# Who'sWho in American Law®

# Who'sWho in American Law®

## 11th Edition

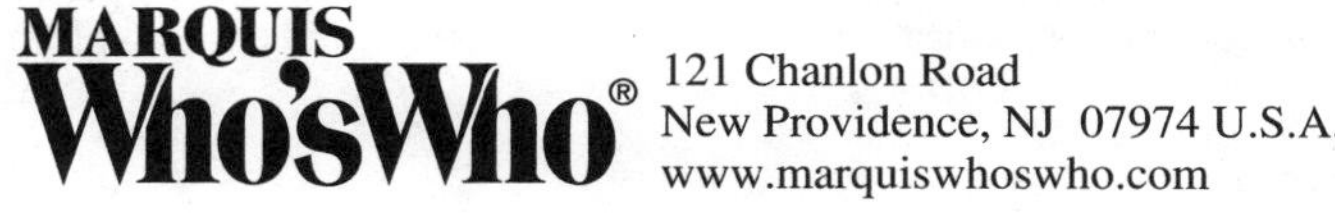
MARQUIS Who'sWho®
121 Chanlon Road
New Providence, NJ 07974 U.S.A.
www.marquiswhoswho.com

# Who'sWho in American Law®




Published by Marquis Who's Who, a member of the Lexis-Nexis Group.

**President and Chief Executive Officer** Lou Andreozzi
**Vice President and Publisher** Randy H. Mysel
**Vice President, Database Production** Dean Hollister





Library of Congress Catalog Card Number 77-79896
International Standard Book Number 0-8379-3516-4 (Classic Edition)
0-8379-3517-2 (Deluxe Edition)
International Standard Serial Number 0162-7880





Manufactured in the United States of America

# Table of Contents

# Preface

The eleventh edition of *Who's Who in American Law* provides biographical information on approximately 23,600 lawyers and professionals in law-related areas including, among others, judges, legal educators, law librarians, legal historians, and social scientists.

The biographical sketches include such information as education, vital statistics, career history, awards, publications, memberships, address(es), and more. In addition, practicing lawyers were asked to include their fields of legal expertise or interest.

In this edition, there are separate indexes for individuals involved actively in the practice of law and for other legal professionals such as judges, law librarians, and legal educators. The "Fields of Practice Index" enables *Who's Who in American Law* users to access practicing lawyers geographically by city and state within fields such as federal or state civil litigation, corporate, taxation, criminal, and approximately 70 other fields of law. The "Professional Index" lists other professionals geographically by type of career such as education, government, or judicial administration.

The selection of the law field codes for the "Fields of Practice Index" was derived from three main sources, beginning with the specialty categories described by the American Bar Association Standing Committee on Specialization. Further information was supplied by state committees and boards on specialization, outlining the specialties recognized by or certified with the respective states. These lists reflect the varying degrees of specialty certification from state to state. Finally, an acknowledged expert on specialization in the legal profession provided valuable information and recommendations for a comprehensive list of recognized areas of law.

Practicing attorneys were asked to select up to three fields that reflected personal practice or interest. The Biographees' sketches reflect these fields. The "Fields of Practice Index" lists these lawyers under their selected fields. Individualized fields not encompassed in the list and newly emerging areas with relatively few practitioners are listed by Biographee name at the end of the index under the category "Other."

As in all Marquis Who's Who biographical volumes, the principle of current reference value determines selection of Biographees. Reference interest is based either on position of responsibility or noteworthy achievement. In the editorial evaluation that resulted in the ultimate selection of the names in this directory, an individual's desire to be listed was not sufficient reason for inclusion.

To supplement the efforts of Marquis researchers, and to ensure comprehensive coverage of important legal professionals, members of the distinguished Board of Advisors have nominated outstanding individuals in their own geographic regions or fields of practice for inclusion in this volume.

Each candidate is invited to submit biographical data about his or her life and professional career. Submitted information is reviewed by the Marquis editorial staff before being written in sketch form, and a prepublication proof of the composed sketch is sent to potential Biographees for verification. Every verified sketch returned by a candidate and accepted by the editorial staff is written in the final Marquis Who's Who format. This process ensures a high degree of accuracy.

In the event that individuals of significant reference interest fail to submit biographical data, the Marquis staff compiles the information through independent research. Sketches compiled in this manner are denoted by asterisks.

Marquis Who's Who editors diligently prepare each biographical sketch for publication. Occasionally, however, errors do appear. We regret all such errors and invite Biographees to notify the publisher so that corrections can be made in a subsequent edition.

# Board of Advisors

Marquis Who's Who gratefully acknowledges the following distinguished individuals who have made themselves available for review, evaluation, and general comment with regard to the publication of the eleventh edition of *Who's Who in American Law*. The advisors have enhanced the reference value of this edition by the nomination of outstanding individuals for inclusion. However, the Board of Advisors, either collectively or individually, is in no way responsible for the final selection of names, or for the accuracy or comprehensiveness of the biographical information or other material contained herein.

**Thomas J. Burke, Jr.**
Partner
Lord, Bissell & Brook
Chicago, Illinois

**Beale Dean**
Partner
Brown, Herman, Dean, Wiseman, Liser & Hart, LLP
Fort Worth, Texas

**Joseph A. DeGrandi**
Former Partner
Beveridge, DeGrandi, Weilacher & Young
Washington, D.C.

**Albert B. Gerber**
Counsel
United National Insurance Company
Philadelphia, Pennsylvania

**Phillip M. Grier**
Former Executive Director
National Association of College and University Attorneys

**Joan M. Hall**
Senior Partner
Jenner & Block
Chicago, Illinois

**James W. Hewitt**
Attorney-at-Law
Lincoln, Nebraska

**David L. Hirsch**
Vice President
Masco Tech./NI Industries, Inc.
Taylor, Michigan

**Joseph H. Johnson, Jr.**
Of Counsel
Lange, Simpson, Robinson & Somerville
Birmingham, Alabama

**Rutledge R. Liles**
President
Liles, Gavin & Costantino
Jacksonville, Florida

**James B. Sales**
Senior Partner
Fulbright & Jaworski
Houston, Texas

# Standards of Admission

Selection of Biographees for *Who's Who in American Law* is determined by reference interest. Such reference value is based on either of two factors: (1) incumbency in a defined position of responsibility or (2) attainment of a significant level of achievement.

Admission based on position includes the following examples:

*Justices of the U.S. Supreme Court*

*Judges of the U.S. Circuit Courts*

*Judges of the U.S. District Courts*

*Attorney General of the United States and other high-ranking federal executive attorneys*

*Chief counsel of congressional committees*

*Justices of state and territorial courts of the highest appellate jurisdiction*

*State and territorial attorneys general*

*Chief judges of selected county courts, based on population*

*Deans and professors at leading law schools*

*General counsel of major corporations and labor unions*

*Officials of the American Bar Association and specialized bar groups*

*Officials of state and territorial bar associations*

*Officials of selected county and city bar associations, based on population*

*Highly rated lawyers in private practice*

*Editors of important legal journals*

Admission by the factor of significant achievement is based on objective criteria for measuring accomplishments within the legal profession.

# Key to Information

**[1] WATTS, BENJAMIN GREENE,** **[2]** lawyer; **[3]** b. May 21, 1935; **[4]** s. George and Sarah (Carson ) W.; **[5]** m. Ellen Spencer, Sept. 12, 1960; **[6]** children: John Allen, Lucy Anne. **[7]** BS, Northwestern U., 1956; JD, U. Chgo., 1965. **[8]** Bar: Ill. 1965, U.S. Supreme Ct. 1980. **[9]** Mem. legal dept. Standard Publs. Corp., Chgo., 1965-73, asst. counsel, 1973-81, counsel, 1981-83; ptnr. Watts, Clayborn, Johnson & Miller, Oak Brook, Ill., 1983-85, sr. ptnr., 1985—; **[10]** lectr. Coll. of DuPage, 1980-94, U. Chgo., 1994—. **[11]** Author: Legal Aspects of Educational Publishing, 1985, Copyright Legalities, 1997. **[12]** Chmn. Downers Grove (Ill.) chpt. ARC, 1982-83; active DuPage council Boy Scouts Am.; trustee Elmhurst (Ill.) Hist. Mus., 1972—, pres. bd. trustees, 1995—. **[13]** Served to lt. USAF, 1959-61. **[14]** Recipient Outstanding Alumnus award Northwestern U., 1971. **[15]** Mem. ABA, Ill. Bar Assn., Chgo. Bar Assn., Am. Mgmt. Assn., Phi Delta Phi, Caxton Club, Tavern Club (Chgo.), Masons **[16]** Democrat. **[17]** Lutheran. **[18]** General practice, Trademark and copyright, General corporate. **[19]** Home: 543 Farwell Ave Elmhurst IL 60126 **[20]** Office: Watts Clayborn Johnson & Miller 1428 Industrial Ct Oak Brook IL 60521

## KEY

- [1] Name
- [2] Occupation
- [3] Vital statistics
- [4] Parents
- [5] Marriage
- [6] Children
- [7] Education
- [8] Professional certifications
- [9] Career
- [10] Career-related activities
- [11] Writings and creative works
- [12] Civic and political activities
- [13] Military service
- [14] Awards and fellowships
- [15] Professional and association memberships, clubs and lodges
- [16] Political affiliation
- [17] Religion
- [18] Fields of legal practice
- [19] Home address
- [20] Office address

# Table of Abbreviations

**The following abbreviations and symbols are frequently used in this book.**

*An asterisk following a sketch indicates that it was researched by the Marquis Who's Who editorial staff and has not been verified by the Biographee.
**A** Associate (used with academic degrees only)
**AA, A.A.** Associate in Arts, Associate of Arts
**AAAL** American Academy of Arts and Letters
**AAAS** American Association for the Advancement of Science
**AACD** American Association for Counseling and Development
**AACN** American Association of Critical Care Nurses
**AAHA** American Academy of Health Administrators
**AAHP** American Association of Hospital Planners
**AAHPERD** American Alliance for Health, Physical Education, Recreation, and Dance
**AAS** Associate of Applied Science
**AASL** American Association of School Librarians
**AASPA** American Association of School Personnel Administrators
**AAU** Amateur Athletic Union
**AAUP** American Association of University Professors
**AAUW** American Association of University Women
**AB, A.B.** Arts, Bachelor of
**AB** Alberta
**ABA** American Bar Association
**ABC** American Broadcasting Company
**AC** Air Corps
**acad.** academy, academic
**acct.** accountant
**acctg.** accounting
**ACDA** Arms Control and Disarmament Agency
**ACHA** American College of Hospital Administrators
**ACLS** Advanced Cardiac Life Support
**ACLU** American Civil Liberties Union
**ACOG** American College of Ob-Gyn
**ACP** American College of Physicians
**ACS** American College of Surgeons
**ADA** American Dental Association
**a.d.c.** aide-de-camp
**adj.** adjunct, adjutant
**adj. gen.** adjutant general
**adm.** admiral
**adminstr.** administrator
**adminstrn.** administration
**adminstrv.** administrative
**ADN** Associate's Degree in Nursing
**ADP** Automatic Data Processing
**adv.** advocate, advisory
**advt.** advertising
**AE, A.E.** Agricultural Engineer
**A.E. and P.** Ambassador Extraordinary and Plenipotentiary
**AEC** Atomic Energy Commission
**aero.** aeronautical, aeronautic
**aerodyn.** aerodynamic
**AFB** Air Force Base
**AFL-CIO** American Federation of Labor and Congress of Industrial Organizations
**AFTRA** American Federation of TV and Radio Artists
**AFSCME** American Federation of State, County and Municipal Employees
**agr.** agriculture
**agrl.** agricultural
**agt.** agent
**AGVA** American Guild of Variety Artists
**agy.** agency
**A&I** Agricultural and Industrial
**AIA** American Institute of Architects
**AIAA** American Institute of Aeronautics and Astronautics
**AIChE** American Institute of Chemical Engineers
**AICPA** American Institute of Certified Public Accountants
**AID** Agency for International Development
**AIDS** Acquired Immune Deficiency Syndrome
**AIEE** American Institute of Electrical Engineers
**AIM** American Institute of Management
**AIME** American Institute of Mining, Metallurgy, and Petroleum Engineers
**AK** Alaska
**AL** Alabama
**ALA** American Library Association
**Ala.** Alabama
**alt.** alternate
**Alta.** Alberta
**A&M** Agricultural and Mechanical
**AM, A.M.** Arts, Master of
**Am.** American, America
**AMA** American Medical Association
**amb.** ambassador
**A.M.E.** African Methodist Episcopal
**Amtrak** National Railroad Passenger Corporation
**AMVETS** American Veterans of World War II, Korea, Vietnam
**ANA** American Nurses Association
**anat.** anatomical
**ANCC** American Nurses Credentialing Center
**ann.** annual
**ANTA** American National Theatre and Academy
**anthrop.** anthropological
**AP** Associated Press
**APA** American Psychological Association
**APGA** American Personnel Guidance Association
**APHA** American Public Health Association
**APO** Army Post Office
**apptd.** appointed
**Apr.** April
**apt.** apartment
**AR** Arkansas
**ARC** American Red Cross
**arch.** architect
**archeol.** archeological
**archtl.** architectural
**Ariz.** Arizona
**Ark.** Arkansas
**ArtsD, ArtsD.** Arts, Doctor of
**arty.** artillery
**AS** American Samoa
**AS** Associate in Science
**ASCAP** American Society of Composers, Authors and Publishers
**ASCD** Association for Supervision and Curriculum Development
**ASCE** American Society of Civil Engineers
**ASHRAE** American Society of Heating, Refrigeration, and Air Conditioning Engineers
**ASME** American Society of Mechanical Engineers
**ASNSA** American Society for Nursing Service Administrators
**ASPA** American Society for Public Administration
**ASPCA** American Society for the Prevention of Cruelty to Animals
**assn.** association
**assoc.** associate
**asst.** assistant
**ASTD** American Society for Training and Development
**ASTM** American Society for Testing and Materials
**astron.** astronomical
**astrophys.** astrophysical
**ATLA** Association of Trial Lawyers of America
**ATSC** Air Technical Service Command
**AT&T** American Telephone & Telegraph Company
**atty.** attorney
**Aug.** August
**AUS** Army of the United States
**aux.** auxiliary
**Ave.** Avenue
**AVMA** American Veterinary Medical Association
**AZ** Arizona
**AWHONN** Association of Women's Health Obstetric and Neonatal Nurses

**B.** Bachelor
**b.** born
**BA, B.A.** Bachelor of Arts
**BAgr, B.Agr.** Bachelor of Agriculture
**Balt.** Baltimore
**Bapt.** Baptist
**BArch, B.Arch.** Bachelor of Architecture
**BAS, B.A.S.** Bachelor of Agricultural Science
**BBA, B.B.A.** Bachelor of Business Administration
**BBB** Better Business Bureau
**BBC** British Broadcasting Corporation

**BC, B.C.** British Columbia
**BCE, B.C.E.** Bachelor of Civil Engineering
**BChir, B.Chir.** Bachelor of Surgery
**BCL, B.C.L.** Bachelor of Civil Law
**BCLS** Basic Cardiac Life Support
**BCS, B.C.S.** Bachelor of Commercial Science
**BD, B.D.** Bachelor of Divinity
**bd.** board
**BE, B.E.** Bachelor of Education
**BEE, B.E.E.** Bachelor of Electrical Engineering
**BFA, B.F.A.** Bachelor of Fine Arts
**bibl.** biblical
**bibliog.** bibliographical
**biog.** biographical
**biol.** biological
**BJ, B.J.** Bachelor of Journalism
**Bklyn.** Brooklyn
**BL, B.L.** Bachelor of Letters
**bldg.** building
**BLS, B.L.S.** Bachelor of Library Science
**BLS** Basic Life Support
**Blvd.** Boulevard
**BMI** Broadcast Music, Inc.
**BMW** Bavarian Motor Works (Bayerische Motoren Werke)
**bn.** battalion
**B.&O.R.R.** Baltimore & Ohio Railroad
**bot.** botanical
**BPE, B.P.E.** Bachelor of Physical Education
**BPhil, B.Phil.** Bachelor of Philosophy
**br.** branch
**BRE, B.R.E.** Bachelor of Religious Education
**brig. gen.** brigadier general
**Brit.** British, Brittanica
**Bros.** Brothers
**BS, B.S.** Bachelor of Science
**BSA, B.S.A.** Bachelor of Agricultural Science
**BSBA** Bachelor of Science in Business Administration
**BSChemE** Bachelor of Science in Chemical Engineering
**BSD, B.S.D.** Bachelor of Didactic Science
**BSEE** Bachelor of Science in Electrical Engineering
**BSN** Bachelor of Science in Nursing
**BST, B.S.T.** Bachelor of Sacred Theology
**BTh, B.Th.** Bachelor of Theology
**bull.** bulletin
**bur.** bureau
**bus.** business
**B.W.I.** British West Indies

**CA** California
**CAA** Civil Aeronautics Administration
**CAB** Civil Aeronautics Board
**CAD-CAM** Computer Aided Design–Computer Aided Model
**Calif.** California
**C.Am.** Central America
**Can.** Canada, Canadian
**CAP** Civil Air Patrol
**capt.** captain
**cardiol.** cardiological
**cardiovasc.** cardiovascular
**CARE** Cooperative American Relief Everywhere
**Cath.** Catholic
**cav.** cavalry
**CBC** Canadian Broadcasting Company
**CBI** China, Burma, India Theatre of Operations
**CBS** Columbia Broadcasting Company
**C.C.** Community College
**CCC** Commodity Credit Corporation
**CCNY** City College of New York
**CCRN** Critical Care Registered Nurse
**CCU** Cardiac Care Unit
**CD** Civil Defense
**CE, C.E.** Corps of Engineers, Civil Engineer
**CEN** Certified Emergency Nurse
**CENTO** Central Treaty Organization
**CEO** chief executive officer
**CERN** European Organization of Nuclear Research
**cert.** certificate, certification, certified
**CETA** Comprehensive Employment Training Act
**CFA** Chartered Financial Analyst
**CFL** Canadian Football League
**CFO** chief financial officer
**CFP** Certified Financial Planner
**ch.** church
**ChD, Ch.D.** Doctor of Chemistry
**chem.** chemical
**ChemE, Chem.E.** Chemical Engineer
**ChFC** Chartered Financial Consultant
**Chgo.** Chicago
**chirurg.** chirurgical
**chmn.** chairman
**chpt.** chapter
**CIA** Central Intelligence Agency
**Cin.** Cincinnati
**cir.** circle, circuit
**CLE** Continuing Legal Education
**Cleve.** Cleveland
**climatol.** climatological
**clin.** clinical
**clk.** clerk
**C.L.U.** Chartered Life Underwriter
**CM, C.M.** Master in Surgery
**CM** Northern Mariana Islands
**CMA** Certified Medical Assistant
**cmty.** community
**CNA** Certified Nurse's Aide
**CNOR** Certified Nurse (Operating Room)
**C.&N.W.Ry.** Chicago & North Western Railway
**CO** Colorado
**Co.** Company
**COF** Catholic Order of Foresters
**C. of C.** Chamber of Commerce
**col.** colonel
**coll.** college
**Colo.** Colorado
**com.** committee
**comd.** commanded
**comdg.** commanding
**comdr.** commander
**comdt.** commandant
**comm.** communications
**commd.** commissioned
**comml.** commercial
**commn.** commission
**commr.** commissioner
**compt.** comptroller
**condr.** conductor
**Conf.** Conference
**Congl.** Congregational, Congressional
**Conglist.** Congregationalist
**Conn.** Connecticut
**cons.** consultant, consulting
**consol.** consolidated
**constl.** constitutional
**constn.** constitution
**constrn.** construction
**contbd.** contributed
**contbg.** contributing
**contbn.** contribution
**contbr.** contributor
**contr.** controller
**Conv.** Convention
**COO** chief operating officer
**coop.** cooperative
**coord.** coordinator
**CORDS** Civil Operations and Revolutionary Development Support
**CORE** Congress of Racial Equality
**corp.** corporation, corporate
**corr.** correspondent, corresponding, correspondence
**C.&O.Ry.** Chesapeake & Ohio Railway
**coun.** council
**CPA** Certified Public Accountant
**CPCU** Chartered Property and Casualty Underwriter
**CPH, C.P.H.** Certificate of Public Health
**cpl.** corporal
**CPR** Cardio-Pulmonary Resuscitation
**C.P.Ry.** Canadian Pacific Railway
**CRT** Cathode Ray Terminal
**C.S.** Christian Science
**CSB, C.S.B.** Bachelor of Christian Science
**C.S.C.** Civil Service Commission
**CT** Connecticut
**ct.** court
**ctr.** center
**ctrl.** central
**CWS** Chemical Warfare Service
**C.Z.** Canal Zone

**D.** Doctor
**d.** daughter
**DAgr, D.Agr.** Doctor of Agriculture
**DAR** Daughters of the American Revolution
**dau.** daughter
**DAV** Disabled American Veterans
**DC, D.C.** District of Columbia
**DCL, D.C.L.** Doctor of Civil Law
**DCS, D.C.S.** Doctor of Commercial Science
**DD, D.D.** Doctor of Divinity
**DDS, D.D.S.** Doctor of Dental Surgery
**DE** Delaware
**Dec.** December
**dec.** deceased
**def.** defense
**Del.** Delaware
**del.** delegate, delegation
**Dem.** Democrat, Democratic
**DEng, D.Eng.** Doctor of Engineering
**denom.** denomination, denominational
**dep.** deputy
**dept.** department
**dermatol.** dermatological
**desc.** descendant
**devel.** development, developmental
**DFA, D.F.A.** Doctor of Fine Arts
**D.F.C.** Distinguished Flying Cross
**DHL, D.H.L.** Doctor of Hebrew Literature
**dir.** director
**dist.** district
**distbg.** distributing
**distbn.** distribution
**distbr.** distributor
**disting.** distinguished
**div.** division, divinity, divorce
**divsn.** division
**DLitt, D.Litt.** Doctor of Literature
**DMD, D.M.D.** Doctor of Dental Medicine
**DMS, D.M.S.** Doctor of Medical Science
**DO, D.O.** Doctor of Osteopathy
**docs.** documents
**DON** Director of Nursing
**DPH, D.P.H.** Diploma in Public Health
**DPhil, D.Phil.** Doctor of Philosophy
**D.R.** Daughters of the Revolution
**Dr.** Drive, Doctor
**DRE, D.R.E.** Doctor of Religious Education
**DrPH, Dr.P.H.** Doctor of Public Health, Doctor of Public Hygiene
**D.S.C.** Distinguished Service Cross

**DSc, D.Sc.** Doctor of Science
**DSChemE** Doctor of Science in Chemical Engineering
**D.S.M.** Distinguished Service Medal
**DST, D.S.T.** Doctor of Sacred Theology
**DTM, D.T.M.** Doctor of Tropical Medicine
**DVM, D.V.M.** Doctor of Veterinary Medicine
**DVS, D.V.S.** Doctor of Veterinary Surgery

**E, E.** East
**ea.** eastern
**E. and P.** Extraordinary and Plenipotentiary
**Eccles.** Ecclesiastical
**ecol.** ecological
**econ.** economic
**ECOSOC** Economic and Social Council (of the UN)
**ED, E.D.** Doctor of Engineering
**ed.** educated
**EdB, Ed.B.** Bachelor of Education
**EdD, Ed.D.** Doctor of Education
**edit.** edition
**editl.** editorial
**EdM, Ed.M.** Master of Education
**edn.** education
**ednl.** educational
**EDP** Electronic Data Processing
**EdS, Ed.S.** Specialist in Education
**EE, E.E.** Electrical Engineer
**E.E. and M.P.** Envoy Extraordinary and Minister Plenipotentiary
**EEC** European Economic Community
**EEG** Electroencephalogram
**EEO** Equal Employment Opportunity
**EEOC** Equal Employment Opportunity Commission
**E.Ger.** German Democratic Republic
**EKG** Electrocardiogram
**elec.** electrical
**electrochem.** electrochemical
**electrophys.** electrophysical
**elem.** elementary
**EM, E.M.** Engineer of Mines
**EMT** Emergency Medical Technician
**ency.** encyclopedia
**Eng.** England
**engr.** engineer
**engring.** engineering
**entomol.** entomological
**environ.** environmental
**EPA** Environmental Protection Agency
**epidemiol.** epidemiological
**Episc.** Episcopalian
**ERA** Equal Rights Amendment
**ERDA** Energy Research and Development Administration
**ESEA** Elementary and Secondary Education Act
**ESL** English as Second Language
**ESPN** Entertainment and Sports Programming Network
**ESSA** Environmental Science Services Administration
**ethnol.** ethnological
**ETO** European Theatre of Operations
**Evang.** Evangelical
**exam.** examination, examining
**Exch.** Exchange
**exec.** executive
**exhbn.** exhibition
**expdn.** expedition
**expn.** exposition
**expt.** experiment
**exptl.** experimental
**Expy.** Expressway
**Ext.** Extension

**F.A.** Field Artillery
**FAA** Federal Aviation Administration
**FAO** Food and Agriculture Organization (of the UN)
**FBA** Federal Bar Association
**FBI** Federal Bureau of Investigation
**FCA** Farm Credit Administration
**FCC** Federal Communications Commission
**FCDA** Federal Civil Defense Administration
**FDA** Food and Drug Administration
**FDIA** Federal Deposit Insurance Administration
**FDIC** Federal Deposit Insurance Corporation
**FE, F.E.** Forest Engineer
**FEA** Federal Energy Administration
**Feb.** February
**fed.** federal
**fedn.** federation
**FERC** Federal Energy Regulatory Commission
**fgn.** foreign
**FHA** Federal Housing Administration
**fin.** financial, finance
**FL** Florida
**Fl.** Floor
**Fla.** Florida
**FMC** Federal Maritime Commission
**FNP** Family Nurse Practitioner
**FOA** Foreign Operations Administration
**found.** foundation
**FPC** Federal Power Commission
**FPO** Fleet Post Office
**frat.** fraternity
**FRS** Federal Reserve System
**FSA** Federal Security Agency
**Ft.** Fort
**FTC** Federal Trade Commission
**Fwy.** Freeway

**G-1 (or other number)** Division of General Staff
**GA, Ga.** Georgia
**GAO** General Accounting Office
**gastroent.** gastroenterological
**GATE** Gifted and Talented Educators
**GATT** General Agreement on Tariffs and Trade
**GE** General Electric Company
**gen.** general
**geneal.** genealogical
**geod.** geodetic
**geog.** geographic, geographical
**geol.** geological
**geophys.** geophysical
**geriat.** geriatrics
**gerontol.** gerontological
**G.H.Q.** General Headquarters
**GM** General Motors Corporation
**GMAC** General Motors Acceptance Corporation
**G.N.Ry.** Great Northern Railway
**gov.** governor
**govt.** government
**govtl.** governmental
**GPO** Government Printing Office
**grad.** graduate, graduated
**GSA** General Services Administration
**Gt.** Great
**GTE** General Telephone and ElectricCompany
**GU** Guam
**gynecol.** gynecological

**HBO** Home Box Office
**hdqs.** headquarters
**HEW** Department of Health, Education and Welfare
**HHD, H.H.D.** Doctor of Humanities
**HHFA** Housing and Home Finance Agency
**HHS** Department of Health and Human Services
**HI** Hawaii
**hist.** historical, historic
**HM, H.M.** Master of Humanities
**HMO** Health Maintenance Organization
**homeo.** homeopathic
**hon.** honorary, honorable
**Ho. of Dels.** House of Delegates
**Ho. of Reps.** House of Representatives
**hort.** horticultural
**hosp.** hospital
**H.S.** High School
**HUD** Department of Housing and Urban Development
**Hwy.** Highway
**hydrog.** hydrographic

**IA** Iowa
**IAEA** International Atomic Energy Agency
**IATSE** International Alliance of Theatrical and Stage Employees and Moving Picture Operators of the United States and Canada
**IBM** International Business Machines Corporation
**IBRD** International Bank for Reconstruction and Development
**ICA** International Cooperation Administration
**ICC** Interstate Commerce Commission
**ICCE** International Council for Computers in Education
**ICU** Intensive Care Unit
**ID** Idaho
**IEEE** Institute of Electrical and Electronics Engineers
**IFC** International Finance Corporation
**IGY** International Geophysical Year
**IL** Illinois
**Ill.** Illinois
**illus.** illustrated
**ILO** International Labor Organization
**IMF** International Monetary Fund
**IN** Indiana
**Inc.** Incorporated
**Ind.** Indiana
**ind.** independent
**Indpls.** Indianapolis
**indsl.** industrial
**inf.** infantry
**info.** information
**ins.** insurance
**insp.** inspector
**insp. gen.** inspector general
**inst.** institute
**instl.** institutional
**instn.** institution
**instr.** instructor
**instrn.** instruction
**instrnl.** instructional
**internat.** international
**intro.** introduction
**IRE** Institute of Radio Engineers
**IRS** Internal Revenue Service
**ITT** International Telephone & Telegraph Corporation

**JAG** Judge Advocate General
**JAGC** Judge Advocate General Corps
**Jan.** January
**Jaycees** Junior Chamber of Commerce
**JB, J.B.** Jurum Baccalaureus

**JCB, J.C.B.** Juris Canoni Baccalaureus
**JCD, J.C.D.** Juris Canonici Doctor, Juris Civilis Doctor
**JCL, J.C.L.** Juris Canonici Licentiatus
**JD, J.D.** Juris Doctor
**jg.** junior grade
**jour.** journal
**jr.** junior
**JSD, J.S.D.** Juris Scientiae Doctor
**JUD, J.U.D.** Juris Utriusque Doctor
**jud.** judicial

**Kans.** Kansas
**K.C.** Knights of Columbus
**K.P.** Knights of Pythias
**KS** Kansas
**K.T.** Knight Templar
**KY, Ky.** Kentucky

**LA, La.** Louisiana
**L.A.** Los Angeles
**lab.** laboratory
**L.Am.** Latin America
**lang.** language
**laryngol.** laryngological
**LB** Labrador
**LDS** Latter Day Saints
**LDS Church** Church of Jesus Christ of Latter Day Saints
**lectr.** lecturer
**legis.** legislation, legislative
**LHD, L.H.D.** Doctor of Humane Letters
**L.I.** Long Island
**libr.** librarian, library
**lic.** licensed, license
**L.I.R.R.** Long Island Railroad
**lit.** literature
**litig.** litigation
**LittB, Litt.B.** Bachelor of Letters
**LittD, Litt.D.** Doctor of Letters
**LLB, LL.B.** Bachelor of Laws
**LLD, L.L.D.** Doctor of Laws
**LLM, L.L.M.** Master of Laws
**Ln.** Lane
**L.&N.R.R.** Louisville & Nashville Railroad
**LPGA** Ladies Professional Golf Association
**LPN** Licensed Practical Nurse
**LS, L.S.** Library Science (in degree)
**lt.** lieutenant
**Ltd.** Limited
**Luth.** Lutheran
**LWV** League of Women Voters

**M.** Master
**m.** married
**MA, M.A.** Master of Arts
**MA** Massachusetts
**MADD** Mothers Against Drunk Driving
**mag.** magazine
**MAgr, M.Agr.** Master of Agriculture
**maj.** major
**Man.** Manitoba
**Mar.** March
**MArch, M.Arch.** Master in Architecture
**Mass.** Massachusetts
**math.** mathematics, mathematical
**MATS** Military Air Transport Service
**MB, M.B.** Bachelor of Medicine
**MB** Manitoba
**MBA, M.B.A.** Master of Business Administration
**MBS** Mutual Broadcasting System
**M.C.** Medical Corps
**MCE, M.C.E.** Master of Civil Engineering
**mcht.** merchant
**mcpl.** municipal
**MCS, M.C.S.** Master of Commercial Science
**MD, M.D.** Doctor of Medicine
**MD, Md.** Maryland
**MDiv** Master of Divinity
**MDip, M.Dip.** Master in Diplomacy
**mdse.** merchandise
**MDV, M.D.V.** Doctor of Veterinary Medicine
**ME, M.E.** Mechanical Engineer
**ME** Maine
**M.E.Ch.** Methodist Episcopal Church
**mech.** mechanical
**MEd., M.Ed.** Master of Education
**med.** medical
**MEE, M.E.E.** Master of Electrical Engineering
**mem.** member
**meml.** memorial
**merc.** mercantile
**met.** metropolitan
**metall.** metallurgical
**MetE, Met.E.** Metallurgical Engineer
**meteorol.** meteorological
**Meth.** Methodist
**Mex.** Mexico
**MF, M.F.** Master of Forestry
**MFA, M.F.A.** Master of Fine Arts
**mfg.** manufacturing
**mfr.** manufacturer
**mgmt.** management
**mgr.** manager
**MHA, M.H.A.** Master of Hospital Administration
**M.I.** Military Intelligence
**MI** Michigan
**Mich.** Michigan
**micros.** microscopic, microscopical
**mid.** middle
**mil.** military
**Milw.** Milwaukee
**Min.** Minister
**mineral.** mineralogical
**Minn.** Minnesota
**MIS** Management Information Systems
**Miss.** Mississippi
**MIT** Massachusetts Institute of Technology
**mktg.** marketing
**ML, M.L.** Master of Laws
**MLA** Modern Language Association
**M.L.D.** Magister Legnum Diplomatic
**MLitt, M.Litt.** Master of Literature, Master of Letters
**MLS, M.L.S.** Master of Library Science
**MME, M.M.E.** Master of Mechanical Engineering
**MN** Minnesota
**mng.** managing
**MO, Mo.** Missouri
**moblzn.** mobilization
**Mont.** Montana
**MP** Northern Mariana Islands
**M.P.** Member of Parliament
**MPA** Master of Public Administration
**MPE, M.P.E.** Master of Physical Education
**MPH, M.P.H.** Master of Public Health
**MPhil, M.Phil.** Master of Philosophy
**MPL, M.P.L.** Master of Patent Law
**Mpls.** Minneapolis
**MRE, M.R.E.** Master of Religious Education
**MRI** Magnetic Resonance Imaging
**MS, M.S.** Master of Science
**MS, Ms.** Mississippi
**MSc, M.Sc.** Master of Science
**MSChemE** Master of Science in Chemical Engineering
**MSEE** Master of Science in Electrical Engineering
**MSF, M.S.F.** Master of Science of Forestry
**MSN** Master of Science in Nursing
**MST, M.S.T.** Master of Sacred Theology
**MSW, M.S.W.** Master of Social Work
**MT** Montana
**Mt.** Mount
**MTO** Mediterranean Theatre of Operation
**MTV** Music Television
**mus.** museum, musical
**MusB, Mus.B.** Bachelor of Music
**MusD, Mus.D.** Doctor of Music
**MusM, Mus.M.** Master of Music
**mut.** mutual
**MVP** Most Valuable Player
**mycol.** mycological

**N.** North
**NAACOG** Nurses Association of the American College of Obstetricians and Gynecologists
**NAACP** National Association for the Advancement of Colored People
**NACA** National Advisory Committee for Aeronautics
**NACDL** National Association of Criminal Defense Lawyers
**NACU** National Association of Colleges and Universities
**NAD** National Academy of Design
**NAE** National Academy of Engineering, National Association of Educators
**NAESP** National Association of Elementary School Principals
**NAFE** National Association of Female Executives
**N.Am.** North America
**NAM** National Association of Manufacturers
**NAMH** National Association for Mental Health
**NAPA** National Association of Performing Artists
**NARAS** National Academy of Recording Arts and Sciences
**NAREB** National Association of Real Estate Boards
**NARS** National Archives and Record Service
**NAS** National Academy of Sciences
**NASA** National Aeronautics and Space Administration
**NASP** National Association of School Psychologists
**NASW** National Association of Social Workers
**nat.** national
**NATAS** National Academy of Television Arts and Sciences
**NATO** North Atlantic Treaty Organization
**NATOUSA** North African Theatre of Operations, United States Army
**nav.** navigation
**NB, N.B.** New Brunswick
**NBA** National Basketball Association
**NBC** National Broadcasting Company
**NC, N.C.** North Carolina
**NCAA** National College Athletic Association
**NCCJ** National Conference of Christians and Jews
**ND, N.D.** North Dakota
**NDEA** National Defense Education Act
**NE** Nebraska
**NE, N.E.** Northeast
**NEA** National Education Association
**Nebr.** Nebraska
**NEH** National Endowment for Humanities
**neurol.** neurological
**Nev.** Nevada
**NF** Newfoundland

**NFL** National Football League
**Nfld.** Newfoundland
**NG** National Guard
**NH, N.H.** New Hampshire
**NHL** National Hockey League
**NIH** National Institutes of Health
**NIMH** National Institute of Mental Health
**NJ, N.J.** New Jersey
**NLRB** National Labor Relations Board
**NM** New Mexico
**N.Mex.** New Mexico
**No.** Northern
**NOAA** National Oceanographic and Atmospheric Administration
**NORAD** North America Air Defense
**Nov.** November
**NOW** National Organization for Women
**N.P.Ry.** Northern Pacific Railway
**nr.** near
**NRA** National Rifle Association
**NRC** National Research Council
**NS, N.S.** Nova Scotia
**NSC** National Security Council
**NSF** National Science Foundation
**NSTA** National Science Teachers Association
**NSW** New South Wales
**N.T.** New Testament
**NT** Northwest Territories
**nuc.** nuclear
**numis.** numismatic
**NV** Nevada
**NW, N.W.** Northwest
**N.W.T.** Northwest Territories
**NY, N.Y.** New York
**N.Y.C.** New York City
**NYU** New York University
**N.Z.** New Zealand

**OAS** Organization of American States
**ob-gyn** obstetrics-gynecology
**obs.** observatory
**obstet.** obstetrical
**occupl.** occupational
**oceanog.** oceanographic
**Oct.** October
**OD, O.D.** Doctor of Optometry
**OECD** Organization for Economic Cooperation and Development
**OEEC** Organization of European Economic Cooperation
**OEO** Office of Economic Opportunity
**ofcl.** official
**OH** Ohio
**OK** Oklahoma
**Okla.** Oklahoma
**ON** Ontario
**Ont.** Ontario
**oper.** operating
**ophthal.** ophthalmological
**ops.** operations
**OR** Oregon
**orch.** orchestra
**Oreg.** Oregon
**orgn.** organization
**orgnl.** organizational
**ornithol.** ornithological
**orthop.** orthopedic
**OSHA** Occupational Safety and Health Administration
**OSRD** Office of Scientific Research and Development
**OSS** Office of Strategic Services
**osteo.** osteopathic
**otol.** otological
**otolaryn.** otolaryngological

**PA, Pa.** Pennsylvania
**P.A.** Professional Association
**paleontol.** paleontological
**path.** pathological
**PBS** Public Broadcasting System
**P.C.** Professional Corporation
**PE** Prince Edward Island
**pediat.** pediatrics
**P.E.I.** Prince Edward Island
**PEN** Poets, Playwrights, Editors, Essayists and Novelists (international association)
**penol.** penological
**P.E.O.** women's organization (full name not disclosed)
**pers.** personnel
**pfc.** private first class
**PGA** Professional Golfers' Association of America
**PHA** Public Housing Administration
**pharm.** pharmaceutical
**PharmD, Pharm.D.** Doctor of Pharmacy
**PharmM, Pharm.M.** Master of Pharmacy
**PhB, Ph.B.** Bachelor of Philosophy
**PhD, Ph.D.** Doctor of Philosophy
**PhDChemE** Doctor of Science in Chemical Engineering
**PhM, Ph.M.** Master of Philosophy
**Phila.** Philadelphia
**philharm.** philharmonic
**philol.** philological
**philos.** philosophical
**photog.** photographic
**phys.** physical
**physiol.** physiological
**Pitts.** Pittsburgh
**Pk.** Park
**Pky.** Parkway
**Pl.** Place
**P.&L.E.R.R.** Pittsburgh & Lake Erie Railroad
**Plz.** Plaza
**PNP** Pediatric Nurse Practitioner
**P.O.** Post Office
**PO Box** Post Office Box
**polit.** political
**poly.** polytechnic, polytechnical
**PQ** Province of Quebec
**PR, P.R.** Puerto Rico
**prep.** preparatory
**pres.** president
**Presbyn.** Presbyterian
**presdl.** presidential
**prin.** principal
**procs.** proceedings
**prod.** produced (play production)
**prodn.** production
**prodr.** producer
**prof.** professor
**profl.** professional
**prog.** progressive
**propr.** proprietor
**pros. atty.** prosecuting attorney
**pro tem.** pro tempore
**PSRO** Professional Services Review Organization
**psychiat.** psychiatric
**psychol.** psychological
**PTA** Parent-Teachers Association
**ptnr.** partner
**PTO** Pacific Theatre of Operations, Parent Teacher Organization
**pub.** publisher, publishing, published
**pub.** public
**publ.** publication
**pvt.** private

**quar.** quarterly
**qm.** quartermaster
**Q.M.C.** Quartermaster Corps
**Que.** Quebec

**radiol.** radiological
**RAF** Royal Air Force
**RCA** Radio Corporation of America
**RCAF** Royal Canadian Air Force
**RD** Rural Delivery
**Rd.** Road
**R&D** Research & Development
**REA** Rural Electrification Administration
**rec.** recording
**ref.** reformed
**regt.** regiment
**regtl.** regimental
**rehab.** rehabilitation
**rels.** relations
**Rep.** Republican
**rep.** representative
**Res.** Reserve
**ret.** retired
**Rev.** Reverend
**rev.** review, revised
**RFC** Reconstruction Finance Corporation
**RFD** Rural Free Delivery
**rhinol.** rhinological
**RI, R.I.** Rhode Island
**RISD** Rhode Island School of Design
**Rlwy.** Railway
**Rm.** Room
**RN, R.N.** Registered Nurse
**roentgenol.** roentgenological
**ROTC** Reserve Officers Training Corps
**RR** Rural Route
**R.R.** Railroad
**rsch.** research
**rschr.** researcher
**Rt.** Route

**S.** South
**s.** son
**SAC** Strategic Air Command
**SAG** Screen Actors Guild
**SALT** Strategic Arms Limitation Talks
**S.Am.** South America
**san.** sanitary
**SAR** Sons of the American Revolution
**Sask.** Saskatchewan
**savs.** savings
**SB, S.B.** Bachelor of Science
**SBA** Small Business Administration
**SC, S.C.** South Carolina
**SCAP** Supreme Command Allies Pacific
**ScB, Sc.B.** Bachelor of Science
**SCD, S.C.D.** Doctor of Commercial Science
**ScD, Sc.D.** Doctor of Science
**sch.** school
**sci.** science, scientific
**SCLC** Southern Christian Leadership Conference
**SCV** Sons of Confederate Veterans
**SD, S.D.** South Dakota
**SE, S.E.** Southeast
**SEATO** Southeast Asia Treaty Organization
**SEC** Securities and Exchange Commission
**sec.** secretary
**sect.** section
**seismol.** seismological
**sem.** seminary
**Sept.** September
**s.g.** senior grade
**sgt.** sergeant
**SHAEF** Supreme Headquarters Allied Expeditionary Forces
**SHAPE** Supreme Headquarters Allied Powers in Europe
**S.I.** Staten Island

**S.J.** Society of Jesus (Jesuit)
**SJD** Scientiae Juridicae Doctor
**SK** Saskatchewan
**SM, S.M.** Master of Science
**SNP** Society of Nursing Professionals
**So.** Southern
**soc.** society
**sociol.** sociological
**S.P.Co.** Southern Pacific Company
**spkr.** speaker
**spl.** special
**splty.** specialty
**Sq.** Square
**S.R.** Sons of the Revolution
**sr.** senior
**SS** Steamship
**SSS** Selective Service System
**St.** Saint, Street
**sta.** station
**stats.** statistics
**statis.** statistical
**STB, S.T.B.** Bachelor of Sacred Theology
**stblzn.** stabilization
**STD, S.T.D.** Doctor of Sacred Theology
**std.** standard
**Ste.** Suite
**subs.** subsidiary
**SUNY** State University of New York
**supr.** supervisor
**supt.** superintendent
**surg.** surgical
**svc.** service
**SW, S.W.** Southwest
**sys.** system

**TAPPI** Technical Association of the Pulp and Paper Industry
**tb.** tuberculosis
**tchg.** teaching
**tchr.** teacher
**tech.** technical, technology
**technol.** technological
**tel.** telephone
**Tel. & Tel.** Telephone & Telegraph
**telecom.** telecommunications
**temp.** temporary
**Tenn.** Tennessee
**Ter.** Territory
**Ter.** Terrace
**TESOL** Teachers of English to Speakers of Other Languages
**Tex.** Texas
**ThD, Th.D.** Doctor of Theology
**theol.** theological
**ThM, Th.M.** Master of Theology
**TN** Tennessee
**tng.** training
**topog.** topographical
**trans.** transaction, transferred
**transl.** translation, translated
**transp.** transportation
**treas.** treasurer
**TT** Trust Territory
**TV** television
**TVA** Tennessee Valley Authority
**TWA** Trans World Airlines
**twp.** township
**TX** Texas
**typog.** typographical

**U.** University
**UAW** United Auto Workers
**UCLA** University of California at Los Angeles
**UDC** United Daughters of the Confederacy
**U.K.** United Kingdom
**UN** United Nations
**UNESCO** United Nations Educational, Scientific and Cultural Organization
**UNICEF** United Nations International Children's Emergency Fund
**univ.** university
**UNRRA** United Nations Relief and Rehabilitation Administration
**UPI** United Press International
**U.P.R.R.** United Pacific Railroad
**urol.** urological
**U.S.** United States
**U.S.A.** United States of America
**USAAF** United States Army Air Force
**USAF** United States Air Force
**USAFR** United States Air Force Reserve
**USAR** United States Army Reserve
**USCG** United States Coast Guard
**USCGR** United States Coast Guard Reserve
**USES** United States Employment Service
**USIA** United States Information Agency
**USMC** United States Marine Corps
**USMCR** United States Marine Corps Reserve
**USN** United States Navy
**USNG** United States National Guard
**USNR** United States Naval Reserve
**USO** United Service Organizations
**USPHS** United States Public Health Service
**USS** United States Ship
**USSR** Union of the Soviet Socialist Republics
**USTA** United States Tennis Association
**USV** United States Volunteers
**UT** Utah

**VA** Veterans Administration
**VA, Va.** Virginia
**vet.** veteran, veterinary
**VFW** Veterans of Foreign Wars
**VI, V.I.** Virgin Islands
**vice pres.** vice president
**vis.** visiting
**VISTA** Volunteers in Service to America
**VITA** Volunteers in Technical Assistance
**vocat.** vocational
**vol.** volunteer, volume
**v.p.** vice president
**vs.** versus
**VT, Vt.** Vermont

**W, W.** West
**WA** Washington (state)
**WAC** Women's Army Corps
**Wash.** Washington (state)
**WATS** Wide Area Telecommunications Service
**WAVES** Women's Reserve, US Naval Reserve
**WCTU** Women's Christian Temperance Union
**we.** western
**W. Ger.** Germany, Federal Republic of
**WHO** World Health Organization
**WI** Wisconsin
**W.I.** West Indies
**Wis.** Wisconsin
**WSB** Wage Stabilization Board
**WV** West Virginia
**W.Va.** West Virginia
**WWI** World War I
**WWII** World War II
**WY** Wyoming
**Wyo.** Wyoming

**YK** Yukon Territory
**YMCA** Young Men's Christian Association
**YMHA** Young Men's Hebrew Association
**YM & YWHA** Young Men's and Young Women's Hebrew Association
**yr.** year
**YT, Y.T.** Yukon Territory
**YWCA** Young Women's Christian Association

**zool.** zoological

# Alphabetical Practices

Names are arranged alphabetically according to the surnames, and under identical surnames according to the first given name. If both surname and first given name are identical, names are arranged alphabetically according to the second given name.

Surnames beginning with De, Des, Du, however capitalized or spaced, are recorded with the prefix preceding the surname and arranged alphabetically under the letter D.

Surnames beginning with Mac and Mc are arranged alphabetically under M.

Surnames beginning with Saint or St. appear after names that begin Sains, and are arranged according to the second part of the name, e.g. St. Clair before Saint Dennis.

Surnames beginning with Van, Von, or von are arranged alphabetically under the letter V.

Compound surnames are arranged according to the first member of the compound.

Many hyphenated Arabic names begin Al-, El-, or al-. These names are alphabetized according to each Biographee's designation of last name. Thus Al-Bahar, Neta may be listed either under Al- or under Bahar, depending on the preference of the listee.

Also, Arabic names have a variety of possible spellings when transposed to English. Spelling of these names is always based on the practice of the Biographee. Some Biographees use a Western form of word order, while others prefer the Arabic word sequence.

Similarly, Asian names may have no comma between family and given names, but some Biographees have chosen to add the comma. In each case, punctuation follows the preference of the Biographee.

Parentheses used in connection with a name indicate which part of the full name is usually deleted in common usage. Hence Chambers, E(lizabeth) Anne indicates that the usual form of the given name is E. Anne. In such a case, the parentheses are ignored in alphabetizing and the name would be arranged as Chambers, Elizabeth Anne. However, if the name is recorded Chambers, (Elizabeth) Anne, signifying that the entire name Elizabeth is not commonly used, the alphabetizing would be arranged as though the name were Chambers, Anne. If an entire middle or last name is enclosed in parentheses, that portion of the name is used in the alphabetical arrangement. Hence Chambers, Elizabeth (Anne) would be arranged as Chambers, Elizabeth Anne.

Where more than one spelling, word order, or name of an individual is frequently encountered, the sketch has been entered under the form preferred by the Biographee, with cross-references under alternate forms.

# Who'sWho in American Law®

## Biographies

**AADALEN, DAVID KEVIN,** lawyer; b. Hamilton, Calif., Dec. 23, 1953; s. Arlie Vernon and Irma Jean (Willig) A.; m. Rhonda Kay Kramer, May 29, 1976; children: Luke David, Amy Johanna, Adam Ross. Student, U. Kans., 1971; BA, Washburn U., 1975, JD, 1979. Bar: Kans. 1980, U.S. Dist. Ct. Kans. 1980. Pvt. practice Topeka, 1980-93; sr. v.p. trust dept. mgr. Mercantile Bank of Topeka, 1993-95; ptnr. Clutter, Hinkel & Aadalen, LLP, 1997—; judge pro tempore Shawnee County Dist. Ct., 1988—. Deacon Topeka Bible Ch., 1981-91; bd. dirs. Cair Paravel Latin Sch., Inc., 1995-98. Named Outstanding Young Man in Am., U.S. Jaycees, 1982. Mem. Kans. Bar Assn., Topeka Bar Assn. (probate com.), Christian Legal Soc. Republican. Probate, Real property, General practice. Home: 3517 SW Oak Pky Topeka KS 66614-3220 Office: Clutter Hinkel & Aadalen LLP 2201 SW 29th St Topeka KS 66611-1908

**AAROE, PAUL MORRIS,** retired superior court judge; b. Oxford, N.J., Dec. 24, 1913; s. Morris and Sadie (Little) A.; m. Marjorie Monroe, July 1, 1952 (div.); m. Eileen O'Rourke Day, May 10, 1958 (dec. Aug. 1979); m. Flora Van Hecke Simmons, Nov. 6, 1983; 1 child, Paul II; 12 stepchildren. AB, Lafayette Coll., Easton, Pa., 1935; LLB, Rutgers U., 1949. Bar: N.J. 1949. Asst. mgr. Sears Roebuck & Co., N.Y.C., 1938-46; assoc. Townsend & Doyle, Jersey City, 1949-52; pvt. practice Warren County, N.J., 1952-72; judge Superior Ct. N.J., Belvidere, 1972-83, 87—; pvt. practice Belvidere, 1983-87. Col. ORD and JAG, U.S. Army, 1942-46, Normandy Invasion, 1944, Battle of the Bulge. Decorated Bronze Star medal. Mem. ABA, JAG Assn., VFW, N.J. Bar Assn., Warren County Bar Assn., Am. Judicature Soc., Am. Legion, Travellers Century Club. Republican. Avocations: travel, chess, music.

**AARON, KENNETH ELLYOT,** lawyer; b. Phila., Nov. 3, 1948; s. Neal L. and Dorothea G. Aaron; m. Phyllis A. Carroll, May 29, 1969; children: Seth Joel, Joshua Scott. BS in Econs., U. Pa., 1970, JD, 1973. Bar: Pa. 1973, U.S. Dist. Ct. (ea. dist.) Pa. 1973, (we. dist.) Pa., 1993, U.S. Ct. Appeals (3rd cir.) 1974, U.S. Supreme Ct. 1977; cert. bus. bankruptcy law specialist, Am. Bankruptcy Bd. Cert. Assoc. Astor & Weiss, Phila., 1973-76; ptnr. Casper & Davidson, P.C., Phila., 1976-80; pvt. practice Phila., 1980-83; ptnr. Garfinkel & Volpicelli, Phila., 1983-86, Mesirov, Gelman, Jaffe, Cramer & Jamieson, Phila., 1986-91, Buchanan Ingersoll P.C., Phila., 1991—. Author: Foreclosure and Repossession, 1989, (chpt.) Bus. Lawyer's Bankruptcy Guide, 1992, BNA's Environmental Due Diligence Guide, 1992, Matthew Bender's Environmental Law Practice Guide, 1992. Commr. Haverford (Pa.) Twp. Planning Bd., 1976-80, mem. lower Merion zoning bd., 1993—; chmn. Indian Creek Homeowners Assn., Wynnewood, Pa., 1985—; mem. Lower Merion steering com., Wynnewood, 1987; campaign chmn. Alan Kessler for Twp. Commr., Wynnewood, 1987, 91, 95; mem. Ea. Dist. of Pa. Bankruptcy Conf., vice chmn. edn. com., 1991, co-chmn. edn. com., 1992, co-chmn. legis. com. 1993; planning commr. Lower Merion Twp. Planning Bd., Ardmore, Pa., 1992; trustee Phila. Bar Found., 1997-99. Recipient Tax Writing award Nat. Assn. Accts., 1970, Am. Jr. award in Creditors' Rights, 1973. Mem. Phila. Bar Assn. (chmn. com. on insolvency issues in real estate 1989—), Phila. Bar Found. (trustee 1997—), Rotary (pres. Haverford Twp. chpt. 1982-83), Hais & Coun. (v.p. 1999—). Avocations: sports, camping, golfing. Bankruptcy, Contracts commercial, Insurance. Office: Buchanan Ingersoll PC Eleven Penn Ctr 14th Fl Philadelphia PA 19103

**AARON, MARCUS, II,** lawyer; b. Pitts., Oct. 24, 1929; s. Marcus Lester and Maxine (Goldmark) A.; m. Barbara Goldman, Feb. 6, 1955; children: Susan, Judith, Barbara. AB, Princeton U., 1950; JD, Harvard U., 1953. Bar: Pa. 1953, D.C. 1953, U.S. Dist. Ct. (we. dist.) Pa. 1956, U.S. Supreme Ct. 1969, U.S. Ct. Appeals (3d cir.) 1971. Assoc. Glick, Berkman & Engel, Pitts., 1956-64; ptnr. Klett, Lieber, Rooney & Schorling, P.C., Pitts., 1965—; asst. solicitor City of Pitts., 1957-67; bd. dirs. Homer Laughlin China Co., Newell, W.Va., 1967—, sec., 1972-88, v.p., 1980-88, pres., treas., 1989—. Trustee Western Pa. Sch. for Blind Children, Pitts., 1969—, pres., 1982-90; bd. dirs. Blue Cross of Western Pa., Pitts., 1972-86, sec., 1984-86; bd. dirs. Centre Engring., Inc., State College, Pa., 1984-92; trustee Rodef Shalom Congregation, Pitts., 1991—, treas., 1996-98, v.p., 1998—. Mem. ABA, Pa. Bar Assn., Allegheny County Bar Assn., Concordia Club, Rivers Club, HYP Pitts. Club. Democrat. Jewish. General corporate, Probate. Home: 1925 Wightman St Pittsburgh PA 15217-1537 Office: Klett Lieber Rooney & Schorling 1 Oxford Ct Fl 40 Pittsburgh PA 15219-1407

**AARONS-HOLDER, CHARMAINE MICHELE,** lawyer; b. Kingston, Jamaica, Jan. 24, 1959; came to U.S., 1982; d. Alan and Berly-Mae Aarons; m. Lisle Anthony Holder, 1982. LLB honors, U. W.I., Barbados, 1980; Cert. Legal Edn., Norman Manley Law Sch., Kingston, 1982; JD cum laude, U. Houston, 1987. Bar: Barbados 1982, Tex. 1987, U.S. Dist. Ct. (so. dist.) Tex. 1988, U.S. Ct. Appeals (5th cir.) 1996. Participating assoc. Fulbright & Jaworski, Houston, 1987-94; atty. Wickliff & Hall, Houston, 1994-99; sr. atty. Equiva Svcs., LLC, Houston, 1999—; bd. dirs. Houston Lawyer Referral Svcs., 1997—. Co-editor, co-author: The Texas Environmental Law Handbook, 1989, 2nd edit., 1990, 3rd edit., 1993. Mem. ABA, Tex. Bar Assn., Houston Bar Assn. (chair campaign for homeless com. 1996-97), Houston Young Lawyers Assn. (chair hunger relief com. 1994-95), Order of Coif, Order of Barons. Democrat. Avocations: swimming, sailing. Environmental, General civil litigation. Office: Equiva Svcs LLC 910 Louisiana St Houston TX 77002-4916

**AARONSON, DAVID ERNEST,** law educator, lawyer; b. Washington, Sept. 19, 1940; s. Edward Allan and May (Rosett) A.; m. Laura Dine, 1991; stepchildren: Dara Prushansky, Jared Prushansky. B.A. in Econs, George Washington U., 1961, M.A., 1964, Ph.D., 1970; LL.B., Harvard U., 1964; LL.M. (E. Barrett Prettyman fellow), Georgetown U., 1965. Bar: D.C. bar 1965, Md. bar 1975, U.S. Supreme Ct. bar 1969. Research asst. Office of Commr., Bur. Labor Stats., U.S. Dept. Labor, Washington, 1961; staff atty. legal intern program Georgetown Grad. Law Center, Washington, 1964-65; research assoc. patent research project dept. econs. George Washington U., Washington, 1966; assoc. firm Aaronson and Aaronson, Washington, 1965-67; ptnr. Aaronson and Aaronson, 1967-70; prof., B.J. Tennery Scholar Am. U. Law Sch., Washington, 1970—; prof. Sch. Justice, Coll. Public and Internat. Affairs, 1981-92; dep. dir. Law and Policy Inst., Jerusalem, Israel, summer, 1978; interim dir. clin. programs Md. Criminal Justice Clinic, 1971-73, founder prosecutor criminal litigation clinic, 1972, co-dir. trial practice litigation program, 1982—; vis. prof. Law Sch. of Hebrew U., Jerusalem, summer, 1978; trustee Montgomery-Prince George's Continuing Legal Edn. Inst., 1983—. Author: Maryland Criminal Jury Instructions and Commentary, 1975, (with N.N. Kittrie and D. Saari) Alternatives to Conventional Criminal Adjudication: Guidebook for Planners and Practitioners, 1977, (with B. Hoff, P. Jaszi, N.N. Kittrie and D. Saari) The New Justice: Alternatives to Conventional Criminal Adjudication, 1977, (with C.T. Dienes and M.C. Musheno) Decriminalization of Public Drunkenness: Tracing the Implementation of a Public Policy, 1981, Public Policy and Police Discretion: Processes of Decriminalization, 1984, (with R. Simon) The Insanity Defense: A Critical Assessment of Law and Policy in the Post-Hinckley Era, 1988, Maryland Criminal Jury Instructions and Commentary, 2d rev. edit., 1988; contbr. articles to legal and public policy jours. Mem. council Friendship Heights Village Council, 1979. Recipient Outstanding Community Service award, 1980; Outstanding Tchr. award Am. U. Law Sch., 1978, 81, Scholar/Tchr. of the Year award Am. U., 1989; Pauline Ruyle Moore scholar in Pub. Law, 1983. Mem. ABA (mem. criminal justice sect. rules of cr. prof. and evid. com. 1991—), D.C. Bar Assn. (chmn. criminal code rev. com. 1971-73), Md. State Bar Assn. (criminal law sect. coun. 1984—, chairperson 1989-90, Robert C. Heeney award 1999), Assn. Am. Law Schs. (elected to sect. coun., criminal justice sect. 1992-97), Montgomery County (Md.) Bar Assn., Soc. for Reform of Criminal Law, Am. Law Inst., Phi Beta Kappa. Office: Am U Law Sch 4801 Massachusetts Ave NW Washington DC 20016-8196

**ABADY, ARLENE,** editor. Editor The Colo. Lawyer, Denver. Office: Colo Bar Assn Inc 1900 Grant St Fl 9 Denver CO 80203-4301

**ABAUNZA, DONALD RICHARD,** lawyer; b. New Orleans, Oct. 25, 1945; s. Alfred E. and Virginia (White) A.; m. Carolyn Thompson; 1 child, Richard. BA, Vanderbilt U., 1966; JD, Tulane U., 1969. Bar: La. 1969, U.S. Dist. Ct. (ea. dist.) La. 1969, U.S. Dist. Ct. (we. dist.) La. 1980, U.S. Supreme Ct. 1986. Assoc. Lemle, Kelleher, Kohlmeyer, Dennery, Hunley, Moss & Frilot, New Orleans, 1969-76; ptnr. Liskow & Lewis, New Orleans, 1977-96, mng. ptnr., 1996—; adj. faculty Tulane Sch. Law, 1981-89. Fellow Am. Coll. Trial Lawyers; mem. La. Bar Assn. (Pres.'s award 1988). Admiralty, Insurance, General civil litigation. Office: Liskow & Lewis 1 Shell Sq 50th Fl 701 Poydras St New Orleans LA 70139-5099

**ABBATT, CANDYCE EWING,** lawyer; b. Dearborn, Mich.. BA, U. Mich., 1979; JD, Wayne State U., 1983. Assoc. Fried & Saperstein P.C., Dearborn, Mich., 1982—. Trustee alumni bd. Law Sch. Wayne State U., Detroit, 1998—; libr. commr. City ofDearborn, Mich., 1998—. Mem. Oakland County Bar Assn., Fairlane Club (mem. athletic com. 1998—), Dearborn Bar Assn. Fax: 248-353-2514. Office: Fried & Saperstein PC 29800 Telegraph Rd Southfield MI 48034-1338

**ABBEY, G(EORGE) MARSHALL,** lawyer, former health care company executive, general counsel; b. Dunkirk, N.Y., July 24, 1933; s. Ralph Ambrose and Grace A. (Fisher) A.; m. Sue Carroll, July 13, 1974; children: Mark, Steven, Michael, Lincoln. BA with high distinction, U. Rochester, 1954; JD with distinction, Cornell U., 1957. Bar: N.H. 1957, Ill. 1965. Atty. McLane, Carleton, Graf, Greene & Brown, Manchester, N.H., 1957-65; atty. Baxter Internat. Inc., Deerfield, Ill., 1965-69, gen. counsel, 1969-72, sec., gen. counsel, 1972-75, v.p., sec., gen. counsel, 1975-82, sr. v.p., gen. counsel, 1985-90, sr. v.p., sec., gen. counsel, 1990-93; pvt. practice, 1993-97; of counsel Bell Boyd & Lloyd, Chgo., 1997—. Editor Cornell Law Rev., 1956-57. Mem. vis. com. Law Sch., U. Chgo., 1978-81; dir. Coun. Puerto Rico-U.S. Affairs, 1988-92; mem. indsl. adv. coun. U. P.R.; dir. P.R.-USA Found., 1975-93, B.U.I.L.D., Chgo., 1980-84, bus. adv. com. B.U.I.L.D. Inc.; bd. dirs. Hundred Club of Lake County, Ill., 1976-86; dir. Food and Drug Law Inst., 1975-93; bd. dirs. Evanston Inventure, 1986-88; former trustee Winnetka Congl. Ch.; dir. Nat. Com. for Quality Health Care, 1988-93; mem. Northwestern U. Corp. Coun. adv. bd., 1976-93; dir. P.R. Cmty. Found., 1986-94; bd. dirs. Better Bus. Bur. Chgo. and No. Ill., 1991-93; mem. Conf. Bd's. Coun. Chief Legal Officers and Legal Quality Coun., 1991-93. Mem. ABA, Ill. Bar Assn., Lake County Bar Assn., Chgo. Bar Assn., Health Industry Mfrs. Assn. (chmn. legal/regulatory affairs 1976-78, bd. dirs. 1978-80, chmn. govt. affairs com. 1980-81), Univ. Club, Exmoor Country Club, Bankers Club (P.R.), Order of the Coif, Phi Beta Kappa. General corporate. Office: Bell Boyd & Lloyd 3 Parkway N Ste 110 Deerfield IL 60015-2548

**ABBOTT, BOB,** state supreme court justice; b. Kans., Nov. 1, 1932. BS, Emporia State U.; JD, Washburn U.; LLM, U. Va. Bar: Kans. 1960. Pvt. practice Junction City, Kans., from 1960; former chief judge Kans. Ct. Appeals; justice Kans. Supreme Ct., 1990—. Office: Kansas Supreme Court 374 Kansas Judicial Ctr Topeka KS 66612-1599*

**ABBOTT, CHARLES FAVOUR,** lawyer; b. Sedro-Wolley, Wash., Oct. 12, 1937; s. Charles Favour and Violette Doris (Boulter) A.; m. Oranee Harward, Sept. 19, 1958; children: Patricia, Stephen, Nelson, Cynthia, Lisa, Alyson. BA in Econs., U. Wash., 1959, JD, 1962. BAr: Calif. 1962, Utah 1981. Law clk. Judge M. Oliver Koelsch, U.S. Ct. Appeals (9th cir.), San Francisco, 1963; assoc. Jones, Hatfield & Abbott, Escondido, Calif., 1964; pvt. practice Escondido, 1964-77, Provo, Utah, 1983-93; of counsel Mueller & Abbott, Escondido, 1997—; ptnr. Abbott, Thorn & Hill, Provo, 1981-83, Abbott & Abbott, Provo, 1993—. Author: How to Do Your Own Legal Work, 1976, 2d edit., 1981, How to Win in Small Claims Court, 1981, How to Be Free of Debt in 24 Hours, 1981, How to Hire the Best Lawyer at the Lowest Fee, 1981, The Lawyers's Inside Method of Making Money, 1979, The Millionaire Mindset, 1987, How to Make Big Money in the Next 30 Days, 1989, Business Legal Manual and Forms, 1990, How to Make Millions in Marketing, 1990, Telemarketing Training Course, 1990, How to Form A Corporation in Any State, 1990, The Complete Asset Protection Plan, 1990, Personal Injury and the Law, 1997, Fen-Phen Fallout--The Medical and Legal Crisis, 1998; mem. editl. bd. Wash. Law Rev. and State Bar Assn. Jour., 1961-62; bd. editors Phen-fen Litigation Strategist, 1998—; contbr. articles to profl. jours. Mem. ATLA, Utah Bar Assn., Calif. Bar Assn., U.S. Supreme Ct. Bar Assn. Personal injury, Administrative and regulatory, General civil litigation. Home: 2830 N Marrcrest Circle Provo UT 84058 Office: Abbott & Abbott 3651 N 100 E Ste 300 Provo UT 84604-4521

**ABBOTT, GREG WAYNE,** state supreme court justice; b. Wichita Falls, Tex., Nov. 13, 1957; s. Calivn Roger and Doris Lacristia (Jacks) Rowley A.; m. Cecilia Therese Phalen, Aug. 15, 1981; 1 child, Audrey. BBA, U. Tex., 1981; JD, Vanderbilt U., 1984. Bar: Tex. 1985, U.S. Dist. Ct. (so. dist.) Tex. 1985. Atty. Butler & Binion, Houston, 1984-92; judge 12th State Dist. Ct., Houston, 1992-96; justice Texas Supreme Ct., 1996—; prof. U. Tex.; mem. com. on Pub. Trust and Confidence in Tex. Cts., Jury Task Force Implementation Project; mem. cert. bd. Tex. Ct. Reporters; exec. com. Family Law 2000 Task Force. Dir. Houston Ctr. for Barrier Free Living, 1986-87; capt. March of Dimes Team Walk, Houston, 1986-87; mem. Gov.'s Com. to Promote Adoption; bd. dirs. Tex. Inst. Rehab. and Rsch., Maywood Children and Family Svcs.; bd. trustees Goodwill Industries; adv. bd. Career and Recovery Resources Inc.;. Named Disabled Person of the Yr. Harris County Com. on Employment of Disabled Persons, 1985, Outstanding Young Texan Tex. Jaycees, 1995; recipient Am. Jurisprudence award Am. Jur, 1983, Named Outstanding Trial Judge, Texas Assn. of Civil Trial and Appellate Specialists, 1995. Mem. State Bar Tex. (com. on legal advt. 1988, Supreme Ct. liason for com. on jud. ethics, jud. conduct commn., code of jud. conduct), Houston Bar Assn. (Houston's Outstanding Young Lawyer 1994), Houston Young Lawyers Assn., Tex. Assn. State Judges (exec. com.). Republican. Roman Catholic. Avocations: snow-skiing, travel, swimming. Home: PO Box 308 Austin TX 78767-0308 Office: Texas Supreme Court PO Box 12248 Austin TX 78711-2248*

**ABBOTT, GUTHRIE TURNER,** law educator. JD, U. Miss., 1967. Fellow in law and humanities Harvard U., Cambridge, Mass., 1975; pvt. practice Gulfport, Miss., 1967-70; mem. faculty Sch. Law U. Miss., 1970—, acting dean, 1985-87, Butler, Snow, O'Mara, Stevens & Cannada endowed lectureship, 1991; vis. scholar Cambridge (Eng.) U., 1987; vice chair adv. com. on the rules of civil practice and procedure Miss. Supreme Ct. Editor Miss. Law Jour. Fellow Miss. Bar Assn. (pres.), Miss. Bar Found.; mem. Am. Inns of Ct. Office: U Miss Law Sch University MS 38677*

**ABBOTT, HIRSCHEL THERON, JR.,** lawyer; b. Clarksdale, Miss., Jan. 11, 1942; s. Hirschel Theron Sr. and Ona Belle (Williamson) A.; m. Mimi Eugenia DuPre, June 14, 1969; children: Barkley, Chip. BBA in Acct., U. Miss., Oxford, 1964; JD, U. Va., Charlottesville, 1971. Bar: La. 1971, Miss. 1971, U.S. Dist. Ct. (ea. dist.) La. 1971, U.S. Ct. Appeals (5th cir.) 1981, U.S. Tax Ct. 1988; bd. cert. tax law specialist. Lawyer Stone, Pigman, Walther, Wittmann & Hutchinson, New Orleans, 1971-75, ptnr., 1975—. Bd. dirs. Episcopal Housing for Srs., Inc., Lambeth House, Inc.; past trustee, sec. Preservation Resource Ctr., New Orleans; past bd. mem., chmn. Trinity Episcopal Sch. Bd. Trustees; past trustee, treas. La. Civil Svc. League; past bd. mem. Uptown Neighborhood Improvement Assn.; past mem., chmn. Jefferson Scholarship Selection Com. U. Va.; past regional chmn. U. Va. Law Sch. Annual Giving Fund; past mem. of vestry Trinity Episcopal Ch.; past mem. Adv. Bd. Jr. League New Orleans. Recipient Monte M. Lemann award, La. Civil Svc. League, 1989. Fellow Am. Coll. Trust and Estate Counsel (mem. charitable planning & exempt orgns. com.), La. Bar Found.; mem. ABA (tax sect., bus. law sect., real property trusts probate sect.), La. Bar Assn. (chmn. tax law specialization commn., tax sect., corp. sect., successions, donations and trusts sect.), Miss. State Bar Assn., New Orleans Estate Planning Coun., Assn. Employee Benefit Planners. Republican. Epicopalian. Taxation, general, General corporate, Estate planning. Office: Stone Pigman Walther et al 546 Carondelet St Ste 100 New Orleans LA 70130-3588

**ABEL, STEVEN L.,** lawyer, mediator; b. N.Y.C., Oct. 2, 1944; s. Wilfred and Lillian Abel; m. Susan J. Abramowitz, Apr. 3, 1966 (div. Apr. 1991); children: Michele, Gregory, Robert; m. Paula Kazdon Davis, July 4, 1991. BA, CCNY, 1966; JD, Bklyn. Law Sch., 1972. Bar: N.Y. 1973. Assoc. atty. Shapiro & Reeder, Spring Valley, N.Y., 1973-76; atty. Reeder & Abel, New City, N.Y., 1976-88, Abel & Brustein-Kampel, New City, 1990—; dir. Ctr. for Family and Divorce Mediation, New City, 1983—; hearing examiner Rockland County Family Ct., 1981-82. Author: Friendly Divorce Guidebook, 1996; editor: Federal Family Law, 1998; contbr. articles to profl. jours. Bd. dirs. Rockland Family Shelter, New City; pres. N.Y. State Coun. on Divorce Mediation, Garden City, 1998-99. Recipient Disting. Svc. award County Legislature, Rockland County, 1986, Achievement award NAACP, 1998. Democrat. Quaker. Avocations: gardening, computers. Family and matrimonial, Alternative dispute resolution. Office: Abel & Brustein-Kampel 2 New Hempstead Rd New City NY 10956-3635

**ABELE, ROBERT CHRISTOPHER,** lawyer; b. Boonville, Mo., Mar. 24, 1958; s. William Arved and Joyce (Gowan) A. AB, U. Mo., 1980; JD, U. Mo., Kansas City, 1983. Bar: Mo. 1983, U.S. Dist. Ct. (we. dist.) Mo. 1983, U.S. Ct. Appeals (8th cir.) 1983, U.S. Ct. Appeals (10th cir.) 1985, U.S. Supreme Ct. 1991, U.S. Ct. Appeals (11th cir.) 1993. Law clk. to judge U.S. Ct. Appeals (8th cir.), 1983-85; assoc. Morrison, Hecker, Curtis, Kuder & Parrish, Kansas City, Mo., 1985-90, ptnr., 1990-91; ptnr. Morrison & Hecker, Kansas City, 1991-95, Badger & Levings, Kansas City, 1995—; adj. prof. U. Mo. Kansas City Sch. Law, 1988. Chmn. Mo. Coun. on Arts, 1989-94; trustee U. Mo.-Kansas City Law Found., 1986-99, pres., 1997-98; bd. dirs. Mid.-Am. Arts Alliance, 1989-98, treas. Nat. Assembly of State Art Agys, 1994-95, 95-96. Recipient Decade award U. Mo.-Kansas City Law Found., 1991. Republican. Avocation: classical vocal music. Federal civil litigation, Product liability, Insurance. Home: 4616 Wyoming St Kansas City MO 64112-1136 Office: Badger & Levings 1101 Walnut St Ste 1207 Kansas City MO 64106-2183

**ABELES, RICHARD ALAN,** lawyer; b. Chgo., June 28, 1937; s. Jerome Guthmann Sr. and Jeanne Katherine (Rosenbacher) Abeles; m. Kathleen Sue Koretz, Jan. 28, 1968; 1 child, Elizabeth Amy. BA, Amherst Coll., 1959; JD, Harvard U., 1963. Bar: Ill. 1963, N.Mex. 1976. Atty. Altheimer & Gray, Chgo., 1963-69; pvt. practice Chgo., 1971-75, Santa Fe, 1976—. Founding pres. Santa Fe Children's Mus., 1987-95; trustee Santa Fe Prep. Sch., 1993-99; elected ofcl. Santa Fe Met. Water Bd., 1988-90. Avocations: skiing, basketball, travel. Fax: 505-984-2040. E-mail: rikal@ibm.net. Real property. Home and Office: 3730 Old Santa Fe Trl Santa Fe NM 87505-4573

**ABELITE, JAHNIS JOHN,** lawyer; b. McMinnville, Tenn., Oct. 10, 1950; s. Augusts and Alexandrine Rita Olga (Tilga) A.; m. Nora Lynn Whitley Baar, May 19, 1990. BA, U. Wash., 1972; JD, U. Puget Sound, 1975. Bar: Wash. 1981, U.S. Dist. Ct. (we. dist.) Wash. 1983. Assoc. Dolack, Hansler et al, Tacoma, 1975-77; legal liaision State of Wash., Olympia, 1977-78; contract specialist State of Wash., Tacoma, 1978-80; contract adminstr. Data I/O Corp., Redmond, Wash., 1980-88; pvt. practice Bothell, Wash., 1981-88; ptnr. Abelite and Gallagher, Seattle, 1988-89; pvt. practice Seattle, 1989—; counsel West Coast Latvian Edn. Ctr., Mountlake Terr., Wash., 1982—; bd. dirs. Latvian Credit Union, Seattle. Mem. ABA, Fed. Bar Assn., Wash. State Trial Lawyers Assn., Seattle-King County Bar Assn. Lutheran. Probate, Family and matrimonial, Contracts commercial. Office: 356 NW Market St Seattle WA 98107-3533

**ABELL, DAVID ROBERT,** lawyer; b. Raleigh, N.C., Nov. 24, 1934; s. De Witt Sterling and Edna Renilde (Doughty) A.; children: David Charles, Elizabeth A. Harrington, Kimberly A. Creasman, Hilary Ayres, Glenn Bryan; m. Ellen Penrod Hackmann, July 27, 1985. BA, Denison U., 1956; JD (Internat. fellow), Columbia U., 1963. Bar: Pa. 1963, Ill. 1973. Assoc. Ballard, Spahr, Andrews & Ingersoll, Phila., 1963-68; sec., counsel Hurst Performance, Inc., Warminster, Pa., 1969-70; sec., gen. counsel STP Corp., Des Plaines, Ill., 1970-72; ptnr. David R. Abell Ltd., Winnetka, Ill., 1974—, Rooks, Pitts & Poust, Chgo., 1996—. Author: Residential Real Estate System, 1977, 2d edit., 1990. Trustee Music Inst. Chgo., 1988-96; bd. govs. Winnetka Cmty. House, 1993-96. Aviator USMCR, 1956-60. Mem. ABA, Ill. Bar Assn., Chgo. Bar Assn., Rotary (pres. Winnetka 1977-78). Episcopalian. Estate planning, Probate, Estate taxation. Home: 740 Oak St Winnetka IL 60093-2521 Office: Rooks Pitts & Poust 560 Green Bay Rd Ste 407 Winnetka IL 60093-2243

**ABELL, RICHARD BENDER,** lawyer, federal judicial official; b. Phila., Dec. 2, 1943; s. Ernest George and Charlotte Amelia (Bender) A.; m. Lucia del Carmen Lombana-Cadavid, Dec. 2, 1968; children: David, Christian, Rachel. BA in Internat. Affairs, George Washington U., 1966, JD, 1974. Bar: Pa. 1974. Vol. Peace Corps, Colombia, 1967-69; assoc. Reilly & Fogwell, West Chester, Pa., 1974-80; asst. dist. atty. Chester County, Pa., 1974-79; staff mem. U.S. Senator Richard Schweiker, Washington, 1979-80; dir. Office of Program Devel. Peace Corp., Washington, 1981-83; dep. asst. atty. gen. U.S. Dept. Justice, Washington, 1983-86, asst. atty. gen., 1986-90; special master U.S. Ct. Fed. Claims, 1991—; mem. adj. faculty Del. Law Sch., Wilmington, 1975-77, West Chester State U., 1976; bd. dirs. Fed. Prison Industries, Inc., 1985-91; chmn. Nat. Crime Prevention Coalition, 1986-90; mem. adv. bd. Nat. Inst. Corrections, 1986-90; co-chmn. adv. com. Nat. Ctr. for State and Local Law Enforcement Tng., 1987-90; vice chmn. rsch. and devel. rev. bd. Dept. Justice, 1987-89; mem. nat. drug policy bd. Enforcement Coordinating Group and Coordinating Group for Drug Abuse Prevention and Health, The White House, Washington, 1988-89. Author: Peter Smith of Westmoreland County, Va. (Died 1741) and Some Descendents, 1996, Sojourns of a Patriot: Field and Prison Papers of An Unreconstructed Confederate, 1998. Chmn. Young Rep. Nat. Fedn., Washington, 1979-81; mem. exec. com. Rep. Nat. Com., 1979-81; mem. fed. coordinating coun. on Juvenile Justice and Delinquency Prevention, 1986-90; mem. Pres.'s Task Force on Adoption, 1987-88; mem. Pres.'s Commn. on Agrl. Workers, 1988-93. With U.S. Army, 1969-71. Decorated Purple Heart, Army Commendation medal for heroism, Air medal. Episcopalian. Home: 8209 Chancery Ct Alexandria VA 22308-1514

**ABELMAN, ARTHUR F.,** lawyer; b. N.Y.C., June 12, 1933; s. Bert and Myra (Dickoff) A. A.B., Harvard U., 1954, J.D., 1957. Bar: N.Y. 1958, U.S. Dist. Ct. (so. and ea. dist.) N.Y. 1958, U.S. Ct. Appeals (2d cir.) 1958. Assoc. Casey Lane & Mittendorf, N.Y.C., 1957-59; counsel Am. Petroleum Inst., N.Y.C., 1959-61; corp. sec. Pocket Books, Inc., N.Y.C., 1961-65; assoc. Weil Gotshal Manges, N.Y.C., 1965-79; counsel Moses & Singer, N.Y.C., 1979—; pres. Millan House, Inc., N.Y.C., 1982—. Pres., Sculpture Ctr., Inc., N.Y.C., 1979-85, trustee, 1971—, exec. com. 1988—, treas., 1991—; trustee Neighbors of the Seventh, Inc., Norman Rockwell Art Collection Trust, E.E. Cummings Trust; trustee James Beard Found., Inc., mem. exec. com., 1995—. Mem. ABA, N.Y. Bar Assn., Assn. of Bar of City of N.Y. Republican. Jewish. Club: Harvard. Libel, Trademark and copyright, Real property. Home: 116 E 68th St New York NY 10021-5905 Office: Moses & Singer LLP 1301 Avenue Of The Americas New York NY 10019-6022

**ABELMAN, HENRY MOSS,** lawyer; b. Lake Charles, La., June 9, 1953; s. Mose and Selma (Moskowitz) A.; m. Andrea Lee Zimmer, Feb. 14, 1985. BA in Econs., Northwestern U., 1975, MM in Bus., 1976; postgrad., NYU, 1977; JD, Fordham U., 1983. Bar: N.Y. 1984, N.C. 1993, U.S. Dist. Ct. (so. and ea. dists.) N.Y. 1985. Br. mgr. Tymshare, Inc., N.Y.C., 1977-82; v.p. Dialogue, Inc., N.Y.C., 1982-85; assoc. Brown, Raysman & Millstein, N.Y.C., 1985-89; assoc. counsel Am. Express Info. Svcs. Corp., N.Y.C., 1989-91; gen. counsel First Data Health Sys. Corp., Charlotte, N.C., 1992—, v.p. procurement, assoc. gen. counsel, 1995—. Contbr. articles to profl. jours.; contbg. columnist Micro Market World, 1986-87. Mem. ABA, Computer Law Assn., N.C. Bar Assn., Nat. Health Lawyers Assn., N.Y. County Lawyers Assn. (chmn. com. sci., tech. and law 1985-88). Republican. Jewish. Computer, Trademark and copyright, General corporate. Home: 8360 Sentinae Chase Dr Roswell GA 30076-4498 Office: First Data Health Sys Corp 10101 Claude Freeman Dr Charlotte NC 28262-4338

**ABENDROTH, DOUGLAS WILLIAM,** lawyer; b. Seattle, Dec. 9, 1952; s. William G. and Doris E. (Bergum) A. BA, UCLA, 1976; JD, Loyola U., L.A., 1982. Bar: Calif. 1982, U.S. Dist. Ct. (cen., so. and no. dists.) Calif. 1982, U.S. Ct. Appeals (9th cir.) 1982. Title examiner Calif. Land Title Co., Santa Ana, 1977-80; assoc. O'Melveny & Myers, Newport Beach, Calif., 1982-89, ptnr., 1990—; bd. dirs. Orange County Bar Found., Santa Ana, 1992—. Petty officer USNR, 1972-78. Mem. Orange County Bar Assn. Presbyterian. General civil litigation, Constitutional, Libel. Office: O'Melveny & Myers 610 Newport Center Dr Ste 1700 Newport Beach CA 92660-6429

**ABLAN, MICHAEL C.,** lawyer, law educator; b. La Crosse, Wis., Mar. 11, 1949; s. Charles J. and Joyce D. (Corey) A.; m. Patti J. Severson-Langer, July 10, 1976 (div. Jan. 1984); children: Alyssa, John, Antony. BABA, Gustavus Adolphus Coll., 1971; JD, Marquette U., 1974. Bar: Wis. 1974, Minn. 1992; U.S. Dist. Ct. (ea. and we. dists.) Wis. 1973, U.S. Tax Ct. 1980, U.S. Ct. Appeals (7th cir.) 1989; cert. arbitrator; Title Ins. lic., Wis. Pvt. practice Michael C. Ablan Law Office, La Crosse, Wis., 1974—; adj. prof. Faculty Bus. Law and Health Care Law Viterbo Coll., La Crosse, 1978—; mem. Alternative Dispute Resolution Panl, Mpls., 1994—; pub. spkr. in field; cons. Small Bus. Devel. Ctr.; lectr. Faculty of Bus. Law, Western Wis. Tech. Coll., La Crosse, U. Wis.-LaCrosse. Bd. dirs. Fauver Hills PTO, No. Hills PTO and Hintgen Sch. PTO; mem., founder St. Elias Eastern Orthodox Ch., La Crosse, 1976—; participant Big Brother/Big Sister Program, La Crosse, adv. bd. mem.; ptnr. Spl. Olympics, 1995; fund raiser, mem. Am. Heart Assn., La Crosse, 1995. Mem. State Bar of Wis. (bus. law sect., entrepreneurial law com., bus. assistance program vol., lawyer referral and info. svc. mem.), State Bar of Minn., Coalition of Wis. aging Groups, La Crosse Area Estate Planning Coun., Wis. Realtors Assn. (affiliate), Tri-State Quality Improvement Network, Greater La Cross Area C. of C. (small bus. coun.), Winona Area C. of C., La Crescent Area C. of C., Caledonia Area C. of C., The Wilderness Soc., Valley View Fitness & Racquet Club, Friends of Hixon Forest Nature Ctr., Greenpeace, Nat. Parks and Conservation Assn., La Crosse Nordic Ski Club, United Temple Assn., Loyal Order of Moose, Grand Lodge Free & Accepted Masons of Wis., Wis. Bow Hunters, La Crosse Cmty. Found., La Crosse County Hist. Soc., Am. Arbitration Assn., Nat. Trust for Hist. Preservation, Native Am. Rights Fund, Am. Task Force for Lebanon, La Cross Riding Club, U.S. Tennis Assn. Avocations: tennis, scuba diving, horseback riding, golf, cross country skiing. General corporate, Probate, Federal civil litigation. Office: 205 5th Ave S Ste 411 La Crosse WI 54601-4059

**ABLES, CHARLES ROBERT,** lawyer, judge; b. South Pittsburg, Tenn., Sept. 13, 1930; s. William McKinley and Iva (Baldwin) A.; m. Rada B. Edmonds, May 20, 1949; children: Patricia Joan, Barbara Elain. B.S., U. Chattanooga, 1964; LL.B., U. Tenn., 1965. Bar: Tenn. 1965, U.S. Dist. Ct. (ea. dist.) Tenn. 1965, U.S. Ct. Appeals (6th cir.) 1977. Sole practice, South Pittsburg, 1971—; judge Manion County Juvenile Ct., Jasper, Tenn., 1980-90. Served with USNG, 1948-50. Mem. Lions, Masons. Republican. Presbyterian. Juvenile, General practice. Home: 105 Lee Hunt Ave South Pittsburg TN 37380-1745 Office: 320 Cedar Ave South Pittsburg TN 37380

**ABLON, KAREN HERRICK,** lawyer; b. Ann Arbor, Mich., Mar. 4, 1966; d. Henry Victor Herrick and Deborah Ruth (Kazdan) Bruckner. BBA, U. Tex., 1988; JD, So. Meth. U., 1991. Bar: Tex. 1991. Lawyer Law Offices Tom Hall, Ft. Worth, 1991—. Mem. ABA, AAUW, Assn. Trial Lawyers Am., Tex. Trial Lawyers Assn., Tarrant County Trial Lawyers Assn., Ft. Worth Young Lawyers Assn. (high sch. mock trial com. 1991—). Jewish. Avocations: dancing, reading. Personal injury, State civil litigation, Product liability. Office: Law Offices Tom Hall 2605 Airport Fwy Ste 100 Fort Worth TX 76111-2373

**ABRAHAM, NICHOLAS ALBERT,** lawyer, real estate developer; b. Boston, Sept. 17, 1941; s. Nicholas and Ida (Kida) A.; m. Evie Stathopoulos, June 30, 1968; children: Annise, Nicholas. BS, Boston U., 1963, JD, 1966. Bar: Mass. 1966, U.S. Dist. Ct. Mass. 1968, U.S. Ct. Appeals (1st cir.) 1971. Sr. ptnr. Abraham-Hanna, P.C., Boston, 1968-88; CEO Boston Investors Fund, Inc., 1988-93; pres., CEO Abraham Properties Inc., Boston, 1993—; CEO., chmn., founder STOR/GARD, Inc., 1996—. Author: Doing Business in Egypt, 1979, Doing Business in Saudi Arabia, 1980, Doing Business in Kuwait, 1982. Bd. of trustees Boston U. Coll. of Bus. Administrn., 1968; chmn. fund raising com. Boy Scouts Am., 1968; coach Weston Little League; founder of Weston Youth Hockey League, 1985. Served with U.S. Army, 1966-67; to lt. comdr. USN, 1967-74. Republican. Eastern Orthodox. State civil litigation, Real property, General corporate. Home: 21 Buckskin Dr Weston MA 02493-1129 Office: Abraham Properties Inc 581 Boylston St Fl 3 Boston MA 02116-3608

**ABRAHAMS, DANIEL B.,** lawyer; b. Norwalk, Conn., Sept. 23, 1955; s. Kwyn and Edna Charik Abrahams; m. Shriley Berry, Apr. 5, 1980; children: David, Michael. BA, Hobart Coll., 1977; MA, Washington U., 1979; JD, George Washington U., 1983. Bar: D.C. 1983, Md. 1984. Investigator Montgomery County Govt., Silver Springs, Md., 1978-80; lawyer Epstein, Becker & Green, P.C., Washington, 1983—; lectr. fed. publs., 1985-98; adj. prof. George Washington U., 1986-93. Author: Fair Labor Standards Handbook, 1985, Employer's Guide to the FLSA, 1993, Government Contracts Compliance Guide, 1994. Democrat. Avocations: children. Government contracts and claims, Labor, General civil litigation. Office: Epstein Becker & Green PC 1227 25th St NW Ste 700 Washington DC 20037-1175

**ABRAHAMS, SAMUEL,** writer, retired lawyer; b. N.Y.C., Dec. 3, 1923; s. Isaac and Ida (Ehrman) A.; m. Ida Savitsky, July 8, 1970. BA, Bklyn. Coll., 1945; MA, Columbia U., 1946; JD, Bklyn. Law Sch., 1956; LLM, NYU, 1961; PhD, Heed U., 1993. Bar: N.Y. 1957, U.S. Dist. Ct. (ea. and so. dists.) N.Y. 1962, U.S. Supreme Ct. 1976. Pvt. practice, Bklyn., 1958-88; arbitrator Civil Ct. N.Y.C., 1982-87; part-time adminstrv. judge parking violations bur., 1976-88; lectr. on fgn. travel, law and politics. Author: Law in Family Conflict, 1970; contbr. articles to profl. and popular jours., newspapers. Mem. Getting Equitable Treatment. With U. S. Army, 1942-43. Mem. ABA, Friends of North Miami Beach Libr., Young Israel of Greater Miami, North Dade Profls. Jewish Fedn. Grtr. Miami, Bklyn. Coll. Alumni Assn. Democrat. Avocations: travel, reading, sports, community involvement. Family and matrimonial, Criminal, Probate.

**ABRAHAMSON, A. CRAIG,** lawyer; b. Washington, May 24, 1954; s. Joseph Labe and Helen Dorothy (Selis) A.; m. Mary Ellen Bernard, Dec. 29, 1979; children: Nicholas Eric, Amy Nicole. BA, U. Minn., 1976; JD, U. Tulsa, 1979. Bar: Minn. 1979, U.S. Dist. Ct. Minn. 1979, Okla. 1982, U.S. Dist. Ct. (no. and ea. dists.) Okla. 1983, Mo. 1991. Assoc. Law Office of Joseph L. Abrahamson, Mpls., 1979-82, Freese & March, Tulsa, 1982-83, Barlow & Cox, Tulsa, 1983-86; pvt. practice Tulsa, 1986-95; ptnr. Levinson, Smith & Abrahamson, Tulsa, 1995—. V.p. program com. Youth Svcs., Tulsa, Inc., Leadership Tulsa Class XVII, 1989-92; sec. Great Expectations Educators, Inc., 1995—. Recipient Am. Jurisprudence Evidence award Lawyers Co-operative Pub. Co. Bancroft-Whitney Co., 1978. Mem. ABA (litigation sect.), Okla. Bar Assn. (family law sect.), Assn. Trial Lawyers Am., Okla. Trial Lawyers Assn., Tulsa County Bar Assn. (profl. responsibility com.). Democrat. Jewish. Lodge: Masons. Avocations: fishing, camping, travel, tennis. Family and matrimonial, State civil litigation, Bankruptcy. Home: 7518 S 107th East Ave Tulsa OK 74133-2530 Office: Levinson Smith & Abrahamson 35 E 18th St Tulsa OK 74119-5201 also: PO Box 3366 Tulsa OK 74101-3366

**ABRAHAMSON, SHIRLEY SCHLANGER,** state supreme court chief justice; b. N.Y.C., Dec. 17, 1933; d. Leo and Ceil (Sauerteig) Schlanger; m. Seymour Abrahamson, Aug. 26, 1953; 1 son, Daniel Nathan. AB, NYU, 1953; JD, Ind. U., 1956; SJD, U. Wis., 1962. Bar: Ind. 1956, N.Y. 1961, Wis. 1962. Asst. dir. Legis. Drafting Research Fund, Columbia U. Law Sch., 1957-60; since practiced in Madison, Wis., 1962-76; mem. firm LaFollette, Sinykin, Anderson & Abrahamson, 1962-76; justice Supreme Ct. Wis., Madison, 1976-96, chief justice, 1996—; prof. U. Wis. Sch. Law, 1966-92; bd. visitors Ind. U. Sch. Law, 1972—, U. Miami Sch. Law, 1982-97, U. Chgo. Law Sch., 1988-92, Brigham Young U., Sch. Law, 1986-88, Northwestern U. Law Sch., 1989-94; chmn. Wis. Rhodes Scholarship Com., 1992-95; chmn. nat. adv. com. on ct.-adjudicated and ct.-ordered health care George Washington U. Ctr. Health Policy, Washington, 1993-95; mem. DNA adv. bd. FBI, U.S. Dept. Justice, 1995—; bd. dirs. Inst. Jud. Adminstrn., Inc., NYU Sch. Law; chair Nat. Inst. Justice's Commn. Future DNA Evidence, 1997—. Editor: Constitutions of the United States (National and State) 2 vols, 1962. Mem. study group program of rsch., mental health and the law John D. and Catherine T. MacArthur Found., 1988-96; mem. coun. fund for rsch. on dispute resolution Ford Found., 1987-91; bd. dirs. Wis. Civil Liberties Union, 1968-72; mem. ct. reform adv. panel Internat. Human Rights Law Group Cambodia Project, 1995-97. Mem. ABA (coun., sect. legal edn. and admissions to bar 1976-86, mem. commn. on undergrad. edn. in law and the humanities 1978-79, standing com. on pub. edn. 1991-95, mem. commn. on access to justice/2000 1993—, mem. adv. bd. Ctrl. and East European law initiative 1994—, mem. consortium on legal svcs. and the public 1995—, vice-chair ABA Coalition for Justice 1997—), Wis. Bar Assn., Dane County Bar Assn., 7th Cir. Bar Assn., Nat. Assn. Women Judges, Am. Law Inst. (mem. coun. 1985—). Home: 2012 Waunona Way Madison WI 53713-1616 Office: Wis Supreme Ct 231 East Capitol PO Box 1688 Madison WI 53701-1688

**ABRAMOVITZ, MICHAEL JOHN,** lawyer; b. N.Y.C., Feb. 7, 1939; s. Max and Anne (Causey) A.; m. Patricia Carson, 1959 (div. 1968); 1 child, Deborah Woodbury; m. Frances Koncilja, Nov. 12, 1972 (div. 1983); 1 child, Nicholas; m. Carol Lay, May 24, 1988; 1 child, Alexandra. AB, Harvard U., 1961; MA in Maths., U. Calif., 1967; postgrad., U. Calif., Berkeley; JD, U. Colo., 1972. Bar: Colo. 1972, U.S. Dist. Ct. Colo. 1972, U.S. Ct. Appeals (10th cir.) 1973, U.S. Tax Ct. 1973, U.S. Supreme Ct. 1975, U.S. Ct. Claims 1977. Law clk. to presiding justice Colo. Supreme Ct., Denver, 1972-73; ptnr. Drexler, Wald & Abramovitz, Denver, 1973-84, Berenbaum & Weinshienk, Denver, 1984-86, Abramovitz, Merriam & Shaw, Denver, 1987-94, Abramovitz & Merriam, Denver, 1994—. Mem. ABA (taxation sect., civil and criminal tax penalties com., litigation sect.), Colo. Bar Assn. Taxation, general, Federal civil litigation, Criminal. Office: Abramovitz & Merriam 1625 Broadway Ste 770 Denver CO 80202-4717

**ABRAMOVSKY, ABRAHAM,** law educator, lawyer; b. Jerusalem, Aug. 12, 1946; came to U.S., 1956; s. Abba and Ahuva (Kruglikov) A.; m. Deborah Lee Wright, Sept. 21, 1970; children: Aviva, Abba, Ari, Dov. BA, Queens Coll., 1967; JD cum laude, SUNY, Buffalo, 1970; LLM, Columbia U., 1971, JSD, 1976. Bar: N.Y. 1971, U.S. Dist. Ct. (so. and ea. dists.) N.Y. 1982, U.S. Supreme Ct. 1982. Pvt. practice N.Y.C., 1971-72, 73-75; asst. prof. Coll. of Law U. Toledo, 1975-77; assoc. prof. Sch. Law Pace U., White Plains, N.Y., 1977-79; prof. Sch. Law Fordham U., N.Y.C., 1979—, dir. Internat. Criminal Law Ctr., 1990—. Editor: Federal Criminal Law and the Corporate Counsel, 1979; columnist N.Y. Law Jour., N.Y.C., 1982—; guest host Cable TV, N.Y.C.; interviewee CBS Nightwatch, ABC News, Daily News, Newsday, L.A. Time, N.Y. Times, San Francisco Chronicle; contbr. articles to profl. jours. Fordham U. grantee, 1987; vis. fellow U. Warwick Sch. of Law, Coventry, Eng., 1976; Charles Evans Hughes fellow Columbia U., 1972-73. Mem. ABA (vice chair internat. criminal law com.), Anti-Defamation League (bd. dirs. L.I. chpt.). Jewish. Office: Fordham U Sch Law 140 W 62nd St New York NY 10023-7407

**ABRAMOWITZ, JOSHUA LON,** lawyer; b. Feb. 21, 1969. BA, Colgate U., 1991; JD, Yale U., 1997. Bar: N.Y. 1998. Assoc. Simpson Thacher & Bartlett, N.Y.C., 1997-99. Editor The Pub. Interest, 1992-94, Yale Law Jour., 1995-97. Mem. ABA, N.Y. State Bar Assn., Assn. of Bar of City of N.Y., Phi Beta Kappa.

**ABRAMOWITZ, ROBERT LESLIE,** lawyer; b. Phila., May, 1950; s. Nathan P. and Lucille H. (Rader) A.; m. Susan Margaret Stewart, Dec. 1, 1974; children: David, Catherine. BA, Yale U., 1971; JD, Harvard U., 1974. Bar: Pa. 1974, N.J. 1975. Assoc. Ballard, Spahr, Andrews & Ingersoll, Phila., 1974-81, ptnr., 1981-90; ptnr. Morgan Lewis & Bockius, LLP, Phila., 1990—; adj. prof. law Villanova U., 1986—. Trustee Moorestown (N.J.) Friends Sch., 1981-90, Rock Sch. of Pa. Ballet, 1990—; pres. Harvard Law Sch. Assn. Greater Phila., 1999—. Mem. ABA, Pa. Bar Assn., Phila. Bar Assn. (exec. com. probate sect. 1982-85, pension com. 1985-94, chair, 1987-89), Yale Club, Merion Cricket Club. Pension, profit-sharing, and employee benefits, Estate planning. Home: 623 Pembroke Rd Bryn Mawr PA 19010-3613 Office: Morgan Lewis & Bockius LLP 1701 Market St Philadelphia PA 19103-2903

**ABRAMS, JEFFREY ALAN,** lawyer; b. Indpls., Mar. 28, 1956; s. Jerome Jeffrey and Barbara (Katz) A.; m. Pamela Flack, July 18, 1981 (div. Mar. 1986); 1 child, Grant Jeffrey; m. Lynn Jacobs, Oct. 21, 1990; children: Joshua David, Rachel Lauren. BS, Miami U., Oxford, Ohio, 1978; JD, Ind. U., 1981. Bar: Ind. 1981, U.S. Dist. Ct. (so. dist.) Ind. 1981. Assoc. Dann Pecar Newman & Kleiman, Indpls., 1981-86, ptnr., 1986—, mng. ptnr., pres., 1998—; lectr. landlord and tenant law, comml. leases, other subjects, 1984—. Bd. dirs. Jewish Cmty. Ctr., 1994—, v.p., 1997—; bd. dirs., exec. com. Ind. chpt. Crohns and Colitis Found. Am., 1996—; grad. Wexact Heritage Found., 1987.. Mem. ABA, Ind. Bar Assn., Indpls. Bar Assn., Broadmoor Club Indpls. (bd. dirs. 1985—, sec. 1986-87, v.p. 1988-91, pres. 1992-93). Republican. Real property, Contracts commercial, Landlord-tenant. Office: Dann Pecar Newman et al Box 82008 Indianapolis IN 46282-0002

**ABRAMS, NANCY,** lawyer; b. Indiana, Pa., Dec. 14, 1954; d. Leonard Allen and Sally (Claster) A.; m. Frederick Segal, Apr. 12, 1987; 1 child, Sara. AB cum laude, Harvard U., 1976; JD, U. Pitts., 1979. Bar: Pa. 1979, Fla. 1980, U.S. Dist. Ct. (mid. and ea. dists.) Pa. 1979. Assoc. Rosenberg & Ufberg, Scranton, Pa., 1979-84, Pechner, Dorfman, Wolffe, Rounick & Cabot, Phila., 1984-87, Myerson & Kuhn, Phila, 1988, Blank, Rome, Comisky & McCauley, Phila., 1988-89; pvt. practice law Phila., 1990-95; with Jablon, Epstein, Wolf & Drucker, Phila., 1996—. Chmn. Red Cross Ctr. City Blood Council, Scranton, 1982-84. Mem. ABA (labor and employment law sect.), Pa. Bar Assn. (labor and employment law sect.), Fla. Bar Assn. (labor and employment law sect.), Phila. Bar Assn., Lackawanna County Bar Assn. (labor and employment law sect.). Avocation: theatre. Labor, Pension, profit-sharing, and employee benefits. Office: Jablon Epstein a Professional Corporation The Bellevue Broad And Walnut St Fl 9 Philadelphia PA 19102

**ABRAMS, NORMAN,** law educator, university administrator; b. Chgo., July 7, 1933; s. Harry A. and Gertrude (Dick) A.; m. Toshka Alster, 1977; children: Marshall David, Julie, Hanna, Naomi. AB, U. Chgo., 1952, JD, 1955. Bar: Ill. 1956, U.S. Supreme Ct. 1967. Assoc. in law Columbia U., 1955-57; rsch. assoc. Harvard U., 1957-59; sec. Harvard-Brandeis Coop. Rsch. for Israel's Legal Devel., 1957-58, dir., 1959; mem. faculty law sch. UCLA, 1959—, prof. law, 1964—, assoc. dean law, 1989-91, vice chancellor acad. pers., 1991—, interim exec. v. chancellor, spring 1998, co-dir. Ctr. for internat. and strategic studies, 1982-83, chmn. steering com., 1985-87, 88-89; vis. prof. Hebrew U., 1969-70, Forchheimer vis. prof., 1986; vis. prof. Bar Ilan U., 1970-71, 78, U. So. Calif., 1972, 73, Stanford U., 1977, U. Calif. at Berkeley, 1977, Loyola U., Los Angeles, summers 1974, 75, 76, 79; spl. asst. to U.S. atty. gen., also prof.-in-residence criminal div. Dept. Justice, 1966-67; reporter for So. Calif. indigent accused persons study Am. Bar Found., 1963; cons. Gov. Calif. Commn. L.A. Riots, 1965, Pres.'s Commn. Law Enforcement and Adminstrn. Justice, 1966-67, Nat. Commn. on Reform of Fed. Criminal Laws, 1967-69, Rand Corp., 1968-74, Ctr. for Adminstrv. Justice, ABA, 1973-77, Nat. Adv. Commn. on Criminal Justice Stds., Organized Crime Task Force, 1976; spl. hearing officer conscientious objector cases Dept. Justice, 1967-68; vis. scholar Inst. for Advanced Studies, Hebrew U., summer, 1994. Author: (with others) Evidence, Cases and Materials, 7th edit., 1983, 8th edit., 1988, 9th edit., 1997, Federal Criminal Law and Its Enforcement, 1986, 2d edit. (with S. Beale), 1993; mem. editorial bd. Criminal Law Forum, 1990—. Chmn. Jewish Conciliation Bd., L.A., 1975-81; bd. dirs. Bet Tzedek, 1975-85, L.A. Hillel Coun., 1979-82, Shalhevet High Sch.; chmn. So. Calif. region Am. Profs. for Peace in Middle East, 1981-83; bd. dirs. met. region Jewish Fedn., 1982-88, v.p. 1982-83; pres. Westwood Kehillah Congregation, 1985. Mem. Soc. for Reform of Criminal Law (mem. exec. com. 1994—), Phi Beta Kappa. Office: UCLA 405 Hilgard Ave Los Angeles CA 90095-9000

**ABRAMS, ROBERT,** lawyer, former state attorney general; b. Bronx, N.Y., July 4, 1938; s. Benjamin and Dorothy (Kaplan) A.; m. Diane B. Schulder, Sept. 15, 1974; children: Rachel Schulder, Becky Schulder. B.A., Columbia U., 1960; J.D., NYU, 1963; LL.D. (hon.), Hofstra U., 1979; Lugum Doctoris (hon.), Yeshiva U., 1984; LLD (hon.), L.I. U., 1989, Pace U., 1991. Mem. N.Y. State Assembly, 1965-69; pres. Borough of Bronx, 1970-78; atty. gen. State of N.Y., 1979-93; ptnr. Stroock & Stroock & Lavan, N.Y.C., 1994—; panel mem. of disting. neutrals CPR Inst. Contbr. articles to profl. publs.; writer column Nat. Law Jour., N.Y. Law Jour., N.Y. Times, N.Y. Newsday, N.Y. Post, N.Y. Daily News, Buffalo News, Albany Times Union, Ganette Suburban Newspapers, The Harvard Environ. Law Rev., NYU Law Rev., Columbia Jour. Environ. Law, Pace Environ. Law Rev., Washburn Law Rev., Albany Law Rev., Pace Law Rev., The Jour. of State Gov. Del. Dem. Nat. Conv., 1972, 76, 80, 84, mem. platform com., 1988; elector Electoral Coll., 1988. Recipient Adam Clayton Powell Pub. Svc. award, Interfaith award Coun. Chs., N.Y.C., Bronx Community Coll. medallion for Svc., Scroll of Honor plaque United Jewish Appeal, Benjamin Cardozo award for legal excellence Jewish Lawyers Guild, Brotherhood award B'nai B'rith, Man of Yr. award NAACP, Alumni Achievement award NYU Sch. Law, Environmentalist of Yr. award Environ. Planning Lobby N.Y., Disting. Pub. Svc. Citation Bus. Coun. N.Y. State, N.Y. State Sheriff's Assn. award, Nat. Crime Victims award, Torch of Liberty award Anti-Defamation League, Anatoly Scharansky Freedom award N.Y. Conf. Soviet Jewry, Environmentalist of Yr. award L.I. Pine Barrens Soc., Il Leone de San Marco Hon. Italian Am. award, Cavaliere medal Pres. Italy, Pres. award Marist Coll., Hubert Humphrey Humanitarian award United Fedn. Tchrs., Law Day award N.Y. State Trial Lawyers Assn., Contbns. to Urban Law award Fordham Law Jour., Deans medal Law Sch. NYU, Margaret Sanger award N.Y. State Family Planning Advocates, Lehman/LaGuardia Civic Achievement award Anti-Defamation League B'nai B'rith and Commn. on Social Justice of the Order of Sons of Italy, Father of the Yr. award Nat. Father's Day Com., B'nai Zion Bill of Rights award, Avodah award Jewish Tchr's. Assn., Man of the Yr. award N.Y. State Consumer Assembly, Rodef Tzedek Pursuer of Justice award Restructionist Rabbinical Coll., Humanitarian award Rochester Labor and Religious Coalition, Special Recognition award Profl. Women in Construction and Allied Industries, Humanitarian award Long Island Assn. for Children with Learning Disabilities, Man of the Yr. award Mental Illness Found., N.Y. State Ct's. Man of the Yr. award Shamrai Tzedek Soc., Grand Marshall award Schenectady Labor Coun. Labor Day Parade, Louis Brandeis award Zionist Orgn. Am., Lubavich Tzivos Hashem award, Chassidius in Am. Exemplary Leadership award Bostoner Chassidum, Recognition for Pub. Svc. award Greater Buffalo AFL-CIO Coun., Effort on Behalf of the Elderly award Workmen's Circle Home & Infirmary For the Aged, Dedication Concerning Reproductive Rights award N.Y. Coun. of Jewish Women, Citation of Appreciation N.Y. State Assn. of Architects, Pesach-Tikvah Hope Developer award, Pub. Svc. award N.Y. Soc. Clin. Psychologists, Cmty. Achievement award Am. Orthodox Fedn., State Svc. award Nat. Columbus Day Com., Environmentalist of the Yr. award Sierra Club, Svc. award N.Y. State Jewish War Veterans, Cadet award N.Y.C. Mission Soc., Disting. Achievement award AMIT Women, Man of the Yr. award Nassau County Police Res. Assn., Ann. award Lubavitch Youth Orgn., Appreciation award Japanese C. of C. of N.Y., Friend of the Cmty. award Empire State Pride Agenda, Roland Smith award Capital Region chpt. N.Y. Civil Liberties Union, Scharansky Freedom award L.I. Com. on Soviet Jewry, Cert. of Honor award N.Y. League of Histadrut, Scouting For the Handicapped Outstanding Svc. award Greater N.Y. Coun. of Boy Scouts of Am., Citizen of the Yr. award We. N.Y. Labor Coalition, Svc. award Citizen's Coun. for the Cmty. of Mentally Retarded, Rockland Hosp. Guild, Man of the Yr. award The Shield Inst. for Retarded Children, Maccabean Svc. award N.Y. Bd. of Rabbis, Thurgood Marshall award Bridge Builders Albany, Pro Choice award Naral N.Y., Dist. Humanitarian award Insts. Applied Human Dynamics, Life-Long Dedication award Holocaust Meml. Com.; named Man of Yr. St. Patrick's Home Aged and Infirm, Man of Yr. State Israel Bonds. Mem. N.Y. State Bar Assn. (Environ. Acheivement award), Nat. Assn. of Attys. Gen. (pres. 1988-89, chmn. environ. protection com. 1982-85, chmn. antitrust com. 1985-88, chmn. civil rights com. 1990-92, chmn. ea. regional conf. of attys. gen. 1983-84, Wyman award for Outstanding Atty. Gen. in the Nation 1991). Democrat. Administrative and regulatory. Office: Stroock & Stroock & Lavan 180 Maiden Ln New York NY 10038-4925

**ABRAMS, ROGER IAN,** law educator, arbitrator; b. Newark, July 30, 1945; s. Avel S. and Myrna (Posner) A.; m. Frances Elise Kovitz, June 1, 1969; children: Jason, Seth. BA, Cornell U., 1967; JD, Harvard U., 1970. Bar: Mass. 1970, U.S. Dist. Ct. Mass. 1971, U.S. Ct. Appeals (1st cir.) 1971. Law clk. to Judge Frank M. Coffin U.S. Ct. Appeals (1st cir.), Boston, 1970-71; assoc. Foley, Hoag & Eliot, Boston, 1971-74; prof. law Law. Sch. Case Western Res. U., Cleve., 1974-86; dean Law Ctr. Nova U., Ft. Lauderdale, Fla., 1986-93; dean Law Sch. Rutgers U., Newark, 1993-1998; prof. law sch. Rutger U., Newark, 1993—; Herbert J. Hannuch scholar Rutgers U., Newark, 1998-99; dean Northeastern U., Boston, 1999—; labor arbitrator Fed. Mediation Svc., 1975—; mem. gender bias report implementation com. Fla. Supreme Ct.; prof. law Law Sch., Rutgers U., 1993—. Author: Legal Bases: Baseball and the Law, 1998; contbr. articles to law jours. Bd. dirs. Inst. for Continuing Legal Edn., N.J., 1993—. Recipient Gen. Counsel's Advocacy award NAACP, Boston, 1974; inductee Union N.J. Hall of Fame, 1995. Mem. Am. Law Inst., Am. Bar Found., Am. Arbitration Assn. (labor arbitrator). Democrat. Jewish. Avocations: swimming, distance walking, reading. Office: Northeastern Univ Sch Law 400 Huntington Ave Boston MA 02115

**ABRAMS, RUTH IDA,** state supreme court justice; b. Boston, Dec. 26, 1930; d. Samuel and Matilda A. BA, Radcliffe Coll., 1953; LLB, Harvard U., 1956; hon. degree, Mt. Holyoke Coll., 1977, Suffolk U., 1977, New Eng. Sch. Law, 1978. Bar: Mass. 1957. Ptnr. Abrams Abrams & Abrams, Boston, 1957-60; asst. dist. atty. Middlesex County, Mass., 1961-69; asst. atty. gen. Mass., chief appellate sect. criminal div., 1969-71; spl. counsel Supreme Jud. Ct. Mass., 1971-72; assoc. justice Supreme Jud. Ct. Mass., Boston, 1977—, Superior Ct. Commonwealth of Mass., 1972-77; mem. Gov.'s Commn. on Child Abuse, 1970-71, Mass. Law Revision Commn. Proposed Criminal Code for Mass., 1969-71; trustee Radcliffe Coll., from 1981. Editor: Handbook for Law Enforcement Officers, 1969-71. Recipient Radcliffe Coll. Achievement award, 1976, Radcliffe Grad. Soc. medal, 1977. Mem. ABA (com. on proposed fed. code from 1977), Mass. Bar Assn., Am. Law Inst., Am. Judicature Soc. (dir. 1978), Am. Judges Assn., Mass. Assn. Women Lawyers. Office: Supreme Jud Ct Mass 1300 New Courthouse Pemberton Square Boston MA 02108*

**ABRAMS, SHERI,** lawyer; b. N.Y.C.. BSBA, Boston U., 1989; JD, George Washington U., 1994. Bar: Va., D.C., U.S. Dist. Ct. (ea. dist.) Va., D.C. Ct. Appeals, U.S. Ct. Appeals (4th cir.). Pvt. practice Fairfax, Va. Bd. dirs. ICON Cmty. Svcs. Mem. ABA, FBA, D.C. Bar Assn., Fairfax County Bar Assn., Alexandria Bar Assn., Nat. Orgn. Social Security Claimant's Reps., Ctrl. Fairfax C. of C. Pension, profit-sharing, and employee benefits, Administrative and regulatory, Estate planning. Office: 11350 Random Hills Rd Ste 800 Fairfax VA 22030-6044

**ABRAMS, STANLEY DAVID,** lawyer; b. Washington, Jan. 30, 1940; s. Norman J. and Sally (Taylor) A.; m. Patricia Dreisen, June 7, 1964; children: Suzanne Bari, Lori Paige. BS, U. Md., 1962, LLB, 1966, JD, 1969. Bar: Md. 1966. Trial atty. FTC, Washington, 1966-67; sr. asst. county atty. Montgomery County, Rockville, Md., 1967-71, adminstrv. hearing examiner, 1971-79; ptnr. Levitan, Ezrin, West & Kerxton, P.C., Bethesda, Md., 1979-84; city atty. City of Gaithersburg, Md., 1979—; ptnr. Abrams, West, Storm, and Diamond P.C., Bethesda, 1984—; cons. Md. Nat. Capital Park and Planning Commn., Silver Spring, 1987, Washington Met. Transit Authority, 1985; mem. faculty ALI/ABA Land Use Inst., Phila., 1981—, Continuing Legal Edn. Inst. Md. Bar, Balt., 1980—. Author: Guide to Maryland Zoning Decisions, 1993, How to Win the Zoning Game, 1978; co-author: Handling the Land Use Case, 1984, Land Use Practice and Forms, 1997; contbg. author: Maryland Appellate Practice Handbook, 1977. With U.S. Army, 1958-62. Mem. ABA, Md. Bar Assn., Montgomery County Bar Assn. (sec. chmn. 1967—), Md. Bar Found., Urban Land Inst., Bethesda-Chevy Chase C. of C. (pres. 1983). Democrat. Jewish. Avocations: travel, writing, lecturing. Land use and zoning (including planning), Real property, Administrative and regulatory. Home: 15101 Emory Ln Rockville MD 20853-1655 Office: Abrams West Storm and Diamond PC 4550 Montgomery Ave Ste 760N Bethesda MD 20814-3379

**ABRAVANEL, ALLAN RAY,** lawyer; b. N.Y.C., Mar. 11, 1947; s. Leon and Sydelle (Berenson) A.; m. Susan Ava Paikin, Dec. 28, 1971; children: Karen, David. BA magna cum laude, Yale U., 1968; JD cum laude, Harvard U., 1971. Bar: N.Y. 1972, Oreg. 1976. Assoc. Paul, Weiss, Rifkind, Wharton & Garrison, N.Y.C., 1971-72, 74-76; fellow Internat. Legal Ctr., Lima, Peru, 1972-74; from assoc. to ptnr. Stoel, Rives, Boley, Fraser & Wyse, Portland, Oreg., 1976-83; ptnr. Perkins Coie, Portland, 1983—. Editor, pub. Abravanel Family Newsletter. Mem., dep. chair Oreg. Internat. Trade Com., Oreg. Dist. Export Coun. Mem. ABA, Portland Met. C. of C. Private international, General corporate, Municipal (including bonds). Office: Perkins Coie 1211 SW 5th Ave Portland OR 97204-3713

**ABRIEL, EVANGELINE G.,** law educator; b. Jacksonville, Fla., Sept. 23, 1954; d. M.S.J. and Jean S. Greek; m. William L. Abriel, Apr. 25, 1981; children: Annie Laurie, William, James. BA in Spanish, Tulane U., 1975, JD, 1978. Bar: La. 1979, Fla. 1979, U.S. Dist. Ct. (ea. dist.) La., U.S. Ct. Appeals (5th cir.). Atty. Gulf Fleet Marine Corp., New Orleans, 1979-81, Ingram Corp., New Orleans, 1981-82, Ecumenical Immigration Svcs., New Orleans, 1982-83; clin. prof. Loyola U. New Orleans Sch. Law, 1983—; vis. assoc. prof. Southwe. U. Sch. Law, L.A., 1990-92; mem. adv. coun. regional office UN High Commr. for Refugees, Washington, 1989-90; mem. adv. coun. La. Ctr. Law and Civic Edn., New Orleans, 1996—; co-convener immigration law subcom. Ninth Cir. Gender Bias Task Force, L.A., 1991—; presenter in field; spkr. in field. Contbr. articles to profl. jours. Mem. legal svcs. subcom. Unity for Homeless, New Orleans, 1993-94; mem. New Orleans pro bono project Homeless Task Force, 1993-94. Mem. Am. Assn. Law Schs., La. State Bar (mem. access to justice com. 1995—), Alpha Lambda Delta, Sigma Delta Pi. Avocations: Spanish, French and Norwegian languages, music, piano, flute. E-mail: abriel@loyno.edu. Office: Loyola U New Orleans Sch Law 7214 Saint Charles Ave New Orleans LA 70118-3538

**ABT, RALPH EDWIN,** lawyer; b. Chgo., Apr. 9, 1960; s. Wendel Peter and Hedi Lucie (Wieder) A. BA, Loyola U., Chgo., 1982; JD, John Marshall Law Sch., Chgo., 1987. Bar: Ill. 1987, U.S. Dist. Ct. (no. dist.) Ill. 1987, U.S. Ct. Appeals (7th cir.) Ill. 1988. Pvt. practice Chgo., 1987-88; staff atty. Sec. of State's Office, Chgo., 1988-95, Ill. Dept. Pub. Aid, Chgo., 1995—. Poll watcher, Chgo., 1981, 83, precinct capt., 1983, 93—. Mem. ABA, Ill. Bar Assn., Chgo. Bar Assn., Trade Law Assn. (charter mem., chmn. charter membership drive 1986), Phi Alpha Delta. Lutheran. Avocations: reading, tennis, bicycling, weight lifting. Home: 5067 W Balmoral Ave Chicago IL 60630-1547 Office: Ill Dept Pub Aid 32 W Randolph St Chicago IL 60601-3405

**ACCARDI, JAMES ROY,** prosecutor; b. Berea, Ohio, Aug. 31, 1949; s. Roy R. Accardi; m. Marian Elizabeth Hollon, June 24, 1989; 1 child, Thomas Burns. BS, U. North Ala., 1971; JD, U. Ala., Tuscaloosa, 1974. Bar: Ala. 1974, U.S. Dist. Ct. (no. dist.) 1975, U.S. Ct. Appeals (11th cir.) 1981. Pvt. practice Huntsville, 1980-81; asst. dist. atty. Madison County Office of Dist. Atty., Huntsville, 1974-80, 81-91, chief trial atty., 1991-93, dep. dist. atty., 1993—. Author: The Abridged Significant Historie, 1979, Amber Aspects, 1988, numerous essays and profiles, 1981—. Pres. bd. dirs. Family Svcs. Ctr., Huntsville, 1991-92. Office: Dist Atty Madison County 100 Northside Sq Huntsville AL 35801-4800

**ACHAMPONG, FRANCIS KOFI,** law educator, consultant; b. Kumasi, Ghana, Feb. 18, 1955; came to U.S., 1981; s. John Wilberforce and Salome (Mensa) A.; m. Nicole Victoria Blache. LLB, U. Ghana, 1976; LLM, U. London, 1977, PhD, 1981; LLM, Georgetown U., 1985. Bar: N.Y. 1986, Va. 1988, U.S. Dist. Ct. (ea. dist.) Va. 1988, U.S. Ct. Appeals (4th cir.) 1988, U.S. Supreme Ct. 1990. Adj. lectr. George Washington U., Washington, 1981-82; asst. prof. Howard U., Washington, 1981-85; prof. Norfolk (Va.) State U., 1985—, chair dept. entrepreneurial studies, 1998—; of counsel Shelton & Malone, Norfolk, 1998—; cons. Aetna Life & Casualty, Hartford, Conn., 1981-82, Profl. Ins. Assn. of Md., Pa., 1986, Shapiro, Meiselman & Greene, P.C., Rockville, Md., 1987, Crowell & Moring, Washington, 1988, Clark & Stant, Virginia Beach, Va., 1988. Author: Workplace Sexual Harassment, 1999; contbr. articles to profl. jours. Mem. Am. Risk and Ins. Assn., Acad. Legal Studies in Bus. Avocations: gospel music, exercise, reading, movies. FAX: 757-683-2506. Home: 1509 Colebrook Dr Virginia Beach VA 23464-7206 Office: Norfolk State U 2401 Corprew Ave Norfolk VA 23504-3993

**ACHEE, ROLAND JOSEPH,** lawyer; b. New Orleans, Dec. 12, 1922; s. Benjamin Elphege and Marie Josephine (Cazenave) A.; m. Jean Winifred Lant, Feb. 19, 1955; 1 child, Marie Alaine Achee Mayo. BA, Centenary Coll., 1944; JD, La. State U., 1949. Bar: La. 1949, U.S. Dist. Ct. (we. dist.) La. 1950, U.S. Ct. Appeals (5th cir.) 1960. Atty. Rountree, Cox, Guin & Achee, Shreveport, La. Editor-in-chief La. Law Review, 1948-49. Chmn. Selective Svc. Bd. No. 10, Shreveport, 1965. Lt. (j.g.) USNR, 1944-46, PTO. Named Outstanding Asst. City Atty. U.S., Nat. Inst. Mcpl. Officers, 1988. Fellow Am. Coll. Trial Lawyers; mem. ABA, Internat. Assn. Def. Counsel, La. Stat Bar Assn. (past chmn. profl. responsibility, legal ethics adv. com. 1991—), Shreveport Bar Assn. (chmn. ethics com. 1975-77, pres. 1984), Harry V. Booth Inn of Ct. (master of bench), Am. Legion (comdr. 1961), Elks (life, Exalted Ruler 1958), Order of Coif. General civil litigation. Home: 182 Bruce Ave Shreveport LA 71105-3711 Office: Rountree Cox Guin & Achee PO Box 1807 400 Travis St Ste 1200 Shreveport LA 71101-5565

**ACHESON, AMY J.,** lawyer; b. Pitts., July 16, 1963; d. Willard Phillips and Patricia Louise (Marshall) A. BA, Haverford Coll., 1984; JD cum laude, U. S.C., 1987. Bar: Pa. 1987, U.S. Dist. Ct. (we. dist.) Pa. 1987, U.S. Ct. Appeals (10th cir.) 1989, U.S. Ct. Appeals (3d cir.) 1988, U.S. Ct. Appeals (4th cir.) 1993. Assoc. Reed, Smith, Shaw & McClay, Pitts., 1987-95; shareholder Berger Law Firm, Pitts., 1995—. Mem. S.C. Law Rev., 1985-87. Fin. officer Ret. Sr. Vol. Program Allegheny County, Pitts., 1990-91; treas. Parents League for Emotional Adjustments, Pitts., 1990-91; mem. adv. bd. Pa. Dept. Correction, Community Svc. Ctr. No. 1, Pitts., 1990-97; bd. mgrs. The Woodwell, Pitts., 1992-97, v.p., 1998—. Mem. ABA (jud. adminstrn. div. com., chmn. subcom. on discipline of fed. judges, 1990-91), Pa. Bar Assn., Allegheny County Bar Assn. (young lawyers sect. coun. 1990-91), Order of the Coif, Order of the Wig and Robe. Federal civil litigation, State civil litigation. Office: Berger Law Firm 912 Frick Bldg Pittsburgh PA 15219

**ACHESON, EDWIN R., JR.,** lawyer; b. Joplin, Mo., Sept. 14, 1955. BS in Mech. and Aerospace Engring., U. Mo., Columbia, 1977; JD, Duke U., 1980. Assoc. Frost & Jacobs, Cin., 1988-94, ptnr., 1994—. Mem. CIPLA (pres. 1997), AIPLA, Rotary Club. Intellectual property. Office: Frost & Jacobs LLP 201 E 5th St Ste 2500 Cincinnati OH 45202-4182

**ACKER, ANN,** lawyer; b. Chgo., July 21, 1948. BA, St. Mary's Coll.; JD, Loyola U. Bar: Ill. 1973. Mem. Chapman and Cutler, Chgo. Office: Chapman and Cutler 111 W Monroe St Ste 1700 Chicago IL 60603-4006

**ACKER, FREDERICK GEORGE,** lawyer; b. Defiance, Ohio, May 7, 1934; s. Julius William and Orah Louise (Dowler) A.; m. Cynthia Ann Wayne, Dec. 1, 1962; children: Frederick Wayne, Mary Katherine, Richard Hoghton, Jennifer Ruth. Student, Ind. U., 1952-54; BA, Valparaiso U., 1956; MA, Harvard U., 1957, JD, 1961; postgrad., U. Manchester (Eng.), 1957-58. Bar: Ill. 1961, Ind. 1961. Ptnr. Winston & Strawn, Chgo., 1961-88, McDermott, Will & Emery, Chgo., 1988—; co-chmn. Joint Prin. and Income Act. com., Chgo., 1976-81. Co-author: (portfolio) Generation-Skipping Tax, 1991; contbr. articles to profl. jours. Bd. dirs. Max McGraw Wildlife Found., Dundee, Ill., 1984—, chmn., pres. 1997—; trustee L.S. Wood Ednl. Trust, Chgo., 1975—, The Nature Conservancy Ill. chpt., Chgo., 1981-90; chmn.1986-90). Danforth Found. fellow, 1956; Fulbright scholar, 1957. Fellow Am. Coll. Trust and Estate Counsel; mem. ABA, Ill. Bar Assn., Trout Unlimited, Fulbright Assn. (bd. dirs. 1994—), Met. Chgo. Club, Anglers Club, Chgo. Farmers Club. Lutheran. Avocations: hunting, fishing. Probate, Estate taxation, Estate planning. Home: 543 N Madison St Hinsdale IL 60521-3213 Office: McDermott Will & Emery 227 W Monroe St Ste 3100 Chicago IL 60606-5096

**ACKER, FREDERICK WAYNE,** lawyer; b. Chgo., Feb. 28, 1966; s. Frederick George and Cynthia Ann (Wayne) A.; m. Anette Kjeldaas, June 3, 1988; children: Chelsea Kirsten, Ingrid Noelle, Stein Frederick. BA, St. Olaf Coll., 1988; JD, U. Notre Dame, 1992; Splty. Degree, U. Oslo, Norway, 1993. Bar: Mich. 1993, Ill. 1994, U.S. Dist. Ct. (no. dist.) Ill. 1995, U.S. Ct. Appeals (7th cir.) 1997, U.S. Ct. Appeals (fed. cir.) 1997. Vis. scholar Notre Dame Law Sch., South Bend, Ind., 1993; atty. Stamos & Trucco, Chgo., 1994-98, Hahn, Loeser & Parks, Columbus, OH, 1998—. Author: The MBA and the Magic Lamp, 1994, (novella) The Curse of Agnes Larsen, 1996; columnist Minn. Spectator, 1988-90; mem. Notre Dame Law Rev. Campaign mgr. Gilbertson for Congress, Mpls., 1988, Fintzen for Rep., Geneva, Ill., 1997; pres. Notre Dame Federalist Soc., 1991-92. Thomas J. White scholar, 1989. Mem. ABA, Chgo. Bar Assn. (internat. fgn. law com. 1995-98, comml. fin. and transactions com. 1995-98, YLS intellectual property law com. 1995-98). Republican. Evangelical Christian. Avocations: fiction and editorial writing, Scandinavian languages and history, fishing, theology. Intellectual property, General civil litigation, Contracts commercial. Office: Hahn Loeser & Parks Ste 1800 One Columbus 10 West Broad St Columbus OH 43215

**ACKER, RODNEY,** lawyer; b. Jacksonville, Tex., Sept. 29, 1949; s. Mike and Dorothy (Kennedy) A.; m. Judy Bruyere, Sept. 2, 1972; children: Amy, Shelley, Rachel, Sam. BBA, U. Tex., Arlington, 1971; JD with honors, Tex. Tech, 1974. Bar: Tex. 1974, U.S. Dist. Ct. (no., so., ea., we. dists.) Tex., U.S. Ct. Appeals (5th and 11th cirs.), U.S. Supreme Ct.; cert. in civil trial law. Law clk. to Hon. Eldon Mahon, U.S. Dist. Ct., Ft. Worth, 1974-76; assoc. Kendrick, Kendrick & Bradley, Dallas, 1976; assoc. Jenkens & Gilcrist, Dallas, 1976-79, ptnr., then shareholder, 1979—. Fellow Am. Bar Found., Tex. Bar Found., Dallas Bar Found.; mem. ABA, Am. Coll. Trial Lawyers, State Bar Tex., Dallas Bar Assn., Patrick Higginbotham Am. Inns of Ct., Phi Delta Phi. Baptist. Federal civil litigation, General civil litigation, Securities. Home: 9639 Hilldale Dr Dallas TX 75231-2705 Office: Jenkens & Gilcrist 1445 Ross Ave Ste 3200 Dallas TX 75202-2799

**ACKER, WILLIAM MARSH, JR.,** federal judge; b. Birmingham, Ala., Oct. 25, 1927; s. William Marsh and Estelle (Lampkin) A.; m. Martha Walters, 1957; children—William Marsh III, Stacey Reed. BA, Birmingham So. Coll., 1949; LLB, Yale U., 1952. Bar: Ala. 1952. Assoc. Graham, Bibb, Wingo & Foster, Birmingham, Ala., 1952-57, Smyer, White, Reid & Acker, 1957-72, Dominick, Fletcher, Yeilding, Acker, Wood & Lloyd, Birmingham, 1972-82; judge U.S. Dist. Ct. (no. dist.) Ala., 1982-96, sr. judge, 1996—. Mem. Ala. Republican Exec. Com.; del. to Repub. Nat. Convention, 1972, 76, 80. Mem. Birmingham Bar Assn. Office: US Dist Ct 481 Hugo L Black Courthouse 1729 5th Ave N Birmingham AL 35203-2000

**ACKERMAN, BRUCE ARNOLD,** law educator, lawyer; b. N.Y.C., Aug. 19, 1943; s. Nathan and Jean (Rosenberg) A.; m. Susan Gould Rose, May 29, 1967; children: Sybil Rose, John Mill. BA summa cum laude, Harvard U., 1964; LLB with honors, Yale U., 1967. Bar: Pa. 1970. Law clk. U.S. Ct. Appeals (2d cir.), New York, 1967-68; law clk. to assoc. justice John M. Harlan U.S. Supreme Ct., Washington, 1968-69; prof. law and public policy analysis U. Pa., Phila., 1969-74; prof. law Yale U., New Haven, 1974-82, Sterling prof. law and polit. sci., 1987—; Beekman prof. law and philosophy Columbia U., N.Y.C., 1982-87. Author: Private Property and the Constitution, 1977, Social Justice in the Liberal State, 1980 (Gavel award ABA), (with Hassler) Clean Coal/Dirty Air, 1981, Reconstructing American Law, 1984, We the People: Foundations, 1991, The Future of Liberal Revolution, 1992, (with Golove) Is NAFTA Constitutional?, 1995, We the People: Transformations, 1998, (with others) The Uncertain Search for Environmental Quality, 1974 (Henderson prize Harvard Law Sch.). Guggenheim fellow, 1985. Fellow Am. Acad. Arts and Scis.; mem. Am. Law Inst. Office: Yale U Law Sch PO Box 208215 New Haven CT 06520-8215

**ACKERMAN, DAVID PAUL,** lawyer; b. Chgo., June 11, 1949; s. Norman Alvin and Ruth (Renberg) A.; m. Deanna Mae Neumayer, Aug. 24, 1972; children: Paul David, Kristin Marie. AB, Princeton U., 1971; JD, Harvard U., 1974. Bar: Ill. 1974, U.S. Dist. Ct. (no. dist.) Ill. 1974. Assoc. McBride, Baker & Coles, Chgo., 1974-80; ptnr. McBride, Baker & Coles, 1980—. Author various articles. Mem. ABA, Ill. Bar Assn., Chgo. Bar Assn., Tower Club. Corporate taxation, Pension, profit-sharing, and employee benefits, Mergers and acquisitions. Office: McBride Baker & Coles 500 W Madison St Ste 40 Chicago IL 60661-2511

**ACKERMAN, HAROLD A.,** federal judge; b. 1928. Student, Seton Hall U., 1945-46, 48; LL.B., Rutgers U., 1951. Bar: N.J. 1951. Adminstrv. asst. to Commr. of Labor and Industry, State of N.J., 1955-56; judge of compensation State of N.J., 1956-62, supervising judge of compensation, 1962-65; judge Union County Dist. Ct., 1965-70, presiding judge, 1966-70; judge Union County Ct., 1970-73, Superior Ct. law div., 1973-75, Superior Ct. Chancery div., 1975-79; judge U.S. Dist. Ct., Dist. of N.J., 1979—, now sr. judge; mem. Supreme Ct. Com. on Revision of Rules, 1967; chmn. Supreme Ct. Com. on County Dist. Cts., 1968; mem. faculty Nat. Jud. Coll., 1978. Sgt. U.S. Army, 1946-48. Recipient Disting. Alumni award Rutgers U. Sch. Law, 1980. Fellow ABA; mem. Order of Coif. Office: US Dist Ct PO Box 999 Newark NJ 07101-0999

**ACKERMAN, KENNETH EDWARD,** lawyer, educator; b. Bronx, N.Y., May 25, 1946; s. Kenneth L. and Anna (McCarthy) A.; m. Kathryn H. Hartnett, July 10, 1972; children—Andrew, Carl, Sheila, Edward, Daniel, Kenneth. Student Talladega Coll., 1966; B.A., Fordham Coll., 1968; J.D. Cornell U., 1971. Bar: N.Y. 1972, Pa. 1994, U.S. Dist. Ct. (no. dist.) N.Y. 1975, U.S. Ct. Appeals (2d cir.) 1975, U.S. Supreme Ct. 1976. Clk. legal dept. Port Authority N.Y. and N.J., 1969; Clk. legal dept. IBM, 1970; ptnr. Mackenzie, Smith, Lewis, Michell & Hughes, Syracuse, N.Y., 1971—; adj. prof. banking law and negotiable instruments Am. Inst. Banking program Onondaga Community Coll., 1984—, Syracuse U. Coll., lectr. Author: Alcoholism-Prognosis for Recovery in the Reconstituted Soviet Republics, 1991; contbr. article to profl. jour. Chmn. Central N.Y. chpt. March of Dimes, 1972-82; mem. A.A.-USSR Travel Group, 1987; bd. dirs. Central N.Y. Health Systems Agy., Inc., 1982-83, Syracuse Sr. Citizens Housing Corp, 1992—. Mem. ABA, N.Y. State Bar Assn. (chmn. com. lawyer alcoholism and drug abuse 1993-95), Onondaga County Bar Assn. (bd. dirs. 1990-93). Banking, Bankruptcy, Contracts commercial. Office: 600 Onondaga Savs Bank Bldg Syracuse NY 13202

**ACKERT, T(ERRENCE) W(ILLIAM),** lawyer; b. N.Y.C., June 8, 1946; s. T.W. and M. Ackert; m. MP. Ackert, July 4, 1970. BA in History, U. West Fla., 1969; JD, U. Fla., 1972. Bar: Fla. 1972, U.S. Dist. Ct. (mid. dist.) Fla. 1972, U.S. Supreme Ct. 1977, U.S. Ct. Appeals (fed. cir.) 1981. Pvt. practice Orlando, Fla., 1972—; counsel Sharks Success, Inc., 1988-93; adj. prof. U. Cen. Fla., Orlando, 1988-93; gen. counsel (Fla.) Morgran Stiftung , Liechtenstein, 1991-95; law lectr. Profl. Skills Inst., Fla., 1981-85. Co-author: Florida Dissolution Manual, 1991; contbr. articles to profl. jours. Chmn. 9th Cir. Grievance Com., Orlando, 1989; mem. Human Svc. Planning Com., Orange County, Fla., 1984. Mem. Seminole County Bar (LAS pres. 1979, Pres. award 1980-83), Orange County Bar (LAS dir. 1980), Fla. Bar (trial lawyers sect., chmn. bar delivery of legal svc. com. 1986-88, chmn. mid-yr. conv. family law 1981, Pres.'s Svc. award 1985, 87). Avocations: pro bono service, travel. Contracts commercial, State civil litigation, Federal civil litigation. Office: PO Box 2548 Winter Park FL 32790-2548 Also: 1133 Louisiana Ave Ste 209 Winter Park FL 32789-2350

**ACKLEY, ROBERT O.,** lawyer; b. Chgo., July 24, 1952; s. William O. and Jeannette E. (Mitchell) A.; m. Patricia Ann Cerney, May 24, 1980; children: Matthew, Allison, Elizabeth, Anne, Kathryn, Kimberly. BA, No. Ill. U., 1974; MA., No. Mich. U., 1977; JD, John Marshall Law Sch., Chgo., 1988. Bar: Ill. 1988, U.S. Dist. Ct. (no. dist.) Ill. 1988. Adminstrv. intern, asst. to city mgr. City of Marquette, Mich., 1976-77; adminstrv. asst. to town mgr. Town of Glastonbury, Conn., 1978; supr. Continental Bank, Chgo., 1979; chief methods analyst dept. fin. City of Chgo., 1980-81, chief supr. ops. dept. revenue, 1981-84; pres. Ackley & Assocs., Chgo., 1984-88; law clk., adminstrv. asst. to chief justice Thomas J. Moran Supreme Ct. of Ill., Lake Forest, 1988-90; atty. Cassiday, Schade & Gloor, Chgo., 1990-91; pvt. practice Chgo., 1991—; bd. dirs. Ill. Pro Bono Ctr.; adj. prof. Roosevelt U., Chgo., 1989-90; mem. panel arbitrators Cir. Ctr. of 19th Jud. Cir., 1991-97, Cir. Ct. Cook County, 1993-97; detention screening atty. pretrial svcs. Cir. Ct. of Cook County, 1991—; drugs panel atty. Office of State Appellate Defender, 1992—. Bd. dirs. Bryn Mawr-Broadway Ridge Mchts. Assn., Chgo., 1984-87; panel mem. Capital Resource Ctr., 1991, Community Econ. Devel. Law Project. Fellow Ill. Bar Found.; mem. ABA, Nat. Assn. Counsel Children, Ill. Bar Assn., Chgo. Bar Assn., Lake County Bar Assn., Ill. Appellate Lawyers Assn., Acad. Polit. Sci. (life). General civil litigation, Juvenile, Family and matrimonial. Home: 606 Buckingham Pl Libertyville IL 60048-3326 Office: 500 N Lake St Ste 109 Mundelein IL 60060-1860

**ACOBA, SIMEON RIVERA, JR.,** judge; b. Honolulu, Mar. 11, 1944; s. Simeon R. and Martina (Domingo) A. BA, U. Hawaii, 1966; JD, Northwestern U., 1969. Bar: Hawaii 1969, U.S. Dist. Ct. Hawaii, U.S. Ct. Appeals (9th cir.). Law clk. Hawaii Supreme Ct., Honolulu, 1969-70; housing officer U. Hawaii, Honolulu, 1970-71; dep. atty. gen., Honolulu, 1971-73; pvt. practice, Honolulu, 1973-80; judge 1st Cir. Ct., State of Hawaii, Honolulu, 1980-94; judge Intermediate Ct. of Appeals, State of Hawaii, 1994—; atty. on spl. contract Div. OSHA, Dept. Labor, Honolulu, 1975-77, Pub. Utilities Div., State of Hawaii, 1976-77, Campaign Spending Com., State of Hawaii, 1976; staff atty. Hawaii State Legislature, 1975. Bd. dirs. Hawaii Mental Health Assn., 1975-77, Nuuanu YMCA, 1975-78, Hawaii Youth at Risk, 1990-91; mem. Gov.'s Conf. on Yr. 2000, Honolulu, 1970, Citizens Com. on Adminstrn. of Justice, 1972, State Drug Abuse Commn., 1975-76, Com. to Consider the Adoption of ABA Model Rules of Profl. Conduct, 1989-91; subcom. chmn. Supreme Ct. Com. Pattern Jury Instrns., 1990-91; mem. Hawaii Supreme Ct. Ad Hoc Com. Jury Master List, 1991-92, Judicial Edn. Com., 1992-93, Hawaii State Bar Assn. Jud. Adminstrn. Com., 1992-94, Permanent Com. Rules of Penal Procedure and Cir. Ct. Rules, 1992-96; instr. criminal law Hawaii Pacific U., 1992—. Recipient Liberty Bell award, 1964. Mem. ABA, ATLA, Hawaii State Bar Assn. (dir. young lawyers sect. 1973), Am. Judicature Soc. Office: Intermediate Ct of Appeals State of Hawaii PO Box 2560 Honolulu HI 96804-2560

**ACOSTA, JULIO CESAR,** lawyer; b. Miami, Fla., Oct. 11, 1967; s. Julio Cesar and Norma Acosta; m. Christine Michele Delgado, June 19, 1993; 1 child, Zachary Taylor. JD, Nova Southeastern U., 1996; BBA, Fla. Internat. U., 1993. Bar: Fla. 1996, U.S. Dist. Ct. (so. dist.) 1998, U.S. Dist. Ct. (mid. dist.) Fla. 1999, U.S. Ct. Appeals (11th cir.) 1999. Assoc. Hightower & Rudd, P.A., Miami, 1996—. Mem. ABA, Dade County Bar Assn. (civil litigation com. 1998—), Cuban Am. Bar Assn. Avocations: golfing, fishing, wieght lifting. Insurance, Personal injury, General civil litigation. Office: Hightower & Rudd PA 100 Biscayne Blvd Ste 2300 Miami FL 33132-2398

**ACOSTA, RAYMOND LUIS,** federal judge; b. N.Y.C., May 31, 1925; s. Ramon J. and Carmen J. (Acha-Jimenez) Acosta-Colon; m. Marie Hatcher, Nov. 2, 1957; children: Regina, Gregory, Ann Marie. Student, Princeton U., 1948; JD, Rutgers U., 1951. Bar: N.J. 1953, U.S. Supreme Ct. 1956, P.R. 1959. Sole practice Hackensack, N.J., 1953-54; spl. agt. FBI, San Diego, Washington, Miami, Fla., 1954-58; asst. U.S. atty. San Juan, P.R., 1958-61; sole practice San Juan, 1961-67; trust officer Banco Credito y Ahorro Ponceno, San Juan, 1967-80; U.S. atty. Dist. P.R., Hato Rey, 1980-82; judge U.S. Dist. Ct. P.R., San Juan, 1982—; Alt. del. U.S.-P.R. Commn. on Status, 1962-63; mem. Gov.'s Spl. Com. to Study Structure and Orgn. Police Dept., P.R., 1969. Contbr. articles to profl. jours. Pres. United Fund, P.R., 1979. Served with USN, 1943-46. Recipient Merit cert. Mayor of San Juan, 1973. Mem. Fed. Bar Assn. (pres., P.R. 1967), P.R. Bankers Assn. (chmn. trust div. 1971, 75, 77), P.R. Bar Assn., Soc. Former Spl. Agts. FBI. Office: US Dist Ct Chase Manhattan Bldg 1200C 254 Ave Munoz Rivera San Juan PR 00918-1900

**ACOSTA, SERGIO ENRIQUE,** lawyer; b. Middletown, N.Y., July 6, 1960; s. Sergio Maria Acosta and Sara Artola; m. Maria Paricia Albornoz, July 2, 1983. Student, Inst. of Am. Univs., Avignon, France, 1980-81; BA, DePaul U., 1982; JD, George Washington U., 1985. Bar: Fla. 1985, U.S. Dist. Ct. (no. dist.) Ill. 1990, U.S. Ct. Appeals (7th cir.) 1990, U.S. Ct. Appeals (D.C. cir.) 1998. Asst. state atty. Dade County Office of State Atty., Miami, 1985-90; asst. U.S. atty. U.S. Atty. Office, Chgo., 1990—, dep. chief, 1994—; adj. prof. law Northwestern U., Chgo., 1998. Fellow Leadership of Greater Chgo.; mem. Nat. Hispanic Prosecutors Assn. (reg. pres., bd. dirs. 1997-98), Hispanic Lawyers Assn. of Ill. Office: Office US Atty 219 S Dearborn St Ste 500 Chicago IL 60604-1703

**ADAIR, DONALD ROBERT,** lawyer; b. Rochester, N.Y., July 24, 1943; s. Robert Voigt and Esca Lois (Naas) A.; m. Susanne Jonsson, Nov. 1969; 1 child, Emily Elsebeth; m. Judith Ann Jameson, Nov. 29, 1975 (div. Nov. 1995); children: Thomas, Abigail, Kathryn Carrie. BA, Harvard U., 1965; JD, Cornell U., 1968. Bar: N.Y. 1968, U.S. Dist. Ct. (we. dist.) N.Y. 1968. Assoc. Nixon, Hargrave, Devans & Doyle, Rochester, 1968-76, ptnr., 1977-87; prin. Adair Law Firm and predecessor firms, Rochester, 1988—; bd. dirs. Detection Sys., Inc., Fairport, N.Y., NetLink Transaction Sys. Corp., Victor, N.Y., Stone Constrn. Equip., Inc., Honeoye, N.Y., Victor Insulators, Inc., Victor, N.Y. Contbr. chpt. to book New York Limited Liability Companies and Partnerships, 1995. Active Greater Rochester chpt. ARC, 1973—, chair, 1991-93; mem. Consumer Credit Counseling Svc. of Rochester, Inc., 1972—, chair, 1994-96. Recipient Spl. Citation for Exceptional Vol. Svc., Greater Rochester chpt. ARC, 1991. Fellow Am. Bar Found. (life); mem. ABA, N.Y. State Bar Assn., Monroe County Bar Assn. General corporate, Finance, Mergers and acquisitions. Office: Adair Law Firm 30 Corporate Woods Rochester NY 14623-1469

**ADAIR, EVAN EDWARD,** lawyer; b. Erie, Pa., Aug. 31, 1950; s. Robert C. and Winifred A. (Ames) A.; m. Rebecca L. Nichols, Nov. 26, 1988; 1 child, Jacqueline. BA, Grove City Coll., 1972; JD, Coll. of William and Mary, 1975. Bar: Pa. 1976, U.S. Dist. Ct. (we. dist.) Pa. 1976, U.S. Ct. Appeals (3d cir.) 1982. Asst. gen. mgr. York St. Inn, Inc., Williamsburg, Va., 1975-76; ptnr. Williams Adair & Ridge, Erie, 1976—; adj. faculty Mercyhurst Coll., Erie, 1982-89; solicitor Harborcreek (Pa.) Twp. Zoning Hearing Bd., 1990—, Summit (Pa.) Twp. Zoning Bd., 1991—, Millcreek (Pa.) Twp., 1992—; asst. solicitor County of Erie (Pa.), 1992—. Field rep. Carter Presdl. campaign, Erie, Toledo, N.W. Pa., 1976; chmn. pub. rels. Erie County Bar Assn., 1979-85; crusade chmn. Am. Cancer Soc., Erie, 1979-85, 92—; pres. Millcreek Youth Athletic Assn., Erie, 1986-97; mem. program com. Boys and Girls Club of Erie, Inc., 1990-92. Mem. ABA, Assn. Trial Lawyers Am., Pa. Bar Assn., Erie Maennerchor Club, East Erie Turners, Phi Delta Phi. Democrat. Presbyterian. Avocation: reading. General practice, Probate, Municipal (including bonds). Office: Williams Adair & Ridge 332 E 6th St Erie PA 16507-1610

**ADAMS, ARLIN MARVIN,** lawyer, arbitrator, mediator, retired judge; b. Phila., Apr. 16, 1921; s. Aaron M. and Mathilda (Landau) A.; m. Neysa Cristol, Nov. 10, 1942; children: Carol (Mrs. Howard Kirshner), Judith A., Jane C. BS in Econs. with highest honors, Temple U., 1941; LLB with honors, U. Pa., 1947, MA in Econs., 1950; DHL (hon.), Temple U., 1964; DSc (hon.), Phila. Coll. Optometry, 1965; LLD (hon.), Phila. Coll. Textiles, 1966, Susquehanna U., 1985, Muhlenberg Coll., 1986, Villanova U., 1987, U. Pa., 1998. Bar: Pa. 1947; U.S. Ct. Appeals (3rd cir.), 1969. Law clk., Chief Justice Horace Stern Pennsylvania Supreme Ct., 1947; assoc. firm Schnader, Harrison, Segal & Lewis, Phila., 1947-50, sr. partner, 1950-63, 66-69; sec. pub. welfare Commonwealth of Pa., Phila., 1963-66; judge U.S. Ct. Appeals (3d cir.), Phila., 1969-87; counsel Schnader, Harrison, Segal & Lewis, Phila., 1987—; apptd. ind. counsel to investigate Dept. HUD, 1990-95; apptd. spl. counsel Pa. Commn. of Police, 1994-95; instr. Am. Inst. Banking, Phila., 1949-52; lectr. fed. practice Law Sch., U. Pa., Phila., 1952-56, lectr. constl. law, 1972-97. Author: Law and Religion, 2 vols., 1991, A Nation Dedicated to Religious Liberty, 1990; Editor-in-chief Law Review U. Penn., 1947; contbr. articles to profl. jours. Pres. Annenberg Inst., 1988-91; chmn. bd. dirs. Moss Rehab. Hosp., Phila., 1962-63; trustee U. Pa., 1985—; chmn. U.S. Supreme Ct. Jud. Fellows Commn., 1987-93, Fels Inst. Govt., Phila., 1967-77, Sch. of Social Work, Bryn Mawr (Pa.) Coll., 1967-78, Diagnostic and Rehab. Ctr., Phila., 1971-72; chmn. overseers U. Pa. Law Sch., 1985-92; trustee Med. Coll. of Pa., 1974-80, hon. trustee, 1981-98; trustee German Marshall Meml. Fund, 1972-84, Lewis H. Stevens Trust, Bryn Mawr Coll., 1972-78, Columbia U. Ctr. for Law and Econ. Studies, U. of Pa. Inst. for Law and Econs., William Penn Found.; hon. trustee Phila. Mus. Art, 1998—. With U.S. Naval Reserve, 1942-45, North Pacific. Recipient Disting. Service award U. Pa. Law Sch., 1981, Justice award Am. Jud. Soc., 1982, John Murray award DePaul U., 1987, Cresset award Rosemont Coll., 1988, Gold Medallion award Chapel of Four Chaplains, Founders award Temple U., 1997, Phila. award, 1997. Mem. ABA (del. ho. of dels. 1966-67, 75-77, chmn. trade assn. com.), Am. Law Inst., Am. Bar Found., Pa. Bar Assn. (pres. 1950, del. ho. of dels. 1967-71), Phila. Bar Assn. (chancellor 1967, Gold Medal award 1999), Am. Judicature Soc. (pres. 1975-77), Am. Philos. Soc. (sec. 1980-83, v.p. 1987-92, pres. 1993-99), Am. Acad. Arts & Scis., Phila. Club, Union League, Sun. Breakfast Club, Legal Club (pres. 1986-91), Jr. Legal Club, Order of Coif, Beta Gamma Sigma. Appellate, Alternative dispute resolution, Constitutional. Office: Schnader Harrison Segal & Lewis LLP 1600 Market St Fl 36 Philadelphia PA 19103-7240

**ADAMS, DANIEL FENTON,** law educator; b. Reading, Pa., July 29, 1922; s. Daniel Snyder and Carrie Betsy (Vought) A.; m. Eloise Williams, Sept. 6, 1968. A.B., Dickinson Coll., 1947; LL.B., Dickinson Sch. Law, 1949. Bar: Pa. 1951, Ark. 1984. Prof. law Sch. Law Dickinson U., Carlisle, Pa., 1949-65, asst. to dean, 1952-54, 56-60, acting dean, 1954-56, asst. dean, 1960-65; prof. Sch. Law U. Ark., Little Rock, 1965-70, 77-93, prof. emeritus, 1993—; asst. dean U. Ark. Sch. Law, Little Rock, 1966-70, acting dean, 1981-82, interim dean, 1989-91; prof. U. Miss. Sch. Law, Oxford, 1970-77; vis. prof. Stetson U. Sch. Law, St. Petersburg, Fla., 1976-77, 99, U. Tenn. Coll. Law, 1993. Contbr. articles to profl. jours. Served with U.S. Army, 1943-44. Mem. ABA, Pa. Bar Assn., Ark. Bar Assn. Home: 32571 River Rd Orange Beach AL 36561-5713

**ADAMS, DANIEL NELSON,** lawyer. AB, Yale U., 1932; LLB, Harvard U., 1935. Bar: N.Y. 1937. Sr. counsel Davis Polk & Wardwell, N.Y.C. Mem. ABA, N.Y. State Bar Assn., Assn. of Bar of City of N.Y., N.Y. County Lawyers Assn., Am. Law Inst. General practice, Corporate taxation. Office: Davis Polk & Wardwell 450 Lexington Ave New York NY 10017-3911

**ADAMS, DAVID HUNTINGTON,** judge; b. Cleve., May 30, 1942; s. Donald Croxton and Nancy (Downer) A.; m. Ann Arendell Rawls, Oct. 2, 1965 (div. 1982); children: Ann Arendell, David Huntington, Susanna Camp; m. Mary Watson, Dec. 4, 1982. AB, Washington and Lee U., 1965, JD, 1968. Bar: Va. 1968, U.S. Dist. Ct. (ea. dist.) Va. 1968, U.S. Ct. Appeals (4th cir.) 1968, U.S. Supreme Ct. 1973. Law clk. U.S. Dist. Ct., Norfolk, Va., 1968-69; assoc. law firm Willcox, Savage, Norfolk, 1969-72; ptnr. law firm Agelasto, Bernard & Adams, Norfolk, 1972-74, Taylor, Walker, Bernard & Adams, Norfolk, 1974-78, Taylor, Walker & Adams, Norfolk, 1974-87, Clark & Stant, P.C., 1987-93; judge U.S. Bankruptcy Ct. (ea. dist. Va.), 1993—; master of the bench James Kent Am. Inn of Ct., 1994—, pres., 1995; lectr. bankruptcy practice joint com. on cont. legal edn. Va. Bar Found., 1981, 89; adminstrv. hearing officer Commonwealth of Va., 1974-89. Author: Virginia Landlord/Tenant Law, 1980. Bd. dirs. Heritage Mus., Norfolk, 1991-94, Virginia Beach Neptune Fest., 1997—, King Neptune XXVI; pres. Bay Colony Civic League, Virginia Beach, 1978, Princess Anne Hills Civic League, Virginia Beach, 1988; mem. 4th Cir. Jud. Conf., 1974—; mem. 2d dist. ethics com. Va. State Bar, 1983-84. Mem. ABA, Am. Bankruptcy Inst., Nat. Conf. Bankruptcy Judges (bd. govs. 1996—), Norfolk-Portsmouth Bar Assn., Virginia Beach Bar Assn., Va. Bar Assn. (bd. dirs. bankruptcy sect. 1990-93, mem. coun. jud. sect. 1995—, chmn. 1997), Hampton Roads Coun. Navy League of U.S. (life mem.). Episcopalian. Clubs: Cavalier Golf and Yacht (commodore 1994, bd. dirs. 1993—), Pyramid, N.Y. Yacht. Avocations: yachting, swimming, cycling. Home: 1533 Quail Point Rd Virginia Beach VA 23454-3115 Office: United States Bankruptcy Ct Walter E Hoffman US Courthouse 600 Granby St Norfolk VA 23510-1915

**ADAMS, DEBORAH ROWLAND,** lawyer; b. Princeton, N.J., July 28, 1952; d. Bernard S. and Natalie S. Adams; m. Charles L. Campbell, June 16, 1990. BA, Colo. Coll., Colorado Springs, 1974; JD, U. Colo., 1978. Bar: Ind. 1978, Colo. 1978, U.S. Dist. Ct. Colo. 1978. Atty. Legal Svcs. Orgn. Ind., Indpls., 1978-79, Pikes Peak Legal Svcs., Colorado Springs, 1979-80, Pub. Defender's Office, Colorado Springs, 1980-81; assoc. Ranson, Thomas, Cook and Livingston, Colorado Springs, 1982-84, Ranson, Thomas, Adams, Petinga and Yukawa, Colorado Springs, 1984; pvt. practice Colorado Springs, 1985—; mem. state Jud. Nominating Commn. for 4th Jud. Dist., 1994-2000; Colo. state grievance com., 1997-2000. Bd. dirs. Domestic Violence Prevention Ctr., 1980-86, pres., 1982-84; bd. dirs. Pikes Peak Legal Svcs., 1983-88, pres., 1986-87, pro bono advocacy sch. faculty, 1990-92; co-chairperson Colo. Springs Devel. Com., Colo. Women's Found., 1987, mem. grant selection com., 1988, 90; bd. dirs. Vis. Nurses Assn., 1989-91; bd. dirs. Chins Up, 1991-97, pres., 1997-98; co-chairperson El Paso County sect. COLTAF Fundraising Com. for benefit of Colo. Legal Aid Found., 1991-99, chairperson, 1994-95; mem. state bd. dirs. Legal Aid Found., 1994—, v.p., 1997-98. Recipient Pro Bono award Pikes Peak Legal Svcs., 1988; named Atty of Yr. El Paso County Legal Secs. Assn., 1990; selected to attend Colo. Springs Leadership Class, Colorado Springs Leadership Inst., 1997. Mem. Colo. Bar Assn. (family law sect. 1991-99, conciliation panel subcom. of profls. com. 1992, bd. govs. 1994-97, exec. com. 1995-97, nominating com. 1996), Colo. Bar Found., Colo. Women's Bar Assn., El Paso County Bar Assn. (pres.-elect 1994-95, pres. 1995-96, Trial Advocacy Sch. faculty 1990, 94, Moot Ct. judge 1992, 95, fee arbitration dispute com. 1990-95), Women Lawyer's Assn. Fourth Jud. Dist.(chairperson jud. nominating com. 1991-93, Portia award 1992), Zonta Club Colorado Springs (pres. 1989-90, co-chairperson dist. 12 regional conf. 1991-92, Zontian of Yr. 1990-91). Democrat. Avocations: reading, skiing, tennis, running, mountain biking. Family and matrimonial. Office: 324 S Cascade Ave Colorado Springs CO 80903-3804

**ADAMS, DEBORAH SUSAN,** laywer; b. Cin., May 17, 1955; d. Vinson and Zada Mae A.; m. Barry N. Stedman, Dec. 19, 1980; children: Kensey Alyn, Gareth Lachlan. BA, U. Cin., 1977; MA, Harvard U., 1979; JD, Harvard Law Sch., 1982. Bar: Ohio 1982, Ky. 1983, U.S. Dist. Ct. (so. dist.) Ohio 1982, U.S. Ct. Appeals (6th cir.) 1986. Assoc. Frost & Jacobs LLP, Cin., 1982-89, ptnr., 1989—. Trustee, chmn. nominating com. Stepping Stones Ctr. for Handicapped, Cin., 1990-96; trustee, sec. Cin. Ballet, 1984-90. Labor. Office: Frost & Jacobs 2500 PNC Ctr 201 E 5th St Cincinnati OH 45202

**ADAMS, DELPHINE SZYNDROWSKI,** lawyer; b. East Chicago, Ind., May 24, 1953; d. Joseph C. and Rachael L. Szyndrowski; m. Dave Adams. BA, Ind. U., 1974; JD, Golden Gate U., 1985. Bar: Calif. 1986, U.S. dist. Ct. (all dists.) Calif. 1986, U.S. Ct. Appeals (9th cir.) 1986. Assoc. Goldberg, Stinnett & Macdonald, San Francisco, 1986-87; assoc. Bronson, Bronson & McKinnon, San Francisco, 1987-91; assoc. Bronson, Bronson & McKinnon, Santa Rosa, Calif., 1991-93, ptnr., 1993-95; ptnr. Bronson, Bronson & McKinnon, San Francisco, 1995-96; atty. pvt. practice, Santa Rosa, 1996—. Co-author: (chpt.) Real Estate Litigation, 1994. Mem. adv. coun. Red Empire Ballet Assn., Santa Rosa, 1992-94. Mem. Engring. Contractors Assn. (adv. coun. 1996—). Avocations: gardening, motorcycling, reading, music. Real property, Construction, General corporate. Office: PO Box 1902 Santa Rosa CA 95402-1902

**ADAMS, EDWARD A.,** legal journalist; b. South Bend, Ind., Sept. 28, 1963; s. Richard E. and Louise M. (Augustine) A.; m. Eliza A. Dolin, Dec. 31, 1988. PhB, Miami U., Oxford, Ohio, 1985; JD, Columbia U., 1988. Metro intern Cin. Enquirer, summer 1983; reporter intern Am. Lawyer, N.Y.C., winter 1984; rschr. intern Cable News Network, Washington, summer 1984; features intern Cleve. Plain Dealer, summer 1985; reporter intern Nat. Law Jour., N.Y.C., summers 1986-87; bus. intern U.S. News & World Report, Washington, summer 1988; TV reporter N.Y. Post, N.Y.C., 1988; law firm reporter N.Y. Law Jour., N.Y.C., 1989-97, on line editor, 1997—. Co-editor book: Inside the Law Schools, 1991. Mem. Investigative Reporters and Editors. Office: NY Law Jour 345 Park Ave S New York NY 10010-1707

**ADAMS, HENRY LEE, JR.,** federal judge; b. 1945. BS in Polit. Sci., Fla. A&M U., 1966; JD, Howard U., 1969. Staff atty. Duval County Legal Aid Assn., 1969-70; asst. pub. defender, pub. defender's office 4th Jud. Cir., 1970-72; with Sheppard, Fletcher, Hand & Adams, Jacksonville, 1972-76, Marshall & Adams, Jacksonville, 1976-79; judge 4th Jud. Cir., 1979-93, U.S. Dist. Ct. (mid. dist.) Fla., 1993—. Active Tots N' Teens; mem. adv. bd. Fla. Augustus Secure Care Unit; mem. Habijax Adv. Bd.; mem. local sch. adv. coun. Mid W. Gilbert Mid. Sch. Mem. NAACP, Nat. Bar Assn., Fla. Bar Assn., Fla. Conf. Circuit Judges (mem. legis. com.), Jacksonville Bar Assn., D.W. Perkins Bar Assn., Kappa Alpha Psi. Office: US Dist Ct Gibbons US Courthouse 801 N Florida Ave Tampa FL 33602-3849

**ADAMS, JOSEPH KEITH,** lawyer; b. Provo, Utah, Apr. 3, 1949; s. Joseph S. and Marian (Bellows) A.; m. Myrle June Overly, Sept. 2, 1971; children: Derek J., Bret K., Stephanie, Julie K., Scott J., Laura. BA summa cum laude, Brigham Young U., 1973; JD, Harvard U., 1976. Bar: Utah 1976, U.S. Dist. Ct. Utah 1976, U.S. Tax Ct. 1983. Assoc. Van Cott, Bagley, Cornwall & McCarthy, Salt Lake City, 1976-82, shareholder, 1982-98; also bd. dirs. Van Cott, Bagley, et al, Salt Lake City, 1993-97, chmn. tax and estate planning sect., 1995-98; ptnr. Stoel, Rives, LLP, Salt Lake City, 1998—; adj. faculty Brigham Young U. Law Sch., Provo, 1993. Co-author: Practical Estate Planning Techniques, 1990. Planned giving com. Restoration Cathedral Madeleine, Salt Lake City, 1991-93; pres. Utah Planned Giving Roundtable, Salt Lake City, 1994, Salt Lake City Estate Planning Coun.; planned giving com. U. Utah Hosp. Found., 1994; bd. dirs. Salt Lake C.C. Found., 1982-98; stake pres. LDS Ch. David O. Mackay scholar Brigham Young U., 1967-73. Fellow Am. Coll. Trust and Estate Counsel; mem. ABA (real property, probate and trust sect., taxation sect.), Utah State Bar (exec. com., past chmn. estate planning probate sect.), Harvard Alumni Assn. Utah (chair bd. dirs. 1980-90), Harvard Law Sch. Assn. Utah (vice chair). Republican. Mem. LDS Ch. Avocations: skiing, reading, golfing. Estate planning, Probate, Estate taxation. Office: Stoel Rives LLP 201 S Main St Ste 1100 Salt Lake City UT 84111-4904

**ADAMS, LEE STEPHEN,** lawyer, banker; b. St. Louis, June 3, 1949; s. Albert L. and Margaret C. (Donoghue) A. A.B., Rutgers Coll., 1971; J.D., Georgetown U., 1974. Bar: D.C. 1975, Mo. 1975, Ohio 1982, Calif. 1995. Asst. dean Georgetown U. Law Ctr., Washington, 1974-76, adj. prof. law, 1973-76; sr. counsel to bd. govs. FRS, Washington, 1976-81; v.p., gen. counsel Fed. Res. Bank, Cleve., 1981-82, sr. v.p., gen. counsel, 1982-86; dep. gen. counsel Bank One Corp., Columbus, Ohio, 1986-95, v.p., gen. counsel, 1986-91; of counsel Morrison & Foerster, San Francisco, 1995-98, Washington, 1999—; lectr. law Cath. U. Law Sch., Washington, 1977-81. Mem. Athletic Club (Columbus), Columbus Country Club. Banking, Administrative and regulatory. Home: 4309 Torchlight Cir Bethesda MD 20816-1846 Office: Morrison & Foerster 2000 Pennsylvania Ave NW Washington DC 20006-1812

**ADAMS, LUDWIG HOWARD,** lawyer; b. Pitts., Dec. 11, 1954; s. Ludwig and Alberta Anne (Howard) A.; m. Lynn Ann Krapcho, Sept. 12, 1981; children: Kimberly Lynn, Justin Andrew. BA, U. Pa., 1976, MA, 1976; JD, Columbia U., 1979; LLM in Taxation, NYU, 1988. Bar: D.C. 1979, N.Y. 1986, U.S. Tax Ct. 1991. Trial atty. tax divsn. U.S. Dept. Justice, Washington, 1979-84; assoc. Cahill Gordon & Reindel, N.Y.C., 1984-90, sr. atty., 1990-96, counsel, 1996—. Editor, author Columbia Jour. Transnational Law, 1978-79. Mem. ABA (tax sect.), N.Y. State Bar Assn. (tax sect.). Methodist. Corporate taxation, Taxation, general, Federal civil litigation. Office: Cahill Gordon & Reindel 80 Pine St Fl 17 New York NY 10005-1790

**ADAMS, LYDIA CECILE,** judge; b. Detroit, Mar. 21, 1960; d. Gerald Ronald and Delores Mae (Claybrooks) Nance; m. Daryl Lamont Adams, Jan. 23, 1980. BBA, Western Mich. U., 1986; JD, Detroit Coll. Law, 1990. Bar: Mich. 1994. Dept. mgr. Dayton-Hudson Dept. Store, Dearborn, Mich., 1986; educator Detroit Pub. Schs., 1987; law clk. Mich. Tax Tribunal, Detroit, 1988; regulation officer corps. and security bur. Mich. Dept. Commerce, Detroit, 1989-90; dept. analyst dept. legal resources Mich. Dept. Commerce, Lansing, 1992-94; regulation agt. BOPR Mich. Dept. Commerce, Detroit, 1994-95; mgr. contracts and copyright WTVS Channel 56 Pub. TV, Detroit, 1994-95; asst. corp. counsel City of Detroit, 1995-96; judge 36th Dist. Ct., Detroit, 1997—. Mem. Mus. African-Am. History, Detroit, Trade Union Leader Conf., Detroit, 1997—. Mem. ABA, State Bar Mich., Wolverine Bar Assn., Women Lawyers Assn. Mich. (dir.-at-large 1995-96), NAACP, Mich. Assn. Black Judges, Nat. Coalition of 100 Black Women, Women's Econ. Club. Democrat. Avocations: gardening, reading, walking, travel. Office: 36th Dist Ct 421 Madison St Ste 4074 Detroit MI 48226-2382

**ADAMS, MARK KILDEE,** lawyer; b. Des Moines, Oct. 8, 1938; s. Walter Bunting and Regina (Kildee) A.; m. Helen von Bachmayr Larsen, May 22, 1982; 1 child, Kirsten. AB, Harvard U., 1960, JD, 1966. Bar: N.Mex. 1966, U.S. Dist. Ct. N.Mex. 1966, U.S. Ct. Appeals (10th cir.) 1970, U.S. Claims Ct., Zuni Pueblo Tribal Ct. Assoc. Rodey, Dickason, Sloan, Akin & Robb, Albuquerque, 1966-70, ptnr., 1970—. Author articles on natural resources and Indian law issues to profl. jours. Capt. U.S. Army, 1960-62. Mem. ABA, Albuquerque Bar Assn. (bd. dirs. 1976-78), Lawyers Club (officer 1980-84). Republican. General corporate, Oil, gas, and mineral. Office: Rodey Dickason Sloan Akin & Robb 201 3d St NW Ste 2200 Albuquerque NM 87102

**ADAMS, MICHAEL JOHN,** lawyer, financial consultant, developer; b. Mpls., Oct. 26, 1945; s. John Franklin and Sylvia Marie (Olson) A.; m. Christine Ellen Peterson, Mar. 1, 1968; children: John, Jeff, Michelle. BA, U. Minn., 1967, JD, 1972. Bar: Minn. 1972. Assoc. Nilva & Frisch, St. Paul, 1972-73; ptnr. Gustafson & Adams, P.A., Edina, Minn., 1973-85; mng. ptnr. Adams & Cesario, P.A., Bloomington, Minn., 1985—; chmn., CEO Olympic Hills Corp., Eden Prairie, Minn., 1973—, MBR/BRI, Mpls., 1973—, ADCO Fin. Svcs., Bloomington, 1974—; CEO North Star Rail, Inc. Bloomington, Minn., 1992—; bd. dirs. Fourth Shift Corp., 1981—. Bd. visitors U. Minn., Mpls., 1982—. Mem. U. Minn. Law Alumni Assn. (bd. dirs. 1985), Olympic Hills Golf Club (pres. 1976-81, treas. 1990). Republican. Avocations: golf, walking, basketball, travel, reading. Office: Adams & Cesario PA 1550 E 79th St Ste 800 Minneapolis MN 55425-3102

**ADAMS, MORGAN GOODPASTURE,** lawyer; b. Nashville, Feb. 2, 1964; s. David Porterfield Jr. and Elizabeth Devereux (Morgan) Spiegel. BA, Bowdoin Coll., 1985; JD, Ga. State U., 1989. Bar: Ga. 1989, Tenn. 1989, D.C. 1990, U.S. Ct. Mil. Appeals 1990, U.S. Dist. Ct. (ea. dist.) Tenn. 1994, U.S. Ct. Vets. Appeals 1994, U.S. Supreme Ct. 1997. Litigation assoc. Luther Anderson Cleary & Ruth, Chattanooga, 1993-95; litig. ptnr. Hatfield, Van Cleave, Akers & Adams, Chattanooga, 1995-97; pvt. practice Chattanooga, 1997—. Contbg. editor ABA Family Law Lit. newsletter. Pres. Advantage Hunter, Hunter Mus., Chattanooga, 1994-95; vice chmn. Hamilton County Rep. Com., Chattanooga, 1997-99. With USMC, 1989-93; maj. USMCR, 1983-89, 93—. Bosch-Duisberg scholar Ga. State U. Coll. Law, Germany, 1989. Mem. Army Navy Club. Pachyderm Club (pres. 1997-98). Avocations: rugby, tennis, running. Personal injury, Family and matrimonial, General civil litigation. Office: 410 McCallie Ave Chattanooga TN 37402-2009

**ADAMS, NATE LAVINDER, III,** lawyer; b. Camp Pendelton, Calif., July 20, 1955; s. Nate Lavinder A. AB, Coll. William & Mary, 1977; MS, Am. U., 1979; JD, Washington & Lee U., 1981. Bar: Va. 1981, D.C. 1982, U.S. Ct. Appeals (4th cir.), U.S. Dist. Ct. (ea. and we. dists.) Va., U.S. Bankruptcy Ct. Law clk. U.S. Dist. Ct., Roanoke, Va., 1981-83; assoc. Bird, Kinder & Huffman, Roanoke, Va., 1983-87; shareholder Hall, Monahan, Engle, Mahan & Mitchell, Winchester, Va., 1987-97, Adams & Kellas, Winchester, Va., 1998—; instr. Shenandoah U., Winchester, Va., 1996—. Co-editor: Virginia State Bar Senior Citizens Handbook, 1993. Chmn. Winchester Bd. of Zoning Appeals. Mem. ABA, Va. Bar Assn., Winchester-Frederick County Bar Assn. Avocations: reading, history, travel, tennis. General civil litigation, Consumer commercial, General practice. Office: Adams & Kellas 21 S Kent St Winchester VA 22601-5049

**ADAMS, RICHARD GLEN,** lawyer; b. West Reading, Pa., Mar. 21, 1941; s. Daniel Snyder and Carrie B. (Vought) A.; m. Merrill Richards, June 13, 1964; children: Rebecca Elizabeth, Rachael Kat. AB, Princeton U., 1963, cert., 1963; LLB, Yale U., 1967, MA in Econs., 1967. Bar: Conn. 1967, U.S. Dist. Ct. Conn. 1967, U.S. Ct. Appeals (2d cir.) 1967. Assoc. Jacobs, Jacobs. Grudberg & Clifford, New Haven, 1967-72; assoc. Ribicoff & Kotkin, Hartford, 1972-73, ptnr., 1973-78; mem. Adams & Tomc, Middletown, Conn., 1978-85; pvt. practice Middletown, 1985-88; ptnr. Adams & Harding, 1988-96; pvt. practice, 1996—; sec., dir. Lyman Farm, Inc., 1968-91; bar exam. reader and grader, 1982. Candidate Conn. Ho. of Reps., 1968; mem. Holiday Project, 1980-95, Hunger Project, 1981-93; mem. Lawyers Alliance Nuclear Arms Control, 1981-90, profl. div. United Way, 1979; bd. dirs. Camp Hazen YMCA, 1984-90; mem. Conn. Legis. Task Force on Environ. Permit Streamlining, 1993-94; mem. Middlefield Rep. Town COm., 1996-99, vice chair, 1995-98; trustee Charles B. Merwin Trust, 1981—. Mem. ABA, Conn. Bar. Assn. (chmn. various coms.), COnn. Sch. Attys. Coun., Middlesex County Bar Assn., Train Collectors Assn., Hist. Assn. Nello Bottle Collectors. Administrative and regulatory, State civil litigation, Real property. Home: 175 Powder Hill Rd Middlefield CT 06455-1133 Office: 163 College St Middletown CT 06457-3238

**ADAMS, SAMUEL FRANKLIN,** lawyer; b. Jacksonville, Fla., Jan. 9, 1958; s. Samuel Eugene and Lucille (Quinn) A.; m. Beverly June Walls, Sept. 27, 1986 (div. 1996); m. Ronda Jean Pence, Sept. 7, 1996; 1 child, Samuel Matthew. BA in Polit. Sci., Stetson U., 1980; JD, Samford U., 1983. Bar: Fla. 1983, S.C. 1987, U.S. Dist. Ct. S.C. 1988. Assoc. Phil Trovillo, P.A., Ocala, Fla., 1983-86; v.p.adminstrn. Good Shepherd Meml. Pk., Spartanburg, S.C., 1986-88, C & C Properties, Spartanburg, 1988—; pvt. practice law Spartanburg, 1988-95; assoc. Dallis Law Firm, PA, Spartanburg, 1995-97; ptnr. Adams & Charles, Attys. at Law, P.A., Spartanburg, 1997—; atty. for City of Chesnee, S.C., 1991-92; magistrate Spartanburg County, 1992—; city judge Pallot Mills, 1992—. Pres. Boiling Springs Jaycees, 1996—. Mem. ABA, Fla. Bar Assn., Am. Assn. Trial Lawyers, Jaycees (v.p. enrollment and growth Spartanburg 1988, legal counsel Boiling Springs 1991-92, 96, pres. 1996-97), Optimists (sec., treas. Ocala chpt. 1984-85). Democrat. Presbyterian. Avocations: hiking, jogging, basketball. General civil litigation, General corporate, Probate.

**ADAMS, STACY WADE,** prosecutor; b. Birmingham, Ala., Apr. 3, 1967; s. Paul Gerald and Emogene (Argo) A.; m. Marjorie Virginia Walker, Aug. 4, 1996. BA, Hampden-Sydney Coll., 1989; JD, Cumberland Sch. Law, Birmingham, 1992. Bar: Ala. 1992, D.C. 1994, U.S. Dist. Ct. (mid. dist.) Ala. 1992. Rsch. asst. dept. medicine U. Ala., Birmingham, 1986-88; accounts rep. Gordon, Silberman, Wiggins & Childs, Birmingham, 1990; law clk., bailiff to Hon. C. Bennett McRae Circuit Ct., Decatur, Ala., 1993-95, law clk., bailiff to Hon. Glenn E. Thompson, 1995; ops. mgr. Joe Money Machinery, Birmingham, 1996; asst. dist. atty. 8th Judicial Dist., Decatur, 1996—. George C. Marshall scholar, 1989. Mem. Nat. Dist. Attys. Assn., Ala. Dist. Attys. Assn., Phi Beta Kappa. Republican. Baptist. Avocation: golf. Home: 393 Jamestown Manor Dr Gardendale AL 35071-2630 Office: Morgan County Dist Attys Office PO Box 668 Decatur AL 35602-0668

**ADAMS, THOMAS LAWRENCE,** lawyer; b. Jersey City, Apr. 14, 1948; s. Lawrence Ignatius and Dorothy Tekla (Halgas) A.; m. Elizabeth Anne Russell, June 14, 1969 (div. 1981); children: Thomas, Katherine; m. Deanna Louise Mollo, July 30, 1983; stepchildren: Kathy, Kerry. BS, N.J. Inst. of Tech., 1969; JD, Seton Hall U., 1975. Bar: N.J. 1975, N.Y. 1976, U.S. Dist. Ct. N.J. 1975, U.S. Patent Office 1975. Systems engr. Grumman Aerospace, Bethpage, N.Y., 1969-71; sr. engr. Weston Instruments, Newark, 1971-74; with patent staff RCA Corp., Princeton, N.J., 1974-75; corp. atty. Otis Elevator, N.Y.C., 1975-77; ptnr. Goebel & Adams, Morristown, N.J., 1978-80, Behr & Adams, Morristown & Edison, N.J., 1981—. Councilman Twp. Council, Livingston, N.J., 1985-88, dep. mayor, 1987; commr. Environ. Commn., Livingston, 1984-87; chmn. Livingston Rep. County com., 1992-98. Mem. N.J. Patent Law Assn., Morris County Bar Assn., Trial Attys. of N.J., N.J. State Bar Assn. (chair patent, trademark, copyright law and unfair competition 1991), Seton Hall Law Rev., Tau Beta Pi, Eta Kappa Nu. Roman Catholic. Lodges: K.C. (Grand Knight 1980). Patent, Trademark and copyright, State civil litigation.

**ADAMS, THOMAS LEWIS,** lawyer; b. Des Moines, May 26, 1934; s. Albert Henry and Dorothy Irene (Potwin) A.; m. Marilyn J. Trout, Aug. 15, 1959 (div. Jan. 1978); children: Sara, Jennifer; m. Kathryn M. Tromly, June 16, 1979. BA, U. Iowa, 1956; MS, Columbia U., 1959; JD, U. Iowa, 1963. Bar: Iowa 1963, Minn. 1964, U.S. Dist. Ct. Minn. 1964. Assoc. Meagher & Geer, Mpls., 1963—. Mem. ABA, Am. Coll. Trial Lawyers, Minn. Def. Lawyers Assn., Phi Beta Kappa. Episcopalian. Avocation: tennis. Construction, Personal injury, General civil litigation. Office: Meagher & Geer 33 S 6th St Ste 4200 Minneapolis MN 55402-3788

**ADAMS, THOMAS TILLEY,** lawyer; b. Orchard Park, N.Y., Oct. 9, 1929; s. Floyd Tilley and Clara Elizabeth (Potter) A.; m. Virginia Rives Smith, Sept. 1, 1956; children: Julia, Janet, Claire, Douglas. BA, U. Buffalo, 1951; JD, Cornell U., 1957. Bar: N.Y. 1957, U.S. Ct. Appeals (2d cir.) 1962, U.S. Supreme Ct. 1962, Conn. 1964. Tchr. Lake Shore Cen. Sch., Angola, N.Y., 1953-54; assoc. Davies, Hardy & Schenck, N.Y.C., 1957-63; prin. Gregory & Adams P.C., Wilton, Conn. and N.Y.C., 1963—; lectr. Cornell U. Law Sch., Ithaca, N.Y., 1962-65, emeritus mem. adv. coun., 1990—; adj. assoc. prof. law Fordham U., N.Y.C., 1973-76; adviser Dana Fund Internat. and Comparative Legal Studies, Toledo, 1976-91; assoc. bd. dirs. Union Trust Co., Stamford, Conn., 1982-94; mem. adv. bd. Norwalk Savs. Soc., 1993-97. Town counsel Town of Wilton, 1966-71; pres. Five Town Found., Norwalk, Conn., 1983-85, trustee, 1989-91; chmn. bldg. com. Wilton High Sch., 1966; bd. dirs. Woodcock Nature Ctr., Wilton-Ridgefield, Conn., 1997—. Recipient Silver Beaver award Boy Scouts Am., 1980, Disting. Alumnus award Cornell Law Sch., 1990. Mem. ABA, Am. Judicature Soc. (dir. 1991-92), Norwalk/Wilton Bar Assn. (pres. 1990), Stamford/Norwalk Regional Bar Assn. (bd. dirs. 1991-93), Conn. Bar Assn. (ethics com. 1970-75, 92-93, mem. coun. bar pres.'s 1988-90), N.Y. Bar Assn., Silver Spring Country Club (gov. 1998—), Cornell Club (N.Y.), Phi Delta Phi. Episcopalian. Fax: 203 834-1628. General practice, Land use and zoning (including planning), Probate. Home: 55 Deer Run Rd Wilton CT 06897-1204 also: Rogers Rock Clb Ticonderoga NY 12883 Office: Gregory & Adams PC 190 Old Ridgefield Rd Wilton CT 06897-4023

**ADAMS, WESLEY P., JR.,** lawyer; b. N.Y.C., Oct. 4, 1935; s. Wesley P. and Dorothy (Campbell) A.; m. Marcia Shaw, June 28, 1957 (div. 1972); m. Amelia Adams, Oct. 13, 1973; children: Denise, Catherine, wesley III, Jennifer. BA, Dartmouth Coll., 1957; JD, U. Va., 1960. Bar: Ky. 1960. Ptnr. Ogden, Robertson & Marshall, Louisville, 1960-82, Goldberg & Simpson, Louisville, 1982-91, Weber & Rose, Louisville, 1991—. Chair Legal Aid. Soc., Louisville, 1968-71; chair attys. divsn. Metro United Way, Louisville, 1966; precinct capt. Dem. Party, Louisville, 1960-66. Mem. ABA, Ky. Bar Assn. (Lawyers Helping Lawyers 1994-96), Louisville Bar Assn. (fed. practice com. 1972). Jewish. Avocations: tennis, gardening, working with alcoholics and homeless. Home: 7306 Wolf Pen Branch Rd Prospect KY 40059-9628 Office: Weber & Rose 2700 Aegon Ctr Louisville KY 40059

**ADAMSON, LARRY ROBERTSON,** lawyer; b. Tucson, Mar. 17, 1935; s. Harold David and Manie (Robertson) A.; m. Florence Anna Obad, May 31, 1969; children—Larry Robertson, Michael Marion. B.S. in Bus. Adminstrn., U. Ariz., 1957, postgrad., 1960-61; J.D., U. San Francisco, 1969; LL.M. in Taxation, NYU, 1970. Bar: Calif. 1970, Ariz., 1971, U.S. Dist. Ct. Ariz. 1971, U.S. Tax Ct. 1970. Staff acct. with various C.P.A. firms in Los Angeles and San Francisco, 1961-69; assoc., then mem. Duffield, Young, Adamson & Alfred, P.C. and predecessors, Tucson, 1970—; guest lectr. U. Ariz. Law Sch., 1974-83, Ariz. Law Inst., 1978-79, So. Ariz. Estate Planning Council, 1976, 83, Tucson Legal Secs. Assn., 1984, State Bar Ariz., 1990, 97, also for various civic, charitable orgns. and tax study groups. Bd. dir. Tucson Airport Authority, 1993-98, pres. 1998; Bd. dirs. Tucson Symphony Soc., 1980-85, mem. exec. com. 1981-84, sec., 1982-84; mem. deferred giving com. Ariz. Sonora Desert Mus., Tucson, 1980-84, bd. dirs. U. Ariz. Found., 1983-88; mem. Tucson Com. on Fgn. Relations, 1984—; bd. dirs. Tucson Med. Ctr. Found., 1985-93, chmn. planned giving com., mem. exec. com., 1985-93, Ariz. Children's Found., 1993-97; exec. com. Planned Giving Roundtable So. Ariz., 1985—, pres., 1997. Served to comdr. USNR, 1953-76. Mem. ABA, Ariz. Bar Assn., Pima County Bar Assn., Am. Inst. C.P.A.s, Ariz. Soc. C.P.A.s, Calif. Soc. C.P.A.s, Am. Assn. Atty.-C.P.A.s, Ariz. Assn. Atty.-C.P.A.s (pres. 1981—), So. Ariz. Estate Planning Council (dir. 1976-84, pres. 1982-83). Clubs: Rotary (dir. club 1975-77, pres. 1985-86, treas. club 1975-76, sec. club 1976-77, dir. and pres. Rotary Club of Tucson Found. 1975—), Tucson Country, Mountain Oyster, U. Ariz. Found. Pres.'s (Tucson). Estate taxation, Estate planning, Personal income taxation. Office: Duffield Young Adamson & Alfred PC 3430 E Sunrise Dr Ste 200 Tucson AZ 85718-3210

**ADANIYA, KEVIN SEISHO,** lawyer; b. San Francisco, Sept. 24, 1968; s. Roy Seijin and Lavern Gay Adaniya. BA in Polit. Sci., U. Calif., Santa Barbara, 1990; JD, U. of the Pacific, Sacramento, 1995. Bar: Hawaii 1996, U.S. Dist. Ct. Hawaii 1997. Law clk. State of Hawaii, Hilo, 1995-96; sole practitioner Honolulu, 1996—. Vol., Kids First Program, Honolulu, 1998-99, Vol. guardian Ad Litem Program, Honolulu, 1998-99. Recipient Edward R. Nakano Meml. award Hawaii Jaycees, 1998, Daniel K. Inouye award, 1999. Mem. ABA (family law sect.), Hawaii State Bar Assn. (family law, bankruptcy law, child and parent advocates sects., dir. Young Lawyers divsn. 1999), Hawaii Bus. Jaycees (v.p. 1997-99, Jaycee of Yr. 1998. Bankruptcy, Family and matrimonial. Office: 33 S King St Ste 140 Honolulu HI 96813-4319

**ADASHEK, JAMES LEWIS,** lawyer; b. Milw., July 5, 1952; s. Floyd M. and Charlotte A.; m. Vivian M., Jan. 3, 1981; children: Beth, Ben. BA in History, U. Md., 1975; JD, Vanderbilt U., 1979. Bar: U.S. Dist. Ct. (ea. dist.) Wis. 1979, (we. dist.) 1986, U.S. Ct. Appeals 7th Cir. 1986. Asst. gen. counsel Bank One Corp., Milw., 1987-97; ptnr. Quarles & Brady, Milw., 1997—. Mem. State Bar Wis., Milw. Bar Assn. Bankruptcy, Banking, Contracts commercial. Office: Quarles & Brady 411 E Wisconsin Ave Ste 2550 Milwaukee WI 53202-4497

**ADDABBO, DOMINIC LUCIAN,** lawyer; b. N.Y.C., Dec. 13, 1951; s. Joseph P. and Grace (Salamone) A.; m. Marianna G. Riverso, Jan. 12, 1980; children: Grace, Lisa, Joseph. BA, St. John's U., 1973, JD, 1976. Bar: N.Y. 1977, Fla. 1978, U.S. Dist. Ct. (ea. and so. dists.) N.Y. 1978. Asst. dist. atty. Queens Dist. Attys. Office, KEw Gardens, N.Y., 1977-81; coun. to pres. Queens Borough Pres., KEw Gardens, N.Y., 1981-83; ptnr. Addabbo & Greenberg, Forest Hills, N.Y., 1983—. Pres. United Exec. Dem. Club, Ozone Park, N.Y., 1981-86, state commiteeman N.Y. State Dem. Party, Queens, 1982-86. Mem. Fla. Bar Assn., N.Y. State Bar Assn., Queens County Bar Assn., Asst. Dist. Attys. Assn. Roman Catholic. Avocations: music, songwriting, Karate. Real property, Criminal, Personal injury. Office: Addabbo & Greenberg 11821 Queens Blvd Forest Hills NY 11375-7201

**ADDIS, RICHARD BARTON,** lawyer; b. Columbus, Ohio, April 9, 1929; s. Wilbur Jennings and Leila Olive (Grant) A.; m. Marguerite C. Christjohn, Feb. 9, 1957; children: Jacqueline Carol, Barton David. BA, Ohio State U., 1954, JD, 1955. Bar: Ohio 1956, U.S. Dist. Ct. (no. dist.) Ohio 1957, N.Mex. 1963, U.S. Dist. Ct. N.Mex. 1963, Laguna Pueblo (N.Mex.) Tribal Ct. 1986. Pvt. practice, Canton, Ohio, 1956-63, Albuquerque, 1963—, Laguna Pueblo, 1986—. Co-developer The Woodlands Subdivsn., Albuquerque; co-owner Cerro del Oro Mine, Valencia County, N.Mex., 1977—. With USMC, 1946-48, 50-52. Mem. Ohio Bar Assn., N.Mex. Bar Assn. General practice, Oil, gas, and mineral. Office: PO Box 25923 Albuquerque NM 87125-0923

**ADDISON, DAVID DUNHAM,** lawyer; b. Richmond, Va., Aug. 23, 1941; s. Grafton Dulany and Anne (Withers) A.; m. Marion Lee Wood, Aug. 21, 1965; children: David Dunham Jr., Marion Lee, Elizabeth Townshend. BA, Hampden-Sydney Coll., 1964; LLB, U. Va., 1967. Bar: Va. 1967. Assoc. Browder, Russell, Morris & Butcher, Richmond, 1967-72; ptnr., dir. Browder & Russell, P.C., Richmond, 1972-90; mem. firm, shareholder Williams, Mullen, Clark & Dobbins, P.C., Richmond, 1990—. Contbr. articles to profl. jours. Fellow Am. Coll. Trust and Estate Counsel (state chmn. 1986-92); mem. ABA (com. chmn. 1987-94), S.R., Va. Bar Assn., Richmond Bar Assn., Estate Planning Coun. Richmond (pres. 1987-88), Richmond Trust Adminstrs. Coun. (pres. 1986-87), Kiwanis Club of Richmond (pres. 1998-99), Country Club of Va., Commonwealth Club. Episcopalian. Avocations: travel, golf. Estate planning, Probate, Taxation, general. Office: Williams Mullen Clark & Dobbins 2 James Center 1021 E Cary St Richmond VA 23219-4000

**ADELE, MICHAEL RAY,** lawyer; b. Calif., July 14, 1963; s. Leon and Sharon A. Bachelor's, U. Calif., Irvine, 1985; JD, Harvard U., 1989. Bar: Calif. Ptnr. Cooley Godward LLP, San Diego, 1996—. Home: 424 Stratford Ct Apt B34 Del Mar CA 92014-2734 Office: Cooley Godward LLP 4365 Executive Dr Ste 1100 San Diego CA 92121-2133

**ADELKOFF, STEVEN J.,** lawyer; b. Pitts., Nov. 15, 1962; s. Stuart Louis and Marilyn Ruth Adelkoff; m. Sherri Konopelski, Mar. 6, 1994. BA in Theatre Arts, Rutgers U., 1985; JD, U. Pitts., 1988. Bar: Pa. 1988, U.S. Dist. Ct. (we. dist.) Pa. 1988, U.S. Tax Ct. 1996. Assoc. Kirkpatrick & Lockhart LLP, Pitts., 1988-96, ptnr., 1997—. Editor-in-chief Jour. Law and Commerce, 1987-88. Real property, Finance. Office: Kirkpatrick & Lockhart LLP 1500 Oliver Bldg Pittsburgh PA 15222

**ADELMAN, MARC D.,** lawyer; b. 1950. BA, Western Ill. U.; JD, Western State U. Bar: Calif. 1978. Pvt. practice San Diego. Mem. ABA, Calif. State Bar Assn. (pres.). General civil litigation. Office: 2718 5th Ave San Diego CA 92103-6329*

**ADELMAN, MICHAEL SCHWARTZ,** lawyer; b. Cambridge, Mass., June 6, 1940; s. Benjamin Taft and Sally Frances (Schwartz) A.; m. Amy Kay, June 14, 1962; children: Robert, Jonathon. Student, Boston U., 1958-59; BA with honors in English, U. Mich., 1962, JD cum laude. Bar: Mich. 1968, Miss. 1974. Assoc. Zwerdling, Miller, Klimist & Maurer, Detroit, 1968-69; ptnr. Philo, Maki, Ravitz, Glotta, Adelman, Cockrel & Robb, Detroit, 1969-70, Glotta, Adelman & Dinges, Detroit, 1970-74, Andalman, Adelman & Steiner P.A., Hattiesburg, Miss., 1974-86, Adelman & Steiner P.A., Hattiesburg, Miss., 1986—; sec., bd. dirs. S.E. Miss. Legal Svcs., Hattiesburg. Contbr. short stories: The Deputy, The Detention Center to New Renaissance. Treas. Hattiesburg Area Equal Rights Coun.; mem. Hattiesburg Biracial Adv. Com., 1987-89, chmn., 1988-89. Recipient Ralph T. Abernathy award Jackson County (Miss.) So. Christian Leadership Conf., 1978. Mem. ABA, South Ctrl. Miss. Bar Assn. (treas.). Criminal, Personal injury, Workers' compensation. Address: 602 Mackwood Dr Hattiesburg MS 39402-2030

**ADELMAN, STANLEY JOSEPH,** lawyer; b. Devils Lake, N.D., May 20, 1942; s. Isadore Russell Adelman and Eva Claire (Robins) Stoller; m. Mary Beth Petchaft, Jan. 30, 1972; children: Laura E., Sarah A. BS, U. Wis., 1964, JD, 1967. Bar: Ill. 1967, U.S. Dist. Ct. (no. dist.) Ill. 1967, Wis. 1968, U.S. Ct. Appeals (7th cir.), U.S. Dist. Ct. (ea. dist.) Wis. 1979, U.S. Supreme Ct. 1982, U.S. Ct. Appeals (10th cir.) 1984, U.S. Ct. Appeals (fed. cir.) 1987. Assoc. Sonnenchein, Carlin, Nath & Rosenthal, Chgo., 1967-75, ptnr., 1975-85; co-chmn. litigation dept. Rudnick & Wolfe, Chgo., 1985-91, 96-97, ptnr., 1985—; profl. responsibility ptnr. Rudnick & Wolfe, 1992-94, mem. mgmt. policy com., 1985-97, co-chmn. complex litigation practices group, 1997-98. Bd. dirs. Legal Assistance Found., Chgo., 1982-83. Fellow Nat. Inst. Trial Advocacy; mem. Chgo. Bar Assn., Chgo. Coun. Lawyers, Am. Inns of Ct. (pres. Markey/Wigmore chpt.), Law Club Chgo., Order of Coif. Jewish. General civil litigation, Federal civil litigation, State civil litigation. Home: 115 Crescent Dr Glencoe IL 60022-1303 Office: Rudnick & Wolfe 203 N La Salle St Ste 1800 Chicago IL 60601-1210

**ADELMAN, STEVEN HERBERT,** lawyer; b. Chgo., Dec. 21, 1945; s. Irving and Sylvia (Cohen) A.; m. Pamela Bernice Kozoll, June 30, 1968; children: David, Robert. BS, U. Wis.-Madison, 1967; JD, DePaul U., 1970. Bar: Ill. 1970, U.S. Dist. Ct. (no. dist.) Ill. 1970, U.S. Ct. Appeals (7th cir.) 1975. Ptnr. Keck, Mahin & Cate, Chgo., 1970-93, Lord, Bissell & Brook, Chgo., 1993—. Contbr. chpts. to books, articles to profl. jours. Bd. dirs. Bur. Jewish Employment Problems, Chgo., 1983—, pres. 1991, 92; employment relations com. Chgo. Assn. Commerce and Industry, 1982-90. Mem. Chgo. Bar Assn. (chmn. labor and employment law com. 1988-89), ABA (Silver Key award 1969), Ill. State Bar Assn., Chgo. Council Lawyers, Decalogue Soc. Labor. Office: Lord Bissell & Brook 115 S La Salle St Ste 3200 Chicago IL 60603-3972

**ADERHOLD, H. RANDOLPH,** prosecutor. U.S. atty. Mid. Dist. Ga., Macon, to 1998, chief civil divsn., 1998—. Office: US Atty Mid Dist Ga 433 Cherry St Macon GA 31201-7919

**ADERHOLD, KATHLEEN,** lawyer; b. Atlanta, Feb. 22, 1962; d. Thomas Carroll and Peggy Aderhold. BA, Vanderbilt U., 1983; JD, Ga. Stae U., 1991. Bar: Ga., U.S. Dist. Ct. (no., so. and mid. dists.) Ga., U.S. Ct. Appeals (11th cir.); cert. civil and domestic mediator. Jud. law clk. to Hon. Perry Brannen, Jr. Savannah, Ga., 1991-92; assoc. Weiner, Shearause, Weitz, et al, Savannah, Ga., 1992-97; pvt. practice Savannah, 1997—. Bd. dirs. Lucas Theatre, Savannah, 1994-98, Savannah Theatre, 1997-99; mem. Leadership Savannah, 1994-96. Mem. Jr. League of Savannah, Savannah Young Lawyers (sec. 1997, pres. 1997-99), Savannah Women Lawyers (v.p. 1995-96, pres. 1996-98), Ga. Younger Lawyers (dist. rep. 1994—). General civil litigation, Family and matrimonial, General practice. Office: PO Box 2232 Savannah GA 31402-2232

**ADERSON, SANFORD M.,** lawyer; b. Pitts., July 15, 1949; s. Sanford C. and Marjorie S. (Stern) A.; m. Leslie S. Sertner, Aug. 12, 1972; children: Benjamin, Jonathan. BSBA, Boston U., 1971, JD, 1974. Bar: Pa. 1974, U.S. Dist. Ct. (we. dist.) Pa. 1974, U.S. Tax Ct. 1978, U.S. Ct. Appeals (3d cir.) 1986. Law clk. to judge Ct. of Common Pleas, Pitts., 1974-83; with Aderson, Frank, Steiner & Blechman, Pitts., 1976—. Bd. dirs. Jewish Cmty. Ctr. of Pitts., 1993-98, chmn. sports, fitness and recreation com., bd. dirs. Mem. ABA, Pa. Bar Assn., Allegheny County Bar Assn. (bankruptcy sect. mem. of coun. 1993-98), Westmoreland Country Club (bd. dirs. 1987—, chmn. legal adv. com., chmn. greens com. 1992-96, v.p. 1997—). Bankruptcy, General corporate, Mergers and acquisitions. Office: Aderson, Frank, Steiner & Blechman 2300 Grant Bldg Pittsburgh PA 15219-2302

**ADKINS, EDWARD JAMES,** lawyer; b. Annapolis, Md., Oct. 18, 1947; s. Lee William and Lottie Elizabeth (Stevenson) A.; m. Cheryl Lynne Walcroft, Aug. 24, 1968; children: Helen Elizabeth, Susan Eileen. AB, U. N.C., 1969; JD, U. Md., 1972. Bar: Md. 1972, D.C. 1988, U.S. Mil. Ct. Appeals 1973, U.S. Dist. Ct. Md. 1974, U.S. Supreme Ct. 1976. Assoc. Smith, Somerville & Case, Balt., 1972-75; assoc. Venable, Baetjer & Howard, Balt., 1975-80, ptnr., 1980-81; ptnr. Miles & Stockbridge, P.C., Balt., 1982-93, prin., 1994—; sr. cons. Yaffe & Offutt Assocs., Balt., 1981-82; adj. prof. Loyola Coll., Balt., 1980-83. Mem. Pension Oversight Commn., Anne Arundel County, Md., 1985; bd. dirs. United Way Cen. Md., Balt., 1980, Children's Home, 1997, Archbishop's Spalding High Sch., 1996; bd. dirs., v.p. YMCA, Anne Arundel County, 1985. Served to capt. USAF, 1973. Named one of Outstanding Young Marylanders Jaycees, 1972. Mem. ABA, Md. Bar Assn., Balt. City Bar Assn., Order of Coif. Democrat. Presbyterian. Pension, profit-sharing, and employee benefits, Personal income taxation, Corporate taxation. Office: Miles & Stockbridge PC 10 Light St Ste 1100 Baltimore MD 21202-1487

**ADKINS, NANCI CHERRY PUGH,** lawyer; b. Chgo., May 12, 1939; d. William and Dorothy Eleanor (Harrison) Cherry; m. Benny James Pugh, Oct. 10, 1964 (div. Nov. 1978); children: William N. Pugh, Pamela D. Pugh; m. Rutherford Hamlet Adkins, Nov. 26, 1992 (dec. Feb. 1998). BA in English, Fisk U., 1975; JD, Vanderbilt U., 1978. Bar: Tenn. 1980. Svc. rep. Ill. Bell Telephone, Chgo., 1957-63; sec., bookkeeper Fred Akard Co., Chgo., 1963-65; law clk. Petway & Blackshear, Chgo., 1976-77, Williams & Dinkins, Chgo., 1978; attorney U.S. Dept. Vet. Affairs, Nashville, 1978—; switchboard operator YWCA, Chgo., 1956-57; mem. policy com. Middle Tenn. Fed. Exec. Assn., Nashville, 1979—; bd. mem. Legal Svcs. of Middle Tenn., Nashville, 1997, adv. bd. mem. Meharry Small Bus. Environ. Adv. Prog., Nashville, 1997. Life mem. Fisk U. Alumni Assn., 1975—; bd. pres. Edgehill Ctr., Nashville, 1989-96. Recipient Thelma Rambo incentive award Fisk U., Nashville, 1975. Mem. NAACP (life), Nat. Bar Assn., Lawyers Assn. for Women (sec. 1982—), Tenn. Assn. for Black Lawyers (charter), Napier-Looby Bar Assn, (treas., 1980—). Democrat. Roman Catholic. Avocations: reading, movies, crossword puzzles, scrabble, crocheting. Home: PO Box 23823 Nashville TN 37202-3823

**ADKINS, ROY ALLEN,** lawyer; b. Georgetown, Ohio, Apr. 13, 1952; s. Roger Wayne Adkins and Mary Ruth Carpenter; m. Karen Sue McClanahan, Aug. 20, 1977; children: Matthew Lindsey, Candice Breanna, Jonathan Zachary, Grant Alexander. BA, U. Cin., 1976; JD, U. Denver, 1979, LLM, 1984. Bar: Colo. 1980, U.S. Dist. Ct. Colo. 1980, U.S. Ct. Appeals (10th cir.) 1998. Mgr. Mountain Bell, Denver, 1977-83; assoc. Eiberger, Stacy, Smith & Martin, Denver, 1984—; ptnr. Eiberger, Stacy, Smith & Martin, 1988-92; atty. pvt. practice, 1992-95; of counsel Antonio Bates Bernard, 1995-98; sr. atty. state & local taxation U.S. West, 1998—. Mem., capt. youth campaign YMCA, 1988-89; pack com. chmn. Boy Scouts Am. Mem. ABA, Colo. Bar Assn. (adminstrv. law sect.), Denver Bar Assn., Denver C. of C., Colo. Assn. Commerce and Industry. Presbyterian. Avocations: fly fishing, hiking, camping. Public utilities, Communications, Administrative and regulatory. Home: 5954 E Geddes Cir Englewood CO 80112-1517 Office: US West Law Dept 1801 California St Ste 3800 Denver CO 80202-2658

**ADKISON, RON,** lawyer; b. Nacogdoches, Tex., Jan. 8, 1955; s. Robert Edward and Doris Ozelle (Pollard) A.; m. Tanya Regina Williamson, June 2, 1979 (div. Dec. 1984); 1 child, Veronica Alexis Adkison; m. Donna Elaine Dennis, Apr. 1, 1990; 1 child, Alexander Aron. BA, Stephen F. Austin U., 1976; JD, Baylor U., 1978. Bar: Tex. 1979, U.S. Dist. Ct. (ea., we., so. and no. dists.) Tex., U.S. Ct. Appeals (5th cir.), U.S. Supreme Ct. Atty. Wellborn & Houston, Henderson, Tex., 1979; ptnr. Wellborn, Houston, Adkison et al., Henderson, Tex., 1980—. Regent Stephen F. Austin State U., Nacogdoches, 1993—; chair bd. regents, 1995-96. Fellow Am. Bd. Trial Advs.; mem. Coll. State Bar Tex. (Disciplinary Rev. com., Adminstrn. Rules Civil Evidence com.), Tex. Trial Lawyers Assn. (dir., chair Toxic Torts com.), Henderson Country Club (pres. 1989-94). Avocations: golf, aviation. General civil litigation, Environmental, Contracts commercial. Office: Wellborn Houston Adkison et 300 W Main St Henderson TX 75652-3109

**ADLER, ALLEN PAUL,** lawyer; b. Cleve., Oct. 21, 1943; s. Luke Bertrum and Pauline Elizabeth A.; m. Karen Jean Welsh, Aug. 7, 1976; 1 child, David Joseph. BA, Ohio U., Athens, 1967; JD, Cleve. State U., 1971. Bar: Ohio, U.S. Dist. Ct. (no. dist.) Ohio, U.S. Dist. Ct. (so. dist.) Ohio, U.S. Ct. Appeals (6th cir.), U.S. Supreme Ct. Asst. atty. gen. State of Ohio, Columbus, 1972—. Office: Atty Gen of Ohio 140 E Town St Columbus OH 43215-5125

**ADLER, ARTHUR S.,** lawyer; b. Bklyn., 1958. BA, Columbia U., 1979, JD, 1982. Bar: N.Y. 1983. Law clk. to Hon. Lenoard B. Sand U.S. Dist. Ct. (so. dist.) N.Y., N.Y.C., 1982-83; assoc. Sullivan & Cromwell, N.Y.C., ptnr. Real property. Office: Sullivan & Cromwell 125 Broad St Fl 33 New York NY 10004-2400

**ADLER, CHARLES DAVID,** lawyer; b. N.Y.C., June 29, 1945; s. Hans J. and Frieda (Nayer) A.; m. Judith Lampert, Mar. 26, 1969; 1 child, Kate Devon. Student, Am. U., 1963-65, Queens Coll., N.Y.C., 1965-67; JD, N.Y. Law Sch., 1970. Bar: N.Y. 1971, U.S. Dist. Ct. (so. and ea. dists.) N.Y. 1975, U.S. Supreme Ct. 1977, U.S. Ct. Appeals (2d cir. 1985), U.S. Ct. Appeals (11th cir.) 1988, Ariz. 1991. Acting dir. law adv. bur., sr. trial atty. N.Y.C. Legal Aid Soc., 1971-76; ptnr. Goltzer & Adler, N.Y.C., 1976—; mem. faculty trial advocacy program Cardozo U. Law Sch., N.Y.C., 1981—, Hofstra U. Law Sch., N.Y.C., 1989, Legal Aid Soc., N.Y.C., 1980—. Mem. Dem. Jud. Screening Com., N.Y.C., 1985; pres. Vol. Com. of Lawyers, Ctr. for Cmty. Alternatives. Mem. Nat. Assn. Criminal Def. Lawyers, N.Y. State Assn. Criminal Def. Lawyers (charter mem.), Bar Assn. City of N.Y. (chair criminal law com.), Ctr. for Cmty. Alternatives (pres.). Avocation: pvt. pilot. Criminal, Aviation. Home: 35 W 9th St New York NY 10011-8901 Office: Goltzer & Adler 598 Madison Ave New York NY 10022-1614

**ADLER, DAVID NEIL,** lawyer; b. Bklyn., Apr. 11, 1955; s. Leonard Howard and Elaine (Holder) A. Student, Colgate U., 1973-75; BA, NYU, 1977; JD, St. John's U., 1980. Bar: N.Y. 1981, U.S. Dist. Ct. (ea. and so. dists.) N.Y. 1986, U.S. Tax Ct. 1989. Pvt. practice Kew Gardens, N.Y., 1982—. Contbr. articles to profl. jours. Mem. Queens County Bar Assn. (com. chmn. 1983—, co-editor Queens Bar Bull. 1987—, bd. mgrs. 1989—, officer 1993—, pres. 1998), N.Y. State Bar Assn. (exec. com. trusts and estates). Probate, Estate taxation. Office: 12510 Queens Blvd Kew Gardens NY 11415-1519

**ADLER, DEREK J.T.,** lawyer; b. N.Y.C., Jan. 12, 1961; s. Lee and Florence Adler; m. Noreen R. Weiss, June 9, 1990; 1 child: Isabel Eden Martha. BA in History, Columbia U., 1984; MS in Urban Affairs, Hunter Coll., 1985; JD, Fordham U., 1988; LLM, London U., 1992. Bar: N.Y. 1989, U.S. Dist. Ct. (so., ea. and no. dists.) N.Y. 1994. Assoc. Skadden, Arps, Slate et al, N.Y.C., 1988-91; asst. solicitor Herbert Smith, London, 1992-94; assoc. Hughes Hubbard & Reed, LLP, N.Y.C., 1994—. Fulbright scholar, London, 1991-92. General civil litigation, Securities. Office: Hughes Hubbard & Reed LLP One Battery Park Plaza New York NY 10004

**ADLER, EDWARD ANDREW KOEPPEL,** lawyer; b. N.Y.C., Apr. 12, 1948; s. H. Henry and Geraldine (Koeppel) A.; m. Karen Stapf, Apr. 15, 1973; children: Heather, Trevor. BA, Trinity Coll., Hartford, Conn., 1969; JD, Columbia U., 1972. Bar: N.Y. 1973, U.S. Dist. Ct. (ea. and so. dists.) N.Y. 1973, U.S. Supreme Ct. 1977. Counsel Koeppel & Koeppel, N.Y.C., 1972—. Trustee Sands Point (N.Y.) Civic Assn., 1982—, also pres., 1986-90; trustee Buckley Country Day Sch., Roslyn, N.Y., 1984—, chmn., 1993-96, also treas., 1987-93; trustee, bldg. commr. Village of Sands Point, 1991—; dir. Port Washington Libr. Found., 1996—; dir. Greenwich House, Inc., 1997—, chmn., 1998—. Mem. ABA, N.Y. State Bar Assn., N.Y. County Lawyers Assn., Manhasset Bay Yacht Club, N.Y. Yacht Club. Avocations: sailing, skiing. Real property, Landlord-tenant. Home: 86 Barkers Point Rd Port Washington NY 11050-1328

**ADLER, ERWIN ELLERY,** lawyer; b. Flint, Mich., July 22, 1941; s. Ben and Helen M. (Schwartz) A.; m. Stephanie Ruskin, June 8, 1967; children: Lauren, Michael, Jonathan. B.A., U. Mich., 1963, LL.M., 1967; J.D., Harvard U., 1966. Bar: Mich. 1966, Calif. 1967. Assoc. Pillsbury, Madison & Sutro, San Francisco, 1967-73; assoc. Lawler, Felix & Hall, L.A., 1973-76, ptnr., 1977-80; ptnr Rogers & Wells, L.A., 1981-83, Richards, Watson & Gershon, L.A., 1983—. Bd. dirs. Hollywood Civic Opera Assn., 1975-76, Children's Scholarships Inc., 1979-80. Mem. ABA (vice chmn. appellate advocacy com. 1982-87), Calif. Bar Assn., Phi Beta Kappa, Phi Kappa Phi. Jewish. General civil litigation, State civil litigation, Insurance. Office: Richards Watson & Gershon 333 S Hope St Bldg 38 Los Angeles CA 90071-1406

**ADLER, IRA JAY,** lawyer; b. N.Y.C., Jan. 1, 1942; s. Ralph and Beatrice (Rosenblum) A.; m. Laraine Sheila Garfinkel, July 4, 1965; children: Jodi, Michael. BA, NYU, 1963, JD, 1966. Bar: N.Y. 1966. Ptnr. Certilman, Balin, Adler & Hyman, LLP, East Meadow, N.Y., 1973—; bd. dirs. Queens County Builders and Contractors, Flushing, N.Y. Contbr. to profl. publs. Mem. ABA, N.Y. State Bar Assn., Nassau County Bar Assn., L.I. Builders Inst. (bd. dirs. 1985—), Real Estate Inst. C.W. Post (bd. dirs. 1986—), N.Y. State Builders Assn. (bd. dirs. 1988—). Real property. Office: Certilman Balin Adler & Hyman LLP 90 Merrick Ave East Meadow NY 11554-1571

**ADLER, JOHN WILLIAM, JR.,** lawyer; b. Washington, June 12, 1936; s. John W. and Cassie E. (Wilder) A.; m. JoAnn P. Smith, May 2, 1970; children: Kathleen E., Kerryann P. BS in Biology, Georgetown U., 1958, LLB, 1961. Bar: D.C. 1962, Ill. 1967, Colo. 1969. Trial atty. U.S. Dept. Justice, Washington, 1962-63, 65-67; judge adv. USAF, Phoenix, 1963-65; gen. atty. United Airlines, Chgo., 1967-70; atty. Lord, Bissell, Brook, Chgo., 1970-75, Conklin, Leahy, Eisenberg, Adler, Chgo., 1975-78, Conklin & Adler, Chgo., 1978-88, Adler, Kaplan & Begy, Chgo., 1988-94, Adler, Murphy & McQuillen, Chgo., 1995—. Capt. USAF, 1963-65. Aviation, General civil litigation, Insurance. Office: Adler Murphy & McQuillen 190 S Lasalle St Chicago IL 60603-3410

**ADLER, KENNETH,** lawyer; b. Queens, N.Y., Aug. 7, 1940; s. Alfred and Florence (Resnick) A.; m. Rita Klein, June 19, 1963; children—Howard, Andrew, Samantha. B.S., L.I. U., 1962; J.D., N.Y. U., 1968. Bar: N.Y. 1969, U.S Dist. Ct. (ea. and so. dists.) N.Y. 1973, U.S. Ct. Appeals (2d cir.) 1975, U.S. Ct. Mil. Appeals, 1980, U.S. Ct. Claims, 1980, U.S. Supreme Ct. 1980. Pub. accts. J.M. Levy & Co., CPAs, N.Y.C., 1961-63, Rashbar & Pokart CPAs, N.Y.C., 1963-64; v.p. Clobar Mfgf. Co., N.Y.C., 1964-69; sr. assoc. Morris H. Halpern, Esq., N.Y.C., 1969-72; founder, sr. ptnr. Kenneth Adler & Assocs., Melville, N.Y., 1972—; fed. ct. arbitrator. Mem., contbr. Coalition of Free Men. Recipient Am. Jurisprudence award, 1969, L.I. U. law award, 1962. Mem. Trial Lawyers Assn. Am., Nassau County Bar Assn., ABA, N.Y. State Bar Assn., Suffolk County Bar Assn., Matrimonial Bar Assn., N.Y. State Trial Lawyers Assn. Suffolk, Assn for Transp. Law Logistics and Policy. Republican. Jewish. Clubs: Hamlet Country Club, K.P. General civil litigation, Insurance, Transportation. Office: Kenneth Adler & Assocs 1 Huntington Quadrangle Melville NY 11747-4401

**ADLER, KRISTIN ELIZABETH,** lawyer; b. Dallas, Mar. 26, 1969. BA, U. Tex., 1991, JD, 1995. Bar: Tex. 1995, U.S. Dist. Ct. (so. dist.) Tex. 1997. Assoc. Williams & Connolly, Washington, 1998—. Office: Williams Connolly 725 12th St NW Washington DC 20005-5901

**ADLER, LEWIS GERARD,** lawyer; b. N.Y.C., Sept. 13, 1960; s. Sherman and Esther (Weiss) A.; m. Kim Adler, Sept. 5, 1988; children: Craig, Stephanie, Katie, Samantha. AS, Vanderbilt U., 1981; JD, Rutgers U., 1985. Bar: N.J. 1986, Pa. 1985, U.S. Dist. Ct. N.J. 1986, U.S. Dist. Ct. Pa. 1990, U.S. Supreme Ct. 1990. Solicitor Gloucester County Constrn. Bd. Appeals, Woodbury, N.J., 1987-88; atty. Gloucester County Sr. Citizen Will Program, Woodbury, 1987-88; pvt. practice Woodbury, N.J., 1989—; spl. counsel Gloucester County, 1990—; pub. defender Deptford Township, 1996, zoning bd. solicitor, 1997—. Designer computer software. Mem. ABA, N.J. Bar Assn., Gloucester County Bar Assn., Phila. Trial Lawyers, Pa. Bar Assn. Democrat. Avocations: water and snow skiing, spelunking, chess, bicycling, rappelling. Environmental, Computer, State civil litigation. Home: 215 Douglass Ave Haddonfield NJ 08033-1626 Office: 57 Euclid St Woodbury NJ 08096-4633

**ADLER, MATTHEW D.,** lawyer; b. Phila., June 15, 1970; s. Gary Leslie and Phyllis (Marder) A. Student, London Sch. Econs., 1991; BA, U. Mich., 1992; JD, Cornell U., 1995. Bar: N.Y. 1995. Atty. Thacher Proffitt & Wood, Washington, 1995—. Pro bono lawyer N.Y. Civil Liberties Union, N.Y.C., 1996; active Big Bfos. of Nat. Capital Area, Washington, 1997. Mem. ABA, Sigma Phi. Jewish. Avocations: sailing, golf.

**ADLER, SARA,** arbitrator, mediator; b. Chgo., Jan. 26, 1942; d. Matthew Michael and Mildred Paula (Eckhaus) Lewison; m. James N. Adler, Aug. 19, 1967; children: Michael, Philip, Matthew. AB, U. Chgo., 1961; JD, UCLA, 1969. Bar: Calif. Cons. Inst. Criminal Justice Adminstrn. U. Calif., Davis, 1969-71; assoc. Law Office of Sara Radin, L.A., 1971-72; assoc. dir. Paralegal Tng. Inst. U. So. Calif., L.A., 1972-74; assoc. Wyman, Bautzer, et al, L.A., 1974-78; arbitrator, mediator Dispute Resolution Svcs., L.A., 1978—. Fellow Coll. Labor and Employment Lawyers; mem. ABA (neutral co-chair ADR in Labor/employment Law 1995-98), Am. Arbitration Assn. (bd. dirs., exec. com., mem. employment law task force), Nat. Acad. Arbitrators (regional chair 1994-96), Indsl. Rels. Rsch. Assn. (pres. so. Calif. 1991-92), L.A. County Bar Assn. (chmn. labor and employment sect. 1997-98). Avocations: travel, theater, bridge. Office: Dispute Resolution Svcs 1034 Selby Ave Los Angeles CA 90024-3106

**ADLER, THEODORE ARTHUR,** lawyer; b. Phila., Aug. 23, 1947; s. George and Gloria Doris (Cantor) A.; m. Shelley Lynn Chirsan, Aug. 21, 1971; children: Jessica Whitney, Bryan Jonathan. BA, Pa. State U., 1969; JD, Dickinson Sch. Law, 1972. Bar: Pa. 1972, U.S. Dist. Ct. (mid. dist.) Pa. 1974, U.S. Supreme Ct. 1977, U.S. Dist. Ct. D.C. 1980; cert. civil trial advocate. Dep. atty. gen. Pa. Dept. Justice, Harrisburg, Pa., 1972-75; gen. counsel Drug & Alchohol Counsel, Harrisburg, Pa., 1975-76; chief counsel Pa. Dept. Gen. Services, Harrisburg, 1976-79; ptnr. Reager, & Adler P.C., Harrisburg, 1979—; cons. Pa. State Gov. Commn., Harrisburg, 1982-84, Pa. Legis. Budget & Fin. Com., 1984; commr. Harrisburg Tax and Rev. Study Commn., 1982-83; adj. prof. law Dickinson Sch. Law, 1986-92. Contbr. articles to law revs. Fin. chmn. Dauphin Co. Dem. Com., Harrisburg, 1982-84. Mem. ABA (cons. model procurement code 1979-82, pub. contract sect., local govt.sect., forum com. on constrn.), Pa. Bar Assn. (vice chmn. pub. contract com. 1982-86, chmn. 1986-88), Dauphin County Bar Assn. Avocations: golf, weight lifting. Construction, Government contracts and claims, General civil litigation. Office: Reager & Adler PC 2331 Market St Camp Hill PA 17011-4642

**ADMIRE, DUANE A.,** lawyer; b. Santa Rosa, Calif., Jan. 6, 1967; s. Neil and Barbara (Johnson) A.; m. Kim E. McCarthy, July 17, 1993. BA in Polit. Sci., Brigham Young U., 1991; JD, Golden Gate U., 1994. Bar: Calif. 1994. Atty. The Admire Law Firm, San Diego, Calif., 1994—. Troop leader Boy Scouts Am., 1994—. Mormon. General civil litigation, Personal injury, General corporate. Office: The Admire Law Firm 12750 Carmel Country Rd San Diego CA 92130-2159

**ADRINE, HERBERT A.,** lawyer; b. Rockmart, Ga., Sept. 1, 1915; s. Wister and Carrie (Russell) A.; m. Laura R. Nellems, Sept. 10, 1947 (div. May 1955); children: Carol A., Parker A.; m. Ethel M. Spencer, Oct. 26, 1956. BBA, Wilberforce U., 1938; LLD, Cleve. State U., 1952. Bar: Ohio 1952, U.S. Dist. Ct. (no. dist.) Ohio 1952, U.S. Supreme Ct. 1971. Legal advisor Tried Stone Baptist Ch.; mem. Ctrl. Area Cmty., Cleve. Sgt. USAF, 1942-46. Recipient Meritorious award Cleve. Bar Assn., 1971, award Cuyahoga County Bar, 1972. Republican. Avocations: bowling, bridge. Probate, Family and matrimonial. Home: 18308 Chagrin Blvd Shaker Heights OH 44122-4847

**ADSIT, JOHN MICHAEL,** lawyer; b. Ft. Atkinson, Wis., May 25, 1961; s. John Miley and Nancy Belle (Philbin) A. BA, U. Mich., 1983; JD, George Washington U., 1987. Bar: Calif. 1988. Legal staff World Bank, Washington, 1986-87; assoc. Zobrist & McCullough, L.A., 1988, Carlsmith, Wichman, L.A., 1989-90; mng. ptnr. Ko & Adsit, Attys. at Law, L.A., 1991, v.p., 1992—. Mem. L.A. County Bar Assn., Fed. Bar Assn. Republican. Presbyterian. Avocations: fitness, animals. General civil litigation, Franchising. Home: 1645 N Holliston Ave Pasadena CA 91104-1434 Office: Ko & Adsit 234 E Colorado Blvd Ste 705 Pasadena CA 91101-2215

**AFFRONTI, FRANCIS CHRISTOPHER,** lawyer; b. Rochester, N.Y., Apr. 30, 1967; s. Francis Alexander and Heather Mary Affronti; m. Lorna Rachel Stead, Jan. 11, 1997. BA, Providence Coll., 1989; JD, Union U., 1992. Bar: N.Y. 1992, U.S. Dist. Ct. (we. dist.) N.Y. 1992. Assoc. Fix Spindelman et al., Rochester, N.Y., 1993-96, Brian J. Barney, Rochester, 1996-98; ptnr. Barney & Affronti, LLP, Rochester, 1999—. Family and matrimonial, Appellate. Office: Barney & Affronti LLP 130 Linden Oaks Ste D Rochester NY 14625-2834

**AFSHAR, CAROLYN MCKINNEY,** lawyer, energy industry executive; b. Decatur, Ga., Oct. 19, 1955; d. Jack Bowie and Margaret Louise (Wilson) McK.; m. Hamid Reza Afshar, July 16, 1978; children: Darian A., Valian A. BA, Ga. Southern Coll., 1979, MA, 1982; JD, Widener U., 1991. Bar: Del. 1991, U.S. Dist. Ct. Del. 1992, U.S. Supreme Ct. 1996. Atty. Columbia Gas Sys. Svc. Corp., Wilmington, Del., 1991-93, 94-95; counsel, corp. sec. Columbia Energy Group Svc. Corp., Herndon, Va., 1995—; corp. sec. Columbia Energy Group, Herndon, 1995—. Editor-in-chief: Del. Jour. Corp. Law, 1990-91. Mem. Great Falls Citizen Assn., Great Falls Athletic Assn., Reston Runners Club. Mem. ABA (chairperson subcom. on leased employees), Am. Corporate Counsel Assn., Am. Soc. Corp. Secs. Avocations: music, travel, literature, marathon running. General corporate, Labor, Pension, profit-sharing, and employee benefits. Home: PO Box 731 Great Falls VA 22066-0731 Office: Columbia Energy Group Svc Corp 13880 Dulles Corner Ln Ste 300 Herndon VA 20171-4600

**AGAPION, BILL,** lawyer; b. Stamford, Conn., Feb. 14, 1926; s. A. Bill and Helen (Theodore) A.; m. Sophia Sitaras, Apr. 28, 1968; children—Irene, Dena, Basil, Emanuel. B.A., U. N.C., 1947, LL.B., 1952. Bar: N.C. 1952, U.S. Dist. Ct. (mid. dist.) N.C. 1952. Sole practice, Greensboro, N.C., 1952-59, 70—; ptnr. Agapion & Agapion, Greensboro, 1960-70. Served to 2d lt. U.S. Army, 1944-46. Decorated Purple Heart (3), Combat Infantry Badge. Mem. Greensboro Bar Assn., N.C. Bar Assn. Democrat. Greek Orthodox. Insurance, Real property, Landlord-tenant. Home: 616 Willoughby Blvd Greensboro NC 27408-3164

**AGATA, BURTON C.,** law educator, lawyer; b. N.Y.C., Feb. 7, 1928; s. Max and Augusta (Steger) A.; m. Dale S. Granirer, Dec. 24, 1955; children: Seth Hugh, Abby Fran. AB, U. Mich., 1947, JD, 1950; LLM in Trade Regulation, NYU, 1951. Bar: N.Y. 1951. Counsel div. N.Y. State Banking Dept., 1955-59; ptnr. firm Burstein & Agata, Mineola and N.Y.C., 1959-61; prof. Mont. U., 1961-62, N.Mex. U., 1962-63, Houston U., 1963-69; counsel Nat. Commn. on Reform Fed. Criminal Laws, 1968-70; prof. law Hofstra U., 1970—, Max Schmertz disting. prof. law, 1982—, interim dean, 1989; mem. faculty Nat. Inst. Trial Advocacy, 1977-81; dir. N.E. Regional Program, 1981-84; spl. counsel N.Y. City Charter Revision Commn., 1987-89, N.Y. State Senate Minority, 1982-87; cons. Fed. Jud. Center, 1972, Inst. Jud. Adminstrn., 1973, HEW, 1971, White House Spl. Action Office Drug Abuse Prevention, 1973, N.Y. State Temp. Com. on Constnl. Revision, 1993-95; Chmn. N.Y. State Task Force, Standards and Go als for Prosecution and Def., 1977-79; cons. Adv. Com. on Qualifications of Counsel, 2d Ct., 1977; bd. dirs. Nassau Economic Opportunity Commn., 1972-73; reporter-cons. action unit on criminal justice system N.Y. State Bar Assn., 1986-90. Contbr. articles to law jours. With JAGC U.S. Army, 1951-54. Food Law fellow NYU, 1951, fellow U. Wis., 1963. Fellow Am. Bar Found. (life); mem. Am. Law Inst., ABA (state antitrust law commn. 1980—, vice chair com. on professionalism sr. lawyers divsn. 1996—), N.Y. State Bar Assn. (exec. com. criminal justice sect., chmn. com. rev. of criminal law 1987—, spl. com. on pre-sentence reports 1989—, Donnelly Act com. 1990—), Assn. of Bar of City of N.Y. (criminal cts. com. 1970-73, penology com. 1973-76, criminal justice council 1983-85, antitrust com. 1986-89), Fed. Jud. Council, Assn. Am. Law Schs. (chmn. criminal law sect. 1973). Home: PO Box 727 Hudson NY 12534-0727 Office: Hofstra U School Law Hempstead NY 11549-0001

**AGGER, JAMES H.,** lawyer; b. 1936; married. A.B., St. Joseph's U., 1958; J.D., U. Pa., 1961. Mem. Krusen, Evans & Byrne, 1965-69; gen. counsel Catalytic Inc., Air Products and Chems. Inc., 1969-77; asst. gen. counsel Air Products and Chems. Inc., Trexlertown, Pa., 1977-80, gen. counsel, 1980—, v.p., 1982-97, corp. sec., 1990, sr. v.p., 1997-99, ret., 1999. General corporate. Office: Air Products & Chems Inc 7201 Hamilton Blvd Allentown PA 18195-1526

**AGHDAMI, FARHAD,** lawyer; b. Tehran, Iran, Jan. 4, 1968; came to U.S., 1971; s. Ali Asghar and Farideh H. Aghdami; m. Amanda North Jones, May 21, 1994. BA, U. Va., 1989; JD, Wake Forest U., 1992; LLM in Taxation, Georgetown U., 1995. Bar: Va. 1992, U.S. Tax Ct. 1997. Assoc. Florance, Gordon and Brown, P.C., Richmond, Va., 1992-97, dir./shareholder, 1997-99; mem. Williams, Mullen, Clark & Dobbins, Richmond, 1999—. Corp. income tax editor Va. Tax Reporter, 1994—; contbr. articles to profl. jours. Mem. ABA (tax sect. estate and gift taxes com., co-chair estate of Hubert task force 1997—), Va. Bar Assn. (tax sect. bd. govs. 1996—). Fax: 804-783-6507. E-mail: faghdami@wmcd.com. Estate taxation, Estate planning, Probate. Home: 1003 West Ave Richmond VA 23220-3717 Office: Williams Mullen Christian & Dobbins Two James Ctr PO Box 1320 1021 E Cary St Richmond VA 23218-1320

**AGNELLO, PATRICIA ANNE,** benefits manager, lawyer; b. N.Y.C., Dec. 7, 1956; d. Patrick Joseph and Josephine Anna Falci; m. Michael A. Ferri, Oct. 16, 1998; 1 child, Michael A. Ferri II. BA, Marymount Manhattan U., 1983; MBA, Adelphi U., 1985; JD, St. John's U. Law, 1995. Bar: N.Y., Conn., D.C. Mgr. exec. benefits Exxon Corp., N.Y.C., 1975-90; mgr. nat. benefits Coopers & Lybrand, N.Y.C., 1991-94, Marsh & McLennan Cos., N.Y.C., 1994—. Mem. ABA, N.Y. State Bar Assn., N.Y.C. Bar Assn. (mem. com.), WEB (bd. dirs., chair comms. 1997—). Office: Marsh & McLennan Cos 1166 Avenue Of The Americas New York NY 10036-2708

**AGNICH, RICHARD JOHN,** lawyer, electronics company executive; b. Eveleth, Minn., Aug. 24, 1943; s. Frederick J. and Ruth H. (Welton) A.; m. Victoria Webb Trescher, Apr. 19, 1969; children: Robert Frederick, Michael McCord, Jonathon Welton. A.B. in Econs., Stanford U., 1965; J.D., U. Tex., 1969. Bar: Tex. 1969. Legis. asst., legal counsel to John G. Tower U.S. Senate, 1969-70, adminstrv. asst. to John G. Tower, 1971-72; asst. counsel Tex. Instruments Inc., Dallas, 1973-78, asst. gen. counsel, 1978-82, v.p., sec., gen. counsel, 1982—, sr v.p., sec. gen. counsel, 1988—. Bd. dirs. U.S. Com. of Pacific Basin Econ. Coun., U.S.-Korea Bus. Coun. Mem. ABA (com. corp. law depts.) Tex. Bar Assn., Dallas Bar Assn., Am. Soc. Corp. Secs., Southwestern Legal Found. (adv. bd. Internat. and Comparative Law Ctr.), Assn. Gen. Counsel (pres.). Republican. Presbyterian. General corporate, Patent. Home: 19 Downs Lake Cir Dallas TX 75230-1900 Office: Tex Instruments Inc PO Box 660199 MS 8658 Dallas TX 75266-0199 also: Tex Instruments Inc 8505 Forest Ln # Ms8658 Dallas TX 75243-4136

**AGOGLIA, EMMET JOHN,** lawyer; b. N.Y.C., Nov. 18, 1930; s. Gerard and Loretta (Clavin) A.; m. K. Carroll Wheeler, Jan. 27, 1957; children: Christine, E. Kevin, Margaret, Michael, Barbara, Elizabeth, Kathleen. BA, St. Francis Coll., 1952; LLB, St. John's Coll., 1958. Bar: N.Y. 1958, U.S. Supreme Ct.1982. Assoc. Lawless & Lynch, N.Y.C., 1959-61, Reilly & Reilly, N.Y.C., 1961-64; ptnr. Crowe, McCoy & Agoglia, Mineola, N.Y., 1964-69, McCoy & Agoglia, Mineola, N.Y., 1969-86, McCoy, Agoglia, Beckett & Fassberg, Mineola, N.Y., 1986-89; lectr. in field; atty. panelist Supreme Ct. State of N.Y. Contbr. articles to profl. publs. Fellow Am. Coll. Trial Lawyers; mem. ABA, N.Y. State Bar Assn., Am. Bd. Trial Advocates, Am. Bd. Profl. Liability Attys. (diplomate), Nassau County Bar Assn. (past bd. dirs., mem. jud. screening com.), N.Y. County Lawyers, Nassau-Suffolk Trial Lawyers, Internat. Acad. Trial Lawyers. Democrat. Roman Catholic. Federal civil litigation, Insurance, Personal injury. Office: McCoy, Agoglia, Beckett & Fassberg 200 Old Country Rd Ste 485 Mineola NY 11501-4298

**AGOSTA, STEVEN S.,** lawyer; b. Richmond, Calif., Dec. 7, 1942; s. Steven S. and Rose J. (Borghi) A.; m. Jan Karen Christensen, Oct. 2, 1971; children: Antony S., Leslie Anne. BA, San Jose (Calif.) State U., 1964; JD, U. Calif., San Francisco, 1967. Bar: Calif. 1968, U.S. Dist. Ct. (no. dist.) Calif. 1970, U.S. Ct. Appeals (9th cir.) 1987. Contracts analyst McDonnel-Douglas Corp., Long Beach, Calif., 1967-69; assoc. Wexler & Wexler Assocs., Millbrae, Calif., 1969-75; minority ptnr. Wexler, Wexler & Agosta, Millbrae, 1976-84, ptnr., 1984-89, sole propr., 1989—. Co-author: The Book of Real Estate Clauses, 1989. Mem. State Bar Calif., Calif. Assn. Realtors (atty. referal panel), San Mateo County Bar Assn., San Mateo County Arbitration (judge pro tem panel, cert. of recognition 1988). Republican. Roman Catholic. Avocations: travel, golf, sports. General practice, General civil litigation. Office: Wexler Wexler & Agosta 485 Broadway Millbrae CA 94030-1923

**AGOSTI, DEBORAH,** judge. Justice Nev. Supreme Court, Carson City. Office: Nevada Supreme Ct Capitol Complex 201 S Carson S Carson City NV 89710-0001*

**AGOSTO, BENNY, JR.,** lawyer; b. N.Y.C., Feb. 28, 1963; s. Beno Sr. and Marino A.; children: Ben III, Jon David. BS, Houston Bapt. U., 1986; JD, So. Tex. Coll. Law, 1986. Bar: Tex. 1995, U.S. Dist. Ct. (so. dist.) Tex. 1995. Atty. Morgan & Assocs., Houston, 1995-96, Barrow & Parrott, Houston, 1996-98, Abraham, Watkins, Nichols & Friend, Houston, 1998—. Fellow Houston Bar Assn.; mem. Houston Trial Lawyers Assn., Houston Trial Lawyers Found., Houston hispanic Bar Assn., Houston Young Lawyers Assn., Mex.-Am. Bar Assn., Alpha Tau Omega. Avocation: golf. Personal injury, General civil litigation. Office: Abraham Watkins Nichols & Friend 800 Commerce St Houston TX 77002-1776

**AGRAN, RAYMOND DANIEL,** lawyer; b. Chgo., June 21, 1957; s. Paul and Esther (Poogach) A.; m. Melinda Carol Finberg, June 8, 1986; children: Alexander Everett, Meredith Bronwyn. BA magna cum laude, Yale U., 1979; JD with highest honors, Columbia U., 1982. Bar: N.Y. 1983, U.S. Dist. Ct. (so. dist.) N.Y. 1983, U.S. Ct. Appeals (2d cir.) 1983, Pa. 1987, N.J. 1995. Assoc. Shearman & Sterling, N.Y.C., 1982-84, Howard, Smith & Levin, N.Y.C., 1984-86; assoc. Wolf, Block, Schorr & Solis-Cohen, Phila., 1986-92, ptnr., 1992-95; ptnr. Ballard Spahr Andrews & Ingersoll LLP, Phila., 1995—; panel chair Ctr. Energy Policy U. Pa., 1992; panelist, Foreign Policy Rsch. Inst., Phila., 1991-92; speaker in field. Contbr. chpt. book Layman's Guide to Venture Capital, 1999, Greater Philadelphia Venture Group Venture Capital Institute, 1999. Bd. dirs., mem. adv. bd. Univ. City Sci. Ctr. Incubator, Phila., 1991-95; bd. dirs. Greater Phila. Venture Group, 1998—. Bates fellow, 1978, Sumitomo fellow of U.S.-Japan Found., 1979; Stone scholar, Kent scholar. Avocations: chess, cooking, reading, outdoors. General corporate, Mergers and acquisitions, Securities. Office: Ballard Spahr Andrews & Ingersoll LLP 1735 Market St Fl 51 Philadelphia PA 19103-7501

**AGRANOFF, GERALD NEAL,** lawyer; b. Detroit, Nov. 24, 1946; s. Carl and Frances (Solomon) A.; children—Lindsay Sara, Dana Jill. B.S., Wayne State U., 1969, J.D., 1972; LL.M., NYU, 1973. Bar: N.Y. 1975, Mich. 1973, U.S. Tax Ct. 1974, U.S. Ct. Claims 1974. Atty.-advisor U.S. Tax Ct., Washington, 1973-75; assoc. law firm Baker & McKenzie, N.Y.C., 1975-79, Baer Marks & Upham, N.Y.C., 1979-80; counsel Pryor, Cashman et al, N.Y.C., 1980-82; gen. counsel Arbitrage Securities Co., Plaza Securities Co., N.Y.C., 1982—; gen. ptnr. Edelman Securities Co., N.Y.C., 1984—, Plaza Securities Co., N.Y.C., 1987-96; trustee, Mgmt. Assistance Inc., Liquidating Trust; bd. dirs. Canal Capital Corp., N.Y.C., Bull Run Corp., Datapoint Corp., Atlantic Gulf Cmtys., Am. Energy Group, Ltd.; adj. instr. NYU Inst. on Fed. Taxation, 1980-81. Bd. dirs. Soho Repertory Theatre, N.Y.C., 1982; mem. N.Y. com. UNICEF. Corporate taxation, Personal income taxation, State and local taxation. Office: The Edelman Cos 717 5th Ave New York NY 10022-8101

**AGRAZ, FRANCISCO JAVIER, SR.,** lawyer, public affairs representative; b. Laredo, Tex., Aug. 21, 1947; s. Jose Jesus and Irene (Garcia-Gomez) A.; m. Rosalinda Varela, Aug. 23, 1969 (div. Feb. 1980); children: Francisco Javier Jr., Raquel Jeanne; m. Ruth Urquidi, Jan. 1, 1984. BA in Journalism, U. Tex. at El Paso, 1970; JD, U. Houston, 1987. Bar: Tex. 1988, U.S. Dist. Ct. (so. dist.) Tex. 1988. Anchor reporter KENS-TV, San Antonio, 1970; corr. ABC Capital Cities Comms., Chgo., Houston, N.Y., 1970-77; pub. affairs analyst Exxon Corp., Houston and Memphis, 1977-83; assoc. Wood, Burney, Cohn & Bradley, Corpus Christi, Tex., 1987-89, Redford, Wray & Woolsey, P.C., Corpus Christi, 1989-91; pres., atty. at law Francisco J. Agraz P.C., Houston, 1991—; gen. mgr. The MRAM Co., Houston, 1996-98; pub. affairs officer FBI, Houston, 1998—. Bd. govs. United Way of Coastal Bend, Corpus Christi, Tex., 1987-91. Mem. State Bar of Tex. (grievance com., pub. rels. com.), Houston Rotary Club. Roman Catholic. Avocations: Spanish translator. E-Mail: Francisco.Agraz@cwixmail.com. General corporate, Private international.

**AHERIN, DARREL WILLIAM,** lawyer; b. Colfax, Wash., July 11, 1946; s. Don Lewis and Leona Margaret (Edwards) A. m. Freda jean Kieffer, June 27, 1968 (dec.); children: Daniel Winston, Dustin Wynne; m. Michelle Rae Messley, June 26, 1982; children: Alex William. BA, Lewis Clark State Coll., 1969; JD, U. Idaho, 1973. Pvt. practice Lewiston, Idaho, 1973—; ptnr. Aherin, Rice & Anegon (formerly Aherin, Rice & Brown), Lewiston, 1973—. Active Planning & Zoning Com., Genesee, Idaho, 1996—. Mem. ATLA (gov. 1996—), Idaho Trial Lawyers Assn. (sec., treas., pres.), Western Trial Lawyers (gov. 1995—), Lewis Clark State Coll. Alumni (pres.). Insurance, Personal injury, Product liability. Home: PO Box 337 Genesee ID 83832-0337 Office: Aherin Rice & Anegon 1212 Idaho St Lewiston ID 83501-1941

**AHERN, THERESA M.,** lawyer; b. Seattle, Mar. 4, 1959; d. Frank James and Dona Jane Ahern; m. John J. Greaney, Oct. 17, 1992; children: Joseph Ahern Greaney, Hannah Rose Greaney. BA magna cum laude, Seattle U., 1981, JD, 1984. Bar: Wash., 1984, U.S. Dist. Ct. (we. dist.) Wash., 1987. Lawyer Olson & Ranes, P.S., Montesano, Wash., 1985-92, Curran Mendoza, P.S., Kent, Wash., 1992—. Pres., bd. dirs. Kent Youth & Family Svcs., 1996-97; sponsor, creator Vol. Family Law Settlement Conf. Program, 1997—; mem. com. Unified Family Ct. Tng. Com., 1998—. Mem. Wash. State Bar Assn., King County Bar Assn., S. King County Bar Assn. (pres. 1996-97). Family and matrimonial. Office: Curran Mendoza PS 555 W Smith St Kent WA 98032-4468

**AHLEN, MICHAEL J.,** law educator; b. St. Louis, Sept. 16, 1943; s. Louis S. and Betty V. A.; m. Mary Ann Ahlen, Sept. 5, 1964 (dec. Feb. 1982); children: Theodore, Jennifer, John. BA, Denison U., 1965; JD, Vanderbilt U., 1968. Bar: Ind. 1968, D.C. 1979, N.D. 1981. Dep. pros. atty. Grant County, Marion, Ind., 1968-70; trial atty. U.S. Dept. Justice, Washington, 1970-78, asst. chief criminal tax div., 1978-81; from asst. to assoc. prof. U. N.D. Law Sch., Grand Forks, 1981-86, Rodney and Betty Webb prof. law, 1996—; mem. jud. planning com. N.D. Supreme Ct., Bismarck, 1989—. Co-editor: North Dakota Trial Manual, 1988, (with E. Myers) Sustained!-The Practitioner's Guide to North Dakota Evidence. Mem. Am. Arbitration Assn. (mem. N.D. com.), State Bar Assn. N.D. (mem. alt. dispute resolution com. 1993-96), Assn. Am. Trial Attys., N.D. Assn. Trial Attys., N.D. Supreme Cts. Continuing Jud. Edn. Commn. Home: 2521 S 40th St Grand Forks ND 58201-5920 Office: U ND Sch Law PO Box 9003 Grand Forks ND 58202-9003

**AHLERS, GLEN-PETER, SR.,** law library director, educator, consultant; b. N.Y.C., Mar. 15, 1955; s. LeGrande Jacob and Joan (Stoltz) A.; m. Sondra Sue Wadley, May 17, 1987; children: Glen-Peter II, Sandia Marie, Gavin Patrick, Sierra Le Ann Rose. BS, U. N.Mex., Albuquerque, 1979; MA, U. of South Fla., 1983; JD, Washburn U., 1987. Bar: Kans. 1987, U.S. Dist. Ct. Kans. 1987, U.S. Ct. Mil. Appeals 1988, D.C. 1990. Reference asst. U. N.Mex. Sch. Law, Albuquerque, 1979-83; asst. dir. Washburn Sch. Law Libr., Topeka, Kans., 1983-87; assoc. libr. dir. Wake Forest U., Winston-Salem, N.C., 1987-90; libr. dir., assoc. prof. D.C. Sch. Law, Washington, 1990-92, U. Ark., Fayetteville, 1992—; computer and libr. cons. Ctr. for R&D in Law-Related Edn., Winston-Salem, 1987-90; adj. prof. Sch. of Law Wake Forest U., Winston-Salem, N.C., 1987-90; bd. dirs. Mid-Am. Law Sch. Libr. Consortium, 1992—, Consortium of Southestern Law Librs., 1988-90. Author: Election Laws of the United States, 1995; co-author: Notary Law and Practice, 1997; editor The Scrivener, 1992—; tech. editor Washburn Law Jour., 1985-86; contbr. articles to profl. jours. Mediator N.C. Neighborhood Justice Ctr., Winston-Salem, 1989-90. Mem. ABA, ALA, Ark. Bar Assn., Am. Assn. Law Librs., Southwestern Assn. Law Librs. (pres. 1995-97), Mid Am. Assn. Law Librs., Scribes (exec. dir. 1997—), Phi Kappa Phi, Kappa Delta Pi, Beta Phi Mu. Avocation: writing. Home: 2139 Revere Ln Fayetteville AR 72701-2711 Office: U Ark Leflar Law Ctr Fayetteville AR 72701-1201

**AHLHEIM, STEPHEN PATRICK,** lawyer; b. June 14, 1968. BA, U. Dayton, 1989; JD, St. Louis U., 1993. Ptnr. Ahlheim & Dorsey LLC, St. Charles, Mo. Mem. Kiwanis (bd. dirs. St. Charles club 1993—), Jaycees (legal counsel St. Charles club 1994—). Roman Catholic. Avocations: brewing, foreign languages, travel. Office: Ahlheim & Dorsey LLC 2209 1st Capitol Dr Saint Charles MO 63301-5809

**AHLSTROM, MICHAEL JOSEPH,** lawyer; b. N.Y.C., June 1, 1953; s. Albert Warren and Bernadette Patricia (Flynn) A.; m. Mary Lou Donnelly, Apr. 19, 1980; 1 child, Courtney Leigh. BS, St. Francis Coll., 1975; JD, U. San Francisco, 1978. Bar: N.Y. 1980, U.S. Dist. Ct. (so. and ea. dists.) N.Y. 1980, Ga. 1982, U.S. Dist. Ct. (no. dist.) Ga. 1983, U.S. Ct. Appeals (11th cir.) 1984, U.S. Supreme Ct. 1987. Counsel Gear Design, Inc., N.Y.C., 1979-80; ptnr. Ahlstrom & Ahlstrom, N.Y.C., 1981-83; gen. counsel Network Rental, Inc., Atlanta, 1984-87; assoc. John Marshall and Assocs., P.C., Atlanta, 1987; ptnr. Marshall & Ahlstrom, P.C., Atlanta, 1987-88; mng. atty. UAW-GM-Ford Chrysler Legal Plan Ga., Atlanta, 1993-96; pvt. practice, Marietta, Ga., 1988-92, 96—; arbitrator NASD. Arbitrator Superior Ct. Fulton County, Ga., 1987—, Ga. Lemon Law, 1991—; panel atty. Cobb County Cir. Defender; spl. master Cobb County Superior Ct., mediator, 1996—, Ga. Registered Neutral, 1997—; mediator, domestic cases, Fulton County Superior Ct., 1998—. Named one of Outstanding Young Men Am. U.S. Jaycees, 1986. Mem. N.Y. Bar Assn., Ga. Bar Assn. (pub. rels. com. 1989-91), Cobb County Bar Assn., Am. Corp.Counsel Assn. (program chmn. 1986-87), Am. Arbitration Assn. (comml. panel 1987—), KC, Phi Delta Phi, Alpha Kappa Psi. Republican. Roman Catholic. Avocations: fishing, hunting, tennis, golf, croquet. General corporate, Contracts commercial, General practice. Home: 613 Fairway Ct Marietta GA 30068-4159

**AHRENSFELD, THOMAS FREDERICK,** lawyer; b. Bklyn., June 30, 1923; s. Frederick Herman and Madeline Florence (Moffett) A.; m. Joan Ann McGowan, Mar. 17, 1944; 1 child, Thomas Frederick. A.B., Bklyn. Coll., 1948; LL.B., Columbia U., 1948. Bar: N.Y. 1948. Assoc., then ptnr. Conboy, Hewitt, O'Brien & Boardman, N.Y.C., 1948-58; sec., assoc. gen. counsel Philip Morris Inc., N.Y.C., 1959-70, v.p., gen. counsel, 1970-76, sr. v.p., gen. counsel, 1976-85; sr. v.p., gen. counsel Philip Morris Cos., Inc., N.Y.C., 1985-88; pvt. practice law Pleasantville, N.Y., 1988—. Trustee Trinity-Pawling Sch. Corp., 1976-98; elder Presbyn. Ch. 1st lt. USAAF, 1942-45. Decorated D.F.C., Air medal with oak leaf clusters. Mem. ABA, N.Y.C. Bar Assn., N.Y. Athletic Club, Mt. Kisco (N.Y.) Country Club, Johns Island (Fla.) Club. General corporate. Home and Office: 85 Nannahagan Rd Pleasantville NY 10570-2314

**AH-TYE, KIRK THOMAS,** lawyer; b. L.A., Mar. 31, 1951; s. Thomas and Ruth Elizabeth (Liu) Ah-T.; m. Deborah Ann Wells, Jan. 31, 1981; 1 child, Torrey Ann. BA, U. Calif., Santa Barbara, 1973; JD, Boston Coll., 1976. Bar: Calif. 1977, U.S. Dist. Ct. (cen. dist.) Calif. 1978, U.S. Dist. Ct. (ea. dist.) Calif. 1994, U.S. Ct. Appeals (9th cir.) 1978, U.S. Supreme Ct. 1981. Co-exec. dir., mng. atty. Channel Counties Legal Svcs. Assn., Santa Barbara, 1977—; expert witness Assembly Com. on Edn., Calif. Legis., Sacramento; panelist Ctr. for the Study of Dem. Instns., Santa Barbara; panelist, instr. CLE approved classes; past legal cons. Santa Barbara chpt. calif. Assn. Bilingual Educators; inaugural prodr., moderator Santa Barbara Law, Sta. KTMS-AM, 1994—. Editor (bar newsletter) The Quibbler, 1992-93, (monthly legal series) Santa Barbara News-Press; contbr. articles to profl. jours. Trustee Montessori Ctr. Sch., Santa Barbara, 1991-93; bd. dirs., v.p. Santa Barbara Internat. Film Festival, 1991-93; chair adv. bd. Santa Barbara Regional Health Authority, 1985; mem. blue-ribbon com. County Bd. Suprs., Santa Barbara, 1988; chair Santa Barbara County Affirmative Action Commn., 1987-88; mem. grant-making com. Fund for Santa Barbara, 1988-92. Recipient Local Hero award Santa Barbara Ind., 1988. Master Santa Barbara Am. Inns of Ct.; mem. State Bar Calif. (state resolutions com. to state bar conf. of dels. 1994-96, exec. com. to conf. dels. 1997, ann. legal svcs. achievement award for so. Calif. 1997, Achievement award for legal svc. 1997), Santa Barbara County Bar Assn. (jud. svc. award com. 1992, chmn. pro bono com. 1993, bd. dirs., sec., CFO 1992—, pres. 1997-98), Lawyer Referral Svc. Santa Barbara (bd. dirs., pres. 1992). Avocations: sports, film, literature, weights, tennis. General civil litigation, Education and schools, Health. Office: Channel Counties Legal Svcs Assn 324 E Carrillo St Ste B Santa Barbara CA 93101-7438

**AIBEL, HOWARD J.,** lawyer; b. N.Y.C., Mar. 24, 1929; m. Katherine Webster, June 6, 1952; children: David Webster, Daniel Walter, Jonathan Brown. AB magna cum laude, 1950; JD cum laude, Harvard U., 1951. Bar:

N.Y. 1952. Assoc. White & Case, N.Y.C., 1952-57; trade regulation counsel GE, 1957-60, spl. litigation counsel elec. equipment antitrust cases, 1960-64; antitrust counsel ITT Corp., N.Y.C., 1964-66, v.p., assoc. gen. counsel, 1966-68, sr. v.p., gen. counsel, 1968-87, exec. v.p., gen. counsel, 1987-92, exec. v.p., chief legal officer, 1992-94; ptnr. LeBoeuf Lamb Greene & MacRae, N.Y.C., 1994-99, of counsel, 1999—; bd. dirs. Farrel Corp., Transparancy, Internat.-USA; vice chmn. Fund for Modern Cts., 1985-95, Conn. Appleseed Ctr. for Law and Justice, 1999—; mem. AAA/ABA/AMA Com. Health Care Dispute Resolution, 1997—. Mem. vis. com. Northwestern U. Law Sch., 1984-90; mem. adv. com. Corp. Counsel Ctr., chmn., 1986-87; bd. dirs. Alliance of Resident Theatres, N.Y.. 1986—, chmn., 1989—; trustee Lawyers Com. for Civil Rights, 1991-95; trustee U. Bridgeport, 1989-91, chmn. adv. com. Sch. Law, 1987-92; cons. trustee Westport Nature Ctr. for Environ. Activities; bd. dirs., 1st v.p. Westport Arts Ctr., 1993-96. Fellow Am. Bar Found. (life); mem. ABA Bus. Law Section Com. on Corporate Governance, Amer. Law Inst. Corporate Governance Project, 1984-94, v.p. Bar Assn. NY, 1988-89, mem. ABA (bus. law com. corp. governance 1994-98), Am. Law Inst., Am. Arbitration Assn. (chmn. exec. com. 1992-95, chmn. bd. dirs. 1995-98), Assn. Gen. Counsel, pres. Harvard Law Sch. Assn. NY, 1992-94, v.p. Harvard Law Sch. Assn., 1994—. General corporate, Alternative dispute resolution. Home: 183 Steep Hill Rd Weston CT 06883-1924 Office: LeBoeuf Lamb Greene & MacRae 125 W 55th St New York NY 10019-5369

**AIDINOFF, M(ERTON) BERNARD,** lawyer; b. Newport, R.I., Feb. 2, 1929; s. Simon and Esther (Miller) A.; m. Celia Spiro, May 30, 1956 (dec. June 28, 1984); children: Seth G., Gail M.; m. Elsie V. Newburg, Nov. 29, 1996. BA, U. Mich., 1950; LLB, Harvard U., 1953. Bar: D.C. 1953, N.Y. 1954. Law clk. to Judge Learned Hand, U.S. Ct. of Appeals, N.Y.C., 1955-56; with Sullivan & Cromwell, N.Y.C., 1956-63, ptnr., 1963-96, sr. counsel, 1997—; dir. Am. Internat. Group Inc., Gibbs & Cox, Inc.; adv. com. to IRS commr., 1979-80, 85-86. Editor in chief The Tax Lawyer, 1974-77. Trustee Spence Sch., 1971-79; mem. adv. com. Gibbs Bros. Fedn., 1965-94; mem. vis. com. Harvard U. Law Sch., 1976-82, 99—; adv. dir. Met. Opera Assn., 1989—; chmn. bd. dirs. St. Luke's Chamber Ensemble, 1988—. 1st lt. JAGC, AUS, 1953-55. Recipient Judge Learned Hand Human Rels. award Am. Jewish Com., 1997. Mem. ABA (vice-chmn. sect. taxation 1974-77, chmn.-elect 1981-82, chmn. 1982-83, chmn. commn. taxpayer compliance 1983-88, Ho. of Dels. 1988-91), N.Y. State Bar Assn., Assn. Bar of City of N.Y. (exec. com. 1974-78, chmn. exec. com. 1977-78, v.p. 1978-79, chmn. taxation com. 1979-81, chmn. govt. ethics com. 1988-90), East Hampton Hist. Soc. (trustee 1983-89, 90-95), Am. Law Inst. (cons. fed. income tax project 1974—, chmn. tax program com. 1988—, John Minor Wisdom award 1995), Found. for a Civil Soc. (bd. dirs. 1994—, vice chmn. 1997-98, chmn. 1999—), Coun. Fgn. Rels., Guild Hall (trustee1989-94, 95—, treas. 1993-94, 95—), Lawyers Com. for Human Rights (bd. dirs. 1986—, treas. 1997—), Confrerie des Chevaliers du Tavestin, Commanderie de Bordeaux, The Parks Coun. (bd. dirs. 1995-97), Century Assn., India House, Met. Club, Phi Beta Kappa. Corporate taxation, Taxation, general. Home: 980 5th Ave New York NY 10021-0126 Office: Sullivan & Cromwell 125 Broad St New York NY 10004-2489

**AIELLO, ROBERT JOHN,** lawyer; b. Bklyn., July 23, 1959; s. John Frank Aiello and Adele Cavaliere; m. Sylvia Stone, Sept. 29, 1996. BA, Trinity Coll., 1981; JD, Fordham U., 1984. Bar: N.Y. 1985, D.C. 1988, U.S. Dist. Ct. (ea. and so. dists.) 1986, U.S. Supreme Ct. 1993. Assoc. Reid & Priest, N.Y.C., 1983; asst. dist. atty. Queens County Dist. Attys. Office, Kew Gardens, N.Y., 1984-91; ptnr. Aiello & Cannick, N.Y.C., 1992—; counsel Assemblyman Joseph R. Lentol, 1992-95. Bd. govs. Columbus Citizens Found., chmn. H.S. scholarship com. Mem. N.Y. State Bar Assn., Columbian Lawyers Assn., Queens Bar Assn. (spkr. 1993—), Don Mont Meml. Rsch. Found. (bd. dirs.), Phi Beta Kappa, Pi Gamma Mu. Roman Catholic. Avocations: running, tennis, boating, skiing, reading. Criminal, Education and schools, Personal injury. Home: 67 Rockcrest Rd Manhasset NY 11030-3416 Office: Aiello & Cannick 233 Broadway Rm 4000 New York NY 10279-4099

**AIKEN, TONIA DANDRY,** lawyer, nurse; b. New Orleans, Mar. 1, 1956; d. Anthony Joseph and Shirley Ann (Jumonville) Dandry; m. James B. Aiken. BSN, La. State U., 1978; JD, Loyola U. 1982. RN, La.; Bar: La. Nurse, La., 1974-81; prin., nurse atty., New Orleans, 1982—. Author, editor: Legal, Ethical and Political Issues in Nursing, 1994; conbtbr. Medical Malpractice in Louisiana; lectr. to health profls., legal and civic groups. Decennial scholar, 1974-75. Mem. Am. Assn. Nurse Attys. (pres. 1993, pres. found. 1994—), Sigma Theta Tau. Personal injury, Health. Office: Ste 3001 3520 General De Gaulle Dr New Orleans LA 70114

**AIKIN, WENDY LISE,** lawyer; b. Brownsville, Tex., Mar. 29, 1952; d. Donald Paul and Renee Marie Aikin; children: Ross Clark, Kyle Lise. BA, U. Fla., 1973, JD, 1978. Bar: Fla. 1979. Atty. Giles, Hedrick & Robinson PA, Orlando, Fla., 1979-82, Robertson, Williams et al, Orlando, 1982-84, Osborne & Aikin, P.A., Orlando, 1985-95; pres., atty. pvt. practice Winter Park, Fla., 1995—. Family and matrimonial, General civil litigation, Personal injury. Office: 288 Park Ave N Winter Park FL 32789-7418

**AIKMAN, ALBERT EDWARD,** lawyer; b. Norman, Okla., Mar. 11, 1922; s. Albert Edwin and Thelma Annette (Brooke) A.; m. Shirley Barnes, June 24, 1944; children: Anita Gayle, Priscilla June, Rebecca Brooke. B.S., Tex. A&M U., 1947; J.D. cum laude, So. Meth. U., 1948, LL.M., 1954. Bar: Tex. (no. dist.) 1948, U.S. Supreme Ct. 1956, U.S. Ct. Appeals (5th dist.), U.S. Tax Ct. Staff atty. Phillips Petroleum Co., Amarillo, Tex., 1948-49; sole practice, Amarillo, 1949-53; tax counsel Magnolia Petroleum Co. (Mobil) Dallas, 1953-56; ptnr. Locke, Purnell, Boren, Laney & Neely, Dallas, 1956-71; sole practice, Dallas, 1973-81; of counsel Pickens Energy Corp., Dallas, 1981-96; couns. Ptnrs. In Exploration, LLC, Dallas, 1997—. Served with inf. U.S. Army, 1943-45. Mem. ABA, Tex. Bar Assn., Dallas Bar Assn. Methodist. Contbr. articles in field to profl. jours. Corporate taxation, Oil, gas, and mineral.

**AILOR, EARL STARNES,** lawyer; b. Newport, Tenn., Jan. 27, 1920; s. Thurman and Lena Belle (Starnes) A.; m. Margaret Aileen Nelson, June 3, 1947; children: Annabell, Albert Earl (dec.), Margaret Pauline, William Thurman. BA, U. Tenn., 1941, JD, 1947. Bar: Tenn. 1946, U.S. Ct. Mil. Appeals 1956, U.S. Supreme Ct. 1960. Pvt. practice Knoxville, Tenn., 1947-60, 87—; ptnr. Asquith, Ailor & Jones, Knoxville, 1961-87; solicitor Knox County, Knoxville, 1954-68. Mem. devel. bd. U. Tenn.; trustee, Sunday sch. tchr. Ch. St. United Meth. Ch., 1978-80; chancellor Holston Conf. United Meth. Ch., 1981-95, del. Southeastern Jurisdictional Conf., 1988, 92, Gen. Conf., 1988—. With U.S. Army, 1941-46, NATOUSA, MTO, JAGC, 1951-52. Decorated Bronze Star with oak leaf cluster, Normandy Jubilee of Liberty medal, 8 battle stars, Combat Inf. badge. Mem. ABA, Tenn. Trial Lawyers Assn., Am. Judicature Soc., Tenn. Bar Assn., Knoxville Bar Assn., U. Tenn. Alumni Assn. (pres. 1963), Lions (life), Masons, Scottish Rite, Omicron Delta Kappa, Phi Delta Phi (life). Democrat. Probate, Estate planning, State civil litigation. Home: 3905 Kenilworth Dr Knoxville TN 37919-6640 Office: 401 Med Arts Bldg Knoxville TN 37902-2603

**AILTS, EVELYN TONIA,** lawyer; b. Abliene, Tex., Oct. 1, 1961; d. Bernard H. Ailts Lucy Testa. BA, U. Tex., 1983; JD with honors, St. Mary's U., San Antonio, 1988. Bar: Tex. 1988, U.S. Ct. Appeals (5th cir.) 1989, U.S. Dist. Ct. (so. dist.) Tex. 1990, U.S. Supreme Ct. 1994. Briefing atty. Tex. Supreme Ct., Austin, 1988-89; assoc. McLeod Alexander Powel & Apffel, Galveston, Tex., 1989-92; pvt. practice Leachman & Ailts, Houston, 1992-93; assoc. Phillips & Akers, Houston, 1993—, also bd. dirs. Assoc. editor (newsletter) Tex. Assn. Def. Counsel, 1996-98. Mem. Tex. Assn. Def. Counsel, Def. Rsch. Inst. (com. appellate advocacy 1998). Appellate. Home: 1123 Bartlett St Apt 8 Houston TX 77006-6435 Office: Phillips & Akers 3200 Southwest Fwy Ste 3400 Houston TX 77027-7528

**AIN, SANFORD KING,** lawyer; b. Glen Cove, N.Y., July 24, 1947; s. Herbert and Victoria (Ben Susan) A.; m. Miriam Luskin, July 12, 1980; children: David Lloyd, Daniel Jason. BA cum laude, U. Wis., 1969; JD, Georgetown U., 1972. Bar: Va. 1972, D.C. 1973, Md. 1982. Ptnr. Sherman, Meehan, Curtin & Ain P.C., Washington, 1972—; mem. faculty continuing legal edn. program State Bar Va., D.C. Bar, Md. Bar. Fellow Am. Acad. Matrimonial Lawyers (pres. D.C. chpt. 1991-94), Am. Coll. Family Trial Lawyers, Va. Trial Lawyers Assn., Md. Bar Assn. Real property, Family and matrimonial. Office: Sherman Meehan Curtin & Ain PC 1900 M St NW Ste 600 Washington DC 20036-3519

**AISENBERG, BENNETT S.,** lawyer; b. Feb. 17, 1931; s. Joseph Samuel and Minna Ruth (Cohan) A. BA, Brown U., 1952; JD, Harvard U., 1955. Bar: Mass. 1955, Colo. 1958, U.S. Dist. Ct. Colo. 1958, U.S. Ct. Appeals (10th cir.) 1958. Ptnr. Gorsuch, Kirgis, Denver, 1958-80; pvt. practice Denver, 1980—. Mem. Nat. Acad. Arbitrators, Colo. Trial Lawyers Assn. (pres. 1984-85), Denver Bar Assn. (trustee 1982-85, 86-89, pres. 1991-92), Colo. Bar Assn. (pres. 1998-99). Personal injury, State civil litigation, Alternative dispute resolution. Office: Colorado State Bank Bldg 1600 Broadway Ste 2350 Denver CO 80202-4921

**AJALAT, SOL PETER,** lawyer; b. Chgo., July 12, 1932; s. Peter S. and Tesbina (Shahadie) Ajalat; m. Lily Mary Roum, Aug. 21, 1960; children: Stephen, Gregory, Denise, Lawrence. BS, UCLA, 1958, JD, 1962. Bar: Calif. 1963, U.S. Dist. Ct. (no., cen., ea. and so. dists.) Calif. 1963, U.S. Claims Ct. 1990. Pvt. practice L.A., 1965—; referee Calif. State Bar Ct., 1984-90. Pres. bd. dirs. St. Nicholas Orthodox Cath. Ch., L.A., 1976-78; pres. Toluca Lake Elem. Adv. Coun., L.A., 1979, L.A. Unified Sch. Dist. Area I Adv. Coun., 1980, Providence High Sch. Adv. Coun., L.A., 1985; bd. dirs. Med. Ctr. North Hollywood, 1991-98, Angels of the Yr. Awards, 1996—, Life Svcs., Inc., 1997—; mem. improvement adv. com. Burbank City media dist., 1997—. Mem. Calif. Bar Assn., L.A. County Bar Assn. (mem. L.A. Superior Ct. bench and bar com. 1987—, chmn. mcpl. ct. com. 1985-86, trustee 1987-88), Calif. Trial Lawyers Assn., L.A. County Trial Lawyers Assn., Lawyers Club L.A. County (pres. 1985-86), Toluca Lake C. of C. (pres. 1997), Wm. A. Neima Rep. Club (pres. 1978-79), Masons, Shriners, Kiwanis. Eastern Orthodox. Avocation: physical fitness. State civil litigation, General practice. Office: 3800 W Alameda Ave Ste 1150 Burbank CA 91505-4340

**AJELLO, MICHAEL JOHN,** lawyer; b. New Haven, Conn., Jan. 13, 1967; s. Joseph Francis and Annajean A.; m. Dana Elizabeth Thompson, July 25, 1992; children: Thomas, Alyssa. BS, Northeastern U., Boston, 1989; JD, Thomas M. Cooley Law Sch., 1995. Bar: Conn. Clk. Judge William Sullivan, New Haven, Conn., 1996-97; atty. Levinson & Cusonelli, New Haven, 1997-98, Bershtein, Lippman, Bachman & McKeon, New Haven, 1998—. Commr. planning and zoning, Hamden, Conn., 1998. Mem. New Haven Young Lawyers (v.p. 1997—), New Haven County Bar, Conn. Trial Lawyers Assn. Consumer commercial, Landlord-tenant, State civil litigation. Office: Bershtein Lippman Bachman & McKeon PC 265 Church St Ste 401 New Haven CT 06510-7012

**AKERS, CHARLES BENJAMIN,** lawyer; b. Leon, Iowa, Jan. 31, 1957; s. Wayne Douglas and Shirley Eileen A.; m. Martha Nan Mailman, May 5, 1989; children: Margaret Frances, Mark Benjamin. BA, Simpson Coll., 1979, BA in Acctg. and BA in Bus. Adminstrn., 1979; JD, U. Houston, 1987. Bar: Tex.; U.S. Tax Ct.; CPA, Tex; cert. estate planning and probate law Tex. Bd. Legal Specialization. Prosecutor Nueces County Atty., Corpus Christie, Tex., 1987-89, Parker County Atty., Weatherford, Tex., 1989-91; assoc. Rohne, Hoodenpyle, et. al., Arlington, Tex., 1991-95; ptnr. Akers & Akers P.C., Weatherford, 1995—. Mem. Parker County Bar Assn., Tex. Bar Assn., State Bar of Tex. (mem. real estate, trust and probate sect. 1993), Epsilon Sigma. Estate planning, Probate, Estate taxation. Office: Akers & Akers PC 111 N Main St Weatherford TX 76086-3240

**AKERS, OTTIE CLAY,** lawyer, publisher; b. Huntsville, Ala., Sept. 4, 1949; s. Merrideth Townsend and Mary Lois (Reed) A.; m. Marcia Bradley Ligon, Mar. 21, 1971; 1 child, Katie Virginia. BA, U. Alabama, Birmingham, 1972, MA, 1976; JD, Samford U., Birmingham, 1985. Bar: Ala. 1985. Assoc. Haskell, Slaughter, Young & Lewis, Birmingham, 1985-86; pub., chief exec. officer Clay-Bradley, Washington, 1986-90; prin. Ottie Akers Law Offices, Birmingham, 1986—. Mem. adminstrv. bd., fin. com. East Lake United Meth. Ch., 1996—; bd. dirs. Bankhead Trail Trust, 1996—. Mem. ABA, Am. Judicature Soc., Assn. Trial Lawyers Am., Ala. Bar Assn., Exch. Club (bd. dirs. Birmingham chpt. 1986, child abuse prevention ctr. 1985-86, 94-96, v.p. fin. 1995-96), Friends of Ala. Sch. Fine Arts Theatre (pres. 1989-90). Communications, General civil litigation, General corporate. Home: PO Box 2038 Buckingham VA 23921 Office: Ottie Akers Law Offices PO Box 610462 Birmingham AL 35261-0462

**AKERS, SAMUEL LEE,** lawyer; b. Chattanooga, Oct. 20, 1943; s. Shelby Russell and Helen Louise (Crumley) A.; m. Mercedes Lilia Vuksanovic, Mar. 13, 1967; children: Bradford Lee, Camby Leigh. BA, Berry Coll., 1966; JD, Memphis State U., 1974. Bar: Tenn. 1974, U.S. Dist. Ct. (ea. dist.) Tenn. 1976, U.S. Ct. Appeals (6th cir.) 1985, U.S. Supreme Ct. 1987, U.S. Dist. Ct. (mid. dist.) Tenn. 1989. Trust examiner Office of the Compt. of the Currency, Memphis, 1975-76; assoc. Luther, Anderson, Cleary & Ruth, Chattanooga, 1976-78, 81-84, ptnr., 1985-93; ptnr. Hatfield Van Cleave & Akers, Chattanooga, 1994, Hatfield Van Cleave Akers & Adams, P.L.C., Chattanooga, 1995-96; spl. agt. FBI, Orlando, Fla., 1978-81; clk. and master Chancery Ct. Hamilton County, 11th Jud. Dist., Chattanooga, 1996—; mem. comml. panel Am. Arbitration Assn., N.Y.C., 1986-96. Asst. instr. SCUBA cert. Lt. comdr. USNR, 1967-71. Named Outstanding Young Man of Am. Jaycees, 1977. Mem. Tenn. Bar Assn., Chattanooga Bar Assn. (bd. govs. 1995-96, sec.-treas. 1997, pres.-elect 1998, pres. 1999—), Soc. Former Spl. Agts. of the FBI (chmn. Chattanooga chpt. 1987-88, 95-96). Republican. Roman Catholic. Avocations: jogging, bicycling, hiking, tennis, scuba diving. State civil litigation, Probate, General civil litigation. Home: 106 Westwood Dr Signal Mountain TN 37377-2525 Office: Chancery Ct Tenn 300 Courthouse Hamilton Co Chattanooga TN 37402

**AKERS-PARRY, DEBORAH,** lawyer; b. Troy, N.Y., Apr. 27, 1949; d. Samuel Lansing and Audrey (Relyea) Rowley. AB, Washington U., St. Louis, 1971; JD, Cleve. State U., 1976. Bar: Ohio 1976. Assoc. Wm. F. Manlove Co., L.P.A.; ptnr. Manlove, Manlove, Rowley & Fuhry, Chagrin Falls, Ohio, 1976-79; pvt. practice Avon Lake, Ohio, 1979-84; assoc. Schwarzwald, Robiner, Wolf & Rock, L.P.A., Cleve., 1984-88; prin. Wolf & Akers, L.P.A., Cleve., 1988—; mem. faculty Ohio CLE Inst., 1985-87, 89-93, Ohio Supreme Ct. Jud. Coll. Teleconf., 1991. Co-author: Disqualification, Family Advocate, vol. 9, #3, 1987; mem. editorial bd. The Domestic Rels. Jour. of Ohio. Trial referee Medina County Ct. of Common Pleas, 1983-84; mem. Profl. Edn. systems, 1990-91; appointee 8th Ohio Appellate Dist. Jud. Conf., 1991, 98, Bench Bar Conf., 1990, 94. Fellow Am. Acad. Matrimonial Lawyers; mem. ABA (family law sect., property divsn. com., 1992—, litigation sect., 1989—, participant Advanced Family Law Advocacy Inst. 1987, faculty 1992-94, 97, vice chmn. family law ethics 1990-91), Nat. Inst. Trial Advocacy (participant Teacher Training Program, Harvard Law Sch., 1993); Ohio State Bar Assn. (vice chmn. family law com. 1992-93, chmn. 1994-96, chmn. legis. drafting subcom. 1989-93, del. coun. of dels. 1990—), Cuyahoga County Bar Assn. (chmn. family law com. 1992-93, trustee 1986-87, mem. grievance com. 1986-96, faculty Trial Advocacy Inst. 1988-89, co-chmn. 1990-91, chmn. 1993), Cleve. Bar Assn. (chmn. family law sect. 1989-90, profl. ethics com. 1986-93), Medina County Bar Assn. (lectr. 1983, 84, 87), Ohio Family Law Inst., Akron Bar Assn., Wayne County Bar Assn., Geauga County Bar Assn., Cleveland-Marshall Coll. of Law Alumni Assn. (trustee 1991-96, chmn. CLE com. 1994-96). Episcopalian. Family and matrimonial. Office: Wolf & Akers LPA 1515 East Ohio Bldg 1717 E 9th St Cleveland OH 44114-2803

**AKHTAR, SHER M.,** lawyer; b. Rawalpindi, Punjab, India, Dec. 15, 1947; m. Fakhrun N. Akhtar; 1 child, Asim J. BSc, Karachi U., 1967; BSChemE, SUNY, Buffalo, 1973; MBA, Western Mich. U., 1977; JD, U. Detroit, 1985. Bar: Mich. 1987. Sales engr. Haviland Products Co., Grand Rapids, Mich., 1974-77, regional mgr., 1977-78; project engr. GM Corp., Lansing, Mich., 1978-80; sr. project engr. GM Corp., Warren, Mich., 1980-89; engring. group mgr. GM Corp., Flint, Mich., 1989-94; pvt. practice law Troy, Mich., 1994—; atty. rep. Site Rev. Bd., State of Mich., 1994—. Mem. Am. Immigration Lawyers Assn., State Bar Mich., Islamic Assn. Greater Detroit (pres. 1986). Avocations: reading, golf. Immigration, naturalization, and customs, General corporate, Family and matrimonial. Office: 755 W Big Beaver Rd Ste 414 Troy MI 48084-4900

**AL, MARC ANDRE,** associate lawyer; b. Leiden, The Netherlands; came to U.S., 1991; s. Bernard P. F. Al and Toop K. Al-Duyster; m. Dawn Marie Mathson, Dec. 28, 1991; 1 child, Juliette Marieke. Law degree, Leiden U., The Netherlands, 1992; JD, William Mitchell Coll. Law, 1994. Bar: Minn. 1994, U.S. Dist. Ct. Minn., 1996, U.S. Dist. Ct. Ariz. 1999, U.S. Ct. Appeals (8th cir.) 1999. Jud. law clk. to Hon. James A. Morrow Anoka, Minn., 1994-95; jud. law clk. to Hon. Jonathan Lebedoff Mpls., 1995-97; assoc. atty. Rider, Bennett, Egan & Arundel, LLP, Mpls., 1997—. Legal advisor Leiden Legal Aid Found., 1990-91. Mem. ABA, Fed. Bar Assn., Minn. State Bar Assn., Hennepin County Bar Assn. Fax: 612-340-7900. E-mail: maal@riderlaw.com. General corporate, Insurance. Office: Rider Bennett Egan & Arundel LLP 333 S 7th St Ste 2000 Minneapolis MN 55402-2431

**ALAIMO, ANTHONY A.,** federal judge; b. 1920. AB, Ohio No. U.; JD, Emory U. Bar: Ga. 1948, Ohio 1948. Assoc. Reuben A. Garland, 1949-51, 53-56; pvt. practice, Atlanta, 1967-63; ptnr. Highsmith, Highsmith, Alaimo & Knox, Brunswick, Ga., 1963-67, Cowart, Sapp, Alaimo & Gale, Brunswick, 1963-67, Alaimo, Taylor & Bishop, Brunswick, 1967-71; judge U.S. Dist. Ct. (so. dist.) Ga., Brunswick, 1971—, now sr. judge. Office: US Dist Ct PO Box 944 Brunswick GA 31521-0944

**ALAN, MATTHEW W. A.,** lawyer; b. Cleve., Nov. 9, 1961. BA in History and Polit. Sci., Cleve. State U., 1984, JD, 1986. Bar: Ohio 1987, D.C. 1992, Pa. 1993. Sr. counsel CBS Corp., Pitts., 1993-98; sec., gen. counsel Westinghouse Safety Mgmt. Solutions, LLC, Aiken, S.C., 1998—. Capt. JAGC, U.S. Army, 1987-93. General corporate, Government contracts and claims, Private international. Office: Westinghouse Safety Mgmt Solutions LLC 1993 S Centennial Ave Aiken SC 29803-7609

**ALAN, SONDRA KIRSCHNER,** lawyer; b. Pitts.; d. Andrew and Lora Hardy Frances Kirschner; m. Riley L. Proffitt, July 9, 1988; children: Gregory Proffitt Alan, Victoria Jade Proffitt Rognerud, Andrew Lawrence Proffitt. BA, SUNY, Buffalo, 1968; JD, Duquesne U., 1980. Bar: Pa. 1980, Va. 1983, U.S. Dist. Ct. (we. dist.) Va. 1982, U.S. Ct. Appeals (4th cir.) 1982. Art tchr. St. Gregory the Gt., Buffalo, 1966-68; mgr. visual arts lab Ind. U. Sch. of Optometry, Bloomington, 1969-71; law clk. to presiding justice Ct. Common Pleas, Waynesburg, Pa., 1979-80; assoc. Law Offices J.D. Bowie, Bristol, Va., 1980-83; pvt. practice Bristol, 1984—. Recipient 2d pl. award Pa. State Art Competition, 1976. Mem. ABA (family sect.), Pa. Bar Assn., Va. Bar Assn., Bristol Bar Assn. (pres. 1984-85). Lutheran. Avocations: pencil sketching, stained glass, home remodeling, gardening. Family and matrimonial, Probate, General practice. Office: 923 Cumberland St Bristol VA 24201-4103

**ALARCON, ARTHUR LAWRENCE,** federal judge; b. L.A., Aug. 14, 1925; s. Lorenzo Marques and Margaret (Sais) A.; m. Sandra D. Paterson, Sept. 1, 1979; children—Jan Marie, Gregory, Lance. B.A. in Polit. Sci, U. So. Calif., 1949, J.D., 1951. Bar: Calif. 1952. Dep. dist. atty. L.A. County, 1952-61; exec. asst. to Gov. Pat Brown State of Calif., Sacramento, 1962-64, legal adv. to gov., 1961-62; judge L.A. Superior Ct., 1964-78; assoc. justice Calif. Ct. Appeals, L.A., 1978-79; judge U.S. Ct. Appeals for 9th Circuit, L.A., 1979—. Served with U.S. Army, 1943-46, ETO. Office: US Ct Appeals 9th Cir 1607 US Courthouse 312 N Spring St Los Angeles CA 90012-4701

**ALBAN, LUDWIG,** lawyer; b. N.Y.C., Dec. 30, 1947. BS, Bradley U., 1969; JD, Tulane U., 1973. V.p. Indusco Rental Inc., N.Y.C., 1969-70; atty., treas. Feinberg & Alban P.C., Brookline, Mass., 1973—; treas. Ferriabough Enterprises Inc. Brookline 1974-77, MVP Assocs. Inc. Brookline, 1978-84. Mem. Mass. Bar Assn., St. John's Lodge (sr. warden). General corporate, Probate, Real property. Office: Feinberg & Alban PC 1051 Beacon St Brookline MA 02446-5685

**ALBER, PHILLIP GEORGE,** lawyer; b. Lansing, Mich., Dec. 10, 1948; s. Phillip Karl and Audrey Irene (Putnam) A.; m. Shari Thornton; children: Emily Nicole, Phillip George, Elisabeth Whitney, Christian Thornton. BA magna cum laude, U. Mich., 1971; JD cum laude, Wayne State U., 1974. Bar: Mich. 1975, U.S. Dist. Ct. (ea. dist.) Mich. 1975, U.S. Ct. Appeals (6th cir.) 1978, U.S. Dist. Ct. (we. dist.) Mich. 1982. Assoc. Harvey, Kruse, Westen & Milan, Detroit, 1975-79, ptnr., 1979-85; ptnr. Mager, Mercer, Scott and Alber, Detroit, 1985—; lectr. Ill. Inst. Continuing Edn., Chgo., 1980. Mem. ABA (torts ins. practice sect., vice chair fidelity and surety law com.), Detroit Bar Assn. (pub. adv. com. 1979—, cir. ct. com. 1978—), Mich. Bar Assn., (rep. assembly 1979-80), Internat. Assn. Def. Counsel (fidelity and surety com. 1984—), Surety Claims Inst., Nat. Bd. Claim Assn. (pres. 1992-94, program chair 1990—), Assn. Def. Trial Counsel. Republican. Roman Catholic. Clubs: Detroit Athletic, Hundred, Goodfellows Old Newsboys (Detroit). Federal civil litigation, State civil litigation, Construction. Home: 655 Rivard Blvd Grosse Pointe MI 48230-1253 Office: Mager Mercer Scott & Alber 755 W Big Beaver Rd Ste 1700 Troy MI 48084-4906

**ALBERT, ROBERT HAMILTON,** lawyer; b. Columbus, Ohio, May 25, 1931; s. Raymond Joseph Albert and Kathryn Mary (Hildebrand) Lett; m. Patricia S. Smith, June 23, 1962; children: Julie Ann Albert Certain, Karen Marie Albert Groeber, Robert H. Jr. BSBA, Ohio State U., 1953; LLB, Franklin U., 1960; JD, Capital U., 1966. Bar: Ohio, 1960, U.S. Tax Ct. 1961, U.S. Dist. Ct. (so. dist.) Ohio, 1962, U.S. Ct. Appeals (6th cir.) 1966, U.S. Ct. Claims 1971, U.S. Supreme Ct. 1971. Indsl. engr. Fairmont Foods Co., Columbus, 1951-52; acct. E.C. Redmund CPA, Columbus, 1953-54, N.Am. Aviation, Columbus, 1956-60; ptnr. Kagay, Albert & Diehl, Columbus, 1961—. Served to capt. USAF, 1954-56. Mem. Ohio State Bar Assn., Columbus Bar Assn. Roman Catholic. Probate, Real property, Taxation, general. Office: Kagay Albert & Diehl 849 Harmon Ave Columbus OH 43223-2411

**ALBERT, RONALD PETER,** lawyer; b. Utica, N.Y., Sept. 10, 1956; s. Raymond J. and Monica (Fischer) A. AB in Econs. magna cum laude, U. Calif., Davis, 1979; JD, U. Calif., Berkeley, 1983; postgrad., Golden Gate U., 1989-91. Bar: Calif. 1983, N.Y. 1985; lic. real estate broker, Calif. Adj. prof. bus. law Syracuse U. Utica Coll., 1988-89; assoc. Griffinger, Levinson, Freed & Heinemann, San Francisco, 1989-93; pvt. practice, Sausalito, Calif., 1994—; lectr. real estate law U. Calif. Haas Sch. Bus., Berkeley, 1992—; pres. Sausalito Exch. Co., 1995—. Supreme Ct. editor U. Calif. Law Rev., 1982-83. Mem. Planning Commn., City of Sausalito, 1997—, chmn., 1999—; active Tax-Aid, San Francisco. Mem. Calif. State Bar, Bar Assn. San Francisco (vol. lawyers svc. program), Equity Asset Mgrs. Assn. Fax: 415-332-9216. Office: 66 George Ln Ste 101 Sausalito CA 94965-1890

**ALBERTS, HAROLD,** lawyer; b. San Antonio, Tex., Apr. 3, 1920; s. Bernard H. and Rose Alberts; m. Rose M. Gaskin, Mar. 25, 1945; children—Linda Rae, Barry Lawrence. LL.B., U. Tex.-Austin, 1942. Bar: Tex. 1943, U.S. Supreme Ct. 1950, U.S. Ct. Mil. Apls. 1959. Tchr., U. Tex. 1942; instr., U. Tex., Austin, 1941-42; legal officer Chase Field, 1944; sole practice, Corpus Christi, Tex. Pres. Jewish Welfare Fund, Corpus Christi, 1948; chmn. Southwest Regional Anti-Defamation League, Tex. and Okla., 1970-71, chmn., 1969-72, chmn. Brotherhood Week, 1957; chmn. Nueces County (Tex.) Red Cross, 1959-61; mem. campaign exec. com., chmn. meetings United Community Services, 1961; v.p. Little Theatre, Corpus Christi, 1964; chmn. Corpus Christi NCCJ, 1967-69, nat. dir., 1974-76; bd. dirs. Tex. State Assn. Mental Health; pres. Combined Jewish Apl., Corpus Christi, 1974-76; moderator Friday Morning Group, 1975, 96. Served to lt. (sr. grade) USNR, 1942-46. Mem. ABA, Tex. Bar Assn., Corpus Christi Bar Assn. Clubs: Kiwanis (pres. 1962), B'nai B'rith (pres. 1955), Mason (32d degree). General practice, State civil litigation, Probate. Home: 5314 Hulen Dr Corpus Christi TX 78413-2247 Office: PO Box 271477 Corpus Christi TX 78427-1477

**ALBERTSON, JACK AARON PAUL,** prosecutor; b. Rantoul, Ill., Apr. 28, 1962; s. Jack Collier and Sandra Lou (Cole) A. BA, U. Redlands, 1984; JD, Willamette U., 1987. Bar: Calif. 1989. Law libr. Riverside County Law Libr., Indio, Calif., 1989-90; dep. Imperial County Dist. Atty., El Centro, Calif., 1990—. Mem. ABA, Nat. Dist. Attorneys Assn., Phi Alpha Delta. Republican. Mem. Ch. of Christ. Avocations: tennis, playing guitar and violin. Office: Imperial County Dist Atty 939 W Main St El Centro CA 92243-2843

**ALBERTY, MICHAEL CHARLES,** lawyer; b. Mt. Lebanon, Pa., Mar. 13, 1959; s. Charles Michael and Georgia (Tsarnas) A.; m. Jacqueline Diakakis,

May 4, 1991. BA, Washington & Jefferson Coll., 1980; MS, Duquesne U., 1981; PhD, U. Pitts., 1987; JD, Duquesne U., 1988. Bar: Pa. 1989, U.S. Dist. Ct. (we. dist.) Pa. 1989, U.S. Tax. Ct. 1989, U.S. SUpreme Ct. 1993. Fin. analyst Ryan Fin. Svcs., Pitts., 1981-84; project mgr. Copperweld Corp., Pitts., 1985-87; human resources coord. Roadway Package System Inc., Pitts., 1987-89; staff atty. Legent Corp., Pitts., 1989—; atty. pvt. practice, Mt. Lebanon, Pa., 1989—, Washington, Pa., 1989—. Atty. for political campaign Dr. Robert Barrickman for Rep., Clarion, Pa., 1992. Recipient award for Saving Life ARC, 1976. Mem. Allegheny County Bar Assn., Pitts. Athletic Assn., Masons. Greek Orthodox. Avocations: fishing, hunting, Karate, ice skating, golf. General corporate, General civil litigation, Family and matrimonial. Home: RR 7 Box 1B Washington PA 15301-9807 Office: 261 Gilkeson Rd Pittsburgh PA 15228-1017

**ALBIN, BARRY G.,** lawyer, rabbi; b. Wichita, Kans., Sept. 6, 1948; s. Frederick Eugene Albin and Eloise Nelda Riley; m. Marianne Kay Olish, Aug. 8, 1970 (div. Feb. 1997); children: Thomas C., Michael A., Benjamin J., Joshua S. BA, U. Kans., 1970, JD, 1973; cert. in data processing, Kansas City C.C., 1981. Bar; Kans. 1973, U.S. Dist. Ct. Kans. 1973. Staff counsel Wyandotte Legal Aid Soc., Kansas City, Kans., 1974-76; pvt. practice Kansas City, 1976-83, 85—; gen. mgr. Chameleon Dental Products, Kansas City, 1983-85; lectr. bus. law Maple Woods C.C., Kansas City, Mo., 1978; staff counsel Kans. State Dept. Social and Rehab. Svcs., Kansas City, 1986-91; legal counsel Mid. Am. Gay Ecumenical Found., Kansas City, Mo., 1975-80, Phylaxis Soc., 1999, N.E. Kans. Valley, AASR. Author: Climbing Jacob's Ladder, 1981, Believers Commentary on Mark, 1985, Believers Commentary on Barnabas, 1986, Catechism of Nasorean Church, 1995. Mebakker rabbi Ha Am Ha Kol, Kansas City, 1985—. Mem. Masons (various offices 1989—), Scottish Rite, Blue Lodge. Democrat. Avocations: computers, reading, hiking, teaching, scripture. Constitutional, Criminal, Appellate.

**ALBRECHTA, JOSEPH FRANCIS,** lawyer; b. Bklyn., Apr. 1, 1957. PhB, Miami U., 1978; JD, U. Toledo, 1984. Bar: Ohio 1984, U.S. Dist. Ct. (no. dist.) Ohio 1984, U.S. Ct. Appeals (5th cir.), U.S. Supreme Ct. 1986. Naturalist Ind. Dunes State Park, Ind. Dept. Natural Resources, Porter, 1978; polit. activist, campaign staff Ohio Alliance for Returns, Columbus, 1979; lobbyist Ohio Sierra Club, Columbus, 1980-81; tech. writer Toledo Met. Area Coun. Govts., 1981-82; legal asst. Gallon, Kalnie & Ivrio Co. LPA, Toledo, 1982-84, assoc., 1984-86; ptnr. Gary and Albrechta, Toledo, 1986-95, Albrechta & Coble, Toledo, Fremont and Perrysburg, Ohio, 1996—; lawyer Otis Elem. Sch. PTO, Fremont, 1994—, St. Johns Luth. Ch., Fremont, 1995—. Vol. Otis Elem. Sch., Fremont, 1990-97; asst. den leader Cub Scouts Pack 312, Fremont, 1991-97; scoutmaster Boy Scouts Troop 400, Fremont, 1997. Mem. ATLA, Ohio Trial Lawyers Assn., Toledo Bar Assn. (grievance investigator 1992—), Sandusky County Bar Assn., Fremont Yacht Club (asst. comdr. 1991—). Democrat. Lutheran. General civil litigation, Personal injury, Product liability. Office: Albrechta & Coble 2255 Christy Rd Fremont OH 43420-9789

**ALBRIGHT, DOUGLAS EATON,** lawyer; b. Sedro Woolley, Wash., Aug. 31, 1948; s. Hubert Wilbur and Reda (Eaton) A.; m. Jan Kristin Halgren, Aug. 15, 1973; children: Kara, Meredith. BA with honors, U. Puget Sound, 1970; JD, U. Wash., 1973. Bar: Wash. 1973; U.S. Dist. Ct. (we. dist.) Wash. 1973. Assoc. Ogden, Murphy, Wallace, Seattle, 1973-76, from ptnr. to mng. ptnr., 1977-94, chmn. bus. dept., 1982-92, chmn. health law sect., 1995—; com. on med. staff and physician rels. Am. Health Lawyers Assn., Chgo., 1991—, peer rev. task force, joint venture task force. Contbr. articles to profl. jours. Dir. Luth. Alliance to Create Housing. Mem. ABA (co-vice chmn. mktg. groups commn. 1987-89, mem. bus. law sect./com. on health), Wash. State Bar Assn. (mem. internat. law sect., com. on Europe), Am. Health Lawyers Assn. Lutheran. Avocations: biking, outdoor activities, flyfishing. Health, General corporate, Mergers and acquisitions. Office: Ogden Murphy Wallace 1601 5th Ave Ste 2100 Seattle WA 98101-1686

**ALBRIGHT, GEORGE MARK,** lawyer; b. San Antonio, June 19, 1955; s. George Vern and Barbara (Carruth) A.; m. Karyn J. Wasden, Dec. 18, 1976; children: Nicole, Steve, Brandon, Michelle, Ashley. BA cum laude, Brigham Young U., 1978; JD, J. Rueben Clark Coll., 1981. Bar: Nev. 1981, U.S. Dist. Ct. Nev. 1981, U.S. Ct. Appeals (9th cir.) 1986, U.S. Supreme Ct. 1993. Law clk. U.S. Bankruptcy Ct., Las Vegas, 1981; assoc. Albright & Stoddard, Las Vegas, 1982; ptnr. Albright Stoddard Warnick & Albright, Las Vegas, 1986—. Author: Construction, 1997; contbr. author (manual) Nev. Civil Practice, 1992; editor, contbg. author Brigham Young U. Law Rev., 1980-81. Varsity scout coach Boy Scouts Am., 1985, explorer scout leader, 1989-90, Eagle Scout, 1969; bishop LDS Ch., 1991-97. Mem. State Bar Nev., Clark County Bar Assn. (com. mem. 1983); charter mem. Phi Delta Phi. Republican. Avocations: water skiing, snow skiing, hunting, fishing. General civil litigation, Insurance, Contracts commercial. Home: 7916 Waterfalls Ave Las Vegas NV 89128-6711 Office: Albright Stoddard Warnick & Albright 9105 Chenin Ave Las Vegas NV 89129-6113

**ALBRIGHT, MARK PRESTON,** lawyer; b. Reading, Pa., Jan. 30, 1958; s. Preston W. and Joan K. Albright; m. Lois Henseler, May 24, 1980; children: Allison S., Meredith J. AB in Polit. Sci. summa cum laude, Albright Coll., 1979; JD, U. Md., 1982. Bar: Pa. 1982, U.S. Dist. Ct. (ea. dist.) Pa. 1982, U.S. Ct. Appeals (3rd cir.) 1992. Assoc. Koch and Koch Attys. at Law, Reading, Pa., 1982-87; sec., gen. counsel Great Valley Savs. Bank, Reading, 1987-89; assoc. Mogel, Speidel, Bobb and Kershner, P.C., Reading, 1989-94; pvt. practice Allentown, Pa., 1994—; course planner, faculty Pa. Bar Inst., Mechanicsburg, Pa., 1998—. Elder, mem. of session First Presbyn. Ch. of Allentown, 1991-96. Mem. Lehigh County Bar Assn., Berks County Bar Assn., Pa. Bar Assn. (tech. task force 1998), Am. Inn of Ct. Labor, General civil litigation, Computer. Office: 2200 W Hamilton St Ste 206 Allentown PA 18104-6329

**ALBRIGHT, TERRILL D.,** lawyer; b. Lebanon, Ind., June 23, 1938; s. David Henry and Georgia Pauline (Doty) A.; m. Judith Ann Stoelting, June 2, 1962; children: Robert T., Elizabeth A. AB, Ind. U., 1960, JD, 1965. Bar: Ind. 1965, U.S. Dist. Ct. (so. dist.) Ind. 1965, U.S. Dist. Ct. (no. dist.) Ind. 1980, U.S. Ct. Appeals (7th cir.) 1981, U.S. Ct. Appeals (3d and D.C. cirs.) 1982, U.S. Supreme Ct. 1972; cert. arbitrator for large complex cse program constrn. and internat. commercial cases Am. Arbitration Assn., cert. mediator. Assoc. Baker and Daniels Law Firm, Indpls., 1965-72; ptnr. Baker and Daniels Law Firm, 1972—. Bd. dirs., pres. Christamore House, Indpls., 1979-86; bd. dirs. Greater Indpls. YMCA, 1980-82; chmn. Jordan YMCA, Indpls., 1982; pres. Community Ctrs. Indpls., 1987-90. 1st lt. U.S. Army, 1960-62. Fellow Am. Bar Found., Ind. Bar Found., Indpls. Bar Found., Am. Coll. Trial Lawyers; mem. Nat. Conf. Bar Presidents (exec. coun. 1995-98), Ind. State Bar Assn. (chmn. young lawyer sect. 1971-72, rep. 11th dist. 1983-85, bd. dirs., v.p. 1991-92, pres. elect 1992-93, pres. 1993-94), Ind. U. Law Alumni Assn. (bd. dirs. 1974-80, pres. 1979-80). Democrat. General civil litigation, Construction, Federal civil litigation. Office: Baker & Daniels 300 N Meridian St Ste 2700 Indianapolis IN 46204-1782

**ALBRITTON, WILLIAM HAROLD, III,** federal judge; b. Andalusia, Ala., Dec. 19, 1936; s. Robert Bynum and Carrie (Veal) A.; m. Jane Rollins Howard, June 2, 1958; children: William Harold IV, Benjamin Howard, Thomas Bynum. A.B., U. Ala., 1959, LL.B., 1960. Bar: Ala. 1960. Assoc. firm Albrittons & Rankin, Andalusia, 1962-66, ptnr., 1966-76; ptnr. firm Albrittons & Givhan, Andalusia, 1976-86; ptnr. Albrittons, Givhan & Clifton, Andalusia, 1986-91; judge U.S. Dist. Ct. (mid. dist.) Ala., Montgomery, 1991-97, chief judge, 1998—. Pres. Ala. Law Sch. Found., 1988-91, Ala. Law Inst. Fellow Am. Coll. Trial Lawyers, Am. Bar Found.; mem. ABA, Fed. Judges Assn. (bd. dirs. 1999—), Ala. State Bar (commr. 1981-89, disciplinary commn. 1981-84, v.p. 1985-86, pres.-elect 1989-90, pres. 1990-91), Am. Judicature Soc., Am. Inns of Ct., Bluewater Bay Sailing Club, Bluewater Bay Country Club, Phi Beta Kappa, Phi Delta Phi, Omicron Delta Kappa, Alpha Tau Omega. Office: US Dist Ct S Court St Rm 311 Montgomery AL 36104-4009

**ALBRITTON, WILLIAM HAROLD, IV,** lawyer; b. Tuscaloosa, Ala., Mar. 21, 1960; s. William Harold III and Jane Rollins (Howard) A.; m. Lucille Smith, July 23, 1983; 1 child, Elizabeth Rollins. BA, U. Ala., Tuscaloosa, 1982, JD, 1985. Ptnr. Albrittons Clifton Alverson and Moody P.C., Andalusia, Ala., 1985—; bd. dirs. Colonial Bank, Andalusia; judge Mcpl. Ct. Andalusia, 1989—. Bd. dirs. Covington County Arts Coun., Andalusia, 1986-90, Andalusia City Schs. Found., 1991—, Andalusia Area C. of C., 1986-89; elder 1st Presbyn. Ch., Andalusia, 1990—. Mem. ABA, Ala. Bar Assn. (sec. pres.'s adv. task force 1986-88, chmn. com. on local bar activities 1990, task force on minority opportunity 1990-96, character and fitness com. 1991-96, chmn. 1993-96, chmn. com. solo practitioners & small firms 1997—), Ala. Def. Lawyers Assn. (bd. dirs. young lawyers sect. 1991-96, amicus curiae com. 1992—), Internat. Assn. Def. Counsel, Am. Inns of Ct., Kiwanis. Avocations: scuba diving, music, photography, travel, sailing. General civil litigation, Insurance, Workers' compensation. Home: 723 Albritton Rd Andalusia AL 36420-4601 Office: Albrittons Clifton Alverson & Moody PC 109 Opp Ave Andalusia AL 36420-3812

**ALBUM, JERALD LEWIS,** lawyer; b. Monroe, La., Oct. 18, 1947; s. Natt B. and Rose Marie (Pickens) A.; m. Joan Abbey Lurie, July 30, 1983; children: Nicole, Jeffrey. BS, Tulane U., 1969, JD, 1973. Bar: La. 1973, Colo. 1990, Tex. 1992, U.S. Dist. Ct. (ea. dist.) La. 1975, U.S. Dist. Ct. (mid. dist.) La. 1980, U.S. Dist. Ct. (we. dist.) La. 1983, U.S. Ct. Appeals (5th cir.) 1976. Assoc. Mmahat, Gagliano, Duffy & Giordano, Metairie, La., 1973-79; assoc. to ptnr. Lemle, Kelleher, Hunley, Moss & Frilot, New Orleans, 1980-85; shareholder Abbott Simses, Album & Knister, New Orleans, 1985-96; ptnr. Album, Stovall, Radecker & Giordano, New Orleans. Mem. La. Assn. of Def. Counsel, New Orleans Bar Assn., La. State Bar Assn. Avocations: golf, volleyball, gardening. Admiralty, Personal injury, General civil litigation. Home: 4637 Southshore Dr Metairie LA 70002-1430 Office: Album Stovall Radecker & Giordano 3850 N Causeway Blvd Ste 1130 Metairie LA 70002-7247

**ALCOX, PATRICK JOSEPH,** lawyer; b. Cleve., Oct. 27, 1946; s. William B. and Helen T. (McKenna) A.; m. Karen Woelfle, Oct. 20, 1979; children: Caitlin M., Molly C. BBA, Cleve. State U., 1970; MBA, Kent State U., 1974; JD, Cleve.-Marshall Coll. Law, 1976. Bar: Ohio, 1976, U.S. Supreme Ct., 1983. Group mgr. IRS, Cleve., 1972-76; fin. account exec. Internat. Mgmt. Group, Cleve., 1976-80; pvt. practice Cleve., 1980—. Ward leader Berea (Ohio) Republican Com., 1985-97; chmn. Berea CSC, 1988-92. Mem. Ohio Bar Assn., Cleve. Bar Assn., Assn. Trial Lawyers Am., Ohio Assn. Trial Lawyers. Roman Catholic. Avocations: jogging, reading, politics. Workers' compensation, Personal injury, Probate. Home: 448 Woodridge Cir Berea OH 44017-2227 Office: 75 Public Sq Ste 650 Cleveland OH 44113-2097

**ALDAG, JEFFREY NOEL,** lawyer; b. Geneva, N.Y., May 16, 1959; s. John Henry and Shirley Anne (Hampton) A. BA, Grinnell Coll., 1984; JD, U. Iowa Law Sch., 1988. Bar: Ill. Rsch. asst. Iowa Protection and Advocacy Svcs., Inc., Iowa City; intern clin. law program U. Iowa, Iowa City; asst. pub. defender Vermilion County Pub. Defenders Office, Danville, Ill., 1989—. Mem. ABA, Ill. Bar Assn., Vermilion County Bar Assn. Avocations: travel, flying, political science, American history. Office: Vermilion County Pub Defenders Office 7 N Vermilion St Danville IL 61832-5806

**ALDAVE, BARBARA BADER,** law educator, lawyer; b. Tacoma, Dec. 28, 1938; d. Fred A. and Patricia W. (Burns) Bader; m. Ralph Theodore Aldave, Apr. 2, 1966; children—Anna Marie, Anthony John. BS, Stanford U., 1960; JD, U. Calif.-Berkeley, 1966. Bar: Oreg. 1966, Tex. 1982. Assoc. law firm Eugene, Oreg., 1967-70; asst. prof. U. Oreg., 1970-73; vis. prof. U. Calif., Berkeley, 1973-74; from vis. prof. to prof. U. Tex., Austin, 1974-89, coholder James R. Dougherty chair for faculty excellence, 1981-82, Piper prof., 1982, Joe A. Worsham centennial prof., 1984-89, Liddell, Sapp, Zivley, Hill and LaBoon prof. banking financial and comml. law, 1989; dean Sch. Law, prof. St. Mary's U., San Antonio, 1989-98, Ernest W. Clemens prof. corp. law, 1996-98; vis. prof. Northeastern U., 1985-88, 98; vis. prof. Boston Coll. 1999; ABA rep. to Coun. Inter-ABA, 1995—; NAFTA chpt. 19 panelist, 1994-96. Pres. NETWORK, 1985-89; chair Gender Bias Task Force of Supreme Ct. Tex., 1991-94; bd. dirs. Tex. Alliance Children's Rights, Assn. Religiously Affiliated Law Schs., Lawyer's com. for Civil Rights Under Law of Tex. Recipient tchg. excellence award U. Tex. Student Bar Assn., 1976, Appreciation awards Thurgood Marshall Legal Soc. of U. Tex., 1979, 81, 85, 87, Tchg. Excellence award Chicano Law Students Assn. of U. Tex., 1984, Hermine Tobolowsky award Women's Law Caucus of U. Tex., 1985, Ethics award Kugle, Stewart, Dent & Frederick, 1988, Leadership award Women's Law Assn. St. Mary's U., 1989, Ann. Inspirational award Women's Advocacy Project, 1989, Appreciation award San Antonio Black Lawyers Assn., 1990, Spl. Recognition award Nat. Conv. Nat. Lawyers Guild, 1990, Spirit of the Am. Woman award J. C. Penney Co., 1992, Sarah T. Hughes award Women and the Law sect. State Bar Tex., 1994, Ann. Tchg. award Soc. Am. Law Tchrs., 1996, Legal Svcs. award Mexican-Am. Legal Def. and Ednl. Fund, 1996, Woman of Justice award NETWORK, 1997, Ann. Peacemaker award Camino a la Paz, 1997, Outstanding Profl. in the Cmty. award Dept. Pub. Justice, St. Mary's U., 1997, Charles Hamilton Houston award Black Allied Law Students Assn. St. Mary's U., 1998, Woman of Yr. award Tex. Women's Polit. Caucus, 1998, award Clin. Legal Edn. Assn., 1998, lifetime achievement award Jour. Law and Religion, 1998. Mem. ABA (com. on corp. laws sect., banking and bus. law 1982-88), Bexar County Women's Bar Assn. (Belva Lockwood Outstanding Lawyer award 1991), San Antonio Bar Assn., World Affairs Coun. San Antonio, Harlan Soc., Tex. Women's Forum, Stanford U. Alumni Assn., Alamo Telecomms. coun., Tex. Appleseed, Tex.-Mexico Bar Assn., San Antonio Bar Found., Order of Coif, Phi Delta Phi, Iota Sigma Pi, Omicron Delta Kappa, Delta Theta Phi (Outstanding Law Prof. award St. Mary's U. chpt. 1990, 91). Roman Catholic. Home: 323 W Woodlawn Ave San Antonio TX 78212-3312 Office: St Mary's U 950 Massachusetts Ave Apt 517 Cambridge MA 02139-3177

**ALDEN, STEVEN MICHAEL,** lawyer; b. Los Angeles, May 19, 1945; s. Herbert and Sylvia Zina (Hochman) A.; m. Evelyn Mae Subotky, Dec. 31, 1977; children: Carissa Louise, Bramley Marshall, Darym Alexander. AB, UCLA, 1967; JD, U. Calif.-Berkeley, 1970. Bar: Calif. 1971, N.Y. 1971. Assoc. Debevoise & Plimpton, N.Y.C., 1971-78, ptnr., 1979—; lectr., seminar panelist Practising Law Inst., N.Y.C., 1981—; panelist, lectr. N.Y. State Bar, Albany, 1984. Contbr. articles to profl. jours., 1982-83. Mem. ABA (real estate fin. com.), Assn. of Bar of City of N.Y. (com. real property law), Am. Land Title Assn. (assoc. lender's counsel group), Am. Coll. Real Estate Lawyers, Order of Coif, Phi Beta Kappa. Republican. Club: Board Room (N.Y.C.). Real property. Office: Debevoise & Plimpton 875 3rd Ave Fl 23 New York NY 10022-6256

**ALDERMAN, JUDITH LORRAINE,** lawyer; b. Syracuse, N.Y., Nov. 13, 1936; d. Samuel R. Levy and Ethel M. Corbeth; m. Edward Alderman (div. 1976); m. Warren Marsula (dec. 1994); children: Steven, James, Tracy. BA, Syracuse U., 1958, JD, 1983. Bar: N.Y. 1984, U.S. Dist. Ct. (no. dist.) N.Y. 1984; cert. hearing officer. Legal clk., assoc. Grasso Law Firm, Syracuse, N.Y., 1983-85; sr. dep. county atty. Onondaga County Atty.'s Office, Syracuse, 1984-98; pvt. practice Fayetteville, N.Y., 1998—. Mem., pres. Fayetteville Manlius Bd. Edn., 1973-80; mem., trustee numerous civic orgns.; mem. County's Execs. Children's Panel, 1990-97. Mem. Onondaga County Bar Assn. Avocations: writing, duplicate bridge. Family and matrimonial, Education and schools, Juvenile. Office: 209 Highbridge St Apt 4 Fayetteville NY 13066-1930

**ALDISERT, RUGGERO JOHN,** federal judge; b. Carnegie, Pa., Nov. 10, 1919; s. John S. and Elizabeth (Magnacca) A.; m. Agatha Maria DeLacio, Oct. 4, 1952; children: Lisa Maria, Robert, Gregory. B.A., U. Pitts., 1941, J.D., 1947. Bar: Pa. bar 1947. Gen. practice law Pitts., 1947-61; judge Ct. Common Pleas, Allegheny County, 1961-68; judge U.S. Ct. Appeals (3d cir.), Pitts., 1968-84, chief judge, 1984-87; sr. judge U.S. Ct. Appeals (3d cir.), Pitts., Sanat Barbara, Calif., 1987—; adj. prof. law U. Pitts. Sch. Law, 1964-87 ; faculty Appellate Judges Seminar, NYU, 1971-85 , assoc. dir., 1979-85 ; lectr. internat. seminar legal medicine U. Rome, 1965, Law Soc. London, 1967, Internat. seminar comparative law, Rome, 1971; chmn. Fed. Appellate Judges Seminar; bd. dirs. Fed. Jud. Center, Washington, 1974-79; mem. Pa. Civil Procedural Rules Com., 1965-84 Jud. Conf. Com. on Adminstrn. Criminal Law, 1971-77; chmn. adv. com. on bankruptcy rules Jud. Conf. U.S., 1979-84; lectr. univs. in U.S. and abroad. Author: Il Ritorno al Paese, 1966-67, The Judicial Process, Readings, Materials and Cases, 1976, Logic for Lawyers: A Guide to Clear Legal Thinking, 1989, Opinion Writing, 1990, Winning on Appeal, 1992. Allegheny dist. chmn. Multiple Sclerosis Soc., 1961-68; pres. ISDA, Cultural Heritage Found., 1965-68; trustee U. Pitts., 1968—; chmn. bd. visitors Pitts. Sch. Law, 1978—. Served to maj. USMCR, 1942-46. Recipient Outstanding Merit award Allegheny County Acad. Trial Lawyers, 1964. Mem. Inst. Jud. Adminstrn., Am. Law Inst., Italian Sons and Daus. of Am. (nat. pres. 1954-68), Italian Sons and Daus. Am. Fraternal Assn. (nat. pres. 1960-68), Phi Beta Kappa, Phi Alpha Delta, Omicron Delta Kappa. Democrat. Roman Catholic. Home: PO Box 3810 Santa Barbara CA 93130-3810 Office: US Ct Appeals 120 Cremona Dr Ste D Santa Barbara CA 93117-5511*

**ALDRICH, ANN,** federal judge; b. Providence, June 28, 1927; d. Allie C. and Ethel M. (Carrier) A.; m. Chester Aldrich, 1960 (dec.); children: Martin, William; children by previous marriage: James, Allen; m. John H. McAllister III, 1986. BA cum laude, Columbia U., 1948; LLB cum laude, NYU, 1950, LLM, 1964, JSD, 1967. Bar: D.C. bar, N.Y. bar 1952, Conn. bar 1966, Ohio bar 1973, Supreme Ct. bar 1956. Research asst. to mem. faculty N.Y. U. Sch. Law; atty. IBRD, 1952; atty., rsch. asst. Samuel Nakasian, Esq., Washington, 1952-53; mem. gen. counsel's staff FCC, Washington, 1953-60; U.S. del. to Internat. Radio Conf., Geneva, 1959; practicing atty. Darien, Conn., 1961-68; asso. prof. law Cleve. State U., 1968-71, prof., 1971-80; judge U.S. Dist. Ct. (no. dist.) Ohio, Cleveland, 1980—; bd. govs. Citizens' Communications Center, Inc., Washington; mem. litigation com.; guest lectr. Calif. Inst. Tech., Pasadena, summer 1971. Mem. Fed. Bar Assn., Nat. Assn. of Women Judges, Fed. Communications Bar Assn., Fed. Judge Assn. Episcopalian. Office: US Dist Ct 201 Superior Ave E Cleveland OH 44114-1201

**ALDRICH, BAILEY,** federal judge; b. Boston, Apr. 23, 1907; s. Talbot and Eleanor (Little) A.; m. Elizabeth Perkins, Aug. 13, 1932; children: Jonathan, David. AB, Harvard U., 1928, LLB, 1932. Bar: Mass. 1932. With Choate, Hall & Stewart, Boston, 1932-54; judge U.S. Dist. Ct. Mass., 1954-59, U.S. Ct. Appeals, 1959-64; chief judge U.S. Ct. Appeals (1st cir.), 1965-72, now sr. judge, 1972—. Mem. Am. Law Inst., Am. Acad. Arts and Scis. Home: 120 Brattle St Cambridge MA 02138-3423 Office: US Courthouse 1 Courthouse Way Ste 8740 Boston MA 02210-3010

**ALDRICH, GEORGE HOOVER,** judge, arbitrator; b. St. Louis, Feb. 25, 1932; s. Emmett Porter and Hettie Barbara (Hoover) A.; m. Rosemary Margaret Balmforth Aldrich, June 6, 1959; children: Edward, Stephen, Robert. BA, DePauw U., 1954; LLB, Harvard Law Sch., 1957, LLM, 1958. Bar: Ind., 1958. Atty. Dept. Navy, Washington, 1959-60, Dept. Def., Washington, 1960-63; legal adv. U.S. Delegation to NATO, Paris, 1963-65; asst. legal adv. Dept. State, Washington, 1965-69, deputy legal adv., 1969-77, amb., deputy spl. rep. to pres., 1977-81; judge Iran-U.S. Claims Tribunal, The Hague, The Netherlands, 1981—; U.S. amb. for Laws of War Negotiations, Geneva, Switzerland, 1974-77; mem. UN Internat. Law Commn., Geneva, Switzerland, 1981, Bd. editors Am. Jour. Internat. Law, 1987—; prof. Leiden U., The Netherlands, 1990-97. Author: The Jurisprudence of the Iran-United States Claims Tribunal, 1996; author, negotiator: The Protocols to the 1973 Vietnam Peace Agreement.; contbr. articles to profl. jours. Pres. Exec. com. of Am. Sch. of The hague, 1987-88. Named Disting. Sr. Exec. President Carter, 1980. Mem. Coun. on Fgn. Rels., Am. Soc. Internat. Law, Internat. Inst. Humanitarian Law. Avocations: tennis, sailing. Home: 24389 Oakwood Park Rd Saint Michaels MD 21663-2543 Office: Iran-US Claims Trib, Parkweg 13, 2585 JH The Hague The Netherlands

**ALDRICH, LOVELL W(ELD),** lawyer; b. Port Chester, N.Y., Dec. 21, 1942; s. Laurence Weld and Leota (Burton) A.; m. Sharon King, Aug. 20, 1966; children: Molly Colleen, Abigail Elizabeth. BBA in Fin., Tex. A&M U., 1965; JD, St. Mary's U., San Antonio, 1968. Bar: Tex. 1968, U.S. Dist. Ct. (so. dist.) Tex. 1971, U.S. Dist. Ct. (ea. dist.) Tex. 1980, U.S. Ct. Appeals (5th cir.) 1981. Assoc. Law Office of Fred Parks, Houston, 1970-72, Lloyd & Hoppess, Houston, 1972-75; sole practice Houston, 1975-78; ptnr. Aldrich & Buttrill, Houston, 1978-81, Aldrich, Buttrill & Kuhn, Houston, 1981-87, Lovell W. Aldrich & Assocs., A Profl. Legal Corp., Houston, 1987—. Served to capt. U.S. Army, 1968-70, Vietnam. Mem. Tex. Bar Assn. (cert. personal injury trial law, bd. cert. legal specialization personal injury trial law), Am. Bd. Trial Advs. Episcopalian. Avocations: travel, golf, photography, reading. Personal injury, General civil litigation, State civil litigation. Home: 1007 Horseshoe Dr Sugar Land TX 77478-3460 Office: Lovell W Aldrich & Assocs PC PO Box 377 Sugar Land TX 77487-0377

**ALDRICH, STEPHEN CHARLES,** judge; b. Mpls., Oct. 28, 1941; s. George Francis and Marjorie Belle (Shimel) A.; m. Myrna Sumption, Sept. 6, 1964; children: Jeffrey Stephen, David George. BA, Grinnell Coll., 1963; JD, U. Minn., 1971. Bar: Minn 1972, U.S. Dist. Ct. Minn. 1975. Staff asst. to Hon. Donald M. Fraser U.S. Congress, Washington, 1965; budget examiner U.S. Office of Mgmt. and Budget, Washington, 1965-67; admissions counselor Grinnell (Iowa) Coll., 1967-68; law clk. to Hon. Philip Neville U.S. Dist. Ct. Minn., Mpls., 1971-72; asst. senate counsel State of Minn., St. Paul, 1972-73; asst. city atty. City of St. Paul, 1973-75; sole practice Mpls., 1975-97; dist. judge Hennepin County, 1997—; mem. Supreme Ct. Bd. on Continuing Legal Edn., St. Paul, 1985-92. Contbr. articles to profl. jours. Mem. City Charter Commn., Mpls., 1972-80; sec., bd. dirs. Powderhorn Devel. Corp. Mpls., 1975-80. Fellow Am. Acad. Matrimonial Lawyers; mem. Hennepin County Bar Assn. (chmn. family law sect. 1985-86, mem. ethics com. 1980-85, 89-96). Mem. United Ch. Christ. Office: Hennepin County Dist Ct C1200 Govt Ctr Minneapolis MN 55497

**ALDRIDGE, BRYANT TAYLOR, JR.,** lawyer; b. Fayetteville, N.C., Jan. 1, 1957; s. Bryant Taylor and Jean Peake A.; m. Susan Castles, Aug. 15, 1981; children: Bryant III, Robert David, Jesse Joseph. BA, Duke U., 1979; JD, Wake Forest U., 1982. Bar: N.C. 1983, U.S. Dist. Ct., U.S. Ct. Appeals (4th cir.) 1983, U.S. Dist. Ct. (ea., mid. and we. dists.) 1983. Ptnr. Harper & Aldridge, Greenville, N.C., 1983-84; police atty. City of High Point, N.C., 1984-86, city atty., 1986-88; ptnr. Bretzmann, Bruner & Aldridge, High Point, N.C., 1988-96, Bretzmann & Aldridge, High Point, N.C., 1996—; bd. dirs. Ctrl. Carolina Legal Svcs., Greensboro, N.C. Bd. dirs. Troop 4 Boy Scouts Am., High Point, 1990—, Y's Men's Club, High Point, 1990—, pres. 2000. Mem. N.C. Bar Assn., N.C. Acad. Trial Lawyers, Inns of Ct. (barrister), Rotary Club of Triad. Democrat. Methodist. Avocation: sports. Personal injury, Workers' compensation, State civil litigation. Home: 2129 Laura Ln High Point NC 27262-7141 Office: Bretzmann & Aldridge LLP 500 E Green Dr High Point NC 27260-6708

**ALESIA, JAMES H(ENRY),** judge; b. Chgo., July 16, 1934; m. Kathryn P. Gibbons, July 8, 1961; children:Brian J., Daniel J. BS Loyola U., 1956; LLB, IIT, Chgo., 1960. Grad. Nat. Jud. Coll., U. Nev.-Reno, 1976. Bar: Ill. 1960, Minn. 1970. Police officer City of Chgo., 1957-60; with Law Office Anthony Scariano, Chicago Heights, Ill., 1960-61; assoc. Pretzel & Stouffer, Chgo., 1961-63; asst. gen. counsel Chgo. & North Western Transp. Co., Chgo., 1963-70; assoc. Rerat Law, Mpls., 1970-71; asst. U.S. atty. No. dist. Ill., Chgo., 1971-73, trial counsel Chessie System, Chgo., 1973; U.S. adminstrv. law judge, 1973-82; ptnr. Reuben & Proctor (firm merged with Isham, Lincoln & Beale), Chgo., 1982-87; judge U.S. Dist., No. Ill., 1987—; faculty Nat. Jud. Coll., U. Nev.-Reno, 1979-80. Mem. Fed. Bar Assn., Justinian Soc. Lawyers, Celtic Legal Soc. Republican. Roman Catholic. Office: US Dist Ct 219 S Dearborn St Chicago IL 60604-1702

**ALESSI, ROBERT JOSEPH,** lawyer, pharmacist; b. Rome, N.Y., Aug. 22, 1958; s. William John and Mary Jean A.; m. Ellen Mary Paczkowski, May 21, 1988; children: Laura C., Grace E. BS in Pharmacy, Union U., 1982; JD cum laude, Albany Law Sch., 1985. Bar: N.Y. 1986, U.S. Dist. Ct. (no. dist.) N.Y. 1986, U.S. Dist. Ct. (we. dist.) N.Y. 1986, U.S. Dist. Ct. (ea. dist.) N.Y. 1993, U.S. Dist. Ct. (so. dist.) N.Y. 1993, U.S. Ct. Appeals (2d cir.) 1995, U.S. Supreme Ct. 1996. Assoc. Nixon, Hargraves, Devans & Doyle, Albany, N.Y., 1985-90; assoc. LeBoeuf, Lamb, Greene & MacRae, Albany, 1990-93, ptnr., 1994—, mng. ptnr., 1999—; adj. prof. law Albany Law Sch., 1989-94. Co-author: Year 2000 Deskbook, 1998. Mem. master plan com. Town of Bethlehem, Delmar, N.Y., 1989-89, mem. planning bd. counsel, 1990-94. Mem. N.Y. State Bar Assn., Albany Law Sch. Environ. Alumni Group, Rockefeller Found. (advisor Pocantico roundtable consensus on brownfields). Avocations: tennis, fitness training, reading. Fax: 518-626-9010. E-mail: ralessi@llgm.com. General civil litigation, Environmental, Public utilities. Home: 8 Partridge Rd Delmar NY 12054-3919 Office:

LeBoeuf Lamb Greene & MacRae LLP One Commerce Plz Ste 2020 99 Washington Ave Albany NY 12210

**ALEXANDER, DONALD G.,** state supreme court justice. Grad., Bowdoin Coll.; JD, U. Chgo. Bar: Maine. Mem. Sen. Edmund Muskie's staff, asst. Maine atty. gen., 1974-76, dep. atty. gen.; judge Dist. Ct., 1978, Maine Superior Ct., 1980-98; justice Maine Supreme Jud. Ct., 1998—. Office: Cumberland County Courthouse PO Box 368 142 Federal St Portland ME 04112-0368*

**ALEXANDER, GEORGE JONATHON,** law educator, former dean; b. Berlin, Germany, Mar. 8, 1931; s. Walter and Sylvia (Grill) A.; m. Katharine Violet Sziklai, Sept. 6, 1958; children: Susan Katina, George Jonathon II. AB with maj. honors, U. Pa., 1953, JD cum laude, 1969; LLM, Yale U., 1965, JSD, 1969. Bar: Ill. 1960, N.Y. 1961, Calif. 1974. Instr. law, Bigelow fellow U. Chgo., 1959-60; instr. internat. relations Naval Res. Officers Sch., Forrest Park, Ill., 1959-60; prof. law Syracuse U. Coll. Law, 1960-70, assoc. dean, 1968-69; prof. law U. Santa Clara (Calif.) Law Sch., 1970—, disting. univ. prof., 1994-95, Elizabeth H. and John A. Sutro prof. law, 1995—, pres. faculty senate, 1996-97, dean, 1970-85, dir. Inst. Internat. and Comparative Law, 1986—, dir. grad. programs, 1997—; dir. summer programs at Oxford, Geneva, Strasbourg, Budapest, Tokyo, Hong Kong, Beijing, Ho Chi Minh City, Singapore, Bangkok, Kuala Lumpur, Seoul, Munich; vis. prof. law U. So. Calif., 1963; vis. scholar Stanford (Calif.) U. Law Sch., 1985-86, 92; cons. in field. Author: Civil Rights, U.S.A., Public Schools, 1963, Honesty and Competition, 1967, Jury Instructing on Medical Issues, 1966, Cases and Materials on Space Law, 1971, The Aged and the Need for Surrogate Management, 1972, Commercial Torts, 1973, 2d edit. 1988, U.S. Antitrust Laws, 1980, Writing A Living Will: Using a Durable Power of Attorney, 1988, (with Scheflin) Law and Mental Disabilities, 1998; author, editor: International Perspectives on Aging, 1992; also articles, chpts. in books, one film. Dir. Domestic and Internat. Bus. Problems Honors Clinic, Syracuse U., 1966-69, Regulations in Space Project, 1968-70; ednl. cons. Comptroller Gen. U.S., 1977—; mem. Nat. Sr. Citizens Law Ctr., 1983-89, pres., 1986-90; co-founder Am. Assn. Abolition Involuntary Mental Hospitalization, 1970, dir., 1970-83. With USN, 1953-56. U.S. Navy scholar U. Pa., 1949-52; Law Bds. scholar, 1956-59; Sterling fellow Yale, 1964-65; recipient Ralph E. Kharas Civil Liberties award, 1970, Owens award as Alumnus of Yr., 1984, Disting. prof. Santa Clara Univ. Faculty Senate, 1994-95. Mem. Internat. Acad. Law Mental Health (mem. sci. com. 1997—), Calif. Bar Assn. (first chmn. com. legal problems of aging), Assn. Am. Law Schs., Soc. Am. Law Tchrs. (dir., pres. 1979), AAUP (chpt. pres. 1962), N.Y. Civil Liberties Union (chpt. pres. 1965, dir., v.p. 1966-70), Am. Acad. Polit. and Social Sci., Order of Coif, Justinian Honor Soc., Phi Alpha Delta (chpt. faculty adviser 1967-70). Home: 11600 Summit Wood Ct Los Altos CA 94022-4500 Office: U Santa Clara Sch Law Santa Clara CA 95053-0001 *I think a primary purpose of law is the protection of individual rights. That requires disproportionate attention to the interests of groups not in the mainstream of our society.*

**ALEXANDER, GERRY L.,** state supreme court justice; b. Aberdeen, Wash., Apr. 28, 1936. BA, U. Wash., 1958, JD, 1964. Bar: Wash. 1964. Pvt. practice Olympia, Wash., 1964-73; judge Wash. Superior Ct., Olympia, 1973-85, Wash. Ct. Appeals Divsn. II, Olympia, 1985-95; justice Wash. Supreme Ct., Olympia, 1995—. Lt. U.S. Army, 1958-61. Mem. ABA, Am. Judges Assn., Wash. State Bar Assn., Thurston-Mason County Assn. (pres. 1973), Puget Sound Inn of Ct. (pres. 1996). Office: Temple of Justice PO Box 40929 Olympia WA 98504-0929

**ALEXANDER, GREGORY STEWART,** law educator; b. 1948. BA, Ill. U., 1970; JD, Northwestern U., 1973; postgrad., U. Chgo., 1974-75. Law clk. to chief judge U.S. Ct. Appeals, 1972-74; asst. prof. law U. Ga., 1975-78, assoc. prof., 1978-84; prof. Cornell U., 1984—; vis. prof. Harvard Law Sch., 1997—. Bigelow fellow U. Chgo., 1974-75; fellow Max-Planck Inst. (Germany), 1995-96. Mem. Am. Soc. Politics and Legal Philosophy, Am. Soc. Legal History. Office: Cornell U Law Sch Myron Taylor Hall Ithaca NY 14853

**ALEXANDER, IAN ROBERT,** lawyer; b. Skokie, Ill., Sept. 5, 1970; s. Joseph David and Rhoda Carol A. BA, U. Ill., Urbana, 1992; JD, Tulane U., New Orleans, 1995. Bar: Ill.; U.S. Dist. Ct. (no. dist.) Ill. 1995, Fed. Trial Bar. Atty. Susan E. Loggans & Assocs., Chgo., 1995-99, Goldberg & Goldberg, Chgo., 1999—. Fellow The Roscoe Pound Found., Assn. Trial Lawyers Am., Ill. Trial Lawyers Assn. Office: Goldberg & Goldberg 33 N Dearborn St Ste 1930 Chicago IL 60602-3108

**ALEXANDER, JAMES PATRICK,** lawyer; b. Glendale, Calif., Oct. 14, 1944; s. Victor Elwin and Thelma Elizabeth (O'Donnell) A.; m. Jeanne Elizabeth Bannerman, June 10, 1967; children: Rene Leigh, Amy Lynne. AB, Duke U., 1966, JD, 1969. Bar: Ala. 1969. Assoc. Bradley, Arant, Rose & White, Birmingham, Ala., 1969-75, ptnr., 1975—; adj. lectr. employment discrimination law U. Ala. Sch. of Law, 1981—; mem. exec. adv. com. spl. studies program U. Ala., Birmingham, 1991-93. Trustee Ala. chpt. Nat. Multiple Sclerosis Soc. (vice chmn. 1987-89, chmn. 1990-91); mem. bd. dirs. Birmingham Civil Right Inst., Inc. Fellow Coll. Labor and Employment Lawyers; mem. Birmingham Bar Assn., Ala. State Bar., ABA, Am. Arbitration Assn. (comml. arbitrator, employment disputes arbitrator), Indsl. Rels. Rsch. Assn. (Ala. chpt.), Sigma Nu, Duke Law Alumni Assn. (pres. Ala. chpt. 1989-90). Federal civil litigation, Labor, Antitrust. Home: 4309 Altamont Rd Birmingham AL 35213-2407 Office: Bradley Arant Rose & White LLP 1400 Park Pl Tower 2001 Park Pl Ste 1400 Birmingham AL 35203-2736

**ALEXANDER, KATHARINE VIOLET,** lawyer; b. N.Y.C., Nov. 19, 1934; d. George Clifford and Violet (Jambor) Sziklai; m. George Jonathon Alexander, Sept. 6, 1958; children: Susan Katina, George J. II. Student, Smith Coll., Geneva, 1954-55; BA, Goucher Coll., 1956; JD, U. Pa., 1959; student specialized courses, U. Santa Clara, 1974-76. Bar: Calif. 1974, U.S. Dist. Ct. (no. dist.) Calif. 1974, U.S. Ct. Appeals (9th cir.) 1974; cert. criminal lawyer Calif. State Bar Bd. Legal Specialization. Research dir., adminstr. Am. Bar Found., Chgo., 1959-60; lectr. law San Jose (Calif.) State U., 1972-74; sr. atty. Santa Clara County, San Jose, 1974-97, ret., 1997. Editor: Mentally Disabled and the Law, 1961; contbg. author: The Aged and the Need for Surrogate Management, 1969-70, Jury Instructions on Medical Issues, 1965-67. Community rep. Office Econ. Opportunity Com., Syracuse, N.Y., 1969-70. Mem. AAUW, Food and Wine Inst., Calif. Bar Assn., Santa Clara County Bar Assn. (trustee 1981-82), Calif. Attys. for Criminal Justice (bd. govs. 1988-92), Jr. League, Anthropology and Stanford Museum of Arts. Presbyterian. Avocations: stock market, gourmet, traveling. Home and Office: 11600 Summit Wood Ct Los Altos CA 94022-4500

**ALEXANDER, KENT B.,** lawyer; b. Atlanta, Nov. 7, 1958. BA in Polit. Sci. magna cum laude, Tufts U., 1980; JD, U. Va., 1983. Bar: Ga. 1983. Assoc. Long & Alridge, Atlanta, 1983-85; asst. U.S. atty. for no. dist. Ga., U.S. Dept. Justice, Atlanta, 1985-92, U.S. atty., 1994-97; of counsel, ptnr. King & Spalding, Atlanta, 1992-94, ptnr., 1997—. Co-founder Hands On Atlanta. Office: King & Spalding 191 Peachtree St SW Atlanta GA 30303-3637

**ALEXANDER, MARY ELSIE,** lawyer; b. Chgo., Nov. 16, 1947; d. Theron and Marie (Bailey) A.; m. Lyman Saunders Faulkner, Jr., Dec. 1, 1984; 1 child, Michelle. BA, U. Iowa, 1969; MPH, U. Calif.-Berkeley, 1975; JD, U. Santa Clara, 1982. Bar: Calif. 1982, U.S. Dist. Ct. (no. dist.), Calif. 1982, U.S. Ct. Appeals (9th cir.) 1982. Rschr. U. Cin., 1969-74; dept. dir., sr. environ. health scientist Stanford Rsch. Inst., Menlo Park, Calif., 1975-80; cons. Alexander Assocs., Ambler, Pa., 1980-82; assoc. Caputo, Liccardo, Rossi, Sturges & McNeil, San Jose, Calif., 1982-84; assoc. Cartwright, Slobodin, Bokelman, et al, San Francisco, 1984-88, ptnr., 1988-96; ptnr. The Cartwright & Alexander Law Firm, 1996—. Com. mem. Cancer Soc., San Jose, 1983; elder Valley Presbyn. Ch., Portola Valley, 1987-90; active Am. Heart Assn., Santa Clara County. Named one of top 10 Trial Lawyers San Francisco Bay Area, San Francisco Chronicle, 1990; Nat. Inst. Occupl. Safety and Health scholar U. Calif., Berkeley, 1975. Mem. ABA, AAS, ATLA (state del., pres. 1996, parliamentarian 1997, treas. 1998, sec. 1999), Consumer Attys. Calif. (formerly Calif. Trial Lawyers Assn. (PAC bd. 1989—, parliamentarian 1991, v.p. 1992, chair mem. com., editor Forum, pres.-elect 1995), San Francisco Trial Lawyers Assn., Trial Lawyers for Pub. Justice, Calif. Women Lawyers, Am. Indsl. Hygiene Assn. (bd. dirs. 1979-81, treas. 1977-79), Santa Clara Trial Lawyers Assn. (bd. dirs. 1983-84). Democrat. Personal injury, Environmental, General civil litigation. Office: The Cartwright & Alexander Law Firm 222 Front St Fl 5 San Francisco CA 94111-4423

**ALEXANDER, RICHARD,** lawyer; b. Cleve., Sept. 26, 1944; m. Nancy L. Biebel, Mar. 16, 1968; children: Marshall, Meredith. BA, Ohio Wesleyan U., 1966; JD, U. Chgo., 1969. Bar: Mich. 1969, U.S. Dist. Ct. (ea. and we. dists.) Mich. 1970, Calif. 1971, U.S. Dist. Ct. (no. dist.) Calif. 1971, U.S. Ct. Appeals (9th cir.) 1971, U.S. Dist. Ct. (ctrl. dist.) Calif. 1972, U.S. Dist. Ct. (ea. dist.) Calif. 1973, U.S. Dist. Ct. D.C. 1980; diplomate Nat. Bd. Trial Advocacy; cert. specialist in trial law. Asst. prof. Grad. Sch. Bus., Mich. State U., 1969-71; assoc. Belli, Ashe, Ellison, Choulos & Lieff, San Francisco, 1971-72, Lieff, Alexander, Wilcox & Hill, San Francisco, 1972-74, Boccardo, Lull, Niland & Bell, San Francisco, San Jose, 1974-80; ptnr. Boccardo Law Firm, San Jose, 1980-87, Alexander & Bohn, San Jose, 1987-91, The Alexander Law Firm, San Jose, 1992-99, Alexander, Hawes & Audet, San Jose, 1999—; lectr. continuing edn. State Bar Calif., 1975, 78, 81-89, mem. com. profl. ethics, 1977-80, spl. master, 1980—, bd. govs., 1985-88, v.p., 1987-88; judge pro tem Santa Clara County Superior Ct., 1976-83, 85-90, arbitrator, 1976-96; mem. Santa Clara County Criminal Justice Adv. Bd., 1978-82, chmn., 1978-80; mem. Santa Clara County Jail Over-crowding Task Force, 1978-81; co-chmn. Superior Ct. Arbitration Adminstrn. Com., 1979—; mem. Santa Clara County Pub. Defender Charter Amendment Task Force, 1980; spkr. legal seminars. Pub. The Consumer Law Page; contbr. articles to profl. jours. Mem. Palo Alto (Calif.) Unified Sch. Dist. Task Force on Spl. Edn., 1975-79; mem. Santa Clara County Data Confidentiality Commn., 1976-78, chmn., 1977-78; vice chmn. sch. improvement program Palo Alto Unified Sch. Dist., 1977-78, mem. found. exploration com., 1984; mem. Santa Clara County Dem. Ctrl. Com., 1978-80; bd. dirs. Japanese Am. Environ. Conf., 1979-81. Recipient Santa Clara County Youth Commn. medal, 1980, Man of Yr. Women's Fund, commendation for disting. svc. Mayor San Jose, 1982, Pro Bono award Ctr. Occupl. Safety Health, 1993; named one of Outstanding Young Men of Am., Man of Yr., The Women's Found., 1989; Roscoe Pound fellow. Mem. NAACP, ATLA, Nat. Assn. Consumer Advs. (founder), Nat. Bd. Trial Advocacy (cert. civil adv. 1980, 85, 90, 95), Nat. Bar Register of Preeminent Lawyers, Consumer Attys. Calif. (v.p. 1995), State Bar Calif. (bd. govs. 1985—, v.p. 1987—), Calif. Attys. for Criminal Justice (founder, treas. 1972-74, gov. 1972-75), Calif. Trial Lawyers Assn. (recognized trial lawyer 1980-89, bd. govs. 1989-94, v.p. 1994-96), San Francisco Bar Assn., Santa Clara County Bar Assn. (pres. 1984), Nat. Trust Hist. Preservation, Alexander Graham Bell Assn. for Deaf, Stanford Alumni Assn., U. Chgo. Alumni Club, Silicon Valley Capital Club. Product liability, Toxic tort, Federal civil litigation. Office: Alexander Hawes & Audet # 600 152 N 3d San Jose CA 95112

**ALEXANDER, RICHARD JOHN,** lawyer; b. Cisco, Tex., June 26, 1948; s. Richard Kenneth and Joan Louise (Thomas) A.; divorced; children: Nathan Thomas, Lauren Kathryn; m. Katherine O'Dowd Alexander. AB in Econs., U. Calif., Berkeley, 1975; JD, Golden Gate U., 1978; postgrad., U.S. Naval War Coll., 1994. Bar: Calif. 1978, U.S. Dist. Ct. (no., cen. and ea. dists.) Calif. 1978, U.S. Ct. Appeals (9th cir.) 1978. Prin. Law Office R.J. Alexander, Point Richmond, Calif., 1978-80, 83-90, 94—; ptnr. Rosenthal, Fullerton & Alexander, Point Richmond, 1981-82; sr. ptnr. Alexander & Brown, Point Richmond, 1991-93. Mem. adv. commn. Conta Costa County Housing Authority, Martinez, Calif., 1982-88; judge pro tem, arbitrator Bay Mcpl. Ct., Richmond, 1983—; bd. dirs. USO No. Calif. Inc., San Francisco, 1990-92. Capt. USNR, 1967—. Mem. Point Richmond Bus. Assn., U.S. Naval Inst. (life), Naval Res. Assn. (life), Richmond Rotary, Richmond C. of C. Avocations: scuba diving, running. General civil litigation, Admiralty, Personal injury. Office: Alexander Law Offices 137 Park Pl Point Richmond CA 94801-3922

**ALEXANDER, ROBERT GARDNER,** lawyer; b. Madison, Wis., May 19, 1949; s. Charles Kohl and Jean (Gardner) A.; m. Karen Lynn Kaminski, Sept. 30, 1989; children: Elizabeth Jean, Sarah Lynn, Rebecca Ann. BA, U. Wis., 1971, JD, 1976; ML in Taxation, DePaul U., 1984. Bar: Wis. 1976, U.S. Dist. Ct. (we. dist.) Wis. 1976, U.S. Dist. Ct. (ea. dist.) Wis. 1978, U.S. Tax Ct. 1982, U.S. Ct. Appeals (7th cir.) 1983. Rsch. atty. U. Wis., Madison, 1976-77; atty. McLario Law Offices, Menomonee Falls, Wis., 1978-87, Alexander Law Offices, S.C., Wauwatosa, Wis., 1987—. Trustee, sec. Falls Bapt. Ch., Inc., Menomonee Falls, 1987—; dir. David Barba Evantelistic Assn., Downers Grove, Ill., 1989—, Preach the Word, Inc., Downers Grove, 1992—; adv. bd. Joy Bapt. Camp, Whitewater, Wis., 1992—. Mem. ABA, Nat. Acad. Elder Law Attys., Wis. State Bar, Milw. Bar Assn., Milw. Estate Planning Counsel, Nat. Assn. Estate Planning Counselors (accredited estate planner), Phi Kappa Phi. Republican. Avocations: music, art, sports. Estate planning, General corporate. Office: Alexander Law Offices SC 2675 N Mayfair Rd Ste 308 Wauwatosa WI 53226-1305

**ALEXANDERSEN, KEVIN CARL,** lawyer; b. Bklyn., Aug. 5, 1959; s. Albert Carl and Veronica F. Alexandersen; m. Becky Blair, Aug. 9, 1986; children: Ashley Elizabeth, Blair Benjamin. BS with high honors, Rochester Inst. Tech., 1981; JD with honors, Ohio No. U., 1986. Bar: Ohio 1986, U.S. Dist. Ct. (no. dist.) Ohio, U.S. Ct. Appeals (6th cir.). Ptnr. Gallagher, Sharp, Fulton & Norman, Cleve., 1986—; lectr. in field of R.R. law and products liability subjects. Federal civil litigation, General civil litigation, State civil litigation. Office: Gallagher Sharp Fulton & Norman 1501 Euclid Ave Fl 7 Cleveland OH 44115-2108

**ALEXIUS, FREDERICK BERNARD,** lawyer; b. Lake Charles, La., Apr. 29, 1941; s. Chauncey August and Helen (Brechtel) A.; m. Mira Boulet, June 15, 1968; children: Nolde Elizabeth, Frederick B. Jr. Student, Tulane U., 1959-60; BA, La. State U., 1963, JD, 1970. Bar: La. 1970, U.S. Dist. Ct. (ea., mid. and we. dists.) La. 1970, U.S. Ct. Appeals (5th cir.) 1971, U.S. Supreme Ct. 1987. Law clk. to assoc. justice Albert Tate Jr. La. Supreme Ct., New Orleans, 1970-71; assoc. Deutsch, Kerrigan & Stiles, New Orleans, 1971-75, Schumacher, McGlinchey, Stafford & Mintz, New Orleans, 1975-76; staff atty. Texaco, Inc., New Orleans, 1976-78; ptnr. Provosty, Sadler & deLaunay, Alexandria, La., 1978—. Trustee Rapides Symphony Orch., Inc., Alexandria, 1979—, pres., 1982-85; trustee Alexandria County Day Sch., 1980-89, Albert Tate Jr. Found., Alexandria Mus. Art, 1990-95, v.p., 1991-93. Mem. ABA, Am. Health Lawyers Assn., La. State Bar Assn. (chmn. mineral law sect. 1986-87), La. Assn. Def. Counsel, La. State U. Law Alumni Assn. (pres. 1986-87), La. Mineral Law Inst. (coun.). Democrat. Episcopalian. Avocations: reading, hunting, roses. Personal injury, Health, Oil, gas, and mineral. Office: Provosty Sadler & deLaunay PO Box 1791 Alexandria LA 71309-1791

**ALEY, CHARLES R.,** lawyer; b. Beaver Falls, Pa., Apr. 3, 1956; s. Charles L. and Lois E. (Teckemeyer) A.; m. Harriet M. Baker, June 21, 1986; 1 child, Christine M. BA in Econs., BSBA in Acctg., Bus, Adminstrn. and Data Processing, BS in Info. Systems, Geneva Coll., 1978; JD, U. Pitts., 1981; LLD (hon.), London Inst. Applied Rsch., 1990. Bar: Pa. 1981, U.S. Dist. Ct. (we. dist.) Pa. 1981, U.S. Tax Ct. 1981, U.S. Ct. Appeals (3d cir.) 1981, U.S. Ct. Appeals (fed. cir.) 1985, U.S. Supreme Ct. 1985, Ohio 1987. Tax atty. Arthur Young & Co., Pitts., 1981-82, Edward J. DeBartolo Corp., Youngstown, 1982-86, Alcan Aluminum Corp., Warren, Ohio, 1986—. Mem. Internat. Parliament for Safety and Peace, 1991—, Republican Senatorial Inner Circle, 1992—. Recipient Disting. Svc. award Geneva Coll., 1991. Mem. ABA, Pa. Bar Assn., Allegheny County Bar Assn., Beaver County Bar Assn., Fed. Cir. Bar Assn., Trumbull County Bar Assn., Assn. Trial Lawyers Am., Internat. Platform Soc., Phi Alpha Delta. Mem. United Meth. Ch. Avocation: pipe organ restoration. Corporate taxation, Personal income taxation, State and local taxation. Home: 1212 6th Ave Beaver Falls PA 15010-4423 Office: Alcan Aluminum Corp 390 Griswold St NE Warren OH 44483-2738

**ALFINI, JAMES JOSEPH,** dean, educator, lawyer; b. Yonkers, N.Y., Oct. 12, 1943; s. James Joseph and Olga (Genish) A.; m. Carol Miller, Dec. 23, 1966; children: David James, Michael Steven. AB, Columbia U., 1965; JD, Northwestern U., 1972. Bar: N.Y. 1973, Ill. 1976, U.S. Dist. Ct. (no. dist.) Ill. 1976, U.S. Ct. Appeals (7th cir.) 1982, U.S. Supreme Ct. 1977. Reginald Heber Smith cmty. lawyer Monroe County Legal Assistance Corp., Rochester, N.Y., 1972-73; asst. dir. research Am. Judicature Soc., Chgo., 1973-77, dir. rsch., 1977-80, asst. exec. dir. programs, 1980-85; adj. prof. law IIT Chgo.-Kent Sch. Law, 1978-85; assoc. prof. of law Fla. State U., Tallahassee, 1985-90, prof. law, 1990-91; dean, prof. No. Ill. U. Coll. Law, 1991-97, prof., 1997—. Co-author: (books) Making Jury Instructions Understandable, 1982, Judicial Conduct and Ethics, 1990, 95; mem. Christian Ch. Bd. Editors Ohio State Jour. Dispute Resolution, 1994—. Mem. governing bd. Cook County Legal Assistance Found., 1981-83; arbitration and mediation rules com. Fla. Supreme Ct., 1988-91; mem. Ill. Jud. Ethics com., 1993-97; chmn. coord. coun. Nat. Ct. Orgns., 1982-83; bd. govs. Chgo. Coun. Lawyers. 1st lt. U.S. Army, 1965-69. Decorated Army Commendation medal. Mem. ABA (sect. dispute resolution, chair), ACLU, Am. Law Inst., Law and Soc. Assn. Democrat. Home: 525 Wing Ln Saint Charles IL 60174-2339

**ALFORD, BARRY JAMES,** lawyer; b. Dallas, Nov. 13, 1965; s. James Arnold and Edwinna Ruth Alford; m. Lora Lyn Smith, Nov. 1, 1992 (div. Aug. 1996); 1 child, Tiffany Marie. BS in Econs., Tex. Christian U., 1988; JD, Oklahoma City U., 1992. Atty. Law Office of Jack Beech, Ft. Worth, 1993-94; pvt. practice law Ft. Worth, 1994—. Mem. Tarrant County Criminal Def. Lawyers Assn., Tarrant County Bar Assn., Tarrant County Young Lawyers Assn. Criminal. Office: Ste 908 One Summit Ave Fort Worth TX 76102

**ALFORD, DUNCAN EARL,** lawyer; b. Spartanburg, S.C., Oct. 17, 1963; s. Earl Curry and Martha Catherine (Van Ness) A.; m. Janet Lynne Gessner, Oct. 6, 1990. BA with high distinction, U. VA., 1985; postgrad., U. Calif., Berkeley, 1987; JD with honors, U. N.C., 1991. Bar: Ga. 1991, N.C. 1991, S.C. 1994. Bus. analyst McKinsey & Co., Inc., Atlanta, 1985-87; distbn. mgr. Eason Publs., Inc., Charlotte, N.C., 1988; law clk. to Hon. Burley B. Mitchell N.C. Supreme Ct., Raleigh, N.C., 1991-92; assoc. Kilpatrick & Cody, Atlanta, 1992-94; atty. Law Offices of Robert A. Hammett, Spartanburg, S.C., 1994-96; assoc. Robinson, Bradshaw & Hinson, P.A., Rock Hill, S.C., 1997—. Contbr. articles to profl. jours. Echols scholar U. Va. Mem. ABA, Phi Alpha Delta. Presbyterian. Avocations: running, golf, racquetball. Probate, Real property, General corporate. Home: 816 Mary Knoll Ct Rock Hill SC 29730-3727 Office: Robinson Bradshaw & Hinson PA 223 E Main St Ste 600 Rock Hill SC 29730-4571

**ALFORD, MARGIE SEARCY,** lawyer; b. Tuscaloosa, Ala., Dec. 20, 1949; d. Joseph Alexander and Margaret Tyler (Zehmer) Searcy; m. Andrew Ray Alford, Sept. 4, 1992. BS, U. Ala., 1967-69, 70-71; student, U. Ams., Mexico City, 1969, Emory U., Atlanta, 1970; JD, U. Ala., 1974. Bar: Ala. 1974; U.S. Dist. Ct. (no. dist.) Ala. 1975. Assoc. univ. counsel U. Ala., Tuscaloosa, 1974-75; pvt. practice Tuscaloosa, 1975-92, Birmingham, Ala., 1992—. Editor-in-chief, prin. author: A Guide to Toxic Torts, 4 vols., 1986; contbg. author: Matthew Bender's Drug Product Liability, 4 vols.; contbr. numerous articles to legal jours.; freelance writer for numerous publs. Active Ea. Area Diabetes Support Group, 1997—; vol. tchr. Ch. Cir., 1996—. Named Most Outstanding Young Career Woman in Ala. Ala. Bus. and Profl. Women, 1986. Mem. ATLA (twice nat. chair environ. and toxic tort law sect., twice nat. chair of women trial lawyers caucus), Ala. Environ. Coun., Ala. Trial Lawyers Assn., Women;s Bus. Ownership Coun. Democrat. Presbyterian. Avocations: collecting antique furniture and paintings, chow chow dog breeder, gardening. Fax: (205) 520-5083. E-mail: margialfor@aol.com. Personal injury, Criminal, Environmental. Office: PO Box 610781 Birmingham AL 35261-0781

**ALFORD, NEILL HERBERT, JR.,** retired law educator; b. Greenville, S.C., July 13, 1919; s. Neill Herbert and Elizabeth (Robertson) A.; m. Elizabeth Talbot Smith, June 26, 1943; children: Neill Herbert III, Margaret Dudley, Eli Thomas Stackhouse. BA, The Citadel-Mil. Coll. S.C., 1940; LLB, U. Va., 1947; JSD, Yale U., 1966. Bar: Va. 1954. Mem. faculty law U. Va. Law Sch., Charlottesville, 1947-61, 62-90; Doherty Found. prof. U. Va. Law Sch., 1966-74, spl. cons. to pres. univ., legal adviser to rector and bd. dirs., 1972-74; Joseph Henry Lumpkin prof., dean Law Sch. U. Ga., Athens, 1974-76; Percy Brown Jr. prof. law U. Va., 1976-90; state reporter Supreme Ct. Va., 1977-84; counsel Woods, Rogers & Hazelgrove, Charlottesville, 1991-97; prof. chair internat. law Naval War Coll., 1961-62, cons. 1962-68; spl. counsel Va. Code Commn. 1954-57; dir. Va. Bankers Assn. Trust Sch., 1958-61; summer tchr. George Washington U., U. N.C.; chmn. bd. dirs. U. Va. Press, 1970-74, 87-89; prof. law emeritus U. Va., 1990—; Lehmann Disting. vis. prof. law Washington U., St. Louis, 1991; Hofstedler prof. Ohio State U. Law Sch., 1992; prof. Washington and Lee Law Sch., 1992. Author: Cases and Materials on Decedents Estates and Trusts, 8th edit, 1993, Modern Economic Warfare: Law and the Naval Participant, 1967; Contbr. articles to profl. jours. Comdr. civil affairs group U.S. Army Res., 1947-66. Lt. col. inf. AUS, 1941-46, ETO; col. inf. AUS; ret. 1968. Decorated Bronze Star, Combat Inf. badge.; Sterling fellow Yale U., 1950-51, Ford fellow U. Wis., 1958. Fellow Va. Law Found., Am. Bar Found.; mem. ABA, Selden Soc., Am. Soc. Legal History, Am. Judicature Soc., Am. Law Inst., Va. State Bar, Va. Bar Assn., Raven Soc., Colonnade Club, Order of Coif, Phi Alpha Delta, Omicron Delta Kappa. Home: 1868 Field Rd Charlottesville VA 22903-1619

**ALFREY, THOMAS NEVILLE,** lawyer; b. New Braunfels, Tex., Oct. 30, 1944; s. Clarence Powhattan and Lilla Carlton (Beadel) A.; m. Rebecca Ann Fruland, June 22, 1979; children: Kimberly, Jessica. BA, Tex. Christian U., 1967; JD, U. Tex., Austin, 1970. Bar: Colo. 1970, U.S. Dist. Ct. Colo. 1970, U.S. Ct. Appeals (10th cir.) 1970. Dep. dist. atty. State of Colo., Denver, 1971-72; asst. dist. atty. 9th jud. dist. State of Colo., Aspen, 1973-74; dir. organized crime strike force Colo. Atty. Gen., Denver, 1974-75; asst. U.S. atty. Dept. Justice, Denver, 1975; assoc. Hall & Evans, Denver, 1975, ptnr., 1976—; cons. Tex. Organized Crime Strike Force, Austin, 1975; lectr. various profl. groups; mem. faculty, Nat. Inst. Trial Advocacy, Denver, 1987-88. 1st lt. U.S. Army, 1970. Mem. ABA, Colo. Bar Assn., Colo. Def. Laywers Assn., Internat. Assn. Def. Counsel, Denver Partnership, Glenmoor Country Club (bd. govs. 1988-92). Avocations: golf, tennis, skiing. General civil litigation, Personal injury.

**ALGEO, ANNEMARIE,** lawyer; b. Darby, Pa., May 3, 1961; d. Thomas M. and Ann Algeo; m. John Tortorella, Feb. 20, 1988 (dec. Dec. 1988); m. James B. Filler, Apr. 24, 1996; children: Aime Filler, Samuel Filler. BA, West Chester U., 1983; JD, Widener U., 1988; MA, St. Charles Sem., Wynwood, Pa., 1999. Bar: Pa. 1988, N.J. 1988, U.S. Dist. Ct. (ea. dist.) Pa. 1989, Virgin Islands 1994. Atty. Shabel, Algeo & Shabel, Mt. Laurel, N.J., 1992-97; pvt. practice Mt. Holly, N.J., 1997—. Personal injury. Home: 13 Moorfield Ln Moorestown NJ 08057-3012 Office: 744 Main St Mount Holly NJ 08060-3069

**ALGORRI, MARK STEVEN,** lawyer; b. L.A., Sept. 25, 1952; s. Ernest Algorri and Ventura Gasulla; m. Pamela, Mar. 1, 1985; three children. AB, UCLA, 1976; JD, U. LaVerne, 1979. Atty. Rossen & Dewitt, L.A., 1978-80; ptnr. Dewitt & Algorri, L.A., 1980-95, Dewitt Algorri & Algorri, L.A., 1996—. Mem. Am. Bd. Trial Advocates, Consumer Attys. of Calif. State civil litigation, Product liability, Personal injury. Office: Dewitt Algorri & Algorri 25 E Union St Pasadena CA 91103-3923

**ALIMARAS, GUS,** lawyer; b. N.Y.C., Oct. 30, 1958; s. Nicholas Constantine and Libby (Keffas) A.; m. Constance N. Siomkos, May 15, 1983; children: Justin Christopher, Alyssa Nicole. BA, CUNY, 1979; JD, Hofstra U., 1982. Bar: N.Y. 1983, U.S. Dist. Ct. (ea. and so. dists.) N.Y. 1985, U.S. Ct. Internat. Trade 1985, U.S. Dist. Ct. (no. and we. dists.) N.Y. 1990, U.S. Supreme Ct. 1994. Assoc. John A. Sotirakis, Astoria, N.Y., 1983, George Kazazis, Astoria, 1983-87; ptnr. Kazazis & Alimaras, LLP, Astoria, 1987—; real estate continuing edn. instr. Queens Coll., CUNY, 1993-97; lectr. Nat. Bus. Inst. Mem. ABA, N.Y. State Bar Assn., Queens County Bar Assn., Long Island City Lawyers Club (pres. 1992-93), Ea. Orthodox Lawyers Assn., Phi Alpha Delta. Real property, Finance, Probate. Office: Kazazis & Alimaras LLP 36-12 34th Ave Ste 200 Long Island City NY 11106-1110

**ALITO, SAMUEL ANTHONY, JR.,** federal judge; b. Trenton, N.J., Apr. 1, 1950; s. Samuel A. and Rose (Fradusco) A.; m. Martha-Ann Bomgardner, 1985; children: Philip Samuel, Laura Claire. AB, Princeton U., 1972; JD, Yale U., 1975. Bar: N.J. 1975, N.Y. 1982, U.S. Dist. Ct. N.J. 1975, U.S. Ct. Appeals (3d cir.) 1977, U.S. Ct. Appeals (2d cir.) 1980, U.S. Ct. Appeals

(D.C. cir.) 1987, U.S. Supreme Ct. 1979. Law clk. to judge U.S. Ct. Appeals (3d cir.), Newark, 1976-77; asst. U.S. atty. U.S. Atty.'s Office, Newark, 1977-81, U.S. atty., 1987-90; asst. to solicitor gen. Office of Solicitor Gen. Dept. Justice, Washington, 1981-85; dep. asst. atty. gen. Office of Legal Counsel Dept. Justice, Washington, 1985-87; judge U.S. Ct. Appeals for 3d Cir., Newark, 1990—. Office: US Courthouse PO Box 999 Newark NJ 07101-0999

**ALLAN, LIONEL MANNING,** lawyer; b. Detroit, Aug. 3, 1943. AB cum laude, U. Mich., 1965; JD, Stanford U., 1968; student, U. Paris. BAr: Calif. 1969, U.S. Supreme Ct. 1972. Law clk. U.S. Dist. Ct. (no. dist.) Calif., 1969-70; pres. Allan Advisors, Inc., legal cons. firm; speaker and writer in field of corp. securities and pvt. internat. law; sec. adv. com. San Jose Fed. Ct., 1969-85; mem. bd. visitors Stanford Law Sch., 1985-88; mem. com. comml. code State Bar Calif., 1974-77, corps. com., 1983-86. Co-author: How to Structure the Classic Venture Capital Deal, 1983, Equity Incentives for Start-up Companies, 1985, Master Limited Partnerships, 1987. Bd. dirs. San Jose Mus. Art, 1983-87; trustee KTEH-TV Channel 54 Found., 1987—; dir. NCCJ, 1995—, Harker Sch., 1998—. Served to capt. JAGC, USAR, 1968-74. Mem. ABA (com. on small bus. 1980—, chmn. internat. bus. subcom. 1985-88, chmn. small bus. com. 1989-93), Santa Clara Bar Assn. (chmn. fed. ct. sect. 1971, 77), Internat. Bar Assn., San Jose C. of C. (dir.), Pi Sigma Alpha, Phi Sigma Iota, Phi Delta Phi. General corporate, Private international, Securities. Office: Allan Advisors Inc 18222 Seebree Ln Monte Sereno CA 95030-3135

**ALLAN, MICHAEL LEE,** lawyer. BA in Internat. Rels., Searford U., 1984; JD, U. Calif., Berkeley, 1989. Bar: Calif., U.S. Dist. Ct. (cen. dist.) Calif., U.S. Ct. Appeals (9th cir.). Pres. Pasadena (Calif.) Area Young Reps., 1994, 95, 98; bd. dirs. Pasadena Rep. Club, 1994, 95. Contracts commercial, General corporate, Trademark and copyright. Office: Allan & Hedges 8th Fl 1545 Wilshire Blvd Los Angeles CA 90017-4501

**ALLAN, RICHMOND FREDERICK,** lawyer; b. Billings, Mont., Apr. 22, 1930; s. Roy F. and Edith (Prater) A.; m. Dorothy Frost, Aug. 9, 1954; children: Richmond P., David F., Michael R. BA, U. Mont., 1954, JD, 1957; postgrad., London Sch. of Econs., 1957-58. Bar: Mont. 1957, U.S. Supreme Ct. 1961, D.C. 1965. Law clk. U.S. Ct. Appeals (9th cir.), San Francisco, 1958-59; ptnr. Kurth, Conner, Jones & Allan, Billings, 1959-61; chief asst. U.S. atty. U.S. Dept. of Justice, Billings, 1961-64; assoc. solicitor U.S. Dept. of Interior, Washington, 1965-67, dep. solicitor, 1968-69; ptnr. Weissbrodt & Weissbrodt, Washington, 1969-77, Casey, Lane & Mittendorf, Washington, 1977-78, Duncan, Weinberg, Miller & Pembroke, P.C., Washington, 1979—. Fulbright Commn. scholar, 1957. Mem. Fed. Bar Assn. (pres. Mont. chpt. 1963-65). Avocations: trap and skeet shooting. Administrative and regulatory, Oil, gas, and mineral, Real property. Office: Duncan Weinberg Genzer & Pembroke PC 1615 M St NW Ste 800 Washington DC 20036-3219

**ALLAN, ROBERT OLAV,** lawyer; b. Albuquerque, Dec. 22, 1960; s. Alexander Olav and Angeline Elsie (Whipple) A.; m. Dawn Marie Gourneau, Aug. 8, 1986; children: Gabrielle, Joshua, Robert. BA, Dartmouth Coll., 1985; JD, U. Colo., 1991. Bar: Navajo Nation 1985, N.Mex. 1994, U.S. Dist. Ct. N.Mex. 1995. Tribal ct. advocate I Navajo Nation Dept. Justice, Window Rock, Ariz., 1985-86, tribal ct. advocate II, 1986-87, tribal ct. advocate III, 1987-88; title examiner II Navajo Land Dept., Window Rock, 1992-94, atty., 1994-95; atty. Navajo Nation Divsn. Natural Resources, Window Rock, 1995—; project dir. Intergovtl. Land Consolidation Project Tri-Party Coop. Agreement Orgn. and Workgroups, 1987-88; pro bono legal counsel Navajo Nation Cts., Window Rock, 1991—; rep. Alliance to Protect Native Rights in Natural Parks Navajo Nation, L.A., 1996—. Mem. Dartmouth Native Am. Coun, Hanover, N.H., 1980-84, Apache County Dems., Window Rock, 1993-96. Am. Indian Grad. Ctr. fellow, 1988-91. Fellow N.Mex. First; mem. ABA, Navajo Nation Bar Assn., N.Mex. Bar Assn. Home: 3209 Grey Hills Ave Gallup NM 87301-6928

**ALLAN, RONALD CURTIS,** lawyer; b. Chgo., Oct. 5, 1937; s. Sven and Stina Allan; m. Ann Gould, Aug. 17, 1963; children: Jennifer, Katherine, Matthew. AB, U. Mich., 1959, JD, 1965. Bar: Ill. 1965, Ohio 1966; U.S. Ct. Appeals (7th cir.) 1965; U.S. Ct. Appeals (6th cir.) 1966. Assoc. Eckhart, McSwain, Hassel & Husum, Chgo., 1965-66; ptnr. Brouse & McDowell, Akron, Ohio, 1967-78; prin. Buckingham, Doolittle & Burroughs, Akron, 1979—; bd. dirs., sec. Yoder Bros., Inc., Barberton, Ohio, Rubber Assocs., Inc., Akron; advisory dir., sec. J.W. Harley, Inc., Twinsburg, Ohio. Editor: Ohio Business Organization Laws and Rules, 4 edits., 1994-98. Trustee, sec. Akron Symphony Orch., 1975-83, Akron Art Mus., 1987-93, Akron Cmty. Found., 1990-96; trustee Akron Gen. Med. Ctr., 1990—; pres. bd. trustees Akron Gen. Med. Found., Old Trail Sch. Found., 1990-97; sec. bd. trustees Akron Rotary Found., 1996—. Capt. USNR, 1959-67. Paul Harris fellow Rotary Internat., 1990. Fellow Akron Bar Found.; mem. ABA, Ohio State Bar Assn. Avocations: classical music, opera, distance running, trout fishing. General corporate, Mergers and acquisitions, Nonprofit and tax-exempt organizations. Office: Buckingham Doolittle & Burroughs 50 S Main St Akron OH 44308-1828

**ALLAN, SHER L.,** lawyer; b. Phoenix, Sept. 22, 1964; d. Earl Rodney Allan Jr. and Janice M. (Rollins) Norton. AA, Gulf Coast C.C., 1982; BS, Fla. State U., 1987, JD, 1989. Bar: Fla. 1990, U.S. Dist. Ct. (no. dist.) Fla. 1995. Asst. state's atty. State's Atty. Office, Quincy, Fla., 1989-92; pvt. practice Panama City, 1992-93; assoc. Law Offices of Charles S. Isler & Assocs., P.A., Panama City, 1993-97. Contbr. articles to profl. publs. Mem. Bay County Bar Assn. (pro bono svc. award 1995), Exch. Club of Panama City (sec.). Avocations: jogging, travel, crafts, needlework. General practice, Criminal, Family and matrimonial. Office: Law Offices of Charles S. Isler & Assocs PA 731 Oak Ave Panama City FL 32401-2560

**ALLEGRA, PETER ALEXANDER,** lawyer; b. N.Y.C., Nov. 19, 1953; s. Edward Colombo and Frances Paula (Masella) A.; m. Karen Lloyd Middleton, July 16, 1983; children: Francesca Paula, Edward Alexander. BA, Boston Coll., 1975; JD, Seton Hall, 1979. Bar: N.J., 1980, Fla., 1980, Tex., 1993, U.S. Supreme Ct., 1986, U.S. Dist. Ct., 1980. Law sec. N.J. Superior Ct., Freehold, 1979-80; ptnr. Allegra, Nebeckopf & DeConca, Red Bank, N.J., 1980—; lectr. Am. Inst. Banking, Long Branch, N.J., 1982-84; adv. trustee Ocean-Monmouth Legal Svcs., Freehold, N.J., 1986-87. Mem. ABA, N.J. Bar Assn. (mock trial coord. 1985-90), Assn. Trial Lawyers Am., Am. Arbitration Assn., Dante Alighieri Club, Figli di Colombo Club. Roman Catholic. Avocations: safari, fishing, music, art collecting. Personal injury, General civil litigation, Criminal. Office: Allegra Nebeckopf & DeConco 286 Broad St Red Bank NJ 07701-2003 also: 2714 John F Kennedy Blvd Jersey City NJ 07306-5711

**ALLEGRUCCI, DONALD LEE,** state supreme court justice; b. Pittsburg, Kans., Sept. 19, 1936; s. Nello and Josephine Marie (Funaro) A.; m. Joyce Ann Thompson, Nov. 30, 1963; children: Scott David, Bowen Jay. AB, Pittsburg State U., 1959; JD, Washburn U., 1963. Bar: Kans. 1963. Asst. county atty. Butler County, El Dorado, Kans., 1963-67; state senator Kans. Legislature, Topeka, 1976-80; mem. Kans. Pub. Relations Bd., 1981-82; dist. judge Kans. 11th Jud. Dist., Pittsburg, 1982-87, adminstrv. judge, 1983-87; justice Kans. Supreme Ct., Topeka, 1987—; instr. Pittsburg State U., 1969-72; exec. dir. Mid-Kans. Community Action Program, Inc. Mem. Dem. State Com., 1974-80; candidate 5th Congl. Dist., 1978; past pres. Heart Assn.; bd. dirs. YMCA. Served with USAF, 1959-60. Mem. Kans. Bar Assn. Democrat. Office: Kansas Supreme Court 374 Kansas Judicial Ctr 301 SW 10th Ave Fl 3 Topeka KS 66612-1599

**ALLEN, BELLE,** management consulting firm executive, communications company executive; b. Chgo.; d. Isaac and Clara (Friedman) A. U. Chgo. Cert. conf. mgr. Internat. Inst. Conf. Planning and Mgmt., 1989. Report, spl. correspondent The Leader Newspapers, Chgo., Washington, 1960-64; cons., v.p., treas., dir. William Karp Cons. Co. Inc., Chgo., 1961-79, chmn. bd., pres., treas., 1979—; pres. Belle Allen Comms., Chgo., 1961—; nat. corr. CCA Press, 1990—; apptd. pub. mem., com. on judicial evaluation Chgo. Bar Assn. 1998—; v.p., treas., bd. dirs. Cultural Arts Survey Inc., Chgo., 1965-79; cons., bd. dirs. Am. Diversified Rsch. Corp., Chgo., 1967-70; v.p., sec., bd. dirs. Mgmt. Performance Systems Inc., 1976-77; cons. City Club Chgo., 1962-65, Ill. Commn. on Tech. Progress, 1965-67; hearing mem. Ill. Gov.'s Grievance Panel for State Employees, 1979—; hearing mem. grievance panel Ill. Dept. Transp., 1985—; mem. adv. governing bd. Ill. Coalition on Employment of Women, 1980-88; spl. program advisor President's Project Partnership, 1980-88; mem. consumer adv. coun. FRS, 1979-82; reporter CCA Press Svc., 1990—; panel mem. Free Press vs. Fair Trial Nat. Ctr. Freedom of Info. Studies Loyola U. Law Sch., 1993, mem. planning com. Freedom of Info. awards, 1993; conf. chair The Swedish Inst. Press Ethics: How to Handle, 1993. Editor: Operations Research and the Management of Mental Health Systems, 1968; contbr. articles to profl. jours. Mem. campaign staff Adlai E. Stevenson II, 1952, 56, John F. Kennedy, 1960; founding mem. women's bd. United Cerebral Palsy Assn., Chgo., 1954, bd. dirs., 1954-58; pres. Dem. Fedn. Ill., 1958-61; pres. conf. staff Eleanor Roosevelt, 1960; mem. Welfare Pub. Rels. Forum, 1960-61; bd. dirs., mem. exec. com., chmn. pub. rels. com. Regional Ballet Ensemble, Chgo., 1961-63; bd. dirs. Soc. Chgo. Strings, 1963-64; mem. Ind. Dem. Coalition, 1968-69; bd. dirs. Citizens for Polit. Change, 1969; campaign mgr. aldermanic election 42d ward Chgo. City Coun., 1969; mem. selection com. Robert Aragon Scholarship, 1991; planning com. mem. Hutchins Era reunion U. Chgo., 1995; mem. reunion planning com. U. Chgo., 1995. Recipient Outstanding Svc. award United Cerebral Palsy Assn., Chgo., 1954, 55, Chgo. Lighthouse for Blind, 1986, Spl. Comms. award The White House, 1961, cert. of appreciation Ill. Dept. Human Rights, 1985, Internat. Assn. Ofcl. Human Rights Agys., 1985; selected as reference source Am. Bicentennial Rsch. Inst. Libr. Human Resources, 1973; named Hon. Citizen, City of Alexandria, Va., 1985. Mem. AAAS, NOW, AAAU, Affirmative Action Assn. (bd. dirs. 1981-85, chmn. mem. and programs com. 1981-85, pres. 1983—), Fashion Group (bd. dirs. 1981-83, chmn. Restrospective View of an Hist. Decade 1960-70, editor The Bull. 1981), Indsl. Rels. Rsch. Assn. (bd. dirs., chmn. pers. placement com. 1960-61), Sarah Siddons Soc., Soc. Pers. Adminstrs., Women's Equity Action League, Nat. Assn. Inter-Group Rels. Ofcls. (nat. conf. program 1959), Publicity Club Chgo. (chmn. inter-city rels. com. 1960-61, Disting. Svc. award 1968), Ill. C. of C. (cmty. rels. com., alt. mem. labor rels. com. 1971-74), Chgo. C. of C. and Industry (merit employment com. 1961-63), Internat. Press Club Chgo. (charter 1992—, bd. dirs. 1992—), Chgo. Press Club (chmn. women's activities 1969-71), U. Chgo. Club of Met. Chgo. (program com. 1993—, chair summer quarter programs 1994), Soc. Profl. Journalists (Chgo. Headline Club 1992—, regional conf. planning com. 1993, co-chair Peter Lisagor awards 1993, program com. 1992—), Assn. Women Journalists, Nat. Trust for Historic Preservation. Office: CCA Press 111 E Chestnut St Ste 36G Chicago IL 60611-6013

**ALLEN, CHARLES CLIFFORD, III,** legal administrator; b. Atlantic City, N.J., Feb. 16, 1947; s. Charles Clifford Allen Jr. and Harriet H. (Clark) Sooy; 1 child, Katharine; m. Cynthia J. Tosi, Feb. 15, 1992. AB, Muhlenberg Coll., 1969; JD, Capital U. Law Sch., 1975. Bar: Mass. Assoc. editor Lawyers Coop. Pub. Co., Rochester, N.Y., 1976-78; editor Equity Pub. Corp., Orford, N.H., 1978-80, mng. editor, 1980-81; staff atty. Mass. Appeals Ct., Boston, 1981-82; asst. reporter of decisions Mass. Supreme Jud. Ct., Boston, 1982-87, dpe. reporter of decisions, 1987-94, reporter of decisions, 1994—. Chmn. bd. trustees Meml. United Meth. Ch., Beverly, Mass., 1989-95; bd. dirs., sec. Beverly Midget Football, Inc., 1989-92; coach Pop Warner Football Program, Beverly, 1989-95; mem. Dem. City Com., 1984-85. Mem. Assn. Reporters of Jud. Decisions (pres. 1998-99). Democrat. Avocations: running, basketball, gardening. Home: 12 Jewett Rd Beverly MA 01915-1906 Office: Mass Supreme Jud Ct New Courthouse Rm 1407 Boston MA 02108

**ALLEN, CHARLES MENGEL,** federal judge; b. Louisville, Nov. 22, 1916; s. Arthur Dwight and Jane (Mengel) A.; m. Betty Anne Cardwell, June 25, 1949; children: Charles Dwight, Angela M. BA, Yale U., 1941; LLB, U. Louisville, 1943. Bar: Ky. 1944. Assoc. Doolin, Helm, Stites and Wood, 1944-45; pvt. practice Louisville, 1946-47; assoc. Farnsley, Hottell and Stephenson, 1947-53; pvt. practice, 1953-55; asst. U.S. atty. Western Dist. Ky., Dept. Justice, 1955-59; ptnr. Booth, Walker & Allen, Louisville, 1959-61; circuit judge Jefferson Cir. Ct., 4th Chancery Br. Jefferson County, 1961-71; dist. judge U.S. Dist. Ct. (we. dist.) Ky., Louisville, 1971-77, chief judge, 1977-85, sr. judge, 1985—. Named Outstanding Alumnus U. Louisville, 1984; recipient Brandeis award U. Louisville Law Sch., 1985, Thomas Hogan Meml. Found award Ky. Civil Liberties Union, 1986, Grauman award U. Louisville, 1986. Mem. ABA, Fed. Bar Assn., Ky. Bar Assn. (Judge of Yr. award 1996), Louisville Bar Assn., Nat. Ry. Hist. Soc. Avocations: tennis, trains, photography, bridge. Office: US Dist Ct 252 US Courthouse 601 W Broadway Ste 450 Louisville KY 40202-2227

**ALLEN, CLIVE VICTOR,** lawyer, communications company executive; b. Montreal, Que., Can., June 11, 1935; s. John Arthur and Norah (Barnett) A.; m. Barbara Mary Kantor, Feb. 22, 1964; children: Drew, Blair. B.A., McGill U., 1956, B.C.L., 1959. Bar: Que. 1960. Mem. firm Hackett, Mulvena, Drummond & Fiske, 1960-63, Fiske, Emery, Allen & Lauzon, 1964-66; v.p., sec. Allied Chem. Can. Ltd., 1966-74; sr. v.p., gen. counsel Northern Telecom Ltd., 1974-97, exec. v.p. law, 1998—; bd. dirs. Allendale Mut. Ins. Co.; mem. adv. bd. Can.-U.S. Law Inst. Mem. ABA, Can. Bar Assn., Bar of Que., Internat. Bar Assn., Assn. Can. Gen. Counsel, Montreal Badminton and Squash Club, St. James' Club (Montreal), Granite Club (Toronto). Communications. Home: 14 Pine Hill Rd, Toronto, ON Canada M4W 1P6 Office: Nortel Networks Corp, 8200 Dixie Rd Ste 100, Brampton, ON Canada L6T 5P6

**ALLEN, DAVID JAMES,** lawyer; b. East Chicago, Ind.. BS, Ind. U., 1957, MA, 1959, JD, 1965. Bar: Ind. 1965, U.S. Dist. Ct. (so. dist.) Ind. 1965, U.S. Ct. Appeals 1965, U.S. Ct. Appeals (fed. and 7th cirs.) 1983, U.S. Tax Ct. 1965, U.S. Supreme Ct. 1965. Ptnr. Hagemier, Allen and Smith, Indpls., 1975—; adminstrv. asst. to Gov. of Ind. Matthew E. Welsh, 1961-65, 65-69; legis. counsel to Gov. of Ind. Roger D. Branigin, 1989-90, Ind. Gov. Bayh; spl. counsel to Gov. Frank O' Bannon State of Ind., 1997—; mem. Spl. Commn. on Ind. Exec. Reorgn., 1967-69; commr. Ind. Utility Regulatory Commn., 1970-75; mem. Ind. Law Enforcement Acad. Bd. and Adv. Coun., 1968-85; mem. Ind. State Police Bd., 1968—; commr. for revision Ind. Adminstrv. Adjudication Act, 1983-87; mem. Ind. Commn. to Recommend Changes in Ind. Legis. Process, 1990—; commr. Ind. Criminal Code Revision Study Commn.; nat. judge advocate Acacia Frat., 1980-86, 92—; chief counsel Ind. Ho. of Reps., 1975-76; spl. counsel Ind. Senate Majority, 1977-78; legis. counsel Ind. Ho. of Reps., Ind. Senate minority parties, 1979-89, Ind. Senate, 1990-97; adj. prof. pub. law Ind. U., Bloomington, 1976—. Author: New Governor In Indiana: Transition of Executive Power, 1965. Mem. ABA, Ind. State Bar Assn. (mem. adminstrv. law com. 1968-77, chmn. adminstrv. law com. 1973-76, mem. law sch. liaison com. 1977-78, criminal justice law exec. com. 1966-72), Indpls. Bar Assn. Administrative and regulatory, Legislative, Public utilities. Office: Hagemier Allen & Smith 1170 Market Tower 10 W Market St Indianapolis IN 46204-2954

**ALLEN, DENISE,** lawyer; b. Boston, June 12, 1957; d. Charles Ambrose and Hazel Helena Allen; m. Herman Tunsil, May 28, 1983 (div. 1992); children: Alexander C. Allen-Tunsil, Nicholas J. Allen-Tunsil. BA, U. Fla., 1978, JD, 1981. Bar: Fla. 1981, U.S. Dist. Ct. (mid. dist.) Fla. 1982, U.S. Ct. Appeals (11th cir.) 1992, Ga. 1993, U.S. Dist. Ct. (no. dist.) Ga. 1993. Atty. Public Defender Office, Jacksonville, Fla., 1981-85, Johnson & Allen Tunsil, Jacksonville, 1985-88, Denise Allen Tunsil, P.A., Jacksonville, 1988-93; prof. bus. law Jones Coll., Jacksonville, 1982-90; atty. Denise Allen, Atty. at Law, Atlanta, 1993-96; atty. Denise Allen, P.C., Decatur, Ga., 1996—, Atlanta, 1997—. Active First African Presbyn. Ch., Lithonia, Ga. Mem. ATLA, Nat. Assn. of Criminal Defense Law, Nat. Bar Assn., Ga. Trial Lawyers Assn., Dekalb Lawyer Assn., Gate City Bar Assn., D.W. Perkins Bar (past pres.). Democrat. Presbyterian. Avocations: racquetball, swimming. Family and matrimonial, Criminal, Personal injury. Office: Denise Allen PC 1745 Mlk Jr Dr NW Atlanta GA 30314-2262

**ALLEN, DUDLEY DEAN,** lawyer; b. Nashville, Mar. 26, 1943; s. John William Jr. and Lois (Davis) A.; m. Lenorah Jane Kinsey, Mar. 8, 1969; children: LeNorah Elizabeth, Dudley D. Jr., John William Stephen. BA, U. Kans., 1965; JD, U. Fla., 1967. Bar: Fla. 1968. Law clk. to presiding justice U.S. Dist. Ct. (so. dist.) Fla., 1968; ptnr. Wilbur & Allen (and predecessor firms), Jacksonville, Fla., 1972—. Lt. USNR, 1968-72. Named John Ise scholar U. Kans., 1964, Summerfield scholar U. Kans., 1963. Mem. Phi Beta Kappa, Order of Coif. General civil litigation, Admiralty, Personal injury. Office: Wilbur & Allen 112 W Adams St Ste 1700 Jacksonville FL 32202-3895

**ALLEN, EDWARD LEFEBVRE,** lawyer; b. Richmond, Va., May 17, 1962; s. Wilbur Coleman and Frances (Gayle) A.; m. Nancy Williams, Sept. 3, 1994; 1 child, Parker Edward. BA, Vanderbilt U., 1984; JD, Washington and Lee U., 1987. Bar: Va. 1987, U.S. Ct. Appeals (4th cir.) 1989, U.S. Claims Ct. 1990, U.S. Ct. Appeals (D.C. cir.) 1996. Assoc. Allen, Allen, Allen & Allen, Richmond, 1987-96, ptnr., 1996—. Mem. ABA, ATLA, Va. Trial Lawyers Assn. (gov. at large 1999—), Va. State Bar (12th cir. rep., young lawyers divsn. 1992-93), Fredericksburg Bar Assn. E-mail: ELA@Allenandallen.com. Personal injury. Home: 401 Chamonix Dr Fredericksburg VA 22405-2029 Office: Allen Allen Allen & Allen 3405 Plank Rd Fredericksburg VA 22407-4959

**ALLEN, F(RANK) C(LINTON), JR.,** lawyer, retired manufacturing executive; b. 1934. BSChE, Tulane U., 1955, JD, 1964. With McDermott, Inc., New Orleans, 1978—, mem. legal staff, 1978-80, asst. gen. counsel, 1980-87, v.p., sec. gen. counsel, 1987-93; v.p. risk mgmt. safety, health and environ. McDermott Internat. Inc., New Orleans, 1993-99, ret., 1999; spl. counsel maritime sect. Jones, Walker Law Firm, New Orleans, 1999—. Environmental, Personal injury, Product liability. Office: Jones Walker Waechter Poitevent Carrere & Denegre 201 St Charles Ave New Orleans LA 70170-5100

**ALLEN, HARRY ROGER,** lawyer; b. Memphis, June 13, 1933; s. Sam J. and Louise (Frazier) A.; children: Julie Ferriss, Steven J., Leslie Loraine Allen Anchor; m. Emily Ann Mason, May 4, 1990; 1 stepchild, Jeremy Myrick. Student, Tulane U., 1951-53; BBA, U. Miss., 1955, LLB, 1959. Bar: Miss. 1959, U.S. Dist. Ct. (so. dist.) Miss. 1961, U.S. Ct. Appeals (5th cir.) 1981, U.S. Supreme Ct. 1981. From assoc. to ptnr. Brunini Everett, Grantam & Quinn, Vicksburg, Miss., 1959-68; ptnr. Bryan, Nelson, Allen, Schroeder, Cobb & Hood, Gulfport, Miss., 1968-91; pres. Allen, Vaughn, Cobb & Hood, P.A., Gulfport, Miss., 1992—; spl. asst. atty. gen. State of Miss., Gulfport, 1989-91; gen. counsel Miss. State Pt. Authority, 1996. Mem. Harrison County com. region XIII commn. Mental Health and Mental Retardation, Gulfport, 1976—; fin. chmn. Miss. Rep. Party, 1982-84; Miss. Elector Bush/Quayle Ticket, Jackson, Miss., 1984; del. Rep. Nat. Conv., Dallas, 1984. Capt. USAF, 1955-58. Named to Best Lawyer in Am. publ., 1988-97. Mem. Internat. Assn. Def. Counsel, Miss. Bar Found. (bd. trustees), Miss. Bar Assn. (pres. Harrison County young lawyers sect. 1969-70, jud. liaison com. 1990-91), Miss. Fed. Bar Assn. (so. dist. commr. 1980-81), Miss. Bar Leadership Conf. (chmn. 1991), Harrison County Bar Assn. (pres. 1990), Lamar Order, Am. Inns of Ct. (pres. Russell 1995-96, Blass-Walker chpt. Republican. Methodist. Avocations: golf, skiing. General civil litigation, Insurance, Personal injury. Office: Allen Vaughn Cobb & Hood P A PO Box 4108 Gulfport MS 39502-4108

**ALLEN, JAMES HENRY,** magistrate; b. Memphis, May 10, 1935; s. Henry L. and Hazel V. A.; m. Charlene Anne Jayroe, July 29, 1961; children—James Henry, Elizabeth Hazel, Luanne Mae. A.B., Memphis State U., 1957; LL.B., Tulane U., 1960. Bar: La. 1960, Tenn. 1961, U.S. Dist. Ct. (we. dist.) Tenn. 1961, U.S. Ct. Appeals (6th cir.) 1973, U.S. Supreme Ct. 1969. Assoc. Tual, Allan, Keltner, and Lee, Memphis, 1960; assoc. Nelson, Norvell & Floyd, Memphis, 1961; claims adjuster State Farm Mut. Automobile Ins. Co., Memphis, 1961-65; adminstrv. asst. law clk. Bankruptcy Ct., Memphis, 1965-67; assoc. Charles G. Black, Memphis, 1967-69; asst. atty. gen. Shelby County (Tenn.), 1969-79; U.S. magistrate, Memphis, 1979—; lectr. on criminal law, recruit class Shelby County Sheriff's Dept., Memphis, 1976; lectr. on fed. rules civil procedure Continuing Legal Edn., Memphis, 1981. Served with USMCR, 1957-65. Tulane U. scholar, 1957-60. Mem. La. State Bar Assn., Memphis and Shelby County Bar Assn., Nat. Council U.S. Magistrates, Phi Alpha Delta. Baptist. Fax: 901-495-1384. Office: US Dist Ct 338 Federal Bldg 167 N Main St Memphis TN 38103-1816

**ALLEN, JEFFREY MICHAEL,** lawyer; b. Chgo., Dec. 13, 1948; s. Albert A. and Miriam (Feldman) A.; m. Anne Marie Guaraglia, Aug. 9, 1975; children: Jason M., Sara M. BA in Polit. Sci. with great distinction, U. Calif., Berkeley, 1970, JD, 1973. Bar: Calif. 1973, U.S. Dist. Ct. (no. and so. dists.) Calif. 1973, U.S. Ct. Appeals (9th cir.) 1973, U.S. Dist. Ct. (ea. dist.) Calif. 1974, U.S. Dist. Ct. (cen. dist.) Calif. 1977, U.S. Dist. Ct. (so. dist.) Calif., U.S. Supreme Ct.; lic. real estate broker. Prin. Graves & Allen, Oakland, Calif., 1973—; teaching asst. dept. polit. sci. U. Calif., Berkeley, 1970-73; lectr. St. Mary's Coll., Moraga, Calif., 1976-90; mem. faculty Oakland Coll. of Law, 1996-98; bd. dirs. Family Svcs. of the East Bay, 1987-92, 1st v.p., 1988, pres., 1988-91; mem. panel arbitrators Ala. County Superior Ct.; arbitrator comml. arbitration panel Am. Arbitration Assn. Mem. editorial bd. U. Calif. Law Rev., 1971-73, project editor, 1972-73; mem. Ecology Law Quar., 1971-72, editor-in-chief Tech. and Practice Guide, chmn. tech. com.; contbr. articles to profl. jours. Treas. Hillcrest Elem. Sch. PTA, 1984-86, pres., 1986-88; past mem. GATE adv. com., strategic planning com. on fin. and budget, dist. budget adv. com., instructional strategy counsel Oakland Unified Sch. Dist., 1986-91; mem. Oakland Met. Forum, 1987-91, Oakland Strategic Planning Com., 1988-90; mem. adv. com. St. Mary's Coll. Paralegal Prog.; bd. dirs. Montera Sports Complex, 1988-89; bd. dirs. Jack London Youth Soccer League, 1988-94; commr. Bay Oaks Youth Soccer, 1988-94; asst. dist. commr. dist. 4 Calif. Youth Soccer Assn., 1990-92, sec. 1993-96, bd. dirs. 1993—, also bd. dirs., pres. dist. 4 competitive league, 1990-93; sec., bd. dirs. Calif. Youth Soccer Assn., 1993-96, chmn. bd. dirs., 1996—; bd. dirs. Calif. Soccer Assn. North, 1996—; mem. U.S. Soccer database mktg. com., 1997—, U.S. Soccer Constl. Commn., 1997-98, U.S. Youth Soccer bylaws com., 1998—, U.S. Youth Soccer Region 4 Regional Coun., 1996—; chmn. U.S. Youth Soccer database mktg. com., 1998—. Mem. ABA (chmn. real property com. gen. practice sect. 1987-91, mem. programs com. 1991-93, chmn. subcom. on use of computers in real estate trans. 1985-86, adv. coord. 1993-96, sect. coun. 1994-98, mktg. bd. 1996—, chmn. tech. com. 1998—, editor Tech. and Practice Guide 1998—), Alameda County Bar Assn. (past vice chmn. com. continuing edn., exec. com. alternative dispute resolution programs, panel mediator, arbitrator), U.S. Soccer Assn. (database mktg. com., constl. commn.), Calif. Bar Assn., Calif. Scholarship Fedn., U.S. Soccer Fedn. (nat. C lic. coach and state referee, state referee instr. and state referee assessor), Calif. North Referee Assn. (referee adminstr. dist. 4 1992-96, state bd. dirs. 1996—), Soc. for Profls. in Dispute Resolution, Oakland C. of C., Rotary (bd. dirs. Oakland 1992-94). Avocations: reading, computers, photography, skiing, baseball, coaching and refereeing youth soccer. Real property, General civil litigation, Bankruptcy. Office: Graves & Allen 436 14th St Ste 1400 Oakland CA 94612-2710

**ALLEN, JEFFREY RODGERS,** lawyer; b. West Point, N.Y., Aug. 15, 1953; s. James R. and Kathryn (Lewis) A.; m. Cynthia Lynn Colyer, Aug. 10, 1975; children: Emily Rodgers, Elizabeth Colyer, Richard Byrd. BA in History, U. Va., 1975; JD, U. Richmond, 1978. Bar: Va. 1978, U.S. Ct. Mil. Appeals 1981, U.S. Ct. Appeals (4th cir.) 1982, U.S. Supreme Ct. 1982. Trial atty. Michie, Hamlett, Donato & Lowry, Charlottesville, Va., 1982-86; chief counsel Va. Dept. Mil. Affairs, Richmond, 1986—; atty., advisor U.S. Army Mobile Air Surg. Transport Team, Savannah, Ga., 1980-82; mem. steering com. X-Car Litigation Group, 1983-85; lectr., organizer Law Everyone Should Know series Piedmont (Va.) C.C., Charlottesville, 1984-86; trial atty., of counsel Thorsen, Marchant & Scher, L.L.P., Richmond, 1986-98; mem. legal adv. com. Va. Gov.'s Mil. Adv. Commn., 1987—, judge advocate adv. coun. N.G. Bur., 1993-96, TJAG Air N.G. judge advocate adv. coun., 1997—, recording sec. ST HQ Liason (East), mem. strategic planning com. Pres. Regency Woods Condominium Assn., Richmond, 1976-78, Ashcroft Neighborhood Assn., Charlottesville, 1983-86; treas. Va. N.G. Found., 1986—. Capt. U.S. Army, 1978-82, lt. col. JAGC, Va. Air N.G., 1982—. Mem. Assn. Trial Lawyers Am., Va. Trial Lawyers Assn., Richmond Bar Assn. Republican. Methodist. Avocations: jogging, mountain climbing, photography, fishing, swimming. Home: 2700 Cottage Cove Dr Richmond VA 23233-3318 Office: Va Dept Mil Affairs Bldg 316 Ft Pickett Blackstone VA 23824-6316

**ALLEN, JOHN THOMAS, JR.,** lawyer; b. St. Petersburg, Fla., Aug. 23, 1935; s. John Thomas and Mary Lita (Shields) A.; m. Joyce Ann Lindsey, June 16, 1958 (div. 1985); children: John Thomas, III, Linda Joyce, Catherine Lee (dec.); m. Janice Dearmin Hudson, Mar. 16, 1987. BS in Bus. Adminstrn. with honors, U. Fla., 1958; JD, Stetson U., 1961. Bar: Fla. 1961,

U.S. Dist. Ct. (mid. dist.) Fla. 1962, U.S. Ct. Appeals (5th cir.) 1963, U.S. Ct. Appeals (11th cir.) 1983, U.S. Supreme Ct. 1970. Assoc. Mann, Harrison, Mann & Rowe and successor Greene, Mann, Rowe, Davenport & Stanton, St. Petersburg, 1961-74, ptnr., 1967-74; sole practice, St. Petersburg, 1974-95; pvt. practice Allen & Maller, P.A., 1996—; counsel Pinellas County Legis. Del., 1974-75; counsel for Pinellas County as spl. counsel on water matters, 1975—. Mem. Com. of 100, St. Petersburg, 1975—. Mem. ABA, Fla. Bar Assn., St. Petersburg Bar Assn., St. Petersburg C. of C., Beta Gamma Sigma. Democrat. Methodist. Club: Lions (St. Petersburg). General practice, Personal injury, State civil litigation. Address: PO Box 13486 Saint Petersburg FL 33733-3486

**ALLEN, KELLER WAYNE,** lawyer; b. Pasco, Wash., June 12, 1959; s. Billy Wayne and Barbara Elizabeth (Cox) A.; m. Katherine Jo Lewis, Sept. 3, 1977; children: Kimberly Jo, Kelsey Marie. BA in Gen. Studies, Ea. Wash. U., 1986; JD, Gonzaga Sch. Law, 1989. Bar: Wash. 1989, Idaho, 1994, U.S. Dist. Ct. (ea. dist.) Wash. 1989, U.S. Dist. Ct. Idaho 1994, U.S. Dist. Ct. (we. dist.) Wash. 1996, U.S. Dist. Ct. Oreg. 1997, U.S. Ct. Appeals (9th cir.) 1996. Staff atty. to Hon. Robert J. McNichols U.S. Dist. Ct., Ea. Dist., Wash., Spokane, 1989-91; assoc. atty. Winston & Cashatt, P.S., Spokane, 1991-93; ptnr. McCormick, Dunn & Black, P.S., Spokane, 1993—. Author: Washington Tort Law and Practice, 1993, Washington Contract Law and Practice, 1998. Bd. dirs. Inland Empire Girl Scouts Coun., Spokane, 1994. Mem. N.W. Human Resource Mgmt. Assn. (bd. dirs. 1993-97), Spokane Area C. of C. Avocations: golf, hunting, fishing. Labor, General civil litigation. Office: McCormick Dunn and Black PS 505 W Riverside Ave Ste 200 Spokane WA 99201-0518

**ALLEN, LAWRENCE RICHARD,** prosecutor; b. Portland, Oreg., May 13, 1952; s. Irving Courtney and Madonna Elizabeth (Walsh) A.; m. Suzanne Elise Chaffey, May 17, 1975 (div. June 1995); children: Rebecca Ann, Sarah Beth; m. Sherrie Lee Setters, Aug. 9, 1997. Student, Treasure Valley C.C., 1972; BS, Willamette U., 1974; JD, John F. Kennedy U., 1980. Bar: Calif. 1980, U.S. Dist. Ct. (no. and ea. dists.) Calif. 1980, U.S. Ct. Appeals (9th cir.) 1985. Clk. Safeway Stores, 1971-80; bus. agt., legal counsel United Foods Comml. Workers Union, Martinez, Calif., 1980-84; assoc. Patrick Beasley Law Office, Redding, Calif., 1984-85, Simpson & Maine, Redding, 1985-87; dep. dist. atty. Shasta County Dist. Atty., Redding, 1987-91, sr. dep. dist. atty., 1991-98; environ. prosecutor Calif. Dist. Atty. Assn., Sacramento, 1998—; instr. Calif. Dept. Fish and Game, 1996, 97, 98, Calif. Dist. Atty.'s Assn., Sacramento, 1996—, Napa Valley Coll. Resource Protection Acad., 1997—. Editor Calif. Dist. Atty. Assn. Case Digest, 1993—. Mem. Family Support Legis. Com., Sacramento, 1995-98; bd. dirs. Wildlife Forensic DNA Found., Sacramento, 1994—, Californians Against Waste, Sacramento, 1981-84. Mem. Moose. Home: 2095 Canal Dr Redding CA 96001-1204 Office: CDAA Environ Prosecution Project 429 Redcliff Dr Ste 225 Redding CA 96002-0102

**ALLEN, LAYMAN EDWARD,** law educator, research scientist; b. Turtle Creek, Pa., June 9, 1927; s. Layman Grant and Viola Iris (Williams) A.; m. Christine R. Patmore, Mar. 29, 1950 (dec.); children: Layman G., Patricia R.; m. Emily C. Hall, Oct. 3, 1981 (div. 1992); children: Phyllip A. Hall, Kelly C. Hall; m. Leslie A. Olsen, June 10, 1995. Student, Washington and Jefferson Coll., 1945-46; AB, Princeton U., 1951; MPub. Admnstrn., Harvard U., 1952; LLB, Yale U., 1956. Bar: Conn. 1956. Fellow Ctr. for Advanced Study in Behavioral Scis., 1961-62; sr. fellow Yale Law Sch., 1956-57, lectr., 1957-58, instr., 1958-59, asst. prof., 1959-63, assoc. prof., 1963-66; assoc. prof. law U. Mich. Law Sch., Ann Arbor, 1966-71, prof., 1971—; sr. rsch. scientist Mental Health Rsch. Inst., U. Mich., 1966—; cons. legal drafting Nat. Life Ins. Co., Mich. Blue Cross & Blue Shield (various law firms); mem. electronic data retrieval com. Am. Bar Assn.; ops. rsch. analyst McKinsey & Co.; orgn. and methods analyst Office of Sec. Air Force.; trustee Ctr. for Study of Responsive Law. Editor: Games and Simulations, Artificial Intelligence and Law Jour.; author: WFF 'N Proof: The Game of Modern Logic, 1961, latest rev. edit., 1973, (with Robin B.S. Brooks, Patricia A. James) Automatic Retrieval of Legal Literature: Why and How, 1962, WFF: The Beginner's Game of Modern Logic, 1962, latest rev. edit., 1973, Equations: The Game of Creative Mathematics, 1963, latest rev. edit., 1973, (with Mary E. Caldwell) Reflections of the Communications Sciences and Law: The Jurimetrics Conference, 1965, (with J. Ross and P. Kugel) Queries 'N Theories: The Game of Science and Language, 1970, latest rev. edit., 1973, (with F. Goodman, D. Humphrey and J. Ross), On-Words: The Game of Word Structures, 1971, rev. edit., 1973; contbr. articles to profl. jours.; co-author/designer: (with J. Ross and C. Stratton) DIG (Diagnostic Instrnl. Gaming) Math; (with C. Saxon) Normalizer Clear Legal Drafting Program, 1986, MINT System for Generating Dynamically Multiple-Interpretation Legal Decision-Assistance Systems, 1991, The Legal Argument Game of Legal Relations, 1997. With USNR, 1945-46. Mem. ABA (coun. sect. sci. and tech.), AAAS, ACLU, Assn. Symbolic Logic, Nat. Coun. Tchrs. Math. Democrat. Unitarian. Home: 2114 Vinewood Blvd Ann Arbor MI 48104-2762 Office: U Mich Sch Law 625 S State St Ann Arbor MI 48109-1215

**ALLEN, LEIGH BRISCOE, III,** lawyer; b. Vicksburg, Miss., Oct. 14, 1938; s. Leigh Briscoe and Margaret Carpenter A.; m. Lynn Yarbrough Allen Haspel, Aug. 10, 1963 (div. Apr. 1984); children: Dorothy, Leigh; m. Lynn McCaa Fielder, Feb. 6, 1988. BA, Washington & Lee U., 1960; LLB, U. Miss., 1964. Bar: Miss. Assoc. Brunini Law Firm, Jackson, Miss., 1964-70, ptnr., 1970—; bd. dirs. The Walker Cos., Jackson, Miss. So. Bank, Port Gibson, Miss. Bd. dirs., chmn. St. Andrews Episcopal Sch., Jackson, 1978-79; bd. dirs. Miss. Children Home Soc., Jackson, 1989-95; pres. Jackson Country Club, 1978; bd. dirs. pres. Annandale Golf Club, 1988-89. 2d lt. inf. U.S. Army, 1960-62. Republican. Episcopal. Avocations: golf, hunting, fishing. Banking, Estate planning, Mergers and acquisitions. Home: 9 East Hill Jackson MS 39216 Office: Brunini Grantham Grower & Hewes 1400 Trustmark Bldg Jackson MS 39201

**ALLEN, LEON ARTHUR, JR.,** lawyer; b. Springfield, Mass., July 15, 1933; s. Leon Arthur Sr. and Elsie (Shoemaker) A.; m. Patricia Mellion, June 23, 1961; 1 child, Christopher L. BEE, Cornell U., 1955; LLB, NYU, 1964. Bar: N.Y. 1964, U.S. Dist. Ct. (so. and ea. dists.) N.Y. 1965. Tech. editor McGraw Hill Pub. Co., N.Y.C., 1958-62; constrn. engr. Gilbert Assocs., N.Y.C., 1962-64; assoc. LeBoeuf, Lamb, Leiby & MacRae, N.Y.C., 1964-70; ptnr. LeBoeuf, Lamb, Leiby & MacRae (name changed to LeBoeuf, Lamb, Greene & MacRae), N.Y.C., 1971—. Served with U.S. Army, 1956-58. Mem. ABA, Assn. of Bar of City of N.Y. (chmn. adminstrv. law com. 1972-74). Clubs: Racquet & Tennis (N.Y.C.); Union (N.Y.C.), Tuxedo (Tuxedo Park, N.Y.). Administrative and regulatory, FERC practice, Private international. Home: 530 E 86th St New York NY 10028-7535 Office: LeBoeuf Lamb Greene MacRae 125 W 55th St New York NY 10019-5369

**ALLEN, LISA JOAN,** lawyer; b. Detroit, Aug. 20, 1964; d. Stephen F. and Suzanne T. A.; m. Michael B. Kril, Aug. 18, 1984 (div. Apr. 1995); children: James Allen, Alexander M.; m. Michael C. Veruto, June 12, 1998; 1 child, Lauren E. BA, SUNY, Binghamton, 1985; JD, SUNY, Buffalo, 1990. Bar: N.Y. 1991. Sr. assoc. Hogan & Willig, Amherst, N.Y., 1989—; adj. prof. SUNY, Buffalo, 1992—; cons. in field. Estate planning, Probate, Family and matrimonial. Office: Hogan & Willig 1 Audubon Pkwy Amherst NY 14228-1145

**ALLEN, NEWTON PERKINS,** lawyer; b. Memphis, Jan. 3, 1922; s. James Seddon and Sarah (Perkins) A.; m. Malinda Lobdell Nobles, Oct. 4, 1947 (dec. Nov. 1986); children: John Lobdell, Malinda Nobles, Newton Perkins, Cannon Fairfax; m. Malinda Lobdell Crutchfield, June 23, 1990. AB, Princeton, 1943; JD, U. Va., 1948. Bar: Tenn. 1947, N.C. 1990. Assoc. Armstrong, Allen, Prewitt, Gentry, Johnston & Holmes, Memphis, 1948, ptnr., 1950-95; assoc. Dann & Allen, 1996—. Contbr. articles to profl. jours. Mem. Chickasaw coun. Boy Scouts Am., 1958-60, exec. bd. mem., 1961-69; trustee LeBonheur Children's Hosp., Memphis, 1964-72, vice chmn. bd., 1965; mem. alumni coun. Princeton, 1954-64, 90-93; pres. bd. trustees St. Mary's Episcopal Sch., 1966-67, v.p., 1972-73; chmn. Greater Memphis Coun. on Crime and Delinquency, 1976-80; co-chmn. Memphis conf. Faith at Work, 1975, bd. dirs., 1976-79; bd. dirs. Memphis Orch. Soc., pres., 1979-81. Mem. ABA (editl. bd. sr. lawyers divsn. 1990, publs. com. chair 1993-95, coun. mem. 1994-95, chair travel and leisure com. 1995-96, vice chair 1996-97, chair-elect 1997-98, chair 1998—), Am. Coll. Trust and Estate Coun., Tenn. Bar Assn., Memphis Bar Assn., Tenn. Def. Lawyers Assn., N.C. Bar Assn., Princeton Alumni Assn. Memphis (pres. 1992), Memphis Lions (pres. 1956). Republican. General practice, General civil litigation, Probate. Office: Dann & Allen 6263 Poplar Ave Ste 1103 Memphis TN 38119-4701

**ALLEN, NOEL LEE,** lawyer; b. Greensboro, N.C., Oct. 23, 1947; s. Simeon Lee and Kathleen (Carnes) A.; m. Sandra Robinson, Aug. 14, 1971; children: Brenner, Jeremy. BA, Elon Coll., 1969; JD, U. N.C., 1973; grad. diploma in law, U. Amsterdam, The Netherlands, 1974. Bar: N.C. 1973, U.S. Supreme Ct. 1978, U.S. Ct. Internat. Trade 1983. Asst. atty. gen. N.C. Dept. Justice, Raleigh, 1974-77; ptnr. Allen & Pinnix, predecessor firms, Raleigh, 1977—; staff cons. Office U.S. Sen. Robert Morgan, Washington, 1978-79; adj. prof. Campbell U., Buie's Creek, N.C., 1980—; vis. lectr. U. N.C., Chapel Hill, 1982. Author: Antitrust and Trade Regulations Law in North Carolina, 1982; cons. editor: European Bankruptcy Laws, 1986; contbr. articles to profl. publs. Trustee Elon Coll., 1986—. Mem. ABA, N.C. Bar Assn. (chmn. internat. law com. 1984-86, 91—). Administrative and regulatory, Antitrust, Private international. Office: Allen & Pinnix Drawer 1270 Raleigh NC 27602-1270

**ALLEN, PATRICK WILLIAM,** lawyer, educator; b. Columbus, Ohio, Aug. 24, 1939; s. Joseph C. and Catherine (Groom) A.; m. Mary R. Mills, June 10, 1961; children: Sarah A., Mary C., William P., Michelle M. BA, U. Dayton, 1961; JD, Ohio No. U., 1965. Bar: Ohio 1965. Assoc. Navarre, Rizor, DaPore & Pettit, Lima, Ohio, 1965-72, ptnr., 1972—; ptnr. E.S. Gallon & Assocs., Dayton, Ohio, 1972-97; dir. E.S. Gallon & Assoc., Dayton, Ohio, 1985-97; assoc. Casper & Casper, Middletown, Ohio, 1997—; adj. prof. U. Dayton Sch. Law, 1976-90. Mem. athletic adv. bd. U. Dayton, 1982-88. Fellow Am. Coll. Trial Lawyers; mem. ATLA, Ohio Bar Assn., Butler County Bar Assn., Dayton Bar Assn. (2d v.p. 1990-91, 1st v.p. 1991-92, pres. 1992-93), Ohio Acad. Trial Lawyers, Montgomery County Trial Lawyers Assn. (sec. 1988, pres. 1990-91). Democrat. Avocations: fishing, gardening. Personal injury, Product liability. Home: 3314 N Us Route 42 Lebanon OH 45036-9732 Office: Casper & Casper 1 N Main St Middletown OH 45042-1904

**ALLEN, PAUL ALFRED,** lawyer, educator; b. New Canaan, Conn., Feb. 18, 1948; s. Alfred J. and Wilma T. (DeWaters) A. BA, Johns Hopkins U., 1970; JD, NYU, 1974; MBA, U. Colo., 1989. Bar: Md. 1974, D.C. 1978, Colo. 1984, Calif. 1992. Exec. dir. Md. Environ. Trust, Balt., 1974-75; assoc. Bergson, Borkland, Margolis & Adler, Washington, 1975-79, ptnr., 1980-82; gen. counsel Plus System, Inc., Denver, 1983-91; counsel Visa USA, Inc., San Francisco, 1991-92, exec. v.p., gen. counsel, 1992—; lectr. Grad. Sch. of Banking, Boulder, Colo., 1984-86, U. Denver Law Sch., 1985-90. Editor: How to Keep Your Company Out of Court, 1984; contbr. articles to profl. jours. Recipient Svc. award Supreme Ct. Colo. Mem. ABA, Calif. Bar Assn., Colo. Bar Assn., Am. Corp. Counsel Assn. Democrat. General corporate, Antitrust, General civil litigation. Office: Visa USA Inc PO Box 8999 San Francisco CA 94128-8999

**ALLEN, PHILLIP STEPHEN,** lawyer; b. Washington, Nov. 20, 1952; s. Robert Mitchell and Edna Beverly (Feldman) A.; m. Cheryl Renée Cohen. BA with honors, U. Md., 1974; JD, George Washington U., 1978; LLM in Taxation, Georgetown U., 1982. Bar: D.C. Ct. Appeals, U.S. Dist. Ct., U.S. Tax Ct., U.S. Ct. Claims, U.S. Supreme Ct. Atty. office assoc. chief counsel IRS, Washington, 1978-84; assoc. tax counsel Met. Life Ins. Co., N.Y.C., 1984—; lectr. World Trade Inst., N.Y.C., 1987—. Mem. ABA (tax sect.), Fed. Bar Assn. (tax sect.), Internat. Tax Assn., Union League Club of N.Y. Republican. Jewish. Avocation: scuba diving. Corporate taxation, Mergers and acquisitions, Private international. Home: 41 Hutton Dr Mahwah NJ 07430-2985 Office: Met Life Ins Co One Madison Ave New York NY 10010

**ALLEN, RANDY LEE,** lawyer; b. Kansas City, Kans., Oct. 19, 1963; s. William Richard and Martha Carol Allen; m. Lori B. Meendering; children: Elizabeth, Henry. BS in Petroleum Engring., Colo. Sch. Mines, 1986; JD, U. Colo., 1990. Bar: Colo. 1990, Ala. 1994. Clk. Astrella & Rice PC, Denver, 1988-90, atty., 1990-94; gen. counsel River Gas Corp., Tuscaloosa, Ala., 1994—. Mem. Ind. Petroleum Assn. Am. (com. mem. 1994—), Ala. Coalbed Methane Assn. (com. mem. 1994—), Rocky Mountain Oil and Gas Assn. (com. mem. 1994—), Rocky Mountain Mineral Law Found. Oil, gas, and mineral, General corporate, Natural resources. Office: River Gas Corp 511 Energy Center Blvd Northport AL 35473-2792

**ALLEN, RICHARD BLOSE,** legal editor, lawyer; b. Aledo, Ill., May 10, 1919; s. James Albert and Claire (Smith) A.; m. Marion Treloar, Aug. 27, 1949; children: Penelope, Jennifer, Leslie Jean. BS, U. Ill., 1941, JD, 1947; LLD, Seton Hall U., 1977. Bar: Ill. 1947. Staff editor ABA Jour., 1947-48, 63-66, exec. editor, 1966-70, editor, 1970-83, editor, pub., 1983-86; pvt. practice Aledo, 1949-57; gen. counsel Ill. State Bar Assn., 1957-63. Editor Sr. Lawyer, 1986-90, 94—; mng. editor Def. Counsel Jour., 1987—. Maj. Q.M.C., AUS, 1941-46. Mem. ABA (mem. ho. of dels. 1996-99), Ill. Bar Assn. (mem. assembly 1972-74), Chgo. Bar Assn., Am. Law Inst., Selden Soc., Scribes, Mich. Shores Club, Sigma Delta Chi, Kappa Tau Alpha, Phi Delta Phi, Alpha Tau Omega. Office: Def Counsel Jour 1 N Franklin St Ste 2400 Chicago IL 60606-2401

**ALLEN, RICHARD MARLOW,** lawyer; b. Chgo., Sept. 26, 1940; s. Vern S. and Naomi C. Allen; children: Amanda, Brian. BS, Purdue U., 1963; LLB, Duke U., 1966. Bar: N.Y. 1967, U.S. Dist. Ct. (so. dist.) N.Y. 1968, U.S. Dist. Ct. Ariz., 1991. Ptnr. Cravath, Swaine & Moore, N.Y.C., 1966—; bd. visitors Duke U. Law Sch.; bd. dirs. various orgns. Mem. Am. Coll. Investment Counsel. Bankruptcy, Contracts commercial, General corporate. Office: Cravath Swaine Moore 3 Garden Rd, 2609 Asia Pac Fin Tower, Hong Kong China

**ALLEN, ROBERT B.,** lawyer; b. Lansing, Mich., Aug. 19, 1945; s. Edward Samuel and Marianne Rose A.; m. Helen Ann Richardson, June 18, 1972; children: Joan, Keith, Christopher. B in Criminology, U. Mich., 1967; JD, U. Chgo., 1975. Bar: Ill. 1975, Mich. 1976. Law clerk to Hon. George Waters U.S. Dist Ct. (no. dist.) Ill., Chgo., 1974-1975; assoc. Filmore, Connors & Black, Lansing, 1976-86; ptnr. Moore, Gennings, Bryant, Stiles & Nash, Grand Rapids, Mich., 1986-94; defender, sr. ptnr. Allen, Allen & Werik, Grand Rapids, 1994—; counsel McNeil Pub., 1989—. Coord. Youth Against Violence program, Grand Rapids, 1980-92, Second Chance program, Ann Arbor, 1974. With U.S. Army, 1968-1972. Mem. ABA, Assn. Legal Assocs., Am. Lawyers Assn., Mich. Criminal Defense Laywers Assn., Soc. Defense Lawyers Mich., Grand Rapids Criminal Defense Lawyers Assn. Presbyterian. Democrat. Avocations: skiing, classic cars, reading. Office: Allen Allen & Werik 800 Lafayette Ave NE Ste 100 Grand Rapids MI 49503-1631

**ALLEN, ROBERT DEE,** lawyer; b. Tulsa, Oct. 13, 1928; s. Harve and Olive Jean (Brown) A.; m. Mary Latimer Conner, May 18, 1957; children: Scott, Randy, Blake. BA, U. Okla., 1951, LLB, 1955, JD, 1970. Bar: Okla. 1955, Ill. 1979, U.S. Dist. Ct. (we., no. and ea. dists.) Okla. 1955, U.S. Dist. Ct. (no. dist.) Ill. 1979, U.S. Ct. Appeals (10th cir.) 1956, U.S. Ct. Appeals (7th cir.) 1980, U.S. Supreme Ct. 1985. Assoc. Abernathy & Abernathy, Shawnee, Okla., 1955; law clk. to judge 10th U.S. Ct. Appeals, Denver, 1956; to judge Western Dist. Okla., 1956-57; asst. ins. commr., gen. counsel Okla. Ins. Dept., 1957-63; partner firm Quinlan, Allen & Batchelor, Oklahoma City, 1963-65, DeBois & Allen, 1965-66; counsel AT&T, Washington, 1966-67; gen. atty. Southwestern Bell Telephone Co., Okla., 1967-79; v.p., gen. counsel Ill. Bell Telephone Co., Chgo., 1979-83; sole practice law Chgo. and Oklahoma City, 1983—; mcpl. counselor Oklahoma City, 1984-89; of counsel Hartzog, Conger & Cason, 1983-90, Kimball, Wilson, Walker and Ferguson, 1990-93, Berry & Durland, 1993-94, Durland & Durland, 1994-96, White, Coffey, Galt & Fite, P.C., 1996-97, Phillips, McFall, McCaffrey, McVay & Murrah, P.C., 1997—; spl. counsel Okla. Mcpl. Power Authority, 1990-94, City of Altus, Okla., 1990—; mem. Gov.'s Ad Valorem Tax Structure and Sch. Fin. Commn., 1972-76; bd. dirs. Taxpayers Fedn. Ill., 1980-83; adv. bd. dirs. Southwestern Legal Found., 1985—; rsch. fellow Southwestern Legal Found., 1994—; adj. prof. ins. law Oklahoma City U. Coll. Law, 1985—, agy. and partnership law, U. Okla. Coll. Law, 1989—; Okla. State chmn. Nat. Inst. Mcpl. Law Officers, 1984-89; apptd. mem. Legis Task Force on Okla. Adminstrv. Code, 1987; founding mem. U. Okla. Assocs., 1980. Bd. dirs. Oklahoma County Legal Aid Soc., 1973—; trustee Oklahoma City Riverfront Redevel. Authority, 1997—. With U.S. Army, 1946-48, 1st lt., 51-53; lt. col. USAR. Fellow Am. Bar Found.; mem. ABA, Fed. Bar Assn. (v.p. Okla. Chpt. 1977—), Okla. Bar Assn., Okla. County Bar Assn., Chgo. Bar Assn., Am. Judicature Soc., Okla. Assn. Mcpl. Attys. (bd. dirs. 1984-89), Order of Coif, Phi Delta Phi, Sigma Phi Epsilon (dir.). Presbyterian. Clubs: Chicago, Oklahoma City Golf and Country, Sunset Ridge Country (Northfield, Ill.). Communications, Administrative and regulatory, Condemnation. Home: 8101 Glenwood Ave Oklahoma City OK 73114-1107

**ALLEN, ROBERT EUGENE BARTON,** lawyer; b. Bloomington, Ind., Mar. 16, 1940; s. Robert Eugene Barton and Berth R. A.; m. Cecelia Ward Dooley, Sept. 23, 1960 (div. 1971); children: Victoria, Elizabeth, Robert, Charles, Suzanne, William; m. Judith Elaine Hecht, May 27, 1979 (div. 1984); m. Suzanne Nickolson, Nov. 18, 1995. BS, Columbia U., 1962; LLB, Harvard U., 1965. Bar: Ariz. 1965, U.S. Dist. Ct. Ariz. 1965, U.S. Tax Ct., 1965, U.S. Supreme Ct. 1970, U.S. Ct. Customs and Patent Appeals 1971, U.S. Dist. Ct. D.C. 1972, U.S. Ct. Appeals (9th cir.) 1974, U.S. Ct. Appeals (10th, and D.C. cirs.) 1984, U.S. Dist. Ct. N.Mex., U.S. Dist. Ct. (no. dist.) Calif., U.S. Dist. Ct. (no. dist.) Tex. 1991, U.S. Ct. Appeals (fed. cir.) 1992, U.S. Dist. Ct. (ea. dist.) Wis. 1995. Ptnr., dir. Allen & Price, Phoenix; spl. asst. atty. gen. Ariz. Ct. Appeals, 1978, judge pro-tem, 1984, 92, 99; Nat. pres. Young Dems. Clubs Am., 1971-73, mem. exec. com. Dem. Nat. Com., 1972-73, Ariz. Gov.'s Kitchen Cabinet working on a wide range of state projects, bd. dirs. Phoenix Bapt. Hosp., 1981-83, Phoenix and Valley of the Sun Conv. and Visitors Bur., United Cerebral Palsy Ariz., 1984-89, Planned Parenthood of Cen. and No. Ariz., 1984-87, Internat. Coun. Ariz. Heart Inst. Found., 1998—, Cordell Hull Found. for Internat. Edn., 1996—, Ariz. Aviation Futures Task Force, chmn. Ariz. Airport Devel. Criteria Subcom., mem. Apache Junction Airport Rev. Com., Am. rep. exec. bd. Atlantic Alliance of Young Polit. Leaders, 1973-77, 77-80, trustee Am. Counsel of Young Polit. Leaders, 1971-76, 81-85, mem. Am. delegations to Germany, 1971, 72, 76, 79, USSR, 1971, 76, 88, France, 1974, 79, Belgium, 1974, 77, Can., 1974, Eng., 1975, 79, Norway, 1975, Denmark, 1976, Yugoslavia and Hungary, 1985, Am. observer European Parlimentary elections, Eng., France, Germany, Belgium, 1979, Moscow Congrssional, Journalist delegation, 1989, NAFTA Trade Conf., Mexico City, 1993, Atlantic Assembly, Copenhagen, 1993, Internat. Coun. Ariz. Heart Inst. Found., 1998—, trustee Environ. Health Found., 1994-97, Friends of Walnut Canyon, 1994-97, Cordell Hull Found. for Internat. Edn., 1996—, spkr. seminars and profl. assns. *Founder of the law firm Allen & Price, Allen practices in the areas of intellectual property and technology, health care, patent and trade secret litigation, antitrust and securities litigation, and general business and personal counseling. The firm of Allen & Price has been the subject of newspaper and magazine articles emphasizing the firm's use of technology to provide prompt and timely business representation at lower cost than the traditional large law firms.* Contbr. articles on comml. litigation to profl. jours. Mem. ABA, Ariz. Bar Assn., Maricopa County Bar Assn., N.Mex. State Bar, D.C. Bar Assn., Am. Judicature Soc., Fed. Bar Assn., Am. Arbitration Assn., Phi Beta Kappa, Harvard Club. Democrat. Episcopalian (lay reader). Intellectual property, Antitrust, General civil litigation. Office: Allen & Price 3131 E Camelback Rd Phoenix AZ 85016

**ALLEN, RUSSELL EARL,** lawyer; b. Petersburg, Va., Jan. 11, 1953; s. Earl L. and Opal R. A.; m. Patricia Sarah Glass, July 4, 1973; children: Jessica Kaitlyn, Flitcher Earl. BS in Sociology, Atlantic Christian Coll., 1975; JD, U. Richmond, 1988. Bar: Va. 1988, U.S. Dist. Ct. (ea. dist.) Va. 1988, U.S. Ct. Appeals (4th cir.) 1988, U.S. Bankruptcy Ct. 1988. Police officer Hopewell, Va., 1977-83, probation officer, 1983-85; atty. pvt. practice, Ashland, Va., 1988—. Mem. ABA, Va. State Bar Assn. Ashland Bar Assn. Mem. Christian Ch. Avocations: guitar, soccer, basketball, computers. Criminal, Family and matrimonial, Juvenile. Office: 112 Thompson St Ashland VA 23005-1512

**ALLEN, WILBUR COLEMAN,** lawyer; b. Victoria, Va., Apr. 30, 1925; s. George Edward and Mary Lee (Bridgforth) A.; m. Frances Brockenbrough Gayle, Sept. 16, 1950; children: Frances Gayle Allen Fitzgerald, Wilbur Coleman Jr., Robert Clayton, Edward Lefebvre, Courtney Bridgforth. BA, U. Va., 1947, JD, 1950. Bar: Va. 1949, D.C. 1954, U.S. Dist. Ct. (ea. and we. dists.) Va. 1951, U.S. Ct. Appeals 1950, U.S. Supreme Ct. 1954. Ptnr. Allen, Allen, Allen & Allen, Richmond, Va., 1950—, pres., 1969-90. Lt. (j.g.) USN, 1942-45, PTO. Sunday Sch. supt. All Saints Episc. Ch., Richmond, 1960-65, vestryman, 1964-68, 70-74, 80-83, sr. warden, 1967-68, chmn. stewardship com., 1980-81; bd. visitors Va. Commonwealth U., 1984-87, property com., 1984-85, audit com., 1984-85. Fellow Am. Coll. Trial Lawyers; mem. ABA, ATLA, Am. Judicature Soc., Va. State Bar, Va. Bar Assn. (chmn. spl. com. on professionalism 1990—), Va. State Bar Council, Va. Trial Lawyers Assn. (chmn. publicity com. 1968, chmn. spl. com. on ins. 1981), N.Y. State Trial Lawyers Assn., Richmond Bar Assn. (pres. 1979, outstanding contbn. award 1981), Country Club of Va., Rotary (pres. 1974-75, Rotarian of Yr. 1980). State civil litigation, Insurance, Personal injury. Home: 4803 Lockgreen Cir Richmond VA 23226-1746 Office: Allen Allen Allen & Allen 1809 Staples Mill Rd Richmond VA 23230-3515

**ALLEN, WILLIAM HAYES,** lawyer; b. Palo Alto, Calif., Oct. 19, 1926; s. Ben Shannon and Victoria Rose (French) A.; m. Joan Webster Emmett, July 16, 1950; children: Edwin Hayes, Neal French, William Kent. Student, Deep Springs Coll., 1942-44; BA with gt. distinction, Stanford U., 1948, LLB, 1956. Bar: D.C. 1958. Corr. AP, Fresno, Calif., 1948-49; newsman AP, Sacramento, 1950-53; law clk. to Chief Justice Earl Warren U.S. Supreme Ct., Washington, 1956-57; assoc. Covington & Burling, Washington, 1957-64, ptnr., 1964-92; ret., 1993—; acting. prof. Stanford U. Law Sch., 1979; adj. prof. Howard U. Law Sch., 1981-83; lectr. George Mason U. Law Sch., 1983-86; practitioner-in-residence Cornell U. Law Sch., 1992; vis. prof. Deep Springs Coll., 1996; chmn. jud. rev. com. Adminstrv. Conf. U.S., 1972-82, sr. conf. fellow, 1982-95; mem. steering com. Nat. Prison Project, 1975-93. Pres. Stanford Law Rev., vol. 8, 1955-56; contbr. articles to legal jours. Trustee Deep Springs Coll., 1984-92, chmn. bd. trustees, 1992; mem. Fair Housing Bd., Arlington County, Va., 1974-79. With U.S. Army, 1945-47. Mem. ABA (mem. coun. adminstrv. law sect. 1969-72, 79-81, chmn. 1982-83), D.C. Bar (chmn. legal ethics com. 1976-78), Am. Law Inst., Nat. Press Club, Am. Acad. of Appellate Practice, Order of Coif. Democrat. Mem. United Ch. of Christ. Administrative and regulatory, Federal civil litigation. Office: Covington & Burling 1201 Pennsylvania Ave NW PO Box 7566 Washington DC 20044-7566

**ALLEN, WILLIAM LEE,** lawyer; b. Duluth, Ga., Feb. 20, 1922; s. William Frederick and Lonnie Lee (Dodd) A.; widower; children: Mary Ellen McCarthy, Melody Anne Spruell. LLB, Drake U., 1952. Bar: Iowa 1952, Ga. 1953, Fla. 1960, U.S. Dist. Ct. (mid. dist.) Fla., U.S. Supreme Ct. Assoc. Mahoney, Hadlow et al, Jacksonville, Fla., 1960-64; asst. counsel City of Jacksonville, 1964-70, chief litig., 1970-89; assoc. Stratford Law Offices, Jacksonville, 1995—. Author: (with others) Florida Appellate Practice, 1977. Mem. charter rev. commn. City of Jacksonville, 1997—. Chief petty officer USN, 1940-48, lt. USNR, 1948-65. Mem. Iowa Bar Assn., Ga. Bar Assn., Fla. Bar Assn., Jacksonville Bar Assn. Democrat. Baptist. Avocations: languages, travel, country music. Condemnation, General civil litigation, Appellate. Home: 3138 Woodtop Dr Jacksonville FL 32277-2631 Office: Stratford Law Office 1301 Riverplace Blvd Ste 1638 Jacksonville FL 32207-9029

**ALLEN, WILLIAM RILEY,** lawyer; b. Coral Gables, Fla., Oct. 24, 1953; s. William George and Winnie (Woodall) A.; m. Mary Faith Ford, June 3, 1989. BA with honors, U. Cen. Fla., 1977; JD with honors, Fla. State U., 1981. Bar: Fla. 1982, U.S. Dist. Ct. (mid. dist.) Fla. 1982, U.S. Ct. Appeals (11th cir.) 1982, U.S. Ct. Appeals (4th cir.) 1988, U.S. Supreme Ct., 1992. With Pitts, Eubank & Ross, P.A., Orlando, 1981-85; prin. W. Riley Allen P.A., Orlando, 1985—. Author: Do Students Know Their Rights?, 1978, Bad Faith Litigation, 1984, Insurance Litigation in Florida, 1992. Recipient Am. Jurisprudence award in criminal law. Mem. ABA (tort and ins. practice com.), ATLA (sustaining, trial lawyer sect.), Fla. Bar Assn. (trial laywers sect.), Acad. Fla. Trial Lawyers (EAGLE, trial lawyers sect.), Orange County Bar Assn. (law and edn., lawyer advt. com., guardian ad litem coms. 1981—, award of excellence 1993, named Guardian Ad Litem of Yr. 1997), Def. Rsch. Inst., Am. Judicature Soc., Cen. Fla. Trial Lawyers (founding dir.), Phi Delta Phi. Republican. Anglican Catholic. Avocations: softball, water and snow skiing, basketball, tennis, running. Federal civil litigation, State civil litigation, Personal injury. Office: W Riley Allen PA 228 Annie St Orlando FL 32806-1208

**ALLEY, JOHN-EDWARD,** lawyer; b. El Dorado, Ark., Dec. 9, 1940; s. Granville Mason and Reyland (Stuppi) A.; m. Mary Elizabeth Conrad, Sept. 10, 1960 (div. 1970); 1 child, John-Edward Jr.; m. Ruth Rice, June 17, 1995. BSBA, U. Fla., 1962, JD, 1965; LLM in Labor Law, NYU, 1968. Bar: Fla. 1966, U.S. Dist. Ct. (so dist.) Fla. 1968, U.S. Supreme Ct. 1971, U.S. Ct. Appeals (5th cir.) 1972, U.S. Ct. Appeals (4th cir.) 1975, U.S. Ct. Appeals (D.C. cir.) 1975, U.S. Dist. Ct. (no. dist.) Fla. 1975, U.S. Ct. Appeals (11th cir.) 1981, U.S. Dist. Ct. (mid. dist.) Fla. 1984. Assoc. Clayton, Arnow, Duncan, Johnston, Clayton & Quincey, Gainesville, Fla., 1966-67, Bruckner & Greene, Miami, Fla., 1968; assoc., then ptnr. Paul & Thomson, Miami, 1969-74; ptnr. Alley & Alley, Chartered, Tampa, Fla., 1974-96, Alley and Alley/Ford & Harrison LLP, Tampa, 1996-98; with Ford & Harrison LLP, Tampa, 1999—; instr. U. Fla., Gainesville, 1965-66, asst. prof., 1966-67; adj. prof. Coll. Law, Stetson U., St. Petersburg, Fla., 1976-85; mem. faculty PTI Mgmt. Ctr., Houston, 1983-88. Contbr. articles to legal jours. Mem. Fla. Bus. Adv. Bd., Labor Lawyers Adv. Com., Coun. for Union-Free Environment. Named Leading Fla. Atty. Am. Rsch. Corp., 1996. Mem. ABA, Fla. Bar Assn. (vice chmn. continuing legal edn. com. 1984-86, 90-91, chmn. elect 1991-92, chmn. 1992-93, chmn. labor and employment law sect. 1973-74, Ralph A. Marsicano award 1988), Am. Arbitration Assn., Am. Employment Law Coun., Dade County Bar Assn., Miami City Club, Univ. Club. Avocations: flying, scuba diving, skiing, classic cars, boating. E-mail: JALLEY@FORDHARRISON.com. Labor, Libel, Federal civil litigation. Office: Ford & Harrison LLP 101 E Kennedy Blvd Ste 900 Tampa FL 33602-5133 also: 25 SE 2d Ave 516 Ingraham Bldg Miami FL 33131

**ALLEY, WAYNE EDWARD,** federal judge, retired army officer; b. Portland, Oreg., May 16, 1932; s. Leonard David and Hilda Myrtle (Blum) A.; m. Marie Winkelmann Dommer, Jan. 28, 1978; children: Elizabeth, David, John; stepchildren: Mark Dommer, Eric Dommer. A.B., Stanford U., 1952, J.D., 1957. Bar: Calif. 1957, Oreg. 1957, Okla. 1985. Ptnr. Williams & Alley, Portland, 1957-59; commd. officer JAGC, U.S. Army, advanced through grades to brig. gen., ret., 1981; dean Coll. Law, dir. Law Ctr. U. Okla., Norman, 1981-85; judge U.S. Dist. Ct. Western Dist. Okla., Oklahoma City, 1985—. Decorated D.S.M., Legion of Merit, Bronze Star. Mem. Fed. Bar Assn., Oreg. Bar Assn., Okla. Bar Assn., Order of Coif, Phi Beta Kappa. Office: US Dist Ct 3102 US Courthouse 200 NW 4th St Rm 1210 Oklahoma City OK 73102-3092

**ALLEYNE, JULIE SUDHIR,** lawyer; b. Hartford, Conn., Jan. 8, 1970; d. Sudhir Ashalal and Jyotsna Sudhir Shah; m. Richard L. Alleyne. BA, Drew U., 1992; JD, Syracuse U., 1995. Bar: Conn. 1995. Assoc. O'Brien, Shafner, Stuart, Kelly & Morris, Norwich, Conn., 1995-96; claim counsel Travelers Property Casualty Corp., Hartford, 1996—. Vice-chair bond com. United Way/Combined Health Appeal Campaign, 1997. Mem. ABA (ins. practices sect.), Conn. Bar Assn. (internat. law sect.). Republican. Jain. Avocations: tennis, fitness, Indian folk dance. Contracts commercial, General corporate, Insurance. Home: 122 Flagg Rd West Hartford CT 06117-2326 Office: Travelers Property Casualty One Tower Sq 3PB Hartford CT 06183-9063

**ALLGOOD, ROBERT LYNELL,** judge; b. Augusta, Ga., Feb. 3, 1954; s. Thomas Forrest Allgood Sr. and Edrie Lyle Ballard; m. Sylvia Terese Allgood, May 20, 1978; children: Sara Terese, Wilson Forrest. BA, U. S.C., 1974; JD, Emory U., 1978. Bar: Ga. 1978, S.C. 1979, U.S. Dist. Ct. (so. dist.) Ga. 1978, U.S. Dist. Ct. S.C. 1980, U.S. Dist. Ct. (no. dist.) Ga. 1980. Ptnr. Allgood & Childs, Augusta, 1978-88; ptnr., founding mem. Allgood & Daniel, Augusta, 1988-95; judge Superior Ct., State Ga., Augusta, 1995—; dir. Sports Performance Products Inc., Augusta, 1997—. Trustee Westminster Schs., Augusta, 1986-89. Baptist. Avocations: golfing, tennis, reading. Office: Superior Ct State GA 530 Greene St Rm 312 Augusta GA 30911-4421

**ALLISON, JAMES PURNEY,** lawyer; b. Paris, Tex., Jan. 16, 1947; s. Ardell and Billie Louise (Parker) A. BS, East Tex. State U., 1967, MS, 1968; JD, U. Tex., 1971. Bar: Tex., U.S. Dist. Ct., U.S. Ct. Appeals (5th and 11th cir.), U.S. Supreme Ct. County atty. Delta County, Cooper, Tex., 1972-79; asst. atty. gen. Atty. Gen., Austin, Tex., 1979-83; ptnr. Allison, Bass & Assocs., Austin, Tex., 1983—; gen. counsel County Judges & Commrs. Assn. Tex., Austin, 1983—. Bd. dirs. Tex. Low-Level Radio-active Waste Disposal Authority, Austin, 1985-91; mem. Indigent Health Adv. Com., Tex. Dept. Human Resources, Austin, 1987-94. Mem. Tex. Assn. Counties (hon. life). Avocations: golf, water skiing. General civil litigation, Legislative, Personal injury. Office: Allison & Assocs 208 W 14th St Austin TX 78701-1645

**ALLISON, JOHN ROBERT,** lawyer; b. San Antonio, Feb. 9, 1945; s. Lyle (stepfather) and Beatrice (Kaliner) Forehand; m. Rebecca M. Picard; 1 child, Katharine. BS, Stanford U., 1966; JD, U. Wash., 1969. Bar: Wash. 1969, D.C. 1973, Minn. 1994, U.S. Supreme Ct. 1973. Assoc. Garvey, Schubert & Barer, Seattle, 1969-73; ptnr., 1973-86; prin. Betts, Patterson & Mines, P.S., 1986-94; sr. counsel Minn. Mining & Mfg. Co., 1994—; lectr. bus. law Seattle U., 1970, U. Wash., 1970-73; judge pro tem, King County Superior Ct., 1983-94. Mem. ABA (vice chmn. toxic and hazardous substances and environ. law com. 1986-91, chair elect 1991-92, chair 1992-93), Minn. Bar Assn., Seattle-King County Bar Assn. (chmn. jud. evaln. polling com. 1982-83), Wash. State Bar Assn. (bd. bar examiners 1984-94), D.C. Bar Assn., Nat. Inst. Pollution Liability (co-chmn. 1988), Order of the Coif, Wash. Athletic (Seattle). State civil litigation, Federal civil litigation, Product liability. Office: Minn Mining & Mfg Co 3 M Ctr Saint Paul MN 55144-0001

**ALLISON, RICHARD CLARK,** judge; b. N.Y.C., July 10, 1924; s. Albert Fay and Anice (Clark) A.; m. Anne Elizabeth Johnston, Oct. 28, 1950; children: Anne Sidney, William Scott, Richard Clark. BA, U. Va., 1944, LLB, 1948. Bar: N.Y. 1948. Practiced in N.Y.C., 1948-52, 54-60; ptnr. Reid & Priest, 1961-87; mem. Iran-U.S. Claims Tribunal, The Hague, 1988—. With USNR, 1942-46. Fellow Southwestern Legal Found., Am. Bar Found. (life); mem. ABA (chmn. com. Latin Am. Law 1964-68, chmn. Internat. Law Sect. 1977, chmn. Nat. Inst. on Doing Bus. in Far East 1972, chmn. internat. legal exchange program 1981-85), Internat. Bar Assn. (chmn. 1986 Conf., ethics com. 1986-89), Société Internat. des Avocats, Inter-Am. Bar Assn., Am. Fgn. Law Assn., Am. Arbitration Assn. (nat. panel), Inst. for Transnational Arbitration, Am. Soc. Internat. Law, Coun. on Fgn. Rels., Assn. Bar City N.Y., Raven Soc., SAR, St. Andrew's Soc. N.Y., Manhasset Bay Yacht Club, Phi Beta Kappa, Omicron Delta Kappa, Pi Kappa Alpha, Phi Delta Phi. Republican. Episcopalian. Home: 224 Circle Dr Manhasset NY 11030-1123 Office: c/o Iran-US Claims Tribunal, Parkweg 13, 2585 JH The Hague The Netherlands

**ALLRED, GLORIA RACHEL,** lawyer; b. Phila., July 3, 1941; d. Morris and Stella Bloom; m. William Allred (div. Oct. 1987); 1 child, Lisa. BA, U. Pa., 1963; MA, NYU, 1966; JD, Loyola U., L.A., 1974; JD (hon.), U. West Los Angeles, 1981. Bar: Calif. 1975, U.S. Dist. Ct. (cen. dist.) Calif. 1975, U.S. Ct. Appeals (9th cir.) 1976, U.S. Supreme Ct. 1979. Ptnr. Allred, Maroko, Goldberg & Ribakoff (now Allred, Maroko & Goldberg), L.A., 1976—. Contbr. articles to profl. jours. Pres. Women's Equal Rights Legal Def. and Edn. Fund, L.A., 1978—, Women's Movement Inc., L.A. Recipient Commendation award L.A. Bd. Suprs., 1986, Mayor of L.A., 1986, Pub. Svc. award Nat. Assn. Fed. Investigators, 1986, Vol. Action award Pres. of U.S., 1986. Mem. ABA, Calif. Bar Assn., Nat. Assn. Women Lawyers, Calif. Women Lawyers Assn., Women Lawyers L.A. Assn., Friars (Beverly Hills, Calif.), Magic Castle Club (Hollywood, Calif.). Labor, Family and matrimonial, General corporate. Office: Allred Maroko & Goldberg 6300 Wilshire Blvd Ste 1500 Los Angeles CA 90048-5217*

**ALLRED, JOHN THOMPSON,** lawyer; b. Mt. Airy, N.C., June 6, 1929; s. Joe Henry and Irene (Thompson) A.; m. Helen Louise Landauer, Apr. 4, 1964; 1 child, John Thompson Jr. BS, U. N.C., 1951, JD with honors, 1959. Bar: N.C., U.S. Dist. Ct. (we., mid., and ea. dists.) N.C., U.S. Ct. Appeals (4th cir.), U.S. Supreme Ct. Assoc. Moore and Van Allen, Charlotte, N.C., 1959-64; from ptnr. to sr. ptnr. Moore and Van Allen, Charlotte, 1964-86; sr. ptnr. Petree Stockton and Robinson, Charlotte, 1986—; mem. N.C. Bd. Law Examiners, Raleigh, 1977-90, chmn., 1989-90. Editor: N.C. Law Rev., 1958-59. tchr. pub. speaking YMCA, Charlotte, 1964; exec. com. Thompson Children's Home, Charlotte, 1970-91; vestry Christ Episc. Ch., Charlotte, 1980. Lt. USNR, 1951-56. Fellow Am. Coll. Trial Lawyers, Am. Bar Found.; mem. Def. Rsch. Inst., ABA, N.C. Bar Assn. (patron), 4th Cir. Jud. Conf., 26th Jud. Dist. Bar Assn. (chmn. 1976). Democrat. Avocation: tennis. Antitrust, Federal civil litigation, Labor. Office: Petree Stockton and Robinson 3500 One First Union Ctr Charlotte NC 28202-6001

**ALLWOOD, JOSEPH CALVIN,** lawyer; b. Louisiana, Mo., July 26, 1963; s. James Calvin and Judyth W. Allwood; m. Kim Marie Cardelli, Mar. 7, 1998. BS in History, N.E. Mo. State U., 1985, BA in Polit. Sci., 1985; JD, U. Mo., 1992. Bar: Mo. 1992. Assoc. atty. Law Office of William W. Cheeseman, Troy, Mo., 1992-95; pvt. practice law Clarksville, Mo., 1996—. Republican. Mem. LDS Ch. Avocations: music, reading. E-mail: jallwood@big-river.net. Fax: 473-242-3738. Office: Ste A 410 S Second St Clarksville MO 63336

**ALM, STEVE,** prosecutor; m. Haunani Ho; 1 child. MEd, U. Oreg., 1979; JD, U. Pacific, 1983. Editor West Pub. Co., 1983-85; dep. prosecuting atty. City and County of Honolulu, 1985-87, line-dep., then felony team supr., 1987-90, dir. dist. and family ct. divsn., 1990-94; U.S. atty. for Hawaii U.S. Dept. Justice, Honolulu, 1994—; adj. prof. Richardson Sch. Law U. Hawaii. Mem. ABA (mem. gov. com. on crime), Hawaii State Bar Assn. (ex-officio mem. domestic violence coordinating coun., v.p. criminal justice and corrections sect.). Office: US Dept Justice Box 50183 300 Ala Moana Blvd Rm 6100 Honolulu HI 96850-6100*

**ALMAN, EMILY ARNOW,** lawyer, sociologist; b. N.Y.C., Jan. 20, 1922; d. Joseph Michael and Cecilia (Greenstone) Arnow; B.A., Hunter Coll., 1948; Ph.D., New Sch. for Social Research, 1963; J.D., Rutgers U., Newark, 1977; m. David Alman, Aug. 1, 1940; children: Michelle Alman Harrison, Jennifer Alman Michaels. Bar: N.J. 1978, U.S. Supreme Ct. 1987. Probation officer, N.Y.C., 1945-48; assoc. prof. sociology Douglass Coll. Rutgers U., Newark, 1960-86, prof. emeritus, 1986—; sr. ptnr. Alman & Michaels, Highland Park, N.J., 1978—. Candidate for mayor, City of East Brunswick, 1972; chmn. Concerned Citizens of East Brunswick, 1970-78; pres. bd. trustees Concerned Citizens Environ. Fund., East Brunswick, 1977-78. Mem. ABA (com. family law) N.J. Bar Assn. (bd. dirs. legal svcs), Middlesex County Bar Assn. (Ann. Aldona Appleton award women lawyers sect. 1990, Ann. Svc. to Families award 1993), Am. Sociol. Assn., Assn. Fed. Bar State of N.J., Assn. Trial Lawyers Am., Trial Lawyers Assn. Middlesex County, Law and Soc. Assn., Am. Judicature Soc., Nat. Assn. Women Lawyers, N.J. Assn. Women Lawyers, ACLU, AAUP, Women Helping Women. Author: Ride The Long Night, 1963; screenplay, The Ninety-First Day, 1963. Family and matrimonial, General civil litigation, Probate. Home: 611 S Park Ave Highland Park NJ 08904-2928

**ALMEIDA, VICTORIA MARTIN,** lawyer; b. Pawtucket, R.I., Oct. 9, 1951; d. Antonio Sanches And Lillian (Martin) A. BA, Salve Regina U., Newport, R.I., 1973; JD, Suffolk U., 1976. Bar: Mass. 1976, R.I. 1976, U.S. Dist. Ct. R.I. 1976, U.S. Ct. Appeals (1st cir.) Mass. 1984, U.S. Supreme Ct. 1987. Law clk. to sr. assoc. justice R.I. Supreme Ct., Providence, 1976; asst. legal counsel Gov. of R.I., Providence, 1977-82; assoc. Gunning, LaFazia & Gnys, Inc., Providence, 1980-87; ptnr. Adler Pollock & Sheehan, Inc., Providence, 1987—; v.p., gen. counsel Quantum Internat. Group, Inc., Providence, 1995—; mem. R.I. Parole Bd., Providence, 1984—. Mem. bd. trustees R.I. chpt. Nat. Multiple Sclerosis Soc., Cranston, 1989-91; mem. corp. Roger Williams Coll., Bristol, R.I., 1977—; chairperson, bd. trustees St. Mary Acad.-Bay View, East Providence, R.I., 1988—; mem. retirement fund for religious Roman Cath. Diocese of Providence, 1988—. Named Woman of Yr., Prince Henry Club, 1977; recipient Disting. Alumna award St. Mary Acad.-Bay View, 1982, appreciation award Am. Cancer Soc., 1979. Fellow R.I. Bar Found.; mem. R.I. Bar Assn. (pub. rels. com., ho. of dels., young lawyers clerkshop com. 1985—), Am. Arbitration Assn. (panel of arbitrators 1984—). Democrat. Avocations: tennis, horseback riding, reading.

**ALMON, RENEAU PEARSON,** state supreme court justice; b. Moulton, Ala., July 8, 1937; s. Nathaniel Lee and Mary (Johnson) A.; m. Deborah Pearson Preer, June 27, 1974; children by previous marriage: Jonathan, Jason, Nathaniel; 1 stepson: Tommy Preer. B.S., U. Ala., 1959; LL.B., Cumberland Sch. Law Samford U., 1964. Bar: Ala. 1964. Price analyst NASA; law clk. to justice Ala. Supreme Ct.; sole practice Moulton; judge 36th Jud. Circuit Ala., 1966-69, Ala. Ct. Criminal Appeals, 1969-75; justice Ala. Supreme Ct., Montgomery, 1974—. Served with U.S. Army. Named one of Outstanding Young Men in Am., 1971. Mem. ABA, Ala. Bar Assn., Lawrence County Bar Assn., Montgomery County Bar Assn., Kappa Alpha, Phi Alpha Delta, Omicron Delta Kappa. Methodist. Office: Ala Supreme Ct 300 Dexter Ave Montgomery AL 36104-3741*

**ALMOND, DAVID RANDOLPH,** lawyer, company executive; b. Richmond, Va., Mar. 8, 1940. BS, U. Va., 1962, LLB, 1967; postgrad. in Exec. Program, MIT, 1981. Assoc. Reid & Priest, N.Y.C., 1967-71; asst. gen. counsel Boise Cascade Corp., Idaho, 1971-77, assoc. gen. counsel and asst. sec., 1977-84; sr. v.p. Wilson Foods Corp., Oklahoma City, 1985-89; sr. v.p., gen. counsel, sec. Fleming Cos. Inc., Oklahoma City, 1989—. Fellow Am. Bar Found. (life); mem. ABA, Okla. Bar Assn., N.Y. State Bar Assa. Bar Assn. Office: Fleming Cos Inc 6301 Waterford Blvd Oklahoma City OK 73118-1198

**ALOE, PAUL HUBSCHMAN,** lawyer; b. Phila., Feb. 2, 1957; s. Paul Edward and Mary (Hubschman) Aloe; m. Barbara Petraglia, Aug. 12, 1984; children: Jessica, Ryan. BA with distinction, George Washington U., 1980; JD with distinction, Hofstra U., 1983. Bar: N.J. 1983, U.S. Dist. Ct. N.J. 1983, N.Y. 1984, U.S. Dist. Ct. so. and ea. dists.) N.Y. 1985, U.S. Ct. Appeals (2d cir.) 1990, U.S. Supreme Ct. 1991, U.S. Ct. Appeals (3d cir.) 1991, Pa. 1991, U.S. Dist. Ct. (no. dist.) N.Y. 1992; U.S. Dist. Ct. (ea. dist.) Pa. 1993. Law clk. N.Y. State Third Dept., Albany, 1983-84; ptnr. Rubin, Baum, Levin et al, N.Y.C., 1984—. Contbr. articles to profl. publs. Mem. ABA, N.Y. State Bar Assn. (chair com. on civil practice law and rules), Assn. Bar City N.Y. Mem. General practice, General civil litigation, Bankruptcy. Office: Rubin, Baum, Levin et al 30 Rockefeller Plz New York NY 10112-0002

**ALONSO, ANTONIO ENRIQUE,** lawyer; b. Havana, Cuba, Aug. 31, 1924; came to U.S., 1959; s. Enrique and Inocencia (Avila) A.; m. Daisy Ojeda, July 20, 1949; children: Margarita, Antonio, Enrique, Jorge. JD, U. Habana, Cuba, 1946; PhD, U. Habana, 1952; student, U. Fla., 1974-76. Bar: Fla. 1976. Pub. defendant High Ct. Las Villas, Cuba, 1946-49; atty. Provincial Gov., Cuba, 1950-52; under sec. Treasury, Cuba, 1952-54; mem. House of Reps. Congress of Cuba, 1954-58; prof. U. Jose Marti, 1952-58, Inst. Soc. Action, 1964-65; prof. modern lang. Coll. St. Teresa, 1968; sole practice Miami, 1976—; adj. prof. St. Mary's Coll., Minn., summers, 1968-73. Author: (with others) Violation of Human Rights in Cuba, 1962, History of the Communist Party of Cuba, 1970; weekly columnist on real estate and law Diario Las Ams. newspaper; contbr. articles to profl. jours. Recipient Field Svc. Program award Nat. Assn. Student Affairs, 1973. Mem. AAUP, Am. Assn. Tchrs. Spanish and Portuguese, Fla. Bar Assn. Republican. Roman Catholic. Real property, General corporate. Home: 1900 SW 12th Ave Miami FL 33129-2613 Office: 1699 Coral Way Ste 315 Miami FL 33145-2860

**ALONSO-ALONSO, RAFAEL,** judge. BA, LLB, U. P.R. Bar: P.R. 1964. Formerly judge U.S. Supreme Ct. P.R., San Juan; sr. counsel Reichard & Escalera Law Firm, San Juan, 1997—. Office: Reichard & Escalera Law Firm PO Box 36148 San Juan PR 00936-4148

**ALSOP, DONALD DOUGLAS,** federal judge; b. Duluth, Minn., Aug. 28, 1927; s. Robert Alvin and Mathilda (Aaseng) A.; m. Jean Lois Tweeten, Aug. 16, 1952; children: David, Marcia, Robert. BS, U. Minn., 1950, LLB, 1952. Bar: Minn. 1952. Pvt. practice New Ulm, Minn.; ptnr. Gislason, Alsop, Dosland & Hunter, 1954-75; judge U.S. Dist. Ct. Minn., St. Paul, 1975—, chief dist. judge, 1985-92, sr. dist. judge, 1992—; mem. 8th cir. jud. coun., 1987-92, Jud. Conf. Com. to Implement Criminal Justice Act, 1979-87; mem. exec. com. Nat. Conf. Fed. Trial Judges, 1990-94. Chmn. Brown County (Minn.) Republican Com., 1960-64, 2d Congl. Dist. Rep. Com., 1968-72, Brown County chpt. ARC, 1968-74. Served with AUS, 1945-46. Mem. 8th Cir. Dist. Judges Assn. (pres. 1982-84), New Ulm C. of C. (pres. 1974-75), Order of Coif. Office: US Dist Ct 754 Fed Bldg 316 Robert St N Saint Paul MN 55101-1495

**ALSTON, SHELDON GIVENS,** lawyer; b. Jackson, Miss., June 11, 1969; s. Alex Armstrong Jr. and Sarah Jane Alston; m. Cassandra Miles Phillips, June 11, 1994; children: Sheldon Givens Jr., Miles Phillips. BA in Polit. Sci., So. Meth. U., 1991; JD, U. Miss., 1994. Assoc. Alston Rutherford and Van Slyke, Jackson, Miss., 1994-97, Alston & Jones, Jackson, Miss., 1997—. Editor Miss. Lawyer. Session mem. Fondren Presbyn. Ch., Jackson; zoning com. mem. Fondren N. Renaissance, Jackson. Pres. award for Vol. Miss. Bar Assn., 1997. Mem. Young Lawyer Assn. (minority involvement com.). Avocations: children, soccer, chess. Home: 3921 Kings Hwy Jackson MS 39216-3328

**ALTEMOSE, MARK KENNETH,** lawyer; b. Easton, Pa., July 21, 1965; s. Richard and Constance Irene (Silfies) A.; m. Jennifer Lou Abram, Nov. 24, 1995; 1 child, Rachel Rebecca. BA in Econ., Lafayette Coll., 1987; JD, Villanova, 1990. Bar: Pa. 1990, N.J. 1990, U.S. Dist. Ct. N.J. 1991, U.S. Dist. Ct. (ea. dist.) Pa. 1991, U.S. Ct. Appeals (3rd cir.) 1991. Assoc. Korn, Kline & Kutner, Phila., 1990-91, Brown, Brown, Scott & Ferretti, Allentown, Pa., 1991-94, Knafo Law Offices, Allentown, Pa., 1994—; hearing com. mem. Disciplinary Bd. Supreme Ct. of Pa., Harrisburg, 1995—, chmn., 1999—. Mem. ATLA, Lehigh County Bar Assn. (co-chmn. Law Day, 1995—), Pa. Trial Lawyers Assn. (bd. govs. 1998—), Pa. Bar Assn., Northampton County Bar Assn. Democrat. Luth. Avocations: weightlifting, running, handball, golf. Personal injury, Product liability, Workers' compensation. Office: Knafo Law Offices 2202 Walbert Ave Allentown PA 18104-1439

**ALTER, ANDREW WILLIAM,** lawyer. BS, Yale Coll., 1983; JD, Harvard U., 1986. Assoc. Cravath, Swaine & Moore, 1986-89, Breed, Abbott & Morgan, 1989-90; dir. in counsel Salomon Brothers Inc., N.Y.C., 1990—. Office: Salomon-Smith Barney Inc 388 Greenwich St New York NY 10013-2339

**ALTER, ELEANOR BREITEL,** lawyer; b. N.Y.C., Nov. 10, 1938; d. Charles David and Jeanne (Hollander) Breitel; children: Richard B. Zabel, David B. Zabel. BA with honors, U. Mich., 1960; postgrad., Harvard U., 1960-61; LLB, Columbia U., 1964. Bar: N.Y. 1965. Atty., office of gen. counsel, ins. dept. State of N.Y., 1964-66; assoc. Miller & Carlson, N.Y.C., 1966-68, Marshall, Bratter, Greene, Allison & Tucker, N.Y.C., 1968-74; mem. firm Marshall, Bratter, Greene, Allison & Tucker, 1974-82, Rosenman & Colin, 1982-97, Kasowitz, Benson, Torres & Friedman, N.Y.C., 1997—; fellow U. Chgo. Law Sch., 1988; adj. prof. law NYU Sch. Law, 1983-87; vis. prof. law U. Chgo., 1990-91, 93; lectr. in field. Editorial bd.: N.Y. Law Jour. Contbr. articles to profl. jours. Trustee Lawyers' Fund for Client Protection of the State of N.Y., 1983—, chmn., 1985—; bd. visitors U. Chgo. Law Sch., 1984-87. Mem. Am. Law Inst., Am. Coll. Family Trial Lawyers, N.Y. State Bar Assn., Assn. of Bar of City of N.Y. (libr. com. 1978-80, com. on matrimonial law 1977-81, 87-88, judiciary com. 1981-84, 94, 95, 96, exec. com. 1988-92), Am. Acad. Matrimonial Lawyers. Family and matrimonial. Office: Kasowitz Benson Et Al 1301 Avenue Of The Americas New York NY 10019-6022

**ALTERMAN, LEONARD MAYER,** lawyer; b. Atlanta, Sept. 27, 1943; s. I. Michael and Evelyn (Blate) A.; m. Susan Diane Moss, Dec. 18, 1966; children: Andrew William, Karen Beth. Student, Emory U., 1961-62; BS, U. Fla., 1965, JD, 1967. Bar: Fla. 1968, U.S. Dist. Ct. (mid. dist.) Fla. 1969. Assoc. William R. Burwell, Gainesville, Fla., 1968, Matthews, Osborne and Ehrlich, Jacksonville, Fla., 1969-71; corp. counsel, corp. sect. Fidelity Mortgage Investors, Jacksonville, 1971-73; pvt. practice Jacksonville, 1974-77, 84—; corp. atty. Lifetime Communities, Inc., Jacksonville, 1977-84. Past mem. bd. dirs., past treas. Children's Home Soc.; past pres., trustee Greenwood Sch.; trustee Congregation Ahavath Chesed; active several community theater orgns., Jacksonville; bd. dirs. Aslan House, Inc., Jacksonville, 1992, Orange Park (Fla.) Community Theatre, 1991-92. With USAR, 1968-74. Mem. Fla. Bar Assn., Jacksonville Bar Assn. Avocations: acting, modeling, biking. General practice, Contracts commercial, General civil litigation. Office: Lifetime Communities, Inc. 9116 Cypress Green Dr Jacksonville FL 32256-1868

**ALTIERI, PETER LOUIS,** lawyer; b. Norwalk, Conn., Dec. 7, 1955; s. John L. and Eileen Mary (Rudden) A.; m. Sandra Shelton White, Sept. 3, 1983; children: Brianna Burr, John Shelton. AB, Georgetown U., 1977; JD, Fordham Sch. Law, 1980. Bar: N.Y. 1981, U.S. Dist. Ct. (so. dist., ea. dist.) N.Y. 1981, U.S. Dist. Ct. (no. dist. and we. dist.) N.Y. 1983, U.S. Dist. Ct. Conn. 1983, U.S. Supreme Ct. 1984, U.S. Ct. Appeals (2d. cir.) 1986, Conn. 1987. Law clk. to judge U.S. Dist. Ct., 1978; intern U.S. Attys. Office, N.Y.C., 1978; assoc. Law Firm Malcolm A. Hoffmann, N.Y.C., 1980-87; ptnr. Epstein, Becker & Green, N.Y.C., 1987—. Mem. ABA, Conn. Bar Assn. (exec. com. antitrust sect. 1988—), Assn. Bar City N.Y. (com. uniform state laws 1985-88, com. on inter-Am. affairs 1997—), The Patterson Club Conn., Union League Club N.Y.C. Antitrust, General civil litigation, Labor. Home: 140 Burr St Fairfield CT 06430-7105 Office: Epstein Becker & Green 250 Park Ave Ste 1201 New York NY 10177-0001

**ALTMAN, BARBARA JEAN FRIEDMAN,** lawyer; b. N.Y.C., Jan. 3, 1947; d. Herbert V. and Marion (Rosenfeld) Friedman; m. Ronald F. Altman, June 13, 1968; children: Andrew Edward, Lynn Alexandra. AB cum laude, Cornell U., 1968; JD, Georgetown U., 1977. Bar: Ill. 1977, U.S. Dist. Ct. (no. dist.) Ill. 1978, U.S. Ct. Appeals (7th cir.) 1978, U.S. Dist. Ct. (we. dist.) Wis. 1983; law clk. U.S. Dist. Ct. (no. dist.) Ill., Chgo., 1977-79; assoc. Hedlund, Hunter & Lynch, Chgo., 1979-83; asst. regional counsel, office of gen. counsel HHS, Chgo., 1983—. Contbr. articles to Georgetown U. Law Jour., 1976-77 (Named Articles Editor, 1976-77).

**ALTMAN, JANE R.,** lawyer; b. Cambridge, Mass., Mar. 14, 1945; d. Nathan and Renee (Owlick) Rotman; m. Robert A. Altman, June 13, 1965; children: Jennifer Anne, John Scott. BA, Barnard Coll., 1966; MS, Bank Street Coll., 1967; JD, Rutgers U., 1978. Bar: N.J. 1978. Assoc. Carchman, Sochor & Carchman, Princeton, N.J., 1978-82; pvt. practice Skillman, N.J., 1982-94; ptnr. Altman & Legband Attys.-at-Law, Skillman, N.J., 1994—; adj. prof. domestic rels. law Mercer C.C., West Windsor, N.J., 1986—; mem. family practice com. N.J. Supreme Ct., 1998—. Advisor Womanspace, Trenton, N.J., 1979—; trustee Millhill Child and Family Devel. Ctr., 1979-83. Mem. ABA, N.J. Bar Assn. (exec. com., family law sect.), Mercer County Bar Assn. (trustee 1983-88). Family and matrimonial. Office: Altman & Legband Attys at Law 148 Tamarack Cir Skillman NJ 08558-2021

**ALTMAN, LOUIS,** lawyer, author, educator; b. N.Y.C., Aug. 6, 1933; s. Benjamin and Jean (Zimmerman) A.; m. Sally J. Schlesinger, Dec. 26, 1955 (dec.); 1 child: Andrew; m. Eleanor Silver, Oct. 30, 1966; 1 child: Robert. AB, Cornell U., 1955; LLB, Harvard U., 1958. Bar: N.Y. 1959, Conn. 1970, Ill. 1973. Assoc. Amster & Levy, N.Y.C., 1958-60; patent atty. Sperry Rand, N.Y.C., 1960-63; chief patent counsel Gen. Time Corp., N.Y.C., 1963-67; ptnr. Altman & Reens, Stamford, Conn., 1967-72; chief patent counsel Baxter Labs, Deerfield, Ill., 1972-76; assoc. prof. John Marshall Law Sch., 1976-79, adj. prof., 1979-96; adj. prof. Loyola Law Sch., 1996-97; of counsel Gerlach, O'Brien & Kleinke, Chgo., 1981-83; ptnr. Laff, Whitesel & Saret, Chgo., 1983—. Author: Callmann on Unfair Competition, Trademarks & Monopolies, 4th edit., 1981, Business Competition Law Adviser, 1983; contbr. Construction Law, 1986, Legal Compliance Checkups, 1985, articles to legal jours. Recipient Gerald Rose Meml. award John Marshall Law Sch., 1988. E-mail: LALTMAN@IBM.net. Patent, Trademark and copyright, Intellectual property. Home: 3005 Manor Dr Northbrook IL 60062-6947 Office: Laff Whitesel & Saret 401 N Michigan Ave Chicago IL 60611-4255

**ALTMAN, WILLIAM KEAN,** lawyer; b. San Antonio, Feb. 18, 1944; s. Marion K. and Ruth (Nunnelee) A.; m. Doris E. Johnson, May 29, 1964; children: Brian, Brad, Blake. BBA, Tex. A&M U., 1965, MBA, 1967; JD, U. Tex., 1979. Bar: Tex. 1970, Okla. 1993, U.S. Dist. Ct. (no. and ea. dists.) Tex., U.S. Ct. Appeals (5th and 11th cirs.), U.S. Supreme Ct. Pres. Altman & Nix, Wichita Falls, Tex., 1970—. Mem. Wichita Falls City Coun., 1998—; bd. dirs. Beacon Ins. Group, 1997—. Mem. ABA, Tex. Bar Assn., Assn. Trial Lawyers Am. (life) (bd. of govs. 1980-83, active coms. and sects.), Tex. Trial Lawyers Assn. (assoc. bd. dirs. 1977-78, bd. dirs. 1978—, active various coms. and sect.). Democrat. Baptist. Personal injury, Insurance, Product liability. Office: Altman & Nix PO Box 500 Wichita Falls TX 76307-0500

**ALTON, JOHN MARSHALL,** lawyer; b. Columbus, Ohio, Mar. 14, 1952; s. Jack R. and Reba J. Alton; m. Peggy Jean Hindenach, Sept. 29, 1979; children: Jeffrey, Jay, Julie. BA, Duke U., 1974; JD, So. Meth. U., 1977. Bar: Ohio 1977, U.S. Dist. Ct. (so. dist.) Ohio 1978, U.S. Supreme Ct. 1988. Assoc. Lane, Alton & Horst, Columbus, 1977-81, ptnr., 1981-94; ptnr. Ray & Alton LLP, Columbus, 1994—. Contbr. articles to profl. jours. Bd. trustees Eastminster Presbyn. Ch., Columbus, Ohio, 1983-86; fundraiser Gahanna-Jefferson Schs., Gahanna, Ohio, 1992. Fellow Am. Bd. Trial Advocates, Nat. Bd. Trial Advocacy, Million Dollar Advocates Forum. Avocations: golf, tennis. Personal injury, Product liability, Professional liability. Office: Ray & Alton LLP Ste 350 175 S 3d St Columbus OH 43215

**ALTSCHUL, MICHAEL F.,** lawyer; b. N.Y.C., May 30, 1949; s. Selig Altschul and Barbara (Field) Roehm. BA, Colgate U., 1971; JD, NYU, 1975. Bar: Ill. 1975, N.Y. 1976, D.C. 1981, U.S. Dist. Ct. (so. dist.) N.Y. 1976, U.S. Dist. Ct. (ea. dist.) N.Y. 1976, U.S. Ct. Appeals (D.C. cir.) 1990, U.S. Supreme Ct. 1979. Assoc. Simpson Thacher & Bartlett, N.Y.C., 1975-80; trial atty. Antitrust div. Dept. Justice, Washington, 1980-90; v.p., gen. counsel Cellular Telecommunications Industry Assn., Washington, 1990—. Mem. Fed. Comm. Bar Assn. (past chmn. wireless practice com.). Antitrust, Communications, Federal civil litigation. Office: Cellular Telecom Ind Assn 1250 Connecticut Ave NW Ste 800 Washington DC 20036-2603

**ALTSCHULER, FREDRIC LAWRENCE,** lawyer; b. Yonkers, N.Y., Feb. 25, 1946; s. David and Doris A.; m. Marjorie R. Olderman, Mar. 9, 1969; children: David, Elizabeth. BA, Syracuse U., 1968; JD, St. John's U., 1972. Bar: N.Y. 1972. Assoc. Milbank Tweed Hadley & McCloy, N.Y.C., 1973-81; assoc. Breed Abbot and Morgan, N.Y.C., 1981-82, ptnr., 1982-87; ptnr. Spengler, Carlson, N.Y.C., 1987-92; of counsel Cadwalader, Wickersham & Taft, N.Y.C., 1992-96, ptnr., 1996—. Mem. ABA, Assn. Bar City N.Y., Urban Land Inst. Real property, Finance. Home: 40 E 80th St New York NY 10021-0237 Office: Cadwalader Wickersham & Taft 100 Maiden Ln New York NY 10038-4818

**ALTSULER, KENT,** lawyer; b. Houston, July 26, 1970; s. Arnold and Joan Altsuler; m. Kimberly Gorel. BA, Duke U., 1993; JD, U. Tex., 1997. Bar: Tex. Atty. Fulbright & Jaworski LLP, Houston. Fulbright scholar, Korea, 1994. General civil litigation. Office: Fulbright & Jaworski LLP 1301 Mckinney St Houston TX 77010-3031

**ALTWIES, JULIE NOREEN,** prosecutor; b. Tiffin, Ohio, Feb. 22, 1958; d. James Eugene and Mary Janet (Wurm) A. BA, U. N.Mex., 1981, JD, 1994. Bar: N.Mex. 1987. Sr. trial pros. atty. Dist. Atty.'s Office, Albuquerque, 1988—. Bd. dirs. Rape Crisis Ctr., Albuquerque, 1996-97. Democrat. Roman Catholic. Office: Dist Atty's Office 111 Union Square St SE Albuquerque NM 87102-3432

**ALVAREZ, ADOLFO, JR.,** lawyer; b. Harlingen, Tex., July 8, 1958; s. Adolfo and Guadelupe (Morales) A.; 1 child, Adolfo Cristobal. BBA, U. Tex., 1982, JD, 1983. Bar: Tex. 1984, U.S. Ct. Appeals (5th cir.) 1987, U.S. Ct. Mil. Appeals 1987, U.S. Supreme Ct. 1988, U.S. Dist. Ct. (so. dist.) Tex. 1991. Spl. asst. atty. U.S. Dept. Justice, Fort Polk, La., 1986-88; asst. atty. gen. State of Tex., Austin, 1988-90; pvt. practice McAllen, Tex. Capt., trial counsel, U.S. Army, 1984-88. Mem. Am. Legion. Roman Catholic. Avocations: golf, running. General civil litigation, Criminal, Family and matrimonial. Office: 4409 N Mccoll Rd Mcallen TX 78504-2464

**ALVAREZ-FARRÉ, EMILIO JOSÉ,** lawyer; b. Havana, Cuba, Sept. 5, 1956; s. Emilio Bonifacio Alvarez and Josefina Farré; m. Martha Isabel Ona, Oct. 1, 1966; children: Nicole Sofia, Natalia Isabel. Student, Yale U., 1974-75; AB, Stanford U., 1978; postgrad., Princeton U., 1979; JD, MBA, U. Chgo., 1986. Bar: Fla. 1986. Assoc. Schutts & Bowen, Miami, Fla., 1986-88; assoc. White & Case, N.Y.C., 1988-97, ptnr., 1998—. Mem. Fla. Bar Assn., Phi Beta Kappa. Christian. Finance, Private international, Mergers and acquisitions. Office: White & Case 200 S Biscayne Blvd Ste 4900 Miami FL 33131-2352

**ALVES, EMANUEL,** lawyer; b. Dakar, Senegal, Feb. 13, 1966; s. Sergio and Isaura Alves; m. Andrea Stoll, May 24, 1991; 1 child, Philip Samuel. BA, Brown U., 1988; JD, Boston U., 1993. Bar: U.S. Dist. Ct. Mass., U.S. Ct. Appeals (1st cir.) 1993. Litigation assoc. Brown, Rudnick, Freed & Gesmer, Boston, 1993-97; fin./credit analyst Bank of New Eng., Boston, 1988-90; assoc. counsel John Hancock Mut. Life Ins. Co., Boston, 1997—. Bd. dirs. Project Place Agy. for Homeless, Boston, 1997—. Avocations: reading, computers, time with son. Insurance, General civil litigation. Home: 42 Emerson Rd Milton MA 02186-5014 Office: John Hancock Mut Life Ins Co 200 Clarendon St Boston MA 02116-5021

**ALWORTH, CHARLES WESLEY,** lawyer, engineer; b. Buenos Aires, Aug. 23, 1943; s. Cecil Dwight and Kathleen Mary (Whitaker) A.; m. Sally Ann Wells, Dec. 21, 1967 (div. Nov. 1981); m. Madeline E. Wilson, Feb. 14, 1983; children: Cecil Dwight II, Barbara Diane. BSEE, U. Okla., 1965, M in Elec. Engring., 1967, PhD, 1969; JD, U. Tulsa, 1992. Bar: U.S. Patent Bar Office 1989, Tex. 1993, U.S. Dist. Ct. (ea. dist.) Tex. 1993; registered profl. engr., La., Okla., Tex. Tchg. asst. elec. engring. U. Okla., Norman, 1965, grad. asst. elec. engring., 1965-67, spl. instr. elec. engring., 1967-68; asst. prof. elec. engring. Tex. A&M U., College Station, Tex., 1968-74; chief, prin. cons. Conoco, Inc., Ponca City, Okla., 1974-90; rsch. assoc. profl. engr. U. Tulsa, Okla., 1990—; chief engr. Alworth Cons., Tyler, Tex., 1990—; of counsel Sefrna & Assocs., Tyler, 1993-95; prin. Charles W. Alworth Engr. & Atty. at Law; assoc. prof. and head elec. engring. U. Tex., Tyler, 1997-98. Patentee in field; contbr. articles to profl. jours. Mem. Phi Delta Phi, Tau Beta Pi, Eta Kappa Nu, Sigma Xi. Episcopalian. Avocations: aviation, woodworking, gardening. Patent, Trademark and copyright, Intellectual property. Home: 502 Cumberland Rd Tyler TX 75703-9324

**AMABILE, JOHN LOUIS,** lawyer; b. N.Y.C., Oct. 13, 1934; s. John A. and Rose (Singer) A.; m. Christina M. Leary, Nov. 23, 1963; children: Tracy Ann, John Christopher. BS cum laude, Coll. Holy Cross, 1956; LLB, St. John's Sch. Law, 1959. Bar: N.Y. 1959, U.S. Dist. Ct. (so. and ea. dists.) N.Y. 1961, U.S. Supreme Ct. 1964, U.S. Ct. Claims 1964, U.S. Ct. Appeals (2d cir.) 1970, U.S. Tax Ct. 1984, U.S. Ct. Appeals (9th cir.) 1984. Assoc. Law Office of Allen Taylor, N.Y.C., 1959-62; assoc. Schwartz & Frohlich, N.Y.C., 1963-69, ptnr., 1969; ptnr. Summit, Solomon & Feldesman (and predecessor firms), N.Y.C., 1971-93, Putney, Twombly Hall & Hirson, N.Y.C., 1993—; faculty mem. ann. seminar Practising Law Inst., 1987-91; mediator so. dist. U.S. Dist. Ct. N.Y., comml. divsn. Supreme Ct., N.Y.; arbitrator ea. dist. U.S. Dist. Ct., Bklyn.; panel chair appellate divsn. Disciplinary Com., 1980-85, 87-92; lectr. in field. Author: Responses to Complaints: Commercial Litigation in New York State Courts, 1995, Warranties: Business and Commercial Litigation in Federal Courts, 1998; editor St. John Law Rev. 1958-59. Regional commr. Am. Youth Soccer Orgn., Chappaqua, N.Y., 1975-84; mem. New Castle Recreation and Parks Commn., 1984-90, chairperson, 1987-89. Mem. ABA, N.Y. State Bar Assn., Assn. Bar City N.Y. (mem. com. on state legis. 1971-74, chair 1975-78, com. on grievances 1979-80, com. on women in cts. 1988-94, com. on judiciary 1989-92, interim mem. 1992, 93, 94, 96, 97, 98, 99, chair com. on gender bias in fed. cts. 1991-93, coun. judicial adminstrn. 1996—, com. on symposium 1997—, chair 1998—), Fed. Bar Coun., Practising Law Inst. (chair winning strategies for depositions in corp. litigation 1991-92, co-chair seminars on art of taking and defending depositions in corp. litigation 1982-85). Democrat. Roman Catholic. Federal civil litigation, State civil litigation. Home: 73 Westorchard Rd Chappaqua NY 10514-1003 Office: Putney Twombly Hall & Hirson 521 5th Ave Fl 10 New York NY 10175-0010

**AMADO, HONEY KESSLER,** lawyer; b. Bklyn., July 20, 1949; d. Bernard and Mildred Kessler; m. Ralph Albert Amado, Oct. 24, 1976; children: Jessica Reina, Micah Solomon, Gabrielle Beth. BA in Polit. Sci., Calif. State Coll., Long Beach, 1971; JD, Western State U., Fullerton, Calif., 1976. Bar: Calif. 1977, U.S. Dist. Ct. (ctrl. dist.) Calif. 1981, U.S. Ct. Appeals (9th cir.) 1981, U.S. Supreme Ct. 1994. Assoc. Law Offices of Jack M. Lasky, Beverly Hills, Calif., 1977-78; pvt. practice Beverly Hills, Calif., 1978—; lectr. in field. Contbr. articles to profl. jours.; mem. editl. bd. L.A. Lawyer mag., 1996—, articles coord., 1999—. Mem. Com. Concerned Lawyers for Soviet Jewry, 1979-90; nat. v.p. Jewish Nat. Fund, 1995-97; bd. dirs. Jewish Nat. Fund L.A., 1990—; sec. L.A. region, bd. dirs. , 1991-94, Am. Jewish Congress, Jewish Feminist Ctr., 1992-99, co-chair steering com., 1994-96; mem. Commn. on Soviet Jewry of Jewish Fedn. Coun. Greater L.A., 1977-83, chmn., 1979-81, commn. on edn., 1982-83, cmty. rels. com., 1979-83. Mem. Calif. Women Lawyers (bd. govs. 1988-90, 1st v.p. 1989-90, jud. evaluations co-chair 1988-90), San Fernando Valley Bar Assn. (family law mediators and arbitrators planel 1983-94, judge pro-tem panel 1987-94), Beverly Hills Bar Assn. (family law mediators panel 1985-94), L.A. County Bar Assn. (family law sect., appellate cts. com. 1987—, chmn. subcom. to examine reorgn. Calif. Supreme Ct. 1990-94, judge pro tem panel 1985-95, appellate jud. evaluations com. 1989—, editl. bd. L.A. Lawyer mag. 1996—, articles coord. 1999—, dist. 2 settlement program 1996—), Calif. State Bar, Calif. Ct. Appeal. Democrat. Jewish. General civil litigation, Appellate, Family and matrimonial. Office: 261 S Wetherly Dr Beverly Hills CA 90211-2515

**AMAN, ALFRED CHARLES, JR.,** dean; b. Rochester, N.Y., July 7, 1945; s. Alfred Charles, Sr. and Jeannette Mary (Czebatul) A.; m. Carol Jane Greenhouse, Sept. 23, 1976. AB, U. Rochester, 1967; JD, U. Chgo., 1970. Bar: D.C. 1971, Ga. 1972, N.Y. 1980. Law clk. U.S. Ct. Appeals, Atlanta, 1970-72; assoc. Sutherland, Asbill & Brennan, Atlanta, 1972-75, Washington, 1975-77; assoc. prof. Sch. Law, Cornell U., Ithaca, N.Y., 1977-82, prof. law, 1983-91, exec. dir. Internat. Legal Studies Program, 1988-90; prof. law, dean Sch. Law, Ind. U., Bloomington, 1991-99, dean, Roscoe C. O'Byrne chair in law, 1999—; cons. U.S. Adminstrv. Conf., Washington, 1978-80, 86—; trustee U. Rochester, 1980—; vis. fellow Wolfson Coll., Cambridge U., 1983-84, 90-91. Author: Energy and Natural Resources, 1983, Administrative Law in a Global Era, 1992, Administrative Law Treatise, 1992. Chmn. Ithaca Bd. Zoning Appeals, 1980-82. Mem. ABA, Am. Assn. Law Schs., D.C. Bar Assn., Ga. Bar Assn., N.Y. State Bar Assn., Phi Beta Kappa. Avocations: music; jazz drumming; piano; composition and arranging. Home: 3703 Chaudion Ct Bloomington IN 47401-4465 Office: Ind U Sch Law Third St and Indiana Ave Bloomington IN 47405

**AMAN, GEORGE MATTHIAS, III,** lawyer; b. Wayne, Pa., Mar. 2, 1930; s. George Matthias and Emily (Kalbach) A.; m. Ellen McMillan, June 20, 1959; children: James E., Catherine E., Peter T. A.B., Princeton U., 1952; LL.B., Harvard U., 1957. Bar: Pa. 1958. Assoc. Townsend Elliot & Munson, Phila., 1960-65; ptnr. Morgan Lewis & Bockius, Phila., 1965-93; of counsel High, Swartz, Roberts & Seidel, Norristown, Pa., 1993—. Commr. Radnor Twp., Pa., 1976-80, 86-92, planning commr., 1981-86; pres. bd. trustees Wayne Presbyn. Ch., Pa., 1981-84. Served to 1st lt. U.S. Army, 1952-54. Mem. ABA, Pa. Mcpl. Authorities Assn., Phila. Regional Mcpl. Fin. Officers Assn. (dir. 1983-87). Republican. Clubs: Merion Cricket (Haverford, Pa.); Princeton (Phila.) (dir 1977-79, treas. 1985-86). General corporate, Municipal (including bonds). Home: 246 Upland Way Wayne PA 19087-4859 Office: High Swartz Roberts Seidel 40 E Airy St Norristown PA 19401-4803

**AMANDES, CHRISTOPHER BRUCE,** lawyer; b. Seattle, Feb. 6, 1955; s. Richard Bruce and Joanne Vivien (Beran) A.; m. Katherine Joan Wildman, Nov. 17, 1990; children: Charlotte Beran Amandes, Grace Monroe Amandes. BA, Rice U., 1976, M of Environ. Engring., 1978; JD, UCLA, 1985. Bar: Tex. 1985, U.S. Dist. Ct. (so. dist.) Tex. 1988, U.S. Ct. Appeals (5th cir. 1988). Engr., project mgr. Espey Huston & Assocs., Houston, 1978-82; jud. clk. U.S. Ct. Appeals 5th Cir., Houston, 1985-86; assoc., ptnr. Vinson & Elkins L.L.P., Houston, 1986—. Author: Texas Environmental Law Handbook, 1997. Co-chmn. City of Houston Land Redevel. Com., Houston, 1996—. Mem. Air and Waste Mgmt. Assn. Environmental. Office: Vinson & Elkins LLP 1001 Fannin St Ste 3300 Houston TX 77002-6706

**AMANN, LESLIE KIEFER,** lawyer, educator; b. Pensacola, Fla., Dec. 21, 1955; d. Robert C. and Marilyn Joan (Franklin) A.; m. Colin B. Amann, Apr. 12, 1985; children: Augustus Kiefer, Nicholas Jacob. BMEd, S.W. Tex. State U., 1976; JD, U. Houston, 1987. Bar: Tex. 1987, U.S. Dist. Ct. (so. dist.) Tex. 1988, U.S. Ct. Appeals (5th cir.), 1991, U.S. Dist. Ct. (no. dist.) Tex. 1992. Legis. aide to Lindon Williams Tex. State Senate, Austin, 1977-81; tchr. The Lincoln Sch., Guadalajara, Mex., 1979-82; legal asst. Koons Rasor Fuller & McCurley, Dallas, 1983-84; clk., assoc., participating assoc. Reynolds, Allen, Cook, Reynolds & Cunningham, Houston, 1984-93; shareholder Cunningham & Amann, Houston, 1993-94; asst. gen. counsel Charter Bank, Houston, 1995-96; fiduciary counsel Nations Bank/Bank of Am., Houston, 1996—; adj. faculty Law Sch., U. Houston, 1988—. Contbr. articles to profl. jours. Mem. adv. bd. Probate and Trust Law Inst., South Tex. Coll. Law, Houston, 1998; vol. Annunciation Orthodox Sch., Houston, 1996—. Fellow Tex. Bar Found.; mem. Houston Bar Assn. (vol. lawyers in pub. schs. 1998), Tex. State Bar., Women Attys. in Tax and Probate. Republican. Methodist. Avocations: writing, reading, book collecting. Probate, General civil litigation, Estate planning. Office: Nations Bank/Bank of Am PO Box 2518 700 Louisiana 6th Fl Houston TX 77252-2518

**AMAR, VIKRAM DAVID,** law educator; b. Walnut Creek, Calif., Feb. 15, 1963; s. Arjan Dass and Kamla Devi (Chambra) A. AB, U. Calif., Berkeley, 1985; JD, Yale U., 1988. Bar: Calif. 1991. Law clk. to Hon. William Norris U.S. Ct. Appeals (9th cir.), L.A., 1988-89; law clk. to Hon. Harry Blackmun U.S. Supreme Ct., Washington, 1989-90; assoc. Gibson, Dunn & Crutcher, Sacramento, 1990-93; prof. law U. Calif., Davis, 1993-98, U. Calif. Hastings Coll. of Law, San Francisco, 1998—; cons. ACLU, L.A., 1996—. Home: 140 Cragmont Dr Walnut Creek CA 94598-2807 Office: U Calif Hastings Coll of Law 200 Mcallister St San Francisco CA 94102-4707

**AMARAL RYAN, ROSA OLINDA,** lawyer; b. Ovar, Portugal, Jan. 18, 1969; came to U.S., 1979; d. Jose and Albertina Amaral; m. John Joseph Ryan IV, July 9, 1993; 1 child, Anna Rebecca. BA, U. Pa., 1991; JD, Temple U., 1995. Bar: N.J. 1995, U.S. Dist. Ct. N.J. 1995, Pa. 1996, U.S. Dist. Ct. (ea. dist.) Pa. 1996. Paralegal Bernstein, Silver & Agins, Phila., 1991-96, assoc., 1996-97; claims counsel ECS Claims Adminstrn., Exton, Pa., 1997—. Mem. ABA, Phila. Bar Assn. Insurance, Professional liability, Personal injury. Office: ECS Claims Adminstrs Inc PO Box 688 600 Eagleview Blvd Exton PA 19341-1121

**AMATO, THERESA ANN,** lawyer; b. Chgo., Mar. 1, 1964; d. Joseph John and Rose Elizabeth (Argo) A. AB, Harvard U., 1986; JD, NYU, 1989. Bar: N.Y. 1990, D.C. 1991, Ill. 1993. Law clk. Hon. Robert W. Sweet U.S. Dist. Ct. (so. dist.) N.Y., N.Y.C., 1990-91; staff atty. Pub. Citizen Litg. Group, Washington, 1991-93; dir. Freedom of Info. Clearinghouse, exec. dir., founder Citizen Advocacy Ctr., Elmhurst, Ill., 1993—. Civil rights. Office: Citizen Advocacy Ctr 238 N York Rd Elmhurst IL 60126-2716

**AMBER, DOUGLAS GEORGE,** lawyer; b. East Chicago, Ind., Apr. 15, 1956; s. George and Margaret (Watson) A. BA in Polit. Sci., Ind. U., 1978; JD, U. Miami, 1985. Bar: Fla. 1985, US. Ct. Claims 1986, U.S. Ct. Internat. Trade 1986, U.S. Tax Ct. 1986, U.S. Ct. Appeals (11th cir.) 1986, U.S. Dist. Ct. (mid. and so. dists.) Fla. 1987, U.S. Ct. Mil. Appeals 1987, U.S. Ct. Appeals (fed. cir.) 1987, Ind. 1988, U.S. Dist. Ct. (no. and so. dists.) Ind. 1988, U.S. Ct. Appeals (7th cir.) 1989, U.S. Supreme Ct. 1989. Dep. prosecutor 31st Jud. Cir. Ind., Crown Point, 1988-93; pvt. practice Munster, 1993—; adj. prof. polit. sci. Purdue U., 1997—. Mem. exec. bd. dirs. Calumet coun. Boy Scouts Am., 1994-96. Mem. ABA, Acad. Legal Studies in Bus., Nat. Dist. Attys. Assn., South Lake County Bar Assn., Ind. State Bar Assn., Lake County Bar Assn. (bd. dirs. 1990-96), Ind. Trial Lawyers Assn., Audio Engring. Soc., Soc. Audio Cons. (cert. video and audio cons.), Mensa, Delta Theta Phi. Avocations: bicycling, weight training. E-mail: amber@axp.calumet.Purdue.edu. Office: Amber & Golding 9250 Columbia Ave Ste 2E Munster IN 46321-3530

**AMBER, LAURIE KAUFMAN,** lawyer; b. N.Y.C., Apr. 15, 1954; d. Martin and Barbara (Schiffman) Kaufman; m. Henry Michael Amber, June 18, 1977; children: Ian, Kyle. BS, Cornell U., 1974, MBA, 1975; JD, U. Miami, 1978. Bar: Fla. 1978, U.S. Dist. Ct. (so. dist.) Fla. 1978, U.S. Tax Ct. 1978, U.S. Ct. Appeals (5th cir.) 1979, U.S. Ct. Customs and Patent Appeals 1979, U.S. Customs Ct. 1979, U.S. Ct. Appeals (11th cir.) 1981, U.S. Ct. Internat. Trade 1981, U.S. Supreme Ct. 1982, U.S. Claims Ct. 1985; cert. civil circuit and family mediator Supreme Ct. Fla. Staff mgr. Proctor & Gamble Mfg. Co., Staten Island, N.Y., 1975; adj. asst. prof. Nova U., Fort Lauderdale, Fla., 1976-77; atty., labor arbitrator Amber & Amber, P.A., South Miami, Fla., 1978—; arbitrator nat. labor panel Am. Arbitration Assn., Miami, 1982—, Grievance Arbitration Panel of Fla. PERC, Tallahassee, 1979—; hearing examiner pers. appeals County of Dade, Miami, 1985-91; pres. Children's Cancer Fund, 1996—. Pres. Office Village Condominium Assn., South Miami, 1994, Children's Cancer Fund, 1996—. Named Woman of Yr. ABWA, 1983. Mem. ABA, Zonta (bd. dirs. Coral Gables, Fla. club 1988). Real property, Probate, General practice. Office: Amber & Amber PA 7731 SW 62nd Ave Ste 202 Miami FL 33143-4908

**AMBERG, STANLEY LOUIS,** lawyer; b. Phila., Oct. 2, 1934; s. Otto Philip and Florence (Bachrach) A.; m. Cynthia Fread, June 18, 1961; children: Stacy, Julie. BSChemE, Rensselaer Poly. Inst., 1956; MS, MIT, 1960; LLB, Harvard U., 1962. Bar: N.Y. 1963, U.S. Ct. Appeals (2d cir.) 1967, U.S. Supreme Ct. 1973. Ptnr. Davis Hoxie Faithfull & Hapgood, N.Y.C., 1962-95; counsel Oerrick, Herrington & Sutcliffe, N.Y.C., 1995—. Contbr. articles to profl. jours. Pres. Temple Beth El of No. Westchester, Chappaqua, N.Y., 1982-83. Lt. U.S. Navy, 1956-58. Mem. ABA, Am. Intellectual Property Law Assn., Assn. of the Bar of City of N.Y., Sigma Xi, Tau Beta Pi. Avocation: photography. Patent, Trademark and copyright, Trade.

**AMBRECHT, JOHN WARD,** lawyer; b. L.A., Jan. 25, 1944. BA in Zoology, UCLA, 1966, MBA, 1968; JD, Loyola U., 1973; LLM in Taxation, NYU, 1974. Bar: Calif. 1974, U.S. Dist. Ct. (ctrl. dist.) Calif. 1983, U.S. Ct. Claims 1986, U.S. Tax Ct. 1976, U.S. Ct. Appeals (9th cir.) 1978. Lawyer Hollister & Brace, Santa Barbara, Calif., 1974-80; pvt. practice Santa Barbara, Calif., 1980—; lectr. Masters in tax Golden Gate U. Law Sch., San Francisco, 1987-88; lectr. estate planning U. Calif., Santa Barbara Ext., 1983-87. Author (jour.) U. So. Calif. Tax Inst., Tax Planning, 1994; reporter: State Bar Calif., Estate Planning, Trust, Probate News, 1993; contbr. articles to profl. jours. Dir., sec. Santa Barbara Club, 1994—; mem. Carpinteria (Calif.) Edn. Found., 1993—; dir. Bishop Diego High Endowment Com., Santa Barbara, 1990-94, Las Contradas Girl Scouts, Santa Barbara, Santa Barbara Estate Planning Coun., 1989—, Santa Barbara City Coll. Found., 1994—; fund raiser Santa Barbara YMCA; pres., dir. Santa Barbara Ballet, 1983; coach Am. Youth Soccer Assn., Santa Barbara. Fellow Am. Coll. Trust and Estate Counsel; mem. Calif. State Bar (chair estate and gift tax sect. 1990-93, estate planning, trust and probate sect. 1994, exec. com. taxation sect. 1993—), Santa Barbara County Bar Assn. (chair tax sect. 1979-83). Estate planning, Probate, Estate taxation. Office: Ambrecht & Cummins LLP 7 W Figueroa St Fl 3D Santa Barbara CA 93101-3189

**AMBROSE, ARLEN S.,** lawyer; b. Pueblo, Colo., Sept. 29, 1937; s. Aubrey and Harriett (Hausman) A.; m. Janet Roseman, July 14, 1963 (div. Apr. 1979); children: David Alan, Judith Maryse; m. Ruth Lurie, July 31, 1988. BS in Bus. Adminstrn., U. Colo., 1959; JD, Georgetown U., 1962. Bar: Colo. 1962, U.S. Dist. Ct. Colo. 1962, U.S. Ct. Appeals (10th cir.) 1962, U.S. Supreme Ct. 1980. Clk. Senator John A. Carroll, Washington, 1959-62; law clk. to Judge William E. Doyle U.S. Dist. Ct. Colo., Denver, 1963-64; assoc. McNichols, Wallace, Nigro & Johnson, Denver, 1964-70, Hays & Thompson, Denver, 1970-73; ptnr. Hays, Patterson & Ambrose, Denver, 1974-78; clk. U.S. Ct. Appeals (10th cir.), Denver, 1979-81; ptnr., shareholder Ambrose Porter & Higgs P.C., Englewood, Colo., 1984-88; sole practitioner Englewood, 1988—; mem. Concerned Lawyers, Inc., Denver, 1978-85. Co-founder, officer, trustee Temple Sinai, Denver, 1967—; co-founder, pres., trustee Rocky Mountain Jewish Hist. Soc., Denver, 1976—; pres., trustee Denver Inst. Jewish Studies, 1984-89. Lt. USNR, 1973-77. Mem. Colo. Bar Assn. (com. on drugs and alcohol related problems 1978—), Arapahoe County Bar Assn., Rocky Mountain Stereo Photography Assn. (v.p. 1998—). Democrat. Jewish. Avocations: stereo photography, travel, genealogy, Colorado history, art. E-mail: Leaagle@aol.com. Real property, General corporate, Family and matrimonial. Home: 3076 S Saint Paul St Denver CO 80210-6761 Office: 3677 S Huron St Ste 105 Englewood CO 80110-3466

**AMBROSE, DONETTA W.,** federal judge; b. 1945. BA, Duquesne U., 1967, JD cum laude, 1970. Law clerk to Hon. Louis L. Manderino Commonwealth Ct. Pa., 1970-71, Supreme Ct. Pa., 1972; asst. atty. gen. Pa. Dept. Justice, 1972-74; pvt. practice atty. Ambrose & Ambrose, Kensington, Pa., 1974-81; asst. dist. atty. Westmoreland County, Pa., 1977-81; judge Ct. Common Pleas Westmoreland County, 1982-93, U.S. Dist. Ct. (we. dist.) Pa., Pitts., 1994—; resident advisor Duquesne U., 1967-70. Scholar Pa. Conf. State Trial Judges, 1992, State Justice Inst., 1993. Mem. ABA, Nat. Assn. Women Judges, Am. Judicature Soc., Pa. Bar Assn., Women's Bar Assn. Western Pa., Pa. Conf. State Trial Judges (sec. 1992-93), Westmoreland County Bar Assn., Italian Sons and Daus. Am., William Penn Fraternal Assn., New Kensington Women's Club, Delta Kappa Gamma. Office: 911 US Courthouse Office 700 Grant St Pittsburgh PA 15219-1906

**AMBROSE, MYLES JOSEPH,** lawyer; b. N.Y.C., July 21, 1926; s Arthur P.. and Ann (Campbell) A.; m. Elaine Miller, June 26, 1948 (dec. Sept. 1975); children: Myles Joseph, Kathleen Anne, Kevin Arthur, Elise Mary, Nora Jeanne, Christopher Miller; m. Lorraine Genovese, June 3, 1994. Grad., New Hampton Sch., N.H., 1944; BBA, Manhattan Coll., 1948, LLD (hon.), 1972; JD, N.Y. Law Sch., 1952. Bar: N.Y. 1952, U.S. Supreme Ct. 1969, D.C. 1973, U.S. Ct. Appeals (fed. cir.) 1970, U.S. Ct. Internat. Trade 1970, D.C. Ct. Appeals 1973. Pers. mgr. Devenco, Inc., 1948-49, 51-54; adminstrv. asst. U.S. atty. So. dist., N.Y., 1954-57; instr. econs. and indsl. rels. Manhattan Coll., 1955-57; asst. to sec. U.S. Treasury, 1957-60; exec. dir. Waterfront Commn. of N.Y. Harbor, 1960-63; pvt. practice law N.Y.C., 1963-69; chief counsel N.Y. State Joint Legislative Com. for Study Alcoholic Beverage Control Law, 1963-65; U.S. commr. customs Washington, 1969-72, spl. cons. to Pres., spl. asst. atty. gen., 1972-73; ptnr. Spear & Hill, 1973-75, Ambrose & Casselman, P.C., 1975-79, O'Connor & Hannan, Washington, 1980-88, Ross and Hardies, Washington, 1988-98; of counsel Arter & Hadden, Washington, 1998—, 1998—; U.S. observer 13th session UN Commn. on Narcotics, Geneva, Switzerland, 1958; chmn. U.S. del. 27th Gen. Assembly, Internat. Criminal Police Orgn., London, 1958, 28th Extraordinary Gen. Assembly, Paris, 1959; U.S. observer 29th Gen. Assembly, Washington, 1960; mem. U.S. del., Mexico City, 1969, Brussels, 1970, Ottawa, 1971, Frankfurt, 1972; chmn. U.S.-Mexico Conf. on Narcotics, Washington, 1960, mem. confs., Washington and; Mexico City, 1969, 70, 71, 72; chmn. U.S.-Canadian-Mexican Conf. on Customs Procedures, San Clemente, Calif., 1970; chmn. U.S. del. Customs Cooperation Coun., Brussels, 1970; chmn., Vienna, 1971, U.S.-European Customs Conf. Narcotics, Paris and; Vienna, 1971; organized drug enforcement DEA, 1973; hon. consul Principality of Monaco, Washington, 1973-98; mem. adv. com. on customs comml. ops. U.S. Treasury Dept., 1988-91; founding organizer Drug Enforcement Adminstrv. Dept. Justice; past chmn. ABA standing com. on customs law. Author: Primer on Customs Law. Bd. dirs. U. Coll. of Dublin-Grad. Bus. Sch., 1996—, Daytop Village; vice chmn. Reagan-Bush Inaugural Com., 1980; mem. adv. bd. Eisenhower Inst. of World Affairs. Decorated Chevalier Ordre Grimaldi, 1999; recipient Presdl. Mgmt. Improvement certificate Pres. Nixon, 1970, Sec. Treasury Exceptional Service award, 1970; decorated knight comdr. Order Merit Italian Republic, 1974; recipient Distinguished Alumnus award N.Y. Law Sch., 1973, Alumni award for pub. service Manhattan Coll., 1972. Fellow Am. Bar Found.; mem. ABA (past chmn. standing com. on customs law), Friendly Sons of St. Patrick, Alpha Sigma Beta, Phi Alpha Delta (hon.). Republican. Roman Catholic. Clubs: Metropolitan (N.Y.C.); University (Washington). Criminal, Immigration, naturalization, and customs, Federal civil litigation. Home: 19385 Cypress Ridge Ter Lansdowne VA 20176-5162 Office: Arter & Hadden 1801 K St NW Washington DC 20006-1301

**AMBROSIO, MICHAEL ANGELO,** judge; b. N.Y.C., Apr. 23, 1945; s. Vincent and Margaret (Carrillo) A.; m. Regina Maria Neal, Sept. 11, 1983. BA, Fordham U., 1966; JD, Harvard U., 1969. Bar: N.Y. 1970. Atty. N.Y. State Mental Hygiene Legal Svc., N.Y.C., 1969-72; atty. grievance com. Assn. of Bar City, N.Y.C., 1972-74; atty. Corp. Counsel N.Y.C., 1974-75; dep. dir. N.Y. State Mental Hygiene Legal Svc., N.Y.C., 1975-83; judge N.Y.C. Family Ct., 1983—; acting justice N.Y. Supreme Ct., 1986—. Mem. Assn. Bar City N.Y., Phi Beta Kappa. Avocations: classical music, reading, swimming. Office: Supreme Ct Kings County 120 Schermerhorn St Brooklyn NY 11201-5108

**AMDAHL, DOUGLAS KENNETH,** retired state supreme court justice; b. Mabel, Minn., Jan. 23, 1919. B.B.A., U. Minn., 1945; J.D. summa cum laude, William Mitchell Coll. Law, 1951, L.L.D. (hon.), 1987. Bar: Minn. 1951, Fed. Dist. Ct. 1952. Ptnr. Amdahl & Scott, Mpls., 1951-55; asst. county atty. Hennepin County, Minn., 1955-61; judge Mcpl. Ct., Mpls., 1961-62, Dist. Ct. 4th Dist., Minn., 1962-80; chief judge Dist. Ct. 4th Dist., 1973-75; assoc. justice Minn. Supreme Ct., 1980-81, chief justice, 1981-89; of counsel Rider, Bennett, Egan & Arundel, Mpls., 1989—; asst. registrar, then registrar Mpls. Coll. Law, 1951-65; moot ct. instr. U. Minn.; faculty mem. and advisor Nat. Coll. State Judiciary; mem. Nat. Bd. Trial Advocacy; chmn. Nat. Ctr. for State Cts. Delay Reduction Adv. Com., 1986-88, Nat. Ctr. for State Cts. Coordinating Coun. on Life-Sustaining Decisionmaking by the Cts., 1989-93. Mem. ABA (chmn. com. on stds. of jud. adminstrn. 1987-96), Minn. Bar Assn., Hennepin County Bar Assn., Internat. Acad. Trial Judges, State Dist. Ct. Judges Assn. (pres. 1976-77), Conf. of Chief Judges (bd. dirs. 1987-88), Delta Theta Phi (assoc. justice supreme ct.). Home: 2322 W 53rd St Minneapolis MN 55410-2501

**AMDAHL, FAITH A.,** lawyer; b. Mpls., Aug. 27, 1961; d. Douglas K. and Phyllis J. Amdahl. BA, St. Olaf Coll., 1983; JD, William Mitchell Coll., 1991. Marshal Minn. Supreme Ct., St. Paul, 1988-92; staff atty. State of Minn., Hon. Smith F. Eggleston, Stillwater, Minn., 1992-97; assoc. McCullough, Smith, Wright and Kempe, P.A., St. Paul, 1997—. Sec., bd. mem. at large Carriage Hills Condo Assn., Eagan, Minn., 1992-98; mental illness task force Mt. Olivet Luth. Ch., Mpls., 1995—. Mem. Douglas K. Amdahl Inn of Ct., Minn. Women Lawyers, Minn. State Bar Assn., Minn. Trial Lawyers Assn. Avocations: fishing, skiing, singing, painting/drawing, reading. Family and matrimonial, Personal injury, Labor. Office: McCullough Smith Wright & Kempe PA 905 Parkway Dr Saint Paul MN 55106-1036

**AMDUR, ARTHUR R.,** lawyer; b. Houston, Jan. 19, 1946; s. Paul S. and Florence Amdur; m. Dora B.; children—Josh, Jonny, Shira. B.A., 1967; J.D., 1970; LL.M., 1974. Bar: Tex. 1970, D.C. 1974; cert. immigration law Tex. Bd. Legal Specialization, 1988 . pvt. practice, Houston and Washington, 1970-76; asst. U.S. atty, Houston, 1976-82; pvt. practice, Houston, 1982—; adj. prof. law South Tex. Coll. Law, Houston. Bd. dirs. YMCA Internat. Refugee Ctr., 1985—; spl. asst. to gen. counsel Republican Nat. Com., Washington, 1974. Named Adj. Law Prof. of Yr., South Tex. Coll. Law, 1983. Mem. Fed. Bar Assn. (pres. 1981), Tex. State Bar Assn., Am. Immigration Lawyers Assn., Immigration Law Examiner, State Bar Tex. (bd. legal specialization 1997—). Jewish. Club: Georgetown U. Alumni (pres. 1984) (Houston). Immigration, naturalization, and customs, Private international, Federal civil litigation. Office: Amdur & Amdur 6161 Savoy Dr Ste 450 Houston TX 77036-3379

**AMDUR, MARTIN BENNETT,** lawyer; b. N.Y.C., Aug. 19, 1942; s. Charles and Helen (Freedman) A.; m. Shirley Bell, May 25, 1975; children—Richard J., Stephen B. A.B., Cornell U., 1964; LL.B., Yale U., 1967; LL.M. in Taxation, NYU, 1968. Bar: N.Y. 1968, U.S. Tax Ct. 1970, U.S. Dist. Ct. (so. and ea. dists.) N.Y. 1971. With Weil, Gotshal & Manges LLP, N.Y.C., 1968—, ptnr., 1975—. Mem. ABA (sect. on taxation), N.Y. State Bar Assn. (taxation sect.), Assn. of Bar of City of N.Y., Am. Coll. Tax Counsel. Corporate taxation, Personal income taxation. Home: 17 Willow Ln Scarsdale NY 10583-3411 Office: Weil Gotshal & Manges LLP 767 5th Ave Fl Concl New York NY 10153-0119

**AMENT, MARK STEVEN,** lawyer; b. Louisville, Sept. 4, 1951; s. Milton and Bernice (Rosenberg) A.; m. Elaine Sue Winkler, Dec. 28, 1976; children: Aaron Samuel, Rachel Lynn. BA, Northwestern U., 1973; JD, Duke U., 1976; LLM in Taxation, U. Miami, 1977. Bar: Ky. 1976, Fla. 1977. Assoc. Greenebaum Doll & McDonald, Louisville, 1977-82, ptnr., 1982-95; mem. Greenebaum Doll & McDonald PLLC, Louisville, 1995—; bd. dirs., sec. Evans Furniture Co., Louisville; lectr. continuing legal edn. seminars, 1978—. Commr., City of Robinswood, Ky., 1986—; mem. Louisville Mayor's Task Force on Low-Income Housing, 1987; v.p. Ctrl. Agy. for Jewish Edn., 1991-94; bd. trustees Congregation Adath Jeshurun, 1995-98. Mem. ABA (com. on comml. fin. svcs.), Ky. Bar Assn., Louisville Bar Assn., Fla. Bar Assn., Am. Health Lawyers Assn., Thoroughbred Owners and Breeders Assn., Jewish Edn. Assn. Louisville (v.p. 1991). Democrat. Avocations: basketball, thoroughbreds. Health, Mergers and acquisitions, Real property. Office: Greenebaum Doll & McDonald 3300 National City Tower Louisville KY 40202

**AMES, EDWARD JAY,** lawyer, public defender; b. Racine, Wis., May 18, 1960; s. Edward James and Patricia Rae Ames; m. Pamela Kim Nutt, Aug. 14, 1982; children: Erica Jaye, Michael William. AA, Spokane (Wash.) Falls C.C., 1983; BA, Ea. Wash. U., 1985; JD, U. Oreg., 1988. Bar: Wash. 1990. Case aide Big Bros. and Sisters Spokane, 1983-85; asst. editor Oreg. Lawyer U. Oreg. Sch. Law, Eugene, 1986-89; legal intern Whatcom County Pub. Defender, Bellingham, Wash., 1989-90; asst. pub. defender Spokane County Pub. Defender, 1990—. Active Spokane County Domestic Violence Consortium, 1993—, past com. chmn. With USN, 1977-80. Mem. Wash. State Bar Assn., Spokane County Bar Assn. (appellate liaison com. 1996—), Psi Chi. Republican. Lutheran. Avocations: automobile racing, fishing. Office: Spokane County Pub Defender W1033 Gardner Ave Spokane WA 99260-0001

**AMES, JOHN LEWIS,** lawyer; b. Norfolk, Va., July 15, 1912; s. Harry Lee and Catherine I. (Betty) A.; m. Margaret Kilbon, Apr. 8, 1939 (dec. Sept. 1996); children: Margaret Lee, John Lewis. AB, Randolph-Macon Coll., 1933; JD, U. Richmond, 1937; postgrad., NYU, 1939-40. Bar: Va. 1936, N.Y. 1940. Mem. tax div. Home Life Ins. Co., N.Y.C., 1937-38; trial atty. Tanner, Sillocks & Friend, N.Y.C., 1938-41; house counsel Ruthrauff & Ryan, Inc., N.Y.C., 1941-42, house counsel and asst. to pres., 1945-48, sec., counsel, 1948-50, v.p., sec., 1950-55, v.p., sec., treas., 1955-57, also dir.; v.p., sec. Erwin, Wassey, Ruthrauff & Ryan, Inc., 1957-59; asst. dir. bus. affairs CBS TV Network, Inc., N.Y.C., 1959-62; v.p., sec. treas. Kudner Agy., Inc., 1962-65, also dir.; sr. v.p. adminstrn. and fin. West, Weir & Bartel, Inc., N.Y.C., 1966, exec. v.p., dir., until 1968; v.p., sec. Lennen & Newell, Inc., 1968-73; v.p. bus. and legal affairs Dancer-Fitzgerald-Sample, Inc., 1973-83, legal cons. Saatchi & Saatchi DFS Inc., 1983-96; dir. Carroll Products, Inc.; spl. agt. FBI, Washington and N.Y.C., 1942-45; spl. dep. atty. gen. N.Y. State, 1946-48; mem. Nassau County N.Y. Crime Commn., 1973-83. Trustee, Randolph-Macon Coll., 1955-85, trustee emeritus, 1985—. Mem. Massapequa Bd. Edn., 1952-79, pres., 1957-78; past pres. Nassau-Suffolk Sch. Bds. Assn. Past chmn. trustees Am. Assn. Advt. Agencies Group Ins; trustee, pres. men's club, chmn. adminstrv. bd. White Stone AM Ch. Mem. N.Y. County Lawyers Assn., Am. Arbitration Assn. (mem. nat. panel), Soc. Former Spl. Agts. FBI (past nat. sec.), Alumni Soc. Randolph-Macon Coll. (past pres.), Lancaster County Crime Solvers, Inc. (pres. 1991-94), Indian Creek Yacht and Country Club, Windmill Point Yacht Club, Phi Kappa Sigma, Omicron Delta Kappa, Tau Kappa Alpha. Methodist. Entertainment, General corporate. Home: PO Box 727 White Stone VA 22578-0727 Office: 375 Hudson St New York NY 10014-3658

**AMES, MARC L.,** lawyer; b. Bklyn., Mar. 14, 1943; s. Arthur L. and Ray (Sardas) A.; m. Eileen Moll, July 12, 1970. JD, Bklyn. Law Sch., 1967; LLM, NYU, 1968. Bar: N.Y. 1967, U.S. Dist. Ct. (ea. and so. dist.) N.Y. 1973, U.S. Ct. Appeals (2nd cir.) 1973, U.S. Supreme Ct. 1973, U.S. Ct. Appeals (3d cir.) 1982, Pa. 1988; lic. radio amateur. Mem. faculty L.I. U., 1968-69, N.Y.C. Community Coll., 1969-70; pvt. practice, 1967—; arbitrator U.S. Dist. Ct. (ea. dist.) N.Y. 1986—, small claims divsn. N.Y.C. Civil Ct., N.Y.C. Civil Ct.; cons. disability retirement and pensions; arbitrator Am. Arbitration Assn.; bd. dirs. Internat. Comms. Concepts, Inc. Contbr. articles to profl. jours.; patentee bridge for billiards, storage materials for sport card collections, auto mirror. Recipient cert. appreciation N.Y. State Trial Lawyers, commendation for disting. svc. as arbitrator. Mem. N.Y. State Trial Lawyers Assn., N.Y. County Lawyers, N.Y. State Bar Assn., Electronic Technol. Soc. N.J. Inc. E-mail: BaseEsq1@aol.com. Labor, Administrative and regulatory, Civil rights. Office: PO Box 272 Pluckemin NJ 07978-0272

**AMESTOY, JEFFREY LEE,** state supreme court chief justice; b. Rutland, Vt., July 24, 1946; s. William Joseph and Diana (Wood) A.; m. Susan Claire Lonergan, May 24, 1980; children: Katherine Leigh, Christina Elizabeth, Nancy Claire. BA, Hobart Coll., 1968; JD, U. Calif., San Francisco, 1972; MPA, Harvard U., 1982; D of Pub. Adminstrn. (hon.), Norwich U., 1994. Bar: Vt. 1973, U.S. Dist. Ct. Vt. 1973. Assoc. Mahady & Klevana, Windsor, Vt., 1973-74; legal counsel Gov.'s Justice Commn., Montpelier, Vt., 1974-77; asst. atty. gen., chief of Medicaid fraud div. State of Vt., Montpelier, 1978-81, commr. labor and industry, 1982-84, atty. gen., 1985-97; chief justice Supreme Ct. Vt., 1997—; pres. Nat. Assn. of Attys. Gen., 1992-98. Trustee Thomas Waterman Wood Gallery, Montpelier, 1986-92. With USAR, 1968-74. Mem. Vt. Bar Assn., Kennedy Sch. Govt. Harvard U. Alumni Exec. Coun., Conf. Chief Justices. Republican. Congregationalist. Home: 503 Loomis Hill Rd Waterbury Center VT 05677-8280

**AMHOWITZ, HARRIS J.,** lawyer, educator; b. N.Y.C., Mar. 19, 1934; s. Samuel and Ruth Amhowitz; m. Melanie Leigh Gale; children: Jennifer Ann, Joshua Seth. AB, Brown U., 1955; LLB, Harvard U., 1961. Bar: N.Y. 1961, U.S. Supreme Ct. 1967. Law clk. to judge U.S. Dist. Ct. N.Y., 1961-63; assoc. Hughes Hubbard & Reed, N.Y.C., 1963-69; gen. counsel Coopers & Lybrand, N.Y.C., 1970-96, dep. chmn., 1991-95, mem. internat. exec. com., 1991-95; of counsel Hughes Hubbard & Reed, 1996—; bd. dirs. ML (Bermuda) Ltd.; adj. prof. NYU Sch. Law, 1975-83; receiver, spl. master U.S. Dist. Ct., 1963-70; pres. bd. dirs. Prosher Group, Ltd., 1970-71; trustee Citizens Budget Commn., Inc., 1983-97. Mem. Assn. Bar City N.Y. (spl. com. on lawyers' role in securities transactions 1975-77, com. profl. and jud. ethics 1983-86, com. profl. discipline 1987-91), Harmonie Club. General corporate. Home: 12600 E Fort Lowell Rd Tucson AZ 85749-9614 Office: Hughes Hubbard & Reed One Battery Park Plz New York NY 10004

**AMICK, STEVEN HAMMOND,** senator, lawyer; b. Ithaca, N.Y., May 13, 1947; s. Arthur Hammond and Marolyn Dee (Hollingshead) A.; m. Helen Louise Masten, Aug. 9, 1969. BA, Washington Coll., 1969; JD, Dickinson Sch. of Law, 1972. Bar: Del. 1972, U.S. Dist. Ct. Del. 1973. Assoc. Daley & Lewis, Wilmington, Del., 1972-74; atty. E.I. Dupont De Nemours and Co., Wilmington, 1974-85, counsel, 1986-96; mem. Del. Ho. of Reps., Newark, 1986-94; mem. Del. Senate, Newark, 1994—, minority leader, 1998—; counsel Cooch & Taylor, Newark, 1996—. Pres. Com. of 39, Wilmington, 1978, Civic League for New Castle County, Wilmington, 1984-86. Mem. Del. Bar Assn. Republican. Presbyterian. Avocation: antique cars. Home: 449 W Chestnut Hill Rd Newark DE 19713-1132 Office: Cooch & Taylor 51 E Main St Ste 1 Newark DE 19711-4695

**AMIDEI, MAURICE ENEAS,** judge; b. Ft. Worth, June 6, 1973; s. Eneas Maurice and Eva Amidei; m. Sara Ann Bryan, Sept. 18, 1959; children: April Sarice Dancer, Anthony Maurice, Angela Margaret Dunn. BBA, So. Meth. U., 1955, LLM, 1966; JD, U. Tex., 1958. Bar: Tex. 1958, N.Y., U.S. Dist. Ct. (all dists.) Tex., U.S. Ct. Appeals (5th cir.), U.S. Supreme Ct. Atty. Law Offices of Ben Gilbert, Ft. Worth, 1958-60, City of Fort Worth, 1959-60; solo law practitioner Ft.Worth, 1960-65; atty. Bryan & Amidei, Ft. Worth, 1965-70; sr. atty. Mobil Oil Corp., Dallas, N.Y.C., Houston, 1970-79; sole practitioner Houston, 1979-94; justice 14th Ct. Appeals/State Appeals Ct., Houston, 1995—. Mem. State Bar Tex., Houston Bar Assn. (appellate sect. liaison 1998-99), Pachyderm Club. Republican. Baptist. Office: 14th Ct of Appeals 1307 San Jacinto St Fl 17 Houston TX 77002-7006

**AMKRAUT, DAVID M.H.,** lawyer, judge; b. N.Y.C.. BS, U. Calif., Santa Cruz, 1974; JD, U. Calif., Berkeley, 1987. Bar: Calif. 1987, U.S. Dist. Ct. (cen. and no. dists.) Calif. 1987, U.S. Ct. Appeals (9th cir.) 1987. Prin. Law Offices of David Amkraut, L.A., 1987—; mcpl. ct. judge, protem Glendale (Calif.), L.A. Mcpl. Cts., 1997—; cons. various pub. and photography mags. and orgns. Author: Guide to the Diversity Visa Program, 1996; contbr. various articles to profl. jours. Mem. L.A. Trial Lawyers Assn., Calif. Trial Lawyers Assn. Avocations: chess (master), writing, travelling. Fax: 213-228-0407. Office: Law Offices Of David Amkraut 900 Wilshire Blvd Ste 230 Los Angeles CA 90017-4703

**AMMEEN, JAMES J(OSEPH), JR.,** lawyer; b. N.Y.C.; s. James Joseph and Judith Ann (Michelsen) A.; m. Sandra Kay Jessup, Mar. 28, 1992; 1 child, Jessup Samuel. AB, Middlebury (Vt.) Coll., 1985; JD, Ind. U., 1995. Sales assoc. Abraham & Strauss, Short Hills, N.J., 1986; asst. buyer Macy's, N.Y.C., 1986-88; dir. retail mktg. CFO Carpet/J.M. Benson, Inc., Windsor, Conn., 1988-89; sales rep. Cole of Calif., L.A., 1989-92; law clk. Indpls., 1994-95; law clk. to Chief Justice Randall T. Shepard Ind. Supreme Ct., Indpls., 1995-97; assoc. Baker & Daniels, Indpls., 1997—. V.p. bd. dirs. Forum for Internat. Profl. Svcs., Indpls., 1996—; bd. dirs. Mapleton-Fall Creek Christian Legal Clinic, Indpls., 1996—, Sheperd Cmty. Devel. Corp., Indpls., 1996—; vol. Meals on Wheels, Indpls. Mem. ABA, Ind. State Bar Assn. (Blackwell award 1994), Indpls. Bar Assn. (program chair for continuing legal edn. profl. responsibility com. 1996—), Indpls. Athletic Club. Roman Catholic. Avocations: bicycling, basketball, camping, hiking. Home: 5018 Central Ave Indianapolis IN 46205-1058 Office: Baker & Daniels 300 N Meridian St Ste 2700 Indianapolis IN 46204-1782

**AMODEO, TINA NIELSEN,** lawyer; b. Phila., June 19, 1965; d. Hans christian and Gloria June (McClure) Nielsen; m. James Edward Amodeo, Aug. 28, 1994 (div. Feb. 1998); 1 child, Kristina Shannon. BA, Rutgers U., 1988; JD, Widener U., 1993. Bar: N.J. 1994, N.Y. 1997, Pa. 1997. Family counselor Child Abuse Prevention, Phila., 1988-89; jud. law clk. N.J. Superior Ct., Camden, N.J., 1994-95; atty. N.J. Legal Rev. Inc., Cherry Hill, N.J., 1995—; mortgage banker James B. Nuttes & Co., Cherry Hill, 1996—; ptnr. Kayton & Amodeo LLC, Cherry Hill, 1996—. Pres. bd. trustees People Against Spouse Abuse, Sewell, N.J., 1998. Avocations: reading, walking, biking, swimming, travel. Real property. Office: Kayton & Amodeo LLC 1040 N Kings Hwy Ste 303 Cherry Hill NJ 08034-1925

**AMON, CAROL BAGLEY,** federal judge; b. 1946. BS, Coll. William and Mary, 1968; JD, U. Va., 1971. Bar: Va. 1971, D.C. 1972, N.Y. 1980. Staff atty. Communications Satellite Corp., Washington, 1971-73; trial atty. U.S. Dept. Justice, Washington, 1973-74; asst. U.S. atty. Ea. Dist. N.Y., 1974-86, U.S. magistrate, 1986-90, dist. ct. judge, 1990—. Recipient John Marshall award U.S. Dept. Justice, 1983. Mem. ABA, Assn. of Bar of City of N.Y., Va. State Bar Assn., D.C. Bar Assn. Office: US District Court 225 Cadman Plz E Brooklyn NY 11201-1818

**AMORY, DANIEL,** lawyer; b. Boston, Dec. 3, 1946; s. Robert and Mary (Armstrong) A.; m. Joan Latchis, Oct. 13, 1973; children: Jonathan, Nathaniel. BA, Harvard U., 1967; JD, Yale U., 1973. Bar: Maine 1973; U.S. Dist. Ct. Maine 1973; U.S. Ct. Appeals (1st cir.). Assoc. Drummond, Woodsum, Plimpton & MacMahon, Portland, Maine, 1973-78, ptnr., 1978—; lectr. in field; mem. adv. com. in local rules, U.S. Dist. Ct. for State of Maine, 1987—; fellow Am. Coll. of Bankruptcy, 1998—. Chmn. bd. dirs. Bd. of Harbor Commrs. for Portland (Maine) Harbor, 1979-86; pres. Saco River Corridor Assn., Portland, 1979-80; vol. Peace Corps, Thailand, 1967-69; trustee Portland Pub. Libr., 1991-95, Portland Stage Co., 1993—, Natural Resources Coun. of Maine, 1997—. Mem. ABA, Maine State Bar Assn. (chmn. bankruptcy and reorgn. sect. 1985-86), Cruising Club of Am. Democrat. Avocations: sailing, history. Bankruptcy, Federal civil litigation, Contracts commercial. Office: Drummond Woodsum & MacMahon PO Box 9781 245 Commercial St Portland ME 04104-5081

**AMSTERDAM, MARK LEMLE,** lawyer; b. N.Y.C., June 10, 1944; s. Leonard M. and Erica (Lemle) A.; children: Lauren, Matthew. AB, Columbia U., 1966, JD cum laude, 1969. Bar: N.Y. 1969, U.S. Dist. Ct. (so., ea. and no. dists.) N.Y. 1972, U.S. Dist. Ct. (no. dist.) Tex., U.S. Supreme Ct. 1973. Assoc. Fried, Frank, Harris, N.Y.C., 1969-70; staff atty. Ctr. Constl. Rights, N.Y.C., 1970-75; atty. pvt. practice, N.Y.C., 1975-76, 81—; ptnr. Rubin Hanley & Amsterdam, N.Y.C., 1976-79, Katz Amsterdam & Lewinter, N.Y.C., 1980, Amsterdam & Lewinter, N.Y.C., 1990—; instr. N.Y. Law Sch., 1982-83. Contbr. articles to profl. jours. Fellow N.Y. State Bar Assn.; mem. Gardeners Bay Country Club. Criminal, Federal civil litigation, State civil litigation. Home: 1220 Park Ave New York NY 10128-1733 Office: 9 E 40th St New York NY 10016-0402

**AMUNDSON, ROBERT A.,** state supreme court justice; m. Katherine Amundson; children: Beth, Amy. BBA, Augustana Coll., 1961; JD, U. S.D., 1964. Asst. atty. gen. Atty. Gen's. Office, 1965-69; mem. firm Belle Fourche and Lead, 1970-89; cir. judge 2d Jud. Cir., 1989-91; justice Supreme Ct. of S.D., Vermillion, 1991—. Office: Supreme Court of South Dakota State Capitol Bldg 500 E Capitol Ave Pierre SD 57501-5070*

**AN, YONG JUN,** prosecutor; b. Seoul, Feb. 10, 1962; came to the U.S., 1974; s. Sang Seong and Jung Ja An; m. Christine Hyang An. BS, U. Md., 1985, JD, 1990; postgrad., U. Houston, 1998—. Bar: Pa. 1990, D.C. 1991, V.I. 1993. Legis. asst. to Spkr. Jim Wright U.S. Ho. Reps., Washington, 1982-91; asst. atty. gen. U.S. V.I. Dept. Justice, 1991-94; asst. U.S. atty. U.S. Dept. Justice, Houston, 1994—. Bd. mem. Mayor's Census 2000 Complete Count Com., Houston, 1998—. Mem. ABA (bd. mem. criminal justice sect. 1997—), Asian-Am. Bar Assn. (pres. 1999—), Leadership Houston Class XVII. E-mail: yongjan@yahoo.com. Home: PO Box 61581 Houston TX 77208-1581 Office: US Attys Office PO Box 61129 Houston TX 77208-1129

**ANAGNOST, THEMIS JOHN,** lawyer; b. Stadion, Arcadia, Greece, June 15, 1913; came to U.S. 1931; s. John and Maria (Psycoson) A.; m. Catherine C., Aug. 15, 1942 (dec. 1990); children: Maria (dec. 1992), Alexander Themis (dec. 1997), James Anthony. AA, U. Chgo., 1935, BA, 1937; JD, Ill. Inst. Tech., 1941; LLM, John Marshall Law Sch., Chgo., 1942. With War Dept. Censorship, 1941-45; ptnr. Anagnost & Anagnost, Chgo., 1948—; instr. Berlitz Sch. Langs.; tutor Ill. Supreme Ct. Law Office Study Provision, 1944-48. Co-founder, past pres. and chmn. bd. The Beverly Farm Found. for Retarded Children; chmn. The Catherine Cook Anagnost Found.; past pres. Students Symphony Orgn. of Chgo.; fin. chmn. Chgo. Girl Scouts U.S.; candidate for Supreme Ct. Justice of Ill., Cook County, 1992, for Atty. Gen. of Ill., 1994. Mem. Hellenic Profl. Soc. Ill. (past pres.), Internat. House Alumni Assn. of U. Chgo. (past dir. and treas.), Panarcadian Fedn. Am. (past supreme legal advisor), Appellate Lawyers Assn. (life), West Suburban Bar Assn. (past v.p.), Women's Bar Assn. of Ill., Nat. Assn. Women Lawyers. Republican. Christian Ch. General civil litigation, General practice. Address: 442 W Wellington Ave # 11W Chicago IL 60657-5804

**ANAST, NICK JAMES,** lawyer; b. Gary, Ind., Apr. 20, 1947; s. James Terry and Kiki (Pappas) A.; m. Linda K. Skirvin, Oct. 28, 1972; children: Jason, Nicole. AB, Ind. U., 1969, JD, 1972. Bar: Ind. 1972, U.S. Dist. Ct. (no. and so. dists.) Ind. 1972, U.S. Ct. Appeals (7th cir.) 1975, U.S. Supreme Ct. 1976. Ptnr. Pappas, Tokarski & Anast, Gary, 1972-74; ptnr. Tokarski & Anast, Gary, 1974-85, Schererville, Ind., 1985—; dep. pros. atty. Lake County Prosecutors Office, Crown Point, Ind., 1973-74; pub. defender Lake County Superior Ct., Gary, 1974-78; atty. Town of Schererville, 1982, 88, 89, Lowell, 1983, City of Lake Station, Ind., 1978. Pres. St. John (Ind.) Twp. Young Dems., 1980. Recipient Service to Youth award YMCA, 1980, Outstanding Service award Schererville Soccer Club, 1985. Fellow Ind. Bar Found.; mem. ABA, Ind. Bar Assn., Lake County Bar Assn. (bd. dirs.) 1983-85, Outstanding Service award 1985). Democrat. Greek Orthodox. Lodge: Lions (pres. Schererville chpt. 1985-86). Avocations: gardening, wood crafts, assisting children. Federal civil litigation, Contracts commercial, General corporate. Office: Tokarski & Anast 7803 W 75th Ave Ste 1 Schererville IN 46375-2655

**ANDERSEN, ANTON CHRIS,** lawyer; b. Salina, Kans., Oct. 3, 1960; s. Anton Jay and Mary Louise (Breitweiser) A. BS in BA, U. Kans., 1983; JD, Washburn U., Topeka, Kans., 1986. Bar: Kans. 1986, U.S. Dist. Ct. Kans. 1986. Ptnr. McAnany Van Cleave & Phillips P.A., Lenexa, Kans., 1986—. Participant Leadership Lenexa, 1987. Mem. Kans. Bar Assn., Phi Delta Phi. Republican. Presbyterian. Avocations: golf, reading, basketball. Workers' compensation, General corporate, Family and matrimonial. Office: McAnany Van Cleave & Phillips PA PO Box 1300 Kansas City KS 66117

**ANDERSEN, DAVID CHARLES,** lawyer; b. Grand Rapids, Mich., Oct. 4, 1955; s. Daniel and Doris (Hoenninger) A.; m. Elestine Whittaker, July 10, 1982 (div. Dec. 1984); 1 child, Joseph; m. Leona L. Lloyd, Apr. 2, 1989. BS, Grand Valley State Coll., 1976; JD, Wayne State U., 1979; cert. paramedic, Davenport Coll., 1987. Bar: Mich. 1979, U.S. Dist. Ct. (we. dist.) Mich. 1979, U.S. Supreme Ct. 1987; cert. paramedic, Mich., 1987; lic. pvt. pilot, 1981. Assoc. Dale R. Sprik, Grand Rapids, 1979-81; ptnr. Sprik & Andersen, Grand Rapids, 1981—; pres., chmn. Grand Rapids Pub. Broadcasting Sta. WEHB-FM, 1982-83. West Mich. Telecommunications Found., Grand Rapids, 1984-88; paramedic instr. Davenport Coll., 1988. Personal injury, Insurance, Environmental. Office: Sprik & Andersen PC 5 Lyon St NW Grand Rapids MI 49503-3114

**ANDERSEN, JAMES A.,** retired state supreme court justice; b. Auburn, Wash., Sept. 21, 1924; s. James A. and Margaret Cecelia (Norgaard) A.; m. Billiette B. Andersen; children: James Blair, Tia Louise. BA, U. Wash., 1949, JD, 1951. Bar: Wash. 1952, U.S. Dist. Ct. (we. dist.) Wash. 1957, U.S. Ct. Appeals 1957. Dep. pros. atty. King County, Seattle, 1953-57; assoc. Lycette, Diamond & Sylvester, Seattle, 1957-61; ptnr. Clinton, Andersen, Fleck & Glein, Seattle, 1961-75; judge Wash. State Ct. of Appeals, Seattle, 1975-84; justice Wash. State Supreme Ct., Olympia, 1984-92, chief justice, 1992-95; ret., 1995. Mem. Wash. State Ho. of Reps., 1958-67, Wash. State Senate, 1967-72. Served with U.S. Army, 1943-45, ETO. Decorated Purple Heart; recipient Disting. Alumnus award U. Wash. Sch. of Law, 1995. Mem. ABA, Wash. State Bar Assn., Am. Judicature Soc. Home: 3008 98th Ave NE Bellevue WA 98004-1817

**ANDERSEN, RICHARD ESTEN,** lawyer; b. N.Y.C., Oct. 26, 1957; s. Arnold and Marianne (Singer) A.; m. Patricia Anne Woods, May 9, 1987; children: Benjamin Singer, David Woods. BA, Columbia U., 1978, JD, 1981; LLM, NYU, 1987. Bar: N.Y. 1982, U.S. Tax Ct. 1982. Ptnr. Jones, Day, Reavis & Pogue, N.Y.C.; mem. bd. advisors Jour. Internat. Taxation, Tax Mgmt. Inc., World Trade Exec. Inc., World Trade Exec. Inc. Author: Foreign Tax Credits, 1996, U.S. Income Tax Withholding (Fgn. Persons), 1997. Mem. ABA, N.Y. State Bar Assn., Internat. Tax Inst., Internat. Fiscal Assn. (mem. N.Y. exec. com.), Internat. Tax Assn. Corporate taxation, Private international, Finance. Office: Jones Day Reavis & Pogue 599 Lexington Ave New York NY 10022-6030

**ANDERSEN, ROBERT MICHAEL,** lawyer; b. Council Bluffs, Iowa, June 4, 1950; s. Howard M. and Muriel Marie (Robinson) A.; m. Natalia Anne Nankovitch, May 1, 1982; children: Erica Nicole, Amelia Marie. BS, U. Iowa, 1972, JD, 1976; MPA, Harvard U., 1986. Bar: Ohio 1976, Iowa 1976, U.S. Ct. Appeals (2d, 6th, and 7th cirs.) 1979, U.S. Supreme Ct. 1979. Assoc. Squire, Sanders & Dempsey, Cleve., 1976-78; pvt. practice Milw.; asst. regional counsel U.S. EPA, Chgo., 1980-82, assoc. regional counsel, 1982-84, dep. regional counsel, regional jud. officer, 1984-86; dep. gen. counsel NSF, Washington, 1986-90; gen. counsel Def. Nuclear Facilities Safety Bd., Washington, 1990-98; chief counsel U.S. Army Corps Engrs., 1998—; adj. prof. lectr. waste mgmt., dept. engring. George Washington U., 1994—; lectr. internat. environ. controls for Antarctica, regulation of sci. fraud and misconduct, and waste mgmt.; mgmt. cons. in field. Articles editor Iowa U. Law Rev., 1975-76; contbr. articles to profl. jours. Recipient Bronze medal EPA, 1982, Meritorious Svc. medal NSF, 1990, Antarctic Svc. medal NSF, 1990, Antarctic medallion, NSF, 1990, Presdl. Meritorious Exec. Rank award Pres. George Bush, 1992, Presdl. Disting. Exec. Rank award Pres. William Jefferson Clinton, 1995, Meritorious Svc. award Def. Nuclear Facilities Safety Bd., 1998. Roman Catholic. Avocations: mountaineering, tennis, chess, writing, mathematics. Home: 7003 Petunia St Springfield VA 22152-3428 Office: USA CE Office of Chief Counsel 20 Massachusetts Ave NW Rm 8220 Washington DC 20314-0001

**ANDERSEN, WAYNE R.,** federal judge; b. Chgo., July 30, 1945; m. Sheila M. O'Brien, Jan. 5, 1991; children: Susan, David, Kristine, Mary, Maureen, Noreen. BA with honors, Harvard Coll., 1967; JD, U. Ill., 1970. Adminstrv. asst. Henry J. Hyde, majority leader Ill. House Reps., 1970-72;

assoc. Burditt & Calkins, Chgo., 1972-76, ptnr., 1977-80; dep. sec. state Ill., 1981-84; judge Cir. Ct. Cook County, 1984-91; supr. judge traffic divsn. First Municipal Dist., 1989-91; dist. judge No. U.S. Courthouse, Ill., 1991—; dir. Rehab. Inst. Chgo.; interviewer schs. com. Harvard Club Chgo. Contbr. articles to profl. jours. Pres., dir., precinct capt. Maine Township Regular Rep. Orgn.; alt. del. Rep. Nat. Conv., Sixth Congrl. Dist. Ill., 1984; Rep. candidate for treas. Cook County, 1974. Mem. Ill. Judges Assn., Chgo. Bar Assn., Fed. Judges Assn. Office: US Courthouse 1486 Dirksen Bldg 219 S Dearborn St Chicago IL 60604-1702

**ANDERSON, ALAN MARSHALL,** lawyer; b. Postville, Iowa, Oct. 23, 1955; s. Hilbert Emil and Wilma Althea (Zummack) A.; m. Ann Marie Luken, Aug. 9, 1980. BA magna cum laude, Coe Coll., 1974-78; MBA with distinction, Cornell U., 1981, JD magna cum laude, 1982; cert. internat. comml. and bus. law, U. Pacific, 1988. Bar: Minn. 1983, U.S. Dist. Ct. Minn. 1983, U.S. Ct. Appeals (4th and 8th cirs.) 1983, U.S. Ct. Appeals (10th cir.) 1985, U.S. Ct. Appeals (fed. cir.) 1987, U.S. Supreme Ct. 1990, U.S. Ct. Appeals (7th cir.) 1992. Law clk. to cir. judge U.S. Ct. Appeals (4th cir.), Richmond, Va., 1982-83; assoc., then ptnr. Faegre & Benson, Mpls., 1983-90; ptnr. Robins, Kaplan, Miller & Ciresi, Mpls., 1990-92; shareholder Larkin, Hoffman, Daly & Lindgren, Mpls., 1992—. Contbr. articles to law revs. Mem. alumni coun. Coe Coll., 1998—. Recipient Chatman Labor Law Prize Cornell Law Sch. Faculty, 1982. Mem. ABA, Minn. Bar Assn. (cert. civil trial specialist, named leading Am. Atty. 1999), Am. Intellectual Property Law Assn., Fed. Cir. Bar Assn., Coe Coll. Alumni Coun., Nat. Assn. Securities Dealers (nat. bd. arbitrators 1990—), Am. Arbitration Assn. (panel of arbitrators 1993—), U.S. Judo Assn. (life mem., nat. bd. legal advisors 1989-94, Silver award), Order of Coif, Phi Beta Kappa, Phi Kappa Phi. Republican. Lutheran. Avocation: judo. General civil litigation, Intellectual property, Appellate. Office: Larkin Hoffman Daly & Lindgren 7900 Xerxes Ave S Ste 1500 Minneapolis MN 55431-1128

**ANDERSON, ALAN WENDELL,** lawyer; b. Kane, Pa., Oct. 29, 1949; s. Herman Laverne and Phyllis Louise (Anderson) A.; m. Deborah Ann Anderson, Dec. 25, 1986; children: Ryan, Morgan. BA magna cum laude, U. No. Colo., 1972; JD, U. Notre Dame, 1975. Bar: Iowa 1975, U.S. Dist. Ct. (no. dist.) Iowa 1976, U.S. Ct. Mil. Appeals 1976, Colo. 1981, U.S. Dist. Ct. Colo. 1981, U.S. Ct. Appeals (10th cir.) 1981, U.S. Supreme Ct. 1995. Ptnr. Rothgerber, Johnson & Lyons, LLP, Denver, 1981—; mem. faculty Nat. Inst. for Trial Advocacy Regional Program, Denver, 1995—. Contbr. articles to law jour. Bd. dirs. Colo. Easter Seal Soc., 1992-95, chmn. bd. dirs., 1995-98. Capt. JAGC, USAF, 1976-81. Mem. Colo. Bar Assn. (litigation com. 1995—), Denver Bar Assn. (professionalism com. 1995-96). Avocations: billiards, fly fishing. Federal civil litigation, Computer, State civil litigation. Office: Rothgerber Johnson & Lyons LLP 1200 17th St Ste 3000 Denver CO 80202-5855

**ANDERSON, ALBERT SYDNEY, III,** lawyer; b. Atlanta, July 7, 1940; s. Albert S. Jr. and Constance S. (Spalding) A.; children: Judith, William. BA in Math., Emory U., 1962; MS in Physics, Stanford (Calif.) U., 1964, PhD in Physics, 1968, JD, 1977. Bar: Ga. 1978, U.S. Patent and Trademark Office 1980, U.S. Supreme Ct. 1981. Assoc. Stokes & Shapiro, Atlanta, 1978-81, Kutak, Rock & Huie, Atlanta, 1981-84; ptnr. Jones & Askew, Atlanta, 1984-96; pvt. practice Norcross, Ga., 1996—; asst. atty. gen. State of Ga., Atlanta, 1984-88. Elder Trinity Presbyn. Ch., Atlanta, 1978-81; chmn. bd. trustees Trinity Sch., Atlanta, 1971-74. Mem. Am. Phys. Soc. Avocations: golf, hiking, music. Patent, Trademark and copyright, Federal civil litigation. Office: Patent Law Offices 35 Technology Pkwy S Ste 170 Norcross GA 30092-2928

**ANDERSON, ANTHONY LECLAIRE,** lawyer; b. Davenport, Iowa, Sept. 15, 1938; s. Frederic Nielsen and Marie Louise (LeClaire) A.; m. Beulah M. Bassham, July 3, 1963; children: Timothy LeClaire, Mark LeClaire, Jonathan Frederic LeClaire. BS with final honors, Washington U., St. Louis, 1967; JD, St. Louis U., 1971. Bar: Mo. 1972, U.S. Dist. Ct. (we. dist.) Mo. 1972, U.S. Dist. Ct. (ea. dist.) Mo. 1972, U.S. Ct. Appeals (8th cir.) 1974, U.S. Ct. Appeals (7th cir.) 1992, U.S. Tax Ct. 1976, U.S. Supreme Ct. 1976. Dir. pub. affairs Key Comm., Inc., St. Louis, 1973-74, Anderson, Wollrab & Wilson, St. Louis, 1974-76, Anderson, Preuss, Mooney & Eickhorst, St. Louis, 1976-82, Anderson, Preuss & Bachman, St. Louis, 1982-87, Anderson & Preuss, St. Louis, 1987—; dir. Shield Fire Ins. Co., St. Louis, 1976-83. Panel atty. Lawyers Reference Svc., St. Louis, 1972-92; mem. Nat. Rep. Congrl. Com., 1998. Served with U.S. Army, 1962-64. Recipient Law Enforcement Assistance cert. Bd. Police Commrs., 1967, Bi-Centennial Comm., Davenport, Iowa, 1976. Mem. ABA, ATLA, Am. Judicature Soc., Ill. Trial Lawyers Assn., Bar Assn. Met. st. Louis, Press (editor 1968-69), Phi Alpha Delta. Episcopalian. Bankruptcy, General corporate, Franchising. Home: 2919 Moniteau Dr Saint Louis MO 63121-4518 Address: Anderson And Preuss 201 S Central Ave Ste 103 Saint Louis MO 63105-3517

**ANDERSON, ARTHUR IRVIN,** lawyer; b. Lexington, Ky., Jan. 19, 1951; s. William Kendrick and Dorothea Amanda (Deffenbaugh) A.; m. Sharon Lee Sisskind, Apr. 15, 1978; children: Jacob Kendrick, Samuel Keith, Melissa Katherine. BA, Northwestern U., 1973; JD, Harvard U., 1978. Bar: Mass. 1978, U.S. Dist. Ct. Mass. 1979, U.S. Ct. Appeals (1st cir.) 1979. Assoc. Gaston & Snow, Boston, 1978-86, ptnr., 1986-91; ptnr. McDermott, Will & Emery, Boston, 1991—. Mergers and acquisitions, Securities, Public utilities. Home: 70 Barnstable Rd Newton MA 02465-2960 Office: McDermott Will & Emery 28 State St Ste 1700 Boston MA 02109-1775

**ANDERSON, AUSTIN GOTHARD,** lawyer, university administrator; b. Calumet, Minn., June 30, 1931; s. Hugo Gothard and Turna Marie (Johnson) A.; m. Catherine Antoinette Spellacy, Jan. 2. 1954; children: Todd, Susan, Timothy, Linda, Mark. BA, U. Minn., 1954, JD, 1958. Bar: Minn. 1958, Ill. 1962, Mich. 1974. Assoc. Spellacy, Spellacy, Lano & Anderson, Marble, Minn, 1958-62; dir. Ill. Inst. Continuing Legal Edn., Springfield, 1962-64; dir. dept. continuing legal edn. U. Minn., Mpls., 1964-70, assoc. dean gen. extension div., 1968-70; ptnr. Dorsey, Marquart, Windhorst, West & Halladay, Mpls., 1970-73; assoc. dir. Nat. Ctr. State Cts., St. Paul, 1973-74; dir. Inst. Continuing Legal Edn. U. Mich., Ann Arbor, 1973-92; dir. Inst. on Law Firm Mgmt., 1992-95; prin. AndersonBoyer Group, Ann Arbor; pres. Network of Leading Law Firms, 1995—; adj. faculty U. Minn., 1974, Wayne State U., 1974-75; mem. adv. bd. Ctr. for Law Firm Mgmt. Nottingham Trent U., Eng.; draftsman ABA Guidelines for Approval of Legal Asst. Programs, 1973, Model Guidelines for Minimum Continuing Legal Edn., 1988; vice chair law practice mgmt. sect. State Bar Mich., 1997—; cons. in field. Co-editor, contbg. author: Lawyer's Handbook, 1975, co-editor 3d edit., 1992; author: A Plan for Lawyer Development, 1986, Marketing Your Practice: A Practical Guide to Client Development, 1986; cons. editor, contbg. author: Webster's Legal Secretaries Handbook, 1981; cons. editor Merriam Webster's Legal Secretarial Handbook, 2d edit., 1996; contbr. chpt. to book and articles to profl. jours. Chmn. City of Bloomington Park and Recreation Adv. Commn., Minn., 1970-72; chmn. Ann Arbor Citizens Recreation Adv. Com., 1981-89, Ann Arbor Parks Adv. Com., 1983-92, chair, 1991-92; rep. Class of '58 U. Minn. Law Sch., 1996—. Recipient Excellence award CLE sect. Assn. of Am. Law Schs., 1992. Fellow Am. Bar Found., State Bar Mich. Found.; mem. ABA (vice chmn. continuing legal edn. com. sect. legal edn. and admission to bar 1988-93, standing com. continuing edn. of bar 1984-90, chmn. law practice mgmt. sect. 1981-82, AII-ABA com. on continuing profl. edn. 1993-96, ALI-ABA com. on continuing profl. edn. 1999—, spl. com. on rsch. on future of legal profession 1998—, sec. Coll. of Law Practice Mgmt. 1993-97, ho. of dels. 1993—, commn. on lawyer advt. 1994-97, futures com.), Internat. Bar Assn., Mich. Bar Assn., State Bar of Mich. (vice chair law practice mgmt. sect.), Ill. Bar Assn., Minn. Bar Assn., Assn. Continuing Legal Edn. Adminstrs., Assn. Legal Adminstrs. (pres. 1969-70), Ann Arbor Golf and Outing Club. Administrative and regulatory. Home: 3617 Larchmont Dr Ann Arbor MI 48105-2855 Office: AndersonBoyer Group 3840 Packard St # 110 Ann Arbor MI 48108-2280

**ANDERSON, BRUCE EDWIN,** lawyer; b. Greeley, Colo., June 21, 1948; s. Maxwell Edward and Anne (Koss) A.; m. Cheryl A. Quinlan, Aug. 30, 1969; 1 child, Nathan Douglas. BA, U. Mo., 1970, JD, 1975. Bar: Mo. 1975, Tex. 1980; cert. in civil trial law and personal injury law Tex. Bd. Legal Specialization. Law clk. to Hon. Albert L. Rendlen, Mo. Ct. Appeals, St. Louis, 1975-76; asst. atty. gen. Mo. Atty. Gen.'s Office, Jefferson City, 1976-79; pvt. practice, Austin, Tex., 1980-84; assoc. Davis & Davis, Austin, 1984-89; assoc. Brin & Brin, San Antonio, 1990, owner, 1991—. Bd. dirs. Am. Cancer Soc., Austin, 1988-89. Lt. (j.g.) USNR, 1970-72. Avocations: running, science fiction, genealogy, political history. Personal injury, General civil litigation. Office: Brin & Brin PC 8200 W Ih 10 Ste 610 San Antonio TX 78230-3878

**ANDERSON, BRUCE HAMILTON,** lawyer; b. Teaneck, N.J., Oct. 13, 1941; s. Oscar Edward Theodore and Edythe Viola (Moats) A.; m. Edith Helen Willis, Aug. 3, 1963; children—Virginia Blair, Lauren Page. BA, Duke U., 1963, JD, 1966. Bar: N.C. 1966, Oreg. 1971, U.S. Dist. Ct. Oreg. 1973, U.S. Ct. Appeals (9th cir.) 1978. Assoc. Butler, Husk & Gleaves, Eugene, Oreg., 1971-75; ptnr. Coons, Cole & Anderson, Eugene, 1975-77, Coons & Anderson, Eugene, 1977-80, Hutchinson, Anderson, Cox & Teising, P.C., Eugene, 1981-85; shareholder Hutchinson, Anderson, Cox, Parrish & Coons, P.C., 1985-92, Hutchinson, Anderson, Cox Coons & DuPriest, P.C., 1992—; vis. instr. environ. law U. Oreg., Eugene, 1976, internat. law, 1998; dir. Solar Energy Assn. Oreg. Mem. Oreg. Small Bus. Adv. Com., Salem, 1982-85; chmn. small bus. adv. com. Lane Community Coll., Eugene, 1983-91; mem. bus. loan adv. com. City of Eugene, 1983-87; co-chair Oreg. del. Pres.'s White House Conf. on Small Bus., 1980; chairperson Oreg. Gov.'s Conf. on Small Bus., 1980; mem. Riverfront Rsch. Park Commission, 1992-96. Co-author: Oregon State Bar, Land Use, 1982; Torts, 1982. Capt. JAGC, USAF, 1969-70. Recipient Resources Def. award Nat. Wildlife Fedn., Washington, 1980; Small Bus. Advocacy award SBA, Portland, 1982. Mem. ABA, Oreg. State Bar (exec. com. internat. law sect., 1988—, chair internat. law sect. 1992-93, chmn. environ. law com. 1974-75, real estate and land use sect. 1982-83), Lane County Bar Assn. (sec.-treas. 1978-79, pres. 1980-81). Presbyterian. General corporate, Environmental, Private international. Home: 4240 Hilyard St Eugene OR 97405-3907 Office: Hutchinson Anderson Cox Coons & DuPriest PC 777 High St Ste 200 Eugene OR 97401-2750

**ANDERSON, BRUCE PAIGE,** lawyer; b. Albany, Ga., Mar. 5, 1952; s. Paul Macon and Ruth Alice (O'neil) A.; m. Sandra Johnston, June 30, 1973; children: Christi Lauren, Sarah Alice. AB in Econs., Ga. So. U., 1973; JD, Loyola U., New Orleans, 1977. Bar: Ga. 1977, La. 1977, Fla. 1978. Asst. atty. gen. State of La., New Orleans, 1981; assoc. John A. Barley & Assocs., Tallahassee, 1981-83; pvt. practice Tallahassee, 1983—; guest lectr. Fla. A&M U. Sch. Architecture, Tallahassee, 1984-85. Bd. dirs., past pres. Killearn Homes Assn. Mem. ABA, Fla. Bar Assn., La. Bar Assn., Ga. Bar Assn., Tallahassee Bar Assn., Jefferson County Bar Assn., Fed. Bar Assn. (pres.). Roman Catholic. General practice, Construction, State civil litigation. Home: 522 N Adams St Tallahassee FL 32301-1112

**ANDERSON, CARL WEST,** judge; b. Monterey Park, Calif., Sept. 11, 1935; s. Carl Ejnar and Mary Madeline (West) A.; m. Margo Hart, Aug. 15, 1964; children: Thomas Hart, Marnie Marie. AB in Pol. Sci., U. Calif., Berkeley, 1957, LLB, 1962; LLM in Jud. Process, U. Va., 1992. Bar: Calif. 1963. Dep. dist. atty. Alameda County (Calif.) Dist. Atty., 1964-72, sr. dep. dist. atty., 1972-75; judge Alameda County Superior Ct., 1975-84; assoc. justice Calif. Ct. Appeals, 1st dist., divsn. 3, San Fransisco, 1984; presiding justice divsn. 4, San Francisco, 1987-97, adminstrv. presiding justice, 1987-97; ret., 1997; pvt. judge, assoc. Am. Arbitration Assn. and alternative adjudication; mem. appellate performance stds. com. Nat. Ctr. for State Cts. Commn., 1994-95. Pres. Piedmont (Calif.) Coun. Boy Scouts Am., 1987, 88, 93. Capt. USAR, 1957-74. Scholar U. Calif. Alumni Assn., 1953; fellow U. Calif. Sch. Law and Ctr. for Study Law and Soc., Germany, 1962-63. Fellow ABA (commn. stds. jud. adminstrn. 1992-93, appellate judges conf. exec. com. JAD 1992, 93, chair-elect 1995—, chair 1996-97), Coun. Chief Judges Cts. Appeal (pres. 1992-93). Avocations: tennis, gardening, golf. Office: Am Arbitration Assn 225 Bush St 18th Fl San Francisco CA 94104-4211

**ANDERSON, CHARLES DAVID,** lawyer; b. Balt., Aug. 4, 1943; s. Charles Quentin and Enid Ruth A.; m. Alison Grey, Apr. 15, 1972 (div. Oct. 1990); children: Charles Thomas, Patrick Grey; m. Kathleen McGuinness, June 8, 1991; 1 child, Alexander James McGuinness. BA, Yale Coll., 1964; JD, U. Chgo., 1967. Capt. USAF, Pentagon, 1967-70; assoc. Caplin & Drysdale, Washington, 1970-72; from assoc. to ptnr. Tuttle & Taylor, L.A., 1972—; lectr. Harvard Law Sch., Cambridge, Mass., 1983, U. So. Calif. Law Sch., L.A., 1976, 78, UCLA Law Sch., 1979, 81, 85. Pres. L.A. Soccer Found., 1994—. Avocations: pens, skiing. Taxation, general, State and local taxation, Corporate taxation. Home: 1164 Madia St Pasadena CA 91103-1960 Office: Tuttle & Taylor 355 S Grand Ave Ste 3900 Los Angeles CA 90071-3176

**ANDERSON, CHARLES HILL,** lawyer; b. Chattanooga, June 16, 1930; s. Ray N. and Lois M. (Entrekin) A.; div.; children: Eric S., Alicia L., Burton H.; m. Shirley Roach, May 17, 1996. JD, U. Tenn., 1953. Bar: Tenn. 1953, U.S. Dist. Ct. Tenn. 1953, U.S. Ct. Appeals (6th cir.) 1956, U.S. Supreme Ct. 1956, U.S. Ct. Mil. 1964. Pvt. practice Chattanooga, 1953-59; assoc. gen. counsel Life & Casualty Ins. Co. Tenn., Nashville, 1960-69; dist. atty. U.S. Dept. Justice, Nashville, 1969-77; pvt. practice Nashville, 1977-79, 87—; asst. adj. gen. State of Tenn., Nashville, 1979-87. Mem. U.S. Atty. Gen. Adv. Com., Washington, 1973-77; del. Tenn. Constl. Conv., Nashville, 1965-66; dir. Nashville Pub. TV Coun., 1994-99; chmn. Met. Bd. of Equalization, 1998—. Brig. gen. USAR, ret., 1987. Mem. ABA, Tenn. Bar Assn., Nashville Bar Assn., Fed. Bar Assn. (pres. Nashville chpt. 1972), Am. Arbitration Assn. (arbitrator), Assn. Life Ins. Counsel, Nat. Fedn. Ind. Bus., Cumberland Club (pres. 1981-82), The Federalist Soc. Presbyterian. Insurance, Labor, General corporate. Home: 221 Diane Dr Madison TN 37115-2565 Office: BNA Corp Ctr Bldg 200 404 Bna Dr Ste 304 Nashville TN 37217-2582

**ANDERSON, CLARE EBERHART,** lawyer; b. Frankfurt, Germany, Aug. 9, 1947; came to U.S., 1947; d. Claude Milton Eberhart and Mary Jean Christopher; m. Bruce C. Lamartine, June 5, 1971 (div. Apr. 1985); children: Ian C. Lamartine, Nicole C. Lamartine; m. Nicholas P. Anderson, Oct. 26, 1985. AB, U. N.C., 1969; MA, Case Western Res. U., 1971; JD, U. Mont. Law Sch., 1997. Audiologist Cleve., Beavercreek, Ohio, 1971-82, Enid, Okla., 1971-82; adolescent outreach coord. Suicide Prevention Ctr., Dayton, Ohio, 1984-87; co-owner, mgr. Big Sky Chili Restaurant, Missoula, Mont., 1988-92; bus. mgr. Heartland Nannies, Missoula, 1993-94; ptnr. Anderson & Anderson, Missoula, 1997—. Mem. ABA, ATLA, Western Mont. Bar Assn., Missoula New Lawyers Assn. (pres. 1998-99). General practice, Family and matrimonial, Personal injury. Home: 19515 Arabian Ln Frenchtown MT 59834-9733 Office: Anderson & Anderson 210 N Higgins Ave Ste 302 Missoula MT 59802-4443

**ANDERSON, CRAIG W.,** lawyer; b. Idaho Falls, Idaho, Aug. 5, 1951; s. Wilford and Betty A.; m. Denise A. Dragoo, Nov. 25, 1977. B.S. magna cum laude, U. Utah, 1973, J.D., 1977. Bar: Utah 1977, U.S. Ct. Appeals (10th cir.), U.S. Supreme Ct. Research assoc. Environ. Law Inst., Washington, 1977; dep. county atty. Salt Lake County, 1978-81; ptnr. Suitter, Axland, Armstrong & Hanson, Salt Lake City, 1981-86, Van Wagoner & Stevens, Salt Lake City, 1986—. Contbr. articles to profl. jours. Editorial bd. Jour. Contemporary Law, 1976-77. Counsel, Children's Service Soc. Utah. U.S. Senate intern, 1974. Mem. Utah Bar Assn., Hinckley Inst. Politics Intern Alumni Assn., Salt Lake County Bar Assn., ABA. Federal civil litigation, State civil litigation. Home: 1826 Hubbard Ave Salt Lake City UT 84108-1362 Office: Dep Dist Atty Salt Lake County 2001 S State St Ste S3600 Salt Lake City UT 84190-0001

**ANDERSON, DAMON ERNEST,** lawyer; b. Minot, N.D., June 20, 1946; s. Melvin Ernest and Maxine I. (Spaulding) A.; m. Julie Kay Severson, Oct. 23, 1982; children: Joshua Daniel, Philip Kyle. BA, Dickinson State U., 1968; JD, U. N.D., 1974. Bar: N.D. 1974, Minn. 1981, U.S. Dist. Ct. N.D. 1974, U.S. Ct. Appeals (8th cir.) 1980, U.S. Supreme Ct. 1980. Pvt. practice Kessler and Anderson, Grand Forks, N.D., 1974-78, Grand Forks, N.D., 1978-98; asst. state's atty. Grand Forks County, N.D., 1978—. Past mem. divsnl. comdr. adv. coun. Salvation Army, Mpls., mem. Salvation Army local adv. bd., Grand Forks. Sgt. U.S. Army, 1968-70. Mem. Am. Legion, Masons. Lutheran. Juvenile. Office: 201 S 4th St Grand Forks ND 58201-4788

**ANDERSON, DAVID ALAN,** lawyer; b. Hutchinson, Minn., Aug. 21, 1955; s. Gordon D. and Irene M. (Falkman) A.; m. Catherine Elizabeth Loftus, Apr. 28, 1984; children; Patricia, Erik, Kevin, Luke, Christopher. BA in Govt. with honors, U. Notre Dame, 1977; JD, U. Colo., 1980. Bar: Colo. 1980, Ind. 1985, Wis. 1985, Ill. 1991. Staff atty. Golden Rule Ins. Co., Indpls., 1986-88, supervising atty., 1988-89, litigation atty., 1989-92, outside counsel/litigator, 1992—; pres. Anderson & Assocs., Indpls., 1992—. Capt. U.S. Army, 1981-86. Recipient ROTC scholarship U.S. Army, 1973-77, Am. Jur. award U. Colo., 1978. Fellow Life Mgmt. Inst.; mem. Assn. Trial Lawyers Am., Ind. State Bar Assn., Ill. State Bar Assn. Federal civil litigation, Insurance.

**ANDERSON, DAVID BOWEN,** lawyer; b. Seattle, Sept. 19, 1948; s. Gordon Browne and Elizabeth Josephine (Bowen) A.; m. Laura Ann Jorgensen, May 23, 1975; children: Elizabeth Christine, Christina Louise. BA with great distinction, Stanford U., 1970; JD, U. Mich., 1974; MBA, Western Wash. U., 1982. Bar: Wash. 1974, U.S. Dist. Ct. (we. dist.) Wash. 1974. Assoc. Bogle & Gates, Seattle, 1974-77; ptnr. Anderson , Connell & Murphy, Bellingham, Wash., 1977—; pres. San Juan Tug & Barge Co., 1979-85; arbitrator Whatcom County, Am. Arbitration Assn.; instr. Pacific N.W. Admiralty Law Inst., Seattle, 1983, Nat. Fishery Law Symposium, Seattle, 1984; lectr. constnl. law Western Wash. U., 1996; mediator U.S. Dist. Ct. (we. dist.) Wash. Mem. adv. com. Bellingham Sch. Bd., 1981-82, Bellingham Vocat. Tech. Inst., 1986; mem. Bellingham Pub. Sch. Found. Bd., 1992, pres., 1992-93. Mem. ATLA, ABA, Wash. State Bar Assn. (spl. dist. counsel, rules of profl. practice com.), Whatcom County Bar Assn. (pres. 1986), Maritime Law Assn. U.S. (proctor), Wash. Atheltic Club (Seattle), Bellingham Rotary Club (chmn. internat. svc. com.), Bellingham Golf and Country Club, Phi Beta Kappa. Presbyterian. Admiralty, Federal civil litigation, Personal injury. Home: 500 16th St Bellingham WA 98225-6315 Office: Anderson Connell & Murphy 1501 Eldridge Ave Bellingham WA 98225-2801

**ANDERSON, DORIS EHLINGER,** lawyer; b. Houston, Dec. 1; d. Joseph Otto and Cornelia Louise (Pagel) Ehlinger; children—Wiley Newton III, Joe E.; m. Wiley Anderson, Jr. (wid.). Permanent high sch. tchr.'s cert. U. Houston, 1948; BA, Rice U., 1946; JD, U. Tex. Law Sch., 1950; MLS in Museology U. Okla. Bar: Tex. 1950, U.S. Supreme Ct. Assoc. Ehlinger & Anderson, Houston, 1950-52, ptnr., 1965—; assoc. Price, Guinn, Wheat & Veltmann, Houston, 1952-55, Wheat, Dyche & Thornton, Houston, 1955-65; life mem. Rice Assocs., Houston, 1984—; dir. Houston Bapt. Mus. Am. Architecture and Decorative Arts, 1980-90, curator costume, 1980; hist. lectr., Harvard Negotiation Seminar, 1992 Edn. for Ministry, U of South, 1999, Editor, Houston, City of Destiny, 1980. Contbr. articles to hist. publs. Partliamentarian Harris County Flood Control Task Force, Houston, 1975—; apptd. ambassador Inst. Texan Culture U. Tex., San Antonio; past pres. gen. San Jacinto Descendants; docent Bayou Bend Mus. Fine Arts, Houston. Recipient best interpretive exhibit award Tex. Hist. Commn., 1983, Outstanding Woman of Yr. award YWCA, Houston, 1983; named adm. Tex. Navy, 1980. Mem. ABA, Assn. Women Attys. Houston, Houston Bar Assn., UDC (pres. Jefferson Davis chpt.) Chaplain Robert E. Lee Chapt., Daus. Republic Tex. (parliamentarian gen.), Am. Mus. Soc., Harris County Heritage Soc., Kappa Beta Pi (pres. lambda alumni). Episcopalian. Oil, gas, and mineral, Real property. Home: 5556 Cranbrook Rd Houston TX 77056-1600 Office: Ehlinger & Anderson 5556 Sturbridge Dr Houston TX 77056-1623

**ANDERSON, EDWARD RILEY,** state supreme court chief justice; b. Chattanooga, TN, Aug. 10, 1932. BS, U. Tenn., 1955, JD, 1957. Bar: Tenn. 1958, U.S. Dist. Ct. (ea. dist.) Tenn. 1965, U.S. Ct. Appeals (4th cir.) 1985, U.S. Ct. Appeals (6th cir.), U.S. Supreme Ct. 1988. Assoc. Joyce & Wilson, Oak Ridge, Tenn., 1957-61; ptnr. Joyce, Anderson & Meredith, Oak Ridge, 1961-87; judge Tenn. Ct. Appeals, Knoxville, 1987-90; justice Tenn. Supreme Ct., Knoxville, 1990—, now chief justice; mem. Tenn. Jud. Conf., 1987—; chmn. Tenn. Jud. Coun., 1990—, Select Senate/House Com. on Ct. Automation, 1990—. Past commr. Oak Ridge City Charter. Fellow Am. Bar Found., Tenn. Bar Found.; mem. ABA, Am. Bd. Trial Advocates (pres. Tenn. chpt. 1987-88), Tenn. Bar Assn., Anderson County Bar Assn. (pres. 1961), Tenn. Def. Lawyers Assn. (pres. 1980-81), Am. Inns of Ct. (pres. Tenn. chpt. 1988-90). Avocations: reading, tennis. Office: Tenn Supreme Ct Supreme Court Bldg 719 Locust St Knoxville TN 37902-2512

**ANDERSON, EDWARD VIRGIL,** lawyer; b. San Francisco, Oct. 17, 1953; s. Virgil P and Edna Pauline (Pedersen) A.; m. Kathleen Helen Dunbar, Sept. 3, 1983; children: Elizabeth D., Hilary J. AB in Econs., Stanford U., 1975, JD, 1978. Bar: Calif. 1978. Assoc. Pillsbury Madison & Sutro, San Francisco, 1978—, ptnr., 1987-94; mng. ptnr., mem. firm mgmt. com. Skjerven Morrill MacPherson Franklin and Friel, San Jose, Calif., 1994—. Editor IP Litigator, 1995—; mem. bd. editors Antitrust Law Devel., 1983-86. Trustee Lick-Wilmerding H.S., San Francisco, 1980—, pres.; trustee Santa Clara Law Found., 1995—, Hamlin Sch. for Girls, San Francisco, 1998—. Mem. ABA, Calif. Bar Assn., San Francisco Bar Assn., Santa Clara Bar Assn. (counsel), City Club San Francisco, Stanford Golf Club, Phi Beta Kappa. Republican. Episcopal. Patent, Intellectual property, Antitrust. Home: 330 Santa Clara Ave San Francisco CA 94127-2035 Office: Skjerven Morrill MacPherson Franklin and Friel 25 Metro Dr Ste 700 San Jose CA 95110-1349

**ANDERSON, ERIC DANIEL,** lawyer; b. Livonia, Mich., Dec. 9, 1965; s. Arthur Francis Jr. and Nacny (Kent) A.; m. Alison Scott Davis, Nov. 29, 1997. BS, Fla. State U., 1989; JD, Thomas Cooley Law Sch., 1993; LLM, Chgo. Kent Cook Sch. Law. Bar: Ill., Mich., U.S. Dist. Ct. (we. dist.) Mich., U.S. Dist. Ct. (no. dist.) Ill. Lawyer Tat Parish Law Office, Watervliet, Mich., 1993--95, Overgaard & Davis, Chgo., 1995—. Asst. sec. gen. of counsel Met. Family Svcs., Chgo., 1996—; gen. counsel Pleasant Dale Park Dist., Burr Ridge, Ill., 1995—, Harris Bank Barrington (Ill.), N.A., 1995—. Mem. Ill. Bar Assn. Avocation: water skiing. Appellate, Banking, General civil litigation. Office: Overgaard & Davis 134 N Lasalle St Chicago IL 60602-1086

**ANDERSON, ERIC SEVERIN,** lawyer; b. N.Y.C., Dec. 16, 1943; s. Edward Severin and Dorothy Elvira (Ekbloom) A. BA in History summa cum laude, St. Mary's U., San Antonio, 1968; JD cum laude, Harvard U., 1971. Bar: Tex. 1971. From assoc. to ptnr. Fulbright & Jaworski, L.L.P., Houston, 1971—. Served with USAF, 1961-65. Mem. ABA, State Bar Tex., Houston Bar Assn. Democrat. Clubs: Houston Ctr., Houston City. Avocations: classical music, theater, sports. General corporate, Securities, Municipal (including bonds). Home: 14 E Greenway Plz Unit 21-o Houston TX 77046-1406 Office: Fulbright & Jaworski LLP 1301 Mckinney St Houston TX 77010-3031

**ANDERSON, GEOFFREY ALLEN,** retired lawyer; b. Chgo., Aug. 3, 1947; s. Roger Allen and Ruth (Teninga) A. BA cum laude, Yale U., 1969; JD, Columbia U., 1972. Bar: Ill. 1972. Assoc. Isham, Lincoln & Beale, Chgo., 1972-79, ptnr., 1980-81; ptnr. Reuben & Proctor, Chgo., 1981-85; dep. gen. counsel Tribune Co., Chgo., 1985-92; gen. counsel Chgo. Cubs, 1986-90, corp. counsel, 1991-92; v.p. Timber Trails Country Club, Inc., 1992—. Elder Fourth Presbyn. Ch., Chgo., chmn. worship and music com., 1990-92, trustee, 1992-95, 99—, v.p., 1993-94; bd. dirs. The James Chorale, Chgo., 1993-96, chmn. program com., 1994-96. Recipient Citizenship award Am. Legion, 1965. Mem. Chgo. Bar Assn. (chmn. entertainment com. 1981-82, Best Performance award 1977), Yale Club (N.Y.C.), Phi Delta Phi. Securities, General corporate.

**ANDERSON, GEORGE ROSS, JR.,** federal judge; b. Anderson, S.C., Jan. 29, 1929; s. George Ross and Eva Mae (Pooler) A.; m. Dorothy M. Downie, Dec. 2, 1951; 1 son, G. Ross. B.Comml. Sci., Southeastern U., 1949; postgrad., George Washington U., 1949-51; LL.B., U. S.C., 1954, LLD (hon.), 1984; LLD (hon.), Anderson Coll., 1998. Bar: S.C. 1954. Mem. identification div. FBI, Washington, 1945-47; clk. to U.S. Senator Olin D. Johnston, Washington, 1947-51, Columbia, S.C., 1953-54; individual practice law Anderson, S.C., 1954-79; U.S. dist. judge Dist. Ct. of S.C., Anderson, 1980—. Asst. editor: U.S. S.C. Law Rev, 1953-54. Bd. dirs. Salvation Army, 1968, YMCA, 1968-79, Anderson Youth Assn., 1978-80. Served with USAF, 1951-52. Recipient War Horse award So. Trial Lawyers Assn., 1990. Fellow Internat. Acad. Trial Lawyers (dir. 1979-81), Internat. Soc. Barristers; mem.

S.C. Bar Assn. (dir. 1977-80, past cir. v.p.), Assn. Trial Lawyers Am. (bd. govs. 1969-71), S.C. Trial Lawyers Assn. (v.p. 1970-71, pres. 1971-72, Outstanding Trial Judge of Yr. 1984), hon. doctor of Laws, U. SC, 1984, bd. dirs.,Federal Judges Assn., 1993-97. Democrat. Baptist. Office: US Dist Ct PO Box 2147 Anderson SC 29622-2147

**ANDERSON, GREGG ALAN,** lawyer, educator; b. Traverse City, MI, Jan. 21, 1957; s. Robert Eugene and Betty Jean Anderson. BS, Ferris State Coll., 1982; JD, U. Fla., 1989. Bar: Fla., 1990. Asst. mgr. Walgreen, Chgo., 1982-85, Clearwater, Fla., 1985-87; law clk. Fine, Farkash & Parlapiano, P.A., Gainesville, Fla., 1987-90; atty. Pub. Defender's Office, Gainesville, Fla., 1990—; adj. lectr. Coll. Law U. Fla., Gainesville, 1995—. Repicipient alumni scholarship Ferris State Coll., 1980. Mem. Fla. Assn. Criminal Def. Lawyers. Avocations: tennis, running, photography, travel. Office: Pub Defender Office 35 N Main St Gainesville FL 32601-5323

**ANDERSON, HERBERT HATFIELD,** lawyer, farmer; b. Rainier, Oreg., Aug. 2, 1920; s. Odin A. and Mae (Hatfield) A.; m. Barbara Stuart Bastine, June 3, 1949; children—Linda, Catherine, Thomas, Amy, Elizabeth, Kenneth. B.A. in Bus. Adminstrn., U. Oreg., 1940; J.D., Yale U., 1949. Exec. trainee U.S. Steel Co., San Francisco, 1940-41; assoc. Spears, Lubersky, Campbell, Bledsoe, Anderson & Young, Portland, Oreg., 1949-54; ptnr. Spears, Lubersky, Bledsoe, Anderson, Young & Hilliard, 1954-90, Lane, Powell, Spears & Lubersky, Portland, 1990—; instr. law Lewis and Clark Coll., Portland, 1950-70. Mem. planning adv. com. Yamhill County, Oreg., 1974-82; bd. dirs. Emanuel Hosp., 1967—; bd. dirs. Flyfisher Found., 1972—, pres., 1972-84; bd. dirs. Multnomah Law Library, 1958—, sec. 1962-68, 77—, pres., 1964-74. Served to maj., parachute inf. U.S. Army, 1942-46, ETO. Fellow Am. Bar Found. (chmn. Oreg. chpt. 1988—); mem. ABA (chmn. governing com. forum on health law 1984-89, chmn. standing com. on jud. selection, tenure and compensation 1978-80, Lawyer's Conf., exec. com. 1980-94, chmn. 1989-90, judicial adminstrn. divsn. coun. 1978-94, sr. lawyer's divsn. coun. 1987-89), Am. Judicature Soc. (bd. dirs. 1981-85), Soc. Law and Medicine, Nat. Health Lawyers Assn., Am. Acad. Hosp. Attys., Oreg. Soc. Hosp. Attys. (pres. 1984-85), Multnomah Bar Found. (bd. dirs. 1955—, pres. 1959-64, 87—), Nat. Bankruptcy Conf. (conferee 1964—, exec. com. 1976-79, chmn. farmer insolvency com. 1985-88), Nat. Assn. R.R. Trial Counsel, Oreg. Bar Assn. (del. to ABA 1966-68), Multnomah Bar Assn. (pres. 1955), Western States Bar Conf. (pres. 1967), Oreg. Asian Pear Coun. (pres. 1989-91), Sigma Chi. Democrat. Lutheran. Clubs: Multnomah Athletic, Michelbook Country, Flyfishers Oreg. (pres. 1972), Willamette Amateur Field Trial (pres. 1968-72). Lodge: Masons. Bankruptcy, Real property, Health. Home: River Meadow Farm 19289 SE Neck Rd Dayton OR 97114-7815 Office: Lane Powell Spears & Lubersky 520 SW Yamhill St Ste 800 Portland OR 97204-1383

**ANDERSON, J. TRENT,** lawyer; b. Indpls., July 22, 1939; s. Robert C. and Charlotte M. (Pfeifer) A.; m. Judith J. Zimmerman, Sept. 8, 1962; children: Evan M., Molly K. BS, Purdue U., 1961; LLB, U. Va., 1964. Bar: Ill. 1965, Ind. 1965. Teaching asst. U. Cal. Law Sch., Berkeley, 1964-65; assoc. Mayer, Brown & Platt, Chgo., 1965-72, ptnr., 1972—; instr. Loyola U. Law Sch., Chgo., 1985. Mem. ABA, Law Club, Union League Club, Mich. Shores Club. Mergers and acquisitions, General corporate, Contracts commercial. Home: 3037 Iroquois Rd Wilmette IL 60091-1106 Office: Mayer Brown & Platt 190 S La Salle St Ste 3100 Chicago IL 60603-3441

**ANDERSON, JAMES E.,** corporate lawyer. AB, Stanford U., 1969, JD, 1972. Bar: Calif. 1972, Tex. 1973, Tenn. 1985. Assoc. Akin, Gump, Strauss, Hauer & Feld, 1972-74, 76-78, ptnr., 1979-83; ptnr. Wald, Harkrader & Ross, 1983-84, Dearborn & Ewing, 1984-91; v.p., gen. counsel Ingram Industries Inc., 1991-96; sr. v.p., sec., gen. counsel Ingram Micro, 1996—. Office: Ingram Micro 1600 E Saint Andrew Pl Santa Ana CA 92705*

**ANDERSON, JAMES FRANCIS,** lawyer; b. Glen Ridge, N.J., June 13, 1965. BA, Seton Hall U., 1987, JD, 1990. Bar: N.J. 1991, U.S. Supreme Ct. 1995. Pvt. practice Spring Lake, N.J., 1991—. Pro bono atty. Ocean-Monmouth Legal Svcs., Freehold, N.J., 1991—; mentor Manasquan (N.J.) H.S., 1994. Mem. ABA, Masons. Criminal, General practice. Office: PO Box 144 Spring Lake NJ 07762-0144

**ANDERSON, JAMES MICHAEL,** lawyer; b. Hazard, Ky., Dec. 27, 1948; s. Naaman Finley Anderson and Eva Lorette (Johnson) Torries; m. Charlotte Gwen Allen, Aug. 23, 1975; children: Leigh Michelle, Laura Elaine. BS, U. So. Miss., 1971; JD, Miss. Coll., 1978. Bar: Miss. 1978. Claim supr. Aetna Casualty & Surety Co., Jackson, Miss., 1971-74; adminstrv. asst. Miss. Workers Compensation Commn., Jackson, 1974-76; claim supr. Home Ins. Co., Jackson, 1976-78; ptnr. McCoy, Wilkins, Noblin, Anderson & Stephens, Jackson, 1978-85, Markow, Walker, Reeves & Anderson, Jackson, 1986-97; gen. counsel, sec. The Am Fed Cos., Ridgeland, Miss., 1998—; lectr. Nat. Bus. Inst. Seminars, Jackson, 1988, 89, Miss. Workers Compensation Commn. Ednl. Conf., Jackson, 1988, Miss. Coll. Sch. Law seminar, Jackson, 1988. Mem. ABA, Miss. State Bar Assn. (officer adminstrv. law and workers compensation sect. 1989—). Republican. Baptist. Administrative and regulatory, Labor, Workers' compensation. Office: The AmFed Cos PO Box 1380 Ridgeland MS 39158-1380

**ANDERSON, JANICE LEE,** lawyer; b. Abington, Pa., July 28, 1957; d. Alfred and Elizabeth J. (Sharer) Munz; m. J. Barry Anderson, June 8, 1985; children: Ryan B., Brett C., Cara E. BS, Kutztown State U., 1979; JD, Dickinson Sch. Law Pa. State U, 1982. Bar: Pa. 1982, N.J. 1983, U.S. Ct. Appeals (3d cir.) 1987, U.S. Supreme Ct. 1988, U.S. Dist. Ct. (mid. and ea. dists.) Pa. 1986, U.S. Dist. Ct. (mid. and ea. dists.) N.J. Law clk. Lebanon (Pa.) County Ct. of Common Pleas, 1982-83; asst. pub. defender Office of the Pub. Defender, Lebanon County, Pa., 1983-85; law clk. Commonwealth Ct. of Pa., Harrisburg, 1985-86; dep. atty. gen. Office of Atty. Gen., Harrisburg, 1986-93, chief dept. atty., 1993-98, sr. dep. atty. gen., 1998-99. Bd. dirs. Nat. Assn. State Charity Ofcls., 1995-97; mem. South Hanover Elem. Sch. Parent-Tchr. Orgn., 1996—. Mem. Pa. Bar Assn. Avocations: raising children, soccer, baseball, skiing. Address: Nonprofit Svc Group 7105 Silver Fox Ct Hummelstown PA 17036 Office: Office of Atty Gen 15th Fl Strawberry Sq Harrisburg PA 17120

**ANDERSON, JILL LYNN,** lawyer; b. Niles, Mich., Apr. 23, 1961. BA, Mich. State U., 1983; JD, Mercer Sch. Law, 1986. Bar: Ga. Ptnr. Kane & Anderson, Atlanta, 1986-90; assoc. Kaufman & Chaiken, Atlanta, 1990-93; pub. defender Douglas County Pub. Defender's Office, Douglasville, Ga., 1994—. Recipient Committment to Excellence award Ga. Indigent Def. Coun., 1996. Mem. Nat. Assn. Criminal Def. Attys., Ga. Assn. Criminal Def. Attys. (bd. dirs., chair indigent def. com. 1996—), Ga. Bar Assn. (young lawyers sect., mock trial com., law awareness for youth com.), Mich. State U. Alumni Assn. (life, bd. dirs. Atlanta alumni 1989-93). Office: Pub Defenders Office 8700 Hospital Dr Douglasville GA 30134-2264

**ANDERSON, JOHN BAYARD,** lawyer, educator, former congressman; b. Rockford, Ill., Feb. 15, 1922; s. E. Albin and Mabel Edna (Ring) A.; m. Keke Machakos, Jan. 4, 1953; children: Eleanora, John Bayard, Diane, Karen, Susan Kimberly. A.B., U. Ill., 1942, JD, 1946; LLM, Harvard U., 1949; hon. doctorates, No. Ill. U., Wheaton Coll., Shimer Coll., Biola Coll., Geneva Coll., North Park Coll. and Theol. Sem., Houghton Coll., Trinity Coll., Rockford Coll. Bar: Ill. 1946. Practice law Rockford, 1946-52; with U.S. Fgn. Service, 1952-55; assigned West Berlin, 1952-55; mem. 87th-95th Congresses from 16th Dist. Ill., mem. rules com.; chmn. Ho. Republican Conf., 1969-79; ind. candidate for Pres. U.S., 1980; vis. prof. Stanford U., spring, 1981, Nova-Southeastern U. Ctr. for Study Law, 1987-99; vis. prof. polit. sci. Brandeis U., 1985, Oreg. State U., spring 1986, U. Mass., 1985—; vis. prof. law Washington Coll. Law Am. U., 1997—; lectr. polit. sci. Bryn Mawr Coll., spring 1985. Author: Between Two Worlds: A Congressman's Choice, 1970, Vision and Betrayal in America, 1976, The American Economy We Need, 1984, A Proper Institution: Guaranteeing Televised Presidential Debates, 1988; editor: Congress and Conscience, 1970. Ind. candidate for Pres. U.S., 1980. Mem. World Federalist Assn. (pres. 1992—), Ctr. for Voting and Democracy (pres. 1996—, co-chair nat. adv. bd. pub. campaign for campaign fin. reform 1997—), Coun. on Fgn. Rels., Phi Beta Kappa. Mem. Evang. Free Ch. (past trustee). Office: 3917 Massachusetts Ave NW Washington DC 20016-5104

**ANDERSON, JON ERIC,** lawyer; b. Jacksonville, N.C., Feb. 1, 1956; m. Lori Jean Schumacher, June 30, 1979; children: Andrew Jon, Elizabeth Ruth, Margaret Mary. BA, U. Wis., 1978; JD, Marquette U., 1981. Bar: Wis. 1981, U.S. Dist. Ct. (ea. and we. dists.) Wis. 1981, U.S. Ct. Appeals (7th cir.) 1996, U.S. Supreme Ct. 1988. Assoc. Mulcahy & Wherry, S.C., Milw., 1981-84; mng. atty. Mulcahy & Wherry, S.C., Sheboygan, Wis., 1984-87, Madison, 1987-90; shareholder Godfrey & Kahn, S.C., Madison, 1991—. Author: (with others) Comparable Worth-A Negotiator's Guide, 1985; contbg. author Pub. Sector Labor Rels., Wis., 1988. Thomas More Soc. scholar, 1979. Mem. ABA, Edn. Law Assn., Wis. Bar Assn. (bd. dirs. labor law sect. 1988-91), Blackhawk Country Club, Wis. Sch. Attys. Assn., Madison Club, Phi Delta Phi, Alpha Sigma Nu. Lutheran. Avocations: woodworking, music. Education and schools, Labor, Administrative and regulatory.

**ANDERSON, JON MAC,** lawyer; b. Rio Grande, Ohio, Jan. 10, 1937; s. Harry Rudolph and Carrie Viola (Magee) A.; m. Deborah Melton, June 1, 1961; children—Jon Gordon, Greta. AB, Ohio U., 1958; JD, Harvard Law Sch., 1961. Bar: Ohio 1961. Law clk. Hon. Kingsley A. Taft Ohio Supreme Ct., Columbus, 1961-62; assoc. Wright, Harlor, Morris & Arnold, Columbus, 1962-67, ptnr., 1968-76; ptnr. Porter, Wright, Morris & Arthur, Columbus, 1977—; adj. prof. law Ohio State U. Law Sch., Columbus, 1975-83; bar examiner State of Ohio, 1971-76, chmn., 1975-76; lectr. tax and estate planning insts.; bd. dirs. White Castle System, Inc., Columbus. Trustee Berea Coll, Ky., 1976—, Pro Musica Chamber Orch., Columbus, 1980-98, Opera Columbus, 1985-88, 1st Congl. Ch., Columbus, 1979-83, Greater Columbus Arts Coun., 1989-99; chmn., 1996-98; mem. adv. council The Textile Mus. Mem. ABA, Ohio State Bar Assn., Columbus Bar Assn., The Columbus Club, Rocky Fork Hunt and Country Club. Democrat. Avocations: music, art, textiles, literature, antique collections. Estate planning, Probate, General corporate. Office: Porter Wright Morris & Arthur 41 S High St Ste 2800 Columbus OH 43215-6194

**ANDERSON, JONATHAN WALFRED,** lawyer; b. New Haven, May 13, 1957; s. Robert W. Anderson and Dorothy (Partington) Barker; m. Leslie D. Vanderveen, Oct. 17, 1981; children: Jeffrey W., Theodore M. BA, Calvin Coll., 1979; JD cum laude, U. Notre Dame, Ind., 1982. Bar: Mich. 1982. Assoc. Varnum, Riddering, Schmidt & Howlett, Grand Rapids, Mich., 1982-88, ptnr., 1988—; lectr. Inst. of Continuing Legal Edn., Ann Arbor, Mich., 1988—, Nat. Bus. Inst., Grand Rapids, 1988—. Bd. dirs. Dwelling Place Grand Rapids, Inc., 1988-93, pres., 1993; bd. dirs. Habitat for Humanity Grand Rapids, Inc., 1988-92, pres. bd. dirs., 1990-91; bd. dirs. Cherry St. Health Svcs., 1995-98, Legal Aid Western Mich., 1998—. Mem. ABA, Internat. Coun. Shopping Ctrs., Bldg. Owners and Mgrs. Assn. Grand Rapids (treas. 1991-92), Constrn. Fin. Mgrs. Assn., State Bar Mich., Grand Rapids Bar Assn. Presbyterian. Avocations: genealogy, opera. Real property. Office: Varnum Riddering Schmidt & Howlett PO Box 352 Grand Rapids MI 49501-0352

**ANDERSON, JOSÉ F.,** law educator, lawyer; b. Balt., Aug. 9, 1960; s. William Armfield Anderson and Aquilla Zenobia (Alaba) Rice; m. Dreama Delores Clarke, May 28, 1983; children: Kristen, Danielle. BA, U. Md., 1981, JD, 1984. Bar: Md. 1985. Appellate atty. Md. Pub. Defender, Balt., 1985-90, spl. asst. pub. defender, 1990-92, supervising atty. appeals divsn., 1992-93; prof. law U. Balt., 1993—. Contbr. articles to profl. jours.; editor-in-chief U. Md. Law Jour., 1983. Chmn. bd. dirs. U. Md. Balt. County Athletic Scholarship Found., 1993-94. Mem. Md. State Bar Criminal Law Coun. (treas. 1997), Md. Criminal Def. Atty.'s Assn. (bd. dirs. 1991—), Optimist, Omicron Delta Kappa. Avocations: golf, classic literature, history, biographics. Office: U Balt 1420 N Charles St Baltimore MD 21201-5720

**ANDERSON, JOSEPH FLETCHER, JR.,** federal judge; b. 1949. BA, Clemson U., 1972; JD, U. S.C., 1975. Pvt. practice law Anderson, Anderson and Anderson, 1977-86; law clk. to presiding justice U.S. Ct. Appeals (4th cir.), 1975-76; mem. Ho. of Reps. 3d Congrl. Dist. S.C., 1980-86; judge U.S. Dist. Ct. S.C., Columbia, 1986—. Chmn. honor coun. U. S.C. Sch. Law, 1976-85, Edgefield Indsl. Devel. Corp., S.C., bd. dirs., 1978-86; mem. local adv. bd. First Citizens Bank and Trust Co., Trenton, S.C., 1983-86; chmn., vol. Edgefield County Re-election Campaign for Sen. Strom Thurmond, 1972, 84; chmn. Edgefield County Campaign for Congressman William Jennings Bryan Dorn for Dem. Nomination for Gov. of S.C.; bd. dirs. Edgefield County United Way, 1983-86; mem. exec. com. Coun. Boy Scouts Am., 1978-86. Named one of Three Outstanding Young Men of S.C., 1980. Mem. ABA, S.C. Bar Assn., S.C. Trial Lawyers Assn., S.C. Law Inst. Coun. Office: US Dist Ct PO Box 447 Columbia SC 29202-0447

**ANDERSON, KARL STEPHEN,** editor; b. Chgo., Nov. 10, 1933; s. Karl William and Eleanor (Grell) a.; m. Saralee Hegland, Nov. 5, 1977; children by previous marriage: Matthew, Douglas, Eric. BS in Editl. Journalism, U. Ill., 1955. Successively advtsg. mgr., asst. to pub., then pub. Crescent Newspapers, Downers Grove, Ill., 1971-73; assoc. pub., editor Chronicle Pub. Co., St. Charles, 1973-80; assoc. pub. Chgo. Daily Law Bull., 1981-88; dir. comms., editor Ill. State Bar Assn., 1988—; past pres. Chgo. Pub. Rels. Forum. Trustee emeritus Chi Psi Ednl. Trust; trustee Leo Sowerby Found. Recipient C.V. Amenoff award No. Ill. U. Dept. Journalism, 1976, award Ill. State Bar Bd. Govs., 1987, Print Media Humanitarian award Coalition Sub Bar Assns., 1987, Robert C. Preble, Jr. award Chi Psi, 1991, Asian-Am. Bar Media Sensitivity award, 1991, Liberty Bell award DuPage County Bar Assn., 1993, Glass Ceiling Busters award Assn. Women Lawyers, 1993, Disting. Svc. award Chgo. Vol. Legal Svcs. Found., 1993, Gratitude award Lawyers Assistance Program, 1993, Outstanding Achievement in Comm. award Justinian Soc., 1994, 3rd prize Nat. Libr. Poetry, 1995, Svc. award Women's Bar Assn. Ill., 1998, Peoria County Bar Assn., 1998, Communicator of Yr. award Justinian Soc., 1999. Mem. Nat. Assn. Bar Execs., Baltic Bar Assn., Chgo. Legal Sec. Assn., Chgo. Press Vets. Assn., Ill. Press assn. (Will Loomis award 1977, 80), Kane County Bar Assn., DuPage Women Lawyers Assn., West Suburban Bar Assn., N. Suburban Bar Assn. (Pub. Svc. award 1997), Bohemian Lawyers Assn. (Liberty award 1999), No. Ill. Newspaper Assn. (past pres.), Pub. Rels. Soc. Ctrl. Ill. (Master Communicator award of achievement 1997), Soc. Profl. Journalists, Headline Club (past pres.), Nordic Law Club, Nellie Fox Soc., Chgo. Athletic Assn., Chi Psi. Home: 3180 N Lake Shore Dr Apt 14D Chicago IL 60657-4851 Office: Ill State Bar Assn 20 S Clark St Ste 900 Chicago IL 60603-1885

**ANDERSON, KATHLEEN GAY,** consultant mediator, hearing officer, arbitrator; b. Cin., July 27, 1950; d. Harold B. and Trudi L. (Chambers) Briggs; m. J.R. Carr, July 4, 1988; 1 child, Jesse J. Anderson. Student, U. Cin., 1971-72, Antioch Coll., 1973-74; cert., Nat. Jud. Coll., U. Nev., Reno, 1987, Inst. Applied Law, 1987, Acad. Family Mediators, 1991. Cert. Am. Arbitration Assn. Comml. Arbitration Panel, Nat. Assn. Securities Dealers Arbitration and Mediation Panels, Lemmon Mediation Inst., Acad. Family Mediators, U.S. Postal Svc. Panel. Paralegal Lauer & Lauer, Santa Fe, 1976-79, Wilkinson, Cragun & Barker, Anchorage, 1981-82; employment law paralegal specialist Hughes, Thorsness, Gantz, Powell & Brundin, Anchorage, 1983-91; investigator, mediator Alaska State Commn. Human Rights, 1991; consultant mediator, arbitrator, trainer The Arbitration and Mediation Group, Anchorage, 1987—; hearing officer Municipality of Anchorage, 1993-99; State of Alaska, 1994—; mem. faculty nat. Jud. Coll., U. Nev., Reno, 1988-89; adj. prof. U. Alaska, Anchorage, 1985—, Alaska Pacific U., 1990-96, Chapman U., 1990; mem. Alaska Supreme Ct. Mediation Task Force, 1991-96; adv. com. Am. Arbitration Assn. for Alaska, 1995-99, ADR subcom. Supreme Ct. Civil Justice Reform task force, 1998-99; trainer mediation svcs. pvt. profit and nonprofit groups, pub. groups, U.S. mil., state and fed. govt.; arbitrator Anchorage Bd. Realtors, 1997—. Author, editor: Professional Responsibility Handbook for Legal Assistants and Paralegals, 1986; contbr. articles to profl. jours. Lectr. Alaska Bar Assn., NLRB, Bus. and Profl. Women, Coun. on Edn. and Mgmt., Small Bus. Devel. Coun., various employers and bus. groups. Mem. Am. Arbitration Assn. (cert. comml. arbitration panel 1996-99, U.S. Postal Svc. Mediation Panel 1999—, U.S. Forest Svc. 1999—), Soc. Profls. in Dispute Resolution, Acad. Family Mediators, Alaska Bar Assn. (assoc., alt. dispute resolution), Alaska Dispute Settlement Assn. (v.p. 1992-93, chair com. on credentialing and stds. of practice, pres. 1997-98). Avocations: jewelry design, antiques, gourmet cooking, rare bead collecting. Home: PO Box 100098 Anchorage AK 99510-0098 Office: PO Box 240783 Anchorage AK 99524-0783

**ANDERSON, KENT TAYLOR,** lawyer; b. Salt Lake City, June 24, 1953; s. Neldon Leroy and Vera Minnie (Taylor) A.; m. Ellis Anderson (div. June 1979); m. Tara Dayle, Apr. 30, 1982; 1 child, Claire Marie. BA, U. Utah, 1975; JD, Georgetown U., 1978. Bar: Utah 1978, Calif. 1987. Assoc. Jones, Waldo, Holbrook & McDonough, Salt Lake City, 1978-83, ptnr., 1983-84; v.p., gen. counsel Am. Stores Properties, Inc., Salt Lake City, 1984-86; v.p., gen. counsel, asst. sec. Am. Stores Co., Salt Lake City, 1987—; sr. v.p., gen. counsel, sec. Alpha Beta Stores, Inc., Anaheim, Calif., 1986-89; exec. v.p., gen. counsel, asst. sec. Am. Stores Co., Salt Lake City, 1989-93, exec. v.p., 1993—; gen. mgr. Am. Stores Properties, Inc., Salt Lake City, 1993-95, COO strategy and devel., mem. exec. coun., 1995—; Mem. staff Georgetown Law Jour., 1976-78. Mem. Utah Bar Assn., Calif. Bar Assn., Phi Beta Kappa. Office: Am Stores Properties Inc 1654 Mohawk Way Salt Lake City UT 84108-3312

**ANDERSON, LAURA ELISABETH,** lawyer; b. Boston, Jan. 30, 1970; d. Winston Anthony and Carol Mamie Anderson; m. Darien Kendall Wright, Sept. 18, 1999. BA, U.N.C., 1991; JD, Washington & Lee U., 1994. Bar: Md. 1995, DC 1996. Univ. counsel U. of Md., College Park, 1995—; Bar: Md. 1995, D.C. 1996. Mem. Nat. Bar Assn., Nat. Coalition of 100 Black Women, Delta Sigma Theta. Avocations: travel, reading. Office: U Md 2101 Main Administration Bldg College Park MD 20742-5021

**ANDERSON, LAUREN WIRTHLIN,** lawyer; b. Verona, N.J., Mar. 4, 1960; d. Donald Richard and Audrey Lilyan (Jacob) Wirthlin; m. James D. Anderson, Apr. 25, 1987; children: Emily Page, Myles Jordan. BA in Polit. Sci., U. Tenn., 1980; student, U. Metz (France), 1982; JD, Duke U., 1985. Bar: Tenn. 1985. Atty. Boult Cummings Conners & Berry, Nashville, 1985-88, Harwell Howard Hyne Gabbert & Manner P.C., Nashville, 1988—; dir. child devel. ctr. Vanderbilt U., Nashville, 1987-92. Active C.A.B.L.E., Nashville, 1990—. Mem. ABA, Tenn. Bar Assn., Nashville Bar Assn. (law practice mgmt. and mock trial coms.). Republican. Presbyterian. Avocations: hiking, white-water rafting, snorkeling, cooking, handcrafts, reading. Mergers and acquisitions, Securities, Trademark and copyright. Office: Harwell Howard Hyne Gabbert & Manner 1800 First American Ctr Nashville TN 37238

**ANDERSON, LAWRENCE ROBERT, JR.,** lawyer; b. Minden, La., Oct. 30, 1945; s. Lawrence Robert and Elnora Dale (Fincher) A.; m. Constance Lorraine Fauver, Oct. 21, 1977; children: Lauren Constance, Frank Lawrence. BS, La. State U., 1967, JD, 1971. Bar: La. 1971, U.S. Dist. Ct. (ea. dist.) La. 1971, U.S. Ct. Appeals (5th cir.) 1971, U.S. Dist. Ct. (mid. dist.) La. 1972, U.S. Dist. Ct. (we. dist.) La. 1975, U.S. Supreme Ct. 1975. Assoc. Sanders, Miller, Downing & Kean, Baton Rouge, 1971, Talley, Anthony, Hughes & Knight, Bogalusa, La., 1971-74; ptnr. Newman, Duggins, Drolla, Gamble & Anderson, Baton Rouge, 1974-76, Anderson & Roberts, Baton Rouge, 1976-79, Anderson, Anderson, Hawsey, Rainach and Stakelum, Baton Rouge, 1979-83, Anderson & Rainach, 1983-88, Anderson & Duncan, 1988-89, Seale, Smith, Zuber & Barnette, Baton Rouge, 1990—. 1st lt. U.S. Army, 1972. Mem. La. Bar Assn., Bar Assn. Fed. 5th Cir., Baton Rouge Bar Assn., Am. Bankruptcy Inst., Comml. Law League Am. Republican. Roman Catholic. Contbr. articles to profl. jours. Bankruptcy, Contracts commercial, Constitutional. Home: 11937 Lake Sherwood Ave N Baton Rouge LA 70816-4340 Office: 8550 United Plaza Blvd Ste 200 Baton Rouge LA 70809-2256

**ANDERSON, LAWRENCE WORTHINGTON,** retired lawyer; b. Dallas, Sept. 27, 1917; s. Frank William and Amelia Kathryn A.; m. Ardene Sarah Boven, June 27, 1942; children: Constance, Lawrence Jr., Carol. JD, U. Tex., 1939. Bar: Ill. 1939, Tex. 1946, U.S. Supreme Ct. 1960. Assoc. Carrington, Gowan, Dallas, 1943-48; ptnr. Harris, Anderson & Henley, Dallas, 1948-60, Anderson, Helley & Shields, Dallas, 1960-80, Ray, Anderson, Shield, Tronti, Dallas, 1980-83; of counsel Anderson, Miller & Sifford, Dallas, 1983-86, Anderson & Miller, Dallas, 1986-1990, Siffod & Anderson, Dallas, 1990—; gen. counsel Internat. Assn. Ins., 1960—, Ladies Profl. Golf Assn., 1970-78; chmn. bd. Am. Intilian Food Co., Dallas, 1978-83, Food Source, Inc., McKinney, Tex., 1985-90; mem. bd. adjustment City of Dallas, 1980-85. With USN, 1943-44. Named to Hall of Fame, Dallas Assn. Def., 1995. Mem. ABA, State Bar Tex., Dallas County Bar Assn., Smith County Bar Assn., Tex. Assn. Def., Hide-Away Lake Club. Republican. Presbyterian. Avocation: golf. Aviation, General civil litigation, Insurance. Home: 1341 Hideaway Ln W Lindale TX 75771

**ANDERSON, LEA E.,** lawyer; b. Clarksburg, W.Va., May 25, 1954; d. Jackson Lawler and Barbara Jean (Sanford) A.; m. Templeton Smith Jr., Aug. 2, 1980; children: Templeton Smith III, Suzanne Lea Smith. BA, W.Va. U., 1976, JD, 1979. Bar: W.Va. 1979, U.S. Dist. Ct. (so. dist.) W.Va. 1979, Pa. 1981, U.S. Supreme Ct. 1982. Assoc. Bowles, McDavid, Graff & Love, Charleston, W.Va., 1979-80; assoc. Goehring, Rutter & Boehm, Pitts., 1980-84, ptnr., 1984-89, mem., 1990—, sec., 1993—; mem. credit com. Alcobar Fed. Credit Union, 1985-87, mem. supervisory com., 1981; mem. vis. com. W.Va. Coll. Law, 1986-89, mem., chmn. W.Va. U. student affairs vis. com., 1996-99. Vol. March of Dimes, 1986, neighborhood coord., 1987-91; chmn. fundraising com. Southminster Nursery Sch., 1989; chmn. Windy Ridge, 1991-93; mem. Performing Arts for Children, South, 1991-94, v.p., membership com. 1993-94; mem. bd. deacons Southminster Presbyn. Ch., Mt. Lebanon, Pa., 1990-93, vice chmn. bd. deacons, 1993, session mem., elder, trustee, 1993-97; active Foster Sch. PTA, 1993-97. Mem. W.Va. Bar Assn., Pa. Bar Assn., Allegheny County Bar Assn. (chmn. edn. com. of young lawyers 1983-84, treas. 1984-85, mem. rules com. family law sect. 1993-94), Child Study Club of Mt. Lebanon (pres. 1989-91), Mt. Lebanon Aqua Club (treas. 1996-98, nominating com. 1997, 98, sec. 1999—), Phi Beta Kappa, Phi Kappa Phi, Phi Delta Phi. Republican. Probate, Estate planning, Family and matrimonial. Office: Goehring Rutter & Boehm 1424 Frick Bldg 437 Grant St Ste 437 Pittsburgh PA 15219-6002

**ANDERSON, LLOYD VINCENT,** lawyer; b. Eau Claire, Wis., Apr. 5, 1943; s. Lloyd V. and Marion (Benner) A.; m. Mary Sue Wilson, June 19, 1965; children: Matthew, Kirsten, Sam. B of Mgmt. in Engring., Rensselaer Poly. Inst., 1965; J.D., Georgetown U., 1969. Bar: Va. 1969, Alaska 1970, Minn. 1972, U.S. Ct. Appeals 1972, U.S. Dist. Ct. Minn. and Alaska 1972, Trust Ter. Pacific Islands 1972, D.C. 1969, U.S. Patent Office 1969. Law clk. Alaska Supreme Ct., Juneau, 1969-70; asst. U.S. atty. Dept. Justice, Agana, Guam, 1970-72; atty. Gray Plant Mooty & Anderson, Mpls., 1972-74; shareholder, dir. Birch Horton Bittner Pestinger & Anderson, Anchorage, 1974-89; pvt. practice, Anchorage, 1989—; bd. dirs. Arrow Leasing, Anchorage. Mem. Anchorage Park Bd., 1976. Mem. ABA, Alaska Bar Assn., Am. Trial Lawyers Assn., Wash. Athletic Club (Seattle) Personal injury, General civil litigation, Product liability. Office: 101 E 9th Ave Ste 9B Anchorage AK 99501-3651

**ANDERSON, MARGRET ELIZABETH,** lawyer; b. Port Chester, N.Y., Oct. 2, 1949; d. Samuel Glover and Evelyn (Oliver) A.; m. Robert T. McDonald, May 16, 1980; children: Christina Anderson-McDonald, Meredith Anderson-McDonald, Melissa Anderson-McDonald. Student, Wellesley Coll., 1967-69; BA, Yale U., 1971; JD, U. Pa., 1974. Bar: Pa. 1974, U.S. Dist. Ct. (ea. dist.) Pa. 1975, U.S. Ct. Appeals (3rd cir.) 1976. Intern Pub. Defender, Phila., 1972-73, U.S. Civil Rights Commn., Washington, 1973; legal writing instr. U. Pa. Sch. Law, Phila., 1973-74; asst. atty. gen. Pa. Dept. of Justice, Phila., 1974-79; sr. atty. Merck & Co., Inc., West Point, Pa., 1979-92; cons. Meadowbrook, Pa., 1992—; of counsel Arnelle & Hastie, Phila., 1993—. Mem. Zoning Hearing Bd., Abington, Pa., 1985-87; vol. March of Dimes, 1987-88, 92, United Way, 1989. Mem. Nat. Bar Assn., Pa. Bar Assn. Episcopalian. Environmental, Product liability. Office: Merck & Co Inc Sumneytown Pike West Point PA 19486

**ANDERSON, MARK ALEXANDER,** lawyer; b. Santa Monica, Calif., Nov. 15, 1953; s. William Alexander and Christina (Murray) A.; m. Rosalie Louise Movius, Nov. 28, 1986; 1 child, Morgan Anderson Movius. AB, U. So. Calif., 1974; JD, Yale U., 1978. Bar: Calif. 1979, U.S. Dist. Ct. (no. dist.) Calif. 1979, U.S. Ct. Appeals (9th cir.) 1979, Oreg. 1982, U.S. Dist. Ct. Oreg. 1982, Wash. 1985, U.S. Dist. Ct. (we. dist.) Wash. 1986, U.S. Supreme Ct. 1989. Law clk. U.S. Ct. Appeals (9th cir.), San Francisco, 1978-79, U.S. Dist. Ct. Oreg., Portland, 1980-82; atty. Miller, Nash, Wiener, Hager & Carlsen, Portland, 1983-92; gen. counsel, asst. sec. Dark Horse Comics, Inc., Milwaukie, Oreg., 1992-98. Chair Raleigh Hills-Garden Home Citizen Participation Orgn., 1992-93. Mem. N.W. Lawyers and Artists (pres. 1988-90), State Bar Calif., Wash. State Bar Assn., Oreg. State Bar (chair antitrust, trade regulation and unfair bus. practices sect. 1991-92), City Club of Portland (chair arts and culture standing com. 1990-92, rsch. bd. 1999—). Antitrust, General corporate, Trademark and copyright. Home: PO Box 8154 Portland OR 97207-8154

**ANDERSON, MELISSA A.,** lawyer; b. Durand, Wis., July 5, 1966; d. Donald L. and Mary A. Anderson. BA in English, Viterbo Coll., 1988; JD, Drake U., 1991. Bar: Iowa 1991. Asst. state pub. defender Ft. Dodge (Iowa) Pub. Defender's Office, 1991-95, Des Moines Adult Pub. Defender's Office, 1995—; adj. instr. Des Moines Area C.C., 1997—. Mem. Nat. Assn. Criminal Def. Lawyers, Iowa Assn. Criminal Def. Lawyers. Office: Des Moines Adult Pub Defenders Office 505 5th Ave Ste 506 Des Moines IA 50309-2320

**ANDERSON, MICHAEL STEVEN,** lawyer; b. Mpls., May 25, 1954; s. Wesley James and Lorraine Kathrine (Sword) A.; m. Gail Karin Miller, June 18, 1977; children: Mark, Steven. BA magna cum laude, Cornell U., 1976; JD, Washington U., St. Louis, 1980. Bar: Wis. 1980, U.S. Dist. Ct. (ea. and we. dists.) Wis. 1980, U.S. Ct. Appeals (7th cir.) 1986, U.S. Supreme Ct. 1991. Ptnr. Axley Brynelson, Madison, Wis., 1980—; gen. counsel DEC, Internat., Inc., 1992—. Editor, author Washington U. Law Quarterly, 1979-80. Apptd. mem. local Bd. Attys. Profl. Responsibility, 1993—. Mem. Am. Corp. Counsel Assn., Lic. Exec. Soc., Order of Coif. Mem. Evangelical Free Ch. Avocation: family. E-mail: manderson@axley.com. General civil litigation, General corporate, Product liability. Home: 5882 Timber Ridge Trail Madison WI 53711-5180 Office: Axley Brynelson 2 E Mifflin St Madison WI 53703-2889

**ANDERSON, P. RICHARD,** lawyer; b. Jacksonville, Fla., Nov. 18, 1947; s. Phillip Richard Anderson and Edith J. Eubanks; m. Marilyn Anne Rodgers, June 14, 1970; children: Jessica Rodgers, Phillip Richard III. BS, U. Md., 1969; JD, Coll. William and Mary, 1973. Bar: Ohio, Ky. Assoc. Calfee Halter & Gilswold, Cleve., 1973-79; mem. Greenbaum Doll & McDonald, Louisville, 1979-98, mng. ptnr., 1994—. Bd. dirs. Louisville Metro United Way, 1994—, Greater Louisville Inc., 1994. Sgt. USMC, 1969-75. Mem. ABA, Cleve. Bar Assn., Louisville Bar Assn. Presbyterian. Avocations: collector antiquarian books of first editions, reading, running. General corporate, Mergers and acquisitions, Private international. Office: Greenbaum Doll & McDonald 3300 National City Tower Louisville KY 40202

**ANDERSON, PAMELA SUE,** contract compliance analyst; b. Ft. Worth, Dec. 15, 1959; d. John Charles and Peggy Ann (Brite) Whisenhunt; m. James Ronald Anderson, May 5, 1978 (div. Aug. 16, 1983, dec. Dec. 4, 1988); 1 child, Jennifer Lea. Grad. high sch., Whitehouse, Tex. Co-owner House of Plants, Devine, Tex., 1980-82; sec. to pres. Leland Petroleum Prodn. Co., Dallas, 1982-84; sec., word processing specialist Contract-ARCO Oil and Gas Co., Dallas, 1984-88; sr. sec. ARCO Oil and Gas Co., Dallas, 1988-89, contract compliance analyst, 1990—; distbr. Amway Corp., Ada, Mich., 1988—. Avocations: fishing, travel, volleyball, sailing, softball, motorcycling.

**ANDERSON, PATRICIA COULTER,** paralegal; b. Washington, Sept. 5, 1965; d. John Kendall and Clare Mary (O'Connor) C.; m. Darrell W. Anderson. AAS summa cum laude, J. Sargeant Reynolds Coll., 1993; BA, William and Mary Coll., 1987. Litigation paralegal Williams, Mullen, Christian and Dobbins, Richmond, Va., 1990-91; paralegal Russell, Cantor, Arkema & Edmonds, P.C., Richmond, 1991-95; litigation paralegal Duane & Shannon, P.C., Richmond, 1995-97; litigatin legal asst. McGuire, Woods, Battle & Boothe, Richmond, 1997—. Paralegal vol. Ctrl. Va. Legal Aid Soc., 1991—. Capt. USAR, 1987—. Mem. Richmond Assn. Legal Assts. (sec. 1994, 95, dir. 1995-97, 2d v.p. 1998, pres. 1999), Va. Assn. Trial Lawyers, Nat. Assn. Legal Assts., Phi Theta Kappa, DGSC Officer's Club. Democrat. Avocations: aerobics, jogging, ice hockey, music. Home: 7062 River Pine Ct Mechanicsville VA 23111-5242 Office: McGuire Woods Battle & Boothe 901 E Cary St Richmond VA 23219-4057

**ANDERSON, PAUL HOLDEN,** state supreme court justice; b. May 14, 1943; m. Janice M.; children: Yovanna, Marina. BA cum laude, Macalester Coll., 1965; JD, U. Minn., 1968. Atty. Vols. in Svc. to Am., 1968-69; spl. asst. atty. gen. criminal divsn. dept. pub. safety Office Minn. Atty. Gen., 1970-71; assoc., then ptnr. LeVander, Gillen & Miller, South St. Paul, Minn., 1971-92; chief judge Minn. Ct. Appeals, 1992-94; assoc. justice Minn. Supreme Ct., 1994—. Deacon, ruling elder House of Hope Presbyn. Ch., St. Paul; mem. PER coms. Ind. Sch. Dist. # 199, 1982-84, mem. and chmn. cmty. svcs. adv. com., bd. dirs., chmn. bd. Mem. Dakota County Bar Assn. (bd. dirs., pres.), South St. Paul/Inver Grove Heights C. of C. (bd. dirs., mem. exec. com.). Avocations: tennis, gourmet cooking, bike riding. Office: Minn Supreme Court 425 Minnesota Judicial Ctr Saint Paul MN 55155-0001

**ANDERSON, PEER LAFOLLETTE,** lawyer, petroleum corporation executive; b. Provo, Utah, 1944. JD, U. Okla., 1969; LLM, George Washington U., 1973. Now v.p., gen. counsel, sec. Citgo Petroleum Corp., Tulsa, 1986—. Office: Citgo Petroleum Corp PO Box 3758 Tulsa OK 74102-3758

**ANDERSON, PHILIP SIDNEY,** lawyer; b. Little Rock, May 9, 1935; s. Philip Sidney and Frances (Walt) A.; m. Rosemary Gill Wright, Sept. 26, 1959; children: Sidney Walt (Mrs. Geoffrey R.T. Kenyon), Philip Wright, Catherine Gill (Mrs. Jess L. Askew III). BA, U. Ark., 1959, LLB, 1959. Bar: Ark. 1960, U.S. Supreme Ct. 1966. Assoc. Wright, Lindsey & Jennings, Little Rock, 1960-65, ptnr., 1965-88; ptnr. Williams & Anderson, Little Rock, 1988—; lectr. Ark. Law Sch., 1963-66; mem. com. on jury instrns. Ark. Supreme Ct., 1962-97; mem. panel for the 8th cir. U.S. Cir. Judge Nominating Commn., 1978-79; mem. fed. adv. com. U.S. Ct. Appeals 8th cir., 1983-88, co-chmn., 1987-88; bd. dirs. Camden News Pub. Co., Little Rock Newspapers, Inc., Winburn Tile Mfg. Co. Co-author: Arkansas Model Jury Instructions, 1965, 74, 89. Pres. Friends of Little Rock Pub. Libr., 1968-69, Little Rock Unltd. Progress, Inc., 1973-74; trustee Cen. Ark. Libr. System, 1981-87, pres. 1984; trustee George W. Donaghey Found., 1976—, pres. 1979-80; trustee Southwestern Legal Found., 1996—. 2d lt. AUS, 1959-60. Fellow Am. Bar Found., Ark. Bar Found. (pres. 1973-74), ABA (chair ho. of dels. 1992-94, bd. govs. 1990-94, 97—, chair coalition for justice 1994-97, pres. 1998-99); mem. Ark. Bar Assn. (spl. award meritorious svc.), Am. Law Inst. (mem. coun. 1982—). Episcopalian. Antitrust, General corporate, Federal civil litigation. Home: 4716 Crestwood Dr Little Rock AR 72207-5436 Office: Williams & Anderson 2200 Stephens Bldg 111 Center St Little Rock AR 72201-4402

**ANDERSON, RICHARD MICHAEL,** lawyer; b. Hollywood, Fla., Dec. 21, 1958; s. R.M. and Rita M. (Kelly) A.; m. Margaret Ruth Hurt, Nov. 3, 1990. Student, Baylor U., 1976-78; BA, U. Fla., 1980; JD, Am. U., 1983. Bar: D.C. 1983, Tex. 1984, U.S. Dist. Ct. (we. dist.) Tex. 1987. Assoc. Kleberg, Dyer, Redford & Weil, Austin, 1983-87, Kleberg & Head, Austin, 1988; assoc., shareholder Redford, Wray & Woolsey, P.C., Austin, 1988-93; shareholder Broyles & Pratt, P.C., Austin, 1993—. Contbr. articles to profl. jours. Public utilities, Administrative and regulatory. Office: Broyles & Pratt PC 6836 Austin Center Blvd Ste 250 Austin TX 78731-3190

**ANDERSON, R(OBERT) BRUCE,** lawyer; b. Effingham, Ill., Feb. 4, 1956; s. Robert Dee and Annalee (Schreiner) A.; m. Shannon Elizabeth Whitcomb, Mar. 19, 1983. BS in Polit. Sci., Ill. State U., 1977; JD, Stetson U., 1981. Bar: Ill. 1981, Fla. 1981. Assoc. Law Offices of James R. DePew, Bloomington, Ill., 1981-82; chief asst. county atty., utilities counsel Collier County, Naples, Fla., 1982-88; ptnr. Young, Van Assendrp & Varnadoe, P.A., Tallahassee and Naples, Fla., 1988—. Mem. editl. adv. com. Local Govt. Law Symposium, Stetson Law Rev., 1986-94. State chmn. Ill. Teenage Rep. Fedn., Springfield, 1974; alt. del. Rep. Nat. Conv., Kansas City, Mo., 1976, 80; mem. exec. com. Collier County Reps., Naples, Fla., 1986, treas. exec. com., 1987-88; active Collier County Devel. Svc. Adv. Com., 1994—, City-County Beach Renourishment Adv. Com., 1994-97, vice-chmn. 1996-97, Leadership Collier Class of 1995. Washington Crossing Found. scholar, 1974. Mem. Fla. Bar Assn., Am. Coll. Trial Lawyers (Excellence in Advocacy medal 1981), Collier County Bar Assn., Nat. Inst. Mcpl. Law (chmn. com. on municipally-owned utilities 1984-86), Naples Area C. of C., Forum Club, Tiger Bay Club, Alpha Kappa Lamda (Holmes award 1978). Republican. Methodist. Land use and zoning (including planning), Public utilities. Office: Young Van Assenderp & Varnadoe 801 Laurel Oak Dr Ste 300 Naples FL 34108-2771

**ANDERSON, ROBERT CHARLES,** lawyer; b. Mt. Clemens, Mich., Nov. 24, 1951; s. Irving Rudolph and Ruth Lorraine A.; m. Sharon Melissa Schreiber, Sept. 9, 1978; children: Robert, Charles, Elizabeth, Ellen. BA, Wayne State U., 1971, U. Tenn., 1973; JD, U. Tenn., 1977. Judge advocate USAF, Biloxi, Miss., Fairbanks, Alaska, 1978-83; asst. dist. atty. Alaska Dept. Law, Fairbanks, 1984-89, 10th Jud. Dist. Tenn., Cleveland, 1989; asst. U.S. atty. U.S. Dept. Justice (mid. dist.) Tenn., Nashville, 1989—; instr. bus. law U. So. Miss., Gulfport, 1978, U. Alaska, Fairbanks, 1980-84. Vol. coach youth tennis, swimming and soccer. Mem. Tenn. Bar Assn. Home: 6323 Wildwood Valley Dr Brentwood TN 37027-4807 Office: US Atty's Office 110 9th Ave S Ste A961 Nashville TN 37203-3870

**ANDERSON, ROBERT EDWARD,** lawyer; b. Spokane, Wash., Sept. 25, 1928; s. Ewald Godfried and Hazel L. A.; m. Audrey May, Nov. 29, 1947; children: Mark, Eric, Kent, Carl. Degree, Gonzaga U., 1950, degree in law, 1954. Bar: Wash., U.S. Dist. Ct. (ea. dist.) Wash., U.S. Supreme Ct. Pvt. practice Spokane, 1954—. Recipient Silver Beaver award Boy Scouts Am., 1976, Lamb award Nat. Luth. Ch. Am., 1980. Lutheran. State civil litigation, Family and matrimonial, General practice. Office: 2032 W Northwest Blvd Spokane WA 99205-3715

**ANDERSON, ROBERT LANIER, III,** federal judge; b. Macon, Ga., Nov. 12, 1936; s. Robert Lanier II and Helen A.; m. Nancy Briska, Aug. 18, 1962; children: Robert, William Hilliar, Browne McIntosh. AB magna cum laude, Yale U., 1958; LLB, Harvard U., 1961. Assoc. Anderson, Walkert, Reichert, Macon, Ga., 1963-79; Judge U.S. Ct. Appeals (11th cir.), 1979—. With USAR, 1058-61, capt. U.S. Army, 1961-63. Mem. ABA, Ga. Bar Assn., Macon Bar Assns., State Bar of Ga., Am. Judicature Soc. Office: US Ct Appeals PO Box 977 Macon GA 31202-0977*

**ANDERSON, ROBERT LEROY,** lawyer; b. Oakland, Calif., Feb. 20, 1924; m. Elisabeth Olney, Dec. 18, 1948; children: Kimberley Riley Clement, Benjamin Olney. AB, U. Calif., Berkeley, 1948; JD, Hastings Coll. of Law, 1951. Bar: Calif. 1952. Dep. dist. atty. County of Alameda, Oakland, Calif., 1952-56; atty. Rankin, Anderson & Geary, Oakland, 1956-63; ptnr. Anderson & Geary, Oakland, 1963-74; ptnr. Anderson, Galloway & Lucchese, Oakland, 1974-86, sr. counsel, 1986—; mem. Med.-Legal Com. Calif., 1970—. 1st lt. U.S. Army Air Corps, 1943-45. Listed in The Best Lawyers in America, 1987—. Mem. Am. Bd. Trial Advocates, Calif. Bar Assn., Alameda County Bar Assn., Contra Costa County Bar Assn. Personal injury. Office: Anderson Galloway & Lucchese 1676 N California Blvd Ste 500 Walnut Creek CA 94596-4183

**ANDERSON, ROBERT MONTE,** lawyer; b. Logan, Utah, Feb. 19, 1938; s. E. LeRoy and Grace (Rasmussen) A.; m. Kathleen Hansen, Aug. 12, 1966; children: Jennifer, Katrina, Alexander. AB, Columbia Coll., 1960; LLB, U. Utah, 1963. Bar: Utah 1963, U.S. Cir. Ct. Appeals (10th cir.) 1967, U.S. Supreme Ct. 1976. Assoc., shareholder, v.p. Van Cott, Bagley, Cornwall & McCarthy, Salt Lake City, 1963-82; pres., shareholder Berman & Anderson, Salt Lake City, 1982-86; v.p., shareholder Hansen & Anderson, Salt Lake City, 1986-90; pres., shareholder Anderson & Watkins, Salt Lake City, 1990-95; pres. Anderson & Smith, Salt Lake City, 1995-97; lawyer, shareholder, pres. Van Cott, Bagley Cornwall & McCarthy, Salt Lake City, 1998—; bd. dirs., mem. exec. com. Anderson Lumber Co., Ogden, Utah. Trustee The Children's Ctr., Salt Lake City, 1973-77; pres. Utah Legal Svcs., Salt Lake City, 1979. Mem. ABA, Utah State Bar Assn. (cts. and judges com. 1991—), Alta Club, Cottonwood Club, Rotary. Avocations: tennis, skiing. Construction, General civil litigation, Real property. Office: Van Cott Bagley Cornwall & McCarthy 50 S Main St Ste 1600 Salt Lake City UT 84144-0103

**ANDERSON, ROSS CARL,** lawyer; b. Logan, Utah, Sept. 9, 1951; s. E. LeRoy and Grace (Rasmussen) A.; 1 child, Lucas Craig Arment. BS in Philosophy magna cum laude, U. Utah, 1973; JD with honors, George Washington U., 1978. Bar: U.S. Dist. Ct. Utah 1978. Assoc. Berman & Giauque, Salt Lake City, 1978-80; v.p., ptnr. Berman & Anderson, Rooker Larsen Kimball & Parr, Salt Lake City, 1980-82; ptnr., sec. Berman & Anderson, Salt Lake City, 1982-85; ptnr., v.p. Hansen & Anderson, Salt Lake City, 1986-89, Anderson & Watkins, Salt Lake City, 1989-92; pres. Anderson & Karrenberg, Salt Lake City, 1992-98, of counsel, 1999—. Columnist Enterprise, 1997-98. Dem. candidate for Congress, Utah 2d Congl. Dist., 1996, candidate for mayor Salt Lake City, 1999; pres. bd. dirs. Citizens for Penal Reform, 1991-94, Guadalupe Ednl. Programs, Salt Lake City, 1985—, ACLU of Utah, 1980-85; bd. dirs. Common Cause of Utah, 1987-89, Planned Parenthood of Utah, 1979-83; mem. Salt Lake Com. on Fgn. Rels., 1983-95. Mem. Utah State Bar Assn. Democrat. Avocations: history, fgn. affairs, skiing. General civil litigation, Civil rights, Personal injury. Home: 418 Douglas St Salt Lake City UT 84102-3231 Office: Anderson & Karrenberg 50 W Broadway Ste 700 Salt Lake City UT 84101-2035

**ANDERSON, RUSSELL A.,** state supreme court justice; b. Bemidji, Minn., May 28, 1942; m. Kristin Anderson; children: Rebecca, John, Sarah. BA, St. Olaf Coll., 1964; JD, U. Minn., 1968; LLM, George Washington U., 1977. Pvt. practice, 1976-82; atty. Beltrami County, 1978-82; dist. ct. judge 9th Jud. Dist., 1982-98; assoc. justice Minn. Supreme Ct., 1998—; mem. Jud. Edn. Adv. Com., Sentencing Guidelines Commn.; liaison State Funding Com., Supreme Ct. Adv. Com. on Rules of Criminal Procedure; chair Supreme Ct. Gender Fairness Implementation Com. Mem. Sch. Dist. 593 Edn. Found., Crookston; mem. Fertile-Beltrami Edn. Found.; past pres., mem. ch. coun., 9th grade Sunday sch. tchr.; mem. Connect U.S.-Russian Domestic Violence Delegation to Russia, 1995, 97. Lt. comdr. USN, 1968-76. Mem. Minn. State Bar Assn., 14th Dist. Bar Assn. Office: Minn Supreme Ct 25 Constitution Ave Saint Paul MN 55155*

**ANDERSON, STANLEY EDWARD, JR.,** lawyer; b. Chgo., Oct. 11, 1940; s. Stanley Edward and Margaret Mary (Turner) A.; m. Louise Ann Perko, July 12, 1968; 1 child, Stephanie Elizabeth. BA, Northwestern U., 1962, MBA, 1964; MS, U. Del., 1966; postgrad., U. Minn., 1967-68; JD, Am. U., 1972. Bar: Va. 1973, D.C. 1974, Ill. 1973, Calif. 1976; registered patent atty. 1973. Chemist E.I. duPont de Nemours & Co., Inc., Wilmington, Del., 1966-67; patent assoc. Hooker Chem. Corp., 1969-70; patent advisor Office of Naval Rsch., Arlington, Va., 73-74; patent atty. Merck & Co., Inc., Rahway, N.J., 1974-76, Harris, Kern, Wallin & Tinsley, L.A., 1977-78; pvt. practice law Thousand Oaks, Calif., 1978—; prof. law So. Calif. Inst. Law, Ventura. With USN, 1958-64. USPHS rsch. fellow, 1965; recipient Book Awards in Agy. and Creditors Rights, Am. U., 1972. Mem. Ill. Bar Assn., D.C. Bar Assn., Va. Bar Assn., State Bar of Calif. Republican. Roman Catholic. Home and Office: 1529 Lynnmere Dr Thousand Oaks CA 91360-1948

**ANDERSON, STEPHEN HALE,** federal judge; b. 1932; m. Shirlee G. Anderson. Student, Eastern Oreg. Coll. Edn., Brigham Young U.; LLB, U. Utah, 1960. Bar: Utah 1960, U.S. Claims Ct. 1963, U.S. Tax Ct. 1967, U.S. Ct. Appeals (10th cir.) 1970, U.S. Supreme Ct. 1971, U.S. Ct. Appeals (9th cir.) 1972, various U.S. Dist. Cts. Tchr. South H.S., Salt Lake City, 1956-57; trial atty. tax div. U.S. Dept. Justice, 1960-64; ptnr. Ray, Quinney & Nebeker, 1964-85; judge U.S. Ct. Appeals (10th cir.), Salt Lake City, 1985—; spl. counsel Salt Lake County Grand Jury, 1975; chmn. fed.-state jurisdiction com. Jud. Conf. U.S., 1995-98; mem. Nat. Jud. Coun. State and Fed. Cts., 1992-96; mem. ad hoc. com. on bankruptcy appellate panels 10th Cir. Jud. Coun., 1995-97; mem. various coms. U.S. Ct. Appeals (10th cir.). Editor-in-chief Utah Law Rev. Cpl. U.S. Army, 1953-55. Mem. Utah State Bar (pres. 1983-84, various offices), Salt Lake County Bar Assn. (pres. 1977-78), Am. Bar Found., Salt Lake Area C. of C. (bd. govs. 1984), U. Utah Coll. Law Alumni Assn. (trustee 1979-83, pres. 1982-83), Order of Coif. Office: US Ct Appeals 4201 Fed Bldg 125 S State St Salt Lake City UT 84138-1102

**ANDERSON, STEVEN ROBERT,** lawyer, consultant; b. Kansas City, Mo., Nov. 1, 1955; s. Bryce Louis and Lorraine R. (Roberts) A.; m. Carole Lynn Twork, Aug. 11, 1979; children: Ryan Matthew, Lauren Marie. BBA, U. Kans., 1978, JD, 1981. Bar: Kans. 1981, U.S. Dist. Ct. Kans. 1981, U.S. Ct. Appeals (10th cir.) 1985, Mo. 1990. Assoc. North, Lancaster & Dickson, Overland Park, Kans., 1981-83, Wagner, Leek & Mullins, Roeland Park, Kans., 1983-85; ptnr. Perry & Hamill, Overland Park, 1985-89, Levy & Craig, Overland Park, 1989—. Pres. Optimist Youth Homes, Overland Park, 1984-88; pres., chmn. bd. Kans. East Youth Svcs., Olathe, 1985-88; mem. Lenexa Bd. Zoning Appeals, 1989—, chmn., 1992-95; mem. Johnson County Transp. Coun., 1990-94, chmn., 1992-94; bd. dirs. Kaw Valley Habitat for Humanity, 1997—. Mem. Optimist (bd. dirs. 1987-94, pres. 1990-91, Optimist of Yr. 1986). Republican. Presbyterian. Real property, General corporate, Contracts commercial. Office: Levy and Craig PC 6310 Lamar Ave Ste 220 Overland Park KS 66202-4284

**ANDERSON, WILLIAM AUGUSTUS,** lawyer; b. L.A., May 22, 1942; s. William A. and M. Patricia (O'Connor) A.; children: David, Mark, Peter, Catherine, Sarah; m. Ruth C. Gannon, June 8, 1994. BS in Fgn. Service, Georgetown U., 1964; JD cum laude, Harvard U., 1967. Bar: Calif. 1968, U.S. Dist. Ct. (cen. dist.) Calif. 1970. Assoc. Gibson, Dunn & Crutcher, L.A., 1970-74; gen. ptnr. North Star Properties Ltd., L.A., 1971—, sole practice, 1975—; v.p., dir. Westwood Ctr. Corp., L.A.1980-84, El Verano Corp., L.A., 1981-84; asst. sec., dir. Haller Schwarz, L.A., 1981—; chmn. Calif. Indsl. Facilities, Inc., 1978-80. Served to lt. USN, 1967-70. Mem. State Bar Calif. (cert. specialist probate, estate planning and trust law 1992—). Republican. Roman Catholic. Estate planning, Probate, Estate taxation. Home: 555 N Lucerne Blvd Los Angeles CA 90004-1204

**ANDERSON, WILLIAM CARL,** lawyer; b. Syracuse, N.Y., July 9, 1958; s. Harold Everett and Mildred Dorothy (Weller) A.; m. Deborah L. Harding, Nov. 3, 1990. BA in History, Washington Coll., Chestertown, Md., 1980; JD, Syracuse U., 1983; postgrad., U. Miami, 1993. Bar: Md. 1984, Fla. 1985. Fin. cons. Merrill Lynch, Miami, Fla., 1984-85; tax cons. Arthur Andersen & Co., Miami, 1985-87; sr. tax specialist Ryder System, Inc., Miami, 1987-90; assoc. tax counsel internat. GE Co., Schenectady, N.Y., 1990-91; tax counsel GE Co., Plainville, Conn., 1991-93; gen. counsel, dir. environ. and quality programs GE Indsl. Sys. Europe, Gent, Belgium, 1993-96; mgr., sr. counsel environ. health and safety GE Co., Plainville, Conn., 1996—; chmn. GE Cmty. Svc. Fund, 1993-94. Treas. Big Bros./Big Sisters of Broward, Inc., Ft. Lauderdale, Fla., 1988-89, d. dirs., 1989-90. Mem. Md. Bar Assn., Fla. Bar Assn., Jaycees (local v.p., treas. 1984, Fla. legal counsel, 1988-89, 90-91). Republican. Lutheran. Avocations: sailing, rowing, cycling. Corporate taxation, Public international, Environmental. Home: 81 Windward Pl Southington CT 06489-3853 Office: GE Legal Ops 41 Woodford Ave Plainville CT 06062-2372

**ANDERSON, WILLIAM CARL,** lawyer; b. Canton, Ohio, Nov. 14, 1941; s. Harry and Carrie (Magee) A.; m. Mary Ellen Graham, June 11, 1962; children: John, Dan, Emily, Adam. BA, Oberlin Coll., 1963; JD, U. Mich., 1966. Bar: Okla. 1966, U.S. Supreme Ct. 1985, U.S. Dist. Ct. (no., ea. and we. dists.) Okla., U.S. Dist. Ct. (no. dist.) Tex., U.S. Dist. Ct. D.C., U.S. Ct. Appeals (5th, 10th, and D.C. cirs.). Clk. to Hon. A.P. Murrah U.S. Ct. Appeals for 10th Circuit, Oklahoma City, 1966-67; ptnr. Doerner, Saunders, Daniel & Anderson, Tulsa, 1967—. Fellow Am. Coll. Trial Lawyers; mem. Am. Inns of Ct. (master Council Oaks chpt.), Order of Coif. Appellate, Environmental, General civil litigation. Office: Doerner Saunders Daniel & Anderson 320 S Boston Ave Ste 500 Tulsa OK 74103-3725

**ANDERSON, WOLFGANG RICHTER,** lawyer; b. Frankfurt, Fed. Republic Germany, June 2, 1941; came to U.S., 1953; s. Vincent O. and Irmgard C. (Happel) A.; m. Maria K. Butenko, Nov. 19, 1972; children: Theodore W., Benjamin J., Andrew C., Daniel A. BA in Prelaw, U. Wash., 1963, JD, 1966. Bar: Wash. 1966, U.S. Supreme Ct. 1971, U.S. Ct. Mil. Appeals. Assoc. Jonson & Jonson, Seattle, 1970-77; sr. ptnr. Anderson & Fields, Inc., P.S., Seattle, 1977—; judge pro tem superior and dist. cts., State of Wash., Seattle; speaker on divorce various tv programs, Seattle. Author: Divorce in Washington; contbr. articles to profl. jours. Prosecutor, NATO liaison fgn. trial observer Fed. Republic of Germany. Served to capt. JAGC, U.S. Army, 1966-70. Republican. Am. Orthodox. Club: Wash. Athletic Club. Lodge: Elks. Avocations: antique collecting, collecting art, stamps, family activities. Family and matrimonial. Office: Anderson & Fields 207 E Edgar St Seattle WA 98102-3191

**ANDERSON-STEPHENS, ANGELITA MARIE,** lawyer; b. New Orleans, Apr. 24, 1961; d. Johnnie E. and Mary Ellen Anderson; m. Charles R. Stephens Jr., July 17, 1999. AB, Columbia U., 1982, JD, 1992; MS, SUNY, Stony Brook. Bar: N.Y. 1995. Sr. systems analyst N.Y.C. Mayor's Office of Mgmt. and Budget, 1986-89; human rights fellow Internat. Ctr. for the Def. of Human Rights, London, 1990; staff atty. Legal Svcs., Corp. B, Bklyn., 1992-94; exec. dir. The City-Wide Task Force on Housing Ct., Inc., N.Y.C., 1994—; mem. adv. com. N.Y. Housing Ct. Online Preparation Educator, N.Y.C., 1998—; instr. Columbia Law Sch.-Profession of Law, 1996, 97. Advisor N.Y. State Legis. Black and Puerto Rican Caucus, Albany, 1995—; steering com. Show Down '97 Rent Regulation Campaign, N.Y., 1996-97; bd. dirs. Met. Coun. on Housing, Inc., N.Y.C., 1995—. Recipient Social Justice award Village Ind. Dems., 1998, Samuel Duboff award The Fund for Modern Cts., 1996; scholarship Met. Black Bar Assn., 1990. Mem. Assn. of the Bar of the City of N.Y. (task force on housing ct. 1997—, com. on minorities 1995-98). Democrat. Soka Gakkai Buddhist. Avocations: swimming, travel, music. Fax: 212-982-3036. Home: 507 49th St E Bradenton FL 34208-5839 Office: City Wide Task Force on Housing Ct Inc 29 John St Rm 1108 New York NY 10038-4005

**ANDO, RUSSELL HISASHI,** lawyer; b. Hilo, Hawaii, Feb. 5, 1955; s. Hiroshi and Pauline Masako (Abe) A.; m. Donna Terumi Muraoka, Aug. 31, 1980; 1 child, Jessica Chie. BA, U. Hawaii, 1977; JD, U. Oreg., 1980. Bar: Hawaii 1980, U.S. Dist. Ct. Hawaii 1980, U.S. Ct. Appeals (9th cir.) 1984. Law clk. Supreme Ct. Hawaii, Honolulu, 1980-81; pvt. practice Honolulu, 1981—; mem. Bd. Examiners Hawaii Supreme Ct., Honolulu, 1994—; mem. arts and scis. adv. coun. U. Hawaii, Honolulu, 1994—. Bd. editors Oreg. Law Rev., 1978-80. Mem. ABA, FBA, Am. Judicature Soc., Am. Arbitration Assn., Hawaii State Bar Assn. General civil litigation, Consumer commercial, Real property. Office: 1001 Bishop St # Pt1570 Honolulu HI 96813-3429

**ANDOLINA, LAWRENCE J.,** lawyer; b. Rochester, N.Y., Apr. 27, 1948; s. Michael Carl and Nina (Formicola) A.; m. Sharon Jean Cemino, Sept. 22, 1973; children: Lindsay, Lauren. BA, Boston Coll., 1970; JD, Albany Law Sch., 1974. Bar: N.Y. 1975, U.S. Dist. Ct. (we. dist.) N.Y. 1976 (no. dist.) 1995, U.S. Ct. Appeals 1980 (2nd cir.). Asst. dist. atty. Monroe County (N.Y.) Dist. Atty. Office, Rochester, 1975-78; atty., assoc. Palmiere, Passero & Crimi, Rochester, 1978-80; atty., ptnr. Affronti, Jesserer, Andolina & Lamb, Rochester, 1980-85, Jesserer, Andolina & Lamb, 1985-87, Jesserer & Andolina, 1987, Harris, Beach & Wilcox, Rochester, 1988—. Mem. Nat. Assn. Crim. Def. Lawyers, New York State Assn. Crim. Def. Lawyers, Monroe County Bar Assn. (past pres. 1991-92). Criminal, Federal civil litigation, Civil rights. Office: Trevett Lenweaver & Salzer 16 E Main St Rochester NY 14614-1808

**ANDREASEN, JAMES HALLIS,** retired state supreme court judge; b. Mpls., May 16, 1931; s. John A. and Alice M. Andreasen; m. Janet Andreasen, June 25, 1961 (dec. July 1985); children: Jon A., Amy E., Steven J.; m. Marilyn McGuire, May 17, 1987. BS in Commerce, U. Iowa, 1953, JD, 1958. Bar: Iowa 1958. Pvt. practice law Algona, Iowa, 1958-75; with Algona City Coun., 1961-68; judge 3d Jud. Dist. Ct., 1975-87; judge Supreme Ct. Iowa, Des Moines, 1987-98, ret., sr. judge, 1998—. Lt. col. USAFR, 1954-75. Mem. ABA, Iowa State Bar Assn., Kossuth County Bar Assn. Republican. Methodist. Office: Kossuth County Courthouse St Capitol Bldg Algona IA 50511

**ANDREASEN, STEVEN W.,** lawyer; b. Salt Lake City, Sept. 17, 1948. BA, U. Utah, 1970, JD, 1974. Bar: Washington 1974. Mem. Davis Wright Tremaine, Seattle, 1974—. Comment Editor: Utah Law Review 1973-74. Mem. Seattle Estate Planning Coun., Order of Coif, Am. Coll. Trust and Estate Counsel. Probate, Estate planning. Office: Davis Wright Tremaine LLP 2600 Century Sq 1501 4th Ave Ste 2600 Seattle WA 98101-1688

**ANDREOFF, CHRISTOPHER ANDON,** lawyer; b. Detroit, July 15, 1947; s. Andon Anastas and Mildred Dimitry (Kolinoff) A.; m. Nancy Anne Krochmal, Jan. 12, 1980; children: Alison Brianne, Lauren Kathleen. BA, Wayne State U., 1969; postgrad. in law Washington U., St. Louis, 1969-70; JD, U. Detroit, 1972. Bar: Mich. 1972, U.S. Dist. Ct. (ea. dist.) Mich. 1972, U.S. Ct. Appeals (6th cir.) 1974, Fla. 1978, U.S. Supreme Ct. 1980. Legal intern Wayne County Prosecutor's Office, Detroit, 1970-72; law clk. Wayne County Cir. Ct., Detroit, 1972-73; asst. U.S. atty. U.S. Dept. Justice, Detroit, 1973-80, asst. chief Criminal Div., U.S. Atty.'s Office, 1977-80, spl. atty. Organized Crime and Racketeering sect. U.S. Dept. Justice, 1980-84, dep. chief Detroit Organized Crime Strike Force, 1982-85, mem. narcotics adv. com. U.S. Dept. Justice, 1979-80; ptnr. Evans & Luptak, Detroit, 1985-93, Jaffe, Raitt, Heuer & Weiss, Detroit, 1995—; lectr. U.S. Atty. Gen. Advocacy Inst., 1984. Recipient numerous spl. commendations FBI, U.S. Drug Enforcement Adminstrn., U.S. Dept. Justice, U.S. Atty. Gen. Mem. ABA, Fed. Bar Assn. (speaker trial advocate and criminal law sect. Detroit 1983—, bd. dirs. 1989-91, chmn. criminal law sect. 1990-91), Mich. Bar Assn., Fla. Bar Assn., Nat Assn. Criminal Def. Lawyers, Detroit Bar Assn. Greek Orthodox. Criminal, Federal civil litigation, State civil litigation. Home: 4661 Rivers Edge Dr Troy MI 48098-4161 Office: Jaffe Raitt Heuer & Weiss One Woodward Ave Ste 2400 Detroit MI 48226

**ANDREOZZI, LOUIS JOSEPH,** lawyer; b. N.J., 1959; m. Lisa Marie Clark, Apr. 12, 1987. BA, Rutgers U., 1981; JD, Seton Hall U., 1984. Bar: N.J. 1984. Asst. gen. counsel Gordon Pub., Inc., Randolph, N.J., 1984-93; dep. gen. counsel Elsevier U.S. Holdings, Morris Plains, N.J., 1985-93; v.p., sec., gen. counsel Reed Elsevier Med. Pub., Belle Mead, N.J., 1994-95; v.p., gen. counsel Lexis-Nexis, Miamisburg, Ohio, 1994-97; chief legal counsel Lexis-Nexis, 1997-98; COO Martindale-Hubbell, New Providence, 1996—, Marquis, NRP, New Providence, 1998—; vice-chmn. Reed Tech. and Info. Svcs., Inc., 1999—; pres., CEO Martindale-Hubbell, Marquis, NRP, New Providence, 1999—; mem. legal adv. bd. Lexis-Nexis, exec. bd. 1994—; mem. Friends of the Law Libr. of Congress; bd. dirs. Am. Assn. of Pub. Named to Dept. Distinction in Bus., Rutgers U., 1981, Nat. Honor Soc. in Econs. and Bus., 1981. Mem. ABA, N.J. Bar Assn., Internat. Bar Assn, Am Corp. Counsel Assn., N.J. Employment Law Assn. Roman Catholic. General corporate, Labor, Trademark and copyright.

**ANDRES, KENNETH G., JR.,** lawyer; b. Trenton, N.J., Nov. 9, 1953; s. Kenneth George and Joan Margaret (Fredericks) A. BA, Swarthmore Coll., 1975; JD, Capital U., 1978. Bar: N.J. 1978, Pa. 1978, U.S. Dist. Ct. N.J. 1978, U.S. Ct. Appeals (3rd cir.) 1981, U.S. Supreme Ct. 1994; cert. civil trial atty., N.J., cert. advocate Am. Bd. Trial Advocates. Ptnr. Andres & Berger PC, Haddonfield, N.J.; adj. prof. law Mercer County C.C., 1983-89; faculty mem. Am. Trial Lawyers Assn. - N.J., 1989—. Contbr. articles to profl. publs. Mem. N.J. Supreme Ct. Dist. III ethics com., 1994-98; mem. N.J. Supreme Ct. Civil Jury Charge Com., 1996—. Named Profl. Lawyer of Yr., N.J. Commn. Professionalism in Law, 1998. Mem. ATLA, ABA, Assn. Trial Lawyers of Am.-N.J. (bd. govs. 1986-90, parliamentarian 1990-91, from asst. sec. to pres. 1990—, N.J. Gold Medal award 1999), Pa. State Bar Assn., N.J. State Bar Assn., Burlington County Bar Assn. (chmn. civil bench and bar com. 1992-94, trustee 1993), Mercer County Bar Assn. (trustee 1982-91). Personal injury, Product liability, State civil litigation. Office: Andres & Berger PC 264 Kings Hwy E Haddonfield NJ 08033-1907

**ANDRESEN, MALCOLM,** lawyer; b. Medford, Wis., July 26, 1917; s. Thomas Whelen and Ethel (Malkson) A.; m. Ann Kimball, 1942 (div. 1968); children: Anthony M., Susan A. Bridges, Abbott K.; m. Barbara Brown, 1971 (div. 1976); m. Nigi Sato, 1979. BA, U. Wis., 1940, LLB, 1941. Bar: Wis. 1941, N.Y. 1946, U.S. Supreme Ct. 1958. Acct. J.D. Miller & Co., N.Y.C., 1946-47; jr. tax acct. Peat Marwick Mitchell & Co., N.Y.C., 1947-48; assoc. Davis Wagner Hallett & Russell, N.Y.C., 1948-52; tax counsel, then sr. tax counsel, sr. govt. rels. adviser Mobil Oil Corp., N.Y.C., 1952-70; dir. tax legal affairs Nat. Fgn. Trade Coun., N.Y.C., 1970-73; of counsel Delson & Gordon, N.Y.C., 1973-77, Whitman & Ransom, N.Y.C., 1977-86; pvt. practice N.Y.C., 1986—. Trustee, fin. v.p. Nat. Urban League, 1959-65; trustee, treas. Cathedral Ch. of St. John the Divine, N.Y.C., 1977-84. Capt. USMCR, 1942-46. Decorated Bronze Star medal. Mem. Assn. of Bar City of N.Y., Internat. Fiscal Assn. (coun. U.S.A. br. pres. 1971-72), Univ. Club (coun. mem. 1985-89, co-chair com. 1988). Democrat. Episcopalian. General corporate, Taxation, general, Real property. Home: 2 Lincoln Sq Apt 24D New York NY 10023-6218 Office: 675 3rd Ave Ste 3004 New York NY 10017-5704

**ANDREU-GARCIA, JOSE ANTONIO,** territory supreme court chief justice. Chief justice Supreme Ct. of P.R. Office: Supreme Ct PR PO Box 9022392 San Juan PR 00902-2392

**ANDREW, LEONARD DELESSIO,** lawyer; b. N.Y.C., Nov. 16, 1941; s. Albert E. and Josephine (DeLessio) A.; m. Helen Fischer, June 25, 1966; children: Elizabeth Jane, Martha Carol. AB in History, Lafayette Coll., 1963; JD, St. John's U., 1969. Bar: N.Y. 1969, D.C. 1973, U.S. Supreme Ct. 1973, Calif. 1975. Staff atty. IBM Corp., Armonk, N.Y., 1969-72, various positions, 1976-99; spl. asst. U.S. Solicitor of Labor, U.S. Dept. of Labor, Washington, 1972-73; regional counsel IBM Corp., Los Angeles, 1974-76; sr. mng. dir., gen. counsel IBM Asia Pacific, Tokyo, N.Y., 1990-94; assoc. gen. counsel IBM Corp., White Plains, N.Y., 1994-99; adj. prof. Temple U. Law Sch., Tokyo, 1993; bd. dirs. Asbury Terr. Housing Corp., Tarrytown, N.Y. Trustee Unitd Meth. Ch. of the Tarrytowns, 1976—. Served to 1st lt. U.S. Army, 1963-65. Fax: (914) 332-4321. Antitrust, Computer, General corporate. Home: 11 Pokohoe Dr Sleepy Hollow NY 10591-1104 Office: IBM Corp 11 Pokahoe Dr Sleepy Hollow NY 10591-1104

**ANDREWS, ALBERT O'BEIRNE, JR.,** lawyer; b. N.Y., Dec. 19, 1939; s. Albert O'Beirne and Frances (Hall) A.; m. Sharon R. Andrews, Aug. 10, 1963 (div. 1984); children: Laura, Albert; m. Lynn A. McEvers, July 30, 1993. BA, U. Mich., 1963; LLB, U. Minn., 1966. Bar: Minn. 1966, Wyo. 1990. Assoc. Wright & West, Mpls., 1966-70; ptnr. Wright, West, Diessner, Mpls., 1971-84; prin. Gray, Plant, Mooty, Mooty & Bennett, P.A., 1985—; lectr. U. Minn. Dept. Bus. Law, 1968-84; chmn. Bus. Law Dept. U. Minn., 1984—; vis. prof. Warsaw Sch. Econs., 1994, 96. Bd. dirs. Guthrie Theater, Mpls., 1969—, pres., chmn., 1976-79; bd. dirs. Minn. Pub. Radio, St. Paul, Greater Yellowstone Coalition, Bozeman, Mont., sec.-treas., 1987—; bd. dirs. Am. Rivers, Washington, 1994—, League of Conservative Voters, Washington, Minn. Gov. Commn. on Arts, 1975-76, Theatre Comm. Group, N.Y.C., 1973-78. Estate planning, General corporate, Taxation, general. Home: 1201 Yale Pl Minneapolis MN 55403-1901

**ANDREWS, ANGUS GRAHAM,** lawyer; b. DeFuniak Springs, Fla., Mar. 19, 1931; s. Edward Leo and Merry Love (Campbell) A.; m. Joyce Spires , Mar. 29, 1953 (div. Feb. 1989); chldren: Angela Kay Andrews Shehee, Angus Graham, Rebecca Joyce Andrews Garea, Ralph Spires; m. Deborah Hardy, June 15, 1996. BS, Davidson Coll., 1953; JD, U. Fla., 1958. Bar: Fla. 1958. Ptnr. Campbell & Andrews Law Frim, DeFuniak Springs, 1958-70, Andrews & Miller Law Firm, DeFuniak Springs, 1970-80; sole practitioner DeFuniak Springs, 1980-98; ptnr. Andrews & Davis, Attys., DeFuniak Springs, 1998—; atty. mem. Health and Human Svc. Bd., Fla., 1996—; mem., chmn. Dist. 1 Adv. Bd., Fla. 1st Dist., 1971-76. 1st lt. U.S. Army, 1953-55. Mem. Walton-Okaloosa County Bar Assn. (pres. 1963), Kiwanis Club (pres. 1965), DeFuniak Springs Bus. and Profl. Assn. (pres. 1995-97). Presbyterian. Avocations: music, gardening, hunting, fishing. Office: Andrews & Davis Attys PO Box 112 Defuniak Springs FL 32435-0112

**ANDREWS, BRANDON SCOTT,** lawyer; b. Ruston, La., Dec. 18, 1971; s. Roger Ensley and Judy Walker Andrews; m. Charlotte Ann Clifford. BA in Polit. Sci., Northwestern State U., 1992; JD, La. State U., 1996. Bar: La. 1996, U.S. Dist. Ct. (mid., we. and ea. dists.) La. 1996, U.S. Ct. Appeals (5th cir.) 1996. Assoc. Dué, Caballero, Price & Guidry, Baton Rouge, 1996—. Recipient Employment Law award CALI, 1996. Mem. ATLA, La. Trial Lawyers Assn., La. Law Rev., Rotary Internat., Order of the Coif, Phi Kappa Phi. Baptist. Personal injury, Admiralty, Product liability. Office: Dué Caballero Price & Guidry 8201 Jefferson Hwy Baton Rouge LA 70809-1623

**ANDREWS, CHERI D.,** lawyer; b. Oakland, Calif., May 29, 1961; m. Jay A. Andrews, Aug. 10, 1985; children: Sarah Renee, Rachel Susanne, Rebecca Anne. BA magna cum laude, Mt. Holyoke Coll., 1983; JD, Temple U., 1987. Bar: Pa. 1987. Atty. Manning, Kinkead, Brooks & Bradbury, Norristown, Pa., 1987-96, High, Swartz, Roberts & Seidel, Norristown, 1996—. Co-author, co-editor: (manual) Montgomery County Civil Practice Manual, 1992— (ABA G.P. Link Project award 1995); editor: Montgomery County Law Reporter, 1994-96. Mary Lyon scholar Mt. Holyoke Coll., 1983. Mem. Montgomery Bar Assn. (bd. dirs. 1996-98), Bucks-Mont Mothers of Multiples (sec. 1997-98). Avocation: quilting. Appellate, General civil litigation, Probate. Office: High Swartz Roberts & Seidel 40 E Airy St Norristown PA 19401-4803

**ANDREWS, DAVID RALPH,** lawyer; b. Oakland, Calif., Jan. 4, 1942; s. David and Mattie (Speeks) A.; m. Rozan McCurdy, July 1, 1962; children: David, Linda. BA, U. Calif., Berkeley, 1968; JD, U. Calif., 1971. Bar: Calif. 1971, D.C. 1986, U.S. Dist. Ct. (no. dist.) Calif. 1971, U.S. Dist. Ct. Hawaii 1991, U.S. Supreme Ct. 1980. Rsch. asst. U. Calif., Berkeley, 1969-71; assoc. McCutchen, Doyle, Brown & Enersen, San Francisco, 1971-75; regional counsel Reg. IX U.S. EPA, San Francisco, 1975-77; legal counsel and spl. asst. for policy U.S. EPA, Washington, 1977-79; dep. gen. counsel Dept. Health and Human Svcs., Washington, 1980-81; ptnr. McCutchen, Doyle, Brown & Enersen, San Francisco, 1981-97, chmn., 1991-95; legal adviser U.S. Dept. State, Washington, 1997—; co-chmn. San Francisco Lawyers' Com. Urban Affairs, 1989-91, ROC Econ. Coun., Ill., 1989-97; steering com. NAACP Legal Def. Fund, Calif., 1989-97. Contbr. articles to profl. jours. Trustee San Francisco Mus. of Modern Art, 1988-97; bd. trustees Golden Gate Nat. Park Assn., 1992-95, Marin Cmty. Found., 1996-97; mem. U.S. Agy. for Internat. Devel. Energy Tng. Program Adv. Com. of the Inst. Internat. Edn. Fellow Max Planck Inst. of Pub. Internat. Law, Heidelberg, Fed. Republic of Germany, 1974; recipient Outstanding Svc. award U.S. EPA, Washington, 1980, Sec.'s Spl. Citation Dept. Health and Human Svcs., Washington, 1981. Mem. ABA (natural resources sect.), Calif. Bar Assn. (vice chair, co-chair subcom. on environ. legis.), San Francisco Bar Assn. Avocations: photography, tennis, running. Environmental, Administrative and regulatory.

**ANDREWS, JOHN,** lawyer; b. Athens, June 22, 1959; s. Constantine and Lily (Gozopolus) A. BS in Criminal Justice cum laude, Northeastern U., 1986, JD, 1989. Bar: Mass. 1989, U.S. Dist. Ct. Mass. 1990, U.S. Ct. Appeals (1st cir.) 1990. Police officer Winthrop (Maine) Police Dept., 1979-84; trial atty., pub. defender Com. for Pub. Counsel Svcs., Salem, Mass., 1989-92; atty. Metaxas, Norman & Pidgeon, Salem, 1992-95; adv. bd. Essex County Bar Assn., Inc., Salem, Mass., 1992—, v.p. 1993—. Mem. Nat. Assn. Criminal Def. Attys., Mass. Assn. Criminal Def. Attys., Mass. Bar Assn., Algonquin Club of Boston (ent. com. 1993-95). Criminal, Personal injury, Family and matrimonial. Home: 252 Commonwealth Ave Boston MA 02116-2401 Office: Metaxas Norman & Pidgeon 8 Front St Salem MA 01970-3744

**ANDREWS, MARY RUTH,** lawyer; b. Bogota, Colombia, May 10, 1965; came to U.S. 1968; BS, Ashland U., 1987; JD, NOVA S.E. U., 1990, MIBA, 1994. Bar: Fla. 1990. Assoc. Krupnick, Campbell, Malone & Roselli et al, Ft. Lauderdale, Fla., 1989-93; supr. dealer credit dept. GMAC, Bogota, 1994-96; assoc. Barwick, Dillian, Lambert & Ice, P.A., Miami, 1996—. Mem. ABA, Fla. Bar Assn., Dade County Bar Assn. (Pro Bono Svc. award 11th jud. cir. 1997, 98). Aviation, Personal injury. Office: Barwick Dillian Lambert & Ice 999 Brickell Ave Ste 555 Miami FL 33131-3041

**ANDREWS, WILLIAM DOREY,** law educator, lawyer; b. N.Y.C., Feb. 25, 1931; s. Sidney Warren and Margaret (Dorey) A.; A.B., Amherst Coll., 1952, LL.D., 1977; LL.B., Harvard U., 1955; m. Shirley May Herrman, Dec. 26, 1953; children: Helen Estelle Andrews Noble, Roy Herrman, John Frederick, Margaret Dorey Andrews Davenport, Susan Louise, Carol Mary Andrews Reid. Bar: Mass. 1959. Practice in Boston, 1959-63; assoc. Ropes & Gray, 1959-63; lectr. Harvard Law Sch., Cambridge, Mass., 1961-63, asst. prof., 1963-65, prof., 1965—, Eli Goldston prof. law, 1986— ; cons. Sullivan & Worcester, 1964—; assoc. reporter for accessions tax proposal Am. Law Inst. Fed. Estate and Gift Tax Project; gen. reporter for subchpt. C, Am. Law Inst. Fed. Income Tax Project, 1974-82, 86-93; cons. U.S. Treasury Dept., 1965-68. Mem. Zoning Bd. Appeals, Concord, 1966-73. Served to lt. USNR, 1955-58. Mem. Am. Law Inst., Am. Bar Assn. Office: Harvard U Law Sch 1545 Massachusetts Ave Cambridge MA 02138-2903

**ANDRIACCHI, DOMINIC FRANCIS,** lawyer; b. Lansing, Mich., Nov. 15, 1943; s. Salvatore D. and Helen M.; m. Linda S. Andriacchi, Apr. 28, 1980; children: Helen, Dominic. BS, No. Mich. U., 1979; JD, Thomas M. Cooley Law Sch., 1983. Bar: Mich. 1983, U.S. Dist. Ct. mich. 1984. Gen. mgr. Andriacchi Magneto Co., Ishpeming, Mich., 1961-77; pvt. practice Ishpeming, 1983—; adj. faculty No. Mich. U. Mem. State Bar Mich., Criminal Defense Attys. of Mich., Marquette County Bar Assn., Marquette County Def. Bar Assn. Criminal, Family and matrimonial, General practice. Office: 321 W Division St Ishpeming MI 49849-2311

**ANDROS, JAMES HARRY,** lawyer; b. Macon, Ga., Nov. 17, 1955; s. Harry and Bessie (Master) A.; m. Janye Evangelia Costarides, June 20, 1992. BA, Emory U., 1977; JD, Mercer U., 1980; LLM in Taxation, U. Fla., 1982. Law clk. Martin, Snow, Grant & Napier, Macon, Ga., 1978-79; assoc. Arnall, Golden & Gregory, Macon, 1980-81; tax mgr. Mauldin & Jenkins, Macon, 1982-85; ptnr. Thrasher & Whitley, Atlanta, 1985-91, Varner, Stephens, Humphries & White, LLP, Atlanta, 1991—; gen. counsel Flint Constrn. Co., Atlanta, 1991—; gen. counsel, bd. dirs. Nu-Way Weiners, Inc., Macon, 1980—, Tetragon Enterprises, Inc., Macon, 1988—, Folsom Techs., Inc., Pittsfield, Mass., 1995, LDM & Assocs., Inc. Atlanta, 1991—. Mem. ABA, Ga. Bar Assn., Atlanta Bar Assn., Lawyers Club of Atlanta, Cobb C. of C., Pi Sigma Alpha. Greek Orthodox. General corporate, Mergers and acquisitions, Taxation, general. Office: Varner Stephens Humphries 3350 Cumberland Cir SE Atlanta GA 30339-3340

**ANGEL, JAMES JOSEPH,** lawyer; b. Racine, Wis., Apr. 1, 1956; s. William J. and Dorothy P. (Potman) A.; m. Catherine Anne Cowan, Oct. 17, 1982; children: Carter Anne, Riley James, Spenser Catherine. BA, W.Va. Wesleyan Coll., 1977; JD, U. Richmond, 1979. Dep. commonwealth atty. City of Lynchburg (Va.) Commonwealth Atty. Office, 1979-84; ptnr. Smith, Angel & Falcone, P.C., Lynchburg, 1984-87; pvt. practice Lynchburg, 1987—. Chmn. Boonsboro-Peakland Neighborhood Assn., Lynchburg, 1990-99. Mem. ATLA, Va. Trial Lawyers Assn., Va. Bar Assn., Va. Coll. Criminal Def. Attys., Lynchburg Bar Assn. (past pres. criminal law sect. 1992). Avocations: golf, whitewater rafting. Criminal, Personal injury, General practice. Office: 725 Church St Lynchburg VA 24504-1481 also: Allied Arts Bldg PO Box 1042 Lynchburg VA 24505-1042

**ANGEL, STEVEN MICHAEL,** lawyer; b. Frederick, Md., Sept. 19, 1950; s. Charles Robert and Laura Emily (Holland) A.; children: Michael Sean, James Curtis; m. Peggy Whitten, May 4, 1996. BS, U. Md., 1972; JD, Oklahoma City U., 1976; LL.M., George Washington U., 1979. Bar: Okla. 1976, U.S. Dist. Ct. Md. 1977, U.S. Dist. Ct. (no. dist.) Tex. 1979, Tex. 1981, U.S. Dist. Ct. (we. dist.) Okla. 1981, U.S. Dist. Ct. (we. dist.) Tex 1981, U.S. Ct. Claims 1981, U.S. Ct. Appeals (5th, 10th, and 11th cirs.) 1981, U.S. Ct. Appeals (D.C. cir.) 1983, U.S. Supreme Ct. 1984, D.C. 1986. Field atty. NLRB, Balt., 1976-79; supervising trial atty. Fed. Labor Rels. Authority, Dallas, 1979-80; mem. Hughes & Nelson, Oklahoma City and San Antonio, 1980-89. Articles editor Oklahoma City U. Law Rev., 1976, 77; contbr. articles to profl. jours. Recipient cert. Spl. Competence in Labor, Law Tex. Bd. Legal Specialization, 1982; various awards Oklahoma City U., 1975, 76; Spl. Achievement cert. Fed. Labor Rels. Authority, 1980. Mem. ABA, Okla. Bar Assn., State Bar Tex., Phi Delta Phi. Democrat. Baptist. Labor, Constitutional. Home: 3314 Sundale Ln Edmond OK 73003-1501 Office: Hughes & Nelson 6488 Avondale Dr # 359 Oklahoma City OK 73116-6404

**ANGELIDIS, STEPHEN ALEXANDER,** lawyer; b. Washington, Oct. 22, 1950; s. Alexander Daniel and Orra (Thomas) A.; m. Holly Anna Zorb, Aug. 10, 1974; children: Matthew Stephen, David Alexander, Daniel Thomas. BA, Wittenberg U., 1973; JD, U. Richmond, 1976. Bar: Va. 1976, U.S. Dist. Ct. (ea. and we. dists.) Va., U.S. Supreme Ct. Ptnr. Steingold & Angelidis PLC, Richmond, Va., 1977—. General civil litigation, Contracts commercial, General practice. Office: Steingold & Angelidis PLC 4905 Radford Ave Ste 100 Richmond VA 23230-3524

**ANGELL, JAMES EDWARD,** lawyer; b. Westfield, Mass., July 26, 1954; s. Carroll S. and Sophie T. Angell. B.A., U. Maine, 1975; J.D., Western New Eng. Coll., 1979. Bar: Mass. 1979, U.S. Dist. Ct. Mass. 1980. Sole practice, Westfield, 1979-92; ptnr. Deleo, Angell, Palmer & Zenkert, 1992—. Mem. Westfield Planning Bd., 1985-86; city prosecutor City of Westfield 1986-89; asst. city solicitor City of Westfield, 1986-89. Mem. ABA, Mass. Bar Assn., Hampden County Bar Assn., Westfield Bar Assn. (treas. 1984-88). Real property, Probate, General practice. Home: 47 Steiger Dr Westfield MA 01085-4929 Office: 48 E Silver St Westfield MA 01085-4449

**ANGELL, M(ARY) FAITH,** federal magistrate judge; b. Buffalo, May 7, 1938; d. San S. and Marie B. (Caboni) A.; m. Kenneth F. Carobus, Oct. 27, 1973; children: Andrew M. Carobus, Alexander P. Carobus. AB, Mt. Holyoke Coll., 1959; MSS, Bryn Mawr Coll., 1965; JD, Temple U., 1971. Bar: Pa. 1971, U.S. Dist. Ct. (ea. dist) Pa. 1971, U.S. Ct. Appeals (3rd cir.) Pa. 1974, U.S. Supreme Ct. 1979; Acad. Cert. Social Workers. Dir. social work, vol. svcs. Wills Eye Hosp., Phila., 1961-64, 65-69; dir. soc. work dept. juvenile divsn. Defender Assoc., Phila., 1969-71; asst. dist. atty. City of Phila., 1971-72; asst. atty. gen. Commonwealth of Pa., Phila., 1972-74, deputy atty. gen., 1974-78; regional counsel ICC, Phila., 1978-80, regional dir., 1980-88; administrv. law judge Social Security Administrn., Phila., 1988-90; U.S. magistrate judge U.S. Dist. Ct. (ea. dist.) Pa., Phila., 1990—; adj. prof. Temple U. Law Sch., Phila., 1976-94, clin. instr., 1973-76; co-chmn. Commn. on Gender, 3d Cir. Task Force on Equal Treatment in Cts., 1994—. Federal trustee Defender Assn. Phila., 1985-90; bd. dirs. Child Welfare Adv. Bd., Phila., 1984-90, Federal Cts. 200 Adv. Bd., Phila., 1987-88, Phila. Woman's Network, 1986-88. Recipient Sr. Exec. Svc. award U.S. Govt., 1980. Mem. NASW, FBA (chair exec. com., pres. 1990-92, recognition 1992), Nat. Assn. Women Judges, Fed. Magistrate Judges Assn. (dist. dir. 1994-98), Phila. Bar Assn. (chmn. com. 1976-77), Temple Am. Inn of Cts. (master 1993-98), Third Circuit Task Force on Equal Treatment in the Courts (co-chair Commn. on Gender 1994-97), Temple Law Alumni Exec. Bd. (Women's Law Caucus Honoree 1996). Office: US District Court 601 Market St 3030 US Courthouse Philadelphia PA 19106

**ANGELO, CHRISTOPHER EDMOND,** lawyer, consultant; b. L.A., Dec. 19, 1949; s. Edmond James and Shirley Ann (Richards) A.; m. Patrice Lonnette Brown, Apr. 26, 1980; 1 child, Alexander Bradshaw. BA, U. Calif., Riverside, 1972; JD, Loyola U., 1975. Bar: Calif. 1976, U.S. Dist. Ct. Calif. 1976. Trial atty. Spray, Gould & Bowers, L.A., 1976-78, Harrington, Foxx, Dubrow & Canter, L.A., 1978-83, Gage & Mazursky, Beverly Hills, Calif., 1983-85; trial atty., ptnr. Gage, Mazursky, Schwartz, Angelo & Kussman, Beverly Hills, Calif., 1986-88; trial atty., gen. ptnr. Mazursky, Schwartz & Angelo, L.A., 1988—; faculty lectr. Calif. Judges Assn., 1989; mem. Loyola Law Sch. Law Review, L.A., 1974-75. Author books and articles in field of tort and ins. bad faith liability. Cons. Bet Tzedak Legal Aid Found., L.A., 1992; counsel Christopher Sampson Non-Profit Found. for Catastrophically Injured, L.A., 1991, dir., founder. Recipient Highlander scholarship U. Calif., 1968-72. Mem. ABA, Italian Am. Lawyers Assn. (bd. govs. 1979-83), Calif. Trial Lawyers Assn. (lectr. 1983—, Cert. of Appreciation), Calif. Bar Assn., Consumer Attys. Assn. L.A. (lectr. 1983—, Cert. of Appreciation). Insurance, Personal injury, Product liability. Office: Mazursky Schwartz & Angelo 10990 Wilshire Blvd Ste 1200 Los Angeles CA 90024-3927

**ANGELOFF, CARL,** lawyer; b. Detroit, Apr. 29, 1930; s. Nick and Louise A.; m. Pamela Blank, Mar. 17, 1971. BA in History cum laude, U. Rochester, 1953; LLB magna cum laude, Harvard U., 1959. Bar: N.Y. 1959, D.C. 1973, Fla. 1985; U.S. Ct. Appeals (2d cir.) 1966, U.S. Ct. Appeals (11th cir.) 1987. Assoc. Nixon Hargrave Devans, Rochester, N.Y., 1959-60; confidential law asst. N.Y. State Supreme Ct. Justice, N.Y.C., 1960-70; assoc. Robinson McCarthy Williams, Rochester, N.Y., 1960-62; ptnr. Robinson Williams Angeloff, Rochester, 1963-66, sr. ptnr., mng. ptnr., 1966-84; sr. ptnr. Edwards & Angell, Palm Beach, Fla., 1985-92; ptnr. Honigman Miller, West Palm Beach, Fla., 1993-95; shareholder Jones Foster Johnston & Stubbs, P.A., West Palm Beach, 1995—. Trustee U. Rochester, N.Y., 1992—; dir. Argus Project, Nat. Alumni and Trustee Coun., Washington, 1996—. Lt. USN, 1954-56. Order St. Andrews, Greek Orthodox, 1972. Mem. Nat. Panel Arbitrators. Avocations: biography, history. Finance. Office: Jones Foster Johnston & Stubbs PA 505 S Flagler Dr West Palm Beach FL 33401-5923

**ANGINO, RICHARD CARMEN,** lawyer; b. McKeesport, Pa., May 2, 1940; s. Carmen and Filomena (Lombardi) A.; m. Alice K. Angino, May 2, 1976; children: Elizabeth, Richard, William. BA in English, Franklin and Marshall Coll., Lancaster, Pa., 1958-62; JD, Villanova U., Pa., 1965. Bar: Pa. 1965, U.S. Supreme Ct. 1968, U.S. Ct. Appeals (3rd cir.) 1975, U.S. Dist. Ct. (ea. and cen. dist.) 1966. Ptnr., civil litigation specialist Angino & Rovner P.C., Harrisburg, Pa., 1965—; pres. Pa. Trial Lawyers Assn., Pa., 1982-83. Co-author: The Pennsylvania No-Fault Motor Vehicle Insurance Act, 1979, Pennsylvania Personal Injury Evidence, 1990. Pres. Leukemia Soc. Am., Ctrl. Pa., 1989-92; v.p. Am. Horticulture Soc., Alexandria. Va., 1990-92, Friends of Wildwood, Harrisburg, Pa., 1989-96; assoc. trustee Franklin and Marshall, 1979—; bd. cons. Villanova Univ. Sch. Law, 1994—, govs. residence preservation com., 1997—. Mem. Internat. Soc. Barristers, Dauphin County Bar Assn., Pa. Bar Assn., Pa. Trial Lawyers Assn., Assn. Trial Lawyers Am. Republican. Roman Catholic. Avocation: ornamental horticulture. Personal injury, Product liability, Professional liability. Home: 2040 Fishing Creek Valley Rd Harrisburg PA 17112-9245 Office: Angino & Rovner PC 4503 N Front St Harrisburg PA 17110-1799

**ANGLE, MARGARET SUSAN,** lawyer; b. Lincoln, Nebr., Feb. 20, 1948; d. John Charles and Catherine (Sellers) Angle. BA in Polit. Sci. with distinciton, U. Wis., 1970, MA in Scandinavian Studies, 1972, JD cum laude, 1976. Bar: Wis. 1977, Minn. 1978. Laaw clk. Madison, Mpls., Chgo., 1974-76; law clk. U.S. Dist. Ct., Mpls., 1977-78; mem. firm Faegre & Bensen, Mpls., 1978-84; sr. atty., asst. gen. counsel, asst. sec. Nat. Car Rental System, Inc., Mpls., 1984-90; corp. sec. Car-Temps; CEO Angle & Assocs., Ltd., Eagan, Minn., 1980—. Note and comment editor U. Wis. Law Rev.; contbr. articles to profl. jours. NDEA fellow, 1972. Mem. ABA, Am. Car Rental Assn. (bd. dirs. 1987-90), Minn. Bar Assn., Wis. Bar Assn., Nennepin County Bar Assn., Alternative Dispute Resolution Com., Niños del Paraguay, Parents of Latin Am. Children, Order of Coif. Alternative dispute resolution, Contracts commercial, Legislative. Office: Angle & Assocs 8425 E Quarterhorse Trail Scottsdale AZ 85258-1365

**ANGLEN, RANDALL S.,** lawyer, judge; b. Kansas City, Mo., Dec. 31, 1957. BA in Journalism, U. Mo., Columbia, 1981; JD, U. Kans., Lawrence, 1990. Bar: Mo., Ark., U.S. Fed. Ct. (we. dist.) Mo. Weather announcer KOMU-TV, Columbia, 1980-82; PM mag. host WPSD-TV, Paducah, Ky., 1982-83; dist. dir. Muscular Dystrophy Assn., Columbia, 1983-85; devel. dir. United Cerebral Palsey, Little Rock, Ark., 1985-86; atty. Branson, Mo., 1991—. Judge City of Hollister, 1993—. Mem. Mo. Assn. Mcpl. Judges, Mo. Assn. Mcpl. Attys. General civil litigation, Criminal, Personal injury. Office: PO Box 1562 Branson MO 65615-1562

**ANGULO, CHARLES BONIN,** foreign service officer, lawyer; b. N.Y.C., Aug. 6, 1943; s. Manuel R. and Carolyn C. (Bonin) A.; m. Penelope Snare, June 28, 1986. BA, U. Va., 1966; cert., U. Madrid, 1966; JD, Tulane U., 1969. Bar: Va. 1969. Assoc. Michael & Dent, Charlottesville, Va., 1969-73; assoc. editor The Michie Pub. Co., Charlottesville, 1973; fgn. svc. officer U.S. Dept. State, Washington, 1973-75; fgn. svc. officer Am. Embassy U.S. Dept. State, Brussels, 1976-78, Santo Domingo, 1981-85; fgn. svc. officer Office of the Legal Advisor, U.S. Dept. State, Washington, 1978-81; exec. dir. office of insp. gen. U.S. Dept. State, Washington, 1985-86; asst. chief protocol U.S. State Dept., Washington, 1986-88, Am. Consulate Gen. U.S. Dept. State, Jeddah, Saudi Arabia, 1988-93; fgn. svc. officer Am. Embassy U.S. Dept. State, Quito, Ecuador, 1993—. Home and Office: 4517 17th Ave W Bradenton FL 34209-4316

**ANKERS, NORMAN C.,** lawyer; b. Detroit, Mar. 18, 1956; s. Chester and Charlotte A.; m. Kathy F. Ankers, Sept. 2, 1989. BA, U. Mich., 1976; JD, Harvard U., 1979. Bar: Mich. 1979, U.S. Dist. Ct. (ea. dist.) Mich. 1979,

U.S. Ct. Appeals (6th cir.) 1982, U.S. Ct. Appeals (9th cir.) 1987. Assoc. Honigman Miller Schwartz & Cohn, Detroit, 1979-83, ptnr., 1984—; instr. trial advocacy Inst. Continuing Legal Edn., Ann Arbor, Mich., 1988—. Mem. Oakland County Bar Assn. (vice-chair profl. com. 1998). Avocation: gardening. General civil litigation, Condemnation. Office: Honigman Miller Schwartz & Cohn 2290 First National Bldg Detroit MI 48226

**ANNARINO, JOHN,** lawyer, educator; b. Newark, Ohio, June 26, 1958; s. Angelo G. and Angela M. (Abbruzzi) A.; m. Glenna A. Keener, May 19, 1988; 1 child, Katie M. BS, U. Dayton, 1980; JD, Capital U., 1983. Magistrate Ct. of Claims Ohio, Columbus, 1990-91, dir., 1991-94; exec. dir. Indsl. Commn., Columbus, 1994-95; chief legal officer Ohio Bur. Workers Compensation, Columbus, 1995—; adj. faculty Columbus State C.C., 1986—; bd. dirs. devel. com. U. Dayton, Ohio, 1996—; chmn. pres.'s leadership coun., 1998—. Exec. bd. The Ohio Found., Columbus, 1992—; trustee Buon Giorno mag., Columbus, 1992—; chmn. devel. com. Cath. Social Svcs., Columbus, 1994—; bd. dirs. United Conservatives Ohio, Columbus, 1995—. Am. Assn. State Compensation Insurance Funds. Avocations: reading, walking, sports. Home: 3411 Sunningdale Way Columbus OH 43221-1434 Office: Ohio Bur Workers Compensation 30 W Spring St # L-29 Columbus OH 43215-2241

**ANNENBERG, NORMAN,** lawyer; b. N.Y.C., Aug. 13, 1912; s. George J. and Jeannette (Lazarus) A. J.D., Harvard U., 1935. Bar: N.Y. 1936, U.S. Ct. Appeals (2d cir.) 1948, U.S. Supreme Ct., 1966. Sole practice, N.Y.C., 1936—. Mem. N.Y. County Lawyers Assn., N.Y. State Bar Assn. Family and matrimonial, General practice, Probate. Office: 145 W 55th St New York NY 10019-5342

**ANNIS, EUGENE IRWIN,** lawyer; b. Shelby, Mont., Apr. 5, 1935; s. J. Dayle and Emogene (Mallette) A.; m. Carol Jean Wilson, Oct. 4, 1975; children: Brian, Jane, Tracy, Joan, Leslie, Nicole, Derek, Selena, Rachel. Student, Gonzaga U., 1953-55, LLB, 1959. Bar: Wash. 1959, U.S. Dist. Ct. Wash. 1960, U.S. Ct. Appeals (9th cir.), U.S. Supreme Ct. 1993. Assoc. Hamblen, Gilbert & Brooke, Spokane, 1960-62; ptnr. Shields, Reiley & Annis, Spokane, 1962-72, Lukins & Annis, Spokane, 1972—. Mem. bd. regents Gonzaga U., Spokane, 1991—, mem. bd. advisors Law Sch., 1990—, pres. bd. advisors, 1991; pres. Ronald McDonald House, Spokane, 1991; chmn. bd. trustees Ft. Wright Coll., Spokane, 1978. 1st lt. U.S. Army, 1960. Recipient Bishop's medal Cath. Diocese of Spokane, 1991. Fellow Am. Coll. Trial Lawyers; mem Wash. State Bar Assn., Spokane County Bar Asn. (pres. 1980). Environmental, General civil litigation, Insurance. Office: Lukins & Annis 1600 Wash Trust Bank Bldg Spokane WA 99201

**ANNOTICO, RICHARD ANTHONY,** legal administration, real estate investor; b. Cleve., Sept. 17, 1930; s. Anthony and Grace (Kovarik) A. AB in Bus. with hons., Ohio U., 1953; LLB, Southwestern Law Sch., 1963; JD, UCLA, 1965. Dir. internat. sales then v.p. Liberty Records, L.A., 1957-64; real estate investment counselor Calif. Land Sales, Beverly Hills, 1964-66; real estate investment counselor R.A. Annotico & Assocs., L.A., 1966-68, real estate investor, 1969—; Spkr. in field.; mem. Bd. of Governors State Calif.; expert witness State Legis. Calif. Contbr. numerous articles to profl. jours. Commr. L.A. Transp. Commn., 1984-88, v.p. 1985-87; commr. L.A. Human Rels. Comm n., 1977-84, pres. 1983-84; mem. Calif. State Senate Small Bus. Adv. Bd., 1978-82, L.A. City County Adv. Commn. on Consolidation, 1976-77; pres. Federated Italian-Americans So. Calif., 1975-76; mem. Mayors Exec. Com. Christopher Columbus Quincentenary 1992. Lt. USAF, 1954-55. Decorated Cavaliere Ufficiale Order of Merit (Italy), Comdr. St. Lazarus Internat. Chivalric, Hospitaller and Mil. Order. Mem. Calif. State Bar Assn. (bd. govs., 1983-86, 86-89, 89-92, v.p. 1986, 89, 92). Office: RA Annotico & Assocs 4267 Marina City Dr Unit 1008 Marina Del Rey CA 90292-5812

**ANSBACHER, BARRY B.,** lawyer; b. Jacksonville, Fla., Jan. 7, 1963; s. Lewis and Sybil Ansbacher; m. Elaine Kenny, Aug. 30, 1992. BA, U. Fla., 1985, JD, 1988. Bar: Fla. 1989, D.C.; bd. cert. real estate atty. Fla. Atty. Ansbacher & Schneider PA, Jacksonville, 1989-97; pvt. practice law Jacksonville, 1997—; pres. Attys. Real Property Coun. NE Fla., Inc., Jacksonville. Author: Complex Real Estate Transactions-Subdivisions, 1994, 96; co-author: Issues of Transboundary Pollution in North America, 1988. Named Outstanding Young Men of Am., 1986. Mem. Fla. Bar Assn. (environ. law sect., exec. coun. cir. rep. real property and trust law sect. 1998), Jacksonville Bar Assn. Jewish. Avocation: equestrian sports. Real property, Land use and zoning (including planning). Office: 1301 Riverplace Blvd Ste 2540 Jacksonville FL 32207-9031

**ANSBACHER, SIDNEY FRANKLYN,** lawyer; b. Jacksonville, Fla., May 28, 1961; 1 child, Benjamin Alexander. BA, U. Fla., 1981; JD, Hamline U., 1985; LLM in Agrl. Law, U. Ark., 1989. Bar: Fla., U.S. Dist. Ct. (mid. dist.) Fla., U.S. Ct. Appeals (D.C. cir.). Atty. Fla. Dept. Natural Resources, Tallahassee, 1986-87; assoc. Turner, Ford, Buckingham, Jacksonville, Fla., 1987-90; ptnr., assoc. Brant, Moore et al, Jacksonville, Fla., 1990-95; ptnr. Mahoney Adams & Criser, Jacksonville, Fla., 1995-97, Upchurch Bailey & Upchurch, St. Augustine, Fla., 1997—. Contbr. articles to profl. jours.; mng. editor Fla. Bar Environ. and Land Use CLE Manual, 1998—. Bd. dirs. Fla. Forestry Found., 1993-96. Recipient Outstanding Achievement award Fla. Wildlife Fedn., 1990. Mem. Fla. Bar Assn. (treas. environ. and land use law sect. 1998—, bd. dirs. 1994-98, Judy Florence Outstanding Svc. award 1992), Jacksonville Bar Assn. (chair environ. and land use law sect. 1994-96). Avocations: bicycling, tennis, reading. Office: Upchurch Bailey & Upchurch PA 780 N Ponce De Leon Blvd Saint Augustine FL 32084-3519

**ANSBRO, JAMES MICHAEL,** lawyer; b. Chgo.; s. Patrick Joseph and Mary Ann (Fogarty) A.; married; children: Ariadne, Brandon. BA, DePaul U., 1967; PhD, Loyola U., Chgo., 1978; JD, John Marshall Law Sch., 1985. Bar: Ill. 1985, U.S. Dist. Ct. (no. dist.) Ill. 1985, U.S. Ct. Appeals (7th cir.) Ill. 1985. Tchr. Chgo. Bd. Edn., 1975-85; pvt. practice law Geneva, Ill., 1985-87, Chgo., 1987-89, Oakbrook Terrace, 1989-91; assoc. Simpson & Cybak, Chgo., 1991-96; pvt. practice law Villa Park, Ill., 1996-97, St. Charles, Ill., 1997—; prof. Loyola U., Chgo., 1975, Waubanse Community Coll., Elburn, Ill., 1985-87; cons. Community Ch. Caucus, Chgo., 1987—. Author: Albion Woodbury Small and Education, 1978, Gunsel, 1988. Mem. ABA, Fed. Bar Assn., Ill. Bar Assn., Chgo. Bar Assn. Avocations: tennis, golf. General civil litigation, General corporate, Personal injury. Office: 4505 E Powers Blvd Decatur IL 62521-2546

**ANSELL, EDWARD ORIN,** lawyer; b. Superior, Wis., Mar. 29, 1926; s. H. S. and Mollie (Rudnitzky) A.; m. Hanne B. Baer, Dec. 23, 1956; children: Deborah, William. BSEE, U. Wis., 1948; JD, George Washington U., 1955. Bar: D.C. 1955, Calif. 1960. Electronic engr. FCC, Buffalo and Washington, 1948-55; patent atty. RCA, Princeton, N.J., 1955-57; gen. mgr. AeroChem. Rsch. Labs., Princeton, 1957-58; patent atty. Aerojet-Gen. Corp., La Jolla, Calif., 1958-63, corp. patent counsel, 1963-82, asst. sec., 1970-79, sec., 1979-82, assoc. gen. counsel, 1981-82; dir. patents and licensing Calif. Inst. Tech., Pasadena, 1982-92; pvt. practice Claremont, Calif., 1992—; co-founder Gryphon Scis., South San Francisco, Calif., 93—, Ciphergen Biosystems, Palo Alto, Calif., 1993—; adj. prof. U. La Verne (Calif.) Coll. Law, 1972-78; spl. advisor, task force chmn. U.S. Commn. Govt. Procurement, 1971. Editor: Intellectual Property in Academe: A Legal Compendium, 1991; contbr. articles to profl. publs. Recipient Alumni Svc. award George Washington U., 1975. Mem. Am. Intellectual Property Law Assn., Assn. Corp. Patent Counsel, Ea. Bar Assn. Los Angeles County, L.A. Intellectual Property Law Assn., Licensing Execs. Soc., Assn. Univ. Tech. Mgrs., State Bar Calif. (exec. com. intellectual property sect. 1983-86), Internet Soc., Athenaeum Club Pasadena, Univ. Club Claremont, Internet Soc. Intellectual property, Trademark and copyright, Alternative dispute resolution. Home and Office: 449 Willamette Ln Claremont CA 91711-2746

**ANSLEY, JAMES RONALD,** lawyer; b. Roanoke Rapids, N.C., Nov. 20, 1961; s. Troy J. and Mildred Ercelle Ansley. BS, N.C. State U., RAleigh, 1984; MAGED, Clemson U., 1988; JD, Miss. Coll., Jackson, 1991. Bar: N.C. 1991, La. 1993. Profl. Law Offices of James R. Ansley, Raleigh. Criminal, Juvenile, Family and matrimonial. Office: Law Offices of James R Ansley 19 W Hargett St Ste 406 Raleigh NC 27601-1350

**ANSLEY, SHEPARD BRYAN,** lawyer; b. July 31, 1939; s. William Bonneau and Florence Jackson (Bryan) A.; m. Boyce Lineberger, May 9, 1970; children-Anna Rankin, Florence Bryan. BA, U. Ga., 1961; LLB, U. Va., 1964. Bar: Ba. 1967. Assoc. Carter & Ansley and predecessor firm Carter, Ansley, Smith & McLendon, Atlanta, 1967-73, ptnr., 1973-84, of counsel, 1984-91; bd. dirs. Prime Bancshares, Inc., Prime Bank, FSB; chmn. bd. dirs., pres. Sodamaster Co. Am.; exec. v.p. Woodridge Realty, Inc.; sr. v.p., ACA Consulting, Inc.; fin. cons. Attkisson, Carter & Akers, Inc.; bd. dirs. Jour. Pub. Law Emory U., 1961-62; bd. dirs., sec. CRM Co., LLC, L.A. County, Calif. Mem. Vestry St. Luke's Episcopal Ch., Atlanta, 1971-74; treas., mem. exec. com., bd. dirs. Alliance Theatre Co., Atlanta, 1974-85; trustee Atlanta Music Festival Assn., Inc., 1975—; v.p., bd. dirs. Atlanta Preservation Ctr. Inc., pres., 1988-90; bd. visitors Lineberger Cancer Rsch. Ctr. U. N.C. at Chapel Hill, 1987-92; pres., bd. dirs. The Study Hall at Emmaus House, Inc.; bd. dirs., The Margaret Mitchell House, Inc.; bd. govs. Ga. Pub. Policy Found., Inc., 1999—. Served to capt. U.S. Army, 1965-67. Mem. ABA, Ga. Bar Assn., Atlanta Bar Assn., Atlanta Lawyers Club, Am. Coll. Mortgage Attys., Atlanta Jr. C. of C. (bd. dirs. 1968-72), Piedmont Driving Club. Real property, Probate.

**ANSPACH, ROBERT MICHAEL,** lawyer; b. Tiffin, Ohio, Feb. 29, 1948; s. William Charles and Evelyn Helen (Smith) A.; m. Jane Evelyn Friedman, Oct. 29, 1983; children: Michael Robert, Robert Joseph, John William. BA, Cornell U., 1970, JD, 1973. Bar: Ohio 1973, U.S. Dist. Ct. (no. dist.) Ohio 1974, U.S. Ct. Appeals (6th cir.) 1976, U.S. Supreme Ct. 1976, U.S. Tax Ct. 1985. Assoc. Shumaker, Loop & Kendrick, Toledo, 1973-79, ptnr., 1979-83, mng. ptnr., 1984, adminstr. trial dept., 1985; founder, mng. ptnr. Robert M. Anspach Assocs., Toledo, 1986—. Co-author: Winning in Court—The Accountant's Role in Litigation, Arbitration and Dispute Resolution, 1986. Trustee Toledo Repertoire Theatre, 1993—, Boys and Girls Clubs Toledo, 1993—; pres. Historic Perrysburg, Inc., 1998-99, pres., 1998—; trustee Toledo Cultural Arts Commn. at the Valentine Theatre. Recipient award of merit Ohio Legal Ctr., 1986. Fellow Ohio State Bar Found.; mem. ABA, Ohio Bar Assn. (vice chmn. jud. adminstrn. and legal reform com. 1982, lawyer's assistance com. 1986—), Toledo Bar Assn., Nat. Assn. R.R. Trial Counsel, Def. Rsch. Inst. Avocations: singing, piano, art collecting, musical composition, tennis. Federal civil litigation, Transportation, Product liability. Home: 29640 Duxbury Ln Perrysburg OH 43551-3414 Office: Robert M Anspach Assocs 405 Madison Ave Ste 2100 Toledo OH 43604-1224

**ANSTEAD, HARRY LEE,** state supreme court justice. Former judge, chief judge U.S. Ct. Appeals. (4th dist.), Fla.; justice Fla. Supreme Ct., Tallahassee, 1994—. Office: Supreme Ct Bldg 500 S Duval St Tallahassee FL 32399-6556*

**ANSTINE, GLEN ROSCOE,** lawyer; b. Omaha, Nebr., Sept. 23, 1952; s. Glenn D. and Phyllis M. (Pawloski) A.; m. Elizabeth Renee Fajardo, Nov. 27, 1958; children: Asia, Kali, Avalon, Sydney, Timothy, Piper, Dylan. BS, Portland State U., 1977; MD, U. Nebr., 1982. Bar: Nebr. 1983, Colo. 1984, U.S. Supreme Ct. 1990, U.S. Ct. Appeals (10th cir.) 1989. Law clk. Nebr. Supreme Ct., Lincoln, 1983-84; pvt. practice law Denver, 1985—; panelist, trustee U.S. Trustee's Office, Denver, 1986—. Criminal, Bankruptcy. Office: 4704 Harlan St Ste 320 Denver CO 80212-7418

**ANTEAU, RONALD W.,** lawyer; b. Detroit, July 26, 1940; s. Larry and Bernice (Abramson) A.; m. Leanne E. Godfrey, Sept. 11, 1965; children: Ronald Todd, Jeffrey Lee. BA, UCLA, 1962, JD, 1965. Bar: Calif. 1966, U.S. Supreme Ct. 1969, U.S. Ct. Mil. Appeals 1969; cert. in family Calif. State Bar Bd. Legal Specialization. Ptnr. Rosen & Anteau, L.A., 1967-69, Trope and Trope, L.A., 1969-82, Simke, Chodos, Silberfeld & Anteau, L.A., 1985-95, Kolodny & Anteau, Beverly Hills, 1995—; pvt. practice Beverly Hills, Calif., 1983-85. Co-author, coord. multi-volume book: Family Law Litigation Guide, 1991; co-author: California Transactions Forms, 1998; editor Calif. State Bar newsletter Family Law News, 1994-95; contbr. articles to profl. jours. Fellow Am. Acad. Matrimonial Lawyers (v.p. membership 1993-94, v.p. programs 1994-95, chpt. pres. 1996-97), Internat. Acad. Matrimonial Lawyers; mem. Am. Coll. Family Trial Lawyers (diplomate). Family and matrimonial. Office: Kolodny & Anteau 9th Fl West Tower 9100 Wilshire Blvd Beverly Hills CA 90212-3415

**ANTHONY, ANDREW JOHN,** lawyer; b. Newark, Jan. 26, 1950; s. Andrew and Mary (Norton) A.; m. Raquel Perez Montoya, Sept. 29, 1990; 1 child, Nicholas. BA, Kean Coll., 1973; JD cum laude, U. Miami, 1976. Bar: Fla. 1977, U.S. Dist. Ct. (so. dist.) Fla. 1977. Assoc. Knight, Peters, Hoeveler, Pickle, Niemaeller & Flynn, Miami, Fla., 1977-79, Vernis & Bowling, Miami, 1979, Ligman, Martin, Shiley & McGee, Coral Gables, Fla., 1979-86; sole practice Coral Gables, 1986—. Mem. ABA, Fla. Bar Assn. Democrat. Roman Catholic. Avocations: numismatics, fishing, reading. State civil litigation, Insurance, Personal injury. Home: 3703 Anderson Rd Coral Gables FL 33134-7052 Office: Ste 1035 999 Ponce De Leon Blvd Coral Gables FL 33134-3037

**ANTHONY, GAYLE DEANNA,** lawyer; b. Dallas, Apr. 27, 1964; d. John Evan Crellin and Dee Arline Grasser; m. Kevin E. Anthony, Aug. 6, 1988; 1 child, Robert Justin Anthony. BA, U. Fla., 1986; JD, Duke U., 1989. Bar: Ky. 1990, Wis. 1993, Ill. 1993, Fla. 1996. Atty. Seiller Havelmacker & Blevins, Paris, Ky., 1991-92; pvt. practice Racine, Wis., 1993—, Pt. Orange, Fla., 1996—. Republican. Avocations: sports, traveling. Estate planning, Family and matrimonial. Office: 800 Sterling Chase Dr Port Orange FL 32124-6999

**ANTHONY, JAMES LLOYD,** lawyer; b. Galveston, Tex., July 22, 1943; m. Sue Krueger, June 3, 1967; children: Hope, Stephen. BA, U. Tex., 1968, JD, 1969. Bar: Tex., 1969; U.S. Dist. Ct. (so. dist.) Tex. 1970, U.S. Dist. Ct. (we. dist.) Tex. 1996, U.S. Ct. of Appeals (5th cir.) 1976; bd. cert. personal injury trial lawyer, Tex. Shareholder McLeod, Alexander, Powel & Apffel, PC, Galveston, Tex., 1969-83; ptnr. Kleberg, Dyer, Redford & Weil, Corpus Christi, Tex., 1983-88; shareholder Redford, Wray & Woolsey, P.C., Corpus Christi, Tex., 1988-93; ptnr. Wray, Woolsey & Anthony, LLP, Corpus Christi, 1993-96, Anthony & Marsh, LLP, Corpus Christi, 1996-97; pvt. practice Corpus Christi, 1997—. Fellow Tex. Bar Found. (sustaining life, trustee 1995-97); mem. Tex. Assn. Def. Counsel, Internat. Assn. Def. Counsel, State Bar of Tex. (mem. grievance com. dist. 11A, 1996-99), Nat. Assn. Railroad Trial Counsel. Methodist. General civil litigation, Contracts commercial, Insurance. Office: 711 N Carancahua St Ste 1001 Corpus Christi TX 78475-0019

**ANTHONY, JOAN CATON,** lawyer, writer; b. South Bend, Ind., July 28, 1939; d. Joseph Robert and Margaret Catherine (McMeel) Caton; m. Robert Armstrong Anthony, Jan. 3, 1980; 1 child, Peter. BA, Marquette U., 1961; MA, Northwestern U., Evanston, Ill., 1963; JD, Catholic U. Am., 1979. Bar: D.C. 1980, Va. 1982. Instr. English Marquette U., Milw., 1963-65; instr. English George Washington U., Washington, 1965-69, asst. prof., 1969-70; spl. asst. student affairs HEW, Washington, 1970-72; dir. Office Student and Youth Affairs U.S. Office Edn., Washington, 1972-74, legis. specialist, 1974-78; chief mgmt. ops. br. Fed. Wildlife Permit Office U.S. Fish and Wildlife Svc., Washington, 1978-81; assoc. Cate and Goodbread, Washington, 1981-86; atty., advisor office legis. counsel U.S. Dept. Interior, 1991-95; staff atty. Interior Bd. Land Appeals, 1995—; mem. U.S. del. to 2d meeting Conf. Parties to Conv. on Internat. Trade in Endangered Species of Wild Flora and Fauna, San Jose, Costa Rica, 1979. Contbr. lit. revs., essays and articles on univ.-cmty. rels., western settlement and internat. negotiations to various publs. Bd. dirs. McLean Citizens Assn., 1982-83, Fairfax County Humane Soc., 1983; pres. Franklin Forest Frolickers, 1985-86; treas. Greater McLean Rep. Women's Club, 1987-88; den leader cub scouts, com. mem. Boy Scouts Am., 1990—; parent vol. Fairfax County Pub. Schs., 1987—. Recipient Spl. Achievement award U.S. Fish and Wildlife Svc., 1981. Mem. D.C. Bar, Va. Bar, DAR (Freedom Hill chpt.). Roman Catholic. Administrative and regulatory, Appellate, Natural resources. Home: 2011 Lorraine Ave Mc Lean VA 22101-5331

**ANTHONY, KENNETH C., JR.,** lawyer; b. Spartanburg, S.C., Jan. 23, 1954; s. Kenneth C. Sr. and Carol Ferguson (Burnside) A.; m. Monta Lorraine Moody, Mar. 15, 1980; children: Jay, Mary Sullivan, Dunk, Grady. Student, Rice U., 1972-74; BA, Wofford Coll., 1975; JD, U. S.C., 1977. Bar: S.C. 1978, U.S. Dist. Ct. S.C. 1978, U.S. Ct. Appeals (4th cir.) 1988, U.S. Supreme Ct. 1996; cert. civil and family mediator; cert. civil arbitrator. Ptnr. The Anthony Law Firm, P.A., Spartanburg, 1978—; adj. prof. Wofford Coll., Spartanburg, 1978-98; bd. advisors U. S.C. Law Sch., Columbia, 1988-92. Fellow S.C. Bar Found. (life); mem. ABA (mem. editl. bd.ABA/BNA Lawyers; Manual on Professonal Conduct), S.C. Bar Assn. (ho. dels. 1985-96, chmn. Law Related Edn. Commn. 1994-96, bd. govs. 1996-99, past chmn. ethic adv. com.), S.C. Trial Lawyers Assn. (bd. govs. 1996-98), Am. Trial Lawyers Assn. E-mail: kanthony@anthonylaw.com. Fax #: 864-583-9772. Personal injury, Product liability, General civil litigation. Office: The Anthony Law Firm PA 250 Magnolia St PO Box 3565 Spartanburg SC 29304-3565

**ANTHONY, ROBERT ARMSTRONG,** law educator, lawyer; b. Washington, Dec. 28, 1931; s. Emile Peter and Martha Graham (Armstrong) A.; m. Ruth Grace Barrons, Feb. 7, 1959 (div.); 1 child, Graham Barrons; m. Joan Patricia Caton, Jan 3, 1980; 1 child, Peter Christopher Caton. BA, Yale U., 1953; BA in Jurisprudence, Oxford U., 1955; JD, Stanford U., 1957. Bar: Calif. 1957, N.Y. 1971, D.C. 1972. Assoc. Pillsbury, Madison & Sutro, San Francisco, 1957-62, Kelso, Cotton & Ernst, San Francisco, 1962-64; assoc. prof. law Cornell U. Law Sch., 1964-68, prof., 1968-75, dir. internat. legal studies, 1964-74; chief counsel, later dir. Office Fgn. Direct Investments, Dept. Commerce, 1972-73; cons. Adminstrv. Conf. U.S., Washington, 1968-71; chmn. Adminstrv. Conf. U.S., 1974-79; ptnr. McKenna, Conner & Cuneo, Washington, 1979-82; sole practice Washington, 1982-83; prof. law George Mason U., Arlington, Va., 1983—; Fulbright lectr., Slovenia, 1994; lectr. Acad. Am. and Internat. Law, Southwestern Legal Found., Dallas, summers 1967-72, instr. Golden Gate U., 1961. Mem. editorial adv. bd. Jour. Law and Tech., 1986-91; contbr. articles to profl. jours. Active Pres.'s Inflation Program Regulatory Coun., 1978-79, Fairfax County (Va.) Rep. Com., 1984-86; chmn. panel U.S. Dept. Edn. Appeal Bd., 1981-83; cons., chmn. pubs. adv. bd. Internat. Law Inst., 1984—; cons. Inst. Pub. Adminstrn., Slovenia, 1994—; bd. dirs. Marin Shakespeare Festival, San Rafael, Calif., 1961-64, Nat. Ctr. for Adminstrv. Justice, 1974-79, Va. Assn. Scholars, 1990-98; commr. Sausalito (Calif.) City Planning Commn., 1962-64. Mem. ABA (coun., sec. sect. adminstrv. law and regulatory practice 1988-94), Assn. Am. Rhodes Scholars, Am. Law Inst., Stanford U. Law Soc. Washington (pres. 1982), Cosmos Club. Home: 2011 Lorraine Ave Mc Lean VA 22101-5331 Office: George Mason U Law Sch 3401 N Fairfax Dr Arlington VA 22201-4411

**ANTIN, MICHAEL,** lawyer; b. Milw., Nov. 30, 1938; s. David Boris and Pauline (Mayer) A.; m. Evelyne Judith Hirsch, June 19, 1960; children: Stephanie, Bryan, Randall. BS, Univ. Calif., 1960; JD, U. Calif., 1963. Bar: Calif. 1963; cert. tax specialist. Tax atty. Cruikshank, Antin & Grebow, Beverly Hills, Calif., 1963-81, Antin, Litz & Grebow, Beverly Hills, 1981-91, Antin & Taylor, L.A., 1993—; bd. dirs. Small Bus. Counsel Am., Washington, The Group, Inc.; speaker in field; instr. Solomon S. Heubner Sch. CLU Studies, 1977-86. Author: How to Operate Your Trust or Probate, 1983; contbr. articles to profl. jours. With U.S. Air Force, 1959-67. Fellow Am. Coll. Tax Counsel, Am. Coll. of Trust & Estate Counsel, L.A. County Bowlers Assn. (bd. dirs. 1996). Avocations: jogging, tennis, cross country skiing, bowling. Estate planning, Taxation, general, Probate. Office: Antin & Taylor 10880 Wilshire Blvd Ste 1010 Los Angeles CA 90024-4111

**ANTOLIN, STANISLAV,** patent lawyer; b. Toronto, Ont., Can., Mar. 27, 1960; came to U.S., 1962; BS, Drexel U., 1983; MS, Carnegie Mellon U., 1985; JD, Widner U., 1994. Bar: Pa., U.S. Patent Office, U.S. Dist. Ct. (we. dist.) Pa. Rsch. engr. Lanxide Corp., Newark, Del., 1985-89, patent agt., 1989-94; patent counsel Kennametal Inc., Latrobe, Pa., 1994-99; assoc. Rhodes & Mason, P.L.L.C., Greensboro, N.C., 1999—. Contbr. articles to profl. jours. Mem. The Minerals, Metals, and Materials Soc. of the AIME, Am. Intellectual Property Law Assn., Pitts. Intellectual Property Law Assn., Allegheny County Bar Assn. E-mail: santolin@rhodesmason.com. Intellectual property, Patent, Trademark and copyright.

**ANTON, JOHN M.,** lawyer; b. Woodland, Calif., Mar. 25, 1947; s. Wellington Baird and Margaret (Musgrove) A. BA, U. Calif., Davis, 1969, JD, 1972. Bar: Calif. 1972, U.S. Dist. Ct. (no. and ea. dists.) Calif. 1982, U.S. Ct. Appeals (9th cir.) 1982. Cons. Senate Judiciary Com. Calif. Legis., Sacramento, 1973-74; defender Pub. Defender's Office Sacramento County, Sacramento, 1974-78; assoc. Eugene C. Treaster, Sacramento, 1979-81, Rodney A. Klein, Inc., Sacramento, 1982-86; ptnr. DeMeo & DeMeo, Santa Rosa, Calif., 1986-93, Boxer Elkind & Gerson, Oakland, Calif., 1993—; active com. confer, com. adminstrs. justice Calif. Med. Assn. Capt. U.S. Army. Mem. Assn. Trial Lawyers Am., Calif. Trial Lawyers Assn. (med. malpractice com. 1991—), Calif. Bar Assn. (com. to confer with Calif. Med. Assn. 1991-93, com. on adminstrn. of justice 1993-97), Redwood Empire Trial Lawyers Assn. (pres. 1992), Sonoma County Trial Lawyers Assn., Internat. Palm Soc., Sierra Club. Democrat. Personal injury, General civil litigation. Office: Boxer & Gerson 171 12th St Ste 100 Oakland CA 94607-4911

**ANTON, RONALD DAVID,** lawyer; b. Phila., Nov. 9, 1933; s. Emil T. Anton and Mary E. Bishara; m. Suzanne J. Winker, Aug. 19, 1976; 1 child, Ronald J. JD, U. Buffalo, 1958; LLM, U. Pa., 1959, Yale U., 1960. Bar: N.Y. 1959. Ptnr. Boniello, Anton, Conti & B., Niagara Falls, N.Y., 1960—; lectr. Univ. Buffalo (N.Y.) Law Sch., 1960-62; cons. N.Y. State Legis., Buffalo, Greater Buffalo (N.Y.) Devel. Found.; past pres. Niagara (N.Y.) County Legal Aid, 1966-68, Niagara Falls (N.Y.) Bar, 1968; past dist. gov. N.Y. State Trial Lawyers, 1984-88; moderator (tv show) The Law For You, N.Y., 1967. Author: Jesus, Saviour, 1992; contbr. articles to profl. jours. Rep. candidate N.Y. State Atty. Gen., 1990; trustee Stella Niagara Edn. Pk., Lewiston, N.Y., 1988—. General civil litigation. Home: 175 White Tail Run Grand Island NY 14072-3223 Office: Boniello Anton Conti & B 770 Main St Niagara Falls NY 14301-1704

**ANTON, S. DAVID,** lawyer; b. Tampa, Fla., Nov. 25, 1958; s. Leonard Morton Anton and Joyce (Schonbrun) Hartmann. BS in Econs., U. Fla., 1981, JD, 1984. Cert. mediator. Pvt. practice family law, dept collection and corp. law Tampa. Mem. Fla. Bar Assn., Hillsborough County Bar Assn. Family and matrimonial, Consumer commercial. Office: Harvey Schonbrun PA 1802 N Morgan St Tampa FL 33602-2328

**ANTONE, NAHIL PETER,** lawyer, civil engineer; b. Baghdad, Iraq, Jan. 17, 1952; came to U.S., 1978; s. Peter and Salima (Kammoo) A. BS in Civil Engring. with highest distinction, U. Baghdad, 1971; MS in Structural Engring., U. Surrey, 1974; JD summa cum laude, Detroit Coll. Law, 1985. Bar: Mich. 1985, U.S. Dist. Ct. (ea. dist.) Mich. 1985; registered profl. engr., Mich. Constrn. engr. Ministry Constrn., Baghdad, 1971-73; project mgr. Ministry Oil, Baghdad, 1974-78; design engr. Harley Ellington Pierce Yee, Southfield, Mich., 1978-79; v.p. Hennessey Engring. Co., Trenton, Mich., 1979-85; assoc. Bodman, Longley & Dahling, Detroit, 1985-88; owner N. Peter Antone Profl. Corp., Southfield, 1988—; ptnr. Antone & Kuhn Law Offices, Farmington Hills, Mich., 1989-93; pvt. practice Southfield, 1993—; lectr. Detroit Coll. Law, 1986-87. Govt. of Iraq scholar, 1974; scholar Det. Coll. Law, 1982. Mem. ABA, Detroit Bar Assn., ASCE (chmn. legis. com. Southeast Mich. chpt. 1981). Avocations: tennis, swimming, exercise, travel, music. Construction, Immigration, naturalization, and customs, Public international. Home: 28935 Murray Crescent Dr Southfield MI 48076-5563 Office: 16445 W 12 Mile Rd Southfield MI 48076-2949

**ANTONETTI-ZEQUEIRA, SALVADOR,** lawyer; b. Arroyo, P.R., Dec. 20, 1941; m. Catherine Stutts; children: Salvador J., Eduardo L. LLB, U. P.R., 1967. Bar: P.R. 1967, U.S. Dist. Ct. P.R. 1968, U.S. Ct. Appeals (1st cir.) 1968, U.S. Supreme Ct. 1975. Sec. univ. bd. U. P.R., San Juan, 1966-68; dean univ. coll. U. P.R., Cayey, 1970-72; from assoc. to ptnr. Nachman & Feldstein, San Juan, 1968-70; ptnr. Fiddler, Gonzalez & Rodriguez, San Juan, 1973-76, from ptnr. to head litigation, 1982—; from ptnr. to mng. ptnr. Goldman, Antonetti & Davila, San Juan, 1977-81; trustee U. P.R., 1992-93, U. P.R. Law Sch. Trust, San Juan, 1986—; mem. adv. com. on local rules U.S. Ct. Appeals (1st cir.) Boston, 1993-97; reporter CJRA adv. group U.S. Dist. Ct., San Juan, 1990-94, mem., 1995—. Contbr. articles to profl. jours. Fellow Am. Coll. Trial Lawyers (pres. P.R. chpt. 1995-97), Internat. Soc. Barristers; mem. Am. Arbitration Assn., ABA. General civil litigation,

Antitrust, Franchising. Office: Fiddler Gonzalez Rodriguez Chase Manhattan Bldg 254 Ave Munoz Rivera San Juan PR 00918-1900

**ANUTA, KARL FREDERICK,** lawyer; b. Menominee, Mich., May 16, 1935; s. Michael J. and Marianne (Strelic) A.; m. Barbara L. Olds Anuta, June 23, 1956; children: Karl Gregory Anuta, Natasha Louise Anuta. BA, Macalester Coll., 1957; LLB, U. Colo. Sch. Law, 1960. Bar: U.S. Supreme Ct., U.S. Dist. Ct., U.S. Ct. Appeals (D.C. and 10th cirs.). Staff atty. Office of Regional Solicitor U.S. Dept. Interior, Denver, 1960-63; staff atty. Frontier Refining Co., Denver, 1963-67, gen. counsel, 1967-68; sr. atty. Husky Oil Co., Denver, 1968-79, chief regional atty., 1979-83, gen. counsel, 1983-84; counsel Duncan, Weinberg & Miller, Denver, 1985-87; atty. pvt. practice, Boulder, Colo., 1987—. Pres., chmn. Interfaith Coun. Boulder, 1964; pres. Hist. Boulder, Inc., 1980; mem. and chmn. City Boulder Landmarks Bd., 1981-91; v.p. Colo. Chautauqua Assn., 1982, Boulder Hist. Soc., 1992; chmn. Boulder Coun. Internat. Visitors, 1986-88; bd. dirs. Spl. Transit Sys. Boulder County, 1988-95, pres. 1995; mem., chmn. County Hist. Preservation Adv. Bd., 1992—; mem. coun. Presbytery of Plains and Peaks. Named Boulder County Pacesetter, Boulder Daily Camera, 1996. Mem. ABA, Colo. Bar Assn. Republican. Presbyterian. Avocations: bicycling, skiing, fishing. Administrative and regulatory, Natural resources, Real property. Office: 1720 14th St PO Box 1001 Boulder CO 80306-1001

**ANUTA, MICHAEL JOSEPH,** lawyer; b. Pound, Wis., Feb. 4, 1901; s. Michael Anuta and Charlotte Zudnochowsky; m. Marianne M. Strelec; children: Mary Hope Milidonis, Nancy Ellen Beauchamp, Janet Grace Dalquist, Michael John, Karl Frederick. LLB, LaSalle Extension U., 1956; LLD (hon.), Alma Coll., 1960; BS (hon.), San Vicinte De Paul, Maracaibo, Venezuela, 1965. Bar: Mich. 1929, U.S. Supreme Ct. 1932, U.S. Dist. Ct. Mich., U.S. Dist. Ct. Wis., Bar of Interstate Commerce Commn. Traffic mgr. M&M Traffic Assn., Menominee, Mich., 1938-48; pros. atty. Menominee County, Menominee, 1938-48; mcpl. judge City of Menominee, 1958-68; reserve judge Menominee, 1929—. Author: East Prussians from Russia, 1979, Ships of our Ancestors, 1983, History of Rotary Clubs in Wisconsin-Michigan, 1993, Anuta Heritage Register, 1993. Dir., v.p. Mich. Children's Aid Soc.; active Boy Scouts Am., 1945—; moderator Synod Presbyn. Ch. Mich., 1953; chmn. Menominee County Def. Council, WWII, 1953. Lt. col. CAP, Mich. Recipient Silver Beaver award Boy Scouts Am., 1945, Silver Antelope, 1967, Disting. Svc. award community svc. Radio Sta. WAGN, 1963, Disting. citation, Govt. Legislature of Mich., 1989; named Man Yr. Menominee Area C. of C., 1971. Mem. ABA, State Bar Mich., Menominee County Bar Assn., Mich. Prosecuting Attys. Assn. (pres. 1945), Menominee County Hist. Soc. (pres. 1967-74, pres. emeritus), Am. Hist. Socs. Germans from Russia (dir. 1978-81), Hist. Soc. Mich. (dir. 1972-78, award merit 1980, Charles Follow award 1983), Am. Arbitrators Assn., Panel Arbitrators Res. Mich. Judge, Rotary (gov. dist. 1963-64, pres. 1934-35), Shriners, Masons (33 degree). Republican. Avocations: pilot, amateur radio. Antitrust, Aviation, General corporate. Home and Office: # 105 1200 Northland Terrace Ln Marinette WI 54143-4193

**ANZMAN, MARK CHARLES,** lawyer; b. Denver, Mar. 1, 1962; s. Joseph Roy and Iris Anzman; m. Laura Elaine Anzman, July 27, 1987; children: Lindsey Elaine, Mark Charles II. B in Bus., Colo. State U., 1989; MBA, JD, U. Dayton, 1992. Bar: Ohio, U.S. Dist. Ct. Ohio, U.S. Ct. Appeals (6th cir.). Atty. Ruschall, Lehman & Hobbs, Miamisburg, Ohio, 1992—. City solicitor Village of Pitsburg, Ohio, 1996—, Village of Ithaca, Ohio, 1996—. With USN, 1981-85. General civil litigation, Criminal, Personal injury. Office: Ruschall Lehman and Hobbs 443 E Central Ave Miamisburg OH 45342-2808

**AOKI, ZACHARY BURKE,** lawyer; b. Lynn, Mass., Nov. 14, 1965; s. Joseph S. and Marguerite Jean (Villa) A.; m. Charisse Marie Adame, Feb. 23, 1991; children: Joshua, Katharine, John. BBA, Baylor U., 1987; JD, Boston Coll., 1990. Bar: Tex. 1990, U.S. Dist. Ct. (we. dist.) Tex. 1991, U.S. Dist. Ct. (no. and so. dists.) Tex. 1995, U.S. Ct. Appeals (5th cir.) 1996. Assoc. Jenkens & Gilchrist, San Antonio, 1990—. Contbr. articles to profl. jours. Recipient Jane Williams scholarshp Data Processing Mgmt. Assn., 1996. Mem. San Antonio Young Lawyers Assn. (v.p., pres.-elect, bd. dirs. 1996—), Tex. Young Lawyers Assn. Avocations: history, woodworking. General civil litigation, Appellate, Computer. Office: Jenkens & Gilchrist 100 W Houston St Ste 1800 San Antonio TX 78205-1457

**APFEL, GARY,** lawyer; b. N.Y.C., June 2, 1952; s. Willy and Jenny (Last) A.; m. Serena Jakobovits, June 16, 1980; children: Alyssa J., I. Michael, Alanna J., Stephen J., Alexander. BA, NYU magna cum laude, 1973; JD, Columbia U., 1976. Bar: N.Y. 1977, Calif. 1988, U.S. Dist. Ct. (so. and ea. dists.) N.Y. 1977, U.S. Dist. Ct. (cen. dist.) Calif. 1988, U.S. Ct. Appeals (9th cir.) 1988. Assoc. Sullivan & Cromwell, N.Y.C., 1976-80; assoc. LeBoeuf, Lamb, Leiby & MacRae, N.Y.C., 1980-84, ptnr., 1985-88; ptnr. Kaye, Scholer, Fierman, Hays & Handler LLP, L.A., 1988-97, Akin, Gump, Strauss, Hauer & Feld, L.L.P., L.A., 1997—. Kent scholar Columbia U., 1976. Mem. ABA, Calif. State Bar Assn. (bus. law sect. corps. com.), Phi Beta Kappa. Mergers and acquisitions, Securities, General corporate. Office: Akin Gump Strauss Hauer & Feld LLP 2029 Century Park E Ste 2600 Los Angeles CA 90067-3012

**APFELBAUM, MARC,** lawyer; b. Phila., Apr. 30, 1955; s. Herbert and Beatrice Bernice (Bitman) A. BA cum laude, U. Pa., 1978; JD magna cum laude, Georgetown U., 1983. Bar: N.Y. 1984, U.S. Dist. Ct. (so. and ea. dists.) N.Y. 1984, Conn. 1991. Assoc. Cravath, Swaine & Moore, N.Y.C., 1983-89; v.p., assoc. gen. counsel, asst. sec. Time Warner Cable, Stamford, Conn., 1989-96, sr. v.p., gen. counsel, sec., 1996—. Editor Georgetown Law Jour., 1982-83. Mem. ABA. Communications, General corporate. Home: 440 W End Ave Apt 14C New York NY 10024-5358 Office: Time Warner Cable 290 Harbor Dr Stamford CT 06902-7475

**APGAR, KENNETH EDWARD,** lawyer; b. Tampa, Fla., Aug. 12, 1946; s. Charles F. and Mary E. (Camp) A.; m. Karen Lynn Von Nida, Apr. 11, 1970; children: Jennifer, Vanessa. BA, U. Fla., 1968, JD, 1970. Bar: Fla. 1971; U.S. Dist. Ct. (mid. dist.) Fla. 1977, U.S. Dist. Ct. (so. and no. dists.) Fla. 1984; U.S. Ct. Appeals (5th and 11 cirs.) 1981; U.S. Supreme Ct., 1975; cert. civil trial advocate, civil trial lawyer. Asst. state atty. State Atty.'s Office, 13th Jud. Cir., Tampa, Fla., 1976-79; assoc. de la Parte & Butler, Tampa, 1979-82; ptnr. Butler & Apgar, Tampa, 1982-90; pvt. practice Tampa, 1990—. Capt. USAF, 1971-76, Fed. Republic of Germany. Mem. ABA, Fla. Bar Assn., Nat. Bd. Trial Advocacy, Assn. of Trial Lawyers of Am., Acad. of Fla. Trial Lawyers, Hillsborough County Bar Assn. Methodist. Avocations: racquetball, computers. General civil litigation, Personal injury, Product liability. Office: 601 E Twiggs St Ste 100 Tampa FL 33602-3921

**APKE, THOMAS MICHAEL,** lawyer, educator; b. Santa Monica, Calif., Jan. 16, 1945; s. Edward Anthony and Harriett (Ruby) A.; m. Virginia Lee Royston, July 17, 1982; children: Daniel Edward, Sarah, Matthew. BS, Pa. State U., 1966; JD, Marquette U., 1969; LLM, U. San Diego, 1983. Bar: Calif. 1971. Assoc. Coombs & Comstock, Culver City, Calif., 1971-74; sole practice Mission Viejo, Calif., 1974-84, Laguna Niguel, Calif., 1985—; prof. bus. law Calif. State U., Fullerton, 1974—. Contbr. articles on bus. law to profl. jours. Mem. Nat. Com. Recipient Disting. Faculty award Calif. State U. Fullerton Alumni Assn., 1982. Mem. Am. Bus. Law Assn., Pacific Southwest Bus. Law Assn., Pa. State Alumni Assn., Beta Gamma Sigma. Roman Catholic. General corporate, Real property, Corporate taxation. Home: 29156 Mira Vis Laguna Niguel CA 92677-4325 Office: Calif State U-Fullerton Dept Mgmt Fullerton CA 92634

**APOLINSKY, STEPHEN DOUGLAS,** lawyer; b. Birmingham, Ala., Dec. 5, 1961; s. Harold Irwin and Sandra Jean (Rubenstein) A. BA, U. Mich., 1983; JD, Emory U., 1987. Bar: Ga. 1987, U.S. Dist. Ct. (no. dist.) Ga. 1987, D.C. 1989, Ala. 1994. Litigation assoc. Bentley, Karesh & Seacrest, Atlanta, 1987-94; mem. Eastman, Stapleton & Apolinsky, LLC, Atlanta, 1995-97, Eastman & Apolinsky, L.L.P., Atlanta, 1997—. Mem. ATLA, Ga. Trial Lawyers Assn., Atlanta Bar Assn., Atlanta Claims Assn., Am.-Israel C. of C. (bd. dirs. S.E. region). Avocations: travel and sports. General civil litigation, Insurance, Personal injury. Office: Eastman & Apolinsky Watkins Bldg 114 E Ponce De Leon Ave Decatur GA 30030-2526

**APPEL, ALBERT M.,** lawyer; b. N.Y.C., May 26, 1945; s. Morris and Belle (Kaplan) A.; m. Irena Uhl, June 10, 1979; 1 child, Elliott. BS in Econs., U. Pa., 1966; JD, NYU, 1969. Bar: N.Y. 1969, U.S. Dist. Ct. (so. and ea. dists.) N.Y. 1971, U.S. Ct. Appeals (2d cir.) 1974, U.S. Ct. Appeals (4th cir.) 1979. Assoc. Spear and Hill, N.Y.C., 1969-75; assoc. Webster & Sheffield, N.Y.C., 1976-80, ptnr., 1981-91; spl. counsel Stroock & Stroock & Lavan LLP, N.Y.C., 1991-97, ptnr., 1998—. Mem. ABA, Am. Health Lawyers Assn., N.Y. State Bar Assn., Assn. of Bar of City of N.Y., Penn Club, Beta Alpha Psi. Health, General civil litigation. Home: 670 W End Ave New York NY 10025-7313 Office: Stroock & Stroock & Lavan LLP 180 Maiden Ln New York NY 10038-4925

**APPEL, GARRY RICHARD,** lawyer; b. Denver, Apr. 13, 1952; s. Robert S. and Virginia S. (Silver) A.; married, May 1, 1982; children: Jonathan, Henry. BA, U. Colo., 1974, JD, 1978. Bar: Colo. 1978, U.S. Dist. Ct. (Colo.) 1978, U.S. Ct. Appeals (10th cir.) 1979. Assoc. Rothgerber, Appel, Powers & Johnson, Denver, 1979-83, ptnr., 1983-92; shareholder Appel, Frey & Lucas, P.C., Denver, 1992-93, Doherty, Rumble & Butler, Denver, 1993—; lectr. Nat. Bus. Inst., P.E.S.I., CLE Internat., various profl. ednl. seminars, 1983—; adj. prof. law U. Colo., Denver U. Contbr. articles to profl. jours. Mem. Colo. Bar Assn. (lectr.), Denver Bar Assn. (chmn. bankruptcy subcom. 1989-91), CLE of Colo. Democrat. Jewish. Avocations: woodworking, hiking, skiing. Bankruptcy, Federal civil litigation. Home: 3110 Cherryridge Rd Englewood CO 80110-6057 Office: Doherty Rumble & Butler 1200 17th St Ste 2400 Denver CO 80202-5858

**APPEL, KENNETH MARK,** lawyer; b. N.Y.C., May 24, 1949; s. Jesse and Rose (Boyarsky) A.; m. Janis Lowe, May 21, 1982; children: Rachael, Matthew. BA with honors in history, NYU, 1972; JD, Cath. U., 1975. Pvt. practice St. Albans, Vt., 1981—. General practice, General civil litigation, Personal injury. Office: 232 N Main St Saint Albans VT 05478-1554

**APPEL, NINA SCHICK,** law educator, dean; b. Feb. 17, 1936, Prague, Czech Republic; d. Leo and Nora Schick; m. Alfred Appel Jr.; children: Karen Oshman, Richard. Student, Cornell U.; JD, Columbia U., 1959. Instr. Columbia Law Sch., 1959-60; adminstr. Stanford U.; mem. faculty, prof. law, 1973—, assoc. dean 1976-83, dean Sch. Law, Loyola U., 1983—, dean Sch. Law, 1983—. Mem. Ill. Compensation Rev. Bd. Mem. Am. Bar Found., Chgo. Bar Found., Ill. Bar Found., Chgo. Legal Club, Chgo. Network. Jewish. Office: Loyola U Sch Law 1 E Pearson St Chicago IL 60611-2055

**APPEL, ROBERT EUGENE,** lawyer, educator; b. Cleve., Oct. 18, 1958; s. Robert Donald and Jean Ann (Crites) A.; m. Margaret Rose Curley, Aug. 24, 1985. BS, Cen. Conn. State U., 1980; JD, U. Bridgeport, Conn., 1982; MBA, U. Conn., 1984; LLM, Boston U., 1984. Bar: Conn. 1983. Asst. mgr. fin. services Lexington Ins. Co., Boston, 1984-85; tax. cons. Touche Ross and Co., Stamford, Conn., 1985-86; asst. dir. nat. design CIGNA Corp., Bloomfield, Conn., 1986-88; dir. nat. design CIGNA Corp., Bloomfield, 1988-98; asst. v.p. Lincoln Nat. Life Ins. Co., Hartford, 1999—; lectr. Real Estate Tng. and Ednl. Svcs., Bridgeport, 1985-88; lectr. real estate Dare Inst., Southbury, 1991—. Div. coord. United Way, 1988. Mem. ABA, Conn. Bar Assn. Republican. Roman Catholic. Avocations: investing, running, weightlifting, motorcycling. Personal income taxation, Estate taxation, Estate planning. Home: 80 Kingston Dr East Hartford CT 06118-2450 Office: Lincoln Fin Group 350 Church St Hartford CT 06103-1106

**APPELBAUM, JOEL ROBERT,** lawyer; b. Liberty, N.Y., Mar. 11, 1949; s. Sidney and Sylvia (Freiman) A.; m. Michelle Joan Gellman, June 8, 1980; 1 child, Edward Andrew. AB in Polit. Sociology, Princeton U., 1971; JD, Union U., 1976. Bar: N.Y., 1977. Ptnr. Appelbaum Bauman and Appelbaum, Liberty, N.Y., 1976—; bd. dirs. Cmty. Gen. Hosp., Harris, N.Y. Mem. alumni sch. com. Princeton U., 1971—. Mem. N.Y. State Bar Assn., Sullivan County Bar Assn., Def. Assn. N.Y. Avocations: professional Latin Jazz musician, vibraphonist, motorcycling, weight training. Office: Appelbaum Bauman & Appelbaum 6 N Main St Liberty NY 12754-1844

**APPENZELLER, PHILLIP CARL, JR.,** lawyer; b. Fennville, Mich., Feb. 18, 1966; s. Phillip Carl Jr. and Anna E. Appenzeller; m. Rhonda J. Brauchler, July 30, 1988; children: Brock P., Zack G. BS, Evangel Coll., Springfield, Mo., 1988; JD, U. Mo., Kansas City, 1992. Assoc. Shughart, Thomson & Kilroy, Kansas City, Mo., 1992-94, McKool Smith, Dallas, 1996—. Capt. JAG, U.S. Army, 1994-96. Mem. Evangel Coll. Alumni Assn. (chmn. bd./pres. 1997—). Republican. Baptist. Avocations: weight lifting, running, basketball. General civil litigation. Office: McKool Smith 300 Crescent Ct Ste 1500 Dallas TX 75201-6970

**APPERSON, BERNARD JAMES,** lawyer; b. Washington, June 28, 1956; s. Bernard James Jr. and Ann Wentworth (Anderson) A. BA in Polit. Sci., Am. U., 1978; JD, Cumberland Sch. Law, 1981; LLM in Internat. Law, Georgetown U., 1985. Bar: Fla. 1981, Ga. 1981, D.C. 1983, U.S. Supreme Ct. 1985. Atty., U.S. trustee for so. dist. N.Y. U.S. Dept. Justice, N.Y.C., 1981; atty. EPA, Washington, 1981-83; atty. civil rights div. U.S. Dept. Justice, Washington, 1983-84, atty. office legis. affairs, 1986-87; asst. U.S. atty. Ea. Dist. Va., Alexandria, 1987-97; counsel to dir. Legal Services Corp., Washington, 1985-86; commr. U.S. Dist. Ct., Ea. Dist. Va., Alexandria, 1996-97; sr. counsel com. on govt. reform and oversight, spl. counsel subcom. Nat. Econ. Growth, Resources etc. U.S. Ho. of Reps., Washington, 1997-98; assoc. ind. counsel Office of the Ind. Counsel, Washington, 1998-99, dep. ind. counsel, 1999—; instr. FBI Tng. Acad., Quantico, Va., 1990; lectr. law U. London and U. Ga., 1990. Assoc. editor Am. Jour. Trial Advocacy Cumberland Sch. Law, 1979-81. County chmn. Paula Hawkins for U.S Senate, Volusia County, Fla., 1974; nat. staff Citizens for Reagan, Fla., Kansas City, Mo., 1976; cons. Reagan for Pres., Detroit, 1980; dep. northeastern regional dir. Reagan-Bush 1984, Washington, 1984. Lewis F. Powell Medal for Excellence in Advocacy Am. Coll Trial Lawyers, 1980. Mem. Federalist Soc. for Law and Pub. Policy Studies, Order of Barristers, St. Andrew's Soc. Republican. Episcopalian. Home: 545 E Braddock Rd Apt 704 Alexandria VA 22314-2171 Office: Office Ind Counsel 1001 Pennsylvania Ave NW Ste 4 Washington DC 20004-2505

**APPLEBAUM, CHARLES,** lawyer; b. Newark, May 19, 1947; s. Harry I. and Francis (Gastwirth) A.; children: Matthew, David, Michael. BA, U. Pa., 1969; JD, Rutgers U., 1973; LLM, NYU, 1978. Bar: U.S. Dist. Ct. N.J. 1973. Law clk. to Hon. Samuel A. Larner Jersey City, 1973-74; assoc., then ptnr. Greenbaum, Rowe, Smith, Ravin & Davis, Woodbridge, N.J., 1974-89; gen. counsel Alfieri Orgn., Edison, N.J., 1989—; adj. prof. law Rutgers Law Sch., Newark, 1985-88. Co-author: New Jersey Real Estate Forms, 1988; contbr. articles to profl. jours. Mem. ABA (real property probate and trust, chmn. significant lit. and publs. 1985-97, co-editor The Acrel Papers 1992, 93, 94), Am. Coll. Real Estate Lawyers (editor publs. 1991—). Real property, Contracts commercial, Land use and zoning (including planning). Office: M Alfieri Co Inc PO Box 2911 399 Thornall St Edison NJ 08837-2236

**APPLEBAUM, HARVEY MILTON,** lawyer; b. Birmingham, Ala., Mar. 1, 1937; s. Oscar Arthur and Evelyn (Stein) A.; m. Elizabeth Bloom, June 23, 1962; children: Anne, Julie Flynn, Kathy. BA summa cum laude, Yale U., 1959; LLB magna cum laude, Harvard U., 1962. Bar: D.C. 1964, Ala. 1962, U.S. Ct. Appeals (D.C.) 1964, U.S. Ct. Internat. Trade 1976, U.S. Ct. Appeals (fed. cir.) 1984. Assoc. Covington & Burling, Washington, 1963-71, ptnr., 1971—; adj. prof. Georgetown U. Law Sch., Washington, 1968-72; lectr. U. Va. Law Sch., Charlottesville, 1975—. Chmn. editorial bd.: ABA Antitrust Law Developments, 1975; contbr. articles to profl. jours. Chmn. fair share dr. Sidwell Friends Sch., Washington, 1982-84; pres. Washington Area Tennis Patrons Found., 1986-90, bd. dirs., 1980—; trustee Levine Sch. of Music, 1983-96. Recipient Service award Sidwell Friends Sch., 1984, Yale medal, 1995; Sheldon traveling fellow Harvard U., 1962. Mem. ABA (chmn. antitrust law sect. 1980-81, mem. task force on global economy 1994—, mem. NAFTA task force 1993—, spl. com. on internat. antitrust 1990-91, D.C. Bar Assn., Ala. Bar Assn., Union Internationale des Avocats (del. 1991-93), Assn. Yale Alumni (bd. govs. 1985-94, chair 1990-92, chair Yale Alumni Mag. 1995—), Yale Club Washington (pres. 1981-82), City Club Washington, Edgemoor Club, Yale Club N.Y.C. Avocations: tennis, travel. Antitrust, Private international. Home: 2912 Albemarle St NW Washington DC 20008-2134 Office: Covington & Burling 1201 Pennsylvania Ave NW PO Box 7566 Washington DC 20044-7566

**APPLEGATE, KARL EDWIN,** lawyer; b. Cicero, Ind., July 21, 1923; s. Karl Raymond and Gladys Mae (Worley) A.; m. Elizabeth Ann Dilts, June 10, 1944; children—Eric Edwin, Raymond Alan, Robert Dale, Beth Ann. B.S., Ind. U., 1946, J.D., 1948. Bar: Ind. 1949, Fed. Ct. (7th cir.); U.S. Supreme Ct., 1968, U.S. Tax Ct., 1983. U.S. commr. So. Dist. Ind., 1953-58, cert. family and civil mediator, Ind. Fla., 1992; dep. prosecutor Monroe County, Ind., 1959; mcpl. judge, Bloomington, Ind., 1960-63; mem. Ind. Ho. of Reps., 1965-66; U.S. atty. So. Dist. Ind., 1967-70; sr. ptnr. Applegate Law Offices, Bloomington, 1970-93, sr. mem., 1991-93; sr. mem. Applegate, McDonald, Koch & Arnold, Bloomington, 1993—, now Applegate McDonald & Koch PC. legal cons. Ind. Masonic Home, Franklin, 1981-82. Trustee 1st United Methodist Ch., 1962-65. Served to staff sgt. AUS, 1941-44, ETO. Decorated Purple Heart. Named Outstanding Young Man of Bloomington, Jaycees, 1956, recipient Disting. Service award U.S. Jr. C. of C., 1956, Good Govt. award, 1961. Mem. Fed. Bar Assn., Ind. Bar Assn. (co-chair com. assistance to lawyers program 1990-94), Monroe County Bar Assn., ABA, Tri-County Bar Assn., Alpha Kappa Psi. Democrat. Clubs: Kiwanis, Elks, Masons. Federal civil litigation, General practice, Personal injury. Home: 509 S Swain Ave Bloomington IN 47401-5129 Office: Applegate McDonald & Koch PO Box 1030 Bloomington IN 47402-1030

**APPLEGATE, WILLIAM RUSSELL,** lawyer; b. Columbia, S.C., Oct. 18, 1946; s. William John and Vera (Lister) A.; m. Jerva Ann Watson, Dec. 20, 1969; children—Jennifer Corey, Amanda Ann. A.B., Wofford Coll., 1968; J.D., U.S.C., 1974, M.A. in Criminal Justice, 1978. Bar: S.C. 1974, U.S. Dist. Ct. S.C. 1974, U.S. Supreme Ct. 1979. Assoc. E. Pickens Rish, Esquire, Lexington, S.C., 1974-75; sole practice, West Columbia, S.C., 1975—; judge Town of Springdale, West Columbia, 1980-90; atty. Town of Gaston, S.C., 1976-90. Vice chmn. Episcopal Ch. Upper Diocese of S.C., Columbia, 1981-97; sr. warden St. Mary's Ch., Columbia, 1979-81. Served to capt. U.S. Army, 1969-71. Mem. S.C. Bar Assn., ABA, Nat. Orgn. Social Security Claimant's Reps. Republican. Episcopalian. Consumer commercial, Family and matrimonial, Personal injury. Home: 123 Woodwinds West Dr Columbia SC 29212-3629 Office: William R Applegate Esquire 1700 Sunset Blvd West Columbia SC 29169-5940

**APPLETON, ALAN B.,** lawyer; b. Frankfort, Ind., Nov. 18, 1945; s. Allen A. and Wilda L. Appleton. BA, Franklin Coll., 1967; JD, U. Louisville, 1970. Bar: D.C. 1975, U.S. Supreme Ct. 1978. Law clk., intern Appleton Law Office, Frankfort, 1970-74, assoc., 1975-89; gen. counsel Appleton Group, Inc., Frankfort, 1975—. Judge Frankfort City Ct., 1972-73. Named Hon. House Parent, The Omaha Home for Boys, 1967, Clinton County Boys Club Bd. Mem. of Yr., Frankfort, 1978. Mem. D.C. Bar Assn., Sigma Alpha Epsilon, Phi Alpha Delta. General corporate. Office: Appleton Group Inc PO Box 541 Frankfort IN 46041-0541

**APPLETON, RICHARD NEWELL,** lawyer; b. Bronx, N.Y., Sept. 1, 1941; s. Harry Newell Appleton and Catherine (Burke) Haddon; m. Kathleen Pauline Sheehan Morrell, Oct. 5, 1963 (div. Apr. 1974); children: Heather, Cheryl; m. Alene Marie Appleton, Aug. 31, 1990; children: Brennan, Adriana. BA, Rutgers Coll., 1964; JD, Western State U., 1983. Bar: Calif. 1984, U.S. Dist. Ct. So. Calif. 1984. Time study engr. E.R. Squibb & Sons, New Brunswick, N.J., 1963-65; plant indsl. engr. Anaconda Wire and Cable, Anderson, Ind., 1965-69; budget analyst Marcona Mining Co., San Juan, Peru, S.A., 1969-73, dir. adminstrv. svcs., 1973-76; internal cons. Iron Ore Can., Sept Iles, Que., 1976-78; mgr. adminstrn. Mullen Engring., Casper, Wyo., 1978-79; consulting engr. Woodward Assocs., San Diego, 1979-81; law clerk Stutz, McCormick, Mitchell & Verlasky, San Diego, 1981-84; assoc. McCormick & Mitchell, San Diego, 1984-91, ptnr., 1991-93, mng. ptnr., 1993—; arbitrator and mediator San Diego County Mcpl. and Superior Ct., 1989—; judge pro tem Small Claims Ct., 1995—. Contbr. articles to profl. jours. and book revs. Precinct committeeman Rep. Party, Anderson, 1966-68. Recipient Cert. Merit award NASA, 1962, Amjur in Evidence award The Lawyers Co-Op Bancroft Whitney, 1983, Most Valuable Reporter award Stats, Inc., 1994. Mem. Calif. Dispute Resolution Coun., Assn. So. Calif. Def. Counsel, San Diego Def. Counsel, Soc. Profls. in Dispute Resolution. Roman Catholic. Avocations: golf, baseball, statistical analysis, fiction and non-fiction writing. State civil litigation, Construction, Personal injury. Office: McCormick & Mitchell 625 Broadway Ste 1400 San Diego CA 92101-5420 Address: 1261 Crystal Springs Dr Chula Vista CA 91915-2154

**APPLEY, ELIZABETH JOAN,** lawyer; b. Queens, N.Y., Apr. 22, 1954; d. George S. Appley and Marlene (Bondy) A.; m. N. Sandy Epstein, June 17, 1984; children: Joseph A. Appley-Epstein, Benjamin M. Appley-Epstein. BA, Hampshire Coll., 1975; JD, Columbia U., 1978. Bar: Ga. 1978, U.S. Dist. Ct. (no. dist.) Ga. 1978, U.S. Ct. Appeals (5th cir. ) 1978, U.S. Ct. Appeals (11th cir.) 1980, U.S. Supreme Ct. 1993. Assoc. Margie Pitts Hames, P.C., Atlanta, 1978-82; pvt. practice Atlanta, 1982—; mem. Ga. Commn. on Gender Bias in Jud. Sys., Atlanta, 1989-91; arbitrator Fulton County Civil Arbitration Program, Atlanta, 1986—; cons. Women's Policy Group, 1996—, Ga. Campaign for Adolescent Pregnancy Prevention, Atlanta, 1996—, Partnership Against Domestic Violence, 1995—. Contbr. articles to legal jours. Bd. dirs. Mental Health Assn. of Metro Atlanta, 1984-88, Ctr. for Black Women's Wellness, 1997—; founding mem., bd. dirs. Vote Choice, A Ga. PAC, Atlanta, 1990—. Recipient Stand Up for Choice award Feminist Women's Health Ctr., 1991. Mem. Nat. Conf. Women's Bar Assns. (bd. dirs. 1990-92), Ga. Assn. for Women Lawyers (pres. 1987-89, chair jud. selection com. 1990-95, Kathleen Kessler award 1995), State Bar Ga. (mem. jud. selection com. 1997—). Federal civil litigation, Alternative dispute resolution, Legislative. Office: 50 Hurt Plz SE Ste 730 Atlanta GA 30303-2915

**APRUZZESE, VINCENT JOHN,** lawyer; b. Newark, Nov. 1, 1928; s. John and Mildred (Cerefice) A.; m. Marie A. Yeager, July 10, 1955; children: Barbara, John, Donald, Lynn, Kathy. BA, Rutgers U., 1950; LLB, U. Pa., 1953. Bar: N.J. 1954, U.S. Dist. Ct. N.J. 1954, U.S. Ct. Appeals (3d cir.) 1962, U.S. Supreme Ct. 1970, U.S. Ct. Appeals (D.C. cir. 1973), U.S. Ct. Appeals (4th cir.) 1973, D.C. 1976, N.Y. 1983. Assoc. Lum, Fairlie & Foster, Newark, 1953-54; sole practice Newark, 1954-55, 58-65; sr. ptnr. Apruzzese & McDermott, Newark, 1965-70; pres. Apruzzese & McDermott, Springfield, N.J., 1970-90, Liberty Corner and Newark; mem. legal adv. bd. Martindale-Hubbell, 1991-98. Bd. dirs. St. Barnabas Hosp., Papermill Playhouse. With JAGC, USAF, 1956-57. Mem. ABA (mem. coun. labor and employment law sect. 1984-94, chair labor & employment law sect. 1992-93, bd. govs. 1988-91), Coll. of Labor and Employment Lawyers, Fed. Bar Assn., Internat. Labor Law Soc. (treas.), Am. Coll. Trial Lawyers, Am. Bar Found., Fed. Bar State N.J., N.J. State Bar Assn. (pres. 1982-84), Essex County Bar Assn., Somerset County Bar Assn., Baltusrol Country Club (Springfield), Chatham (Mass.) Beach and Tennis Club, Eastward Ho Country Club (Chatham). Labor, General practice. Office: Apruzzese McDermott Mastro & Murphy PO Box 112 25 Independence Blvd Liberty Corner NJ 07938

**AQUILA, ALBERT,** lawyer; b. Mineola, N.Y., Sept. 13, 1968. BBA, Hofstra U., 1990; JD, St. Johns U., 1993. Atty. Sullivan & Liapakis, N.Y.C., 1993—. Personal injury, General civil litigation, Product liability. Office: Sullivan & Lapakis 120 Broadway New York NY 10271-0002

**AQUILINO, THOMAS JOSEPH, JR.,** federal judge, law educator; b. Mt. Kisco, N.Y., Dec. 7, 1939; s. Thomas Joseph and Virginia Burr (Doughty) A.; m. Edith Luise Berndt, Oct. 27, 1965; children: Christopher T., Philip A., Alexander B. Student, Cornell U., 1957-59, U. Munich, 1960-61; BA, Drew U., 1962; postgrad., Free U., Berlin, 1965-66; JD, Rutgers U., 1969. Bar: N.Y. 1972, U.S. Dist. Ct. (so., ea. and no. dists.) N.Y. 1973, U.S. Ct. Appeals (2nd cir.) 1973, U.S. Supreme Ct. 1976, U.S. Ct. Appeals (3rd cir.) 1977, Interstate Commerce Commn. 1978, U.S. Ct. Claims 1979, U.S. Ct. Internat. Trade 1984. Law clk. to judge U.S. Dist. Ct. (so. dist.) N.Y., N.Y.C., 1969-71; atty. Davis Polk & Wardwell, N.Y.C., 1971-85; judge U.S. Ct. Internat. Trade, N.Y.C., 1985—; adj. prof. law Benjamin N. Cardozo Sch. of Law, 1984-95; mem. bd. visitors Drew U., 1997—. With U.S. Army, 1962-65. Mem. N.Y. State Bar Assn., Fed. Bar Coun. Roman Catholic. Avocations: sports, travel, linguistics, cinema. Office: US Ct Internat Trade 1 Federal Plz New York NY 10278-0001

**ARABIA, PAUL,** lawyer; b. Pittsburg, Kans., Mar. 28, 1938; s. John K. and Melva (Jones) A. B.A., Kans. State Coll.; J.D., Washburn U. Bar: Kans. 1966, U.S. Dist. Ct. Kans. 1966, U.S. Ct. Appeals (10th cir.) 1968. Ptnr., Fettis & Arabia, Wichita, 1968-74, Arabia & Wells, Wichita, 1974-78; pvt. practice, Wichita, 1978—. Program host Sta. KAKE-TV: Peoples Lawyer; TV host/producer: Legal Point. Mem. Kans. Bar Assn., Wichita Bar Assn. General civil litigation, Civil rights, General corporate. Office: PO Box 275 Wichita KS 67201-0275

**ARABIAN, ARMAND,** arbitrator, mediator, lawyer; b. N.Y.C., Dec. 12, 1934; s. John and Aghavnie (Yalian) A.; m. Nancy Arabian, Aug. 26, 1962; children: Allison Ann, Robert Armand. BSBA, Boston U., 1956, JD, 1961; LLM, U. So. Calif., L.A., 1970; LLD (hon.), Southwestern Sch. Law, 1990, Pepperdine U., 1990, U. West L.A., 1994, We. State U., 1997, Thomas Jefferson Sch. of Law, 1997. Bar: Calif. 1962, U.S. Supreme Ct. 1966. Dep. dist. atty. L.A. County, 1962-63; pvt. practice law Van Nuys, Calif., 1963-72; judge Mcpl. Ct., L.A., 1972-73, Superior Ct., L.A., 1973-83; assoc. justice U.S. Ct. Appeal, L.A., 1983-90, U.S. Supreme Ct. Calif., San Francisco, 1990-96; ret., 1996; adj. prof. sch. law Pepperdine U., 1996—. 1st lt. U.S. Army, 1956-58. Recipient Stanley Litz Meml. award San Fernando Valley Bar Assn., 1986, Lifetime Achievement award San Fernando Valley Bar Assn., 1993; Pappas Disting. scholar Boston U. Sch. Law, 1987; Justice Armand Arabian Resource and Comm. Ctrs. named in honor of Van Nuys and San Fernando Calif. Courthouses, 1999. Republican. Fax no.: (818) 781-6002; e-mail: honarabian@AOL.com. Office: 6259 Van Nuys Blvd Van Nuys CA 91401-2711

**ARAGON, RAYMOND GEORGE,** lawyer; b. L.A., Mar. 19, 1953; s. Juan Bautista and Connie (Martinez) A.; m. Virginia Sive, July 29, 1978; children: Andrea, David. BA in Polit. Sci., San Diego State U., 1975; JD, U. Calif., Davis, 1980. Bar: Calif. 1980, U.S. Dist. Ct. (so. dist.) Calif. 1980; cert. specialist in criminal law, Calif.; cert. real estate broker, Calif. Sr. trial atty. South Bay br. Sr. Citizens Legal Svcs., San Diego, 1980-88; supervising atty. San Diego County Dept. Pub. Defender, San Diego, 1988—; mem. faculty Nat. Inst. for Trial Advocacy, San Diego, 1997—. Bd. dirs. San Diego Chicano Fedn., 1984-86. Mem. San Diego County Bar Assn. (bd. dirs. 1997—), Consumer Attys. of San Diego (bd. dirs. 1998—), San Diego La Raza Lawyers Assn. (pres. 1995-96), San Diego County Bar Found. (bd. dirs. 1998—), Nat. Hispanic Media Coalition (chair San Diego chpt. 1997—), Am. Inn of Ct. Office: Dept Pub Defender County of San Diego 233 A St Ste 400 San Diego CA 92101-4097

**ARAMBURU, JOHN RICHARD,** lawyer; b. Spokane, Wash., Mar. 8, 1945; s. Victor B. Aramburu and Virginia (Westacott) Scarpelli; m. Lesa Rae French, Aug. 23, 1991. BA, U. Wash., 1967, JD, 1970. Bar: Wash. 1970, U.S. Dist. Ct. (we. dist.) Wash. 1970, U.S. Ct. Appeals (9th cir.) 1970, U.S. Dist. Ct. (ea. dist.) Wash. 1973. Assoc. Irving M. Clark, Jr., Seattle, 1970-78; prin. Law Offices of J. Richard Aramburu, Seattle, 1978—. Author: Real Property Deskbook, 1985, rev. edit., 1996. Bd. dirs. Allied Arts of Seattle, 1987-89; legal chair Wash. Environ. Coun., Seattle, 1982-88. Mem. Wash. State Bar (chairperson CLE com. 1977, chairperson environ. and land use law sect. 1978),. Avocations: squash, skiing, river rafting. Land use and zoning (including planning), Environmental. Office: Law Offices of J Richard Aramburu 505 Madison St Ste 209 Seattle WA 98104-1138

**ARANGO, EMILIO,** lawyer; b. Havana, Cuba, Mar. 4, 1927; came to U.S., 1960; s. Enrique Jose and Nyla Eulalia (Nuñez-Mesa) A.; m. Sylvia Fromm, Dec. 8, 1956 (div. June 1984); children: Sylvia Maria, Vivianne Victoria, Carolina Natalia. LLD, U. Havana, 1950. Assoc. Nuñez-Mesa & Machado, Havana, 1950-56; house counsel Standard Oil Ind., Havana, 1956-59, Standard Oil Calif., Havana, 1959-61; assoc. Reid & Priest, N.Y.C., 1961-69; gen. atty. Schlumberger, Caracas, Venezuela, 1969-78; asst. gen. counsel United Fruit Co., N.Y.C., 1978—; counsel Douglas M. Case, Atty. at Law, Cin.; cons. Chiquita Brands Internat. Coordinator ABA com. to help Cuban Lawyers, N.Y., 1962-64. Mem. Council of Ams. Republican. Roman Catholic. Contracts commercial, General corporate, Public international. Home: 415 Bond Pl Cincinnati OH 45206-1872 Office: Douglas M. Case Atty at Law 8700 Old Indian Hill Rd Cincinnati OH 45243-3724

**ARANT, EUGENE WESLEY,** lawyer; b. North Powder, Oreg., Dec. 21, 1920; s. Ernest Elbert and Wanda (Haller) A.; m. Juanita Clark Flowers, Mar. 15, 1953; children: Thomas W., Kenneth E., Richard W. B.S. in Elec. Engring, Oreg. State U., 1943; J.D., U. So. Calif., 1949. Bar: Calif. 1950. Mem. engring. faculty U. So. Calif., 1947-51; practiced in Los Angeles, 1950-51; patent atty. Hughes Aircraft Co., Culver City, Calif., 1953-56; pvt. practice, L.A., 1957-97, Ventura, Calif., 1997—. Author articles. Mem. La Mirada (Calif.) City Council, 1958-60; trustee Beverly Hills Presbyn. Ch., 1976-78. Served with AUS, 1943-46, 51-53. Mem. ABA, Am. Intellectual Property Law Assn., State Bar Calif., Ala. State Bar, Santa Barbara Rotary, Univ. Club Santa Barbara. Democrat. Patent, Trademark and copyright. Home: 15711 W Telegraph Rd Spc G89 Santa Paula CA 93060-4095 Office: 674 County Square Dr Ste 205 Ventura CA 93003-9023

**ARBER, HOWARD BRUCE,** lawyer; b. N.Y.C., Sept. 7, 1949; s. Jack Charles and Rita (Cohen) A.; m. Linda Ellen Trapani, Oct. 2, 1983; one child: Jillian. B.S., NYU, 1972; J.D., Hofstra U., 1975. Bar: N.Y. 1976, U.S. Dist. Ct. (so. and ea. dists.) 1983. Engaged in real estate mgmt. Rose Assocs., N.Y.C., 1976-78; assoc. Entin & Rosenthal, N.Y.C., 1978-79, Jacobson & Goldberg, N.Y.C., 1979-81; sole practice, West Hempstead, N.Y., 1981-86, ptnr. Gerson & Arber, 1986-88; sole prac., Hempstead, NY, 1988—; gen. counsel Eastern Motor Racing Assn., N.Y.C., 1981—, L.I. Sports Car Assn., N.Y.C., 1981—; arbitrator Nassau County Dist. Cts., 1982—. Mem. Nassau County Bar Assn. (assigned counsel plan com.), Am. Arbitration Assn. (arbitrator 1986—). State civil litigation, Family and matrimonial, Real property.

**ARBES, JAKE,** lawyer; b. Indpls., July 9, 1951; s. Max and Genia Jed A.; m. Tina R. Perchik, May 24, 1980; children: Max Daniel, Ross Eli. AB, Harvard U., 1973; JD, NYU, 1978; MPA, Princeton U., 1978. Bar: Ga. 1978, U.S. Dist. Ct. (no. dist. ) Ga. 1978, U.S. Ct. Appeals (5th cir.) 1978, U.S. Ct. Appeals (11th cir.) 1981, U.S. Ct. Appeals (4th cir.) 1983, U.S. Supreme Ct. 1992, U.S. Ct. Appeals (6th cir.) 1989, U.S. Ct. Appeals (10th cir.) 1992. Law clk. U.S. Ct. Appeal s(11th cir.), Atlanta, 1979-80; asst. U.S. atty. U.S. Dist. Ct. (no. dist.) Ga., 1980-82; ptnr. Abbott & Arbes, 1982-85; atty. pvt. practice, 1985—. Author: Criminal Appeals in Georgia, 1998. Past pres. Congregation Shaerith Israel, Atlanta. NAt. Inst. Trial Advocacy (instr. 1983—), Lawyers Club Am., Nat. Assn. Criminal Def. Lawyers, State Bar Ga., Ga. Assn. Criminal Def. Lawyers, Atlanta Bar Assn. Jewish. Avocations: collecting compact discs and old concert posters. Criminal. Home: 1597 E Sussex Rd NE Atlanta GA 30306-3038 Office: 233 Peachtree St NE Ste 2300 Atlanta GA 30303-1509

**ARBETMAN, JEFFREY FARRELL,** lawyer; b. Chgo., Jan. 23, 1941; s. Charles and Evelyn Mae (Honigberg) A.; m. Sara M. Amarilla, Apr., 1997. BA, U. Wis., 1963; JD, Loyola U., 1967. Bar: Ill. 1967, Calif. 1973, Ariz. 1978, U.S. Dist. Ct. (ea. dist.) Ill. 1968, U.S. Ct. Appeals (7th cir.) 1968, U.S. Ct. Appeals (9th cir.) 1972, U.S. Dist. Ct. (so. dist.) Calif. 1972, U.S. Dist. Ct. Ariz. 1982. Asst. house counsel Aldens Inc., Chgo., 1967-68; asst. U.S. atty. ea. dist. U.S. Dept. Justice, East St. Louis, Ill., 1968-72; asst. U.S. atty. so. dist. U.S. Dept. Justice, San Diego, 1972-78; asst. atty. gen. State of Ariz. Atty. Gen., Phoenix, 1978-86; atty. pvt. practice, Phoenix, 1986—. Co-author: Arizona Appellate Handbook, 1970-98. Mem. State Bar Ariz., State Bar Calif., Maricopa County Bar Assn. Independent. Avocations: classic and antique cars, collecting antiques. Administrative and regulatory, Consumer commercial, Labor. Home: 107 E Myrtle Ave Phoenix AZ 85020-4837 Office: 2702 N 3rd St Ste 3020 Phoenix AZ 85004-4607

**ARBIT, BERYL ELLEN,** legal assistant; b. L.A., Aug. 16, 1949; d. Harry A. and Norma K. (Michelson) A. BA, UCLA, 1970. From legal asst. to sr. legal asst. O'Melveny & Myers, L.A., 1977—; guest lectr. atty. asst. tng. program UCLA, 1991. Mem. UCLA Atty. Asst. Alumni Assn. (bd. dirs. 1980-82), Alpha Omicron Pi (treas. West L.A. alumnae chpt. 1993—), Nu Lambda (corp. bd. pres. 1978-80, chpt. adv. 1976-78). Avocations: travel, theater, needlework, bridge. Office: O'Melveny & Myers 400 S Hope St Los Angeles CA 90071-2899

**ARBIT, TERRY STEVEN,** lawyer; b. Chgo., May 11, 1958; s. Jack and Sandra (Dwork) A.; m. Rhona Sue Schwartz, July 21, 1985; children: Julie Lyn, Michael Colin. BA, U. Pa., 1980, MA, 1980; JD, U. Chgo., 1983. Bar: Ill. 1983, Mich. 1984, U.S. Dist. Ct. (no. dist.) Ill. 1985, U.S. Ct. Appeals (7th and 9th cirs.) 1988. Law clk. to justice Mich. Supreme Ct., Southfield, 1983-84; assoc. Karon, Savikas & Horn, Ltd., Chgo., 1984-88, Goldberg, Kohn, Bell, Black, Rosenbloom & Moritz Ltd., Chgo., 1989-90; counsel profl. liability sect. FDIC, Washington, 1991-95; trial atty. divsn. of enforcement Commodity Futures Trading Commn., Washington, 1996—. Mem. ABA, Phi Beta Kappa, Pi Gamma Mu, Pi Sigma Alpha. Avocations: polit. studies, swimming, cycling. Home: 8 Botany Ct North Potomac MD 20878-4208 Office: Commodity Futures Trading Commn 1155 21st St NW Washington DC 20036-3308

**ARBOLEYA, CARLOS JOAQUIN,** lawyer, broker; b. Havana, Cuba, Aug. 16, 1958; came to U.S., 1960; s. Carlos Jose and Marta Aurora (Quintana) A. ABA, Miami Dade C.C., 1977; BBA in Fin., U. Miami, 1980, MBA in Fin., 1981, JD, 1987. Bar: Fla. 1989, U.S. Ct. Appeals (D.C. cir.) 1990. From teller to br. mgr. Barnett Bank South Fla. N.A., North Miami Beach, 1975-84; realtor, assoc. Cervera Real Estate, 1980—; pres. Owner's Box Promotions, 1993-95; owner Carlos J. Arboleya, Jr., P.A., Coconut Grove, 1988—; adv. bd. Exec. Nat. Bank, 1994—, Linda Ray Infant Ctr., 1990—; bd. dirs. Pvt. Industry Coun. Jobs for Miami; Hispanic adv. com. U. Miami Sports Mktg., 1992-95. Bd. dirs. Greater Miami Tennis Found., 1995, U. Miami Ear Inst., 1993; vice chma. planning adv. bd. City of Miami, 1993-95, 98-99, chmn. 1995-98, chmn. code enforcement bd., 1990-91, vice chmn. 1989-90; asst. scoutmaster Boy Scouts Am.; participant joint civilian orientation conf. U.S. Dept. Def., 1995. Mem. ABA, Nat. Soc. Hispanic MBAs, Nat. Eagle Scout Assn., Cuban Am. Bar Assn., Builders Assn. South Fla., Am. Title Ins. Co., Attys. Title Ins. Fund, Inc., Fla. Bar Assn., Latin Bus. Assn., Latin Builders Assn., Hispanic Law Students Assn., Coral Gables C. of C., Greater Miami C. of C. (sports coun., chmn., homestead motorsports complex com., 1994-97, co-chmn. existing events com., 1992-94), Leadership Miami (exec. com. 1990-93, task force 1984-88, Coconut Grove Jaycees, Phi Delta Phi, Delta Sigma Pi (Outstanding Alumni award 1982). Republican. Roman Catholic. Real property, Banking, General corporate. Office: Carlos J Arboleya Jr PA 2550 S Dixie Hwy Coconut Grove FL 33133-3137

**ARBUCKLE, JESS W.,** lawyer; b. Hutchinson, Kans., Feb. 8, 1960; s. Robert W. and Alice Darlyn Arbuckle; m. Kimberlee J. Bannon, Sept. 2, 1989; children: Charlie, Jeni, Sam. BS in Bus. Adminstrn., U. Kans., 1982; JD, U. Tulsa, 1985. Bar: Okla. 1985, Kans. 1990, U.S. Dist. Ct. (no. and ea. dists.) Okla., U.S. Dist. Ct. Kans., U.S. Ct. Appeals (10th cir.), U.S. Supreme Ct. 1991. Assoc. Law Offices of David L. Sobel, Tulsa, Okla., 1985-88, 89-90, Norman & Wohlgemuth, Tulsa, 1988-89; ptnr. Martindell, Swearer & Shaffer, LLP, Hutchinson, Kans., 1990-98; corp. counsel Alliance Ins. Cos., McPherson, Kans., 1998—. Pres. bd. dirs. Boys and Girls Club Hutchinson, 1997, 98; bd. mem. McPherson County United Way, 1998—. Recipient Leadership Hutchinson award Hutchinson C. of C., 1992. Mem. Kans. Assn. Def. Counsel. Republican. Fax: 316-241-5482. E-mail: jess-arbuckle@fami.com. Office: Alliance Ins Cos PO Box 1401 Mcpherson KS 67460-1401

**ARBUTHNOT, ROBERT MURRAY,** lawyer; b. Montreal, Quebec, Can., Oct. 23, 1936; s. Leland Claude and Winnifred Laura (Hodges) A.; m. Janet Marie O'Keefe, Oct. 6, 1968; children: Douglas, Michael, Mary Kathleen, Allison Anne. BA, Calif. State U., San Francisco, 1959; JD, U. Calif., San Francisco, 1966. Bar: Calif. 1967, U.S. Dist. Ct. (no. and cen. dists.) Calif. 1967, U.S. Ct. Appeals (9th cir.) 1967, U.S. Supreme Ct. 1975. Assoc. trial lawyer Rankin & Craddick, Oakland, Calif., 1967-69; assoc. atty. Ericksen, Arbuthnot, Brown, Kilduff & Day, Inc., San Francisco, 1970-73, ptnr., 1973-80, chmn. bd., mng. dir., 1980—; gen. counsel CFS Ins. Svcs., San Francisco, 1990—; pro tem judge, arbitrator San Francisco Superior Ct., 1990—; lectr. in field. Bd. regents St. Mary's Coll. High Sch., Berkeley, Calif., 1988-91. With U.S. Army, 1959-62. Recipient Honors plaque St. Mary's Coll. High Sch., 1989. Mem. Internat. Assn. of Ins. Counsel, No. Calif. Assn. of Def. Counsel, Def. Rsch. Inst., Assn. Trial Lawyers Am., San Francisco Lawyers Club. Avocations: boating, family activities. General civil litigation, Personal injury, Product liability. Office: Ericksen Arbuthnot Brown Kilduff & Day Inc 260 California St Ste 1100 San Francisco CA 94111-4300

**ARBUZ, JOSEPH ROBERT,** lawyer; b. N.Y.C., Nov. 23, 1949; s. Jose Hernan Cortes and Rachel Dweck Arbuz; m. Millicent Luck Fornah July, 1978 (div.); 1 child, Christina. BA, Fla. State U., 1972, MS in Pub. Adminstrn., 1975; JD, Howard U., 1977; MDiv, Southwestern Bapt. Sem., 1981; postgrad. in theology, Westminster Theol. Sem., 1995. Bar: Fla. 1978, U.S. Ct. Mil. Appeals 1983, U.S. Dist. Ct. (so. dist.) Fla. 1986; lic. min. So. Bapt. Ch., 1983—. EEO investigator Smithsonian Instn., Washington, 1985; asst. atty. gen. Atty. Gen., Miami, Fla., 1986; pvt. practice Miami, Fla., 1987-90, Miami Beach, Fla., 1994—. Evangelism Gambrell St. Bapt. Ch., Ft. Worth, 1980; campaign vol. Dem. Party, Miami Beach, 1987; pastor Biscayne Bapt. Ch., Miami, 1989; choir mem. U. Bapt. Ch., Coral Gables, Fla., 1994-97; performer Miami Christmas Pageant, Miami, 1994, 96. 1st lt. Signal Corps., U.S. Army, 1972-74; capt. USAF, 1982-84. J.F.K. Tchg. scholar Miami-Dade C.C., Miami, 1969. Mem. Delta Theta Phi. Democrat. Presbyterian. Avocations: exercise, theatre, reading, church activities. E-mail: Jarbuz@cs.com. Fax: 305-535-0964. Personal injury, General practice, Insurance. Office: 1400 Lincoln Rd Apt 304 Miami Beach FL 33139-2189

**ARCARA, RICHARD JOSEPH,** federal judge; b. Buffalo, June 6, 1940; s. Philip and Angela (Arcara); m. Gwendolyn White, July 1, 1976. B.A. in History, St. Bonaventure U., 1962; J.D., Villanova U., 1965. Bar: N.Y. bar 1966. Law clk. Legal Aid Bur., Buffalo, 1965; asso. firm Lipsitz, Green, Fahringer, Roll, Schuller & James, Buffalo, 1968-69; asst. U.S. atty. Western Dist. N.Y., 1969-73, 1st asst. U.S. atty., 1973-74, U.S. atty., after 1975; Erie County dist. atty., 1982-88; judge U.S. Dist. Ct. N.Y., Buffalo, 1988—. Capt. M.P., U.S. Army, 1966-68. Mem. Erie County Bar Assn., N.Y. State Bar Assn., Am. Bar Assn. Republican. Roman Catholic. Club: Buffalo Yacht. Office: US Dist Ct 609 US Courthouse 68 Court St Buffalo NY 14202-3405

**ARCENEAUX, ADAM,** lawyer; b. Cambridge, Md., Jan. 12, 1966; s. André and Mary Slocum A.; m. Margaret Rose Brockman, Aug. 11, 1990; children: Austin Emerson, Audrey Rose. BS in Mktg. and Bus. Analysis, Ind. U., 1988, JD summa cum laude, 1993. Bar: Ind. 1993, U.S. Dist. Ct. (no. and so. dists.) 1993. Atty. Ice, Miller, Donadio & Ryan, Indpls., 1993—. Mem. Ind. Bar Assn., Indpls. Bar Assn., Def. Rsch. Inst., Ind. U. Sch. Law Indpls. Alumni Assn. (bd. dirs. 1996—, mem. capital campaign steering com. 1998—), Columbia Club. Republican. Roman Catholic. General civil litigation, Appellate, Product liability. Office: Ice Miller Donadio & Ryan One American Sq 1 American Sq # Indianapolis IN 46282-0001

**ARCHER, GLENN LEROY, JR.,** federal judge; b. Densmore, Kans., Mar. 21, 1929; s. Glenn LeRoy and Ruth Agnes (Ford) A.; m. Carole J. Thomas, 1990; children: Susan, Sharon, Glenn, Thomas. B.A., Yale U., 1951; J.D. with honors, George Washington U., 1954. Bar: D.C. 1954. Asst. atty. gen. U.S. Dept. Justice, Washington, 1981-85; circuit judge U.S. Ct. Appeals (fed. cir.), Washington, 1985-94, chief judge, 1994-97, sr. cir. judge, 1997—. Republican. Methodist. Office: US Ct of Appeals Fed Circuit 717 Madison Pl NW Washington DC 20439-0002

**ARCHIBOLD, JOHN EWING,** lawyer; b. Denver, Mar. 15, 1933; s. Robert French and Eleanor Eileen (Ewing) A.; m. Mary Ellen Ogelsby, Sept. 12, 1964; children: John Christopher, Stephen Ewing, Mary Elizabeth Eileen, Sarah Ellen Dean. AB, Princeton U., 1955; LLB, U. Denver, 1959; LLM, Georgetown U., 1965. Bar: Colo. 1960, D.C. 1964, U.S. Supreme Ct. 1965. Spl. liaison asst. U.S. Dept. State, Washington, 1960; trial atty. U.S. Dept. Justice, Washington, 1960-66; assoc. Grant, Shafroth, Toll & McHendrie, Denver, 1966-68; ptnr. Casey, Klene, Horan & Archibold, Denver, 1968-69; asst. atty. gen. Colo. Dept. Law, Denver, 1970-72; assoc. counsel Colo. Pub. Utilities Commn., Denver, 1972-74, chief counsel, 1974-90; of counsel Kelly, Stanfield & O'Donnell, Denver, 1991-1993; v.p. Info-Media, Inc., Denver, 1990—. Contbr. articles to legal publs. Precinct committeeman Denver Rep. Party, 1958-59; chmn. Citizenship Day Com., Denver, 1967; dir. Rude Park Nursery, 1957-59; chancellor Anglican Cath. Ch. 1979-80, Diocese of Holy Trinity, 1977-90. Col. U.S. Army, 1955-86. Mem. Denver Bar Assn., Colo. Bar Assn. Avocations: reading, travel. Home: 1624 S Steele St Denver CO 80210-2940

**ARCONTI, RICHARD DAVID,** lawyer; b. Danbury, Conn., Nov. 16, 1952; s. Gino Joseph and Patricia Helen (Olmstead) A.; m. Deborah Ann Wolter, Sept. 10, 1983; children: Meghan Phelan, Richard Joseph. BA, U. Notre Dame, 1974; JD, U. Conn., 1977. Bar: Conn. 1977, U.S. Dist. Ct. Conn. 1977. Assoc. Nahley and Sullivan, Danbury, Conn., 1977-78; asst. states atty. State's Attys. Office Jud. Dist. Danbury, 1978-84; ptnr. Secor, Cassady & McPartland, P.C., Danbury, 1984; adj. prof. Western Conn. State U., Danbury, 1989—; ptnr. Pinney, Payne, Van Lenten, Burrell, Wolfe & Dillman PC, Danbury. Dir. West Conn. State U. Found.; dir. ARC, 1990—. Mem. ATLA, Conn. Bar Assn., Conn. Trial Lawyers Assn., Danbury Bar Assn. (pres.), Nat. Bd. Trial Adv. (diplomate). Democrat. Roman Catholic. Avocations: baseball, golf, saxophone. Criminal, Personal injury. Home: 15 Raquel Dr Danbury CT 06811-3205 Office: Pinney Payne Van Lenten Burrell Wolfe & Dillman PC 83 Wooster Heights Rd Danbury CT 06810-7548

**AREEN, JUDITH CAROL,** law educator, university dean; b. Chgo., Aug. 2, 1944; d. Gordon Eric and Pauline Jeanette (Payberg) A.; m. Richard M. Cooper, Feb. 17, 1979; children: Benjamin Eric (dec.), Jonathan Gordon. AB, Cornell U., 1966; JD, Yale U., 1969. Bar: Mass. 1970, D.C. 1972. Program planner for higher edn. Mayor's Office City of N.Y., 1969-70; dir. edn. voucher study Ctr. for Study Pub. Policy, Cambridge, Mass., 1970-72; mem. faculty Georgetown U., Washington, 1971—, assoc. prof. law, 1972-76, prof., 1976—, prof. cmty. and family medicine, 1980-89, assoc. dean Law Ctr., 1984-87; dean, exec. v.p. for law affairs Georgetown U, Washington, 1989—; gen. counsel, coord. domestic reorgn. pres.' reorgn. project Office of Mgmt. and Budget, Washington, 1977-80; spl. counsel White House Task Force on Regulatory Reform, Washington, 1978-80; cons. NIH, 1984; cons. NRC, 1985, mem. com. film badge dosimetry; bd. dirs. MCI World Comm., Safeguard Sci. Author: Youth Service Agencies, 1977, Cases and Materials on Family Law, 4th edit., 1999, Law, Science and Medicine, 1984, 2d edit., 1996. Mem. Def. Adv. Com. Women In Svcs., Washington, 1979-82; trustee Cornell Univ. Woodrow Wilson Internat. Ctr. for Scholars fellow, 1988-89, Kennedy Inst. Ethics Sr. Rsch. fellow, Washington, 1982—. Mem. ABA, D.C. Bar Assn., Am. Law Inst.

**ARENCIBIA, RAUL ANTONIO,** lawyer; b. N.Y.C., Dec. 18, 1955; s. Raul and Elba (Petrovitch) A.; m. Patricia Lucia Moore, Mar. 22, 1987; children: Adam Loell, Aaron Francis, Andrea GeorgeAnn. BA cum laude, NYU, 1977; JD, Harvard U., 1980. Bar: Fla. 1980, U.S. Dist. Ct. (so. dist.) Fla. 1980, U.S. Ct. Appeals (5th and 11th cirs.) 1981, U.S. Dist. Ct. (mid. dist.) Fla. 1985. Assoc. Paul & Thomson, Miami, Fla., 1980-81, Mahoney, Hadlow, et al, Miami, 1981-82, Frates & Novey, Miami, 1983-84, Dady, Siegfried, et al, Coral Gables, Fla., 1984-85; pvt. practice Miami, 1985-89; of counsel Goytisolo & Saez, Miami, 1988-89; mng. ptnr. Goytisolo, Saez & Arencibia, Miami, 1989-90; pvt. practice Miami, 1990-91; with Bailey, Harper & Arencivia, Miami, 1991—. Contbg. author: Bonds: The Protective Layer in the Construction Process, 1987. Recipient NYU Founders Day award, 1977, NYU scholar, 1973. Mem. ABA, Fla. Bar Assn., Dade County Bar Assn., Cuban Am. Bar Assn. Republican. Roman Catholic. Avocation: chess. Appellate, Federal civil litigation, General civil litigation.

**ARENSTEIN, GILBERT GREGORY,** lawyer, associate; b. Cin., Jan. 3, 1969; s. Gerald Leslie and Ileane (Roberts) A.; m. Debra Ann Janes, Sept. 4, 1994. BA, Tulane U., 1991; JD, Capital U., 1994, ML in Tax and Bus., 1994. Bar: Ohio 1994, U.S. Dist. Ct. (so. dist.) Ohio 1995. Assoc. Dysinger & Stewart, LPA, Tipp City, Ohio, 1995—; mem. Dayton Trust & Estate Planning Group, 1996—. Mem. Miami County Bar Assn. (rules com. 1995-98, probate law com. 1998—), Tipp City Rotary (sgt. at arms 1997—), Tipp City Area C. of C. (bd. dirs. 1998—). Avocations: amateur soccer, golf, tennis, skiing, softball. Estate planning, Probate, General corporate. Office: Dysinger & Stewart, LPA 249 S Garber Dr Tipp City OH 45371-1183

**ARESTY, JEFFREY M.,** lawyer; b. Framingham, Mass., Dec. 31, 1951; s. Victor Joseph and Pola (Granek) A.; m. Ellen Louise Gould, Aug. 15, 1976; children: Joshua, Abigail, Joanne. BA, Johns Hopkins U., 1973; JD, Boston U., 1976, LLM in Taxation, 1978, LLM in Internat. Banking, 1993. Bar: Mass. 1977, D.C. 1982. Tax specialist Coopers & Lybrand, Boston, 1976-78; assoc. Meyers, Goldstein & Crossland, Brookline, Mass., 1978-79; ptnr. Crossland, Aresty & Levin, Boston, 1979-87, Aresty & Levin, Boston, 1987-91; ptnr. Aresty Internat. Law Offices, Boston, 1992—. Cons. editor Tax Shelter Investment Rev., 1981-85. Recipient Disting. Achievement award Boston Safe Deposit and Trust, 1976, Grad. Banking Alumni Achievement award Boston U. Law Sch., 1993. Mem. ABA (membership chmn. 1981-84, coun. 1985-91, vice chmn. computer div. 1985-90, sect. law practice mgmt. 1985-91, chmn. internat. interest group 1992-96, chmn. internat. negotiations task force 1992-95, chmn. Mass. state membership com. 1985-91, internat. law sect., chair law practice com. 1995-98, co-editor ABA Guide Internat. Bus. Negotiations 1994, prodr. ABA/AT&T CD-Rom on Cross-Cultural Comm., 1997), Am. Bar Found., Mass. Bar Assn. (bd. dels., exec. com. 1981-83, chmn. law practice sect. 1983-85), Am. Bar Found. (standing com. tech. and info. svcs., 1998—, pub. bd. gen. practice, 1998—), Mass. Bar Found. Contracts commercial, Private international, Real property. Home: 35 Three Ponds Rd Wayland MA 01778-1732 Office: Aresty Internat Law Offices Bay 107 Union Wharf Boston MA 02109

**ARFMANN, DENNIS L.,** lawyer. BA, U. Nebr., 1974, JD, 1979; LLM, George Washington U., 1991. Bar: Nebr. 1980, Colo. 1988. Ptnr. Winner Nichols, Douglas, Kelly & Arfmann, Scottsbluff, Nebr., 1980-91, Bradley Cmapbell, Carney & Madsen, Golden, Colo., 1991-95, Holme Roberts & Owen LLP, Denver, 1995—; chair air quality com. Colo. Assn. Commerce and Industry; chair air subcom. Rocky Mtn. Oil and Gas Assn., 1992-95; adv. bd. Clean Air Act Reporter; mem. Denver Regional Air Coun., Western Regional Air Partnership's Market Trading Forum. Mem. ABA (natural resources, environ. & energy law sect.). Environmental. Office: Holme Roberts & Owen 1700 Lincoln St Ste 4100 Denver CO 80203-4541

**ARGENTO, VICTORIA M(ARIE),** lawyer; b. Rochester, N.Y., May 21, 1962; d. Francis C. Sr. and Elaine A. (Busico) A. BA, St. John Fisher Coll., 1984; JD, SUNY, Buffalo, 1987. Bar: N.Y. 1988, U.S. Bankruptcy Ct. (we. dist.) N.Y. 1989, U.S. Dist. Ct. (we. dist.) N.Y. 1989. Sole practice Rochester, 1988-90; ptnr. LePore & Argento, Rochester, 1990-93, mng. ptnr., 1993—. Panel spkr. (seminar) Going Solo, 1994. Mem. East Rochester Rep. Com., 1984-91, dep. leader, 1990-91; vol. Lawyers for Learning, Rochester, 1994-96, Maplewood Neighborhood Assn. Mem. ABA, N.Y. State Bar Assn., Monroe County Bar Assn. Republican. Roman Catholic. Avocations: youth football volunteer, little league coach. Family and matrimonial, Real property, General practice. Office: LePore & Argento One E Main St Rochester NY 14614

**ARGERIS, GEORGE JOHN,** lawyer; b. Ten Sleep, Wyo., May 12, 1931; s. John Brown and Martha (Wilsonoff) A. BA, U. Colo., 1954; JD, U. Wyo., 1959. Bar: Wyo. 1959, U.S. Dist. Ct. Wyo. 1959, U.S. Supreme Ct. 1968. Asst. atty. gen. State of Wyo., Cheyenne, 1960-63; supervisory atty. Fgn. Claims Commn. U.S., Washington, 1963-68; dep. gen. counsel U.S. Info. Agy., Washington, 1972-74; ptnr. Guy, Williams, White & Argeris, Cheyenne, 1974-94; of counsel Orr, Buchhammer & Kehl (was Guy, Williams, White & Argeris), 1994-98. Assoc. editor U. Wyo. Law Rev., 1957-58. Mem. ABA, Assn. Def. Trial Lawyers, Wyo. Def. Lawyers Assn., Wyo. Trial Lawyers Assn., Omicron Delta Kappa, Chi Gamma Iota. Insurance, Product liability, Personal injury. Home: 3619 Carey Ave Cheyenne WY 82001-1227 Office: Orr Buchhammer & Kehl (was Guy Williams White & Argeris) 1600 Van Lennen Ave Cheyenne WY 82001-4636

**ARGEROS, ANTHONY GEORGE,** lawyer; b. Moline, Ill., Dec. 1, 1964; s. George Anthony and Helen (Tsakanikas) A. BS, Ill. State U., 1987; JD, DePaul U., Chgo., 1990. Bar: Ill. 1990, U.S. Dist. Ct. (no. dist.) Ill. 1990, U.S. Dist. Ct. (cen. dist.) Ill. 1991, U.S. Dist. Ct. Ill. (trial bar) 1992, U.S. Ct. Appeals (7th cir.). Assoc. Elliott & McClure, P.C., Bourbonnais, Ill., 1990-93, Jack Samuel Ring & Assocs., Ltd., Chgo., 1993-97, Dennis T. Schoen, P.C., Chgo., 1997—. Mem. editl. bd. Jour. Health and Hosp. Law, 1988-89. V.p. membership devel. Kankakee (Ill.) Area Jaycees, 1991-92, v.p. community devel., 1992-93; bd. dirs. Kankakee Air Festival, 1991-92, Contemporary Coun. for Econ. Devel., Bourbonnais, Ill., 1992-93. Mem. ABA, ATLA (adv. Nat. Coll. of Advocacy 1991—), Ill. Trial Lawyers Assn., Chgo. Bar Assn., Ill. Bar Assn., Ill. State U. Alumni Assn. (bd. dirs. Chgo. Downtown and Northshore chpt. 1998-99), Order of Barristers, Phi Alpha Delta. Republican. Orthodox. Avocations: computers, hunting, fishing, golf, archery. General civil litigation, Product liability, Personal injury. Office: Dennis T Schoen PC 221 N Lasalle St Ste 663 Chicago IL 60601-1223

**ARGETSINGER, CAMERON R.,** lawyer; b. Youngstown, Ohio, Mar. 1, 1921; s. James Cameron and Louise May (Williams) A.; m. Jean Rose Sause, July 26, 1941; children: James Cameron II, Louise B. (Mrs. Thomas J. Kanaley), Michael R., Marya J. (Mrs. Arthur B. Smith Jr.), Margretta E., Peter O., Robert C., Samuel W., Philip R. AB, Youngstown U., 1951; JD, Cornell U., 1954. Bar: N.Y. 1954, U.S. Dist. Ct. (we. dist.) N.Y. 1977, U.S. Dist. Ct. (no. dist.) N.Y. 1980, U.S. Supreme Ct. 1958. Pvt. practice Watkins Glen, N.Y., 1955-70; exec. dir. Sports Car Club of Am., Inc., Denver, 1971-77; ptnr. Lape & Argetsinger, Montour Falls, N.Y., 1977-80; pvt. practice law Montour Falls, 1980—; commr. Internat. Motor Sports Assn., Inc., Tampa, 1985-92. Founder, race dir., exec. dir. Watkins Glen Grand Prix and U.S. Grand Prix, Watkins Glen, 1948-70. 2d lt. U.S. Army, 1942-45. Recipient Woolf Barnato trophy Sports Car Club of Am., Inc., 1948, Best Organized World Championship Grand Prix, Grand Prix Drivers Assn., London, 1965. Mem. NRA, N.Y. Bar Assn. (ho. dels. 1981-82, 96-97), Schyler County Bar Assn. (pres. 1980-83). Republican. Presbyterian. Avocations: books, guns and hunting, cars. Probate, Estate taxation, Real property. Office: 412 W Main St Montour Falls NY 14865

**ARGHAVANI, FIROOZEH (FAY),** lawyer; b. Mar. 31, 1968; m. Sean Toranji, Jan. 7, 1994. BS, U. Calif., Irvine, 1990; JD, Western State U., 1994. Bar: Calif. 1995, U.S. Dist. Ct. (cen. dist.) Calif. Pvt. practice Santa Ana, Calif., 1995—. Mem. L.A. County Bar Assn., Orange County Bar Assn. Bankruptcy, Landlord-tenant, Personal injury. Office: 401 Civic Center Dr W Ste 800 Santa Ana CA 92701-7502

**ARGIROPOULOS, ANTHONY,** lawyer; b. Vineland, N.J., Oct. 30, 1971; s. Anthony and Frances Argiropoulos. BA in English, West Chester (Pa.) U., 1993; JD, Temple U., 1997. Bar: Pa. 1998, N.J. 1998, U.S. Dist. Ct. N.J. 1998. Jud. intern to Hon. Jerome B. Simardle U.S. Dist. Ct. N.J., Camden, 1995; tcht. asst. legal rsch. and writing Temple U. Sch. Law, Phila., 1996; litigation assoc. Fox, Rothschild, O'Brien & Frankel, Lawrenceville, N.J., 1997—. Mem. staff Temple U. Sch. Law Polit. and Civil Rights Law Rev., 1995-97. Recipient various awards. Mem. Princeton Bar Assn., Mercer County Bar Assn., N.J. Bar Assn. (young lawyers divsn. and fed. practice sect.), Phi Sigma Tau. General civil litigation. Office: Fox Rothschild et al Princeton Pike Corp Ctr 997 Lenox Dr Bldg 3 Lawrenceville NJ 08648-2317

**ARGUE, JOHN CLIFFORD,** lawyer; b. Glendale, Calif., Jan. 25, 1932; s. J. Clifford and Catherine Emily (Clements) A.; m. Leah Elizabeth Moore, June 29, 1963; children: Elizabeth Anne, John Michael. AB in Commerce and Fin., Occidental Coll., 1953, LLD (hon.), 1987; LLB, U. So. Calif., 1956. Bar: Calif. 1957. Since practiced in Los Angeles; mem. firm Argue & Argue, 1958-59, Flint & MacKay, 1960-72; mem. firm Argue, Pearson, Harbison & Myers, 1972-89, of counsel, 1990—; bd. dirs. Avery Dennison, Apex Mortgage Capital, TCW Convertible Fund, Nationwide Health Properties, Compensation Resource Group; mem. adv. bd. LAACO, Ltd., Mellow Fin. West Coast bd., TCW/DW Mut. Funds, TCW Galileo Funds; chmn. The Rose Hills Found., Amateur Athletic Found., L.A. Sports Coun., Criminal Justice Legal Found., 1994-99, L.A. 2012 Bid Com. Pres. So. Calif. Com. Olympic Games, 1972—; founding chmn. L.A. Olympic Organizing Com., 1978-79; trustee Pomona Coll., U. So. Calif.; vice chmn. Occidental Coll., Mus. Sci. and Industry; mem. nat. adv. coun. Autry Mus. Western Heritage; chmn. bd. Greater L.A. affiliate Am. Heart Assn., 1982; chmn. Verdugo Hills Hosp., 1979; pres. Town Hall of Calif., 1985, U. So. Calif. Assocs., 1988-93; chmn. PGA Championship, 1983, chmn. adv. bd., 1995; vice chmn., sec. L.A. 2000 Com., 1991 Olympic Sports Festival, 1993 Superbowl, 1994 World Cup. Mem. L.A. Bar Assn., Calif. Bar Assn., Southern Calif. Golf Assn. (pres. 1979), Calif. Golf Assn. (v.p. 1979), Calif. State Srs. Golf Assn. (v.p.), L.A. Area C. of C. (chmn. 1989), Chancery Club (pres. 1985-86), Calif. Club (pres. 1983-84), L.A. Athletic Club, Riviera Country Club, Oakmont Country Club (pres. 1972), L.A. Country Club, Rotary, Phi Delta Phi, Alpha Tau Omega. General corporate, Taxation, general, Real property. Home: 1314 Descanso Dr La Canada Flintridge CA 91011-3149 Office: Argue Pearson Harbison & Myers 801 S Flower St Ste 5000 Los Angeles CA 90017-4625

**ARGUEDAS, CRISTINA C.,** lawyer; b. 1953. BA, U. N.H.; JD, Rutgers U., 1979. Bar: Calif. 1979. Dep. fed. defender U.S. Dist. Ct. (no. dist.) Calif.; ptnr. Cooper, Arguedas & Cassman, Emeryville, Calif.; lawyer rep. U.S. Ct. Appeals (9th cir.) Jud. Conf. Named one of 50 Top Lawyers Nat. Law Jour., 1998. Mem. Calif. Attys. for Criminal Justice (past pres.). Office: Cooper Arguedas & Cassman 5900 Hollis St Ste N Emeryville CA 94608-2008*

**ARIEL, FRANK Y.,** lawyer; b. Tehran, Iran, Mar. 1, 1966; came to U.S., 1982; children: Joshua, Jordan. BA, UCLA, 1989; JD, Whittier Coll., 1992. Bar: Calif. 1992. Pvt. practice L.A., 1992—; cons. in field, L.A., 1992—. Mem. Consumer Atty. Group of L.A., Calif. Atty. Assn. Contracts commercial, Personal injury, General practice. Office: 1801 Century Park E Ste 2400 Los Angeles CA 90067-2326

**ARIS, JOHN LYNNWOOD,** lawyer; b. Ann Arbor, Mich., Dec. 5, 1965; s. Leslie Lynnwood and Virginia Baldwin A.; m. Lana Marie Howe, Sept. 2, 1995; children: Mark Benjamin, Amy Lynne. BA in Econs., Coll. William and Mary, 1988; JD, U. Mich., 1991. Bar: Pa. 1991, U.S. Dist. Ct. (ea. dist.) Pa. 1992, U.S. Ct. Appeals (3rd cir.) 1993. Assoc. Duane, Morris & Heckscher LLP, Phila., 1991—. Vol. Vols. for Indigent, Phila., 1991—; home meeting leader Living Word Cmty., Phila., 1994-95, 1997—. Mem. Phila. Bar Assn. (mem. problems homeless com. 1995-97, mem. compulsory arbitration com. 1997—). , Phila. Assn. Def. Counsel. Avocations: Bible, tennis, softball, singing, trumpet. Insurance, Personal injury, General civil litigation. Office: Duane Morris & Heckscher LLP 1650 Market St Fl 37 Philadelphia PA 19103-7396

**ARIS, JORAM JEHUDAH,** lawyer; b. Haderah, Israel, Feb. 6, 1953; came to U.S., 1957; s. Joseph Koenigstein and Shoshanah (Lemberger) Aris; m. Gloria Bakash, Sept. 22, 1984; children: Giselle Dina, Danielle Lisa, Noah Elliot, Jonathan Joseph. Student, York U., Eng., 1972; BA magna cum laude, CUNY, 1973; JD, N.Y. Law Sch., 1978. Bar: N.J. 1978, N.Y. 1979. Assoc. U.S. Attys. Office (so. dist.) N.Y., N.Y.C., 1977, N.Y. State Atty. Gens. Office, N.Y.C., 1978; atty. First & First, N.Y.C., 1978-79, Empire Mut. Ins. Co., N.Y.C., 1979-80; law sec. N.Y. State Supreme Ct., N.Y.C., 1980-81; sole practice N.Y.C., 1981—; chmn. Collective, N.Y.C., 1971-72. Mem. Riverdale Dem. Club, Bronx, N.Y., 1975-86, N.Y.C. Community Bd. #8, Bronx, 1980-86, Pub. Safety Com., Bronx, 1980-84, Environ. Safety and Sanitation, Bronx, 1985-86, Housing Com., Bronx, 1980-82, law com. 1984-86, ethics com. 1984-86; pres. Windsor Tenants Assn., Bronx, 1985-86; vol. N.Y.C. Adopt-A-Hwy.; active Hebrew Inst. Riverdale, N.Y.C., Conservative Synagogue Adath Israel, N.Y.C., Riverdale Temple, N.Y.C., Bene Naharayim (Iraqi) Synagogue, N.Y.C. Mem. ABA (elder care section), N.Y. State Bar Assn. (elder care sect.), N.Y. County Lawyers Assn. (trial atty.), Bronx County Bar Assn., Am.-Sephardic Orgn., Phi Delta Phi. Democrat. Jewish. E-mail: LawyerAris@aol.com. General civil litigation, Personal injury, Probate. Home and Office: 3671 Hudson Manor Ter Bronx NY 10463-1137

**ARISTEI, J. CLARK,** lawyer, educator; b. Washington, Sept. 6, 1948; s. Jerome and Eleanor Ruth (Clark) A. AA, L.A. Harbor Coll., 1968; BA cum laude, Calif. State U., Long Beach, 1971; JD, U. San Diego, 1975. Bar: Calif. 1975, U.S. Dist. Ct. (so. dist.) Calif. 1975, U.S. Dist. Ct. (cen. dist.) Calif. 1979, U.S. Dist. Ct. (ea. dist.) Calif. 1993, U.S. Dist. Ct. (no. dist.) N.Y. 1996, U.S. Ct. Appeals (7th cir.) 1997. Pvt. practice San Diego, 1975; assoc. Bennett Olan Law Office, Beverly Hills, Calif., 1976-77, Fogel, Feldman, Kingler, Ostrov & Klevens, L.A., 1977-92, Kananack, Murgatroyd, Baum & Hedlund, L.A., 1993-94; shareholder Baum, Hedlund, Aristei et al, L.A., 1994—; adj. prof. law U. of West L.A., 1986-97. Mem. faculty libr. com. U. West L.A., 1995-97. Mem. State Bar Calif., Consumer Attys. Calif., Consumer Atty. Assn. L.A. Avocations: architecture, bicycling. Personal injury, Product liability, Aviation. Office: Baum Hedlund Aristei Guilford & Downey 12100 Wilshire Blvd Ste 950 Los Angeles CA 90025-7107

**ARIZAGA, LAVORA SPRADLIN,** retired lawyer; b. Garvin County, Okla., Apr. 29, 1927; d. Gervase Eugene and Donah Lavorah (Eddings) Spradlin; m. Francisco DePaula Arizaga, Aug. 10, 1946; children: F.D. III, Lavora Cristina Arizaga Ewan, Rebecca Maria Arizaga Armour, Nicolas Antonio. BA, U. Okla., 1952; JD, U. Houston, 1979. Bar: Tex. 1979. Sole practitioner Houston, 1979-92. Pres. United Meth. Women, St. Luke's United Meth. Ch., Midland, 1996-98; chmn. Affirmative Action Adv. Bd., City of Houston, 1984-86. Mem. AAUW, LWV (pres. Beaumont, Tex. 1960-61, v.p. Tex. 1983-85, pres. Houston 1985-87, Midland, Tex. 1997-99), UN Assn.-USA (bd. dirs.). Personal income taxation, Estate taxation, Corporate taxation. Home: 1809 Kensington Ln Midland TX 79705-1706

**ARKIN, ROBERT DAVID,** lawyer; b. Washington, Feb. 15, 1954; s. William Howard and Zenda Lillian (Lieberman) A.; m. Rose Morgenstern, Dec. 29, 1974; children: Chelsea Morgenstern-Arkin, Nora Morgenstern-Arkin, Rose Morgenstern-Arkin. BA, U. Pa., 1976, MA, 1976; JD, U. Va., 1979. Bar: Minn. 1980, Ga. 1987. Law clk. to chief justice Supreme Ct. Minn., St. Paul, 1979-80; assoc. Leonard, Street and Deinard, Mpls., 1980-84, ptnr., 1985-86; spl. asst. atty. gen. State of Minn., St. Paul, 1981; of counsel Trotter, Smith & Jacobs, Atlanta, 1986-89; ptnr. Minkin & Snyder, Atlanta, 1989—; mem. Tech. Rev. Com. Seed Money Venture Capital Product Loan Program, Minn. Office of Software Tech. Devel., St. Paul, 1985-86; vice chmn. Minn. Software Tech. Commn. (gubernatorial appointee), St. Paul, 1985-86. Exec. editor: Va. Jour. Internat. Law, Charlottesville, 1978-79; contbr. articles to profl. jours. Participant Leadership Mpls. of Greater Mpls. C. of C., 1984-85; mem. steering com. Young Leadership Devel., Mpls. Fedn. for Jewish Service, 1982-85; bd. dirs., mem. exec. com. Community Housing and Service Corp., Mpls., 1981-85. Mem. ABA (health law, computer law, bus. law and internat. sects.), Minn. Bar Assn. (chmn. internat. contracts com. 1985-86), Ga. Bar Assn. (computer, corp., health care and internat. law sects.), Atlanta Bar Assn., Computer Law Assn., Minn. Software Assn. (bd. dirs. 1986), Image Film and Video Assn. (bd. dirs. 1988-90), Am. Israel Chamber of Commerce & Industry S.W., Inc. (founder, bd. dirs., sec. 1991—), Pi Gamma Mu. Jewish. Avocations: film, photography, writing. Computer, Mergers and acquisitions, Securities. Home: 20 Battle Ridge Dr NE Atlanta GA 30342-2451

**ARLEN, JENNIFER HALL,** law educator; b. Berkeley, Calif., Jan. 7, 1959; d. Michael John and Ann (Warner) A.; m. Robert Lee Hotz, May 21, 1988; children: Michael Arlen Hotz, Robert Arlen Hotz. BA, Harvard U., 1982; JD, NYU, 1986; PhD in Econs., NYU, 1992. Bar: N.Y. 1987, U.S. Ct. Appeals (11th cir.) 1987. Summer clk. U.S. Dist. Ct. (ea. dist.) N.Y., Bklyn., 1984; summer assoc. Davis Polk & Wardwell, N.Y.C., 1985; law clk. U.S. Cir. Judge, 11th cir., Savannah, Ga., 1986-87; asst. prof. law Emory U., Atlanta, 1987-91, assoc. prof. law, 1991-93; prof. law U. So. Calif., L.A., 1994—, Iradelle and Theodore Johnson prof. law and bus., 1997—; vis. prof. law U. So. Calif., 1993. Olin fellow U. Calif. Sch. Law, Berkeley, fall 1991. Mem. ABA, Am. Assn. Law Schs. (chair remedies sect. 1994, chair elect 1993, mem. exec. com. 1990-91, 95, chair torts sect. 1995, chair elect 1994, treas. 1991, sec. 1992-93, exec. com. bus. assns. sect. 1995-96, chair law and econ., sect. 1996, chair elect law and econs. sect. 1995, chair 1996), Am. Law and Econ. Assn. (bd. dirs. 1991-93), Am. Econ. Assn., Order of Coif, Am. Law Inst. Democrat. Office: U So Calif Law Ctr Los Angeles CA 90089-0001

**ARMBRECHT, WILLIAM HENRY, III,** retired lawyer; b. Mobile, Ala., Jan. 13, 1929; s. William Henry and Katherine (Little) A.; m. Dorothy Jean Taylor, Sept. 1, 1951; children—Katherine Handley, William Taylor, Alexander Paterson. B.S., U. Ala., 1950, J.D., 1952. Bar: Ala. 1952, U.S. Supreme Ct. 1972. Assoc. Inge, Twitty, Armbrecht & Jackson, Mobile, 1952-56; ptnr. Armbrecht, Jackson, McConnell & DeMouy, Mobile, 1956-65, Armbrecht, Jackson & DeMouy, Mobile, 1965-75, Armbrecht, Jackson, DeMouy, Crowe, Holmes & Reeves, Mobile, 1976-94, Armbrecht, Jackson, DeMouy, Crowe, Holmes & Reeves, LLC, 1994-96. Served to 1st lt. JAGC, AUS, 1952-54. Mem. ABA, Ala. Bar Assn. (chmn. grievance com. 1973-74, chmn. sect. corp. banking and bus. law 1976-78), Mobile Bar Assn., Mobile Area C. of C. Found. (bd. dirs. 1990-92), Southeastern Corp. Law Inst. (mem. planning com. 1967-96), Phi Delta Phi, Delta Kappa Epsilon. Episcopalian. Oil, gas, and mineral, Estate planning, General practice. Home: 600 Fairfax Rd E Mobile AL 36608-2931 Office: Armbrecht Jackson DeMouy Crowe Holmes & Reeves LLC 1300 AmSouth Ctr PO Box 290 Mobile AL 36601-0290

**ARMENTI, JOSEPH ROCCO,** lawyer, writer; b. Neptune, N.J., Sept. 11, 1950; s. Rocco Carmen and Lucie (Taranta) A.; m. Maria Elizabeth Masters, June 6, 1982. BA, Villanova U., 1972; PhD, Dropsie U., 1982; JD, Temple U., 1986. Bar: Pa. 1986, U.S. Dist. Ct. (ea. dist.) Pa. 1986, U.S. Ct. Appeals (3d cir.) 1986, N.J. 1987. Ptnr. Joseph R. Armenti & Assoc., Phila., 1987—. Author: Elements of Divine Power, 1983; author, editor: Transcendence and Immanence, 1972, Wisdom and Knowledge, 1976, The Human Religious Quest, I-IV, 1986—; contbr. articles to profl. jours. Active ARC Disaster Relief Team, AHEPA. Fellow Dropsie U. for Hebrew and Cognate Studies, Phila., 1974-80. Mem. ABA, ACLU, N.J. Bar Assn., Pa. Bar Assn., Phila. Bar Assn. (edn. com. criminal div. 1989—), Assn. Trial Lawyers Am., Pa. Trial Lawyers Assn., Phila. Trial Lawyers Assn., Nat. Assn. Criminal Def. Lawyers, Internat. Soc. for Neo-Platonic Studies, Am. Acad. Religion, Soc. Bibl. Lit., Justinian Soc., Hellenic Lawyers Club, Phila. Lawyers Club, Hellenic Univ. Club, Lions, Tau Epsilon Rho, Phi Alpha Delta. Roman Catholic. Criminal, General civil litigation, Personal injury. Office: Joseph R Armenti & Assoc 303 Chestnut St Ste 100-204 Philadelphia PA 19106-2702 also: 601 Haddon Ave Ste 117 Collingswood NJ 08108-3703

**ARMOUR, GEORGE PORTER,** lawyer; b. Bryn Mawr, Pa., June 10, 1921; s. Charles Joseph and Florence (Eagle) A.; m. Isabel Blondet, Nov. 22, 1958; children: Luis O., Carlos O. BA, Temple U., 1943, JD, 1949. Bar: Pa. 1949, N.Y. 1969, Calif. 1975. Assoc. Bennett & Bricklin, Phila., 1949-59; atty. Atlantic Richfield Co., 1959-83; gen. atty. Phila., 1965-68; assoc. gen. counsel Phila., N.Y.C., L.A., 1968-78; dep. gen. counsel L.A., 1978-83; pvt. practice law, 1983—; chmn. Internat. and Comparative Law Ctr., Southwestern Legal Found., Dallas, 1980-82. Mem. Assocs. Calif. Inst. Tech., 1981—; mem. Soc. of Fellows Huntington Libr. and Art Gallery, San Marino, Calif., 1982—. With USAAF, 1943-46. Mem. ABA, Calif. Bar Assn., Calif. Club (L.A.), Valley Hunt Club (Pasadena). Republican. Episcopalian. General corporate, Oil, gas, and mineral, Private international. Home and Office: 1621 Orlando Rd Pasadena CA 91106-4130

**ARMOUR, JAMES LOTT,** lawyer; b. Jackson, Tenn., May 19, 1938; s. Quintin and Frances (Breeden) A.; m. Nancy Stokes Johnson, Mar. 17, 1962; 1 son, John Lawson. BA, Vanderbilt U., 1961, LLB, 1964; LLM, So. Meth. U., 1967. Bar: Tenn. 1964, Tex. 1965, U.S. Supreme Ct. 1967, N.Y. 1969, Okla. 1972. Assoc. firm Turner Rodgers Winn Scurlock & Terry, Dallas, 1965-67; internat. atty. Mobil Corp., N.Y.C. and London, 1967-71, Phillips Petroleum Co., Bartlesville, Okla., 1971-74; asst. gen. counsel Conoco, Inc., Stamford, Conn., 1974-83; ptnr. firm Locke Liddell & Sapp LLP, Dallas, 1984—. chair adv. bd. oil and gas SW Legal Fedn.; mem. Dallas Com. on Fgn. Rels.; former mem. alumni bd. Vanderbilt Law Sch. Mem. ABA, Assn. of Bar of City of N.Y., State Bar Tex., Dallas Bar Assn., Petroleum Club, Phi Delta Phi, Kappa Sigma. Episcopalian. FERC practice, Oil, gas, and mineral, Private international. Home: 4541 Belfort Pl Dallas TX 75205-3618 Office: Locke Liddell & Sapp LLP 2200 Ross Ave Ste 2200 Dallas TX 75201-2748

**ARMSTRONG, ALAN LEIGH,** lawyer; b. L.A., Apr. 25, 1945; s. Don Leigh and Barbara Caroline (Hayes) A.; m. Margie Jean Lehner, July 1, 1972; children: Don Leigh, Mark Leigh. BA, U. Calif., Riverside, 1967; JD, Western State U., Fullerton, Calif., 1984. Bar: Calif. 1984, U.S. Dist. Ct. (cen. dist.) Calif. 1985, U.S. Ct. Appeals (9th cir.) 1985, U.S. Tax Ct. 1987, U.S. Supreme Ct. 1988. Physicist USN, Pomona, Calif., 1967-74; engr. USN, Seal Beach, Calif., 74-93; pvt. practice Alan Leigh Armstrong, Atty. At Law, Huntington Beach, Calif., 1985—; adj. prof. law Trinity Law Sch., 1992—. Lay reader St. James Episcopal Ch., Newport Beach, Calif., 1991—, vestryman, 1985-88; cubmaster Boy Scouts Am., Huntington Beach, 1988-92, asst. scoutmaster, 1992-94, com. chair, 1994-97, com. mem. 1998—. Mem. ABA, Christian Legal Soc. Republican. Avocations: sailing, automatic musical instrument collecting. Estate planning, Probate, General corporate. Office: Alan Leigh Armstrong Atty At Law 18652 Florida St Ste 225 Huntington Beach CA 92648-6006

**ARMSTRONG, EDWIN ALAN,** lawyer; b. Atlanta, June 20, 1950; s. Carl Edwin and Betty (Hawkins) A.; m. Marlene Bryant, Aug. 12, 1978. BA, Berry Coll., 1972; JD, Emory U., 1976. Bar: Ga. 1976, U.S. Dist. Ct. (no. dist.) Ga. 1977, U.S. Ct. Appeals (5th cir.) 1981, U.S. Ct. Appeals (11th cir.) 1982, U.S. Supreme Ct. 1989, U.S. Dist. Ct. (so. dist.) Ga., U.S. Ct. Appeals (4th cir.), U.S. Ct. Appeals (D.C. cir.) 1992, U.S. Ct. Appeals (6th cir.) 1992, U.S. Dist. Ct. (mid. dist.) Ga 1992. Atty. Flynt Jud. Cir. Pub. Defenders Office, McDonough, Ga., 1976-77; assoc. Neely, Neely & Player, Atlanta, 1977; pvt. practice, Atlanta, 1977-79, 81—; assoc. Stolz, Shulman & Loveless, Atlanta, 1979-81. Contbr. articles to profl. jours. Mem. ABA (forum com. on air and space law, tort and ins. practice sect.), ATLA, Atlanta Bar Assn., Decatur-DeKalb Bar Assn., State Bar Ga. (chmn. aviation law sect. 1998—), Ga. Trial Lawyers Assn., Nat. Transp. Safety Bd. Bar Assn. (founding, com. legis. and regulatory activity 1989—, editor newsletter 1991-92), Lawyer-Pilots Bar Assn. Episcopalian. Avocation: flying. State civil litigation, Aviation, Personal injury. Home: 4098 Northlake Creek Cv Tucker GA 30084-3416

**ARMSTRONG, GENE LYNDON,** lawyer, utilities executive; b. Waterloo, Iowa, Dec. 29, 1940; s. Oscar J. and Violet A. Armstrong; m. Ann Marwood Haberman, Sept. 12, 1964; children: David A., Matthew P. BS, U. Wis., 1963, MS in Econs., 1964; LLB, Stanford U., 1967. Bar: Ill. 1967, U.S. Dist. Ct. (no. dist.) Ill. 1967, U.S. Ct. Appeals (7th cir.) 1996. Assoc. Isham, Lincoln & Beale, Chgo., 1967-74; ptnr. Roan & Grossman, Chgo., 1975-80; ptnr., shareholder Cichocki & Armstrong, Ltd., Oak Park, Ill., 1980-97; shareholder, prin. Gene L. Armstrong & Assoc., Oak Park, Ill., 1997—; chmn., pres. Dame Co., Oak Park, 1984—, New Landing Utility, Inc., Oak Park, 1984—; ptnr., mgr. CAM Properties, Oak Park, 1989—. Pres. Oak Park-River Forest Cmty. Chest, 1979-80; bd. dirs. Oak Park Housing Ctr., 1974-77; pres. Great Am. Lighthouse Assn., Oak Park, 1974—. Republican. Avocations: gardening, photography, snow skiing, travel. General civil litigation, Appellate, Public utilities. Home: 1113 N Elmwood Ave Oak Park IL 60302-1246 Office: Gene L Armstrong & Assocs PC 1111 South Blvd Oak Park IL 60302-2838

**ARMSTRONG, GORDON GRAY, III,** lawyer; b. Mobile, Ala., Jan. 13, 1964; s. Gordon Gray Jr. and Margaret Claire A.; m. Simone Delaine Manley, Mar. 19, 1994; 1 child, Gordon Gray IV. BA, U. Ala., 1986, JD, 1989. Bar: Ala. 1989, U.S. Dist. Ct. (so. dist.) Ala. 1991, U.S. Ct. Appeals (11th cir.) 1992, U.S. Supreme Ct. 1995. Assoc. Clark, Deen & Copeland, Mobile, Ala., 1989-92; atty pvt. practice, Mobile, Ala., 1992—. Mem. ABA (del. young lawyers divsn. 1993—), Nat. Assn. Criminal Def. Lawyers, Assn. Trial Lawyers Am., Am. Collectors Assn. (atty. program 1997—), Ala. State Bar Assn. (exec. com. young lawyers sect. 1992—, treas. 1995-96, sec. 1996-97, v.p. 1997-98, pres. 1998-99), Ala. Criminal Def. Lawyers Assn., Mobile Bar Assn. Avocations: fishing, golf, hunting, recreational sports, gardening. Criminal, Personal injury, Consumer commercial. Office: 205 Congress St Mobile AL 36603-6407

**ARMSTRONG, JACK GILLILAND,** lawyer; b. Pitts., Aug. 10, 1929; s. Hugh Collins and Mary Elizabeth (Gilliland) A.; m. Ellen Lee Gliem, June 10, 1951 (dec.); children: Thomas G., Elizabeth Armstrong Pride; m. Elizabeth Lacewll White, March 27, 1993. AB, U. Mich., 1951, JD, 1956. Bar: Pa. 1956, Mich. 1956, U.S. Supreme Ct. 1968, Fla. 1981. Assoc. Buchanan, Ingersoll, Rodewald, Kyle & Buerger, Pitts., 1956-65; ptnr. Buchanan, Ingersoll, P.C., Pitts., 1965-90; counsel Buchanan, Ingersoll, P.C., 1990-94, of counsel, 1995; of counsel Rothman Gordon, P.C., 1996—; dir. Standard Steel Splty. Co., Greer, S.C. Trustee Union Dale Cemetery, 1972—, pres., 1992-95. Dir. Sigma Nu Ednl. Found., 1998—. Lt. U.S. Army, 1951-53. Mem. ABA (sects. taxation, real property, probate and trust law), Pa. Bar Assn. (real property, probate, and trust law sect., mem. coun. 1981-84, treas. 1985, vice chmn. probate divsn. 1986-88, chmn. 1988-89, tax law sect.), Fla. Bar (real property, probate and trust law sect., tax sect.), Allegheny County Bar Assn. (probate and trust law), Palm Beach County Bar Assn., Estate Planning Coun. Pitts., Am. Coll. Trust and Estate Counsel (Pa. state chmn. 1990-95), Am. Coll. Tax Counsel, U. Mich. Alumni Assn. (Disting. Alumni Svc. award 1981), Am. Arbitration Assn. (nat. panel 1965—), Order of Coif, Duquesne Club, Univ. Club (pres. 1988-89), St. Clair Country Club, Town Club Jamestown, Delray Beach Club, Chautauqua Golf Club, Pine Tree Golf Club, Masons, Shriners, Royal Order Jesters, Phi Alpha Delta, Signa Nu. Estate taxation, Probate, Estate planning. Home: 4376 Pine Tree Dr Boynton Beach FL 33436-4818

**ARMSTRONG, JAMES F.,** lawyer; b. Jamestown, N.Y., Dec. 29, 1969; s. Donald Frank and Elizabeth Ann A.; m. Janice C. Minnuto, Nov. 29, 1997. BA, Canisius Coll., 1992; JD, SUNY, Buffalo, 1995. Bar: N.Y. 1996, U.S. Dist. Ct. (we. dist.) N.Y. 1996. Assoc. Jasen, Jasen & Sampson, P.C., Buffalo, 1996-99, Underberg & Kessler, LLP, 1999—. Mem. N.Y. Bar Assn., Erie County Bar Assn., Def. Rsch. Inst. Democrat. Roman Catholic. Avocation: golf. Product liability, Insurance, General civil litigation. Home: 3510 Heatherwood Dr Hamburg NY 14075-2103 Office: Jasen Jasen & Sampson PC 69 Delaware Ave Rm 700 Buffalo NY 14202-3805

**ARMSTRONG, JAMES LOUDEN, III,** lawyer; b. Miami, Fla., Jan. 7, 1932; s. James Louden and Jean Macrea (Cawley) A.; m. Mary Elizabeth McCall, Aug. 25, 1955; children: Patricia Payan, James L. IV. BA, Yale U., 1955, LLB, 1958. Bar: Fla. 1958, U.S. Dist. Ct. (so. dist.) Fla. 1958, U.S. Dist. Ct. (middle dist.) Fla. 1960, U.S. Dist. Ct. (no. dist.) Fla. 1964, U.S. Ct. Appeals (5th and 11th cir.) 1962, U.S. Supreme Ct. 1962. Assoc. Smathers & Thompson, Miami, 1958-64, ptnr., 1964-87; ptnr. Kelley Drye & Warren LLP, Miami, 1987—. Pres. Orange Bowl Com., Miami, 1976; co-chmn. Cmty. Partnership for Homeless, Inc., 1994—. Fellow Am. Coll. Trial Lawyers, Internat. Acad. Trial Lawyers; mem. Dade County bar Assn.(pres. 1972), Yale Club (pres. 1966). Republican. Presbyterian. Avocation: golf. Federal civil litigation, General civil litigation, Antitrust. Home: 4911 Alhambra Cir Coral Gables FL 33146-1600 Office: Kelley Drye & Warren LLP 2400 Miami Ctr 201 S Biscayne Blvd Ste 400 Miami FL 33131-2378

**ARMSTRONG, JAMES SINCLAIR,** foundation director, retired lawyer; b. N.Y.C., Oct. 15, 1915; s. Sinclair Howard and Katharine Martin (LeBoutillier) A.; m. Charlotte Peirce Horwood Faircloth, Nov. 22, 1978. Student, Milton (Mass.) Acad., 1934; AB cum laude, Harvard, 1938; JD, Harvard U., 1941; postgrad., Northwestern U., 1942-44, 46-48. Bar: Ill. 1941, N.Y. 1959. Assoc. Isham, Lincoln & Beale, Chgo., 1941-45, 46-49; ptnr. Isham, Lincoln & Beale, 1950-53; commr. SEC, Washington, 1953-57; chmn. SEC, 1955-57; asst. sec. navy for fin. mgmt., also compt. Dept. Navy, 1957-59; exec. v.p. U.S. Trust Co. of N.Y., 1959-80; ptnr. Whitman & Ransom, N.Y.C., 1980-84, of counsel, 1984-93; of counsel Whitman Breed Abbott & Morgan, N.Y.C., 1993-94, ret., 1995; bd. dirs., sec., treas. The Reed Found., Inc.; bd. dirs. The Bramwell Growth Fund, Inc. Chmn. emeritus English-Speaking Union U.S.; trustee emeritus, past pres. Gunnery Sch., Washington, Conn.; chmn. emeritus Nat. Inst. Social Scis.; sr. warden emeritus L'Eglise Francaise du St. Esprit; trustee Am. Friends Brit. Libr. Lt. (j.g.) USNR, 1945-46. Decorated officer Order Orange-Nassau (The Netherlands), comdr. Order of the Brit. Empire (U.K.). Mem. Am. Law Inst. (life), Practicing Law Inst. (mem. faculty The SEC Speaks program), Assn. of Bar of City of N.Y., Harvard Law Sch. Assn. (life), Navy League of U.S. (life), N.Y. Hist. Soc. (life), N.Y. Soc. Libr. (life), Am. Soc. Venerable Order St. John of Jerusalem, Pilgrims of U.S., St. Andrews Soc. State of N.Y. (life, past pres.), Huguenot Soc. Am. (life, past pres.), St. Nicholas Soc. City of N.Y. (life), Scottish Heritage USA (life), Soc. Colonial Wars of N.Y. (life), Squadron A Assn. (life), Victorian Soc. in Am. (life), Century Assn., Ch. Club of N.Y. (life, past pres.), Harvard Club, N.Y. Yacht Club, Thurs. Evening Club, Union Club, Chevy Chase (Md.) Club, Washington (Conn.) Club, Washington Garden Club, Edgartown (Mass.) Yacht Club, Edgartown Reading Rm. Securities, Land use and zoning (including planning), Banking. Home: 501 E 79th St

Apt 3C New York NY 10021-0731 Office: The Reed Found Inc 444 Madison Ave Rm 2901 New York NY 10022-6903

**ARMSTRONG, KENNETH,** lawyer; b. Chgo., Mar. 25, 1949. BS in Bus. Adminstrn., Sussex (Eng.) U., 1971; JD with distinction, Pacific Coast U., 1989. Cert. real estate appraiser, Nat. Assn. Real Estate Appraisers; cert. review appraiser, Nat. Assn. Review Appraisers; registered locksmith, Nat. Assn. Associated Locksmiths Am.; registered beer judge; lic. real estate broker Calif. Pvt. practice Mt. Shasta, Calif.; legal cons. student body Calif. State U., Long Beach, 1991; internat. spkr. asset protection. Author continuing edn. course for attys.; contbr. articles to profl. jours. Mem. City of Long Beach Downtown Redevel. Agy. PAC, 1982; performing mem. Magic Castle, Hollywood, Calif., 1989—. Recipient Corpus Juris Suecundum award West Legal Pub. Co., 1985-86, 1st and 3d pl. awards Am. Homebrewers Assn. Nat. Homebrewer Competition, Calif. and Nev., 1997. Mem. ABA, Calif. State Bar Assn., Long Beach Bar Assn., L.A. County Bar Assn., L.A. Trial Lawyers Assn., Siskiyou County Bar Assn. (past pres.), Cow Counties Bar Assn., Elks (past exalted ruler), Masons. Avocations: magician, philosophy, musician, taco bender. Fax: (916) 926-9817. Real property, General practice, Private international. Office: 326 N Mount Shasta Blvd Ste 2 Mount Shasta CA 96067-2283

**ARMSTRONG, KENNETH,** lawyer; b. Washington, June 25, 1955; s. Henry Kenneth and Ann (Bauman) A.; m. Deborah Baumgartner, Feb. 18, 1984 (div. Dec. 1993); 1 child, Caitlin; m. Trina Blandford-Hader, July 22, 1995. BA, Clark U., 1976; JD, Am. U., 1979. Bar: Md. 1979, D.C. 1980, U.S. Dist. Ct. Md. 1980, U.S. Dist. Ct. D.C. 1981. Assoc. Donahue, Ehrmantraut & Montedonico, Rockville, Md., 1979-83, ptnr., 1984-87; ptnr. Armstrong, Donohue, Ceppos & Voughan, Rockville, Md., 1987—. Author: (with others) Medical Malpractice in Maryland, 1987. Fellow Internat. Acad. Trial Lawyers, Am. Coll. Trial Lawyers; mem. Am. Bd. Trial Advocates, Bar Assn. D.C., Bar Assn. of Montgomery County, Md. Bar Assn., Am. Inns of Ct. (Montgomery County chpt. master 1991-96). Democrat. Roman Catholic. General civil litigation, Personal injury, Insurance. Home: 13412 Cleveland Dr Rockville MD 20850-3603 Office: Armstrong Donohue Ceppos & Vaughan 204 Monroe St Ste 101 Rockville MD 20850-4434

**ARMSTRONG, ORVILLE,** judge; b. Austin, Tex., Jan. 21, 1929; s. Orville Alexander and Velma Lucille (Reed) A.; m. Mary Dean Macfarlane; children: Anna Louise Glenn, John M., Paul Jefferson. BBA, U. Tex., Austin, 1953; LLB, U. So. Calif., 1956. Bar: Calif., 1957, U.S. Ct. Appeals (9th cir.) 1958, U.S. Supreme Ct. 1980. Ptnr., Gray, Binkley & Pfaelzer, 1956-61, Pfaelzer, Robertson, Armstrong & Woodard, L.A., 1961-66, Armstrong & Lloyd, L.A., 1966-74, Macdonald, Halsted & Laybourne, L.A., 1975-88, Baker & McKenzie, 1988-90; judge Superior Ct. State of Calif., 1991-92, assoc. justice ct. appeal State of Calif., 1993—; lectr. Calif. Continuing Edn. of Bar. Served with USAF, 1946-49. Fellow ABA, Am. Coll. Trial Lawyers; mem. State Bar Calif. (gov. 1983-87, pres. 1986-87), L.A. County Bar Assn. (trustee 1971-72), Chancery Club (pres. 1988), Calif. Club. Baptist. Office: 300 S Spring St Los Angeles CA 90013-1230

**ARMSTRONG, OWEN THOMAS,** lawyer; b. Sheboygan, Wis., July 13, 1923; s. Dewey Thomas and Esther Marie (DeVille) A.; m. Jane Bowe Roessel, Sept. 3, 1949; children: Owen Thomas, Jr., William Dewey. BA, U. Wis., 1947, LLB, 1949; LLM, Harvard U., 1950. Bar: Wis. 1949, Mo. 1951, U.S. Dist. Ct. (ea. dist.) Mo. 1952, U.S. Ct. Appeals (8th cir.) 1953, U.S. Supreme Ct. 1958. Asst. prof. law Washington U., St. Louis, 1949, U. N.Mex., Albuquerque, 1950-51; assoc. Lowenhaupt & Chasnoff, St. Louis, 1951-58; ptnr. Lowenhaupt, Chasnoff, Armstrong & Mellitz, St. Louis, 1958-94; mem. Lowenhaupt & Chasnoff, L.L.C., St. Louis, 1994-96, of counsel, 1996—. Dem. twp. committeeman, Clayton, Mo., 1968-72. Served to 1st lt. (j.g.) USNR S.C., 1943-46, PTO. Mem. ABA, Mo. Bar Assn., St. Louis Bar Assn. Roman Catholic. General corporate, Pension, profit-sharing, and employee benefits, State and local taxation. Home: Apt 106 420 S Kirkwood Rd Saint Louis MO 63122 Office: Lowenhaupt & Chasnoff LLC 10 S Broadway Saint Louis MO 63102-1712

**ARMSTRONG, PAUL WHITE,** lawyer, educator; b. Manchester, N.H., Mar. 30, 1945; s. Paul William and Ruth Marie (White) A.; m. Maria Luken, Apr. 26, 1975. MA, U. Dayton, 1969; JD, U. Notre Dame, 1972; LLM, NYU, 1978. Bar: N.J. 1973, Mich. 1974, U.S. Dist. Ct. N.J. 1973, U.S. Supreme Ct. 1976. Assoc. Rhoades, Mckee & Boer, Grand Rapids, Mich., 1973-74, Legal Aid Soc., Morristown, N.J., 1975; sole practitioner Bedminster, N.J., 1976-85; of counsel Weiner & Weiner, Morristown, 1986-93, Timmins, Larsen, Beacham & Hughes, Livingston, N.J., 1994-96, Kern, Augustine, Conroy & Schoppmann, Bridgewater, N.J., 1996—; adj. prof. Rutgers Law Sch., Newark, 1985—, Robert Wood Johnson Med. Sch., New Brunswick, N.J., 1985—; lectr. nat. and internat. law and bioethics, 1976—. Author publs. in field. Chmn. N.J. Bioethics Commn., Princeton, 1990—; chmn. Gov.'s Coun. on AIDS, Trenton, N.J., 1989-92; chmn. N.J. Health Decisions, Princeton, 1994—; pres. Samaritan Homeless Interim Program, 1990—; trustee, founder, Karen Ann Quinlan Hospice, 1976—. Recipient Disting. Citizen award Acad. of Medicine (N.J.), 1989, Am. Law and Health award Boy Scouts Am., 1996; Victoria fellow Rutgers U., 1990. Home: 1051 Tall Oaks Dr Bridgewater NJ 08807-1237 Office: Kern Augustine et al 120 Route 22 West Bridgewater NJ 08807

**ARMSTRONG, PHILLIP DALE,** lawyer; b. Waukegan, Ill., Mar. 27, 1943; s. James Leonard and Bernice Frances (Nader) A.; m. Leila Robson; children: Leonard Hart, Theodore Nader, Leila VIII. BS in Chem. Engring., U. Mo., 1966; JD, Gonzaga U., 1978; LLM, U. Mo., Kansas City, 1979. Bar: N.D. 1979, U.S. Dist. Ct. N.D. 1979, U.S. Dist. Ct. Ariz. 1991, U.S. Tax Ct. 1980, U.S. Ct. Appeals 1983, U.S. Supreme Ct. 1984. Mktg. trainee Dow Chem. Co., Midland, Mich., 1966-68; chem. engr. Clark Oil and Refining, Hartford, Ill., 1968-70; life guard, pool attendant, pool mgr. various hotels and condominiums, Miami Beach, Fla., 1970-75; assoc. McCutcheon Law Firm, Minot, N.D., 1979-81; sole practice Minot, 1981—, Mandan, N.D., 1995—; founder, pres. Producers Oil & Gas Corp., 1992—; trustee in bankruptcy for chpts. 7, 12, and 13, N.W. and S.W. divs. Dist. of N.D., 1980-95; founder Armstrong Oilwell Ops., 1996. Mem. ABA, N.D. Bar Assn., Nat. Assn. Bankruptcy Trustees, Am. Bankruptcy Inst., Exch. Club (Minot). Republican. Episcopalian. Home: 1006 Valley View Dr Minot ND 58703-1642 Office: Armstrong Law Firm 12 Main St S Minot ND 58701-3871 also: 402 1st St NW Mandan ND 58554-3118

**ARMSTRONG, SAUNDRA BROWN,** federal judge; b. Oakland, Calif., Mar. 23, 1947; d. Coolidge Logan and Pauline Marquette Brown; m. George Walter Armstrong, Apr. 18, 1982. B.A., Calif. State U.-Fresno, 1969; J.D. magna cum laude, U. San Francisco, 1977. Bar: Calif. 1977, U.S. Supreme Ct. 1984. Policewoman Oakland Police Dept., 1970-77; prosecutor, dep. dist. atty. Alameda County Dist. Atty., Oakland, 1978-79, 80-82; staff atty. Calif. Legis. Assembly Com. on Criminal Justice, Sacramento, 1979-80; trial atty. Dept. Justice, Washington, 1982-83; vice chmn. U.S. Consumer Product Safety Commn., Washington, 1984-86; commr. U.S. Parole Commn., Washington, 1986-89; judge Alameda Superior Ct., 1989-91, U.S. Dist. Ct. (no. dist.) Calif., San Francisco, 1991—. Recipient commendation Calif. Assembly, 1980. Mem. Nat. Bar Assn., ABA, Calif. Bar Assn., Charles Houston Bar Assn., Black C. of C., Phi Alpha Delta. Republican. Baptist. Office: US Dist Ct 1301 Clay St Ste 400S Oakland CA 94612-5225

**ARMSTRONG, STEVEN HOLM,** lawyer. AB in History and Lit., Harvard U.; JD, Columbia U., 1990. Bar: Conn. 1990, N.Y. 1991. Asst. city editor Miami (Fla.) Herald, 1982-87; atty. Townley & Updike, 1990-94; regulatory atty. in antitrust, contracts and govt. rels. Colgate Palmolive Co., N.Y.C., 1995—. Office: Colgate Palmolive Co 300 Park Ave Fl 8 New York NY 10022-7499

**ARMSTRONG, VICTORIA ELIZABETH,** law educator, small business owner, real estate broker; b. San Francisco, Mar. 30, 1950; d. William Tracy and Virginia Lois (Hoessel) A. Student, Stanford U., 1970, Trinity U., Dublin, Ireland, 1970-71; BA with honors, U. Calif., Santa Cruz, 1972; JD, U. Calif., San Francisco, 1975; LLM, U. Calif., Berkeley, 1980. Lic. real estate broker, Calif.; credentialed community coll. tchr., supr., adminstr., Calif. Pvt. practice property mgr. Stockton, Calif., 1968—; atique shop owner Stockton, 1977—; part-time instr. bus., law, and adminstrn. of justice San Joaquin Delta C.C., Stockton, 1977-80, instr. law and real estate, 1980—, mem. acad. senate, 1985-90, parliamentarian of senate, 1986-88, mem. exec. bd., 1986-90, 1st v.p., 1988-90; vis. prof. Sch. Bus. and Pub. Adminstrn., U. of Pacific, Stockton, 1987. Author: Business Law Syllabus, 1980, 2d edit., 1984, Foundations of Business Law, 1986, 2d edit., 1987, Business Law Tutorial (curriculum package), 1989; co-author: Contemporary Business Law Principles and Cases Test Bank, 5th edit., 1993; mng. editor Hastings Law Jour., 1974-75; also articles. Mem. Leadership Stockton, Greater Stockton C. of C., 1981-82; bd. dirs. Stockton Community Forum, 1983-85, Leadership Stockton Alumni Assn., 1986-88; mem. San Joaquin Gen. Hosp. Aux., 1981—; mem. Dameron Hosp. Found., Stockton, 1982—. Recipient 1st ann. Marian Adult Leadership award Cath. Diocese of Stockton, 1988; award for outstanding achievement and accomplishment in ednl. leadership Alpha Gamma Sigma, 1989, award for outstanding teaching performance, 1990; Vesta J. Skehan scholar, 1973; 1066 Found. scholar, 1974-75. Mem. Western Bus. Law Assn. (2d v.p., program chair 1990-91, 1st v.p. 1991-92, editor Proc. 1991, pres.-elect 1992-93, pres. 1993-94), Calif. Tchrs. Assn. (sec. 1982-83, treas. 1984-85, exec. com. 1982-83, 84-85, New Educator award 1982), Women Lawyers San Joaquin County, Calif. Real Estate Edn. Assn., Internat. Platform Assn., Am. Acad. Legal Studies in Bus. (pres.- elect Western region 1992-93), Mensa, AAUW, Ladies Aux. Calif. Pioneer Soc., Phi Alpha Delta (clk., mem. exec. com. 1972-75), Delta Kappa Gamma (parliamentarian, exec. bd. 1986-90). Roman Catholic. Avocations: travel, writing, spectator sports, computers, reading. Home: 2904 Kensington Way Stockton CA 95204-4314 Office: San Joaquin Delta CC 5151 Pacific Ave Stockton CA 95207-6304

**ARMSTRONG, WILLIAM TUCKER, III,** lawyer; b. Houston, Nov. 13, 1947; s. William Tucker Jr. and Jess (Nettles) A.; m. Nancy Bayliss Armstrong, Feb. 18, 1978; children: Will, Anne, Daniel. BA, Am. U., 1969; JD with honors, U. Tex., 1972. Bar: Tex. 1972, U.S. Ct. Appeals (5th cir.) 1972, U.S. Dist. Ct. (so. & we. dists.) Tex. 1978, U.S. Ct. Appeals (11th cir.) 1982, U.S. Ct. Appeals (D.C. cir.) 1983. Staff counsel for inmates Tex. Dept. Corrections, Huntsville, 1972-73; assoc. Foster, Lewis, Langley, Gardner & Banack, San Antonio, 1973-76, shareholder, 1976-96; shareholder Jeffers & Banack, 1996—. Active South Tex. Leukemia Soc., bd. dirs., 1989-92. Mem. Tex. State Bar Assn. (mem. coun. sch. law sect. 1985-87), San Antonio Longhorn Club (pres. 1993-94), San Antonio Tex. Exes (pres. 1995-96), Oak Hills Country Club (dir. 1998—). Methodist. Avocation: golf. E-mail: warmstrong@jeffersbanack.com. Civil rights, General civil litigation. Office: Jeffers & Banack Inc 745 E Mulberry Ave Ste 900 San Antonio TX 78212-3154

**ARNASON, JOEL FREDERICK,** lawyer; b. Grand Forks, N.D., Nov. 11, 1955; s. A. Fred and Helen M. (Rousseau) A.; m. Laurie J. Steinbar, July 30, 1983; children: Joel William, Ann Carroll, Patrick John, James Frederick. BA in Govt., Harvard U., 1978; JD, U. N.D., 1981. Bar: N.D. 1981, Minn. 1982, U.S. Dist. Ct. N.D. 1981, U.S. Ct. Appeals (8th cir.) 1988, U.S. Dist. Ct. Minn. 1992. Pvt. practice Grand Forks, 1981—. Mem. dist. com. Lake Agassiz dist. Boy Scouts Am., 1985—; bd. dirs. Red River Valley chpt. ARC, 1987—, YMCA, Grand Forks, 1988—. Mem. ABA, N.D. Bar Assn., Minn. Bar Assn., K.C., Delta Theta Phi (N.D. chancellor 1983—). Roman Catholic. Avocations: marathon running, road racing. General practice, Criminal, Personal injury. Office: 215 S 4th St Grand Forks ND 58201-4737

**ARNETT, DEBRA JEAN,** lawyer; b. Horton, Kans., July 15, 1956; d. Ralph E. and Margaret J. (Parry) A.; 1 child, Taylor Margaret Arnett. BSW, U. Kans., 1979, JD, 1982. Bar: Kans. 1982, U.S. Dist. Ct. Kans. 1982, U.S. Ct. Appeals (10th cir.) 1985. Atty., dir. McDonald, Tinker, Skaer, Quinn & Herrington, P.A., Wichita, Kans., 1982-91; judge pro tem State of Kans. 6th Judicial Dist., Miami County, 1993—; dir. Hartley, Nicholson, Hartley & Arnett, P.A., Paola, Kans., 1991-99; Law Offices of Debra J. Arnett, Paola, Kans., 1999—; adj. assoc. prof. law Wichita State U., 1984-90. Rsch. asst. (book) Jurisdiction in Civil Actions, 1983. Vol., bd. dirs. Christmas in Oct., Miami County, Kans., sec. 1992—; bd. dirs., sec. Paola Free Libr. Found., 1992—, Lakemary Ctr., 1999—. Recipient Justice Lloyd Kagey Leadership award U. Kans. Sch. Law, 1982, Robert C. Foulston & George Siefkin prize for excellence in appellate advocacy, 1981; mem. Nat. Moot Ct. Team, U. Kans. Sch. Law, 1981; invited Hague (The Netherlands) Treaty Roundtable on Internat. Adoptions, U.S. State Dept., 1993. Mem. ABA (litigation, family law, and ins. practice sects.), Nat. Assn. Women Bus. Owners (sec. Wichita chpt. 1988-89, v.p. 1989-90, pres. 1990-91), Def. Rsch. Inst., Kans. Bar Assn. (sec. litigation sect. 1991-92, pres.-elect 1992-93, pres. 1993-94), Kans. Assn. Def. Counsel (bd. govs. 1983—), Miami County Bar Assn. (treas. 1995—), Wichita Bar Assn., Jenny Mitchell Kellogg Circle (bd. dirs. 1995—), Rotary (Paola chpt.). Family and matrimonial, General civil litigation, General practice. Office: Law Offices of Debra J Arnett 1 W Shawnee PO Box 211 Paola KS 66071-0211

**ARNETT, FOSTER DEAVER,** lawyer; b. Knoxville, Tenn., Nov. 28, 1920; s. Foster Greenwood and Edna (Deaver) A.; m. Jean Medlin, Mar. 3, 1951; children: Melissa Lee Arnett Campbell, Foster Jr. BA, U. Tenn., 1946; LLB, U. Va., 1948. Bar: Va. 1948, Tenn. 1948, U.S. Dist. Ct. (ea. dist.) Tenn. 1949, U.S. Ct. Appeals (6th cir.) 1954, U.S. Supreme Ct. 1958, U.S. Dist. Ct. (ea. dist.) Ky. 1978, U.S. Dist. Ct. (mid. dist.) Tenn. 1983, U.S. Dist. Ct. (ea. and we. dists.) Va. 1990. In practice Knoxville, 1948—; ptnr. Arnett, Draper & Hagood (and predecessors), 1954—; mem. Nat. Conf. Commrs. on Uniform State Laws, 1980-83; life mem. U.S. Ct. Appeals (6th cir.) Jud. Conf. Contbr. articles to profl. jours. Pres. Knox Children's Found., 1959-61, 75-76, East Tenn. Hearing and Speech Ctr., 1963-65, Knoxville Teen Ctr., 1969-71, Knoxville News-Sentinel Charities Inc., 1985—; v.p. Ft. Loudon Assn., 1972-75; del. Rep. Nat. Conv., 1964; bd. dirs., exec. com. Tenn. Mil. Inst., 1973-75; formerly active ARC, Am. Cancer Soc., United Fund. With AUS, 1942-46, PTO; to lt. col. USAR, ret. Decorated Silver Star, Bronze Star, Purple Heart. Fellow Am. Coll. Trial Lawyers (former chair legal ethics com., mem. atty.-client relationship com., mem. other coms.), Internat. Acad. Trial Lawyers (trustee Acad. Found. 1984-91, dean 1988-89, pres. 1992-93, mem. Found. Bd. 1983-92), Internat. Soc. Barristers, Am. Bar Found. (life), Tenn. Bar Found. (charter); mem. ATLA, ABA (mem. standing coms. on unauthorized practice of law and assn. comm., aviation and space law, state cert. legal specialist), Am. Bd. Trial Advs. (adv., charter, 1st pres. Tenn. chpt. 1985-86), Am. Inns of Ct. (charter, master of the bench emeritus Hamilton S. Burnett chpt.), Southea. Legal Found. (legal adv. bd.), Tenn. Bar Assn. (pres. 1968-69), Knoxville Bar Assn. (pres. 1959-60, Govs. award 1989), Internat. Assn. Def. Counsel (sec.-treas. 1981-84), S.E. Def. Counsel Assn. (v.p. 1966), Am. Acad. Hosp. Attys. of Am. Hosp. Assn. (charter), Tenn. Hosp. Assn., Am. Soc. Law, Medicine and Ethics, Fedn. Ins. and Corp. Counsel, Def. Rsch. Inst. (charter), U.S. Supreme Ct. Hist. Soc. (founder), Tenn. Supreme Ct. Hist. Soc. (founder), Federalist Soc., SAR, Scribes, U. Tenn. Nat. Alumni Assn. (pres. 1961-62, chmn. nat. ann. giving program 1961-63), Scabbard and Blade, Scarrabbean, Torchbearer, U. Va. Law Sch. Alumni Assn. (pres. 1991-93, nat. chmn. appeals Law Sch. Found. 1986-88), Raven Soc., 511th Parachute Infantry Regiment Assn., Civitan Club, Farmington Country Club, Charlottesville, Va.), Cherokee Country Club, LeConte Club, Univ. Club (hon.), Men's Cotillion (bd. dirs. 1960-61, 63-64, 66-68, trustee 1962—), Appalachian Club (pres. 1974-76), 511th Parachute Infantry Regiment Assn., Phi Gamma Delta, Phi Delta Phi (hon.), Omicron Delta Kappa (hon.). Presbyterian. General civil litigation, Aviation, Health. Home: 4636 Alta Vista Way Knoxville TN 37919-7605 Office: Arnett Draper & Hagood Ste 2300 First Tennessee Plaza Knoxville TN 37929-2300

**ARNKRAUT, JOE,** legal administrator, writer; b. Newark, Jan. 3, 1960; s. Sam F. and Jill E. Arnkraut. BS in Fin., UCLA, 1990. Legal adminstr. Santa Monica, Calif., 1990—, writing cons., trainer, 1990—. Demorat. Roman Catholic. Avocations: freelance writing, skydiving, spelunking, cross-country and super marathon races. Office: 900 Wilshire Blvd Ste 230 Los Angeles CA 90017-4703

**ARNOFF, FRED JAY,** lawyer; b. Cleve., Oct. 4, 1950; s. Bernard D. and Shirley (Siegelman) A.; m. Gail Fidelholtz, Sept. 1, 1974; children: Steven, Debra. BS, Miami U., Oxford, Ohio, 1972; JD, U. Akron, Ohio, 1975. Bar: Ohio 1975, U.S. Dist. Ct. (no. dist.) Ohio 1975. Assoc. Kenen & Snider, Cleve., 1975-77; ptnr. Persky Shapiro et al, Cleve., 1977—. Vice pres. Jewish Nat. Fund, Cleve., 1987-97. Mem. ABA, Ohio Bar Assn., Cleve. Bar Assn., Cuyahoga County Bar Assn. Bankruptcy, General corporate, Contracts commercial. Office: Persky Shapiro et al 1410 Terminal Tower Cleveland OH 44113

**ARNOLD, CRAIG ANTHONY (TONY ARNOLD),** law educator; b. Montreal, Que., Can., May 22, 1965; came to U.S., 1968; s. Lloyd Edison and Shirley Ann (Gossett) A. BA with highest distinction, U. Kans., 1987; JD with distinction, Stanford U., 1990. Bar: Mo. 1990, U.S. Ct. Appeals (10th cir.) 1990, Tex. 1992, U.S. Dist. Ct. (we. dist.) Tex. 1992, U.S. Ct. Appeals (5th cir.) 1993. Law clk. to James K. Logan, U.S. Ct. Appeals for 10th Cir., Olathe, Kans., 1990-91; assoc. Matthews & Branscomb, P.C., San Antonio, 1991-95; vis. prof. U. P.R. Sch. of Law, 1995; tchg. fellow Stanford Law Sch., 1995-96; asst. prof. Law Sch. Chapman U., 1996-99, assoc. prof., 1999—; dir. Ctr. for Land Resources, 1999—; adj. faculty Trinity U., 1995. Exec. editor Stanford Law and Policy Rev., 1988-90; contbr. articles to legal jours. Organizer, chmn. Jefferson Bicentennial Meeting on Constn., Lawrence, Kans., 1987; mem. Willie Velasquez Book Fund Com., San Antonio, 1992; ordained deacon First Presbyn. Ch., San Antonio, 1994-95, worship leader, 1994-95, strategic planning com., 1994-95, leader classes and Bible studies, 1992-95; co-leader, participant Mission trips to Mex. and Kenya; bd. dirs. Good Samaritan Ctr.; bd. dirs. Fedn. Ecuménica Fe y Accion, San Antonio, 1992-95, Lawyers Com. for Civil Rights Immigrant and Refugee Rights Project, 1993-95; adv. bd. careers in law program North Orange County Regional Occupl. Program, 1998—; adv. bd. Raymond Nichols League of Former Student Leaders, U. Kans., 1999—. Recipient Time Mag. Achievement award; Harry S Truman scholar Truman Scholarship Found., 1985; Rosemary Ginn fellow Mortar Board Nat. Found., 1987. Mem. ABA, State Bar Tex. (Pro Bono Coll.), Phi Beta Kappa. Avocations: hiking, running, horseback riding. Environmental, Real property, Land use and zoning (including planning).

**ARNOLD, FRED ENGLISH,** lawyer; b. Mexico, Mo., May 10, 1938; s. Charles P. and Mary E. (Blackman) A.; m. Dorothy P. Offutt, Dec. 31, 1966; children: Jane E., Charles P. III, Susan J. AB, Harvard U., 1960, LLB, 1963. Bar: Mo. 1963, U.S. Dist. Ct. (ea. dist.) Mo. 1964, U.S. Supreme Ct. 1966. Assoc. Thompson Coburn, St. Louis, 1964-70, ptnr., 1971—. Trustee Mary Inst., St. Louis, 1981-87, v.p., 1985-86; bd. dirs. Repertory Theatre of St. Louis, 1982-88; bd. dirs. Whitfield Sch., St. Louis, 1990-96, pres., 1991-93, Arts & Edn. Coun. Greater St. Louis, 1991-97, vice chmn., 1996-97; adv. com. Jordan Charitable Found., St. Louis, 1975—; bd. curators Ctrl. Meth. Coll., 1997—. Mem. ABA, Mo. Bar Assn., Am. Coll. Real Estate Lawyers, Noonday Club, The Racquet Club. Democrat. Methodist. Real property, General corporate. Home: 6400 Wydown Blvd Saint Louis MO 63105-2200 Office: Thompson Coburn 1 Mercantile Ctr Saint Louis MO 63101-1643

**ARNOLD, GARY D.,** lawyer; b. L.A., July 20, 1951; s. Daryl and Shirley Ann (Haymore) A.; m. Mary Elizabeth Wilcox, Aug. 3, 1974; children: Bonnie, Jeffrey, James. BS, U.S.C., 1973, JD, 1976. Calif. 1976, U.S. Dist. Ct. (south, ea., cen., no. dists.), U.S. Supreme Ct. Assoc. Nordman Camany, Hair & Compton, Oxnard, Calif., 1976-81; ptnr. Nordman Camany, Hair & Compton, Oxnard, 1981-89, Arnold & Back, Thousand Oaks, Calif., 1989-90, Arnold, Mathews, Wojkowski & Zirbel LLP, Thousand Oaks, 1990—. Chmn. Southeast Ventura County YMCA, 1994-96. Recipient Order of the Coif, 1976. Mem. Ventura County Bar Assn. Real property, General corporate, Taxation, general. Office: Arnold Mathews Wojkowski & Zirbel LLP 2901 N Ventura Rd # 240 Oxnard CA 93030-1150

**ARNOLD, GAYLE EDWARD,** lawyer; b. Celina, Ohio, June 24, 1950; s. William Floyd and Mary Ellen (Fast) A.; m. Rebecca Gentile, Aug. 9, 1975 (div. Feb. 1989); m. Sue Anne Cannell, Oct. 27, 1989; children: Leah, Joshua, Elissa, Natalie, Katie, Cameron. BS, Taylor U., 1972; MS, Ball State U., 1975; JD, U. Notre Dame, 1980. Bar: Ohio 1980, U.S. Dist. Ct. (so. dist.) Ohio 1980, U.S. Ct. Appeals (6th cir.) 1987, U.S. Dist. Ct. (no. dist.) Ohio 1993. Tchr. Connersville (Ind.) Pub. Schs., 1972-73; residence hall dir., football coach Taylor U., Upland, Ind., 1973-76; tchr. Eastbrook Pub. Schs., Marion, Ind., 1974-76; assoc. Lane, Alton & Horst, Columbus, Ohio, 1980-85; assoc. Jacobson, Maynard, Tuschman & Kalur, Columbus, 1985-87, mng. ptnr., 1988-97; mng. ptnr. Arnola & Assocs. Co. LPA, 1997—. E-mail: garnold@arnoldlaw.net. Professional liability, Personal injury, General civil litigation. Home: 1370 Wingate Dr Delaware OH 43015-9200 Office: Arnola & Assocs Co LPA 115 W Main St # 200 Columbus OH 43215-5041

**ARNOLD, J. KAREN,** lawyer; b. Cleve.. B in Music Edn., James Madison U., 1969; M in Music, U. Cin., 1971; JD, U. Pitts., 1983. Bar: Pa. 1983, U.S. Dist. Ct. (we. dist.) Pa. 1983, Va. 1990, U.S. Supreme Ct. 1995, U.S. Dist. Ct. (mid. dist.) Pa. 1996; cert. NREMT. Music tchr. Russell Co. Pub. Schs., Lebanon, Va., 1971-72, Laurel (Del.) Pub. Schs., 1972-73, Pitts. Pub. Schs., 1973-77; paralegal Nernberg & Laffey, Pitts., 1977-80; pvt. practice Pitts., 1983-86; asst. pub. defender Centre County Pub. Defender's Office, Bellefonte, Pa., 1987-88; child abuse prosecutor Centre County Dist. Attys. Office, Bellefonte, 1988—; arbitrator Allegheny County Ct. Common Plea, Pitts., 1984-87; spkr. Pa. Optometric Assn., Harrisburg, Pa., 1993; class presenter Pa. State U., State Coll., 1997. Notes and comments editor U. Pitts. Law Rev., 1982-83. Vol. ambulance svc. B.E.M.S., Bellefonte, 1993—; vol. organist various chs., State Coll., 1990—. Full Performance scholar U. Cin., 1969-71. Mem. Nat. Dist. Atty. Assn., Pa. Dist. Attys. Assn., Pa. Bar Assn., Centre County Bar Assn., PDAI Child Abuse Prosecutors Coalition (facilitator trial adv. cause 1994). Office: Centre County Dist Attys Office Fl 4 Courthouse Bellefonte PA 16823

**ARNOLD, LARRY MILLARD,** lawyer; b. L.A., Oct. 22, 1949; s. Daryl and Shirley Ann Arnold; m. Lorelei Krieger, Sept. 13, 1980; children: Alison Marie, Brady David. BA, U. So. Calif., 1971; JD, Calif. Western U., San Diego, 1974. Bar: Calif. 1974, U.S. Dist. Ct. (ctrl. dist.) Calif. 1974, U.S. Dist. Ct. (no. dist.) Calif. 1979, U.S. Ct. Appeals (9th cir.) 1981, U.S. Dist. Ct. (so. dist.) Calif. 1987, U.S. Dist. Ct. Ariz. 1993, U.S. Dist. Ct. Nebr. 1999. Atty. Cummins, White & Brendfubach, L.A., 1974-78; sr. ptnr. Cummins & White, LLP, Newport Beach, Calif., 1978—. Chmn. support com. Orange County 4-H, 1985—. Mem. Young Execs. of Am., Santa Ana Country Club, Balboa Bay Club. Republican. General civil litigation, Insurance, Real property. Office: Cummins & White LLp 2424 SE Bristol St Ste 300 Newport Beach CA 92660-0764

**ARNOLD, MORRIS SHEPPARD,** judge; b. Texarkana, Tex., Oct. 8, 1941. BSEE, U. Ark., 1965, LLB, 1968; LLM, Harvard U., 1969, SJD, 1971; MA (hon.), U. Pa., 1977, JD (hon.), 1986; LLD (hon.), U. Ark., Little Rock. Bar: Ark. 1968, Pa. 1985. Tchg. fellow law Harvard U., 1969-70; from asst. prof. to prof. Ind. U. Law Sch., 1971-76, prof., 1976-77, dean, 1985; prof. law, history U. Pa., 1977-81; Ben J. Altheimer disting. prof. law U. Ark., Little Rock, 1981-84; judge U.S. dist. Ct. (we. dist.) Ark., Ft. Smith, 1985-92, U.S. Cir. Ct. (8th cir.), 1992—; vis. fellow commoner Trinity Coll., Cambridge U., 1978; v.p., dir. office of pres., U. Pa., 1980-81; vis. prof. Stanford (Calif.) U. Law Sch., 1985. Author: Old Tenures and Natura Brevium, 1974, Yearbook 2 Richard II, 1378-79, 1975, On the Laws and Customs of England, 1980, Unequal Laws Unto a Savage Race, 1985, Select Cases of Trespass from the King's Courts, 1307-1399, 2 vols., 1985, 87, Arkansas Colonials, 1986, Colonial Arkansas 1686-1804: A Social and Cultural History, 1991. Rep. gen. counsel, Ark., 1982, chmn., 1983; bd. dirs. Nature Conservancy of Ark., 1982-87, Ark. Arts Ctr., 1981-84. Decorated Chevalier Ordre Palmes Acad. (France); Frank Knox fellow Harvard U., U. London, 1970-71, Mus. Sci. Natural History, 1986. Fellow Am. Soc. Legal History (hon.), Athenaeum Club London, Union League Club Phila., Country Club Little Rock. Office: US Cir Judge PO Box 2060 Little Rock AR 72203-2060

**ARNOLD, REBECCA WILLIAMS,** lawyer, accountant; b. Bandana, Ky., July 5; m. Thomas Laurence Arnold, June 4, 1984; 1 child, Matthew Laurence. BS, Murray (Ky.) State U., 1978, MBA, 1982; JD, Washington U., St. Louis, 1987. Bar: Mo. 1987, Idaho 1988. Acct. Comptroller of Treasury, Nashville, Tenn., 1978-81, Jackson Purchase RECC, Paducah, Ky., 1982-84; atty. Givens Pursley & Huntley, Boise, Idaho, 1988-94, Albertson's Inc., Boise, 1994—. Mem. Jr. League of Boise, 1989—. Mem. Idaho State Bar, Mo. Bar. Real property, Land use and zoning (including planning), General corporate. Home: 3973 Erick Ln Boise ID 83704-4658

**ARNOLD, RICHARD SHEPPARD,** federal judge; b. Texarkana, Tex., Mar. 26, 1936; s. Richard Lewis and Janet (Sheppard) A.; m. Gale Hussman,

June 14, 1958 (divorced); children: Janet Sheppard, Arnold Hart, Lydia Palmer, Arnold Turnipseed; m. Kay Kelley, Oct. 27, 1979. BA summa cum laude, Yale U., 1957; LLB magna cum laude, Harvard U., 1960; LLD, U. Ark., 1992, U. Richmond, 1998. Bar: D.C. 1961, Ark. 1960. Pvt. practice Washington, 1961-64, Texarkana, Ark., 1964-74; law clk. to justice Brennan U.S. Supreme Ct., 1960-61; assoc. Covington & Burling, 1961-64; ptnr. Arnold & Arnold, 1964-74; legis. sec. Gov. of Ark., 1973-74, staff coord., 1974; legis. asst. Senator Bumpers of Ark., Washington, 1975-78; judge U.S. Dist. Ct. (ea. and we. dists.) Ark., 1978-80, U.S. Ct. Appeals (8th cir.), Little Rock, 1980—; chief judge U.S. Ct. Appeals (8th cir.), 1992-98; part-time instr. U. Va. Law Sch., 1962-64; mem. Ark. Constl. Revision Study Commn., 1967-68. Case editor: Harvard Law Rev., 1959-60; contbr. articles to profl. jours. Gen. chmn. Texarkana United Way Crusade, 1969-70; pres. Texarkana Community Chest, 1970-71; mem. vis. com. Harvard Law Sch., 1973-79, U. Chgo. Law Sch., 1983-86, 94-97; candidate for Congress 4th Dist. Ark., 1966, 72; del. Democratic Nat. Conv., 1968, Ark. Constl. Conv., 1969-70; chmn. rules com. Ark. Dem. Com., 1968-74, mem. exec. com., 1972-74; mem. Com. on Legis. Orgn., 1971-72; trustee U. Ark., 1973-74; chmn. budget com. Jud. Conf. of U.S., 1987-96. Fellow Am. Bar Found.; mem. Am. Law Inst. (coun.), Jud. Conf. U.S. (exec. com. 1992-98), Cum Laude Soc., Phi Beta Kappa. Episcopalian. Office: 600 W Capitol Ave Ste 208 Little Rock AR 72201-3321*

**ARNOLD, ROY WILLIAM,** lawyer; b. Pitts., Oct. 9, 1968; s. Roy Henry and Janet Louise (Lee) A.; m. Diana Lynn Whipps, Aug. 19, 1995. BA, U. Pa., 1990; JD, U. Pitts., 1993. Bar: Pa. 1993, U.S. Dist. Ct. (we. dist.) Pa. 1993, U.S. Ct. Appeals (3d cir.) 1995. Law clk. to Hon. Alan N. Bloch Pitts., 1993-95; assoc. Reed, Smith, Shaw & McClay, Pitts., 1995—; dir. Pa. Consumers Bd., Phila., 1989-90; econ. rsch. asst. Greater Phila. Econ. Devel. Coalition, Phila., 1989. Mem. Leadership Devel. Initiative, Pitts., 1996-97, North Hills Estate Civic Assn., Pitts., 1996-97; vol. Pitts. Cares, 1996-97. Mem. ABA, Allegheny County Bar Assn., Pi Kappa Phi, Pi Gamma Mu. General civil litigation, Securities, Contracts commercial. Office: Reed Smith Shaw & McClay 435 6th Ave Ste 2 Pittsburgh PA 15219-1886

**ARNOLD, W. H. (DUB ARNOLD),** state supreme court justice. BA, Henderson State U., 1957; LLB, Ark. Law Sch., 1962. Dep. prosecuting atty. Clark County, Ark., 1965-66; prosecuting atty. 8th Jud. Dist., State of Ark., 1969-72; chmn.hief justice Ark. Workers Compensation Commn., 1973-77; prosecuting atty. 9th Jud. Dist. East, State of Ark., 1981-90; mcpl. judge Clark County, 1979-80; cir./chancery judge 9th Jud. Dist. East, State of Ark., 1991-96; chief justice Ark. Supreme Ct., 1997—; law educator Ouachita Bapt. U., Arkadelphia, Ark., 1975-76, Ark. Law Enforcement Acad., 1990, Garland County C.C., 1993; lectr. Ark. Prosecuting Atty.'s Assn., 1988. Office: Justice Bldg 625 Marshall St Ste 1230 Little Rock AR 72201-1052*

**ARNOLD, WILLIAM MCCAULEY,** lawyer; b. Waco, Tex., May 3, 1947; s. Watson Caulfield and Mary Rebecca (Maxwell) A.; m. Karen Axtell, May 17, 1980; children: Margaret McCauley, William Axtell. BA, Duke U., 1969; JD, U. Tex., 1972. Bar: Tex. 1973, Va. 1975, D.C. 1977, Md. 1983, U.S. Dist. Ct. (ea. dist.) Va. 1975, U.S. Ct. Appeals (4th cir.) 1977, U.S. Ct. Claims 1977, U.S. Supreme Ct. 1978. Spl. atty. U.S. Dept. Justice, Newark, 1973-75; asst. county atty. County of Fairfax, Va., 1975-78; ptnr. Cowles, Rinaldi & Arnold, Ltd., Fairfax, 1978-95; ptnr. McCandlish & Lillard, Fairfax, 1995—; instr. No. Va. Community Coll., Alexandria. Pres. Clifton Betterment Assn., Va., 1979-81; chmn. Clifton Planning Commn., 1980-85; mem. Clifton Town Council, 1985—; bd. dirs. Clifton Gentlemen's Social Club, 1981-84. Mem. ABA, Va. State Bar Assn., Fairfax County Bar Assn., Va. Trial Lawyers Assn., Am. Arbitration Assn. (arbitrator), Associated Builders and Contractors (counsel to bd. dirs.). State civil litigation, Construction. Office: McCandlish & Lillard PC 11350 Random Hills Rd Ste 500 Fairfax VA 22030-6044

**ARNSDORFF, FRANCES GEORGE,** court administrator; b. Savannah, Ga., Nov. 26, 1957; d. Frank Vreeland and Allene Elizabeth (Wilkie) George; m. Glenn Andrew Arnsdorff, Mar. 9, 1985. BS in Math. Scis., Armstrong State Coll., 1980. Programmer/analyst Chatham County MIS, Savannah, 1980-87, systems analyst, 1987-92; deputy ct. adminstr. Superior Ct., Ea. Jud. Cir., Savannah, 1992—. Grad. Leadership Savannah; treas. Savannah Bus. and Profl. Women, 1991—; mem. Jr. League, Savannah; pres. Girl Scout Coun. of Savannah, 1995-99. Young Careerist, Savannah BPW, 1991, Disting. Svc. award nominee Savannah Jaycees, 1993, others. Mem. AAUW (sec. 1993—), Ga. Assn. Ct. Mgmt., Nat. Assn. for Ct. mgmt., Nat. Assn. Pretrial Svcs. Agys., Armstrong Atlantic State U. Alumnae (pres. 1992-94, Outstanding Alumni Svc. award 1994), Alpha Gamma Delta (province dir. 1992—). Avocations: crafts, studying history, travel. Office: Superior Ct Adminstrn 133 Montgomery St Rm 116 Savannah GA 31401-3238

**ARON, JERRY E.,** lawyer; b. Lancaster, Pa., Oct. 1, 1951. BS, Drexel U., 1974; JD, Stetson U., 1977. Bar: Fla. 1977. Lawyer Gunster, Yoakley, Valdes-Fauli & Stewart, West Palm Beach, Fla.; teaching asst. legal rsch. and writing Stetson Coll. Law, 1975-76; chmn. Palm Beach County Realtor/ Atty. Joint Com., 1983-84. Editor-in-chief Stetson Law Rev., 1976-77. Mem. ABA (real property, probate and trust law sect., econs. of law practice sect., chmn. standing com. lawyers' title guaranty funds), Am. Coll. Real Estate Attys., Fla. Bar (exec. coun. real property probate and trust law sect. 1980—, exec. com. 1985—, sec. 1985-88, dir. real property divsn. 1988-90, chmn.-elect. 1990-91, chmn. 1991-92, chmn. publs. 1980-85, co-chair action line com. 1984-85, liason with title insurers 1984-85, energy law com., environ. land use sect., pub. utilities law com., Annual Svc. award), Palm Beach County Bar Assn., Blue Key, Phi Delta Phi. Real property, Contracts commercial, Construction. Office: Gunster Yoakley Valdes-Fauli & Stewart Phillips Pt 777 S Flagler Dr Ste 500 West Palm Beach FL 33401-6161

**ARON, MARK G.,** lawyer, transportation executive; b. Hartford, Conn., Jan. 27, 1943; s. Samuel H. and Florence A.; m. Cindy Sondik, June 1, 1966; 1 child, Samantha. B.A. summa cum laude, Trinity Coll., 1965; LL.B., Harvard U., 1968. Bar: Va., Mass., D.C. Asst. prof. law Osgood Hall Law Sch., York U., Toronto, 1968-70; assoc. Goulston & Storrs, Boston, 1970-71; atty., asst. gen. counsel then dep. gen. counsel U.S. Dept. Transp., Washington, 1971-81; asst. gen. counsel CSX, Richmond, Va., 1981-83, gen. counsel spl. projects, 1983-85; sr. v.p. corp. svcs. Chessie System R.R., Balt., 1985-86; sr. v.p. law and pub. affairs CSX Corp., Richmond, 1986-95, exec. v.p. law and pub. affairs, 1995—. Trustee Va. Union U.; bd. dirs. Va. Literacy Found., Theatre IV, Ctrl. Va. Pub. Broadcasting; mem. Or Ami Cong. Mem. Va. Bar Assn., Mass. Bar Assn., D.C. Bar Assn., Country Club Va. Office: CSX Corp One James Ctr PO Box 85629 901 E Cary St Richmond VA 23285-5629

**ARON, ROBERTO,** lawyer, writer, educator; b. Mendoza, Argentina, Nov. 1, 1915; s. David and Catalina (Trostanetzky) A.; m. Catalina Berstein, May 1, 1940 (dec. Oct. 1965); children: Jaim, Sylvia, Daniel; m. Eva Coriat, Dec. 14, 1968; stepchildren: Sonia, Aileen (twins). BA in Law, U. Chile, 1943; LLM in Internat. Law, NYU, 1977, LLM in Corp. Law, 1979, M in Hebrew and Judaic Studies, 1995. Bar: Israel 1960. Sr. ptnr. Aron and Cia, Santiago, Chile, 1943-57, Arón, Tamir and Arón, Tel Aviv, 1960—; adj. tchr. NYU, 1983; lectr. Tel Aviv U., 1985—, bd. govs., 1982; vis. prof. faculty of law U. Chile, 1991; bd. dirs. Otzar Itiashvut Hayeudim Bank, Tel Aviv; mem. Israeli del. to UN, 1975; participant Oxford Trial Advocacy Program. Co-author: How To Prepare Witnesses for Trial, 1985, Trial Communications Skills, 1986, Cross-Examination and Impeachment of Witnesses, 1989. Mem. Nat. Inst. Trial Advocacy (participant workshops on teaching trial advocacy Harvard Law Sch.), Advocates Assn., Assn. Trial Lawyers Am. Avocations: golf, pipe collecting. Contracts commercial, General civil litigation, Criminal. Home: 985 5th Ave Apt 12A New York NY 10021-0142 Office: Arón, Tamir and Arón 630 3rd Ave New York NY 10017-6705 also: Arón and Arón, 48 Derech Petach Tikva Bldg B, Tel Aviv 66184, Israel

**ARONBERG, DAVID ANDREW,** lawyer; b. Miami Beach, Fla., May 4, 1971. BA, Harvard U., 1993, JD, 1996. Bar: Fla. 1996, D.C. 1999. Assoc. Steel Hector & Davis LLP, Miami, 1996—. General civil litigation. Office: Steel Hector & Davis LLP 200 S Biscayne Blvd Ste 4000 Miami FL 33131-2310

**ARONOVITZ, CORY JAY,** lawyer; b. Phila., Mar. 15, 1968; s. Arnold and Arlene Aronovitz; m. Cynthia Gayle Aronovitz, Oct. 12, 1997. BA, Muhlenberg Coll., 1990; JD, John Marshall Law Sch., 1993. Bar: Ill. 1993, U.S. Dist. Ct. (no. dist.) Ill. 1993, U.S. Dist. Ct. N.J. 1995. Legal counsel Ill. Gaming Bd., Chgo., 1993-94; atty. Cooper, Perski, et al, Atlantic City, N.J., 1994-98, Rudnick & Wolfe, Chgo., 1998—. Author: Casino Gaming: Policy, Economics and Regulation, 1996, Gambling Public Policies and Social Sciences, 1997; contbr. articles to profl. jours. Recipient The John Rosecrance gambling rsch. paper competition award, The Inst. for Study Gambling and Comml. Gaming, U. Nev., 1994. Mem. Internat. Assn. Gambling Attys., Casino Mgmt. Assn., Coun. Problem Gambling. Entertainment, Legislative, General civil litigation. Office: Rudnick & Wolfe 203 N Lasalle St Ste 1800 Chicago IL 60601-1210

**ARONOVSKY, RONALD GEORGE,** lawyer; b. San Francisco, Oct. 1, 1955; s. George N. and Eleanor (Milovich) A. BA in History, U. Calif., Berkeley, 1977; JD, U. Calif., 1980. Bar: Calif. 1980, U.S. Dist. Ct. (no. dist.) Calif. 1980, U.S. Ct. Appeals (9th cir.) 1981, U.S. Dist. Ct. (ea. dist.) Calif. 1982, U.S. Dist. Ct. (cen. dist.) Calif. 1988, U.S. Supreme Ct. 1985. Jud. extern Calif. Supreme Ct., San Francisco, 1979; law clk. to Judge Alfred T. Goodwin U.S. Ct. Appeals (9th cir.), Portland, Oreg., 1980-81; assoc. Orrick, Herrington & Sutcliffe, San Francisco, 1982-86, ptnr., 1987-95; ptnr. Alden, Aronovsky & Sax, San Francisco, 1995—. Contbr. articles to profl. publs. Mem. ABA, Am. Judicature Soc., 9th Cir. Hist. Soc., Order of Coif, Phi Beta Kappa. General civil litigation, Securities, Environmental. Office: Alden Aronovsky and Sax 235 Montgomery St Fl 28 San Francisco CA 94104-3115

**ARONS, MARK DAVID,** lawyer; b. Durham, N.C., Apr. 26, 1958; s. Marvin Shield Arons and Cyvia (Russian) Peters. BA, Vanderbilt U., 1980; JD, Case Western Res. U., 1983. Bar: Conn. 1983, U.S. Dist. Ct. Conn. 1983, U.S. Ct. Appeals (2d cir.) 1984, U.S. Supreme Ct. 1988; diplomate Nat. Inst. Trial Advocacy; bd. cert. civil trial lawyer Nat. Bd. Trial Advocacy. Ptnr. Willinger Shepro Tower and Bucci, P.C., Bridgeport, Conn. Notes editor Case Western Res. Jour. Internat. Law, 1983. Bd. dirs. B'nai B'rith Youth Orgn., New Haven, Congregation B'nai Jacob, Woodbridge, Conn., The Children's Ctr., Hamden; bd. dirs., coord. coun. Children in Crisis; mem. Jewish Fedn.-Young Leadership, New Haven, 1987-88; organizing com. Spl. Olympics World Games, New Haven, Conn., 1995. Mem. ABA, Conn. Bar Assn., Assn. Trial Lawyers Am., Conn. Trial Lawyers Assn. (pub. rels. com.), New Haven Young Lawyers (program chmn. 1991-92), New Haven Jaycees (bd. dirs. 1985-87), Alpha Epsilon Pi (asst. regional gov.). Democrat. General civil litigation, Personal injury, General practice. Office: Willinger Shepro Tower and Bucci PC 855 Main St Bridgeport CT 06604-4915

**ARONSKY, JEFFREY ADAM,** lawyer; b. N.Y.C., Aug. 10, 1969; s. Theodore Steven and Sharon Rose Aronsky; m. Jill Suzanne Wolfman, July 2, 1998. BA, U. Md., 1990; JD, U. Fla., 1993. Atty. Newman & Okun, P.C., N.Y.C., 1994-98; pvt. practice law N.Y.C., 1998—. Fax: 212-577-6776. E-mail: JefArons@aol.com. Office: 170 Broadway Rm 1002 New York NY 10038-4154

**ARONSON, MARK BERNE,** consumer advocate; b. Pitts., Aug. 24, 1941; s. Richard J. and Jean (DeRoy) A.; m. Ellen Jane Askin, July 20, 1970 (div. Oct. 1993); children: Robert M., Andrew A., Michael D. BS in Econs., U. Pa., 1962; JD, U. Pitts., 1965. Pvt. practice Pitts., 1965-90; sr. ptnr. Behrend & Aronson, Pitts., 1967-80, Behrend, Aronson & Morrow, Pitts., 1980-83; pres. Current Concepts Corp., Pitts., 1992—; real estate broker, 1972-94; cons. to attys., 1991—; pvt. consumer advocate, 1991—. Past pres. Community Day Sch., Pitts., Rodef Shalom Jr. Congregation; trustee Rodef Shalom Congregation, Pitts, 1979-87, Pitts. Child Guidance Found., 1987-90; mem. Pitts. Coun. on Edn., 1986-89. Mem. Am. Arbitration Assn. (mem. nat. panel arbitrators), Masons (master). Republican. Jewish. State civil litigation, Real property, General practice. Address: Ste 506-507 Churchill Mansions 2525 Greensburg Pike Pittsburgh PA 15221-3684

**ARONSTEIN, MARTIN JOSEPH,** law educator, lawyer; b. N.Y.C., Jan. 25, 1925; s. William and Mollie (Mintz) A.; m. Sally K. Rosenau, Sept. 18, 1948; children: Katherine Aronstein Porter, David M., James K. BE, Yale U., 1944; MBA, Harvard U., 1948; LLB, U. Pa., 1965. Bar: Pa. 1965. Bus. exec. Phila., 1948-65; assoc. firm Obermayer, Rebmann, Maxwell & Hippel, Phila., 1965-67; partner Obermayer, Rebmann, Maxwell & Hippel, 1968-69; assoc. prof. law U. Pa., 1969-72, prof., 1972-78; counsel firm Ballard, Spahr, Andrews & Ingersoll, Phila., 1978-80; partner Ballard, Spahr, Andrews & Ingersoll, 1980-81; prof. law U. Pa., 1981-86, prof. emeritus, 1986—; of counsel firm Morgan, Lewis & Bockius, Phila., 1986-95. Contbr. articles to law revs.; mem. Permanent Editorial Bd. Uniform Comml. Code, 1978-80, counsel, 1980-87, counsel emeritus, 1987—. Served with USN, 1943-46. Mem. Am. Law Inst., ABA (reporter com. on stock certs. 1973-77, chmn. subcom. on investment securities 1982-84), Phila. Bar Assn., Order of Coif, Sigma Xi, Tau Beta Pi. Home: 1820 Rittenhouse Sq Philadelphia PA 19103-5832 Office: Morgan Lewis & Bockius 1701 Market St Philadelphia PA 19103-2903

**ARP, RANDALL CRAIG,** lawyer; b. Luverne, Minn., Jan. 1, 1957; s. Richard Christian and Ruth Ann (Kadinger) A.; m. Jean Ellen Pickard, Apr. 9, 1983; children: Ryan C., Richard C. BA, Moorhead State U., 1979; JD, U. Colo., 1982. Bar: Colo. 1982, U.S. Dist. Ct. Colo. 1982. Assoc. Miller, Makkai & Dowdle, Denver, 1982-88, ptnr., 1988—. Mem. Colo. Bar Assn., Colo. Trial Lawyers Assn., Adams County Bar Assn. Democrat. Roman Catholic. Avocations: golf, raquet ball, softball, hunting, woodworking. Bankruptcy, Family and matrimonial, Consumer commercial. Office: Myers Bradley Devitt & Arp 2201 Ford St Golden CO 80401-2425

**ARPEN, TRACEY I., JR.,** lawyer; b. Jacksonville, Fla., Oct. 29, 1947; s. Tracey I. and Martha T. Arpen; m. Sandra H. Heiss, Aug. 29, 1970; children: Matthew T., Katherine J. BA, U. Fla., 1969, JD, 1972. Bar: Fla. 1973. Assoc., then ptnr. Marks, Gray, Conroy & Gibbs, Jacksonville, 1979-93; asst. gen. counsel City of Jacksonville, Office of Gen. Counsel, 1993-98, dep. gen. counsel, 1998—; chmn. State Atty.'s select com. on environ. crime, Jacksonville, 1991-92. Pres. Jacksonville Cmty. Coun., 1991-92, Greenscape of Jacksonville, 1991; mem. Jacksonville 2010 Comprehensive Plan Adv. Com., 1989-90. Capt. U.S. Army, 1973-76. Mem. Fla. Planning and Zoning Assn. Lutheran. Avocations: skiing, travel. Home: 3489 Loretto Rd Jacksonville FL 32223-1910 Office: Jacksonville Gen Counsel Office 117 W Duval St Ste 480 Jacksonville FL 32202-3700

**ARQUIT, KEVIN JAMES,** lawyer; b. Ithaca, N.Y., Sept. 11, 1954; s. Gordon James and Nora (Harris) A. BA cum laude, St. Lawrence U., 1975; JD cum laude, Cornell U., 1978. Bar: Ohio 1978, N.Y. 1980, U.S. Dist. Ct. (so. and ea. dists.) N.Y. 1980, U.S. Dist. Ct. (we. dist.) N.Y. 1983, U.S. Dist. Ct. (no. dist.) Calif. 1983, U.S. Ct. Appeals (3d cir.) 1983,, U.S. Dist. Ct. (no. dist.) N.Y. 1985, U.S. Ct. Appeals(2d cir.) 1985, U.S. Supreme Ct. 1989. Assoc. Arter & Hadden, Cleve., 1978, Fish & Neave, N.Y.C., 1978-83, Harris, Beach & Wilcox, Rochester, N.Y., 1983-86; atty. advisor to chmn. FTC, Washington, 1986-87, chief staff, 1987-88, gen. counsel, 1988-89; dir. Bur. Competition, Washington, 1989-92; ptnr., head Rogers & Wells Antitrust Practice Group, N.Y.C., 1992—. Republican. Roman Catholic. Antitrust. Office: Rogers & Wells 200 Park Ave Fl 8E New York NY 10166-0800

**ARRAIZA, MANUEL F.,** lawyer; b. 1937. BA, U. P.R.; LLB. Bar: P.R. 1960. Pvt. practice Vega Baja, P.R. Mem. P.R. Bar Assn. (pres.). General civil litigation, Criminal. Office: PO Box 4603 Vega Baja PR 00694-4603*

**ARRINGTON, JAMES EDGAR, JR.,** lawyer; b. Richlands, Va., Aug. 3, 1947; s. James and Daisy (Morefield) A. BS, East Tenn. State U., 1969; JD, U. Richmond, 1975. Bar: Va. 1976. Atty. Browning, Morefield, Schelin & Arrington, Lebanon, Va., 1975-84; mgmt. cons. Arrington Cons. Inc., Lebanon, 1984-87; atty., mng. ptnr. Arrington Schelin & Herrell, P.C., Bristol, Va., 1987—; substitute judge 29th Cir., Va., 1979-81, spl. justice, 1978-81. Dir. South West Va. Legal Aid, Castlewood, Va., 1979-82; advisor Boys Scouts, Grundy, Va., 1969—; dir. Mental Health, Lebanon, 1989-92. Sgt. U.S. Army, 1969-71. Fellow So. Trial Lawyers Assn; mem. Am. Trial Lawyers Assn. (advocate), Va. State Bar Assn. (advt. com.), Va. Trial Lawyers Assn. Democrat. Avocations: commercial pilot, advanced scuba diver, karate. General civil litigation, Personal injury, Contracts commercial. Office: Arrington Schelin & Herrell 1315 Euclid Ave Bristol VA 24201-3830

**ARRINGTON, JOHN LESLIE, JR.,** lawyer; b. Pawhuska, Okla., Oct. 15, 1931; s. John Leslie and Grace Louise (Moore) A.; m. Elizabeth Anne Waddington, 1956 (div.); children: Elizabeth Anne, John Leslie III, Winifred L., Katherine M.; m. Linda Vance, 1972. Grad., Lawrenceville Sch., 1949; AB, Princeton U., 1953; JD, Harvard U., 1956, LLM, 1957. Bar: Okla. 1956, U.S. Supreme Ct. 1960. Assoc. Arrington, Kihle, Gaberino & Dunn and predecessor firms, Tulsa, 1957-61, ptnr., 1961-93, chmn., CEO, 1994-96; gen. counsel ONEOK, Inc., 1997-98; of counsel Gable & Gotwals, Tulsa, 1998—; chmn. bd. dirs. Woodland Bank of Tulsa, 1979-94. Prin. draftsman Okla. Supreme Ct. rules governing disciplinary proceedings, 1980-81; bd. dirs. Tulsa County Legal Aid Soc., 1965-70, pres. 1967-70; bd. dirs. Tulsa Family Mental Health Ctr., 1982-89. Named Outstanding Young Man, Tulsa Jaycees, 1963. Mem. ABA, Tulsa County Bar Assn. (Young Lawyer award 1962, pres. 1970, Pres.'s award 1984, Professionalism award 1993), Okla. Bar Assn. (mem. profl. responsiblity commn. 1977-84, vice chmn. 1983-84, Disting. svc. award 1984, Golden Gavel award 1985, Pres.'s award 1991, Masonic award for ethics 1995), So. Hills Country Club (Tulsa), Princeton Club (N.Y.C.). Republican. Episcopalian. General corporate, Public utilities, General civil litigation. Home: 2300 Riverside Dr Unit 3E Tulsa OK 74114-2402 Office: 100 W 5th St Ste 1000 Tulsa OK 74103-4293

**ARSENAULT, GARY JOSEPH,** lawyer, accountant; b. Bayshore, N.Y., June 16, 1956; s. Eudore Joseph and Alice Marie (Desautels) A.; m. Reneé Bennett, Jan. 21, 1984 (div. Nov. 1987). AA, Suffolk C.C., Seldon, N.Y., 1976; BS in Acctg., La. State U., 1979; JD cum laude, So. U., 1994. Bar: La. 1994, U.S. Dist. Ct. (we. and mid. dists.) La. 1995. Acct. Otto Danielson, Ltd., Copenhagen, 1979, Hannis T. Bourgeois, CPA's, Baton Rouge, 1980-84; ptnr. Bosch & Arsenault, CPA's, Baton Rouge, 1984-91; pvt. practice acctg., Gary J. Arsenault, CPA, Baton Rouge, 1991-94; assoc. Neblett, Beard & Arsenault, Alexandria, La., 1994—. Contbr. article to profl. jour. Amb. Friendship Force, Baton Rouge, 1987-89; chmn. Internat. Assn. Students in Econs. and Bus. Mgmt., La. State U., Baton Rouge, 1988-91. Mem. ATLA, Soc. La. CPA's, Alexandria Bar Assn. Roman Catholic. Avocations: cycling, skiing, tennis, racquetball, hunting. Admiralty, Personal injury, Workers' compensation. Office: Neblett Beard & Arsenault PO Box 1190 Alexandria LA 71309-1190

**ARSENAULT, RICHARD J.,** lawyer; b. Aug. 2, 1954. BA, SUNY; JD, La. State U. Bar: La., Tex., Colo., Washington, U.S. Dist. Ct. (ea. and we. dists.) La., U.S. Ct. Appeals (5th and 11th cirs.), U.S. Supreme Ct. Sr. ptnr. Neblett, Beart & Arsenault, Alexandria, La.; mem. faculty La. State U. Law Ctr., Baton Rouge, 1991—. Mem. editorial bd. The Forum, 1982-86, Maritime Law Reporter, 1987—. Eucharistic minister, lector, St. Frances Xavier Cathedral, 1993—, mem. stewardship com., 1994; co-chmn. Ann. Hope House, 1994; vice chmn. ann. function Arthritis Found., Alexandria, 1994. Mem. ABA (admiralty and maritime law com., port watch subcom.), ATLA (chmn.-elect sect. on ins., negligence, worker's compensation and admiralty law 1994-95, chmn. admiralty sect. 1995-96), La. Bar Assn. (jour. editor 1983—, chmn. sect. insu., negligence, compensation and admiralty law 1986-87, governanc com. 1995-96, continuing legal edn. program com. 1996, ho. dels. 9th jud. dist. 1996-98, long range planning com. 1996—, others), Alexandria Bar Assn. (jour. editor 1983, pres. 1991-92), La. Trial Lawyers Assn. (editor monthly publ., pres.'s adv. com. 1983), So. Trial Lawyers Assn. (bd. govs. 1988—), Am. Inns of Ct. (mem. exec. com. 1992-95, pres. 1992-93), Miss. Trial Lawyers Assn., Southeastern Admiralty Law Inst., Tex. Trial Lawyers Assn. Office: Neblett Beart & Arsenault PO Box 1190 Alexandria LA 71309-1190

**ARTERBURN, DAVID K.,** prosecutor; b. Gothenburg, Nebr., June 13, 1957; s. Keith Lock and Hazel Lorraine Arterburn; m. Cindy Lynn Sheldon, May 24, 1980; children: Jeffrey, Kaitlyn, Chad. AA, York Coll., 1977; BA, U. Nebr., 1978, MA, 1982, JD, 1985. Bar: Nebr., U.S. Dist. Ct. Nebr. Grad. tchg. asst. U. Nebr., Lincoln, 1980-81; law clk. Lancaster County Dist. Ct., Lincoln, 1984-85; ptnr. Freeman and Arterburn, McCook, Nebr., 1986-91; chief dep. county atty. Red Willow County Attys. Office, McCook, 1986-91; atty., advisor U.S. Dept. Health and Human Svcs., Omaha, 1991-92; asst. atty. gen. Nebr. Dept. Justice, Lincoln, 1992—; instr., adj. faculty McCook C.C., 1987-91. Mem. Red Willow County Child Protection Team, McCook, 1986-90, York (Nebr.) Coll. Bd. Advisors, 1987-97; bd. dirs. Cornhusker Christian Children's Found., McCook, 1991—. Recipient Law Enforcement Coordinating Com. award State Nebr., 1997. Mem. Nat. Dist. Attys. Assn., Nebr. State Bar Assn., Nebr. County Attys. Assn. Avocation: coaching youth soccer and baseball. Office: Nebr Dept Justice 2115 State Capitol Lincoln NE 68509

**ARTERTON, JANET BOND,** judge; b. 1944. BA, Mt. Holyoke Coll., 1966; JD, Northeastern U., 1977. Law clk. to Hon. Herbert J. Stern U.S. Dist. Ct. N.J., 1977-78; ptnr. Garrison & Arterton, 1978-95; judge U.S. Dist. Ct. Conn., New Haven, 1995—. Fellow Am. Bar Found., Conn. Bar Found.; mem. ATLA, Nat. Employment Lawyers Assn., Conn. Employment Lawyers Assn., Conn. State Trial Lawyers Assn. (bd. govs. 1990-95), Conn. Bar Assn. (mem. adv. com. state ct. rules 1992, mem. fed. jud. selection com. 1991-93, mem. exec. com. women and the law sect. 1990-93, chairperson fed. practice sect. 1993-95. Office: US Dist Ct Conn 141 Church St New Haven CT 06510-2030

**ARTHER, RICHARD OBERLIN,** polygraphist, educator; b. Pitts., May 20, 1928; s. William Churchill Sr. and Florence Lind (Oberlin) A.; m. Mary-Esther Wuensch, Sept. 12, 1951; children: Catherine, Linda, William III. BS, Mich. State U., 1951; MA, Columbia U., 1960. Chief assoc. John E. Reid and Assocs., Chgo., 1951-53; dir. N.Y.C. office John E. Reid and Assocs., 1953-58; pres. Sci. Lie Detection, Inc., N.Y.C., 1958—, Nat. Tng. Ctr. Polygraph Sci., N.Y.C., 1958—. Author: Interrogation for Investigators, 1958, The Scientific Investigator, 1964, 6th edit., Arther Polygraph Reference Guide, 1964—; editor: Jour. Polygraph Sci., 1966—. Fellow Acad. Cert. Polygraphists (exec. dir. 1962—), Am. Polygraph Assn. (founding mem.), Am. Assn. Police Polygraphists (founding mem., Polygraphist of Yr. 1980), N.Y. State Polygraphists (founder), N.J. Polygraphists (founder). Office: Sci Lie Detection Inc 200 W 57th St Ste 1400 New York NY 10019-3211

**ARTHUR, LINDSAY GRIER,** retired judge, author, editor; b. Mpls., July 30, 1917; s. Hugh and Alice (Grier) A.; m. Jean Johansen, Sept. 19, 1940; children: Lindsay G., Mollie K., Julie A. AB, Princeton U., 1939; postgrad., Harvard U., 1939-40; LLB, JD, U. Minn., 1946. Bar: Minn. 1946, U.S. Dist. Ct. Minn. 1948, U.S. Supreme Ct. 1964. Lawyer Nieman, Bosard & Arthur, Mpls., 1946-54; alderman Mpls. City Coun., 1951-54; judge Mcpl. Ct., Mpls., 1954-61; chief judge juvenile div. Dist. Ct., Mpls., 1961-79, 87-93, judge felony, civil div., 1979-83; chief judge mental health div. Dist. Ct., 1983-87; mediator, 1987—; arbitrator civil and family cts., 1991—. Author: Twin Cities Uncovered, 1996, A Manual for Mediators, 1995; editor: Digest of Juvenile and Family Law, 1983-93; contbr. articles to profl. jours. Bd. dirs. Nat. Ctr. State Cts., Williamsburg, 1974-77, Metro YMCA, Mpls. area, 1981-85; chmn. trustees Bethlehem Luth. Ch., 1979-80. Lt. USNR, 1942-45, PTO. Mem. Nat. Coun. Juvenile Ct. Judges (pres. 1972-73, Jud. scholar 1985—), ABA (disabilities com. 1984-89), Am. Law Inst. (advisor divorce law 1989-93). Avocations: writing, walking. Home: 1201 Yale Pl Apt 205 Minneapolis MN 55403-1955

**ARTIGLIERE, RALPH,** lawyer, educator; b. Morristown, N.J., Mar. 1, 1947; s. Fiore Joseph and Mary (Bolcar) A.; m. Gale Anderson, June 14, 1969; children: William Michael, Adam Robert. BS in Engring., U.S. Mil. Acad., 1969; JD, U. Fla., 1977. Bar: Fla. 1977, U.S. Dist. Ct. (mid. dist.) Fla. 1978, U.S. Ct. Appeals (11th cir.) 1981, U.S. Dist. Ct. (no. dist.) Fla. 1984. Project mgr. Ryder System, Inc., Miami, Fla., 1974-75; cons. Ryder System, Inc., Gainesville, Fla., 1975-77; atty. Holland & Knight, Lakeland, Fla., 1977-81, Lane, Trohn, Clarke, Bertrand & Williams, Lakeland, Fla., 1981-91, Anderson & Artigliere, P.A., Lakeland, Fla., 1991—; mem. jury instrn. com. Fla. Supreme Ct., Tallahassee, 1990—; aj. prof. U. South Fla., Tampa, 1991-92; instr. legal writing U. Fla. Law Sch., Gainesville, 1976-77. Author: (chpt.) Florida Forms of Jury Instruction, 1990, Drafting and Using

Jury Instructions in Civil Cases, 1998. Pres. Santa Fe High Sch. Bd., Lakeland, 1985; chmn. 10th Cir. Jud. Nominating Commn., Polk County, Fla., 1985-86; bd. dirs. Polk Pub. Mus., Lakeland, 1987-89, United Cerebral Palsy of Polk County, Lakeland, 1980-82. Capt. U.S. Army, 1969-74, Vietnam. Decorated Bronze Star, Air medal with "V"; recipient Fla. Bar Pro Bono award Fla. Supreme Ct., 1982. Fellow Am. Coll. Trial Lawyers; mem. ABA, FBA, Fla. Bar (cert. civil trial lawyer 1993—, chmn. CLE com. 1996-97), Polk County Trial Lawyers Assn. (pres. 1995-96), Phi Kappa Phi, Order of Coif. Republican. Avocations: fly fishing. Personal injury, General civil litigation, Insurance. Home: 138 Sands Point Dr Tierra Verde FL 33715-2211 Office: Anderson & Artigliere PA 4927 Southfork Dr Lakeland FL 33813-2043

**ARTIMEZ, JOHN EDWARD, JR.,** lawyer; b. Wheeling, W.Va., Aug. 20, 1956; s. John Edward and Wilma Mae (Wilson) A.; m. Linda Rae Richmond, Apr. 11, 1981; 1 child, Brittany Rae. BA magna cum laude, W.Va. U., 1978, JD, 1981. Bar: W.Va. 1981, U.S. Dist. Ct. (no. and so. dists.) W.Va. 1981. Assoc. Bachmann, Hess et al, Wheeling, 1981-85, ptnr., 1986-89; pvt. practice Artimez Law Offices, Moundsville, W.Va., 1989—. Mem. ABA, Assn. Trial Lawyers Am., W.Va. Trial Lawyers Assn., Moundsville Country Club, Elks. Republican. Methodist. Avocations: skiing, golf, scuba diving. Federal civil litigation, State civil litigation, Personal injury. Home: 100 Leatherwood Dr Moundsville WV 26041-1017 Office: Artimez Law Offices 409 Morton Ave Moundsville WV 26041-1616

**ARTMAN, ERIC ALAN,** lawyer; b. Jacksonville, Ill., Dec. 22, 1956; s. H. Dean and Cornelia Isabel (Green) A. BS in Math., Computer Sci., U. Ill., Urbana, 1978; JD, U. Ill., Champaign, 1981. Bar: Ill. 1981, U.S. Dist. Ct. (cen. dist.) Ill. 1983. Staff atty. Ill. Ho. of Reps., Springfield, 1981-83; assoc. Gramlich & Morse, Springfield, 1983-85, Saul J. Morse and Assoc., Springfield, 1985-87; dir. industry affairs Tele-Sav Inc., Springfield, 1987—; bd. dirs. State Bank of Auburn, Ill. Mem. Ill. Commerce Commn. Steering Com. on Ill. Universal Service Fund. Mem. ABA, Competetive Telecommunications Assn., (legal affairs coms., fed. affairs com.), Ill. Bar Assn., Sangamon County Bar Assn. Republican. Club: Island Bay Yacht. Lodge: Lions. Avocation: boating. Administrative and regulatory, State civil litigation, Legislative. Office: Tele-Sav Inc PO Box 20490 2375 W Monroe St Springfield IL 62708

**ARVEY, JAMES TERRENCE,** lawyer; b. Chgo., Aug. 1, 1946; s. Erwin B. and Sunny M. (Ainsworth) A.; children: Jason, Allison. BA, U. Miami, 1970; JD, DePaul U., 1975. Bar: Ill. 1975, U.S. Dist. Ct. (no. dist.) Ill. 1977. Prosecutor City of Chgo., 1975-77; assoc., then ptnr. Arvey, Hodes, Costello & Burman, Chgo., 1977-90; ptnr. Schwartz & Freeman, Chgo., 1990-95. Pres. LaSelle Street Assn., Chgo., 1983; v.p. Lincoln Park Conservation Assn., Chgo., 1984. With U.S. Army, 1970-71. Bankruptcy, Consumer commercial, Land use and zoning (including planning). Home: 21 E Division St Apt 3N Chicago IL 60610-5212 Office: Schwartz & Freeman 47 W Division St # 206 Chicago IL 60610-2220

**ASAI-SATO, CAROL YUKI,** lawyer; b. Osaka, Japan, Oct. 22, 1951; came to U.S., 1953; d. Michael and Sumiko (Kamei) Asai; 1 child, Ryan Makoto Sato. BA cum laude, U. Hawaii, 1972; JD, Willamette Coll. Law, 1975. Bar: Hawaii 1975. Assoc. firm Ashford & Wriston, Honolulu, 1975-79; counsel Bank of New Eng., Boston, 1979-81; assoc. counsel Alexander & Baldwin, Honolulu, 1981-83, sr. counsel, 1984-88; of counsel Rush, Moore, Craven, Sutton, Morry, Beh, 1988-89, ptnr., 1989-97; ptnr. Alston Hunt Floyd & Ing, 1997—; lawyer; b. Osaka, Japan, Oct. 22, 1951; came to U.S., 1953; d. Sumiko (Kamei) Asai; 1 child, Ryan Makoto Sato. BA cum laude, U. Hawaii, 1972; JD, Willamette Coll. Law, 1975. Bar: Hawaii 1975. Assoc. firm Ashford & Wriston, Honolulu, 1975-79; counsel Bank of New Eng., Boston, 1979-81; assoc. counsel Alexander & Baldwin, Honolulu, 1981-83, sr. counsel, 1984-88; of counsel, Rush, Moore, Craven, Sutton, Morry, Beh, 1988-89, ptnr., 1989-97; ptnr. Alston Hunt Floyd & Ing, 1997—. Willamette Coll. Law Bd. Trustees scholar, 1972-73. Mem. ABA, Hawaii Bar Assn., Hawaii Women Lawyers, Phi Beta Kappa, Phi Kappa Phi. Democrat. Willamette Coll. Law Bd. Trustees scholar, 1972-73. Mem. ABA, Hawaii Bar Assn., Hawaii Women Lawyers, Phi Beta Kappa, Phi Kappa Phi. Democrat. Contracts commercial, General corporate, Real property. Office: Alston Hunt Floyd & Ing Pacific Tower 18th Fl 1001 Bishop St Ste 1800 Honolulu HI 96813-3689

**ASARO, V. FRANK,** lawyer; b. San Diego, July 28, 1935; s. Frank B. and Josephine (Quinci) A.; m. Barbara A. Mansfield, Aug. 16, 1958 (div. Mar., 1988); children: Dean, Valerie, Stephanie, Audrey. BA, San Diego State U., 1957; postgrad., Loyola U., L.A., 1957-60; JD, LLB, Southwestern U., L.A., 1961. Bar: Calif. 1962; U.S. Dist. Ct. (so. dist.) Calif. 1962, U.S. Dist. Ct. Ala. 1990; U.S. Ct. Appeals (9th cir.) 1965, U.S. Ct. Appeals (6th cir.) 1983. Clk. to the Hon. Justice Coughlin Calif. Dist. Ct. Appeal (4th dist.), San Diego, 1961-62; assoc. atty. Jenkins & Perry, San Diego, 1962-65, partner, 1965-70; partner Gant & Asaro, San Diego, 1970-80; sr. partner Asaro, Gattis & Sullivan, San Diego, 1980-82, Asaro & Long, San Diego, 1982-85, V Frank Asaro and Assocs., San Diego, 1985—; judge pro-tem San Diego Superior Ct., 1975—; arbitrator, San Diego Superior Ct., 1975, 1997; lectr. Practicing Law Inst. Author: Balance Between Order and Chaos, 1988, A Primal Wisdom, 1997; contbr. columnist Dicta County Bar Journal, 1965-70. Chairman Harborview Redevelopment Com., San Diego, 1975-85; mem. County Airport relocation SANPAT Com., San Diego County, 1970-75, City Center Planning Com., San Diego, 1986-90. Recipient citation for pub. svc., Mayor San Diego, 1989. Mem. Calif. State Bar Assn. (del.), San Diego County Bar Assn., Rotary Club (program chair 1996—, pres. 1998—), Barristers Club San Diego (dir.). Achievements include patent for avalanche rescue markers. Avocations: writing, music, philosophy. Real property. Office: V Frank Asaro and Assocs 4370 La Jolla Village Dr San Diego CA 92122-1251

**ASCHERMANN, MARK L.,** lawyer; b. Decatur, Ill., Dec. 23, 1958; s. Lawrence H. and Sylvia Arlene Aschermann; m. Leneva Leigh Lackey, 1985; children: Taylor, Luke. BS, U. Ill., 1981; JD, South Tex. Coll. Law, Houston, 1984. Bar: Tex. 1984, U.S. Dist. Ct. (so. dist.) Tex. 1984, U.S. Dist. Ct. (no. and we. dists.) Tex. 1990, U.S. Ct. Appeals (5th cir.) 1991. Assoc. Sears & Burns, Houston, 1984-86, Mark Ascherman, Atty. at Law, Houston, 1986-88, Axelrod, Smith, Komiss & Kirshbaum, Houston, 1989-92; atty. Aschermann Atty. At Law, Houston, 1992—. Contbr. articles to profl. jours. Mem. speaker com. Houston Livestock Show and Rodeo, 1988—; mem. Leadership Houston, 1987, Tex. Agrl. Lifetime Leadership; active St. Luke's Meth. Ch. Republican. Consumer commercial, State civil litigation, Federal civil litigation. Office: Aschermann Atty At Law 3730 Kirby Dr Ste 520 Houston TX 77098-3979

**ASH, WALTER BRINKER,** lawyer; b. Wichita, Kans., June 8, 1932; s. Walter Bonsall and Gladys Elvira (Brinker) A.; m. Fern Ostrom, Sept. 16, 1986; children: Paul B., Allison L., Carolyn A. BA, U. Kans., 1955, BL, 1957. Bar: Kans. 1957, Colo. 1959. Personal asst. to Solicitor Gen. U.S. Dept. Justice, Washington, 1957-58, trial atty., 1958-59; assoc. Davis, Graham & Stubbs, Denver, 1959-63, ptnr., 1964-82; ptnr. Wade Ash Woods Hill & Guthery P.C., Denver, 1982-91, Wade Ash Woods & Hill P.C., Denver, 1991-93, Wade Ash Woods Hill & Farley, P.C., Denver, 1993—. Fellow Am. Coll. Trust and Estate Counsel; mem. ABA, Colo. Bar Assn., Denver Bar Assn., Internat. Acad. Estate and Trust Law. Estate planning, Probate, Estate taxation. Home: 6814 N Trailway Cir Parker CO 80134-6200 Office: Wade Ash Woods Hill & Farley 360 S Monroe St Ste 400 Denver CO 80209-3709

**ASHBY, KIMBERLY A.,** lawyer; b. Plainfield, N.J., Sept. 9, 1957; d. John L. and Patricia (Andrews) A. BA with high honors, U. Fla., 1978, JD, 1980. Bar: Fla. 1981. Research aide U.S. Ct. Appeals (2d cir.), Lakeland, Fla., 1981; assoc. Maguire, Voorhis & Wells, P.A., Orlando, Fla., 1981-86, ptnr., 1986—. Contbr. articles to profl. jours. Elder, trustee Park /Lake Presbyn. Ch., Orlando, 1984-86. Mem. Fla. Bar Assn. (mem. young lawyers jud. relations com. 1983-84, appellate rules com. 1985-86), Fla. Def. Lawyers (Amicus brief writer 1984). Republican. Avocation: marathon running. Fax: 407-843-6610. E-mail: kashby@akerman.com. Construction, Landlord-tenant, Consumer commercial. Office: Akerman Senterfitt & Eidson PA Citrus Ctr PO Box 231 255 S Orange Ave Orlando FL 32802-0231

**ASHCRAFT, DAVID BEE,** lawyer; b. Clarksburg, W.Va., July 9, 1947; s. Donald Bee and Patty JoAnn (Smith) A.; m. Sandra Stroud, Sept. 15, 1990; children: William, Robert, James, Kristen, Kara, Kameron. BS in Math., Wake Forest U., 1969, JD, 1974. Bar: N.C. 1974. With Haworth Riggs Kuhn Haworth & Miller, High Point, N.C., 1974-86; assoc. Wyatt Early Harris & Wheeler, High Point, 1986—; adv. bd. dir. First Union Nat. Bank, High Point, 1992-96. Mem. High Point Rotary (pres. 1994). Methodist. Avocations: tennis, hiking. General corporate, Mergers and acquisitions. Office: Wyatt Early Harris & Wheeler LLP 1912 Eastchester Dr High Point NC 27265-3501

**ASHDOWN, CHARLES COSTER,** lawyer; b. N.Y.C., 1961; s. Cecil Spanton Jr. and Marie Antoinette Ashdown; m. Philomena Saldanha, Sept. 16, 1989; children: Marygrace, Helen. BA magna cum laude, Fordham U., 1983; JD, U. Notre Dame, 1986. Bar: Ohio 1986, U.S. Dist. Ct. (so. dist.) Ohio 1987, U.S. Ct. Appeals (6th cir.) 1994. Student law clk. to Hon. John E. Sprizzo U.S. Dist. Ct. (so. dist.) N.Y., N.Y.C., 1984; ptnr. Strauss & Troy, Cin., 1986—. Trustee Cin. Opera Assn., 1987-93, mem. adv. bd., 1998—; judge Midwest Concours d'Elegance, Cin., 1992-95, chief judge, 1997—; planned giving adv. com. Episcopal Retirement Homes, Inc., 1998—. Mem. ABA, Cin. Bar Assn., Black Lawyers Cin. Roundtable, Univ. Club Cin., Alpha Sigma Nu, Phi Kappa Phi. General civil litigation, Contracts commercial, Land use and zoning (including planning). Home: 1739 Churchwood Dr Cincinnati OH 45238-1901 Office: Strauss & Troy The Fed Reserve Bldg 150 E Fourth St 4th Fl Cincinnati OH 45202-4018

**ASHE, BERNARD FLEMMING,** arbitrator, educator, lawyer; b. Balt., Mar. 8, 1936; s. Victor Joseph Ashe and Frances Cecelia (Johnson) Flemming; m. Grace Nannette Pegram, Mar. 23, 1963; children: Walter Joseph, David Bernard. BA, Howard U., 1956, JD, 1961. Bar: Va. 1961, D.C. 1963, Mich. 1964, N.Y. 1971. Tchr. Balt. Pub. Schs., 1956-58; atty. NLRB, Washington, 1961-63; asst. gen. counsel Internat. Union United Auto Workers, Detroit, 1963-71; gen. counsel N.Y. State United Tchrs., Albany, 1971-96, arbitrator, 1996—; mem. adj. faculty Cornell Sch. Indsl. and Labor Rels., Albany div., 1981, 87, Fordham U. Law Sch., 1996—, Roger Williams U. Law Sch., 1996-98. Contbr. articles on labor and constnl. law to profl. jours. Bd. dirs. Urban League Albany, 1979-85, 1st v.p., 1981-85; trustee N.Y. Lawyers Fund for Client Protection, 1981—, Adelphi Univ., Garden City, N.Y., 1997—. Fellow Am. Bar Found. (life), Coll. Labor and Employment Lawyers (emeritus); mem. ABA (chmn. sect. labor and employment law sect. 1982-83, consortium on legal svcs. and the pub. 1979-84, commn. on pub. understanding about the law 1987-91, mem. standing com. on group and prepaid legal svcs. 1996-97, ho. of dels. 1985-96, 97—, nominating com. 1988-91, bd. govs. 1991-94, exec. com. 1993-94, accreditation com. sect. legal edn. and admission to the bar 1994-98, chmn. standing com. on group and prepaid legal svcs. 1996-97, sr. lawyers divsn. coun. 1996—, chair drafting com. 1998—), Am. Law Inst., Nat. Bar Assn., Am. Arbitration Assn. (bd. dirs. 1982-98, Whitney North Seymour Sr. medal 1989), N.Y. State Bar Assn., Albany County Bar Assn.

**ASHFORD, DOROTHY M.,** lawyer; b. Columbia, S.C., June 1, 1947; d. Moses and Mary (Bell) A.; 1 child, Kiah Leigh. BA, Clemson U.; JD, Seton Hall U. Bar: N.J. 1977, Pa. 1977; lic. real estate agt., N.J. Sr. mgr. IBM, White Plains, N.Y., 1969-93; sr. counsel Geotek, Montvale, N.J., 1993-98; sr. bus. cons. IBM Global Svcs., 1998—. Home: 12320 Alameda Trace Cir Apt 409 Austin TX 78727-6461

**ASHLEY, FRED TURNER,** lawyer, mediator, arbitrator; b. Hawthorne, Calif., Apr. 20, 1950; s. John Parkinson and Dorothy Mae (Burks) A.; m. Patricia Ann Jones, June 15, 1975; children: Erin Ann, Robert Ryan. BA, U. Calif., Santa Barbara, 1972; MPA, U. Calif., L.A., 1975; JD cum laude, Loyola U., 1978. Bar: Calif. 1978, U.S. Dist. Ct. (ctrl. dist.) Calif. 1978, U.S. Ct. Appeals (9th cir.) 1978, U.S. Supreme Ct. 1981. Assoc. Hill, Farrer & Burrill, L.A., 1978-82; ptnr. Ashley & Honn, L.A., 1982-83; assoc. Paul, Hastings, Janofsky & Walker, Costa Mesa, Calif., 1983-87; prin. Law Offices of Fred T. Ashley, Orange County, Calif., 1987—; spkr. in field. Contbr. articles to profl. jours. Dir. Fair Housing Coun. Orange County, 1996-97. Recipient Disting. Svc. award Nat. Employment Lawyers Assn., Can. Mem. Calif. Employment Lawyers Assn. (chair 1993-95, Disting. Svc. award 1990), Calif. Dispute Resolution Coun., So. Calif. Mediation Assn. (co-chair labor and employment law sect. 1997—), Orange County Bar Assn. (chair labor and employment law sect. 1990), Orange County Indsl. Rels. Rsch. Assn. Avocations: fishing, golf, tennis. Labor, General civil litigation, Civil rights. Office: Law Office of Fred T Ashley 2201 Dupont Dr Ste 710 Irvine CA 92612-7508

**ASHLEY, JAMES PATRICK,** lawyer; b. Terre Haute, Ind., May 5, 1953; s. Cornelius Ellis and Ruth LaVerne A.; m. Lisa Ann Larsson, Aug. 2, 1975; children: Alison Elisabeth, Amanda Suzanne. BSBA, Ill. State U., 1975; JD, Drake U., 1991. Bar: Minn. 1991; U.S. Dist. Ct. Minn. 1992; U.S. Ct. Appeals (8th cir.) 1993. Claim supr., claim examiner and claim rep. Ill. Employers Ins. of Wausau, River Forest, Ill., 1976-80; casualty claim mgr. Brotherhood Mut. Ins. Co., Fort Wayne, Ind., 1980-88; law clk. Hanson, McClintock & Riley, Des Moines, 1989-91; assoc. Chadwick, Johnson & Condon, Mpls., 1991-96; shareholder Chadwick & Assocs., Chanhassen, Minn., 1996-99; trial atty. Allstate Ins. Co., Edina, Minn., 1999—. Recipient acad. scholarship Drake Law Sch., Des Moines, 1989. Roman Catholic. Avocations: reading, winemaking. General civil litigation, Insurance, Product liability. Home: 12771 Gerard Dr Eden Prairie MN 55346-3129 Office: Allstate Ins Co 7401 Metro Blvd Ste 510 Edina MN 55439-3033

**ASHLEY-FARRAND, MARGALO,** lawyer, mediator, private judge; b. N.Y.C., July 26, 1944; d. Joel Thomas and Margalo (Wilson) Ashley; m. Marvin H. Bennett, Mar. 5, 1964 (div. June 1974),; children: Marc, Aliza; m. Thomas Ashley-Farrand, Dec. 11, 1981. Student, UCLA, 1962-63, U. Pitts., 1972-74; BA cum laude, NYU, 1978; JD, Southwestern U., 1980. Bar: D.C. 1981, Md. 1981, Calif. 1983, U.S. Dist. Ct. (ctrl. and no. dists.) Calif. 1984; cert. family law specialist Calif. State Bar. Pvt. practice law Washington, 1981-82; ptnr. Ashley-Farrand & Smith, Glendale, Calif., 1983-87; pvt. practice law, 1987-95; pvt. practice Pasadena, Calif., 1995—; v.p. Legal Inst. Fair Elections, 1995—; settlement officer L.A. Mcpl. Ct., 1990—; judge pro tem L.A. Mcpl. Ct., 1989—, L.A. Superior Ct., 1993—. Convenor, pres. East Hills chpt. NOW, 1972-74, mem. Pa. state bd., 1972-74, pres. Hollywood chpt. 1974-75, mem. bd. N.Y.C. chpt. 1975-78; convenor, coord. L.A. Women's Coalition for Better Broadcasting, 1974-75; Dem. nominee Calif. State Assembly, 1994. Themis soc. scholar, 1980; named one of Outstanding Young Women of Am., 1980. Mem. ABA, ACLU, NOW, NWPC, League of Conservation Voters, Calif. Women Lawyers, Women Lawyers Assn. L.A., Pasadena Interracial Women's Club (pres. 1993-94). Family and matrimonial, Appellate, Probate. Office: 215 N Marengo Ave Fl 3 Pasadena CA 91101-1504

**ASHTON, MARK RANDOLPH,** lawyer; b. Abington, Pa., Sept. 10, 1955; s. Frank E. and Charlotte (Wagenbaur) A. BA in Internat. Affairs, George Washington U., 1977; JD, John Marshall U., 1980. Bar: Pa. 1980. Law clk. to Hon. Mason Avrigian Ct. of Common Pleas of Montgomery County, Norristown, Pa., 1980-81; assoc. Abrahams & Loewenstein, Norristown, 1982-87; dept. chmn. Riley, Riper, Hollin & Colagreco, 1987-90; ptnr. Fox, Rothschild, O'Brien & Frankel, Exton, Pa., 1990—. Mem. Montgomery Bar Assn. (bd. dirs. 1985-87), Chester County Bar Assn. (chmn. family law sect. 1988-90), Wissahickon Valley Hist. Soc. (pres.), D.J. Freed Am. Inn of Ct. (v.p.). Republican. Episcopalian. Family and matrimonial. Home: 413 Stratford Ave Collegeville PA 19426-2553 Office: Fox Rothschild O'Brien & Frankel 760 Constitution Dr Ste 104 Exton PA 19341-1149

**ASHTON, ROBERT W.,** lawyer, foundation administrator; b. Memphis, Jan. 26, 1937; s. Robert Wilson and Ina Louise (Jones) A.; m. Jean Isabel Willoughby; children: Katherine, Susanna, Emily, Isabel. BA, U. Mich., 1960; LLB, Vanderbilt U., 1964. Bar: N.Y. 1965. Assoc., Beekman & Bogue, N.Y.C., 1964-73, ptnr., 1973-81; ptnr. Gaston Snow Beekman & Bogue, N.Y.C., 1981-89; counsel, 1989-91; pvt. practice 1991—; exec. dir. The Bay Found., 1977—, Josephine Bay Paul and C. Michael Paul Found., 1977-87; bd. dirs. St. Matthew's & St. Timothy's Neighborhood Ctr., N.Y.C., 1973—, The Fund for Artists Colonies, 1983-90, St. Luke's Orch., N.Y.C., 1988—, Marine Biol. Lab., Woods Hole, Mass., 1980-89, Alumni Bd. Vanderbilt Law Sch., 1980-88, The Millay Colony for the Arts, 1991—. Mem. Assn. of Bar of City of N.Y., Estate Lawyers Club, Century Assn. Democrat. Estate planning, Estate taxation, Non-profit and tax-exempt organizations. Home: 300 W 108th St New York NY 10025-2757 Office: 17 W 94th St New York NY 10025-7116

**ASHWORTH, BRENT FERRIN,** lawyer; b. Albany, Calif., Jan. 8, 1949; s. Dell Shepherd and Bette Jean (Brailsford) A.; m. Charlene Mills, Dec. 16, 1970; children: Amy, John, Matthew, Samuel (dec.), Adam, David, Emily, Luke, Benjamin. BA, Brigham Young U., 1972; JD, U. Utah, 1975. Bar: Utah 1977. Asst. county atty. Carbon County, Price, Utah, 1975-76; assoc. atty. Frandsen & Keller, Price, Utah, 1976-77; v.p. legal affairs, sec., gen. counsel Nature's Sunshine Products, Provo, Utah, 1977—. Bd. dirs., gen. counsel Carbon County Nursing Home, Prize, 1976-77; mem. Provo Landmarks Commn., 1997—, co-chair sesquicentennial com., 1998—; chmn. Utah County Cancer Crusade Com., 1981-83; chmn. Provo LCOC Arts subcom.; city councilman Payson City, Utah, 1980-82, mem. planning commn., 1980-82, mayor pro tem, 1982; bd. dirs. ARC, Utah County chpt., 1988-94, Springville Mus. Art, 1998—; pres. Deseret Village Spani Fork, Utah, 1988-90; gen. counsel Brigham Young Acad. Found., 1995—; co-chair Provo Utah Sesquecentennial com., 1998—. Mem. ABA, SAR (pres. Utah County chpt. 1989-90, state chpts. 1st v.p. 1990-91, state soc. pres. 1991-92, chancellor 1992-94), ATLA, Southeastern Utah Bar Assn. (sec. 1977), Utah State Bar, Am. Corp. Counsel Assn. (sec. Intermountain chpt. 1990-91), Emily Dickinson Soc. Utah (pres. 1995-97), Sons Utah Pioneers, Kiwanis Club (v.p. 1995-96, pres. 1997-98), Phi Kappa Phi, Phi Eta Sigma. General corporate, Private international. Home: 1965 N 1400 E Provo UT 84604-2106 Office: Natures Sunshine Products 1655 N Main St Spanish Fork UT 84660-1007

**ASKEY, WILLIAM HARTMAN,** magistrate, lawyer; b. Williamsport, Pa., June 21, 1919; s. Charles Fisher and Marguerite Kirlin (Hartman) A.; m. Betty Arlene Moore, July 3, 1942; 1 dau., Elizabeth Powell. BA, Bucknell U., 1941; JD, U. Pitts., 1951. Bar: Lycoming County Cts., 1951, Pa. 1952, U.S. Dist. Ct. (mid. dist.) Pa. 1952, U.S. Supreme Ct. 1960. Sole practice Williamsport, Pa., 1951—; U.S. commr. U.S. Dist. Ct. (mid. dist.) Pa., 1964-71; part-time U.S. magistrate, judge, 1971—; with AAA, North Penn. Bd. dirs. Appalachia Ednl. Lab., Charleston, W.Va., 1967-85; mem. Vestry Episcopal Ch., Williamsport, Pa., jr. warden, 1989. Served to maj. USAAF, 1941-46. Mem. Lycoming Law Assn. (pres. 1968-69), Pa. Bar Assn., ABA (Nat. Conf. Spl. Ct. Judges), Fed. Bar Assn. (hon.), Fed. Magistrate Judges Assn., Masons, Ross Club (Williamsport).

**ASKIN, MARILYN,** law educator, lawyer; b. N.Y.C.; d. Simon and Lena (Merker) Klein; m. Frank Askin, Aug. 6, 1960; children: Andrea, Jonathan, Daniel. B.S. in Edn., CCNY, 1954; postgrad. Russian Inst., Columbia U., 1958-60; J.D., Rutgers U., 1970. Bar: N.J. 1970. U.S. Dist. Ct. N.J. 1970, U.S. Supreme Ct. 1977, N.Y. 1983; cert. in elder law, 1995. Journalist The Record, Hackensck, N.J., 1956-62; tchr. high sch. English, Newark, 1964-67; regional dir. Am. Jewish Congress, Newark, 1971-76; counsel Pub. Documents Com., Washington, 1976-77; sr. atty. Essex Newark Legal Services, Orange, N.J., 1978-93; of counsel, Fein, Such, Kahn & Shepard, Parsippany, N.J., 1993-95; lectr. Inst. Continuing Legal Edn., 1983, 87—; adj. faculty Rutgers Law Sch., 1984—; mem. ethics com. Supreme Ct. Dist., 1985—, adj. faculty Seton Hall U. Law Sch., 1992—; mem. Supreme Ct. Com. on Rels. with Media, 1990—, Supreme Ct. Com. on Women in the Cts., 1994—; Editl. bd. N.J. Lawyer Mag., 1987—. Rev. bd. Children in Placement, Essex County, 1980—; bd. trustees Chr-Ill. (home health non-profit), 1983—. Author: ABC's of Elder Law, 1990, Elder Law, 1993, Elder Law Made Easy!, 1995, Elder Law for Neophytes, 1997, Long-Term Care Insurance, 1995, Reverse Mortgages, 1993, Nursing Home Residents As Clients, 1994, Elder Law for Neophytes. Mem. Nat. Acad. Elder Law Attys. Essex County Bar Assn. (chair com. on rights of elderly 1981—), N.J. State Bar Assn. (chair aging and the law com. 1985-89), N.J. Women Lawyers (pres. 1997—), Essex County Women Lawyers (pres. 1989-91), Nat. Legal Aid and Defender Assn. (chair sr. citizen sect. 1986-89), Rutgers Law Sch. Alumni Assn. (pres. 1993-94). Office: 193 Zeppi Ln West Orange NJ 07052-4129

**ASKINS, KNOX WINFRED,** lawyer; b. Houston, July 19, 1937; s. Elgie Joseph and Geneva (Rulison) A.; m. Augusta Ann Thomas, Sept. 13, 1958; children: Diane, Suzanne, Sally Ann, James, Paul, Clark. BFA, U. Houston, 1958, JD, 1962. Bar: Tex. 1962, U.S. Dist. Ct. (so. dist.) Tex. 1962, U.S. Supreme Ct. 1970. Assoc. Kiibler and Kiibler, LaPorte, Tex., 1962-65; ptnr. Askins and Armstrong, P.C., LaPorte, 1965—; gen. counsel, bd. dirs. Bay Bancshares, Inc. and Bayshore Nat. Bank, LaPorte; city atty. City of LaPorte, 1965—. Bd. dirs. Houston Area Rapid Transit, 1973; pres. LaPorte Bayshore C. of C., 1973-74. Fellow Tex. Bar Found.; mem. State Bar Tex., Houston Bar Assn., Christian Legal Soc., LaPorte Rotary Club (pres. 1973-74), Order of Barons, Delta Theta Phi. Republican. Avocations: photography, amateur radio. Banking, General corporate, Probate. Home: 1022 Oak Leaf St La Porte TX 77571-6930 Office: Askins and Armstrong PC PO Box 1218 702 W Fairmont Pkwy La Porte TX 77571-6217

**ASMAR, LAILA MICHELLE,** lawyer; b. Laurel, Miss., July 23, 1957; d. Mitchell and Marie Jeannette Asmar. BS in BA, U. So. Miss., 1979; JD cum laude, So. Tex. Coll. Law, Houston, 1985. Bar: Tex. 1985; CPA, Tex., Miss.; bd. cert. estate planning and probate lawyer; cert. mediator; cert. arbitrator N.Y. Stock Exch. and Nat. Assn. Securities Dealers. Acct. Peat Marwick Mitchell, Jackson, Miss., 1979-80, Houston Oil Internat., Houston, 1980-81; tax analyst Tenneco Inc., Houston, 1981-84; assoc. atty. Clark Thomas Winters & Newton, Austin, Tex., 1985-87; fin. cons. Linscomb & Williams, Houston, 1988-89; pvt. practice law, Houston, 1989—; guest expert The Ron Stone Show, Sta. KPRC-TV, Houston, 1990-92, guest reporter Morning News, 1992. Co-author of ABA pub.: Federal Income Taxation of Life Insurance, 1989; contbr. articles to profl. jours. Trustee Theater Under Stars, Houston, 1989-91. Mem. Tex. Bar Assn. Republican. Episcopalian. Estate planning, Securities, Probate.

**ASPEN, MARVIN EDWARD,** federal judge; b. Chgo., July 11, 1934; s. George Abraham and Helen (Adelson) A.; m. Susan Alona Tubbs, Dec. 18, 1966; children: Jennifer Marion, Jessica Maile, Andrew Joseph. BS in Sociology, Loyola Univ., 1956; JD, Northwestern U., 1958. Bar: Ill., 1958. Individual practice Chgo., 1958-59; draftsman joint com. to draft new Ill. criminal code Chgo. Bar Assn.-Ill. Bar Assn., 1959-60; asst. state's atty. Cook County, Ill., 1960-63; asst. corp. counsel City of Chgo., 1963-71; pvt. practice law, 1971; judge Cir. Ct. Cook County, Ill., 1971-79; judge U.S. Dist. Ct. (ea. dist.) Ill., Chgo., 1979-95, chief judge, 1995—; Edward Avery Harriman adj. prof. law Northwestern U. Law Sch.; past chmn. new judges, recent devels. in criminal law, and evidence coms. Ill. Judicial Conf., adv. bd. Inst. Criminal Justice, John Marshall Sch. Law; past mem. Ill. Law Enforcement Commn., Gov. Ill. Adv. Commn. Criminal Justice, Cook County Bd. Corrections; past chmn. assoc. rules com. Ill. Supreme Ct., com. on ordinance violation problems; past vice chmn. com. on pattern jury instrns. in criminal cases; lectr. at judicial confs. and trial advocacy programs nationally and internationally; planner, participant in legal seminars at numerous schools including Harvard U., Emory U., U. Fla., Oxford U. (Eng.), U. Bologna, Nuremberg (Germany) U., U. Cairo, Egypt, U. Zimbabwe, U. Malta, U. The Philippines, U. Madrid; past mem. Georgetown U. Law Ctr. Project on Plea Bargaining in U.S., spl. faculty NITA advanced Trial Advocacy Program introducing Brit. trial techniques to experienced Am. litigators, spl. faculty of ABA designed to acquaint Scottish lawyers with modern litigation and tech.; frequent faculty mem. Nat. Judiciary Coll., Fed. Judicial Ctr., U. Nev. (Reno), Nat. Inst. for Trial Advocacy, Colo.; bd. dir. Fed. Judicial Ctr.; past mem. Judicial Conf. Com. on Adminstrn. of the Bankruptcy System, Trial Bar Implementation Com. on Civility of the 7th Fed. Cir.; exec. bd. Fed. Jud. Ctr. Co-author Criminal Law for the Layman-A Citizen's Guide, 2d edit., 1977, Criminal Evidence for the Police, 1972, Protective Security Law, 1983; contbr. over two dozen articles to legal publs. Past mem. vis. com. Northwestern U. Sch. Law, chmn. adv. com. for short courses (post law sch. ednl. program); mem. vis. com. U. Chgo. Law Sch.; organizer, past pres. Northwestern Univ. Sch. of Law chpt. Amincourt Program U.S. Judicial Conf; past mem. Cook County Bd. Corrections, John Howard Assn. With USAF, 1958-59; trustee Am. Inns Ct. Recipient Nat. Ctr. Freedom of Info. Studies award, Ctr. for Pub. Resources award, Nat. Ctr. for Freedom of Info. Studies award, Merit award Northwestern U. Alumni Assn.; named Person of Yr. Chgo. Lawyer, 1995. Mem. Am. Bar Found. (bd. dirs.), Judicature Soc. Ill. (past chmn. coms.), Chgo. Bar Assn.

(bd. mgrs. 1978-79, past chmn. criminal law com., past bd. editors Chgo. Bar Record, mem. commn. on criminal justice. coms. on cont. legal edn., devel. of law, civil disorder and others), Ill. State Bar Assn. (past chmn. pub. rels., corrections, fair trial/free press, criminal law coms., mem. others), Northwestern U. Law Alumni Assn. (past pres., Merit award), ABA (past mem. ABA bd. govs., mem. house dels., past chmn. exec com., mem. bd. editors ABA Jour.), Nat. Conf. Fed. Trial Judges (past mem. coun. sect. litigation, past chmn., coun. sect. criminal justice, past co-chmn. liason jud. com. sect. litigation, mem. jury comprehension study com., pres., ho. dels., standing com. fed. jud. improvements, co-chmn. sect. litigation Inst. Trial Practice Task Force), Am. Inns Ct. Office: US Dist Ct 2548 US Courthouse 219 S Dearborn St Chicago IL 60604-1702

**ASPERO, BENEDICT VINCENT,** lawyer; b. Newton, N.J., Sept. 3, 1940; s. Umberto S. and Rose (Cerreta) A.; m. Sally Hennen, June 26, 1971; children: Benedict Vincent Jr., Alexander Morgan. AB, U. Notre Dame, 1962, J.D., 1966. Bar: N.J. 1970, N.Y. 1982, D.C. 1983, U.S. Dist. Ct. N.J. 1970, U.S. Supreme Ct. 1981. Assoc., then ptnr. Meyers, Lesser & Aspero, Sparta, N.J., 1971-76, Benedict V. Aspero, Sparta and Morristown, N.J., 1976-82; ptnr. Broderick, Newmark, Grather & Aspero, Morristown, N.J., 1982-89, Courter, Kobert, Laufer, Purcell & Cohen, 1989-91; prin. Benedict V. Aspero, Morristown, 1992-96; ptnr. Aspero & Aspero, P.C., Morristown, 1996-97, Benedict V. Aspero, Esq., P.C., 1997—; mem. adv. bd. Summit Bank. Trustee, pres. Harding Twp. Civic Assn., 1982-85; trustee, pres. Craig Sch., Loyola Retreat House. Mem. ABA, N.J. Bar Assn., Morris County Bar Assn., Sussex County Bar Assn., Sorin Soc. Republican. Roman Catholic. Clubs: Morristown, Essex Hunt. Contracts commercial, General corporate, Probate. Office: 222 Ridgedale Ave PO Box 1573 Morristown NJ 07962-1573

**ASSAEL, MICHAEL,** lawyer, accountant; b. N.Y.C., July 20, 1949; s. Albert and Helen (Hope) A.; m. Eiko Sato. BA, George Washington U., 1971; MBA., Columbia U. Grad. Sch. Bus., 1973; JD, St. John's Law Sch., 1977. Bar: N.Y. 1978, U.S. Dist. Ct. (so. and ea. dists.) N.Y. 1980, U.S. Supreme Ct. 1982; CPA, N.Y. Tax sr. Price Waterhouse & Co., N.Y.C. and Tokyo, 1977-78; pvt. practice law, N.Y.C., 1978—; pvt. practice acctg., N.Y.C., 1978—. Author: Money Smarts, 1982. Pres. bd. dirs. 200 Block East 74th Street Assn., 1982; bd. dirs. 200 E 74 Owners Corp., 1981—, treas., 1983-84, pres., 1984-85; mem. Yorkville Civic Council, tenant adv. com. Lenox Hill Neighborhood Assn., 1981-82. Recipient N.Y. Habitat/Citibank mgmt. achievement award, 1985. Mem. ABA, N.Y. State Bar Assn., N.Y. County Lawyers Assn., Am. Inst. CPA's, Am. Assn. Atty. CPA's, Inc., Nat. Assn. Accts., N.Y. State Soc. CPA's, Aircraft Owners and Pilots Assn. Clubs: N.Y. Road Runners, Columbia Bus. Sch. (N.Y.). Real property, Personal income taxation, Landlord-tenant.

**ASSELIN, JOHN THOMAS,** lawyer; b. Manshester, Conn., May 13, 1951; s. Oliver Joseph and MaryRose Mildred (Dondero) A.; children: Jessica Lynn, Kristina Anne. BA, U. Conn., 1973, JD, 1976. Bar: Conn. 1976, U.S. Dist. Ct. Conn. 1976. Pvt. practice Willimantic, Conn., 1976—; lectr. Practicing Law Inst. N.Y., Profl. Edn. Systems Inc. Author: Connecticut Workers' Compensation Practice Manual, The Trial Handbook for Connecticut Lawyers; contbr. articles to profl. jours. served Conn. gov. Thomas J. Meskill, U.S. Rep. Robert Steele. Grantee Deerfield Found. Mem. ABA (lectr.), Conn. Bar Assn. (exec. com. civil justice sect.), Assn. Trial Lawyers Am., Conn. Trial Lawyers Assn. (bd. govs. 1981—), Phi Beta Kappa, Phi Kappa Phi, Pi Sigma Alpha. Roman Catholic. Avocations: horses, team penning. Personal injury, Workers' compensation, Family and matrimonial. Office: 661 Windham Rd South Windham CT 06266-1100

**ASSERSON, BRIAN MICHAEL,** lawyer; b. N.Y.C., Dec. 28, 1951; s. Arthur and Mina Asserson; m. Lori Robin Marshall, July 4, 1981; children: Derek Bradley, Ilana Erin. BA, Hofstra U., 1973, JD, 1976. Bar: N.Y. 1977, U.S. Dist. Ct. (so. and ea. dists.) N.Y. 1978, D.C. 1979, U.S. Supreme Ct. 1984. Assoc. atty. Metro. Transp. Authority, N.Y.C., 1976-83; mng. atty. The Hertz Corp., Parsippany, N.J., 1983-86; sr. counsel Marsh & McLennan Cos., N.Y.C., 1986-92; chief counsel The Home Ins. Co., N.Y.C., 1992-93; CEO The Robert Plan, Bethpage, N.Y., 1993-96; asst. v.p. GAB Robins N.Am., Parsippany, 1996-97; sr. counsel Cendant Corp., Parsippany, 1997—. Trustee Washington Commons, N.J., 1987-97. Mem. ABA, Am. Mgmt. Assn., D.C. Bar Assn., N.Y. State Bar Assn. General civil litigation, Franchising, Insurance. Office: Cendant Corporation 1 Sylvan Way Parsippany NJ 07054-3878

**ATCHERLEY, LINDA FRANCESCA,** lawyer; b. Hong Kong, Apr. 25, 1959; d. Flavio Antonino and Martha June Esposito; m. Wilbur Wade Atcherley, Jan. 7, 1981 (div. Aug. 1983); 1 child, Christopher; m. Paul Ernest Vincent, Apr. 27, 1996. BS, U. Calif., San Diego, 1981; AS, Coleman Coll., 1982; JD, Western State U., 1989. Bar: Calif. 1998, U.S. Dist. Ct. (so. dist.) Calif., U.S. Ct. Appeals (9th cir.). Swim instr., lifeguard YWCA Downtown, San Diego, 1978-81; customer svc. rep. Mitsubishi Foods, San Diego, 1983-87; assoc. Ludecke, Denton & Burns, San Diego, 1987-95; pvt. practice San Diego, 1995—. Contbr. articles to profl. jours. Sec., v.p., historian PTA Jurez Lincoln Sch., San Diego, 1990-94, pres. Booster's Club, 1992-94; pres. Aux. Parkview Little League, Chula Vista, 1990-92. Mem. Calif. Applicante Attys. Assn. (pres. 1995-97, bd. dirs., dir. com. 1997-98, co-chair consumer info. svc. 1998—), San Diego County Bar Assn., Consumers Attys. Calif. (bd. govs. 1995—), Lawyers for Literacy. Republican. Roman Catholic. Avocation: playing the piano. Workers' compensation, Pension, profit-sharing, and employee benefits, Personal injury. Office: Law Offices of Linda F Atcherley 2333 1st Ave Ste 204 San Diego CA 92101-1540

**ATCHISON, RODNEY RAYMOND,** lawyer, arbitrator; b. Hanford, Calif., Nov. 14, 1926; s. Clyde Raymond and Velma May (Watts) A.; m. Evaleen Mary McFadden, June 27, 1948; children: Cathlin Atchison, Susan Barisone, Kerry Dexter, Brian. Student, San Jose State Coll., 1946-49; JD, U. Santa Clara, 1952. Bar: Calif. 1953, U.S. Dist. Ct. (all dists.) Calif. 1953, U.S. Ct. Appeals (9th cir.) 1953, U.S. Supreme Ct. 1971. Assoc. Mullen & Filippi, Attys., San Francisco, 1953-55; dep. county counsel Santa Clara Calif. County Counsel, San Jose, 1955-57; city atty. City of Mountain View, Calif., 1957-62, City of Santa Cruz, Calif., 1962-90; pres. Atchison, Anderson, Hurley & Barisone, Profl. Law Corp., Santa Cruz, 1980-96; of counsel Atchison & Barisone, Profl. Law Corp., Santa Cruz, 1996—, Law Offices of Rodney R. Atchison, 1996—; arbitrator Am. Arbitration Assn., San Francisco, 1970—. Pres. Rotary Club Mountain View, Calif., 1961-62, Santa Cruz (Calif.) County Bar Assn., 1973. With USNR, 1944-46. Mem. ABA, Santa Cruz Rotary Club, Elks Lodge (life). Roman Catholic. Avocations: skiing, travel, golf. Real property, Contracts commercial, Alternative dispute resolution. Office: Law Offices of Rodney R Atchison 333 Church St Santa Cruz CA 95060-3811

**ATES, J. ROBERT,** lawyer; b. New Orleans, Sept. 12, 1945; s. Loten Arthur Jr. and Eugenia Lea (Carpenter) A. BA, Tulane U., 1967; JD, Loyola U., New Orleans, 1972. Bar: La. 1973, U.S. Dist. Ct. (ea., mid. and we. dists.) La., U.S. Ct. Appeals (5th cir.), U.S. Supreme Ct., Colo. 1990. Prof., chmn. sci. dept. East Jefferson High Sch., Metairie, La., 1967-72; law clk. to judge La. Ct. Appeals (4th cir.), New Orleans, 1972-73; assoc. Kierr, Gainsburgh, Benjamin, Fallon & Lewis, New Orleans, 1974-78, ptnr., 1979-87; ptnr. Gainsburgh, Benjamin, Fallon, David & Ates, New Orleans, 1987-94; prin. J. Robert Ates, A Profl. Law Corp., New Orleans, 1994-95, Ates & Assocs., A Profl. Law Corp., New Orleans, 1996—; lectr. in field; mem. adj. law faculty and skills faculty, Continuing Legal Edn. Programs, Tulane U., Loyola Law Schs. Mem. ATLA, FBA, La. Bar Assn. (vice chmn. civil law sect. 1986-87, chmn. 1987—, sec., treas. 1985—, chmn. pub. rels. and edn. com. 1987—, mem. ho. of dels. 1987-94, bd. govs. 1993—, gen. sec. and editor La. Bar Jour. 1993—), Orleans Bar Assn., Jefferson Bar Assn., La. Trial Lawyers Assn. (pres.'s adv. com.), Soc. Am. Law Tchrs., Am. Soc. Law and Medicine. Democrat. Baptist. Avocations: photography, snow skiing, water skiing, hunting, fishing. Personal injury, Admiralty, Product liability. Home: 29 Turnberry Dr La Place LA 70068-1617 Office: Ates & Assocs A Profl Law Corp 4004 Magazine St Ste A New Orleans LA 70115-2762

**ATKIN, GARY EUGENE,** lawyer; b. Salt Lake City, Oct. 7, 1946; s. Henry Eugene and Dolores Heckman (Dykes) A.; m. Marsha Selin, June 12, 1967; children: Kathryn Dawn, Kenneth Eugene. BS in Acctg., U. Utah, 1967, JD, 1970. Bar: Utah 1970, U.S. Dist. Ct. Utah 1970, U.S. Ct. Appeals (10th cir.) 1978, U.S. Supreme Ct. 1978. Assoc. Rawlings, Roberts & Black, Salt Lake City, 1970-74; assoc. counsel Utah State Legislature, Salt Lake City, 1974-79; ptnr. Gustin, Adams, Kesting & Liapis, Salt Lake City, 1979-81, of counsel, 1981-82; ptnr. Atkin & Anderson, Salt Lake City, 1982-91, Atkin & Assocs., Salt Lake City, 1992—. Mem. Assn. Trial Lawyers Am., Fed. Bar Assn., Utah Trial Lawyers Assn. (bd. dirs. 1980-90, pres. 1984-85). Avocation: announcer. Bankruptcy, General corporate, Personal injury. Home: 4498 Adonis Dr Salt Lake City UT 84124-3923 Office: Atkin & Assocs 311 S State St Ste 380 Salt Lake City UT 84111-5215

**ATKINS, AARON ARDENE,** lawyer; b. Du Quoin, Ill., July 17, 1960; s. Thornton A. and Venita Lee (Thornton) A. BA, So. Ill. U., 1982, JD, 1985. Bar: Ill. 1985, U.S. Dist. Ct. (so. dist.) Ill. 1986. Ptnr. Miller & Atkins, Du Quoin, 1985-87; pvt. practice Du Quoin, 1987—; city atty. City of Du Quoin, Ill.; village atty. Village Dowell, Ill.; atty. Consol. Pub. Water Dist., Perry County Housing Authority, 1995—. Bd. dirs. Boys Club, Du Quoin, 1986-87, United Way, Du Quoin, 1987-94; cons. Sacred Heart Endowment Fund, Du Quoin, 1987-94; active in Sacred Heart Parish Coun., 1987-94, organist, 1974—. Mem. Ill. State Bar Assn., Perry County Bar Assn. (sec.-treas. 1995—), Du Quoin Bus. Assn., K.C. (4th degree), Elks (organist Du Quoin club 1992-94). Roman Catholic. Avocation: antiques. Banking, Probate. Home: 2372 Magnolia Rd Du Quoin IL 62832-3609 Office: 18 N Oak St Du Quoin IL 62832-1615

**ATKINS, C(ARL) CLYDE,** federal judge; b. Washington, Nov. 23, 1914; s. C. C. and Marguerite (Criste) A.; m. Esther Castillo, Jan 18, 1937; children: Julie A. Landrigan, Carla A. Schulte (dec.), Carl Clyde (dec.). Student, U. Miami, Fla., 1931-32; LLB, U. Fla., 1936; LLD, Barry Coll. (now Barry U.), Miami Shores, 1966; JD, U. Fla., 1967; LLD (hon.), U. Miami, Miami Shores, 1970; LLD, St. Thomas of Villanova U. (formerly Biscayne Coll.), Miami, 1970. Bar: Fla. 1936. Pvt. practice Stuart, Fla., 1936-41, Miami, Fla., 1941-66; ptnr. firm Walton, Lantaff, Schroeder, Atkins, Carson & Wahl (and predecessors), 1941-66; judge U.S. Dist. Ct. (so. dist.) Fla., 1966—, chief judge, 1977-82, sr. judge, 1983—; founder-trustee Lawyers Title Guaranty Fund (now Atty.'s Title Ins. Fund, Inc.), 1948-66, treas., 1963-66. Contbr. articles to profl. jours. Pres. St. Augustine Diocesan Union of Holy Name Societies, 1950-51, Miami Archdiocesan Coun. Cath. Men, 1959-70. Recipient Outstanding Cath. award NCCJ, 1959, Lifetime Achievement award Attys. divsn. Greater Miami Jewish Fed., 1997; establishment of C. Clyde Atkins Moot Ct. Series by U. Miami Sch. Law, 1997. Fellow Am. Coll. Trial Lawyers; mem. ABA, (jud. adminstrv. divsn. Ho. of Dels., 1960-66, 79-80), Dade County Bar Assn. (pres. 1953-54), The Fla. Bar (bd. govs. 1954-59, pres. 1960-61), Nat. Conf. Fed. Trial Judges (chmn. exec. com. 1975-77, del. Jud. Adminstrn. Coun. 1979-82), Nat. Conf. Christians and Jews (chmn. Miami region 1989-95), Miami Kiwanis Club (past dir.), Coral Gables Country Club, Century Club of Coral Gables (past dir.), Serra Club (pres. 1965-66, 91-92), Tau Kappa Alpha, Phi Kappa Tau, Phi Alpa Delta. Office: US Dist Ct Rm 417 301 N Miami Ave Miami FL 33128-7705

**ATKINS, PETER ALLAN,** lawyer; b. N.Y.C., June 29, 1943; m. Lorraine Marilyn Feuerstadt, Apr. 3, 1966; children: Aileen Debra, Karen Jennifer. BA magna cum laude, CUNY, 1965; LLB cum laude, Harvard U., 1968. Bar: N.Y. 1969. Assoc. Skadden, Arps, Slate, Meagher & Flom LLP, N.Y.C., 1968-74, ptnr., 1975—; mem. dean's adv. com. Harvard Law Sch.; bd. dirs. A Better Chance, Inc. Contbr. articles to profl. jours. Mem. ABA, N.Y. State Bar Assn., Assn. of Bar of City of N.Y. General corporate, Securities, Mergers and acquisitions. Office: Skadden Arps Slate Meagher & Flom LLP 919 3rd Ave New York NY 10022-3902

**ATKINS, RONALD RAYMOND,** lawyer; b. Kingston, N.Y., Mar. 8, 1933; s. A. Raymond and Charlotte S. A.; m. Mary-Elizabeth Empringham, June 23, 1956; children: Peter Herrick, Timothy Barnard, Suzanne Elizabeth. BS in Econs., U. Pa., 1954; JD, Columbia U., 1959. Bar: N.Y. 1959. Assoc. Pell, Butler, Curtis & LeViness, N.Y.C., 1959-61, ptnr., 1962-67; ptnr. Bisset & Atkins, N.Y.C., 1967—, also Greenwich, Conn., 1982—; also of counsel Davidson, Dawson & Clark, LLP, N.Y.C.; trustee Mianus Gorge Preserve, Inc., chmn., 1984-94. 1st lt. U.S. Army, 1954-56. Fellow Frick Collection, Piermont Morgan Libr.; mem. ABA, N.Y. State Bar Assn., Assn. Bar City N.Y. Republican. Episcopalian. Club: University (N.Y.C.), Grolier Club (N.Y.C.), Field Club (Greenwich, Conn.), U. Pa. Club (N.Y.C.). Probate, Estate taxation, General corporate. Home: Hobby Hill Farm Mianus River Rd Bedford NY 10506 also: 777 North St Greenwich CT 06831-3105

**ATKINS, SPENCER BERT,** lawyer, real estate developer; b. Alamogordo, N.Mex., Aug. 20, 1951; s. Spencer Wyatt and Donnetta Jo (Reeves) A.; m. Eve M. Luteyn, Dec. 12, 1970; children: Mardelle, Erinna, Alissandra. BA in Univ. Studies, U. N.Mex., 1972, JD, 1977. Bar: N.Mex. 1981, U.S. Dist. Ct. N.Mex. 1981, U.S. Ct. Appeals (10th cir.) 1981. Asst. dist. atty. 12th jud. dist. State of N.Mex, Alamogordo, 1981-83, dist. pub. defender 12th jud. dist., 1983-88, dist. atty. 12th Jud. Dist., 1988-96, appt. interm dist. atty., 1988; pvt. practice Alamorgordo, 1997—; real estate developer Alamogordo, 1979—; adv. dir. 1st Nat. Bank, Alamogordo, 1997—. Contbr. articles to profl. jours., 1977. Chmn. planning and zoning commn., Alamogordo, 1982-86; vice chmn. Young Dems. Otero County, Alamogordo, 1985, chmn., 1986-87; mem. N.Mex. Street Gang Task Force, Gov.'s Task Force for Improvement N.Mex. Criminal Justice Records, Gov.'s Task Force Drug Abuse Prevention. Mem. N.Mex. Dist. Attys. Assn. (pres. 1991-92), Nat. Assn. Justice Info. Systems, N.Mex. Jud. Info. Systems Coun., Masons, Elks, Rotary, Delta Theta Phi, Sigma Phi Epsilon. Avocations: music, electronics. Criminal. Home: PO Box 255 Alamogordo NM 88311-0255 Office: 1007 New York Ave Alamogordo NM 88310-6921

**ATKINS, THERESA,** corporate lawyer; b. Seoul, Republic of Korea, Apr. 11, 1953; came to U.S., 1958; d. Stanley Atkins and Elizabeth Severson; divorced; children: Michael Berezansky, Adrian Berezansky. BA in Psychology, SUNY, Oneonta, 1974; JD, Union U., Albany, 1990. Bar: N.Y., U.S. Dist. Ct. (so., no. and ea. dists.) N.Y. Sr. atty. N.Y. State Ct. Appeals, Albany, 1990-92; assoc. Hiscock & Barclay, Albany, 1992-93; adj. prof. law Albany Law Sch., Albany, 1994-96; asst. counsel Gov. of N.Y., Albany, 1993-94; assoc. LeBoef, Lamb, Albany, 1994-97; v.p. of law Telergy, Albany, 1997—. Communications. Office: Telergy One Telergy Pky East Syracuse NY 13057

**ATKINS, THOMAS HERMAN,** lawyer; b. Richmond, Va., Jan. 13, 1939; s. J. Herman Jr. and Elizabeth S. (Lowdermilk) A.; m. Karin-Heide Bach, Feb. 15, 1964; children: Tanja Alexandra, Tiffany Nichole. BA, U. Richmond, 1960; JD, U. Va., 1963. Bar: Va. 1963, U.S. Dist. Ct. (ea. dist.) Va. 1970, U.S. Ct. Appeals (4th cir.) 1970, Ohio 1972. Ptnr. Stallard, Levit & Atkins, Richmond, 1969-70; assoc. May, Garrett & Miller, Richmond, 1970-72; assoc. counsel Cooper Tire & Rubber Co., Findlay, Ohio, 1972-76; from asst. to assoc. counsel ARMCO Inc., Middletown, Ohio, 1976-86; assoc. counsel ARMCO Inc., Parsippany, N.J., 1986-90; assoc. gen. counsel Ebasco Svcs. Inc., N.Y.C., 1990-95, Raytheon Engrs. & Constn., Lyndhurst & Princeton, N.J., 1995—. Served to maj. U.S. Army, 1963-69. Mem. Internat. Bar Assn., Va. Bar Assn., Ohio Bar Assn., Phi Beta Kappa, Omicron Delta Kappa. Republican. Presbyterian. Lodge: Masons (sr. warden 1972). Avocations: scuba diving, traveling, photography. General corporate, Private international, Contracts commercial. Home: 31 Warren Cutting Chester NJ 07930-2728 Office: Raytheon Engrs & Constrn 508 Carnegie Ctr Princeton NJ 08540-6249

**ATKINSON, JEFF JOHN FREDERICK,** law educator, lawyer, writer; b. Mpls., Nov. 12, 1948; S. Frederick Melville Atkinson and Patricia (Bauman) Atkinson Farnes; m. Janis Pressendo, Dec. 22, 1982; children: Tara, Abigail, Grant, Kelsey. BS, Northwestern U., 1974; JD summa cum laude, DePaul U., 1977. Bar: Ill. 1977, U.S. Ct. Appeals (7th cir.) 1977, U.S. Dist. Ct. (no. dist.) Ill. 1978, U.S. Supreme Ct 1982. Editor, reporter various Chgo. area newspapers and radio stas., 1967-71; assoc. Jenner & Block, Chgo., 1977-80; pvt. practice Evanston, Wilmette and Chgo., 1980—; vis. prof., instr. Loyola U. Law Sch., Chgo., 1982-91; adj. prof. DePaul U. Coll. Law, Chgo., 1991—. Author: Modern Child Custody Practice (2vols.) 1986, Am. Bar Assn. Guide to Family Law; contbr. articles on criminal, family, constl. law, health law and ethics to various publs. Elected bd. mem. Avoca Sch., 1999—. Mem. ABA (chmn. child custody com. 1983-84, 86-87, 89-92, mem. editl. bd. Family Advocate 1988-96, mem. publs. devel. bd. 1984-89, mem. task force on needs of children 1983-85, chmn. rsch. com. 1987-88, Merit awards 1984, 86-94), ACLU (bd. dirs. Ill. div. 1972-74), Ill. Bar Assn., Am. Health Lawyers Assn., Northwestern U. Coll. Alumni Assn. (v.p. 1987-89). Home: 3514 Riverside Dr Wilmette IL 60091-1050

**ATKINSON, MICHAEL PEARCE,** lawyer; b. Ft. Worth, Feb. 19, 1946; s. Charles Pearce and Nancy Lou (Thompson) A.; m. Melissa Jan Potter, July 17, 1976; children: Charles Travis, Kellen Elizabeth. BA, U. Okla., 1968, JD, 1972; MS, U. Tex., 1975. Bar: Okla. 1972, U.S. Dist. Ct. (we. and ea. dists.) Okla. 1972, U.S. Dist. Ct. (no. dist.) Okla. 1975, U.S. Ct. Appeals (10th cir.) 1981. Ptnr. Jones, Atkinson, Williams, Bane & Klingenberg, Enid, Okla., 1972, Best Sharp Thomas Glass & Atkinson, Tulsa, 1980-87, Thomas Glass Atkinson Haskins Nellis & Boudreaux, Tulsa, 1980-93, Atkinson, Haskins, Nellis, Boudreaux, Holeman, Phipps & Brittingham, Tulsa, 1994—; asst. pub. defender Office of Oklahoma County Pub. Defender, Oklahoma City, 1973; asst. dist. atty. Office of Oklahoma County Dist. Atty., Oklahoma City, 1974; asst. adj. prof. Coll. of Law U. Tulsa, 1976-77. With USAR, 1970-72. Master Am. Inns of Ct. (emeritus); fellow Am. Coll. Trial Lawyers; mem. Internat. Assn. Def. Counsel (faculty trial acad. 1986), Am. Bd. Trial Advocates (pres. Okla. chpt. 1995, diplomate). Presbyterian. Avocations: hunting, fishing, running. Product liability, Insurance, Personal injury. Home: 2440 E 28th St Tulsa OK 74114-5611 Office: Aktinson Haskins Nellis Boudreaux Holeman Phipps & Brittingham 525 S Main St Tulsa OK 74103-4509

**ATKINSON, RUSSELL DEAN,** federal bureau of investigation agent, consultant; b. San Jose, Calif.. BA in Math., U. Calif., Santa Barbara, 1969; JD, U. Calif., Berkeley, 1973. Bar: Calif. Spl. agt. FBI, San Jose, Calif., 1973—; probation monitor State Bar of Calif., San Jose, 1992-95. Mem. High Tech. Crimes Investigation Assn. (chmn. legis. com. Silicon Valley chpt. 1992—). Achievements include successful completion of the first federal trade secret theft case in California; successful rescue of kidnapped executive. Avocations: running, computing, cryptology. Office: 950 S Bascom Ave Ste 3011 San Jose CA 95128-3539

**ATKINSON, SHERIDAN EARLE,** lawyer; b. Oakland, Calif., Feb. 14, 1945; s. Arthur Sheridan and Esther Louise (Johnson) A.; m. Margie Ann Lehtin, Aug. 13, 1966. 1 son, Ian Sheridan. BS, U. Calif.-Berkeley, 1966, MBA, 1971; JD, U. San Francisco, 1969. Bar: Calif. 1970. Prin. Atkinson & Assocs., fin. and mgmt. cons., corp. and bus. valuations, San Francisco, 1968—; assoc. Charles O. Morgan, Jr., San Francisco, 1972-76; pvt. practice, San Francisco Bay Area,1976—. With USAR, 1970-76. Mem. Calif. Bar Assn. Republican. State civil litigation, General corporate, General practice.

**ATLASS, THEODORE BRUCE,** lawyer, educator; b. Chgo., June 2, 1951; s. Ralph Louis Atlass and Opal Jeanne Collins. BSBA, U. Denver, 1972; JD, DePaul U., 1975; LLM, U. Miami, Coral Gables, Fla., 1976. Bar: Colo. 1975, U.S. Tax Ct. 1976, U.S. Supreme Ct. 1982. Shareholder Theodore B. Atlass, P.C., Denver, 1976-83, Atlass Profl. Corp., Denver, 1986—; ptnr. Welborn, Dufford, Brown & Tooley, Denver, 1983-85; lectr. Colo. Soc. CPAs, 1977—, Coll. Law U. Denver, 1976—. Chmn. Advanced Estate Planning Symposium U. Denver, 1982—; bd. dirs. St. Joseph Hosp. Found., Denver, 1982-97, Colo. Ballet, Denver, 1985-92. Fellow Am. Coll. Tax Counsel, Am. Coll. Trust & Estate Counsel (Colo. state chair 1996—; fiduciary income tax com. chair 1997—); mem. Denver Estate Planning Coun. (pres. 1991-92), Denver Tax Assn. (pres. 1985), Centennial Estate Planning Coun. (pres. 1993-94). Republican. Presbyterian. Estate planning, Probate, Estate taxation. Office: Atlass Profl Corp Ste 100 3665 Cherry Creek North Dr Denver CO 80209-3712

**ATNEY, IRENE P.,** lawyer; b. Buenos Aires, Mar. 28. BS, CCNY; JD, Hofstra U., 1987; LLM in Environ. Laws, Pace U., 1990. Assoc. Bower & Gardner, N.Y.C., 1987-89; counsel U.S. Dept. Energy/Brookhaven Nat. Lab., Upton, N.Y., 1990—; mem. environ. adv. com. Pace U., White Plains, N.Y., 1992—. Mem. N.Y.C. Bar Assn. (com. nuclear tech. and the law 1994-96, internat. environ. law com. 1999—). Environmental, Government contracts and claims, Private international. Office: US Dept Energy Brookhaven Nat Lab 53 Bell Ave Upton NY 11923

**ATNIP, JOSEPH PRIESTLEY,** lawyer, judge, minister; b. Memphis, Feb. 15, 1955; s. Robert Lee and Nancy (Priestley) A.; m. Kathy Lynn Clark, July 16, 1983; children: Katie Elizabeth, Rebekah Suzanne. BA, U. Tenn., 1979; JD, Vanderbilt U., 1982. Bar: Tenn. 1982, U.S. Dist. Ct. (we. dist.) Tenn. 1988, U.S. Ct. Appeals (6th cir.) 1987, U.S. Ct. Claims 1990. Pvt. practice Obion and Weakley County, 1982-90; dist. pub. defender 27th Jud. Dist. State of Ten., 1990—; city judge Greenfield and Sharon, Tenn., 1986—; bd. advisors Freed Hardeman U., Henderson, Tenn., 1997; mem. exec. com. Dist. Pub. Defenders Conf., Nashville, 1993-94. Bd. dirs. Westate Corrections Network, Union City, Tenn., 1996—. with USN Ceremonial Guard, 1975-77. Mem. Am. Legion, Rotary (pres. Greenfield chpt. 1989-90). Home: 366 Priestly Rd Greenfield TN 38230-3925 Office: Dist Pub Defender 111 Main St Dresden TN 38225

**ATOR, LLOYD GEORGE, JR.,** lawyer, writer, photographer; b. Bozeman, Mont., Feb. 18, 1944; s. Lloyd George and Anna (Beckham) A.; m. Nancy Almand, Feb. 4, 1963; 1 child, Sara Melissa. BA in Polit. Sci., Millsaps Coll., 1966; JD, Vanderbilt U., 1969. Bar: D.C. 1970. Sr. counsel U.S. Senate Legis. Counsel Office, Washington, 1969-80; tax counsel Am. Bankers Assn., Washington, 1980-83; ptnr. Price Waterhouse, Washington, 1983-90; pvt. practice Washington, 1990-91; counsel Alston & Bird, Washington, 1991; prin. Legis. Drafting Svcs., Washington, 1992-94; legis. counsel U.S. Senate Com. Commerce, Sci. & Transp., Washington, 1994—. Co-author: Federal Income Taxation of Banks and Financial Institutions, 1990; author: Federal Income Taxation, 1971, Criminal Procedure, 1970, Blackstone Law Summaries; editorial advisor, columnist jour. Bank Taxation, 1988-91; contbr. articles to profl. jours. Mem. ABA (chmn. internat. tax subcom. banking com. tax sect. 1990-91, chmn. bank and savs. and loan com. tax sect. 1988-89), Internat. Fiscal Assn., Am. Soc. Media Photographers. Avocations: cooking, music, fiction. Corporate taxation, Legislative. Home: 1404 Highland Dr Silver Spring MD 20910-1524 Office: US Senate Com Commerce Sci & Transp Sd 512 Washington DC 20510-0001

**ATTANASIO, JOHN BAPTIST,** dean, law educator; b. Jersey City, N.J., Oct. 19, 1954; s. Gaetano and Madeline (Germinario) A.; m. Kathleen Mary Spartana, Aug. 20, 1977; children: Thomas, Michael. BA, U. Va., 1976; JD, NYU, 1979; diploma in law, Oxford U., 1982; LLM, Yale U., 1985. Bar: Md. 1979, U.S. Dist. Ct. Md. 1980, U.S. Ct. Appeals (4th cir.) 1980, U.S. Supreme Ct. 1983. Pvt. practice Balt., 1979-81; vis. asst. prof. law U. Pitts., 1982-84; assoc. prof. law U. Notre Dame, Ind., 1985-88, prof. law, 1988-92; Regan dir. Kroc Inst. for Internat. Peace Studies, 1991-92; dean Sch. of Law St. Louis U., 1992-98; dean, William Hawley Atwell chair constnl. law So. Meth. U. Sch. Law, Dallas, 1998—. Co-author: Constitutional Law 1989. Chair adv. bd. Ctr. for Civil and Human Rights, 1990-92; mem. Fulbright awards area com., 1994-96; bd. dirs. Legal Svcs. Ea. Mo., 1996-98; bd. dirs. Ctr. for Internat. Understanding, 1993—. Recipient Legal Teaching award Sch. of Law, NYU, 1994. Mem. Ctrl. States Law Sch. Assn. (v.p. 1992-94), Phi Beta Kappa, Alpha Sigma Nu. Democrat. Roman Catholic. Office: So Meth U Sch Law PO Box 750116 3315 Daniel Ave Dallas TX 75275-0116

**ATTER, HELEN SOFGE,** lawyer; b. Orlando, Fla., June 30, 1954; d. John Thomas and Helen Lucille Sofge; m. Michael Anthony Atter, Aug. 27, 1983; children: Lenorae, Brittany. AA, Lake Sumter C.C., Leesburg, Fla., 1974; BA, Fla. State U., 1976; JD, U. Fla., 1980. Bar: Fla. Assoc. Schneider, Dunay, Ryan & Marks, Jacksonville, Fla., 1980-84; v.p., house counsel First Am. Title of Fla., Jacksonville, 1984-87; assoc. gen. counsel PGA Tour, Inc., Ponte Vedra Beach, Fla., 1988-93, v.p. human resources, 1994-96, v.p. corp. compliance, 1996-97; v.p. World Golf Found. Mgmt. Svcs. PGA Tour, Inc., St. Augustine, Fla., 1997—; advisor to bd. TPC Village, Inc., Jacksonville, 1993-97. Vol. counsel Jacksonville Legal Aid, 1982-84; bd. dirs. Vol. Jacksonville, 1998—. Mem. ABA, Fla. Bar Assn. Labor, Real property, General corporate. Office: PGA Tour-WGFMS 21 World Golf Pl Saint Augustine FL 32092-2724

**ATTERBURY, ROBERT RENNIE, III,** lawyer; b. Englewood, N.J., July 11, 1937; s. Robert Rennie Jr. and Beatrice May (Tether) A.; m. Lynda Duer Smith, Sept. 14, 1963; children: Stockton Ward, Kendall C. B. BA, U. Pa.,

1960, LLB, 1963. Bar: N.Y. 1963, Ill. 1966. Assoc. Donovan, Leisure, Newton & Irvine, N.Y.C., 1963-66; atty. Caterpillar Tractor Co., Peoria, Ill., 1966-73; sr. atty. Caterpillar Overseas S.A., Geneva, Switzland, 1973-78; gen. atty. Caterpillar Tractor Co., Peoria, 1978-83; assoc. gen. counsel Caterpillar Inc., Peoria, 1983-91, v.p., sec., gen. counsel, 1991—; mem. planning com. Ray Garrett Jr. Corp. and Securities Law Inst., Chgo., 1991—; mem. adv. coun. Asia/Pacific Ctr. for Resolution of Internat. Bus. Disputes, San Francisco, 1991—; mem. Mfrs. Alliance Law Coun. I., Arlington, Va., 1992-98, vice chair, 1998—; mem. The Forum for U.S.-European Union Legal-Econ. Affairs, Boston, 1995—, large law dept. coun., 1996—; mem. corp. counsel com. Nat. Ctr. for State Cts., 1998—. Pres. AMC Found., 1991—; bd. dirs. Peoria Symphony Found., 1991—; bd. dirs. Lakeview Mus. Arts and Scis., 1995-98, vice chmn., 1998—; bd. dirs., sec. Lakeview Mus. Found., 1998—. Mem. ABA, SAR, Am. Corp. Counsel Assn., Am. Soc. Corp. Secs., Assn. Gen. Counsel, Country Club Peoria (dir.), Rotary. Contracts commercial, General corporate, Private international. Home: 315 W Crestwood Dr Peoria IL 61614-7328 Office: Caterpillar Inc 100 NE Adams St Peoria IL 61629-0002*

**ATWOOD, JACK MCLEAN,** lawyer; b. Boston, Sept. 19, 1946; s. Bernard Phillips and Dorothy Velda Atwood; m. Susan Ava Ingram Monteo, Sept. 1, 1968 (div. 1974); m. Christine M. Farrell, Jan. 11, 1975 (div. 1992); children: Alyssa, Joshua. BA, U. N.H., 1968; JD, Suffolk U., 1971. Bar: Mass. 1972, U.S. Dsit. Ct. Mass. 1972. Staff atty. Mass. Defenders Com., Brockton, 1972-75; sole practitioner Plymouth, Mass., 1975—. Capt. U.S. Army, 1968-72. Avocations: skiing, reading, home repair. Criminal, Personal injury.

**ATWOOD, JAMES R.,** lawyer; b. White Plains, N.Y., Feb. 21, 1944; s. Bernard D. and Joyce Rose A.; m. Wendy Fisler, Aug. 22, 1981 (div. July 1993); children: Christopher Charles, Carl Fisler. BA, Yale U., 1966; JD, Stanford U., 1969. Bar: Calif. 1969, D.C. 1970. Law clk. to judge U.S. Ct. Appeals, L.A., 1969-70; law clk. to Chief Justice Warren Burger U.S. Supreme Ct., 1970-71; mem. Covington & Burling, Washington, 1971-78, ptnr., 1977-78, 81—; dep. asst. sec. for transp. affairs U.S. Dept. State, Washington, 1978-79, dep. legal adviser, 1979-80; acting prof. Law Sch. Stanford U., 1980. Author: (with Kingman Brewster) Antitrust and American Business Abroad, 2nd edit, 1981. Mem. bd. visitors Law Sch. Stanford U., 1995-97. Mem. ABA, Am. Soc. Internat. Law, Washington Inst. Fgn. Affairs, D.C. Bar Assn. Antitrust, Private international, Federal civil litigation. Home: 8020 Greentree Rd Bethesda MD 20817-1304 Office: Covington & Burling PO Box 7566 1201 Pennsylvania Ave NW Washington DC 20044-7566

**ATWOOD, RAYMOND PERCIVAL, JR.,** lawyer; b. Ossining, N.Y., June 25, 1952; s. Raymond Percival and Berniece Lucille (Beach) A.; m. Theresa Carol Goeken, Aug. 13, 1977; children: Shannon, Heather, Sarah, Raymond III, Jennifer. BS cum laude, U. Nebr., 1972, J.D., 1974; cert. Trial Advocacy, Hastings Coll. Law, U. Calif.-San Francisco, 1978, Advanced Trial Advocacy, Harvard U. Law Sch., 1988. Bar: Nebr. 1975, U.S. Dist. Ct. Nebr. 1975, U.S. Bankruptcy Ct. 1975, Mo. 1978, U.S. Ct. Appeals (8th cir.) 1979. Agy. legal counsel Nebr. Workmen's Compensation Ct., Lincoln, 1975-77; staff counsel Hartford Ins. Co., Kansas City, Mo., 1977-78; ptnr. McCord, Janssen & Atwood, Lincoln, 1978-80, Healey, Wieland, Kluender, Atwood Geier & Bartle, Lincoln, 1980—; educator Lincoln Sch. Commerce, Nebr., 1978-81; bd. dir. legal studies Lincoln Sch. Commerce, Nebr., 1979-81; educator U. Nebr. Coll. Law, Lincoln, 1982—; legal seminar lectr., 1976-91. Contbr. articles to profl. jours. Organizer United Way, Lincoln, 1975-77; campaign chmn. Larson for Legislature, Lincoln, 1984. Mem. ABA, Nebr. Order Barristers, Nebr. Trial Lawyers Assn., Assn. Trial Lawyers Am., Nebr. State Bar, Delta Theta Phi. Unitarian. Workers' compensation. Office: Healey Wieland Atwood Geier & Bartle PO Box 83104 1141 H St Lincoln NE 68508-3256

**ATWOOD, ROY TRESS,** lawyer; b. Streator, Ill., Sept. 21, 1957; s. Roy Crawford and June Tress A.; m. Holly Gene Beggs, Aug. 28, 1981; children: Roy Garrett, Brandon Gregory, Adam Grayson, Andrew Gerard. BS, U. Ill., 1979; JD, So. Meth. U., 1988. Bar: Tex. 1988. Acctg. and fin. mgr. Cargill, Inc., Ft. Worth, 1981-85; atty. Liddell, Sapp, Zivley, Hill & LaBoon, Dallas, 1988-90, Gibson, Dunn & Crutcher, Dallas, 1990-92, Herbert, Adams, Crawford & Atwood, Dallas, 1992-94, Jones, Day, Reavis & Pogue, Dallas, 1994—; Coach nat. mock trial teams So. Meth. U., Dallas, 1992—; mem. faculty Nat. Inst. Trial Advocacy, Dallas, 1997—. Editor-in-chief Jour. Air Law and Commerce, 1987-88 (Best article award 1987); contbr. articles to profl. jours. Mem. Carrollton Zoning Bd. Adjustment, 1995—. Recipient Trial Advocacy award Orgain, Bell & Tucker, 1988. Mem. Am. Inns Ct. (barrister). Republican. Methodist. State civil litigation, Federal civil litigation. Office: Jones Day Reavis & Pogue 2001 Ross Ave Ste 2300 Dallas TX 75201-8001

**AUCHTER, JOHN RICHARD,** lawyer; b. Springfield, Mass., May 1, 1922; s. Frank and Alfaretta (Thurston) A.; m. Norma Jean Ledger Wood; children: Susan Adrienne (dec.), Richard Hagen, Ellen Laura, John Lovejoy, Sarah Jean. BA, Amherst Coll., 1947; JD, Northeastern U., 1950. Bar: U.S. Supreme Ct. 1964, U.S. Dist. Ct. Mass. 1965. Agt. and title atty. Commonwealth Land Title Ins. Co., First Am. Title Ins. Co.; title atty. Lawyers Title Ins. Co.; ptnr. Auchter, Bozenhard, Socha & Ely and predecessor firms, Springfield and Palmer, Mass., 1959-85; counsel Bozenhard, Socha, Ely & Kolber, West Springfield, Mass., 1985—; pvt. practice Palmer, 1985-94; ptnr. Auchter & Thompson, Palmer, 1995—; instr. real estate law Western New Eng. Coll., Springfield, Mass., 1966-69; land ct. examiner, 1956—; justice of peace, 1974—. Contbr. articles to profl. jours. Bd. dirs. Goodwill Industries of Springfield/Hartford Area, Inc., 1952-75, 77—, pres. 1961-67, 73, chmn bd. 1974-75, counsel 1966—; bd. dirs. Alcoholism Services of Greater Springfield, 1973-75, hon. dir. 1975—; bd. dirs. Palmer Ambulance Service, 1984—. Served to cpl. CAC, AUS, 1943-46. Mem. ABA, Mass. Bar Assn., Hampden County Bar Assn., Am. Judicature Soc., Mass. Conveyancers Assn., Estate Planning Coun. Hampden County, Quaboag Valley C. of C., Inc. (bd. dirs. 1978—, pres. 1978-81, chmn. legis. com. 1981—), Exch. Club (co-founder Suburban Springfield 1985—), Home Builders Assn. Greater Springfield (bd. dirs. 1956-58, counsel), Theta Delta Chi. Club: Exchange (Springfield)(pres. 1959-60, bd. dirs. New Eng. dist. 1982-85). Real property, Estate planning, Probate. Home: 39 Meadowbrook Ln Palmer MA 01069-1134 Office: Auchter & Thompson PO Box 967 39 Meadowbrook Ln Palmer MA 01069-1134

**AUCUTT, RONALD DAVID,** lawyer; b. St. Paul, Dec. 28, 1945; s. Howard Lewis and Eleanor May (Malcolm) A.; m. Grace Diane Kok, Apr. 3, 1976; children: David Gerard, James Andrew. BA, U. Minn., 1967, JD, 1975. Bar: Minn. 1975, D.C. 1976, Va. 1978, Tex. 1999, U.S. Supreme Ct. 1978, U.S. Tax Ct. 1980, U.S. Dist. Ct. D.C. 1980, U.S. Ct. Appeals (D.C. cir.) 1980, U.S. Ct. of Claims 1980, U.S. Claims Ct. 1982, U.S. Ct. Appeals (fed. cir.) 1982, U.S. Dist. Ct. (ea. dist.) Va. 1986, U.S. Ct. Appeals (4th cir.) 1986. Assoc. Miller & Chevalier, Chartered, Washington, 1975-81, ptnr., 1982-98; ptnr. McGuire, Woods, Battle & Boothe, L.L.P., McLean, Va., 1998—; mem. bd. advisors IRS Practice Alert, N.Y.C., 1987-93; adj. prof. Sch. Law U. Va., 1998—. Mem. bd. advisors Jour. Taxation Exempt Orgns., 1989—, Bus. Entities, N.Y.C.; mem. editl. bd. Estate Planning, N.Y.C., 1993—, mem. adv. bd. Tax Mgmt. Estates, Gifts, and Trusts Jour., 1999—; editl. adv. bd. Judges and Lawyers Bus. Valuation Update, Portland, Oreg., 1999—; contbr. articles to profl. publs. Sec.-treas. Miller and Chevalier Charitable Found., Washington, 1980-82, pres., 1993-97; bd. dirs. Evang. Free Ch. Am., Mpls., 1986-92, vice moderator, chmn. bd. dirs., 1993-95, moderator, 1995-97; bd. dirs. Coun. for Ct. Excellence, Washington, 1993—, Advocates Internat., Fairfax, Va., 1997—, vice chmn. 1999—; Orgn. Security and Coop. in Europe internat. observer Bulgarian Parliamentary election, 1997; mem. adv. bd. Trinity Law Sch., Santa Ana, Calif., 1998—; bd. visitors U. Minn. Law Sch., 1998—. Lt. USN, 1970-73. Fellow Am. Bar Found., Am. Coll. Tax Counsel, Am. Coll. Trust and Estate Counsel (bd. regents 1996—, chmn. bus. planning com. 1997—, sec. 1999—); mem. ABA (chair taxation sect., com. on estate and gift taxes 1986-88, vice chmn. com. on govt. submissions 1989-91, chmn. 1991-93, coun. 1993-97, liaison to sect. real property, probate and trust law 1990—, vice chair com. ops. 1998—), Internat. Acad. Estate and Trust Law (academician), Christian Legal Soc., Met. Club Washington, Univ. Minn. Law Alumni Assn. (bd. dirs. 1998—). E-mail: rdaucutt@mwbb.com. Taxation, general, Estate planning, Estate taxation. Home: 3417 Silver Maple Pl Falls Church VA 22042-3545 Office: McGuire Woods Battle & Boothe LLP 1750 Tysons Blvd Ste 1800 Mc Lean VA 22102-4215

**AUERBACH, ERNEST SIGMUND,** lawyer, company executive, writer; b. Berlin, Dec. 22, 1936; s. Frank L. and Gertrude A.; m. Jeanette Taylor, 1990; 1 child, Hans Kevin. AB, George Washington U., 1958, JD, 1961; postgrad., U.S. Army Gen. Staff Coll., 1975. Bar: D.C. 1962, Pa. 1978. Atty. So. Ry. Co., Washington, 1961-62; commd 1st lt. U.S. Army, 1962, advanced through grades to col.; served in Germany, Vietnam, Pentagon; div. counsel Xerox Corp., Stamford, Conn., 1970-75; mng. atty. NL Industries, Inc., N.Y.C., 1975-77; from asst. to assoc. gen. counsel, staff v.p. INA Corp., Phila., 1977-79; sr. v.p. INA Svc. Co., 1979-82; sr. v.p., chief of staff INA Internat., 1982-83; pres. internat. life and group ops. CIGNA Worldwide Corp. div. CIGNA Corp., 1984-89; mng. dir. Crusader Life Ins. PLC, Reigate, Eng., 1984-86, chmn., 1986-89; pres., COO N.Y. Life Worldwide Holding, Inc., N.Y.C., 1989-90; pres., CEO Paperless Claims, Inc., N.Y.C., 1991-92; dir. gen. Seguros Azteca Ins. Co., Mexico City, 1992-93; sr. cons. Anderson Consulting, Mexico City, 1993-95; sr. v.p. United Ins. Cos., Inc., Irving, Tex., 1995-97, also pres., CEO student ins. divsn., 1996-97, pres., CEO ins. group, 1997; pres., COO Software Testing Assurance Corp., N.Y.C., 1998; pres., CEO Paperless Adjudication, LLC, N.Y.C., 1998—. Author: Joining the Inner Circle: How To Make It As A Senior Executive, 1990; contbg. author: The Wall St. Jour. on Mng., 1990; contbr. articles to legal, fin., news, and def. jours. Mem. Am. Coun. on Germany; computer sys. tech. adv. com. Dept. Commerce, 1974-76; mem. bd. adv. dirs. Salvation Army, Mexico City, 1993-94; commr. bd. adjustment City of Coppell, Tex., 1996-97. Ret. col. USAR, 1985. Decorated Legion of Merit with oak leaf cluster, Bronze Star. Mem. ABA, Westchester-Fairfield Corp. Counsel Assn. (founding officer), Audubon Soc. (bd. dirs. Greenwich chpt. 1999—), Univ. Club, Nat. Arts Club (N.Y.C.), Army and Navy Club (Washington chpt.). Private international, General corporate, Public international. Home: 36 E Lyon Farm Dr Greenwich CT 06831-4349

**AUERBACH, HILLEL JOSHUA,** lawyer; b. N.Y.C., Dec. 7, 1936; s. Philip and Bernice Lillian (Ackerman) A.; m. Sara-Ann Rosner, July 30, 1961; children-Ellen, Jonathan, Stephen. B.S., MIT, 1958; LL.B., Yale U., 1961; LL.M. in Taxation, NYU, 1962. Bar: N.Y. 1962, Conn. 1967, U.S. Dist. (so. and ea. dists.) N.Y. 1962, U.S. Dist. Ct. Conn. 1967, U.S. Ct. Appeals (2d cir.) 1967. Assoc. Casey Lane & Mittendorf, N.Y.C., 1962-66; ptnr. Winnick Resnik Skolnick & Auerbach, P.C., New Haven, Conn., 1966-87; sole practice, 1987—. Fellow Conn. Bar Found. (chmn. grant com. 1996—, mem. exec. bd. 1998—); mem. ABA, Conn. Bar Assn., New Haven County Bar Assn. Probate, Personal income taxation, General corporate. Office: 60 Commerce Dr Trumbull CT 06611-5403

**AUERBACH, JEFFREY IRA,** lawyer; b. N.Y.C., Mar. 21, 1953; s. Robert Frank and Jo Ann (Kitt) A.; m. Terry Harriet Tretter, June 17. 1984; children: Andrew Daniel, Michael Harrison. BS, Cornell U., 1975; MPhil, Yale U., 1977, PhD, 1981; JD, George Washington U., 1989. Bar: D.C. 1989, U.S. Dist. Ct. D.C. 1989, Md. 1990, U.S. Ct. Appeals (fed. cir.) 1990, U.S. Ct. Appeals (D.C. cir.) 1990. Postdoctoral fellow Nat. Cancer Inst., Bethesda, Md., 1981-82; assoc. sr. investigator SmithKline & French Lab., Phila., 1982-84; rsch. geneticist W.R. Grace & Co., Columbia, Md., 1984-86; patent examiner U.S. Patent & Trademark Office, Washington, 1986; law clk. to assoc. Saidman, Sterne et al., Washington, 1986-90; ptnr. Myers, Rose & Liniak, Bethesda, 1990-91; assoc. Weil, Gotshal & Manges, Washington, 1991-93; ptnr. Howrey & Simon, Washington, 1993—; pres., founder Replicon, Inc., 1995—. Inventor externalization of products of bacteria, methods for the isothermal amplification of nucleic acid molecules. Postdoctoral fellow Am. Cancer Soc., 1981. Mem. ABA, Am. Intellectual Property Law Assn., Md. State Bar Assn., Fed. Cir. Bar Assn. Republican. Avocations: stained glass, bicycling, skiing. Patent, Biotechnology, Federal civil litigation. Home: 13109 Jasmine Hill Ter Rockville MD 20850-3662 Office: Howrey and Simon 1299 Pennsylvania Ave NW Washington DC 20004-2400

**AUERBACH, JOSEPH,** lawyer, educator; b. Franklin, N.H., Dec. 3, 1916; s. Jacob and Besse Mae (Reamer) A.; m. Judith Evans, Nov. 10, 1941; children: Jonathan L., Hope B. Pym. AB, Harvard U., 1938, LLB, 1941. Bar: N.H. 1941, Mass. 1952, U.S. Ct. Appeals (1st, 2d, 3d, 5th, 7th and D.C. cirs.), U.S. Supreme Ct. 1948. Atty. SEC, Washington and Phila., 1941-43, prin. atty., 1946-49; fgn. service staff officer U.S. Dept. State, Dusseldorf, W. Ger., 1950-52; ptnr. Sullivan & Worcester, Boston, 1952-82, counsel, 1982—; lectr. Boston U. Law Sch., 1975-76; lectr. Harvard Bus. Sch., Boston, 1980-82, prof., 1982-83, Class of 1957 prof., 1983-87, prof. emeritus, 1987—; prof. Harvard Extension Sch., 1988, 91-95; bd. dirs. Nat. Benefit Life Ins. Co., N.Y.C., Inacom Corp., Omaha, Auerbach, Christenson, Tagiuri, Inc., Boston; past dir. The Williams Cos., Old Colony Trust Co., Manhattan Fund, Liberty Fund, Hemisphere Fund, Harvard Bus. Sch. Pub. Co. Author: (with S.L. Hayes, III), Investment Banking and Diligence, 1986, Underwriting Regulation and Shelf Registration Phenomenon in Wall Street and Regulation, 1987, also chpt. to book, papers and articles in field. Trustee Mass. Eye and Ear Infirmary, Boston, 1981—, chmn. devel. com., 1985-88, chmn. nominating com., 1993-94; mem. adv. bd., former chmn. devel. com. Am. Repertory Theatre, Cambridge, Mass., 1985—; bd. dirs., past pres. Friends of Boston U. Librs., 1972—; past v.p., bd. dirs. Shakespeare Globe Ctr., N.A., 1983-90; overseer New Eng. Conservatory of Music, 1992-98, mem. fin. com.; bd. dirs. English Speaking Union, Boston, 1995-98; chair 1938 Harvard Pres. Assn.; active Harvard Coll. Fund, Harvard Law Sch. Fund. Decorated Army Commendation medal; recipient Disting. Svc. award Harvard Bus. Sch., 1996, Disting. Teaching award 1993, Exemplary Svc. award Harvard Extension Sch., 1995. Mem. ABA, Mass. Bar Assn., Boston Bar Assn., Harvard Mus. Assn., St. Botolph Club, Harvard Club N.Y.C., Shop Club, Downtown Club. General corporate, Securities, Mergers and acquisitions. Home: 300 Boylston St Apt 512 Boston MA 02116-3923 Office: Sullivan & Worcester 1 Post Office Sq Ste 2300 Boston MA 02109-2129 also: Harvard Bus Sch Cumnock Hall Rm 300 Boston MA 02163

**AUERBACH, MARSHALL JAY,** lawyer; b. Chgo., Sept. 5, 1932; s. Samuel M. and Sadie (Miller) A.; m. Carole Landsberg, July 3, 1960; children—Keith Alan, Michael Ward. Student, U. Ill.; J.D., John Marshall Law Sch., 1955. Bar: Ill. 1955. Sole practice Evanston, Ill., 1955-72; ptnr. in charge matrimonial law sect. Jenner & Block, Chgo., 1972-80; mem. firm Marshall J. Auerbach & Assocs., Ltd., Chgo., 1980—; mem. faculty Ill. Inst. Continuing Legal Edn. Author: Illinois Marriage and Dissolution of Marriage Act, enacted into law, 1977; Historical and Practice Notes to Illinois Marriage and Dissolution of Marriage Act, 1980-88; contbr. chpts. to Family Law, Vol. 2. Fellow Am. Acad. Matrimonial Lawyers; mem. Ill. State Bar Assn. (chmn. family law sect. 1971-72), ABA (vice-chmn. family law sect. com. for liaison with tax sect. 1974-76). Family and matrimonial. Home and Office: 180 N La Salle St Ste 2307 Chicago IL 60601-2703

**AUERBACH, PAUL IRA,** lawyer; b. N.Y.C., Dec. 30, 1932; s. Joseph and Fannie (Steingard) A.; children: Stuart Andrew, Beth Royce; m. Diane Carol Sennet, Feb. 19, 1987. LLB, Bklyn. Law Sch., 1954; CLU, Am. Coll., 1980, ChFC, 1982. Bar: N.Y. 1955, Fla. 1991, U.S. Dist. Ct. (so. and ea. dists.) N.Y., U.S. Dist Ct. (so. dist.) Fla. 1991. Trial counsel Cosmopolitan Mutual Ins. Corp., N.Y.C., 1955-57, Hertz Corp., N.Y.C., 1957-59; ptnr. Brent, Phillips, Auerbach & Dranoff, Rockland, N.Y., 1959-63; prin. Paul I. Auerbach, Atty. at Law, N.Y.C. and Bronx, 1963—, Palm Beach Gardens, Fla., 1990—. Founder Young Dem. Com., Bronx, 1955-60; committeeman Rep. Com., South Orangeton, N.Y., 1970-76. Mem. ABA, KP, N.Y. Bar Assn., N.Y. Criminal Bar Assn., Bronx Bar Assn. (chmn. criminal law com. 1990-91), Nat. Assn. Criminal Def. Lawyers, Internat. Assn. Fin. Planners, Rotary (chmn. drug prevention 1970-74), Palm Beach County Bar Assn., North Palm Beach Bar Assn., Nat. Acad. Elder Law Attys., Sunrise W. Palm Beach Rotary Club, Masons. Avocations: tennis, gourmet food, golf. Criminal, Family and matrimonial, Probate. Home: 11215 Curry Dr Palm Beach Gardens FL 33418 Other: PGA Nat 7 Aiden Ct Palm Beach Gardens FL 33418-7018

**AUERBACH, PHILIP GARY,** lawyer; b. Irvington, N.J., Sept. 26, 1932; s. Sam and Nettie (Walsh) A.; m. Cynthia Auerbach, June 30, 1962; children: Lisa, Jon, Lauren. BS, Ohio State U., 1954; JD, U. Pa., 1959. Atty. Plone & Tomar, Camden, N.J., 1959-60; ptnr. Drazin, Warshaw, Auerbach & Rudnick, Red Bank, N.J., 1960-71; sr. ptnr. Auerbach, Rudnick, Waldman, Ford, Addonizio & Pappa, Red Bank, 1971-86; pvt. practice Red Bank, 1986-88; ptnr. Auerbach, Melody & Cox, Red Bank, 1988-92, Auerbach & Cox, Red Bank, 1992-94; pvt. practice, 1994—; adj. prof. Rutgers Law Sch., Newark, 1971—; vis. prof. Ct. Practice Inst., Chgo., Willamette Sch. Law, Salem, Oreg.; speaker nationally; keynote speaker Willamette U., Salem, Oreg., 1991. Author: Try It, 1976, Try It Again, 1992; contbr. articles to profl. jours., chpts. to books. Atty. Bd. Adjustment, Red Bank, 1968-69, Millstone, N.J., 1973-74; mem. Supreme Ct. Com. Civil Procedure. Mem. ABA, N.J. State Bar Assn., N.J. Trial Attys. (pres. 1970-71, chmn. 1971-72, Trial Bar award 1992), Inns of Ct. (pres. Monmouth County Haydn proctor 1994-95). Avocations: skiing, jogging, tennis. General civil litigation, Criminal, Personal injury. Office: 231 Maple Ave Red Bank NJ 07701-1727

**AUFILL, BENNETT BRANTLEY, III,** lawyer; b. Hillsboro, Tex., Feb. 15, 1943; s. Bennett Brantley II and Lucille (Pinkerton) A.; m. Mary Ella Keeter; children: Bennett Brantley IV, Benjamin Arthur. BA in Chemistry, Tex. Christian U., 1965; MS in Mech. Engring., U. N.Mex., 1971; JD, South Tex. Coll. Law, Houston, 1974; MBA, So. Meth. U., 1987. Bar: Tex. 1975. Registered profl. engr. Tex. 1975. Physicist USAF Weapons Lab., Albuquerque, 1967-71; prin. engr. Houston Lighting & Power, 1971-76; environ. coord. Exxon (Carter Mining Co.), Gillette, Wyo., 1977-80; atty. Ctrl. & Southwest, Dallas, 1980-90; assoc. Burleson Pate & Gibson, Dallas, 1991-93; pvt. practice Dallas and Hillsboro, 1993—; adj. prof. Cox Sch. of Bus., So. Meth. U., 1990-94; tchr. Southeastern Paralegal Inst., Dallas, 1988—;. Spkr. 20th annual Tex. Oil & Gas Inst., 1994. Mem. Am. Legion (past comdr. Hillsboro Post 4, 1995-97), panel of arbitrators N. Y. Stock Exch., 1993—. Capt. USAF, 1967-71. Recipient E.E. Townes award South Tex. Coll. Law, 1975. Mem. Tex. Supr.'s Assn., S.W. adv. com. Am. Arbitration Assn. Meth. Avocation: ranching. General civil litigation, Criminal, Environmental. Office: PO Box 731 Hillsboro TX 76645-0731

**AUFRECHT, DAVID BRADLEY,** lawyer; b. Chgo., Aug. 19, 1970; s. Michael and Marlene Aufrecht. BS in Bus., Ind. U., 1992; JD, Washington U., St. Louis, 1995. Bar: Ill. 1995, U.S. Dist. (no. dist.) Ill. 1995. Assoc. Shaw Gussis & Domanskis, Chgo., 1996-97, of counsel, 1998; pvt. practice, Chgo., 1998—. Mem. Chgo. Bar Assn. (real estate law com. 1995—). Real property. Office: 55 W Monroe St Ste 3550 Chicago IL 60603-5020

**AUGUSTINI, MICHAEL CHARLES,** lawyer; b. Denver, Sept. 28, 1967; m. Hope Hall, Nov. 18, 1995. BA, Bowdoin Coll., Brunswick, Maine, 1989; JD, U. Maine, 1995. Bar: Maine 1995, U.S. Ct. Appeals (1st cir.) 1996, D.C. 1996. Law clk. U.S. Ct. Appeals, 1st Cir., Bangor, Maine, 1995-96; assoc. Arnold and Porter, Washington, 1996—. Product liability, Federal civil litigation. Office: Arnold and Porter 555 12th St NW Washington DC 20004-1206

**AUGUSTYNSKI, ADAM J.,** lawyer; b. Chgo., June 16, 1965; s. Marian Marcin and Genowefa (Jedrzejek) A.; m. Michele Honora Thorne, Sept. 28, 1991; 1 child, Alexander Thorne. AB with honors, Harvard U., 1986; JD, Northwestern U., 1990. Bar: Ill. 1990. Asst. legis. office U.S. Senator Alan Dixon, Washington, 1984; asst. office of chief of staff U.S. Senator Paul Simon, Washington, 1985; spl. asst. to pres. Polish Nat. Alliance, Chgo., 1989-94; pvt. practice Chgo., 1991—. Democrat. Roman Catholic. Avocations: sports, international politics. General practice, General civil litigation, Real property. Office: 5850 W Bryn Mawr Ave Chicago IL 60646-6226

**AUKLAND, DUNCAN DAYTON,** lawyer; b. Delaware, Ohio, July 6, 1954; s. Merrill Forrest and Elva Sampson (Dayton) A.; m. Diane Sue Clevenger, Aug. 7, 1982. BA, Va. Polytech. Inst., 1978; JD, Capital U., 1982. Bar: Ohio 1982, U.S. Dist. Ct. (so. dist.) Ohio 1982. Legal intern Ohio EPA, Columbus, 1982, staff atty., 1982-83, legal cons., 1983; sole practice Columbus, 1983-90; judge adv. USNG, Columbus, 1990—. Atty. Clean Up and Recycling Backers of Clintonville, Columbus, 1983-89; deacon Overbrook Presbyn. Ch., Columbus, 1986-89. With JAGC, USAR, 1984-90. Mem. Ohio Bar Assn., Va. Poly. Alumni Assn. Cen. Ohio (pres. 1984-85), Ohio Gamma Alumni Corp. (trustee 1983-88, 91-95). Republican. Avocations: golf, home repairs. Home: 5789 Crescent Ct Worthington OH 43085-3804 Office: Ohio Adj Gen's Dept Attn: AGOH-JA 2825 W Dublin Granville Rd Columbus OH 43235-2712

**AULGUR, ROBERT DAVIS,** lawyer; b. Kansas City, Mo., July 16, 1954; s. Robert Morris and Susan Ann A.; m. Nancie Divilbiss Hawke (div.; 1 child, David Andrew; m. Linda Jean McKay, Mar. 30, 1991; stepchildren: Heather McKay, Graham McKay. BA, Westminster Coll., 1976; JD, U. Mo., 1979. Bar: Mo. 1979. Co-editor Missouri Prosecutors Trial Casebook, 1982-84; co-author Missouri Criminal Code-A handbook for law enforcement officers, 1989, 90. Active mem. Muscular Dystrophy Assn., Columbia, 1993; bd. dirs., vice-chair U. Mo. Polit. Action Com., Columbia, 1996—; Chmn. Cmty United Methodist Fin. Commn., 1995; mem. Cmty. United Methodist Bldg. Commn., 1996—; active several Dem. campaigns, 1972—. Named Mo. Prosecutor of Yr., Mo. Assn. Pros. Attys., 1983. Mem. Boone County Bar Assn., Columbia C. of C. (ambassador 1993—, mem. govtl. affairs commn. 1994—, co-chair gov. affairs commn. 1996-97). Methodist. Avocations: traveling, reading, movie watching, collections. Criminal, Family and matrimonial, Juvenile. Home: 3813 Bray Ct Columbia MO 65203-5336 Office: Shurtleff Froeschner Bunn & Aulgur LLC 25 N 9th St Columbia MO 65201-4845

**AUMOEUALOGO, SOLI SALANOA,** public defender; b. Faga'alu, Am. Samoa, May 25, 1939; s. Salanoa S.P. and Faa'alo (Lepogafaiga) A.; m. Fialupe Fiaui, Dec. 7, 1964 (div.); children: Freda Anoni, Robin Peteroni, Sofia Leilani. BS, Okla. Christian Co., Oklahoma City, 1964; JD, Calif. Western Coll., San Diego, 1973. Bar: Am. Samoa 1973. Asst. atty. gen. Dept. Legal Affairs, Pago Pago, Am. Samoa, 1973-77; dir. Pub. Defender's Office, Govt. Am. Samoa, Pago Pago, 1978-95; senator Am. Samoa Legislature, 1995-97, asst. legis. counsel, 1997—; chmn. Am. Samoa Devel. Corp., 1989-92. Chmn. Immigration Bd., 1973-77, Parole Bd., 1973-77, House Rules Com. Legislature, 1966-68; mem. Criminal Justice Adv., 1973-86; candidate for Rep. U.S. Congress, 1986, 88. Mem. Am. Samoa Bar Assn. (pres. 1987-88), Calif. Western Alumni Assn. (pres. 1985-87). Avocations: lawn tennis, fishing. Home: PO Box 4437 Pago Pago AS 96799-4437 Office: Pub Defender's Office PO Box 4030 Pago Pago AS 96799-4030

**AUSHERMAN, LARRY PRICE,** lawyer; b. July 1, 1952. B in Gen. Studies, U. Kans., 1974; M in Natural Resources, U. Mich., 1978; JD, U. N.Mex., 1979. Bar: N.Mex. 1979. Shareholder Modrall, Sperling, Roehl, Harris & Sisk, Albuquerque, 1979—. Mem. ABA (past chair SONREEL hard minerals com.), N.Mex. State Bar Assn. (past chair sect. natural resources, energy and environ. law), Nature Conservancy (trustee, chmn. N.Mex. chpt.). Environmental, Natural resources. Office: Modrall Sperling Roehl Harris & Sisk 500 4th St NW Ste 1000 Albuquerque NM 87102-2186

**AUSNEHMER, JOHN EDWARD,** lawyer; b. Youngstown, Ohio, June 26, 1954; s. John Louis and Patricia Jean (Liguore) A.; m. Carole Marie Ausnehmer; children: Jill Ellen, Amber Layne. BS, Ohio State U., 1976; JD, U. Dayton, 1980. Bar: Ohio 1980, U.S. Dist. Ct. (no. dist.) Ohio 1981, U.S. Supreme Ct. 1984, U.S. Ct. Appeals (6th cir.) 1984. Law clk. Ohio Atty. Gen., Columbus, 1978, Green, Schiavoni, Murphy, Haines & Sgambati Co., L.P.A., 1978; assoc. Dickson Law Office, Petersburg, Ohio, 1979-85 ; sole practice, Youngstown, Ohio, 1984—; asst. prosecuting atty. Mahoning County, Ohio, 1986-89, 92—. Mem. Ohio Acad. Trial Lawyers, ABA, Ohio State Bar Assn., Mahoning County Bar Assn., Columbiana County Bar Assn., Phi Alpha Delta. Democrat. Roman Catholic. Club: Mahoning Valley Soccer (rep. 1982-84). General practice, Personal injury, Workers' compensation. Home: 51 S Shore Dr Boardman OH 44512-5926 Office: PO Box 3965 721 Boardman Poland Rd Ste 201 Youngstown OH 44512-5105

**AUSTIN, ANN SHEREE,** lawyer; b. Tyler, Tex., Aug. 25, 1960; d. George Patrick and Mary Jean (Brookshire) A. BA cum laude, U. Houston, 1983; JD, South Tex. Coll., 1987. Bar: Tex. 1987, U.S. Dist. Ct. (no. dist.) Tex. 1988, U.S. Ct. Appeals (5th cir.) 1989, U.S. Dist. Ct. (we. dist.) Tex. 1990, U.S. Ct. Appeals (D.C. cir.) 1992, U.S. Supreme Ct. 1992, U.S. Dist Ct. (ea. dist.) Tex. 1993. With First City Ops. Ctr., Houston, 1980-85; law clk. Lipstet, Singer, Hirsch & Wagner, Houston, 1985-86, Pizzitola, Hinton & Sussman, Houston, 1986-87; briefing atty. Hon. Hal M. Lattimore Ct. Appeals, 2d Jud. Dist., Ft. Worth, 1987-88; assoc. Cantey & Hanger, Ft. Worth and Dallas, 1988-93, Smith, Ralston & Russell, Dallas, 1993-94, Russell, Austin & Henschel, Dallas, 1994-95; pvt. practice Arlington, 1995-96; prin. Landau, Omahana & Kopka, Ltd., Dallas, 1996-97; asst. city atty. City of Dallas, 1997—; tchr. Project Outreach State Bar of Tex., 1992. Chpt. editor: Cases and Materials on Civil Procedure, 1987. Mem. Ft. Worth Hist. Preservation Soc., com. mem., 1992; fundraiser Nat. Com. Prevention Child Abuse, 1988—, Women's Haven. Mem. Tex. Young Lawyers Assn. (women in the profession com. 1992-94, profl. ethics and grievance awareness com. 1992-94, jud. rev. com. 1990), Dallas Bar Assn. (jud. com. 1992-94, 99—, ethics com. 1999—, comty. involvement com. 1999—), Dallas Assn. Young Lawyers, Dallas Women's Bar Assn. (continuing legal edn. com. 1999—), Ft. Worth Tarrant County Young Lawyers Assn. (treas. 1989-90, dir. 1989, judge Teen Ct., co-chair Adopt-A-Sch. program), Tarrant County Women's Bar Assn., Am. Inns. of Ct. Methodist. Avocations: walking, reading, sky diving. Municipal (including bonds), Labor, Federal civil litigation. Office: City Hall 7DN City Atty's Office 1500 Marilla St Dallas TX 75201-6300

**AUSTIN, DANIEL WILLIAM,** lawyer; b. Springfield, Ill., Feb. 24, 1949; s. Daniel D. and Ruth A. (Ahrenkiel) A.; m. Lois Ann Austin, June 12, 1971; 1 child, Elizabeth Ann. BA, Millikin U., 1971; JD, Washington U., 1974. Bar: Ill. 1974, U.S. Dist. Ct. (cen. dist.) Ill. 1979, U.S. Ct. Appeals (7th cir.) 1980, U.S. Supreme Ct. 1980, U.S. Tax Ct. 1986. Assoc. Miley & Meyer, Taylorville, Ill., 1974-78; ptnr. Miley, Meyer & Austin, Taylorville, 1978-81; prin. Meyer, Austin & Romano P.C., Taylorville, 1981—. Pres. United Fund, Taylorville, 1980, Christian County YMCA, Taylorville, 1983-85, St. Vincent Meml. Hosp. Found., 1998—. Named one of Outstanding Young Men Am., 1985, Outstanding Citizen of City of Taylorville, 1993. Mem. ABA, Ill. Bar Assn., Christian County Bar Assn., Order of Barristers. Democrat. Presbyterian. Club: Taylorville Country (pres. 1985). Lodge: Sertoma (Taylorville pres. 1976). Avocations: golf, photography. Real property, Probate, General corporate. Home: 14 Westhaven Ct Taylorville IL 62568-9064 Office: Meyer Austin & Romano PC 210 S Washington St Taylorville IL 62568-2245

**AUSTIN, J. RUDY,** lawyer; b. Bluefield, W.Va., Aug. 23, 1942; s. James Olin and Vera Elizabeth (Cox) A.; m. Betty Joyce Smoot, June 25, 1965; children: James Andrew, Edward Scott, Bethany Campbell. BA, U. Va., 1964, LLB, 1967. Bar: Va., U.S. Dist. Ct. (we. dist.) Va., U.S. Ct. Appeals (4th cir.). Ptnr. Gentry Locke Rakes & Moore, Roanoke, Va., 1970—; mem. disciplinary bd. Va. State Bar, 1990-96, chmn., 1995-96. Bd. dirs. United Way Roanoke Valley, 1993-96. Fellow Am. Coll. Trial Lawyers, Va. Law Found. Am. Bar Found.; mem. Roanoke Bar Assn. (pres. 1986-87). Insurance, Construction, Intellectual property. Office: Gentry Locke Rakes & Moore PO Box 40013 Roanoke VA 24022-0013

**AUSTIN, JOHN DELONG,** judge; b. Cambridge, N.Y., May 31, 1935; s. John DeLong and Mabel Cowles (Bascom) A.; m. Marcia Kay Behan, Aug. 15, 1969 (dec.); children: John DeLong, Susan Behan. AB, Dartmouth Coll., 1957; postgrad., u. Minn., 1959; JD, Albany Law Sch., 1969. Bar: N.Y. 1970. Editl. dir. Glens Falls (N.Y.) Times, 1960-66; sole practice Glens Falls, 1970-79; law asst. Warren County Judge and Surrogate, 1975-79, N.Y. State Supreme Ct., 1980-84; judge Warren County Family Ct., N.Y., 1984-99, Warren County Ct. and Surrogate's Ct., 1999—; judge; b. Cambridge, N.Y., May 31, 1935; s. John DeLong and Mabel Cowles (Bascom) A.; m. Marcia Kay Behan, Aug. 15, 1969 (dec.); children: John DeLong, Susan Behan. AB, Dartmouth Coll., 1957; postgrad. U. Minn., 1959; JD, Albany Law Sch., 1969. Bar: N.Y. 1970. Editorial dir. Glens Falls (N.Y.) Times, 1960-66; sole practice, Glens Falls, 1970-79; law asst. Warren County Judge and Surrogate, 1975-79; law asst. N.Y. State Supreme Ct., 1980-84; judge Warren County Family Ct. (N.Y.), 1984-99; judge Warren County Court and Surrogates Court, 1999— ; instr. Adirondack Community Coll., Glens Falls. Councilman, Town of Queensbury (N.Y.), 1969-71, supr., 1972-74; budget officer Warren County, N.Y., 1974; mem. N.Y. State Local Govt. Records Adv. Coun. Editor New Eng. Hist. and Geneal. Register, 1970-73; contbr. hist. and geneal. articles to various periodicals. Served with U.S. Army, 1958-60. Recipient Adminstrv. Law prize Albany Law Sch., 1969. Fellow Am. Soc. Genealogists; mem. N.Y. State Bar Assn., Warren County Bar Assn., Mohican Grange, Elks. Republican. Editor New Eng. Hist. and Geneal. Register, 1970-73; contbr. hist. and geneal. articles to various periodicals. Councilman Town of Queensbury, N.Y., 1969-71, supr., 1972-74; budget officer Waren County, N.Y., 1974; mem. N.Y. State Local Govt. Records Adv. Coun. With U.S. Army, 1958-60. Recipient Adminstrv. Law prize Albany Law Sch., 1969. Fellow Am. Soc. Genealogists; mem. N.Y. State Bar Assn., Warren County Bar Assn., Mohican Grange, Elks. Republican. Office: Warren County Mcpl Ctr Lake George NY 12845

**AUSTIN, RAYMOND DARREL,** judge; b. Chilchinbeto, Ariz., Dec. 18, 1953; s. Dan and Alice (Yellowhair) A.; m. Diane Wakeman, Aug. 9, 1980; children: Nabahe, Daniel, Joseph, Taylor. BS in Psychology, Ariz. State U., 1979; JD, U. N.Mex., 1983. Bar: Navajo Nation 1983, Ariz. 1984, Utah 1984, U.S. Dist. Ct. Utah 1984, U.S. Dist. Ct. Ariz. 1984. Atty. Navajo Nation Dept. Justice, Window Rock, Ariz., 1983-85; assoc. justice Navajo Nation Supreme Ct., Window Rock, 1985—; Herman Phleger disting. vis. prof. law Stanford Law Sch., 1995; vis. prof. Ariz. State U. Law Sch., 1996, 98, U. Utah Law Sch., 1996; trainer Indian judges Navajo Jud. Br., Window Rock, 1985—, Nat. Indian Justice Ctr., Petaluma, Calif., 1988—; lectr. on Indian law and tribal ct. systems to law schs. and legal assns.; bd. dirs. Sexual Abuse Tng. Devel. Project for Tribal Judges, Albuquerque, 1986-88; bd visitors U. N.Mex. Law Sch., Albuquerque, 1989. Mem. adv. coun. Indian Legal Programs, Ariz. State U. Coll. of Law, Tempe, 1989-98; bd. dirs. Nat. Indian Justice Ctr., Petaluma, Calif., 1992-98. Recipient letter of commendation Tuba City (Ariz.) Dist. Ct., 1984, Outstanding Contbns. to Indian Ct. Systems award Indian Bar Assn. N.Mex., 1985, Harvard U. Found. medal for outstanding contbns. to Native Am. law, 1999. Mem. Nat. Am. Indian Ct. Judges Assn. (bd. dirs. 1991-94), Ariz. Bar Assn., Utah Bar Assn., Navajo Nation Bar Assn., Navajo Tribe Indians. Democrat. Avocations: reading, running, racquetball, hunting, Navajo language. Office: Navajo Nation Supreme Ct PO Box 520 Window Rock AZ 86515-0520

**AUSTIN, ROBERT EUGENE, JR.,** lawyer; b. Jacksonville, Fla., Oct. 10, 1937; s. Robert Eugene and Leta Fitch A.; children: Robert Eugene, George Harry Talley; m. Carolyn Rhea Songer. BA, Davidson Coll., 1959; JD, U. Fla., 1964. Bar: Fla. 1965, D.C. 1983, U.S. Supreme Ct. 1970; cert. in civil trial law Nat. Bd. Trial Advocacy, Fla. Bar. Legal asst. Fla. Ho. Reps., 1965; assoc. Jones & Sims, Pensacola, Fla., 1965-66; ptnr. Warren, Warren & Austin, Leesburg, Fla., 1966-68, McLin, Burnsed, Austin & Cyrus, Leesburg, 1968-77, Austin & Burleigh, Leesburg, 1977-81; sole practice Leesburg, 1981-83, Leesburg and Orlando, Fla., 1984-86; ptnr. Austin & Lockett P.A., 1983-84, Austin, Lawrence & Landis, Leesburg and Orlando, 1986-92, Austin & Pepperman, Leesburg, 1992—; asst. state atty., 1972; mem. Jud. Nominating Commn. and Grievance Com. 5th Dist. Fla.; gov. Fla. Bar, 1983; trustee U. Fla. Law Ctr. Chmn. Lake Dist. Boy Scouts Am.; asst. dean Leesburg Deanery Diocese Cen. Fla.; trustee Fla. House, Washington, U. Fla. Law Ctr., 1983—, chmn., 1988-90. Mem. Acad. Fla. Trial Lawyers, Am. Arbitration Assn., Am. Law Inst., Nat. Inst. Trial Advocacy, Lake County Bar Assn., Roscoe Pound Am. Trial Found., Timuquana Country Club (Jacksonville), Kappa Alpha, Phi Delta Phi. Democrat. Episcopalian. Home: PO Box 490200 Leesburg FL 34749-0200 Office: Austin & Pepperman 1321 Citizens Blvd Ste C Leesburg FL 34748-3946

**AUSTIN, SCOTT RAYMOND,** lawyer; b. Newark, Ohio, Jan. 14, 1956; s. Frank W. and Donna J. (Essig) A.; m. Jilise B. Bushling, May 27, 1989; children: Alec Steven, Luke William. BS summa cum laude, Ohio U., 1979, MBA, 1981; JD, Georgetown U., Washington, 1984. Bar: Fla. 1984, U.S. Dist. Ct. (so. dist.) Fla. 1986, U.S. Dist. Ct. (mid. dist.) Fla. 1991, U.S. Ct. Appeals (11th cir.) 1995. Law clk. Nat. Assn. Broadcasters, Washington, 1982-83; assoc. Ruden, Barnett et al., Ft. Lauderdale, Fla., 1984-92; ptnr. Houston & Shahady, P.A., Ft. Lauderdale, 1992-97, English, McCaughan & O'Bryan, P.A., Ft. Lauderdale, 1997—. Sr. editor, mem. exec. editl. bd. Law and Policy in Internat. Bus., 1983-84; contbr. articles to profl. jours. Mem. ABA (mem. corp., banking and bus. law sect., chmn. ltd. liability co. legis. revisions com.), Fed. Bar Assn., Broward County Bar Assn., The Fla. Bar, Georgetown Club (pres. 1994—), Beta Gamma Sigma. Avocations: computer music development, programming, international travel. Computer, Mergers and acquisitions, Securities. Office: English McCaughan & O'Bryan 100 NE 3rd Ave Ste 1100 Fort Lauderdale FL 33301-1144

**AUTEN, DAVID CHARLES,** lawyer; b. Phila., Apr. 4, 1938; s. Charles Raymond and Emily Lillian (Dickel) A.; m. Suzanne Crozier Plowman, Feb. 1, 1969; children: Anne Crozier, Meredith Smedley. BA, U. Pa., 1960, JD, 1963. Bar: Pa. 1963. Ptnr. Reed Smith Shaw & McClay (and predecessor), Phila., 1963—. Author articles in field. V.p. N.E. Cmty. Mental Health Ctr., 1971-72; vice chmn. alumni ann. giving U. Pa., 1975-77, 81-82, chmn., 1982-84, trustee, 1977-80, 83-88; pres. Gen. Alumni Soc., 1977-80; chmn. Benjamin Franklin Assocs., 1975-77, 81-82, bd. overseers Sch. Arts and Scis., 1983-96; trustee U. Pa. Health Sys., 1995—, Springside Sch., 1985-88, v.p., 1987-88; pres. Soc. of Coll., 1975-77; v.p. Assn. Reps. for Educated Action, 1971-79; bd. mgrs. Presbyn.-U. Pa. Med. Ctr., 1980—, vice chmn., 1983-85, 88-95; trustee Presbyn. Found. for Phila., 1986—, vice chm., 1996-98, chmn., 1998—; bd. mgrs. Phila. City Inst., 1981—, treas., 1990-99; bd. dirs. Kearsley Home, 1974—, treas., 1990-96, chmn., 1996—; bd. mgrs. St. Peter's Sch., 1975-88, pres., 1978-79; bd. dirs. Greater Phila. Internat. Network, 1989-94, Com. of Seventy, 1990—, Courtland Found., Del Pres Health Care Inc., Courtland Health Care, chmn., 1998—; mem. econ. devel. com. Greater Phila. First Corp.; rector's warden Christ Ch., Phila., 1996—. Mem. ABA, Pa. Bar Assn. (vice chmn. real property sect. 1985-87, chmn. 1987-88), Am. Land Title Assn., Phila. Bar Assn. (vice chmn. young lawyers sect. 1971-72), Juristic Soc. (pres.), Am. Coll. Real Estate Lawyers, Interfrat. Alumni Coun. U. Pa. (pres. 1970-74), French Am. C. of C. (bd. dirs. 1989—), Phi Beta Kappa, Theta Xi (pres. 1974-76, chmn. found. 1977-86), Rittenhouse Club (pres. 1979-82), Union League (bd. dirs., v.p., pres. 1993-94, chmn. Lincoln Found. 1996—), Fourth St. Club (bd. dirs. 1998—), Phila. Club. Episcopalian (vestryman). Real property, Banking, Finance. Home: 120 Delancey St Philadelphia PA 19106-4303 Office: Reed Smith Shaw & McClay 2500 One Liberty Pl Philadelphia PA 19103

**AUTON, LINDA MAY EISENSCHMIDT,** lawyer, nurse; b. Alexandria, Va., Sept. 14, 1952; d. Clyde Raymond and Katherine Mae (Flewelling) Eisenschmidt; m. William G. Auton, May 26, 1973. ADN, Laramie County C.C., Cheyenne, Wyo., 1979; BS magna cum laude, Bridgewater State Coll., 1983; JD, Suffolk U., 1988. Bar: Mass. 1988, U.S. Dist. Ct. Mass. 1989, Ga. 1990, U.S. Supreme Ct. 1994; RN, Mass. Staff and charge nurse VA Med. Ctr., Boston, 1979-80, Cardinal Cushing Gen. Hosp., Brockton, Mass., 1980-85; paralegal Powers & Hall, Boston, 1985-88, assoc., 1988-89; ptnr. Dunn & Auton, Boston, 1989-91; pvt. practice, Abington, Mass., 1991—; developer innovative geropsychiat. unit, unit mgr. Provident Nursing Home, Boston, 1983-84; created AdvoGuard charitable guardianship orgn., 1996; mem. Cranberry Spl. Ethics, Middleboro, Mass., 1993—. Author: Legal, Ethical and Political Issues in Nursing, 1994, So You've Fired RN Magazine, 1995. Trustee Am. Assn. Nurse Atty.'s Found., 1995—, pres. 1997. Mem. Am. Assn. Nurse Attys. (bd. dirs., exec. com. 1984—, pres. 1994), Am. Psychiat. Nurses Assn. (pres. N.E. region 1997-98), Mass. Nurses Assn. (legis. com. dist. III, entrepreneur coun. 1994, steering com. on statewide campaign for safe care), Plymouth Dist. Bar Assn. (sec. 1999), Rockland C. of C., Nat. Acad. of Elder Law Attys., Phi Delta Phi. Avocations: ballroom dancing, equestrian activities. General practice, Health, Landlord-tenant. Office: Advoguard Inc 319 Centre Ave Ste 163 Rockland MA 02370-2613

**AUTRY, EDWARD THOMAS,** lawyer; b. Stone Mountain, Ga., Sept. 6, 1971; s. Amos Randolph and Margaret B. Autry; m. Mary Ellen Gustaitis, Apr. 18, 1998. BS in Acctg., Berry Coll., Rome, Ga., 1993; JD, U. Memphis, 1996. Bar: Tenn. 1996, Miss. 1997, Ala. 1998. Assoc. atty. Williams, McDaniel, Wolfe & Womack, P.C., Memphis, 1995—. Mem. Greater Memphis Planned Giving Coun., 1996—. Mem. Tenn. Bar Assn., Miss. Bar Assn., Ala. Bar Assn., Memphis Bar Assn. Estate planning, Probate, Estate taxation. Office: Williams McDaniel et al 5521 Murray Rd Memphis TN 38119-3717

**AVAGLIANO, FRANCIS ANTHONY,** law educator, secondary education educator; b. Corning, N.Y., Nov. 4, 1947; s. Frank Francis and Frances Margaret (Conzo) A. AS in Bus. Adminstn., Corning Cmty. Coll., 1968; BS in Bus. and Distributive Edn., SUNY, Albany, 1970, MS in Bus. and Distributive Edn., 1974; cert. driver and traffic safety edn., SUNY, Cortland, 1978, C.A.S. supervisory and adminstrn., 1979; cert. in alcohol studies, Rutgers U., 1983. Tchr. bus. and math. Corning Northside Blodgett Jr. H.S., 1970-71; tchr. bus. edn., instr. driver edn. Corning East H.S., 1971—; instr. N.Y. State Drinking and Driving program, 1981—; part-time adj. instr. bus. Corning Cmty. Coll., 1971—, Tompkins-Cortland Cmty. Coll., 1980—; cons. various schs., N.Y.; presenter in field; diversity tng. facilitator Corning-Painted Post Sci. Dist./Corning Inc., 1991—. Recipient Tchr. of Mo. award Rotary Club, 1977, recognition from The Leader newspaper, 1977. Mem. N.Y. State Secondary Principal's Assn., N.Y. State Bus. Tchrs. Assn., Ea. Bus. Tchrs. Assn., Corning Tchrs. Assn., Criminal Justice Soc. Corning Cmty. Coll., YMCA, Elks. Home: 17 W 1st St Corning NY 14830-2629 Office: CPP East HS 201 Cantigny St Corning NY 14830-2018

**AVANT, DANIEL L.,** lawyer; b. Baton Rouge, Feb. 12, 1952; s. John L. and Genevieve R. A.; m. Kathryn Hays, Nov. 1, 1980; 1 child, Jami. BA, La. State U., 1975, JD, 1977. Bar: U.S. Dist. Ct. (mid., ea, and we. dists.) La. 1977, U.S. Supreme Ct. 1981. Ptnr. Avant & Falcon, Baton Rouge, 1977—. Deacon Chapel on Campus, Baton Rouge, 1992—. Appellate, General civil litigation, Labor. Office: Avant & Falcon 429 Government St Baton Rouge LA 70802-6114

**AVANT, GRADY, JR.,** lawyer; b. New Orleans, Mar. 1, 1932; s. Grady and Sarah (Rutherford) A.; m. Katherine Willis Yancey, Feb. 23, 1963; children: Grady M., Mary Willis Yancey. B.A. magna cum laude, Princeton U., 1954; J.D., Harvard U., 1960. Bar: N.Y. 1961, Ala. 1962, Mich. 1972. Assoc. Bradley, Arant, Rose & White, Birmingham, Ala., 1961-63; assoc., ptnr. Long, Preston, Kinnaird & Avant, Detroit, 1972-87; ptnr. Dickinson, Wright, Moon, Van Dusen & Freeman, Detroit, 1988-94; sr. v.p. investment banking North Am. Capital Advisors, Inc., Bloomfield Hills, Mich., 1995-96; pvt. practice Grosse Pointe, Mich., 1996—. Contbr. articles to legal jours. Served to lt. USMC, 1954-57. Mem. ABA (bus. law sect., fed. regulation of securities com.), Am. Law Inst., Assn. of Bar of City of N.Y., State Bar of Mich. (coun. sect. antitrust law 1978-85, chmn. sect. 1983-84, bus. law sect.), Detroit Com. on Fgn. Rels. (exec. com. 1979—, chmn. 1986-88), Grosse Pointe Club, Mountain Brook Club, Knickerbocker Club, Met. Club, Princeton Club of Mich. (pres. 1976-77, 94-95). Episcopalian. Fax: 313-886-6556. Securities, Antitrust, General corporate. Home and Office: 406 Lincoln Rd Grosse Pointe MI 48230-1607

**AVDEEF, THOMAS,** lawyer; b. N.Y.C., Dec. 16, 1940; s. Alexis and Marie Ann Avdeef; m. Lucille Arlene Cardwell, May 8, 1965; children: Christine, Rachel, Andrea. AA, Orange Coast Coll., 1968; BA, Long Beach State U., 1971; JD, Am. Coll. Law, Anaheim, Calif., 1978. Bar: Calif. 1979, U.S. Dist. Ct. (ctrl. dist. ), Calif. 1980, U.S. Dist. Ct. (so. dist.) Calif. 1994, U.S. Dist. Ct. (ea. dist.) Calif. 1995. Police officer Santa Ana (Calif.) Police Dept., 1964-69; investigator Orange County Dist. Atty. Office, Santa Ana, 1969-81, dep. dist. atty., 1981-91; pvt. practice Orange, 1991—. With USN, 1959-63. Mem. Am. Legion, Elks, Moose. Republican. Roman Catholic. Avocations: golf, fishing. Criminal. Office: Law Offices of Thomas Avdeef 158 N Center St Orange CA 92866-1502

**AVERA, TROY G., JR.,** lawyer, pilot; b. Nashville, Ga., May 12, 1947; s. Troy G. Sr. and Margaret R. Avera; divorced; children: Stephanie Elizabeth, Kevin Scott. BSEE, Fla. State U., 1970; MS in Aviation Sys., U. West Fla., 1972; JD, Nova U., 1986. Bar: Fla., U.S. Dist. Ct. (so. and mid. dists.) Fla. Pilot Air Fla., Miami, 1979-84, Midway Airlines, Chgo., 1986-91, United Airlines, Chgo., 1995—; atty. Barwick Dillian Lambert & Ice, Miami, 1992—. Comdr. USNR, 1971-79. Mem. ABA, Fla. Bar Assn. (aviation law com. 1986—). Aviation. Office: Barwick Dillian Lambert & Ice 999 Brickell Ave Ste 555 Miami FL 33131-3041

**AVERY, BRUCE EDWARD,** lawyer; b. Boonville, N.Y., Aug. 16, 1949; s. Edward Cecil and Marian Alma (Pierce) A.; m. Margaret Calvert, June 21, 1969; children: Sarah, Prudence. BA in Sociology, Polit. Sci., Hobart Coll., 1971; JD, U. Louisville, 1976. Bar: Ky. 1976, U.S. Ct. Mil. Appeals 1977, U.S. Army Ct. Mil. Rev. 1984, U.S. Supreme Ct. 1984, Md. 1992, D.C., 1993, U.S. Ct. Vet. Appeals 1992, U.S. Dist. Ct. Md. 1993. Commd. capt. U.S. Army, 1976, advanced through grades to maj., 1983; rschr. U.S. Army Rsch. Inst., Ft. Knox, Ky., 1972-76, atty., 1976-77; atty. U.S. Army, Camp Zama, Japan, 1977-80, U.S. Army Recruiting, Ft. Meade, Md., 1980-83, U.S. Army Claims Svc., Ft. Meade, 1984-87, U.S. Armed Forces Claims Svc., Seoul, Korea, 1987-89; chief claims V Corps, Frankfort, Germany, 1989-91; pvt. practice Rockville, Md., 1991—. Mem. Ft. Knox Bd. Edn., Ky., 1975-76. Mem. ABA, ATLA, FBA, D.C. Bar, Md. State Bar., Ky. Bar Assn. Personal injury, Military, General practice. Office: 51 Monroe St Ste 1509 Rockville MD 20850-2414

**AVERY, EMERSON ROY, JR.,** judge; b. Cortland, N.Y., Mar. 28, 1954; s. Emerson Roy, Sr. and Phyllis Marie (Unold) A.; m. Marilyn Joan Weiss, July 17, 1977; children: Emerson Roy III, Michael Aaron. AB, Syracuse U., 1976; JD, Widener U., 1980. Bar: N.Y. 1981. Assoc. Emerson R. Avery Law Offices, Cortland, 1981-87; asst. pub. def. Cortland County Pub. Def. Office, Cortland, 1982-83, pub. def., 1983-84; asst. dist. atty. Cortland County Dist. Atty. Office, Cortland, 1984-86; corp. counsel dept. law City of Cortland, Cortland, 1988-91; ptnr. Avery & Avery Law Offices, Cortland, 1988-96; asst. dist. atty. Cortland County Dist. Atty.'s Office, 1992-96; judge Cortland County Family and Surrogate Ct., 1996—; adj. prof. bus. law SUNY, Cortland, 1991-96. Bd. dirs. Coop. Extension Cortland County, v.p., 1980-84; bd. dirs. 1879 Houst Mus., Cortland, 1984-86, 93—, United Fund Cortland, 1986-87. Mem. ABA, ATLA, N.Y. State Bar Assn., Cortland County Bar Assn. (past pres.), N.Y. State Trial Lawyers Assn. Republican. Presbyterian. Avocations: reading, coin and stamp collecting, downhill skiing, water skiing, scuba diving.

**AVERY, JAMES THOMAS, III,** lawyer, management consultant; b. Richmond, Va., July 21, 1945; s. James Thomas Jr. and Hester Vail (Kraemer) A.; m. Nancy Carolyn Hoag, June 22, 1968; children: James Thomas IV, Carolyn Sears, John Dolph II. AB magna cum laude, Princeton U., 1967; MBA, JD, Harvard U., 1975. Bar: Mass. 1975, U.S. Dist. Ct. Mass. 1975, U.S. Ct. Appeals (1st cir.) 1975. Assoc. Choate, Hall & Stewart, Boston, 1975-79; dir. Cambridge (Mass.) Research Inst., 1979-85; pres. The Avery Co., Boston, 1985—; prin. Symmetrix, Inc., Lexington, Mass., 1992-94; pres., CEO PHH Fantus Cons., Inc., Hunt Valley, Md., 1995-97; bd. dirs. Boston Pub. Co. Treas. All Saints Ch., Brookline, Mass., 1976-78; vestryman Ch. of Redeemer, Chestnut Hill, Mass., 1985-89. Capt. U.S. Army, 1967-71, Vietnam. Decorated Bronze Star, Air medal. Mem. ABA, Phi Beta Kappa. Republican. Episcopalian. Clubs: Somerset, Harvard, The Second (trustee, sec. 1980-85) (Boston); Brookline Thursday. Avocations: tennis, golf, skiing. Antitrust, General corporate, Securities.

**AVERY, JAMES WILLIAM,** lawyer; b. Brockport, N.Y., July 23, 1957; s. L. Donald and Janice E. Avery; m. Meegan Avery, Nov. 28, 1988; children: Meredith, William. BA, Austin Coll., 1979; JD, U. Denver, 1982. Bar: N.Y. 1982, Colo. 1983, U.S. Ct. Appeals (10th cir.) 1983, U.S. Ct. Appeals (2d cir.) 1989, U.S. Dist. Ct. Colo. 1983, U.S. Dist. Ct. (we. dist.) N.Y. 1989. Lawyer Hansen & Breit, P.C., Denver, 1982-84, Madden & Strate, P.C., Wheat Ridge, Colo., 1984-87, Greengard & Senter, P.C., Denver, 1987-89; pvt. practice Denver, 1989-90; ptnr. Avery & Howe, P.C., Denver, 1990-95; lawyer James W. Avery & Assocs., Denver, 1995—. Mem. adv. bd. Rochester (N.Y.) Found. for Brain Injury, 1990—, HCF Flames Track & Field Club, Aurora, Colo., 1997—, Persecuted Christians Task Force, Highland Ranch, Colo., 1996—. General civil litigation, Personal injury, Professional liability. Home: 10173 Quarry Hill Pl Parker CO 80134-3748 Office: James W Avery & Assocs Ste 700 4600 S Ulster St Denver CO 80237

**AVERY, JOHN ORVAL,** lawyer; b. Idaho Falls, Idaho, June 25, 1951; s. Orval Eames and Lucile (Wheeler) A.; m. Betty Rae Bird, May 15, 1970 (div. May 2, 1997); children: Jonathon Mark, Christopher John, Shelly Ann, Charles B., Tracie Lee, Jacqueline, Stephanie, Alex. Assoc. in Bus., Ricks Coll., 1971; BS in Acctg., Brigham Young U., 1973; JD, U. Idaho, 1985. Bar: Idaho 1985, U.S. Dist. Ct. Idaho 1985, U.S. Tax Ct. 1985. Atty. intern Idaho Legal Aid Clinic, Moscow, 1984-85; dep. prosecuting atty. Bingham County Dep. Atty.'s Office, Blackfoot, Idaho, 1985-86; assoc. atty. Moss & Luke P.A., Blackfoot, 1985-86, Jenkins Law Office, Idaho Falls, 1986-89; ptnr. Cooper Wetzel Avery & Lee P.A., Idaho Falls, 1989—; mem. Ea. Idaho Estate Planning Coun., Idaho Falls, 1993—. Bd. dirs. Bonneville Joint Sch. Dist. 93, 1993—, chmn., 1996—. Mem. Idaho State Bar Assn. (family law sect. 1993—). Republican. Mem. Ch. LDS. Avocations: skiing, sailing, golfing, hiking, horseback riding. Contracts commercial, Estate planning, Family and matrimonial. Office: Cooper Wetzel Avery & Lee PA 770 S Woodruff Ave Idaho Falls ID 83401-5285

**AVERY, REIGH KESSEN,** legal assistant; b. Cin., Sept. 16, 1949; d. Henry Charles and Margaret Elizabeth (Dam) Kessen; m. Gerald L. Poe, Oct. 5, 1968 (div. Nov. 1989); children: Amy Kathleen, Michael Lee; m. Melvin L. Avery, May 6, 1996. AAS, El Centro Coll., Dallas, 1988. Legal sec. Victor C. McCrea Jr. & Co., Dallas, 1983-84, legal asst., 1986-90; legal sec. Fanning, Harper & Martinson, Dallas, 1984-86, Thompson & Knight, Dallas, 1986; legal asst. Nacol, Wortham & Assocs., Dallas, 1990-91; sr. legal asst. Snelling and Snelling, Inc., Dallas, 1992-93; free-lance legal asst. Tex., 1993-95; sr. legal asst. Nationwide Mutual Ins. Co., 1995—. Chair comm. Fox Meadow Farms Homeowners Assn., Loveland, Ohio, 1972-74; pro bono vol. Child Support Clinic, Dallas, 1988, North Ctrl. Tex. Legal Svcs. Found., Inc., Dallas, 1988—; vol. Ramses The Gt. Exhbn. Dallas Mus. Nat. History Assn., 1989. Mem. Nat. Assn. Legal Assts., State Bar Tex. (legal assts. div.), Dallas Assn. Legal Assts. (litigation sect., com. nat. affairs 1988-89), Phi Theta Kappa, Phi Beta Lambda. Avocations: computers, Greek mythology, logic problems, crossword puzzles. Home and Office: 725 Pinoak Dr Grand Prairie TX 75052-6522

**AVGERIS, GEORGE NICHOLAS,** lawyer; b. Chgo., Apr. 18, 1939; s. Charles and Theodora (Thouas) A.; m. Demetra Datsopoulos, Nov. 19, 1967; children: Charles Christopher, Theodora Demetra. BA, North Cen. Coll., 1961; JD, U. Ill., 1964. Bar: Ill. 1964. Assoc. John R. Collis, Hinsdale, Ill., 1964-67, Sweeney & Riman, Chgo., 1967-69; pvt. practice Hinsdale, 1969—. Mem. Ill. State Bar Assn., Ill. Trial Lawyers Assn., Assn. Trial Lawyers Am., Chgo. Bar Assn., DuPage County Bar Assn. (lectr. seminars, chmn. med. legal com., civil practice com.). Republican. Greek Orthodox. Avocations: children, reading, baseball. Personal injury. Home: 801 S County Line Rd Hinsdale IL 60521-4728 Office: 29 E 1st St Hinsdale IL 60521-4115

**AWERDICK, JOHN HOLMES,** lawyer; b. Tarrytown, N.Y., Nov. 28, 1947; s. John Henry and Grace Evelyn (Lawrence) A.; m. Susan Marie McIntosh Awerdick, Mar. 21, 1950; children: Jason, Megan. BS, Georgetown U. Sch. Fgn. Svc., Washington, 1969; JD, Fordham U. Law Sch., N.Y.C., 1974. Bar: N.J., U.S. Dist. Ct. 1974. Assoc. Williams, Caliri, Miller, Otley & Horn, 1974-76; atty. law dept. CBS, Inc., 1976-77; from dir. to v.p. mktg. svcs. Columbia House, 1977-90; of counsel Ferguson, Gille & Romaine, Montclair, N.J., 1990-93; counsel, ptnr. Stryker, Tams & Dill LLP, Newark, N.J., 1993-98; counsel Williams, Caliri, Miller & Otley, Wayne, N.J., 1998—; dir. Parcel Shippers' Assn., 1981-86; legal affairs com. Direct Mktg. Assn., 1996-98; govt. affairs com. 1980-86; co-chair Am. Publishers and Recording Industry Assn. Am., 1980-86; trustee Montclair Hist. Soc., 1987-92, 1997-99. Mem. ABA, N.J. State Bar Assn. (dir. entertainment and arts law sect. 1992-97), The Copyright Soc. U.S., Computer Law Assn. Intellectual property, Trademark and copyright, Advertising. Office: Williams Caliri Miller & Otley 1428 Route 23 Wayne NJ 07470-5826

**AWSUMB, ROBERT ARDIN,** lawyer; b. St. Paul, Minn., Nov. 26, 1959; s. Roger Leonard Awsumb and Paula Ann Downs. BA, U. Minn., 1982; JD magna cum laude, William Mitchell Coll. Law, St. Paul, 1986. Bar: Minn. 1986. Assoc. atty. Rider, Bennett, Egan & Arundel, Mpls., 1986-91; pres., founding ptnr. Rambow & Awsumb, Bloomington, Minn., 1991-98; founder, chief mgr. R.A. Awsumb & Assocs., St. Paul, 1998—; adj. prof. William Mitchell Coll. Law, 1993—; mediator Minn. Supreme Ct., St. Paul, 1994—. Avocations: camping, fishing, travel. Alternative dispute resolution, General civil litigation, Insurance. Home: 645 Montcalm Pl Saint Paul MN 55116-1732 Office: RA Awsumb & Assocs 1525 Landmark Towers 345 Saint Peter St Saint Paul MN 55102-1211

**AXE, NORMAN GOLD,** lawyer; b. Phila., May 15, 1932; s. Morton and Anne Helen (Gold) Axe; m. Geraldine Schaeffer, Aug. 28, 1960 (div.); m.

Eleanor Ruth Klein, Aug. 10, 1969; children—Jason, Audrey, Holly. B.S., Temple U., 1953; J.D. 1958. Bar: Pa. 1959, D.C. 1965, Calif. 1969, U.S. Supreme Ct. 1969, U.S. Ct. Appeals (9th cir.) 1970. Estate tax examiner IRS, Phila., 1959-61, lawyer, Washington, 1961-65; lawyer Am. Trucking Assn., Washington, 1965-66; assoc. various law firms, Los Angeles, 1968-70; sole practice, Santa Monica, Calif., 1970—; instr. Adult Schs., Los Angeles, 1970—, UCLA, 1979-80; referee Calif. State Bar Ct., Los Angeles, 1978-81; arbitrator Los Angeles Superior Ct., 1979—. Served to 1st lt. U.S. Army, 1953-55, col. Res. Mem. Calif. State Bar Assn. Personal income taxation, Estate planning, Probate. Home and Office: 915 Georgina Ave Santa Monica CA 90402-2023

**AXELRAD, ALEXIS SARAH,** lawyer; b. N.Y.C., Aug. 18, 1972; d. Herbert Louis and Rita (Stockler) A. BA, U. Md., 1994; JD, N.Y. Law Sch., 1997. Bar: N.Y. 1998. Intern Gay Men's Health Crisis, N.Y.C., summer 1995; law clk. Equal Employment Opportunity Commn., N.Y.C., summer 1996; rsch. asst. NYLS NYU, N.Y.C., 1996-97; contract litig. asst. Skadden, Arps, Slate, Meagher & Flom, N.Y.C., 1998; assoc. Barst & Mukamal LLP, N.Y.C., 1998—. V.p. N.Y. Law Sch. chpt. N.Y. Civil Liberties Union, N.Y.C., 1995-97. Mem. ABA, Am. Immigration Lawyers Assn., N.Y. State Bar Assn., Assn. of the Bar of the City of N.Y. (com. on immigration and nationality law sect. 1998—), Legal Assn. Women (sec. 1996-97), Phi Alpha Delta. Avocations: books, pets, movies, music. Appellate. Office: Barst & Mukamal LLP 2 Park Ave Fl 19 New York NY 10016-5675

**AXELROD, CHARLES PAUL,** lawyer; b. N.Y.C., Oct. 23, 1941; s. Abraham and Lillian Rose (Neidetch) A.; m. Gail Y. Buksbaum, June 24, 1965; children: Seth Jordan, Tracy Brooke. BS, NYU, 1963; JD, Bklyn. Law Sch., 1966. Bar: N.Y. 1966, U.S. Ct. Appeals (2d cir.) 1967, U.S. Dist. Ct. (so. dist.) N.Y. 1970, U.S. Supreme Ct. 1974, U.S. Dist. Ct. (ea. dist.) N.Y. 1975, U.S. Ct. Appeals D.C. 1979. Assoc. Kane, Kessler & Proujansky, N.Y.C., 1970-72, Law Offices of Richard Frank P.C., N.Y.C., 1972-79; ptnr. Goldstein & Axelrod, N.Y.C., 1980-94, Camhy, Karlinsky & Stein LLP, N.Y.C., 1994—; chmn. legis. sub-com. study of securities laws N.Y. State Assembly, 1972; adj. prof. law Pace U., Pleasantville, N.Y., 1976-77. Vol. atty. City of N.Y. Com. on Human Rights, 1972. Mem. ABA, N.Y. State Trial Lawyers Assn., N.Y. County Lawyers Assn., N.Y. State Bar Assn., Nat. Assn. Securities Dealers (bd. arbitrators), Com. on Securities and Exchs. (N.Y.C.). Democrat. Jewish. Lodge: B'Nai Brith. Securities, General corporate, Contracts commercial. Office: Camhy Karlinsky & Stein LLP 1740 Broadway Fl 16 New York NY 10019-4315

**AXELROD, PETER,** lawyer; b. N.Y.C., Aug. 11, 1948; s. George and Gloria (Washburn) A.; m. Dulcie Jan Pridgeon, June 20, 1970 (div. 1978); m. Joanna R. Kotcher, Apr. 7, 1979 (div. 1998). AB, U. Calif., Berkeley, 1970; JD, U. Calif., 1973. Bar: Calif. 1973, U.S. Dist. Ct. (no. and ea. dist.) Calif. 1973, U.S. Ct. Appeals (9th cir.) 1973. Assoc. Neil D. Reid, Inc., San Francisco, 1973-78; ptnr. Reid & Axelrod, San Francisco, 1978-87, Corte Madera, Calif., 1987-90; mng. ptnr. Reid, Axelrod, Ruane, Kearney & McCormack, Corte Madera, 1991—. Author: (with others) California Torts, 1984, 2d edit., 1997. Mem. Nat. Transp. Safety Bd. Bar Assn. (sec. 1987—), Internat. Soc. Air Safety Investigators (pres. 1991—), Lawyer-Pilots Bar Assn., Def. Rsch. Inst., Aviation Ins. Assn., Helicopter Assn. Internat. Democrat. Avocations: flying, cattle ranching. Aviation, Insurance. Office: Reid Axelrod Ruane Kearney & McCormack 1018 E St San Rafael CA 94901-2823

**AXINN, STEPHEN MARK,** lawyer; b. N.Y.C., Oct. 21, 1938; s. Mack N. and Lili H. (Tannenbaum) A.; m. Stephanie Chertok, May 12, 1963; children: Audrey, David, Jill. BS, Syracuse U., 1959; LLB, Columbia U., 1962. Bar: N.Y. 1962, U.S. Supreme Ct. 1962. Assoc. Cahill & Gordon, N.Y.C., 1963-64, Malcolm A. Hoffman, N.Y.C., 1964-66; assoc. Skadden, Arps, Slate, Meagher & Flom, N.Y.C., 1966-69, ptnr., 1970-97; ptnr. Axinn, Veltrop & Harkrider LLP, N.Y.C., 1997—; adj. prof. Law Sch. NYU, 1981-83, Law Sch. Columbia U., 1983-85. Author: Acquisitions Under H-S-R, 1980; contbr. articles to profl. jours. Chmn. lawyers div. United Jewish Appeal, N.Y.C., 1985-87; mem. exec. com., treas. Jewish Theol. Sem. Am., 1984-96; mem. bd. visitors Columbia Law Sch., 1993—; mem. adv. panel on environ. crimes by orngs. U.S. Sentencing Commn., 1992-94. Capt. U.S. Army, 1965-68. Mem. ABA (council antitrust sect. 1983-85), N.Y. State Bar Assn. (chmn. antitrust sect. 1982-83). Antitrust, Securities, Federal civil litigation. Office: Axinn Veltrop & Harkrider LLP 1633 Broadway New York NY 10019-6708

**AXTELL, CLAYTON MORGAN, JR.,** lawyer; b. Deposit, N.Y., Aug. 4, 1916; s. Clayton Morgan and Olive Aurora (Vosburgh) A.; m. Margaret Williamson RitchieApr. 24, 1943; children: Margaret R. Axtell Stevenson, Clayton Morgan III, Karen R. Axtell Arnold, Susan R. Axtell. AB, Cornell U., 1937, JD, 1940. Bar: N.Y. 1940, U.S. Dist. Ct. (no. dist.) N.Y. 1941, U.S. Supreme Ct. 1964. Assoc. Hinman, Howard & Kattell, Binghamton, N.Y., 1940-48; ptnr. Hinman, Howard & Kattell, Binghamton, 1948—; former mem. adv. bd. First-City Nat. Bank, Binghamton; bd. dirs. Farmers Nat. Bank, Deposit, N.Y., First City Nat. Bank, Binghamton. Pres. N.Y. State Sch. Bd. Attys., Albany, 1962-63, Broome County Bar Assn., Binghamton, 1967-68, Conrad and Virginia Klee Found.; mem. N.Y. State Rep. Com., Binghamton, 1988-93. 1st lt. US Army, 1942-46 ETO. Decorated Bronze Star U.S. Army, 1945, Croix de Guerre, Govt. of France, 1945; recipient Disting Svc. award U.S. Jr. C. of C., 1942; named Young Man of Yr. Binghamton Jr. C. of C., 1949. Mem. ABA, N.Y. State Bar Assn., Hillcrest -Port Dick Kiwanis (pres.), Binghamton Club. Republican. Lutheran. Home: 1338 Chenango St Binghamton NY 13901-1539 Office: Hinman Howard & Kattell 80 Exchange St Ste 700 Binghamton NY 13901-3490

**AYCOCK, CHARLES,** lawyer; b. 1941; m. Margaret Aycock; children: Chris, Karen. BBA, Tex. Tech. U.; LLB, U. Tex. Bar: Tex. 1967. Ptnr. Aldridge, Aycock, Actkinson & Rutter, Farwell, Tex. Mem. ABA, State Bar Tex. (pres. 1999—). Office: Aldridge Aycock Actkinson & Rutter PO Box 286 402 3d St Farwell TX 79325-0286*

**AYE, WALTER EDWARDS,** lawyer; b. Washington, Mar. 24, 1947; s. Ralph Claxton and Elizabeth Ann (Schuchardt) A.; m. Sara Miller, Jan. 16, 1995. BA, U. Pa., 1969; JD with honors, U. Fla., 1975; LLM, NYU, 1976. Bar: Fla. 1975, U.S. Dist. Ct. (mid. dist.) Fla. 1976, U.S. Ct. Appeals (5th and 11th cirs.) 1976, U.S. Tax Ct. 1976, U.S. Ct. Claims 1976. Assoc. Tranam, Simmons, Kempker, Scharf, Barkin, Frye & O'Neill, Tampa, 1976-80, MacFarlane, Ferguson, Allison & Kelly, Tampa, 1980-81; pvt. practice Tampa, 1982—. Contbr. articles to profl. jours. Bd. dirs. Japan Am. Soc. Fla., 1990-95; mem. City of Tampa Barrio Latino Commn., 1988-93; past v.p. Tampa Internat. Trade Coun.; mem. Tampa Bay Area Coun. on Fgn. Rels. Mem. ABA (labor and employee law sect., practice mgmt. sect.), Fed. Bar Assn. (co-chair adminstrv. and standing orders coms.), Nat. Employment Lawyers Assn. (Fla. pres.-elect), Acad. Fla. Trial Lawyers, Fla. Bar Assn. (editor-in-chief, chair practice mgmt. and devel. sect., past v.p. youth and law sect., adv. dir. LOMAS, special tech. adv. com.), Hillsborough County Bar Assn., Tampa Bay PC Users Group, Tampa Yacht and Country Club, Tampa Yacht and Mallet Club, Hyde Park Men's Club, Ye Mystic Krewe of Gasparilla (vice-chmn. Marshalls, chmn. Point Marshalls), Bloomingdale Golfers Club. Avocations: computer activities, golf, tennis, croquet, cooking. Labor, General civil litigation, Taxation, general. Office: 610 W Azeele St Tampa FL 33606-2206

**AYERS, JAMES CORDON,** lawyer; b. Raleigh, N.C., Aug. 2, 1934; s. Edwin White and Laura Cordon (Stedman) A.; m. Leona Bell Weston, Aug. 1, 1965; children: James Cordon Jr., Alan Andrew. BSBA, U. N.C., 1958; JD, Ohio State U., 1977. Bar: Ohio 1977, U.S. Dist. Ct. (so. dist.) 1978, U.S. Ct. Appeals (6th cir.) 1983, U.S. Supreme Ct. 1992. Dist. sales mgr. Gen. Tel. Dir. Co., 1965-71; pres. Cols. Advt. co., 1971-74; sr. v.p. Assoc. Ind. Dir., 1972-74, exec. v.p. univ. dir., 1972-74; asst. atty. gen. workers' compensation sect. State of Ohio, Columbus, 1977-79; pvt. practice James C. Ayers Law Office, Columbus, 1979—; ind. hearing examiner Ohio Dept. Pub. Safety, 1993—; mem. Armed Forces Disciplinary Bd., N.C. 1960; bd. dirs. Post Exch., Camp Lejeune, 1960; summary ct. martial jurisdiction USMC Camp Lejeune, 1960. Chmn. Columbus County March of Dimes, 1961; pres. SBA; jud. panelist Ohio Mock Trial, 1995—. Recipient Dean's award, 1977. Mem. Ohio Bar Assn., Internat. Law Soc. (co-founder 1976), Men's Golf Assn. (dir. 1990-92, treas. 1990-91, v.p. 1992), Scarlet and Gray (dir. 1988, v.p. 1989), The Gang, Phi Delta Phi (Grad. of Yr.). Avocation: golf. General civil litigation, Workers' compensation, Personal injury. Home: 3870 Lyon Dr Columbus OH 43220-4907 Office: Ohio Dept Pub Safety 165 N High St Columbus OH 43215-2402

**AYERS, JEFFREY DAVID,** lawyer; b. Grant, Nebr., Nov. 30, 1960; s. William D. and Lela R. (Gilmore) A.; m. Shelly Jo Dodds, June 11, 1988; children: Sydney Elizabeth, Bailey Anne. BS, Graceland Coll., 1982; MBA, JD, U. Iowa, 1985. Bar: Mo. 1985. Assoc. Stinson, Mag & Fizzell, Kansas City, Mo., 1985-88, Bryan, Cave, McPheeters & McRoberts, Kansas City, 1989-92; ptnr. Blackwell Sanders Peper Martin LLP, Kansas City, Mo., 1992—; mayor City of Lake Tapawingo, Mo., 1993-96. Trustee Little Blue Valley Sewer Dist., 1994-95. Democrat. Reorganized Ch. Latter-Day-Saints. Finance, Banking, Securities. Office: Blackwell Sanders et al 2300 Main St Ste 1100 Kansas City MO 64108-2416

**AYLSWORTH, ROBERT REED,** lawyer; b. Evansville, Ind., Oct. 24, 1953; s. Robert Earl and Loraine L. (Simmons) A.; m. Carolyn Sue Cundiff, Mar. 5, 1976; children—Beth Anne, Benjamin Reed. BS, U. So. Ind., 1975; JD magna cum laude, Ind. U.-Indpls., 1979. Bar: Ind. 1979, U.S. Dist. Ct. (so. dist.) Ind. 1979, U.S. Ct. Appeals (7th cir.) 1992. Assoc. Phillips and Long, Boonville, Ind., 1979-82; dep. pros. atty. Warrick County-2d Jud. Cir. Ind., Boonville, 1980-93; pvt. practice law, Boonville, 1982-93; judge Warrick Superior Ct. 2, Warrick County, Ind., 1993—. Mem. ABA, Ind. State Bar Assn., Warrick County Bar Assn. (pres. 1983), Evansville Bar Assn. Democrat. Office: PO Box 567 112 E Main St Boonville IN 47601-1649

**AYLSWORTH, TONY,** corporation executive; b. Sept. 14, 1963; m. Jodi R. Aylsworth. BS, U. So. Ind., 1986; JD, U. Louisville, 1990; grad., Grad. Sch. Banking, Colo., 1998. Pvt. practice Ind., 1991-93; asst. v.p. Peoples Trust and Savings Bank, Boonville, Ind., 1992-94, trust officer, 1994—, COO, 1998; Pres. Warrick County Bar Assn., 1995-96, BHS/CJHS Bldg. Corp., 1998. Mem. bd. pub. works City of Boonville, 1996-98. Mem. Ind. Bar Assn., Ky. Bar Assn. Office: Peoples Trust and Savings Bank PO Box 307 Boonville IN 47601-0307

**AYLWARD, GRETCHEN PHILLIPS,** lawyer; b. Buffalo, Dec. 20, 1956; d. James Francis and Marcella Anne Phillips; m. Myles Hannan, June 18, 1982 (div. June 1990); 1 child, Kerry Elizabeth; m. Ansgarius Joseph Aylward, Oct. 6, 1990; 1 child, Alexander Joseph. BA, SUNY, Buffalo, 1979, JD, 1995. Bar: N.Y. 1995, U.S. Dist. Ct. (we. dist.) N.Y. Assoc. Griffith & Yost, Buffalo, 1995—. Mem. jr. bd. Buffalo Gen. Hosp., 1986-90; bd. dirs. Buffalo Coun. on World Affairs, 1997—. Mem. ABA, Am. Immigration Lawyers Assn., N.Y. State Bar Assn. Avocations: skiing, travel, reading. Immigration, naturalization, and customs. Office: Griffith & Yost Key Ctr 50 Fountain Plz Buffalo NY 14202-2212

**AYLWARD, J. PATRICK,** lawyer; b. Walla Walla, Wash., Aug. 20, 1951; s. James F. and Mary Jane (Little) A.; m. Peggy D. Deobald, Feb. 13, 1982; children: Alana Nicole, Sean Patrick. BA, Stanford U., 1973; JD, U. Wash., 1976. Bar: Wash. 1976, U.S. Dist. Ct. (ea. dist.) Wash. 1980, U.S. Tax Ct. 1984, U.S. Ct. Appeals (9th cir.) 1984, U.S. Dist. Ct. (we. dist.) 1987. Assoc. Hughes, Jeffers and Danielson, Wenatchee, Wash., 1976-81; prin. Jeffers, Danielson, Sonn and Aylward, P.S., Wenatchee, 1981—; mem. Ltd. Practice Bd., Olympia, Wash., 1985-90; tchr., panel mem. Continuing Edn. Seminars for Attys. and Ltd. Practice Officers, 1981—; mem. Pacific Real Estate Inst., 1997—. Vol. Wash. State Centennial Games, Wenatchee, 1989. Mem. ABA (real property, probate and trust sect.), Am. Coll. Real Estate Lawyers, Wash. State Bar Assn. (exec. com. real property, probate and trust sect. 1991-93, legis. com. 1988—, chair legis. com. 1994-95, Pres. award 1996), Chelan-Couglas County Bar Assn. (pres. 1990-91, v.p. 1988-90, past sec., participant legal aid and edn. programs 1976—), Aircraft Owners and Pilots Assn., Exch. Club. Avocations: flying, skiing, hunting, golfing. Real property, Land use and zoning (including planning). Office: Jeffers Danielson Sonn & Aylward PS 317 N Mission St Wenatchee WA 98801-2005

**AYOUB, PAUL JOSEPH,** lawyer; b. Boston, Nov. 4, 1955; s. Joseph and Eleanore Ayoub; m. Jane Cronin; 1 child, Elizabeth Eleanore. BA magna cum laude, Brown U., 1978; JB, Boston Coll., 1982. Bar: Mass. 1982, U.S. Dist. Ct. Mass. 1984, U.S. Ct. Appeals (1st cir.) 1984, U.S. Tax Ct. 1986. Assoc. Gasten & Snow, Boston, 1982-90, ptnr., 1990-91; ptnr. Peabody & Arnold, Boston, 1991—; mem. steering com. Peabody & Arnold, Boston, 1997—. Chair alumni ann. fund Noble and Greenough Sch., Dedham, Mass., 1988-90, mem. capital campaign com., 1992-96; bd. dirs. St. Jude Children's Rsch. Hosp., Memphis, 1992—, chmn. legal com., 1996-98; mem. adv. com. to exec. bd. St. John of Damascus Ch., Dedham, 1995-98, exec. mgmt. bd. 1997—; mem. capital campaign com. Park Sch., Brookline, Mass., 1996-98; co-chair Alumni Ann. Found., 1998—. Mem. Mass. Bar Assn., Mass. Conveyancers Assn. (pres. 1984—), Mortgage Bankers Assn. Am. (legal affairs com. 1996—), Boston C. of C. (devel. and transp. com. 1997—), Boston Local Devel. Corp. Avocations: piano, running, golf. Banking, Real property, General corporate. Office: Peabody and Arnold LLP 50 Rowes Wharf Fl 7 Boston MA 02110-3342

**AYRES, CAROLINE PATRICIA,** lawyer; b. Charlottesville, Va., June 9, 1957; d. James Clifford and Ruth Deborah (Harris) Ayres. BA, U. Va., 1978, JD, 1981. Bar: Del. 1985, Md. 1991, D.C. 1991, Va. 1993, U.S. Dist. Ct. Del., U.S. Ct. Appeals (3d cir.) D.C., U.S. Supreme Ct. Legis. asst. U.S. House Jud. Com., Washington, 1981; legal cons. John B. Lowe Assocs., Temple Hills, Md., 1982-83; legis. asst. U.S. Senator Charles Percy, Washington, 1983-85; dep. atty. gen. State of Del., Wilmington, 1986-87, asst. New Castle County atty., 1987-88; assoc. Jacobs & Crumplar, P.A., Wilmington, 1988-93; ptnr. Law Offices Caroline Patricia Ayres, Hockessin, Del., 1993—; bd. dirs. United Way, Wilmington, So. Chester Community Med. Ctr., West Grove, Pa. Minority fellow, Va. State Coun. Higher Edn., 1974. Mem. Assn. Trial Lawyers Am., Del. State Bar Assn., Md. Bar Assn., Va. Bar Assn., Va. Trial Lawyers Assn., Del. Trial Lawyers Assn., D.C. State Bar Assn., D.C. Women's Bar Assn. Avocations: playing piano, aerobics, swimming, poetry reading. Environmental, Personal injury, General corporate.

**AYRES, GUY ROBINS, III,** lawyer; b. Salisbury, Md., June 25, 1945; s. Guy Robins Ayres and Marjolane (Reilly) Hopkins; m. Mar. 1, 1969; children: S. Courtney, Chase R., Charles R. BS, U. Md., 1967; JD, U. Balt., 1970. Bar: Md. 1971, U.S. Dist. Ct. Md. 1971, U.S. Ct. Appeals (4th cir.) 1984, U.S. Supreme Ct. 1974. Assoc. Hennesey Law Office, Towson, Md., 1971-72, Goodman Meagher & Enoch, Ocean City, Md., 1972-73; ptnr. Ayres, Jenkins, Gordy & Almand, Ocean City, 1973—; solicitor Mayor and City Coun. of Ocean City, 1982—, city councilman, 1978-82. Avocations: travel, golf, reading. General civil litigation, Municipal (including bonds), Real property. Office: Ayres Jenkins Gordy & Almand 5200 Coastal Hwy # B Ocean City MD 21842-3117

**AYRES, RICHARD EDWARD,** lawyer; b. Salem, N.J., Feb. 2, 1942; s. John Lecroy and Mary Sayre (Fogg) A.; m. Margaret Alice Miles, Aug. 29, 1964; (div. 1985); children: Alice Elizabeth Hutchinson, Richard Alden; m. Merribel Symington, May 17, 1986. AB, Princeton U., 1964; MA in Politics, LLB, Yale U., 1969. Bar: N.Y. 1971, U.S. Ct. Appeals (D.C. cir.) 1971, U.S. Ct. Appeals (1st, 2nd, 5th, 9th, and 10th cirs.) 1972, U.S. Ct. Appeals (8th cir.) 1973, D.C. 1975, U.S. Supreme Ct. 1976. Atty. Vera Inst. Justice, N.Y.C., 1969-70; co-founder, sr. atty. Natural Resources Def. Coun., N.Y.C., 1970-73; sr. atty. Natural Resources Def. Coun., Washington, 1973-91; ptnr. O'Melveny & Myers, Washington, 1991-96; chmn. Nat. Clean Air Coalition, 1975-91; commr. Nat. Commn. Air Quality, 1978-81; mem. Clean Air Act adv. com. U.S. EPA, 1995—; mem. adv. coun. Gas Rsch. Inst., 1991-93; mem. Carnegie Commn. Sci., Tech. and Govt. Task Force Sci. and Tech. in Jud. and Regulatory Decision Making, 1991-93; mem. mayor's environ. adv. coun., Washington, D.C., 1999—. Contbr. articles to profl. jours. Bd. dirs. League Conservation Voters, 1975-94; mem. bd. trustees Natural Resources Def. Coun., 1992—; mem. bd. Clean Air Action Corp., 1993—, New Century Fund, 1993—, Breakthrough Technologies Inst., 1993—. Recipient citation Outstanding Svc. to Pub. Interest, Yale Law Sch., for role in creating pub. interest law movement, 1989; trustee Keystone Ctr., 1998—. Mem. ABA (chmn. environ. values com. sect. adminstrv. law and regulatory practice 1991—, sect. natural resources, energy and environ. law 1995—). Democrat. Environmental. Office: Howrey & Simon 1299 Pennsylvania Ave NW Ste 1 Washington DC 20004-2420

**AYRES, TED DEAN,** lawyer, academic counsel; b. Hamilton, Mo., July 14, 1947; m. Marcia Sue Busselle; children: John Corbett, Jackson Frazer, Joseph Dean. BSBA, Ctrl. Mo. State Coll., 1969; JD, U. Mo., 1972. Bar: Mo. 1972, U.S. Dist. Ct. (we. dist.) Mo. 1972, U.S. Ct. Appeals (8th cir.) 1977, U.S. Supreme Ct. 1977, Colo. 1984, U.S. Dist. Ct. Colo. 1984, U.S. Ct. Appeals (10th cir.) 1984, Kans. 1987. Law clk. to presiding justice Mo. Supreme Ct., Jefferson City, 1972-73; ptnr. Stubbs & Ayres, Chillicothe, Mo., 1973-74; atty. Southwestern Bell Tel. Co., St. Louis, 1974-76; counsel U. Mo., Columbia, 1976-84; univ. counsel U. Colo., Boulder, 1984-86; gen. counsel Kans. Bd. Regents, Topeka, 1986-92, gen. counsel, dir. govtl. rels., 1992-96; acting pres. Pitts. State U., 1995; gen. counsel, assoc. to pres. Wichita (Kans.) State U., 1996—; adj. asst. prof. coll. bus. adminstrn. U. Colo., Denver, 1984-85, adj. assoc. prof., 1985-86; spl. asst. atty. gen. State of Colo., 1984-86, State of Kans., 1987—; presenter region II conf. Assn. Coll. Unions Internat., U. Mo., Rollas, 1983; spkr. Soc. Colo. Archivists, U. Colo., Boulder, 1985; adj. prof. Washburn U., Topeka, 1989; adj. prof. kinesiology and sport studies Wichita State U., 1999—. Contbr. articles to profl. jours. Active adv. com. Boone County (Mo.) Cmty. Svcs.; mem. com. social concerns Mo. United Meth. Ch., 1979-81, supervisory com. Mothers' Morning Out program, 1980-84; adminstv. bd., com. on fin. and stewardship 1st United Meth. Ch., Topeka, 1989-91, family life coun., 1994-95; trustee Mid-Mo. chpt. Nat. Multiple Sclerosis Soc., 1981-84; mem. bd. mgrs. Topeka YMCA-Downtown Br., 1991-96, fedn. coun. Indian Guides program, 1988-91; treas. pack 175 Cub Scouts, 1990-95; bd. dirs. Innovative Tech. Enterprise Corp., 1991-94, S.W. Youth Athletic Assn., Inc., 1994-96, Friends of Topeka Zoo, 1995—, Wichita Tech. Corp., 1997—, Wichita State U. Hist. Preservation Commn., 1998—, parents coun. Truman State U., 1997-99. Curator scholar, 1969-70, Omar E. Robinson scholar, 1970-71, John M. Dalton Ednl. Trust scholar 1971-72. Mem. Mo. Bar Assn., Nat. Assn. Coll. and Univ. Attys. (chairperson Southwestern region 1979-81, bd. dirs. 1985-88, various coms. 1979—, del. and presenter numerous CLE workshops), Friends of Topeka Zoo, U. Mo. Alumni Assn. (life). Education and schools, Constitutional, Labor. Home: 2214 SW Brookfield St Topeka KS 66614-4236 Office: Wichita State Univ 201 Morrison Hl Wichita KS 67260-0001

**AZAR, EDWARD P.,** lawyer; b. Paterson, N.J., Oct. 2, 1952; s. Philip E. and Tess Azar; m. Cyntia M. Azar, Oct. 8, 1977; children: Lauren, Ryan. BS, Seton Hall U., 1974; JD, Widener U., 1977. Bar: N.J., U.S. Dist. Ct. N.J., U.S. Supreme Ct. Sole practitioner Newfoundland, N.J., 1977—. Recipient PBA Silver award Butler (N.J.) Police Dept., 1996. Mem. Passaic County Bar Assn. (trustee 1994-97), Masons, Phi Delta Phi. Republican. Avocations: fishing, boating. Home: 19 Enli St Wayne NJ 07470 Office: 2840 Rte 23 Newfoundland NJ 07435

**BAB, ANDREW LAURANCE,** lawyer; b. N.Y.C., June 2, 1965; s. Donald Stuart and Ryna Thrope B.; m. Cheryl Milone, Dec. 7, 1996; 1 child, Jason Nathaniel. BA, Yale U., 1986; JD, Columbia U., 1992. Bar: N.Y. 1993. Assoc. Lazard Freres & Co., N.Y.C., 1986-89; clk. Chief Judge Thomas J. Meskill, N.Y.C., 1992-93; assoc. Cravath Swaine & Moore, N.Y.C., 1993-97, Debevoise & Plimpton, N.Y.C., 1997—. Mem. Yale Club N.Y. Avocations: piano, tennis, travel, chess. General corporate, Mergers and acquisitions, Construction. Office: Debevoise & Plimpton 875 3d Ave New York NY 10022

**BABB, ALFRED WARD,** lawyer; b. Pitts., Feb. 18, 1940; s. John Donald and Thelma Jean Babb; m. Sherie Ellen Braun, Mar. 25, 1977; children: Paul, Mitch, Michelle, David, Katie, Brandon. JD, U. Calif., San Francisco, 1972. Bar: Calif. 1972, Pa. 1975. Assoc. Bray Baldwin Egan Brietwieser, Martinez, Calif., 1972-74; gen. counsel Nat. Contractors Group, Pitts., 1974-80; ptnr. Babb, Alfred W., Pitts., 1980—; pres. Babb & Assocs., P.C., Pitts, Wexford, New Castle, 1989—. Dir. ARC Allegheny, Pitts., 1998. 1st lt. U.S. Army, 1961-63. Mem. Indsl. Sales (dir., chair 1989). Republican. Labor, Personal injury, Probate. Office: Babb & Assocs PC Ste 401 Temple Bldg New Castle PA 16101

**BABB, DONALD LYNN,** lawyer; b. Stillwater, Okla., Dec. 29, 1953; s. Donald Wayne and Norma Lou (McCleskey) B.; m. Darla Karen Scott, Apr. 9, 1974; children: Derek Kencade, Zachery Vincent. Student, USAF Acad., 1972-73; BA, Okla. State U., 1977; JD, U. Okla., 1980. Bar: Okla. 1980, U.S. Dist. Ct. (we. dist.) Okla. 1980, U.S. Dist. Ct. (ea. dist.) Okla. 1981, U.S. Dist. Ct. (no. dist.) Okla. 1986, U.S. Ct. Appeals (10th cir.) 1982, U.S. Supreme Ct. 1993. Assoc. Pierce, Couch, Hendrickson, Baysinger & Green, Oklahoma City, 1980-86, ptnr., 1987—; lectr., speaker in field. Mem. ABA, Okla. Bar Assn., Oklahoma County Bar Assn., Internat. Assn. Def. Counsel, Def. Rsch. Inst., Internat. Assn. Arson Investigators, Okla. Assn. Def. Counsel. Democrat. Insurance, Personal injury, Product liability. Office: Pierce Couch Hendrickson Baysinger & Green 1109 N Francis Ave Oklahoma City OK 73106-6871

**BABBIN, JED LLOYD,** lawyer; b. N.Y.C., Mar. 16, 1950; s. Harold H. and Pearl (Bander) B.; m. Frances Kloker, June 22, 1975 (div. 1990); children: Jacob Harold, Norman Tyler; m. Sharon Cohen. BE, Stevens Inst. Tech., Hoboken, N.J., 1970; JD, Samford U., 1973; LLM, Georgetown U., 1978. Bar: Ala. 1973, D.C. 1978. Assoc. McKenna, Connor & Cuneo, Washington, 1977-81; v.p., gen. counsel Shipbuilders Coun., Washington, 1977-81; dir. contract policy Lockheed Corp., Washington, 1985-90; dep. under sec. of def. acquisition planning Office Sec. of Def., Washington, 1990-91; ptnr. McGuire, Woods, Battle & Boothe, Washington, 1991-94, Tighe, Patton, Tabackman & Babbin, Washington, 1994—. Capt. USAF, 1973-77. Fellow Nat. Contract Mgmt. Assn.; mem. ABA, Am. Mensa Ltd. Republican. Jewish. Avocations: fishing, bird hunting. Government contracts and claims, Criminal, Administrative and regulatory.

**BABBIN, JEFFREY R.,** lawyer; b. Queens, N.Y., Apr. 6, 1960; s. Saul A. Babbin and Elaine Montrose Usdane; m. Marlene B. Schwartz, May 31, 1992; 1 child, Anna S. BS in Econs., U. Pa., 1981; JD, Stanford U., 1984. Bar: D.C. 1984, U.S. Dist. Ct. D.C. 1985, U.S. Ct. Appeals (3rd cir.) 1986, U.S. Ct. Appeals (9th cir.) 1987, U.S. Dist. Ct. Conn. 1992, Conn. 1993, U.S. Ct. Appeals (D.C., 8th and 2d cirs.) 1996, U.S. Supreme Ct. 1996. Assoc. Pierson Semmes & Finley, Washington, 1984-89, Spiegel & McDiarmid, Washington, 1989-91; assoc. Wiggin & Dana, New Haven, 1992-96, ptnr., 1997—. Co-author: Litigation Issues in the Distribution of Securities: An International Perspective, 1997. Com. chmn. Vision for Greater New Haven, 1994-96. Mem. ABA, Conn. Bar Assn. Democrat. Jewish. General civil litigation, Administrative and regulatory, Appellate. Home: 28 High St Guilford CT 06437-3410 Office: Wiggin & Dana 1 Century Tower New Haven CT 06510-7013

**BABBY, LON S.,** lawyer; b. Bklyn., Feb. 21, 1951. BA, Lehigh U., 1973; JD, Yale U., 1976. Bar: Conn. 1976, D.C. 1977, U.S. Supreme Ct. 1981, U.S. Claims Ct., 1986; cert. agt. Nat. Basketball Players Assn., Nat. Football League Players Assn. Law clk. to Hon. M. Joseph Blumenfeld Dist. Conn., 1976-77; mem. Williams & Connolly, Washington, 1977—; adj. faculty George Washington U. Law Sch., 1991-92. Editor Yale Law Jour., 1974-76; contbr. articles to profl. jours. Mem. ABA, D.C. Bar, Conn. Bar Assn., Phi Beta Kappa, Omicron Delta Kappa. Sports, Contracts commercial. Office: Williams & Connolly 725 12th St NW Washington DC 20005-5901

**BABCOCK, BARBARA ALLEN,** law educator, lawyer; b. Washington, July 6, 1938; d. Henry Allen and Doris Lenore (Moses) B.; m. Thomas C. Grey, Aug. 19, 1979. AB, U. Pa., 1960; LLB, Yale U., 1963. Bar: Md. 1963, D.C. 1964, JD (hon.), U. San Diego 1983, U. Puget Sound, 1988. Law clk. U.S. Ct. Appeals D.C., 1963; assoc. Edward Bennett Williams, 1964-66; staff atty. Legal Aid Agy., Washington, 1966-68; dir. Pub. Defender Svc. (formerly Legal Aid Agy.), 1968-72; assoc. prof. Stanford U., 1972-77, prof., 1977—; asst. atty. gen. U.S. Dept. Justice, 1977-79. Ernest W. McFarland Prof. Law, 1986-97; Judge John Crown Prof. of Law, 1997—. Democrat. Author: (with others) Sex Discrimination and The Law, 1975, Sex Discrimination and The Law: History, Theory and Practice, 1996; (with Carrington) Civil Procedure, 1977, (with Massaro) Babcock, Civil Procedure: Problems and Cases, 1997;

contbr. articles to profl. jours. Home: 835 Mayfield Ave Palo Alto CA 94305-1052 Office: Stanford U Sch Law Stanford CA 94305

**BABCOCK, CHARLES LYNDE, IV,** lawyer; b. Bklyn., June 23, 1949; s. Charles Lynde III and Dorothy (Yates) B.; m. Janet Judd Laughlin, June 12, 1976; children: Katherine Kester, Barbara Yates. AB, Brown U., 1971; JD, Boston U., 1976. Bar: Tex. 1977, U.S. Dist. Ct. (no. dist.) Tex. 1977, U.S. Dist. Ct. (so. dist.) Tex. 1979, U.S. Ct. Appeals (5th and 11th cirs.) 1979, U.S. Supreme Ct. 1980, U.S. Dist. Ct. (we. dist.) Tex. 1981, U.S. Ct. Appeals (9th and 10th cirs.) 1982, U.S. Dist. Ct. (ea. dist.) Tex. 1982. Sportswriter Phila. Inquirer, 1971-73; law clk. to presiding justice U.S. Dist. Ct. (no. dist.) Tex., Dallas, 1976-78; assoc. Jackson, Walker, Winstead, Cantwell & Miller, Dallas, 1978-83, ptnr., 1983—. Author: Business Law for Executives, 1977, Texas Media Law handbook, 1984; contbr. articles to legal jours. Bd. dirs. Freedom of Info. Found. Tex., 1986—. Recipient Disting. Pro Bono Svc. award North Tex. Legal Svcs. Found., 1986. Fellow Tex. Bar Found.; mem. ABA, Tex. Bar Assn. Mem. Soc. of Friends. Avocation: sports. Federal civil litigation, State civil litigation, Libel. Office: Jackson & Walker LLP 6000 Nations Bank Pla 901 Main St Dallas TX 75202-3797 also: Jackson & Walker LLD 1100 Louisiana St Ste 4200 Houston TX 77002-5219

**BABCOCK, CHARLES WITTEN, JR.,** lawyer; b. Kansas City, Mo., Dec. 6, 1941; s. Charles W. and Esther L. (Marcy) B.; m. Sharon K. Chamberlain, June 26, 1976; children: David, William, Susan, Stephen. BA with honors, U. Mo., 1963; JD, Harvard U., 1966. Bar: Mo. 1966, Mich. 1971. Judge advocate USMC, various locations, 1966-69; assoc. Blackwell, Sanders, Kansas City, 1969-71; staff atty. Gen. Motors Corp., Detroit, 1971—. Contbr. articles to profl. jours. Bd. dirs. Mothers Against Drunk Driving, 1992—. Avocation: amateur radio. Administrative and regulatory, General corporate, Product liability. Home: 917 Grand Marais St Grosse Pointe MI 48230-1867 Office: Gen Motors Corp PO Box 33122 Detroit MI 48232-5122

**BABCOCK, JEFFERY ALAN,** lawyer; b. Orlando, Fla., Dec. 12, 1955; s. Dexter Blunt Jr. and Mildred Lucile (Naegelin) B. BA in Econs. cum laude, Tex. Luth. U., 1978; JD, St. Marys U., San Antonio, 1980. Intern civil sect. U.S. Attys. Office, San Antonio, 1980; briefing atty. U.S. Ct. Appeals (4th cir.), San Antonio, 1981-82; asst. dist. atty., trial supr. Dist. Attys. Office, Corpus Christi, Tex., 1982-87; asst. dist. atty. Dist. Attys. Office, Kingsville, Tex., 1985-87; asst. U.S. atty. Laredo, Tex., 1987-89, Houston, 1989—. Mem. campaign for Fred Biery, San Antonio, 1977-78; co-chmn. campaign for Gary Hart, Corpus Christi, 1984. Mem. ABA, Kleberg-Kennedy County Bar Assn., Nueces County Bar Assn., San Antonio Bar Assn., Nueces County Dist. Attys., Tex. Dist. Attys. and County Attys. Assn. (cert. criminal law), Tex. Bar Assn. Office: US Attys Office PO Box 61129 Houston TX 77208-1129

**BABCOCK, KEITH MOSS,** lawyer; b. Camden, N.J., Aug. 5, 1951; s. William Strong Jr. and Dinah Leslie (Moss) B.; m. Jacquelyn Sue Dickman, Aug. 16, 1975; children: Michael Arthur, Max William. AB, Princeton U., 1973; JD, George Washington U., 1976. Bar: S.C. 1977, U.S. Dist. Ct. S.C. 1977, U.S. Ct. Appeals (4th cir.) 1977, U.S. Supreme Ct. 1980. Staff atty. S.C. Atty. Gen.'s Office, Columbia, 1977-78, state atty., 1978-79, asst. atty. gen., 1979-81; ptnr. Barnes & Austin, Columbia, 1981-82, Austin & Lewis, Columbia, 1982-84, Lewis, Babcock & Hawkins, Columbia, 1984—; mem. civil justice adv. com. for dist. S.C., 1991-94. Bd. dirs. Columbia Jewish Community Pre-Sch., 1984, chmn., 1985-86; bd. dirs. Columbia Jewish Community Ctr., 1986-88. Mem. ABA, S.C. Bar Assn. (chmn. prof. resp. com. 1985-86), Richland County Bar Assn., Princeton Alumni Assn. of S.C. (v.p. 1980-86, 88-89, pres. 1990-93, 96-98), George Washington U. Law Sch. Alumni Assn. (bd. dirs. 1983-87), Summit Club, Spring Valley Country Club (Columbia). Democrat. Episcopalian. Federal civil litigation, State civil litigation, Condemnation. Home: 233 W Springs Rd Columbia SC 29223-6912 Office: Lewis Babcock & Hawkins 1513 Hampton St Columbia SC 29201-2928

**BABCOCK, LEWIS THORNTON,** federal judge; b. 1943. BA cum laude, U. Denver, 1965, JD, 1968; LLM, U. Va., 1968. Ptnr. Mitchell and Babcock, Rocky Ford, Colo., 1968-76; atty. City Las Animas, Colo., 1969-74, City Rocky Ford, 1970-76; asst. dist. atty. 11th Jud. Cir., La Junta, Colo., 1973-76, dist. judge, 1978-83; judge Colo. Ct. Appeals, 1983-88, U.S. Dist. Ct. Colo., Denver, 1988—; escrow and loan closing agt. FHA, Rocky Ford, 1973-76. Bd. dirs. Colo. Rural Legal Svcs. Inc., 1974-76. With Colo. N.G., 1968-74. Named to Order St. Ives. Mem. ABA, Colo. Bar Assn., Denver Bar Assn., Colo. Bar Found., North Ind. Dist. Bar Assn. Office: US Dist Ct C-502 US Courthouse 1929 Stout St Rm C550 Denver CO 80294-1929

**BABER, WILBUR H., JR.,** lawyer; b. Shelby, N.C., Dec. 18, 1926; s. Wilbur H. and Martha Corinne (Allen) B.; BA, Emory U., 1949; postgrad. U. N.C., 1949-50, U. Houston, 1951-52; JD, Loyola U., New Orleans, 1965. Bar: La. 1965, Tex. 1966. Sole practice, Hallettsville, Tex., 1966—. Trustee Raymond Dickson Found. Served with U.S. Army. Mem. ABA, ASCE, La. Bar Assn., Tex. Bar Assn., La. Engring. Soc., Tex. Surveyors Assn. Methodist. Lodge: Rotary. Probate, Oil, gas, and mineral, State civil litigation. Office: PO Box 294 Hallettsville TX 77964-0294

**BABIRAK, MILTON EDWARD, JR.,** lawyer; b. Blue Island, Ill., Sept. 27, 1946; s. Milton and Mildred Babirak; B.S., U. Ill., 1968; J.D., John Marshall Law Sch., 1973; LL.M., Georgetown U., 1979. Bar: Ill. 1973, D.C. 1976, Va. 1987, Md., 1997, U.S. Dist. Ct. Md., U.S. Dist. Ct. (ea. dist.) Va. Assoc. Billig Sher & Jones, Washington, 1979-81; pvt. practice Washington, 1981-83; ptnr. Babirak & Fisher, Washington, 1983-90; ptnr. Babirak, Albert & Vangellow, P.C., 1990—. Editor JohnMarshall Law Rev., 1970-72. Mem. D.C. Bar Assn. (dir. com. on emerging bus.), Va. Bar Assn. (estate planning litigation and bus. law), Md. State Bar (estate, litigation and bus. law sect.), Va. Bar Assn., Montgomery County Bar Assn. (estate planning, litigation and bus. law), Fairfax County Bar Assn. General civil litigation, Estate planning, General corporate. Home: 2100 Huntington Ave Alexandria VA 22303-1534 Office: Babirak Albert & Vangellow PC 47539 Coldspring Pl Sterling VA 20165-7446

**BABLER, WAYNE E.,** lawyer, retired telephone company executive; b. Orangeville, Ill., Dec. 8, 1915; s. Oscar E. and Mary (Bender) B.; m. Mary Blome, Dec. 27, 1940; children: Wayne Elroy Jr., Marilyn Anne Monson, Sally Jane Sperry. BA, Ind. Cen. Coll., 1935; JD, U. Mich., 1938; LLD, Ind. Cen. U., 1966. Bar: Mich. 1938, N.Y. 1949, Mo. 1955, Wis. 1963, U.S. Supreme Ct. 1963. Assoc. Bishop & Bishop, Detroit, 1938-42; ptnr. Bishop & Bishop, 1945-48; atty. AT&T, 1948-55; gen. solicitor Southwestern Bell Tel. Co., St. Louis, 1955-63; v.p., gen. counsel, sec. Southwestern Bell Tel. Co., 1965-80, ret., 1980; v.p., gen. counsel Wis. Tel. Co., Milw., 1963-65. Bd. dirs., chmn. St. Louis Soc. Crippled Children; bd. dirs. St. Louis Symphony Soc. Mem. ABA (chmn. pub. utility sect. 1978-79), Fed. Communications Bar Assn., Wis. Bar Assn., Mo. Bar. Assn., Delray Dunes Country Club, Ocean Club. Antitrust, Federal civil litigation, Administrative and regulatory. Home: 11943 Date Palm Dr Boynton Beach FL 33436-5534

**BABLITCH, WILLIAM A.,** state supreme court justice; b. Stevens Point, Wis., Mar. 1, 1941. B.S., U. Wis., Madison, 1963, J.D., 1968. Bar: Wis. 1968. Pvt. practice law Stevens Point, Wis.; mem. Wis. Senate, 1972-85, senate majority leader, 1976-82; justice Wis. Supreme Ct., Madison, 1985—; dist. atty. Portage County, Wis., 1969-72. Mem. Nat. Conf. State Legislators (exec. com. 1979). Office: Wis Supreme Ct PO Box 1688 Madison WI 53701-1688*

**BACA, JOSEPH FRANCIS,** state supreme court justice; b. Albuquerque, Oct. 1, 1936; s. Amado and Inez (Pino) B.; m. Dorothy Lee Burrow, June 28, 1969; children: Jolynn, Andrea, Anna Marie. BA in Edn., U. N.Mex., 1960; JD, George Washington U., 1964; LLM, U. Va., 1992. Asst. dist. atty. 1st Jud. Dist., Santa Fe, 1965-66; pvt. practice Albuquerque, 1966-72; dist. judge 2d Jud. Dist., Albuquerque, 1972-88; justice N.Mex. Supreme Ct., Santa Fe, 1989—, chief justice, 1995-97; spl. asst. to atty. gen. Office of N.Mex. Atty. Gen., Albuquerque, 1966-71. Dem. precinct chmn., albuquerque, 1968; del. N.Mex. Constl. Conv., Santa Fe, 1969; bd. dirs. State Justice Inst., 1994—, V.Chmn. 1999—. Recipient Judge of Yr. award Peoples Commn. for Criminal Justice, 1989, Quincentennial Commemoration Achievement award La Hispanidad Com., 1992, Luchando por la Justicia award Mex. Am. Law Students Assn. U. N.Mex. Law Sch., 1993; J. William Fulbright Disting. Pub. Svc. award George Washington U. Alumni Assn., 1994, Recognition and Achievement award Commn. on Opportunities for Minorities in the Profession, 1992, others; named one of 100 most influential Hispanics Hispanic Bus. Mag., 1997, 98. Mem. ABA, Hispanic Nat. Bar Assn., N.Mex. Bar Assn. (outstanding jud. svc. award 1998), Am. Law Inst., Scribes, Am. Jud. Soc., Albuquerque Bar Assn., Santa Fe Bar Assn., N.Mex. Hispanic Bar Assn., Alumni Assn. (pres. 1980-81), Kiwanis (pres. Albuquerque chpt. 1984-85), KC (dep. grand knight 1968). Roman Catholic. Avocation: reading history. Office: Supreme Ct NMex Supreme Court Bldg PO Box 848 Santa Fe NM 87504-0848

**BACCINI, LAURANCE ELLIS,** lawyer; b. Darby, Pa., Nov. 16, 1945; m. Tracey Judith Lane, Dec. 20, 1969; 1 child, Allyson Alexandra Lane. BS, Drexel U., 1968; JD, Villanova U., 1971. Bar: Pa. 1971, U.S. Dist. Ct. (ea. dist.) Pa. 1973, U.S. Ct. Appeals (3d cir.) 1979. Law clk. to chief judge U.S. Dist. Ct. (ea. dist.) Pa., 1971-73; assoc. Schnader, Harrison, Segal & Lewis, Phila., 1973-78, ptnr., 1979—, mem. exec. com., 1990-91; ptnr. Wolf, Block, Schorr and Solis-Cohen, 1991—; speaker, faculty mem. on labor law Practising Law Inst., N.Y.C.; trustee Phila. Bar Found., 1986—; bd. dirs. Interest on Lawyers Inst. Account Bd. Author: NLRA Supervisor's Handbook; assoc. editor Villanova Law Rev. Recipient Drexel One Hundred honor award, 1992. Mem. Phila. Bar Assn. (bd. govs. 1978—, chmn. 1982, vice chancellor 1986, chancellor-elect 1987, chancellor 1988, commn. on jud. selection, retention and evaluation 1978-79), chmn. exec. com. young lawyers sect., chmn. long range planning com.), Pa. Bar Assn. (ho. of dels. 1983—), ABA (former chair, and dir. young lawyers div. 1981-82, chair long-range planning com., young lawyers div.'s Fed. practice com., fed. jucicial standards com., judicial conf. for 3d cir., house of dels. 1988—, mem. editorial bd. The Labor Lawyer), Greater Phila. C. of C.(bd. dirs. 1988). Labor. Office: Wolf Block Schorr and Solis-Cohen Packard Bldg 12th Flr SE Corner 15 St & Chestnut St Philadelphia PA 19102

**BACETICH, DOMINIC LEE,** lawyer; b. Mt. Vernon, Wash., Oct. 8, 1955; s. Albert Anthony and Norma Jean (Wudtke) B. BA with honors cum laude, Gonzaga U., 1977, JD, 1980. Bar: Wash. 1980, U.S. Dist. Ct. (we. dist.) Wash. 1982. Assoc. Law Offices Michael W. Smith, Anacortes, Wash., 1980-81; ptnr. Smith & Bacetich, Anacortes, 1982-83; assoc. Hutchinson & Foster, Lynnwood, Wash., 1983; ptnr. Law Offices Paul Stocker, Everett, Wash., 1984-85, Bacetich & Wilson, Everett, 1985-86; pvt. practice Everett, 1986-95; prin., owner Bacetich-Duffy, Inc. P.S., Everett, 1995—; bd. dirs. Cuff, Ltd., Seattle, 1992—. Commr., bd. dirs. Emerald City Softball Assn., Seattle, 1983—; bd. dirs., v.p. Anacortes Sch. Bd. Dirs., 1981-82; pres. Kiwanis, 1982. Mem. Skagit County Bar Assn., Snohomish County Bar Assn. (bd. dirs. 1994-96). Democrat. Roman Catholic. Avocations: golf, gardening, cooking, softball. Personal injury, Insurance. Office: Bacetich-Duffy Inc PS 1604 Hewitt Ave Ste 505 Everett WA 98201-3536

**BACH, THOMAS HANDFORD,** lawyer, investor; b. Vineland, N.J., Dec. 25, 1928; s. Albert Ludwig and Edith May (Handford) B. A.B., Rutgers U., 1950; LL.B., Harvard U., 1956. Bar: N.Y. State bar 1957. Asso. firm Hawkins, Delafield & Wood, N.Y.C., 1956-61, Reed, Hoyt, Washburn & McCarthy, N.Y.C., 1961-62; ptnr. Bach & Condren, N.Y.C., 1963-71, Bach & McAuliffe, N.Y.C., 1971-79, Stroock & Stroock & Lavan, N.Y.C., 1979-88, Sullivan & Donovan, N.Y.C., 1989—; co-counsel N.Y. State Senate Housing and Urban Devel. Com., 1971; fiscal cons. N.Y.C. Fin. Adminstrn., 1967-70; asst. counsel State Fin. Com., N.Y. State Constl. Conv. of, 1967; del. U.S./Japan Bilateral Session, 1988, Moscow Conf. on Law and Bilateral Econ. Rels., 1990; spkr. Practicing Law Inst., Mcpl. Bond Workshop, N.Y., 1995-97. Contbr. articles to profl. jours.; co-author: A Guide to Certificates of Participation, 1991, the Handbook of Municipal Bonds, 1994. Mem. N.Y. State Commn. to Study Constl. Tax Limitations, 1974-75; chmn. subcom. Pub. Securities Assn.; dir. Citizens Union of N.Y. Served with U.S. Army, 1951-53, 1st lt. U.S. Army, 1952-53, Japan. Mem. Am. Bar Assn., N.Y. State Bar Assn. (internat. law. sect.), Assn. of Bar of City of N.Y., N.J. Bar Assn., N.Y. Mcpl. Analysts Group (chmn. 1973-74), Mcpl. Forum of N.Y., Tax Collectors and Treas. Assn. of N.J., Market Technicians Assn., Internat. Fin. Svcs. Vol. Corps. Episcopalian. Municipal (including bonds), Securities. Home: 4 E 89th St New York NY 10128-0636 also: 615 W Oak Rd Vineland NJ 08360-2262 Office: Sullivan & Donovan 415 Madison Ave New York NY 10017-1111

**BACHHUBER, MICHAEL JOSEPH,** lawyer; b. Milw., Jan. 15, 1959; s. Martin L. and Marie C. Bachhuber; m. Teddi M. Beam, Aug. 1983 (div. Dec. 1988); children: Karl A., Andrea J. BA, U. Wis., Milw., 1983; postgrad., Antioch U., 1985-86; JD, U. Wis., Madison, 1987. Bar: Wis. 1988, U.S. Dist. Ct. (ea. and we. dists.) Wis. 1988, U.S. Ct. Appeals (7th cir.). Law clk., atty. Podell, Ugent & Cross, S.C., Milw., 1987-88; pvt. practice Milw., 1988-98; advocacy specialist Wis. Coalition for Advocacy, Milw., 1997—. Dir., treas. Milw. Mob for Survival/Peace Action, 1994-96; dir. 20/20 Vision Milw., 1990-97. Mem. Wis. Employment Lawyers Assn. General civil litigation, Administrative and regulatory, Pension, profit-sharing, and employee benefits. Office: Wis Coalition for Advocacy 2040 W Wisconsin Ave Ste 678 Milwaukee WI 53233-2098

**BACINO, BIRGER GREG,** lawyer; b. Loves Park, Ill., Apr. 1, 1959; s. Birger and Fonda Bacino. BS, Western Ill. U., Macomb, 1983; JD, Calif. Western Sch. Law, San Diego, 1990. Bar: Calif. 1990, Tex., Calif. Owner, atty. Law Offices of Birger Greg Bacino, San Diego, 1990—. Mem. ABA, ATLA, San Diego County Bar Assn., Consumer Attys. of San Diego, Consumer Attys. of Calif. Avocations: writing, golf, legal education. Office: Law Offices of Birger Greg Bacino 3033 5th Ave Ste 301 San Diego CA 92103-5873

**BACK, MICHAEL WAYNE,** lawyer; b. Gary, Ind., Oct. 27, 1949; s. Virlan and Eunice Inez (Dooley) B.; m. Deborah Lynn Martinez, Oct. 1, 1988; children: Michael Christiaan, Amelia Michelle, Mark W., Hillary E. BS, Purdue U., 1976; postgrad., John Marshall Law Sch., 1979; 1979. Bar: Ind. 1979, U.S. Dist. Ct. (no. and so. dists.) Ind. 1979. Pvt. practice (atty.) Crown Point, Ind., 1979-87; hearing officer Lake County Circuit Ct., Crown Pl., 1980-87; pvt. practice Lake County Circuit Ct., 1987--. Sargeant USAF, 1969-71. Ind. State Bar Assn., Lake County Bar Assn. (bd. dirs. 1996—), Fed. Bar (bd. govs.), Ind. Trial Lawyers Assn. (bd. govs. 1996—). Democrat. Roman Catholic. Club: Innsbrook Country, Merrillville (sec. 1986-87, bd. dirs. 1985-93, pres. 1991-93). Avocations: golf, tennis. Office: Lake County Circuit Ct 1 Professional Ctr Ste 204 Crown Point IN 46307-1882

**BACKES, JON WILLIAM,** lawyer; b. Grand Forks, N.D., Dec. 3, 1960; s. Orlin William and Mildred L. Backes; m. Karla M. Keller, Sept. 15, 1984; children: Alexandria Ann, Katelyn Keller, Brieann Leigh. BS in Acctg., Minot State U., 1984; JD with distinction, U. N.D., 1990. Bar: Colo. 1990, U.S. Dist. Ct. Colo. 1990, N.D. 1993, U.S. Dist. Ct. N.D. 1993, U.S. Ct. Appeals (8th cir.) 1998. Assoc. Moye Giles O'Keefe Vermeire & Gorrell, Denver, 1990-93; assoc. McGee Hankla Backes & Dobrovolny, Minot, 1993-95, ptnr., 1995—. Editor N.D. Law Rev., 1989-90. Bd. dirs. St. Joseph's Cmty. Health Found., Minot, 1995—, Minot Cath. Schs. Found., 1995—, Minot Art Assn., 1994—. Mem. ABA, Colo. Bar Assn., Denver Bar Assn., Ward County Bar Assn. (pres. 1996), N.D. Bar Assn., Nat. Health Lawyers Orgn., Order of the Coif. Avocations: horses, skiing, hunting, family. General civil litigation, Health, General corporate. Office: McGee Hankla Backes & Dobrovolny 15 2d Ave SW #305 Minot ND 58701

**BACKMAN, GERALD STEPHEN,** lawyer; b. N.Y.C., Apr. 16, 1938; s. Morris and Marion (London) B.; m. Susan Pergament, Sept. 3, 1961 (dec. May 1978); children: Jonathan A., Kenneth S.; m. Barbara Fried Kaynes, Nov. 3, 1979; children: Jonathan J. Kaynes, Adam R. Kaynes. BA, U. Pa., 1959; LLBcum laude, Harvard U., 1962. Assoc. Weil, Gotshal & Manges LLP, N.Y.C., 1962-70, ptnr., 1970—; house counsel The Associated Merchandising Corp., N.Y.C., 1965-68; lectr. N.Y.U., 1973, Irving Trust Co., N.Y.C., 1981-88; mem. Blue Ribbon Commission on Audit Coms. of Nat. Assn. Corp. Dirs. Bd. dirs. Hewlett-East Rockaway (N.Y.) Jewish Ctr., 1976-97, chmn. legal com., 1974-85, sec., 1980-82; bd. dirs. 25 E. 86th St. Corp., N.Y.C., 1996-99. Mem. ABA, Am. Arbitration Assn. (arbitrator), N.Y. State Bar Assn. (trustee bus. law sect.), Assn. Bar N.Y.C., Masons. Republican. Jewish. Avocations: golf, skiing, tennis, fishing. General corporate, Securities, Mergers and acquisitions. Home: 25 E 86th St Apt 9G New York NY 10028-0553 Office: Weil Gotshal & Manges LLP 767 5th Ave Fl Concl New York NY 10153-0119

**BACON, BRETT KERMIT,** lawyer; b. Perry, Iowa, Aug. 8, 1947; s. Royden S. and Aldeen A. (Zuker) B.; m. Bonnie Jeanne Hall; children: Jeffrey Brett, Scott Michael. BA, U. Dubuque, 1969; JD, Northwestern U., 1972. Bar: Ohio 1972, U.S. Ct. Appeals (6th cir.) 1972, U.S. Supreme Ct. 1980. Assoc., Thompson, Hine & Flory, Cleve., 1972-80, ptnr., 1980—; speaker in field. Author: Computer Law, 1982, 1984. V.p. profl. sect. United Way, Cleve., 1982-86; pres. Shaker Heights Youth Ctr., Inc., Ohio, 1984-86; elder Ch. of Western Res., 1996—. Mem. Fedn. Ins. and Corp. Counsel, Bar Assn. Greater Cleve., Cleve. Play House Club (officer 1986-94, pres. 1991-93, pres. men's com. 1993-96), Pepper Pike Civic League (trustee and treas. 1994-97). General civil litigation, Contracts commercial, Personal injury. Home: 33076 Woodleigh Rd Cleveland OH 44124-5257 Office: Thompson Hine & Flory 3900 Key Ctr 127 Public Sq Cleveland OH 44114-1216

**BACON, JENNIFER GILLE,** lawyer; b. Kansas City, Kansas, Dec. 26, 1949. BA with honors, U. Kansas, 1971, JD, 1976; MA, Ohio State U., 1973. Bar: Mo. Ptnr. Shughart, Thompson & Kilroy, Kansas City, Mo. Contbr. articles to profl. jours. Mem. ABA, Mo. Bar (pres.), Kansas City Metro. Bar Assn., Lawyers Assn. Kansas City. Office: Shughart Thompson & Kilroy 12 Wyandotte Plz 120 W 12th St Ste 1500 Kansas City MO 64105-1929

**BADEN, EARL W., JR.,** lawyer; b. Bradenton, Fla., Jan. 31, 1939; s. Earl W. Sr. and Daisy (Brown) B.; m. Ina Holley, April 23, 1964; children: Holley M., Heather N. BS, Fla. State U., 1965; JD, Stetson U., 1968. Bar: Fla. 1969, U.S. Dist. Ct. (mid. dist.) Fla. 1969, U.S. Supreme Ct. 1982. Assoc. Pratt Atty., Palmetto, Fla., 1969-70; sole practice Bradenton, Fla., 1970—. Mem. Manatee County Hist. Commn. Mem. 4-H, Kiwanis. Republican. Methodist. Avocations: hunting, fishing, welding. Home: 1210 99th St NW Bradenton FL 34209-9730 Office: 1101 6th Ave W Bradenton FL 34205-7727

**BADER, ANGELA MARIE,** lawyer; b. Sunbury, Pa., Sept. 15, 1970; d. John Paul and Carol Diane Koletar; m. Darryl John Bader Jr., June 5, 1993. BS in Bus. Adminstrn. with distinction, U. Nev., Reno, 1992; JD with distinction, U. of the Pacific, Sacramento, 1995. Bar: Nev. 1995, Calif. 1996, U.S. Dist. Ct. Nev. 1995. Law clk. to Hon. Steven R. Kosach 2d Jud. Dist. Ct./State of Nev., Reno, 1995-96; assoc. atty. Laxalt & Nomura Ltd., Reno, 1996—. Avocations: backpacking, skiing, rollerblading, mountain biking, tennis. General civil litigation, Insurance, Personal injury. Office: Laxalt & Nomura Ltd 50 W Liberty St Ste 700 Reno NV 89501-1947

**BADER, GERALD LOUIS, JR.,** lawyer; b. St. Louis, Mar. 15, 1934; s. Gerald L. and Mabel A. (Stephens) B.; (div.); children: Gerald L. III, Stephanie, Cynthia, Carlie, Deborah; m. Barbara Anne Lien, June 2, 1979; children: Matthew Stephen, Mary Rachel. BA, Washington U., 1956; LLB, U. Mich., 1959. Bar: Colo. 1960, Mo. 1960, N.Y. 1961, U.S. Supreme Ct. 1972. Assoc. White & Case, N.Y.C., 1960-62, 64-65, Hodges, Silverstein & Harrington, Denver, 1965-68; pres. Bader and Assocs. P.C., Denver, 1969—. Sec. Denver City Rep. Ctrl. Com., 1969-73; pres. Rocky Mountain Child Devel. Fedn., Denver, 1982-90; dir. Ctrl. City Opera House Assocs., Denver, 1984—, The Legal Ctr., Denver, 1992-98. 1st lt. U.S. Army, 1960-62. Republican. Roman Catholic. Avocations: golf, running, skiing. Fax: (303) 534-0725. E-Mail: glBader@GLBader.com. Federal civil litigation, General corporate, Real property. Office: Bader and Assocs PC 1660 Wynkoop St Denver CO 80202-1115

**BADER, GREGORY VINCENT,** lawyer; b. Puyallup, Wash., Feb. 6, 1948; s. Frederick A. and Patricia W. (Burns) B. BA, Mont. State U., 1970; MA, Washington State U., 1972; JD, Harvard U., 1978. Bar: Tex. 1979, Idaho 1980, U.S. Dist. Ct. (so. dist.) Tex. 1981, U.S. Dist. Ct. (ea. dist.) Tex. 1982, U.S. Ct. Appeals (5th cir.) 1982. Assoc. Foreman & Dyess, Houston, 1978-79; counsel Boise (Idaho) Cascade Corp., 1979-81; atty. Texaco Inc., Houston, 1981-84, Conoco Inc., Houston, 1984-85; atty. Am. Gen. Corp., Houston, 1985-86, sr. atty., 1986—. Author: The Civil Rights Act of 1991, 1992. Del. Idaho State Dem. Conv., Pocatello, 1980; mem. Cath. League Religious & Civil Rights, Fedn. Am. Immigration Reform. NSF fellow, 1970-73. Mem. MENSA, Sierra Club, U.S. English, Nat. Right to Life Com., Am. Athletic Club (Houston). Roman Catholic. Avocations: traveling, stamp collecting, running, polit. affairs. General corporate, Labor, Pension, profit-sharing, and employee benefits. Office: Am Gen Corp Law Dept 2929 Allen Pky Houston TX 77019-2197

**BADER, IZAAK WALTON,** lawyer; b. N.Y.C., June 20, 1922; s. Maximillian Bader and Ida (Sussman) R.; m. Betty Sands Bader, Mar. 26, 1972. AB in Chemistry, NYU, 1942, JD, 1968. Bar: N.Y., D.C., U.S. Supreme Ct. Atty., FTC, Washington, 1948-50; asst. counsel N.Y. State Rent Com., N.Y.C., 1950-54; patent counsel Swingline Inc., 1954-72; sr. ptnr. Bader & Bader, White Plains, N.Y., 1972—; counsel Heart Disease Found., 1970-76, Ind. Investment Protective League, N.Y.C., 1972—; spl. counsel La. State Employees' Retirement System, Tchrs.' Retirement System of La., State Bd. Adminstrn. Fla., Lindner Fund, Inc., Shriners Hosps. for Children. Mem. ABA, N.Y. State Bar Assn., Westchester County Bar Assn. Democrat. Securities, Patent, General civil litigation. Home: 2980 Riverside Dr Coral Springs FL 33065-1008 Office: 65 Court St White Plains NY 10601-4200

**BADGER, DAVID HARRY,** lawyer; b. Indpls., June 16, 1931; s. David Henry and Mayme Pearl (Wright) B.; m. Donna Lee Bailey, June 24, 1954; children: David Mark, Lee Ann, Steven Michael. BEE, Rose Poly. Inst., 1953; JD, Ind. U., 1964. Bar: Ind. 1964, U.S. Dist. Ct. (so and no. dists.) Ind. 1964, U.S. Patent Office 1964, U.S. Ct. Customs and Patent Appeals 1971, U.S. Ct. Appeals (fed. cir.) 1982. Engr. GE, 1953-56, Ransburg Corp., Indpls., 1956-62; chief elec. engr. Rex Metal Craft, Inc., Indpls., 1963-64; patent counsel Ransburg Corp., Indpls., 1964-74, sec., 1974-76; legal counsel Ball Corp., Muncie, Ind., 1976-77; ptnr. Jenkins, Coffey, Hyland, Badger & Conard, Indpls., 1977-82; mng. ptnr. Brinks, Hofer, Gilson & Lione, Indpls., 1982-98. Contbr. articles to profl. jours.; patentee in U.S. and fgn. countries. With USN, 1953-55, lt. comdr. USNR. Named Hon. Alumnus Rose Hulman Inst. Tech., 1987. Mem. ABA (various coms.), IEEE, Ind. Bar Assn. (various coms.), Am. Intellectual Property Law Assn. (various coms.), Licensing Execs. Soc. (various coms.), Indpls. Bar Assn., Internat. Assn. Intellectual Property Law, Indpls. Jazz Club (bd. dirs. 1983-85, 95-97), Junto of Indpls. (bd. dirs. 1997—). Patent, Trademark and copyright, Federal civil litigation. Home: 938 E 58th St Indianapolis IN 46220-2606 Office: Brinks Hofer Gilson & Lione 1 Indiana Sq Ste 2425 Indianapolis IN 46204-2045

**BADGER, RONALD KAY,** lawyer; b. Horton, Jabs., Aug. 24, 1933; s. Clarence E. and Josephine L. (Rick) B.; m. Janet L. Horner, Feb. 16, 1963; children: Hellen J. Badger Haag, Ronald K. Jr., Laura J. Badger Davis. BS in Bus., U. Kans., 1958, BS in Law, 1961, JD, 1968. Bar: Kans. 1961, U.S. Dist. Ct. Kans. 1961, U.S. Ct. Appeals (10th cir.) 1973, U.S. Supreme Ct. 1982, U.S. Ct. Claims 1990. Law clk. to Judge Arthur J. STanley, U.S. Dist. for Kans., Kansas City, 1961-62; spl. asst. to U.S. atty. for dist. of Kans., Dept. Justice, Topeka, 1962-64; assoc. Foulston & Siefkin, Wichita, Kans., 1964-66; atty. in contract adminstrn. Boeing Co., Wichita, 1966-68; pvt. practice, Wichita, 1968—. Bd. dirs. Kans. Bar Jour., 1966-82; contbr. articles to legal jours. Bd. dirs. Wichita Symphony Soc., 1970—. Mem. FBA (pres. Kans. chpt. 1978-80), Kans. Bar Assn., Wichita Bar Assn., Wichita Estate Planning Coun. (sec. 1996-97, pres. 1997-98), Lions (pres. Wichita 1984-85). Republican. Methodist. Probate, Environmental, Personal injury. Office: 343 N Market St Ste 200 Wichita KS 67202-2009

**BADGEROW, JOHN NICHOLAS,** lawyer; b. Macon, Mo., Apr. 7, 1951; s. Harry Leroy Badgerow and Barbara Raines (Buell) Novaria; m. Teresa Ann Zvolanek, Aug. 7, 1976; children: Anthony Thornton, Andrew Cameron, James Terrill. BA in Bus. and English with honors, Principia Coll., 1972; JD, U. Mo., Kansas City, 1975. Bar: Kans. 1976, U.S. Dist. Ct. Kans. 1976, U.S. Ct. Appeals (10th cir.) 1977, U.S. Ct. Appeals (4th cir.)

1979, U.S. Supreme Ct. 1982, U.S. Ct. Appeals (fed. cir.) 1985, U.S. Ct. Appeals (8th cir.) 1986, Mo. 1986, U.S. Dist. Ct. (we. dist.) Mo. 1986. Ptnr. McAnany, VanCleave & Phillips, P.A., Kansas City, Kans., 1975-85; ptnr.-in-charge Spencer, Fane, Britt & Browne, Kansas City, Mo. and Overland Park, Kans., 1986—; Co-author, co-editor: Kansas Lawyer Ethics, 1996. Co-author: Kansas Employment Law, 1992. Co-chmn. Civil Justice Reform Act Commn., Dist. of Kans., 1995-96. Mem. ABA, Kans. Jud. Coun., Kans. Bar Assn. (employment seminars, bd. editors 1982-88, CLE com. 1989-95, Outstanding Svc. award 1995, mem. ethics adv. opinion com. 1997—), Kans. Met. Bar Assn. (chmn. civil rights com.), Lawyers' Assn. Kansas City, Kans. Assn. Def. Counsel (age discrimination seminar), Mission Valley Hunt Club (Stilwell, Kans.). Republican. Christian Scientist. Avocations: horseback riding, carpentry, reading. Federal civil litigation, Civil rights, General civil litigation. Office: Spencer Fane Britt & Browne 9401 Indian Creek Pkwy Ste 700 Shawnee Mission KS 66210-2007

**BADR, GAMAL MOURSI,** legal consultant; b. Helwan, Egypt, Feb. 8, 1924; came to U.S., 1970; s. Ahmad Moursi and Aisha Morshida (Al-Alaily) B.; m. Fatima al-Zahraa Barakat, June 18, 1950; children: Hefni, Hussein. LLB, U. Alexandria, Arab Republic of Egypt, 1944, LLD summa cum laude, 1954; diploma in econs., U. Cairo, 1945, diploma in pvt. law, 1946. Asst. dist. atty. Mixed Cts. Egypt, Alexandria, 1945-49; from assoc. to ptnr. Vatimbella, Catzeflis, Garrana & Badr, Alexandria, 1949-63; legal advisor UN Congo Operation, Kinshasa, Congo, 1963-64; justice Supreme Ct. Algeria, Algiers, 1965-69; from mem. to dep. dir. legal dept. UN Secretariat, N.Y.C., 1970-84; legal advisor Mission of Qatar to UN, N.Y.C., 1984-94; advisor Mission of Saudi Arabia to UN, N.Y.C., 1998—; permanent bur. mem. Pan-Arab Lawyers' Fedn., Cairo, 1959-61; adj. prof. law NYU, 1982—; lectr. The Hague Acad. Internat. Law, 1984. Author: Agency, 1980, State Immunity, 1984; gen. editor Commercial Law of the Middle East; contbr. articles to profl. jours. Mem. Internat. Law Assn. (London), Am. Soc. Internat. Law, Am. Arbitration Assn. (panel of arbitrators), Am. Fgn. Law Assn. (v.p. 1985-87, 89-92), Egyptian-Am. Assn. (pres. 1987-90), Rotary (pres. Alexandria Club 1962-63). Muslim. Home: 18 Peter Lynas Ct Tenafly NJ 07670-1115

**BAE, FRANK S. H.,** law educator, law librarian; b. Chung King, Szechuan, China, Dec. 19, 1941; came to U.S., 1967; s. Tse H. and Yu F. (Wang) B.; m. Anne Rita Donavan, March 15, 1975; children: Stephen, David, Marie, Elizabeth. LLB, Nat. Chung Shing U., Taipei, Taiwan, 1965; MCL, U. Miami, Fla., 1968; MS, U. Wis., 1970; JurD (hon.), New England Sch. Law, Boston, 1977. Dir. law libr. New England Sch. Law, 1970—, asst. prof. law, 1970-73, assoc. prof. law, 1973-74, prof. law, 1974—. Co-author: Searching the Law, 2nd edit., 1999. Mem. New England Law Libr. Consortium (bd. dirs.). Office: New Eng Sch Law Libr 154 Stuart St Boston MA 02116-5616

**BAENA, SCOTT LOUIS,** lawyer; b. N.Y.C., Sept. 15, 1949; s. I. Alexander and Rose (Snofsky) B.; m. Regine Chesna, Apr. 8, 1984; children: Jeffrey Lance, Brad Alexander. BBA in Acctg., Geogre Washington U., 1970, JD with honors, 1974. Bar: Fla. 1974. Ptnr. Helliwell, Melrose & DeWolf, Miami, Fla., 1974-79; mng. ptnr. Stroock & Stroock & Lavan, Miami, 1974-79; adj. prof. U. Miami Sch. of Law, 1983-89. Mem. Pres. Com. on Econ. Devel., 1970; pres. Coral Gables-Riviera Homeowners Assn., 1986; mem. Coral Gables Zoning and Planning Bd., Code Enforcement Bd., Hist. Preservation Task Force. Fellow Am. Bar Found.; mem. ABA (com. on comml. fin. svcs., corp., banking and bus. law sect. 1983—), Fla. Bar Assn. (chair bus. law sect. 1986-87, bd. govs.), Dade County Bar Assn. (bd. dirs. young lawyers div. 1977-79), Am. Law Inst. Jewish. Avocations: golf, woodworking. Bankruptcy, Contracts commercial. Office: Stroock & Stroock & Lavan First Union Financial center 200 S Biscayne Blvd Ste 3300 Miami FL 33131-2385

**BAER, H. CARL, III,** lawyer; b. Oakland, Calif., June 21, 1945; s. H. C. and Jessie Baer; m. Terry L. Baer, Apr. 8, 1967; children: Marc, Erin. BA, Bemidji State U., 1972; JD, U. Minn., 1975. Bar: Minn. 1975, U.S. Dist. Ct. Minn. 1976, U.S. Supreme Ct. 1981. Assoc. Powell, Drahos, Baer & Anderson, Bemidji, 1975-78; shareholder, ptnr. Kief, Fuller, Baer & Wallner, Bemidji, 1979-97, Fuller, Baer, Wallner & Anderson, Bemidji, 1998—; bd. dirs. Security State Bank, Bemidji, Minn. State Bd. Law Examiners, St. Paul, 1983-97; bd. visitors U. Minn. Sch. Law, 1991-96. Contbr. articles to profl. jours. Bd. dirs. Bemidji State U. Found., 1993-98, pres., 1998; bd. dirs. Headwaters Sch. Music and Art, Bemidji, 1998—; dir. Mayor's Blue Ribbon Com. to Build Libr., Bemidji, 1995, 1st Luth. Ch. Coun., Bemidji. Recipient Advocacy of Achievement award Legal Svcs. of Minn., 1992; named Leading Atty. 1995-98 Am. Rsch. Peer Survey. Mem. ABA, ATLA, Minn. State Bar Assn., Minn. Trial Lawyers Assn. Avocations: songwriting, singing, fishing, golf, traveling. State civil litigation, Personal injury, Workers' compensation. Office: Fuller Baer Wallner & Anderson Box 880 514 America Ave Bemidji MN 56619

**BAER, JOHN RICHARD FREDERICK,** lawyer; b. Melrose Park, Ill., Jan. 9, 1941; s. John Richard and Zena Edith (Ostreyko) B.; m. Linda Gail Chapman, Aug. 31, 1963; children: Brett Scott, Deborah Jill. BA, U. Ill., Champaign, 1963, JD, 1966. Bar: Ill. 1966, U.S. Dist. Ct. (no. dist.) Ill. 1967, U.S. Ct. Appeals (7th cir.) 1969, U.S. Ct. Appeals (D.C. cir.) 1975, U.S. Ct. Appeals (9th cir.) 1979, U.S. Supreme Ct. 1975. Assoc. Keck, Mahin & Cate, Chgo., 1966-73, ptnr., 1974-97; of counsel Sonnenschein Nath & Rosenthal, Chgo., 1997—; mem. Ill. Atty. Gen.'s Franchise adv. bd., 1992-94, 96—, chair 1996—. Mem editl. bd. U. Ill. Law Forum, 1964-65, asst. editor, 1965-66; contbg. editor: Commercial Liability Risk Management and Insurance, 1978. Mem. Plan Commn., Village of Deerfield (Ill.), 1976-79, chmn., 1978-79, mem. Home Rule Study Commn., 1974-75, mem. home rule implementation com., 1975-76. Mem. ABA (topics and articles editor Franchise Law jour. 1995-96, assoc. editor 1996—), Internat. Franchise Assn. (legal/legis. com. 1990—), Inter-Pacfic Bar Assn., Ill. Bar Assn. (competition dir. region 8 nat. moot ct. 1974, profl. ethics com. 1977-84, chmn. 1982-83, spl. com. on individual lawyers advt. 1981-83, profl. responsibility com. 1983-84, standing com. on liaison with atty. registration and disciplinary commn. 1989-93), Internat. Bar Assn. E-mail: jrb@sonnenschein.com. Administrative and regulatory, Franchising, Contracts commercial. Office: Sonnenschein Nath & Rosenthal 8000 Sears Tower 233 S Wacker Dr Chicago IL 60606-6404

**BAER, JOSEPH RICHARD,** lawyer; b. Downey, Calif., Oct. 28, 1957; s. Samuel Joseph and Margaret Elizabeth Baer; m. Laura I. Ignacio, Apr. 29, 1989; children: Alec, Taryn, Justin. AA, Fullerton (Calif.) Coll., 1978; BA, Calif. State U., Fullerton, 1982; JD, L.A., 1986. Bar: Calif., U.S. Dist. Ct. (So. and Ctrl. dists.) Calif., U.S. Ct. Appeals, U.S. Supreme Ct. Law clk. Murchison & Cummings, L.A., 1983-92, assoc., 1993-96; assoc., ptnr. Keller, Price & Moorhead, Redondo Beach, Calif., 1991-96; lawyer pvt. practice, Manhattan Beach, Calif., 1996—. Democrat. Roman Catholic. General civil litigation, Personal injury, Product liability. Office: Law Offices Joseph R Baer 317 Rosiecans Ave 2d Fl Manhattan Beach CA 90266

**BAER, LUKE,** lawyer; b. Portage La Prairie, Man., Can., Aug. 7, 1950; came to U.S., 1951; s. Allan and Edna (Brubacher) B.; m. Leslie Ann Swazee, Sept. 11, 1982; children: Jessica Ann, Edward Allan. Student, U. Wis., Whitewater, 1971-73; BA in German and History, U. Wis., 1974; student, Rheinische F. Willhelms U., Bonn, Fed. Republic of Germany, 1973-74; JD, William Mitchell Coll. Law, 1978. Bar: Minn. 1979, U.S. Dist. Ct. Minn. 1979, Nev. 1985, U.S. Dist. Ct. Nev. 1985, U.S. Ct. Appeals (9th cir.) 1984. Law clk. to chief judge U.S. Dist. Ct., St. Paul, 1979-81; assoc. Dorsey & Whitney, Mpls., 1981-86; v.p., gen. counsel Porsche Cars N.Am., Inc., Reno, 1986-92, dir. human resources, 1989-92; v.p., gen. counsel, sec. Robert Bosch Corp., Broadview, Ill., 1992—. Del. U.S.-China Joint Session on Trade, Investment and Econ. Law. Recipient West Pub. Book award, 1976, 1977, Am. Jurisprudence Book award, 1977, , Hornhood award, 1977; CJS scholar, 1977, Space Ctr. Acad. scholar, 1977, Richard C. Schall scholar, 1977, 3M Acad. scholar, 1978. Mem. ABA, Internat. Platform Assn., Minn. Bar Assn., Nev. Bar Assn., Hennepin County Bar Assn., Nat. Order Barristers (Excellence in Appellate Adv. award). Republican. Avocations: pvt. pilot, reading and speaking German, skiing. General corporate. Office: Robert Bosch Corp 2800 S 25th Ave Broadview IL 60153-4594

**BAER, ZENAS,** lawyer; b. Fordville, N.D., Nov. 11, 1951; s. Allan and Edna (Brubacher) B.; m. Julia Suits, Dec. 30, 1988. BA in Polit. Sic. and German, U. Minn.,, 1976; JD, Hamline U., 1980. Bar: Minn. 1980, U.S. Dist. Ct. Minn. 1980, U.S. Ct. Claims, 1985, U.S. Dist. Ct. N.D. 1988, U.S. Ct. Appeals (8th cir.) 1996, U.S. Supreme Ct. 1997. Mng. ptnr. Wefald & Baer, Hawley, Minn., 1980-95; ptnr. Zenas Bear & Assocs., Hawley, 1996—; councilman City of Hawley, 1981-89; city atty. City of Hawley, Minn, 1990—; examiner titles Clay Co., 1984—; gen. coun. for White Earth Band of Chippewa Indians; mem. Minn. Bd. Med. Practice, 1994-98. Alt. sevice as consciencious objector, 1969-72. Recipient 2 awards for excellence Lawyers Coop., Bancroft-Whitney, 1979. Mem. ABA, ATLA, Minn. Trial Lawyers Assn. (past pres.), Hawley C. of C. Personal injury, General civil litigation, Criminal. Home: 812 6th Ave S Moorhead MN 56560-3502 Office: Zenas Bear & Assocs 331 6th St Hawley MN 56549-4020

**BAEZ, JULIO A.,** lawyer; b. Santo Domingo, Dominican Republic, July 6, 1954; came to U.S. 1962; s. Julio A. and Maria Carmela (Fland) B. BA, SUNY, Stony Brook, 1976; JD, U. Aix-Marseille III, 1978; LLM, Sch. of Law and Polit. Sci., Aix-en-Provence, France, 1979; postgrad., various. Law intern, Office of Legal Affairs UN, N.Y.C., 1979-80, legal officer, Office of Legal Affairs, 1981-85, 88—; escort interpreter U.S. Dept. State, Washington, 1980; law cons., Ctr. on Transnat. Corps. UN, N.Y.C., 1980-81; legal officer, Food and Agrl. Orgn. UN, Rome, 1985-87; asst. sec., Former Yuguslavia War Crimes Comn. UN, Geneva, 1992-94; ind. jurist, Western Sahara Referendum UN, 1994-96; legal officer, Divsn. Ocean Affairs, Law of the Sea, Office Legal Affairs UN, N.Y.C., 1994-96; legal officer, Internat. Trade Law Branch UN Office UNCITRAL, Vienna, 1996-99; legal officer, Divsn. Ocean Affairs, Law of the Sea, Office Legal Affairs UN, N.Y.C., 1999—. Pro bono counselor Tenants' Union of the West Side, N.Y.C., 1980-85. Mem. Madrid Bar, New York State Bar. Democrat. Roman Catholic. Home: 41 Jane St New York NY 10014-5127 Office: United Nations Secretariat Office of Legal Affairs S-3200G New York NY 10017

**BAGARAZZI, JAMES MICHAEL,** lawyer; b. Englewood, N.J., Sept. 29, 1951; s. Michael Joseph and Dolores Marie (Barbieri) G. BS cum laude, Fairfield (Conn.) U., 1973; JD with honors, George Washington U., 1980. Bar: D.C. 1980, N.J. 1982, U.S. Ct. Appeals (Fed. cir.) 1982, S.C. 1985, U.S. Supreme Ct. 1986. Law clk. to trial judge U.S. Ct. Claims, Washington, 1980-81; assoc. Finnegan, Henderson, Farabow et al, Washington, 1981-85, Dority and Manning, P.A., Greenville, S.C., 1985-87; shareholder Dority and Manning, P.A., Greenville, S.C., 1988—. Contbr. articles to profl. jours. Mem. ABA, S.C. Bar Assn., Greenville County Bar Assn., Carolina Patent Trademark and Copyright Law Assn. (pres. 1995-96). Roman Catholic. Patent, Trademark and copyright. Office: Dority and Manning PA 700 E North St Ste 15 Greenville SC 29601-3000

**BAGARIA, GAIL FARRELL,** lawyer; b. Detroit, Oct. 6, 1942; d. Vincent Benjamin and Inez Elizabeth (Coffey) Farrell; m. William James Bagaria, Nov. 28, 1964; children: Bridget Ann, William James, Benjamin George. BA, U. Detroit, 1964; JD, Cath. U. Am., 1980. Bar: Md. 1980, U.S. Dist. Ct. Md., 1982. Cons. Miller & Webster, Clinton, Md., 1980-82; pvt. practice Bowie, Md., 1982—. Mem. Prince George's Women's Lawyers Caucus (sec. 984, pres. 1986, treas. 1997), Md. State Bar Assn., Women's Bar Assn. Md., Prince George's County Bar Assn., Soroptimist Internat. (Bowie-Crofton chpt., pres. 1988-89, 93-94), Greater Bowie C. of C. (bd. dirs. 1995-97, 99—, sec. 1997-98, 98-99, Outstanding Bus. Person 1997). Democrat. Roman Catholic. Probate, Estate planning, Elder. Office: PO Box 759 Bowie MD 20718-0759

**BAGBY, GLEN STOVALL,** lawyer; b. Memphis, Sept. 1, 1944; s. Steadman Thomas and Sarah Frances (Rhodes) B.; m. Terri Stovall; children: Sarah Jane, Elizabeth Anne. AB, Transylvania U., 1966; JD, U. Ky., 1969. Bar: Ky. 1969, U.S. Ct. Claims 1975, U.S. Tax Ct. 1972, U.S. Supreme Ct. 1972. Assoc. Brock & Brock, Lexington, Ky., 1969-71; ptnr. Brock, Brock & Bagby, Lexington, Ky., 1971-98, Woodward, Hobson & Fulton, Lexington, Ky., 1999—; chmn. Bd. Constrn. Appeals, Bd. Rev., Lexington, 1979-81. Bd. dirs. Julius Marks Home for Elderly, Lexington, 1975-88; chmn. bd. trustees Ky. Conf. United Meth. Ch., 1993-96, chancellor, 1976—; bd. dirs. Magee Christian Edn. Found., 1989—; vice chmn. Good Samaritan Hosp., Lexington, 1980-92. Fellow Am. Coll. Trust and Estate Counsel, Ky. Bar Found.; mem. ABA, Ky. Bar Assn. (probate com. 1974—, ho. of dels. 1985-92), Fayette County Bar Assn., Blue Grass Estate Planning Coun. (pres. 1987-88), Lexington C. of C., U. Ky. Alumni Assn. Probate, Family and matrimonial, General civil litigation. Office: Woodward Hobson & Fulton 200 W Vine St Fl 5 Lexington KY 40507-1620

**BAGBY, WILLIAM RARDIN,** lawyer; b. Grayson, Ky., Feb. 19, 1910; s. John Albert and Nano A. (Rardin) B.; m. Mary Carpenter, Sept. 3, 1939; 1 child, John Robert; m. Elizabeth Hinkel, Nov. 22, 1975. AB, Cornell U., 1933; JD, U. Mich., 1936; postgrad., Northwestern U., 1946-47. Bar: Ky. 1937, Ohio 1952, U.S. Tax Ct. 1948, U.S. Supreme Ct. 1950, U.S. Ct. Appeals (6th cir.) 1952. Pvt. practice Grayson, 1937-43; atty., judge City of Grayson, 1939-43; counsel Treasury Dept., Chgo., Cleve. and Cin., 1946-54; pvt. practice Lexington, Ky., 1954—; prof. U. Ky., 1956-57; gen. counsel Headley-Whitney Mus., 1974-84; mem. Bd. of Adjustment, Lexington-Urban County City Govt., 1965-97, chmn., 1980-97. Trustee Bagby Found. Musical Arts, N.Y.C., 1963-74; trustee, gen. counsel McDowell Cancer Found., 1979-91, pres., 1988-91. Lt. USN, 1943-46. Mem. ABA (hon. life), Am. Judicature Soc., Ky. Bar Assn. (hon. life), Fayette County Bar Assn., Lexington Club, U. Ky. Faculty Club, Rotary. Democrat. Probate, Taxation, general. Home: 228 Market St Lexington KY 40507-1030 Office: 1107 1st National Bldg Lexington KY 40507

**BAGGETT, STEVEN RAY,** lawyer; b. Fayetteville, Ark., July 3, 1963; s. Harold Ray and Norma June (King) B.; m. Amy Lynn Griggs, Jan. 2, 1999. BA, U. Ark., 1985; JD, So. Meth. U., 1988. Bar: Tex. 1988, U.S. Dist. Ct. (no. dist.) Tex. 1988, U.S. Ct. Appeals (5th cir.) 1992. Assoc. Thompson & Knight, Dallas, 1988-95, shareholder, 1996—. Recipient Am. Jurisprudence awards Bancroft-Whitney Co., 1985-86. Mem. Tex. Bar Assn., Dallas Bar Assn. (spkrs. com. 1997, state fair trial by jury com. 1998—, jud. com. 1999, cmty. involvement com. 1999, law in the schs. and cmtys. com. 1999), Ark. U. Alumni Assn., So. Meth. U. Alumni Assn., Phi Beta Kappa. Avocations: weight training, running, ice skating, music. Federal civil litigation, General civil litigation, State civil litigation. Office: Thompson & Knight 1700 Pacific Ave Ste 3300 Dallas TX 75201-4693

**BAGGOTT, THOMAS MCCANN,** lawyer; b. Dayton, Ohio, Feb. 10, 1943; s. Horace Worman and Dorothy B.; m. Mary Louise Ricker, Dec. 20, 1969; children: Roland W., Porsha M. BA, Ohio State U., 1967; JD, Ohio No. U., 1971. Bar: Ohio 1971, U.S. Dist. Ct. (so. dist.) Ohio 1971, U.S. Supreme Ct. 1997. Referee Montgomery County Probate Ct., Dayton, 1971-73; prosecuting atty. City of Vandalia, Ohio, 1974; assoc. Baggott Logan & Gianuglou, Dayton, 1975-80; ptnr. Baggott Law Offices Co., Dayton, 1980-87; prin. Thomas M. Baggott Co., Dayton, 1987-91; ptnr. Altick & Corwin, Dayton, 1991—. Mem. Assn. Trial Lawyers Am., Ohio State Bar Assn., Ohio Acad. Trial Lawyers (trustee 1977-84), Dayton Bar Assn. (treas. 1985-86, chmn.), Miami Valley Trial Lawyers Assn. General civil litigation, Personal injury, Probate. Office: Altick & Corwin 1700 One Dayton Centre Dayton OH 45402-1108

**BAGLEY, CHARLES FRANK, III,** lawyer; b. Dec. 3, 1944; m. Kirsten L., Aug. 19, 1967; children: Charles F. IV, Gordon T. BA, Southwestern U., 1966; JD, Washington & Lee U., 1969. Judge advocates gen. ct. lt. U.S. Navy, 1969-74; ptnr. Campbell, Woods, Bagley, Emerson, McNeer & Herndon, 1974—. pres. bd. dirs. tri state coun. Boy Scouts of Am., 1982-85; mem. bd. dirs. Contact Huntington, Hospice Huntington, chmn. 1987-89; active Huntington Area C. of C., Enslow Park Presbyn. Ch. Mem. ABA, Va. Bar Assn., W.Va. State Bar Assn. (mem. bd. govs. 1986-93, pres. 1991-92), W.Va. Bar Assn. (mem. exec. coun. 1986-95, pres. 1993-94), Def. Trial Coun. W.Va. (mem. bd. govs. 1985-90), Cabell County Bar Assn. (pres. 1985-86), Internat. Assn. Ins. Coun., Def. Rsch. Inst., Inc. (state chmn. 1985-90). Alternative dispute resolution, Insurance, Toxic tort. Address: 1123 12th Ave Huntington WV 25701-3423

**BAGLEY, CONSTANCE ELIZABETH,** law educator, lawyer; b. Tucson, Dec. 18, 1952; d. Robert Porter Smith and Joanne Snow-Willstadter. AB in Polit. Sci. with distinction, with honors, Stanford U., 1974; JD magna cum laude, Harvard U., 1977. Bar: Calif. 1978, N.Y. 1978. Tchg. fellow Harvard U., 1975-77; assoc. Webster & Sheffield, N.Y.C., 1977-78, Heller, Ehrman, White & McAuliffe, San Francisco, 1978-79; assoc. McCutchen, Doyle, Brown & Enersen, San Francisco, 1979-84, ptnr., 1984-90; lectr. bus. law Stanford (Calif.) U., 1988-90, lectr. mgmt., 1990-91, lectr. law and mgmt., 1991-95, sr. lectr. law and mgmt., 1995—, GBS Trust faculty fellow, 1997-98, lectr. Stanford Exec. Program; lectr. Stanford Mktg. Mgmt. Exec. Program; bd. dirs. Alegre Enterprises, Inc., Latina Publ. LLC; corp. practice series adv. bd. Bur. Nat. Affairs, 1984—; faculty adv. bd. Stanford Jour. Law, Bus. and Fin., 1994—; editl. bd. Jour. Internet Law, 1997—; lectr., planning com. Calif. Continuing Edn. Bar, L.A., San Francisco, 1983, 85-87; lectr. So. Area Conf., Silverado, 1988, Young Pres. Orgn. Internat. U. for Pres., Hong Kong, 1988. Author: Mergers, Acquisitions and Tender Offers, 1983, Managers and the Legal Environment: Strategies for the 21st Century, 1991, 3rd edit., 1999; co-author: Negotiated Acquisitions, 1992, Cutting Edge Cases in the Legal Environment of Business, 1993, 2d edit. 1998, Proxy Contests and Corporate Control: Strategic Considerations, 1997, Proxy Contests and Corporate Control: Conducting the Proxy Campaign, 1997, The Entrepreneur's Guide to Business Law, 1998; contbg. editor: Calif. Bus. Law Reporter, 1984-95. Vestry mem. Trinity Episcopal Ch., San Francisco, 1984-85; vol. Moffit Hosp. U. Calif., San Francisco, 1983-84; bd. dirs. Youth and Family Assistance, Redwood City, Calif., 1996-99. Mem. ABA, Acad. Legal Studies in Bus., Stanford Faculty Club, Cap and Gown Soc., Phi Beta Kappa. Republican. Office: Stanford U Grad Sch Bus 518 Memorial Way Stanford CA 94305-5009

**BAGLEY, SHANA ANGELA,** lawyer; b. Marin County, Calif., Jan. 10, 1968; d. William T. and Diane L. Bagley. BA in Rhetoric, U. Calif., Davis, 1990; postgrad., Inst. Internat. and Comp. Law, Oxford, Eng., 1991; JD, Santa Clara U., 1993. Bar: Calif. 1993, U.S. Dist. Ct. (no. dist.) Calif. 1993, U.S. Dist. Ct. (ea. dist.) Calif. 1994. Assoc. atty. Thayer, Harvey, Hodder & Gregerson, Modesto, Calif., 1994-98, Damrell, Nelson, Schrimp, Pallios & Ladine, Modesto, 1998—. Mem. Stanislaus County Bar Assn. (client rels. com. 1998—), Stanislaus County Women's Lawyer Assn. (vice chair newsletter 1998), Stanislaus Rugby Football Club (tournament dir.), NRA, Alpha Phi (v.p. 1989-90), East Bay Bulldogs Rugby Football Club. Republican. Avocations: rugby, hockey, hunting, fishing, soccer. Insurance, General civil litigation. Office: Damrell Nelson et al 1601 I St Modesto CA 95354-1110

**BAGSHAW, BRADLEY HOLMES,** lawyer; b. Salem, Mass., Mar. 26, 1953; s. James Holmes and Hope (Bradley) B.; m. Suzanne LuBien, Aug. 23, 1975. AB summa cum laude, Bowdoin Coll., 1975; JD cum laude, Harvard U., 1981. Bar: Wash. 1981, U.S. Dist. Ct. (we. dist.) Wash. 1981, U.S. Dist. Ct. (ea. dist.) Wash. 1989, U.S. Ct. Appeals (9th cir.) 1989. Assoc. Helsell Fetterman, Seattle, 1981-88, ptnr., 1988—, mng. ptnr., 1991-97, ptnr., 1997—. Federal civil litigation, State civil litigation, Admiralty. Home: 6240 27th Ave NE Seattle WA 98115-7114 Office: Helsell Fetterman 1325 4th Ave Ste 1500 Seattle WA 98101-2569

**BAHLER, GARY M.,** lawyer. BA, Houghton Coll., 1973; JD, Cornell U., 1976. Bar: N.Y. 1977. Sec., dep. gen. counsel Venator Group, Inc. (formerly Woolworth Corp.), N.Y.C., 1991-93, sr. v.p., 1993-98, sr. v.p., gen. counsel, sec., 1998—. Office: Venator Group Inc 233 Broadway Fl 3N New York NY 10279-0399

**BAHLS, STEVEN CARL,** law educator, dean; b. Des Moines, Sept. 4, 1954; s. Carl Robert and Dorothy Rose (Jensen) B.; m. Jane Emily Easter, June 18, 1977; children: Daniel David, Timothy Carl, Angela Emily. BBA, U. Iowa, 1976; JD, Northwestern U., Chgo., 1979. Bar: Wis. 1979, Mont. 1989, Ohio 1994; CPA, Iowa. Assoc. Frisch, Dudek & Slattery, Milw., 1979-84, dir., 1985; assoc. dean and prof. U. Mont. Sch. of Law, Missoula, 1985-94; dean., prof. law sch. Capital U. Law Sch., Columbus, Ohio, 1994—. Coordinating exec. editor Northwestern U. Law Rev., 1979. Vice chair Columbus Works. Mem. ABA, Am. Agrl. Law Assn. (pres.-elect), Wis. Bar Assn., Mont. Bar Assn., Ohio Bar Assn., Columbus Bar Assn. (bd. govs.), Order of Coif. Republican. Methodist. Avocations: photography, travel, hiking. Home: 499 N Columbia Ave Bexley OH 43209-1003 Office: Capital U Law Sch 303 E Broad St Columbus OH 43215-3200

**BAHNER, S. BRENT,** lawyer; b. Ardmore, Okla., Aug. 8, 1957; s. Donald W. and Wanda S. Bahner; m. Susan K. Daniel, June 2, 1986; children: Sara Elizabeth, Ann Kathleen, Katherine Susanne. BBA in Mgmt., Baylor U., 1979; JD, U. Okla., 1982. Bar: Okla. 1982, U.S. Dist. Ct. (ea., no., and we. dists.) Okla., U.S. Ct. Appeals (10th cir.). Ptnr. Fischl Culp McMillin Chaffin & Bahner, Ardmore, Okla., 1982—; mem. Def. Rsch. Inst., Chgo., 1986—. Mem. bd. edn. Ardmore City Sch., 1991—; mem. Lake Murray Chapel Assn., 1995—. Mem. Am. Bd. Trial Advocates (assoc.), Okla. Assn. Def. Counsel (bd. dirs., v.p. 1986-94), Ardmore C. of C. (bd. dirs. 1998). General civil litigation, Insurance, Oil, gas, and mineral. Home: 214 E St SW Ardmore OK 73401-4945 Office: Fischl Culp McMillin Chaffin & Bahner PO Box 1766 Ardmore OK 73402-1766

**BAHS, JESS ALLEN,** lawyer; b. Hastings, Mich., Jan. 12, 1967; s. John Edward and Susan Katheryne (Maurer) B.; m. Denise May Burch, July 1, 1989; children: Jessica, Evan. BS in Social Sci., Mich. State U., 1989; JD, Wayne State U., 1992, LLM in Taxation, 1998. Bar: Mich. 1992, U.S. Dist. Ct. (ea. dist.) Mich. 1992, U.S. Tax Ct. 1992. Sr. assoc. Foster Swift Collins and Smith, Lansing, Mich. Bd. mem. Saginaw County Art Mus., 1993-97. Mem. Saginaw County Bar Assn. (treas. 1996-97). Taxation, general, Corporate taxation, State and local taxation. Office: Foster Swift Collins & Smith 313 S Washington Sq Lansing MI 48933-2172

**BAICKER-MCKEE, STEVEN F.,** lawyer; b. N.Y.C., Mar. 22, 1958; s. Joseph A. and Maxine H. Baicker; m. Carol K. McKee, May 28, 1983; children: Kyle S., Eric W., Sara M. BA, Yale U., 1980; JD, Coll. William and Mary, 1987. Bar: Pa., U.S. Dist. Ct. (we. dist.) Pa., U.S. Dist. Ct. (mid. dist.) Pa. Law clk. U.S. Dist. Ct. (we. dist.) Pa., Pitts., 1987-89; litig. shareholder Babst, Calland, Clements & Zomnir, P.C., Pitts., 1989—; Mem. rules com. Pa. Discovery, 1997; chmn. Tech. Com., 1997—. Author: Federal Civil Rules Handbook, A Student's Guide to the Federal Rules of Civil Procedure; editor: The Tech. Bulletin, 1998—; contbr. articles to profl. jours. Mem. ABA (mem. litig. sect. 1989—), ATLA, Pa. Bar Assn. (mem. civil litig. sect. 1989—, mem. environ. mineral and natural resources law sect. 1989—), Allegheny County Bar Assn. Environmental, Federal civil litigation, Computer. Office: Babst Calland Clements & Zomnir PC Two Gateway Ctr Fl 8 Pittsburgh PA 15222

**BAIL, LISA A.,** lawyer; b. Boston, Feb. 16, 1968; d. Richard N. and Arlynne L. B.; m. Wai Y. Lee, July 20, 1997. BA, Boston U., 1990, JD, 1993. Bar: Hawaii 1993, Mass. 1994, U.S. Dist. Ct. Hawaii 1993, U.S. Ct. Appeals (9th cir.) 1996. Atty. Goodsill Anderson Quinn & Stifel, Honolulu, 1993—. Mem. ABA, Hawaii State Bar Assn. Environmental, Product liability, Federal civil litigation. Office: Goodsill Anderson Quinn & Stifel 1099 Alakea St Ste 1800 Honolulu HI 96813-4512

**BAILEY, BRIDGET,** lawyer; b. Chgo., May 7, 1963; d. Marvin Oscar and Florence Veronica (Kimbrough) B. BA, Grambling State U., 1985, MPA, 1987; JD, U. Tenn., 1994. Bar: Tenn. 1994. Intern WLS Radio, Chgo., 1985; intern talk show host Centel Cable, Matteson, Ill., 1985; TV model, spokesperson Designer Mart, Chgo., 1986-88; computer programmer AMCCOM, Rock Island, Ill., 1987-88; computer programmer/analyst U.S. Railroad Retirement Co., Chgo., 1988-91; law clk. Lewis, King, Krieg & Waldrop, Knoxville, Tenn., 1993-94; assoc. Lewis, King, Krieg, Waldrop & Catron, Knoxville, Tenn., 1994—; mem. continuing legal edn. com., H.S. mock trial competition com., U. Tenn. Coll. of Law mentor program; exec. bd. profl. responsibility Supreme Ct. Tenn.; mem. disciplinary hearing bd. Tenn. Bd. Profl. Responsibility. Active Big Bros./Big Sisters, 1983-84; bd. dirs. Diversity Outreach br. Am. Heart Assn. Recipient Cmty. Svc. award YWCA, 1995. Mem. Knoxville Bar Assn., ETLAW (v.p.), Women and Minorities Com., Barristers (exec. bd. 1994—), Hamilton Burnett Am. Inn of Ct. (exec. bd. dirs.), Knoxville Quarterback Club, Black Achievers, Alpha Kappa Alpha, Alpha Kappa Mu. Democrat. Avocations: communicating, speaking, meeting people. State civil litigation, Entertainment, Insurance. Office: Lewis King Krieg & Waldrop PO Box 2425 Knoxville TN 37901-2425

**BAILEY, FRANCIS LEE,** lawyer; b. Waltham, Mass., June 10, 1933; m. Florence Gott (div. 1961); m. Froma Portney (div. 1972); m. Lynda Hart, Aug. 26, 1972 (div. 1980); m. Patricia Shiers, June 10, 1985. Student, Harvard U., 1950-52, 57; LL.B., Boston U., 1960. Bar: Mass. 1960, U.S. Dist. Ct. Mass., 1961, U.S. Ct. Appeals (1st cir.) 1963, U.S. Tax Ct. 1964, U.S. Ct. Appeals (6th cir.) 1964, U.S. Supreme Ct. 1964, U.S. Ct. Appeals (2d cir.) 1967, U.S. Ct. Appeals (10th cir.) 1968, U.S. Ct. Appeals (3d cir.) 1969, U.S. Ct. Appeals (9th cir.) 1970, U.S. Ct. Appeals (4th and 7th cirs.) 1971, U.S. Dist. Ct. (we. and no. dists.) Tex. 1980, U.S. Ct. Mil. Appeals 1981, U.S. Ct. Appeals (8th and 11th cirs.) 1984, U.S. Ct. Appeals (5th cir.) 1985, Fla. 1989, U.S. Dist. Ct. (ea. dist.) Wis. 1991. Prin. Law Offices of F. Lee Bailey, West Palm Beach, Fla. Author: (with Harvey Aronson) The Defense Never Rests, 1971, Cleared for the Approach, 1977, (with John Greenya) For the Defense, 1976; novel Secrets, 1979; How to Protect Yourself Against Cops In California and Other Strange Places, 1982, To Be a Trial Lawyer, 1983; numerous works in field of criminal law (with Henry Rothblatt). Lt. USMC, 1952-56. Mem. ABA, ATLA. Criminal, General civil litigation, Aviation.

**BAILEY, GEORGE SCREVEN,** lawyer; b. Columbia, S.C., Feb. 7, 1951; s. Edward E. and Mary S. (Simpson) B. BA in Econs., Wofford Coll., 1972; JD, U.S.C., 1975; LLM in Taxation, NYU, 1976. Bar: S.C. 1976, U.S. Tax Ct. 1979, U.S. Ct. Appeals (4th cir.) 1982. Cert. tax specialist. Assoc. Johnson, Smith et al, Sparantanburg, S.C., 1976-77, Law Offices R. Young, Columbia, S.C., 1976, O'Connor & Young, Columbia, 1976-79; sec.-treas. O'Connor & Bailey, P.A., Columbia, 1979-84; ptnr. Nelson, Mullins, Riley & Scarborough, L.L.P., Columbia, 1984—; state rep. to spl. liaison tax com. of southeastern region, Atlanta, 1980-83. Mem. Am. Coll. Tax Counsel, S.C. Bar Assn. (chmn. tax sect. 1986-87, sect. estate planning, probate and trust law, chmn. taxation law specialization adv. bd. 1990-91), So. Fed. Tax Inst. (trustee 1994—), Richland County Bar Assn., Forest Lake County Club, Columbia Cotillion Club, Pine Tree Hunt Club, Palmetto Club, Columbia Taxation Study Group. Estate planning, Corporate taxation, Personal income taxation. Office: Nelson Mullins Riley & Scarborough LLP 1330 Lady St Columbia SC 29201-3300

**BAILEY, GORDON FREEBORN, JR.,** lawyer; b. Huntsville, Ala., July 24, 1944; s. Gordon F. and Carridelle G. B.; m. Anne Paulk, Mar. 18, 1967; children—Gordon F. III, Clark, Allison. B.A., Birmingham So. Coll., 1966; J.D., U. Ala., 1969. Bar: Ala. 1969, D.C. 1973. Pub. defender program, Mobile, Ala., 1969; ptnr. Isom, Jackson & Bailey, Anniston, Ala., 1973—; spl. asst. atty. gen. State Ala., 1981—. Mem. alumni bd. dirs. Birmingham So. Coll., mem. State Child Support Enforcement Com., 1980—; pres. bd. dirs. Vol. Action Ctr., 1980-81; mem. recreation adv. commn. City of Anniston, 1979—; pres.-elect Eastern regional conf. U/FSA. Served to capt. JAGC, U.S. Army, 1969-73. Mem. Nat. Reciprocal and Family Support Assn., ABA, D.C. Bar Assn., Ala. Bar Assn., Ala. State Bar (family law sect. pres. 1997-98), Calhoun/Cleburne County Bar Assn. (pres. 1981-82), Ala. Jud. Coll. Faculty Assn. (hon.). Democrat. Methodist. Club: Kiwanis (pres. 1981-82) (Anniston, Ala.). Family and matrimonial, Juvenile. Office: 822 Leighton Ave Anniston AL 36207-5748

**BAILEY, HOWARD WILLIAM (BILL BAILEY),** lawyer; b. Iowa City, Iowa; s. Lee Bailey and Myrtle Eddy; m. Bernice Danshaw, Sept. 1941; m. Agnes Sexton, Feb. 15, 1959; 1 child, Lee R.; m. Isabella Kayori, Aug. 28, 1998; children from previous marriage Sandra Gary (dec.), Craig. BA, Iowa U., 1940, JD, 1942. Bar: Iowa 1942, Calif. 1954. Lt. U.S. Army, 1940. Republican. Lutheran. Criminal, Juvenile, General practice. Home: 3795 N Fresno St Fresno CA 93726-5527

**BAILEY, J. DENNIS,** lawyer; b. Danville, Va., Sept. 6, 1960; s. John M. and Bess M. (Freeman) B.; m. Laurie Newman, Dec. 22, 1961; children: Austin, James. BA in Philosophy, Elon Coll., 1982; JD, Wake Forest U., 1985. Bar: N.C. 1985; U.S. Dist. Ct. (mid. dist.) N.C. 1986; U.S. Ct. Appeals (4th cir.) 1986. Clk. to presiding judge Hon. Frank Bullock U.S. Dist. Ct. Mid. Dist. of N.C., Greensboro, 1985-86; dir. Bell, Davis & Pitt, P.A., Winston-Salem, N.C., 1987—; barrister Inn of Ct., Winston-Salem, N.C., 1992-94. Bd. dirs. Assembly Terrace Sr. Housing Project, Winston-Salem, 1995—, Elon Coll. Trustees, 1982-84. Mem. N.C. Bar Assn. State civil litigation, Personal injury, Professional liability.

**BAILEY, K. RONALD,** lawyer; b. Sandusky, Ohio, July 30, 1947; s. Kenneth White and Virginia McClung (Sheddan) B.; m. Sara Ann Geary Bressler, Mar. 14, 1969 (div. June 1973); 1 child, Matthew Scott; m. Lynn Darlene Kammer, Aug. 31, 1973; children: Thomas Keith, Kenneth Richard. B in Liberal Studies summa cum laude, Bowling Green State U., 1979; JD, Cleveland-Marshall Law Sch., 1982; grad., Gerry Spence's Trial Lawyers Coll., 1994. Bar: Ohio 1983, U.S. Dist. Ct. (no. dist.) Ohio 1983, U.S. Ct. Appeals (6th cir.) 1985, U.S. Supreme Ct. 1992. Tool, diemaker Gen. Motors, Sandusky, 1968-84; sole practice Huron, Ohio, 1983-87; sr. trial atty. K. Ronald Bailey & Assocs. Co., Legal Profl. Assn., Sandusky, 1987—; chmn. Charter Rev. Com. of Huron, 1984. Mem. ATLA, Nat. Assn. Criminal Def. Lawyers, Ohio Bar Assn. (coun. dels. 1998—), Erie County Bar Assn., Ohio Assn. Criminal Def. Lawyers (bd. dirs. 1988—, v.p. publs. 1991-93, 97-98, treas. 1994, pres. 1995-96, chmn. capital litigation 1997—, Pres.'s award 1989-95, 97-98, v.p. CLE 1997-98). Democrat. Pentecostal. Avocations: reading, photography, painting, swimming, drag racing. Criminal, Personal injury, General civil litigation. Home: 513 Williams St Huron OH 44839-2535 Office: K Ronald Bailey & Assocs Co, Legal Profl Assn 220 W Market St Sandusky OH 44870-2515

**BAILEY, MARYANN GEORGE,** lawyer; b. Citronelle, Ala., Jan. 30, 1951; d. William Edwin Deese and Mary Alma Webb; m. Ronald F. George, Dec. 26, 1975 (div. Jan. 1983); 1 child, Kristen Leigh. BS, U. S. Ala., 1975; JD, U. Houston, 1980. Bar: Tex. 1980, U.S. Dist. Ct. (so. dist.) Tex. 1981, U.S. Dist. Ct. (we. dist.) Tex. 1991. Pvt. practice Houston, 1980-88; assoc. then ptnr. Thornton, Summers, Biechlin, Dunham & Brown, LC, San Antonio, 1988—. Bd. dirs. Alamo Children's Adv. Ctr., San Antonio. Fellow Tex. Bar Found.; mem. San Antonio Bar Assn. Roman Catholic. Personal injury, Contracts commercial, Construction. Office: Thornton Summers Biechlin Dunhan & Brown 10100 Reunion Pl Ste 300 San Antonio TX 78216-4128

**BAILEY, MICHAEL KEITH,** lawyer; b. Washington, Feb. 19, 1956; s. Alda Merrill and Joan (Moyers) B.; m. Linda Ann Braswell, Dec. 18, 1982; children: Julia Anne, David Allen. AB in Econs. and Polit. Sci., Coll. William and Mary, 1978; JD, Stetson U., 1981. Bar: Fla. 1981, U.S. Dist. Ct. (mid. dist.) Fla. 1982, U.S. Ct. Appeals (11th cir.) 1982, U.S. Supreme Ct. 1986. Assoc. Pitts, Eubanks, et al, Orlando, Fla., 1981-86; ptnr. Parrish, Bailey & Myers, P.A., Orlando, 1986-98, Bailey & Myers, P.A., Maitland, Fla., 1998—. Mem. ABA, ATLA (charter; pres.'s club), So. Trial Lawyers Assn., Def. Rsch. Inst., Orange County Bar Assn., Acad. Fla. Trial Lawyers (eagle patron), Nat. Bd. Trial Adv. (cert. civil trial advocate), Fla. Bar Bd. Ctr. (civil trial atty.). Republican. Baptist. Personal injury, Insurance, General civil litigation. Home: 701 E Lake Sue Ave Winter Park FL 32789-5804 Office: Bailey & Myers PA 100 E Sybelia Ave Ste 375 Maitland FL 32751-4777

**BAILEY, STEPHEN ROBERT,** lawyer; b. Dallas, Apr. 27, 1964; s. John Allison and Jane (Beasley) B. Student, Franklin Coll., Lugano, Switzerland, 1985, U. Valencia, Spain, 1985; BA, U. Tex., 1986; JD, So. Meth. U., 1989. Bar: Tex. 1989. Assoc. Andrews & Kurth, LLP, Houston, 1989-93; assoc. Cruse, Scott, Henderson & Allen, LLP, Houston, 1993-96, ptnr., 1006—. Editor Jour. Air Law and Commerce, 1988-89. Vol. atty. Houston Vol. Lawyers Program, Houston, 1990—. Mem. State Bar Tex., D.C. Bar, Houston Bar Assn., Houston Young Lawyers Assn. General civil litigation, Professional liability. Home: 6611 Westchester St Houston TX 77005-3755 Office: Cruse Scott et al 600 Travis St Ste 3900 Houston TX 77002-2910

**BAILEY, THOMAS CHARLES,** lawyer; b. Rochester, N.Y., Nov. 26, 1948; s. Charles George and Teckla Barbara (Driscoll) B.; m. Rosalie Stoll, Sept. 24, 1974; children: Leah Isabelle, Molly Driscoll, Elizabeth Rose. BA, Princeton U., 1970; JD, SUNY, Buffalo, 1974. Bar: N.Y. 1975, Fla. 1977. Assoc. Little & Burt, Buffalo, 1974-78, ptnr., 1978-80; ptnr. Saperston & Day, PC, Buffalo, 1980-92; pvt. practice Buffalo, 1992-97; mem. Albrecht Maguire Heffern and Gregg PC, Buffalo, 1997—; bd. dirs., sec. Buffalo Therapeutic Riding Ctr. Inc., 1999—. Pres. St. Thomas Moore Guild, 1981; trustee Shea's O'Connell Preservation Guild, 1986-96, chmn., 1994. Mem. ABA, N.Y. State Bar Assn. (exec. com. of real property law sect.), Fla. Bar Assn., Am. Assn. Franchisees and Dealers (fair franchising standards com.), Saturn Club, Mathais Soc., Princeton U. Alumni Assn. Western N.Y. (pres. 1990-91), Brookhaven Trout Club. Avocations: fly fishing, boating, horses. Franchising, General corporate, Real property. Office: Albrecht Maguire Heffern and Gregg PC 2100 Main Place Tower Buffalo NY 14202-3721

**BAILIN, DEBORAH M.,** lawyer; b. San Francisco, Sept. 19, 1964; d. Richard H. and Sarah W. (Dawes) B.; m. William A. Loginov, Oct. 13, 1991. BA, Colgate U., 1987; JD, Cornell U., 1990; LLM, Boston U., 1992. Bar: Mass. 1990, N.H. 1991, U.S. Dist. Ct. N.H. 1991. Assoc. Pennington & Marshall, Boston, 1991, Laboe & Assocs., Concord, N.H., 1991-92, Cleveland, Waters & Bass, Concord, 1992-94, Lotter & Bailin, P.C., Manchester, N.H., 1994—; instr. Am. Coll., Bethlehem, Pa., 1994—. Mem. N.H. Estate Planning Coun., N.H. Bar Assn. Avocations: racquetball, cross-country skiing, bicycling. Estate planning, Estate taxation, Corporate taxation.

**BAILLIE, CHARLOTTE LYNN,** lawyer; b. San Pablo, Calif., May 2, 1968; d. Donald Stewart and Marilyn Louise Baillie; m. Robert Shaw Nield, Feb. 8, 1997; children: Shawn, Curtis. BS in Econs. magna cum laude, U. Pacific, 1990; JD, U. Calif., Davis, 1994. Dep. dist. atty. Placer County Dist. Atty., Auburn, Calif., 1994-99. Mem. ABA, Placer County Bar Assn. Avocations: Civil War reenactor, classic car shows, flying, tatting. E-mail: cbaillie@placer.ca.gov. Office: Placer County Dist Atty 11562 B Ave Auburn CA 95603-2605

**BAILLIE, JAMES LEONARD,** lawyer; b. Mpls., Aug. 27, 1942; s. Leonard Thompson and Sylvia Alfreda (Fundoerg) B.; m. Constance Samson, June 19, 1965; children: Jennifer, Craig, John. AB in History, 1964; JD, U. Chgo., 1967. Bar: Minn. 1967, U.S. Dist. Ct. Minn. 1968, U.S. Ct. Appeals (8th cir.) 1969, U.S. Ct. Appeals (5th cir.) 1980. Law clk. to presiding justice U.S. Dist. Ct., Mpls., 1967-68; assoc. Fredrikson & Byron, P.A., Mpls., 1968-73, shareholder, 1973—. Mem. ABA (litigation sect. co-editor Bankruptcy Litigation 1998, bus. law sect. editl. bd. Bus. Law Today 1993-98, bus. sect. chair pro bono com. 1999—, standing com. on lawyer pub. svc. responsibility 1991-96, chmn. 1993-96, nat. pro bono award 1984, John Minor Wisdom award 1999), Minn. State Bar Assn. (chmn. bankruptcy sect. 1985-88), Hennepin County Bar Assn. (sec. 1992-93, treas. 1993-95, pres.-elect 1995-96, pres. 1996-97). Bankruptcy, Contracts commercial, General civil litigation. Home: 2851 E Lake Of The Isles Pky Minneapolis MN 55408-1055 Office: Fredrikson & Byron PA 1100 Internat Ctr 900 2nd Ave S Minneapolis MN 55402-3314

**BAIN, C. RIDLEY,** lawyer; b. Richmond, Va., Sept. 21, 1951; s. H. Lee Jr. and Ann R. Bain; m. Lenore K. Bain; children: Lauren Elizabeth, Karen Bennett, David Ridley. BA, Randolph-Macon Coll., 1973; JD, U. Va., 1978. Ptnr. Slayton, Bain & Clary, Lawrenceville, Va., 1979—. Sec.-treas., bd. dirs. Va. Legal Aid Soc., Lynchburg, 1993—; bd. dirs., past pres. Southside Va. C.C., Alberta, 1988-96; trustee Lawrenceville United Meth. Ch., 1992—, Brunswick Acad., Lawrenceville, 1995—. Mem. Va. Bar Assn., Va. Trial Lawyers Assn., Brunswick County Bar Assn. (pres.). Real property, Family and matrimonial, General civil litigation. Office: Slayton Bain & Clary 411 S Hicks St Lawrenceville VA 23868-2115

**BAIN, JAMES WILLIAM,** lawyer; b. Suffern, N.Y., Dec. 19, 1949; s. William James and Agnes (Hoey) B.; m. Colleen K., Mar. 23, 1974; children: Rebecca, Meghan. BA, U. Conn., 1972; JD, U. Fla., 1976. Bar: Fla. 1977, U.S. Dist. Ct. (ea. dist. ) Tenn. 1980, Tenn. 1984, U.S. Ct. Appeals (11th cir.) 1984, U.S. Ct. Appeals (D.C. cir.) 1984, Colo. 1986, U.S. Dist. Ct. Colo 1986, U.S. Ct. Appeals (10th cir.) 1988, U.S. Supreme Ct. 1998. Atty. trial Tenn. Valley Authority, Knoxville, 1977-85; atty. dir. Roath & Brega, P.C., Denver, 1985-89, Brega & Winters, P.C., Denver, 1989—; instr. U. Fla., Gainesville, 1976, U. Colo., Boulder, 1987-90; seminar chmn. Inst. for Advanced Legal Study, Denver, 1987. Contbr. articles to profl. jours.; editor constrn. law column Colo. Lawyer. Recipient Civil Litigation Writing award for 1986-87, Denver Colo. Bar Assn., 1987. Mem. ATLA, Colo. Bar Assn., Fla. Bar Assn., Am. Judicature Soc., Am. Arbitration Assn. (arbitrator 1986), Internat. Platform Assn. Avocations: soccer, skiing, biking, basketball. Federal civil litigation, Construction, State civil litigation. Office: Brega & Winters PC 1700 Lincoln St Ste 2222 Denver CO 80203-4522

**BAINBRIDGE, JOHN SEAMAN,** retired law school administrator, law educator, lawyer; b. N.Y.C., Nov. 1, 1915; s. William Seaman and June Ellen (Wheeler) B.; m. Katharine Barker Garrett, Feb. 3, 1943 (div. July 24, 1968); 1 son, John Seaman; m. 2d, Elizabeth Kung-Ji Liu, May 13, 1978. B.S., Harvard U., 1938; LL.B., J.D., Columbia U., 1941. Bar: N.Y. 1941, Md. 1946, U.S. Dist. Ct. Md. 1946, U.S. Supreme Ct. 1946, U.S. Dist. Ct. (so. dist.) N.Y. 1948. Gen. practice law, Md. and N.Y., 1945-56; asst. dean Columbia U. Law Sch., 1956-65, assoc. dir. Internat. Fellows Program, 1960-62, asst. to pres. Columbia U., 1965-66; dir. Project on Staffing of African Instns. of Legal Edn. and Research, 1962-72; assoc. dir. Ctr. for Adminstrn. of Justice, Wayne State U., Detroit, 1972-74; dir. planning Sch. Law, Pace U., Westchester County, N.Y., 1974-76; assoc. dean, dean, prof. law No. Ill. U. Coll. Law, Glen Ellyn, 1976-81; vis. prof., assoc. dean Del. Law Sch., Wilmington, 1981-82; dean, prof. law Touro Coll. Sch. Law, Huntington, N.Y., 1982-85; cons. Edward John Noble Found., 1959-61, Inst. Internat. Edn., 1962-67; mem. adv. com. Peace Corps Lawyers Project, 1963; founder, dir. African Law Assn. in Am., Inc., 1965-72. Served to lt. comdr. USNR, 1940-46. Mem. ABA, Sons of Revolution, S.R. Presbyterian. Club: Harvard (N.Y.C.). Author: The Study and Teaching of Law in Africa, 1972. Home: 17 Ringfield Rd Chadds Ford PA 19317-9130

**BAINE, KEVIN T.,** lawyer; b. N.Y.C., Aug. 18, 1949. AB cum laude, Princeton U., 1971; JD magna cum laude, U. Pa., 1974. Bar: D.C., N.Y., Md. Comment editor Law Review U. Pa., 1973-74; law clerk Judge Edward Weinfield, U.S. Dist. Ct. (so. dist.) N.Y., 1974-75, Assoc. Justice Thurgood Marshall, U.S. Supreme Ct., 1975-76; mem. Williams & Connolly, Washington. Mem. ABA (co-chair first amendment and media litig. com., sect litig. 1989-92, co-chair resource devel. com., sect. litig. 1995-96), Order of Coif. Constitutional, Libel, General civil litigation. Office: Williams & Connolly 725 12th St NW Washington DC 20005-5901

**BAINTON, DENISE MARLENE,** lawyer; b. Trenton, N.J., June 12, 1949; d. Milford C. and Anne M. (Docherty) Smith; m. Raymond Port McKinster, Dec. 26, 1987. MusB, U. Ariz., 1971, MusM, 1974, JD highest distinction, 1983. Bar: Ariz. 1983, U.S. Dist. Ct. Ariz. 1984, U.S. Ct. Appeals (9th cir.) 1985, U.S. Supreme Ct. 1988. Music tchr. Flowing Wells Pub. Schs., Tucson, 1971-80; piano instr. Pima Community Coll., Tucson, 1974-77; law clk. to judge U.S. Dist. Ct. Ariz., Phoenix, 1983-84; ptnr. DeConcini McDonald Yetwin & Lacy, Tucson, 1984—. Editor Ariz. Law Rev., 1982-83. Mem. Ariz. Bar Assn., Pima County Bar Assn., Nat. Coun. Sch. Attys., Nat Assn. Coll. and U. Attys., Order of Coif. Education and schools, Civil rights, Labor. Office: DeConcini McDonald Yetwin & Lacy 2525 E Broadway Blvd Ste 200 Tucson AZ 85716-5300

**BAINTON, J(OHN) JOSEPH,** lawyer; b. Long Branch, N.J., May 21, 1947; s. Robert L. and Elizabeth (Dowling) B.; 1 child, John Joseph Jr. BA, Kenyon Coll., 1969; JD, Rutgers U., Newark, 1973. Bar: N.Y. 1973. Assoc. Burke & Burke, N.Y.C., 1972-76; ptnr. Reboul, MacMurray, Hewitt, Maynard & Kristol, N.Y.C., 1976-89, Shea & Gould, N.Y.C., 1989-90, Whitman & Ransom, N.Y.C., 1991-92, Ross & Hardies, N.Y.C., 1993-98, Bainton McCarthy & Siegel, LLC, N.Y.C., 1998—. Contbr. articles to legal jours. Mediator Mandatory Mediation Program So. Dist. N.Y. Mem. U.S. Trademark Assn. (editor 1976), Internat. Anticounterfeiting Coalition (bd. dirs. 1986-92), Products Liability Adv. Coun., Nat. Inst. Trial Advocacy (faculty). Avocation: yacht racing. General civil litigation, Product liability, Trademark and copyright. Office: Bainton McCarthy & Siegel LLC 130 E 35th St New York NY 10016-3815 also: 400 Main St Stamford CT 06901-3004

**BAIR, BRUCE B.,** lawyer; b. St. Paul, May 26, 1928; s. Bruce B. and Emma N. (Stone) B.; m. Jane Lawler, July 19, 1952; children: Mary Jane, Thomas, Susan, Barbara, Patricia, James, Joan, Bruce, Jeffrey. BS, U. N.D., 1950, JD, 1952. Bar: N.D. 1952, U.S. Dist. Ct. N.D. 1955, U.S. Ct. Appeals (8th cir.) 1971, U.S. Supreme Ct. 1974. Assoc. Lord and Ulmer, Mandan, N.D., 1955-57; ptnr. Bair, Bair & Garrity and predecessors, Mandan, 1957—; spl. asst. atty. gen. State of N.D., 1967—; chmn. bd. Bank of Tioga, 1984—, also dir. Rep. precinct committeeman, 1956-70, chmn. Morton County Rep. Com., 1958-62, mem. N.D. Rep. State Cen. Com., 1962-67; pres. sch. bd. St. Joseph's Cath. Ch., 1967-68; mem. bd. Mandan Pub. Sch. Dist. #1, 1971-77; mem. exec. com. Internat. Assn. Milk Control Agys., 1970—; mem. bd. regents U. Mary, Bismarck, N.D., 1984—. Served to 1st lt. JAG Corps USAF, 1952-55. Fellow Am. Coll. of Trust and Estate Counsel; mem. ABA, N.D. Bar Assn., Big Muddy Bar Assn., Am. Legion, Rotary, Elks. Roman Catholic. General civil litigation, Estate planning, Probate. Home: 901 3rd St NW Mandan ND 58554-2537 Office: 210 1st St NW Mandan ND 58554-3115

**BAIR, JOEL EVAN,** lawyer; b. Mishawaka, Ind., Nov. 14, 1949; s. James E. B.; m. Susan Trimmer, June 19, 1971; children: Noelle, Jonathan, Katie. BS Ae. E., Ind. Inst. Tech., 1971; JD, U. Notre Dame, 1974, MS, 1975. Patent atty. U.S. Patent and Trademark Office. Pvt. practice Corpus Christi, Tex., 1978-87; assoc. Varnum, Riddering, Schmidt & Howlett, LLP, Grand Rapids, 1987-93, ptnr., 1993-97; ptnr. Raden, Fishman, Graven & McGarry, Grand Rapids, 1997—; mem., chmn. intellectual property law sect. State Bar Mich., Lansing, 1991-97. Lt. JAG USN, 1975-78; lt. USNR, 1975-7. Mem. ABA (mem. intellectual property law sect. 1989—), Internat. Trademark Assn., State Bar Tex., State Bar Mich. (mem. intellectual property sect., chmn. 1996-97), Grand Rapids Bar Assn. Avocations: sailing, model shipbuilding. Fax: (616) 742-1010. E-mail: jeb@raderfishman.com. Intellectual property. Office: Rader Fishman Grauer & McGarry 171 Monroe Ave NW Ste 600 Grand Rapids MI 49503-2634

**BAIRD, CHARLES BRUCE,** lawyer, consultant; b. DeLand, Fla., Apr. 18, 1935; s. James Turner and Ethelyn Isabelle (Williams) B.; m. Barbara Ann Fabian, June 6, 1959 (div. Dec. 1979); children: C. Bruce Jr., Robert Arthur, Bryan James; m. Byung-Ran Cho, May 23, 1982; children: Merah-Iris, Haerah Violet. BSME, U. Miami, 1958; postgrad UCLA, 1962-64; MBA, Calif. State U., 1966; JD, Am. U., 1971. Bar: Va. 1971, U.S. Dist. Ct. (ea. dist.) Va. 1971, D.C. 1973, U.S. Dist. Ct. D.C. 1973, U.S. Ct. Appeals (4th cir.) 1974, U.S. Supreme Ct. 1975. Rsch. engr. Naval Ordnance Lab., Corona, Calif., 1961-67; aerospace engr. Naval Air Systems Command, Washington, 1967-69; cons. engr. Bird Engring. Rsch. Assts., Vienna, Va., 1969-71; prof. Def. Systems Mgmt. Coll., Ft. Belvoir, Va., 1982; spl. asst. for policy compliance USIA Voice of Am., Washington, 1983-84; cons. Booz, Allen & Hamilton, Inc., Bethesda, 1975-82, IBM, Bethesda, Md., 1984, Logistics Mgmt. Inst., McLean, Va., 1986-98; adj. prof. Fla. Inst. Tech., 1988. Contbr. articles to profl. jours. Inventor computer-based communications systems for the gravely handicapped. Bd. govs. Sch. Engring. U. Miami, 1957; trustee Galilee United Meth. Ch., Arlington, Va., 1983-87. Mem. ATLA, Internet Soc., Fed. Comm. Bar Assn., United We Stand Am. (founding mem.), Sigma Alpha Epsilon. Republican. General civil litigation, Communications, Computer. Home and Office: 5396 Gainsborough Dr Fairfax VA 22032-2744

**BAIRD, CHARLES F.,** state supreme court justice; b. Texas, Mar. 3, 1955; m. Elizabeth Margaret Garcia Baird. Student, Kilgore Jr. Coll., 1973-74; BBA, U. Tex., 1976; student, Georgetown U., 1976-77; graduated, So. Tex. Coll. of Law, 1980; M of Laws in the Judicial Process, U. Va. Law Sch., 1995. Pvt. practice Houston, 1980-90; judge Tex. Ct. Criminal Appeals, Austin, 1990—. Contbr. articles to profl. jours. Regional adv. com. Am. Acad. Jud. Edn.; mem. Austin Rape Crisis Ctr. Adv. Bd., St. Luke United Meth. Ch. (v.p., trustee); co-chair implementation com. Tex. Supreme Ct.'s Gender Bias Task Force. Recipient So. Tex. Coll. Law Disting. Alumnus award, 1993, Harris County Dems. State Jud. award, 1992. Mem. State Bar of Tex. (past mem. ct. cost, efficiency and delay com., past mem. continuing legal edn. com.), Tex. Bar Found., State Bar Coll., Travis County Bar Assn. Methodist. Office: Tex Ct Criminal Appeals PO Box 12248 Capitol Sta Austin TX 78711-2308 Office: Tex Ct Criminal Appeals Supreme Court Bldg 201 W 14th St Austin TX 78701-1614

**BAIRD, DENISE COLLEEN,** lawyer; b. Kansas City, Kans., May 21, 1956; d. William Coleman and Jay Nees Baird; m. Alan Leo Harkness, June 24, 1990; 1 child, Bridget Baird Harkness. BA in Philosophy, Ripon Coll., 1978; JD, U. Idaho, 1984. Bar: Idaho, U.S. Dist. Ct. Idaho, U.S. Ct. Appeals (9th cir.). Jud. clk. Idaho Supreme Ct., Boise, 1984-86; atty. Moffatt Thomas, Boise, 1986-90; corp. counsel Hewlett-Packard Co., Boise, 1990—; chair young lawyers sect. Idaho Bar Assn., Boise, 1990; pres. Idaho Law Found., Boise, 1996-98. Bd. dirs. Hays Shelter Home, Boise, 1986-97, Learning Lab., Boise, 1998—; mem. Idaho Govs. Welfare Reform Task Force, Idaho, 1995-96. Recipient Outstanding Svc. award Idaho State Bar, Boise, 1990; named Idaho Statesman Disting. Citizen, Boise, 1991. Avocations: soccer, skiing, hiking. Computer, Contracts commercial, Antitrust. Office: Hewlett Packard Co 11413 Chinden Blvd Boise ID 83714-1023

**BAIRD, DOUGLAS GORDON,** law educator, dean; b. Phila., July 10, 1953; s. Henry Welles and Eleanora (Gordon) B. BA, Yale U., 1975; JD, Stanford U., 1979; LLD, U. Rochester, 1994. Law clk. U.S. Ct. Appeals (9th cir.), 1979, 80; asst. prof. law U. Chgo., 1980-83, prof. law, 1984—, assoc. dean, 1984-87, Bigelow prof. law, 1988—, dean, 1994-99. Author: (with others) Security Interests in Personal Property, 1984, 2d edit., 1987, Bankruptcy, 1985, 2d edit., 1990, Elements of Bankruptcy, 1992, (D. Baird, R. Gertner, R. Picker) Game Theory and the Law, 1994. Mem. AAAS, Order of Coif. Office: U Chgo Sch Law 1111 E 60th St Chicago IL 60637-2776

**BAIRD, LINDSAY DARE,** lawyer; b. Nürnburg, Germany, July 8, 1959; came to U.S., 1960; d. Niven James and Joan Gard B.; m. Steven Roy Osborn, May 20, 1995. BS, Wilson Coll., 1989; JD, Dickinson Sch. Law, 1993. Mgr., instr. Wilson Coll., Chambersburg, Pa., 1982-89; pvt. practice Carlisle, Pa., 1994—. Mem. Am. Horse Show Assn., U.S. Combined Tng. Assn., Therapeutic Riding Assn. Cumberland County (atty., bd. dirs.), Federalist Soc. Republican. Avocations: training horses, instruction, art. General practice, Family and matrimonial, Juvenile. Office: 37 S Hanover St Carlisle PA 17013-3307

**BAIRD, LOURDES G.,** federal judge; b. 1935. BA with highest honors, UCLA, 1973, JD with honors, 1976. Asst. U.S. atty. U.S. Dist. Ct. (ctrl. dist.) Calif., L.A., 1977-83, U.S. atty., 1990-92; ptnr. Baird & Quadros, 1983-84, Baird, Munger & Myers, 1984-86; judge East L.A. Mcpl. Ct., 1986-87; adj. prof. law Loyola U., L.A., 1986-90; judge L.A. Mcpl. Ct., 1987-88, L.A. Superior Ct., 1988-90; U.S. atty. ctrl. dist. Calif., 1990-92; judge U.S. Dist. Ct. (ctrl. dist.) Calif., L.A., 1992—; faculty civil RICO program Practicing Law Inst., San Francisco, 1984-85, western regional program Nat. Inst. Trial Advocacy, Berkeley, Calif., 1987-88; adj. prof. trial advocacy Loyola U., L.A., 1987-90. Recipient Silver Achievement award for the professions YWCA, 1994; named Woman of Promise, Hispanic Womens' Coun., 1991, Alumnus of Yr., UCLA Sch. Law, 1991. Mem. Mexican-Am. Bar Assn., Calif. Women Lawyers, Hispanic Nat. Bar Assn., UCLA Sch. Law alumni Assn. (pres. 1984). Office: US Dist Ct Ctrl Dist Calif Edward R Roybal Bldg 255 E Temple St Ste 770 Los Angeles CA 90012-3334

**BAIRD, THOMAS BRYAN, JR.,** lawyer; b. Newport News, Va., June 21, 1931; s. Thomas Bryan and Mary Florence (Rieker) B.; m. Mildred Katherine Clark, June 23, 1956; children: Sarah, Thomas Bryan III, William, Laura. BA, U. Va., 1952; LLB, U. Tenn., 1960. Bar: Tenn. 1964, Va. 1969, U.S. Dist. Ct. (we. dist.) 1970. With State Farm Ins., Knoxville, Tenn., 1960-68; asst. commonwealth atty., Wytheville, Va., 1969-71; commonwealth atty. Wythe County, 1972-99; prin. Thomas B. Baird, Jr. Trustee, Simmerman Home for the Aged, 1972-83. Served with U.S. Army, 1953-55. Mem. ABA, ATLA, Nat. Dist. Attys. Assn., Va. Bar Assn., Am. Judicature Soc., Va. Trial Lawyers Assn., Va. Commonwealth Attys. Assn., Phi Alpha Delta. Democrat. Presbyterian. Criminal, Insurance, Real property. Home: 875 N 18th St Wytheville VA 24382-1022

**BAIRD, ZOË,** foundation administrator, lawyer; b. Bklyn., June 20, 1952; d. Ralph Louis and Naomi (Allen) B.; m. Paul Gewirtz, June 8, 1986; 1 child, Julian Baird Gewirtz. AB, U. Calif., Berkeley, 1974, JD, 1977. Bar: Washington, 1979, Calif. 1977, Conn. 1989. Law clk. Hon. Albert Wollenberg, San Francisco, 1977-78; atty., advisor Office Legal Counsel U.S. Dept. Justice, Washington, 1979-80; assoc. counsel to the Pres. The White House, Washington, 1980-81; assoc., then ptnr. O'Melveny & Myers, Washington, 1981-86; counsellor, staff exec. GE, Fairfield, Conn., 1986-90; v.p., gen. counsel Aetna Life & Casualty, Hartford, 1990-93, sr. v.p. gen. coun., 1993-96; pres. John & Mary R. Markle Found., N.Y.C., 1998—; bd. dirs. Sci. Pk. Devel. Corp., New Haven, So. New Eng. Telecom. Corp., mem. bd. contbrs. Mem. Am. Lawyer Media, N.Y.C. (bd. contbrs.). Office: John & Mary Markle Found 75 Rockefeller Plz Rm 1800 New York NY 10019-6908*

**BAIRSTOW, FRANCES KANEVSKY,** labor arbitrator, mediator, educator; b. Racine, Wis., Feb. 19, 1920; d. William and Minnie (DuBow) Kanevsky; m. Irving P. Kaufman, Nov. 14, 1942 (div. 1949); m. David Steele Bairstow, Dec. 17, 1954; children: Dale Owen, David Anthony. Student U. Wis., 1937-42; BS, U. Louisville, 1949; student Oxford U. (Eng.), 1953-54; postgrad. McGill U., Montreal, Que., 1958-59. Rsch. economist U.S. Senate Labor-Mgmt. Subcom., Washington, 1950-51; labor edn. specialist U. P.R., San Juan, 1951-52; chief wage data unit WSB, Washington, 1952-53; labor rsch. economist Canadian Pacific Ry. Co., Montreal, 1956-58; asst. dir. indsl. rels. ctr. McGill U., 1960-66, assoc. dir., 1966-71, dir., 1971-85, lectr., indsl. rels. dept. econs., 1960-72, asst. prof. faculty mgmt., 1972-74, assoc. prof. faculty mgmt., 1974-83, prof., 1983-85; lectr. Stetson Law Sch., Fla. spl. master Fla. Pub. Employees Rels. Commn., 1985-97; dep. commr. essential svcs. Province of Que., 1976-81; mediator So. Bell Telephone, 1985—, AT&T and Comm. Workers Am., 1986—; cons. on collective bargaining arbitrator to OECD, Paris, 1979; cons. Nat. Film Bd. of Can., 1965-69; arbitrator Que. Consultative Coun. Panel of Arbitrators, 1968-83, Ministry Labour and Manpower, 1971-83, United Airlines and Assn. Flight Attendants, 1990-95, Am. Airlines and Transport Workers Union, 1997-98, State U. System of Fla., 1990-97; FDA, 1996-98, Social Security Adminstrn., 1996-97, Am. Airlines, 1997—; arbitrator Tampa Gen. Hosp., 1996—, mediator Canadian Public Svc. Staff Rels. Bd., 1973-85; contbg. columnist Montreal Star, 1971-85. Chmn. Nat. Inquiry Commn. Wider-Based Collective Bargaining, 1978. Fulbright fellow, 1953-54. Mem. Canadian Indsl. Rels. Rsch. Inst. (exec. bd. 1965-68), Indsl. Rels. Rsch. Assn. Am. (mem. exec. bd. 1965-68, chmn. nominating com. 1977), Nat. Acad. Arbitrators (bd. govs. 1977-80, program chmn. 1982-83, v.p. 1986-88, nat. coord. 1987-90), Ctrl. Fla. Indsl. Rels. Rsch. Assn. (pres. 1999). Home and Office: 1430 Gulf Blvd Apt 507 Clearwater FL 33767-2856

**BAIRSTOW, RICHARD RAYMOND,** retired lawyer; b. Waukegan, Ill., Sept. 26, 1917; s. Fred Raymond and Mildred (Wright) B.; m. Mary Kelley, Aug. 8, 1942 (dec. June 19, 1979); children: Kathleen Bairstow Young, Suzanne Bairstow Hicks, Mary Bairstow Neely; m. Agnes Macaitis Caldwell, July 22, 1980 (dec. July 22, 1995). AB, U. Ill., 1939, JD, 1947; postgrad., George Washington U., 1939-41. Bar: Ill. 1947, U.S. Dist. Ct. (no. dist.) Ill. 1964, U.S. Ct. Mil. Appeals 1963, U.S. SUpreme Ct. 1963. Assoc. Hall, Meyer & Carey, Waukegan, 1947-49; asst. state's atty. Lake County, Waukegan, 1949-53; ptnr. McClory & Bairstow, Waukegan, 1953-60, McClory, Bairstow, Lonchar & Nordigan, Waukegan, 1960-66; prin. Richard R. Bairstow & Assocs., Waukegan, 1966-98; ret., 1998; dist. atty. Fox Lake Fire Protection Dist., Ingleside, Ill., 1948-98; adminstrv. law judge Ill. Dept. Revenue, Chgo., 1953-87. Bd. dirs. ARC, Lake County, 1947-73; mem., pres. Salvation Army, Waukegan, 1954-66; bd. dirs. Lake County Family YMCA, 1990-91. Col. AUS, 1941-46, ETO, USAR, 1946-71, ret. U.S. Army Command and Gen. Staff Coll., 1965. Mem. ABA, Ill. Lake County Bar Assn., Assn. U.S. Army, The Ret. Officers Assn., Am. Legion, Glen Flora Country Club, Waukegan City Club, Delta Tau Delta, Phi Alpha Delta. Republican. Episcopalian. General practice, Probate, Real property. Home: 2122 Ash St Waukegan IL 60087-5033

**BAKER, ANITA DIANE,** lawyer; b. Atlanta, Sept. 4, 1955; d. Byron Garnett and Anita (Swanson) B.; m. Thomas Johnstone Robison III, Sept. 26, 1995. BA summa cum laude, Oglethorpe U., 1977; JD with distinction, Emory U., 1980. Bar: Ga. 1980. Assoc. Hansell & Post, Atlanta, 1980-88, Kitchens, Kelley, Gaynes, Huprich & Shmerling, 1989-90; asst. gen. counsel NationsBank Corp., 1991-97; v.p., gen. counsel Adaris Corp., 1997—. Mem. Ga. Bar Assn., Atlanta Bar Assn., Southeastern Software Assn., Atlanta Hist. Soc., pace Acad. Alumni Assn. (bd. dirs.), Oglethorpe U. Alumni Assn. (bd. dirs.), Order of Coif, Phi Alpha Delta, Phi Alpha Theta, Alpha Chi, Omicron Delta Kappa. Banking, General corporate, Computer. Office: Adaris Corp Glenridge 400 Bldg 3 5825 Glenridge Dr NE Ste 101 Atlanta GA 30328-5387

**BAKER, BEVERLY POOLE,** lawyer; b. Fairfield, Ala., Jan. 14, 1944; d. Grafton Chester and Minda Lee (Ingersoll) Poole; m. James Keaton Baker; children: Paige, Paula Baker Carroll, Leslie Baker Housman. BA summa cum laude, U. Ala., 1982; JD, Samford U., 1985. Assoc. McMillan & Spratling, Birmingham, 1985-86; assoc. Haskell Slaughter & Young, Birmingham, 1986-89, ptnr., 1989—. Fellow AAUW; mem. ABA, Nat. Bar Assn., Nat. Assn. Bond Lawyers, Ala. State Bar Assn., Birmingham Bar Assn., Magic City Bar Assn., Birmingham Inns of Ct. Avocations: breeding show dogs, rose cultivation. Labor, Alternative dispute resolution, Federal civil litigation. Office: Haskell Slaughter & Young LLC 1901 6th Ave N Ste 1200 Birmingham AL 35203-2621

**BAKER, BRUCE JAY,** lawyer; b. Chgo., June 18, 1954; s. Kenneth and Beverly (Gould) B. Student, U. Leeds, Eng., 1974-75; BS, U. Ill., 1976; JD, Washington U., 1979. Bar: Ill. 1979, U.S. Dist. Ct. (no. dist.) Ill. 1984. Asst. atty. gen. antitrust divsn. State of Ill., Chgo., 1979-83; assoc. Mass, Miller & Josephson Ltd., Chgo., 1983-86; sr. counsel Discover Card Services Inc., Riverwoods, Ill., 1986-89; sr. legis. counsel Dean Witter Fin. Svcs. Group, Riverwoods, 1989-91; gen. counsel Ill. Commr. Banks and Trust Cos., Chgo., 1991-94; ptnr. Schiff Hardin & Waite, Chgo., 1994-99, of counsel, 1999—; sr. v.p., gen. counsel Ill. Bankers Assn., 1999—. Contbr. articles to profl. jours. Registered lobbyist Ill. Legislature, Springfield, 1985-91, 94—. Named Ill. State scholar, 1972. Mem. ABA (antitrust com., banking com., chmn. state banking law devels. task force 1998—), Ill. State Bar Assn. (comml. banking and bankruptcy sect.), Chgo. Bar Assn. (fin. insts. com.), Ill. Bankers Assn. (legis. counsel 1985-86, gen. counsel 1994—, Disting. Bank Counsel award 1991, 97). Banking, General corporate, Administrative and regulatory. Office: Ill Bankers Assn 111 W Jackson Blvd Ste 910 Chicago IL 60604-3502 also: Schiff Hardin & Waite 7200 Sears Tower Chicago IL 60606

**BAKER, CAMERON,** lawyer; b. Chgo., Dec. 24, 1937; s. David Cameron and Marion (Fitzpatrick) B.; m. Katharine Julia Solari, Sept. 2, 1961; children: Cameron III, Ann, John. Student, U. Notre Dame, 1954-57; AB, Stanford U., 1958; LLB, U. Calif., Berkeley, 1961. Bar: Calif. 1962, U.S. Dist. Ct. (so. dist.) Calif. 1962, U.S. Dist. Ct. (no. dist.) Calif. 1963, U.S. Ct. Appeals (9th) 1963. With Adams, Duque & Hazeltine, Los Angeles, 1961-62; with Pettit & Martin, San Francisco, 1962-95, mng. ptnr., 1972-81, 84-87, mem. exec. com, 1971-82, 84-88; with Farella, Braun & Martel, San Francisco, 1995—; mayor City of Belvedere, Calif., 1978-79; arbitrator Am. Arbitration Assn.; owner Larkmead Vineyards, Napa Valley, Calif. Dir. Lassen Nat. Park Found., 1992—; trustee Belvedere Cmty. Found. Mem. ABA (sects. on bus. law and internat. law and practice), Calif. Bar Assn. (sect. bus., real property and internat. law), Bar Assn. San Francisco (bd. dirs. 1966, 72-73), Boalt Hall Alumni Assn. (dir. 1982-84), Bohemian Club, Tiburon Peninsula Club. General corporate, Mergers and acquisitions, Private international. Home: 38 Alcatraz Ave Belvedere CA 94920-2504 Office: Farella Braun & Martel 235 Montgomery St Fl 31 San Francisco CA 94104-3159

**BAKER, CARL LEROY,** lawyer; b. Woodland, Calif., Nov. 9, 1943; s. Elmer L. and Lucea G. (Tickner) B.; m. Suzon L. Lockhart, June 13, 1966; children: Michele S., Eric L. BA, Sacramento State Coll., 1965; JD, Ind. U., 1968. Bar: Ind. 1968, U.S. Dist. Ct. (no. and so. dists.) Ind. 1968, U.S. Supreme Ct. 1978. Atty. Lincoln Nat. Corp., Ft. Wayne, Ind., 1968-74, asst. gen. counsel, 1974-77, assoc. gen. counsel, 1977-81, 2d v.p., 1979-85, v.p., 1985—, v.p., deputy gen. counsel, 1992—; mem. assoc. faculty Ind.-Purdue U. at Ft. Wayne, 1976—. Mem. staff Law Jour. Ind. U. Sch. Law, 1966-67. Bd. dirs., v.p. Garrett (Ind.) Pub. Libr., Ch. Builders, Inc., Ft. Wayne, 1986—, pres., 1994; pro bono atty. indigent clients, Ft. Wayne, 1968—; mem. adv. bd. Lincoln Mus. Mem. Ind. Bar Assn. (conf. speaker 1988), Am. Coun. Life Ins. (legal sect. 1972—), Assn. Life Ins. Counsel, Am. Judicature Soc., Ind. Trial Lawyers Assn., Am. Corp. Counsel Assn., Nat. Lawyers Club (Washington), Delta Theta Phi, Sigma Phi Epsilon. Avocations: trout fishing, splitting firewood, hiking, Indiana U. basketball. Civil rights, Insurance, Labor. Office: Lincoln Nat Corp 1300 S Clinton St Fort Wayne IN 46802-3506

**BAKER, CARL TENEYCK,** lawyer; b. Gloversville, N.Y., Jan. 15, 1951; s. Henry TenEyck and Virginia (Tasheff) B; m. Sandra A. Stoffolano, Oct. 12, 1975; children: Christopher T., Jessica A. BA, Cornell U., 1973; JD, Albany U., 1978. Bar: N.Y. 1979; U.S. Dist. Ct. (no. dist.) N.Y. 1979. Assoc. LaPann, Reardon, Fitzgerald & Firth, P.C., Glens Falls, N.Y., 1978-83; ptnr. LaPann, Reardon, Morris, Fitzgerald & Firth P.C., Glens Falls, N.Y., 1983-90, Fitzgerald, Morris, Baker & Firth P.C., 1990—; pres. Estate Planning Coun. Northeastern N.Y., 1993—; lectr. N.Y. State Bar Assn. Continuing Legal Edn. Contbg. author: (book) The New York Estate Tax; author course materials in field. Treas. Widowed Persons Svc., Glens Falls, 1984-97, pres., 1997—; bd. govs., chmn. planned giving coun. Glens Falls Hosp.; dir., vice chair Compre-Care Inc., 1993—; bd. dirs. Hudson Headwaters Health Network. Mem. ABA (real property, probate and trust law sect.), Nat. Acad. Elder Law Attys., N.Y. State Bar Assn. (trusts and estates sect., chair com. on practice and ethics), Kiwanis (pres. Glens Falls chpt. 1985-86). Estate planning, Probate, Estate taxation. Office: FitzGerald Morris Baker Firth PC 1 Broad St # 2017 Glens Falls NY 12801-4301

**BAKER, CATHERINE HAYMES,** lawyer, consultant; b. L.A., Aug. 20, 1958; d. Bertram and Bette Jane (Baum) Haymes; m. Christopher Royal Baker, Sept. 13, 1987. Student, Pomona Coll., 1976-77; BA, U. Calif., Berkeley, 1980; JD, UCLA, 1983. Bar: Calif. 1984. Campaign rep. Proposition X of Santa Monica, Calif., 1984; rsch. assoc., prodn. NBC Studios, Burbank, Calif., 1984-85; corp. assoc. Loeb & Loeb, L.A., 1984-85; v.p. Lee, Jackson & Bowe, Inc., Beverly Hills, Calif., 1985-90; pres. Advantage Legal Search and Consulting, L.A., 1990—; expert witness Kirtland & Packard, L.A., 1991. Mem., lobbyist Californians for Nonsmokers' Rights, L.A., 1981-84; vol. Concern II, Beverly Hills, 1982-86; participant DES Action (DESAD Project), Oakland, Calif., 1992; mem. Citizens Against Tobacco Smoke (CATS), 1987—. Mem. Calif. State Bar Assn., L.A. County Bar Assn., L.A. County Barristers (vol.), Women Lawyers of L.A., Nat. Assn. of Legal Search Cons., Phi Alpha Delta, Phi Beta Kappa, Gamma Phi Beta (Panhellenic del. 1978-80), Omicron Delta Epsilon. Avocations: international travel, computers, hiking, pet ownership, attending conferences. Office: Advantage Legal Search & Cons # 4 329 S Mccarty Dr Beverly Hills CA 90212-3718

**BAKER, DAVID REMEMBER,** lawyer; b. Durham, N.C., Jan. 17, 1932; s. Roger Denio and Eleanor Elizabeth (Ussher) B.; m. Myra Augusta Mullins, Nov. 2, 1955. PhB, U. Chgo., 1949; BA, Birmingham-So. Coll., 1951; JD, Harvard U., 1954. Bar: Ala. 1954, N.Y. 1963, U.S. Supreme Ct. 1972. Assoc. Cabaniss & Johnston, Birmingham, Ala., 1957-62; assoc. Chadbourne, Parke, Whiteside & Wolff, N.Y.C., 1962-66, ptnr., 1967-86; ptnr. Jones, Day, Reavis & Pogue, N.Y.C., 1986-93, ret. ptnr., 1993—; ptnr. Afridi, Angell & Baker, N.Y.C., 1993-96, Gersen, Baker & Wood LLP, N.Y.C., 1997-98; gen. counsel Baker, Johnston & Wilson LLP, Birmingham, Ala., 1998—; counsel Afridi & Angell, 1997—; gen. counsel Econ. Club of N.Y., N.Y.C., 1977—; pres. Remember Baker Corp. Co-editor Due Diligence, Disclosures and Warranties in the Corporate Acquisition Practice, 1988, 2d edit., 1992; author articles and book chpts. Pres. N.Y. Legis. Svc., N.Y.C., 1975-98, chmn., 1998—; mem. adv. com. to Sec. of State of N.Y. on Access to Corps. Database, 1988-92; sec., dir. Jr. Achievement of N.Y., 1973-99; dir. Jr. Achievement of Greater Birmingham, 1999—; trustee Birmingham-So. Coll., 1985—. With U.S. Army, 1954-57. Mem. ABA (liaison com. fin. acctg. stds. bd.), Am. Arbitration Assn. (nat. panel), Am. Law Inst., Am. Fgn. Law Assn., Am. Soc. Internat. Law, Am. Judicature Soc., Assn. Bar City N.Y. (chmn. com. on state legis. 1968-70), Ala. Bar Assn., Birmingham Bar Assn., Internat. Bar Assn. (vice chmn. bus. orgn. com. 1986-90, chmn. com. on trusts for bus. 1990-94, rep. to U.S. members N.Y. area 1988—, prin. rep. to UN in N.Y. 1993—), Internat. Law Assn., Assn. Lloyd's Mems. (N.Am. adv. bd.), N.Y. State Bar Assn. (exec. com. bus. law sect. 1987-89, exec. com. internat. law and practice sect. 1991-92, chmn. internat. investment and devel. com. 1991-92), Internat. Ins. Soc., Musica Viva N.Y. (pres. 1994-96), Harvard Club, Met. Club. Democrat. Unitarian. Avocation: bridge (life master Am. Contract Bridge League). Mergers and acquisitions, Securities, Private international. Home: 1200 Beacon Pkwy E Apt 500 Birmingham AL 35209-1041 also: 315 E 72d St Apt 2-J New York NY 10021 Office: Baker Johnston & Wilson LLP 1 Independence Plz Ste 322 Birmingham AL 35209-2634 also: 126 E 56th St Fl 17 New York NY 10022-3613

**BAKER, FREDERICK MILTON, JR.,** lawyer; b. Flint, Mich., Nov. 2, 1949; s. Frederick Milton Baker and Mary Jean (Hallitt) Rarig; m. Irene Taylor; children: Jessica, Jordan. BA, U. Mich., 1971; JD, Washington U., St. Louis, 1975. Bar: Mich. 1975, U.S. Dist. Ct. (we. dist.) Mich. 1980, U.S. Dist. Ct. (ea. dist.) Mich. 1981, U.S. Ct. Appeals (6th cir.) 1983, U.S. Supreme Ct. 1986. Instr. law Wayne State U., Detroit, 1975-76; research atty. Mich. Ct. Appeals, Lansing, 1976-77, law clk. to chief judge, 1977; asst. prof. T.M. Cooley Law Sch., Lansing, Mich., 1978-80; ptnr. Willingham & Cote, Lansing, 1980-86, Honigman, Miller, Schwartz & Cohn, Lansing, 1986—. Author: Michigan Bar Appeal Manual, 1982; editor Mich. Bar Jour., 1984-89; contbr. articles to profl. jours. Founder, pres. Sixty Plus Law Ctr., Lansing, 1978-87, bd. dirs., 1987—; mem. community adv. bd. Lansing Jr. League, 1983-90; co-founder, dir., sec.-treas. John D. Voelker Found., 1989—; bd. dirs. Lansing chpt. ACLU, 1997—, bd. dirs. Greater Lansing chpt., 1997—; treas. Kehillat Israel, 1996-98. Fellow Mich. State Bar Found.; mem. ABA (Outstanding Single Project award 1980, Disting. brief award 1988), Mich. Bar Assn. (vice chmn. jour. adv. bd. 1984-87, chmn. jour. adv. bd. 1987—, young lawyers sect. coun. 1980-84, grievance com. 1982-84, John W. Cummiskey award 1984), Ingham County Bar Assn. Unitarian. Club: Big Oak (Baldwin, Mich.). Avocations: photography, fishing, running, frisbee, squash. Federal civil litigation, State civil litigation, Insurance. Home: 640 Oakwood Dr East Lansing MI 48823-3031 Office: Honigman Miller Schwartz & Cohn 222 N Washington Sq Ste 400 Lansing MI 48933-1800

**BAKER, GAIL DYER,** lawyer; b. West Point, N.Y, Mar. 16, 1954; s. Hillier Locke Jr. and Miriam Jane (Dyer) B. BA magna cum laude, U. Minn., 1978; JD, Suffolk U., 1981. Bar: Minn. 1981, U.S. Dist. Ct. Minn. 1981. Assoc. R.C. Ploetz & Assocs., Mpls., 1981-82; exec. dir., staff atty. Legal Assistance of Olmsted County, Rochester, Minn., 1982-85; assoc. Steward, Perry, Mahler & Bird, P.A., Rochester, 1985-87, Ryan & VanDerHeyden, Rochester, 1987-88, Ryan & Grinde Ltd., Rochester, 1988-89; ptnr. Baker Law Offices, Rochester, 1989—. Class agt. Suffolk U. Law Sch.; mem. task force on adoption and foster care Minn. Supreme Ct., 1996-97; co-chair Children in Need of Protection and Svcs. Rules Commn., 1997-99. Mem. ABA (young lawyers divsn. dist. rep. 1985-87, publs. chmn. 1987-90, child adv. vice chmn. 1985-90, family law sect. pub. devel. bd. 1989—, mediation com. 1989-90, children and law task force 1989—, task force devel. standards of practice for attys. representing children in dependency and neglect cases 1994-96), Minn. Bar Assn. (family law sect., coahc h.s. mock trials 1990—), Olmsted County Bar Assn. (treas. 1984-86, chair law day 1983-84 chair Bicentennial of Const. 1988, v.p. 1996-97, pres. 1997-98), U. Minn. Alumni Assn., Phi Beta Kappa, Phi Delta Phi. Republican. Presbyterian. Family and matrimonial, General practice, Juvenile. Home: 1412 Berkman Ct SE Rochester MN 55904-4934 Office: Baker Law Offices 2212 2nd St SW Rochester MN 55902-0824

**BAKER, GEORGE WALTER,** lawyer; b. N.Y.C., Apr. 25, 1948; s. George W. and Una (O'Reilly) B.; m. Susan Keane, Sept. 5, 1981; children: Jane, Thomas. BA, Columbia U., 1969, JD, 1973. Bar: Conn. 1973. Ptnr. Bentley Mosher & Babson, Stamford, Conn., 1973-94, Hawthorne Ackerly & Dorrance, New Canaan, Conn., 1994—. Councilman Town of New Canaan, 1989—; founder, dir. Laurel House, Inc., Stamford, Conn., 1983-93. Mem. Conn. Bar Assn. (employment at will com. 1996—), New Canaan Rotary Club (pres. 1993-94). Democrat. Episcopalian. Avocation: playing the piano. Labor. Office: Hawthorne Ackerly & Dorrance 25 South Ave New Canaan CT 06840-5485

**BAKER, H. NICHOLAS,** lawyer; b. Hazard, Ky., Apr. 10, 1937; s. Mark H. and Roberta (Brashear) B.; m. Susan Henson, July 12, 1974; children—Hank, Sarah, Matthew. B.A., Georgetown Coll., Ky., 1959; J.D., U. Louisville, 1966. Bar: Ky. 1966, U.S. Dist. Ct. (we. dist.) Ky. 1968, U.S. Dist. Ct. (ea. dist.) Ky. 1971, U.S. Supreme Ct. 1971. Sole practice, Louisville, 1966—. Mem. Ky. Senate, 1970-78. Served with U.S. Army, 1959-60. Mem. Ky. Bar Assn. Democrat. Episcopalian. State civil litigation, Personal injury, Probate. Home: 2300 Phoenix Hill Dr Louisville KY 40207-1227 Office: 702 Starks Bldg Louisville KY 40202

**BAKER, HAROLD ALBERT,** federal judge; b. Mt. Kisco, N.Y., Oct. 4, 1929; s. John Shirley and Ruth (Sarmiento) B.; m. Dorothy Ida Armstrong, June 24, 1951; children: Emily, Nancy, Peter. A.B., U. Ill., 1951, J.D., 1956. Bar: Ill. bar 1956. Practiced in Champaign, Ill., 1956-78; partner firm Hatch & Baker, 1960-78; chief judge U.S. Dist. Ct. (cen. dist.) Ill., Danville, 1978-94, sr. judge, 1994—; adj. mem. faculty Coll. Law, U. Ill., 1972-78; sr. counsel Presdl. Commn. on CIA Activities within U.S., 1975. Pres. Champaign Bd. Edn., 1967-76, pres., 1967-76. Served to lt. j.g. USN, 1951-53. Mem. ABA, Ill. Bar Assn. Democrat. Episcopalian. Office: US Dist Ct 201 S Vine St Rm 338 Urbana IL 61802-3369

**BAKER, JAMES A.,** state supreme court justice; b. Evansville, Ind., Mar. 30, 1931. BBA, So. Meth. U., 1953, LLB, 1958. Bar: Tex. 1958, U.S. Dist. Ct. (no. dist.) Tex. 1958, U.S. Ct. Appeals (5th cir.) 1961, U.S. Ct. Appeals (11th cir.) 1981, U.S. Supreme Ct. 1980. Atty. Goldberg, Alexander and Baker, 1958-72, Weber, Baker and Allums, 1972-79; prin. Law Office of James A. Baker, 1979-86; judge U.S. Ct. Appeals (5th cir.), Dallas, 1986-95; justice Supreme Ct. of Tex., Austin, 1995—; lectr. State Bar of Tex. Profl. Devel. Program; guest lectr. So. Meth. U. Sch. Law, Dallas Bar Assn., El Centro Dalls C.C. Contbg. author Tex. Collection Manual, 1980. Fellow Tex. Bar Found., Dallas Bar Found.; mem. ABA (mem. task force on appellate delay reduction 1991-92), State Bar Tex., Dallas Bar Assn. (former chair bankruptcy and comml. law sect. 1974, bd. dirs. 1995), Coll. of State Bar Tex., Am. Judicature Soc., Inst. Judicial Adminstrn., William Mac Taylor Jr. Inn of Ct. Office: Supreme Ct Bldg 201 W 14th Rm 104 PO Box 12248 Austin TX 78711-2248*

**BAKER, JAMES EDWARD SPROUL,** retired lawyer; b. Evanston, Ill., May 23, 1912; s. John Clark and Hester (Sproul) B.; m. Eleanor Lee Dodgson, Oct. 2, 1937 (dec. Sept. 1972); children: John Lee, Edward Graham (dec. Aug. 1988). A.B., Northwestern U., 1933, J.D., 1936. Bar: Ill. 1936, U.S. Supreme Ct. 1957. Practice in Chgo., 1936—; assoc. Sidley & Austin, and predecessors, 1936-48, ptnr., 1948-81; of counsel Sidley & Austin, 1981-93; lectr. Northwestern U. Law Sch., 1951-52; nat. chmn. Stanford U. Parents Com., 1970-75; mem. vis. com. Stanford Law Sch., 1976-79, 82-84, Northwestern U. Law Sch., 1980-89, DePaul U. Law Sch., 1982-87. Served to comdr. USNR, 1941-46. Fellow Am. Coll. Trial Lawyers (regent 1974-81, sec. 1977-79, pres. 1979-80); mem. ABA, Bar Assn. 7th Fed. Circuit, Ill. State Bar Assn., Chgo. Bar Assn., Soc. Trial Lawyers Ill., Northwestern U. Law Alumni Assn. (past pres.), Order of Coif, Phi Lambda Upsilon, Sigma Nu. Republican. Methodist. Clubs: John Evans (Northwestern U.) (chmn. 1982-85); University (Chgo.); John Henry Wigmore (past pres.); Midday (Chgo.), Legal (Chgo.), Law (Chgo.) (pres. 1983-85); Westmoreland Country (Wilmette, Ill.), Pauma Valley Country (Calif.). Federal civil litigation, Antitrust, State civil litigation. Home: 1300 N Lake Shore Dr Chicago IL 60610-2169 Office: Sidley & Austin 1 First Natl Plz Chicago IL 60603-2003

**BAKER, LESA KAY,** legal secretary; b. Pitts., Oct. 9, 1967; d. Kenneth Jay and Kay Lea (Whipkey) Baker; m. Keith Nair, Apr. 28, 1990 (div. Oct. 1997). A.Gen.Studies, Allegany Coll., Somerset, Pa., 1995; postgrad., Allegany Coll. Legal sec. J.L. Hajduk, Somerset, 1988-93, W.H. Beachy III, Somerset, 1993-94; part time reporter, typist Sargarent's Ct., 1994—. Sec. Rep. Com., Somerset, 1994. Ch. of God. Avocation: Nascar racing. Home: 615 Kircher Pl Boswell PA 15531-1060

**BAKER, LINDI L.,** lawyer; b. San Antonio, Jan. 1, 1952; d. Louis R. and R. Jean Brandt; m. Buck N. Baker, Aug. 26, 1972. BS, S. Oreg. State U., 1974, MS, 1978; JD, U. San Francisco, 1984. Bar: Calif. 1984, Oreg. 1991. Staff atty. Calif. Supreme Ct., San Francisco, 1984-85; assoc. Heller Ehrman White & McAuliffe, San Francisco, 1985-91; of counsel Schultz Salisbury Cauble & Dole, Grants Pass, Oreg., 1997—. Precinct rep. Rep. Party, Josephine County, Oreg., 1998-99; pres. Grants Pass Mus. Art; bd. dirs. Coalition for Kids. Mem. Oreg. Bar Assn., Calif. Bar Assn. General practice, General civil litigation, Real property. Office: Schultz Salisbury Cauble & Dole 111 SE 6th St Grants Pass OR 97526-2403

**BAKER, LLOYD HARVEY,** retired lawyer; b. Sept. 17, 1927; s. George William and Marion (Souville) B.; m. Barbara I. Gustafson, Sept. 4, 1955; children: Laurie, Jeffrey. Student, Colgate U., 1945-48; LLB, NYU, 1951. Bar: N.Y. 1951, U.S. Dist. Ct. (so. and ea. dists.) N.Y. 1953, U.S. Ct. Appeals (2d cir.) 1970. Assoc. Milligan, Reilly, Lake & Schneider, Babylon, N.Y., 1952-53; staff Fgn. Claims Commn., Washington, 1954; spl. attorney windfall investigations FHA, Washington, 1955; asst. U.S. atty. for Ea. Dist. N.Y., 1955-59; sole practice Bayshore and Islip, N.Y., 1959-67; atty. Suffolk County (N.Y.) Legal Aid Soc., 1967-69; dep. chief civil div. U.S. Atty.'s Office for Ea. Dist. N.Y., 1969-74; asst. counsel met. region Penn Central R.R. and Conrail, N.Y.C., 1975-81; ptnr. Bleakley, Platt, Remsen, Millham and Curran, N.Y.C., 1982-87; asst. town atty. Town of Islip, N.Y., 1987-97, retired, 1997—. Mem. Suffolk County Republican Com., 1963-71. Mem. Suffolk County Bar Assn. (chmn. fed. ct. com.), Bay Shore (N.Y.) Yacht Club. Episcopalian. Federal civil litigation, State civil litigation. Home: 5 Mulberry Rd Islip NY 11751-3707 Office: Town Hall of Islip Main St Islip NY 11751

**BAKER, LOREN LEONARD,** lawyer; b. Oklahoma City, Aug. 5, 1946; s. Homer Leonard and Carolyn Jane (Kerr) B.; m. Deborah Ann Shock, Aug. 29, 1969 (div. 1972); m. Felisa L. Brown, Nov. 15, 1994. BA, U. Okla., 1972, JD, 1975. Bar: Okla. 1976, U.S. Dist. Ct. (we. dist.) Okla. 1976, U.S. Ct. Appeals (10th cir.) 1979. Pvt. practice Oklahoma City, 1977-89; gen. counsel Libertarian Party Okla., Oklahoma City, 1979-89; state treas., 1983-85. Sgt. USAF, 1964-68. Mem. Assn. Libertarian Lawyers, Phi Alpha Delta. Libertarian. Environmental, Government contracts and claims, Labor. Home: PO Box 1881 Petersburg VA 23805-0881 Office: HQ Def Commissary Agy USAF Fort Lee VA 23801

**BAKER, LYNN DALE,** lawyer, educator; b. Miles City, Mont., Jan. 11, 1946; s. Robert Franklin and June D. (Babcock) B.; m. Imogene D. Baker, Oct. 8, 1967 (div. 1987); children: Channing Treavor, Chanelle Tete, Cory Justin. BA, U. Mont., 1968, JD, 1986; MA, U. of the Ams., 1970. Bar: Mont. 1986, U.S. Dist. Ct. (fed. dist.) 1986, U.S. Ct. Appeals (9th cir.) 1987. H.s. tchr. The Glenham (S.D.) Sch., 1970-71; linguist, title VII Rocky Boy (Mont.) Schs., 1971-74; prof. edn. U. Alberta, Edmonton, 1974-78; paralegal Hartelius & Ferguson, Great Falls, Mont., 1979-83; atty. Hartelius & Ferguson, Great Falls, 1986-87; ptnr. Hartelius, Ferguson & Baker, Great Falls, 1987-95, Hartelius, Howard, Crosswhite & Baker, LLP, Lakeside, Mont., 1995—; adj. prof. Coll. of Great Falls, 1991—; cons. bilingual edn. N.W. Regional Ednl. Lab., Portland, Oreg., 1972-74; dir. Far North Ednl. Lab., Edmonton, 1974-79. Nat. Indian Bilingual Edn. Conf., Billings, Mont., 1974; mem. Province of Alberta Cross Cultural Edn. Com., 1974-78; paralegal program adv. com. May Coll., Great Falls, Mont., 1994—. State bd. mem. MS Soc. of Great Falls, 1993—; com. mem. Am. Cancer Soc. Jail-A-Thon, Great Falls, 1987-92; vol. atty. Am. Radio Relay League, Newington, Conn., 1990—; mem. Cascade County Dem. Com., 1992—. mem. ABA (com. on women and minorities 1992—), Mont. Bar Assn., Am. Trial Lawyers Assn., Mont. Trial Lawyers Assn., Cascade County Bar Assn. Democrat. Avocations: amateur radio (K7LUH), paragliding, fishing, teaching, auto racing. Personal injury, Labor. Office: Hartelius Ferguson Baker & Kazda 600 Central Ave Great Falls MT 59401-3179

**BAKER, MARK ROBERT,** lawyer; b. Buffalo, Aug. 27, 1954; s. Jack R. and Barbara A. (Mussen) B.; m. Diane Price, Jan. 3, 1977. AB, Columbia Coll., 1976; JD, Columbia U., 1979. Bar: N.Y. 1980, U.S. Dist. Ct. (so. dist.) N.Y. 1980. Assoc. Dewey, Ballantine, Bushby, Palmer & Wood, N.Y.C., 1979-87, ptnr., 1987-97; corp. sr. v.p., chief legal officer Continental Grain Co., 1997—. Exec. and contbr. editor Columbia Journ. Law and

Social Problems, 1978-79. Mem. Assn. of Bar of City of N.Y. Securities, Mergers and acquisitions, General corporate. Office: Continental Grain Co 277 Park Ave Rm 3701 New York NY 10172-0178

**BAKER, PATRICIA (JEAN),** lawyer, mediator; b. June 28, 1948. BS summa cum laude, Wright State U., Dayton, Ohio, 1973; MBA, Northeastern U., Boston, 1989; JD, Calif. Western U., San Diego, 1993. Bar: Calif. 1993; cert. mediator. With GenRad Inc., Boston, 1974-82; mktg./sales staff GE Co., Boston, 1982-84; major accounts mgr. Fluke Mfg. Co., Boston, 1984-89; pub. rels. mgr. Racal Dana, Irvine, Calif., 1989-90; legal intern Pub. Defenders Dependancy, San Diego, 1992; law clk. Civil divsn. U.S. Atty., San Diego, 1992; personal injury atty. L.H. Parker, Long Beach, Calif., 1993; mediator/atty. Baker & Assocs., San Diego, 1993-94; dir. Orange County region Am. Arbitration Assn., Irvine, 1994-97; v.p. govt. programs Am. Arbitration Assn., Washington, 1997—; mediator San Diego Mediation Ctr., 1993-97; trainer mediation skills Am. Arbitration Assn., 1994—; adj. prof. Western State U., Irvine, 1995-96; MCLE presenter San Diego County Bar, 1994, State Bar of Calif., 1996, ABA, 1997; mediator Superior Ct., San Diego, 1994-97, U.S. Bankruptcy Ct. (cen. dist.) Calif., 1995-97; adj. prof. Columbus Sch. of Law, Washington, 1997—. Bd. dirs. Legal Aid Soc., San Diego, 1994, T. Homann Law Assn., San Diego, 1994. Recipient Am. Jurisprudence awards, 1992/. Mem. ABA (ADR sect.), D.C. Bar Assn., State Bar of Calif., San Diego County Bar Assn. (ADR sect.), So. Calif. Mediation Assn. Avocations: tennis, golf.

**BAKER, RICHARD SOUTHWORTH,** lawyer; b. Lansing, Mich., Dec. 18, 1929; s. Paul Julius and Florence (Schmid) B.; m. Kathleen E. Yull, 1956 (dec. 1964); m. Marina J. Vidoli, 1965 (div. 1989); children: Garrick Richard, Lydia Joy; m. Barbara J. Walker, 1997. Student, DePauw U., 1947-49; A.B. cum laude, Harvard, 1951; J.D., U. Mich., 1954. Bar: Ohio 1957, U.S. Dist. Ct. (no. dist.) Ohio 1958, U.S. Tax Ct. 1960, U.S. Supreme Ct. 1971, U.S. Ct. Appeals (6th cir.) 1972. Since practiced in Toledo; mem. firm Fuller & Henry, and predecessors, 1956-91; pvt. practice Toledo, 1991—; Chmn. nat. com. region IV Mich. Law Sch. Fund, 1967-69, mem.-at-large, 1970-85. Bd. dirs. Asso. Harvard Alumni, 1970-73; mem. Epworth Assembly, Ludington, Mich.. Served with AUS, 1954-56. Fellow Am. Coll. Trial Lawyers; mem. ABA, Ohio Bar Assn., Toledo Bar Assn., Lawyer-Pilots Bar Assn., Toledo Club, Harvard Club (pres. Toledo chpt. 1968-77), Capital Club, Phi Delta Theta, Phi Delta Phi. General civil litigation, Environmental, Workers' compensation. Office: 2819 Falmouth Rd Toledo OH 43615-2215

**BAKER, ROBERT KENNETH,** lawyer; b. Anderson, Ind., Mar. 20, 1940; s. James Leslie and Bernadine (Bright) B.; m. Sally Jean Kauffman, Dec. 13, 1971 (div.); children: Alexis Bright, Sarah Elizabeth. AB in Econs., Stanford U., 1962, LLB, 1965. Bar: Calif. 1966, N.Y., 1971, U.S. Dist. Ct. (cen. dist.) Calif. 1966, U.S. Dist. Ct. (so. dist.) N.Y. 1972, U.S. Dist. Ct. (ea. dist.) N.Y., 1974, U.S. Dist. Ct. (so. dist.) Calif. 1979, U.S. Dist. Ct. (ea. dist.) Calif. 1983, U.S. Ct. Appeals (2d cir.) 1972, U.S. Ct. Appeals (5th cir.) 1976, U.S. Ct. Appeals (9th cir.) 1976, U.S. Supreme Ct. 1976. Instr. Columbia Law Sch., N.Y.C., 1965-66; staff mem. Antitrust div. U.S. Dept. Justice, Washington, 1966-67, spl. asst. to Dep. Atty. Gen., 1967-68; dep. gen. counsel, co-dir. Media Task Force, Nat. Commn. on Causes Prevention of Violence, Washington, 1968-69; assoc. Cravath, Swaine & Moore, N.Y.C., 1970-76; ptnr. Agnew, Miller & Carlson, Los Angeles, 1976-79, Alef, Baker, Grunfeld & Wilson, Beverly Hills, Calif., 1980-86, Kindel & Anderson, Los Angeles, 1988—. Mem. Calif. State Bar Assn., Los Angeles County Bar Assn., ABA. Club: Regency (Los Angeles). Federal civil litigation, Antitrust, General corporate. Home: 234 S Figueroa St Los Angeles CA 90012-2541

**BAKER, ROBERT W., JR.,** lawyer; b. Balt., June 29, 1948; s. Robert W. B. and Jeanne Chalmers (Patton) Hobbs; m. Sandra G. Baker, Aug. 20, 1977; children: Emily T., Peter W. BA, Wesleyan U., 1970; JD, U. Md., 1974. Bar: Md. 1974, Vt. 1990. Assoc. Merriman, Crowther & Mann, Balt., 1974-79, Thomas L. Hennessey, Towson, Md., 1979-80; assoc. Weinberg and Green, Balt., 1980-83, ptnr., 1984-89; v.p., gen. counsel IDX Systems Corp., Burlington, Vt., 1989—. Trustee adv. Notre Dame Coll. Md., Balt., 1987-89; trustee, treas. Lake Champlain Waldorf Sch., Shelburne, Vt., 1994-97; dir. Evergreen House, Balt., 1993—. Mem. ABA, Am. Corp. Counsel Assn., Computer Law Assn., New Eng. Legal Found. (mem. Vt. adv. bd. 1992—, bd. dirs. 1997—). Avocations: skiing, reading, triathlete. General corporate, Computer, Contracts commercial. Home: 5402 Lake Rd Charlotte VT 05445-9487 Office: IDX Systems Corp 1400 Shelburne Rd Burlington VT 05403-7754

**BAKER, ROY GORDON, JR.,** lawyer; b. San Antonio, June 19, 1953; s. Roy Gordon and Carolyn Blanch (Slinkert) B.; m. Cynthia Lynn Lee, July 6, 1977; children: Teri Diane, Amanda Christine. BA magna cum ladue, Pepperdine U., 1974; JD, U. Calif., San Francisco, 1977; LLM in Taxation, Golden Gate U., 1989. Bar: Calif. 1977, U.S. Dist. Ct. (no. dist.) Calif. 1977, U.S. Dist. Ct. (ctrl. dist.) Calif. 1984, U.S. Ct. Appeal (9th cir.) 1977, U.S. Tax Ct. 1984; accredited estate planner. Dep. atty. gen. Calif. Dept. Justice, San Francisco, 1977-79; atty., assoc. Stark, Stewart, Wells, Rahl, Field & Schwartz, Oakland, Calif., 1979-83, atty., ptnr., 1983-85; atty., ptnr. Stark, Stewart, Wells, Rahl, Field & Schwartz, Walnut Creek, Calif., 1985-89, Field, Baker & Rchardson, Walnut Creek, 1990-94; atty., shareholder R. Gordon Baker, Atty. At Law, P.C., Walnut Creek, 1994—. Contbr. articles to profl. jours. Participant Leadership Contra Costa, Walnut Creek C. of C., 1993. Mem. ABA (taxation sect., real property, probate and trust law sect.), State Bar Calif. (taxation sect.), Contra Costa County Bar Assn., Nat. Assn. Estate Planners and Counsels, Diablo Valley Estate Planning Coun. (bd. dirs. 1993—). Avocations: fishing, gardening, sailing, canoeing. Estate planning, Probate, General corporate. Office: R Gordon Baker Atty At Law PC 2033 N Main St Ste 750 Walnut Creek CA 94596-3728

**BAKER, THOMAS EDWARD,** lawyer, accountant; b. Washington, July 24, 1923; s. John Thad and Angelina E. (Rappa) B.; m. Mildred M. Younglove, Dec. 26, 1944 (dec. May 1995); children: Jean Ann Baker Holland, Cindy Baker Goralewicz, Linda Hogan; m. Helen Draughon, Nov. 3, 1996. BS, U. Okla., 1950, JD, 1950. Bar: Okla. 1950; CPA, Okla. Pvt. practice Oklahoma City, 1950; agt., spl. agt. IRS, 1951-53; ptnr. Shutler Baker Simpson & Logsdon, Kingfisher, Okla., 1953-79, Baker Logsdon & Schulte, Kingfisher, 1979—. Trustee U. Okla. Found., Inc., 1987-89. WithAUS, 1943-46. Mem. Am. Legion (past svc. officer), Elks, Rotary (pres. Kingfisher club 1957). Democrat. Mem. Christian Ch. (Disciples of Christ). General practice, Probate, Oil, gas, and mineral. Home: 1211 Regency Ct Kingfisher OK 73750-4251 Office: Baker Logsdon & Schulte 302 N Main St Kingfisher OK 73750-2799

**BAKER, THURBERT E.,** state attorney general; b. Rocky Mount, N.C., Dec. 16, 1952; m. Catherine Baker; children: Jocelyn, Chelsea. BA in Polit. Sci., U. N.C.; JD, Emory U., 1979. Mem. Ga. Ho. of Reps., 1988-90, asst. adminstrn. floor leader, 1990-93, adminstrn. floor leader, 1993-97; atty. gen. State of Ga., 1997—. Trustee DeKalb County (Ga.) Libr. Bd.; vice chmn. DeKalb County Bd. of Appeals; trustee Statewide Ga. Diabetes Bd.; trustee Ebenezer Bapt. Ch., Atlanta, DeKalb Coll. Found. Mem. DeKalb County C. of C. (bd. dirs.), Nat. Med. Soc.-Emory U. Office: Atty Gen Law Dept 40 Capitol Sq SW Atlanta GA 30334-9003

**BAKER, TIM A.,** lawyer; b. Miami, Fla., Aug. 5, 1962; s. Thomas Justin Baker and Mary Anne (McDougal) Wood; m. Cynthia Anne Oppliger, June 8, 1991. BA in Journalism, Ind. U., 1984; JD with honors, Valparaiso U., 1989. Bar: Ind. 1989, U.S. Dist. Ct. (so. and no. dists.) Ind. 1989, U.S. Ct. Appeals (7th cir.) 1991. Law clk. Hon. Larry J. McKinney U.S. Dist. Ct. (so. dist.), Indpls., 1989-91; assoc. Barnes & Thornburg, Indpls., 1991-95; asst. U.S. Atty. Office of U.S. Atty., Indpls., 1995—. Columnist Ind. Lawyer, 1991—. Mem. Indpls. Bar Assn. (sec. labor and employment law sec.). Avocations: weight lifting, racquetball. Federal civil litigation, Civil rights, Labor. Office: Office of US Atty US Courthouse 5th Fl 46 E Ohio St Indianapolis IN 46204-1903

**BAKER, WALTER WRAY, JR.,** lawyer; b. Raleigh, N.C., July 27, 1942; s. Walter Wray and Maggie Lee (Holland) B.; m. Jane Marlyn Green, June 14, 1964; children: Susan, Valerie, Walter. AA, Campbell Coll., 1962; AB, U. N.C., 1964, JD, 1966. Bar: N.C. 1966, U.S. Dist. Ct. (ea. and mid. dists.) N.C., U.S. Supreme Ct. 1974. Rsch. asst. to chief justice N.C. State Supreme Ct., Raleigh, 1966-67; pvt. practice High Point, 1967-94; ptnr. Baker & Boyan, PLLC, High Point, 1994—; writer, lectr. continuing legal edn. personal injury & ethics. Mem. N.C. Acad. Trial Lawyers (pres. 1985-86), High Point Bar Assn. (pres. 1985), N.C. State Bar (councillor 18th jud. dist.), Am. Bd. Trial Advocates, Guilford Inn of Ct., Million Dollar Advocates Forum. Democrat. Mem. Wesleyan Ch. Personal injury, General civil litigation. Office: Baker & Boyan PLLC 820 N Elm St High Point NC 27262-3920

**BAKER, WILLIAM COSTELLO, JR.,** lawyer; b. Mobile, Ala., Sept. 15, 1959; s. William C. and June B. BA, Fla. State U., 1981; JD, Stetson U., 1983. Bar: Fla. 1984. Assoc. Levin, Middlebrooks et al, Pensacola, Fla., 1984-85; pvt. practice Pensacola, 1986-94, Baker and Baker, 1995—. Mem. Acad. Fla. Trial Lawyers, Escambia-Santa Rosa Bar Assn., Fla. Bar Assn. Democrat. Roman Catholic. Personal injury, General civil litigation. Office: Baker and Baker 300 E Government St Pensacola FL 32501-6021

**BAKER, WILLIAM PARR,** lawyer; b. Balt., Sept. 5, 1946; s. George William and Jane (Parr) B.; m. Christine Corbett, Oct. 23, 1982; children: William Corbett, Brendan Parr, Laura Elizabeth. BA, St. Francis Coll., Loretto, Pa., 1968; JD, U. Md., 1971. Bar: Md. 1971, U.S. Dist. Ct. Md. 1972, U.S. Tax Ct. 1978, U.S. Supreme Ct. 1980, U.S. Ct. Appeals (4th cir.) 1982. Law clk. Md. Ct. Appeals, 1971-72; ptnr. Baker and Baker, PA and predecessors, Balt., 1972—; civil case mediator Cir. Ct. for Balt. County; adj. prof. U. Md. Sch. Law. Co-author: Maryland Elder Law, 1996, Keys to Success in a Real Estate Transaction in Maryland, 1998; contbr. articles to profl. jours. V.p. bd. dirs. Santa Claus Anonymous, 1973-76; bd. dirs. Balt. Assn. Retarded Citizens, 1981—. Mem. ABA, Md. Bar Assn., Bar Assn. Balt. City, Golfers Charitable Assn. (bd. dirs. 1989—), Balt. Country Club. Roman Catholic. Contracts commercial, General practice, Federal civil litigation. Office: Baker and Baker PA and predecessors 1000 Mercantile Trust Bldg 409 Washington Ave Baltimore MD 21204-4920

**BAKKEN, GORDON MORRIS,** law educator; b. Madison, Wis., Jan. 10, 1943; s. Elwood S. and Evelyn A. H. (Anderson) B.; m. Erika Reinhardt, Mar. 24, 1943; children: Angela E., Jeffrey E. BS, U. Wis., 1966, MS, 1967, PhD, 1970, JD, 1973. From asst. to assoc. prof. history Calif. State U., Fullerton, 1969-74, prof. history, 1974—, dir. faculty affairs, 1974-86; cons. Calif. Sch. Employees Assn., 1976-78, Calif. Bar Commn. Hist. Law., 1985—; mem. mgmt. task force on acad. grievance procedures Calif. State Univ. and Colls. Systems, 1975; mem. Calif. Jud. Coun. Com. Trial Ct. Records Mgmt., 1992—. Author 5 books on Am. legal history; contbr. articles to profl. jours. Placentia Jusa referee coord., 1983. Russell Sag resident fellow law, 1971-72, Am. Bar Found. fellow in legal history, 1979-80, 84-85; Am. Coun. Learned Socs. grantee-in-ai d, 1979-80. Mem. Orgn. Am. Historians, Am. Soc. Legal History, Law and Soc. Assn., Western History Assn., Calif. Supreme Ct. Hist. Soc. (v.p.), Phi Alpha Theta (v.p. 1994-95, pres. 1996-97). Democrat. Lutheran. Office: Calif State U 800 N State College Blvd Fullerton CA 92834-6846

**BAKKENSEN, JOHN RESER,** lawyer; b. Pendleton, Oreg., Oct. 4, 1943; s. Manley John and Helen (Reser) B.; m. Ann Marie Dahlen, Sept. 30, 1978; children: Michael, Dana, Laura. AB magna cum laude, Harvard U., 1965; JD, Stanford U., 1968. Bar: Oreg. 1969, Calif. 1969, U.S. Dist. Ct. Oreg. 1969. Ptnr. Miller, Nash, Wiener, Hager & Carlsen, Portland, Oreg., 1968—; lawyer del. 9th Cir. Jud. Conf., San Francisco, 1980-82. Author: (with others) Advising Oregon Businesses, 1979. Past bd. dirs. Assn. for Retarded Citizens, Portland; advisor Portland Youth Shelter House; mem. and counsel to bd. dirs. Friends of Pine Mountain Observatory, Portland. Mem. ABA (forum on constrn. industry and sect. pub. contract law and sci. and tech.), Fed. Comm. Bar Assn., Oreg. State Bar, Oreg. Assoc. Gen. Contractors (legal com. 1991, counsel to bd. dirs. 1992), Multnomah Athletic Club. Avocation: astronomy. Construction, Federal civil litigation, State civil litigation. Office: Miller Nash Wiener Hager & Carlsen 111 SW 5th Ave Portland OR 97204-3699

**BALABER-STRAUSS, BARBARA,** lawyer; b. N.Y.C., July 30, 1938; d. Philip Balaber and Clara (Rund) Balaber; children—Nancy C., Elizabeth A. A.B. cum laude, Hunter Coll., 1960; J.D. Brooklyn Law Sch., 1978. Bar: N.Y. 1979, U.S. Dist. Ct. (so. and ea. dists.) N.Y. 1979. Law clk. to presiding justices U.S. Bankruptcy Ct., 1977-78; law asst., assoc. Law Office of R. Dryer, N.Y.C., 1978-79; sole practice, N.Y.C., 1979—; apptd. bankruptcy trustee U.S. Trustee Panel, U.S. Dist. Ct. (so. dist.) N.Y., N.Y.C., 1979—. Mem. Bankruptcy Lawyers Bar Assn., Comml. Law League, bd. dirs., Natl. Assn. Bankruptcy Trustees (NABT), com. chmn.-CLL Women's Bar Assn. of State of NY (WBASNY), Westchester Bar Assn., Gender Bins Task Force-2nd cir., (com. on bankruptcy), Phi Beta Kappa. Bankruptcy, General corporate, Contracts commercial. Home: 20 Irene Ct Demarest NJ 07627-1207 Office: 81 Main St Unit 501 White Plains NY 10601-1720

**BALDANTE, JOHN W.,** lawyer; b. Newark, Feb. 1, 1958; s. John William and Roberta Baldante; m. Marie Riley, Nov. 8, 1986; 1 child, Paris. BA, U. MD., 1980; JD, Widener U., 1983. Bar: Pa. 1983, N.J. 1983, U.S. Dist. Ct. (ea. dist.) Pa. 1983, U.S. Dist. Ct. N.J. 1983, U.S. Ct. Appeals (3d cir.) 1983. Assoc. LaBrum & Doak, P.C., Phila., 1983-87, Mozenter, Molloy & Durst, P.C., Phila., 1987-88; assoc. Levy, Angstreich, Finney, Baldante, Rubenstein & Coren, P.C., Phila., 1988-89, ptnr., 1989—; lectr. in field. Mem. ATLA, Pa. Trial Lawyers Assn., Phila. Trial Lawyers Assn. (bd. dirs. 1993-95), N.J. Trial Lawyers Assn., Pa. Bar Assn., N.J. Bar Assn., Phila. Bar Assn., Camden Bar Assn., Law PAC, Justinian Soc., Omicron Delta Kappa. Office: Levy Angstreich Finney Baldante Rubenstein & Coren 1616 Walnut St Fl 18 Philadelphia PA 19103-5319

**BALDAUF, KENT EDWARD,** lawyer; b. Pitts., Feb. 6, 1943; s. Walter William and Esther (Burr) B.; m. Kathleen Dian Abels, June 10, 1967; children: Kent Edward Jr., Krista K., Kara K. BS in Metall. Engring., Carnegie Mellon U., 1964; JD, Cleve. State U., 1970. Bar: Pa. 1970, U.S. Patent and Trademark Office 1971, U.S. Ct. Appeals (Fed. cir.) 1990, U.S. Supreme Ct. 1977. Shareholder, v.p., dir. Webb Law Firm, Pitts., 1988—. Editor Cleve. State U. Law Rev., 1969-70. Mem. ABA, Pa. Bar Assn., Allegheny County Bar Assn., Am. Intellectual Property Law Assn. (pres. 1998-99), Pitts. Intellectual Property Law Ass n., Engrs. Soc. Western Pa., Valley Brook Country Club, Duquesne Club. Patent, Trademark and copyright, Federal civil litigation. Home: 480 Clubview Dr McMurray PA 15317-3023 Office: The Webb Law Firm 436 7th Ave Pittsburgh PA 15219-1826

**BALDI, ROBERT OTJEN,** lawyer; b. Phila., Aug. 3, 1949; s. Joseph F. M. II and Caroline (Otjen) B.; m. Cheryl Ervin, Apr. 15, 1973; children: Elizabeth DuBois, Meredith Otjen. BA, Lycoming Coll., 1971; JD, U. Tulsa, 1974. Bar: Pa. 1975, U.S. Ct. Claims 1975, U.S. Supreme Ct. 1978, U.S. Dist. Ct. (ea. dist.) Pa. 1979, U.S. Ct. Appeals (3d cir.) 1985. Law clk. to judge Bucks County Ct. Common Pleas, Doylestown, Pa., 1975-76; pub. defender Bucks County Pub. Defenders Office, Doylestown, 1976-79; assoc. Cordes, King & Assocs., Newtown, Pa., 1979-81; founding ptnr. Baldi & Cepparulo, & Williams, P.C., New Hope, Pa., 1981—; solicitor Bucks County Dept. Mental Health and Mental Retardation, Doylestown, 1979—, Bucks County Dept. Consumer Protection, Doylestown, 1981-84; lectr. mental health law, consumer protection law; apptd. to Gov.'s Trial Ct. Nominating Commn. by Gov. Robert P. Casey, 1991, 92. Pres. bd. dirs. Vols. in Teaching Alternatives, Doylestown, 1981, 82; bd. dirs. Big Sisters Bucks County, 1981, Buckingham Friends Elem. Sch., 1988; v.p. Big Bros. Bucks County, 1982. Mem. ABA, Pa. Bar Assn., Bucks County Bar Assn., Assn. Trial Lawyers Am., Pa. Trial Lawyers Assn., KP, Phi Delta Phi. Republican. Presbyterian. Avocations: scuba diving, sailing. General civil litigation, Federal civil litigation, State civil litigation. Home: 270 Iron Hill Rd Doylestown PA 18901-2015 Office: Baldi & Cepparulo PC 123 W Bridge St New Hope PA 18938-1401

**BALDIGA, JOSEPH HILDING,** lawyer; b. Woonsocket, R.I., Dec. 18, 1962; s. Robert S. and Lois E. (Wickstrom) B.; m. Mary P. Baldiga, June 9, 1990; 1 child, Lucy Porter. BA, Boston Coll., 1984, JD, 1987. Bar: Mass. 1987, U.S. Dist. Ct. Mass. 1988. Assoc. Peabody & Brown, Boston, 1987-88, Goodwin Procter & Hoar, Boston, 1988-94; ptnr. Mirick O'Connell, Worcester, Mass., 1994—. Trustee Dynamy, Worcester, 1997—, Chestnut St. Mktg. House Assn., Millville, Mass,. 1992—. Mem. Mass. Bar Assn., Boston Bar Assn., Worcester Bar Assn., Am. Bankruptcy Inst., Comml. Law League, Turnaround Mgmt. Assn. Fax: 508-791-8502. E-mail: jhbaldiga@modl.com. Bankruptcy, Contracts commercial, Banking. Office: Mirick O'Connell 100 Front St Worcester MA 01608-1402

**BALDOCK, BOBBY RAY,** federal judge; b. Rocky, Okla., Jan. 24, 1936; s. W. Jay and S. Golden (Farrell) B.; m. Mary Jane (Spunky) Holt, June 2, 1956; children: Robert Jennings, Christopher Guy. Grad., N.Mex. Mil. Inst., 1956; JD, U. Ariz., 1960. Bar: Ariz. 1960, N.Mex. 1961, U.S. Dist. Ct. N.Mex., 1965. Ptnr. Sanders, Bruin & Baldock, Roswell, N.Mex., 1960-83; adj. prof. Eastern N.Mex. U., 1962-81; judge U.S. Dist. Ct. N.Mex., Albuquerque, 1983-86, U.S. Ct. Appeals (10th cir.), 1986—. Mem. N.Mex. Bar Assn., Chaves County Bar Assn., Ariz. Bar Assn., Phi Alpha Delta. Office: US Ct Appeals PO Box 2388 Roswell NM 88202-2388

**BALDWIN, ALLEN ADAIL,** lawyer, writer; b. St. Augustine, Fla., July 15, 1939; s. Larrie Paul and Bertha Mae (Capallia) B. BA, Brigham Young U., 1969; JD, So. U., Baton Rouge, 1975. Bar: Fla. 1975. Tchr. Putnam County Sch. Bd., Palatka, Fla., 1969-71; pvt. practice Palatka, 1975—. Author: Tricks to Make the Angels Weep, 1986, Call It Not Heaven, 1991, Redeem Us From Virtue, 1992. Mem. Latter-day Saints Ch. Avocations: reading, swimming, hiking. Family and matrimonial, General practice, Probate. Office: 308 Saint Johns Ave Palatka FL 32177-4723

**BALDWIN, BRENT WINFIELD,** lawyer; b. Wichita, Kans., July 10, 1952; s. Howard Stewart and Marguerite (Winfield) B.; m. Karen M. Altshuler, Sept. 27, 1974 (div. Apr. 1987); 1 child, Geoffrey W.; m. Scarlett J. Whitener, Aug. 17, 1991. BBA magna cum laude, U. Tex., 1974, JD, 1977. Bar: Mo. 1977, U.S. Dist. Ct. (ea. and we. dists.) Mo. 1977, Ill. 1978, U.S. Ct. Appeals (8th cir.) 1980, U.S. Ct. Appeals (7th cir.) 1981, U.S. Dist. Ct. (cen. dist.) Ill. 1981, U.S. Supreme Ct. 1982. Pvt. practice St. Louis, 1977—; mng. ptnr. Baldwin & Hess, St. Louis, 1984-95, Hinshaw & Culbertson, St. Louis, 1995—. Contbr. articles to profl. jours. Chmn. bd. Deaconess Med. Ctrs. North & West, Deaconess Found. Mem. ABA, ATLA, Mo. Bar Assn., Bar Assn. Met. St. Louis, Lawyers Assn. St. Louis, Mo. Orgn. Def. Lawyers, Am. Ins. Attys., Def. Rsch. Inst., Rotary (pres., Paul Harris fellow), Solar Found (bd. dirs.), Mo. Athletic Club. Personal injury, Professional liability, Product liability. Office: Hinshaw & Culbertson 1010 Market St Ste 1400 Saint Louis MO 63101-2046

**BALDWIN, CHARLES SELDEN, IV,** lawyer; b. Winston-Salem, N.C., May 30, 1968; s. Charles Selden III and Beth Dixson Baldwin; m. Devon Starr Davis, May 31, 1997. BA in English, U. N.C., 1990; JD, Am. U., 1993, MA, 1994; LLM in Internat. Law with distinction, Georgetown U., 1996. Bar: N.C. 1993, D.C. 1994, U.S. Dist. Ct. (ea. dist.) N.C. 1996, U.S. Dist. Ct. (we. dist.) N.C. 1997, U.S. Ct. Appeals (4th cir.) 1997. Assoc. Rountree & Seagle, LLP, Wilmington, N.C., 1996-98; ptnr. Rountree & Seagle, LLP, Wilmington, 1999—. Author: International Litigation Guide to Jurisdiction Practice and Strategy, Transnational Publishers, 1998. Bd. dirs. Covenant Moravian Ch., Wilmington, 1998—; coord. Interfaith Hospitality Network, Wilmington, 1998—. Mem. N.C. Bar Assn., New Hanover County Bar Assn. Federal civil litigation, Private international, Admiralty. Office: Rountree & Seagle LLP 2419 Market St Wilmington NC 28403-1135

**BALDWIN, GLEN S.,** lawyer; b. Glenridge, N.J., Aug. 22, 1947; s. O. Russell and Anne Baldwin; m. Maureen E. Touhey, Nov. 22, 1970; children: Alyson, Emily. BA in Polit. Sci., The Citadel, 1970; JD, U. S.C., 1975. Bar: S.C. 1975, U.S. Dist. Ct. S.C. 1979. Law clk. S.C. Supreme Ct., Columbia, 1975-76; asst. county atty. Greenville County, Greenville, S.C., 1976-77; city atty. City of Greenville, 1977-79; sr. counsel E.I. duPont de Nemours & Co., Wilmington, Del., 1979—; mem. legis. affairs com. N.J. Chem. Industry Coun., Trenton, 1984-86, Calif. Chem. Industry Coun., Sacramento, 1984-86, S.C. State C. of C., Columbia, 1982-86. Contbg. author: (program manual) State Ground Water Management, 1987. Rep., New Castle County (Del.) Civic Assn., 1984-87; pres. Shipley Woods Civic Assn., New Castle County, 1984-87. Capt. U.S. Army Res., 1970-78. Mem. ABA (environ. com., subcom. on pesticides), S.C. Bar Assn., The Citadel Alumni Assn. (dist. dir., pres.), Del. Valley Alumni Assn. Avocations: fly fishing, photography. Antitrust, Administrative and regulatory, Mergers and acquisitions. Office: DuPont Co Legal Dept Rts 48 and 141 Wilmington DE 19805

**BALDWIN, GORDON BREWSTER,** law educator, lawyer; b. Binghamton, N.Y., Sept. 3, 1929; s. Schuyler Forbes and Doris Ambeline (Hawkins) B.; m. Helen Louise Hochgraf, Feb., 1958; children: Schuyler, Mary Page. LLB, Cornell U., 1953; BA, Haverford Coll., 1950. Bar: N.Y. 1953, Wis. 1965. Pvt. practice Rochester and Rome, N.Y., 1953-57; prof. law U. Wis., Madison, 1957-99, Evjue-Bascom profl. law, 1991-99; emeritus prof. U. Wis., Masidon, 1999—; assoc. dean law U. Wis., Madison, 1968-70; dir. officer edn. U. Wis., 1972-99; of counsel Murphy & Desmond, S.C., Madison, Wis., 1986-95; chmn. internat. law U.S. Naval War Coll., 1963-64; Fulbright prof., Cairo, 1966-67, Tehran, Iran, 1970-71; lectr. State Dept., Cyprus, 1967, 1969, 1971; counselor internat. law U.S. Dept. State, Washington, 1975-76, cons., 1976-77; vis. prof. Chuo U., Tokyo, 1984, Giessen U., Fed. Republic Germany, 1987, 92, Thommasat U., Thailand, 1997; cons. U.S. Naval War Coll., 1961-65; chmn. screening com. on law Fulbright Program, 1974; mem. constl. law com. Multi-State Bar Exam, 1972-82; chmn. State Pub. Def. Bd., 1980-83, Wis. Elections Bd., 1991-96; cons., rep. Marshall Island Constn. Conv., 1990. Mem. Wis. Bd. Elections, 1991-95, Wis. head coun., 1998—. Ford Found. fellow, 1962-63. Fellow Am. Bar Found.; mem. AAUP (nat. coun. 1975-78, pres. Wis. conf. 1986-87), Bar Assn. (vice chmn. sect. on individual rights 1973-75), Fulbright Alumni Assn. (dir. 1979-82), Am. Law Inst., Order of Coif, Madison Club, Madison Lit. Club (pres. 1985-86), Univ. Club, Rotary (pres. Madison 1980, dist. gov. 1999—), Phi Beta Kappa. Home: 3958 Plymouth Cir Madison WI 53705-5212 Office: U Wis 975 Bascom Mall Sch Law Madison WI 53706-1399

**BALDWIN, HOWARD,** lawyer; b. Phoenix, July 28, 1937; s. Judson and Helen Mary (Phillips) B.; m. Annette Joyce Hils, June 19, 1959; 1 child, Denise Renee. BS, Ariz. State U., 1969; JD, U. Ariz., 1972. Bar: Ariz. 1973, U.S. Dist. Ct. Ariz. 1973, U.S. Ct. Appeals (9th cir.) 1989, U.S. Supreme Ct. 1979. Dep. county atty. Pima County, Tucson, 1973-80; pvt. practice, Tucson, 1980—; legal adviser Pima County Bd. Health, Tucson, 1973-80, Kino Cmty. Hosp., Tucson, 1973-80. Bd. dirs. Cmty. Orgn. Personal Enrichment, Tucson, 1977-80; bd. dirs., treas. La Frontera Ctr., Inc., Tucson, 1977-83. Recipient Cert. of Appreciation, Pima County Bd. Health, 1980, Pima County Atty., 1980, Kino Cmty. Hosp., 1980, La Frontera Ctr., Inc., 1983. Mem. Ariz. State Bar Assn., Pima County Bar Assn. Democrat. General practice, General civil litigation, Health. Office: 22 E University Blvd Tucson AZ 85705-7737

**BALDWIN, JEFFREY KENTON,** lawyer, educator; b. Palestine, Ill., Aug. 8, 1954; s. Howard Keith and Annabelle Lee (Kirts) B.; m. Patricia Ann Mathews, Aug. 23, 1975; children: Matthew, Katy, Timothy, Philip R. BS summa cum laude, Ball State U., 1976; JD cum laude, Ind. U., 1979. Bar: Ind. 1979, U.S. Dist. Ct. (so. dist.) Ind. 1979, U.S. Ct. Appeals (7th cir.) 1979, U.S. Dist. Ct. (no. dist.) Ind. 1984. Mem. majority leader's staff Ind. Senate, Indpls., 1976; instr. Beer Sch. Real Estate, Indpls., 1977-78, Am. Inst. Paralegal Studies, Indpls., 1987—; dep. Office Atty. Gen., Indpls., 1979-81; mng. ptnr. Baldwin & Baldwin, Danville, Ind., 1979—; agt. Nat. Attys. Title Assurance Fund, Vevay, Ind., 1983—; officer, bd. dirs. Baldwin Realty, Inc., Danville; conf. participant White House Conf. on Small Bus. (Ind. meeting 1994), congl. appointee, 1995; bd. dirs. Small Bus. Coun. Bd. dirs. Hendricks Civic Theatre, Inc.; organizer, Hendricks County Young Republicans, 1972; sec. Hendricks County Rep. Com., 1978-84; bd. dirs. Hendricks County Assn. for Retarded Citizens, Danville, 1982-86; cons. Hendricks County Right for Life, Brownsburg, Ind., 1984—; mem. philanthropy adv. com. Ball State U., Muncie, Ind., 1987—; judge Hendricks County unit Am. Cancer Soc., 1987; coordinator region 2 Young Leaders for Mutz, Indpls., 1987-88; cubmaster WaPaPh dist. Boy Scouts Am., 1988, S.M.E. chmn., 1988-89; steering com. Ind. Lawyers Bush/Quayle; founder, chmn. Christians for Positive Reform; candidate for Congress 7th Congl. Dist. of Ind.; del. to Annual Conf. South Ind. Conf. of United Meth. Ch., 1993, 95-98; host com. Midwest Rep. Leadership Conf., 1997; dist. coord. Hoosier Families for John Price for U.S. Senate; v.p. Danville Little League Baseball, 1998—. Recipient Presdl. award of honor Danville Jaycees, 1980; named hon. sec. State Ind., 1980. Mem. ABA, Ind. Bar Assn., Hendricks County Bar Assn., Indpls. Bar Assn., Internat. Platform Assn., Nat. Assn.

Realtors, Ind. Assn. Realtors, Met. Indpls. Bd. Realtors (Hendricks County div.), Federalist Soc., Ind. Farm Bur., Nat. Fedn. Ind. Bus., Ind. C. of C., Danville C. of C. (sec. 1986), Moot Ct. Soc., Blue Key, Phi Soc. Methodist. General civil litigation, Legislative, General practice. Home: PO Box 63 Danville IN 46122-0063

**BALDWIN, JOHN,** legal association administrator, lawyer; b. Salt Lake City, Feb. 9, 1954. BA, U. Utah., 1977, JD, 1980. Bar: Utah 1980, U.S. Dist. Ct. Utah 1980, U.S. Ct. Appeals (10th cir.) 1984. Assoc. Jardine, Linebaugh, Brown & Dunn, Salt Lake City, 1980-82; asst. atty. gen. Utah Atty. Gen.'s Office, Salt Lake City, 1982-85; dir. Utah Divsn. Securities, Salt Lake City, 1985-90; exec. dir. Utah State Bar, Salt Lake City, 1990—; adj. assoc. prof. mgmt. Eccles Sch. Bus., U. Utah. Mem. N.Am. Securities Adminstrs. Assn. (bd. dirs. 1987-90, pres. 1988-89), U. Utah Young Alumni Assn. (bd. dirs. 1987-90), U. Utah Beehive Honor Soc. (bd. dirs. 1993-97), U. Utah Alumni Assn. (bd. dirs. 1995-97). Office: Utah State Bar 645 S 200 E # 310 Salt Lake City UT 84111-3837

**BALDWIN, KELLEY YEAGER,** lawyer; b. Bloomington, Ind., May 30, 1963; d. Roy Robert and Judith Ann Yeager; m. Warren Robert Good6; chiren: Alexander Tyler, Nicholas Robert. BS, Ind. U., Bloomington, 1985; JD, Ind. U., Indpls., 1988. Bar: Ind.; U.S. Supreme Ct. (no. and so. dist.) 1988. Ptnr. Robinson, Yeager, Good, Baldwin & Apsley, Shelbyville, Ind., 1988—. Mem. ABA, Ind. State Bar Assn. Criminal, Family and matrimonial. Office: Robinson Yeager Good Baldwin & Apsley 45 W Washington St Shelbyville IN 46176-1243

**BALESTER, VIVIAN SHELTON,** legal research consultant, retired lawyer; b. Pine Bluff, Ark., Dec. 10, 1931; d. Marvin W. and Mary Lena (Burke) Shelton; m. James Beverly Standerfer, Aug. 1, 1951 (dec. 1952); 1 child, Walter Eric; m. Raymond James Balester, Oct. 19, 1956; children: Carla Maria, Mark Shelton. BA cum laude, Vanderbilt U., 1955; MLS, Case Western Res. U., 1972, JD, 1975. Bar: Ohio 1975, U.S. Dist. Ct. (no. dist.) Ohio 1975. Ind. bibliographic and legal rsch. cons. Cleve., Washington, Nashville, 1959—; head law libr. Squire, Sanders & Dempsey, Cleve., 1975-86; Ohio del. White House Conf. Librs./Info. Svcs., 1979; spkr. Law Librs. Nat. Conf., 1978, 80, 82; mem. adv. com. on profl. ethics Case Western Res. U., 1982-85. Lay reader St. Alban's Episc. Ch., 1978—, mem. vestry, 1977-79, 84-86, 98—, warden, 1979, 84; mem. coun. Diocese of Ohio, 1980-82, chmn. racial justice com., 1980-86, chmn. nominating com., 1982, del. Nat. Confs. on Faith Pub. Policy, Racism, 1982; dep. gen. Conv. of Episc. Ch. in U.S., 1985; mem. Women's Polit. Caucus, 1978-86; founder, co-chmn. Greater Cleve. Ann. Martin Luther King Celebration, 1980-86; convener AIDS Interfaith Coalition of Greater Cleve., 1987-94; mem. County Commrs. Adv. Com. on Handicapped, 1980-84; chmn. adolescent health coalition Fedn. Cmty. Planning, 1979-81, mem. health concerns commn., 1981-96, vice chairperson, 1986-96; regional chmn. alumni edn. Vanderbilt U., 1982-83; mem. cmty. adv. com. Cleve. Orch., 1983-95; bd. dirs. Hospice Coun. No. Ohio, 1979-81, vol. atty., 1982-85; bd. dirs. Interch. Coun. Greater Cleve., 1978-84, 86-88, 92, sec. bd., 1993-97, AIDS Housing Coun., 1987-94, Health Issues Task Force, 1988-94, Stopping AIDS is My Mission, 1993-96; mem. Ohio Com. Nat. Security, 1983; bd. dirs. WomenSpace, 1979-83. Recipient Merit Svc. award Cleve. Bar Assn., 1979, Outstanding Cmty. Svc. award Fedn. Cmty. Planning, 1980, Woman of Profl. Excellence award YWCA, 1983, Cleve. Mayor's award for volunteerism, 1984, Interchurch Coun. Ecumenical Adv. award, 1988, Western Res. Hist. Soc. Cmty. Leader award, 1989; NEH fellow, 1980. Democrat. Home and Office: 2460 Edgehill Rd Cleveland OH 44106-2408

**BALICK, HELEN SHAFFER,** retired judge; b. Bloomsburg, Pa.; d. Walter W. and Clarissa K. (Bennett) Shaffer; m. Bernard Balick, June 29, 1967. JD, Dickinson Sch. Law, 1966, LLD, 1997. Bar: Pa. 1967, Del. 1969. Probate adminstr. Girard Trust Bank, Phila., 1966-68; pvt. practice law Wilmington, Del., 1969-74; staff atty. Legal Aid Soc. Del., Wilmington, 1969-71; master Family Ct. Del., New Castle County, 1971-74; bankruptcy judge, U.S. magistrate Dist. Del., Wilmington, 1974-80; bankyupcy judge Dist. Del., 1974-94; chief judge Dist. Del., Wilmington, 1994-98; guest lectr. Dickinson Sch. Law, 1981-87; lectr. Dickinson Forum, 1982. Pres. bd. trustees Cmty. Legal Aid Soc., Inc., 1972-74; truste Dickinson Sch. Law, 1985—; mem. Citizens Adv. Com., Wilmington, 1973-74, Wilmington Bd. Edn., 1974. Recipient Women's Leadership award Del. State Bar Assn., 1997; named to Hall of Fame of Del. Women, 1994. Mem. Del. Bar Assn., Fed. Bar Assn., Nat. Conf. Bankruptcy Judges (bd. govs. 1986), Nat. Assn. Women Lawyers, Del. Alliance Profl. Women (Trailblazer award 1984), Nat. Assn. Women Judges, Wilmington Women in Bus. (bd. dirs. 1980-83), Am. Judges Assn., Am. Coll. Bankruptcy, Am. Bankruptcy Inst., Turnaround Mgmt. Assn. (bd. dirs. 1995-97), Dickinson Sch. Law Gen. Alumni Assn. (exec. bd. 1977-80, 87—, v.p. 1981-84, pres. 1984-87, Outstanding Alumni award 1991, Career Achievement award 1998), Phi Alpha Delta. Home: 2319 W 17th St Wilmington DE 19806-1330

**BALIDO, CARLOS A.,** lawyer; b. L.A., Feb. 28, 1965; s. Carlos M. and Leslie F. Balido; m. Jennifer Jackson, May 25, 1991; children: Elizabeth, Catherine. BA, Trinity U., 1987; JD, Tex. Tech. U., 1990. Bar: Tex. 1990, U.S. Dist. Ct. (no. dist.) Tex. 1993, U.S. Dist. Ct. (we. dist.) Tex. 1996. Assoc. Touchstone, Bernays, Johnston, Brall & Smith, Dallas, 1990-96, ptnr., 1997—. Mem. Tex. Assn. Def. Counsel, Dallas Assn. Def. Counsel. Personal injury, Insurance, Workers' compensation. Office: Touchstone Bernays Johnston Beall & Smith 4700 Renaissance Twr Dallas TX 75270

**BALINT, ELLEN BARNEY,** deputy attorney general; b. Albany, N.Y., Mar. 11, 1966; d. Robert Holmes and Judith Kienit Barney; m. Thomas John Balint, Jr., Oct. 1, 1994; 1 child, Christopher. BA, Smith Coll., 1988; JD, Rutgers U., 1992. Bar: N.J., Pa. U.S. Dist. Ct. N.J. Assoc. Quinlan, Dunne, et al, Merchantville, N.J., 1992-95, Mason Griffin & Pierson, Princeton, N.J., 1995-99; dep. atty. gen. divsn. of law N.J. State Atty. Gen., Princeton, 1999—. Mem., vol. Sunshine Found., Mercer County, N.J., 1994—; bd. mem. Glendale Civic Assn., Ewing, N.J., 1995—. Office: Mason Griffin & Pierson 101 Poor Farm Rd Princeton NJ 08540-1941

**BALITIS, JOHN JAMES, JR.,** lawyer; b. Heidelberg, Germany, Mar. 20, 1962; came to the U.S., 1965; s. John James and Rose Balitis; m. Tammy Albright, Jan. 21, 1989. BA summa cum laude, Dickinson Coll., 1984; JD, U. Va., 1987. Bar: Ariz. 1988, Ariz. Supreme Ct. 1988, U.S. Dist. Ct. Ariz. 1988, U.S. Ct. Appeals (9th cir.) 1989. Summer assoc. McNees, Wallace & Nurick, Harrisburg, Pa., 1985, LeBoeuf, Lamb, Leiby & MacRae, Washington, 1986; summer assoc. Fennemore Craig, Phoenix, 1987, assoc., 1987-93, dir., shareholder, 1994—. Contbr. articles to profl. jours. Bd. mem. Florence Crittenton Svcs. Ariz., Phoenix, 1994—, Chrysalis Shelters for Victims of Domestic Violence, Phoenix, 1994—; arbitrator Nat. Assn. Securities Dealers, Chgo., 1996—; judge pro tem Ariz. Superior Ct., Phoenix, 1996—; spkr. in field. Mem. ABA (litigation and labor sects.), State Bar Ariz. (labor and employment sect.), Maricopa County Bar Assn., Ariz. Assn. Def. Counsel. Federal civil litigation, State civil litigation, Labor. Office: Fennemore Craig 3003 N Central Ave Ste 2600 Phoenix AZ 85012-2913

**BALKA, SIGMUND RONELL,** lawyer; b. Phila., Aug. 1, 1935; s. I. Edwin and Jane (Chernicoff) B.; m. Elinor Bernstein, May 29, 1966. AB, Williams Coll., 1956; JD, Harvard U., 1959. Bar: Pa. and D.C. 1961, N.Y. 1969, U.S. Supreme Ct. 1966. Sr. atty. Lilco, Mineola, N.Y., 1969-70; v.p., gen. counsel Brown Boveri Corp., North Brunswick, N.J., 1970-75; asst. gen. counsel Power Authority State N.Y., N.Y.C., 1975-80; gen. counsel Krasdale Foods, Inc., N.Y.C., 1980—; pres. Graphic Arts Coun. N.Y., 1980—. Chmn. Hunts Point Environ. Protection Coun., N.Y.C., 1980—; chmn. law com. N.Y.C. Community Bd. 6, Queens, 1980-88, chmn. econ. devel. com., 1988-99; chmn. Soc. for a Better Bronx, 1985—; bd. dirs. Bronx Arts Coun., 1981—, Greater N.Y. Met. Food Coun., 1986—, Jewish Repertory Theatre, 1987—; chmn. Bronx Borough Pres.'s Adv. Com. on Resource Recovery, 1988-90; chair fellows, mem. vis. com. Williams Coll. Mus. of Art, 1996-99. Fellow Am. Bar Found.; mem. ABA (co-chmn. pro bono project corp. law dept. 1986-88, chmn. 1988-90, com. of corp. gen. counsel 1974—, planning chmn. 1994-96, membership chmn. 1996-98), FBA, Am. Corp. Counsel Assn. (bd. dirs. Met. N.Y. chpt., bd. dirs. Found. 1992—), Assn. Bar City N.Y. General corporate. Office: Krasdale Foods Inc 400 Food Center Dr Bronx NY 10474-7098

**BALKAN, KENNETH J.,** lawyer; b. N.Y.C., Oct. 18, 1948; s. Robert and Leona (Brenner) B.; m. Berta Hochman, Aug. 16, 1970; children: Richard, Lauren, Adam. BA, Fairleigh Dickinson U., 1969; JD, St. John's U., 1972. Bar: N.Y. 1973, U.S. Dist. Ct. (so. and ea. dists.) N.Y. 1974, U.S. Ct. Appeals (2d cir.) 1975, U.S. Supreme Ct. 1978. Law intern Dist. Atty.'s Office County of Queens, N.Y.C., 1971; assoc. Kroll, Edelman, Elser & Wilson, N.Y.C., 1972-77; ptnr. Wilson, Elser, Edelman & Dicker, N.Y.C., 1977-81, L'Abbate & Balkan, Garden City, N.Y., 1981-94; ptnr. L'Abbate, Balkan, Colavita & Contini, L.L.P., Garden City, 1995-98, of counsel, 1999—; mem. editorial bd. Profl. Liability Reporter; mem. St. John's Law Rev., 1971-72; mediator for U.S. Dist. Ct. (ea. and so. dists.) N.Y.; lectr. in field. Contbr. articles to profl. jours. Mem. Def. Rsch. Inst. Mem. ABA (tort and ins. practice law and litigation subcoms., nat. reporter ins. coverage, profl. officer and dirs. law com., constrn. industry com.), N.Y. State Bar Assn. (former mem. com. profl. discipline, mem. ins. negligence and compensation law com., trial lawyers com.), Nassau County Bar Assn. (coms. ethics, ins. law, fee conciliation). Insurance, Professional liability, General civil litigation. Office: L'Abbate Balkan Colavita & Contini LLP 1050 Franklin Ave Rm 400 Garden City NY 11530-2929

**BALKANY, CARON LEE,** lawyer; b. Miami, Fla., Apr. 4, 1950; d. John W. and Marilyn R. Balkany. AA, U. Fla., 1970; BA, George Washington U., 1972; JD, U. Miami, 1977. Bar: Fla. 1977, D.C. 1979, Colo. 1980. Ptnr. Caron Balkany, P.A., Coral Gables, Fla.; intern Dade County Pub. Defender's Office, 1974; cons. Dade County, 1973; atty. Dade County Rape Treatment Ctr., Safe Space for Battered Women; chairperson White Ho. Conf. on Youth, 1970; mem. Rape Treatment Ctr. Task Force; youth dir. women's bus. U.S. Dept. Labor, 1971. Contbr. articles to profl. jours. State civil litigation, Personal injury. Office: 1806 Milford Cir Sun City Center FL 33573-5231

**BALKIN, JEFFREY GILBERT,** lawyer; b. Chgo., Mar. 29, 1943; s. David R. and Sari S. (Sol) B.; children: Stephanie, Jeremy. PhB, Wayne State-Monteith Coll., 1965; JD with honors, Wayne State U., 1968. Bar: Mich. 1968, D.C. 1972, Calif. 1975, U.S. Sup. Ct. 1982; cert. tax specialist, Calif.; C.P.A., Calif. Atty. office internat. ops. IRS, Washington, 1970-73; dir. internat. tax ops. Touche Ross & Co., Los Angeles, 1974-77; sole practice, Los Angeles, 1977-81; ptnr. Bronson, Bronson & McKinnon, Los Angeles, 1981-85; sole practice, Los Angeles, 1985—; mem. tax mgmt. editorial adv. bd. Fgn. Income Portfolio series Bur. Nat. Affairs, 1977—; instr. Sch. Public Adminstrn. U. So. Calif., 1978-85, Grad sch. pub. adminstrn. Golden Gate U., 1987-88; mem. Inst. for Tax Adminstrn., 1989—, mem. Industry Sector Adv. Com. on services for Trade Policy Matters, Dept. Commerce and U.S. Trade Rep., 1982-86. Mem. Calif. Bar Assn., Braemar Country Club (Tarzana, Calif.). Jewish. Contbr. articles to profl. jours. Private international, Corporate taxation, State and local taxation. Home: 19534 Greenbriar Dr Tarzana CA 91356-5423

**BALKO, GEORGE ANTHONY, III,** lawyer, educator; b. Bklyn., June 22, 1955; s. George Anthony Jr. and Settimia (Palumbo) B. AB, Yale U., 1977; JD, U. Calif., San Francisco, 1986. Bar: Mass. 1986, U.S. Dist. Ct. Mass. 1987, U.S. Ct. Appeals (1st cir.) 1987, D.C 1990. Assoc. Swartz & Swartz, Boston, 1986-87, Bowditch & Dewey, Worcester, Mass., 1987-95; ptnr. Bowditch & Dewey, Worcester, 1996—; adj. prof. Anna Maria Coll., Paxton, Mass., 1988—, mem. paralegal studies adv. bd., 1988-95. Author: Risk Management for Nursing Homes: A Primer In Long-Term Care Adminstration Handbook, 1993, Ambulatory Care and the Law: Lien Claims Where None Exist As of Right, 1995; legal columnist Jour. of Workers Compensation, 1996—. Mem. Rice Sch. PTA, Holden, Mass., 1989-93; bd. health Town of Holden, 1995—, chmn. 1996—; moderator, 1999—; pres., bd. dirs. Elm Park Ctr. for Early Childhood Edn., 1994-96, mem. 1993-97. Recipient Am. Jurisprudence award for Ins. Law Lawyers Coop. Pub. Co. and Bancroft Whitney Co., 1985. Roman Catholic. Avocations: history, travel, tennis. Personal injury, Product liability, Insurance. Home: 4 Chestnut Hill Rd Holden MA 01520-1603 Office: Bowditch & Dewey 311 Main St Worcester MA 01608-1552

**BALL, HAYWOOD MORELAND,** lawyer; b. Jacksonville, Fla., June 29, 1939; s. John Willis and Margaret Ann (Moreland) B.; m. Anne Towers, June 16, 1962; children: William Tucker, Sarah Anne Sheffield, David Winchester. BA, Washington and Lee U., 1961; JD, U. Fla., 1964. Bar: Fla. 1964, U.S. Dist. Ct. (mid. dist.) Fla. 1964, U.S. Ct. Appeals (11th cir.) 1964. Ptnr. Ulmer, Murchison, Ashby and Ball, Jacksonville, 1964-83, Donahoo, Ball, McMenamy & Johnson, Jacksonville, 1983—. Mem. Fla. Bar Assn. (bd. govs. young lawyers sect. 1970-74). Democrat. Episcopalian. Avocation: golf. Estate planning, Probate, Real property. Home: 270 5th St Atlantic Beach FL 32233 Office: Donahoo Ball McMenamy & Johnson Ste 2925 50 N Laura St Jacksonville FL 32202-3677

**BALL, JAMES HERINGTON,** lawyer; b. Kansas City, Mo., Sept. 20, 1942; s. James T. Jr. and Betty Sue (Herington) B.; m. Wendy Anne Wolfe, Dec. 28, 1964; children: James H. Jr., Steven Scott. AB, U. Mo., 1964; JD cum laude, St. Louis U., 1973. Bar: Mo. 1973. Asst. gen. counsel Anheuser-Busch, Inc., St. Louis, 1973-76; v.p., gen. counsel, sec. Stouffer Corp., Solon, Ohio, 1976-83; sr. v.p., gen. counsel Nestle Enterprises, Inc., Solon, 1983-91; gen. counsel, sr. v.p. Nestle USA, Inc., Glendale, Calif., 1991—. Editor-in-chief St. Louis U. Law Jour., 1972-73. Bd. dirs. Alliance for Children's Rights, L.A., 1992—, Am. Swiss Found., N.Y.C., 1996—. Lt. comdr. USN, 1964-70, Vietnam. Mem. Mo. Bar Assn. General corporate, Mergers and acquisitions, Real property. Office: Nestle USA Inc 800 N Brand Blvd Rm 1045 Glendale CA 91203-3213

**BALL, OWEN KEITH, JR.,** lawyer; b. Louisville, Feb. 19, 1950; s. Owen Keith and Martha Katherine (Guntherberg) B.; m. Shirley Marie Galinski, Sept. 16, 1972. BSCE, U. Kans., 1972, JD, 1980. Bar: Mo. 1980, U.S. Dist. Ct. (we. dist.) Mo. 1980, Kans. 1988, U.S. Dist. Ct., Kans., 1988. Ptnr. Smith, Gill, Fisher & Butts P.C., Kansas City, Mo., 1980-87; pvt. practice as a loan broker Lawrence, 1987-88, pvt. practice, 1988-91; legal counsel Marian Merrell Dow Inc., Kansas City, Mo., 1991-92; corp. counsel Marion Merrell Dow Inc., Kansas City, Mo., 1992-95, Hoechst Marion Roussel, Inc., Kansas City, Mo., 1995—. Mem. staff Hyatt Regency Hotel com. to investigate safety of the Hyatt Regency Hotel, Kansas City C. of C., 1981. Lt. USN, 1972-77. Mem. Am. Corp. Counsel Assn., Mo. Bar Assn., Kansas City Met. Bar Assn. Avocation: classical music. Securities, General corporate, Mergers and acquisitions. Office: Hoechst Marion Roussel Inc 10236 Marion Park Dr Kansas City MO 64137-1405

**BALLAN, STEVEN G.,** lawyer; b. N.Y.C., May 5, 1951; s. Abraham and Sylvia B.; m. Sara Smith, Nov. 21, 1986 (div. 1995). BS, Cornell U., 1983; JD, Golden Gate U., 1993. Bar: N.Y. 1994. Legal rschr. Vol. Employment Law Ctr., San Francisco, 1993; law clk./student intern Calif. Dept. Indsl. Rels., San Francisco, 1993; law clk./legal rsch. asst. Robert H. Ballan Law Office, Norwood, N.Y., 1990-93; atty. Norwood, 1993-96; pvt. practice Potsdam, N.Y., 1996—. Bd. dirs. Tompkins County chpt. ARC, Ithaca, N.Y., 1986-90 (chmn. 1988-90); mem. St. Lawrence County Dem. Com., Potsdam, 1994—; vol. Spl. Programs for the Handicapped, 1978-80, Meadow House, 1978-79, Big Brothers Big Sisters, 1977-81. Recipient James Gibbs Group Human Rights award Tompkins County Human Rights Commn., 1986. Mem. ABA, N.Y. State Bar Assn., St. Lawrence County Bar Assn. Avocations: hunting, fishing, watching hockey and football, cooking Chinese food. General practice, Family and matrimonial. Office: PO Box 5047 6 Canal St Potsdam NY 13676-1112

**BALLANTINE, BEVERLY NEBLETT,** lawyer; b. Sweetwater, Tex., Oct. 3, 1941; d. William Parks and Inez (Crenshaw) Neblett; m. John Ballantine, Dec. 31, 1970; children: William John, Christopher Robert. BA, Duke U., 1964; MA, Emory U., 1965; JD, So. Meth. U., 1969. Bar: Tex. 1969, U.S. Dist. Ct. (no. dist.) Tex. 1969, Colo. 1972, U.S. Ct. Appeals (10th cir.) 1972, U.S. Dist. Ct. Colo. 1972. Law clk. to judge U.S. Dist. Ct. (no. dist.) Tex., Dallas, 1969-70; assoc. Mullin and Wells, P.C., Dallas, 1970-72; assoc., then ptnr. Criswell, Patterson, Ballantine, Englewood, Colo., 1972-77; pvt. practice Littleton, Colo., 1977—. Mem. Colo. Bar Assn. (elected to bd. govs. 1988-90), Arapahoe County Bar Assn. (pres. 1987-88). Democrat. Methodist. Labor, Probate, General civil litigation. Office: 6601 S University Blvd Ste 100 Littleton CO 80121-2913

**BALLANTINE, DOUGLAS CAIN,** lawyer; b. Louisville, Ky., Oct. 28, 1958; s. John Tilden Ballantine and Mary January Strode Elder; m. Mariam Zena, Apr. 26, 1997. BA, Am. U., 1984; JD, Ind. U., 1988. Bar: Ky. 1988, U.S. Ct. Appeals (3d cir.) 1989, U.S. Dist. Ct. (ea. and we. dists.) Ky. 1990, V.I. 1994, U.S. Dist. Ct. V.I. 1994, U.S. Ct. Appeals (6th cir.) 1994, U.S. Supreme Ct. 1994. Contractor Louisville, 1980-81; charter sailboat capt. William Kimball Charters, Tortola, V.I., 1981-82, The Moorings, Tortola, V.I., 1982-83, Sadler Yachts, Easton, Md., 1983; law clk. to Hon. David O'Brien U.S. Dist. Ct., St. Croix, V.I., 1988-90; assoc. Odgen, Newell & Welch, Louisville, 1990-96, ptnr., 1997; bd. dirs. Legal Aid Soc., Louisville, 1995—, chmn. Wheels of Justice Bike Ride, 1994, 95, 96. Vol. Future Fund Land Trust, Louisville, 1996—. Mem. ABA, Ky. Bar Assn. (ethics com. 1995—, professionalism com. 1993-95), Louisville Bar Assn., Focus Louisville Alumni Group (bd. dirs. 1997—). Avocations: sailing, outdoor activities, woodworking. General civil litigation, Professional liability, Environmental. Office: Ogden Newell & Welch 1700 Citizens Plaza Louisville KY 40202

**BALLANTINE, JOHN TILDEN,** lawyer; b. Louisville, Feb. 26, 1931; s. Thomas Austin and Anna Marie (Pfeiffer) B.; m. Mary January Strode, May 15, 1954 (div. 1964); children: John T. Jr., William Clayton, Douglas C.; m. Beverley Jo Hackley, Dec. 8, 1967; 1 child, Susan Marie. BA with high distinction, U. Ky., 1952; JD, Harvard U., 1957. Bar: Ky. 1957, U.S. Ct. Appeals (6th cir.) 1958, U.S. Supreme Ct. 1982. Law clk. to presiding judge U.S. Dist Ct. (we. dist.) Ky., 1957-58; assoc. then ptnr. Ogden Newell & Welch, Louisville, 1958—; mem. civil rules com. Ky. Supreme Ct., 1988-96. Bd. dirs. Family and Children Agy., Louisville, 1965-75, pres., 1971-74; bd. dirs. Our Lady of Peace Hosp., Louisville, 1968-73, 88—, chmn., 1968-69, 91-93; bd. dirs. Met. United Way, Louisville, 1975-81; mem. Hist. Landmarks and Preservation Dists. Commn., Louisville, 1976-88; bd. dirs. Ky. Derby Festival, Louisville, 1975-81, v.p., 1975. 1st lt. USAF, 1952-54. Recipient Outstanding Young Man in Field of Law award Louisville Jaycees, 1966. Fellow Am. Coll. Trial Lawyers; mem. ABA, Ky. Bar Assn. (bd. govs. 1996—, ho. of dels. 1985-86, 89—, clients' security fund 1993-96, Ky. evidence rules rev. commn. 1995—), Louisville Bar Assn. (bd. dirs. 1969-71, 88, 89, 92, 93, 96—, pres. 1970, profl. responsibility com. 1988-93, past chmn. physician-atty. com.), U.S. 6th Cir. Ct. Appeals Jud. Conf. (life), Am. Bd. Trial Advs., Fed. Ins. and Corp. Counsel, Ky. Def. Counsel (pres. 1981-82), Louis D. Brandeis Am. Inn of Ct., Ky. Character and Fitness Com., Pendennis Club, The Law Club, Lawyers Club. General civil litigation, Personal injury, Insurance. Office: Ogden Newell & Welch 1700 Citizens Plaza 500 W Jefferson St Ste 1700 Louisville KY 40202-2874

**BALLANTYNE, RICHARD LEE,** lawyer; b. Evanston, Ill., Dec. 10, 1939; s. Frank and Grace (Bowles) B.; children: Richard L. Jr., Brant. BS in Engring., U. Conn., 1965, MBA, 1967; JD with honors, George Washington U., 1969. Bar: Mass., 1970, Fla. 1994, U.S. Dist. Ct. Mass. 1976, U.S. Patent Office 1982. Dir. corp. devel. Itek Corp., Lexington, Mass., 1969-73, assoc. counsel, 1973-75; corp. counsel, sec. Goodhope Industries, Springfield, Mass., 1975-77; gen. counsel, asst. treas., sec. Compugraphic Corp., Wilmington, Mass., 1977-82; v.p., gen. counsel, sec. Prime Computer Inc., Natick, Mass., 1982-89, Harris Corp., Melbourne, Fla., 1989—. Served with U.S. Army, 1958-61. Mem. ABA, N.E. Corp. Counsel Assn. Inc. (pres. 1984-86), Licensing Execs. Soc., Am. Soc. Corp. Secs, Computer Law Forum. Republican. Avocations: jogging, golf. General corporate, Computer, Patent. Office: Harris Corp 1025 W Nasa Blvd Melbourne FL 32919-0002

**BALLARD, ELIZABETH ANN,** lawyer; b. Ada, Okla., Apr. 18, 1969; d. James R. and H. Arlene Treas; m. Christopher B. Ballard. BS in Journalism, Okla. State U., 1991; JD, U. Okla., 1993. Bar: Okla. 1994, U.S. Dist. Ct. (we. and no. dists.) Okla. 1994, U.S. Ct. Appeals (10th cir.). Assoc. Shelton Law Firm, Oklahoma City, Okla., 1994-96, Wilburn, Masterson & Smiling, Tulsa, 1997—. Pres. Tulsa Christian Legal Soc., 1998-99. Baptist. Insurance, Product liability, Alternative dispute resolution. Office: Wilburn Masterson & Smiling 7134 S Yale Ave Ste 560 Tulsa OK 74136-6337

**BALLARD, MICHAEL EUGENE,** lawyer; b. Mobile, Ala., Jan. 24, 1953; s. John T. and Dolores (Hall) B. BS, U. Ala., 1975, MBA, 1977, JD, 1978; LLM in Taxation, Emory U., 1980. Bar: Ala. 1978. Assoc. Stokes, Clark & McAtee, Mobile, 1978-80, Hamilton, Butler, Riddick, Tarlton & Sullivan, Mobile, 1981-86; atty. Cooper & Worsham, CPA's, Atlanta, 1980; pvt. practice law Mobile, 1986-90; mem. firm Drinkard, Ulmer, Hicks & Leon, Mobile, 1990-93, Drinkard, Ulmer & Hicks, Mobile, 1993-94, Whitfield & McAlpine, P.C., Mobile, 1994-98, Ulmer, Hillman & Ballard, Mobile, 1998—; lectr. U. So. Ala., 1986—. Mem. Ala. Bar Assn. (client security fund com. 1985—, vice chmn. 1995-98), Mobile Bar Assn. (vice chmn. constrn. com. 1990, probate com. 1985-87, 89-90, 96—, constrn. and bylaws com. 1983-86, 89—, bankruptcy sect. 1996—), Estate Planning Coun. Mobile (exec. bd. 1987-89), Athelstan Club. Episcopalian. Taxation, general, Probate, General practice. Office: Ulmer Hillman & Ballard 63 S Royal St Ste 1107 Mobile AL 36602-3238

**BALLARD, NANCER H.,** lawyer; b. Buffalo, N.Y., May 20, 1954; d. Robert L. and Frances H. Ballard; 1 child, Andrew. BA in Creative Writing, Ithaca U., 1975; MA in Counseling, Goddard Grad. Sch., 1977; JD, Northeastern U., 1984. Coop. intern Nat. Consumer Law Ctr., Boston, fall 1982; clk. to staff attys. office U.S. Ct. Appeals 9th Cir., spring 1983; clk. to hon. Hugh Bownes U.S. Ct. Appeals 1st Cir., 1984-85; assoc. Goodwin, Procter & Hoar, Boston, 1985-91, ptnr., 1991—; tchg. asst. Ithaca (N.Y.) Coll., spring 1975, instr., 1975-76; dir. edn. Counseling Svcs., Inc., 1976-78, interim exec. dir., 1977; instr. Boston Ctr. for Adult Edn., 1976-78; tchg. asst. criminal law Northeastern U. Coll. Criminal Justice, Boston, 1983-84; chairperson ins. practice group Goodwin, Procter & Hoar, Boston, 1990-98, co-chair environ. dept., 1996-97; vis. rsch. scholar Wellesley (Mass.) Ctrs. for Women, 1996-98; vis. scholar Brandeis U. Women's Studies Program, Waltham, Mass., 1998—; spkr. in field. Contbr. articles to profl. jours. Mem. ABA (tort and ins. practice sect. 1989—, sect. litigation 1990—, sect. law practice mgmt. 1994—), Mass. Bar Assn., Boston Bar Assn. (co-chair task force on profl. challenges and family needs 1998-99), Women's Bar Assn. Mass. (appts. com. 1990—, 1995 Gala fundaising com., co-chair appts., endorsements and awards com. 1996—, employment issues com. 1997—, bd. dirs. 1997—). Environmental, General civil litigation, Insurance. Office: Goodwin Procter & Hoar Exchange Pl Boston MA 02109-2803

**BALLARD, WADE EDWARD,** lawyer; b. Tallassee, Ala., Feb. 20, 1957; s. Kay B. and Alice Nelson (Lawless) B.; m. Karen Cecile Studstill, Oct. 6, 1984. BA, Wofford Coll., 1979; JD, Duke U., 1982. Bar: N.C. 1982, S.C. 1983, U.S. Dist. Ct S.C. 1984, U.S. Dist. Ct. (ea. dist.) N.C. 1986, U.S. Dist. Ct. (we. and mid. dists.) N.C. 1992, U.S. Dist. Ct. S.C., U.S. Ct. Appeals (5th cir.) 1985, U.S. Ct. Appeals (4th cir.) 1986. Assoc. Haynsworth, Baldwin, Miles, Johnson, Greaves & Edwards, Greenville, S.C., 1982-89; shareholder, founding mem. Edwards, Ballard, Bishop, Sturm, Clark and Keim, P.A., 1989—. Editor (book) Florida Employment Law Manual, 1987, 88. Mem. N.C. Bar Assn., S.C. Bar Assn., Greenville Young Lawyers Club (social chmn. 1984, v.p. 1985, pres. 1986), Phi Beta Kappa. Avocations: reading, hunting, fishing, golf. Civil rights, Labor, Environmental. Home: 201 Muirfield Dr Spartanburg SC 29306-6631

**BALLEW, JEFFREY LYNN,** lawyer; b. Washington, July 26, 1955; s. Harry Lee and Iris Marie (Young) B.; m. Melissa Carol Brown; children: Lauren, Sam. BA, Emory U., 1977; JD, U. Ga., 1981. Bar: Ga., U.S. Ct. Appeals (11th cir.). Chief asst. dist. atty. Tallapoosa Jud. Cir., Buchanan, Ga., 1982-95; asst. dist. atty. Douglas Jud. Cir., Douglasville, Ga., 1995—. Office: Douglas County Dist Attys Office 8700 Hospital Dr Douglasville GA 30134-2264

**BALMER, THOMAS ANCIL,** lawyer; b. Longview, Wash., Jan. 31, 1952; s. Donald Gordon and Elisabeth Clare (Hill) B.; m. Mary Louise McClintock, Aug. 25, 1984; children: Rebecca Louise, Paul McClintock. AB, Oberlin Coll., 1974; JD, U. Chgo., 1977. Bar: Mass. 1977, D.C. 1981, U.S. Dist. Ct. Mass. 1977, Oreg. 1982, U.S. Dist. Ct. Oreg. 1982, U.S. Ct. Appeals (9th cir.) 1982, U.S. Ct. Appeals (D.C. cir.) 1983, U.S. Supreme Ct. 1987. Assoc. Choate, Hall & Stewart, Boston, 1977-79, Wald, Harkrader & Ross, Washington, 1980-82; trial atty. antitrust div. U.S. Dept. Justice, Washington, 1979-80; assoc. Lindsay, Hart, Neil & Weigler, Portland, Oreg., 1982-84; ptnr. Lindsay, Hart, Neil & Weigler, Portland,

1985-90, Ater Wynne LLP, Portland, 1990-93, 97—; dep. atty. gen. State of Oregon, Salem, 1993-97; adj. prof. of law Northwestern Sch. Law Lewis and Clark Coll., 1983-84, 90-92. Contbr. articles to law jours. Active mission and outreach com. United Ch. of Christ, Portland, 1984-87, Met. Svc. Dist. Budget Com., Portland, 1988-90; bd. dirs. Multnomah County Legal Aid Svc., Inc., 1989-93, chair 1992-93; bd. dirs. Chamber Music Northwest, 1997—. Mem. ABA, Oreg. Bar Assn. (chmn. antitrust sect. 1986-87). Democrat. Home: 2521 NE 24th Ave Portland OR 97212-4831 Office: Ater Wynne LLP 222 SW Columbia St Ste 1800 Portland OR 97201-6618

**BALOG, DOUGLAS ALLAN,** lawyer; b. Geneva, Ill., Mar. 26, 1963; m. Gina Balog; children: Matthew, Eric, Jason. BS in Aero.-Aircraft Maintenance Engring, St. Louis U., 1985; MS in Aero. Sci., Embry-Riddle Aero. U., 1990; JD, Pace U., 1997. Bar: Ill., 1997, Fla., 1998, U.S. Ct. Appeals (Fed., 11th cirs.), 1998, U.S. Ct. Internat. Trade, 1998, U.S. Patent and Trademark Office, 1998, U.S. Dist. Ct. (mid. dist.) Fla. 1999. Atty. Harris Semiconductor, Palm Bay, Fla., 1998—. General corporate, Contracts commercial. Office: Harris Corp Semiconductor Sector 2401 Palm Bay Rd NE Palm Bay FL 32905-3398

**BALTHASER, ANITA YOUNG,** legal assistant; b. Ft. Benning, Ga., Aug. 24, 1951; d. Burnham James and Mary Kenyon (Brown) Young; m. James Lee Balthaser, July 14, 1979. BA, Hofstra U., 1973; MSLS, Case Western Reserve U., 1977. Libr. Ohio Legis. Ref. Bur., Columbus, 1977-79, Parsons Behle & Latimer, Salt Lake City, 1979-82; legal asst. Kimball Parr Waddoups & Gee, Salt Lake City, 1982-84, Watkiss & Saperstein, Salt Lake City, 1984-92, Ballard, Spahr Andrews & Ingersoll, Salt Lake City, 1992—. Mem. Nat. Assn. Bond Lawyers, Utah State Bar Assn. (legal assts. divsn.). Lutheran. Avocations: hiking, camping, cross country skiing, travel. Office: Ballard Spahr Andrews & Ingersoll 201 S Main St Ste 1200 Salt Lake City UT 84111-2210

**BALTHASER, JAMES HARVEY,** lawyer; b. Columbus, Ohio, Oct. 7, 1954; s. James R. and Kathryn F. (Herman) B.; m. Dianne A. Davis, June 21, 1975; 1 child, Kathryn Dee. BA, Ohio State U., 1975, JD, 1978. Bar: Ohio 1978, U.S. Tax Ct. 1984. Supr. Touche Ross & Co., Columbus, 1978-82; mem. Schwartz, Warren & Ramirez, Columbus, 1982-96; ptnr. Thompson, Hine & Flory, Columbus, 1996—. Mem. ABA, Columbus Bar Assn., Am. Inst. of CPA's (cert.). E-mail: jbalthaser@thf.com. Taxation, general, Estate planning, General corporate. Home: 9417 Avemore Ct Dublin OH 43017-9672 Office: Thompson Hine & Flory 10 W Broad St Ste 700 Columbus OH 43215-3435

**BAMBACE, PETER JOSEPH,** lawyer; b. Houston, July 11, 1963; s. Robert Shelly and Medeline Constance (Saxer) B.; m. Mary Maydell Burkhalter, May 22, 1994; 1 child, Alexandra. BBA, Tex. Tech. U., 1985; JD, U. Houston Law Ctr., 1989. Bar: Tex., U.S. Dist. Ct. (so., ea., we. and no. dists.) Tex., U.S. Ct. Appeals (5th cir.). From assoc. to dir. Coats, Rose, Yale, Holm, Ryman & Lee, Houston, 1990—. Vol. Houston Livestock Show and Rodeo, 1992—. Mem. ABA, Tex. Bar Assn., Tex. Young Lawyer's Assn., Houston Bar Assn. Republican. Roman Catholic. Fax: 713-652-9702. Office: Holm Bambace Cotton LLP 1301 Mckinney St Ste 3150 Houston TX 77010-3031

**BAMBERGER, MICHAEL ALBERT,** lawyer; b. Berlin, Feb. 29, 1936; s. Fritz and Kate (Schwabe) B.; m. Phylis Skloot, Dec. 19, 1965; children—Kenneth A., Richard A. AB magna cum laude, Harvard U., 1957, LLB magna cum laude, 1960. Bar: N.Y. 1960, D.C. 1982. Assoc. Proskauer Rose Goetz & Mendelsohn, N.Y.C., 1960-69; assoc. Finley, Kumble, Wagner, Heine, Underberg, Manley, Myerson & Casey, N.Y.C., 1970, ptnr., 1971-87; ptnr. Sonnenschein Nath & Rosenthal, N.Y.C., 1987—; mem. faculty various legal seminars and insts.; mem. joint editl. bd. on uninc. orgn. acts. ABA/Nat. Conf. Commrs. on Uniform State Laws, 1994—; chmn. bd. Transcontinental Music Publs., New Jewish Music Press. Co-editor: State Limited Partnership Laws, 7 vols. and supplements, 1987—, State Limited Liability Company and Partnership Laws, 5 vols. and supplements, 1993—; editor Harvard Law Rev., 1958-60; contbr. articles to profl. jours. Vice chair bd. overseers Hebrew Union Coll.-Jewish Inst. Religion, N.Y.C.,; v.p., bd. dirs. Leo Baeck Inst., Selfhelp Cmty. Svcs.; bd. dirs. Ctr. Jewish History. Mem. ABA (com. on ltd. partnerships 1980—, chair com. on tech. and intellectual property 1992-95, chair, ad hoc com. on security interests in intellectual property 1990-98), First Amendment Lawyers Assn., N.Y. State Bar Assn. (exec. com. comml. and fed. litigation sect. 1989-93), Assn. Bar City N.Y. (com. on fed. legislation 1979-82, com. on civil rights 1982-86, chmn. 1983-86), N.Y. County Lawyers Assn. (securities com. 1980-82). Jewish. General corporate, Libel, Constitutional. Home: 172 E 93rd St New York NY 10128-3711 Office: Sonnenschein Nath & Rosenthal Ste 2401 1221 Avenue Of The Americas New York NY 10020-1089

**BAMBERGER, PHYLIS SKLOOT,** judge; b. N.Y.C., May 2, 1939; d. George Joseph and Martha (Wechselblatt) S.; m. Michael A. Bamberger, Dec. 19, 1965; children: Kenneth, Richard. BA, Bklyn. Coll., 1960; LLB, NYU, 1963. Bar: N.Y. 1963, U.S. Supreme Ct. 1967, U.S. Ct. Appeals (2d cir.) 1965, U.S. Dist. Ct. (so. dist.) N.Y. 1966, U.S. Dist. Ct. (ea. dist.) N.Y. 1979. Assoc. Legal Aid Soc., N.Y.C., 1963-67; assoc.-in-charge criminal appeals Bur. Legal Aid Soc., N.Y.C., 1967-72; atty.-in-charge, fed. def. svcs. unit/appeal Legal Aid Soc., N.Y.C., 1972-88; judge N.Y. State Ct. Claims designated to sit in the N.Y. State Supreme Ct., Bronx County, 1988—; mem. N.Y. State Chief Judge's Jury Project, 1993-94; mem. com. on alts. to incarceration Office of Ct. Adminstrn., 1994-96, mem. criminal law and procedure adv. com., 1994-98, co-chair 1998—. Author: Criminal Appeals Handbook, 1984; editor, contbr. Practice Under the Federal Sentencing Guidelines, 1988, 90, 93 (also supplements); author, compiler Recent Developments in State Constitutional Law, 1985; contbr. numerous articles to publs. Mem. ABA, N.Y. State Bar assn. (co-chair presdl. com. on problems in criminal justice sys. 1986-88, mem. com. on the future of the profession), Assn. of Bar of City of N.Y. (chair com. on provision of legal svcs. to persons of moderate means 1995-98, 21st century com. 1992-95, chair com on probation 1993-94), Phi Beta Kappa. Office: Bronx County Courthouse 851 Grand Concourse Bronx NY 10451-2937

**BANBURY, J. HUNTER,** lawyer, tool manufacturing company executive; b. Denver, Nov. 5, 1969; s. Brooke Wellington and Mary Jo Banbury; m. Kris Proctor, Aug. 7, 1992. BA, Occidental Coll., 1990; MBA, Cornell U., 1994, JD, 1995. Bar: Colo. 1995, U.S. Dist. Ct. Colo. 1995. Asst. to chmn. Blaw-Knox Corp., Pitts., 1994; assoc. Berenbaum, Weinshiusk & Eason, Denver, 1995-97; v.p. Park Corp., Cleve., 1997—; pres. Cone-Blanchard Corp., machine tool mfrs., Windsor, Vt., 1997—. Achievements include career as turn around specialist. Avocations: skiing, golf, scuba, tennis, biking. Office: Cone-Blanchard Corp PO Box 757 Windsor VT 05089-0757

**BANCROFT, JUDITH GAIL,** lawyer; b. Cherokee, Iowa, Dec. 9, 1949; d. Mark William and Edna Pauline B.; m. Kenneth M. Socha, Dec. 28, 1986. BA magna cum laude, St. Olaf Coll., 1972; JD with honors, U. Iowa, 1976. Bar: N.Y. 1977, Washington 1995. Assoc. Brown & Wood, N.Y.C., 1976-84; v.p. Morgan Stanley & Co., N.Y.C., 1984-87; counsel Kaye, Scholer, Fierman, Hays & Handler, N.Y.C., 1989-92, Fried, Frank, Harris, Shriver & Jackbson, Washington, 1992-96; ptnr. Powell, Goldstein, Frazer & Murphy, Washington, 1996—; cons. in field. Mem. ABA, D.C. Bar Assn., Assn. of Bar of City of N.Y., Women's Bar Assn. D.C., Internat. Bus. Law Com. Avocations: golf, sailing. General corporate, Computer, Intellectual property. Home: 7010 Armat Dr Bethesda MD 20817-2104 Office: Powell Goldstein Frazer & Murphy Ste 600 1001 Pennsylvania Ave NW Washington DC 20004-2505

**BANCROFT, WEBB ERNEST,** lawyer; b. Webster, S.D., May 2, 1957. BA, U. Nebr., 1979, JD, 1983. Lawyer Assoc. Students U. Nebr., Lincoln, Nebr., 1984-86, Bancroft Law Office, Lincoln, 1984-89; dep. pub. defender Lancaster County Pub. Defender, Lincoln, 1989—. Office: Lancaster County Pub Defender 555 S 10th St Lincoln NE 68508-2874

**BAND, JORDAN CLIFFORD,** lawyer; b. Cleve., Aug. 15, 1923; s. Samuel Melville and Helen Rita (Krause) B.; m. Alice Jeanne Glickson, Apr. 27, 1946; children: Terril R., Stefanie Band Allweiss, Claudia Band McCord. Student, U. Ala., 1943-44; BBA, Case Western Res. U., 1947, LLB, 1948. Bar: Ohio 1948, U.S. Dist. Ct. (no. dist.) Ohio 1948. Assoc. Ulmer & Berne, Cleve., 1948-56, ptnr., 1956-94, ret., 1994—; bd. dirs. numerous cos. Chmn. Greater Cleve. Conf. on Religion and Race, 1964-66, Greater Cleve. Project, 1978-81; nat. chmn. Nat. Jewish Community Rels. Adv. Coun., N.Y.C., 1967-70; presiding officer Cleve. Community Rels. Bd., 1970-90; nat. vice chmn. Am. Jewish Com., 1976-79; legal counsel Jewish Community Fedn. Cleve., 1984-87, also trustee, officer numerous civic and non-profit orgns. Recipient Kane Leadership award Jewish Community Fedn., 1961, Bronze medal, 1978, Cert. of Appreciation, City of Cleve., 1970-88, Cert. of REcognition, Ohio Senate, 1987. Mem. ABA, Ohio Bar Assn., Cuyahoga County Bar Assn., Cleve. Bar Assn., Order of Coif. Democrat. Avocations: community relations, civic activities, tennis. General corporate, Real property, Mergers and acquisitions. Office: Ulmer & Berne 1300 E 9th St Ste 900 Cleveland OH 44114-1583

**BANDON, WILLIAM EDWARD, III,** lawyer; b. Bklyn., June 12, 1961; s. William Edward Jr. and Lila Marie (Arida) B.; m. Patricia Linden McKeogh, Sept. 18, 1993; 1 child, John Robert. AB in History, Princeton U., 1983; JD, NYU, 1987. Bar: N.Y. 1988, U.S. Dist. Ct. (so. and ea. dists.) N.Y. 1988. Summer assoc. Cullen and Dykman, Bklyn., 1986, assoc., 1987-96; assoc. Brown Raysman Millstein Felder & Steiner LLP, N.Y.C., 1996-99, ptnr., 1999—. Trustee Lotte Kauski Found. for Gifted Children, Inc., N.Y.C., 1996—; mem. Somers (N.Y.) Hist. Soc., 1989—, Katonah (N.Y.) Hist. Mus., 1996—. Mem. ABA, N.Y. County Lawyers Assn. (chair com. tech. and automation 1997—), Computer Law Assn. Democrat. Avocation: local history. Computer, Intellectual property, General corporate. Home: 5 Quicks Ln Katonah NY 10536-1005 Office: 120 W 45th St New York NY 10036-4041

**BANDY, JACK D.,** lawyer; b. Galesburg, Ill., June 19, 1932; s. Homer O. and Gladys L. (Van Winkle) B.; m. Betty McMillan, Feb. 18, 1956; children: Jean A. Bandy Abramson, D. Michael, Jeffery K. *Great-great grandparents, Reuben and Sibby Adkisson Bandy were among the first settlers of Knox County, Illinois in 1837. They bought 160 acres near Galesburg, and started the family farm. After Reuben's death (1861), it was operated by their son, George, and his wife, Narcissa Holland Bandy. When George retired, his son, George Albert "Burt" and his wife Mattie Mears Bandy, continued the farm until 1907 when they sold it and moved to Galesburg. Their son, Homer Oliver, married Gladys Lillian Van Winkle Bandy. They were parents of Jack D. Bandy, subject of this biography.* BA, Knox Coll., 1954; LLB, U. La Verne, 1967. Bar: Calif. 1972. Safety engr. Indsl. Indemnity Co., L.A., 1960-65, sr. safety engr., 1965-69, resident safety engr., 1969-72; trial atty. Employers Ins. of Wausau, L.A., 1972-79; mng. atty. Wausau Ins. Cos., L.A., 1979-92; arbitrator, mediator L.A. Superior Mcpl. Ct., 1992—. Contbr. articles to profl. jours. Youth leader YMCA, Mission Hills, Calif., 1965-72. Served with U.S. Army, 1954-56. Mem. Calif. State Bar, Am. Soc. Safety Engrs. (cert. safety profl.). Personal injury, Alternative dispute resolution, Insurance.

**BANGEL, HERBERT K.,** lawyer; b. Norfolk, Va., May 29, 1928; m. Carolyn Kroskin; children: Nancy Jo, Brad J. BS in Commerce, U. Va., 1947, JD, 1950. Bar: Va. 1949, U.S. Dist. Ct. (ea. dist.) Va., U.S. Ct. Appeals (4th cir.), U.S. Tax Ct., U.S. Bd. Immigration Appeals, D.C., U.S. Supreme Ct. Ptnr. Bangel, Bangel & Bangel, Portsmouth, Va., 1950—; bd. dirs. Portsmouth Enterprises, Inc., Dominion Bank Greater Hampton Roads, Tidewater Profl. Sports Inc.; substitute judge Portsmouth Gen. Dist. Ct., 1979-84; mem. U.S. Ct. Appeals (4th cir.) Jud. Conf. Commr. Eastern Va. Med. Authority (named changed to Med. coll of Hampton Rds.), 1983-91, vice chmn., 1987-88; pres., chmn. Portsmouth Area United Fund, 1971-73; bd. dirs. Portsmouth Indsl. Found., 1968-90, bd. dirs. Urban League Tidewater (Va.), 1978-79, Tidewater chpt. Am. Heart Assn., 1983-84, Portsmouth Community Trust Distbn. Com., 1977-87, chmn., 1985-86; bd. dirs. Maryview Hosp., 1969-87; trustee Portsmouth-Chesapeake Area Found., 1968-72, United Community Funds and Councils Va., 1970-71, others; chmn. Portsmouth Redevel. and Housing Authority, 1977-83. Named First Citizen, City of Portsmouth, 1974. Mem. ABA, Va. Bar Assn., Portsmouth Bar Assn. (pres. 1964), Norfolk Bar Assn., Tidewater Trial Lawyers Assn. (bd. dirs. 1968-73), Va. Trial Lawyers Assn. (bd. govs. 1970), Assn. Trial Lawyers Am., Suburban Country Club (pres. 1961-62), Oceans Club (bd. dirs. 1973-76), Town Point Club (bd. govs. 1983—), Portsmouth Sports Club, Moose, Elks, B'nai B'rith. Democrat. Jewish. Personal injury. Home: 1 Crawford Pkwy Apt 1702 Portsmouth VA 23704-2613 Office: Bangel Bangel & Bangel PO Box 760 Portsmouth VA 23705-0760

**BANK, MARK ALBERT,** lawyer; b. Manhasset, N.Y., Aug. 15, 1966; s. Michael Alan and Nancy (Hoffman) B.; m. Cathy Kahn, July 10, 1993; children: Mac Alec, Merrick Abram. BA, U. Mich., 1988; JD, George Washington U., 1991. Bar: Va. 1991, Md. 1992, D.C. 1992, Mich. 1993, U.S. Ct. Appeals (4th cir.) 1992. Lawyer Schwartz & Ellis, Arlington, Va., 1991-93, Law Office of Mark A. Bank, Southfield, Mich., 1993-94; lawyer, of counsel Williams, Schaefer, Ruby & Williams, P.C., Birmingham, Mich., 1994-96; lawyer The Law Firm of John F. Schaefer, Birmingham, 1996—; adj. prof. law Detroit Coll. of Law, 1998—. Family and matrimonial, Estate planning, General civil litigation. Office: Law Firm of John F Schaefer 380 N Old Woodward Ave Ste 320 Birmingham MI 48009-5322

**BANKOWSKI, CAROLYN ANN,** lawyer; b. Boston, June 7, 1968; d. Paul Francis and Rita Emma Bankowski. BS, Emerson Coll., 1990; JD, Suffolk U., 1995. Bar: Mass. 1995, U.S. Dist. Ct. Mass. 1996. Assoc. Coffey & Shea, Boston, 1995-97, Curran Coffey & Moran LLP, Boston, 1997—. Mem. Internat. Women's Insolvency & Restructuring Confedn., Mass. Bar Assn. (dial-a-lawyer vol. 1997—), Boston Bar Assn. Democrat. Roman Catholic. Bankruptcy, Consumer commercial, Contracts commercial. Office: Curran Coffey & Tavenner LLP 85 Merrimac St Boston MA 02114-4728

**BANKS, ERIC KENDALL,** lawyer; b. St. Louis, Aug. 21, 1955; s. Willie James Banks Jr. and Grace (Kendall) Palmer; children: Brittany Renee, Bryson Kendall. BSBA, U. Mo., St. Louis, 1977; JD, U. Mo., Columbia, 1980. Bar: Mo. 1980, Ill. 1988, U.S. Dist. Ct. (we. dist.) Mo. 1980, U.S. Dist. Ct. (ea. dist.) Mo. 1984, U.S. Ct. Appeals (8th cir.) 1984, U.S. Ct. Appeals (D.C. cir.) 1998, U.S. Tax Ct. 1988, U.S. Supreme Ct. 1996. Asst. gen. counsel Mo. Pub. Svc. Commn., Jefferson City, 1980-84; asst. atty. Office Circuit Atty., St. Louis, 1984-87; pvt. practice, St. Louis, 1987-91, Clayton, Mo., 1991-92; corp. counsel Siegel-Robert, St. Louis, 1992-97; city counselor City of St. Louis, 1997-99; ptnr. Thompson, Coburn, 1999—, Thompson Coburn, St. Louis, 1999—; adj. prof. civil law St. Louis U. Law Sch., 1987-92, Washington U. Sch. law, 1991; sec. bd. dirs. Black Leadership Tng. Program, St. Louis, 1975-77. Sec. bd. dirs. Wesley House Assn.; bd. trustees Mo. U. Law Sch. Found. St. Louis Met. Leadership Program fellow, 1975-77. Mem. ABA (labor and employment com.), Nat. Bar Assn., Bar Assn. Met. St. Louis, Mo. Bar Assn. (adminstrv. law com., com. counsel), Mound City Bar Assn., Bar Assn. Met. St. Louis. Lutheran. Club: Toastmasters Internat. (adminstrv. v.p. 1983, William Tellman award 1982). Avocations: karate, reading, photography, public speaking, community work. Fax: (314) 552-7256. E-mail: ebanks@thompsoncoburn.com. Home: 2755 Russell Blvd Saint Louis MO 63104-2137 Office: Thompson Coburn One Mercantile Ctr Saint Louis MO 63101

**BANKS, FRED LEE, JR.,** state supreme court judge; b. Jackson, Miss., Sept. 1, 1942; s. Fred L. and Violet (Mabry) B.; m. Taunya Lovell, June 5, 1967 (div. 1975); children: Rachel R., Jonathan L.; m. Pamela Gipson, Jan. 28, 1978; 1 child, Gabrielle G. BA, Howard U., 1965, JD cum laude, 1968. Bar: Miss. 1968, U.S. Dist. Ct. (no. and so. dists.) Miss. 1968, U.S. Ct. Appeals (5th cir.) 1968, D.C. 1969, U.S. Supreme Ct. 1971. Ptnr. Banks, Owens & Byrd and predecessor firms Anderson, Banks, Nichols & Stewart; Anderson, Banks, Nichols & Leventhal; Anderson & Banks, Jackson, 1968-85; rep. Miss. Ho. of Reps., 1975; judge Miss. 7th Cir. Ct., Hinds County and Yazoo County, 1985-91; assoc. justice Miss. Supreme Ct, Jackson, 1991—; mem. Miss. Bd. Bar Admissions, 1978-81; pres. State Mut. Fed. Savs. and Loan, Jackson, 1976-89; mem. minority adv. com. U. Miss. Sch. of Law. Bd. dirs. NAACP, 1981—; mem. Nat. Adv. Com. for the Edn. of Disadvantaged Children, 1978-80; del. Dem. Nat. Conv., 1976, 1980; co-mgr. Miss. Carter-Mondale presidl. campaign, 1976; legislator Miss. Ho. of Reps., Jackson, 1976-85; bd. visitors Miss. Coll. Sch. of Law. Mem. ABA, Magnolia Bar Assn., Nat. Bar Assn., Hinds County Bar Assn., Am. Inns of Ct., Charles Clark Inn, Miss. Bar Assn. (chair criminal justice task force), D.C. Bar Assn., Sigma Pi Phi, Am. Inns of Ct., Chalres Clark Inn. Roman Catholic. Home: 976 Metairie Rd Jackson MS 39209-6948 Office: Mississippi Supreme Court 450 High St Jackson MS 39201-1006*

**BANKS, JOHN ROBERT, JR.,** lawyer; b. Balt., Mar. 15, 1958; s. John Robert and Ida Carol (Cromer) B. BA, Coll. William and Mary, Williamsburg, Va., 1980; JD, U. Houston, 1983. Bar: Tex. 1983, U.S. Dist. Ct. (so. dist.) Tex. 1983; cert. bus. bankruptcy law Tex. Bd. Legal Specialization. Assoc. Levin & Kasner, P.C. fka Levin, Roth & Kasner, P.C., Houston, 1983-96; pvt. practice Houston, 1997; ptnr. Mason, Coplen & Banks, LLP, Houston, 1998—. Dir. Cmty. Assn. Inst. Greater Houston, 1995-97, chmn. amb.'s subcom., 1995-97, chmn. legal com., 1995, vice chmn. legal com., 1994, chmn. mem. svc. com., 1998; mem. adminstrv. bd. Chapelwood United Meth. Ch., 1997—, trustee, 1998—. Mem. Fed. Bar Assn. Republican. Avocation: stamp collecting. Telecopier: (713) 785-8651. Bankruptcy, Consumer commercial, General civil litigation. Office: Mason Coplen & Banks LLP Attys at Law 7500 San Felipe St Ste 700 Houston TX 77063-1709

**BANKS, ROBERT SHERWOOD,** lawyer; b. Newark, Mar. 28, 1934; s. Howard Douglas and Amelia Violet (Del Bagno) B.; m. Judith Lee Henry; children—Teri, William; children by previous marriage—Robert, Paul, Stephen, Roger, Gregory, Catherine. A.B., Cornell U., 1956, LL.B., 1958. Bar: N.J. 1959, N.Y. 1968. Practice law Newark, 1958-61; atty. E.I. duPont, Wilmington, Del., 1961-67; with Xerox Corp., Stamford, Conn., 1967-88; v.p., gen. counsel Xerox Corp., 1975-88; sr. counsel Latham & Watkins, N.Y.C., 1988-89; gen. counsel Keystone Holdings, 1989-92; bd. dirs. Cornell U. Found.; mem. panel of mediators, neutral advisors Ctr. for Pub. Resources. Mem. adv. coun. Cornell Law Sch.; past trustee U.S. Supreme Ct. Hist. Soc.; past bd. dirs. Ctr. for Pub. Resources. Mem. ABA, N.Y. Bar Assn., Am. Arbitration Assn. (panel arbitrators), Am. Judicature Soc. (exec. com., bd. dirs., pres. 1989-91), Cornell Law Assn., Am. Corp. Counsel Assn. (bd. dirs., chmn. 1982-83), Atlantic Athletic Club, Jonathan's Landing Club. General corporate.

**BANNER, ROBERT ALAN,** lawyer; b. N.Y.C., Oct. 14, 1954; s. Harold and Bernice (Miller) B.; m. Colleen O'Hora, June 24, 1995. BA summa cum laude, U. Pa., 1976, JD, 1979. Bar: N.Y. 1980, U.S. Dist. Ct. (so. and ea. dists.) N.Y. 1981. Assoc. Milbank Tweed Hedley & McCloy, N.Y.C., 1980-85; ptnr. Lepatner Block Pawa & Rivelis, N.Y.C., 1989-94; founding ptnr. Kalin & Banner, N.Y.C., 1995-97; ptnr. Berman, Paley, Goldstein & Kannry LLP, N.Y.C., 1997—; mem. N.Y. Bldg. Congress, N.Y.C., 1996—; mem. faculty NYU, 1994; design profl. Pratt Sch. of Design, N.Y.C., 1992. Author: New York Forms of Jury Instruction: Officer and Director Liability, 1994. Mem. AIA (com. on edn.). General civil litigation, Construction. Home: 137 Riverside Dr New York NY 10024-3702 Office: Berman Paley Goldstein & Kannry LLP 500 5th Ave Fl 43 New York NY 10110-0375

**BANNISTER, J. ALAN,** lawyer; b. Birmingham, Ala., Mar. 29, 1962; s. James William and Mary Lois Bannister; m. Robin B. Buchanan, Feb. 8, 1986; children: Julien Buchanan, Sophia Buchanan. BS in Acctg., Auburn U., 1984; JD, U. Ala., Tuscaloosa, 1988. Bar: N.Y. 1988. Assoc. Cravath, Swaine & Moore, N.Y.C., 1988-90, Debevoise & Plimpton, N.Y.C., 1990-93; assoc. Clifford Chance, N.Y.C. and London, 1993-98, ptnr., 1998—. Contbr. articles to law jours. Mem. N.Y.C. Rep. Com., 1988—. Mem. Assn. Bar City N.Y., Univ. Club. Avocations: golf, hiking. Securities, General corporate, Mergers and acquisitions. Office: Clifford Chance One New York Plaza Fl 39 New York NY 10004-2004

**BANNISTER, SHELLEY ASHLEY,** law educator; b. Rochester, N.Y., Sept. 22, 1952; d. Dan Wesley and Audrey Marie B. BA, Western Ill. U., 1974; JD, Loyola U., 1978; MA, U. Ill., Chgo., 1987, PhD in Sociology, 1996. Bar: Ill. 1978. Ptnr. Bannister & Block, Chgo., 1978-80, Bannister, Block & Spevack, Chgo., 1980-83, Bannister & Byrne, Chgo., 1983-86; asst. prof. Northeastern Ill. U., Chgo., 1987-93, assoc. prof., 1993—; vis. tchr. Cool County Jail, Chgo., 1998—. Co-author: (chpt.) It's a Crime: Women and Justice, 1992. Vice chair Ill. Clemency Project Battered Women, Chgo., 1996—. Office: Northeastern Ill U 5500 N Saint Louis Ave Chicago IL 60625-4679

**BANNISTER, T(HOMAS) SCOTT,** lawyer; b. Des Moines, June 8, 1949; s. Thomas M. and Margaret (Mulock) B.; m. Janet R. Smeltzer, June 5, 1971; children—Thomas Ryan, Christopher Scott. m. Kathy L. Pickell, May 24, 1996. B.A., U. Iowa, 1971; J.D., Drake U., 1974. Bar: Iowa 1974, U.S. Dist. Ct. (no. dist.) Ill., U.S. Dist. Ct. (no. and so. dists.) Iowa 1974, U.S. Ct. Appeals (8th cir.) 1974, U.S. Ct. Appeals (7th cir.) 1978. Mem. Gamble, Riepe, Burt, Webster & Fletcher, Des Moines, 1974-76; gen. counsel Iowa Dept. Transp., Des Moines, 1976-80; mem. Bump & Haesemeyer, Des Moines, 1980-84; ptnr. Hanson, Bjork & Russell, Des Moines, 1984-87; ptnr. Bannister & Assocs., Des Moines, 1987— ; sec. Heartland Rail Corp., Des Moines, 1983—, Iowa Interstate Railroad, Fillmore Weston Railway, Iowa Northern Railing Co. Pres. bd. dirs. Iowa Pub. TV, Des Moines, 1982-84. Mem. Assn. Interstate Commerce Commn. Practitioners, ABA, Iowa Bar Assn., Polk County Bar Assn., Omicron Delta Kappa. Republican. Episcopalian. Club: Des Moines. Administrative and regulatory, Contracts commercial, General corporate. Home: 111 56th St Des Moines IA 50312-2149 Office: Bannister & Assocs 1300 Des Moines Bldg 405 6th Ave Des Moines IA 50309

**BANOFF, SHELDON IRWIN,** lawyer; b. Chgo., July 10, 1949. BSBA in Acctg., U. Ill., 1971; JD, U. Chgo., 1974. Bar: Ill. 1974, U.S. Tax Ct. 1974. Ptnr. Katten Muchin & Zavis, Chgo., 1974—; chmn. tax conf. planning com. U. Chgo. Law Sch., 1993-94. Co-editor Jour. of Taxation, 1984—; contbr. articles to profl. jours. Mem. ABA, Chgo. Bar Assn. (fec. taxation com., mem. exec. coun. 1980—), Chgo. Fed. Tax Forum, Am. Coll. Tax Counsel. Taxation, general, Personal income taxation, Corporate taxation. Office: Katten Muchin & Zavis 525 W Monroe St Ste 1600 Chicago IL 60661-3693

**BANSTETTER, ROBERT J.,** lawyer; b. 1940. BS, St Louis U., 1963; JD, U. Ill., 1966. Bar: Mo. 1967, Ill. 1966. Atty. Labor Rels. Internat. Shoe, 1966-70; v.p., gen. coun. & sec. Gen. Am. Life Ins. Co., 1992—. Labor, Insurance. Office: Gen Am Life Ins Co 700 Market St Saint Louis MO 63101-1829

**BANTA, DON ARTHUR,** lawyer; b. Chgo., Mar. 10, 1926; s. George A. and Grace Regina (Donnelly) B.; m. Mickey Edwards, Mar. 31, 1951; children: Stephanie, Meredith, John, Hillary. BS, Northwestern U., 1948, LLB, 1950. Bar: Ill. 1950, U.S. Ct. Appeals (7th cir.) 1951, U.S. Dist. Ct. (no. dist.) Ill. 1953, U.S. Ct. Appeals (6th cir.) 1963, U.S. Supreme Ct. 1967, U.S. Ct. Appeals (3d cir.) 1972, U.S. Ct. Appeals (11th cir.) 1982. Assoc. Vogel & Bunge, Chgo., 1950-51; atty. Montgomery Ward & Co., Chgo., 1951-53; assoc. Pruitt & Grealis, Chgo., 1953-55; ptnr. Naphin Banta & Cox and predecessor firms, Chgo., 1956-90, Banta Hennessy & Graefe, Chgo., 1990-99, Michael Best & Friedrich, Chgo., 1999—; vol. cons. Chgo. Vol. Legal Svcs. Found., 1983—. Author: (with others) Labor Arbitration-A Practical Guide for Advocates. 1990, Supplement to How Arbitration Works 1985-89, 1991, How Arbitration Works, 5th edit., 1997, Discipline and Discharge in Arbitration, 1998. Mem. bd. edn. Deerfield (Ill.) Sch. Dist., 1964-70, pres., 1968-69. With U.S. Army, 1944-46, ETO. Fellow Coll. Labor and Employment Lawyers; mem. ABA (labor sect. com. on alternative dispute resolution in labor and employment law), Ill. State Bar Assn., Chgo. Bar Assn., Phi Delta Phi, Delta Tau Delta, Union League Club. Roman Catholic. Federal civil litigation, General civil litigation, Labor. Home: 1000 Lake Shore Chicago IL 60611-1310 Office: Michael Best & Friedrich 77 W Wacker Dr Chicago IL 60601-1604

**BANWO, OPEOLU,** lawyer; b. Lagos, Nigeria, Apr. 30, 1964; came to the U.S., 1995; s. Omotayo and Comfort Banwo; m. Olunike Banwo, Feb. 20, 1993; children: Femi, Temitope, Mayowa. LLB, U. Ife, Nigeria, 1985; barrister at law, Nigerian Law Sch., Lagos, 1986; LLM, U. Lagos, 1989. Bar: Nigeria 1986, N.Y. 1997, N.Y. Supreme Ct. 1997, U.S. Dist. Ct. Nebr. 1997. Assoc. Okechukwu, Bello & Assocs., Enugu, Nigeria, 1986-88; ptnr. Banwo, Abidakun & Co., Lagos, 1988-95; mng. ptnr. Midwest Immigration Attys., Omaha, 1997—; pres. Midwest Cons., Inc., Omaha, 1996—; chmn. Specialty Pers. Svcs., Omaha, 1997—; bd. dirs. Noblehouse Inc., Lagos. Mem. Concerned Profls. for Justice, Lagos, 1993-95. Mem. ABA, Am. Immigration

Lawyers Assn., Internat. Bar Assn., N.Y. Bar Assn., Jr. Chamber Internat. (founding pres. Ikoyi Jr. Chamber local chpt. 1994—). Avocations: golf, chess, net surfing. Immigration, naturalization, and customs, Bankruptcy, Personal injury. Office: Midwest Immigration Attys 319 S 17th St Ste 600 Omaha NE 68102-1917

**BANZHAF, JOHN F., III,** legal association administrator, lawyer; b. N.Y.C., July 2, 1940; s. John F., Jr. and Olga (Mischenko) B.; m. Ursula Maag, 1971. B.S. in Elec. Engring, M.I.T., 1962; J.D. magna cum laude, Columbia U., 1965. Civilian research asst. Signal Corps Engring. Labs., 1957; research engr., cons. Lear Siegler Corp., 1959-62; editor Columbia Law Rev., 1964-65; research fellow Nat. Municipal League, 1965; law clk. to U.S. Dist. Judge Spottswood W. Robinson III, 1965-66; asso. firm Watson, Leavonworth, Kelton & Taggart, N.Y.C., 1967; founder, exec. dir. Action on Smoking and Health, Washington, 1968—, Nat. Inst. Legal Activism, 1980—; prof. law and legal activism Nat. Law Center, George Washington U., 1968—; exec. dir. Action on Safety and Health, 1971-80, Open America, 1975-80; founder Nat. Center for Law and the Deaf, 1975—; Bd. dirs. Consumers Union, 1971. Recipient 17th ann. Sat. Rev. award distinguished TV programming in pub. interest, 1969; Advt. Age award, 1967, 68; those who made advt. news, 1967, 68; Benjamin Franklin Lit. and Med. Soc. award, 1981. Mem. Sigma Xi, Eta Kappa Nu, Tau Beta Pi. Home: 2810 N Quebec St Arlington VA 22207-5215 Office: Nat Center for Law and the Deaf 2013 H St NW Washington DC 20006-4207 *Despite the increasing complexity of society, and the seemingly overwhelming power of large institutions both public and private, one determined individual can still have a significant and beneficial impact on society. (I was responsible, as an individual, for over 200 million dollars worth of free radio and television time for anti-smoking commercials which led to the ban on cigarette commercials.).*

**BARACK, DEBORAH ELISE,** lawyer; b. Madison, Wis., Oct. 22, 1970; d. Stephan Floyd and Renee Jeane Barack. BA, U. Mo., 1992; JD, Northeastern U., 1995. Bar: Hawaii 1995, U.S. Dist. Ct. Hawaii 1997. Law clk. to Hon. Corinne K.A. Watanabe Intermediate Ct. Appeals Hawaii, Honolulu, 1995-96; assoc. Carlsmith Ball, Honolulu, 1997—. Vol. reader Kapiolani Hosp. for Women and Children, Honolulu, 1998. Mem. ABA, Hawaii Bar Assn. Democrat. Jewish. Avocations: reading, running, aerobics, politics. Admiralty, Federal civil litigation, Insurance. Office: Carlsmith Ball 444 S Flower St Fl 9 Los Angeles CA 90071-2901

**BARAM, ART,** lawyer; b. Russia, Sept. 1, 1969; came to U.S., 1988; s. Roman and Bella (Baram) Sitnyakovsky. BA cum laude, UCLA, 1991, JD, 1995. Bar: Calif. 1995. Internat. tax advisor Coopers & Lybrand, L.A., 1995-97; tax atty. Buchalter, Nemer, Fields & Younger, L.A., 1997—. Contbr. articles to profl. jours. Republican. Jewish. Corporate taxation, Taxation, general, Personal income taxation. Office: Buchalter Nemer Fields & Younger 601 S Figueroa St # 2300 Los Angeles CA 90017-5704

**BARAN, JAN WITOLD,** lawyer, educator; b. Ingolstadt, Germany, May 14, 1948; came to U.S., 1951; s. Jerzy Leopold and Leonce Sidonie (Vanden Bussche) B.; m. Kathryn Kavanagh, June 16, 1979; children: Brendan Jerzy, Maria Leonce, Elise Jett, Anna Margaret. BA, Ohio Wesleyan U., 1970; JD, Vanderbilt U., 1973. Bar: Tenn. 1973, D.C. 1976, U.S. Dist. Ct. D.C. 1980, U.S. Ct. Appeals D.C. 1980, U.S. Ct. Appeals (10th cir.) 1994, U.S. Supreme Ct. 1980. Legal counsel Nat. Rep. Congl. Com., Washington, 1975-77; exec. asst. Fed. Election Commn., Washington, 1977-79; assoc. Baker & Hostetler, Washington, 1979-81, ptnr., 1981-85; ptnr. Wiley, Rein & Fielding, Washington, 1985—; gen. counsel, George Bush for Pres., Inc., 1987-88; gen. counsel, Bush-Quayle, Inc., 1988; lectr. Practicing Law Inst., Washington, 1978—. Author: The Election Law Primer for Corporations, 1984, 88, 92, 99. Chmn. nat. adv. bd. Jour. of Law and Politics, 1983—; gen. counsel Am. bicentennial Presdl. Inaugural Inc., 1989, Rep. Nat. Com., 1989-92; mem. Pres. Commn. Fed. Ethics Law Reform; amb., head U.S. del. World Adminstrv. Radio Conf. WARC, Malaga, Spain, 1992; trustee Citizens Rsch. Found., 1995—; gen. counsel, dir. Bus.-Industry Polit. Action Com., 1996—. Patrick Wilson scholar, 1970-73. Mem. ABA (chmn. com. election law 1981—), D.C. Bar Assn., FBA (chmn. polit. campaign and election law com. 1981-83). Roman Catholic. Administrative and regulatory, Federal civil litigation. Home: 1608 Walleston Ct Alexandria VA 22302-3928 Office: Wiley Rein & Fielding 1776 K St NW Ste 900 Washington DC 20006-2332

**BARASCH, DAVID M.,** prosecutor. U.S. atty. U.S. Dist. Ct. (mid. dist.) Pa. Office: US Attorney Mid District of PA Federal Bldg PO Box 11754 Harrisburg PA 17108-1754

**BARASCH, MAL LIVINGSTON,** lawyer; b. N.Y.C., May 14, 1929; s. Joseph and Ernestine (Livingston) B.; m. S. Ann Beckley, May 19, 1962; children: Amy Pitcairn Barasch, Jody Taylor Barasch. B.S. in Econs. with distinction, U. Pa., 1951; LL.B., Yale U., 1954. Bar: N.Y. 1957, U.S. Dist. Ct. (so. dist.) N.Y. 1960, U.S. Tax Ct. 1960. Assoc. Mudge Rose Guthrie Alexander & Ferdon, N.Y.C., 1957-62; assoc. Rosenman & Colin, N.Y.C., 1962-67; ptnr. Rosenman & Colin, 1968—; mem. exec. com., 2d v.p. library N.Y. Law Inst., 1979—. Dist. leader, mem. exec. com. N.Y. County Dem. Com., 1961-65; treas., bd. dirs. Lenox Hill Neighborhood House; bd. dirs. Visions, Svcs. for the Blind and Visually Impaired. With U.S. Army, 1954-56. Fellow N.Y. Bar Found., Am. Coll. Trust and Estate Counsel; mem. ABA, N.Y. State Bar Assn., Assn. of Bar of City of N.Y., Internat. Acad. Estate and Trust Law (academician), Beta Gamma Sigma. Club: University (N.Y.C.). Estate planning, Probate, Estate taxation. Home: 1088 Park Ave New York NY 10128-1132

**BARBADORO, PAUL J.,** federal judge; b. Providence, June 4, 1955; s. Donald James and Elizabeth B.; m. Inez E. McDermott, Aug. 16, 1986; children: Katherine E., John James. BA cum laude, Gettysburg Coll., 1977; JD magna cum laude, Boston Coll., 1980. Bar: N.H. 1980. Asst. atty. gen. N.H. Atty. Gen., Concord, 1980-84; legal counsel U.S. Sen. Warren B. Rudman, Washington, 1984-86, Orr & Reno, Concord, 1986-87; dep. chief counsel U.S. Senate Iran-Contra Com., Washington, 1987; dir. Rath, Young, Pignatelli and Oyer, Concord, 1987-92; judge U.S. Dist. Ct., Concord, 1992-97, chief judge, 1997—; mem. adv. group for dist. of N.H., Civil Justice Reform Act, Concord, 1992-94; mem. long range planning com. N.H. Supreme Ct., 1989-90; mem. 1st Cir. Jud. Coun., 1994-96; adj. prof. Franklin Pierce Law Ctr., 1997-98. Mem. N.H. Bar Assn. (chmn. unauthorized practice of law com. 1982-84, jud. conf. com. on automation and tech. 1996—, com. on cooperation with the cts. 1997—), U.S. Dist. Ct. N.H. Bar, 1st Cir. Ct. Appeals Bar, Order of Coif. Office: WB Rudman Courthouse 55 Pleasant St Rm 409 Concord NH 03301-3938

**BARBAGALLO, RALPH A.,** lawyer; b. Lawrence, Mass., Nov. 13, 1942; s. Ralph A. and Mary (Zappardi) B.; m. Marie E. Consoli, Aug. 8, 1971; children: Anne Marie, Ralph A. III. BS, St. Anselm Coll., Manchester, N.Y., 1964; JD, Boston U., 1967. Bar: Mass. 1968, N.H. 1988. Intern atty. gen. Edward Brooke State of Mass., 1966; atty. Essex County Pub. Defender, Mass., 1972-74; master Essex County Probate Ct., 1980; gen. counsel Lawrence Redevel. Authority, 1978-83; spl. town counsel Town of N. Andover (Mass.), 1983; pvt. practice Lawrence and N.Andover, Mass., 1988—; founder Alfred Realty Trust, 1977, Remington Realty, 1985;. Mem. Andover Rep. Com., 1979—; campaign mgr. Lawrence Mayoral Candidate Kathleen Pappalardo, 1971; candidate for Mass. Ho. Reps., 1973, 75; coord. Francis Hatch for Gov., 1978; campaign worker Senator Edward Brooks, 1966, 72, 78; chmn. No. Andover Charter Commn., 1985. Mem. ABA (ins. law sect., entertainment law sect.), ASCAP, Mass. Bar Assn., Lawrence Bar Assn., Mass. Acad. Trial Lawyers, N.H. Bar Assn., N.H. Trial Lawyers Assn. (gov. Rickingham County sect.), Am. Trial Lawyers Assn., Eastern Dist. Jud. Nominations Coun. (Mass.), Italian Am. Sons of Italy., Lawrence Musicians Union (elected del. 12 times), Justinian Law Soc., Italian Am. Civic Assn.. Roman Catholic. Avocations: tennis, song writing. Personal injury. Office: 231 Sutton St Ste 2C North Andover MA 01845-1620

**BARBAS, STEPHEN MICHAEL,** lawyer; b. Tampa, Fla., July 16, 1954; s. Carlos Francis and Gloria B.; m. Scheznarda Eva Luque, Aug. 2, 1980; children: Terin Marie, Amy Lauren. Student, Stetson U.; BS, Fla. State U., 1976; JD, Loyola U., New Orleans, 1979. Bar: Fla. 1979, U.S. Dist. Ct. (mid. dist.) Fla. 1980, U.S. Ct. Appeals (5th cir.) 1980, U.S. Ct. Appeals (11th cir.) 1981. Asst. city atty. City of Tampa, 1979—; ptnr. Barbas, Weed, Glenn, Morgan & Wheeley, Tampa, 1982—. Contbg. author Loyola Law Rev., 1978. Pres. Bright Horizons of Tampa Bay, Inc., 1979-81, Tampa Day Preschool and Kindergarten, Tampa, 1989-91. Mem. ABA (litigation sect.), Fla. Bar Assn. (workers' compensation sect.), Hillsborough County Bar Assn. Democrat. Roman Catholic. Avocations: golfing, fishing, reading, interior designing, antiques. Workers' compensation, Personal injury, Insurance. Home: 2916 W Hawthorne Rd Tampa FL 33611-2830 Office: Barbas Weed Glenn Morgan & Wheeley 1802 W Cleveland St Tampa FL 33606-1852

**BARBEE, JOE ED,** lawyer; b. Pharr, Tex., Feb. 27, 1934; s. Archie Allen and Concha (Leal) B.; m. Yolanda Margaret Atonna, Feb. 17, 1962; children—Cynthia M., Adam A., Walter J. BSEE, U. Ariz., 1961; JD, Western New Eng. Coll., 1973. Bar: Mass. 1973, U.S. Patent Office 1973, U.S. Ct. Appeals (fed. cir.) 1982. Engr. Gen. Electric Co., Pittsfield, Mass., 1961-73; patent atty. Fort Wayne, Ind., 1973-75, Magnavox, Fort Wayne, 1975-76, Motorola, Inc., Phoenix, 1976—. Sgt. U.S. Army, 1953-56. Recipient Outstanding Performance award U.S. Civil Svc., 1960. Mem. ABA, Am. Patent Law Assn., Am. Intellectual Property Law Assn. Republican. Methodist. Avocations: tennis, hunting, fishing. Patent, Trademark and copyright. Home: 7611 N Mockingbird Ln Paradise Valley AZ 85253 Office: Motorola Inc 8220 E Roosevelt St # B3 Scottsdale AZ 85257-3804

**BARBEOSCH, WILLIAM PETER,** banker, lawyer; b. N.Y.C., Nov. 25, 1954; s. Peter Joseph and Marie Delores (Slesiona) B.; m. Marta B. Varela, Sept. 6, 1986. AB magna cum laude, Brown U., 1976; JD, Columbia U., 1979; MBA, Yale U., 1989. Bar: N.Y. 1980, U.S. Tax Ct. 1985. Atty. Casey, Lane and Mittendorf (and successor firms), N.Y.C., 1979-86, Milbank, Tweed, Hadley and McCloy, N.Y.C., 1986-87; mgmt. assoc. Swiss Bank Corp., N.Y.C., 1989-90; v.p. The Chase Manhattan Pvt. Bank, N.Y.C., 1990-99, mng. dir., 1999—. Mem. N.Y. State Bar Assn., Assn. of the Bar of City of N.Y., Stone House Club, Brown U. Club, Phi Kappa Psi (sec. R.I. Alpha chpt. 1974-75). Republican. Roman Catholic. Avocations: swimming, history, politics. Home: 545 W 111th St Apt 7E New York NY 10025-1965 Office: The Chase Manhattan Bank 1211 Ave of the Ams New York NY 10036-8890

**BARBER, BARBARA LENISE,** assistant attorney general; b. Cin., Mar. 3, 1962; d. John L. and Barbara J. (Bennent) B. BBA, Xavier U., 1986; JD, Salmon P. Chase Coll. Law, 1997. Bar: Ohio 1997. Br. ops. specialist The Fifth Third Bank, Cin., 1980-86; ops. adminstr. Gen. Electric Capital Corp., Cin., 1986-92; paralegal Graydon, Head & Ritchey, Cin., 1992-97; asst. atty. gen. State of Ohio, 1997—. Bd. dirs. (pub. and moot ct. competitions) No. Ky. Law Rev., No. Ky. Moot Ct. Avocations: sewing, the performing arts. Office: Atty Gen/Taxation State Office Tower 30 E Broad St Fl 16 Columbus OH 43215-3414

**BARBER, JENSEN E.,** lawyer, author; b. Asheville, N.C., May 22, 1945; s. Donald McArthur Barber and Frances Peeble Phillips. MA in Criminal Justice, George Washington U., 1978; JD, Cath. U. Bar: D.C. Pvt. practice Washington, 1984—; NITA prof. Emory U. Law Sch., Atlanta; cons. in field. Mem. U. Club, Georgetown Club. Avocations: sailing, skiing, opera, travel. Fax: 202-628-0249. E-mail: jebarber@juno.com. Office: 400 7th St NW Ste 400 Washington DC 20004-2242

**BARBER, MARK EDWARD,** lawyer; b. Enumclaw, Wash., Dec. 30, 1952; s. Earl Marion Barber and Delila Mae Willis Lontz; m. Pamela Johnson, Aug. 30, 1974; 1 child, Matthew Edward. BA, U. Wash., 1975; JD, Pepperdine U., 1978. Bar: Wash. 1978, U.S. Dist. Ct. Wash. 1978, U.S. Ct. Appeals (9th cir.) 1980, U.S. Supreme Ct. 1985. Atty. Heavey & Woody, Inc. P.S., Seattle, 1978-79; sole practitioner Seattle, 1979-81; atty., prin. shareholder Warren Barber Dean & Fontes, P.S., Renton, Wash., 1981—. Bd. dirs. Justice Polit. Action Com., Tacoma, 1993-95, Sunset Valley Farms Homeowners Assn., Issaquah, Wash., 1991-92, 95-96. Mem. ATLA, Wash. State Bar Assn., King County Bar Assn., Wash. State Trial Lawyers Assn. (pres. 1995-96). Personal injury, Product liability, Professional liability. Office: Warren Barber et al 100 S 2nd St Renton WA 98055-2013

**BARBER, PHILLIP MARK,** lawyer; b. Pitts., Apr. 7, 1944; s. Armour G. and Irene Estelle (Doyle) B.; m. Barbara Jean Jennings, Aug. 6, 1966 (div. Dec. 1981); children: Heather C., Jessica L., Melissa A.; m. Penelope Louise Constantikes, Apr. 15, 1989 (div. Nov. 1991). BA, U. Mich., 1966; JD, Harvard U., 1969. Bar: Idaho 1969, Calif. 1971, U.S. Ct. Appeals (9th cir.) 1974, U.S. Supreme Ct. 1977. Law clk. Supreme Ct. Idaho, Boise, 1969-70; assoc. Nossaman, Waters, Scott, Krueger & Riordan, L.A., 1970-71; asst. atty. gen. State of Idaho, Boise, 1971-72; assoc. Elam, Burke, Jeppesen, Evans & Boyd, Boise, 1972-76, ptnr., 1977-81; ptnr. Hawley, Troxell, Ennis & Hawley, Boise, 1981—; mem. select com. on bar examination Idaho Supreme Ct., 1973-74, select com. on appellate rules, 1976-77, standing com. 1977-84; mem. Idaho Code Commn., 1978-96. Contbr. articles to profl. jours. Chmn. rules com. Idaho Dem. Comm., 1976; chmn. Boise Area Econ. Devel. Coun., 1985-88; leadership coun., N.W. Policy Ctr., 1988-97; vice chmn. N.W. Bus. Coalition, 1987-89; mem. exec. com. Idaho Bus. Coun., 1986-94. Recipient Disting. Citizen award Idaho Stateman Newspapers, 1985. Mem. ABA, Idaho State Bar (exam. com. 1983-85), State Bar Calif., Boise Bar Assn., Boise Area C. of C. (bd. dirs. 1980-81, 83-88, pres., chmn. bd. 1985). Roman Catholic. Avocations: golf, skiing, photography. Administrative and regulatory, Legislative, Real property. Home: 1196 Shenandoah Dr Boise ID 83712-7451 Office: Hawley Troxell Ennis & Hawley 877 Main St Ste 1000 Boise ID 83702-5884

**BARBER, STEVEN THOMAS,** lawyer; b. Evansville, Ind., Apr. 13, 1948; s. Raymond Shirley and Betty Lou (Wilzbacher) B.; m. Mary Ann Hughes, May 17, 1975; children: Kathryn Alissa, Michael Steven. AB, Ind. U., 1970, JD, 1974. Bar: Ind. 1974, U.S. Ct. Appeals (7th cir.) 1974, U.S. Dist. Ct. (so. dist.) Ind. 1983, U.S. Ct. Appeals (fed. cir.) 1983. Ptnr. Lockyear & Barber, Evansville, Ind., 1974-84, Barber, Levco & Williams, Evansville, Ind., 1984-87; adj. prof. U. Evansville, 1978-93; ptnr. Barber & Hamilton, 1987—. Author: (textbook) Legal Writing for Paralegals, 1993, Legal Research for Paralegals, 1995. Bd. dirs. Evansville (Ind.) ARC, 1988—, chmn. of bd., 1993-94; bd. dirs. Family & Children's Svc., Evansville, 1989—, pres., 1992-93; bd. dirs. Ozanam Family shelter, Evansville, 1988-90. Mem. Evansville Bar Assn. (bd. dirs. 1994—), Ind. State Bar Assn., Order of the Coif, Phi Beta Kappa. General civil litigation, Labor, General practice. Home: 209 S Fairlawn Ave Evansville IN 47714-1364 Office: Barber and Hamilton 123 NW 4th St Rm 402 Evansville IN 47708-1713

**BARBERY, PAUL SAUNDERS,** lawyer; b. Keystone, W.Va., Dec. 5, 1936; s. Edwin Carrico and Mildred Marshall Barbery; m. Margaret Harris, July 21, 1961 (dec. July 1975); m. Sarah Davis, May 22, 1976; 1 child, Kevin Saunders. BS in Mining Engring., Va. Poly. Inst. and State U., 1959; LLB, U. Richmond, 1964. Bar: Va. 1964, W.Va. 1993, N.C. 1994, U.S. Dist. Ct. (ea. dist.) Va. 1964, U.S. Ct. Appeals (4th cir.) 1968, U.S. Dist. Ct. (so. dist.) W.Va. 1983. Ptnr. Martin Hopkins & Lemon, Roanoke, Va., 1964-74; gen. counsel PittstonCoal Group, Lebanon, Va., 1974-75; gen. counsel, corp. sec. Va. Iron and Coke, Roanoke, 1975-76; sr. v.p., gen. counsel A.T. Massey Coal Co., Richmond, 1976-94; pvt. practice Richmond, 1994-97, Charlotte, N.C., 1997—; v.p., gen. counsel Am. Metals and Coal Internat., 1994—; chmn. bd. Elk Run Coal Co., Sylvester, W.Va., 1976-94; cons. in field. Trustee Eastern Mineral Law Found., Morgantown, W.Va., 1985-94; advisor Marshall U. Higher Edn. Learning Program, 1992-95; bd. dirs. Stonehenge County Club, Richmond, 1989-92. Named Disting. Alumni, Dept. Mines and Minerals, Va. Poly. Inst. and State U., 1990. Mem. McNeil Law Soc., Tau Beta Pi. Avocations: golf, boating. Contracts commercial, General corporate, General practice. Home: 481 Bay Harbour Rd Mooresville NC 28117-9059 Office: BB&T Center 200 S College St Ste 620 Charlotte NC 28202-2065

**BARBIN, RYTHER LYNN,** lawyer; b. Port Arthur, Tex., July 15, 1943; s. L.B. and Edna Mae (Ryther) B.; m. Marla Egbert Sankey, Dec. 24, 1987; children: Jordan Ross, Gabriel, Nathaniel. BBA, Tex. Tech. U., 1966; JD, Baylor U., 1968. Bar: Tex. 1968, Hawaii 1976, U.S. Dist. Ct. Hawaii 1976; lic. realtor, Hawaii. Law clk. U.S. Dept. Justice, Washington, 1967; officer trust dept. Bank of Am., San Francisco, 1968-71; officer Investors Bank & Trust Co., Boston, 1972-74; sole practice Wailuku, Hawaii, 1974-82, 84—; ptnr. Barbin & Ball, Wailuku, 1982-84; arbitrator Hi Supreme Ct. Bd. dirs. Maui United Way, 1980-88, v.p., 1987-88, pres., 1989-90; mem. sch. bd. Maui Dist. Sch., 1980-84; state del., dist. coun. Hawaii Dems., Wailuku, 1978-84; field rep. for U.S. Senator Daniel K. Inouye; campaign mgr. Dem. Presdl. Campaigns Maui County, 1983; vice-chmn. Maui County Dem. Party, 1986-87; chmn. Maui County Dem. Party, 1997-98; bd. dirs. Maui Humane Soc., Maui Kokua Svc. Recipient cert. of appreciation Gov. State of Hawaii, 1981. Mem. ABA, Hawaii Bar Assn. (bd. dirs.) Maui Bar Assn. (pres. 1984-86), Upcountry Jaycees Makawao (officer 1979-83), Rotary (pres. Wailuku club 1986-87). Episcopalian. Bankruptcy, Immigration, naturalization, and customs, General practice. Home: 555 Iao Valley Rd Wailuku HI 96793-3007 Office: 24 N Church St Ste 407 Wailuku HI 96793-1608

**BARBOR, JOHN HOWARD,** lawyer; b. Pitts., Mar. 4, 1952; s. Thomas Sharp and Irene (Park) B.; m. Gretchen Suzanne Kunst, Mar. 20, 1982; children: Peter Howard, Katherine Suzanne. AB, Dartmouth Coll., 1974; JD, Boston Coll., 1977. Bar: Pa. 1977. Ptnr. Barbor and Barbor, Indiana, Pa., 1978-89, Barbor & Cicola, Indiana, 1989-93; Barbor & Vaporis, Indiana, 1993—. Bd. dirs., solicitor Indiana County YMCA, 1985-94; solicitor Indiana County Red Cross, 1979—; bd. dirs. Indiana Arts Coun., 1986-89; bd. dirs. Indiana County Zoning Appeals Bd., 1995—, chmn., 1998—. Mem. ABA, Pa. Bar Assn., Pa. Bar Inst. (bd. govs. 1995-97), Ind. County Bar Assn. (exec. bd. 1988, 95), Ind. Country Club, Phi Beta Kappa. Republican. Lutheran. Real property, Probate, State civil litigation. Home: 18 Daugherty Dr Indiana PA 15701-2222 Office: Barbor and Vaporis 917 Philadelphia St Indiana PA 15701-3911

**BARBOUR, WILLIAM H., JR.,** federal judge; b. 1941. BA, Princeton U., 1963; JD, U. Miss., 1966; postgrad, NYU, 1966. Bar: Miss. Ptnr. Henry, Barbour & DeCell, Yazoo City, Miss., 1966-83; judge U.S. Dist. Ct. (so. dist.) Miss., 1983—, chief judge, 1989-96, judge, 1996—. Youth counselor Yazoo City, 1971-82. Office: US Dist Ct 245 E Capitol St Ste 430 Jackson MS 39201-2414

**BARCELO, JOHN JAMES, III,** law educator; b. New Orleans, Sept. 23, 1940; s. John James Jr. and Elfrida Margaret (Bisso) B.; m. Lucy L. Wood, July 14, 1974; children—Lisa, Amy, Steven. B.A., Tulane U., 1962, J.D., 1966; S.J.D., Harvard U., 1977. Bar: La. 1967, D.C. 1974, U.S. Supreme Ct. 1974, N.Y. 1975. Fulbright scholar U. Bonn, Fed. Republic Germany, 1966-67; research assoc. Harvard U. Law Sch., Cambridge, Mass., 1968-69; prof. law Cornell U. Law Sch., Ithaca, N.Y., 1969—, A. Robert Noll. prof. of law, 1984-96, dir internat. legal studies, 1972-88, 90—, William Nelson Cromwell prof. internat. and comprative law, 1996—; cons. Import Trade Adminstrn., Dept. Commerce. Author: (with others) Law: Its Nature, Functions and Limits, 3rd edit., 1986, International Commercial Arbitration, 1999; contbr. articles to profl. jours. Mem. Am. Assn. for Comparative Study of Law (bd. dirs.), Am. Soc. Internat. Law, Soc. Comprative Law, Maritime Law Assn. U.S. Office: Cornell U Law Sch Myron Taylor Hall Ithaca NY 14853

**BARCLAY, CRAIG DOUGLAS,** lawyer; b. Zanesville, Ohio, Oct. 19, 1948; s. Robert Wilson and Letha Leota B.; m. Charlene Prout, Jan. 2, 1983; children: Amanda, Douglas, Grant. BS in Mktg., Ohio State U., 1970, JD, 1973. Bar: Ohio 1973, U.S. Dist. Ct. Ohio 1973. Assoc. Wright, Harlor, Morris & Arnold, Columbus, 1973-79; ptnr. Porter, Wright, Morris & Arthur, Columbus, 1979-90, Maloon, Maloon & Barclay, Columbus, 1990-94, Wolske & Blue, Columbus, 1994—; mem., commr. bd. commrs. for unauthorized practice of law Supreme Ct., Columbus, 1992-95. Bd. dirs. Lifecare Alliance, Columbus, 1984-90; usher Broad St. Presbyn. Ch., Columbus, 1984-90. Mem. Am. Bd. Trial Advs. (Ohio chpt.), Ohio State Bar Assn. Avocations: golf, sports. Personal injury, General civil litigation. Home: 3082 Elbern Ave Columbus OH 43209-2030 Office: Wolske & Blue 580 S High St Ste 300 Columbus OH 43215-5672

**BARCLAY, H(UGH) DOUGLAS,** lawyer, former state senator; b. N.Y.C., July 5, 1932; s. Hugh and Dorothy Barclay; m. Sara Seiter, Aug. 15, 1959; children: Kathryn D., David H., Dorothy G., Susan M., William A. BA, Yale U., 1955; JD, Syracuse U., 1961; DSc (hon.), St. Lawrence U., 1985; LLD, SUNY, 1990. Bar: N.Y. 1962. Ptnr. Hiscock & Barclay and predecessors, Syracuse, N.Y., 1961—; sec., gen. counsel KeyCorp and subs., Albany, N.Y., 1971-89; mem. N.Y. State Senate, 1965-84, chmn. Judiciary com., chmn. Select Task Force on Ct. Reorgn., chmn. senate codes com.; dir., chmn. bd. Syracuse Supply Co; chmn. bd. Eagle Media, Inc. Mem. N.Y. State Econ. Power Allocation Bd., N.Y. Racing Assn., bd. trustees; pres. Met. Devel. Assn.; trustee, former chmn. Syracuse U., chair chancellor search com.; vice chmn. N.Y. State George Bush for Pres., 1988; chmn. N.Y. State Bush-Quayle campaign, 1992; mem. policy coun. Gov. Pataki's Transition Team; bd. visitors Syracuse U. Coll. Law; mem. Onondaga C.C. Found. Lt. arty. U.S. Army, 1955-57, Korea. Mem. ABA, N.Y. State Bar Assn. Banking, General corporate. Office: Hiscock & Barclay PO Box 4878 221 S Warren St Syracuse NY 13202-1633

**BARCLAY, JOHN ALLEN,** lawyer; b. L.A., Feb. 14, 1951; s. George H. and Shirley Iris (Handler) B. AA, L.A. Valley Coll., 1970; BA, U. Southern Calif., 1972, JD, 1975. Bar: Calif. 1975, U.S. Dist. Ct. (cen., ea., and no. dists.) Calif. 1976, U.S. Ct. Appeals (9th cir.) 1976, U.S. Tax Ct. 1976, U.S. Ct. Claims, 1995. Prin. Barclay & Brestoff, Encino, 1978-80, Barclay & Moskatel, Beverly Hills, Calif., 1980-82, Barclay Law Corp., Newport Beach, Calif., 1982—; instr. U. Calif.-Irvine, 1985-87, UCLA, 1982-85, L.A. Valley Coll., Van Nuys, 1980-82. Author: Exchanging in the '80's, 1986, Accumulating Wealth, 1987, Insurance for Environmental Claims Against Bankruptcy Estates, 1992, Deducting Your Down Payment, 1984; contbr. articles to profl. jours. Mem. adv. bd. Calif. State U.; dir., sec. Orange County Nat. Conf. Christians and Jews; dir. Parent Help USA. Mem. ABA, Legion Lex (bd. dirs. Orange County chpt. 1987-95, pres. 1992), Masons (master Hollywood chpt. 1982). Jewish. Avocations: sailing, scuba. Real property, Contracts commercial, Franchising. Office: Barclay Law Corp 5000 Birch St Ste 2900 Newport Beach CA 92660-2139 *Notable cases include: Palmdale redevel. agy. vs. Germano, eminent domain case, represented property owner; Pasante v. McWilliams represented shareholder against former attorney claiming an interest in Upper Deck Company, affirmed on appeal.*

**BARCLAY, STEVEN CALDER,** lawyer; b. Phoenix, Ariz., Jan. 17, 1956; s. Leslie Calder and Ruth (Lindke) B.; m. Janice Marie Reno, Sept. 25, 1982; 1 child, Jordan Nicole. BA magna cum laude, Oral Roberts U., 1977; JD cum laude, Notre Dame U., 1980. Bar: Ariz. 1980, U.S. Dist. Ct. Ariz. 1980, U.S. Ct. Appeals (9th cir.) 1980. Assoc. Snell & Wilmer, Phoenix, 1980-83; corp. counsel S.W. divsn. CIGNA Healthplans, Inc., Phoenix, 1983-85; ptnr. Barclay & Reece, Phoenix, 1985-87; pvt. practice Phoenix, 1987-90; shareholder, pres. Barclay & Goering, PC, Phoenix, 1990—. Mem. editl. bd. Today's Health Care Mag., 1994—. Mem. State Bar Ariz., Ariz. Assn. HMOs (counsel, lobbyist 1987-96), Ariz. Assn. Health Care Lawyers, Am. Health Lawyers Assn., Pub. Affairs Profls. Ariz. (dir., pres.), The Samaritans, Ariz. Sports Coun. (counsel). Republican. Avocations: camping, hiking, jogging, scuba diving, tennis. Health, Insurance, Legislative. Office: Barclay & Goering PC 1001 N Central Ave Ste 600 Phoenix AZ 85004-1947

**BARCUS, BENJAMIN FRANKLIN,** lawyer; b. Tacoma, June 24, 1960; s. George Eldon Barcus and Gwendolyn (Evans) Johnson. BBA, U. Wash., 1982; JD, U. Puget Sound, 1985. Bar: Wash. 1986, U.S. Dist. Ct. (we. dist.) Wash. 1986, U.S. Ct. Appeals (9th cir.) 1986, U.S. Supreme Ct. 1991. Customer svc. rep. Tacoma News Tribune, 1979-80; claims rep., investigator Office Atty. Gen. State of Wash., Seattle, 1980-81; ind. svc. contractor Am. Express Co. Inc., Seattle, 1981-85; assoc. Talbot, Orlandini, Waldron & Hemmen, Tacoma, 1986-88; pvt. practice, Tacoma, 1989—. Precinct committeeman Wash. Dem. Com., Tacoma, 1982-88. Mem. ABA, ATLA, Wash. State Bar Assn., Wash. State Trial Lawyers Assn., Wash. Assn. Criminal Def. Lawyers, Tacoma-Pierce County Bar Assn., Mopars Unltd. (treas. Tacoma chpt. 1982-88), Ferrari Owner's Club, Ferrari Club Am., Mercedes Benz Club Am., Rolls Royce Owners Club, Fircrest Golf Club, Tacoma Yacht Club. Congregational. Avocations: collecting and restoring automobiles, soccer, running, water skiing, tennis. Personal injury, Criminal, General corporate. Home: 2223 E Day Island Blvd W Tacoma WA 98466-1816 Office: 4303 N Ruston Way Tacoma WA 98402-5313

**BARDACK, PAUL ROITMAN,** lawyer; b. N.Y.C., Nov. 13, 1953; s. Lawrence Stanley and Charlotte (Sebold) B.; m. Esther Roitman, May 27,

1979; children: David, Avi, Daniella. BA, Yale U., 1975; JD, Am. U., 1978. Bar: D.C. 1980. Atty. U.S. Dept. HUD, Washington, 1978-79; gen. counsel to U.S. congressman Robert Garcia, Washington, 1979-81; atty. Barrett Smith Schapiro Simon & Armstrong, N.Y.C., 1981-83; mgr. econ. devel. dept. City of Cleve., 1983-84; chief exec. officer, gen. counsel Econ. Devel. Resources, Inc., Phila. and Washington, 1984-86; sr. policy advisor Gov. Thomas Kean, Trenton, N.J., 1986-89; dep. asst. sec. for econ. devel. HUD, Washington, 1989-93; v.p. Nat. Mentoring Partnership, Washington, 1993-99; cons. Booz Allen & Hamilton, McLean, Va., 1999—. Mem. ABA, D.C. Bar Assn. Jewish. Computer, Education and schools, Legislative. Home: 14833 Melfordshire Way Silver Spring MD 20906-5745 Office: Booz Allen & Hamilton 8251 Greensboro Dr Ste 1 Mc Lean VA 22102-3812

**BARDACKE, PAUL GREGORY,** lawyer, former attorney general; b. Oakland, Calif., Dec. 16, 1944; s. Theodore Joseph and Frances (Woodward) B.; children: Julie, Brynn, Francheska, Chloe. BA cum laude, U. Calif.-Santa Barbara, 1966; JD, U. Calif.-Berkeley, 1969. Bar: Calif. 1969, N.Mex. 1970. Lawyer Legal Aid Soc., Albuquerque, 1969; assoc. firm Sutin, Thayer & Browne, Albuquerque, 1970-82; atty. gen. State of N.Mex., Santa Fe, 1982-86; ptnr. Sutin, Thayer & Browne, 1987-90, Eaves, Bardacke, Baugh, Kierst & Kiernan, P.A., 1991—; adj. prof. N.Mex. Law Sch., Albuquerque, 1973—; mem. faculty Nat. Inst. Trial Lawyers Advocacy, 1978—. Bd. dirs. All Faiths Receiving Home, Albuquerque; bd. dirs. Friends of Art, 1974, Artspace Mag., 1979-80, Legal Aid Soc., 1970-74. Reginald Heber Smith fellow, 1969. Fellow Am. Coll. Trial Lawyers; mem. ABA, Calif. Bar Assn., N.Mex. Bar Assn., Am. Bd. Trial Advocates (pres. N.Mex. chpt. 1992-93). Democrat. Antitrust, Federal civil litigation, State civil litigation. Office: Eaves Bardacke Baugh Kierst & Kiernan PA PO Box 35670 Albuquerque NM 87176-5670

**BARDEN, KENNETH EUGENE,** lawyer, educator; b. Espanola, N.Mex., Nov. 21, 1955; s. Lloyd C. and Beverly A. (Coverdale) B. BA cum laude, Ind. Ctrl. U., 1977; JD, Ind. U., 1977; cert., Harvard U., 1983. Bar: Ind. 1981, U.S. Dist. Ct. (so. dist.) Ind. 1981, U.S. Tax Ct. 1983, U.S. Ct. Mil. Appeals 1983, U.S. Ct. Appeals (6th and 7th cirs.) 1983, U.S. Ct. Internat. Trade 1983, U.S. Ct. Claims Ohio 1990, Rep. of Palau, 1998. Law clk. Marion County Prosecutor's Office, Ind., 1976-78, Krieg Devault Alexander & Capehart, Indpls., 1978-79; baliff Marion County Mcpl. Ct. 7, 1979-81, commr.-judge pro tem, 1981; pub. defender criminal divsn. 1 Marion County Superior Ct., 1981; asst. to U.S. magistrate U.S. Dist. Ct. (so. dist.) Ind., Indpls., 1982-84; city atty. City of Richmond, Ind., 1984-89; pres. Bd. Pub. Works and Safety, 1988-89; corp. counsel Richmond Power & Light Co., 1984-89; pres. City of Richmond Bd. Pub. Works and Safety, Ohio, 1988-89; chief gen. counsel City of Dayton, Ohio, 1989-98; tax atty., asst. atty. gen. Rep. of Palau, 1998—; adj. prof. law Ind. Ctrl. U., Indpls., 1983. Contbr. articles to profl. jours. Nat. v.p. Coll. Dems. of Am., 1979-82; ward chmn. Marion County Dems., 1977-81; precinct committeeman Wayne County Dems., 1985-89, treas. 2d dist., 1986-89; del to NATO European Youth Leadership Conf., 1980; co-founder Hubert H. Humphrey Tng. Inst. for Campaign Politics, 1980; treas. Perry Twp. Dem. Club, 1980-83; alt. del. Dem. Nat. Conv., 1980; del. White House forum on Domestic and Econ. Policy, 1975; del Youth Conf. on Nat. Security and the Atlantic Alliance, Mt. Vernon Coll., Washington, 1976, Am. Coun. Young Polit. Leaders Fgn. Policy Conf., 1987; mem. U.S. Youth Coun. under Pres. Carter, 1980; mem. Ind. Gov.'s Cmty. Corrections Com., 1973-75; mem. adv. coun. Friends of the Battered, 1985-88; mem. pers. policies forum Bur. Nat. Affairs, 1985-88; mem. Dem. Leadership Coun., 1987—, Am. Coun. of Young Polit. Leaders, 1986—; founding mem., bd. dirs. Richmond (Ind.) Cmty. Devel. Corp., 1987-89; legal counsel Richmond Greater Progress Com., 1987-89. Recipient Youth in Govt. award Optimist Club, 1972; named one of Outstanding Young Men in Am., 1986. Mem. ABA (com. on industry regulation, Young lawyers divsn. labor law com., urban, state and local govt. sect., vice chair Town Hall com. 1985-87, chair 1987-88, vice chair citizenship edn. com. 1987-88, victims com. sect. of criminal justice 1985—, lawyers and arts com., chmn. town hall com. 1987-91, vice chmn. citizenship edn. com. 1987-94, chair Arson Law Project 1993-94, contbr. editor Arson Law Reporter), Fed. Bar Assn., Ind. State Bar Assn., Indpls. Bar Assn., Wayne County Bar Assn., Ind. Coun. on World Affairs, Fed. Energy Bar Assn., Ind. Assn. Cities and Towns, Nat. League of Cities, Am. Soc. Pub. Adminstrs., Athenaeum Club (Indpls.), World Trade of Ind. Club, Kiwanis, Phi Alpha Delta, Epsilon Sigma Alpha, Alpha Phi Omega. Methodist. E-mail: kbarden@palaunet.com. Family and matrimonial, Private international. Home: PO Box 6011 Palau PW 96940-0841 Office: Tax Counsel Rep of Palau PO Box 6011 Palau PW 96940-0841

**BARDI, HENRY J.,** lawyer; b. Bklyn., July 26, 1947; s. Joseph a. and Margaret B.; m. Maryann Ra, Jan. 11, 1975; children: Joseph H., Philip J., Rosemary. BS in Econ., St. John's U., 1971, JD, 1974. Bar: N.Y. 1975, U.S. Dist. Ct. (ea. and so. dists.) N.Y. 1976, Fla. 1988, U.S. Dist. Ct. (mid. dist.) Fla. 1989, U.S. Ct. Appeals (11th cir.) 1993. Assoc. counsel N.Y.C. Conciliation and Appeals Bd., 1975-76; trial atty. Legal Aid Soc.--Criminal, Bklyn., 1976-78; pvt. practice Levittown, N.Y., 1978-82; dep. county atty., chief litig. Nassau County Atty.'s Office, Mineola, N.Y., 1982-89; trial atty. Alpert, Josey & Grilli, P.A., Tampa, Fla., 1989-90; mng. atty. staff counsel office Progressive Ins. Co., Tampa, 1990—; assoc. counsel East Coast Abstract Title Co., Mineola, N.Y.; counsel Seaford (N.Y.) Fire Dept., 1985-89. Mem. sch. bd. St. William the Abbot, Seaford; committeeman Nassau County (N.Y.) Rep. Party; pres. Seaford Rep. Club, 1988-89. Mem. N.Y. State Bar Assn., Hillsborough County Bar Assn. Roman Catholic. Avocation: golf. General civil litigation, Personal injury, Insurance. Office: Progressive Ins Co 500 N West Shore Blvd Ste 630 Tampa FL 33609-1953

**BARDOTT, HEATHER KATHLEEN,** lawyer; b. Woodbury, N.J., May 23, 1969; d. Joseph Walter and Dorothy Kay McGinnis; m. Dwight Steven Bardot, June 16, 1990; children: Madison, Ileana. BS with distinction, U. Va., 1991; JD, George Mason U., 1994. Bar: Va. 1994, U.S. Dist. Ct. (ea. dist.) Va. 1994, U.S. Dist. Ct. (we. dist.) Va. 1998. Law clk. U.S. Dist. Ct., Richmond, Va., 1994-95; atty. Trichilo Bancroft McGavin Horvath & Judkins, Fairfax, Va., 1995—. Bd. dirs. Saybrooke Homeowners Assn., Bristow, Va., 1998—. Mem. Va. Assn. Def. Attys. (chair young lawyers divsn. 1998—), No. Va. Def. Attys. Avocations: running, hiking. Insurance, Workers' compensation, Personal injury. Office: Trichilo Bancroft 4117 Chain Bridge Rd # 400 Fairfax VA 22030-4117

**BARELA, JONATHAN LEWIS,** lawyer; b. Las Cruces, N.Mex., June 5, 1960; s. John Zamora and Edna Mae (Alvidrez) B.; m. Regina Villareal, July 5, 1986; children: John Paul, Christiana Nicole. BS, Georgetown U., 1982, JD, 1987. Bar: N.Mex. 1988, U.S. Dist. Ct. N.Mex. 1989, U.S. Ct. Appeals (10th cir.) 1989. Asst. atty. gen., dir. civil div. N.Mex. Atty. Gen., Santa Fe, 1989-90; assoc. Modrall, Sperling, Roehl, Harris & Sisk, Albuquerque, 1987-89, 91—; bd. dirs. N.Mex. Mortgage Fin. Authority, Albuquerque, 1989-90. State ctrl. com. N.Mex. Rep., Albuquerque, 1988—; mem. Albuquerque/Bernalillo County Private Industry Coun., 1993—. Recipient Disting. Svc. award Villa Santa Maria, Inc., 1991. Mem. ABA, KC, Kiwanis. Roman Catholic. Avocations: sports, antiques. General civil litigation, Administrative and regulatory, Legislative. Office: Modrall Sperling Roehl Harris & Sisk 10101 Corona Ave NE Albuquerque NM 87122-3009

**BARENHOLTZ, CELIA GOLDWAG,** lawyer; b. Washington, Dec. 11, 1955; d. Herbert and Anita Charlotte Goldwag; m. Paul K. Barenholtz, Aug. 28, 1983; children: Jeanne, Madeleine. BA, Grinnell (Iowa) Coll., 1979; JD, Columbia U., 1979. Bar: N.Y. 1980, U.S. Dist. Ct. (so. and ea. dist.) N.Y. 1980, U.S. Ct. Appeals (2d cir.) 1985, U.S. Ct. Appeals (9th cir.) 1990, U.S. Supreme Ct. 1992, U.S. Ct. Appeals (11th cir.) 1998. Law clk. Hon. Eugene H. Nickerson, Bklyn., 1979-80; assoc. Paul, Weiss, Rifkind, Wharton & Garrison, N.Y.C., 1983-89; asst. U.S. atty. criminal divsn. U.S. Atty.'s Office, So. Dist. N.Y., N.Y.C., 1983-89; ptnr. Kronish Lieb Weiner & Hellman LLP, N.Y.C., 1989—. Federal civil litigation, State civil litigation, Criminal. Office: Kronish Lieb Weiner & Hellman LLP 1114 Ave of Americas New York NY 10036

**BARGER, KATHLEEN CARSON,** lawyer; b. Tacoma, Apr. 15, 1948; d. Ralph Anthony and Bertaleigh (Pyle) C.; m. James V. Barger, Aug. 31, 1968 (div. Aug. 1985); children: Julia L., Jonathan C. BA, Duquesne U., 1968; MA, U. Pitts., 1972; JD, U. N.C., 1976. Bar: N.C. 1976, U.S. Dist. Ct. (mid. dist.) N.C. 1976, U.S. Ct. Appeals 1988. Atty. Western Electric, Greensboro, N.C., 1976-80; atty. AT&T, Basking Ridge, N.J., 1980-84, Washington, 1984-89; atty., ptnr. Thompson & Mitchell, Washington, 1989-92; ptnr. Wickwire Gavin, P.C., Vienna, Va., 1992—; lectr. Fed. Publs., Washington, 1988—, mem. adv. bd., 1988—; mem. adv. bd. BNA-Fed. Contracts Report, Washington, 1990—. Mem. ABA (coun. pub. contract sect. 1989—, chmn. acctg., cost & pricing com. 1986—). Roman Catholic. Avocation: Irish history. Government contracts and claims, Communications, Administrative and regulatory. Home: 905 St Stephens Rd Alexandria VA 22304-1724 Office: Wickwire Gavin PC 8100 Boone Blvd Ste 700 Vienna VA 22182-7732

**BARIL, LYNDA KATHERINE,** lawyer; b. Billings, Mont., Jan. 3, 1948; d. Armond and Mary Ann (Green) B.; m. Robert R. Garrison, June 4, 1988. MBA, Univ. Puget Social, 1974; JD, Am. Univ., 1984. Investigator Federal Trade Commn., Seattle, 1979-84; dir. Northwest Water Resources, Seattle, 1984-87; water quality agent Washington State Univ., Port Townsend, 1990-93, dir. cmty. learning ctr., 1993—. Home: 201 W Patison St Port Hadlock WA 98339-9751

**BARKEN, BERNARD ALLEN,** lawyer; b. St. Louis, July 20, 1924; s. Gottlieb and Hattie E. (Rubin) B.; m. Jocelyn Moss Kopman, Sept. 1, 1948; children: Thomas L., Dale Susan. JD, Washington U., 1947. Bar: Mo. 1947, U.S. Dist. Ct. (ea. dist.) Mo. 1947, U.S. Ct. Appeals (8th cir.) 1954, U.S. Tax Ct. 1966, U.S. Ct. Appeals 2nd cir.) 1985, U.S. Supreme Ct. 1984. Sole practice St. Louis, 1947-80; ptnr. Shifrin & Treiman, St. Louis, 1980-88; pres. Bernard A. Barken, St. Louis, 1988-91; ptnr. Barken & Bakewell L.L.P., St. Louis, 1991—. With USAAF, 1943-44. Mem. ABA, Bar Assn. Met. St. Louis (v.p. 1958, chmn. young lawyers 1953). Jewish. Avocations: piano, tennis, gardening. General practice, General corporate, General civil litigation. Home: 30 Vouga Ln Saint Louis MO 63131-2628 Office: Barken & Bakewell LLP 500 N Broadway Ste 2000 Saint Louis MO 63102-2130

**BARKER, APRIL ROCKSTEAD,** lawyer; b. Harlingen, Tex., Apr. 22, 1969; d. Roger Gerald and Maxine Ann (McCarthy) Rockstead; m. David M. Barker, Aug. 5, 1995. BA in Journalism, U. Wis., 1990; JD, Harvard U., 1995. Bar: Ill. 1995, Wis. 1996, U.S. Dist. Ct. (no. dist.) Ill. 1995, U.S. Dist. Ct. (ea. and we. dist.) Wis. 1996. Assoc. Jenner & Block, Chgo., 1995-96, Liebmann, Conway, Olejniczak & Jerry S.C., Green Bay, Wis., 1996—; vice chair State of Wis. Com. on the Participation of Women in the Bar, 1999—; mem. media law rels. com. State Bar Wis., 1999—; mem. Cmty. Cooordinated Care, Green Bay, 1997-99. Mem. adv. bd. Bay Bus. Jour., Green Bay, 1997-98. Mem. Leadership Green Bay Class 1998, 1997-98. Mem. ABA, Wis. Bar Assn., Ill. Bar Assn., Chgo. Bar Assn., Phi Beta Kappa. Roman Catholic. Avocations: music, literature. Insurance, General civil litigation, Libel. Home: 712 Northern Ave Green Bay WI 54303-3902 Office: Liebmann Conway Olejniczak & Jerry PO Box 23200 Green Bay WI 54305-3200

**BARKER, CHRIS A(LLEN),** lawyer; b. Sheffield, Ala., July 24, 1965; s. Allen Dean and Martha Carol (Weatherby) B. BA magna cum laude in History, Birmingham-So. U., 1987; JD, U. Ala., 1990. Bar: Ala. 1990, U.S. Dist. Ct. (mid. dist.) 1992, U.S. Dist. Ct. (so. dist.) 1991, Fla. 1991, U.S. Dist. Ct. (no. dist.) 1991, U.S. Dist. Ct. (mid. dist.) 1993, U.S. Ct. Appeals 1991. Assoc. Trimmier, Atchison & Hayley, Birmingham, 1990-93; ptnr. Alpert, Barker & Calcutt, P.A., Tampa, 1993—; approved counsel Nat. Ctr. for Auto Safety, Washington. Co-author: Florida Practice Handbook-Workers' Compensation, 1994, 95; asst. author: Flordia Practice Handbook-Damages, 1993; editor-in-chief (legal newspaper) The Column, 1989-90. Mem. Rep. Nat. Com., Washington, 1993—; sponsor Paralyzed Vets. Am., Tampa, 1993—. Mem. ABA, Fla. Bar Assn. (workers' compensation sect. 1994-96, Hillsborough County Bar Assn., Corporate Counsel of Hillsborough County. Republican. Methodist. Avocations: sports, investment and money mgmt., fiction, fgn. langs. (Japanese, Spanish). General civil litigation, Securities, Insurance. Office: Alpert Barker & Calcutt PA 100 S Ashley Dr Ste 2000 Tampa FL 33602-5313

**BARKER, CLAYTON ROBERT, III,** lawyer; b. Statesville, N.C., Aug. 27, 1957; s. Clayton Robert Jr. and Alta Jo Barker; m. Sandra Ann Mills, June 30, 1990. AB with distinction, Stanford U., 1979; postgrad., Tufts. U., 1982; JD, U. Va., 1983. Bar: N.Y. 1984, Ga. 1995. Assoc. Shearman & Sterling, N.Y.C., 1983-85, Skadden, Arps, Slate, Meagher & Flom, N.Y.C., 1985-91; counsel The Coca-Cola Co., Atlanta, 1991—. Contbr. articles to profl. jours. Mem. Am. Coun. on Germany. Mem. Internat. Bar Assn., Am. Soc. Internat. Law, N.Y. State Bar Assn. (internat. law and practice sect., fgn. investment in U.S. bus. com.), Am. Coun. on Germany (young leader 1992), Assn. for Corp. Growth (dir. Atlanta chpt.), Federalist Soc., Omicron Delta Kappa. Republican. Presbyterian. General corporate, Private international, Banking. Office: The Coca-Cola Co 1 Coca Cola Plz NW Atlanta GA 30313-2499

**BARKER, DOUGLAS ALAN,** lawyer; b. Martinsville, Va., Oct. 25, 1957; s. Cecil Ray and Virginia Adeline (Bryant) B.; children: Daryn Ruth, Dylan Victoria. BS, Va. Tech., 1981; MBA, The Citadel, 1988; JD cum laude, Pepperdine U., 1993. Bar: Calif. 1993, U.S. Dist. Ct. (ctrl. dist.) Calif. 1993, S.C. 1996, U.S. Dist. Ct. S.C. 1996. Assoc. Haight, Brown & Bonesteel, Santa Monica, Calif., 1993-96, Young Clement Rivers & Tisdale, Charleston, S.C., 1996-97; individual practice law Charleston, 1997—. Lt. comdr. USN, 1981-87. Decorated Expeditionary medal USN, Beirut, Lebanon, 1983. Mem. ABA, L.A. Bar Assn., Charleston County Bar Assn., Assn. Bus. Trial Lawyers, L.A. JD/MBA Assn., Phi Delta Phi (magister 1992-93). Avocation: military history. General civil litigation, Intellectual property, Trademark and copyright. Home: 1253 Sam Snead Dr Mount Pleasant SC 29466-6923 Office: 3 Broad St Charleston SC 29401-3001

**BARKER, GREGORY KIMBALL,** lawyer; b. Topeka, Oct. 28, 1946; s. Gerald K. and Lois (Billet) B. BA, Kans. U., 1970; JD, Washburn U., 1977. Bar: Kans. 1977, U.S. Ct. Appeals (10th cir.) 1977, U.S. Supreme Ct. 1984. Trust officer Goodland (Kans.) State Bank, 1977-79; assoc. Holbrook & Ellis, Kansas City, Kans., 1979-81; city atty. Junction City, Kans., 1982-88; spl. prosecutor Geary County, Junction City, 1986-88; ptnr. Barker & Collett, Junction City, 1987—; mcpl. judge City of Wichita, Kans., 1997—. Dist. commr. Boy Scouts Am., Junction City, 1985-87; dir. Junction City Little Theater, 1986-87. Maj. Kans. N.G., 1974-92. Mem. Rotary. Republican. Methodist. Office: 455 N Main St Wichita KS 67202-1600

**BARKER, ROBERT OSBORNE (BOB BARKER),** mediator, property management and global marketing consultant, educator; b. Cleve., June 13, 1932; m. Sharon Ann; children: Debra, Stephen Robert, Dawn, Michael, Colleen. Student, Henry Ford C.C., 1950; BA in Comm. Arts and Sci., Mich. Ste U., 1954; postgrad., LaSalle U., 1966-68, U. Wis., 1989, U. Fla., 1996. Lic. cmty. assn. mgr., real estate agent., notary public; registered lobbyist. With pub. rels. dept. Ford Motor Co., Dearborn, Mich., 1953; mgr. Kaiser Aluminum Co., Chgo., 1956-58; advt. mgr. Bastian Blessing Co., Chgo., 1958-59; mgr. Sun Co., Ohio and Detroit, 1959-71, Goodyear Tire & Rubber Co., Detroit, 1971-72; mgr., v.p. NAM, Washington, Boston and Southfield, Mich., 1972-87; pres., CEO Barker Cons. Inc., 1987-96; mgr., v.p. seminars and materials dept. Am. Supplier Inst., 1987-90; nat. mdse. mgr. Costa del Mar Sunglasses, Ormond Beach, Fla., 1990-91; resort mgr. Oceanside 99 Condo, 1992-93, 96—, Outrigger Beach Club, 1994-95; adj. facutly mktg., advtsg., retailing, sales fundamentals, internat. mktg. Daytona Beach C.C., 1994—; owner Dolphin Beach Club Condo, 1981—; ct. and pvt. mediator. Twp. trustee, Findlay, Ohio, 1962; lay min. Episcopal ch., 1960-85, vestry, 1981; mem. St. James Episcopal Ch.; mem. exec. bd. dirs. Volusia County Rep., 1991-99; bd. dirs. Am. Cancer Soc., 1991, chmn. pub. issues, lobbyist; bd. dirs. Dearborn Civic Theatre, 1980-84, Volusia Presdl. forum, 1991-99, Dearborn City Beautiful commr. emeritus, 1970-90; commr. Ormond Beach Quality of Life, Beautification and Planning bd., 1990—; mem.adv. coun. bd. Habitat Humanity; res. police officer, Dearborn, 1968-88; pres. Dearborn High and Lindbergh Elem. PTA; bd. dirs. Bldg. Assn. Mgrs., 1991-95, Cmty. assoc. Inst., 1993-97, Volusia County Pers. Bd., 1991-93; mem. adv. ocun. bd. Coun. of aging; active Fla. Police Benevolent Assn., Fla. Sheriffs Assn., Daytona and Ormond Beach Rep. Club, bd. dirs., 1991-99, Ormond Meml. Art Mus., heritage mem.; amb. Daytona Internat. Airport; team selection scout Fla. Citrus Sports for New Year's Bowl football game, Orlando, Fla., 1997—. Served with USNR, 1949-58, AFROTC, 1951-54. Recipient Vol. of Yr. award Am. Cancer Soc., 1991—. Mem. Meeting Planners Internat., Assn. Execs., Fla. Pub. Rels. Soc. (Volusia chpt., former v.p. bd. dirs.), Am. Legion (life), Mich. State U. Alumni (past. pres.), Mich. State U. S. Alumni Club, Ormond Beach C. of C. (amb., former chmn. pub. rels., Beatification, JazzMatazz, social com.), Ormond Shrine Club (pres. 1994-95), Elks, Exch. Club, Rotary (pres. 1987-88), Masons, Moose-Legion, Shriners (dir. pub. rels. 1984, provost unit, Fez on Wheels and Vets. unit), Jaycees (Findlay, Ohio Spoke award, v.p. Findlay, Ohio 1960-64), Delta Tau Delta. Home: 19 Riverview Dr Ormond Beach FL 32174-7056

**BARKER, RONALD C.,** lawyer; b. Newton, Utah, Sept. 28, 1927; s. Stephen Waldo and Hazel Vilate (Larsen) B.; married Apr. 2, 1952; children: Stephen, Bart, LuAnn, Mitchell, Beth, Sterling, Heather, Dawn, Marshall. BS in Acctg., Utah State U., 1949; JD in Law, U. Utah, 1955. Bar: Utah, U.S. Ct. Appeals (10th cir.), U.S. Supreme Ct. Acct. Jones and Atwood, Ogden, Utah, 1949-50; CPA Burnett & Humphries, Idaho Falls, Idaho, 1950-52; CPA Salt Lake City, 1952—, atty. self employed, 1956—. Lt. U.S. Army Corps Engrs., 1946. LDS. Contracts commercial, General civil litigation, Personal injury. Home: 5655 W 3500 S Salt Lake City UT 84128-2601 Office: 2870 S State St Salt Lake City UT 84115-3692

**BARKER, SARAH EVANS,** judge; b. Mishawaka, Ind., June 10, 1943; d. James McCall and Sarah (Yarbrough) Evans; m. Kenneth R. Barker, Nov. 25, 1972. BS, Ind. U., 1965; JD, Am. U., 1969; LLD (hon.) U. Indpls., 1984; Doctor Pub. Svc. (hon.) Butler U., 1987; LLD (hon.) Marian Coll., 1991; LHD U. Evansville, 1993. Bar: Ind., 1969, U.S. Dist. Ct. (so. dist.) Ind., 1969, U.S. Ct. Appeals (7th cir.), 1973, U.S. Supreme Ct., 1978. Legal asst. to senator U.S. Senate, 1969-71, spl. counsel to minority, govt. ops. com., permanent investigations subcom., 1971-72; dir. rsch., scheduling and advance Senator Percy Re-election Campaign, 1972; asst. U.S. atty. So. Dist. Ind., 1972-76, 1st asst. U.S. atty., 1976-77, U.S. atty., 1981-84; judge U.S. Dist. Ct. (so. dist.) Ind., 1984-94, chief judge, 1994—; assoc., then ptnr. Bose, McKinney & Evans, Indpls., 1977-81; mem. long range planning com. Jud. Conf. U.S., 1991-96, exec. com., 1989-91, standing com. fed. rules of practice and procedure, 1987-91, dist. judge rep., 1988-91; mem. jud. coun. 7th cir. Ct. Appeals, 1988—, jud. fellows commn. U.S. Supreme Ct., 1993-98; jud. adv. com., sentencing commn., 1995-97, bd. advisors, Ind. U., Purdue U., Indpls.; mem. pres.'s cabinet Ind. U.; bd. visitors Ind. U. Sch. of Law, Bloomington. Mem. Ind. Hist. Soc. ; bd. dirs. Clarian Health Ptnrs. Recipient Peck award Wabash Coll., 1989, Touchstone award Girls Club of Greater Indpls., 1989, Leach Centennial 1st Woman award Valparaiso Law Sch., 1993, Most Influential Women award Indpls. Bus. Jour., 1996, Paul Buchanan award of excellence Indpls. Bar Found., 1998; named Ind. Woman of Yr., Women in Comm., 1986, Ind. Univ. Disting. Alumni, 1996. Mem. ABA, Ind. Bar Assn., Indpls. Bar Assn. (Antoinette Dakin Leach award 1993), Fed. Judges Assn., Nat. Assn. Former U.S. Attys., Am. Judicature Soc., Lawyers Club, Kiwanis. Republican. Methodist. Office: US Dist Ct 210 US Courthouse 46 E Ohio St Indianapolis IN 46204-1903*

**BARKER, WILLIAM M.,** state supreme court justice; b. Chattanooga, Sept. 13, 1941; married; 3 children. BS, U. Chatanooga, 1964; JD, U. Cin., 1967. Bar: Tenn. 1967. Pvt. practice, 1967-83, cir. ct. judge, 1983-95; justice Ct. of Appeals, 1995-98, Tenn. Supreme Ct., 1998—; adj. prof. U. Tenn., Chatanooga, 1984—. Chmn. bd. deacons 1st Presbyn. Ch. Chattanooga, 1995-97. With USAMC, 1967-69. Fellow Tenn. Bar Found., Chattanooga Bar Found.; mem. Am. Legion, Alpha Soc., U. Tenn. Chattanooga Alumni Coun., Chattanooga Rotary Club. Office: Tenn Supreme Ct Ste 410 540 McCallie Ave Chattanooga TN 37402-2096*

**BARKER, WILLIAM W.,** lawyer; b. Sacramento, Sept. 20, 1961; s. Wesley Lawton and Mary Jo Deane (Haden) B. AB in English, U. Calif., Berkeley, 1983; JD, U. of the Pacific, Sacramento, 1986, LLM in Bus. and Taxation, 1987. Bar: Calif. 1987, Wash. 1998. Lawyer Graham & James, Sacramento, 1987-89; sr. counsel SEC, Washington, 1989-97; lawyer Graham & James, Seattle, 1997—. Author: SEC Registration of Public Offerings Under the Securities Act Of 1933, 1996. Mem. ABA (subcom. on fed. regulation of securities 1997—, subcom. on pub. co. disclosure practices). Securities. Office: Graham & James 1001 4th Ave Fl Plz44 Seattle WA 98154-1119

**BARKETT, ROSEMARY,** federal judge; b. Ciudad Victoria, Tamaulipas, Mex., Aug. 29, 1939; came to U.S., 1946, naturalized, 1958; BS summa cum laude, Spring Hill Coll., 1967; JD, U. Fla., 1970. Bar: Fla., U.S. Dist. Ct. (so. dist.) Fla., U.S. Ct. Appeals (5th cir.), U.S. Supreme Ct. Pvt. practice West Palm Beach, Fla., 1971-79; judge 15th Jud. Cir. Ct., Palm Beach County, Fla., 1979-84, 4th Dist. Ct. Appeal, West Palm Beach, Fla., 1984-85; assoc. justice Supreme Ct. Fla., Tallahassee, Fla., 1985-92, chief justice, 1992-94; judge U.S. Ct. of Appeals (11th cir.) Fla., Miami, 1994—; mem. faculty U. Nev., Reno, Fla. Jud. Coll. Mem. editorial bd. The Florida Judges Manual. Mem. vis. com. Miami U. Law Sch.; mem. bd. visitors St. Thomas U. Recipient Woman of Achievement award Palm Beach County Commn. on Status of Women, 1985; named to Fla. Women's Hall of Fame, 1986. Fellow Acad. Matrimonial Lawyers; mem. ABA, Fla. Bar Assn. (family law sect., chairperson ct. stats. and workload com. and study commn. on guardianship law, lectr. on matrimonial media and criminal law continuing legal edn.), Palm Beach County Bar Assn., Am. Acad. Matrimonial Lawyers (award 1984), Fla. Assn. Women Lawyers (Palm Beach chpt.), Nat. Assn. Women Judges, Palm Beach Marine Inst. (former chairperson, bd. trustees), Acad. Fla. Trial lawyers (Achievement award 1988), Assn. Trial Lawyers Am. (Achievement award 1986). Office: US Ct of Appeals (11th cir) Fla 99 NE 4th St Rm 1223 Miami FL 33132-2140*

**BARKMAN, JON ALBERT,** lawyer; b. Somerset, Pa., Oct. 8, 1947; s. Blair Albert and Billie (Dietz) B.; m. Annette E. Shaulis, Dec. 1, 1983. BA, Washington and Jefferson U., 1969; JD, Duquesne U., 1975. Bar: Pa. 1975, U.S. Dist. Ct. (we. dist.) Pa. 1975, U.S. Supreme Ct. 1984, U.S. Ct. Appeals (3rd cir.) 1989. Mem. claims dept. Liberty Mut. Ins. Co., Pitts., 1969-71; dist. justice Commonwealth of Pa., Somerset, 1973-93; pvt. practice Somerset, 1975—; pres. Barkman Realty, Inc., Somerset County Settlement and Abstract Co. Inc. Advisor Com. Against Sexual Assault, Somerset, Pa., 1984; Pa. del. Nat. Spl. Ct. Judges Conv., Honolulu, 1989, Atlanta, 1991. Paul Harris fellow, 1989. Mem. ABA, ATLA, Pa. Trial Lawyers Assn., Somerset County Bar Assn. (pres. 1990—), Allegheny County Bar Assn., Elks, Rotary. Republican. Methodist. Home: 388 High St Somerset PA 15501-1301 Office: 116-118 N Center Ave Somerset PA 15501-2027

**BARKOFF, RUPERT MITCHELL,** lawyer; b. New Orleans, May 7, 1948; s. Samuel and Martha (Lewis) B.; m. Susan Joyce Levitt, May 31, 1970; children: Stuart, Jeffrey, Lisa. BA in Econs. with high distinction, U. Mich., 1970, JD magna cum laude, 1973. Bar: Ga. 1973. Assoc. Kilpatrick Stockton LLP, Atlanta, 1973-80, ptnr., 1980—. Contbr. articles to profl. jours. Mem. ABA (bus. law sect., antitrust sect., forum on franchising, panelist ann. forums 1980-92, chmn. 1989-92, assoc. editor Franchise Law Jour. 1981-86), Ga. Bar Assn. (corp. and banking sect.), Atlanta Bar Assn., Phi Beta Kappa. Democrat. Jewish. General corporate, Franchising. Home: 5215 Vernon Springs Trl NW Atlanta GA 30327-4511 Office: Kilpatrick Stockton LLP 1100 Peachtree St NE Ste 2800 Atlanta GA 30309-4501

**BARKSDALE, MICHAEL SCOTT,** lawyer; b. Memphis, June 16, 1952; s. Andrew Lee and Aimee Joy (Shofner) B.; m. Suzanne Croft Southard, Oct. 27, 1979; children: Michael Scott Jr., James Matthew, Andrew Taylor. BA, Vanderbilt U., 1974; JD, U. Ga., 1977. Bar: Ga. 1977, U.S. Dist. Ct. (so., mid. and no. dists.) Ga. 1977, U.S. Ct. Appeals (11th cir.) 1981, U.S. Supreme Ct. 1990. Assoc. Greer, Klosik & Daugherty, Atlanta, 1977-81; assoc., ptnr. Gray, Gilliland & Gold, Atlanta, 1981-86; mng. trial atty. Home Ins. Co., Atlanta, 1986-95; mng. atty. Hartford Ins. Co., 1995—; mem. State Bar Fee Arbitration Panel, Atlanta, 1986-87. Mem. Atlanta Bar Assn., S.E. Claims Exec. Assn., Def. Rsch. Inst., Jaycees (pres. 1986-87, Jaycee of Yr. 1987), Rotary. Methodist. Avocations: tennis, landscaping, travel. Alternative dispute resolution, Insurance, Professional liability. Home: 555 Burridge Trl Alpharetta GA 30022-5211 Office: Barksdale & Assoc 50 Glenlake Pkwy NE Ste 301 Atlanta GA 30328-3489

**BARKSDALE, RHESA HAWKINS,** federal judge; b. Jackson, Miss., Aug. 8, 1944; s. John Woodson Jr. and Mary Bryan (Saunders) B. BS, U.S. Mil. Acad., 1966; JD, U. Miss., 1972. Law clk. to Hon. Byron R. White U.S. Supreme Ct., 1972-73; assoc., then ptnr. Butler, Snow, O'Mara, Stevens & Cannada, Jackson, 1973-90; judge U.S. Ct. Appeals (5th cir.), Jackson,

1990—; instr. U. Miss. Sch. Law, Jackson, 1975-76, Miss. Coll. Sch. Law, Jackson, 1976. Chmn. Miss. Vietnam Vets. Leadership Program, Jackson, 1982-85; del. Rep. Nat. Conv., New Orleans, 1988; elector election of Pres. of U.S., Jackson, 1988. Capt. U.S. Army, 1966-70, Vietnam. Decorated Silver Star, Bronze Star for Valor, Purple Heart; Cross of Gallantry with silver star (Republic of Vietnam). Mem. Am. Inn of Ct. (Charles Clark chpt.), Phi Delta Phi (Nat. Grad. of Yr. 1972). Episcopalian. Office: US Ct Appeals 5th Cir James O Eastland Courthouse 245 E Capitol St Ste 200 Jackson MS 39201-2414*

**BARLEY, JOHN ALVIN,** lawyer; b. Jacksonville, Fla., Oct. 16, 1940; s. Lewis Alvin Barley and Catherine Alberta (Curran) McKendree; m. Mary Freida Szarowicz, Nov. 30, 1974 (div. Dec. 1991); children: Jared Scott, Jessica Lauren; m. Debora Ann Barber Brown, July 11, 1998. BS, Fla. State U., 1963; JD, U. Fla., 1968. Bar: Fla. 1969, U.S. Dist. Ct. (mid. and no. dists.) Fla. 1973, U.S. Ct. Appeals (5th and 11th cirs.) 1973, U.S. Supreme Ct. 1973. Law clk. to judge U.S. Dist. Ct. (so. dist.), Miami, Fla., 1968-69; exec. asst. to Hon. Ray C. Osborne Lt. Gov. Fla., Tallahassee, 1969-70; asst. dir. div. of labor Fla. Dept. Commerce, Tallahassee, 1971; assoc. Maguire, Voorhis & Wells, Orlando, Fla., 1972-73; asst. atty. gen. Dept. of Legal Affairs, Tallahassee, 1974-75; gen. counsel Dept. of Gen. Services, Tallahassee, 1976-78; pvt. practice, Tallahassee, 1978—. Mem. Tallahassee Leon County Architectural Rev. Bd., 1994, 96. Mem. ABA, Fla. Bar Assn. (pub. contract law com., bd. govs. young lawyers div. 1974, rules of civil procedure com. 1974-88, 91-92), Tallahassee Bar Assn., Am. Judicature Soc., Phi Delta Phi. Roman Catholic. Avocations: camping, hunting, fishing, swimming, running. Construction, General civil litigation, Contracts commercial. Home: 4927 Heathe Dr Tallahassee FL 32308-2134 Office: 400 N Meridian St Tallahassee FL 32301-1254 also: PO Box 10166 Tallahassee FL 32302-2166

**BARLIANT, RONALD,** federal judge; b. Chgo., Aug. 25, 1945; s. Lois I. Barliant; children: Claire, Anne. BA in History, Roosevelt U., Chgo., 1966; postgrad., Northwestern U., Chgo., 1966-67; JD, Stanford U., 1969. Bar: Ill. 1969, U.S. Dist. Ct. (no. dist.) Ill., U.S. Ct. Appeals (7th cir.). VISTA vol., staff atty. Cook County Legal Assistance Found., Chgo., 1969-72; assoc. Miller, Shakman, Hamilton and Kurtzon, Chgo., 1972-76, ptnr., 1976-88; judge U.S. Bankruptcy Ct. (no. dist.) Ill., Chgo., 1988—; adj. prof. debtor-creditor rels. John Marshall Law Sch., 1991-92; bd. dirs. Cook County Legal Assistance Found., 1975-82; gen. counsel Chgo. Coun. Lawyers, 1983-86. Mem. Fed. Bar Assn. (bd. dirs. 1992-94), Nat. Conf. Bankruptcy Judges (bd. govs. 1997—). Avocations: opera, theatre, golf, Cubs baseball. Office: US Bankruptcy Ct 219 S Dearborn St Rm 738 Chicago IL 60604-1702

**BARLOW, JOHN ADEN,** lawyer; b. Columbus, Ohio, June 8, 1942; s. William Willard and Eleanore (Johnson) B.; m. Patricia Ann Mowry, Oct. 17, 1970 (div. Aug. 1982); children: William P., Allison J., Jonathan A.; m. Patricia Marion Palmer, Sept. 3, 1982. BSc in Edn., Ohio State U., 1963, JD cum laude, 1968. Bar: Ohio 1969, Wash. 1969, U.S. Dist. Ct. (we. dist.) Wash. 1969, U.S. Dist. Ct. (ea. dist.) Wash. 1992. Assoc. Skeel McKelvey Henke Evenson & Betts, Seattle, 1968-70; ptnr. Walstead Mertsching Husemoen Donaldson & Barlow, Longview, Wash., 1970—; mem. Wash. State Ins. Commr.'s Tort Reform Com., 1987. Contbg. author to 2 books. Named Boss of Yr., Cowlitz County Legal Secs. Assn., 1989. Fellow Am. Coll. Trial Lawyers; mem. Wash. State Trial Lawyers Assn. (bd. dirs. 1981-90, v.p. for west 1989-90), Cowlitz County Bar Assn. (pres. 1974-75), Longview C. of C. (bd. dirs. 1977-80), Kiwanis (pres. Longview 1973). Democrat. Avocations: golf, antiques. Personal injury, Insurance. Home: 1506 23d Ave Longview WA 98632-3616 Office: Walstead Mertsching Husemoen Donaldson & Barlow 1000 12th Ave Ste 2 Longview WA 98632-2500

**BARLOW, W. P., JR.,** lawyer; b. Washington, July 29, 1945; s. W.P. and Elaine Virginia (Zweifel) B.; m. Kathryn L. Prescott, June 13, 1977; children: Ashley Prescott, Matthew Wallace. BA, U. Wis., 1967; JD, Marquette U., 1970. Bar: Wis. 1970, Tex. 1981, U.S. Ct. Appeals (5th, 7th, 11th cirs.) 1971, U.S. Dist. Ct. (ea. and we. dists.) Wis. 1970, U.S. Dist. Ct. (no. and so. dists.) Tex. 1981. Assoc., Ames, Riordan, Crivello & Sullivan, Milw., 1970-74; sr. ptnr. Barlow, Russo & Felker, Milw., 1974-78, Dallas, 1978-83; sr. ptnr. Barlow & Lippe, Dallas, 1983-84; pres. W.P. Barlow Jr., P.C., Dallas, 1984—; chmn. bd. dirs. 1st Savs. & Loan, Burkburnett, Tex.; bd. dirs. 1st Nat. Group, Houston, 1st Nat. Bank, Tom Bean, 1st Nat. Indemnity, 1st Nat. Life Ins., Dallas. Mem. Fellowship of Christian Athletes, Friends Pub. Library, Dallas, 1983—; bd. dirs. Tex. Spl. Olympics, Austin, 1984—. Served to lt. comdr. USN, 1971-74. Recipient Most Disting. Vol. award Tex. Spl. Olympics, 1986. Fellow Sequoyah, Am. Indian Sci. and Engring. Soc.; mem. ABA, Fed. Bar Assn., Assn. Trial Lawyers Am., Tex. Trial Lawyers Assn., Tex. Bar Assn., Dallas Bar Assn., Dallas Trial Lawyers Assn., Houston Bar Assn., Houston Trial Lawyers Assn., Nat. Interfraternity Conf. (bd. dirs. 1985—), Sigma Tau Gamma (dir. 1972-84, pres. 1978-80, Ellsworth C. Dent award 1967), Sigma Tau Gamma Found. (dir., pres. 1984—, Wilson C. Morris award 1982, Marvin M. Millsap award 1983), Delta Theta Phi, Alpha Epsilon Rho. Clubs: Lincoln City, Energy. Legislative, Administrative and regulatory, Banking. Office: 8080 N Central Expressway 13th Floor PO Box 13 Dallas TX 75221-0013

**BARMANN, BERNARD CHARLES, SR.,** lawyer; b. Maryville, Mo., Aug. 5, 1932; s. Charles Anselm and Veronica Rose (Fisher) B.; m. Beatrice Margaret Murphy, Sept. 27, 1965; children: Bernard Charles Jr., Brigit. PhD, Stanford U., 1966; JD, U. San Diego, 1974; MPA, Calif. State U., Bakersfield. Bar: Calif. 1974, U.S. Dist. Ct. (so. dist.) Calif. 1974, U.S. Dist. Ct. (ea. dist.) Calif. 1978, U.S. Ct. Appeals (9th cir.) 1984, U.S. Supreme Ct. Asst. prof. Ohio State U., Columbus, 1966-69, U. Toronto, Ont., Can., 1969-71; dep. county counsel Kern County, Bakersfield, Calif., 1974-85; county counsel Kern County, Bakersfield, 1985—; adj. prof. Calif. State U., Bakersfield, 1986—. Editor: The Bottom Line, 1991-93, contbr. articles to profl. jours. Mem. exec. bd. So. Sierra coun. Boy Scouts Am., Bakersfield, 1986—; bd. dirs. Kern County Acad. Decathlon, Bakersfield, 1988—. Danforth Found. fellow, 1963-65; grantee Fulbright Found., 1963-65. Mem. Calif. Bar Assn. (law practice mgmt. sect. exec. com.), County Counsel Assn. Calif. (bd. dirs. 1990—, chair 1993-94), Rotary. Avocations: golf, skiing, travel, photography. Office: Kern County Office of County Counsel 1115 Truxtun Ave Bakersfield CA 93301-4639

**BARMETTLER, JOSEPH JOHN,** lawyer; b. Omaha, Sept. 10, 1933; s. William Thomas and Dorothy Lucy (Flynn) B.; m. Jeanne Waller, June 21, 1958; children: Joseph Jr., Gregory, Richard, Katie, Peggy Carbullido, Timothy, Michael. BSC, Creighton U., 1956, JD, 1959. Bar: Nebr. 1959, U.S. Dist. Ct. Nebr. 1959, U.S. Ct. Appeals (8th cir.) 1963, U.S. Ct. Claims 1963. Assoc. Fitzgerald, Hamer, Brown & Leahy, Omaha, 1959-64; ptnr. Fitzgerald, Schorr, Barmettler & Brennan, Omaha, 1964—, CEO, 1988—; gen. counsel Metro. Community Coll., Omaha, 1974—, Village of Boys Town, Nebr., 1991—, City of La Vista, Nebr., 1993—. Mem. devel. coun. Omaha Legal Aid Soc., 1989—; pres.'s coun. Creighton U., Omaha, 1990—. Fellow Nebr. Bar Found.; mem. Nebr. Bar Assn. (chmn. ways, means and planning com. 1993-94, ho. of dels. 1986—, chmn. budget and adminstrn. com. 1993-94), Omaha Bar Assn., Omaha Downtown Rotary (dir. 1986-89, Paul Harris fellow). Republican. Avocations: boating, golf, photography. General corporate, Municipal (including bonds), Real property. Office: Fitzgerald Schorr Barmettler & Brennan PC Ste #1100 Woodmen Tower Omaha NE 68102

**BARNA, JAMES FRANCIS,** lawyer; b. Brentwood, N.Y., May 4, 1969; s. Thomas John and Ellen Veronica (Byrne) B.; m. Jennifer Baggett, Aug. 22, 1992; 1 child, Helen Veronica. BA in Multidisciplinary Studies, SUNY, Stony Brook, 1992; JD, Washington U., 1996. Bar: Tenn. 1996, U.S. Dist. Ct. (we. dist.) Tenn. 1998, U.S. Ct. Appeals (6th cir.) 1998. Law clk. Mary Anne Sedey & Assocs., St. Louis, 1994, Stokes & O'Malley, St. Louis, 1995-96; assoc. Ford & Harrison, LLP, Memphis, 1996-98; pvt. practice Memphis, 1998-99; assoc. Weintraub, Stock, Bennett, Grisham & Underwood, Memphis, 1999—. Articles editor Washington U. Jour. Urban and Contemporary Law, 1994-96. Rschr. So. Justice Inst., Durham, N.C., 1992. Sgt. USAR, 1990-93. Mem. ABA, Tenn. Bar Assn., Memphis Bar Assn., Phi Delta Phi. Democrat. Roman Catholic. Avocations: fly fishing, camping, cooking. Labor, General civil litigation, Civil rights. Office: Weintraub Stock Bennett Grisham & Underwood Ste 2560 One Commerce Sq Memphis TN 38103

**BARNABEO, SUSAN PATRICIA,** lawyer; b. Plainfield, N.J., July 27, 1960; d. Austin E. and Patricia F. B. BA magna cum laude, Bucknell U., 1982; JD magna cum laude, U. Mich., 1985. Bar: N.Y. 1986, N.J. 1986. Assoc. Milbank, Tweed, Hadley & McCloy, N.Y.C., 1985-90; assoc. counsel film programming HBO, N.Y.C., 1990-93, sr. counsel film programming, 1993-95; v.p., sr. counsel film programming, 1995—. Mem. ABA, Assn. of Bar of City of N.Y. Entertainment, Intellectual property, General corporate. Office: 1100 Ave Of The Americas New York NY 10036-6712

**BAR-NADAV, MEIRON,** lawyer. Bar: N.J. Sole practice law Hackensack, N.J., 1987—; assoc. McCarter & English, Newark, 1987-96; in-house counsel Bergen Med. Imaging, L.L.C., Paramus, N.J., 1996—; admissions advisor Fairleigh Dickinson U., Teaneck, N.J., 1998; legal cons., editor View Point mag. Mem. ATLA, N.J. Bar Assn., Bergen County Bar Assn., Nat. Assn. Criminal Def. Lawyers, ABA. Republican. Avocations: scuba, rock climbing. General practice, Health, Personal injury. Office: Bergen Med Imaging LLC 84 Main St Hackensack NJ 07601-7132

**BARNARD, ALLEN DONALD,** lawyer; b. Williston, N.D., Feb. 22, 1944; s. Donald J. and Ruth E. (Franklin) B.; m. Andra Lynn Lebsock, Nov. 24, 1962; children: Alana, Aaron. BA in Social Scis., U. N.D., 1965; JD, U. Notre Dame, 1968. Bar: Minn. 1968, U.S. Dist. Ct. Minn. 1968, U.S. Ct. Appeals (8th cir.) 1971, U.S. Supreme Ct. 1973. Assoc. Best & Flanagan, Mpls., 1968-72, ptnr., 1972—, mng. ptnr., 1991-93; city atty. City of Golden Valley, Minn., 1988—, housing and redevel. authority atty., 1978—. Mem. ABA, Hennepin County Bar Assn., Mpls. Athletic Club, Madeline Island Yacht Club (bd. dirs. 1991-97). Avocations: sailing, skiing. General civil litigation, Condemnation, Land use and zoning (including planning). Office: Best & Flanagan 4000 US Bank Pl 601 2nd Ave S Minneapolis MN 55402-4331

**BARNARD, GEOFFREY W.,** judge; b. 1945. Magistrate judge for V.I., U.S. Magistrate Ct., Charlotte Amalie, St. Thomas, 1986—. Office: US Magistrate Ct 345 US Courthouse 5500 Veterans Dr Charlotte Amalie VI 00802-6424*

**BARNARD, GEORGE SMITH,** lawyer, former federal agency official; b. Opelika, Ala.; s. George Smith and Caroline Elizabeth (Dowdell) B.; m. Muriel Elaine Outlaw, July 26, 1945; children: Elizabeth Elaine Barnard Crutcher, Charles Dowling, Beverly Laura Barnard Parker, Andrew Carey. BA, U. Ala., 1948, LLB, 1950. Bar: Fla. 1978, Ala. 1950, U.S. Tax Ct. 1950, U.S. Dist. Ct. Ala. 1950, U.S. Dist. Ct. Fla. 1978, U.S. Dist. Ct. (so. dist. trial bar) Fla. 1995, U.S. Supreme Ct. 1965, U.S. Ct. Claims 1979, U.S. Ct. Appeals (Fed. cir.) 1984, U.S. Ct. Appeals (11th cir.) 1985. Pvt. practice Opelika, 1950-51; with IRS, 1951-78; attache, revenue service rep. Sao Paulo Brazil, 1965-71, Mexico City, 1971-77; ptnr. Barnard, P.A., Miami, Fla., 1978-87; of counsel Barnard, P.A., 1987-91; lectr. taxation U. Ala., 1958-60. Pres. Rocky Ridge Vol. Fire Dept., 1956-58, Rocky Ridge Civic Club, 1959, Ala. chpt. Nat. Assn. Internal Revenue Employees, 1962; commr. Rocky Ridge Civic Water Works, 1960-62; bd. dirs. S.E.Pompano Homeowners Assn., 1996-99. With USAAF, 1942-46. Recipient Albert Gallatin award U.S. Treasury Dept., 1978; named Hon. Citizen of Tex., 1979, Hon. Admiral in Tex. Navy, 1979. Mem. Fgn. Svc. Retirees Assn. of Fla. (advisor/dir. for S.E. Fla. 1987-98, dir. emeritus 1998—, original incumbent historian 1998—), Kappa Sigma. Republican. Personal income taxation, Estate taxation, Private international. Home: 651 SW 6th St VT-912 Pompano Beach FL 33060 Office: Barnard PA 3940 N Andrews Ave Fort Lauderdale FL 33309-5240

**BARNARD, MORTON JOHN,** lawyer; b. Chgo., Mar. 22, 1905; s. Julius and Martha (Wittman) B.; m. Eleanor Spivak, Aug. 16, 1936; 1 child, James W. PhB, U. Chgo., 1926, JD, 1927. Bar: Ill. 1927, U.S. Supreme Ct. 1949, U.S. Ct. Mil. Appeals 1954, U.S. Dist. Ct. (no. dist.) Ill., U.S. Ct. Appeals (7th cir.). Ptnr. Barnard and Barnard, Chgo., 1934-41, 46-84, Foss, Schuman, Drake & Barnard, Chgo., 1985-88; ptnr. Gottlieb & Schwartz, Chgo., 1989-90, of counsel, 1990-93; of counsel Miller, Shakman, Hamilton, Kurtzon & Schlifke, Chgo., 1993-97; adj. prof. John Marshall Law Sch., Chgo., 1947-64; pres. Ill. State Bar Assn., 1971-72; lectr. in field. Author: Contested Estates, 1985, 93; contbr. articles to profl. jours. Life mem. Chgo. Hist. Soc. Lt. col. U.S. Army, 1942-46. Recipient Certs. of Appreciation Ill. State Bar Assn., 1972, Chgo. Bar Assn., 1986, Bd. Govs.' award Ill. State Bar Assn., 1988, Austin Fleming Disting. Svc. award Chgo. Estate Planning Coun., 1993, Addis E. Hull award Ill. Inst. for Continuing Legal Edn., 1996. Fellow Am. Coll. Trust and Estate Counsel (bd. regents 1968-74), Am. Bar Found., Am. Bar Assn. (life), Ill. Bar Found., Chgo. Bar Found.; mem. Union League Club (Chgo.). Republican. Avocations: singing and acting in Bar Assn. Christmas Spirits, 1932-95. Probate, Estate planning, Estate taxation. Home: 228 Woodlawn Ave Winnetka IL 60093-1553

**BARNARD, ROBERT C.,** lawyer; b. 1913; s. Robert C. and Elsie (Francis) B.; m. Helen Hurd, Dec. 25, 1939; children—Robert Christopher, Mary Anne. BA, Reed Coll., 1935; postgrad. Columbia U. Law Sch. 1935-36; BA, Oxford (Eng.) U., 1938, BCL (Rhodes scholar), 1939, MA, 1951. Bar: Wash., 1940, D.C., 1947, U.S. Sup. Ct., 1943. Chief app. sect. antitrust div., chief legal adv. Office of Asst. Solicitor Gen., Dept. Justice, Washington, 1939-47; assoc. Cleary, Gottlieb, Steen & Hamilton, Washington, 1947-49, in charge Paris office, 1949-52, Washington, after 1952, sr. ptnr., 1961-84, counsel, 1984—. Recipient Internat. Achievement award Internat. Soc. for Regulatory Toxicology and Pharmacology, 1995. Mem. ABA, Am. Indsl. Health Coun. (sci. advisor), Fed. Bar Assn., D.C. Bar Assn., Washington Bar Assn. Contbr. articles to profl. jours. Administrative and regulatory, Antitrust, Environmental. Home: 5409 Dorset Ave Chevy Chase MD 20815-6627 Office: 2000 Pennsylvania Ave NW Washington DC 20006-1812

**BARNDOLLAR, LIVIA DEFILIPPIS,** lawyer. Of counsel Marvin and Ferro, New Canaan, Conn. Family and matrimonial. Office: Marvin and Ferro 34 Elm St New Canaan CT 06840-5501

**BARNEBEY, MARK PATRICK,** lawyer; b. Bradenton, Fla., June 30, 1957; s. Kenneth Alan Barnebey and Jane Marie (Wolf) Naumann; m. Marianne Elaine Phillips, Aug. 20, 1983; children: Matthew Patrick, Christopher Conlan. BS in Fin. cum laude, Fla. State U., 1978, MSP in Urban and Regional Planning, 1983, JD with honors, 1983. Bar: Fla. 1983, U.S. Dist. Ct. (mid. dist.) Fla. 1984, U.S. Ct. Appeals (11th cir.) 1984, U.S. Supreme Ct. 1992. Assoc. Harllee, Porges, Hamlin & Brownell, Bradenton, 1983-86; asst. county atty. Manatee County, Bradenton, 1986-87, sr. asst. county atty., 1988-97, chief asst. county atty., 1997-99; shareholder Kirk-Pinkerton, Sarasota, 1999—. Co-author: Development Impact Fees, 1987. Bd. dirs. Manatee River Fair Assn. Recipient Legal Writing award Fla. Bar, Tallahassee, 1992, Outstanding Contbn. to Local Govt. Law award, 1994. Mem. ABA, Am. Planning Assn., Manatee County Bar Assn., Fla. Bar (cochmn. land use seminar 1992-96, mem. environ. and land use sect., exec. coun. city, county and local govt. law sect. 1994—, sec.-treas. 1997-98, chmn.-elect 1998-99, chair 1999—, mem. grievance com. 12B 1996-98, chmn. 1997-98), Fla. Planning and Zoning Assn. (pres. Gulf Coast chpt. 1988-89, 91-92, bd. dirs. 1984—, state conf. dir. 1990-91, v.p. policy affairs 1991-92, pres. 1993-94). Methodist. Avocations: raising children, sports, travel. Land use and zoning (including planning), Municipal (including bonds), Administrative and regulatory. Office: Manatee County Attys Office 1112 Manatee Ave W Bradenton FL 34205-7804

**BARNES, ALISON,** law educator; b. Phila.; d. Russell A. and Edna (Wiegner) Nelson. BA in History, U. Fla., 1978, Cert. in Gerontology, 1982, JD, 1985; diploma in Law, U. Cambridge, Eng., 1992. Dir. Fla. Cmty. Care for Elderly Dist. III Older Ams. Coun. Alachua County, Gainesville, Fla., 1979-83; policy analyst U. Fla. Pub. Policy Project, Gainesville, 1985-89; sr. policy analyst U.S. Senate Spl. Com. on Aging, Washington, 1989-90, George Washington U. Health Policy Project, Washington, 1992-93; asst. prof. Marquette U. Sch. Law, Milw., 1993-95, assoc. prof., 1995—; cons. jud. trainer Ctr. for Health Policy Rsch., Washington, 1994-95; faculty sponsor Habitat for Humanity, Milw., 1993—, Pub. Interest Law Soc., Milw., 1994—, Health Law Soc., Milw., 1994—; founding adv. bd. dirs. Jour. Law, Medicine and Ethics, Milw., 1995; mem. Fla. Ho. of Reps. Ad Hoc Com. on Aging Task Force on Guardianship; lectr. in field. Co-author: Elderlaw, 1992, Counseling Older Clients, 1997; contbr. articles to profl. jours. Bd. dirs. Alachua County Older Ams. Coun., Gainesville, 1986-90, long term care ombudsman, 1985-87; libr. adv. bd. Santa Fe Regional Libr., Gainesville, 1980-83. Recipient grant German Marshall Fund, 1990, grant State Justice Inst., 1989-90, grant Am. Bar Found., 1988. Mem. Soc. for Health and Human Values, Soc. for Law, Medicine and Ethics, Nat. Health Lawyers' Assn., Fla. Bar, U.S. Supreme Ct. Bar, Am. Soc. for Law, Medicine and Ethics, Am. Soc. on Aging, Gerontol. Soc. Am. Office: Marquette Univ Law Sch 1103 W Wisconsin Ave Milwaukee WI 53233-2381

**BARNES, BELINDA SUE,** lawyer; b. Miami, Fla., Oct. 7, 1963; d. Paul G. Barnes and Marilyn (Kinneer) Vore; m. Timothy Preston Jackson, May 22, 1992. BS in Econs., Ohio State U., 1984, JD, 1987. Bar: Ohio 1987. Assoc., ptnr. Enz, Jones & Legrand, Columbus, Ohio, 1987-95, Lane, Alton & Horst, Columbus, Ohio, 1995—. Mem. Ohio State Bar Assn., Columbus Bar Assn. (jud. com., chairperson 1996-97, jud. campaign adv. com.). Republican. Methodist. Avocation: antiquing. State civil litigation, Insurance, Personal injury. Office: Lane Alton & Horst 175 S 3rd St Ste 700 Columbus OH 43215-5100

**BARNES, BRAY B.,** lawyer; b. Jersey City, Dec. 24, 1950; s. Douglass Charles and Lottie Josephine (Bonowicz) B.; m. Patricia Jean Savage, May 21, 1977; children: Brian, Kathleen, Kelly. Grad., N.J. State Police Acad., 1972; AS, Brookdale C.C., 1977; BA summa cum laude, CUNY, 1980; MA, John Jay Coll., 1980; JD, Seton Hall U., 1984. Bar: N.J. 1985, U.S. Dist. Ct. N.J. 1985, U.S. Ct. Appeals (3d cir.) 1986, U.S. Supreme Ct. 1989. Police officer Matawan and Monmouth County Prosecutor's Office, 1972-84; pvt. detective, 1978-85; assoc. Teich, Groh, Frost, Trenton, N.J., 1985-86; assoc, ptnr. Hiering, Dupignac & Barnes, Toms River, N.J., 1986-92; ptnr. Carton Witt, Asbury Park, 1992-93, Picco Mack Herbert, Trenton, 1993-94, Warshaw & Barnes, Red Bank and Toms River, N.J., 1994—; counsel 200 Club, Ocean County, 1990—; adj. prof. Trenton State Coll., 1986-88, Ocean County Coll., Toms River, 1989—. Contbr. articles to profl. jours. Bd. dirs. Boy Scouts Am., Monmouth and Ocean County, N.J., 1985—; trustee, chmn. Diocese of Trenton, Cath. Charities, 1990—; trustee NCCJ, 1994—; trustee Lakewood Prep., 1994—. 1st lt. U.S. Army, 1970-71, 73-78. Recipient Silver Beaver award Boy Scouts Am. Monmouth Coun., 1991. Mem. CBA Alumni Assn. (pres., trustee). Republican. Roman Catholic. Avocation: karate. Bankruptcy, Franchising, Banking. Office: Warshaw & Barnes 10 W Bergen Pl Ste 202 Red Bank NJ 07701-1500

**BARNES, CAROLYN S.,** lawyer; b. Victoria, Tex., Jan. 12, 1957; d. Samuel J. Slone and Sadie Marie Roell Machalec; children: William Zimmer Barnes, Charles Austin Lee Bednorz. BA, Tex. Luth. Coll., Seguin, 1979; JD, U. Tex., 1984. Bar: Tex. 1984. Atty. Fly, Moeller & Seel, Victoria, 1984-86, C.S. Machalec Barnes, Victoria, 1986-92; ptnr. Barnes Bednorz, P.C., Austin, Tex., 1993—. Lutheran. Avocations: camping, travel, gardening. Home: 419 Indian Trail Liberty Hill TX 78642 Office: Barnes Bednorz PC 610 Brazos St Ste 107 Austin TX 78701-3244

**BARNES, DEBORAH BROWERS,** lawyer; b. July 31; d. Clyde Edward and Lucille Ann Browers; m. Ronald Barnes, Aug. 16, 1974; 1 child, Grayson. BA in Journalism, U. Okla., 1976; JD with distinction, Oklahoma City U., 1983. Bar: Okla. 1984. Legal assoc. Crowe & Dunlevy, P.C., Oklahoma City, 1983-85; jud. asst. Supreme Ct. Okla., Oklahoma City, 1985-89; assoc. Stack & Barnes, P.C., Oklahoma City, 1989-91; atty. Transok, Inc., Tulsa, 1991-96, v.p. human resources and adminstrn., 1996-97; corp. sec., assoc. gen. counsel ONEOK, Inc., Tulsa, 1997—. Mem. governing bd. dirs. Jasmine Moran Found., Seminole, Okla., 1997. Mem. ABA, Okla. Bar Assn. (bd. mem. mineral law sect. 1997—), Tulsa County Bar Assn. (chmn., vice chmn. ct. ops. com. 1995-96), Tulsa Bar Assn. (chmn. ct. ops. com. 1996-97), Am. Inns of Ct. Republican. Methodist. Avocations: interior design, boating. General corporate, Securities, Labor. Office: ONEOK Inc 100 W 5th St Tulsa OK 74103

**BARNES, DONALD MICHAEL,** lawyer; b. Hazleton, Pa., June 15, 1943; s. Donald A. and Margaret (Resuta) B.; m. Mary Catherine Gibbons, June 3, 1967; children: Donald M., Stephanie A., Susan E. BS in Indsl. Engring., Pa. State U., 1965; JD cum laude, George Washington U., 1970. Bar: D.C. 1970, U.S. Dist. Ct. D.C. 1970, U.S. Ct. Appeals (D.C. cir.) 1970, U.S. Ct. Appeals (5th cir.) 1975, U.S. Ct. Appeals (4th cir.) 1980, U.S. Ct. Appeals (8th cir.) 1981, U.S. Ct. Appeals (6th cir.) 1993, U.S. Supreme Ct. 1975. Assoc. Arent, Fox, Kintner, Plotkin & Kahn, Washington, 1970-78; ptnr. Arent, Fox, Kintner, Plotkin & Kahn, 1978-97; mng. shareholder Jenkens & Gilchrist, Washington, 1997—. Notes editor George Washington Law Rev., 1969-70. Mem. ABA (criminial justice, antitrust, litigation and adminstrv. law sects.), Fed. Bar Assn., D.C. Bar Assn., Order of Coif, Phi Delta Phi. Antitrust, Federal civil litigation, Administrative and regulatory. Office: Jenkens & Gilchrist 1919 Pennsylvania Ave NW Washington DC 20006-3404

**BARNES, HARRY F.,** federal judge; b. 1932. Student, Vanderbilt U., 1950-52; BS, U.S. Naval Academy, 1956; LLB, U. Ark., 1964. With Pryor & Barnes, Camden, Ark., 1964-66, Barnes & Roberts, Camden, 1966-68, Gaughan, Laney, Barnes & Roberts, Camden, 1968-78, Gaughan, Laney & Barnes, Camden, 1978-82; mcpl. judge Camden and Ouachita Counties, 1975-82; circuit judge 13th jud. dist. State of Ark., 1982-93; judge U.S. Dist. Ct. (we. dist.) Ark., 1993—; mem. Ark. Jud. Discipline and Disability Commn. With USMC, 1956-86, col. res. ret. Named Outstanding Trial Judge in Ark., Ark. Trial Lawyers Assn., 1986. Mem. ABA, Ark. Bar Assn., Ark. Jud. Coun. (bd. dirs.). Office: US Dist Ct (we dist) Ark PO Box 1735 El Dorado AR 71731-1735

**BARNES, HERSHELL LOUIS, JR.,** lawyer; b. Dublin, Tex., June 4, 1943; s. Hershell Louis and Dell (Walker) B.; m. Gayle Pierson, Oct. 17, 1970; children—Hershell Louis III, Jessica Lynn. B.B.A. with honors, Tex. Tech U., 1967, J.D. with honors, 1970. Bar: Tex. 1970. Assoc. Proctor & Jones, Austin, Tex., 1970-71; ptnr. Seay, Gwinn, Crawford, Mebus & Blakeney, Dallas, 1971-82, Haynes & Boone, Dallas, 1982—; lectr. Tex. Assn. Bus., Council on Edn. in Mgmt., Tex. Assn. Risk Mgmt. Trustee Tex. Tech Law Sch. Found. Served to capt. Tex. Army N.G., 1969-74. Mem. ABA (practice and procedure sect., labor law sect., individual rights sect.), Fed. Bar Assn. (labor law sect.), Dallas County Bar Assn., State Bar Tex. (labor law sect.), Tex. Tech Law Sch. Alumni Assn. (pres. 1982), Beta Gamma Sigma, Phi Kappa Phi, Sigma Iota Epsilon. Republican. Methodist. Clubs: Texas, LAncers, Red Raider, Royal Oaks Country. Note editor Tex. Tech Law Rev., 1969-70. Labor. Home: 8380 County Road 130 Celina TX 75009-2966 Office: Haynes & Boone 3200 International Plz Dallas TX 75202

**BARNES, JAMES JEROME,** lawyer; b. Trenton, N.J., Nov. 16, 1961; s. James Edward and Sarah Ann (Shuman) B.; m. Elizabeth Johnson, Aug. 1988; children: Sarah, Jerome, Justin. BA, Dartmouth Coll., 1984; JD, Howard U., 1988. Bar: Pa., U.S. Dist. Ct. (we. dist.) Pa. Ptnr. Buchanan Ingersoll, P.C., Pitts., 1988—. Trustee Carnegie Libr. Pitts., 1994—; bd. dirs. Friends of the Carnegie, Pitts., 1994—, ARC Allegheny, Pitts., 1994—, Womanspace East, 1993—, Neighborhood Housing Svcs., Inc., 1995—. Fellow Am. Bar Found.; mem. ABA, Nat. Bar Assn., Pa. Bar Assn. (mem. judiciary com. 1994, comm. adv. 1994), Nat. Assn. Stock Plan Profls. (charter), Homer S. Brown Law Assn. Securities, General corporate, Finance. Home: 320 Richland Ln Pittsburgh PA 15208-2731 Office: Buchanan Ingersoll PC One Oxford Ctr 20th Fl Pittsburgh PA 15219

**BARNES, JENNIFER REON,** lawyer; b. Colorado Springs, Colo., May 18, 1956; d. Duane E. and Barbra (Harvey) B. BS, U. Wis., LaCrosse, 1978; JD, Ariz. State U., 1987. Bar: Ariz. 1987, U.S. Dist. Ct. Ariz. 1987. Lawyer Treon, Strick, Lucia & Aquirre, Phoenix, 1987-97; pvt. practice Jennifer R. Barnes, P.C., Phoenix, 1997—; adj. prof. Ariz. State U. Coll. Law, 1997-98. Mem. Ariz. Trial Lawyers Assn. (seminar com. 1995—, legis. com. 1996—, co-chair legis. com. 1998—, bd. dirs. 1997—). Democrat. Avocations: sculpture, opera, theater, golf, music, skiing. Personal injury, Product liability, General civil litigation. Home: 102 W Alameda Dr Tempe AZ 85282-3506

**BARNES, MARY ANN,** lawyer; b. Glens Falls, N.Y., Nov. 3, 1961; d. Roy H. Barnes and Mary E. Gregory; m. Russell Warren Potter, Dec. 7, 1990. BA, James Madison U., 1983; JD, Del. Law Sch. Bar: Va. 1989, Del. 1989, D.C. 1997. Assoc. Chandler, Franklin & O'Bryan, Charlottesville, Va., 1988-97, jr. ptnr., 1997—; chmn. Mercy House Com., Harrisburg, Va., 1996-97. Mem. Va. Trail Lawyers Assn., Am. Trial Lawyers Assn., Va. Womens Attys. Assn., Harrisonburg Rockingham County Bar Assn. (Pro Bono award 1996), Charlottesville Bar Assn. Democrat. Avocations: downhill skiing, hiking, reading, cooking. Product liability. Office: Chandler Franklin & O'Bryan 2564 Ivy Rd Charlottesville VA 22903-4616

**BARNES, NATASHA LYNN,** lawyer; b. Woodward, Okla., Aug. 24, 1971; d. Lex V. and Bonnie A. Barnes. BS, Okla. State U., 1993; JD, U. Okla., 1996. Bar: Tex. 1996. Atty. Thornton, Summers, Biechlin, Dunham and Brown, Austin, Tex., 1996—. Mem. Austin Young Lawyer's Assn., Travis County Bar Assn. Fax: 512-327-4694. Insurance, Personal injury. Office: Thornton Summers Biechlin et al Ste C-100 916 S Capital Texas Hwy Austin TX 78746

**BARNES, ROBERT BRYAN,** lawyer; b. Birmingham, Ala., Aug. 20, 1960; s. Robert Carson Jr. and Judith Brown B.; m. Janet Elizabeth Wood, July 11, 1987; children: Robert, Carson, Jennifer. BA, Furman U., 1982; JD, U. S.C., 1986. Bar: S.C. 1986, U.S. Dist. S.C. 1987, U.S. Ct. Appeals 1987. Law clk. Hon. James E. Moore, Greenwood, S.C., 1986, Hon. Joe F. Anderson, Greenville, S.C., 1987; assoc. Tompkins, McMaster & Thomas, Columbia, S.C., 1987-88; assoc. Rogers, Townsend & Thomas (and predecessors), Columbia, 1988-94, shareholder, 1994—. Columnist Mechanic's Lien Bull., 1993; contbr.: (chpt.) Credit Manager's Survival Kit. Active First Bapt. Ch., Columbia. Mem. ABA, S.C. Bar, Richland County Bar Assn., Phi Beta Kappa. Avocation: licensed private pilot. Construction, Federal civil litigation. Office: Rogers Townsend & Thomas PO Box 100200 1441 Main St Columbia SC 29202-3200

**BARNES, SUSAN ELIZABETH,** lawyer; b. Mt. Carmel, Ill., Sept. 25, 1955; d. Allen Dean and Audrey Leola Dorris; m. Thomas B. Barnes; 1 child, Nicholas Allen. BA in English and Humanities, Case Western Res. U., 1978; JD, U. Tulsa, 1982. Bar: Fla. 1987, U.S. Dist. Ct. (mid. dist.) Fla. 1990. Asst. pub. defender (9th cir.), Orlando, Fla., 1987-95; pvt. practice Orlando, 1995—. Mem. Fla. Assn. Criminal Def. Lawyers, Ctrl. Fla. Criminal Def. Atty. Assn., Fla. Assn. Women Lawyers, Orange County Bar Assn. Criminal. Office: 1 S Orange Ave Ste 304 Orlando FL 32801-2625

**BARNES, THOMAS ARTHUR, JR.,** lawyer; b. Los Angeles, Jan. 4, 1949; s. Thomas Arthur and Katherine Marian (Gillman) B.; m. Mary Therese Grant, Aug. 10, 1974; children: Grant Thomas, Hope Ellen. B.A., U. Colo., 1971; J.D., Ohio Northern U., 1974. Bar: Colo. 1975, U.S. Dist. Ct. Colo. 1975, U.S. Ct. Appeals (10th cir.) 1981, U.S. Supreme Ct. 1980. Atty., VISTA, Denver, 1976-77; dep. dist. atty. Dist. Atty.'s Office, Colorado Springs, Colo., 1977-81; sole practice, Colorado Springs, 1981—; instr. criminal justice Pikes Peak Community Coll., 1978; juvenile ct. magistrate, 1990; instr. Denver Paralegal Inst., 1994—. Mem. Gov.'s Juvenile Justice Council, Denver, 1976-80, Colorado Springs Human Rels. Commn., 1991-97; organizer Shape-Up Prison Visitation Program, Canon City, Colo., 1980-81; advisor Minority Council for Arts, 1983-85. Recipient Commendation award Colo. Gov., 1980. Mem. Colo. Bar Assn., El Paso County Bar Assn., Colo. Trial Lawyers Assn., Inn of Ct. Democrat. Personal injury, Criminal, Juvenile. Office: 431 South Cascade Ave Colorado Springs CO 80903-3805

**BARNES, TOM R., II,** lawyer; b. Hays, Kans., Feb. 1, 1963; s. Tom R. and Mary C. Barnes; m. Barbara A. Robbins, Aug. 5, 1989 (div. Apr. 1998); children: Joshua A., Joy C., Jared T. BA, Ft. Hays State U., Hays, 1985; JD, Washburn U., 1988. Bar: Kans. 1988, U.S. Dist. Ct. Kans. 1988. Sole practitioner Hays, 1988; assoc. atty. Clinkscales & Clinkscales, Hays, 1988-89, Stumbo, Hanson & Hendricks LLP, Topeka, 1989—; asst. city atty. Perry, Lecompton, Auburn and Silver Lake, Kans., 1989—; city atty. Harveyville, Kans., 1999—; mem. Topeka Areawide Bankruptcy Coun., 1997-98. Mem. Kans. Bar Assn., Topeka Bar Assn. Republican. Roman Catholic. Bankruptcy, Probate, Real property. Office: Stumbo Hanson & Hendricks 2887 SW Macvicar Ave Topeka KS 66611-1704

**BARNES, WILLIE R.,** lawyer; b. Dallas, Dec. 9, 1931; M. Barbara Ann Bailey; children: Michael, Sandra, Traci, Wendi, Brandi. BA, UCLA, 1953, JD, 1959. Bar: Calif. 1960, U.S. Dist. Ct. (cen. dist.) Calif. 1960. Various atty. positions Calif. Dept. of Corps., L.A., 1960-70, asst. commr. of corps., 1970-75, commr. of corps., 1975-79; ptnr., chmn. corp. dept. Manatt, Phelps, Rothenberg & Phillips, L.A., 1979-88; ptnr. Wyman, Bautzer, Kuchel & Silbert, L.A., 1989-91, Katten Muchin Zavis & Weitzman, L.A., 1991-92, Musick, Peeler & Garrett, L.A., 1992—; chmn. svc. plan com. Knox-Keene Health Care, 1976-79; mem. securities regulatory reform com. State of Calif., 1979-81; mem. shareholders rights and securities transactions Calif. Senate Commn. on Corp. Governances, 1986—; chmn. Leveraged Real Estate Task Force, Inst. Cert. Planners, 1985-86; gen. counsel UCLA Alumni Assn., 1982-86. Co-mng. editor: Calif. Bus. Law Reporter, 1982-83. With U.S. Army , 1954-56. Named Law Alumnus of Year UCLA, 1976; recipient Resolution of Commendation Calif. Senate, 1979, Calif. Assembly, 1979. Mem. ABA (fed. regulation of securities and state regulation of securities coms., franchise forum, futures regulation com.), State Bar Calif. (bus. law sect. 1979, exec. com. 1983-86, vice chmn. 1985-86, com. on corps. 1982-83, ad hoc com. on corp. governance and takeovers 1986-88), Beverly Bar Assn. (corp. and comml. law sect.) Century City Bar Assns., L.A. Bar Assn., M.W. Securities Commrs. Assn., N.Am. Securities Assn., Ind. Commn. on L.A. Police Dept. Democrat. Avocations: tennis, basketball, photography. General corporate, Franchising, Securities. Office: Musick Peeler & Garrett One Wilshire Blvd Ste 2000 Los Angeles CA 90017

**BARNES-BROWN, PETER NEWTON,** lawyer; b. Rutland, Vt., Aug. 22, 1948; s. Rufus Enoch and Julia Pottwin (Morgan) Brown; m. Susan Linda Barnes, Aug. 11, 1974; children: Diana Morgan, David Alexander, Julia Elizabeth. AB, Brown U., 1970; JD, U. Pa., 1976. Bar: Ga. 1978, N.Y. 1979, Mass. 1985. Law clk. Assoc. Justice Alfred H. Joslin R.I. Supreme Ct., Providence, 1977-78; assoc. Olwine, Connelly, Chase, O'Donnell & Weyher, N.Y.C., 1978-84, Goodwin, Procter & Hoar, Boston, 1984-86; internat. counsel Cullinet Software, Inc., Westwood, Mass., 1986-89; prin. Van Wert & Zimmer, P.C., Lexington, Mass., 1989-93; co-founder, mem. Morse, Barnes-Brown & Pendleton, P.C., Waltham, Mass., 1993—; dir., clk. New England-Latin Am. Bus. Council, Inc., Boston, 1992—. Contbr. articles to profl. jours. Mem. ABA, Mass. Bar Assn., N.Y. State Bar Assn., State Bar Ga., Boston Bar Assn. General corporate, Private international, Computer. Office: Morse Barnes-Brown & Pendleton PC Reservoir Place 1601 Trapelo Rd Waltham MA 02451-7333

**BARNETT, BARRY CRAIG,** lawyer; b. Corsicana, Tex., Jan. 19, 1959; s. Donald Wayne and Patricia (Anderson) B.; married, Aug. 31, 1985; children: Caroline Robbins, James Edward. BA, Yale U., 1981; JD, Harvard U., 1984. Bar: Tex. 1985, U.S. Dist. Ct. (no. dist.) Tex. 1988, U.S. Dist. Ct. (so. dist.) Tex. 1986, U.S. Supreme Ct. 1990. Law clk. Judge Jerre S. Williams U.S. Ct. Appeals (5th cir.), Austin, Tex., 1984-85; from assoc. to ptnr. Susman Godfrey L.L.P., Houston and Dallas, 1985—. Fellow Dallas Bar Found.; mem. ATLA, ABA, Dallas Bar Assn., Houston Bar Assn. Federal civil litigation, State civil litigation. Office: Susman Godfrey LLP 2323 Bryan St Ste 1400 Dallas TX 75201-2663

**BARNETT, EDWARD WILLIAM,** lawyer; b. New Orleans, Jan. 2, 1933; s. Phillip Nelson and Katherine (Wilkinson) B.; m. Margaret Mauk, Apr. 3, 1933; children: Margaret Ann Stern Edward William. B.A., Rice U., 1955; LL.B., U. Tex.-Austin, 1958. Bar: Tex. 1958. Mem. Baker & Botts, Houston, 1958—, mng. ptnr., 1984-98; bd. dirs. Tex. Commerce Bancshares; bd. dirs., chmn. Cen. Houston, Inc., 1989-91. Trustee Rice U., Houston, 1991—, chmn. bd. trustees, 1996—; trustee Baylor Coll. Medicine, St. Luke's Episcopal Health System; life trustee U. Tex. Law Sch. Found.; bd. dirs. Tex. Rsch. League, Tex. Assn. Taxpayers; chmn. Greater Houston Partnership, 1992. Fellow Am. Coll. Trial Lawyers; mem. ABA (chmn. sect. antitrust law 1981-82), State Bar Tex., Houston Bar Assn., Coronado Club (pres. 1989), Houston Country Club, Old Baldy Club. Antitrust, General civil litigation. Office: Baker & Botts 3000 One Shell Plaza Houston TX 77002

**BARNETT, GARY,** lawyer; b. Chgo., Dec. 20, 1955; s. Lawrence Barnett and Deena Mae Goldberg; m. Shirley Y. Moh, May 23, 1986; children: Matthew, James. BS, U. Tulsa, 1978, JD, 1981; LLM, NYU, 1986. Bar: Okla. 1981, N.Y. 1986, Calif. 1989. Legal intern Gordon & Gordon, Claremore, Okla., 1980-81; assoc. Sublett, McCormick, Andrew & Keefer, Tulsa, 1981-82; prin. Barnett & Assocs., Claremore and Tulsa, 1982-85; assoc. Cadwalader, Wickersham & Taft, N.Y.C., 1986-92, ptnr., 1993-95; ptnr. O'Melveny & Myers LLP, N.Y.C., 1995—; chmn. confs. on new devel. in securitization Practising Law Inst., N.Y.C., 1995—. Contbr. articles to profl. jours. Securities, Finance. Office: O'Melveny & Myers LLP 153 E 53rd St Fl 54 New York NY 10022-4611

**BARNETT, HUGH,** lawyer; b. Springfield, Ohio, July 2, 1935; s. Hugh W. Barnett and Dorothy Deaton; m. Roberta Otstat, Aug. 24, 1963; children: Hugh W., Samuel M., Daniel J. AB, Princeton U., 1957; LLB, U. Mich., 1962. Ptnr. Martin, Browne, Hull & Harper, Springfield, 1962—. Trustee Springfield Cmty. Hosp., 1990-96. Lt. USN, 1957-59. Fellow Am. Bar Found.; mem. ABA, Ohio State Bar Assn., Clark County Bar Assn. (pres. 1998-99), Rotary (pres. 1995-96). General corporate, Estate planning. Office: Martin Browne Hull & Harper One S Limestone St 8th fl Springfield OH 45501-0140

**BARNETT, MARK WILLIAM,** state attorney general; b. Sioux Falls, S.D., Sept. 6, 1954; s. Thomas C. and Dorothy Ann (Lievrance) B.; m. Deborah Ann Barnett, July 14, 1979. BS in Govt., U. S.D., 1976, JD, 1978. Bar: S.D. Pvt. practice law Sioux Falls, 1978-80; asst. atty. gen. State of S.D., Pierre, 1980-83, spl. prosecutor, 1984-90, atty. gen., 1990—; ptnr. Schmidt, Schroyer, Colwill and Barnett, Pierre, 1984-90; mem. S.D. Law Enforcement Tng. Commn., 1987—; mem. S.D. Bar Commn., 1986-88, 89-92, S.D. Corrections Commn., 1987. Bd. dirs. D.A.R.E., S.D. drug prevention prog., 1987—. Mem. S.D. Bar Assn. (pres. young lawyers' sect. 1985), Am. Judicature Soc. (nat. bd. dirs. 1984-88), State's Atty. Assn. (bd. dirs. 1987-90). Republican. Avocations: golf, weight lifting, snowmobiling. Office: Office Atty Gen 500 E Capitol Ave Pierre SD 57501-5070*

**BARNETT, MARTHA WALTERS,** lawyer; b. Dade City, Fla., June 1, 1947; d. William Haywood and Helen (Hancock) Walters; m. Richard Rawls Barnett, Jan. 4, 1969; children: Richard Rawls, Sarah Walters. BA cum laude, Tulane U., 1969; JD cum laude, U. Fla., 1973. Bar: Fla. 1973, U.S. Dist. Ct. (mid. and so. dists.) Fla. 1973, U.S. Ct. Appeals (3d, 4th and 11th cirs.) 1975, D.C. 1989. Assoc. Holland & Knight LLP, Tallahassee, Fla., 1973-78, ptnr., 1979—; bd. dirs., v.p. Fla. Lawyers Prepaid Legal Svc. Corp., 1978-80, pres., 1980-82, legis. com., 1983-84, mem. commn. on access to justice, 1984-86, exec. coun. tax sect., 1987-88, exec. coun. pub. interest sect., 1989-91; active Fla. Commn. Ethics, 1984-87, chairperson, 1986-87, Fla. Taxation and Budget Reform Commn., 1989—; Legal adv. bd. Martindale-Hubbell, 1990—; chair Ho. of Dels., 1994-96. Mem. Fla. Coun. Econ. Edn., Fla. Edn. Found.; bd. dirs. Lawyers Com. Civil Rights Under Law. Nominated candidate for pres. elect of the Amer. Bar Assn., 1999—. Fellow Am. Bar Found. (life); mem. ABA (exec. coun. sect. on individual rights and responsibility 1974-86, bd. govs. 1986-89, task force on minorities in profession 1984-86, commn. on women in profession 1987-90, long range planning com. 1988-91, chair bd. govs. fin. com. 1988-89, bd. editors ABA Jour. 1990-94, exec. coun. sect. legal edn. and admission to bar 1990-94, chairperson commn. on pub. understanding about the law 1990-93, pres.-elect 1999—, others), Nat. Inst. Dispute Resolution (sec.-treas. 1988-94, bd. dirs. 1988-94, Gov. appt. Fla. Constitution revision Commn., 1997-98), Am. Law Inst., Fla. Bar Assn. (exec. coun. pub. interest law sect. 1989-91), Tallahassee Bar Assn. Administrative and regulatory, Legislative, State and local taxation. Office: Holland & Knight LLP PO Box 810 Tallahassee FL 32302-0810

**BARNETT, MICHAEL JAMES,** lawyer; b. Greenville, S.C., June 6, 1948; s. James Long and Hester (Dickson) B.; m. Patricia Tyler, Aug. 13, 1972; children: Jennifer Lee, Madison James, Tyler Dickson. BA, Furman U., 1970; JD, U. S.C., 1973. Bar: S.C. 1973, U.S. Dist. Ct. S.C. 1979, U.S. Ct. Appeals (4th cir.) 1980, U.S. Supreme Ct. 1980. Ptnr. McCrackin, Barnett, Richardson & Clemmons, L.L.P., Myrtle Beach, S.C., 1977—; pres. Horry County Bar Assn., Myrtle Beach, 1985-86. Pres. Am. Cancer Soc., Horry County, 1983-84, Myrtle Beach Civitan Club, 1977-79; bd. dirs. United Way Horry County, 1982-89; trustee Furman U., 1990-94, S.C. Found. Ind. Colls., 1990-93, S.C. Bapt. Retirement Homes, 1983-88. 1st lt. U.S. Army, 1973. Mem. ABA, Assn. Trial Lawyers Am., S.C. Bar. Avocations: fishing, golf, hunting. Banking, General civil litigation, Real property. Office: McCrackin Barnett Richardson & Clemmons LLP 1000 21st Ave N Myrtle Beach SC 29577-7415

**BARNETT, ROBERT BRUCE,** lawyer; b. Waukegan, Ill., Aug. 26, 1946; s. Bernard and Betty Jane (Simon) B.; m. Rita Lynn Braver, Apr. 10, 1972; 1 child, Meredith Jane. BA, U. Wis., 1968; JD, U. Chgo., 1971. Bar: D.C. 1971. Law clk. to Hon. John Minor Wisdom U.S. Ct. Appeals (5th cir.), 1971-72; law clk. to assoc. justice Byron R. White U.S. Supreme Ct., Washington, 1972-73; legis. asst. Sen. Walter F. Mondale, Washington, 1973-75; assoc. Williams & Connolly, Washington, 1975-78, ptnr., 1979—; adj. prof. Georgetown Law Sch., 1973-80. Bd. trustees John F. Kennedy Ctr. for Performing Arts, 1994—; bd. visitors Sanford Inst. of Pub. Policy, Duke U., 1998—. Democrat. Entertainment, General civil litigation, General corporate. Office: Williams & Connolly 725 12th St NW Washington DC 20005-5901

**BARNETT, ROBERT GLENN,** lawyer; b. Oxford, Miss., July 30, 1933; s. Arden and Vera (Turner) B.; m. Rae Ragsdale, Apr. 21, 1962; children: Laura Lee, Mary Melissa. BA, U. Miss., 1959, JD, 1961. Ptnr. Houston & Barnett, Southaven, Miss., 1961-63, Neal, Houston, Elliott & Barnett, Jackson, Miss., 1963-65, Barnett & Barnett, Jackson, Miss., 1965-70; legal counsel Deposit Guaranty Nat. Bank, Jackson, 1970-79, gen. counsel, sec. to bd., 1979-95; counsel Butler, Snow, O'Mara, Stevens and Cannada, Jackson, 1996—; vis. prof. U. Miss. Law Sch., Oxford, Miss., 1978-79, 85; banking law course coord., lectr. Sch. Banking of the South, Baton Rouge, 1978-79. Pres. Family Services Assn., Jackson, 1970-71; bd. dirs. Community Services Assn., 1968-70; bd. govs. Jackson Symphony Orch. Assn., 1981-85. Lt. (j.g.) USNR, 1954-58; capt. USNR, 1979. Fellow Young Lawyers of Miss. Bar (pres. 1995-96); mem. ABA (banking law com. 1982—), Miss. Bar Assn. (2d v.p. 1968-69), Jackson Legal Aid Bd. Trustees (pres. 1965-67), Miss. Bankers Assn. (chmn. bank lawyers com.), Miss. Jr. Bar Assn. (pres. 1967-68), Miss. Corp. Counsel Assn. (pres. 1988), So. Conf. Bank House Counsel (chmn. 1989), Lions (pres. North Jackson chpt. 1967-68), River Hills Tennis Club (dir. 1979-82, Patrick Farm Golf Club, Whisper Lake Golf Club. Baptist. Banking. Office: Butler Snow O'Mara Stevens and Cannada PO Box 22567 Jackson MS 39225-2567

**BARNETT, STEPHANIE BLAIR,** lawyer; b. Ft. Wainwright, Alaska, July 17, 1961; d. Paul Wayne Barnett and Sharon Barnett McCann. BA, Southwest Tex. State U., 1983; JD, U. Houston, 1989. Bar: Tex. 1989, U.S. Dist. Ct. (so. dist.) Tex. 1990. Clk., assoc. Law Offices of Oscar Nipper, Houston, 1987-90; intern Harris County Dist. Atty.'s Office, Houston, 1988; assoc. Law Office of Wilbur H. (Pete) Dunten, Dickinson, Tex., 1990-93; pvt. practice Houston and Galveston, 1993—. Mem. Galveston County Bar Assn., Houston Assn. Debtors Attys., Galveston County Criminal Def. Lawyers, San Leon-Bacliff-Bayview C. of C. (chmn. 4th July), Lions. Republican. Avocations: church choir, dogs, host/mentor/tutor, antiques, gardening. Bankruptcy, Criminal, General civil litigation. Home: 4728 W Bayshore Dr Bacliff TX 77518-1424 Office: 17300 El Camino Real Ste 110 Houston TX 77058-2744

**BARNETT, WILLIAM A.,** lawyer; b. Chgo., Oct. 13, 1916; s. Leo James and Anita (Olsen) B.; m. Evelyn Yates, June 23, 1945 (dec. Nov. 4, 1988); children: William, Mary Leone, Therese, Kathleen. LLB, Loyola U., Chgo., 1941. Admitted to Ill. bar, 1941. With IRS, 1948-54; atty. chief counsel's office Chgo., 1948-52; dist. counsel penal div. Detroit, 1952-54; chief tax atty. U.S. Atty's Office, Chgo., 1955-60; practitioner before the 6th Circuit Ct. Appeals, since 1954; practitioner 7th Circuit Ct. Appeals, 1955—, U.S. Supreme Ct., 1959—; lawyer; b. Chgo., Oct. 13, 1916; s. Leo James and Anita (Olsen) B.; LL.B., Loyola U., Chgo., 1941; m. Evelyn Yates, June 23, 1945 (dec. Nov. 4, 1988); children: William, Mary Leone, Therese, Kathleen. Admitted to Ill. bar, 1941; with IRS, 1948-54, atty. chief counsel's office, Chgo., 1948-52, dist. counsel penal div., Detroit, 1952-54; chief tax atty. U.S. Atty's Office, Chgo., 1955-60; practitioner before the 6th Circuit Court of Appeals, since 1954, 7th Circuit Ct. Appeals, 1955—, U.S. Supreme Ct., 1959—. Fellow Internat. Acad. Trial Lawyers; mem. ABA, Fed. Bar Assn., Ill. Bar Assn., Nat. Assn. Criminal Def. Lawyers, Ill. Trial Lawyers Assn. Fellow Internat. Acad. Trial Lawyers; mem. ABA, Fed. Bar Assn., Ill. Bar Assn. Criminal, Federal civil litigation, Taxation, general. Home: 1448 W Norwood St Chicago IL 60660-2404 Office: 135 S La Salle St Chicago IL 60603-4159

**BARNETT, WILLIAM MICHAEL,** lawyer; b. New Orleans, June 15, 1925; s. Herman Lyon Barnett and Irma Samson; m. Audrey Steinert, Mar. 17, 1954; children: Robert Alan, James Michael. BA, Yale U., 1950; LLB, Tulane U., 1953. Assoc. Guste, Barnett & Redmann, New Orleans, 1953-57; ptnr. Guste, Barnett & Little, New Orleans, 1957-70; mng. ptnr. Guste, Barnett & Colomb, New Orleans, 1970-75, Guste, Barnett & Shushan, New Orleans, 1975—. Pres. Madonna Manor, Jefferson Parish, La., 1964-65, Upper Audubon Assn., New Orleans, 1986-88; trustee Boy Scouts of Am., New Orleans, 1970-75, Pharm. Mus., New Orleans, 1985-93; dir. La. Civil Svc. League, New Orleans, 1985—, La. Landmark Soc., New Orleans, 1963-65, Continental Savs. & Loan Assn., New Orleans, 1971-82, 1st v.p. Cultural Attractions Fund, New Orleans, 1966-68; pres. New Orleans Jr. C. of C., 1960-61; chmn. New Orleans Civil Svc. Commn., City of New Orlans, 1963-75. Sgt. U.S. Army Infantry, 1943-44, ETO. Decorated Bronze star; recipient M.M. Lemann award City of New Orleans, 1982. Mem. La. Bar Assn. (del. ho. of dels. 1961-64), Nat. Assn. Yale Alumni (dir. 1973-75), Yale Alumni Assn. La. (pres. 1968-70), Exeter Acad. Alumni Assn. of La. (pres. 1968-75), Soc. Escargot Orleanais (master chancellor 1990-92), Chevalier de Tastevin. Republican. Unitarian. General civil litigation, Consumer commercial, Probate. Home: 7227 Benjamin St New Orleans LA 70118-3505 Office: Guste Barnett & Shushan 25th Fl 639 Loyola Ave New Orleans LA 70113-3125

**BARNETTE, CURTIS HANDLEY,** steel company executive, lawyer; b. St. Albans, W.Va., Jan. 9, 1935; s. Curtis Franklin and Garnett Drucella (Robinson) B.; m. Loris Joan Harner, Dec. 28, 1957; children: Curtis Kevin, James David. AB with High Honors, W.Va. U., 1956; postgrad. (Fulbright scholar), U. Manchester, 1956-57; J.D., Yale U., 1962; grad. advanced mgmt. program, Harvard U., 1974-75; LLD (hon.), W.Va. U., 1995, Allentown Coll., 1996, U. Charleston, 1998, Lehigh U., 1999. Bar: Conn. 1962, Pa. 1968, D.C. 1988, W.Va. 1990. Atty. Wiggin & Dana, New Haven, Conn., 1962-67; atty. Bethlehem (Pa.) Steel Corp., 1967-92, sec., 1976-92, gen. counsel, 1977-92, sr. v.p., 1985-92, chmn., CEO, 1992—, also bd. dirs., 1986—; lectr. U. Md., 1958-59; law tutor Yale U., 1962-67; chmn., bd. dirs. Am. Iron and Steel Inst., 1997, dir., 1992—; bd. dirs. Met. Life Ins. Co., Owens Corning, Lehigh Valley Partnership; chmn. Internat. Iron and Steel Inst., 1994-95, dir. 1992—. Trustee Lehigh U., 1993—, Pa. Soc., 1993—; mem. Adminstrv. Conf. U.S., 1988-89; dir. W.Va. U. Found., 1982—, chair, 1987-88; mem. adv. com. on Trade Policy and Negotiations, 1989—, Coal Commn., 1990. With U.S. Army Counterintelligence Corps, 1957-59; major USAR, 1959-67. Mem. ABA, Fed. Bar Assn., Pa. Bar Assn., Conn. Bar Assn., Northampton County Bar Assn., D.C. Bar Assn., W.Va. Bar Assn., Assn. Gen. Counsel (pres. 1988-90), Am. Soc. Corp. Secs. (chmn. 1986), Am. Law Inst., Pa. Chamber Bus. and Industry (dir. 1985-93), Bus. Coun., Bus. Roundtable (policy com. 1992—), Pa. Bus. Roundtable (dir. 1986—, chmn. 1994-95, Loblolly Bay and Loblolly Pines, Links, Saucon Valley Country Club, Bet hlehem Club, Blooming Grove Hunting and Fishing Club, Yale Club of N.Y.C., Univ. Club of Washington, Phi Beta Kappa, Beta Theta Pi, Phi Alpha Theta, Phi Delta Phi. Administrative and regulatory, Federal civil litigation, General corporate. Home: 1112 Prospect Ave Bethlehem PA 18018-4914 Office: Bethlehem (Pa) Steel Corp 1170 8th Ave Bethlehem PA 18016-7600

**BARNHARDT, ZEB ELONZO, JR.,** lawyer; b. Winston-Salem, N.C., Dec. 28, 1941; s. Zeb Elonzo and Katie Sue (Taylor) B.; m. Pam Hall; children: Daniel Black, Kathleen Martin. AB, Duke U., 1964; JD, Vanderbilt U., 1969. Bar: N.C. 1969. Assoc. Womble Carlyle Sandridge & Rice, PLLC, Winston-Salem, 1969-75, mem., 1975-97, of counsel, 1997-98; owner, mgr., cons. Barnhardt & Assocs., Inc., Winston-Salem, 1998—; pvt. practice law, Winston-Salem, 1998—. Alumni admissions adv. com. Duke U., 1970-72; bd. dirs. Industries for Blind, Winston-Salem, 1973-85, vice chmn., 1983-84, chmn., 1985; bd. dirs. Goodwill Industries, Winston-Salem, 1973-80; bd. dirs. The Little Theatre, Winston-Salem, 1979-85, asst. treas., 1980, treas., 1981-82, v.p., 1983-84, pres., 1984-85; adv. bd. Salvation Army, Winston-Salem, 1973-85, chmn., 1979-80; bd. dirs. Leadership Winston-Salem, 1984-92, v.p. adminstrn., 1988-89, pres. 1989-90; com. mem. Winston-Salem Found., 1975-84, vice chmn., 1978-80, chmn., 1983-84; trustee High Point U., 1984-96. With USN, 1964-66. Recipient Disting. Service award as Young Man of Yr. Winston-Salem Jaycees, 1974; Disting. Alumni award Duke U., 1979. Mem. ABA (fed. regulation securities laws com., law firms com., com. on law and accounting, bus. law sect.), N.C. Bar Assn. (chmn. securities regulation com. 1985-87, vice chmn. bus. law sect. 1987-89, chmn. bus. law sect. 1989-91, bd. govs. 1991-94, chmn. membership recruitment and retention com. 1997—), Forsyth County Bar Assn., Winston-Salem Jaycees (life, pres. 1973-74), N.C. Jaycees (regional dir. 1974-75, legal counsel 1975-77), Greater Winston-Salem C. of C. (bd. dirs. 1973-74), Forsyth Country Club, Rotary. Democrat. Methodist. Securities, General corporate. Home: 4389 Winterberry Ridge Ct Winston Salem NC 27103-9738 Office: Barnhardt & Assocs Inc 4389 Winterberry Ridge Ct Winston Salem NC 27103-9738

**BARNHART, FORREST GREGORY,** lawyer; b. Alpine, Tex., Sept. 11, 1951; s. F. Neil and Jody (Ogg) B. AB, Vassar Coll., 1973; JD, Cornell U., 1976. Bar: Fla. 1976, U.S. Dist. Ct. (so. dist.) Fla. 1977, U.S. Ct. Appeals (5th and 11th cirs.) 1977; cert. civil trial lawyer. Assoc. Levy, Plisco, Perry, Shapiro, Kneen & Kincade, West Palm Beach, Fla., 1976-78; assoc. Montgomery Searcy & Denney, P.A., West Palm Beach, 1978-81, ptnr., 1981-89; ptnr. Searcy, Denney, Scarola, Barnhart & Shipley, P.A., West Palm Beach, 1989—; lectr. in field; moderator TV show Call the Lawyer, 1983-85; dir. WXEL-TV and FM, Pub. Radio and TV, West Palm Beach. Contbr. chpt. to The Advocates Primer, 1991. Spkr., com. mem. Floridians Against Constnl. Tampering, 1984; mem. Jud. Nominating Commn., 1986-90; trustee Fla. Lawyers Action Group; bd. dirs. 1000 Friends of Fla., Legal Aid Soc. Palm Beach County. Recipient Al J. Cone award; mem. Eagle Hall of Fame, 1991. Fellow ATKA, ABA, FBA (treas. 1983-84, sec., v.p. 1984-85, pres. 1986-87), Fla. Bar, Palm Beach County Bar Assn. (vice chmn. fed. ct. practice com. 1981-82, media law com. 1981-82, bench bar com. 1980-81, chmn. pub. rels. com. 1983-84, TV com. 1984—), Palm Beach Trial Lawyers Assn. (founding dir.), Acad. Fla. Trial Lawyers (sec. 1990-91, treas. 1991-92, pres.-elect 1992-93, pres. 1993—, bd. dirs. 1986-90, chmn., key man legis. com. 1986—, mem. coll. of diplomates, steering counsel continuing edn. com., Eagle Benefactor, Disting. Lectr. in Jurisprudence 1988, sec. 1990-91), Fla. Lawyers Action Group (chair bd. trustees), Cornell Club. General civil litigation, Personal injury, Product liability. Home: 236 Miraflores Dr Palm Beach FL 33480-3618 Office: Searcy Denney Scarola Barnhart & Shipley 2139 Palm Beach Lakes Blvd West Palm Beach FL 33409-6601

**BARNHART, KATHERINE LOUISE,** lawyer; b. Detroit, Mar. 18, 1940; d. Joseph D. and Mae (MacNeill) B.; m. Feliciano Colista, Oct. 31, 1968; children: Gian A. Colista, Celia Diana Colista, Joseph Aaron Colista. BA, U. Mich., 1962; postgrad. in urban planning, Wayne State U., 1969-70, JD, 1976. Bar: Mich. 1976, U.S. Dist. Ct. (ea. dist.) Mich. 1976. Sr. social planner City of Detroit, 1964-67; sole practice Detroit, 1977—. Mem. ABA, Mich. Bar Assn. (past chair family law sect.), Detroit Bar Assn. (past chair family law com.), Women Lawyers Assn. (treas. 1978-80), Am. Acad. Matrimonial Lawyers (chair-elect), Detroit NOW (sec. 1983). Democrat. Family and matrimonial. Office: 36800 Woodward Ave Bloomfield Hills MI 48304-0915

**BARNHILL, DAVID STAN,** lawyer; b. Washington, N.C., May 10, 1949; s. Arthur David and Ida Bea (Cox) B.; m. Katherine C. Felger, July 26, 1975; children: Hannah Katherine, Mary Rachel. BS, Va. Poly. Inst., 1971, MS, 1973; doctoral studies, U. Va., 1976-79; JD magna cum laude, Washington and Lee U., 1983. Bar: Va. 1983, U.S. Ct. Appeals (4th cir.) 1983, U.S. Supreme Ct. 1990, Federal Ct. Claims 1994. Asst. prof. social sci. Va. Intermont Coll., Bristol, Va., 1973-76; soc. sci. researcher U. Va., Charlottesville, Va., 1979-80; assoc. Woods, Rogers & Hazlegrove, Roanoke, Va.,

1983-88, ptnr., 1989—. Author of several profl. articles. Bd. dirs. Total Action Against Poverty, Roanoke, 1987-90, DePaul Children's Svcs., Roanoke, 1985-95, Legal Aid Roanoke Valley, 1990-92. Sgt. USNG, 1972-78. Named Lead Articles Editor Washington & Lee Law Review, 1982-83. Mem. ABA (forum on constrn. industry, civil litigation sect.), Va. State Bar (chmn. 6th dist. ethics com. 1990-91, bd. govs. constrn. law sect. 1991—, chair, 1998, state bar coun. 1995—, state bar disciplinary bd. 1995—, vice chair bench-bar and media rels. com. 1996— ), Va. Bar Assn. (constrn. law coun., civil litigation coun.), Roanoke Bar Assn. (bd. dirs. 1992-94), Va. Assoc. Gen. Contractors (legal affairs and contract documents coms. 1992—), Va. Tech. Alumni Assn., Order of the Coif. Democrat. Baptist. Avocations: middle distance running, writing. General civil litigation, Construction, Communications. Home: 5145 Falcon Ridge Rd Roanoke VA 24014-5720 Office: Woods Rogers & Hazlegrove 10 S Jefferson St Ste 1201 Roanoke VA 24011-1319

**BARNHILL, DONALD EARL,** lawyer; b. Borger, Tex., Apr. 27, 1951; s. C.M. and Dorthy (Taylor) B.; m. Denise A. Westbrook, Nov. 10, 1973; children: Jennifer, Ashley, Catherine. BBA, Tex. Tech U., 1973; JD, St. Mary's Coll., San Antonio, 1978. Bar: Tex. 1979, D.C. 1992, U.S. Dist. Ct. (we. dist.) Tex. 1981, U.S. Ct. Appeals (5th and 11th cirs.) 1981, U.S. Ct. Appeals (fed. cir.) 1989, U.S. Claim Ct. 1985, U.S. Tax Ct. 1981, U.S. Supreme Ct. 1985. Systems engr. EDS, Dallas, 1973-76; asst. dist. atty. Bexar County, San Antonio, 1976; sole practitioner San Antonio, 1973-86; ptnr. East & Barnhill, San Antonio, 1986-98; mng. ptnr. Douglas & Barnhill, P.C., San Antonio, 1998—; spkr. in field. Author: The Federal Competitor (newsletter); author seminar manual. Mem. San Antonio Bar Assn., Bd. of Contracts Bar Assn., U.S. Claims Ct. Bar Assn., U.S. Fed. Cir. Ct. Appeals Bar Assn. Avocations: tennis, golf. Government contracts and claims, General civil litigation, Labor. Office: Douglas & Barnhill PC 8024 Vantage Dr Ste 700 San Antonio TX 78230-4731

**BARNHILL, HENRY GRADY, JR.,** lawyer; b. Buena Vista, Ga., Aug. 24, 1930; s. Henry Grady and Imogene (Hogg) B.; m. Sarah Carolyn Haire, Oct. 29, 1953; children: Grady Michael, Stephen Drew, Kevin Scott, Carol Kelly. JD, Wake Forest U., Winston-Salem, N.C., 1958. Bar: N.C. 1958, U.S. Dist. Ct. (ea., mid. and we. dists.) N.C. 1958, U.S. Ct. Appeals (4th cir.) 1961, U.S. Supreme Ct. 1983, U.S. Ct. Appeals (fed. cir.) 1985. Assoc. Womble Carlyle Sandridge & Rice, Winston-Salem, 1958-61, ptnr., 1961—. Mem. bd. visitors Sch. of Law Wake Forest U. Lt. USAF, 1951-55. Fellow Am. Coll. Trial Lawyers (state chmn. 1986-88); mem. Am. Bd. Trial Advs., N.C. Assn. Def. Attys., N.C. Bar Assn. (litigation sect.), 4th Cir. Jud. Conf., Forsyth County Bar (pres. 1979-80), Inns of Ct. (Chief Justice Joseph Branch). Democrat. Presbyterian. Avocation: tennis. Federal civil litigation, State civil litigation, Product liability. Home: 3121 Robinhood Rd Winston Salem NC 27106-5610 Office: Womble Carlyle Sandridge & Rice PLLC PO Drawer 84 1600 BB&T Financial Ctr Winston Salem NC 27102

**BARNHILL, ROBERT EDWIN, III,** lawyer; b. Lubbock, Tex., Dec. 29, 1956; s. Robert Edwin Jr. and Karen Sue (Green) B.; m. Jana Susan Barnett, Aug. 9, 1980. BBA, Tex. Tech U., 1976, MBA, JD, 1980. Bar: Tex. 1980, U.S. Dist. (no. dist.) Tex. 1980; CPA; personal fin. specialist; CFP. Staff acct. Peat, Marwick & Mitchell, Dallas, 1980-82; assoc. Blackledge Law Offices, Lubbock, 1982-83, Walters and Assocs., Lubbock, 1983-85; sole practice Lubbock, 1985—; instr. Lubbock Christian Coll., 1982-83, So. Plains Coll., Lubbock, 1982-83, Tex. Tech. U., Lubbock, 1986—; sec., treas. Innovative Money Adv. Inc., 1985-94; pres. Live Spkrs., Inc., 1995—. Bd. dirs. So. Plains chpt. ARC, Lubbock, 1984-95, Big Bros./Big Sisters, Lubbock, 1984-95. Mem. ABA (tax sect., real estate, probate, trust), AICPAs, Tex. Bar Assn. (tax sect., real estate, probate, trust), Tex. Soc. CPAs, Internat. Assn. for Fin. Planning (pres. Tex. chpt. 1988-89), Nat. Spkrs. Assn., Toastmasters Club (dist. gov. 1986-87, sr. v.p. 1995-96, internat. pres. 1996-97, accredited spkr.). Republican. Mem. Christian Ch. Personal income taxation, Estate taxation, Probate. Home: 2506 61st St Lubbock TX 79413-5648 Office: PO Box 2583 Lubbock TX 79408-2583

**BARNHOLDT, TERRY JOSEPH, JR.,** lawyer, real estate executive; b. Charlotte, N.C., Nov. 30, 1954; s. Terry Joseph and Martha Frances (Cannon) B. BA, Duke U., 1977; JD, Wake Forest U., 1982. Bar: N.C. 1986. Assoc. Forsyth Legal Assocs., Winston-Salem, N.C., 1986; real estate negotiator JCP Realty, Inc., N.Y.C., 1986-89; sr. asset mgr. N.Y. Life Ins. Co., N.Y.C., 1989-91; v.p., asset mgr. Citicorp Real Estate, Inc., N.Y.C. and Dallas, 1991-95; v.p. lease transactor Citicorp Realty Svcs., 1995—. Recipient Am. Jurisprudence award, 1982; William B. McMannis scholar, 1980-82. Mem. ABA, N.C. Bar Assn., Internat. Coun. Shopping Ctrs., Nat. Retail Mchts. Assn., N.Y. Real Estate Brokers, Urban Land Inst., Internat. Platform Assn., Washington Duke Club, Phi Delta Theta (pres. 1976). Real property, Contracts commercial. Home: 3011 Netherland Ave Bronx NY 10463-3406 Office: Citicorp Corp Realty Svcs One Court Square 8th Fl Long Island City NY 11120

**BARNICK, HELEN,** retired judicial clerk; b. Max, N.D., Mar. 24, 1925; d. John K. and Stacy (Kankovsky) B. BS in Music cum laude, Minot State Coll., 1954; postgrad., Am. Conservatory of Music, Chgo., 1975-76. With Epton, Bohling & Druth, Chgo., 1968-69; sec. Wildman, Harrold, Allen & Dixon, Chgo., 1969-75; part-time assignments for temporary agy. Chgo., 1975-77; sec. Friedman & Koven, Chgo., 1977-78; with Lawrence, Lawrence, Kamin & Saunders, Chgo., 1978-81; sec. Hinshaw, Culbertson et al., Chgo., 1982; sec. to magistrate judge U.S. Dist. Ct. (we. dist.) Wis., Madison, 1985-91; dep. clk., case adminstr. U.S. Bankruptcy Ct. (we. dist.) Wis., Madison, 1992-94; ret., 1994. Mem. chancel choir 1st Bapt. Ch., Mpls.; mem. choir, dir. sr. high choir Moody Ch., Chgo.; mem. chancel choir Fourth Presbyn. Ch., Chgo., Covenant Presbyn. Ch., Madison; dir. chancel choir 1st Bapt. Ch., Minot, N.D.; bd. dirs., sec.-treas. Peppertree at Tamarack Owners Assn., Inc., Wisconsin Dells, Wis.; mem. Festival Choir, Madison. Mem. Christian Bus. and Profl. Women (chmn.), Bus. and Profl. Women Assn., Participatory Learning and Tchg. Orgn., Sigma Sigma Sigma. Home: 7364 Old Sauk Rd Madison WI 53717-1213

**BARNIER, DAVID JOHN,** lawyer; b. San Diego, Mar. 16, 1970; s. John Francis Barnier and Barbara Elizabeth Allen. BS in Psychology, U. Calif., Berkeley, 1992; JD, U. So. Calif., 1995. Bar: Calif. 1995, Nev. 1996, U.S. Dist. Ct. (so. dist.) Calif. 1996, U.S. Ct. Appeals (9th cir.) 1998. Law clk. 2d Jud. Dist. Nev., Reno, 1995-96; assoc. Ault, Deuprey, Jones & Gorman, San Diego, 1996-97, Parnell & Assocs., Las Vegas, Nev., 1997-98, Barker, Thomas & Walters, San Diego, 1998—. Construction, General civil litigation.

**BARNUM, JEANNE SCHUBERT,** lawyer; b. Phila., Aug. 11, 1950; d. Richard George and Mildred Emma (Leh) Schubert; m. Gary C. Barnum, June 21, 1980; children: Matthew, Sarah. AB magna cum laude, Wilson Coll., Chambersburg, Pa., 1972; JD, Dickinson Sch. Law, 1976. Bar: N.J. 1976, U.S. Dist. Ct. N.J. 1976, Pa. 1975, U.S. Dist. Ct. (ea. dist.) Pa. 1975, U.S. Ct. Appeals (3d cir.) 1979. Assoc. Pelino Wasserstrom Chucas & Monteverde, Phila., 1975-77; assoc. Pelino & Lentz, Phila., 1977-83, dir., 1983—; mng. dir. N.J. office Pelino & Lentz, Haddonfield, N.J., 1984—. Elder First Presbyn. Ch., Somerdale, N.J., 1983, 92-95. Davison-Foreman fellow Wilson Coll., 1972. Mem. ABA, Nat. Assn. Women Lawyers (pres. 1990-91, chmn. mid-yr. meeting 1988, 94, exec. bd. 1988-93), Assn. Trial Lawyers Am., Pa. Bar Assn., N.J. Bar Assn. (ADR com. mem. 1990-91), Camden County Bar Assn. (fed. cts. com. 1990—), Phila. Bar Assn., Phi Beta Kappa. Presbyterian. Avocations: golfing, tennis, music, reading. General civil litigation, Contracts commercial, Banking. Office: Pelino & Lentz One Liberty Pl 32nd Fl Philadelphia PA 19103-7393 also: 30 S Haddon Ave Haddonfield NJ 08033-1860

**BARON, MARK,** lawyer; b. Detroit, Mar. 20, 1944; s. Fred and Lucille (Lumberg) B.; m. Charlotte R. Oberin, Oct. 20, 1973 (div. Mar. 1982); children: Jossef D., Miriam; m. Carol Richards, Dec. 15, 1985; stepchildren, Gordon Richards, Bradley Richards. BA, Kalamazoo Coll., 1966; JD, Mich. State U., 1969. Bar: Mich. 1969, U.S. Dist. Ct. (eas. dist.) Mich. 1979, U.S. Ct. Appeals (6th cir.) 1974, U.S. Supreme Ct. 1980, Va. 1983, U.S. Ct. Appeals (4th cir.) 1987, U.S. Dist. Ct. (ea. dist.) Va. 1987. Various legal svc. atty. positions Mich., 1969-74; ptnr. Baron & Ellenbogen, Saginaw, Mich., 1974-85, Loucks & Baron, Saginaw, 1974-85; pvt. practice Saginaw, Richmond, Va., 1988—; staff atty. Va. Dept. for Rights for the Disabled, Richmond, 1985-88; instr. in criminal law Saginaw Valley State Coll., 1979. Contbg. editor newsletter Pers. Policy Solutions, 1994-96; author, pub. newsletter Common Sense Employer, 1987-89. Bd. dirs. Richmond Office Cmty. Corrections, 1996—. Reginald Heber Smith Cmty. Lawyer fellow Howard U. Sch. of Law, 1969-71. Jewish. Avocations: tennis, reading, travel, plays. Labor, Civil rights, Administrative and regulatory. Office: 1523 Edram Forest Dr Richmond VA 23233-4902

**BARONE, GUY T.,** lawyer; b. San Demetrio, Italy, Sept. 9, 1946; Came to the U.S., 1951; s. Victor and Paula (Carosa) B.; m. Mary Susan E., July 11, 1970; children:Juliane E., Benjamin M., Katherine S. BS, U. Dayton, Toledo, 1968; JD, U. Toledo, Ohio, 1972. 'ar: Ohio, U.S. Dist. Ct. Atty. M.L. Okun, Toledo, 1973, Toledo Legal Aid Soc., Toledo, 1973-76; asst. prosecutor Lucas Cty. Prosecutor's Office, Toledo, 1976-78, Frank W. Cubbon, Jr. & Assocs., Co. L.P.A., Toledo, 1978-97; assoc. Barone & Driscoll, Toledo, 1997—; mem. bd. trustees Toledo Legal Aid Soc., 1976-89; mem. grievance com. Toledo Bar Assn., 1994—. Pres. parish coun. St. Piux Ch., Toledo; mem. parent's assn. Ladyfield Sch. Mem. Assn. Trial Lawyers of America, Toledo Bar Assn., Toledo Women's Bar Assn., Toledo Trial Lawyer's Assn., Lucas Cty. Bar Assn., Ohio State Bar Assn., Ohio Acad. Trial Lawyers. Avocations: golf, reading. Personal injury, Product liability, Real property. Home: 4951 Skelly Rd Toledo OH 43623-2740 Office: Law Offices Barone & Driscoll 320 N Michigan St Fl 4 Toledo OH 43624-1632

**BARONE, JOHN A.,** judge; b. N.Y.C., July 31, 1948; s. Guiseppe and Yolanda C. B.; m. Paula Capella, Apr. 20, 1975 (dec. Feb. 1981); m. Rosemary Novella, Oct. 18, 1986; 1 child: Joseph. BA, Fordham U., 1970; JD, Harvard U., 1973. Asst. counsel N.Y.C. Planning Commn., 1974-76; assoc. Blanc & Spielberg, N.Y.C., 1977-79, Moore, Berson, Lifflander & Mewhinney, N.Y.C., 1979-81; law sec. Justice Harold Silverman, Bronx, N.Y., 1982-88; ptnr. Baker, Nelson & Williams, N.Y.C., 1989-92; judge Bronx Criminal Ct., 1992—. Author: A View from the Bronx; contbr. articles to profl. jours. Bd. dirs. Alcoholism Coun. N.Y.C., Bronx YMCA; adv. bd. Congress Italian Am. Orgn., Bklyn. Captain U.S. Army. Recipient Bishop Pernicone, Role Model awards Italian Big Sisters, Bronx, 1992. Mem. N.Y.C. Bar Assn., Bronx County Bar Assn., N.Y. County Lawyers. Roman Catholic. Avocations: playing piano, fishing. Office: Bronx Municipal Court 215 E 161st St Bronx NY 10451-3511

**BARR, CARLOS HARVEY,** lawyer; b. Greeley, Colo., Oct. 12, 1936; s. Charles Allen B. and Zelma Arvilla (Sechler) Turner; m. Martha Lucía Sánchez-Morales, May 10, 1985. BA in Polit. Sci., U. Wash., 1959, MA in Polit. Sci., 1967; JD, George Wash. U., 1971. Bar: Wash. 1971, U.S. Dist. Ct. (ea. dist.) Wash. 1972, U.S. Dist. Ct. (we. dist.) Wash. 1979, U.S. Ct. Appeals (9th cir.) 1973, U.S. Supreme Ct. 1981, U.S. Tax Ct. 1985; cert. Spanish-English interpreter, Wash. Mgmt. intern U.S. Dept of Army, Ft. Lewis, Wash., 1960; joined Fgn. Svc., Dept. State, 1960, officer, 1960-61; vice consul U.S. Consulate Gen., Monterrey, Mex., 1961-64; consular officer, third sec. Am. Embassy, Khartoum, Sudan, 1964-66; analyst Latin Am. Bur., Washington, 1967-68; personnel officer Washington, 1968-70, consular affairs officer, 1970-71, resigned; dir. legal svcs. Community Action Com. OEO, Pasco, Wash., 1971-72; lawyer Spokane (Wash.) County Legal Svc., 1972-73; pvt. practice Kennewick, Wash., 1973-75, Richland, Wash., 1975—. Mem. ABA, ATLA, Wash. Bar Assn., Wash. Trial Lawyers Assn., Fed. Bar Assn., Hispanic Bar Assn. Wash., Inter-Am. Bar Assn., Nat. Hispanic Bar Assn., Acad. Polit. Sci. Avocation: Spanish literature. Product liability, Workers' compensation, Personal injury. Office: 1207 George Washington Way Richland WA 99352-3411

**BARR, CHARLES F.,** lawyer, reinsurance company executive. BA, Boston Coll., 1972; JD, Suffolk U., 1976. Bar: Mass. 1977, Conn. 1993; CPCU. Counsel Comml. Union Ins. Cos., 1977-81; asst. gen. counsel Reliance Ins. Cos., 1981-87; v.p., gen. counsel United Pacific Life Ins. Co., 1984-87, Gen. Accident Ins. Co., 1987-89; asst. gen. counsel Gen. Reins. Corp., Stamford, Conn., 1989-90, v.p., asst. gen. counsel, 1990-94, sr. v.p., gen. counsel, sec., 1994—. Office: Gen Reins Corp 695 Main St Stamford CT 06901-2141

**BARR, CULVER KENT,** lawyer; b. Rochester, N.Y., Jan. 27, 1936; s. Culver Anthony and Clara Kent B.; m. Barbara Allen Burnham Peaslee, July 15, 1957 (div. 1974); children: Julia B. Barr, Kristin K. Hood, Culver A. Barr II, Randolph K. Barr; m. Kathleen Marie Geraghty, May 17, 1981. BA, Syracuse U., 1957; LLB, Union U., 1960, JD, 1968. Bar: N.Y. 1961, U.S. Dist. Ct. (we. dist.) N.Y. 1961, U.S. Supreme Ct. 1964. Atty. Wilson, Trinker & Gilbert, Rochester, 1960-62, Traynor & Skehan, Rochester, 1962-67; judge Rochester City Ct., 1968-72, Monroe County Ct., Rochester, 1973-82; atty. Barr & Conaty, Rochester, 1983—; Bd. dirs. Pre-Trial Svcs. Corp., Rochester, 1995—. Bd. dirs. Friendship Nursery, Inc., Rochester, 1970-76. Recipient Charles F. Crimi award Monroe County Bar Assn., 1993; named youngest Judge elected in Rochester history. Mem. SAR, Humane Soc. (mem. adv. bd. 1972—), Irish Am. Cultural Inst. (patron 1980—). Avocations: traveling, collecting stamps, coins, sports items, political items. Criminal, Real property, Probate. Home: 76 Yarmouth Rd Rochester NY 14610-1943 Office: Barr & Conaty 16 E Main St Rochester NY 14614-1808

**BARR, JAMES HOUSTON, III,** lawyer; b. Louisville, Nov. 2, 1941; s. James Houston Jr. and Elizabeth Hamilton (Pope) B.; m. Sarah Jane Todd, Apr. 16, 1970 (div.); 1 child, Lynn Jamison, m. Cindy Ann Jeffries, May 31, 1997; one child, Worden Washington. Student, U. Va., 1960-63, U. Tenn., 1963-64; BSL, JD, U. Louisville, 1966. Bar: Ky. 1966, U.S. Ct. Appeals (6th cir.) 1969, U.S. Supreme Ct. 1971, U.S. Ct. Mil. Appeals 1978. Law clk. Ky. Ct. Appeals, Frankfort, 1966-67; asst. atty. gen. Ky. Frankfort, 1967-71, 79-82; asst. U.S. atty. U.S. Dept. Justice, Louisville, 1971-79, 83—; 1st asst. U.S. Atty., 1978-79; asst. dir. counsel U.S. Army C.E., Louisville, 1982-83. Lt. comdr. USNR, 1967-81, lt. col. USAR, 1981-91. Mem. Fed. Bar Assn. (pres. Louisville chpt. 1975-76, Younger Fed. Lawyer award 1975), Ky. Bar Assn., Louisville Bar Assn., Soc. Colonial Wars, SAR, Soc. Ky. Pioneers, Pendennis Club, Louisville Boat Club, Filson (Louisville) Club, Delta Upsilon. Republican. Episcopalian. Home: 100 Westwind Rd Louisville KY 40207-1520 Office: US Atty 510 W Broadway Ste 1000 Louisville KY 40202-2281

**BARR, JAMES NORMAN,** federal judge; b. Kewanee, Ill, Oct. 21, 1940; s. James Cecil and Dorothy Evelyn (Dorsey) B.; m. Trilla Anne Reeves, Oct. 31, 1964 (div. 1979); 1 child, James N. Jr.; m. Phyllis L. DeMent, May 30, 1986; children: Renae, Michele. BS, Ill. Wesleyan U., 1962; JD, Ill. Inst. Tech., 1971. Bar: Ill. 1972, Calif. 1977. Assoc. Pretzel, Stouffer, Nolan & Rooney, Chgo., 1974-76; claims counsel Safeco Title Ins. Co., L.A., 1977-78; assoc. Kamph & Jackman, Santa Ana, Calif., 1978-80; lawyer pvt. practice Law Offices of James N. Barr, Santa Ana, 1980-86; judge U.S Bankruptcy Ct. Ctrl. Dist. Calif., Santa Anna, 1987—; adj. prof. Chapman U. Sch. Law, 1996—. Lt. (s.g.) USN, 1962-67, Vietnam. Mem. Fed. Bar Assn. (Orange County chpt. bd. dirs. 1996—), Orange County Bar Assn. (cmty. outreach com.), Nat. Conf. Bankruptcy Judges, Orange County Bankruptcy Forum (bd. dirs. 1989—), Peter M. Elliott Inn Ct. (founder, first pres. 1990-91). Office: US Bankruptcy Ct 411 W 4th St Santa Ana CA 92701-4500

**BARR, JOHN MONTE,** lawyer; b. Mt. Clemens, Mich., Jan. 1, 1935; s. Merle James and Wilhelmina Marie (Monte) B.; student Mexico City Coll., 1955; BA, Mich. State U., 1956; JD, U. Mich., 1959; m. Marlene Joy Bielenberg, Dec. 17, 1954; children: John Monte, Karl Alexander, Elizabeth Marie. Admitted to Mich. bar, 1959, since practiced in Ypsilanti; mem. Ellis B. Freatman, Jr., 1959-61; ptnr., chief trial atty. Freatman, Barr, Anhut & Moir and predecessor firm, 1961-63; pres. Barr, Anhut, Assoc. PC, 1963-94; pres. Barr, Anhut & Assocs., 1994—; city atty. City of Ypsilanti, 1981. Lectr. bus. law Eastern Mich. U., 1968-70. Pres., Ypsilanti Family Service, 1967; mem. Ypsilanti Public Housing Com., 1980-84; sr. adviser Explorer law post Portage Trail council Boy Scouts Am., 1969-71, commr. Potawatomi dist., 1973-74, commr. Washtenong dist., 1974-75, dist. committeeman, 1984, wolverine coun. v.p., 1992, v.p. Great Sauk Trail coun., 1995—; bd. dirs. Mich. Mcpl. League Legal Def. Fund., pres. 1989-90. Served with AUS, 1959-60. Recipient Silver Beaver award Boy Scouts Am., 1992, Mich. Mcpl. League award of Merit Mcpl. League Legal Def., 1992. Mem. State Bar Mich. (grievance bd. hearing panel 1969-97, state rep. assembly 1977-82, bd. commrs. 1993—), Am., Ypsilanti, Washtenaw County (pres. 1975-76, Profl. and Civility award 1998) Bar Assns., Washtenaw County Trial Lawyers Assns., Mich. Mcpl. Attys. Assn. (pres. 1989-90, MAMA dist. mcpl. atty. award, 1993), U.S. (instr. piloting, seamanship, sail), Ann Arbor (comdr. 1972-73) power squadrons. Lutheran. Club: Washtenaw Country. Contbr. articles to boating mags. General practice. Home: 1200 Whittier Rd Ypsilanti MI 48197-2152 Office: 105 Pearl St Ypsilanti MI 48197-2611

**BARR, JON-HENRY,** lawyer; b. Livingston, N.J., Sept. 1, 1970; s. Gary and Susan Barr. BA, Lehigh U., 1992; JD, Seton Hall U., 1995. Bar: N.J. 1996, D.C. 1998, U.S. Dist. Ct. N.J. 1996, U.S. Ct. Appeals (3d cir.) 1997. Jud. law clk. Superior Ct. N.J., Freehold, N.J., 1995-96; assoc. Law Offices of Robert Blackman, Edison, N.J., 1996-98; ptnr. Barr & Canada, LLC, Clark, N.J., 1998—. Sec. Union Middlesex REACT, Woodbridge, N.J., 1989—; councilman Twp. of Clark, N.J., 1993-94; mem. Clark Rep. Civic Assn., 1996—. Named one of Outstanding Young Men of Am., 1998. Mem. ABA, N.J. State Bar Assn., Union County Bar Assn. Jewish. Avocations: politics, travel. General practice, Criminal, General civil litigation. Home: 69 Fairview Rd Clark NJ 07066-2904 Office: Barr and Canada LLC 21 Brant Ave Clark NJ 07066-1512

**BARR, JUNE HATTON,** lawyer; b. Wash., May 17, 1953; d. Gerald William and Etta Carrie (Jones) Hatton; m. Timothy Dwight Barr, Aug. 29, 1981; 1 child, Timothy Randolph. BA, Wesleyan U., Middletown, Conn., 1975; JD, U. Mich. Sch. Law, 1978. Atty. Nationwide Mut. Ins. Co., Columbus, Ohio, 1978-81, sr. atty., 1981-84, asst. counsel, 1984-88, assoc. counsel, 1988-89; pvt. practice, 1988—; adj. prof. Prince Georges Cmty. Coll., Largo, Md., 1994—. Mem. Bd. Franklin County Bd. Mental Retardation and Devel. Disabilities Residential Services Bd., Ohio 1980-86; bd. govs. Holy Trinity Day Sch., Bowie, Md., 1994—, chmn., 1998—. Mem. ABA, Md. State Barn Assn., Prince George's County Bar Assn., D.C. Bar Assn. Baptist. Avocation: piano. Probate, General practice, General civil litigation. Office: PO Box 5070 Laurel MD 20726-5070

**BARR, MICHAEL BLANTON,** lawyer; b. Freeport, N.Y., July 24, 1948; s. Harry Kyle and Rosemary (Blanton) B.; m. Nancy Nickeson, Aug. 11, 1979; children: Nicholas Upton, Jessica Nickeson, Alice Primrose. B.S., Georgetown U., 1970; J.D., George Washington U., 1973. Bar: D.C. 1973. U.S. Dist. Ct. D.C. 1973, U.S. Ct. Appeals (D.C. cir.) 1974, U.S. Ct. Appeals (3d cir.) 1979, U.S. Ct. Appeals, (4th cir.) 1976, U.S. Ct. Appeals (6th cir.) 1981, U.S. Supreme Ct. 1980. Assoc. LeBoeuf, Lamb, Lieby & McRae, Washington, 1973-76, Hunton & Williams, Washington, 1976-80; ptnr. Hunton & Williams, Washington, 1980—, mng. ptnr. Washington office, 1985—. Contbr. articles to profl. jours. Bd. trustees Georgetown Day Sch.; bd. dirs. Am. Sch. of Tangier, Morocco, 1989—. Mem. ABA, Internat. Bar Assn., D.C. Bar Assn. Clubs: City Tavern (Washington), Union League (N.Y.). General corporate, Private international. Home: 8004 Glendale Rd Chevy Chase MD 20815-5903 Office: Hunton & Williams 1900 K St NW Washington DC 20006-1110

**BARR, WILLIAM PELHAM,** lawyer, former attorney general of United States; b. N.Y.C., May 23, 1950; s. Donald and Mary (Ahern) B.; m. Christine Moynihan, June 23, 1973; 3 children. AB, Columbia U., 1971, MA, 1973; JD, George Washington U., 1977. Bar: Va. 1977, D.C. 1978. Staff officer CIA, Washington, 1973-77; law clk. to presiding judge Cir. Ct., Washington, 1977-78; assoc. Shaw, Pittman, Potts & Trowbridge, Washington, 1978-82, 83-84, ptnr., 1985-89, 93-94; dep. asst. dir. domestic policy staff The White House, Washington, 1982-83; asst. atty. gen. Office Legal Counsel, U.S. Dept. Justice, Washington, 1989-90, dep. atty. gen., 1990-91, atty. gen., 1991-93; exec. v.p., gen. counsel G.T.E. Corp., Washington, 1994—. Mem. ABA, Va. State Bar Assn., D.C. Bar Assn., KC. Republican. Roman Catholic. Office: GTE Corp 1850 M St NW Ste 1200 Washington DC 20036-5823*

**BARRAD, CATHERINE MARIE,** lawyer; b. Moscow, Idaho, Dec. 12, 1953; d. Richard Gary and Hazel Mae (Hollon) Morrison; m. Mark William Barrad, Dec. 29, 1974 (div. June 1997); children: Joshua, Samuel, Rachel. Student, Saddleback Coll., 1971-72, UCLA, 1972-73, U. Calif., Irvine, 1973-74, Calif. State U., Long Beach, 1976-77; BS in Law, JD, Western State U., 1980. Bar: Calif. 1980, Hawaii 1993. Pvt. practice Law Offices of Catherine M. Barrad, Long Beach, 1980-93, Maui, 1993—; arbitrator court annexed arbitration program 2d Cir. Ct. Hawaii, 1993—. Del. Coun. Jewish Fedns., Long Beach, 1990, bd. dirs., 1983-93; del. Jewish Community Rels. Coun., 1987-92; cubmaster Pack 111 Boy Scouts Am., Long Beach, 1989-93; v.p. Jewish Arts and Edn. Coun. Maui, 1994-97. Recipient Neuberger Young Leadership award Jewish Fedn. Long Beach, 1990, Chai Vol. award Jewish Community Ctr., Long Beach, 1990. Mem. Women Lawyers of Long Beach (sec. 1981-82, pres. 1982-83), Hawaii State Bar Assn, Maui County Bar Assn., Aloha House (bd. dirs. 1995-97), Rotary Maui Upcountry (pres. 1994-96, bd. dirs. 1994-97). Democrat. Jewish. Fax: 808-573-0853. Family and matrimonial, Personal injury, General civil litigation. Office: PO Box 1591 Makawao HI 96768-1591

**BARRAZA, HORACIO,** lawyer; b. El Paso, Tex., June 11, 1967; s. Jorge and Carmen T. Barraza. BS, U. Tex., El Paso, 1989; JD, Western State U., 1993. Bar: Calif. 1995, U.S. Dist. Ct. (so. dist.) Calif. 1995. Assoc. Singleton & Dean, Escondido, Calif., 1995-97, Singleton & Assocs., Escondido, 1997—. Mem. ABA, ATLA, San Diego County Bar Assn., North San Diego County Bar Assn., San Diego Trial Lawyers Assn., Consumer Attys. of Calif., Am. Inns. of Ct. (assoc.). Personal injury, Product liability, General civil litigation. Office: Singleton & Assocs 120 Woodward Ave Escondido CA 92025-2637

**BARRE, ERWAN,** lawyer; b. Saint-Malo, France, July 21, 1968; came to the U.S., 1998; s. Yvonnick and Marcelle Barre; m. Virginie Dinkian, Oct. 4, 1997. Diplome, Ecole Supérieure de Commerce Reims, France, 1990; licence, maitrise, Diplome d'Etudes Approfondies, Sorbonne U., Paris, 1993; LLM, Columbia U., 1996. Bar: Paris 1996, N.Y. 1998. Fin. auditor KPMG, Paris, 1990-93; fin. analyst Credit Indsl. et Commercial, London, 1990-95; lawyer Sullivan & Cromwell, Paris, 1996-98, N.Y.C., 1998—. Avocations: wine tasting, French literature. Mergers and acquisitions. Office: Sullivan & Cromwell 125 Broad St Fl 28 New York NY 10004-2489

**BARRECA, CHRISTOPHER ANTHONY,** lawyer; b. Pittsfield, Mass., Sept. 15, 1928; s. Christopher Joseph and Jennie (Cannici) B.; m. Alice Hazlehurst, Sept. 5, 1953. AA, Boston U., 1950, JD, 1953; LLM, Northwestern U., 1968. Bar: Mass. 1954, Ky. 1969, Mass. 1995, U.S. Ct. Appeals (6th cir.) 1970, Conn. 1988. With Gen. Electric Co., Fairfield, Conn., 1953-93, labor arbitration and litigation counsel, 1971-80, sr. labor and employment law counsel, 1980-93; ptnr., office chair, sr. counsel Paul, Hastings, Janolsky & Walker LLP, Stamford, Conn., 1993-99, sr. counsel, 1999—; mem. arbitration services adv. com. Fed Mediation and Conciliation Service, 1973—; adj. prof. U. Louisville, 1970-71, U. Bridgeport (Conn.) Sch. of Law, 1986—; selectman Weston, 1997—. Co-author, editor: Labor Arbitrator Development, 1983, A Practical Guide for Advocates, 1990; contbr. articles to profl. jours. Chmn. Weston (Conn.) Bd. Edn., 1977-82; trustee, vice chair exec. com., chmn. com. legal affairs Boston U., 1977—. Served with AUS, 1946-47. Mem. ABA (chmn. labor and employment law sect. com. labor arbitration advocacy, elected to governing council of labor and employment law sect. 1986—, chair 1996-97), Boston U. Sch. Law Alumni Assn. (Silver Shingle award 1982), Aspetuck Valley Country Club (Weston, pres. 1995-96). Labor, Administrative and regulatory, General corporate. Home: 6 Aspetuck Hill Ln Weston CT 06883-2601 Office: Paul Hastings Janolsky & Walker LLP 1055 Washington Blvd Stamford CT 06901-2216

**BARREIRA, BRIAN ERNEST,** lawyer; b. Fall River, Mass., Sept. 1, 1958; s. Ernest R. and Lillian (Rego) B. BS in Ops. Mgmt., Boston Coll., 1980; JD, Boston U., 1984, LLM in Taxation, 1990. Bar: Mass. 1985. Estate settlement specialist State Street Bank and Trust Co., Boston, 1985-87; assoc. Barron & Stadfeld, Boston, 1987-88, Winokur, Winokur, Serkey, Rosenberg, & Hingham, P.C., Plymouth, 1988-96; sole practice Plymouth, Mass., 1996—. Contbr. articles to profl. jours. Mem. ABA (chmn. elder law com. 1990-95, chmn. long-term health care issues com. 1992-96), Nat. Acad. Elder Law Attys., Mass. Bar Assn. (mem. probate sect. coun. 1993-94, 95-97). Estate planning, Probate, Estate taxation. Home: 1525 Tremont St Duxbury MA 02332-3313 Office: 225 Water St Ste 212 Plymouth MA 02360-4026

**BARRETT, BRUCE ALAN,** lawyer; b. Pitts., Aug. 9, 1950; s. Hugh Horner and Ethel (McCrea) B.; m. Gayle Gray, Sept. 7, 1974; children: Eric, Sarah, Brian. BA, U. Pitts., 1972; JD, Cleve. State U., 1975. Bar: Pa. 1975, U.S. Dist. Ct. (we. dist.) Pa. 1978. Ptnr. Magee & Barrett, Meadville, Pa., 1975-79; sole practice Meadville, 1979-85; ptnr. Barrett & Dratler, Meadville, 1985—; 1st asst. pub. defender Crawford County, Meadville, 1978—. Chmn. parade com. Meadville Meml. Day Celebration, 1980-82. Named one of Outstanding Young Men Am., 1986. Mem. Pa. Bar Assn., Crawford County Bar Assn. (treas. 1988, 89, 90, 91), Pa. Jaycees (parliamentarian 1988, assoc. legal counsel 1989, legal counsel 1990), Meadville Jaycees (pres. 1979-80, Amb. award 1988, Senatorship award 1990). Republican. Presbyterian. State civil litigation, General practice, Criminal. Office: Barrett & Dratler 965 S Main St Meadville PA 16335-3273

**BARRETT, CAROLYN HERNLY,** paralegal; b. Geneva, Ill., Jan. 17, 1954; d. Wayne Francis and Genevieve (Moyer) Hernly; m. Bradley Clayton Barrett, June 20, 1976; children: Heather Hernly, Lance Clayton, Colin Courtney. Grad., Moser Bus. Coll., 1975; BS in Bus. Mgmt., Nat.-Louis U., 1996. Legal sec. Rathje, Woodward, Dyer & Burt, Wheaton, Ill., 1975-77; paralegal Chadwell, Kayser, Ruggles, McGee & Hastings, Chgo., 1978-80, Patrick James Perretti, Glen Ellyn, Ill., 1992-95; adminstrv. asst. Charles C. Snyder, PC, Oak Brook, Ill., 1996—; adminstr. Bedrava, Lyman & Van Epps, Oak Brook, Ill., 1998—. Pres. Forest Glen PTA, Glen Ellyn, 1988-90; mem. Rep. Senatorial Innter Cir., Washington, 1991—, Nat. Trust for Hist. Preservation; chair ways and means com. Glen Ellyn Hist. Soc., 3d v.p., 1992—. Recipient Medal of Freedom, Rep. Senatorial Inner Cir., 1994. Mem. DAR, Nat. Fedn. Rep. Women, Women in Arts (charter). Presbyterian. Avocations: collecting antiques, travel, scuba, restoring homes. Home: 675 N Main St Glen Ellyn IL 60137-4045

**BARRETT, DAVID A.,** lawyer; b. Altoona, Pa., Aug. 12, 1950; s. Arthur L. and Mary (Bell) B.; m. Diane DeWitt, May 23, 1981; children: Alexander, Annabel. AB, Harvard U., 1971; JD, Columbia Law Sch., 1974. Bar: N.Y. 1975, U.S. Dist. Ct. (so. dist.) N.Y. 1975, U.S. Dist. Ct. (ea. dist.) N.Y. 1987, U.S. Dist. Ct. (no. dist.) N.Y. 1992, U.S. Ct. Appeals (2d cir.) 1975, U.S. Ct. Appeals (6th cir.) 1979, U.S. Ct. Appeals (D.C. cir.) 1980, U.S. Ct. Appeals (3d cir.) 1987, U.S. Ct. Appeals (5th cir.) 1993, U.S. Ct. Appeals (11th cir.) 1994, U.S. Supreme Ct. 1979. Law clk. to Hon. Wilfred Feinberg U.S. Ct. Appeals (2d Cir.), N.Y.C., 1974-75; Karpatkin fellow ACLU, N.Y.C., 1975-76; law clk. to Hon. Thurgood Marshall U.S. Supreme Ct., Washington, 1976-77; spl. counsel U.S. Dept. Justice, Office Legis. Affairs, Washington, 1977-79; assoc. Cravath, Swaine & Moore, N.Y.C., 1979-85; assoc. prof. Rutgers U. Law Sch., Newark, 1985-87; ptnr. Barrett Gravante Carpinello & Stern LLP, N.Y.C., Albany, 1987—. Author: (with others) NYU Inst. State and Local Taxation, 1987, Reforming Libel Law, 1992. Mem. Senator Charles Schumer's Judicial Screening Comm., 1999—; counsel N.Y. Choice Pac, N.Y.C., 1984—. Mem. Columbia Law Sch. Bd. Vis., 1996—. General civil litigation, Antitrust, Securities. Office: 1585 Broadway New York NY 10036-8200 also: 100 State St Albany NY 12207

**BARRETT, DAVID EUGENE,** judge; b. Hiawassee, Ga., June 25, 1955; s. Homer and Laura Arispah (Wilson) B.; children: Laura Elizabeth, Thomas Jeffrey. BA summa cum laude, U. Ga., 1977, JD cum laude, 1980. Assoc. Erwin, Epting, et al, Athens, Ga., 1980-84, Blasingame, Burch, et al, Athens, 1984; pvt. practice Hiawassee, 1984-92; judge Recorders Ct., 1986-92, Superior Ct., Enotah Cir., 1992—; counsel Towns County Humane Soc., Hiawassee, 1985-92; counselor Alzheimer Support, Hiawassee, 1985. Mem. ABA, Ga. Bar Assn., Mountain Bar Assn. (sec. 1987-88, v.p. 1988-89, pres. 1989-90), Western Bar Assn. (sec. 1983-84), Trial Lawyers Assn. Am., Towns County C. of C. (bd. dirs. 1986-87, 90-92, pres. 1988), Demosthenian Lit. Soc. (bd. dirs., sec. bd. trustees 1978-89, chmn. bd. 1986-89), Athens Jaycees (v.p. 1983-84). Home: 924 Mining Gap Ln Young Harris GA 30582-2324 Office: Superior Ct Enotah Cir 59 S Main St Ste K Cleveland GA 30528-1376

**BARRETT, DAVID OLAN,** lawyer; b. Indianapolis, May 25, 1970; m. Jacqueline R. Barrett. BA in Polit. Sci. and Journalism, Ind. U., 1992, JD, 1995. Bar: Ind. 1995, U.S. Dist. Ct. (no. and so. dists) Ind., U.S. Ct. Appeals (7th cir.), U.S. Supreme Ct. Assoc. Ice Miller Donadio & Ryan, Indpls., 1995-99; counsel Emmis Comm. Corp., Indpls., 1999—. Mem. bd. editors Ind. Law Jour.; contbr. numerous articles to lay publs. and profl. jours; presenter on topics relating to corp. and comm. law. Bd. dirs. Jewish Comty Rels. Coun., Indpls., 1995—; mem. Indpls. New Leaders Project, 1997—. Mem. ABA, Defense Rsch. Inst., Ind. State Bar Assn., Indpls. Bar Assn., Order of Barristers, Sherman Minton Moot Ct. Bd. General corporate, Communications, General civil litigation. Home: 9679 Troon Ct Carmel IN 46032-9373 Office: Emmis Comm Corp One Emmis Plaza 40 Monument Cir Ste 700 Indianapolis IN 46204-2941

**BARRETT, GEORGE EDWARD,** lawyer; b. Nashville, Oct. 19, 1927; s. George E. and Annie (Conroy) B.; m. Eloise McBride Barrett, Sept. 14, 1957; (div. 1988); children: Anne-Louise, Mary Eloise, Kathryn Conroy. BS, Spring Hill Coll., 1952; diploma, Oxford U., Eng., 1953; JD, Vanderbilt U., Nashville, 1957. Bar: Tenn., U.S. Ct. Appeals (6th cir.), U.S. Supreme Ct. Atty. Barrett, Johnston & Parsley, Nashville. Civil rights, Labor. Office: Barrett Johnston & Parsley 217 2nd Ave N Nashville TN 37201-1601

**BARRETT, JAMES EMMETT,** federal judge; b. Lusk, Wyo., Apr. 8, 1922; s. Frank A. and Alice C. (Donoghue) B.; m. Carmel Ann Martinez, Oct. 8, 1949; children: Ann Catherine Barrett Sandahl, Richard James, John Donoghue. Student, U. Wyo., 1940-42, LLB, 1949; student, St. Catherine's Coll., Oxford, Eng., 1945, Cath. U. Am., 1946. Bar: Wyo. 1949. Mem. firm Barrett and Barrett, Lusk, 1949-67; atty. Niobrara Sch. Dist., 1950-64; county and pros. atty. Niobrara County, Wyo., 1951-62; atty. Town of Lusk, 1952-54; atty. gen. State of Wyo., 1967-71; judge U.S. Circuit Ct. Appeals (10th cir.), 1971—, now sr. judge. Active Boy Scouts Am.; sec.-treas. Niobrara County Republican Central Com.; trustee St. Joseph's Children's Home, Torrington, Wyo., 1971-85. Served as cpl. AUS, 1942-45, ETO. Recipient Distinguished Alumni award U. Wyo., 1973. Mem. VFW, Am. Legion, Order of Coif (hon. mem. Wyo. Coll. Law/U. Wyo. chpt.). Office: US Ct Appeals PO Box 1288 Cheyenne WY 82003-1288

**BARRETT, JANE FRANCES,** lawyer; b. Monterey, Calif., Sept. 13, 1952; d. Harle V. Barrett and Lucille M. Richstatter. BA in Polit. Sci., Loyola Coll., Balt., 1973; JD, U. Md., 1976. Bar: Md., D.C., U.S. Dist. Ct. Md. 1986, U.S. Ct. Appeals (4th cir.) 1987, U.S. Dist. Ct. Washington 1998. Atty. gen. U.S. Environ. Protection Agy., Washington, 1976-86; asst. atty. gen. State of Md., Balt., 1981-86; asst. U.S. atty. U.S. Atty. Office Dist. Md., Balt., 1986-97; ptnr. Dyer Ellis & Joseph, Washington, 1998—; adj. prof. U. Md., Balt., 1990-97. Contbr. articles to profl. jours. Mem. adv. working group environ. sanctions U.S. Sentencing Commn., Washington, 1992-93; bd. dirs. Women's Housing Coalition, Balt., 1998-99. Recipient Bronze medal U.S. EPA, 1997, Commdrs. award Army Corps. Engrs., 1998. Mem. ABA (vice-chair environ. crimes enforcement subcom. 1995—), WISTA. Environmental, Criminal, Federal civil litigation. Office: Dyer Ellis & Joseph 600 New Hampshire Ave NW Washington DC 20037-2403

**BARRETT, JANE HAYES,** lawyer; b. Dayton, Ohio, Dec. 13, 1947; d. Walter J. and Jane H. Barrett. BA, Calif. State U.-Long Beach, 1969; JD, U. So. Calif., 1972. Bar: Calif. 1972, U.S. Dist. Ct. (cen. dist.) Calif. 1972, U.S. Ct. Appeals (9th cir.) 1982, U.S. Supreme Ct. Assoc. Arter, Hadden, Lawler, Felix & Hall, L.A., 1972-79, ptnr., 1979-94, mng. ptnr., 1984-93; ptnr. Preston, Gates & Ellis, 1994—; mng. ptnr. Preston, Gates & Ellis, L.A., 1994—; lectr. bus. law Calif. State U., 1973-75. Mem. adv. bd. Harriet Buhai Legal Aid Ctr., 1991-96, mem. bd. pub. counsel, 1996-98; pres. Pilgrim Parents Orgn. 1990-91. Named Outstanding Grad. Calif. State U., Long Beach, 1988, Outstanding Alumnae Polit. Sci., 1993. Fellow Am. Bar Found.; mem. ABA (bd. govs. 1980-84, chmn. young lawyers divsn. 1980-81, com. on delivery of legal svcs. 1985-89, exec. coun. legal edn. and admissions sects. 1985-89, fin. sec. torts and ins. practice 1982-83, adv. mem. fed. judiciary com. 1994-96, v.p. 1997—, v.p. Am. Bar Endowment 1984-90, bd. dirs. 1990—, sec. 1993-95, v.p. 1998-99, pres., 1999—, bd. fellows young lawyers divsn. 1992—), Calif. State Bar (com. adminstrn. of justice, editl. bd. Calif. Lawyers 1981-84), Legion Lex (bd. dirs. 1990-93), Los Feliz Homeowners Assn. (bd. dirs.). Democrat. Federal civil litigation, General civil litigation, Intellectual property. Office: Preston Gates & Ellis 725 S Figueroa St Ste 2100 Los Angeles CA 90017-5421

**BARRETT, JOHN J(AMES), JR.,** lawyer; b. Phila., May 19, 1948; s. John J. and Carmela (DiJohn) B.; m. Rosemary A. Campagna, Aug. 23, 1969; children: Jeffrey, Kristin, Jacqueline. BA, Temple U., 1970, JD, 1973. Bar: Pa. 1973, N.J. 1987, U.S. Dist. Ct. (ea. dist.) Pa. 1973, U.S. Ct. Appeals (3rd cir.) 1975, U.S. Dist. Ct. (mid. dist.) Pa. 1986, U.S. Supreme Ct. 1986, U.S. Dist. Ct. N.J. 1987. Assoc. Saul, Ewing, Remick & Saul, Phila., 1973-80; ptnr. Saul, Ewing, Remick & Saul, 1980—. Mem. Nat. Assn. R.R. Trial Counsel, Phila. Assn. Def. Counsel. Federal civil litigation, Product liability, State civil litigation. Office: Saul Ewing Remick & Saul 3800 Centre Sq W Philadelphia PA 19102

**BARRETT, JOHN RICHARD,** lawyer; b. N.Y.C., Nov. 26, 1928; m. Marie Louise Barrett; children: William, Brian. BA cum laude, Notre Dame U., 1952; JD, U. Va., 1955. Bar: Va. 1955, Fla. 1957, U.S. Dist. Ct. (so. dist.) Fla. 1961, U.S. Supreme Ct. 1972, U.S. Ct. Appeals (5th and 11th cir.) 1981. Legal asst. to chief judge N.Y. Ct. Appeals, 1955-56; corp. counsel Gen. Aniline & Film Corp., N.Y.C., 1957; mcpl. judge City Miami, Fla., 1959-63, city atty., 1963-66; sr. ptnr. Barrett & Rogers, P.A. predecessor, Miami, 1974—; chmn. grievance com. Fla. Bar 1967-70; bd. dirs. Amscort Internat., San Francisco; vice chmn. Redwood Securities Group, Inc., San Francisco. Mem. adminstrv. bd. trustees St. Thomas U., 1981, gen. counsel, 1981—; bd. dirs. Greater Miami Philharm. Soc., Inc., 1968-69; mem. diocesan bd. edn. Roman Cath. So. Diocese, 1967-71; v.p. bd. dirs. Miami Chamber Symphony, 1982-84; trustee Miami Country Day Prep. Sch., 1981-84. Mem. ABA, Fla. Bar Assn. (chmn. grievance com. 1967-70, co-chmn. legis. com. 1971), Dade County Bar Assn., Fed. Bar Assn., Am. Judicature Soc., Am. Judges Assn., Fla. Bar Found. General corporate, General practice, Probate. Office: Barrett & Rogers PA predecessor Internat Place 100 SE 2nd St Miami FL 33131-2100 also: Amvest Bldg One Boar's Head Pl Charlottesville VA 22903

**BARRETT, MICHAEL D.,** lawyer; b. Bloomsberg, Pa., July 5, 1956; m. Dana M. Barrett, Nov. 13, 1982; children: Lauren, Matthew. BS cum laude, U. Minn., 1977; JD cum laude, William Mitchell Coll. of Law, St. Paul, 1987; postgrad., U. Minn., 1980—. Bar: Minn. 1987; U.S. Dist. Ct. Minn. 1987. Law clk. Cousineau, McGuire & Anderson, Mpls., 1984-87, assoc., 1987-95, officer, sr. atty., 1996—. Mem. Hennepin County Bar Assn., Minn. State Bar Assn., Casco Point Assn. (pres., co-founder 1996—). Avocations: woodworking, hunting, fishing. Personal injury, Insurance, Workers' compensation. Office: Cousineau McGuire & Anderson 1550 Utica Ave S # 600 Minneapolis MN 55416-5318

**BARRETT, ROBERT MATTHEW,** law educator, lawyer; b. Bronx, N.Y., Mar. 18, 1948; s. Harry and Rosalind B. AB summa cum laude, Georgetown U., 1976, MS in Fgn. Service, JD, 1980. Bar: Calif. 1981. Assoc. Latham & Watkins, L.A., 1980-82, Morgan, Lewis & Bockius, L.A., 1982-84, Skadden, Arps, Slate, Meagher & Flom, L.A., 1984-86, Shea & Gould, L.A., 1986-87, Donovan, Leisure, Newton & Irvine, L.A., 1988-90; ptnr. Barrett & Zipser, L.A., Calif., 1991-93; prof. law U. LaVerne Law Sch., Woodland Hills, Calif., 1993—. Civilian vol. L.A. Sheriff's Dept., 1997—. Mem. State Bar Calif. (standing com. on profl. responsibility and conduct 1995-99, chair 1997-98, spl. advisor 1998-99), L.A. Bar Assn. (bd. advisors vols. in parole com. 1981—). Fax: 818-883-8142. Address: Univ La Verne Coll Law 21300 Oxnard St Woodland Hills CA 91367-5016

**BARRETT, VIRGINIA M.,** lawyer; b. Hackensack, N.J., Feb. 18, 1953; d. James Joseph and Marjorie Helen (Hennessey) B.; m. Ronald J. Hurley, Aug. 15, 1981; children: Beth Barrett Hurley, Lynn Barrett Hurley. BA, Ramapo Coll., 1975; JD, So. Ill. U., 1978. Bar: Ill. 1979, N.J. 1980, U.S. Dist. Ct. N.J. 1980. Assoc. Travis, Tucker & Assocs., Oaklawn, Ill., 1978-79, Morgan, Melhuish, Monaghan, Arvitson, Abrutyn & Lisowski, Livingston, N.J., 1980-86, Law Office of Robert A. Auerbach, Fairlawn, N.J., 1986-87, Thomas J. Haynes, Maywood, N.J., 1987-88; ptnr. Karcher, Salmond, Rainone & Barrett, Edison, N.J., 1989-95, Kroll & Tract, Newark, 1995—. Bus. editor: Law Jour., So. Ill. U., 1977-78. Dir. girls basketball Maywood Youth Athletic Assn., Maywood, 1994—, coach girls basketball, 1990-95. Mem. Am. Arbitration Assn. (arbitrator 1989—), N.J. Bar Assn., Bergen County Bar Assn., Middlesex County Bar Assn. Avocations: canoeing, skiing, hiking. State civil litigation, Civil rights, Product liability. Office: Kroll & Tract 1 Gateway Ctr Newark NJ 07102-5311

**BARRETT, WILLIAM L. D.,** lawyer; b. Winsted, Conn., July 30, 1938; s. William L. and Virginia (Deming) B.; children: Alicia, Jennifer, Christopher, Sarah; m. Erika Izakson, Jan. 17, 1987. BA, Yale U., 1960; LLB, Harvard U., 1963. Bar: N.Y. 1964. Assoc. Webster & Sheffield, N.Y.C., 1963-71, ptnr., 1971-86; ptnr. Hollyer, Brady, Smith, Troxell, Barrett, Rockett, Hines & Mone, N.Y.C., 1987—; dir. Metropolis Mag., N.Y.C. Trustee, v.p. Leopold Schepp Found., N.Y.C. Mem. ABA, N.Y. State Bar Assn., Assn. Bar City N.Y., Am. Arbitration Assn. (bd. dirs. 1988—, exec. com. 1992—, Whitney North Seymour medal for disting. svc. 1993), Harvard Club. Roman Catholic. Avocations: harpsichord, hiking, photography, French literature. General corporate, Securities. Home: 5 Riverside Dr New York NY 10023-2534 Office: Hollyer Brady Smith Troxell Rockett Hines & Mone 551 5th Ave New York NY 10176-0001

**BARRIENTES, JOHN CHARLES,** insurance claims executive, lawyer; b. Hondo, Tex., Feb. 19, 1944; s. Robert and Auralia (Medina) B.; m. Rebecca Ann Spence, July 16, 1946; children: Diana, Lisa, John-David. BA in Math., St. Mary's U., San Antonio, 1967; JD in Law, U. West L.A. Sch. Law, 1981. Bar: Calif. 1982, U.S. Dist. Ct. (ctrl. dist.) Calif. 1983; CPU. Claim rep. State Farm Ins. Co., L.A., 1969-76, claims supt., 1976-80; divisional claim supt. State Farm Ins. Co., Torrance, Calif., 1980-84; claim mgr. State Farm Ins. Co., Houston, 1984-88; asst. v.p. BI claims State Farm Ins. Co., Bloomington, Ill., 1988-92, asst. v.p. casualty claims, 1992—. 1st lt. U.S. Army, 1967-69. Mem. ABA, Ctrl. Ill. Chpt. CPCU. Avocations: golfing, tennis. Insurance. Home: 1107 E Monroe St Bloomington IL 61701-3328 Office: State Farm Ins Co 112 E Washington St # Fb-11 Bloomington IL 61701-1002

**BARRON, HAROLD SHELDON,** lawyer; b. Detroit, July 4, 1936; s. George Leslie and Rose (Weinstein) B.; m. Roberta Yellin, Nov. 17, 1963; children: Lawrence Ira, Jean Louise. A.B., U. Mich., 1958, J.D., 1961. Bar: N.Y. 1963, Mich. 1961, Ill. 1983, Pa. 1992. Pvt. practice N.Y.C., 1962-68; practice in Southfield, Mich., 1968-83, Chgo., 1983-93, Pa., 1991—; atty. Hughes Hubbard & Reed, 1962-68; corp. counsel Bendix Corp., 1968-69, sec., assoc. gen. counsel, 1969-72, sec., gen. counsel, 1972-83, v.p., 1974-83; ptnr. Arnstein, Gluck, Lehr, Barron & Milligan, Chgo., 1983-86, Seyfarth, Shaw, Fairweather & Geraldson, Chgo., 1986-91; v.p., gen. counsel Unisys Corp., Blue Bell, Pa., 1991-92, sr. v.p., gen. counsel, 1992-94; sr. v.p., gen. counsel, sec., 1994—; mem. nat. adv. coun. and faculty Practising Law Inst., N.Y.C.; bd. dirs. Royal Maccabees Life Ins. Co., Southfield, 1983-94; chmn. bd. F.A. Tucker Group, Inc., 1991-95. Com. visitors U. Mich. Law Sch.; trustee Children's Hosp. Mich., Detroit, 1976-84; mem. Census Adv. Com. on Privacy and Confidentiality, 1975-76; mem. governing bd., adv. coun. Purdue U. Info. Privacy Rsch. Ctr.; bd. dirs. Citizens Rsch. Coun. of Mich., 1982-83, Greater Phila. Econ. Devel. Coalition. Served with AUS, 1961-62. Mem. ABA (chmn. bus. law sect., sec. bus. law sect., chmn. com. of corp. gen. counsel, sect. bus. law coun., com. corp. law and taxation, internat. bus. law com., com. devels. in investment svcs., com. long-range issues affecting bus. law practice, com. on corp. laws), Am. Arbitration Assn., Am. Soc. Corp. Secs. (securities law com.), Mich. Bar Assn., Assn. Bar City N.Y. (com. corp. law depts.), Carlton Club, Chgo. Club, Bryn Mawr Country Club (Chgo.), Green Valley Country Club (Phila.). General corporate, Securities, Mergers and acquisitions. Office: Unisys Corp PO Box 500 Blue Bell PA 19424-0001

**BARRON, JEROME AURE,** law educator; b. Tewksbury, Mass., Sept. 25, 1933; s. Henry and Sadie (Shafmaster) B.; m. Myra Hymovich, June 18, 1961; children—Jonathan Nathaniel, David Jeremiah, Jennifer Leah. A.B. magna cum laude, Tufts Coll., 1955; JD, Yale U., 1958; LL.M., George Washington U., 1960. Bar: Mass. 1959, D.C. 1960. Law clk. to chief judge U.S. Ct. Claims, Washington, 1960-61; assoc. firm Cross, Murphy & Smith, Washington, 1961-62; asst. prof. law U. N.D., Grand Forks, 1962-64; vis. assoc. prof. U. N.Mex., Albuquerque, 1964-65; assoc. prof. George Washington U., from 1965, prof., 1973—, dean, 1979-88, Lyle T. Alverson prof. law, 1987—; dean Syracuse U. Coll. Law, 1972-73. Author: (with Donald Gillmor and Todd Simon) Mass Communication Law, Cases and Comment, 6th edit., 1997, First Amendment in a Nutshell, 1993, Constitutional Law: Principles and Policy, 5th edit., 1996, (with C. Thomas Dienes) Constitutional Law In A Nutshell, 4th edit., 1998; contbr. articles, chpts. to profl. publs. Served with U.S. Army, 1959-60. Mem. ABA, D.C. Bar, Cosmos Club, Phi Beta Kappa. Office: George Washington U 2000 H St NW Washington DC 20006-4234

**BARROW, CLISBY HALL,** lawyer; b. Macon, Ga., Sept. 20, 1965; s. Fletcher Kennedy and Anne Kite Hall; children: John Costley Barrow IV. BA, Davidson Coll., 1987; JD, Vanderbilt U., 1991. Law clk. to U.S. Dist. Judge Thomas A. Wiseman Nashville, Tenn., 1991-92; assoc. Baker, Worthington, Crossley, Stansberry & Woolf, Nashville, 1993-94, Bass, Berry & Sims, PLC, Nashville, 1994—. Personal injury, Product liability, Intellectual property. Office: Bass Berry & Sims PLC 2700 First American Ctr Nashville TN 37238

**BARROW, JOHN J.,** lawyer; b. Athens, Ga., Oct. 31, 1955; s. James and Phyllis (Jenkins) B.; m. Victoria Pentlarge, Dec. 19, 1953. AB, U. Ga., 1976; JD, Harvard U., 1979. Bar: Ba., U.S. Dist. Ct. (no. and mid. dists.) Ga., U.S. Ct. Appeals (11th cir.), U.S. Ct. Appeals (5th cir.). Clk. to Hon. Tom Clark U.S. Ct. Appeals, Tampa, Fla., 1979-81; assoc. Winburn & Assocs., Athens, Ga., 1981-83; ptnr. Winburn, Lewis & Barrow, Athens, Ga., 1983—; mem. rev. panel State Bar Disciplinary Bd., 1997-99; mem. Ga. Com. on Continuing Lawyer Competency, 1984-87. Commr. Athens-Clarke County Commn., Athens, 1991—. Named Boss of the Yr., Athens Legal Secs. Assocs., 1987. Mem. Ga. Trial Lawyers Assn., Assn. Trial Lawyers Am. Democrat. Baptist. Avocations: govt., tennis, backpacking, spectator sports. Personal injury, Product liability, General practice. Home: 255 Milledge Hts Athens GA 30606-4927

**BARROWS, RONALD THOMAS,** lawyer; b. Detroit, Jan. 19, 1954; s. Harland Wayne and Jeanette Edith (Authier) B. BA in English and Polit. Sci. magna cum laude, Oakland U., 1976; JD, Wayne State U., 1979. Bar: Mich. 1979, U.S. Dist. Ct. (ea. dist.) Mich. 1979, U.S. Ct. Appeals (6th cir.) 1983, U.S. Tax Ct. 1986; lic. real estate broker, Mich; cert. comml. investment mem. Realtors Nat. Mktg. Inst. Assoc. Abbott, Nicholson, Quilter, Esshaki & Youngblood, P.C., Detroit, 1979-80; counsel Lindon Land Co., Inc., Harper Woods, Mich., 1980-82; pvt. practice St. Clair Shores, Mich., 1981-87; ptnr. Barrows & Alt, P.C., Troy, Mich., 1987-90; sole practice Grosse Pointe, Mich., 1990—; cons./counselor to corp. and pvt. real estate investors and developers; adj. prof. Oakland U. Paralegal Program, 1989-90. Contbr. articles to profl. jours. Mem. Mich. Comml. Investment Coun.; chmn. adv. com. Mich. chpt. Nat. Multiple Sclerosis Soc., co-chair coun. adv. com., mem. client programs com. Mem. ABA, ATLA, Mich. Bar Assn. (title stds. com. 1985—, real property coun. 1987-97, treas. 1994-97, chmn. water law com. 1985-90), Nat. Assn. Realtors, Mich. Assn. Realtors (sr. instr. 1980-91), Macomb County Assn. Realtors (lawyer realtor com. 1984-88), Nat. Order Barristers. Republican. Presbyterian. Avocations: sailing, billiards, theater, photography. Real property, Finance. Office: PO Box 36958 Grosse Pointe MI 48236-0958

**BARRUS, ALFRED EMERY,** lawyer; b. Wendell, Idaho, Mar. 8, 1947; s. Joseph Eugene and Ruth T. (Hopkin) B.; m. Kathleen Anderson, June 10, 1971; children: Spencer, Amanda, Kelsey, Sam, Kylie. BA, Brigham Young U., 1971; JD, U. Idaho, 1974. Bar: Idaho 1974, U.S. Dist. Ct. Idaho 1974. Pros. atty. Cassia County, Burley, Idaho, 1974-84, dep. pros. atty., 1984-96; pvt. practice Burley, 1974—. Leader Boy Scouts Am., Burley, 1975-92; pres. PTA, 1982, Burley. Mem. Am. Acad. Adoption Attys., Kiwanis (pres. 1980). Republican. Mem. LDS Ch. Family and matrimonial. Home: 205 W 200 S Burley ID 83318-5011 Office: 1918 Overland Ave Burley ID 83318-2439

**BARRY, DAVID F.,** ; b. Marblehead, Mass., Mar. 3, 1940; s. Donald and Eileen E. (Kirchthurn) B.; m. Ann Marie Seward, June 15, 1968. BS, Salem (Mass.) State Coll., 1963; JD, Suffolk U., 1968, MBA, 1978. Bar: Mass. 1968, U.S. Dist. Ct. Mass. 1970, U.S. Ct. Appeals (3d cir.) 1978, U.S. Supreme Ct. 1979, U.S. Tax Ct. 1980. Tchr. pub. schs. Long Beach, Calif., 1963-64; pvt. practice Marblehead, 1968—; adjudicator U.S. Govt., Boston, 1970-73; prof. bus. adminstrn. Salem (Mass.) State Coll., 1974—; cert. mediator and arbitrator; cons. SBA, Salem, 1982—. Bd. dirs. Market Sq. Assocs., Inc., Marblehead, 1979—; mem. U.S. Service Acad. selection com., Salem, 1983—. Mem. Mass. Bar Assn., Essex County Bar Assn., NEA. Republican. Roman Catholic. General practice, Probate, Condemnation.

**BARRY, DESMOND THOMAS, JR.,** lawyer; b. N.Y.C., Mar. 26, 1945; s. Desmond Thomas and Kathryn (O'Connor) B.; m. Patricia Mellicker, Aug. 28, 1971; children: Kathryn, Desmond Todd. AB, Princeton U., 1967; JD, Fordham U., 1973. Bar: N.Y. 1974, U.S. Dist. Ct. (so. and ea. dist.) N.Y. 1974, U.S. Ct. Appeals (2d cir.) 1974, U.S. Ct. Appeals (9th cir.) 1980, U.S. Ct. Appeals (5th cir.) 1983, U.S. Ct. Appeals (3d cir.) 1984, U.S. Supreme Ct. 1985. Assoc. Condon & Forsyth, N.Y.C., 1973-79, ptnr., 1979—. Trustee Canterbury Sch., New Milford, Conn., 1970-80. Capt. USMC, 1967-70, Vietnam. Decorated Navy Commendation medal with combat V, Combat Action medal, 1969, Vietnamese Cross of Gallantry, 1969. Mem. ABA (chmn. aviation & space law com. 1996-97), N.Y. State Bar Assn., Assn. of Bar of City of N.Y., Internat. Assn. Def. Counsel (exec. com. mem.), Univ. Club N.Y.C., Winged Foot Golf Club. Republican. Roman Catholic. Aviation, Insurance. Home: 9 Thomas Pl Norwalk CT 06853-1500 Office: Condon & Forsyth LLP 685 3rd Ave Fl 14 New York NY 10017-4024

**BARRY, ELIZABETH J.,** lawyer; b. San Antonio, Jan. 29, 1955; d. John Reagan and Marian Ellen (Combs) B.; m. Sanford P. Rabinowitch, Aug. 18, 1984; children: Jessica, Laura. AB magna cum laude, U. Ga., 1974, JD cum laude, 1978. Bar: Ga. 1978, Alaska 1981, U.S. Dist. Ct. Ga., U.S. Dist. Ct. Alaska, U.S. Ct. Appeals (9th cir.), Fed. Ct. Claims, U.S. Supreme Ct. Atty. Dept. Interior, Arlington, Va., 1978-80; atty. Solicitor's Office Dept. Interior, Anchorage, Alaska, 1980-83; asst. atty. gen. human svcs. sect. State of Alaska, Anchorage, 1983-85, asst. atty. gen. natural resources sect., 1985-93, supervising atty. natural resources sect., 1993—. Bd. dirs. SaaKaaya Children's Ctr., Anchorage, 1991-95; mem. Anchorage Platting Bd., Municipality of Anchorage, 1984-89; commr., state rep. Alaska Women's Commn., 1989-91. Mem. Alaska Bar Assn. Avocations: hiking, skiing, kayaking, reading, music. Office: Alaska Dept Law 1031 W 4th Ave Ste 200 Anchorage AK 99501-5903

**BARRY, MARYANNE TRUMP,** federal judge; b. N.Y.C., Apr. 5, 1937; d. Fred C. and Mary Trump; m. John J. Barry, Dec. 26, 1982; 1 child, David W. Desmond. BA, Mt. Holyoke Coll., 1958; MA, Columbia U., 1962; JD, Hofstra U., 1974, LLD (hon.); LLD (hon.), Seton Hall U., Caldwell Coll. Bar: N.J. 1974, N.Y. 1975, U.S. Ct. Appeals (3d cir.), U.S. Supreme Ct. Asst. U.S. Atty., 1974-75, dep. chief appeals div., 1976-77, chief appeals div., 1977-82, exec. asst. U.S. Atty., 1981-82, 1st asst., 1981-83; judge U.S. Dist. Ct., N.J., 1983—; chmn. Com. on Criminal Law Jud. Conf. of U.S., 1994-96. Fellow Am. Bar Found.; mem. ABA, N.J. Bar Assn., Am. Judicature Soc. (bd. dirs.), Assn. Fed. Bar State of N.Y. (pres. 1982-83). Office: US Dist Ct PO & Courthouse Bldg Rm 333 PO Box 999 Newark NJ 07101-0999

**BARRY, WILLIAM HENRY, JR.,** federal judge; b. Nashua, N.H., Feb. 3, 1930; s. William H. and Mabel Sidney (Monica) B.; m. Nancy Collins, Aug. 10, 1958; children: William, Julia, Maura. BS, Holy Cross Coll., Worcester, Mass., 1956; JD, Suffolk U., Boston, 1961. Bar: N.H., 1961. Adjuster Liberty Mutual Ins., Worcester, 1956-61; atty. Harkaway, Barry & Gall, Nashua, 1961-65, Small Bus. Adminstrn., Concord, N.H., 1965-66; asst. U.S. atty. U.S. Dept. Justice, Concord, 1966-68; clerk U.S. Dist. Ct., Concord, 1968-72, U.S. magistrate judge, 1972-95; of counsel Barry Law Office, Nashua, 1995—. Candidate 2d dist. U.S. Congress, N.H., 1966; dir. Big Bros./Big Sisters, Nashua, 1990-97. Sgt. U.S. Army, 1950-52, Korea. Fellow N.H. Bar Assn. Democrat. Roman Catholic. Office: Barry Law Office 255 Main St Nashua NH 03060-2929

**BARSAMIAN, J(OHN) ALBERT,** lawyer, lecturer, educator, criminologist, arbitrator; b. Troy, N.Y., May 1, 1934; s. John and Virginia (Tachdjian) B.;m. Alice Missirilan, Apr. 21, 1963; children: Bonnie, Tamara. BS in Psychology with honors, Union Coll., 1956; JD, 1968; LLB, Albany Law Sch., 1959; postgrad., Nat. Jud. Coll., 1997. Bar: N.Y. 1961, U.S. Dist. Ct. (no. dist.) N.Y. 1961, U.S. Supreme Ct. 1967; fire tng. cert. N.Y. State Exec. Dept. Pvt. practice, 1961—; dir. criminal sci., chmn. dept. Russell Sage Coll., 1970-88, assoc. prof. criminal sci., 1977-82, prof., 1982-87, prof. emeritus, 1987—; lectr. office local govt. divsn. criminal justice svcs. State N.Y., 1964-72, N.Y. State Police Acad., 1970; judge adminstrv. law N.Y. State Pub. Employment Rels. Bd., 1996—; faculty pub. affairs and policy pub. svc. tng. program Nelson A. Rockefeller Coll., 1986-91, Sch. Labor Rels. Extension divsn. Cornell U., 1986; gaming cons. Gov.'s Office Indian Rels., N.Y., 1991-92; spl. counsel Office of Police Chief, Cohoes, N.Y., 1986—, to city mgr., Troy, N.Y., 1993; counsel Watervliet Police Assn., 1967-74, Cohoes Police Assn., 1967-74, Colonie Police Assn., 1977-80, Troy Police Command Officers Assn., 1981-85, North Greenbush Police Assn., 1985-90, Office of the Police Chief, Syracuse, N.Y., 1985-90, Fire Dept. Union, Albany, N.Y., 1986, Schenectady Fire Fighters Union, 1992-95; gen. counsel Internat. Narcotic Enforcement Officers Assn., 1982-84, Troy Uniformed Firefighters Assn., 1977-97; spl. investigator Rensselaer County Dist. Atty., 1959-61; mem. law guardian panel N.Y. State Family Ct., 1967-77; mem. mediation panel N.Y. State Pub. Employment Rels. Bd., 1968-73. Founder, chmn. dept. police sci. Hudson Valley C.C., 1961-69; mem. adv. bd. History Ctr. Skidmore Coll., 1993—; bd. dirs. Rensselaer County ARC, 1966-70; memm. alumni coun. Union Coll., 1981-86; mem. parish coun. St. Peter Armenian Ch., Watervliet, N.Y., 1979-83, chmn., 1981-83, vice chmn., 1984; evaluator office of non-collegiate programs N.Y. State Dept. Edn., 1985—; hon. dep. sheriff St. Mary Parish (La.). Tarzian scholar Union Coll., 1952-56, Porter scholar, 1956-59; decorated chevalier, knight comdr. Sovereign Order of Cyprus; recipient Police Sci. Students' award Hudson Valley C.C., 1968, award for meritorious svc. to law enforcement Law Enforcement Officers Soc., 1969, Archbishop's cert. merit Armenian Ch. Am., 1973, Lawyers Coop. Pub. Co. prize in cirminal law, 1957. Mem. ABA (com. on police selection and tng. 1967-69, mem. Rensselaer county criminal justice coord. coun., 1976-78), N.Y. Bar Assn. (chmn. com. on police 1970-72, trial lawyers sect. com. cont. legal edn. 1977-97), Assn. Trial Lawyers Am., Nat. Assn. Adminstrv. Law Judges, Am. Arbitration Assn., Acad. Criminal Justice Scis., Am. Assn. Criminology, Union Coll. Alumni Assn. (Silver medal 1956), Les Amis d'Escoffier Soc., Masonic Vet. Assn. Troy (life), N.Y. State Trial Lawyers Assn., N.Y. Vet. Police Assn. (life, hon., counsel), Royal Order of Jesters, Shriners, Rose Croix (most wise master Delta chpt. 1986), Phi Delta Theta, Alpha Phi Sigma, Lambda Epsilon Chi. Criminal, Labor, Administrative and regulatory. Home and Office: 5 Sage Hill Ln Albany NY 12204-1315

**BARTA, JAMES JOSEPH,** judge; b. St. Louis, Nov. 5, 1940; BA, St. Mary's U., 1963; JD, St. Louis U., 1966. Bar: Mo. 1966, U.S. Supreme Ct. 1969. Spl. agt. FBI, Washington, Cleve. and N.Y.C., 1966-70; chief trial atty. St. Louis Circuit Atty., 1970-76; assoc. Guilfoil, Symington & Petzall, St. Louis, 1976-77; asst. U.S. atty. Eastern Dist. Mo., 1977-78; lectr. Greater St. Louis Police Acad., 1970-76; spl. asst. atty. gen. Mo., St. Louis, 1974-75; spl. asst. atty. (circuit), St. Louis, 1976-78; judge bankruptcy ct. U.S. Dist. Ct. for Eastern Dist. Mo., 1978—, chief judge bankruptcy ct., 1986-89, 95—; mem. U.S. Supreme Ct. Adv. Com. on Bankruptcy Rules, 1987-94, chmn. tech. subcom.. 1990-94, style subcom., 1992-94; mem. tech. adv. com. St. Louis Council on Criminal Justice, 1972-74; dir. Organized Crime Task Force, St. Louis, 1972-74; project dir. St. Louis Crime Commn., 1975-77. Fellow Am. Coll. Bankruptcy (cir. chmn. 1990-94, bd. dirs. 1994-97, sec. bd. dirs. 1995-97); mem. ABA, Am. Bankruptcy Inst. (bd. dirs. 1989-94), Am. Judicature Soc., Mo. Bar Assn., St. Louis Bar Assn., St. Louis Bar Assn. CLE Inst. (at large 1989-93), Former Spl. Agts. FBI. Office: US Bankruptcy Ct 1 Met Sq 211 N Broadway Fl 7 Saint Louis MO 63102-2733

**BARTELS, DIANE J.,** lawyer; b. Morristown, N.J., 1958. BA, Ursinus Coll., 1980; JD, Dickinson Sch. Law, Carlisle, Pa., 1983. Insurance. Office: 1807 N Market St Wilmington DE 19802-4810

**BARTEMES, AMY STRAKER,** lawyer; b. Steubenville, Ohio, July 17, 1968; d. Ralph John and Martha Rose Straker; m. Brian Michael Bartemes, Oct. 5, 1996; 1 child, Cole Philip. BA, Purdue U., 1990; JD, Vanderbilt U., 1993. Bar: Ohio, 1993, U.S. Dist. Ct. (so. dist.) Ohio, 1996, U.S. Ct. Appeals (6th cir.), 1996, U.S. Dist. Ct. (no. dist.) Ohio, 1997. Assoc. atty. Shayne & Greenwald Co., LPA, Columbus, Ohio, 1993-97, Bricker & Eckler, LLP, Columbus, 1997—. Mem. Ohio State Bar Assn., Columbus Bar Assn., Phi Beta Kappa, Phi Delta Phi. Federal civil litigation, State civil litigation, Labor. Office: Bricker & Eckler LLP 100 S 3d St Columbus OH 43215

**BARTH, J. EDWARD,** lawyer, shareholder; b. Oklahoma City, Oct. 24, 1937; s. Richard L. and Vera S. Barth; m. Gene Bloomston, Apr. 15, 1972; children: Lance Rothstein, Rodney Rothstein, Lee P. Barth. BA, Yale U., 1959; JD, U. Mich., 1962. Bar: Okla. 1962, U.S. Dist. Ct. (we. dist.) Okla., U.S. Dist. Ct. (no. dist.) Tex., U.S. Ct. Appeals (5th and 10th cirs.). Law clk., Chief Judge A.P. Murrah U.S. Ct. Appeals 10th Cir., Oklahoma City, 1963-64; ptnr. Bohanon & Barth, Oklahoma City, 1964-79; shareholder, dir. Andrews Davis Legg Bixler Milsten & Price, Oklahoma City, 1979—; chmn. com. on admissions and grievances, U.S. Dist. Ct. (we. dist.) Okla., 1987—; judge Okla. Temporary Ct. Appeals, Oklahoma City, 1991-92. Chmn. Met. Area Projects Oversight Bd., Oklahoma City, 1994—; pres., trustee Oklahoma City Cmty. Found., 1989-98; chmn., dir. ARC, Oklahoma County, 1979—. Mem. ABA, Okla. Bar Assn. (Lawyer of Month 1994), Oklahoma County Bar Assn. (dir. 1975-77). General corporate, Contracts commercial, Real property. Home: 6020 Riviera Dr Oklahoma City OK 73112-7356 Office: Andrews Davis Legg Bixler Milsten & Price 500 W Main St Ste 500 Oklahoma City OK 73102-2275

**BARTH, KAREN ANN,** lawyer; b. Dubuque, Iowa, Dec. 8, 1966; d. Henry Victor and Janet Marie Barth. BA, Colo. State U., 1989; JD, U. Calif., Davis, 1995. Bar: Calif. 1995. Law clk. Colo. Atty. Gen.'s Office, Denver, 1993; law clk. to Justice Davis, Calif. 3d Dist. Appellate Ct., Sacramento, 1994; legal intern Calif. Atty. Gen.'s Office, Sacramento, 1994, Sacramento Dist. Atty.'s Office, Sacramento, 1995; assoc. Baum, Hedlund, Anstei, Guilford & Downey, L.A., 1995—. Mem. Barrister Ptnrs. for Success Com., 1995—. Mem. ABA, Nat. Assn. Women Lawyers, L.A. Women Lawyers Assn., The Barristers, George McBurney Complex Litigation Inn of Ct. Avocations: rock climbing, diving, skiing, basketball, volleyball. Appellate, Consumer commercial, Product liability. Office: Baum Hedlund et al 12100 Wilshire Blvd Ste 950 Los Angeles CA 90025-7107

**BARTHOLD, CLEMENTINE B.,** retired judge; b. Odessa, Russia, Jan. 11, 1921; came to U.S., 1925; d. Joseph Anton and Magdalene (Richter) Schwan; m. Edward Brendel Barthold, July 5, 1941 (dec.); children: Judith Anne Barthold DeSomone, John Edward. Student, Aberdeen Bus. Coll., 1940; BGS, Ind. U. S.E., 1978; JD, Ind. U., Indpls., 1980. Bar: Ind. 1980, U.S. Dist. Ct. (so. dist.) Ind. 1980. Sec., asst. to mgr. Clark County C. of C., Ind., 1959-60; chief probation officer Clark Cir. and Superior Cts., Jeffersonville, 1960-72; rsch. cons. Pub. Action Correctional Effort, Clark and Floyd Counties, 1972-75; instl. parole officer Ind. Women's Prison, Indpls., 1975-80; atty. State of Ind., 1980-83; judge Clark Superior Ct. No. 1, Jeffersonville, 1983-95; ret., 1995; ptnr. Barthold & De Simone Attys. at Law, 1998—. Councilwoman Clark County, Jefferson, 1997—. Recipient Good Govt. award Jeffersonville Jaycees, 1966, Good Citizenship award, 1967, Wonder Woman award, 1984, Robert J. Kinsey award, 1986, Sagamore of Wabash award, 1986, Outstanding Cmty. Svc. award Social Concerns League, 1966, Disting. Svc. award, Outstanding Contbn. to Field of Correction award, Women of Achievement award, Jeff BPW Appreciation award, Juvenile Justice award, Disting. Contemporary Women in History award, Disting. Leadership award, Women of Achievement award, 1982-83, Appreciation award VIPO, 1983, Children and Youth Recognition award, 1984, Gov.'s Exemplary award, 1984, 88, 89, 92, Commitment to Youth award, 1987, Warren W. Martin award, 1973, 87, Outstanding Child Advocacy in Ind. award, 1987, Cmty. Svc. award, 1988, Orgnl. Renewal award, 1988, Parents Without Ptnrs. award, 1989, Ind. Youth Investment award, 1992, Excellence in Pub. Info. and Edn. award, 1992. Mem. LWV, Ind. Bar Assn., Clark County Bar Assn., Ind. Correctional Assn. (pres. 1971, Disting. Svc. award 1967, 85), Ind. Judges Assn., Ind. Juvenile Justice Task Force, Ind. U. Alumni Assn., Howard Steamboat Mus., Bus. Profl. Women's Club, Ladies Elks Aux. Roman Catholic. Home: 948 E 7th St Jeffersonville IN 47130-4106

**BARTHOLD, WALTER,** lawyer; b. Toronto, Ont., Can., June 8, 1924; came to U.S., 1924; s. Walter and Josephine (Salmon) B.; m. Denise Buffington, May 2, 1957 (div. 1996); children: Charles F., David F., Nancy L.; m. Dorothy True LaValle, Sept. 7, 1996. BS, Northwestern U., 1948; LLB, Yale U., 1951. Bar: N.Y. 1952, U.S. Supreme Ct. 1963, U.S. Ct. Appeals (2d cir.) 1955. Assoc. Arthur, Dry & Kalish, N.Y.C., 1952-60, ptnr., 1961-78; ptnr. Barthold & McGuire, N.Y.C., 1978-81, Kissam, Halpin & Genovese, N.Y.C., 1981-82, Barthold & Eikenberry, N.Y.C., 1983-84; pvt. practice N.Y.C., 1984—; counsel Leaf Sternklar & Drogin, N.Y.C., 1988-89, Ferber, Greilsheimer, Chan & Essner, 1989-92. Author: Attorney's Guide to Effective Discovery Techniques, 1965. With U.S. Army, 1943-46, ETO. Fellow Am. Coll. Trial Lawyers, Am. Bar Found., N.Y. Bar Found.; mem. ABA, Assn. Bar City N.Y., N.Y. State Bar Assn., Yale Club. Democrat. Episcopalian. Avocations: music, biking, stamp collecting. General civil litigation, Antitrust. Home: 323 Stevens Ave Ridgewood NJ 07450-5203 Office: 489 5th Ave New York NY 10017-6105

**BARTIMUS, JAMES RUSSELL,** lawyer, educator; b. Trenton, Mo., Oct. 21, 1949; s. James Leeper and Dixie Lee (Swearingen) B.; m. Mary Dana Quick, Sept. 8, 1979; children: Adam James, Philip David, Ian Christian. BA, U. Mo., Columbia, 1971; JD, U. Mo., Kansas City, 1977; postgrad., Med. Sch., 1978-80. Bar: Mo. 1977, U.S. Dist. Ct. (we. dist.) Mo. 1977, U.S. Dist. Ct. Colo. 1992, U.S. Supreme Ct. 1994. Pvt. practice Frickleton & Presley, Kansas City, 1977—; adj. prof. sch. law U. Mo.-Kansas City, mem. adj. grad. faculty sch. nursing, lectr. sch. nursing and sch. law; lectr. numerous other law and health related groups. Contbr. articles to profl. jours., chpts. to books. Lt. USNR, 1971-74, Vietnam, Japan. Mem. ABA, ATLA, Am. Coll. Legal Medicine, Am. Bd. Profl. Liability Attys., Am. Bd. Trial Attys., Am. Soc. Law and Medicine, Am. Bar Found., Mo. Inst. Justice, Mo. Bar Assn., Mo. Assn. Trial Lawyers, Ariz. Trial Lawyers Assn., Kans. trial Lawyers Assn., Colo. Trial Lawyers Assn., Pitts. Inst. Legal Medicine, Kansas City Met. Bar Assn., Kansas City Bar Found., Internat. Soc. Barristers, Lawyer-Pilot's Bar Assn., U. Mo.-Kansas City Law Found., Kansas City Club, Blue Hills country Club, Shadow Glen Club, Phi Delta Phi. Personal injury, Product liability. Office: Frickleton & Preselye 1100 Main St Ste 2300 Kansas City MO 64105-5187

**BARTKUS, ROBERT EDWARD,** lawyer; b. Kearny, N.J., Sept. 30, 1946; s. Edward Charles and Dorothy Agnes (Konschott) B.; m. Mary Bartkus. BA with honors, Swarthmore Coll, 1968; JD, Stanford U., 1976. Bar: Calif. 1976, N.J. 1977, N.Y. 1977, U.S. Supreme Ct. (3d, 2d cirs.), U.S. Dist. Ct. N.J., U.S. Dist. Ct. (so. and ea. dist.) N.Y. Spl. counsel Schulte, Roth & Zabel, N.Y.C., 1985-88; tchg. asst. Stanford U. Law Sch., 1976; mem. Dist. X Ethics Com., 1992-97; lectr. N.J. Inst. for Continuing Edn., 1988—; master John J. Gibbons Intellectual Property Inn of Ct. Articles coeditor Stanford Law Rev., 1974-76; author Innovation Competition 28 Stanford Law Rev. 1976; author, editor: New Jersey Federal Civil Practice, 1992, N.J. Federal Civil Procedure, 1999; mem. editl. bd. N.J. Law Jour. (Alfred C. Clapp award 1995). Atty. Community Law Offfice, 1976-79, Legal Aid Soc., 1979-87; mem. alumni coun. Swarthmore Coll., 1977-78. Lt. USNR, 1968-73. Mem. ABA (ethics com. Dist. X), Nat. Assn. Securities Dealers (arbitrator), N.J. Bar Assn. (chair fed. practice com.), Assn. Fed. Bar of State of N.J., Morris County Bar Assn., Am. Arbitration Assn. (arbitrator), Delta Upsilon. Federal civil litigation, State civil litigation. Home: 6 Terrill Dr Califon NJ 07830-3443 Office: Profl Corp 90 Maple Ave Morristown NJ 07960-5221

**BARTLE, HARVEY, III,** federal judge; b. Bryn Mawr, Pa., June 6, 1941; s. Harvey Jr. and Dorothy L. (Baker) B.; m. Nathalie Akin Vanderpool, June 12, 1993; children: Elizabeth Louisa Masterson, Harvey IV, Peter Dixon Baker. AB in History, Princeton U., 1962; LLB, U. Pa., 1965. Bar: Pa. 1965, U.S. Dist. Ct. (ea. dist.) Pa. 1965, U.S. Ct. Appeals (3d cir.) 1969, U.S. Supreme Ct. 1978. Law clk. to Hon. John Morgan Davis U.S. Dist. Ct. (ea. dist.) Pa., 1965-67; assoc. Dechert, Price & Rhoads, 1967-73, ptnr., 1973-79, 81-91; Pa. Ins. Commr., 1979-80, Pa. Atty. Gen., 1980-81; judge U.S. Dist. Ct. (ea. dist.) Pa., 1991—. Editor Law Review U. Pa. Capt. U.S. Army Res. Mem. ABA, Phila. Bar Assn., Am. Law Inst. Episcopalian. Office: US Dist Ct 601 Market St Philadelphia PA 19106-1713

**BARTLETT, D. BROOK,** federal judge; b. 1937. BA, Princeton U., 1959; LLB, Stanford U., 1962. Assoc. Stinson, Mag, Thomson, McEvers & Fizzell, 1962-67, ptnr., 1967-69; asst. atty. gen. State of Mo., 1969-73, 1st asst. atty. gen., 1973-77; assoc. Blackwell, Sanders, Matheny, Weary & Lombardi, 1977-78, ptnr., 1978-81; judge U.S. Dist. Ct. (we. dist.) Mo., Kansas City, 1981-95, chief judge, 1995—. Office: US Dist Ct 400 E 9th St Ste 8552 Kansas City MO 64106-2681

**BARTLETT, EDWARD,** lawyer, legal association administrator; b. 1945. BS, U. Mont., JD. Bar: Mont. 1970. Pvt. practice Butte. Mem. ABA, State Bar Mont. (pres.-elect 1998-99). Natural resources, General corporate. Office: 40 E Broadway St Butte MT 59701-9350 also: State Bar Mont PO Box 577 Helena MT 59624-0577*

**BARTLETT, JAMES WILSON, III,** lawyer; b. Pasadena, Calif., Mar. 21, 1946; s. James Wilson Jr. and Helen (Archbold) B.; m. Jane Edmunds Graves; children: Matthew Archbold, Polly Graves. BA, Washington & Lee U., 1968; JD, Vanderbilt U., 1975. Bar: Md. 1975, U.S. Dist. Ct. Md. 1975, U.S. Dist. Ct. (no. dist.) Ohio, 1992, U.S. Ct. Claims 1984, U.S. Ct. Appeals (4th cir.) 1976, U.S. Ct. Appeals (6th cir.) 1992, U.S. Supreme Ct. 1995. Assoc. Semmes, Bowen & Semmes, Balt., 1975-85; pvt. practice Balt., 1985-86; ptnr. Kroll & Tract, Balt., 1986-87; ptnr. Wilson, Elser, Moskowitz, Edelman & Dicker, Balt., 1987-98, mng. ptnr., 1998—; permanent mem. jud. conf. 4th Cir. Assoc. editor: Am. Maritime Cases, 1997—; contbr. articles to profl. jours. Chmn. law firm campaign United Fund, Balt., 1979; bd. dirs. Roland Park Civic League, 1987-90. 1st lt. U.S. Army, 1969-71. Mem. ABA (chmn. admiralty and maritime litigation com. litigation sect. 1997-99, vice chmn. 1985-88, chmn. admiralty and maritime law com. tort and ins. practice sect. 1990-91, vice chmn. 1992-95), Md. Bar Assn., Balt. City Bar Assn., Maritime Law Assn. U.S. (proctor, bd. dirs. 1998—), Def. Rsch. Inst., Md. Assn. Def. Trial Counsel, Assn. Average Adjusters (Eng.), Assn. Average Adjusters U.S., Am. Boat and Yacht Coun., St. Andrews Soc., Md. Club, Propeller Club U.S. (gov. Balt. chpt. 1984-87, 97—, v.p. 1987-88, exec. v.p. 1988-89, pres. 1989-90, nat. regional v.p. 1991-92, nat. 3d v.p. 1995-96). Republican. Presbyterian. Admiralty, Professional liability, Product liability. Home: 307 Edgevale Rd Baltimore MD 21210-1913 Office: Wilson Elser Moskowitz Edelman & Ducker 400 E Pratt St Fl 7 Baltimore MD 21202-3116

**BARTLETT, JOSEPH WARREN,** lawyer; b. Boston, June 14, 1933; s. Charles W. and Barbara (Hastings) B.; m. May Parish, Apr. 28, 1956 (div.); children: Charles, Susan, Henry; m. Barbara Bemis, Sept. 20, 1980. AB, Harvard U., 1955; LLB, Stanford U., 1960. Bar: Mass. 1962, D.C. 1969, N.Y. 1981. Law clk. Chief Justice Warren, U.S. Supreme Ct., 1960-61; pvt. practice Boston, 1961-66; ptnr. Gaston & Snow, Boston, 1966-80; ptnr. Gaston & Snow (formerly Gaston Snow Beekman & Bogue), N.Y.C., 1980-90, of counsel, 1990-91; ptnr. Mayer, Brown & Platt, 1991-96, Morrison & Foerster, N.Y.C., 1996-; counsel Mass. Commn. Adminstrn., 1964-65; gen. counsel, under sec. Dept. Commerce, Washington, 1967-69; prin. adviser on universal social security coverage Sec. of HEW, Washington, 1978-79; acting prof. Stanford U., 1978; trustee, mem. fin. com. Montefiore Med. Ctr.; mem. Council on Fgn. Relations; adj. prof. NYU Law Sch. Served to 1st lt. U.S. Army, 1956-57. Fellow Am. Bar Found.; mem. Am. Law Inst., Am. Bar Assn., Boston Bar Assn. (pres. 1977-78). Democrat. Episcopalian. General corporate, Securities. Home: 200 E 71st St Apt 16C New York NY 10021-5147 Office: Morrison & Foerster Ste 306 1290 Avenue Of The Americas Fl 41 New York NY 10104-0050

**BARTLETT, ROBERT WILLIAM,** lawyer, publishing executive; b. Chgo., Nov. 11, 1941; s. Robert C. and Rita E. Bartlett; m. Mary Lou Holtzman, Mar. 8, 1988. AB, Stanford U., 1963; LLB, U. Va., 1966. Bar: Ill. 1966. Assoc. counsel U.S. League Savs. Instns., Chgo., 1970-77, assoc. gen. counsel, editor legal bull., 1977-81, sr. v.p., 1981-91; exec. editor bus. and fin. group Commerce Clearing House, Riverwoods, Ill., 1991—. Mem. ABA (mem. com. on savs. instns. 1973--). Roman Catholic. Avocation: running. Banking. Home: 8 Anglican Ln Lincolnshire IL 60069-3316 Office: Commerce Clearing House 2700 Lake Cook Rd Deerfield IL 60015-3888

**BARTLEY, BRIAN JAMES,** lawyer; b. Bossier City, La., Apr. 11, 1955; s. Robert Paul and Joan Ann (Leahy) B.; m. Kathleen Dorothy Skove, Aug. 11, 1979 (div. Feb. 1984); children: Kimberly Karen, Ryan Matthew; m. Marilynn Ann Kyritsis, Dec. 8, 1990; children: Sara Leahy, Elizabeth Joan. BA in Philosophy, U. Del., 1977; JD, Del. Law Sch., 1980. Bar: Pa. 1980, U.S. Dist. Ct. (ea. dist.) Pa. 1980, Del. 1981, U.S. Dist. Ct. Del. 1981, U.S. Supreme Ct. 1984, U.S. Ct. Appeals (3d cir.) 1991. Law clk. Del. State Pub. Defender, Wilmington, Del., 1978-79; law clk. Lawrence M. Sullivan, Wilmington, Del., 1979-81, atty., 1981-83, 83-88; atty. pvt. practice, Wilmington, Del., 1983-85; solicitor Town of Bellefonte (Del.), 1983-92; ptnr. Sullivan and Bartley, Wilmington, 1988-93, 95-99; atty. pvt. practice, Wilmington, 1993-95, 99—, Del. State Pub. Defender, Wilmington, 1981—; instr. State of Del. Probation and Parole Office, Wilmington, 1990—; mem. tng. subcom. Del. Sentencing Accountability Commn., Wilmington, 1987-88. Mem. Del. Commn. Women. Wilmington, 1994—, chmn. strategic planning com., 1994-95, legis. com., 1996—; mem. legis. subcom. Del. Trauma System Planning Group, Dover, 1994-95; campaign dir. Dennis B. Phifer Dem. Candidate for State Treas., Wilmington, 1994; mem. Dem. State Coordinated Campaign Com., 1994; mem. Del. Roundtable, 1990-94; fundraiser Oberly for Senate Campaign, 1993-94, Butler for Atty. Gen. Campaign, 1994; vol. Thomas B. Carper Campaign for Gov., 1992, Ruth Ann Minner Campaign for lt. gov., 1992, Carper for Congress, 1982, 84, 86, 88, 90, William Quillen Campaign fot Gov., 1984; counsel Dem. State Hdqs., Election Day, 1990, 92, 94; candidate Dem. Nomination for State Atty. Gen., 1986. Mem. Am. Soc. Safety Engrs. (assoc.), Del. State Bar Assn., Del. Trial Lawyers Assn. (chmn. criminal law com. 1993-95, mem. legis. com. 1994-95). Democrat. Roman Catholic. Avocations: elective politics, poetry. Criminal, Personal injury, Workers' compensation. Home: 704 W 23rd St Wilmington DE 19802-3933 Office: Del State Pub Defender 1214 King St Ste 200 Wilmington DE 19801-3218

**BARTO, CHARLES O., JR.,** lawyer; b. Altoona, Pa., Aug. 12, 1946; s. Charles O. and Ernestine I. (Styers) B.; m. Marsha D. Packer, July 31, 1971; 1 child, Megan Suzanne. BA, Pa. State U., 1968; JD, Dickinson Sch. of Law, 1971. Bar: Pa. 1971, U.S. Dist. Ct. (mid. dist.) Pa. 1971, U.S. Supreme Ct. 1975, U.S. Ct. Appeals (3d cir.) 1979, U.S. Tax Ct. 1985. Asst. pub. defender Dauphin County Pub. Defender's Office, Harrisburg, Pa., 1971-73; assoc. Killian, Gephart & Snyder, Harrisburg, 1971-74; ptnr. Killian & Gephart, Harrisburg, 1975-83; prin. Charles O. Barto, Jr. & Assocs., Harrisburg, 1983—; gen. counsel Pa. Health Care Assn., Harrisburg, 1971—; conflicts counsel Hosp. Assn. Pa., Harrisburg, 1990—. Contbr. articles to books in field. V.p. St. Thomas Civic Assn., Linglestown, Pa., 1976-87; pres. consistory St. Thomas United Ch. of Christ, Linglestown, 1989, 92; chair constn. com. Pa. Coun. Chs., Harrisburg, 1990—, parliamentarian, 1990—; mem. Pa. Forestry Assn. Recipient Better Life award Pa. Health Care Assn., 1988, award of merit Health Care Facilities Assn. Pa., 1977, Boss of Yr. award Dauphin County Legal Secs. Assn., 1985-86. Mem. ABA, Pa. Bar Assn., Dauphin County Bar Assn., Assn. Trial Lawyers Am., Pa. Trial Lawyers Assn., Nat. Health Lawyers Assn. (bd. dirs. 1994—, pres. 1997-98), Kiwanis, Koons Pool and Swim Club (pres. 1994—). Democrat. Avocations: tennis, skiing, coaching softball, computer programming, collecting pens. Administrative and regulatory, State civil litigation, Health. Office: Charles O Barto Jr & Assocs 608 N 3rd St Harrisburg PA 17101-1102

**BARTOL, ERNEST THOMAS,** lawyer; b. Mineola, N.Y., Feb. 2, 1946; s. Frank Henry and Mary Ann (Kretlein) B.; m. Christine Ann Pillis; children: Jacqueline Marie, Aimee Elizabeth, Suzanne Melissa. BS in Acctg., Fordham U., 1967; JD, Villanova U., 1970. Bar: N.Y. 1971, U.S. Dist. Ct. (ea. and so. dists.) N.Y. 1973, U.S. Ct. Appeals (2d cir.) 1975, U.S. Supreme Ct. 1974. Staff acct. Pustorino, Puglisi, Behan & Co., N.Y.C., 1965-70; tax specialist Arthur Young & Co., Phila., 1970; acct. Arthur Andersen & Co., N.Y.C., 1970-71; assoc. Gehrig, Ritter, Coffey et al, Hempstead, N.Y., 1971-78; founder, sr. ptnr. Murphy, Bartol & O'Brien, LLP, Mineola, N.Y., 1978—; bd. dirs. numerous cos.; counsel to senator N.Y. State Senate, Garden City, 1985-90. Exec. leader Nassau County Rep. Com., Westbury, N.Y., 1978—, Oyster Bay Rep. Com., 1978—; sec., mem. parish coun. and spl. sch. com. St. Edward Roman Cath. Ch., Syosset, N.Y., 1978-80; mem. exec. com. United Cerebral Palsy Assn. Nassau County, 1978—, chmn. forget-me-not ball, 1987-92; pres., founder cmty. adv. coun. Syosset Cmty. Hosp., 1987-92; bd. dirs. L.I. Children's Mus., 1996-99 bd. trustees NY Inst. Tech., 1997-99. Named Man of Yr., United Cerebral Palsy Assn. Nassau County, 1993. Mem. ABA, N.Y. State Bar Assn. (trusts and estates law com. 1983—, lectr. on estate topics), Nassau County Bar Assn. (estates and trusts law com. 1975—), profl. ethics com. 1980-86, 89-93), Criminal Cts. Bar Assn., Nassau Lawyers Assn. L.I. (bd. dirs. 1977—, chmn. 1992-93, rec. sec. 1993-94, corr. sec. 1994-95, 1st v.p. 1995-97, pres. 1997-98), Fed. Bar Coun., N.Y. State Trial Lawyers Assn., Cath. Lawyers Guild Diocese Rockville Centre, Chaminade H.S. Alumni Assn. (class rep. 1971, class dir. 1971-72, 1st v.p. 1972-74, pres. 1974-76), Rotary (sec.-treas. Syosset club 1980-90), Alpha Kappa Psi. Roman Catholic. Avocations: racquetball, tennis, fishing, softball, stamp collecting. Probate, Estate planning, General civil litigation. Office: Murphy Bartol & O'Brien LLP 22 Jericho Tpke Mineola NY 11501-2937

**BARTOLINI, DANIEL JOHN,** lawyer, educator; b. Trenton, N.J., Aug. 7, 1935; s. Ermindo and Katherine (Iorio) B.; m. Kay Jean Lee, Dec. 19, 1958; children: Debra L., Daniel John Jr., Alyssa D., Wilmin P. AB in Philosophy, Villanova U., 1957; postgrad., Cath. U. Am., 1958; JD, U. Md., Balt., 1969. Bar: Md. 1970, U.S. Dist. Ct. Md. 1974, U.S. Ct. Appeals (4th cir.) 1977, U.S. Supreme Ct. 1977. Analyst Social Security Adminstrn., Balt. and, N.J., 1958-84; assoc. Burke Gerber Wilen & Francomano, Balt., 1983-87; ptnr. Bartolini & Seaman, Balt. and Ellicott City, Md., 1989—; prof. law Villa Julie Coll., Stevenson, Md., 1987—. With USMC, 1957-59. Recipient performance awards Social Security Adminstrn., 1960-80, Undersec.'s award Dept. Health and Human Resources, 1971; named Citizen of Yr. KC Coun. 3960, 1992. General civil litigation, Criminal, General practice. Home: 10512 Marriottsville Rd Randallstown MD 21133-1308 Office: Bartolini & Seaman 1643 Liberty Rd Sykesville MD 21784-6544

**BARTON, BERNARD ALAN, JR.,** lawyer; b. Glens Falls, N.Y., Aug. 13, 1948; s. Bernard A. Sr. and Geraldine (Bushey) B.; children: Lindsey, Kylie. BA, U. Fla., 1969, JD, 1975, LLM, 1976. Bd. cert. tax lawyer. Ptnr. Holland & Knight, Tampa, Fla., 1976—. Editor, contbg. author Florida Taxation, State Taxation Series, 1994. Mem. ABA, Nat. Assn. Bond Attys., Fla. Bar Assn. (exec. coun. tax sect., chmn. various coms. 1980-99). Republican. Episcopalian. Taxation, general, State and local taxation, Corporate taxation. Office: Holland & Knight 400 N Ashley Dr PO Box 1288 Tampa FL 33601-1288

**BARTON, BRUCE ANDREW,** lawyer; b. Detroit, May 30, 1934; s. Michael Andrew and Mary Watson (Strain) B.; m. Barbara Ann Haener, Feb. 3, 1962; children: Anne M. Blackport, Colleen M. Davis, Scott A. Barton, Kevin A. Barton. B of Philosophy, U. Detroit, 1958, JD, 1961. Bar: Mich. 1961, U.S. Dist. Ct. (ea. dist.) Mich. 1973, U.S. Supreme Ct. 1973, U.S. Dist. Ct. (we. dist.) Mich. 1974, U.S. Claims Ct. 1990. Pvt. practice Jackson, Mich., 1962, 77-79; asst. prosecuting atty. County of Jackson, 1962-65, prosecuting atty., 1965-76; ptnr. Barton Benedetto & Bishop, Jackson, 1979-93, shareholder, 1994-95; pvt. practice Jackson, 1996—. Dist. adminstr. Mich. Little League Dist. 3, S.E. Mich., 1987—; chmn. Jackson Rep. Party, 1995-96; pres. Exch. Club of Jackson, 1988-89. Roman Catholic. General practice, Criminal, Probate. Office: 414 S Jackson St Jackson MI 49201-2217

**BARTON, ELLEN LOUISE,** lawyer, educator, consultant; b. Harrisburg, Pa., Jan. 17, 1946; d. George Michael and Irene Catherine (Gregor) Schmeltzer; m. Norman W. Barton, Nov. 28, 1987; children: William Michael, Ian Christopher, Michael Alexander. A.B. in Psychology, Rosemont Coll., 1972; J.D., U. Cin., 1978. Dist. Fellow Am. Soc. Healthcare Risk Mgmt. Bar: Ohio 1978, U.S. Dist. Ct. (so. dist.) Ohio 1979, Pa. 1985, U.S. Ct. Appeals (3d cir. 1985), Maryland 1989; CPCU. Occupational analyst Commonwealth of Pa., Harrisburg, 1972-74; ins. adjuster Lloyd

Deist, Inc., Cin., 1977-78; asst. editor FC&S Bulls, Nat. Underwriter Co., Cin., 1978-81; assoc. dir. risk mgmt. U. Cin., 1981-84, dir. risk mgmt., 1984-85; dir. risk mgmt. U. Pa., 1985-87; ptnr. Fischer, Klimon, Salman & Harpster, Cin., 1984-85, Klimon, Salman, Greve & Harpster, Phila., 1985-89, Barton & Salman, Balt., 1990-91; pres. Neumann Ins. Co., 1987-97; corp. dir. risk mgmt. Franciscan Health System, Aston, Pa., 1987-97; sr. v.p., legal svcs. gen. counsel Franciscan Health System, 1993-97; dir., chairperson Alternative Ins. Mgmt. Svcs., Inc., 1989-97; dir., chmn. Preferred Physicians Ins. Co., 1988-97; dir., chairperson Consol. Cath. Casualty Risk Retention Group, Inc., 1987-97; CEO, gen. counsel New Am. Health, L.L.C., Glen Burnie, Md., 1997-98; health care practice leader Aon Risk Svcs., Inc., Balt., 1998; v.p. risk mgmt. MedStar Health, Columbia, Md., 1999—; cons. Don Malecki & Assocs., Fort Thomas, Ky., 1983-85; asst. atty. gen. State of Ohio, Columbus, 1983-85; asst. prof. family medicine U.Cin., 1984-85; legal advisor Children's Internat. Summer Villages, Cin., 1984-85. Editor: Insuring the Lease Exposure, Part II, 1981; contbr. articles to profl. jours. Mem. Our Lady of Rosary Sch. Bd., Greenhills, Ohio, 1974-81; v.p. Covered Bridge Civic Assn., Cin., 1979-81, area rep., 1979-82; pres. Nat. Underwriter Co. Fed. Credit Union, Cin., 1980-81. Pa. Higher Edn. Assistance Agy. scholar Rosemont Coll., Phila., 1971-72. Mem. ABA, Ohio Bar Assn., Pa. Bar Assn., Md. Bar Assn., Soc. CPCUs, Am. Soc. Law and Medicine, Nat. Health Lawyers Assn., Am. Soc. Healthcare Risk Mgrs., Risk and Ins Mgmt. Soc. (pres. 1990-91), Am. Inst. for Property and Liability Underwriters (chartered property and casualty underwriter 1981). Republican. Roman Catholic. Insurance, Personal injury, Health. Office: MedStar Health 5565 Sterrett Pl Fl 5 Columbia MD 21044-2665

**BARTON, JAMES CARY,** lawyer; b. Raymondville, Tex., Sept. 1, 1940; s. Dewey Albert and Dorothy Marie (Keene) B.; m. Isabel Pattee Critz, Sept. 12, 1964 (div. June 1975); children: Hamilton Keene, James Albert, John Franklin; m. Carolyn Ann Cox, Dec. 20, 1975; stepchildren: Holly Ann Adams, Laura Lee Adams, Jennifer Lynn Adams. BA, Baylor U., 1962; LLB, Harvard U., 1965. Bar: Tex. 1965, U.S. Dist. Ct. (so. dist.) Tex. 1972, U.S. Tax Ct. 1977. Trial atty. FPC, Washington, 1965-67; atty.-advisor U.S. Tax Ct., Washington, 1967-68; assoc. to ptnr. Kleberg, Mobley, Lockett & Weil, Corpus Christi, Tex., 1969-75, Brown, Maroney, Rose, Baker & Barber, Austin, Tex., 1975-82; ptnr. to of counsel Johnson & Swanson, Austin and Dallas, 1982-88; dir. Smith, Barshop, Stoffer & Millsap, Inc., San Antonio, 1988-91; prin. J. Cary Barton, P.C., San Antonio, 1991-93; prin Barton & Schneider, L.L.P., San Antonio, 1993—; speaker in field. Sgt. USAF, 1968-69. Mem. ABA, State Bar Tex. (mem. coun. of real estate probate and trust law sect. 1982-85, mem. real estate forms com. 1986—), Am. Coll. Real Estate Lawyers, Tex. Bd. legal Specialization (cert. in comml. real estate law), Tex. Coll. Real Estate Attys. Democrat. Episcopalian. Real property. Office: Barton & Schneider LLP 700 N Saint Marys St Ste 1825 San Antonio TX 78205-3596

**BARTON, JUDITH MARIE,** lawyer, lobbyist; b. Grosse Pointe, Mich., Feb. 19, 1953; d. Joseph J. and Shirley (Fisher) B.; m. A. Scott MacGuidwin, Sept. 19, 1980; children: Stephen Fisher, Richard Joseph, Elizabeth Ashley, James Scott, Scott Thomas. BA, U. Mich., 1975; JD, Thomas M. Cooley Sch. Law, 1979. Bar: Mich. 1981, U.S. Dist. Ct. (we. and ea. dists.) Mich. 1982. Mgr. bus. and circulation Football News/Basketball Weekly, Grosse Pointe, 1975-77; legis. asst. Mich. Ho. of Reps., Lansing, 1977-80, legal specialist, 1980-81; staff dir. Mich. State Senate, Lansing, 1981-83; pvt. practice Lansing, 1983-93; majority gen. coun. Mich. House of Reps., 1993—, chief policy and legal counsel, 1994—; lobbyist Mich. Rental Housing Assn., 1989-93. Bd. dirs. Common Cause, Lansing, 1983-89, state chairperson, Mich., 1987-89; bd. dirs. Landlords of Mid-Mich., Lansing, 1985-89. Mem. ABA, Mich. Bar Assn., Ingham County Bar Assn., Women's Law Assn., Pub. Action Com., Capitol Area Women's Network (bd. dirs. 1983-84), Civitan Internat., Pi Beta Phi. Republican. Roman Catholic. Real property, Legislative, Family and matrimonial. Home: 4317 Manitou Dr Okemos MI 48864-2715

**BARTON, ROBERT L., JR.,** judge, educator; b. Ballston Spa, N.Y., June 19, 1943; s. Robert L. Sr. and Bertha (Di Pasquale) B.; m. Jean M. Adamchic, Aug. 14, 1965; children: Robert Joseph, Katherine Anne. BA, U. Pitts., 1965; JD, Boston Coll., 1969. Bar: Mass. 1969, R.I. 1970, D.C. 1972, U.S. Ct. Appeals (1st cir.) 1970, U.S. Ct. Appeals (D.C. cir.) 1973, U.S. Dist. Ct. R.I., 1971, U.S. Dist. Ct. D.C. 1973, U.S. Dist. Ct. Md. 1973. Law clk. U.S. Dist. Ct. R.I., Providence, 1969-70; staff atty. R.I. Legal Svcs., Providence, 1970-71; spl. asst. to solicitor U.S. Dept. Labor, Washington, 1971-72; assoc. Sherman, Dunn, Cohen & Leifer, Washington, 1972-75; trial atty. FTC, Washington, 1975-88; judge Pa. Office of Hearing & Appeals, Pitts., 1988-90, Office of Hearings, Washington, 1990-95, Office of Adminstr. Law Judges, Washington, 1995—; trial instr. Nat. Inst. Trial Advocacy, Washington, 1982-86, U.S. Dept. Justice, Washington, 1986-96. Chair com. Cath. League for Religious Rights, Milw., 1983-84. Master Am. Inn of Ct.; mem. Fed. Bar Assn. (co-chair adminstrv. jud. com.), Fed. Adminstrn. Law Judges Assn. (mem. exec. com.), Nat. Lawyers Assn. Roman Catholic. Avocations: travel tennis, swimming. Office: Office Adminstrv Law Judges 5107 Leesburg Pike Ste 1905 Falls Church VA 22041-3234

**BARTON, ROBIN LISA,** lawyer; b. Staten Island, N.Y., Mar. 18, 1968; d. Alan Herbert and Joan Miriam Barton. BA in Polit. Sci., Purdue U., 1989; JD, NYU, 1992. Bar: N.Y. 1993, U.S. Dist. Ct. (so. dist.) N.Y. 1997. Asst. dist. atty, Manhattan Dist. Atty.'s Office, N.Y.C., 1992-94, Office of Spl. Narcotics, N.Y.C., 1994-98, Rackets Bur., Manhattan Dist. Atty.'s Office, N.Y.C., 1998—. Avocations: sports, reading, needlework, pets. Office: NY County Dist Atty's Office 1 Hogan Pl New York NY 10013-4311

**BARTON, ROGER E.,** lawyer; b. Dec. 28, 1962; s. Gerald C. and Lenore Barton; m. Kathryn Barton; children: Gregory, Matthew. Bar: N.Y. 1988. Atty. Dreyer & Traub, N.Y.C., 1987-88, Sidley & Austin, N.Y.C., 1988-91; atty., head corp. and internat. dept. Barton & Zasky, N.Y.C., 1991—. Mem. fund raising com. The Fisher Ctr. for Alzheimer Rsch. Found., N.Y.C.; chmn. N.Y.-Budapest Sister City Program, N.Y.C.; pres. 201 W. 89th Owners Corp., N.Y.C.; bd. dirs. Culligan-Hungary Rt., Transbridge, Inc. General corporate, Personal injury. Office: Barton & Zasky 420 Lexington Ave Rm 2618 New York NY 10170-0135

**BARTON, THOMAS MCCARTY,** lawyer; b. Atlanta, Nov. 27, 1964; s. Earl G. and Ansley B. (Boyd) B.; m. Elizabeth Hudson, Aug. 20, 1988; children: Haley Elizabeth, Katherine India. BS in History, Presbyn. Coll., Clinton, S.C., 1986; JD magna cum laude, U. Ga., 1989. Bar: Ga. 1989, U.S. Ct. Appeals (11th cir.) 1989, U.S. Dist. Ct. (no. and mid. dist.) Ga. 1989. Ptnr. Smith, Gambrell & Russell, Atlanta, 1989—. Editl. bd. Ga. Law Rev., 1988. Smith Gambrell Merit scholar, 1989. Mem. ABA, Ga. Bar Assn. Am. Inns of Ct. (mem., barrister 1993-94), Order of the Coif. General civil litigation. Office: Smith Gambrell & Russell 1230 Peachtree St NE Ste 3100 Atlanta GA 30309-3592

**BARTOSIC, FLORIAN,** law educator, lawyer, arbitrator; b. Danville, Pa., Sept. 15, 1926; s. Florian W. and Elsie (Woodring) B.; m. Eileen M. Payne, 1952 (div. 1969); children: Florian, Ellen, Thomas, Stephen; m. Alberta C. Chew, 1990. B.A., Pontifical Coll., 1948; B.C.L., Coll. William and Mary, 1956; LL.M., Yale U., 1957. Bar: Va. 1956, U.S. Supreme Ct. 1959. Asst. instr. Yale U., 1956-57; assoc. prof. law Coll. William and Mary, 1957, Villanova U., 1957-59; atty. NLRB, Washington, 1956, 57, 59; counsel Internat. Brotherhood of Teamsters, Washington, 1959-71; prof. law Wayne State U., 1971-80, U. Calif., Davis, 1980-92; recalled to tchg., 1994—; prof. emeritus law U. Calif., Davis, 1993—, dean law, 1980-90; adj. prof. George Washington U., 1966-71, Cath. U. Am., 1960-71; mem. panel arbitrators Fed. Mediation and Conciliation Service, 1972—; hearing officer Mich. Employment Relations Commn., 1972-80, Mich. Civil Rights Commn., 1974-80; bd. dirs. Mich. Legal Services Corp., 1973-80, Inst. Labor and Indsl. Relations, U. Mich., Wayne State U., 1976-80; mem. steering com. Inst. on Global Conflict and Cooperation, 1982-83; mem. adv. bd. Assn. for Union Democracy Inc., 1980—, adv. coms. Calif. Jud. Council, 1984-85, 87; vis. scholar Harvard Law Sch., 1987, Stanford Law Sch., 1987; sr. rsch. scholar ILO, 1990-91; acad. visitor Oxford U., London Sch. Econs., 1991; mem. exec. bd. Pub. Interest Clearinghouse, 1988-90. Co-author: Labor Relations Law in the Private Sector, 1977, 2d edit., 1986; contbr. articles to law jours. Mem. ABA (sec. labor relations law sect. 1974-75), Fed. Bar Assn., Am. Law Inst. (acad. mem. labor law adv. com. on continuing profl. edn.), Soc. Profls. in Dispute Resolution (regional v.p. 1979-80), Indsl. Rels. Rsch. Assn., Internat. Soc. Labor Law and Social Legis., Internat. Indsl. Rels. Assn., Am. Arbitration Assn. (panel), Nat Lawyers Guild, ACLU (dir. Detroit chpt. 1976-77), Order of Coif (hon.), Scribes. Home: 235 Ipanema Pl Davis CA 95616-0253 Office: U Calif Sch Law Mrak Hall Dr Davis CA 95616

**BARTUNEK, ROBERT R(ICHARD), JR.,** lawyer; b. Cleve., July 2, 1946; s. Robert Richard and Clare Elizabeth (Lonsway) B.; 1 child, Kathryn Elizabeth. BS, Bucknell U., 1968; MBA, Ohio State U., 1974, JD, 1975; LLM, U. Mo., Kansas City, 1986. Bar: Mo. 1975, Kans. 1997, U.S. Dist. Ct. (we. dist.) Mo. 1975, U.S. Tax Ct. 1981, U.S. Dist. Ct. Kans. 1997. Ptnr. Beckett, Lolli & Bartunek, Kansas City, 1975-96, Swanson, Midgley, Gangwere, Kitchin & McLarney, Kansas City, 1997—. Mem. Men's Sr. Baseball League. Decorated Bronze Star. Mem. ABA, Lawyers Assn. Greater Kansas City, Kansas City Met. Bar Assn. (chmn. tax law com.). Roman Catholic. General corporate, Taxation, general, Estate taxation. Home: 608 W Dartmouth Rd Kansas City MO 64113-2029 Office: Swanson Midgley Gangwere Kitchin & McLarney 922 Walnut 1500 Commerce Trust Bldg Kansas City MO 64106

**BARTZ, DAVID JOHN,** lawyer; b. Appleton, Wis., Feb. 15, 1955; s. Frederick Carl and Dorothy Lucille (Weckwerth) B. BA, U. Wis., 1976; MA in Pub. Affairs, U. Minn., 1979; JD, Ariz. State U., 1985. Bar: Ariz. 1985, U.S. Dist. Ct. Ariz. 1985, U.S. Ct. Appeals (9th cir.) 1985, Wis. 1989, U.S. Dist. Ct. (we. dist.) Wis. 1996, U.S. Dist. Ct. (ea. dist.) Wis. 1997. Policy analyst Minn. Dept. Transp., St. Paul, 1978-79; office dir. Wis. Senate, Madison, 1979-82, 86; pvt. practice, Phoenix, 1985-86; adminstr. Wis. Dept. Justice, Madison, 1987-91; pvt. practice, Madison, 1991—. Mem. ASPA (sec. Wis. Capital chpt. 1981-82), Ariz. Bar Assn., Wis. Bar Assn., Dane County Bar Assn. General corporate, Criminal, Labor.

**BARUSCH, LAWRENCE ROOS,** lawyer; b. Oakland, Calif., Aug. 23, 1949; s. Maurice Radston and Phyllis (Rose) B.; m. Susan Amanda Smith, Aug. 7, 1983; children: Nathaniel M., Ariana G. BA summa cum laude, Harvard U., 1971, JD cum laude, 1975. Bar: Calif. 1975. Assoc. Cotton, Seligman & Ray, San Francisco, 1975-77; gen. counsel Jones & Guerrero Co., Inc., Agana, Guam, 1977-82; ptnr. Klemm, Blair & Barusch, P.C., Agana, Guam, 1982-85; assoc. Davis, Graham & Stubbs, Salt Lake City, 1986-87; counsel Parsons, Behl & Latimer, Salt Lake City, 1987-89, shareholder, 1989—; counsel Guam Tax Code Commn., 1990-94; adj. prof. U. Utah Coll. Law, 1998-99, vis. assoc. prof., 1999—; mem. com. U.S. activities of foreigners and tax treaties, tax sect. ABA, 1994—. Contbr. articles to Guam Bar Jour., Utah Bar Jour. and Tax Notes. Chmn Dem. Party, Davis County, Utah, 1997-99. Sheldon fellow Harvard U., 1971. Mem. Guam Bar Assn. (pres. 1982-84), No. Marianas Bar Assn., Utah Bar Assn. (chmn. tax sect. 1994-95), Calif. Bar Assn., Phi Beta Kappa. Corporate taxation, Natural resources, Real property. Office: Parsons Behle & Latimer 201 S Main St Ste 1800 Salt Lake City UT 84111-2218

**BARWELL, CINDY ANN,** lawyer; b. Bklyn., Aug. 3, 1957; d. Walter E. and Ingeborg (Rodenkerchen) B. BSBA, U. Denver, 1977; MBA, U. Miami, Fla., 1978; JD, U. Toledo, 1984. Bar: Fla. 1984, Colo. 1994, U.S. Dist. Ct. (so. dist.) Fla. 1987, U.S. Ct. Appeals (11th cir.) 1992, U.S. Supreme Ct. 1989. Assoc. Martz and McClure, St. Augustine, Fla., 1984-85, Novey and Mendelson, Tallahassee, Fla., 1985, Reynolds and Reynolds, Boca Raton, Fla., 1985-88; prin. Cindy A. Barwell, P.A., Boca Raton, Fla., 1988—; traffic magistrate County of Palm Beach, Fla.; arbitrator, mediator; spl. master Collections Ct., Palm Beach County. Mem. ABA, Fla. Bar Assn. Republican. General civil litigation, General practice, Landlord-tenant. Office: Cindy A Barwell PA 1300 SW 20th St Boca Raton FL 33486-6643

**BASCONI, PAMELA BRAY,** lawyer; b. Louisville, Sept. 10, 1951; d. Walter Andrew and Roberta Lee (Schrodt) Wimberg; children: Zachary Andrew, Michael D. BBA, U. Ky., 1973, JD, 1976. Atty. Fowler Measle & Bell, Lexington, Ky., 1976-84, Gallion Baker & Bray, Lexington, Ky., 1984—; instr., land transfer, U. Ky. Coll. Law, Lexington, 1991-92; dir. Fayette County Bar Assn., Lexington, 1995—. Pres., dir. Providence Montessori Sch., Lexington, 1991-95; bd. dirs. Family Care Ctr., Lexington, 1991-95; Leadership Lexington C. of C., 1990-91. Mem. Ky. Bar Assn. (chair partnership com. 1986), Lexington Jour. Club, Bluegrass Estate Planning Coun. (dir. 1978-81). Avocations: biking, skiing. Health, Estate planning, General corporate. Office: Gallion Baker & Bray 200 W Vine St Ste 710 Lexington KY 40507-1641

**BASEFSKY, STUART MARK,** law reference librarian, information specialist; b. Denver, Oct. 31, 1949; s. Stanley S. and Ilene U. (Sunshine) B.,; m. Claire M. Germain, Aug. 16, 1976; 1 child, Nicolas. Student, U. Erlangen, Fed. Republic of Germany, 1969-70; BA, U. Colo., 1971; MA in Teaching, Duke U., 1975; MSLS, U. N.C., 1979. Info. specialist N.C. Sci. & Tech. Rsch. Ctr., Research Triangle Park, N.C., 1980; documents libr. N.C. State U., Raleigh, 1980-83, Duke U., Durham, N.C., 1983-93; reference libr. Sch. Indsl. & Labor Rels., Cornell U., Ithaca, N.Y., 1993—; adj. instr. sch. info. and libr. sci. U. N.C., Chapel Hill, 1990-92; mem. adv. bd. Washington Alert Svc. of Congl. Quar. Inc., 1990—, pres. Ithaca Pub. Ed. Initiative, 1996—; mem. adv. bd. HR Advisor of Ria/Alignmark, 1998—. Contbr. numerous articles to profl. jours.; TV interviewee on pub. documents and telecaptioning, 1985-87. Pres. Ithaca Pub. Edn. Initiative, 1996—. Recipient Key Vol. award Durham County, 1978, ILR Recognition award, 1999. Mem. ALA, N.C. Libr. Assn. (lobbyist 1987, mem. exec. bd. 1984-85), Patent Documentation Soc., Am. Assn. Law Librs. (founder, chmn. citation reform com. 1980-83), Internat. Platform Assn. Democrat. Avocation: swimming. Home: 10 Wedgewood Dr Ithaca NY 14850-1063 Office: Cornell U Sch Indsl & Labor Rels Catherwood Lib Ives Hall Ithaca NY 14853-3901

**BASHAW, STEVEN BRADLEY,** lawyer; b. Chgo., Mar. 2, 1951; s. Raymond P. and Neila M. (Booth) B.; m. Laura L. Liptrot, Mar. 18, 1972; children: Jennifer, Kimberly, Andrew, Daniel. B.A. in History, U. Ill. 1973; J.D., Chgo. Kent Coll. Law, 1976. Bar: Ill. 1976, U.S. Dist. Ct. (no. dist.) Ill. 1976. Atty. Shapiro & Kreisman, Northbrook, Ill., 1974-77, Denis B. Pierce, Atty., Chgo., 1977-78; ptnr. Pierce & Bashaw, Chgo., 1978-83, Bashaw & Assocs., Hinsdale, Ill., 1983-93; ptnr. McBride Baker & Coles, Chgo., 1993—; teaching asst. Chgo. Kent Coll. Law, 1975-77; lectr. U.S. League of Savs., Chgo., 1979—; instr. Coll. DuPage Real Estate Law, 1990—; arbitrator DuPage and Cook County Ct. Annexed Arbitratio; mediator DuPage Ct. Annexed Mediator; lectr., panelist Mortgage Bankers Assn. Am., Washington, 1980—; panelist Ill. Mortgage Bankers Assn., Chgo., 1982—, Ill. Continuing Legal Edn., Ill. Inst. Tech., Chgo., 1985-86, Personal Computers for Lawyers, Representing the Mortgagee under the Ill. Morgage Foreclosure Law, 1987-89; mem. Cook County jud. com. Implementation of Ill. Mortgage Foreclosure, 1987, DuPage County jud. com., 1987; instr. Inst. Fin. Edn. Coorespondence. Study Dept., 1986—. Sect. chmn. Hinsdale Village Caucus, 1983-85. Mem. ABA, Ill. State Bar Assn. (past chair alternative dispute resolution sect.; mem. coun. real estate sect.), Porsche Club Am. Republican. Roman Catholic. Real property, State civil litigation, Contracts commercial. Office: McBride Baker & Coles 1 Mid America Plz Oakbrook Terrace IL 60181

**BASHWINER, STEVEN LACELLE,** lawyer; b. Cin., Aug. 3, 1941; s. Carl Thomas and Ruth Marie (Burlis) B.; m. Arden J. Lang, Apr. 24, 1966 (div. 1978); children: Heather, David; m. Donna Lee Gerber, Sept. 13, 1981; children: Margaret, Matthew. AB, Holy Cross Coll., 1963; JD, U. Chgo., 1966. Bar: Ill. 1966, U.S. Dist. Ct. Ill. 1967, U.S. Ct. Appeals (7th cir.) 1968, U.S. Supreme Ct. 1970. Assoc. Kirkland & Ellis, Chgo., 1966-72, ptnr., 1972-76; ptnr. Friedman & Koven, Chgo., 1976-86, Katten Muchin & Zavis, Chgo., 1986—. Served to sgt. USAFR, 1966-72. Mem. ABA, Fed. Bar Assn., Chgo. Bar Assn., Chgo. Inn of Ct., Legal Club Chgo., Law Club Chgo, Tavern Club. Securities, Federal civil litigation, Labor. Home: 834 Green Bay Rd Highland Park IL 60035-4630 Office: Katten Muchin & Zavis 525 W Monroe St Ste 1600 Chicago IL 60661-3693

**BASILE, PAUL LOUIS, JR.,** lawyer; b. Oakland, Calif., Dec. 27, 1945; s. Paul Louis and Roma Florence (Paris) B.; m. Linda Lou Paige, June 20, 1970; m. 2d Diane Chierichetti, Sept. 2, 1977. BA, Occidental Coll., 1968; postgrad., U. Wash., 1969; JD, UCLA, 1971. Bar: Calif. 1972, U.S. Dist. Ct. (cen. dist.) Calif. 1972, U.S. Dist. Ct. (no. dist.) Calif. 1985, U.S. Ct. Appeals (9th cir.) 1972, U.S. Tax Ct. 1977, U.S. Ct. Claims. 1978, U.S. Customs Ct. 1979, U.S. Ct. Customs and Patent Appeals 1979, U.S. Ct. Internat. Trade 1981, U.S. Supreme Ct. 1977; cert. specialist in taxation law Bd. of Legal Specialization, State Bar of Calif. Assoc. Parker, Milliken, Kohlmeier, Clark & O'Hara, L.A., 1971-72; corp. counsel TFI Cos., Inc., Irvine, Calif., 1972-73; pvt. practice L.A., 1973-80, 90-96, 98—; mem. Basile & Siener, L.A., 1980-86, Clark & Trevithick, L.A., 1986-90; ptnr. Wolf, Rifkin & Shapiro, L.A., 1990, of counsel, 1990-92; ptnr. Basile & Lane, LLP, L.A., 1996-97; of counsel Shaffer, Gold & Rubaum, L.L.P., L.A., 1996—; gen. counsel J.W. Brown, Inc., L.A., 1980—, asst. sec., 1984-92; sec., gen. counsel Souriau, Inc., Valencia, Calif., 1981-90; v.p., sec., dir., gen. counsel Pvt. Fin. Assocs., L.A., 1983-94; gen. counsel Quest Relocation Group, Toluca Lake, Calif., 1994-97, v.p. real estate, 1996—. Trustee, sec. Nat. Repertory Theatre Found., 1975-94, mem. exec. com., 1976-94, chmn. bd. dirs., 1991-94; mem. fin. com., bd. dirs. Calif. Music Theatre, 1988-92; bd. dirs. March of Dimes Birth Defects Found., Los Angeles County, 1982-87, mem. exec. com., 1983-86, sec., 1985-86; dist. fin. chmn. L.A. Area coun. Boy Scouts Am., 1982-83; trustee Occidental Coll., L.A., 1989-94; active L.A. Olympic Organizing Com., Ketchum Downtown YMCA, Vols. Am. L.A., others. Mem. ABA (taxation sect., corp. tax com., vice chmn. closely held bus. com. 1992-94, chair, 1994-96, chmn. subcom. on continuing legal edn. 1990-94, chmn. subcom. on estate planning 1992, sec. 1996-97, small firm lawyers com., bus. law sect., real property sect., probate and trust law sect., spl. problems of bus. owners com., estate planning and drafting, pre-death planning issues com.), State Bar Calif. (bus. law sect., nonprofit and unicorporated orgns. com. 1989-92, taxation sect., estate planning, trust and probate sect., taxation law adv. commn. 1994-97, vice chmn. 1995-96, chair 1996-97, mem. bd. legal specialization 1996-97), L.A. County Bar Assn. (taxation sect., com. on closely-held and pass-through entities, bus. and corps. law sect., sole practitioner section exec. com. 1995-99), Beverly Hills Bar Assn. (probate, trust & estate planning section, taxation section, vice chmn. Estate and Gift Tax Com., 1998—, law practice mgmt. section), Can. Calif. C. of C. (dir. 1980-89, 2d v.p. 1983-84, 1st v.p. 1984-85, pres. 1985-87), L.A.-Vancouver Sister City Assn. (dir., exec. com. 1987-92, treas. 1987-89, pres. 1989-92), French-Am. C. of C. (councilor 1979-84, v.p. 1980, 82-84), L.A. Area C. of C. (dir. 1980-81), Occidental Coll. Alumni Assn. (pres. 1979-80, v.p. 1978-79, alumni bd. govs. 1977-81, chmn. annual fund campaign 1990-91), Grand People (bd. dirs. 1985-92, chmn. bd. 1986-92), Rotary Club of L.A. (dir. 1994-96, sergeant-at-arms 1986-87, chmn. gateway com. 1993-94, chmn. world cmty. svc. com. 1991-93, chmn. vols. Am. of L.A. com. 1988-90, chmn. golf com. 1986-87, vice-chmn. pres. com. 1985-86), Rotary Internat. (chmn. club extension com. 1995-96, cmty. svc. dir. 1993-95, chmn. gift of life com. 1992-93), Small Bus. Coun. of Am., Inc. (legal adv. bd. 1989—), The Group, Inc., Attorneys for Family Held Enterprises. Democrat. Baptist. General corporate, Estate planning, Taxation, general. Home: 3937 Beverly Glen Blvd Sherman Oaks CA 91423-4404 Office: Shaffer Gold & Rubaum LLP 11400 W Olympic Blvd Ste 350 Los Angeles CA 90064-1558

**BASINGER, RICHARD LEE,** lawyer; b. Canton, Ohio, Nov. 24, 1941; s. Eldon R. and Alice M. (Bartholomew) B.; m. Rita Evelyn Gover, May 14, 1965; children: David A., Darron M. BA in Edn., Ariz. State U., 1963; postgrad. Macalester Coll., 1968-69; JD, U. Ariz., 1973. Bar: Ariz. 1973, U.S. Dist. Ct. Ariz. 1973, U.S. Tax Ct. 1977, U.S. Ct. Appeals (6th cir.) 1975, U.S. Ct. Appeals (9th cir.) 1976, U.S. Supreme Ct. 1977; cert. arbitrator. Assoc. law offices, Phoenix, 1973-74; pvt. practice, Scottsdale, Ariz. 1974-75; pres. Basinger & Assocs., P.C., Scottsdale, 1975—, also bd. dirs. Contbr. articles to profl. jours. Bd. dirs. Masters Trail Ventures, Scottsdale, 1984-85, Here's Life, Ariz., Scottsdale, 1976—; precinct committeeman Republican Party, Phoenix, 1983—; bd. dir. Ariz. Coll. of the Bible, 1992-93. NSF grantee, 1968-69. Mem. ABA, Ariz. Bar Assn., Maricopa County Bar Assn., Ariz. State Horseman's Assn. (bd. dirs. 1984-86, 1st v.p. 1986), Scottsdale Bar Assn., Western Saddle Club (bd. dirs. 1983-86, pres. 1985-86), Scottsdale Saddle Club, Saguaro Saddle Club. Baptist. Real property, General corporate, Probate. Office: Mohave County Atty Dep County Atty Civil Divsn PO Box 7000 Kingman AZ 86402-7000

**BASKERVILL, CHARLES THORNTON,** lawyer; b. South Boston, Va., May 26, 1953; s. William Nelson and Julia Alice (Moore) B.; m. Pamela Temple Shell, July 17, 1976; children: Ann Cabell, Susannah Thornton. BA, Hampden-Sydney Coll., 1975; JD, U. Richmond, 1978. Bar: a. 1978, U.S. Dist. Ct. (ea. dist.) Va. 1978. Assoc. White, Hamilton, Wyche & Shell, P.C., Petersburg, Va., 1978-96; asst. commonwealth's atty Petersburg, 1985—; assoc. Shell, Johnson, Andrews, Baskervill & Baskervill, P.C., Petersburg, 1996—; commr. of accts. City of Petersburg, Va., 1996—. Former dir. Petersburg Crime Prevention Found. Named to Athletic Hall of Fame, Hampden-Sydney Coll., 1988. Mem. Prince George County Bar Assn. (sec.-treas. 1990-91, pres. 1991-92), Petersburg Bar Assn. Methodist. Avocations: golf, tennis. Estate planning, Probate, Family and matrimonial. Office: Shell Johnson Andrews Baskervill & Baskervill PC 43 Rives Rd Petersburg VA 23805-9255

**BASKIN, SUSAN DAICOFF See DAICOFF, SUSAN**

**BASKIN, WILLIAM MAXWELL, SR.,** lawyer; b. Birmingham, Ala., Aug. 12, 1921; s. Joel L. and Edith Mae (Eichenberger) B.; m. Betty Jane Jones, May 25, 1947; children: William Maxwell Jr., Becky Lee Warner. AA, 1948; AB, George Washington U., 1948, LLB, 1950. Bar: Va. 1950, U.S. Dist. Ct. (ea. dist.) Va. 1951, U.S. Supreme Ct. 1955. Substitute judge Mcpl. Ct., Falls Church, Va., 1950-53; city atty. Falls Church, 1953-57; ptnr. Baskin, Baskin & Jackson, Falls Church, 1950-92; retired, 1992; commr. in chancery cir. ct. Fairfax County, Va., 1955-87; bd. dirs. 1st Va. Bank, Falls Church, dir., 1969-96. Trustee Va. Intremont Coll., 1971-76; bd. dirs. Child Devel Ctr., Falls Church, 1962-63, United Cerebral Palsy of No. Va., 1962, pres. 1963. Served to capt. USMC, 1942-46. Recipient Disting. Service award, George Washington U., 1979. Fellow Va. Bar Law Found. (charter); mem. ABA, Va. Bar Assn., Va. State Bar (pres. 1979-80), Fairfax County Bar Assn. (pres. 1966-67), Am. Judicature Soc., Washington Golf and Country Club, Lions (pres. 1961-62). Presbyterian. Avocations: tennis, golf, travel. General practice, Real property, Probate. Office: Baskin Baskin Jackson & Hansbarger 301 Park Ave Falls Church VA 22046-3335

**BASON, GEORGE F., JR.,** lawyer; b. Chapel Hill, N.C., June 30, 1931; s. George Francis and Mary Isabel (Reuther) B.; m. Sheilah Margaret Weavis, Oct. 12, 1961; children—Neil William, Iain George. A.B. cum laude, Davidson Coll., 1953; J.D. cum laude, Harvard U., 1956. Bar: NC 1956, D.C. 1958, U.S. Supreme Ct. 1961, Md. 1989. Assoc. Royall, Koegel and Harris, Washington and N.Y.C., 1958-61, Martin, Whitfield and Thaler, Washington, 1962-66; asst. prof. law Am. U., 1966-69, assoc. prof., 1969-72; sole practice, Washington, 1972-78, 88—; pres. George F. Bason Jr. P.C., Washington, 1978-84; judge U.S. Bankruptcy Ct. for D.C., 1984-88; chmn. bankruptcy and reorgn. com. D.C. Bar, 1974-75; standing trustee for D.C. Wage Earner Plans Under Chapter XIII Bankruptcy Act, 1972-75. Author: Debtor and Creditor Relations, Bankruptcy and Non-bankruptcy Rights and Remedies, 1984, vols. 9, 10 and 11 West's Legal Forms 2d. Recipient Am. Bar Found. Constl. Law Essay Contest 1st prize, 1973. Mem. ABA, D.C. Bar Assn. Contbr. articles to profl. jours. Bankruptcy. Office: Ste 223 4910 Massachusetts Ave NW Washington DC 20016-4300

**BASS, DONNA BLACKWELL,** lawyer; b. Forest, Miss., Dec. 8, 1958; d. Carl F. and Ora S. Blackwell; m. Gerald L. Bass Jr.; children: Dylan, Caitlin. BS in Social & Rehab. Svcs., U. So. Miss., 1980, MS in Criminal Justice, 1981, JD, 1989. Bar: Fla. 1989, U.S. Dist. Ct. (no. dist. Fla.) 1997, U.S. Dist. Ct. (so. dist. Fla.) 1997. Counselor Columbia (Miss.) Tng. Sch., 1981-83; dist. single intake counselor, Dept. Health & Rehab. Svcs. State of Fla., Madison, 1983-86; atty. Dept. Health & Rehab. Svcs. State of Fla., Tallahassee, 1989-95, sr. atty. Dept. Bus. & Profl. Registration, 1995-97; pvt. practice Tallahassee, 1997—. Avocations: fishing, boating. General civil litigation, General practice, Labor. Office: PO Box 759 Crawfordville FL 32326-0759

**BASS, JAY MICHAEL,** lawyer; b. Valdosta, Ga., Aug. 27, 1963. BA, Valdosta State Coll., 1985; JD, U. Ga., 1988. Bar: Ga. 1988, U.S. Dist. Ct. (mid. dist.) Ga. Asst. solicitor Ga. State Solicitor's Office, Athens, 1989-90; ptnr. Closson, Bass & Tomberlin, Valdosta, 1991—; bd. dirs. Lowndes County Criminal Liaison/So. Jud. Cir. Ct., 1995—, Nat. Criminal Def. Coll., 1992. Mem. Nat. Assn. Criminal Def. Lawyers, Ga. Assn. Criminal Def.

Lawyers (v.p. 1998—), Valdosta Assn. Criminal Def. Lawyers (founder, pres. 1998-99). Avocations: golf, fishing, model rocketry, family activities. General civil litigation, Criminal, Workers' compensation. Office: Closson Bass & Tomberlin PO Box 112-114 W Valdosta GA 31603-0159

**BASS, JOHN A.,** lawyer; b. Pitts., Mar. 16, 1962; s. Lee Weil and Marian (Seif) B.; m. Amy Chefitz, May 30, 1987; children: Samuel, Madison. BA, Emory U., 1984; JD, Duquesne U., 1988. Bar: Pa. 1988, U.S. Dist. Ct. (we. dist.) Pa. 1988. Assoc. Grogan Graffam McGinley & Luchino, Pitts., 1988-94, shareholder, 1995—; gen. counsel Pitts. Ctr. Found., 1998—. Personal injury, General civil litigation. Office: Grogan Graffan McGinley Luchino 3 Gateway Ctr Fl 22D Pittsburgh PA 15222-1000

**BASS, WILLIAM MORRIS,** lawyer; b. Crowley, La., Jan. 10, 1942; s. William T. and Rebecca (Hulkahy) B.; divorced 1994; children: Aaron, Casey, James; m. Penelope McCollum, June 5, 1995. BS, La. State U., Baton Rouge, 1966; JD, Loyola U., New Orleans, 1969. Bar: La. 1969, U.S. Dist. Ct. (ea., we. and mid. dists.) 1969, U.S. Ct. Appeals (5th cir.) 1969, U.S. Superior Ct. Sole practitioner Lafayette, La.; mediator, 1997. Fellow La. State Bar Found.; mem. La. Bar Assn. (sect. law and medicine, 1996), LLA (chpt. pres. 1994-96, state pres. 1998-99, nat. bd. dirs. 1995—). Republican. Episcopalian. Admiralty, Product liability, Professional liability. Office: 700 Saint John St Lafayette LA 70501-6768

**BASSECHES, ROBERT TREINIS,** lawyer; b. N.Y.C., Jan. 24, 1934; s. Jacob Thomas and Paula (Treinis) B.; m. Harriet Itkin, July 6, 1958; children: K.B., Joshua, Jessica. BA, Amherst Coll., 1955; LLB, Yale U., 1958. Bar: D.C. 1962, U.S. Ct. Appeals (D.C. cir.) 1962, U.S. Ct. Appeals (2d cir.) 1978, U.S. Ct. Appeals (4th cir.) 1998. Law clk. to judge David L. Bazelon U.S. Ct. Appeals (D.C. cir.), Washington, 1958-59; law clk. to justice Hugo L. Black U.S. Supreme Ct., Washington, 1959; assoc. Shea & Gardner, Washington, 1959-63, ptnr., 1963—, adminstrv. ptnr., 1980-86, chmn., exec. com., 1988-93. Trustee Green Acres Sch., Rockville, Md., 1971-76, pres., chmn. bd. trustees, 1973-75; pres. Chevy Chase (Md.) Village Citizens Assn., 1976. Mem. Maritime Adminstrv. Bar Assn. (pres. 1969-71, sec. 1967-69), Phi Beta Kappa. Administrative and regulatory, Transportation. Office: Shea & Gardner Ste 800 1800 Massachusetts Ave NW Washington DC 20036-1872

**BASSEN, NED HENRY,** lawyer; b. N.Y.C., June 8, 1948; s. Harold Russell and Annette (Frankfeldt) B.; m. Susan Millington Campbell, July 2, 1999; children: Amanda Lee, Susannah Spence. BS, Cornell U., 1970, JD, 1973. Bar: N.Y. 1974, U.S. Dist. Ct. (so. and ea. dists.) N.Y. 1974, U.S. Ct. Appeals (11th cir.) 1984, U.S. Dist. Ct. (ea. dist.) Mich 1990. Assoc. Baer Marks & Upham, N.Y.C., 1975-80; assoc. Kelley Drye & Warren, N.Y.C., 1973-75, 80-83, ptnr., 1983-92; ptnr. and labor group head Mudge Rose Guthrie Alexander & Ferdon, N.Y.C., 1993-95; ptnr., co-chair labor and employment group Hughes Hubbard & Reed LLP, N.Y.C., 1995—. Note and comment editor Cornell Law Rev., 1972-73. V.p. local condominium assn., 1988-93. Mem. ABA (labor and employment law sect.), U.S. Coun. for Internat. Bus., Indsl. Rels. Com., Indsl. Rels. Rsch. Assn., N.Y. State Bar Assn. (labor law sect., com. on equal employment opportunity law), N.Y. State Mgmt. Attys. Conf. Labor. Office: Hughes Hubbard & Reed LLP 1 Battery Park Plz Fl 12 New York NY 10004-1482

**BASSETT, EDWARD CALDWELL, JR.,** lawyer; b. Newton, Mass., July 4, 1952; s. Edward C. and Marie A. (Querfurth) B.; m. Nancy A. Bassett, May 17, 1981; children: Andrew, Allison, Christopher. AB, Boston Coll., 1974, JD, 1977. Bar: Mass. Ptnr., mem. mgmt. com. Mirick, O'Connell DeMallie & Lougee, Worcester, Mass., 1977—. Editor: Benders UCC Reporter Digest, 1977; contbr. articles to profl. jours. Chmn. Southboro (Mass.) Bd. Appeals, 1985-94; exec. com., trustee Anna Maria Coll., Paxton, Mass., 1992-94. Avocation: tennis. Personal injury, Product liability, Condemnation. Office: Mirick O'Connell et al 1700 Bank of Boston Twr Worcester MA 01608

**BASSETT, JOHN WALDEN, JR.,** lawyer; b. Roswell, N.Mex., Mar. 21, 1938; s. John Walden Sr. and Evelyn (Thompson) B.; m. Patricia Lubben, May 22, 1965 (dec. Apr. 1995); children: John Walden III, Loren Patricia; m. Nolana Knight, May 2, 1998. AB in Econs., Stanford U., 1960; LLB with honors, U. Tex., 1964. Bar: Tex. 1964, N.Mex. 1964. Assoc. Atwood & Malone, Roswell, 1964-66; White House fellow, spl. asst. to U.S. Atty. Gen., Washington, 1966-67; ptnr. Atwood, Malone, Mann & Turner and predecessors, Roswell, 1967-95, Bassett & Copple, LLP, Roswell, 1995—; bd. dirs. A.H. Belo Corp., Dallas, AMMA Found., Washington. Assoc. editor U. Tex. Law Rev., 1962. Mem. N.Mex. State Bd. Edn., 1987-91; pres., chmn. bd. United Way of Chaves County, N.Mex., 1973; bd. dirs. Ednl. Achievement Found., Roswell, 1992—, N.Mex. Found. for Ednl. Excellence, Albuquerque. 1st lt. U.S. Army, 1961-68. Mem. ABA, Tex. Bar Assn., N.Mex. Bar Assn., Chaves County Bar Assn., Order of Coif, Rotary (pres. 1976), N.Mex. Amigos, Phi Delta Phi. Republican. Episcopalian. General practice, Real property, Probate. Home: 5060 Bright Sky Rd Roswell NM 88201-8800 Office: Bassett & Copple 400 N Pennsylvania Ave Ste 250 Roswell NM 88201-4788

**BASSETT, ROBERT ANDREWS,** lawyer; b. Pitts., Dec. 7, 1946; s. Ralph Harris and Mary (Andrews) B.; m. Victoria Ann Panettiere, June 15, 1969; children: Robert Anthony, Christopher James. Student, San Diego State U., 1964-65; BS in Engring., U.S. Mil. Acad., 1969; postgrad., MIT, 1974-75; JD, Quinnipiac Sch. Law, 1991. Bar: Conn. 1991. Commd. 2d lt. U.S. Army, 1969, advanced through grades to capt., 1971; assigned to Air Def. Arty., El Paso, Tex., 1969, Ansbach, Germany, 1969-72, Kunsan and Osan, Republic of Korea, 1972-73, Stewart AFB, N.Y., 1973-74; resigned, 1974; mktg. mgr., product mgr. Linde divsn. Union Carbide Corp., N.Y.C., 1975-82; bus. mgr. Linde divsn. Union Carbide Corp., Danbury, Conn., 1982-92; corp. counsel, asst. sec. Praxair, Inc., Danbury, 1992—; mem. proxy fees adv. com. N.Y. Stock Exch., 1995. Contbr. articles on corp. governance to law jours. Chmn. goals com. Newtown (Conn.) Bd. Edn., 1986; chmn. music devel. adv. com. C.H. Booth Pub. Libr., Newtown, 1998—. Mem. Am. Soc. Corp. Secs. (corp. practices com. 1993—, chmn. publs. subcom. 1994—). General corporate, Securities, Contracts commercial. Home: 10 Monitor Hill Rd Newtown CT 06470-2243 Office: Praxair Inc 39 Old Ridgebury Rd Ste M-1 Danbury CT 06810-5108

**BASSITT, JANET LOUISE,** lawyer; b. Macomb, Ill., Oct. 8, 1941; d. James Russell Hoover and Louise Loretta (Lawrence) Hoover Reed; children: Teri Beth, William Jefferson, Margaret Louise. BA in Psychology with honors, U. Ill., Chgo., 1976; JD, John Marshall Law Sch., 1980. Bar: Ill. 1981, U.S. Dist. Ct. (no. dist.) Ill. 1982, U.S. Ct. Appeals (7th cir.) 1982, U.S. Tax Ct. 1983, U.S. Supreme Ct. 1985. Sole practice Roselle, Ill., 1982—; instr. Harper Coll., Palatine, Ill., 1983-88, Coll. Fin. Planning, Denver, 1985-88. Author: Attorney Conduct, 1985, Trust Yourself, 1990; contbr. articles to profl. jours. Vol. lawyer Constl. Rights Found., Chgo., 1982—; chmn. March of Dimes, Wenatchee, Wash., 1971-72; bd. dirs. United Way Schaumburg-Hoffman Estates, 1986-89; leader Wenatchee area Boy Scouts Am., 1971-72. Mem. ABA, Ill. Bar Assn. Entertainment. Address: PO Box 72277 Roselle IL 60172-0277

**BASSLER, WILLIAM G.,** federal judge; b. 1938. BA, Fordham Univ. Coll., 1960; JD, Georgetown U., 1963; LLM, NYU, 1969. Law sec. to Hon. Mark A. Sullivan N.J. Superior Ct., 1963-64; with Parsons, Canzona, Blair & Warren, 1964-70; ptnr. Labrecque, Parsons & Bassler, 1970-83, Evans, Koelzer, Osborne, Kreizman & Bassler, 1983-84, Carton, Nary, Witt & Arvantis, 1984-88; judge Superior Ct. State of N.J., 1988-91; fed. judge U.S. Dist. Ct. (N.J. dist.), Newark, 1991—. Mem. ABA, N.J. State Bar Assn., Monmouth County Bar Assn. Office: Martin Luther King Fed CourtHouse PO Box 999 50 Walnut St Rm 5060 Newark NJ 07101

**BASTEDO, WAYNE WEBSTER,** lawyer; b. Oceanside, N.Y., July 13, 1948; s. Walter Jr. and Barbara Catherine (Manning) B.; m. Bina Shantilal Mistry, Dec. 29, 1978. AB in Polit. Sci. cum laude, Princeton U., 1970; postgrad., NYU, 1977-78; JD, Hofstra U., 1978; LLM, NYU, 1988; postgrad., Fairleigh Dickinson U., 1988—. Bar: N.Y. 1980. Mgr. adminstrv. Law Jour. Seminars Press, N.Y.C., 1978-79; editor decisions and legal digests N.Y. Law Jour., N.Y.C., 1979-81; sole practice N.Y.C., 1981-82; atty. Western Union Corp., Upper Saddle River, N.J., 1983—; cons. litigation Exxon Corp., N.Y.C., 1982; cons. litigation Western Union Corp., Upper Saddle River, 1983, mem. corp. restructuring staff 1986-91. Author: A Comparative Study of Soviet and American World Order Models, 1978, Who Has the Edge on Justice? Computer Services Alter Fair Play, 1979; assoc. editor Hofstra U. Law Rev. 1976-77; editor (directory series) Outside Counsel: Inside Director, 1976-81; contbr. articles to profl. jours. Mem. policy com. Roosevelt Island (N.Y.) Residents Assn., 1981-82. Served to lt. USN, 1970-75, Vietnam. N.Y. State Regents scholar, 1966-70, USN Officer Tng. scholar, 1967-70. Mem. ABA, N.Y. County Lawyers Assn. Democrat. Methodist. Avocations: internat. law and politics, cinema, writing. General corporate, Contracts commercial, Communications. Home: Riviera Towers 6040 Boulevard E Apt 26D West New York NJ 07093-3857 Office: Western Union Corp Office Gen Counsel 1 Lake St Saddle River NJ 07458-1813

**BASTIAANSE, GERARD C.,** lawyer; b. Holyoke, Mass., Oct. 21, 1935; s. Gerard C. and Margaret (Lally) B.; m. Paula E. Paliska, June 1, 1963; children: Elizabeth, Gerard. BSBA, Boston U., 1960; JD, U. Va., 1964. Bar: Mass. 1964, Calif. 1970. Assoc. Nutter, McClennen & Fish, Boston, 1964-65; counsel Campbell Soup Co., Camden, N.J., 1965-67; gen. counsel A&W Internat. (United Fruit Co.), Santa Monica, Calif., 1968-70; ptnr. Kindel & Anderson, Los Angeles, 1970—. Mem. ABA, Calif. Bar Assn., Mass. Bar Assn., Japan Am. Soc., Asia Soc., World Trade Ctr. Assn. Clubs: California (Los Angeles); Big Canyon Country (Newport Beach, Calif.). General corporate, Private international. Home: 2 San Sebastian Newport Beach CA 92660-6828 Office: Kindel & Anderson 2030 Main St Ste 1300 Irvine CA 92614-7220

**BATA, RUDOLPH ANDREW, JR.,** lawyer; b. Akron, Ohio, Jan. 9, 1947; s. Rudolph Andrew and Margaret Eleanor (Ellis) B.; m. Genevieve Ruth Brannan, Aug. 25, 1968 (div. May 1985); 1 child, Seth Andrew; m. Linda Lee Waldo, May 7, 1985; 1 child, Sarah Ariel. BS, So. Coll., Collegedale, Tenn., 1969; JD, Emory U., 1972. Bar: D.C. 1973, N.C. 1978, U.S. Dist. Ct. N.C. 1991, U.S. Ct. Appeals (4th cir.) 1991; cert. mediator AOC. Assoc. ICC, Washington, 1972-73; in house counsel B.F. Saul Real Estate Investment Trust, Chevy Chase, Md., 1973-74; staff atty. Martha, Cafferky, Powers & Jordan, Washington, 1974-75; asst. corp. counsel Hardee's Food Systems, Inc., Rocky Mount, N.C., 1975-78; ptnr. Bata & Blomeley, Murphy, N.C., 1978-87, 88-90, Bata & Sumpter, Murphy, 1987-88; sole practice, 1990—. Bd. dirs. Cherokee County United Fund, Murphy, 1981-83. Mem. ABA, N.C. Bar Assn., D.C. Bar Assn., 30th Jud. Dist. Bar Assn., So. Soc. of Adventist Attys. (pres. 1984-85), Cherokee County C. of C. (bd. dirs. 1980-82). Avocations: golf, tennis, hiking. Real property, Banking, Probate. Office: 225 Valley River Ave Ste A Murphy NC 28906-3000

**BATAVIA, ANDREW I.,** law educator, lawyer; b. Bklyn., June 15, 1957; m. Cheryl Nicholson; children: Joseph, Katerina. BA, U. Calif., Riverside, 1980; MS, Stanford U., 1983; JD, Harvard U., 1984. Bar: Calif. 1984, DC, 1988, U.S. Supreme Ct. 1991, Fla. 1996. Assoc. dir. for health svcs. rsch. Nat. Rehab. Hosp. Rsch. Ctr., Washington, 1986-90; spl. asst. to atty. gen. U.S. Dept. Justice, Washington, 1990-91; assoc. dir. White House Domestic Policy Coun., Washington, 1991-92; rsch. dir. for disability and rehab. policy Abt Assocs., Bethesda, Md., 1992-93; exec. dir. U.S. Nat. Coun. on Disability, Washington, 1993; legis. asst. Office of U.S. Senator John McCain, Washington, 1993-95; counsel McDermott, Will & Emery, Miami, Fla., 1995-97; assoc. prof. law Fla. Internat. U., North Miami, 1997—; mem. adv. com. various fed. agys., Washington, 1990—; dir./cons. various fed. rsch. projects, Washington, 1990—. Author: The Payment of Medical Rehabilitation Services, 1989; founding assoc. editor Jour. Disability Policy Studies, 1991—; contbr. articles to profl. jours. Mem. sr. adv. group Bush for Pres. Campaign, Washington, 1992; dep. chairperson disability coalition Dole for Pres. Campaign, Washington, 1995; co-chairperson Barrier-Free Environment Com., City of Miami, Miami Beach, Fla., 1997—; bd. dirs. Death with Dignity Nat. Ctr., Calif., 1998—. Recipient Chancellor's award U. Calif., Riverside, 1995; named Mary Switzer Disting. Rsch. fellow Nat. Inst. on Disability and Rehab. Rsch., Washington, 1986-87, internat. fellow U.S. Dept. Edn., Washington, 1987, White House fellow Pres. Commn. on White House Fellowships, Washington, 1990-91. Fellow Washington Acad. Scis.; mem. Kennedy Inst. Ethics. Republican. Fax: 305-919-5848. E-mail: batavia1957@hotmail.com. Home: 2845 Prairie Ave Miami Beach FL 33140-3408 Office: Fla Internat Univ Sch Policy & Mgmt Biscayne Blvd North Miami FL 33261

**BATCHELDER, ALICE M.,** federal judge; b. 1944; m. William G. Batchelder III; children: William G. IV, Elisabeth. BA, Ohio Wesleyan U., 1964; JD, Akron U., 1971; LLM, U. Va., 1988. Tchr. Plain Local Sch. Dist., Franklin County, Ohio, 1965-66, Jones Jr. High Sch., 1966-67, Buckeye High Sch., Medina County, 1967-68; assoc. Williams & Batchelder, Medina, Ohio, 1971-83; judge U.S. Bankruptcy Ct., Ohio, 1983-85, U.S. Dist. Ct. (no. dist.) Ohio, Cleve., 1985-91, U.S. Ct. of Appeals (6th cir.), Cleveland, 1991—. Mem. ABA, Fed. Judge's Assn., Fed. Bar Assn., Medina County Bar Assn. Office: US Ct of Appeals (6th cir) 143 W Liberty St Medina OH 44256-2215

**BATCHELOR, JAMES KENT,** lawyer; b. Long Beach, Calif., Oct. 4, 1934; s. Jack Morrell and Edith Marie (Ottinger) B.; m. Jeanette Lou Dyer, Mar. 27, 1959; children: John, Suzanne; m. Susan Mary Leonard, Dec. 4, 1976. AA, Sacramento City Coll., 1954; BA, Calif. State U., Long Beach, 1956; JD, Hastings Coll. Law, U. Calif., 1959. Bar: Calif. 1960, U.S. Dist. Ct. (cen. dist.) Calif. 1960, U.S. Supreme Ct. 1968; cert. family law specialist Calif. Bd. Legal Specialization, 1980. Dep. dist. atty., Orange County, Calif., 1960-62; assoc. Miller, Nisson, Kogler & Wenke, Santa Ana, Calif., 1962-64; ptnr. Batchelor, Cohen & Oster, Santa Ana, 1964-67, Kurilich, Ballard, Batchelor, Fullerton, Calif., 1967-72; pres. James K. Batchelor, Inc.; tchr. paralegal sect. Santa Ana City Coll.; judge pro-tem Superior Ct., 1974—; lectr. family law Calif. Continuing Edn. of Bar, 1973—. Contbr. articles to profl. jours. Fellow Am. Acad. Matrimonial Lawyers (pres. So. Calif. chpt. 1989-90); mem. ABA, Calif. State Bar (placque chmn. family law sect. 1975-76, advisor 1976-78), Orange County Barristers (founder, pres., placque 1963), Calif. State Barristers (placque 1965, v.p.), Orange County Bar Assn. (plaque sec. 1977, pres. family law sect. 1968-71, Best Lawyers in Am. 1989-90, 91-92, 93-94, 95-96, 97-98, 99—). Republican. Methodist. Family and matrimonial. Office: 765 The City Dr S Ste 270 Orange CA 92868-4942

**BATEMAN, DAVID ALFRED,** lawyer; b. Pitts., Jan. 28, 1946; s. Alfred V. and Ruth G. (Howe) B.; m. Trudy A. Heath, Mar. 13, 1948; children: Devin C., Mark C. A.B. in Geology, U. Calif.-Riverside, 1966; J.D., U. San Diego, 1969; LL.M., Georgetown U., 1978. Bar: Calif. 1970, U.S. Dist. Ct. (so. dist.) Calif. 1970, U.S. Ct. Mil. Appeals 1972, Wash. 1973, U.S. Dist. Ct. (we. dist.) Wash. 1973, U.S. Supreme Ct. 1974, D.C. 1976, U.S. Dist. Ct. D.C. 1977, U.S. Ct. Claims 1979, U.S. Ct. Appeals (9th cir.) 1981. Assoc. Daubney, Banche, Patterson and Nares, Oceanside, Calif., 1969-72; asst. atty. gen. State of Wash., Olympia, 1977-81; ptnr. Bateman & Woodring, Olympia, 1981-85, Woodring, Bateman & Westbrook, 1985-89, Hanemann & Bateman, 1989-92, Hanemann, Bateman & Jones, 1992—; instr. Am. Inst. Banking, San Diego, 1972, U. Puget Sound, Olympia campus, spring, 1979. Served to capt. JAGC, USAF, 1972-77; col. JAGC, USAFR, 1977-97. Mem. Calif. State Bar Assn., D.C. Bar Assn., Wash. State Bar Assn., Rotary (past chmn. internat. svcs. com.). Roman Catholic. Real property, Private international, Land use and zoning (including planning).

**BATEMAN, HEIDI S.,** lawyer; b. Spokane, Wash., June 17, 1965; d. John Alan and Carole L. Havens; children: Ryan Downey, Matthew Downey; m. David Alan Bateman, Mar. 26, 1998. BA with honors, Gonzaga U., 1987; JD, U. Wash., 1990. Bar: Wash. 1990, U.S. Dist. Ct. (we. dist.) Wash. 1994. Assoc. Bogle & Gates, PLLC, Seattle, 1990-96, sr. litigation atty., 1997-98; ptnr. Miller Bateman, LLP, Seattle, 1999—. Active Guardian Ad Litem Program, Seattle, 1990—; fund raiser U. Wash. Alumni Orgn., Seattle, 1990—. Mem. ABA (comml. and corp. litigation coms. 1998—), Wash. State Bar Assn. (legis. coms. 1995-96), King County Bar Assn. (jud. screening com. 1996-97). Avocations: travel, reading, skiing. Federal civil litigation, Real property, State civil litigation. Office: Miller Bateman LLP 1426 Alaskan Way Ste 301 Seattle WA 98101-2016

**BATES, BEVERLY BAILEY,** lawyer; b. Atlanta, Jan. 23, 1938; d. Fred Eugene and Justine Elizabeth (Marques) B. AB, Mercer U., 1959, LLB, 1961. Bar: Ga. 1961, U.S. Ct. Mil. Appeals 1963, U.S. Supreme Ct. 1965, D.C. 1966, U.S. Dist. Ct. (no. dist.) Ga. 1966, U.S. Ct. Appeals (5th cir.) 1967, U.S. Ct. Appeals (11th cir.) 1981, U.S. Ct. Appeals (fed. cir.) 1982, U.S. Dist. Ct. (so. dist.) Ga. 1982, U.S. Dist. Ct. (mid. dist.) Ga. 1985. Asst. U.S. atty. No. dist. Ga. U.S. Dept. Justice, Atlanta, 1966-74; ptnr. Bates & Baum, Atlanta, 1974—; spl. master Ga. Commn. on Equal Employment, 1986—. Contbr. articles to profl. jours. Rep. Buckhead Neighborhood Planning Unit, Atlanta, 1982-85; v.p., bd. dirs. Pine Hills Civic Club, Atlanta, 1982-85. Served to capt. U.S. Army, 1961-66. Mem. ABA, Fed. Bar Assn. (pres. 1972-73, named Younger Fed. Lawyer of Yr. Atlanta chpt. 1972), Atlanta C. of C. (pres. downtown coun. 1982-83, bd. dirs. 1982-83), Mercer U. Law Sch. Alumni Soc. (pres. 1971-72), Mercer U. Alumni Soc. (pres. Atlanta chpt. 1974-75), Atlanta Lawyers Club, Resurgens Atlanta (pres. 1981-82). General civil litigation, Contracts commercial, Personal injury. Office: Bates & Baum 3151 Maple Dr NE Atlanta GA 30305-2503

**BATES, DAVID ALLEN,** lawyer, management consultant; b. Oct. 6, 1953; m. Beth Bates, Oct. 7, 1990; 1 child, Anna. BA in Psychology and Sociology, UCLA, 1976; JD, We. State U., 1978. Dist. atty. Orange County Dist. Atty.'s Office, Santa Ana, Calif., 1979-85; developer, cons. Real Estate Devel. Partnerships, L.A., 1985-94; lawyer pvt. practice, S. Lake Tahoe, Calif., 1994—; conflict panels atty., El Dorado County S. Lake Tahoe, Calif., 1997-98. Mem. Calif. State Bar Assn. Avocations: author, speaker on constitution. Personal injury, Real property. Office: 2250 Elm Ave South Lake Tahoe CA 96150-3435

**BATES, HAROLD MARTIN,** lawyer; b. Wise County, Va., Mar. 11, 1928; s. William Jennings and Reba (Williams) B.; m. Audrey Rose Doll, Nov. 1, 1952 (div. Mar. 1978); children—Linda, Carl. m. Judith Lee Farmer, June 23, 1978. B.A. in Econs., Coll. William and Mary, 1952; LL.B., Washington and Lee U., 1961. Bar: Va. 1961, Ky. 1961. Spl. agt. FBI, Newark and N.Y.C., 1952-56; tech. sales rep. Hercules Powder Co., Wilmington, Del., 1956-58; investigator U.S. Def. Dept., Lexington, Va., Louisville, 1959-62; practice law, Louisville, 1961-62; sec.-treas., dir., house counsel Life Ins. Co. of Ky., Louisville, 1962-66; practice law, Roanoke, Va., 1966—; sec., dir. James River Limestone Co., Buchanan, Va., 1970-96; sec. Eastern Ins. Co., Roanoke, 1984-87. Pres., Skil, Inc., orgn. for rehab. Vietnam vets., Salem, Va., 1972-75; freshman football coach Washington and Lee U., 1958-60. Served to cpl. U.S. Army Airborne, 1946-47, PTO. Mem. Va. Bar Assn., Roanoke Bar Assn., William and Mary Alumni Assn. (bd. dirs. 1972-76), Soc. Former Spl. Agts. of FBI (chmn. Blue Ridge chpt. 1971-72). Republican. General corporate, Corporate taxation, Estate planning. Home: 2165 Laurel Woods Dr Salem VA 24153-1807 Office: 406 Professional Arts Bldg Roanoke VA 24011

**BATES, JOHN WYTHE, III,** lawyer; b. Richmond, Aug. 22, 1941; s. John Wythe, Jr. and Virginia (Wellington) B.; m. Beverly Jane Estes, June 20, 1964; children: Elizabeth Puller, Kathryn Wellington. BS, Va. Tech., 1963; LLB, U. Va., 1966. Assoc. McGuire Woods Battle & Boothe, L.L.P., Richmond, 1966-71, pntr., 1971—, mng. ptnr., 1989-96; mem. Va. Racing Commn., 1997—. Chmn. United Way Gtr. Richmond, 1975-76; pres. Family and Children's Svc. Richmond, 1978-80; trustee St. Paul's Coll., 1989-96, Va. Found. Ind. Colls., 1994—; sr. warden St. Stephen's Ch., 1985-86. Va. Law Found. fellow, 1997. Mem. Am. Coll. Real Estate Lawyers, Richmond Real Estate Group, Forum Club, River Rd. Citizens Assn. (pres. 1983-84), Country Club Va. (pres. 1987-88), Bull and Bear Club (pres. 1980-81), Commonwealth Club. Episcopalian. Avocations: golf, waterfowl hunting. Real property, Land use and zoning (including planning), Landlord-tenant. Office: McGuire Woods Battle & Boothe LLP One James Ctr 901 E Cary St Richmond VA 23219-4057

**BATES, JULIA REINBERGER,** prosecutor; b. Cleve., Sept. 6, 1950; d. William Charles and Mary Ann (Maecker) R.; m. James Douglas Bates, July 31, 1982; children: William Lee, Lee Ann. BA, Wittenberg U., 1972; JD, U. Toledo, 1976. Bar: Ohio 1977. Asst. prosecutor Lucas County, Toledo, 1976-96, prosecutor, 1996—; lectr. in field. Sch. bd. mem. Trinity Luth. Sch., Toledo, 1992—, chmn., 1995; trustee Crimestoppers, Inc., Toledo, 1995—, Police Athletic League, Toledo, 1997—; active Domestic Violence Task Force, Toledo, 1995—, Criminal Justice Coordinating Counsel, Toledo, 1996—, Lucas County Dem. Party Exec. Com., 1996—. Mem. Nat. Dist. Attys. Assn., Ohio Pros. Attys. Assn. (exec. com., treas. 1999), Ohio Womens Bar, Ohio Bar, Toledo Womens Bar Assn., Toledo Bar. Home: 3718 River Rd Toledo OH 43614-4330 Office: Lucas County Prosecutors Office 700 Adams St Ste 250 Toledo OH 43624-1680

**BATES, ROGER LEE,** lawyer; b. Clanton, Ala., Jan. 20, 1957; s. John Ed and Billie (Litaker) B.; m. Sandra Cooper, Aug. 11, 1977; children: Brandon, Alan. BS, Auburn U., 1979; JD, Cumberland Sch. Law, 1982. Bar: Ala. 1982. Law clk. to sr. judge Fed. Dist. Ct., Birmingham, Ala., 1982-83; assoc. McDaniel Hall, Birmingham, 1983; from assoc. to ptnr. Barnett Tingle Noble, Birmingham, 1983-87; ptnr. Tingle, Watson & Bates, PC, Birmingham, 1988-95; mem. Hand Arendall, L.L.C., Birmingham, 1996—; city atty. City of Hoover, Ala., 1998—; dep. atty. gen., Montgomery, Ala., 1995-99. State coord. Fob James for Gov. Campaign, Ala., 1998. Mem. ABA, Ala. State Bar Assn. Baptist. Office: Hand Arendall LLC 2001 Park Pl Ste 900 Birmingham AL 35203-4803

**BATISTA, ALBERTO VICTOR,** lawyer; b. N.Y.C., May 1, 1963; s. Santiago and Juana (Garcia) B. BA, St. Thomas U., Miami, Fla., 1984; JD, U. Miami (Fla.), 1987. Bar: Fla. 1988. Pvt. practice Miami, Fla., 1989—. Recipient Children First award, 1992-97, Put Something Back award, 1991-97. Mem. Dade County Bar Assn. (Vol. Lawyers award 1989-97, Pub. Svc. award 1997), Fla. Bar Assn. Avocation: bicycling. Fax: 305-576-1805. E-mail: aubatista@aol.com. Family and matrimonial, Criminal, Personal injury. Address: 3550 Biscayne Blvd Ste 206 Miami FL 33137-3833

**BATLA, RAYMOND JOHN, JR.,** lawyer; b. Cameron, Tex., Sept. 1, 1947; s. Raymond John and Della Alvina (Jezek) B.; m. Susan Marie Clark, Oct. 1, 1983; children: Sara, Charles, Michael, Traci. BS with highest honors, U. Tex., 1970, JD with honors, 1973. Bar: Tex. 1973, D.C. 1973, U.S. Dist. Ct. (so. dist.) Tex. 1982, U.S. Ct. Appeals (D.C. cir.) 1974, U.S. Ct. Appeals (5th cir.) 1982, U.S. Ct. Appeals (10th cir.) 1978, U.S. Supreme Ct. 1977. Structural engr. Tex. Hwy. Dept., Austin, 1970; assoc. Hogan & Hatson, Washington, 1973-82, gen. ptnr., 1983—; mem. Am. Endowment for Democracy Internat. Observer Del. to Czechoslovakia, 1990; sec. Coun. on Alt. Fuels, 1987-97. Author: Petroleum Regulation Handbook, 1980, Natural Gas Yearbook, 1991; columnist, mem. editorial bd. Natural Gas mag., 1984-91, Energy Law Jour., 1991-93; contbr. articles to profl. jours. Mem. ABA (mem. spl. com. for energy fin., vice chmn. energy com. 1981, cen. and Ea. Europe law inst. internat. law com., spl. com on energy fin. 1989—), Fed. Energy Bar Assn. (chmn. internat. energy transactions com. 1993-94), Fed. Bar Assn., D.C. Bar Assn., State Bar Tex., City Club of Wash., London Capital Club, Order of Coif, Chi Epsilon, Tau Beta Pi. Private international, Public international, Public utilities. Home: 12406 Shari Hunt Grv Clifton VA 20124-2056 also: 5 Half Moon St, London W1Y 7RA, England Office: Hogan & Hatson 555 13th St NW Washington DC 20004-1109 also: Hogan & Hartson, 21 Garlick Hill, London EC4V 2AU, England

**BATOR, CHRISTINE VICTORIA,** lawyer; b. Linden, N.J., June 9, 1949; d. Walter Peter and Frances Mary (Padlo) B.; m. Norman Alfred Lehoullier, Jan. 19, 1975. BA, Seton Hall U., 1970, JD, 1975; LLM, NYU, 1982. Bar: N.J. 1975, U.S. Dist. Ct. 1975, N.Y. 1982. Law clk. to presiding justice Superior Ct. N.J., Flemington, 1975-76; dir. office legal affairs N.J. Dept. Health, Trenton, 1976—; ptnr. Carella, Byrne, Bain & Gilfillan, Roseland, N.J., 1982-88, Hannoch Weisman, Roseland, N.J., 1988-91; of counsel Kobert, Lauter & Cohen, Princeton, NJ, 1991—. Dir., NJ Lawyer Newspaper. Mem. ABA, N.J. Bar Assn. (trustee, 1996-99, chair banking law sect., 1994, chair edn. subcom. 1987-89, health and hosp. law sect.), Pres., Exec. Women N.J, 1992-94, commnr., NJ Highway Authority, 1996-99 (chmn. bd., appointments com.). Office: Hannoch Weisman 4 Becker Farm Rd Ste 11 Roseland NJ 07068-1734

**BATSON, DAVID WARREN,** lawyer; b. Wichita Falls, Tex., Jan. 4, 1956; s. Warren M. Batson and Jacqueline (Latham) Rhone. BBA, Midwestern State U., 1976; JD, U. Tex., 1979. Bar: Tex. 1980, U.S. Dist. Ct. (no. dist.) Tex. 1981, U.S. Tax Ct. 1981, U.S. Ct. Appeals (5th cir.) 1983, U.S. Ct. Appeals (D.C. cir.) 1983, U.S. Ct. Claims 1984, U.S. Supreme Ct. 1984.

Atty. Arthur Andersen & Co., Ft. Worth, 1980-81; tax atty. The Western Co. of N.Am., Ft. Worth, 1981-85; sr. tax atty. Alcon Labs., Inc., Ft. Worth, 1985; gen. counsel Data Tailor, Inc., Ft. Worth, 1985-87; sr. tax atty. Arco, 1988-90; atty. pvt. practice, Wichita Falls, Tex., 1990—; lectr. U. of Tex., Arlington, 1984-85; of counsel Means & Means, Corsicana, Tex., 1985-86. Contbr. articles to profl. jours. Speaker A Wish With Wings, Arlington, Tex., 1984-85, Habitat for Humanity. Mem. Assn. Trial Lawyers Am., Tex. Bar Assn., Christian Legal Soc., Tex. Trial Lawyers Assn., State Bar at Tex. Coll., Phi Delta Phi. Avocations: negotiations, camping, self improvement. Contracts commercial, Mergers and acquisitions, Private international. Address: PO Box 1887 Wichita Falls TX 76307-1887

**BATSON, RICHARD NEAL,** lawyer; b. Nashville, May 1, 1941; s. John H. and Mildred (Neal) B.; children: John Hayes, Richard Davis. BA cum laude, Vanderbilt U., 1963, JD, 1966. Bar: Ga. 1967. Law clk. to Judge Griffin B. Bell U.S. Ct. Appeals (5th cir.), Atlanta, 1966-67; assoc. Alston & Bird (formerly Alston, Miller & Gaines), Atlanta, 1967-71, ptnr., 1971—; spkr. Nat. Conf. Bankruptcy Judges, 1982, 86, 87, 88, 94, 96, Bank Lending Inst., 1986-87, also other instns. and assns.; adj. prof. Emory U. Sch. Law, 1994-95; co-lectr. Ga. State U., fall 1984; mem. bankruptcy rules com. Jud. Conf. U.S., 1993—. Co-author: Problem Loan Strategies, 1985, rev. 1998; contbg. author Bankruptcy Litigation Manual, 1990—; contbg. editor Norton Bankruptcy Law and Practice, 1990—. Sgt. USAF, 1967-73. Fellow Am. Coll. Trial Lawyers, Am. Coll. Bankruptcy (bd. dirs., pres. 1997—); mem. Atlanta Bar Assn. (pres. 1979-80), Am. Law Inst., Southeastern Bankruptcy Law Inst. (bd. dirs., pres. 1986-87), Nat. Bankruptcy Conf. (exec. com.). Avocations: hiking, outdoor activities. Office: Alston & Bird One Atlantic Ctr 1201 W Peachtree St NW Ste 4200 Atlanta GA 30309-3424

**BATT, NICK,** property and investment executive; b. Defiance, Ohio, May 6, 1952; s. Dan and Zenith (Dreher) B. BS, Purdue U., 1972; JD, U. Toledo, 1976. Asst. prosecutor Lucas County, Toledo, 1976-80, civil divsn. chief, 1980-83; village atty. Village of Holland, Ohio, 1980-91; law dir. City of Oregon, Ohio, 1984-91; spl. counsel State of Ohio, 1983-93; pres. Property & Mgmt. Connection, Inc., Toledo, 1993—. Mem. Maumee Valley Girl Scout Coun., Toledo, 1977-80; bd. mem. Bd. Cmty. Rels., Toledo, 1975-76; mem. Lucas County Dem. Exec. Com., 1981-83. Named One of Toledo's Outstanding Young Men, Toledo Jaycees, 1979. Mem. KC, Elks. Democrat. Roman Catholic. Office: Property & Mgmt Connection Inc 1732 Arlington Ave Toledo OH 43609-3050

**BATTAGLIA, BRIAN PETER,** lawyer; b. St. Petersburg, Fla., Oct. 10, 1960; s. Anthony S. and Virginia A. (Knopick) B.; m. Nancy L. Pateras, Sept. 27, 1986; children: Jason Michael, Matthew Brian. BS in Criminology, Fla. State U., 1982; JD, Drake U., 1985; LLM in Health Law, Loyola U., Chgo. Bar: Fla. 1986, U.S. Dist. Ct. (mid. dist.) Fla. 1987, U.S. Ct. Appeals (11th cir.) 1992, U.S. Supreme Ct. 1993. Cert. mediator cir. and county ct., Fla., 1995—. Assoc. Battaglia, Ross, Dicus and Wein, P.A., Tampa, St. Petersburg, 1986-90, shareholder litigation dept., 1990—, chair health law practice group; adj. prof. St. Petersburg Jr. Coll. People's Law Sch., 1988-92, Stetson U. Coll. of Law, 1997-99; mem. 6th cir. unlicensed practice of law com. Fla. Supreme Ct., 1993-95, chmn., 1995. Contbr. articles to law jours. Bd. dirs. Pinellas Opportunity Coun., 1988-92, pres., 1990-92; bd. dirs. Head Start, 1989-91, Bay Area Legal Svcs., 1994-97; v.p. Comty. Law Program, 1990-92, pres., 1992-95. Recipient pro bono cert. of appreciation Cmty. Law Program, 1993. Mem. ABA (com. on condemnation, zoning and land use litigation 1991-95), Am. Health Lawyers Assn., Fla. Bar (vice chmn. eminent domain com. 1994-95, health law sect. 1996-99, Pres.'s Pro Bono Svc. award 6th jud. cir. 1994), Am. Judicature Soc., Hillsborough County Bar Assn., St. Petersburg Bar Assn. (exec. com. 1993-95, 99—, Pro Bono award 1990, chair law day com. 1999), Delta Theta Phi, Alpha Phi Sigma. BPBlaw@aol.com. Condemnation, Health, General civil litigation. Office: Battaglia Ross Dicus and Wein PA 980 Tyrone Blvd N Saint Petersburg FL 33710-6333

**BATTAGLIA, JOHN JOSEPH,** lawyer; b. Jersey City, Sept. 16, 1959; s. John Joseph and Caterina Maria Battaglia; m. Lisa Sherry Tiback Toback, May 27, 1991; children: Joshua, Jenna. BA in Psychology, Rutger's U., 1981; MS in Indsl. Psychology, Stevens Inst. of Tech., 1984; JD, Fordham U., 1995. Bar: N.J. 1995, N.Y. 1996. Test and measurement specialist Dept. of Personnel, City of N.Y., 1984-87, divsn. chief, police svcs. divsn., 1987-95; assoc. Winthrop, Stimson, Putnam & Roberts, N.Y.C., 1995—. Assoc. editor Fordham Law Rev., 1994-95; contbr. articles to profl. jours. Mem. ABA (tax sect.), N.Y. State Bar Assn., Assn. of Bar of City of N.Y., Order of Coif. Republican. E-mail: Battagliaj@winstim.com. Pension, profit-sharing, and employee benefits, Taxation, general. Office: Winthrop Stimson Putnam & Roberts One Battery Park Plaza New York NY 10004

**BATTAGLIA, LYNNE ANN,** prosecutor. U.S. atty. Md., 1993—; chief of staff Office of U.S. Sen. Barbara A. Mikulski. Office: US Attys Office US Courthouse Rm 6625 101 W Lombard St Baltimore MD 21201-2626

**BATTEY, RICHARD HOWARD,** judge; b. Aberdeen, S.D., 1929; m. Shirley Ann Battey; children: David, Russell, Dianne. BA, U. S.D., 1950, JD, 1953. Bar: S.D. 1953. Atty. City of Redfield, S.D., 1956-63; state's atty. Spink County, S.D., 1959-65, 81-84; chief judge U.S. Dist. Ct. S.D., Rapid City, 1994—, sr. judge, 1999—; practicing atty., Redfield, 1956-85; mem. criminal laaw com. Jud. Conf. U.S., 1993-99; adj. prof. U. S.D., 1973-75. Served with AUS, 1953-55. Mem. Dist. Judges Assn. 8th Cir. Ct. Appeals (past pres.). Office: US Dist Ct 318 Fed Bldg 515 9th St Rapid City SD 57701-2626

**BATTISTE, PAUL A.,** lawyer; b. N.Y.C., Aug. 17, 1943; s. John and Annette (Grande) B.; m. Kathleen M. Dwyer, Oct. 31, 1965; children: Katherine A., Paul A. BA, CCNY, 1965; JD, Bklyn. Law Sch., 1971. Asst. dist. atty. Dist. Atty. Kings County, Bklyn., 1972-80, Dsit. Atty. Bronx, N.Y., 1980-84; sole practitioner Bklyn., 1984-97; mng. attorney Battiste, Aronowsky & Suchow, Inc., Staten Island, 1997—; treas. Kings County Criminal Bar, Bklyn., 1986-91, v.p., 1991-96, pres., 1996-97. 'em. Bklyn. Bar Assn. (chair criminal law sect. 1987-89, vice chair assigned counsel screening com. 1989-97), Columbian Lawyers Assn. Criminal. Office: Battiste Aronowsky & Suchow Inc 358 Saint Marks Pl Staten Island NY 10301-2417

**BATTLE, LEONARD CARROLL,** lawyer; b. Toronto, Ont., Can., Oct. 25, 1929; s. Leonard Conlon and Beatrice Hester B.; m. Marjory Estelle Holland, Dec. 28, 1953; children: David, Tracy, Thomas, Patricia, John, Mary. AB, U. Mich., 1950; JD, Ind. U., 1958. Bar: Mich. 1961, Ind. 1961, U.S. Ct. Mil. Appeals 1964, U.S. Supreme Ct. 1964. Claims adjuster State Farm Ins. Co., 1959-61; asst. pros. atty. Midland County (Mich.), 1961-67; sole practice, Midland, Mich., 1967—. Served to lt. col. JAG USAFR, 1950-84, USAFRR, 1984—. Mem. ATLA, Midland County Bar Assn. (pres.), Mich. State Bar Assn. (mil. law com.), Judge Advs. Assn. Clubs: Kiwassee Kiwanis, Elks (Midland). Federal civil litigation, State civil litigation, Bankruptcy. Home: 408 Harper Ln Midland MI 48640-7321 Office: 200 E Main St Midland MI 48640-6510

**BATTLE, LESLIE ANNE ELIZABETH,** lawyer; b. Orchard Park, N.Y.. BA, Wellesley Coll., 1990, MIT, 1990; JD, Syracuse U., 1993. Bar: Mass. 1994. Counsel MetLife Auto & Home, Warwick, R.I., 1995—. Andrews scholar Syracuse U. Coll. of Law, 1993, 94, 95, Dorothy Denis scholar Wellesley Coll., 1986-90, Stecher scholar, 1989. Mem. R.I. In-House Counsel Assn. Avocations: body building, skiing, classical violin. Insurance, General corporate. Office: MetLife Auto & Home 700 Quaker Ln Warwick RI 02886-6681

**BATTLE, TIMOTHY JOSEPH,** lawyer; b. San Francisco, May 20, 1953; s. Joseph Emmett and Mary Gertrude (McCarthy) B.; m. Lonnell Susan Freeman, Apr. 28, 1979; children: Ann, Megan, Mary Katharine. BA cum laude, U. Notre Dame, 1975; JD, U. Va., 1978. Bar: Va. 1979, D.C. 1980. Assoc. Miles & Stockbridge, Washington, 1986-87; ptnr. Krupin, Carr, Morris & Graeff, Washington, 1988-89, Carr, Morris & Graeff, Washington, 1990, Battle & Battle, Alexandria, Va., 1991—. Mem. Va. State Bar Assn. (lectr.), No. Va. Def. Lawyers. General civil litigation, Insurance, Personal injury. Home: 4400 Ferry Landing Rd Alexandria VA 22309-3150 Office: Battle & Battle PO Box 19631 112 S Alfred St Alexandria VA 22320-9631

**BATTLES, JOHN MARTIN,** lawyer; b. Pitts., Pa., May 10, 1957; s. John and Rosemarie B.; m. Mary Ann Battles; children: John David, Katherine Rose. BA, U. Pitts., 1978; MA in Bus. Adminstrn., U. Cin., 1980, JD, 1990. Asst. corp. counsel Cincom Systems, Cin.; now corp. counsel Lexis-Nexis Group, divsn. Reed Elsevier Inc., Dayton, Ohio. Intellectual property, Computer, Contracts commercial. Home: 7 Crescent Ct Fort Thomas KY 41075 Office: Lexis Nexis Group 9443 Springboro Pike Miamisburg OH 45342

**BATTS, DEBORAH A.,** judge; b. Phila., Apr. 13, 1947; d. James A., Jr. and Ruth Violet (Silas) Batts; 2 children. BA, Radcliffe Coll., 1969; JD, Harvard U., 1972. Summer atty. Foley, Hoag & Eliot, Boston, Mass., 1970, Kaye, Scholer, Fierman, Hays & Handler, N.Y.C., 1971; law clerk to Hon. Lawrence W. Pierce U.S. Dist. Ct. (so. dist.) N.Y., N.Y.C., 1972-73; assoc. atty. Cravath, Swaine & Moore, N.Y.C., 1973-79; asst. U.S. atty. criminal divsn. U.S. Dist. Ct. (so. dist.) N.Y., N.Y.C., 1979-84; assoc. prof. law Fordham U., 1984-94, adj. prof. law, 1994—; spl. assoc. counsel dept. investigation N.Y.C., 1990-91; commr. law revision com. State of N.Y., 1990-94; judge U.S. Dist. Ct. (so. dist.) N.Y., N.Y.C., 1994—; Bd. trustees Cathedral Sch., N.Y.C., 1990-96; mem. faculty Corp. Counsel Trial Advocacy Program, 1988-94. Contbr. articles to legal jours. Trustee Spence Sch., 1987-95. Mem. Second Cir. Fed. Bar Coun., Assn. Bar. City N.Y., Lesbian and Gay Law Assn. Greater N.Y., Met. Black Bar Assn. Office: US Courthouse 500 Pearl St Rm 2510 New York NY 10007-1316

**BATZLI, TERRENCE RAYMOND,** lawyer; b. Dec. 28, 1946; s. Marion Raymond and Kathryn Velma (Hudran) B.; m. Sharon Lee Heinatz, Aug. 2, 1969; children: Catherine Barrett, Jonathan Raymond. BS, U. Richmond, 1974, JD, 1975. Bar: Va. 1975, U.S. Dist. Ct. (ea. dist.) Va. 1975, U.S. Dist. Ct. (we. dist.) Va. 1983, U.S. Ct. Appeals (4th cir.) 1984. Mem. Mays & Valentine and predecessor firms, Richmond, 1982-93, Durrette, Irvin & Bradshaw, Richmond, 1993-96; prin. Barnes & Batzli, PC, 1996—; mediator Access Family Mediation-McCammon Group; adj. prof. law Reynolds Community Coll., Richmond, 1980-82. Mem. adv. bd. VA Head Injury Found., 1990-91, Nat. Head Injury Found., 1988—. Capt. U.S. Army, 1966-70. Named one of Top Three Family Law Lawyers in Richmond, Richmond Mag., 1999. Fellow Am. Acad. of Matrimonial Lawyers; mem. Richmond Bar Assn. (chmn. family law sect. 1982-83, exec. com. 1982-83), Hanover County Bar Assn. (treas. 1997, sec. 1998, pres.-elect 1999), Metro Richmond Family Law Bar Assn. (founding pres.), Va. State Bar (bd. govs. family law sect. 1996—, sec. 1997, vice-chair 1999), Hanover Assn. Bus. (pres. 1989, bd. dirs.), Ruritan Club (club pres., zone gov., dist. sec.), Burkwood Club (bd. dirs.), Rotary (bd. dirs. 1980-84). Republican. Methodist. Family and matrimonial. Home: 10997 Sugarloaf Dr Mechanicsville VA 23116 Office: Barnes & Batzli PC 4701 Cox Rd Ste 207 Glen Allen VA 23060-6802

**BAUCH, THOMAS JAY,** lawyer, educator, former apparel company executive; b. Indpls., May 24, 1943; s. Thomas and Violet (Smith) B.; m. Ellen L. Burstein, Oct. 31, 1982; children: Chelsea Sara, Elizabeth Tree. BS with honors, U. Wis., 1964, JD with highest honors, 1966. Bar: Ill. 1966, Calif. 1978. Assoc. Lord, Bissell & Brook, Chgo., 1966-72; lawyer, asst. sec. Marcor-Montgomery Ward, Chgo., 1973-75; spl. asst. to solicitor Dept. Labor, Washington, 1975-77; dep. gen. counsel Levi Strauss & Co., San Francisco, 1977-81, sr. v.p., gen. counsel, 1981-96, counsel, 1996—; pvt. practice, Tiburon, Calif., 1996—; cons. prof. Stanford (Calif.) U. Law Sch., 1997—; ptnr. Ika Enterprises; mng. dir. Doughnet.com Inc.; mng. dir., gen. counsel Marine Desalinazation Corp. Mem. U. Wis. Law Rev., 1964-66. Bd. dirs. Urban Sch., San Francisco, 1986-91, San Francisco Psychoanalytic Inst., Gateway H.S., San Francisco, Charles Armstrong Sch., Belmont, Calif.; bd. visitors U. Wis. Law Sch., 1991-95. Mem. Am. Assn. Corp. Counsel (bd. dirs. 1984-87), Bay Area Gen. Counsel Assn. (chmn. 1994), Univ. Club, Villa Taverna Club, Corrinthian Yacht Club, Order of Coif, San Francisco Yacht Club. General corporate. Office: 49 Main St Tiburon CA 94920-2507

**BAUCKHAM, JOHN HENRY,** lawyer; b. Royal Oak, Mich., Mar. 16, 1923; s. Henry Charles and Mabel Lillian (Stratford) B.; m. Nancy Lee Bassett, Aug. 5, 1943 (div. 1972); children: Thomas, Laura Bauckham Callander, David, Robert; m. Dorothy Ann Kobussen, Jan. 29, 1973 (div. 1988); m. Rosalie Kirklin, Feb. 14, 1993. JD, U. Mich., 1949. Bar: Mich. 1949, U.S. Dist. Ct. (we. dist.) Mich. 1953, U.S. Ct. Appeals (6th cir.) 1971, U.S. Dist. Ct. (ea. dist.) Mich. 1977, U.S. Supreme Ct. 1978. Assoc. Adams Smith & Yenner, Kalamazoo, 1949-50; ptnr. Harry F. Smith,, 1950-55, Bauckham & Enslen, Kalamazoo, 1957-60, Bauckham, Reed, Lang, Shaefer & Travis, Kalamazoo, 1960-79; with Bauckham, Sparks Rolfe, Lohrstorfer & Thall PC/predecessors, 1979—; pres. Bauckham, Sparks Rolfe, Lohrstorfer & Thall PC, 1999—. Author: Duties and Responsibilities of Michigan Townships Officials, Boards, and Commissioners. With USAF, 1943-45. Mem. ABA, Mich. Bar Assn., Kalamazoo County Bar Assn. (pres. 1966-67, chmn. state grievance panel 1982—, mem. state character and fitness com. 1987—), Elks. Republican. Episcopalian. Avocations: golf, travel, sports. Land use and zoning (including planning), Real property, Municipal (including bonds). Home: 259 Ballantrae Ct Kalamazoo MI 49006-4349 Office: Bauckham Sparks et al 458 W South St Kalamazoo MI 49007-4621

**BAUER, CHARLES WIDMAYER,** lawyer, judge; b. Hartford, Conn., Nov. 26, 1943; s. Phillip John and Ruth Olive (Widmayer) B.; m. Sophia Godfrey, Feb. 27, 1978; children: Stephanie Widmeyer, Justin Frederick. BA, Hamilton Coll., 1965; JD, U. Conn., 1968. Bar: Conn., U.S. Dist. Ct. Conn., U.S. Ct. Appeals (2d cir.), U.S. Supreme Ct. Assoc. Eisenberg & Anderson, New Britain, Conn., 1975-81; staff atty. Pub. Interest Law Firm Phila., 1972-73; vol. U.S. Peace Corps, Botswana, Africa, 1968-71; judge probate Town of Burlington (Conn.), 1978—, town counsel, 1981—; ptnr. Eisenberg, Anderson, Michalik & Lynch, New Britain, 1981—. Mem. Dem. Town Com., Burlington, 1988—; pres. Leadership New Britain, 1989-90; bd. dirs. United Community Svc., New Britain, 1989—; incorporator New Britain Meml. Hosp., 1989—. Mem. U.S. Trial Lawyers Assn., New Britain Bar Assn., New Britain C. of C. (v.p. membership 1990—). Municipal (including bonds), Land use and zoning (including planning), Probate. Home: 7 Hart Ridge Dr Burlington CT 06013-1817 Office: Eisenberg Anderson Michalik & Lynch PO Box 2950 Burlington CT 06050

**BAUER, GENE MARC,** lawyer; b. Baldwin, N.Y., May 15, 1949; s. Sidney F. and Elvira S. Bauer. BA cum laude, Williams Coll., 1971; JD cum laude, Harvard U., 1974. Bar: N.Y. 1975, U.S. Dist. Ct. (so. and ea. dists.) N.Y. 1975, U.S. Ct. Appeals (2d cir.) 1975, U.S. Supreme Ct. 1980, Mass. 1996. Assoc. Rogers & Wells, N.Y.C., 1974-77, Patterson, Belknap, Webb & Tyler, N.Y.C., 1977-80; assoc. gen. counsel Gen. Instrument Corp., N.Y.C., 1981-92, The Cooper Cos. Inc., Ft. Lee, N.J., 1993-95; exec. v.p., gen. counsel, sec. Copley Pharm. Inc., Canton, Mass., 1995—; mediator U.S. Dist. Ct. (so. dist.) N.Y., 1992-95, Small Claims Ct., N.Y.C., 1990-95. Mem. Assn. of Bar of City of N.Y. (com. on state cts. 1986-88, antitrust com. 1991-93), Nat. Cable Television Assn. (coalition opposing signal theft 1985-91), Satellite Television and Broadcasting Assn. (antipiracy task force 1986-91). General corporate, Health, General civil litigation. Office: Copley Pharm Inc 25 John Rd Canton MA 02021-2827

**BAUER, HENRY LELAND,** lawyer; b. Portland, Oreg., June 7, 1928; s. Henry and Emma L. (Peterson) B.; m. Doris Jane Philbrick, Sept. 11, 1952 (dec.); children: Henry Stephen, Thomas Leland. BS in Bus., Oreg. State U., 1950; JD, U. Oreg., 1953. Bar: Oreg. 1953, U.S. Dist. Ct. Oreg. 1956, U.S. Ct. Appeals (9th cir.) 1960. Mem. Bauer & Bauer, Portland, 1955-70, Bauer, Murphy, Bayless & Fundingsland, and successor firms, Portland, 1970-75; prin. Henry L. Bauer & Assocs., P.C., Portland, 1975—; past mem. adv. coun. Oreg. State U. Coll. Bus. Past mem. adv. coun. Oreg. State U. Coll. Bus.; past bd. dirs., vice chmn. St. Vincent Hosp. and Med. Ctr.; mem., past pres. coun. trustees St. Vincent Med. Found.; lifetime trustee Kappa Sigma Endowment Fund; bd. dirs., past pres. Nat. Interfrat. Conf.; trustee Nat. Interfrat. Found.; past pres. Columbia Pacific coun. Boy Scouts Am.; past pres. Portland Civic Theatre; bd. visitors U. Oreg. Sch. Law, 1979-83; trustee Oreg. State U. Found.; chmn. Oreg. State U. Pres.'s Club. 1st lt. USAF, 1953-55. Recipient Silver Antelope award Boy Scouts Am.; named Disting. Alumnus, Oreg. State U., 1994. Mem. ABA, Oreg. Bar Assn., Multnomah County Bar Assn., Am. Judicature Soc., Lang Syne Soc., German-Am. Soc., Oreg. State U. Alumni Assn. (bd. dirs.), Delta Theta Phi, Kappa Sigma (past nat. pres.), Multnomah Athletic Club, Arlington Club, Masons. Republican. Presbyterian. Estate planning, Probate, Real property. Office: Henry L Bauer & Assocs PC 5440 SW Westgate Dr Ste 250 Portland OR 97221-2422

**BAUER, KEITH JAY,** lawyer; b. Portland, Oreg., Sept. 24, 1947; s. Eugene Walter and Viola LaVerne (Davidson) B.; m. Madge Hastings Baughman, May 31, 1969; children: Katherine Amelia, John Hastings. BA in Econs. and Polit. Sci., Willamette U., 1969, JD, 1973. Bar: Oreg. 1973, U.S. Dist. Ct. 1973, U.S. Ct. Appeals (9th cir.) 1973. Ptnr. Rhoten, Rhoten & Speerstra, Salem, Oreg., 1973-80, Parks, Bauer & Sime, Salem, 1980—. Pres. Salem Art Assn., 1976-83; bd. dirs. Benedictine Nursing Ctr., Mt. Angel, Oreg., 1973-76, Vols. for Srs., Salem, 1977-81; bd. visitors Willamette U. Mem. Oreg. Bar Assn. (exec. com. antitrust sect. 1979-81, continuing legal edn. com. 1976-79, chmn. exec. com. Salem chpt. 1982-87, litigation com. exec. com. and chmn. 1988-91, health law sect. exec. com. 1996—), Oreg. Assn. Def. Coun. (sec., treas., pres. exec. com. 1988—, author handbooks, editor jour., pres.), Multnomah Athletic Club, Illahee Country Club, Def. Rsch. Inst. (Oreg. state rep. 1995-98). Episcopalian. Avocations: photography, skiing, gardening. Health, Insurance, Personal injury. Office: Parks Bauer & Sime 494 State St Ste 440 Salem OR 97301-3656

**BAUER, MARVIN AGATHER,** lawyer; b. Milw., June 28, 1940; m. Gray Bauer; children: Laura, Andrew. BS, U. Wis., 1962; JD, U. Chgo., 1965. Bar: Calif. 1966. Dep. atty. gen. State of Calif., Los Angeles, 1965-69; ptnr. Archbald & Spray, Santa Barbara, Calif., 1969-82, Bauer, Harris Clinkenbeard & Nava, Santa Barbara, 1982—; lectr. U. Calif., 1975-77. Bd. dirs. Carpinteria Valley Assn., Calif., 1980-83, Carpinteria Boys Club, 1983-84. Mem. Am. Coll. Trial Lawyers, Am. Bd. Trial Advocates, Santa Barbara Bar Assn. (pres. 1978-79, bd. dirs. 1974-80), Calif. Med.-Legal Com., Santa Barbara Med. Legal Com. State civil litigation, Insurance, Personal injury. Home: PO Box 1307 Summerland CA 93067-1307 Office: Bauer Harris Clinkenbeard & Nava 925 De La Vina St Santa Barbara CA 93101-3243

**BAUER, PAUL ANTHONY, III,** lawyer; b. Phila., Sept. 23, 1967; s. Paul A. Jr. and Joan Veronica Bauer; m. Molly Beth McNab, June 9, 1995; 1 child, Sarah Jayne. MBA, Widener U., 1992, JD, 1992. Bar: Pa. 1992, N.J. 1992, U.S. Dist. Ct. (ea. dist.) Pa. 1993. Asst. dist. atty. Montgomery County Dist. Atty.'s Office, Norristown, Pa., 1992-96; ptnr. Breidenbach, Breidenbach, Troncelliti & Bauer, Norristown, 1996-98; founding ptnr. Garner & Bauer, Pottstown, Pa., 1998—. Criminal. Office: Garner & Bauer 1976 E High St Pottstown PA 19464-3277

**BAUER, SYDNEY MEADE,** lawyer; b. Seguin, Tex., Sept. 18, 1957; s. Sydney Moore and Dorothy Meade (Bruns) B.; m. Ann Thompson, Dec. 18, 1982. B.B.A., U. Tex., 1979, J.D., 1982. Bar: Tex. 1982. Shareholder Clark, Thomas & Winter, Austin, Tex., 1989—; mem. Pro-Bono Law Project, San Antonio, 1983—. Mem. steering com. John Connally Presdl. Campaign, Guadalupe County, Tex., 1980; mem. exec. heart club Am. Heart Assn., San Antonio, 1984; mem. BSA Friends of Scouting; election judge Precinct 237, 1994-97. Mem. ABA (real estate financing com. 1985—), Tex. Bar Assn. Travis County Bar Assn., San Antonio Bar Assn., State Bar Tex. (constn. com. 1985), Tex. Exes. Alumni Assn., Pi Kappa Alpha (pres. 1978-79), Phi Delta Phi. Republican. Episcopalian. Banking, Contracts commercial, Real property. Office: Clark Thomas & Winter PC 700 Lavaca St Ste 900 Austin TX 78701-3102

**BAUER, WILLIAM JOSEPH,** federal judge; b. Chgo., Sept. 15, 1926; s. William Francis and Lucille (Gleason) B.; m. Mary Nicol, Jan. 28, 1950; children—Patricia, Linda. A.B., Elmhurst Coll., 1949, LLD, 1969; JD, DePaul U., 1952, LLD (hon.), 1993; John Marshall Law Sch., 1987; LLD (hon.), Roosevelt U., 1994. Bar: Ill. 1951. Ptnr. Erlenborn, Bauer & Hotte, Elmhurst, Ill., 1953-64; asst. state's atty. Du Page County, Ill., 1952-56; 1st asst. state's atty., 1956-58, state's atty., 1959-64; judge 18th Jud. Cir. Ct., 1964-70; U.S. dist. atty. No. Ill. Chgo., 1970-71; judge U.S. Dist. Ct. (no. dist.), Chgo., 1971-75; judge U.S. Ct. Appeals (7th cir.), 1975-86, chief judge, 1986-93; senior judge U.S. Ct. Appeals (7th cir.), Chicago, 1994-; instr. bus. law Elmhurst Coll., 1952-59; adj. prof. law DePaul U., 1978-91; former mem. Ill. Supreme Ct. Com. on Pattern Criminal Jury Instrns.; chmn. Fed. Criminal Jury Instrn. Com. 7th Cir. Trustee Elmhurst Coll., 1979—, De Paul U., 1984—, DuPage Meml. Hosp.; bd. advisors Mercy Hosp. Served with AUS, 1945-47. Mem. ABA, Ill. Bar Assn., Du Page County Bar Assn. (past pres.), Chgo. Bar Assn., Fed. Bar Assn. (former bd. dirs.). Roman Catholic. Clubs: Union League, Law, Legal (Chgo.). Office: US Ct Appeals 219 S Dearborn St Ste 2754 Chicago IL 60604-1803*

**BAUGH, JERRY PHELPS,** lawyer; b. Evansville, Ind., July 20, 1933; s. Emmanuel Henry and Elva Lorene (Winkler) B.; m. Mary Frances Jones, July 16, 1960; children: David E., Matthew K., Carolyn G. Student, Exeter (Eng.) U., 1953-54; AB, DePauw U., 1955; JD, U. Mich., 1958. Bar: Ind. 1958, U.S. Dist. Ct. (so. dist.) Ind. 1958, U.S. Supreme Ct. 1971. Fgn. service officer U.S. Dept. State, Washington, 1958-66; ptnr. Baugh & Baugh, Evansville, Ind., 1966-74; asst. city atty. City of Evansville, 1967-70, city atty., 1970-71; ptnr. Lacey, Terrell, Annakin, Heldt & Baugh, Evansville, 1974—, Terrell, Baugh, Salmon & Born LLP, Evansville, 1998—; asst. sec., dir. Cen. Ind., Evansville, 1982-91, sec., 1991-98. Mem. ABA, Ind. State Bar Assn., Evansville Estate Planning Coun. (pres. 1982-83), Evansville Bar Assn. (pres. 1983-84), Order of Coif. Democrat. Episcopalian. Probate, Estate planning, General corporate. Home: 100 NW 1st St Apt 104 Evansville IN 47708-1223 Office: Terrell Baugh Salmon & Born 5011 Washington Ave Evansville IN 47715-4865

**BAUGH, MARK ANTHONY,** lawyer; b. Maypen, Clarendon, Jamaica, Sept. 29, 1967; came to U.S. 1985; s. Carlton Vivian and Jane Rebecca B.; m. Nancy Vincent, Aug. 30, 1995. BS, Tenn. State U., 1989; JD, Vanderbilt U., 1992. Bar: Tenn. 1993, U.S. Dist. Ct. (mid. dist.) Tenn. 1993. Atty. Booker Baugh & Grant, Nashville, 1993—. Treas. Com. to Re-elect Supreme Ct. Justice A.A. Birch, 1998; pres. Poplar Creek Homeowners Assn., 1998. With Tenn. NG, 1989-92. Mem. Harry Phillips Am. Inn of Cts., Tenn. Commn. on Tech., Tenn. Bd. Profl. Responsibility (hearing com. 1997—). Roman Catholic. Bankruptcy, Labor, Workers' compensation. Office: Booker Baugh & Grant 315 Deaderick St Ste 1280 Nashville TN 37238-1280

**BAUGHMAN, LEONORA KNOBLOCK,** lawyer; b. Bad Axe, Mich., Mar. 21, 1956; d. Lewie L. and Jannette A. (Krajenka) K.; m. Jene W. Baughman, Dec. 5, 1981; children: Wesley J. and Adrianne J. Student, Cen. Mich. U., 1973-75; AB, U. Mich., 1977; JD, U. Notre Dame, 1981. Bar: Mich. 1981, U.S. Dist. Ct. (ea. dist.) Mich. 1982. Assoc. Foster, Swift, Collins & Coey, P.C., Lansing, Mich., 1981-86; staff atty. Chrysler Fin. Corp., Troy, Mich., 1987—. Mem. ABA, Mich. Bar Assn., Nat. Assn. Women Lawyers, Am. Bankruptcy Inst., State Bar Mich. (sec. bus. law sect., speaker 4th ann. comml. law seminar). Bankruptcy, General civil litigation, Contracts commercial. Office: Chrysler Financial Corp 27777 Franklin Rd Southfield MI 48034-2337

**BAUGHMAN, R(OBERT) PATRICK,** lawyer; b. Zanesville, Ohio, Nov. 18, 1938; s. Robert G. and Kathryn E. B.; m. Joyce Hall, June 17, 1959; 1 dau., Patricia. B.S., Ohio State U., 1960, J.D., 1963. Bar: Ohio 1963. Assoc. firm Sindell & Sindell, Cleve., 1964-71, Jones, Day, Reavis & Pogue, Cleve., 1972-73; asst. atty. gen. State of Ohio, Columbus, 1971-72; pres., prin. firm Baughman & Assocs., Cleve., 1973—. Mem. ABA, Ohio Bar Assn., Cuyahoga County Bar Assn., Nat. Council Self-Insurers, Internat. Assn. Indsl. Accident Bds. and Commns., Internat. Platform Assn. Episcopalian. Club: Columbia Hills Country. Admiralty, Product liability, Workers' compensation. Office: Baughman & Assocs 55 Public Sq Cleveland OH 44113-1901

**BAUGHN, ALFRED FAIRHURST,** lawyer; b. Florence, Ariz., May 1, 1912; s. Otis James and Mary Holman (Fairhurst) B.; m. Barbara Hobbs, June 17, 1935; children: Brent F., Barbara E. AB, U. So. Calif., 1935, JD, 1938. Bar: Calif. 1938, U.S. Dist. Ct. (so. dist.) Calif. 1939, U.S. Ct. Appeals (9th cir.) 1945, U.S. Dist. Ct. Ariz. 1948, Ariz. 1959, U.S. Supreme Ct. 1967. With Title Guarantee & Trust, L.A., 1937-41; corp. counsel Pacific Western Oil Co., 1942-43; pvt. practice law, L.A. and Hollywood, Calif., 1943-56; head Ariz. atty. Signal/Garrett Co., 1956-77, ret., 1977; pvt. practice law, Ariz. and Calif., 1977-94; Ariz. Assn. Industries spl. atty. utility rate hearings Ariz. Corp. Commn., 1977-80; bd. dirs. EPI-HAB, Inc., 1974-90. Adopted by Hopi Indian Chief Seletstewa and Squaw (2d Mesa), 1967; Pres. scholar U. So. Calif., 1931-35. Mem. L.A. Philanthropic Found. (life), Skull and Scales (U. So. Calif.), Phi Alpha Delta (chpt. pres. 1938), Kappa Sigma (pres. L.A. alumni 1945, pres. Phoenix Alumni 1960). Republican. Mem. Christian Ch. Clubs: Hollywood Exch. (pres. 1947); Kiwanis (Phoenix pres. club 1965); Hopi Kachina Klub (organizer, charter v.p. 1974), Hon. Order Ky. Cols. (pres. Phoenix chpt. 1980—), Phoenix Teocali of Order Quetzalcoatl (pres. 1984), Ariz. Bola Tie Soc., Masons (Master 1953), Shriners (Potentate 1971), Jesters (head Phoenix Ct. 1969), Internat. Gorillas (chief 1971—).

**BAUM, DONALD HIRAM,** lawyer; b. Cin., Mar. 12, 1963; m. Elona Lipschitz. BS in Bus., Ind. U., 1985; JD, U. San Francisco, 1990. Bar: Calif. 1990, U.S. Dist. Ct. (no. dist.) Calif. 1990, U.S. Dist. Ct. (ctrl. dist.) Calif. 1997, U.S. Ct. Appeals (9th cir.) 1990. Ter. mgr. W.H. Brady Co., Chgo. and Detroit, 1985-87; extern to Hon. Ira A. Brown, Jr. San Francisco Superior Ct., 1989-90; assoc. Miller, Stall & Regalia, Walnut Creek, Calif., 1990-97; asst. gen. counsel Marcus & Millicnap, 1997-99; gen. counsel Pacific Property Co., 1997—; vis. h.s. tchr. street law program U. San Francisco, 1989. Regional semi-finalist nat. appelate advocacy competition ABA, San Francisco, 1989. Mem. Home Builder's Assn., Phi Delta Theta. Avocations: skiing, camping, travel, golf. Real property, Construction. Office: Pacific Property Co 777 S California Ave Palo Alto CA 94304-1102

**BAUM, E. HARRIS,** lawyer; b. Phila., June 20, 1933; s. Albert I. and Rose Blanche (Nathanson) B.; m. Joyce L. Blumberg, June 24, 1957 (dec. Jan. 1981); children: Sharon, Susan, Lewis; m. Myrna Field, Mar. 25, 1983. BS, Temple U., 1954, LLB, 1957. Bar: Phila. 1958, Pa. 1958, U.S. Cir. Ct. (3rd cir.) 1958, U.S. Supreme Ct. Assoc. Harry Norman Ball, Esq., Phila., 1958-62; sr. ptnr. Zarwin, Prince & Baum, Phila., 1962-68, Zarwin & Baum, Phila., 1968-94; sr. ptnr., chief litigation dept. Zarwin, Baum, DeVito, Kaplan & O'Donnell, Phila., 1995—; lectr. in field. Pres. Keneseth Israel Synagogue, Elkins Park, Pa., 1996-98; exec. bd. Headhouse Conservancy, Phila., 1993—; adv. bd. Phila. Blind Assn.; active ASSIST Disabled Police Fire Fighters, Phila., 1994. With USAR, 1954-56. Mem. Pa. Trial Lawyers, Phila. Trial Lawyers, Athenaeum of Phila., Lawyer's Club, Bala Country Club, Million Dollar Adv. Forum. Avocations: cycling, traveling, sailing, golfing. General civil litigation, Contracts commercial, General corporate. Office: Zarwin Baum DeVito Kaplan & O'Donnell 1515 Market St Ste 1200 Philadelphia PA 19102-1981

**BAUM, ERIC IVAN,** lawyer; b. Oakland, Calif., July 8, 1954; s. Paul and Willa Baum; m. Christine E. Mitges, Dec. 13, 1992; children: Emelia Lynn, Harrison Paul. BA, U. Calif., Berkeley, 1980; JD, U. Calif., San Francisco, 1987. Bar: Calif. 1987. Assoc. Law Office Allan Schwartz, San Francisco, 1987-88, Law Office Sam Perlmutter, L.A., 1988-94; corp. counsel, v.p. bus. and legal affairs Sony Pictures Entertainment, Inc., Culver City, Calif., 1994—; adj. prof. grad. prodrs. program UCLA, 1997—.

**BAUM, GORDON LEE,** lawyer, non-profit organization administrator; b. St. Louis, Aug. 24, 1940; s. James Paul and Johnnie Thelma (Thompson) B.; m. Georgia Dee Thompson, Sept. 12, 1959 (div. 1977); children: Gordon Lee II, Mark Evans Sterling, Duane Russell Stuart; m. Linda Gaye Gulledge, Feb. 10, 1978; children: Laura Leigh, Renee Gabrielle. *Descended from Pennsylvania Dutch/German (Pennsylvaani Deitsch) pioneer Johann Theobald Baum (1693-1762), German Lutheran refugee from Elsass (Alsace), immigrated to America prior 1720. Among the first settlers in Reading, Pennsylvania area, he donated land and in 1738 helped establish Alsace Church and cemetery, now twin churches Alsace Lutheran and Grace Alsace (Reform). His son, Johannes (1725-1808), was a courtmartial man in Berks County militia during the Revolution. His son, Jonas (1765-1825), guard at Reading POW prison for captured British and Hessian soldiers. Henry Van Reed (1779-1829), was founder of Van Reed Paper Mills in Reading.* Grad., U. Mo., 1965; JD, St. Louis U., 1969. Bar: Mo. 1969, U.S. Dist. Ct. Mo. 1969. Sr. inspection clk. Chevrolet Divsn. GM Corp., St. Louis, 1961-65, work standards engr., 1965-69; field dir. mid-west Citizens Coun. Am., Jackson, Miss., 1969-84; pvt. practice civil law St. Louis, 1969—; chief exec. officer, Coun. Conservative Citizens, St. Louis, 1985—, Conservative Citizens Found., St. Louis, 1985—; dir. St. Louis Met. Area Citizens Coun. Assoc. editor (newspaper) Citizens Informer, 1971—; talk show host WGNU Radio, St. Louis, 1995—. State Coord. Wallace Presdl. Campaign, Mo., 1972, 76; del. Dem. Party State Conv., 1976. Yeoman 2d class petty officer USN, 1958-61. Mem. Mo. Bar Assn., Phi Alpha Delta, MENSA, NRA, Sons of Confederate Vets., Hist. Soc. Berks County, Pa., Ger.-Am. Heritage Soc., Am. Legion. Lutheran. Avocations: politics, history, hunting, gardening, travel. Personal injury, Non-profit and tax-exempt organizations. Home: 4219 Celburne Ln Bridgeton MO 63044-1502 Office: Coun of Conservative Citizens PO Box 221683 Saint Louis MO 63122-8683

**BAUM, PETER ALAN,** lawyer; b. Jamaica, N.Y., Sept. 22, 1947; s. Morris and Elsa (Sturtz) B.; m. Barbara Hartman, Nov. 29, 1969; children: Benjamin, Lisa, Alexander. BA, Colgate U., 1969; JD, Syracuse U., 1972. Bar: N.Y. 1973, U.S. Dist. Ct. (no. dist.) N.Y. 1974. House counsel William Porter Real Estate Co., Syracuse, N.Y., 1972-73; pvt. practice Syracuse, 1973-82; ptnr. DiStefano and Baum, Syracuse, 1983-85, Baum and Woodard, Syracuse, 1985-90; prin. Peter A. Baum Law Offices, Chittenango, N.Y., 1990-96; ptnr. Iaconis, Iaconis and Baum, Chittenango, 1997—; lectr. Onondaga C.C., Syracuse, 1976-79. Chmn. bd. dirs. Syracuse Area Landmark Theater, 1982-83; bd. dirs. Syracuse Opera Co., 1979-85. Mem. N.Y. State Bar Assn. (ho. of dels. 1992-93), Madison County Bar Assn. (pres. 1993), Onondaga County Bar Assn. (continuing edn. chmn. 1977-78), Onondaga Title Assn. Real property, Landlord-tenant. Office: Iaconis Iaconis & Baum 282 Genesee St Chittenango NY 13037-1705

**BAUM, STANLEY DAVID,** lawyer; b. Bklyn., Feb. 22, 1954; s. Irwin and Muriel A. (Margolis) B.; m. Ilyne Rhona Fried, June 9, 1979; children: Andrew, Miranda. BS, U. Pa., 1976, JD, 1980; LLM, NYU, 1984. Bar: N.Y. 1981, U.S. Tax Ct. 1993. Assoc. Carter, Ledyard & Milburn, N.Y.C., 1988-98, Swidler, Berlin, Shereff, Friedman, LLP, N.Y.C., 1998—. Contbr. numerous articles to profl. jours. Mem. N.Y. State Bar Assn. (tax sect., com. on employee benefits). Pension, profit-sharing, and employee benefits.

**BAUM, STANLEY M.,** lawyer; b. Bronx, N.Y., Mar. 6, 1944; s. Abraham S. and Mae (Weiner) B.; m. Louise Rae Iteld, Aug. 30, 1970; children: Rachel Jennifer, Lauren Amy. BS in Commerce, Rider Coll., 1966; JD summa cum laude, John Marshall Law Sch., 1969. Bar: Ga. 1970, U.S. Dist. Ct. (no. dist.) Ga. 1970, U.S. Ct. Appeals (5th cir.) 1970, U.S. Supreme Ct. 1973, U.S. Ct. Appeals (11th cir.) 1981, U.S. Tax Ct. 1983. Law clk. to U.S. atty. No. Dist. Ga., 1969; legal aide Ga. Gen. Assembly, 1970-71; asst. U.S. atty. No. Dist. Ga., 1971-74; ptnr. Bates & Baum, 1974—. Pres. Congregation Shearith Israel, 1976-78; chmn. Rep. Party of DeKalb County, 1983-85, 4th Dist. Rep. Party, 1985-89; pres. Resurgens, Atlanta, 1987-88, Electoral Coll., 1988; del. Rep. Nat. Conv., 1992; mem. DeKalb County Bd. Ethics, 1991—, chair 1993; mem. Met. Atlanta Rapid Transit Authority Bd. Ethics, 1993—. Mem. ABA (criminal justice sect. white collar com.), Ga. Bar Assn., Atlanta Bar Assn. (chmn. criminal law sect. 1985-86, bd. dirs. 1986-87), Fed. Bar Assn. (pres. Atlanta chpt. 1976-77, nat. council 1974-77), Dekalb Bar Assn. (pres. 1989-90), Am. Judicature Soc., Nat. Dist. Attys. Assn. Clubs: Atlanta Lawyers. Lodge: Masons. Office: 3151 Maple Dr NE Atlanta GA 30305-2503

**BAUMAN, FREDERICK CARL,** lawyer; b. Harrisburg, Pa., July 31, 1952; s. Carl Frederick Jr. and June Edna (Roeder) B. BA, U. Del., 1974; JD, Harvard U., 1977. Bar: N.Y. 1978, Pa. 1985, Tex. 1988, N.J. 1989, Ariz. 1996. Assoc. Davis Polk & Wardwell, N.Y.C., 1977-81, Hawkins Delafield & Wood, N.Y.C., 1981-83; atty. Bell Atlantic Corp., Phila., 1983-86; v.p., counsel Bell Atlantic Compushop, Dallas, 1986-88; v.p., spl. counsel Bell Atlantic Capital Corp., Paramus, N.J., 1988; v.p., counsel, sec. Bell Atlantic TriCon Leasing Corp., Paramus, 1989, sr. v.p., gen. counsel, sec., 1990-94; sr. v.p., gen. counsel, sec. TriCon Capital Corp., Paramus, 1993-94; v.p., assoc. gen. counsel FINOVA Capital Corp. (f/k/a Greyhound Fin. Corp.), Phoenix, 1994—. Vice chmn. U.S. Olympic Com., Ariz., 1998—. C. Rodney Sharp scholar, 1970, Harvard Club of Del. scholar, 1976. Mem. ABA, Am. Corp. Counsel Assn. (Ariz. chpt. bd. dirs.), Tex. Bar Assn., Ariz. Bar Assn., Phi Beta Kappa. Presbyterian. General corporate, Finance, Mergers and acquisitions. Office: FINOVA Capital Corp 1850 N Central Ave Phoenix AZ 85004-4527

**BAUMANN, CRAIG WILLIAM,** lawyer; b. Lakewood, Ohio, Sept. 1, 1959; s. Robert William and Miriam (Norton) B.; m. Ann Marie Niece; children: Samuel Matthew, Madeline Olivia. BA, Luther Coll., Decorah, Iowa, 1982; JD, Hamline U., St. Paul, 1986. Bar: Minn. 1986, U.S. Ct. Appeals (8th cir.) 1987, U.S. Dist. Ct. Minn. 1987. Atty., ptnr. Steigauf & Baumann, Woodbury, Minn., 1986—. Lutheran. General practice, Probate, Real property. Office: Steigauf & Baumann 1937 Woodlane Dr Woodbury MN 55125-3926

**BAUMANN, JULIAN HENRY, JR.,** lawyer; b. Ft. Leavenworth, Kans., Feb. 20, 1943; s. Julian Henry and Helene (Claiborne) B.; B.S., Clemson U., 1965; postgrad. U. Tenn., 1966; J.D., U. S.C., 1968; LL.M. in Taxation, N.Y. U., 1975; m. Karen Ann Hofmann, July 14, 1973; children—Andrew H., Allison C. Admitted to S.C. bar, 1968, Del. bar, 1976, assoc. firm Richards, Layton & Finger, Wilmington, Del., 1975-80, dir., 1980—. Served to capt., JAGC, U.S. Army, 1969-74. Fellow Am. Coll. Tax Counsel; mem. Am. Bar Assn., S.C. Bar Assn., Del. State Bar (chmn., sec. taxation 1990-91), Wilmington Tax Group (chmn. 1988-89), The Com. of 100 (pres. 1994-96); Bd. of Mgrs., The Nemours Found., Wilmington Club, Greenville Country Club. Democrat. Roman Catholic. Taxation, general, Corporate taxation, Personal income taxation. Home: 8 Brendle Ln Wilmington DE 19807-1300 Office: Richards Layton & Finger One Rodney Sq 10th & King Sts Wilmington DE 19801

**BAUMBERGER, CHARLES HENRY,** lawyer; b. Port Huron, Mich., Sept. 13, 1941; s. Peter Julius and Evelyn Margaret (Jackson) B.; m. Martha Carolyn Megathlin, Aug. 8, 1969; children: Peter Scott, Charles Henry Jr. BA, Vanderbilt U., 1963; JD, U. Fla., 1966. Bar: Fla. 1966, U.S. Dist. Ct. (so. dist.) Fla. 1967; cert. civil trial lawyer. Atty. Stephens, Demos & Magill, Miami, Fla., 1967-68; ptnr. Hastings, Goldman & Baumberger, Miami, 1969-74; founding ptnr. Rossman & Baumberger P.A., Miami, 1974—; lectr. various continuing legal edn. programs; guest on numerous radio, TV talk shows, 1987—. Contbr. articles to profl. jours. Mem. Gov's. Task Force on Emergency Room and Trauma Care, 1987; So. Fla. Health Action Coalition, Inc., 1984; task force on trauma and trauma systems Dept. Transp., 1987—. Served to 1st lt. U.S. Army Res., 1966-72. Mem. ABA, ATLA (past chair of Profl. Negligence Sect.), Fed. Bar Assn., Dade County Bar Assn. (bd. dirs. 1977-88, pres. 1989-90), Fla. Bar (exec. coun. trial lawyers sect. 1983-89, chmn. 1990-91), Acad. Fla. Trial Lawyers (bd. dirs. 1980-89), Dade County Trial Lawyers Assn. (founding mem. bd. dirs. 1981-84), Am. Bd. Trial Advocates (Miami chpt. past pres.), Fla. Lawyers Action Group, So. Trial Lawyers Assn., Trial Lawyers for Pub. Justice (founding mem. 1982—), Am. Coll. Trial Lawyers, Coral Reef Yacht Club, Univ. Club. Democrat. Methodist. Personal injury. Home: 5755 Suncrest Dr Miami FL 33156-5704 Office: Rossman Baumberger & Reboso 44 W Flagler St Fl 23 Miami FL 33130-1808

**BAUMGARDNER, JOHN ELLWOOD, JR.,** lawyer; b. Balt., Jan. 6, 1951; s. John Ellwood and Nancy G. (Brandenburg) B.; m. Astrid Rehl, Sept. 7, 1974; children: Jeffrey Mark, Julia Alexis. Bar: N.Y. 1976. Assoc. Sullivan & Cromwell, N.Y.C., 1975-83, ptnr., 1983—; supervisory dir. The Turkish Pvt. Equity Investment Co., 1991-93; trustee JPM Advisor Funds, 1996. Mem. ABA, N.Y. State Bar Assn., Assn. of Bar of City of N.Y., Nat. Dance Inst. (bd. dirs. 1988-89), Princeton Club. General corporate. Office: Sullivan & Cromwell 125 Broad St Fl 28 New York NY 10004-2489

**BAUMGARTNER, GREGORY S.,** lawyer; b. Scottsbluff, Nebr., Apr. 23, 1955; s. R.W. and D.J. B.; m. Stacy Lynn Riddle, Oct. 1, 1994; children: Brett, Ty. BS, U. Nebr., 1978, JD, 1982; LLM, Denver U., 1983. Sole practice law Houston, 1984-94; ptnr. Riddle & Baumgartner L.L.P., Houston, 1994—. Mem. ABA, ATLA, Tex. Trial Lawyers Assn. Office: Riddle & Baumgartner LLP 6810 Fm 1960 Rd W Ste 200 Houston TX 77069-3804

**BAUMKEL, MARK S.,** lawyer; b. Flint, Mich., Feb. 17, 1951; s. Sherwood and Marilyn (Schiff) B.; m. Julie A. Kimbrell, Oct. 20, 1978; 1 child, Molly. BA cum laude, Oakland U., Rochester,Mich., 1973; JD cum laude, Wayne State U., 1977. Bar: Mich. 1977, U.S. Dist. Ct. Mich. 1977, U.S. Ct. Appeals (6th cir.) 1985. Assoc. dist. counsel U.S. SBA, Detroit, 1977-78; asst. pros. atty. Ingham County Prosecutor's Office, Lansing, Mich., 1978-79; assoc. atty. Shifman & Goodman, P.C., Southfield, Mich., 1979-81, Kaufman & Friedman, Southfield, 1981-84; sole practitioner Troy, Mich., 1984-94; ptnr. Provizer & Phillips, P.C., Southfield, 1994—. Mem. Assn. Trial Lawyers Am. (sustaining), Mich. Trial Lawyers Assn. (PAC contbr.), Oakland County Bar Assn., Wayne County Mediation Tribunal (mediator), Am. Arbitration Assn. (arbitrator), Oakland County Mediation (mediator). Avocations: long-distance running and biking, guitar. General civil litigation, Personal injury, Product liability. Home: 3826 Lakecrest Dr Bloomfield Hills MI 48304-3040 Office: Provizer & Phillips PC 6785 Telegraph Rd # 400 Bloomfield Hills MI 48301-3135

**BAUR, SUSAN IRENE,** prosecutor; b. Seattle, July 26, 1957; d. Leonard William and Betty Lorraine Baur; children: Eleanor, Emily. BA, Seattle U.; JD, U. Puget Sound, 1985. Bar: Wash. 1985. Dep. prosecutor Cowlitz County Prosecutor's Office, Kelso, Wash., 1986-94; chief criminal dep. prosecutor Cowlitz County Prosecutor's Office, Kelso, 1994—. Office: Cowlitz County Prosecutors Office 312 SW 1st Ave Rm 110 Kelso WA 98626-1799

**BAUSCH, JANET JEAN,** lawyer; b. Wahoo, Nebr., May 25, 1942; d. Roy L. and Agnes (Rezek) Meyers; m. Dean J. Taylor, Apr. 4, 1964 (div. Dec. 1979); children: Tracy J., Krista J., Jay D.; m. Lawrence C. Bausch, May 11, 1988; children: Cris, Tim. BA, U. Nebr., 1964; MA, Stanford (Calif.) U., 1976; JD, Western Sch. of Law, 1979. Bar: Calif. 1980, U.S. Dist. Ct. (cen. dist.) Calif. 1980. Corp. counsel Lastomerics, Ltd., Gardena, Calif., 1980-87; legis. liaison and adminstrv. law judge Dept. Labor, Lincoln, Nebr., 1987-90; asst. gen. counsel Gen. Dynamics, Pomona, Calif., 1990—; lectr. U. Nebr., Lincoln, 1988; del. U.S./Japan Bilateral Session on Econ. and Legal Issues, Tokyo, 1988. Amb. People to People, Japan and Republic of China, 1989; bd. dirs. Lancaster County Child Advocacy, Lincoln, 1987-90; co-chair Lancaster County Am. Cancer Soc., Lincoln, 1989-90. Mem. ABA, L.A. County Bar Assn., AMA Aux., Calif. Bar Assn., Nebr. Bar Assn., Bear Creek Golf Club Assn. (bd. dirs.), Stanford Profl. Women. Avocations: skiing, tennis, golf, fishing, travel. Labor, Government contracts and claims, General corporate. Home: 38405 Oaktree Loop Murrieta CA 92562-3009 Office: Gen Dynamics 1675 Mission Blvd Pomona CA 91766

**BAVIELLO, MICHAEL ANGELO, JR.,** lawyer; b. Bronx, N.Y., Dec. 4, 1951; s. Michael Angelo and Anna (Morena) B. BS in Fin., Suffolk U., 1987; JD, Nova U., 1990. Control officer Nat. Bank Westchester, Eastchester, N.Y., 1973; corp. loan auditor Nat. Bank N.Am., N.Y.C., 1973-76; account supr. Comml. Credit Bus. Svcs., N.Y.C., 1976-77; v.p. Baviello Industries, Inc., Bronx, N.Y., 1977-78; mgr. M.A. Baviello Co. Inc., Naples, Fla., 1977-81; broker, owner Baviello Investment Groups, Naples, 1981-85, 87; law clk. Jerome H. Wolfson, Profl. Assn., Miami, Fla., 1988-89; rsch. asst. Nova U. Law Ctr., Ft. Lauderdale, Fla., 1989; freelance legal and tax rsch. svcs. profl., 1990-91; pvt. practice law Naples, Fla., 1991—. Mem. ABA (tax sect., real property, probate and trust sect., bus. sect.), Assn. Trial Lawyers Am., Fla. Bar Assn., Collier County Bar Assn., Phi Delta Phi, Rotary. Avocations: cycling, chess, computers, cooking, fishing, running. Office: 1027 5th Ave N Naples FL 34102-5818

**BAXENDALE, JAMES CHARLES LEWIS,** lawyer, corporate professional; b. Batley, Yorkshire, Eng., Dec. 1, 1945; came to Can., 1953; came to U.S., 1961; s. Stanley and Dora Maria (Day) B. BA in Econs., Rutgers U., 1967, JD, 1970, MBA, 1975; postgrad. law, Magdalen Coll., Oxford U., Eng., 1971-72. Bar: N.J. 1971, U.S. Dist. Ct. N.J. 1971, Oreg. 1981, U.S. Ct. Appeals (9th cir. ) 1982, U.S. Supreme Ct. 1983. Law clk. Div. Chancery N.J. Superior Ct., 1970-71; sr. law clk. to judge U.S. Dist. Ct. N.J., 1973; dep. pub. adv. State of N.J., 1974-77; dir. ptnr. Strauss, Wills & Baxendale, Princeton, N.J., 1977-78; sr. trial atty., office sec. U.S. Dept. Transp., Washington, 1978-80; ptnr. Stoll, Stoll & Baxendale, Portland, Oreg., 1980-81; mem. legal dept. Portland Gen. Elec. Co., 1981-88; assoc. gen. counsel Portland Gen. Corp., 1988—; pres., chief exec. officer Oreg. World Trade Ctr. Corp., Portland, 1988—. Founder, 1st editor-in-chief Rutgers Jour. Computers and the Law, 1970; contbr. articles to profl. jours. mem. joint conf. com. United Hosps. of Newark, 1972-75; bd. dirs. West Coast Chamber Orch., Portland, 1982-86, mem. exec. com., 1984-86; trustee Pacific Ballet Theatre, Portland, 1984—, pres., 1984-86, mem. exec. com. 1984—, chmn. ballet com., 1987—, disting. service award, 1987; mem. bd. for correction of mil. records USCG, Washington, 1979-80. Served to 1st lt. USAR, 1967-71. Mem. ABA (standing com. law and tech. 1970-74), Oreg. Bar Assn. (chmn. pub. utility law sect. 1987-88), N.J. Bar Assn. (gen. council 1974-75, chmn. com. ct. applications of electronic data processing 1972-73). Republican. Episcopalian. Club: Riverplace Athletic (Portland). Administrative and regulatory, General corporate, FERC practice. Home: 1209 SW 6th Ave # 603 Portland OR 97204-1089 Office: Portland GE Corp 121 SW Salmon St Portland OR 97204-2901

**BAXTER, GEORGE T.,** lawyer; b. Passaic, N.J., Mar. 13, 1952; s. Fred Calvert and Rosemarie Baxter. BA, William Paterson Coll., 1977; MA, John J. Coll., 1979; JD, Rutgers U., 1983. Bar: N.J. 1984, U.S. Dist. Ct. (3d cir.) 1984, Tex. 1990. Pvt. practice Ridgewood, N.J., 1984—; cons. numerous attys. on transfusion-associated AIDS cases, throughout U.S. Sgt. USMC, 1969-72. Mem. Am. Trial Lawyers Assn. Personal injury. Office: 20 W Ridgewood Ave Ridgewood NJ 07450-3117

**BAXTER, GREGORY STEPHEN,** lawyer; b. Long Branch, N.J., Mar. 26, 1948; s. George Washington and Doris Louise (Bogart) B.; m. Katherine Ruth Nilsen, Apr. 15, 1972; children: David Stephen, Kevin Scott, Stephen Gregory. BBA, Wake Forest U., 1969; JD, Seton Hall U., 1972. Bar: N.J. 1972, U.S. Dist. Ct. N.J. 1972, U.S. Supreme Ct. 1982. Law sec. to judges Aikins & Arnone, Freehold, N.J., 1972-73; assoc. Saling, Moore, O'Mara & Coogan, Eatontown, N.J., 1973-79; prin., ptnr. Caruso & Baxter (formerly Saling, Gassert, Caruso & Baxter), Shrewsbury, N.J., 1979—; bd. dirs. Ocean-Monmouth Legal Svcs., Red Bank, N.J., 1983-86; trustee Monmouth Bar Found., Freehold, 1988-94, 97—. Mem. West Long Branch Zoning Bd. Adjustment, 1980-84, Long Branch and West Long Branch County Rep. Com., 1974—. Mem. N.J. Bar Assn., Monmouth Bar Assn. (pres. 1987-88, chair jud. evaluations and reappointments com. 1995—), Legal Aid Soc. Monmouth County (pres. 1982-85, trustee 1978—). Methodist. Avocation: tennis. Family and matrimonial, Municipal (including bonds), Real property. Home: 45 Parker Rd West Long Branch NJ 07764-1136 Office: Caruso & Baxter PA 1129 Broad St Shrewsbury NJ 07702-4333

**BAXTER, HOWARD H.,** lawyer; b. Cleve., July 31, 1931; s. Harold H. and Bessie (Bovee) B.; m. Ona Mae Miller, June 25, 1955; children: Kevin, Douglas, John, Susan. BS, Iowa State Coll., 1953; JD, Case Western Res. U., 1956. Bar: Ohio 1956, D.C. 1982; U.S. Dist. Ct. (no. dist.) Ohio 1962, U.S. Ct. Appeals (3rd cir.) 1978, U.S. Supreme Ct. 1978, U.S. Ct. Appeals (fed. cir.) 1982. Assoc. McNeal & Schick, Cleve., 1956-60; group counsel Harris Corp., Cleve., 1960-76; sec., gen. counsel Molins USA Inc., Richmond, Va., 1976-79; v.p., gen. counsel The Langston Co., Inc., Cherry Hill, N.J., 1976-79, Cuyahoga County Hosp. System, Cleve., 1979-81; v.p., sec., gen. counsel Macey Machine Co., Inc., Cleve., 1981-88, exec. v.p., 1988-91; ptnr. Kasdan & Baxter Co., Cleve., 1992—. Chmn. zoning com. Lakewood (Ohio) Rep. Club, 1959-60; vestry, sr. warden St. Stephens Episcopal Ch., Beverly, N.J., 1977-79, Lakewood, 1981—, Ch. of the Ascension, Lakewood. Mem. NRA, Ohio State Bar Assn., Cleve. Bar Assn., Great Lakes Hist. Soc. (vice chmn. 1981-88, exec. v.p. 1968-76, trustee 1968—, chmn. exec. com. 1982-94), Ohio Gun Collectors Assn., Inc., Edgewater Yacht Club. Avocations: Marine history, sailing, shooting sports, scale model railroading. Contracts commercial, General corporate, Private international. Home: 18107 Clifton Rd Lakewood OH 44107-1024 Office: Kasdan & Baxter Co Superior Bldg 815 Superior Ave E Ste 1920 Cleveland OH 44114-2701

**BAXTER, JAMES THOMAS, III,** lawyer; b. Columbus, Miss., Nov. 23, 1947; s. James Thomas Jr. and Doris Gaynell (Gaither) B.; m. Sharon Kay Smith, Aug. 7, 1971; children: Katherine, Jennifer. BSBA, Auburn U., 1970; JD cum laude, Samford U., 1973. Bar: Ala. 1973, U.S. Dist. Ct. (no. dist.) Ala. 1973, U.S. Ct. Appeals (5th cir.) 1977, U.S. Ct. Appeals (11th cir. 1981), U.S. Dist. Ct. (mid. dist.) Ala. 1989, U.S. Dist. Ct. (ea. dist.) Tenn. 1989. Assoc. Cloud, Berry, Ables, Blanton & Tatum, P.C., Huntsville, Ala., 1973-75, ptnr., 1975-78; ptnr. Berry, Ables, Tatum, Little & Baxter, P.C., Huntsville, 1978-93, Berry, Ables, Tatum, Baxter, Parker & Hall P.C., Huntsville, 1995—. Co-author: (handbooks) Foreclosure and Repossession, 1989, Basic Bankruptcy, 1989, Protection of Security Interests in Bankruptcy, 1988. Capt. USAFR, 1970—. Mem. ABA (litigation and family law practice mgmt. sect.), ATLA, Nat. Assn. Retail Collection Attys., Ala. State Bar Assn., Comml. Law League, Am. Arbitration Assn. Democrat. Methodist. General civil litigation, Bankruptcy, Consumer commercial. Home: 1206 Kennamer Dr SE Huntsville AL 35801-1633 Office: Berry Ables Tatum Baxter Parker & Hall PC 315 Franklin St SE # 165 Huntsville AL 35801-4208

**BAXTER, MARVIN RAY,** state supreme court justice; b. Fowler, Calif., Jan. 9, 1940; m. Jane Pippert, June 22, 1963; children: Laura, Brent. BA in Econs., Calif. State U., 1962; JD, U. Calif.-Hasting Coll. Law, 1966. Bar: Calif. 1966. Appointments sec. to Gov. George Deukmejian, 1983-88; dep. dist. atty. Fresno County, Calif., 1967-68; assoc. Andrews, Andrews, Thaxter & Jones, 1968-70, ptnr., 1971-82; apptd. sec. to Gov. George Deukmejian, 1983-88; assoc. justice Calif. Ct. Appeal (5th dist.), 1988-90, Calif. Supreme Ct., 1991—; mem. Jud. Coun. of Calif., chmn. policy coord. and liaison com., 1996—. Mem. Fresno County Bar Assn. (bd. dirs. 1977-82, pres. 1981), Calif. Young Lawyers Assn. (bd. gov. 1973-76, sec.-treas. 1974-75), Fresno County Young Lawyers Assn. (pres. 1973-74), Fresno County Legal Svcs., Inc. (bd. dirs. 1973-74), Fresno State U. Alumni Assn. (pres. 1970-71), Fresno State U. Alumni Trust Coun. (pres. 1970-75). Office: Calif Supreme Ct 350 Mcallister St San Francisco CA 94102-4712

**BAXTER, RALPH H., JR.,** lawyer; b. San Francisco, 1946. AB, Stanford U., 1968; MA, Cath. U. Am., 1970; JD, U. Va., 1974. Chmn. Orrick, Herrington & Sutcliffe LLP, San Francisco, 1990—; mem. adv. bd. nat. Employment Law Inst. Author: Sexual Harassment in the Workplace: A Guide to the Law, 1981, 2nd. rev. edit., 1989, 94, Manager's Guide to Lawful Terminations, 1983, rev. edit., 1991; mem. editorial bd. Va. Law Rev., 1973-74; mem. editorial adv. bd. Employee Rels. Law Jour. Mem. ABA (mgmt. co-chair com. on employment rights and responsibilities in workplace labor and employment law sect. 1987=90). Office: Orrick Herrington & Sutcliffe LLP Old Fed Res Bank Bldg 400 Sansome St San Francisco CA 94111-3143

**BAXTER, RANDOLPH,** judge; b. Columbia, Tenn., Aug. 15, 1946; s. Lenon Pillow and Willie Alexine (Hood) B.; m. Yvonne Marie Williams, Nov. 26, 1980; children: Mark, Melissa, Scott; m. Rebecca Terrell, Oct. 10, 1968; (div. Apr. 1976); 1 child, Kimberly Lynn. BS, Tuskegee Inst., 1967; JD, U. Akron, 1974. Bar: Ohio 1976, U.S. Dist. Ct. (no. dist.) Ohio 1978, U.S. Ct. Appeals (6th cir.) 1978, U.S. Supreme Ct. 1980. Salary analyst B.F. Goodrich Co., Akron, 1971-73; courts planner Criminal Justice Commn., Akron, 1973-76; dep. dir., pub. service dept. City Akron, 1976-78; asst. U.S. atty. U.S. Dept. Justice, Cleve., 1978-85, chief appellate litigation, 1982-85; judge U.S. Bankruptcy Court (no. dist.) Ohio, 1985-96, judge bankruptcy appellate panel U.S. Ct. Appeals for 6th Cir., 1996—; instr. real estate law Kent State U., 1974-78; adj. prof. U. Akron Coll. Law; v.p., dir. Alpha Phi Alpha Homes, Inc., Akron, 1971-85. Bd. dirs. Western Res. Hist. Soc., 1988-92, Christian Radio Fellowship, Tuskegee U., 1989—, Akron Auto Assn., 1990—, Children's Svcs. Inc., 1993—, Salvation Army, Akron, 1993—, Emmanuel Christian Acad., 1994—, Stan Hywet Found., 1995—, trustee, 1995—. Served to capt. AUS, 1968-71, Vietnam. Named Man of Yr., Akron Jaycees, 1977; recipient Disting. Service award City Akron, 1978, Spl. Achievement award U.S. Dept. Justice, 1981, 82, Disting. Vets. award Fed. Exec. Bd. Cleve., 1982. Mem. ABA, Akron Barristers Club (pres. 1978-79), Fed. Bar Assn., Nat. Bar Assn., Akron Bar Assn., Nat. Conf. Bankruptcy Judges, Am. Bankruptcy Inst., Comml. Law League Am., Akron City Club, Alpha Phi Alpha. Home: 4133 Evergreen Ln Richfield OH 44286-9595 Office: US Bankruptcy Ct 127 Public Sq Ste 3205 Cleveland OH 44114-1216

**BAXTER-SMITH, GREGORY JOHN,** shareholder; b. Davenport, Iowa, Sept. 27, 1949; s. James Sanford Baxter and Doris Arlene (Olson) Smith; m. Carolyn Imes, June 10, 1975 (div. Oct. 1980); children: Bradley Imes, Brian McBride; m. Karen Ruth Thomas, Dec. 12, 1986. BA in English, Bucknell U., 1971; JD, U. Mo., 1974. Bar: Mo. 1974, U.S. Dist. Ct. (we. dist.) Mo. 1975, U.S. Tax Ct. 1975. Clk. Hon. Charles Shangler Mo. Ct. Appeals, Kansas City, 1974-75; assoc. Miller & Poole, Springfield, Mo., 1975-76; shareholder Poole & Smith, P.C., Springfield, 1976-78, Gregory J. Smith, P.C., Springfield, 1978-86, Poole, Smith & Wieland, P.C., Springfield, 1986-90, Smith & Fels, P.C., Springfield, 1990—. Mem. Springfield Met. Bar Assn., Greene County Estate Planning Coun., Elks. Republican. Lutheran. Avocation: golf. General corporate, General civil litigation, Estate taxation.

**BAYARD, MICHAEL JOHN,** lawyer; b. San Bernardino, Calif., May 6, 1953; s. William Morgan and Barbara June (Maguire) B.; m. Randy June Thomas, Dec. 10, 1976; children: Michael, Janelle, Ashley, Luke. AB in Polit. Sci., U. Calif., Berkeley, 1976; JD, U. Calif., San Francisco, 1979. Assoc. Shapiro & Maguire, Beverly Hills, Calif., 1979-84; assoc., then ptnr. Wickwire Gavin & Gibbs, L.A., 1984-88; ptnr. Lillick McHose/Pillsbury Madison & Sutro, L.A., 1988-94; ptnr., of counsel Sonnenschein Nath & Rosenthal, L.A., 1994—; founder, owner Constrn. ADR Svcs., Pasadena, Calif., 1997—. Contbr. over 25 articles to profl. publs. Bd. dirs. La Canada Edn. Found., 1990-96; mem. com. La Canada Serv-A-Thon, 1995—. Mem. L.A. County Bar Assn. (chair constrn. law subsect. 1984-85, co-chair constrn. law subsect. 1985-86, vice chair real property sect. 1998—), Foreman Constrn. Industry. Avocations: kids sports, Victorian architecture. Construction. Home: 3615 Hampstead Rd La Canada Flintridge CA 91011-3910 Office: Sonnenschein Nath & Rosenthal 601 S Figueroa St Ste 1500 Los Angeles CA 90017-5720

**BAYBAYAN, RONALD ALAN,** lawyer; b. Paia, Hawaii, July 4, 1946; s. Celedonio Ladresa and Carlina (Domingo) B.; m. Dianne Lea, June 14, 1969 (div. June 1985); children: Alycia Kay, Amber Lea; m. Sharyn Dee Huckins, Dec. 31, 1985 (div. Oct. 1996). BA, Coe Coll., 1968; JD, Drake U., 1974. Bar: Iowa 1977, U.S. Dist. Ct. (so. dist.) Iowa 1977, U.S. Tax Ct. 1978, U.S. Dist. Ct. (no. dist.) Iowa 1980, U.S. Ct. Appeals (8th cir.) 1985, U.S. Supreme Ct. 1985, U.S. Dist. Ct. Hawaii 1986. Asst. law librarian Drake U., Des Moines, 1974-77; assoc. Law Office Mike Wilson, Des Moines, 1977-78; sole practice Des Moines, 1978—; bd. dirs. Berkley & Co. Amb.; presenter in field. Co-author: Paralegals in Family Law Practice in Iowa, 1995, How to Draft Wills and Trusts in Iowa, 1996, 99, A Practical Guide to Estate Administration in Iowa, 1997. Bd. dirs. Wakonda Christian Ch., 1989-90; dir. communique Victory Christian Ctr., 1991—; mem. bd. counselors Drake U. Law Sch., 1997—. Served with USAF, 1969-73. Mem. ABA, Iowa Bar Assn., Polk County Bar Assn., Am-Filipino Assn. Iowa (bd. dirs. 1986), Bass Anglers Sportsman Soc. (Iowa chpt. pres. 1979-82), Iowans for Better Fisheries (bd. dirs. 1991), Mid-Iowa Bassmasters (past pres., past v.p., past sec.). Republican. State civil litigation, Family and matrimonial, General practice. Home: 6217 Urbandale Ave Des Moines IA 50322-3541 Office: 4921 Douglas Ave Ste 3 Des Moines IA 50310-2749

**BAYKO, EMIL THOMAS,** lawyer; b. Pitts., Mar. 5, 1947; s. Emil and Ruth (Alberti) B.; m. Ruth Ann Loucks, Nov. 5, 1967; children: Anthony M., Keith C., Paul S. BA in Polit. Sci., Kent State U., 1970; JD cum laude, U. Ill., Champaign, 1973. Bar: Ill. 1973, U.S. Dist. Ct. (no. dist.) Ill. 1973, U.S. Ct. Appeals (7th cir.) 1974, D.C. 1975, N.Y. 1975, U.S. Ct. Appeals (2d cir.) 1975, U.S. Ct. Claims 1976, U.S. Dist. Ct. (so. dist.) N.Y. 1976, U.S. Ct. Appeals (D.C. cir.) 1976, U.S. Supreme Ct. 1976, U.S. Dist. Ct. (ea dist.) Pa. 1978, U.S. Ct. Appeals (3d cir.) 1978, Tex. 1980, U.S. Dist. Ct. (so. dist., no. dist., ea. dist., we. dist.) Tex. 1981, U.S. Ct. Appeals (5th cir.) 1981. Assoc. Chapman & Cutler, Chgo., 1973-74, White & Case, N.Y.C., 1975-80; ptnr. Liddell, Sapp, Zivley, Hill & LaBoon, Houston, 1981, Holtzman Urquhart Bayko & Moore, Houston, 1982-95, Bayko Gibson Carnegie Hagan Schoonmaker & Meyer, Houston, 1995—. Co-author: Essays on American Law, 1971, Home Rule, 1972. Harno fellow U. Ill., 1971-73. Mem. ABA, Assn. of Bar of City of N.Y., Houston Bar Assn., Chgo. Bar Assn., Tex. Bar Assn., D.C. Bar Assn., Order of Coif. Democrat. Presbyterian. Clubs: Tex., Houston. Federal civil litigation, State civil litigation, Environmental. Office: Bayko Gibson Carnegie Hagan Schoonmaker Chase Twr 65th Fl 600 Travis St Houston TX 77002-3002

**BAYLESS, RICHARD VERN,** lawyer; b. Los Angeles, June 3, 1931; s. Vern V. and Margie (Johnson) B.; m. Marlene V. Little, June 14, 1953 (div. 1970); children—Sally Jo, Molly J., Richard J., Joanne, John P. B.S., Oreg. State U., 1953; LL.B., Lewis & Clark Northwestern Coll. Law, 1960. Bar: Oreg. 1960, U.S. Dist. Ct. Oreg. 1960. Ptnr. law firm Murphy & Bayless, Portland, 1966-68, Bauer, Murphy, Bayless & Fundingsland, Portland, 1968-76, Hampson Bayless, Murphy & Stiner, 1976-87, Bayless, Stiner, Rueppell & Lawrence, 1987-94, Bayless & Murphy, 1994—. 1st lt. USAF, 1954-56. Republican. Clubs: Multnomah Athletic, Riverside Golf and Country Club. General corporate, State civil litigation, Contracts commercial. Home: 7049 SW Windemere Loop Portland OR 97225-6166 Office: Bayless & Murphy 1300 SW 5th Ave Ste 3035 Portland OR 97201-5646

**BAYLIFF, EDGAR W.,** lawyer; b. Hazelwood, Ind., Feb. 23, 1927; s. Henry A. and Grace Eva (Bourn) B.; m. Betty L. Whitman, June 4, 1949; children: Bradford W., Dixie L. BA, Ind. U., 1951; JD, Ind. U., Indpls., 1954. Bar: Ind. 1954, U.S. Dist. Ct. (so. and no. dists.) Ind. 1954; diplomate Nat. Bd. Trial Advocacy. Ptnr. Bayliff, Harrigan, Cord & Maugans, Kokomo, Ind., 1955—. Contbr. articles to profl. jours. Recipient Disting. Alumni Svc. award Ind. U. Sch. Law, 1990. Mem. ABA, Assn. Trial Lawyers Am. (gov. 1969-72), Ind. Trial Lawyers Assn. (pres. 1965, life dir. coll. fellow, Hoosier Freedom award 1983, Trial Lawyer of Yr. 1993, Lifetime Achievement award 1995), Ind. Bar Assn. Fax: 765-459-3974. General civil litigation, Personal injury. Home: 1901 Greytwig Dr Kokomo IN 46902-4516 Office: Bayliff Harrigan Cord & Maugans PO Box 2249 Kokomo IN 46904-2249

**BAYLINSON, CHRISTOPHER MICHAEL,** lawyer; b. Atlantic City, N.J., Aug. 31, 1962; s. Roy S. and Florence B.; m. Marlena, July 18, 1992; children: Christopher Stone, Jackson Graham. BA, Rollins Coll., 1984; JD, Quinnipac Sch. Law, 1988. Bar: N.J. 1988. Law clk. Atlantic County Civil Divsn., Atlantic City, N.J., 1988-89; ptnr. Cooper, Perskie, April, Niedelman, Wagenheim & Levenson, Atlantic City, N.J., 1989-99, Perskie Nehmad & Perillo, Atlantic City, 1999—; master Haneman Inns Ct., Atlantic City, 1998; bd. dirs. Cape Atlantic Legal Svcs. Bd. dirs. Atlantic City Art Ctr. Mem. N.J. State Bar Assn., N.J. Defense Inst., N.J. Defense Assn., Atlantic County Bar Assn. (trustee 1997-98, Outstandin Young Lawyer award 1998), Boardwalk Runners Club. Avocations: running, surfing. General civil litigation, Real property, Land use and zoning (including planning). Office: Perskie Nehmad & Perillo 1125 Atlantic Ave Atlantic City NJ 08401-4806

**BAYLY, JOHN HENRY, JR.,** judge; b. Washington, Jan. 26, 1944; s. John Henry and Salome Carole (Winters) B.; m. Barbara Jean Downey, Feb. 16, 1974 (dec. Jan. 1977); 1 child, Anne Louise; m. Katherine Bridget Kenny, Dec. 1, 1979; children: Johanna, Georgia. AB, Fordham U., 1966; JD, Harvard U., 1969. Bar: U.S. Dist. Ct. D.C. 1969, U.S. Ct. Appeals (D.C. cir.) 1969, D.C. 1971, U.S. Supreme Ct. 1974. Atty., advisor FCC, Washington, 1969-71; asst. atty. Office of U.S. Atty., Washington, 1971-75, 78-85; dep. minority counsel Senate Select Com. on Intelligence, Washington, 1975-76; acting asst. gen. counsel Corp. for Pub. Broadcasting, Washington, 1976-78; gen. counsel Legal Services Corp., Washington, 1985-87, pres., 1987-88; of counsel Stein, Mitchell & Mezines, Washington, 1988-90; judge D.C. Superior Ct., 1990—. Mem. D.C. Bar Assn., John Carroll Soc., Counsellors, Bryant Inn of Ct., Lawyers Club Washington, Phi Beta Kappa. Republican. Roman Catholic. Home: 3512 Runnymede Pl NW Washington DC 20015-2420 Office: DC Superior Ct 500 Indiana Ave NW Ste 1 Washington DC 20001-2191

**BAYORGEON, JAMES THOMAS,** judge; b. Kaukauna, Wis., May 7, 1935; s. Joseph F. and Lorraine (DeBrue) B.; m. Jeanne Marie Collins, Aug. 27, 1983. JD, Marquette U., 1958. Bar: U.S. Dist. Ct. (ea. dist.) Wis. 1958, U.S. Ct. Mil. Appeals, 1958, U.S. Ct. Appeals (7th cir.) 1961. Pvt. practice Appleton, Wis., 1962-83; judge Wis. Cir. Ct., Appleton, 1983—. With U.S. Army, 1958-61. Mem. ABA, Assn. Trial Lawyers Am., Outagamie County Bar Assn. Roman Catholic. Office: Outagamie County Br One Wis Cir Ct 410 S Walnut St Appleton WI 54911-5920

**BAZERMAN, STEVEN HOWARD,** lawyer; b. N.Y.C., Dec. 12, 1940; s. Solomon and Miriam (Kirschenberg) B.; m. Christina Ann Gray, Aug. 28, 1981 (div. June 1988). BS in Math., BS in Engring., U. Mich., 1962; JD, Georgetown U., 1966. Bar: D.C. 1967, N.Y. 1968, U.S. Dist. Ct. (so. dist.) N.Y. 1970, U.S. Dist. Ct. (ea. dist.) N.Y. 1973, U.S. Claims Ct. 1976, U.S. Ct. Appeals (2d cir.) 1978, U.S. Cts. Customs and Patents Appeals 1981-82, U.S. Ct. Appeals (fed. cir.) 1982. Assoc. Arthur, Dry & Kalish, N.Y.C., 1967-80, Offner & Kuhn, N.Y.C., 1980-83; ptnr., head litigation dept. Kuhn, Muller & Bazerman, N.Y.C., 1983-87; ptnr. Moore, Berson, Lifflander, Eisenberg & Mewhinney, N.Y.C., 1987-88; of counsel Lerner, David, Littenberg, Krumholz & Mentlik, Westfield, N.J., 1988, Sutton, Basseches, Magidoff & Amaral, N.Y.C., 1988-90, Graham, Campaign & McCarthy P.C., N.Y.C., 1990-96, Bazerman & Drangel, P.C., N.Y.C., 1996—; governing counsel Community Law Offices Legal Aid Soc., N.Y.C., 1974-83, treas., 1979-82. Author: Guide to Treatment Regulation; co-author: Guide to Registering Trademarks; contbr. articles to profl. jours. Vol. counsel community law offices Legal Aid Soc., N.Y.C., 1974-82, treas., 1979-82. Mem. Assn. of Bar of City of N.Y., Am. Intellectual Property Law Assn., N.Y. Patent, Trademark & Copyright Law Assn. Jewish. Avocations: horses, classic automobiles. Patent, Trademark and copyright, Federal civil litigation. Office: Bazerman & Drangel PC 60 E 42nd St Rm 1158 New York NY 10165-1132

**BAZLER, FRANK ELLIS,** retired lawyer; b. Columbus, Ohio, Jan. 17, 1930; s. Frank Hayes and Minnie Maybrum (Rucker) B.; m. Virginia Ann Hutchison, Oct. 17, 1954. BSBA, Ohio State U., 1951, JD, 1953. Bar: Ohio 1953, U.S. Dist. Ct. (we. dist.) Ohio 1956, U.S. Ct. Mil. Appeals 1957, U.S. Supreme Ct. 1957, U.S. Ct. Appeals (6th cir.) 1964. Assoc. Robert S. Miller, Atty., Troy, Ohio, 1955-57; ptnr. Miller, Bazler & Schlemmer, Troy, 1957-71; asst. corp. counsel Hobart Mfg. Co., Troy, 1971-74; corp. atty., asst. sec. Hobart Corp., Troy, 1974-95; ret., 1995; of counsel Dungan & LeFevre, Troy, 1995—; v.p. Bazler Transfer & Storage, Inc., Columbus, Ohio, 1950-58; sec., bd. dirs. Golden Triangle Farms, Inc., Troy, 1972—. Pres. Troy United Fund, Inc., 1960, Troy Mus. Corp., 1990; chmn. Miami County chpt. ARC, 1955-59, Miami County (Ohio) Rep. Fin. Com., 1981-84; mem. Miami County Gen. Bd. Health, 1992—; commn. on cert. of Attys. as Specialists of Supreme Ct. of Ohio, 1994-99, chmn., 1994-96. Capt. JAG, USAFR, 1953-61. Named one of Outstanding Young Men in Troy and Ohio, Troy Jaycees, 1957, Ohio Jaycees, 1961; recipient Disting. Citizen award Troy C. of C., 1985, Citizenship award Ohio State U., 1993. Fellow Am. Bar Found. (Ohio chair 1995—), Ohio State Bar Found. (pres. 1992); mem. ABA (ho. of dels. 1984—, mem. gen. practice sect. 1976-80, mem. standing com. on specialization 1999—), Ohio State Bar Assn. (pres. 1984-85, coun. of dels. 1979-88, Ohio Bar medal 1990), Miami County Bar Assn. (pres. 1966, Meritorious Svc. award 1985), Nat. Coun. Bar Pres. (exec. coun. 1988-91), Kiwanis (pres. 1964), Brukner Nature Ctr. (trustee 1998—, pres. 1999—), Indsl. Heritage Mus. of Miami County (trustee, sec. 1997—), Masons, Scottish Rite. Republican. Presbyterian. Avocations: photography, travel, golf. General corporate, General practice. Home: 741 Gloucester Rd Troy OH 45373-1223 Office: Dungan & LeFevre 210 W Main St Troy OH 45373-3287

**BEA, BARBARA ANN,** legal secretary; b. Richmond, Va., Nov. 26, 1957; d. Arthur and Edith (Thompson) B.; 1 child, Michael T. Sec. IEEE, Washington, 1981-83, Greenhoot, Inc., Washington, 1983-85; legal sec. Friedlander, Misler, Friedlander, Sloan & Herz, Washington, 1985-88, Arnold & Porter, Washington, 1988-97, Dickstein, Shapiro, Morin & Olshinsky, Washington, 1997-99, Hale and Dorr, Washington, 1999—. Democrat. Mem. Seventh-Day Adventist Ch. Home: 2329 White Owl Way Suitland MD 20746-1063

**BEACH, ARTHUR O'NEAL,** lawyer; b. Albuquerque, Feb. 8, 1945; s. William Pearce and Vivian Lucille (Kronig) B.; BBA, U. N.Mex., 1967, JD, 1970; m. Alex Clark Doyle, Sept. 12, 1970; 1 son, Eric Kronig. Bar: N.Mex. 1970. Assoc. Smith & Ransom, Albuquerque, 1970-74; assoc. Keleher & McLeod, Albuquerque, 1974-75, ptnr., 1976-78, shareholder Keleher & McLeod, P.A., Albuquerque, 1978—; teaching asst. U. N. Mex., 1970. Bd. editors Natural Resources Jour., 1968-70. Mem. ABA, State Bar N.Mex. (unauthorized practice of law com., adv. opinions com., med.-legal panel, legal-dental-osteo.-podiatry com., jud. selection com., specialization bd.), Albuquerque Bar Assn. (dir. 1978-82). Democrat. Mem. Christian Sci. Ch. General civil litigation, Insurance, Personal injury. Home: 2015 Dietz Pl NW Albuquerque NM 87107-3240 Office: Keleher & McLeod PA PO Drawer AA Albuquerque NM 87103

**BEACH, BARBARA PURSE,** lawyer; b. Washington, June 12, 1947; d. Clifford John and Lillian (Natarus) B. BA, U. Ky., 1968; MSW, U. Md., 1972; JD, Am. U., 1980. Bar: D.C. 1980, Va. 1980. Law clk. to presiding justice benefit rev. bd. U.S. Dept. Labor, Washington, 1980; asst. city atty. City of Alexandria, Va., 1981-85; atty. Ross, Marsh, Foster, Myers & Quiggle, Alexandria, 1985-90, Beach, Butt & Assocs., P.C., Alexandria, 1990-92; prin. Beach & Assocs., Alexandria, 1992—; town atty. Town of Herndon (Va.), 1992-94. Vice chmn. Va. Health Svcs. Cost Rev. Coun., 1989-92; mem. Va. Commn. on Women and Minorities, 1990-92; bd. divs. Am. Heart Assn., Alexandria, 1996—, divsn. pres., 1998-99. Mem. Va. Trial Lawyers Assn., Alexandria Bar Assn. (pres. 1987-88), Kiwanis (bd. dirs.). General practice, General corporate, Land use and zoning (including planning). Office: Beach & Assocs 416 Prince St Alexandria VA 22314-3114

**BEACH, CHARLES ADDISON,** lawyer; b. Albany, N.Y., Apr. 21, 1945; s. Charles A.W. and Eleanor (Johnston) B.; m. Jane L. Shlionsky, June 8, 1968; children: James E. and Jonathan M. BA, Hamilton Coll., 1967; JD, Cornell U., 1973. Bar: N.Y. 1974, U.S. Dist. Ct. (no., ea., we. and so. dists.) N.Y. 1974, U.S. Ct. Appeals (2d and 10th cirs.) 1975, U.S. Supreme Ct. 1982, Tex. 1991, U.S. Dist. Ct. (no. dist.) Tex. 1993, U.S. Ct. Appeals (5th cir.) 1995, U.S. Ct. Appeals (6th cir.) 1998. Assoc. Shearman & Sterling, N.Y.C., 1973-81; counsel Exxon Corp., N.Y.C., 1981-90, Irving, Tex., 1990—; mem. adv. bd. Inst. Transnat. Arbitration, S.W. Legal Found.; mem. adv. coun. Cornell Law Sch. Vol. Peace Corps., Libya and Tunisia, 1968-71; adv. coun. Cornell Law Sch. Fellow Tex. Bar Found. (life); mem. ABA, N.Y. State Bar Assn., Assn. of Bar of City of N.Y., Am. Arbitration Assn. (Dallas adv. coun.), U.S. Coun. Internat. Bus./Internat. C. of C. (arbitration com. and S.W. com. on arbitration), Inst. for Trasnational Arbitration of the Southwestern Legal Found. (adv. bd.). Private international, General civil litigation. Home: 1431 N Travis Cir Irving TX 75038-6238 Office: Exxon Corp 5959 Las Colinas Blvd Irving TX 75039-2298

**BEACH, DOUGLAS RYDER,** lawyer, educator; b. Kittery, Maine, Sept. 20, 1948; s. Raymond Homer and Carolyn (Ryder) B.; m. Deborah C.M. Henry; children: Lindsay Alison, Garrett Wesley, Katherine Henry. BS, Central Conn. State U., 1970; JD cum laude, New Eng. Sch. Law, 1973; grad. with honors, U.S. Army Judge Sch., U. Va., 1976. Bar: Mass. 1973, Mo. 1977, U.S. Dist. Ct. (ea. and we. dists.) Mo. 1977, U.S. Ct. Mil. Appeals, 1973. Gen. ptnr. Paule & Beach, Inc., Clayton, Mo., 1977-81, Kaveney, Beach, Russell, Bond & Mittleman, Clayton, 1981-88, Beach, Burcke & Helfers, P.C., 1988—; instr. bus. law Washington U., St. Louis, 1980-89; city atty. Cit y Chesterfield, Mo. Contbr. chpt. to Medical Records, Property Distribution, Trial Tactics in Domestic Relations, 1984, Elder Bonhomme Presbyterian Ch., Chesterfield, Mo., 1984. Treas. Y's Men's Internat., St. Louis, 1977-80; mem. exec. bd. John Marshall Rep. Club, 1969-72. Lt. col. USMCR, 1973-91. Mem. ABA, Am. Acad. Matrimony Lawyers (pres. Mo. chpt., Best Atty. U.S. Am. 1990-91, 92-93, 94-95, 96-97, 98-99), St. Louis County Bar Assn. (named Outstanding Young Lawyer 1983, pres. 1984-85), Met. Bar St. Louis, Trial Lawyers Assn. St. Louis. Family and matrimonial, State civil litigation, General practice. Home: 1535 Walpole Dr Chesterfield MO 63017-4614 Office: Beach Burcke & Helfers PC 222 S Central Ave Ste 900 Saint Louis MO 63105-3575

**BEACH, STEPHEN HOLBROOK,** lawyer; b. Highland Park, Mich., June 3, 1915; s. Stephen Holbrook and Katherine Jean (Campbell) B.; m. Mary Frances Mulvihill, July 6, 1951; children: Jennifer Katherine Beach Buda, Stephen Holbrook III. AB with honors in Polit. Sci, Kalamazoo Coll., 1936; LLB cum laude, U. Detroit, 1941; postgrad., Georgetown U., 1945, Columbia U., 1970. Bar: Mich. 1941, U.S. Dist. Ct. (ea. dist.) Mich., 1941, U.S. Supreme Ct. 1944, N.Y. 1947, U.S. Dist. Ct. (so. dist.) N.Y. 1947, U.S. Dist. Ct. (ea. dist.) N.Y. 1949, D.C. 1949, Conn. 1975. Assoc. Winthrop, Stimson, Putnam & Roberts, N.Y.C., 1946-48, Cann, Lamb & Kittelle, N.Y.C., 1948-56, Willkie, Farr, Gallagher, Walton and Fitzgibbon, N.Y.C., 1956-60; staff atty. IBM Corp., N.Y.C., 1960-61; of counsel supplies div. IBM Corp., N.Y.C. and Dayton, N.J., 1961-65; v.p., gen. counsel, sec. The Svc. Bur. Corp., N.Y.C., 1965-75; v.p., gen. counsel Data Svcs. Control Data Corp., Greenwich, Conn., 1976-78; gen. counsel Computer Co. Control Data Corp., Mpls., 1979-80, v.p., assoc., gen. counsel, 1980-82, sr. v.p. telecommunications policy, corp. sec., 1983-85; of counsel Rogers, Hoge & Hills, White Plains, N.Y., 1985-86; pvt. practice law Greenwich and Stamford, Conn., 1986—; bd. dirs., corp. sec. Dataware Techs., Inc. Editor-in-chief U. Detroit Law Jour., 1937-41. Capt. U.S. Army, 1943-46. Mem. ABA (sci. and tech. sect., banking and bus. law sect.), Conn. Bar Assn. (intellectual property and computer law sects.), N.Y. State Bar Assn. (banking and bus. law sect.), D.C. Bar Assn., Assn. of Data Processing Svcs. Orgns. (v.p. govt. rels., bd. dirs. 1978-84), The Wee Burn Country Club, Delray Dunes Golf and Country Club. Republican. Episcopalian. Avocation: golf. Computer, Communications, General corporate. Home: 52 Brushy Hill Rd Darien CT 06820-6007 Office: PO Box 1202 Darien CT 06820-1202

**BEACHLER, EDWIN HARRY, III,** lawyer; b. Pitts., Nov. 21, 1940; s. Edwin H. and Mercedes S. BA, Georgetown U., 1962; JD, U. Pitts., 1965. Bar: Pa. 1965, U.S. Dist. Ct. (we. dist.) Pa. 1965, U.S. Ct. Appeals (3d cir.) 1966. Assoc. McArdle, McLaughlin, Paletta & McVay, Pitts., 1966-72; ptnr. Caroselli, Beachler, McTiesman and Conboy, Pitts., 1972—; adj. prof. U. Pitts. Law Sch. Mem. ATLA, ABA, Allegheny County Bar Assn., Allegheny County Acad. Trial Lawyers, Pa. Trial Lawyers Assn. (gov. 1982-83). Federal civil litigation, State civil litigation, Personal injury. Home: 5660 Darlington Rd Pittsburgh PA 15217-1510

**BEAHM, FRANKLIN D.,** lawyer; b. Independence, Kans., Jan. 18, 1953; s. Edgar Hiram and Dorothy S.; m. Tawny L. McIntyre, Jan. 7, 1994; children: F. David, Patrick Stuart, Kristin Sanders, Stephen McWilliams. BBA, So. Methodist U., 1975; JD, Tulane U., 1977. Bar: La. 1977, Colo. 1993, U.S. Dist. Ct. (ea. dist.) La. 1977, U.S. Dist. Ct. (mid. dist.) La. 1980, U.S. Dist. Ct. (we. dist.) La. 1985, U.S. Ct. Appeals (5th cir.), U.S. Tax Ct. 1989, U.S. Supreme Ct. 1993. Assoc. Manard & Schoenberger, New Orleans, 1977-80, Bourgeois, Bennett, Metairie, La., 1980; assoc. Hammett, Leake & Hammett, New Orleans, 1980-83, ptnr., 1983-85; ptnr. Thomas, Hayes & Beahm, New Orleans, 1985-95, Chehardy, Sherman, Ellis, Breslin, Murray, Metairie, 1995-97, Beahm & Green, New Orleans, 1997—. Mem. Am. Health Lawyers Assn., Am. Soc. Law and Medicine, La. Assn. Def. Counsel, La. Bar Assn. (Interprofl. com. 1997-98), La. Med. Soc. (Interprofl. com. 1997-98), La. Soc. Hosp. Attys. of the La. Hosp. Assn., Denver Bar Assn., Def. Rsch. Inst. (med. malpractice com., product liability com.), Beta Alpha Psi. Health, Professional liability, General corporate. Office: 145 Robert E Lee Blvd Ste 408 New Orleans LA 70124-2581

**BEAIRD, JAMES RALPH,** law educator, dean; b. 1925. BS, U. Ala., 1949, LLB, 1951; LLM, George Washington U., 1953. Bar: Ala. 1951, D.C. 1973. Atty. U.S. Dept. Labor, 1951-56, asst. solicitor, 1956-59; assoc. gen. counsel NLRB, 1959-60; assoc. solicitor U.S. Dept. Labor, 1960-65; vis. prof. U. Ga., 1965-66, prof. law, 1967-89, prof. emeritus, dean, 1976-87, dean emeritus; John Sparkman Vis. Disting. Prof., U. Ala., 1988—; mem. Sec. Labor's Adv. Council on Welfare and Pension Plans, 1968—. Mem. adv. com. for Ga. SBA, 1969—. Mem. Farrah Order Jurisprudence. Office: U Ga Sch Law Athens GA 30602

**BEAL, CAROL ANN,** lawyer; b. N.Y.C., Aug. 8, 1962; d. Harry Steven and Margot Sanders; m. Kenneth I. Beal, Dc. 4, 1988; children: Zachary, Eric. BA in Psychology, SUNY, Binghamton, 1983; JD, St. John's U., 1986. Bar: N.Y. 1987, U.S. Dist. Ct. (ea. dist.) Conn. Assoc. A.F. Pennisi, Forest Hills, N.Y., 1986-88, jr. ptnr., 1988-90; ptnr. C.A. Beal, Forest Hills, 1990-93, Beal & Beal, Jericho, N.Y., 1993—; lectr. on landlord-tenant law, co-operatives and condominiums, wills, trusts and estates, 1986—. Mem. Queens Bar Assn., Landlord Tenant Assn., Nassau Bar Assn., Syosset Tennis Acad. Avocations: tennis, skiing. Landlord-tenant, Probate, Bankruptcy. Office: Beal & Beal 34 Birchwood Pk Crescent Jericho NY 11753-2343

**BEALE, ROBERT LYNDON,** lawyer; b. Port Angeles, Wash., Sept. 10, 1936; s. Fred G. and Dorothy (Auld) B.; m. Elaine Brown, May 30, 1958 (div. May 1966); children: Tammy, John; m. Marilyn Fijalka, Nov. 4, 1967; children: William, Joseph, Anne. BA, Coll. Puget Sound, 1958; LLB, U. Wash., 1963. Bar: Wash. 1964, U.S. Dist. Ct. (we. dist.) Wash. 1964, U.S. Ct. Appeals (9th cir.) 1989. Assoc. Murray, Scott, McGavick, Tacoma, 1964-66; ptnr., then shareholder McGavick, Graves, P.S., Tacoma, 1966—. Contbr. chpt. to book: Community Property Deskbook, 1977. Bd. dirs. Pacific Harbors coun. Boy Scouts Am., Tacoma, 1984—, pres., 1987-90. Recipient Silver Beaver award Mt. Rainier coun. Boy Scouts Am., 1991. Mem. Wash. State Bar Assn. (bd. bar examiners 1977-91), Tacoma Club (pres. 1990-91), Fircrest Golf Club (bd. dirs. 1988-89), Order of Coif. Fax: (253) 627-2247. E-mail: rlb@megawick.com. Avocations: golf, skiing. Real property, Contracts commercial. Office: McGavick Graves PS 1102 Broadway Tacoma WA 98402-3525

**BEAM, CLARENCE ARLEN,** federal judge; b. Stapleton, Nebr., Jan. 14, 1930; s. Clarence Wilson and Cecile Mary (Harvey) B.; m. Betty Lou Fletcher, July 22, 1951; children—Randal, James, Thomas, Bradley, Gregory. BS, U. Nebr., 1951, JD, 1965. Feature writer Nebr. Farmer Mag., Lincoln, 1951; with sales dept. Steckley Seed Co., Mount Sterling, Ill., 1954-58, advt. mgr., 1958-63; from assoc. to ptnr. Chambers, Holland, Dudgeon & Knudsen, Berkheimer, Beam, et al, Lincoln, 1965-82; judge U.S. Dist. Ct. Nebr., Omaha, 1982-87, chief judge, 1986-87; cir. judge U.S. Ct. Appeals (8th cir.), 1987—; mem. com. on lawyer discipline Nebr. Supreme Ct., 1974-82; mem. Conf. Commrs. on Uniform State Laws, 1979—, chmn. Nebr. sect., 1980-82; mem. jud. conf. com. on ct. and jud. security, 1989-93, chmn., 1992-93. Contbr. articles to profl. jours. Mem. Nebr. Rep. Cen. Com., 1970-78. Capt. U.S. Army, 1951-53, Korea. Regents scholar U. Nebr., Lincoln, 1947, Roscoe Pound scholar U. Nebr., Lincoln, 1964. Mem. Nebr. State Bar Assn. Office: US Ct Appeals 8th Cir 435 Federal Bldg 100 Centennial Mall N Lincoln NE 68508-3859

**BEAMER, DIRK ALLEN,** lawyer; b. Findlay, Ohio, July 9, 1967; s. Duane Allen and Donna Kay (Kieffer) B.; m. Jessica Faith Becker, Aug. 8, 1992. BA, Kenyon Coll., 1990; JD, U. Mich., 1993. Bar: Ohio 1993, U.S. Dist. Ct. (no. dist.) Ohio 1994, U.S. Ct. Appeals (6th cir.) 1994, Mich. 1995, U.S. Dist. Ct. (ea. dist.) Mich. 1996. Law clk. to hon. Sam Bell U.S. Dist. Ct. (no. dist.) Ohio, Akron, 1993-95; shareholder Wright Penning, P.C., Farmington Hills, Mich., 1995—. Mem. Phi Beta Kappa. General civil litigation. Office: Wright Penning PC 27655 Middlebelt Rd Ste 170 Farmington Hills MI 48334

**BEAN, JAMES ROY,** judge; b. Saginaw, Mich., Jan. 16, 1948; s. James Roy and Rella Mae (Cannon) B.; m. Kathleen A. Martz, June 30, 1973; 1 child, James Roy IV. BA with high honors, Mich. State U., 1970; JD, Wayne State U., 1973. Bar: Fla. 1974, U.S. Dist. Ct. (so. dist.) Fla. 1976, U.S. Dist. Ct. (no. dist.) Fla. 1980, U.S. Dist. Ct. (mid. dist.) Fla. 1986, U.S. Ct. Appeals (5th cir.) 1977. Law clk., assoc. Smith and Portman P.A., Savannah, Ga., 1973; instr. bus. law Valdosta (Ga.) State Coll., 1974; asst. pub. defender Office of Pub. Defender, 15th Jud. Cir. Fla., West Palm Beach, 1975-77; asst. state atty., br. office supr. Office of State Atty., 3d Jud. Dist. Fla., Perry, 1977-92; cir. judge Fla. Judiciary, 3d Jud. Cir. Fla., Perry, 1992, 94—; asst. state atty. spl. pros. unit Office of State Atty., 3d Jud. Cir. Fla., Live Oak, 1993. Mem. Taylor County Bar Assn. and Found. (pres. 1990-92), Rotary Internat., Elks. Presbyterian. Avocations: fishing, classic cars, golf, antiques. Home: PO Box 107 3397 Azalea Dr Perry FL 32348 Office: Office of Circuit Judge PO Box 1000 Perry FL 32348-1000

**BEANE, JERRY LYNN,** lawyer; b. Winnsboro, Tex., Mar. 3, 1944; s. Von Rhea and Charlene (Hawkins) B.; children from previous marriage: Lucynda, Todd. BA, Baylor U., 1965, JD, 1967. Bar: Tex. 1967, U.S. Dist. Ct. (no. dist.) Tex. 1968, U.S. Dist. Ct. (ea. dist.) Tex. 1972, U.S. Dist. Ct. (so. dist.) Ga. 1971, U.S. Ct. Appeals (5th cir.) 1970, U.S. Ct. Appeals (11th cir.) 1982, U.S. Ct. Appeals (10th cir.) 1979, U.S. Supreme Ct. 1972. Assoc. Strasburger & Price, Dallas, 1967-73, ptnr., 1974—; adj. prof. law Southern Methodist U. Law Sch., 1989-94. Mem. Dallas Commn. on Children and Youth, 1977-78, Dallas County Health Com., 1978. Mem. ABA, Dallas Assn. Young Lawyers (pres. 1973, chmn. continuing legal edn. com. 1979, chmn. bar activities com. 1980), Baylor Ex-Editors Assn., Baylor Law Sch. Alumni Assn., Tex. Bar Assn. Baptist. Clubs: City, DAC Country. Contbr. articles to profl. jours.; editor in chief Baylor Law Rev. 1967. Federal civil litigation, Antitrust, State civil litigation. Office: Strasburger & Price PO Box 50100 901 Main St Ste 4300 Dallas TX 75202-3714

**BEAR, HENRY LOUIS,** lawyer; b. Kansas City, Kans.; s. Max and May (Kagon) B.; m. Betty Jean Isenhart, Jan. 4, 1951; 1 dau., Dinah. J.D., U. Mo., 1939. Bar: Mo. 1939, Calif. 1949, U.S. Dist. Ct. (so. dist.) Calif. 1949, U.S. Supreme Ct. 1959. Assoc., O'Hern & O'Hern, Kansas City, Mo., 1939-42; ptnr. Bear, Kotob, Ruby & Gross, and predecessors, Downey, Calif., 1949—; sec., dir. Pyrotronics Corp.; dir. Bank of Irvine. Chmn. Midland dist. council Boy Scouts Am., 1954; active Community Chest, Lynwood, Calif. Served to lt. USAF, 1942-46. Named Lynwood Man of Yr. 1952. Fellow Am. Coll. Probate Counsel; mem. Mo. Bar Assn., Calif. Bar Assn., Los Angeles County Bar Assn., Calif. Trial Lawyers Assn. Clubs: Rotary (Downey); Exec. Dinner (Pres. Lynwood, Calif.); Elks. Author: California Law of Corporations, Partnerships and Associations, 1970. Banking, General corporate, Probate. Office: Bear Kotob Ruby & Gross 10841 Paramount Blvd PO Box 747 Downey CA 90241-0747

**BEAR, JEFFREY LEWIS,** lawyer; b. L.A., Apr. 16, 1947; s. Bernard and Rhoda B.; m. Linda Grodman Bear Snibbe (div.); 1 child, Ryan Steven; m. P. Renee LoCascio, Aug. 9, 1997. BA in Polit. Sci., Calif. State U., Northridge, 1968; JD, Loyola U., 1971. Bar: Calif. 1972, U.S. Dist. Ct. (cen. dist.) Calif. 1972, U.S. Ct. Appeals (9th cir.) 1972. Dep. atty. gen. Calif. Atty. Gen., L.A., 1971-73; dep. pub. defender L.A. County Pub. Defender, L.A., 1973-77; ptnr. Sommer & Bear, Beverly Hills, Calif., 1977—; mem. arbitrator panel L.A. Superior Ct.; mem. pro tem panel L.A. Mcpl. Ct., Beverly Hills Mcpl. Ct.; spkr. in field. Co-author: Drunk Driving Trial Seminar Syllabus, 1977, 78, 79, Defense of Drunk Driving Cases, 1978—. Fellow Loyola U. Sch. Law, 1968. Mem. State Bar Calif. (mem. litig. sect.), L.A. County Bar Assn. (mem. litig. sect.), Beverly Hills Bar Assn., Consumer Attys. Assn. L.A., Porsche Club Am. (L.A. region), Profl. Assn. Diving Instrs. Criminal, Personal injury, Product liability. Office: Sommer & Bear 9777 Wilshire Blvd Ste 512 Beverly Hills CA 90212-1905

**BEAR, LARRY ALAN,** lawyer, educator; b. Melrose, Mass., Feb. 28, 1928; s. Joseph E. and Pearl Florence B.; m. Rita Maldonado, Mar. 29, 1975; children: Peter, Jonathan, Steven. BA, Duke U., 1949; JD, Harvard U., 1953; LLM, (James Kent fellow), Columbia U., 1966. Bar: Mass. 1953, P.R. 1963, N.Y. 1967. Trial lawyer Bear & Bear, Boston, 1953-60; cons. legal medicine P.R. Dept. Justice, 1960-65; prof. law sch. U. P.R., 1960-65; legal counsel, then commr. addiction svcs. City of N.Y., 1967-70; dir. Nat. Action Com. Drug Edn. U. Rochester, N.Y., 1970-77; pvt. practice N.Y.C., 1970-82; pub. affairs radio broadcaster Sta. WABC, N.Y.C., 1970-82; U.S. legal counsel Master Enterprises of P.R., 1982-90; pres. Found. for a Drug Free Pa., 1991-92; adj. prof. markets, ethics and law Stern Sch. Bus., NYU, 1986-99, vis. prof. profl. responsibility, 2000—; lectr. in legislation and ethics Wharton Sch., U.a., 1996—; vis. prof. legal medicine Rutgers U. Law Sch., 1969; vis. prof. legal, social and ethical context of bus. Athens Lab. for Bus. Adminstrn., Greece, 1996; mem. alcohol and drug com. Nat. Safety Coun., 1972-82; cons. in field of substance abuse prevention, edn. programming, 1980—; mem. Atty. Gen.'s Med./Legal Adv. Bd. on Drug Abuse, Pa., 1992. Author: Law, Medicine, Science and Justice, 1964, The Glass House Revolution: Inner City War for Interdependence, 1990, Free Markets, Finance, Ethics, and Law, 1994; contbr. articles to profl. jours. Mem. adv. com. on pub. issues Advt. Coun., 1972-95; mem.-at-large Nat. coun. Boy Scouts Am., 1972-85; chmn. Bd. Ethics, Twp. of Mahwah (N.J.), 1990-91; mem. alumni admissions adv. com. Duke U., 1987—. Mem. ABA, N.Y. State Bar Assn., Forensic Sci. Soc. Great Britain, Acad. Colombiana de Ciencias Medico-Forenses, Harvard Club (N.Y.C.). Legislative, Education and schools, Finance. Home: 95 Tam Oshanter Dr Mahwah NJ 07430-1526 Office: Dept Fin Mgmt Edn Ctr 44 W 4th St Ste 9-190 New York NY 10012-1106

**BEARAK, COREY B(ECKER),** lawyer; b. Forest Hills, N.Y., Oct. 7, 1955; s. Stephen Irwin Bearak and Phyllis (Stone) Stark; m. Rachelle Pamela Confino, Mar. 24, 1985; children: Jonathan Marc, Marisa Jean. BA in Polit. Sci., Hofstra U., 1977, JD, 1981. Bar: N.Y. 1982. Asst. to sec. of state N.Y. State, Albany and N.Y.C., 1978; pvt. practice Queens, N.Y., 1982—; counsel, chief staff Councilman Sheldon S. Leffler, N.Y.C., 1982-99; legis. counsel to Bronx Borough Pres. Fernando Ferrer, N.Y.C., 1999—; mem. bd. edn., chair legal, budget and legis. coms. N.Y.C. Cmty. Sch. Dist. 26, 1989-93. Contbr. publs. to law digest. Mem. Cmty. Planning Bd. 13, Queens, N.Y.C., 1980-88; mem. nat. bd. N.Y. State Dem. Action; chmn., mem. Nat. Jewish Dem. Coun., 1994-97; Dem. Liberal candidate for State Assembly from 25th dist., 1988; alt. del. Dem. Nat. Conv., 1984—; bd. dirs. Queens Jewish Cmty. Coun., 1987-94, fin. sec., 1994, v.p., 1995—; del. N.E. Queens Jewish Cmty. Coun., 1986, legis. chmn., 1987-95, sec., 1989-91, pres., 1991-98, chair exec. com., 1998—; v.p. Ea. Queens Civic Coun., 1994-97; co-chmn. Cmty. Advocates for Pub. Edn., 1995; founder, v.p. Queens Civic Congress, 1997—; co-chair Fedn. Civic Councils the Borough Queens, 1995-97; pres. North Bellerose Civic Assn., 1991-97, v.p. 1997—; 1st v.p. Queens County Line Dem. Assn., Glen Oaks, N.Y., 1980-82, pres., 1982-84, 93—, exec. sec., 1985-93; trustee Hofstra Law Sch. Alumni Bd., 1994—, v.p., 1996-98, 1st v.p., 1999—. Recipient Cert. of Merit Boy Scouts Am., 1983, Cmty. Svc. award Young Israel New Hyde Park, 1997, Outstanding Svc. to Cmty. N.E. Queens award Queens Jewish Coun., 1998. Mem. N.Y. State Bar Assn. (legis. policy com., environ. law sect.), Queens Bar Assn. (assoc. editor jour. 1983-86, real property com., legis. and law reform com.). Avocations: family, friends, softball, music, football. Legislative, General practice, Environmental. Home: 82-35 251st St Bellevue NY 11426-2527 Office: 250 Broadway Fl 22 New York NY 10007-2516

**BEARD, BRUCE E.,** lawyer; b. Jacksonville, Fla., Apr. 11, 1959; s. John Richard and Mary Helen (Sheehan) B.; m. Karen M. Schlechta, Aug. 29, 1992; children: Jared Joseph, Allison Vivian. BA, Ea. Ill. U., 1981; JD, So. Ill. U., 1984. Jud. clk. Ill. Supreme Ct., Springfield, 1985-86; assoc. Thompson & Mitchell, St. Louis, 1986-88; atty. Southwestern Bell Tel., St. Louis, 1988-94; atty. Southwestern Bell Wireless, Dallas, 1994-96; atty. Southwestern Bell Wireless, St. Louis, 1996-97, sr. counsel, 1997-98, gen. atty., 1998—. Recipient Best Regulatory Brief award SBC, Dallas, 1994, 95. Mem. Fed. Comm. Commn., Mo. Bar (adminstrv. law com.). Administrative and regulatory, Communications, General corporate. Office: Southwestern Bell Mobile Sys Inc 17330 Preston Rd Ste 100A Dallas TX 75252-5619

**BEARD, MARK G.,** lawyer; b. Ilwaco, Wash., Jan. 20, 1953; m. Oleta Jay Batchelder, Aug. 28, 1976; children: Nathan John, Milan Ray. BS in Psychology, U. Wash., 1977, BA in History, 1977; JD, U. Puget Sound, 1981. Bar: Wash. 1981, U.S. Dist. Ct. (we. dist.) Wash. 1981, U.S. Ct. Appeals (9th cir.) 1981, U.S. Supreme Ct. 1991; cert. Nat. Bd. Trial Advocacy. Dep. prosecutor Snohomish County, Everett, Wash., 1981-82; law clk. to Hon. William T. Weeks U.S. Dist. Ct., Seattle, 1982-83; assoc. Schawabe, Williamson, Wyatt, Moore & Roberts, Seattle, 1983-84; ptnr. Lane Powell Spears Lubersky, Seattle, 1984—. Served with USAF, 1971-72. Mem. ABA, Maritiome Law Assn. U.S. (proctor 1989), Def. Rsch. Inst., Wash. Def. Trial Lawyers Assn. Office: Lane Powell et al 1420 5th Ave Seattle WA 98101-4087

**BEARDSLEY, ERICA SWECKER,** lawyer; b. Louisburg, N.C., July 22, 1968; d. Hubert Earl and Vicki (McQuarry) Swecker; m. Lewis Sudlow Beardsley, Sept. 14, 1996. BA in Psychology, U. Va., 1990; JD, William & Mary Law Sch., Williamsburg, Va., 1995. Bar: Va. 1995, D.C. 1998. Press sec. U.S. Congressman William Lipinski, Washington, 1990-92; law clk. U.S. Fed. Magistrate Judge, Newport News, Va., 1995-96; atty. Watt, Tieder, Hoffar & Fitzgerald, L.L.P., McLean, Va., 1996—. Mem. ABA, Va. Bar Assn. (co-chair domestic violence project young lawyer's divsn.), Va. Women Atty.'s Assn., Fairfax Bar Assn., Va. State Bar.

**BEARMON, LEE,** lawyer. BBA, U. Minn., JD. Bar: Minn. 1956. Sr. v.p., gen. counsel, sec. Carlson Cos., Inc, Mpls. Office: Carlson Cos Inc PO Box 59159 Minneapolis MN 55459-8200

**BEASLEY, JAMES EDWIN,** lawyer; s. James Edwin and Margaret Ann (Patterson) B.; children: Pamela Jane, Kimberly Ann, James Edwin. BS, Temple U., 1953, JD, 1956. Bar: Pa. 1956. Law clk. U.S. Dist. Ct. (ea. dist.) Pa., Phila., 1954-56; prin., owner Beasley, Casey & Erbstein, Phila., 1966—; instr. law Temple U., 1976-80, adj. prof., 1994; permanent del. 3d Cir. Jud. Conf.; chmn. standard civil jury inst. Pa. Supreme Ct.; bd. dirs. NATA; bd. trustees Pop Warner Little Scholars. Author: Products Liability and the Unreasonably Dangerous Requirement; contbr. articles to profl. jours. With USN, 1943-45, USAR, 1951-57. Mem. ABA, ATLA, FBA, Am. Jucicature Soc., Pa. Bar Assn., Phila. Bar Assn., Am. Law Inst., Am. Bd. Trial Advocates, Phila. Trial Lawyers Assn. (pres. 1970-71, Justice Michael Musmanno award), Pa. Trial Lawyers Assn. (pres. 1969-70), Inner Cir. Advs., Am. Bd. Profl. Liability Attys., Temple U. Gen. Alumni Assn. (cert. of honor), Pa. Soc., Aircraft Owners and Pilots Assn. (cert. flight instr. single-multi engine airplane and instrument FAA), Six Diamonds Aerobatic Flight Team, Nat. Air Racing Group, Union League. Episcopalian. Fax: 215-592-8360. E-mail: lawyers tortlaw.com. Personal injury, Libel. Office: 1125 Walnut St Philadelphia PA 19107-4918

**BEASLEY, JAMES W., JR.,** lawyer; b. Atlanta, July 13, 1943; s. James W. and Sara Capal (Tucker) B.; m. Elizabeth Barno Marshall-Beasley, Nov. 28, 1986. AB cum laude, Davidson Coll., 1965; LLB cum laude, Harvard U., 1968. Bar: N.Y. 1969, D.C. 1971, Fla. 1972, U.S. Supreme Ct. 1973. Assoc. Sullivan & Cromwell, N.Y.C., 1968, Wilmer, Cutler & Pickering, Washington, 1970-72; assoc., then ptnr. Paul & Thomson, Miami, Fla., 1972-78; mng. ptnr. Beasley, Olle & Downs, Miami, 1978-88; ptnr. Tew , Jordan, Schulte & Beasley, Miami, 1988-89, Cadwalader, Wickersham & Taft, Palm Beach, Fla., 1989-94, Tew & Beasley LLP, Palm Beach, 1994-97, Beasley, Leacock & Hauser, P.A., Palm Beach, 1997—. Author: Florida Corporations, 1985; contbr. articles to profl. jours. Mem. Urban Land Inst.; chmn. County Conv. Ctr. Adv. Bd., 1994-96. Capt. U.S. Army, 1968-70. Mem. ABA, ATLA, Fla. Bar Assn. (chmn. securities regulation com. bus. law sect. 1975-77), Acad. Fla. Trial Lawyers. General civil litigation, Securities, Appellate.

**BEASLEY, JOSEPH WAYNE,** lawyer; b. Sylacauga, Ala., Feb. 10, 1943; s. William Ocie and Alice Lorraine (Blackmon) B.; m. Gerri Gay Aldrich, Aug. 26, 1966. BS in Aerospace Engring., U. Fla., 1966, JD with high honors, 1973; MS in Aeronautics & Astronautics, U. Wash., 1970. Bar: Fla. 1974, U.S. Dist. Ct. (so. dist.) Fla. 1974, U.S. Ct. Appeals (5th cir.) 1981, U.S. Ct. Appeals (11th cir.) 1982, U.S. Dist. Ct. (mid. dist.) Fla. 1982. From engr. to lead engr. Boeing Aircraft Co., Seattle, 1966-71; instr. legal writing, rsch. U. Fla., Gainesville, 1973-74; assoc. litigator Mershan Sawyer Johnston Dunwoody & Cole, Miami, Fla., 1974-78; ptnr., shareholder Kelly Black Black Byrne & Beasley P.A., Miami, 1978—. Mem. ABA, Fla. Bar Assn. (environ. com., comml. litigation com., chair 11th judicial cir. grievance com.), Coral Reef Yacht Club, Coconut Grove Civic Club (past bd. dirs.). Republican. Baptist. Avocations: marathon running, snow skiing, handball, sailing, karate. General civil litigation, Condemnation. Office: Kelly Black Black Byrne & Beasley PA 1400 Alfred I Dupont Bldg Miami FL 33131

**BEASLEY, OSCAR HOMER,** lawyer, educator; b. Denver, Sept. 30, 1925; m. Shirlee Beasley; 4 children. BA, U. Omaha, 1949; JD, U. Iowa, 1950. Bar: Iowa 1949, N.Mex. 1952, Calif. 1964, Hawaii 1982. Assoc. Joseph L. Smith, Albuquerque, 1955-59; ptnr. Ertz & Beasley, Albuquerque, 1959-62, Beasley & Colberg, Albuquerque, 1962-64; atty. 1st Am. Title Ins. Co., Santa Ana, Calif., 1964-70, sr. v.p., sr. title counsel, 1970—; mem. N.Mex. Ho. of Reps., 1958-62; instr. Western State U. Coll. Law, Fullerton, Calif., 1970-96, also mem. adv. bd. Mem. N.Mex. Ho. of Reps., 1958-62. Mem. ABA, Calif. Bar Assn., Orange County Bar Assn., L.A. County Bar Assn., N.Mex. Bar Assn., Iowa Bar Assn., Am. Coll. Real Estate Lawyers, Am. Land Title Assn. (hon. Indian Land Claims Com.). E-mail: obeasley@firstam.com. Real property. Home: 1100 Irvine Blvd # 511 Tustin CA 92780-3529 Office: First Am Title Ins Co 114 E 5th St Santa Ana CA 92701-4642

**BEATIE, RUSSEL HARRISON, JR.,** lawyer; b. Lawrence, Kans., Jan. 20, 1938; m. Julia Ferguson DuVall; children: Benjamin Wilson Parkhill, Amy Wilder. BA cum laude, Princeton U., 1959, LLB cum laude Columbia U., 1964. Bar: N.Y. 1964, U.S. Dist. Ct. (so. and ea. dists.) N.Y., U.S. Ct. Appeals (2d, 3d, 5th, 6th, 7th, 9th and 10th cirs.), U.S. Supreme Ct. Assoc. Dewey, Ballantine, Bushby, Palmer & Wood, N.Y.C., 1964-66, 68-72, Rogers & Wells, 1966-68; ptnr. Dewey Ballantine, 1972-83; pvt. practice, 1983-88; ptnr. Brown & Wood, N.Y.C., 1989-93, Beatie, King & Abate, N.Y.C., 1993-97, Beatie and Osborn, 1997—. 1st lt., arty. U.S. Army, 1959-61. Mem. Assn. of Bar of City of N.Y., Union Club. Republican. Author: Road to Manassas—The Growth of Union Command in the Eastern Theatre from the Fall of Fort Sumter to the First Battle of Bull Run, 1961. Federal civil litigation, State civil litigation. Office: 599 Lexington Ave New York NY 10022-6030

**BEATTIE, JAMES RAYMOND,** lawyer; b. Passaic, N.J., Aug. 31, 1935; s. James R. Sr. and Emma (Mihalisin) B.; m. Irene Jacq, May 12, 1962; children: James R. III, Janice C. BA, Rutgers U., 1957; LLB, U. Notre Dame, 1960. Bar: N.J. 1960, U.S. Dist. Ct. N.J. 1960, U.S. Supreme Ct. 1978, U.S. Tax Ct. 1981, U.S. Ct. Appeals (D.C. cir.) 1982. Ptnr. Neal and Beattie, Hackensack, N.J., 1961-63, Sheridan and Beattie, Hackensack, 1967-68; pvt. practice Hackensack, 1964-67, 68-72; ptnr. Beattie Padovano, Montvale, N.J., 1972-84, mng. ptnr., 1984—; vice chmn., bd. dirs. Found. for Free Enterprise, Paramus, N.J., 1990—, chmn., 1994-96; bd. trustee Bergen County Legal Svcs. Corp., 1975-80; bd. govs. Hackensack Hosp., 1997—. Bd. dirs. St. Joseph's H.S., Montvale, 1983—; trustee Bergen C.C. Found., Paramus, N.J., 1986—, co-pres., 1995-96; trustee Hackensack Hosp. Found., 1989—, treas., 1995—; bd. govs. Hackensack Hosp., 1997—; pres. bd. dirs. Tri-Boro Ambulance Corps, 1980-83; trustee The Acad. Decathlon of N.J., 1997; pres. Greater Montvale Businessman's Assn., 1988-89. Named Man of Yr. Park Ridge Rotary, 1988, Citizen of Yr., Greater Pascack Valley C. of C., 1995; honoree March of Dimes, 1990. Mem. Commerce and Industry Assn. No. N.J. (bd. dirs. 1991—). Real property, Banking, Land use and zoning (including planning). Office: Beattie & Padovano 50 Chestnut Ridge Rd Montvale NJ 07645-1830

**BEATTY, ANDREW HYLAND,** lawyer; b. Winnipeg, Man., Can., Sept. 19, 1964; s. James Hyland and Hazel Irene (McTeer) B. BA, U. Man., 1984; JD, N.Y. Law Sch., 1989. Bar: N.Y. 1990, U.S. Dist. Ct. (so. & ea. dists.) N.Y. 1993. Assoc. Shea & Gould, N.Y.C., 1989-91, Whitman & Ransom, N.Y.C., 1991-93, Ross & Hardies, N.Y.C., 1993—. Chpt. editor: Products Liabilitiy Desk Reference, 1991. Mem. ABA, N.Y. County Lawyers Assn. Avocations: skiing, rock climbing. General civil litigation, Product liability. Office: Ross & Hardies 65 E 55th St New York NY 10022-3219

**BEATTY, MICHAEL L.,** lawyer; b. 1947; s. Herbert Francis and Lola (Stuewe) B.; m. Kathleen Murphy; children: Erin, Piper. BA, U. Calif., 1969; JD, Harvard U., 1972. Bar: Tex. 1972. Assoc. mem. Vinson and Elkins, 1972-74; prof. U. Idaho, 1974-79; vis. prof. law U. Wyo., 1980-81; atty. Colo. Interstate Gas Co., 1981-84, gen. counsel, 1984-85; with The Coastal Corp., Houston, 1985-93, exec. v.p., gen. counsel, 1989-93; with Akin, Gump, Strauss, Hauer & Feld LLP, Houston, 1993-98; prin. Michael L. Beatty & Assocs., P.C., Denver, 1998—. FERC practice, General civil litigation. Office: Michael L Beatty & Assocs PC 1401 17th St Ste 1600 Denver CO 80202-1239

**BEATTY, TINA MARIE,** legal assistant; b. Charlotte, N.C., Dec. 21, 1955. BA, Winthrop Coll., 1976; MBA, U. N.C., Charlotte, 1984; cert., The Nat. Ctr. for Paralegal Tng., 1976; MLiberal Arts, Winthrop Coll., 1992. Legal asst. Whitesides and Robinson, Gastonia, N.C., 1979-80, Garland and Alala, P.A., Gastonia, 1980-81, Kennedy Covington Lobdell & Hickman, Charlotte, 1981-88; documentation policy supr. Corp. Banking Group, First Union Nat. Bank N.C., Charlotte, 1988-93; legal asst. Moore & Van Allen, PLLC, Charlotte, 1993—; asst. state dir. Am. Inst. for Paralegal Studies, Inc., Charlotte, 1990-91. Charlotte area alumni steering com. Winthrop Coll., 1984, alumni ann. fund class agt., 1991-92, 92-93. Alumni Grad. scholar Winthrop Coll., 1991-92. Avocations: travel, photography, pottery. Office: Moore & Van Allen PLLC NationsBank Corp Ctr 100 N Tryon St Fl 47 Charlotte NC 28202-4000

**BEATTY, WILLIAM LOUIS,** federal judge; b. Mendota, Ill., Sept. 4, 1925; s. Raphael H. and Teresa A. (Collins) B.; m. Dorothy Jeanne Starnes, June 12, 1948; children: William S., Steven M., Thomas D., Mary C. Student, Washington U., St. Louis, 1945-47; LL.B., St. Louis U., 1950. Bar: Ill. 1950. Gen. practice law Granite City, 1950-68; circuit judge 3d Jud. Circuit Ill., 1968-79; U.S. dist. judge So. Dist. Ill., 1979—. Served with AUS, 1943-45. Mem. Madison County Bar Assn., Tri-City Bar Assn. Roman Catholic. Office: So Dist Ct 750 Missouri Ave Rm 377 East Saint Louis IL 62201-2954

**BEATY, JAMES ARTHUR, JR.,** judge; b. 1949. BA cum laude, Western Carolina U., 1971; JD, UNC, 1974; postgrad., U. Nev., 1985-91. With Richard C. Erwin, Winston-Salem, N.C., 1974-77; atty. at law Ewrin and Beaty, Winston-Salem, 1977-78, Beaty and Friende, Winston-Salem, 1980-81; pvt. practice Winston-Salem, 1978-79; judge N.C. Superior Ct., 1981-94; dist. judge U.S. Dist. Ct. (mid. dist.) N.C., 1994—. Mem. ABA, N.C. State Bar, Forsyth County and 21st Judicial Dist. Bar, Winston-Salem Bar Assn., N.C. Acad. Trial Lawyers (outstanding trial ct. judge of the yr., 1990), N.C. Assn. Black Lawyers (sec. 1976, v.p. 1978), NAACP (life), Alpha Phi Alpha, Sigma Pi Phi, Rotary Club. Office: 251 N Main St Rm 248 Winston Salem NC 27101-3914

**BEAUSANG, MICHAEL FRANCIS, JR.,** lawyer; b. Phila., June 9, 1936; s. Frank M. and Betty Jane (Barnum) B.; m. Jane Graves (div. Dec. 1984); children: Michael F. III, Suzanne A., Elizabeth Jane; m. Deborah Deavers, June 21, 1986. BS in Mech. Engring., U. Pa., 1958; LLB, Georgetown U., 1964; LLM, NYU, 1967. Bar: Ill. 1965, Pa. 1966. Assoc. McCoy, Evans & Lewis, Phila., 1964-67; pvt. practice Phila., 1967-69; ptnr. Butera, Beausang, Cohen & Brennan, King of Prussia, Pa., 1969—; bd. dirs. Jefferson Bank, Phila. Contbr. numerous articles on taxation to profl. jours. Lt. USN, 1958-62. Mem. ABA, Pa. Bar Assn., Montgomery County Bar Assn. Republican. Episcopalian. Avocations: fishing, tennis. Taxation, general, Insurance, Banking. Office: Butera Beausang Cohen & Brennan 630 Freedom Business Ctr Dr King Of Prussia PA 19406

**BEAUZAY, VICTOR H(ILTON),** lawyer; b. Waverly, N.Y., Mar. 28, 1924; s. Eugene Louis and Edith (Peet) B.; m. JoEllen, Apr. 17, 1946; children—Victor H. II, Victoria Ellen Beauzay. Student Syracuse U., 1947; A.B. in Polit. Sci., Stanford U., 1948, J.D., 1951. Bar: Calif. 1952, U.S. Sup. Ct. 1957. Lectr. in workers' compensation law; chmn. Workers' Compensation Adv. Commn., Calif. State Bar Specialization Program; exec. com. State BarCalif., conf. of dels. 1984-87. Served with U.S. Army, 1943-46. Recipient Golden Banana award P & L Seminar Soc., 1979, Gene Marias Lifetime Achievement award. Mem. Santa Clara County Bar Assn. (pres. 1981), Calif. Applicants' Attys. Assn. (pres. 1968-69, chmn. legis. com. 1968-71). Clubs: Century (pres.), Masons (San Jose). Workers' compensation. Office: 101 Park Center Plz Ste 900 San Jose CA 95113-2205

**BEBB, RICHARD S.,** lawyer; b. L.A., July 22, 1952; s. Robert Stanley and Sue (Williams) B.; m. Christine K. Bebb, June 29, 1974; children: Michelle, David. AB, Stanford U., 1974; JD, U. Calif., San Francisco, 1977. Bar: Calif. Assoc. Reinjohn, Catlin & Clements, L.A., 1977-79, Ruffo, Ferrari & McNeil, San Jose, Calif., 1979-81; assoc. Ferrari Alvarez Olsen & Ottoboni, P.C., San Jose, 1981-84, ptnr., 1984-96; ptnr. Ferrari Olsen Ottoboni & Bebb, P.C., San Jose, 1996-98, Ferrari Olsen Ottoboni & Bebb, L.L.P., San Jose, 1998—. Mem. audit com. City Team Ministries, San Jose, 1994—; mem. bd. advisors Green Pastures, 1984—; youth athletic coach to 16 teams, 1984-96. Mem. Attys. for Family Held Enterprises, Am. Coll. CLU, The Exec. Coun. (assoc.), Inst. Cert. Bus. Counselors, San Jose Rotary, Decathlon Club, Silicon Valley Capital Club, Los Altos Golf and Country Club. E-mail: rbebb@ferrari.calaw.com. General corporate, Mergers and acquisitions, Estate planning. Office: Ferrari Olsen Ottoboni & Bebb LLP 333 W Santa Clara St Ste 700 San Jose CA 95113-1716

**BEBCHICK, LEONARD NORMAN,** lawyer; b. New Bedford, Mass., Dec. 11, 1932; s. Samuel and Frances (Hait) B.; m. Gabriela Meyerhoff, Aug. 31, 1968; children: Ilana, Brian. AB, Cornell U., 1955; LLB, Yale U., 1958. Bar: Mass. 1958, D.C. 1960, Md. 1989. Atty. CAB, Washington, 1959-60; assoc. Ginsburg & Leventhal, Washington, 1960-64; ptnr. Bebchick, Sher & Kushnick, Washington, 1964-74, Martin, Whitfield, Smith & Bebchick, Washington, 1974-82; pres. Leonard N. Bebchick P.C., Washington, 1982-88; ptnr. Leva, Hawes, Mason, Martin & Bebchick, Washington, 1988-89; pvt. practice as lawyer Washington, 1989—;; joint co. sec. Brit Caledonian Airways, Eng., 1963-88; bd. dirs. British Caledonian Group, Eng., 1978-88, London Transport Internat. Cons., U.S., 1990-92; spl. counsel D.C. Pub. Svc. Commn., Washington, 1965-66, V.I. Pub. Utilities Commn., 1967-70. Pres. Congregation Beth El of Montgomery County, 1993-95; bd. dirs. United Synagogue of Conservative Judaism, 1993—, United Israel Appeal, 1998—, Jewish Fedn. Greater, Washington, 1996—; bd. govs. coms. Jewish Agy. Israel, 1998—; v.p. Muss H.S., Israel, 1997—. Mem. ABA (chmn. adv. com. on aero. law 1982-83), FBA, Internat. Bar Assn., Inst. of Dirs. (London), U.S. Nat. Student Assn. (v.p. internat. affairs 1953-54). Democrat. Jewish. Federal civil litigation, Administrative and regulatory, General corporate. Home: 6321 Lenox Rd Bethesda MD 20817-6023 Office: 888 16th St NW Washington DC 20006-4103

**BEBER, ROBERT H.,** lawyer, financial services executive; b. N.Y.C., Aug. 17, 1933; s. Morris and Martha (Pollock) B.; m. Joan Parsons, June 14, 1957; children: Andrea, Judith, Deborah. A.B. in Econs, Duke U., 1955, J.D., 1957. Bar: N.Y., N.C. With Everett, Everett & Everett, N.C., 1957-58; atty. SBA, Washington, 1961-63; with RCA, 1963-81; sr. v.p., gen. counsel, sec. GAF Corp., N.Y.C., 1981-83, exec. v.p., dir., 1983-84, dir. subs.; sr. v.p., gen. counsel, sec. Phlcorp, Inc. (formerly Baldwin United Corp.), Phila., 1984-88; asst. gen. counsel litigation W.R. Grace & Co., N.Y.C., 1988-89, v.p., dir. litigation, 1989-91, sr. v.p., gen. counsel, 1991-93, exec. v.p., 1993-98, ret., 1999, cons., 1999—. Bd. vis. Sch. Law, Duke U., 1996—; chmn. bd. Health Care Plan N.J., 1975-78; v.p. South Jersey C. of C., 1974-77. Served with U.S. Army, 1958-61. Mem. ABA. Republican. Jewish. General corporate, General civil litigation. Home: 7228 Queenferry Cir Boca Raton FL 33496-5953 Office: WR Grace & Co 1 Town Center Rd Boca Raton FL 33486-1050

**BECERRA, ROBERT JOHN,** lawyer; b. Jersey City, Jan. 26, 1962; s. Joseph Hercules and Blanche (Rosado) B.; m. Christiana Marie Carroll, Oct. 30, 1993. BBA, U. Miami, 1986, JD, 1990. Bar: Fla. 1990, U.S. Dist. Ct. (so. dist.) Fla. 1991, (mid. dist.) Fla. 1991, (ea. dist.) Mich. 1994, U.S. Ct. Appeals (11th cir.) 1991, U.S. Supreme Ct. 1994, U.S. Ct. Appeals (3d cir.) 1997. Assoc. Raskin & Raskin, Miami, Fla., 1990-96, ptnr., 1997—. Mem. Fed. Bar Assn., Dade County Bar Assn. (fed. cts. com., Certificate of Merit 1993), Phi Kappa Phi. Democrat. Roman Catholic. Avocations: sailplane pilot, scuba diving, boating, skiing. Criminal, Federal civil litigation, Aviation. Office: Raskin & Raskin 2937 SW 27th Ave Ste 206 Miami FL 33133-3772

**BECH, DOUGLAS YORK,** lawyer, resort executive; b. Seattle, Aug. 18, 1945; s. Albert Richard and Vera Evelyn (Peterson) B.; m. Sheryl Annette Tucker, Aug. 9, 1968; children: Kristen Elizabeth, Allison York. BA, Baylor U., 1967; JD, U. Tex., 1970. Bar: Tex. 1970, N.Y. 1993. Ptnr. Andrews & Kurth, Houston, 1970-93, Akin, Gump, Strauss, Hauer & Feld, 1994-97; mng. dir. Raintree Capital Co., Houston, 1994—; chmn. Raintree Resorts Internat., Inc., Club Regina Resorts, Inc.; bd. dirs. Frontier Oil, efax.com, Pride Cos., Drexler Found. Sgt. USAR, 1968-74. Republican. Baptist. Avocations: running, snowskiing, travel, big game hunting, golf. Securities, General corporate, Mergers and acquisitions. Office: Raintree Resorts Internat 10000 Memorial Dr Ste 480 Houston TX 77024-3409

**BECHER, ANDREW CLIFFORD,** lawyer; b. Evanston, Ill., Jan. 24, 1946; s. Clifford C. and Ardeth M. (Johnson) B.; m. Deborah M. Bell, Jan. 18, 1969; children: Cory, Megan, Adam J. BS, Purdue U., 1968; JD, U. Ill., 1971. Bar: Ill. 1971, Minn. 1977, Tex. 1998. Assoc. McDermott, Will & Emery, Chgo., 1972-76; stockholder Briggs & Morgan, Mpls., 1976-87; sr. v.p. Dain Bosworth, Inc., Mpls., 1987-89; ptnr. Robins, Kaplan, Miller &

Ciresi, Mpls., 1989-96; sr. v.p. Cal Dive Internat. Inc., Houston, 1996—; bd. dirs. Fantasy Flight Pub., Inc., Minn., Tri-Point Ptnrs., L.L.C., Houston, Energy Resource Technology, Inc., Houston, Hour Glass Golf, Inc., S.C.; lectr. in law Chgo. Kent Coll. Law-Ill. Inst. Tech., 1973-75; assoc. prof. Hamline U., St. paul, 1978-80. Chair local and state govt. com. St. Paul C. of C., 1978-80. Capt. U.S. Army, 1971-79, USAR. Mem. ABA, Minn. Bar Assn., Ill. Bar Assn., Tex. Bar Assn. Presbyterian. Avocations: family, travel, investments, golf, cars. Mergers and acquisitions, Securities, General corporate. Office: Cal Dive Internat Inc 400 N Sam Houston Pkwy E Houston TX 77060-3548

**BECHTLE, LOUIS CHARLES,** federal judge; b. Phila., Dec. 14, 1927; s. Charles R. and Gladys (Kirchner) B.; m. Margaret Beck, Sept. 7, 1978; children: Barbara, Nancy, Amy; 1 stepchild, Samuel. B.S., Temple U., 1951, LL.B., 1954. Bar: Pa. 1954. Asst. U.S. atty. U.S. Dept. Justice, Phila., 1957-59, U.S. atty., 1969-72; pvt. practice law Jacoby & Maxmin, Phila., 1959-62; pvt. practice Wisler, Pearlstine, Talone, Gerber, Norristown, Pa., 1962-69; U.S. dist. judge U.S. Dist. Ct., Phila., 1972—; now sr. judge U.S. Dist. Ct. (Eastern Dist.), Phila.; adj. faculty Temple U. Law Sch., Phila., 1974-93, Villanova Law Sch., 1985-89; mem. Jud/ Panel on Multidist. Litigation, 1994—. Served with U.S. Army, 1946-47. Mem. Montgomery County Bar Assn., Fed. Bar Assn. Republican. Presbyterian. Office: US Dist Ct 17613 US Courthouse 601 Market St Philadelphia PA 19106-1713

**BECK, ANDREW JAMES,** lawyer; b. Washington, Feb. 19, 1948; s. Leonard Norman and Frances (Greif) B.; m. Gretchen Ann Schroeder, Feb. 14, 1971; children: Carter, Lowell, Justin. BA, Carleton Coll., 1969; JD, Stanford U., 1972; MBA, Long Island U., 1975. Bar; Va. 1972, N.Y. 1973, Pa., 1992. Assoc. Casey, Lane & Mittendorf, N.Y.C., 1972-80, ptnr., 1980-82; mng. ptnr. Haythe & Curley, N.Y.C., 1982—; gen. counsel Nat. Stroke Assn., 1992—. Bd. dirs. Allied Devices Corp., 1994-98; trustee Bklyn. Heights Synagogue, 1980-81, Bklyn. Heights Montessori Sch., 1988-92, treas., 1990-92. Mem. ABA, Va. State Bar Assn., N.Y. Stat Bar Assn., Pa. Bar Assn., Assn. of Bar of City of N.Y., Nat. Stroke Assn. (gen. counsel 1992—). Avocations: squash, bridge. General corporate, Securities. Home: 71 Willow St Apt 1 Brooklyn NY 11201-1657 Office: Haythe & Curley 20th Flr 237 Park Ave New York NY 10017-3140

**BECK, BRUCE LENNART,** lawyer; b. Harvey, N.D., Dec. 11, 1946; s. Charles Joel and Gertrude A. (Waits) B.; m. Lynne Christine Richards, Oct. 18, 1969; children: Emily, Brian, Lauren. BA, Cornell Coll., Mt. Vernon, Iowa, 1968; JD, U. Minn., 1973. Bar: Minn. 1973, U.S. Dist. Ct. Minn. 1973. Pvt. practice North St. Paul, Minn., 1973-75; ptnr. Memmer Caswell Parks & Beck, St. Paul, 1975-83, Galena & Beck, Maplewood, Minn., 1983—. Author Ramsey County Probate Procedure, 1988. With U.S. Army, 1968-70. Mem. North St. Paul-Maplewood Rotary Club (pres. 1988-89, Dist. 5090 sec. 1989-90, Paul Harris fellow 1991), Minn. Bar Assn. Presbyterian. Avocations: bicycling, book collecting. Probate, Real property, Criminal. Home: 5260 Hilltop Ave N Lake Elmo MN 55042-9591 Office: Becks & Marks PLLP 2785 White Bear Ave N Maplewood MN 55109-1307

**BECK, DANA KENDALL,** lawyer; b. Bklyn.. BA, SUNY, Albany, 1987; JD, U. Bridgeport, 1991. Bar: Conn. 1992, U.S. Dist. Ct. Conn. 1998. Law clk. Conn. Superior Ct., Bridgeport, 1990-91; assoc. Schiavetti, Geisler et al, Garden City, N.Y., 1991-94; mng. atty. Beck & Beck, Monroe, Conn., 1995—; asst. dir. The Entrepreneurial Ctr., U. Hartford, Bridgeport, Conn., 1998—; instr. Women's Bus. Devel. Ctr., Stamford, Conn., 1996—, The Entrepreneurial Ctr., Bridgeport, 1998—; legal expert Home-Based Working Moms, 1997—. Mem. Nat. Assn. Women Bus. Owners (dir.-at-large 1998—), Entrepreneurial Women's Network (v.p. 1995—). E-mail: DKBeck@prodigy.net. Contracts commercial, General practice, General civil litigation. Office: Beck & Beck LLC PO Box 881 Monroe CT 06468-0881 also: PO Box 1228 Scarsdale NY 10583-9228

**BECK, DAVID CHARLES,** lawyer; b. Kansas City, Mo., July 11, 1954; s. W. Morton and Jane Lillian (Partridge) B.; m. Susan Jane Kessler, Oct. 7, 1978; children: Miranda Jillian, Jonathan "Jake" Guthrie, S. Spencer. BA in English, U. Oreg., 1978; JD, U. Va., 1982. Atty. Peabody & Brown, Boston, 1982-85, Powers Pyles Sutter & O'Hara, Washington, 1985-86, McDermott Will & Emery, Washington, 1986-88; ptnr. Casson Harking & Lapallo, Washington, 1988-93; spl. counsel Proghauer Rose, Washington, 1993-96; ptnr. Powers Pyles Sutter & Verville, Washington, 1996—; pres. bd. dirs. St. John's Cmty. Svc., Washington, 1995-97. Mem. D.C. Health Care Assn. (exec. dir. 1993—). Health, Administrative and regulatory, General civil litigation. Office: Powers Pyles Sutter Verville 1875 Eye St NW Ste 1200 Washington DC 20006-5420

**BECK, DENNIS L.,** judge; b. Belen, N.Mex., Dec. 7, 1947; m. Christine T. Beck, Mar. 2, 1968. BA, Coll. William & Mary, 1969, JD, 1972. Bar: Calif. 1972, U.S. Dist. Ct. (ea. dist.) Calif. 1978, U.S. Ct. Appeals (9th cir.) Calif. 1978. Asst. dist. atty. Fresno (Calif.) County, 1972-78, 79-83, 1987-90; assoc. Crossland Crossland Caswell & Bell, Fresno, 1978-79; judge Kings County Superior Ct., Hanford, Calif., 1983-85; assoc. Thomas, Snell, et al., Fresno, 1985-87; magistrate judge U.S. Dist. Ct. (ea. dist.) Calif., Fresno, 1990—. Office: US Dist Ct 1130 O St Rm 3489 Fresno CA 93721-2201

**BECK, GREGORY MICHAEL,** lawyer; b. San Diego, Aug. 31, 1952; s. Frances Joseph and Dora Youman (Chenault) B.; m. Jennifer Beck; children: Mallory, Allison, MacKenzie, Jonathan. BA in Acctg. and Econs., Loyola U., L.A., 1974; JD, U. Calif., 1978. Ptnr. Beck & Christian, APC, Laguna Hills, Calif.; mem. The Source Group, Laguna Hills. Tribal chief YMCA, Mission Viejo, 1997; mem. tech. com. Barcelona Hills Elem. Sch., Mission Viejo, 1996-97. Mem. Orange County Venture Network, Decision Makers, Monday Club, Law Firm Adv. Group. Roman Catholic. Avocations: mountain biking, swimming, camping, skiing. Office: Beck & Christian 23041 Mill Creek Dr Laguna Hills CA 92653-1257

**BECK, HENRY M., JR.,** lawyer; b. N.Y.C., Mar. 17, 1951; s. Henry M. and Althea H. Beck; m. Margaretta MacIntyre Foulk; children: Aaron, Emily. BS summa cum laude, Duke U., 1973; JD cum laude, Harvard U., 1976. Bar: Mass. 1977, Conn. 1978. Assoc. Hale & Dorr, Boston, 1976-78, Hoppin, Carey & Powell, Hartford, Conn., 1978-82; ptnr. Hoppin, Carey & Powell, 1982-87; prin. Danaher, Tedford, Lagnese & Neal, P.C., Hartford, 1987-95; ptnr. Halloran & Sage, LLP, Hartford, 1995—; lectr. bus. planning U. Conn. Sch. Dentistry. Contbr. articles to profl. jours. Mem. adv. com. UCC article 6 Conn. Law Revision Commn.; active Boy Scouts Am.; bd. dirs., exec. com. Sci. Ctr. Conn., 1995—. Recipient Charles A. Dukes award for Svc., Duke U., 1985. Mem. Conn. Bar Assn. (chmn., lectr. continuing edn. programs 1986-98, mem. exec. com. corp. and other bus. orgns. sect., mem. comml.), Duke U. Alumni Assn. (bd. dirs. 1985-88, exec. com. 1986-88, pas t pres. No. Conn. chpt.), Assn. Comml. Fin. Attys., Greater Hartford C. of C. (bd. dirs. exec. com., chmn. bus. coun. 1988-90). Democrat. Avocations: sailing, skiing, water sports, tennis. General corporate, Contracts commercial, Securities. Home: 58 Woodpond Rd West Hartford CT 06107-3526 Office: Halloran & Sage LLP 225 Asylum St Ste 7 Hartford CT 06103-1516

**BECK, JAMES HAYES,** lawyer; b. Canton, Ohio, Aug. 29, 1935; s. Harry W. and Helen (Hayes) B.; m. Denise, Dec. 22, 1995; children: Barbara Elizabeth, James Rolf. AB, Wittenberg U., 1956; LLB, U. Va., 1959, JD, 1970. Bar: Ohio 1959, U.S. Dist. Ct. (no. dist.) Ohio 1960, U.S. Supreme Ct. 1971. Pvt. practice Cleve., 1959-63; jr. ptnr. Leanza, Longano, Farina & Mendelson, Cleve., 1963-66; assoc. Nadler & Nadler, Youngstown, Ohio, 1966-73; ptnr. Beck & Tyrrell, Canfield, Ohio, 1973-83; sr. ptnr. Beck & Vaughn, Canfield, 1984-87; pvt. practice Canfield, 1987—. v.p. Canfield Civic Assn., 1972-74. Mem. Am. Arbitration Assn., Assn. Trial Lawyers Am., Mahoning County Bar Assn. (chmn. profl. econs. com. 1979-82, chmn. unauthorized practice of law com. 1976-79, grievance com. 1983-84, ins. com. 1984-85, inquiry com. 1987—), Ohio State Bar Assn., ACLU, Youngstown Power Squadron (comdr. 1985, exec. com. 1983—), Canfield Lions Club (bd. dirs. 1978-79), Point Yacht Club, Boardman Tennis Ctr. Democrat. Lutheran. Avocations: boating, tennis, bridge, gourmet cooking. Bankruptcy, General corporate, Real property. Office: James H Beck Olde Courthouse Bldg Canfield OH 44406-1407

**BECK, JAN SCOTT,** lawyer; b. Newark, May 5, 1955; s. Robert William and Dorothy (Warhaftig) B.; m. Marla Terri Klein, Sept. 27, 1981; children: Jamie Kyle, Bryan Michael, Sean Jason. BA in Acctg., Rider Coll., 1977; JD, Villanova U., 1980, LLM in Taxation, 1985. Bar: N.J. 1980, U.S. Dist. Ct. N.J. 1980, N.Y. 1981, U.S. Tax Ct. 1981, D.C. 1985, U.S. Supreme Ct. 1986. Pvt. practice Westfield, N.J., 1980-86; atty. Inspiration Resources Corp., N.Y.C., 1986-88; dir. taxation ADT Inc., Boca Raton, Fla., 1988-89, v.p., gen. counsel, 1989-96; sr. v.p., dir. ADT Security Svcs., Inc., 1996-97; mng. dir. The Turbary Group, Boca Raton, Fla., 1997—; atty. Laventhol & Horwath, Phila., 1979-80, Touche Ross & Co., N.Y.C., 1980-86; bd. dirs. taxation Inspiration Resources Corp., N.Y.C. Author: The Strike: Student Involvement, 1975. Mem. ABA, N.Y. State Bar Assn., N.J. Bar Assn., AICPA, N.J. Soc. CPAs, Tax Exec. Inst., Omicron Delta Epsilon, Delta Epsilon Kappa. Avocations: camping, backpacking, mountain climbing, writing, skiing. Corporate taxation, Mergers and acquisitions, General corporate. Home: 20988 Solano Way Boca Raton FL 33433-1621 Office: The Turbary Group 7280 W Palmetto Park Rd Boca Raton FL 33433-3422

**BECK, LAUREN LYNN,** lawyer; b. Houston, Sept. 26, 1965. BA, U. Tex., 1987; JD, Baylor U., 1990. Bar: Tex. 1990, U.S. Dist. Ct. (so. dist.) Tex., U.S. Ct. Appeals (5th cir.), U.S. Supreme Ct.; bd. cert. in civil appellate law, Tex. Assoc. McFall, Sherwood & Sheehy, P.C., Houston, 1990-97, shareholder, 1998—. Mem. Jr. League of Houston, Inc., 1991—. Fellow Tex. Bar Found.; mem. Internat. Assn. Def. Counsel, Tex. Assn. Def. Counsel. Appellate. Office: McFall Sherwood & Sheehy PC 909 Fannin St Houston TX 77010-1001

**BECK, LELAND S.,** lawyer; b. Newark, May 6, 1931; s. Stanely S. and Jennie Beck; m. Phyllis Mae Krawitz, Aug. 21, 1954; children: Hillary, Matthew, Susan, Joan. BA, Cornell U., 1953, JD, 1955. Bar: N.Y., 1955, U.S. Dist. Ct. (so. and ea. dists.) N.Y., 1956, U.S. Cir. Ct. (2nd cir.), 1975, U.S. Claims Ct., 1994. Trial lawyer Liberty Mut. Ins. Co., N.Y.C., 1955-57; ptnr. Whiting & Beck, N.Y.C., 1957-60; pvt. practice Mineola, N.Y., 1960-63; ptnr. Rothenberg & Beck, Mineola, 1963-68, Cooperstein & Beck, Garden City, N.Y., 1973-95, Beck & Rubin, Garden City, Beck, Salvi, Gewurz & Strauss, Garden City, 1995—. Mem. ABA, N.Y. State Bar Assn., N.Y. St. Assn. Trial Lawyers, Nassau County Bar Assn. (bd. dirs. 1991-92, 98—). General civil litigation, Personal injury, Professional liability. Office: Beck Salvi Gewurz & Strauss 595 Stewart Ave Garden City NY 11530-4787

**BECK, PAUL AUGUSTINE,** lawyer; b. Pitts., Aug. 16, 1936; s. August W. and Agnes (Heyl) B.; m. Nancy Flaherty; children: Jennifer, Bradford, Michael. BS, Carnegie-Mellon U., 1957; LLB, Duquesne U., 1962. Bar: Pa. 1962, U.S. Ct. Appeals (4th cir.) 1963, U.S. Supreme Ct. 1966, U.S. Ct. Appeals (2d and 3d cirs.) 1971, U.S. Ct. Appeals (7th cir.) 1974, U.S. Ct. Appeals (Fed. cir.) 1982. Ptnr. Buell, Ziesenheim, Beck & Alstadt, Pitts., 1962-88, Buchanan Ingersoll, Pitts., 1988-95; propr. Paul A. Beck & Assocs., Pitts., 1995—; del. U.S. Ct. Appeals (3d cir.) Jud. Conf., 1983. Chmn. alumni forum com. Carnegie-Mellon U., Pitts., 1966-67. Capt. U.S. Army, 1957-59. Mem. ABA, Pa. Bar Assn. (ho. of dels. 1984—), Nat. Coun. Pat. Law Assn., Allegheny County Bar Assn. (gov. 1977-79, chmn. intellectual property law sect. 1979-84), Pitts. Intellectual Property Law Assn. (bd. dirs., pres. 1989-90), Duquesne U. Law Sch. Alumni Assn. (v.p. 1997-98, pres. 1999—). Patent, Trademark and copyright, Intellectual property. Office: Paul A Beck & Assocs 1106 Frick Bldg 437 Grant St Pittsburgh PA 15219-6002 *Man must set principles as guided by his conscience under which he will live. He will then be accountable to mankind and God in meeting that standard.*

**BECK, RONALD JERRY,** judge; b. Kingsport, Tenn., Sept. 22, 1941; s. Victor R. and Anna P. Beck; m. Louise Bundy, Oct. 11, 1970; children: Robyn, Gabriel. BA, Emory & Henry Coll., 1965; postgrad., Emory U., 1965-66; JD, U. Tenn., 1968. Bar: Tenn. 1969, U.S. Dist. Ct. (ea. dist.) Tenn. 1970. Ptnr. Mitchell & Beck, Kingsport, 1969-72; asst. dist. atty. Sullivan County, Offic of Dist. Atty., Blountville, Tenn., 1972-93; judge Cir. Ct., Kingsport, 1993—. Mem. Rotary, Masons. Democrat. Office: Cir Ct Panel II 200 Shelby St Kingsport TN 37660-4256

**BECK, RUDY DALE,** lawyer; b. Mexico, Mo., Aug. 9, 1949; s. Phillip L. and Loretta B. (Byrns) B.; m. Becky S. Black, July 28, 1972; children: Jessica Lynn, Rachel Renee. AB, Knox Coll., 1971; JD, U. Mo., 1974. Bar: Mo. 1974, U.S. Dist. Ct. (ea. dist.) Mo. 1975, U.S. Tax Ct. 1984. Founder, prin. Beck, Tieweyer & Zerr, P.C., St. Charles, Mo., 1974—; adv. dir. Enterprise Bank, St. Louis; presenter confs. and orgns. in field. Author: Estate Planning Basics, 1988. Bd. dirs., past pres. Boys & Girls Club, St. Charles County, Mo., 1974—; planned giving bd. dirs. Duchesne H.S., St. Charles, 1995—, Acad. of the Sacred Heart, St. Charles, 1995—, Cardinal Glennon Hosp., St. Louis, 1997—. 1st lt. USAR, 1974. Mem. KC, Estate Planning Coun. of St. Louis, Bar Assn. of Met. St. Louis (small bus. com.), Kiwanis (past chmn. scholarship com. St. Charles chpt.). Avocations: golf, flying, skiing. Probate, Estate taxation, General corporate. Home: 47 Forest Lake Ct Saint Charles MO 63301-8720

**BECK, STEPHANIE G.,** lawyer; b. Endicott, N.Y., Jan. 10, 1964; d. Ray A. and Donna E. (Geesey) B. BA with honors, SUNY, Binghamton, 1986; JD, Syracuse U., 1989. Bar: N.Y. 1990, U.S. Dist. Ct. (no. dist.) N.Y. 1990. Atty. Young & Paniccia, Binghamton, 1990—. Advisor/vol. Drama Club for Mentally and Physically Impaired, Binghamton, 1992-96; mem. ch. coun. Our Saviour Luth. Ch., Endwell, N.Y., 1990-94, 96; asst. coach Boys and Girls Club, Endwell, 1986-91. Mem. N.Y. State Bar Assn., Broome County Bar Assn. Democrat. Lutheran. Avocations: softball, volleyball. General practice, Family and matrimonial, Probate. Office: Young and Paniccia 22 Riverside Dr Binghamton NY 13905-4612

**BECK, STUART EDWIN,** lawyer; b. Phila., Aug. 12, 1940; s. Louis M. and Anna (Cooper) B.; m. Elaine Kushner, June 20, 1964; children: Adam, Barry, Caroline. BSME, Drexel U., 1964; JD, George Washington U., 1968. Bar: Va. 1968, U.S. Dist. Ct. D.C. 1969, Pa. 1970, U.S. Dist. Ct. (ea. dist.) Pa. 1971, U.S. Ct. Appeals (3d cir.) 1971, U.S. Supreme Ct. 1980, U.S. Ct. Appeals (4th cir.) 1989, U.S. Patent and Trademark Office. Assoc. Seidel, Gonda & Goldhammer, Phila., 1969-73; atty. pvt. practice, Phila., 1974-79, 91—; ptnr. Trachman, Jacobs & Beck, Phila., 1979-88, Weinstein, Trachtman, Beck & Kimmelman, Phila., 1988-91; adj. prof. patent law Rutgers U. Law Sch., Camden, N.J.; instr. patent, trademark and copyright law The Phila. Inst. Capt. Am. Cancer Soc., 1974, 75; bd. dirs. Jewish Family and Children Svc. Phila., 1973-89, legal, fin. and budget com., 1979—, spkrs. com., 1979—, bldg. and grounds com., 1980-82, trustee, 1989; bd. dirs., by-laws revision com., bldgs. and grounds com., edn. com. Temple Beth Hillel; bd. dirs. Phila. Vol. Lawyers for Arts, 1980-84, treas., 1980-82. Mem. ABA (patent trademark and copyright law sect., litigation sect., anti-trust law sect.), Am. Intellectual Property Law Assn. (com. patent contracts other than govt. 1971-75), Pa. Bar Assn., Phila. Bar Assn. (com. profl. responsibility 1975-93, com. election procedures 1976-84, com. law and arts 1976-80), Phila. Patent Law Assn. (com. ethics 1977-83, com. pub. rels. 1974-77, com. profl. responsibility 1975-79). Avocations: sailing, travel. Intellectual property, Patent, Trademark and copyright.

**BECK, WENDY LYNN,** lawyer; b. Falmouth, Mass., Sept. 2, 1971; d. Ronald Phillip and Zina Bea Beck. BA in Criminology, U. Fla., 1992, JD, 1995. Bar: Fla. 1996, U.S. Dist. Ct. (so. dist.) Fla. 1996, U.S. Dist. Ct. (no. and mid. dists.) Fla. 1999. Assoc. Colodny Fass & Talenfeld, Ft. Lauderdale, Fla., 1996—. Mem. ATLA, Broward County Bar Assn. General civil litigation, Probate, General corporate. Office: Colodny Fass & Talenfeld PA 2000 W Commercial Blvd Ste 232 Fort Lauderdale FL 33309-3060

**BECK, WILLIAM G.,** lawyer; b. Kansas City, Mo., Mar. 4, 1954; s. Raymond W. Beck and Wanda Williams; 1 child, Collin M. BA in Econs., U. Mo., Kansas City, 1974, JD, 1978. Bar: Mo. 1978, U.S. Dist. Ct. (we. dist.) Mo. 1978, U.S. Dist. Ct. (no. dist.) Ill. 1991, U.S. Dist. Ct. (ea. dist.) Mich. 1991, U.S. Dist. Ct. (ea. dist.) Wisc. 1997, U.S. Ct. Appeals (5th cir.) 1988, U.S. Ct. Appeals (6th cir.) 1993, U.S. Ct. Appeals (2d cir.) 1997, U.S. Ct. Appeals (10th cir.) 1997, U.S. Supreme Ct. 1997. Shareholder Field, Gentry, Benjamin & Robertson, P.C., Kansas City, 1978-89; ptnr. Lathrop & Norquist, Kansas City, 1989-95, Lathrop & Gage, L.C., Kansas City, 1996—. Commr. Human Rels. Commn., Jackson County, Mo., 1985-89; chmn. Citizens Assn., Kansas City, 1991-92, 95—; mem. Pub. Improvement Adv. Com., Kansas City, 1991—, vice chmn., 1995-98, chmn. 1998—, fin. chmn. cmty. infrastructure com., 1996—; mem. Waste Minimization Com., Kansas City, 1990-91. Environmental, Federal civil litigation, Toxic tort. Office: Lathrop & Gage LC 2345 Grand Blvd Ste 2500 Kansas City MO 64108-2603

**BECK, WILLIAM HAROLD, JR.,** lawyer; b. Clarksdale, Miss., Aug. 18, 1928; s. William Harold and Mary (McGaha) B.; m. Nancy Cassity House, Jan. 30, 1954; children—Mary, Nancy, Katherine. BA, Vanderbilt U., 1950; JD, U. Miss., 1954. Bar: Miss. 1954, La. 1960. Atty., Clarksdale, Miss., 1954-57; asst. prof. Tulane U., 1957-59; ptnr. Foley & Judell, New Orleans, 1959-88; of counsel, 1988—. Served to capt., AUS, 1951-53. Mem. La. Bar Assn., Miss. Bar Assn., SAR, Soc. Colonial Wars, S.R., Mil. and Hospitaller Order of St. Lazarus of Jerusalem, Huguenot Soc., Mil. Order Fgn. Wars. Municipal (including bonds). Office: Foley & Judell 1 Canal Pl 365 Canal St Ste 2600 New Orleans LA 70130-1138

**BECKER, ALISON LEA,** lawyer; b. Covington, Ky., Apr. 5, 1963; d. Richard L. and Rosalind M. (Schuppert) Ante; m. Patrick J. Becker, Apr. 4, 1992; 1 child, Christopher P. BA, No. Ky. U., 1984, JD, 1987. Bar: Ohio 1988, Fla. 1998, U.S. Dist. Ct. (so. dist.) Ohio 1988, U.S. Ct. Appeals (6th cir.) 1988, U.S. Army Ct. Mil. Rev. 1990, U.S. Ct. Mil. Appeals 1992, U.S. Supreme Ct. 1992, Fla. 1998, U.S. Dist. Ct. (mid. dist.) Fla. 1998, U.S. Ct. Appeals (11th cir.) 1999. Sole practice Cin., 1988-89; trial def. atty. U.S. Army JAG Corps, Goeppingen, Germany, 1990-91; trial counsel, legal assistance atty. U.S. Army JAG Corps, Stuttgart, Germany, 1991-92; def. appellate counsel U.S. Army JAG Corps, Falls Church, Va., 1992-94; chief claims and adminstrv. law U.S. Army JAG Corps, Atlanta, 1994-97; sr. atty. Office Atty. Gen., Tampa, Fla., 1998—; coord. for appellate def. before U.S. Supreme Ct., U.S. Army, Falls Church, 1992-94. Office: Office Atty Gen 2002 N Lois Ave Fl 7 Tampa FL 33607-2386

**BECKER, ANDREW N.,** lawyer; b. San Mateo, Calif., May 11, 1954; s. Leo H. and M. Blossom Becker; m. Donna R. Fisher, Aug. 10, 1986; children: Matthew, Samuel. BA, U. Calif., Berkeley, 1976; JD cum laude, U. Puget Sound, Seattle, 1984. Bar: Wash. 1985, U.S. Dist. Ct. (we. dist.) Wash. 1985, U.S. Ct. Appeals (9th cir.), 1986. Assoc. Dan R. Dubitzky, Seattle, 1984-85; pub. defender Kipsap County Office Assigned Counsel, Port Orchard, Wash., 1985-86; pvt. practice, Port Orchard, 1986—; city atty. City of Gig Harbor, Wash., 1986-95. Coach PAA Baseball, Gig Harbor, 1993-98. Mem. Wash. State Bar Assn. (disciplinary bd. 1992-95), Wash. Trial Lawyers Assn. (sustaining), Kitsap County Bar Assn. (trustee 1993-94, treas. 1995, sec. 1996, v.p. 1997, pres. 1998). Fax: 360-895-1445. Personal injury. Office: Tremont Profl Bldg 104 Tremont St Ste 220 Port Orchard WA 98366-3765

**BECKER, BRUCE ERWIN,** lawyer; b. Wadena, Minn., May 6, 1990; s. Erwin H. and Peggy J. Becker; m. Vicki L. Roberts, Oct. 27, 1980 (div. Dec. 1994) remarried, July 19, 1996; children: Barbara L., Brooke A. BA, U. Mont., 1972, JD, 1976. Bar: Mont. 1976, U.S. Dist. Ct. Mont. 1976. Law clk. 16th Jud. Dist., Forsyth, Mont., 1976-78; atty. Park County, Livingston, Mont., 1978-82; pvt. practice law Moses Law Firm, Billings, Mont., 1983-86; city atty. Bozeman, Mont., 1986-91; pvt. practice law Livingston, 1991-96, city atty., 1996—. Pres. Livingston Roundup Assn., 1998. Mem. Mont. Bar Assn., Elks (exhalted ruler 1996). Home: 614 N 14th St Livingston MT 59047-1502 Office: 203 S Main St Livingston MT 59047-3016

**BECKER, DOUGLAS WESLEY,** lawyer; b. St. Louis, July 12, 1950; s. Donald William and Joetta Lea (Greer) B. m. Deborah Ackerman, June 10, 1972 (div. Oct. 1985); children: Laura Marie, MacKenzie Brooke; m. Kimberly Dinsdale, Apr. 30, 1989. BBA, So. Meth. U., 1972, JD, 1976. Bar: Tex. 1976, U.S. Supreme Ct. 1979; cert. residential and comml. real estate law Tex. Bd. Legal Specialization. Ptnr. Gresham, Davis, Gregory, Worthy & Moore, San Antonio, 1976-82; mem. Kaufman, Becker, Reibach & Richie, Inc., San Antonio, 1983-94, Cauthorn, Hale, Hornberger, Fuller, Sheehan & Becker Inc., San Antonio, 1994—. Editor Real Estate, Probate and Trust Law Sect., Reporter Jour., State Bar of Tex., 1997—; contbr. articles to profl. jours. Pres. Vis. Nurse Assn., San Antonio, 1982; trustee, chmn. San Antonio Regional Hosp., 1993-94. Staff sgt. USAR, 1971-77. Mem. State Bar Tex. (coun. mem. real estate, probate and trust law sects. 1993-97), Tex. Coll. Real Estate (bd. dirs.), Tex. Assn. Bank Counsel, San Antonio Young Lawyers Assn. (pres. 1984), Am. Coll. real Estate Lawyers, San Antonio Bd. Realtors (bd. dirs. cert. comml. investment mem. chpt. 1992-93, 98—), San Antonio Real Estate Coun. (chmn. govt. affairs com. 1993-94, sec. 1994-95, v.p. 1995-96), Oak Hills Country Club (bd. dirs. 1993-97). Avocations: golf, skiing, trivia, reading, real estate. Contracts commercial, General corporate. Office: Cauthorn Hale Hornberger Fuller Sheehan & Beck 700 N Saint Marys St Ste 620 San Antonio TX 78205-3510

**BECKER, EDWARD ROY,** federal judge; b. Phila., May 4, 1933; s. Herman A. and Jeannette (Levit) B.; m. Flora Lyman, Aug. 11, 1957; children: James Daniel (dec. 1969), Jonathan Robert, Susan Rose, Charles Lyman. BA, U. Pa., 1954; LLB, Yale U., 1957. Bar: Pa. 1957. Ptnr. Becker, Becker & Fryman, Phila., 1957-70; U.S. Dist. Judge, 1970-82; judge U.S. Ct. Appeals (3d cir.), 1982—, chief judge, 1998—; counsel Rep. City Com., Phila., 1965-70; mem. task force on implementation of new jud. article Joint State Govt. Commn., 1969; lectr. law U. Pa. Law Sch., 1978-83; mem. edn. adv. com. concerning Comprehensive Crime Control Act, Fed. Jud. Ctr., 1981-90, Fed. Jud. Ctr. Com. on Sentencing, Probation and Pretrial Svcs., 1985-90; bd. dirs. Fed. Jud. Ctr., 1991-95; mem. faculty sr. appellate judges seminar Inst. Jud. Adminstrn., N.Y.C., 1992-94. Bd. editors Manual for Complex Litigation, 1981-90; contbr. articles to profl. jours. Trustee Magna Carta Found., Phila.; vis. com. U. Chgo. Law Sch., 1988-91; chair Rhodes Scholarship Selection Com. Dist. II (Pa., N.Y., Vt., N.H.), 1996-98. Fellow Am. Bar Found.; mem. ABA (jud. rep. antitrust sect. 1983-86), Phila. Bar Assn., Am. Judicature Soc., Am. Law Inst. (adv. com. restatement conflict of laws 2d, mem. ALI-ABA com. 1992—, chmn. program subcom. 1996—), Jud. Conf. U.S. (com. on adminstrn. probation system 1979-87, chmn. com. on criminal law and probation adminstrn. 1987-90, com. on long range planning 1991-96, exec. com. 1999—), Phi Beta Kappa. Jewish. Home: 936 Herbert St Philadelphia PA 19124-2417 Office: US Ct Appeals 19613 US Courthouse 601 Market St Philadelphia PA 19106-1713

**BECKER, ERIC L.,** lawyer; b. Racine, Wis., June 13, 1949; married, June 15, 1974; children: Erin M., Eric N. BA, U. Wis., Whitewater, 1971; JD, Marquette U., 1974. Bar: Wis. 1974. Trust officer Midland Nat. Bank, Milw., 1973-75; shareholder Quincey, Becker & Schuessler, S.C., Beaver Dam, Wis., 1975—; bd. dirs. M&I Bank South Ctrl., Watertown, Wis., Nancy's Notion, Ltd., Beaver Dam, Wis. Bd. dirs. Beaver Dam Unified Sch. Dist. Bd. Edn., 1984—, pres., 1987, 96; trustee Beaver Dam Scholarship Found., Inc., 1991—, bd. pres., 1996-98; bd. dirs. YMCA, Beaver Dam, 1982-90, pres., 1987-89. Mem. ABA, State Bar of Wis. (gov. 1989-91), Kiwanis (Beaver Dam club). Avocations: golf, volunteer. Estate planning, Probate, State civil litigation. Office: Quincey Becker & Schuessler SC 130 Park Ave Beaver Dam WI 53916-2108

**BECKER, NANCY ANNE,** state supreme court justice; b. Las Vegas, May 23, 1955; d. Arthur William and Margaret Mary (McLoughlin) B. BA, U.S. Internat. U., 1976; JD, George Washington U., 1979. Bar: Nev. 1979, D.C. 1980, Md. 1982, U.S. Dist. Ct. Nev. 1987, U.S. Ct. Appeals (9th cir.) 1987. Legis. cons. D.C. Office on Aging, Washington, 1979-83; assoc. Goldstein & Ahalt, College Park, Md., 1980-82; pvt. practice Washington, 1982-83; dep. city atty., prosecutor criminal div. City of Las Vegas, 1983; judge Las Vegas Mcpl. Ct., 1987-89, Clark County Dist. Ct., Las Vegas, 1989—; now assoc. judge Nev. Supreme Ct.; cons. MADD, Las Vegas, 1983-87. Contbr. articles to profl. publs. Pres. Clark County Pro Bono Project, Las Vegas, 1984-88. Mem. So. Nev. Assn. Women Attys. (past officer), Am. Businesswomen's Assn. (treas. Las Vegas chpt. 1985-86), NCCJ, Las Vegas and Latin C. of C., Vietnam Vets Am., Soroptimist Internat. Office: Nevada Supreme Court Capital Complex 201 S Carson St Carson City NV 89701-4702*

**BECKER, THEODORE MICHAELSON,** lawyer; b. Chgo., Feb. 18, 1949; s. Michael and Hazel Becker; m. Tamara B. Kaplan, June 11, 1983; children: Adam Michael, Alex Jordan, Ian David. AB summa cum laude, Washington U., St. Louis, 1970; MA in Sociology, Northwestern U., 1972, JD summa cum laude, 1974, PhD in Sociology, 1981. Bar: Ill. 1975, U.S. Dist.

Ct. (no. and so. dist.) Ill. 1975, U.S. Ct. Appeals (7th and 10th cirs.) 1975, U.S. Ct. Appeals (9th cir.) 1976, U.S. Supreme Ct. 1978, U.S. Dist. Ct. (cen. dist.) Ill. 1979, U.S. Dist. Ct. (no. dist. trial bar) Ill. 1982, U.S. Ct. Appeals (Fed. cir.) 1983. Russell Sage fellow, instr. Yale U., New Haven, 1974-75; pvt. practice Chgo., 1975—. *Theodore Becker represents clients ranging from individuals and small companies to financial institutions and the largest multinational corporations. He has obtained a number of multi-million dollar recoveries for his clients and has successfully defended multi-million dollar actions against his clients. Mr. Becker achieved national recognition when he obtained a verdict of $52 million on behalf of a small Chicago ice cream supplier against the fast food giant McDonald's Corporation for breach of a "handshake agreement. The verdict was the largest in Cook County (Chicago) Court history. That case is presently included in the curricula of major law schools and colleges.* Contbr. articles to books and profl. jours. Mem. ABA, Ill. Bar Assn., Chgo. Bar Assn., Phi Beta Kappa, Order of Coif. General civil litigation. Office: Becker Assocs 19 S La Salle St Ste 1500 Chicago IL 60603-1407

**BECKERMAN, DALE LEE,** lawyer; b. Omaha, Feb. 7, 1949; s. Harold Frank and Marjorie Jane (Butler) B.; m. Kathryn Jane Barr, Nov. 20, 1971; children: Clare, Harold. BA, Amherst Coll., 1971; JD with honors, George Washington U., 1975. Bar: D.C. 1976, Mo. 1976, U.S. Dist. Ct. (we. dist.) Mo. 1976, U.S. Ct. Appeals (8th cir.) 1979, U.S. Ct. Appeals (10th cir.) 1990, Kans. 1993. Assoc. Deacy & Deacy, Kansas City, Mo., 1975-80, ptnr., 1980—; mem. Cir. Ct. Bench Bar Com., Kansas City, 1985, advisor, 1986. Mem. ABA, Mo. Bar, Kansas City Met. Bar Assn., Lawyers Assn. Kansas City, Internat. Assn. Def. Counsel, Johnson County Kans. Bar Assn. General civil litigation, Civil rights, Insurance. Home: 4509 W 82d St Shawnee Mission KS 66208 Office: Deacy & Deacy Nations Bank Ctr 920 Main St Ste 1900 Kansas City MO 64105-2010

**BECKETT, THEODORE CHARLES,** lawyer; b. Boonville, Mo., May 6, 1929; s. Theodore Cooper and Gladys (Watson) B.; m. Daysie Margaret Cornwall, 1950; children: Elizabeth Gayle, Theodore Cornwall, Margaret Lynn, William Harrison, Anne Marie. BS, U. Mo., Columbia, 1950, JD, 1957. Bar: Mo. 1957. Since practiced in Kansas City; mem. firm Beckett Law Firm; instr. polit. sci. U. Mo., Columbia, 1956-57; asst. atty. gen. State of Mo., 1961-64. Former mem. bd. dirs. Kansas City Civic Ballet; mem. City Plan Commn., Kansas City, 1976-80; mem. bd. curators U. Mo., 1995—, pres. 1998. 1st lt. U.S. Army, 1950-53. Mem. Am., Mo., Kansas City bar assns., Lawyers Assn. Kansas City, Newcomen Soc. N.Am., SAR, Order of Coif, Sigma Nu, Phi Alpha Delta. Presbyterian. Clubs: Kansas City (Kansas City, Mo.), Blue Hills Country (Kansas City, Mo.). Federal civil litigation, State civil litigation. Office: 1400 Commerce Trust Bldg 922 Walnut St Kansas City MO 64106-1809

**BECKETT, THEODORE CORNWALL,** lawyer; b. Heidelberg, Fed. Republic of Germany, Nov. 21, 1952; (parents Am. Citizens); s. Theodore Charles and Daysie Margaret (Cornwall) B.; m. Patricia Anne McKelvy, June 18, 1983; children: Anna Kathleen, Kerry Christine, Cooper Charles. BA, U. Mo., 1975, JD, 1978. Bar: Mo. 1978, U.S. Dist. Ct. (we. dist.) Mo. 1978. Ptnr. Beckett & Hensley L.C., Kansas City, Mo., 1994—. Bd. dirs. Kans. Spl. Olympics, 1979-84, legal advisor, 1984—, Kans. City Metro Spl. Olympics, 1993—. Mem. ABA, Mo. Bar Assn., Kansas City Bar Assn., Mo. Assn. Trial Attys., Assn. Trial Lawyers Am., Kansas City Club, Carriage Club, Beta Theta Pi. Democrat. Presbyterian. General civil litigation, Personal injury, Construction. Office: Beckett & Hensley LC PO Box 13185 610 Commerce Tower Kansas City MO 64199

**BECKETT, WILLIAM HENRY MILLER,** lawyer; b. Newton, Mass., May 3, 1940; s. Ralph G. and Elizabeth (Bartlett) B.; m. Sally Wadsworth, Jan. 25, 1963 (dec.); children: William H.M. Jr., Alexander F.W., Elizabeth B.; m. Virginia Morgan, June 15, 1997. BA, Harvard U., 1962; JD, Boston U., 1965. Bar: Mass. 1965, N.H. 1966, U.S. Dist. Ct. N.H. 1966, U.S. Dist. Ct. Mass. 1966, U.S. Ct. Appeals (1st cir.) 1966, U.S. Supreme Ct. 1966. Law clk. to chief justice and judges Superior Ct. of the Commonwealth of Mass., Boston, 1965-66; assoc. Perkins, Holland and Donovan, Exeter, N.H., 1966-70; ptnr. Holland, Donovan, Beckett, Hermans & Davison, P.A., Exeter, 1970—; bar examiner N.H. Com. of Bar Examiners, Concord, 1978-88; master N.H. Superior Ct., Concord. Mem. Exeter Sch. Bd., 1971-74; trustee Exeter Hosp., 1987—, N.H. Hosp. Assn., Concord, 1990—, Seacoast Hospice, 1999—. Mem. ABA, Assn. Trial Lawyers Am., N.H. Bar Assn., Mass. Bar Assn., U.S. Supreme Ct. Hist. Soc. (N.H. chairperson). Avocations: sailing, tennis, golf, squash. Fax: 603-772-5956. General civil litigation, Family and matrimonial, Estate planning. Office: Holland Donovan Beckett Hermans & Davison PO Box 1090 151 Water St Exeter NH 03833-2456

**BECKHAM, WALTER HULL, JR.,** lawyer, educator; b. Albany, Ga., Apr. 18, 1920; m. Ethel Koger, Mar. 13, 1943; children: Barbara, Walter III, James K. AB, Emory U., 1941; LLB cum laude, Harvard U., 1948. Bar: Fla. 1949, U.S. Supreme Ct. 1956, D.C. 1978. Assoc. prof. law U. Miami, Fla., 1948-49; ptnr. Nichols, Gaither, Beckham et al, 1950-67; of counsel Podhurst, Orseck, Josefsberg, Eaton, Meadow, Olin & Perwin P.A., Miami, 1967—; prof. law U. Miami, 1967-82, prof. emeritus, 1982—. Editor Harvard Law Rev. Pres. Greater Miami YMCA, 1963-68, Crippled Children's Soc. Dade County, 1968-69; mem. Dade County Mental Health Bd., 1971-73; chmn. bd. trustees YMCA Blue Ridge Assembly, 1977-79; trustee Nat. Jud. Coll., 1990-96, trustee, chmn., 1995-96, chmn. emeritus, 1996—. With USNR, 1941-46; capt. USNR, ret. Recipient The Perry Nichols award, Acad. Fla. Trial Lawyers, 1984. Mem. ABA (spl. com. on tort liability system 1979-84, spl. commn. on assn. governance 1983-84, chmn. tort and ins. practice sect. 1974-75, Ho. of Dels. 1979-85, 87-95, sec.-elect 1986-87, sec. 1987-90), Am. Bar Found., Am. Coll. Trial Lawyers, Am. Law Inst., Assn. Trial Lawyers Am. (chmn. aviation sect. 1966-68), Fla. Bar Assn. (past mem. bd. of govs. jr. bar sect.), Dade County Bar Assn. (pres. jr. bar sect. 1952-53, exec. com. 1953-54), Internat. Acad. Trial Lawyers (pres. 1973), Internat. Acad. Law and Sci., Law Sci. Inst., Maritime Law Assn. U.S., Nat. Inst. Trial Adv. (trustee 1976-86, chmn. 1983-85), Inner Circle of Advs., Med. Inst. for Attys. (dir. 1968-83), Nat. Bd. Trial Adv. (founding mem.), Phi Beta Kappa, Omicron Delta Kappa, Phi Alpha Delta, Chi Phi, Kiwanis. General civil litigation, Personal injury, Product liability. Home: 1111 Crandon Blvd Apt B1105 Key Biscayne FL 33149-2766 Office: Podhurst Orseck Josefsberg Eaton Meadow Olin & Perwin PA City Nat Bank Bldg 25 W Flagler St Ste 800 Miami FL 33130-1720

**BECKHAM, WALTER HULL, III,** lawyer; b. Boston, Feb. 12, 1948; s. Walter Hull Jr. and Ethel Brooks (Koger) B. BA, Emory U., 1970, JD, 1977; MBA, U. Mich., 1972. Bar: Ga. 1977, U.S. Dist. Ct. (no. dist.) Ga. 1978, U.S. Dist. Ct. (so. dist.) Ga. 1980, U.S. Dist. Ct. (mid. dist.) Ga. 1988, U.S. Ct. Appeals (11th cir.) 1982. Investment analyst, portfolio mgr. Life of Ga., Atlanta, 1972-74; assoc. Jessee, Ritchie & Duncan, P.C., Atlanta, 1977-81, ptnr., 1981-82; pvt. practice, Atlanta, 1982—. Bd. dirs. Cmty. Outreach YMCA, Atlanta, 1973-75, Brookhaven Boys Club, Atlanta, 1976; pres. Emory U. Sr. Honor Soc., Atlanta, 1984-85; mem. Emory U. Law Sch. Coun., 1993—. Mem. ABA (tort and ins. practice sect., long range planning com. 1986-90, chmn. satellite seminars and videotapes com. 1990-92, chmn. pub. rels. com. 1993, com. coord. 1993, coun. 1990-93, sect. chmn. 1995-96), Ga. Bar Assn. (co-chmn. com. on professionalism 1997—), Atlanta Bar Assn. (state ct. com. 1985), Internat. Acad. Trial Lawyers, Ga. Trial Lawyers Assn. (long range planning com. 1982-86), Kappa Alpha (Hardeman Province Ct. of Honor). Avocations: hunting, fishing, skiing. General civil litigation, Personal injury, Securities. Home: 1208 Village Run NE Atlanta GA 30319-5303 Office: 2600 GLG Grand 75 14th St Atlanta GA 30309

**BECKISH, RICHARD MICHAEL,** lawyer; b. Scranton, Pa., Aug. 7, 1961; s. Richard Michael Sr. and Hessie Helen Beckish; m. Patricia Irene Hamm, Sept. 3, 1994. Student, Ga. Inst. Tech., 1979-82; AA in Pub. Adminstrn., Golden Gate U., 1985; BS in Bus., U. N.Y., Albany, 1987. Bar: Ala. 1992, U.S. Ct. Appeals (11th cir.) 1993, U.S. Dist. Ct. (so. dist.) Ala. 1993. Securities broker First Tenn. Bank, Mobile, 1987-88; asst. to fundraising chmn. U.S. Ho. of Reps., Birmingham, Ala., 1990; assoc. C.S. Chiepalich PC, Mobile, 1993-94; sole practice Mobile, 1994—. Active Mobile Young Republicans, 1993—; vice-chancellor St. Thomas Moore Soc., Mobile, 1998. With USN, 1984-89. Mem. Ala. Trial Lawyers Assn., Tillman's Corner (Ala.) C. of C., Phi Kappa Tau, Phi Alpha Delta (vice-chancellor 1991—). Roman Catholic. Avocation: Soo Bakh Do. General civil litigation, Criminal, Consumer commercial. Home: 252 Rapier Ave Mobile AL 36604-2940 Office: 951 Government St Ste 406 Mobile AL 36604-2427

**BECKLEY, JAMES EMMETT,** lawyer; b. St. Joseph, Mo., Aug. 30, 1941; s. Emmett and Marguerite (Brebant) B.; m. Nena M. Gaines; children: Sarah, James Michael, Marguerite. AB cum laude, Rockhurst Coll., 1964; JD, Northwestern U., 1967. Bar: Ill., 1968, N.D., 1968, U.S. Dist. Ct. (no. dist.) Ill. Assoc. Kirkland & Ellis, Chgo., 1967-69, Law Offices of Frank Lunding Jr., Chgo., 1969-71; ptnr. Roan and Grossman, Chgo., Ill., 1972-78, Adler, Kaplan & Begy, Chgo., 1989; founder, ptnr. James E. Beckley & Assocs., Wheateh, IL, 1991—; pub. mem. Secutities Industry Conf. on Arbitration; arbitrator N.Y. Stock Exchange and CBOT; expert witness in litigation against securities dealers. Contbr. articles to profl. jours. and chpts. to books including: Discovery in Broker-Dealer Litigation, Blue Sky Laws and Common Law Remedies., Class Actions; lectr. to profl. and ednl. orgns. and instns. Chmn. Wheaton Band Commn., 1996—. Mem. ABA (sects. antitrust law and gen. litigation, subcoms. on profl. issues and SEC enforcement), Chgo. Bar Assn., Pub. Investors Arbitration Bar Assn. (bd. dirs.), Illinois State Bar Assn. (sects. on tort law, litigation, antitrust law). Roman Catholic. Avocations: creative writing, tennis. Antitrust, General civil litigation, Securities. Home: 201 W Union Ave Wheaton IL 60187-4126 Office: James E Beckley & Assoc 528 W Roosevelt Rd Ste 200 Wheaton IL 60187-2300

**BECKMAN, DAVID,** lawyer; b. Burlington, Iowa, 1950. BSIE, Iowa State U., 1973; MBA, JD, U. Iowa, 1976. Bar: Iowa 1976; CPA, Iowa. Ptnr. Beckman and Hirsch, Burlington, Iowa; mem. Iowa Supreme Ct. Commn. on Cts. in the 21st Century, team co-chair, mem. steering com. Fellow Iowa State Bar Found.; mem. ABA (chair lotus notse interest group 1994-98), AICPA, Iowa Soc. CPAs (bd. dirs., sec., exec. com. 1985-88, ethics com. 1988—, chair by laws com. 1987-89, continuing profl. edn. com. 1983-86), Iowa State Bar Assn. (bd. govs. 1990-96, pres. 1998-99), Des Moines County Bar Assn. (pres. 1994-95), Gamma Epsilon Sigma. E-mail: ddb@iowalaw.com. Corporate taxation, Probate. Office: Beckman and Hirsch 314 N 4th St Burlington IA 52601-5314*

**BECKMAN, DEBORAH HUBBARD,** law firm administrator; b. Newport Beach, Calif., July 18, 1962; d. John and Janet Hubbard; m. David Beckman, May 9, 1992; children: Diandrea, Taryn. BA, Pomona Coll., 1984; MBA, Northwestern U., 1988. Asst. acct. officer Union Bank, L.A., 1984-86; from sr. cons. to mgr. Price Waterhouse, West L.A., 1988-90; v.p. DAG Mgmt., Inc. (subs. 1st Interstate Bancorp), Denver, 1990-94; dir. adminstrn. Phelan, Cahill & Quinlan, Chgo., 1995-96; COO Cahill, Christian & Kunkle, Chgo., 1996—. Mem. Assn. Legal Adminstrs., Bus. Vols. for the Arts. Avocations: running, cycling, photography, cooking. Office: Cahill Christian & Kunkle 224 S Michigan Ave Ste 1300 Chicago IL 60604-2589

**BECKMAN, MICHAEL,** lawyer; b. N.Y.C., Oct. 8, 1945; s. Albert Beckman and Cecille Bronson; m. Susan Liebowitz, June 26, 1970 (separated Dec. 1987); children: Andrew D., Jason D. Bar: N.Y. 1969, U.S. Dist. Ct. (so. dist.) N.Y. 1972. Atty. Gordon Brady Keller & Ballen, N.Y.C., 1969-71; ptnr. Wolkowitz & Beckman, N.Y.C., 1971-74; sr. ptnr. Bell Kalnick Beckman Klee & Green, N.Y.C., 1974-88; sole practice N.Y.C., 1988-92; sr. ptnr. Beckman & Millman PC, N.Y.C., 1992-96, Beckman Millman & Sanders LLC, N.Y.C., 1996—; adj. prof. law NYU, 1981-93; bd. dirs. Amilite Corp. Dir. N.Y. Jr. Tennis League, N.Y.C., 1986-95, Sports & Arts in Schs. Found. Mem. West Side Tennis Club. Avocations: tennis, skiing. General corporate, Real property, Securities. Home: 437 W 24th St New York NY 10011-1253 Office: Beckman Millman & Sanders LLC 116 John St New York NY 10038-3300

**BECKSTEAD, JOHN ALEXANDER,** lawyer; b. Murray, Utah, July 23, 1950; s. Farol W. and Ruth I. (Elieson) B.; m. Deborah Heiner, June 28, 1972; children: Alexander, Spencer, Taylor, Christopher. BA, U. Utah, 1972, JD, 1975. Bar: Ariz. 1975, U.S. Dist. Ct. Ariz. 1975, Utah 1977, U.S. Dist. Ct. Utah 1977, U.S. Ct. Appeals (10th cir.) 1977. Dep. county atty. Maricopa County Atty.'s Office, Phoenix, 1975-77; spl. dep. county atty. Organized Crime Bur., Maricopa County (Ariz.) Atty.'s Office, Phoenix, 1977-79; mem. Callister, Nebeker & McCullough, Salt Lake City, 1977—, shareholder, dir., 1981—, exec. com., exec. v.p., 1991-97, adminstrv. shareholder, mng. atty., 1991-94; trustee Utah Legal Svcs., Inc., 1994— (pres. 1998—); mentor Utah Tech. Fin. Corp., 1994-97. Scoutmaster Boy Scouts of Am., Salt Lake City, 1992-95. Mem. ABA (subcom. creditors rights, inventory and accounts receivable financing factor, comml. fin. svcs. com.), Utah State Bar Assn. (sec. banking and fin. sect. 1983-84, vice chmn. 1984-85, chmn. 1985-86, chmn. subcom. on contracts/secured transactions/sales, model Utah jury instructions, section of litigation 1987—, 10th Circuit subcom. of the commercial bnkg. and fin. transactions com. of the litigation section 1989-90). Contracts commercial, General civil litigation, Intellectual property. Office: Callister Nebeker & McCullough Gateway Tower East # 900 10 E South Temple Salt Lake City UT 84133-1101

**BECKSTROM, CHARLES G.,** lawyer; b. Jamestown, N.Y., July 14, 1940; s. Charles Wilbert and Dorothy Helen (Carlson) B.; m. Marie Jane Trebilcock, Nov. 28, 1964; children: Kimberly Leigh, Erika Lynne, Kristyn Marie, Stephanie Rae. B.A., Mich. State U., 1962; M.B.A., Wayne State U., 1966; J.D., SUNY-Buffalo, 1969. Bar: Mich. 1969, N.Y. 1971, Pa. 1997. Ptnr. Johnson, Peterson, Tener & Anderson, Jamestown, 1970-89, Beckstrom & Plumb, Jamestown, 1989—; fin. analyst Fisher Body div. Gen. Motors Corp., Warren, Mich., 1963-66; lawyer Ernst & Ernst, Detroit, 1969-70; town atty. Town of Ellery, N.Y., 1972-83; bd. dirs. Dowcraft Corp.; bd. dirs., asst. sec. Bur. Veritas Quality Internat. (N.Am.) Inc. Trustee, chmn. 1st Covenant Ch. Jamestown, 1976-82; chmn., bd. pensions Evangelical Covenant Ch. Nat. Pension Plan, Chgo., 1979-84; mem. exec. bd. Evangelical Covenant Ch., 1986-92. Served with U.S. Army, 1963-64. Mem. Jamestown Bar Assn., N.Y. Assn. Sch. Attys., Jamestown Estate Planning Coun. (pres., v.p., sec.), Internat. Found. Employee Benefit Plans, Norden Club. Republican. Labor, Pension, profit-sharing, and employee benefits, General corporate. Home: 125 Westminister Dr Jamestown NY 14701-4438 Office: PO Box 579 Jamestown NY 14702-0579

**BECKWITH, MICHAEL V.,** lawyer; b. Mpls., May 30, 1947; s. Owen W. and Elna E. Beckwith; m. Patricia Flores, May 17, 1998; children: John P., Michael O., Joseph P. AA, Santa Monica City Coll., 1972; BS, U. West L.A., 1974; JD, Midvalley Coll. Law, 1977. Assoc. Oxnard, Calif., 1978-80; ptnr. Oxnard, 1980-86, pvt. practice, 1986—. With USN, 1966-70. Mem. Calif. Applicants Atty. Assn., L.A. Bar Assn., Ventura Bar Assn. Avocations: building autos, woodworking, home improvements. Workers' compensation. Office: 309 S A St Oxnard CA 93030-5820

**BECKWITH, SANDRA SHANK,** judge; b. Norfolk, Va., Dec. 4, 1943; d. Charles Langdale and Loraine (Sterneberg) Shank; m. James Beckwith, Mar. 31, 1965 (div. June 1978); m. Thomas R. Ammann, Mar. 3, 1979. BA, U. Cin., 1965, JD, 1968. Bar: Ohio 1969, Ind. 1976, Fla. 1979, U.S. Dist. Ct. (so. dist.) Ohio 1971, U.S. Dist. Ct. Ind. 1976, U.S. Supreme Ct. 1977. Sole practice Harrison, Ohio, 1969-77, 79-81; judge Hamilton County Mcpl. Ct., Cin., 1977-79, 81-86, commr., 1989-91; judge Ct. Common Pleas, Hamilton County Divsn. Domestic Rels., 1987-89; assoc. Graydon, Head and Ritchey, 1989-91; judge U.S. Dist. Ct. (so. dist.) Ohio, 1992—; mem. Ohio Chief Justice's Code of Profl. Responsibility Commn., 1984, Ohio Gov.'s Com. on Prison Crowding, 1984-90, State Fed. Com. on Death Penalty Habeas Corpus, 1995—; pres. 6th Cir. Dist. Judges Assn., 1998-99; chair So. Dist. Ohio Automation Com., 1997-99. Office: Potter Stewart US Courthouse Ste 810 Cincinnati OH 45202

**BECKWORTH, LINDLEY GARY, JR.,** lawyer; b. Washington, Apr. 29, 1943; s. Lindley and Eloise (Carter) B.; m. Martha Brindley, Aug., 1966; children: Melissa Love, Allison Louise. BA, U. Tex., Austin, 1966, LLB, 1968. Bar: Tex. 1968, U.S. Dist. Ct. (ea. dist.) Tex. 1974, U.S. Dist. Ct. (we. dist.) La. 1977, U.S. Ct. Appeals (5th cir.) 1980. Asst. counsel Consumer Credit Commn. State of Tex., Austin, 1968; asst. dist. atty. Gregg County, Longview, Tex., 1969; ptnr. Whitehead-Beckworth Law Firm, Longview, 1973-85; pvt. practice Longview, 1985—; vis. com. dept. botany U. TEx., 1988—; v.p. Gregg Bus. Incubator, Inc., Longview, 1991—; founder record labels Making Tex. Music, Code of the West Pub. Chmn. Water Adv. Commn. City of Longview, 1981-93. Mem. Gregg County Bar Assn. (sec. 1970, v.p. 1971), State Bar of Tex. (bar jour. com., vice chmn. 1974-86), Tex. Trial Lawyers Assn., Univ. Tex. Law Alumni Assn. (dist. dir. 1987-89), Univ. Tex. Alumni Assn. (dist. dir. 1989-91), Ex-Students Assn. U. Tex. (dist. coun. mem. dist. 7 1988-91), Gregg County U. Tex. Ex-Students Assn. (pres. 1975), Coun. State Govts., Washington (yr. two participant Japan environ. study. 1991). Methodist. General civil litigation, Entertainment, Private international. Office: 700 Glencrest Ln Ste A Longview TX 75601-5187

**BECRAFT, CHARLES D., JR.,** lawyer; b. Corning, N.Y., June 1, 1939; s. Charles D. and Mary A. (Szepansky) B. BS in Bus. Adminstrn., Syracuse U., 1961; LLB, JD, Union U., 1964. Bar: N.Y. 1967. Assoc. Flynn Law Offices, Bath, N.Y., 1967-68, Nasser Law Offices, Corning, N.Y., 1968-70; prin., owner Becraft Law Offices, Corning, N.Y., 1970-75, 80—; ptnr. Becraft, Knox & Kahl, Corning, N.Y., 1975-80. Asst. dist. atty. County of Steuben, N.Y., 1970-73; city judge City of Corning, 1977-80. With U.S. Army, 1965-67. Mem. N.Y. Bar Assn., Steuben County Bar Assn. (pres. 1981-83), Corning City Bar Assn., Kiwanis, Lions. Republican. Methodist. Avocations: tennis, skiing, wine making. Estate planning, General practice, Real property. Office: 135 Cedar St Corning NY 14830-2634

**BECTON, CHARLES L.,** lawyer; b. Morehead City, N.C., May 4, 1944; s. Edith Becton Nibbs; m. Brenda Carole Brown, Aug. 15, 1970; m. Nicole, Kevin, Michelle. BA, Howard U., 1966; JD, Duke U., 1969; LLM, U. Va., 1986. Bar: N.C., U.S. Dist. Ct. (ea., mid., we. dists.) N.C., U.S. Ct. Appeals (4th cir.), U.S. Supreme Ct. Atty. NAACP Legal Def. and Edn. Fund, Inc., N.Y.C., 1969-70, Chambers, Stein, Ferguson & Becton, Charlotte, N.C., 1970-80; judge N.C. Ct. Appeals, Raleigh, 1981-90; atty. Fuller, Becton, Slifkin & Bell, Raleigh, 1990—. State civil litigation, Personal injury. Home: 3011 Wade Rd Durham NC 27705-5630 Office: Fuller Becton Slifkin & Bell PA 4020 Westchase Blvd Ste 375 Raleigh NC 27607-3964

**BEDDOW, RICHARD HAROLD,** judge; b. Springfield, Mass., Jan. 3, 1932; s. Richard Harold and Elizabeth Christine (Geehern) B.; m. Trudy C. Howells, Jan. 14, 1967; children: Catherine Elizabeth Almand, Elissa Christine. BS, U. Mass., 1953; LLB, Boston Coll, 1959. Bar: Mass. 1960. Atty. ICC, Washington, 1959-69, mem. rev. bd., 1969-73, adminstrv. law judge, 1973-81; adminstrv. law judge NLRB, Washington, 1981—. With USN, 1953-55. Roman Catholic. Avocation: landscape gardening. Home: 2406 Rockwood Rd Accokeek MD 20607-9584 Office: NLRB 1099 14th St NW Washington DC 20570-0001

**BEDORE, JESS C.,** lawyer; b. San Francisco, Jan. 26, 1949; s. Jess C. and Genevieve B. Bedore; m. Jayne M. Bedore, Aug. 17, 1985. BA in Govt., Calif. State U., 1972; JD, Lincoln U., 1976. Bar: Calif. Asst. pub. defender Sacramento (Calif.) County Pub. Defender's Office, 1976-78; assoc.aww Law Offices of Leo M. O'Connor, Sacramento, 1978-81; sr. dep. dist. atty. Placer Co. Dist. Atty.'s Office, Auburn, Calif., 1981-90; trial atty., ptnr. Sinclair, Wilson & Bedore, Roseville, Calif., 1990—. Mem. Placer County Rep. Ctrl. Com., 1989-93. Mem. ATLA, Consumer Attys. Calif., Consumer Attys. Sacramento. Criminal, Personal injury, Professional liability. Office: Sinclair Wilson & Bedore 2390 Professional Dr Roseville CA 95661-7745

**BEEBE, WALTER H.,** lawyer; b. N.Y.C., May 24, 1940; s. Frederick Sessions and Liane Beebe; (div. 1981); children: John, Kathryn, Andrew; m. Carol Lois McDaniel, June 30, 1985; children: Frederick, Galen. BA cum laude, Harvard U., 1962; LLB, Stanford U., 1965. Bar: N.Y. 1966, U.S. Supreme Ct. 1976. Assoc. Olwine, Connelly, Chase, N.Y.C., 1966-76; ptnr. Davis & Cox, N.Y.C., 1976-82; sr. ptnr. Jacobs Persinger & Parker, N.Y.C., 1982—. Founder, pres. N.Y. Open Ctr., N.Y.C., 1983—; dir., sec. Interfaith Ctr., N.Y., 1998—. Mem. Assn. Bar City N.Y., Univ. Club. Avocation: philosophy. General corporate, Estate planning. Office: Jacobs Persinger & Parker 77 Water St Fl 17 New York NY 10005-4498

**BEECH, JOHNNY GALE,** lawyer; b. Chickasha, Okla., Sept. 18, 1954; s. Lovell Gale and Lucille L. (Phillips) B.; m. Judy Carol Schroeder, Dec. 31, 1977. BS, Southwestern Okla. State U., 1977; JD, U. Ark., Little Rock, 1980; LLM in Energy-Environment, Tulane U., 1985. Bar: Okla. 1980, U.S. Dist. Ct. (we. dist.) Okla. 1982, U.S. Dist. Ct. (no. dist.) Tex. 1983, U.S. Dist. Ct. (no. dist.) Okla. 1986, U.S. Dist. Ct. (ea. dist.) Okla. 1997. Assoc. Meacham, Meacham and Meacham, Clinton, Okla., 1980-84, Ford & Brown, Enid, Okla., 1985-86, Wright & Sawyer, Enid, 1986-88, Phillips, McFall, McCaffrey, McVay, Sheets and Lovelace, Oklahoma City, 1988-90; ptnr., mng. dir. Lester & Bryant, Oklahoma City, 1990-96; mgr. Beech Edwards and Percival PLLC, 1996—; mcpl. judge Town of Arapaho, Okla., 1982-84; assoc. gen. counsel Proserv Basketball, 1996—. Bd. dirs. Jr. Achievement Garfield County, Enid, 1986-88; commr. Little League Baseball; bd. dirs., treas. Edmond All Sports, Inc., 1999; mem. Bus. Sch. adv. coun. Southwestern U. Mem. ABA (real property, probate and trusts sect.), ATLA, Okla. Bar Assn. (law sch. com. 1989-91, uniform laws com. 1994-96, chmn. desk manual com. young lawyers div., uniform laws com. 1994—), Okla. Assn. Def. Counsel, Garfield County Bar Assn. (treas. 1988-89), Am. Bus. Club, Southwestern Okla. State U. Alumni Assn. (pres. 1983-86, parliamentarian 1992, exec. counsel 1986—, pres. 1997—), Southwestern Sch. Bus. Alumni Assn. (v.p. 1980-92, pres. 1992-93), Jaycees, Am. Bus. Club, Phi Alpha Delta (sec. 1979). Democrat. Methodist. Avocations: reading, bike racing. Banking, State civil litigation, Sports. Home: 702 N Cook St Cordell OK 73632-3002 Office: Beech Edwards & Percival PLLC 4901 Richmond Sq Ste 102 Oklahoma City OK 73118-2000

**BEECH, KRISTEN LEE,** lawyer, educator; b. Balt., May 10, 1966; d. Scott and Jane Elizabeth Beech. BA cum laude, Towson (Md.) State U., 1989; JD, Dickinson Sch. Law, Carlisle, Pa., 1992. Bar: Pa. 1992, U.S. Dist. Ct. (mid. dist.) Pa. 1992. Assoc. atty. Post & Schell, P.C., Harrisburg, Pa., 1992-95, McGuckin & Assocs., Lancaster, Pa., 1995-96, Marshall & Farrell, Camp Hill, Pa., 1996-97, Galli, Reilly & Stellato, Phila., 1997—; adj. prof. Dickinson Sch. Law, 1997—. Mem. Dauphin County Bar Assn., Phila. County Bar Assn. Professional liability, Personal injury. Office: 1845 Rittenhouse Sq Philadelphia PA 19103

**BEEGHLEY, STEVEN RAY,** lawyer; b. Long Beach, Calif., Sept. 22, 1970; s. William Clyde Beeghley and Carol Elizabeth Mellen. BS in Bus. Adminstrn., U. Ariz., 1993; JD, U. Houston, 1996. Bar: Ariz. 1996, U.S. Dist. Ct. 1996. Assoc. Holloway, Odegard & Sweeney, Phoenix, 1996—. Mem. exec. coun. Miracle Makers-Phoenix Children's Hosp., 1997-99. Mem. Ariz. Assn. Def. Counsel, Def. Rsch. Inst. Democrat. Insurance, Personal injury, Construction. Office: Holloway Odegard & Sweeney 3101 N Central Ave Ste 1200 Phoenix AZ 85012-2699

**BEEK, BARTON,** lawyer; b. Pasadena, Calif., Jan. 23, 1924; s. Joseph Allan and Carroll (Brewster) B.; m. Linda McCarter, Dec. 28, 1978; children: Charles, Carroll, Barbara, Barton Jr., Joseph. BS, Calif. Poly. U., 1944; MBA, Stanford U., 1948; JD, Loyola U., L.A., 1955. Bar: Calif. 1955. Ptnr. O'Melveny & Myers, L.A., 1955—; Bd. dirs. Wynns Internat., Orange, Calif., JMC Group, Inc., La Jolla, Calif. Lt. (j.g.) USN, 1943-46. Mem. Newport Harbor Yacht Club. Office: O'Melveny & Myers 610 Newport Center Dr Newport Beach CA 92660-6419

**BEELNER, KEN PHILLIP,** investigator, legal assistant; b. Dubuque, Iowa, July 2, 1936; s. Matthias and Agnes (Schmitz) B.; divorced; children: Kenneth M., Kristine E. Student, Loras Coll., Dubuque, 1955-56. Claims adjuster Arnold & Watts, West Palm Beach, Fla., 1965-68; field claims State Farm Claims, West Palm Beach, 1968-79, atty.-negotiator, 1979-83; legal asst. Slawson & Burman, West Palm Beach, 1983-85; investigator, legal asst. Farish, Farish & Romani, West Palm Beach, 1985—. Mem. Plaintiff/Paralegal Assn. (pres. 1989-90), Acad. Fla. Trial Lawyers, Rotary Internat., Palm Beach Claims Assoc. (pres. 1971, honorary lifetime mem. 1985), K.C., Loyal Order of Moose. Avocations: tennis, skiing. Office: Farish Farish & Romani 316 Banyan Blvd West Palm Beach FL 33401-4658

**BEEMER, JOHN BARRY,** lawyer; b. Scranton, Pa., Sept. 4, 1941; s. Ellis and Rose Mary (Costello) B.; m. Diane Montgomery Fletcher, July 18, 1964; children: David, Bruce. BS, U. Scranton, 1963; LL.B., George Washington U., 1966. Bar: Pa. 1966, U.S. Supreme Ct. 1980; cert. civil trial adv. Nat.

Bd. Trial Advocacy. Law clk. U.S. Ct. Claims, 1966-67; clk. to judge U.S. Dist. Ct. (mid. dist.) Pa., 1967-68; assoc. Warren, Hill, Henkelman & McMenamin, Scranton, 1968-72; ptnr. Beemer, Brier, Rinaldi & Fendrick, 1972-77; pres. Beemer, Rinaldi, Fendrick & Mellody, P.C., Scranton, 1977-83; ptnr. Beemer & Beemer, Scranton, 1984—; lectr. in law U. Scranton, 1969-70. Chmn. com. constn. and by-laws revision Lackawanna (county Pa.) United Fund., 1971; nat. chmn. U. Scranton Alumni Fund Drive, 1972. Mem. ABA, Pa. Bar Assn., Lackawanna Bar Assn. (bd. dirs. 1988—), Assn. Trial Lawyers Am., Pa. Trial Lawyers Assn., Phi Delta Phi. Criminal, Federal civil litigation, State civil litigation. Office: 114116 N Abington Rd Clarks Summit PA 18411

**BEENS, RICHARD ALBERT,** lawyer; b. Tracy, Minn., Sept. 7, 1941; s. Albert Charles and Dolores (Burnham) B.; m. Lynn Margaret Baker, Aug. 20, 1966 (dec. June 1973); 1 child, Jennifer Lois; m. Laura Lee Marie Geraghty, Aug. 9, 1974. BA, Coll. St. Thomas, St. Paul, 1965; JD, U. Minn., 1968. Bar: Minn. 1968, U.S. Ct. Appeals (8th cir.) 1968. From assoc. to ptnr. Babcock & Locher, Anoka, Minn., 1968-77; ptnr. Steffen, Munstenteiger, Beens & Peterson, Anoka, 1977—; instr. U. Minn. Law Sch., Mpls., 1972-73; asst. pub. defender State of Minn., Anoka, 1977-83, State Bd. PUb. Defenders 1986—. Vol. Peace Corps, West Pakistan, 1962-64; commr. Met. Waste Control Com., St. Paul, 1974-83; mem. Aviation Adv. Task Force, St. Paul, 1984-85; chmn. adv. com. Met. Council Solid Waste, St. Paul, 1986—. Mem. Assn. Trial Lawyers Am., Minn. Trial Lawyers Assn., Minn. Bar Assn., Anoka County Bar Assn. (chmn. ethics com. 1982—, chmn. judicial evaluation com. 1987—), Am. Arbitration Assn. (arbitrator 1970—). Avocations: reading, hunting, fishing. Federal civil litigation, State civil litigation, Criminal. Office: 403 Jackson St Anoka MN 55303-2372

**BEER, LOUIS DELAMARE,** lawyer, industrial developer, consultant; b. Washington, Mar. 3, 1945; s. Howard Louis and Jane Alfreda (Flickinger) B; m. Patience Dyas Carden, June 25, 1966; children—Jocelyn, Mary, Michael, A.B. cum laude, Harvard U., 1966; J.D. U. Mich., 1968. Bar: Mich. 1969, U.S. Dist. Ct. (ea. dist) Mich. 1971, U.S. Supreme Ct. 1972, U.S. Ct. Appeals (6th cir.) 1972. Exec. dir. Flint (Mich.) Edn. Assn., 1968-70; exec. sec. Mich. State Senate Minority Caucus, 1969; assoc. Riley and Rounell, Detroit 1971-73; sr. ptnr. Beer and Boltz, 1973-78; sr. ptnr. Kemp, Klein, Endelman and Beer, 1978-89; chmn. 1st Pub. Corp., Farmington Hills, Mich., 1989—; owner, operator Saginaw Indsl. Ctr.; chmn. Saginaw Indsl. Machinery; econ. devel. cons. in field. Chmn. Ralls for Gov. Com., 1978. Active Harvard Club, Mich. Mem. ABA (mem. sect. coms.), Mich. Bar Assn. Democrat. Episcopalian. Clubs: Detroit Athletic, Renaissance (Detroit); Oakland (Pontiac Mich.); Bloomfield Open Hunt (Bloomfield Hills, Mich.). Contbr. articles to profl. jours. Labor, Real property, Land use and zoning (including planning). Home: 9100 Foxhollow Ct Clarkston MI 48348-1965 Office: 1010 Hess Ave Saginaw MI 48601-3729 also: 31513 Northwestern Hwy Ste 201 Farmington Hills MI 48334

**BEER, PETER HILL,** federal judge; b. New Orleans, Apr. 12, 1928; s. Mose Haas and Henret (Lowenburg) B.; children: Kimberly Beer Bailes, Kenneth, Dana Beer Long-Innes; m. Marjorie Barry, July 14, 1985. BBA, Tulane U., 1949, LLB, 1952; LLM, U. Va., 1986. Bar: La. 1952. Successively assoc., ptnr., sr. ptnr. Montgomery, Barnett, Brown & Read, New Orleans, 1955-74; judge La. Ct. Appeal, 1974-79, U.S. Dist. Ct. (ea. dist.) La., New Orleans, 1979—; vice chmn. La. Appellate Judges Conf.; apptd. by chief justice of U.S. to state-fed. com. Jud. Conf. U.S., 1985-89; apptd. by chief justice of U.S. to Nat. Jud. Coun. State and Fed. Cts., 1993—. Mem. bd. mgrs. Touro Infirmary, New Orleans, 1969-74; mem. exec. com. Bur. Govtl. Rsch., 1965-69; chmn. profl. divsn. United Fund New Orleans, 1966-69; mem. New Orleans City Coun., 1969-74, v.p., 1972-74. Capt. USAF, 1952-55. Decorated Bronze Star. Mem. ABA (mem. ho. dels.), Am. Judicature Soc., Fed. Bar Assn., La. Bar Assn., Fed. Judges Assn. U.S. (bd. dirs. 1985, 5th cir. rep. bd. govs.), Nat. Lawyers Club, So. Yacht Club, St. John Golf Club. Jewish. Home: 133 Bellaire Dr New Orleans LA 70124-1008 also: 204 3rd Ave Pass Christian MS 39571-3214 Office: US Dist Ct US Courthouse 500 Camp St New Orleans LA 70130-3313

**BEERY, PAUL FREDERICK,** lawyer; b. Marion, Ohio, Oct. 31, 1931; s. Walter Thornton and Mable Louella (Jones) B.; m. Diane Kay Bero, June 7, 1958; children: Kimberly Kay, Eric Walter. BS in Acctg., Ohio State U., 1954; JD, Georgetown U., 1959. Bar: Ohio. Ptnr. George, Freck, King & McMahon, Columbus, Ohio, 1960-67; prin. Paul F. Beery Orgn., Columbus, 1968-71; pres. Beery & Spurlock Co., L.P.A., Columbus, 1972—. 1st lt. U.S. Army, 1955-56. Mem. Columbus Bar Assn., Transp. Lawyers Assn., Transp. Practitioners, Athletic Club of Columbus, Catawba Island Club. Transportation. Office: Beery & Spurlock Co LPA 275 E State St Columbus OH 43215-4330

**BEETEM, A. PAGE,** lawyer; b. Covington, Ky., Oct. 23, 1970. BA in Comms., No. Ky. U., Highland Heights, 1992; JD, Salmon P. Chase Coll. Law, Highland Heights, 1995. Bar: Ohio 1995, Ky. 1996; U.S. Dist. Ct. (we. and ea. dist.), Ohio (so. dist.), 1999. Atty. Condit, McDermott & Stewart, Covington, Ky., 1995-96, Paul J. Schacher & Assocs., Ft. Mitchell, Ky., 1996—. Personal injury, Pension, profit-sharing, and employee benefits, Workers' compensation. Office: 250 Grandview Dr Ste 500 Fort Mitchell KY 41017-5657

**BEEZER, ROBERT RENAUT,** federal judge; b. Seattle, July 21, 1928; s. Arnold Roswell and Josephine (May) B.; m. Hazlehurst Plant Smith, June 15, 1957; children: Robert Arnold, John Leighton, Mary Allison. Student, U. Wash., 1946-48, 51; BA, U. Va., 1951, LLB, 1956. Bar: Wash. 1956, U.S. Supreme Ct. 1968. Ptnr. Schweppe, Krug, Tausend & Beezer, P.S., Seattle, 1956-84; judge U.S. Ct. Appeals (9th cir.), Seattle, 1984-96, sr. judge, 1996—; alt. mem. Wash. Jud. Qualifications Commn., Olympia, 1981-84. 1st lt. USMCR, 1951-53. Fellow Am. Coll. Trust and Estate Counsel, Am. Bar Found.; mem. ABA, Seattle-King County Bar Assn. (pres. 1975-76), Wash. Bar Assn. (bd. govs. 1980-83). Clubs: Rainier, Tennis (Seattle). Office: US Ct Appeals 802 US Courthouse 1010 5th Ave Seattle WA 98104-1195

**BEGAM, ROBERT GEORGE,** lawyer; b. N.Y.C., Apr. 5, 1928; s. George and Hilda M. (Hirt) B.; m. Helen C. Clark, July 24, 1949; children—Richard, Lorinda, Michael. B.A., Yale U., 1949, LL.B., 1952. Bar: N.Y. bar 1952, Ariz. bar 1956, U.S. Dist. Ct. Ariz. 1957, U.S. Ct. Appeals (9th cir.) 1958, U.S Supreme Ct. 1973. Assoc. firm Cravath, Swaine & Moore, N.Y.C., 1952-54; spl. counsel State of Ariz., Colorado River Litigation in U.S. Supreme Ct., 1956-58; pres. Begam, Lewis Marks & Wolfe, P.A., Phoenix. Author: Fireball, 1987. Pres. Ariz. Repertory Theater, 1960-66, trustee Atla Roscoe Pound Found.; bd. dirs. Phoenix Theater Ctr., 1955-60, 87-92, Boys Clubs of Met. Phoenix; bd. govs. Welzmann Inst. Sci., Rehovot, Israel; pres. Am. Com. for Welzmann Inst. of Sci. Fellow Internat. Soc. Barristers; mem. Assn. Trial Lawyers Am. (pres. 1976-77, chmn. polit. action com. 1979-86), Western Trial Lawyers Assn. (pres. 1970), Am. Bd. Trial Advocates (bd. dirs.), State Bar Ariz. (cert. specialist in injury and wrongful death litigation). Clubs: Yale (N.Y.C.), Desert Highlands Country (Scottsdale, Ariz.), Pinetop Country (Pinetop, Ariz.), Wig and Pen (London). Avocations: writing, theater, golf. Personal injury, Product liability. Office: Begam Lewis Marks & Wolfe 111 W Monroe St Ste 1400 Phoenix AZ 85003-1787

**BEGGS, HARRY MARK,** lawyer; b. Los Angeles, Nov. 15, 1941; s. John Edgar and Agnes (Kentro) B.; m. Sandra Lynne Mikal, May 25, 1963; children: Brendan, Sean, Corey, Michael. Student, Ariz. State U., 1959-61, Phoenix Coll., 1961; LL.B., U. Ariz., 1964. Bar: Ariz. 1964, U.S. Dist. Ct. Ariz. 1964, U.S. Ct. Appeals (9th cir.) 1973, U.S. Ct. Appeals (fed. cir.) 1995, U.S. Supreme Ct. 1991. Assoc. Carson Messinger Elliott Laughlin & Ragan, Phoenix, 1964-69, ptnr., 1969-93; mem., mng. lawyer Carson Messinger Elliott Laughlin & Ragan, P.L.L.C., Phoenix, 1994—. Mem. editorial bd. Ariz. Law Rev. 1963-64; contbr. articles to profl. jours. Recipient award for highest grade on state bar exam. Atty. Gen. Ariz., 1964; Fegtly Moot Ct. award, 1963, 64; Abner S. Lipscomb scholar U. Ariz. Law Sch., 1963. Fellow Ariz. Bar Found. (founder); mem. State Bar Ariz., Ariz. Acad., Maricopa County Bar Assn. State civil litigation, Federal civil litigation, Antitrust. Office: PO Box 33907 Phoenix AZ 85067-3907

**BEGHE, RENATO,** federal judge; b. Chgo., Mar. 12, 1933; s. Bruno and Emmavve (Frymire) B.; m. Bina House, July 10, 1954; children: Eliza Ashley, Francesca Forbes, Adam House, Jason Deneen. B.A., U. Chgo., 1951, J.D., 1954. Bar: N.Y. 1955. Practiced in N.Y.C.; assoc. Carter, Ledyard & Milburn, 1954-65, ptnr., 1965-83; ptnr. Morgan, Lewis & Bockius, 1983-89; judge U.S. Tax Ct., Washington, 1991—; lectr. N.Y. U. Fed. Tax Inst., 1967, 78, U. Chgo. Fed. Tax Conf., 1974, 80, 86, also other profl. confs. Mng. editor U. Chgo. Law Rev., 1953-54; contbr. articles to profl. jours. Mem. ABA, Internat. Bar Assn., N.Y. State Bar Assn. (chmn. tax sect. 1977-78), Assn. of Bar of City of N.Y. (chmn. art law com. 1980-83), Am. Law Inst., Internat. Fiscal Assn., Am. Coll. Tax Counsel, America-Italy Soc. Inc. (bd. dirs. 1980-92), Phi Beta Kappa, Order of Coif, Phi Gamma Delta. Home: 633 E St SE Washington DC 20003-2716 Office: US Tax Ct 400 2nd St NW Washington DC 20217-0002

**BEGLEITER, MARTIN DAVID,** law educator, consultant; b. Middletown, Conn., Oct. 31, 1945; s. Walter and Anne Begleiter; m. Ronni Ann Frankel, Aug. 17, 1969; children: Wendy Cara, Hilary Ann. BA, U. Rochester, 1967; JD, Cornell U., 1970. Bar: N.Y. 1970, U.S. Dist. Ct. (ea. dist.) N.Y. 1971, U.S. Ct. Appeals (2d cir.) 1975. Assoc. Kelley Drye & Warren, N.Y.C., 1970-77; assoc. prof. Law Sch., Drake U., Des Moines, 1977-80, prof., 1980-87, 93—, Richard M. and Anita Calkins disting. prof. law, 1987-93. Contbr. articles to legal jours. Mem. ABA (com. on estate and gift taxes, taxation sect. 1980—, com. on tax legislation and regulations, lifetime transfers, real property, probate and trust law sect. 1980—, study com. law reform 1996—, chmn. task force on spl. use valuation 1988-93, advisor Nat. Conf. Commns. on Uniform State Laws 1988-93), Iowa Bar Assn. (adviser, resource person, probate, trust sect. 1983-89, 93—), Am. Law Inst. (adviser restatement 3d trusts 1994—). Jewish. Avocations: science fiction, golf. Office: Drake U Sch Law 27th & Carpenter Sts Des Moines IA 50311

**BEGLEITER, RONNI FRANKEL,** lawyer; b. Tupper Lake, N.Y., July 7, 1948; d. Samuel and Ruth (Kaplan) Frankel; m. Martin David Begleiter, Aug. 16, 1969; children: Wendy Cara, Hilary Ann. BA, Cornell U., 1969; MLS, Columbia U., 1971; JD, Drake U., 1982. Bar: Iowa 1983, U.S. Tax Ct. 1977. Libr. Fried Frank Harris Shriver & Jacobson, N.Y.C., 1971-74, Proskauer Rose Goetz & Mendelsohn, N.Y.C., 1974-77; reference libr. Drake U. Law Libr., Des Moines, 1977-81; clk. Iowa Supreme Ct., Des Moines, 1983-84; assoc. Davis, Hockenberg, Wine, Brown & Koehn, Des Moines, 1984-87; assoc., shareholder Pingel & Templer PC, West Des Moines, Iowa, 1987—; adj. prof. Drake U. Law Sch., Des Moines, 1992, 95, 97. Chmn. Clive (Iowa) Mayor's Libr. Com., 1995-98; chairperson, bd. trustees Clive Pub. Libr., 1999—. Nominated for Clive Citizen of Yr., 1999. Mem. ABA, Iowa State Bar Assn., Polk County Bar Assn., ERISA Forum, West Des Moines Tax Forum. Estate planning, Pension, profit-sharing, and employee benefits, Probate. Office: Pingle & Templer PC 3737 Woodland Ave Ste 437 West Des Moines IA 50266-1937

**BEGLEY, THOMAS D., JR.,** lawyer; b. Phila., May 2, 1938; s. Thomas Devlin and Margaret (Moore) B.; m. Anne E. Glass, June 24, 1961 (dec. Feb. 1977); children: Thomas D. III, Sharon A., Mark L., Colleen I. Student, Georgetown U., 1959, Georgetown U., 1962. Pvt. practice Begley, Begley & Fendrick, P.C., Moorestown, N.J., 1962—; senator Georgetown U. Senate, Washington, 1962—. Author: How to Develop and Manage a Successful Trust & Estates/Elde-Law Practice, 1997; (with others) New Jersey Elder Law Practice, 1997. V.p. South N.J. Alzheimers Assn.; bd. dirs. Moorestown Bd. Edn. Found. Fellow Nat. Acad. Elder Law Attys. (bd. dirs.); mem. N.J. Bar Assn. (past chmn. elder law sect., past chmn. bd. consultors real property probate and trust law sect. 1989—). Republican. Roman Catholic. Avocations: swimming, boating, travel. Estate planning, Probate, Elder. Office: Begley Begley & Fendrick PC 509 S Lenola Rd Ste 7 Moorestown NJ 08057-1561

**BEHAR, JEFFREY STEVEN,** lawyer; b. Phila., Nov. 20, 1952; s. Joseph and Helene (Richmond) B.; m. Lori R. Wolfe, July 30, 1977; children: Alexander J., Mallory R. BA magna cum laude, UCLA, 1974; JD, Loyola U., L.A., 1978. Bar: Calif. 1978, U.S. Dist. Ct. (ctrl. dist.) Calif. 1978. Ptnr. Shield & Smith, L.A., 1978-91; founding ptnr. Ford, Walker, Haggerty & Behar, Long Beach, Calif., 1991—. Mem. Am. Bd. Trial Advocates, Internat. Assn. Def. Counsel, Def. Rsch. Inst., Assn. So. Calif. Def. Counsel (bd. dirs. 1994—), Phi Beta Kappa. Avocations: race cars, volleyball, golf. Aviation, Construction, Insurance. Office: Ford Walker Haggerty & Behar One World Trade Ctr Long Beach CA 90831

**BEHR, LAURENCE DONALD,** lawyer; b. Rochester, N.Y., Aug. 9, 1951; s. Gervin Thomas Behr and Mary Berenice Doxtater; m. Marlene Jeanette DeGeorge, Aug. 7, 1981. BA cum laude, SUNY, Buffalo, 1973, JD magna cum laude, 1981. Bar: N.Y. 1982, U.S. Dist. Ct. (no. dist.) N.Y. 1982, U.S. Dist. Ct. (we. dist.) N.Y. 1982, U.S. Dist. Ct. (no. dist.) N.Y. 1985, U.S. Dist. Ct. (so. dist.) N.Y. 1988, U.S. Supreme Ct. 1988. Litig. ptnr. Saperston & Day, P.C., Buffalo, 1983-90, Lustig & Brown, LLP, Buffalo, 1990-91, Casey, Sanchez, et al, Buffalo, 1991-92; pvt. practice Buffalo, 1992-98; ptnr. Barth, Sullivan & Behr, Buffalo, 1998—; arbitrator/mediator Am. Arbitration Assn., Syracuse, N.Y., 1987—, Resolute Sys. Inc., Brookfield, Wis., 1995—, Arbitration and Medin Svcs., Mineola, N.Y., 1998; mem. nominating com. Buffalo Bd. Ethics, 1988-97. Contbr. articles to profl. jours. Mem. Nat. Bar Assn., N.Y. State Bar Assn., Erie County Bar Assn. (chair ins. com. 1988-91), We. N.Y. Lawyers for Life (pres. 1993—). Roman Catholic. Avocations: philosophy, poetry, golf. Personal injury, Insurance, Professional liability. Office: Barth Sullivan & Behr 43 Court St Ste 530 Buffalo NY 14202-3101

**BEHR, RALPH STEVEN,** lawyer; b. June 19, 1951. BA cum laude, SUNY, Albany, 1973; JD, Hofstra U., 1976. Bar: Oreg. 1976, N.Y. 1977, Fla. 1988, U.S.Dist. Ct. (so. dist.) Fla. 1991, U.S. Dist. Ct. (middle dist.) Fla. 1991, U.S. Dist. Ct. (we. dist.) Fla. 1991, U.S. Supreme Ct. 1991; cert. real estate broker, N.Y.; lic. commodity futures trading advisor. Legis. aide N.Y. State Assembly, Albany, 1971-73; dist. atty. Nassau County (N.Y.) Dist. Atty.'s Office, 1975-76; pvt. practice Portland, Oreg., 1976-77, Deerfield Beach, Fla., 1988—; legal editor Pvt. Label mag., N.Y.C., 1978-82; v.p., counsel Foods Oils Corp., Carlstadt, N.J., 1977-88; instr. legal rsch. and writing Hofstra U., 1975-76. Legal editor Pvt. Label Mag., 1978-82. Vol. atty. N.Y. Family Ct.; commr. Housing Authority Deerfield Beach, 1988—; treas. campaign Lisa G. Trachman County Ct. Judge, 1994. Goethe Inst. scholar West German Govt., 1969, N.Y. State Regents scholar, 1969. Mem. Broward Assn. Criminal Def. Lawyers (bd. dirs.), Broward County Bar Assn. (ethics com.), Pvt. Label Mfrs. Assn. (bd. dirs. 1980-83, legal affairs com. 1983-86). Avocations: sailing, golf. Fax: 954-761-1524. E-mail: behr@aksi.net. Criminal, General corporate, Public international. Office: 101 SE 10th St Fort Lauderdale FL 33316-1023

**BEHRENDT, JOHN THOMAS,** lawyer; b. Syracuse, Kans., Oct. 26, 1945; s. Thomas Franklin and Anna Iola (Carrithers) B.; children: Todd Thomas, Gretchen Jean; m. Theresa Ann Elmore, Oct. 27, 1985. BA, Sterling Coll.; JD cum laude, U. Minn. Bar: Calif. 1971, Tex. 1973, N.Y. 1989. Assoc., then sr. ptnr. Gibson, Dunn & Crutcher, L.A., 1970-71, 1974—; lectr. Practicing Law Inst., Acctg. for Lawyers. Capt. JAGC, U.S. Army, 1971-74. Mem. ABA (law and acctg. com.), L.A. County Bar Assn, Order of Coif. Republican. Presbyterian. Clubs: Jonathan (L.A.); Union League (N.Y.); The Tuxedo (Tuxedo Park, N.Y.). Federal civil litigation, General corporate, Private international. Office: Gibson Dunn & Crutcher 200 Park Ave Fl 47 New York NY 10166-0193

**BEHRENS, BRIAN CHARLES,** lawyer, associate; b. St. Louis, Sept. 9, 1969; s. Kenneth Charles Behrens and Patricia Ann Osterberg; m. Laura Lee Sak, June 29, 1996. BSBA, U. Mo., Columbia, 1991; MBA, St. Louis U., 1995, JD, 1995. Bar: Mo. 1995, Kans. 1996, U.S. Dist. Ct. (we. dist.) Mo. 1995, U.S. Dist. Ct. Kans. 1996. Assoc. Wallace, Saunders, Austin, Brown & Enochs, Overland Park, Kans., 1995-97, Suelthaus & Walsh, P.C., St. Louis, 1997—. Contbr. articles to profl. jours.; staff mem. St. Louis U. Pub. Law Rev., 1993-94. Mem. ABA, Mo. Bar, Kans. Bar Assn. Roman Catholic. Avocations: travel, golf, hockey. General corporate, Intellectual property, Real property. Office: Suelthaus & Walsh PC 7733 Forsyth Blvd Fl 12 Saint Louis MO 63105-1817

**BEHRMANN, LAWRENCE JAMES,** lawyer; b. San Francisco, July 31, 1960; s. Lawrence Amos and Barbara Jean B.; m. Maria Hurst, Aug. 24, 1988; children: Laurie Anne, David Aaron, Steven Alexander. BA, Brigham Young U., 1985, JD, 1988. Bar: Tex. 1989, U.S. Ct. Mil. Appeals 1989, U.S. Dist. Ct. (so. dist.) Tex. 1993,. Judge adv. USMC, Okinawa, Japan, 1988-93; owner, pres. Lawrence J. Behrmann & Assocs., Houston, 1993—; fgn. area officer USMC, Okinawa, 1991-94, dep. staff judge adv. III Marine Expeditionary Force, 1992. Contbr. articles to profl. jours. Scoutmaster Boy Scouts Am., Okinawa, 1992, mem. cub scout com., Houston, 1999. Capt. USMC, 1989-93, past mem. USMCR. Mem. Tex. Bar Assn. (family law, appellate practice and advocacy sects.), Okinawa Bench and Bar Assn. Mem. LDS Ch. Family and matrimonial, Federal civil litigation, State civil litigation. Office: 10301 Northwest Fwy Ste 400 Houston TX 77092-8228

**BEIGHTOL, SCOTT CHRISTOPHER,** lawyer; b. Sioux City, Iowa, May 16, 1963; s. Richard Eugene and JoAnn (Lichty) B.; m. Desiree Kristin Erickson, June 29, 1991; children: Quinn, Ari. BA in English, Holy Cross Coll., 1985; JD, U. Wis., 1988. Bar: Wis., U.S. Dist. Ct. (ea. and we. dists.) Wis. 1988, U.S. Dist. Ct. (so. dist.) Ind. 1998, U.S. Ct. Appeals (7th cir.) Ill. 1988. Assoc. U.S. Dept. Justice, Washington, summer 1987; atty. Michael, Best & Friedrich, Milw., 1988—; dir. Nat. Worksite Benefits, LLC, Mequon, Wis., 1996—. Sr. editor Wis. Law Review, 1986-88. Dir. Friends of Milw. Pub. Mus., 1994-98, Guest House, 1995-98; mem. Milw. Curling Club, 1994—; trustee Village of Whitefish Bay, Wis., 1998—. Mem. Wis. State Bar (dir. employment sect. 1996—). Republican. Roman Catholic. Avocations: distance running, reading. Labor, Civil rights, General civil litigation. Office: Michael Best and Friedrich LLP 100 E Wisconsin Ave Ste 3300 Milwaukee WI 53202-4108

**BEIMFOHR, DOUGLAS ALAN,** lawyer; b. Manhasset, N.Y., Oct. 11, 1960; s. Edward G. and Joella J. (White) B.; m. Jennifer Ann Groel, July 22, 1989. BA, U. Va., 1982, JD, 1986. Bar: N.Y. 1988, N.J. 1994. Assoc. Thacher, Proffitt & Wood, N.Y.C., 1986-89, Kelley Drye & Warren, N.Y.C., 1989-95, Robinson, St. John & Wayne, N.J., 1995-96; shareholder Buchanan, Ingersoll, P.C., N.J., 1996—. General corporate, Contracts commercial, Banking. Office: Buchanan Ingersoll 500 College Rd E Princeton NJ 08540-6635

**BEINECKE, CANDACE KRUGMAN,** lawyer; b. Paterson, N.J., Nov. 26, 1946; d. Martin and Sylvia (Altshuler) Krugman; m. Frederick W. Beinecke II, Oct. 2, 1976; children: Jacob Sperry, Benjamin Barrett. BA, NYU, 1967; JD, Rutgers U., 1970. Bar: N.Y. 1971. Assoc., then ptnr., then chair Hughes, Hubbard & Reed, N.Y.C., 1970—. Bd. dirs. Merce Cunningham Found., N.Y.C., Jacob's Pillow Dance Festival, Lee, Mass., First Eagle Fund; mem. vis. com. Met. Mus. Art Watson Libr. Mem. ABA, Assn. Bar City of N.Y., River Club, Women's Forum. General corporate, Private international, Mergers and acquisitions. Office: Hughes Hubbard & Reed One Battery Park Plaza New York NY 10004-1466

**BEININ, WILLIAM J.,** lawyer; b. N.Y.C., Mar. 8, 1945; s. George and Flora (Friedman) B.; m. Jane Schwat, July 3, 1973; children—Gregg C., Kimberly A. B.A., CCNY, 1965; J.D., N.Y. Law Sch., 1968. Bar: N.Y. 1969, U.S. Dist. Ct. (so. and ea. dists.) N.Y. 1972. Sole practice, N.Y.C., 1969-71; ptnr. Herman & Beinin, N.Y.C., 1971—. Recipient Am. Jurisprudence award N.Y. Law Sch., 1967, 68. Personal injury, General civil litigation, General practice. Office: Herman & Beinin 185 Madison Ave New York NY 10016-4325

**BEIRNE, MARTIN DOUGLAS,** lawyer; b. N.Y.C., Oct. 24, 1944; s. Martin Douglas and Catherine Anne Beirne; m. Kathleen Harrington; children: Martin, Shannon, Kelley. BS, Spring Hill Coll., 1966; JD with honors, St. Mary's U., 1969. Bar: Tex. 1969, U.S. Dist. Ct. (ea. dist.) Tex. 1972, U.S. Dist. Ct. (so. dist.) Tex. 1971, U.S. Dist. Ct. (no. dist.) Tex., U.S. Dist. Ct. (we. dist.) Tex., U.S. Ct. Appeals (5th and 11th cirs.) 1974, U.S. Dist. Ct. (ea. dist.) Calif., U.S. Supreme Ct. 1975. Ptnr. Fulbright & Jaworski, Houston, 1971-85; mng. ptnr. Beirne, Maynard & Parsons, Houston, 1985—. Editor-in-chief St. Mary's Law Rev. Bd. dirs. St. Thomas U., Houston Law Rev. Found., Nat. Conf. Christians and Jews. Capt. U.S. Army, 1969-71. Fellow Tex. Bar Found.; mem. ABA, Tex. Bar Assn., Houston Bar Assn., Coronado Club, The Houstonian Club, Legatus-U. Houston Law Sch. Found. Roman Catholic. Federal civil litigation, State civil litigation, General corporate. Office: Beirne Maynard & Parsons LLP Wells Fargo 1300 Post Oak Blvd Fl 24 Houston TX 77056-3028

**BEISNER, JOHN HERBERT,** lawyer; b. Salina, Kans., Feb. 24, 1953; s. Herbert J. and Matilda (Cordel) B.; m. Diane G. Klinke, Apr. 26, 1980; 1 child, Laura Ann. BA, U. Kans., 1975; JD, U. Mich, 1978. Bar: Calif. 1978, D.C. 1980. Assoc. O'Melveny & Myers, Washington, 1978-85, ptnr., 1985—, mgmt. com., 1996—. Mem. State Colls. Coord. Com. Kans. Bd. Regents, 1974-75. Mem. ABA, Am. Law Inst., Fed. Comm. Bar Assn. Federal civil litigation, Communications, Administrative and regulatory. Office: O'Melveny & Myers 555 13th St NW Ste 500W Washington DC 20004-1159

**BEISWANGER, GARY LEE,** lawyer; b. Billings, Mont., May 31, 1938. BA in Philosophy, History-Polit. Sci., U. Mont., 1960, LLB, 1963. Bar: Mont. 1963, U.S. Dist. Ct. Mont. 1963, U.S. Ct. Appeals (9th cir.) 1987. Pvt. practice, Billings, 1965—. Mem. ABA, ATLA, State Bar Mont., Mont. Trial Lawyers Assn., Yellowstone County Bar Assn. General corporate, General civil litigation, Real property. Office: Rocky Village Ctr I 1500 Poly Dr Billings MT 59102-1748

**BEIZER, LANCE KURT,** lawyer; b. Hartford, Conn., Sept. 8, 1938; s. Lawrence Sidney and Victoria Merriam (Kaplan) B. BA in Sociology, Brandeis U., 1960; MA in English, San Jose State U., 1967; JD, U. San Diego, 1975. Bar: Calif. 1975. Selective svc. affairs coord. U. Calif., 1969-73, vet. affairs coord., 1973-75; vet. outreach coord. San Diego Community Coll. Dist., 1975-76; dep. dist. atty. Santa Clara County, Calif., 1976—. Bd. mgrs. Santa Clara Valley S.W. YMCA, Saratoga, Calif., 1988—, chair, 1991-93; bd. dirs. The Lumen Found., San Francisco, 1985—. Bd. dirs. Fedn. Cmty. Ministries, Calif., 1992—, chair, 1996—; bd. dirs. South Bay Homeless Teenagers Alliance, 1997—, chair, 1997—. Lt. USNR, 1961-65. Mem. Calif. Dist. Attys. Assn., Santa Clara County Bar Assn., Am. Profl. Soc. on Abuse of Children, Nat. Assn. Counsel for Children, Am. Weil Soc., Mensa, Commonwealth Club. Republican. Episcopalian. Home: 1197 Capri Dr Campbell CA 95008-6002 Office: Santa Clara County Dist Atty 70 W Hedding St San Jose CA 95110-1768

**BEJNAR, THADDEUS PUTNAM,** law librarian, lawyer; b. Carmel, Calif., Aug. 19, 1948; s. Waldemere and Katherine (Marble) B.; m. Susan Mavis Richards, Mar. 25, 1976 (div. Jan. 1986); m. Catherine Slade Baudoin, Apr. 10, 1988 (div. Apr. 1995). AB in Philosophy, U. So. Calif., 1971; JD, Georgetown U., 1978; MLIS, U. Tex., 1986. Bar: N.Mex. 1978, U.S. Dist. Ct. N.Mex. 1980, U.S. Ct. Appeals (10th cir.) 1981. Atty. Indian Pueblo Legal Svcs., Zuni, N.Mex., 1978-80; pvt. practice law Albuquerque, 1980-84; legal rsch. libr. U. N.Mex., Albuquerque, 1984-87; law libr. Supreme Ct. Law Libr. State of N.Mex., Santa Fe, 1987—; tchr. legal admissibility electronic records Advanced Legal Rsch. C.L.E., 1984-97 ; bd. dirs. Waldemere, Bejnar & Assocs. Author: Jurisdictional Guide to Jury Instructions, 1986; editor N.Mex. Jud. Conduct Handbook, 1989-93, Manual of Citation for the Ctrs. of the State of N.Mex., 1991-92, 2d edit., 1997; sr. editor N.Mex. Legal Forms, 1991-94. Chmn. N.Mex. del. White House Conf. Librs., 1991; chmn. N.Mex. Adv. Com. on Rules and Publs., 1992-96; prin. Legal Informatics, an internat. cons. firm, 1992—. Lt. USAF, 1971-74. Mem. ALA, Am. Assn. Law Librs., N.Mex. Libr. Assn., Adirondack Mt. Club, Order of Coif, Spec. Libr. Assn., Phi Kappa Phi, Phi Alpha Delta, Beta Phi Mu. Mem. Soc. of Friends. Avocations: philately, hiking, conservation. Home: Rt 2 Box 94 Socorro NM 87801 Office: Supreme Ct Law Libr PO Drawer L 237 Don Gaspar Ave Santa Fe NM 87501-2178

**BEKES, GREGORY E.,** lawyer; b. Phila., Feb. 15, 1950; s. Walter Thomas and Ethel Florence (Finger) B.; m. Kathleen Robin Moore, Feb. 12, 1972; children: Jason, Matthew, Melissa. BA, Glassboro State Coll., 1971; MBA, So. Ill. U., 1978; JD with honors, U. Louisville, 1988. Bar: Ind. 1988, U.S. Dist. Ct. (no. and so. dists.) Ind. 1988, U.S. Ct. Appeals (7th cir.) 1988, Ky.

1989, U.S. Dist. Ct. (we. dist.) Ky. 1989. Prodn. supr. Campbell Soup Co., Camden, N.J., 1971-78; quality control supr. William Underwood Co., Hannibal, Mo., 1978-79; pers. mgr. Orville Redenbacker Popcorn, Valparaiso, Ind., 1979-81; pers. assoc. Gen. Foods, Inc., Chgo., 1981-85; dir. human rels. Ferraley, Salem, Ind., 1985-88; assoc. Rogers Fuller & Pitt, Louisville, 1988-90; ptnr. Grotke & Bekes, Greenwood, Ind., 1990—. Mem. Ind. Bar Assn., Ky. Bar Assn., Washington County Bar Assn. Avocation: astronomy. General corporate, Labor. Office: Grotke & Bekes PC 748 S State Road 135 Greenwood IN 46143-9410

**BEKRITSKY, BRUCE ROBERT,** lawyer; b. Utica, N.Y., Nov. 9, 1946; s. Morris and Dorothy (Horowitz) B.; m. Helene Marcia Andrews, June 23, 1968; children: Brett Jonathan, Amy Beth, Seth Benjamin. BA, Yeshiva U., 1968; JD, Bklyn. Law Sch., 1973. Bar: N.Y. 1974, U.S. Dist. Ct. (ea. and so. dists.) N.Y. 1975, U.S. Ct. Appeals (2d cir.) 1975, U.S. Supreme Ct. 1978. Atty. Legal Services Bklyn., 1974-81; assoc. Law Offices of Richard Hartman, Little Neck, N.Y., 1981-86; sole practice Mineola, N.Y., 1986—. Mem. ABA, N.Y. State Bar Assn., Nassau County Bar Assn. Democrat. Jewish. Consumer commercial, Family and matrimonial, Juvenile. Office: 1551 Kellum Pl Mineola NY 11501-4811

**BELAFSKY, BETTY MATILDA,** lawyer; b. Detroit, July 7, 1941; d. Charles and Blanche Forman; m. Mark Lewis Belafsky, Dec. 25, 1962; children—Caryn, Peter. B.S., U. Pa., 1962; J.D., Rutgers U., 1983. Bar: N.J. 1983. Assoc. firm Supnick et al, Haddonfield, N.J., 1988—. Fellow N.J. Bar Assn., Pa. Bar Assn.; mem. Fla. Bar Assn.

**BELANGER, ROBERT EUGENE,** lawyer; b. Pitts., June 10, 1958; s. Eugene Edward and Patricia Mickle (Pelikan) B.; m. Gale Elizabeth Lynam, May 21, 1988; children: Sean Robert, Katharine Anne. BA, John Carroll U., 1981; JD, Cleve.-Marshall Coll. of Law, 1986; cert. with honors, Naval Justice Sch., Newport, R.I., 1988. Bar: Ohio 1986, U.S. Ct. Mil. Appeals 1989, U.S. Dist. Ct. (no. dist.) Ohio 1990, U.S. Supreme Ct. 1992, Fla. 1993. Assoc. Svete McGee & Carrabine, L.P.A., Chardon, Ohio, 1990-94; supervising asst. state atty. 19th Jud. Cir., Stuart, Fla., 1994—. Bd. dirs. Geauga County Bd. Mental Health and Drug Addiction, Chardon, 1991-94; sustaining mem. Rep. Nat. Com., Washington, 1990—; chmn. Martin County (Fla.) Rep. Exec. Com. Capt. USMC, 1986-90. Mem. ABA, Fla. Bar Assn., SAR (compatriot Western Res. chpt. 1990—). Roman Catholic. Avocations: running, karate. Criminal, Admiralty. Home: 3698 SW Thistlewood Ln Palm City FL 34990-7718 Office: Office of State Atty Constnl Bldg 4th Fl 120 E Ocean Blvd Stuart FL 34994-2206

**BELAY, STEPHEN JOSEPH,** lawyer; b. Joliet, Ill., May 30, 1958; s. Donald L. and Miriam A. (Madden) B.; m. Trudy L. Patterson, Nov. 7, 1987; children: Jacob, Katherine. BA, U. Iowa, 1980, JD, 1983. Bar: Iowa 1983, U.S. Dist. Ct. (no. dist.) Iowa 1985. Pvt. practice Cedar Rapids, Iowa, 1983-88; asst. county atty. State of Iowa, Burlington, 1988-89, Decorah, 1989-92, 95—; assoc. Anderson, Wilmarth & Van Der Maaten, Decorah, 1993-96; ptnr. Anderson, Wilmarth, Van Der Maaten & Belay, Decorah, 1997—. Chair Winneshiek County Rep. Party, Decorah, 1992-94. Mem. ABA (chair juvenile justice com. young lawyers divsn. 1992-93), Iowa State Bar Assn. (chair juvenile law com. young lawyers divsn. 1992-94), Lions (bd. dirs. 1991-93). Roman Catholic. Avocations: trout fishing, bicycling, camping. General civil litigation, Family and matrimonial. Home: 903 Pine Ridge Ct Decorah IA 52101-1135 Office: Anderson Wilmarth Van Der Maaten & Belay PO Box 450 Decorah IA 52101-0450

**BELCHER, CHRISTINE VICTORIA,** paralegal; b. Perth Amboy, N.J., Sept. 21, 1956; d. Stephen Edward and Irene Marie (Doucet) B. BA, New Eng. Coll., 1979. Dir. theatre publicity Colby-Sawyer Coll., New London, N.H., 1979-80; bus. mgr. Arlington (Va.) Dance Theatre, 1981-82; restaurant mgmt. Hyatt Regency Crystal City (Va.), 1982-86; bookkeeper Clyde's of Tyson's, Tyson's Corner, Va., 1986-88; paralegal Blooston, Mordkofsky, Jackson & Dickens, Washington, 1989-95; technical specialist Troy Systems, Inc., Fairfax, Va., 1995—. Mem. Jaycees (regional dir. Va. Jaycees 1986-87, dist. dir. 1985-86, Otto Jeff Gibson award 1986, Seiji Hiorochi award U.S. Jaycees 1989, mem. U.S. Jaycee Internat. Senate 1989—). Home: 5815 Apple Wood Ln Burke VA 22015-2727 Office: Troy Systems Inc 3701 Pender Dr Ste 500 Fairfax VA 22030-6045

**BELCHER, DENNIS IRL,** lawyer; b. Wheeling, W.Va., Aug. 24, 1951; s. Finley Duncan Belcher and Ellen Jane (Huffman) Good; m. Vickie Marie Early, Aug. 2, 1975; children: Sarah Anne, Matthew Irl, Benjamin Scott. BA, Coll. William and Mary, 1973; JD, U. Richmond, 1976. Bar: Va. 1976, U.S. Tax Ct. 1978. Assoc. McGuire, Woods, Battle & Boothe, Richmond, Va., 1976-83, ptnr., 1983—, mem. exec. com., 1996—; adj. prof. taxation Va. Commonwealth U., Richmond, 1985-88. Co-author: Business Tax Planning Forms for Businesses and Individuals, 1985. Chmn. Richmond chpt. Am. Heart Assn., 1984-85; mem. House of Delegates, 1998-99; mem., bd. trustees St. Christopher's Sch., 1993—. Fellow Am. Coll. Trust and Estate Counsel (bd. regents. 1999—); mem. ABA (real property and probate sect., sec. 1997-98, chmn. marital deduction com., vice chmn. lifetime transfers com., ho. of dels. 1998-99, vice chair probate divsn. 1999—), Va. Bar Assn. (wills and trusts and taxations sects.), Bull and Bear Club, Country Club of Va. Presbyterian. Avocations: golf, farming. Estate taxation, Probate, General corporate. Office: McGuire Woods Battle & Boothe 1 James Ctr 901 East Cary St Richmond VA 23219

**BELDOCK, MYRON,** lawyer; b. N.Y.C., Mar. 27, 1929; s. George J. and Irene (Goldstein) B.; m. Elizabeth G. Pease, June 28, 1953 (div. 1969); children: David, Jennifer, Hannah, Benjamin, Adam Schmalholz; m. Karen L. Dippold, June 19, 1986. BA, Hamilton Coll., 1950; LLB, Harvard U., 1958. Bar: N.Y. 1958, U.S. Dist. Ct. (ea. and so. dists.) N.Y. 1960, U.S. Ct. Appeals (2d cir.) 1960, U.S. Supreme Ct. 1973, U.S. Dist. Ct. (no. dist.) N.Y. 1983, U.S. Ct. Appeals (3d cir.) 1985, U.S. Ct. Appeals (5th cir.) 1992. Asst. U.S. Atty. U.S. Atty's Office, Eastern Dist., N.Y., 1958-60; assoc. Geist, Netter & Marx, N.Y.C., 1960-62; sole practice N.Y.C., 1962-64; ptnr. Beldock Levine & Hoffman LLP, N.Y.C., 1964—. Bd. dirs., v.p. Brotherhood-In-Action, N.Y.C., 1972—; bd. dirs. Brookdale Revolving Fund., N.Y.C., 1973-76. Served with U.S. Army, 1951-54. Mem. Assn. of Bar of City of N.Y. (spl. com. penology 1974-80), N.Y. County Lawyers Assn., Bklyn. Bar Assn., Kings County Criminal Bar Assn., N.Y. County Criminal Bar Assn., N.Y. State Assn. Criminal Def. Lawyers, Nat. Assn. Criminal Def. Lawyers, Nat. Lawyers Guild. Criminal, Civil rights, General civil litigation.

**BELFORT, DAVID ERNST,** lawyer; b. New Port Beach, Calif., July 6, 1970; s. Georges and Marlene Belfort; m. Kimberley Weyl, Aug. 31, 1997. BA, Hobart Coll., 1992; JD, Franklin Pierce Law Ctr., 1996; cert. internat. law, Sheffield U., 1997. Bar: Mass. 1996, U.S. Dist. Ct. Mass. 1996, U.S. Ct. Appeals (D.C. cir.) 1998. Assoc. Law Offices Frank N. Dardeno, Somerville, Mass., 1996—. Mem. Mass. Bar Assn., Boston Bar Assn., Health Care for All (vol., network atty.). Avocations: outdoor activities, politics, chess, basketball, travel. General civil litigation, Labor, Workers' compensation. Office: Law Offices Frank N Dardeno 424 Broadway Somerville MA 02145-2619

**BELIN, DAVID WILLIAM,** lawyer; b. Washington, June 20, 1928; s. Louis I. and Esther (Klass) B.; m. Constance Newman, Sept. 14, 1952 (dec. June 1980); children: Jonathan L., James M., Joy E., Thomas R., Laura R.; m. Barbara Hauben Ross, May 2, 1992. BA, U. Mich., 1951, MBA, 1953, JD, 1954. Bar: Iowa 1954. Ptnr. Herrick & Langdon, 1955-62, Herrick, Langdon, Sandblom & Belin, 1962-66; sr. ptnr. Belin. Harris, Langdon & Helmick, 1966-78, Belin Lamson McCormick Zumbach Flynn, Des Moines, 1978—; trustee Kemper Mut. Funds; bd. dirs. Outdoor Techs. Group; counsel Pres.'s Commn. on the Assassination of President Kennedy (Warren Commn.), 1964; exec. dir. Commn. on CIA Activities within the U.S. (Rockefeller Commn.), 1975; mem. Pres.'s Com. on Arts and the Humanities, 1984-90. Author: November 22, 1963: You Are the Jury, 1973, Final Disclosure: The Full Truth About the Assassination of President Kennedy, 1988, Leaving Money Wisely: Creative Estate Planning for Middle- and Upper-Income Americans for the 1990s, 1990. Bd. dirs. Des Moines Comty. Drama Assn., 1961-64, Des Moines Symphony, 1968-70; mem. adv. bd. Nat. Assn. Gifted Children, 1993—; bd. dirs. Phi Beta Kappa Assocs. With AUS, 1946-47. Recipient Henry M. Bates Meml. award U. Mich. Law Sch., Brotherhood award NCCJ, 1978; hon. orator U. Mich., 1950. Mem. Soc. Barristers, Michigamua Club, Order of Coif, Phi Beta Kappa Assocs., Phi Beta Kappa, Phi Kappa Phi, Delta Sigma Rho, Beta Alpha Psi. Federal civil litigation, General corporate, Estate planning. Home: 666 Walnut St Ste 2000 Des Moines IA 50309-3909 *Knowledge is important because it leads to wisdom, and wisdom is important because it leads to deed.*

**BELINSKY, ILENE BETH,** lawyer; b. Boston, Jan. 30, 1956; d. Harry Lewis and Ann Natalie (Rubin) B. B.A., Simmons Coll., 1977; J.D. cum laude, New Eng. Sch. Law, Boston, 1980. Bar: Mass. 1980, U.S. Dist. Ct. Mass. 1981, U.S. Ct. Appeals (1st cir.) 1981, U.S. Supreme Ct. 1984. Reservitz, Steinberg & Belinsky P.C., Brockton, Mass., 1980-85; ptnr., 1985—; bd. dirs. Southeastern Mass. Legal Assistance Corp., New Bedford, 1982-86. Bd. dirs. Brockton unit Am. Cancer Soc., 1983, 84. Mem. Mass. Bar Assn. (dir. young lawyers div. 1984-86), Mass. Women's Bar Assn., ABA, Plymouth County Bar Assn., Assn. Trial Lawyers Am., Mass. Acad. Trial Lawyers. Republican. Jewish. Personal injury, Family and matrimonial, Criminal. Office: 528 Pleasant St Brockton MA 02301-2515

**BELK, FRED M., JR.,** lawyer; b. Memphis, Aug. 20, 1937; s. Fred McKinney and Letitia Fielding (Ellis) B.; m. Linda Kay Moore, Feb. 3, 1961; children: Fred III, Fielding, Jonathan, Tish Summerlin. BA, U. Miss., 1961, LLB, 1963, JD, 1972. Bar: Miss., Tenn. Mem. Senate State of Miss., 1968-71; pros. atty. Marshall County, Miss., 1976—; master in chancery Miss., 1977-90; chancery judge 18th Chancery Dist., Miss., 1996. Recipient Disting. Svc. award, Jaycees, 1965; named Outstanding Young Men Am. Jaycees, 1968. Mem. Marshall County Bar Assn. (pres. 1978-81), Nat. Dist. Atty. Assn. (state dir. 1982-88), Miss. State Pros. Assn. (past pres.), Marshall County C. of C. (past pres.), Jr. C. of C. (past pres. 1968), Lions (past pres.), Rotary (past pres.). Office: Belk Law Office PO Box 307 Holly Springs MS 38635-0307

**BELL, ALLEN ANDREW, JR.,** lawyer; b. Paris, Ill., June 23, 1951; s. Allen Andrew and Mary Elizabeth (Charley) B.; m. Carol Anne Larson, June 15, 1974; children: Sara Elizabeth, Emily Anne, David Allen, Elizabeth Anne. BA, DePauw U., 1973; JD cum laude, Ind. U.-Indpls., 1980. Bar: Ill. 1980, Ind. 1980, U.S. Dist. Ct. (so. dist.) Ind. 1980, U.S. Dist. Ct. (ctrl. dist.) Ill. 1980, (so. dist.) Ill. 1990, U.S. Ct. Appeals (7th cir.) 1988, U.S. Supreme Ct., 1994. Underwriter Am. States Ins. Co., Indpls., 1973-80; assoc. Dillavou Overaker Asher & Smith, Paris, Ill., 1980-85; ptnr. Ruff, Garst & Bell, Paris, 1985-87, Ruff & Bell, 1987-94, Jones & Jones Law Office, P.C., 1994—; asst. state's atty. Edgar and Clark Counties, 1987; pub. defender Edgar and Clark Counties, 1982-84, 87-91; mem. City of Paris Planning Commn., 1985-94, City of Paris Police Pension Bd., 1988-93; treas. Edgar County Hist. Soc., 1984-87; mem. Wabash Valley coun. Boy Scouts Am., 1994—. Mem. Ill. State Bar Assn., Ind. State Bar Assn., Edgar County Bar Assn. (pres. 1982-83), Comml. Law League, KC. Republican. Catholic. General practice, Bankruptcy, Consumer commercial. Office: PO Box 8 110 E Washington St Paris IL 61944-2257

**BELL, AMY CLIFTON,** lawyer; b. Little Rock, Aug. 2, 1970; d. Mason William and Betty Anne Clifton; m. Carroll Wood Bell III, Sept. 16, 1995. BA, Hendrix Coll., 1992; JD, U. Ark., 1995. Bar: Ark. Assoc. atty. Schieffler Law Firm, West Helena, Ark., 1996—. Mem. Phillips County Bar Assn. (v.p. 1998), Phillips County C. of C. (bd. dirs. 1997-98). Avocations: collecting antiques, reading, baking. Family and matrimonial, General practice. Office: Schieffler Law Firm 426 Plaza West Helena AR 72390-2541

**BELL, ASA LEE, JR.,** lawyer; b. Tarboro, N.C., Sept. 26, 1965; s. Asa Lee Sr. (dec.) and M.R. Bell; m. Angela Ross, Sept. 5, 1992; children: Asa Bell III, Allison Christine. BA, U. N.C., 1987, JD/MBA, 1991. Bar: N.C. 1991, U.S. Dist. Ct. (mid. and ea. dists.) N.C. 1994. Lawyer Fuller, Becton, Slifkin & Bell, Raleigh, N.C., 1991—. Mem. ATLA (gov. 1994-97), N.C. Assn. Black Lawyers (first v.p. 1996-98, pres. 1998—, Lawyer of the Yr. 1997). Personal injury, Condemnation.

**BELL, BRIAN MAYES,** lawyer; b. Columbus, Tex., Aug. 21, 1940; s. Robert Harvey and Edith Virginia (Kimball) B.; m. Karen Ann Roof, May 25, 1962 (div. 1973); m. Charlotte Jean Starks, Dec. 28, 1973 (div. 1980); m. Sue Ann Curry, July 25, 1980; children: Robin L., Susan L., Michael K., Miles A. Franz, Alex F. Franz. BS, So. Meth. U., 1962; JD, U. Denver, 1968. Bar: Colo. 1969, U.S. Dist. Ct. Colo. 1969, U.S. Ct. Appeals (10th cir.) 1969. Assoc. Rovira, DeMuth & Eiberger, Denver, 1968-72; atty., asst. sec. Mountain Bell Tele. Co., Denver, 1972-83; sr. corp. counsel, asst. sec. U.S. West, Inc., Englewood, Colo., 1983-93; adj. prof. U. Colo., Denver, 1974-83; legal cons. 1993—. Mem. ABA, Am. Soc. Corp. Secs. (bd. dirs. 1990-93, pres. Colo. chpt. 1988-89), Am. Corp. Counsel Assn. (bd. dirs. Colo. chpt. 1989-95), Met. Club, Valley Country Club. Republican. Presbyterian. General corporate, Securities. Home: 3233 Country Club Pkwy Castle Rock CO 80104-8300

**BELL, CHARLES D.,** lawyer; b. McKeesport, Pa., Jan. 23, 1923; s. Charles R. and Bertha Beatrice (Davis) B.; m. Mary Porter Wilkin, Mar. 17, 1945 (dec. 1971); children—Betty Bell Williams, Peggy Jean Hrach, Charles William, Julie Bell Caldwell; m. Marjorie Wicks, Mar. 26, 1977. BS in Chemistry, Bethany Coll., 1944; JD, U. Mich., 1949. Bar: W.Va., 1951. Assoc. Schroeder, Merriam, Hofgren & Brady, Chgo., 1950-51, Bell, McMullen, Wellsburg, W.Va., 1951—; asst. pros. atty. Brooke County, Wellsburg, 1960-68, 72-76, 81-90; bd. dirs., sec. Banner Fibreboard Co., Wellsburg. Past bd. dirs. W.Va. Rehab. Found., North Ctrl. region Boy Scouts Am.; mem. W.Va. Ind. Coll. Found., chmn., 1992-95; bd. trustees Bethany Coll., 1976-97, chmn., 1977-97. Served with AUS, 1944-46. Mem. ABA, Brooke County Bar Assn., W.Va. State Bar Assn., Wheeling Country Club, Masons, Elks. Republican. General practice, General civil litigation. Home: 1222 Pleasant Ave Wellsburg WV 26070-1345 Office: Bell McMullen 67 Town Sq Wellsburg WV 26070

**BELL, DERRICK ALBERT,** law educator, author, lecturer; b. Pitts., Nov. 6, 1930; s. Derrick Albert and Ada Elizabeth (Childress) B.; m. Jewel Allison Hairston, June 26, 1960 (dec. Aug. 1990); m. Janet Dewart, June 28, 1992; children: Derrick Albert III, Douglass Dubois, Carter Robeson. AB, Duquesne U., 1952; LLB, U. Pitts., 1957; hon. degree in law, Toogaloo Coll., 1983, Northeastern U., 1985, Mercy Coll., 1988, Allegheny Coll., 1989, Howard U., 1995, Bates Coll., 1997. Bar: D.C. 1957, Pa. 1959, N.Y. State 1966, Calif. 1969. Atty. civil rights div. Dept. Justice, Washington, 1957-59; 1st asst. counsel NAACP Legal Def. Edn. Fund, N.Y.C., 1960-66; dep. dir. Office Civil Rights, HEW, Washington, 1966-68; exec. dir. Western Ctr. on Law and Poverty, 1968-69; lectr. law Harvard U., Cambridge, Mass., 1969-71; prof. law Harvard U., Cambridge, 1971-80, 86-92; dean U. Oreg. Law Sch., 1981-85;, 1991-93; vis. prof. NYU Sch. Law, 1991—, scholar-in-residence, 1993-94. Author: Race, Racism and American Law, 1973, 3d edit., 1992, Shades of Brown: New Perspectives on School Desegregation, 1980, And We Are Not Saved: The Elusive Quest for Racial Justice, 1987, Faces at the Bottom of the Well: The Permanence of American Racism, 1992, Confronting Authority: Reflections of an Ardent Protester, 1994. Mem. gospel choirs Psalms of Survival in an Alien Land Called Home, 1996, Constitutional Conflicts, 1997. 1st lt. USAF, 1952-54. Grantee Ford Found., 1972, 75, 91, 93, 94-96, NEH, 1980-81. Home: 444 Central Park W Apt 14B New York NY 10025-4358 Office: NYU Sch Law 40 Washington Sq S New York NY 10012-1005

**BELL, GREGORY S.,** lawyer; b. Lincoln, Nebr., May 7, 1948; s. Forest O. and Joyce A. Bell; m. Kristine K. Karstens, Sept. 1, 1968; children: Geoffrey, Gretchen. BA, U. Ill., 1970, MEd, 1974, JD, 1975. Bar: Ill. 1975, U.S. Dist. Ct. (cen. dist.) Ill. 1977, U.S. Ct. Appeals (7th cir.) 1980. Law clk. Supreme Ct. Ill., 1975-76; assoc. Swain, Johnson & Gard, Peoria, Ill., 1976-80, ptnr., 1980-83; assoc. Sutkowski & Washkuhn, Peoria, 1983-84, ptnr., 1984; ptnr. Hasselberg, Rock, Bell & Kuppler, Peoria, 1994—; atty. Village of Germantown Hills, Ill., 1982—. Mem. Lincoln Inn of Ct. (Master of Bench 1997—), Phi Beta Kappa, Phi Eta Sigma, Phi Kappa Phi. General civil litigation, Appellate, Municipal (including bonds). Home: 320 W Eagle Nest Rd Dunlap IL 61525-9428 Office: Hasselberg Rock Bell & Kuppler 4600 N Brandywine Dr Ste 200 Peoria IL 61614-5512

**BELL, HARRY FULLERTON, JR.,** lawyer; b. Charleston, W.Va., Nov. 17, 1954; s. Harry Fullerton and Kathryn Laura (Lewis) B. BS in Econs. cum laude, W.Va. U., 1977, JD, 1980. Bar: W.Va. 1980, U.S. Dist. Ct. (so. dist.) W.Va. 1980, U.S. Dist. Ct. (no. dist.) W.Va. 1986, U.S. Ct. Appeals (4th cir.) 1986. Asst. pros. atty. Kanawha County, Charleston, 1980-82; assoc. Kay, Casto, Chaney, Love & Wise, Charleston, 1982-85, ptnr., 1986-92; ptnr. Bell and Assocs., Charleston, 1992—; instr. Marshall U., Huntington, W.Va., 1984-86. Contbr. articles to profl. jours. Pres. fireman's civil svc. commn. City of Charleston, 1985-86; mem. adminstrv. bd. Christ Meth. Ch., Charleston, 1985-87, bd. trustees, 1986-87; bd. dirs. Charleston Civic Ctr., 1987-91, chmn., 1989-91. Mem. W.Va. Bar Assn. (vice chmn. com. on lawyers profl. liability ins. 1984-85, 90—, chmn. 1985-87, young lawyers bd. 1985, cert. merit 1985, young lawyers sect. 1985), Kanawha County Bar Assn. (chmn. courthouse renovation com. 1984-85), Def. Trial Counsel of W.Va., Def. Rsch. Inst., W.Va. U. Alumni Assn. (treas. 1985, v.p. Kanawha County chpt. 1986, pres. 1986-88), Berry Hills Country Club, Beta Gamma Sigma, Omicron Mu Epsilon. Republican. Avocations: sports car racing, flying, golf, tennis, skiing. Federal civil litigation, State civil litigation, Insurance. Home: 1235 Upper Ridgeway Rd Charleston WV 25314-1427 Office: Bell & Assocs PO Box 1723 Charleston WV 25326-1723

**BELL, JAMES FREDERICK,** retired lawyer; b. New Orleans, Aug. 5, 1922; s. George Bryan and Sarah Barr (Perry) B.; m. Jill Cooper Arden, Apr. 14, 1951; children: Bradley Cushing, Sara Perry, Ashley Arden. A.B. cum laude, Princeton U., 1943; LL.B., Harvard U., 1948. Bar: D.C. 1949. Assoc. Pogue & Neal, Washington, 1948-53, ptnr., 1953-88, cons., 1988-89; ret., 1988; gen. counsel Conf. State Bank Suprs., 1951-87. Chmn. com. on canons and other bus. Episcopal Diocese of Washington, 1960-78; pres. Episc. Ctr. for Children, Washington, 1966-67. Lt. USNR, 1943-46. Mem. ABA, D.C. Bar Assn. Home: 2103 R St NW Washington DC 20008-1933 *The fragmentation of human thought into an increasing number of disciplines has proliferated standards of judgment as to the rightness or wrongness of human conduct to a point where consensus as to viable guidelines becomes impossible.*

**BELL, JAMES LEE,** lawyer; b. Tuscaloosa, Ala., July 8, 1947; s. Archie and Margaret B. BA in Internat. Studies, U. S.C., 1970, JD, 1973. Bar: S.C., U.S. Dist. Ct. S.C., Fla., U.S. Tax Ct., U.S. Ct. Appeals (4th, 5th and 11th cirs.), La., U.S. Dist. Ct. (no., so. and mid. dists.) Fla. Sr. ptnr. The Bell Law Firm, P.A., Charleston, S.C.; gen. counsel S.C. Homeowners Assn., Chopstick Theater, Inc.; counsel S.C. Disabled Am. Vets., Tacht Cove, Lowco Concrete Pumping, Inc.. Contbr. articles to profl. jours. Pension, profit-sharing, and employee benefits, Personal injury, Product liability. Office: The Bell Law Firm PA 184 E Bay St Ste 303 Charleston SC 29401-2142

**BELL, JANETTE MOORE,** prosecutor; b. Cleve., June 13, 1965; d. Clyde Lynn and Mary Ann (Wolfram) Moore; m. Steven Paul Bell, May 26, 1989; 1 child, Abigail Evelyn. BS, Miami U., 1987; JD, Cleve.-Marshall Coll. Law, 1990. Asst. prosecuting atty. Lake County Prosecutor's Office, Painesville, Ohio, 1990—; instr. legal rsch. and writing Lakeland Cmty. Coll., Kirtland, Ohio, 1992-93. Home: 47 N Park Pl Painesville OH 44077-3416

**BELL, JASON B.,** lawyer; b. Beardstown, Ill., Feb. 12, 1970; s. Harold and Kay Bell. BA in English, Vanderbilt U., 1992; JD, U. Louisville, 1995. Bar: Ind., Ky., U.S. Dist. Ct. (we. dist.) Ky. Assoc. Fine & Hatfield, Evansville, Ill., 1995-96, Kerrick Grise & Stivers, Elizabethtown, Ky., 1996—. Mem. Leadersip Elizabethtown, Ky., 1996—; trustee Severns Valley Bapt. Ch., Elizabethtown, 1998—. Mem. Ky. Bar Assn., Ky. Def. Counsel. Republican. So. Baptist. Insurance, Personal injury. Home: 1311 Heritage Ct Elizabethtown KY 42701-2046 Office: Kerrick Grise & Stivers 2935 Dolphin Dr Ste 103 Elizabethtown KY 42701-7105

**BELL, JOHN ALTON,** lawyer, judge; b. Greer, S.C., Dec. 1, 1958; s. Dallas Frank Sr. and Una Merle (Gay) B.; m. Vida Ivy, June 30, 1984; children: Luke, Meredith. BA, Carson-Newman Coll., 1980; JD, Memphis State U., 1982. Bar: Tenn. 1983, U.S. Dist. Ct. (we. dist.) Tenn. 1983, U.S. Army Ct. Mil. Rev. 1984, U.S. Ct. Mil. Appeals 1987, U.S. Dist. (ea. dist.) Tenn. 1988. Assoc. Litigation Support, Inc., Memphis, 1983; officer ops. and tng. U.S. Army, Ft. Knox, Ky., 1983-84; legal assistance atty. U.S. Army, Ft. Knox, 1984-86, defense counsel, 1986-87; assoc. King & King, Greeneville, Tenn., 1987-89; ptnr. King, King & Bell, Greeneville and Newport, Tenn., 1989-90, Bell & Bell P.C., Newport, 1990-98; judge Cooke County Sessions and Juvenile Ct., Newport, 1998—; instr. bus. law Sullivan Jr. Coll., Ft. Knox, 1986-87; adj. prof. bus. law Walter State C.C., 1989-90, 97—. Columnist It's The Law, Newport Plain Talk, 1984-85, 89-98. Bd. dirs. Extended Sch. Program, Greeneville, 1988; co-vice chmn. Rep. Com. Cocke County, Tenn., 1989-95. Named Ky. Col., Gov. Ky., 1986. Mem. ABA, Fed. Bar Assn., Tenn. Bar Assn., Assn. Trial Lawyers Am., Judge Advocate Gen.'s Assn. Republican. Baptist. Avocations: sports, church activities. Personal injury, General practice, Military. Office: Cooke County Sessions Ct 111 Court Ave Newport TN 37821-3102

**BELL, JOHN ANDREW,** lawyer; b. Greenfield, Mass., Oct. 10, 1951; s. George E. and Louise A. B. BA in Journalism cum laude, U. Maine, 1974, JD, 1982. Bar: Maine 1982, U.S. Dist. Ct. Maine 1982, N.H. 1986, U.S. Dist. Ct. N.H. 1989. Assoc. Lloyd P. Lafountain, Biddeford, Maine, 1982-84; ptnr. Boone & Bell, Biddeford, Maine, 1984-86; assoc. Green McMahon & Heed, Keene, N.H., 1986-90, ptnr., 1990-98; atty. pvt. practice, Keene, N.H., 1998—. Pres. Samaritans, Keene, 1990-91. Hasler scholar, U. Maine, Portland, 1981. Fellow N.H. Bar Found.; mem. N.H. Lawyers Assn., N.H. Assn. Criminal Def. Attys. Criminal, Personal injury, Family and matrimonial. Office: 41 School St Keene NH 03431-3389

**BELL, JOHN WILLIAM,** lawyer; b. Chgo., May 3, 1946; s. John and Barbara Bell; m. Deborah Bell, Aug. 25, 1974; children: Jason, Alicia. Student, U. So. Calif., 1964-65; BA, Northwestern U., 1968; JD cum laude, Loyola U., Chgo., 1971. Bar: Ill. 1971. Assoc. Kirkland & Ellis, Chgo., 1972-75; ptnr. Johnson & Bell, Ltd. (formerly Johnson, Cusak & Bell, Ltd.), Chgo., 1975—. Mem. ABA (vice chmn. products, gen. liability and consumer law com. sect. tort and ins. practice 1986-87, 88—, com. on torts and ins. practice sect.), Ill. Bar Assn., Chgo. Bar Assn. (tort liability sect., aviation com. 1982—, chmn. med.-legal rels. com. 1994-95), Internat. Assn. Ins. Def. Counsel, Ill. Def. Coun. (faculty mem. trial acad. 1994), Soc. Trial Lawyers Am., Ill. Trial Lawyers Assn., Am. Coll. Trial Lawyers, Fed. Trial Bar. Personal injury, Insurance, General civil litigation.

**BELL, JOSEPH JAMES,** lawyer; b. Kansas City, Mo., Sept. 30, 1947; s. James Joseph and Mary Beatrice (O'Rourke) B. BA in Polit. Sci., U. Nev., Reno, 1969; JD, New Coll. of Calif., San Francisco, 1979. Bar: Calif. 1980, U.S. Dist. Ct. (no.dist.) Calif. 1980, U.S. Dist. Ct. (ea. dist.) Calif. 1981, U.S. Dist. Ct. (ctrl. dist.) Calif. 1988, U.S. Ct. Appeals (9th cir.) 1988. Law clk. Pub. Advocates, Inc., San Francisco, 1977-79, San Francisco Neighborhood Legal Assistance Found. Litigation unit, San Francisco, 1977-79, Law Offices of Thomas E. Horn, 1979-80; supervising atty. Nevada County Legal Assistance, Inc. and Lawyer Referral Svc., 1980-81; pvt. practice Grass Valley, Calif., 1982—; pro tem judge Nevada County Superior Ct., Nevada City, Calif., 1988-91, Nevada County Small Claims Ct., 1989—; lectr. Sierra Coll., Grass Valley, 1997—; bd. govs. dist 1 State Bar of Calif., 1994; mem. family adv. com. Calif. Jud. Coun., 1998—. Bd. dirs. Legal Svcs. No. Calif., Inc., Sacramento, 1981-84; mem. Dem. Ctrl. Com., Nevada County, Calif., 1982-86; vol. firefighter Ophir Hill Fire Dept., pres., 1991-92, bd. dirs., 1993—. Recipient Pro Bono award State Bar Calif., 1982, 87-88. Mem. Nevada County Bar (pres. 1986-87, family law sect., pro tem judge fee arbitration com. 1988—), Sacramento County Bar, Placer County Bar, Sierra Club (Sierra Nevada Group, officer Mother Lode chpt., Conservationist award 1991), Kiwanis. Democrat. Avocations: travel, rafting, skiing, biking, piano. Fax: 530-272-7340. E-Mail: bellslaw@oro.net. Family and matrimonial, State civil litigation, Environmental. Office: 350 Crown Point Cir Ste 250 Grass Valley CA 95945-9524

**BELL, MILDRED BAILEY,** law educator, lawyer; b. Sanford, Fla., June 28, 1928; d. William F. and Frances E. (Williford) Bailey; m. j. Thomas Bell, Jr., Sept. 18, 1948 (div.); children: Tom, Elizabeth, Ansley. AB, U. Ga., 1950, JD cum laude, 1969; LLM in Taxation, N.Y. U., 1977. Bar: Ga. 1969. Law clk. U.S. Dist. Ct. No. Dist. Ga., 1969-70; prof. law Mercer U.,

Macon, Ga., 1970-94; prof. emeritus Mercer U., 1994—; mem. Ga. Com. Constl. Revision, 1978-79. Bd. editors Ga. State Bar Jour., 1974-76; contbr. articles to profl. jours., chpts. in books. Mem. ABA, Ga. Bar Assn., Phi Beta Kappa, Phi Kappa Phi,. Republican. Episcopalian. Home: 615 Laurel Lake Dr Apt A-233 Columbus NC 28722-7420

**BELL, PAUL ANTHONY, II,** lawyer; b. Latrobe, Pa., Mar. 12, 1954; s. Paul Anthony and Marcia Chloe (Martin) B.; m. Arlene Rotella, Aug. 19, 1978; children: Montgomery Vincent, Elyse Maureen, Alexa Marie. AB cum laude, Princeton U., 1975; JD, U. Pitts., 1978. Bar: Pa. 1978, U.S. Dist. Ct. (we. dist.) Pa. 1978. Assoc. Scales and Shaw, Greensburg, Pa., 1978, Laurel Legal Services, Indiana, Pa., 1978-81; sole practice Blairsville, Pa., 1981-88; asst. public defender Indiana County, Pa., 1982-85, asst. dist. atty., 1985-87; ptnr. Simpson, Kablack & Bell, Indiana, Pa., 1987—; bd. dirs. Laurel Legal Services. Pres. Saints Simon and Jude Council, Blairsville, 1982-85; dir. rights com. Torrance (Pa.) State Hosp., 1984-86; dir. Blairsville-Saltburg Sch. Dist., 1996—, pres., 1997—. Mem. ABA, Pa. Bar Assn., Indiana County Bar Assn. (dir. 1995—). Republican. Roman Catholic. Lodge: Rotary. Avocations: golf, bridge, reading, basketball. Real property, Personal injury, Probate. Office: Simpson Kablack & Bell 20 N 7th St Indiana PA 15701-1804

**BELL, PAUL BUCKNER,** lawyer; b. Charlotte, N.C., July 29, 1922; s. George Fisher and Carrie (Savage) B.; m. Betty Sue Trulock, May 3, 1952; children: Paul B., Morris Trulock, Betty Fisher, Douglas Savage. BS, Wake Forest U., 1947, JD cum laude, 1948. Bar: N.C. 1948. Pres. Bell, Seltzer, Park & Gibson, Charlotte, 1948-97; of counsel Alston & Bird LLP, 1998—; dir. Southland Investors Inc., Idlewild Farms, Inc.; pres., dir. Charpat Investment Corp.; lectr. Practising Law Inst., 1974, N.C. Bar, 1985; adj. prof. patent law Wake Forest U. Sch. Law, 1974—; prof. patent law U. N.C. Sch. Law, 1995—. Trustee Mecklenburg Presbytery, Alexander Children's Ctr., Presbyn. Home of Charlotte, Mountain Retreat Assn.; chmn. Presbyn. Ch. Found. Served to 1st lt. USAAF, 1943-46. Mem. ABA, N.C. Bar Assn. (v.p. 1988—), Mecklenburg Bar Assn., Am. Intellectual Property Assn., Licensing Execs. Soc., Federation Internationale Des Conseils Propriete Industrielle (pres. U.S.A.), Charlotte City Club (past pres.), Charlotte Country Club, Charlotte Textile club (past pres.), Grandfather Golf and Country Club, Union League (N.Y.C.), Sigma Phi Epsilon, Phi Alpha Delta. Presbyterian. Federal civil litigation, Patent, Trademark and copyright. Home: 322 S Canterbury Rd Charlotte NC 28211-1838 Office: 1211 E Morehead St Charlotte NC 28204-2816

**BELL, PETER A.,** lawyer; b. Olean, N.Y., May 14, 1955; s. Seth E. and Josephine A. B.; m. Janet L. Wright, Apr. 23, 1983; children: Rebekah L. Eckman, Meegan M. Johnston, Joshua D., Seth C., Joanna M., Petra L. AA, Hillsborough C.C., Tampa, Fla., 1974; BA, U. South Fla., 1976; JD, South Tex. Coll. Law, Houston, 1981. Bar: Fla. 1982, U.S. Dist. Ct. (mid. dist.) Fla. 1990. Assoc. atty. John M. Hathaway, Punta Gorda, Fla., 1982-83; asst. state atty. State Atty.'s Office, Bartow, Fla., 1984-85; atty. in pvt. practice, Punta Gorda, 1986—; chmn. bylaws rev. com. Legal Svcs. of Charlotte County, Punta Gorda, 1990, chmn. legal aid devel. com., 1997-98; hearing officer 20th Jud. Cir., Punta Gorda, 1991-94, gen. master, 1998—. Bd. dirs. Punta Gorda Housing Authority, 1992-96, chmn., 1993-96; mem. coun. Peace Luth. Ch., 1995-98, pres., 1997-98. Mem. Charlotte County Bar Assn. (sec.-treas. 1998—). Achievements include organization and funding of a legal aid office for Charlotte County. Avocations: raising children, coaching youth sports, community choir. Family and matrimonial, Probate, Bankruptcy. Office: 322 Tamiami Trl Ste 20 Punta Gorda FL 33950-4868

**BELL, REBECCA MORGAN,** lawyer; b. Charleston, W.Va., July 6, 1960; d. Richard Lee and Charlotte Ariel (Hager) M.; children: Morgan Alexandra, Zachary John. BA in Psychology, U. W.Va., 1981, JD, 1987. Bar: W.Va. 1987, U.S. Dist. Ct. (no. and so. dist.) W.Va. 1987. Pvt. practice Princeton, W.Va., 1987-91; assoc. Bell & Griffith L.C., Princeton, 1991—. Personal injury, Family and matrimonial, Criminal. Office: Bell & Griffith LC 1625 N Walker St Princeton WV 24740-2624

**BELL, RICHARD G.,** lawyer; b. Billings, Mont., Sept. 16, 1947; s. George A.W. and Mary Helen (Sharp) B.; m. Linda Carol Riggs, June 21, 1969; children: Stephen, Geoffrey. AB, Stanford U., 1969; JD, U. Calif., San Francisco, 1972. Bar: Calif.; U.S. Supreme Ct., 1990; U.S. Ct. Appeals Calif. (9th cir.) 1973; U.S. Dist. Ct. Calif. (no. dist., 1972, cen. dist., 1976). Assoc. Finch, Sauers, Player & King, Palo Alto, Calif., 1972-76; ptnr. Finch, Sauers, Player & Bell, Palo Alto, 1976-83; gen. counsel Watkins-Johnson Co., Palo Alto, 1983-90; v.p., gen. counsel Watkins-Johnson Co., 1990-97; ptnr. Corp. Advisory Law Group, Los Altos, Calif., 1998—. Bd. dirs. Family Svc. Assn., Palo Alto, 1981-87; trustee Mountain View Los Altos Union H.S. Dist., 1990-98; pres. bd. Los Altos Conservatory Theater, 1991-95. Mem. ABA, Calif. Bar Assn., Santa Clara County Bar Assn., Palo Alto Area Bar Assn. Republican. Episcopalian. General corporate, Government contracts and claims, Labor. Office: Corp Adv Law Group 40 Main St Los Altos CA 94022-2902

**BELL, ROBERT CHARLES,** lawyer; b. St. Paul; s. Charles N. and Esther C. (Carlsten) B.; m. Carmen Florence Anderson, Sept. 10, 1954; children: Caroline Florence Beckman, Alison McGinnity. BSc, U. Minn., 1949, LLB, 1950. Bar: Minn. 1951, U.S. Dist. Ct. Minn. 1953, U.S. Ct. Appeals (8th cir.) 1990. Ptnr. Robins, Davis & Lyons, St. Paul, 1953-61, Peterson, Bell & Converse, St. Paul, 1962—; city atty. City of Roseville, Minn., 1968—. With U.S. Army, 1944-46, PTO. Mem. ABA, Minn. State Bar Assn.; mem. Minn. Ho. of Reps., St. Paul, 1967-74. Avocations: golf, hunting, fishing, forestry. General civil litigation, Insurance, Municipal (including bonds). Home: 807 Heinel Dr Roseville MN 55113 Office: Petersen Bell & Converse 30 7th St E Saint Paul MN 55101-4914

**BELL, ROBERT CHRISTOPHER,** lawyer; b. Abilene, Tex., Nov. 23, 1959; s. Peter Frank Arundel and Dorothy (Hyde) B.; m. Burkely Wells, July 13, 1987 (div. apr. 1988); m. Alison Ayres, Nov. 14, 1992; children: Atlee Christopher, Connally Ayres. BJ in Journalism, U. Tex., 1982; JD, South Tex. Coll. Law, 1992. Bar: Tex. 1992, U. S. Dist. Ct. (so. dist.) Tex. 1992. Reporter, photographer Sta. KXII-TV, Ardmore, Okla., 1982-83; reporter, anchorperson Sta. KVII-TV, Amarillo, 1983-88; rerter Sta. KTRH Radio, Houston, 1989-91; law clk. Hinton, Sussman & Bailey, Houston, 1991-92; assoc. Alexander & McEvily, Houston, 1992-93; pvt. practice Houston, 1993-95; ptnr. Bell & Henry LLP, Houston, 1995—. Mem. govt. rels. bd. United Way, Houston, 1998—; mem. adv. bd. Trees for Houston, Houston, 1997—; mem. Houston City Coun., 1997—; vol. Houston Taping for the Blind, 1991—; bd. dirs. Big Bros./Big Sisters, Houston, 1996—. Democrat. Episcopalian. Avocations: tennis, running, writing, reading. Securities, General civil litigation, Criminal. Home: 4103 Underwood St Houston TX 77025-1719 Office: Bell & Henry LLP 3212 Smith St Ste 100 Houston TX 77006-6622

**BELL, ROBERT HOLMES,** federal judge; b. Lansing, Mich., Apr. 19, 1944; s. Preston C. and Eileen (Holmes) B.; m. Helen Mortensen, June 28, 1968; children: Robert Holmes Jr., Ruth Eileen, Jonathan Neil. BA, Wheaton Coll., 1966; JD, Wayne State U., 1969. Bar: Mich. 1970, U.S. Dist. Ct. (we. dist.) Mich. 1970. Asst. prosecutor Ingham County Prosecutor's Office, Lansing, Mich., 1969-72; state dist. judge Mich. State Cts., 1973-78; state cir. judge Mich. State Cts., Mason, 1979-87; judge U.S. Dist. Ct. Mich., Grand Rapids, Mich., 1987—. Office: US Dist Ct 411 Fed Bldg 110 Michigan St NW Grand Rapids MI 49503-2363

**BELL, ROBERT M.,** judge; b. Rocky Mount, N.C., July 6, 1943. AB with honors, Morgan State Coll., 1966; JD, Harvard U., 1969. Bar: Md. 1969. Judge Md. Dist. Ct. Dist. 1, Balt., 1975-79; former judge Cir. Ct. Md. 8th Jud. Cir.; assoc. judge Md. Ct. Spl. Appeals, 1980-91; assoc. judge Md. Ct. Appeals, Balt., 1991-96, chief judge, 1996—. Mem. ABA, Nat. Bar Assn., Md. State Bar Assn., Inc., Bar Assn. Balt. City, Monumental City Bar Assn. Office: Court of Appeals 634 Courthouse East 111 N Calvert St Baltimore MD 21202-1904 Office: Court of Appeals 361 Rowe Blvd Annapolis MD 21401-1672*

**BELL, ROBERT MORRALL,** lawyer; b. Graniteville, S.C., Feb. 15, 1936; s. Jonathan F. and Ruby Lee (Carpenter) B.; m. Cecelia Richardson Coker, June 11, 1965 (dec.). AB, U. S.C., 1958, LLB, 1965. Bar: S.C. 1965, U.S. Dist. Ct. S.C. 1965, U.S. Ct. Appeals (4th cir.) 1970. With Watkins, Vandiver, Kirven & Long, Anderson, S.C., 1965-67; sr. law clk. to chief judge U.S. Dist. Ct. S.C., Greenville, 1967-69; mem. Abram, Bowen & Townes, Greenville, 1969-71, Bell, Surasky and Anderson, P.A., Langley, S.C., 1971-76, sr. ptnr., 1976—; county atty. Aiken County (S.C.), 1982—. Mem. S.C. Hwy. Commn., 1982-86; state exec. committeeman S.C. Dem. Com., 1980-86; mem. S.C. Bd. Chiropractic Examiners, 1978-80; mem. Svc. Coun. of Aiken County, 1976-82, Aiken County Planning Commn., 1976-80, Chmn. Aiken County Transportation Com., 1993-96; bd. dirs. Aiken County Crippled Children's Soc., 1976-82, Gregg-Graniteville Found., 1984—, chmn., 1998—; del. gen. & jurisdictional confs. United Meth. Ch., 1988-92. With USAR, 1959-60. Mem. ABA, ATLA, Aiken County Bar Assn., S.C. Bar Assn., S.C. Trial Lawyers Assn., Masons, Shriners, Kappa Sigma Kappa, Tau Kappa Alpha, Phi Delta Phi, Chi Psi. Democrat. Methodist. Personal injury, Workers' compensation. Office: Bell Surasky and Anderson PA PO Box 1890 2625 Jefferson Davis Hwy Langley SC 29834

**BELL, SAMUEL H.,** federal judge; b. Rochester, N.Y., Dec. 31, 1925; s. Samuel H. and Marie C. (Williams) B.; m. Joyce Elaine Shaw, 1948 (dec.): children: Henry W., Steven D.; m. Jennie Lee McCall, 1983. BA, Coll. Wooster, 1947; JD, U. Akron, 1952. Pvt. practice Cuyahoga Falls, Ohio, 1956-68; asst. pros. atty. Summit County, Ohio, 1956-58; judge Cuyahoga Falls Mcpl. Ct., Ohio, 1968-73, Ct. of Common Pleas, Akron, Ohio, 1973-77, Ohio Ct. Appeals, 9th Jud. Dist., Akron, 1977-82, U.S. Dist. Ct. (no. dist.) Ohio, Akron, 1982—; adj. prof. Coll. Wooster; adj. prof., adv. bd. U. Akron Sch. Law, past trustee Dean's club; bd. dirs. Jos. R. Miller Found. Coauthor: Federal Practice Guide 6th Cir., 1996. Recipient Disting. Alumni award U. Akron, 1988, St. Thomas More award, 1987. Fellow Akron Bar Found. (trustee 1989-94, pres. 1993-94); mem. Fed. Bar Assn., Ohio Bar Assn., Akron Bar Assn., Fed. Judges Assn. (bd. dirs.), Akron U. Sch. Law Alumni Assn. (Disting. Alumni award 1983), Charles F. Scanlon Akron Inn Ct. (pres. 1990-92), Ohio Hist. Soc., Supreme Ct. Hist. Soc., Akron City Club, Masons, Phi Alpha Delta. Republican. Presbyterian. Office: US Dist Ct 526 Fed Bldg & US Courthouse 2 S Main St Akron OH 44308-1813

**BELL, STEVEN DENNIS,** lawyer; b. Akron, Ohio, Feb. 11, 1953; s. Sam H. and Joyce E. (Shaw) B.; m. E. Jane White (div. Feb. 1995); children: Colleen, Patrick. BA, U. Notre Dame, 1975; JD, U. Akron, 1978. Bar: Ohio 1979, D.C. 1989, U.S. Dist. Ct. (no. dist.) Ohio 1980, U.S. Ct. Appeals (6th cir.) 1980, U.S. Ct. Appeals (D.C. cir.) 1987, U.S. Supreme Ct. 1989, U.S. Dist. Ct. (so. dist.) Ohio 1990, U.S. Dist. Ct. (ea. dist.) Mich. 1996. Pvt. practice Akron, 1979-81; chief trial atty. City of Akron, 1981-84; asst. U.S. atty. no. dist. Ohio U.S. Atty.'s Office, Cleve., 1984-88, chief civil divsn., 1986-88, chief appellate litigation, 1987; ptnr. Janik & Bell, Cleve., 1988-91, Ulmer & Berne LLP, Cleve., 1991—. Mem. ABA, Ohio State Bar Assn., Nat. Health Lawyers Assn. Federal civil litigation, Criminal, Environmental. Office: Bond Ct Bldg 1300 E 9th St Lbby 9 Cleveland OH 44114-1503

**BELL, STEWART LYNN,** lawyer; b. L.A., Feb. 6, 1945; s. Jack C. and Kathryn Arline (Winn) B.; m. Karen Virginia Davis, Dec. 23, 1966 (div. Feb. 1974); 1 child, Linda Marie; m. Jeanne Dorothy Brick, June 8, 1974; children: Kristin Denise, Stephen Jeffrey, Gregory Matthew. BS, U. Nev., Las Vegas, 1967; JD, UCLA, 1970. Bar: Calif. 1970, Nev. 1971, U.S. Dist. Ct. Nev. 1971, U.S. Dist. Ct. (cen. dist.) Calif. 1973, U.S. Supreme Ct. 1976, U.S. Ct. Appeals (9th cir.) 1990. Legal asst. to Hon. Judge Howard W. Babcock 8th Judicial Dist. Ct., Nev., 1970-71; lawyer Clark County Pub. Defender's Office, Nev., 1971-72; sr. ptnr. Bell, Leavitt & Greer, Chtd., 1974-83, Stewart L. Bell, Chtd., Las Vegas, Nev., 1983-89, Bell & Davidson, Nev., 1990-94; dist. atty. Clark County Dist. Atty. Office, Nev., 1995—; alt. judge City of North Las Vegas, 1981-88; coroner's inquest judge Clark County, 1979—; referee Juvenile Ct., 1988—; mental commitment judge, 1981—; small claims judge, 1990—. Mem. ABA, Assn. Trial Lawyers Am., Nev. Bar Assn. (bd. govs. 1981-92, v.p. 1989-90, pres. elect 1990-91, pres. 1991-92), Nev. Trial Lawyers Assn., Clark County Bar Assn. (sec. 1978, v.p. 1979, pres. 1980), State Bar Calif., Nat. Dist. Atty's Assn. (bd. dirs. 1995—, child support enforcement com. 1995—, juvenile justice adv. com. 1995—, metropolitan prosecutors com. 1995—, co-chmn. 1996—), Nev. Dist. Atty's Assn., Nev. Adv. Coun. Prosecuting Atty's. Democrat. Lodge: Elks. Criminal, Personal injury. Office: 601 Bridger Ave Las Vegas NV 89101-5805

**BELL, TROY NATHAN,** lawyer; b. New Orleans, Sept. 5, 1962; s. Robert Marshall Jr. and Geraldine (Johnson) B. BA in Polit. Sci., Loyola U., 1985; JD, So. U., 1990. Bar: La. 1990, U.S. Dist. Ct. (ea., mid., we. dists.) La. 1990. Dep. clerk bailiff U.S. Ct. Appeals 5th Cir., New Orleans, 1985-86; teaching asst. Coun. on Legal Edn., Columbia, Mo., 1987; law clerk Barbara Harris Pape, P.C., Columbia, 1987-88, Cobb and Cobb, Baton Rouge, La., 1989-90; assoc. atty. Carter and Cates, New Orleans, 1991-93; law clk. to Justice Revius Ortique Supreme Ct., La., 1994; assoc. atty. Aultman, Tyner, McNeese, & Laird, 1994-98; ptnr. Aultman Tyner Ruffin & Yarborough, New Orleans, 1998—. Speaker Orleans Parish Sch. Vols., New Orleans, 1990—; mentor Boys to Men, New Orleans, 1992—. Recipient scholarship Mortimer Rosecan Found., 1986-88, Circardo award for best law rev. article Circardo Found., 1989-90. Fellow Coun. Legal Edn. Opportunities; mem. La. State Bar Assn. (minority involvement and labor law coms.), Nat. Coll. Advocacy (advocate). Toxic tort, Product liability, General civil litigation.

**BELL, VENETIA DARLENE,** lawyer, associate; b. Bklyn., 1959. BA, Calif. State U., Stanislaus, Turlock, 1981, MA with distinction, 1984; JD with honor, U. Md., Balt., 1996. Bar: Md. 1997, U.S. Dist. Ct. Md. 1997, U.S. Ct. Appeals (D.C. cir.) 1998, U.S. Ct. Appeals (4th cir.) 1999. Social worker Washoe City Dept. Social Svcs., Sparks, Nev., 1990-94; law clk. Howard County Cir. Ct., Ellicott City, Md., 1993-94; atty. Ober, Kaler, Grimes & Shriver, Balt., 1997—; mem. ctrl. Md. regional adv. bd., Md. Alternative Dispute Resolution Commn., 1998; mediator Balt. County Cir. Ct. Named Pro Bono Atty. of Month, Bar Assn. Balt. City, Balt., Feb., 1998. Mem. ABA, ATLA. Alternative dispute resolution, State civil litigation, Labor. Office: Ober Kaler Grimes & Shriver 120 E Baltimore St Ste 800 Baltimore MD 21202-1643

**BELL, WAYNE STEVEN,** lawyer; b. L.A., June 24, 1954; s. Joseph and Jane Barbara (Barsook) B.; m. M. Susan Modzelewski, Apr. 1, 1989; 1 child, Seth Joseph Bell. BA magna cum laude, UCLA, 1976; JD, Loyola U., L.A., 1979; Advanced Mgmt. Program, Rutgers U., 1992. Bar: Calif. 1980, U.S. Dist. Ct. (cen. dist.) 1981, U.S. Tax Ct. 1981, U.S. Ct. Appeals (9th cir.) 1981, U.S. Dist. Ct. (so. and no. dists.) Calif. 1983, U.S. Supreme Ct. 1984, D.C. 1986, Tex. 1995; lic. real estate broker, Calif. Intern office of gov. State of Calif., Sacramento, summer 1976; assoc. Levinson, Rowen, Miller, Jacobs & Kabrins, L.A., 1980-82; sr. assoc. Montgomery, Gascou, Gemmill & Thornton, L.A., 1982-84; counsel, project developer Thomas Safran & Assocs., L.A., 1984-85; of counsel Greenspan, Glasser & Medina, Santa Monica, Calif., 1984-86; assoc. gen. counsel Am. Diversified Cos., Costa Mesa, Calif., 1985-88; legal cons. Project Atty., L.A., 1988-89; sr. counsel, asst. sec. Ralphs Grocery Co., L.A., 1989-99, v.p., sr. counsel, asst. sec., 1999—; judge pro tem Mcpl. Ct. South Bay Jud. Dist., 1987, L.A. Superior Ct., 1991, 94, 97; settlement officer L.A. Mcpl. Ct., Settlement Officer Program, 1990-92; spl. master State Bar Calif., 1991-92. Chief note and comment editor Loyola U. Law Rev., 1978-79; contbr. articles to profl. jours. and gen. pubs. Vol. atty. Westside Legal Svcs., Santa Monica, 1982-87; legal ombudsman Olympics Ombudsman Program L.A. County Bar Assn., 1984; gov. apptd. mem. Calif. adv. coun. Legal Svcs. Corp., 1982-88, Autism Soc. Am., Amnesty Internat.; contbg. mem. Dem. Nat. Com.; mem. leadership coun. So. Poverty Law Ctr.; charter mem. presdl. task force Ams. for Change; bd. dirs. Am. Theatre Arts, Hollywood, Calif., 1983-84; pres., exec. com., bd. dirs. Programs for the Developmentally Handicapped, Inc., L.A., 1987-92; chmn. bd. appeals handicapped accommodations City of Manhattan Beach, 1986-88; bd. dirs. The Foodbank of So. Calif., 1991-94, sec., 1993; legal oversight com. Legal Corps L.A., 1995-97; sec. bd. trustees The Ralphs/Food 4 Less Found., 1995—; vol. L.A. County Bar Assn., Barristers Homeless Shelter Advocacy Project, 1996—. Mem. Calif. Bar Assn. (legal svcs. sect. standing com. legal problems of aging 1983-86, chmn. legis. subcom. 1984-86, conf. dels. alternate 1987), D.C. Bar Assn. (real estate sect. on comml. real estate), Legal Assistance Assn. Calif. (bd. dirs., mem. exec. com., legis. strategy com. 1984-86), Loyola Law Sch. (advocate), Los Angeles County Bar Assn. (mem. exec. com. labor and employment law sect. 1997-99). Democrat. Avocations: sailing, hiking, human behavior study, photography, travel. General corporate, Labor, State civil litigation. Office: Ralphs Grocery Co PO Box 54143 Los Angeles CA 90054-0143

**BELL, WILLIAM HALL,** lawyer; b. Greeneville, Tenn., July 16, 1951; s. Charles B. and Peggy (Hall) B.; m. Ellen Bell, July 3, 1981; children: Burnley, Bethany. BA in Psychology, BA in Polit. Sci. with honors, U. Tenn., 1975, JD, 1978; LLM, Cambridge (Eng.) U., 1979; cert. d'Assiduite, Hague (The Netherlands) Acad. Internat. Law, 1984. Bar: Tenn 1978, U.S. Dist. Ct. Tenn. 1980. Ptnr. Bell & Mills, Greeneville, 1979—; adv. com. Macro Engrng. Group, MIT Sch. Engrng.; co-counsel on Macro-Engrng. Law, Internat. Law Collaborative, Cambridge, Mass.; legal advisor to solicitor-at-law in Cambridge U., Eng., 1978-79; law lectr. Cambridge Inst. Arts and Techs., 1978-79. Mem. Tenn. Trial Lawyers Assn. (bd. dirs.), Greeneville Bar Assn. (pres.). Private international, Public international, General corporate. Office: 114 S Main St Greeneville TN 37743-9490

**BELL, WILLIAM WOODWARD,** lawyer; b. May 15, 1938; s. Charles Smith and Janie Mae (Woodward) B.; m. Mary Elizabeth Beniteau, May 31, 1969; children: Susan Elizabeth, Carol Ann. BBA, Baylor U., 1960, JD, 1965. Bar: U.S. Dist. Ct. (we. dist.) Tex. 1967, U.S. Supreme Ct. 1971. Ptnr. Sleeper, Boynton, Burleson, Williams & Johnson, Waco, Tex., 1965-68, Holloway, Slagle & Bell, Brownwood, 1968-71, Johnson, Slagle & Bell, Brownwood, 1971-74; pvt. practice Brownwood, 1974-80; atty. City of Brownwood, 1980-99; ptnr. Bell and Ellis, Brownwood, 1980-89, Bell, Franklin & Morelock and Investment Co., Brownwood, 1962-86. Capt. USMC, 1960-63. Named Vol., 1991, Developer of Yr., Tex. Indsl. Devel. Coun. Fellow Tex. Bar Found.; mem. Tex. Bar Assn. (chmn. dist. 15B grievance com. 1986-87), Brown County Bar Assn., Am. Judicature Soc., Phi Alpha Delta. Baptist. General practice, State civil litigation. Home: PO Box 1564 Brownwood TX 76804-1564 Office: PO Box 1726 Brownwood TX 76804-1726

**BELLAC, PATRICIA SHARMAN,** lawyer; b. N.Y.C., May 8, 1961; d. Alphonse Heinz and Doreen (Prete) B.; m. Jonathan L. Kates, May 26, 1990; children: Benjamin, Daniel, Gregory. BA, McGill U., 1983; JD, Fordham U., 1991. Bar: N.J. 1991, Colo. 1993. Employee benefits cons. Alexander & Alexander Consulting Group, N.Y.C., 1986-87; paralegal Proskaver, Rose, Goetz & Mendelsohn, N.Y.C., 1987-89; summer assoc. atty. Carpenter, Bennett & Morrissey, Newark, 1990, atty., 1991-93; atty. Berenbaum, Weinshienk & Eason, P.C., Denver, 1993-98, Jung & Assocs., P.C., Boulder, 1998—. Bd. dirs. NOW (dir. fundraising and programs, N.Y.C., 1986-91). Mem. Colo. Bar Assn., Denver Bar Assn., Colo. Women's Bar Assn. Avocations: skiing, hiking, swimming, running. General civil litigation, Labor, Pension, profit-sharing, and employee benefits. Home: 4566 Robinson Pl Boulder CO 80301-3143

**BELLACOSA, JOSEPH W.,** state supreme court justice; b. Bklyn., Sept. 1, 1937; s. Frank and Antoinette Bellacosa; m. Mary Bellacosa; children: Michael, Peter, Barbara. BA in English, St. John's U., 1959, LLB, 1961. Bar: N.Y. 1961. With N.Y. Life Ins. Co., 1961-63; law asst., law sec. to Hon. Marcus G. Christ N.Y. Cts. Appellate Divsn., 1963-70; assoc. prof. law St. John's U., 1970-75, asst. dean academics and admissions, 1970-73; prof. law, dir. govt. law ctr. Union U., 1970-75, 83-85; chief clk., counsel N.Y. Ct. Appeals, 1975-83; judge N.Y. Ct. Claims, 1985-87; chief adminstrv. judge N.Y. State Cts., 1985-87; assoc. judge N.Y. Ct. Appeals, Albany, 1987—; vis. prof. St. John's U., 1979-83; chmn. N.Y. State Sentencing Guidelines Com., 1983-85; mem. Chief Judge's Media Adv. Com. on TV and Cts. Author: Criminal Procedure Law of the State of New York, 1974-85; assoc. editor St. John's Law Rev. Mem. Albany chpt. Fund for Modern Cts. Bd. and Strategic Planning Com. City of Albany; communicant, law scripture reader, lay eucharistic min. St. Madeleine Sophie, Guilderland, N.Y. Mem. Am. Law Inst., Assn. of Bar of City of N.Y. (arbitration com. 1965-69, ethics com. 1969-73), N.Y. State Bar Assn. (criminal justice sect., Outstanding Contbn. to Criminal Justice Edn. criminal justice sect. 1981). Office: NY Ct of Appeals Court of Appeals Hall 20 Eagle St Albany NY 12207-1009*

**BELLAH, C. RICHARD,** lawyer; b. San Antonio, Jan. 11, 1955; s. Max and Charlotte (Arant) B.; m. Erin P. Jones, Oct. 1987. BS in Gen. Bus. Adminstrn., Ariz. State U., 1977; JD, U. Ariz., 1980. Bar: U.S. Dist. Ct. Ariz. 1980, U.S. Ct. Appeals (9th cir.) 1981, U.S. Tax Ct. 1985, U.S. Supreme Ct. 1985. Law clk. to presiding justice Ariz. Supreme Ct., Phoenix, 1980-81; assoc. Crotts & Laird, Phoenix, 1981-82; ptnr. Charles, Smith & Bellah, Glendale, Ariz., 1982-86; pvt. practice Glendale, 1986-88; ptnr. Bellah & Harrian, Glendale, 1988—; councilman City of Glendale, 1984-92, vice mayor, 1991-92; justice of peace pro tem Maricopa County Justice Ct., Glendale, 1985-90. Committeeman precinct Maricopa County Reps.; bd. dirs. Glendale Youth Ctr., Faith House Women's Shelter, Fiesta Bowl, Phoenix Christian H.S., 1993—; mem. fin. com. and policy com. N.W. Cmty. Christian Sch.; deacon Bapt. Ch. Recipient Outstanding Service award Am. Legion, 1979, Cert. of Appreciation Ariz. State Legis., 1979, Maricopa Services Commn., 1985, Phoenix of Realtors, 1985, Soroptimist Internat., 1985, City of Glendale, 1985, Glendale Sr. Ctr., 1986. Mem. ATLA, ABA (Silver Key award 1979), Ariz. Bar Assn., Ariz. Trial Lawyers Assn., Phi Alpha Delta (chpt. justice, vice justice alumni assn.), Sigma Phi Epsilon (Hall of Honor). Avocation: jogging. Family and matrimonial, General practice, Juvenile. Home: 6301 W Aster Dr Glendale AZ 85304-1638 Office: Bellah and Harrian 5622 W Glendale Ave Glendale AZ 85301-2525

**BELLAH, KENNETH DAVID,** lawyer; b. Aug. 17, 1955; s. Virgil and Joyce (Allen) B. BA, Augustana Coll., 1977; JD Chgo. Kent Coll. Law, Ill. Inst. Tech., 1980. Bar: Ill. 1980, U.S. Dist. Ct. (no. dist.) Ill. 1980, U.S. Ct. Appeals (7th cir.) 1980. Assoc. Matthias & Matthias, Chgo., 1980-83; ptnr. Matthais & Bellah, Chgo., 1983-99, Fox and Grove, Chartered, Chgo., 1999—; lawyer; b. Joliet, Ill., Aug. 17, 1955; s. Virgil and Joyce (Allen) B.; m. Lori Ann Piazza, Nov. 26, 1983. B.A., Augustana Coll., 1977; J.D., Chgo. Kent Coll. Law, Ill. Inst. Tech., 1980. Bar: Ill. 1980, U.S. Dist. Ct. (no. dist.) Ill. 1980, U.S. Ct. Appeals (7th cir.) 1980. Assoc. Matthias & Matthias, Chgo., 1980-83; ptnr. Matthias & Bellah, Chgo., 1983—. Republican. Methodist. State civil litigation, Federal civil litigation, Insurance. Office: Fox and Grove Chartered 311 S Wacker Dr Ste 6200 Chicago IL 60606-6695

**BELLAMY, WERTEN F. W., JR.,** lawyer; b. Washington, Sept. 22, 1964. AB, Princeton U., 1986; JD, U. Va., 1989. Bar: Pa. 1990. Sr. atty. Merck & Co., Inc., Whitehouse Sta., N.J.; sr. counsel Genetics Inst. Am. Home Products. 1st Lt. USAR, 1986. Mem. ABA (mem. sect. natural resources, energy, environ. law), Nat. Assn. Securities Profls., Pa. Bar Assn. (mem. sect. natural resources, energy, environ. law). General corporate. Office: Am Home Products Genetics Inst 87 Cambridge Park Dr Cambridge MA 02140*

**BELLAS, GEORGE STEVEN,** lawyer; b. Chgo., May 8, 1948; s. Steven C. and Demetra Bellas; m. Linda M. Boznos. BS in Psychology, Loyola U., 1971, JD, 1973. Asst. state's atty. Will County State's Atty., Joliet, Ill., 1973-75; assoc. Law Offices of Joseph Singer, Joliet, 1975-76, Murges & Johnson, Chgo., 1976-78; ptnr. Bellas & Murray, Chgo., 1978-80; assoc. Sidney Kleinman, Ltd., Chgo., 1980-82; prin. George Bellas & Assocs., Chgo., 1982-90, Bellas & Wachowski, Des Plaines, Ill., 1990—. Mem. ATLA, N.W. Suburban Bar Assn. (pres. 1990-91), Des Plaines C. of C. (dir. 1996-98). Contracts commercial, General civil litigation, Probate. Office: Bellas & Wachowski 1550 N Northwest Hwy Park Ridge IL 60068-1411

**BELLER, GARY A.,** lawyer, insurance company executive; b. N.Y.C., Oct. 16, 1938; s. Charles W. and Jeanne A. B.; m. Carole P. Wrubel, Nov. 22, 1967; 1 child, Jessie Melissa. BA, Cornell U., 1960; LLB, NYU, 1963, LLM, 1971. Bar: N.Y. 1963. Various positions gen. counsel's office Am. Express Co., N.Y.C., 1968-82, exec. v.p. and gen. counsel, 1983-94; exec. v.p., chief legal officer Met. Life Ins. Co., N.Y.C., 1995—. Bd. dirs. Lenox Hill Neighborhood Assn.; bd. dirs., chmn. Citizens' Crime Commn. N.Y. Mem. ABA, Assn. Bar City N.Y. General corporate. Office: Met Life Ins Co 1 Madison Ave Ste 10A New York NY 10010-3642*

**BELLER, HERBERT N.,** lawyer; b. Ill., 1943. BSBA, Northwestern U., 1964, JD cum laude, 1967. Bar: Ill. 1967, D.C. 1969; CPA, Ill. Law clk. to Hon. Theodore Tannenwald, Jr. U.S. Tax Ct., 1967-68; ptnr. Sutherland, Asbill & Brennan, Washington; adj. prof. law Georgetown U., Washington, 1972-81. Editor-in-chief: The Tax Lawyer, 1993-96. Mem. ABA (mem. sect. taxation, vice chair 1993-96, mem. coun. 1989-92, liaison to Am. Law Inst. fed. income tax project on integration of individual and corp. income taxes 1990—, chmn. govt. submissions com. 1988-89, chmn. closely held corps. com. 1981-83), Am. Coll. Tax Counsel, D.C. Bar Assn., Ill. State Bar Assn. Office: Sutherland Asbill & Brennan LLP 1275 Pennysylvania Ave NW Washington DC 20004

**BELLEVILLE, PHILIP FREDERICK,** lawyer; b. Flint, Mich., Apr. 24, 1934; s. Frederick Charles and Sarah (Adelaine) B.; m. Geraldean Bickford, Sept. 2, 1953; children—Stacy L., Philip Frederick II, Jeffrey A. BA in Econs. with high distinction and honors, U. Mich., 1956, J.D., 1960, MS in Psychology CCU, 1997. Bar: Calif. 1961. Assoc. Latham & Watkins, LA., 1960-68; ptnr. Latham & Watkins, L.A. and Newport Beach, Calif., 1968-98; ptnr., chmn. litigation dept. Latham & Watkins, L.A. and Newport Beach, 1973-80; ptnr. Latham & Watkins, L.A., Newport Beach, San Diego, Washington, 1980-98, Chgo., 1983-98, N.Y.C., 1985-98, London and San Francisco, 1990-98, Moscow, 1992-98, Hong Kong, 1995-98, Tokyo, 1995-98, Singapore, 1997-98, Silicon Valley, 1997-98. Asst. editor Mich. Law Rev., Ann Arbor, 1959-60. Past mem. So. Calif. steering com. NAACP Legal Def. Fund, Inc., L.A.; mem. cmty. adv. bd. San Pedro Peninsula Hosp., Calif., 1980-88. James B. Angell scholar U. Mich., 1955-56. Mem. ABA (antitrust and trade regulation and bus. law sects.), L.A. County Bar Assn. (bus. trial lawyers sect.), Assn. Bus. Trial Lawyers, Order of Coif, Portuguese Bend (Calif.) Club, Palos Verdes (Calif.) Golf Club, Caballeros, Phi Beta Kappa, Phi Kappa Phi, Alpha Kappa Psi. Republican. Avocations: antique and classic autos, public service, sports, art, antiques. Federal civil litigation, State civil litigation, Antitrust. Office: Latham & Watkins 633 W 5th St Ste 4000 Los Angeles CA 90071-2005

**BELLHOUSE, CAROL,** lawyer; b. Brantford, Ont., Can., Oct. 14, 1953; came to U.S., 1960, naturalized, 1980; d. Gerald LaVerne and Irma (Vansickle) Bellhouse; m. James K. Horstman, July 2, 1980 (div.); children: Whitney Sarah, Michael Andrew. BA, Wesleyan U., 1976; JD, Washington U., St. Louis, 1980. Bar: Ill. 1981, U.S. Dist. Ct. (cen. dist.) Ill. 1981, Colo. 1991. Assoc. Costello, Young & Metnik, Springfield, Ill., 1980-82; sole practice Springfield, 1982—. Office: PO Box A Leadville CO 80461-1017

**BELLINGER, EDGAR THOMSON,** lawyer; b. N.Y.C., Sept. 23, 1929; s. John and Margaret (Thomson) B.; children from previous marriage: Edgar Jr., Robert, Margaret; m. Ann Clark, Feb. 25, 1989. BA, Haverford Coll., 1951; JD with honors, George Washington U., 1955. Bar: D.C. 1955, Md. 1955. Law clk. to chief judge U.S. Dist. Ct. D.C., 1955-57; asst. U.S. atty. for Washington, 1957-59; ptnr. Pope, Ballard & Loos, Washington, 1959-81, Zuckert, Scoutt and Rasenberger, Washington, 1981-94; ptnr. Bellinger & Assocs., Washington and Md., 1995—; chmn. unauthorized practice com. D.C. Ct. Appeals, 1972-78; mem. D.C. jud. conf., 1972-90; bd. mgrs. Chevy Chase Village, 1983-86. Mem. ABA, D.C. Bar Assn. (D.C. Ct. Appeals orgn. com. 1972), Md. Bar Assn., Talbot County Bar Assn., Am. Arbitration Assn. (panel of arbitrators), Nat. Assn. Securities Dealers (panel of arbitrators), Met. Club, Chevy Chase Club (bd. govs. 1972-77, pres. 1976-77), Barristers. State civil litigation, Insurance, Probate. Home: 27497 West Point Rd Easton MD 21601-8439 Office: 888 17th St NW Washington DC 20006-3939 also: PO Box 739 Easton MD 21601-0739

**BELLINGER, JOHN BELLINGER, III,** lawyer; b. Paris, Mar. 28, 1960; s. John B. Bellinger Jr. and Anne Taliaferro (Tynes) B.; m. Caroline Dawn Renzy, June 9, 1984; children: Catharine Meade, Ann Thomson. AB, Princeton U., 1982; JD, Harvard U., 1986; MA, U. Va., 1991. Assoc. Shaw, Pitman, Potts & Trowbridge, Washington, 1986-88; spl. asst. to dir. CIA, Washington, 1988-91; assoc., then spl. counsel Wilmer, Cutler & Pickering, Washington, 1991-95; gen. counsel, commn. on the roles and capatilities of U.S. Intelligence Cmty., Washington, 1995-96; spl. counsel senate select com. on intelligence U.S. Senate, Washington, 1996; sr. counsel for nat. security matters criminal divsn. Dept. Justice, Washington, 1997—. Vestryman St. Mary's Episcopal Ch., Arlington, Va., 1991-94, sr. warden, 1993-94; bd. govs. St. Albans Sch., Washington, 1997—; mem. Coun. on Fgn. Rels., Am. Coun. on Germany. Banking, Public international. Office: Dept Justice 950 Pennsylvania Ave NW Rm 2113 Washington DC 20530-0001

**BELLISARIO, DOMENIC ANTHONY,** lawyer; b. Pitts., May 14, 1953; s. Domenic and Mary (Murgia) B.; m. Barbara Marie Johns, May 25, 1990. BA, U. Pitts., 1975, JD, 1978. Bar: Pa. 1978; U.S. Dist. Ct. (we. dist.) Pa., 1978; U.S. Ct. Appeals (3d cir.) 1985. Trial atty. Nat. Labor Rels. Bd., Pitts., 1978-83; human resource counsel Western Res. Care Sys., Youngstown, Ohio, 1986-89; ptnr. Bellisario & Pontier, Pitts., 1984-90; pvt. practice Pitts., 1991—. Author: Preventing and Defending Sexual Harassment Claims in Pennsylvania, 1996, Basic Wage and Hour Law in Pennsylvania, 1997. Mem. coun. Nat. Italian Am. Found., Washington, 1991. Mem. ABA, Pa. Bar Assn., Allegheny County Bar Assn., Pa. Trial Lawyers Assn., Italian Cultural Heritage Soc. West Pa. Avocations: travel, skiing. Labor, Personal injury. Office: 1000 Law & Finance Bldg Pittsburgh PA 15219

**BELLIVEAU, JAMES DENNIS,** lawyer; b. Atlanta, Aug. 1, 1949; s. James Dennis and Marian Norris (Kennihan) B.; m. Janet Ann Liebel, Oct. 11, 1980; children: Jennifer Eve, Michael James, David Warren. BS in Petroleum/Natural Gas Engring., Pa. State U., 1972, BA in Gen. Arts and Scis., 1972; JD, U. Pitts., 1975. Bar: Pa. 1976, W.Va. 1990, U.S. Supreme Ct. 1991, U.S. Ct. Appeals (3d cir.) 1978, U.S. Dist. Ct. (we. dist.) Pa. 1976; cert. civil trial advocate. Spl. asst. county solicitor Allegheny County Health Dept., Pitts., 1975-77; staff atty. Neighborhood Legal Svcs. Assn., Pitts., 1977-80, mng. atty., 1980-83; trial atty. Stokes, Lurie, Tracy & Cole, Pitts., 1983-85; trial atty., mgr. personal injury litigation, ptnr. Edgar Snyder & Assocs., Pitts., 1985—. Elder, clk. of session Meml. Pk. Presbyn. Ch., Wesford, Pa., 1996—; bd. dirs. Huntington Woods Homeowners Assn., Wexford, 1992-96; soccer coach North Allegheny Soccer Club, Ingomar, 1991—; vol. leader Boy Scouts Am.; vol. men. Sch. Band Parents Orgn. Mem. ATLA, Western Pa. Trial Lawyers Assn. (bd. dirs. 1990-93), Allegheny County Bar Assn. (civil litigation sect., coun. mem. 1995—), Pa. Bar Assn., Million Dollar Advocates Forum. Democrat. Avocations: downhill skiing, gardening. Personal injury, Product liability, General civil litigation. Office: Edgar Snyder & Assocs 1600 Gulf Twr 707 Grant St Pittsburgh PA 15219-1908

**BELLIVEAU, KATHRIN PAGONIS,** lawyer; b. Fall River, Mass., Aug. 25, 1968; d. Constantine Peter and Betty (Jamoulis) Pagonis; m. James Joseph Belliveau, June 20, 1998. BA magna cum laude, Wellesley Coll., 1990; JD, Boston Coll., 1993. Bar: R.I. 1993, U.S. Dist. Ct. R.I. 1994. Assoc. Tillinghast Collins & Graham, Providence, 1993-96, Adler Pollock & Sheehan, Providence, 1996-97; counsel Hasbro, Inc. Pawtucket, R.I., 1997—. Bd. dirs. Children's Mus., Providence, 1998—, Caritas House, Pawtucket, 1997—. Mem. ABA, Wellesley Club of R.I. (bd. dirs. 1996—), Phi Beta Kappa. Greek Orthodox. Avocations: tennis, golf, skiing, cooking. General corporate, Product liability, Labor. Office: Hasbro Inc 1027 Newport Ave Pawtucket RI 02861-2500

**BELLIZZI, JOHN J.,** law enforcement association administrator, educator, pharmacist; b. N.Y.C., July 26, 1919; s. Francis X. and Carmela (Bruno) B.; m. Celeste Morga, Sept. 1, 1942; children: John J. Jr., Robert F. PhG, St. John's U., N.Y.C., 1939; LLB, Albany Law Sch., 1960; JD, Union U., 1968; LLD, St. John's U., 1981. Pharmacist St. Luke's Hosp., N.Y.C., 1939-44; police officer N.Y.C. Police Dept., 1944-53; narcotics agt. N.Y. Bur. Narcotics Enforcement, N.Y.C., 1953-59; dir. N.Y. Bur. Narcotics Enforcement, Albany, 1959-81; exec. dir. N.Y. State Drug Abuse Commn., Albany, 1981-84, Internat. Narcotics Enforcement Assn., Albany, 1984—; prof. pharmacy law St. John's U., N.Y.C., 1962-76; lectr. in field. Contbr. articles to profl. jours. Recipient Papal medal Vatican, 1965. Mem. Internat. Narcotics Enforcement Officers Assn. (pres. 1960-62, Anslinger medal 1979, chmn. law enforcement com. Paramount Pictures, 1972-75, Svc. award 1975), Ft. Orange Club, Albany Country Club, Univ. Club (Albany), Phi Alpha Delta, Phi Sigma Chi (pres. 1939), Sigma Chi (fellow). Office: Internat Narcotics Enforcement Officers Assn 112 State St Albany NY 12207-2005

**BELLO, CHRISTOPHER ROBERT,** lawyer; b. Stamford, Conn., Jan. 14, 1962; s. Robert Sammy and Frances Marion Bello. BA, Dickinson Coll., 1983; JD, U. Bridgeport, 1987. Bar: Conn. 1987, U.S. Ct. Mil. Appeals, 1989, U.S. Dist. Ct. Conn., 1997. Assoc. Bello Lapine and Cassone, Stamford, Conn., 1983-90, sr. assoc., 1991-96; asst. staff judge advocate U.S. Army 411th Eng. Bde., Dharan, Saudi Arabia, 1990-91; asst. gen. counsel Gen. Reins. Corp., Stamford, Conn., 1996—. Capt. USAR, 1988-96. Democrat. General corporate, Securities, Insurance. Office: Gen Reins Corp 695 East Main St Stamford CT 06904

**BELLOMO, SALVATORE,** lawyer; b. Palermo, Italy, June 27, 1959; came to U.S., 1965; s. Gioacchino and iolanda (Calistro) B. BA, Marquette U., 1981; JD, Calif. We. Sch. of Law, 1985. Bar: N.J. 1985, U.S. Dist. Ct. N.J. 1985. Asst. prosecutor County of Passaic, Paterson, N.J., 1986—. Roman Catholic. Home: 205 13th St Palisades Park NJ 07650-2006 Office: Passiac County Prosecutors 77 Hamilton St Paterson NJ 07505-2018

**BELLONI, ROBERT CLINTON,** federal judge; b. Riverton, Oreg., Apr. 4, 1919; s. John Edward and Della (Clinton) B.; children: James L., Susan K. BA, U. Oreg., 1941, LLB, 1951. Bar: Oreg. 1951. Practiced in Coquille, Oreg., 1951-52, Myrtle Point, Oreg., 1952-57; judge Oreg. Circuit Ct., Coos and Curry Counties, Coquille, 1957-67; U.S. dist. judge Dist. Oreg., 1967-89, chief judge, 1971-76, sr. judge, 1989—. Councilman, Myrtle Point, 1953-57, mayor, 1957; chmn. Coos County Democratic Central Com., 1957; Hon. trustee Boys and Girls Aid Soc. Oreg., 1960. Served to 1st lt. AUS, 1942-46. Robert C. Belloni Boys Forest Ranch dedicated in his honor Coos County Bd. Commrs., 1969. Mem. ABA, Oreg. Bar Assn., Am. Judicature Soc., Oreg. Juvenile Ct. Judges Assn. (pres. 1963), Circuit Ct. Judges Assn. Oreg. (pres. 1966), 9th Circuit Dist. Judges Assn. (pres. 1980-81), Sigma Alpha Epsilon, Delta Theta Phi. Episcopalian. Office: US District Ct Libr 827 Courthouse 1000 SW 3rd Ave Portland OR 97204-2937*

**BELNICK, MARK ALAN,** lawyer; b. Elizabeth, N.J., Oct. 30, 1946; s. Ben B. and Rhoda Helen (Dubrowsky) B.; m. Randy Lee Birer, Mar. 23, 1974; children: Kelly Ann, Cory Frances, Jason Todd. BA cum laude, Cornell U., 1968; JD, Columbia U., 1971. Bar: N.Y. 1972, U.S. Tax Ct., 1972, U.S. Ct. Appeals (2d cir.) 1972, U.S. Dist. Ct. (so. dist.) N.Y. 1973, U.S. Supreme Ct. 1975, U.S. Dist. Ct. (ea. dist.) N.Y. 1978, U.S. Ct. Appeals (9th cir.) 1980, D.C. 1981, U.S. Ct. Appeals (4th cir.) 1982. Assoc. Marshall, Bratter, Greene et al, N.Y.C., 1971-72; assoc. Paul, Weiss, Rifkind, Wharton & Garrison, N.Y.C., 1972-79, ptnr., 1979-98; exec. v.p., chief corp. counsel Tyco Internat. Ltd., N.Y.C., 1998—; adj. prof. law Benjamin N. Cardozo Sch. Law, N.Y.C., 1982-86; cisiting prof. Cornell U., 1999—; mem. panel mediators and fact finders N.Y. State Pub. Employment Rels. Bd., Albany, 1972-79; deputy chief counsel U.S. Senate select com. on secret mil. assistance to Iran and Nicaraguan opposition, 1987-88; chief counsel select com. on structure and governance Nat. Assn. Security Dealers, 1994-96; bd. visitors Columbia Law Sch., 1996—; dir. Cornell U. prelaw program, 1999—. Mem. com. on alumni trustee nominations Cornell U., 1993-97, mem. coun., 1992-96, 98—, mem. adv. coun. Coll. Arts and Scis., 1993—, dir. prelaw program, 1999—; mem. adminstrv. bd. Cornell Coun., 1999—; bd. trustees Ethical Culture Fieldston Schs., 1999—. Harlan Fiske Stone scholar, 1971. Fellow Am. Coll. Trial Lawyers (downstate N.Y. com., fed. civil procedure com.); mem. ABA, N.Y. State Bar Assn., Assn. Bar City N.Y., Univ. Club N.Y.C. General civil litigation, Criminal, Public international. Office: Tyco Internat Ltd 712 5th Ave Fl 48 New York NY 10019-4108

**BELSKY, MARTIN HENRY,** law educator, lawyer; b. Phila., May 29, 1944; s. Abraham and Fannie (Turnoff) B.; m. Kathleen Waits, Mar. 9, 1985; children: Allen Frederick, Marcia Elizabeth. BA cum laude, Temple U., 1965; JD cum laude, Columbia U., 1968; cert. of study Hague (Netherlands) Acad. Internat. Law, 1968; diploma in criminology Cambridge (Eng.) U., 1969. Bar: Pa. 1969, Fla. 1983, N.Y., 1987, U.S. dist. ct. (ea. dist.) Pa. 1969, U.S. Ct. Appeals (3d cir.) 1970, U.S. Supreme Ct. 1973. Chief asst. dist. atty. Phila. Dist. Atty.'s Office, 1969-74; assoc. Blank, Rome, Klaus & Comisky, Phila., 1975; chief counsel U.S. Ho. of Reps., Washington, 1975-78; asst. adminstr. NOAA, Washington, 1979-82; dir. Ctr. for Govtl. Responsibility, assoc. prof. law U. Fla. Holand Law Ctr., 1982-86; dean Albany Law Sch., 1986-91, dean emeritus, prof. law, 1991-95; dean U. Tulsa Coll. of Law, 1995—; chair Select Commn. on Disabilities, N.Y., Spl. Commn. on Fire Svcs.; bd. advs. Ctr. Oceans Law and Policy; mem. corrections task force Pa. Gov.'s Justice Commn., 1971-75; adv. task force on cts. Nat. Adv. Commn. on Criminal Justice Standards and Goals, 1972-74; mem. com. on proposed standard jury instrns. Pa. Supreme Ct., 1974-81; lectr. in law Temple U., 1971-75; mem. faculty Pa. Coll. Judiciary, 1975-77; adj. prof. law Georgetown U., 1977-81. Chmn. Phila. council Anti-Defamation League, 1975, N.Y. region, mem. D.C. bd., 1977-78, chair N.Y. region, mem. nat. leadership Coun.; exec. v.p. Urban League Northeastern N.Y.; bd. dirs. Coun. on Aging & Disability. Stone scholar and Internat. fellow Columbia U. Law Sch. Mem. N.Y. State Bar Assn., Albany County Bar Assn., Phila. Bar Assn. (chmn. young lawyers sect. 1974-75), Pa. Bar Assn. (exec. com. young lawyers sect. 1973-75), ABA (del. young lawyers sect. exec. bd. 1973-75), Fla. Bar Assn., Fed. Bar Assn., Am. Judicature Soc., Nat. Dist. Attys. Assn., Am. Soc. Internat. Law, Am. Arbitration Assn. (referee N.Y. State Commn. on Jud. Discipline), Temple U. Liberal Arts Alumni Assn. (v.p. 1971-75), Am. Law Inst., Fund for Modern Cts. (bd. dirs.), Hudson-Mohawk Assn. Colls. and Univs. (v.p.), Sword Soc. Jewish. Club: B'nai B'rith (v.p. lodge 1973-75), Cardoto Soc., United Jewish Fedn. Northeastern N.Y. (v.p., pres. elect). Author: (with Steven H. Goldblatt) Analysis and Commentary to the Pennsylvania Crimes Codes, 1973; Handbook for Trial Judges, 1976, Oceans and Capital Law and Policy, 1994; contbr. articles to legal publs.; editor in chief Jour. Transnat. Law, Columbia Law Sch., 1968; mem. bd. advisors Territorial Sea Jour. Office: U Tulsa Coll Law 3120 E 4th Pl Tulsa OK 74104-2418

**BELSON, JAMES ANTHONY,** judge; b. Milw., Sept. 23, 1931; s. Walter W. and Margaret (Taugher) B.; m. Rosemary P. Greenslade, Jan. 11, 1958; children: Anthony James, Marie Taylor, Elizabeth Ann, Stephen Griffin. AB cum laude, Georgetown U., 1953, JD, 1956, LLM, 1962. Bar: D.C. 1956, Md. 1962. Law clk. U.S. Ct. Appeals (D.C. cir.), 1956-57; assoc. Hogan & Hartson, Washington, 1960-67, ptnr., 1967-68; trial judge D.C. Superior Ct., 1968-81, presiding judge civil divsn., 1978-81; assoc. judge D.C. Ct. Appeals, Washington, 1981-91, sr. judge, 1991—; faculty mem. Nat. Jud. Coll., 1973-80; bd. dirs. Coun. for Ct. Excellence, 1982—, Cath. Legal Immigration Network, Inc., 1994-98; bencher Am. Inn of Ct. VI, 1983-90. Bd. editors Georgetown Law Jour., 1955-56. Bd. dirs. Project SHARE D.C., Inc., 1992—, chmn., 1997—. With JAGC, U.S. Army, 1957-60. Mem. ABA, Bar Assn. of D.C. (bd. dirs. 1966-67, chmn. jr. bar 1965-66), Am. Judicature Soc. (bd. dirs. 1980-85), Am. Bar Found., John Carroll Soc. (bd. govs. 1978-85, 1st v.p. 1989-91), Sovereign Mil. Order of Malta Fed. Assn. (pres. 1991-94, bd. dirs. 1988-95, 97—, chmn. task force on Cuba 1994—). Home: 12 W Severn Ridge Rd Annapolis MD 21401-5844 Office: DC Ct Appeals 500 Indiana Ave NW Rm 5510 Washington DC 20001-2131

**BELT, DAVID LEVIN,** lawyer; b. Wheeling, W.Va., Jan. 13, 1944; s. David Homer and Mae Jean (Duffy) B.; m. Carolyn Emery Copeland Belt, July 22, 1967; children: David Clifford, Amy Elizabeth. BA, Yale U., 1965, LLB, 1970. Bar: Conn. 1970. Assoc. Jacobs, Grudberg, Belt & Dow, P.C., New Haven, Conn., 1970-74, mem., 1974—. Co-author: The Connecticut Unfair Trade Practices Act, 1994; contbr. articles to profl. jours. 1 lt. USAR, 1965-67, Vietnam. Fellow Conn. Bar Found.; mem. Conn. Bar Assn. (exec. com. antitrust and trade regulation sect. 1978—), Conn. Trial Lawyers Assn., Yale Club N.Y.C. General civil litigation, Antitrust, Federal civil litigation. Office: Jacobs Grudberg Belt & Dow PC 350 Orange St New Haven CT 06511-6415

**BELT, SCOTT M.,** lawyer; b. Morris, Ill., Sept. 15, 1962; s. Gerald Roger and Elizabeth (Delight) B.; m. Cynthia L. Belt, Sept. 2, 1990; children: Tara, Jessica, Jenna, Monica. AS in Law Enforcement, So. Ill. U., 1986, B in Profl. Photography, 1986; JD cum laude, Thomas M. Cooley Law Sch., 1990. Bar: Ill. 1990, N.D. 1991. Law clk. U.S. Dept. Justice, Grand Rapids, Mich., 1989-90; assoc. McKeown Law Firm, Joliet, Ill., 1990-91; ptnr. Peacock, McFarland & Belt, Morris, 1991-98; pvt. practice Morris, 1998—. Mem. Assn. Trial Lawyers of Am., Ill. State Bar Assn. Personal injury, Product liability. Office: 105 1/2 W Washington St Morris IL 60450-2144

**BELTHOFF, RICHARD CHARLES, JR.,** lawyer; b. Denville, N.J., Jan. 28, 1958; s. Richard Charles and Barbara Ann (Erdmann) B.; m. Vicki Shannon Alligood, June 13, 1981; children: Ashley Nicole, Jason Michael. BSP, East Caroline U., 1980; JD, U. N.C., 1984. Bar: N.C. 1984, U.S. Dist. Ct. (we. dist.) N.C. 1984, U.S. Ct. Appeals (4th cir.) 1987. Assoc. Grier & Grier, Charlotte, N.C., 1984-89; ptnr. Grier Belthoff & Furr PA, Charlotte, N.C., 1989-98; sr. corp. counsel, asst. sec. Compass Group USA, Inc., Charlotte, N.C., 1998—. Contbr. articles to legal jours. Mem. ABA, N.C. Bar Assn., Mecklenburg County Bar Assn. Environmental, Labor, General corporate. Home: 426 Shasta Ln Charlotte NC 28211-4054 Office: Compass Group Legal Dept 2400 Yorkmont Rd Charlotte NC 28217-4511 *Notable cases include: Raritan River Steel Co. vs. Cherry, Bekaert & Holland, 1986, the first case in N.C. determining accountant's liability for negligently prepared audits.*

**BELTON, JOHN THOMAS,** lawyer; b. Yonkers, N.Y., Feb. 24, 1947; s. Harry James and Anne Marie (Kupko) B.; m. Linda Susanne Cheugh, jan. 6, 1973; 1 child, Joseph Timothy. BA, Ohio State U., 1972, postgrad. in bus. adminstrn., 1972-73; JD, Ohio No. U., 1976. Bar: Ohio 1977, U.S. Ct. of Claims. Sole practice Columbus, Ohio, 1976-83; ptnr. Belton & Marlin, and predecessor firm Belton, Goldwin & Cheugh, Columbus, 1983—; arbitrator Franklin County Ct. Common Pleas, 1983—; dir. Weeks-Finneran Inc. Rep. precinct chmn., 1983; v.p. Far Northwest Coalition, 1984. Mem. ch. coun. St. Peter's Parish, 1984—, Pub. Bd. Zoning Appeals, 1991—; pres. Dublin Youth Athletics, 1985—. With USAF, 1968-71. Mem. ABA, ATLA, Columbus Bar Assn. (com. chmn. 1976—), U.S. Dist. Ct. Fed. Bar, U.S. Supreme Ct. Bar, Ohio Bar Assn. (bd. govs. 1993—), Dublin Jr. C. of C., The Pres., Ohio State Alumni, Republican Glee, Columbus Shamrock, K.C., Order of Barristers, Omicron Delta Kappa, Phi Alpha Delta (justice 1975). Roman Catholic. Avocations: reading, chess, golfing, racquetball, recreational activities. State civil litigation, Criminal, Personal injury. Home: 8649 Dunsinane Dr Dublin OH 43017-8757 Office: Belton Wherry & Marlin 2066 Henderson Rd Columbus OH 43220-2452

**BELTRE, LUIS OSCAR,** lawyer; b. Azua, Dominican Republic, Apr. 30, 1954; came to U.S., 1966; s. Rafael Euribiades and Maria Remedios (Ramirez) B.; m. Olga Maria Martinez, Oct. 5, 1975; children: Yadira Eurisa, Luis Oscar Jr., Zeus Oscar. BS, Pace U., 1977; JD, Case Western Res. U., 1981. Bar: N.Y. 1982, N.J. 1982, Fla. 1982, U.S. Dist. Ct. (so. and ea. dists.) N.Y. 1982, U.S. Dist. Ct. N.J. 1982, U.S. Supreme Ct. 1986. Assoc. Kaplan, Russin, Vecchi & Kirkwood, N.Y.C., 1981-82, Kaplan, Russin, Vecchi & Heredia-Bonetti, Santo Domingo, Dominican Republic, 1982-83; sole practice N.Y.C., 1983—; bd. dirs. Banco Dominico Hispano, Dominican Republic. Cons. Desfile Fiestival Dominicano, N.Y.C., 1984—, Assn. Prensa Turistica, N.Y.C., 1984—; bd. dirs. Fed. Com. Ind. Dominicano, N.Y.C., 1983—. Mem. Assn. Trial Lawyers Am., N.Y. State Trial Lawyers Assn. Republican. Roman Catholic. Avocations: trumpet, swimming, tennis. Contracts commercial, Criminal, Immigration, naturalization, and customs. Home: 198 Nimitz Rd Paramus NJ 07652-4612 Office: 4845 Broadway New York NY 10034-3134

**BELTZ, CHARLES ROBERT,** lawyer; b. Chgo., Dec. 18, 1937; s. Charles Robert and Amy Margaret (Ferguson) B.; m. Anna Kerns, Mar. 30, 1980; children: Kathleen Beltz Glowski, Cynthia Beltz Beltowski, Charles R. III. BA cum laude, Alma Coll., 1959; JD, U. Mich., 1961. Bar: Mich. 1961, U.S. Dist. Ct. (ea. and we. dists.) Mich. 1961, U.S. Ct. Mil. Appeals 1962, U.S. Supreme Ct. 1966, U.S. Dist. Ct. (no. dist.) Ind. 1968, U.S. Ct. Appeals (6th cir.) 1983; bd. cert. civil trial advocate. Trial lawyer Beltz & Assocs., Flint, Mich., 1961—. Author: (book) L, 1975, Best Poems of -90s (Editor's Choice 1996), Between the Raindrops, 1995 (Editor's Choice 1995). Pres. Linden (Mich.) Cmty. Schs. PTA, 1965-67; sponsor Flint Cmty & Cultural Ctr., Flint, 1985—; trustee Alma (Mich.) Coll., 1970-72, pres. alumni assn., 1970-71. Recipient Men's Nat. High Point Driving award Mercedes-Benz Club of Am., 1988, 92, 96, Mem. of Yr. (Internat. Stars sect.), 1990, Officer of Yr., 1988. Fellow Roscoe Pound-Am. Trial Lawyers Found.; mem. State Bar of Mich. (mem. ethics com. 1987-89), Assn. Trial Lawyers of Am. (chpt. pres. 1969-72), Genessee County Bar Assn. (chmn. Bench & Bar Com. 1976-89, pres. 1979-80, mediator 1975—, Flint Trial Lawyers Assn. (pres. 1969-72), Mercedes-Benz Club Am. (legal counsel 1986—, nat. pres. 1990-92), Tau Kappa Alpha, Alpha Psi Omega. Avocations: writing, playing hockey, pvt. pilot. Office: Beltz & Assocs 444 Church St Flint MI 48502-1324

**BELTZER, HOWARD STEWART,** lawyer; b. N.Y.C., Dec. 6, 1957; s. Herman Martin and Cynthia Marilyn B.; m. Alison Colette Lindsay-Beltzer, June 16, 1985; children: Clifford Benjamin, Miranda Leigh. BA magna cum laude, Harvard Coll., 1979; JD, Yale U., 1982. Ptnr., head of workouts and bankruptcy group White & Case, LLP, N.Y.C., 1982—. Contbr. articles to profl. jours. Recipient Edwards Whitaker award Harvard U., 1976-79, others. Mem. Assn. of Bar of City of N.Y. (com. on bankruptcy and corp. reorganization), ABA (mem. bus. bankruptcy com.), Phi Beta Kappa. Bankruptcy. Office: White & Case LLP 1155 Avenue Of The Americas New York NY 10036-2711

**BELZ, EDWIN J.,** lawyer; b. Latnobe, Pa., Feb. 28, 1936; s. Carl Stephen and Elizabeth Muhr B.; m. Suzanne Mary Schwarz, July 8, 1967; children: Daniel, Jeanine, Christopher, Luke. BA, St. Vincent Coll., 1958; JD, DePaul Coll., 1961. Bar: Ill. 1961, U.S. Dist. Ct. Ill. 1967. Asst. state's atty. Cook County, Chgo., 1961-64; atty. Vacarello Law Office, Chgo., 1965; ptnr. Belz & Huhl, Chgo., 1965-85, Belz & McWilliams, Chgo., 1985—. Sponsor Norwood PK. Little League, Chgo., 1973—; mem. Norwood Hist. Soc., 1980—. With U.S. Army, 1961. Mem. Chgo. Bar Assn., Northwest Bar Assn. Avocations: reading, golfing, traveling. General civil litigation. Home: 6125 NE Circle Dr Chicago IL 60631-2417 Office: Belz & McWilliams 4407 N Elston Ave Chicago IL 60630-4418

**BENAK, JAMES DONALD,** lawyer; b. Omaha, Jan. 22, 1954; s. James R. and Norma Lea (Roberts) B.; Patricia Ann Duffy, Mar. 1995; 1 child, James Duffy. BA, U. Nebr., 1977; JD, Creighton U., 1980. Bar: Nebr. 1980, U.S. Dist. Ct. Nebr. 1980, U.S. Ct. Appeals (7th cir.) 1988, U.S. Ct. Appeals (6th cir.) 1989, Ill. 1990, U.S. Dist. Ct. (no. and ctrl. dists.) Ill. 1991. Assoc. Kennedy, Holland, DeLacy & Svoboda, Omaha, 1980-84; asst. gen. atty. Union Pacific R.R. Co., Omaha, 1984-87, gen. atty., 1987-90; ptnr. Jenner & Block, Chgo., 1990—. Bd. dirs. Combined Health Agys. Drive/Nebr., 1985-90, Automated Monitoring and Control Internat., Inc., 1987-90, Coll. World Series, 1989-90. Mem. ABA (litigation sect.), Nebr. Bar Assn., Chgo. Bar Assn. (pub. utility and ins. law com.). Republican. Roman Catholic. General civil litigation, Transportation, Intellectual property. Home: 225 Ravine Rd Hinsdale IL 60521-3713 Office: Jenner & Block One IBM Plz Chicago IL 60611

**BENAKIS, GEORGE JAMES,** lawyer; b. N.Y.C., June 24, 1971; s. James G. and Voula (Aneson) B. BA, Brooklyn Coll., 1992; JD, Fordham U., 1995. Bar: N.Y. Legal asst. Wachtell, Lipton, Rosen & Katz, N.Y.C., 1992-94; intern N.Y. State Atty. Gen., N.Y.C., 1994; case mgr. Paine Webber, Inc., Weehawken, N.J., 1995-96; contract atty. Cleary, Gottleib, N.Y.C., 1996-97; assoc. Ateshoglou, Kavourias & Chrysanthem, P.C., N.Y.C., 1997-98, Capitol Lease Funding L.P., N.Y.C., 1998—. Mem. ABA, N.Y. State Bar Assn., Assn. Bar City of New York, New York County Lawyer's Assn., Ea. Orthodox Lawyers Assn., N.Y. State Hellenic-Am. Rep. Assn. (mem. pub. rels. sect. 1997), Pan-Imbrian Benevolent Assn. (pres. 1995-98). Greek Orthodox. Avocations: fishing, basketball. Appellate, Real property, General civil litigation. Office: Capital Lease Funding LP 111 Maiden Ln Fl 36 New York NY 10038-4813

**BENAVIDES, FORTUNATO PEDRO (PETE BENAVIDES),** federal judge; b. 1947. BBA, U. Houston, 1968, JD, 1972. Atty. Rankin, Kern & Martinez, McAllen, Tex., 1972-74, Cisneros, Beery & Benavides, McAllen, 1974, Cisneros, Brown & Benavides, McAllen, 1975, Cisneros & Benavides, McAllen, 1976; pvt. practice McAllen, 1977; judge Hidalgo County Ct.-at-Law # 2, Edinburg, Tex., 1977-79; prin. Law Offices of Fortunato P. Benavides, McAllen, 1980-81; judge 92nd Dist. Ct. of Hidalgo County, Tex., 1981-84, 13th Ct. Appeals, Corpus Christi, Tex., 1984-91, Tex. Ct. Criminal

Appeals, Austin, 1991-92; atty. Atlas & Hall, McAllen, 1993-94; judge U.S. Ct. Appeals (5th cir.), Austin, 1994—; commr. Tex. Juvenile Probation Commn., 1983-89; vis. judge to cts. in Tex., 1993. Active Mex.-Am. Dems. of Tex., 1990-92, Mustangs of Corpus Christi, 1990-91, hon. mem., 1992, St. Michael Episc. Ch., Austin, 1992—. Mem. ABA, State Bar Tex., Hidalgo County Bar Assn. Office: US Ct Appeals 5th cir Homer Thornberry Judicial Bldg 903 San Jacinto Blvd Ste 450 Austin TX 78701-2450*

**BENDER, JOHN CHARLES,** lawyer; b. N.Y.C., May 17, 1940; s. John H. and Cecilia B.; m. Helen Hadjiyannakis; 1 child, Marianna Celene. BSME, Northea. U., 1964; JD, NYU, 1968, LLM, 1971. Bar: N.Y. 1968, U.S. Dist. Ct. (so. dist.) N.Y. 1972, U.S. Supreme Ct. 1997. Atty. Marshall, Bratter, Greene, Allison and Tucker, 1968-69; asst. dir, NYU Ctr. for Internat. Studies, N.Y.C., 1969-71; atty. Poletti Freidin Prashker Feldman & Gartner, N.Y.C., 1971-75; spl. counsel Moreland Act Commn. on Nursing Homes and Residential Facilities, N.Y.C., 1975-76; gen. counsel N.Y. State Fin. Control Bd., N.Y.C., 1976-80; v.p., gen. counsel News Am. Pub. Inc., N.Y.C., 1980-85; group v.p., gen. counsel Simon & Schuster Inc., N.Y.C., 1985-90; sr. v.p., dir., gen. counsel Maxwell Macmillan Group, 1991-95; dir. Black Book Mktg. Group, Inc., 1994-96. Chmn., trustee Trust for Cultural Resources of City of N.Y., 1981—; chmn., trustee Mary McDowell Ctr. for Learning, 1993—. Mem. ABA, Assn. of Bar of City of N.Y. (mem. com. on comm. law 1981-85, mem. spl. com. on edn. and the law 1982-85). Communications, General corporate, Intellectual property. Home: 27 W 67th St New York NY 10023-6258 Office: 150 E 58th St New York NY 10155-0002

**BENDER, LAURIE,** lawyer; b. Seattle, July 29, 1959; d. Dean Bender and Karen Arol Bender-Evanson; m. John P. Annand, Oct. 28, 1988; children: Alexander, Quinn. BS, We. Wash. U., 1982; JD, Lewis and Clark Coll., 1988. Bar: Oreg. Lawyer Met. Pub. Defender, Inc., Portland, Oreg., 1988-94, Bakker, Bender & Kappinski, Portland, 1994—. Coach S.E. Soccer Club, Portland, 1995—. Mem. Oreg. State Bar Assn., Multnoma Bar Assn., Oreg. Criminal Def. Lawyer Assn. Democrat. Avocations: soccer, book club, hiking. Criminal, Juvenile, Family and matrimonial. Office: Bakker Bender & Karpinski 621 SW Alder St Ste 621 Portland OR 97205-3621

**BENDER, MICHAEL LEE,** state supreme court justice; b. N.Y.C., Jan. 7, 1942; s. Louis and Jean (Waterman) B.; m. Judith Jones, Feb. 27, 1967 (div. Mar. 1977); children: Jeremy, Aviva; m. Helen H. Hand, Sept. 10, 1977; children: Maryjean Hand-Bender, Tess Hand-Bender, Benjamin Hand-Bender. BA in Philosophy, Dartmouth Coll., 1964; JD, U. Colo., 1967. Bar: Colo. 1967, D.C. 1967, U.S. Supreme Ct. 1980. Pub. defender City and County Denver, 1968-71; assoc. regional atty. EEOC, 1974-75; supr. atty. Jefferson County Pub. Defender, 1975-77; divsn. chief Denver Pub. Defender, Denver, 1977-78; atty. Gibson, Dunn & Crutcher, L.A., 1979-80; ptnr. Bender & Treece P.C., Denver, 1983-93; pres., shareholder Michael L. Bender PC, 1993-97; also pres. Bender & Treece P.C.; justice Colo. Supreme Ct., 1997—; adj. faculty U. Denver Coll. Law, 1981-86, chair. ABA Criminal Justice sect., Washington, 1990-91, NACD Lawyers Assistant Com., 1989-90; dir. Nat. Assn. Criminal Def. Lawyers, 1984-90; mem. practitioner's adv. com. U.S. Sentencing Com., 1990-91; mem. com. for Criminal Justice Act for Dist. Colo. U.S. Dist. Ct., 1991-93, domestic rels. reform com.; liason mem. Colo. Pub. Edn. com., Ct. Svcs., 1998—, atty. regulation adv. com., 1998-99; co-chair civil justice com. Supreme Ct., 1998—. Contbr. articles to profl. jours. Bd. govs. Colo. Bar, 1989-91. Recipient Fireman award Colo. State Pub., 1990; Robert C. Heeney Meml. award Nat. Assn. Criminal Def. Lawyers, 1990; named Vol. of Yr. Denver Bar Assn., 1988. Mem. Colo. Bar Assn. (ethics com. 1980—), ABA (chair criminal justice sect. 1990-91, criminal justice standards com. 1997—). Democrat. Jewish. Avocations: aerobics, skiing, bicycling, camping. Office: Colo Supreme Ct State Jud Bldg 2 E 14th Ave Fl 4 Denver CO 80203-2115*

**BENDER, MICHAEL SETH,** lawyer, partner; b. N.Y.C., May 26, 1954; s. Murray and Maxine B.; m. Sophie Marie Caroline Haas, May 29, 1994; children: Miles Haas, Tess Sylvia. BA, Boston U., 1976; JD, Emory U., 1979. Bar: N.Y. Mem. Stokes and Bender, Decatur, Ga., 1980-83, Rosenburg Mine & Armstrong, N.Y.C., 1984-94, Argyropoulos & Bender, Astoria, N.Y., 1994—. Mem. Assn. Trial Lawyers Am., N.Y. State Bar Assn. Democrat. Jewish. Avocations: skiing, sailing, outdoor activities. Personal injury, Product liability. Home: 353 E 83rd St Apt 22A New York NY 10028-4342 Office: Argyropoulos & Bender 31 01 Broadway Astoria NY 11106

**BENDER, PAUL EDWARD,** lawyer; b. Decatur, Ill., June 5, 1951; s. Kenneth Donald and Martha Rosalie (Heinzelmann) B.; m. Anne Marie Scartabello, Dec. 31, 1976 (div. 1978). B.A., Millikin U., 1973; J.D. cum laude, Hamline U., 1976; MBA, U. Phoenix, 1997. Bar: Minn. 1976, Ill. 1977, U.S. Dist. Ct. (cen. dist.) Ill. 1982. Assoc. Halloran & Alfuby, Mpls., 1976-77; sole practice Bender Law Office, Arthur, Ill., 1977-79; sr. title atty. Chgo. Title Ins. Co., Peoria, Ill., 1979-82; ptnr. Cordis & Bender, Princeville, Ill., 1982-84; sr. title atty., Chgo. Title Co., Champaign, Ill., 1984-88, asst. v.p., mgr., 1990-92, resident v.p., Champaign County mgr., 1992-96, mgr. McLean County Title Co., 1996—, Decatur Title, 1997—. Pres. Peoria Evening Optimist Club, 1981-82, lt. gov. zone 6 Ill. Optimists, 1982-83. Mem. ABA, Peoria Bar Assn. (chmn. real estate com. 1983-84, mem. continuing legal edn. 1981-83), Champaign County Bar Assn., Ill. Bar Assn., Bloomington YMCA Svc. Club, Champaign C. of C. (zoning com. 1990-96), Lions, Masons, Shriners. Republican. Methodist. Real property, Bankruptcy. Home: 303 N Cottage Ave Normal IL 61761-4264

**BENDER, RONALD ANDREW,** lawyer; b. Butte, Mont., Sept. 29, 1946; s. John A. and Mary R. (Sullivan) B.; m. Jane K. Pozega, June 28, 1969; children: Andrew P., Kelly B. BA, Carroll Coll., Helena, Mont., 1968; JD, U. Mont., 1971. Bar: Mont. 1971, U.S. Dist. Ct. (fed. dist.) Mont. 1971, U.S. Ct. Appeals (9th cir.) 1974. Law clk. to Hon. Russell E. Smith U.S. Dist. Ct., Missoula, Mont., 1971-73; atty. Worden, Thane & Haines, P.C., Missoula, 1973—. Contbr. articles to law rev. Bd. dirs. Five Valleys Land Trust, Missoula, 1990-96. Recipient Am. Jurisprudence Achievement award, 1969, 70, 71. Mem. ABA, Mont. Bar Assn., Mont. Inst. Continuing Legal Edn., Am. Bd. Trial Advocates, Assn. Trial Lawyers Am., Mont. Def. Trial Lawyers, Def. Rsch. Inst., Missoula C. of C. (bd. dirs. 1990-93), Rotary (bd. dirs. 1990-93). General civil litigation, Banking, Labor. Office: Worden Thane & Haines PC 111 N Higgins Ave Ste 600 Missoula MT 59802-4494

**BENDER, STEVEN A.,** lawyer; b. White Plains, N.Y., Aug. 11, 1954; s. Louis and Jean (Waterman) B.; m. Audrey H. Ingber, Apr. 2, 1982; children: Sarah, Gabriel. AB, Ohio Wesleyan U., 1976; LLB cum laude, N.Y. Law Sch., N.Y.C., 1981. Bar: N.Y. 1981, U.S. Dist. Ct. (so. dist.) N.Y. 1981, U.S. Ct. Appeals (2d cir.) 1981. Assoc. Bender & Frankel, P.C., N.Y.C., 1981-84; asst. dist. atty. Westchester County Dist. Atty., White Plains, N.Y., 1984-88, dep. bur. chief, trial divsn., 1988-97, bur. chief, homicide bur., 1997—. Contbr. articles to profl. jours. Avocations: nonfiction reading, writing, excercise, family. Office: Westchester County Dist Atty 111 Martin Luther King Blvd White Plains NY 10601-2509

**BENDES, BARRY JAY,** lawyer; b. N.Y.C., Sept. 8, 1950; s. Arnold R. and Shirley B.; m. Tamara Shulman, Jan. 14, 1984; children: David Laurence, Jessica Haley. BA cum laude, Queens Coll., 1971; JD, NYU, 1974, cert. in real property law, 1980. Bar: N.Y. 1975, N.J. 1988; U.S. Dist. Ct. (so. dist.) N.Y. 1975, U.S. Dist. Ct. (ea. dist.) N.Y. 1975, U.S. Dist. Ct. N.J. 1988, U.S. Ct. Internat. Trade 1985, U.S. Tax Ct. 1988, U.S. Ct. Appeals (2d cir.) 1975, U.S. Supreme Ct. 1978, U.S. Ct. Appeals (7th cir.) 1997. Assoc. Leon, Weill & Mahony, N.Y.C., 1974-78; assoc. Certilman Haft Balin Buckley Kremer & Hyman and predecessor firms, N.Y.C., L.I., N.J. and Boca Raton, Fla., 1978-82, ptnr. 1983-88; ptnr. Rivkin, Radler, Dunne & Bayh, N.Y.C., L.I., Washington, Chgo., L.A., 1988-89; shareholder, coun. Parker Duryee Rosoff & Haft, P.C. 1989-93; ptnr. Kane Kessler, P.C., N.Y.C., 1994—, ptnr. Vedder Price Kaufman & Kammholz, N.Y.C., Chgo., Livingston, N.J., 1997—; sr. v.p. adminstrn. and gen. counsel Emerson Computer Corp. & Emerson Tech. L.P., 1989-92, gen. coun., 1990-92, sec., 1991-92, Emerson Radio Corp. Rsch. editor NYU Rev. Law and Social Change, 1972-74. Organizing new bus., N.J. Bar Found., 1994. Mem. ABA (com. on computer contracting, sect. sci. and tech. 1983—), Am. Arbitration Assn. (nat. panel arbitrators), Assn. Bar City N.Y. (computer law com. 1986-89, chmn. sub-com. software liability 1987-89, uniform state laws 1990-94, 97—, sec. 1993-94, task force ltd. liability companies 1993-94), N.Y. State Bar Assn., N.J. State Bar Assn. (com. on third party opinions 1989—, computer related law 1993—, third party legal opinions in acquisitions and mergers 1995, in secured financings under and outside ABA accord 1993, author, spkr.), Am. Corp. Counsel Assn. (dir. greater N.Y. chpt. 1990—, sec. 1995—, chair com. on third party legal opinions, 1992-97, moderator corp. counsel roundtable 1993—, v.p. 1998—, spkr., lectr.), Am. Soc. Corp. Secs. (corp. practice com. 1992—). Contracts commercial, Securities, Computer. Office: Vedder Price Kaufman & Kammholz 805 3rd Ave New York NY 10022-7513 also: 345 Eisenhower Pkwy Livingston NJ 07039-1722

**BENDICH, JUDITH ELLEN,** lawyer; b. N.Y.C., Jan. 17, 1945; m. Arnold J. Bendich, Aug. 2, 1964; 1 child, Justin Bendich. BA, U. Md., 1966; JD, U. Wash., 1975. Bar: Wash. 1975, U.S. Dist. Ct. (we. dist.) Wash. 1975, U.S. Ct. Appeals (9th cir.) 1975, U.S. Ct. Appeals (D.C. cir.) 1986, U.S. Supreme Ct. 1979. Ptnr. Bendich, Stobaugh & Strong, Seattle, 1975—; lectr. U. Wash., Seattle, 1975-76; commr. Seattle Civil Svc. Commn., 1985-87; pres. ACLU of Wash., Seattle, 1980-83; bd. dirs. Nat. ACLU, N.Y.C., 1983—, mem. exec. com., 1987-97. Mem. FBA, King County Bar Assn. Mentor Program, Washington Women Lawyers, Washington State Trial Lawyers Assn., Nat. Employment Lawyers Assn. Labor, Pension, profit-sharing, and employee benefits. Office: Bendich Stobaugh & Strong PC 900 4th Ave Ste 3800 Seattle WA 98164-1044

**BENEDICT, ANTHONY WAYNE,** lawyer; b. Perry, Okla., Aug. 18, 1956; s. Billy Lee and Kathryn Enola (Dowell) B. BA in political sci., Sul Ross State U., 1981; JD (hons.), U. Tex., 1984. Bar: Tex. 1984, Okla. 1998; U.S. Dist. Ct. (no. dist.) Tex. 1984, U.S. Ct. Appeals (5th cir.), Okla. 1998. Atty. Phillips Petroleum Co., Amarillo, Tex., 1984-99. Mem. ABA. Republican. Avocations: golf, travel, computers. General civil litigation, General corporate. Home: PO Box 1502 Bartlesville OK 74005-1502

**BENEDICT, GREGORY BRUCE,** business administration and finance professional, legal consultant; b. San Antonio, Tex., June 16, 1955; s. Bruce Oren and Joan (Baker) B.; m. Rita Marie Willefsky, Nov. 25, 1978; children: Elizabeth Culhane, Zoe Katherine, Erin Fisher. BS in Fin., U. Colo., 1977; JD, U. N.Mex., 1984. Bar: N.Mex. 1984, U.S. Dist. Ct. N.Mex. 1987. Atty. Erwin & Davidson, P.C., Raton, N.Mex., 1984-87; pvt. practice Albuquerque, 1987; v.p. Fisher Automatic Svc., Inc., Bryan, Ohio, 1988-96, pres., 1997, 1997—; lectr. N.Mex. Bar Assn., Santa Fe, 1987. bd. dirs. Black Swamp Coun. Boy Scouts Am., Findlay, Ohio, 1989—. Recipient Pro Bono award N.M. Lawyer Referral for Elderly, 1986, Am. Jurisprudence award Am. Jurisprudence, 1983. Mem. ABA, N.M. Bar Assn., Williams County Bar Assn. (pres. 1995-96), Nat. Automatic Merchandising Assn., Ohio Automatic Merchandising Assn., Bryan Rotary Club (treas. 1992—), First Presbyn. Ch. (elder 1996—). Avocations: skiing, fishing, Am. history, computers. E-mail: fasico@bright.net. Home: PO Box 852 Bryan OH 43506-0852 Office: Fisher Automatic Svc Inc PO Box 447 Bryan OH 43506-0447

**BENEDICT, JAMES NELSON,** lawyer; b. Norwich, N.Y., Oct. 6, 1949; s. Nelson H. and Helen (Wilson) B.; m. Janet E. Fagal, May 8, 1982. B.A. magna cum laude, St. Lawrence U., 1971; J.D., Albany Law Sch. of Union U., 1974. Bar: N.Y. 1975, U.S. Dist. Ct. (no., ea. and so. dists.) N.Y. 1975, U.S. Ct. Appeals (2d cir.) 1975, U.S. Ct. Appeals (8th cir.) 1977, U.S. Ct. Appeals (10th cir.) 1978, U.S. Ct. Appeals (11th cir.) 1982, U.S. Supreme Ct. 1978. Assoc. Rogers & Wells, N.Y.C., 1974-82, ptnr., 1982—. Mem. bd. contbg. editors and advisors The Corp. Law Rev., 1976-86. Contbr. articles to profl. jours. Bd. dirs. Reece Sch., N.Y.C., 1984-89, Stanley Isaacs Neighborhood Ctr., N.Y.C., 1984-89; trustee St. Lawrence U., Canton, N.Y., 1985-91. Mem. ABA (chmn. securities litigation subcom. on 1940 Act matters 1984-86, 96—), Fed. Bar Council, N.Y. State Bar Assn., Assn. Bar City N.Y. (mem. com. on securities regulation, fed. legislation com., fed. cts. com.) Am. Soc. Writers on Legal Subjects, Sky Club (N.Y.C.), Scarsdale Golf Club, Phi Beta Kappa. Federal civil litigation, State civil litigation, Securities. Home: 26 Kensington Rd Scarsdale NY 10583-2217 Office: Rogers & Wells 200 Park Ave Fl 8E New York NY 10166-0800

**BENESCH, KATHERINE,** lawyer; b. Balt., Jan. 18, 1946; d. Isaac and Jane (Van Praag) B.; m. Thomas Romer, Oct. 21, 1977. BA, Wheaton Coll., Norton, Mass., 1968; MPH, Yale U., 1970; JD, Duquesne U., 1979. Bar: Pa., 1980, U.S. Ct. Appeals (3rd cir.) 1981, U.S. Supreme Ct. 1985, N.J. 1991, U.S. Dist. Ct. 1991, U.S. Dist. Ct. N.J. 1991, U.S. Ct. Appeals D.C. 1992. Assoc. Dickie, McCamey and Chilcote, Pitts., 1979-80; asst. exec. dir., legal counsel Presbyn. U. Hosp., Pitts., 1980-81; assoc. Specter & Buchwach, P.C., Pitts., 1982-84; atty. Mellon Bank Corp., Pitts., 1984-86; pvt. practice Pitts., 1986-88; prin. Katherine Benesch & Assoc., Pitts., 1989-91; ptnr. Hannoch Weisman, Trenton, N.J., 1991-93; prin. Law Offices of Katherine Benesch, Princeton, 1994-96, 98; ptnr. Benesch & Obade, Princeton, 1997, Archer & Greiner, Princeton, 1999—; past pres. N.J. Bar Assn. in Health and Hosp. Law Sect.; adj. asst. prof. anesthesiology and critical care sch. medicine U. Pitts., mem. ctr. med. ethics; advisor Princeton U. Bioethics Forum. Editor: Medicolegal Aspects of Critical Care, 1986; contbr. chpts. to books and articles to profl. jours. Fellow Am. Bar Found.; mem. ABA, Assn. Trial Lawyers Am., Am. Arbitration Assn., Amer. Health Lawyers Assn., Pa. Bar Assn. (del.) Allegheny County Bar Assn. (bd. govs.), Pa. Trial Lawyers Assn., Western Pa. Soc. Hosp. Attys., N.J. Bar Assn., Mercer County Bar Assn., vice pres., Princeton Bar Assn. Health, General civil litigation, Personal injury. Office: Archer & Greiner PC 993 Lenox Dr Ste 108 Lawrenceville NJ 08648-2316

**BENESH, WILLIAM STEPHEN,** lawyer, partner; b. San Antonio, July 24, 1961; s. G. A. and Betty Jo (Humphries) B.; m. Jennifer Loraine Kulcak, Apr. 27, 1985; children: William Stephen, Jr., Austin Humphries. BBA, U. Tex., 1984, JD, 1987. Bar: Tex. 1988, U.S. Ct. Appeals (5th cir.) 1989, U.S. Dist. Ct. (so. dist.) Tex. 1988, U.S. Dist. Ct. (ea. dist.) Tex. 1992, U.S. Dist. Ct. (no. dist.) Tex. 1993, U.S. Dist. Ct. (we. dist.) Tex. 1997. Assoc. Bracewell & Patterson, L.L.P., Houston, 1988-96, ptnr., 1996—. Deacon Second Bapt. Ch., Houston, 1989—; scout leader, Boy Scouts of Am., Houston, 1989—; legal counsel, Meml. Bend Civil Assn., Houston, 1990—. Fellow, Tex. Bar Found., Houston Bar Found.; mem. State Bar Grievance Com. (Panel Chair 1993—). Republican. Avocations: scouting, camping, U. Tex. athletics. Contracts commercial, General civil litigation, Product liability. Home: 12810 Traviata Dr Houston TX 77024-4727 Office: Bracewell & Paterson LLP 711 Louisiana St Ste 2900 Houston TX 77002-2721

**BENHAM, ROBERT,** state supreme court justice; m. Nell (Dodson) B.; children: Corey Brevard, Austin Tyler. BS in Polit. Sci. with honors, Tuskegee U.; JD, U. Ga.; LLM, U. Va. Judge Ga. Ct. Appeals, Ga., 1984-89; justice Supreme Ct., State of Ga., Atlanta, 1989—, presiding justice, chief justice; mem. adv. bd. 1st So. Bank. Chmn. Gov.'s Commn. on Drug Awareness and Prevention, State of Ga.; mem. Ga. Hist. Soc.; trustee Fa. Legal Hist. Found.; bd. dirs. Cartersville (Ga.) Devel. Authority, Cartersville-Bartow C. of C.; deacon, former Sunday Sch. supt. The Greater Mt. Olive Bapt. Ch.; notably one of first black individuals elected to a statewide position in the history of Ga. Mem Atlanta Bar Assn. (bd. dirs. jud. sect.), Ga. Bar Found., Lawyers Club Atlanta, Masons, Shriners, Elks. Office: Ga Supreme Ct 244 Washington St SW Rm 572 Atlanta GA 30334-9007

**BENIGNO, THOMAS DANIEL,** lawyer; b. Queens, N.Y., July 29, 1954; s. John Baptiste and Ernesta Mary (Yannaco) B.; m. Maria Angelica Vasquez, Jan. 26, 1980; children: Diana Maria, Laura Michelle, John Frederick. BA with honors, Hofstra U., 1976; JD, Benjamin Cardozo Law Sch., 1979. Bar: N.Y. 1981, U.S. Dist. Ct. (so. and ea. dists.) N.Y. 1985. Atty. Legal Aid Soc., Bronx, N.Y., 1979-84; ptnr. Benigno, Cassisi & Casissi, Floral Park, N.Y., 1984-87; mng. ptnr., gen. counsel Benigno/Gurrieri Real Estate Mgmt. and Devel., Bklyn., 1984-95; pres. Gurben Properties, Inc., Floral Park, 1987-88, Movies for Kids Inc., Valley Stream, N.Y., 1989-90; gen. counsel Our Gang Assocs. Inc. (doing bus. as Thin White Line), Cedarhurst, N.Y., 1988-90. Mem. N.Y. Bar Assn., Rotary Internat. Real property, Contracts commercial, Construction. Office: 269 Hempstead Ave Ste 2 Malverne NY 11565-1224

**BENINATI, NANCY ANN,** lawyer; b. West Islip, N.Y., Apr. 2, 1969; d. Salvatore James and Phyllis Ellen (Quig) B. BA, Cornell U., 1991; JD, Golden Gate U. Sch. Law, 1995. Bar: Calif. 1995, U.S. Dist. Ct. (ea. and no. dists.) Calif. 1995. Law clk. Moore & Lafferty, Bklyn., 1993, Hinton & Alfert, Walnut Creek, Calif., 1994-95; assoc. Hinton & Alfert, Walnut Creek, 1995-97; pvt. practice Law Offices of Nancy A. Beninati, Oakland, 1997—; assoc. Baryton, Purcell, Curtis & Geagan, 1998—. Rsch. asst. Wis. Law Rev., 1995. Recipient Writing & Rsch. award Am. Jurisprudence/Bancroft Whitney, 1992, Cmty. Property award, 1995. Mem. ABA, Consumer Attys. of Calif., Alameda Contra Costa Trial Lawyers Assn., Contra Costa County Bar Assn. Avocations: fitness instruction, pottery, hiking, films, cooking. General civil litigation, Labor, Personal injury. Office: 3946 La Cresta Ave Oakland CA 94602-1729

**BENJAMIN, EDWARD BERNARD, JR.,** lawyer; b. New Orleans, Feb. 11, 1923; s. Edward Bernard and Blanche (Sternberger) B.; m. Adelaide Wisdom, May 11, 1957; children: Edward Wisdom, Mary Dabney, Ann Leith, Stuart Minor. BS, Yale U., 1944; JD, Tulane U., 1952. Bar: La. 1952. Practiced in New Orleans, since 1952; ptnr. Jones, Walker, Waechter, Poitevent, Carrere & Denegre, New Orleans, 1967—; pres. Am. Coll. Probate Counsel, 1986-87, Internat. Acad. Estate and Trust Law, 1976-78; vice chmn. bd. trustees Southwestern Legal Found., 1980-88, bd. dirs., 1988-90; chmn. bd. Starmount Co., Greensboro, N.C., 1968-88, chmn. emeritus, 1988—. Editor-in-chief Tulane U. Law Rev., 1951-52; mem. editorial bd. Community Property Jour., 1974-89. Trustee Hollins Coll., 1966-87; chancellor Episcopal Diocese of La., 1984—, Trinity Episcopal Ch., New Orleans, 1974-92; mem. adv. bd. CCH Estate & Fin. Planning Svc., 1982-88; chmn. Salavation Army City Commd. Adv. Bd., 1965-68; pres. New Orleans Jr. C. of C., 1953. 1st lt., F.A. pilot, U.S. Army, 1943-46. Mem. Am. Coll. Tax Counsel, Am. Law Inst., ABA (sec. taxation sect. 1967-68, coun. 1976-79, coun. real property, probate and trust law sect. 1978-81), La. Bar Assn. (chmn. taxation sect. 1959-60), La. Law Inst., La. Bar Found. (trustee 1998-99), New Orleans Country Club, Southern Yacht Club, New Orleans Lawn Tennis Clu. Estate planning, Estate taxation, Corporate taxation. Home: 1837 Palmer Ave New Orleans LA 70118-6215 Office: Jones Walker Waechter Poitevent Carrere & Denegre 201 Saint Charles Ave Fl 51 New Orleans LA 70170-1000

**BENJAMIN, EVAN,** account executive; b. N.Y.C., May 29, 1957; s. Donald S. and Geri Benjamin; m. Susan Safdeye, Sept. 11, 1982; children: Victoria, Donnie, Edward. BA cum laude, U. Albany, 1979; JD, Boston U., 1982. Bar: N.Y. 1983, Commonwealth of P.R. 1983. Atty. McConnell Valdas Kelley Sifre, San Juan, P.R., 1982-86; sr. acct. exec. E.S. Originals Inc., N.Y.C., 1986—. Office: ES Originals 450 W 33d St New York NY 10001

**BENJAMIN, GARY ADAMS,** lawyer; b. Rockford, Ill., Feb. 9, 1951; s. Robert Owen and Lorraine Evelyn (Adamson) B.; m. Alison Choate, Sept. 28, 1975; children: Nicholas Alden, Kirsten Mara. BA, Ohio Weslyan U., 1973; JD, Wayne State U., 1978. Bar: Mich. 1978, U.S. Dist. Ct. (ea. dist.) Mich. 1978, U.S. Ct. Appeals (6th cir.) 1981, U.S. Dist. Ct. (we. dist.) Mich. 1992. Assoc. Reosti & Assocs., Detroit, 1978-82, Shrauger, Dunn & Aronson, Detroit, 1982-93; pvt. practice Detroit, 1993—; mediator Wayne County Cir. Ct. Bd. dirs. Southwest Community Mental Health Ctr., Detroit, 1976-77, Downtown Sr. Citizens Ctr., Detroit, 1977-82, Golightly Sch. Community Orgn., Detroit, 1987-92; bd. dirs. Bridging Communities Inc., 1990-95, pres. 1996—; active Caring Together, Inc., 1992—. Mem. Assn. Trial Lawyers Am. (com. co-chmn. 1987-88, 90-95), Am. Arbitration Assn. (arbitrator med. malpractice sect. 1985—), Nat. Lawyers Guild (bd. dirs. Detroit chpt. 1981-82), NAACP (Detroit chpt.), Detroit Athletic Club. General civil litigation, Labor, Personal injury. Office: 3270 Penobscot Bldg Detroit MI 48226

**BENJAMIN, JACK CHARLES,** lawyer; b. New Orleans, Sept. 15, 1927; s. Isaiah Cerf Benjamin and Gladys Turk; m. Emily Ann Stein, Jan. 5, 1958; children: Jan Carole, Jack C. Jr. BA, Tulane U., 1948, LLB, 1950. Bar: La. 1950, U.S. Dist. Ct. (ea. and mid. dists.) La. 1950, U.S. Ct. Appeals (5th cir.) 1959, U.S. Dist. Ct. (we. dist.) La. 1970, U.S. Supreme Ct. 1972, U.S. Ct. Appeals (11th cir.) 1981. Ptnr. Holbrook & Benjamin, New Orleans, 1950-52; pvt. practice New Orleans, 1953-54; asst. U.S. atty. U.S. Dept. Justice, New Orleans, 1955-57; assoc. Law Offices Raymond H. Kierr, New Orleans, 1958-61, Kierr & Gainsburgh, New Orleans, 1962-71; ptnr. Kierr, Gainsburgh & Benjamin, New Orleans, 1972-73, Kierr, Gainsburgh, Benjamin, Fallon & Lewis, New Orleans, 1974-87, Kierr, Gainsburgh, Benjamin, Fallon, David & Ates, New Orleans, 1987-88, Gainsburgh, Benjamin, Fallon, David & Ates, New Orleans, 1988-94, Gainsburgh, Benjamin, Fallon & David, New Orleans, 1994-95; of counsel Gainsburgh, Benjamin, David, Meunier, Noriea & Warshauer, New Orleans, 1995-97, Gainsburgh, Benjamin, David, Meunier & Warshauer, New Orleans, 1997—; Mem. adv. bd. Tulane Maritime Law Ctr., New Orleans, 1987—; pres. La. Ctr. Law and Civic Edn., New Orleans, 1997-98; bd. dirs. hist. soc. U.S. Dist. Ct. (ea. dist.) La., New Orleans, 1997—. Contbr. articles to profl. jours. Mem. World Trade Ctr., La. Civil Svc. League, New Orleans Mus. Art, Contemporary Art Ctr., League Women Voters, Audubon Inst. Sgt. U.S. Army, 1946-47. Recipient Pres. award New Orleans Bar Assn., 1996. Fellow Am. Coll. Trial Lawyers, La. Bar Found. (life), Am. Inn of Ct. Found.; mem. Am. Judicature Soc., Maritime Law Assn. U.S., Tex. Trial Lawyers Assn., Met. Crime Commn. (mem. exec. com. 1979—, past pres. 1990-92), Vis. Nurses Assn. (bd. dirs. 1957—, past pres. 1960-66), Jewish Endowment Found. (bd. dirs. 1998—), La. Orgn. Jud. Excellence (regional v.p. 1987-96, pres. 1997—), Jewish Welfare Fedn., Tulane Emeritus Club (bd. govs. 1998—), New Orleans Lawn Tennis Club. Democrat. Jewish. Avocations: tennis, swimming, reading. General civil litigation, Admiralty, Personal injury. Office: Gainsburgh Benjamin David Meunier & Warshauer 2800 Energy Ctr 1100 Poydras St New Orleans LA 70163-1101

**BENJAMIN, JAMES SCOTT,** lawyer; b. Miami Beach, Fla., Aug. 28, 1954; s. Julian R. Benjamin and June Lois Garvin; m. Laura Cipolla, Mar. 5, 1989; children: Kaitlyn, Courtney. BS in Advt., U. Fla., 1976; JD, Samford U., 1979. Bar: Fla. 1980, U.S. Dist. Ct. (so. dist.) Fla. 1981, U.S. Dist. Ct. (mid. dist.) Fla. 1989, U.S. Ct. Appeals (11th cir.) 1989, U.S. Dist. Ct. (we. dist.) Tex. 1993, U.S. Supreme Ct. 1994. Assoc. Krause Reinhard & Pozen, Miami, Fla., 1980-81; asst. state atty. 17th Jud. Cir. Broward County, Ft. Lauderdale, Fla., 1981-84; shareholder Benjamin & Aaronston P.A., Ft. Lauderdale, 1984—; presenter/lectr. in field. Author, columnist Xcitement Mag., 1990—, Screw Mag., 1998—. Bd. dirs. Arthritis Found., Ft. Lauderdale, 1998, treas., 1999—. Mem. Fla. Assn. Criminal Def. Attys. (bd. dirs. 1998—), Broward County Assn. Criminal Def. Lawyers (v.p. 1997-98, pres. 1998-99), First Amendment Lawyers Assn., Free Speech Coalition, Inns of Ct. Avocation: fly fishing. Criminal, Constitutional, Entertainment. Office: Benjamin & Aaronson PA Ste 1615 One Financial Plaza Fort Lauderdale FL 33394

**BENJAMIN, JEFF,** lawyer, pharmaceutical executive; b. Bklyn., Dec. 28, 1945; s. Haskell and Lillian (Sikofski) B.; m. Betty Gae Meckler, Mar. 21, 1971; children: Lily Meckler, Ross Meckler. B.A., Cornell U., 1967; J.D. cum laude, NYU, 1971. Bar: N.Y. 1971, U.S. Dist. Cts. (so. and ea. dists.) N.Y. 1972. Assoc., Kronish, Lieb, Shainswit, Weiner & Hellman, N.Y.C., 1971-74; atty. Ciba-Geigy Corp., Ardsley, Tarrytown, N.Y., 1974—, counsel for regulatory affairs, 1976—, div. counsel, 1978—, asst. gen. counsel, 1985—; dir. legal dept. and assoc. gen. counsel, 1986-89, v.p., assoc. gen. counsel, 1989-96, v.p. gen. counsel, 1996-97; v.p. assoc. gen. counsel, compliance with law officer Novartis Corp., Summit, N.J., 1997—. Contbr. law articles to profl. jours.; lectr. in the field. Mem. Citizens Adv. Com., Town of Ramapo, N.Y. Served with USAR, 1969-74. Eagle Scout. Mem. ABA, Order of Coif, Cornell U. Alumni Assn. (admissions amb.). Antitrust, General corporate, Environmental. Home: 13 Park Ave New City NY 10956-1107 Office: Novartis Corp 564 Morris Ave Summit NJ 07901-1315

**BENKERT, JOSEPH PHILIP, JR.,** lawyer; b. Phila., Apr. 16, 1958; s. Joseph Philip Sr. and Caroline Beatrice (Whitehouse) B.; m. Mary Russell Doherty, Oct. 22, 1988. BS cum laude, James Madison U., 1979; MS, JD cum laude, Syracuse U., 1981. Bar: D.C. 1982, Colo. 1987, U.S. Ct. Appeals (fed. cir.) 1983, U.S. Ct. Appeals (D.C. cir.) 1984. Pvt. practice Haligman and Lottner, P.C., Denver, 1996—, Littleton, Colo., 1996-97; sr. fellow, bd. advisors Inst. Info. Law and Policy, Ctr. for the New West, 1994-95; spkr. in field. Mem. ABA, D.C. Bar Assn., Colo. Bar Assn., Denver Bar Assn., Denver C. of C., Fed. Commn. Bar Assn., Rocky Mountain Home-Based and Bus. Assn. (founder, bd. dirs. 1995-96, Outstanding Friend of Home-

Based Bus. award 1994). Communications, General civil litigation. Office: Haligman & Lottner PC 5712 S Sheridan Blvd Littleton CO 80123-2736

**BENN, NILES S.,** lawyer; b. Phila., Feb. 18, 1945; s. Samuel and Rose (Singer) B.; m. Joyce Barmach, June 30, 1968; children—Merrick Jordan, Evan Samuel. BS Temple U., 1967; JD, Dickinson Sch. of Law, 1972. Bar: Pa. 1972, U.S. Dist. Ct. (mid. dist.) Pa. 1973, U.S. Supreme Ct. 1983. Ptnr., Wiley & Benn, Dillsburg, Pa., 1973-90; prin. Law Offices of Niles S. Benn, Esq., York, Pa., 1990-99, Benn & Robinson, York, 1999—. Bd. mgrs. Holy Spirit Hosp., 1978—, 1995—, mem. fin. com., 1983—, asst. treas., 1983-90, 90-93, vice chmn. mental health ctr., 1983—, treas., 1990—, vice chmn. bd. dirs., 1993-95, chmn., 1995—; chmn. Holy Spirit Health Sys., 1999—; mem. legis. com. Phila. sect. Am. Cancer Soc., 1982-87, bd. dirs. York unit, 1977-90, pres., 1985-95, mem. exec. com. Pa. div., 1981-95, bd. dirs., 1981-85, chmn. legacy and planned giving com., 1985-88, chmn. pub. affairs com., 1982-85, vice chmn. Pa. div. bd., 1985-87, chmn., 1987-89; chmn. Dillsburg Community Health Ctr., 1977-87; bd. dirs. York Council Jewish Charities, 1985—, Capitol Engring. Corp., 1985-87; solicitor Lake Meade Mcpl. Authority, 1975-77, Carroll Twp. Zoning and Hearing Bd., 1980-82, Carroll Twp. Planning Commn., 1980-84, Carroll Twp. Bd. Suprs., 1983-84, No. York County Sch. Dist., 1973-84, Monaghan Twp. Planning Commn., 1973-98, Monaghan Twp. Bd. Suprs., 1973-98; vice chmn. Am. Cancer Soc., Pa., 1985-89, chmn. bd., 1987—. Named Vol. of Yr., Pa. div. Am. Cancer Soc., 1984. Mem. ABA (family law sect.), Pa. Bar Assn. (family law sect., com. on legal edn. and bar admission), York County Bar Assn. (chmn. ins. com., divorce rules com., chmn. fee dispute com. 1996—, chmn. 1999—), Am. Cancer Soc. (nat. bd. dirs. 1989-96, recipient St. George's Medalm 1993, hon. bd. mem. Penn. divsn. 1997—), York-Adams Bd. Realtors (mediator 1997—). General corporate, Real property, Libel. Home: 1295 Detwiler Dr York PA 17404-1107

**BENNETT, DAVID HINKLEY,** lawyer; b. Portage, Wis., Sept. 18, 1928; s. Ross and Helen (Hinkley) B.; m. LaVonne Wilson, Feb. 3, 1955; children: Mark H., Todd W., John D. BBA, U. Wis., 1952, LLB, 1956. Bar: Wis. 1956, U.S. Ct. Appeals (7th cir.) 1962, U.S. Supreme Ct. 1966. Ptnr. Bennett & Bennett, Portage, 1956—; dist. atty. Columbia County, Wis., 1959-67; regent Wis. State Univs., 1965-71. Served to 2d lt. AUS, 1953-56. Mem. ABA, Wis. Bar Assn. Republican. Presbyterian. Lodge: Masons. General practice, Personal injury, Estate planning. Home: 215 W Franklin St Portage WI 53901-1643 Office: Bennett and Bennett 135 W Cook St # 30 Portage WI 53901-2103

**BENNETT, EDWARD JAMES,** lawyer; b. Newton, Iowa, Dec. 27, 1941; s. Erskine Francis and Malvina Esther (Goodhue) B.; m. Virginia Lee Cook, Jan. 30, 1965; children: Susan Elizabeth, Edward James. BA, U. Iowa, 1964, JD, 1966. Bar: Iowa 1966, U.S. Dist. Ct. (so. dist.) Iowa 1967. Atty. Diehl, Clayton & Cleverley, Newton, 1966-70; atty. The Maytag Co., Newton, 1970-74, sr. atty., 1974-80, assoc. counsel, 1980-85, asst. sec., asst. gen. counsel, 1985-86; asst. sec., asst. gen. counsel Maytag Corp. (formerly The Maytag Co.), Newton, 1986-90; sec., asst. gen. counsel Maytag Corp., Newton, 1990—; sec. The Hoover Co., 1990—, Dixie-Narco Inc., 1990—, Maytag Internat. Inc., 1990—, Hoover Holdings Inc., 1990—, Maytag Fin. Svcs. Corp., 1990—, Maytag Corp. Found., 1990—; dir. Progress Industries, 1993—, sec., 1994—. Mem. Civil Svc. Commn., Newton, 1980-86; mem. Newton Zoning Bd. Adjustment, 1978-96, chmn., 1978-85; sec., trustee Newton Cmty. Ctr., Inc., 1976-94; trustee Newton Cmty. Schs. Found., 1994—, v.p., 1996, pres., 1997; bd. dirs. Des Moines Metro Opera, 1998—, sec. 1998—. Mem. ABA, Iowa State Bar Assn. (mem. trade regulation com. 1981-92, 93-97), Iowa Assn. Bus. and Industry (chmn. unemployment compensation com. 1976-94), Assn. Home Appliance Mfrs. (mem. product safety com. 1975-92)25457961. Republican. Presbyterian. Antitrust, General corporate, Securities. Home: 203 Foster Dr Des Moines IA 50312-2539 Office: Maytag Corp 403 W 4th St N Newton IA 50208-3034

**BENNETT, GEORGE H., JR.,** lawyer, healthcare company executive. BS, U. Miami, 1975; JD, Ohio State U., 1978. Bar: Ohio 1978. Assoc. Mortiz McClure Hughes & Kerscher, 1978-80, Baker & Hostetler, 1980-83; gen. counsel Cardinal Distbn. Inc., 1984-86, v.p., 1986-91, v.p., chief adminstrv. officer, 1991-94; exec. v.p., gen. counsel Cardinal Health Inc., Dublin, Ohio, 1994—. Office: Cardinal Health Inc 5555 Glendon Ct Dublin OH 43016-3249

**BENNETT, GRAY WESTON,** lawyer, dairyman; b. Dayton, Ohio, Aug. 12, 1960; s. Herd L. and Louise F. (Stilwell) B. AB, Duke U., 1983; JD, U. Akron, 1990. Bar: Ohio 1991. Ptnr. Bennett & Bennett, Eaton, Ohio, 1991—; coach mock trial Ohio Ctr. for Law Related Edn., Columbus, Ohio, 1991-92. Co-author: (3 vols.) Advanced Torts, 1989. Chmn. county re-election campaign C.J. Thomas Moyer, Eaton, 1992; chmn. county campaign James Walsh, Ohio 12th dist. Ct. Appeals, 1990; charter mem. Young Reps. Com., Preble County, Ohio, 1992. Recipient Bracton's Inn award U. Akron Law Sch., 1990. Mem. ABA, Ohio Bar Assn. (chmn. gen. practice sect. legis. com. 1991), Preble County Bar Assn. (trustee 1992—), Rotary (chmn. co-gourd 1992—), Phi Alpha Delta. Avocations: dairy cattle, hunting, golf. General practice, Criminal, Family and matrimonial. Office: Bennett & Bennett 200 W Main St Eaton OH 45320-1748

**BENNETT, HERD LEON,** lawyer; b. Portsmouth, Ohio, Oct. 17, 1934. BA, Duke U., 1956; JD, Cornell U., 1959. Bar: Ohio 1959. Ptnr. Bennett & Bennett, Eaton, Ohio, 1959—; asst. atty. gen. of Ohio, 1962-63; spl. counsel to atty. gen. of Ohio, 1963-70; trustee Ohio State Bar Found., 1984-92, chair planning and rsch. com., 1986-92, awards com., 1988-90, pres. 1991-92; trustee Preble County Law Libr. Assn., 1970-72; trustee Ohio Legal Continuing Edn. Inst., 1990-91, 93-99, treas., 1993-94, vice chmn., 1994-95, chmn., 1995-96; trustee Eaton Found., 1978—, v.p., 1980—; trustee Nat. Hummel Found. and Mus., 1982—; bd. dirs. Ohio Bar Title Ins. Co., 1991-98, Northedge Shopping Ctr., Inc., Miller's Super Markets, Inc. Trustee Eaton Cmty. Improvement Corp., 1981-94 (v.p. 1987-94), trustee Preble County Area Cmty. Improvement Corp., 1994— (pres. 1994—); mem. Eaton Area C. of C., 1959—; mem., moderator, Sunday Sch. tchr. Concord United Ch. of Christ, Eaton H.S. Alumni Assn. (pres. 1983-84, permanent advisor); exec. officer Duke U. Offie Devel., 1956-90, admissions interview chmn. for S.W. Ohio, 1994-97. Mem. ABA (real property, probate and trust law sect.), Nat. Assn. Criminal Def. Lawyers, Am. Judicature Soc., Ohio State Bar Assn. (mem. bd. govs. 1997—, mem. legal ethics and profl. conduct com. 1981—, coun. dels. 1981—), Preble County Bar Assn. (v.p. 1972-74, pres. 1974-76). Office: Bennett & Bennett 200 W Main St Eaton OH 45320-1748

**BENNETT, JAMES H.,** lawyer; b. Montclair, N.J., July 30, 1937; s. Richard Holcombe and Dorothea (Seller) B.; m. Mary Ellen Smith, Sept. 13, 1963 (div. Apr. 1979); children: Stephen Carroll, Kristy Lorraine; m. Lynnette Margaret Buchanan, July 14, 1979; children: John Sukwon, Margaret MiYong. AB summa cum laude, Princeton U., 1959; LLB, Stanford U., 1962. Bar: N.J. 1963, U.S. Dist. Ct. N.J. 1963, U.S. Supreme Ct. 1969, Conn. 1974, U.S. Dist. Ct. Conn. 1991. Law sec. Supreme Ct. of N.J., Newark, 1962-63; assoc. McCarter & English, Newark, 1963-66; internat. atty. Warner-Lambert, Morris Plains, N.J., 1966-68; sr. atty. internat., divsn. counsel Allied Chem. Corp., N.Y.C., 1968-70; sr. internat. atty. Richardson-Merrell Inc., Wilton, Conn., 1970-75; counsel, L.Am. bus. divsn. GE Co., Westport, Conn., 1975-78; v.p., internat. counsel Revlon Health Care Group, Tuckahoe, Tarrytown, N.Y., 1978-85; pvt. practice law New Canaan, Conn., 1985—; v.p., sec. Palladium (USA) Inc. New Canaan planning and zoning rep. Southwestern Reg. Plan Assn., 1996—; dir., mem. exec. com.; elder First Presbyn. Ch. of New Canaan, 1997—; mem. New canaan Planning and Zoning Commn., 1985-96, chmn., 1993-96; alt. Essex county to N.J. State Rep. Com., Trenton, 1964-66; counsel, campaign mgr. Montclair Cmty. Com., 1964, 68; mem. fin. com. S.W. coun. Girl Scouts U.S.A.; mem. soc. justice task force Presbytery of S.N.E. Edward John Noble Found. fellow, 1959-62. Mem. Conn. Bar Assn., Westchester-Fairfield Corp. Counsel Assn. (sec. 1984-85, chmn. exec. com. planning and zoning sect. 1988-91), Phi Beta Kappa. Republican. Avocation: swimming. General corporate, Private international, Real property. Home and Office: 137 Old Kings Hwy New Canaan CT 06840-6411

**BENNETT, JEFFREY,** lawyer; b. Portland, Maine, Apr. 6, 1962; s. Herbert Howard and Elaine Sheila (Leve) B.; m. Dale Lori Fishbein, Jan. 24, 1991. BA in Polit. Sci., U. N.H., 1986; JD, Boston U., 1989. Bar: Mass. 1989, Maine 1991, U.S. Dist. Ct. Mass. 1989, U.S. Dist. Ct. Maine 1991, U.S. Ct. Appeals (1st cir.) 1990. Atty. Goldstein & Manello, Boston, 1989-91, H.H. Bennett & Assocs., P.A., Portland, 1991—. Recipient Am. Jurisprudence (Evidence) award Lawyers Coop. Pub. Co., 1987, Am. Jurisprudence (Comml. Code) award, 1988. Mem. Assn. Trial Lawyers Am. (state del. 1992-93, comml. litigation com. 1992—, young lawyers com. 1992—), Maine Trial Lawyers Assn. (bd. govs. 1992-93). General civil litigation, Contracts commercial, Environmental. Office: H H Bennett & Assocs PA PO Box 7799 Portland ME 04112-7799

**BENNETT, JESSIE F.,** lawyer; b. Bridgeport, Conn.; d. Cornelius T. and Jessie F. (Sutcliffe) B.; m. Ronald J. Canuel, Nov. 3, 1990. BS in Fin. with honors, Fairfield U., 1980; JD magna cum laude, Quinnipiac Coll., 1986. Bar: Conn., 1986; U.S. Dist. Ct. Conn., 1987, U.S. Dist. Ct. (so. and ea. dists.) N.Y. 1989, U.S. Ct. Appeals (2d cir.) 1989, D.C. Ct. of Appeals, 1989, U.S. Supreme Ct., 1989. Jud. clk. to Judge Ellen Bree Burns U.S. Dist. Ct., New Haven, 1986; atty. Cohen & Wolf, Danbury, Conn., 1987-88, Davidson & Naylor, Norwalk, Conn., 1988-92; law clk. Jud. Dept. State of Conn., Waterbury, 1992-96; asst. state's atty. State of Conn. Divsn. Criminal Justice, 1996—. Mem. ABA, ATLA, Conn. Bar Assn., Nat. Dist. Attys. Assn., Conn. Trial Lawyers Assn., D.C. Bar Assn., Phi Delta Phi, Phi Alpha Delta (Am. Jurisprudence award in Remedies and Family Law, Kristin Ann Carveth Meml. Scholastic award, Code Enforcement Ofcl. of Yr. 1999, Pres. award 1999, Cert. Appreciation award 1999). Roman Catholic. Avocations: exercise, music, cooking, travel. Criminal. Office: States Attys Office 80 Washington St Hartford CT 06106-4405

**BENNETT, JOHN HENRY, JR.,** lawyer; b. Charleston, S.C., Apr. 26, 1945; s. John H. B. and Leonora B. Stack. Student, Dartmouth Coll.; BA, George Washington U., 1968; JD, U. S.C. Bar: S.C. 1971. Page S.C. Ho. of Reps., 1964; staff to U.S. Senator Richard B. Russell, 1966; staff atty. Neighborhood Legal Assistance Program, 1971-73. Author: Intestacy and Real Property in South Carolina, 1970. Bd. dirs. Christian Family; exec. dir. Clariosophic Found. Recipient Gedney M. Howe award for pub. svc. Charleston County Bar Assn., 1986, 87. Mem. S.C. Soc., Charleston Concert Assn. (bd. dirs.), S.C. Acad. Authors (bd. govs.), Yeamans Hall Club, St. Cecilia Soc., Carolina Yacht Club, Soc. Cin., Soc. Colonial Wars, Sea Is. Yacht Club, Hibernian Soc., Sons of Confederate Vets., St. David's Soc., Sigma Nu, Phi Delta Phi. Episcopalian. Home: 95 Rutledge Ave Charleston SC 29401-1722 Office: 16 Fulton St Charleston SC 29401-1921

**BENNETT, JOHN K.,** lawyer; b. Newark, N.J., Apr. 4, 1955. BA magna cum laude, Lafayette Coll., 1977; JD cum laude, Seton Hall U., 1980; LLM in Labor Law with honors, NYU, 1988. Bar: N.J. 1980, U.S. Dist. Ct. N.J., U.S. Dist. Ct. N.Y. (ea., so. and no. dists.), U.S. Ct. Appeals (2d and 3d cirs.), U.S. Supreme Ct. Law sec. to Hon. Robert L. Clifford Supreme Ct. N.J., 1980-81; assoc. to sr. ptnr. Carpenter, Bennett & Morrissey, Newark, 1981-98; ptnr., chair labor and employment law practice Connell, Foley & Geiser LLP, 1998—. Articles editor Seton Hall Law Rev., 1979-80; contbr. articles to profl. jours. Mem. ABA (litigation and labor and employment law sects., state labor law devel. com.), N.J. State Bar Assn. (exec. com. labor and employment law sect.), Essex County Bar Assn. Fax: 973-535-9217. Labor, General civil litigation. Office: Connell Foley & Geiser LLP 85 Livingston Ave Roseland NJ 07068-3702

**BENNETT, PAUL WILLIAM,** lawyer; b. Tyler, Tex., Aug. 19, 1967; s. Paul Amon and Altha Jeanette (Rouse) B.; m. Janet Elizabeth Risley, July 25, 1992. BA, Austin Coll., Sherman, Tex., 1989; JD, Tex. Tech U., 1993. Bar: Tex. 1993, U.S. Dist. Ct. (no. dist.) Tex. 1995. Legis. asst. Tex. Ho. of Reps., Austin, 1989; law clk. Office of Staff Judge Advocate USAF, Lubbock, Tex., 1992-93; law cl. Office of Tex. Atty. Gen., Lubbock, 1993; atty. Corley & Corley, L.L.P., Dallas, 1993-95, Law Offices of Ira Thomas King, Dallas, 1995-99, Fletcher & Springer, LLP, Dallas, 1999—. Mem. governing coun. Austin Coll., 1986-87. Mem. ABA, Def. Rsch. Inst., Dallas Bar Assn. (history and meml. com.). Republican. Baptist. General civil litigation, Insurance, Professional liability. Home: 120 Spyglass Dr Coppell TX 75019-3162 Office: Fletcher & Springer LLP 9400 N Central Expy Fl 14 Dallas TX 75231-5027

**BENNETT, RICHARD D.,** lawyer; b. Memphis, Jan. 29, 1961; m. Cindy Gallaher, Oct. 27, 1990. BS, U. Tenn., Martin, 1984; JD, U. Memphis, 1988. Bar: U.S. Dist. Ct. (we. dist.) Tenn. 1988, U.S. Dist. Ct. (ea. dist.) Ark. 1988, U.S. Ct. Appeals (6th and 8th cirs.) 1991. Ptnr. Weintraub, Stock, Bennett, Grisham & Underwood PC, Memphis, 1988—. Bd. dirs. U. Memphis Law Alumni Bd., 1996—; chpt. atty. Associated Builders and Contractors, West Tenn., 1989—. Mem. ABA (sect. labor and employment law), Tenn. Bar Assn. (sect. labor and employment law, bd. dirs. young lawyers divsn. 1996-97), Memphis Bar Assn. (bd. dirs. young lawyers divsn. 1993-94), Kiwanis. Labor, Construction, General civil litigation. Office: Weintraub Stock Bennett Grisham & Underwood 2560 One Commerce Sq Memphis TN 38103

**BENNETT, ROBERT WILLIAM,** law educator; b. Chgo., Mar. 30, 1941; s. Lewis and Henrietta (Schneider) B.; m. Harriet Trop, Aug. 19, 1979. B.A., Harvard U., 1962, LL.B., 1965. Bar: Ill. bar 1966. Legal asst. FCC commr. Nicholas Johnson, 1966-67; atty. Chgo. Legal Aid Bur., 1967-68; asso. firm Mayer, Brown & Platt, Chgo., 1968-69; faculty Northwestern U. Sch. Law, Chgo., 1969—; prof. law Northwestern U. Sch. Law, 1974—, dean, 1985-95. Author: (with LaFrance, Schroeder and Boyd) Hornbook on Law of the Poor, 1973. Knox Meml. fellow London Sch. Econs., 1965-66. Fellow Am. Bar Fedn. (bd. dirs., treas.); mem. Chgo. Council Lawyers (pres. 1971-72), Am. Law Inst., ABA. Home: 2130 N Racine Ave Chicago IL 60614-4002 Office: Northwestern U Sch Law 357 E Chicago Ave Chicago IL 60611-3059

**BENNETT, STEVEN ALAN,** lawyer; b. Rock Island, Ill., Jan. 15, 1953; s. Ralph O. and Anne E. B.; m. Jeanne Aring; children: Preston, Spencer, Hunter, Whitney. BA in Art History, U. Notre Dame, 1975; JD, U. Kans., 1982. Bar: Tex. 1983, Ohio 1995, U.S. Dist. Ct. (no. dist.) Tex. 1983, U.S. Ct. Appeals (5th cir.) 1983, U.S. Supreme Ct. 1995. Atty. Freytag, Marshall, et al, Dallas, 1982-84, Baker, Mills & Glast, Dallas, 1984-87; ptnr. Shank, Irwin, Conant et al, Dallas, 1987-89; gen. counsel Bank One, Tex., N.A., Dallas, 1989-94; sr. v.p., gen. counsel, sec. Banc One Corp., Columbus, Ohio, 1994-99; exec. v.p., chief legal officer, sec. Cardinal Health, Inc., Dublin, Ohio, 1999—. City councilman, mayor pro tem Mesquite, Tex., 1984-86; trustee Meadowview Sch., Mesquite, 1985-92; chair fin. com. St. Brendan Ch., Hilliard, Ohio, 1998—; pres., bd. dirs. Dallas Dem. Forum, 1993-94; bd. dirs. Ohio Hunger Task Force, Columbus, 1995—; trustee Woodrow Wilson Internat. Ctr. for Scholars, Washington, 1996—, vice-chmn., 1999—. Fellow, Ohio State Bar Found.; mem. ABA (banking law com.), Tex. Assn. Bank Counsel, Dallas Bar Assn., Ohio State Bar Assn., Columbus Bar Assn., St. Thomas More Soc. (Dallas bd. dirs. 1990-94), Am. Corp. Counsel Assn. (bd. dirs. 1996—, chair policy com. 1997—), The Bankers Roundtable (lawyers' coun. 1994-98), Phi Beta Kappa. Avocation: landscape photography. Administrative and regulatory, Banking, General corporate. Office: Cardinal Health Inc 7000 Cardinal Pl Dublin OH 43017-1092

**BENNETT, THOMAS WESLEY,** lawyer; b. Hawkinsville, Ga., Mar. 21, 1936; s. Thomas Jerome and Nora Lee (Smith) B.; m. Sherry Julia Lindsey, July 8, 1974; children: Wendy, Jennifer, Deanne, April. BA, Mercer U., 1961; JD, U. Ga., 1964. Bar: Ga. 1964, U.S. Dist. Ct. (mid. dist.) Ga. 1964, U.S. Dist. Ct. (so. dist.) Ga. 1983. Pvt. practice Macon, Ga., 1968—. Author: Georgia Medical Torts-Physician, 1981. Rep. 81st Dist., Ga. Gen. Assembly, 1971-72; v.p. Ga. Assn. Area Planning and Devel. Commn., 1973-74, pres., 1974-75, govs. adv. bd. 1973-74; bd. dirs. Middle Ga. Area Planning and Devel. Commn., 1973-77, Ga. Planning Commn., 1974-75. With U.S. Army, 1954-57. Mem. Elks. Methodist. Personal injury, Professional liability, Real property. Office: PO Box 7328 Macon GA 31209-7328

**BENNETT, WILLIAM PERRY,** lawyer; b. Inglewood, Calif., Aug. 28, 1938; s. George William and Lenora (Perry) B.; m. Linda L. Schneider, Aug. 19, 1961; children: Greg, Mark, Carin. BA, Calif. State U., Long Beach; MA in Specialized Ministry, Grace Theol. Sem.; JD, U. So. Calif.; DMin, Reformed Theol. Sem. Bar: Calif. 1965, U.S. Ct. Appeals (9th cir.) 1965, U.S. Supreme Ct. 1993; lic. real estate broker; cert. real estate investment specialist, real estate mgmt. specialist, family law specialist; lifetime tchg. credential specialized subject. Ptnr. Powars, Tretheway & Bennett Law Corp., 1965-78; sr. ptnr. William P. Bennett Law Corp., 1978-97; sr. real estate atty. Wise, Wiezorek, Timmons & Wise, 1991-94; owner, broker Century 21 Pacific Coast Realty, 1979-88, Pacific Coast Properties, Long Beach, 1988—; assoc. prof. bus. and real estate law Calif. State U., Long Beach, 1965-86; exec. dir. Grandparents Rights Ctr., 1998—; gen. counsel Campus Crusade for Christ, 1991-93; alumni pres., univ. adv. bd. Calif. State U., Long Beach; real estate arbitrator Am. Arbitration Assn. Panel, 1965—, L.A. County Superior Ct. Arbitrator/Pro Tem Judge, Christian Conciliation Svc., L.A. and Orange Counties; bus. adv. bd. Long Beach City Coll.; spl. counsel numerous chs. and religious orgns. including Chs. Uniting in Global Mission, Crystal Cathedral Ministries, Calvary Chapel; adj. prof. of law Simon Green Leaf/Trinity U. Bd. dirs., leagl advisor Long Beach Area March of Dimes, 1973-90; exec. dir. Legal Ministry Campus Crusade for Christ, dir. property mgmt. Campus Crusade, exec. mgmt. team Arrowhead Springs Conf Ctr., 1991-94; dir. Grandparents Rights Ctr. Mem. Long Beach Bar Assn. (bd. govs. 1970-76), Long Beach Area C. of C. (bd. dirs. 1985-86, Bus. Person of Yr. award 1987), Seal Beach C. of C. (pres. 1985-86, 89-90), Kiwanis Internat. (pres., lt. gov., Kiwanian of Yr.), Century 21 Orange County Brokers Coun. (pres. 1984), So. Calif. Investment Soc. (pres. 1988). Republican. Avocations: academics, speaking, religion. Family and matrimonial, Non-profit and tax-exempt organizations, Consumer commercial. Home and Office: 723 W Chapman Ave Orange CA 92868-2820

**BENNION, DAVID JACOBSEN,** lawyer; b. Glendale, Calif., Jan. 29, 1940; s. Donald Clark and Margaret (Jacobsen) B.; m. Constance Wilson, Jan. 27, 1966; children—Marian, Margaret, Elizabeth, David, Sarah, Heidi. B.A., Stanford U., 1964, J.D., 1966. Bar: Calif. 1966. Ptnr. Boccardo Law Firm, San Jose, Calif., 1966-79; mission pres. Ch. of Jesus Christ of Latter-day Saints, Geneva, Switzerland, 1979-82; ptnr. Packard, Packard and Bennion, Palo Alto, Calif., 1982-90; ptnr. Bohn, Bennion & Niland, 1993-98; law offices of David J. Bennion, 1998—; instr. continuing edn. of bar, personal injury trial. Mem. ABA, Calif. State Bar, Assn. Trial Lawyers Am., Am. Bd. Trial Advs., Am. Inns. Ct. (treas., mem. exec. com. Sara Clara County), Republican. Personal injury, Product liability, General civil litigation. Home: 1357 Woodland Ave Menlo Park CA 94025-2849 Office: 95 S Market St # 360 San Jose CA 95113-2301

**BENOLIEL, JOEL,** lawyer; b. Seattle, June 11, 1945; s. Joseph H. and Rachel (Maimon) B.; m. Maureen Alhadeff, Mar. 1971; 1 child, Joseph D. BA in Polit. Sci., U. Wash., 1967, JD, 1971. Bar: Wash., U.S. Dist. Ct. (we. dist.) Wash., U.S. Ct. Appeals (9th cir.), U.S. Mil. Ct. Appeals. Assoc. atty. MacDonald, Horgue & Bayless, Seattle, 1971-73, ptnr., 1973-78; v.p., gen. counsel Jack A. Benaroya Co., Seattle, 1978-84; ptnr. Trammell Crow Co., Seattle, 1985-87, Spieker Ptnrs., Bellevue, Wash., 1987-92; sr. v.p. law and real estate, gen. counsel Price Costco, Inc., Issaquah, Wash., 1992—. Bd. dirs. Overlake Sch., Redmond, Wash., 1995—, Congregation Ezra Bessaroth, Seattle, 1992-95. With U.S. Army, 1968-74. Avocations: tennis, boating, skiing, reading fiction. Real property, General corporate, Contracts commercial. Office: Price Costco Inc 999 Lake Dr Issaquah WA 98027-5367

**BENSHOOF, JANET LEE,** lawyer, association executive; b. Detroit Lakes, Minn., May 10, 1947; m. Richard Klein; children: David, Eli. BA summa cum laude, U. Minn., 1969; JD, Harvard U., 1972. Dir. law reform South Bklyn. Legal Svcs., 1972-77; dir. reporductive freedom project ACLU, N.Y.C., 1977-92; founder, pres. Ctr. Reproductive Law & Policy, N.Y.C., 1992—; guest lectr. Yale U., Columbia U., Rutgers U., Case Western Reserve U. Contbr. articles to profl. jours. Recipient Margaret Sanger award, 1986, Christopher Tietze Humanitarian award Nat. Abortion Fedn., 1988, Gloria Steinem award Ms. Found. Women, N.Y.C., 1989, 10 for 10 award Ctr. Population Optiums, 1990; named one of 100 Most Influential Lawyers in Am. Nat. Law Jour., 1991, 94; MacArthur Found. Fellowship grant, 1992—. Mem. ABA, Am. Pub. Health Assn., N.Y.C. Bar Assn. Office: Ctr Reproductive Law & Policy 120 Wall St New York NY 10005-3904

**BENSON, BARBARA SARA,** lawyer; b. N.Y.C., July 30, 1951. BS, Cornell U., 1973; MS, U. Wis., 1977; JD, U. Calif., Davis, 1982. Bar: Calif. 1992. Assoc. Maloney, Chase, Fisher & Hurst, San Francisco, 1982-83, LeBoeuf, Lamb, Leiby & MacRae, San Francisco, 1983-86; atty. Pacific Gas Transmission Co., San Francisco, 1987-89, Pacific Gas and Electric Co., San Francisco, 1989—. Bd. dirs., vice-chair, chair Strawberry Design Rev. Bd., Mill Valley, Calif., 1988-95; vice -chair Strawberry Recreation Dist., Mill Valley, 1997—; bd. dirs. Marin County chpt. ARC, Marin County, Calif., 1996—. Mem. State Bar of Calif., Bar Assn. of San Francisco. Office: Pacific Gas and Elec Co PO Box 7442 San Francisco CA 94120-7442

**BENSON, JOHN SCOTT,** lawyer; b. Atlanta, Sept. 17, 1947; s. Lawrence Walker and Betty Lamar (Chick) B.; m. Louise Kathryn Sweet, July 22, 1984; children: Nathaniel Scott, Elisabeth Sweet. BA magna cum laude, Vanderbilt U., 1969; JD, U. Va., 1974. Bar: Fla. 1974, Colo. 1988. Assoc. Martin, Ade, Birchfield & Johnson, Jacksonville, Fla., 1974-78, ptnr., 1978-88; ptnr. Kraemer, Kendall & Benson, P.C., Colorado Springs, Colo., 1988—; bd. dirs. Associated Unit Cos., Inc.; adj. prof. U. Colo. Coll. Bus., Colorado Springs, 1996-98. Bd. dirs. Cerebral Palsy of Jacksonville, 1980-88, pres., 1986; mem. Fedn. Council YMCA Indian Guides, 1985-86; bd. dirs. Children's Services of Jacksonville, 1986-88. Served to 1st lt. U.S. Army, 1969-71, Vietnam. Decorated Air medal; named one of Outstanding Young Men in Am., 1979. Mem. Colo. Bar Assn., El Paso County Bar Assn., Colorado Springs Estate Planning Coun., Christian Legal Soc., Christian Mgmt. Assn., Phi Beta Kappa, Phi Kappa Sigma. Republican. Avocations: sunday school teaching, camping, skiing. Real property, General corporate, Estate planning. Office: 430 N Tejon St Ste 300 Colorado Springs CO 80903-1167

**BENSON, SCOTT MICHAEL,** lawyer; b. West Bend, Wis., Apr. 28, 1963; m. Lisa Louise Autio, Oct. 3, 1987; children: Sarah M., Scott M. II, Joseph E. BA, Carroll Coll., 1985; JD, Marquette U., 1991. Bar: Wis.; U.S. Dist. Ct. (ea. and we. dists.) Wis., U.S. Ct. Appeals Fed. Cir. Assoc. Gutglass, Erickson & Bonville, Milw., 1991-92, Law Offices of Robert L. Pavlic, S.C., Brookfield, Wis., 1993-95; shareholder Hutchison & Benson, S.C., Brookfield, 1996—. Mem. ABA, State Bar of Wis., Waukesha County Bar Assn. Republican. Lutheran. Real property, General civil litigation. Office: Hutchison & Benson SC 200 Regency Ct Ste 101 Brookfield WI 53045-6185

**BENTLEY, ANTHONY MILES,** lawyer; b. N.Y.C., July 16, 1945; s. Herbert A. and Dorothy Dene (Hyman) B. BA, U. Pa., 1967; JD, Fordham U., 1971. Bar: N.Y. 1971, U.S. Ct. Appeals (2d cir.) 1971, Pa. 1973, U.S. Dist. Ct. (so. and ea. dists.) N.Y. 1973, U.S. Tax Ct. 1976, U.S. Supreme Ct. 1976, U.S. Ct. Appeals (fed. cir.), 1995, U.S. Claims Ct. 1996, U.S. Dist. Ct. Ariz. 1996, U.S. Ct. Internat. Trade 1996. Assoc. Hughes Hubbard & Reed, N.Y.C., 1970, Cahill Gordon & Reindel, N.Y.C., 1971-75, Goldstein Shames Hyde, N.Y.C., 1975-76; sole practice N.Y.C., 1977—; spl. master N.Y. County Supreme Ct., 1977—, N.Y. County Civil Ct., 1994—; arbitrator N.Y.C. Ct. N.Y. Coun. Editor Fordham Law Rev., 1970-71; founding editor Fordham Urban Law Jour., 1971. Trustee Am. Judges Found. With U.S. Army, 1963-65. Recipient Disting. Svc. award FTC, 1976, 79. Mem. ABA, Assn. of Bar of City of N.Y., Assn. Trial Lawyers Am., Pa. Bar Assn., Phila. Bar Assn., Mensa, Intertel, Am. Judges Assn. (N.Y. del.), N.Y. County Lawyers Assn., N.Y. Civil and Criminal Cts. Bar Assn. Jewish. Landlord-tenant, Federal civil litigation, Bankruptcy. Address: 116 W 72nd St New York NY 10023-3315

**BENTLEY, FRED DOUGLAS, SR.,** lawyer; b. Marietta, Ga., Oct. 15, 1926; s. Oscar Andrew and Ima Irene (Prather) B.; children from previous marriage: Fred Douglas, Robert Randall; m. Jane Morrill McNeel, Nov. 7, 1997. BA, Presbyn. Coll., 1949; JD, Emory U., 1948. Bar: Ga. 1948. Sr. mem. Bentley & Dew, Marietta, 1948-51; ptnr. Bentley, Awtrey & Bartlett, Marietta, 1951-56, Edwards, Bentley, Awtrey & Parker, Marietta, 1956-75, Bentley & Schindelar, Marietta, 1975-80, Bentley, Bentley & Bentley, Marietta, 1975-80, 1980—; pres. Beneficial Investment Co., Newmarket, Inc., Happy Valley, Inc., Bentley & Sons, Inc.; founder, chmn. bd. Charter Bank and Trust Co.; founder, trustee emeritus Kennesaw Coll. Mem. Ga. Ho. Reps., 1951-57, Ga. Senate, 1958; past pres. Cobb County (Ga.) C. of C.; founder, hon. curator Bentley Rare Book Galleries-Brenau U., Kennesaw State U.; mem., past chmn. Ga. Coun. Arts, 1976-89; mem. Gov.'s Fine Arts

Com., 1990-92, Cummer Mus. of Art (hon. life); attache Ghana Olympic Com.; founder Cobb Emergency Svcs., bd. advisors Emory U-Woodruff. Served with USN. Recipient Blue Key Cmty. Svc. award, Founder's award, 1992, Clarisse Baquell award for outstanding svc., Spl. Svc. award Kennesaw State Coll., Robert Cleveland award for lifetime achievement in law; named Citizen of Yr., C. of C., 1951, Leader of Tomorrow, Time mag., 1953, Vol. Citizen of Yr., Atlanta Jour./Constn., 1981, Kennesaw Historical Soc. Man of Yr., 1996, Brenau Univ. Man of Yr., 1996; fellow J. Pierpont Morgan Libr.; Oct. 15 Fred Bentley Day City & Coun. Mem. ABA, Ga. Bar Assn., Ga. Mus. Art (bd. advisors, hon. life mem.), Nat. PTA (hon. life), Cobb Landmarks Soc. (founder), Kennesaw Mountain Jaycees (founder), Rotary (hon. life), Georgian Club (bd. dirs.), The Grolier Club (hon.), Fellows of Marietta Cobb Mus. of Art (founder, chmn.), Ga. Mus. (life, bd. advisors). Republican. Methodist. General practice. Home: 1441 Beaumont Dr Kennesaw GA 30152-3201 Office: 241 Washington Ave NE Marietta GA 30060-1958

**BENTLEY, JOSHUA MARK,** lawyer; b. San Francisco, Feb. 27, 1965; s. John Martin and Ruth Catherine (Marshall) B.; m. Emily Elaine Blanchard, Aug. 15, 1990; children: Kaitlin Meredith, Olivia Roxanne. BA, U. Calif., Santa Barbara, 1983-88; JD, U. Santa Clara, Calif., 1991. Bar: Calif. 1991, U.S. Dist. Ct. Calif. 1991. Dep. dist. atty. San Mateo County Dist. Atty.'s Office, Redwood City, Calif., 1991-93; gen. ptnr. Smith, Bentley & Hartnett, Redwood City, 1993—. Recipient Congl. Recognition, Congresswoman Anna Eshoo, 1996. Mem. ABA, Calif. State Bar. Republican. Roman Catholic. Office: Smith Bentley & Hartnett 777 Marshall St Redwood City CA 94063-1818

**BENTON, ANTHONY STUART,** lawyer; b. Decatur, Ill., Jan. 28, 1949; s. Paul Stewart and Allene Juanita (Jones) B.; m. Peggy Ann Miller, Aug. 6, 1977; children: Allison Renee, Emily Elizabeth, Anne McKinley. BA cum laude, U. Ill., 1971; JD summa cum laude, Ind. U., 1976. Bar: Ill. 1976, Ind. 1976, U.S. Dist. Ct. (so. and no. dists.) Ind. 1976, U.S. Ct. Appeals (7th cir.) 1978, U.S. Supreme Ct. 1993. Assoc. Stuart & Branigin, Lafayette, Ind., 1976-80; ptnr. Stuart & Branigin, Lafayette, 1980—; prof. in environ. Purdue U. Sch. Civil Engring., 1993—. Bd. dirs. Lafayette C. of C., 1993—, treas., 1998, chair-elect, 1999; bd. dirs. New Directions, Lafayette, 1978-80, Clegg Found., Lafayette, 1980-83, Wabash Ctr., Lafayette, 1984-86; mem. pres. coun. Purdue U., 1990—, convocations bd. dirs., 1991-97. With USNR, 1971-77. Fellow Ind. Bar Found. (bd. dirs. 1998—); mem. Nat. Assn. R.R. Trial Counsel, Ind. State Bar Assn. (sec. sect. on environ. law 1992), Ill. State Bar Assn., Am. Judicature Soc., Environ. Law Inst., Masons. Environmental, Labor, Construction. Office: Stuart & Branigin PO Box 1010 Lafayette IN 47902-1010

**BENTON, DONALD STEWART,** publishing company executive, lawyer; b. Marlboro, N.Y., Jan. 2, 1924; s. Fred Stanton and Agnes (Townsend) B. Student, U. Leeds, Eng., 1945; BA, Columbia U., 1947, JD, 1949; LLM, NYU, 1953. Bar: N.Y. 1953. Practiced in N.Y.C., 1953-56; atty. N.Y. State Banking Dept., 1954-55; v.p. Found. Press, Inc., Bklyn., 1957-60; exec. asst. to exec. v.p. N.Y. Stock Exchange, 1960-61; dir. reference book dept. and spl. projects editor Appleton Century Crofts, N.Y.C., 1962-71; sr. editor Matthew Bender & Co., Inc., N.Y.C., 1974-77; sr. legal editor Warren, Gorham & Lamont, Inc., N.Y.C., 1977-89. Author: Thorndike Encyclopedia of Banking and Financial Tables, 3rd edit., 1999 yearbook, Federal Banking Laws, 3rd edit., 1987, Real Estate Tax Digest, 1984, Criminal Law Digest, 3rd edit., 1983, Modern Real Estate and Mortgage Checklists, 1979. Mem. Cresskill (N.J.) Zoning Bd. Adjustment, 1969-71, 82-83, 86—, Cresskill Planning Bd., 1971-74; councilman City of Cresskill, 1972-74. With AUS, 1943-46, 50-52. Decorated Bronze Star. Mem. Phi Delta Phi. Mem. Reformed Ch. in Am. Home: 117 Heatherhill Rd Cresskill NJ 07626-1020 Office: AS Pratt & Sons Warren Gorham & Lamont 395 Hudson St New York NY 10014-3669

**BENTON, EDWARD HENRY,** lawyer; b. Norwalk, Conn., Dec. 1, 1950; s. Edward Failing and Margaret Theresa (Sabo) B. BA, Yale U., 1974; JD, Vanderbilt U., 1981. Bar: N.Y. 1982. Pres. POS Corp., New Haven, 1974-76; asst. account exec. Benton & Bowles Inc., N.Y.C., 1976-78; assoc. Simpson Thacher & Bartlett, N.Y.C., 1981-85, Skadden, Arps, Slate, Meagher & Flom, N.Y.C., 1985-86, Cadwalader, Wickersham & Taft, N.Y.C., 1987; chmn. bd. dirs. Video Cave, Inc., Hudson, N.Y., egalxz, Inc.; bd. dirs. Columbia County Indsl. Devel. Agy. Mem. Vanderbilt U. Law Rev., 1980-81. Patrick Wilson scholar, 1978-81. Mem. Yale Club (N.Y.C.), Royal Hong Kong Yacht Club. Episcopalian. E-mail: edwardbenton@mail.com. General corporate, Private international, Alternative dispute resolution. Home and Office: 88 Richmond Rd PO Box 88 Malden Bridge NY 12115-0088

**BENTON, LEE RIMES,** lawyer; b. Birmingham, Ala., Sept. 5, 1951; s. William Dallas and Elizabeth (Rimes) B.; m. Sharon Brenneman; children: Sarah Elizabeth, James Bradley. BA, Auburn U., 1974; JD, Samford U., 1977. Bar: U.S. Dist. Ct. (no. dist.) Ala. 1978, U.S. Dist. Ct. (mid. dist.) Ala., U.S. Dist. Ct. (so. dist.) Ala., U.S. Ct. Appeals (5th cir.), U.S. Ct. Appeals (11th cir.). Clk. Justice Richard L. Jones, Ala. Supreme Ct., Montgomery, 1977-78; assoc. Denaburg, Schoel, Meyerson & Ogle, Birmingham, Ala., 1978-81; ptnr. Najjar & Denaburg, Birmingham, 1981-87, Schoel, Ogle, Benton & Centeno, Birmingham, 1987-98; with Benton & Centeno, LLP, Birmingham, 1998—; mem. adv. com. Ala. Law Inst.-Ala. Fraudulent Transfer Act, Tuscaloosa, 1986-87; lectr. Nat. Bus. Inst., Altoona, Wis., 1991-92, Ala. Law Inst.-ABA, Tuscaloosa, 1988-89, 94. Dir. Ala. Goodwill Industries, Birmingham, 1987; trustee, elder, chmn. bd. deacons South Highland Presbyn. Ch., Birmingham, 1985-86, 87-90, 93-95, 96-98; treas. Birmingham Bar Found., 1996-98. Mem. ABA, Ala. Trial Lawyers Assn. (lectr. CLE 1988), Ala. Bar Assn. (chmn. bankruptcy comml. law sect. 1990-91), Birmingham Bar Assn. (chmn. grievance com. 1989-90, treas. young lawyers sect. 1982, exec. com. 1993-95). Avocations: landscaping. Bankruptcy, Federal civil litigation, State civil litigation. Office: Benton & Centeno 550 Landmark Ctr 2100 157 Ave N Birmingham AL 35203

**BENTON, W. DUANE,** judge; b. Springfield, Mo., Sept. 8, 1950; s. William Max and Patricia F. (Nicholson) B.; m. Sandra Snyder, Nov. 15, 1980; children: Megan Blair, William Grant. BA in Polit. Sci. summa cum laude, Northwestern U., 1972; JD, Yale U., 1975; MBA in Accounting, Memphis State U., 1979; student Inst. Jud. Adminstrn., NYU, 1992; LLD (hon.), Ctrl. Mo. State U., 1994; LLM, U. Va., 1995; LLD (hon.), Westminster Coll., 1999. Bar: Mo. 1975; CPA, Mo. Ensign USN, 1972; advanced through grades to capt., 1993; judge advocate USN, Memphis, 1975-79; chief of staff for Congressman Wendell Bailey, Washington, 1980-82; pvt. practice Jefferson City, Mo., 1983-89; dir. revenue Mo. Dept. of Revenue, Jefferson City, 1989-91; judge Mo. Supreme Ct., Jefferson City, 1991—, chief justice, 1997-99; adj. prof. Westminster Coll., U. Mo.-Columbia Sch. Law. Contbr. articles to profl. jours.; mng. editor Yale Law Jour., 1974-75. Chmn. Multistate Tax Commn. Washington, 1990-91; chmn. Mo. State Employees Retirement System, Jefferson City, 1989-93; regent Ctrl. Mo. State U., 1987-89; dir. Coun. for Drug Free Youth, Jefferson City, 1989—; mem. Mo. Mil. Adv. Com., 1989-91; mem. Mo. Commn. Intergovernmental Coop., Jefferson City, 1989-91; trustee, deacon 1st Bapt. Ch., Jefferson City. Danforth fellow JFK Sch. Govt. Harvard U., 1990. Mem. ABA (tax com. 1975—), Mo. Bar Assn. (tax com. 1975—), AICPA (tax com. 1983—), Mo. Soc. CPA's (tax com. 1983—), Navy League, Mil. Order of World Wars, Vietnam Vets of Am., VFW, Am. Legion, Phi Beta Kappa, Beta Gamma Sigma, Rotary (sgt. at arms 1990—). Baptist. Lt. USN, 1975-80. Capt. JAGC USNR. Office: Supreme Court PO Box 150 Jefferson City MO 65102-0150

**BENZ, WILLIAM J.,** lawyer; b. Phila., Nov. 7, 1954; s. William Joseph and Margaret Virginia (Hiller) B.; m. Donna Ann Horne, Oct. 16, 1981; children: William, Sean, Kristian. BA, LaSalle Coll., Phila., 1976; JD, U. of the Pacific, 1979. Bar: Pa. Legal intern Sacramento County Dist. Atty., 1979; assoc. Victor Lipsky, P.C., Phila., 1979-80, McCoy & Auchinleck, P.C., Newtown, Pa., 1980-82, Lipsky & Brandt, P.C., Phila., 1982-86; sole practice Southampton, Pa., 1986—. Bd. dirs. LaSalle Coll. High Sch. Alumni Bd., Springfield, Pa., 1987—; bd. dirs. Northampton (Pa.) Twp. Zoning Hearing Bd., 1988—. Mem. Phila. Bar Assn., Bucks County Bar Assn., Feasterville Businessmen's Assn. (pres. 1992). Republican. Roman Catholic. Avocation: golf. Personal injury, Probate, General corporate. Office: 307 Lakeside Park Southampton PA 18966-4050

**BENZAN, JOHN PATRICK,** lawyer; b. Cambridge, Mass., Dec. 12, 1963; s. Rafael and Grace Beatrice Benzan; m. Kimberly Henrietta Kelley, May 30, 1992; children: Patrick, Katharine. BA, Coll. Holy Cross, Worcester Mass., 1985; JD, Suffolk U., 1989. Bar: Mass., 1990, R.I., 1990, U.S. Dist. Ct. Mass., 1990. Asst. atty. gen. Atty. Gen.'s Office, Boston, 1994-96; asst. dist. atty. Middlesex County Dist. Atty.'s Office, Cambridge, Mass., 1996-98; assoc. Lane, Altman & Owens, Boston, 1998—. Bd. dirs. YMCA, 1994—. Mem. ABA (mem. criminal litig. sect. coun. 1998—), Holy Cross Gen. Alumni Assn. Roman Catholic. Avocations: physical fitness, reading. Criminal, Real property. Office: Lane Altman & Owens 101 Federal St Fl 26 Boston MA 02110-1842

**BERALL, FRANK STEWART,** lawyer; b. N.Y.C., Feb. 10, 1929; s. Louis J. and Jeannette F.; m. Christiana Johnson, July 5, 1958 (dec. July 1972); children: Erik Dustin, Elissa Alexandra; m. Jenefer M. Carey, Sept. 1, 1980. BS, Yale U., 1950, JD, 1955; LLM in Tax, NYU, 1959. Bar: N.Y. 1955, Conn. 1960; accredited estate planner. Assoc. firm Mudge, Stern, Baldwin & Todd, N.Y.C., 1955-57, Townley, Updike, Carter & Rodgers, N.Y.C., 1957-60; atty. Conn. Gen. Life Ins. Co., Bloomfield, Conn., 1960-65; atty. trust dept. Hartford Nat. Bank & Trust Co., Conn., 1965-67; assoc. Cooney & Scully, Hartford, Conn., 1968-70; ptnr. Copp & Berall and predecessors, Hartford, 1970—; v.p., sec., gen. counsel, bd. dirs. John M. Blewer, Inc., Essex, Conn., 1969-86; asst. in instrn. Yale U. Law Sch., 1954-55; lectr. U. Conn. Sch. Ins., 1964-72, Law Sch., 1972-73; instr. estate planning Am. Coll. Life Ins., 1968-69; adj. asst. prof. grad. tax program U. Hartford, 1973-74; counsel Conn. Gov.'s Strike Force for Full Employment, 1971-72, Conn. Gov.'s Commn. on Tax Reform, 1972-73, State Tax Commr.'s Commn., 1972-75, Com. on Tax Law Clarification, 1984-88; lectr. in field. Co-author: A Practitioners Guide to the Tax Reform Act of 1969, 1970, Estate Planning and the Close Corporation, 1970, Planning Large Estates, 1970, Revocable Inter Vivos Trusts, 1985, The Migrant Client: Tax, Commnity Property, and Other Considerations, 1994; sr. editor Conn. Bar Jour., 1969—; mem. editl. bd. Estate Planning mag., 1973—, Practical Tax Lawyer, 1988—, Jour. Taxation of Trusts and Estates, 1988-92. Bd. dirs. Bloomfield Interfaith Homes, 1967-71; mem. adv. council U. Hartford Tax Inst., 1970-82; co-chmn. adv. council Hartford Tax Inst., 1986-94; co-chmn. Notre Dame Estate Planning Inst., 1977—; trustee Culver Ednl. Found., 1997—. 1st lt., F.A. U.S. Army, 1951-52. Fellow Am. Coll. Trust and Estate Counsel (chmn. Conn. chpt. 1975-81, editl. bd. 1975-87, chmn. estate and gift tax com. 1976-81, chmn. accessions tax com. 1984-88, regent 1977-83), Am. Coll. Tax Counsel; mem. ABA (chmn. com. estate planning and ins. 1979-85, chmn. task force on retroactivity and constitutionality of tax law changes 1985-89, vice chmn. comm. estate planning and drafting 1992-96, co-chmn. com. non-tax issues in drafting wills and recovable trusts and co-chmn. tax litig. and controversy of real property probate and trust sect. 1995—, chmn. mem. com. 1977-79, chmn. com. on income of estates and trusts 1983-85, chmn. com. econ. tax practice 1987-89, chmn. CLE com. tax sect., co-founder, convener estate planning seminar group 1972-78), Conn. Bar Assn. (exec. com., estates and probate sect. 1973—, chmn. 1984-86, chmn. tax sect. 1969-72, exec. com. 1969—, vice chmn. com. on specialization 1974-77), Hartford County Bar Assn. (chmn. com. liaison with IRS 1972-74, com. charter and by-laws 1975), Am. Law Inst. (tax adv. group 1980-89), Internat. Acad. Estate and Trust Law (exec. coun. 1978-82, spkr. numerous seminars), Tax Club of Hartford (pres. 1975-76), Culver Summer Schs. Alumni Assn. (v.p. 1975-85, pres. 1997—, bd. dirs. 1985-91, 93—), Culver Club (pres. 1996—), Yale Club of Harford (dir. 1998—, pres. 1999—). Probate, Estate taxation, State and local taxation. Home: 9 Penwood Rd Bloomfield CT 06002-1520 Office: Copp & Berall LLP 55 Farmington Ave Ste 703 Hartford CT 06105-3790 *As a tax lawyer, I view my job as helping to keep the system going by seeing to it that my clients pay the government all it is legally entitled to receive in taxes, but no more, and doing pro bono work for the improvement of the entire federal and state tax law system.*

**BERANBAUM, JOHN A.,** lawyer; b. N.Y.C., Feb. 9, 1955; s. Samuel Louis and Betty (Samson) B.; m. Nancy Coates, Jan. 16, 1994; 1 child, Sarah Elizabeth Fuller. BA magna cum laude, Yale U., 1977; JD, NYU, 1981. Bar: N.Y. 1982, N.J. 1983, Pa. 1989, U.S. Dist. Ct. (so. and ea. dist.) N.Y., U.S. Dist. Ct. (ea. dist.) Pa., U.S. Ct. Appeals (2d and 3d cirs.), U.S. Supreme Ct. Atty. Hunterdon County Legal Svcs., Flemington, N.J., 1981-85, N.J. Dept. Pub. Advocate, Trenton, 1985-89; assoc. Galfand, Lurie & March, Phila., 1989-92, Vladeck, Waldman, Elias & Engelhard, N.Y.C., 1992-95; ptnr. Law Office of John A. Beranbaum, N.Y.C., 1995-98, Beranbaum, Menken, Ben-Asher & Fishel, N.Y.C., 1998—; mediator U.S. Dist. Ct. for Ea. Dist. N.Y., 1994—. Mem. ABA, N.Y. State Bar Assn., Assn. Bar City N.Y., Nat. Employees Lawyers Assn. Labor, Federal civil litigation. Office: Beranbaum Menken Et Al 3 New York Plz New York NY 10004-2442

**BERARD, DOUGLAS CLAY,** lawyer; b. Lynn, Mass., Aug. 30, 1945; s. Anthony Dwight and Lucille (Clay) B.; m. Linda Margaret Allison, June 28, 1968. BA in History and Polit. Sci., The Citadel, 1968; JD, Southwestern U., L.A., 1978. Bar: Calif. 1979, U.S. Dist. Ct. (cen. dist.) Calif. 1980, U.S. Ct. Appeals (9th cir.) 1980. Assoc. Revere, Citron and Wallace, L.A., 1979-81, Law Office of Barry Zalma, L.A., 1981-85; ptnr. Zalma and Berard, Culver City, Calif., 1985-87, Berard and Mavogos, 1987-89; of counsel Berger, Kahn, Shafton & Moss, 1989-91, ptnr., 1991—. Served to capt. USAF, 1968-73, Vietnam. Mem. ABA, Calif. Bar Assn., Los Angeles County Bar Assn., Internat. Assn. Property Ins. Counsel (past pres., founding mem.). Democrat. Office: Berger Kahn Sharton & Moss 23161 Ventura Blvd Ste 102 Woodland Hills CA 91364

**BERCHEM, ROBERT LEE, SR.,** lawyer; b. Milford, Conn., Aug. 17, 1941; s. Robert W. and Barbara (Maher) B.; m. Lee Contrucci, Feb. 19, 1966; children: Kerry, Robert L. Jr., Jonathan. AB, Fairfield U., 1962; LLB, Villanova U., 1965; LLM, U. Mich., 1967. Bar: Conn. 1965. Law clk. U.S. Dist. Ct., Conn., 1965-66; prin. Berchem, Moses & Devlin, P.C., Milford, 1967—. Trustee Fairfield (Conn.) U.; chmn. Milford Hist. Dist. Commn., 1976—. Mem. ABA, Conn. Bar Assn., New Haven County Bar Assn., Milford Bar Assn. Democrat. Roman Catholic. Avocations: golf, skiing. Contracts commercial, Bankruptcy, Real property. Home: 125 W River St Milford CT 06460-3420 Office: Berchem Moses & Devlin PC 75 Broad St Milford CT 06460-3331

**BERCOVICI, MARTIN WILLIAM,** lawyer; b. Omaha, Nov. 7, 1942; s. Jacob and Ethelyn (Kramer) B.; m. Ellen Pokress, Aug. 7, 1971; children: Jason M., Lauren P., Nicole J. BS, U. Mo., 1964; JD, NYU, 1967. Bar: D.C. 1968, Calif. 1969, U.S. Ct. Appeals (D.C. cir. 1969), U.S. Supreme Ct. 1973, U.S. Ct. Appeals (5th cir.) 1980, U.S. Ct. Appeals (fed. cir.) 1985, U.S. Ct. Appeals (7th cir.) 1987, U.S. Ct. Appeals (6th cir.) 1990. Teaching fellow George Washington U. Law Sch., Washington, 1967-68; law clk. to Hon. Joseph C. Waddy U.S. Dist Ct. D.C., 1968; asst. prof. San Diego State Coll., 1968-69; assoc. Keller & Heckman, Washington, 1969-73, ptnr., 1973—; v.p. legal Waterway Comms. System, Inc., Jeffersonville, Ind., 1986-93; mem. U.S. Del. to World Adminstrv. Radio Conf. for the Mobile Svcs.; vice-chmn. Fed. Adv. Comm. for the World Adminstrv. Radio Conf. for the Mobile Svcs., Washington, 1985-87, Fed. Comms. Commn., Geneva, 1987; exec. dir. Alliance for Rail Competition, Washington. Mem. ABA. Communications, Transportation, Administrative and regulatory. Office: Keller & Heckman 1001 G St NW Ste 500W Washington DC 20001-4545

**BERDON, ROBERT IRWIN,** state supreme court justice; b. New Haven, Dec. 24, 1929; s. Louis J. and Jean (Cohen) B.; m. Nancy Tarr, Aug. 30, 1964 (dec. Mar. 1992); 1 child, Peter A. BS, U. Conn., 1951, JD, 1957; LLM in Jud. Process, U. Va., 1988. With Bank of Manhattan, 1953-54; pvt. practice New Haven, 1957-73; treas. State of Conn., 1971-73; judge Superior Ct., State of Conn., New Haven, 1973-91; justice Supreme Ct., State of Conn., 1991—; adj. prof. law U. Bridgeport Sch. Law, 1986-91; lectr. in law U. Conn. Sch. of Law, 1993; assoc. fellow Saybrook Coll., Yale U., 1986—; lectr. Am. Bd. Trial Advs., 1986; mem. Conn. Bd. Pardons, 1991-92. Contbr. articles to profl. jours. Recipient Judiciary award Conn. Trial Lawyers Assn., 1976, Disting. Alumni award U. Conn., 1977, Outstanding State Trial Judge in U.S. award Assn. Trial Lawyers in Am., 1982, Pub. Svc. award U. Conn. Sch. Law Alumni Assn., 1989, Judiciary award Conn. Bar Assn., 1991. Home: 245 Pleasant Point Rd Branford CT 06405-5609 Office: Conn Supreme Court Drawer Z Sta A 231 Capitol Ave Hartford CT 06106-1548

**BERENBERG, DANNY BOB,** lawyer; b. Mpls., Sept. 10, 1944; s. Morris and Theresa Clara B.; children: Jake Robert, Jena Thompson. BA, U. Minn., 1966; JD, 1970. Bar: Minn. 1970, U.S. Supreme Ct. 1976. Mem. firm Schermer, Schwappach, Borkon & Ramstead, Mpls., 1970-75; mgr. Lincoln Dels Restaurants, Bloomington, Minn., 1975-77, sr. exec., 1981-90; vice chmn. Lincoln Baking Co., 1981—, Lincoln Dels Inc., 1981-89; founding ptnr. Eichhorn-Hicks & Beredberg Attys. at Law, 1989—; chmn. Highwayman's, Inc., 1990; chmn. Highwayman's Inc., 1991 . Founder Kaiser Roll Found. and Kaiser Roll, wheelcair and able-bodied race; bd. dirs. Bloomington Hospitality Assn., A.M. Miller & Assocs., Inc., Minn. chpt. U.S. Olympic Com., 1985—, Sister Kenny Inst., 1990, Shattuck Sch., chmn. devel. com.; founder S.W. Hospitality Assn.; founder, pres., bd. dirs. 494 Ministry, 1982—, Cancer Kids Found., 1985—; mem. Minn. Conv. Facility Commn., 1984—, Minn. Internat. Trade Commn., 1984—; mem. Minn. Hwy. Beautification Commn., 1989—; dir. devel. Shattuck St. Mary's Sch. Served to 1st lt. AUS, 1968. Named Bloomington Man of Yr., Bloomington mag. 1982, Small Bus. of Yr. award, 1982; recipient Teamsters Law Enforcement Recognition award, 1982, merit award Minn. N.G., 1982, Omar Bonderud-Human Rights award City of Bloomington, 1983, Minn. Human Rights award, 1985, Good Neighbor award WCCO, 1986, Disting. Community Citizen award March of Dimes, 1986, Community Svc. award, 1990. Mem. Conv. Bur. (dir.), Minn. Restaurant Assn., Hennepin County Bar Assn., Minn. Bar Assn., Norwegian Home Guard Friends (founder). Jewish. Club: U. Minn. Touchdown (v.p.).

**BERENDT, ROBERT TRYON,** lawyer; b. Chgo., Mar. 8, 1939; s. Alex E. and Ethel L. (Tryon) B.; m. Sara Probert, June 15, 1963; children: David, Elizabeth, Katherine. BA, Monmouth Coll., 1961; JD with distinction, U. Iowa, 1965. Bar: Iowa 1965, Ill. 1968, U.S. Dist. Ct. (no. dist.) Ill. 1968, U.S. Ct. Appeals (7th cir.) 1968, Mo. 1979, U.S. Dist. Ct. (ea. dist.) Mo. 1979. Assoc. Schiff Hardin & Waite, Chgo., 1968-73, ptnr., 1973-78; litigation counsel Monsanto Co., St. Louis, 1978-83, asst. gen. counsel, 1983-85, assoc. gen. counsel, 1986-96; of counsel Thompson Coburn, St. Louis, 1996—; Disting. Neutral, Ctr. for Pub. Resources; editl. adv. bd. Alternatives, Inside Litigation, Product Safety and Liability Reporter-Bur. Nat. Affairs. Contbr. articles to profl. jours. Lt. USNR, 1965-68. Mem. ABA (litigation sect., coun. mem. 1993-96), Mo. Bar Assn., Ill. Bar Assn., Iowa Bar Assn., Bar Assn. Met. St. Louis, Product Liability Adv. Coun. (bd. dirs., exec. com., Inst. for the Judiciary, pres.-trustee Found. 1992-98). Avocations: golf, tennis, reading. General civil litigation, Antitrust, Environmental. Office: Thompson Coburn 1 Mercantile Ctr Saint Louis MO 63101-1643

**BERENSON, WILLIAM KEITH,** lawyer; b. Nashville, Nov. 23, 1954; s. Leon and Lorraine Florence (Keiles) B; m. Mara Lynn Rubinton; 1 child, Marissa Laurel. BA with honors, U. Tex., 1976; JD, So. Meth. U., 1979. Bar: Tex. 1979, U.S. Dist. Ct. (no. dist.) Tex., U.S. Ct. Appeals (5th and 11th cirs.), U.S. Supreme Ct.; cert. personal injury trial law, Tex. Bd. Legal Specialization. mem. Supreme Ct. Jury Task Force. Author: Evaluating Settlement Offers, 1990, Texas Automobile Injury Guide, 1993, Trying the Automobile Injury Case in Texas: Plaintiff's Perspective, 1995, Automobile Injury Cases in Texas, 1996, Quantification of Personal Injury Claims, 1997; mem. editl. bd. Ins. Settlement and Litigation Reporter; mem. editl. adv. bd. Ins. Issues Annotated. Chmn. Longhorn Coun. Boy Scouts Am., Ft. Worth; bd. dirs. So. Meth. U. Alumni Assn., AIDS Interfaith Network; dir. Regional Coun. of Parents and Alumni, So. Meth. U.; vol. atty. North Tex. Humane Soc. Fellow Tarrant County Bar Found.; mem. ABA, ATLA (sustaining mem. pub. interest group com.), State Bar Tex., Tex. Bar Assn., Tarrant County Bar Assn. (jud. evaluation com., fee arbitration com.), Tarrant County Lawyrs Assn. (bd. dirs. 1994-99), Tex. Trial Lawyers Assn., Coll. State Bar Tex., Nat. Coll. Advocacy, Roscoe Pound Found., Phi Alpha Delta. Avocations: golf, snow skiing. Personal injury, General civil litigation. Office: 900 River Plaza Tower 1701 River Run Fort Worth TX 76107-6579

**BERENZWEIG, JACK CHARLES,** lawyer; b. Bklyn., Sept. 29, 1942; s. Sidney A. and Anne R. (Dubowe) B.; m. Susan J. Berenzweig, Aug. 8, 1968; children: Mindy, Andrew. B.E.E., Cornell U., 1964; J.D., Am. U., 1968. Bar: Va. 1968, Ill. 1969. Examiner U.S. Pat. Off., Washington, 1964-66; pat. adviser U.S. Naval Air Systems Command, Washington, 1966-68; ptnr. Brinks, Hofer, Gilson & Lione and predecessor firm, Chgo., 1968—. Editorial staff Am. U. Law Rev., 1966-68; contbr. articles to profl. jours. Mem. ABA, Chgo. Bar Assn., Ill. State Bar Assn., Bar Assn. 7th Fed. Cir., Va. State Bar, Internat. Trademark Assn. (bd. dirs. 1983-85), Brand Names Edn. Found. (bd. dirs. 1993-98), Meadow Club (Rolling Meadows, Ill.), Miramar Club (Naples, Fla., Delta Theta Phi. Patent, Trademark and copyright, Federal civil litigation. Home: 4119 Terramere Ave Arlington Heights IL 60004-1359 Office: Brinks Hofer Gilson & Lione Ltd Ste 3600 455 N Cityfront Plaza Dr Chicago IL 60611-5599

**BERESFORD, DOUGLAS LINCOLN,** lawyer; b. Washington, June 1, 1956; s. Spencer Moxon and Ann (Lincoln) B.; m. Lori Anne Mainous, Sept. 22, 1990; children: Alexander Gould, Erik Mainous. AB cum laude, Harvard U., 1978; JD, Georgetown U., 1982. Bar: D.C. 1982, U.S. Ct. Appeals (D.C. cir.) 1984, U.S. Supreme Ct. 1986. Assoc. Morgan, Lewis & Bockius, Washington, 1982-83; assoc. Newman & Holtzinger, P.C., Washington, 1983-89, ptnr., 1989-94; ptnr. Long, Aldridge & Norman, Washington, 1994—. Administrative and regulatory, General civil litigation, FERC practice. Office: Long Aldridge & Norman 701 Pennsylvania Ave NW Ste 600 Washington DC 20004-2692

**BEREZNOFF, GREGORY MICHAEL,** lawyer; b. Grand Rapids, Mich., Aug. 10, 1951; s. Walter and Marjorie Ann (Nash) B. BA with high honors, Mich. State U., 1974; JD, U. Detroit, 1978. Bar: Mich. 1978, U.S. Dist. Ct. (ea. dist.) Mich. 1978. Assoc. Schureman, Frakes, Glass & Wulfmeier, Detroit, 1978-85, ptnr., 1986-87; prin. Zamler Mellen & Shiffman, P.C., Southfield, Mich., 1987—. Mem. ABA, Assn. Trial Lawyers Am., Wayne County Bar Assn., Oakland County Bar Assn., Mich. Trial Lawyers Assn. Avocations: tennis, golf, fly casting, photography. State civil litigation, Personal injury, Labor. Home: 725 River Bend Dr Rochester MI 48307-2726 Office: Zamler Mellen & Shiffman PC 23077 Greenfield Rd Southfield MI 48075-3709

**BERG, DAVID HOWARD,** lawyer; b. Springfield, Ohio, Mar. 4, 1942; s. Nathan Stewart Berg and Mildred (Besser) Berg-Filion; children: Geoffrey Alan, Gabriel Adam, Caitlin Hannah; m. Kathryn Page, July 10, 1994. Student, Tulane U., 1963; BA in English, U. Houston, 1964, JD, 1967. Bar: Tex. 1967, U.S. Dist. Ct. Tex. 1967, N.Y. 1989, U.S. Dist. Ct. (so. dist.) N.Y. 1990, U.S. Ct. Appeals (2d, 4th, 5th, 8th and 11th cirs.) 1990, U.S. Supreme Ct. 1990. Law clk. NLRB, Washington, 1967-68; ptnr. David Berg & Assocs., Houston, 1968-77, Berg & Androphy, 1977-98, Berg Androphy & Wilson, 1998—; mem. fed. ct. lawyers adv. com. U.S. Dist. Ct. (so. dist.) Tex.; mem. U. Houston Law Found., 1996—; spl. counsel commn. on lawyer discipline, Tex. State Bar, 1996—. Contbr. articles and essays to mags. Issues staff Jimmy Carter Campaign, Atlanta, 1976; adviser Jimmy Carter Transition Govt., Washington, 1976; adviser Mayor Kathy Whitmire campaigns, 1980-91; patron Friends of Menil Collection, 1990-91; adviser campaign Mayor Bob Lanier, 1991; chmn. City of Houston's "Imagine Houston"; bd. dirs. "Camp for All"; bd. dirs. U. Houston Law Found., 1996. Recipient 1st pl. for best feature article in a scholarly jour. Nat. Assn. Publ., 1991. Fellow Internat. Acad. Trial Lawyers, Houston Bar Found.; mem. ATLA, Tex. Bar Assn. (chmn. grievance com. 1984-85), Tex. Bar Found., N.Y. State Bar Assn., Tex. Trial Lawyers Assn., Houston Trial Lawyers Assn., U. Houston Law Alumni Assn. (bd. dirs. 1992-95), Am. Bd. Trial Advocates (assoc.). Democrat. Jewish. Avocations: writing, running, fishing. Criminal, Personal injury. Home: 16 Sunset Blvd Houston TX 77005-1838 Office: Berg Androphy & Wilson 3704 Travis St Houston TX 77002-9550

**BERG, HANS FREDRIK,** lawyer; b. St. Paul, Mar. 28, 1936; s. Ejner and Alphild (Hortelius) B.; m. Gail Andrews, Nov. 11, 1971; children: Heather, Sonja. BA, Fairleigh Dickinson U., 1961; LLB, Blackstone Sch. Law, Chgo., 1973. Bar: Calif. 1973, U.S. Dist. Ct. (cen. dist.) Calif. 1976, U.S. Supreme

Ct. 1985. Sr. appraiser L.A. County Assessor, 1964-74; sr. dep. dist. atty. Los Angeles County, Calif., 1974-89; pvt. practice law, Lancaster, Calif., 1989-97; mem. faculty Trade Tech. Coll., L.A., 1974-76. Chmn. Quartz Hill Sch. Site Coun., 1982-83, chmn. ad hoc com., 1983; v.p. AV Criminal Def. Bar Assn., 1993-94; pres. AV Dependency Bar Assn., 1994-95. Served with U.S. Army, 1954-56. Honored by resolution Calif. Assembly, 1980, Westside Union Sch. Bd. Quartz Hill, 1983, L.A. City Bd. Suprs., 1989. Mem. AV Bar Assn., Calif. Dist. Attys. Assn., Assn. Dep. Dist. Attys., Smithsonian Inst., Nat. Geog. Soc., Ocean Soc., Fairwind Yacht Club (L.A.).

**BERG, JEFFREY A.,** lawyer, mediator; b. Mpls., Apr. 20, 1956; s. Boyd L. and Majel C. Berg; m. Patricia K. Berg, Sept. 26, 1981; 1 child, Eric J. BA, Hamline U., St. paul, 1978, JD, 1981. Bar: Minn. 1981. Atty. Corrick & Sondrall, Chartered, Robbinsdale, Minn., 1983-84, Berg, Henderson, Hass & Nyquist, Brooklyn Center, Minn., 1984-86, Jensen & Weyland, Brooklyn Park, Minn., 1986-90; atty., shareholder Thorson & Berg, P.A., Maple Grove, Minn., 1990-99; with Henningson & Snoxell, Ltd., Mpls., 1999—; officer and dir., panel mediator Mediation Ctr., St. Paul and Mpls., 1985-98, North Hennepin Mediation Project, Brooklyn Center, 1985-92; officer, mem. cabinet North Hennepin Leadership Acad., Brooklyn Park, 1992-97. Mem. Maple Grove Rotary Club (pres. 1993-94, asst. dist. gov. 1996—, Svc. Above Self award 1997). Lutheran. Avocations: golf, skiing, snowmobiling, sailing, fishing. Family and matrimonial, Labor, Alternative dispute resolution. Office: Henningson & Snoxell Ltd 6160 Summit Dr N Ste 640 Minneapolis MN 55430-4001

**BERG, WILLIAM GERARD,** lawyer; b. Lafayette, Ind., Apr. 1, 1961; s. William James and Charlene Marie Berg; m. Jean Marie Moran, Oct. 14, 1989; children: Aileen Marie, Kelly Moran, Liam Gerard. BS, U. Ill., 1983; JD, DePaul U., 1986. Assoc. Law Office of James Keating, Chgo., 1986-93, Schaffenegger, Watson & Peterson, Chgo., 1993-95, Brydges Riseborough, Chgo., 1995-96; ptnr. French, Kezelis & Kominarek, Chgo., 1996—; spkr. Nat. Bus. Inst., Chgo., 1998. Author (manual) Premises Liability in Illinois—Trial of a Difficult Case, 1998. Active Project Insight, Project H.U.M.E., Chgo. Mem. ABA, Ill. State Bar Assn., Ill. Def. Counsel, Chgo. Bar Assn. Roman Catholic. Avocation: community volunteer. Transportation, Personal injury, Product liability. Office: French Kezelis & Kominarek 33 N Dearborn St Fl 7 Chicago IL 60602-3102

**BERGAN, EDMUND PAUL, JR.,** lawyer; b. N.Y.C., May 6, 1950; s. Edmund Paul and Alice (Gordon) P. B.; m. Patricia Ann Gallagher, Jan. 31, 1987; children: Annabel (dec.), Caroline. BA, Holy Cross Coll., 1971; JD, Fordham U., 1975. Bar: N.Y. 1976. Staff atty. SEC, Washington, D.C., 1975-77; v.p., assoc. gen. counsel Securities Industry Assn., N.Y.C., 1977-81; v.p., asst. gen. counsel Alliance Capital Mgmt. LP, N.Y.C., 1981-88; v.p. gen. counsel Alliance Fund Distbrs., N.Y.C., 1988-94; v.p., gen. counsel Alliance Fund Svc. Subs., N.Y.C., 1988-94; sr. v.p., gen. counsel Alliance Fund Distbrs. and Alliance Fund Svcs., N.Y.C., 1994—. Mem. ABA (mem. fed. securities com. 1982—, investment advisers and cos. subcom. 1999—), Investment Co. Inst. (SEC rules com. 1986—, closed-end fund com. 1989—, chmn. 1992-97, various subcoms.). Republican. Roman Catholic. Avocations: historical studies, athletics. Securities. Office: Alliance Capital Mgmt LP 1345 Ave of Americas New York NY 10105-3198

**BERGAN, MARSHA ANN,** lawyer; b. Decorah, Iowa, Oct. 14, 1951; d. Donald Enos and Helen Mae (Ellingson) B. BA, Luther Coll., Decorah, Iowa, 1973; student, Am. U., 1972; JD, U. Iowa, 1977. Bar: Iowa 1977, U.S. Dist. Ct. (no. and so. dists.) Iowa 1977, U.S. Ct. Appeals (8th cir.) 1979. Acctg. technician GPO, Washington, 1973; Reginald Heber Smith fellow Legal Services Corp. Iowa, Iowa City, 1977-79, staff atty., 1979-80, co-mng. atty., 1980-81; ptnr., Bergan & Weyer, Iowa City, 1981—, judicial magistrate, Johnson Co., 1988—. Mem. edit. bd. Iowa Law Rev., 1976-77. Bd. dirs. Domestic Violence Project, Iowa City, 1982-85, Willow Creek Neighborhood Center, 1978-81, Student Legal Services, 1982; commr. Iowa City Human Rights Commn., 1986. Mem. Iowa Bar Assn., Johnson County Bar Assn., Iowa Orgn. Women Attys. Democrat. Lutheran. General practice. Office: Bergan & Weyer PO Box 3188 Iowa City IA 52244-3188

**BERGAN, PHILIP JAMES,** lawyer; b. White Plains, N.Y., Apr. 13, 1938; s. Raymond Patrick and Marjorie (Ward) B. m. Susan Ellen Bancroft, Sept. 18, 1965; children: David Andrew, Jeffrey Matthew. AB, Holy Cross Coll., 1960; MA, Stanford U., 1963; LLB, Yale U., 1964. Bar: N.Y. 1966, U.S. Ct. Appeals (2d cir.) 1966, U.S. Supreme Ct. 1971, U.S. Dist. Ct. (so. dist.) N.Y 1973. Assoc. Shearman & Sterling, N.Y.C., Paris, London, 1964-77; gen. counsel merchant banking group Citicorp/Citibank, N.A., N.Y.C., 1978-82; v.p. gen. counsel's office Citicorp/Citibank N.A., N.Y.C., 1982-84; assoc. gen. counsel Citicorp/Citibank, N.A., N.Y.C., 1984-91; from counsel to ptnr. D'Amato & Lynch, N.Y.C., 1992—; bd. dirs. Household Bank, Prospect Heights, Ill., 1993—; 1st Ctrl. Nat. Life Ins. Co. of N.Y., N.Y.C., 1998—. Contbr. articles to prof. jours. Mem. ABA (banking law com. bus. law sect. 1992—), N.Y. State Bar Assn., Assn. Bar City N.Y. (banking law com. 1993-96, legal history com. 1995-98), Down Town Assn. Banking, Finance, Securities. Banking, Finance, Securities. Home: 935 Park Ave New York NY 10028-0212 Office: D'Amato & Lynch 70 Pine St Fl 47 New York NY 10270-0002

**BERGER, ALAN I.,** lawyer; b. St. Louis, Aug. 23, 1933; s. Sam and Evelyn Ruth (Wittner) B.; m. Harriette Sue Ofstein, Feb. 19, 1961; children: Rochelle Lynn, Rachel Lea. BA, Washington U., St. Louis, 1954, JD, 1959. Bar: Mo. 1959, U.S. Dist. Ct. (ea. dist.) Mo. 1959, U.S. Ct. Appeals (8th cir.) 1965, U.S. Ct. Appeals (2d cir.) 1967, U.S. Ct. Appeals (4th cir.) 1968, U.S. Ct. Appeals (5th cir.) 1969, U.S. Ct. Appeals (6th and 7th cirs.) 1972. Assoc. Guffey & McMahon, St. Louis, 1959-60, John R. Stockham, St. Louis, 1960-61; ptnr. McMahon & Berger (now McMahon, Berger, Hanna, Linihan, Cody and McCarthy), St. Louis, 1961-80; sr. ptnr. McMahon, Berger, Hanna, Linihan, Cody and McCarthy, St. Louis, 1980—; instr. labor law St. Louis U., 1961-66. Contbg. editor: The Developing Labor Law, 1975—. 1st lt. U.S. Army, 1954-56. Mem. ABA, Bar Assn. Met. St. Louis (chmn. labor law sect. 1978), Univ. Club (bd. dirs. 1985-94), Media Club. Avocations: tennis, art. Labor. Home: 900 S Hanley Rd Apt 8E Saint Louis MO 63105-2668 Office: McMahon Berger Hanna Linihan Cody & McCarthy 2730 N Ballas Rd Saint Louis MO 63131-3039

**BERGER, BARRY STUART,** lawyer; b. Houston, May 22, 1942; s. Herman and Anna (Seidler) B. BS, U. Houston, 1964, JD, 1967; LLM, Georgetown U., 1969. Bar: Tex. 1967, U.S. Ct. Appeals (D.C. cir.) 1971, U.S. Supreme Ct. 1973, U.S. Dist. Ct. (so. and ea. dists.) Tex., U.S. Ct. Appeals (5th cir.). Asst., then assoc. prof. law U. Balt., 1969-72; counsel select com. on crime U.S. Ho. of Reps., Washington, 1972-73; gen. counsel, asst. v.p. Green Internat., Balt., 1973-75; gen. atty. Dresser Industries, Inc., Houston, 1976-81; assoc. gen. counsel Geosource Inc., Houston, 1982-84; pres. Barry S. Berger, P.C., Houston, 1984—; cons. Jud. Conf. D.C., Washington, 1968-69, Jud. Conf. Md., Balt., 1970-72; instr. S.W. Legal Asst. Inst., Houston, 1980-81. Ford Found. fellow, 1967-69. Mem. ATLA, Tex. Bar Assn., Houston Bar Assn., Tex. Trial Lawyers Assn., Houston Trial Lawyers Assn. (bd. dirs. 1996-97), Phi Beta Kappa, Phi Kappa Phi, Omicron Delta Kappa. Avocations: golf, tennis, fishing, reading. Admiralty, Personal injury, Product liability. Office: 2828 Bammel Ln Apt 1111 Houston TX 77098-1132

**BERGER, CAROLYN,** judge; BA, U. Rochester, 1969; MEd, Boston U., 1971, JD, 1976. Bar: Del. 1976, U.S. Dist. Ct. Del. 1976, U.S. Ct. Appeals (3d cir.) 1981, U.S. Supreme Ct. 1981. Dep. atty. gen. Del. Dept. Justice, Wilmington, 1976-79; assoc. Prickett, Ward, Burt & Sanders, Wilmington, 1979, Skadden, Arps, Slate, Meagher & Flom, Wilmington, 1979-84; vice-chancellor Ct. of Chancery, Wilmington, 1984-94; justice Del. Supreme Ct., 1994—. Mem. ABA, Del. Bar Assn. Office: Carvel State Bldg 820 N French St Fl 11 Wilmington DE 19801-3509*

**BERGER, CHARLES LEE,** lawyer; b. Evansville, Ind. Oct. 14, 1947; s. Sydney L. and Sadelle (Kaplan) B.; m. Leslie Lilly, Apr. 20, 1973; children—Sarah, Rebecca, Leah. B.A., U. Evansville, 1969; J.D. cum laude, Ind. U., 1972. Bar: Ind. 1972, U.S. Dist. Ct. (so. dist.) Ind. 1972, U.S. Ct. Appeals (7th cir.) 1972, U.S. Ct. Appeals D.C. 1975, U.S. Supreme Ct. 1977, U.S. Dist. Ct. (we. dist.) Ky. 1981, U.S. Ct. Appeals (6th cir.) 1984. Ptnr., Berger & Berger, Evansville, 1972—; mem. study com. Ind. Supreme Ct. Rules of Evidence, 1993—; mem. Ind. Jud. Qualifications Disciplinary Commn., 1998—. Bd. dirs. Leadership Evansville, 1977. Fellow Ind. Bar Found.; mem. Ind. Bar Assn. (chmn. trial lawyers sect. 1982-83), Am. Bd. Trial Advocates, Ind. Trial Lawyers Assn. (bd. dirs. 1973-77, 77-84, v.p. 1984—). Jewish. Personal injury, Federal civil litigation, State civil litigation. Home: 7408 E Sycamore St Evansville IN 47715-3762 Office: Berger & Berger 313 Main St Evansville IN 47708-1485

**BERGER, DAVID,** lawyer; b. Archbald, Pa., Sept. 6, 1912; s. Jonas and Anna (Raker) B.; children—Jonathan, Daniel. AB cum laude, U. Pa., 1932, LLB cum laude, 1936. Bar: Pa. 1938, D.C., N.Y. Asst. to prof. U. Pa. Law Sch., Phila., 1936-38, spl. asst. to dean; law clk. Pa. Supreme Ct., Phila., 1939-40; spl. asst. to dir. enemy alien identification program U.S. Dept. Justice, Washington, 1941-42; law clk. U.S. Ct. Appeals, 1946; pvt. practice Phila., Washington and N.Y.C.; city solicitor Phila., 1956-63; founder, chmn. Berger & Montague, P.C., Phila.; former counsel Sch. Dist. Phila.; former chmn. adv. com. Pa. Superior Ct.; mem. drafting com. fed. rules evidence U.S. Supreme Ct.; lectr. on legal subjects. Author numerous articles on law. Nat. commr. Anti-Defamation League; assoc. trustee U. Pa., mem. bd. overseers Law Sch.; Presdl. appointee U.S. Holocaust Meml. Coun.; dir. Internat. Tennis Hall of Fame; trustee Game Conservancy USA; bd. dirs. ARC, Palm Beach, Fla.; founder, mem. Friends of Art and Preservation in Embassies. Decorated Silver Star and Presdl. Unit Citation; Fellow Duke of Edinburgh's Award World Fellowship; David Berger chair of law for the improvement of the adminstrn. of justice established at U. Pa. Law Sch.; enshrined in U. Pa. Tennis Hall of Fame, 1997. Fellow Am. Coll. Trial Lawyers, Internat. Acad. Trial Lawyers, Internat. Soc. Barristers; mem. ABA (vice-chair tort and ins. practice sect. com. on comml. torts 1988-89), Phila. Bar Assn. (pres., bd. govs., chancellor), Phila. Bar Found. (past pres.), The Athenaeum Phila., Penn Club (N.Y.C., founder), Order of Coif, The Queens Club (London), Royal Ascot Racing Club (Ascot, Eng.). Antitrust, Bankruptcy, Federal civil litigation. Home: Elephant Walk 109 Jungle Rd Palm Beach FL 33480-4809 Office: Berger & Montague PC 1622 Locust St Philadelphia PA 19103-6305

**BERGER, HAROLD,** lawyer, engineer; b. Archbald, Pa., June 10, 1925; s. Jonas and Anna (Raker) B.; m. Renee Margareten, Aug. 26, 1951; children: Jill Ellen, Jonathan David. BS in Elec. Enging, U. Pa., 1948, JD, 1951. Bar: Pa. 1951. Practiced in Phila.; judge Ct. of Common Pleas, Phila. County, 1971-72; chmn., moderator Internat. Aerospace Meetings Princeton U., 1965-66; chmn. Western Hemisphere Internat. Law Conf., San Jose, Costa Rica, 1967; chmn. internat. Confs. on Aerospace and Internat. Law, Coll. William and Mary; permanent mem. Jud. Conf. 3d Circuit Ct. of Appeals; mem. County Bd. Law Examiners, Phila. County, 1961-71; chmn. World Conf. Internat. Law and Aerospace, Caracas, Venezuela, Internat. Conf. on Environ. and Internat. Law, U. Pa., 1974, Internat. Confs. on Global Interdependence, Princeton U., 1975, 79; mem. Pa. State Conf. Trial Judges, 1972-80, Nat. Conf. State Trial Judges, 1972—; chmn. Pa. Com. for Independent Judiciary, 1973—; adv. coun. Biddle Law Libr., U. Pa., 1991—; mem. bd. overseers Sch. Engring. & Applied Scis., U. Pa., 1998—. Mem. editorial advisory bd.: Jour. of Space Law, U. Miss. Sch. of Law, 1973—; contbr. articles to profl. jours. Mem. We the People 200 Com. for Constn. Bicentennial, 1991. Served with Signal Corps, AUS, 1944-46. Recipient Alumnus of Year award Thomas McKean Law Club, U. Pa. Law Sch., 1965, Gen. Electric Co. Space award, 1966, Nat. Disting. Achievement award Tau Epsilon Rho, 1972, Spl. Pa. Jud. Conf. award, 1981. Mem. Inter-Am. Bar Assn. (past chmn. aerospace law com.), Fed. Bar Assn. (past nat. chmn. com. on aerospace law, pres. Phila. chpt. 1983-84, mem. nat. exec. coun., past nat. chmn. fed. jud. com., Presdl. award 1970, Nat. Disting. Svc. award 1978, nat. com. 1987 bi-centennial of U.S. Constn., chmn. class action and complex litigation com. 3d cir. 1990—, nat. chmn., alternate dispute resolution com. 1992-95, pres. eastern dist. Pa. chpt. 1996—), ABA (Spl. Presdl. Program medal 1975, past chmn. aerospace law com., mem. state and fed. ct. com., nat. conf. of state trial judges), Phila. Bar Assn. (past chmn. jud. liaison com. 1975, chmn. internat. law com. 1977), Assn. U.S. Mems. Internat. Inst. Space Law Internat. Astronautical Fedn. (former bd. dirs.), Internat. Acad. Astronautics Paris. Alternative dispute resolution, Federal civil litigation, Entertainment. Office: 1622 Locust St Philadelphia PA 19103-6305

**BERGER, JAIME BENJAMIN,** lawyer; b. Mexico City, July 18, 1949; s. Lazaro and Sura Blima (Stender) B.; m. Esther Rosenberg, Nov. 21, 1971 (div. May 10, 1985); children: Abraham, Joseph, Ann Myriam; m. Marcia Glukenhous, Sept. 9, 1986; children: Alissa, Daniel. Diploma, Nat. U. Mex., Mexico City, 1971. Bar: Mex. 1971. With Bufete Vuridico & Berger, Tijuana, Mex. Author: Practice and Dictionary of Mercatile, 1983, Juicio de Amparo, 1984, Panoramic View of Mexican Law, 1987. Mem. Inter-Am. Bar Assn. Admiralty, General civil litigation, Contracts commercial. Office: Bufete Vuridico & Berger, 1909 6th St Ste 301, Tijuana Mexico 22000

**BERGER, LAWRENCE HOWARD,** lawyer; b. Phila., May 19, 1947; s. Howard Merrill Berger and Doris Eleanor Cummins; m. Julie Mitchell Collins, Aug. 8, 1970; children: Colby Shaw, Ryan Lawrence, Lindsey Wade. BS, Mich. State U., 1969; JD, U. Va., 1972. Bar: Pa. 1972, U.S. Dist. Ct. (ea. dist.) Pa. 1973, U.S. Ct. Appeals (3d cir.) 1986. Assoc. Morgan, Lewis & Bockius LLP, Phila., 1972-79, ptnr., 1979—; bd. dirs. INROADS/Phila., Lacrosse Found. Trustee Agnes Irwin Sch., 1984-86, Naomi Wood Charitable Trust-Woodford Mansion Mus., 1986—, Fairmount Park Coun. for Hist. Sites, 1989-95, Fairmont Park Hist. Trust, 1993-95; dir. Phila. Lacrosse Assn., 1992—. Recipient Frank Carr Community Svc. award, 1991. Fellow Am. Bar Found.; mem. ABA (sec. com. on nonprofit corps. 1980-90), Pa. Bar Assn. (chmn. com. on uniform comml. code 1978-80), Phila. Bar Assn., Pa. Bar Inst., Banking Law Inst. (lectr. 1985), Pa. Bankers Assn. (lectr. 1980, 89), Martins Dam Club, Blue Key, Omicron Delta Kappa. Banking, General corporate, Non-profit and tax-exempt organizations. Home: 360 Pond View Rd Devon PA 19333-1732 Office: Morgan Lewis & Bockius LLP 1701 Market St Philadelphia PA 19103-2903

**BERGER, LELAND ROGER,** lawyer; b. N.Y.C., Feb. 3, 1956; s. Albert and Audrey Sybil (Ellenbogen) B.; m. Lisa M. Burk, Feb. 15, 1987 (div. Dec. 1998) ; 1 child, Robert Samson. Student, Am. U., 1977; BA, Dickinson Coll., 1978; JD, Lewis & Clark Coll., 1982. Bar: Oreg. 1983, U.S. Dist. Ct. Oreg. 1983, U.S. Ct. Appeals (9th cir.) 1990. Pvt. practice Portland, Oreg., 1983-84; assoc. Rieke, Geil & Savage, P.C., Portland, 1984-94; pvt. practice Portland, 1995—; mem. legal com. NORML. Mem. Oreg. Bar Assn. (ad hoc com. to study multi-state bar exam. 1983-84, uniform criminal jury instrn. com. 1989-90, sec. 1990-91, criminal law sect., appellate law sect.), Multnomah County Bar Assn. (corrections com. 1987), Oreg. Young Attys. Assn. (bd. dirs. 1983-84), Nat. Lawyers Guild (co-chair criminal justice com. Portland chpt. 1983-84), Oreg. Criminal Def. Lawyers Assn. (rep. to Oreg. Health Divsn. adv. com. on med. marijuana 1999), Nat. Criminal Def. Lawyers Assn. Democrat. Jewish. Appellate, Constitutional, Criminal. Home: 3427 NE 11th Ave Portland OR 97212-2240 Office: 950 Lloyd Ctr PMB 3 Portland OR 97232-1262

**BERGER, MARC JOSEPH,** lawyer; b. Chgo., June 28, 1947; s. Lawrence and Esther Berger; m. Eileen Neiberg, Aug. 29, 1971. MA in Music Theory, U. Chgo., 1973; MusD, Northwestern U., 1984; JD, Southwestern U., 1989. Bar: Calif. 1989, U.S. Dist. Ct. (ctrl. Calif.) 1989, U.S. Ct. Appeals (9th cir.) 1989. Prof. music Am. Conservatory Music, Chgo., 1973-79; assoc. Yusim Stein & Hanger, Encino, Calif., 1989-91, Howarth & Smith, L.A., 1991-97, Michael P. Stone P.C., Pasadena, Calif., 1997—. Composer (opera) Der Gruftwächter, 1998. Wildman scholar Southwestern U., 1985-89. Avocations: music, theater, chess. Labor, Appellate, General civil litigation.

**BERGER, MELVIN GERALD,** lawyer; b. Bklyn., June 13, 1943; s. Louis and Lillian (Shapiro) B.; m. Ellen Terry Chelmow, Jan. 24, 1965 (dec. 1991); children—Michael R., Andrew R., Lee M.; m. Joyce Goldstein, Nov. 26, 1992. B.S., CCNY, 1965; M.S., NYU, 1967; J.D., George Washington U., 1971, LL.M., 1975. Bar: Md. 1972, U.S. Ct. Claims 1973, U.S. Ct. Customs and Patent Appeals 1972, D.C. 1986, U.S. Ct. Appeals (fed. cir.) 1989, (4th cir.) 1992, Fla. 1994. Patent examiner U.S. Patent Office, Washington, 1967-69; patent advisor Dept. of Navy, Naval Ordnance Lab., White Oak, Silver Spring, Md., 1969-72, patent atty., 1972-73; law clk. U.S. Ct. Claims, Washington, 1973-74; trial atty. Antitrust div. Dept. of Justice, Washington, 1974-79; trial atty. Office of Gen. Counsel, Fed. Energy Regulatory Commn., Washington, 1979-84; atty. Brand, Beeny, Berger & Whitler (formerly Brand & Leckie), 1984-86, ptnr. 1987-93; of counsel 1993—. Cub Scout leader, 1977-79, 81-82; com. mem. Boy Scouts Am., 1979-86. Recipient Superior Performance award Dept. of Navy, 1973; Spl. Achievement award Dept. of Justice, 1976; Superior Job Performance award Fed. Energy Regulatory Commn., 1980, 82. Mem. ABA, Phi Beta Kappa, Order of Coif. Club: B'nai B'rith. Home: 941 Paddington Ter Lake Mary FL 32746-5316 Office: 1730 K St NW Washington DC 20006-3868

**BERGER, MICHAEL GARY,** lawyer; b. New Haven, Apr. 16, 1946; s. Jacob and Edith (Axelrod) B.; m. Miriam Janet Haines, July 24, 1977; children: Richard, Daniel. BS, Yale Coll., 1968; JD, Columbia U., 1973. Asst. dist. atty. New York County Office of Dist. Atty., N.Y.C., 1973-76; pvt. practice N.Y.C., 1981—; counsel Epstein, Becker & Green, P.C., N.Y.C., 1987—; arbitrator Am. Arbitration Assn., 1994—; mem. Criminal Justice Act Panel, N.Y.C., 1976-79; legal rep. clients in various fields icluding bus., medicine, profl. sports and entertainment; spkr. at cmty. client and bar groups. Mem. cons. bd.: Lawyers Cooperative Practice Guide—Handling a Criminal Case in New York, 1994; commentator on legal matters for Ct. TV, CNBC, Fox News, nat. and local TV programs; contbr. book revs. to law publs. Criminal Justice Act atty. for indigent clients accused of fed. crimes. Mem. ABA, Nat. Assn. Criminal Def. Lawyers, N.Y. State Bar Assn., Assn. of Bar of City of N.Y. Avocation: tennis. General civil litigation, Criminal, Entertainment. Office: Law Offices 20th fl 250 Park Ave New York NY 10177-0001

**BERGER, ROBERT BERTRAM,** lawyer; b. N.Y.C., Sept. 1, 1924; s. Edward William and Sophie (Berkowitz) B.; m. Phyllis Ann Korona, June 14, 1947; children: Barry Robert, Mark Alan, Karen Elizabeth Berger Adametz, James Michael; m. 2d, Arlene Kidder Wills, Dec. 27, 1980; 1 stepchild, Kimberly Kidder Wills Campbell. BS, Georgetown U., 1948; JD, U. Conn., 1952. Bar: Conn. 1952, U.S. Dist. Ct. Conn. 1953, U.S. Tax Ct. 1967, U.S. Ct. Appeals (2d cir.) 1968. Sole practice, 1952-56; ptnr. Berger & Alaimo, Enfield, Conn., 1956-82, Berger, Alaimo, Santy & McGuire, 1982-91, Berger, Santy & McGuire, 1991-94, Berger & Santy, 1994—; judge Probate Dist. of Enfield, 1989-94; dir. Enfield Vis. Nuses Assn., 1993-96; bd. dirs., mem. exec. com. Conn. Attys. Title Ins. Co., Rocky Hill. Chmn. Enfield Dem. Town Com., 1979-87, Conn. Psychiat. Security Review Bd., 1985—; pres. United Way of N. Cen. Conn., 1981-84; trustee St. Bernard's Roman Cath. Ch., 1977-90, 99—; trustee, exec. bd. mem. Johnson Meml. Hosp. and Johnson Meml. Corp., Stafford, Conn.; bd. dirs. United Way of Capitol Area, 1981-85, United Way N. Cen. Conn., 1977—. With USMCR, 1942-45. Decorated Purple Heart; recipient Disting. Svc. award Enfield Jr. C. of C., 1955, Clayton Frost award U.S. Jr. C. of C., 1959-60. Mem. ABA, Conn. Bar Assn., Hartford County Bar Assn., Enfield Lawyers Assn. (pres. 1973-74), Am. Judicature Soc. Club: Enfield Rotary (pres. 1970-71, Paul Harris fellow 1984). Contbr. monthly polit. column Enfield Press, 1980-84. Probate, Real property, General corporate. Office: PO Box 1163 Enfield CT 06083-1163

**BERGER, STEVEN R.,** lawyer; b. Miami, Aug. 23, 1945; s. Jerome J. and Jeanne B. B.; m. Francine Blake, Aug. 20, 1966; children: Amy, Charlie. BS, U. Ala., 1967; JD, 1969. Bar: Fla. 1969, Nev. 1991, U.S. Dist. Ct. (no. dist.) Fla. 1969, U.S. Dist. Ct. (so. dist.) Fla. 1971, U.S. Dist. Ct. (mid. dist.) Fla. 1989, U.S. Dist. Ct. Nev. 1991, U.S. Ct. Appeals (5th cir.) 1971, U.S. Ct. Appeals (11th cir.) 1981, U.S. Ct. Appeals (2nd and 9th cirs.) 1991, U.S. Supreme Ct. 1972, U.S. Ct. Claims 1977. Assoc. W. Dexter Douglass, Tallahassee, Fla., 1969-71, William R. Dawes, Miami, 1971; ptnr. Carey, Dwyer, Cole Selwood & Bernard, Miami, 1971-81; sole practice Steven R. Berger, P.A., 1981-89; ptnr. Wolpe, Leibowitz, Berger & Brotman, 1989-94, Berger & Chafetz, 1994—; mem. faculty Nat. Appellate Advocacy Inst., Washington, 1980; vice chmn. bench and bar adv. com. Ct. Appeals. 4th Dist., 1986-92. Chmn. City Miramar Planning Bd., 1975-76. Mem. ABA (vice chmn. app. practice com. litigation sect. 1981-83, chmn. 5th cir. subcom. appellate practice com. 1978-81), Am. Judicature Soc., Am. Arbitration Assn., Tallahassee Bar Assn., Kendall-South Miami Dist. Bar Assn., Dade County Def. Bar Assn., Fla. Def. Lawyers Assn. (vice chmn. appellate rules com. 1989), Def. Rsch. Inst., Rep. Nat. Lawyers Assn., Internat. Assn. Def. Counsel, N.Y. State Bar Assn., State Bar Nev., N.Y. State Trial Lawyers Assn. Appellate, Labor, General civil litigation. Office: Berger & Chafetz PO Box 1627 Miami FL 33256

**BERGER, VIVIAN OLIVIA,** lawyer, educator; b. N.Y.C., July 22, 1944; d. Jacob and Rita (Both) Berger; m. Curtis Jay Berger, June 17, 1973. BA, Harvard U., 1966; JD, Columbia U., 1973. Bar: N.Y. 1974, U.S. Dist. Ct. (so. and ea. dist.) N.Y. 1974, U.S. Ct. Appeals (2d cir.) 1974, U.S. Supreme Ct. 1979, U.S. Dist. Ct. (no. dist.) N.Y. 1980, U.S. Ct. Appeals (10th cir.) 1986. Law clk. to judge U.S. Ct. Appeals (2d cir.), N.Y.C., 1973-74; asst. prof. law Columbia U., N.Y.C., 1975-77, assoc. prof. law, 1977-80, prof. law, 1983—; vice dean Columbia U., 1989-93, Nash prof. law, 1993—; asst. dist. atty. N.Y. County, N.Y.C., 1977-83; of counsel Hoffinger Friedland Dobrish Bernfeld & Stern, P.C., N.Y.C., 1994—; mem. adv. commn. 1st dept. N.Y. Appellate Div., N.Y.C., 1984—; asst. counsel Legal Def. Fund NAACP, N.Y.C., 1986—. Contbr. articles to profl. jours. Vol. mediator Queens Mediation Ctr., 1985-86; arbitrator small claims N.Y.C. Civil Ct., 1986—; nat. bd. dirs. ACLU, N.Y.C., 1980—, gen. counsel, 1986—; bd. dirs. First Dept. Assigned Counsel Corp., 1991—, So. Ctr. for Human Rights, 1990—. Mem. ABA, Assn. of Bar of City of N.Y. (civil rights com. 1979-82, criminal cts. com. 1983-86, 91-94, criminal advocacy com. 1986-89, coun. on criminal justice 1991—, spl. com. on capital representation 1994—, coun. on jud. adminstrn. 1989-91), N.Y. Women's Bar Assn., N.Y. State Dist. Atty.'s Assn., Am. Law Inst., N.Y. Lawyers Against the Death Penalty. Avocations: reading, sketching, hiking, jogging. Criminal, Alternative dispute resolution, Appellate. Office: Columbia Law Sch 435 W 116th St New York NY 10027-7297 also: Hoffinger Friedland Dobrish Bernfeld & Stern 100 E 59th St New York NY 10022-1301

**BERGERSON, DAVID RAYMOND,** lawyer; b. Mpls., Nov. 23, 1939; s. Raymond Kenneth and Katherine Cecille (Langworthy) B.; m. Nancy Anne Heeter, Dec. 22, 1962; children—W. Thomas C., Kirsten Finch, David Raymond. BA, Yale U., 1961; JD, U. Minn., 1964. Bar: Minn. 1964. Assoc. Fredrikson Law Firm, Mpls., 1964-67; atty. Honeywell Inc., Mpls., 1967-74, asst. gen. counsel, 1974-82, v.p., asst. gen. counsel, 1983-84, v.p., gen. counsel, 1984-92; pvt. practice law Mpls., 1992-94; v.p., sec. Telcom Sys. Svcs., Inc., Plymouth, Minn., 1994-96, dir., cons., 1996-97; v.p. bd. dirs. Hogan Bergerson, Inc., Mpls., 1997—. Bd. dirs. Pillsbury Neighborhood Svcs., Inc., Mpls., 1983-92. Republican. Club: Minneapolis. Avocations: tennis; bird-hunting. General corporate, Securities, Mergers and acquisitions. Home: 2303 Huntington Point Rd E Wayzata MN 55391-9740 Office: Hogan Bergerson Inc 4040 IDS Ctr Minneapolis MN 55402

**BERGHOFF, PAUL HENRY,** lawyer; b. Chgo., Aug. 25, 1956; s. John Colerick Sr. and Doris Margaret (Anderson) B.; m. Kathryn Elaine Thompson, May 30, 1981. B.A. cum laude in Chemistry, Lawrence U., 1978; J.D. cum laude, U. Mich., 1981. Bars: Ill. 1981, U.S. Dist. Ct. (no. dist.) Ill. 1981, U.S. Ct. Appeals (fed. cir.) 1983, U.S. Supreme Ct. 1986. Assoc. Allegretti & Witcoff, Ltd., Chgo., 1981-85, ptnr. 1985-96; founding ptnr. McDonnell Boehnen Hulbert & Berghoff, Chgo., 1996—. Mem. ABA, Ill. Bar Assn., Chgo. Bar Assn., Patent Law Assn. Chgo. Mem. United Ch. of Christ. Avocation: music. Federal civil litigation, Patent, Trademark and copyright. Office: McDonnell Boehnen Hulbert & Berghoff 300 S Wacker Dr Chicago IL 60606-6680

**BERGIN, JEFFREY THOMAS,** lawyer; b. Phoenix, Sept. 13, 1962; s. Daniel Timothy and Ann (Edmunds) B.; m. Margaret Gail Cartledge, Nov. 28, 1992; children: Christopher, Jennifer. BS in BA, U. Ariz., 1985, JD with distinction, 1991. Bar: Ariz. 1991, U.S. Dist. Ct. Ariz. 1991. Atty. Jones, Skelton and Hochuli, Phoenix, 1991-95, Lewis and Roca, Phoenix, 1995-97, Jones, Skelton and Hochuli, Tucson, 1997—. Asst. editor DRI Alternative Dispute Resolution Choices, 1997. Vol., Habitat for Humanity, Tucson, 1998. Mem. ABA, Def. Rsch. Inst., Ariz. Assn. Def. Counsel. Avocations: marathon racing, triathlons. State civil litigation, Insurance, Professional liability. Office: Jones Skelton and Hochuli 202 E Wetmore Rd Ste 105 Tucson AZ 85705-1736

**BERGKVIST, THOMAS A.,** lawyer; b. Des Moines, Aug. 20, 1960; s. Carl Ivar and Else (Bon Jespersen) B.; m. Laurie Varlotta, May 4, 1991; children: Kristen Nicole, Carolyn Paige. BA, Trinity Coll., 1982; JD magna cum laude, Boston U., 1985. Bar: Pa. 1985, N.J. 1987. Atty. Saul Ewing Remick & Saul, Phila., 1985-93, Law Office of Thomas A. Bergkvist, Phila., 1993—; of counsel Kahn Greenberg & Blau, Malvern, 1996—. Mem. ABA, Pa. Bar Assn., Phila. Bar Assn., Phila. Estate Planning Coun., Germantown Cricket Club, Pi Gamma Mu. Estate planning, Probate, Estate taxation.

**BERGMAN, EDWARD JONATHAN,** lawyer, educator; b. Jersey City, Aug. 10, 1942; s. Abe and Ethel (Leitner) B.; m. Jennifer Shapiro, Feb. 1, 1969 (div.); children: Peter Jeremy, Jennifer Amy. BA, U. Pa., 1963; JD, Columbia U., 1966. Bar: N.J. 1974, U.S. Dist. Ct. N.J. 1974, U.S. Supreme Ct. 1989; cert. comml. mediator N.J. Assn. of Profl. Mediators. Ptnr. Bergman & Barrett, Princeton, N.J., 1975—; pub. defender Princeton Borough, 1986—, Princeton Twp., 1988—; fed. mediator U.S. Dist. Ct., N.J., 1992—; mediator N.J. Superior Ct., 1995—; lectr. Woodrow Wilson Sch., Princeton U., 1990-92; affiliated faculty U. Pa. Wharton Sch. of Bus. Dept. of Legal Studies, Phila., 1995—; vis. lectr. U. Calif. at Berkeley, St. Petersburg U. Joint Mgmt. Program, Russia, 1995—; official dispute resolver NHLA/AAHA; affiliate Bickerman Dispute Resolution Group, Washington, 1998—. Author: (with J. Bickerman) Court-Annexed Mediation: Perspectives on Selected State & Federal Programs, 1998. Trustee Princeton Ballet, 1942-92, Arts Coun. Princeton, 1998—. Mem. ABA (sec. on dispute resolution, mediation com., chmn. subcom. on ct.- annexed mediation), N.J. Bar Assn., Mercer County Bar Assn., Princeton Bar Assn. (pres. 1986-87), Nat. Inst. for Dispute Resolution, Soc. Profl. in Dispute Resolution, Penn Basketball Club (exec. bd. 1995—), Penn Club N.Y. Avocations: wine food, travel, sports, art and architecture. General civil litigation, General practice. Home: 95 Wilson Rd Princeton NJ 08540-2601 Office: Bergman & Barrett PO Box 1273 Princeton NJ 08542-1273

**BERGMAN, NORA RIVA,** lawyer, mediator. AA, St. Petersburg Jr. Coll., 1987; BA, U. South Fla., 1989; JD, Stetson U., 1992. Bar: Fla. 1992, U.S. Dist. Ct. Fla. 1992, U.S. Ct. Appeals (11th cir.) 1997; cert. civil mediator. Atty. Nora Riva Bergman, P.A., St. Petersburg, Fla., 1992—, mediator, 1997—. Vol. mediator Clearwater (Fla.) Human Rels., 1997—. Mem. Fed. Bar Asn., Nat. Inst. for Dispute Resolution, Soc. for Profls. in Dispute Resolution. Alternative dispute resolution, Labor. Office: 360 Central Ave Ste 1220 Saint Petersburg FL 33701-3838

**BERGMAN, ROBERT IRA,** laywer; b. N.Y.C., May 9, 1954; s. Morris and Frances R. BA, Bklyn. Coll., 1977; JD, Bklyn. Law Sch., 1980. Bar: N.Y. 1981, Fla. 1982, U.S. Dist. Ct. (so. and ea. dists.) N.Y. 1982. Assoc. Isaacson Robustelli Fox et al, N.Y.C., 1980-87, ptnr., 1987-92; ptnr. Fogelgaren and Bergman, N.Y.C., 1992-98, Fogelgaren, Forman & Bergman LLP, N.Y.C., 1998—. Mem. N.Y. State Bar Assn., Workers Compensation Bar Assn. (bd. dirs. 1988—), N.Y. State Trial Lawyers Assn. Workers' compensation, Personal injury, Pension, profit-sharing, and employee benefits. Home: 5 Horizon Rd Fort Lee NJ 07024-6651 Office: Fogelgaren Forman & Bergman LLP 277 Broadway New York NY 10007-2001

**BERGNER, JANE COHEN,** lawyer; b. Schenectady, N.Y., Apr. 6, 1943; d. Louis and Selma (Breslaw) Cohen; m. Alfred P. Bergner, May 30, 1968; children: Laura, Justin. AB, Vassar Coll., 1964; LLB, Columbia U., 1967. Bar: D.C. 1968, U.S. Dist. Ct. D.C. 1968, U.S. Ct. Appeals (D.C. cir.) 1968, U.S. Ct. Fed. Claims 1969, U.S. Ct. Appeals (fed. cir.) 1969, U.S. Tax Ct. 1979, U.S. Supreme Ct. 1992. Trial atty. tax divsn. U.S. Dept. Justice, Washington, 1967-74; assoc. Arnold & Porter, Washington, 1974-76, Rogovin, Huge & Lenzner, Washington, 1976-83; of counsel Arter & Hadden, 1983-86; ptnr. Spriggs & Hollingsworth, 1986-89, Feith & Zell, P.C., 1989-93; pvt. practice Washington, 1993—; mem. jud. confs. U.S. Ct. Fed. Claims, U.S. Tax Ct. Author: Tax Court Practice and Court of Federal Claims Practice; contbg. author: West's Federal Forms, vol. 8, 1997; contbr. articles to profl. jours. Bd. dirs. Jewish Social Svc. Agy., Washington, Jewish Coun. for the Aging, Washington; former mem. cmty. adv. bd. Sta. WAMU-FM, Washington. Mem. ABA (sect. taxation, govt. rels. com., ct. procedure com., civil and criminal penalties com., chmn. subcom. important devels. 1991-93, chmn. regional liaison meetings com. 1993-95, sect. litigation); Vassar Coll. Class Alumnae (chair spl. gifts com. 25th reunion), D.C. Bar (chair taxation sect. 1985-90, chair tax audits and litigation com. 1990-93, Best Sect. Cmty. Outreach award 1993), Fed. Bar Assn., Women's Bar Assn. D.C., Nat. Partnership for Women and Families, Women's Tax Luncheon Group, Columbia U. Law Sch. Alumni Assn., Svc. Guild Washington, Vassar Club. E-mail: jbergnerlaw@abanct.org. Taxation, general, Estate planning, Federal civil litigation. Home: 5659 Bent Branch Rd Bethesda MD 20816-1049 Office: 1133 Connecticut Ave NW Washington DC 20036-4305

**BERGREEN, MORRIS HARVEY,** lawyer, business executive, private investor; b. Passaic, N.J., Sept. 28, 1917; s. Harold and Jennie (Dolgen) B.; m. Adele G. Bergreen, Sept. 1, 1947; children: Laurence, John. Student, NYU, 1935-38; LLB, Fordham U., 1941; postgrad., NYU. Bar: N.Y. 1942. Sr. ptnr. Bergreen & Bergreen, N.Y.C., 1953-86, 95—; ret. of counsel Milbank, Tweed, Hadley & McCloy, N.Y.C., 1986-95; sr. ptnr. Bergreen & Bergreen, N.Y.C., 1995—; pres. Croydon Co., Inc., Westminster Broadcasting Corp., Claridge Broadcasting Corp.; gen. mgr. Grosvenor Investment Co., Skirball Investment Co. Pres. The Skirball Found.; bd. dirs., founding mem. bd. trustees Skirball Mus. and Cultural Ctr.; mem. adv. bd. Skirball Inst. on Am. Values; trustee, bd. dirs. Audrey Skirball Kenis Theatre, Inc.; life trustee NYU, mem. acad. affairs com., mem. devel. com., trustee NYU Sch. Med., trustee NYU Sch. Med. Found., trustee health initiatives com., trustee Bronfman Ctr. for Jewish Student Life; life trustee Mt. Sinai-NYU Med. Ctr.; bd. govs. Oxford Ctr. for Hebrew and Jewish Studies Oxford U.; trustee, mem. investment com. NCCJ, Inc.; bd. dirs., v.p. Grand St. Settlement; trustee Jewish Home and Hosp. for Aged; bd. dirs. Sarah R. Neuman Nursing Home, others. 1st lt. USAAF, 1942-46. Recipient Albert Gallatin medal for outstanding contbn. to society NYU, 1995. Mem. ABA, N.Y. State Bar Assn., Assn. Bar of City of N.Y., Fordham Law Rev. Assn., Harmonie Club (N.Y.C.), Sunningdale Country Club (Scarsdale, N.Y.), Club at Morningside (Rancho Mirage, Calif.), Tamarisk Country Club (Rancho Mirage, Calif.), Hillcrest Country Club (L.A.), N.Y. Athletic Club. General corporate, Estate planning, Estate taxation. Home: 24 Highland Farm Rd Greenwich CT 06831-2606 also: 980 Fifth Ave New York NY 10021-0126 Office: Bergreen & Bergreen 767 Fifth Ave Fl 43 New York NY 10153-0023

**BERGSCHNEIDER, DAVID PHILIP,** legal administrator; b. Springfield, Ill., Nov. 19, 1951; s. Fred J. and Ruby A. (Martin) B.; m. Dawn E. Combes, Sept. 23, 1989; children: Alec, Bryant, Cale. Student, Bradley U., 1969-71; BA, Ill. Coll., 1973; JD, Marquette U., 1976. Bar: Ill. 1976, Wis. 1976, U.S. Ct. Appeals (7th cir.) 1990, U.S. Supreme Ct. 1980. Mem. legis. staff Ill. Gen. Assembly, Springfield, 1976-77; asst. defender Office State Appellate Defender, Springfield, 1977-93, legal dir., 1993—. Co-author: Defending Illinois Criminal Cases, 1988, Illinois Criminal Practice, 1980, Brief Writing and Oral Argument Handbook, 1988, 94, 97; author: Illinois Handbook of Criminal Law Decisions, 1993, 2d edit., 1998; also articles. Recipient Award of Excellence Ill. Pub. Defender Assn., 1989. Mem. ABA, Ill. Bar Assn. (criminal justice sect. coun. 1987-91, 94-98, sec. 1995-96, chmn. 1996-97), Ill. Attys. for Criminal Justice, Aircraft Owners and Pilots Assn. Office: Office State Appellate Def PO Box 5780 Springfield IL 62705-5780

**BERGSTEDT, ANDERS SPENCER,** lawyer; b. Södertälje, Sweden, May 15, 1963; came to U.S., 1965; s. Jan-Eric Oskar and Vivianne (Sanfridsson) B. BA cum laude, U. Wash., 1985, JD, 1988. Bar: Wash. 1990, U.S. Dist. Ct. (we. dist.) Wash. 1990. Exec. dir. The Tenants Union, Seattle, 1988-90; mng. atty. Hyatt Legal Svcs., Seattle, 1990-92; pvt. practice Seattle, 1992—. Author: Translegalities: A Legal Guide for Transsexuals, 1997. Co-founder, treas. FTM Conf. and Edn. Project, Seattle, 1996—; mem. Vol. Attys. for People with AIDS, 1992—; bd. dirs. The Pride Found, 1993-95, Internat. Conf. Transgender Law & Employment Policy, 1996—; co-chair Seattle Commn. Lesbians and Gays, 1989-91; mem. adv. bd. Office Crime Victim Advs., Olympia, Wash., 1989-92. Mem. Wash. State Bar Assn., Wash. State Trial Lawyers Assn., Golden Key, Pi Sigma Alpha, Phi Beta Kappa. Bankruptcy, Estate planning, Entertainment. Office: 2133 3rd Ave Ste 106 Seattle WA 98121-2387

**BERGTRAUM, HOWARD MICHAEL,** lawyer; b. N.Y.C., Jan. 8, 1946; s. Murry and Edith (Katz) B.; m. Susan Levitan, July 27, 1969; children: Jordan, Matthew, Andrea. BS, Queens Coll., 1966; JD, Cornell U., 1969; LLM, Georgetown Law Ctr., 1972. Bar: N.Y. 1970. Atty. adviser SEC, Washington, 1969-72; ptnr. O'Sullivan, Graev & Karabell LLP, N.Y.C., 1975—. Mem. ABA, N.Y. State Bar Assn. Securities, Corporate taxation, General corporate. Home: 10 I U Willets Rd Old Westbury NY 11568-1519 Office: O Sullivan Graev & Karabell LLP 30 Rockefeller Plz Fl 41 New York NY 10112-0198

**BERK, ALAN S.,** law firm executive; b. N.Y.C., May 11, 1934; s. Phil and Mae (Buchberg) B.; m. Barbara Binder, Dec. 18, 1960; children—Charles M., Peter M., Nancy M. BS in Econs., U. Pa., 1955; MS in Bus., Columbia U., 1956. CPA, 1960. Staff acct. Arthur Young & Co., N.Y.C., 1956-62; mgr., prin. Arthur Young & Co., 1962-67; sr. v.p. Avco Corp., Greenwich, Conn., 1967-75; dir. Arthur Young & Co., 1975—, ptnr., 1976—, chief fin. officer, 1979-89; nat. dir. fin., treas. Ernst & Young, 1989-92; exec. dir. Kelley, Drye & Warren, N.Y.C., 1993-94. Mem. nat. adv. group Nat. Tech. Inst. for the Deaf, Rochester, N.Y.; chmn. bd. dirs. Jewish Home for the Elderly of Fairfield County, Inc., 1997—; 1st v.p., treas. Bruce Mus., Greenwich, Conn., 1996—; trustee, treas. Fund for Peace, Washington; mem. golf bd. Town of Greenwich, Conn.. With U.S. Army, 1957. Mem. AICPA, N.Y. State Soc. CPAs, Fin. Execs. Inst., Landmark Club, Stockbridge (Mass.) Golf Club, Stockbridge Sportmen's Club, Lake Dr. Homeowner's Assn. Home: 14 Cornelia Dr Greenwich CT 06830-3906

**BERK, BRIAN D.,** lawyer; b. N.Y.C., Dec. 6, 1961; s. Howard Ira and Phyllis Jane B.; m. Sarah Hazi, Apr. 2, 1990; children: Talia, Eric, Daniel. BA cum laude, SUNY, Albany, 1983; JD cum laude, Pace U., 1986. Bar: N.Y. 1987, U.S. Dist. Ct. (so. and ea. dists.) 1987. Assoc. Rosenman & Colin, N.Y.C., 1987-91; assoc. Franklin Weinrib Rudell & Vassallo P.C., N.Y.C., 1991-95, ptnr., 1996—; mem. joint com. of Bar Assn. of N.Y. and N.Y. Court Lawyers Assn. which oversees legal referral svc., 1995-97. Family and matrimonial, Contracts commercial, Entertainment. Office: Franklin Weinrib Rudell & Vassallo PC 488 Madison Ave New York NY 10022-5702

**BERKELHAMMER, ROBERT BRUCE,** lawyer; b. Providence, Oct. 27, 1949; s. Cyril Lester and Anne Louise (Rossman) B.; m. Miriam June Finkelstein, Mar. 9, 1975; children: Jessi, Max, Abby. BA, U. Rochester, 1971; JD, Boston U., 1974. Bar: R.I. 1975, U.S. Dist. Ct. R.I. 1977, Mass. 1998. Atty. NLRB, Pitts., 1974-77; ptnr. Licht & Semonoff, Providence, 1977-97, Chace, Ruttenberg & Freedman, Providence, 1997—. Pres. Jewish Family Service, Inc., Providence, 1988-91. Mem. ABA, R.I. Bar Assn. Jewish. Real property, Contracts commercial, General corporate. Home: 131 Laurel Ave Providence RI 02906-4622 Office: Chace Ruttenberg & Freedman 1 Park Row Ste 300 Providence RI 02903-1235

**BERKMAN, ALLEN H.,** lawyer; b. Canton, Ohio, Jan. 7, 1912; s. Hyman and Sarah B.; m. Selma Wiener, Mar. 20, 1938 (dec. Nov. 1995); children: Barbara B. Ackerman, Susan B. Rahm, Richard L., Helen B. Habbert, James S. AB, U. Mich., 1933; JD, Harvard Law Sch., 1936; LHD (hon.), Hebrew Union Coll., 1993. Lawyer Pitts., 1937—; founder Berkman Ruslander Pohl Lieber & Engel, Pitts., 1965-89; atty. Kirkpatrick & Lockhart, LLP, Pitts., 1989—. Trustee Pitts. Trust for Cultural Resources, 1983—, exec. com.; adb. com. Benedum Ctr. Performing Arts; bd. dirs. Bedford Internat. Festival Found., 1991—, Pitts. Symphony Soc., 1978-94, bd. dirs. 1998—; pres. Rodef Shalom Congregation, 1976-82; bd. dirs. Montefiore Found. (now Jewish Healthcare Found. Pitts.), audit fin. com. 1990—; adv. bd. The Salvation Army Pitts., 1967-82; bd. dirs. United Jewish Fedn. Greater Pitts.; nat. bd. govs. Am. Jewish Com., nat. exec. coun. (Human Rels. award Pitts. chpt., 1994); bd. dirs. Nat. Conf. for Community & Justice; trustee, chair Winchester-Thurston Sch. for Girls; bd. dirs. Am. Friends Hebrew U.; hon. mem. nat. bd. govs. Hebrew Union Coll.-Jewish Inst. Religion; dir. emeritus World Affairs Coun. Pitts. Recipient David Glick award World Affairs Coun. Pitts., 1997. Fellow Pa. Bar Found.; mem. ABA, Pa. Bar Assn., Am. Law Inst., Am. Arbitration Assn., U.S. Supreme Ct. Hist. Soc., Am. Jud. Soc., Allegheny County Bar Assn., Phi Beta Kappa. Office: Kirkpatrick & Lockhart 1500 Oliver Building Pittsburgh PA 15222-2312

**BERKOFF, MARK ANDREW,** lawyer; b. Boston, Aug. 8, 1961; s. Marshall Richard and Bebe R. B.; m. Susan Lynn Ochalek; children: Alexander, Rachel. BA with honors, U. Wis., 1983; JD, U. Chgo., 1986. Bar: Ill. 1987, U.S. Dist. Ct. (no. dist. Ill.) 1987, U.S. Ct. Appeals (7th cir.) 1990. Ptnr. Rudnick & Wolfe, Chgo., 1986—. Vol. Am. Cancer Soc., Chgo., 1993-96, Make-A-Wish Found. No. Ill., 1998—. Mem. ABA, Chgo. Bar Assn. Avocations: sports, collecting Currier & Ives prints, numismatics, family. Bankruptcy, Consumer commercial. Office: Rudnick & Wolfe 203 N Lasalle St Ste 1500 Chicago IL 60601-1293

**BERKOWITE, JEFFREY,** lawyer; b. N.Y.C., Jan. 9, 1966; s. Marvin and Judith Berkowite; m. Emily Berkowite, Nov. 15, 1992; 1 child, Matthew. BA, Union Coll., 1985; JD, Bklyn. Law Sch., 1992. Bar: N.J. 1992, N.Y. 1993. Assoc. Thurm & Heller, N.Y.C., 1992-93, Dambin & Assocs., N.Y.C., 1993-97, Proskauer Rose LLP, Washington, 1997-98; sr. comml. counsel Schering-Plough Corp., Kenilworth, N.J., 1998—. Mem. Nat. Health Lawyers Assn., N.Y. State Bar Assn. Health, Contracts commercial, Administrative and regulatory. Office: Schering Plough Corp 2000 Galloping Hill Rd Kenilworth NJ 07033

**BERKOWITZ, ALAN ROBERT,** lawyer; b. Atlantic City, Sept. 17, 1942; s. Myer and Ida Mae (Subin) B.; m. Ellen Schwarz, Aug. 15, 1965; children: Adam, Erik. BA, Drake U., 1964; JD, Am. U., 1967. Bar: U.S. Dist. Ct. D.C. 1968. U.S. Ct. Appeals (fed. cir.) 1969, Calif. 1972, U.S. Dist. Ct. (no. dist.) Calif. 1972, U.S. Ct. Appeals (9th cir.) 1972, U.S. Dist. Ct. (ea. dist.) Calif. 1975, U.S. Supreme Ct. 1987. Atty. Nat. Labor Rels. Bd., Washington, 1967-69; trial specialist Nat. Labor Rels. Bd., San Francisco, 1969-75, supervisory atty., 1975-77; regional atty. Nat. Labor Rels. Bd., Oakland, Calif., 1977-81; ptnr. Schachter, Kristoff, Orenstein & Berkowitz, San Francisco, 1982—; mng. ptrn. Schachter, Kristoff, Orenstein & Berkowitz, 1991—; corp. sec. Equal Employment Ednl. Programs, Larkspur, Calif., 1981-87; chmn. Comparative Indsl. Rels. Conf., Sydney, Australia, 1988. Chmn. Parks & Recreation Commn., Tamalpais Valley, Calif., 1975-77. Mem. ABA (labor and employment law sect., com. of devel. of the law under the Nat. Labor Rels. Act), Calif. Bar Assn. (chmn. program com. labor and employment sect. 1982-84, pvt. sector labor rels. com. 1984-86, exec. com. 1987-91), Bar Assn. San Francisco (labor and employment sect.). Avocations: running, fly fishing. Labor. Office: Schachter Kristoff Orenstein & Berkowitz 505 Montgomery St Fl 14 San Francisco CA 94111-2552

**BERKOWITZ, HERBERT MATTIS,** lawyer; b. N.Y.C., June 23, 1947; m. Gloria E. Deems, June 16, 1968; 1 child, Peter Aaron. BA, Bklyn. Coll., 1967; JD, U. Wis., 1971. Bar: Wis. 1971, Ohio 1972, Fla. 1979, U.S. Supreme Ct. 1974, U.S. Ct. Appeals (D.C. cir. 1974), U.S. Ct. Appeals (6th cir.) 1976, U.S. Ct. Appeals (5th cir.) 1981, U.S. Ct. Appeals (11th cir.) 1981. Law clk. Ohio Ct. Appeals, Cleve., 1971-73; atty. antitrust div. U.S. Dept. Justice, Cleve., 1973-74, asst. U.S. Atty., 1975-78; atty. organized crime strike force U.S. Dept. Justice, Tampa, 1978-80; assoc. Levine, Freedman, Hirsch & Levinson, Tampa, 1980-84; ptnr. Oster & Berkowitz, Tampa, 1984-90; mng. sr. ptnr. Berkowitz & Almerico, Tampa, 1990-94, Berkowitz & Assocs., Tampa, 1994—. Mem. ABA, Fla. Bar Assn., Hillsborough County Bar Assn. (In the Trenches award 1997), ATLA (sustaining), Fla. Trial Lawyers Assn., Am. Bd. Trial Advocates, Am. Inns of Ct. Personal injury, Insurance, General civil litigation. Office: Berkowitz & Assocs 4809 E Busch Blvd Tampa FL 33617-6019

**BERKOWSKY, PETER ARTHUR,** lawyer, retired military officer; b. Cornwall, N.Y., Mar. 29, 1942; s. Samuel Nathan and Sydell Berkowsky; m. Dolores Ethel Finder, Aug. 3, 1980; children: Daniel Benjamin, Jesse Samuel. AB in History, Brandeis U., 1964; JD, Cornell U., 1967. Bar: N.Y., U.S. Dist. Ct. (so. and ea. dists.) N.Y., U.S. Ct. Appeals (2d cir. and Armed Forces), U.S. Supreme Ct. Spl. agt., Office Spl. Investigations USAF, Beale AFB, Calif., 1967-71; asst. atty. gen., Dept. Law N.Y. State, N.Y.C., 1972-77; prin. ct. atty., Appellate Divsn., 1st. Dept. Supreme Ct., N.Y.C., 1977-79, 87-91, prin. law clk. to Hon. Justice Arnold L. Fein, 1979-86, prin. law clk. to Hon. Justice Richard W. Wallach, 1991—; asst. staff judge adv. USAFR, McGuire AFB, N.J., Hanscom AFB, Mass., Pentagon, D.C., 1973-98; admissions liaison officer U.S. Air Force Acad., 1992—; mem. law dept. adv. panel for bus. sch. Baruch Coll., N.Y.C., 1998—. Founder, dir. Internat. Minyan for N.Y.C. Marathoners, 1983—. Col. USAF, 1967-71, USAFR, 1991, Desert Storm. Decorated Legion of Merit. Mem. Internat. Assn. Jewish Lawyers and Jurists, N.Y. County Lawyers' Assn. (law-related edn. com.). Democrat. Jewish. Avocation: running. Home: 16 Fredon Dr Livingston NJ 07039-3136 Office: Supreme Ct Appellate Divsn 1st Dept 27 Madison Ave New York NY 10010-2201

**BERKSON, JACOB BENJAMIN,** lawyer, author, conservationist; b. Washington County, Md., Dec. 6, 1925; s. Meyer and Ida Evelyn (Berman) B.; m. Ann Goldstein, June 25, 1955 (div.); children: Daniel Jeremy, Susan Kay, James Meyer. BA, U. Va., 1947, LLB, 1949, JD, 1970; grad., Fed. Exec. Inst., Charlottesville, Va., 1972. Bar: Md. 1949, Va. 1949, U.S. Supreme Ct. 1965, Calif. 1975. Sole practice Hagerstown, Md., 1949-52, 54-64; ptnr. McCauley, Cooey, Berkson & Wright, Hagerstown, 1964-70; dep. gen. counsel U.S. GSA, Washington, 1970-76; pvt. practice law Hagerstown, 1976—; instr. Law Hagerstown Bus. Coll., 1986; trial magistrate, Hagerstown and Washington County, Md., 1951-52; mem. Legis. Coun. Md., 1955-58; del. Md. Legislature, 1955-58; trial magistrate, Hagerstown, 1958-59. Recipient commendation for svc. to U.S. Naval Acad. and pub. interest Chief of Naval Personnel, 1956. Lt. USNR, 1944-46, 52-54. Author: Shingahi Saburo and Short Stories, 1978, Comin' Home, 1993, A Canary's Tale, 1996; case editor, co-founder Va. Law Weekly, 1948; contbr. articles to profl. jours., address to Congrl. Record. Scoutmaster local coun. Boy Scouts Am.; organizer, dir. County Youth Conservation Corps; active Big Bros.; bd. dirs. Doub's Woods County Park, Devil's Backbone County Park; assisted in establishment of C&O Canal Nat. Histo. Park, 1954-70; camp sponsor YMCA; adv. Model Youth Legis.; pres. PTA; chmn. Washington County Park Commn., 1961-66; bd. dirs. Rachel Carson Coun., Inc., Chevy Chase, Md., 1996—. Mem. ABA, Calif. Bar Assn., Va. Bar Assn., Md. Assn. County Civil Attys. (pres., award for svc. as pres. 1966), Washington County Bar Assn. (pres.), Am. Legion, Hagerstown Club, Lions (pres.), Speakers Soc., Elks, Torch Club (Hagerstown). Republican. Jewish. Environmental, General practice, Personal injury. Home and Office: 1419 Potomac Ave Hagerstown MD 21742-3315

**BERLAGE, JAN INGHAM,** lawyer; b. Lewiston, N.Y., Nov. 17, 1969; s. Jan Coxe and Gai Elizabeth (Ingham) B. BA, Wesleyan U., Middletown, Conn., 1992; postgrad., Oxford U., 1992; JD, U. Va., 1995. Law clk. to Hon. E. Stephen Derby U.S. Bankruptcy Ct. Dist. Md., Balt., 1995-96; assoc. Day, Berry & Howard, Hartford, Conn., 1996—. Exec. editor Jour. of Law and Politics, Charlottesville, 1994-95, editl. bd., 1993-94; author: (short story) Aguilar Expression, 1990. Deacon Avon Congl. Ch., 1997—; mem. Rep. Town Com., Avon, 1998—. Mem. Federalist Soc. (pres. U. Va. chpt. 1994-95, co-chmn. Hartford chpt. 1997—), Conn. Young Lawyers Assn. (co-chmn. comml. law and bankruptcy sect. 1997—), N.Y. Bar Assn. (mem. comml. law and fed. litigation sects., intellectual property subcom. 1998—), Jefferson Literary and Debating Soc., N.Am. Securities Adminstrn. Assn. (task force mem. 1994), Oxford U. Legal Soc., United Oxford/Cambridge U. Club, Phi Delta Phi, Psi Upsilon, Phi Beta Kappa. Bankruptcy, General civil litigation, Intellectual property. Office: Day Berry & Howard LLP City Place I Hartford CT 06103-3499

**BERLAND, SANFORD NEIL,** lawyer; b. N.Y.C., Aug. 12, 1950; s. Stephen Isaiah and Alice Lydia (Greenfield) B.; m. Susan A. Winston, Nov. 4, 1989; children: Laurence, Noah, Stephanie, Alexander, Schuyler, Grant. BA magna cum laude, SUNY, Buffalo, 1972, JD magna cum laude, 1977. Bar: N.Y. 1978, U.S. Ct. Appeals (2d, 10th and 11th cirs.), U.S. Dist. Ct. (ea., so. and no. dists.) N.Y., U.S. Supreme Ct. Law clk. to Hon. E.R. Neaher U.S. Dist. Ct. (ea. dist.) N.Y., 1977-79; assoc. Dewey, Ballantine, Bushby, Palmer & Wood, N.Y.C., 1979-83; assoc., ptnr. Law Offices of Russel H. Beatie, Jr., N.Y.C., 1983-88; counsel Kellner, Chehebar & Deveney, N.Y.C., 1988-90; corp. counsel-litigation Pfizer Inc., N.Y.C., 1990-93, sr. corp. counsel, 1993-99, dir. corp. risk mgmt., asst. sec., 1999—; tchg. fellow Washington U., St. Louis, 1973-74; guest lectr. Pace U. Law Sch., 1989. Editor-in-chief Buffalo Law rev., 1976-77; contbr. articles to profl. jours. Mem. Huntington (N.Y.) Town Dem. Com., 1996—. Mem. ABA, N.Y. Bar Assn., Assn. Bar City N.Y., Phi Beta Kappa. Avocations: tennis, cycling. General civil litigation, Product liability, General practice. Home: 16 Wildwood Dr Dix Hills NY 11746-6041 Office: Pfizer Inc 235 E 42nd St New York NY 10017-5755

**BERLAND, SUSAN AMY,** lawyer; b. Jericho, N.Y., May 27, 1961. Student, Mich. State U., 1979-81; BA, SUNY, Albany, 1982; JD, Hofstra U., 1986. Bar: N.Y. 1986, Fla. 1989. Assoc. Meltzer, Lippe & Goldstein, P.C., Mineola, N.Y., 1986-87, Law Offices Russel H. Beatie, Jr., N.Y.C., 1987-89; ptnr. Berland & Winston, Albertson, N.Y., 1989-95; asst. Atty. Gen. for State of N.Y., 1989-95; ast. town atty. Town of Huntington, N.Y., 1996—; sec., treas. Herb Winston Assocs., Inc., Jericho, 1983—. Assoc. editor Hofstra U. Labor Law Jour., 1985-86. Bd. dirs. Birchwood Civic Assn., Jericho, 1982-86. Mem. N.Y. County Lawyers Assn., Assn. of Bar of City of N.Y., N.Y. State Bar Assn., Fla. Bar Assn. Democrat. Jewish. Avocations: tennis, guitar, bowling, aerobics, reading. Home: 16 Wildwood Dr Dix Hills NY 11746-6041 Office: Town of Huntington 100 Main St Huntington NY 11743-6904

**BERLAT, WILLIAM LEONARD,** lawyer; b. N.Y.C., Oct. 26, 1937; s. Daniel and Miriam (Kamnin) B.; m. Patricia A. Strack; children: Kimberly, Eden, Kathryn, Jessica. BS, U. Ariz., 1961, JD, 1964. Bar: Ariz. 1964, U.S. Dist. Ct. Ariz. 1964, U.S. Supreme Ct. 1969, U.S. Cir. Ct. of Appeals (9th cir.) 1977. Sole practice Tucson, 1964—; cons. atty., office in Saudi Arabia, 1978-79; judge pro tempore Ariz. Superior Ct., 1982-85. Author: (pamphlet) Revocable Trusts, 1984. Served with USAF, 1955-59. Mem. State Bar of Ariz., Ariz. Trial Lawyers, Pima County Bar Assn., Nat. Rifle Assn. Republican. Clubs: Safari. Lodge: Elks. Avocations: hunting, flying, gun dogs. Personal injury, General corporate, General civil litigation. Office: 3100 N Campbell Ave Ste 101 Tucson AZ 85719-2315

**BERLEY, DAVID RICHARD,** lawyer; b. Bklyn., Apr. 9, 1942; s. Alexander and Ruth (Ginsburg) B.; m. Sharon Lee Freeman, Aug. 10, 1964 (div. 1975); children: Steven N., Barbara Robin; m. Katalin Fine, Feb. 14, 1992. BS, Boston U., 1963; JD, Boston Coll., 1966. Bar: Mass. 1966, U.S. Dist. Ct. Mass. 1966, U.S. Ct. Claims 1970, Fla. 1977, U.S. Dist. Ct. (so. dist.) Fla. 1977, U.S. Tax Ct., U.S. Ct. Appeals (11th cir.). Pvt. practice, 1966-77; gen. counsel Econocar Internat. Inc., Miami, Fla., 1976-77; v.p., gen. counsel Emergency Med. Services Assn., Inc., Miami, 1977-79, pvt. practice, 1979-85; ptnr. Berley & Littman, PA, Miami, 1985-94; pvt. practice Miami, 1994—. Active Greater Miami Heart Assn., Jewish Fedn. Greater Miami, Bus. Vols. for Arts; past chmn. City of Miami Waterfront adv. bd., Coconut Grove Playhouse Soc. of Stars; mem. citizens' adv. bd. Sta.-WLRN Pub. Radio. Mem. ABA, ATLA, Mass. Bar Assn., Fla. Bar Assn. (grievance com.), Fla. Internat. Bankers Assn., Boston Coll. Law Sch. Alumni Assn., Greater Miami C. of C., Coconut Grove C. of C., Coconut Grove Playhouse Soc. Stars. Banking, General corporate, Private international. Office: 848 Brickell Ave Ste 200 Miami FL 33131-2915

**BERLIN, ALAN DANIEL,** lawyer, international energy and legal consultant; b. Bklyn., Oct. 20, 1939; s. Joseph Jacob and Rose (Smith) B.; m. Renee Wellinger, Dec. 22, 1962; children—Nicole Suzanne, Allison Leigh. BBA, CCNY, 1960; LLB, NYU, 1963, LLM, 1968. Bar: N.Y. 1963. Assoc. Aranow, Brodsky, Bohlinger, Einhorn & Dann, N.Y.C., 1965-68; asst. counsel Gen. Electric Co., N.Y.C., 1968-70; tax counsel Norton Simon Inc., N.Y.C., 1970-77; asst. prof. Pace U. Grad. Sch. Bus., 1977-85; pres. Belco Petroleum Corp., N.Y.C., 1977-88, The Crown Group, White Plains, N.Y., 1988-95; ptnr. Aitken Irvin Lewin Berlin Vrooman & Cohn L.L.P., 1995—; spl. cons. to UN Dept. Tech. Cooperation for Devel., 1989—, UN Ctr. for Transnat. Corps., 1990—; hon. assoc. Ctr. for Petroleum and Mineral Law & Policy, U. Dundee, Scotland, 1993—; bd. dirs. Chapparal Resources, Inc., Belco Oil & Gas Corp. Author monographs on fed. income tax. With U.S. Army, 1963-65. Mem. ABA, Internat. Bar Assn., N.Y. State Bar Assn., Assn. of Bar of City of N.Y., Inter-Am. Bar Assn., Assn. Internat. Petroleum Negotiators. Lodge: Masons. General corporate, Taxation, general, Oil, gas, and mineral. Office: Aitken Irwin Lewin Berlin Vrooman & Cohn LLP 2 Gannett Dr White Plains NY 10604-3403

**BERLIN, MARK A.,** lawyer; b. Bklyn., Nov. 1, 1944; s. Roy and Bess (Wolfe) B.; m. Renee D., June 7, 1970; children: Robert, Brian, Steven. BS in Econs., N.Y.U., 1966; LLM, 1973; JD, Bklyn. Law Sch., 1969. Bar: N.Y. 1970, Fla. 1979. With Touche Ross & Co., 1969-73; asso. Seidman & Seidman, N.Y.C., 1973-75; with Schulman & Berlin P.C., N.Y.C., 1975-89, mng. atty.; sole practice, 1990—. Mem. ABA, N.Y. State Bar Assn., Fla. Bar Assn., Am. Inst. C.P.A.s, N.Y. State Soc. C.P.A.s. Personal income taxation, Probate. Home: 23433 Alzira Cir Boca Raton FL 33433-8232

**BERLIN, PATRICIA,** lawyer; b. N.Y.C., Aug. 13, 1949; d. Irving and Muriel (Kashinsky) B.; m. Victor R. Goldmerstein, Sept. 22, 1974; 1 child, Blake. BA, CUNY, 1976; JD, U. Bpl., Conn., 1984. Clk. State of Conn., Middletown, 1984-85; pvt. practice Stratford, Conn., 1985—. Alt. Zoning Bd. Appeals, Easton, Conn., 1990—. Mem. ABA, Conn. Bar Assn., Greater Bpl. Bar Assn. Democrat. Jewish. Avocations: reading, exercise, travel, golf. Family and matrimonial, Real property, General practice. Office: 3288 Main St Stratford CT 06614-4800

**BERLINER, ALAN FREDERICK,** lawyer; b. Columbus, Ohio, Feb. 26, 1951; s. Israel and Lotte (Phillips) B.; m. Barbara Jean Watson, Aug. 17, 1974; children: Alyssa, Brett; m. Karen P. Connett, Feb. 21, 1998. BS in Econs., Case Western Res. U., 1973; JD, Ohio State U., 1976. Bar: Ohio 1976, U.S. Dist. Ct. (so. dist.) Ohio 1976, U.S. Ct. Appeals (6th cir.) 1976. Assoc. Carlile, Patchen, Murphy & Allison, Columbus, 1976-80, ptnr., 1980—; mng. ptnr. Carlile Patchen & Murphy, Columbus, 1989-97; asst. dir., chief legal counsel Ohio Dept. Ins., Columbus, 1997-99; bd. dirs. CBS Agy., Inc. Bd. dirs., bd. trustees Huckelberry Ho., Columbus, 1976-87, pres. 1983-85; bd. dirs. YMCA/Camp Willson Cons. Bd., Columbus, 1981-87. Mem. ABA (torts and ins. practice com. 1976—), Ohio Bar Assn. (ins. com.), Columbus Bar Assn. (common pleas ct. com.). Federal civil litigation, State civil litigation, Insurance. Office: Thompson Hine & Flory LLP One Columbus 10 W Broad St Columbus OH 43215-3435

**BERLOW, ROBERT ALAN,** lawyer; b. Detroit, Feb. 11, 1947; s. Henry and Shirley (Solovich) B.; m. Elizabeth Ann Goldin, Sept. 20, 1972; children: Stuart, Lisa. BA, U. Mich., 1968; JD, Wayne State U., 1971. Bar: Mich. 1971, U.S. Supreme Ct. 1978. Asst. to dean, instr. law sch. Wayne State U., Detroit, 1971-72; mem. Radner, Radner, Shefman, Bayer and Berlow, P.C., Southfield, Mich., 1972-78; gen. counsel Perry Drug Stores, Inc., Pontiac, Mich., 1978-80, gen. counsel, sec., 1980-82, v.p., gen. counsel, sec., 1982-88, sr. v.p., gen. counsel, sec., 1988-93, sr. v.p., chief adminstrn. officer, gen. counsel, sec., 1993-94, exec. v.p., gen. counsel, sec., 1994-95; sr. mem. Dykema Gossett, PLLC, 1995—. Pres. Agy. for Jewish Edn., Metro Detroit, 1993-95, v.p., 1987-93; bd. dirs. Jewish Cmty. Ctr. Met. Detroit, 1989—, v.p., 1992-93, treas., 1996-97, sec., 1997—. Mem. ABA, Bar of Supreme Ct. of U.S., Mich. Bar Assn. (chair comml. leasing and mgmt. of real estate com. of real property sect. 1993-98, mem. real property sect. coun. 1995—, frequent spkr. continuing legal edn. programs), Internat. Coun. Shopping Ctrs. (roundtable leader nat. law conf. 1986, 88-90, 93-98). Avocations: sports, photography. General corporate, Landlord-tenant, Contracts commercial. Office: Dykema Gossett PLLC 1577 N Woodward Ave Bloomfield Hills MI 48304-2837

**BERMAN, ANDREW HARRIS,** judge; b. Washington, Oct. 11, 1949; s. Julian L. and Joan S. Berman; m. Pamela A. Kaul; children: Zoe, Eli, Cody. BA (hons.), Univ. Wis., 1971; JD, Univ. Ill., 1975. Bar: Ill. 1975, U.S. Dist. Ct. (no. dist.) Ill. 1975, U.S. Ct. Appeals (7th cir.) 1976, U.S. Supreme Ct. 1979. Asst. appellate defender Office of The State Appelalte Defender, Chgo., 1975-79; asst. pub. defender Cook County Public Defender, Chgo., 1979-96; circuit ct. judge State Ill., Chgo., 1996—. Office: Circuit Ct Cook County 1100 S Hamilton Ave Chicago IL 60612-4207

**BERMAN, BERNARD MAYER,** lawyer; b. Phila., May 9, 1940; s. Henry and Mildred (Ginsburg) B.; m. Mona Halpern, June 7, 1964; children: Minda, Kyle, Joshua. BA, Swarthmore (Pa.) Coll., 1962; LLB, Columbia U., 1965, JD, 1969. Bar: Pa. 1965, U.S. Dist. Ct. (ea. dist.) Pa. 1966, U.S. Ct. Appeals (3d cir.) 1966, U.S. Supreme Ct. 1969. Jud. law clk. Ct. of Common Pleas, Phila., 1965-66; pvt. practice Phila., 1965-66; pub. defender trial atty. Delaware County, 1966-77; jud. law clk. Ct. of Common Pleas, Delaware County, Pa., 1967-74; pvt. practice Delaware County, 1966-89; ptnr. Scallan, March, Berman & Hurwitz and predecessor firms, Media, Pa., 1966-88, Scallan and Berman, Media, 1988-89, Bernard M. Berman and Assocs., Media, 1989-97; mng. ptnr. Berman Asbel & Berman, 1997—; mem. Spl. Com. to Revise Rules and Civil Procedures, Delaware County, 1974-75; arbitrator Am. Arbitration Assn., 1968—; mediator Fee Dispute Resolution Com., Delaware County, 1987—. Mem., Guy G. DeFuria Amer. Inn of Ct., 1997—, sec. young men's com. Phila. Fedn. Jewish Agys., 1966, 67; pres. B'nai B'rith Simon Wolf Lodge, Wallingford, Pa., 1978-80, Southeastern Pa. and Del. coun., 1984-86, bd. govs. dist. 3, Phila., 1984-89. Mem. ABA, Pa. Bar Assn., Delaware County Bar Assn., Rose Valley Chorus (parliamentarian 1986-87), Phi Sigma Kappa (grand coun. 1983-91, grand pres. 1991-95, Ct. of Honor, 1995—). Avocations: tennis, sailing, amateur theater, gardening, singing. E-mail: bmb@BermanLaw.com. General civil litigation, Family and matrimonial, Personal injury. Home: 28 Furness Ln Media PA 19086-6059 Office: Berman Asbel & Berman LLP 20 W Third St Media PA 19063-2824

**BERMAN, DAVID,** lawyer, poet; b. N.Y.C., Sept. 11, 1934; s. Joseph and Sophie (Hersh) B. BA with honors, U. Fla., 1955; postgrad. Johns Hopkins U., 1955-56; JD, Harvard U., 1963. Bar: Mass. 1963. Teaching fellow Harvard Coll., 1962-63, 66-67; law clk. to justice Mass. Supreme Ct., 1963-64; asst. atty. gen. Commonwealth of Mass., 1964-67; assoc. Zamparelli & White, 1967, ptnr., 1968-74; pvt. practice, 1974-82, 1990—; ptnr. Berman & Moren, Medford, Mass., 1982-89. Author: Future Imperfect, 1982, Slippage, 1996, Early Mandamus in Massachusetts, Massachusetts Legal History, 1998. Trustee Cantata Singers, 1981—. Mem. ABA, Mass. Bar Assn., Mass. Bar Found., Middlesex Bar Assn. (Most Outstanding Trial Lawyer Appelate award, 1998), Harvard Club (Boston), Signet Soc., Confrerie de la Chaine des Rotisseurs, Ordre Mondial, Masons. Republican. Unitarian. Federal civil litigation, General civil litigation, State civil litigation. Home: 33 Birch Hill Rd Belmont MA 02478-1729 Office: 100 George P Hassett Dr Medford MA 02155-3264

**BERMAN, ELIHU H.,** lawyer; b. Hartford, Conn., July 20, 1922; s. Saul and Emma (Kaplan) B.; m. Muriel Goldman, Jan. 18, 1945 (div. 1975); chldren: Rachel Rabinowitz, Jonathan; m. Susan A. Slamowitz, Dec. 19, 1975. BA, Harvard Coll., 1944; JD, Harvard Law Sch., 1948. Bar: Conn. 1948, Mass. 1948, Israel 1972, Fla. 1974, U.S. Dist. Ct. Conn. 1949, U.S. Dist. Ct. Fla. 1977, U.S. Ct. Appeals 1979, U.S. Supreme Ct. 1985; bd. cert. civil trial lawyer. Ptnr. Hurwitz and Berman, Hartford, 1950-62, Ritter and Berman, Hartford, 1962-71, Krug, Berman & Silverman, Clearwater, Fla., 1980—; assoc. prof. Stetson Law Sch., St. Petersburg, Fla., 1975-77. Editor-in-chief: Conn. Bar Jour., 1954-56. Asst. corp. counsel City of Hartford, 1956-58; pres. Jewish Nat. Fund Coun. of Greater Hartford, 1961-71, Conn. Region, Zionist Orgn. of Am., 1968-70; bd. dirs. Pinellas County (Fla.) Jewish Fedn., 1991—. Mem. ATLA, Fla. Bar Assn., Clearwater Bar Assn., Acad. Fla. Trial Lawyers. General civil litigation, Family and matrimonial, Personal injury. Home: 2918 Mill Stream Ct Clearwater FL 33761-3341 Office: Krug Berman & Silverman PA 1525 S Belcher Rd Clearwater FL 33764-7603

**BERMAN, ERIC M.,** lawyer, musician; b. Bklyn., Apr. 1, 1948; s. Bernard and Florence (Grier) B.; m. Christine Beck, Aug. 5, 1973 (div. Apr. 1986); m. Sheri Klein, July 31, 1988. BS in Music Edn., Hofstra U., 1970; MA in Music, NYU, 1971, PhD in Music, NYU, 1981; JD, St. John's U., 1981. Bar: N.Y. 1982, U.S. Dist. Ct. (so. and ea. dists.) N.Y. 1982. Instr. pub. schs., N.Y., 1970-71, 73-84; prin. tubaist San Antonio Symphony, 1971-73; musician, bus. mgr. Kapelye Klezmer Band, N.Y.C., 1981—; sole practice, N.Y.C., 1982-87; ptnr. Smith Carroad Levy and Victor, 1987-89; head litigation collection div. Finkelstein, Borah, Schwartz, Altschuler & Goldstein, 1990; pvt. practice Eric M. Berman, P.C., 1991—; dir., counsel Nassau Symphony Orch., Garden City, N.Y., 1982—, New Classical Consort, N.Y.C., 1983-86, Melville (N.Y.) Brass Ensemble, 1983-84; impartial hearing officer N.Y. State Dept. Edn., 1996—. Contbr. Music Sound Output, 1983-88, Modern Musician and Recording, 1983-88, Music and the Law, 1983-84; musician: (recs.) Levine and His Flying Machine, 1985, Kapelye's Chicken, 1987, Kapelye's On the Air, 1995. Mem. ABA, Nat. Assn. Retail Collection Attys. (comml. law league), N.Y. State Bar Assn. (exec. com., entertainment arts and sports law sect., editor of sect. pubs., comml. and fed. litigation sect., com. on comml. litigation), Am. Arbitration Assn. (panelist 1987—), Assn. of Bar of City of N.Y., N.Y. State Sch. Music Assn. Avocations: antiques, tennis, table tennis. Entertainment, Consumer commercial. Office: Eric M Berman PC 185 Willis Ave Mineola NY 11501-2622

**BERMAN, JOSHUA MORDECAI,** lawyer, manufacturing company executive; b. Rochester, N.Y., Aug. 4, 1938; s. Jeremiah Joseph and Rose (Rappaport) B.; m. Ruth Freed, Mar. 17, 1996; children: Marc Ethan, Eve. BBA summa cum laude, CCNY, 1958; JD cum laude, Harvard U., 1961. Bar: Mass. 1961, N.Y. 1984. With Goodwin, Procter & Hoar, Boston, 1961-80, ptnr., 1969-80; pres. Berman Engel P.C., 1980-85; counsel Kramer, Levin, Naftalis & Frankel, 1985—; adviser Fidelity Investments, 1971—, Brierley Investments Ltd., Wellington, New Zealand, 1988—; chmn. bd., CEO Tyco Internat. Ltd., 1970-73, bd. dirs., v.p. Founder, pres. Boston Children's Sch., 1965-66. General corporate, Mergers and acquisitions, Securities.

**BERMAN, LEONARD KEITH,** lawyer; b. Dearborn, Mich., Mar. 30, 1963; s. Hyman Jack and Doris (Grushky) B.; m. Sharon Elizabeth Williams, Oct. 8, 1988; children: Sarah, Rebbeca. BA, Mich. State U., 1985; JD cum laude, Wayne State U., 1988. Bar: Mich. 1988, U.S. Dist. Ct. (ea. and we. dists.) Mich. 1988. Assoc. Bodman, Longley & Dahling P.C., Troy, Mich., 1987-91; staff atty. Elias Bros. Restaurants Inc., Warren, Mich., 1991-94; assoc. Hainer & Demorest P.C., Troy, 1994—; of counsel Fin. Law Assocs., Troy, 1994—, Robert Riely P.C., Dearborn, 1996—. Pres. Cedar Springs Homeowners Assn., Novi, Mich., 1992—. Mem. ABA, State Bar Mich. Republican. Contracts commercial, Labor, General practice. Office: Hainer & Demorest PC 888 W Big Beaver Rd Ste 1400 Troy MI 48084-4738

**BERMAN, MARTIN SAMUEL,** lawyer; b. Boston, May 30, 1933; s. Walter and Tillie (Cherkofsky) B. BS, Boston U., 1956; JD, New Eng. Sch. of Law, Boston, 1965. Bar: Mass., 1965, U.S. Supreme Ct., 1970. Pres. Berman & Sons, Inc., Boston, 1960-87, chmn., 1988—; atty. pvt. practice Boston, 1965—. Pres. Jewish Big Bros. and Sisters Assn., Boston, 1985-88; chmn. disaster svc. ARC, Boston, 1966-69, bd. dirs., 1967-80; trustee Beth Israel Hosp., Boston, 1980-97, Emerson Coll., 1990-94; chmn. fin. devel. Massachusetts Bay unit ARC; trustee New Eng. Eng. Sch. Law, 1975-93; trustee Lakes Region Conservation Trust, 1994—; overseer Beth Israel-Deaconess Hosp., 1997—. Mem. Rental Housing Assn. (pres. 1960-62), Inst. Real Estate Mgmt. (past pres.), Greater Boston Real Estate Bd. (v.p.1965), Lambda Alpha (pres. Boston chpt. 1998). Jewish. General practice, Landlord-tenant. Office: 15 Court Sq Boston MA 02108-2503 Address: PO Box 1312 Bridgehampton NY 11932-1312

**BERMAN, MICHAEL BARRY,** lawyer; b. N.Y.C., Apr. 10, 1942; s. Mark S. and Roslyn (Roberts) B.; m. Rochelle Holland, June 7, 1969; 1 child, Michele. BA, Iowa Wesleyan U., 1964; MAT, Trenton State Coll., 1973; MA in Indsl. Rels., Rutgers U., 1977; JD, Cardozo Sch. Law, N.Y.C., 1984. Bar: N.J. 1985, D.C. 1985, U.S. Ct. Appeals (3d cir.) 1985, U.S. Supreme Ct. 1989. Assoc. Jerome A. Gertner, Lakewood, N.J., 1984-86; staff atty. Ocean-Monmouth Legal Svcs., Toms River, N.J., 1986-87; assoc. Cohen, Meshulam & Cohen, Verona, N.J., 1987-89, Krieger & Ferrara, Jersey City, 1989; pvt. practice Lakewood, N.J., 1989-90; ptnr. Collins & Berman, Toms River, N.J., 1990—; asst. to chmn. N.J. Pub. Employment Rels. Com., Trenton, 1973-81; gen. counsel Nat. Mus. of Am. Jewish Mil. History, 1992-98. V.p. Lakewood Community Sch. Bd., 1984-87; active Lakewood Bd. Edn., 1984-87, 89, Rep. Cen. Com., Lakewood, 1987-88; pres. Lakewood Rep. Club, 1992-93; mem. adv. bd. Ocean County Cath. Charities; pres. Congregation Ahavat Shalom, 1993-95. With U.S. Army, 1968-70. Mem. Ocean County Bar Assn., N.J. Bar Assn. (subcom. alimony support 1987), Jewish War Vets (state comdr. N.J. chpt. 1985-86, nat. com. 1985-89, nat. judge advocate 1992-98, nat. quartermaster 1996-98, nat. comdr. 1998-99), Vietnam Vets Am. (N.J. chpt. v.p. 1990-92), Masons. Family and matrimonial, Labor, Workers' compensation. Office: Collins & Berman 18A Robbins St Toms River NJ 08753-7629

**BERMAN, MYLES LEE,** lawyer; b. Chgo., July 11, 1954; s. Jordan and Eunice (Berg) B.; m. Mitra Moghimi, Dec. 19, 1981; children: Elizabeth, Calvin, Justin. BA, U. Ill., 1976; JD, Chgo.- Kent Coll. of Law, 1979. Bar: Ill. 1980, Calif. 1987, U.S. Dist. Ct. (no. dist.) Ill. 1980, U.S. Dist. Ct. (cen. dist.) Calif. 1988, U.S. Supreme Ct. 1992. Asst. state's atty. Cook County State's Atty.'s Office, Chgo., 1980-82; pvt. practice Offices of Myles L. Berman, Chgo., 1982-91; pvt. practice, L.A., 1988—; founder Nat. Drunk Driving Def. Task Force; traffic ct. judge pro tem Beverly Hills Mcpl. Ct., 1990—; traffic ct. judge pro tem adminstr. Culver Mcpl. Ct., 1991—; probation monitor State Bar Calif., 1992—. Editor: Century City Lawyer, 1992—. Mem. ABA, Santa Monica Bar Assn., Los Angeles County Bar Assn., Calif. Attys. for Criminal Justice, Nat. Assn. Criminal Def. Lawyers, Beverly Hills Bar Assn., Century City Bar Assn. (chmn. criminal law sect. 1989—, bd. govs. 1991—, Outstanding Svc. award 1990, 92, 93, 94, Spl. Recognition 1994, treas. 1994, sec. 1995, v.p. 1996, pres.-elect 1997, pres. 1998), Criminal Cts. Bar Assn. (evaluation profl. stds. and state bar com. 1996-97), Orange County Bar Assn., South Orange County Bar Assn., Cyberspace Bar Assn. Avocations: family, sports. Criminal. Office: 9255 Sunset Blvd Ste 720 Los Angeles CA 90069-3304 also: 2659 Townsgate Rd Ste 101-24 Westlake Vlg CA 91361-2710

**BERMAN, RICHARD BRUCE,** lawyer; b. Freeport, N.Y., Sept. 26, 1951; s. Nathan and Helen Dorothy (Raiden) B.; m. Laurie Michael, Nov. 2, 1985. BA in Speech Communication, Am. U., 1973; JD, U. Miami, 1976. Bar: Fla. 1976, U.S. Dist. Ct. (so. dist.) Fla. 1976, D.C. 1978. Atty. Travelers Ins. Co., Ft. Lauderdale, Fla., 1977-84; assoc. Frank & Flaster P.A., Sunrise, Fla., 1984-88, DeCasare & Salerno, Ft. Lauderdale, Fla., 1988-89; pvt. practice, 1989—; bd. dirs. Frosch Health Care Cons., Inc., Landerhill; mem. worker's compensation rules com. Fla. Bar, 1991-94; mem. Fla. Workers Advs., 1991—, bd. dirs., 1997—. Mem. panel health care Dem. Legis. Task Force, Ft. Lauderdale, 1985-87; mem. adv. bd. Reflex Sympathetic Dystrophy Syndrome Assn. Fla., 1992—; mem. B'nai Brith. Mem. ABA, ATLA, D.C. Bar, Fla. Bar Assn., Broward County Trial Lawyers Assn., B'nai Brith. Avocations: writing and performing music, theatre. Personal injury, Workers' compensation, Insurance.

**BERMAN, RONALD CHARLES,** lawyer, accountant; b. Chgo., July 7, 1949; s. Joseph and Helen Berman; m. Kristine K. Topp, May 1, 1993; children: Daniel J. Lohr, Joseph James. BBS with highest honors, U. Ill., 1971, JD with honors, 1974. Bar: Ill. 1974, Wis. 1976; CPA, Wis. Mem. tax staff Grant Thornton, Chgo., 1974-76; tax supr. Grant Thornton, Madison, Wis., 1976-78, tax mgr., 1978-81, ptnr. tax dept., 1991-94; assoc. Neider & Boucher, Madison, 1995-96, shareholder, 1997—. Mem. editl. adv. bd. Physician's Tax Advisor Newsletter, 1986-89, Physician's Tax and Investment Advisor, 1989-93. Scoutmaster Boy Scouts Am., Middleton, Wis., 1978—, fin. chmn. Mohawk Dist. Four Lakes coun., Madison, 1981-85, chmn. endowment fund, 1984-92, v.p. fin., 1992-94, exec. bd., 1982—, treas., 1994-96, nat. rep., 1996—; bd. dirs. Scouts on Stamps Soc. Internat., 1986-96, v.p., 1996-98; bd. dirs. Madison Pension Coun., 1986-98, pres., 1988-89. Recipient Silver Beaver award Boy Scouts Am., 1981. Mem. ABA (employee benefits com. taxation sect.), AICPA, Wis. Soc. CPAs (chmn. fed. tax com. 1990-92), State Bar Wis., Ill. Bar Assn., Madison Estate Coun. (bd. dirs. 1991-97), Wis. Planned Giving Coun., Nat. Com. Planned Giving, Web Network Benefits Profls., Optimists, Order of Coif, Alpha Pi Omega, Phi Kappa Phi, Phi Alpha Delta. Avocations: photogrphy, philately, camping. Estate planning, Pension, profit-sharing, and employee benefits, Taxation, general. Home: 3906 Rolling Hill Dr Middleton WI 53562-1224

**BERMAN, TONY,** lawyer; b. N.Y.C., Dec. 31, 1933; s. Murray T. and Lillian L. (Levine) B.; children: Julie A., Nina A. JD cum laude, NYU, 1957. Bar: N.Y. 1958, U.S. Ct. Appeals (2d cir.) 1960, U.S. Dist. Ct. (so. and ea. dists.) N.Y. 1961. Asst. atty. gen. State of N.Y., N.Y.C., 1957-63; ptnr. Berman Paley Goldstein & Kannry, N.Y.C., 1963—. Co-author: Construction Business Handbook, 1978, Avoiding Liability in Architecture Design and Construction, 1983. Mem. ABA, N.Y. State Bar Assn., Assn. of Bar of City of N.Y., The Moles. Construction, General civil litigation, Federal civil litigation. Address: 417 E 24th St New York NY 10013 Office: Berman Paley Goldstein & Kannry LLP 500 5th Ave Fl 43 New York NY 10110-0375

**BERMINGHAM, JOSEPH DANIEL,** lawyer; b. Lackawanna, N.Y., July 26, 1938; s. Joseph Daniel and Marian Rita (Mahon) B.; m. Ann Barbara Goslin, Aug. 20, 1966; children: Christopher, David, Sarah, Elizabeth. BA, Canisius Coll., 1959; JD, Boston Coll., 1962. Bar: N.Y. 1962, U.S. Dist. Ct. (we. dist.) N.Y. 1964, U.S. Ct. Appeals (2d cir.) 1970, U.S. Supreme Ct. 1977. Assoc. Vincent E. Doyle, Esquire, Buffalo, 1964-67; ptnr. Doyle, Diebold & Bermingham and successor firms, Buffalo, 1967-88, Bermingham, Cook & Mahoney, P.C., Buffalo, 1988-93, Bermingham & Cook, P.C., 1993-98; prin. law clk. Erie County Surrogate Ct., Buffalo, 1998—. Co-author: Course Handbook, New York State Director of Criminal Justice Service, 1980. Pres. Amherst (N.Y.) Soccer Assn., 1984; bd. dirs. Neighborhood Legal Svcs., Inc., Buffalo, 1984-86. 1st lt. U.S. Army, 1962-64. Mem. Erie County Bar Assn. (v.p. and pres. 1986-88, bd. dirs. 1981-84, Lawyer of Yr. 1993), Western N.Y. Trial Lawyers Assn. (v.p. and pres. 1984-85), N.Y. State Bar Assn. (ho. of dels. 1986-90, 8th jud. dist. v.p. 1991-97). General civil litigation, Personal injury, Product liability. Office: Erie County Surrogate's Ct 92 Franklin St Buffalo NY 14202-3902

**BERN, MARC JAY,** lawyer; b. Milw., June 19, 1950; s. James Ellis and Harriet (Kramer) B.; children—Lindsay, Jesse, Noah; m. Roberta Roth, May 20, 1984; 1 child, Erica. B.A., with distinction, U. Wis., 1972; J.D., Ill. Inst. Tech., 1975. Bar: Wis. 1975, U.S. Dist. Ct. (ea. and we. dists.) Wis. N.Y. 1983, U.S. Dist. Ct. (so. and ea. dists.) N.Y., U.S. Dist. Ct. (we. dist.) N.Y. 1990. Assoc. Habush, Gillick, Habush, Davis & Murphy, Milw., 1975-79; ptnr. Gillick, Murphy, Gillick, Bern & Wicht, Milw., 1979-82; assoc. Lipsig, Sullivan, Liapakis, N.Y.C., 1983-84; sr. trial assoc. Julien & Schlesinger, P.C., N.Y.C., 1984-86, Trolman & Glaser, P.C., 1986-88; pvt. practice law, 1988-91; counsel Weitz & Luxembourg PC 1992—; lectr. Milw. Area Tech. Coll., 1979-80, Continuing Edn. State Bar Wis., 1978—, Melvin Belli Seminar, Am. Trial Lawyers Assn., 1982—, Hahneman Med. Coll., 1980, Practicing Law Inst., 1984—, Wis. Acad. Trial Lawyers, Madison, 1981—, NYU Sch. Continuing Edn., 1985—, Inst. Continuing Profl. Edn., 1981-82, N.Y. State Trial Lawyers Assn., 1986-88. Mem. Am. Trial Lawyers Assn., State Bar Wis., State Bar N.Y., Am. Judicature Soc., Am. Soc. Law and Medicine, N.Y. State Trial Lawyers Assn., Assn. Trial Lawyers Am. (ann. conv. lectr 1991), Delta Theta Phi. Personal injury, General civil litigation, Product liability. Home: 25 E 86th St Apt 3E New York NY 10028-0553 Office: 315 5th Ave Fl 5 New York NY 10016-6510

**BERNABEI, LYNNE ANN,** lawyer; b. Highland Park, Ill., Apr. 11, 1950; d. Guy and Anna (Tamarri) B. BA, Harvard U., 1972, JD, 1977. Bar: D.C. 1979, U.S. Supreme Ct. 1988, U.S. Dist. Ct. D.C. 1977, U.S. Ct. Appeals (D.C. cir.) 1979, U.S. Ct. Appeals (3d cir.) 1985, U.S. Ct. Appeals (fed. cir.) 1988, U.S. Ct. Appeals (4th cir.) 1992, U.S. Ct. Appeals (6th cir.) 1990. Clk. U.S. Dist. Ct. Judge William Bryant, Washington, 1977-78; assoc. Tigar & Buffone, Washington, 1978-80; clin. instr. Georgetown U., Washington, 1980-81; gen. counsel Govt. Accountability Project, Washington, 1981-85; ptnr. Newman, Sobol, Trister & OWens, Washington, 1985-87, Bernabei & Katz, Washington, 1987—. Co-author: The High Citadel: On the Influence of Harvard Law School, 1978; author articles. Recipient Achievement award Lambda Legal Defense and Edn. Fund, Washington, 1990. Mem. ABA, ATLA, Nat. Lawyers Guild (bd. dirs. D.C. chpt. 1992-95). Civil rights, Labor, General civil litigation. Office: Bernabei & Katz 1773 T St NW Ste 100 Washington DC 20009-7139

**BERNARD, BARTON WILLIS,** lawyer; b. Lafayette, La., May 29, 1969; s. Garland Paul and Elaine Anne Bernard; m. Elizabeth Montgomery, Aug. 23, 1996. B in Fin., U. Southwestern La., 1992; JD, La. State U., 1995. Bar: La., U.S. Dist. Ct. (all dists.) La., U.S. Ct. Appeals (5th cir.). Law clk. U.S. Bankruptcy Ct. (we. dist.) La., Opelousas, 1995-96; atty. William H. Patrick, APLC, Baton Rouge, 1996-97, Paul J. Hebert, Ltd., Lafayette, La., 1998—. Mem. La. Bar Assn., South La. Bankruptcy Bar assn. (sec. 1998). Avocations: golf, tennis. Bankruptcy, Federal civil litigation, State civil litigation. Home: 200 S Mall St Lafayette LA 70503-2254 Office: Paul J Hebert Ltd 301 Rue Beauregard Ste B Lafayette LA 70508-3265

**BERNARD, BRUCE WILLIAM,** lawyer; b. Erie, Pa., Feb. 3, 1951; s. Barney and Barbara Jean (Wurst) B.; m. Valerie Jean Noziglia, June 2, 1978 (div.); children: Elizabeth Anne, Brandon Wallace, Brittany Lynn; m. Catherine Ann Blore, May 4, 1984. BA, Case Western Res. U., Cleve., 1972, JD, 1975. Bar: Pa. 1975, U.S. Dist. Ct. (we. dist.) Pa. 1975, U.S. Supreme Ct. 1980, U.S. Ct. Fed. Claims 1989. Assoc. Silin, Eckert & Burke, Erie, 1975-77; ptnr. Ely & Bernard, Erie, 1978-85, Bernard, Stuczynski & Bonanti, Erie, 1985—; instr. Am. Inst. Banking, Erie, 1981-82. Bd. dirs., Erie Civic Music Assn., 1976-83, Florence Crittendon Svcs., Erie, 1978-84, Meth. Towers, Erie, 1979—. Named Vol. of Yr., Erie chpt. ARC, 1982. Mem. Pa. Bar Assn., Erie County Bar Assn., Assn. Trial Lawyers Am., Pa. Trial Lawyers Assn., Phi Delta Phi. Republican. Methodist. Club: Kiwanis (bd. dirs. 1978-81, 90-91, Disting. Service award 1976, 79). Personal injury, Real property, Workers' compensation. Home: 6720 Manchester Farms Rd Fairview PA 16415-1649 Office: Bernard Stuczynski & Bonanti 234 W 6th St Erie PA 16507-1319

**BERNARD, DONALD RAY,** law educator, international business counselor; b. San Antonio, June 5, 1932; s. Horatio J. and Amber (McDonald) B.; children: Doren, Kevin, Koby; m. Elizabeth Priscilla Gilpin, 1986. Student, U. Mich., 1950-52; JD, U. Tex., 1958, BA, 1954, JD, 1958, LLM, 1964. Bar: Tex. 1958, U.S. Ct. Mil. Appeals, 1959, U.S. Supreme Ct. 1959; lic. comml. pilot. Commd. ensign U.S. Navy, 1954, advanced through grades to commdr., 1956-75, retired, 1975; briefing atty. Supreme Ct. Tex., Austin, 1958-59; asst. atty. gen. State of Tex., Austin, 1959-60; ptnr. Bernard & Bernard, Houston, 1960-80; pvt. practice law Houston, 1980-94; prof. internat. law U. St. Thomas, Houston, 1991-94; guest lectr. Sch. Bus. Mont. State U., 1995-96; mem. faculty S.W. Sch. Real Estate, 1968-77. Author: Origin of the Special Verdict As Now Practiced in Texas, 1964; co-author: (novel) Bullion, 1982. Bd. dirs. Nat. Kidney Found., Houston, 1960-63; chmn. Bd. Adjustment, Hedwig Village, Houston, 1972-76; bd. regents Angeles U. Found., The Philippines; chmn. of the bd. Metro Verde Devel. Corp., The Philippines;; bd. dirs. Gloria Dei Luth. Ch., Endowment Found. Comdr. USN, 1950-92; ret., air show pilot Confederate Air Force, 1970-80. Mem. Lawyers Soc. Houston (pres. 1973-74), Houston Bd. Realtors, ABA, Inter-Am. Bar Assn., Tex. Bar Assn. (com. liaison Mex. legal profession), Houston Bar Assn. (chairperson emeritus internat. law sect.), Internat. Bar Assn. (del. to 1st seminar with Assn. Soviet Lawyers, Moscow, 1988), Assn. Soviet Lawyers , Lawyer-Pilot Bar Assn., Sons of the Republic of Tex., Lic. Execs. Soc., St. James's Club, Masons, Shriners, Alpha Tau Omega, Phi Delta Phi. Lutheran.

**BERNARD, JOHN MARLEY,** lawyer, educator; b. Phila., Feb. 6, 1941; s. Edward and Opal (Marley) B.; children: John Marley Jr., Kendall M., Katherine M., James M.; m. Esther L. von Laue, May 31, 1986. BA, Swarthmore Coll., 1963; LLB, Harvard U., 1967. Bar: Pa. 1967. Assoc. Montgomery McCracken Walker & Rhoads, Phila., 1967-73, ptnr., 1973-86; ptnr. Ballard Spahr Andrews & Ingersoll, LLP, Phila., 1986—; lectr. Temple U. Law Sch., Phila., 1975-95; instr. Phila. Acad. for Employee Benefits Tng., 1996-99; guest instr. U.S. Dept. Labor, Washington, 1984-96; instr. U. Pa. Wharton Sch., Phila., 1989-90; bd. dirs. PENJERDEL Employee Benefits Assn., Phila. Contbg. author: Handbook of Employee Benefits, 1989. Mem. ABA, Pa. Bar Assn. Pension, profit-sharing, and employee benefits, Corporate taxation, Labor. Office: Ballard Spahr Andrews & Ingersoll LLP 1735 Market St Fl 51 Philadelphia PA 19103-7501

**BERNARD, MICHAEL MARK,** lawyer, city planning consultant; b. N.Y.C., Sept. 5, 1926; s. H.L. and Henryetta (Siegel) B.; m. Laura Jane Pincus, Aug. 28, 1958; 1 dau., Daphne Michelle. AB, U. Chgo., 1949; JD, Northwestern U., 1953; MCity Planning, Harvard U., 1959. Bar: Ill. 1952, U.S. Dist. Ct. (no. dist.) Ill. 1953, N.Y. 1955, U.S. Ct. Appeals (1st cir.) 1956. Pvt. practice law Chgo. and N.Y.C., 1953-55; rsch. asst. Law Sch. Harvard U., 1955-56; city planning cons., atty.-adviser Puerto Rico, 1956-58; rsch. atty. Model Laws Project Am. Bar Found., 1959-60; city planner, legal adviser Chgo. Dept. City Planning, 1960-64; cons. planning and land regulation, 1964—; cons. Chgo. Area Transp. Study, 1965; mem. exec. faculty Boston Archtl. Ctr., 1967—; adv. to Gov.'s Exec. Office on reorgn. Commonwealth Mass., 1968-72; chmn. 1st Nat. Transp. Needs Study Mass.; cons. A.I.A. Rsch. Corp., 1974; cons. Mass. Atty. Gen., 1981—; mem. com. urban devel. and housing World Peace Through Law Ctr., 1965—; mem. com. transp. law transp. research bd. NRC-NAS, 1966—; cons. White House Policy Adv. Com. to D.C., 1966; del. World Congress Housing and Planning, Paris, France, 1962, Tokyo, Japan, 1966; fellow Ctr. Advanced Visual Studies, M.I.T.; prin. investigator Northwestern U. Transp. Ctr.; lectr. in field; vis. prof. urban and regional planning U. Iowa, 1969-70; vis. lectr. Harvard U., MIT, U. Mich.; mem. faculty Am. Law Inst., 1978—. Author: Constitutions, Taxation and Land Policy, 2 vols., 1979-80, Airspace in Urban Development, 1963; co-editor: Policy Studies Jour.; editor, pub.: Reflections on Space; revision project mgr.: Constitutional Uniformity & Equality in State Taxation, 2 vols., 1984, Transformation of Property Rights in the "Space Age", 1993; spl. editor: Urban Law Ann. Washington U. Sch. Law; columnist: Jour. Real Estate Devel.; bd. editors: Real Estate Fin.; contbr. articles to profl. jours. Patron Hull House Assn., Chgo., 1965; v.p., trustee Cambridge Community Art Ctr., 1971-73; mem. standing com. Unitarian Ch.; mem. founding site com. Mus. Contemporary Art, Chgo. With USN, 1944-46. Recipient cert. of commendation for teaching Boston Archtl. Ctr., 1984; grantee NRC-NAS, 1964-66. Fellow Lincoln Inst. Land Policy; mem. ABA (land use, planning and zoning com., chmn. T.D.R. subcom. 1984-89, air and space com.), Internat. Fedn. Housing and Planning, Am. Arbitration Assn. (cert., bldg. and constrn. arbitrator),Am. Soc. Pub. Adminstrn., Policy Studies Orgn., Am. Planning Assn. (chmn. legis. com. Met. Chgo. sect. 1963-65, Mass. state report planning and law div. 1990—), Boston Soc. Architects (affiliate), Nat. Space Soc. (bd. dirs., space law com. Boston chpt.), Am. Underground Space Assn., Internat. Ctr. for Land Policy Studies, Urban Affairs Assn. (jour. rev. editor), Am. Crafts Coun., Mass. Assn. Craftsmen (v.p. 1975-78). Boston Visual Artists Union (hon., sec.-gen. 1971-72), New England Poetry Club (life), U. Chgo. Club Boston (bd. dirs.), Boston Athenaeum (life, dir. Poetry program). Land use and zoning (including planning), Municipal (including bonds), Real property. Home: 25 Stanton Ave Newton MA 02466-3005 *It seems to me that man's random, specialized intervention in the universe will prove to be the most constant cause for concern in the future. The problem might be seen not so much as how to keep the earth whole, but as how man may keep whole himself: this remains the role and strength of creative, intuitive endeavor, the source of everything I find of true value. Hopefully, ours will not become the "Age of the Idiot Savant."*.

**BERNARD, STEVEN MARTIN,** lawyer; b. N.Y.C., Dec. 14, 1946; s. Louis and Osne (Rubin) B.; m. Jean Marie Castle, Feb. 15, 1969; children: Aric, Matthew, Alexandria, Jordana. BA, CCNY, 1967; JD, Bklyn. Law Sch., 1972. Bar: N.Y. 1973, Calif. 1973. Atty., sect. of fin. ICC, Washington, 1972-73; assoc. Rhodes & Sherrod, Fremont, Calif., 1973-74; ptnr. Rhodes, McKeehan & Bernard, Fremont, 1974-76, McKeehan, Bernard & Wood, Fremont, 1976-89; with Bernard & Wood, Fremont, 1989-96, Bernard, Balglev & Bonaccorsi, Newark, Calif., 1997—. Sec. G.I. Forum, Fremont, 1975; pres. Temple Beth Torah, Fremont, 1976-79. Mem. Assn. Trial Lawyers Am., N.Y. Bar Assn., Calif. Bar Assn., Washington Twp. Bar Assn. Democrat. Jewish. Avocations: sports, skiing, reading, coaching youth sports. General civil litigation, Land use and zoning (including planning), Contracts commercial. Home: 40358 Canyon Heights Dr Fremont CA 94539-3009 Office: Bernard Balglev & Bonaccorsi 3900 Newpark Mall Fl 3 Newark CA 94560-5243

**BERNAUER, THOMAS A.,** lawyer; b. Culver City, Calif., Sept. 4, 1942; m. Kathleen Bernauer; children: Donovan, Logan. BA, U. So. Calif., 1964, JD, 1967. Bar: Calif. 1968, U.S. Dist. Ct. (ctrl. dist.) Calif. 1968, U.S. Supreme Ct. 1979. With . Harwood, Adkinson & Bernauer, Newport Beach, Calif., 1968-84; pvt. practice Newport Beach, 1985—; lectr. in field; lectr. Nat. Bus. Inst., Inc.; mem. judge pro tem program Orange County Superior Ct., 1980—. With U.S. Army. Decorated Bronze Star (2), Army Commendation medals (2). Fellow Am. Acad. Matrimonial Lawyers (cert. specialist-family law); mem. ABA, State Bar of Calif., Orange County Bar Assn. Family and matrimonial. Office: 500 Newport Center Dr Ste 950 Newport Beach CA 92660-7018

**BERNHARD, ALEXANDER ALFRED,** lawyer; b. New Orleans, Sept. 20, 1936; s. John Helanus and Dora (Solosko) B.; m. Martha Ruggles, Nov. 21, 1959 (div.); children: John, Jason, Frederic; m. Joyce Harrington, Dec. 30, 1976 (div.); m. Myra Mayman, Nov. 2, 1986. BS, MIT, 1957; LLB, Harvard U., 1964. Bar: Calif. 1964, Oreg. 1965, Mass. 1966, N.H. 1991. Law clk. to judge U.S. Ct. Appeals (9th cir.), 1964-65; assoc. Johnson, Johnson & Harrang, Eugene, Oreg., 1965-66, Bingham, Dana & Gould, Boston, 1966-71; assoc. Hale and Dorr, Boston, 1971-73, jr. ptnr., 1973-75, sr. ptnr., 1975—. Trustee, bd. dirs. Mass. Eye and Ear Infirmary, chmn., 1992-96, chmn. emeritus, 1996—. Lt. submarines USNR, 1957-61. Mem. ABA, Boston Bar Assn., Union Boat Club, Longwood Cricket Club. Democrat. General corporate, Private international, Corporate taxation. Office: Hale and Dorr 60 State St Ste 25 Boston MA 02109-1816

**BERNHARD, CHRISTINE A.,** lawyer; b. Boston; d. William Francis and June Lucille (Horne) B.; m. Anthony J. Rusciano, Aug. 23, 1980 (div. 1992); children: Alexander Rusciano, Jennifer Rusciano. BA, Newton Coll., 1975; JD, New Eng. Sch. Law, 1978. Bar: Mass. 1979, Mich. 1981. Law clk., rsch. atty. Oakland County Cir. Ct., Pontiac, Mich., 1979-80; assoc. Goldstein, Serlin & Eserow, Southfield, Mich., 1980-86; corp. staff atty. Auto Club Ins. Assn., Dearborn, Mich., 1986-88, asst. corp. sec. and counsel, 1988-95, dir. office of gen. counsel, 1995—; lectr. in field. City commr. Birmingham (Mich.) City Commn., 1986-89; zoning appeal mem. Birmingham Bd. Zoning Appeals, 1989-91. Mem. Am. Soc. Corp. Secs., Am. Corp. Counsel Assn. (pres. Mich. chpt. 1994-95, pres. scholarship found. Mich. chpt. 1995—), Mich. Bar Assn., Mass. Bar Assn., Mich. Women's Bar Assn. Avocation: learning to play golf. Insurance. Office: Auto Club Ins Assn 1 Auto Club Dr Dearborn MI 48126-4213

**BERNICK, ALAN E.,** lawyer, accountant; b. St. Paul, June 20, 1958; s. Herbert Jay and Marcia Bernick; m. Elisa Kim Neff, Aug. 24, 1986; children: Joshua Norton, Daniel Noah, Matthew David. BA, U. Minn., 1980, JD, 1983. Bar: Minn. 1983, U.S. Dist. Ct. Minn. 1983, U.S. Tax Ct. 1985; CPA, Minn. Ptnr. Oppenheimer Wolff & Donnelly LLP, St. Paul, 1983—. Mem. exec. bd. Indianhead coun. Boy Scouts Am., 1993—. Mem. AICPA, Minn. State Bar Assn. (chair tax sect. 1995-97), Minn. Soc. CPAs (chair 1995-96). Avocations: family, outdoor activities, golf. Corporate taxation, State and local taxation, General corporate. Home: 621 Hampshire Dr Mendota Hts MN 55120-1935 Office: Oppenheimer Wolff & Donnelly LLP 332 Minnesota St Ste 1700 Saint Paul MN 55101-1314

**BERNIER, MARCEL J.,** lawyer; b. Miami, Fla., Jan. 6, 1958; s. Jean G. and Annette D. Bernier; m. Martha Rowland, Aug. 29, 1992; children: Andre, Monique. BA, Fla. State U., 1979; JD, U. Conn., 1982; LLM, Boston U., 1985. Bar: Conn. 1982, U.S. Dist. Ct. Conn. 1983, U.S. Tax Ct. 1983. Assoc. Danaher, O'Connell, Attmore, Tedford & Flaherty, Hartford, Conn., 1982-84, Copelon, Schiff & Zangari, Hartford, Conn., 1985; assoc., ptnr. Andros, Floyd & Miller, P.C., Hartford, Conn., 1985—; spkr. in field. Author: Limited Liability Companies in Connecticut, 1994. Mem. ABA (taxation and bus. law sects. 1985—), Conn. Bar Assn. (tax sect. exec. com. 1992—), Ltd. Liability Co. Subcom. (com. 1995—). Avocations: running, golf, skiing. General corporate, Mergers and acquisitions, Estate planning. Office: Andros Floyd and Miller PC 864 Wethersfield Ave Hartford CT 06114-3184

**BERNING, PAUL WILSON,** lawyer; b. Marceline, Mo., Apr. 22, 1948; s. Harold John and Doris (Wilson) B. BJ, U. Mo., 1970; JD with honors, U. San Francisco, 1986. Bar: Calif. 1986, U.S. Dist. Ct. (no. dist., ea. dist., so. dist.) Calif. 1986, U.S. Dist. Ct. (cen. dist.) Calif. 1989, U.S. Ct. Appeals (9th cir.) 1986, U.S. Ct. Claims 1992, U.S. Supreme Ct. 1992. Copy editor Chgo. Sun-Times, 1970-74, nat., fgn. editor, 1974-78; asst. news editor San Francisco Examiner, 1978-83; law clerk San Francisco dist. atty. Consumer Fraud Divsn., 1984; extern Calif. Supreme Ct., San Francisco, 1985, San Francisco Superior Ct., 1986; assoc. Thelen, Marrin, Johnson & Bridges, San Francisco, 1986-94, ptnr., 1995-98; ptnr. Thelen Reid & Priest, San Francisco, 1998—. Co-author: (book chpt.) Proving and Pricing Construction Claims, 1990; contbr. speeches and papers to profl. confs. Mem. ABA (forum on constrn. industry 1986—), State Bar Assn. Calif., Bar Assn. San Francisco (coord. legal assistance for mil. pers. 1991-92, assoc. liaison to San Francisco lawyers com. for urban affairs 1987-92), High Speed Ground Transp. Assn., Modern Transit Soc. Avocations: horseback riding, sailing, reading. Construction, Transportation, General civil litigation. Office: Thelen Reid & Priest LLP 2 Embarcadero Ctr Ste 2100 San Francisco CA 94111-3995

**BERNING, RANDALL KARL,** lawyer, consultant, educator, publisher; b. Highland Park, Ill., Apr. 13, 1950; s. Karl Ives and Alpha (Mikkelsen) B.; m. Carol Ann Bublitz, Oct. 22, 1983. BA, U. Ill., 1973; JD, Golden Gate U., 1977; LLM in Health Law, Loyola U., Chgo., 1989. Bar: Ill. 1977, D.C. 1980. Asst. atty. gen. State of Ill., Chgo., 1977-79, contractural hearing officer Ill. sec. of state, 1981-83; pvt. practice law Chgo., 1979—, Washington, 1986—; pvt. practice cons. Burlingame, Calif., 1979—, Naples, Fla., 1997—; cons. to coun. on dental practice ADA, Chgo., 1987—; clin. asst. prof., Dept. Oral Health Care Delivery, U. Md., Balt., 1992—; mem. nat. adv. coun. for nursing rsch., dept. health and human svcs., Nat. Inst. Health, 1994-98; dir. practice adminstrn., adj. prof. dental jurisprudence U. Ill. at Chgo. Coll. of Dentistry, 1993—; clin. instr., dept. pub. health and hygiene U. Calif. at San Francisco Sch. of Dentistry, 1992—; also affiliated with Gardner, Carton & Douglas health law dept. and Arthur Andersen LLP, higher edn. cons. practice. Editl. bd. Jour. Law and Ethics in Dentistry, 1987-92; pub. The Expert Series for Dentists, The Expert Series for Physicians; originator, sponsor Ann. Dentistry and the Law Conf., 1988-94. Active Rep. Com.; vol. various civic activities; bd. deacons United Ch. of Christ, 1990-93. Mem. APHA, ABA, Ill. Bar Assn., D.C. Bar Assn., Am. Assn. Dental Schs. Health. Home: 5850 Cloudstone Ct Naples FL 34119-4606 Office: 3400 Tamiami Trl N Ste 201 Naples FL 34103-3717 also: Ste 600 312 W Randolph Chicago IL 60606

**BERNS, MICHAEL ANDREW,** lawyer; b. Urbana, Ill., Jan. 22, 1968; s. Thomas Bernhard and Jeannie Marie B.; m. Kelly Janelle Welty, Dec. 6, 1997. BS, U. Ill., 1990; JD, Washington U., St. Louis, 1993. Atty., engr. Berns Clancy & Assocs., Urbana, Ill., 1993-98; atty. pvt. practice, Urbana, Ill., 1993-98, 98—. Mem. Rotary. Intellectual property, Patent, Trademark and copyright. Office: 107 W Goose Aly Urbana IL 61801-2756

**BERNS, PHILIP ALLAN,** lawyer; b. N.Y.C., Mar. 18, 1933; s. Milton Benjamin and Rose (Aberman) Bernstein; m. Jane Klaw, June 7, 1959; children: David, Peter, Jay. BS in Marine Transp., N.Y. State Maritime Coll., 1955; LLB, Bklyn. Law Sch., 1960. Bar: N.Y. 1960, Calif. 1990, U.S. Ct. Appeals (2d cir.) 1962, U.S. Ct. Appeals (9th cir.) 1982. Admiralty atty. admiralty sect. U.S. Dept. Justice, N.Y.C., 1960-71, asst. atty. in charge admiralty sect., 1971-77; atty. in charge torts br. U.S. Dept. Justice, San Francisco, 1977—; adj. prof. McGeorge Law Sch., Sacramento, 1978-88; bd. dirs. Pacific Admiralty Seminar, San Francisco. Assoc. editor Am. Maritime Cases, 1978—. Chmn. exec. com. S.I. (N.Y.) Community Bds., 1969-70, 1st vice chmn. no. 3 bd., 1975-77, treas. no. 3 bd., 1973-74; chmn. 122d Precinct, Community Counsel, S.I., 1968-71; pres. Walnut Creek (Calif.) Little League, 1984-85, v.p. 1978-83; pres. Chestnut Hill Civic Assn., S.I., 1968-74, Congregation B'nai Jeshurun, S.I., 1973-76, v.p., 1971-73; cub pack leader Boy Scouts Am., S.I., 1969-70; bd. dirs. Mid-Island Little League, S.I., 1972-77, Jewish Community Ctr., S.I., 1976, Little League Dist. 4, Contra Costa (Calif.) County, 1984-90. Lt. USN, 1955-57. Named United Jewish Appeal Man of Yr., Congregation B'Nai Jeshurun, 1976. Mem. ABA (admiralty and maritime law com. 1991-94), Maritime Law Assn. U.S. (exec. com. 1991-94, vice chmn. practice and rules com. 1976-91, chmn. govt. liaison com. 1994—, no. dist. Calif. admiralty rules com. 1998—). Avocations: athletics, volunteer work. Home: 3506 Sugarberry Ln Walnut Creek CA 94598-1746 Office: US Dept Justice Torts Br PO Box 36028 450 Golden Gate Ave San Francisco CA 94102-3661

**BERNS, SHELDON,** lawyer; b. Cleve., Dec. 13, 1932; s. Myron J. and Florence (Lamden) B.; m. Barbara Begun, Aug. 11, 1957; children: Jamie, Jonathan, Jordan, Justin. BBA, Ohio State U., 1958; JD, Case Western Res. U., 1960. Prin. Kahn, Kleinman, Yanowitz & Arnson Co., L.P.A., Cleve., 1960—. Councilman City of Beachwood, Ohio, 1970-77; mem. Cuyahoga County Rep. Exec. Com., 1968—, vice chmn., 1980-88. Mem. ABA, Greater Cleve Bar Assn., 8th Jud. Conf. (life), Order of Coif. Jewish. Avocations: camping, cycling. General civil litigation, Land use and zoning (including planning), Construction. Office: Kahn Kleinman Yanowitz & Arnson Co LPA The Tower at Erieview # 2600 1301 E 9th St Cleveland OH 44114-1800

**BERNSTEIN, BARRY JOEL,** lawyer; b. Charleston, S.C., Feb. 11, 1961; s. Charles Stanley Bernstein and Sara Blum Baumwand; m. Charlene Wilkins, May 29, 1998. BA, U. S.C., 1983, JD, 1995. Bar: S.C., U.S. Dist. Ct. S.C. Security mgr. Boeing, Wichita, Kans., 1986-88; pres. Security Cons., Inc., Charleston, S.C., 1988-92; law clk. Bernstein and Bernstein, P.A., Charleston, 1992-95; ptnr. Breland and Bernstein, Greenville, S.C., 1995-97; owner, pres. Bernstein Law Firm, Greenville, 1998—. Dir. Homeless Animal Res. and Placement, Greenville, 1995—. 1st lt. U.S. Army, 1983-86. Helen Gullickson scholarship U. S.C. Sch. of Law, 1994. Mem. S.C. Trial Lawyers Assn., Shriners, Mason, Comms. Law League of Am., Phi Delta Phi (Province pres. 1996-98). Jewish. Alternative dispute resolution, Family and matrimonial, Military. Home: 7 Double Oak Ct Taylors SC 29687-6601 Office: Bernstein Law Firm PO Box 10001 Greenville SC 29603-0001

**BERNSTEIN, BARRY SELWYN,** lawyer; b. N.Y.C., Sept. 18, 1946; s. Sidney I. and Anne (Ness) B.; m. Leslie Beth Prager, June 5, 1988; 1 child, Jared Douglas. BA, CUNY, 1967; JD, Bklyn. Law Sch., 1971. Bar: N.Y. 1972, U.S. Dist. Ct. (ea. and so. dists.) N.Y. 1974. Atty. Corp. Counsel's Office, N.Y.C., 1972-75; assoc. Schneider, Kleinick & Wietz, N.Y.C., 1975-76; asst. corp. counsel City of N.Y., 1976-77; ptnr. Judge, Livoti & Bernstein, N.Y.C., 1977-87, Livoti, Bernstein & Moraco, N.Y.C., 1987—; arbitrator U.S. Dist. Ct. (ea. dist.) N.Y., 1988—. Mem. N.Y. State Trial Lawyers, N.Y. State Bar Assn., Am. Arbitration Assn., K.P. Democrat. Jewish. Avocations: scuba diving, travel, reading. General civil litigation, Personal injury, Family and matrimonial. Home: 2 Bay Club Dr Flushing NY 11360-2917

**BERNSTEIN, BERNARD,** lawyer, corporate executive; b. Bklyn., Feb. 9, 1929; s. Irving and Esther (Schriro) B.; m. Carmel Roth, June 24, 1973. AB, Syracuse U., 1950; JD, Harvard U., 1953. Bar: N.Y. 1955. With Philipp Bros., Inc. subs. Salomon Inc. (formerly Minerals and Chems. Philipp, Englehard Minerals & Chems. Corp., Phibro-Salomon, Inc.), N.Y.C., 1965—; now sr. legal cons. Philipp Bros., Inc. subs. Citigroup, Inc., N.Y.C.; also bd. dirs. Philipp Bros., Inc. subs. Salomon Inc. (formerly Phibro-Salomon, Inc.), N.Y.C. Chmn. Speculum Musicae. With AUS, 1953-55. Mem. ABA, Am. Arbitration ASsn. (bd. dirs.). Contracts commercial, General corporate, Private international. Home: 25 E 86th St New York NY 10028-0553 Office: Philipp Bros Inc 7 World Trade Ctr Fl 28 New York NY 10048-1102

**BERNSTEIN, BRENDA JOY,** lawyer; b. Columbia, S.C., Nov. 16, 1963; d. Arnold and Willardean Bernstein. BA in History, Emory U., 1984; JD, U. Ga., 1987. Bar: Ga. 1987. Assoc. Bovis Kyle & Burch, Atlanta, 1987-89; asst. dist. atty. Piedmont Jud. Cir., Winder, Ga., 1989-91, Gwinnett Jud. Cir., Lawrenceville, Ga., 1991-95; pvt. practice Atlanta, 1995—; tchr. Am. Paralegal Inst., Atlanta, 1994—; lectr. in field. Author: Georgia Jurisprudence, 1995; contbr. articles to profl. jours. Mem., past bd. dirs. Am. Jewish Com., Atlanta; chmn. Younger Lawyers Alumni Com. U. Ga., 1998-99; bd. dirs. YLAC, 1995—. Mem. State Bar of Ga. (co-chmn. criminal law com. younger lawyer sect. 1996-97, bd. dirs., 1995-96), Ga. Assn. Criminal Def. Lawyers. Criminal. Office: 800 Grant Bldg 44 Broad St NW Atlanta GA 30303-2327

**BERNSTEIN, CHARLES BERNARD,** lawyer; b. Chgo., June 24, 1941; s. Norman and Adele (Shore) B.; A.B., U. Chgo., 1962; J.D., DePaul U., 1965; m. Roberta Luba Lesner, Aug. 7, 1968; children—Edward Charles, Louis Charles, Henry Jacob. Admitted to Ill. bar, 1965, U.S. Supreme Ct. bar, 1972; asso. firm Axelrod, Goodman & Steiner, Chgo., 1966-67, Max & Herman Chill, Chgo., 1967-74, Bellows & Assos., Chgo., 1974-81, Marvin Sacks Ltd., Chgo., 1981; individual practice law, 1981—; basketball press dir. U. Chgo., 1967-74. Officer Congregation Rodfei Zedek, 1979-93, bd. dirs., 1978-93. Recipient Am. Jurisprudence award, 1963; citation meritorious service Dist. Grand Lodge 6 B'nai B'rith, 1969; My Brothers Keeper award Am. Jewish Congress, 1977. Mem. Chgo. Bar Assn., Ill. State Bar Assn., Chgo. Jewish Hist. Soc. (treas. 1977-79, v.p. 1979-82, dir. 1977—), Chgo. Pops Orch. Assn. (treas., exec. com. 1975-81), Am. Jewish Hist. Soc., Art Inst. of Chgo., Chgo. Hist. Soc., Jewish Geneal. Soc. (dir. 1977—), Nu Beta Epsilon. Club: B'nai B'rith. Author: (with Stuart L. Cohen) Torah and Technology: The History and Genealogy of the Anixter Family, 1986, (with Neil Rosenstein) From King David to Baron David: The Genealogical Connections Between Baron Guy de Rothschild and Baroness Alix de Rothschild, 1989, The Rothschilds of Nordstetten: Their History and Genealogy, 1989; contbr. articles to mags., profl. jours. Landlord-tenant, Probate, General practice. Home: 5400 S Hyde Park Blvd Chicago IL 60615-5828 Office: One N LaSalle Chicago IL 60602

**BERNSTEIN, DAVID WILLIAM,** lawyer; b. Bklyn., Feb. 13, 1938; s. Sidney Abraham B. and Carol Elsa Silverman; m. Carol Ellen Lamberg, June 16, 1959 (div. 1977); m. Melissa Lewis, Mar. 7, 1980; children: Andrew, Donna, Lauren. BA magna cum laude, Harvard U., 1959, LLB magna cum laude, 1962. Bar: N.Y. 1962. Assoc. atty. Rogers & Wells, N.Y.C., 1962-67, ptnr., 1967—, chmn. corp. dept., 1989-97. Contbr. numerous articles to Fin. Law Rev., 1996—. Bd. dirs. Internat. Preschs., 1966—. Mem. Inwood Country Club (sec. 1982-91). Republican. Jewish. Avocation: golf. Fax: 212-878-8375. E-mail: bernsted@rw.com. Office: Rogers & Wells 200 Park Ave Fl 8E New York NY 10166-0800

**BERNSTEIN, DONALD SCOTT,** lawyer; b. Bklyn., July 11, 1953; s. Emanuel and Shirley (Smithline) B.; m. Jo Ellen Finkel, May 31, 1987; children: Daniel Emanuel, Julia Clare. BA, Princeton U., 1975; JD, U. Chgo., 1978. Bar: N.Y. 1979, U.S. Dist. Ct. (ea. and so. dists.) N.Y. 1979. Assoc. Davis Polk & Wardwell, N.Y.C., 1978-86, ptnr., 1986—; panelist Practicing Law Inst., N.Y.C., 1983—, Am. Law Inst., ABA, 1991—, Am. Bankruptcy Inst., 1991—; mem. vis. com. U. Chgo. Law Sch., 1995-98, chmn., 1997-98. Bd. dirs. Altro Health and Rehab. Svcs., Bronx, N.Y., 1988-90, N.Y. chpt. Am. Diabetes Assn., 1992-96; mem. exec. com. bankruptcy lawyers div. United Jewish Appeal Fedn., 1985—. Mem. ABA (bus. bankruptcy com., com. on legal opinions), Am. Coll. Bankruptcy, New York County Lawyers Assn. (bd. dirs. 1992-94), Nat. Bankruptcy Conf. (exec. com. 1996—), Am. Bankruptcy Inst., Assn. Bar City N.Y. (com. on bankruptcy and corp. reorgn. 1979-83, 85-88, chmn. 1993-96, mem. tribar opinion com. 1988—, chmn. 1998—). Banking, Bankruptcy, Contracts commercial. Office: Davis Polk & Wardwell 450 Lexington Ave New York NY 10017-3911

**BERNSTEIN, EDWIN S.,** judge; b. Long Beach, N.Y., Aug. 15, 1930; s. Harry and Lena (Strizver) B.; children: Debora, Andrea, David. BA, U. Pa., 1952; LLB, Columbia U., 1955. Bar: N.Y. 1955, U.S. Ct. Appeals (2d cir.) 1962, U.S. Dist. Ct. (ea. and so. dists.) N.Y. 1962, U.S. Tax Ct. 1962, U.S. Supreme Ct. 1964, Md. 1981, D.C. 1982. Mem. bd. contract appeals Dept. Army, Heidelberg, Fed. Republic Germany, 1968-72; regional counsel U.S. Navy, Quincy, Mass., 1972-73; adminstrv. law judge U.S. Dept. Labor, Washington, 1973-79, Fed. Mine Safety and Health Rev. Commn., Washington, 1979-81, U.S. Postal Svc., Washington, 1981-87, USDA, Washington, 1987—; liaison rep. Administrv. Conf. of U.S., Washington, 1983-84; guest lectr. SUNY-Albany, 1978, U. Md., 1982, George Washington U., 1984. Author: U.S. Army Procurement Handbook, 1971; Establishing Federal Administrative Law Judges as an Independent Corps, 1984, also articles. Bd. dirs. Washington Hebrew Congregation, 1985-88. Recipient Meritorious Civilian Svc. award Dept. Army, 1972. Mem. ABA, Fed. Bar Assn., D.C. Bar Assn., Fed. Adminstr. Law Judges Conf. (pres. 1983-84), Papermill Assn. (pres. 1980-81). Lodge: Masons. Avocations: golf; bridge; sailing; wines; opera. Home: 5702 Balsam Grove Ct Rockville MD 20852-5551 Office: USDA 1049 South Bldg Independence Ave and 14th St SW Washington DC 20250

**BERNSTEIN, ERIC MARTIN,** lawyer; b. Passaic, N.J., May 5, 1957; s. Abbot Alan and Jean Hausman (Schwartz) B. BA, Drew U., 1979; JD, U. Okla., 1982; MS in Indsl. and Labor Rels., Cornell U., 1985. Bar: N.J. 1982, U.S. Dist. Ct. N.J. 1982, D.C. 1985, U.S. Ct. Appeals (3d cir.) 1985, U.S. Supreme Ct. 1986. Assoc. Mandelbaum Salsburg Gold & Lazaris, East Orange, N.J., 1982-83; pvt. practice Clifton, N.J., 1983-84; sr. assoc. Gerald L. Dorf, P.A., Rahway, N.J., 1984-87; of counsel Vaida & Vaida, P.C., Flemington, N.J., 1987-88; pvt. practice Bridgewater, Clifton and Three Bridges, N.J., 1988-92; ptnr. Weiner Lesniak, Parsippany, N.J., 1992-97, Mauro Savo Camerino & Grant, Somerville, N.J., 1998—; lectr. Bur. Govt. Rsch., Rutgers U., New Brunswick, N.J., 1983—; mem. adj. faculty Raritan Valley C.C., Somerville, N.J., 1988-90; city atty. City of Passaic, N.J., 1990-92; mcpl. atty. Washington Twp.-Warren County, 1991—, Hardwick Twp.-Warren County, 1992—, West Windsor-Mercer County, 1993-97, North Plainfield-Somerset County, 1997—, Bethlehem Twp.-Hunterdon County, 1998—, Stillwater Twp.-Sussex County, 1998—, Paramus Borough-Bergen County, 1999—, Franklin Township-Hunterdon County, 1999—, Union City-Hudson County, 1999—; bd. atty. Englewood Bd. Edn.-Bergen County, 1996-99, Lincoln Park Bd. Edn.-Morris County, 1997—. Asst. editor, co-author: Governing New Jersey Municipalities, 1984, co-editor, author, 6th edit., 1995; asst. editor N.J. Mcpl. Attys. Mag., 1984-92; editor N.J. State Bar Assn. Local Govt. Law Newsletter, 1995—. Vol. atty. Lawyers for the Arts, N.J., 1986—. Mem. ABA, Fed. Bar Assn., N.J. Bar Assn. (1st vice chair local govt. law sect. 1995—), D.C. Bar Assn., Passaic County Bar Assn., Somerset County Bar Assn. Republican. Jewish. Avocations: tennis, golf, stamp collecting, classical and jazz music. Labor, Education and schools, Municipal (including bonds). Home: 10 Timberline Dr Bridgewater NJ 08807-1204 Office: PO Box 1277 77 N Bridge St Somerville NJ 08876-1918

**BERNSTEIN, GEORGE L.,** lawyer, accountant; b. Phila., Feb. 22, 1932; s. Leon B. and Elizabeth (Seidman) B.; m. Phyllis Wagner, June 27, 1954; children: Harris, Lisa. BS in Econs., U. Pa., 1953, JD cum laude, 1956. Bar: Pa. 1957; CPA, Pa. Accountant Laventhol & Horwath, Phila., 1950-90, exec. ptnr., chief exec. officer, 1980-90; chief oper. officer Dilworth, Paxon, Attys., Phila., 1991-94; CFO, CAO HFA, Inc., Exec. Search Cons., Phila., 1994—. Nat. chmn. profl. divsn. State of Israel Bonds, 1988-90; co-chmn. bd. trustees Am. Jewish Congress, Phila., 1988-90; bd. dirs. Mann Ctr. for Performing Arts, Phila.; trustee Einstein Health Care Network, Phila. Recipient Humanitarian award State of Israel Bonds, 1989. Mem. AICPA (coun. 1976-79, 81-87, strategic planning com. 1986-90, v.p. 1986-87, bd. dirs. 1981-84, com. small and medium sized firms 1978-80, MAS exec. com. 1971-75), Pa. Inst. CPAs (pres. 1976-77, com.m on past pres., chmn. MAS com., long-range objectives com., budget and fin. com.), Locust Club (pres. 1990-92, exec. com., bd. dirs.). Democrat. Avocations: golf, walking, music, theatre.

**BERNSTEIN, JACOB,** lawyer; b. Glen Cove, N.Y., Dec. 23, 1932; s. David and Ida (Miller) B.; m. Eva Belle Smolokoff, June 28, 1959; children: Diane Susan, Neal Robert. AB, U. Rochester, 1954; JD, U. Mich., 1957. Bar: N.Y. 1957, U.S. Supreme Ct. Mem. Ralph J. Marino, 1959-64, Marino & Bernstein, 1964-73, Marino, Bernstein & La Marca, Oyster Bay, N.Y., 1973—; lectr. in field. Actor Sagamore Players, 1972—. Founding mem., trustee Cmty. Found., 1962—; trusztee Oyster Bay Jewish Ctr., 1962—, pres., 1965-67; sec. bd. dirs. oyster Bay youth and Family Counseling Agy., 1975—; pres. Oyster Bay E. Norwich Youth Coun., 1976-78; divsn. chmn. United Jewish Appeal, 1965-74; bd. dirs., counsel America's Sail, 1994—; mem. EPTL-SCPA adv. com. to N.Y. State Legis., 1990—. With U.S. Army, 1958-59. Recipient United Jewish Appeal award of honor, 1972; named Man of Yr. Oyster Bay Jewish Ctr., 1986. Mem. ABA, N.Y. Bar Assn., U.S. Dist. Ct. Bar Assn., Nassau County Bar Assn., Nassau Lawyers Assn., North Shore Lawyers Assn., Rotary (pres. 1967-68, dist. parliamentarian 1986-87, govs. aide 1999—), Sagamore Yacht Club (chief legal officer 1973—). Republican. Estate planning, Probate, Real property. Office: PO Box 180 Oyster Bay NY 11771-0180

**BERNSTEIN, JAN LENORE,** lawyer; b. N.Y.C., Apr. 24, 1957; d. James Hanley and Joan Mathilda (Wertheimer) B. BA magna cum laude, U. Pa., 1979; JD, Rutgers U., 1982. Bar: N.J. 1982, Pa.1983, N.Y. 1990. Law clk. to hon. Herbert S. Glickman Newark, 1982-83; ptnr. Riker, Danzig, Scherer, Hyland and Perretti LLP, Morristown, N.J., 1983—; mem. jud. performance com., women in the cts. com., econ. consequences of dissolution com., dis. X fee arbitration com. N.J. Supreme Ct.; mem. exec. com. family law sect.; past mem. family practice com.; presenter in field. Mem. editl. bd. N.J. Lawyer mag.; bd. dirs. N.J. Lawyer newspaper; contbr. articles to profl. jours. Dem. committeeperson; assoc. trustee U. Pa., chair woemn's atheltic bd., mem. trustee coun. Penn Women, bd. of athletic advisors. Mem. N.J. Bar Assn. (past chair women's rights sect.), Morris County (N.J.) Bar Assn. (family law com.). Fax: 973-538-1984. E-mail: info@riker.com. Family and matrimonial. Office: Riker Danzig Scherer Hyland & Perreti LLP Headquarters Plaza Speedwell Ave Morristown NJ 07962 also: 50 W State St Ste 1010 Trenton NJ 08608-1220

**BERNSTEIN, JEREMY MARSHALL,** lawyer; b. Denver, Dec. 29, 1952; s. Harry S. and Belle R. (Sperling) B.; m. Elyse A. Elliott, Aug. 23, 1985. BA with honors and distinction, Stanford U., 1975; JD, Boston U., 1979. Bar: Colo. 1979, U.S. Dist. Ct. D.C. 1979, U.S. Ct. Appeals (10th cir.) 1986. Law clk. to presiding justice Colo. Ct. Appeals, Denver, 1979-80; assoc. Grant, McHendrie, Haines & Crouse, Denver, 1980-82, Cogswell & Wehrle, Denver, 1982-84; assoc. and head of litigation Garfield & Hecht, P.C., Aspen, Colo., 1984-87; pvt. practice law Aspen, 1988—. Mem. ABA, Colo. Trial Lawyers' Assn., Colo. Bar Assn., Pitkin County Bar Assn. (sec. 1985-86), Phi Beta Kappa. Avocations: skiing, fly fishing. Family and matrimonial, Personal injury, General civil litigation. Office: 300 E Hyman Ave Ste D Aspen CO 81611-1947

**BERNSTEIN, JOSEPH,** lawyer; b. New Orleans, Feb. 12, 1930; s. Eugene Julian and Lola (Schlemoff) B.; m. Phyllis Maxine Askanase, Sept. 4, 1955; children: Jill, Barbara, Elizabeth R, Jonathan Joseph. BS, U. Ala., 1952, LLB, Tulane U., 1957. Bar: La., 1957. Clk. to Justice E. Howard McCaleb of La. Supreme Ct., 1957; assoc. Jones, Walker, Waechter, Poitevent, Carrere & Denegre, 1957-60, ptnr., 1960-65; pvt. practice New Orleans, 1965—; former gen. counsel Alliance for Affordable Energy. Past pres. New Orleans Jewish Community Ctr., Met. New Orleans chpt. March of Dimes. Trustee New Orleans Symphony Soc.; past mem. adv. council New Orleans Mus. Art; past nat. exec. com. Am. Jewish Com. 2d lt. AUS, 1952-54. Mem. ABA, La. Bar Assn., New Orleans Bar Assn., Phi Delta Phi, Zeta Beta Tau. Republican. Jewish. General corporate, General practice, Public utilities. Home: 708 Explanade Ave Bay Saint Louis MS 39520

**BERNSTEIN, MARK R.,** retired lawyer; b. York, Pa., Apr. 7, 1930; s. Phillip G. Bernstein and Evelyn (Greenfield) Spielman; m. E. Louise Bernstein, May 10, 1955; children: Phillip, Cary, Adam, Andrew, Jonathan, Evan. BA, U. Pa., 1952; JD, Yale U., 1957. Bar: N.C., U.S. Dist. Ct. (we. dist.) N.C., U.S. Ct. Appeals, U.S. Custom Ct. Atty. Kennedy, Covington, Lobdell, & Hickman, Charlotte, N.C., 1957-60, Haynes, Graham, Bernstein & Baucom, Charlotte, N.C., 1960-67; atty. Parker, Poe, Adams & Bernstein, Charlotte, N.C., 1968-98, chmn., 1963-68; bd. dirs. Family Dollar Stores, Inc., Nat. Welders Supply Co., Inc. Bd. dirs., vice-chmn. The Found. of the Carolinas, Inc., Charlotte Symphony Orchestra, The Wildacres Found.; past pres. Charlotte Symphony Assn.; past chmn. mayor's com. for a Performing Arts Ctr., 1983-85, com. mem. Performing Arts Ctr. Task Force, 1987; chmn. N.C. Econ. Devel. Bd.; past pres. Temple Beth El, Charlotte Jewish Cmty. Ctr., Charlotte Civitan Club, Am. Symphony Orch. League, Golden Circle Theatre, Found. of Shalom Park; past mem. exec. com. Yale Law Sch.; past mem. bd. N.C. Blumenthal Performing Arts Ctr. Recipient Disting. Svc. award Jaycees, 1961, State of Israel Humanitarian award, 1981, Charlotte Fedn. of Jewish Charities A Man of the Ages award, 1985, Silver Medallion award NCCJ, 1995, Israel Humanitarian award, The Vanguard award for personal svcs. Arts and Sci. Coun., 1998. Mem. Mecklenburg County Bar Assn. (past pres.), Charlotte City Club, The Tower Club (bd. dirs.), Olde Providence Racquet Club (past pres.). Democrat. General corporate, Mergers and acquisitions. Home: 5300 Hardison Rd Charlotte NC 28226-6426

**BERNSTEIN, MERTON CLAY,** law educator, lawyer, arbitrator; b. N.Y.C., Mar. 26, 1923; s. Benjamin and Ruth (Frederica (Kleeblatt)) B.; m. Joan Barbara Brodshaug, Dec. 17, 1955; children: Johanna Karin, Inga Saterlie, Matthew Curtis, Rachel Libby. B.A., Oberlin Coll., 1943; LL.B., Columbia U., 1948. Bar: N.Y. 1948, U.S. Supreme Ct. 1952. Assoc. Schlesinger & Schlesinger, 1948; atty. NLRB, 1949-50, 50-51, Office of Solicitor, U.S. Dept. Labor, 1950; counsel Nat. Enforcement Commn., 1951, U.S. Senate Subcom. on Labor, 1952; legis. asst. to U.S. Sen. Wayne L. Morse, 1953-56; counsel U.S. Senate Com. on R.R. Retirement, 1957-58; spl. counsel U.S. Senate Subcom. on Labor, 1958; assoc. prof. law U. Nebr., 1958-59; lectr., sr. fellow Yale U. Law Sch., 1960-65; prof. law Ohio State U., 1965-75; Walter D. Coles prof. law Washington U., St. Louis, 1975-96, Walter D. Coles prof. emeritus, 1997—; mem. adv. com. to Sec. of Treas. on Coordination of Social Security and pvt. pension plans, 1967-68; prin. cons. Nat. Commn. on Social Security Reform, 1982-83; vis. prof. Columbia U. Law Sch., 1967-68, Leiden U., 1975-76; mem. adv. com. rsch. U.S. Social Security Adminstrn., 1967-68, chmn., 1969-70; cons. Adminstrv. Conf. of the U.S., 1989, Dept. Labor, 1966-67, Russell Sage Found., 1967-68, NSF, 1970-71, Ctr. for the Study of Contemporary Problems, 1968-71. Author: The Future of Private Pensions, 1964, Private Dispute Settlement, 1969, (with Joan B. Bernstein) Social Security: The System That Works, 1988; contbr. articles to profl. jours. Mem. Bethany (Conn.) Planning and Zoning Commn., 1962-65, Ohio Retirement Study Commn., 1967-68; co-chmn. transition team for St. Louis Mayor Freeman Bosley Jr., 1993; bd. dirs. St. Louis Theatre Project, 1981-84; pres. bd. Met. Sch. Columbus, Ohio, 1974-75; del. White House Conf. Aging, 1995. With AUS, 1943-45. Fulbright fellow, 1975-76, Elizar Wright award, 1965. Mem. ABA (sec. sect. labor rels. law 1968-69), Internat. Assn. for Labor Law and Social Security (bd. dirs. U.S. chpt. 1973-83, 88-91), Fulbright Alumni Assn. (bd. dirs. 1976-78), Indsl. Rels. Rsch. Assn., Nat. Acad. Arbitrators, Am. Arbitration Assn. (mem. adv. com. St. Louis region 1987—), Nat. Acad. Social Ins. (founding mem., bd. dirs. 1986-91). Democrat. Jewish. E-mail: bernstem@wu-law.wustl.edu. Office: Washington U Sch Law Campus Box 1120 Saint Louis MO 63130

**BERNSTEIN, MICHAEL IRWIN,** lawyer; b. Bklyn., Mar. 31, 1938; s. Samuel Bernard and Fay Louise (Barotz) B.; m. Janice Esther Reisner, Sept. 2, 1961; children: Lynne, Marci, Susan. BA in Econs., U. Mich., 1959; LLB, Columbia U., 1962. Bar: N.Y. 1963, U.S. Dist. Ct. (so. and ea. dists.) N.Y. 1963, U.S. Ct. Appeals (2d cir.) 1963, U.S. Supreme Ct. 1974. Atty. NLRB, N.Y.C., 1962-65; assoc. Nordinger, Riegelman, Benetar & Charney, N.Y.C., 1965-70; ptnr. Aranow, Brodsky, Bohlinger, Benetar & Einhorn, N.Y.C., 1971-78, Benetar, Isaacs, Bernstein & Schair, N.Y.C., 1979-89, Benetar Bernstein Schair & Stein, N.Y.C., 1989—; lectr. in field. Contbr. numerous articles to profl. jours. Fellow N.Y. State Bar Found ; mem. ABA (chmn. fed. labor standards legis. com. 1985-88, past. chmn. subcom. on occupational health and safety, past. chmn. subcoms. on age discrimination and equal pay), N.Y. State Bar Assn. (past chmn. labor and employmeny law sect. 1990—, past chmn com. on intake and investigation, task force of reviewing practices), N.Y.C. Bar Assn. (past chmn. on labor law, past chmn. spl. com. on non-legal pers.), Coll. Labor and Employment Lawyers. Labor, Alternative dispute resolution. Home: 35 South Pl Chappaqua NY 10514-3612 Office: Benetar Bernstein Schair & Stein 330 Madison Ave New York NY 10017-5001

**BERNSTEIN, MITCHELL HARRIS,** lawyer; b. N.Y.C., Sept. 19, 1949; s. Melvin and Gladys (Weissman) B.; m. Barbara Veitch, Oct. 8, 1978; children: Jonathan, Matthew, Emily. AB, U. Pa., 1970; JD, Yale U., 1973. Bar: N.Y. 1974, U.S. Ct. Appeals (2d cir.) 1974, U.S. Dist. Ct. (so. and ea. dists.) N.Y. 1974, U.S. Ct. Appeals (5th and D.C. cirs.) 1980, U.S. Supreme Ct. 1980, D.C. 1981, U.S. Ct. Appeals (4th cir.) 1981, U.S. Dist. Ct. D.C. 1982, U.S. Ct. Appeals (3d cir.) 1985. Assoc. Breed, Abbott & Morgan, N.Y.C., 1974-77; sr. atty. U.S. EPA, Washington, 1977-81; assoc. Skadden, Arps, Slate, Meagher & Flom, Washington, 1981-83, ptnr., 1983-93; mem. Van Ness Feldman, Washington, 1994—. Bd. advisors Chem. Waste Litigation Reporter, Washington, 1985—. Mem. ABA, D.C. Bar. Assn. Environmental, Administrative and regulatory. Office: Van Ness Feldman Ste 7 1050 Thomas Jefferson St NW Washington DC 20007-3837

**BERNSTEIN, ROBERT ALAN,** lawyer; b. Charleston, S.C., Mar. 30, 1958; s. Charles Stanley Bernstein and Sara Marjorie (Blum) Baumwald; m. Mary Deann Phillips, Sept. 4, 1983; children: Benjamin Daniel, Preston Manning. BS cum laude, U. S.C., 1980, JD cum laude, 1983. Bar: S.C. 1983, U.S. Dist. Ct. S.C. 1983. Law clk. to judge U.S. Dist. Ct. S.C., Columbia, 1983-85; assoc. Turner, Padget, Graham & Laney, P.A., Columbia, 1985-92; shareholder Bernstein & Bernstein, P.A., Charleston, S.C., 1992—. Contbr. notes S.C. Law Rev., 1984. Recipient Am. Jurisprudence award, 1982, 83. Mem. ABA, S.C. Bar Assn., Charleston County Bar Assn., Comml. Law League Am., Order of Coif, Order of Wig and Robe, Rotary, Phi Beta Kappa, Zeta Beta Tau (trustee Alpha Theta chpt. 1984—). Jewish. Avocations: tennis, basketball, jogging. Federal civil litigation, Consumer commercial, General practice. Office: Bernstein & Bernstein PA 5416 Rivers Ave Charleston SC 29406-6165

**BERNSTEIN, STEPHEN RICHARD,** lawyer; b. Detroit, July 14, 1947; s. Samuel J. and Alice B. Student, Wayne State U., Detroit, 1965-69; JD, Detroit Coll. Law, E. Lansing, Mich., 1973. Staff atty. Am. Title Ins. Co., Oak Park, Ill., 1972-73; supervising atty. Oakland County Legal Aid, Pontiac, Mich., 1973-75; ptnr. Bernstein & Rabinouitz, PC, Troy, Mich., 1975-86; sole practitioner pvt. practice, Farmington Hills, Wis., 1986-98; ptnr. Swistak, Levine, Partouich & Bernstein, PC, Farmington Hills, Wis., 1998—; hearing panel mem. Atty. Discipline Bd., Detroit, 1989—; rep. assembly State Bar Mich., Lansing, 1976-84; mediator Mediation Tribunal Assn., Detroit, 1991—. Dir. U. Mich. Student Buyers Assn., Ann Arbor, 1997—. Recipient Cert. Appreciation Detroit Pub. Schs., 1993; named Hall of Honour Alpha Epsilon Pi U. Western Ontario, London, Ontario, Can., 1998. Mem. Southeast Mich. Officials Assn., Detroit Maccabi Club, Alpha Epsilon Pi. Family and matrimonial, General civil litigation, Sports. Office: Swistak Levine Partovich & Bernstein PC 30445 Northwestern Hwy Ste 140 Farmingtn Hls MI 48334-3174

**BERNSTEIN, STUART,** lawyer; b. Chgo., Nov. 23, 1919; m. Doris Golding. A.B., U. Chgo., 1942, J.D., 1947. Bar: Ill. 1947. Assoc. Mayer, Brown & Platt, Chgo., 1947-58, ptnr., 1958-90, sr. counsel, 1991—; mem. United Air Lines Pilots System Bd., 1958-72, 86—; trustee emeritus, mem. bd. trustees Chgo. Ednl. Television Assn. Pres. Dist. 113 Bd. Edn., Lake County, Ill., 1970-72; mem. Plan Commn. and Zoning Bd. Appeals, Highland Park, Ill., 1966-72. Served to 1st lt. USAAF, 1942-46. Decorated Air medal (5). Mem. ABA, Ill. Bar Assn., Chgo. Bar Assn., Chgo. Council Lawyers, Order of Coif, Phi Beta Kappa. Clubs: Law, Standard (Chgo.). Editor-in-chief U. Chgo. Law Rev., 1947. Labor, Federal civil litigation. Office: Mayer Brown & Platt 190 S La Salle St Ste 3100 Chicago IL 60603-3441

**BERNSTINE, DANIEL O'NEAL,** law educator, university president; b. Berkeley, Calif., Sept. 7, 1947; s. Annias and Emma (Jones) B.; m. Nancy Jean Tyler, July 27, 1971 (div. Mar. 1986); children: Quincy Tyler, Justin Tyler. BA, U. Calif., Berkeley, 1969; JD, Northwestern U., Chgo., 1972; LLM, U. Wis., 1975. Bar: D.C. 1970, Wis. 1979. Prof. law Howard U. Law Sch., Washington, 1975-78, gen. counsel, interim dean, 1987-90; prof. law U. Wis. Law Sch., Madison, 1978-97, dean, 1990-97; pres. Portland (Ore.) State Univ., 1997—. Author: Wisconsin and Federal Civil Procedure, 1986. Bd. dirs. Madison Cmty. Found., 1990-94, Portland Urban League, Legacy Health Sys.; mem. Portland Multnomah Progress Bd., 1998—, Kellogg Commn. on the Future of State and Land-Grant Univs., 1997—. Mem. Am. Law Inst. Office: Portland State Univ PO Box 751 Portland OR 97207-0751

**BERNZ, DAVID,** lawyer; b. N.Y.C., Nov. 26, 1958. BA, Boston U., 1980; JD, CUNY, Queens, 1991. Bar: N.Y. 1992, U.S. Fed. Dist. Ct. 1994. Staff atty. Middletown (N.Y.) Hudson Legal Svcs., 1992; ptnr. Bacon & Bernz Attys. at Law, Newburgh, N.Y., 1993-96; pvt. practice Newburgh, 1997—. Avocations: music, performance, songwriting. Family and matrimonial, Real property, Landlord-tenant. Office: 10 Little Britain Rd Newburgh NY 12550-5100

**BEROLZHEIMER, KARL,** lawyer; b. Chgo., Mar. 31, 1932; s. Leon J. and Rae Gloss (Lowenthal) B.; m. Diane Glick, July 10, 1954; children: Alan, Eric, Paul, Lisa. BA, U. Ill., 1953; JD, Harvard U., 1958. Bar: Ill. 1958, U.S. Ct. Appeals (7th cir.) 1964, U.S. Ct. Appeals (9th cir.) 1969, U.S. Supreme Ct. 1976. Assoc. Ross & Hardies, Chgo., 1958-66, ptnr., 1966-76, of counsel, 1993—; v.p. legal Centel Corp., Chgo., 1976-77, v.p., gen. counsel, 1977-82, sr. v.p., gen. counsel, 1982-88, sr. v.p., gen. counsel, sec., 1988-93; v.p., gen. counsel, sec., 1988-93; mem. nat. adv. bd. Ctr. for Informatics Law, John Marshall Law Sch., Chgo., 1988-93; mem. Corp. Counsel Ctr., Northwestern U. Law Sch., 1987-93, mem. emeritus, 1993—; mem. adv. bd. Litigation Risk Mgmt. Inst., 1989-95; bd. dirs. Milton Industries, Chgo., Devon Bank, Chgo.; cons. Mt. Pulaski Tel. and Elec. Co., Lincoln, Ill., 1981-86; sec., gen. counsel Consol. Water Co., Chgo., 1968-72; mem. human rels. task force Chgo. Cmty. Trust, 1988-90. Bd. dirs. The Nat. Conf. Commn. and Justice, Chgo., presiding co-chmn., 1987-90, mem. nat. exec. bd. dirs., 1988-98, chair investment com., 1991-94, nat. co-chair, 1992-95, pres., 1993-94, chair, 1995-98; mem. exec. bd. Internat. Coun. Christians and Jews, 1996—, v.p., 1998—; bd. dirs. Evanston (Ill.) Mental Health, 1975-82, chair, 1978-80; dir. Evanston Comty. Found., 1996—, vice chair, chair grants com., 1996-98, chair, 1999—; bd. dirs. Beth Emet Found., 1997; trustee Northlight Theatre, Evanston, 1992—, vice-chair, 1993-99; mem. coun. The Communitarian Network, 1993-96; trustee Beth Emet Synagogue, Evanston, 1985-87, 89, sec., 1985-89; chair Capital Campaign Plan com., 1994-97; mem. discrimination priority com. United Way, 1990-97, vice-chair, 1993; mem. assembly Parliament of the World's Religions, 1993; mem. Ill. atty. gen.'s ad hoc com. for creation of justice commn., 1994; mem. adv. com. Ill. Justice Commn., 1995-96; mem. adv. bd. Nat. Underground R.R. Freedom Ctr., 1997—. 1st lt. U.S. Army, 1953-55. Fellow Am. Bar Found.; mem. ABA (chair telcom. com. bus. law sect. 1982-86, dispute resolution com. 1986-90, office com. 1991-95, mem. Coalition for Justice 1993-97, bd. editors Bus. Law Today 1995-97, co-chair conflicts of interest com. 1997—), Chgo. Bar Assn. (mem. devel. of law com. 1963-67, chair 1971-73), Chgo. Coun. Lawyers. Democrat. General corporate, Securities, Public utilities. Home: 414 Ashland Ave Evanston IL 60202-3208 Office: Ross & Hardies 150 N Michigan Ave Ste 2500 Chicago IL 60601-7567

**BERREY, ROBERT WILSON, III,** retired judge; b. Dec. 6, 1929; s. Robert Wilson and Elizabeth (Hudson) B.; m. Katharine Rollins Wilcoxson, Sept. 5, 1950; children: Robert Wilson IV, Mary Jane, John Lind. AB, William Jewell Coll., 1950; MA, U. S.D., 1952; LLB, Kansas City U., 1955; LLM, U. Mo., Kansas City, 1972; grad. Trial Judges Coll., U. Nev., 1972; postgrad., Ariz. State U., U. Nev. Bar: Mo. 1955, Kans. 1955. Assoc. Shugert and Thomson, 1955-56, Clark, Krings & Bredehoft, 1957-61, Terry and Welton, 1961-62; judge 4th Dist. Magistrate Ct., Jackson County, Mo., 1962-79; assoc. cir. judge 16th Cir. Ct., Jackson County, 1979-81, cir. judge, 1981-83, mem. mgmt.-exec. com., 1979-83; judge Mo. Ct. Appeals (we. dist.), Kansas City, 1983-97, chief judge, 1994, chmn. rules com., 1990-91, mem., 1993-95, conf. sec., 1992-93, mem. security com., 1992-94; ret., 1997; mem. Supreme Ct. Com. to Draft Rules and Procedures for Mo.'s Small Claims Ct., 1976-86. Vol. legal cons. Psychiat. Receiving Ctr. Del. Atlantic Coun. Young Polit. Leaders, Oxford, Eng., 1965; Kansas City rep. to Pres.'s Nat. Conf. on Crime Control; del.-at-large White House Conf. on Aging, 1972; former pack chmn. Cub Scouts Am.; counselor, com. mem. Boy Scouts Am., sponsor Eagle Scouts; vice chmn. water fowl com. Mo. Conservation Fedn., 1968-69, chmn. water fowl com., 1971-73; v.p. Cook PTA, 1967-68; mem. cts. and judiciary com. Mo. Bar, 1969-73; mem. Midwest region adv. com. Nat. Pks. Svcs., 1973-78, chmn., 1973-78; mem. Mo. State Judicial Planning Commn., 1977; chmn. Senatorial Redistricting Com., Mo., 1991; bd. dirs., founder Kansas City Open Space Found., 1976; regional dir. Young Rep. Nat. Fedn., 1957-59, gen. counsel, 1959-61, nat. vice-chmn.; chmn. Mo. Young Rep. Fedn., 1960, nat. committeeman, 1959-60, 61-64; Mo. alt.-at-large Rep. Nat. Conv., 1960, asst. gen. counsel, 1964, del. state and dist. convs., 1960, 64, 68; bd. dirs. Naturalization Coun., Kansas City, pres., 1973—, Native Sons of Kansas City, 1987—, chmn. long-range planning com., 1992, 1st v.p., 1994, pres., 1995; trustee Kansas City Mus., 1972-73, Hyman Brand Hebrew Acad., 1983—, Woods Meml. Christian Ch., 1988—, chmn., deacon, 1988-91, elder, 1991-94, 96—, chmn. trustees, 1992—, chmn. property, 1991-97, vice chmn. bd. dirs., 1998-99, chmn. bd. dirs., 1998-99, chmn. strategic and bldg. planning com., 1995, chmn. ofcl. bd., 1998-99; mem. status coun. LEAA, 1993-96; hon. life dir. Rockhurst Coll. Mem. Mo. Bar (Disting. Svc. award 1973, agr. law com., com. coun. 1980-81), Kansas City Bar Assn., Urban League (past exec. com. dir.), SAR (registrar 1998-99), Kansas City Mus. Natural Sci. Soc. (charter), Tex. Longhorn Breeders Assn. (life), Am. Royal (bd. govs.), Am. Forestry Assn. (life), Mo. Longhorn Breeders Assn. (life), Mo. Farm Bur., Clay County Lodge (life, Mo. Marshall 1993, jr. warden 1994, sr. warden 1995, worshipful master 1995-97), Nat. Soc. SAR (law commendation medal 1995, 98), Shrine, Ararat Temple (hon. life, provost), DeMolay Legion Honor (life), Waldo Optimist Club (v.p. 1967-68), Ducks Unltd. (life, nat. trustee 1986-89, state trustee/nat. del. 1992, 94, nat. spl. projects com. 1990-95, trustee emeritus 1993, life sponsor U.S., Can., Mex., state coun. 1985—, Sportsman of Yr. 1985, Conservation Svc. award 1992, Absentee Conservation Farmer Lubbock County Soil and Water Conservation Dist. 1994), The Explorers Club, Kansas City Club, Hartwell Hunt Club (dir. 1994-97), U. Club Kansas City, J Club, William Jewell Coll., Alpha Phi Omega, Delta Theta Phi (life, Toast 1990), Pi Gamma Mu, Tau Kappa Epsilon (Hall of Fame 1986). Family and matrimonial, State civil litigation. Home: 31694 W 132d St Excelsior Springs MO 64024-9402 also: RR 2 Battle Lake MN 56515-9802

**BERRIDGE, GEORGE BRADFORD,** retired lawyer; b. Detroit, June 9, 1928; s. William Lloyd and Marjorie (George) B.; m. Mary Lee Robinson, July 6, 1957; children: George Bradford, Elizabeth A., Mary L., Robert L. AB, U. Mich., 1950, MBA, 1953, JD, 1954. Bar: N.Y. 1954. Assoc. Chadbourne & Parke, N.Y.C., 1954-61; gen. atty., v.p. law Am. Airlines, Inc., N.Y.C., 1961-71; sr. v.p., gen. counsel Americana Hotels, Inc., N.Y.C., 1971-74, Nat. Westminster Bank U.S.A., N.Y.C., 1975-89, Nat. Westminster Bancorp, N.Y.C., 1989-93; ret., 1993. Contbr. articles to U. Mich. Law Rev. Served to lt. (j.g.) USN, 1951-53. Recipient Howard P. Coblentz prize U. Mich. Law Sch., 1954. Episcopalian. Banking, Private international, Administrative and regulatory. Home: 2 Circle Ave Larchmont NY 10538-4219

**BERRIGAN, HELEN GINGER,** federal judge; b. 1948. BA, U. Wis., 1969; MA, Am. U., 1971; JD, La. State U., 1977. Staff rschr. Senator Harold E. Hughes, 1971-72; legis. aide Senator Joseph E. Biden, 1972-73; asst. to mayor City of Fayette, Miss., 1973-74; law clk. La. Dept. Corrections, 1975-77; staff atty. Gov. Pardon, Parole and Rehab. Commn., 1977-78; prin. Gravel Brady & Berrigan, New Orleans, 1978-94, Berrigan, Litchfield, Schonekas, Mann & Clement, New Orleans, 1984-94; judge U.S. Dist. Ct. (ea. dist.) La., New Orleans, 1994—; active La. Sentencing Commn., 1987. Active Com. of 21, 1989, pres., 1990-92, ACLU of La., 1989-94, Forum for Equality, 1990-94, Amistad Rsch. Ctr. Tulane U., 1990-95. Mem. La. State Bar Assn. (mem. fed. 5th cir. 1986—), La. Assn. Criminal Def. Lawyers, New Orleans Assn. Women Attys. Office: US Dist Ct 500 Camp St C-556 New Orleans LA 70130-3313

**BERRIGAN, PATRICK JOSEPH,** lawyer; b. Niagara Falls, Ont., Can., Nov. 3, 1933; came to U.S., 1950; s. Thomas Joseph and Florence Cecilia (Glynn) B.; m. Shirley Mae Snyder, July 6, 1957; children: Carolyn, Deborah, Patrick Jr., Susan, Ann, Mary, James, Tara. BA in English, Holy Cross Coll., 1954; LLB, Notre Dame U., 1957. Bar: N.Y. 1958, U.S. Dist. Ct. (we. dist.) N.Y. 1960, U.S. Dist. Ct. (we. dist.) Pa. 1976, U.S. Ct. Appeals (2d cir.) 1962, U.S. Ct. Appeals (3rd cir.) 1977. Lawyer Runals, Broderick, Shoemaker, et al, Niagara Falls, N.Y., 1959-78; pvt. practice Niagara Falls, 1978—; spl. investigator City of Niagara Falls, 1972; spl. dist. atty. County of Niagara N.Y., Lockport, 1974-76; mem. judicial conf. Judicial Conf. of the State of N.Y., 1978-80; counsel N.Y. State Assembly Com. on mortgages, Albany, 1960-63. Mem. Niagara U. Adv. Bd., Lewiston, N.Y., 1978-82; bd. dirs. Nat. Conf. of Christian and Jews, Niagara Falls, 1977; mem. Youth Bd., Niagara Falls, 1965-68. Sgt. U.S. Army, 1957-59; pres. Mount St. Mary's Adv. Bd., 1982—, bd. trustees, 1990-97; bd. dirs. Health System Niagara, 1997-99; bd. trustees Mount St. Mary's Hosp., 1999—, v.p. Mem. ABA (gen. practice sect. labor law 1991-92), Niagara Falls Country Club (bd. govs.), Niagara Falls Bar Assn., Niagara County Bar Assn., N.Y. Bar Assn. Republican. Roman Catholic. Avocations: hockey player (old timers), golf. Labor, General civil litigation, General corporate. Home: 790 Thornwood Dr Lewiston NY 14092-1167 Office: PO Box 712 Niagara Falls NY 14302-0712

**BERRING, ROBERT CHARLES, JR.,** law educator, law librarian, former dean; b. Canton, Ohio, Nov. 20, 1949; s. Robert Charles and Rita Pauline (Franta) B.; m. Barbara Rust, June 20, 1975; children: Simon Robert, Daniel Fredrick. B.A. cum laude, Harvard U., 1971; J.D., U. Calif.-Berkeley, 1974, M.L.S., 1974. Asst. prof. and reference librarian U. Ill. Law Sch., Champaign, 1974-76; assoc. librarian U. Tex. Law Sch., Austin, 1976-78; dep. librarian Harvard Law Sch., Cambridge, Mass., 1978-81; prof. law, law librarian U. Wash. Law Sch., Seattle, 1981-82; prof. law, law librarian U. Calif., Boalt Hall Law Sch., Berkeley, Calif., 1982—, dean sch. library and info. scis., 1986-89, Walter Perry Johnson chair, 1998—; mem. Westlaw Adv. Bd., St. Paul, 1984-91; cons. various law firms; mem. on Legal Exch. with China, 1983—, chmn., 1991-93.; vis. prof. U. Cologne, 1993. Author: How to Find the Law, 8th edit., 1984, 9th edit., 1989, Great American Law Revs., 1985, Finding the Law, 1999; co-author: Authors Guide, 1981; editor Legal Reference Svc. Quar., 1981—; author videotape series Commando Legal Rsch., 1989. Chmn. Com. Legal Ednl. Exch. with China, 1991-93. Robinson Cox fellow U. Western Australia, 1988; named West Publishing Co. Acad. Libr. of Yr., 1994. Mem. Am. Assn. Law Libraries (pres. 1985-86), Calif. Bar Assn., ABA, ALA, Am. Law Inst. Office: U Calif Law Sch Boalt Hall Rm 345 Berkeley CA 94720-0001

**BERRINGTON, CRAIG ANTHONY,** lawyer; b. Chgo., Aug. 9, 1943; s. Leo and Geraldine (Dale) Berrington; m. Susan Dale Olsen, Sept. 3, 1967; children: Jennifer, Emily, Lacy. BA, Am. U., 1965; JD, Northwestern U., 1968. Bar: D.C. 1969, U.S. Supreme Ct. 1989. Atty. U.S. Dept. Labor, Washington, 1968-75, assoc. solicitor, 1975-77, exec. asst. to under sec., 1977-79, dep. asst. sec. Employment Standards Adminstrn., 1979-86; sr. v.p., gen. counsel Am. Ins. Assn., Washington, 1986—. Mem. ABA, U.S. Supreme Ct. Bar, D.C. Bar. Insurance, Administrative and regulatory, Corporate taxation. Home: 5920 Granby Rd Rockville MD 20855-1419 Office: Am Ins Assn 1130 Connecticut Ave NW Washington DC 20036-3904

**BERRITT, HAROLD EDWARD,** lawyer; b. N.Y.C., Jan. 3, 1936; s. Philip H. and Anne L. (Rimer) B.; m. Charlotte Bayer, July 1957 (div. Nov. 1976); children: Gail J., Richard E.; m. Nancy A. Brown, Jan. 8, 1977; children: Matthew P., Alexis C. BBA, U. Mich., 1957, JD, 1960. Bar: N.Y. 1961. Assoc. Stroock & Stroock & Lavan, N.Y.C., 1961-69; ptnr. Pryor, Cashman, Sherman & Flynn, N.Y.C., 1969-95, Rubin Baum Levin Constant & Friedman, N.Y.C., 1995-97; shareholder Greenberg Traurig, Miami, 1997—; bd. dirs. Claire's Stores, Inc., Pembroke Pines, Fla. Trustee Nat. Found. for Advancement in the Arts, Miami. Mem. ABA, Fresh Meadow Country Club, Commanderie De Bordeaux. Avocations: classical music, wine, golf, tennis. General corporate, Securities. Office: Greenberg Traurig 1221 Brickell Ave Miami FL 33131-3224

**BERRY, ANDERS TAYLOR,** lawyer; b. Hyannis, Mass., Jan. 9, 1954; s. John Raymond Jr. and Ruth (Anderson) B.; m. Barbara Sutherland, Aug. 27, 1994. BA in History, Colgate U., 1976; JD, U. Mont. Sch. Law, 1994. Bar: Mont., 1994. Supr. retail acctg. Merrill Lynch & Co., N.Y.C., 1982-89; internal auditor Gruntal & Co., Inc., N.Y.C., 1989-91; dep. county atty. Hill County, Havre, Mont., 1994-96; assoc. Smith, Walsh, Clarke & Gregoire, Great Falls, Mont., 1996-97; assoc. gen. counsel DADCO, Inc., Great Falls, 1997—. Vol. Ch. of Ascension Homeless Shelter, N.Y.C., 1983-91, Poverello Ctr., Missoula, Mont., 1991-94; dir. Bear Paw Youth Guidance Home, Havre, 1994-96. Mem. ABA, Mont. Bar Assn., Cascade County Bar Assn. Republican. Episcopalian. Avocations: Reading, golf, bird hunting. General corporate, Securities. Office: DA Davidson & Co 8 3d St N Great Falls MT 59401

**BERRY, BRADLEY CARL,** prosecutor; b. L.A., Mar. 3, 1954; s. Carl and Barbara Mae Berry; m. Lou Flowers, Mar. 10, 1990; children: R. Casey Hill, Renee' Hill. BS, Oreg. State U., 1976; JD, Gonzaga Sch. of Law, 1979. Bar: Oreg. Assoc. Patrick F. Boileau, Atty. at Law, Portland, Oreg., 1980-81; dep. dist. atty. Yamhill County Dist. Atty.'s Office, McMinnville, Oreg., 1981-84, dist. atty., 1996—; assoc. Brown & Tarlow, P.C., Newberg, Oreg., 1984-89; shareholder Brown, Tarlow & Berry, P.C., Newberg, 1989-96; Chmn. Yamhill County Domestic Violence Coun., McMinnville, 1997—; chair, bd. dirs. Oreg. Downtown Devel. Assn., Portland, 1987-96; bd. dirs., chair-elect United Way of Yamhill County, McMinnville, 1997—. Mem. Newberg Active 20130, KP, Lions. Home: PO Box 191 Newberg OR 97132-0191 Office: Yamhill County Dist Atty's Office 535 E 5th St Mcminnville OR 97128-4526

**BERRY, CARL DAVID, JR.,** lawyer; b. N.Y.C., Mar. 18, 1963; s. Carl David Sr. and Elsie M. Berry; m. Simone Odetta, May 16, 1998; 1 child, Justin Tamerat. Grad., N.Y. State Police Acad., 1987; BA, SUNY, New Paltz, 1992; JD, N.C. Ctrl. U., 1995. Bar: Fla. 1999. Adminstrv. asst. Kidder Peabody & Co., N.Y.C., 1983-87; trooper N.Y. State Police, Fishkill, 1987-93; assoc. Lexis/Nexis-Mead Data Ctrl., Durham, N.C., 1993-95, McCrary & Mosley, Miami, Fla., 1996-98; pvt. practice Lauderhill, Fla., 1999—; bd. advisors In Focus Mag., Miami, Fla., 1997—; bd. dirs. Black Archives, Miami. Cpl. USMCR, 1985-93. Decorated Nat. Def. medal USMC, 1991. Fellow Battery; mem. ABA (entertainment and sports law sect., bus. law sect.), Nat. Bar Assn. (Fla. chpt.), Fla. Bar Assn. (entertainment arts and sports law sect., bus. law sect.), Broward County Bar Assn., Kappa Alpha Psi. Avocations: fitness, motorcycling, fishing. E-mail: CarlúDúBerry@abanet.org. Fax: 954-742-5571. Entertainment, General corporate, Contracts commercial. Office: 6730A W Commercial Blvd Lauderhill FL 33319-2115

**BERRY, CHARLES RICHARD,** lawyer; b. Louisville, Apr. 19, 1948; s. Charles Russell and Lillie Juanita (Crady) B.; m. Joan Phyllis Rosenberg, Aug. 29, 1970; children: Kevin Charles, Ryan Andrew. BA, Northwestern U., 1970, JD, 1973. Bar: Ariz. 1973, U.S. Dist. Ct. Ariz. 1973, U.S. Ct. Appeals (9th cir.) 1983. Assoc. Snell & Wilmer, Phoenix, 1973-77; ptnr. Tilker, Burke & Berry, Scottsdale, Ariz., 1978-80, Norton, Berry, French & Perkins, P.C. and predecessor firm Norton, Burke, Berry & French, P.C., Phoenix, 1980-86; dir. Fennemore Craig, Phoenix, 1986-90; ptnr. Titus, Brueckner & Berry, Scottsdale, 1991—. Mem. Ariz. Bar Assn. (chmn. securities regulation sect. 1996-97), Paradise Valley Rotary Club (pres. 1995-96). Mem. Unitarian Ch. E-mail address: tbandb@uswest.net. Fax: 480-483-3215. Securities, General corporate, Real property. Home: 6148 E Mountain View Rd Scottsdale AZ 85253-1807 Office: Titus Brueckner & Berry 7373 N Scottsdale Rd Ste B252 Scottsdale AZ 85253-3513

**BERRY, DAWN BRADLEY,** lawyer, writer; b. Peoria, Ill., Mar. 11, 1957; d. Raymond Coke and Clarette (Williams) Bradley; m. William Lars Berry, July 12, 1980. BS, Ill. State U., 1979, MS, 1982; JD, U. Ill., 1988. Bar: N.Mex. 1988, U.S. Dist. Ct. N.Mex. 1988, U.S. Ct. Appeals (10th cir.) 1993. Assoc. Modrall, Sperling, Roehl, Harris and Sisk, Albuquerque, 1988-90; pvt. practice Tijeras and Albuquerque, 1990—; assoc. Hinkle Law Offices, Albuquerque, 1995-96. Author: Equal Compensation for Women, 1994, The Domestic Violence Sourcebook, 1995, The Divorce Sourcebook, 1995, The Fifty Most Influential Women in American Law, 1996, The Divorce Recovery Source Book, 1998, The Estate Planning Sourcebook, 1999. Pres., bd. dirs. Talking Talons Youth Leadership, Tijeras, 1993-98, v.p., 1998—. Recipient Outstanding Young Alumni award Ill. State U., 1996; Rickert scholar for pub. svc. U. Ill., 1988. Mem. NAFE, ACLU, N.Mex. Women's Bar Assn., S.W. Writer's Workshop, Parrot Heads of N.Mex., Communication Artists of N.Mex., F. Scott Fitzgerald Soc. Avocations: travel, dance, falconry, gardening, Renaissance fairs. Civil rights. Home and Office: 222 Raven Rd Tijeras NM 87059-8016

**BERRY, HENRY NEWHALL, III,** lawyer; b. Boston, Sept. 25, 1930; s. Henry Newhall Jr. and Mary Antoinette Berry; m. Elizabeth Lee Kononen, Mar. 31, 1956 (div. June 1983); children: Henry, Wendy, Bethany, Melissa; m. Susan Jane Deitchman, Oct. 6, 1990. BA, U. Maine, Orono, 1955; LLB, U. Maine, Portland, 1964. Bar: Maine 1964, U.S. Dist. Ct. Maine, 1964, U.S. Ct. Appeals (1st cir.) 1969, U.S. Supreme Ct. 1967. Title atty. Maine Dept. Transp., Augusta, 1964-65; law clk. U.S. Bankruptcy Ct., Portland, 1965-66; pvt. practice Portland, 1966-72; legal aid atty. Pine Tree Legal Assistance, Portland, 1967; county atty. Cumberland County, Portland, 1973-74, dist. atty., 1975-83; pvt. practice South Portland, 1984—; fed. hearing examiner U.S. Govt., Portland, 1969-70. Town councilor Cape Elizabeth (Maine) Coun., 1967-71, 97—; mem. budget com. Cumberland County, Portland, 1997—. Cpl. U.S. Army, 1952-54. Mem. Cumberland Bar Assn. Republican. Roman Catholic. General practice. Office: 169 Ocean St S Portland ME 04106-3636

**BERRY, JAMES FREDERICK,** lawyer, biology educator; b. Washington, Dec. 22, 1947; s. James Frederick and Joyce (Drummond) B.; m. Lynn M. Latzel, Aug. 2, 1997; children: Jennifer, Andrea L. BS, Fla. State U., 1970, MS, 1973; PhD, U. Utah, 1978; JD, Chgo.-Kent Law Sch., 1990. Bar: Fla. 1990, Ill. 1991, U.S. Dist. Ct. (mid. dist.) Fla. 1991, U.S. Dist. Ct. (no. dist.) Ill. 1991, U.S. Ct. Appeals (11th cir.) 1991. Teaching asst. Fla. State U., Tallahassee, 1969-73; chemist Fla. Dept. Agr., Tallahassee, 1973-74; teaching fellow U. Utah, Salt Lake City, 1974-78; rsch. assoc. Carnegie Mus., Pitts., 1983—; prof. biology Elmhurst (Ill.) Coll., 1978—; assoc. Burke, Bosselman & Weaver, Chgo., 1990-93; cons. ENCAP, Inc., DeKalb, Ill., 1983-84; rsch. asst. IIT Chgo.-Kent Law Sch., 1989-90; instr. law Am. Planning Assn., Chgo., 1992-94; adj. prof. Stuart Sch. Bus., Ill. Inst. Tech., 1995—. Contbr. articles to profl. jours. Bd. trustees Chgo. String Ensemble, 1989-94. Rsch. grantee U.S. Fish and Wildlife Svc., Washington, 1983-85, Elmhurst Coll., 1979-86. Mem. ABA, Ill. State Bar Assn., Sigma Xi, Phi Kappa Phi. Roman Catholic. Avocations: environmental protection activities, classical music. Environmental, Land use and zoning (including planning), General civil litigation. Office: Elmhurst Coll 190 Prospect Ave Elmhurst IL 60126-3271

**BERRY, JAN VANCE,** lawyer; b. Ames, Iowa, Mar. 14, 1951; s. Burl V. and Helen I. (Messer) B. BA, Drake U., 1973, JD, 1977. Bar: Iowa 1978, U.S. Dist. Ct. (so. dist.) Iowa 1978, U.S. Ct. Appeals (8th cir.) 1978, U.S. Dist. Ct. (no. dist.) Iowa 1986. Asst. Polk County Atty., Polk County Attys. Office, Des Moines, 1978-81; ptnr. Handley, Berry & Eisenhauer, Ankeny, Iowa, 1981-85, Handley & Berry, Ankeny, 1985-88; counsel Iowa Pub. Employment Rels. Bd., Des. Moines, 1988—. Mem. Iowa Bar Assn. Labor, Administrative and regulatory. Office: Pub Employment Rels Bd 514 E Locust St Ste 202 Des Moines IA 50309-1912

**BERRY, JANIS MARIE,** lawyer; b. Everett, Mass., Dec. 20, 1949; d. Joseph and Dorothy I. (Barbato) Sordillo; m. Richard G. Berry, Dec. 27, 1970; children: Alexis, Ashley, Lindsey. BA magna cum laude, Boston U., 1971, JD cum laude, 1974. Bar: Mass. 1974, U.S. Dist. Ct. Mass. 1975, U.S. Ct. Appeals (1st cir.), 1980, U.S. Supreme Ct. 1982. Law clk. Mass. Supreme Jud. Ct., Boston, 1974-75; assoc. Bingham, Dana & Gould, Boston, 1975-80; asst. U.S. atty. Boston, 1980-81; spl. atty. dept. justice N.E. Organized Crime Strike Force, Boston, 1981-84; chief atty. dept. justice N.E. Organized Crime Drug Task Force, Boston, 1984-86; ptnr. Ropes & Gray, Boston, 1986-94; pvt. practice, 1995; ptnr. Roche, Carens & DeGiacomo, 1996-97, Rubin & Rudman LLP, 1997—; instr. Harvard Law Sch., 1983-86, Inst. Trial Advocacy, Boston, 1984-87; lectr. Dept. Justice Advocacy Inst., 1986; mem. Mass. Bd. of Bar Overseers, 1989-93; bd. mem. Mass. Housing Fin. Agy., 1995—; chmn. merit selection panel U.S. Magistrate, 1989, Mass. Jud. Nominating Coun., 1991-92; trustee Social Law Libr., 1999—. Author: Defending Corporations Public Contracts Jour., (with others) Federal Criminal Practice, 1987. Candidate Mass. Atty. Gen., 1994; mem. Mass. Com. for Pub. Counsel Svcs., Boston, 1986-91; v.p. Boston Inn of Ct., 1990-91; trustee Atlanticare Hosp., 1990-94. Spl. Commendation award Dept. of Justice, Washington, 1983. Mem. Mass. Bar Assn., Boston Bar Assn., Am. Law Inst., Women's Bar Assn., Phi Beta Kappa. General civil litigation, Criminal, Personal injury. Office: Rubin & Rudman LLP 50 Rowes Wharf Fl 3 Boston MA 02110-3319

**BERRY, L. CLYEL,** lawyer; b. Twin Falls, Idaho, July 17, 1949; s. Clyel J. and Nellie B.; m. Jill Brunzell, July 17, 1970; children: Jacob Clyel, Matthew Robert. BABA, Wash. State U., 1973; JD, U. Idaho, 1975. Bar: Idaho 1976, U.S. Dist. Ct. (dis. Idaho) 1976, U.S. Ct. Appeals (ninth cir.) 1982. Assoc. Emil F. Pike, Twin Falls, 1976-78; ptnr. Pike and Berry, Twin Falls, 1978-83; prin. Twin Falls, 1983—; sec., dir. Theisen Motors, Inc., Twin Falls. Mem. Idaho State Bar Assn., Idaho Trial Lawyer Assn. (regional dir. 1981-82), Assn. Trial Lawyers of Am., Fifth Jud. Dist. Bar Assn. (sec.-treas. 1977-78). Avocations: whitewater rafting, kayaking, lic. Alaska guide, skiing, fishing, travel. General practice, Personal injury, Workers' compensation. Office: PO Box 302 Twin Falls ID 83303-0302

**BERRY, MARGARET ANNE,** lawyer; b. Terre Haute, Ind., Jan. 2, 1950; d. David Warren and SHirley J. Martin; m. Howard H. Berry, Jan. 2, 1981. BA, Ind. U., Bloomington, 1973, JD, 1976. Bar: Ind. 1976; U.S. Dist. Ct. (so. dist.), Ind. 1976; U.S. Supreme Ct., 1984. Assoc. Eugene Weaver Atty., Brazil, Ind., 1976-81; sole practitioner pvt. practice, Brazil, Ind., 1981—; chief deputy prosecutor 13th Jud. Cir., Brazil, Ind., 1978-81, deputy prosecuting atty., 1977-94; com. on character and fitness Superme Ct. Ind., Indpls., 1988—; pres. bd. dirs. YMCA Clay County, Brazil, Ind., 1992-97, I.U. Residence Hall Alumni Assn., Bloomington, Ind., 1991-93. Co-chair Capital Campaign YMCA Clay County, Brazil, Ind., 1993—; bd. mem. Preservation Assn. Clay County, Brazil, Ind., 1995—; candidate for Judge Rep. Party Clay County, Brazil, Ind., 1994. Mem. Ind. State Bar Assn., Clay County Bar Assn., Natural Athlete Strength Assn., All Natural Physique and Power Conf. Republican. Avocations: powerlifting, antique collecting, gardening. Real property, Probate, Estate planning. Office: 13 W National Ave Brazil IN 47834-2536

**BERRY, MAX NATHAN,** lawyer; b. Cushing, Okla., Dec. 29, 1935; m. Heidi Jacqueline Lehrman; children: Elizabeth, Stefanie, David. BA, U. Okla., 1958, LLB, 1960; LLM, Georgetown U., 1963; diploma, Nat. Assn. Danish Enterprises, Denmark. Bar: Okla., 1960, D.C., 1967; U.S. Ct. Mil. Appeals, 1960; U.S. Ct. Internat. Trade, U.S. Ct. Customs and Patent Appeals, 1964. Lawyer, Internat. Affairs Div./Judge Advocate Generals Corps U.S. Army, Washington; counsel Office of Gen. Counsel, Dept. U.S. Treasury, Washington, 1963-67; pvt. practice Washington, 1967—; owner The New Playwrights Theatre, Washington. Contbr. articles to profl. jours. Bd. dirs., chmn. Pa. Ave. Devel. Corp., 1980; chmn. Mayor's Internat. Task Force, Washington; bd. dirs., chmn. exec. com. Close Up Found.; bd. dirs. Cmty. Found. of Greater Washington; past co-chmn. Mayor's Downtown Blue Ribbon Commn., Washington; trustee, pres. Archieves of Am. Art; trustee Smithsonian Instn.; bd. dirs. Phillips Collection, Washington; chmn. Georgetown Waterfront Arts Commn., Filmfest/DC, 1987, 88; active numerous other bds. and civic orgns. Capt. U.S. Army, 1960-63. Recipient Communiy Leadership award, Anti-Defamation League, 1989, John Singleton Copley medal, Nat. Portrait Gallery, Smithsonian Instn., Mayor's Art award, Washington, 1987, Decoration of Merit of the Knight First Class, Order of Lion of Finland, Merit Agricole medal France, Prince Henrik's Medal of Honor, Denmark, Disting. Svc. medal, Sao Paulo, Brazil, Merit of Sculpture award, Colombia, others. Mem. ABA, Fed. Bar Assn., others. Democrat. Public international, Administrative and regulatory. Office: 3213 O St NW Washington DC 20007-2843

**BERRY, PHILLIP SAMUEL,** lawyer; b. Berkeley, Calif., Jan. 30, 1937; s. Samuel Harper and Jean Mobley (Kramer) B.; m. Michele Ann Perrault, Jan. 16, 1982; children: David, Douglas, Dylan, Shane, Matthew. AB, Stanford U., 1958, LLB, 1961. Bar: Calif. 1962. Ptnr., Berry, Davis & McInerney, Oakland, Calif., 1968-76; owner Berry & Berry, Oakland, 1976—, pres., 1977—. Mem. adv. com. Coll. Natural Resources, U. Calif., Berkeley; mem. Calif. State Bd. Forestry, 1974-86, vice-chmn., 1976-86; trustee So. Calif. Ctr. for Law in Pub. Interest, 1970-87, Sierra Club Legal Def. Fund, 1975-90, Pub. Advs., 1971-86, chmn. bd., 1981-82; dir. Pacific Environment Resources Ctr., 1997—. Served with AUS, 1961-67. Mem. ABA, Calif. State Bar Assn., Sierra Club (nat. pres. 1969-71, 91-92, v.p. conservation law 1971—, v.p. polit. affairs 1983-85, John Muir award), Am. Alpine Club. General civil litigation, Personal injury, Product liability. Office: Berry & Berry 1300 Clay St Fl 9 Oakland CA 94612-1425

**BERRY, ROBERT WORTH,** lawyer, educator, retired army officer; b. Ryderwood, Wash., Mar. 2, 1926; s. John Franklin and Anita Louise (Worth) B. B.A. in Polit. Sci., Wash. State U., 1950; J.D., Harvard U., 1955; M.A., John Jay Coll. Criminal Justice, 1981. Bar: D.C. 1956, U.S. Dist. Ct. (D.C.) 1956, U.S. Ct. of Appeals (D.C. cir.) 1957, U.S. Ct. Mil. Appeals 1957, Pa. 1961, U.S. Dist. Ct. (ea. dist.) Pa. 1961, U.S. Dist. Ct. (ctrl. dist.) Calif. 1967, U.S. Supreme Ct. 1961, Calif. 1967, U.S. Ct. Claims 1975, Colo. 1997, U.S. Dist. Ct. Colo. 1997, U.S. Ct. Appeals (10th cir.) 1997. Research assoc. Harvard U., 1955-56; atty. Office Gen. Counsel U.S. Dept. Def., Washington, 1956-60; staff counsel Philco Ford Co., Phila., 1960-63; dir. Washington office Litton Industries, 1967-71; gen. counsel U.S. Dept. Army, Washington, 1971-74, civilian aide to sec. army, 1975-77; col. U.S. Army, 1978-87; prof., head dept. law U.S. Mil. Acad., West Point, N.Y., 1978-86; ret. as brig. gen. U.S. Army, 1987; mil. asst. to asst. sec. of army, Manpower and Res. Affairs Dept. of Army, 1986-87; asst. gen. counsel pub. affairs Litton Industries, Beverly Hills, Calif., 1963-67; chair Coun. of Def. Space Industries Assns., 1968; resident ptnr. Quarles and Brady, Washington, 1971-74; dir., corp. sec., treas., gen. counsel G.A. Wright, Inc., Denver, 1987-92, dir., 1987—; pvt. practice law Fort Bragg, Calif., 1993-96; spl. counsel Messner & Reeves LLC, Denver, 1997—; foreman Mendocino County Grand Jury, 1995-96. Served with U.S. Army, 1944-46, 51-53, Korea. Decorated Bronze Star, Legion of Merit, Disting. Service Medal; recipient Disting. Civilian Service medal U.S. Dept. Army, 1973, 74, Outstanding Civilian Service medal, 1977. Mem. FBA, Bar Assn. D.C., Calif. Bar Assn., Pa. Bar Assn., Colo. State Bar Assn., Army-Navy Club, Army-Navy Country Club, Phi Beta Kappa, Phi Kappa Phi, Sigma Delta Chi, Lambda Chi Alpha. Protestant. General corporate, Contracts commercial, Private international.

**BERRY, WILLIAM WELLS,** lawyer; b. Nashville, Sept. 10, 1917; s. Allen Douglas and Agnes Wilkie (Vance) B.; m. Mary John Atwell, May 31, 1941 (dec.); children: William W., Edith Allen Berry Collier; m. Virginia N. Buntin, Jan. 4, 1986. B.A., Vanderbilt U., 1938, LL.B., 1940. Bar: Tenn. 1940. Pvt. practice law Nashville, 1940-42, 46—; ptnr. Bass, Berry & Sims, 1965—. Mem. Tenn. Inheritance Tax Study Com., 1977, 82; mem. adv. com. dental divsn. Tenn. Dept. Pub. Health, 1953-57; pres. Bill Wilkerson Hearing and Speech Ctr., 1959-67; bd. dirs. Noel Meml. Found., 1954-68; trustee Tenn. Fed. Tax Inst., 1973-79, pres., 1976-77; trustee Monroe Harding Home, 1971-93, Washington Found., 1978—, Nashville Found., 1965-82, Nelson Found., 1997—. Capt. AUS, 1942-46. Decorated Air medal with oak leaf cluster. Fellow Am. Coll. Estate and Trust Counsel (chmn. Tenn. chpt. 1975-81, bd. regents 1979-85), Internat. Acad. Trial Lawyers, Am. Bar Found., Tenn. Bar Found., Nashville Bar Found.; mem. ABA, Tenn. Bar Assn., Nashville Bar Assn. (bd. dirs. 1969-72, v.p. 1971-72), Am. Judicature Soc., Nashville Srs. Golf Assn. (pres. 1978-80), Nat. Soc. SAR, English Speaking Union (bd. dirs., past pres. Nashville chpt. 1991-93), 200 Club (bd. dirs., past comdr.), Belle Meade Country Club, Highlands Country Club. Democrat. Presbyterian (deacon, elder). General corporate, Probate, Estate taxation. Home: 5110 Boxcroft Pl Nashville TN 37205-3702 also: 312 Pipers Ct Highlands NC 28741-6634 Office: Bass Berry & Sims 2700 First American Ctr Nashville TN 37238

**BERRYMAN, LARRY BRENT,** lawyer; b. St. Louis, Feb. 5, 1944; s. Carl and Dora (Hyatt) B.; m. Katherine E. Shutz, Feb. 23, 1966; children: Bradley P., Anne M.; m. Crystel E. Henkel, Feb. 15, 1991; children: Chandra E., Lance M., Erich C. BS in Edn., Northwest Mo. U., 1966; J.D., U. Wyo., 1974. Bar: Wyo. 1974, Fla. 1978, U.S. Dist. Ct. Wyo. 1980. Ptnr. Scott-Shelledy & Berryman, Worland, Wyo., 1978-82; dep. county atty. County of Washakie, Wyo., 1978-82; county atty. County of Washakie, 1982-91; pvt. practice Worland, Wyo., 1991—; pub defender State of Wyoming, Worland, 1998—. Chmn. adv. bd. Bethesda Care Ctr., Worland, Wyo. 1980; bd. dirs. Washakie County Mental Health Bd., 1982. Served to lt. USN, 1975-78. Recipient Lyman Advocate award U. Wyo., 1974. Mem. Worland C. of C. (bd. dirs.), Wyo. County Attys. Assn., Nat. Assn. Dist. Attys. Republican. Mem. Ch. of Jesus Christ of Latter Day Saints. Lodge: Kiwanis (pres. Worland chpt.). Home: 111 Country Dr Worland WY 82401-3110 Office: PO Box 853 Worland WY 82401-0853

**BERRYMAN, RANDALL SCOTT,** lawyer; b. Atlanta, Apr. 9, 1966; s. Emory Ellis Berryman and Jacqueline Marie Campbell; m. Michele Whittington, June 25, 1988; 1 child, Ian Connor. AA, Emory U., 1986, BA, 1988; JD, U. Ga., 1991. Bar: Ga. 1991, U.S. Dist. Ct. (no. dist.) Ga. 1991. Assoc. Johnson & Montgomery, Atlanta, 1991-94, Caldwell & Watson, Atlanta, 1994-97, Warner, Mayoue & Bates, P.C., Atlanta, 1997—; bd. dirs. Adoption Info. Svcs., Inc., Lawrenceville, Ga. Mem. Atlanta Bar Assn. Family and matrimonial. Office: Warner Mayoue & Bates PC Riverwood 100 Bldg Ste 2300 3350 Riverwood Pkwy Atlanta GA 30339

**BERRYMAN, RICHARD BYRON,** lawyer; b. Indpls., Aug. 16, 1932; s. Herbert Byron and Ruth Katherine (Mayerhoefer) B.; m. Virginia Marie Asti, June 9, 1957; children: Steven, Susan, Kenneth. BA, Carleton Coll., 1954; JD, U. Chgo., 1957. Bar: D.C. 1957. Atty. bur. of aeronautics U.S. Dept. Navy, Washington, 1957-59, atty. office gen. counsel, 1959-62; assoc. Cox, Langford & Brown, Washington, 1962-65, ptnr., 1965-68; ptnr. Fried, Frank, Harris, Shriver & Jacobson, Washington, 1968-90; pvt. practice Washington, 1990—. Mem. vis. com. Law Sch. U. Chgo., 1978-82; trustee Carleton Coll., Northfield, Minn., 1982-86; dir. Pericles Inst., Washington, 1996—. Mem. ABA. Administrative and regulatory, General corporate, Private international. Office: 1225 I St NW Ste 500 Washington DC 20005-3914

**BERSHTEIN, HERMAN SAMMY,** lawyer; b. New Haven, Sept. 2, 1925; s. William and Bessie (Burke) B.; children: Joy, Richard, Jan. BA, Yale U., 1950; LLB, U. S.C., 1954. Bar: Conn. 1954, S.C. 1954, U.S. Dist. Ct. Conn. 1955. Pvt. practice law Hamden, Conn., 1954-69; pres. Bershtein Bershtein & Bershtein, Hamden, 1969—; arbitrator Am. Arbitration Assn., Hamden, 1969—. Judge advocate for Jewish War Vets, Hamden, 1955-75. 2d lt. U.S. Army, 1943-46. Personal injury, General civil litigation, Product liability. Office: Bershtein Bershtein & Bershtein 1188 Dixwell Ave Hamden CT 06514-4732

**BERSI, ANN,** lawyer. BA, MA, San Diego State U.; JD, Calif. Western Sch. of Law; PhD in Higher Edn. Adminstrn., U. Conn. Past mem. law firms Morris, Brignone & Pickering, Lionel, Sawyer & Collins, Las Vegas; dir. employee rels. State of Nev., 1981-83; exec. dir. State Bar Nev., 1983-89; dep. dist. atty. civil divsn. Clark County Dist. Atty.'s Office, Las Vegas; past instr. pub. adminstrn. Pace U., N.Y.; legal counsel Clark County Sch. Dist. Bd. Trustees. Mem. State Bar Nev. (pres. bd. govs. 1999—). Office: District Attorneys Office PO Box 552215 Las Vegas NV 89155-2215*

**BERSIN, ALAN DOUGLAS,** lawyer, school system administrator; b. Bklyn., Oct. 15, 1946; s. Arthur and Mildred (Laikin) B.; m. Elisabeth Van Aggelen, Aug. 17, 1975 (div. Dec. 1983); 1 child, Alissa Ida; m. Lisa Foster, July 20, 1991; children, Madeleine Foster, Amalia Rose. AB magna cum laude, Harvard U., 1968; student, Oxford U., 1968-71; JD, Yale U., 1974. Bar: Calif. 1975, U.S. Dist. Ct. (ctrl. dist.) Calif. 1975, U.S. Ct. Appeals (9th cir.) 1977, Alaska 1983, U.S. Dist. Ct. Alaska 1983, U.S. Dist. Ct. Hawaii 1992, U.S. Dist. Ct. (so. dist.) Calif. 1992, U.S. Supreme Ct., 1996. Exec. asst. Bd. Police Commrs., L.A., 1974-75; assoc. Munger, Tolles & Olson, L.A., 1975-77, ptnr., 1978-92; spl. dep. dist. atty. Counties of Imperial and San Diego, Calif., 1993-98; supt. pub. edn. San Diego City Schs., 1998—; adj. prof. of law U. So. Calif. Law Ctr.; vis. prof. Sch. Law U. San Diego, 1992-93; named spl. rep. for U.S. s.w. border by U.S. Atty. Gen., 1995-98; mem. Atty Gen.'s adv. com. of U.S. Attys., 1995-98; tech. adv. panel Nat. Inst. of Justice Law Enforcement, adv. com. FCC/NTIA Pub. Safety Wireless; founder U.S./Mex. Binat. Lab. Program; chmn. bd. dirs. U.S. Border Rsch. Tech. Ctr., S.W. Border Coun. Named Rhodes scholar 1968; recipient Resolution of Merit award Mayor and City Coun. L.A., 1991, Spl. Achievement award Hispanic Urban Ctr., 1992, Peacemaker's award San Diego Mediation Assn., 1997, Morgan award San Diego LEAD, 1998. Mem. Assn. Bus. Trial Lawyers (bd. govs. 1986-88), Inner City Law Ctr. (chmn. bd. dirs. 1987-90). Democrat. Jewish. Avocations: scuba diving, skiing, travel. Fax: 619-291-7182. E-mail: abersin@mail.sandi.net. Federal civil litigation, State civil litigation, Securities.

**BERSON, MARK IRA,** lawyer; b. Boston, May 13, 1943; s. Barnet J. and Sadye (Levine) B.; m. Ellen Marjorie Gordon, Dec. 21, 1969; children: Julie, Steven, Michael. BA, U. Vt., 1965; LLB, Suffolk U., 1968; LLM, NYU, 1969. Bar: Mass. 1968, U.S. Dist. Ct. Mass. 1969, U.S. Dist. Ct. Vt. 1974, U.S. Ct. Appeals (1st dist.) 1972, U.S. Supreme Ct. 1974. Asst. atty. gen. Commonwealth of Mass., Boston, 1970-72; assoc. Levy, Winer & Hodos, Greenfield, Mass., 1972-74; ptnr. Levy, Winer, Hodos & Berson, Greenfield, 1974-93; mng. ptnr. Levy, Winer, P.C., Greenfield, 1993—. Pres. Tapestry Health Systems, Inc., Northampton, 1973—; vice chair clients security bd. Supreme Jud. Ct., 1995. Recipient Margaret Sanger award Family Planning Coun. We. Mass., Northampton, 1975, 88, Pro Bono Publico award Mass. Bar Assn., 1992. Mem. Am. Acad. Matrimonial Lawyers (past pres. Mass. chpt.), Franklin County Bar Assn. (pres. 1989-91). Democrat. Jewish. Family and matrimonial, Health, General civil litigation. Office: Levy Winer PC PO Box 1538 Greenfield MA 01302-1538

**BERSON, SUSAN A.,** lawyer; b. Omaha, Nebr., July 28, 1965. BA, U. Nebr., 1987, JD, 1990; postgrad., Georgetown U., 1994. Bar: D.C., Mo., Kans., U.S. Supreme Ct., U.S. Ct. Appeals (8th and 10th cirs.). Sr. trial atty. tax divsn. U.S. Dept. Justice, Washington, 1990-98; of counsel Shook, Hardy & Bacon LLP, Kansas City, Mo., 1998—; instr., lectr., judge Legal Edn. Inst., Washington, 1996-98; judge Regional Moot Ct. Competition for Law Schs., Kansas City, Mo., 1998; spkr. Tax Controversy Practice Group, Bankruptcy Practice Group. Vol. Habitat for Humanity, Kansas City, Mo., 1998, Bread for City, Washington, 1991-98. Recipient Outstanding Atty. award U.S. Atty. Gen., 1996. Mem. Yr. 2000 Group (spkr.). Federal civil litigation, Bankruptcy, Taxation, general. Office: Shook Hardy & Bacon LLP 1200 Main St Ste 4200 Kansas City MO 64105-2122

**BERTAIN, G(EORGE) JOSEPH, JR.,** lawyer; b. Scotia, Humboldt County, Calif., Mar. 9, 1929; s. George Joseph and Ellen Veronica (Canty) B.; m. Bernardine Joy Galli, May 11, 1957; 1 child, Joseph F. AB, St. Mary's Coll. Calif., 1951; JD, Cath. U. Am., 1955. Bar: Calif. 1957. Assoc. Hon. Joseph L. Alioto, San Francisco, 1955-57, 59-65; asst. U.S. Atty. No. Dist. Calif., 1957-59; pvt. practice of law San Francisco, 1966—; panel mem. Theodore Granik's Am. Forum of The Air, Washington, 1955. Editor-in-Chief, Law Rev. Cath. U. Am. (vol. 5), 1954-55. Mem. bd. regents St. Mary's Coll. Calif., 1980—; chmn. San Francisco Lawyers Com. for Ronald Reagan, 1966-78, San Francisco lawyers com. for elections of Gov./U.S. Pres. Ronald Reagan, 1966, 70, 80, 84; spl. confidential advisor to Gov. Reagan on jud. selection, San Francisco, 1967-74; chmn. San Francisco Lawyers for Better Govt., 1978—; confidential advisor to Senator Hayakawa on judicial selection, 1981-82, to Gov. Deukmejian, 1983-90, to Gov. Wilson, 1991-92; bd. dirs. St. Anne's Home, Little Sisters of the Poor, San Francisco. Recipient De La Salle medal St. Mary's Coll. Calif., 1951, Signum Fidei award, 1976. Mem. ABA, Calif. Bar Assn., Fed. Bar Assn. (del. to 9th cir. jud. conf. 1967-76), St. Thomas More Soc. San Francisco, U.S. Supreme Ct. Hist. Soc., Assn. Former U.S. Attys and Asst. U.S. Attys. No. Calif. (past pres.), Commonwealth Club, Wester Assn., Knights of Malta, KC. Republican. Roman Catholic. Antitrust, Federal civil litigation, General civil litigation. Address: 2314 9th Ave San Francisco CA 94116-1937

**BERTANI-TOMCZAK, AMY M.,** judge; b. Joliet, Ill., Apr. 1, 1957; d. Louis and Doris M. (Agazzi) Bertani; m. Jeffery J. Tomczak, July 13, 1996. BA in Polit. Sci., St. Mary's U., San Antonio, 1979; JD, Thomas M. Cooley Law Sch., 1985. Bar: Mich., Ill. Asst. state's atty. Will County State's Atty., Joliet, 1986-92; asst. atty. gen. Ill. Atty. Gen., Chgo., 1993-94; judge Will County Cir. Ct., Joliet, 1994—. Mem. nominating com. Trailway coun. Girls Scouts U.S. Mem. Will County Bar Assn., Exch. Club of Joliet. Roman Catholic. Office: Will County Ct House 14 W Jefferson St Ste 464 Joliet IL 60432-4300

**BERTELSEN, MICHAEL WILLIAM,** lawyer; b. July 7, 1951; s. Harvey William and Georgianna (Frankberg) B. BA, U. Minn., Morris, 1974; JD, Hamline U., 1978. Bar: Minn. 1978, U.S. Dist. Ct. Minn. 1978. Ptnr. Bell, Bertelsen & Bright, Shoreview, Minn., 1984—; conciliation ct. referee Ramsey County Dist. Ct., St. Paul; family ct. mediator Ramsey County Dist. Ct., St. Paul. Mme. Minn. State Bar Assn. Family and matrimonial, Probate, General practice. Office: Bell Bertelsen & Bright 300 Harbor Pl 500 Highway 96 W Shoreview MN 55126-1944

**BERTELSMAN, WILLIAM ODIS,** federal judge; b. Cincinnati, Ohio, Jan. 31, 1936; s. Odis William and Dorothy (Gegan) B.; m. Margaret Ann Martin, June 13, 1959; children: Kathy, Terri, Nancy. B.A., Xavier U., 1958; J.D., U. Cin., 1961. Bar: Ky. 1961, Ohio 1962. Law clk. firm Taft, Stettinius & Hollister, Cin., 1960-61; mem. firm Bertelsman & Bertelsman, Newport, Ky., 1962-79; judge U.S. Dist. Ct. (ea. dist.) Ky., Covington, 1979—, chief judge, 1991-98; instr. Coll. Law U. Cin., 1965-72; city atty., prosecutor Highland Heights, Ky., 1962-69; adj. prof. Chase Coll. of Law, 1989—. Contbr. articles to profl. jours. Served to capt. AUS, 1963-64. Mem. ABA, Ky. Bar Assn. (bd. govs. 1978-79), U.S. Jud. Conf. (standing com. on practices and procedure 1989-95, liaison mem. adv. com. on civil rules 1989-95), No. Ky. C. of C. (pres. 1974, bd. dirs. 1969-77). Republican. Roman Catholic. Club: Optimist.

**BERTHELSEN, RICHARD GLEN,** lawyer; b. Oklahoma City, Feb. 23, 1957; s. Donald Melvin and Alice May (Lynde) B. BBA in Mgmt., Tex. A&M U., 1980, MBA in Fin., 1982; JD, South Tex. Coll. Law, 1989. Bar: Tex. 1990, Kans. 1991, U.S. Dist. Ct. Kans. 1991, U.S. Supreme Ct. 1997. Agt., broker Berthelsen Ins. Agy., Houston, 1982-87; law clk., then assoc. Edwards & Assocs., Houston, 1987-91; in-house counsel Alliance Ins. Cos., McPherson, Kans., 1991—. Asst. editor Law Rev. South Tex. Coll. Law, 1987-89. V.p., bd. dirs. chmn. deed restriction Sharpstown Civic Assn., Houston, 1990-91; risk mgmt. con. YMCA, McPherson, 1997—; active Big Bros.-Little Bros. Mem. Kans. Claims Assn., CPCU Soc. (evening instr. ins. law Houston chpt. 1989-91), McPherson County Bar Assn. (sec.-treas. 1997—), Kiwanis, Phi Delta Phi. Republican. Methodist. Avocations: sailing, softball, ballroom dancing. Insurance. Home: 9010 Brae Ridge Dr San Antonio TX 78249-3846 Office: Alliance Ins Cos 1122 N Main St Mcpherson KS 67460-2846

**BERTLES, JAMES BILLET,** lawyer; b. New Rochelle, N.Y., May 16, 1955; s. William Matthew and Eileen (Billet) B.; m. Lisa Conger Preston, Aug. 15, 1981; children: Katherine Conger, Preston Elizabeth, Alexander Harrison. BA, Amherst Coll., 1977; JD, Fordham U., 1981. Bar: Conn. 1981, Fla. 1982; bd. cert. in wills, trusts and estate law, Fla. Assoc. Cummings & Lockwood, Stamford, Conn., 1981-85, Palm Beach, Fla., 1985-89; assoc. Cadwalader, Wickersham & Taft, Palm Beach, Fla., 1989-90, ptnr., 1990-94; ptnr. Gunster, Yoakley, Valdes-Fauli & Stewart, P.A., West Palm Beach, Fla., 1994—; bd. dirs. Wilmar Corp. Author (with others) International Trust Laws, 1993. Bd. dirs. Palm Beach Civic Assn., Beach Club; chmn. planned giving com., bd. dirs. Norton Mus. Art; mem. Town of Palm Beach Zoning Commn.; chancellor, mem. vestry Bethesda By-the-Sea Episcopal Ch., Palm Beach, Fla. Mem. ABA, Fla. Bar Assn., Palm Beach County Bar Assn., The Beach Club (bd. dirs.). Republican. Avocations: sports, travel. Estate planning, Probate, Estate taxation. Office: 777 S Flagler Dr West Palm Beach FL 33401-6161

**BERTONI, FERNANDO RAUL,** lawyer; b. Buenos Aires, Aug. 9, 1967; came to U.S., 1992; m. Paola Biressi, Nov. 27, 1998. LLM, Am. U., Washington, 1993; JD cum laude, U. Buenos Aires, 1990. Bar: Buenos Aires 1991, N.Y. 1994. Assoc. Di Iorio & Iglesias, Buenos Aires, 1991-92; fgn. assoc. Werbel & Carnelutti, N.Y.C., 1993-94; corp. assoc. King & Spalding, Atlanta, 1994-96, Fried, Frank, Harris, Shriver & Jacobson, N.Y.C., 1996—. Avocations: traveling, reading, soccer, skiing. General corporate, Finance, Private international. Office: Fried Frank Harris Shriver & Jacobson 1 New York Plz Fl 22 New York NY 10004-1980

**BERTRAM, MANYA M.,** retired lawyer; b. Denver; d. Samuel and Ruby (Feiner) Boran; m. Barry Bertram, June 19, 1938; children: H. Neal, Carel. *Husband Barry retired in 1980 as Assistant Insurance Commissioner of the State of Calif. Son H. Neal, Phi Beta Kappa, 1963 Reed College, PhD Physics 1967 Harvard University, is currently a professor at the UC San Diego, Department of Magnetic Recording Graduate Program. Daughter-in-law Ann Pollock Bertram, BA 1983 San Jose State, English Literature. Daughter Carel Bertram, BA 1965 UC Berkeley, Phi Beta Kappa, MA 1988 Art History, University of California at Los Angeles, PhD 1998 Art History, is currently teaching Art History at the University of Texas at Austin. Grandchildren: Alanya, BA Rhetoric, 1996 UC California; Rumeli, BA Arts, 1998 Hampshire College; Seth Aaron, UOP.* JD magna cum laude, Southwestern U., 1962. Ptnr. Most and Bertram, L.A., 1963-83; of counsel Levin, Ballin, Plotkin, Zimring & Goffin, North Hollywood, Calif., 1983-92, Janice Fogg, 1993-97; ret. Former trustee Southwestern U. Sch. Law, former pres. Southwestern U. Sch. Law Alumni Assn.; former bd. advisors Whittier Coll. of Law, L.A., Beverly Coll. Law; commr. Calif. Commn. on Aging, Sacramento, 1977-82; bd. dirs. Jewish Family Svc., L.A. Mem. ABA, Calif. State Bar Assn., L.A. County Bar Assn., Federacion Internac. de Abagados, Iota Tau Tau, B'nai B'rith (life mem.), Hadassah (life mem.). Avocation: geneology. Probate.

**BERTRAM, PHYLLIS ANN,** lawyer, communications executive; b. Long Beach, Calif., July 30, 1954; d. William J. and Ruth A. Bertram; AA, Long Beach City Coll., 1975, BS in Acctg., U. So. Calif., 1977; MBA, Calif. State U., Long Beach, 1978; JD, Western State U., 1982. Bar: Calif. 1982, U.S. Ct. Appeals (9th cir.), U.S. Dist. Ct. Instr., lifeguard City of Long Beach, Calif., 1972-78; sports ofcl. swimming, softball, volleyball, and basketball, 1972—; asst. commr. Met. Conf. Community and Jr. Colls., Long Beach, 1978-84; instr. seamanship, fire sci. and bus. adminstrn. Long Beach City Coll., 1977—; mgmt. cons., 1978—; mgr. Pacific Bell, 1983—, Spl. Access Tariffs, Local Competition Tariffs, Interconnection/Collocation Tariffs, Individual Case Basis Tariffs, Local Competition Tariffs, Long Distance Application Case Mgmt.; instr./lectr. Regulatory Rels./Policy/Requirements; guest lectr. sports officiating camps and tng. sessions. Instr. CPR, water safety, small craft, first aid ARC, 1972—; mem. Rep. Nat. Com. Recipient resolutions Calif. Senate and Assembly, Long Beach City Council; numerous service awards ARC; Ednl. research grantee, City of Long Beach, 1972. Mem. U. So. Calif. Alumni Assn., U. So. Calif. Commerce Assocs., Assn. of MBA Execs., Bay Area Career Women, Inc. (corp. sec., bd. dirs., leadership adv. coun.), So. Calif. Volleyball Ofcls. Assn., Nat. Assn. Sports Ofcls., So. Calif. Basketball Ofcls. Assn., Women's Basketball Ofcls. Assn., Women's Swim Ofcls. Assn. (pres.), So. Calif. Softball Umpires Assn., State Bar Calif., ABA, Fed. Bar Assn. Los Angeles, Internat. Platform Assn., Town Hall Calif., Commonwealth Club of Calif., Los Angeles County Bar Assn., Calif. State U. at Long Beach Alumni Assn., U. So. Calif. Alumni Assn., Delta Theta Phi. Republican. Club: Seal Beach Yacht. Communications, Public utilities, Sports. Office: Ste 1715 140 New Montgomery St San Francisco CA 94105-3705

**BERTSCHY, TIMOTHY L.,** lawyer; b. Pekin, Ill., Nov. 12, 1952. AB magna cum laude, U. Ill., 1974; JD, George Washington U., 1977. Bar: Ill. 1977, U.S. Dist. Ct. (cen. dist.) Ill., U.S. Ct. Appeals (7th cir.) 1982, U.S. Supreme Ct. Ptnr. Heyl, Royster, Voelker & Allen, Peoria, Ill., 1977—. Editor Bus. Torts Newsletter. Fellow Ill. State Bar Found., Am. Bar Found.; mem. ABA (ho. dels. 1995—), Ill. State Bar Assn. (pres. 1998-99), Peoria County Bar Assn. E-mail: tbertschy@hrva.com. General civil litigation. Office: Heyl Royster Voelker & Allen PC 124 SW Adams St Ste 600 Peoria IL 61602-1352*

**BERZOW, HAROLD STEVEN,** lawyer; b. Bklyn., Oct. 22, 1946; s. Julius and Lillian (Hershkowitz) Brzozowsky; m. Lynore Kushner, Aug. 22, 1970; children: Alan, Jason, Rachel. BA, Bklyn. Coll., 1968; JD, Bklyn. Law Sch., 1971. Bar: N.Y. 1972, U.S. Dist. Ct. (so. and ea. dists.) N.Y. 1973, U.S. Ct. Appeals (2d cir.) 1975, U.S. Supreme Ct. 1978. Assoc. Finkel, Nadler & Goldstein, N.Y.C., 1971-77; ptnr. Finkel, Goldstein, Berzow, Rosenbloom & Nash, LLP, N.Y.C., 1977—. Mem. ABA, N.Y. County Bar Assn., N.Y. State Bar Assn., Am. Bankruptcy Inst. Jewish. Bankruptcy, Contracts commercial, General corporate. Home: 15 Acorn Ln Plainview NY 11803-1901 Office: Finkel Goldstein Berzow Rosenbloom & Nash LLP 26 Broadway New York NY 10004-1703

**BESHAR, PETER JUSTUS,** lawyer; b. N.Y.C., Nov. 20, 1961; s. Robert Peter and Christine (Wedemeyer) B.; m. Sarah Jones, Jan. 5, 1991; children: Isabel Emma, Henry Frederick, Sophie Charlotte. BA, Yale U., 1984; JD, Harvard U., 1989. Bar: N.Y. 1989. Law clerk the Hon. Vincent L. Broderick, N.Y.C., 1989-90; spl. asst. to the Hon. Cyrus Vance Internat. Conf. on the Former Yugoslavia, 1992-93; asst. atty. gen. Office of Atty. Gen., N.Y.C., 1994; ptnr. Gibson, Dunn & Crutcher, N.Y.C., 1995—. Trustee Jay Heritage Soc., 1995. Mem. Coun. on Fgn. Rels. Office: Gibson Dunn & Crutcher 200 Park Ave Fl 47 New York NY 10166-0193

**BESHAR, ROBERT PETER,** lawyer; b. N.Y.C., Mar. 3, 1928; m. Christine von Wedemeyer, Dec. 20, 1953; children: Cornelia, Jacqueline, Frederica, Peter. AB honors with exceptional distinction, Yale U., 1950, LLB, 1953. Bar: N.Y. 1954. Asst. gen. counsel Waterfront Commn. N.Y. Harbor, 1954-55; law sec. Hon. Charles D. Breitel, Appellate div. 1st dept. N.Y. Supreme Ct., N.Y.C., 1956-58; spl. hearing officer Justice Dept., 1967-68; dep. asst. sec. Commerce; dir. Bur. Internat. Commerce; nat. export expansion coordinator Commerce Dept., Washington, 1971-72; pvt. practice, N.Y.C., 1972—; pres. various family enterprises, 1993—; bd. dirs. Nat. Semicondr. Corp. (audit and dir's. affairs coms., counsel to bd. dirs. 1972-98); mem. bus. adv. panel Nat. Commn. for Rev. of Antitrust Laws, 1978-79; mem. Mcpl. Securities Rulemaking Bd., 1982-85; bd. govs. Fgn. Policy Assn., 1991—. Author: Current Legal Aspects of Doing Business With Sino-Soviet Nations, 1973; editor: Manhattan Auto Study, 1973. Trustee Westchester Coll. Found., 1992—; mem. Planning Bd. of Somers, 1984-97. Scholar of the House, Yale U., 1950. Mem. ABA (chmn. corp. and antitrust law com. 1982-85), N.Y. State Bar Assn., Elizabethan and Gypsy Trail Clubs, Phi Beta Kappa. General practice, General corporate. Home: 120 E End Ave New York NY 10028-7552 Office: 1513 1st Ave at 79th St New York NY 10021-0901 also: PO Box 533 Somers NY 10589-0533

**BESHEAR, STEVEN L.,** lawyer; b. Dawson Springs, Ky., Sept. 21, 1944. A.B., U. Ky., Lexington, 1966, J.D., 1968. Bar: N.Y. 1969, Ky. 1971. Assoc. White and Case, N.Y.C., 1968-70; later ptnr. Beshear, Meng and Green, Lexington; mem. Ky. Ho. of Reps., 1974-79; atty. gen. State of Ky., Frankfort, 1979-83, lt. gov., 1983-87; ptnr. Stites & Harbison, Lexington, 1987—. Bd. editors, Ky. Law Jour., (1967-68.). Mem. Fayette County Bar Assn., Ky. Bar Assn., ABA, Order of Coif, Phi Beta Kappa, Phi Delta Phi, Omicron Delta Kappa. Administrative and regulatory, General civil litigation, Government contracts and claims. Office: Stites & Harbison 2300 Lexington Fin Ctr 250 W Main St Ste 2300 Lexington KY 40507-1758

**BESHEARS, CHARLES DANIEL, III,** lawyer; b. Kansas City, Kans., June 15, 1952; s. Charles Daniel and Mildred F. Beshears; m. Karen Sue McCown, Oct. 16, 1982; 1 child, Charles Scott. BA in Anthropology, BA in Psychology, Occidental Coll., 1974; JD, Lewis and Clark Coll., 1979. Bar: Oreg. 1979, U.S. Dist. Ct. Oreg. Adminstr. L.A. C.C. Dist., 1975-76; ptnr. Brown and Beshears, Tigard, Oreg., 1979-81, Galton, Popick & Scott, Portland, Oreg., 1981-83, Carney, Buckley & Kasameyer, Portland, 1983-89; pvt. practice, Portland, 1989—; CLE guest spkr. Oreg. Law Inst., Portland, 1989. Contbr. author: Consumer Law in Oregon, 1996. Mem. Oreg. State Bar (guest spkr., contbr. to book), Multnomah County Bar Assn. Democrat. Avocations: hiking, travel, bicycling. Personal injury, Family and matrimonial, General practice. Office: 1600 SW 1st Ave Ste 1150 Portland OR 97201-5704

**BESING, RAY GILBERT,** lawyer, writer; b. Roswell, N.Mex., Sept. 14, 1934; s. Ray David and Maxine Mable (Jordan) B.; m. Heather McEachern; children: Christopher, Gilbert, Andrew, Paul. Student, Rice U., 1952-54; B.A., Ripon Coll., 1957; postgrad., Georgetown U., 1957; J.D., So. Methodist U., 1960. Bar: Tex. 1960. Ptnr. Geary, Brice, Barron, & Stahl, Dallas, 1960-74; sr. ptnr. Besing, Baker & Glast, Dallas, 1974-77; prin. Law Offices of Ray G. Besing, P.C., Dallas, 1977—; lectr. trial procedures So. Meth. Sch. of Law, 1966-68; guest lectr. comms. law and policy, univs. and industry confs., 1984—; lectr. Bologna Ctr. of Johns Hopkins U., Nitze Sch. Advanced Internat. Studies. *Served as trial attorney representing Carter Electronics in the landmark case of Carterphone vs. AT&T (FCC 1968), opening the telephone equipment market to competition. Represented MCI Telecommunications Corporation in a series of regulatory agency and court cases against AT&T and the Bell Operating Companies, which provided key evidence to MCI and the U.S. Department of Justice in their antitrust suits against AT&T, leading to the 1984 breakup of the AT&T and Bell Telephone System monopolies over equipment and long distance services. Author: The Thirty Years War: The Defeat of the AT&T Monopoly to be published in 2000. Lecturer and adjuct professor on U.S. and European telecommunications history and policy.* Mng. editor, So. Methodist U. Law Jour., 1959-60. Pres. Dallas Cerebral Palsy Found., 1970; bd. dirs. Dallas Symphony, 1972, Dallas Theatre Center, 1971; trustee Ripon Coll., 1969-76; mem. Tex. Gov.'s Transition Team on Telecom., 1982. Tex. Moot Ct. champion, 1958. Mem. Tex. Bar Assn., Dallas Bar Assn., Dallas Jr. C. of C. (v.p. 1964), Sigma Chi. Democrat. Episcopalian (mem. exec. council diocese Dallas, 1969-72). E-mail: rbesing@roadrunner.com. Home and Office: 400 Graham Ave Santa Fe NM 87501-1658

**BESOZZI, PAUL CHARLES,** lawyer; b. N.Y.C., Aug. 22, 1947; s. Alfio Joseph and Lucy Agnes (Ducibella) B.; m. Caroline Lisa Hesterberg, Oct. 7, 1978; 1 child, Christina Claire. BS cum laude in Fgn. Service, Georgetown U., 1969, JD, 1972; MBA in Bus./Govt. Rels., George Washington U., 1977. Bar: Va. 1972, D.C. 1973, U.S. Ct. Mil. Appeals 1972, U.S. Supreme Ct. 1977, U.S. Ct. Appeals (4th cir.) 1978, U.S. Ct. Appeals (3d cir.) 1996. Assoc. Arnold & Porter, Washington, 1977-80; gen. counsel, minority counsel U.S. Senate Com. on Armed Services, Washington, 1980-84; ptnr. Hennessey, Stambler & Siebert, P.C., Washington, 1984-86, ptnr., Besozzi & Gavin, 1987-93; ptnr., Besozzi, Gavin & Craven, Washington, 1993-95, Besozzi, Gavin, Craven, & Schmitz, 1995-96, Patton Boggs LLP, Washington, 1996—. Contbr. articles and revs. to legal jours. Editor Georgetown Law Jour., 1971-72. Alumni interviewer Georgetown U. Alumni Assn., Washington, 1981—, dir. procurement roundtable, 1991—, Georgetown U. Alumni Assn. (bd. gov., 1993—). Served as capt. JAGC, U.S. Army, 1972-76. Mem. ABA, Fed. Comms. Bar Assn., Phi Beta Kappa, Phi Alpha Theta, Pi Sigma Alpha. Communications, Legislative, Public utilities. Office: Patton Boggs LLP 2550 M St NW Ste 400 Washington DC 20037-1301

**BESSER, BARRY I.,** lawyer; b. L.A., June 21, 1952; s. Ben and Alline Besser; m. Sandra Andrea Casanova, Feb. 27, 1982. BS, Calif. State U., Northridge, 1974; JD, Western State U., 1977. Bar: Calif. 1979, U.S. Dist. Ct. (cen. dist.) Calif., 1980. Assoc. Law Offices of Ward Mikkelson, Orange, Calif., 1979-80, Jacoby & Meyers, Mission Viejo, Calif., 1980-82, Klein & Cutler, Inc., Santa Ana, Calif., 1982-85; pvt. practice Orange, Calif., 1985—. Mem. Orange County Bar Assn. (bd. dirs. 1988, 89), Orange County Trial Lawyers Assn. (bd. dirs. 1993-95), Orange County Barristers (prse. 1989), Rotary. Avocations: travel, sports. Family and matrimonial, Personal injury, Criminal. Office: 333 City Blvd W Ste 1600 Orange CA 92868-2933

**BEST, CHARLES WILLIAM, JR.,** lawyer; b. Atlanta, Aug. 18, 1936; s. Charles William and Virginia C. (Clark) B.; m. Kate Livingstone Ewing, Aug. 23, 1958 (div. Feb. 1976); children: Charles William III, Karen L. Habighorst, Thomas Ewing; m. Mary Ewing Fears, Apr. 12, 1980; 1 child, Michael Allen. BSEE, Va. Mil. Inst., Lexington, 1958; JD, U. Va., 1971. Bar: Va. 1971. Ptnr. Kaufman & Canoles, Norfolk, Va., 1971-90, Wilks, Best & Alper, Norfolk, Va., 1990-95, Best & Best, PLC, Norfolk, Va., 1995-98; sole practitioner Norfolk, 1998—. Capt., USAF, 1958-63. Mem. ABA, Va. State Bar ASsn., Norfolk Portsmouth Bar Assn., Order of Coif. Presbyterian. Avocation: offshore fishing. General corporate, Estate planning. Home: 1485 Trading Point Ln Virginia Bch VA 23452-4733 Office: 500 E Main St Ste 1619 Norfolk VA 23510-2206

**BEST, FRANKLIN LUTHER, JR.,** lawyer; b. Lock Haven, Pa., Dec. 14, 1945; s. Franklin L. and Hazel M. (Yearick) B.; m. Kimberly R., May 1, 1982. BA, Yale U., 1967; JD, U. Pa., 1970; postgrad., Columbia U., 1994. Bar: Pa. 1970. Assoc. MacCoy, Evans & Lewis, Phila., 1970-74; asst. counsel Penn Mut. Life Ins. Co., Phila., 1974-77, asst. gen. counsel, 1978-84, assoc. gen. counsel, 1985-99, corp. counsel, 1999—; counsel, asst. sec. Penn Ins. and Annuity Co., Phila., 1983-96, counsel, sec., 1996—, corp. counsel, 1999—; lectr. Pa. Bar Inst., 1976-84. Author: Pennsylvania Insurance Law, 1991, 2d edit., 1998; contbr. articles to profl. jours. Bd. dirs. Ctr. City South Neighborhood Assn., 1979-80, pres., 1978-79; mem. Com. of Seventy, 1978-84; sec. Washington Sq. Assn., 1977-87; mem. 30th Ward Rep. Exec. Com., 1972-84, West Pikeland Twp. Open Spaces Com., 1987—, chairperson, 1995—, planning commn., 1994—, chairperson, 1996—. Mem. ABA, Internat. Claim Assn. (sec. 1995—, exec. com. 1979-81, 85-88), Phila. Bar Assn., Yale Club of Phila. Baptist. Insurance, General civil litigation, Probate. Office: Penn Mut Life Ins Co Independence Sq Philadelphia PA 19172-0001

**BEST, JUDAH,** lawyer; b. N.Y.C., Sept. 4, 1932; s. Sol and Ruth (Landau) B.; m. Sally Joan Dial, June 29, 1962; 1 child, Stephen Andrew. AB, Cornell U., 1954; LLB, Columbia U., 1959. Bar: N.Y. 1959, D.C. 1961, U.S. Supreme Ct. 1963. Trial atty. Solicitor's Office, U.S. Dept. Labor, Washington, 1960-61; asst. U.S. atty. for D.C., 1961-64; assoc., then ptnr. Chapman, DiSalle & Friedman, Washington, 1964-70; ptnr. Dickstein, Shapiro & Morin, Washington, 1970-80, Steptoe & Johnson, Washington, 1980-87, Debevoise & Plimpton, Washington, 1987—; participant trial advocacy program U. Va. Sch. Law, 1981—. Contbr. articles to profl. publs. Served with U.S. Army, 1954-56. Fellow Am. Coll. Trial Lawyers; mem. ABA (coun., litigation sect. 1977-81, chmn. subcom. on litigation 1982-84, mem. fed. regulation securities com., corp. bank and bus. law sect., pub. contracts sect., vice chmn. ABA Task Force Report on RICO 1983-85, chmn. litigation sect. 1988-89, sect. del. 1989—, mem. standing com. on fed. judiciary 1990-93, chmn. 1996-97, mem. spl. com. on governance 1993-95), Fed. Bar Assn., D.C. Bar Assn., Am. Bar Found., Am. Law Inst., Cosmos Club, Washington Golf and Country Club, City Club of Washington. Criminal, Federal civil litigation. Home: 2808 Woodland Dr NW Washington DC 20008-2742 Office: Debevoise & Plimpton 555 13th St NW Ste 1100E Washington DC 20004-1163 also: 875 3rd Ave New York NY 10022-6225

**BEST, KAREN MAGDALENE,** legal secretary; b. Worden, Ill., Oct. 10, 1947; d. Royal H. and Doris (Klausing) Lueker; m. Rodger R. Best, Mar. 29, 1975; 1 child, Jill Marie. Grad. H.S., Edwardsville, Ill., 1965. Claims sec. Madison County Mutual, Edwardsville, 1965-75; legal sec. Young, Welsch, Young & Hall, Danville, Ill., 1975-77, Mudge, Riley & Lucco, Edwardsville, 1977-79, Droste & Price, Mt. Olive, Ill., 1979-95; clk. Wolff Oil Co., Litchfield, Ill., 1995-96; legal sec. Lucco, Brown & Mudge, Edwardsville, 1996-98, Scharf Law Office, Litchfield, Ill., 1998—. Mem. Zion Lutheran Ladies Aid, pres. 1997-99. Lutheran. Avocations: reading, travel. Home: 5324 Niemanville Trl Litchfield IL 62056-4614

**BETTAC, ROBERT EDWARD,** lawyer; b. Ashland, Ohio, Aug. 13, 1949; s. Donald Albert and Ruth Lavina (Foos) B.; m. Suzanne Lee Shepherd, June 30, 1979; children: Jacqueline Lee, Robert Mitchell. BA in Polit. Sci., Ashland U., 1972; JD, U. Cin., 1979. Bar: U.S. Dist. Ct. (we. and so. dists.) Tex. 1983, U.S. Dist. Ct. (no. dist.) Tex. 1989, U.S. Ct. Appeals (5th and 11th cirs.) 1981. Assoc. Foster & Assocs., Inc., San Antonio, 1979-84; ptnr. Foster, Bettac & Heller, P.C., San Antonio, 1984-89, Akin Gump Strauss Hauer & Feld, San Antonio, 1989—. Author: (with others) Texas Practice Guide, 2d ed., 1983. Mem. Witte Mus. Coun., San Antonio, 1984—. Labor. Home: 126 Rosemary Ave San Antonio TX 78209-3841 Office: Akin Gump Strauss Hauer & Feld 300 Convent St Ste 1500 San Antonio TX 78205-3732

**BETTS, BARBARA LANG,** lawyer, rancher, realtor; b. Anaheim, Calif., Apr. 28, 1926; d. W. Harold and Helen (Thompson) Lang; m. Roby F. Hayes, July 22, 1948 (dec.); children: John Chauncey IV, Frederick Prescott, Roby Francis II; m. Bert A. Betts, July 11, 1962; 1 child, Bruce Harold; stepchildren: Bert Alan, Randy W., Sally Betts Joynt, Terry Betts Marsteller, Linda Betts Hansen, LeAnn Betts Wilson. BA magna cum laude, Stanford U., 1948; LLB, Balboa U., 1951. Bar: Calif. 1952, U.S. Supreme Ct. 1978. Pvt. practice Oceanside, Calif., 1952-68, San Diego, 1960—, Sacramento, 1962—; ptnr. Roby F. Hayes & Barbara Lang Hayes, 1952-60; city atty. Carlsbad, Calif., 1969-68; v.p. Isle & Oceans Marinas, Inc., 1970-80, W.H. Lang Corp., 1964-69; sec. Internat. Prodn. Assocs., 1968—, Margaret M. McCabe, M.D., Inc., 1977-78. Co-author: (with Bert A. Betts) A Citizen Answers. Chmn. Traveler's Aid, 1952-53; pres. Oceanside-Carlsbad Jr. Chambrettes, 1955-56; vice chmn. Carlsbad Planning Commn., 1959; mem. San Diego Planning commn., 1959; v.p. Oceanside Diamond Jubilee Com., 1958; candidate Calif. State Legislature, 77th Dist., 1954; mem. Calif. Dem. State Ctrl. Com., 1958-66, co-chmn. 1960-62; co-chmn. 28th Congl. Dist.; alt. del. Dem. Nat. Conv., 1960; co-sponsor All Am. B-24 Liberator Collings Found. Named to Fullerton Union H.S. Wall of Fame, 1986; recipient Block S award Stanford U. Mem. ABA, AAUW (legis. com. 1958-59, local pres. 1959-60, asst. state legis. chmn. 1958-59), DAR (regent Oceanside chpt. 1960-61), DFC Soc. (assoc.), Am. Judicature Soc., Nat. Inst. Mcpl. Officers, Calif. Bar Assn., San Diego County Bar Assn., Oceanside C. of C. (sec. 1957, v.p. 1958, dir. 1953-54, 57-59), Heritage League (2d divsn. 8th Air Force), No. San Diego County Assn. Cs. of C. (sec.-treas.), Bus. and Profl. Women's Club (so. dist. legislation chmn. 1958-59), San Diego C. of C., San Diego Hist. Soc., Fullerton Jr. Assistance League, Calif. Scholarship Fedn. (life), Loyola Guild of Jesuit H.S., Soroptimist Internat. (pres. Oceanside-Carlsbad 1958-59, sec. pub. affairs San Diego and Imperial Counties 1954, pres. pres.'s coun. San Diego and Imperial Counties, Mex. 1958-59), Barristers (Stanford, Sacramento), Disting. Flying Cross Soc. (assoc.), Stanford Mothers, Phi Beta Kappa. Probate, Pension, profit-sharing, and employee benefits, Real property. Home: 441 Sandburg Dr Sacramento CA 95819-2559 Office: Betts Ranch 8701 E Levee Rd Elverta CA 95626 also: 1830 Avenida Del Mundo Coronado CA 92118-3018

**BETTS, KIRK HOWARD,** lawyer; b. Jersey City, Mar. 5, 1951; s. Fred Semour and Mary Elizabeth (Morrell) B.; m. Christine Marlene Sheridan, Mar. 19, 1976; 1 child, Abigail Sheridan. BA, George Washington U., 1973; JD, Am. U., 1979. Bar: D.C. 1980, U.S. Dist. Ct. (D.C. dist.) 1980, U.S. Ct. Appeals (D.C., 5th and 11th cirs.) 1980, U.S. Supreme Ct. 1984, Md. 1986, U.S. Ct. Appeals (6th cir.) 1989. Assoc. Northcutt Ely, Washington, 1979-82; mng. ptnr. Ely, Ritts, Pietrowski & Brickfield, Washington, 1982-84, Ely, Ritts, Brickfield & Betts, Washington, 1984-86; counsel Dickinson, Wright, Moon, Van Dusen & Freeman, Washington, 1986-87, ptnr., 1987-96, ptnr. in charge Washington office, 1993-95; mng. ptnr. Betts & Holt, Washington, 1996—; asst. counsel U.S. Senate subcom. on intergovtl. rels., Washington, 1974-76; legis. aide to Hon. William V. Roth, Washington, 1973-74. Chmn. bd. mgrs. for Hallowood Conf. Ctr., St. Luke Luth. Ch., Silver Spring, Md., 1985—, ch. coun., 1987-90, v.p., 1989; chmn. Carl E. and Nathalia B. Rantzow Endowment for Sem. Edn., 1989—; mem. pres.'s cabinet Luth. Theol. Sem., Gettysburg, 1995—; bd. dirs. Luth. World Relief, 1998—. Named to Hon. Order Ky. Cols., 1988; awarded key to City of Vanceburg, Ky., 1987. Mem. ABA (sects. on pub. utility law, law practice mgmt., trust and real property, govt. contracts, Best Article in Series award 1980), D.C. Bar Assn., Md. State Bar Assn., Fed. Energy Bar Assn., Wash. Coll. of Law/Am. U. (alumni rels. com. 1987-88, devel. coun. 1989—, chmn. 1993-95, deans adv. coun. 1995—), Podickory Yacht Club (Annapolis, Md.) (vice commodore 1975-76). Republican. Lutheran. Avocations: sailing, woodworking, collecting lit. about Chesapeake Bay. E-mail: kbetts@bett-sandholt.com. FERC practice, Public utilities. Home: 6412 Goldleaf Dr Bethesda MD 20817-5830 Office: Betts & Holt 815 Connecticut Ave NW Washington DC 20006-4004

**BETTS, REBECCA A.,** lawyer. BA, Dickinson Coll., 1972; JD, W.Va. U., 1976. BAr: W.V., U.S. Dist. Ct. (so. dist.) W.Va. 1976, U.S. Ct. Appeals (4th cir.) 1978, U.S. Supreme Ct. 1984. Assoc. Spilman, Thomas, Battle & Klostermeyer, Charleston, W.Va., 1976-77; asst. U.S. atty. U.S. Atty.'s Office, 1977-81, chief civil divsn., 1979-81; founding ptnr. King, Betts & Allen, Charleston, W.Va.; U.S. atty. U.S. Dist. Ct. (So. Dist.), W.Va., 1994—; mem. 4th Cir. adv. com. on rules & procedures, com. for local rules and subcom. on criminal rules for So. Dist. W.Va., mem. civil justice reform act adv. com. Assoc. editor: W.Va. Law Rev. Mem. W.Va. State Bar (past mem. com. on legal ethics), The Legal Aid Soc. of Charleston (bd. dirs.), Order of the Coif. Office: US Attorney for South Dist WV US Courthouse Rm 4000 300 Virginia St E Charleston WV 25301-2503

**BETZ, GILBERT CALVIN,** lawyer; b. Jacksonville, Fla., Apr. 21, 1948; s. Gilbert Robert and Argene Frazier (Lucas) B.; m. Deborah A. Scott, Jan. 21, 1974 (div. Dec. 1987); children: Robert Scott, Kimberly Ayn; m. Debra L. Vess, June 28, 1994; 1 child, David Alan. BS, U. Fla., 1970; MA, Ctrl. Mich. U., 1976; JD, Stetson U., 1980. Bar: Fla. 1980, D.C. 1988, U.S. Dist. Ct. (mid. and so. dists.) Fla. 1980, U.S. Ct. Appeals (11th cir.) 1990. Asst. corp. counsel The Deltona Corp., Miami, Fla., 1980-86; ptnr. Mancilla & Betz, P.A., Coral Gables, Fla., 1986-90; prin. Gilbert C. Betz, P.A., Miami, Fla., 1990—. Exec. editor Stetson U. Law Rev., 1980. Vice chmn. Metro-Dade Unsafe Structures, Miami, 1994—; treas., exec. com. Citizens for a Better So. Fla., Miami, 1993—; pro bono guardian atty. Fla. Guardian Ad Litem Program, Miami, 1993—. Capt. USAF, 1971-77, lt. col. USAFR, 1983—. Mem. Air Force Assn., Res. Officers Assn. U.S., Phi Alpha Delta (local pres. 1978), Kappa Sigma (local pres. 1967). Republican. General corporate, Family and matrimonial, Real property. Home: 610 Conde Ave Coral Gables FL 33156-4226 Office: 2025 SW 32nd Ave Miami FL 33145-2211

**BEUKEMA, JOHN FREDERICK,** lawyer; b. Alpena, Mich., Jan. 30, 1947; s. Christian F. and Margaret Elizabeth (Robertson) B.; m. Cynthia Ann Parke, May 25, 1974; children: Frederick Parke, David Christian. BA, Carleton Coll., 1968; JD, U. Minn., 1971. Bar: Minn. 1971, U.S. Ct. Mil. Appeals 1974, U.S. Dist. Ct. Minn. 1975, U.S. Ct. Appeals (8th cir.) 1981, U.S. Ct. Appeals (fed. cir.) 1984, U.S. Supreme Ct. 1988, U.S. Dist. Ct. (we. dist.) Wis. 1997. Assoc. Faegre & Benson, Mpls., 1971, 75-79, ptnr., 1980—. Vestryman Cathedral Ch. St. Mark, Mpls., 1983-86; bd. dirs. Neighborhood

Involvement Program, Mpls., 1986-90, pres., 1989-90; bd. dirs. Ronald McDonald House of Twin Cities, 1991-97, sec., 1995-97. Lt. JAGC, USNR, 1972-75. Mem. ABA, Minn. State Bar Assn., Hennepin County Bar Assn. Republican. Episcopalian. Antitrust, General civil litigation, Appellate.

**BEUMLER, HENRY WEBER,** lawyer; b. Douglas, Ariz., May 27, 1913; s. Henry Conrad Andrew and Susan Alberta (Weber) B.; m. Mary Estelle Collins, June 11, 1939; children: Henry Collins, Timothy Collins, Edward Collins, Candyce Collins. BA, U. Ariz., 1934, JD, 1936; postgrad., U. Mex., 1937, Ariz. State U., 1960. Bar: Ariz. 1936, U.S. Dist. Ct. (Ariz.) 1936. Ptnr. Beumler & Beumler, Douglas, 1936-58; pvt. practice, Douglas, 1958-78, Portal, Ariz., 1978—; tchr. Douglas High Sch., 1958-78; mayor City of Douglas, 1950-60; city atty. Douglas, 1939-42; dep. atty. Cochise County, Ariz., 1940-42; commr. U.S. Dist. Ct., Tucson, 1948-68. Mem. Ariz. Devel. Bd., 1954-58, Ariz. Civil Rights Commn., 1956-58, San Simon Unified Dist. Sch. Bd., pres., 1985-88. Served to lt. col. AUS, 1942-46. Paul Harris fellow Rotary Internat. Mem. ABA, Ariz. Bar Assn., Cochise County Bar Assn., Ret. Tchrs. Assn., Masons, Phi Delta Kappa. Probate. Address: PO Box 16166 Portal AZ 85632-1166

**BEUSTRING, GLENN ROLAND,** lawyer; b. Tulsa, Aug. 17, 1941; s. Roland J. and Flora M. (Strain) B.; single;children—Kimberly Kate, Becca Lynn, Donald Glenn, Jessica Mae. B.S. in Bus. Adminstrn., Abilene Christian Coll., 1963; J.D., U. Tulsa, 1966. Bar: Okla. 1967. Assoc. Kothe, Eagleton & Hall, 1967-70; sole practice, Tulsa, 1970—; guest lectr. div. continuing edn. U. Tulsa Coll. Law. Mem. Okla Trial Lawyers Assn. (exec. com. 1983, v.p. 1984, pres.-elect 1985, pres. 1986), Assn. Trials Lawyers Am. Deomcrat. Personal injury, Federal civil litigation, State civil litigation. Office: 2624 E 21st St Ste 1 Tulsa OK 74114-1718

**BEUTTENMULLER, RUDOLF WILLIAM,** lawyer; b. St. Louis, Dec. 20, 1953; s. Paul A. and Doris R. (Henle) B.; m. Ragina Lee Winters, July 14, 1984. AB cum laude, Princeton U., 1976; JD with distinction, Duke U., 1980. Bar: Tex. 1980, U.S. Dist. Ct. (no. dist.) Tex. 1980. Assoc. Jenkens & Gilchrist, Dallas, 1980-83; ptnr. Gregory, Self & Beuttenmuller, Dallas, 1983-88, Bradley, Bradley & Beuttenmuller, Irving, Tex., 1988-93; dir. Thomas & Self, Dallas, 1994—. Articles editor Duke Law Jour., Durham, 1979-80. Mem. Rep. Nat. Com., Washington, 1984. Mem. ABA, Dallas Bar Assn., Duke Law Alumni Assn., Princeton Alumni Assn. Banking, General corporate, Real property. Home: 4417 Amherst Ave Dallas TX 75225-6907 Office: Thomas & Self 5339 Spring Valley Rd Dallas TX 75240-3009

**BEVAN, ROBERT LEWIS,** lawyer; b. Springfield, Mo., Mar. 23, 1928; s. Gene Walter and Blanche Omega (Woods) B.; m. Ronice Diane Gartin, Jan 25, 1977; children: Matthew Gene, Lisa Ann. AB, U. Mo., 1950; LLB, U. Kansas City, 1957. Bar: Mo. 1957, D.C. 1969. Adminstrv. asst. U.S. Senator T. Hennings Jr., Washington, 1957-60; legis. asst. U.S. Senator E.V. Long, Washington, 1960-69; sr. govt. relations counsel Am. Bankers Assn., Washington, 1970-84; ptnr. Hopkins & Sutter, Washington, 1984-95; of counsel Stinson, Mag and Fizzell, Kansas City, Mo., 1995—. Ghost author: The Intruders, 1967; contbg. editor U.S. Banker, 1985-88. Fieldman Dem. Nat. Com., 1968. Served with U.S. Army, 1946-47, 1951-53. Mem. ABA (bus. law sect., chmn. banking law com. 1988-92, commn. on IOLTA, co-chmn. joint comm. com.), Echequer Club. Avocations: art and antiques. Banking, Administrative and regulatory, Legislative. Office: 1201 Walnut St Fl 28 Kansas City MO 64106-2117

**BEWLEY, PETER DAVID,** lawyer; b. Atlantic City, N.J., Aug. 4, 1946; s. Philip Bessor and Gladys Elizabeth Bewley; m. Barbara L. Sell, June 1, 1968 (dec. June 25, 1971); 1 child, Peter David Jr.; m. Lee D. Catanese, Aug. 12, 1972; 1 child, Stephen Philip. BA in Politics cum laude, Princeton U., 1968; JD, Stanford U., 1971. Bar: Calif. 1971, D.C. 1972, U.S. Ct. Appeals (D.C. cir.) 1972, U.S. Supreme Ct. 1976. Assoc. Wilmer, Cutler & Pickering, Washington, 1972-76; gen. atty., from asst. to assoc. gen. counsel Johnson & Johnson, New Brunswick, N.J., 1977-94; sr. v.p., gen. counsel, sec. Nova Care, Inc., King of Prussia, Pa., 1994-98, The Clorox Co., Oakland, Calif., 1998—; dir. Non Prescription Drug Mfrs. Assn., Washington, 1991-94, Access World Wide Comms., Alexandria, Va., 1998—. Mem. editl. adv. bd. Food and Drug Law Jour., 1992-94. City councilman City of Gladstone, N.J., 1993-94. Capt. USAF, 1971-72. Mem. ABA, Am. Corp. Counsel Assn., Am. Soc. Corp. Secs., Order of the Coif. Avocations: travel, skiing, reading. General corporate, Mergers and acquisitions, Securities. Home: 6066 Mazuela Dr Oakland CA 94611-2208 Office: The Clorox Co 1221 Broadway Fl 13 Oakland CA 94612-1888

**BEYER, GARRETT JOSEPH,** lawyer; b. San Francisco, June 26, 1964; s. Joseph Philip and Joanne Elaine B.; m. Pauline Diane, May 29, 1994. BA in Bus. Adminstrn., U. Puget Sound, 1988; MBA, Gonzaga U., 1989, JD, 1993; LLM in Taxation, U. Wash., 1997. Bar: Wash. 1994, U.S. Dist. Ct. (ea. dist.) Wash. 1994. Assoc. Robert B. Henderson, Spokane, Wash., 1991-95, Lemargie & Whitaker, Ephrata, Wash., 1995-96; of counsel Monahan & Biagi, Seattle, 1997—. Mem. Wash. State Bar Assn. (tax sect., internat. law sect.), Wash. State Trial Lawyers Assn., King County Bar Assn. (internat. sect.). Republican. Lutheran. Private international, Corporate taxation, Public international. Office: Monahan & Biagi PLLC 701 5th Ave Ste 5701 Seattle WA 98104-7003

**BEYER, JENNIFER ELMER,** lawyer; b. Alexandria, La., Sept. 3, 1963; d. Richard Anthony Elmer and Priscilla (Escude) Allums. BS, La. Coll., 1984; JD, La. State U., 1987. Bar: La. 1987, U.S. Dist. Ct. (we. and mid. dists.) La. 1988, U.S. Ct. Appeals (5th cir.) 1988, U.S. Dist. Ct. (ea. dist.) La. 1990. Ptnr. Preis, Kraft & Roy, Lafayette, La., 1987—. Mem. ABA, La. Assn. Def. Counsel, La. Bar Assn., Lafayette Parish Bar Assn. Admiralty, Insurance, General civil litigation. Home: 305 Marguerite Blvd Lafayette LA 70503-3133 Office: Preis Kraft & Roy 102 Versailles Blvd Ste 400 Lafayette LA 70501-6703

**BEYER, VICKI WOODY,** lawyer; b. Park Ridge, Ill., Dec. 11, 1966; d. Ronald Wayne and Susan (Haggitt) Woody; m. William Blane Beyer, Jan. 1, 1994; 1 child, Hope Anastasia. BBA, U. Iowa, 1988; JD, N.Y. Law Sch., 1992. Lawyer Daniel A. D'Alessandro, Jersey City, N.J., 1993-95, Stark & Stark, Lawrenceville, N.J., 1995—. Vol. reader Recording for the Blind & Dyslexic, Princeton, N.J., 1996; vol. Del. Valley Girl Scouts, East Brunswick, N.J., 1996, mem. Women of Distinction award dinner com., 1996. Mem. Zonta Internat. Avocations: hand-made crafts, baking, hiking, beach-going. Workers' compensation, Pension, profit-sharing, and employee benefits, Administrative and regulatory. Office: Stark & Stark 993 Lenox Dr Ste 101 Lawrenceville NJ 08648-2389

**BEYER, WAYNE CARTWRIGHT,** lawyer; b. Bklyn., Feb. 21, 1946; s. Gerhard Robert and Barbara Janeway (Fein) B. AB, Dartmouth Coll., 1967; MAT, Harvard U., 1970; Jd, Georgetown U., 1977. Bar: N.H. 1978, U.S. Dist. Ct. N.H. 1978, U.S. Tax Ct. 1986, U.S. CT. Appeals (1st cir.) 1979, U.S. Supreme Ct. 1986, D.C. 1996. Mem. staff U.S. Ho. of Reps., Washington, 1973-75; atty. McLane, Graf, Raulerson, P.A., Manchester, N.H., 1978-83; chief of staff GSA, Washington, 1983-84, dep. gen. counsel, 1984-86; atty. Cleveland, Waters & Bass, P.A., Concord, N.H., 1986-94; pvt. practice Manchester, N.H., 1994-96; asst. corp. counsel Dist. of Columbia, 1996—; lectr. civil rights. Contbr. articles to profl. jours. Mem. ABA, N.H. Bar Assn., Assn. Trial Lawyers Am., Def. Rsch. Inst., Internat. Assn. Chiefs of Police, Harvard Club. Federal civil litigation, Constitutional, Civil rights. Home: 1501 Porter St NW Apt 527 Washington DC 20008 Office: Office Corp Counsel 441 4th St NW 6th Flr S Washington DC 20001

**BEZANSON, THOMAS EDWARD,** lawyer; b. Hartford, Conn., Aug. 1, 1945; s. Philip Thomas and Lillian (Carlson) B.; m. Janie R. Bezanson, Aug. 10, 1969; children: Philip, Jeffrey. BA, Grinnell, 1967; MA, Rutgers U., 1971, JD, 1974. Bar: N.Y. 1975, U.S. Dist. Ct. (ea. dist.) 1975, U.S. Dist. Ct. (so. dist.) N.Y. 1975, U.S. Ct. Appeals (2d cir.) 1975, U.S. Ct. Appeals (6th cir.) 1980, U.S. Supreme Ct. 1991. Assoc. Chadbourne & Parke, N.Y.C., 1974-81, ptnr., 1981—. Author: 42 Poems, 1993. Bd. dirs. Westchester Philharm., 1992-98, N.Y. Lawyers for the Public Interest, Inc., 1997—. Served in U.S. Army, 1967-69, Thailand. Mem. ABA, N.Y. State Bar Assn., Assn. of Bar of City of N.Y. Product liability, Federal civil litigation, State civil litigation. Office: Chadbourne & Parke 30 Rockefeller Plz New York NY 10112-0002

**BHATNAGAR, MARY ELIZABETH,** lawyer; b. Nashville, July 8, 1943; d. Thomas A. and Elizabeth D. (Levine) Kelly; m. Rajendra S. Bhatnagar, Feb. 27, 1966; children: Ranjit, Rajiv. BA, Duke U., 1965; MA, Northwestern U., 1968; JD, San Mateo Law Sch., 1979. Bar: Calif. 1979, U.S. Dist. Ct. (no. dist.) Calif. 1979. Pvt. practice, San Mateo, Calif., 1979—; prof. bus. law Coll. San Mateo, 1979—. Bd. dirs. LWV of Cen. San Mateo county, 1989—. Mem. ABA, Calif. State Bar, San Mateo County Bar Assn. Democrat. Contracts commercial, Estate planning, Alternative dispute resolution. Office: Bovet Profl Ctr 177 Bovet Rd Ste 600 San Mateo CA 94402-3191

**BIALKIN, KENNETH JULES,** lawyer; b. N.Y.C., Sept. 9, 1929; s. Samuel and Lillian (Kastner) B.; m. Ann Eskind, Aug. 19, 1956; children: Lisa Beth, Johanna. AB, U. Mich., 1950; cert. of attendance, London Sch. Econ., 1952; JD, Harvard U., 1953. Bar: N.Y. 1953, U.S. Dist. Ct. (ea. dist.) N.Y. 1955, U.S. Supreme Ct. 1964, U.S. Dist. Ct. (so. dist.) N.Y. 1972, U.S. Ct. Appeals (2d cir.) 1976. Assoc. Willkie Farr & Gallagher, N.Y.C., 1953-60, ptnr., 1960-88; ptnr. Skadden, Arps, Slate, Meagher & Flom, N.Y.C., 1988—; adj. prof. law NYU, 1967-87; lectr., commentator legal and fin. symposia; mem. N.Y. Stock Exch. Legal Adv. Commn., 1983-92, 98—, chmn. internat. securities subcom., 1989-98; bd. dirs. Citigroup Inc., Travelers Property & Casualty Corp., Oshap Techs., Mcpl. Assistance Corp. City of N.Y., Sapiens Internat., Ltd., Tecnomatix Techs., Ltd.; mem. Adminstrv. Conf. of U.S., 1987-92; chmn. Com. on Fin. Svcs.; vis. com. grad. faculty New Sch. for Social Rsch., 1992—. Editor: The Business Lawyer, 1980; bd. editors Corp. Governance Jour., 1992—; contbr. articles on corp., fin. investment law to profl. jours. Chmn. Conf. Pres. Major Am. Jewish Orgns., 1984-86; chmn. Am.-Israel Friendship Leaque, 1995—; nat. chmn. Anti-Defamation League B'nai Brith, 1982-86; pres. Jewish Cmty. Rels. Coun. N.Y., 1989-92; vice-chmn., dir. Jerusalem Found., Inc., 1975—. Mem. ABA (chmn. fed. regulation securities com. 1974-79, chmn. com. to study fgn. investment in U.S. 1978-80, chmn. ad hoc com. on insider trading regulation 1988—, chmn. sect. corp. banking and bus. law 1981-82, 88), Am. Jewish Hist. Soc. (pres. 1997—), N.Y. County Lawyers Assn. (pres. 1986-88), Am. Bar Retirement Assn. (dir. 1981-84), Coun. Fgn. Rels., Harvard Club. General corporate, Mergers and acquisitions, Securities. Home: 211 Central Park W New York NY 10024-6020 Office: Skadden Arps Slate Meagher & Flom 919 3rd Ave New York NY 10022-3902

**BIALKOWSKI, STEPHEN WALTER,** lawyer; b. Englewood, N.J., Sept. 25, 1961. AB in History/Govt., Muhlenberg Coll., 1983; JD, Seton Hall U., 1986. Bar: N.J. 1986, N.Y. 1988, U.S. Dist. Ct. N.J. 1986, U.S. Dist. Ct. (so. and ea. dists.) N.Y. 1987, U.S. Ct. Appeals (2d and 3d cirs.) 1988, U.S. Supreme Ct. 1994. Assoc. Condon & Forsyth, 1986-88, Shanley & Fisher, PC, 1988-89, Peckar & Abramson, PC, 1989-93; gen. ptnr. McLellan & Bialkowski, 1993—; prof. NYU, 1993—; expert on constrn. law, 1998—; dir., coord. and instr. legal studies program Bergen C.C., 1994-95; guest lectr. Cmty. Builders Assn., 1998, Builders Assn. No. N.J., 1997, Midlantic Nat. Bank. Mem. Am. Arbitration Assn. (constrn. arbitrator). Fax: 201-487-0441. E-mail: sbialkowski@worldnet.att.net. Construction, Contracts commercial, General civil litigation. Address: 87 Essex St Hackensack NJ 07601-4090

**BIALLA, ROWLEY,** lawyer; b. N.Y.C., Aug. 13, 1914; s. Edward and Amy (Rowley) B.; m. Marian L. Dunham, Mar. 23, 1945 (div. Mar. 1951); children: Margeret L., Jean B. Murphy; m. Mary S. Wilson, Aug. 21, 1954; 1 child, Nancy R. AB, Dartmouth Coll., 1937; LLB, Yale U., 1940. Bar: N.Y. 1940; U.S. Supreme Ct. 1945. Assoc. White & Case, N.Y.C., 1940-41, 46-51; house counsel Guggenheim Interests, N.Y.C., 1952-79; pvt. practice, Northport, N.Y., 1979—; sec. Daniel and Florence Guggenheim Found., N.Y.C., 1979—; sec., bd. dirs. Lavanberg Found., N.Y.C., 1981—. Capt. U.S. Army, 1941-45. Mem. ABA. Avocations: history, genealogy. Probate, Real property, Estate taxation. Home and Office: 43 Highland Ave Northport NY 11768-1611

**BIALO, KENNETH MARC,** lawyer; b. N.Y.C., Nov. 21, 1946; s. Walter and Mildred (Miller) B.; m. Katherine Ann Burghard; children: Darren Andrew, Caralyn Alyssa, Jacquelyn Anne, Matthew Joseph Geronimo, Kelsey Elizabeth Ariel. BS, U. Rochester, 1968; JD cum laude (note &comment editor. law review, Order of the Coif, Univ. Scholar), NYU, 1971; LLM, London Sch. Econs., 1973. Bar: N.Y. 1972, U.S. Ct. Appeals (2d cir.) 1974, U.S. Ct. Appeals (fed. cir.) 1988, U.S. Supreme Ct. 1975. Law clk. Hon. L.W. Pierce U.S. Dist. Ct. (so. dist.) N.Y., 1971-72; assoc. Sullivan & Cromwell, N.Y.C., 1973-80; counsel, sr. counsel Exxon Corp., N.Y.C., 1980-90; sr. counsel, chief litigation atty. Exxon Chem. Co., Darien, Conn., 1990-91; ptnr. Baker & Botts, N.Y.C., 1992—; lectr. Practicing Law Inst., N.Y.C., 1982, 88, N.Y. State Bar Assn., 1997. Contbg. editor: Family Legal Guide, 1974; note, comment editor: Law Rev. Univ. Scholar; contbr. articles to profl. jours.; note and comment editor NYU Law Rev. Trustee Village of Larchmont, N.Y., 1991—; mem. PLI Adv. Com. on Litig., 1994—; v.p. bd. dirs. Little League, Larchmont, 1985-94, mem. recreation com., 1987-89; pres., bd. govs. Univ. Club of Larchmont, 1995—. Mem. ABA (litig. sect. task force on client concerns 1994-95, subcom. class action, litig. sect.), N.Y. State Bar (antitrust com., fed. and comml. litig. sect., former chmn. corp. counsel com. 1989-91), Assn. of Bar of City of N.Y. (arbitration com.), Fed. Bar Coun. (com. 2d cir. cts.), Am. Arbitration Assn. (mem. arbitrator's panel), Order of Coif. Avocations: tennis, baseball, opera, symphony. Federal civil litigation, Antitrust. Office: Baker & Botts 599 Lexington Ave New York NY 10022-6030

**BIANCHI, DAVID WAYNE,** lawyer; b. Amsterdam, N.Y., June 12, 1950; s. Fred and Palma (Biasi) B.; m. Frances Shekter, Apr. 12, 1981; 1 child, Nicholas David. BS, Fla. State U., 1972; JD, San Fernando Valley Coll., 1979. Bar: Califr. 1979, U.S. Dist. Ct. (cen. dist.) Calif. 1981, U.S. Dist. Ct. (ea. dist.) Calif. 1992; cert. specialist in family law Calif. Bd. Legal Specialization. Dep. city atty. City of Lancaster, Calif., 1984-87; ptnr. Michelizzi, Schwabacher, Ward & Bianchi, Lancaster, 1980—; instr. bus. law Antelope Valley C.C., Lancaster, 1983—; judge pro tem L.A. County Superior Ct., Antelope Mcpl. Ct. Mem. adv. bd. Salvation Army, 1991—. Mem. Antelope Valley Bar Assn. (pres. 1988, chmn. fee arbitration com. 1994—), Kiwanis Club Antelope Valley (bd. dirs. 1984—, pres. 1998-99), Elks (exalted ruler 1986-87). Avocations: golf, fishing, sports, coaching soccer. Family and matrimonial, Estate planning, Probate. Office: Michelizzi Schwabacher Ward & Bianchi 767 W Lancaster Blvd Lancaster CA 93534-3118

**BIANCO, S. ANTHONY,** lawyer; b. Bklyn., Aug. 12, 1949; s. Vincent and Rose Bianco; m. Mary Ellen Stoltz, Jan. 2, 1983; children: Anna Rose, Maria Louisa. BE in Chem. Engring., Pratt U., 1971; JD, Columbia U., 1974. Bar: N.Y. 1975, U.S. Dist. Ct. (so. dist.) 1976, U.S. Ct. Appeals (2d cir.) 1977. Assoc. Chadbourne & Park, N.Y.C., 1974-79; v.p., assoc. gen. counsel Booz Allen & Hamilton Inc., N.Y.C., 1979—; dir. Profl. Cons. Ins. Co., Burlington, Vt., 1994—. With U.S. Army, 1970-74. Mem. N.Y. Athletic Club. General practice, Contracts commercial, Labor. Home: 25 E 86th St New York NY 10028-0553 Office: Booz Allen & Hamilton Inc 101 Park Ave Fl 21 New York NY 10178-0053

**BIAS, DANA G.,** lawyer; b. Lexington, Ky., Mar. 12, 1959; d. Cyrus Dana and Betty Jo (Haddox) B. BA with highest honors, U. Louisville, 1981; JD magna cum laude, Boston U., 1984. Bar: Mass. 1985, N.Y. 1985, U.S. Dist. Ct. (so. and ea. dists.) N.Y. 1986, Ky. 1995. Counselor Mass. Half-Way Houses, Inc., Boston, 1982-83; sr. trial atty. Criminal Def. div. Legal Aid Soc., N.Y.C., 1984-89, mng. atty., 1989-94; sole practitioner Hauppauge, N.Y., 1995; sr. trial atty. Louisville-Jefferson County Pub. Defender Corp., 1995-97; asst. public advocate, capital trial atty. Dept. of Public Advocacy, 1997—; lectr. N.Y.C. Pub. Schs., 1989. Contbr. articles to profl. jours. Mem. ABA, ACLU, N.Y. State Bar Assn., Nat. Assn. Criminal Def. Lawyers, Mass. Bar Assn., Ky. Bar Assn., N.Y. Civil Liberties Union, Woodcock Soc., Mortar Bd., Phi Kappa Phi, Phi Eta Sigma. Democrat. Criminal, Constitutional, Civil rights. Office: Dept Public Advocacy Capital Trial Unit 100 Fair Oaks Ln Ste 302 Frankfort KY 40601-1108

**BIBERAJ, BUTA,** lawyer; b. Plav, Yugoslavia, June 25, 1964; came to U.S., 1967; d. Hisen and Ajshe Biberaj. JD, George Mason U., 1993. Bar: N.Y., Md., Va., U.S. Dist. Ct. (ea. dist.) Va., U.S. Ct. Appeals (4th cir.), U.S. Supreme Ct. Law clk. Alexandria (Va.) Pub. Defender's Office, 1992-93; front end mgr. Price Club, Fairfax, Va., 1987-95; mem. Biberaj & O'Reilly, P.L.C., Leesburg, Va., 1994-96; ptnr. Biberaj & Assocs., P.C., Leesburg, Va., 1997—. Avocations: sports, reading. Criminal, Family and matrimonial, General practice. Office: Biberaj & Assocs PC 19 E Market St Leesburg VA 20176-3001

**BIBUS, THOMAS WILLIAM,** lawyer; b. Cin., July 13, 1949; s. Howard Fred and Ernestine G. (Bross) B.; children: Thomas Bradley, William Jason, Rebecca Lynn, Barbara Ann. BA in Econs., U. Cin., 1971; JD, Chase Coll. of Law, 1976. Bar: Ohio 1976, U.S. Dist. Ct. (so. dist.) Ohio 1976. Expediter, dispatch inspector ILSCO Corp., Cin., 1971-72; mgmt. trainee trust dept. Provident Bank, Cin., 1972-73; purchasing agent Cin. Butcher Supply Co., 1973-76; sole practice, Cin., 1976—. Mem. membership adv. panel Choicecare, Cin., 1983-87, past vice chmn.; profl. adviser Parents without Ptnrs, Cin., 1998-99 mem. dir., 1999—; founder, leader Coping with Separation; active Young Friends of Cin. Zoo, New Visions, Single Parent Ctr., also facilitator, mem. legal focus com.; bd dirs. Sunday Night Singles of Hyde Park Community United Meth. Ch., 1989; speaker coping with divorce program Hamilton County Domestic Rels. Ct. Mem. Cin. Bar Assn. (speakers bur., probate, estate planning, domestic relations, sole practice comm.), Cheviot Westwood Bus. Assn. (v.p., bd. dirs. 1987-89), Profls. Networking for Kids, Cin. Vegetarian Soc., West Side Lawyers (founder), Greater Cincinnati C. of C. (updowntowners div. of Downtown coun.), Sierra Club (Miami group, sub-chmn. family outings 1989-91), Mercedes Benz Club (sec. Cin. Dayton sect.), Ohio Bar Assn (named bd. govs. solo small firm sect.). Family and matrimonial, Bankruptcy, Probate. Office: 2962 Harrison Ave Cincinnati OH 45211-6724

**BICE, SCOTT HAAS,** dean, lawyer, educator; b. Los Angeles, Mar. 19, 1943; s. Fred Haas and Virginia M. (Scott) B.; m. Barbara Franks, Dec. 21, 1968. B.S., U. So. Calif., 1965, J.D., 1968. Bar: Calif. bar 1971. Law clk. to Chief Justice Earl Warren, 1968-69; successively asst. prof., assoc. prof., prof. law., Carl Mason Franklin prof. U. So. Calif., Los Angeles, 1969—; assoc. dean U. So. Calif., 1971-74, dean Law Sch., 1980—; vis. prof. polit. sci. Calif. Inst. Tech., 1977; vis. prof. U. Va., 1978-79; bd.dirs. Western Mut. Ins. Co., Residence Mut. Ins. Co., Imagine Films Entertainment Co., Jenny Craig, Inc. Mem. editl. adv. bd. Calif. Lawyer, 1989-93; contbr. articles to law jours. Bd. dirs. L.A. Family Housing Corp., 1989-93, Stone Soup Child Care Programs, 1988—. Affiliated scholar Am. Bar Found., 1972-74. Fellow Am. Bar Found. (life); mem. Am. Law Inst., Calif. Bar, Los Angeles County Bar Assn., Am. Law Deans Assn. (pres. 1997-99), Am. Judicature Soc., Calif. Club, Chancery Club, Long Beach Yacht Club. Home: 787 S San Rafael Ave Pasadena CA 91105-2326 Office: U So Calif Sch Law Los Angeles CA 90089-0071

**BICHLER, HOWARD JOSEPH,** lawyer, educator; b. Port Washington, Wis., July 6, 1951; s. Joseph W. and Delores M. (Binsfield) B.; m. Lydia M. Vitort, June 9, 1984; 1 child, Seth Joseph. BA in English and Polit. Sci., U. Wis., 1973; JD, Marquette U., 1976. Bar: Wis. Atty., planner Southeastern Wis. Regional Planning Commn., Waukesha, 1976-79; staff atty. Wis. Judicare, Wausau, Wis., 1979-85; gen. consel St. Croix Chippewa Indians of Wis., Hertel, 1985—; assoc. lectr. U. Wis., Eau Claire, 1990—, U. Wis. Barron County, Rice Lake, Wis., 1991—. Chmn. Burnett County Hist. Soc., Siren, Wis., 1992-94; mem. com. Wis. legis. study com. Fed. Tax Exempt Lands, Madison, 1996—; asst. scoutmaster Troop 28, Boy Scouts Am., Rice Lake, 1996—. Recipient Ann. Svc. award Gt. Lakes Intertribal Coun., 1996. Mem. State Bar of Wis. (chair Indian law sect. 1996—). Roman Catholic. Avocations: hunting, fishing, cross-country skiing. Native American. Home: 1843 23rd Ave Rice Lake WI 54868-9114

**BICK, ROBERT STEVEN,** lawyer; b. N.Y.C., Apr. 11, 1961; s. Daniel Marvin and Marilyn (Tankus) B. BBA with distinction, U. Mich., 1983, JD, 1986. Bar: Mich. 1986, U.S. Dist. Ct. (ea. dist.) Mich. 1986. Law clk. 45-B Dist. Ct. Mich., Oak Park, 1979; intern Nat. Law Ctr., Washington, 1980; summer assoc. Vandeveer, Garzia, Tonkin, Kerr, Heaphy, Moore, Sills & Poling, P.C., Detroit, 1984, Dykema Gossett, Detroit, 1985; assoc. Schlussel, Lifton, Simon, Rands, Galvin & Jackier, P.C., Southfield, Mich., 1986-88; assoc. Williams, Schaefer, Ruby & Williams, Birmingham, Mich., 1988-92, ptnr., 1992—. Intern Nat. Park Service Student Conservation Assn., Inc., Yosemite Nat. Park, 1979. Mem. ABA, Am. Arbitration Assn. (arbitrator 1991—), Fed. Bar Assn., Oakland County Bar Assn. (bus. law com. 1988—, continuing legal edn. com. 1989-91), Nat. Assn. Securities Dealers Assn., Inc. (arbitrator 1989—), Nat. Futures Assn. (arbitrator 1990—), Golden Key Hornor Soc. (life), FMA Honor Soc. of the Fin. Mgmt. Assn. (life, U. Mich. chpt.). Democrat. Avocations: golf, skiing. General corporate, Securities, Mergers and acquisitions. Home: 31700 Briarcliff Rd Franklin MI 48025-1273 Office: Williams Williams Ruby & Plunkett PC 380 N Old Woodward Ave Ste 300 Birmingham MI 48009-5322

**BICKEL, DAVID ROBERT,** lawyer; b. Pawnee City, Nebr., Feb. 8, 1944; s. Myron Overton and Jane (Sawyer) B.; m. Nancy Marshall Robinson, Jan. 10, 1981; children: Alexandra, Maria, Nancy Marshall. AB, U. N.C., 1967; JD, U. Houston, 1972; LLM in Taxation, Georgetown U., 1977; EFM, U. South (Sewanee), 1990. Bar: Tex. 1972, D.C. 1985, U.S. Dist. Ct. (no. and so. dists.) Tex., U.S Ct. Appeals (5th cir.). Sr. trial atty. antitrust div. Dept. Justice, Washington, 1972-78; asst. U.S. atty. U.S. Dist. Ct. (no. dist.) Tex., Dallas, 1978-81; assoc. Locke, Purnell, Dallas, 1982-83; of counsel Colton & Boykin, Washington, 1985-89; exec. v.p., gen. counsel Exec. Plans Corp., Washington, 1989-95; sr. trial atty. U.S. Dept. of Justice Anti-trust, 1995—. Contbr. articles to profl. jours. Coordinator Houston Shakespeare Soc., 1972. With USMCR, 1963-69. Mem. ABA, D.C. Bar Assn., Tex. Bar Assn., Antitrust Div. Profl. Assn. (pres. 1977-78), Chevy Chase Club, Met. Club, City Tavern Club, Phi Gamma Delta. Taxation, general, Insurance, Antitrust. Home: 7703 Chatham Rd Chevy Chase MD 20815-5052 Office: 1401 H St NW Ste 3000 Washington DC 20005-2110

**BICKEL, JOHN W., II,** lawyer; b. Champaign, Ill., Sept. 9, 1948; s. John William and Virginia Bickel; children: Hannah, Molly, Sarah. BS, U.S. Mil. Acad., 1970; JD, So. Meth. U., 1976. Bar: N.Y. 1988, Tex. 1976, U.S. Ct. Appeals (5th and 11th cirs.) 1980, U.S. Supreme Ct. 1983. Assoc. Thompson & Knight, Dallas, 1980-83; ptnr. Brown, Thomas, Karger & Bickel, Dallas, 1983-84; co-mng., co-founder, ptnr. Bickel & Brewer, Dallas, 1984—; co-founding ptnr. Bickel & Brewer Storefront, PLLC, Dallas; adv. mem. Tex. Supreme Ct. Jury Charge Task Force, 1992; mem. com. for qualified judiciary. Mem. exec. bd. So. Meth. U. Sch. Law; mem. Hiram A. Boaz Soc. So. Meth. U.; mem. Tex. Com.: A Time to Lead--The Campaign for So. Meth. U.; mem. adv. com. Southwestern Ball, 1997—. Fellow Tex. Bar Found., Dallas Bar Found. (sustaining life); mem. ABA, State Bar Tex. (past chmn. litigation com. of environ. and natural resource law sect.), N.Y. Bar Assn., Dallas Bar Assn., Markey/Wigmore Inns of Ct. (Chgo. chpt.), West Point Assn. Grads. (trustee 1997-98, 99—, mem. strategic planning com. 1997—), West Point Soc. North Tex. (bd. dirs.). Federal civil litigation, General civil litigation, State civil litigation. Office: Bickel & Brewer 4800 Bank One Ctr 1717 Main St Ste 4800 Dallas TX 75201-4651

**BICKERMAN, PETER BRUCE,** lawyer; b. Flushing, N.Y., May 10, 1952; s. Hylan A. and Evelyn (Apogi) B.; m. Karen D. Levesque, Sept. 5, 1981; children: Joshua M., Kalyn E. BA, Union Coll., Schenectady, 1973; JD, NYU, 1976. Bar: Maine 1977, U.S. Supreme Ct. 1981, U.S. Ct. Appeals (1st cir.) 1989, U.S. Dist. Ct. Maine 1977. Staff atty. State Maine, Dept. Atty. Gen., Augusta, 1977; asst. atty. gen. State Maine, Dept. Atty. Gen., 1977-87; atty., shareholder Lipman & Katz, Augusta, 1987-95; sole practice Augusta, 1995-99; counsel Verrill & Dana, LLP, Augusta, 1999—; adv. com. Maine Rules of Civil Procedure, 1991—. Bd. dirs. Pine Tree Legal Assistance, 1998—, Maine Civil Liberties Union, 1999—. Mem. Maine Bar Assn., Maine Trial Lawyers Assn. General civil litigation, Administrative and regulatory, Federal civil litigation. Office: Verrill & Dana LLP 45 Memorial Cir Ste 4 Augusta ME 04330-6430

**BICKFORD, NATHANIEL JUDSON,** lawyer; b. N.Y.C., Jan. 6, 1940; s. Albert Conde and Esther (Horan) B.; m. Jewelle Ann Wooten, Feb. 1, 1962; children—Laura Conde, Emily Allen Lansbury. A.B., Harvard U., 1961;

LL.B., Columbia U., 1964. Bar: N.Y., 1964. Assoc. Cahill, Gordon & Reindel, N.Y.C., 1964-70; ptnr. Lankenau, Kovner & Bickford, N.Y.C., 1970-92; ptnr. Lane & Mittendorf, N.Y.C., 1993—; dir. various corps. and investment groups. Mem. ABA, N.Y. State Bar Assn., N.Y.C. Bar Assn., Fed. Bar Council. Democrat. Episcopalian. Clubs: Century Assn., Knickerbocker (N.Y.C.), River. General corporate, Finance, Private international. Office: Lane & Mittendorf 320 Park Ave Fl 10 New York NY 10022-6815

**BICKS, PETER ANDREWS,** lawyer; b. Washington, Dec. 5, 1959; s. Robert Alan and Patricia (Hughes) B.; m. Linda Danovitch, Nov. 16, 1997; 1 child, Avery Andrews. BA, Pomona Coll., 1982; LLB, Georgetown U., 1986. Bar: N.Y. 1987, U.S. Dist. Ct. (so. dist.) N.Y. 1990, U.S. Dist. Ct. (ea. dist.) N.Y. 1993, U.S. Dist. Ct. Ariz. 1994, U.S. Ct. Appeals (2nd cir.) 1998. Asst. press sec. John Anderson Presdl. Campaign, Washington, 1980; lead advance person Mayor Ed Koch, N.Y.C., 1981-82; mgmt. analyst N.Y.C. (N.Y.) Dept. Sanitation, 1982-83; ptnr. Donovan Leisure Newton Irvine, N.Y.C., 1995-98, Orrick, Herrington & Sutcliffe, LLP, N.Y.C., 1998—. Pres. 175 E. 73d St. Corp., N.Y.C., 1987-97. Mem. ABA, N.Y. State Bar Assn., Seawanhaka Corinthian Yacht Club, Castine Golf Club. Republican. Avocations: sailing, tennis, golf. Fax: 212-506-5151. E-mail: pbicks@orrick.com. General civil litigation, Securities, Entertainment. Home: 1150 5th Ave Apt 6C New York NY 10128-0724 Office: Orrick Herrington & Sutcliffe LLP 666 5th Ave Rm 203 New York NY 10103-1798

**BIDOL, JAMES ALEXANDER,** lawyer; b. Jackson, Mich., Feb. 24, 1944; s. Alexander and Helen Harriet Bidol; m. Margaret Elma Davison; children: Jonathon S., Molly J., Oliver J. AA, Jackson Jr. Coll., 1964; BA, U. Mich., 1966, JD, 1969. Bar: Mich. 1969, U.S. Dist. Ct. (we. dist.) Mich. 1970. Assoc. Lokker Boter & Dalman, Holland, Mich., 1969-70, Boter Dalman & Murphy P.C., Holland, 1970-74; ptnr. Boter Dalman Murphy & Bidol P.C., Holland, 1974-90, Cunningham Dalman P.C., Holland, 1990—. Bd. dirs. Holland Cmty. Action House, 1991-96. Fellow Mich. State Bar Found.; mem. Holland Lions Club (pres. 1977-78). Avocations: Michigan history, tennis, racketball, travel. Fax: 616-396-7106. E-mail: cunndalm@crossover.net. Personal injury, Federal civil litigation, State civil litigation. Home: 16632 James St Holland MI 49424-6045

**BIDWELL, JAMES TRUMAN, JR.,** lawyer; b. N.Y.C., Jan. 2, 1934; s. James Truman and Mary (Kane) B.; m. Gail S. Bidwell, Mar. 6, 1965 (div.); children: Hillary Day Bidwell Mackay, Kimberley Wade, Cortney E.; m. Katherine T. O'Neil, July 15, 1988. BA, Yale U., 1956; LLB, Harvard U., 1959. Bar: N.Y. 1959. Atty. USAF, Austin, Tex., 1959-62; assoc. Donovan, Leisure, Newton & Irvine, N.Y.C., 1962-68, ptnr., 1968-84; ptnr. White & Case, N.Y.C., 1984-98; sr. counsel Linklaters & Paines, N.Y.C., 1998—. Pres. Youth Consultation Svc., 1973-78; trustee Berkeley Divinity Sch. Mem. ABA, Fed. Bar Assn., N.Y. State Bar Assn., N.Y. County Lawyers Assn. Episcopalian. General corporate, Private international, Contracts commercial. Office: Linklaters & Paines 1345 Avenue Of The Americas New York NY 10105-0302

**BIDWELL, MARK EDWARD,** lawyer; b. Atlanta, Oct. 30, 1956; s. donald Wellwood and Carmen Edilia Bidwell. BS in Mgmt., Syracuse U., 1982, MBA in fin., 1989, JD cum laude, 1989. Bar: Mass. 1989, N.Y. 1990, U.S. Dist. Ct. (no. dist.) N.Y. 1990. Salesman Cadillac, Olds, Toyota, Ithaca, N.Y., 1979; sys. analyst Gen. Electric, Stamford, Conn., 1983-85; assoc. Menter Law Office, Syracuse, N.Y., 1988-91; sole practitioner Bidwell Law Office, Syracuse, 1991—. Mem. ABA, N.Y. Bar Assn. Avocations: teaching skiing, teaching water skiing. Bankruptcy, Family and matrimonial, General practice. Home: 8011 Falls Rd Trumansburg NY 14886-9127 Office: 60 Presidential Plz Syracuse NY 13202-2292

**BIEBEL, PAUL PHILIP, JR.,** lawyer; b. Chgo., Mar. 24, 1942; s. Paul Philip Sr. and Eleanor Mary (Sweeney) B.; divorced; children: Christine M., Brian E., Jennifer A., Susan E. AB, Marquette U., 1964; JD, Georgetown U., 1967. Bar: Ill. 1967, U.S. Dist. Ct. (no. dist.) Ill. 1967, U.S. Ct. Appeals (6th cir.) 1985, U.S. Supreme Ct. 1972. Asst. dean of men Loyola U., Chgo., 1967-69; asst. state's atty. Cook County State's Atty., Chgo., 1969-75, dep. state's atty., 1975-81; 1st asst. atty. gen. Ill. Atty. Gen., Chgo., 1981-85; pub. defender Cook County Pub. Defender, Chgo., 1986-88; ptnr. Winston & Strawn, Chgo., 1985-86, 88-94, Altheimer & Gray, Chgo., 1994-96; judge Cir. Ct. Cook County, Ill., 1996—. Contbr. articles to profl. publs. Mem. Fed. Bar Assn. (bd. dirs. 1988—, pres. 1994-95), Cath. Lawyers Guild (bd. dirs. 1988—, Cath. Lawyer of Yr. 1988), Ill. Appellate Lawyers, 7th Cir. Bar Assn., Chgo. Bar Assn. (chmn. com. 1991-93), Georgetown Law Alumni Assn. (bd. dirs. 1991-96). Roman Catholic. Avocations: reading, golf. State civil litigation. Home: 5415 N Forest Glen Ave Chicago IL 60630-1523 Office: Cir Ct Cook County Child Protection Divsn 1100 S Hamilton Ave Chicago IL 60612-4207

**BIEBELBERG, KEITH N.,** lawyer; b. Newark, Feb. 29, 1960; s. Les and Roselyn B.; m. Tracy L. Biebelberg, Sept. 14, 1997. Law clk. to Hon. Alfred M. Wolin Judge Superior Ct. N.J., Elizabeth, 1983-84; ptnr. Biebelberg & Martin, Millburn, N.J.; master Joseph Halpern Inn of Ct., Somerset, N.J., 1997—. Mem. N.J. State Bar Assn., Assn. Criminal Def. Lawyers N.J. Federal civil litigation, State civil litigation, Criminal. Office: Biebelberg & Martin 374 Millburn Ave Millburn NJ 07041-1343

**BIEDERMAN, DONALD ELLIS,** lawyer; b. N.Y.C., Aug. 23, 1934; s. William and Sophye (Groll) B.; m. Marna M. Leerburger, Dec. 22, 1962; children: Charles Jefferson, Melissa Anne. AB, Cornell U., 1955; JD, Harvard U., 1958; LLM in Taxation, NYU, 1970. Bar: N.Y. 1959, U.S. Dist. Ct. (so. dist.) N.Y. 1967, Calif. 1977. Assoc. Hale, Russell & Stentzel, N.Y.C., 1962-66; asst. corp. counsel City of N.Y., 1966-68; assoc. Delson & Gordon, N.Y.C., 1968-69; ptnr. Roe, Carman, Clerke, Berkman & Berkman, Jamaica, N.Y., 1969-72; gen. atty. CBS Records, N.Y.C., 1972-76; sr. v.p. legal affairs and adminstrn. ABC Records, L.A., 1977-79; ptnr. Mitchell, Silberberg & Knupp, L.A., 1979-83; exec. v.p., gen. counsel Warner/Chappell Music Inc. (formerly Warner Bros. Music), L.A., 1983—; adj. prof. Sch. Law Southwestern U., L.A., 1982—, Pepperdine U., Malibu, Calif., 1985-87, Loyola Marymount U., L.A., 1992; lectr. Anderson Sch. Mgmt. UCLA, 1993, U. So. Calif. Law Ctr., 1995-97. Editor: Legal and Business Problems of the Music Industry, 1980; co-author: Law and Business of the Entertainment Industries, 1987, 2nd edit., 1991, 3d edit., 1995. Bd. dirs. Calif. Chamber Symphony Soc., L.A., 1981-92; dir. Entertainment Law Inst. U. So. Calif., 1993—. 1st lt. U.S. Army, 1959. Recipient Hon. Gold Record, Recording Industry Assn. Am., 1974, Trendsetter award Billboard mag., 1976, Gold Triangle award Am. Acad. Dermatology, 1999. Mem. N.Y. Bar Assn., Calif. Bar Assn., Riviera Country Club, Cornell Club. Democrat. Jewish. Avocations: golf, skiing, travel, reading. Entertainment, Intellectual property. Home: 2406 Pesquera Dr Los Angeles CA 90049-1225 Office: Warner/Chappell Music Inc 10585 Santa Monica Blvd Los Angeles CA 90025-4921

**BIEHL, KATHY ANNE,** lawyer; b. Pitts., Jan. 27, 1956; d. Edward Robert and Julianne (Addis) B. BA with highest honors, So. Meth. U., 1976; JD with honors, U. Tex., 1979. Bar: Tex. 1979, U.S. Dist. Ct. (so. dist.) Tex. 1986, U.S. Ct. Appeals (5th cir.) 1986. Assoc. Schlanger, Cook, Cohn, Mills & Grossberg, Houston, 1979-82; sole practice Houston, 1982-98; lectr. Rice U., Houston, 1982; adj prof. U. Houston, 1988; owner, mgr. Metaphysiques Tapes, Houston, 1988—; co-owner, mgr. Mantic Door Music, Houston, 1992-97. Contbr. articles to profl. jours. Vol. Tex. Accts. and Lawyers for Arts, Houston, 1981-98, Orange Show Found., Houston, 1985-98. Mem. Tex. Bar Assn., Phi Beta Kappa. Democrat. Mem. Unitarian Ch. General practice, Probate, General corporate. Office: PO Box 313194 Jamaica NY 11431-3194

**BIELASKA, MARY GERALDINE,** lawyer, entertainment company executive; b. Derby, Conn., Sept. 18, 1958; d. Edward Thaddeus Bielaska and Carol Louise (Biggs) Starkey. BA in English, Legal Studies summa cum laude, Quinnipiac Coll., 1980; JD, Fordham U., 1985. Bar: N.Y. 1985, U.S. Dist. Ct. (so. and ea. dist.) N.Y. 1994. Legal asst. Wiggin & Dana, New Haven, Conn., 1978-82, Am. Elec. Power Svc. Corp., N.Y.C., 1983; assoc. Hawkins, Delafield & Wood, N.Y.C., 1985-87, Dewey Ballantine, N.Y.C., 1987-95; CEO Zanicorn Entertainment, Ltd., N.Y.C., 1995—; speaker Investment Mgmt. Inst. Seminar on Corp. Governance, N.Y.C., 1994. Assoc. editor Urban Law Jour., Fordham U., N.Y.C., 1984-85. Mem. ABA (bus. law sect. com. on partnerships, unincorp. assns. 1986—, com. on devels. in bus. planning, 1993-94), N.Y. State Bar Assn., N.Y. County Lawyers Assn., Assn. of Bar of City of N.Y. (interdisciplinary com. to rev. the proposed uniform limited liability company act 1993-96, corp. law com. 1992-96, chair subcom. rev. uniform partnership act 1992-96, subcom. limited liability company act 1992-96), Fin. Women's Assn. of N.Y., Inc. (bd. dirs. 1993-95, entrepreneurs com., co-chair ann. entrepreneurs dinner 1994), Nat. Women's Econ. Alliance Found. (dirs. resource coun. 1994-95). Democrat. Roman Catholic. Avocations: auto racing, skiing, scuba diving, horseback riding. Home: 240 W 73rd St Apt 1410 New York NY 10023-2798 Office: Zanicorn Entertainment Ltd 355 W 52nd St Fl 6 New York NY 10019-6239

**BIELE, HUGH IRVING,** lawyer; b. Bridgeport, Conn., July 28, 1942; s. Ray James and Blanche (McClellan) B.; m. Pamela Althea Johnson, Aug. 21, 1965 (div.); children: Jonathan Christopher, Melissa Lynne. BA, St. Lawrence U., Canton, N.Y., 1965; JD, U. Utah, 1968. Bar: Utah 1968, U.S. Dist. Ct. Utah 1968, Calif. 1972, U.S. Dist. Ct. Calif. 1972, U.S. Ct. Appeals (9th and 10th cirs.). Instr. San Francisco Law Sch., 1971-73; atty. United Calif. Bank, San Francisco, 1971-74; v.p., sr. counsel First Interstate Bank, L.A., 1974-81; ptnr. Biele & Stuehrmann, L.A., 1981-83; sr. ptnr. Biele, Stuehrmann & Lapinski, L.A., 1983-84; founding ptnr. Biele & Lapinski, L.A., 1985-89; ptnr. Barton, Klugman & Detting, L.A., 1989-91; ptnr., dir. comml. law and litigation Grace, Skocypec, Cosgrove & Schirm, L.A., 1992-95; bd. govs. Fin. Lawyer Conf., L.A., 1976—, pres. 1984-85, original developer, ptnr. Engine Co. No. 28 rehabilitation, 1982—, ptnr. Engine Co. No. 28 Restaurant, 1988—, owner Biele Enterprises, bd. dirs. Vege-Kurl, Inc., 1990—. Author screenplay: Corporate Cancer, 1989, Hedge of Thorns, 1990. Bd. dirs. Community Counseling Svc., L.A., 1989—, pres., 1993-95, chmn. bd. dirs., 1995—; bd. dirs. Casa de Rosa and the Sunshine Mission, 1997—; bd. dirs., v.p., sec. Project New Hope, Inc., L.A., 1990-92; commr. Episc. Diocese AIDS Ministry, L.A., 1988-93; chmn. Vols. in Parole, L.A., 1979-80, 89-90, Lawyers for Human Rights, 1988—, co-pres. elect, 1999. Maj. U.S. Army, 1968-70. Decorated Bronze Star with oak leaf cluster, Army Commendation medal. Mem. ABA, Fed. Bar Assn., Internat. Bar Assn., L.A. County Bar Assn. (internat. sect. exec. com. 1978-97, chmn. 1981-82, exec. com. comml. law and bankruptcy sect. 1986—, chair 1992-93), Calif. State Bar (fin. inst. com.), Internat. Bankers Assn. Calif., St. Lawrence U. Alumni Assn. (pres. 1979-91). Republican. Episcopalian. Avocations: skiing, jogging, aerobics, travel. Banking, Contracts commercial, Bankruptcy. Home and Office: 3016 Hollycrest Dr Los Angeles CA 90068-1802

**BIELENBERG, LEONARD HERMAN,** lawyer; b. Genesee, Idaho, July 14, 1927; s. Herman Christian and Rosella Elizabeth (Roth) B.; m. Alta Fern Claney, Oct. 31, 1953; children: Terry, Anne, Paul, Mary. BS in Bus., U. Idaho, 1950, JD, 1952. Bar: Idaho 1952, U.S. Dist. Ct. Idaho 1952. Asst. atty. gen. State of Idaho, Boise, 1952-54; ptnr. Felton & Bielenberg, Moscow, Idaho, 1954-69; pros. atty. Latah County, Moscow, 1961-67; sr. ptnr. Felton, Bielenberg & Anderson, Moscow, 1969-73, Bielenberg & Anderson, Moscow, 1973-75, Bielenberg, Anderson & Walker, Moscow, 1975-97; ret., 1998; lectr. U. Idaho Law Sch., Moscow, 1960-67. Pres. Moscow Jaycees, 1958-59; bd. dirs. Moscow Hosp. Assn., 1970-82. With USNR, 1945-46, PTO. Recipient Disting. Service award Moscow Jaycees, 1957. Mem. Idaho State Bar, Latah County Bar Assn. (exec. sec. 1964), Clearwater Bar Assn., Moscow C. of C. (bd. dirs. 1958-59), Lions (pres. Moscow 1971-72), K.C. (grand knight 1957-58), Elks, Moose. Republican. Roman Catholic. Avocations: snow and water skiing, fishing, motorcycling. Estate planning, Probate, Estate taxation. Home: 1039 Virginia Ave Moscow ID 83843-9455

**BIELORY, ABRAHAM MELVIN,** lawyer, financial executive; b. Modena, Italy, Sept. 20, 1946; came to U.S., 1948; s. Motel and Basia (Spielberg) B.; m. Beverly B. Berkowitz, Jan. 26, 1969; children: Jennifer Rebecca, Debra Elizabeth, David Ethan. BS, N.J. Inst. Tech., 1968; JD, U. Denver, 1973. Bar: N.J. 1974, U.S. Dist. Ct. N.J. 1974, U.S. Supreme Ct. 1979. Field engr. Control Data Corp., Mpls., 1968-69; assoc. Paschon & Feurey, Toms River, N.J., 1973-77, ptnr., 1978; ptnr. VanSicle & Bielory, Toms River, 1978-88, Babcock, Hennes & Bielory, P.C., Bricktown and Toms River, N.J., 1989-96; owner ABEV Fin. Svc., Lakewood, 1976—; ptnr. Bielory & Hennes, PC, Bricktown, Toms River, 1996—. V.p. Lakewood Hebrew Day Sch., N.J., 1975-82, pres., 1982-86; trustee Hillel High Sch., Deal, N.J., 1983—; v.p. Congregation Sons of Israel, Lakewood, 1984-86, pres. 1986-88. Sgt. USAF, 1969-73. Fellow ABA; mem. ATLA, N.J. State Bar Assn., Trial Atty. N.J., Ocean County Bd. Realtors, Women's Coun. of Realtors (assoc.), Ocean County Bar Assn. (chmn. ins. com. 1975), Hudson County Bar Assn. (sr. citizen com. 1984), Internat. Lawyers Assn., Jewish War Vets. Republican. Consumer commercial, Real property, Probate. Home: 1422 14th St Lakewood NJ 08701-1504

**BIELUCH, WILLIAM CHARLES,** judge; b. Hartford, Conn., Nov. 12, 1918; s. Joseph and Catherine (Galazka) B.; m. Nellie Sidor, July 4, 1942 (dec. Dec. 1982); children: William Charles Jr., Virginia M., Philip J.; m. Pauline O'Connor, Nov. 25, 1983. AB magna cum laude, Brown U., 1939; JD, Yale U., 1942. Bar: Conn. 1942. Assoc. Covington, Burling, Rublee, Acheson & Shorb, Washington, 1942-43; ptnr. Bieluch, Barry & Ramenda and predecessors, Hartford, 1946-68; judge Cir. Ct. Conn., 1968-73, Ct. Common Pleas Conn., 1973-76; judge Superior Ct. Conn., 1976-85, Appellate Session, 1979-83, Appellate Ct. Conn., 1985-88, ret. 1988; judge trial referee, 1988—. Trustee emeritus S. S. Cyril and Methodius Roman Catholic Ch., Hartford; corporator St. Francis Hosp. and Med. Ctr., Hartford. Served to lt. (j.g.) USCG, World War II. Decorated Knight St. Gregory (Pope Paul VI); recipient Merit award Polish Legion Am. Vets., 1952, Man of Yr. award United Polish Socs., 1968, Archdiocesan medal of appreciation Archbishop John F. Whealon, 1970, Disting. Grad. award Nat. Cath. Elem. Sch., 1995. Mem. Conn. Bar Assn. (chmn. Jr. Bar Sect. 1948-49), Hartford County Bar Assn., KC, Phi Beta Kappa. Republican. Office: 95 Washington St Hartford CT 06106-4406 *The achievements of life are but the prelude to success.*

**BIEN, ELLIOT LEWIS,** lawyer; b. N.Y.C., Dec. 26, 1945; s. Morris and Ruth B.; m. B. Anne Zishka, Oct. 12, 1974; children: Jordan, Adam. AB, Columbia Coll., N.Y.C., 1967, JD, 1971; LLM, Harvard, Cambridge, 1972. Bar: Mass. 1971, Ill. 1975, U.S. Supreme Ct. 1978, Calif. 1979. Asst. prof. DePaul Sch. Law, Chgo., 1972-75; assoc. Friedman & Koven, Chgo., 1976-79, Cullinan & Brown, San Francisco, 1980-81; assoc., ptnr. Bronson, Bronson, & McKinnon, San Francisco, 1982-90; ptnr. Bien & Summers, San Francisco, Novato, 1990—; legal counsel Ill. Gov.'s Commn. to Revise Mental Health Codes., 1973. Contbr. articles to profl. jours. Nat. commr. Anti-Defamation League, N.Y.C., 1990-96; trustee Larkspur Sch. Bd., Larkspur, Calif., 1991-92. Recipient Award of Merit Bar Assn. San Francisco, 1989. Fellow Am. Acad. Appellate Lawyers; mem. Calif. Acad. Appellate Lawyers, Marin County Bar Assn. Appellate. Office: Bien & Summers LLP PO Box 2626 Novato CA 94948-2626

**BIENVENU, JOHN CHARLES,** lawyer; b. Modesto, Calif., Sept. 11, 1957; s. Robert Charles and Martha Louise (Beard) B.; m. Sarah Luciene Brick, May 10, 1983; children: Reed Charles, Loren John. Student, U. Calif., Berkeley, 1975-78; BA summa cum laude, U. N.Mex., 1985; JD with distinction, Stanford U., 1988. Bar: Calif., 1988, N.Mex., 1990; U.S. Ct. Appeals (9th cir.) 1988, U.S. Ct. Appeals (10th cir.) 1990; U.S. Ct. Fed. Claims, 1991. Assoc. Brobeck, Phleger & Harrison, San Francisco, 1988-90, Rothstein, Walther, Donatelli, Hughes, Dahlstrom & Cron, Santa Fe, N.Mex., 1990-93; prin. Santa Fe, 1993—. Mem. N.Mex. State Bar (legal svcs. com.), Am. Trial Lawyers Assn., ACLU (cooperating atty. N.Mex.). Democrat. General civil litigation, Civil rights. Home: 1580 Cerro Gordo Rd Santa Fe NM 87501-6143 Office: PO Box 2455 310 Mckenzie St Santa Fe NM 87501-1883

**BIERCE, JAMES MALCOLM,** retired judge; b. Columbus, Ohio, July 5, 1931; s. Bruce Wallace and Glyde Vivian (Brown) B.; m. Frances Marilyn Ruth, June 19, 1953 (div. Sept. 1963); children—James M., Teresa Anne; m. 2d, Fern C., July 22, 1967. LL.B., U. Akron, 1963. Bar: Ohio 1965, Mich. 1971, U.S. Dist. Ct. (no. dist.) Ohio 1969, U.S. Ct. Appeals (6th cir.) 1966, U.S. Supreme Ct. 1972. Employment officer Trans World Airlines, Kansas City, Mo., 1955-58; asst. dir. law City of Cuyahoga Falls (Ohio), 1966-68; sr. mng. ptnr. Bierce, Holland, Manning, Metz & Wilson, Akron, 1968-77; judge Cuyahoga Falls Mcpl. Ct., 1977-95; instr. Ohio Jud. Coll., 1979-95; faculty adviser Nat. Jud. Coll., 1983—; chmn. mentor com. Ohio Jud. Conf., 1992—, vice chmn. ret. judges com., 1996-97. Bd. dirs. Am. Diabetes Assn., 1982-83; pres. Cuyahoga Valley Community Mental Health Center, 1983-85, Cuyahoga Falls Fraternal Order of Police Assn., 1977; trustee Cuyahoga Falls Sch. Found., 1985-86; pres. Akron Crime Clinic, 1993. With USNR, 1953-57. Mem. ABA, Ohio Bar Assn., Akron Bar Assn., Am. Judges Assn., Am. Judicature Assn., Akron Area Mcpl. Judges Assn. (pres. 1982-84), Am. Diabetes Assn., Lions, Phi Alpha Delta (officer 1969-78, named Outstanding Alumni 1985). Republican. Avocations: power boating, travel, computers.

**BIERLEY, JOHN CHARLES,** lawyer; b. Portsmouth, Ohio, Oct. 12, 1936; s. C. Harold and Mildred R. (Turner) B.; m. Ruth Lykes Webb, Sept. 26, 1964; 1 son, John Charles. B.A., U. Fla., 1958, J.D. (Fla. Law Center Assn. scholar, Bigelow Meml. scholar Am. Legion), 1963. Bar: Fla. 1964, U.S. Dist. Ct. (mid. dist.) Fla., U.S. Ct. Appeals (11th cir.), U.S. Supreme Ct. Practiced in Tampa, 1964—; assoc. Fowler, White, Gillen, Humpkey & Trenam, Tampa, 1964-66; ptnr. Macfarlane, Ferguson, Allison & Kelly, Tampa, 1966-92, Macfarlane Ferguson & McMullen, Tampa, 1992-97, Smith Clark Delesie Bierley Mueller & Kadyk, Tampa, 1997—; pres. Internat. Cultural and Econ. Ctr., Inc., 1975-78; lectr. internat. studies U. South Fla., Tampa, 1964-72; adj. prof. Stetson Coll. Law, 1984; bd. dirs. Cayman Nat. Bank & Trust Co., Ltd., Bay Cities Bank, Caymanx Trust Co., Ltd.; chmn. Fla. Coun. Internat. Devel., 1974-75, 95-97, Fla. Gov.'s Conf. on World Trade, 1980, 85; pres. Tampa World Trade Coun., 1971-73; chmn. hurricane disaster com. ARC, 1968-71; dir. Tampa Bay Area Com. Fgn. Rels., 1971-91, chmn., 1991—; mem. Asian R & D Coun., State of Fla., 1986; trustee U. Fla. Law Ctr. Assn., 1981—; chmn. Southeast U.S./Japan Assn., 1991-93. Mem. external internat. adv. bd. U. Fla., 1992—; bd. dirs. Tampa Bay Rsch. Inst., U. Fla. Found., 1997—. Served to capt., USMCR, 1958-61. Recipient Fla. Blue Key award Fla. Hall of Fame, 1958; named Tampa Bay Internat. Bus. Person of Yr., 1990. Mem. ABA, Fla. Bar Assn. (chmn. internat. law com. 1972-74), Inter-Am. Bar Assn. (bd. dirs., silver medal 1983), Am. Soc. Internat. Law, Internat. Fiscal Assn., Coun. Fgn. Rels., Soc. Internat. Bus. Fellows (bd. dirs. 1987—), Internat. Bar Assn., Ye Mystic Krewe of Gasparilla, Univ. Club, Merrymakers Club, Phi Delta Phi, Kappa Sigma. Democrat. Presbyterian. Private international. Office: Smith Clark Delesie Bierley Mueller & Kadyk PO Box 2939 100 N Tampa St Ste 2120 Tampa FL 33602-5809

**BIERMACHER, KENNETH WAYNE,** lawyer; b. Hartford, Conn., Oct. 15, 1953; s. Donald David and Ethel Pearl (Biermacher) Lawton; m. Joan; children: Carl Joseph II (dec.), Matthew Robert, Michelle Renee; 1 step child Brent Cohen. BS summa cum laude, U. New Haven, 1976; JD with honors, Drake U., 1979. Bar: Iowa 1980, Tex. 1985, U.S. Dist. Ct. (so. dist.) Iowa 1980, U.S. Dist. Ct. (no. dist.) Iowa, 1981, U.S. Ct. Appeals (8th cir.) 1981, U.S. Supreme Ct. 1983, U.S. Dist. Ct. (no. dist.) Tex. 1984, U.S. Dist. Ct. (so. and we. dists.) Tex. 1985, U.S. Dist. Ct. (ea. dist.) Tex. 1993, U.S. Ct. Appeals (5th cir.) 1985. Assoc. Whitfield, Musgrave, Selvy, Kelly, Eddy, Des Moines, 1980-84; shareholder Geary, Stahl & Spencer, P.C., Dallas, 1984-89, Leonard Marsh Hurt Terry & Blinn, Dallas, 1989-90; ptnr.-in-charge Dallas office Small, Craig & Werkenthin, P.C., Dallas, 1990-93; v.p., ptnr., dir. Kane, Russell, Coleman & Logan, P.C., Dallas, 1993—; pres., dir. Frontrunner Capital Corp., Dallas, 1999—; lectr. Iowa Defense Counsel Assn. Annual Meeting, 1982, Des Moines Area Community Coll. Legal Asst. Program, 1981-82, Human Resources Forum, Am. Electronics Assn., Dallas, 1986; legal research asst. Iowa State Bar Assn. Com. on Study Fed. Rules Evidence, 1982; chmn. spl. com. on Friends of Moot Ct. Drake Law Sch. Bd. Counsellors, 1983-84. Contbg. author: Understanding Iowa Law, 1984; editor: Energy and Nat. Resources Guide for Iowa, 1979; contbr. articles to law jours. Adv. U. New Haven Law Enforcement Explorers Post Boy Scouts Am., 1975; coach Johnston Sr. High Sch. Mock Trial Teams, Iowa, 1984; del. Polk County Rep. Conv., Des Moines, 1980, Iowa Rep. State Conv., 1980; deacon Canyon Creek Bapt. Ch., 1986-87; chmn. scholarship and fin. aid com. Canyon Creek Christian Acad., 1985-87; trustee Boys and Girls Clubs of Greater Dallas, Inc., 1997—, chmn. circus com., 1998—, chmn. resource devel. com., 1999—; bd. dirs. Henry C. Lee Inst. Forensic Sci., 1996—. Recipient Acad. Scholarship U. New Haven, 1973-76; semi-finalist Midwest Regional Moot Ct. Competition, 1979. Mem. ABA (sub-com. on fraudulent and deceptive trade practices, sect. tort and ins. practice 1985-86, vol. atty. post-conviction death penalty representation project 1988-89), ATLA, FBA, Iowa State Bar Assn. (mem. Young Lawyer Sect. ethics com. 1981, law schs. panel com. 1982, law-related edn. com. 1983-84), Def. Rsch. Inst., Iowa Assn. Trial Lawyers (founding dir., chmn. Drake U. Law Sch. student bd. dirs. 1978-79, ex-officio mem. bd. dirs. 1978-79), Dallas Bar Assn. (mock trial com., law in changing soc. com. 1985, speech com. 1985-86, bus. litigation sect. ethic and courtesy com. 1988, qualified mediator 1989—, mem. cts. com. 1995, mem. fee dispute com. 1995), State Bar Tex. (legal assts. com. 1988-91), Dallas Assn. Young Lawyers (liaison with other profls., fed. opinions com. 1986), Order of Barristers, Atty.-Mediator Assn., Drake U. Law Sch. bd. counselors (regional v.p. for Tex. and Okla. 1986-89), Alpha Chi (vice chmn. Conn. chpt. 1975-76). E-mail: kbiermacher@krcl.com. Federal civil litigation, State civil litigation, Personal injury. Home: 4324 Hollow Oak Dr Dallas TX 75287-6847 Office: Kane Russell Coleman & Logan PC 1601 Elm St Ste 3700 Dallas TX 75201-4798

**BIERMAN, JAMES NORMAN,** lawyer; b. St. Louis, Nov. 23, 1945; s. Norman and Margaret (Loeb) B.; m. Catherine Best, Apr. 10, 1983; 1 child, James Norman. AB magna cum laude, Washington U., 1967; JD, Harvard Law Sch., 1970. Assoc. Hogan & Hartson, Washington, 1970-72; asst. dean Harvard Law Sch., Cambridge, Mass., 1973-75; assoc. Foley & Lardner, Washington, 1975-79, ptnr., 1979-85, ptnr. in charge, 1985—, mem. mgmt. com., 1989-98. Mng. editor Harvard Jour. Legis., 1969-70. Mem. Civil Rights Reviewing Authority HEW, Washington, 1979-80. Mem. ABA, Fed. Bar Assn., D.C. Bar Assn., Supreme Ct. Bar, Washington Lawyers Com. for Civil Rights and Urban Affairs (bd. dirs.), Phi Beta Kappa, Omicron Delta Kappa, Pi Sigma Alpha, Phi Eta Sigma, City Club (Washington). Administrative and regulatory, Private international, Mergers and acquisitions. Home: 906 Peacock Station Rd Mc Lean VA 22102-1021 Office: Foley & Lardner 3000 K St NW Fl 5 Washington DC 20007-5143

**BIERY, EVELYN HUDSON,** lawyer; b. Lawton, Okla., Oct. 12, 1946; d. William Ray and Nellie Iris (Nunley) Hudson. BA in English and Latin summa cum laude, Abilene (Tex.) Christian U., 1968; JD, So. Meth. U., 1973. Bar: Tex. 1973, U.S. Dist. Ct. (we. dist.) Tex. 1975, U.S. Dist. Ct. (so. dist.) Tex. 1977, U.S. Dist. Ct. (no. dist.) Tex. 1979, U.S. Ct. Appeals (5th cir.) 1979, U.S. Ct. Appeals (11th cir.) 1981, U.S. Supreme Ct. 1981. Atty. Law Offices of Bruce Waitz, San Antonio, 1973-76; mem. LeLaurin & Adams, PC, San Antonio, 1976-81; ptnr. Fulbright & Jaworski, San Antonio, 1981—, head bankruptcy, reorganization and creditors' rights sect., 1990—; policy com. Fulbright & Jaworski, San Antonio, 1996-98; speaker on creditors' rights, bankruptcy and reorganization law; lectr. Southwestern Grad. Sch. Banking, Dallas, 1980, La. State U. Sch. Banking, 1994; presiding officer, U. Tex. Sch. of Law Bankruptcy Conf., 1976, 94, State Bar Tex. Creditors' Rights Inst., 1985, State Bar Tex. Advanced Bus. Bankruptcy Law Inst., 1985, State Bar Tex. Inst. on Advising Officers, Dirs. and Ptnrs. in Troubled Bus., 1987, State Bar Tex. Advanced Creditors Rights Inst., 1988; pres. San Antonio Young Lawyers Assn., 1979-80; mem. bankruptcy adv. com. fifth cir. jud. coun., 1979-80; vice-chmn. bankruptcy com. Comml. Law League Am., 1981-83; mem. exec. bd. So. Meth. U. Sch. Law, 1983-91. Editor: Texas Collections Manual, 1978, Creditor's Rights in Texas, 2d edit., 1981; author: (with others) Collier Bankruptcy Practice Guide, 1993. Del. to U.S./Republic of China joint session on trade, investment and econ. law, Beijing, 1987; designated mem. Bankruptcy Judge Merit Screening Com. State of Tex. by Tex. State Bar Pres., 1979-82; patron McNay Mus., San Antonio; rsch. ptnr. Mind Sci. Found., San Antonio; diplomat World Affairs Coun., San Antonio. Recipient Outstanding Young Lawyer award San Antonio Young Lawyers Assn., 1979. Fellow Soc. of Internat. Bus. Fellow, Am. Coll. Bankruptcy Attys., Tex. Bar Found. (life), San Antonio Bar Found.; mem. Tex. Bar Assn. (chair bankruptcy com. 1982-83, chair corp., banking and bus. law sect. 1989-90), Tex. Assn. Bank Counsel (bd. dirs. 1988-90), San Antonio Young Lawyers Assn. (pres. 1979-80), Plaza Club San Antonio (bd. dirs. 1982—), Zonta (Chair Z club com. 1989-90), Order of Coif. Bankruptcy, Federal civil litigation, General corporate. Office: Fulbright & Jaworski 300 Convent St Ste 2200 San Antonio TX 78205-3792 also: 1301 Mckinney St Ste 5100 Houston TX 77010-3031

**BIERY, FRED,** judge; b. McAllen, Tex., Nov. 11, 1947; s. Samuel F. and Clara Belle (Martin) B.; m. Marcia Mattingly, May 25, 1989; children: Anna Lisa, Molly. BA, Tex. Luth. Coll., 1970; JD, So. Meth. U., 1973. Bar: Tex., U.S. Dist. Ct. (fed. dist.) Tex. 1974. From assoc. to shareholder Biery, Biery, Davis & Myers, P.C., San Antonio, 1973-78; judge County Ct. Two, San Antonio, 1979-82, 150th Dist. Ct., San Antonio, 1983-88, 4th Ct. of Appeals, San Antonio, 1989-94, U.S. Dist. Ct. (we. dist.) Tex., San Antonio, 1994—. Regent Tex. Luth. Coll., Seguin, 1970—. Served USAR, 1970-76. Recipient Disting. Alumni award Tex. Luth. Coll., 1980; named Outstanding Young Dem., Bezar County Dems., 1978. Mem. ABA, State Bar Tex., San Antonio Bar Assn. (pres. 1987-88, Outstanding Young Lawyer 1980), Am. Inns of Ct. (pres. 1990-92). Avocations: basketball, gardening. Office: US Dist Ct 655 E Durango Blvd 1st Fl San Antonio TX 78206-1102

**BIGELOW, ROBERT WILSON,** trial lawyer; b. L.A., Oct. 22, 1964; s. William Phillips and Dona (Heath) B.; m. Madeline Garcia, Sept. 24, 1995; children: William, Emma. Student, UCLA, 1982-84; BA with distinction, U. N.Mex., 1990; JD, Georgetown U., 1993. Bar: N.Y. Intern FTC, Washington, 1992; mem. Georgetown Criminal Justice Clinic, Washington, 1992-93; sr. staff aty. Criminal Def. divsn. Legal Aid Soc., Bronx, N.Y., 1993—; mentor John Jay Legal Svcs., Inc., White Plains, N.Y., 1997—. Mem. ABA (criminal justice sect. 1996—, def. function/svcs. com. 1996—), Assn. Legal Aid Attys. (rep. 1997—). Democrat. Episcopalian. Avocation: baseball research. Criminal. Home: 154 Ferry St Newark NJ 07105-2111 Office: Legal Aid Soc Criminal Def Divsn 1020 Grand Concourse Bronx NY 10451-2605

**BIGGERS, NEAL BROOKS, JR.,** federal judge; b. Corinth, Miss., July 1, 1935; s. Neal Brooks and Sara (Cunningham) B.; 1 child, Sherron. BA, Millsaps Coll., 1956; JD, U. Miss., 1963. Sole practice Corinth, 1963-68; pros. atty. Alcorn County, 1964; dist. atty. 1st Jud. Dist. Miss., 1968-75, cir. judge, 1975-84; judge U.S. Dist. Ct. (no. dist.) Miss., Oxford, 1984—. Contbr. articles to profl. jours. Office: US Dist Ct PO Box 1238 911 Jackson Ave Oxford MS 38655-1238

**BIGLOW, ROBERT R.,** lawyer; b. Ashland, Wis., June 14, 1922; s. Craque Chester and Mildred Maria (Byrne) B.; m. Genevieve Johanna Jaeger, Sept. 3, 1953; children: Michael J., Mark W., Crague C., John B., Jennifer A., Laura A., Mary, Eileen. BS, Duluth (Minn.) State U., 1942; BSL, LLB, JD, U. Minn, 1948. Bar: Minn., U.S. Dist. Ct., U.S. Ct. Appeals, U.S. Supreme Ct. Pvt. practice, Mpls., 1949—. With USAAF, WWII, ETO, USAF, Korea; col. USAFR ret. Avocations: music, sports, hunting, fishing. Personal injury, Probate, Alternative dispute resolution. Home: 1621 Hillsboro Ave S Saint Louis Park MN 55426-1828 Office: 401 2d Ave S Minneapolis MN 55401

**BIGUS, EDWARD LOWELL,** lawyer; b. Kansas City, Mo., Mar. 3, 1958; s. Kenneth E. and Elma B. (Weaver) B.; m. Ellyn K. Bergmann, Mar. 9, 1989; children: Jacob M., Samuel J. BS, U. Kans., 1981, JD, 1984. Bar: Kans. 1984. Pvt. practice Overland Park, Kans., 1984—. Mem. Johnson County Bar Assn., Johnson County Barristers. Jewish. Avocation: sailing. Family and matrimonial, Criminal, General civil litigation. Office: 11900 W 87th Street Pkwy #240 Lenexa KS 66215-4517

**BIGWOOD, ROBERT WILLIAM,** lawyer; b. Fergus Falls, Minn., June 30, 1956; s. Robert M. and Barbara I. (Barr) B.; m. Gretchen K. Brink, July 8, 1978; children: Maria, Daniel, Mark. BA cum laude, U. Minn., 1977, JD, 1980. Bar: Minn. 1980, U.S. Dist. Ct. Minn. 1983. Ptnr. Pemberton Sorlie and Rufer, Fergus Falls, 1980—. Pres., Campaign chmn. Fergus Falls United Fund, 1987-88; pres., Lakeland Hospice, Inc., Fergus Falls, 1985-87. Mem. ABA, Minn. State Bar Assn., Kiwanis, Phi Kappa Phi. Republican. Methodist. General practice, Probate, Real property. Home: 618 N Ann St Fergus Falls MN 56537-1717 Office: Perberton Sorlie and Rufer 110 N Mill St Fergus Falls MN 56537-2135

**BILANDIC, MICHAEL A.,** state supreme court justice, former mayor; b. Chgo., Feb. 13, 1923; s. Matthew and Domenica (Lebedina) B.; m. Heather Morgan, July 15, 1977; 1 son, Michael Morgan. JD, DePaul U., 1948. Bar: Ill. 1949. Master in chancery Cir. Ct. Cook County, Ill., 1964-67; spl. asst. to atty. gen., 1965-68; ptnr. Anixter, Bilandic & Pigott and predecessors, Chgo., 1963-77; acting mayor Chgo., 1976, mayor, 1977-79; ptnr. Bilandic, Neistein, Richman, Hauslinger and Young, Chgo., 1979-84; justice Ill. Appellate Ct., 1984-90, Ill. Supreme Ct., 1990—. Mem. Chgo. City Coun., 1969-76, chmn. com. on environ. control, 1970-74, chmn. fin. com., 1974-76. 1st lt. USMC, 1942-46. Mem. Am., Ill., Chgo. bar assns., Cath. Lawyers Guild. Democrat. Roman Catholic. Office: 160 N La Salle St Fl 20 Chicago IL 60601-3103

**BILBY, RICHARD MANSFIELD,** federal judge; b. Tucson, May 29, 1931; s. Ralph Willard and Marguerite (Mansfield) B.; m. children: Claire Louise, Ellen M. Moore; m. Elizabeth Alexander, May 25, 1996. BS, U. Ariz., 1955; JD, U. Mich., 1958. Bar: Ariz. 1959. Since practiced in Tucson; law clk. to Chief Judge Chambers, 9th Circuit Ct. Appeals, San Francisco, 1958-59; mem. firm Bilby, Thompson, Shoenhair & Warnock, 1959-79, partner, 1967-79; judge U.S. Dist. Ct., Dist. Ariz., Tucson, 1979-96; chief judge U.S. Dist. Ct., Dist. Ariz., 1984-90, sr. judge, 1996—; conscientious objector hearing officer Dept. Justice, 1959-62; chmn. Pima County Med.-Legal panel, 1968-70; Mem. Tucson Charter Revision Com., 1965-70. Chmn. United Fund Profl. Div., 1968; chmn. Spl. Gift Div., 1970, St. Joseph Hosp. Devel. Fund Drive, 1970; Republican state chmn. Vols. for Eisenhower, 1956; Rep. county chmn., Pima County, Ariz., 1972-74; Past pres. Tucson Conquistadores; bd. dirs. St. Josephs Hosp., 1969-77, chmn., 1972-75. Served with AUS, 1952-54. Fellow Am. Coll. Trial Lawyers; mem. Ariz. Acad., Town Hall (dir. 1976-79). Office: US Dist Ct 55 E Broadway Blvd Rm 426 Tucson AZ 85701-1719

**BILDER, MARSHALL D.,** lawyer; b. Bklyn., Nov. 2, 1964; s. Seymour and Beverly Bilder; m. Anne Elisabeth Bilder, Aug. 13, 1989; 1 child, Nicole Hayley. BA, U. Fla., 1985; JD with honors, Rutgers U., Newark, 1989. Bar: N.J. 1989, U.S. Dist. Ct. N.J. 1989, U.S. Ct. Appeals (D.C. cir.) 1991, Colo. 1992. Law to hon. Michael P. King Superior Ct. N.J. Appellate Divsn., 1989-90; assoc. Sterns & Weinroth, Trenton, N.J., 1990-97; ptnr. Sterns & Weinroth, Trenton, 1997—. Recipient Morris Gann prize in evidence. Mem. Order of the Coif. Product liability, Federal civil litigation, General civil litigation. Home: 74 Murray Dr Neshanic Station NJ 08853-3042 Office: Sterns & Weinroth 50 W State St Ste 1400 Trenton NJ 08608-1220

**BILDERBACK, JAMES WILLIAM, II,** lawyer; b. Fresno, Calif., Oct. 21, 1963; s. Dean Loy Bilderback and Florence Elizabeth (Gillmore) Ellsworth; m. Leslie Ann Reed, July 15, 1989; children: Emma Christine, Claire Elizabeth. BA, U. Calif., Berkeley, 1985; JD cum laude, U. San Francisco, 1992. Bar: Calif. 1992, U.S. Dist. Ct. (no. dist.) Calif. 1992, U.S. Dist. Ct. (ctrl. dist.) Calif. 1993, U.S. Ct. Appeals (9th cir.) 1993, U.S. Supreme Ct. 1998. Deputy atty. gen. Calif. Dept. Justice, L.A., 1992—. Mem. L.A. County Bar Assn., L.A. County Bar Assn. Barristers (pres. 1999—, sec. 1996-98). Office: Calif Dept Justice 300 S Spring St Fl 5 Los Angeles CA 90013-1230

**BILDERSEE, ROBERT ALAN,** lawyer; b. Albany, N.Y., Jan. 22, 1942; s. Max U. and Hannah (Marks) B.; m. Ellen Bernstein, June 9, 1963; 1 child, Jennifer M. A.B., Columbia Coll., 1962, M.A., 1964; LL.B., Yale U., 1967. Assoc. Wolf Block Schorr & Solis-Cohen, Phila., 1967-72; sole practice, Phila., 1972-73; assoc., then ptnr. Fox Rothschild, O'Brien & Frankel, Phila., 1973-80; ptnr. Morgan Lewis & Bockius LLP, Phila., 1980-97; founding ptnr. Bildersee and Silbert, LLP, Phila., 1997—; lectr. Temple U. Sch. Law, Phila., 1978-91; asst. in instrn. Yale U. Law Sch., New Haven, 1966. Author: Pension Regulation Manual, Pension Administrator's Forms and Checklists, 1987; contbg. author: Employee Benefits Handbook, 1982—; editor: Beyond the Fringes; contbr. articles to profl. jours. Woodrow Wilson fellow, 1962. Mem. ABA, Pa. Bar Assn., Phila. Bar Assn. Avocation: wildlife photography. E-mail: erisaplus@aol.com. Pension, profit-sharing, and employee benefits, Corporate taxation, Labor. Office: Bildersee and Silbert LLP 1617 Jfk Blvd Ste 1111 Philadelphia PA 19103-1821

**BILGER, BRUCE R.,** lawyer; b. Balt., Feb. 27, 1952. BA, Dartmouth Coll., 1973; MBA, JD, U. Va., 1977. Bar: Tex. 1977. Mem. Vinson & Elkins, L.L.P., Houston. Mem. Phi Beta Kappa. Mergers and acquisitions, Private international, Finance. Office: Vinson & Elkins LLP 2300 First City Tower 1001 Fannin St Houston TX 77002-6760

**BILINKAS, EDWARD J.,** lawyer; b. Kearny, N.J., May 20, 1954; s. Edward William and Mary B.; m. Dolores D., May 6, 1984; children: Jacquline, Edward, Jennifer. BA, Ashland Coll., 1976; JD, Calif. We. Sch. Law, 1981. Bar: N.J., N.Y., U.S. Dist. Ct. N.J., U.S. Dist. Ct. (so. and ea. dists.) N.Y. Trial atty. Essex County Attys. Office, Newark, 1981-83; asst. U.S. atty. U.S. Attys. Office, Newark, 1983-85; 1st asst. pros. atty. Essex County Prosecutors Office, Newark, 1985-88; ptnr. Lorber, Schneider, Nuzzi, Bilinkas & Mason, Fairfield, N.J., 1988—. Criminal. Office: Lorber Schneider Nuzzi Bilinkas & Mason 310 Passaic Ave Fairfield NJ 07004-2523

**BILL, ARTHUR HENRY,** lawyer; b. Cleve., Sept. 18, 1941; s. Herbert Edward and Virginia (Salisbury) B.; m. Janet Francis Stewart, Aug. 30, 1969; children: Colin, James, Carolyn. BA in Econs., Rutgers U., 1963; JD, Boston U., 1969. Bar: D.C. 1969, Md. 1970. Mgmt. asst. Gen. Electric Corp., Pittsfield, Mass., 1965-66; staff atty. U.S. SEC, Washington, 1969-72; assoc. Freedman, Levy, Kroll & Simonds, Washington, 1972-75, ptnr., 1975—. Served to 1st lt. U.S. Army, 1963-65, Korea. Mem. ABA, D.C. Bar Assn., Md. Bar Assn. General corporate, Mergers and acquisitions, Securities. Home: 6844 Glenbrook Rd Bethesda MD 20814-1219 Office: Freedman Levy Kroll & Simonds 1050 Connecticut Ave NW #825 Washington DC 20036

**BILLAUER, BARBARA PFEFFER,** lawyer, educator; b. Aug. 9, 1951; d. Harry George and Evelyn (Newman) Pfeffer. BS with honors, Cornell U., 1972; JD, Hofstra U., 1975; MA, NYU, 1982; cert. in risk scis. and pub. policy, Johns Hopkins U., 1999. Bar: N.Y. 1976, Fed. Dist. Ct. N.Y. 1977, U.S. Ct. Appeals (2d cir.) 1978, U.S. Supreme Ct. 1984. Assoc. Bower & Gardner, N.Y.C., 1974-78; sr. trial atty. Joseph W. Conklin, N.Y.C., 1978-80; assoc. dept. head Curtis, Mallet-Prevost, Colt & Mosle, N.Y.C., 1980-82; ptnr. Anderson, Russell, Kill & Olick, N.Y.C., 1982-86, Stroock & Stroock & Lavan, N.Y.C., 1986-90; ptnr., chair environ. and toxic tort practice Keck, Mahin, Cate & Koether, 1990-93; prin. Barbara P. Billauer & Assocs., Lido Beach, N.Y., 1993—; vis. scholar Johns Hopkins U. Sch. Pub. Health, 1998-99; faculty SUNY Stony Brook Med. Sch.; adj. assoc. prof. NYU Grad. Sch., 1982-88; lectr. Rutger's U. Med. Sch.; jud. screening com. Coordinated Bar Assn., 1983-86; mem. spl panel Citywide Ct. Adminstrn. 1982-85; bd. dirs. Weizmann Inst., Am. Com. Co-author: The Lender's Guide to Environmental Law: Risk and Liability, 1993. Fellow Am. Bar Found.; mem. AAAS, ABA (comml. leasing sect. indoor air polution 1990-93), Met. Womens Bar Assn. (v.p. 1981-83, pres. 1983-85, chmn. bd. 1985-87), Nat. Conf. Womens Bar Assn. (bd. dirs., v.p. 1989-95), Internat. Coun. Shopping Ctrs. (environ. com.), Am. Soc. Microbiology, Brit. Occupl. Hygiene Soc., N.Y. Acad. Scis., Am. Soc. Safety Engrs. Environment Personal Injury, Toxic Torts. Personal injury, Environmental, Health. Office: 146 Eva Dr Lido Beach NY 11561-4818

**BILLEK, MAXWELL L.,** lawyer; b. Bayonne, N.J., June 22, 1968; s. Andrew Edward Billek and Carol Wynn Carlson; m. Abigail A. Donington, June 18, 1994. BA, Rutgers U., 1990; JD, Am. U., 1993. Bar: N.J. 1993, Pa. 1993, U.S. Dist. Ct. N.J. 1993. Law sec. Judge N. Stroumtsos, Newark, 1993-94; assoc. Donington LeRoe, Edison, N.J., 1994-95, Michael Lazarus, P.A., Edison, 1995-97; ptnr. Lazarus & Billek, P.A., Edison, 1997—. Personal injury, Insurance. Office: Lazarus & Billek PA 10 Parsonage Rd Ste 306 Edison NJ 08837-2429

**BILLER, HOLLY M.,** lawyer, legal administrator; b. Bklyn., Mar. 15, 1955; d. Murray and Frym (Graber) B. BA summa cum laude, Bklyn. Coll., 1976; JD, Fordham U., 1983. Bar: N.Y. 1984. Counsel, legal advisory Merril Lynch, N.Y.C., 1983-85; ptnr. Biller & Biller, Esqs., N.Y.C., 1989-93; atty. N.Y.C. Bd. Edn., 1993-95; dir. disciplinary unit N.Y.C. Homeless Svcs., 1995-96; dir. employment law, assoc. gen. counsel N.Y.C. Children's Svcs., 1996—; tchg. asst. Fordham Law Sch., N.Y.C., 1983; instr. law Bklyn. Coll., 1987-95. Vol. Congressman Schumer, Bklyn., City Councilman Baron, Bklyn. Regents scholar Sheepshead Bay H.S., 1972. Mem. N.Y. Bar Assn., Mensa, Psi Chi. Avocations: violin, piano, guitar, accordion, composing.

**BILLINGS, FRANKLIN SWIFT, JR.,** federal judge; b. Woodstock, Vt., June 5, 1922; s. Franklin S. and Gertrude (Curtis) B.; m. Pauline Gillingham, Oct. 13, 1951; children: Franklin, III, Jireh Swift, Elizabeth, Ann. S.B., Harvard U., 1943; postgrad., Yale U. law Sch., 1945; J.D., U. Va., 1947. Bar: Vt. 1948, U.S. Supreme Ct., 1958. With dept. electronics Gen. Electric Co., Schenectady, N.Y., 1943; bldg. dept. Vt. Marble Co., Proctor, 1945-46; pvt. practice law Woodstock, 1948-52; mem. firm Billings & Sherburne, Woodstock, 1952-66; asst. sec. Vt. Senate, 1949-55, sec., 1957-59; sec. civil and mil. affairs State of Vt., 1959-61; exec. clk. to gov., 1955-57; judge Hartford Mcpl. Ct., 1955-63; mem. Vt. Ho. of Reps., 1961-66, chmn. jud. com., 1961, speaker of ho., 1963-66; judge Vt. Superior Ct., 1966-75; assoc. justice Vt., Montpelier, 1975-83; chief justice Bar Vt., Montpelier, 1983-84; judge U.S. Dist. Ct. Vt., 1984-94, chief judge, 1988-92, sr. ct. judge, 1994—. Active, Town of Woodstock, 1948-72. Served as warrant officer 1st class attached Brit. Army, 1944-45. Decorated Purple Heart; Brit. Empire medal. Mem. Vt. Bar Assn., Delta Theta Phi. Office: US Dist Ct PO Box 598 Woodstock VT 05091-0598

**BILLINGSLEY, LANCE W.,** lawyer; b. Buffalo, Apr. 18, 1940; m. Carolyn Gouza Billingsley, Aug. 25, 1962; children: Lance II, Brant, Ashlynn. BA, U. Md., 1961; JD, U. Buffalo, 1964; state and local, Harvard U., 1988. Pntr., assoc. Nylen & Gilmore, Riverdale, Md., 1964-75; ptnr. Meyers, Billingsley, Rodbell & Rosenbaum, P.A., Riverdale, 1975—; chmn. bd. of regents Univ. Sys. of Md., 1995-99; vice-chmn. U. of Md. Found., 1985—; bd. dirs. U. Md. Med. Sys.; asst. atty. gen. State of Md., 1967-68; city atty. Hyattsville, Md., 1976—; chmn. Nat. Wildlife Visitors Ctr., 1989-94; chmn. bd. Econ. Devel. Corp., Landover, Md., 1983-92; bd. dirs. Cmty. Bank Md. Contbr. articles to numerous law publications. Chmn. Dem. State Cen. Com., 1970-74, Dem. Com. Prince George's County, 1974-80. Named One of Outstanding Young Men Am., 1975-80. Mem. ABA (young lawyers exec. com. 1972-74, editorial bd. Barrister mag. 1973-75), Md. Bar Assn. (bd. govs. 1970-72), Terrapin Club (bd. dirs. 1983—, pres. 1998-99), Columbia Country Club (Chevy Chase, Md.), Omicron Delta Kappa. Avocations: skiing, tennis. E-mail: lbillingsley@mbrriaw.com. General corporate, Municipal (including bonds). Home: 7102 College Heights Dr Hyattsville MD 20782-1154 Office: Meyers Billingsley Rodbell & Rosenbaum PA 6801 Kenilworth Ave Ste 400 Riverdale MD 20737-1385

**BILLINGTON, BARRY E.,** lawyer; b. Bruceton, Tenn., June 24, 1940; s. Charles Raymond and Edith Virginia (Bowles) B.; m. Bonnie Leslie Johnson; Oct. 16, 1971 (div. Mar. 23, 1990); children: Erin Alexis, Barry E., Jr. AB in Econs., Davidson Coll., 1964; JD, Emory U., 1968. Bar: Calif. 1969, Ga. 1971, U.S. Dist. Ct. (ctrl. dist.) Calif. 1969, U.S. Dist. Ct. (no. dist.) Ga. 1971. Assoc. Surr & Hellyer, San Bernardino, Calif., 1968-70; with Mfrs. Life Ins. Co., Atlanta, 1970-71; assoc. Carter, Ansley, Smith & McClendon, Atlanta, 1971-72; of counsel Raiford & Hills, Decatur, Ga., 1972-75; ptnr. Raiford, Hills, Billington & McKeithen, Atlanta, 1975-77, Rich, Bass, Kidd, Witcher & Billington, Decatur, 1977-82, Billington & Beasley, Decatur, 1982-83, Billington & Turner, Atlanta, 1983-85, Barry E. Billington & Assocs., Atlanta, 1985—. Editor: Ga. Rep. Party Newsletter, 1968. Rep. publicity dir. San Bernardino County, 1969-70, San Bernardino County for Ronald Reagan Com., 1970; alt. del. Rep. Ctrl. Com. of Calif., 1969-70; chmn. 4th dist. Conservative Caucus, 1977-79; candidate for Ga. Ho. Reps., 52nd dist., 1978, U.S. Congress, 4th dist., Ga., 1980. With U.S. Army Mil. Police Corps, 1958-60. Mem. Atlanta Bar Assn. (spkr.'s com., litigation, family law, criminal law sects. 1974-77), Decatur-DeKalb Bar Assn. (chmn. spkr.'s com. 1977-78), ABA (litigation sect. 1969-88), Ga. Trial Lawyers Assn., Assn. Trial Lawyers Am. Family and matrimonial, Personal injury, Criminal. Home: 878 Sherwood Cir Forest Park GA 30297-3035 Office: 3 Dunwoody Park Ste 103 Atlanta GA 30338-6709

**BILLINGTON, GLENN EARLE,** lawyer; b. Ithaca, N.Y., Nov. 8, 1943; s. Earle K. and Jean (Powell) B.; m. Anne Toth, Dec. 27, 1967; children: Peter J., Karen L., Steven J. AB, Cornell U., 1965; JD, Cleve. State U., 1970. Bar: Ohio 1970, U.S. Dist. Ct. (no. dist.) Ohio 1970, U.S. Ct. Appeals (6th cir.) 1972, U.S. Supreme Ct. 1975. Civil dir. Legal Aid Soc. Cleve., 1973-75; pvt. practice law Cleveland Heights, Ohio, 1975—. Chmn. Cuyahoga County Bd. Mental Retardation, Cleve., 1978-83; acting judge Cleveland Heights Mcpl. Ct., 1978-93; ctrl. committeeman Cuyahoga County Dems., Cleve., 1976—. Mem. ABA, Ohio Bar Assn., Cleve. Bar Assn., Kiwanis. Methodist. Avocations: flying, political campaign management. General civil litigation, General corporate, Probate. Home: 2584 Exeter Rd Cleveland OH 44118-4244 Office: 1991 Lee Rd #102 Cleveland OH 44118-2571

**BILSTAD, BLAKE TIMOTHY,** lawyer; b. Silver Spring, Md., Feb. 21, 1970. BA in History magna cum laude, Duke U., 1991; JD cum laude, Harvard U., 1996. Bar: Calif. 1996, U.S. Dist. Ct. (so. dist.) Calif. 1996, D.C. 1999. Assoc. Cooley Godward LLP, San Diego, 1995, assoc. dept. bus., 1996—. Mem. ABA, San Diego County Bar Assn. General corporate, Securities, Intellectual property. Office: Cooley Godward LLP 4365 Executive Dr Ste 1100 San Diego CA 92121-2133

**BILY, KIRKLAND JARRARD,** lawyer; b. Houston, Sept. 25, 1965; s. Richard C. and C. Sue Bily; m. Leslie Ann Bily, Apr. 10, 1993; children: Emily Elaine, Kyle Jacob. BS in Biochemistry cum laude, Tex. A&M U., 1987; JD cum laude, U. Houston, 1990. Bar: Tex. 1990. Assoc. Vinson & Elkins LLP, Houston, 1990-95, Am. Ref-Fuel Co., Houston, 1995—. Mem. Coastal Conservation Assn., Ducks Unltd. General corporate, Contracts commercial, Mergers and acquisitions. Office: Am Ref-Fuel Co Ste 200 15990 N Barkers Land Houston TX 77079

**BINDER, DAVID FRANKLIN,** lawyer, author; b. Beaver Falls, Pa., Aug. 1, 1935; s. Walter Carl and Jessie Maivis (Bliss) B.; m. Deana Jacqueline Pines, Dec. 25, 1971; children: April, Bret. BA, Geneva Coll., 1956; JD, Harvard U., 1959. Bar: Pa. 1960, U.S. Ct. Appeals (3rd cir.) 1963, U.S. Supreme Ct. 1967. Law clk. to chief justice Pa. Supreme Ct., 1959-61; counsel Fidelity Mut. Life Ins. Co., Phila., 1964-66; ptnr. Bennett, Bricklin & Saltzburg, Phila., 1967-68; mem. Richter, Syken, Ross, and Binder, Phila., 1969-72, Raynes, McCarty, Binder, Ross and Mundy, Phila., 1972—; mem. faculty Pa. Coll. Judiciary; judge pro tempore Phila. Common Pleas Ct., 1991-97; lectr., course planner Pa. Bar Inst.; mem. civil procedural rules com., ad hoc. com. on evidence Supreme Ct. Pa. Author: Hearsay Handbook, 1975, ann. supplements, 2nd edit., 1983, 3rd edit., 1991. Recipient Disting. Alumnus award Geneva Coll., 1981. Mem. ABA, Pa. Bar Assn., Phila. Bar Assn., Assn. Trial Lawyers Am. (lectr.), Pa. Trial Lawyers Assn., Harvard Law Sch. Assn., Am. Bd. Trial Advs., Am. Coll. Trial Lawyers, Union League. Federal civil litigation, State civil litigation, Personal injury. Home: 1412 Flat Rock Rd Penn Valley PA 19072-1216 Office: Raynes McCarty Binder Ross and Mundy 1845 Walnut St Ste 2000 Philadelphia PA 19103-4767

**BINDOCK, MARK,** lawyer; b. Bedford, Ohio, Mar. 14, 1948. JD, St. Mary's U., San Antonio. Bar: Tex. 1978, U.S. Dist. Ct. (we. dist.) Tex. 1985. Pvt. practice law San Antonio. Office: 8023 Vantage Dr San Antonio TX 78230-4769

**BINES, HARVEY ERNEST,** lawyer, educator, writer; b. Winthrop, Mass., Nov. 25, 1941; s. Carl and Lillian (Cooper) B.; m. Joan Carol Paller, Dec. 27, 1964; children: Jonathan W., Joel T., Susanne R., Benjamin E. BS, MIT, 1963; JD, U. Va., 1970. Bar: Mass 1971, Va. 1971, U.S. Dist. Ct. Mass., U.S. Dist. Ct. (ea. dist.) Va., U.S. Ct. Appeals (1st, 3d, 4th, 7th and D.C. cirs.), U.S. Supreme Ct. Law clk. to hon. John D. Butzner Jr. U.S. Ct. Appeals (4th cir.), Richmond, Va., 1970-71; asst. prof. Law Sch. U. Va., Charlottesville, 1971-74, assoc. prof. Law Sch., 1974-76; assoc. Sullivan & Worcester, Boston, 1976-79, ptnr., 1980—; adj. prof. Boston Coll. Law Sch., Chestnut Hill, Mass., 1981-88, bd. dirs., treas. Schweitzer Fellowship, Boston. Author: Law of Investment Management, 1978, 1991. Lt. USNR, 1963-67. Mem. Am. Law Inst., Internat. Bar Assn., Boston Bar Assn. Email: heb@sandw.com. General corporate, Securities, Private international. Home: 36 Clarke St Lexington MA 02421-4916 Office: Sullivan & Worcester 1 Post Office Sq Ste 2300 Boston MA 02109-2129

**BINFORD, GREGORY GLENN,** lawyer; b. Canton, Ohio, Oct. 8, 1948; s. Edwin and Helen Marie B. BA, Case Western Res. U., 1970, JD, 1973. Bar: Ohio 1973. Ptnr. Guren, Merritt, Cleve., 1973-84, Benesch, Friedlander, Cleve., 1984—. Mem. men's com. Cleve. Playhouse, 1980—. Mem. ABA, Nat. Health Lawyers Assn., Cleve. Bar Assn. (chair health law sect.), Ohio State Bar Assn. Health, Administrative and regulatory. Office: Benesch Friedlander America Bldg 200 Public Sq 2300 Cleveland OH 44114-2378

**BING, RICHARD MCPHAIL,** lawyer; b. Lewes, Del., Aug. 23, 1950; s. Arden E. and Ellen Louise (Judd) B.; m. Valerie Lynn Wasson, Dec. 18, 1971; children: Jennifer Lynn, Kristin Tyler. BA, U. Richmond, 1972, JD, 1978. Bar: Va. 1979, U.S. Dist. Ct. (ea. and we. dists.) Va. 1979, U.S. Dist. Ct. (we. dist.) Pa. 1990, U.S. Dist. Ct. (no. dist.) N.Y. 1990, U.S. Dist. Ct. (ctrl. dist.) Ill. 1996, U.S. Ct. Appeals (4th cir.) 1979, U.S. Ct. appeals (2d cir.) 1990, U.S. Supreme Ct. 1994, U.S. Dist. Ct. (ctrl. dist.) Ill. 1996. Dir. ins. Bur. of Ins., Richmond, Va., 1978-79; resident gen counsel Va. Gasoline Retailers Assn., Richmond, 1979-83; ptnr. Pearce & Bing, Richmond, 1983-93, Bing & Assocs., P.C., Richmond, 1993—; adj. prof. law J. Sargent Reynolds Community Coll., Richmond, 1984-85. Mem. Henrico County Rep. Com; bd. dirs. Three Chopt PTA, Richmond, 1984-85. Mem. ABA, Va. Bar Assn., Va. Bar, Richmond Bar Assn., Fed. bar Assn., Assn. Trial Lawyers Am., Va. Trial Lawyers Assn., Nat. Lawyers Club, Tcukahoe Jaycees (pres. 1981-82), Bull and Bear Club, Hermitage Country Club, Tobacco Co. Club, The Spider Club (bd. dirs.), Am. Assn. of Franchisees and Dealers, Svc. Sta. Dealers of Am., Inc., Affiliate Attys. Group. Avocations: golf, bicycling, photography. Federal civil litigation, General civil litigation, Contracts commercial. Home: 1701 Habwood Ln Richmond VA 23233-4451 Office: Bing & Assocs PC 300 Arboretum Pl Ste 140 Richmond VA 23236-3465

**BINGHAM, PAMELA MARY MUIR,** lawyer, consultant; b. Dallas, Aug. 14, 1948; d. William Lane and Virginia Potter Bingham; m. Stephen Clooney Broussard, Apr. 24, 1988 (div. Dec. 1994). AA, Bennett Coll., 1968; BA, Vassar Coll., 1971; JD, U. Memphis, 1986. Bar: Tenn. 1986, U.S. Dist. Ct. (we. dist.) Tenn. 1988, D.C. 1989. Gen. counsel Tenn. Treasury Dept., Nashville, 1986-88; asst. state atty. gen. Office of the State Atty. Gen., Nashville, 1988-95; pvt. practice law Nashville, 1995-97; laywer, cons. Mcpl. Tech. Adv. Svc. U. Tenn., Nashville, 1997—; legal advisor Brandreth Park Assocs., L.P., Ossining, N.Y., 1996—; compliance cons. Bridgestone/Firestone Corp., Nashville, 1996; cons. Tenn. Mcpl. Attys. Assn., Nashville, 1997—. Author: Tennessee Municipal Handbook, 1997. Com. mem., advisor Brandreth Park Assn., Ossining, 1995—; v.p. Villages of Brentwood Homeowners' Assn., Nashville, 1995—. Mem. Nashville Bar Assn. (mem. ADR com. 1997—), Middle Tenn. Hunter Jumper Assn. (3rd high point champion 1994, 1st low working hunter champion 1997). Episcopalian. Avocations: riding and training show horses, professional musician, songwriter, skiing. Municipal (including bonds), State and local taxation, General corporate. Office: U Tenn Mcpl Tech Adv Svc 226 Capitol Blvd Ste 402 Nashville TN 37219-1807

**BINNING, J. BOYD,** lawyer; b. N.Y.C., July 7, 1944; s. James Edward and Lillian (Doughty) B.; m. Penelope Elizabeth Lancione, July 22, 1977; children: Alicia, Peter. AA, Wesley Coll., 1964; BS cum laude, Urbana Coll., Ohio, 1970; MA in Polit. Sci., Eastern Ky. U., 1971; JD, Ohio No. U., 1974. Bar: Ohio 1976, U.S. Dist. Ct. (so. dist.) Ohio 1977, U.S. Ct. Appeals (6th cir.) 1977, U.S. Dist. Ct. (no. dist.) Ohio 1979, U.S. Supreme Ct. 1979. Dep. sheriff Miami County, Troy, Ohio, 1971-74; investigator, legal intern Miami County prosecutor's office, Troy, 1973-75; spl. counsel for the Ohio Senate Jud. Com.; instr., advisor Iowa State Law Enforcement Acad., Des Moines, 1976; pvt. practice law, Columbus, 1976—; spl. counsel jud. com. Ohio Senate; judge moot ct. Capital Law Sch., Columbus. Author: Civil Rights and the Federal Courts, 1971. Grad. scholar Eastern Ky. U., 1970-71. Mem. Ohio State Bar Assn., Columbus Bar Assn., Columbus Bar Found., Ohio Acad. Trial Lawyers, Nat. Assn. Criminal Def. Lawyers. General civil litigation, Criminal, Personal injury. Office: 592 S 3rd St Columbus OH 43215-5754

**BIOLCHINI, ROBERT FREDRICK,** lawyer; b. Detroit, Sept. 22, 1939; s. Alfred and Erma (Barbetti) B.; m. Frances Lauinger, June 5, 1965; children: Robert F., Douglas C., Frances E., Tobin m., Thomas A., Christine M. BA, U. Notre Dame, 1962; LLB, George Washington U., 1965. Bar: Okla., Mich., 1965. Assoc. Doerner, Stuart, Saunders, Daniel, Anderson & Biolchini, Tulsa, 1968-71, ptnr., 1971-94; ptnr. Stuart, Biolchini, Turner & Givray, Tulsa, 1994—; bd. dirs. Pennwell Corp., Lawrence Electronics Inc., Lumen Energy Corp., Bank of The Lakes, Bank of Jackson Hole; chmn. bd. Valley Nat. Bank; mem. Lloyds of London, 1979—. Bd. dirs. Thomas Gilcrease Mus., past pres., chmn. bd., 1977-80, dir. emeritus, 1980—; bd. dirs., sec., legal clk. Tulsa Ballet Theatre, Inc., 1976-84; trustee, pres. Monte Cassino Endowment, 1978—; chmn. Christ the King Parish Coun., 1974-75; mem. adv. coun. U. Notre Dame Law Sch., 1982—; chmn. Cath. Diocese Tulsa Fund for Future, 1998—; bd. dirs. legal counsel Tulsa Area United Way, 1986—; mem. pres.'s coun. Regis Coll., 1986—. Served as capt. U.S. Army, 1965-67. Mem. Okla. Bar Assn., Mich. Bar Assn., Met. Tulsa C. of C. (bd. dirs. 1992—), Summit Club, Southern Hills Country Club, Club Ltd., Knights of Malta, Knights of the Holy Sepulchre. Roman Catholic. General corporate, Securities, Federal civil litigation. Home: 1744 E 29th St Tulsa OK 74114-5402 Office: First Place Tower 15 E 5th St Ste 3300 Tulsa OK 74103-4340

**BIONDI, JOHN MICHAEL,** lawyer; b. Ellwood City, Pa., July 14, 1968; s. John Mario Biondi and Elizabeth Jean Carsele; m. Andrea Marie Cantelmi, Sept. 24, 1994; children: Grace Alexandra, Sebastian Lucas. BA, Gannon U., 1990; JD, Ohio No. U., 1993. Bar: Pa. 1993, U.S. Dist. Ct. (we. dist.) Pa. 1994. Atty. Pomerico Leymarie Clark & Puntureri, Ellwood City, Pa., 1993-95; law clk. Ct. of Common Pleas, New Castle, Pa., 1995-96; atty. Stepanian & Muscatello, Butler, Pa., 1996—. mem. Pa. Bar Assn., Butler County Bar Assn., Lawrence County Bar Assn. Republican. Roman Catholic. Avocation: house restoration. Insurance, General civil litigation, Public utilities. Home: 344 4th St Beaver PA 15009-2349 Office: 222 S Main St Butler PA 16001-5930

**BIRCH, ADOLPHO A., JR.,** state supreme court justice; b. Washington, Sept. 22, 1932. BA, Howard U., 1956, JD, 1956. Bar: Tenn. 1957. Pvt. practice Nashville, 1958-66, asst. pub. defender, 1964-66, asst. dist. atty., 1966-69; judge Davidson County Gen. Sessions Ct., 1969-78, Tenn. Criminal Ct. (20th jud. dist.), 1978-87; former judge Tenn. Ct. Criminal Appeals; chief justice Tenn. Supreme Ct., Nashville, 1996-97, assoc. justice, 1997—; assoc. prof. Nashville Sch. of Law. Served USNR, 1956-58. Mem. ABA, Nat. Bar Assn., Tenn. Bar Assn., Nashville Bar Assn., Napier Lobby Bar Assn. (past pres.). Office: 401 7th Ave N Ste 304 Nashville TN 37219-1406*

**BIRCH, STANLEY FRANCIS, JR.,** federal judge; b. 1945. BA, U. Va., 1967; JD, Emory U., 1970, LLM in Taxation, 1976. Law clk. to Hon. Judge Sidney O. Smith Jr. U.S. Dist. Ct. (no. dist.) Ga.; mem. firm Greer, Sartain & Carey, Gainesville, Ga., 1974-76, Deal, Birch, Jarrard & Link, Gainesville, 1976-83, Birch, Hartness & Link, Gainesville, 1983-85, Vaughan, Davis, Birch & Murphy, Atlanta, 1985-90; judge U.S. Ct. Appeals (11th cir.), Atlanta, 1990—. Lt. U.S. Army 1970-72. Mem. State Bar Ga., Ga. Bar Found., Atlanta Bar Assn., Gainesville Northeastern Bar Assn., 11th Cir. Hist. Soc., Lawyers Club Atlanta, Ga. Legal History Found., U. Va. Alumni Assn., Emory U. Sch. Law Alumni Assn., Calvert Hall Alumni Assn., Old Warhorse Lawyers Club, Theta Delta Chi. Office: US Ct Appeals 11th Cir 56 Forsyth St NW Atlanta GA 30303-2205*

**BIRCHER, EDGAR ALLEN,** lawyer; b. Springfield, Ohio, Apr. 28, 1934; s. John Clark and Ethel Ann (Speakman) B.; m. Lavinia Brock, Sept. 30, 1978; children: Douglas, Stephen, Todd, Karen. BA, Ohio Wesleyan U., 1956; JD, Ohio State U., 1961; postgrad., Columbia U., 1974, Stanford U., 1975. Bar: Ohio 1962, Tex. 1973. Assoc. Fuller, Seney, Henry & Hodge, Toledo, 1962-64; with Cooper Industries, Inc., Houston, 1964-88, v.p., 1977-88, gen. counsel, 1977-88; pres. Flex Law, Inc., Houston, 1988—; of counsel Evans Kosut & Kasprzak, Houston, Tex., 1995—. With USAF, 1956-59. Mem. Tex. Bar Assn., Yacht Club Galveston, Phi Delta Theta, Phi Delta Phi. Public international, Labor. Home: 1501 Harbor View Cir Galveston TX 77550-3119 Office: 16945 Northchase Dr Ste 1600 Houston TX 77060-2153

**BIRD, FRANCIS MARION, JR.,** lawyer; b. Atlanta, Jan. 14, 1938; s. Francis Marion Sr. and Mary Adair (Howell) B.; m. JoAnn Galvin, Aug. 1994; children from previous marriage: Barbara, Michael. AB, Princeton U., 1959; LLB, Emory U., 1964; LLM, Harvard U., 1966. BAr: Ga. 1964, U.S. Ct. Appeals (3d cir. and 11th cir.), U.S. Dist. Cts. (no. dist. and mid. dist.) Ga. Officer USN, 1959-62; assoc. Jones Bird & Howell, Atlanta, 1964-70, ptnr., 1971-82; ptnr. Alston & Bird, Atlanta, 1982-88; pvt. practice Atlanta, 1988—; dir., sec. Summit Industries, Inc., 1980—. Adv. bd. mem. The Devereux Ctr., Kennesaw, Ga., 1989—. Mem. ABA, State Bar of Ga. (chmn. Standing Com. on Publs. 1977-78), Atlanta Bar Assn. (chmn. small firm/sole practitioner sect. 1995-96), Lawyers Club of Atlanta, Old War Horses Lawyers Club. Avocations: writing, outdoor adventure programs, walking. Probate, Estate planning, Alternative dispute resolution. Home: 110 Montgomery Ferry Dr NE Atlanta GA 30309-2713 Office: 400 Colony Sq NE Ste 1750 Atlanta GA 30361-6307

**BIRD, JOHN COMMONS,** arbitrator, educator; b. Chgo., Nov. 16, 1922; s. Francis Henry and Harriet Mackay (Smith) B.; m. Irene Elizabeth Grogloth, June 12, 1948; children: Elizabeth Anne Bird Gellert, John Traill, Bruce Mackay. AB, Dartmouth Coll., 1943; JD, U. Cin., 1948. Bar: Ohio 1948, Pa. 1950, Ky. 1956, U.S. Dist. Ct. (we. dist.) Ky. 1957, U.S. Supreme Ct. 1971. Atty. U.S. Steel Corp., Pitts., 1948-52, 58-66; asst. sec. U.S. Steel Corp., various locations, 1952-83; atty. homes div. U.S. Steel Corp., New Albany, Ind., 1952-58; gen. atty. U.S. Steel Corp., Birmingham, Ala., 1966-75, sr. gen. atty., 1975-83; sec. Birmingham Forest Products, Cordova, Ala., 1970-74; arbitrator Birmingham, 1983—; adj. prof. Birmingham-So. Coll., 1987—; mem. roster of arbitrators Am. Arbitration Assn., 1983—, Fed. Mediation and Conciliation Svc., 1992—, Better Bus. Bur., 1983—. Precinct clk. Bd. Elections, Mountain Brook, Ala., 1980—. Lt. USNR, 1943-46, PTO. Ky. Col. Gov. of Ky., 1978. Mem. Birmingham Bar Assn., Kiwanis (bd. dirs. 1992-93), Delta Upsilon, Phi Delta Phi. Republican. Episcopalian. Avocations: fishing, walking, reading, writing, teaching. Home and Office: 3125 Guilford Rd Birmingham AL 35223-1216

**BIRD, WENDELL RALEIGH,** lawyer; b. Atlanta, July 16, 1954; s. Raleigh Milton and R. Jean (Edwards) B. BA summa cum laude, Vanderbilt U., 1975; JD, Yale U., 1978. Bar: Ga. 1978, Ala. 1980, Calif. 1981, Fla. 1982, U.S. Ct. Appeals (2d, 3d, 4th, 5th, 6th, 7th, 8th, 9th, 10th and 11th cirs.) 1979-83, U.S. Supreme Ct. 1983. Law clk. to judge U.S. Ct. Appeals (4th cir.), Durham, N.C., 1978-79, U.S. Ct. Appeals (5th cir.), Birmingham, Ala., 1979-80; pvt. practice San Diego, 1980-82; atty. Parker, Johnson, Cook & Dunlevie, Atlanta, 1982-86; sr. ptnr. Bird & Assocs., P.C., Atlanta, 1986—; adj. prof. Emory U. Law Sch., Atlanta, 1985—; lectr. Washington Non-Profit Tax Conf., 1982—. Author: The Origin of Species Revisited, 2 vols., 1987; contbg. author: Federal Taxation of Exempt Organizations, 1994, CCH Federal Tax Service, 1988—; mem. bd. editors Yale U. Law Jour., 1977-78, others; contbr. articles to profl. jours. Bd. govs. Coun. for Nat. Policy, Washington, 1983—. Recipient Egger prize Yale U., 1978, Vanderbilt U. award, 1972. Mem. ABA (litigation sect., taxation sect., com. on exempt orgns., past chmn. subcom. on religious orgns., past chmn. subcom. on state and local taxes, chmn. subcom. on charitable contbns., sect. on real property probate and trust, com. charitable gifts), Am. Law Inst., Ga. Bar Assn., Fla. Bar Assn., Calif. Bar Assn., Ala. Bar Assn., Assn. Trial Lawyers Am., Phi Beta Kappa. Republican. Avocations: science, skiing, photography, genealogy, piano, architecture. Constitutional, Non-profit and tax-exempt organizations. Home: 92 Blackland Rd NW Atlanta GA 30342-4420 Office: Bird & Assocs PC 1150 Monarch Plz 3414 Peachtree Rd NE Atlanta GA 30326-1153

**BIRG, YURI M.,** lawyer; b. Minsk, Belorus, Aug. 12, 1966; came to U.S., 1979; s. Michael and Elizabeth B.; m. Ilana Taitler, July 16, 1989; children: Rebecca S., Jessica A. BA in Polit. Sci., U. Ill., 1988; JD, DePaul U., 1991. Bar: Ill. 1991, U.S. Dist. Ct. Ill. 1992. Prin. Birg Law Firm, Lincolnwood, Ill., 1991—; dir. Immigrant Def. Com., Lincolnwood, 1997—. Mem. Am. Immigration Lawyers Assn., Assn. Trial Lawyers Am., Chgo. Bar Assn. Avocations: soccer, chess, collecting model cars. Immigration, naturalization, and customs, Personal injury, Real property. Office: 4433 W Touhy Ave Ste 460 Lincolnwood IL 60712-1881

**BIRKBECK, A.J. KOERTS,** lawyer; b. Flushing, Mich., May 31, 1960; s. Benj H. and Gretchen Anne (Gettel) B.; m. Catherine Mary Margaret Battel, Aug. 10, 1985; children: Allison, Sarah. BS, U. Mich., 1983, MBA, 1985; JD, U. Chgo., 1991. Bar: Ill. 1991; U.S. Dist. Ct. (no. dist.) Ill. 1991. Closing officer Great Lakes Fed. Savings, Ann Arbor, Mich., 1983-85; sr. fin. analyst Amoco Corp., Chgo., 1985-88; atty. Winston & Strawn, Chgo., 1991-93; mng. atty. Zevnik, Horton, Guibord & McGovern, Chgo., 1993-97; mng. ptnr. Fulcrum Environ. Law, Chgo., 1997—. Contbr. to profl. jours. Com. mem. Oak Park Energy & Environ. Commn. Ill., 1998—; com. mem. Barne Park Remediation Com., Oak Park. Mem. ABA, Ill. State Bar Assn. (environ. sect. coun. 1999—), Lake Calumet Cluster Group, Amer. Assn. Petroleum Geologists, Chgo. Bar Assn. Presbyterian. Avocations: flying, sailing, skiing. Environmental, Real property, Toxic tort. Home: 1000 Belleforte Ave Oak Park IL 60302-1304

**BIRMINGHAM, PATRICK MICHAEL,** lawyer; b. St. Paul, Apr. 2, 1947; s. George Thomas and Nona Birmingham; m. Karen Ann Moir, Oct. 17, 1992. BS, Portland State U., 1970; JD, Western State U., 1975. Bar: Oreg., Calif., U.S. Dist. Ct. Oreg., U.S. Dist. Ct. Calif., U.S. Dist. Ct. Wash., U.S. Supreme Ct. With Riverside County (Calif.) Office of Pub. Defender, 1975-78; pvt. practice Portland, Oreg., 1978—. With U.S. Army N.G., 1970-75. Named in Best Lawyers in Am. and Nar. Directory Criminal Def. Lawyers. Mem. Oreg. Criminal Def. Lawyers (life), Calif. Attys. for Criminal Justice, Nat. Assn. Criminal Def. Lawyers, Multnomah Defenders Inc. (bd. dirs. 1990-92), Multnomah County Bar Assn. (mentor program 1994-99). Criminal. Office: 1001 SW 5th Ave Ste 1625 Portland OR 97204-1132

**BIRMINGHAM, RICHARD JOSEPH,** lawyer; b. Seattle, Feb. 26, 1953; s. Joseph E. and Anita (Loomis) B. BA cum laude, Wash. State U., 1975; JD, Seattle U., 1978; LLM in Taxation, Boston U., 1980. Bar: Wash. 1978, Oreg. 1981, U.S. Dist. Ct. (we. dist.) Wash. 1978, U.S. Tax Ct. 1981. Ptnr. Davis Wright Tremaine, Seattle, 1982-93; shareholder Birmingham Thorson & Barnett, P.C., Seattle, 1993—; mem. King County Bar Employee Benefit Com., Seattle, 1986, U.S. Treasury ad hoc com. employee benefits, 1988—. Contbg. editor: Compensation and Benefits Mgmt., 1985—; contbr. articles to profl. jours. Mem. ABA (employee benefits and exec. compensation com. 1982—), Wash. State Bar Assn. (speaker 1984-86, tax sect. 1982—), Oreg. State Bar Assn. (tax sect. 1982—), Western Pension Conf. (speaker 1986), Seattle Pension Round table. Democrat. Avocations: jogging, bicycling, photography. Pension, profit-sharing, and employee benefits, Personal income taxation. Home: 505 Belmont Ave E Apt 204 Seattle WA 98102-4862 Office: Birmingham Thorson & Barnett PC 3315 Two Union Square 601 Union St Seattle WA 98101-2341

**BIRMINGHAM, WILLIAM JOSEPH,** lawyer; b. Lynbrook, N.Y., Aug. 7, 1923; s. Daniel Joseph and Mary Elizabeth (Tighe) B.; m. Helen Elizabeth Roche, July 23, 1955; children: Deirdre, Patrick, Maureen, Kathleen, Brian. ME, Stevens Inst. Tech., 1944; MBA, Harvard U., 1948; JD, DePaul U., Chgo., 1953. Bar: Ill. 1953, U.S. Patent and Trademark Office, 1955, U.S. Dist. Ct. (no. dist.) Ill. 1960, U.S. Supreme Ct. 1961, U.S. Ct. Appeals (7th cir.) 1962, U.S. Ct. Appeals (3d cir.) 1968, U.S. Ct. Appeals (D.C. cir.) 1973, U.S. Ct. Mil. Appeals 1973, U.S. Ct. Appeals (fed. cir.) 1982, U.S. Ct. Claims 1986; registered profl. engr., Ill., Ind. Chem. engr. Standard Oil Co. Ind., Chgo., 1948-53, patent atty., 1953-59; assoc. Neuman, Williams, Anderson & Olson, Chgo., 1959-60, ptnr., 1961-91, Leydig, Voit & Mayer, Ltd., Chgo., 1991-93, of counsel, 1994-96. Served to capt. USNR, 1942-75. Mem. ABA, ASME, Fed. Cir. Bar Assn., Am. Intellectual Property Law Assn., Intellectual Property Law Assn. Chgo. Patent, Trademark and copyright, Federal civil litigation. Home: 233 Pine St Deerfield IL 60015-4853

**BIRN, HAROLD M.,** lawyer; b. Bronx, N.Y., Mar. 2, 1969; s. Lawrence E. and Susan E. Birn. BA, SUNY, Binghamton, 1991; JD, Bklyn. Law Sch., 1994. Bar: N.J. 1994, N.Y. 1995, U.S. Dist. Ct. (so. and ea. dists.) N.Y. 1995, U.S. Dist. Ct. (no. dist.) N.Y. 1998. Atty. LeSchack & Grodensky, P.C., N.Y.C., 1994—. Mem. N.Y. State Bar Assn., N.Y. County Lawyers Assn. Consumer commercial, Public utilities, General practice. Office: LeSchack & Grodensky PC 20 Thomas St Fl 1 New York NY 10007-1190

**BIRNBAUM, IRWIN MORTON,** lawyer; b. Bklyn., July 15, 1935; s. Sol N. and Rose (Cohen) B.; m. Arlene R. Burrows, June 8, 1957; children: Bruce J., Leslie R. Birnbaum Ventura, Amy G. Birnbaum Heath. BS in Acctg., Bklyn. Coll., 1956; JD, NYU, 1961. Bar: N.Y. 1962. Budget officer Montefiore Med. Ctr., Bronx, N.Y., 1962-70, v.p., chief fin. officer, 1970-86; counsel Proskauer & Rose LLP, N.Y.C., 1986-89, ptnr., 1989-97; COO Yale Univ. Sch. Medicine, New Haven, Conn., 1997—; bd. dirs. N.Y. Regional Transplant Program, N.Y.C., treas., exec. com.; bd. dirs. FFH/N.E. Ins. Com., MCIC Vt., Inc.; adj. prof. Robert Wagner Sch. Pub. Svc., NYU; lectr. pub. health, health policy, adminstrn. Sch. Medicine Yale U. Editor: Health Care Law Treatise, 1990. Bd. trustees, treas., exec. com. Malmonides Med. Ctr., Bklyn., 1988—; sec./treas., exec. com. Hosp. Trustees N.Y. State, 1990-97. Fellow N.Y. Acad. Medicine; mem. Assn. of Bar of City of N.Y. (sec. com. on medicine and law 1989-90, sec. health law com. 1995-96), Am. Acad. Hosp. Attys. (spl. com. in health care systems). Avocations: sailing, tennis, reading, travel. Health. Office: Yale Univ Sch Medicine 333 Cedar St I-209 SHM PO Box 208049 New Haven CT 06520-8049

**BIRNBAUM, JULIAN R.,** lawyer; b. Boise, Idaho, May 1, 1948; s. Milton and Audrey (Roossin) B.; m. Andrea Jean Pfeiffer, Jan. 5, 1980; children: Susan Adele, Molly Jean. AB, Harvard U., 1970; JD, U. Chgo., 1975. Bar: Ill. 1975, W.Va. 1981, N.Y. 1984, U.S. Dist. Ct. (no. dist.) Ill. 1975, U.S. Dist. Ct. (no. and so. dists.) W.Va. 1981, U.S. Dist. Ct. (so. dist.) N.Y. 1986, U.S. Dist. Ct. (ea. dist.) N.Y. 1987, U.S. Ct. Appeals (2d cir.) 1989, U.S. Ct. Appeals (3d cir.) 1995. Staff atty. Legal Assistance Found. Chgo., 1975-80, Legal Aid Soc., Bklyn., 1983-86; civil rights atty. Appalachian Rsch. and Def. Fund, Charleston, W.Va., 1980-83; assoc. Vladeck, Waldman, Elias & Engelhard, P.C., N.Y.C., 1986-88, ptnr., 1988—. Contbr. articles to profl. publs. Mem. Nat. Lawyers Guild. Labor, Civil rights. Home: 468 E 16th St Brooklyn NY 11226-6501 Office: Vladeck Waldman Elias & Engelhard PC 1501 Broadway Ste 800 New York NY 10036-5560

**BIRNBAUM, SHEILA L.,** lawyer, educator; b. 1940. B.A., Hunter Coll., 1960, M.A., 1962; LL.B., NYU, 1965. Bar: N.Y. 1965. Legal asst. Superior Ct., N.Y.C., 1965; assoc. Berman & Frost, N.Y.C., 1965-70, ptnr., 1970-72; prof. Fordham U., N.Y.C., 1972-78; prof. NYU, N.Y.C., 1978-86, assoc. dean, 1982-84; ptnr. Skadden, Arps, Slate, Meagher & Flom, 1984—. Author: (with Rheingold) Products Liability, Law, Practice Science, 1974. Mem. N.Y.C. Bar Assn. (mem. exec. com. 1978—, jud. com. 1977), ABA (chmn. product gen. liability, consumer land coms.), Assn. of Bar of City of N.Y. (exec. com. 1978—, 2d century com. 1984-86), Phi Beta Kappa, Phi Alpha Theta, Alpha Chi Alpha. Office: Skadden Arps Slate Meagher & Flom 919 3rd Ave New York NY 10022-3902

**BIRNE, KENNETH ANDREW,** lawyer; b. Englewood, N.J., Apr. 2, 1956; s. Alvin Aaron and Rita May (Gorsky) B.; m. Pamela Beth Ross; children: Jennafer Sara, Allison Francie, Jonathan Ross. BA in Polit. Sci., Ohio State U., 1978; JD, Case Western Res. U., 1981. Bar: Ohio 1981, U.S. Dist. Ct. (no. dist.) Ohio 1981. Sole practice Cleve., 1981-85; ptnr. Peltz & Birne, Cleve., 1985—; instr. Am. Inst. Paralegal Studies, Cleve., 1982-93, pers. dir. Cleve. area, 1984-93; cons. in field. Mem. Ohio Bar Assn., Cleve. Bar Assn. (chmn. practice and procedure clinic 1984-86, vol. Call for Action 1986, meritorious service award 1986), Cuyahoga County Bar Assn., Phi Eta Sigma, Zeta Beta Tau, Phi Delta Phi. Lodge: Masons. Personal injury, Workers' compensation, State civil litigation. Office: Peltz & Birne Midland Bldg Ste 1880 Cleveland OH 44115-1093

**BIRNEY, PHILIP RIPLEY,** lawyer; b. Canton, Ohio, June 25, 1940; s. Forrest Earl and Jean Lois (Ripley) B.; m. Susanne Elaine St. John, July 11, 1964; children: Julie Michelle, Laurie Catherine, Nicole Susanne. BS in Bus. Adminstrn., Northwestern U., 1962; JD, Hastings Coll. Law, 1965. Bar: Calif. 1966, U.S. Dist. Ct. (all dists.) Calif., U.S. Ct. Appeals (9th and 11th cirs.), U.S. Supreme Ct. 1975; diplomate Am. Coll. Trial Lawyers; diplomate, cert. specialist med. profl. liability Am. Bd. Profl. Liability Attys. Dep. atty. gen. State of Calif., Sacramento, 1966-68; dep. dist. atty. Sacramento County, 1968-70; sr. ptnr., chief trial lawyer Wilke, Fleury, Hoffelt, Gould & Birney, Sacramento, 1970—. Mem. ABA, Calif. State Bar Assn., Sacramento County Bar Assn. (judiciary com. 1991-94, jud. rev. com. 1992—, chmn. 1995—), Am. Bd. Trial Advs. (bd. dirs. Sacramento Valley chpt. 1994—, pres. Sacramento Valley chpt. 1998-99, Civility award 1995), Calif. Med.-Legal Com., No. Calif. Assn. Def. Counsel (bd. dirs. 1986-88). Professional liability. Home: 832 Senior Way Sacramento CA 95831-2129 Office: Wilke Fleury Hoffelt Gould & Birney 400 Capitol Mall Fl 22 Sacramento CA 95814-4407

**BIRNKRANT, HENRY JOSEPH,** lawyer; b. Phila., Jan. 24, 1955; s. Harry Philip and Myra Arlene (Hendler) B.; m. Lynn Rachel Goldin, Oct. 23, 1983; children: Aviva Michelle, Beth Elana. BA magna cum laude, U. Rochester, 1976; JD, Columbia U., 1979; LLM, NYU, 1983. Bar: D.C. 1979, U.S. Dist. Ct. D.C. 1980; U.S. Ct. Appeals (D.C. cir.) 1980, U.S. Tax Ct. 1984. Assoc. Bergson, Borkland, Margolis & Adler, Washington, 1979-82, Covington & Burling, Washington, 1983-88; assoc. Cole, Corette & Abrutyn, Washington, 1988-90, ptnr., 1991-96; ptnr. Alston & Bird, Washington, 1997—. Author: (with others) Butterworth's International Taxation of Financial Instruments and Transactions, 1989; editor: Columbia Jour. Law and Social Problems, 1979; contbr. articles to profl. jours.; bd. advisors Jour. Internat. Taxation. Mem. ABA (tax section). Taxation, general, Corporate taxation, Personal income taxation. Home: 5506 Durbin Rd Bethesda MD 20814-1012 Office: Alston & Bird North Bldg 11th Fl 601 Pennsylvania Ave NW Washington DC 20004-2601

**BIRNKRANT, SHERWIN MAURICE,** lawyer; b. Pontiac, Mich., Dec. 20, 1927. BBA, U. Mich., 1949; MBA, 1951; JD with distinction, Wayne State U., 1954. Bar: Mich. 1955, U.S. Dist. Ct. (ea. dist.) 1960, U.S. Supreme Ct. 1960, U.S. Ct. Appeals (6th cir.) 1966. Mem. Oakland County Bd. Suprs., 1967-68; asst. atty. City of Pontiac, 1956-67, city atty., 1967-83; of counsel Schlussel, Lifton, Simon, Rands, Galvin & Jackier, Southfield, Mich., 1983-90, Sommers, Schwartz, Silver & Schwartz, Southfield, Mich., 1990-95; shareholder Birnkrant & Birnkrant P.C., Farmington Hills, Mich., 1995—. Mem. ABA (chmn. urban, state and local govt. law sect. 1987-88, Mich. chmn. pub. contract law sect. 1979-97, ho. of dels. 1990-93, alternate del. to ho. of dels., 1993-96, vice chmn. coordinating com. for model procurement code for state and local govt. 1974—), State Bar Mich. (chmn. pub. corp. law sect. 1973-74, coun. adminstrv. law sect. 1975-76), Oakland County Bar Assn. (chmn. ethics and unauthorized practices com. 1961-62), Am. Judicature Soc., Mich. Assn. Mcpl. Attys. (pres. 1975, coun. of pres. 1992—). Government contracts and claims, Land use and zoning (including planning), Municipal (excluding bonds). Office: Birnkrant & Birnkrant PC 31555 W 14 Mile Rd Ste 201 Farmington Hills MI 48334-1287

**BIRREN, JEFFREY EMMETT,** lawyer; b. Chgo., Jan. 28, 1951; s. James E. and Elizabeth Ann (Solomon) B. AB, U. So. Calif., 1974, MA, 1980; JD, Southwestern U., Los Angeles, 1985. Bar: Calif. 1985, U.S. Dist. Ct. (so. dist.) Calif. 1985, U.S. Dist. Ct. (no., ea. and cen. dists.) Calif. 1986, U.S. Ct. Appeals (9th cir.) 1986. Asst. dir. mini coll. U. So. Calif., L.A., 1970-79, instr., 1979; with legal staff L.A. Raiders, 1980-85, gen. counsel, 1985—; adj. prof. Southwestern U. Sch. Law. Mem. ATLA. Unitarian. General practice, Antitrust. Office: Oakland Raiders 1220 Harbor Bay Pkwy Alameda CA 94502-6570

**BIRTCH, GRANT EACRETT,** lawyer; b. Boston, Dec. 9, 1959; s. Alan G. and Elaine G. B.; m. Susan Sprung, June 14, 1981; children: Banjamin, Madeline, Christopher. BA, Beloit Coll., 1981; JD, U. Wis., 1990. Bar: Wis. 1990, U.S. Dist. Ct. (ea. and we. dists.) Wis. 1990. Assoc. Adams & Woodrow, Neenah, Wis., 1990-95, Direnzo & Bomier, Neenah, Wis., 1995-98, Hesson & Assoc., Neenah, Wis., 1998—. Bd. dirs. Regional Domestic Abuse Svcs., Oshkosh, Wis., 1992-98, pres., 1996-97. Mem. Winnebago County Bar Assn. (pres. 1999—), Beta Theta Pi. Contracts commercial, Probate, Real property. Office: Hesson & Assocs 244 E Doty Ave Neenah WI 54956-3032

**BISCEGLIE, ANTHONY PATRICK,** lawyer; b. N.Y.C., July 22, 1952; s. Patrick and Margaret (Hanly) B.; m. Bonny Sue Lundy, Mar. 5, 1983; children: Alexander, Sarah. BA, U. Colo., 1974; JD, Antioch Law Sch., 1978. Bar: D.C. 1979, U.S. Ct. Appeals (D.C. cir.) 1979, U.S. Dist. Ct. D.C. 1979, U.S. Supreme Ct. 1990, Md. 1991. Law clk. U.S. Dept. Justice/U.S. Atty.'s Office, Washington, 1976-78; law clk. Hon. Robert M. Scott D.C. Superior Ct., Washington, 1978-79; assoc. Verner, Liipfert, Bernhard & McPherson, Washington, 1979-80, Canan, Burns & O'Toole, Washington, 1980-84; ptnr. Bisceglie & Walsh, Washington, 1984—; arbitrator N.Y. Stock Exch., 1989—; mem. adv. bd. Corp. Counsel Lawlast, 1994—, Civil Rico Report, Washington, 1987—. Contbr. articles to profl. publs. Gen. counsel Greenwood PTA, Brookeville, Md., 1992—; asst. scoutmaster Boy Scouts Am., Ashton, Md., 1996—. Named to Top 50 Heavy Hitters, Washingtonian Mag., 1997. Mem. ABA (Hero of the Day award 1996), Nat. Assn. Criminal Def. Lawyers. Avocations: white water canoeing, mountain biking, skiing. General corporate, Criminal. Office: Bisceglie & Walsh 1130 17th St NW Washington DC 20036-4604

**BISHAR, JOHN JOSEPH, JR.,** lawyer; b. N.Y.C., Jan. 22, 1950; s. John Joseph Sr. and Mildred (Marron) B.; m. Noreen Ellen Leddy, Aug. 5, 1972; children: Kimberly, Kelly, Lauren. BA, Georgetown U., 1971; JD, Fordham U., 1974. Bar: N.Y. 1975, U.S. Dist. Ct. (ea. dist.) N.Y. 1975. Assoc. Cullen & Dykman, Garden City, N.Y., 1974-80; sr. v.p., gen. counsel North Am. Bancorp., Garden City, 1980-87; mng. ptnr. Cullen & Dykman, Garden City, 1987—. Bd. dirs. YMCA of Long Island, Huntington, N.Y., 1981—; bd. of trustees Family Life Ctr., Garden City, 1985—; gov. Cath. Sch. of St. Mary, Garden City, 1985—. Named Man of Yr. YMCA of Long Island, 1986. Mem. ABA, N.Y. State Bar Assn., Nassau County Bar Assn., N.Y. State Bankers Assn. (lawyers adv. com.), Assn. Bank Holding Cos. (lawyers com.). Republican. Roman Catholic. Clubs: Cherry Valley (Garden City), Atlantic Beach (N.Y.). Avocations: sports, golf, basketball, tennis, coaching kids. Banking, General corporate. Home: 53 Chestnut St Garden City NY 11530-6334

**BISHIN, WILLIAM ROBERT,** lawyer, legal consultant, educator; b. N.Y.C., Sept. 1, 1939; s. Arthur Abraham and Jean (Dashevsky) B.; m. Sharlee Field, Jan. 23, 1967 (div.); children: Benjamin, Susannah; m. Adeline Safyan, Apr. 6, 1976. AB cum laude, Columbia U., 1960; LLB magna cum laude, Harvard U., 1963. Bar: Wash. 1978, N.Y. 1964, Calif. 1965, U.S. Dist. Ct. (cen. dist.) Calif. 1965, U.S. Dist. Ct. (we. dist.) Wash. 1978, U.S. Ct. Appeals (9th cir.) 1980, U.S. Supreme Ct. 1981. Am. history editor Columbia Ency., 1960; assoc. Paul, Weiss, Rifkind, Wharton & Garrison, N.Y.C., 1960; asst. prof. law U. So. Calif. Law Ctr., Los Angeles, 1963-65, assoc. prof., 1965-67, prof., 1967-80; sole practice, Seattle, 1980—; syndicated columnist Los Angeles Times, 1968-70; juvenile ct. referee Superior Ct. County of Los Angeles, 1971-75; ptnr. Edwards & Bishin, Los Angeles, 1973-76; litigator Pacht, Ross, Warne, Bernhard & Sears, Inc., Los Angeles, 1977-78; prof. law U. Puget Sound Law Sch., 1978-80; arbitrator comml. panel Am. Arbitration Assn., 1980—. Editor Harvard Law Rev., 1961-63. Am. Council Learned Socs. fellow, 1968; Columbia U. scholar, 1968; recipient Dart award U. So. Calif., 1969. Mem. ABA, Fed. Bar Assn. (pres. 1984-85), Western Wash. (sec., chmn. continuing legal edn. com.), Am. Arbitration Assn., Wash. State Bar Assn. (chmn. subcom. continuing legal edn. goals), N.Y. State Bar Assn. Contbr. to The Weekly, 1981-82; author: (with C. Stone) Law, Language and Ethics, 1972, Advocacy and Analysis in Contract Interperation Cases, 1988, Litigating the Meaning of Statutes, 1994; contbg. author Mass Media and the Supreme Court, 2d edit., 1976; contbr. articles to legal jours. Federal civil litigation, State civil litigation. Office: 1111 3rd Ave Ste 1865 Seattle WA 98101-3217

**BISHOP, ALFRED CHILTON, JR.,** lawyer; b. Alexandria, Va., Oct. 3, 1942; s. Alfred Chilton and Margaret (Marshall) B.; divorced; 1 son, Alfred Chilton III; m. 2d Catherine Ann Keppel, May 17, 1980. B.A. with distinction, U. Va., 1965, LL.B., 1969; LL.M. in Taxation, Georgetown U., 1974. Bar: N.Y. 1970, U.S. Ct. Appeals (2d cir.), 1970, U.S. Tax Ct. 1971, U.S. Ct. Claims 1971, D.C. 1977. Assoc. Shearman and Sterling, N.Y.C., 1969-70; assoc. trial atty., Office of Chief Counsel IRS, Washington, 1970-74, sr. trial atty., 1974-80, sr. technician reviewer, 1980-81, br. chief, 1981—. Recipient

Am. Jurisprudence award 1968, 1968. Mem. ABA (tax sec.), D.C. Bar Assn., Sr. Exec. Service Candidate Network (v.p. 1980-81, pres. 1981-82, dir. 1983), Sr. Exec. Assn., Phi Delta Phi. Episcopalian. Home: 7523 Thistledown Trl Fairfax Station VA 22039-2207

**BISHOP, BRUCE TAYLOR,** lawyer; b. Hartford, Conn., Sept. 13, 1951; s. Robert Wright Sr. and Barbara (Taylor) B.; m. Sarah M. Bishop, Aug. 31, 1974; children: Elizabeth, Margaret. BA in Polit. Sci., Old Dominion U., 1973; JD, U. Va., Charlottesville, 1976. Bar: Va. 1977, U.S. Supreme Ct., Va. 1976, U.S. Dist. Ct. (ea. dist.) Va., U.S. Dist. Ct. (we. dist.) Va., U.S. Ct. Appeals (4th cir.); diplomate Am. Bd. Trial Advocates. Law clk. to chief judge U.S. Dist. Ct. (ea. dist.) Va., 1976-77; assoc. Willcox & Savage, P.C., Norfolk, Va., 1977-82; ptnr. Willcox & Savage, P.C., Norfolk, 1983—; bd. dirs. Nautical Adventures, Inc., Norfolk FestEvents, Ltd., 1981—, pres., 1982-85; pres. Va. OpSail 2000 Found.; mem. bd. visitors Old Dominion U., 1972-83, sec., 1979-81, chmn., mem. various coms.; speaker in field. Treas. Norfolk Reps., 1978-82, also mem. numerous coms.; bd. dirs., chmn. regional Key Club campaign United Way South Hampton Roads; chmn., co-chmn. United Negro Coll. Fund, 1981, Four Cities United Way Campaign; trustee Va. Stage Co., 1982; pres. Community Promotion Corp.; commr. Norfolk Redevel. and Housing Authority; active numerous other community orgns. Named Outstanding Young Man, Norfolk Jaycees; recipient Disting. Alumni award Old Dominion U., Dominion Vol. of Yr. award, 1993. Mem. ABA (mem. various sects.), Fed. Bar Assn. (pres. Tidewater chpt. 1980-81), Am. Bd. Trial Advocates, Va. Assn. Def. Lawyers, Va. Bar Assn., Va. Trial Lawyers Assn., Norfolk-Portsmouth Bar Assn., Def. Rsch. Inst., Internat. Assn. Def. Counsel, Assn. Def. Attys., Def. Rsch. Inst., Old Dominion U. Alumni Assn. (bd. dirs. 1978-83), Old Dominion U. Ednl. Found. (bd. dirs. 1987—), Norfolk C. of C. (chmn. downtown devel. com. 1980-81), James Keat Am. Inn of Ct. (master). Avocations: basketball, tennis, gardening. Aviation, Product liability, Toxic tort. Office: Willcox & Savage PC One Commercial Place Norfolk VA 23510

**BISHOP, BRYAN EDWARDS,** lawyer; b. Providence, Nov. 29, 1945; s. Charles Frederick Jr. and Emma Kirtley (Edwards) B.; m. Martha Jo Maben, June 12, 1970; children: Jennifer, Adam. BSME, U. Tex., Arlington, 1968; JD, Harvard U., 1972. Bar: Tex. 1972, U.S. Ct. Appeals (5th cir.) 1972. Ptnr. Rain, Harrell, Emery, Young & Doke, Dallas, 1972-87, Locke Purnell Rain Harrell, Dallas, 1987-98, Locke Liddell & Sapp LLP, Dallas, 1999—. Mem. ABA, State Bar Tex. (corp. law com., corp. banking and bus. law sect.), Tex. Bus. Law Found. (bd. dirs.). Club: Dallas Petroleum. Mergers and acquisitions, Securities, Banking. Home: 7031 Roundrock Rd Dallas TX 75248-5144 Office: Locke Liddell & Sapp LLP 2200 Ross Ave Ste 2200 Dallas TX 75201-2748

**BISHOP, JAMES DODSON,** lawyer, mediator; b. Washington, Sept. 28, 1957; s. James William and Jane Lillian (Dodson) B. BA magna cum laude in Polit. Sci., Lincoln (Pa.) U., 1979; JD, Howard U., Washington, 1982. Bar: Pa. 1985. Dir. Atty./Client Arbitration Bd. D.C. Bar, Washington, 1987-93; dir. Archdioscesan Legal Network of Cath. Charities, Washington, 1993—. Mediator, D.C. Superior Ct., Washington, 1987—; lay reader St. Georges Episcopal Ch., Washington, 1984—. Mem. ABA (vice chmn. State and Local Bar Dispute Resolution Com., 1993). Democrat. Episcopalian. Avocation: church activities. Home: 5157 33rd St NW Washington DC 20008-2011 Office: Catholic Charities 1221 Massachusetts Ave NW Washington DC 20005-5302

**BISHOP, LES, JR.,** lawyer; b. Huntindon, Tenn., Jan. 25, 1966; s. Lester and Bettie Bishop; m. Rachel Bishop, Dec. 28, 1979; children: Jake, Ben. BA in Psychology, Union U., Jackson, Tenn., 1977; JD, U. Tenn., Knoxville, 1984. Atty. Fed. Express Corp., Memphis. Office: Fed Express Corp 1980 Nonconnah Blvd Memphis TN 38132-2103

**BISHOP, MAHLON LEE,** lawyer, consultant, arbitrator; b. Pekin, Ill., Apr. 2, 1930; m. Joyce Ann Bresee, Apr. 27, 1952. BS, U. Ill., 1951, JD, 1956. Bar: Ill. 1956. Assoc. Winston & Strawn, Chgo., 1956-59; v.p., gen. counsel Wilson Foods Corp., Oklahoma City, 1958-77; sr. v.p. John Morrell & Co., Chgo., 1977-85; of counsel Isham, Lincoln & Beale, Chgo., 1985-87; pvt. practice, Winnetka, Ill., 1987—; founding chmn. Meat Industry Safety Com., Chgo., 1970-75; founding mem. Employee Retirement Ins. Com., Washington, 1975-77. Maj. USMC, 1951-54. Labor, Pension, profit-sharing, and employee benefits, Administrative and regulatory. Office: 722 Oak St Winnetka IL 60093-2521

**BISHOP, ROBERT WHITSITT,** lawyer; b. Atlanta, Jan. 7, 1949; s. James Clarence and Dorothy Davis (Whitsitt) B.; m. Cynthia Graham, Aug. 23, 1970; children: Jessica Levesque, Joshua Davis, Amanda Joyce, Alexandra Kelt. Student, Duke U., 1966-68; BA with high distinction, U. Ky., Lexington, 1973; postgrad. George Washington U., 1973-74; JD, U. Ky., 1976. Bar: Ohio 1976, Ky. 1981. Mem. Squire, Sanders & Dempsey, Cleve., 1976-80, Barnett & Alagia, Louisville, 1980-84; ptnr. Greenebaum, Young, Treitz & Maggiolo, Louisville, 1984-87; founding mem. Friedman, Evans & Bishop, Louisville, 1987-88; ptnr. Amshoff, Amshoff, Evans, Bishop & Masters, Louisville, 1988; founding mem., ptnr. Evans, Bishop, Masters & Mullins, Louisville, 1989-93; founding mem., ptnr. Bishop & Wilson, Louisville, 1993—; founder, dir., officer Indoor Soccer of Louisville Inc., (The Louisville Thunder), 1984-85; bd. dirs., officer Louisville Thunder, Inc., 1985-87, Cen. Indoor Soccer League, 1984. Author: The Interdict. Bd. dirs., mem. pers. and fin. coms. Louisville Central Community Ctrs. Inc., 1985. Mem. ABA, Ky. Bar Assn., Ohio Bar Assn., Louisville Bar Assn. (chmn. fed. practice sect. 1987-88), Cleve. Bar Assn., Order of Coif, Phi Beta Kappa, Sigma Alpha Epsilon. Avocations: mountain and rock climbing, soccer, creative writing. Federal civil litigation, State civil litigation. Home: 3901 Glen Bluff Rd Louisville KY 40222-5911 Office: Bishop & Wilson 6520 Glenridge Park Pl Ste 6 Louisville KY 40222-3412

**BISSELL, JOHN W.,** federal judge; b. Exeter, N.H., June 7, 1940; s. H. Hamilton and Sarah W. B.; m. Caroline M.; July 15, 1967; children—Megan L., Katharine W. AB, Princeton U., 1962; LLB, U. Va., 1965. Law clk. U.S. Dist. Ct., N.J., 1965-66; assoc. Pitney, Hardin & Kipp, Newark and Norristown, N.J., 1966-69, ptnr., 1972-78; asst. U.S. atty. N.J., 1969-71; judge Essex County, N.J., 1978-81, N.J. Superior Ct., 1981-82, U.S. Dist. Ct. N.J., Trenton and Newark, 1983—. Office: US Dist Ct Federal Square PO Box 999 Newark NJ 07101-0999

**BISSELL, ROLIN PLUMB,** lawyer; b. Yokosuka, Japan, Sept. 19, 1960; came to U.S., 1961; s. Elliston Perot III and Edith R. Bissell; m. Avery Boling, Sept. 12, 1987. BA in Philosophy and Econs., Columbia Coll., 1982; JD, U. Va., 1985. Law clk. to Chief Justice Richard Neely Supreme Ct. of W.Va., Charleston, 1985-86; assoc. Dewey Ballantine Bushby, Palmer & Wood, N.Y.C., 1986-88; assoc. Schnader Harrison Segal & Lewis LLP, Phila., 1988-93, ptnr., 1994—. Contbr. articles to law jours. Dir. Chestnut Hill Hist. Soc., Phila., 1993-98, Landmarks Soc., Phila., 1998—; mem. Com. of Seventy, Phila., 1998—. Antitrust, Federal civil litigation, Securities. Office: Schnader Harrison Segal & Lewis 1600 Market St Fl 34 Philadelphia PA 19103-7286

**BISSINGER, MARK CHRISTIAN,** lawyer; b. Steubenville, Ohio, June 4, 1957; s. Emerson Melvin and Nancy (Osbun) B.; m. Julie Furber, Sept. 28, 1985; children: Lucas Christian, Nathan Kenneth. BS in Civil Engring., Purdue U., 1979; JD, U. Cin., 1983. Bar: Ohio 1983, U.S. Dist. Ct. (so. dist.) Ohio 1983, U.S. Ct. Appeals (6th cir.), Ky. 1993. Assoc. Dinsmore & Shohl, Cin., 1983-90, ptnr., 1990—; spkr. Ohio Continuing Legal Edn., Cin., 1990—; lectr. Nat. Bus. Inst., 1990—; commn. cert. attys. as splsts. Supreme Ct. Ohio; mem. Supreme Ct. Ohio's Bd. Bar Examiners; lectr. Lorman Edn. Svcs. Pres. Ctr. for Comprehensive Alcoholism Treatment, Cin., 1989-92. Named Order of Coif, Cin., 1983; inducted class of 1999 Cin. Acad. of Leadership for Lawyers. Mem. ABA, Cin. Bar Assn., Ohio Bar Assn., No. Ky. Bar Assn., Ky. Bar Assn. Avocations: family, travel, sports. General civil litigation, Construction, Bankruptcy. Office: Dinsmore & Shohl 255 E 5th St Cincinnati OH 45202-4700

**BITENSKY, SUSAN HELEN,** law educator; b. N.Y.C., Jan. 3, 1948; d. Reuben Bitensky; m. Elliott Lee Meyrowitz, Apr. 17, 1982; 1 child, William N. BA magna cum laude, Case Western Res. U., 1971; JD, U. Chgo., 1974. Bar: Pa. 1974, U.S. Dist. Ct. (we. dist.) Pa. 1974, U.S. Ct. Appeals (3d cir.) 1975, U.S. Ct. Appeals (2d cir.) 1977, N.Y. 1979, U.S. Dist. Ct. (so. and ea. dists.) N.Y. 1979, Mich. 1988. Asst. gen. counsel United Steelworkers Am., Pitts., 1974-77; assoc. Cohen, Weiss and Simon, N.Y.C., 1977-81; assoc. counsel N.Y.C. Bd. Edn., Bklyn., 1981-87; assoc. prof. law Detroit Coll. Law at Mich. State U., 1988-93, prof. law, 1993—. Contbg. author: Children's Rights in America: UN Convention on the Rights of the Child Compared with U.S. Law; contbr. articles to profl. jours. Mem. ABA, Phi Beta Kappa. Office: Detroit Coll Law at Mich State U 447 Law College Bldg East Lansing MI 48824-1300

**BITNER, RICHARD H.,** lawyer, educator; b. Yonkers, N.Y., Jan. 16, 1968; s. Richard Frank and Mary Ellen Bitner; m. Alison Appich, June 4, 1994. BA, Auburn U., 1990; JD, So. Meth. U., 1993. Bar: Fla., U.S. Dist. Ct. (mid. dist.) Fla. 1994, U.S. Ct. Appeals (11th cir.) 1994, U.S. Supreme Ct. 1998. Legis. clk. U.S. Senator Connie Mack, Washington, 1991; atty. Taraska, Grower, Unger & Ketchum, Orland, Fla., 1994-95, Unger Willis Cacciatore & Swartwood, Orland, 1995-96, Hannah, Estes & Ingram, Orlando, 1996—; prof. U. Phoenix, Orlando, 1998. Contbr. articles to profl. jours. Judge, Teen Ct., Orlando, 1997—. Recipient Pro Bono award Legal Aid, Orlando, 1997, 98. Avocations: golf, wine, travel, theatre. Health, General civil litigation, Personal injury. Office: Hannah Estes & Ingram 37 N Orange Ave Ste 300 Orlando FL 32801-2439

**BITTERMAN, GREGORY VAL,** lawyer; b. Bklyn., June 15, 1960; s. Arnold David and Pearl (Wornow) B. BA, U. Rochester, 1982; JD, Case Western Res. U., 1985. Bar: N.Y. 1986, N.J. 1986, U.S. Dist. Ct (so. and ea. dists.) N.Y., U.S. Dist. Ct. N.J. 1986, U.S. Ct. Appeals (2nd cir.) 1989, U.S. Dist. Ct. (no. dist.) N.Y., 1998. Assoc. Leon F. Entin, Esq., Syosset, N.Y., 1985-86, Goldberg & Connolly, Rockville Centre, N.Y., 1986-88, Schwarzfeld, Ganfer & Shore, N.Y.C., 1988-89, Kroll & Tract, N.Y.C., 1989-90, D'Amato & Lynch, N.Y.C., 1990-92; ptnr. Law Offices of Gregory V. Bitterman, N.Y.C., 1992—. Pension, profit-sharing, and employee benefits. Home: 139 E Choir Ln Westbury NY 11590-5734 Office: 32 Court St Ste 904 Brooklyn NY 11201-4404

**BITTICK, PEGGY SUE,** lawyer; b. Pasadena, Tex., Jan. 14, 1965; 1 child, Gavin Nicholas. BS, U. Tex., 1988; JD, S. Tex. Coll. Law, Houston, 1995. Bar: Tex. 1995, U.S. Dist. Ct. (so. and ea. dists.) Tex. 1995, U.S. Dist. Ct. (no. and we. dists.) 1996, U.S. Ct. Appeals (5th cir.) 1995. Tchr. Pearland (Tex.) Ind. Sch. Dist., 1988-92; assoc. Hirsch & Westheimer, P.C., Houston, 1994-97; pvt. practice Pearland, 1997—. Active sch. bd. Pearland Ind. Sch. Dist., 1999—. Mem. Rotary (bd. dirs.). Democrat. Labor, Education and schools, General practice. Office: Law Offices Peggy S Bittick 2113 Grand Blvd Pearland TX 77581-3401

**BITZEGAIO, HAROLD JAMES,** retired lawyer; b. Coalmont, Ind., Jan. 29, 1921; s. Nicholas Gilbert and Dora Belle (Burns) B.; m. Betty Jean Law, Apr. 15, 1950; children: Judith L. Bitzegaio Wallin, Gail Ann Bitzegaio Wright, Susan R. Bitzegaio Denyer, James R., Jane E. BS, Ind. State U., 1948; JD, Ind. U., 1953; grad., Ind. Jud. Coll., 1980. Bar: Ind. 1953, U.S. Dist. Ct. (so. dist.) Ind. 1953, U.S. Ct. Appeals (7th cir.) 1956. Sole practice Terre Haute, Ind., 1953-58, 81-97; judge Vigo Superior Ct., Terre Haute, 1959-80; of counsel Anderson & Nichols Law Office. Editor, contbr.: Indiana Pattern Jury Instructions, 1966. Mem. Ind. Adv. Com. Civil Rights, Indpls., 1961-70, Mayor's Com. Civil Rights, Terre Haute, 1967-68; bd. dirs. Wabash Valley Council Boy Scouts Am., Terre Haute, 1960-80. Served to lt. comdr. USN, 1941-46, PTO. Decorated D.F.C. with gold star, Air medal with two gold stars, Purple Heart; named Sagamore of the Wabash, Gov. of Ind., 1990. Mem. ABA, Ind. Bar Assn., Terre Haute Bar Assn., Ind. Judges Assn. (bd. mgrs. 1961-80, pres. 1977-78), Ind. U. Law Alumni Assn. (pres. 1973-74, recipient disting. service award 1974), VFW (life), Nat. Rifle Assn. (life), Ducks Unltd. (nat. trustee, emeritus). Democrat. Club: Terre Haute Country (bd. dirs. 1974-76). General practice. Home and Office: 2703 E Springhill Dr Terre Haute IN 47802-8406

**BIVANS, ROGER WAYNE,** lawyer; b. Melbourne, Fla., Apr. 4, 1966; s. Richard W. and Helen T. Bivans; m. Beth W. Bivans, Apr. 19, 1997. BS in Ocean Engring., U.S. Naval Acad., 1988; JD, U. Tex., 1996. Bar: Tex. 1996, U.S. Dist. Ct. (no. dist.) Tex. 1996, U.S. Dist. Ct. (so. dist.) Tex. 1998. Atty. Gibson, Dunn & Crutcher LLP, Dallas, 1996—. Lt. USN, 1988-93. Mem. ABA, Dallas Bar Assn., Dallas Assn. Young Lawyers. General corporate, Securities, Intellectual property. Office: Gibson Dunn & Crutcher LLP 1717 Main St Ste 5400 Dallas TX 75201-7390

**BIVENS, DONALD WAYNE,** lawyer, judge; b. Ann Arbor, Mich., Feb. 5, 1952; s. Melvin Donley and Frances Lee (Speer) B.; children: Jody, Lisa. BA magna cum laude, Yale U., 1974; JD, U. Tex., 1977. Bar: Ariz. 1977, U.S. Dist. Ct. Ariz. 1977, U.S. Ct. Appeals (9th cir.) 1977, U.S. Ct. Appeals (fed. cir.) 1984, U.S. Supreme Ct. 1982. Ptnr. Meyer, Hendricks & Bivens, P.A., Phoenix, 1977—; judge pro tem Maricopa County Superior Ct., Ariz., 1987—, Ariz. Ct. Appeals, Phoenix, 1999—; bd. dirs. Ctr. for Law in Pub. Interest, Phoenix, 1983-85. Note & Comment editor Tex. Law Rev., Austin, 1976-77. Pres. Ariz. Young Dems., 1980-82, Scottsdale Men's League, 1980-82; v.p., bd. dirs. Phoenix Symphony Assn., 1980-86; bd. dirs. Scottsdale Arts Ctr. Assn., 1981-84, Planned Parenthood Cen. and No. Ariz., 1989-92; adv. bd. Ariz. Theater Co., 1987-88. Recipient Consul award U. Tex. Sch. Law, 1977, Three Outstanding Young Men award Phoenix Jaycees, 1981. Mem. ABA (coun. litigation sect. 1995-98, chmn. computer litigation com. 1989-92, resource devel. com. litigation sect. 1992—, tech. task force 1998—, state del. to Ho. of Dels. 1999—), Am. Bar Found., Ariz. Bar Found., State Bar Ariz. (bd. govs. 1993-2000, pres. 1998-99—, peer rev. com. 1992—), Ariz. Trial Lawyers Assn., Maricopa County Bar Assn. (bd. dirs., chmn. Trial Adv. Inst. 1986-87, Mem. of Yr. 1998), Thurgood Marshall Inn of Ct. (pres. 1992-93). Democrat. Avocations: music, theater. Federal civil litigation, Computer, Securities. Home: 4929 E Cochise Rd Paradise Valley AZ 85253-1044 Office: Meyer Hendricks & Bivens PA 3003 N Central Ave Ste 1200 Phoenix AZ 85012-2921

**BIX, BRIAN,** law educator; b. Mpls., Aug. 1, 1962; s. Harold Charles and Helen (Helman) B. BA, Washington U., St. Louis, 1983; JD, Harvard U., 1986; DPhil, Oxford (Eng.) U., 1991. Bar: Mass. 1994, Conn. 1995. Jud. clk. to Justice A. Handler N.J. Supreme Ct., Trenton, 1986-87; jud. clk. to Judge S. Reinhardt 9th Circuit Ct. of Appeals, L.A., 1987-88; lectr. in law Kings Coll., U. London, 1991-93; jud. clk. to Justice Benjamin Kaplan Mass. Appeals Ct., Boston, 1993-95; assoc. prof. law Quinnipiac Law Sch., Hamden, Conn., 1995-98, prof., 1998—; vis. prof. of law George Wash. Law Sch., 1999. Author: Law, Language and Legal Determinacy, 1993, Jurisprudence: Theory and Context, 1996, 2d edit., 1999; editor: Analyzing Law, New Essays in Legal Theory, 1998. Mem. Am. Law Inst. Office: Quinnipiac Law Sch 275 Mount Carmel Ave Hamden CT 06518-1950

**BIXBY, DAVID MICHAEL,** lawyer; b. Pensacola, Fla., Aug. 10, 1954; s. Harry Lewellyn and Ann Olivia B.; m. Karen Louise Schroeder, Sept. 5, 1981; children: Laura, Elizabeth. BA, Harvard Coll., 1976, U. Cape Town, 1977; JD, Yale Law Sch., 1980. Bar: Ariz. 1981, U.S. Dist. Ct. Ariz. 1981, U.S. Ct. Appeals (9th cir.) 1981. Law clk. Hon. David W. Williams U.S. Dist. Ct., L.A., 1980-81; ptnr. Lewis & Roca, LLP, Phoenix, 1981-98; sr. v.p., gen. counsel Samaritan Health Sys., Phoenix, 1998—. Mem. Assn. Am. Health Lawyers. Health, General corporate, Finance. Office: Samaritan Health Sys 1441 N 12th St Phoenix AZ 85006-2837

**BIXLER, JOHN MOURER,** lawyer; b. Washington, Oct. 14, 1927; s. John S. and Elsie (Mourer) B.; m. Miriam Calhoun, Aug. 16, 1952; children: Allyson Sue Switzer, Stephen J., Mary Lynn Frye. BS, U. Pa., 1949; LLB, Harvard U., 1954. Bar: D.C. 1954, Md. 1960. Staff mem. Charles S. Rockey & Co. CPAs, Phila., 1949-51; assoc. Miller & Chevalier, Washington, 1954-61; mem. Miller & Chevalier, Chartered, Washington, 1962-98; ptnr. Ross, Marsh & Foster, Washington, 1998—; lectr. local estate planning couns. Am. Law Inst. ABA, NYU Inst. Fed. Taxation. Trustee D.C. Legal Aid Soc., Washington, 1975-92, U. Pa., Phila., 1975-80, Concord-St. Andrew's United Meth. Ch., Bethesda, Md., treas., 1986—, Meth. Home of D.C., 1982—; trustee Miller and Chevalier Charitable Found., Washington, 1969—, pres., 1969-94, v.p., 1990—, treas., 1993—. Recipient Joseph Wharton award Wharton Sch. Club of Washington, 1982. Fellow Am. Bar Found.; mem. The Met. Club of City of Washington, Lawyers Club, The Barristers, Am. Coll. Trust and Estate Counsel (regent 1987-94, D.C. state chmn. 1983-87, Washington rep. 1987—), Am. Coll. Tax Coun., Confrerie des Chevaliers du Tastevin (grand chamberlain hon., commanderie d'Amerique, dir. Tastevin Found., treas. sous-commanderie de Washington). Republican. Methodist. Avocations: wine growing, gardening, travel. Estate taxation, Estate planning, Probate. Home: 5304 Moorland Ln Bethesda MD 20814-1334 Office: Ross Marsh & Foster 2001 L St NW Ste 400 Washington DC 20036-4946

**BIZAR, IRVING,** lawyer; b. N.Y.C., June 30, 1932; s. Samuel Bizar and Julia Weinberg; m. Beverly J. Goldstein, Sept. 1, 1960 (div. June 1982); children: Steven E., Carolyn S.; m. Eileen Joy Schwartz, June 30, 1985. BA in Acctg., CUNY, 1953; JD cum laude, Bklyn. Law Sch., 1956. Bar: N.Y. 1957, U.S. Ct. Appeals (2d cir.) 1958, U.S. Ct. Appeals (5th cir.) 1974, U.S. Supreme Ct. 1977, U.S. Ct. Appeals (11th cir.) 1985, U.S. Ct. Appeals (4th cir.) 1986. Assoc. Pomerantz, Levy & Haudek, N.Y.C., 1957-62, Cravath, Swaine & Moore, N.Y.C., 1962-63, Demov & Morris, N.Y.C., 1963-68; ptnr. Demov, Morris, Levin & Shein, N.Y.C., 1968-77, Pincus, Ohrenstein, Bizar & D'Alessandro, N.Y.C., 1978-83, Bizar D'Alessandro Shustak & Martin, 1985-90, Bizar, Martin & Schneider, N.Y.C., 1990-95, Bizar & Martin LLP, N.Y.C., 1995—. Dem. dist. leader 84th Assembly Dist., N.Y.C., 1966-68. Mem. Assn. of Bar of City of N.Y., N.Y. State Bar Assn. (fed. judiciary com. litigation comml. sect.). Federal civil litigation, State civil litigation, Securities. Office: Bizar Martin and Taub LLP 1350 Ave of Americas New York NY 10019

**BIZOT, JOHN ERIC,** lawyer; b. Charlottesville, Va., May 28, 1962; s. Richard Byron and Joyce Hellmann Bizot; m. Tracy Binius, Apr. 20, 1991; 1 child, Raymond Binius. BA in History and Internat. Affairs, Fla. State U., 1983; MA in History, Columbia U., 1984, JD, 1987. Bar: Fla. 1988. Assoc. Bedell Law Firm, Jacksonville, Fla., 1987-88; asst. regional counsel U.S. Dept. HHS, Chgo., 1988—. Office: US Dept HHS Office of the Gen Counsel 105 W Adams St Fl 19 Chicago IL 60603-4109

**BIZUB, JOHANNA CATHERINE,** library director; b. Denville, N.J., Apr. 13, 1957; d. Stephen Bernard and Elizabeth Mary (Grizzle) B.; m. Scott Jeffrey Smith, 1992. BS in Criminal Justice, U. Dayton, 1979; MLS, Rutgers U., 1984. Law libr. Morris County Law Libr., 1981-83, Clapp & Eisenberg, Newark, 1984-86; dir. libr. Sills Cummis, 1986-94; libr. dir. Montville (N.J.) Twp. Pub. Libr., N.J., 1994-97; libr. dir. law dept. Prudential Ins. Co. Am., Newark, 1997—. Mem. ALA, N.J. Law Librs. Assn. (treas. 1987-89, v.p./pres.-elect 1989-90, 99—, pres. 1990-91), Am. Assn. Law Librs. (pvt. law librs. SIS, vice chair 1992-93, chair 1993-94, past chair 1994-95), N.J. Libr. Assn., Assoc. Libr. of Morris County (v.p. 1995, pres. 1996, treas. 1997-01), Spl. Libr. Assn. N.J. (treas. 1990-92), Am. Legion Aux. (treas. Rockden unit 175 1983-93). Democrat. Roman Catholic. Home: 11 Elm St Rockaway NJ 07866-3108 Office: Prudential Ins Co Am 22 Plz 751 Broad St Newark NJ 07102-3714

**BJORK, ROBERT DAVID, JR.,** lawyer; b. Evanston, Ill., Sept. 29, 1946; s. Robert David and Lenore Evelyn (Loderhose) B.; m. Linda Louise Reese, Mar. 27, 1971; children: Heidi Lynne, Gretchen Anne. BBA, U. Wis., 1968; JD, Tulane U., 1974. Bar: La. 1974, U.S. Dist. Ct. (ea. dist.) La. 1974, U.S. Ct. Appeals (5th cir.) 1974, U.S. Dist. Ct. (mid. dist.) 1975, U.S. Supreme Ct. 1977, U.S. Dist. Ct. (we. dist.) 1978, U.S. Ct. Appeals (11th cir.) 1981, Calif. 1983, U.S. Dist. Ct. (no. dist.) Calif. 1983, U.S. Dist. Ct. (ea. dist.) Calif. 1984. Ptnr. Adams & Reese, New Orleans, 1974-83; assoc. Crosby, Heafey, Roach & May, Oakland, Calif., 1983-85; ptnr. Bjork, Lawrence, Poeschl & Kohn, Oakland, 1985—; instr. paralegal studies Tulane U., New Orleans, 1979-82. Mem. Tulane U. Law Rev., 1973-74; editor Med. Malpractice newsletter, 1983—. Bd. dirs. Piedmont (Calif.) Coun. Camp Fire, 1984-92, pres., 1987-89; treas. Couhig Congl. Com., New Orleans, 1980-82; bd. dirs. Camp Augusta Trust, 1990—. Lt. USNR, 1968-71. Mem. ABA, Internat. Assn. Def. Counsel, Calif. Bar Assn., La. Bar Assn. (chmn. young lawyers sect. 1982-83), Am. Soc. Law and Medicine. State civil litigation, Federal civil litigation, Personal injury. Home: 1909 Oakland Ave Piedmont CA 94611-3706 Office: Bjork Lawrence Poeschl & Kohn 1901 Harrison St # 1630 Oakland CA 94612-3574

**BJORNSON, ERIK,** lawyer; b. Tacoma, Wash., July 13, 1966. BS, U. Wash., 1991; JD, Seattle U., 1995. Bar: Wash. 1995, U.S. Dist. Ct. (we. dist.) Wash. 1995, U.S. Ct. Appeals (9th cir.) 1995. Atty. Kandrowski, Bjornson, Platter, Bellingham, Wash., 1995—. Office: Konorowski Bjornson Platter 1145 Broadway Ste 1300 Tacoma WA 98402-3524

**BLACHLY, JACK LEE,** lawyer; b. Dallas, Mar. 8, 1942; s. Emery Lee and Thelma Jo (Budd) B.; m. Lucy Largent Rain, Jan. 15, 1972; 1 son, Michael Talbot. BBA, So. Meth. U., 1965, JD, 1968. Bar: Tex. 1968, U.S. Ct. Appeals (5th cir.) 1969, U.S. Supreme Ct. 1975, U.S. Tax Ct. 1977. Trust officer First Nat. Bank in Dallas, 1968-70; ptnr. firm Reese & Blachly, Dallas, 1970-71; assoc. firm Rain Harrell Emery Young & Doke, Dallas, 1971-76; staff atty. Sabine Corp., Dallas, 1976-77, mgr. legal dept., 1977-80, v.p., gen. counsel, 1980-89; asst. gen. counsel Pacific Enterprises Oil Co. USA (merger Sabine Corp. and Pacific Enterprise Oil Co. USA), Dallas, 1989-90; pvt. practice Dallas, 1990—. Mem. Tex. Bar Assn., Dallas Bar Assn., Dallas Gun Club, Northwood Club. Baptist. General corporate, Oil, gas, and mineral, Securities. Office: 16012 Red Cedar Trl Dallas TX 75248-3901

**BLACHMAN, MICHAEL JOEL,** lawyer; b. Portsmouth, Va., Aug. 16, 1944; s. Zalmon I. and Rachel G. (Grossman) B.; m. Paula D. Levine, Nov. 23, 1969; children: Dara R., Erica Dale. BS, Am. U., 1966; JD, U. Tenn., 1969. Bar: Va. 1969, U.S. Dist. Ct. (ea. dist.) Va. 1971, U.S. Supreme Ct. 1974, U.S. Ct. Appeals (4th cir.) 1977. Asst. commonwealth's atty. Commonwealth of Va., Portsmouth, 1970-72; assoc. Bangel, Bangel & Bangel, Portsmouth, 1972-77, ptnr., 1977—; chmn. Portsmouth Juvenile Adv. Com., 1975-78. Mem. Va. Dem. Steering Com. 1980-85; vice chmn. Indsl. Devel. Authority and Port and Indsl. Commn., Portsmouth, 1987-89, chmn. 1989-93; bd. dirs. United Jewish Fedn. Tidewater, 1980—, v.p. 1989—. With USCGR, 1966-72. Recipient Young Leadership award United Jewish Fedn. Tidewater, 1983. Mem. ABA, Assn. Trial Lawyers Am., Va. Bar Assn., Va. Trial Lawyers Assn. (v.p. 1985-88, pres. 1989-90), So. Trial Lawyers Assn. (bd. dirs. 1991—), Portsmouth Bar Assn., Portsmouth C. of C., Kiwanis (bd. dirs. Portsmouth club 1973-75), B'nai B'rith. Jewish. Avocations: tennis, travel, reading. Personal injury. Office: Bangel Bangel & Bangel PO Box 760 Portsmouth VA 23705-0760

**BLACK, BARBARA ARONSTEIN,** legal history educator; b. Bklyn., May 6, 1933; d. Robert and Minnie (Polenberg) A.; m. Charles L. Black, Jr., Apr. 11, 1954; children—Gavin B., David A., Robin E. BA, Bklyn. Coll., 1953; LLB, Columbia U., 1955; MPhil, Yale U., 1970, PhD, 1975; LLD (hon.), N.Y. Law Sch., 1986, Marymount Manhattan Coll., 1986, Vt. Law Sch., 1987, Coll. of New Rochelle, 1987, Smith Coll., 1988, Bklyn. Coll., 1988, York U., Toronto, Can., 1990, Georgetown U., 1991. Assoc. in law Columbia U. Law Sch., N.Y.C., 1955-56; lectr. history Yale U., New Haven, 1974-76, asst. prof. history, 1976-79, assoc. prof. law, 1979-84; George Welwood Murray prof. legal history Columbia U. Law Sch., N.Y.C., 1984—, dean faculty of law, 1986-91. Editor Columbia Law Rev., 1953-55. Active N.Y. State Ethics Commn., 1992-95. Recipient Fed. Bar Assn. prize Columbia Law Sch., 1955. Mem. Am. Soc. Legal History (pres. 1986-90), Am. Acad. Arts and Scis., Am. Philos. Soc., Mass. Hist. Soc., Supreme Ct. Hist. Soc., Selden Soc., Century Assn. Office: Columbia U Sch Law 435 W 116th St New York NY 10027-7201

**BLACK, BARBARA JEAN,** lawyer; b. Moses Lake, Wash., Sept. 1, 1960; d. George E. and Judith C. B. BA, Wash. State U., 1982; JD, Gonzaga U. Sch. Law, 1993. Lawyer Fitterer & Moberg, Moses Lake, Wash., 1993-95; sole practice law Moses Lake, 1994—. Pres. bd. dirs. Our Place domestic violence victim's agy., Moses Lake, 1998—. Mem. ABA, Wash. State Bar Assn., Grant County Bar Assn. Avocation: water sports. Family and matrimonial. Office: PO Box 1118 Moses Lake WA 98837-0169

**BLACK, BARBRA I.,** lawyer; b. Boston, Mar. 16, 1966; d. Allan Stephen and Sharon Madeline (Garber) B. BA, Brandeis U., 1988; JD, Suffolk U., 1992. Bar: Mass. 1992—. Pvt. practice Framingham, Mass. Mem. Mass.

Bar Assn., Boston Bar Assn. Jewish. Avocations: travel, dancing, working out. Office: 161 Worcester Rd Ste 309 Framingham MA 01701-5300

**BLACK, BERT,** lawyer; b. Chgo., Dec. 28, 1945; s. Simon and Dorothy (Gottlieb) B.; m. Judy Finchum, Dec. 9, 1977. BS, U. Md., 1974; MS, Ga. Inst. Tech., 1975; JD, Yale U., 1982. Bar: Md. 1982. Staff engr. Exxon Rsch. & Engring. Corp., Florham Park, N.J., 1975-76; project engr. Law Environ., Inc., Marietta, Ga., 1976-79; assoc. Venable, Baetjer & Howard, Balt., 1982-89, Smith Gambrell & Russell, Atlanta, 1989-91; ptnr. Weinberg & Green, Balt., 1991—. Editor Shepard's Expert and Scientific Evidence Quar., 1993—; edtl. adv. bd. Toxics Law Reporter, 1990—. 1st lt. USMC, 1965-70, Vietnam. Mem. ABA (chair-elect sci. and tech. sect. 1995-96). Avocations: gardening, hiking, travelling. Office: Weinberg & Green 100 S Charles St Ste 1500 Baltimore MD 21201-2770

**BLACK, BLANE ALAN,** lawyer; b. North Charleroi, Pa., Feb. 2, 1956; s. Ronald Arthur and Viola Wren (Vess) B.; m. Kim Michelle Vercamen, Nov. 22, 1980; children: Shannon, Megan, Kellyn, Matthew. Student, U. Pitts., 1978, U. Pitts., 1981. Bar: Pa. 1981, U.S. Dist. Ct. (we. dist.) Pa. 1981. Ptnr. Marcus & Black, Monongahela, Pa., 1981—; solicitor Boroughs of Roscoe and Dunlevy, Pa., 1983—. Mem. ABA, Pa. Bar Assn., Washington County Bar Assn., Allegheny County Bar Assn., Monongahela Rotary (pres. 1989-90), Monongahela Area C. of C. (bd. dirs. 1990—), Univ. Pitts. Golden Panthers. Democrat. Baptist. Avocations: golf, basketball. Personal injury, Bankruptcy, General practice. Home: 318 Quarry Rd Washington PA 15301-3022 Office: Marcus & Black 204 W Main St # 652 Monongahela PA 15063-2408

**BLACK, CLINTON RUTHERFORD,** lawyer; b. N.Y.C., Oct. 24, 1946; s. Clinton Rutherford III and Patricia Murphy Black; m. Caroline Black, June 30, 1979; children: Clinton V, Emily. BA, New Eng. Coll., 1972; JD, U. Balt., 1982. Asst. atty. gen. Office of the Mayland Atty. Gen., Balt., 1982-85; assoc. Thomas & Libowitz, Balt., 1985-88, ptnr., 1988—. Mem. ABA, Md. State Bar Assn., Balt. City Bar Assn. Office: Thomas & Libowitz PA 100 Light St Ste 110 Baltimore MD 21202-1036

**BLACK, D(EWITT) CARL(ISLE), JR.,** lawyer; b. Clarksdale, Miss., Aug. 17, 1930; s. DeWitt Carlisle Sr. and Alice Lucille (Hammond) B.; m. Ruth Buck Wallace, June 6, 1970; children: Elizabeth B. Smithson, D. Carl Black III. BA, Miss. Coll., 1951, LLB, 1963; MPA, Princeton U., 1953; LLM in Taxation, NYU, 1965. Bar: Miss. 1963, U.S. Dist. Ct. (so. dist.) Miss. 1963, U.S. Ct. Appeals (5th cir.) 1965. Rsch. asst. Pub. Affairs Rsch. Coun., Baton Rouge, 1956-57; asst. mgr., dir. rsch. Miss. Econ. Coun., Jackson, 1957-64; ptnr. Butler, Snow, O'Mara, Stevens & Cannada, Jackson, 1965-98, of counsel, 1999—; chair Miss. Tax Inst., Jackson, 1987. Treas. New Stage Theatre, Jackson, 1965-69; pres. Miss. Symphony Orch. Assn., Jackson, 1985-86, Miss. Symphony Found., Jackson, 1989-92. Cpl. U.S. Army, 1953-55. Fellow Am. Coll. Tax Counsel; mem. Miss. Bar Assn. (chair tax sect. 1989-90), Univ. Club, River Hills Club. Episcopalian. Avocations: fishing, reading. Taxation, general, Pension, profit-sharing, and employee benefits, Estate planning. Home: 1704 Poplar Blvd Jackson MS 39202-2119 Office: 1700 Deposit Guaranty Plz Jackson MS 39201

**BLACK, FREDERICK A.,** prosecutor; b. July 2, 1949; s. John R. and Dorothy (Todd) B.; m. Katie Kaliangara, Oct. 27, 1976; children: Shane, Shanthini, Sheena. BA, U. Calif., Berkeley, 1971; JD, Lewis and Clark Coll., 1975. Bar: Oreg. 1975, Guam 1976, U.S. Ct. Appeals (9th cir.) 1976. Dir. Office of Guam Pub. Defender, 1975-78; dep. dir. Office of Oreg. Fed. Defender, 1981-84; asst. U.S. atty. Dist. Guam and No. Mariana Islands, 1978-81, 84-89, 1st asst. U.S. atty., 1989-91; U.S. atty. Dept. Justice Dist. Agana, Guam and No. Mariana Islands, 1991—. Author: Oregon Search and Seizure Manual. Leader Boy Scouts Am. Recipient Spl. award Chief Postal Inspector, 1986, Drug Enforcement Adminstrn. award, 1986, 89. Mem. Guam Water Polo Team. Avocation: sailing. Office: US Atty's Office Pacific News Bldg 108 Hernan Cortez Ave Ste 500 Agana GU 96910-5009

**BLACK, HERBERT ALLEN,** lawyer; b. Boston, Sept. 3, 1957; s. Herbert Allen III and Norma Diane B.; m. Katherine Fischer, Apr. 25, 1981; childre: Peter F., Allen S., Katherine C. BS, USCG Acad., 1979; JD, Coll. William & Mary, 1991. Bar: Va. 1991, U.S. Ct. Appeals (4th cir.) 1991, U.S. Ct. Appelas Armed Forces 1996, Md. 1996, U.S. Dist. Ct. Md. 1996. Commd. 1st lt. USCG, 1979, advanced through grades to comdr., 1986; comdg. officer Cutter Cape Starr USCG, Atlantic City, N.J., 1981-83; sr. ops. contr. 5th. Dist. USCG, Portsmouth, Va., 1983-86; comdg. officer Cutter Aquideck USCG, Portsmouth, 1986-88; intern, law clk. White House, Washington, 1990; prin. legal asst. 14th Dist. USCG, Honolulu, 1991-93; instr. Coast Guard Naval Justice Sch., Newport, R.I., 1993-95; asst. to chief counsel USCG, Washington, 1995-96; retired USCG, 1996; atty. Ober, Kaler, Grimes & Shriver, Balt., 1996—; adj. instr. Defense Inst. Internat. Legal Studies, Newport, 1993—, U. Balt., 1996—. Author: Coast Guard Law Specialist Manual, 1993; co-author: (chpt.) Coastguardsmen's Manual, 1990; contbr. articles to profl. jours. Mem. ABA, Maritime Law assn., Marine Trades Assn. Md. (pres.), Retired Officer's Assn., Am. Legion. Republican. Presbyterian. Avocations: sailing, writing, martial arts, family. Admiralty, General civil litigation, Private international. Office: Ober Kaler Grimes & Shriver 120 E Baltimore St Ste 800 Baltimore MD 21202-1643

**BLACK, JAMES ISAAC, III,** lawyer; b. Lakeland, Fla., Oct. 26, 1951; s. James Isaac Jr. and Juanita (Feemster) B.; m. Vikki Harrison, June 15, 1973; children: Jennifer Leigh, Katharine Ann, Stephanie Marie. BA, U. Fla., 1973; JD, Harvard U., 1976. Bar: Fla. 1976, N.Y. 1977, U.S. Tax Ct. 1984. Assoc. Sullivan & Cromwell, N.Y.C., 1976-84, ptnr., 1984—. Mem. ABA, N.Y. State Bar Assn. (persons under disability com. trusts and estates law sect. 1984-90), Assn. of Bar of City of N.Y. (sec. 1980-81, trusts estates and surrogates ct. com. 1980-83), Scarsdale Golf Club. Real property, Estate planning, Probate. Home: 23 Chesterfield Rd Scarsdale NY 10583-2205 Office: Sullivan & Cromwell 125 Broad St Fl 28 New York NY 10004-2489

**BLACK, LOUIS ENGLEMAN,** lawyer; b. Washington, Aug. 5, 1943; s. Fischer Sheffey and Elizabeth (Zemp) B.; m. Cecelia Whidden, Sept. 5, 1966; 1 child, Kerrison Todd. BA, NYU, 1968, JD, 1971, LLM in Taxation, 1978. Bar: N.Y. 1972. Assoc. Carter, Ledyard & Milburn, N.Y.C., 1972-79; ptnr. Van Ginkel & Benjamin, N.Y.C., 1979-83; of counsel Zimet, Haines, Moss & Friedman, N.Y.C., 1983-84; of counsel DeForest & Duer, N.Y.C., 1984-86, ptnr., 1986—; vice-chmn. bd. dirs. MacMillan Ring-Free Oil Co., Inc., 1986-87; chmn. bd. Lee's Gourmet Farms, Inc., 1993-97. Editor: NYU Jour. Internat. Law and Politics, 1970-71; author: Partnership Buy/Sell Agreements, 1977. Mem. ABA, N.Y. State Bar Assn. General corporate, Taxation, general, Computer. Home: 220 E 65th St Apt 24M New York NY 10021-6629 Office: DeForest & Duer 90 Broad St Fl 18 New York NY 10004-2276

**BLACK, MARTHA L.,** lawyer; b. Dixon, Ill., Nov. 4, 1947; d. Robert Smock and Jean F. Winston. BA, U. Calif., Riverside, 1970; JD, U. Detroit, 1980. Bar: Mich. 1980, U.S. Dist. Ct. (ea. dist.) Mich. 1982, U.S. Ct. Appeals (6th cir.) 1982. Staff atty. U.S. Dist. Ct. (ea. dist.) Mich., Detroit, 1980-82, law clk. to judge Thomas Thornton, 1982-84; assoc. Sommers, Schwartz, Silver, Schwartz, Southfield, Mich., 1984-85; atty. water bd. City of Detroit, 1985-87; asst. regional counsel U.S. EPA, San Francisco, 1987-95; founding ptnr. Kohler & Black PLC, Traverse City, Mich., 1995—. Fax: 231-929-9476. E-mail: mlblack@traverse.com. Office: Kohler & Black PLC PO Box 1031 104 S Union St Ste 206 Traverse City MI 49684-2518

**BLACK, PAMELA WYNNE,** paralegal; b. Mexico City, Sept. 1, 1971; d. Howard Goodner, Jr. and Dracilla Margaret (Chichester) Chilton; m. Peter Willis Black, Dec. 30, 1994; 1 child, Kathryn Wynne. BS in Bus. Adminstrn., Regis U., 1993. Case clerk Leonrd, Street & Dienard, Mpls., 1994-95, paralegal, 1995-96; pres. Tavis Inc., Eden Prairie, Minn., 1996—. Home: 5535 Westwood Ave Minnetrista MN 55364

**BLACK, ROBERT ALLEN,** lawyer; b. Ocala, Fla., Aug. 15, 1954; s. Allen Harrison and Rose Marie (Dupree) B. BA, U. Tex., El Paso, 1977; JD summa cum laude, Tex. Tech U., 1980. Bar: Tex. 1980, U.S. Ct. Appeals (5th and 11th cirs.) 1980, U.S. Supreme Ct. 1985. Ptnr. Mehaffy & Weber, Beaumont, Tex., 1980—; mng. ptnr. Mehaffy & Weber, 1998—; adj. prof. law Lamar U., Beaumont, Tex., 1981-84. Case note editor Tex. Tech Law Rev., 1979-80; editor Jefferson County Bar Jour., 1991-93. Pres. Humane Soc. S.E. Tex., Beaumont, 1983-89; bd. dirs. YMCA, Beaumont, 1985-87, Beaumont Cmty. Players, 1989-91; host TV show Pets on Parade, Beaumont, 1986-87; mem. Beaumont City Planning and Zoning Commn., 1987-90; mem. Beaumont Hist. Landmark Commn., 1989-90. Named one of Outstanding Young Men of Am., Jaycees, 1982. Mem. ABA, Jefferson County Bar Assn. (treas. 1994-95, v.p. 1995-96, pres.-elect. 1996-97, pres. 1997-98)), Tex. Bar Assn., Am. Contract Bridge League (bd. govs. 1992-96, pres. unit 201, 1991-93, 94-96). Democrat. Avocations: book collecting, tennis, history. Federal civil litigation, Libel, Personal injury. Home: 601 22nd St Beaumont TX 77706-4915 Office: Mehaffy & Weber 2615 Calder St Ste 800 Beaumont TX 77702-1993

**BLACK, ROBERT L., JR.,** retired judge; b. Cin., Dec. 11, 1917; s. Robert L. and Anna M. (Smith) B.; m. Helen Chatfield, July 27, 1946; children: William C., Stephen L., Luther F. AB, Yale U., 1939; LLB, Harvard U., 1942. Bar: Ohio 1946, U.S. Ct. Appeals (6th cir.) 1947, U.S. Supreme Ct. 1955. pvt. practice, Cin., 1946-53; ptnr. Graydon, Head & Ritchey, Cin., 1953-72; judge Ct. Common Pleas, Cin., 1973-77, Ct. Appeals, Cin., 1977-89, vis. and assigned judge, 1989-92; mem. jury instrns. com. Ohio Jud. Conf. 1973—, chmn. 1986-92. Councilman Village Indian Hill (Ohio), 1953-65, mayor, 1959-65; mem. standing com. Diocese of So. Ohio, Episcopal Ch., 1958-64, lay del. to gen. assembly, 1966, 69; vestryman, warden Indian Hill Episcopal Ch.; chmn. Cin. Human Rels. Commn., 1967-70. Served to capt. U.S. Army, 1942-45. Decorated Bronze Star. Mem. Cin. Bar Assn., Ohio Bar Assn., ABA, Am. Judicature Soc., Nat. Legal Aid and Defender Assn., Phi Beta Kappa. Republican. Episcopalian. Clubs: Queen City, Camargo, Commonwealth (Cin.). Contbr. articles on law to profl. jours. Home: 5900 Drake Rd Cincinnati OH 45243-3306

**BLACK, ROY,** lawyer; b. N.Y.C., Feb. 17, 1945; s. Richard and Minna (Benett) B. BA, U. Miami, Fla., 1967, JD, 1970. Bar: Fla. 1970. Sr. asst. pub. defender Dade County, Miami, 1971-76; ptnr. Roy E. Black, P.A., Miami, 1976-79, Black and Furci, P.A., Miami, 1979-93, Black & Seiden, Miami, 1993-96, Black, Srebnick & Kornspan, Miami, 1996—. Author: Black's Law: A Criminal Lawyer Reveals his Strategies in Four Cliffhanger Cases, 1999. Recipient Nelson Potyner award ACLU, 1982, Criminal Justice award Dade County Bar Assn., 1991. Criminal. Office: Black Srebnick & Kornspan 201 S Biscayne Blvd Ste 1300 Miami FL 33131-4311

**BLACK, SUSAN HARRELL,** federal judge; b. Valdosta, Ga., Oct. 20, 1943; d. William H. and Ruth Elizabeth (Phillips) Harrell; m. Louis Eckert Black, Dec. 28, 1966. BA, Fla. State U., 1965; JD, U. Fla., 1967; LLM, U. Va., 1984. Bar: Fla. 1967. Atty. U.S. Army Corps of Engrs., Jacksonville, Fla., 1968-69; asst. state atty. Gen. Counsel's Office, Jacksonville, 1969-72; judge County Ct. of Duval County, Fla., 1973-75; judge 4th Jud. Cir. Ct. of Fla., 1975-79; judge U.S. Dist. Ct. (mid. dist.) Fla., Jacksonville, 1979-90, chief judge, 1990-92; judge U.S. Ct. Appeals (11th cir.) Fla., Jacksonville, 1992—; faculty Fed. Jud. Ctr.; mem. U.S. Judicial Conf. Com. on Judicial Improvements; bd. trustees Am. Inns. Ct. Found. Trustee emeritus Law Sch. U. Fla.; past pres. Chester Bedell Inn of Ct. Mem. Am. Bar Assn., Fla. Bar Assn., Jacksonville Bar Assn. Episcopalian. Office: US Dist Ct PO Box 53135 311 W Monroe St Jacksonville FL 32201-3135*

**BLACK, WALTER EVAN, JR.,** federal judge; b. Balt., July 7, 1926; s. Walter Evan and Margaret Luttrell (Rice) B.; m. Catharine Schall Foster, June 30, 1951; children: Walter Evan III, Charles Foster, James Rider. A.B. magna cum laude, Harvard U., 1947, LL.B., 1949. Bar: Md. 1949. Assoc. Hinkley & Singley, Balt., 1949-53; ptnr. Hinkley & Singley, 1957-67; asst. U.S. atty. Dist. Md., Balt., 1953-55; U.S. atty. Dist. Md., 1956-57; ptnr. Clapp, Somerville, Black & Honemann, Balt., 1968-82; U.S. dist. judge Dist. Md., Balt., 1982—, chief judge, 1991-94; sr. status, 1994—; Sec.-treas. Parkwood Cemetery Co., Balt., 1967-82; also dir.; sec. So. Mech. Inc., Balt., 1971-82; also dir.; pres. Charles T. Brandt Inc., Balt., 1972-82; also dir. Chmn. Bd. Municipal and Zoning Appeals, Balt., 1963-67; mem. Jail Bd., Balt., 1971-73, Atty. Grievance Commn., 1978-82, Rev. Bd., 1975-78, chmn., 1975-76; mem. Gov.'s Commn. to Revise Annotated Code, 1975-82. Alt. Md. del. Republican Nat. Conv., 1960; chmn. Rep. City Com., Balt., 1962-66; Md. del. Rep. Nat. Conv., 1964; bd. dirs. Balt. Urban League, 1963-69, 76-82; bd. dirs. Union Meml. Hosp.; dir. Hosp. for Consumptives of Md. Mem. Bar Assn. Balt. City, ABA, Md. Bar Assn., Rule Day Club, Lawyers' Round Table. Baptist. Office: US Dist Ct 101 W Lombard St Ste 404 Baltimore MD 21201-2626

**BLACK, WILLIAM REA,** lawyer; b. N.Y.C., Nov. 4, 1952; s. Thomas Howard and Dorothy Chambers (Dailey) B.; m. Kathleen Jane Owen, June 24, 1978; children: William Ryan, Jonathan Wesley. BSBA, U. Denver, 1978, MBA, 1981; JD, Western State U., Fullerton, Calif., 1987. Bar: Calif., U.S. Ct. Appeals (fed. cir.), U.S. Dist. Ct.; lic. real estate broker. Bus. mgr. Deere & Co., Moline, Ill., 1979-85; dir. Mgmt. Resource Svcs. Co., Chgo., 1985-86; sr. v.p. Geneva Corp., Irvine, Calif., 1986-91; pvt. practice Newport Beach, Calif., 1991-92; gen. counsel Sunclipse, Inc., 1992-98; spl. counsel Amcor, Ltd., 1992-98; dir. gen. Amcor de Mex., S.A. de C.V., 1993-98; secretario KHL de Mex. S.A. de C.V., 1995-98; CEO Kuroi Kiku Corp., Kuroi Ryu Corp., First Reconnaissance Co.; v.p., gen. cousnel Sextant Avionique, 1999—; bd. dirs. Mann-Craft, Inc., Pyraponic Industries, Arkenol Asia, Inc., Anle Paper Co.; sec. Krasner Group, TCJC, Inc., Charisma Mfg. Co., Inc., KGI Fashions, Inc., Dermasci. Labs., Inc., Raymark Container, Inc., Georgetown Collection, Inc., Magic Attic Press, Inc., The LL Knickerbocker Co. (Thailand), Ltd., Harlyn Internat. Co., Ltd., S.L.S. Trading Co., Ltd., Am. Employers Def., Inc., United Studios Self Def., Inc. Mng. editor Western State U. Law Rev., Fullerton, 1984-87. Instr. Pai Lum Kung Fu Karate, Hartford, Conn., 1970-75, U.S. Judo Assn., Denver, 1975-80, United Studios Kenpo, L.A., 1995—. Recipient Am. Jurisprudence award Bancroft-Whitney Co., 1984, 85, 86; Pres.'s scholar full acad. merit scholarship, 1983. Mem. ABA, Am. Soc. Appraisers, Inst. Bus. Appraisers, Assn. Productivity Specialists, Am. Employment Law Coun., Profls. in Human Resources Assn., Am. Mgmt. Assn., Orange County Bar Assn., L.A. County Bar Assn., Mu Kappa Tau. Avocations: karate (2d degree black belt), skiing, scuba, golf. General corporate, Labor, Mergers and acquisitions. Office: 369 San Miguel Dr Ste 350 Newport Beach CA 92660-7852

**BLACKBURN, JAMES B., III,** lawyer; b. Pitts., Nov. 16, 1946; s. James B. Jr. and Ethel Louise (Herrod) B.; m. Cynthia Jan Coote, Aug. 10, 1974; children: Sarah Louise, James B. IV, Natalie Alice. BA, Princeton U., 1969; MPA, N.C. State U., 1974; JD, Duke U., 1980. Bar: N.C. 1980. Staff atty. Gen. Rsch. Divsn, N.C. Gen. Assembly, Raleigh, 1980-84; gen. counsel N.C. Assn. County Commrs., Raleigh, 1984—. Sgt. U.S. Army, 1970-72. Mem. Internat. Mcpl. Lawyers Assn., N.C. Bar Assn. Home: 1100 W Forest Hills Blvd Durham NC 27707-1626 Office: NC Assn County Commrs PO Box 1488 Raleigh NC 27602-1488

**BLACKBURN, JOHN GILMER,** lawyer; b. Opelika, Ala., Oct. 21, 1927; s. John A. and Vera (Isley) B.; m. Phyllis Blackburn, May 12, 1951; children: Gay Blackburn Maloney, Allison Blackburn Akins, Lisa Blackburn Ayerst. BS in Acctg., Auburn U., 1950; JD, U. Ala., 1954; LLM in Taxation, NYU, 1956. Bar: Ala. 1954. Sole practice Decatur, Ala., 1955-79; ptnr. Blackburn, Maloney & Schuppert, P.C., Decatur, 1979—; lectr. various tax seminars. Mayor, City of Decatur, 1962-68; mem. exec. com. Ala. Dems.; chmn. Auburn U. Found.; chmn. Ala. Rev. Com. on Higher Edn. With U.S. Army, 1946-47, to 1st lt., 1951-52, ETO. Mem. ABA (com. on life ins., cos. sect. taxation), Ala. Bar Assn. (chmn. tax sect.). Methodist. Lodge: Kiwanis. Estate planning, Corporate taxation, Estate taxation. Office: PO Box 1469 Decatur AL 35602-1469

**BLACKBURN, MICHAEL PHILIP,** lawyer; b. East St. Louis, Ill., June 7, 1945; s. Thomas Doyle and Erma Jeanette (Macke) B.; m. Phyllis Ann Macke, Feb. 10, 1972 (div. 1983). BA, So. Ill. U., 1967; JD, Western State U., Fullerton, Calif., 1982. Bar: Calif. 1983, U.S. Ct. Appeals (9th cir.) 1984, U.S. Dist. Ct. (cen. dist.) Calif. 1984, U.S. Tax Ct. 1984, U.S. Supreme Ct. 1992, U.S. Dist. Ct. (no. dist.) Calif. 1992, U.S. Dist. Ct. (ea. dist.) Calif. 1993. Lawyer pvt. practice, Long Beach, Calif., 1983-85; house counsel TransAmerica, Torrance, Calif., 1985-88; assoc. Mercer & Zinder, Orange, Calif., 1988-91; ptnr. Mercer & Zinder, Orange, 1991; mgr. bay area office Mercer & Zinder, Walnut Creek, Calif., 1991-98; v.p. bd. dirs. Zinder, Blackburn, Park, Clements & Keenan, Walnut Creek, Calif., 1998—, v.p., mem. exec. com. Dem. candidate U.S. House Reps., 42nd Congl. Dist., 1986. Capt. USAF, 1967-72. Recipient scholarship So. Ill. Univ., 1963. Roman Catholic. Avocations: pocket billiards, reading. Product liability, Insurance, Personal injury. Office: Zinder Blackburn Park Clements & Keenan 205 Lennon Ln # 210 Walnut Creek CA 94598-2420

**BLACKBURN, RICHARD WALLACE,** lawyer; b. Detroit, Apr. 21, 1942; s. Wallace Manders and E. Jean (Beetham) B.; m. Dede Frances Reid, Aug. 29, 1964; children: David Thomas, Jeffrey Manders, Megan Louise. Student, Baldwin-Wallace Coll., 1960-62; A.B., Mich. State U., 1964; J.D., George Washington U., 1967; grad. advanced mgmt. program, Harvard Bus. Sch., 1988. Labor atty. Chesapeake & Potomac Telephone Co., Washington, 1967-70; gen. corp. atty. Chesapeake & Potomac Telephone Co., Richmond, Va., 1970-74; regulatory atty. AT&T, N.Y.C., 1974-76; gen. atty. New Eng. Telephone Co., Boston, 1976-81; v.p., gen. counsel New Eng. Telephone Co., 1981—; exec. v.p., gen. counsel, sec. Duke Energy, Charlotte, N.C. Dir. New Eng. Legal Found., 1988; mem. Concord (Mass.) Zoning Bd. Appeals, chmn., 1984, 87; trustee Mass. Eye and Ear Infirmary. Mem. Fed. Communications Bar Assn., Am. Bar Assn., Newcomen Soc. N.Am., Boston Bar Assn. Republican. Episcopalian. Office: Duke Energy Corp 422 S Church St PO Box 1244 Charlotte NC 28201-1244*

**BLACKBURN, ROGER LLOYD,** lawyer; b. Mobile, Ala., Mar. 18, 1946; s. Rogers Hammock and Louise (Megahee) B.; m. Linda McNulty, Mar. 29, 1969. BA, U. Fla., 1968, JD, 1971. Bar: Fla. 1971, U.S. Dist. Ct. (so. dist.) Fla. 1972, U.S. Tax Ct. 1979. Ptnr. Blackwell, Walker & Gray, Miami, Fla., 1971-76, Leesfield & Blackburn, P.A., Miami, 1976-92; pvt. practice North Ctrl. Fla., 1992—; of counsel Hicks & Anderson, P.A., Miami, 1995—. Mem. ATLA, Fla. Bar Assn., Dade County Bar Assn. (bd. dirs. 1974-86), Acad. Fla. Trial Lawyers (bd. dirs. 1985-91, exec. com. 1989-91), Dade County Trial Lawyers Assn. (pres. 1985-86), Am. Bd. Trial Advocates (pres. Miami chpt. 1991-92, nat. bd. dirs., chmn. seminar com., diplomate), Eighth Jud. Cir. Bar Assn., U. Fla. Law Ctr. Assn. (trustee 1986-95, trustee emeritus 1995—), U. Fla. Coll. Law Alumni Coun. (pres. 1984), Fla. Acad. Cert. Mediators, Fla. Blue Key. Democrat. Personal injury, General civil litigation, Federal civil litigation. Office: 100 Biscayne Blvd Miami FL 33132-2304

**BLACKBURN, SHARON LOVELACE,** federal judge; b. 1950. BA, U. Ala., 1973; JD, Samford U., 1977. Law clk. to Hon. Robert Varner U.S. Dist. Ct. Ala., 1977-78; staff atty. Birmingham Area Legal Svcs., 1979; asst. U.S. atty. U.S. Atty's. Office, 1979-91; judge U.S. Dist. Ct. (no. dist.) Ala., Birmingham, 1991—. Mem. Birmingham Bar Assn. Office: US Dist Ct 730 US Courthouse 1729 5th Ave N Birmingham AL 35203-2000

**BLACKFORD, JASON COLLIER,** lawyer; b. Findlay, Ohio, Oct. 30, 1938; s. Emerson Miller and Isabel (Collier) B.; ;m. Jane Edith Howells; children: Thomas, Melinda. BA, Denison U., 1960; LLB, Yale U., 1963. Bar: Ohio 1964, U.S. Dist. Ct. (no. dist.) Ohio 1966, U.S. Ct. Appeals (10th cir.) 1974, U.S. Ct. Appeals (6th cir.) 1985, U.S. Supreme Ct. 1985. Assoc. Weston, Hurd, Fallon, Paisley & Howley, Cleve., 1964-69, ptnr., 1969—; adj. prof. Cleve. Marshall Sch. of Law. Author: Ohio Corporation Law and Practice, 2 vols., Organizing an Ohio Corporation, Business Organizations, 2 vols.; editor: Ohio Legal Form. Mem. Fairmount Presbyn. Ch. 1st lt. USAR, 1963-69. Mem. Ohio Bar Assn. (corp. law com. 1969—), Cleve. Bar Assn. (trustee 1978-81), Am. Arbitration Assn. (comml. and securities panel, chmn. regional adv. coun., nat. securities com.), Nat. Assn. Securities Dealers (panel of arbitrators). Avocations: writing, antique weapons. General corporate, Securities, Mergers and acquisitions. Office: Weston Hurd Fallon Paisley & Howley 2500 Terminal Towers Cleveland OH 44113

**BLACKFORD, ROBERT NEWTON,** lawyer; b. Cin., Feb. 5, 1937; s. Robert Criley and Virginia Pendleton (Yowell) B.; m. Margaret Ann Williams, July 22, 1961; children: William Pendleton, John Whitner. BSBA, U. Fla., 1960; JD, Emory U., 1968. Bar: Fla. 1968, Ga. 1968. Mem., dir. Maguire, Voorhis & Wells, P.A., Orlando, Fla., 1972-98, sec., treas., 1972-95; ptnr. Holland & Knight LLP, Orlando, 1998—; dir. Hughes Supply, Inc., Orlando, 1970—, sec., 1972-96, asst. sec., 1996-98; dir., sec. Princeton Fin. Corp., 1987-94. Mem. Orlando Mcpl. Planning Bd., 1969-75, Orlando Downtown Devel. Bd., 1972-77, chmn., 1975-77, bd. dirs. Crime Commn., Inc., 1985-88; mem. Orange County's Refuse Disposal Citizens Coordination Com., 1988-90, Orange County Solid Waste Adv. Bd., 1992-96; mem. neighborhood concerns com. Orlando Naval Tng. Ctr. Base Closing Commn., 1994-96; trustee Chelsey G. Magruder Found., Inc., 1981—, pres., 1982-85, 92-94, sec., 1998—; trustee Orlando Mus. Art, 1980-82, 85-91, pres. 1985-86, chmn. bd., 1986-87, v.p. 1989-91; ruling elder First Presbyn. Ch., Orlando, 1989—, tchr., 1970—. Mem. ABA, Fla. Bar Assn., Ga. Bar Assn., Orange County Bar Assn., Orlando Area C. of C. (pres. 1980, chmn. bd. dirs. 1981), Orange County Hist. Soc. (bd. dirs. 1980-83), Country Club Orlando (bd. dirs. 1994-97, sec. 1994-96). Democrat. General corporate, Securities. Home: 2931 Nela Ave Orlando FL 32809-6178 Office: Holland & Knight LLP 200 S Orange Ave Ste 2600 Orlando FL 32801-3449

**BLACKLIDGE, RAYMOND MARK,** lawyer; b. Ft. Belvoir, Va., May 17, 1960; s. Martin H. and Carol Ann (Fiarito) B.; m. Karen Marie Tennis, June 19, 1982; children: Robert Mark, Jonathon Michael, Sara Kathryn. BA, So. Ill. U., 1982; JD, John Marshall Law Sch., 1985. Bar: Ill. 1986, U.S. Dist. Ct. (no. dist.) Ill. 1986. Sole practice West Chicago, Ill., 1986, 92—; ptnr., corp. sec. Grief, Bus & Blacklidge, P.C., Ill., 1987-92; bd. dirs., sr. v.p., gen. counsel, sec. The Jerger Co., Inc., Mobile Homeowners Ins. Agys., Inc., Jerger & Sons, Inc.; bd. dirs., gen. counsel, sec. Mobile USA Ins. Co., Inc., Mobile United Property & Casualty Ins. Co., Inc.; bd. dirs., sr. v.p., gen. counsel, sec., treas. MHIA Premium Fin. Co.; dir., sr. v.p., sec., treas. Mobile Adjustment Co., Inc.; arbitrator 18th Jud. Cir.; reg. lobbyist, Fla., 1994—; of counsel Edward J. Boltz, Christopher C. Benfante and David E. Caddigan, 1993-94; regional mgr. and counsel Alliance of Am. Insurers, 1992-96; title ins. agent Atty.'s Title Ins. Fund, 1994—. Editor-in-chief Marshall Opinion, 1985. Pres., bd. dirs. West Chicago Clean and Proud, Inc.; bd. dirs. West Chicago R.R. Days, Inc., 1988-94; alderman City of West Chicago, 1989-94; Rep. precinct committeeman Winfield Twp. Precinct, DuPage County, 1991-94. Mem. Fla. Ins. Coun. (bd. dirs. 1996—), Alliance Am. Insurers (mem. govt. affairs com., alliance so. regional advisory com.), Gavel Soc., Columbian Club (v.p.), KC (trustee West Chicago 1985—, Knight of Yr. award 1987). Republican. Roman Catholic. Avocations: travel, religious studies, family, sports, roller blading. General corporate, Insurance, Legislative. Office: 7785 66th St N Pinellas Park FL 33781-3113

**BLACKMAN, DAVID MICHAEL,** lawyer; b. Oakland, Calif., Jan. 29, 1943; s. Sidney Joshua and Pauline (Golson) B.; m. Ardis Blackman; children: Jeremy, Rebekah, Kyra, Stephanie. BA cum laude, San Francisco State U., 1968; JD, U. Calif., Davis, 1972. Bar: Calif. 1972, U.S. Dist. Ct. (ea. dist.) Calif. 1972, U.S. Tax Ct. 1974, U.S. Ct. Appeals (9th cir.) 1987; cert. Am. Bd. Profl. Liability Attys., Nat. Bd. Trial Advocacy. Dep. atty. gen. State of Calif., Sacramento, 1972-73; staff State Pub. Defender, Sacramento, 1978-79; ptnr. Blackman & Blackman, Sacramento, 1973—; adj. prof. U. Calif., Davis., 1982-84; arbitrator Am. Arbitration Assn.; judge pro-tem Superior Ct.; lectr. in field; founding sponsor Civil Justice Found.; mem. Dept. of Ins. Task Force on Consumer Complaints and Unfair Practices. Author practice manuals. Mem. ATLA, Calif. Trial Lawyers Assn. (Chpt. Pres. of Yr. award 1988), Sacramento County Bar Assn. (coun. 1978-80), Capitol City Trial Lawyers Assn. (pres. 1988). Personal injury, Product liability. Home: 3585 Montclair Rd Cameron Park CA 95682-9031 Office: Blackman & Blackman 7750 College Town Dr Ste 300 Sacramento CA 95826-2361

**BLACKMAN, JEFFREY WILLIAM,** lawyer; b. L.A., Oct. 24, 1948; s. Ralph Leonard and Judith Esther (Glantz) B. BA, U. Ariz., 1970, JD, 1976. Bar: Ariz. 1976, U.S. Dist. Ct. Ariz. 1977, U.S. Ct. Appeals (9th cir.) 1980, U.S. Supreme Ct. 1980, U.S. Dist. Ct. (no. dist.) Calif. 1988. Pvt. practice law Oracle, Ariz., 1977-85; assoc. with several law firms Phoenix, Tucson, 1986-87; pvt. practice law Tucson, 1988—. Participant March for the Animals, Washington, 1990, 96. 2d lt. ROTC, U.S. Army, 1968-69. Recipient Cert. of Appreciation, Ctr. for Environ. Edn. Whale Protection Fund, 1984, UNICEF, Defenders of Wildlife, Nat. Humane Edn. Soc.,

ASPCA, Nation of Israel, Wine Diploma, San Francisco Wine Inst. Wine Adv. Bd., 1964; named Ptnr. for Life, Cal Farley's Boy Ranch, Amarillo, Tex., 1982. Mem. State Bar Ariz., Mensa, Alliance Francaise. Democrat. Jewish. Avocations: rock drummer, tennis, desert hiking, gardening, animal welfare. Criminal, General civil litigation, General practice. Office: PO Box 41624 Tucson AZ 85717-1624

**BLACKMAN, KENNETH ROBERT,** lawyer; b. Providence, May 19, 1941; s. Edward and Beatrice (Wolf) B.; m. Meryl June Rosenthal, June 7, 1964; children: Michael, Susan, Kevin. AB, Brown U., 1962; LLB, Columbia U., 1965, MBA, 1965. Bar: N.Y. 1966. Law clk. to U.S. Dist. Judge, 1965-66; ptnr. Fried, Frank, Harris, Shriver & Jacobson, N.Y.C., 1966—. Mem. ABA, N.Y. Bar Assn., Assn. Bar City of N.Y., Phi Beta Kappa, Beta Gamma Sigma. General corporate, Securities, Bankruptcy. Office: Fried Frank Harris Shriver & Jacobson 1 New York Plz Fl 22 New York NY 10004-1980

**BLACKMAN, PAUL H.,** criminologist, political scientist; b. Chgo., July 12, 1944; s. Julius and Phyllis Rena (Waldman) B.; m. Susan Ruth Maclay, Aug. 11, 1971. BA, U. Calif., Riverside, 1964; MA, Johns Hopkins U., 1966; PhD, U. Va., 1970. Asst. prof. polit. sci. U. N.D., Grand Forks, 1968-71; lectr. Univ. Coll. U. Md., College Park, 1972-78; cons. Am. Polit. Rsch. Corp., Bethesda, Md., 1973-74; v.p. Media Rsch., Inc., Bethesda, 1974-75; cons. Heritage Found., Washington, 1975-76; rsch. coord. NRA Inst. for Legis. Action, Fairfax, Va., 1977—. Author: Third Party President?, 1975; co-author: No More Wacos, 1997. Recipient Thomas S. Szasz award for outstanding contbns. to cause of civil liberties Ctr. for Ind. Thought, 1997. Mem. Am. Soc. Criminology, Homicide Rsch. Working Group. Jewish. Avocations: ultradistance and trail running, home brewing. Office: NRA Inst for Legis Action 11250 Waples Mill Rd Fairfax VA 22030-7400

**BLACKMAR, CHARLES BLAKEY,** state supreme court justice; b. Kansas City, Mo., Apr. 19, 1922; s. Charles Maxwell and Eleanor (Blakey) B.; m. Ellen Day Bonnifield, July 18, 1943 (dec. 1983); children: Charles A. (dec.), Thomas J., Lucy E. Blackmar Alpaugh, Elizabeth S., George B.; m. Jeanne Stephens Lee, Oct. 5, 1984. AB summa cum laude, Princeton U., 1942; JD, U. Mich., 1948; LLD (hon.), St. Louis U., 1991. Bar: Mo. 1948. Pvt. practice law Kansas City; ptnr. Swanson, Midgley, Jones, Blackmar & Eager, and predecessors, 1952-66; profl. lectr. U. Mo. at Kansas City, 1949-58; prof. law St. Louis U., 1966-82, prof. emeritus; judge Supreme Ct. Mo., 1982-89, 1991—, chief justice, 1989-91, sr. status, 1992; spl. asst. atty. gen. Mo., 1969-77, labor arbitrator, active sr. judge, 1992—; chmn. Fair Pub. Accommodations Commn. Kansas City, 1964-66; mem. Commn. Human Rels. Kansas City, 1965-66. Author: (with Volz and others) Missouri Practice, 1953, West's Federal Practice Manual, 1957, 71, (with Devitt) Federal Jury Practice and Instructions, 1970, 3d edit., 1977, (with Devitt, Wolff and O'Malley) 4th edit., 1988-92; contbr. numerous articles on probate and corp. law to profl. publs. Mem. Jackson County Rep. Com., 1952-58; mem. Mo. Rep. Com., 1956-58. 1st lt., inf. AUS, 1943-46. Decorated Silver Star, Purple Heart. Mem. Am. Law Inst., Nat. Acad. Arbitrators, Mo. Bar (spl. lectr. insts.), Disciples Peace Fellowship, Scribes (pres. 1986-87), Order of Coif, Phi Beta Kappa. Mem. Disciples of Christ Ch. Home (winter): 2 Seaside Ln Apt 402 Belleair FL 33756-1989 also (summer): 612 Hobbs Rd Jefferson City MO 65109

**BLACKMON, WILLIE EDWARD BONEY,** lawyer; b. Houston, Apr. 16, 1951; s. A.L. and Florence (Joseph) B. BBA in Mktg., Tex. A&M U., 1973; JD, Tex. Southern U., 1982. Bar: Nebr. 1984, Mich. 1985, U.S. Dist. Ct. (ea. dist.) Mich., 1984, U.S. Ct. Mil. Appeals 1984, U.S. Supreme Ct. 1987, Tex. 1989, U.S. Dist. Ct. (no. dist.) Tex. 1990, U.S. Dist. Ct. (so. dist.) Tex. 1993. Terr. sales mgr. Gillette Co., 1977-79; sales and mktg. coord. Drilco divsn. Smith Internat., 1973-77; legal intern Gulf Coast Legal Found., Houston, 1982; intern/ind. counsel City of Detroit, 1982-84; judge advocate USAF, Ellsworth AFB, Offutt AFB, S.D., 1984-89, USAFR, Reese AFB, Randolph AFB, Tex., 1989-94; dep. staff judge advocate Tex. Air N.G., Ellington Field, Tex., 1994—; asst. criminal dist. atty., Lubbock County, Tex., 1990-91; asst. criminal dist. atty., Harris County, Tex., 1991-92; pvt. practice, Houston, 1992-97; assoc. mcpl. judge City of Houston, 1995-97, mcpl. judge, 1997—; admissions liaison officer USAF Acad., 1990—; internat. election supr. Orgn. for Security and Coop. in Europe (OSCE), Bosnia, 1997; adj. instr. Judge Advocate Gen.'s Sch. Air Univ., Maxwell AFB, Ala., 1996—; guest spkr., lectr. Tex. Tech. U., U. Nebr., Creighton U., Tex. A&M U., Tex. So. U. Named to Tex. A&M U. Athletic Hall of Fame, 1994. Mem. ABA, NAACP, State Bar Tex., Nebr. Bar Assn., State Bar Mich., Nat. Bar Assn. (Living Legend award 1990), Tex. Assn. African Am. Lawyers, Houston Lawyers Assn., Wolverine Bar Assn., Am. Judges Assn., Tex. Mcpl. Cts. Assn., , Mexican-Am. Bar Assn., Houston Bar Assn., Tex. Coalition Black Dems., Aggie Officers Assn., Masons. Baptist. Avocations: scuba diving, skiing, hiking, biking, dancing. Home: 8766 Pattibob St Houston TX 77029-3334 Office: 1400 Lubbock St Ste 214 Houston TX 77002-1526

**BLACKSHEAR, A. T., JR.,** lawyer; b. Dallas, July 5, 1942; s. A.T. and Janie Louise (Florey) B.; m. Stuart Davis Blackshear. B.B.A. cum laude, Baylor U., 1964, J.D. cum laude, 1968. Bar: Tex. 1968, U.S. Ct. Appeals (5th cir.) 1970, U.S. Tax Ct. 1970; C.P.A., Tex. Acct. Arthur Andersen & Co., Dallas, 1964-66; assoc. Fulbright & Jaworski, Houston, 1969-75; ptnr. Fulbright & Jaworski, 1975—, chmn. exec. com., 1992—. Trustee Baylor Coll. Medicine, Meml./Hermann Healthcare Sys.; bd. dirs. Ctrl. Houston, Inc. Mem. ABA, State Bar Tex., Houston Bar Assn., Houston Ctr. Club, Coronado Club, Houston Country Club. Baptist. Corporate taxation, Personal income taxation, Health. Office: Fulbright & Jaworski 1301 Mckinney St Fl 51 Houston TX 77010-3031

**BLACKSTOCK, LEROY,** lawyer; b. El Reno, Okla., Apr. 19, 1914; s. Herbert Austin and Ethel Mae (Gwin) B.; m. Virginia Lee Lowman, Dec. 29, 1939; children: Craig, Priscilla, Birch, Lore, Trena. Grad., Draughon's Bus. Inst., Tulsa, 1933; LL.B., U. Tulsa, 1938. Bar: Okla. 1938. With Phillips Petroleum Co., Tulsa, 1933-41; asst. credit mgr. Phillips Petroleum Co., 1939-41; practiced in Tulsa, 1941-74; counsel Blackstock & Montgomery; dir., gen. counsel Tulsa Homebuilders Assn., 1959-68; dir. Fourth Nat. Bank, Tulsa, 1969-76, Owasso 1st State Bank, Okla., 1967-70; pres. Skelly Stadium Corp., 1964-70; pres., trustee Gt. Western Investment Trust; mem. nat. adv. com. Practising Law Inst., 1969-70; pres. Jud. Reform Inc., 1966-70; lectr. law office mgmt., econs. U. Tulsa Coll. Law, 1970-75; chmn. Okla. Coun. on Jud. Complaints, 1974-84; pres. Tulsa Sci. Center, 1968-73; chmn. Tulsa U. Law Schs. Com., 1960-74, Citizens Adv. Com. County Commrs., 1963-66; pres., bd. dirs. Tulsa County Bar Found., 1962-66; patron Okla. Bar Found., trustee, 1966; mem. Gov.'s Acad. for State Govt., 1966-68; chmn. Okla. Supreme Ct. Bar Com., 1966. Author: Managing Partner Approach, Paper Dolls and Lawyers' Fees. Pres. Tulsa council Camp Fire Girls, 1971-72; pres. Tulsa Baptist Laymen's Corp., 1962-66; Bd. dirs. Tulsa County Mental Health Assn., 1963-70, Tulsa Psychiat. Found., 1964-67; pres. Tulsa County Legal Aid Soc., 1961-62, bd. dirs., 1958-66. Served with USNR, 1943-46. Recipient Disting. Citizens award Okla. Psychol. Assn., 1963; Disting. Alumni award U. Tulsa, 1969, 78; Disting. Alumni award Tulsa U. Coll. Law, 1978; Boss of Year award Tulsa County Assn. Legal Secs., 1978. Fellow Am. Coll. Probate Counsel; mem. ABA (ho. dels. 1965-67, mem. spl. com. on nat. coordination of disciplinary enforcement 1969-72, standing com. profl. discipline 1973-77), Okla. Bar Assn. (bd. govs. 1965-67, pres. 1966), Tulsa County Bar Assn. (pres. 1962, Outstanding Atty. award 1961), World Assn. Lawyers (charter mem.), Tulsa County Hist. Soc. (founding mem.), Photog. Soc. Am., Soc. Amateur Cinematographers, Phi Alpha Delta. Republican. Baptist (chmn. deacons 1962, chmn. bldg. com. 1951-53). Club: Petroleum (dir. 1974-77). Real property, Taxation, general, Probate. Home: 7213 S Atlanta Tulsa OK 74136 Office: 320 S Boston Ave Ste 2000 Tulsa OK 74103-4709

**BLACKWELL, BRUCE BEUFORD,** lawyer; b. Gainesville, Fla., July 23, 1946; s. Benjamin B. and Doris Juanita (Heagy) B.; m. Julie McMillan, July 12, 1969; children: Blair Allison, Brooke McMillan. BA, Fla. State U., 1968, JD with honors, 1974. Bar: Fla. 1975, Ga. 1977, U.S. Supreme Ct. 1979, N.Y. 1980. Atty. So. Bell Tel. & Telegraph Co., Charlotte, N.C., 1975-76, Atlanta, 1976-78; antitrust atty. AT&T, Orlando and N.Y.C., 1978-80; atty. Sun Banks, Inc., Orlando, Fla., 1980; assoc. Peed & King, P.A., Orlando, 1981-84; shareholder King & Blackwell, P.A., Orlando, 1984-97, King, Blackwell & Downs, P.A., 1997—; counselor to First Ctrl. Fla. Inns of Ct., 1999—. Bd. dirs. Legal Aid Soc., Orlando, 1986-88; chmn. Winter Park (Fla.) Civil Svc. Bd., 1992-94; trustee Fla. State U. Found., 1985-86. Capt. USAF, 1968-72. Recipient award of excellence Legal Aid Soc., 1993, Judge J.C. Stone Pro Bono Disting. Svc. award, 1996, Annual Friend of FAWL award Fla. Assn. Women Lawyers, 1998. Mem. Fla. Bar (chmn. 9th cir. grievance com. 1985-87, chmn. mid-yr. meeting 1986, chmn. 9th cir. fee arbitration com. 1992-94, bd. govs. 1994-98, vice chair statewide disciplinary rev. com. 1995-96, co-chair 1997-98, vice-chmn. access to cts. com. 1995-97, chmn. annual meeting com. 1997, mem. supreme ct. spl. com. on pro bono svcs. 1996-97, mem. com. to determine need for a new DCA 1998, Fla. Bar Presidents' Pro Bono Svc. award 1997, chair spl. com. on solo/small firm practice 1997-98, mem. rules com. 1997-98, mem. edn. work force 1996-97), Fla. Bar Found. (bd. dirs. 1998-2001), Orange County Bar Assn. (exec. coun. 1983-86, pres. 1987-88), Fla. State U. Alumni Assn. (nat. pres. 1985-86), Orlando Touchdown Club (pres. 1996-97), Gold Key, Order of Omega, Omicron Delta Kappa. Democrat. Presbyterian. Avocation: study of China. General civil litigation, Family and matrimonial, Personal injury. Home: 1624 Roundelay Ln Winter Park FL 32789-4042 Office: PO Box 1631 Orlando FL 32802-1631

**BLACKWELL, THOMAS FRANCIS,** lawyer; b. Detroit, Nov. 25, 1942; m. Sandra L. Kroczek; children: Robert T., Katherine M. BA, U. Notre Dame, Ind., 1964; JD, U. Mich., 1967. Bar: Mich and U.S. Dist. Ct. (we. and ea. dists.) Mich. 1968, U.S. Ct. Appeals (6th cir.) 1969. Assoc. Smith, Haughey, Rice & Roegge, Grand Rapids, Mich., 1967-71, ptnr., 1971—, treas., 1979-85, 89—, exec. com., 1985-89; spl. asst. atty. gen. State of Mich., 1972-82. Fellow Mich. State Bar Found.; mem. ABA, State Bar Mich., Grand Rapids Bar Assn., FBA, Products Liability Adv. Coun., Mich. Def. Trial Attys., Peninsular, Kent Country Club. General civil litigation, Personal injury, Product liability. Office: Smith Haughey Rice & Roegge 250 Monroe Ave NW Ste 200 Grand Rapids MI 49503-2251

**BLACKWOOD, EILEEN MORRIS,** lawyer; b. West Chester, Pa., Sept. 4, 1958; d. Matthew Temple and Helen Stokes (Morris) B. AB, Dartmouth Coll., 1980; JD cum laude, Cornell U., 1986. Bar: Vt. 1987, U.S. Dist. Ct. Vt. 1987. Law clk. to Judge Franklin S. Billings, Jr., U.S. Dist. Ct. for Vt., Rutland, 1986-87; assoc. Paul, Frank & Collins, Inc., Burlington, Vt., 1987-92; ptnr. Blackwood & Kraynak, Burlington, 1992-98; owner Blackwood Assocs., P.C., Burlington, 1998—. Contbr. articles to legal publs. Bd. dirs. Childcare Resource and Referral Ctr., Williston, Vt., 1989-95; bd. dirs. Vt. ACLU, Montpelier, 1989-92, v.p., 1991-92; mem. Williston Planning Commn., 1990—, chair, 1994-98; mem. Vt. Jud. Nominating Bd., 1997—; bd. dirs. Samara Found. Vt., 1998—. Mem. ABA, Vt. Bar Assn. (chair women's sect. 1990-91, chair employment law com. 1996—), Vt. Employment Lawyers Assn. (vice chair 1994-95, chair 1996-96), Am. Inns of Ct. (sec. No. Vt. chpt. 1995-96). Labor, Education and schools, General civil litigation. Office: PO Box 875 90 Main St Burlington VT 05402

**BLADEN, EDWIN MARK,** lawyer, judge; b. Detroit, Feb. 2, 1939; s. Philip and Ruth Sara (Millstein) B.; m. Paula Dee Maskin, Sept. 2, 1962; children: Philip, Sara, Jeffrey. BA, Wayne State U., 1962, JD, 1965. Asst. atty. gen. State of Mich., Lansing, 1965-86; mng. atty. Moran & Bladen, Lansing, 1987-93; pvt. practice, East Lansing, Mich., 1994-97; adminstrv. law judge USCG, 1999—. Author: Consumer Law of Michigan, 1978. Mem. Dem. Polit. Reform Comm., Mich., 1968. With U.S. Army Security, 1957-60, Korea. Recipient Alexander Freeman scholarship Wayne State U., Detroit, 1962-65. Mem. State Bar Mich. (chmn. anti-trust sect., treas./sec. 1990-94), Nat. Assn. Fraud Units (pres. 1985-86). Office: 1314 Fairoaks Ct East Lansing MI 48823-1810

**BLADES, G(ENE) GRANVILLE,** lawyer, accountant; b. Easton, Md., Nov. 17, 1965; s. Gene William and Jean (Wise) B. BA, Washington Coll., Chartertown, Md., 1986; PhD, Catholic U., Washington, 1990; JD, U. Md., 1994. Bar: Md. 1994, D.C. 1995, U.S. Ct. Appeals (4th and fed. cirs.) 1994, U.S. Dist. Ct. Md. 1995, U.S. Ct. Internat. Trade 1995, U.S. Tax Ct. 1994, U.S. Ct. Claims 1995. Instr. Chesapeake Coll., Wye Mills, Md., 1990-93; ptnr. Kent & Blades, Denton, Md., 1994-95; pvt. practice Easton, 1995—; legal counsel Trappe (Md.) Vol. Fire Dept., 1995—; dir. North Choptank Corp., Easton, 1997—; cons., legal counsel Blades Design, LLC, Trappe, 1994—. Author: Politics of Sectional Avoidance, 1990, Brief History of White Marsh Parish, 1997; editor The Epistle, 1995. Treas. Habitat for Humanity Talbot Co., Easton, 1997—; dir. Talbot Co. Humane Soc., Easton, 1996—; sec. Old White Marsh Cemetary Corp., Trappe, 1997—. Mem. ABA, AICPA, Md. State Bar Assn., Talbot County Bar Assn., Caroline County Bar Assn. (sec. 1994-95), Nat. Acad. Elder Law Attys. Republican. Episcopal. Avocations: photography, travel. Estate planning, Family and matrimonial, Real property. Home: 2814 Ocean Gtwy Trappe MD 21673-1764 Office: 127 N West St Ste E Easton MD 21601-2758

**BLAES, STEPHEN MATHIAS,** lawyer; b. Wichita, Kans., July 16, 1938; s. Omer W. and Catherine Jane (Maher) B.; m. Mary Colleen Cavanaugh, July 6, 1961; children: Matthew, Lori, Brian, Michael. BS in Commerce and Fin., St. Louis U., 1960; JD with distinction, U. Kans., 1963. Bar: Kans. 1963, U.S. Dist. Ct. Kans., U.S. Ct. Appeals (10th cir.), U.S. Supreme Ct. Law clk. U.S. Dist. Ct. Kans., Kansas City, 1963-64; ptnr. Jochems, Sargent & Blaes, Wichita, 1964-69, Blaes & Heath, Wichita, 1969-89; spl. counsel Foulston & Siefkin, Wichita, 1989-93; gen. counsel Cath. Health Assn. U.S., St. Louis, 1979-93; chmn. bd., sr. cousnel CSJ Health Sys., Wichita, 1986-93, pres., CEO, 1993-95; chmn., CEO N.Am. Health Alliance, Cape Girardeau, Mo., 1995—; del. Congress Hosp. Trustees, Chgo. Mem. Am. Acad. Hosp. Attys. (pres. 1984-85), Am. Hosp. Assn. (ho. of dels. 1992-95, governing coun. on healthcare sys. 1992-95), Crestview Country Club (pres. 1992). Republican. Roman Catholic. Avocations: golf, photography, travel. Health. Office: NAm Health Alliance 280 S Mount Auburn Rd Cape Girardeau MO 63703-4918

**BLAGG, JAMES W.,** prosecutor; m. Nancy Sanford; 3 children. BA in Govt., St. Mary's U., Tex., 1968, JD, 1972. Bar: Tex. 1972. Asst. dist. atty. Bexar County, Tex., 1973-80; asst. U.S. Atty., 1981-84; chief criminal divsn. U.S. Atty. for Western Dist. Tex., 1984-85, first asst., 1984-85, U.S. atty., 1996—; pvt. practice law, 1985-95. Served to capt., inf. U.S. Army. Recipient Prosecutor of Yr. award Texans' War on Drugs, 1984. Office: US Atty Western Dist Tex 601 NW Loop 410 Ste 600 San Antonio TX 78216-5597*

**BLAHER, NEAL JONATHAN,** lawyer; b. Lowell, Mass., Nov. 6, 1960. BA in Psychology, U. Pa., 1981; JD, Villanova U., 1986. Bar: Pa. 1986, N.J. 1986, U.S. Dist. Ct. N.J. 1986, Fla. 1987, U.S. Dist. Ct. (ea. dist.) Pa. 1987, U.S. Ct. Appeals (3rd cir.) 1987, U.S. Ct. Appeals (11th cir.) 1988, U.S. Dist. Ct. (mid. dist.) Fla. 1988, U.S. Supreme Ct. 1997. Intern law clk. to presiding justice Cir. Ct., Phila., 1984-85; paralegal Fineman & Bach, Phila., 1982-83, assoc., 1986-88; assoc. Allen, Dyer, Doppelt, Franjola & Milbrath, P.A., Orlando, Fla., 1988-93; pvt. practice Orlando, 1993—. Mem. Fla. Bar, Orange County Bar Assn., Pub. Investors Arbitration Bar Assn. Avocation: music. Securities, Trademark and copyright, Franchising. Home and Office: PO Box 804 Orlando FL 32802-0804

**BLAIN, PETER CHARLES,** lawyer; b. Milw., Nov. 15, 1949; s. Emile Octave and Mary Catherine (Usalis) B.; m. Katherine Stauber, June 12, 1971; children: Thomas Peter, Timothy Charles, Katherine Elizabeth, Peter James. BS, Wis. State U., Stevens Point, 1971; JD, Georgetown U., 1978. Bar: Wis. 1978. Budget analyst VA, Washington, D.C., 1974-78; atty. Reinhart, Boerner, Van Deuren, Norris & Rieselbach S.C., Milw., 1978—; chmn. Wis. State Bar Insolvency Sect., 1995-97; lectr. U. Wis., Milw., 1984—. Contbr. articles to profl. jours. 2d Lt. U.S. Army, 1972-74. Listed Best Lawyers in Am., Woodward/White, 1987—. Mem. Milw. Bar Bankruptcy Sect. (prog. chmn. 1984-85, sect. chmn. 1986-87, co-chair bankruptcy sect. bench/bar com. 1998—). Democrat. Roman Catholic. Avocation: reading. Bankruptcy. Office: Reinhart Boerner Van Deuren Norris & Rieselbach SC 1000 N Water St Ste 1800 Milwaukee WI 53202-6650

**BLAINE, STEVEN ROBERT,** lawyer; b. Tulsa, Aug. 24, 1969; s. Kent Robert and Barbara Ellen (Loftus) B. BA, Bellarmine Coll., 1992; JD, U. Dayton, 1995. Bar: Ky. 1995. Contract atty. Brown, Todd & Heyburn, PLLC, Louisville, 1996—. Mng. editor Dayton Intellectual Property Law Jour., 1994-95. Ky. Gov.'s scholar. Mem. ABA, Ky. Bar Assn., Fed. Bar Assn., Louisville Bar Assn. Avocations: tennis, yoga, Celtic music, Impressionist art, Woody Allen films, all things Celtic. E-Mail: blainesr@iglou.com. Intellectual property, Trademark and copyright, General civil litigation. Home: 747 Yorkwood Pl Louisville KY 40223-3555

**BLAIR, DAVID BELMONT,** lawyer; b. Oslo, Norway, July 4, 1963; came to U.S., 1963; s. David William and Rosemary Blair; m. Bernice Blair, Aug. 5, 1989; children: David S., Edith C., John M. AB, Georgetown U., 1985; JD, Cornell U., 1989. Bar: Mass. 1990, D.C. 1996. Law clerk, Hon. Frank M. Johnson, Jr. U.S. Ct. Appeals 11th Cir., Montgomery, Ala., 1989-90; trial atty., tax div. U.S. Dept. Justice, Washington, 1990-95; assoc. Miller & Chevalier, Washington, 1995-98; mem. Miller & Chevalier, 1999—. Mem. ABA, Fed. Bar Assn. Taxation, general, Corporate taxation. Office: Miller & Chevalier 655 15th St NW Ste 900 Washington DC 20005-5799

**BLAIR, EDWARD EUGENE,** lawyer; b. Great Falls, Mont., Nov. 28, 1963; s. Roy Eugene and Mary Ann (Hammett) B. BA, Birmingham-So. Coll., 1987; JD, Samford U., 1990. Bar: Ala. 1990, U.S. Dist. Ct. (no. dist.) Ala. 1991. Law clk. Jefferson County Office of the Dist. Atty., Birmingham, Ala., 1989-90, Hon. Robert E. Austin, Oneonta, Ala., 1990; assoc. Smith, Gaines, Gaines & Sabatini, Huntsville, Ala., 1991—; pvt. practice, 1994—. Bd. dirs. Huntsville-Madison County Daycare Assn., 1991—, Child Care Mgmt. Agy. No. Ala., Huntsville, 1992—, Mental Health Assn. Madison County, Huntsville, 1992—. Mem. Assn. Trial Lawyers Am., Ala. Trial Lawyers Assn., Ala. State Bar Assn., Huntsville-Madison County Bar Assn. (law day com. 1991-92, bench and bar rels. com. 1992—), Birmingham-So. Coll. Alumni Assn. (pres. 1992—, no. regional dir.). Avocations: book collecting, scuba diving, phys. fitness, karate, oriental art collecting. Family and matrimonial, Bankruptcy, Entertainment. Home: PO Box 2855 Huntsville AL 35804-2855 Office: Ste 103 200 W Court Sq Huntsville AL 35801-4225

**BLAIR, GRAHAM KERIN (KERRY BLAIR),** lawyer; b. Aug. 20, 1951; s. Joseph William and Ruth Marilyn (Shore) B.; m. Melanie Ann Offield, Sept. 12, 1998; children: Elizabeth, Austin. BA, So. Meth. U., 1973; JD, U. Tex., 1976. Bar: Tex. 1976, U.S. Ct. Appeals (5th cir.) 1977, U.S. Dist. Ct. (so. dist.) Tex. 1977. Assoc. Bracewell & Patterson, Houston, 1976-79; ptnr., co-chmn. litigation sect. Chamberlain, Hrdlicka, White, Williams & Martin, Houston, 1979-82; sr. ptnr. Norton & Blair, Houston, 1982-93; shareholder, head Houston litigation group Verner, Liipfert, Bernhard, McPherson and Hand, Chtd., Houston, 1993—; author, lectr. on banking and constrn. litigation and alternative dispute resolution procedures; dir. advocacy, bd. advs. U. Tex. Sch. Law, Austin, 1976. *Mr. Blair has over twenty-three years of experience and leadership in complex business litigation, successfully representing clients in disputes alleging damages in the hundreds of millions of dollars. His clients have included major oil and gas companies, insurers, energy developers, large banks and borrowers, public universities, hotel owners, construction and manufacturing concerns, public ac counting and law firms. Kerry Blair's articles and comments have been featured in the Wall Street Journal, ABA Journal, The American Banker, National Law Journal, The Texas Lawyer and various other domestic and international newspapers and business journals.* Contbr. articles to profl. jours. Lt. USNR, 1973-76. Fellow Houston Bar Found.; mem. ABA, Tex. Bar Found., Houston Bar Assn. (mem. adminstrn. justice com.), State Bar Tex., Alpha Tau Omega. Republican. Methodist. Federal civil litigation, State civil litigation, Construction. Address: Verner Liipfert Bernhard McPherson and Hand Chtd 1111 Bagby St Fl 47 Houston TX 77002-2551

**BLAIR, JAMES NEWELL,** lawyer; b. Washington, July 29, 1940; s. Newell and Greta (Flinterman) B.; m. Wendy Ann Miller, Apr. 22, 1978; 1 child, Hilary Ann. AB, Dartmouth Coll., 1962; JD, Harvard U., 1970. Bar: N.Y. 1971, U.S. Dist. Ct. (so. dist.) N.Y. 1974, U.S. Ct. Appeals (2d cir.) 1975. Assoc. White & Coch, N.Y.C., 1970-71; assoc. Rogers Hoge & Hills, N.Y.C., 1972-80, ptnr., 1980-86; pvt. practice N.Y.C., 1987-88; ptnr. Teitler & Teitler, N.Y.C., 1988-91, Loselle, Greenawalt, Kaplan, Blair, N.Y.C., 1991-99, Wolman, Babitt & King, 1999—; arbitrator small claims div. N.Y.C. Civil ct. Bd. dirs., treas. 600 West End Ave. Owner's Corp., N.Y.C., 1980—; mem. vestry Ch. of Christ the King, Stone Ridge, N.Y., 1991-96; mem. coun. Episcopal Diocese N.Y. Lt. USN, 1962-67. Mem. N.Y. State Bar Assn. (fed. cts. com. 1986-89, exec. com. comml. and fed. litigation sect. 1989—, chair civil practice law and rules com. 1991-95, mem. 1995—, adv. com. civil practice to chief adminstr. ctrs. 1995—), Assn. of Bar of City of N.Y. (com. on nuclear energy and the law 1989-92, others), Harvard Club of N.Y.C. Democrat. Episcopalian. Avocations: chamber music, cross-country skiing, rebuilding farmhouse. General civil litigation, Bankruptcy. Home: 600 W End Ave New York NY 10024-1610 Office: 521 5th Ave New York NY 10175-0003

**BLAIR, JANYCE KEIKO IMATA,** lawyer; b. Honolulu, Sept. 22, 1942; d. Yutaka and Bessie Tomiyo Imata. BA, Mich. State U., 1964; JD, Golden Gate U., 1981. Bar: Calif. 1982, U.S. Dist. Ct. (cen. dist.) Calif. 1986, U.S. Ct. Appeals (9th cir.) 1987, U.S. Supreme Ct. 1987. Editor Mich. State U., East Lansing, 1964-68; chief com. clk. Hawaii State Legislature, Honolulu, 1970-78; acquisitions editor U. Hawaii Press, Honolulu, 1970-78; assoc. Law Offices M.J. Bleckman, Gardena, Calif., 1982-88; ptnr. Bleckman & Blair, Gardena, 1988—; instr. Whittier Coll. Sch. Law, L.A., 1985-87, San Fernando Valley Coll. Law, L.A., 1986. Literacy tutor L.A. Urban League, 1990-91, El Segundo Libr. Literacy, Calif., 1993-94. Mem. State Bar Calif. (mem. various coms.), L.A. County Bar Assn. (mem. appellate cts. com. 1985-87, 97-98). Avocations: reading, traveling, gardening. Appellate, Criminal. Office: Bleckman & Blair 302 W Grand Ave Ste 3 El Segundo CA 90245-5108

**BLAIR, M. WAYNE,** lawyer; b. Spokane, Washington, Oct. 17, 1942. BS in Elec. Engr., U. Washington, 1965, JD, 1968. Bar: Wash. 1968. With USAF, 1968-72. Recipient Helen M. Geisness award, 1987, President's award, 1990. Mem. ABA (Ho. of Dels. 1988-91), Seattle-King County Bar Assn. (trustee 1981-83, pres. 1987-88), Washington State Bar Assn. (bd. govs. 1991-94, pres. 1998-99), Am. Judicature Soc. General corporate, Real property, Alternative dispute resolution. Office: 5800 Columbia Ctr 701 5th Ave Seattle WA 98104-7097

**BLAIR, RICHARD BRYSON,** lawyer; b. Athens, Ohio, Oct. 1, 1945; s. Richard Holmes and Doris Ruth Blair; m. Ellen A. Riehl, Aug. 24, 1968; children: Heather Ann, Heidi Lynn, Richard Holmes II, Molly Jane. BA, Franklin and Marshall Coll., 1967; JD, Ohio Northern U., 1970. Bar: Ohio 1970, U.S. Dist. Ct. (no. dist.) Ohio 1972. Assoc. Roth and Stephens, Youngstown, Ohio, 1970-75; ptnr. Roth and Stephens, Youngstown, 1976-77; ptnr., v.p. Roth, Stephens, Blair and Co. LPA, Youngstown, 1977—, Roth, Blair, Roberts, Strasfeld & Lodge, LPA, Youngstown. Bd. dirs. Greater Youngstown Coalition of Christians, 1994-98, co-chmn., 1996-98; trustee, mem. bd. edn. Eagle Hts. Acad. Mem. Ohio Bar Assn., Mahoning County Bar Assn., Internat. Assn. Ins. Counsel, Ohio Assn. Civil Trial Attys., Def. Rsch. Inst., Nat. Assn. R.R. Trial Counsel. Avocations: family, church activities, golf, sailing, jogging. General civil litigation, Insurance, Personal injury. Home: 253 Wildwood Dr Youngstown OH 44512-3340 Office: Roth Blair Roberts Strasfeld & Lodge LPA 1100 Bank 1 Bldg Youngstown OH 44503

**BLAIR, RICHARD EUGENE,** lawyer; b. Loudon, Tenn., Mar. 7, 1923; s. John Thomas and Minnie Laura (Jones) B.; m. Marjorie Ann Bechtel, Apr. 17, 1954; children: Catherine Elizabeth, Marilynne B. BA, U. Wash., 1948; JD, Georgetown U., 1956; LLM, So. Meth. U., 1962. Bar: Va. 1956, U.S. Supreme Ct. 1962, U.S. Dist. Ct. (ea. dist.) Va. 1972, U.S. Ct. Appeals (4th cir.) 1981. Commd. ensign, U.S. Navy, 1944, advanced through grades to capt., 1967, ret., 1972; sole practice, Fairfax, Va., 1972-79, Mc Lean, Va., 1979-82; of counsel Harrison, Golden & Hughes, P.C., Mc Lean, 1982-86; dir. Mc Lean Savs. & Loan Assn., 1977-88, gen. counsel, 1975-82; dir. McLean Fin. Corp., 1982-87; chmn. bd. dirs. Unifed Land Title Co., 1986-87; adj. prof. oil and gas law Georgetown U., 1962-75; vis. prof. Duke U. Law Sch., 1964-68. Contbr. articles to profl. jours. Recipient Navy Lawyer award Navy League U.S., 1961. Mem. Va. Bar Assn., Fairfax County Bar Assn., Georgetown U. Law Sch. Alumni Assn. Republican. Presbyterian. Oil, gas, and mineral, Estate planning, Family and matrimonial. Office: 20530 Falcons Landing Cir #3304 Sterling VA 20165-3583

**BLAIR, ROBERT ALLEN,** business executive, lawyer; b. Suffolk, Va., June 25, 1946; s. Thomas Francis Jr. and Ossie (Southern) B.; m. Linda Britt, Dec. 27, 1970; children: Robert Allen II, Thomas Edward. BA in Math., Coll. William and Mary, 1968; JD, U. Va., 1973. Bar: Mass. 1974, U.S. Dist. Ct. Mass. 1974, U.S. Ct. Appeals (D.C. cir.) 1976, U.S. Dist. Ct. D.C. 1980. Assoc. Goodwin, Procter & Hoar, Boston, 1973-74; assoc. Surrey & Morse, Washington, 1974-78, ptnr., 1979-81; mng. ptnr. Anderson, Hibey & Blair, Washington, 1981-95; ptnr., chair govt. practice group Manatt, Phelps & Phillips, 1995-99; co-chmn., gen. counsel GlobalOptions, LLC, Washington, 1999—; dir. Palmer Tech. Services, Inc., Washington, 1983-93. Mem. editorial bd. Law Rev. U. Va., 1971-73. Chmn. bd. Inst. on Terrorism and Subnat. Conflict, Washington, 1982-95; co-counsel Citizens for Dem. Alternatives in 1980, Washington, 1979-81; mem. adv. panel on fgn. policy, def. and arms control Dem. Nat. Com., Washington, 1982-85; mem. drafting team for fgn. policy, def. and arms control issue workshop Dem. Nat. Conf., Phila., 1982, mem. bus. coun., 1988-90, 94—, mng. trustee, 1994-95; mem. Senate Dem. Roundtable, Washington, 1983—; mem. Senate Dem. Leadership Circle, Washington, 1983—; vice chmn. Potomac Group, Washington, 1983-84, chmn., 1984-85; mem. adv. council Dem. Platform Com., Washington, 1984; spl. counsel 1984 Dem. Nat. Conv., San Francisco, 1984; spl. counsel to nat. fin. chmn. Dem. Nat. Com., Washington, 1984-85, mem. fin. bd. dirs., 1983-85, 88; mem. Nat. Dem. Club, Senate Dem. Majority Trust, 1992—; vice chmn. Washington Fgn. Affairs Soc., 1984-87; mem. Gov.'s Econ. Adv. Council, Va., 1986-94; commr. Va. Port Authority, Commonwealth Va., 1991-96, vice chmn. finance/planning com., 1992-94, chmn., 1994-96; chmn. S Corp. Assn., Washington 1996—, chmn. reform project, 1993-96; advisory bd. Thomas Jefferson Program Pub. Policy William and Mary, 1996—; bd. dirs. Everybody Wins, 1997—, Youth Leadership Inst., Washington, 1984-86. Named to Outstanding Young Men Am., U.S. Jaycees, 1976. Mem. ABA, Univ. Club (Washington). General corporate, Private international, Administrative and regulatory. Home: 4936 Rodman St NW Washington DC 20016-3239 Office: GlobalOptions LLC 1615 L St NW Ste 1350 Washington DC 20036-5655

**BLAIR, SAMUEL RAY,** lawyer; b. Aurora, Ill., June 19, 1941; s. Donald R. and Jeanette E. (Quirin) B.; m. Jean Jordan, Nov. 25, 1964 (div. 1977); children: Alissa Lynn Motzfeldt, Jason Jordan. BA, U. Denver, 1963; JD, Lewis & Clark Coll., 1969. Bar: Oreg. 1969, Hawaii 1990. Assoc. Hershizer, Mitchell et al, Portland, Oreg., 1970-73; pvt. practice law Salem, Oreg., 1973—, Koloa, Hawaii, 1990—; adj. prof. law Willamette U., Salem, 1985—. Mem. Marion County Bar Assn. (pres. 1985), Oreg. State Bar Assn., Kauai Bar Assn., Hawaii Bar Assn., Hawaii Def. Counsel Assn., Hawaii Trial Lawyers Assn., Assn. Trial Lawyers Am., Hospice, Million Dollar Advocates Forum. Avocations: travel, reading, trekking, martial arts (Aikido). General civil litigation, Personal injury, Product liability. Office: 2360 Kiahuna Plantation Dr Koloa HI 96756-9713

**BLAIR, WARREN EMERSON,** retired federal judge; b. Chgo., June 23, 1916; s. Henry Allan and Mae Idella (Spratt) B.; m. Madeline Mary Sheehan, 1947 (dec. 1997). J.D., DePaul U., 1940; M.B.A., George Washington U., 1958. Bar: Ill. bar 1940, Republic of Korea bar 1951, U.S. Supreme Ct. bar 1954, Ohio bar 1954, N.Y. State bar 1964. Mem. firm Blair, Chiara & Blair, Chgo., 1940-42; atty. SEC, Cleve., 1947-54; chief enforcement atty. trading and exchanges div. SEC, Washington, 1954-60; asst. regional adminstr. SEC, N.Y.C., 1960-64; adminstrv. law judge SEC, Washington, 1964-70; chief adminstrv. law judge SEC, 1970-94; mem. Adminstrv. Conf. U.S., 1972-74. Served to 1st lt. U.S. Army, 1942-46; to capt. 1950-52, ETO, Korea. Decorated Silver Star, Purple Heart with oak leaf cluster. Mem. ABA, Fed. Bar Assn., Am. Judicature Soc., Fed. Adminstrv. Law Judges Conf., Pi Gamma Mu, Delta Kappa Epsilon. Home: 2440 Virginia Ave NW Washington DC 20037-2601

**BLAIS, ROBERT HOWARD,** lawyer; b. Muskegon, Mich., May 14, 1955. BA with high honors, Mich. State U., 1977; JD cum laude, U. Notre Dame, 1980. Ptnr. Bogle & Gates, Seattle, 1988-93; shareholder Gores & Blais, Seattle, 1993—; adj. prof. estate and tax planning Seattle U., 1982-83; chairperson Wash. State U. Planned Giving Adv. Bd., 1989-96. Mem. ABA, Wash. State Bar Assn. (real property, probate and trust coun. 1987-88), , Seattle-King County Bar Assn., Estate Planning Coun. Seattle (pres. 1996-97), Am. Coll. Trust and Estate Counsel. Estate planning, Probate. Office: Gores & Blais 1420 5th Ave Ste 2600 Seattle WA 98101-1357

**BLAKE, DANIEL L.,** lawyer; b. Oakland, Calif., Apr. 10, 1950; s. Kenneth E. and Kathleen Hosford Blake; m. Paulette Lowe, Jan. 1996. BA in Psychology, Antioch Coll., Yellow Springs, Ohio, 1975; MA in Psychology, Columbia Pacific U., 1982, PhD in Anatomy, 1983; JD, U. S.C., 1995. Bar: S.C. 1995, U.S. Dist. Ct. S.C. 1995, U.S. Ct. Appeals (4th cir.) 1995, U.S. Supreme Ct. 1999. Asst. solicitor 4th Cir. S.C., Darlington, 1995-96, 3d. Cir. S.C., Sumter, 1996; assoc. Gardner Law Firm, Darlington, 1997; pvt. practice Hartsville, S.C., 1998—. Mem. ABA, ATLA, Nat. Assn. Criminal Def. Lawyers. Avocation: kayaking. Bankruptcy, Criminal, Personal injury. Home: 412 Haven Dr Hartsville SC 29550-5018 Office: 450 W Carolina Ave Hartsville SC 29550-4524

**BLAKE, DAVID GORDON,** lawyer; b. Bryn Mawr, Pa., July 27, 1946; s. Alton David and Eleanore (Lavery) Gordon; m. Barbara Clemens Trimble, Aug. 7, 1976; children: Chad G., Scott B. BA, Tulane U., 1969; JD, Temple U., 1973. Bar: Pa. 1973, U.S. Supreme Ct. 1979. Ptnr. Cramp, D'Iorio, McConchie & Forbes, Media, Pa., 1973-96, Beatty, Cramp, Kauffman and Lincke, Media, 1996—. Editor Del. County Legal Jour., 1980. Pres. Responsible Living Ltd., Media, 1980-81; bd. dirs. Fox Valley Community Assn., Glen Mills, Pa., 1984-86; mem. Rep. com., Radnor Twp., Pa., 1988—; v.p. Ithan PTO, 1989-90; pres. Radnor Soccer Club, 1989-96; treas. Radnor-Wayne Little League, 1989; mem. Nat. Rep. Presdl. Task Force. Named Man of Yr. Wayne area Jaycees, 1976. Mem. Del. County Bar Assn. (bd. dirs. 1986-88, 98—), Guy de Furia Am. Inns of Ct. Avocations: reading, coaching. General civil litigation, Insurance, Personal injury. Home: 673 Mill Rd Villanova PA 19085-1219 Office: Beatty Cramp Kauffman & Lincke PO Box 901 Media PA 19063-0901

**BLAKE, JONATHAN DEWEY,** lawyer; b. Long Branch, N.J., June 14, 1938; s. Edgar Bond and Haven (Johnstone) B.; m. Prudence Anne Rowsell, Dec. 22, 1964 (div. June 1977); children: Juliet Haven, Deborah Anne, Susanna Rowsell; m. Elizabeth L. Shriver, Dec. 9, 1977; children: Jonathan Shriver-Blake, Molly Shriver-Blake. BA magna cum laude, Yale U., 1960, LLB cum laude, 1964; BA, MA, Oxford U., Eng., 1962. Bar: D.C. 1965, U.S. Supreme Ct. 1973, U.S. Dist. Ct. D.C. 1965, U.S. Dist. Ct. Md. 1985, U.S. Ct. Appeals (D.C. cir.) 1965, U.S. Ct. Appeals (2d cir.) 1973. Assoc. Covington & Burling, Washington, 1964-72, ptnr., 1972—, chmn. mgmt. com., 1996—; tchr. Howard U., Washington, 1965-70, U. Va., Charlottesville, 1965-70. Contbr. articles to profl. jours. Pres. Great Falls Citizens Assn., Va., 1967-68; exec. com., bd. dirs. Deerfield Acad, Mass., 1980-85. Rhodes scholar, 1960; recipient Gordon Brown prize, 1959. Mem. ABA (chair internat. telecomm. com. 1993-99), Fed. Comm. Bar Assn. (pres. 1980-85). Administrative and regulatory, Communications, Private international. Home: 4926 Hillbrook Ln NW Washington DC 20016-3208 Office: Covington & Burling PO Box 7566 1201 Pennsylvania Ave NW Washington DC 20044-7566

**BLAKE, TAMRA A.,** legal business manager; b. Cambridge, Mass., Aug. 11, 1958; d. Donald L. and Edna C. Greene; m. Trevor P. Blake, Aug. 20, 1988; children: Symore A., Austin T. BA, Wellesley Coll., 1980. Asst. v.p. comml. real estate loan adminstrn. Citicorp, N.Y.C., 1980-85; v.p., head loan adminstrn. real estate Bank of New Eng., Boston, 1985-91; v.p., MIS mgr. comml. real estate Fleet Bank, Boston, 1991-96, sr. v.p., corp. legal bus. mgr., 1996—. Trustee of endowments St. Peters Episcopal Ch., Cambridge, Mass., 1992-98; bd. dirs. Big Bros. Assn. Greater Boston, 1996—; trustee Buckingham Browne & Nichols Sch., Cambridge, 1998—. Avocations: reading, finance, tennis. Administrative and regulatory. Office: Fleet Bank 75 State St Mabof 10C Boston MA 02109

**BLAKE, WILLIAM GEORGE,** lawyer; b. Lamoni, Iowa, Dec. 10, 1949; s. George Charles and Mildred Lucille (Norman) B.; m. Barbara Kay Holseid, May 28, 1972; children: Jennifer Christine, Angela Sue. BA, Graceland Coll., Lamoni, 1972; JD, U. Nebr., 1975. Bar: Nebr. 1975, U.S. Dist. Ct. Nebr. 1975. Asst. city atty. City of Lincoln (Nebr.), 1975-79, chief asst. city atty., 1979-84; assoc. Pierson, Ackerman Fitchett, Akin & Hunzeker, Lincoln, 1984-85; ptnr. Pierson, Fitchett, Hunzeker, Blake & Loftis, Lincoln, 1986—. Vice chmn. Lincoln Parks and Recreation Bd., 1987-88, chmn., 1989-91; mem. Lincoln Parks and Recreation Found., bd. dirs. 1992-95, chmn. 1996-97. Mem. ABA, Nebr. Bar Assn., Lincoln-Lancaster County Bar Assn. Democrat. Reorganized Ch. of Jesus Christ of Latter-day Saints. Avocation: mountaineering. General civil litigation, Condemnation, Real property. Office: Pierson Fitchett Hunzeker Blake & Loftis PO Box 95109 Lincoln NE 68509-5109

**BLAKELY, JOHN T.,** lawyer; b. Beloit, Wis., May 26, 1944; s. Walter Edwin and Virginia (Treleaven) B.; m. Ellen Ford, Dec. 27, 1968 (div. Apr. 1988); children: Sara, Ford; m. Pamela Rose Westmoreland, Mar. 16, 1991. BA, Duke U., 1966; JD, U. Mich., 1969. Bar: Fla., U.S. Ct. Appeals (11th cir.), U.S. Dist. Ct. (mid. dist.) Fla., U.S. Supreme Ct.; bd. cert. personal injury lawyer; bd. cert. Nat. Bd. Trial Advocacy. Instr. law U. Wis., Madison, 1969-70; assoc. Carlton, Fields, Ward et al., Tampa, Fla., 1970-73; ptnr. Johnson, Blakely, Pope, Bokor, Ruppel & Burns, P.A., Clearwater, Fla., 1973—. Mem. ABA, ATLA, Fla. Bar (bd. cert. civil trial law), Acad. Fla. Trial Lawyers, Nat. Bd. Trial Advocacy. Personal injury, Probate, General civil litigation. Office: Johnson Blakely Pope Bokor Ruppel & Burns PA 975 6th Ave S Naples FL 34102-6753

**BLAKELY, ROBERT GEORGE,** lawyer; b. Beloit, Wis., Aug. 21, 1947; s. George Knowlton and Catherine Lucille (Mitchell) B.; m. Susan Bradford Amsler; children: Robert, Alison; m. Louise A. Delahoyde. BA, Denison U., 1969; JD, Marquette U., 1972. Bar: Wis. 1972, U.S. Dist. Ct. (ea. and we. dists.) Wis. 1972. Assoc. Blakely & Long, Beloit, Wis., 1972-74, Hansen Law Firm, Beloit, 1974-80; ptnr. Hansen, Eggers & Blakely, Beloit, 1980—; instr. real estate law and continuing edn. Mem. Wis. State Bar (joint realtors com. 1997—), Beloit Jaycees (pres. 1972-84, Outstanding Young Man 1975). Republican. Congregationalist. Avocations: skiing, mountain biking. Real property, Family and matrimonial, Contracts commercial. Office: Hansen Eggers & Blakely 416 College St Ste A Beloit WI 53511-6310

**BLAKEMAN, BRUCE ARTHUR,** lawyer; b. Oct. 2, 1955; s. Robert M. and Betty Ellen (Harris) B.; m. Nancy Shevell, May 28, 1984; 1 child, Arlen. BS in Polit. Sci., Ariz. State U., 1980; JD, Calif. Western U., San Diego, 1983. Bar: N.Y. 1984, N.J. 1984, U.S. Dist. Ct. (so. dist.) N.Y. 1987, U.S. Dist. Ct. (ea. dist.) N.Y. 1987, U.S. Ct. Appeals (4th cir.) 1989, U.S. Supreme Ct. 1991. Ptnr. Robert M. Blakeman & Assocs., Valley Stream, N.Y., 1984—; gen. counsel New Eng. Motor Freight, Inc., Eastern Freight Ways, Inc., Phoenix Motor Express, Inc. and Carrier Logistics, Inc., Elizabeth, N.J.; dir. North Sea Ins. Co., Valley Stream; mem. devel. bd. Franklin Hosp. Med. Ctr., Valley Stream, 1988—. Councilman Town Bd., Hempstead, N.Y., 1993—; elected mem. 1st session Nassau County Legislature, 1995-97, elected presiding officer, majority leader, 1996, 98-2000; dir. Tempo, Inc., Woodmere, N.Y., 1993—; chmn. Ben Franklin Club of Franklin Hosp. Med. Ctr., Valley Stream, 1990-92; hon. sheriff City of N.Y., 1997; hon. police chief Hempstead, N.Y., 1997. Named Man of Yr., Yeshiva of South Shore, 1996, Man of Yr., Superior Officers Assn. Nassau County Police Dept., 1996, Man of Yr., Jewish Lawyers Assn. of Nassau County, 1996, Man of yr., Woodmere Merchant's Assn., 1997; recipient President's award Ct. Officers Assn., 1996, Spirit of Life award South Shore chpt. City of Hope, 1997, Cmty. Achievement award Am. Com. Shaare Zedek Med. Ctr. in Jerusalem, 1997, Bernard M. Bloom Meml. award for disting. pub. svc. OTSAR, 1998, Pub. Affairs award for work in child care North Shore Child and Guidance Ctr., 1998, Spl. Recognition award Child Care Coun. Nassau County, 1998, Pub. Affairs award for outstanding legis. leadership North Shore Child and Family Guidance Assn., 1998, First Cmty. Achievement award Congregation Ahavat Yisrael, 1998; honored by 1 in 9 Long Island Breast Cancer Action Coalition, Parents for Advancement of Conductive Edn., 1998, N.Y. State Assn. on Health, Phys. Edn., Recreation, Dance and Athletics, 1998, Nat. Tennis Assn. for Disabled, 1998. Mem. Nassau Lawyers' Assn. L.I. Inc. (pres. 1994, dir. 1988—), Nassau County Bar Assn., N.J. Bar Assn., Phi Delta Phi (majister 1983—, Outstanding Mem. 1983). Republican. Jewish. Avocations: basketball, tennis, sports cars. General civil litigation, Real property, Transportation. Home: 39 Clubside Dr Woodmere NY 11598-1365 Office: Robert M Blakeman & Assocs 108 S Franklin Ave Valley Stream NY 11580-6105 also: 1-71 No Ave E Elizabeth NJ 07201

**BLAKESLEE, WESLEY DANIEL,** lawyer, consultant; b. Wilkes-Barre, Pa., May 28, 1947; s. Daniel Leo and Anne Blakeslee; m. Georgia Carroll Croft, July 28, 1973; children—Jaime Kiersten, Christopher Justin, Shaun Michael. B.S., Pa. State U., 1969; J.D. (hon.), U. Md.-Balt., 1976. Bar: Md. 1976, U.S. Dist. Ct. Md. 1977, U.S. Tax Ct. 1984. Systems analyst NASA, Greenbelt, Md., 1969-76; assoc. Semmes, Bowen & Semmes, Balt., 1976-78; assoc. Dulany & Davis, Westminster, Md., 1978-83, ptnr., 1983; sole practice, Westminster, 1984—; Assoc. Gen. Couns., Johns Hopkins Univ., 1999—, lectr., dir. computer devel. U. Md. Law Sch., Balt., 1984-89. Contbg. author, editor; Maryland District Court Practice, 1981, revised 1983. Author: Understanding Computers, 1984. Contrbg. author: Computers, 1984. Rep. Carroll County, Md. State Employment and Tng. Council, 1980-82; bd. dirs. Carroll County chpt. Am. Heart Assn., Westminster 1981-87; bd. mgrs. Carroll County YMCA, 1987-95; bd. govs. Md. Law Sch. Fund, Balt., 1982—. Mem. ABA, Fed. Bar Assn. (treas. Balt. chpt. 1984-90), Md. Bar Assn. (young lawyers sect. council 1982-84, Outstanding Service award 1984, litigation sect. coun. 1982—, Chair 1995), Carroll County Bar Assn. (treas. 1984), Order of Coif, Delta Theta Phi, Carroll County Dem. Club, Westminster Rotary. Roman Catholic. Personal injury, Contracts commercial, Intellectual property. Home: 980 Hook Rd Westminster MD 21157-7335 Office: 104 E Main St Westminster MD 21157-5003

**BLAKLEY, BENJAMIN SPENCER, III,** lawyer; b. DuBois, Pa., Sept. 1, 1952; s. Benjamin Spencer Jr. and Mary Jane (Campney) B.; m. Kathleen M. Ellermeyer, Oct. 20, 1989; children: Benjamin Spencer IV, Kevin Charles, Kyra Jane. BA, Grove City Coll., 1974; JD, Duquesne U., 1977. Bar: Pa. 1977. Ptnr. Blakley, Jones & Mohney, DuBois, 1977—; pub. defender Clearfield (Pa.) County, 1977-84; instr. Pa. State U., DuBois, 1979-85. Mem. adv. bd. Salvation Army Pa. Corp., DuBois, 1978-98, chmn., 1988-91; mem. DuBois Area Youth Aid Panel, 1984-87; mem. Citizens for Effective Govt., DuBois, 1985-97; trustee DuBois Vol. Fire Dept., 1986-87, treas., 1987-90; mem. DuBois Ednl. Found., 1990—, Cath. Counseling and Adoption Svcs., 1996—; bd. dirs. DuBois Sr. and Cmty. Ctr., 1992-97. Mem. Pa. Bar Assn., Clearfield County Bar Assn., DuBois Vol. Fire Dept. Relief Assn. (pres. 1998). Democrat. Methodist. Family and matrimonial, Criminal, General practice. Office: Blakley Jones & Mohney PO Box 6 90 Beaver Dr Du Bois PA 15801-2440

**BLAN, KENNITH WILLIAM, JR.,** lawyer; b. Dec. 15, 1946; s. Kennith William and Sarah Shirley (Shane) B.; 1 child, Noah Winton; m. Lyndy r. Ervin, Sept. 1, 1995. BS, U. Ill., 1968, JD, 1971. Bar: Ill. 1972, U.S. Supreme Ct. 1978. With Office State's Atty., Vermilion County, Ill., 1971-72; atty. Chgo. Title & Trust Co., 1972; assoc. Graham, Meyer, Young, Welsch & Maton, Ill., Chgo., Springfield, Danville, 1972-74; pvt. practice Danville, 1975—; spl. asst. atty. gen. Ill., 1974-76; atty. City of Georgetown, Ill., 1985-92, Village of Belgium, Ill., 1987-89, Village of Westville, Ill., 1988-91. Contbr. chpts. to books. Chmn. Vermilion County Young Rep. Club, 1975-77; founding sponsor Civil Justice Found.; mem. Christian Business-men's Com., Christian Legal Soc. Capt. CAP. Mem. ABA, ATLA, Ill. Bar Assn., Vermilion County Bar Assn., Lawyer-Pilots Bar Assn., Ill. Trial Lawyers Assn. (bd. mgrs.), Ind. Trial Lawyers Assn., Am. Soc. Law and Medicine, Christian Legal Soc., Gideons Internat., Aircraft Owners and Pilots Assn., Elks. E-mail: blanlaw@aol.com. Personal injury, Federal civil litigation, State civil litigation. Office: PO Box 1995 Danville IL 61834-1995

**BLANCHARD, BRIAN WHEATLEY,** lawyer; b. State College, Pa., Nov. 7, 1958; s. Converse Herrick and Margaret (Wheatley) B.; m. Mary Willoughby; children: Will, Ben, Allison. BA, U. Mich., 1980; JD, Northwestern U., 1989. Bar: Ill. 1989, Wis. 1997, U.S. Dist. Ct. (we. dist.) Wis., U.S. Dist. Ct. (no. dist.) Ill., U.S. Ct. Appeals (7th cir.). Reporter Miami Herald, 1980-86; law clk. Hon. Walter J. Cummings U.S. Ct. Appeals (7th cir.), Chgo., 1989-90; asst. U.S. atty. Office of the U.S. Atty., Chgo., 1990-97; assoc. Quarles & Brady, Madison, Wis., 1997—. Editor-in-chief Northwestern U. Law Rev. Mem. Dane County Bar Assn. (law for pub. com. 1998—), Chgo. Coun. Lawyers (bd. govs. 1994-96), Order of Coif. General civil litigation, Criminal. Office: Quarles & Brady 1 S Pinckney St Ste 600 Madison WI 53703-2808

**BLANCHARD, ERIC ALAN,** lawyer; b. 1956. BBA, U. Mich., 1978; JD, Harvard U., 1981. Bar: Ill. 1981. Atty. Schiff, Hardin & Waite, 1981-86; corp. atty. Dean Foods Co., Franklin Park, Ill., 1986-88, gen. coun., sec., v.p., pres. dairy divsn., 1988—. General corporate, Securities, Finance. Office: Dean Foods Co 3600 N River Rd Franklin Park IL 60131-2185

**BLAND, JAMES THEODORE, JR.,** lawyer; b. Memphis, June 16, 1950; s. James Theodore and Martha Frances (Downen) B.; m. Pattie L. Martin, Apr. 12, 1974. BBA magna cum laude, Memphis State U., 1972, JD, 1974. Bar: Tenn. 1975, U.S. Dist. Ct. (we. dist.) Tenn. 1976, U.S. Tax Ct. 1976, U.S. Supreme Ct. 1983, U.S. Ct. Claims 1987; cert. Estate Planning specialist. Estate tax atty. IRS, Memphis, 1974-76; of counsel Armstrong, Allen, Braden, Goodman, McBride & Prewitt, Memphis, 1976-91; prin. James T. Bland, Jr. and Assocs., Memphis, 1991—; instr. in taxation, bus. law State Tchr.'s Inst., Memphis, 1975-83; bd. dirs. Thomas W. Briggs Found., Memphis. Fellow Am. Coll. Trust and Estate Counsel; mem. ABA (legis. initiatives com., taxation sect., specialization in estate planning real property, probate and trust sect., Achievement award 1983, 85), Fed. Bar Assn. (pres. 1987-88, 1st v.p. 1985-86, nat. coun. 1979—, bd. dirs. young lawyers divsn. 1979-84, pres. Memphis mid south chpt. 1979-80), Tenn. Bar Assn. (chmn. tax sect. 1984-85, bd. govs. 1984-85, 89-90, 90-91), Tenn. Young Lawyers Conf. (pres. 1985), Memphis Bar Assn. (bd. dirs. 1990-91), Tenn. Soc. CPA's. Republican. Methodist. Probate, Taxation, general, General civil litigation. Office: 4646 Poplar Ave Ste 320 Memphis TN 38117-4433

**BLAND, JOHN L.,** lawyer; b. Wichita Falls, Tex., Sept. 20, 1944. Student, Vanderbilt U.; BA, U. Tex., 1967, JD with honors, 1969. Bar: Tex. 1969. Mem. Bracewell & Patterson, LLP, Houston, 1969—. Mem. State Bar Tex., Houston Bar Assn., Phi Delta Phi. General corporate, Mergers and acquisitions, Securities. Office: Bracewell & Patterson LLP 2900 S Tower Pennzoil Pl 711 Louisiana St Houston TX 77002-2781

**BLAND, J(OHN) RICHARD,** lawyer; b. Denver, Oct. 30, 1946; s. Harry Edward and Julia Lenora (Bjelland) B.; m. Carole Jeanne Martin, Aug. 25, 1968. BS, Augustana Coll., 1968; JD, Drake U., 1971. Bar: Iowa 1971, Minn. 1971, U.S. Supreme Ct. 1976. Assoc. Meagher & Geer PLLP, Mpls., 1971-75, ptnr., 1975—; lectr. Minn. Inst. of Legal Edn., Mpls., 1985—. Fellow Am. Coll. Trial Lawyers; mem. Minn. Bar Assn., Minn. Def. Lawyers Assn. (bd. dirs. 1986-88). Professional liability, Personal injury, General civil litigation. Home: 17225 5th Ave N Plymouth MN 55447-3593 Office: Meagher & Geer PLLP 33 S 6th St Ste 4200 Minneapolis MN 55402-3722

**BLAND, RICHARD NORMAN,** lawyer; b. Phila., Apr. 29, 1959; s. Howard Jerome and Mollie (Sterling) B.; m. Emily Hawkes, Sept. 1, 1984; children: Zachary Davis, Alexandra Hawkes, Theodore Sterling. BA, U. Vt., 1982; JD, Washington U., 1985. Bar: Vt. 1985, U.S. Dist. Ct. Vt. 1986, U.S. Ct. Appeals (2nd cir.) 1989, U.S. Supreme Ct. 1989. Assoc. Downs, Rachlin & Martin, Burlington, Vt., 1985-91; v.p., general counsel Vt. Mutual Ins. Co., Montpelier, Vt., 1991—; dir. Granite Mutual Ins. Co., Barre, Vt., 1994—. Contbr. articles to profl. jours. Mem. work group Vt. Lead Paint Hazard Commn., Burlington, 1994. Recipient Order of Barristers Washington U. Sch. Law, St. Louis, 1985. Mem. Def. Rsch. Inst., ABA, Vt. Bar Assn. (co-chmn. ins. law com. 1994—), Phi Beta Kappa. Avocations: golf, squash, snow mobile, chess, hiking. Insurance, General corporate, Personal injury. Office: Vt Mutual Ins Co 89 State St Montpelier VT 05602-2954

**BLANK, ALAN ROBERT,** lawyer; b. Cleve., Oct. 8, 1956; s. Gerald and Lois Barbara (Bernstein) B.; m. Ellyn Leslie Sternfield, Oct. 25, 1981; children: Michael Adam, Stephanie Gayle. AB, Washington U., St. Louis, 1978, JD, 1981. Bar: Mo. 1981. Assoc. Popkin, Stern, Heifetz, Lurie, Sheehan & Cheritz, St. Louis, 1981-85; ptnr. Popkin & Stern, St. Louis, 1986-88; mng. ptnr. St. Louis Office, Stoel Rives LLP (formerly Stoel Rives Boley Jones & Grey), 1988—. Mng. editor Washington U. Law Quar., 1980-81. Active Vol. Lawyers Program, St. Louis, 1984—; com. mem. adv. coun. Internat. Valuation Scis. Inst., Lindenwood Coll., St. Louis, 1987—. Washington U. hon. scholar, 1974-78. Mem. ABA, Mo. Bar, Bar Assn. Met. St. Louis, Nat. Assn. Bond Lawyers, Omicron Delta Kappa. Home: 4147 SW Westdale Dr Portland OR 97221-3152 Office: Stoel Rives LLP 700 NE Multnomah St Ste 950 Portland OR 97232-4109

**BLANK, A(NDREW) RUSSELL,** lawyer; b. Bklyn., June 13, 1945; s. Lawrence and Joan B.; children—Adam, Marisa. Student U. N.C., 1963-64; BA, U. Fla., 1966, postgrad. Law Sch., 1966-68; JD, U. Miami, 1970. Bar: Ga. 1971, Fla. 1970; cert. civil trial advocate Nat. Bd. Trial Advocacy. Law asst. Dist. Ct. Judge, Atlanta, 1970-72; ptnr. A Russell Blank & Assocs., P.C., 1985—. Contbr. articles to profl. jours. Mem. pub. adv. com. Atlanta Regional Commn., 1972-74. Recipient Merit award Ga. Bar Assn., 1981. Mem. Atlanta Bar Assn., Ga. Bar Assn., Ga. Trial Lawyers Assn. (officer), Lawyers Club Atlanta, ABA, ATLA, Fla. Bar Assn., Am. Bd. Trial Advocates (advocate, pres. Ga. chpt.), Xenix Soc. (bd. dirs.). Federal civil litigation, State civil litigation, Personal injury. Office: 230 Peachtree St NW Ste 800 Atlanta GA 30303-1512

**BLANK, GARRY NEAL,** lawyer; b. Boston, May 12, 1957; s. Marvin and Marjorie (Cohen) B.; m. Lynnette Louise Walker, June 9, 1996. BA in Econs., U. Pa., 1979; JD in Law, Boston Coll., 1982. Bar: Mass. 1982, U.S. Dist. Ct. (ea. dist.) Mass. 1983, U.S. Dist. Ct. (so. dist.) N.Y. 1990. Founding ptnr. Blank and Solomon, Boston and Sandwich, Mass., 1984—. Moderator Town of Sandwich, 1990—, mem. bylaw rev. com., 1989-91. Mem. Mass. Acad. Trial Attys., Mass. Moderators Assn., Mass. Bar Assn., Barnstable Bar Assn., BBB of Ea. Mass., Maine and Vt., Hyannis Yacht Club. Avocations: sailing, swimming, skating, building, rowing. General corporate, Personal injury, General civil litigation. Home: 449 Route 130 Sandwich MA 02563-2339 Office: Blank and Solomon 148 State St Boston MA 02109-2506

**BLANK, HELENE E.,** lawyer; b. Bklyn., Aug. 9, 1953; d. Sam and Miriam Blank; m. Marc M. Dittenhoefer, Dec. 17, 1994. BA, Queens Coll., 1974; JD, N.Y. Law Sch., 1977. Bar: N.Y. 1977. Asst. gen. counsel N.Y.C. Transit Authority, 1977-82; atty. of record Home Ins. Co., N.Y.C., 1982-85; sr. trial atty. Law Offices of Philip M. Damashek, N.Y.C., 1985-94, Schneider Kleinick Weitz and Damashek, N.Y.C., 1994; sole practitioner Bklyn., 1995—. Named Woman of Yr., Inst. Jewish Humanities, Bklyn., 1997. Mem. N.Y. State Bar Assn., N.Y. State Women's Bar, Met. Women's Bar Assn. (past pres., bd. dirs., officer, chair bd.), N.Y. State Trial Lawyers Inst. (dean 1994—). Avocation: tennis. Personal injury, Product liability, General civil litigation. Office: 2741 Atlantic Ave Brooklyn NY 11207-2803

**BLANKE, RICHARD BRIAN,** lawyer; b. St. Louis, Oct. 28, 1954; s. Robert H. and Phyllis I. (Kessler) Schaffler. BA, U. Pa., 1977; JD, U. Mo., 1980. Bar: Mo. 1980, U.S. Dist. Ct. (ea. and we. dists.) Mo. 1980. Ptnr. Blanke & Assocs., St. Louis County, Mo., 1980-90, Uthoff, Graeber, Bobinette & O'Keefe, St. Louis, 1991—; lawyer; b. St. Louis, Oct. 28, 1954; s. Robert H. and Phyllis I. (Kessler) Schaffler. BA, U. Pa., 1977; JD, U. Mo., 1980. Bar: U.S. Dist. Ct. (ea. and we. dists.) Mo. 1980, Mo. 1980. Ptnr. Blanke & Assocs., St. Louis County, Mo., 1980-90, Uthoff, Graeber, Bobinette & O'Keefe, St. Louis, 1991—. Mem. ABA, Assn. Trial Lawyers Am., Mo. Bar Assn., Mo. Assn. Trial Attys., St. Louis Met. Bar Assn. Mem. ABA, ATLA, Mo. Bar Assn., Mo. Assn. Trial Attys., St. Louis Met. Bar Assn. General practice, Personal injury, Family and matrimonial. Office: Uthoff Graeber Bobinette & O'Keefe 906 Olive St Ste 300 Saint Louis MO 63101-1426

**BLANKER, ALAN HARLOW,** ; b. Montague, Mass., Sept. 15, 1951; s. William Charles and Ann (Harlow) B.;. B.A., Colby Coll., 1973; J.D., Georgetown U., 1976. Bar: Mass. 1977, U.S. Dist. Ct. Mass. 1977. Ptnr. Levy, Winer, Greenfield, Mass., 1977—; dir., clk. Esleeck Mfg. Co., Inc., Montague, 1980—, also dir.; bd. dirs. Valley Tire Co., Ltd., Greenfield; incorporator Heritage Bank for Savs., Greenfield, 1980-86, Greenfield Savs. Bank, 1986—; trustee Greenriver Cemetery Co., 1997—. Editor Georgetown

Law Jour., 1975-76. Mem. Greenfield Fin. Com., 1980-84; chmn. Greenfield Sch. Bldg. Com., 1977-81; mem. Greenfield Republican Town Com., 1976-85, Greenfield Town Coun., 1992-95, Greenfield Sch. Bldg. Com., 1996-99; incorporator Franklin Med. Ctr., 1979—, pres., treas.; bd. dirs., clk. Greenfield Indsl. Devel. Area Corp.; dir. Greenfield Cmty. YMCA, 1995—. Mem. Franklin County C. of C. (chmn. tech. services com. 1982—), Phi Beta Kappa, Pi Sigma Alpha. Congregationalist. Lodge: Kiwanis. General corporate, Estate planning, Banking. Home: 840 Colrain Rd Greenfield MA 01301-9763 Office: Levy Winer et al PO Box 1538 Greenfield MA 01302-1538

**BLANKMEYER, KURT VAN CLEAVE,** lawyer; b. Springfield, Ill., Sept. 10, 1937. BA, Harvard Coll., 1959; JD, Yale U., 1972. Bar: N.Y. 1973, Conn. 1983, U.S. Dist. Ct. (so. dist.) 1973, U.S. Dist. Ct. (ea. dist.) N.Y. 1975, U.S. Ct. Appeals (2d cir.) 1973. Assoc. Webster & Sheffield, N.Y.C., 1972-78; v.p., assoc. gen. counsel Lone Star Industries, Stamford, Conn., 1978-94; pvt. practice Wilton, Conn., 1994—; cons. in field, Wilton, 1994—; lectr. in field. Mem. Corp. Bar Assn., Conn. Bar Assn., Bar Assn. of City of N.Y. General corporate, Contracts commercial, Antitrust. Office: 144 Signal Hill Rd Wilton CT 06897-1932

**BLANTON, DARRELL DREW,** lawyer; b. Jacksonville, Fla., Mar. 1, 1960; s. Harry Clark Jr. and Patsy Gayle Blanton; m. Amelia Anne Norman, Sept. 26, 1987; children: Lillie Wetherington, Amelia Drew, Avery Redding. BA, Carson-Newman Coll., 1982; JD, Memphis State U., 1985. Bar: Tenn. 1985, U.S. Ct. Appeals (6th cir.) 1985, U.S. Dist. Ct. (we. dist.) Tenn. 1985. Atty. Picard & Caywood, Memphis, 1985-94, Causey Caywood Taylor McManus & Bailey, Memphis, 1994-99; pvt. practice, 1999—. Pres. elect, program dir. Highland Hundred U. Memphis, 1998. Mem. Memphis Bar Assn. (bd. dirs. 1992). Avocation: collecting historical documents and signatures. Family and matrimonial, General practice. Office: 5350 Poplar Ave Ste 725 Memphis TN 38119-3697

**BLANTON, HOOVER CLARENCE,** lawyer; b. Green Sea, S.C., Oct. 13, 1925; s. Clarence Leo and Margaret (Hoover) B.; m. Cecilia Lopez, July 31, 1949; children: Lawson Hoover, Michael Lopez. JD, U. S.C., 1953. Bar: S.C. 1953. Ordained deacon, Bapt. Ch. Assoc. Whaley & McCutchen, Columbia, S.C., 1953-66; ptnr. McCutchen, Blanton, Rhodes and Johnson and predecessors, Columbia, 1967—; dir. Legal Aid Service Agy., Columbia, chmn. bd., 1972-73. Gen. counsel S.C. Rep. Conv., 1962; del. Rep. State Conv., 1962, 64, 66, 68, 70, 74; bd. dirs. Midlands Cmty. Action Agy., Columbia, vice chmn., 1972-73; bd. dirs. Wildewood Sch., 1976-78; mem. Gov.'s Legal Svcs. Adv. Coun., 1976-77, Commn. on Continuing Legal Edn. for Judiciary, 1977-84, Commn. on Continuing Lawyer Competence, 1988-92, Commn. on Continuing Legal Edn. and Specialization, 1992-99, sec. 1995, chmn., 1996-99. Mem. ABA. S.C. Bar (ho. of dels. 1975-76, chmn. fee disputes bd. 1977-81), Richland County Bar Assn. (pres. 1980), S.C. Def. Trial Attys. Assn., Def. Rsch. Inst., Assn. Def. Trial Attys. (state chmn. 1971-77, 80-95, exec. coun. 1977-80), Am. Bd. Trial Advs. (pres. S.C. chpts. 1989), Toastmasters Club (pres. 1959), Palmetto Club, Phi Delta Phi. General civil litigation, Personal injury, Workers' compensation. Home: 3655 Deerfield Dr Columbia SC 29204-3730 Office: 1414 Lady St Columbia SC 29201-3304

**BLANTON, W. C.,** lawyer; b. LaRue County, Ky., Apr. 13, 1946; s. Crawford and Lillian (Phelps) B. BS in Math., Mich. State U., 1968, BA in Social Sci., 1968; MEd, U. Vt., 1970; JD, U. Mich., 1975. Bar: Ind. 1975, U.S. Dist. Ct. (no. and so. dists.) Ind. 1975, U.S. Ct. Appeals (7th cir.) 1977, Minn. 1996, U.S. Dist. Ct. Minn. 1996. Residence hall dir. U. Wis., Madison, 1970-72; assoc. Ice Miller Donadio & Ryan, Indpls., 1975-81, ptnr., 1982-94; ptnr. Popham, Haik, Schnobrich & Kaufman, Ltd., 1995-97, Oppenheimer Wolff & Donnelly LLP, Mpls., 1997—. Mem. ABA. Democrat. Avocations: skiing, travel, bridge. Environmental, General civil litigation, Natural resources. Office: Oppenheimer Wolff & Donnelly LLP 3400 Plaza VII 45 S 7th St Ste 3400 Minneapolis MN 55402-1609

**BLASCHAK, THOMAS R.,** lawyer; b. Johnstown, Pa., Mar. 16, 1967; m. Kimberli S. Goodall, June 18, 1994; children: Alexander T., Brittney S. BA in Fin., U. Pitts., 1989, BA in Polit. Sci., 1989; JD, U. Dayton, 1992. Bar: Ohio, 1992. Atty. Hyatt Legal Svc., Dayton, Ohio, 1993-95, mng. atty., 1995-97; pvt. practice Dayton, 1997—. Asst. text editor U. Dayton Law Rev., 1992. Family and matrimonial, Probate. Office: 5568 Airway Rd Dayton OH 45431-1505

**BLASGEN, SHARON WALTHER,** lawyer; b. Bremerton, Wash., Apr. 12, 1942; d. William Edwin and Helen Walther; m. Michael William Blasgen, Sept. 10, 1965; children: Alexandra Helen, Nicholas William McKenna. BA, Scripps Coll., Claremont, Calif., 1964; JD, U. Calif., Berkeley, 1967. Bar: Calif. 1969, N.Y. 1970, D.C. 1983, U.S. Ct. Appeals (9th cir.), U.S. Dist. Ct. (no. and so. dists.) Calif., U.S. Dist. Ct. (so. dist.) N.Y. Law clk. Calif. Ct. Appeal, San Francisco, 1967-69; atty. IBM Corp., Armonk, N.Y., 1969-72; counsel, asst. sec. IBM World Trade Corp., N.Y.C., 1972-74; area counsel IBM Corp., San Jose, Calif., 1974-79; regional counsel IBM Corp., Washington, 1979-83; div. counsel IBM Corp., White Plains, N.Y., 1983-86, asst. group counsel, 1986-88; assoc. gen. counsel IBM Corp., Somers, N.Y., 1988-93; gen. coun. SSD, San Jose, Calif., 1993—; bd. dirs., exec. com. Calif. Employment Law Coun. Bd. dirs. Boy Scouts of Westchester/Putnam, White Plains, 1989-91, Opera San Jose, 1997—. Elected to YWCA Internat. Acad. Women Achievers, 1993. Mem. Silicon Valley Assn. Gen. Counsels. Antitrust, Computer, Contracts commercial. Home: 17418 Paseo Carmelo Los Gatos CA 95030-7559 Office: 5600 Cottle Rd San Jose CA 95123-3696

**BLASKE, E. ROBERT,** lawyer; b. Battle Creek, Mich., June 4, 1945; s. Edmund Robert and Wilma Jayne (Hill) B.; m. Vicki Lyn Rayner, Aug. 11, 1968. BA with distinction, U. Mich., 1966, JD cum laude, 1969. Bar. Mich. 1969, U.S. Dist. Ct. (we. dist.) Mich. 1970, U.S. Ct. Appeals (6th cir.) 1983. Ptnr. Blaske & Blaske, Battle Creek, 1969—; mem. Mich. Bd. Law Examiners, 1976-89, drafting com. for rules to implement Mich. mental health code, 1978-79, multi-state bar exam. com. Nat. Conf. Bar Examiners, 1983-85, multi-state profl. responsibility exam. com., 1985—; instr. trial advocacy program steering com. U.S. Dist. Ct. (we. dist.) Mich., 1982—; lectr. Inst. Continuing Legal Edn., 1983—; mediator U.S. Dist. Ct. (we. dist.) Mich., 1985-86, Calhoun County Cir. Ct. Mich., 1984—; arbitrator U.S. Dist. Ct. (we. dist.) Mich., 1987—. Mem. U. Mich. Law Rev., 1968-69. Bd. dirs. Calhoun County Legal Aid Soc., Battle Creek, 1976, Mich. Audubon Soc., Kalamazoo, 1981, Blaske-Hill Found., Battle Creek, 1983—; bd. govs. Lawyers Club U. Mich. Law Sch., 1985—. Mem. ABA, ATLA, State Bar Mich., Calhoun County Bar Assn. (pres. 1977-78), MIch. Trial Lawyers Assn., Order of Coif. Roman Catholic. Personal injury, State civil litigation. Home: 25001 Battle Creek Hwy Bellevue MI 49021-9603 Office: Blaske & Blaske 1509 Hertiate Tower Battle Creek MI 49017

**BLATT, RICHARD LEE,** lawyer; b. Oak Park, Ill., May 24, 1940; s. B. Lee Gray and Madelyn Gertrude (Bentley) B.; m. Carol Milner Jenkinson, May 21, 1965 (div. Dec. 1984); children: Christopher Andrew Lee, Katherine Lee, Susannah Lee; m. Carolyn Elizabeth LeBlanc, Jan. 31, 1987; 1 child, Jennifer Lee DeNux Blatt. BA, U. Ill., 1962; JD, U. Mich., 1965. Bar: Ill. 1968, U.S. Dist. Ct. (no. dist.) Ill. 1968, U.S. Ct. Appeals (7th cir.) 1968, U.S. Supreme Ct. 1974, U.S. Dist. Ct. (so. dist.) Ill. 1977, U.S. Ct. Appeals (4th cir.) 1987, N.Y. 1989, U.S. Ct. Appeals (3rd cir.) 1990, U.S. Dist. Ct. (ea. and so. dists.) N.Y., 1998. Assoc. Peterson, Lowry, Rall, Barber & Ross, Chgo., 1968-75; ptnr. Peterson, Ross, Schloeb & Seidel, Chgo., 1975-91, Peterson & Ross, Chgo., 1991-94; sr. ptnr. Blatt, Hammesfahr & Eaton, Chgo., 1994—. Author: (with Robert G. Schloerb, Robert W. Hammesfahr, Lori S. Nugent) Punitive Damages: A Guide to the Insurability of Punitive Damages in the United States and Its Territories, 1988, (with Robert W. Hammesfahr and Lori S. Nugent) Punitive Damges: A State-by-State Guide to Law and Practice, 1991 (in Japanese 1995). Capt. inf. USAR, 1965-67, Korea. Fellow Chartered Inst. Arbitrators; mem. ABA, SAR, Ill. State Bar Assn., Soc. Mayflower Desc. State Ill., N.Y. State Bar Assn., Chgo. Bar Assn., Chgo. Club, Racquet Club Chgo., Phi Beta Kappa, Phi Kappa Phi. General civil litigation, Insurance, Private international. Home: 70 E Cedar St Apt 1101 Chicago IL 60611-1135 Office: Blatt Hammesfahr & Eaton 333 W Wacker Dr Ste 1900 Chicago IL 60606-1293

**BLATT, SOLOMON, JR.,** federal judge; b. Sumter, S.C., Aug. 20, 1921; s. Solomon and Ethel (Green) B.; m. Carolyn Gayden, Sept. 12, 1942; children: Gregory, Sheryl Blatt Hooper, Brian. AB, U. S.C., 1941, LLB, 1946, LLD (hon.), 1987; LLD (hon.), The Citadel, 1990, Coll. of Charleston, 1992. Bar: S.C., 1946. Ptnr. Blatt & Fales, Barnwell, S.C., 1946-71; judge U.S. Dist. Ct. S.C., Charleston, 1971-86, chief judge, 1986-90; sr. judge U.S. Dist. Ct. S.C., 1990—. Office: US Dist Ct SC PO Box 835 Charleston SC 29402-0835

**BLATZ, KATHLEEN ANN,** state supreme court justice, state legislator; B.A. summa cum laude, U. Notre Dame, 1976; M.S.W., U. Minn., 1978; J.D. cum laude, U. Minn., 1984. Psychiat. social worker, 1979-81; mem. Minn. Ho. of Reps., St. Paul, 1978—, chmn. crime and family law, fin. instns. and ins. coms.; justice Minn. Supreme Ct., 1996—, chief justice, 1998— Office: Minn Judicial Ctr 25 Constitution Ave Rm 424 Saint Paul MN 55155-1500*

**BLAUGRUND, DAVID SCOTT,** lawyer; b. Cleve., Feb. 1, 1953; s. Marvin Jerome and Ellen Ann (Goodman) B.; m. Kathy Jo Harman, Dec. 9, 1977; children: Michael Curtis, Jordan Spencer. BA cum laude, Miami U., Oxford, Ohio, 1974; JD, Ohio State U., 1976. Bar: Ohio 1977. Staff atty. State personnel Bd. of Rev. State of Ohio, Columbus, 1977, exec. dir., 1977-80; v.p., legal counsel CN&A, Inc., Columbus, 1980-87, exec. v.p., gen. counsel, 1987-89; pvt. practice Dublin, Ohio, 1989—; instr. seminars in field. Trustee Dublin Unitarian Universalist Ch., 1988-91; cubmaster pack 295 Boy Scouts Am., Upper Arlington, Ohio, 1987-89, asst. scoutmaster troop 200, Dublin, 1989-90, scoutmaster, 1990-96, com. chmn., 1996-98, dist. com. chmn., 1999—; baseball coach Dublin Youth Athletics, 1989-95. Recognition award for svc. in labor rels. Ohio Assn. of County Bds. of Mental Retardation and Devel. Disabilities, 1985, Buckeye Dist. and Simon Kenton Coun., 1995, 96. Mem. ABA, Columbus Bar Assn., Ohio Bar Assn., Heritage Golf Club, Phi Beta Kappa. Avocations: backpacking, tennis, golf, music, reading. Labor, Administrative and regulatory, General practice. Office: 5455 Rings Rd Ste 500 Dublin OH 43017-7527

**BLAWIE, JAMES LOUIS,** law educator; b. Newark, Mar. 26, 1928; s. Louis Paul and Cecelia Ruth (Grish) B.; m. Marilyn June Beyerle, May 30, 1952; children: Elias J., Cecelia R., Christiana L. BA, U. Conn., 1950; AM, Boston U., 1951, PhD, 1959; JD, U. Chgo., 1955. Bar: Conn. 1956, Calif. 1965, U.S. Dist. Ct. (no. dist.) Calif. 1965, U.S. Ct. Appeals (9th cir.) 1967, U.S. Supreme Ct. 1968. Instr. polit. sci. Mich. State U., East Lansing, 1955; assoc. prof. U. Akron, Ohio, 1956-57, Kent State U., 1956-57; asst. prof. bus. law U. Calif., Berkeley, 1958-60; assoc. prof. law Santa Clara U., Calif., 1960-63, prof. law, 1963—; vis. prof. polit. sci. Calif. State U., Hayward, 1966-67; adminstrv. law judge U.S. Equal Employment Opportunity Commn., Washington, 1982-85; complaints examiner U.S. Equal Employment Opportunity Agy., Office Equal Employment Opportunity; cons. in field. Author: (handbook) The Michigan Township Board, 1957; contbr. articles to profl. jours. Mem. Citizen's Adv. Com. on Capital Improvements, 1962-65; bd. dirs. Washington Hosp., 1964-68. Maj. U.S. Army, 1963-74. Boston U. Faculty fellow, 1951-53; U. Chgo. Law Sch. scholar, 1953-55; grantee Mich. State U. grantee, 1955-56, Helsinki Govt. Ministry Edn. grantee, 1980-81. Mem. ABA, Fairfield County Bar Assn., Mensa. Republican. Avocations: computers, photography, travel, rare diseases databases. Home: 41752 Marigold Dr Fremont CA 94539-4779 also: PO Box 1102 Fremont CA 94538-0110 Office: Santa Clara U Sch Law Santa Clara CA 95053-0001

**BLAZEWICK, ROBERT B.,** lawyer, educator, military officer; b. Rural Geneva, Wis., Apr. 25, 1962; s. Robert George and Jacqueline Rose (Gourley) B. BA, Marquette U., 1984, JD, 1987. Bar: Wis. 1987, U.S. Dist. Ct. (ea. and we. dists.) Wis. 1987, U.S. Ct. Appeals (7th cir.) 1988, U.S. Supreme Ct. 1993, U.S. Armed Forces Ct. of Appeals 1998. Assoc. atty. Scanlan & Hartigan, Chgo., 1987; commd. ensign USN, 1986, advanced through grades to lt. comdr., 1994; assoc. atty. Scanlan & Hartigan, Chgo., 1987; criminal def. U.S. Navy, Great Lakes, Ill., 1987-89; staff judge adv. USS Lincoln U.S. Navy, Norfolk, Va., 1989-91, Alameda, Calif., 1989-91; fed. tort atty. U.S. Navy, Washington, 1991-93; criminal def. U.S. Navy, Naples, Italy, 1993-95; law educator Naval Justice Sch. U.S. Navy Naval War Coll., Newport, R.I., 1995-99; staff judge adv. cruiser Destroyer Group 3, San Diego, 1999—. Editor Naval Law Rev., 1998. Mem. ABA, FBA, Wis. Bar Assn. Roman Catholic. Avocations: theater, cars, fitness. Military, Criminal, Administrative and regulatory. Home: 3150 Front St San Diego CA 92103 Office: Staff Judge Advocate Cruiser-Destroyer Group 3 FPO AP 96601-4702

**BLEAU, DENISE J.,** lawyer; b. Jacksonville, Fla., Aug. 30, 1960; d. Arthur Joseph and Joan G. Bleau. BA in Speech Comm., U. South Fla., 1982; JD, U. Fla., 1986. Assoc. Ford & Assocs., P.A., Tavares, Fla., 1986-90; ptnr. Ford & Bleau, P.A., Tavares, 1990-91; asst. county atty. Palm Beach County Atty.'s Office, West Palm Beach, Fla., 1991-97; pvt. practice Boca Raton, Fla., 1997—. Mem. Lantana (Fla.) Town Coun., 1996-97, mayor pro-tem, 1997—, mayor, 1997-99. Office: 400 S Dixie Hwy Ste 420 Boca Raton FL 33432-6023

**BLECHER, JONATHAN BURTON,** lawyer; b. N.Y.C., Nov. 18, 1957; s. Melvin Blecher and Doris Rita Bacolas; m. Noelia Edith Moreno, Oct. 28, 1989; 1 child, Jordan Alexander. BA, U. Fla., 1978, JD, 1981. Asst. states atty. Fla. State Attys. Office, Dade County, 1981-84; assoc. Entin, Schwartz, P.A., Miami, 1984-86; sr. assoc. Essen and Essen, Miami, 1986-92; sr. ptrn. Jonathan B. Blecher, P.A., Miami, 1992—. Recipient Eagle Scout Boy Scouts Am., 1973. Mem. Fla. Assn. of Criminal Def. Lawyers, Cuban-Am. Bar Assn., Fla. Bar Assn. (traffic ct. rules com. 1993—). Avocations: bicycle riding, computers, frisbee, travel, wine collecting. Criminal. Office: Jonathan B Blecher PA 9130 S Dadeland Blvd Ste 1510 Miami FL 33156-7850

**BLECKLEY, JEANETTE A.,** lawyer; b. Columbia, S.C., Feb. 2, 1943; d. Thomas Marcus and Amanda Elizabeth (Cobb) B.; m. Nathan G. Pearce, Dec. 3, 1967 (div. 1979); 1 child, Angelique Nicole Pearce. AA, Young Harris (Ga.) Coll., 1963; student, American River Coll., Sacramento, 1966-67; JD, Lincoln U., Sacramento, 1974. Bar: Calif., U.S. Dist. Ct. (3d dist.) Calif.; cert. tchr., Calif. Gen. office staff Procter & Gamble, Atlanta, 1962-64; contract negotiator, adminstr., purchasing agt., pub. rels. Am. Cable Elec. Supply, Inc., Sacramento, 1965-74; engring. asst. R&D,s. Ban Electronics, Sacramento, 1970; pvt. practice Sacramento, 1974—. Contbr. articles to Reflections; author, writer, composer album Willows, Wisps and Wishes, 1994. Mem. Calif. Bar Assn., Sacramento Bar Assn., Calif. Women Lawyers, Sacramento Valley Legal Svcs., Sigma Beta Sigma. Avocations: music, antique cars, writing, dancing, football. General civil litigation, Family and matrimonial, Personal injury. Office: 2501 Darwin St Sacramento CA 95821-5509

**BLEICH, JEFFREY LAURENCE,** lawyer, law educator; b. Neubreuke, Germany, May 17, 1961; came to U.S., 1964; s. Charles Allen Bleich and Linda Sue Caplan; m. Rebecca Lee Pratt, Aug. 12, 1984; children: Jacob, Matthew, Abigail. BA in Polit. Sci., Amherst Coll., 1983; MA in Pub. Policy, Harvard U., 1986; JD, U. Calif., Berkeley, 1989. Bar: Calif. 1989, D.C. 1990, U.S. Ct. Appeals (D.C. cir.) 1990, U.S. Dist. Ct. (no. dist.) Calif. 1992, U.S. Ct. Appeals (4th cir.) 1993, U.S. Supreme Ct. 1993, U.S. Ct. Appeals (9th cir.) 1994. Law clk. U.S. Ct. Appeals, Washington, 1989-90, U.S. Supreme Ct., Washington, 1990-91; legal asst. Iran-U.S. Claims Tribunal, The Hague, 1991-92; ptnr. Munger, Tolles & Olson LLP, San Francisco, 1992—; adj. prof. U. Calif., Berkeley, 1993—. Editor-in-chief Calif. Law Rev., Nat. Debt; columnist San Francisco Atty. Mem. adv. bd. Coalition on Homelessness, San Francisco. Recipient James Madison award Soc. Profl. Journalists, 1998. Mem. ABA (chair amicus com., award 1996, Pro Bono Publico award 1996), Bar Assn. San Francisco (bd. dirs. 1998—), Lawyers' Com. Civil Rights of San Francisco Bay Area (co-chair), Lawyers Com. Human Rights (bd. dirs. 1998—), Legal Aid Soc. (bd. dirs. 1998—), Barristers Club San Francisco (pres.). Democrat. Avocations: short story writer, tennis, kayaking, camping. General civil litigation, Intellectual property. Office: Mungor Tolles & Olson 33 New Montgomery St Fl 19 San Francisco CA 94105-4506

**BLEIER, MICHAEL E.,** lawyer. BA, U. Tulsa, 1962; JD, Georgetown U., 1965. Bar: Pa, D.C. Atty. Office of Gen. Counsel, Bd. Govs. Fed. Reserve System, 1971-78, sr. counsel, 1979-81, asst. gen. counsel, 1981-82; mng. counsel Mellon Bank Corp., Pitts., 1982-88, asst. gen. counsel, 1989-91, dep. gen. counsel, 1991-92, gen. counsel, 1992—, sr. mgmt. com. Mem. Am. Bankers Assn. (vice chmn. bank counsel com. 1996—), Lawyers Coun. Bankers Roundtable (chmn. 1993-98). Banking, Administrative and regulatory, Mergers and acquisitions. Office: Mellon Bank Corporation One Mellon Bank Ctr 19th Flr Pittsburgh PA 15258

**BLEILER, CHARLES ARTHUR,** lawyer; b. Boston, Mar. 16, 1945; s. Charles Edward and Grace Rita Bleiler; m. Joyce Ann Kohlmyer, Oct. 6, 1972; children: Charles Edward. BS, Tufts U., 1967; JD, U. San Diego, 1973. BAr: Calif. 1973, U.S. Dist. Ct. (so. dist.) Calif. 1973. Commd. ensign U.S. Navy, 1967, advanced through grades to lt. comdr., resigned, 1978; ptnr. Williams, Clodig & Bleiler, San Diego, 1974-85, Bleiler & Reiter, San Diego, 1985-91, Malowney, Chialtas & Bleiler, San Diego, 1991-93; pres. Charles A. Bleiler A.P.C., San Diego, 1987—; lectr. San Diego Trial Lawyers Assn., 1982. Bd. dirs. Rancho Santa Fe (Calif.) Cmty. Ctr., 1990-94, pres., 1993-94; mem. San Dieguito Soccer Bd., Encinitas, Calif., 1991-92; bd. dirs. Torrey Pines H.S. Found., Del Mar, Calif., 1996-98, pres., 1997-98; founding mem., lector Nativity Ch., Rancho Santa Fe; fundraiser for charitable orgns.; bd. dirs. Rancho Santa Fe Little League, 1989-92. Mem. ATLA, Calif. State Bar, San Diego County Bar Assn., Optimist Club (charter pres. Kearny Mesa club 1987-89). Republican. Roman Catholic. Avocations: sailing, horseback riding, skiing, coaching youth baseball and soccer. Personal injury, Labor, Construction. Home: PO Box 1653 Rancho Santa Fe CA 92067-1653 Office: 12770 High Bluff Dr Ste 380 San Diego CA 92130-2060

**BLEIWEISS, SHELL J.,** lawyer; b. Chgo., Mar. 7, 1950; s. Ben and Berte (Melin) B.; m. Patricia Lynn Heck, Dec. 19, 1970 (div. 1976); m. Jo Ellen Rosencrans, May 21, 1985; children: Michael Lawrence, Lowell Rosencrans. BA, So. Ill. U., 1971, MS, 1974; JD, Northwestern U., 1982. Bar: Ill. 1982, U.S. Dist. Ct. (no. dist.) Ill. 1982. Wildlife ecologist Jack McCormick & Assoc., Devon, Pa., 1973-76; project mgr. Betz Converse Murdoch, Plymouth Meeting, Pa., 1976-78; cons. McGraw Hill Publ., N.Y.C., 1978-79; assoc. Sidley & Austin, Chgo., 1981-85, Coffield, Ungaretti, Harris & Slavin, Chgo., 1985-88; ptnr. McDermott, Will & Emery, Chgo., 1988-97; atty. pvt. practice, 1998—. Environ. advisor Roland Burris for Atty. Gen. Campaign, Ill., 1986. NSF fellow, 1970. Mem. ABA (chair environ. ADR com.), Chgo. Bar Assn. Environmental, Health, Administrative and regulatory. Office: 321 S Plymouth Ct Ste 1200 Chicago IL 60604-3996

**BLENCOWE, PAUL SHERWOOD,** lawyer; b. Amityville, N.Y., Feb. 10, 1953; s. Frederick Arthur and Dorothy Jeanne (Ballenger) B.; m. Mary Frances Faulk, Apr. 11, 1992; 1 child, Kristin Amanda. BA with honors, U. Wis., 1975; MBA, U. Pa., 1976; JD, Stanford U., 1979. Bar: Tex. 1979, Calif. 1989. Assoc. Fulbright & Jaworski, Houston, 1979-86; assoc. Fulbright & Jaworski, London, 1986-87, ptnr., 1988-89; ptnr. Fulbright & Jaworski L.L.P., L.A., 1989—. Editor: China's Quest for Independence: Policy Evolution in the 1970s, 1980; editor-in-chief Stanford Jour. of Internat. Law, 1978-79; contbr. articles on U.S. securities and corp. law to profl. jours. Mem. ABA, The Calif. Club, Phi Beta Kappa, Phi Kappa Phi, Beta Theta Pi. Securities, Mergers and acquisitions, General corporate. Office: Fulbright & Jaworski LLP 865 S Figueroa St Fl 29 Los Angeles CA 90017-2543

**BLENKO, WALTER JOHN, JR.,** lawyer; b. Pitts., June 15, 1926; s. Walter J. and Ardis Leah (Jones) B.; m. Joy Kinneman, Apr. 9, 1949; children: John W., Andrew W. BS, Carnegie-Mellon U., 1950; JD, U. Pitts., 1953. Bar: Pa. 1954. Pvt. practice law Pitts., 1954—; ptnr. Eckert, Seamans, Cherin & Mellott, Pitts., 1984-93, of counsel, 1993—; mem. adv. bd. dept. mech. engrng. Carnegie-Mellon U., 1992—. Active Churchill Vol. Fire Co., 1970-82; charter and hon. mem. Wilkinsburg Emergency Med. Svc.; sec. Hampton Twp. Zoning Hearing Bd., 1991-92, vice-chmn., 1993; mem. Hampton Twp. Sch. Bd., 1993-97, pres. 1996. With U.S. Army, 1944-46, ETO. Decorated Bronze Star; recipient Disting. Svc. award Carnegie-Mellon U. Alumni Assn., 1993. Fellow Am. Coll. Trial Lawyers; mem. ASME, Pa. Bar Assn., Allegheny County Bar Assn., Assn. Bar of City of N.Y., Pitts. Intellectual Property Law Assn. (pres. 1977-78), Engrs. Soc. Western Pa., Internat. Patent and Trademark Assn., Carnegie-Mellon U. Alumni Assn. (exec. bd. 1996—, exec. com. 1997—), Duquesne Club, Univ. Club, Princeton Club (N.Y.), Rolls-Royce Owners Club (bd. dirs. 1982-84, v.p. publs. 1984-87, treas. 1987-89). Avocation: old cars. Patent, Trademark and copyright, Federal civil litigation. Home: 4073 Middle Rd Allison Park PA 15101-1207 Office: Eckert Seamans Cherin & Mellott 600 Grant St Pittsburgh PA 15219-2702

**BLEVINS, JEFFREY ALEXANDER,** lawyer; b. Forest Hills, N.Y., June 18, 1955; s. William E. and Mary J. Blevins; m. Pamela A. Manos, Nov. 26, 1983 (div. Mar. 1995); 1 child, Mary; m. Diane L. Banno, June 12, 1999. BA, Denison U., 1977; JD, DePaul U., 1981. Bar: Ill. 1981, U.S. Dist Ct. (no. dist.) Ill. 1981, U.S. Dist. Ct. (we. dist. Wis. 1984, U.S. Ct. Appeals (7th cir.) 1984, U.S. Supreme Ct. 1990. Personnel specialist Comerica Bank, Detroit, 1979-80; assoc. Bell, Boyd & Lloyd, Chgo., 1981-88, ptnr., 1988—; lectr., author Ill. Inst. Continuing Legal Edn., 1989. Editor in chief DePaul Law Rev., 1980. Mem. Ill. State Bar Assn. (labor and employment coun. 1992-95), Chgo. Bar Assn., Mid-day Club, Omicron Delta Epsilon. Republican. Lutheran. Labor, Federal civil litigation, State civil litigation.

**BLEWS, WILLIAM FRANK,** lawyer; b. Pensacola, Fla., Dec. 21, 1940; s. Frank Edward and Ruby Blews; children—Michelle, Sabrina, Deborah. BA, Baylor U., 1964; JD, Stetson U., 1966. Bar: Fla., 1966, U.S. Supreme Ct. 1970; cert. trial lawyer, Fla. Bar; cert. civil trial adv. Nat. Bd. Trial Advocacy, Am. Bd. Trial Advocates. Assoc. Mann, Harrison, Mann & Rowe, St. Petersburg, Fla., 1966-70, Chambers & Blews, 1970-71; pvt. practice, St. Petersburg, Fla., 1971—. Mem. adv. bd. Ret. Sr. Vol. Program, 1977-78; trustee Stetson U.; mem. bd. overseers coll. law Stetson U., 1991—; bd. dirs. YMCA, 1975, Center Against Spouse Abuse, Inc., 1981-82; trustee Fla. Supreme Ct. Hist. Soc., 1990—. Recipient Ben Willard award Stetson U., 1990. Fellow Am. Coll. Trial Lawyers, Am. Bar Found.; mem. ABA, Am. Bd. Trial Advs., Fla. Bar Assn. (trial lawyers sect., mem. unauthorized practice law com. 6th jud. cir. 1972-74, chmn. 1973-74, bd. govs. 1988-93, pres.-elect 1993, pres. 1994-95), Fla. Coun. Bar Assn. Pres., St. Petersburg Bar Assn. (pres. 1981-82), Fed. Bar Assn., Pinellas Trial Lawyers Assn. (pres. 1975-76), Acad. Fla. Trial Lawyers (diplomate, bd. dirs. 1972-79, pres. 1976-77), Am. Judicature Soc., Assn. Trial Lawyers Am. (bd. govs. 1977-79), Stetson Lawyers Assn. (pres. 1992), St. Petersburg C. of C., Am. Inns Ct., Phi Delta Phi. State civil litigation, Insurance, Personal injury. Office: 696 1st Ave N Saint Petersburg FL 33701-3610

**BLINDER, ALBERT ALLAN,** judge; b. N.Y.C., Nov. 27, 1925; s. William and Sarah (Gold) B.; m. Meredith Zaretzki, Nov. 16, 1961 (dec.); 1 son, Adam Z.; m. Joan Goodman, Jan. 20, 1985. A.B., N.Y. U., 1944, postgrad., 1944-45; J.D., Harvard U., 1948. Bar: N.Y. 1949, U.S. Dist. Ct. (so. dist.) N.Y. 1953, U.S. Ct. Appeals (2d cir.) 1953; U.S. Supreme Ct. 1967. Asst. U.S. atty. so. dist. N.Y., 1950-53; asst. dist. atty. County of Bronx, N.Y., 1954-60; ptnr. Saxe, Bacon & O'Shea, N.Y.C., 1960-64; ptnr. Blinder, Steinhaus & Hochhauser, N.Y.C., 1965-73; judge N.Y. State Ct. Claims, N.Y.C., 1973-96; jud. hearing officer N.Y. State Supreme Ct., 1996—; asst. counsel N.Y.C. Bd. High Edn., 1953-54; research counsel N.Y. Commn. on the Law of Estates, 1965; assoc. counsel N.Y. Commn. Revision of Penal Law, 1966-70; asst. counsel N.Y. Commn. on Eminent Domain, 1970-73; rsch. asst. N.Y. Commn. State Ct. System, 1971-73. Mem. ABA, Internat. Bar Assn., N.Y. State Bar Assn., Assn. Bar City N.Y., N.Y. County Lawyers Assn., Am. Arbitration Assn. (mem. nat. panel arbitrators 1965-73). Assoc. editor: Am. Criminal Law Quarterly, 1968-70; mem. adv. bd. Am. Criminal Law Quarterly, 1969-70. Office: 115 Broadway New York NY 10006-1604

**BLINKEN, SALLY S.,** lawyer; b. N.Y.C., May 5, 1961; d. David Graystein and Jane Brickman; m. David A. Blinken, May 31, 1984; 1 child, Allegra. BA, Conn. Coll., 1983; JD cum laude, Bklyn. Law, 1991. Bar: Conn., U.S. Dist. Ct. (so. and ea. dist.) N.Y. Rsch. assoc. Della Femina Travisand, N.Y.C., 1984-88; assoc. Breed Abbott & Morgan, N.Y.C., 1991—. General civil litigation, Probate. Office: Whitman Breed Abbott & Morgan 200 Park Ave New York NY 10166-0005

**BLISH, JOHN HARWOOD,** lawyer; b. Racine, Wis., May 9, 1937; s. Wesley Wainwright and Lois Margaret (Jensen) B.; m. Edith Josephine Smith, Aug. 5, 1961; children: Geoffrey Harwood, Catherine Elizabeth. AB, Brown U., 1959; JD, U. Mich., 1965. Bar: R.I. 1965, U.S. Dist. Ct. R.I. 1967, U.S. Ct. Appeals (1st cir.) 1973, U.S. Ct. Appeals (Fed. cir.) 1985. Assoc. Edwards & Angell, Providence, 1965-73, ptnr., 1973-86, Blish & Cavanagh, Providence, 1986—. Bd. overseers Moses Brown Sch., Providence, 1978-81; bd. dirs., past pres. Sophia Little Home, Cranston, R.I.; trustee, past pres. Providence Country Day Sch., East Providence, R.I. Served to lt. j.g. USN, 1959-62. Fellow Am. Coll. Trial Lawyers; mem. R.I. Bar Assn., ABA, Am. Judicature Soc., Assoc. Alumni Brown U. (past bd. dirs., sec.), Univ. Club (trustee, past pres.), Brown of R.I. Club (trustee, past pres., Providence), Acoaxet Club (Westport, Mass.), Order of Coif, Phi Delta Phi. Federal civil litigation, State civil litigation. Home: 66 Catlin Ave Rumford RI 02916-2329 Office: Blish & Cavanagh 30 Exchange Ter Ste 8 Providence RI 02903-1765

**BLISS, RICHARD JON,** lawyer; b. Rice Lake, Wis., Apr. 27, 1951; s. Richard Burt and Lolly (Davis) B.; m. Susan Elizabeth Ramage, June 19, 1976; children: Jon, Steve, Brock. BA, Wheaton (Ill.) Coll., 1973; JD, U. Wis., 1976. Bar: Wis. 1976, U.S. Dist. Ct. (ea. dist.) Wis. 1976. Assoc. Godfrey & Kahn, S.C., Milw., 1976-82, shareholder, 1983—, mng. ptnr., pres., 1996—; bd. dirs. Ripon (Wis.) Foods, Inc. Note editor U. Wis. Law Rev., 1975-76. Bd.dirs. Vine and Brs. Found., Inc., Milw., 1996—, Milw. Ctr. for Independence, 1993-98. Mem. Univ. Club of Milw., Town Club, Milw. Club. Avocations: aviation, tennis. General corporate, Mergers and acquisitions. Home: 706 E Lexington Blvd Whitefish Bay WI 53217-5338 Office: Godfrey & Kahn SC 780 N Water St Ste 1500 Milwaukee WI 53202-3590

**BLITZ, CHARLES AKIN,** lawyer; b. Honolulu, Sept. 2, 1949; s. Howard Samuel and Marjorie C. (Cooke) B.; m. Karen Lee Sherwood, May 6, 1976; children: C. Tyler, Derek A., Colby S. BA, Willamette U., 1972; JD, Lewis & Clark Coll., 1975; LLM in Labor and Employment, Georgetown U., 1979. Bar: Ore. Supreme Ct., 1975, U.S. Dist. Ct. (Ore.), 1975, U.S. Dist. Ct. (9th cir.), 1975, U.S. Mil. Ct. Appeals, 1976, U.S. Ct. Appeals (4th cir.), 1977, U.S. Ct. Appeals (DC cir.), 1978, U.S. Supreme Ct., 1979. Assoc. Cass Scott Woods & Smith, Eugene, Oreg., 1979-82; asst. atty. gen. Oreg. Dept. Justice, Salem, 1982-83; assoc. Spears Lubersky Law Firm, Portland, 1983-85; ptnr. Lane Powell Spears Lubersky, Portland, 1985-98, Bullard Korshoj Smith & Jernstedt, Portland, 1998—. Author: Model Policies and Procedures for Special Districts, Including Administrative Rules, 1994, 2nd edit., 1996. Chmn. Civil Svc. Reform Task Force for the City of Portland, 1985-86, Enhanced Sheriff's Patrol Dist. Bd., Washington County Sheriff's Office, Hillsboro, Oreg., 1988-91; asst. scoutmaster, coun. chmn. risk mgmt. and Butte Creek Ranch com. Cascade Pacific Coun., Boy Scouts Am., Portland, 1988—; mem. Citizens Crime Commn., Portland, 1992—; exec. bd. mem. Cascade Pacific Coun., Boy Scouts Am., Portland, 1993—; trustee Charitable Trust Rotary Club Portland, 1994-97; ski patroller Mount Hood Ski Patrol, Portland, 1996—. Capt. USMC, 1975-79, maj. USMCR, 1982. Recipient Vigil Honor, Boy Scouts Am.-Cascade Pacific Coun., Portland, 1996, Silver Beaver award Boy Scouts Am., Portland, 1998; James E. West fellow Boy Scouts Am., Portland, 1996, Paul Harris fellow Rotary Internat., Portland, 1994, 97. Mem. Oreg. State Bar (chmn. labor law sect. 1995-96), Oreg. Assn. Chiefs of Police and Oreg. State Sheriff's Assn. (legal counsel 1987—, Presdl. award of merit 1990, 91, 93), Rotary Club Portland (dir. 1995-98). Republican. Episcopalian. Avocations: skiing, western trail riding. E-mail: ablitz@bksjlaw.com. Fax: 503-224-8851. Labor, Municipal (including bonds), Civil rights. Office: Bullard Korshoj Smith & Jernstedt 1000 SW Broadway Ste 1900 Portland OR 97205-3071

**BLITZER, SIDNEY MILTON, JR.,** lawyer; b. Baton Rouge, May 25, 1944. AB in Econs., Duke U., 1966; JD, La. State U., 1969. Bar: La. 1969; bd. cert. estate planning and adminstrn. specialist; bd. cert. tax atty. Assoc. Kantrow, Spaht, Weaver & Blitzer, Baton Rouge, 1969-72; prin. Kantrow, Spaht, Weaver & Blitzer APLC, Baton Rouge, 1972—; spl. advisor continous revision trust com. La. Law Inst., 1975-76, mem. trust com., 1992—, mem. successions and donations com., 1990—; adj. prof. La. State U. Law Ctr., 1975-76, 83—. Contbr. articles to profl. jours. Former bd. dirs. Baton Rouge Assn. Retarded Citizens, La. Easter Seal Soc., Baton Rouge Easter Seal Soc. Fellow Am. Coll. Trust and Estate Coun.; mem. ABA, Internat. Acad. Trust and Estate Law, La. Bar Assn. (lcetr.), Baton Rouge Bar Assn., Baton Rouge Estate and Bus. Planning Coun. Estate planning, Probate, Estate taxation. Office: Kantrow Spaht Weaver & Blitzer APLC PO Box 2997 Baton Rouge LA 70821-2997

**BLIWISE, LESTER MARTIN,** lawyer; b. Phila., Dec. 22, 1945; s. Sanford and Mollie (Cohen) B.; m. Ilene Estelle Hisiger, June 23, 1968; children: Matthew Scott, Howard Michael. BA, Rutgers U., 1967; JD, Bklyn. Law Sch., 1970. Bar: N.Y. 1971, U.S. Dist. Ct. (no. dist.) N.Y. 1971, U.S. Dist. Ct. (so. dist.) N.Y. 1975. Law asst. appellate div. 3d dept. N.Y. State Supreme Ct., Albany, 1970-71, law sec. appellate div. 3d dept., 1971-72; assoc. Burstein and Marcus, White Plains, N.Y., 1972-73; assoc. Trubin Sillcocks Edelman & Knapp, N.Y.C., 1973-78, ptnr., 1978-84; ptnr. Milgrim Thomajan Jacobs & Lee, N.Y.C., 1984-85, Curtis, Mallet-Prevost, Colt & Mosie, N.Y.C., 1985-87, Schulte Roth & Zabel, LLP, N.Y.C., 1987-97, LeBoeuf, Lamb, Greene & MacRae LLP, N.Y.C., 1997—; mem. coun. advisors Ticor Title Ins. Co., N.Y.C., 1990—. Contbr. chpts. in books Real Estate Titles, 1984, rev., 1988, 2d edit., 1994, rev. edit., 1998, Foreign Investment in the U.S., 1989, rev. 1990, 92; notes editor Bklyn. Law Rev., 1969-70. Mem. planning bd. Town of Mamaroneck, N.Y., 1984-88. Mem. N.Y. Sate Bar Assn. (del. to Ho. of dels., 1992-94, chair real estate financing and liens com., real property law sect. 1980-88, 98—, chair real property law sect. 1991-92, sec. 1988-89, 2d vice chair 1989-90, 1st vice chair 1990-91), Am. Coll. Real Estate Lawyers. Real property, Finance. Home: 155 Franklin St New York NY 10013-2936 Office: LeBoeuf Lamb Greene & MacRae LLP 125 W 55th St New York NY 10019-5369

**BLOCH, ALAN NEIL,** federal judge; b. Pitts., Apr. 12, 1932; s. Gustave James and Molly Dorothy B.; m. Elaine Claire Amdur, Aug. 24, 1957; children: Rebecca Lee, Carolyn Jean, Evan Amdur. B.S. in Econs, U. Pa., 1953; J.D., U. Pitts., 1958. Bar: Pa. 1959. Indsl. engr. U.S. Steel Corp., 1953; practice law Pitts., 1959-79; judge U.S. Dist. Ct. (we. dist.) Pa., Pitts., 1979-96, sr. judge, 1997—; mem. Jud. Conf. U.S. Com. on Ct. Security, 1987—; chmn. joint task force on death penalty representation Supreme Ct. Pa.-Ct. Appeals; past mem. Rule 11 task force Ct. Appeals (3d cir.). Contbr. articles to legal publs. Vice chmn. Stadium Authority Pitts., 1970-80; bd. dirs. St. John's Gen. Hosp., Pitts., 1975-80. Served with AUS, 1953-55. Mem. Am. Bar Assn., Acad. Trial Lawyers Allegheny County, Phi Delta Phi. Jewish. Club: River. Office: US Dist Ct We Dist US Post Office and Courthouse 700 Grant St Ste 837 Pittsburgh PA 15219-1934

**BLOCH, DONALD MARTIN,** lawyer; b. Lynn, Mass., May 16, 1939; s. Meyer James and Bertha (Berman) B.; m. Ellen Ann Green, June 18, 1961; children: Andrew Louis, Linda Phyllis, David Michael. BA, Bowdoin Coll., 1960; LLB, Harvard U., 1963. Bar: Mass. 1963, U.S. Dist. Ct. Mass. 1974. Assoc. Lane, Altman & Owens LLP, Boston, 1966-71; ptnr. Lane, Altmon & Owens LLP, Boston, 1972—. Mem. Framingham (Mass.) Town Meeting, 1970-95, Town Charter Commn., Framingham, 1978-79; bd. dirs. South Middlesex Assn. for Retarded, Framingham, 1980-86, Metrowest Mental Health Assn., Framingham, 1983-95, Mary Morse Healthcare inc., 1997—; mem. Mass. Adv. Com. to U.S. Civil Rights Commn., 1991-93. Capt. U.S. Army, 1963-65. Named one of Outstanding Citizens, Greater Framingham Jewish Fedn., 1983. Mem. Harvard Club Boston, Bowdoin Club Boston (officer, bd. dirs.), Phi Beta Kappa. Republican. Real property, Landlord-tenant, General corporate. Office: Lane Altman & Owens LLP 101 Federal St Fl 26 Boston MA 02110-1842

**BLOCH, STEFANIE Z.,** lawyer; b. Phila., Feb. 17, 1950; div. July 1985; children: Jennifer Ann, Michael Todd. BS in Edn., U. Md., 1972; JD, Rutgers U., 1993. Bar: N.J. 1993, Pa. 1993, U.S. Dist. Ct. N.J. 1993, U.S. Ct. Appeals (3d cir.) 1996. Tchr. 5th grade Riverside, N.J., 1972-76; owner flower bus. Scent-inient, Cherry Hill, N.J., 1983-91; assoc. Steinberg & Ginsberg, Voorhees, N.J., 1993-95, Sufrin, Zucker, Steinberg, Waller & Wixted, P.C., Blackwood, N.J., 1995—; lectr. N.J. Inst. for Continuing Legal Edn., Whippany, 1998—; atty., guest Legal Line T.V. show, 1998—. Recipient Am. Jurisprudence award Lawyers Coop. Pub., 1992, Outstanding Acad. Achievment award Am. Acad. of Matrimonial Lawyers, 1992, 93. Mem. ABA, N.J. State Bar, Camden County Bar Assn. (mem. family law com. 1996—). Avocations: travel, boating. Family and matrimonial, Personal injury, Juvenile. Office: Sufrin Zucker Steinberg Waller & Wixted PC 1650 Blackwood Clementon Rd Blackwood NJ 08012-4632

**BLOCH, STUART MARSHALL,** lawyer; b. Detroit, Nov. 5, 1942; s. A. Howard and Pauline Betty (Rappaport) B.; m. Julia Chang, Dec. 21, 1968. AB, U. Miami, 1964; LLB, Harvard U., 1967. Bar: Mich. 1968, D.C. 1968. Ptnr. Ingersoll and Bloch, Washington, 1972—; chmn. Real Estate Reporter, Ltd., Washington, 1978—. Author: A Periodical Guide to FIRREA, 1989, The Workout Game, 1987, 90, The Liability Game, 1988; editor State Digest of Land Sales, 1977—, D.C. Real Estate Reporter, 1979—; fellow Salzburg Seminar, 1988. Chmn. Land Devel. Inst., Washington, 1974—; trustee Arena Stage, 1983, Black Student Fund, Washington, 1983; major gifts chmn. Harvard U. Law Sch., 1983; 25th reunion chmn. U. Miami, 1989; pres. Internat. Found. for Timesharing, 1983; mem. corp. Northeastern U., Boston, 1983; mem, bd. individual vol. svc. Jewish Nat. Fund, 1994. Recipient spl. citation Am. Land Devel. Assn., 1980; citation D.C. City Coun., 1982, Jewish Nat. Fund Tree of Life award, 1991. Mem. ABA, D.C. Bar Assn., Mich. Bar Assn., Univ. Club (Washington). Real property, Administrative and regulatory. Office: Ingersoll & Bloch 1300 N St NW Washington DC 20005-3600

**BLOCK, DAVID JEFFREY,** lawyer; b. Bklyn., Aug. 22, 1951; s. Herbert and Ruth Block. BA in Polit. Sci., SUNY, Buffalo, 1973; JD, Emory U., 1976. Bar: N.Y. 1977, D.C. 1978, Calif. 1979. Atty. advisor U.S. Comptroller of the Currency, Washington, 1977-79; assoc. Rosenblum, Parish and Bacigalupi, San Francisco, 1979-81; ptnr. Rosen Wachtell & Gilbert, San Francisco, 1983-86; pvt. practice law San Francisco, 1981-83, 86-90; of counsel Adams, Sadler & Hovis, San Francisco, 1990-94, Leland Parachini Steinberg Matzger & Melnick, San Francisco, 1994—; lectr. in field. Contbr. articles to profl. jours. Avocations: golf, cooking, wine collecting. Banking, Securities, Mergers and acquisitions. Office: 333 Market St San Francisco CA 94105-2102

**BLOCK, DENNIS JEFFREY,** lawyer; b. Bronx, N.Y., Sept. 1, 1942; s. Martin and Betty (Berger) B.; m. Lauren Elizabeth Troupin, Nov. 27, 1967; children: Robert, Tracy, Meredith. BA, U. Buffalo, 1964; LLB, Bklyn. Law Sch., 1967. Bar: N.Y. 1968, U.S. Dist. Ct. (ea. dist.) N.Y., U.S. Dist. Ct. (so. dist.) N.Y., U.S. Ct. Appeals (2d, 3d, 5th, 6th, 7th, 8th, 9th, 10th and 11th cirs.), U.S. Supreme Ct. Br. chief SEC, N.Y.C., 1967-72; assoc. Weil, Gotshal & Manges, L.L.P., N.Y.C., 1972-74, ptnr., 1974-98; ptnr. Cadwalader, Wickersham & Taft, N.Y.C., 1998—. Co-author: The Business Judgment Rule: Fiduciary Duties of Corporate Directors and Officers, Law & Business, Inc., 1987, 5th edit., 1998; co-editor: The Corporate Counselor's Desk Book, 1982, 5th edit., 1999; contbr. articles to profl. jours. Chmn. major gifts lawyers div., United Jewish Appeal Fedn., 1987-89, chmn. lawyers div., 1989-91. Mem. ABA (coun. litigation sect., com. on corp. laws sect. bus. law), Assn. of Bar of City of N.Y., Am. Law Inst.

**BLOCK, JESSICA,** lawyer; b. N.Y.C., June 10, 1952; d. Irvin and Doris (Senk) B.; m. Bob Allen Jacobson, Dec. 13, 1992; 1 child, Leah Claire. BA, SUNY, Stony Brook, 1974; MA, U. Toronto, 1976; JD, Northeastern U. Sch. Law, 1982. Assoc. Shapiro & Grace, Boston, 1982-83, Csaplar & Bok, Boston, 1983-90, Gaston & Snow, Boston, 1990-91, Choate, Hall & Stewart, Boston, 1991-92; prin. Heidlage & Reece, Boston, 1992-98; of counsel Field & Roos, 1998—; hearing officer Bd. Bar Overseers, Boston, 1996—; panelist, faculty MCLE Seminars, Boston, 1996—. Mem. ABA, Mass. Bar Assn., Boston Bar Assn., Women's Bar Assn. Professional liability, State civil litigation.

**BLOCK, MARCENE BURGESS,** lawyer; b. Salina, Kans., May 15, 1954; d. Richard Benton and Marcene (Reynolds) Burgess; m. Frank Emmanuel Block Jr., Nov. 15, 1975; children: Frank Emmanuel III, Richard Burgess, John Burckhardt. Student, Smith Coll., 1972-74; BA, U. Va., Charlottesville, 1976, JD, 1979. Bar: N.C. 1980, Fla. 1984. Assoc. Everett, Creech & Hancock, Durham, N.C., 1981-82; sole practice Durham, 1982-83, Vero Beach, Fla., 1984-87. Mem. N.C. State Bar Assn., Fla. State Bar Assn. Republican. Anglican. Address: 141 El Dorado Dr Little Rock AR 72212-2763

**BLOCK, MARTIN,** lawyer; b. N.Y.C., July 14, 1937; s. Leonard and Rose (Tenzer) B.; m. Linda Zuckerman, Dec. 25, 1965 (div. 1979); children: Sarin, Bryson; m. Ann Block, July 15, 1990. Student Bklyn. Coll., 1959-61, NYU, 1962-63; LL.B., Bklyn. Law Sch., 1965. Bar: N.Y. 1965, U.S. Dist. Ct. (so. and ea. dists.) N.Y. 1966, U.S. Ct. Appeals (2d cir. 1979). Assoc. Seymour L. Colin, N.Y.C., 1965-70; assoc. then ptnr. Queller, Fisher, Block & Wisotsky, N.Y.C., 1970-85; ptnr. Sanders, Sanders, Block & Woycik, P.C. 1985—; instr. Hofstra U. Trial Adv. Program, 1994—; guest lectr. Lawline-Cable TV, N.Y.C., 1984. Served as staff sgt. USNG, 1959-64. Recipient Cert. in Civil Trial Adv. Nat. Bd. Trial Adv., 1993. Mem. ATLA, Nassau County Bar Assn. (chair Plaintiffs Roundtable com.), Assn. Trial Lawyers of City of N.Y., N.Y. State Trial Lawyers Assn. (lectr. 1984), Nassau-Suffolk Trial Lawyers Assn. (treas. 1998 sect., bd. dirs. 1994-97), Pres. Club, Am. Arbitration Assn. Democrat. Jewish. Personal injury, State civil litigation, Federal civil litigation. Office: Sanders Sanders Block & Woycik PC 100 Herricks Rd Mineola NY 11501-3652

**BLOCK, MAUREEN SHANGHNESSY,** lawyer; b. Pitts., Mar. 5, 1966; d. Michael John and Carol Jean Shanghnessy; m. Steven Joseph Block, May 7, 1994. BA in Polit. Sci., Spanish, Duke U., 1988; JD, U. Pa., 1991; postgrad., Columbia U., 1990-91. Bar: N.Y., Conn. Assoc. Fulbright & Jawarski, LLP, N.Y.C., 1991-93; v.p., counsel Donaldson, Lufkin & Jennette, N.Y.C. and San Francisco, 1993—. Avocation: equestrian. Securities, General corporate, Private international. Office: Donaldson Lufkin & Jennette 600 California St San Francisco CA 94108-2704

**BLOCK, MITCHELL STERN,** lawyer; b. Dallas, May 31, 1953; s. Richard E. Block and Phyllis (Katz) Harp; m. Sara Whitney Block, Apr. 7, 1984. BA, So. Meth. U., 1976, JD, 1980. Bar: Tex. 1980, U.S. Dist. Ct. (no. dist.) Tex., 1980. Law clk. A. J. Pope III, Esquire, Corpus Christi, Tex., 1971; law clk., then assoc. James A. Gandy, Esquire, Dallas, 1978-81; asst. county atty. Nolan County Atty.'s Office, Sweetwater, Tex., 1981; ptnr. Clark & Block, Snyder, Tex., 1981-82; pvt. practice Austin, Tex., 1982-83; assoc. Halperin & Marcus, N.Y.C., 1984, W. C. Roberts, Jr., Esquire, Dallas, 1985-86; asst. corp. atty. Wyatt Cafeterias, Inc., Dallas, 1986-88, corp. atty., 1989-91, gen. counsel, v.p. real estate, sec., 1991-93; real estate atty. Morrison Restaurants Inc., Mobile, Ala., 1993-95; v.p., gen. counsel, sec. Morrison Fresh Cooking, Inc. (now Morrison Restaurants Inc.), Atlanta, 1996—. Mem. Am. Soc. Corp. Secs., State Bar Tex. (corp. counsel sect., labor and employment law sect.), Dallas Bar Assn. (corp. counsel sect.), Internat. Coun. Shopping Ctrs. Real property, Landlord-tenant, General corporate. Office: Morrison Restaurants Inc PO Box 2467 Baton Rouge LA 70821-2467

**BLOCK, NELSON R(ICHARD),** lawyer; b. San Antonio, Tex., Mar. 24, 1951; s. Norman and Ethel (Poliakoff) B. BA, Johns Hopkins U., 1973; JD, U. Tex., 1976. Bar: Tex. 1976. Law clk. 14th Ct. Appeals, Houston, 1976-77; assoc. Sheinfeld, Maley & Kay, P.C., Houston, 1977-83; shareholder Sheinfeld, Maley & Kay, P.C., Houston, 1983—; speaker various insts. Author: Commercial Law Manual: Ch. 40 Contractural Subordination, 1991: pub. The Jour. of Scouting History. Mem. bd. dirs., legal counsel Sam Houston Area coun. Boy Scouts Am., 1984—, mng. trustee The Hillcourt Found.; mem. Baden-Powell World Fellowship. Mem. ABA, Tex. Bar Assn. (chmn. uniform comml. code com. 1982-84), Houston Bar Assn., Tex. Bar Found., Selden Soc. (state corr. 1978—), Houston Comml. Fin. Lawyers Forum (founder), Am. Coll. of Comml. Fin. Lawyers. Avocations: camping, hiking, reading, history, sketching. Banking, Contracts commercial. Office: 1001 Fannin St Ste 3700 Houston TX 77002-6709

**BLOCK, RICHARD RAPHAEL,** lawyer, arbitrator; b. Phila., Nov. 9, 1938; s. Harry and Ida (Brandes) B.; m. Joanne Kramer, July 1, 1943 (div. Jan. 1973); 1 child, Jeffrey. AB, Dickinson Coll., 1959; LLB cum laude, U. Pa., 1962. Bar: Pa. 1963, N.J. 1980, D.C. 1982. Assoc. Folz & Bard, Phila., 1963-64; ptnr. Melzer & Schiffrin, Phila., 1964-75, Beitch & Block, Phila., 1975-90; dir. community rels. Dist. Atty. of Phila., 1991-96; chief tech. officer Phila. Dept. of Commerce, 1996—; chmn. hearing com Disciplinary Bd. Supreme Ct. Pa., 1982-90. Contbg. author: Handbook of Pennsylvania Courts, 1970, Divorce Mediation, 1985, Prenuptial Agreements, 1989, Encyclopedia on Matrimonial Practice, 1991; assoc. editor U. Pa. Law Rev.; contbr. articles to profl. jours. Vice pres. Am. Jewish Congress, Phila., 1975; campaign mgr. Elect Joan Specter to City Coun., Phila., 1978, 82, 86. Mem. Pa. Bar Assn. (arbitrator Inter-Atty. Dispute Resolution 1987—, speaker 1988) Am. Arbitration Assn., Phila. Coll. Judiciary (lectr. 1984). Republican. Avocations: horse racing, computers, music.

**BLOCK, STEVEN WILLIAM,** lawyer; b. Fayetteville, N.C., May 10, 1960; s. Franklin Lee and Wendy Barshay Block; m. Leslie Silverman, Apr. 8, 1990; children: Graham, Jessica. BA, U. N.C., 1982; MA, Middlebury Coll., 1985; JD, Am. U., 1986; LLM in Admiralty, Tulane U., 1994. Bar: N.Y. 1986, D.C. 1989, Wash. 1994, U.S. Dist. Ct. (we. dist.) Wash. 1994, Alaska 1995, U.S. Dist. Ct. Alaska 1995, U.S. Dist. Ct. (ea. dist.) Wash. 1996, U.S. Ct. Appeals (9th cir.) 1996, U.S. Dist. Ct. (so. dist.) N.Y. 1998. Atty. Betts, Patterson & Mines, Seattle, 1997—. Author: Kooperativ, 1997. Admiralty, Transportation, General civil litigation. Office: Betts Patterson & Mines 800 Financial Ctr 1215 4th Ave Ste 700 Seattle WA 98161-1090

**BLOCK, WILLIAM KENNETH,** lawyer; b. N.Y.C., Oct. 23, 1950; s. Louis and Catherine Veronica (Kerr) B. BA, Colgate U., 1973; JD, Union U., Albany, N.Y., 1976. Bar: N.Y. 1977. Gen. counsel N.Y.C. Tax Commn., 1978-81; asst. commn. fin. N.Y.C. Dept. Fin., 1981-84, dep. commr. fin., 1984-89; assoc. Schwartz, Weiss, Steckler & Hoffman, P.C., N.Y.C., 1989-91; pvt. practice, William K. Block, P.C., N.Y.C., 1992—; adj. lectr. real estate NYU, 1992—. Contbr. articles on real property tax law and procedure to profl. jours. Mem. ABA, Internat. Assn. Assessing Officers (chmn. met. jurisdiction coun. 1987-88, presdl. citation 1986, McCareen award 1988), N.Y. State Assessors Assn., N.Y. State Bar Assn., New York County Bar Assn. (com. on City of N.Y., real property com., govt. counsel com.), Real Estate Rev. Bar Assn., dir. 1995—), Assn. Bar City of N.Y. (com. on tax certiorari), Real Estate Bd. N.Y. (com. on taxation). Democrat. Roman Catholic. Administrative and regulatory, Real property, State and local taxation. Home: 115 E 34th St Apt 20K New York NY 10016-4631 Office: 295 Madison Ave Fl 38 New York NY 10017-6304

**BLOEDE, VICTOR CARL,** lawyer, academic executive; b. Woodwardville, Md., July 17, 1917; s. Carl Schon and Eleanor (Eck) B.; m. Ellen Louise Miller, May 9, 1947; children—Karl Abbott, Pamela Elena. A.B., Dartmouth Coll., 1940; J.D. cum laude, U. Balt., 1950; LL.M. in Pub. Law, Georgetown U., 1967. Bar: Md. 1950, Fed. Hawaii 1958, U.S. Supreme Ct. 1971. Pvt. practice Balt., 1950-64; mem. Goldman & Bloede, Balt., 1959-64; counsel Seven-Up Bottling Co., Balt., 1958-64; dep. atty. gen. Pacific Trust Ter., Honolulu, 1952-53; asst. solicitor for ters. Office of Solicitor, U.S. Dept. Interior, Washington, 1953-54; atty. U.S. Justice, Honolulu, 1955-58; assoc. gen. counsel Dept. Navy, Washington, 1960-61, 63-64; spl. legal cons. Md. Legislature, Legis. Council, 1963-64, 66-67; assoc. prof. U. Hawaii, 1961-63, dir. property mgmt., 1964-67; house counsel, dir. contracts and grants U. Hawaii System, 1967-82; house counsel U. Hawaii Research Corp., 1970-82; legal counsel Law of Sea Inst., 1978-82; legal cons. Rsch. Corp. and grad. rsch. divsn. U. Hawaii, 1982-92; spl. counsel to Holifield Congl. Commn. on Govt. Procurement, 1970-73. Author: Hawaii Legislative Manual, 1962, Maori Affairs, New Zealand, 1964, Oceanographic Research Vessel Operations, and Liabilities, 1972, Hawaiian Archipelago, Legal Effects of a 200 Mile Territorial Sea, 1973, Copyright-Guidelines to the 1976 Act, 1977, Forms Manual, Inventions: Policy, Law and Procedure, 1982; writer, contbr. Coll. Law Digest and other publs. on legislation and pub. law. Mem. Gov.'s Task Force Hawaii and The Sea, 1969, Citizens Housing Com. Balt., 1952-64; bd. govs. Balt. Cmty. YMCA, 1954-64; bd. dirs. U. Hawaii Press, 1964-66, Coll. Housing Found., 1968-80; appointed to internat. rev. commn. Canada-France Hawaii Telescope Corp., 1973-82, chmn., 1973, 82; cofounder, incorporator First Unitarian Ch. Honolulu. Served to lt. comdr. USNR, 1942-45, PTO. Grantee ocean law studies NSF and NOAA, 1970-80. Mem. ABA, Balt. Bar Assn., Fed. Bar Assn., Am. Soc. Internat. Law, Nat. Assn. Univ. Attys. (founder & 1st chmn. patents & copyrights sect. 1974-76). Home: 635 Onaha St Honolulu HI 96816-4918

**BLOEMER, DONNA MICHELLE,** lawyer; b. Covington, Ky., Nov. 8, 1969. AA, BA, Thomas More Coll., Crestview Hills, Ky., 1991; JD, No. Ky. U., 1994. Bar: Ky. 1994, Ohio 1995, U.S. Dist. Ct. (ea. dist.) Ky. 1998, U.S. Dist. Ct. (so. dist.) Ohio 1998. Law clk. Ky. Supreme Ct., Frankfort, 1995-97; assoc. The Lawrence Firm, Cin., 1997—; adj. prof. legal writing No. Ky. U. Chase Coll. Law, Highland Heights, 1995-98. Mem. alumni bd. dirs. Thomas More Coll., 1995—. Mem. Covington-Kenton County Jaycees, Salmon P. Chase Inn of Ct. General civil litigation. Office: The Lawrence Firm 425 Walnut St Cincinnati OH 45202-3923

**BLOM, DANIEL CHARLES,** lawyer, investor; b. Portland, Oreg., Dec. 13, 1919; s. Charles D. and Anna (Reiner) B.; m. Ellen Lavon Stewart, June 28, 1952; children: Daniel Stewart (dec.), Nicole Jan Heath. BA magna cum laude, U. Wash., 1941, postgrad., 1941-42; JD, Harvard U., 1948; postgrad., U. Paris, 1954-55. Bar: Wash. 1949, U.S. Supreme Ct. 1970. Tchg. fellow speech U. Wash., 1941-42; law clk. to justice Supreme Ct. Wash., 1948-49; since practiced in Seattle; assoc. Graves, Kizer & Graves, 1949-51; gen. counsel Northwestern Life Ins. Co., 1952-54; ptnr. Case & Blom, 1952-54; assoc., ptnr., of counsel Ryan, Swanson & Cleveland, 1956—; exec. v.p., gen. counsel Family Life Ins. Co., 1977-85, spl. counsel, 1985-91; vice chmn. Wash. Bd. Bar Examiners, 1970-72, chmn., 1972-75; mem. industry adv. com. Nat. Assn. Ins. Commrs., 1966-68; pres. Wash. Ins. Coun., 1971-73, gen. counsel, 1975-78; mediator Arbitration Forums, Inc. Editor Wash. State Bar Jour., 1951-52; assoc. editor The Brief, 1975-76; author: Life Insurance Law of the State of Washington, 1980, Banking and Insurance, Deregulatory Cross-Currents, 1985, Hostile Insurance Company Takeovers: New Frontier of the Law, 1990, Administrative Finality Under the Washington Insurance Code, 1991, Business and Professionalism, 1994, The Civility Problem, 1995, Technics and the Civilization of Law Practice, 1997, Varieties of Regulatory Experience, 1998. Chmn. jury selection Wash. Gov.'s Writer's Day Awards, 1976; bd. dirs. Crisis Clinic; trustee Bush Sch., 1971-79, v.p., 1976-77; trustee, v.p. Frye Mus., Seattle, 1976-82, World Affairs Coun. Seattle, 1972-94, Friends of Seattle Pub. Libr., 1982-87; bd. visitors U. Wash. Libr., 88-92, Friends of U. Wash. Librs., bd. dirs., 1991-95, pres., 1991-92. 2d lt. AUS, 1942-45, PTO. Decorated Bronze Star; Rhodes scholarship finalist, 1949. Mem. ABA (vice chmn. com. on life ins. law, sect. tort and ins. practice 1971-76, chmn. 1976-78, sect. program chmn. 1978-79, mem. coun. 1979-83, chmn. pub. rels. com. 1981-83, chmn. com. on profl. independence of the lawyer 1984-85, chmn. com. on scope and correlation 1985-86, chmn. com. on handbook and bylaws 1987-88, chmn. hist. com. 1991-94, del. ABA to Union Internat. Des Avocats 1986-91, policy coord. tort and ins. practice sect. 1986-90), Wash. Bar Assn. (award of merit 1975, chmn. legal edn. liason com. 1977-78), Seattle Bar Assn., Union Internat. Des Avocats (v.p. 1987-92), N.Am. Found. for Internat. Legal Practice (dir. 1987-95, pres. 1987-89, chmn. 1990-95), Am. Judicature Soc., Assn. Life Ins. Counsel, Harvard Law Sch. Assn., Am. Coun. Life Ins. (legis. com. 1982-85), Am. Arbitration Assn., Found. UIA (coun. 1990-97), Fedn. Regulatory Counsel, (dir. 1995-97), Harvard Assn. Seattle and Western Wash. (trustee 1976-77), Phi Beta Kappa, Tau Kappa Alpha. Insurance, General corporate, Administrative and regulatory. Home: 100 Ward St # 602-3 Seattle WA 98109-5613 Office: Ryan Swanson & Cleveland 1201 3rd Ave Ste 3400 Seattle WA 98101-3034

**BLOMQUIST, ERNEST RICHARD, III,** lawyer; b. Chgo., July 20, 1946; s. Ernest R. Jr. and Olga Ann (Nemcek) B.; m. Roberta L. Blomquist, Aug. 9, 1969; children: Britt, Carrie, Tracy. BA in History, Western Ill. U., 1968; JD, Ill. Inst. Tech., 1973. Bar: Ill. 1973, U.S. Dist. Ct. (no. dist.) Ill. 1973, U.S. Supreme Ct. 1976. Trial atty. Cook County States Atty., Chgo., 1973-77; corp. counsel, village atty. Village of Arlington Heights, Ill., 1977—; ptnr. Massucci, Blomquist, Brown, Arlington Heights, 1979—; lectr., author Ill. Inst. Continuing Legal Edn., 1986—, Ill. Traffic Law Conf., Bradley U., 1986, Northwest Mcpl. Police Tgn. Inst., seminars on criminal law, 1980—; lectr., mem. faculty So. Ill. Sch. Law, Nat. Jud. Coll., U. Nev., Reno, Ill. Dept. Pub. Health/DWI Breath Testing, Prosecutors and Pub. Defenders

Tng. Insts., Mo. Police Tng. Inst., Northwestern U. Traffic Inst., ABA, Nat. Assn. Criminal Def. Attys., Ill. Bar Assn. Mem. Gov.'s Task Force on Jud. Merit Selection, Ill., 1987—, Commn. on Evaluation Jud. Performance, Ill. Supreme Ct., 1986—; mem. alumni bd. dirs. Western Ill. U., 1989-90. Recipient Alumni Achievement award Western Ill. U., 1997—. Mem. Fed. Trial Bar Assn., N.W. Suburban Bar Assn. (pres. 1986-87., chm. com. criminal law, jud. liason, chmn. jud. screening com.), Ill. State Bar Assn., Ill. Trial Lawyers Assn., Chgo. Bar Assn., Ill. Inst. Continuing Legal Edn. (bd. dirs.), Rotary. Criminal. Office: Massucci Blomquist Brown 750 W Northwest Hwy Arlington Heights IL 60004-5343

**BLOODWORTH, A(LBERT) W(ILLIAM) FRANKLIN,** lawyer; b. Atlanta, Sept. 23, 1935; s. James Morgan Bartow and Elizabeth Westfield (Dimmock) B.; m. Elizabeth Howell, Nov. 24, 1967; 1 child, Elizabeth Howell. AB in History and French, Davidson Coll., 1957; JD magna cum laude with 1st honors, U. Ga., 1963. Bar: Ga. 1962, U.S. Supreme Ct. 1971. Asst. dir. alumni and pub. relations Davidson Coll., N.C., 1959-60; assoc. Hansell & Post, Atlanta, 1963-68, ptnr., 1969-84; ptnr. Bloodworth & Nix, Atlanta, 1984-95, Bloodworth & McSwain, Atlanta, 1996—; counsel organized crime com. Met. Atlanta Commn. on Crime, 1965-67; asst. sec., counsel Met. Found. Atlanta, 1968-76. Bd. dirs. Atlanta Presbytery, 1974-78; trustee Synod of S.E., Presbyn. Ch. in U.S.A., Augusta, Ga., 1982-87; trustee Big Canoe Chapel, Ga., 1983-86, 88-91, chmn. bd. trustees, 1985-86, 90-91; mem. pres.'s adv. coun. Presbyn. Homes, 1989—; mem. president's adv. coun. Thornwell Home and Sch. for Children, 1998—. elder North Ave Presbyn. Ch., Atlanta. 1st lt. Intelligence Corps, USAR, 1957-59. Recipient Jessie Dan MacDougal Scholarship award U. Ga. Found., 1963, Outstanding Student Leadership award Student Bar Assn., U. Ga., 1963. Fellow Am. Coll. Trust and Estate Counsel; mem. ABA, State Bar Ga., Atlanta Bar Assn., Atlanta Estate Planning Coun., North Atlanta Estate Planning Coun., Capital City Club, Lawyers Club, Sphinx Club, Gridiron Club, Phi Beta Kappa, Phi Kappa Phi, Omicron Delta Kappa, Alpha Tau Omega (pres. chpt. 1957), Phi Delta Phi (grad. of yr. 1963, pres. chpt. 1963). Republican. Presbyterian. Probate, Estate planning, Estate taxation. Home: 3784 Club Dr NE Atlanta GA 30319-1108 Office: 706 Monarch Plz 3414 Peachtree Rd NE Atlanta GA 30326-1153

**BLOOM, ALLEN JERRY,** lawyer; b. St. Louis, May 6, 1930; d. Morris K. and Dorothy Marie (Barken) B.; m. Jeanne Akers, Nov. 23, 1960; children: Lisa S., Michael W. BSBA in Acctg., Wash. U., St. Louis, 1953; JD, St. Louis U., 1957. Bar: Mo. 1957, Ill. 1991, U.S. Dist. Ct. Mo. 1957, U.S. Dist. Ct. (so. dist.) Ill., 1990. Pvt. practice St. Louis, 1957—. Sgt. USAF, 1948-49. Mem. ABA, Met. Bar Assn., Mo. Bar Assn. Consumer commercial, General practice, Probate. Home: 24 Spoede Woods Saint Louis MO 63141-7828 Office: 1620 S Hanley Rd Saint Louis MO 63144-2906

**BLOOM, BARRY MARSHALL,** lawyer; b. Dallas, Sept. 24, 1946; s. Louis M. and Rosalie Mae (Brown) B.; m. Susan Reneé Roseé, Feb. 1, 1970; children: Lissa Alayne, Farra Julianne, Brennan Irwin. BBA, U. Tex., 1969; JD, So. Meth. U., 1972; LLM in Taxation, Georgetown U., 1975. Bar: Tex. 1972, U.S. Dist. Ct. (no. dist.) Tex. 1978, U.S. Tax Ct. 1975. Atty. interpretative div. Office of Chief Counsel for IRS, Washington, 1972-75; atty. Regional Counsel's Office for IRS S.W. region, Dallas, 1975-78; assoc. Freytag, Marshall, Beneke, LaForce, Rubinstein & Stutzman, Dallas, 1978-80; ptnr. Freytag, LaForce, Rubinstein & Teofan, Dallas, 1981-87, Fugit, Hubbard, Woolley, Bloom & Mersky, Dallas, 1987-90; pres. Barry M. Bloom, P.C., Dallas, 1990—. Lt. USAR, 1969-72. Recipient Am. Jurisprudence award Bancroft-Whitney, 1970, 71. Mem. ABA, Tex. Bar Assn., Dallas Bar Assn. Taxation, general, General corporate, Estate planning.

**BLOOM, CHARLES JOSEPH,** lawyer; b. Pitts., July 7, 1946; s. Israel C. and Ida (Lample) B.; m. Susan Halsey Potts, May 14, 1971; children: Zachary B., Amanda H., Theodore L. BA, Princeton U., 1967; JD magna cum laude, U. Pa., Phila., 1971. Bar: Pa. 1971, U.S. Dist. Ct. (ea. dist.) Pa. 1971, U.S. Ct. Appeals (3d cir.) 1972, U.S. Supreme Ct. 1978. Law clk. U.S. Ct. Appeals (3d cir.), Phila., 1971-72; assoc. Pepper, Hamilton & Scheetz, Phila., 1972-78, ptnr., 1978-80; ptnr. Hunt, Kerr, Bloom & Hitchner, Phila., 1980-85, Kleinbard, Bell & Brecker, Phila., 1985-92, Stevens & Lee, P.C., Wayne, Pa., 1992—. Bd. dirs. Main Line Art Ctr., 1997—, Cloister Inn Princeton, 1980-89, chmn., 1983-85; commr. Lower Merion Twp., 1998—; v.p. Haverford (Pa.) Civic Assn. (1989—). With U.S. Army, 1968-71. Mem. Phila. Bar Assn. (fed. cts. com. 1975—, chmn. unauthorized practice law com. 1985, bench-bar conf. com. 1985-90), Order of Coif. Avocations: numismatics, collecting antique toy trains. Contracts commercial, Federal civil litigation, Libel.

**BLOOM, MICHAEL ANTHONY,** lawyer; b. Phila., Sept. 4, 1947; s. Edward Bloom and Edythe (Weiss) Barbour; m. Debra Sue Lobis, Aug. 15, 1971; 1 child, Alexis Rachael. AB, Dickinson U., 1969; JD, Villanova U., 1974. Bar: Pa. 1974, U.S. Dist. Ct. (ea. dist.) Pa. 1974, U.S. Tax Ct. 1976, U.S. Ct. Appeals (3d cir.) 1977, U.S. Ct. Appeals (4th cir.) 1979, U.S. Supreme Ct. 1980. Assoc. Pelino, Wasserstrom, Chucas & Monteverde, Phila., 1974-77, Wasserstrom & Chucas, Phila., 1977-79; ptnr. Wasserstrom, Chucas, Sirlin & Bloom, Phila., 1980-82, Cohen, Shapiro, Polisher, Shiekman and Cohen, Phila., 1982-88, Morgan, Lewis & Bockius, Phila., 1988—; chmn. Hearing Commn. Disciplinary Bd., Pa. Supreme Ct., 1987-89; co-founder, past chmn., mem. steering com. Ea. Dist. Pa. Bankruptcy Conf., Phila., 1989, 94-95. Contbr. articles to profl. jours. Bd. dirs. Jewish Community Ctrs. of Greater Phila., 1987-91; bd. dirs., pres. Gershman YM-YWHA, Phila., 1987-90; co-chmn. Share Our Strength, Phila, 1987-90; v.p., bd. dirs. Pa. Ballet Asssn., 1987—; mem. adv. bd. Pa. Vol. Lawyers for Arts, 1990—. Recipient Fidelity award Fidelity Bank, Phila., 1983, Joseph and Sylvia Daroff award Jewish Y's and Community Ctrs., Phila., 1984. Fellow Am. Bar Found., Pa. Bar Found.; mem. ABA (com. on counsel responsibility sect. bus. law 1990), Am. Bankruptcy Inst., Pa. Bar Assn. (chmn. legal ethics and profl. responsibility com. 1985-91, com. on specialization 1989—, publs. com. 1986—, ho. of dels. 1983—, co-chair, mem. com. Amicus Curiae Brief com. 1991-94, Spl. Achievement award 1986, 87, 88), Phila. Bar Assn. (bd. govs. 1982-84, chmn. spl. com. on ethics in govt. 1988—). Avocation: middle and long distance running. Bankruptcy, Ethics. Office: Morgan Lewis & Bockius 1701 Market St Philadelphia PA 19103-2903

**BLOOM, ROBERT AVRUM,** lawyer; b. N.Y.C., Jan. 24, 1930; s. Samuel and Rose (Ladenheim) B; m. Joan Pivar, Apr. 19, 1959; children: Jonathan, Matthew. BA summa cum laude, Princeton U., 1951; LLB, Harvard U., 1957; PhD, N.Y.U., 1974. Bar: N.Y. 1957, U.S. Dist. Ct. (ea. dist.) N.Y. 1958. Assoc. Senator Edward J. Speno, Mineola, N.Y., 1957-59; sole practice Great Neck, N.Y., 1959-62; ptnr. Martin Bloom & Van De Walle, Great Neck, 1962-75, Hollenberg Levin Marlow & Bloom, Mineola, N.Y., 1975-79, Bloom & Amrod, Garden City, 1979-85; pres. Bloom & Esterces, P.C., Garden City, 1985-87; with Blodnick Pomeranz Schultz & Abromowitz, P.C., N.Y.C., 1987-88; of counsel Bivona & Cohen, P.C., N.Y.C., 1988—. Pres. Pederson-Krag Mental Health Clinic, Huntington, N.Y., 1978-80; sec., treas. Found. for the Establishment of an Internat. Criminal Ct., Boston, 1972-79. Served as lt. j.g. USN, 1954-57. Mem. N.Y. State Trial Lawyers Assn. Democrat. Jewish. Personal injury, General civil litigation, Probate. Home: 377 Rector Pl Apt 7M New York NY 10280-1435

**BLOOMER, HAROLD FRANKLIN, JR.,** lawyer; b. N.Y.C., Nov. 4, 1933; s. Harold Franklin and Allene (Cress) B.; m. Mary Jane Lloyd, July 16, 1955 (div. June 1976); children: Sarah Allene, Margaret Gail, Leslie Lloyd; m. Freya Donald, Nov. 30, 1985; children: Katharine Roma, Alice Donald. AB, Amherst Coll., 1956; LLB, Columbia U., 1967. Bar: Conn. 1967, N.Y. 1968, U.S. Dist. Ct. Conn. 1968, U.S. Dist. Ct. (so. and ea. dists.) N.Y. 1974, U.S. Ct. Appeals (2d cir.) 1974. Assoc. Debevoise, Plimpton, Lyons & Gates, N.Y.C., 1967-77; counsel Burlington, Underwood & Lord, Jeddah, Saudi Arabia, 1977-78; chief internat. counsel Saudi Rsch. & Devel. Corp., London, 1978-80; counsel Morgan, Lewis & Bockius LLP, London and N.Y.C., 1980-81, ptnr., 1981—; adj. prof.Pepperdine U. Sch. Law, London, 1985. Mem. Rep. Town Meeting, Greenwich, Conn., 1964-74, 92—, chmn. pub. works com., 1971-74, chmn. land use com., 1998—; mem. Rep. Town Com., Greenwich, 1973-74; trustee San. Products Trust, Riverside, Conn., 1965-74. Lt. (j.g.) USNR, 1957-60. Kent scholar Columbia U., 1965-66, Stone scholar Columbia U., 1966-67. Mem. ABA, Am. Arbitration Assn. (panel of arbitrators 1990—), Assn. of Bar of City of N.Y., Riverside Yacht Club. Republican. Episcopalian. Avocations: sailing, canoeing, skiing, biking, running. Contracts commercial, Finance, Private international. Office: Morgan Lewis & Bockius LLP 101 Park Ave Fl 44 New York NY 10178-0060

**BLOOMER, WILLIAM JOHN,** lawyer; b. Rutland, Vt., Apr. 22, 1952; s. Robert Asa and Mary Elizabeth Bloomer; m. Margery Elizabeth Pierce, June 9, 1973; children: Matthew A., Mary Katelin, Aaron P., Geoffrey E. BA, U. Vt., 1973; JD, Boston U., 1976. Bar: Vt. 1976, U.S. Dist. Ct. Vt. 1977. Attorney, officer Bloomer & Bloomer, P.C., Rutland, 1976—; city atty. City of Rutland, 1981-83; justice of peace, Rutland. Alderman City of Rutland, 1979-81, pres. bd. aldermen, 1980-81; freshman baseball coach Rutland H.S., 1994—. Mem. Rotary. Roman Catholic. Probate, Municipal (including bonds). Office: 22 Cottage St Rutland VT 05701-3404

**BLOOMFIELD, NEIL JON,** lawyer, law educator, real estate broker; b. N.Y.C., July 25, 1945; s. Elmer Joel and Charlotte (Orlov) B.; children—Jennifer, Violet. B.A. cum laude, Princeton U., 1966; J.D. cum laude, Harvard U., 1969. Bar: N.Y. 1969, Calif. 1972. Assoc., Willkie, Farr & Gallagher, N.Y.C., 1969-73, ptnr. Bloomfield & Greene, 1974-80; pres. Bloomfield White & Whitney, Inc., Sausalito, Calif., 1974-77, Law Offices of Neil Jon Bloomfield, 1980—; bd. dirs. Vol. Lawyers for the Arts, N.Y.C., 1970-72; adj. prof. law U. San Francisco, 1982-83; cert. expert in real estate law and trusts related to real estate Calif. Superior Ct. Mem. Marin County Bar Assn., San Francisco Bar Assn., Clolsrer Inn, Lincolns Inn Soc. (Cambridge). Editor: Community and Racial Crises, 1966. Real property, Taxation, general, General civil litigation. Office: 900 5th Ave Ste 202 San Rafael CA 94901-2928

**BLOOMQUIST, AMY PETERSON,** lawyer; b. Grand Rapids, Mich., Jan. 28, 1961; d. Stephen Earl Peterson and Patricia Elizabeth (Hollinger) Respondek; m. Lawrence Randall Bloomquist, July 7, 1990; 1 child, Randall Holt. BBA, Tex. A&M U., 1983; JD, U. Tex., 1986. Bar: Tex. 1987; CPA Tex. 1988. Law clk. Reischman & Kimes, Austin, Tex., 1980-84, Kimes & Spears, Austin, Tex., 1984-86; tax sr. Arthur Andersen & Co., Austin, Tex., 1986-89; assoc. Hilgers & Watkins, Austin, Tex., 1989—. Contbr. articles to profl. jours. Dir. Austin Lawyers & Accts. for Arts, 1987-93, Estates Barton Creek Property Owners Assn., Austin, 1994—; Austin Respite Care Ctr., 1993-94. Tex. A&M U. undergrad. fellow, 1982-83. Mem. State Bar Tex., Tex. Soc. CPAs (advanced estate planning conf. com. 1992-93), Estate Planning Coun. Ctrl. Tex. (dir. 1993-95), Travis County Bar Assn. (dir. 1993-94, chmn. estate planning and probate comm. 1993-94). Independent. Presbyterian. Avocations: jogging, reading, family, church. Estate planning, Probate, Estate taxation. Home: 3404 Winding Creek Dr Austin TX 78735-1477 Office: Hilgers & Watkins 98 San Jacinto Blvd Ste 1300 Austin TX 78701-4289

**BLOOMQUIST, DENNIS HOWARD,** lawyer; b. Mpls. Sept. 18, 1942; s. Howard Richard and Ingrid Marit (Brostrom) B.; m. Shirley Anne Ruemele, Aug. 22, 1964; children—Michael Dennis, Eric William. B.A., Albion Coll., Mich., 1964; M.B.A., Mich. State U., 1965; J.D. cum laude, Wayne State U., 1968; LL.M., NYU, 1975. Bar: Mich. 1968, U.S. Dist. Ct. (ea. dist.) Mich. 1968, N.Y. 1971, Va. 1995. Assoc. Parsons, Tennent, Hammond, Hardig & Ziegelman, Detroit, 1968-70, Alexander and Green, N.Y.C., 1970-73; tax counsel Mobil Oil and Mobil Corp., N.Y.C., 1973-81, gen. counsel Mobil Land Devel. Corp., N.Y.C., 1981-88, real estate and land devel., Mobil Corp., 1984-88, asst. gen. tax counsel, Fairfax, Va., 1988—; lectr. continuing legal edn. Mem. ABA, Bar Assn. Mich., N.Y. State Bar Assn. Congregationalist. Corporate taxation, Real property, General corporate. Home: 11136 Rich Meadow Dr Great Falls VA 22066-1417 Office: 3225 Gallows Rd Fairfax VA 22037-0001

**BLOOMSTON, BRETT MICHAEL,** lawyer, educator; b. Birmingham, Ala., June 29, 1971; s. Robert Norman and Rochelle (Lassen) B. BA, U. Ala., 1993, JD, 1996. Bar: Ala. 1996, U.S. Dist. Ct. (no. and mid. dists.) Ala. 1996, U.S. Ct. Appeals (11th cir.) 1997. Assoc. Lloyd, Schreiber & Gray, Birmingham, Ala., 1996-97, Johnson, Liddon, Bear & Tuggle, Birmingham, Ala., 1997—; asst. prof. U. Ala., Birmingham, 1998. Mem. NACDL, ATLA, Birmingham Bar Assn., Greater Birmingham Criminal Def. Attys. Assn. Avocations: hiking, canoeing, reading. General civil litigation, Criminal. Office: Johnson Liddon Bear & Tuggle 2100 1st Ave N Ste 700 Birmingham AL 35203-4223

**BLOSSER, DAVID JOHN,** lawyer; b. auburn, Ind., July 6, 1950; s. Clarence W. and Joyce A. B.; 1 child, Aaron. AB, Ind. U., 1974; JD, U. Toledo, 1982. Bar: Ind., 1984, Mich., 1984. Staff atty. N.Am. Van Lines, Inc., Ft. Wayne, Ind., 1982-88; asst. gen. counsel Ark. Best Coop., Ft. Smith, 1988-89; gen. counsel NSK Corp., Ann Arbor, Mich., 1989-96; shareholder, atty. David J. Blosser & Assocs., Angola, Ind., 1996—. Mem. Ind. State Bar Assn., Mich. State Bar Assn., Steuben County Bar Assn. Transportation, General corporate, General civil litigation. Office: 207 Hoosier Dr Ste 6 Angola IN 46703-9315

**BLOUNT, CHARLES WILLIAM, III,** lawyer; b. Independence, Mo., Nov. 14, 1946; s. Charles William and Mary Marguarette (Van Trump) B.; m. Susan Penny Smith Turner, Dec. 20, 1969 (div. Nov., 1987); children: Charles William IV, Chaille Elizabeth; m. Bonnie M. Harp., Jan. 1, 1991. BS in Journalism, U. Kans., 1968; JD cum laude, U. Toledo, 1981. Bar: Mo. 1981, U.S. Dist. Ct. (we. dist.) Mo. 1981, Tex. 1985, U.S. Dist. Ct. (no. dist.) Tex. 1988, U.S. Ct. Appeals (5th cir.) 1995, U.S. Supreme Ct. 1997; cert. in civil appellate law Tex. Bd. Legal Specialization. Litigation assoc. Shugart, Thomson & Kilroy, Kansas City, Mo., 1981-84, Hughes & Luce, Dallas, 1984-87; litigation assoc. Simpson & Dowd L.L.P., Dallas, 1987-91, ptnr., 1991-94; mem. Dowd & Blount, Dallas, 1994-99; ptnr. Perry-Miller & Blount, L.L.P., Dallas, 1999—; mem. West Group Tex. Editl. Bd., 1999. Bd. govs. U. Toledo Coll. Law, 1980-81; trustee Episcopal Diocese We. Mo., Kansas City, 1983-84; mem., chmn. com. Boy Scouts of Am., Kansas City, 1983-84, Richardson, Tex., 1984-92. 1st lt. U.S. Army, 1968-72. Mem. Phi Kappa Phi, Phi Kappa Tau (pledge pres., social chmn., activities chmn., 1965—). Avocations: music, reading. State civil litigation, Appellate, General corporate. Office: Perry-Miller & Blount LLP 3300 Oak Lawn Ave Ste 675 Dallas TX 75219-4292

**BLOUNT, DAVID LAURENCE,** lawyer; b. Columbia, Mo., July 14, 1954; s. Don H. and Carol (Middleton) B.; m. Laurie Susan Lucker, Dec. 30, 1978 (dec. 1980); m. Paula Lynn Abrams, Oct. 8, 1982; children: Madeline Avram, Justine Ariel. BS, Coll. William and Mary, 1975; JD, Lewis and Clark Coll., 1980. Bar: Oreg. 1980, U.S. Dist. Ct. Oreg. 1982, U.S. Ct. Appeals (9th cir.) 1987. Assoc. U.S. EPA, Washington, 1980-82, Clackamas County Dist. Atty.'s Office, Oregon City, Oreg., 1983, Acker, Underwood & Smith, Portland, Oreg., 1983-85; ptnr. Adler & Blount, Portland, 1985-89, Copeland, Landye, Bennett & Wolf, LLP, 1989—. Contbr. articles to profl. jours. Bd. dirs. Burnside Projects for Homeless, Portland, 1983-85. Mem. Fed. Bar Assn., Oreg. State Bar. Assn. (environ. law sect. 1986-89, chair 1989, state of Oreg. environ. cleanup adv. com., 1989—, chair 1991), Multnomah Bar Assn., Oreg. Trial Lawyers Assn., Assn. Trial Lawyers Am., Multnomah Athletic Club. Democrat. Avocations: travel, hiking, skiing, basketball. Environmental, General civil litigation, Administrative and regulatory.

**BLOUNT, DAVID RUSSELL,** lawyer, risk manager; b. Sasebo, Japan, Mar. 19, 1968; s. Donald Wallace and Patricia Ann Blount; m. Amy Denise Adams, Mar. 14, 1998. BS in Criminal Justice, U. Ala., 1992, JD, 1995. Bar: Ala. Supr. Byers Engrng. Co., Birmingham, Ala., 1991-96; mgr. Underground Utility Locating, Birmingham, 1996-98; risk mgr. Ctrl. Locating Svc., Syracuse, N.Y., 1998. Mem. Ala. Bar Assn., Birmingham Bar Assn. Home: 8764 Drumlin Heights Dr Baldwinsville NY 13027-1458

**BLUCHER, PAUL ARTHUR,** lawyer; b. Youngstown, Ohio, Aug. 1, 1958; s. Arthur E. and Lillian L. (McQuillan) B.; m. Brenda Lee Kilgore, Aug. 25, 1990. AS with honors, Youngstown State U., 1984, BS magna cum laude, 1986; JD, U. Pitts., 1990. Bar: Fla. 1990, U.S. Dist. Ct. (mid. dist.) Fla. 1997, U.S. Ct. Appeals (11th cir.) 1998. Police officer Mahoning County Sheriff, Youngstown, 1979-85, police detective, 1985-87; assoc. Brigham, Moore, et al., Sarasota, Fla., 1990-96; ptnr. Brigham, Moore, et al., Sarasota, 1996-97; sole practice law Sarasota, 1997—. Mem. allocations & admissions com. United Way, Sarasota, 1996— (Pathfinder Club Recognition award 1996); mem. Amyotrophic Lateral Sclerosis Assn. 1995—. Mem. ABA (state and local gov. com. 1990-99, real property sect. condemnation com. 1999—), Fla. Bar Assn. (stress mgmt. com. 1997—, young lawyers 1990-95, eminent domain com. 1990—), Fla. Restaurant Assn., Assn. Eminent Domain Profls. Democrat. Roman Catholic. Avocations: scuba diving, boating, flying. E-mail: pblucher@fifthamendment.com. Condemnation, Constitutional, State civil litigation. Office: 1800 2nd St Ste 803 Sarasota FL 34236-5986

**BLUE, JAMES MONROE,** lawyer; b. St. Petersburg, Fla., Oct. 5, 1941; s. James Monroe and Mildred (Hobbs) B.; m. Barbara Ann Alderson, Jan. 3, 1981; children: Tammy Marlene, Kelli Christine, Shannon Kathlene. BA, Fla. State U., 1963; JD with honors, Stetson Coll., 1967. Bar: Fla. 1967, U.S. Dist. Ct. (mid. dist.) Fla. 1968, U.S. Ct. Appeals (11th cir.) 1968, U.S. Supreme Ct. 1978. Assoc. Carlton, Fields, Ward, Emmanuel, Smith & Cuttler, Tampa, Fla., 1967-69; ptnr. Alley, Alley & Blue, Miami, Fla., 1969-75, Smith, Young & Blue, Tallahassee, 1975-79, Allen, Norton & Blue, Tampa, 1979—. Mem. ABA, Fla. Bar Assn., Fla. Bar (chmn. labor law sect. 1978-79, Fla. C. of C. (human resources com. 1989—), Tampa C. of C. (com. of 100, 1987—), Hunters Green Country Club. Republican. Presbyterian. Avocations: golf, boating, reading. Labor. Office: 324 S Hyde Park Ave Ste 350 Tampa FL 33606-4110

**BLUESTEIN, EDWIN A., JR.,** lawyer; b. Hearne, Tex., Oct. 16, 1930; s. Edwin A. and Frances Grace (Ely) B.; m. Marsha Kay Meredith, Dec. 21, 1957; children: Boyd, Leslie. B.B.A., U. Tex., 1952, J.D., 1958. Bar: Tex. 1957, U.S. Ct. Appeals (5th cir.) 1960, U.S. Dist. Ct. (so. dist.)Tex. 1959, U.S. Dist. Ct. (ea. dist.)Tex. 1965, U.S. Supreme Ct. 1967, U.S. Ct. Appeals (11th cir.) 1982. Law clk. U.S. Dist. Ct., Houston, 1958-59; assoc. Fulbright & Jaworski, Houston, 1959-65, participating atty., 1965-71, ptnr., 1971-97; head admiralty dept. Fulbright & Jaworski, 1984-93; sr. ptnr. Fulbright & Jaworski, Houston, 1990-97; of counsel Fulbright & Jaworski, 1998—; mem. permanent adv. bd. Tulane Admiralty Law Inst., New Orleans, 1983—; mem. planning com. Houston Marine Ins. Seminar, 1970-76; lectr. profl. seminars. Assoc. editor: American Maritime Cases; contbr. articles to profl. jours. Mem. Tex. Coastal Mgmt. Adv. Com., Austin, 1975-78; bd. dirs. Barbour's Cut Seafarers Ctr., 1992—, Houston Internat. Seafarers Ctr., 1993—. Served with U.S. Army, 1952-54. Recipient Yachtsman of Yr. award Houston Yacht Club, 1978; Eagle Scout, Boy Scouts Am., 1944. Mem. Tex. Bar Found., Maritime Law Assn. U.S. (mem. exec. com. 1980-83), Houston Mariners Club (pres. 1970), Southeastern Admiralty Law Inst. (dir. 1983-85, Houston C. of C. (chmn. ports and waterways com. 1978-79), Propeller Club U.S., Theta Xi (chpt. pres. 1952). Methodist. Club: Houston Yacht (commodore 1979-80). Admiralty, Insurance. Home: 603 Bayridge Rd La Porte TX 77571-3512 Office: Fulbright & Jaworski 1301 Mckinney St Houston TX 77010-3031

**BLUESTEIN, MARGARET MILES,** lawyer; b. Florence, S.C., Mar. 22, 1968; d. James Robert and Anne (Godwin) Miles; m. Bryan Hyman Bluestein, May 3, 1997. BA in Polit. Sci., Furman U., 1990; JD, U. S.C. Sch. Law, 1993. Bar: S.C., U.S. Dist. Ct. S.C., U.S. Ct. Appeals (4th cir.). Atty. Suggs & Kelly, Columbia, S.C., 1993—. Vol. Jr. League of Columbia, 1998; pro bono vol. S.C. Bar Pro Bono Program, Columbia, 1993—. Avocations: volleyball, basketball, reading, travel. Workers' compensation, Pension, profit-sharing, and employee benefits. Office: Suggs & Kelly PO Box 8113 Columbia SC 29202-8113

**BLUESTEIN, S. SCOTT,** lawyer; b. Charleston, S.C., Sept. 2, 1967; s. Nathan J. and Ettaleah Bluestein; m. Natalie R. Parker, Feb. 7, 1998. BA, U. Fla., 1989; JD, U. S.C., 1992; LLM in Maritime and Admiralty, Tulane U., 1993. Bar: S.C. 1992, La. 1993, U.S. Dist. Ct. (ea., mid. and we. dist.) La. 1996, U.S. Ct. Appeals (5th cir.) 1996, U.S. Dist. Ct. S.C. Mem. ABA, ATLA, Maritime Law Assn. Avocations: sailing, baseball, exercise, travel. E-Mail: boatinglaw@charliston.net. Admiralty, Private international, Personal injury. Office: Raley & Bluestein PA 145 King St Ste 311 Charleston SC 29401-2230

**BLUESTONE, ANDREW LAVOOTT,** lawyer; b. N.Y.C., Feb. 16, 1951; s. Henry Robert and Joan (Lavoott) B.; m. Janet Francesca Whelehan, May 1987; 1 child, Gabrielle. BA, Alfred U., 1973; MA, SUNY, Oswego, 1975; JD, Syracuse U., 1978. Bar: N.Y. 1979, U.S. Dist. Ct. (so. and ea. dists.) N.Y. 1979. Sr. trial asst. dist. atty. Kings County Dist. Atty., Bklyn., 1978-84; sr. assoc. Davis & Hoffman, N.Y.C., 1984-86, Donald Ayers, N.Y.C., 1986, Alexander, Ash, Schwartz & Cohen, N.Y.C., 1986-88, Trolman & Glaser, N.Y.C., 1988-89; pvt. practice, N.Y.C., 1989—; arbitrator Small Claims Civil Ct. City of N.Y. Bd. dirs. Scandia Symphony, N.Y.C., St. Luke's AME Ch., N.Y.C. Mem. ABA, N.Y.C.T.L.A., Def. Assn. N.Y., Assn. Trial Lawyers Am., N.Y. State Trial Lawyers Assn., Bklyn. Bar Assn. General civil litigation, Personal injury, Contracts commercial. Office: 233 Broadway Fl 51 New York NY 10279-5199

**BLUM, BAMBI G.,** lawyer; b. N.Y.C., Sept. 11, 1956; d. I. Charles and Barbara Baron Groff; m. Jeffrey D. Blum, Mar. 10, 1978; 1 child, Michael Hadley. BA, Brandies U., 1977; JD magna cum laude, Nova U., 1983. Ptnr. Hicks Anderson & Blum, Miami, Fla., 1986-96; atty. pvt. practice, Miami, Fla., 1997—. Appellate. Office: 46 SW 1st St Fl 4 Miami FL 33130-1610

**BLUM, GARY BERNARD,** lawyer; b. Brighton, Eng., Feb. 1, 1946; came to U.S., 1947; s. Peter and Alice (Fenchel) B.; m. Marsha Weinberg, Sept. 9, 1973; children: Annette, Jesse, Alyce. BA, U. Colo., 1968, JD, 1971. Bar: Colo. 1971, U.S. Dist. Ct. Colo. 1971, U.S. Ct. Appeals (10th cir.) 1971, U.S. Supreme Ct. 1975. Dep. pub. defender State of Colo., Denver, 1971-74, asst. atty. gen., 1975-78; shareholder Long & Jaudon P.C., Denver, 1978—; lectr. law U. Colo.; mem. grievance com. Colo. Supreme Ct., 1988-93, mem. civil justice com.; mem. com. on lawyer conduct Fed. Ctr., 1995—; mem. Fed. Faculty of Advocates. Mem. ATLA, Colo. Bar Assn. (chmn. ethics com. 1985—), Denver Bar Assn., Colo. Def. Lawyers Assn. Democrat. Jewish. Avocations: jogging, reading, skiing, tennis. Health, Administrative and regulatory, Alternative dispute resolution. Office: Long & Jaudon PC 1600 Ogden St Denver CO 80218-1414

**BLUMBERG, EDWARD ROBERT,** lawyer; b. Phila., Feb. 15, 1951. BA in Psychology, U. Ga., 1972; JD, Coll. William and Mary, 1975. Bar: Fla., 1975, U.S. Dist. Ct. Fla., 1975, U.S. Ct. Appeals, 1975, U.S. Supreme Ct., 1979. Assoc., Knight, Peters, Hoeveler & Pickle, Miami, Fla., 1977-76; ptnr. Deutsch & Blumberg, P.A., Miami, 1978—; adj. prof. U. Miami Sch. Paralegal Studies. Author: Proof of Negligence, Mathew Bender Florida Torts, 1988. Mem. ABA (ho. of dels. 1997—), ATLA, Dade County Bar Assn., Fla. State Bar (bd. govs., pres. elect 1996-97, pres. 1997-98), Acad. Fla. Trial Lawyers, Nat Bd. Trial Advocacy (cert. civil trial adv.), Fla. Bar Found. (bd. dirs. 1996—). Personal injury, State civil litigation, Federal civil litigation. Office: Deutsch & Blumberg PA 100 Biscayne Blvd Fl 28 Miami FL 33132-2304

**BLUMBERG, GRACE GANZ,** law educator, lawyer; b. N.Y.C., Feb. 16, 1940; d. Samuel and Beatrice (Finkelstein) Ganz; m. Donald R. Blumberg, Sept. 9, 1959; 1 dau., Rachel. B.A. cum laude, U. Colo., 1960; J.D. summa cum laude, SUNY, 1971; LL.M., Harvard U., 1974. Bar: N.Y. 1971, Calif. 1989. Confidential law clk. Appellate Div., Supreme Ct., 4th Dept., Rochester, N.Y., 1971-72; teaching fellow Harvard Law Sch., Cambridge, Mass., 1972-74; prof. law SUNY, Buffalo, 1974-81, UCLA, 1981—; reporter Am. Law Inst., Prins. of the Law of Family Dissolution. Author: Community Property in California, 1987, rev. edit., 1999, Blumberg's California Family Code Annotated (ann.); contbr. articles to profl. jours. Office: UCLA Sch Law Box 951476 Los Angeles CA 90095-1476

**BLUMBERG, JOHN PHILIP,** lawyer; b. Mpls., Dec. 6, 1949. BA cum laude, Calif. State U., Long Beach, 1972; JD, Western State U., Fullerton, Calif., 1976. Bar: Calif. 1976, U.S. Dist. Ct. (cen. dist.) Calif. 1978, U.S. Ct. Appeals (9th cir.); cert. civil trial specialist Nat. Bd. Trial Advocacy. Pvt. practice, L.A., Long Beach and Orange County, Calif., 1976—; dir. Dispute Resolution Ctr., Long Beach, 1993—; judge pro tem Long Beach-L.A., 1979-92; arbitrator Los Angeles County and Orange County Superior Cts., civil litigation settlement officer; del. Calif. State Bar Conf., 1985-90; pres. Legal

Aid Found., Long Beach, 1986-87, 92-93, also bd. dirs.; lectr. various profl. and edn. groups; mem. faculty Hastings Ctr. for Trial Advocacy, 1988-89. Assoc. editor Western State U. Law Review, 1975-76; contbr. articles to profl. jours. Mem. Consumer Attys. of Calif., Long Beach Bar Assn. (bd. govs., arbitrator atty.-client disputes, mem. legis. and legal aid coms., dir. trial advocacy inst.), Am. Bd. Trial Advs., Los Angeles County Bar Assn., Consumer Attys. L.A., Am. Arbitration Assn., Orange County Bar Assn., Calif. State Bar (former chmn. com. on rules and procedures of ct. 1992-93). Avocations: music, theater. State civil litigation, Personal injury. Office: 100 Oceangate Ste 1100 Long Beach CA 90802-4344

**BLUMBERG, PHILLIP IRVIN,** law educator; b. Balt., Sept. 6, 1919; s. Hyman and Bess (Simons) B.; m. Janet Helen Mitchell, Nov. 17, 1945 (dec. 1976); children: William A.M., Peter M., Elizabeth B., Bruce M.; m. Ellen Ash Peters, Sept. 16, 1979. AB, Harvard U., 1939, JD, 1942; LLD (hon.), U. Conn., 1994. Bar: N.Y. 1942, Mass. 1970. Assoc. Willkie, Owen, Otis, Farr & Gallagher, N.Y.C., 1942-43, Szold, Brandwen, Meyers and Blumberg, N.Y.C., 1946-66; pres., chief exec. officer United Ventures Inc., 1962-67; pres., chief exec. officer, trustee Federated Devel. Co., N.Y.C., 1966-68, chmn. fin. com., 1968-73; prof. law Boston U., 1966-74; dean U. Conn. Sch. Law, Hartford, 1974-84, prof. law, 1984-89, dean and prof. law emeritus, 1989—; bd. dirs. Verde Exploration Ltd.; mem. legal adv. com. to bd. dirs. N.Y. Stock Exch., 1989-93; advisor corp. governance project, restatement of suretyship and restatement of agy. Am. Law Inst.; vis. lectr. U. Brabant, Tilburg, Netherlands, 1985, U. Internat. Bus. and Econs., Beijing, 1989, U. Sydney, 1992, Jagiellonian U., Cracow, Poland, 1992. Author: Corporate Responsibility in a Changing Society, 1972, The Megacorporation in American Society, 1975, The Law of Corporate Groups: Procedure, 1983, The Law of Corporate Groups: Bankruptcy, 1985, The Law of Corporate Groups: Substantive Common Law, 1987, The Law of Corporate Groups: General Statutory Law, 1989, The Law of Corporate Groups: Specific Statutory Law, 1992, The Multinational Challenge to Corporation Law, 1993, The Law of Corporate Groups: State Statutory Law, 1995, The Law of Corporate Groups: Enterprise Liability, 1998; mem. editl. bd. Harvard Law Rev., 1940-42, treas., 1941-42; contbr. articles to profl. jours. Trustee Black Rock Forest Preserve, Inc.; trustee emeritus Conn. Bar Found. Capt. USAAF, 1943-46, ETO. Decorated Bronze Star. Mem. ABA, Conn. Bar Assn., Am. Law Inst., Hartford Club, Harvard Club (Boston), Army & Navy Club (Washington), Phi Beta Kappa, Delta Upsilon. Home: 791 Prospect Ave Apt B-5 Hartford CT 06105-4224 Office: U Conn Sch Law 65 Elizabeth St Hartford CT 06105-2213

**BLUME, JAMES DONALD,** lawyer, consultant; b. St. Louis, Feb. 17, 1950; s. Donald David and Elizabeth Ann (Reitter) B.; m. Marilyn Rose Ender, Nov. 17, 1985. BA in Econs. cum laude, Cornell U., 1972; JD, U. Tex., 1975. Bar: Tex. 1975, U.S. Dist. Ct. (no., so., we. and ea. dists.) Tex. 1975, U.S. Ct. Appeals (5th and 11th cirs. 1975), U.S. Supreme Ct. 1989. Dir. rsch. charter revision com. City of Austin, Tex., 1975-76; staff atty. Tex. Dept. Comptroller, 1976-77, dir. claims, 1977-78, assoc. dep. comptroller, 1978-79; ptnr. Albach, Gutow, Rosenberg & Blume, Dallas, 1979-84, Gutow & Blume, P.C., Dallas, 1984-86, Mauro, Wendler, Sheets, Blume & Gutow, Dallas, 1986-90; pvt. practice, Dallas, 1990—; mem. State Unauthorized Practice Law Com., Dallas, 1986-90, regional chmn., 1987-90, state chmn., 1991—. Author: Hotel Occupancy Tax, 1984, Miscellaneous Occupation Tax, 1984, Federal Restrictions on Sales Tax, 1984. Pres. congregation St. Paul's Evang. and Ref. Ch., Dallas, 1984-85, 90-92; pres. NB, Tex. Assn. United Ch. of Christ, Dallas, 1987-89. Mem. ABA, Assn. Trial Lawyers Am., Tex. Trial Lawyers Assn., Texoma Sailing Club. Democrat. Avocation: sailing. General civil litigation, State and local taxation.

**BLUME, JOSHUA SHAI,** lawyer; b. Newark, Jan. 3, 1968; s. David Marvin and Gila (Markovsky) B. BS summa cum laude, Georgetown U., 1990, LLM in Internat. Law with distinction, 1996; JD, NYU, 1993. Bar: N.J. 1993, D.C. 1996, U.S. Dist. Ct. N.J. 1993, U.S. Ct. Vet. Claims 1999; cert. small claims and landlord-tenant mediator. Jud. law clk. to judge Hon. Roger F. Mahon Superior Ct. N.J., Flemington, 1993-94; assoc. Ulrichsen, Amarel & Eory, Skillman, N.J., 1994-95; atty.-advisor Bd. Vets. Appeals/ U.S. Dept. Vets. Affairs, Washington, 1996-99; appellate atty., gen. counsel U.S. Dept. Vet. Affairs, Washington, 1999—. Mem. Internat. Biogenic Soc., Phi Beta Kappa. Avocations: politics, creative writing, religion, philosophy, reading. Appellate. Home: 4501 Connecticut Ave NW Washington DC 20008-3710 Office: 625 Indiana Ave NW Ste 633 Washington DC 20004-2923

**BLUME, NETTIE LYNN,** lawyer; b. New Orleans; d. Harry and Doris (Klein) Cohen; m. Gary Lee Blume, Nov. 19, 1978; children: Zachary, Rachel. BA, Goucher Coll., 1976; JD, U. Ala., 1980. Bar: Ala. 1980. Asst. dist. atty. Tuscaloosa (Ala.) County Dist. Atty. Office, 1980-88; ptnr. Blume & Blume, Tuscaloosa, 1988—. Mem. Partlow Advocacy Com., Tuscaloosa, 1994—. Mem. Ala. State Bar Assn. (worker's compensation sect.), Tuscaloosa County Bar Assn. Criminal, General civil litigation, Family and matrimonial. Office: Blume & Blume 2300 University Blvd E Tuscaloosa AL 35404-4136

**BLUME, PAUL CHIAPPE,** lawyer; b. Omaha, Oct. 11, 1929; s. Herman Alexander and Marie (Simoni) B.; m. Mary Lou Higgins, June 28, 1958; children—Nancy, Julia, Paul II, William. BS in Commerce, Loyola U., Chgo., JD. Bar: Ill. 1957. Legal sect. mgr. Aldens Inc., 1957-58; assoc. Lord, Bissell & Brook, 1959-63, of counsel, 1983—; v.p., gen. counsel Nat. Assn. Ind. Insurers, Des Plaines, Ill., 1963-83, Ill. Ins. Info. Svc., 1987-96, Ill. Ins. Conf., Chgo., 1984-96; pres. Ins. Briefs, Inc., 1984—. Capt. U.S. Army, 1951-53. Mem. Ill. State Bar Assn., Chgo. Bar Assn., Fedn. Ins. Counsel, Turnberry Country Club (Crystal Lake, Ill.). Insurance, Administrative and regulatory, Legislative. Office: 115 S La Salle St Chicago IL 60603-3801

**BLUME, PETER KEEFE,** lawyer; b. Pitts., July 21, 1956; s. Robert Paul and Elizabeth Blume; m. Patricia Marie Williams, Sept. 17, 1988; children: Margaret, Robert, Emily, Michael, Catherine, Therese. BA, Yale U., 1978; JD, U. Notre Dame, 1981. Bar: Pa. 1981, U.S. Dist. Ct. (we. dist.) Pa. 1981. Assoc. Buchanan Ingersoll, Pitts., 1981-86; ptnr. Babst, Calland, P.C., Pitts., 1986-90, Yukevich, Blume, P.C., Pitts., 1990-97, Thorp, Reed & Armstron, Pitts., 1998—. Pres., trustee Aquinas Acad., Pitts., 1996—; bd. dirs. Cath. Action League, Pitts., 1996—. Mem. Harvard-Yale-Princeton Club, Yale Club Pitts. (bd. dirs. 1994-96). Roman Catholic. General corporate, Securities. Home: 405 Church Ln Allison Park PA 15101-1127 Office: Thorp Reed & Armstron One Riverfront Ctr Pittsburgh PA 15222

**BLUMENFELD, JEFFREY,** lawyer, educator; b. N.Y.C., May 13, 1948; s. Martin and Helen Kay (Smith) B.; m. Laura Madeline Ross, June 11, 1970; children: Jennifer Ross Blumenfeld, Joshua Ross Blumenfeld. AB in Religious Thought cum laude, Brown U., 1969; JD, U. Pa., 1973. Bar: D.C. 1973. Asst. U.S. atty. U.S. Atty. for D.C., Washington, 1975-79; trial atty. Antitrust div. U.S. Dept. of Justice, Washington, 1973-75, sr. trial atty. U.S. versus AT&T staff, 1979-82, asst. chief spl. regulated industries, 1982-84, chief U.S. versus AT&T staff, 1984; ptnr. Blumenfeld & Cohen, Washington, 1984—; v.p., gen. counsel Rhythms Net Connections, 1997—; adj. prof. Georgetown U. Law Ctr., Washington, 1983—. Bd. dirs. Charles E. Smith Jewish Day Sch., Washington, 1991-93. Democrat. Jewish. Antitrust, Communications, Federal civil litigation. Office: Blumenfeld & Cohen 1615 M St NW Ste 700 Washington DC 20036-3214

**BLUMENREICH, GENE ARNOLD,** lawyer; b. Washington, Apr. 1, 1943; s. Sidney M. and Dorothy N. Blumenreich; m. Margaret Jacobs, Sept. 4, 1966; children: Megan, Stephen, Kate. BA, U. Va., 1964; JD, Harvard U., 1967. Bar: Mass. 1969. Assoc. Surrey, Karasik, Gould & Greene, Washington, 1967-68; assoc. Fine & Ambrogne, Boston, 1968-73, ptnr., 1973-90; dir. Powers & Hall, Boston, 1990-95; ptnr. Nutter, McClennen & Fish, LLP, Boston, 1995—. Pres. League Sch. of Boston, Newton, 1979-81; chmn. Newton Ambulance Com., 1973-76; dir. Friends of Longfellow House, Cambridge, 1996—. Banking, Computer, Health. Office: Nutter McClennen & Fish LLP One International Pl Boston MA 02110

**BLUMENTHAL, JEFFREY MICHAEL,** lawyer; b. Putnam, Conn., Apr. 5, 1960; s. Bernard Saunders and Sheila (Molans) B.; m. Catherine Gallo, Sept. 20, 1987; children: Matthew Samuel, Scott Benjamin. BA summa cum laude, U. Hartford, 1981; JD, U. Va., 1985. Bar: Mass. 1985, Conn. 1986, U.S. Dist. Ct. Conn. 1986, U.S. Dist. Ct. (so. and ea. dists.) N.Y. 1988. Law clk. to Chief Judge T.F. Gilroy Daly, U.S. Dist. Ct. for Conn., 1985-87; assoc. Debevoise & Plimpton, N.Y.C., 1987-89; atty. for law and regulatory affairs Aetna Life & Casualty Co., Hartford, Conn., 1989-90, counsel, 1990-96; counsel Aetna/U.S. Healthcare, Hartford, 1996-98; corp. bus. unit year 2000 project mgr. Aetna, Inc., Hartford, 1998—. Mem. Defense Rsch. Inst., 1997—, Economic Development Comm., 1996—, vice-chair, 1999—; bd. dirs. Main St. Partnership, 1996-97, co-chair Economic Restructuring Comm., 1996-97, co-dir. Hartford Area Mediation Program, 1991-93, mem.; mem. mediation program Weaver High Sch., Hartford; com. mem. State of Conn. Study of Mediation Programs, 1992-93; chmn. Town of Simsbury Recycling Com., 1993-94; mem. Conn. Lawyers Clearinghouse on Affordable Housing, 1990-92; mem. bd. visitors U. Hartford Coll. Arts and Scis., West Hartford, Conn., 1989-90. Hardy C. Dillard legal writing fellow U. Va., 1983-84. Mem. Raven Soc. Federal civil litigation, State civil litigation, Health. Office: Aetna Inc 151 Farmington Ave Rm RE2L Hartford CT 06156-0002

**BLUMENTHAL, RICHARD,** state attorney general; m. Cynthia Blumenthal; 4 children. BA, Harvard Coll.; JD, Yale U., 1973. Law clk. Justice Harry A. Blackmun, 1974-75; U.S. atty. State of Conn., 1977-81, former rep., 1984-87, senator, 1987-90, state atty. gen., 1991—. Sgt. USMCR. Office: Atty Gen Office 55 Elm St Hartford CT 06106-1797*

**BLUMENTHAL, WILLIAM,** lawyer; b. White Plains, N.Y., Nov. 4, 1955; s. Louis and Mary (Meyer) B.; m. Marjory Susan Spodick, Dec. 30, 1979; 1 child, Deborah Louise. AB, Brown U., 1977, MA, 1977; JD, Harvard U., 1980. Bar: D.C. 1980, U.S. Dist. Ct. D.C. 1986. Cons. Policy & Mgmt. Assocs., Inc., Boston, 1977-80; teaching fellow Harvard U., Cambridge, Mass., 1978-80; assoc. Jones, Day, Reavis & Pogue, Washington, 1980-83; assoc. Sutherland, Asbill & Brennan, Washington, 1983-87, ptnr., 1988-93; ptnr. Kelley Drye & Warren, Washington, 1993-95, King & Spalding, Washington, 1995—. Editor Horizontal Mergers: Law and Policy, 1986; contbr. to book: The Merger Review Process, 1995, Mergers & Acquisitions Handbook, 1986. Harvey A. Baker fellow Brown U., 1977. Mem. ABA (chmn. Clayton Act com. 1992-94, chmn. monograph com. 1989-92, vice chmn. antitrust sect. 1997-98). Antitrust, Mergers and acquisitions, Federal civil litigation.

**BLUMROSEN, ALFRED WILLIAM,** law educator; b. Detroit, Dec. 14, 1928; s. Sol and Frances (Netzorg) B.; m. Ruth L. Gerber, July 3, 1952; children: Steven Marshall, Alexander Bernet. BA, U. Mich., 1950, JD, 1953. Bar: Mich. 1953, N.J. 1961, N.Y. 1981. Sole practice Detroit, 1953-55; mem. faculty Rutgers Law Sch., Newark, 1955—, prof., 1961—, acting dean, 1974-75, Herbert J. Hannoch scholar, 1984, Thomas A. Cowan prof., 1986—; dir. fed.-state rels., chief conciliations U.S. EOOC, 1965-67, cons. to chmn., 1977-79; advisor U.S. Dept. Justice, HUD, 1968-72, U.S. Dept. Labor, 1995-96; of counsel Kaye, Scholer, Fierman, Hays & Handler, N.Y.C., 1979-82; dir. Ford Found. intentional discrimination project Rutgers U., Law Sch., 1998—. Author: Black Employment and the Law, 1971, Modern Law: The Law Transmission System and Equal Employment Opportunity, 1993; contbr. articles to profl. jours. Fulbright scholar, South Africa, 1993, Rockefeller Inst. Resident scholar Bellagio Conf. Ctr., 1995. Mem. ABA (Ross essay prize 1983), Internat. Soc. for Labor Law and Social Security, Indsl. Relations Rsch. Assn., Order of Coif. Office: Rutgers U Sch Law 15 Washington St Newark NJ 07102-3105

**BLUMROSEN, RUTH GERBER,** lawyer, educator, arbitrator; b. N.Y.C., Mar. 7, 1927; d. Lipman Samuel and Dorothy (Finklebrand) Gerber; m. Alfred William Blumrosen, July 3, 1952; children: Steven Marshall, Alexander B. BA in Econs., U. Mich., 1947, JD, 1953. Bar: Mich. 1953, U.S. Supreme Ct. 1967, U.S. Ct. Appeals (3d cir.). pvt. practice law, Detroit, 1953-55; cons. civil rights litigation, 1958-65; acting chief advice and analyses, acting dir. compliance EEOC, Washington, 1965; asst. dean Howard U., Washington, 1965-67; consul to chmn. EEOC, 1979-80; expert EEO HHS, Washington, 1980-81; assoc. prof. Grad. Sch. Mgmt., Rutgers U., Newark, 1972-87; adj. prof. Rutgers Law Sch., 1994—; resident scholar Rockefeller Found., Bellagio, Italy, 1995. Adviser, N.J. Commn. on Sex Discrimination in the Statutes, 1983-85; commr. N.J. Gov.'s Study Commn. on Discrimination in Pub. Works Procurement and Constrn. Contracts, 1990-93. Gen. advisor, Rutgers Law Sch. Intentional Discrimination Proj., three year study of employment discrimination funded by The Ford Found.- 1998—, Fulbright scholar So. Africa, 1993. Mem. ABA, Fed. Bar Assn., Indsl. Rels. Rsch. Assn., Nat. Com. Pay Equity. Author: (with A. Blumrosen) Layoff or Worksharing: The Civil Rights Act of 1964 in the Recession of 1975; (with A. Blumrosen, et. al.) Downsizing and Employee Rights, 50 Rutgers Law Review 943, 1998; The Duty to Plan for Fair Employment Revisited: Worksharing in Hard Times, 1975; Wage Discrimination, Job Segregation and Title VII of Civil Rights Act of 1964, 1979; Wage Discrimination and Job Segregation: The Survival of a Theory, 1980; An Analysis of Wage Discrimination in N.J. State Service, 1983; Worksharing, STC and Affirmative Action in Shortime Compensation: A Formula for Worksharing; Remedies for Wage Discrimination., 1987. Office: 15 Washington St # 915 Newark NJ 07102-3105

**BLUMSTEIN, ANDRÉE KAHN,** lawyer; b. Poughkeepsie, N.Y., Oct. 5, 1945; d. Ludwig Werner and Tatyana (Uffner) Kahn; m. James Franklin Blumstein, June 25, 1971. BA, Vassar Coll., 1967; MPhil, Yale U., 1970, PhD, 1973; JD, Vanderbilt U., 1981. Bar: Tenn. 1981, U.S. Dist. Ct. (mid. dist.) Tenn. 1981, U.S. Ct. Appeals (6th cir.) 1982, U.S. Supreme Ct. 1985, N.Y. 1988. Vis. lectr. in German Duke U., Durham, N.C., 1974-75; asst. prof. German Vanderbilt U., Nashville, 1975-78; assoc. Trabue, Sturdivant and DeWitt, Nashville, 1981-86, ptnr., 1987-93; ptnr. Sherrard & Roe, 1993—; lectr. law Vanderbilt U. Sch. Law, 1993—; reporter on state and local tax Tax Analysts, 1991—; mem. civil justice reform act group Mid. Dist. of Tenn.; pres. Tenn. Health Decisions, 1997—. Author: Misogyny and Idealization, 1977; contbr. articles to profl. pubs. Bd. dirs. League for Hearing Impaired,Nashville, 1983—, sec., 1984, pres., 1985, 86, 87; pres. Am. Jewish Nashville chpt. 1998—. Mem. ABA, Fed. Bar Assn., Tenn. Bar Assn. (chmn. antitrust sect. 1986-90), Nashville Bar Assn. (chmn. appellate practice sect. 1992, 97, 99), Lawyers Assn. Women, Tenn. Lawyers Assn. for Women, Am. Inns of Cts. (Harry Phillips chpt. 1995), Order of Coif, Phi Beta Kappa. Antitrust, General civil litigation, Health. Office: Sherrard & Roe 424 Church St Ste 2000 Nashville TN 37219-3304

**BLUMSTEIN, EDWARD,** lawyer; b. Phila., Aug. 24, 1933; s. Isaac and Mollye (Rodofsky) B.; m. Susan Perloff, Aug. 13, 1983; 1 child, Daniel Blumstein. BS in Econs., U. Pa., 1955; JD, Temple U., 1958. Bar: U.S. Dist. Ct. (ea. dist.) Pa. 1959, U.S. Ct. Appeals (3rd cir.) 1959. Sole practice Phila., 1959-85; ptnr. Blumstein, Block & Pease, Phila., 1985—; adj. prof. Sch. Law Temple U., 1994—. Gen. Counsel to North American Ski Journalists Assn. With U.S. Army, 1958-64. Mem. ABA, Pa. Bar Assn., Phila. Bar Assn. (bd. govs. 1984-85, past chmn. family law sect. 1984). Assn., Phila. Trial Lawyers Assn., Acad. Family Mediators and Family Mediation Assn. Del. Valley (pres. 1990-91). Republican. Jewish. Lodge: B'nai B'rith.. Avocations: skiing, sailing, reading, photography. Family and matrimonial, Personal injury, Alternative dispute resolution. Office: Blumstein Block & Pease 1518 Walnut St Fl 4 Philadelphia PA 19102-3403

**BLUMSTEIN, JEFFREY PHILLIP,** lawyer; b. N.Y.C., June 27, 1947; s. Harold and Esther Blumstein; m. Vivien Verbeek, Jan. 22, 1983; children: Rene Marie, Allison. BA cum laude, Syracuse U., 1969; JD, Columbia U., 1973. Bar: N.J. 1974, U.S. Dist. Ct. N.J. 1974, U.S. Ct. Appeals (3rd cir.) 1986. Dep. atty. gen. N.J. Atty. Gen.'s Office, Trenton, 1973-77; ptnr. Szaferman, Lakind, Blumstein, Watter & Blader, P.C., Lawrenceville, N.J., 1977—. Mem. Assn. Trial Lawyers N.J., Mercer County Bar Assn. Avocations: tennis, reading biographies and histories. Federal civil litigation, State civil litigation, Appellate. Office: Szaferman Lakind Blumstein Watter & Blader PC 101 Grovers Mill Rd Ste 104 Lawrenceville NJ 08648-4706

**BLUNK, CHRISTIAN RAYMOND,** lawyer; b. Omaha, Oct. 14, 1958; s. Raymond C. and Barbara Nell (Allen) B.; m. Ann Elizabeth Gaines, July 30, 1983; children: Morgan Whitney, Lauren Elizabeth. BSBA with distinction, U. Nebr., 1980, JD, 1984. Bar: Nebr. 1984, U.S. Dist. Ct. Nebr. 1984. Pvt. practice, Omaha, 1984-86; ptnr. Bachman & Blunk, P.C., Omaha, 1986-90, Chatelain, Blunk & Maynard, Omaha, 1991-96, Andersen, Berkshire, Lausitsen & Brower, Omaha, 1996—. Mem. ABA, Nebr. Bar Assn., Omaha Bar Assn., Assn. Trial Lawyers Am., Nebr. Assn. Trial Attys., Masons, Kiwanis. Republican. Congregationalist. Avocation: sports. Securities, Personal injury, General corporate. Office: Anderson Berkshire Lauritsen & Brower 8805 Indian Hills Dr Ste 200 Omaha NE 68114-4077

**BLY, ROBERT MAURICE,** lawyer; b. Connersville, Ind., Oct. 31, 1944; s. Karl H. and Faye Virginia (DeHoff) B.; m. Ann Patrice Gleason, Aug. 24, 1968; 1 child, Thomas Robert. BS, Ball State U., 1966; JD, U. Tenn., 1973. Bar: Ill. 1973, Ind. 1974, U.S. Dist. Ct. (so. dist.) Ind. 1974, U.S. Dist. Ct. (no. dist.) Ind. 1978, U.S. Supreme Ct. 1981, Tenn. 1991, U.S. Dist. Ct. (ea. dist.) Tenn. 1992. Pub. sch. tchr. pub. schs., Ind., 1966-71; regional counsel's staff Chgo. (Ill.) Title & Trust Co., 1973-75; dep. prosecutor Porter County Ind., Valparaiso, 1975-76; pvt. practice law Valparaiso and Kokomo, Ind., 1976-91, Knoxville, 1992—; adj. instr. Ind. U., Kokomo, 1987-91; del. Ho. of Dels., Ind. Bar Assn., Indpls., 1988; founder Southeast Estate Planning Inst.; guest lectr. in field. Columnist Fairfield Glade Sun, 1993-94; contb. author: Generations Planning Your Legacy, 1999. Pres. Vols. in Cmty. Svc., Kokomo, 1980-85; del. Ind. State Rep. Conv., Indpls., 1986; mem. Nat. Rep. Senatorial Com., Washington, 1993-96. Fellow Esperti Peterson Inst. for Wealth Strategies, Offshore Inst., Mid South Estate Planning Forum (founding mem., pres. 1997—); mem. Nat. Network Estate Planning Attys., Tenn. Bar Assn. (tax, probate and trusts sect.). Episcopalian. Avocations: collecting and restoring classic automobiles, traveling. Estate planning, Estate taxation, Private international. Office: 9111 Cross Park Dr Ste D200 Knoxville TN 37923-4521

**BLYDENBURGH, DONALD RICHARD,** judge, educator; b. Huntington, N.Y., Feb. 20, 1952; s. Joseph Louis and Margaret Cora (Chapman) B.; m. Mary Kathleen Long, July 5, 1975; children: Donald Patrick, Jessica Michelle, Meghan Elizabeth. AA in Social Sci., Suffolk (N.Y.) C.C., 1972; BA in History and Polit. Sci., L.I. U., 1974; JD, Hofstra U., 1978. Bar: N.Y. 1979, U.S. Dist. Ct. (ea. and so. dists.) N.Y. 1979, U.S. Ct. Appeals (2nd cir.) 1982, U.S. Supreme Ct. 1984. Asst. county atty. Suffolk County Atty. Office, Hauppauge, N.Y., 1979-80; asst. town atty. Smithtown (N.Y.) Town Atty., 1980-83, town atty., 1983-86; pvt. practice law Hauppauge, 1986-96; justice N.Y. State Supreme Ct., Central Islip, 1997—; legislator Suffolk County, Hauppauge, 1986-96, presiding officer, 1990-96. Mem. N.Y. State Bar Assn., Suffolk County Bar Assn., Pi Gamma Mu. Office: NYS Supreme Ct Cohalan Ct Complex 400 Carleton Ave Central Islip NY 11722-4504

**BLYTH, JOHN E.,** lawyer, educator; b. Rochester, N.Y., Oct. 19, 1931; s. Ray G. and Ruby Luella (Spaulding) B.; m. Joanna E. Jennings, Aug. 23, 1963; children: Geoffrey E., Jennifer E., Jane Blyth Warren, James E. AB, Colgate U., 1953; LLB, NYU, 1960; JD, Goethe U., 1962. Bar: N.Y. 1961. Ptnr. Harter, Secrest & Emery, Rochester, 1961-93, Hiscock & Barclay, Rochester, 1994-95, Blyth & Lamb, Rochester, 1995—; speaker in field; adj. prof. Cornell U. Law Sch., Ithaca, N.Y., 1990—; former trustee Keuka Coll., Keuka Park, N.Y., 1986—. Contbr. articles to profl. jours. Pres. Palmyra (N.Y.) Macedon Sch. Bd., 1969-72, Citizen's Tax League, Rochester, 1984-86. Sgt. U.S. Army, 1954-57, ETO. Named Internat. Exec. of Yr., Rochester C. of C., 1994. Mem. N.Y. State Bar Assn. (chair real property law sect. 1990-91), Am. Coll. Real Estate Lawyers. Avocation: organist. Real property, Private international. Home: 1428 Hidden Pond Ln Walworth NY 14568-9538 Office: Blyth & Lamb 510 Wilder Bldg 1 E Main St Rochester NY 14614-1807

**BLYTHE, JAMES DAVID, II,** lawyer; b. Indpls., Oct. 20, 1940; s. James David and Marjorie M. (Horne) B.; m. Sara S. Frantz, Nov. 21, 1974; 1 child; Amanda Renee. BS, Butler U., 1962; JD, Ind. U., 1966. Bar: Ind. 1966, U.S. Supreme Ct. (so. dist.) Ind., 1966, U. S. Supreme Ct. 1980, U.S. Ct. Appeals (7th cir.), 1993. Diplomate, U.S. congl. staff asst. Ct. Practice Inst., 1965-69; majority atty. Ind. Ho. of Reps., 1967, 69; dep. prosecutor Marion County Prosecutor's Office, 1966, 68; pvt. practice Indpls., 1966—; sr. ptnr. Blythe & Ost, 1994—; mem. com. on character and fitness Ind. Supreme Ct., 1974-94; host TV show Ask a Lawyer, 1977-79. Bd. dirs. Marion County chpt. Am.Cncer Soc., 1971-76 (pres. 1975-76), Cen. Ind. coun. Boy Scouts Am., 1969-72, exec. com., 1969-71, Crossroads of Am. Coun., 1972-87, executive com. 1976-84, pres., 1979-81, life mem 1987, Salvation Army, 1975—, vice chmn., 1986, chmn., 1987, 88; Ind. chmn. West Indies Ambassador Exchange, Jaycees, 1972-73; pres. N.Crl. H.S. Alumni, 1996-98; mem. lawyers fund raising com. Indpls. Mus. Art., 1973-74; co-membership chmn, Friends of Channel 20, 1975;. Recipient cert. of Merit Am.Cancer Soc., 1971, 74-75, Outstanding Service award Indpls. br. Am. Cancer Soc., 1972-73, Richard E. Rowland award Jaycees, 1971-72, Stanley K. Lacy Meml. award Jaycees, 1974, Disting. Service award Jaycees, 1974, Silver Beaver award Boy Scouts Am., 1981, Live Mem. award Nat. Eagle Scout Assn., 1996; commendation Gov. State of Ind., 1973; named Man of Yr. Am. Cancer Soc., 1974; Jim Blythe Day named in his honor, Mayor of Indpls., 1976; named Sagamore of the Wabash, 1981, North Central Hall of Fame, 1999.. Mem. Indpls. Bar Assn. (bd. mgrs. 1978-81, 89-90, chmn. grievance com. 1980-88),Kiwanis (v.p. Indpls 1986-87, pres. 1987-88, found pres. 1988-89, Ind. dist. found. 1989—, pres. 1995-98, ptrd. Indpls. found. 1989, civic award, 1991, Abe Lincoln Fellow, 1993, named Kiwanis Man of the Year, 1997), Kappa Sigma, PHi Delta Phi. Republican. Presbyterian. General corporate, Family and matrimonial, General civil litigation. Home: 11028 E Lakeshore Dr Carmel IN 46033-4402 Office: 10585 N Meridian St Ste 200 Indianapolis IN 46290-1067

**BOACKLE, K.F.,** lawyer, writer, educator; b. Jackson, Miss., Mar. 13, 1944; s. Abraham Milton and Clara Josephine Boackle; m. Sheila Marie Ashker; children: David, Paul, Mark. BBA, Loyola U., 1966; JD, Jackson Sch. Law, 1972. Real estate broker Jackson, 1971—, pvt. law practice, 1979—. Author: Mississippi Real Estate Contracts and Closings, 1991, Mississippi Real Estate Foreclosure Law, 1994, Real Estate Closing Deskbook, 1997. Mem. ABA, Miss. Bar Assn., Tri-County Real Estate Attys. Assn. (pres. 1989-90), Hinds County Bar Assn. Real property, General civil litigation, Contracts commercial. Office: 16 Northtown Dr Ste 102 Jackson MS 39211-3058

**BOARDMAN, HAROLD FREDERICK, JR.,** lawyer, corporate executive; b. Darby, Pa., Nov. 23, 1939; s. Harold Frederick and Juanita (Sorzano) B.; m. Martha Eltie, May 23, 1987; children: Kimberly, Leslie. BS, Trinity Coll., Hartford, Conn., 1961; JD with honors, George Washington U., 1964; grad. advanced mgmt. program, Duke U., 1988. Bar: D.C. 1965, Hawaii 1971, N.J. 1974, U.S. Dist. Ct. D.C. 1965, U.S. Ct. Appeals (D.C. cir.) 1965, U.S. Ct. Mil. Appeals 1965, U.S. Supreme Ct. 1974. Gen. atty. Fed. Home Loan Bank Bd., Washington, 1964-66; atty. Hoffmann-LaRoche, Inc., Nutley, N.J., 1966; with Hoffmann-LaRoche, Inc., Nutley, 1973-94, sec., 1979-94, assoc. gen. counsel, 1981-88, v.p., gen. counsel, bd. dirs. exec. com., 1988-94, mem. pharms. mgmt. com., ret., 1995; of counsel Crummy, Del Deo, Dolan, Griffinger & Vecchione, Newark, 1995-96; exec. v.p., gen. counsel Rhone-Poulenc Inc., Princeton, N.J., 1996-98; bd. dirs. Rhone Poulenc Inc., 1996; exec. v.p., gen. counsel Rhone Poulenc Rorer, Collegeville, PA, 1998; bd. advisors N.J. Econ. Devel. Ctr., Newark; corp. counsel faculty Seton Hall U. Cabinet mem. United Way Passaic Valley, N.J., 1991-93. Capt. JAGC, USAF, 1966-73. Mem. ABA, N.J. Bar Assn., Hawaii Bar Assn., D.C. Bar Assn., N.J. Corp. Counsel Assn., Am. Corp. Counsel Assn., Pharm. Mfrs. Assn. (exec. com. law sect. 1991-94), Internat. Assn. Def. Counsel. Republican. Episcopalian. Avocations: golf, boating. General corporate. Home: 1225 Denbigh Ln Radnor PA 19087-4646

**BOARDMAN, MARK SEYMOUR,** lawyer; b. Birmingham, Ala., Mar. 16, 1958; s. Frank Seymour and Flora (Sarinopoulos) B.; m. Cathryn Dunkin, 1983; children:Wilson Paul, Joanna Christina. BA cum laude, U. Ala., 1979, JD, 1982. Bar: Ala. 1982, U.S. Dist. Ct. (no. dist.) Ala. 1982, U.S. Ct. Appeals (11th cir.) 1983, U.S. Supreme Ct. 1987. Assoc. Spain, Gillon, Riley, Tate & Etheredge, Birmingham, 1982-84; ptnr. Porterfield, Scholl, Bainbridge, Mims and Harper, P.A., Birmingham, 1984-93, Boardman Carr & Weed, P.C., Birmingham, 1993—. Pres. Holy Trinity Holy Cross Greek Orthodox Cathedral, 1991, 92, sec., 1987, asst. treas., 1986, treas., 1988, 89, v.p., 1990, 96, 97, 98, 99, bd. auditors, 1994; mem. coun. Greek Orthodox Diocese of Atlanta, 1992-95; mem. Shelby County (Ala.) Work Release Commn., sec., 1996. Mem. ABA, Ala. State Bar, Shelby County Bar Assn. (treas. 1992-93, sec. 1994, v.p. 1995, pres. 1996), Birmingham Bar Assn. (co-chmn. econs. of law com. 1997, local bar liaison com. 1997), Am. Jud. Soc., Ala. Def. Lawyers Assn., Def. Rsch. Inst., Ala. Claims Assn., Order of Barristers, Phi Beta Kappa, Delta Sigma Rho-Tau Kappa Alpha, Pi Sigma Alpha. Greek Orthodox. Insurance, General civil litigation, Personal injury. Home: 1915 Wellington Rd Birmingham AL 35209-4026 Office: Boardman Carr & Weed PC PO Box 59465 Birmingham AL 35259-9465

**BOARDMAN, MICHAEL NEIL,** lawyer; b. N.Y.C., Jan. 7, 1942; s. Martin Vincent and Hannah (Greisman) B.; m. Constance Hallie Kramer, Aug. 28, 1966; children: Adam Lawrence, Amy Suzanne. AB, Syracuse U., 1964; JD, Seton Hall U., 1967. Bar: N.J. 1968, U.S. Dist. Ct. N.J. 1968, U.S. Supreme Ct. 1971. Assoc. Liebowitz, Krafte & Liebowitz, Englewood, N.J., 1968-69; ptnr. Boardman & Epstein, Saddle Brook, N.J., 1969-75; pvt. practice Saddle Brook and Ridgewood, N.J., 1975—; designated counsel State of N.J. Office of Pub. Defender, 1970-77; mem. skills tng. course faculty Inst. Continuing Legal Edn., Newark, 1976—; vice-chmn. Bergen County dist. fee arbitration com. Supreme Ct. N.J., 1987-88, chmn. 1988-89, mem. Bergen County dist. ethics com., 1991.; lectr. Inst. Continuing Legal Edn., Newark, 1979—. Dem. committeeman County of Bergen, N.J., 1974-76; mem. Citizens Com. to Study Declining Enrollment, Glen Rock, N.J., 1975-77; panelist Matrimonial Early Settlement Program, Bergen County, 1978—; mem. Glen Rock Jewish Ctr., Soc. of the Valley Hosp., Ridgewood, N.J.; mem. profl. adv. bd. Nat. Hypoglycemia Assn., Inc., 1985—. Mem. ABA, N.J. State Bar Assn., Bergen County Bar Assn., Am. Judicature Soc., NOW, Adoptive Parents Orgn. Bergen County Club. General practice, Family and matrimonial, Real property. Home: 48 Glen Blvd Glen Rock NJ 07452-1626 Office: 4 Franklin Ave Ridgewood NJ 07450-3202

**BOARDMAN, RICHARD JOHN,** lawyer; b. Newton, Mass., Mar. 28, 1940; s. Raymond Everett and Miriam Lucile (Temperley) B.; 1 child, Lawrence Luke. BA, U. Mass., 1962; JD, U. N.D., 1965; LLM, Yale U., 1966. Bar: N.D. 1965, Mo. 1970, U.S. Dist. Ct. (ea. dist.) Mo. 1970, U.S. Ct. Appeals (8th cir.) 1970, U.S. Supreme Ct. 1968. Asst. prof. law Cath. U. of Am. Law Sch., Washington, 1966-69; assoc. dir., atty. Legal Aid Soc., St. Louis, 1969-74; asst. prof. of comm. med. St. Louis U. Med. Sch., 1974-78; pvt. practice, 1978—; pres. Lafayette Title Co., 1980—; v.p. Gateway Legal Svcs., St. Louis, 1997—; bd. dirs. Bar Plan Title Ins. Co. Pres. Singer Inst., St. Louis, 1982-85; bd. dirs. Kids in the Middle, Inc., St. Louis, 1980-82, Places for People, Inc., St. Louis, 1973-75. Mem. ABA, ACLU, Mo. Ind. Title Assn., Mo. Bar Assn. (subcom. chair property com. 1988-90, chair property law com. 1996-98), St. Louis Met. Bar Assn. (co-chair title ins. sect., 1990—, chair real property sect. 1987-89), Am. Land Title Assn., Nat. Network Estate Planning Attys. (charter). Real property, Probate, Estate planning. Office: 4526 S Grand Blvd Saint Louis MO 63111-1039

**BOARDMAN, ROBERT A.,** lawyer; b. 1947. BA, Muskingum Coll., 1969; JD, Case Western Reserve U., 1972. Bar: Ohio 1972, Colo. 1976. Assoc. atty. Roetzel & Andress, 1972-75, atty., 1975-83; asst. gen. coun., sec. Manville Corp., Denver, 1983-87, v.p., sec., 1988-90; sr. v.p., gen. coun. Navistar Internat. Transp. Corp., Chgo., 1990—. E-mail Address: RABG@NAVISTAR.com. General corporate, Securities, Finance. Office: Navistar Internat Transp Corp 455 N Cityfront Plaza Dr Chicago IL 60611-5503

**BOAS, FRANK,** lawyer; b. Amsterdam, North Holland, The Netherlands, July 22, 1930; came to U.S., 1940; s. Maurits Coenraad and Sophie (Brandel) B.; m. Edith Louise Bruce, June 30, 1981 (dec. July 1992); m. Jean Scripps, Aug. 6, 1993. AB cum laude, Harvard U., 1951, JD, 1954. Bar: U.S. Dist. Ct. D.C. 1955, U.S. Ct. Appeals (D.C. cir.) 1955; U.S. Supreme Ct. 1958. Atty. Office of the Legal Adviser U.S. State Dept., Washington, 1957-59; pvt. practice, Brussels and London, 1959-79; of counsel Patton, Boggs & Blow, Washington, 1975-80; pres. Frank Boas Found., Inc., Cambridge, Mass., 1980—. Mem. U.S. delegation to UN confs. on law of sea, Geneva, 1958, 60; vice chmn. Commn. for Ednl. Exch., Brussels, 1980-87; mem. vis. com. Harvard Law Sch., 1987-91, Ctr. for Internat. Affairs, 1988—; dir. Found. European Orgn. for Research and Treatment of Cancer, Brussels, 1978-87, Paul-Henri Spaak Found., Brussels, 1981—, East-West Ctr. Found., Honolulu, 1990—, Law of the Sea Inst., Honolulu, 1992-97, Pacific Forum CSIS, Honolulu, 1996—, Honolulu Acad. Arts, 1997—; hon. sec. Am. C. of C. in Belgium, 1966-78. With U.S. Army, 1955-57. Decorated Officer of the Order of Leopold II, comdr. Order of the Crown (Belgium), comdr. Order of Merit (Luxembourg); recipient Tribute of Appreciation award U.S. State Dept., 1981, Harvard Alumni Assn. award, 1996. Mem. ABA, Fed. D.C. Bar Assn., Pacific and Asian Affairs Coun. (pres.), Honolulu Com. Fgn. Relations, Pacific, Outrigger Canoe (Honolulu), Travellers (London), Am. and Common Market (Brussels pres. 1981-85), Honolulu Social Sci. Assn. Private international, Public international, Education and schools. Home: 4463 Aukai Ave Honolulu HI 96816-4858

**BOBAY, CRAIG JOHN,** magistrate; b. Ft. Wayne, Ind., Sept. 21, 1956; s. Thomas Eugene and Joan F. (Alspaugh) B.; m. Nancy Ann Verstynen, Aug. 13, 1977; children: Elizabeth V., Mollie A., Anne M. BA, Ind. U., Ft. Wayne, 1980; JD cum laude, Ind. U., Bloomington, 1991. Bar: Ind. 1991, U.S. Dist. Ct. (no. and so. dists.) Ind. 1991, U.S. Ct. Appeals (7th cir.) 1992. Law clk. U.S. Dist. Ct. (no. dist.), Ft. Wayne, 1991-93; atty. Hunt Suedhoff LLP, Ft. Wayne, 1993-97; dir. ct. ops. Allen Superior Ct., Ft. Wayne, 1985-88, referee, 1995-97, magistrate, 1997—. Bd. dirs. Bishop Bishop Dwenger H.S., Ft. Wayne, 1998—; pres., charter mem. Ind. Fedn. Cath. Schs., Indpls., 1995-97; bd. dirs., pres. St. Jude Sch. Bd., Ft. Wayne, 1991-95. Mem. ABA, Allen County Bar Assn. Roman Catholic. Avocations: hiking, running, skiing, brewing. Office: Allen Superior Ct Allen County Courthouse 715 S Calhoun St Rm 208 Fort Wayne IN 46802-1805

**BOBBITT, RONALD ALBERT,** lawyer; b. Chgo., Dec. 23, 1953; s. Booker T. and Clara M. Bobbitt; married; 2 children. BS, U. Ill., 1976; JD, Antioch U., 1979. Bar: Ill. 1979, U.S. Dist. Ct. (no. dist.) Ill. 1979, U.S. Ct. Appeals (7th cir.) 1979. Clk. to adminstrv. asst. to chief justice, 1978; sr. ptnr. Bobbitt & Assocs., Chgo., 1979—. Mem. NAACP, Chgo., 1990. Recipient Key to City Mayor's Office, Birmingham, 1980, Goodwill Community Svc. award Chgo. Heights, Ill., 1981. Mem. ABA, Nat. Bar Assn., Nat. Bus. Execs., Nat. Urban League, Chgo. Bar Assn., Cook County Bar Assn., Psi Chi, Phi Eta Sigma. Avocation: horseback riding. Office: Bobbitt & Assocs 155 N Michigan Ave Chicago IL 60601-7511

**BOBIS, DANIEL HAROLD,** lawyer; b. N.Y.C., May 1, 1918; s. Morris N. and Sarah C. Bobis; m. Selma Linder, May 15, 1960; children: Jodee E. Bobis Verbow, Stacee M. Bobis Miccio. LLB, St. Lawrence U., 1939; BS, Columbia U., 1947. Bar: N.Y. 1949, U.S. Patent and Trademark Office 1950, U.S. Supreme Ct. 1961, U.S. Ct. Appeals (3d cir.) 1963, N.J. 1964, U.S. Dist. Ct. N.J. 1964, U.S. Ct. Appeals (fed. cir.) 1982. Patent atty. Worthington Corp. (later Studebaker-Worthington Corp.), Harrison, N.J., 1946-1952, patent counsel, until 1969; mem. firm Popper, Bain, Bobis, Gilfillan & Rhoades, Newark, N.J., 1969-74, Popper & Bobis, Newark, N.J., 1974-79, Popper, Bobis & Jackson, Newark, N.J., 1979-88; of counsel Lerner, David, Littenberg, Krumholz & Mentlik, Westfield, N.J., 1988—; a founder Ann. Outstanding Patent Award, N.J. Coun. for R & D, 1966; former instr. on intellectual property matters and causes Horizon Sch. for Parlegal Tng., Linden, N.J. Capt. pilot AC, AUS, 1943-46; ETO. Decorated Air medal with one silver and 3 bronze oak leaf clusters, Purple Heart. Mem. ABA (chmn., mem. intellectual property coms.), N.J. Bar Assn. (chmn., mem. intellectual property coms.), N.J. Patent Law Assn. (pres. 1966, chmn., mem. intellectual property coms.), various N.J. county bar assns. (chmn., mem. intellectual property coms.). Intellectual property, Patent, Trademark and copyright. Home: 30 Burnham Ct Scotch Plains NJ 07076-3147 Office: Lerner David Littenberg Krumholz & Mentlik 600 South Ave W Ste 300 Westfield NJ 07090-1497

**BOBROWSKY, KIM RUSSELL,** lawyer, songwriter, mediator, arbitrator; b. Ann Arbor, Mich., Jan. 1, 1951; d. Alfred R. and Elaine (Elkind) B.; married (div. Apr. 21, 1992); 1 child, Joshua. BA with honors, Penn State U., 1972; JD, Duquesne U., 1976. Bar: Pa. 1976, U.S. Dist. Ct. (we. dist.) Pa. 1977, U.S. Ct. Appeals (3d cir.) 1989, U.S. Supreme Ct. 1992. Plaintiff trial atty. Evans, Ivory & Evans, Pitts., 1976-83; def. trial atty. Continental Ins. Co., Pitts., 1983-90; plaintiff, def. trial atty. Cipriani & Werner, Pitts., 1990-95, of counsel, 1995-96; pvt. practice mediation & arbitration, 1995-96; ptnr. Bowes & Bobrosky, Pitts., 1996—; adj. cert. settlement judge and arbitrator, U.S. Dist. Ct. Writer (songs) Magic Moments, 1993, My Fantasy, 1993, We've Got This Love, 1993. Mem. Pa. Trial Lawyers Assn., Def. Rsch. Inst., Am. Arbitration Assn. (mem. panel neutrals), Masonic Lodge (past master 1980). Avocations: tai chi, piano, bridge, guitar. Product liability, Personal injury, Insurance. Home: 3005 Eastview Rd Bethel Park PA 15102-1629

**BOCCARDO, JAMES FREDERICK,** lawyer; b. San Francisco, July 1, 1911; s. John Humbert and Erminia Gemma (Ferrando) B.; m. Lorraine Dimmett, Nov. 21, 1936; children: Leanne Boccardo Rees, John Humbert II. AB, San Jose State U., 1931; JD, Stanford U., 1934. Bar: Calif. 1934, D.C. Sole practice San Jose, Calif., 1934—. Mem. ABA, Calif. Bar Assn., D.C. Bar Assn., Internat. Acad. Trial Lawyers, Assn. Trial Lawyers Am., Calif. Trial Lawyers Assn., Santa Clara County Trial Lawyers Assn., Inner Circle Advs. (past pres.). Republican. Avocations: golf, aviation. Fax: 408-354-1021. Personal injury, Condemnation, General civil litigation. Office: 111 W St John St San Jose CA 95113-1113 also: 985 University Ave Ste 12 Los Gatos CA 95032-7639

**BOCCHI, LINDA ROSA,** lawyer; b. Bklyn., June 14, 1957; d. Arcadio and Doris Esther (Vega) Figueroa; m. Gregory J. Bocchi, May 30, 1987; 1 child, Matthew Gregory. BA in Econs., Harper Coll., 1977; JD, Cornell U., 1980. Bar: D.C. 1980. Atty. F.C.C., Washington, 1980-88; sr. assoc. Baker & Hostetler, Washington, 1988-92; gen. counsel Copywright Royalty Tribunal, Washington, 1992-93; v.p., assoc. gen. counsel Recording Industry Assn., Washington, 1993—. Office: RIAA 1330 Connecticut Ave NW Ste 300 Washington DC 20036-1725

**BOCCIA, BARBARA,** lawyer; b. Bklyn., Dec. 16, 1957; d. Daniel and Marie Boccia. BS with honors, U. Tenn., 1980; JD, U. of the Pacific, 1983. Bar: Calif. 1983, D.C. 1983. Litigation lawyer, ptnr. Mullen & Filippi, San Francisco, 1983-86; litigation lawyer Jones, Brown, Clifford & McDevitt, San Francisco, 1987-88; litigation lawyer, mng. lawyer Crymes, Hardie & Heer, San Francisco, 1988-89; pvt. practice Daly City, Calif., 1989-92; sr. trial atty., supervising atty. Akin & Carmody, San Francisco, 1992-94; prin. Law Office of Barbara Boccia, Inc., Daly City, Calif., 1994—; arbitrator, corp. cons., writer, educator, speaker in field. Vol. Hotline and Spks. Bur., San Francisco AIDS Found., 1987-90; mem. founding bd. dirs. Northeast Ark. Regional AIDS Network; HIV instr. ARC, 1991. Named One of Outstanding Young Women in Am., 1980. Mem. San Francisco Bar Assn., Indsl. Claims Assn., Ins. Edn. Assn., Queen's Bench, Italian Welfare Agy. Avocations: jogging, basketball, aerobics, writing, being a mom. State civil litigation, Workers' compensation, Insurance. Office: PO Box 2210 Daly City CA 94017-2210

**BOCCIA ROSADO, ANN MARIE,** paralegal; b. San Pedro, Calif., Apr. 23, 1958; d. Franklin S. and Julia (Mattera) Boccia; m. Robert Daniel Rosado. AA, Harbor Coll., 1983; paralegal cert., Continental Tech. Inst., L.A., 1986. Invoicing/sales rep. Bronson of Calif., Gardena, 1976-78; traffic mgr. GSC Athletic Equipment, San Pedro, 1978-81; exec. legal sec. Stein, Shostak, Shostak & O'Hara, L.A., 1981; paralegal, computer adminstr. Stolpman, Krissman, Elber, Mandel & Katzman LLP, Long Beach, Calif., 1981—; cons. San Pedro Chiropractic Ctr., 1989-96; instr. Michaels Stores, Inc., 1997—. Recipient Presdl. award Calif. Trial Lawyers Assn., 1988; named Legal Sec. of the Yr., 1998. Mem. Nat. Paralegal Assn., Assn. Trial Lawyers Am., L.A. Trial Lawyers Assn. (speaker 1989-92, moderator 1991, voter registration com. 1988-89, Ann. Law Day participant 1991-92), L.A. Paralegal Assn., Long Beach Legal Secs. Assn. (chmn. benefits 1995—, chmn. day-in-ct. 1998—, treas. 1998, v.p. 1999). Democrat. Roman Catholic. Avocations: computer programming, walking, reading, boating, needlepoint. Office: Stolpman Krissman Elber Mandel & Katzman LLP 111 W Ocean Blvd Flr 19 Long Beach CA 90802-4632

**BOCHETTO, GEORGE ALEXANDER,** lawyer; b. Bklyn., Oct. 7, 1952; m. Paula Agins, Aug. 6, 1987; children: David, Evan. BA, SUNY, Albany, 1975; JD cum laude, Temple U., 1978. Bar: Pa. 1978, N.Y. 1995, U.S. Dist. Ct. (ea. dist.) Pa. 1979, U.S. Supreme Ct. 1992, U.S. Tax Ct. 1986. Pvt. practice, 1979-90; assoc. Pelino & Lentz, P.C., Phila., 1978-79, Monteverde & Hemphill, P.C., Phila., 1990-93, Bochetto & Lentz, P.C., Phila., 1993—. Contbr. articles to profl. jours. Bd. dirs. Pa. Spl. Olympics, 1986—; mem. Rep. State Com., Pa., 1992—; appt. Pa. State Athletic Commr. Gov. Ridge, 1995—. Mem. ABA, Pa. Bar Assn., Phila. Bar Assn. (subcom. chairperson profl. responsibility com. 1978—). Avocations: amateur boxing, boating, sports. General civil litigation, Contracts commercial, Professional liability. Office: Bochetto & Lentz PC 1524 Locust St Philadelphia PA 19102-4401

**BOCHICCHIO, VITO SALVATORE,** lawyer; b. Pitts.; s. Richard John and Francesca (Romano) B.; m. Giovanna Febbraro, Nov. 21, 1992; children: Richard, Giosue, Francesco. BA, MA, Duquesne U., 1984, JD, 1987. Bar: Pa. 1987, U.S. Dist. Ct. (we. dist.) Pa. 1987. Asst. dist. atty. Office Allegheny County Dist. Atty., Pitts., 1988-90; assoc. Rothman Gordon, Pitts., 1990-94; ptnr. O'Brien, Rulis & Bochicchio, Pitts., 1994—; sec. Big Jim's Inc., Pitts., 1992—. Committeeman Allegheny County Dem. Com., Pitts., 1981—. Mem. Allegheny County Bar Assn., Small Mfrs. Coun., Calabria Club. Roman Catholic. Avocation: karate. Workers' compensation, Insurance, Personal injury. Office: O'Brien Rulis & Bochicchio 100 5th Ave Ste 5 Pittsburgh PA 15222-1821

**BOCK, VALERIE L.,** lawyer; b. Bloomington, Ind., Dec. 31, 1968; d. Loren V. and Dorothy F. Bock; m. Arnaud Georges Tisserand, Jan. 27, 1996. BA in Liberal Studies, Ky. State U., 1991; JD, U. Louisville, 1994. Bar: Ky., U.S. Dist. Ct. (we. dist.) Ky. Assoc. atty. Law Offices of Steve P. Robey, Providence, Ky., 1996—. General civil litigation, Personal injury, Appellate. Office: Law Offices of Steve P Robey 508 E Main St Providence KY 42450-1210

**BOCKELMAN, JOHN RICHARD,** lawyer; b. Chgo., Aug. 8, 1925; s. Carl August and Mary (Ritchie) B. Student, U. Wis., 1943-44, Northwestern U., 1944-45, Harvard U., 1945, U. Hawaii, 1946; BSBA, Northwestern U., 1946; MA in Econs., U. Chgo., 1949, JD, 1951. Bar: Ill. 1951. Atty.-advisor Chgo. ops. office AEC, 1951-52; asso. firm Schradzke, Gould & Ratner, Chgo., 1952-57, Brown, Dashow & Langeluttig, Chgo., 1957-59, Antonow & Weissbourd, Chgo., 1959-61; partner firm Burton, Isaacs, Bockelman & Miller, Chgo., 1961-69; pvt. practice Chgo., 1970—; prof. bus. law Ill. Inst. Tech., Chgo., 1950-82; lectr. econs. DePaul U., Chgo., 1952-53; bd. dirs., sec. Arlington Engring. Co.; bd. dirs., v.p., Universal Distbrs., Inc. Pres. 1212 Lake Shore Dr. Condo Assn., Chgo., Near North Assn. of Condo Pres., Chgo. Served with USNR, 1943-46. Mem. ABA, Ill. Bar Assn., Chgo. Bar Assn., Cath. Lawyers Guild Chgo., Lake Point Tower Club, Barclay Ltd. Club, Whitehall Club, Internat. Club, Anvil Club (East Dundee, Ill.), Univ. Club (San Diego), Tavern Club (Chgo.), Phi Delta Theta. General corporate, Probate, Real property. Home: 1212 N Lake Shore Dr Chicago IL 60610-2371 Office: 1212 N Lake Shore Dr # 24b-5 Chicago IL 60610-2371

**BODANSKY, ROBERT LEE,** lawyer; b. N.Y.C.. BA cum laude, Syracuse U., 1974; JD with honors, George Washington U., 1977; cert. postgrad. studies, Ctr. Internat. Legal Studies, Salzburg, Austria, 1978. Bar: Md. 1978, D.C. 1978, U.S. Dist. Ct. Md. 1978, U.S. Ct. Appeals (D.C. cir.) 1980, U.S. Dist. Ct. D.C. 1980, U.S. Ct. Appeals (4th cir.) 1981, U.S. Supreme Ct. 1982. First assoc., then ptnr. Feldman, Krieger, Goldman & Tish, Washington, 1978-83; ptnr. Feldman, Bodansky & Rubin, Washington, 1984-95; prin. Freer, McGarry, Bodansky & Rubin, P.C., Washington, 1995-97; ptnr. Nixon, Hargrave, Devans & Doyle, LLP (now Nixon Peabody LLP), Washington, 1997—; advisor internat. bus. law and taxation programs McGeorge Sch. Law, Sacramento, Calif., 1985—. Author: Special Problems of Subcontractors and Suppliers, 1987. Legal advisor Parkwood Resident's Assn., Kensington, Md., 1984; bd. dirs. Ridgeleigh Residents' Assn., 1987—, Congregation Har Shalom, 1989-91; tchr. Adas Israel Congregation, Washington, 1975-91. Mem. ABA (chmn. subcom. internat. and foreign bus. law young lawyers div. 1978-80), Md. State Bar Assn., D.C. Bar Assn. Contracts commercial, General corporate, Real property. Office: Nixon Peabody LLP 1 Thomas Cir NW Ste 700 Washington DC 20005-5802

**BODAS, MARGIE RUTH,** lawyer; b. Virginia, Minn., Mar. 15, 1954; d. William Elmer and Delia (Isaacson) Bodas. BA in Comms., U. Minn., Duluth, 1976; JD, William Mitchell Coll. Law, St. Paul, 1986. Bar: Minn. 1986, U.S. Dist. Ct. Minn. 1986. News editor Mesabi Dailey News, Virginia, 1976-80; exec. dir. Quad Cities Drug Commn., Virginia, 1980-82; with customer svc. West Pub., St. Paul, 1982-84; law clk. Hon. Hyam Segell, Ramsey County, St. Paul, 1984-86; assoc. Hanft, Friede, Swelbar & Burns, P.A., Duluth, Minn., 1986-87; lawyer, shareholder Lommen Nelson Cole & Stageberg, P.A., Mpls., 1988—. Author column on trends. Mem. steering com. Leadership Mpls., 1997—, co-chair steering com., 1999—. Mem. ABA, Minn. Bar Assn. (chair publs. com. 1990-92), Hennepin County Bar Assn. (chair workers compensation sect. 1998—), C. of C. Mpls. Lutheran. Avocations: black and white photography, writing, gardening, sewing. General civil litigation, Workers' compensation. Office: Lommen Nelson Cole & Stageberg PA 1800 IDS Ctr 80 S 8th St Minneapolis MN 55402-2100

**BODDEN, THOMAS ANDREW,** lawyer; b. Lafayette, Ind., Dec. 18, 1945; s. William A. and Dorothy (Schlacks) B.; m. Irene S. Hiye; children: Wendee, Todd, Christopher. AB, Cornell U., 1968; JD, U. Miami, 1974. Bar: Hawaii 1975. Assoc. Torkildson, Katz et al, Honolulu, 1975-78, ptnr., 1978-81; pres. Bodden & Muraoka Law Corp., Maui and Wailuku, Hawaii, 1981—. Author: Taxation of Real Estate in Hawaii, 1979, Taxation of Real Estate in U.S., 1982, Selling DPP Programs, 1983. Pres. Kihei Community Assn., 1984-86. Served to lt. USN, 1969-72. Mem. ABA (tax, real property, probate and trust sects.), Hawaii Bar Assn., Nat. Assn. Realtors/RESSI (pres. 1987), Hawaii Assn. Realtors (pres. 1989). Lodge: Rotary. Estate planning, Probate, Real property. Office: 24 N Church St Ste 200 Wailuku HI 96793-1606

**BODDIE, REGINALD ALONZO,** lawyer; b. New Haven, June 14, 1959; s. Gladys Geraldine (Harrell) B. BA, Brown U., 1981; JD, Northeastern U., 1984. Bar: N.Y., U.S. Dist. Ct. (ea. and so. dists.) N.Y. 1986, D.C. 1987, U.S. Ct. Appeals (2d cir.) 1989, U.S. Supreme Ct. 1990. Staff atty. Legal Aid Soc., N.Y.C., 1984-86, Harlem Legal Svcs., N.Y.C., 1986-88; asst. counsel Ctr. for Law and Social Justice Medgar Evers Coll. CUNY, 1988-95; pvt. practice Law Offices of Reginald A. Boddie, N.Y.C., 1995—; arbitrator Lemon Law, N.Y. Atty. Gen. and Am. Arbitration Assn., N.Y.C., 1986-94. Founder, pres., exec. dir. United Youth Enterprises, Inc., New Haven, 1976—; founder, dir. Coll. Prep. program Ctrl. H.S., Providence, 1980-81; bd.dirs. Claremont Neighborhood Ctrs., Inc., Bronx, N.Y., 1994-96; vol. instr. ARC, New Haven, 1975-90; bd. dirs. Boys and Girls' Clubs of Union County, Union, N.J., 1996-97; vol. law edn. instr. N.Y.C. Pub. Schs., 1998—. Recipient Good Citizenship award Civitan Internat. Club, New Haven, 1977, 2 commendations Brown U., 1981, Outstanding Cmty. Svc. award New Haven Police Dept., 1984, Cmty. Svc. award Pub. Sch. 21, Bklyn., 1993, others. Mem. N.Y. State Bar Assn., N.Y.C. Bar Assn., Bklyn. Bar Assn., Optimist Internat. Club. General civil litigation, Civil rights, General practice. Office: Ste 2035 19 Fulton St Rm 408 New York NY 10038-2100

**BODENSTEIN, IRA,** lawyer; b. Atlantic City, Nov. 9, 1954; s. William and Beverly (Grossman) B.; m. Julia Elizabeth Smith, Mar. 9, 1991; children: Sarah Rose, George William, Jennie Kathryn. Student, Tel Aviv U., 1974-75; BA in Govt., Franklin & Marshall Coll., 1977; JD in Econs., U. Miami, 1980. Bar: Ill. 1980, U.S. Dist Ct. (no. dist.) Ill. 1980, U.S. Ct. Appeals (7th cir.) 1982, Fla. 1983. Assoc. James S. Gordon Ltd., Chgo., 1980-85, mem., 1985-89; mem. Portes, Sharp, Herbst & Fox, Ltd., Chgo., 1990-91; shareholder Towbin & Zazove, Ltd., Chgo., 1991-93; ptnr. D'Ancona & Pflaum, Chgo., 1993-98; U.S. trustee Region 11, Chgo., 1998—. Pres., bd. dirs., benefit chmn. Gus Giordano Jazz Dance, Chgo., 1990—; treas. Chgo. Pub. Art Group, 1995-99. Mem. ABA (bus. law sect., rep. young lawyers divsn. dist. 15, 1986-87, ann. meeting adv. com. 1990, spkr. spring meeting 1996, 97), Chgo. Bar Assn. (bd. dirs. young lawyers sect. 1985-87, chmn.-elect 1987-88, chmn. 1988-89, antitrust com., chmn. athletics com. 1984-85, bd. mgrs. 1990-92, chmn. pub. affairs and media rels. com., chmn. assn. meetings com., memberships com. 1996, cert. of appreciation 1984-93, 96-97). Democrat. Jewish. Home: 2848 W Wilson Ave Chicago IL 60625-3743 Office: Office US Trustee 227 W Monroe St Ste 3350 Chicago IL 60606-5099

**BODENSTEINER, WILLIAM LEO,** lawyer; b. Austin, Minn., Dec. 10, 1947; s. William Henry and Mildred Marie (Dibble) B.; divorced; 1 child, Kari. BS, Mankato State U., 1980; JD, Valparaiso U., 1983. Bar: Minn. 1983, U.S. Dist. Ct. Minn. 1985. Pvt. practice, Austin, 1983—. With U.S. Army, 1968-70, Vietnam. Mem. Mower County Bar Assn. (pres. 1988-89), 10th Dist. Bar Assn. (pres. 1987-88). Roman Catholic. Avocation: trout fishing. Bankruptcy, Consumer commercial, Family and matrimonial. Home: 307 S Main St Austin MN 55912-4432 Office: 309 N Main St Austin MN 55912-3407

**BODINE, JOSEPH IRA,** lawyer; b. Greeley, Colo., June 4, 1950; s. Olen Doyle Sr. and Muriel Joy Roberts; m. LeAnne Marie Kontz, Dec. 14, 1973; children: Sabrina, Jared, Adam. BA, U. S.C., 1980; MPA, Golden Gate U., 1986; JD, Brigham Young U., 1995. Bar: Utah 1995, U.S. Dist. Ct. Utah 1995, Colo. 1996, U.S. Dist. Ct. Colo. 1996. Enlisted USAF, 1968, advanced through grades to commd. officer 2nd Lt., 1981, ret., 1992; pvt. practice law. Mem. transp. adv. com. City Greeley, 1997-99, chair budget adv. com., 1997-99, budget adv. com. City Greeley, 1997—, chair 1998-99. Decorated Air Force Commendation medal Hdqrs. Tactical Air Command, 1988, Air Force Achievement medal Hdqrs. Tactical Warfare Ctr., 1990, Meritorious Svc. medal Hdqrs. Tactical Warfare Ctr., 1992. Mem. ABA, Colo. Bar Assn. (co-chair law edn. com. 1998-99), Weld County Bar Assn., Am. Legion. Avocation: umpiring high school baseball. Bankruptcy, Family and matrimonial, General practice. Office: 1129 10th St Greeley CO 80631-3809

**BODKIN, HENRY GRATTAN, JR.,** lawyer; b. L.A., Dec. 8, 1921; s. Henry Grattan and Ruth May (Wallis) B.; m. Mary Louise Davis, June 28, 1943; children: Maureen L. Dixon, Sheila L. McCarthy, Timothy Grattan. B.S. cum laude, Loyola U., Los Angeles, 1943, J.D., 1948. Bar: Calif. 1948. Pvt. practice Los Angeles, 1948-51, 53-95; ptnr. Bodkin, McCarthy, Sargent & Smith (predecessor firms), L.A.; of counsel Sullivan, Workman & Dee, L.A., 1995—. Mem. L.A. Bd. Water and Power Commrs., 1972-74, pres., 1973-74; regent Marymount Coll., 1962-67; trustee Loyola-Marymount U., 1967-91, vice chmn., 1985-86. With USNR, 1943-45, 51-53. Fellow Am. Coll. Trial Lawyers; mem. Calif. State Bar (mem. exec. com. conf. of dels. 1968-70, vice chmn. 1969-70), California Club, Riviera Tennis Club, Tuna Club, Chancery Club (pres. 1990-91), Phi Delta Phi. Republican. Roman Catholic. Federal civil litigation, State civil litigation, Insurance. Home: 956 Linda Flora Dr Los Angeles CA 90049-1631 Office: Sullivan Workman & Dee 800 S Figueroa St Fl 12 Los Angeles CA 90017-2521

**BODKIN, ROBERT THOMAS,** lawyer; b. Anderson, Ind., Jan. 26, 1945; s. Robert G. and Marggie Jean (Whelchel) B.; m. Penny Ann Nichols, June 17, 1967; children: Beth Ann, Bryan Thomas. BS, Ind. U., Bloomington, 1967; JD, Ind. U., Indpls., 1973. Bar: Ind. 1973, U.S. Dist. Ct. (so. dist.) Ind. 1973, U.S. Dist. Ct. (no. dist.) Ind. 1975, U.S. Ct. Appeals (7th cir.) 1974, U.S. Supreme Ct. 1977. Law clk. U.S. Dist. Ct., Indpls., 1973-75; assoc. Bamberger Foreman Oswald & Hahn, Evansville, Ind., 1975-80, ptnr., 1980—; town atty., Newburgh, Ind., 1984—; city atty. City of Boonville, Ind., 1988-91. Bd. dirs. Evansville Dance Theatre, 1983, Evansville Philharm. Orch., 1983-85; trustee Evansville Day Sch., 1983-86; chmn. bd. St. Mary's Warrick Hosp. Found. Named Vol. of Yr. Hist. Newburgh, Inc., 1983; fellow Ind. Bar Found., 1983. Mem. ABA, Def. Rsch. Inst., Ind. Bar Assn., Evansville Bar Assn., Bar Assn. of 7th Fed. Cir., Ind. Mcpl. Lawyers Assn. (bd. dirs. 1986—), Def. Trial Counsel Ind. (dir. 1999—), Ind. Def. Trial Counsel (diplomat). Democrat. E-mail: tbodkin@bamberger.com. Federal civil litigation, State civil litigation, Personal injury. Home: 100 W Water St Apt 3 Newburgh IN 47630-1174 Office: Bamberger Foreman Oswald & Hahn 708 Hulman Bldg Evansville IN 47708

**BODNAR, ALEXANDRA A.,** lawyer. BA, Dartmouth Coll., 1991; JD, U. So. Calif., L.A., 1996. Bar: Calif. Supreme Ct. 1996, U.S. Dist. Ct. (ctrl. dist.) Calif. 1996, Calif. Ct. Appeals 1996. Paralegal Davis, Polk & Wardwell, N.Y.C., 1991-93; law clk. Ernst & Young, L.A., 1994; jud. extern judge Rafeedie U.S. Dist. Ct., L.A., 1994; cert. law clk. L.A. County Dist. Atty.'s Office, L.A., 1995; atty. Freshman, Marantz, Orlanski, Cooper &

Klein, Beverly Hills, Calif., 1997-98, Graham & James, LLP, L.A., 1998—. Mem. ABA (labor and employment sect.), L.A. County Bar Assn. (labor and employment sect.), Women Lawyers Assn. L.A., Dartmouth Club L.A. (young alumni chairperson). Labor. Office: Graham & James LLP 801 S Figueroa St Los Angeles CA 90017-2573

**BODNAR, PETER O.,** lawyer; b. Queens, N.Y., Mar. 19, 1945; s. John and Edith (Schultz) B. BA in Govt., NYU, 1966; JD, Fordham U., 1970. Bar: N.Y. 1971, U.S. Dist. Ct. (so. dist.) N.Y. 1973. Confidential law sec. to Hon. Evans V. Brewster Family Ct. and County Ct. Westchester County, N.Y., 1970-73; pvt. practice White Plains, N.Y., 1973-77; ptnr. Bodnar & Greene, P.C., White Plains, N.Y., 1977-80, Bender & Bodnar, White Plains, N.Y., 1980-98; prin. Law Offices of Peter O. Bodnar, White Plains, NY, 1998—; pres., CEO P.A.J. Am. Ltd./The Olo Corp., 1990-97, CEO Organica, USA, Inc., 1998—. Trustee Village of Ossining, N.Y., 1975-77. Fellow Am. Acad. Matrimonial Lawyers; mem. ABA (family law sect.), N.Y. State Bar Assn. (family law sect.), Westchester County Bar Assn. (family law sect., exec. com. 1992—). Family and matrimonial. Office: 140 Grand St White Plains NY 10601-4831

**BODNEY, DAVID JEREMY,** lawyer; b. Kansas City, Mo., July 15, 1954; s. Daniel F. and Retha (Silby) B.; m. Sarah Hughes; children: Christian Steven, Anna Claire. BA cum laude, Yale U., 1976; MA in Fgn. Affairs, U. Va., 1979, JD, 1979. Bar: Ariz. 1979, U.S. Dist Ct. Ariz. 1980, U.S. Ct. Appeals (9th cir.) 1980, U.S. Supreme Ct. 1983. Legis. asst., speechwriter U.S. Senator John V. Tunney, Washington, 1975-76; sr. editor Va. Jour. of Internat. Law, 1978-79; assoc. Brown and Bain PA, Phoenix, 1979-85, ptnr., 1985-90; gen. counsel New Times, Inc., Phoenix, 1990-92; ptnr. Steptoe & Johnson, Phoenix, 1992—; vis. prof. Ariz. State U., Tempe, 1985, 94—. Co-author: Libel Defense Resource Center: 50-State Survey, 1982—. Bd. dirs. Ariz. Ctr. for Law in the Pub. Interest, Phoenix, 1983—, pres., 1989-90; chmn. Yale Alumni Schs. Com., Phoenix, 1984-87; vice chmn. City of Phoenix Solicitation Bd., 1986-88, chmn., 1988-89; bd. dirs. Children's Action Alliance, 1995—, v.p., 1998—; mem. adv. panel on Civil Liberties to White House Commn. on Aviation Safety and Security, 1997. Mem. ABA (forum com. on communication law 1984—, concerned correspondents network com. 1979—), Ariz. Bar Assn. Democrat. Clubs: Yale (bd. dirs. Phoenix club 1979—), Ariz. Acad. General civil litigation, Libel, Communications. Office: Steptoe & Johnson 40 N Central Ave Ste 2400 Phoenix AZ 85004-4453

**BODOFF, JOSEPH SAMUEL UBERMAN,** lawyer; b. Bryn Mawr, Nov. 2, 1952; s. Bernard David and Ruth Irma (Uberman) B. BS, Pa. State U., 1974; JD, Villanova U., 1977. Bar: Pa. 1977, U.S. Dist. Ct. (ea. dist.) Pa. 1979, U.S. Ct. Appeals (3d cir.) 1980, U.S. Supreme Ct. 1988, Mass. 1987, U.S. Dist. Ct. Mass. 1988, U.S. Ct. Appeals (1st cir.) 1988, R.I. 1998, U.S. Dist. Ct. R.I. 1999. Jud. law clk. Phila. County Ct. of Common Pleas, 1977-79; assoc. Pincus, Verlin, Hahn & Reich, Phila., 1979-86; ptnr. Kaye, Fialkow, Richmond & Rothstein, Boston, 1986-91, Gaston & Snow, Boston, 1991, Warner & Stackpole, Boston, 1991-94, Hinckley, Allen & Snyder, Boston, 1994-98, Shechtman & Halperin, Boston, 1998—; dir. Am. Bankruptcy Inst., Alexandria, Am. Bd. of Certification, Alexandria, Coun. of Cert. Bankruptcy Specialists; co-chair ABI Unsecured Trade Creditor com., Alexandria, 1993-98, ABI Creditors' Com. Manual Task Force, 1993-94, chair ABI Task Force on Preferences, 1995-97; chair NACM Bankruptcy and Insolvency Group, Portland, 1998—. Author: Cramdown: The Ultimate Chapter 11 Threat, 1992, (with others) Bankruptcy Business Acquisitions, 1998; contbr. articles to profl. publs. Mem. Mus. Coun. of Mus. of Fine Arts, Boston, 1997-99. Mem. ABA, Am. Bankruptcy Inst. (dir. 1995—), Coun. of Cert. Bankruptcy Specialists (dir. 1995—), Am. Bd. of Certification (dir. 1996—), Boston bar Assn., Nat. Assn of Credit Mgmt. Avocations: skiing, tennis, wine collecting, piano. Bankruptcy, Consumer commercial, Contracts commercial. Home: 64 Forest St Chestnut Hill MA 02467-2930 Office: Shechtman & Halperin 265 Franklin St Boston MA 02110-3113

**BODOVITZ, JAMES PHILIP,** lawyer; b. Evanston, Ill., Aug. 20, 1958; s. Philip Edward and Dosha (Laurman) B. BS, U. So. Calif., 1980, JD, 1984. Bar: N.Y. 1985, D.C. 1989, Calif. 1990. Assoc. Shearman & Sterling, N.Y.C., 1984-89, San Francisco, 1989-92; br. chief divsn. broker-dealer enforcement U.S. Securities Exch. Commn., N.Y.C., 1992-96; v.p., counsel law dept. The Equitable Life Assurance Soc. of U.S., N.Y.C., 1996—. Mem. ABA, Assn. Bar City N.Y. (Thurgood Marshall award 1998). Democrat. Securities, Federal civil litigation, General civil litigation. Office: The Equitable Cos 1290 Ave of Americas 12 Flr New York NY 10104

**BODOW, WAYNE R.,** lawyer; b. Bklyn., Apr. 25, 1943; s. Charles G. and Rosalind L. B.; m. Alice Turski, Aug. 29, 1971 (div. Dec. 1977); 1 child, Amy Ellen; m. Linda S. Taylor, Dec. 16, 1988 (div. Oct. 1994); 1 child, Elana Sara; m. Lillian Stienmann, June 7, 1998. BA, Rockford Coll., 1965. Bar: N.Y. 1975; U.S. Dist. Ct. (no. and we. dists.) N.Y. 1975; cert. in consumer bankruptcy law Am. Bankruptcy Bd. Cert. Pvt. practice; mem. alternate dispute resolution panel U.S. Bankruptcy Ct. No Dist N.Y., 1999—. Contbr. articles to profl. jours. Active mem. Coalition of Medicaid Advocates of Western N.Y. Mem. Am. Bankruptcy Inst., Nat. Assn. Consumer Bankruptcy Attys. (founder), Nat. Assn. Chpt. 13 Trustees (assoc.), Ctrl. N.Y. Bankruptcy Bar Assn., Turnaround Mgmt. Assn., Nat. Assn. Consumer Advocates, Nat. Coun. Exchangors, Onondaga County Bar Assn. (chmn. consumer law sect., lectr.). Fax: 315-422-9113. Office: 1925 Park St Ste 1 Syracuse NY 13208-1080

**BOE, MYRON TIMOTHY,** lawyer; b. New Orleans, Oct. 30, 1948; s. Myron Roger and Elaine (Tracy) B. BA, U. Ark., 1970, JD, 1973; LLM in Labor, So. Methodist U., 1976. Bar: Ark. 1974, Tenn. 1977, U.S. Ct. Appeals (4th, 5th, 6th, 7th, 8th, 9th, 10th, 11th cirs.) 1978, U.S. Supreme Ct. 1978. City atty. City of Pine Bluff, Ark., 1974-75; sec.-treas. Ark. City Atty. Assn., 1975; sr. ptnr. Rose Law Firm, Little Rock, 1980—. Author: Handling the Title VII Case Practical Tips for the Employer, 1980. Served to 2d lt. USAR, 1972-73. Recipient Florentino-Ramirez Internat. Law award, 1975. Fellow Coll. Labor and Employment Lawyers, Inc., Ark. Bar Found., Ark. Bd. Legal Specialization (sec. 1982-85, chmn. 1985-89, labor, employment discrimination, civil rights).; mem. ABA (labor sect. 1974—, employment law com. 1974—), Ark. Bar Assn. (sec., chmn. labor sect. 1978-81, ho. of dels. 1979-82, Golden Gavel award 1983), Def. Rsch. Inst. (employment law com. 1982—), Am. Employment Law Coun. (charter), Ark. Assn. Def. Counsel. Labor, Civil rights. Office: Rose Law Firm 120 E 4th St Little Rock AR 72201-2893

**BOEDIGHEIMER, ROBERT DAVID,** lawyer; b. Mpls., Nov. 13, 1962; s. David Eugene and Phyllis Kay (Bylander) B.; m. Wendi Suzanne Lusk. BA in Philosophy, Polit. Sci. and Speech Comm. with distinction, U. Minn., 1985, JD, 1988. Bar: Minn. 1990, U.S. Dist. Ct. Minn. 1990. Law clk. to Hon. Lynn C. Olson Anoka, Minn., 1989-90; assoc. Adams & Cesario, P.A., Bloomington, Minn., 1990-95; ptnr. McCloud & Boedigheimer, Bloomington, Minn., 1995—. Mem. ABA, Minn. State Bar Assn., Anoka County Bar Assn., Bloomington C. of C. Republican. Roman Catholic. Avocations: racquetball, golf, weight training, skiing, watercolor painting. General civil litigation, Family and matrimonial, Personal injury. Office: McCloud & Boedigheimer 5001 W 80th St Ste 201 Bloomington MN 55437-1110

**BOEHM, THEODORE REED,** judge; b. Evanston, Ill., Sept. 12, 1938; s. Hans George and Frances (Reed) B.; children from previous marriage: Elisabeth, Jennifer, Sarah, Macy; m. Margaret Stitt Harris, Jan. 27, 1985. AB summa cum laude, Brown U., 1960; JD magna cum laude, Harvard U., 1963. Bar: D.C. 1964, Ind. 1964, U.S. Supreme Ct. 1975. Law clk. to Chief Justice Warren, Justice Reed, Justice Burton, U.S. Supreme Ct., Washington, 1963-64; assoc. Baker & Daniels, Indpls., 1965-70, ptnr., 1970-88, 95-96, mng. ptnr. 1980-87; gen. counsel major appliances GE, Louisville, 1988-89; v.p., gen. counsel GE Aircraft Engines, Cin., 1989-91; dep. gen. counsel Eli Lilly & Co., 1991-95; justice Ind. Supreme Ct., 1996—. Pres. Ind. Sports Corp., 1980-88; chmn. organizing com. 1987 Pan Am. Games, Indpls. Mem. ABA, Ind. Bar Assn., Am. Law Inst. Office: Indiana Supreme Ct State House Rm 311 Indianapolis IN 46204-2728

**BOEHNEN, DAVID LEO,** grocery company executive, lawyer; b. Mitchell, S.D., Dec. 3, 1946; s. Lloyd L. Boehnen and Mary Elizabeth (Buche) Roby; m. Shari A. Bauhs, Aug. 9, 1969; children: Lesley, Michelle, Heather. AB, U. Notre Dame, 1968; JD with honors, Cornell U., 1971. Bar: Minn. 1971. Assoc. Dorsey & Whitney, Mpls., 1971-76, ptnr., 1977-89; sr. v.p. law and external rels. Supervalu Inc., Mpls., 1991-97, exec. v.p., 1997—; vis. prof. law Cornell U. Law Sch., Ithaca, N.Y., fall 1982; bd. dirs. ATM Med. Inc.. Mem. adv. coun. on arts and letters U. Notre Dame, 1993—; mem. adv. Coun. Cornell U. Law Sch., 1983-92, chmn. coun. 1986-90. Mem. Minn. Bar Assn. (chmn. bus. law sect., 1986), Greater Mpls. C. of C. (bd. dirs. 1988-90), Minikahda Club (Mpls.), Spring Hill Golf Club. Roman Catholic. Securities. Home: 71 Otis Ln Saint Paul MN 55104-5645

**BOEHNER, LEONARD BRUCE,** lawyer; b. Council Bluffs, Iowa, Apr. 19, 1930; s. Bruce and Flora (Kruse) B. AB, Harvard U., 1952, JD, 1955. Bar: N.Y. 1956, U.S. Dist. Ct. (so. dist.) N.Y. 1963, U.S. Ct. Appeals (2d cir.) 1963, U.S. Supreme Ct. 1964. Assoc. Dewey, Ballantine, Bushby, Palmer & Wood, N.Y.C., 1959-66; ptnr. Clare & Whitehead, N.Y.C., 1966-73, Morris & McVeigh LLP, N.Y.C. 1973—. Served to lt. USN, 1955-59. Mem. Assn. Bar City N.Y. Club: Union (N.Y.C.). Estate planning, Securities, General corporate. Office: Morris & McVeigh 767 3rd Ave New York NY 10017-2023

**BOENSCH, ARTHUR CRANWELL,** lawyer; b. Charleston, S.C., Nov. 9, 1933; s. Frank Neville and Mary Alice (Cranwell) B.; m. Katherine Hume Lucas, June 16, 1956; children: Arthur Cranwell, Katherine Breland, Alice Metzendorf, Frances Murdaugh, Benjamin; m. 2d, Annelle Yvonne Beach, July 27, 1979. BS in Gen. Engring., U.S. Naval Acad., 1956; JD, U. S.C., 1970. Bar: S.C. 1970, U.S. Dist. Ct. (so. dist.) Ga. 1970, U.S. Dist. Ct. S.C. 1971. Ptnr. Ackerman & Boensch, Walterboro, S.C., 1970-73, Bogoslow & Boensch, Walterboro, S.C., 1973-75; pvt. practice Walterboro, S.C., 1976—; city recorder, mcpl. ct. judge, Walterboro, 1973-78. Chmn. Colleton County Alcohol and Drug Abuse Commn., 1991-96; dist. chmn. Boy Scouts Am., 1988-95, mem. exec. bd. Coastal Carolina coun., 1978—; vestryman St. Jude's Episcopal Ch.; lay rector Cursillo Episcopal Diocese of S.C., 1989; del. Episcopal conv. Diocese of S.C., 1995-96, 98-99, standing com., 1997—. Lt. Comdr. USN, 1956-57. Recipient Silver Beaver award and Dist. Merit award Boy Scouts Am., 1982; James West fellow, 1996. Mem. S.C. Bar Assn. (chmn. lawyers caring about lawyers com. 1989-91), Rotary, Phi Alpha Delta. General practice. Address: PO Box 258 Waterboro SC 29488-0003

**BOER, ROGER WILLIAM,** lawyer; b. Holland, Mich., July 2, 1934; s. William H. and Frances (Hulst) B.; m. Judith L. Jaqua, June 21, 1957; children; William, James, Charles, Martha, Karen. BA, Calvin Coll., 1956; JD, Wayne State U., 1960. Bar: Mich. 1961, U.S. Dist. Ct. Mich. 1961, U.S. Tax Ct. 1966. Atty. Mitts, Smith, Haughey & Packard, Grand Rapids, Mich., 1960-61; founding ptnr. McKee & Boer, Grand Rapids, Mich., 1961-63; asst. prosecuting atty., dep. prosecuting atty. Kent County Office, Grand Rapids, Mich., 1961-62, 63-64; founding ptnr. Rhoades, Garlington, McKee & Boer, Grand Rapids, Mich., 1963-65, Rhoades, McKee & Boer, Grand Rapids, Mich., 1965-87; founding shareholder Rhoades, McKee, Boer, Goodrich & Titta, Grand Rapids, Mich., 1987—, pres., 1994-99; spl. counsel Mich. Joint House Senate Investigating Com. on Worker's Compensation, 1964-65; spl. prosecutor one-man grand jury, 1977-78; sec. Grand Rapids Pub. Edn. Fund, 1989; bd. dirs., sr. shareholder Rhoades, McKee, Boer, Goodrich & Titta. Bd. dirs. Wedgewood Acres Home for Boys, 1969-71; bd. trustees Pine Rest Christian Hosp., 1971-83. bd. pres., 1981-83; study com. on abortion Christian Reformed Ch., 1973-74; bd. dirs. BBG Corp. Mem. State of Mich. Bar Assn., Grand Rapids Bar Assn. (trustee 1980-82, adv. com. in family law for Grand Rapids social agencies), Am. Trial Lawyers Assn., Green Ridge Country Club (bd. dirs. 1977-79), Egypt Valley Country Club, Peninsular Club. General civil litigation, General corporate, Family and matrimonial. Home: 961 Gladstone Dr SE Grand Rapids MI 49506-3392 Office: Rhoades Mckee Boer Goodrich & Titta 161 Ottawa Ave NW Grand Rapids MI 49503-2701

**BOERINGER, GRETA,** librarian; b. Vermillion, S.D., Jan. 19, 1960; d. James Leslie and GraceNocera B. BA, Susquehanna U., 1981; JD, Tulane U., 1985; MS in Libr. & Info. Sci., U. N.C., 1989. Bar: La. 1985. Reference documents computer libr. U. Ark., Little Rock, 1989-92; fed. depository libr. inspector U.S. Govt. Printing Office, Washington, 1992-96; legal reference specialist Law Libr. Congress Reading Room, Washington, 1996-97; reference documents, non-print libr. Pace U., White Plains, N.Y., 1997—; cmty. legal resources network libr. CUNY Law Sch., Flushing, N.Y., 1999—. Democrat. Mem. Soc. of Friends. Avocation: acting Shakespeare. Fax: 914-422-4139. E-mail: gboeringer@law.pace.edu. Office: Pace U Law Sch Libr 78 N Broadway White Plains NY 10603-3710

**BOERSIG, THOMAS CHARLES, JR.,** lawyer; b. St. Louis, July 11, 1956; s. Thomas Charles and Mary Louise (Schmitt) B.; m. Glenda JoAnn Worley, Dec. 29, 1984; children: Thomas C. III, Leah Marie, Samuel. BA, S.E. Mo. U., 1980; JD, St. Louis U., 1983. Bar: Mo. 1983. Law clk. Mo. Ct. Appeals-Ea. Dist., St. Louis, 1982; editl. asst. St. Louis U. Law Sch., 1982-83; compliance/sr. compliance atty. Edward D. Jones & Co., St. Louis, 1983-95, investment rep. devel. midwest, 1995—; arbitrator Nat. Assn. Securities Dealers, 1985—, Am. Arbitration Assn., St. Louis, 1990—, Nat. Futures Assn., Chgo., 1992—. Asst. editor: Products Liability in Missouri, 1984. V.p., pres. Sappington Sch. PTO, St. Louis, 19944-96. With U.S. Army, 1974-76. Mem. ABA (sect. on corp., banking and bus. law), Mo. Bar Assn. (alt. dispute resolution com. 1985—). Avocations: hiking, fishing, reading, golfing, hunting. Securities, Alternative dispute resolution, Administrative and regulatory.

**BOES, LAWRENCE WILLIAM,** lawyer; b. Bklyn., Aug. 3, 1935; s. Lawrence and Elizabeth (Schaefer) B.; m. Joan Mary Elward, Oct. 2, 1965; children: Lawrence, Siobhan, Thomas. AB, Columbia Coll., 1961; JD, Columbia U., 1964. Bar: N.Y. 1965, U.S. Dist. Ct. (ea. dist.) N.Y. 1968, U.S. Dist. Ct. (so. dist.) N.Y. 1968, U.S. Ct. Appeals (2d cir.) 1971, U.S. Ct. Appeals (8th cir.) 1974, U.S. Supreme Ct. 1974, U.S. Ct. Appeals (9th cir.) 1982, U.S. Ct. Appeals (3d cir.) 1988. Law clk. to judge U.S. Ct. Appeals (2d cir.), 1964-65; assoc. Reavis & McGrath, N.Y.C., 1965-70, ptnr., 1970-88; ptnr. Fulbright & Jaworski L.L.P., N.Y.C., 1989—. Revs. editor Columbia Law Rev., 1963-64. Mem. Village of Westbury Code Rev. Commn., N.Y., 1983—, chmn., 1991—. Cpl. U.S. Army, 1958-60. Pulitzer scholar N.Y.C. Bd. Edn., 1954; nat. scholar Columbia U., 1962. Mem. ABA, N.Y. State Bar Assn. (com. on stds. of atty. conduct 1999—), Bar Assn. Nassau County (chair 1998—, profl. ethics com.), Univ. Glee Club N.Y.C. (sec. 1998—). Avocations: gardening, baseball, glee club singing. Antitrust, General civil litigation, Appellate. Office: Fulbright & Jaworski LLP 666 5th Ave Fl 31 New York NY 10103-3198

**BOESKY, JULIE A.,** lawyer; b. Detroit, Feb. 8, 1963; d. Malcolm Dale and Elaine Beryl Boesky; m. Jonathan Shapiro, Apr. 1, 1990; children: Madeline, Benjamin. BA with high honors, U. Mich., 1984; JD with high honors, George Washington U., 1987. Assoc. Akin Gunz Stinness Haver & Feld, Washington, 1987-88, Rogovin Huge & Schiller, Washington, 1988-90; trial atty. U.S. Dept. Justice, Washington, 1990-91; cons. Moon, Moss, McGill, Portland, Maine, 1991-95; atty. Bennett, Bennett & Troiano, Portland, 1997—. Jewish. Labor. Office: Bennett Bennett & Troiano 121 Middle St Portland ME 04101-4156

**BOESPFLUG, JOHN FRANCIS, JR.,** lawyer; b. 1944. AB, Whitman Coll., 1966; JD, U. Wash., 1969. Bar: Wash. 1969. Of counsel Bogle & Gates, Bellevue, Wash., 1994—. Mem. ABA. Construction, Land use and zoning (including planning). Office: Bogle & Gates 10500 NE 8th St Ste 1500 Bellevue WA 98004-4398

**BOESTER, ROBERT ALAN,** lawyer; b. Cleve., Aug. 6, 1951; s. Elmer Frederick and Beatrice Mae (Zerby) B.; m. Dorothy Jean Keller, Aug. 17, 1974; children: Jennifer Brooke, Allison Keller. BA, Wittenberg U., 1973; JD, Boston U., 1976. Bar: Va. 1976, U.S. Dist. Ct. (ea. dist.) Va. 1984, U.S. Ct. Appeals (4th cir.) 1988. Asst. commonwealth's atty. Commonwealth of Va., Hampton, 1976-80, dep. commonwealth's atty., 1981-83; ptnr. James, Richardson & Quinn, P.C., Hampton, 1983-86, Hawkins, Burcher & Boester, P.C., Hampton, 1986—; chmn. bd. dirs. Hampton (Va.) Coliseum, 1988-91, 94—. Pres. Hampton (Va.) Frolics, Inc., 1988-92; soccer and basketball coach Phillips Athletic Assn., Hampton, 1990—. Avocation; sitting on the beach. Insurance, Personal injury, Criminal. Office: Hawkins Burcher & Boester PC One E Queens Way Hampton VA 23669-3503

**BOGAARD, WILLIAM JOSEPH,** lawyer; b. Sioux City, Iowa, Jan. 18, 1938; s. Joseph and Irene Marie (Hensing) B.; m. Claire Marie Whalen, Jan. 28, 1961; children: Michele, Jeannine, Joseph, Matthew. BS, Loyola Marymount U., L.A., 1959; JD with honors, U. Mich., 1965. Bar: Calif. 1966, U.S. Dist. Ct. (ctrl. dist.) Calif. 1966. Ptnr. Agnew, Miller & Carlson, L.A., 1970-82; exec. v.p., gen. counsel 1st Interstate Bancorp, L.A., 1982-96; vis. prof. securities regulation and banking Mich. Law Sch., Ann Arbor, 1996-97; lectr. securities regulation and corps. U. So. Calif. Law Sch., L.A., 1997—; mem. Calif. Commn. on Jud. Nominees Evaluation, 1997-99. Mem. city coun., mayor City of Pasadena, Calif., 1978-86, 99—. Capt. USAF, 1959-62. Mem. ABA, Calif. State Bar, Los Angeles County Bar Assn. (Corp. Counsel of Yr. award 1988). Avocations: jogging, French and Spanish languages, hiking. Administrative and regulatory, Mergers and acquisitions, Securities. Office: U So Calif Law Sch 699 Exposition Blvd # 442 Los Angeles CA 90089-0040

**BOGART, WILLIAM HARRY,** lawyer; b. Sayre, Pa., Mar. 5, 1931; s. Harry M. and Luella C. Bogart; AB, Duke U., 1953; AAA, The Hague Acad. Internat. Law, 1962; JD, Syracuse U., 1963; m. Karin Rudolph, Dec. 12, 1962 (div. Dec. 1987); children: Barbara, Silke. Bar: N.Y., 1964. Mem. firm Ali, Gerber, Parr & Bogart, Syracuse, N.Y., 1966-67, Bogart & Andrews, Syracuse, 1967-77; mem. firm Bogart & Assocs., P.C., Syracuse, 1977—; cons. in field to various govts, fin. instns., ednl. instns.; lectr. in field. Contbr. articles to profl. jours. Drafted civil rights laws for Czechoslovak Constn. Mem. missionary com. Presbyterian Ch., 1974-77; active with Acad. Scis. and Russian Govt. drawing comml., ins. and banking laws. Served with USMC, 1951-52. Mem. ABA, Am. Arbitration Assn., N.Y. State Bar Assn., N.Y. State Trial Lawyers Assn., Onondaga County Bar Assn., Assn. of Attenders and Alumni, Lawyers Intergroups, World Ct., Assn. Atty. and Advocates, UN Assn., Univ. Club, Army and Navy Club, Witte Soc. Dem Hague Club, Masons (32d degree). Democrat. Contracts commercial, Private international, Personal injury. Home: 110 E Lake Rd Skaneateles NY 13152-9110 Office: 1600 State Tower Bldg 109 S Warren St Syracuse NY 13202-1798

**BOGDAN, EDWARD ANDREW, JR.,** lawyer, partner; b. Amsterdam, N.Y., July 4, 1930; s. Edward A. Sr. and Valeria A. (Olbrycht) B.; m. Florence N. Bishop, Sept. 10, 1960; children: Agnes B. Lancaster, Edward A. III, Valerie A., Stephen A. AB, Harvard U., 1952; JD, Albany Law Sch., 1959. N.Y. 1959. Trial atty. U.S. Dept. Justice, Washington, D.C., 1959-61; assoc. Plowden, Wardlaw & Littlefield, Albany, N.Y., 1961-63; ptnr. Littlefield & Bogdan, Albany, 1963-76, Bogdan Fivel & Volk, Albany, 1976-78, McNamee, Lochner, Titus & Williams, Albany, 1978-91, Bogdan, Marsh & Faist P.C., Albany, 1991-93, Bogdan & Faist, P.C., Albany, 1993—; Bd. dirs. Ballston Knitting Co., Ballston Spa, N.Y., 1970-90. With USN, 1954-56. Avocations: fly fishing, platform tennis, golf. Legislative, Administrative and regulatory. Office: Bogdan & Faist PC 111 Washington Ave Ste 750 Albany NY 12210-2238

**BOGE, SAMANTHA,** lawyer; b. Dubuque, Iowa, Sept. 22, 1948; d. Cyril Francis Boge and Isabelle Marie Hanten; m. Frederic Alan Cummings, Dec. 20, 1977 (div. Apr. 1993); children: Christian, Sara, Alice Kate. BS, Iowa State U., 1970; JD, Fla. State U., 1975. Bar: Fla. 1975, U.S. Dist. Ct. (no. dist.) Fla. 1975, U.S. Ct. Appeals (11th cir.) 1978, U.S. Dist. Ct. (mid. dist.) Fla. 1980. Ptnr. Judelle & Boge, Tallahassee, Fla., 1975-79; assoc. gen. counsel Fla. Dept. Adminstrn., Tallahassee, 1979-82; sec., treas. Cummings, Lawrence & Vezina, Tallahassee, 1986-91; of counsel Stowell, Anton & Kraemer, Tallahassee, 1992—. Pres., bd. dirs. Ronald McDonald House, Tallahassee, 1992—; bd. trustees Leon H.S. Mem. Am. Inns. of Ct. (barrister 1994-97), Am. Arbitration Assn. (arbitrator 1986—). Alternative dispute resolution, Construction, Contracts commercial. Office: Stowell Anton & Kraemer 211 E Call St Tallahassee FL 32301-7607

**BOGEN, MARK DAVID,** lawyer; b. Chgo., Aug. 15, 1959; s. Gilbert and Rosalyn B.; m. Victoria S. Sanders, children: Michael, Laura. BS, U. Ill., Champaign, 1980; JD, Loyola U., 1983. Bar: Ill. 1983, Fla. 1990. Attorney Anes Ozmon Lewin and Assocs., Chgo., 1983-84; gen. counsel Pacific Investment Corp., Chgo., 1984-85, also bd. dirs.; v.p. gen. counsel The Rockefeller Group, Ltd., Chgo., also bd. dirs.; ptnr., atty. Bogen, Rosenblum and Assoc., 1986-89; pvt. practice, 1989—; prof. bus. law Fla. Atlantic U., Boca Raton, 1991-92; bd. dirs. Atlanta Gold Corp., Vancouver, B.C., Can., Bogen Group, Inc., Champ Products, Inc., Internat. Prodns., Ltd.; legal counsel GuldCoast Pubs., Inc.; former asst. state atty Broward County, Fla., 1991. Author law column Sun-Sentinel Newspaper, Fla., 1992. Mem. ABA, Chgo. Bar Assn., Ill. Bar Assn., Fla. Bar Assn., Ill. Trial Lawyers Assn. Avocations: tennis, golf, baseball. Home: 980 N Federal Hwy Ste 206 Boca Raton FL 33432-2711

**BOGENSCHUTZ, J. DAVID,** lawyer; b. Covington, Ky., May 15, 1944; s. John Francis and Virginia Margaret (Dugan) B.; m. Mary H. McCleary, Oct. 24, 1981; children: Kathleen, Emily. BA, Miami U., Oxford, Ohio, 1966; JD, U. Cin., 1969. Bar: Ohio 1969, U.S. Dist. Ct. (so. dist.) Ohio 1970, U.S. Ct. Appeals (6th cir.) 1971, Fla. 1971, U.S. Dist. Ct. (so. dist.) Fla. 1972, U.S. Ct. Appeals (5th cir.) 1980, U.S. Dist. Ct. (mid. dist.) Fla. 1981, U.S. Ct. Appeals (4th and 11th cirs.) 1981, U.S. Dist. Ct. (ea. dist.) Wis. 1989, U.S. Ct. Appeals (3d cir.) 1999. Instr. Criminal Justice Inst. Nova U., 1977; instr. Broward County Criminal Justice Inst., 1972; asst. solicitor County of Broward, 1971, chief asst. state's atty., 1974-77; ptnr. Bogenschutz & Dutko, P.A., Ft. Lauderdale, Fla.; mem. Gov.'s Com. on Criminal Justice Standards and Goals, 1975-76; mem. bench bar liaison com. U.S. Dist. Ct. (so. dist.) Fla., 1985—. Mem. ATLA, NACDL, Broward County Bar Assn. (criminal law sect. chmn. 1980-81, exec. com. 1981-86, sec., treas. 1985-86), Ohio Bar Assn., Fla. Bar Assn. (criminal law sect., grievance com. 17th jud. cir. 1982-84), Fed. Bar Assn., Greene County Bar Assn., Fla. Pros. Atty.'s Assn., Nat. Dist. Atty.'s Assn. Democrat. Roman Catholic. Criminal, Appellate. Office: Bogenschutz & Dutko PA Colonial Bank Bldg 600 S Andrews Ave Ste 500 Fort Lauderdale FL 33301-2851

**BOGER, KENNETH SNEAD,** lawyer; b. Concord, N.C., Sept. 8, 1946; s. Charles E. Jr. and Mary (Snead) B.; m. Robin Zaverl, Oct. 10, 1969; children: Adam S., Hallie S., Fiona G. AB, Duke U., 1968; MBA, U. Chgo., 1973; JD, Boston Coll., 1976. Bar: Mass. 1977. Assoc. Warner & Stackpole, Boston, 1976-82, ptnr., 1983—. 1st lt. inf. U.S. Army, 1968-71, Vietnam. General corporate, Intellectual property, Securities. Home: 200 Church St Rear Newton MA 02458-1906 Office: Warner & Stackpole 75 State St Ste 600 Boston MA 02109-1808

**BOGGS, BETH CLEMENS,** lawyer; b. Dubuque, Iowa, July 28, 1967; d. Theodore Alan and Mary Ann (Fleckenstein) Clemens; m. T. Darin Boggs, Mar. 9, 1991. BA, Govs. State U., 1987; JD, So. Ill. U., 1991. Bar: Ill. 1991, Mo. 1992, U.S. Dist. Ct. (so. dist.) Ill. 1991, U.S. Dist. Ct. (ea. dist.) Mo. 1992. Clk. R. Courtney Hughes & Assocs., Carbondale, Ill., 1990-91; lawyer Sandberg Phoenix & von Gontard, St. Louis, 1991-93; assoc. LaTourette, Schlueter & Byrne, St. Louis, 1993-95; mng. ptnr. Landau, Omahana & Kopka, P.C., St. Louis, 1995-99; mng. and founding ptnr. Boggs, Backer & Bates, LLC, St. Louis, 1999—; adj. faculty Webster U., 1995—. Editor student articles So. Ill. U. Law Jour., 1991; contbr. articles to profl. jours. Mem. Young Lawyers divsn. of ABA (vice chair corp. counsel com. 1991-92, editor Corp. Counsel Newsletter 1991-92), Bus. Women St. Louis, Women Lawyers Assn. Avocations: tennis, softball, golf. General civil litigation, General corporate, Insurance. Office: BBB 7912 Bonhomme Ave Ste 400 Saint Louis MO 63105-3512

**BOGGS, DANNY JULIAN,** federal judge; b. Havana, Cuba, Oct. 23, 1944; s. Robert Lilburn and Yolanda (Pereda) B.; m. Judith Susan Solow, Dec. 23, 1967; children: Rebecca, David, Jonathan. A.B., Harvard Coll., Cambridge, Mass., 1965; J.D., U. Chgo., 1968; LLD (hon.), U. Detroit Mercy, 1994. Dep. commr. Ky. Dept. Econ. Security, 1969-70; legal counsel, adminstrv. asst. Gov. Ky., 1970-71; legis. counsel to Rep. legislators Ky. Gen. Assembly, 1972; asst. to solicitor gen. U.S. Dept. Justice, Washington, 1973-75; asst. to chmn. FPC, Washington, 1975-77; dep. minority counsel Senate Energy Com., Washington, 1977-79; of counsel Bushnell, Gage, et al., Washington, 1979-80; spl. asst. to Pres. White House, Washington, 1981-83; dep.

sec. U.S. Dept. Energy, Washington, 1983-86; judge U.S. Ct. Appeals (6th cir.), Cin., 1986—; mem. adv. com. on appellate rules Jud. Conf. U.S., 1991-94, com. on automation and tech., 1994—. Mem. vis. com. U. Chgo. Law Sch., 1984-87, 99—; del. Republican Nat. Conv., 1972; staff dir. energy subcom. Rep. Platform Com., 1980; trustee Lexington Sch., 1999—. Mem. ABA, Ky. Bar Assn., Mont Pelerin Soc., Phila. Soc., Order of Coif, Phi Delta Phi. Office: US Ct Appeals US Courthouse 601 W Broadway Ste 220 Louisville KY 40202-2227

**BOGGS, JAMES DOTSON,** lawyer; b. Kansas City, Mo., Aug. 31, 1949; s. William C. and Helen C. (Harbison) B.; m. Vickie R. Boggs, May 27, 1972; children: William Christian, Meghan Raye. BA, U. Mo., Columbia, 1971; JD, U. Mo., Kansas City, 1975. Bar: Mo. 1975, U.S. Dist. Ct. (we. dist.) Mo., U.S. Ct. Appeals (8th cir.), U.S. Supreme Ct. Assoc. Witt and Shafer, Platte City, Mo., 1975-78; ptnr. Witt and Boggs, Platte City, Mo., 1979-81, Witt, Boggs & Shaw, Platte City, Mo., 1982-85, Witt, Boggs, Shaw & Van Amburg, Platte City, Mo., 1985-87; pvt. practice Kansas City, Mo., 1987—. Chmn. Platte County Dem. PArty, 1985-86; commr. Platte County Jud. Commn., 1987-93, 93—. Mem. Mo. Bar Assn. (gov. 1992—), Mo. Assn. Trial Attys. (govs., 1985—, exec. com. 1994—), Reach Out Am. (dir. 1994—). Office: 6406 N Cosby Ave Kansas City MO 64151-2377

**BOGGS, JUDITH SUSAN,** lawyer, health policy expert; b. Bklyn., Feb. 11, 1946; d. Robert Henry and Ethel (Shapiro) Solow; m. Danny Julian Boggs; children: Rebecca, David, Jonathan. BA cum laude, Bklyn. Coll., 1966; JD, U. Chgo., 1969. Bar: Ky. 1970. Human rights rep. Ky. Human Rights Commn., Frankfort, Ky., 1969; legal counsel Ky. Dept. Mental Health, Frankfort, 1970-73; sr. legal advisor Social and Rehabilitation Service, Washington, 1973-77; dir., health systems div. Health Care Fin. Adminstrn., Washington, 1978-82, special asst. to assoc. adminstr. for policy, 1982-86, spl. asst. to adminstr., 1986-87; sr. policy analyst The White House, Washington, 1987-89; of counsel Alagia, Day, Trautwein & Smith, Louisville, 1989-93; sr. v.p., gen. counsel Ky. Hosp. Assn., 1993-94; pvt. practice, 1994—. Mem. ABA, Ky. Bar Assn., Nat. Health Lawyers Assn., Louisville Bar Assn. Health, Administrative and regulatory.

**BOGGS, STEVEN EUGENE,** lawyer; b. Santa Monica, Calif., Apr. 28, 1947; s. Eugene W. and Annie (Happe) B. BA in Econ., U. Calif., Santa Barbara, 1969; D of Chiropractic summa cum laude, Cleveland Chiropractic, L.A., 1974; PhD in Fin. Planning, Columbia Pacific U., 1986; JD in Law, U. So. Calif., 1990. Bar: Calif. 1990, U.S. Dist. Ct. (cen. dist.) Calif. 1990, Hawaii 1991, U.S. Ct. Appeals (9th cir.); CFP; lic. chiropractor Hawaii, Calif.; lic. radiography X-ray supr. and operator. Faculty mem. Cleveland Chiropractic Coll., 1972-74; pres. clinic dir. Hawaii Chiropractic Clinic, Inc., Aiea, 1974-87; pvt. practice Honolulu, 1991—; mem. faculty Hawaii Pacific U., 1997-99; cons. in field; seminar presenter 1990—. Contbr. articles to profl. jours. Recipient Cert. Appreciation State of Hawaii, 1981-84. Fellow Internat. Coll. of Chiropractic; mem. ABA, Am. Trial Lawyers Assn., Consumer Lawyers of Hawaii, Am. Chriopractic Assn., Hawaii State Chiropractic Assn. (pres. 1978, 85, 86, v.p. 1977, sec. 1979-84, treas. 1976, other coms., Valuable Svc. award 1984, Cert. Appreciation 1986, Cert. Achievement 1986, Chiropractor of Yr. 1986, Outstanding Achievement award 1991), Consumer Lawyers of Hawaii (bd. dirs.). Democrat. Avocations: sailing, scuba, snorkling, boogie boarding, bicycling. Personal injury, Insurance. Office: 1188 Bishop St Ste 1705 Honolulu HI 96813-3307

**BOGRAD, SANDRA LYNN,** lawyer; b. Newark, Oct. 16, 1958; d. Arnold Jack and Mildred (Gaby) B. BA, Rutgers Coll., 1980; JD, Vt. Law Sch., 1983. Bar: N.J. 1983, U.S. Dist. Ct. N.J. 1983, U.S. Ct. Appeals (3d cir.) 1990, U.S. Supreme Ct. 1990, D.C. 1993. Law clk. Essex County Prosecutor's Office, Newark, 1982; jud. clk. to judge Philip M. Freedman Newark, 1983; asst. prosecutor Essex County Prosecutor's Office, Newark, 1984-87; assoc. Shanley & Fisher P.C., Morristown, N.J., 1988-93, Pitney, Harden, Kipp & Szuch, Morristown, N.J., 1993—. Contbr. articles to profl. jours. Mem. Nat. Assn. Criminal Def. Attys., N.J. State Bar Assn. Democrat. Jewish. Avocations: biking, painting, travel. Criminal, Labor. Office: Pitney Harden Kipp & Szuch Morristown NJ 07960

**BOGUCKI, RAYMOND SPENCER,** lawyer; b. Hammond, Ind., Aug. 14, 1951; s. Raymond L. Bogucki & Bette J. Spencer; m. Vicki Kincheloe; children: Chant Graham, Anthony Dean. BA in Comms., U. Ky., 1976; JD, No. Ky. U., Highland Heights, 1980. Bar: Ky. 1980. Lawyer in pvt. practice Florence, Ky., 1980—, Augusta, Ky., 1981—, Maysville, Ky., 1994—; prof. No. Ky. U., Highland Heights, 1981-94. Served with USN, 1969-72. Mem. ABA, ATLA, Ky. Acad. Trial Attys. Roman Catholic. Personal injury, Criminal. Office: PO Box 6206 Florence KY 41022-6206

**BOGUE, ANDREW WENDELL,** federal judge; b. Yankton, S.D., May 23, 1919; s. Andrew S. and Genevieve Bogue; m. Florence Elizabeth Williams, Aug. 5, 1945; children—Andrew Stevenson, Laurie Beth, Scott MacFarlane. B.S., S.D. State U., 1941; LL.B., U. S.D., 1947. Bar: S.D. 1947. States atty. Turner County, S.D., 1952-67; judge 2d Jud. Cir., S.D., 1967-70; judge U.S. Dist. Ct. S.D., Rapid City, 1970—, chief judge, from 1980, sr. judge, 1985—. Mem. S.D. Bar Assn., Fed. Judges Assn. Episcopalian. Office: US Courthouse Fed Bldg Rm 244 515 9th St Rapid City SD 57701-2626

**BOGUS, CARL THOMAS,** law educator; b. Fall River, Mass., May 14, 1948; s. Isidore E. and Carolyn (Dashoff) B.; m. Dale Shepard, Sept. 5, 1970 (div. 1987); children: Elizabeth Carol, Ian Troy; m. Cynthia J. Giles, Nov. 5, 1988; 1 child, Zoe Churchill. AB, Syracuse U., 1970, JD, 1972. Bar: Pa. 1973, U.S. Dist. Ct. (ea. dist.) Pa. 1973, U.S. Ct. Appeals (3d cir.) 1976, U.S. Supreme Ct. 1977. Assoc. Steinberg, Greenstein, Gorelick & Price, Phila., 1973-79, ptnr., 1979-83; assoc. Mesirov, Gelman, Jaffe, Cramer & Jamieson, Phila., 1983-84, ptnr., 1985-91, assoc. prof. Roger Williams U. Sch. Law, 1996—; vis. prof. Rutgers U. Sch. Law, Camden, 1992-96; mem. bd. Visitors Coll. Law, Syracuse U., N.Y., 1976—; mem. nat. adv. panel Violence Policy Ctr., 1993—. Contbr. articles to profl. jours. Bd. dirs. Handgun Control, Inc., 1987-89, bd. govs., 1992-93; bd. dirs. Ctr. to Prevent Handgun Violence, 1989-92, Lawyers Alliance for Nuclear Arms Control, 1987-89. Mem. ABA (Ross Essay award 1991), Syracuse Law Coll. Assn. (exec. sec. 1979-83, 2d v.p. 1983-85). Democrat. Jewish. Office: Roger William U Sch Law 10 Metacom Ave Bristol RI 02809-5103

**BOGUT, JOHN CARL, JR.,** lawyer; b. Billings, Mont., July 31, 1961; s. Jack Carl and Joan E. (Gibson) B. BA, Denison U., 1983; JD, Duquesne U., 1986. Bar: Pa. Supreme CT., U.S. Dist. Ct. (we. dist.) Pa., U.S. Ct. Appeals (3d cir.), U.S. Supreme Ct. Law clk. Meyer, Darragh, Buckler, Bebenek & Eck, Pitts., 1985; asst. dist. atty. County of Allegheny, Pitts., 1986-89; litigation atty. Swensen, Perer & Johnson, Pitts., 1989—; Magistrate's Ct. prosecutor Pitts. Dist Atty.'s Office, 1988; cons. Bogut, Inc., Pitts., 1986—. Cons. Civic Light Opera Guild, Pitts., 1986—. Mem. ABA, Pa. Bar Assn., Allegheny County Bar Assn., Pa. Dist. Atty.'s Assn., Pitts. Ski Club, Young Republicans, Alpha Tau Omega. Lutheran. Avocations: skiing, sailing, ice hockey, lacrosse. General civil litigation, Criminal, General practice. Office: Wayman Irvin & McAuley 1624 Frick Bldg Pittsburgh PA 15219

**BOGUTZ, JEROME EDWIN,** lawyer; b. Bridgeton, N.J., June 7, 1935; s. Charles and Gertrude (Lahn) B.; m. Helene Carole Ross, Nov. 20, 1960; children: Marc Lahn, Tami Lynne. BS in Fin., Pa. State U., 1957; JD, Villanova U., 1962. Bar: Pa., U.S. Dist. Ct. (ea. dist.) Pa., U.S. Ct. Appeals (3d cir.), U.S. Supreme Ct. Assoc. Dash & Levy, Phila., 1962-63, Abrahams & Loewenstein, Phila., 1963-64; dep. dir., chief of litigation Community Legal Svcs., Phila., 1964-68, dir., 1966-78; emeritus, 1978—; pvt. practice law Phila., 1968-71; ptnr. Bogutz & Mazer, Phila., 1971-81, Fox Rothschild O'Brien & Frankel, Phila., 1981-98; judge Pro Tem Phila. Ct. Common Pleas, 1992—; ptnr. Christie, Pabarue, Mortensen & Young, P.C., Phila., 1998—; adj. clin. prof. law Villanova (Pa.) U., 1969-72, lectr., 1987—, bd. consultors Law Sch., 1983—; pres. Internat. Mobile Machines, Phila., 1980-81, Interdigital Comm., 1980-81, also bd. dirs. ABA-JAD Lawyers Conf., 1987-92,em. exec. coun., 1986-92, vice chmn., 1987-88, chmn., 1989-90, chmn. nominating com., 1989-90, mem. long range planning com., 1989-90; bd. dirs. Jefferson Park Hosp., Phila. Bd. dirs. Am. Friends of Hebrew U., 1988-93, chmn. exec. com., 1991-93, pres., 1993-95, chmn. bd. 1995-98, chair steering com., pres. Pa. Futures Commn. on Justice in the 21st Century, 1993—, chmn. of bd., 1993-97. With USAR, 1956-60. Fellow Am. Bar Found. (life), Pa. Bar Found. (life, pres. 1986-88, bd. dirs. 1983—, lifetime dir. 1991—), Am. Judicature Soc. (life, bd. dirs. 1990—); mem. ABA (ho. of dels. 1980-84, 86-96, credentials and admissions com. 1987-88, nominating com. 1992, 93, chair ABA/JAD bench bar com., vice chmn. lawyer's conf. 1987-89, chair 1988-90, co-chair mid-yr. meeting com. 1987-88, planning com., conf. sect. officers, 1988-90, bd. mem. consortium on legal svcs. and pub. 1987-91, mem. disaster relief task force, bd. dirs., commr., chmn. ABA Commn. on Advt. 1988-91), Pa. Bar Assn. (pres. 1985-86, bd. dirs. 1983-90, chair Governance Com., 1996-98), Phila. Bar Found. (pres. 1981), Phila. Bar Assn. (v.p. 1978, pres.-elect 1979, chancellor 1980, sec. 1975-78, trustee 1979—), Pa. Bar Trust (chair 1993—), Pa. House of Dels. (life; chair governance com. 1996-98), Nat. Met. Bar Leaders (founder, pres. 1979-82, pres. emeritus 1983—), Nat. Conf. Bar Pres. (exec. coun. 1981-84), Phila. C. of C. (bd. dirs. 1980-83). Republican. Jewish. Avocations: golf, sailing. General corporate, General civil litigation, Communications. Home: 110 S Somerset Ave Ventnor City NJ 08406-2848 Office: Christie Pabarue Mortensen & Young 1880 Jfk Blvd Fl 10 Philadelphia PA 19103-7424

**BOHANNON, CHARLES TAD,** lawyer; b. Dallas, June 25, 1964; s. Charles Spencer and Donna Pauline (Smith) B.; m. Gayle Renee Alston, July 26, 1986. BA, Hendrix Coll., 1986; JD, U. Ark., Little Rock, 1992; LLM, Washington U., St. Louis, 1993. Bar: Ark. 1992, Tex. 1993, U.S. Dist. Ct. (ea. and we. dists.) Ark. 1992, U.S. Dist. Ct. (no. dist.) Tex. 1994, U.S. Ct. Appeals (5th and 8th cirs.) 1994, U.S. Tax Ct. 1994. Staff atty. U.S. Ct. Appeals (8th cir.), St. Louis, 1992-94; assoc. Gill Law Firm, Little Rock, 1994-98, Wright, Lindsey & Jennings, LLP, Little Rock, 1998—. Contbr. articles to profl. jours. Mem. ABA, Ark. Bar Assn., Pulaski County Bar Assn., Nat. Transp. Safety Bd., Bar Assn. Fifth Cir., Bar Assn. State Bar of Tex., Am. Judicature Soc., Nat. Assn. Bond Lawyers, Ark. State Soccer Assn., Ctrl. Ark. Referees Assn., Aircraft Owners and Pilots Assn. Avocations: soccer (player, referee, coach), flying, fly fishing, home renovation. Taxation, general, Municipal (including bonds), Aviation. Office: Wright Lindsey & Jennings 200 W Capitol Ave Ste 2200 Little Rock AR 72201-3699

**BOHANON, LUTHER L.,** federal judge; b. Ft. Smith, Ark., Aug. 9, 1901; s. William Joseph and Artelia (Campbell) B.; m. Marie Swatek, July 17, 1933; 1 son, Richard L. LLB, U. Okla., 1927; LLD (hon.), Oklahoma City U., 1991. Bar: Okla. 1927, U.S. Supreme Ct. 1937. Gen. practice law Seminole, Okla. and Oklahoma City, 1927-61; judge U.S. Dist. Ct. Okla. (no., ea., and we. dists.), 1961-74, sr. judge, 1974—. Mem. platform com. Democratic Nat. Conv., 1940. Served to maj. USAAF, 1942-45. Recipient citations and awards including citation from Okla. Senate and Ho. of Reps., 1979, Okla. County Bar Assn. and Jour. Record award, 1987, Humanitarian award NCCJ, 1991; Luther Bohanon Am. Inn of Ct. named in his honor Am. Inn of Ct. XXIII/U. Okla., 1991. Mem. U.S. Dist. Judges Assn. (10th cir.), Fed. Judges Assn., Okla. Bar Assn., Oklahoma County Bar Assn., Oklahoma City C. of C., Sigma Nu, Phi Alpha Delta. Methodist. Clubs: Mason (Shriner, 32 deg.), K.T, Jester, Kiwanis, Com.of 100, Men's Dinner Club. Home: 1617 Bedford Dr Oklahoma City OK 73116-5406 Office: US Dist Ct PO Box 1514 200 NW 4th St Ste 2001 Oklahoma City OK 73102-3028

**BOHLEN, CHRISTOPHER WAYNE,** lawyer; b. Decatur, Ill., July 24, 1949; s. Martin Orlando and Mamie Virginia (Andrews) B.; m. Rosemary Pistorius, June 4, 1972; children: Harper Pistorius, Andrew Pistorius, Elizabeth Pistorius. BA, U. Ill., 1970; JD, Northwestern U., 1973. Bar: Ohio 1973, U.S. Dist. Ct. Ohio 1974, Ill. 1977, U.S. Dist. Ct. (cen. dist.) Ill. 1977, U.S. Supreme Ct., 1977, U.S. Dist. Ct. (no. dist.) Ill. 1986, U.S. Ct. Appeals (7th cir.) 1986. Atty. Legal Aid/Pub. Defender's Office, Cleve., 1973-77; assoc. Blanke & Blanke, Kankakee, Ill., 1977-78; ptnr. Blanke, Norden, Barmann & Bohlen P.C., Kankakee, 1978—. Mem. exec. bd. Kankakee YMCA, 1984-90; mem. exec. bd. Kankakee Valley Park Dist., 1983—, pres., 1986—; precinct committeeman Kankakee Rep. Com., 1985—; mem. Kankakee Planning Commn., 1986—, Kankakee County Pub. Bldg. Commn., 1986—. Recipient Claude E. Clarke award, 1976; named Kankakee County Outstanding Vol., 1989. Mem. Ill. State Bar Assn., Ill. Trial Lawyers Assn., Riverview Hist. Dist. Mem. United Ch. Christ. Federal civil litigation, Personal injury, State civil litigation. Home: 949 S Chicago Ave Kankakee IL 60901-5236 Office: Blanke Norden Barmann & Bohlen PC PO Box 428 Monee IL 60449-0428

**BOHLKE, GARY LEE,** lawyer, playwright; b. Yakima, Wash., Mar. 9, 1941; s. Francis Douglas and Laura Mae (Bianchi) B. BA, U. Wash., 1963; JD, Am. U., 1966; LLM, U. London, 1967; diploma, London Inst. World Affairs, 1967. Bar: DC 1967. Assoc. Mason, Fenwick & Lawrence, Washington, 1967-70; atty., adv. U.S. C.E., Washington, 1972-74; ast. solicitor environ. law U.S. Dept. Interior, Washington, 1974-83; sr. atty. environ. protection U.S. Dept. Interior, 1983-86; assoc. gen. counsel litigation and enforcement Farm Credit Adminstrn., 1988-90; dir. Ackerson & Feldman Chartered, 1991-93; ptnr. Semmes, Bowen & Semmes, 1993-97; mem. mgmt. com. Internat. Law Practice Group, 1995-97; prin. Oppenheimer, Wolff, Donnelly & Bayth (and predecessor firm), 1997-98; shareholder Ablondi, Foster, Sobin & Davidow PC, 1998—. Author: (plays) Echoes, 1988, The Crime Tetraology consisting of Double Cross, 1982, Obsession, 1984, Judgment, 1985, Act of Justice, 1987; (novel) Forever a Stranger, 1990, (screenplay) Double Cross, 1992. Vice chmn. com. on environ. and transp., Washington; advisor Neighborhood Commn. 4C, 1980-88. Mem. ABA, D.C. Bar Assn. (chmn. environ. law com. 1977-78). Lutheran. Home: 1716 Eutaw Pl Baltimore MD 21217-3730 Office: 1150 18th St NW Ste 900 Washington DC 20036-3846

**BOHM, JACK NELSON,** lawyer; b. Sharon, Pa., July 5, 1924; s. Joseph and Irene (Bohm) B.; m. Elizabeth Viscofsky, Sept. 27, 1947; children: Robert Mark, Richard Darrell, Lorie Joyce Klumb. Student, U. Pa., 1942-43, U. Ga., 1943-44; JD, Washington U., St. Louis, 1948. Bar: Mo. 1948, U.S Dist. Ct. (we. dist.) Mo. 1948, U.S. Ct. of Mil. Appeals 1955, U.S. Supreme Ct. 1955, U.S. Ct. of Appeals (8th Cir.) 1960, Kans. 1985, U.S. Dist. Ct. Kans. 1985. Assoc. Hall Bresler & Cohn, Kansas City, Mo., 1948-61; ptnr. Glass Bohm & Hirschman, Kansas City, Mo., 1961-71, Stoup & Bohm, Kansas City, Mo., 1971-81; chmn. bd. Buck Bohm & Stein, P.C., Kansas City/Leawood, Kans., 1981-97; sr. counsel Morrison & Hecker LLP, Overland Park, Kans., 1997—; chief judge U.S. Army Ct. of Mil. Appeals, 1977-80, Mobilization Designation. Editor: State Variations of Commercial Law, 1985. Pres. Dist. 2 B'nai B'rith, 1964; co-chmn., NCCJ, Kansas City, 1968-71. With U.S. Army 1943-46, USAR, 1948-84, brigadier gen. AUS, ret. 1977-84. Legion of Merit U.S. Army, 1984. Mem. ABA, Mo. Bar Assn. (chmn. commr. law com. 1977-79), Kans. Bar Assn., Meadowbrook Country Club, Phi Alpha Delta. Bankruptcy, General corporate, Probate. Home: 11300 Fontana St Shawnee Mission KS 66211-1751 Office: 9200 Indian Creek Pkwy Ste 450 Overland Park KS 66210-2017 also: 2600 Grand Blvd Kansas City MO 64108-4613

**BOHN, ROBERT HERBERT,** lawyer; b. Austin, Tex., Sept. 2, 1935; s. Herbert and Alice B.; m. Gay P. Maloy, June 4, 1957; children: Rebecca Shoemaker, Katherine Bernat, Robert H., Jr.. BBA, U. Tex., 1957, LLB, 1963. Bar: Tex. 1963, Calif. 1965. Ptnr. Boccardo Law Firm, San Jose, Calif., 1965-87, Alexander & Bohn, San Jose, 1987-91; Bohn, Bennion & Niland, 1992-97, Bohn & Bohn, 1998—; spkr. Calif. Continuing Edn. of Bar; judge pro tem Superior Ct. of Calif., San Jose, 1975-96. Mem. Consumer Attys. Calif., Am. Bd. Trial Advocates, ATLA, Santa Clara County Bar Assn., Calif. State Bar Assn., Trial Lawyers Pub. Justice, Roscoe Pound Found., Million Dollar Advocates Forum, Lawyers Arbitration Mediation Svc. (pres.), Commonwealth Club Calif., Silicon Valley Capital Club, Exec. Golfers (dir. gen.), Texas Cowboys Assn., Phi Gamma Delta. Alternative dispute resolution, Labor, Product liability. Home: 14124 Pike Rd Saratoga CA 95070-5380 Office: 152 N 3rd St Ste 200 San Jose CA 95112-5515

**BOHNE, EDWARD DANIEL,** lawyer; b. Springfield, Ill., May 27, 1956; s. Edward Herman and Virginia Viola (Strand) B.; m. Christine Mary Gillespie, Dec. 23, 1978; children: Amanda Marie, Rebecca Anne. BA in Polit. Sci., Western Ill. U., 1979; JD, Washington U., St. Louis, 1986. Bar: Ill. 1987, Mo. 1988, U.S. Dist. Ct. (we. dist.) Mo. 1988, U.S. Dist. Ct. (so. dist.) Ill. 1988, U.S. Ct. Appeals (7th cir.) 1991, U.S. Ct. Vets. Appeals 1992, U.S. Ct. Appeals (fed. cir.) 1994. Assoc. Talbert & Mallon, P.C., Alton, Ill., 1988-89; pvt. practice Alton, 1990—. Maj. USAR, 1979—. Mem. ABA, NRA (life), Res. Officers Assn. (life), Assn. Trial Lawyers Am., U.S. Armor Assn., Nat. Orgn. Social Security Claimants Reps., Nat. Orgn. Vets Advocates, Ill. State Bar Assn. Republican. Roman Catholic. Pension, profit-sharing, and employee benefits, Probate, Family and matrimonial. Office: 2854 Homer Adams Pky PO Box 1107 Alton IL 62002-1107

**BOHNEN, MICHAEL J.,** lawyer; b. Buffalo, Mar. 9, 1947; s. Joyce B. Oppenheim, June 19, 1969; children—Sharon, Deborah. B.A., Harvard U., 1968, J.D., 1972. Bar: Mass. 1972. Assoc. Nutter, McClennen & Fish, LLP, Boston, 1972-80, ptnr., 1980—; lectr. Boston U. Law Sch., 1981-85. Pres., Solomon Schechter Day Sch., Newton, 1980-82; pres. Jewish Community Rels. Council, Boston, 1991-93; chmn. Combined Jewish Philanthropies, 1993-95, New Jewish H.S., 1995—; vice chmn. Jewish Coun. for Pub. Affairs., 1995-99. Co-author: Mass. Corporate Forms, 1990. Mem. Boston Bar Assn. (chmn. corp. law com. 1997-99). General corporate, Mergers and acquisitions, Securities. Home: 60 Nathan Rd Newton MA 02459-1105 Office: Nutter McClennen & Fish LLP One International Pl Boston MA 02110

**BOHNHOFF, HENRY M.,** lawyer; b. Albuquerque, Dec. 25, 1956; s. Herman Carl William and Lois Marie (Jacobsen) B.; m. Jennifer Lynn Swedberg, June 7, 1980; children: H. Matthew, J. Christopher, J. Thomas. BS with honors, Stanford U., 1978; JD, Columbia U., 1982. Bar: N.Mex. 1982, U.S. Dist. Ct. N.Mex. 1983, U.S. Ct. Appeals (10th cir.) 1983, U.S. Supreme Ct. 1987. Law clk. to chief judge U.S. Dist. Ct. N.Mex., Albuquerque, 1982-83; assoc. Rodey, Dickason, Sloan, Akin & Robb, Albuquerque, 1983-87; chief asst. atty. gen. N.Mex. Atty. Gen.'s Office, Santa Fe, 1987-88; dept. atty. gen. N.Mex. Atty. Gen., Santa Fe, 1988-89; ptnr. Rodey, Dickason, Sloan, Akin & Robb, Albuquerque, 1989—. Exec. editor Columbia Jour. Environ. Law, 1981-82. Pres. Redeemer Luth. Ch., Albuquerque, 1987-89. Mem. ABA, N.Mex. Bar Assn., Phi Beta Kappa. Republican. Avocations: rock climbing, woodworking, sailing, tennis. Federal civil litigation, Construction, Professional liability. Office: Rodey Dickason Sloan Akin Robb PA 200 3rd St NW Ste 2200 Albuquerque NM 87102-3334

**BOHREN, MICHAEL OSCAR,** lawyer; b. Appleton, Wis., Feb. 27, 1947; s. Oscar Robert and Martha (Anderson) B.; m. Mary Joset Morse, Nov. 26, 1977; children: Juliana Rose, Katherine Elizabeth. AB, Ripon Coll., 1969; JD, Marquette U., 1975. Bar: Wis. 1978, U.S. Dist. Ct. (ea. and we. dists.) Wis. 1975, U.S. Ct. Appeals (5th and 7th cirs.) 1976, U.S. Supreme Ct. 1978. Atty. USDA, Washington, 1975; gen. counsel Aries Ltd., Milw., 1975-78; atty. Marola & Bohren, Milw., 1978—. Bd. dirs. Kettle Moraine Sch. Dist., Wales, Wis., 1982—, pres., 1986—; bd. dirs. Waukesha (Wis.) Symphony; v.p. Greenfield (Wis.) Sch. Dist., 1977-81. Mem. ABA, ATLA, Wis. Bar Assn., Wis. Trial Lawyers Assn., Masons. Republican. Avocations: geology, politics, reading. General civil litigation, Civil rights, Contracts commercial. Home: 315496 SW Christopher Way Delafield WI 53018 Office: Marola & Bohren PO Box 27771 Milwaukee WI 53227-0771

**BOIES, WILBER H.,** lawyer; b. Bloomington, Ill., Mar. 15, 1944; s. W. H. and Martha Jane (Hutchison) B.; m. Victoria Joan Steinitz, Sept. 17, 1966; children: Andrew Charles, Carolyn Ursula. AB, Brown U., 1965; JD, U. Chgo., 1968. Bar: Ill. 1968, U.S. Dist. Ct. (no. dist.) Ill. 1968, U.S. Dist. Ct. (ea. dist.) Wis. 1973, U.S. Ct. Appeals (7th cir.) 1974, U.S. Ct. Appeals (5th cir.) 1975, U.S. Ct. Appeals (3d cir.) 1977, U.S. Supreme Ct. 1978, U.S. Ct. Appeals (8th cir.) 1994, U.S. Ct. Appeals (9th cir.) 1995. Assoc. Altheimer & Gray, Chgo., 1968-71; ptnr. McDermott, Will & Emery, Chgo., 1971—. Contbr. articles to profl. jours. Active CPR Inst.for Dispute Resolution. Mem. ABA, Legal Club Chgo., Law Club Chgo., Bar Assn. 7th Fed. Cir., Chgo. Bar Assn. (chmn. class litigation com. 1991-92), Chgo. Coun. Lawyers, Monroe Club, Chgo. Bar Found. Federal civil litigation, State civil litigation, Alternative dispute resolution. Office: McDermott Will & Emery 227 W Monroe St Ste 3100 Chicago IL 60606-5096

**BOINSKI, PATRICIA MARIE,** lawyer; b. Blossburg, Pa., May 23, 1951; d. Francis Louis and Delores Ann (Petroski) B. BA, Lycoming Coll., 1973; MA, George Washington U., 1978, JD, 1985. Bar: Pa. 1986. Staff asst. Joseph M. McDade M.C., Washington, 1972-73; dir. membership svcs. Nat. Apartment Assn, Washington, 1973-74; from legis. asst. to assoc. dir. fed. govt. rels. ARCO, Washington, 1974-87, dir. fed. govt. rels., 1987—. Dir. USO Met. Washington, 1993—. Avocations: walking, reading. Office: ARCO 601 Pennsylvania Ave NW # 400 Washington DC 20004-2601

**BOISSEAU, RICHARD ROBERT,** lawyer; b. Phila., Sept. 6, 1944; s. Robert Bartholomew and Anne Cecilia (Tierney) B.; m. Jo-Ann Elizabeth Tompkins, Jan. 20, 1970; children: Richard Andrew, Thomas, Kristen. BS cum laude, Drexel U., 1968; JD cum laude, Temple U., 1974. Bar: Ga. 1974, U.S. Dist. Ct. (no. dist.) Ga. 1974, U.S. Ct. Appeals (4th cir.) 1980, U.S. Ct. Appeals (11th cir.) 1981, U.S. Supreme Ct. 1984, U.S. Ct. Appeals (9th cir.) 1986. Ptnr. Kilpatrick Stockton LLP, Atlanta, 1974—. Contbg. author: How Arbitration Works, 1987, 93, 97; contbr. articles to numerous profl. publs. Bd. dirs. Vis. Nurse Health Sys., Atlanta, 1976—. Mem. Ga. Bar Assn., Atlanta Bar Assn. Republican. Roman Catholic. Avocations: golf, running. Labor, Civil rights. Office: Kilpatrick Stockton LLP 1100 Peachtree St NE Ste 2800 Atlanta GA 30309-4501

**BOK, DEREK,** law educator, former university president; b. Bryn Mawr, Pa., Mar. 22, 1930; s. Curtis and Margaret (Plummer) B.; m. Sissela Ann Myrdal, May 7, 1955; children: Hilary Margaret, Victoria, Tomas Jeremy. B.A., Stanford U., 1951; J.D., Harvard U., 1954; M.A., George Washington U., 1958. Fulbright scholar Paris, 1954-55; faculty Harvard U. Law Sch., Cambridge, Mass., 1958—, prof., 1961—, dean, 1968-71; pres. Harvard U., Cambridge, 1971-91; 300th anniversary univ. prof. Harvard U., 1991—. Editor: (with Archibald Cox) Cases and Materials on Labor Law, 1962; author: (with John T. Dunlop) Labor and the American Community, 1970, Beyond the Ivory Tower: Social Responsibilities of the Modern University, 1982, Higher Learning, 1986, Universities and the Future of America, 1990, The Cost of Talent, 1993, (with William G. Bowen) The Shape of the River, 1998; contbr.: In the Public Interest, 1980, The State of the Nation, 1997. Bd. dirs., nat. chmn. Common Cause, 1999—, Overseas Cts. Inst. Music, 1997—. Fellow Ctr. for Advanced Studies in the Behavioral Scis., 1991-92. Fellow Am. Acad. Arts and Scis., mem. Inst. Medicine, Am. Philos. Soc., Phi Beta Kappa. Office: Harvard U JFK Sch of Govt Cambridge MA 02138

**BOLAÑOS, ANITA MARIE,** lawyer; b. Berwyn, Ill., Apr. 20, 1964; d. Jose M. and Anita Marie (Loycano) Bolaños. AB, U. Mich., 1986; JD, DePaul U., 1989. Bar: Ill. 1990. Ptnr. Schiller DuCanto & Fleck, Chgo., 1990—. Fellow Am. Acad. Matrimonial Lawyers; mem. ABA, Ill. Bar Assn. Roman Catholic. Avocations: running, piano. Family and matrimonial. Office: Schiller DuCanto & Fleck 200 N La Salle St Ste 2700 Chicago IL 60601-1099

**BOLDT, MICHAEL HERBERT,** lawyer; b. Detroit, Oct. 11, 1950; s. Herbert M. and Mary Therese (Fitzgerald) B.; m. Margaret E. Clarke, May 25, 1974; children: Timothy (dec.), Matthew. Student, U. Detroit, 1968-70; B.A., Wayne State U., 1972; J.D., U. Mich., 1975. Bar: Ind. 1975, U.S. Dist. Ct. (so. dist.) Ind. 1975, U.S. Ct. Appeals (7th cir.) 1979, U.S. Supreme Ct. 1980, U.S. Ct. Appeals (D.C. cir.) 1983. Assoc. Ice, Miller, Donadio & Ryan, Indpls., 1975-81, ptnr., 1982—; bd. dirs. Star Alliance, Inc. Contbr. articles to profl. jours. Mem. ABA, Ind. State Bar Assn., Indpls. Bar Assn., Highland Golf and Country Club, Skyline Club. Labor, Pension, profit-sharing, and employee benefits. Office: Ice Miller Donadio & Ryan Box 82001 1 American Sq Indianapolis IN 46282-0001

**BOLEN, JAMES AUBREY, JR.,** lawyer; b. Alexandria, La., Nov. 15, 1937; s. James Aubrey and Dorothy Deane (Durham) B.; m. Diann Ransbottom, Aug. 19, 1967; children—Alysia, James Aubrey III, Jonathan. B.A., La. State U., 1961, LL.B., 1965. Bar: La. Assoc., Irving Ward-Steinman, Alexandria, 1965, Mansour & Lauve, Alexandria, 1965-66, Stafford & Pitts, Alexandria, 1966-70; ptnr. Stafford, Pitts & Bolen, Alexandria, 1970-72; pres. Bolen & Erwin, Ltd., Alexandria, La., 1972—. Spkr. seminars for Allstate, Dresser Industries. Councilman-at-large Alexandria City Council, 1977-84,

88. Mem. ABA, Def. Research Inst., La. Assn. Def. Coun. (spkr.), Internat. Assn. Def. Coun., La. Bar Assn. (spkr.), Alexandria Bar Assn. Democrat. Baptist. Product liability, Professional liability, Personal injury. Home: 608 Welwyn Way Alexandria LA 71303-2619 Office: 709 Versailles Blvd Alexandria LA 71303-2352

**BOLES, EDGAR HOWARD, II,** lawyer; b. Cleve., Mar. 2, 1947; s. Laurence Huey and Blossom (Miller) B.; m. Elizabeth Young, Dec. 27, 1974; children—Gwendolyn H., Edgar H. III, Mary H., Elizabeth A. B.A., Ohio Wesleyan U., 1969; J.D., Case Western Res. U., 1973. Bar: Ohio 1973. Law clk. Ct. of Appeals of Ohio, Cleve., 1973-75; asst. county prosecutor Cuyahoga County, Cleve., 1975-76; mem. firm Calfee, Halter & Griswold, 1976-84; ptnr. Thomas & Boles, Chagrin Falls, 1985-97; ptnr. Buckley, King & Bluso, 1998—. Mem. bd. govs. Case Western Res. U. Sch. Law, Cleve., 1981-89. Mem. ABA, Ohio Bar Assn., Greater Cleve. Bar Assn. Republican. Episcopalian. Club: Kirtland, Tavern. Federal civil litigation, State civil litigation. Home: 621 Falls Rd Chagrin Falls OH 44022-2560 Office: Buckley King & Bluso 1400 Bank One Center Cleveland OH 44114-2652

**BOLES, RICHARD JOSEPH,** lawyer; b. Cambridge, Mass., Sept. 8, 1936; s. Frances Farrel and Mildred Lawrence (Plunket) B.; m. Sue Edgarton, Sept. 27, 1959; children: Richard J. Jr., Thomas E. BS in Marine Engring., Mass. Maritime Acad., 1957; JD, U. N.C., 1966. Bar: N.C., U.S. Tax Ct. U.S. Dist. Ct. N.C. Ptnr. Spears, Barnes, Baker & Boles, Durham, N.C., 1968-74; v.p. ops., gen. counsel The Aviation Group, Inc., Raleigh, N.C., 1974-81; ptnr. Beischer, Boles & Beischer, Durham, 1981—; pres. Croasdaile Farm, Durham, 1986—. Contbr. articles to profl. jours. Lt. USN, 1957-60. Mem. ABA, Internat. Bar Assn., N.C. Bar Assn. (chmn. com. internat. taxation 1994—, coun. mem. sect. internat. law, 1993—, treas. 1995—). Democrat. Avocations: philosophy. Taxation, general, Private international. Office: Beischer Boles & Beischer 2726 Croasdaile Dr Ste 101 Durham NC 27705-2500

**BOLLA, WILLIAM JOSEPH,** lawyer; b. Chester, Pa., Aug. 2, 1947; s. William Andrew and Margaret Mary (Campbell) B.; divorced; children: Christopher Campbell, Gregory Gibson. BS in Psychology, Pa. State U., 1969; JD, Dickinson Sch. Law, 1972. Bar: Pa. 1972, U.S. Supreme Ct. 1986. Assoc. McGavin DeSantis & Koch, Reading, Pa., 1973; asst. dist. atty. Bucks County, Doylestown, Pa., 1973-76; ptnr. Heckler & Bolla, Doylestown, 1976-85, McNamara, Heckler & Bolla, Doylestown, 1986-98, McNamara & Bolla, Doylestown, 1998—. Minority counsel state govt. com. Pa. Senate, Harrisburg, 1976-77, mem. fin. com., 1978-81; bd. dirs. Bucks County chpt. Am. Cancer Soc., Doylestown, v.p., 1991-92, pres., 1993-95; bd. dirs. Bucks County Symphony Soc., 1995-96; pres. Doylestown Twp. Pks. and Recreation Bd., 1992-95; founder, pres. Bucks County Challenger Baseball Program for Handicapped Children, 1994-99; mem. adv. bd. Big Bros./Big Sisters Bucks County, Doylestown, 1987-93. Mem. Pa. Bar Assn. (ho. dels. 1997-98), Bucks County Bar Assn. (bd. dirs., chmn. young lawyers com. 1976-77, chmn. real estate sect. 1987-88, chmn. merit selection of judges 1984-85, chmn. bench and bar com. 1992-95, chmn. realtor legal com. 1991—, v.p./pres.-elect 1995-96, pres. 1996-97). Republican. Avocations: Civil war, traveling. E-mail address: wjbolla@pil.net. Real property, Family and matrimonial, General practice. Office: McNamara & Bolla 122 E Court St Doylestown PA 18901-4321

**BOLLES, DONALD SCOTT,** lawyer; b. Buffalo, Dec. 17, 1936; s. Theodore H. and Marie (Heth) B.; m. Jean Waytulonis Oct. 24, 1963 (dec. May 1983); children: Scott, Matthew; m. Geraldine Novinger, Feb. 14, 1988. BA, Alfred U., 1960; JD cum laude, U. San Diego, 1970. Bar: Calif. 1971, U.S. Dist. Ct. (so. and no. dists.) Calif. 1971. Ptnr. Hutton, Foley, Anderson & Bolles, Inc., King City, Calif., 1971-95, Anderson & Bolles, Inc., King City, Calif., 1995—; prof. Monterey Coll. Law, Calif. Editor lead articles San Diego Law Rev., 1969-70. Trustee Mee Meml. Hosp., King City, 1974-78, chmn., 1978-80; chmn. King City Recreation Commn., 1974-77; candidate mcpl. ct. judge primary and gen. election, Monterey County, Calif., 1986; sec., founding mem. bd. dirs. Project Teen Ctr. Inc., 1986-90; bd. dirs. Sun St. Ctrs., 1991-99, Monterey Coll. Law, 1995—; pres. Corral de Tierra Homeowners Assn., 1996-98. Served to capt. U.S. Army, 1961-67, Vietnam. Decorated Combat Infantryman's badge, Army Commendation medal. Mem. Monterey County Bar Assn. (exec. com. 1985-86). Republican. Club: Toastmasters (King City) (pres. 1972-74). Lodge: Lions (pres. 1975-76, sec. 1984-86 King City club). Avocations: application of computer science to practice of law, tennis, golf, bridge, choir. General practice, State civil litigation, Family and matrimonial. Home: 23799-1B Monterey Salinas Hwy Salinas CA 93908-9328 Office: Anderson & Bolles Inc PO Box 26 523 Broadway St King City CA 93930-3230

**BOLLING, WALTER HARRISON, JR.,** lawyer; b. Dalton, Ga., Apr. 14, 1948; s. Walter Harrison Sr. and Elizabeth Ann (Wilfong) G.; m. Alice Vivian Hullender, Dec. 6, 1972; 1 child, Laura Elizabeth Bolling Delius. BA, U. Tenn., Chattanooga, 1971; JD, U. Tenn., Knoxville, 1975. Bar: Tenn. 1976, U.S. Dist. Ct. (ea. dist.) Tenn. 1976, Ga. 1976, U.S. Dist. Ct. (no. dist.) Ga. 1976, U.S. Ct. Appeals (11th cir.) 1976. Assoc. Arvin Reingold, Chattanooga, 1976, James L. Banks, Chattanooga, 1976; ptnr., owner Bolling & Bolling Assocs. P.C., Dalton, Ga., 1976—; mentor Students Involved in Free Enterprise, Dalton Coll. Mem. Dalton C. of C., Dalton Civitan Club, Dalton Golf and Country Club. Democrat. Baptist. Avocations: golf, fishing, pool, reading, fitness. Fax: 706-226-6283. Family and matrimonial, Bankruptcy, Personal injury. Home: 31 Aspen Ct Ringgold GA 30736-5229 Office: Bolling & Bolling Assocs PC 113 N Hamilton St Dalton GA 30720-4213

**BOLLINGER, LEE CARROLL,** law educator; b. 1946. B.S., U. Oreg., 1968; J.D., Columbia U., 1971. Law clk. to Judge Wilfred Feinberg U.S. Ct. Appeals (2nd cir.), 1971-72; law clk. Chief Justice Warren Burger U.S. Supreme Ct., 1972-73; asst. prof. law U. Mich., 1973-76, assoc. prof., 1976-78, prof., 1978-94, dean, 1987-94; provost Dartmouth Coll., 1994-96, prof. govt., 1994-96, pres. U. Mich., 1997, prof. law, 1997—; rsch. assoc. Clare Hall, Cambridge U., 1983. Author: (with Jackson) Contract Law in Modern Society, 1980; The Tolerant Soc., 1986, Images of a Free Press, 1991. Fellow Am. Acad. Arts and Scis. Recipient Rockefeller Humanities fellowship. Office: U Michigan 2074 Fleming Adminstrn Bldg Ann Arbor MI 48109-1340

**BOLOCOFSKY, DAVID N.,** lawyer, psychology educator; b. Hartford, Conn., Sept. 29, 1947; s. Samuel and Olga Bolocofsky; m. Debra Stein, June 25, 1994; children: Vincent, Daniel, Charly. BA, Clark U., 1969; MS, Nova U., 1974, PhD, 1975; JD, U. Denver, 1988. Bar: Colo. 1988; cert. sch. psychologist, Colo. Tchr. high sch. Univ. Sch., Ft. Lauderdale, Fla., 1972-73; ednl. coord. Living and Learning Ctr., Ft. Lauderdale, 1972-75; asst. prof. U. No. Colo., Greeley, 1975-79, assoc. prof., 1979-90, dir. sch. psychology program, 1979-82; assoc. Robert T. Hinds Jr. & Assocs., Littleton, Colo., 1988-93; hearing officer State of Colo., 1991—; pres. David N. Bolocofsky, P.C., Denver, 1993—; psychol. cons. Clin. Assocs., Englewood, Colo., 1978—. Author: Enhancing Personal Adjustment, 1986, (chpts. in books) Children and Obesity, 1987, Obtaining and Utilizing a Custody Evaluation, 1989; contbr. numerous articles to profl. jours. Mem. Douglas-Elbert Bar Assn., Arapahoe Bar Assn., Nat. Assn. Sch. Psychologists (ethics com. 1988-91), Colo. Soc. Sch. Psychologists (bd. dirs. 1978-96, treas. 1993-96), Interdisciplinary Commn. on Child Custody (pro bono com. 1988-93), Colo. Bar Assn. (family law sect., sec. juvenile law sect. 1990-92), Colo. Soc. Behavioral Analysis Therapy (treas. 1990-96), Arapmhc (bd. mem. 1993—, bd. pres.1995-97). Avocations: sailing, golf, skiing. Family and matrimonial, Juvenile. Home: 9848 E Maplewood Cir Englewood CO 80111-5401 Office: 7887 E Belleview Ave Ste 1275 Englewood CO 80111-6094

**BOLT, JOHN ROBERT,** lawyer; b. Everett, Mass., Oct. 31, 1948; s. Charles and Marguerite Rosemary (DiVenuti) B.; m. Barbara Reyes, April 4, 1970 (div. Aug. 1994); 1 child, Michael Anthony. BA, U. Ariz., 1970, JD, 1973. Bar: Ariz. 1973. Ptnr. Donau, Bolt, Hickle & Whitley, Tucson, Ariz., 1973-77, Donau, Bolt & Hickle, Tucson, 1977-80, Donau & Bolt, Tucson, 1980—; judge pro tempore Pima County Superior Court, Tucson, 1983—; lectr. family matters various orgns. Fellow Am. Acad. Matrimonial Lawyers; mem. Pima County Bar Assn. Family and matrimonial. Office: Donau & Bolt 3505 N Campbell Ave Ste 501 Tucson AZ 85719-2033

**BOLTER, HOWARD LEE,** lawyer; b. Mpls., Dec. 20, 1962; s. Burton Allen and Jane Natalie Bolter; m. Linda Jean Soranno; children: Andrew, Julia. Bar: Minn. 1988, U.S. Dist. Ct. Minn. 1990, U.S. Ct. Appeals (8th cir.) 1997. Law clk. Hennepin county Dist. Ct., Mpls., 1988-90; assoc. Harvey, Thorfinniso et al, Eden Prairie, Minn., 1990-91, Weinblatt & Davis, St. Paul, 1991, Sandra Boehm & Assocs., St. Paul, 1991-94; ptnr. Borkon, Ramstead, Mariani & Letourneau, Mpls., 1994—. Mem. ABA, Minn. State Bar Assn., Nat. Employment Lawyers Assn. (bd. dirs., sec.-treas. Midwest chpt. 1994-97), Hennepin County Bar Assn. (vice chmn., chmn. program com. 1996—, governing coun. 1998—). Labor, Civil rights. Office: Borkon Ramstead Mariani & Letourneau 608 2d Ave #485 Minneapolis MN 55402

**BOLTON, STEPHEN TIMOTHY,** lawyer; b. San Antonio, Nov. 11, 1946; s. Grant Erwin Bolton and Mary Ann (Sedgwick) Aukerman; m. Deborah Dixon, July 7, 1973; children: Margaret D., William G., Melinda A., Clay E. BA, U. Va., 1969, LLB, 1972. Bar: Ohio 1972, U.S. Dist. Ct. (no. dist.) Ohio 1973, U.S. Tax Ct. 1984, U.S. Ct. Appeals (3rd cir.) 1988, U.S. Ct. Appeals (6th cir.) 1988, U.S. Supreme Ct. 1989. Assoc. Manchester, Bennett, Powers & Ullman, Youngstown, Ohio, 1972-77, ptnr., 1978—, exec. com., 1985—, pres., 1993—. Bd. dirs. N.E. Ohio Legal Svcs., Youngstown, Ohio, 1974-76, Mahoning County Bd. of Mental Retardation and Developmental Disabilities, Youngstown, 1985-86; mem. Leadership Youngstown, 1986-87. Mem. Ohio State Bar Assn. (media law com. 1990—, coun. of dels. 1991—). General civil litigation, Insurance, Libel. Home: 56 Poland Mnr Poland OH 44514-2057 Office: Manchester Bennett Powers & Ullman 201 E Commerce St Ste 200 Youngstown OH 44503-1641

**BOMAN, MARC ALLEN,** lawyer; b. Cleve., Sept. 4, 1948; s. David S. and Shirley T. (Freier) B.; m. Leah Eilenberg, June 10, 1984; children: Autumn, Heidi, Jane, David. Student, Purdue U., 1966-68; BA, Case Western Res. U., 1971, JD, 1974. Bar: Ohio 1974, Wash. 1978, D.C. 1978, U.S. Dist. Ct. (we. dist.) Wash. 1980, U.S. Ct. Appeals (9th cir.), U.S. Dist. Ct. (ea. dist.) Wash. 1985, U.S. Ct. Appeals (fed. cir.) 1986. Atty.-advisor Office of Gen. Counsel U.S. Gen. Acctg. Office, Washington, 1974-78; dep. prosecuting atty. Office of Prosecuting Atty., King County, Wash., 1978-81; assoc. Perkins Coie, Seattle, 1981-86, ptnr., 1986—; spl. ind. dep. prosecutor ethics investigation of county execs., 1994; mem. Seattle Ethics and Elections Commn., 1995-98; spkr. in field. Bd. dirs. Perkins Coie Cmty. Svcs. Fellowship, 1987-97, co-chmn., 1994-97; former bd. dirs. Totem coun. Girl Scouts U.S., Seattle Day Ctr. for Adults, Madrona Neighborhood Coun.; trustee Herzl-Ner Tamid Congregation, 1987-98, pres., 1994-96; mem. Leadership Tomorrow, United Way King County-Seattle C. of C., 1987-88; trustee King County Bar Found., 1995—, v.p., 1997-98, pres., 1998-99. Recipient Pres.'s award King County Bar Assn., 1999. Mem. Seattle King Bar Assn. (trustee 1986-89, chmn. divsn. young lawyers 1984-85). General civil litigation, Construction, Government contracts and claims. Office: Perkins Coie 1201 3rd Ave Fl 40 Seattle WA 98101-3029

**BOMBERGER, RUSSELL BRANSON,** lawyer, writer; b. Lebanon, Pa., May 1, 1934; s. John Mark and Viola (Aurentz) B.; divorced; children—Ann Elizabeth, Jane Carmel. BS, Temple U., 1955; MA, U. Iowa, 1956, M.A., 1961, PhD, 1962; MS, U. So. Calif., 1960; LLB, JD, LaSalle U.; grad., U.S. Marine Corps Command and Staff Coll., 1987, U.S. Naval War Coll., 1991. Bar: Calif. 1970, U.S. Supreme Ct. 1975. Mem. editorial staff Phila. Inquirer, 1952-54; lectr. U. Iowa, 1955-57, U. So. Calif., 1957-58; asst. prof. U.S. Naval Postgrad. Sch., Monterey, Calif., 1958-62; assoc. prof. U.S. Naval Postgrad. Sch., 1963-75, prof., 1975-89, prof. emeritus, 1989—; practice law, 1970—; free lance writer, 1952—, communications cons., 1963—; safety cons. internat. program U. So. Calif. Inst. Safety and Systems Mgmt., 1983—; cons. Internat. Ctr. for Aviation Safety, Lisbon, 1984—. Author: (novel) The Alternate Candidate, (broadcast series) The World of Ideas, (motion picture) Strokes and Stamps, (stage play) Closely Held; abstracter-editor: Internat. Transactional Analysis Assn. Capt. USNR, 1966-94. Decorated Meritorious Civilian Svc. medal, 1989; Am. Psychol. Found. fellow Columbia U., 1954-55, CBS fellow U. So. Calif., 1957-58. Aviation, Probate, Intellectual property. Office: PO Box 8741 Monterey CA 93943-8741

**BOMBINO, ISABEL PINERA,** lawyer; b. Havana, Cuba, Jan. 6, 1954; came to U.S., Jan. 1971; d. Osvaldo V. Piñera and Lidia (Ayala) Molina; m. Hector L. Bombino, June 9, 1972 (div. Apr. 1980). AA with honors, Hillsborough Community Coll., 1974; BA with honors, U. S. Fla., 1977; postgrad., Nova Law Ctr., 1977-78; JD with honors, Fla. State U., 1980. Legal intern to chief justice Fla. Supreme Ct., Tallahassee, Fla., 1979; intern Pub. Defender's Office, Orlando, Fla., 1979; asst. states atty. Dade County States Atty. Office, Miami, 1980-81; lawyer pvt. practice Miami, Fla., 1981—. Spl. master Dade County Value Adjustment Bd., 1995-99. Recipient Am. Jurisprudence award in Criminal Law, 1977, Fed. Jurisdiction, 1978, Adminstrv. Law, 1978. Mem. ABA, Cuban-Am. Bar Assn., Fla. Trial Lawyers Assn., Phi Alpha Delta. Republican. Roman Catholic. Criminal, Personal injury, Family and matrimonial. Home: 1412 Ortega Ave Miami FL 33134-2252 Office: 330 SW 27th Ave Ste 609 Miami FL 33135-2968

**BOMSER, ALAN H.,** lawyer; b. N.Y.C., Sept. 11, 1931; s. Sol Bomser and Henrietta Dundes; m. Anne Elizabeth Sullivan, Oct. 13, 1984 (dec. Nov. 1995); m. Betsy S. Gould, July 20, 1997; children: Jennifer Bomser Dryden, Michael C. Degree, Columbia Coll., 1952; JD, Columbia U., 1954. Bar: N.Y. 1955, U.S. Dist. Ct. N.Y. 1955. Assoc. Nottingham & McEniry, N.Y.C., 1955-59, Paul Weiss Rifkind Wharton and Garrisen, N.Y.C., 1959-63; ptnr. Marshall Vigoda & Bomser, N.Y.C., 1963-67, Barovick, Konecky & Bomser, N.Y.C., 1967-70, Bomser & Oppenheim, N.Y.C., 1970-74, Bomser & Messing, N.Y.C., 1975-79, Weiss Meibach & Bomser, N.Y.C., 1980-88, Gottleb Schiff Bomser & Sendroff, N.Y.C., 1989-93, Marshall & Bomser, N.Y.C., 1993-95, Solovay, Marshall and Edlin, N.Y.C., 1995-97; pvt. practice N.Y.C., 1997—. Contbr. articles to profl. jours. With U.S. Army, 1954-56. Mem. N.Y. State Bar Assn., Assn. of Bar of City of N.Y., Copyright Soc. U.S.A. Democrat. Jewish. Avocations: cooking, baking, carpentry, skiing, sailing. E-mail: abomser@pipeline.com. Intellectual property, Entertainment. Home: 415 E 52d St #2CB New York NY 10022 Office: 853 Broadway Ste 1711 New York NY 10003-4703

**BONACORSI, MARY CATHERINE,** lawyer; b. Henderson, Ky., Apr. 24, 1949; d. Harry E. and Johanna M. (Kelly) Mack; m. Louis F. Bonacorsi, Apr. 23, 1971; children: Anna, Kathryn, Louis. BA in Math., Washington U., St. Louis, 1971; JD, Washington U., 1977. Bar: Mo. 1977, Ill. 1981, U.S. Dist. Ct. (ea. dist.) Mo., U.S. Dist. Ct. (so. dist.) Ill., U.S. Ct. Appeals (8th cir.), U.S. Supreme Ct. Ptnr. Thompson Coburn, St. Louis, 1977—; chairperson fed. practice com. eastern dist., St. Louis, 1987—, eight cir. jud. conf. com., St. Louis, 1987—. Mem. ABA, Assn. Trial Lawyers of Am., Mo. Bar Assn., Met. St. Louis Bar Assn., Order of Coif. Federal civil litigation, Labor. Office: Thompson Coburn One Mercantile Ctr Saint Louis MO 63101

**BONACQUIST, HAROLD FRANK, JR.,** lawyer; b. Schenectady, N.Y., June 14, 1948; s. Harold F. Sr. and Janice (Piper) B.; m. Lucy Carol Walters, Jan. 14, 1984; 1 child, Lucy Piper. BA, Cornell U., 1971; JD cum laude, Albany (N.Y.) Law Sch., 1974. Bar: N.Y., 1975. Litigation assoc. Lynn & Lynn, P.C., Albany, 1974-75, Weil, Gotshal & Manges, N.Y.C., 1976-81; legal rsch. clerk appellate divsn. 3d dept. Albany, 1975-76; counsel Offices of Willard DaSilva, Garden City, N.Y., 1981-82; counsel Traub, Bonacquist & Fox, N.Y.C., 1995—, mem., 1982-95; mem. Leaf, Sternklar & Drogin, N.Y.C., 1987-88; lectr. N.Y. State Commn. Corrections, Albany, 1973-74; legal writing instr. Albany Law Sch., 1973-74; mediator U.S. Bankruptcy Ct. So. Dist., N.Y.C., 1994—. Comments editor Albany Law Rev., 1973-74; contbr. articles to profl. jours. V.p., nat. legal advisor The Holiday Project, San Francisco, 1984-87; com. mem. The Presbyn. Ch., Mt. Kisco, N.Y., 1994—. Mem. Justinian Soc. Republican. General civil litigation, Bankruptcy. Home: 19 Sun Valley Dr North Salem NY 10560-1049 Office: Traub Bonacquist & Fox 655 3rd Ave New York NY 10017-5617

**BOND, JILL KAWA,** lawyer; b. Buffalo, N.Y., Nov. 29, 1961; d. Stanley and Harriett Stiegler Kawa; m. Keith N. Bond, July 26, 1986; children: Jonathan, Christine, Andrew. BA, Canisius Coll., 1982; JD, SUNY, Buffalo, 1985. Bar: N.Y. 1986. Assoc. Hurwitz & Fine, PC, Buffalo, 1985-88; corp. counsel Rich Products, Buffalo, 1988-99, dep. gen. counsel, 1999—. Dir. Clarkson Ctr., Buffalo, 1996—; mem. Leadership Buffalo, 1996—. Named to 40 Under 40, Bus. First, Buffalo, 1996. Mem. Women's Bar Assn. State N.Y. (dir. western N.Y. chpt. 1996—), Erie County Bar Assn. (mem. labor com. 1996—), Niagara Frontier Corp. Counsel Assn. (dir., sec. 1992—). Labor, Contracts commercial, Product liability. Home: 21 Chapel Woods W Williamsville NY 14221-1851 Office: Rich Products Corp 1150 Niagara St Buffalo NY 14213-1797

**BOND, RANDALL SCOTT,** lawyer; b. Bryan, Tex., Sept. 27, 1969; s. James Burnett and Mary Beth Bond; m. Laura Marie Restivo, Dec. 17, 1994. BA, Tex. A&M U., 1993; JD, U. So. Tex., 1996. Bar: Tex. 1996. Asst. dist. atty. Galveston County Dist. Atty., Galveston, Tex., 1996-97; assoc. Bruchez & Goss, P.C., Bryan, Tex., 1998—. Active March of Dimes, Bryan-College Station, Tex., 1998—; mem. College Station Zoning Bd. of Adjustments, 1999—. Mem. ABA (young lawyers divsn.), State Bar Tex. (litigation sect.). Republican. Roman Catholic. Avocations: reading, athletics, travel. Criminal, Banking, Consumer commercial. Home: 502 Bolton Ave College Station TX 77840-2506 Office: Bruchez & Goss PC 4343 Carter Creek Pkwy Bryan TX 77802-4455

**BONDI, HARRY GENE,** lawyer; b. Sheridan, Wyo., Apr. 3, 1948; s. Gene and Elizabeth (Poynter) B; divorced; 1 child, Bert Gene. BS in sci., fin., Fairfield U., 1970; JD, U. Wyo., 1974; postgrad., Georgetown U. Law Ctr., 1977. Bar: Wyo. 1974, U.S. Dist. Ct. D.C. 1976, U.S. Tax Ct. 1976, U.S. Ct. Claims 1975, U.S. Supreme Ct. 1980, D.C. 1975, Colo. 1988, U.S. Dist. Ct. Wyo. 1977, U.S. Ct. Appeals (10th cir.) 1980. Trial atty. U.S. Renegotiation Bd., Washington, D.C., 1974-77; pub. defender Wyo. State Pub. Defender Office, Casper, 1978-79; pvt. practice Harry G. Bondi, P.C., Casper, 1977—. Author: Wyoming Labor and Employment Law, 1992, Workers Compensation in Wyoming, 1993, Wrongful Discharge Claims Under Wyoming Law, 1994, 95. Chmn. City of Casper Housing and Cmty. Devel. Commn., 1977-81; past pres. Natrona County Meals of Wheels, Inc., 1988-90, Meals on Wheels Found., 1991-94; bd. dirs. Casper Jr. Baseball League, 1994—. Mem. Wyo. Bar Assn., Natrona County Bar Assn., Am. Trial Lawyers Assn., Wyo. Trial Lawyers Assn., Wyo. Criminal Defense Lawyers Assn., Colo. Bar Assn., D.C. Bar Assn., Federal Bar Assn., Criminal Justice Adminstrn. Panel Dist. Wyo. Avocations: hiking, biking, soccer. Personal injury, General civil litigation, Criminal.

**BONDOC, ROMMEL,** lawyer; b. Pomona, Calif., June 23, 1938; s. Nicholas Rommel and Gladys Sue (Buckner) B.; m. Ariel Guiberson, Aug. 20, 1960 (div. 1963); m. Alberta Linnea Young, Dec. 13, 1967; children—Daphne, Patience, Margaret, Nicholas. A.B., Stanford U., 1959, J.D., 1963. Bar: Calif. 1964, U.S. Ct. Appeals (9th cir.) 1965, U.S. Supreme Ct. 1969. Assoc. Melvin Belli, San Francisco, 1964-66, Vincent Hallinan, San Francisco, 1966-69; sole practice, San Francisco, 1969—. Mem. San Francisco Bar Assn. (judiciary com. 1982-85), No. Calif. Criminal Trial Lawyers Assn. (bd. dirs. 1972—, pres. 1978-79), Calif. Attys. for Criminal Justice (bd. dirs. 1975-80). Democrat. Methodist. Criminal. Home: 509 Canyon Rd Novato CA 94947-4330 Office: 819 Eddy St San Francisco CA 94109-7701

**BONDY, JOSEPH AARON,** lawyer; b. N.Y.C., Jan. 18, 1968; s. Frederick and Joan Marie Bondy; m. Meeka Jun, Sept. 6, 1997. BA in Psychology, Columbia U., 1991; JD, Bklyn. Law Sch., 1994. Bar: N.Y. 1995, U.S. Dist. Ct. (ea. and so. dist.) N.Y. 1995, U.S. Ct. Appeals (1st and 2d cirs.) 1996, U.S. Ct. Appeals (11th cir.) 1998, U.S. Ct. Appeals (4th cir.) 1999. Assoc. Law Offices of Richard Canton and Richard Jasper, N.Y.C., 1994-96; pvt. practice N.Y.C., 1996—; mem. nat. legal com. Nat. Orgn. for Reform Marijuana Laws, Washington, 1996—; faculty mem. Nat. Criminal Def. Coll., Macon, Ga., 1998—. Mem. Nat. Assn. Criminal Def. Lawyers (life), N.Y. State Assn. Criminal Def. Lawyers (bd. dirs.), Nat. Eagle Scout Assn. Jewish. Avocations: long-distance running, camping, fishing, skiing. E-mail: bondylaw@aol.com. Criminal, Civil rights, Appellate. Office: 475 Park Ave S Ste 3300 New York NY 10016-6901

**BONEE, JOHN LEON, III,** lawyer; b. Hartford, Conn., Dec. 16, 1947; s. John Leon, Jr. and M. Elaine (Sheridan) B. BA, Trinity Coll., Hartford, 1970; JD, Suffolk U., Boston, 1974; postgrad., Hague Acad. Internat. Law, The Netherlands, 1975. Bar: Conn. 1974, U.S. Dist. Ct. Conn. 1974; U.S. Ct. Appeals (2d cir.) 1975, U.S. Supreme Ct. 1979. Assoc. McCook, Kenyon and Bonee, Hartford, 1974-78; ptnr. The Bonee Law Offices, Hartford, Conn., 1979—. Contbr. articles to profl. jours. Mem. bd. edn. Town West Hartford, 1981-83, corp. counsel, 1983, mem. community planning adv. com., 1984, mem. town coun., 1985-89; bd. dirs. World Affairs Coun., Hartford, 1980-91. Mem. ABA (gen. practice and internat. law sects., mem. ho. dels. 1996—), Conn. Bar Assn. (editor-at-large jour. 1978-84, probate and family law sects., mem. ho. of dels. 1995—), Hartford County Bar Assn. (bd. dirs. 1991-97, treas. 1992-93, sec. 1993-94, pres. elect 1994-95, pres. 1995-96, past pres. 1996-97, co-chair bench/bar leadership conf. com. 1992-93). General civil litigation, Probate, General practice. Office: 1 State St Hartford CT 06103-3100

**BONER, ELEANOR KATZ,** lawyer; b. N.Y.C., Jan. 20, 1922; d. Louis and Della (Cherry) Katz; m. Mitchell Boner, June 14, 1942; children: Ethel, Alexander, Lawrence. BA cum laude, Hunter Coll., 1941; LLB, St. Lawrence U., 1943; D in Jud. Sci. cum laude, Bklyn. Law Sch., 1945, JD, 1967; PhD, Columbia U., 1967. Bar: N.Y. 1943, U.S. Dist. Ct. D.C. 1972, U.S. Ct. Appeals D.C. 1972, U.S. Supreme Ct. 1971, U.S. Customs Ct. 1978, U.S. Ct. Internat. Trade 1981. Pvt. practice N.Y.C., 1943-71; ptnr. Boner & Glod, Washington, 1972-75, Boner, Gold & Oesch, St. Gallen, Switzerland; gen. counsel to Mark Berger, N.Y.C., 1975-80; pvt. practice New Rochelle, N.Y., 1981—. Author: The Hypothetical Question in the Law of Evidence, 1945, Alexander, Child of Love, 1990. Mem. ABA, N.Y. Bar Assn., Assn. Bar of City of N.Y., Westchester County Bar Assn., Phi Beta Kappa. Avocation: art. General practice, Private international, Public international.

**BONESIO, WOODROW MICHAEL,** lawyer; b. Hereford, Tex., Dec. 27, 1943; s. Harold Andre and Elizabeth (Ireland) B.; m. Michaele Ann Dougherty; children: Elizabeth Eaton, Jo Kristin, William Michael. B.A., Austin Coll., 1966; J.D., U. Houston, 1971. Bar: Tex. 1971, U.S. Dist. Ct. (we., no., so., and ea. dists.) Tex. 1973, U.S. Ct. Appeals (5th cir.) 1973, U.S. Ct. Appeals (11th cir.) 1981. Law clk. to U.S. dist. Judge Western Dist. Tex., San Antonio, 1971-73; ptnr. Akin, Gump, Strauss, Hauer & Feld, Dallas, 1973-92, Kuntz & Bonesio LLP, Dallas, 1992—; speaker profl. confs. Democratic precinct chmn. Dallas County; ruling elder, First Presbyterian Ch., Dallas, 1999—; bd. dirs. Grace Presbytery Devel. Bd., 1986-88. Fellow Tex. Bar Found.; mem. ABA, Fed. Bar Assn., Am. Judicature Soc., Dallas Bar Assn., Tex. Bar Coll., Dallas Bar Found., Dallas Assn. Def. Counsel, Order of Barons, Austin Coll. Alumni Assn. (bd. dirs. 1983), U. Houston Law Alumni Assn. (chpt. pres. 1982), Vocal Majority (bd. dirs. 1990—), Soc. for Preservation and Encouragement Barber Shop Quartet Singing in Am. (internat. chorus champions 1975, 79, 82, 85, 88, 91, 94, 97), Lake Highlands Exch. Club, Phi Alpha Delta. E-mail: kbllp@connect.net. General civil litigation, Consumer commercial, State and local taxation. Office: Kuntz & Bonesio LLP 1717 Main St Ste 4050 Dallas TX 75201-7303

**BONHAM, JOHN DWIGHT,** retired lawyer; b. Tuscaloosa, Ala., Sept. 13, 1928; s. Harry Dwight and Mamie Marie (Griffith) B.; m. Bobbye Claire Maxwell, Sept. 13, 1952; 1 child, Mary Bonham Ward. BS in Commerce, U. Ala., 1950, JD, 1952. Bar: Ala. 1952, U.S. Dist. Ct. (so. dist.) Ala. 1960. Staff atty. Legis. Ref. Svc., Montgomery, Ala., 1952-55; ptnr. Hare & Bonham Attys., Monroe County, Ala., 1955-60; asst chief, trial atty. Ala. Conservation Dept., Montgomery, 1960-70; asst. dir., chief atty. Ala. Legis. Ref. Svc., Montgomery, 1970-95. 1st lt. USAR, 1953-60. Presbyterian. Avocations: hunting, fishing.

**BONHAM-YEAMAN, DORIA,** law educator; b. Los Angeles, June 10, 1932; d. Carl Herschel and Edna Mae (Jones) Bonham; widowed; children: Carl Q., Doria Valerie-Constance. BA, U. Tenn., 1953, JD, 1957, MA, 1958; EdS in Computer Edn., Barry U., 1984. Instr. bus. law Palm Beach Jr. Coll., Lake Worth, Fla., 1960-69; instr. legal environment Fla. Atlantic U., Boca Raton, 1969-73; lectr. bus. law Fla. Internat. U., North Miami, 1973-83, assoc. prof. bus. law, 1983—. Editor: Anglo-Am. Law Conf., 1980; Developing Global Corporate Strategies, 1981; editorial bd. Attys. Computer Report, 1984-85, Jour. Legal Studies Edn., 1985—. Contbr. articles to profl. jours. Bd. dirs. Palm Beach County Assn. for Deaf Children, 1960-63; mem.

Fla. Commn. on Status of Women, Tallahassee, 1969-70; mem. Broward County Democratic Exec. Com., 1982—; pres. Dem. Women's Club Broward County, 1981; mem. Marine Coun. of Greater Miami, 1978-94, Svc. award, 1979. Recipient Faculty Devel. award Fla. Internat. U., Miami, 1980; grantee Notre Dame Law Sch., London, summer 1980. Mem. AAUW (pres. Palm Beach county chpt. 1965-66), U.S. Coun. for Internat. Bus., No. Dade C. of C., Acad. Legal Studies in Bus., Alpha Chi Omega (alumnae club pres. 1968-71), Tau Kappa Alpha. Episcopalian. Office: Fla Internat U Coll Bus Adminstrn Bus Law Dept North Miami FL 33181

**BONHAUS, LAURENCE ALLEN,** lawyer, urban planner; b. Cin., May 27, 1949; s. Alphonse Lawrence and Mary Kathryn (Muchmore) B.; 1 child, Andrew Laurence; m. Hildy Marcia (Kuznof). B.S. in Architecture cum laude, U. Cin., 1973, J.D., 1976. Bar: Ohio 1976, U.S. Supreme Ct. 1982. Draftsman, designer Arend & Arend Architects, Cin., 1969-72; designer Kral, Zepf, Frietag and Assos., Architects & Engrs., Cin., 1972-73; designer, OSHA specialist offices Robert Harter Snyder, Cin., 1973-76; OSHA and bldg. code specialist, Project Designer AEDES Assos., Inc., 1973-76; individual practice archtl. and planning law, Cin., 1976—; v.p., urban planner Citysystems, Inc., Cin., 1976—; arbitrator Am. Arbitration Assn.; Arbitrator Ct. of Common Pleas; sec. P.D.A., Inc. Co-chmn. Ohio Confederation, 1970-72, lobbyist for state and state affiliated univs.; mem. Gradison Campaign com., N.Avondale Neighborhood Assn.; past pres., treas., trustee NAPA; v.p. Fairview/Clifton Heights housing devel. corp.; v.p. Asbury property mgmt. non-profit housing corp.; mem. Greater Cin. Beautiful Com., Contemporary Arts Center; condr., music dir. The Cin. Civic Orch., concert master emeritus; mus. dir., condr. Gilbert and Sullivan Soc., Cin., also bd. dirs.; condr. Cin. Young Peoples Theater; co-chmn., treas., bd. dirs., exec. com. Ohio Solar Resources Adv. Panel; v.p. Cin. Archtl. Found.; keynote speaker State Solar Design competition, 1986; sustaining mem. Republican Nat. Com. Mem. AIA (co-chmn. nat. conv. com. 1980, nat. codes and standards com., Henry Adams cert., 1973, chmn. Cin. chpt. speakers bur., by-laws com.), ABA, Cin. Bar Assn. (chmn. OSHA com., mem. constrn. and engrng. law com., real property law com., mus. dir. for ann. meeting), Architects Soc. Ohio, Lawyers Club of Cin., Southwest Ohio Alt. Energy Assn. (founding mem., dir., exec. com.), Ohio Solar Energy Assn. (pres. dir.), Nat. Passive Solar Conf. Planning Com., Energy Network (co-founder), Queen City Engrs. Club (founder, past pres., bd. dirs.), SCARAB (v.p., 1970-71), Greater Cin. C. of C. (energy com.), Phi Alpha Delta (alumni justice Cin. chpt., dep. internat. justice, Outstanding Service cert. 1980, 82). Methodist (mem. adminstrv. bd.). Clubs: Updowntowners (Oktoberfest planning com.), Cincinnatus, Metro. Works include interior design and execution of mosaic panel Forest Chapel United Meth. Ch., 1969, restoration Fleischman mansion, 1974-76, Conroy mansion, 1977-79; Guest lectr., U. of Cin. Coll. of Engrg. ion Liability Law; new zoning code and land use plan Union Twp., Clermont County, Ohio, 1977-78; handicapped accessibility study Montgomery County, Ohio, 1979-81; urban renewal study Newark, Ohio, 1977-78; ind. living facility Total Living Concepts, Inc., Cin., 1980-81, solar zoning ordinances, 1982-83. Construction, Land use and zoning (including planning), Real property. Home: 948 Dana Ave Cincinnati OH 45229-2215

**BONIN, ALBERT M.,** lawyer; b. N.Y.C., Dec. 10, 1953; s. Adolph E. and Geraldine (Genovese) B.; children: Lauren E., Jessica L. B in Econ., Queens Coll., 1975; JD, William Mitchell Coll. Law, 1979. Bar: Colo. 1981. Assoc., v.p. Robert T. Hinds Jr. & Assocs., PC, Denver, 1983-94; assoc. Quade, Fontana & Bonin, Denver, 1994—; v.p., chmn. bd. Nat. Ctr. for Continuing Legal Edn., Denver, 1979-81. Co-author: Colorado Domestic Relations Forms, 1999. Mem. ABA, Colo Bar Assn. (pres. family law sect.), Arapahoe County Bar Assn., Denver Bar Assn. Family and matrimonial. Office: Quade Fontana & Bonin 5353 W Dartmouth Ave Ste 301 Denver CO 80227-5516

**BONNER, JOHN RYCKMAN,** lawyer; b. Greenwich, Conn., May 24, 1929; s. George Remington and Edith Hazen (Walbridge) B.; m. Jane Brownfield, Apr. 5, 1950 (dec. 1984); children—Janice Bonner Case, John Ryckman; m. Nancy Wallace Royster, Jan. 12, 1985; 1 child, Ashley Bonner Tully. B.A. with highest honors, U. Fla., 1949, J.D., 1950. Bar: Fla. 1950, U.S. Supreme Ct. 1973. Ptnr. Bonner & Hogan, P.A. and predecessor firms, Clearwater, Fla.; city judge Clearwater, 1954-66; city atty. Largo (Fla.), 1959-73. Served to capt. USAF, 1952-53. Mem. Clearwater Bar Assn. (pres. 1959-60), Fla. Bar, Phi Alpha Delta. Probate, Estate planning. Home: 415 Poinsettia Rd Clearwater FL 33756-1026 Office: 611-B S Myrtle Clearwater FL 33756-5666

**BONNER, ROBERT CLEVE,** lawyer; b. Wichita, Kans., Jan. 29, 1942; s. Benjamin Joseph and Caroline (Kirkwood) B.; m. Kimiko Tanaka, Oct. 11, 1969; 1 child, Justine M. BA, Md. U., 1963; JD, Georgetown U., 1966. Bar: D.C. 1966, Calif. 1967, S. Ct. Appeals (4th, 5th, 9th, 10th cirs.), U.S. Supreme Ct. Law clk. to judge U.S. Dist. Ct., L.A., 1966-67; asst. U.S. atty. U.S. Atty's Office (cen. dist.) Calif., L.A., 1971-75, U.S. atty., 1984-89; judge U.S. Dist. Ct. (cen. dist.) Calif., L.A., 1989-90; ptnr. Kadison, Pfaelzer, et al, Los Angeles, 1975-84; dir. Drug Enforcement Adminstrn., Washington, 1990-93; ptnr. Gibson, Dunn & Crutcher, L.A., 1993—; chair Calif. Commn. on Jud. Performance, 1997—. Served to lt. comdr. USN, 1967-70. Fellow Am. Coll. Trial Lawyers, Fed. Bar Assn. (pres. Los Angeles chpt. 1982-83). Republican. Roman Catholic. Office: Gibson Dunn & Crutcher 333 S Grand Ave Ste 4400 Los Angeles CA 90071-3197

**BONNER, WALTER JOSEPH,** lawyer; b. N.Y.C., Nov. 18, 1925; s. Walter John and Marie Elizabeth (Guerin) B.; m. Maureen O'Malley; 1 child, Justin R.; children from previous marriage: Kevin P., Keith M., Barbara A., Susan E. A.B. cum laude, Cath. U. Am., 1951; J.D., Georgetown U., 1955. Bar: U.S. Supreme Ct., D.C., Va. Law clk. to judge U.S. Ct. Appeals D.C. Circuit, 1954-55; judge U.S. Dist. Ct., Washington, 1955-56; asst. U.S. dist. atty. for D.C., 1956-60; ptnr. firm Michaels, Wishner & Bonner, Washington; adj. prof. Georgetown U. Law Ctr., 1957-58, 67-83. Trustee Lawrence E. Dean Meml. Scholarship Fund, Georgetown U. Med. Ctr. Served with USNR, 1943-85, capt. Res. ret. Fellow Am. Coll. Trial Lawyers; mem. ABA, Fed. Bar Assn., Bar Assn. of D.C., Va. State Bar, Va. Trial Lawyers Assn., Res. Officers Assn., Naval Res. Lawyers Assn., Naval Res. Assn., Phi Delta Phi. Clubs: Officers and Faculty (U.S. Naval Acad.). Federal civil litigation, Criminal, State civil litigation. Office: 1140 Connecticut Ave NW Ste 900 Washington DC 20036-4009

**BONNESON, PAUL GARLAND,** lawyer; b. Milw., May 12, 1959; s. Garland Waldemar and Marilyn Adah (Giese) B. BA cum laude, Marquette U., 1981; JD, Drake U., Des Moines, 1984. Bar: Wis. 1984, U.S. Dist. Ct. (ea. dist.) Wis. 1984, U.S. Ct. Appeals (7th cir.) 1991, U.S. Supreme Ct. 1992. Assoc. Riemer Law Offices, Delavan, Wis., 1984-87, Tikalsky, Raasch & Tikalsky, Waukesha, Wis., 1987-90, Rudolph Law Offices, Elm Grove, Wis., 1990-91; pvt. practice Wauwatosa, Wis., 1991—; mem. Badger State Vettes, Ltd., 1997—. Mem. Rep. Party of Waukesha County, 1996—; active Elmbrook Ch., Brookfield, Wis. Mem. State Bar of Wis. (pres. young lawyers divsn. 1994-95, exec. com. 1995-96, bd. govs. 1995-96, continuing legal edn. com. 1996—), Waukesha County Bar Assn. (bd. dirs. 19986), Corvette Club. Republican. Personal injury, Criminal, Family and matrimonial. Home: 20185 A Independence Dr Brookfield WI 53045-5385 Office: 631 N Mayfair Rd Ste 2 Wauwatosa WI 53226-4249

**BONNEY, HAL JAMES, JR.,** federal judge; b. Norfolk, Va., Aug. 27, 1929; s. Hal J. and Mary (Shackelford) B.; m. Marie McBee, July 4, 1963 (div. 1979); children: David James, John Wesley. BA, U. Richmond, 1951, MA, 1953; JD, Coll. William and Mary, 1969. Bar: Va. 1969. Instr. Norfolk public schs., 1951-61; supt. Douglas MacArthur Acad., 1961-67; practiced law, 1969-71; law clk. U.S. Dist. Ct., 1969; prof. U. Va., 1964-71, Coll. William and Mary, 1969-71; U.S. bankruptcy judge Norfolk, 1971-95; ret., 1995; adj. prof. law Regent U. Sch. Law, 1987—. Tchr. Wesleymen Bible class Sta. WTAR-AM, 1962-98, tchr. emeritus, 1998; tchr. Good News TV Network, 1989—; treas. Wesleymen Found., Inc., Billy Graham Crusades, 1974-76; pres. adv. coun. CBN U., 1986-95; vice-chmn. Va. Meth. Bd. Edn., Inc., 1991—; bd. visitors Duke Div. Sch., 1991—; bd. dirs. Norfolk Union Mission, 1994—, The Tidewater Winds; mem. City of Norfolk Task Force on Pub. Housing, 1995-96; advisor Film Sch., Regent U., 1996—; mem. rules com. Va. United Meth. conf., 1996—; bd. ordained ministry United Meth. Ch., Va. Recipient S.A.R. Good Citizenship medal, Woodmen of the World History medal, U. Richmond Gold medal, George Washington honor medal Freedoms Found., Alli award Cultural Alliance Greater Hampton Rds., 1998; Judge Hal Bonney Day named in honor by City of Norfolk, Jan. 27, 1998. Mem. Nat. Conf. Bankruptcy Judges (pres. 1983, chmn. editl. bd. The Am. Bankruptcy Law Jour.), Va. State Bar, Norfolk and Portsmouth Bar Assn., Nat. Film Soc., Am. Film Inst., Brit. Film Inst., Am. Cinematheque, James Kent Inn of Ct. (pres. 1994-96, hon. mem.), Phi Alpha Theta, Pi Sigma Alpha, Phi Alpha Delta, Mason, Shriners, Elks. Methodist. Home: 1357 Windsor Point Rd Norfolk VA 23509-1311 Office: The Wesleymen 408 Boush St Norfolk VA 23510-1215

**BONOMI, JOHN GURNEE,** retired lawyer; b. N.Y.C., Aug. 13, 1923; s. Felix A. and Bessie (Gurnee) B.; m. Patricia Updegraff, Aug. 22, 1953; children: Kathryn, John. B.A., Columbia U., 1947; J.D., Cornell U., 1950; LL.M., N.Y.U., 1957. Bar: N.Y. 1952, U.S. Supreme Ct. 1966, U.S. Dist. Ct. (so. dist.) N.Y. 1975, U.S. Ct. Appeals (2d cir.) 1978. Asst. dist. atty. N.Y. County, 1953-60; spl. counsel subcom. antitrust and monopoly, for hearings on organized crime and monopoly in profl. boxing, Kefauver Com. U.S. Senate, 1960-61; spl. asst. atty. gen. investigating 1961 N.Y.C. mayor race N.Y. State, 1961-62; chief counsel com. grievances Assn. Bar City N.Y., 1963-76; vis. scholar Harvard U. Law Sch., 1976-77; counsel firm Anderson, Russell, Kill & Olick, N.Y.C., 1977-80; practice law N.Y.C., 1980-96; mem. com. grievances and admissions U.S. Ct. Appeals (2d cir.), 1983—; lectr. Fordham U. Law Sch., 1973; mem. N.Y. state judicial conf. com. on disciplinary enforcement, 1971-72. Columnist: N.Y. Law Jour. 1978-83; contbr. articles to legal jours. Trustee Village of Tarrytown, N.Y., 1965-67, 68-72; councilman, dep. supr. Town of Greenburgh, 1974; spl. counsel to Village of Irvington, N.Y., 1972. With USAAF, 1943-45, ETO. Mem. ABA (spl. com. on evaluation disciplinary enforcement Clark Com. 1967-70, cons. spl. com. on evaluation ethical stds. 1967-69), N.Y. State Bar Assn. (vice-chmn. com. grievances 1970-71, com. profl. discipline 1988-93), Am. Law Inst. (spl. com. peer rev. 1978-80), New York County Lawyers Assn. (com. profl. discipline 1993—), Assn. of Bar of City of N.Y. (cons. spl. com. on free press and fair trial, Medina com. 1966-67, com. profl. discipline 1983-88), Inst. Jud. Adminstrn., Nat. Orgn. Bar Counsel (pres. 1970-71, chmn. spl. com. on Watergate discipline 1974-76). Democrat. Club: Harvard (N.Y.C.). Administrative and regulatory. Home: 131 Deertrack Ln Irvington NY 10533-1013

**BONOVITZ, SHELDON M.,** lawyer. BS, U. Pa.; JD, Harvard U. Bar: Pa. Ptnr. Duane, Morris & Heckscher LLP, Phila., 1969—, chmn. tax dept., 1972-93, mem. ptnrs. bd., 1976—, vice chmn., 1994-97, chmn., 1998—; atty.-advisor to Honorable Arnold Raum, U.S. Tax Ct.; bd. dirs. Comcast corp., Surg. Laser Tech., Inc., WWF Paper Corp., The Graham Co., Sandhurst Venture Fund; lectr. in law U. Pa. Law Sch., 1979-86, 93, 95, Temple U. Sch. Law, 1967-78; speaker in field. Contbr. articles to profl. jours. Fellow Am. Coll. Tax Counsel; mem. ABA (chair com. on corp. tax 1987-88), Pa. Bar Assn. (tax law sect.), Phila. Bar Assn. (chair tax sect. 1987-88), Am. Law Inst. (tax adv. group). Taxation, general, General corporate, Estate planning. Office: Duane Morris & Heckscher LLP One Liberty Pl Philadelphia PA 19103-7396

**BOOCHEVER, ROBERT,** federal judge; b. N.Y.C., Oct. 2, 1917; s. Louis C. and Miriam (Cohen) B.; m. Lois Colleen Maddox, Apr. 22, 1943; children: Barbara K., Linda Lou, Ann Paula, Miriam Deon. AB, Cornell U., 1939, JD, 1941; HD (hon.), U. Alaska, 1981. Bar: N.Y. 1944, Alaska 1947. Law clk. Nordlinger, Riegel & Cooper, 1941; asst. U.S. atty. Juneau, 1946-47; partner firm Faulkner, Banfield, Boochever & Doogan, Juneau, 1947-72; asso. justice Alaska Supreme Ct., 1972-75, 78-80, chief justice, 1975-78; judge U.S. Ct. Appeals (9th cir.), Pasadena, Calif., 1980-86; sr. judge U.S. Ct. Appeals, Pasadena, Calif., 1986—; mem. 9th cir. rules com. U.S. Ct. Appeals, 1983-85, chmn. 9th cir. libr. com., 1995—; chmn. Ala. Jud. Coun., 1975-78; mem. appellate judges seminar NYU Sch. Law, 1975; mem. Conf. Chief Justices, 1975-79, vice chmn., 1978-79; mem. adv. bd. Nat. Bank of Ala., 1968-72; guest spkr. Southwestern Law Sch. Disting. Lecture Series, 1992. Contbr. articles to profl. jours. Chmn. Juneau chpt. ARC, 1949-51, Juneau Planning Commn., 1956-61; mem. Alaska Devel. Bd., 1949-52, Alaska Jud. Qualification Commn., 1972-75; mem. adv. bd. Juneau-Douglas Community Coll. Served to Capt. U.S. Army, 1941-45. Named Juneau Man of Year, Rotary, 1974; recipient Disting. Alumnus award Cornell U., 1989. Fellow Am. Coll. Trial Attys.; mem. ABA, Alaska Bar Assn. (pres. 1961-62), Juneau Bar Assn. (pres. 1971-72), Am. Judicature Soc. (dir. 1970-74), Am. Law Inst., Juneau C. of C. (pres. 1952, 55), Alaskans United (chmn. 1972), Cornell Club L.A., Altadena Town and County. Office: US Ct Appeals PO Box 91510 125 S Grand Ave Pasadena CA 91105-1652

**BOOCOCK, STEPHEN WILLIAM,** lawyer; b. Wilkinsburg, Pa., Sept. 25, 1948; s. William Samuel and Zelda Elizabeth (Heginbotham) B.; m. Carol Ann Bennett, July 11, 1970; children: Eric Alan, Allison Anne, Megan Leigh. BS in Acctg., Pa. State U., 1970; JD, U. Pitts., 1973. Bar: Pa. 1974, U.S. Dist. Ct. (we. dist.) Pa. 1973. Supervising tax specialist Coopers & Lybrand, Pitts., 1973-76; tax counsel Incom Internat., Inc., Pitts., 1977-81; asst. treas., dir. tax Allegheny Ludlum Corp., Pitts., 1981-93, asst. v.p. taxes, 1994-96; asst. v.p. taxes, chief tax officer Allegheny Teledyne Inc., Pitts., 1996—. Treas. Meadow Wood Homeowner's Assn., 1990—. Served to capt. U.S. Army, 1970-79; with USAR. Mem. ABA, AICPA, Pa. Bar Assn., Allegheny County Bar Assn., Pa. Inst. CPAs, Pa. Chamber Bus. and Industry (tax subcom.), Pitts. C. of C. (tax subcom.), Com. on State Taxation, Splty. Steel Industry N.Am. (chmn. tax subcom. 1993—), Tax Execs. Inst. (treas. Pitts. chpt. 1985-86, sec. 1986-87, sr. v.p. 1987-88, pres. 1988-89, nat. inst. dir. 1989-91, v.p. region VI 1992-93, mem. IRS adminstrv. affairs com. 1993—, vice chmn. 1995-97, chmn. 1997—, membership com. 1993-97, mem. alternative tax sys. com. 1995-97, tax info. sys. com. 1995-97, nominating com. 1994-95, 97-98, 50th ann. task force 1993-95). Republican. Avocations: golf, hunting, fishing. Corporate taxation, Taxation, general, State and local taxation. Home: 2625 Woodmont Ln Wexford PA 15090-7978 Office: Allegheny Teledyne Inc 1000 Six PPG Pl Pittsburgh PA 15222-5479

**BOOHER, ALICE ANN,** lawyer; b. Indpls., Oct. 6, 1941; d. Norman Rogers and Olga (Bonke) B. BA in Polit. Sci., Butler U., 1963; LLB, Ind. U., 1966, JD, 1967. Bar: Ind. 1966, U.S. Dist. Ct. (so. dist.) Ind. 1966, U.S. Tax Ct. 1970, U.S. Ct. Customs and Patent Appeals 1969, U.S. Ct. Mil. Appeals 1969, U.S. Ct. Appeals (D.C. cir.) 1969, U.S. Supreme Ct. 1969; cert. tchr., Ind. Rsch. asst., law clk. Supreme and Appellate Cts. Ind., Indpls., 1966; legal intern, atty., staff legal advisor Dept. State, Washington, 1966-69; staff legal adviser Bd. Vets. Appeals, Washington, 1969-78, sr. atty., 1978—, counsel, 1991—; former counselor D.C. Penal Facilities and Shelters. Author: The Nuclear Test Ban Treaty and the Third Party Non-Nuclear States, also children's books; contbr. articles to various publs., chpts. to Whiteman Digest of International Law; exhibited crafts, needlepoint in juried artisan fairs; originator U.S. postage stamps Women in Mil. Svc., 1980-97, POWs/MIAs, 1986-96. Bd. dirs. numerous community groups, including D.C. Women's Commn. for Crime Prevention, 1980-81; pres., legal adviser VA employees Assn. Recipient various awards; named Ky. Col., 1988. Mem. DAV (life), VFW Aux. (life), LWV, Women's Bar Assn. D.C., D.C. Sexual Assault Coalition (chmn. legal com.), Butler U. Alumni Assn., Nat. Mus. Women in Arts, Kennedy Ctr. Stars, Sackler Gallery (patron), Women in Mil. Svcs. to Am. Found. (charter), Bus. and Profl. Women (pres. D.C. 1980-81, nat. UN fellow 1974, nat. bd. dirs. 1980-82, 87—, Woman of Yr. award D.C. 1975, Marguerite Rawalt award D.C. 1986), USO, Women Officers Profl. Assns., Navy League U.S.A., Am. Legion Aux. (life), Nat. Task Force on Women of the Mil. and Women Mil. POWS (chair Esther Peterson Tribute 1995, panel, paper moderator conf. 1997, book reviewer, contbr. to Stars & Stripes, Ex POWs Bull., others), U.S. Naval Inst.

**BOOKIN, DANIEL HENRY,** lawyer; b. Ottumwa, Iowa, Oct. 16, 1951. BA, U. Iowa, 1973; JD, Yale U., 1976. Bar: Calif. 1978. Law clk. U.S. Dist. Ct. (no. dist.) Calif., 1976-77; asst. U.S. atty. U.S. Dist. Ct. (so. dist.) N.Y., 1978-82; ptnr. O'Melveny & Myers, San Francisco, 1982—. Mem. bd. editors Yale Law Jour., 1975-76. Fellow Am. Coll. Trial Lawyers, Phi Beta Kappa. Office: O'Melveny & Myers Embarcadero Ctr W Tower 275 Battery St San Francisco CA 94111-3305

**BOONE, CELIA TRIMBLE,** lawyer; b. Clovis, N.Mex., Mar. 3, 1953; d. George Harold and Barbara Ruth (Foster) T.; m. Billy W. Boone, Apr. 21, 1990. BS, Ea. N.Mex. U., 1976, MA, 1977; JD, St. Mary's U., San Antonio, 1982. Bar: Tex. 1982, U.S. Dist. Ct. (no. dist.) Tex. 1983, U.S. Ct. Appeals (5th cir.) 1985, U.S. Supreme Ct. 1986. Instr. English, Eastern N.Mex. U., Portales, 1977-78; editor Curry County Times, Clovis, 1978-79; assoc. Schulz & Robertson, Abilene, Tex., 1982-85, Scarborough, Black, Tarpley & Scarborough, 1985-87; ptnr. Scarborough, Black, Tarpley & Trimble, Abilene, Tex., 1988-90, Scarborough, Black, Tarpley & Boone, 1990-94, of counsel Scarborough, Tarpley, Boone & Fouts, 1994-96; prin. Law Office of Celia Trimble Boone, , Abilene, 1996—; instr. legal rsch. and writing St. Mary's Sch. Law, 1981-82. Legal adv. to bd. dirs. Abilene Kennel Club, 1983-85; mem. landmarks commn. City of Abilene, 1989-90. Recipient Outstanding Young Lawyer of Abilene, 1988. Mem. ABA, State Bar Tex. (mem. disciplinary rev. com. 1989-93), Am. Trial Lawyers Assn., Tex. Trial Lawyers Assn., Tex. Criminal Def. Lawyers Assn., Tex. Acad. Family Law Specialists, Tex. Bd. Legal Specialization (cert. 1987), Abilene Bar Assn. (bd. dirs. 1985-86, 87-88, sec./treas. 1985-86), Abilene Young Lawyers Assn. (bd. dirs. 1985-86, 87-89, treas. 1985-86, pres.-elect 1987-88, pres. 1988-89), NOW, ACLU, Phi Alpha Delta. Democrat. Avocations: needlework, gardening. Family and matrimonial, General civil litigation, Bankruptcy. Office: 104 Pine St Ste 705 Abilene TX 79601-5934

**BOONE, LABARRON N.,** lawyer; b. Mobile, Ala., Aug. 14, 1967; s. William Dillard and Shirley Spears Boone. BS in Indsl. Engring., Auburn U., 1990; JD, U. Ala., 1995. Project engr. BCM Engrs., Mobile, 1985-88, 91-92, Argo & Co., Birmingham, 1988-91; law clk. Sirote & Permut, Birmingham, 1992-93, Miller, Hamilton, Snider & Odom, Mobile, 1993-94, Pierce, Carr & Alford, Mobile, 1993-94; assoc. Beasley, Wilson, Allen, Main & Crew, Montgomery, 1995—. Mem. Assn. Trial Lawyers Am. (legis. exec. com. 1997—), Ala. Trial Lawyers Assn. (gov. 1997—), Fed. Bar Assn. (chair spl. activity com. 1997—), C. of C. Avocations: running, tennis, basketball, golf, theater. Product liability, Personal injury, Insurance. Home: 5755 Willas Ln Apt H Montgomery AL 36116-6145 Office: Beasley Wilson Allen Main & Crew 218 Commerce St Montgomery AL 36104-2540

**BOONE, RICHARD WINSTON, SR.,** lawyer; b. Washington, July 19, 1941; s. Henry Shaffer and Anne Catherine (Huehne) B.; m. Jean Knox Logan, Dec. 17, 1966; children: Elizabeth Anne, Richard Winston, Jr., Katheryn Jeanne. BA with honors, U. Ala., 1963; JD, Georgetown U., 1970. Bar: Va. 1970, D.C. 1970, Md. 1984, U.S. Ct. Appeals (D.C. cir.) 1970, U.S. Ct. Appeals (2nd cir.) 1973, U.S. Ct. Appeals (4th cir.) 1972, U.S. Supreme Ct. 1974, U.S. Ct. Claims 1975. Ptnr. Carr, JOrdan, Coyne & Savits, Washington, 1977-81; shareholder, dir. Wilkes, Artis, Hedrick & Boone, P.C., McLean, Va., 1984-95; pres. Richard W. Boone, P.C., McLean, 1984-95, The Law Offices of Richard W. Boone, 1995-97, Boone & Assocs., P.C., 1998—. Capt. USAR, 1964-67. Mem. D.C. Def. Lawyers Assn., Va. Trial Lawyers Assn., Va. Assn. Def. Attys., Barristers Assn. Avocations: model railroading, personal computer. Personal injury, General civil litigation, Health.

**BOONE, THEODORE SEBASTIAN,** lawyer; b. Urbana, Ill., Jan. 7, 1961; s. William Werner and Eileen Georgeanna (Herweh) B. BA cum laude with highest deptl. distinction, U. Ill., 1983; JD, Columbia U., 1987. Bar: N.Y. 1988, D.C. 1989. Assoc. Arnold & Porter, Washington, 1991—; translator, speaker in field. Contbr. book revs., articles to profl. jours. Grantee Internat. Rsch. and Exchs. Bd., Budapest, 1987-88, Fulbright and Bavarian State, Munich, 1983-84; Fgn. Lang. Area Studies/U.S. Dept. Edn., 1986-87. Mem. ABA (vice chmn. com. internat. investment, devel. and privatization), Am. Soc. Internat. Law, Am. C. of C. in Hungary (bd. govs. 1989-93, pres. 1991-93), N.Y. Bar Assn., D.C. Bar Assn., Phi Beta Kappa. Avocations: German and Hungarian language. General corporate, Private international, Legislative. Office: Arnold and Porter 555 12th St NW Washington DC 20004-1206

**BOONSTRA, MARK THOMAS,** lawyer; b. Muskegon, Mich., May 20, 1957; s. John Robert and Dorothy Pearl (Walhout) B; m. Julie Lynn Trusewicz, Aug. 27, 1988. BA in Polit. Sci., Mich. State U., 1979; JD, M Applied Econs., U. Mich., 1983. Bar: Mich. 1983, U.S. Dist. Ct. (ea. dist.) Mich. 1985, U.S. Dist. Ct. (we. dist.) Mich. 1992, U.S. Ct. Appeals (6th cir.) 1987. Law clk. to Hon. Ralph B. Guy, Jr. judge U.S. Dist. Ct. (ea. dist.) Mich., Detroit, 1983-85; assoc. Miller, Canfield, Paddock & Stone P.L.C., Detroit, 1985-90; prin. Miller, Canfield, Paddock & Stone, Detroit, 1991—. Recipient Mich. Competitive Scholarship; named to Outstanding Young Men of Am., 1988. Mem. ABA, Fed. Bar Assn., Washtenaw County Bar Assn., Oakland County Bar Assn. (task force on alternative dispute resolution 1986), Nat. Audubon Soc., Nature Conservancy, Earthwatch, Washington Cty. Econ. Club, Phi Beta Kappa. Republican. Mem. United Church of Christ. Avocations: photography, travel, sports. Antitrust, General civil litigation, Securities. Office: Miller Canfield Paddock & Stone 150 W Jefferson Ave Fl 25th Detroit MI 48226-4432

**BOOS, ROBERT WALTER, II,** lawyer; b. Lawton, Okla., Sept. 18, 1954; s. Robert W. and Martha Boos. BA with honors, U. Notre Dame, 1976; JD, UCLA, 1979. Bar: Ill. 1979, Fla. 1986. Ptnr. Arnstein, Gluck, Weitzenfeld & Minow, Chgo., 1979-85; atty. Taub & Williams, P.A., Tampa, Fla., 1986-88; ptnr. Honigman, Miller, Schwartz & Cohn, Tampa, 1988-97, Ruden McClosky Smith Schuster & Russell, P.A., Tampa, 1997—. Federal civil litigation, General civil litigation, State civil litigation. Office: Ruden McClosky Smith et al 401 E Jackson St Ste 2700 Tampa FL 33602-5230

**BOOTH, EDGAR CHARLES,** lawyer; b. Gainsville, Fla., July 13, 1934; s. Clyde V. and Bertha H. Booth; m. Anne Cawthon, Sept. 6, 1958; children: Rainey, John. BBA, U. Fla., 1956, JD, 1962. Bar: Fla. 1962. Pvt. practice Tallahassee, 1962—; judge small claims ct. Tallahassee, 1963-64; city judge Tallahassee, 1964-70. Capt. USAF, 1957-60. Mem. Fla. Bar Assn. (continuing legal edn. com. 1975—), Tallahasse Bar Assn. (sec., treas. 1970-71), Fla. Def. Lawyers Assn., Def. Research Inst., Fla. Mcpl. Judges Assn. (pres. 1969-70). Democrat. Episcopalian. Avocations: sailing, tennis, hiking, camping. Fax: 850-224-7442. Civil rights, Federal civil litigation, Administrative and regulatory. Home: 900 High Rd Tallahassee FL 32304-1819 Office: PO Box 840 Tallahassee FL 32302-0840

**BOOTH, GORDON DEAN, JR.,** lawyer; b. Columbus, Ga., June 25, 1939; s. Gordon Dean and Lois Mildred (Bray) B.; m. Katherine Morris Campbell, June 17, 1961; children: Mary Katherine Williams, Abigail Kilgore Curvino, Sarah Elizabeth, Margaret Campbell, Celecia. BA, Emory U., 1961, JD, 1964, LLM, 1973. Bar: Ga. 1964, D.C. 1977, U.S. Supreme Ct. 1973. Pvt. practice Atlanta, 1964-96; ptnr. Schreeder, Wheeler & Flint, Atlanta, 1995—; bd. dirs., v.p. Stallion Music Inc., Nashville, BAA USA, Inc.; chmn. CPS Systems, Inc., Dallas; trustee, sec. Inst. for Polit. Econ., Washington. Contbr. articles to profl. jours. Trustee Met. Atlanta Crime Commn., 1977-80, chmn., 1979-80; mem. assembly for arts and scis. Emory Coll., 1971-86, chmn., 1983. Mem. Internat. Bar Assn. (coun. sect. bus. law 1974-88, chmn. aero. law com. 1971-86), State Bar Ga., Capital City Club, Piedmont Driving Club, Univ. Club (N.Y.C.), Advocates Club, Sigma Chi. Federal civil litigation, Private international, Transportation. Home: 3226 Paces Mill Rd SE Atlanta GA 30339-3787

**BOOTH, HAROLD WAVERLY,** lawyer, finance and investment company executive; b. Rochester, N.Y., Aug. 8, 1934; s. Herbert Nixon and Mildred B. (Anderson) B.; m. Flo Rae Spelts, July 4, 1957; children: Rebecca, William, Eva, Harold, Richard. B.S., Cornell U., 1955; J.D., Duke U., 1961. Bar: Nebr. 1961, Ill. 1967, Iowa 1974; CLU; chartered fin. counselor; cert. fin. planner. Staff atty. Bankers Life Nebr., Lincoln, 1961-67; pres. First Nat. Bank, Council Bluffs, Iowa, 1970-74; exec. v.p., treas. Blue Cross-Blue Shield Ill., Chgo., 1974-77; pres., chief exec. officer, chmn. Bankers Life Nebr., Lincoln, 1977-84; exec. v.p. Colonial Penn Group, Phila., 1985-87; chmn., chief exec. officer VGVR Cos., 1985—. Served to 1st lt. USAF, 1955-58. Fellow Life Mgmt. Inst. (pres. 1981-84); mem. Ins. Fedn. Nebr. (past pres.). Finance, Insurance. Home: 1000 Stony Ln Gladwyne PA 19035-1128

**BOOTH, JOHN W. (BILL BOOTH),** lawyer; b. Baton Rouge, Dec. 27, 1946; s. Luther Lambert and Blanche Dorothy Booth; m. Ingrid Mary Jones, Aug. 5, 1972; children: Erin Alisal, Benjamin Nelson. BA in Govt., Centenary Coll., 1968; JD, So. Meth. U., 1971. Bar: Tex. 1983, U.S. Dist. Ct. (no. dist.) Tex. 1984, U.S. Dist. Ct. (ea. dist.) Tex. 1996. Assoc. Worsham Forsythe, Dallas, 1971-72; asst. dist. atty. Dallas County Dist. Atty.'s Office, 1972-80, chief felony prosecutor, 1980-83; pvt. practice, Dallas, 1984—.

Mem. NACDL, Tex. Assn. Criminal Def. Attys., Dallas Assn. Criminal Def. Attys. Methodist. Avocations: snow skiing, long-distance running. Criminal, Personal injury, Product liability. Office: Abrams Centre Bank Bldg 9330 Lbj Fwy Ste 900 Dallas TX 75243-3443

**BOOTH, MICHAEL A.,** lawyer; b. Cin., May 15, 1967; s. Robert James and Shirley Ann Booth; m. Patricia S. Adams, Oct. 3, 1997. BS, Miami U., 1989; JD, U. Cin., 1995. Lawyer Sebaly, Shillito & Dyer, Dayton, Ohio, 1995—. Mem. Order of Barristers, Order of Coif. General corporate. Office: Sebaly Shillito & Dyer 1300 Courthouse Plaza NE Dayton OH 45402

**BOOTHBY, CAROL ANN,** lawyer; b. Redwood City, Calif., Sept. 9, 1956; d. William Ancil Jr. and Marjory (Dow) B. BA, Calif. State U., Bakersfield, 1977; JD, U. Wash., 1980. Bar: Wash. 1980, U.S. Dist. Ct. (we. dist.) Wash. 1981. Staff atty. Wash. State Supreme Ct., Olympia, 1981-89, sr. staff atty., 1989-97, lead staff atty., 1997—. Mem. ABA (com. appellate staff attys.). Office: Wash State Supreme Ct PO Box 40929 Temple of Justice Olympia WA 98504-0929

**BOPP, JAMES, JR.,** lawyer; b. Terre Haute, Ind., Feb. 8, 1948; s. James and Helen Marguerite (Hope) B.; m. Cheryl Hahn, Aug. 8, 1970 (div.); m. Christine Marie Stanton, July 3, 1982; children: Kathleen Grace, Lydia Grace, Marguerite Grace. BA, Ind. U., 1970; JD, U. Fla., 1973. Bar: Ind. 1973, U.S. Supreme Ct. 1977. Dep. atty. gen. State of Ind., Indpls., 1973-75; ptnr. Bopp & Fife, Indpls., 1975-79, Brames, Bopp, Abel & Oldham, Terre Haute, Ind., 1979-92, Bopp, Coleson & Bostrom, 1992—; of counsel, Webster, Chamberlain and Bean, Washington D.C., 1997—, dep. prosecutor Vigo County, Terre Haute, 1979-86; gen. counsel Nat. Right to Life Com., Washington, 1978—; pres. Nat. Legal Ctr. for Medically Dependent and Disabled, 1984—; gen. counsel James Madison Ctr. Free Speech, 1997—; instr. law Ind. U., 1977-78. Mem. Pres.'s Com. on Mental Retardation, 1984-87, mem. congl. biomed. ethnics adv. com., 1987-89; Vigo County Election Bd., 1991-93; vice chmn. Early for Gov., 1995-96. Del. Republican State Conv., Indpls., 1980, 82, 84, 86, 90, 92, 94, 96, 98; alt. del. Republican Nat. Conv., 1992, 96; chmn. Vigo County Republican Ctrl. Com., 1993-97, White House Conf. on Families, Washington, 1980, White House Conf. on Aging, Mpls., 1981; bd. dirs. Leadership Terre Haute, 1986-89, Nat. Republican Pro-Life Com., Washington, 1983-91, Alliance for Growth and Progress, Terre Haute, 1993-97; chmn. bd. dirs. Hospice of Wabash Valley, Terre Haute, 1982-88; mem. The Federalist Soc., Free Speech & Election Law Practice Group (chmn. election law subcom.), 1996—. Editor: Human Life and Health Care Ethics, 1985; Restoring the Right to Life: The Human Life Amendment, 1984; editor-in-chief Issues in Law and Medicine, 1985—. Mem. Ind. State Bar Assn., Terre Haute Bar Assn. Republican. Catholic. Lodge: Terre Haute Rotary (bd. dirs. 1984-86). Constitutional, General civil litigation, Non-profit and tax-exempt organizations. Home: 1124 S Center St Terre Haute IN 47802-1116 Office: Bopp Coleson & Bostrom 1 S 6th St Terre Haute IN 47807-3510

**BORCHARD, WILLIAM MARSHALL,** lawyer; b. N.Y.C., Nov. 19, 1938; s. Bernard Philip and Helen (Marshall) B.; m. Myra Cohen, Dec. 13, 1969; children: Jillian, Thomas. BA, Princeton U., 1960; JD, Columbia U., 1964. Bar: N.Y. 1964, U.S. Dist. Ct. (so. and ea. dists.), U.S. Ct. Appeals (2d, 3d, fed. cirs.), U.S. Supreme Ct. Assoc. Kaye, Scholer, Fierman, Hays and Handler, N.Y.C., 1964-74, ptnr., 1974-83; ptnr. Cowan, Liebowitz and Latman, N.Y.C., 1983—; mem. editorial bds. Art and the Law, 1982—, The Trademark Reporter, 1983-99. Author: A Trademark Is Not a Copyright or a Patent, 1999, Trademarks and the Arts, 1999. Staff sgt. USAFR, 1961-67. Stone scholar Columbia Law Sch. N.Y.C., 1962. Mem. ABA (coun. 1987-90), Am. Law Inst. (adv. com. 1986-92), Internat. Trademark Assn. (legal counsel 1988-91). Democrat. Jewish. Avocations: tennis, boating, biking. Trademark and copyright. Office: Cowan Liebowitz and Latman 1133 Ave of Americas New York NY 10036-6799

**BORDELON, ALVIN JOSEPH, JR.,** lawyer; b. New Orleans, Nov. 1, 1945; s. Alvin Joseph and Mildred (Quarella) B.; m. Melanie Rose Bond; children by previous marriage: Peter Jude, Emily Aprill; m. Melanie Rose Bond. BA in English, U. New Orleans, 1968; JD, Loyola U., New Orleans, 1973. Bar: La. 1973, U.S. Ct. Appeals (5th cir.) 1975, U.S. Supreme Ct. 1983. Landman Chevron Oil Co., New Orleans, 1973-74; pvt. practice New Orleans, 1974-75; ptnr. Douglas, Favre & Bordelon, New Orleans, 1975-76, Monroe & Lemann, New Orleans, 1976-81; sr. ptnr. Bordelon, Hamlin & Theriot, New Orleans, 1981—; labor negotiator St. Tammany Parish Sch. Bd., Covington, La., 1991—, St. Bernard Parish Sch. Bd., Chalmette, La., 1986—; instr. criminal justice Loyola City Coll., 1975-76, Loyola U. Sch. Law, 1976-77. Mng. editor Loyola Law Rev., 1972-73. Chmn. Alcoholic Beverage Control Bd., New Orleans, 1983-84; mem. Mayor's Commn. on Crime, New Orleans, 1979; pres. Faubourg St. John Neighborhood Assn., New Orleans, 1977-80. With U.S. Army, 1968-70. Recipient Outstanding Civic Leadership award La. State Senate, Baton Rouge, 1982; named Short Story Competition 1st Place winner Writer's Digest, 1993. Mem. Profl. Assn. of Dive Instrs., La. Bar Assn. Republican. Roman Catholic. Avocations: poetry and short story writing, fishing, diving. Federal civil litigation, General civil litigation, State civil litigation. Office: Bordelon Hamlin & Theriot 701 S Peters St New Orleans LA 70130-1588

**BORDEN, DAVID M.,** state supreme court justice; b. Hartford, Conn., Aug. 4, 1937. BA magna cum laude, Amherst Coll., 1959; LLB cum laude, Harvard U., 1962. Bar: Conn. 1962, U.S. Dist. Ct. Conn. 1962, U.S. Ct. Appeals (2d cir.) 1965, U.S. Supreme Ct. 1969. Pvt. practice Hartford, Conn., 1962-77; judge Conn. Ct. Common Pleas, 1977-78, Conn. Superior Ct., 1978-83, Conn. Appellate Ct., 1983; assoc. justice Conn. Supreme Ct., 1990—; chief counsel joint com. on judiciary Conn. Gen. Assembly, 1975-76; lectr. Law U. Conn. Sch. Law, 1970-73; exec. dir. Conn. Commn. to Revise Criminal Statutes, 1963-71. Mem. Conn. Bar Assn., Hartford County Bar Assn., Phi Beta Kappa. Democrat. Jewish. Avocations: hiking, reading. Office: Conn Supreme Ct Drawer N Sta A Hartford CT 06106-1548*

**BORDEN, DIANA KIMBALL,** lawyer; b. Boston, Sept. 23, 1956; d. Robert Borden and Barbara Adams; m. William W. Crawford Jr., Sept. 4, 1981. BA magna cum laude, Harvard and Radcliffe Colls., 1979; JD with honors, U. Tex., 1983. Bar: Tex. 1983, U.S. Dist. Ct. (we. dist.) Tex. 1986. Assoc. McGinnis, Lochridge & Kilgore, Austin, 1983-89, ptnr., 1989-91; assoc. prof. law St. Mary's U., San Antonio, 1991-93; v.p., gen. counsel Evolutionary Technologies Internat. Inc., Austin, 1993-97; shareholder Graves, Dougherty, Hearon & Moody, Austin, 1998—. Computer, General corporate, Contracts commercial. Office: Graves Dougherty Hearon & Moody 515 Congress Ave Ste 2300 Austin TX 78701-3503

**BORDOFF, JASON ERIC,** consultant; b. Bklyn., Aug. 27, 1972; s. Fred and Ninette B. BA with honors, Brown U., 1994; MLitt, Oxford (Eng.) U., 1998. News dir. WBRU-FM, Providence, 1992, v.p., gen. mgr., 1993; legis. asst. Union Am. Hebrew Congregations, Washington, 1994-95; legal asst. Skadden, Arps, Slate, Meagher & Flom, Washington, 1995; assoc. McKinsey & Co., Inc., N.Y.C., 1997—. British Marshall scholar, Oxford, 1995-97. Avocations: tennis, opera. Office: 55 E 52nd St New York NY 10022-5907

**BORDY, MICHAEL JEFFREY,** lawyer; b. Kansas City, Mo., July 24, 1952; s. Marvin Dean and Alice Mae (Rostov) B.; m. Marjorie Enid Kanof, Dec. 27, 1973 (div. Dec. 1983); m. Melissa Anne Held, May 24, 1987; children: Shayna Robyn, Jenna Alexis, Samantha Falyn. Bar: Calif., 1986, U.S. Dist. Ct. (cen. dist.) Calif., 1986, (so. dist.) Calif., 1987, U.S. Ct. Appeals (9th cir.), 1986. Tchg. asst. biology U. Kans., Lawrence, 1975-76, rsch. asst. biology, 1976-80; post-doctoral fellow Johns Hopkins U., Balt., 1980-83; tchg. asst. U. So. Calif., L.A., 1984-86; assoc. Thelen, Marrin, Johnson & Bridges, L.A., 1986-87, Wood, Lucksinger & Epstein, L.A., 1987-89, Cooper, Epstein & Hurewitz, Beverly Hills, Calif., 1989-93; ptnr. Jacobson, Runes & Bordy, Beverly Hills, 1994-96, Jacobson, Sanders & Bordy, LLP, Beverly Hills, 1996-97, Jacobson White Diamond & Bordy, LLP, Beverly Hills, 1997—. Bd. govs. Beverly Hills (Calif.) Bar Barristers, 1988-90, Cedars-Sinai Med. Ctr., L.A., 1994—; bd. dirs. Sinai Temple, 1998—; cabinet United Jewish Fund/Real Estate, L.A., 1995—; mem. planning com. Am. Cancer Soc., 1996—; mem. Guardians of the Jewish Home for the Aging, 1995—, Fraternity of Friends, 1997—; active Lawyers Against Hunger, 1995—. Pre-Doctoral fellow NIH, Lawrenee, 1977-80; post-doctoral fellow Mellon Found., Balt., 1980-83. Mem. ABA, State Bar Calif., L.A. County Bar Assn., Beverly Hills Bar Assn. (gov., barrister 1988-92, chair real estate sect. 1998—), Profl. Network Group. Democrat. Jewish. Avocations: running, reading. Real property, General corporate, Environmental. Office: Jacobson White Diamond & Bordy LLP 9777 Wilshire Blvd Ste 918 Beverly Hills CA 90212-1902

**BOREL, STEVEN JAMES,** lawyer; b. Kansas City, Mo., Nov. 12, 1947; s. Mark and Margaret (Gibson) B.; m. Nancy Jean Dunaway, Aug. 31, 1967; children: Lindsay Kay, Emily Jean, Amy Lynn. BSBA, Pitts. State U., 1969; JD, U. Mo., Kansas City, 1972. Bar: Mo. 1972, Kans. 1989. Assoc. Stubbs, Epstein & Mann, Kansas City, 1972-79; pvt. practice Kansas City, 1979—. Rsch. editor U. Mo.-Kansas City Law Rev., 1971-72. Capt. U.S. Army, 1969-74. Mem. ATLA, Mo. Assn. Trial Attys., Kans. Trial Lawyers Assn., Kansas City Met. Bar Assn. (chmn. workers' compensation com. 1991-93). Personal injury. Office: 1101 Walnut St Ste 900 Kansas City MO 64106-2182

**BOREN, BARRY MARC,** lawyer; b. N.Y.C., Apr. 16, 1950; s. Arthur Jay and Corrine Jawitz; m. Caryn J. Tanis, Dec. 16, 1989; children: Brett, Margot. BA, U. Wis.-Madison, 1972; JD, John Marshall Law Sch., 1976. Bar: Ill. 1976, U.S. Dist. Ct. (no. dist.) Ill. 1976, U.S. Ct. Internat. Trade 1977, Fla. 1978, U.S. Dist. Ct. Trial Bar (so. dist.) Fla. 1978, U.S. Ct. Appeals (7th cir.) 1978, U.S. Ct. Appeals (5th cir.) 1979, U.S. Supreme Ct. 1980, U.S. Ct. Appeals (fed. cir.) 1991, U.S. Dist. Ct. (mid. dist.) Fla. 1994, U.S. Ct. Appeals (11th cir.) 1994. Spl. asst. atty. gen. State of Ill., Chgo., 1975-77; atty. Robbins, Coe, et al, Chgo., 1977-80; pres. Ventura Ltd., Miami, Fla., 1980-90; atty. Sandler, Travis, Rosenberg, Miami, Fla., 1990-91, Andrew Parish Law Office, Miami, Fla., 1991-92, pvt. practice, Miami, Fla., 1992—; pres. Ixora Ltd., Miami, 1988-91. Mem. Am. Assn. Exporters & Importers, Fla. Bar Assn. (internat. law sect. 1992—), Fla. Customs Brokers & Forwarding Assn. Private international, Trademark and copyright, General civil litigation. Office: 9200 S Dadeland Blvd Ste 412 Miami FL 33156-2712

**BOREN, JAMES EDGAR,** lawyer; b. New Orleans, Nov. 16, 1949; s. John E. and Katherine (Savage) B.; m. Teresa Anne Berlin, Mar. 7, 1971; children: Anna Blynn, Katherine Lenore, Rebecca Camille. BA, La. Tech U., 1971; JD, La. State U., 1975. Bar: La. 1975, U.S. Dist. Ct. (mid. dist.) La. 1975, U.S. Ct. Appeals (5th cir.)1975, U.S. Dist. Ct. (we. dist.) La. 1976, U.S. Dist. Ct. (ea. dist.) La. 1977, U.S. Supreme Ct. 1979, U.S. Ct. Appeals (11th cir.) 1981. Asst. dist. atty. Parish of East Baton Rouge, 1975-76; ptnr. Boren, Holthaus & Perez, Baton Rouge, 1976-88; pvt. practice Baton Rouge, La., 1988—. Contbr. articles to profl. publs. Mem. ACLU (bd. dirs. 1988-92), La. Assn. Criminal Def. Lawyers (bd. dirs. 1985—, pres. commendation 1986, pres. 1990-91), Nat. Assn. Criminal Def. Lawyers (bd. dirs. 1992-95, chmn. death penalty com. 1994—). Democrat. Criminal. Home: 2035 E Lakeshore Dr Baton Rouge LA 70808-1464 Address: 830 Main St Ste A Baton Rouge LA 70802-5597

**BORENSTEIN, MILTON CONRAD,** lawyer, manufacturing company executive; b. Boston, Oct. 21, 1914; s. Isadore Sidney and Eva Beatrice B.; m. Anne Shapiro, June 20, 1937; children: Roberta, Jeffrey. AB cum laude, Boston Coll., 1935; JD, Harvard U., 1938. Bar: Mass. 1938, U.S. Dist. Ct. 1939, U.S. Ct. Appeals 1944, U.S. Supreme Ct. 1944. Pvt. practice law Boston, 1938—; officer, dir. Sweetheart Paper Products Co., Inc., Chelsea, Mass., 1944-61; pres. Sweetheart Paper Products Co., Inc., Chelsea, 1961-83, chmn. bd., 1984; with Sweetheart Plastics, Inc., Wilmington, Mass., 1958—; v.p. Sweetheart Plastics, Inc., Wilmington, 1958-84, also dir.; v.p. Md. Cup Corp., Owings Mills, 1960-77, exec. v.p., treas., 1977-84, also dir. Bd. dirs. Am. Assocs. Hebrew U., 1968—; trustee Combined Jewish Philanthropies, Boston, 1969—, N.E. Sinai Hosp., Stoughton, Mass., 1974—, Ben-Gurion U., 1975-85, 87—, Boston Coll., 1979-87, chmn. estate planning coun., 1981-83, mem. coun. exec. com. 1984—, assoc. trustee, 1987-96; mem. pres.'s coun. Sarah Lawrence Coll., 1970-79; bd. overseers Jewish Theol. Sem. Am., 1971—; mem. pres. Congregation Kehillath Israel, Brookline, Mass., 1977-79, hon. pres., 1979—; mem. pres's coun. Brandeis U., 1979-81, fellow, 1981—; v.p. Assoc. Synagogues of Mass., 1980-81; exec. com. New Eng. region Anti-Defamation League, 1980—; bd. dirs., nat. governing coun. Am. Jewish Congress, 1984—; assoc. chmn. scholarship com. Harvard Law Sch., 1964-66, mem. spl. gifts com., 1990, mem. Langdell com., 1991, 92, 93, 94, 95, 96, 97, 98, 99, Boston regional campaign com., 1992, chmn. class reunion gift, 1993, 98. Recipient Community Svc. award Jewish Theol. Sem. Am., 1970, Am. Jewish Congress, 1993, Bald Eagle Outstanding Alumnus award Boston Coll., 1991; named Rofeh Internat. Man of Yr., 1996. Fellow Mass. Bar Found.; mem. ABA, Mass. Bar Assn., Boston Bar Assn. (mem. bicentennial com. 1986-87), Harvard Club (Boston and N.Y.C.), Harvard Faculty Club. General corporate. Home: 273 Eliot St Chestnut Hill MA 02467-1445 Office: Concorde Assocs 1 Devonshire Pl Ste 2912 Boston MA 02109-3533

**BORGER, JOHN PHILIP,** lawyer; b. Wilmington, Del., Apr. 19, 1951; s. Philip E. and Jane (Smyth) B.; m. Judith Marie Yates, May 24, 1974; children: Jennifer, Christopher, Nicholas. BA in Journalism with high honors, Mich. State U., 1973; JD, Yale U., 1976. Bar: Minn. 1976, U.S. Dist. Ct. Minn. 1976, U.S. Ct. Appeals (8th cir.) 1979, U.S. Supreme Ct. 1982, N.D. 1988, U.S. Dist. Ct. N.D. 1988, Wis. 1993. Editor-in-chief Mich. State News, East Lansing, 1972-73; assoc. Faegre & Benson, LLP, Mpls., 1976-83, ptnr., 1984—; bd. dirs. Milkweed Edits.; adj. prof. U. Minn. Sch. Journalism and Mass Comm., 1999. Mem. ABA (chmn. media law and defamation torts com. torts and ins. practice sect. 1996-97), Minn. Bar Assn., State Bar Assn. N.D., Wis. Bar Assn., Hennepin County Bar Assn. Libel, Appellate, General civil litigation. Office: Faegre & Benson LLP 2200 Norwest Ctr 90 S 7th St Ste 2200 Minneapolis MN 55402-3901

**BORGESON, EARL CHARLES,** law librarian, educator; b. Boyd, Minn., Dec. 2, 1922; s. Hjalmer Nicarner and Doris (Danielson) B.; m. Barbara Ann Jones, Sept. 21, 1944; children—Barbara Gale, Geoffrey Charles, Steven Earl. BS in Law, U. Minn., 1947, LLB, 1949; BA in Law Librarianship, U. Wash., 1950. Libr. Harvard U. Law Sch. Libr., 1952-70; assoc. dir. Stanford U. Librs., 1970-75; assoc. law libr. Los Angeles County (Calif.) Law Libr., 1975-78; prof. and law libr. So. Meth. U., Dallas, 1978-88, prof. emeritus of law, 1988; lectr. UCLA Grad. Sch. Libr. Sci., 1975-78; adj. prof. Tex. Women's U., 1979-80; adj. prof. U. North Tex., Denton, 1988-90; librarian AccuFile, Inc., 1992—; cons. in field. With USNR, 1943-46. Mem. Am. Assn. Law Librs. Home: 1D Village Way Sherborn MA 01770-1536

**BORISOFF, RICHARD STUART,** lawyer; b. Rochester, N.Y., May 4, 1945; s. Samuel M. and Ida B.; m. Risa W. Polgar, Aug. 17, 1967; children: Mindy, Dara. BA, U. Pa., 1967; JD, Columbia U., 1970. Bar: N.Y. 1971, D.C. 1981, U.S. Dist. Ct. (so. dist.) N.Y. 1973, U.S. Ct. Appeals (2nd cir.) 1973. Assoc. Paul, Weiss, Rifkind, Wharton & Garrison, N.Y.C., 1970-78, ptnr., 1978—. Office: Paul Weiss Rifkind Wharton & Garrison Ste 2330 1285 Avenue Of The Americas New York NY 10019-6028

**BORISON, SCOTT CRAIG,** lawyer; b. N.Y.C., Feb. 8, 1961; s. E.B. and Joan B. Borison; m. Janet S. Legg, May 22, 1988; children: Ian, Madison. BA in Russian Studies, Fairleigh Dickinson U., 1982; JD, U. Okla., 1987. Bar: Okla. 1987, D.C. 1994, Md. 1995, U.S. Dist. Ct. Md., U.S. Dist. Ct. D.C., U.S. Ct. Appeals (4th and 10th cirs.), U.S. Tax Ct., U.S. Ct. Vets. Appeals. Law clk. Okla. Ct. Appeals, Oklahoma City, 1987-89; counsel Centurion Oil, Inc., Oklahoma City, 1989-93; atty., mem. Legg Law Firm, LLC, Frederick, Md., 1994—. Mem. Nat. Assn. Consumer Bankruptcy Attys., Frederick County Bar Assn., Bankruptcy Bar Dist. Md. Bankruptcy. Office: Legg Law Firm LLC 5500 Buckeystown Pike Frederick MD 21703-8331

**BORJA, ARTHUR,** lawyer; b. Mexico City, Apr. 7, 1965; s. Arthur and Maria Teresa (Velarde) B.; m. Martha Elizabeth Poe, Oct. 7, 1988; children: Alexander, William, Gregory. Student, U.S. Naval Acad., 1983-84; BS, Tulane U., 1987; JD, Thomas M. Cooley Law Sch., Lansing, Mich., 1994. Bar: Mich. 1994, U.S. Dist. Ct. (we. dist.) Mich. 1994, Kent County Cir. Ct. Mich., 1994. Tchg. asst. Thomas M. Cooley Law Sch., Lansing, 1991-94; assoc. Moch & Assocs. P.C., Grand Rapids, Mich., 1992-94; pvt. practice Grand Rapids, Holland, Lansing, Mich., 1994—. Author: Litigating Child Restraint Cases, 1993, Pharmacy Law, 1995, Helmet Litigation, 1995; contbr. articles to profl. jours. Bd. dirs. Childsafe, Grand Rapids, 1993—. Lt. USN, 1987-91. Fellow Scribes; mem. ATLA (vice-chair 1991-94, bd. govs. 1994-95, pub. svc. award 1994), Non-commissioned Officers' Assn., Mich. Trial Lawyer's Assn., State Bar Mich. (consumer law com., advt. specialization com. 1994-95), Grand Rapids Jaycees, Phi Delta Phi. Avocations: sailing, computers, travel. Product liability, Family and matrimonial, Immigration, naturalization, and customs. Home: 2001 Ontario Ave NE Grand Rapids MI 49505-4470 Address: PO Box 140861 Grand Rapids MI 49514-0861

**BORK, ROBERT HERON,** lawyer, author, educator, former federal judge; b. Pitts., Mar. 1, 1927; s. Harry Philip and Elizabeth (Kunkle) B.; m. Claire Davidson, June 15, 1952 (dec. 1980); children: Robert Heron, Charles E., Ellen E.; m. Mary Ellen Pohl, Oct. 30, 1982. BA, U. Chgo., 1948, JD, 1953; LLD (hon.), Creighton U., 1975, Notre Dame Law Sch., 1982; LHD, Wilkes-Barre Coll., 1976; JD (hon.), Bklyn. Law Sch., 1984; ThD, DeSales Sch. Theology, 1990; LLD honoris causa, Adelphi U., 1990. Bar: Ill. 1953, D.C. 1977. Assoc., then ptnr. Kirkland, Ellis, Hodson, Chaffetz & Masters, Chgo., 1955-62; assoc. prof. Yale Law Sch., 1962-65, prof. law, 1965-75, on leave, 1973-75; solicitor gen. U.S. Dept. Justice, Washington, 1973-77, acting atty. gen., 1973-74; Chancellor Kent prof. law Yale Law Sch., 1977-79, Alexander M. Bickel prof. pub. law, 1979-81; ptnr. Kirkland & Ellis, Washington, 1981-82; judge U.S. Ct. Appeals for D.C. Cir., 1982-88, resigned, 1988; resident scholar Am. Enterprise Inst. for Pub. Policy Rsch., Washington, 1977, adj. scholar, 1977-82, John M. Olin scholar in legal studies, 1988—; mem. Presdl. Task Force on Antitrust, 1968; cons. Cabinet Com. on Edn., 1972; trustee Woodrow Wilson Internat. Ctr. for Scholars, 1973-78; nominated for position assoc. justice U.S. Supreme Ct., 1987, confirmation denied by U.S. Senate. Author: The Antitrust Paradox: A Policy at War with Itself, 1978, 2d edit., 1993, The Tempting of America: The Political Seduction of the Law, 1990, Slouching Towards Gomorrah: Modern Liberalism and American Decline, 1996. Mem. bd. govs. Smith Richardson Found., 1988; bd. dirs. Inst. for Ednl. Affairs, 1988; apptd. Permanent Com. for the Oliver Wendell Holmes Devise, 1989. With USMCR, 1945-46, 50-52. Recipient Francis Boyer award Am. Enterprise Inst., 1984, Henry Salvatori prize Intercollegiate Svcs. Inst., 1998. Fellow AAAS; mem. Federalist Soc. (co-chmn., bd. trustees).

**BORKER, WALLACE JACOB,** lawyer; b. N.Y.C., Dec. 11, 1919; s. David and Jennie (Siff) B.; m. Bettie Mae Harper, July 14, 1945; 1 child, David. AB, Cornell U., 1940; LLB, Columbia U., 1948. Bar: N.Y. 1948, U.S. Dist. Ct. (so. dist.) N.Y. 1948, U.S. Dist. Ct. (ea. dist.) N.Y. 1965, U.S. Ct. Appeals (2d cir.) 1965. Assoc. Cravath, Swaine and Moore, N.Y.C., 1948-52; sr. counsel Union Bag & Paper Corp., N.Y.C., 1952-55, Am. Elec. Power Service Corp., N.Y.C., 1955-61; ptnr. Borden and Ball, N.Y.C., 1961-76; of counsel Morgan, Lewis and Bockius, N.Y.C., 1976-84; counsel Rubin, Gross, Harris, Fischl and Roth, N.Y.C., 1985-89; ptnr. Borker & Sussman, N.Y.C., 1989-96, Lebensfeld Borker & Sussman, N.Y.C., 1996—; sec. Balchem Corp., Slate Hill, N.Y., 1983—, Transnuclear Inc., Hawthorne, N.Y., 1993—. Editor: Columbia Law Review, 1947-48. Served to lt. comdr. USN, 1941-46. Mem. ABA, Assn. of Bar of City of N.Y., N.Y. State Bar Assn. Democrat. Avocation: gardening. Club: University (N.Y.C.). General corporate, General civil litigation, Securities. Home: 6 Evon Ct Scarsdale NY 10583-5548 Office: Lebensfeld Borker & Sussman LLP 342 Madison Ave New York NY 10173-0002

**BORKOWSKI, JOHN JOSEPH,** lawyer; b. Detroit, June 30, 1952; s. John Joseph and Virginia Frances (Bergel) B.; m. Carmen Ana Cintron, May 29, 1982 (div. 1993). BA in Govt. and Internat. Studies, U. Notre Dame, 1973, JD, 1976. Bar: Ohio 1976, U.S. Dist. Ct. (no. dist.) Ohio 1976, U.S. Ct. Appeals (6th cir.) 1977, U.S. Ct. Appeals (D.C. cir.) 1985, U.S. Supreme Ct. 1980. Dir. debate U. Notre Dame, Ind., 1974-76; law clk. to justice U.S. Dist. Ct. (no. dist.), Cleve., 1976-78; lawyer FCC, Washington, 1978-80; assoc. Fly, Shuebruk, Gaguine, Boros, Schulkind and Braun, Washington, 1980; lawyer FCC, 1981—; asst. for pvt. land mobile radio, 1996-97; chief, policy and rules br. Pub. Safety and Pvt. Wireless divsn. Wireless Comms. Bur., 1997—. Recipient Performance award FCC, 1983, 84, 85, 88, 91, 92, 95, 97, 98. Mem. Train Collectors Assn. Roman Catholic. Avocations: computers, model trains, numismatics, science fiction. Administrative and regulatory, Communications, Public utilities. Office: FCC 1919 M St NW Washington DC 20554-0001

**BORMAN, CHANNA ERIN,** lawyer; b. New Braunfels, Tex., Feb. 22, 1969; d. Charles Elmo and Mary Louise (Schaefer) B.; m. Thomas Jeffrey Eckert, Jan. 31, 1998. BA, Tex. Tech U., 1990, JD, 1994. Bar: Tex. 1994. Assoc. Meece & Kohn, Bryan, Tex., 1994-96, Searcy & Gandy PC, College Station, Tex., 1996—. Fellow Tex. Bar Found.; mem. Tex. Young Lawyers Assn. (dir. dist. 2 1997—, mem. various coms.), Brazos County Bar Assn. (social chair 1994—, Pro Bono award 1998), Brazos Valley Young Lawyers Assn. (pres. 1997—). Democrat. Episcopalian. E-mail: ceborman@txcyber.com. Family and matrimonial, General practice, Personal injury. Home: 4614 Harrow Ct Bryan TX 77802-5618 Office: Searcy & Gandy PC 2405 Texas Ave S Ste 301 College Station TX 77840-4602

**BORMAN, JOHN,** lawyer, trial specialist, arbitrator, mediator; b. Little Falls, Minn., Mar. 21, 1946; s. Myron Francis and Bernadette Mary (Burggraff) B.; 1 child, Mac A. Nelson II. BA in Political Sci., U. Minn., 1973; JD, Notre Dame, 1979. Bar: Minn. 1979, Wis. 1987, U.S. Dist. Ct. Minn. 1980, U.S. Dist. Ct. (we. dist.) Wis. 1990, U.S. Dist. Ct. (we. dist.) Mich. 1996, U.S. Ct. Appeals (8th cir.) 1986, U.S. Ct. Appeals (6th cir.) 1996, U.S. Supreme Ct. 1986; cert. civil trial specialistt Minn. State Bar Assn. Law clk. to Hon. Glenn E. Kelley Minn. Dist. Ct., Winona, 1979-80; ptnr. Robins, Kaplan, Miller & Ciresi LLP, Mpls., 1981-97, Streater & Murphy PA, Winona, Minn., 1997—; researcher, organizer Minn. Pub. Interest Research Group, Mpls., 1973-76; pres. bd. govs. Minn. Consumer Alliance, Mpls., 1995-97; bd. dirs. Minn. Advocates for Human Rights, Mpls., 1991-94. Contbr. to profl. jours. Troop com. chair Boy Scouts of Am., Golden Valley, Minn., 1990-95; Served to sgt. USMC, 1964-68. Named Super Lawyer Minn. Jour. Law & Politics, 1998, Leading Am. Atty. Am. Rsch. Corp. Mem. ABA, Minn. Bar Assn., Ramsey County Bar Assn., Winona County Bar Assn., Hennepin County Bar Assn., Assn. Trial Lawyers Am., Minn. Trial Lawyers Assn. (bd. govs. 1981—, excellence award, 1997), Acad. Cert. Trial Lawyers. Personal injury, Product liability, Professional liability. Office: Streater & Murphy PA 64 E 4th St Winona MN 55987-3508

**BORMAN, PAUL DAVID,** judge. BA, U. Mich., 1959, JD, 1962; LLM, Yale U., 1964. Staff atty. U.S. Commn. on Civil Rights, 1962-63; asst. U.S. atty. U.S. Atty. Office, 1964-65; spl. counsel Mayor's Devel. Team, 1967-68; asst. prosecuting atty. Wayne County Prosecutor's Office, 1974-75; dist. judge U.S. Dist. Ct. (ea. dist.) Mich., Detroit, 1994—. Mem. ABA, Fed. Bar Assn., State Bar Mich., Oakland County Bar Assn. Office: US Courthouse 740 240 W Lafayette Blvd Detroit MI 48226-2704

**BORN, BROOKSLEY ELIZABETH,** lawyer; b. San Francisco, Aug. 27, 1940; d. Ronald Henry and Mary Ellen (Bortner) B.; m. Alexander Elliot Bennett, Oct. 9, 1982; children: Nicholas Jacob Landau, Ariel Elizabeth Landau, Andrew E. Bennett, Laura F. Bennett, Peter J. Bennett. AB, Stanford U., 1961, JD, 1964. Bar: D.C. 1966. Law clk. U.S. Ct. Appeals, Washington, 1964-65; legal rschr. Harvard Law Sch., 1967-68; assoc. Arnold and Porter, Washington, 1965-67, 68-73, ptnr., 1974-96, 99—; chair U.S. Commodity Futures Trading Commn., Washington, 1996-99; lectr. law Columbus Sch. Law, Cath. U. Am., 1972-74; adj. prof. Georgetown U. Law Center, Washington, 1972-73. Pres. Stanford Law Rev, 1963-64. Chmn. bd. visitors Stanford Law Sch., 1987; bd. dirs. Nat. Legal Aid and Defenders Assn., 1972-79, Washington Legal Clinic for Homeless, 1993-96, Lawyers Com. for Civil Rights Under Law, 1993-96, Am. Bar Found., 1989-99, Washington Lawyers Com. for Civil Rights and Urban Affairs, 1992-96, Nat. Women's Law Ctr., 1981—; trustee Ctr. for Law and Social Policy, Washington, 1977-96, Women's Bar Found., 1981-86. Mem. ABA (chair sect. ind. rights and responsibilities 1977-78, chair fed. judiciary com. 1980-83, chair consortium on legal svcs. and the pub. 1987-90, bd. govs. 1990-93, chair resource devel. coun. 1993-95, chair coun. Fund for Justice and Edn. 1995-96, state del. from D.C. 1994—), D.C. Bar (sec. 1975-76, mem. bd. govs. 1976-79), Am. Law Inst., Southwestern Legal Found. (trustee 1993-96), Order of Coif. Office: Arnold & Porter 555 12th St NW Washington DC 20004-1206

**BORN, DAWN SLATER,** lawyer. BA in Pub. Justice summa cum laude, SUNY, Oswego, 1977; JD summa cum laude, U. Houston, 1981. Assoc. Wood, Campbell Moody & Gibbs, Houston, 1981-83; assoc. Bracewell & Patterson, LLP, Houston, 1983-88, ptnr., 1988-94; dir. corp. devel. Enron Capital & Trade Resources subs. Enron Corp., Houston, 1994-95, dir. restructuring, 1995-96; v.p., gen. counsel GNI Group, Inc., Houston, 1996-98; ptnr. LaBoeuf, Lamb, Greene & MacRae, LLP, Houston, 1998—; bd. dirs., mem. fin. planning com. Queensland Alumina Ltd., bd. dirs. Healthcare Techs. Inc.; spkr. in field. Bd. dirs., exec., mem. nominating and endowment coms. Boys and Girls Country of Houstin, Inc., 1996—; mem. edn. com. River Oaks Bapt. Sch., 1994-97, gender com., 1994—, chair gender com. 1995—, chair ad hoc com. to address mid. sch. disciplinary sys., 1996-97, mem. ad hoc com. to revise honor roll requirements, 1996-97, ad hoc com. for diversity and equity, 1998—. Mem. ABA (bus. law and corp. counsel sects.), NAFE, State Bar Tex. (bus. law and corp. counsel sects., chair franchise and distbn. law com. 1993-94), D.C. Bar Assn., Houston Bar Assn., Coll. of State Bar Tex., Tex. Exec. Women (mentor and round table discussion group leader). General corporate, Mergers and acquisitions, Securities. Address: 3704 Plumb St Houston TX 77005-2810 Office: LeBoeuf Lamb Greene & MacRae LLP 1000 Louisiana St Houston TX 77002-5000

**BORN, SUZANNE,** lawyer; b. Waseca, Minn., Apr. 23, 1946. BA, U. Minn., 1977; JD, Hamline U., 1980. Bar: Minn. 1980, U.S. Dist. Ct. Minn. 1980, U.S. Ct. Appeals (8th cir.) 1980, U.S. Supreme Ct. 1997. Law clk. Hon. John F. Thoreen, Stillwater, Minn., 1980-83; ptnr. Stone & Zander, Mpls., 1983-85; pvt. practice, Mpls., 1985—; adminstrv. law judge Minn. State Office of Adminstrv. Hearings, Mpls., 1989—. Editor Hamline Law Review, 1979-80. Mem. Mpls. Commn. on Civil Rights, 1987-92; mem. Minn. Supreme Ct. Parental Cooperation task force, Hamlin Univ. Sch. Law adv. bd. Mem. Minn. Women Lawyers (pres. 1985-86, Myra Bradwell award for promoting the interests of women in the legal prof. 1998), Minn. State Bar Assn. (family law sect. chair 1999—), Henn. County Bar Assn. (family law sect. exec. com.). Family and matrimonial, Juvenile. Office: 333 Washington Ave N Minneapolis MN 55401-1377

**BORNHEIMER, ALLEN MILLARD,** lawyer; b. Brewer, Maine, June 10, 1942; s. Millard Genthner and Gertrude Evelyn (Kinney) B.; m. Deborah Russell Hill, June 17, 1967; children: Anneliese, Charles, Elizabeth. Student, Phillips Exeter Acad., 1961; AB, Harvard U., 1965, LLB, 1968. Bar: Mich. 1968, Mass. 1971. Assoc. Dickinson, Wright, McKean & Cudlip, Detroit, 1968-70; assoc. Choate, Hall & Stewart, Boston, 1970-76, ptnr., 1976—, mng. ptnr., 1988-95; bd. dirs. Cargex Properties, Inc. and affiliated cos., Portland, Maine. Town moderator, Duxbury, Mass., 1982—, chmn. fin. com., 1974-76, mem. capital budget com., 1977; bd. dirs. Jordan Hosp., Plymouth, Mass., 1974-81; trustee North Yarmouth (Maine) Acad., 1976-79. Mem. ABA, Mass. Bar Assn., Boston Bar Assn., Am. Coll. Investment Counsel, Mass. Moderators Assn., Duxbury Yacht Club (bd. dirs. 1982-84), Harvard Club (Boston). Republican. Avocations: golf, piano, sailing. General corporate, Finance, Banking. Home: 76 Upland Rd Duxbury MA 02332-3930 Office: Choate Hall & Stewart Exchange Pl 53 State St Boston MA 02109-2804

**BORNMANN, CARL MALCOLM,** lawyer; b. Somerville, N.J., Aug. 13, 1936; s. John Carl Bornmann and Dorothy Louise (Balliet) Capparelli; children: Carl, Gregory, Melissa. BS, Ohio U., 1958; JD with distinction, Ind. U., 1961; MA, Columbia U., 1989. Bar: Ind. 1961, N.Y. 1962, U.S. Dist. Ct. (so. and ea. dists.) N.Y. 1962, U.S. Ct. Appeals (2d cir.) 1962, U.S. Supreme Ct. 1965. Assoc. Cahill, Gordon, Reindel & Ohl, N.Y.C., 1961-69; ptnr. Cahill, Gordon & Reindel, N.Y.C., 1970—. dir. Residents for the Future of Briarcliff Manor, 1994-96; del. USSR People to People Internat., 1990. Mem. ABA (bus. law sect.), N.Y. State Bar Assn., Japan Soc. of N.Y.C., Collier County (Fla.) Bar Assn. (assoc.), Order of Coif. General practice, Banking, General corporate. Home: 4419 Rosea Ct Naples FL 34104-4445

**BOROWIEC, WILLIAM MATTHEW,** lawyer; b. Sierra Vista, Ariz., Dec. 21, 1962; s. Matthew William and Margaret Lynn Borowiec. BA, U. Ariz., 1987; JD, Hamline U., 1989. Bar: Ariz. 1991, U.S. Dist. Ct. Ariz. 1995. Atty. Blaser & Assocs., Tucson, 1991-93, Monroe & Assocs., Tucson, 1993, Felix & Holohan, Tucson, 1993-97; mng. ptnr. Borowiec & Borowiec, Sierra Vista, Ariz., 1997—. Com. mem. Forgach House Charity Tennis Tournament, Sierra Vista. Mem. ABA, Ariz. Trial Lawyers Assn. Avocations: golf, tennis, hunting, fishing. Appellate, State civil litigation, Personal injury. Office: Borowiec and Borowiec 2700 E Fry Blvd Ste B8 Sierra Vista AZ 85635-2828

**BOROWY, FRANK RHINE,** lawyer; b. Glen Ridge, N.J., Mar. 2, 1948; s. Frank Stanley and Alenna (Rhine) B.; m. Karen Judith Wallace, Sept. 27, 1975; children: Laura, William. BA, Gettysburg Coll., 1970; JD, U. Conn., 1973. Bar: Conn. 1973, U.S. Dist. Ct. Conn. 1974, U.S. Ct. Appeals (2d cir.) 1975, U.S. Ct. Appeals (fed. cir.), U.S. Supreme Ct. 1977. Ptnr. Nassau, Borowy & Griffith, Newington, Conn., 1980—; asst. atty. Town of Newington, 1985—. Author: (play) The Way to Philadelphia, 1987. Active, Newington Town Coun., 1977-79, Newington Rep. Town Com., 1977—; vice chmn. Town of Newington Standing Ins. Commn., 1977-79; chmn. Salvation Army Adv. Bd., New Britain, Conn., 1996—. Mem. Conn. Bar Assn., Conn. Trial Lawyers Assn., Fed. Bar Assn. Methodist. Personal injury, Real property. Office: Nassau Borowy & French 66 Cedar St Newington CT 06111-2633

**BORRELL, MARK STEVEN,** lawyer; b. Ventura, Calif., May 11, 1960; s. Roger W. and Mary Jane Borrell; m. Cindy Robin Borrell, Nov. 7, 1998. BS in Fin., U. Colo., 1982; JD, U. Pacific, 1986. Bar: Calif. 1986, U.S. Dist. Ct. (ea. dist.) Calif. 1986, U.S. Dist. Ct. (ctrl. dist.) Calif. 1987, U.S. Ct. Appeals (9th cir.) 1987. Ptnr. Borrell & Borrell, Ventura, 1986-93; shareholder Benton, Orr, Duval & Buckingham, Ventura, 1994—; mem. bar liaison com. Ventura County Cts., 1993—; arbitrator Ventura County Superior and Mcpl. Cts., 1995—. Mem. Assn. So. Calif. Def. Counsel, Ventura County Bar Assn. (law libr. com. 1988-91), Ventura County Trial Lawyers Assn. (bd. dirs. 1995—, sec.-treas. 1997-98), Ventura County Criminal Def. Bar Assn. (bd. dirs. 1988-92, v.p. 1989, pres. 1990), Traynor Soc., Order of Coif. Avocation: cycling. State civil litigation, Personal injury, Criminal. Office: Benton Orr Duval & Buckingham 39 N California St Ventura CA 93001-2620

**BORSOS, ROBERT BRUCE,** lawyer; b. Kalamazoo, Mich., Aug. 19, 1951; s. Robert Louis and Shirley (Isabelle) B.; m. Sandra Sue Asquini, Aug. 3, 1974; children: Mark, Eric. BS, Western Mich. U., 1973; JD, Notre Dame U., 1976. Bar: Mich. 1985, U.S. Dist. Ct. (we. dist.) Mich. 1985, U.S. Ct. Appeals (6th cir.). Ptnr. Kreis, Enderle, Callander & Hudgins, Kalamazoo, 1976—. Mem. Ambucs Club, Rotary, County C. of C. (chmn.). Bankruptcy, General corporate, Estate planning. Office: Kreis Enderle Callander & Hudgins One Moors Bridge Kalamazoo MI 49002

**BORTNICK, BLAINE H.,** lawyer; b. Washington, Dec. 24, 1963. BA, Duke U., 1986; JD, Emory U., 1989; LLM, NYU, 1990. Bar: N.Y. 1991, Va. 1991, U.S. Dist. Ct. (ea. dist.) Va. 1991, D.C. 1992, U.S. Ct. Appeals (4th cir.) 1992, U.S. Dist. Ct. D.C. 1992, U.S. Dist. Ct. (so. and ea. dists.) N.Y. 1993, U.S. Supreme Ct. 1996. Atty. Sandground, Barondess & West, Vienna, Va., 1991-93; assoc. Liddle & Robinson, LLP, N.Y.C., 1993-97, ptnr., 1998—. Mem. Assn. Bar City N.Y. (mem. fed. legis. com. 1995-98). General civil litigation, Family and matrimonial, Labor. Office: Liddle & Robinson LLP 685 3rd Ave New York NY 10017-4024

**BOSS, AMELIA HELEN,** law educator, lawyer; b. Balt., Apr. 3, 1949; d. Myron Theodore and Loretta (Oakjones) B.; m. Roger S. Clark, Mar. 3, 1979; children: Melissa, Seymour, Edward, Ashley. Student, St. Hilda's Coll., England, 1968; BA in Sociology, Bryn Mawr, 1970; JD, Rutgers U., 1975. Bar: N.J. Pa., U.S. Dist. Ct. (ea. dist.) N.J., U.S. Dist. Ct. (ea. dist.) Pa., U.S. Supreme Ct., U.S. Ct. Appeals (3d cir.). Law clk. Hon. Milton B. Cranford N.J. Supreme Ct., 1975-76; assoc. Pepper, Hamilton & Scheetz, Phila., 1976-78; assoc. prof. law Rutgers U. Sch. Law, Camden, N.J., 1983-87, Temple U., Phila., 1989-91; prof. law Temple U. Sch. Law, Phila., 1991—; vis. prof. law U. Miami Sch. Law, Coral Gables, Fla., 1985-86; Leo Goodwin disting. vis. prof. law Nova U., Sch. Law, 1998; mem. coms. Nat. Conf. Commrs. on Uniform State Laws; U.S. rep. to UN Commn. on Internat. Trade Law. Author: (books) Electronic Data Interchange Agreements: A Guide and Sourcebook, 1993, ABCs of the UCC: Article 2A, ABCs of the UCC: Article 5; editor-in-chief The Data Law Report, 1993-97, The Business Lawyer, 1998-99, ABCs of the UCC; mem. permanent editl. bd. Uniform Comml. Code; contbr. articles to profl. jours. Named among top 50 women lawyers in U.S. Nat. Law Jour., 1998. Fellow Am. Bar Found.; mem. ABA (chmn.-elect bus. law sect.), Am. Law Inst., Am. Bankruptcy Inst., Am. Coll. Comml. Fin. Lawyers, Nat. Assn. Women Lawyers. Home: 309 Westmont Ave Haddonfield NJ 08033-1714 Office: Temple U Sch Law 1719 N Broad St Philadelphia PA 19122-6002

**BOSS, LENARD BARRETT,** lawyer; b. Passaic, N.J., Mar. 6, 1960; s. Lawrence Steven and Laura (Ziegler) B. BA in Rhetoric, Bates Coll., 1982; JD with high honors, George Washington U., 1985. Bar: Pa. 1985, D.C. 1986, Md. 1995, U.S. Ct. Appeals (4th and 11th cirs.) 1986, U.S. Ct. Appeals (D.C. cir.) 1987, U.S. Dist. Ct. D.C. 1987, U.S. Ct. Appeals (3d cir.) 1988, U.S. Supreme Ct. 1989. Assoc. Asbill, Junkin, Myers & Buffone, Washington, 1986-91; ptnr. Asbill, Junkin & Myers, Washington, 1991-95; asst. fed. pub. defender Fed. Pub. Defender's Office, Washington, 1995—. Avocations: films, music, sports. Criminal, General civil litigation. Office: 625 Indiana Ave NW Ste 550 Washington DC 20004-2901

**BOSSER, STEVEN JOHN,** prosecutor; b. Yonkers, N.Y., Dec. 27, 1952; s. John Joseph and Margaret Frances (Flanagan) B.; m. Susan Virginia Coggins, Oct. 17, 1981; children: Timothy, Katharine. BA in Econ., SUNY, Albany, 1977; JD, St. John's U., Jamaica, N.Y., 1984. Bar: N.Y. 1985, N.J. 1985, U.S. Dist. Ct. N.J. 1985, Tex. 1986, U.S. Dist. Ct. (no. dist.) Tex. 1988, U.S. Supreme Ct. 1989, DC Ct. Appeals, 1989. Asst. city atty. City Atty's. Office, Ft. Worth, 1986-87; asst. criminal dist. atty. Tarrant County Dist. Atty's Office, Ft. Worth, 1987—; lectr. Tex. Dept. Pub. Safety, Austin, 1993-97, Tarrant County Auto Theft Task Force, Ft. Worth, 1994-97. Com. chair Boy Scouts Am., 1994-96, various other positions, 1995—. With U.S. Army, 1973-76. Recipient Prosecutor Yr. award Tex. Assn. Vehicle Theft Investigators, 1994; named to Outstanding Young Men of Am., 1987. Mem. Tex. State Bar Assn., Tex. Dist. and County Attys. Assn., D.C. Bar Assn. Republican. Avocations: camping, hiking, computers. Office: Tarrant County Dist Atty 401 W Belknap St Fl 4 Fort Worth TX 76102-1913

**BOSSES, STEVAN J.,** lawyer; b. Bronx, N.Y., July 29, 1937; s. Fred and Frieda (Picard) B.; m. Abbye Z. Bosses, May 24, 1964; children: Donna Lynne, David Keith, Gary Philip. BME, Cornell U., 1960; LLB, Columbia U., 1963. Bar: N.Y. 1963, U.S. Dist. Ct. (so. dist.) N.Y. 1964, U.S. Dist. Ct. (ea. dist.) N.Y. 1964, U.S. Patent Office 1964, U.S. Ct. Appeals (2d cir.) 1970, U.S. Ct. Appeals (3rd cir.) 1979, U.S. Ct. Appeals (fed. cir.) 1982, U.S. Supreme Ct. 1989. Assoc., Watson Leavenworth Kelton & Taggart, N.Y.C., 1963-71, ptnr., 1972-81; ptnr. Fitzpatrick, Cella, Harper & Scinto, N.Y.C., 1981—. Mem. ABA, ASME, N.Y. State Bar Assn., Am. Intellectual Property Law Assn., Fed. Bar Coun. (trustee 1989-94), Fed. Cir. Bar Assn., N.Y. Intellectual Property Law Assn. Patent, Trademark and copyright, Federal civil litigation. Home: 19 Springdale Rd Scarsdale NY 10583-7330 Office: 30 Rockefeller Plz New York NY 10112-0002

**BOSSI, MARK VINCENT,** lawyer; b. Arkansas City, Kans., July 28, 1962; s. Thomas Richard and Norma Jean (Heffner) B. BS/BA, U. Kans., 1984; JD, George Washington U., 1987. Bar: Mo. 1987, Ill. 1988, Kans. 1988; U.S. Dist. Ct. (ea. and we. dist.) Mo. 1987, U.S. Dist Ct. Kans. 1988, U.S. Dist. Ct. (so. dist.) Ill., 1988, U.S. Ct. Appeals (8th cir.) 1990. Assoc. Thompson and Mitchell, St. Louis, 1987-95, ptnr., 1996; ptnr. Thompson Coburn, St. Louis, 1996—; adj. prof. law St Louis U., 1998—. Lawyer St. Louis Vol. Lawyers, 1989—; bd. dir. The Lighthouse For The Blind, Inc., 1994—, sec. 1996—. Mem. ABA, Mo. Bar Assn., Ill. Bar Assn., Kans. Bar Assn., Bar Assn. Met. St. Louis (bus. law sect.), Am. Bankruptcy Inst. Bankruptcy, General civil litigation, Contracts commercial. Office: Thompson Coburn 1 Mercantile Ctr Ste 3400 Saint Louis MO 63101-1623

**BOST, THOMAS GLEN,** lawyer; b. Oklahoma City, July 13, 1942; s. Burl John and Lorene Bell (Croka) B.; m. Sheila K. Pettigrew, Aug. 27, 1966; children: Amy Elizabeth, Stephen Luke, Emily Anne, Paul Alexander. BS in Acctg. summa cum laude, Abilene Christian U., 1964; JD, Vanderbilt U., 1967. Bar: Tenn. 1967, Calif. 1969. Instr. David Lipscomb Coll., Nashville, 1967; asst. prof. law Vanderbilt U., Nashville, 1967-68; ptnr. Latham & Watkins, Los Angeles, 1968—; lectr. on taxation subjects. Chmn. bd. regents, law sch. bd. visitors Pepperdine U., Malibu, Calif., 1980—. Mem. ABA (chmn. standards of tax practice com., sec. taxation 1988-90), State Bar of Calif., Los Angeles County Bar Assn. (chmn. taxation sect. 1981-82). Republican. Mem. Ch. of Christ. Club: Calif. (Los Angeles). Personal income taxation, Corporate taxation, State and local taxation.

**BOSTON, DERRICK OSMOND,** lawyer; b. Georgetown, Guyana, May 31, 1964; came to U.S., 1980; s. Derrick Osmond and Stella Hyacinth (Benjamin) B. BA, Harvard U., 1984, JD, 1987. Bar: Calif. 1990. Assoc. Irell & Manella, L.A., 1989—; alt. dir. L.A. County Metro. Transp. Authority, 1993; Asst. to Mayor Bradley on Rebuild L.A., 1992; counsel The Ind. Commn. on the Police Dept. (Christopher Commn.), 1991. Securities, General corporate, Mergers and acquisitions. Office: Irell & Manella 1800 Avenue Of The Stars Los Angeles CA 90067-4276

**BOSTON, WILLIAM CLAYTON,** lawyer; b. Hobart, Okla., Nov. 29, 1934; s. William Clayton and Dollie Jane (Gibbs) B.; m. Billie Gail Long, Jan. 20, 1962; children: Kathryn Gray, William Clayton III. BS, Okla. State U., 1958; LLB, U. Okla., 1962; LLM, NYU, 1967. Bar: Okla. 1961. Assoc. Mosteller, Fellers, Andrews, Snider & Baggett, Oklahoma City, 1962-64; ptnr. Fellers, Snider, Baggett, Blankenship & Boston, Oklahoma City, 1968-69, Andrews, Davis, Legg, Bixler, Milsten & Murrah, Oklahoma City, 1972-86; pvt. practice Oklahoma City, 1986—. Contbr. articles to profl. jours.; mem. adv. bd. The Jour. of Air Law and Commerce, 1995—. Past pres. and trustee Ballet Okla.; past v.p., bd. dirs. Oklahoma City Arts Coun.; past trustee Nichols Hills (Okla.) Methodist Ch.; past trustee, chmn. Okla. Found. for the Humanities; past trustee, vice-chmn., sec. Humanities in Okla., Inc., 1992-95. With U.S. Army, 1954-56. Mem. ABA (former chmn. subcom. on aircraft fin., former chmn. aircraft fin. and contract divsn. forum on air and space law), FBA, Internat. Bar Assn., Inter-Pacific Bar Assn., Okla. State Bar Assn., Oklahoma County Bar Assn. General practice. Home: 1701 Camden Way Oklahoma City OK 73116-5121 Office: 4005 NW Expressway St Oklahoma City OK 73116-1691

**BOSTWICK, DONALD W.,** lawyer; b. Wichita, Aug. 25, 1943; s. Edgar Plato and Pauline Mildred (Varner) B.; m. Jillayne Deanne Weickert, June 15, 1969. BS in Bus. Acctg., U. Kans., 1965, JD, 1968. Shareholder Adams, Jones, Robinson and Malone, Wichita, 1968—; chair U.S. magistrate sel. panel, 1993, co-chair civil justice reform act com., 1995—; mem. Tenth Cir. Adv. Com., 1995—. Chair bd. editors Kans. Bar Jour., 1991-94; mng. editor U. Kans. LAw Review, 1967-68. Officer, bd. dirs. Big Bros.-Big Sisters, Wichita, 1974-79; chmn. Rural Water Dist. No. 5, Benton, Kans., 1987—. Recipient Outstanding Svc. award Kans. Bar Assn., Topeka, 1994. Fellow Am. Coll. Trial Lawyers, Am. Bar Found., Kans. Bar Found. (life); mem. Order of Coif, Kans. U. Law Soc. (pres. 1996-97). Republican. Methodist. Avocations: reading, history, gardening. Federal civil litigation, FERC practice, General civil litigation. Home: 2962 SW Indianola Rd Benton KS 67017-9178 Office: Adams Jones Robinson Malone 155 N Market St Ste 600 Wichita KS 67202-1820

**BOSTWICK, FREDERICK DEBURLO, III,** lawyer; b. Midland, Tex., Mar. 14, 1953; s. Fred. D. and Jane (Holt) B.; m. Linda Watts, May 28, 1977; children: Ellie, Doran, Will. BA, Vanderbilt U., 1975; JD, Baylor U., 1978. Bar: Tex. 1978, Wash. 1979 U.S. Dist. Ct. (we. dist.) Wash. 1979, U.S. Dist. Ct. (we. dist.) Tex. 1981, U.S. Ct. Appeals (5th cir.) 1983, U.S. Supreme Ct. 1984, U.S. Dist. Ct. (so. dist.) Tex. 1986, U.S. Dist. Ct. (no. dist.) Tex. 1990. Assoc. Kayce & Fleck, Seattle, 1978-80, Naman, Howell, Smith & Lee, Waco, Tex., 1980-85; ptnr. Naman, Howell, Smith & Lee, P.C., Waco, 1985—; adj. prof. Baylor U. Law Sch., 1991—. Bd. dirs. Caritas Food for People, Waco, 1980—; bd. dirs. Heart of Tex. Legal Svcs., 1981-86, pres., 1984; bd. dirs. Evangelia Settlement, 1981-84, pres., 1984; trustee Waco Ind. Sch. Dist., 1986-92, pres., 1990-91; mem. bd. govs. Waco Found., 1995—. Mem. ABA, State Bar of Tex., Wash. State Bar Assn., Waco-McLennan county Bar Assn., Tex. Assn. Defense Counsel, Defense Rsch. Inst. Avocations: running, sailing, camping, reading. General civil litigation, Civil rights, Product liability. Home: 2624 Cedar Ridge Rd Waco TX 76708-2353 Office: Naman Howell Smith & Lee PC 900 Washington Ave Ste 700 Waco TX 76701-1294

**BOSTWICK, RICHARD RAYMOND,** retired lawyer; b. Billings, Mont., Mar. 17, 1918; s. Leslie H. and Maude (Worthington) B.; m. Margaret Florence Brooks, Jan. 17, 1944; children: Michael, Patricia, Ed, Dick. Student, U. Colo., 1937-38; A.B., U. Wyo., 1943, J.D., 1947. Bar: Wyo. 1947. Claim atty. Hawkeye Casualty Co., Casper, Wyo., 1948-49; ptnr. Murane & Bostwick, Casper, 1949-91; ret., 1991; lectr. U. Wyo. Coll. Law. Contbr. articles profl. jours. Past trustee Casper YMCA; dep. dir. Civil Def., 1954-58; chmn. local SSS, 1952-70; mem. curriculum coordinating com. Natrona Co. Sch. Dist. 2, High Sch. Dist.; Wyom. rep. adv. com. U.S. Tenth Circuit Ct. Appeals, 1985-87; mem. U. Wyo. Coll. Law Adv. Com., 1987-91. Capt. AUS, 1943-46. Decorated Bronze Star medal; recipient Silver Merit awards Am. Legion. Mem. ABA (Harrison Tweed award 1968), Am. Coll. Trial Lawyers, Wyo. Bar Assn. (pres. 1964-65, 1st Pro Bono award 1987), Natrona County Bar Assn. (pres. 1956), Am. Judicature Soc. (exec. com. 1973-75, sec. 1975-77 Herbert Harley award), Internat. Assn. Def. Counsel, Fedn. Ins. and Corp. Counsel, Nat. Conf. Bar Pres. (exec. council 1970-72), Internat. Soc. of Barristers (dir. 1971-76, pres. 1975), Am. Legion (dir. 1951-58, post comdr. 1953-54), Wyo. Alumni Assn. (trustee 1955-57), Casper C. of C. (chmn. legis. com. 1955-57, dir. 1959-62, v.p.). Presbyterian. Lodges: Masons, Shriners, KT. Personal injury, Federal civil litigation, State civil litigation. Home: 1137 Granada Ave Casper WY 82601-5932 *I was fortunate enough to select a profession which I find I have liked from the beginning and with which I am still fascinated. This makes it easy to work hard and to maintain a high standard of pride in the profession and to donate and devote time to the upgrading of it over and above daily routine. To be able to work hard, to create a job well done, and to experience satisfaction over and above the mere elements of a livelihood is a goal worthy of effort.*

**BOSWELL, DAVID A.,** lawyer; b. Wilmington, Del., Aug. 2, 1966; s. Paul H. and Jeanne B. BA in English with honors, Coll. William & Mary, 1988; JD, U. Pa. Sch. Law, 1992. Bar: Del. 1993, U.S. Dist. Ct. Del. dist. 1994, U.S. Ct. of Appeals (3d cir.) 1996. Jud. law clk. Hon. Carl Goldstein, Superior Ct. Del., Wilmington, 1992-93; assoc. Schmittinger & Rodriguez, P.A., Wilmington, 1993-95; house atty. House Reps., Del. Gen. Assembly, Dover, 1994-96; ptnr., branch mgr. Schmittinger & Rodriguez, P.A., Wilmington, 1996—. Recipient Dist. Pro Bono Svc. award Del. Vol. Legal Svcs., Inc., 1988. Labor, Personal injury, Legislative. Office: Schmittinger & Rodriguez PA 1300 N Market St Ste 205 Wilmington DE 19801-1813

**BOSWELL, JOHN HOWARD,** lawyer; b. Houston, Mar. 22, 1932; s. Henry Oliver and Opal Everest (Wineburg) B.; m. Sharon Lee Ueckert, Dec. 19, 1959; children—John Brooke, Mark Richard. B.B.A., U. Houston, 1955; J.D., U. Houston, 1963. Bar: Tex. 1962, U.S. Supreme Ct. 1970, U.S. Ct. Appeals (5th cir.) 1970; cert. civil trial advocate Nat. Bd. Trial Advocacy, Tex. Bd. Legal Specialization. Sr. shareholder Boswell and Hallmark, P.C., Houston; lectr. State Bar Tex. Continuing Legal Edn. Program, 1978-84, Pepperdine U. Coll. Law; faculty Tex. Coll. of Trial Advocacy, 1980-90. Served to lt. USNR, 1955-58. Mem. Am. Bd. Trial Advocates, Internat. Assn. Ins. Counsel, Tex. Assn. Def. Counsel, Def. Research Inst. Personal injury, Federal civil litigation, State civil litigation. Home: 405 Chapelwood Ct Houston TX 77024-6737 Address: Boswell & Hallmark 1010 Lamar St Ste 900 Houston TX 77002-6314

**BOSWELL, WILLIAM DOUGLAS,** lawyer; b. Harrisburg, Pa., June 7, 1918; s. Ralph Everett and Edna Stansberry (Heller) B.; m. Doris M. Lutz, June 9, 1945; children: William D. Jr., Jeffrey R., Nancy Jeanne, Joanne Elizabeth. PhB, Dickinson Coll., 1940, LLB, 1943. Bar: Pa. 1943, U.S. Dist. Ct. (mid. dist.) Pa. 1946, U.S. Dist. Ct. (ea. dist.) Pa. 1965, U.S. Ct. Appeals (3d cir.) 1966, U.S. Ct. Appeals (4th cir.) 1982, U.S. Supreme Ct. 1962. Ptnr. Compton, Handler, Berman & Boswell, Harrisburg, Pa., 1946-71, Berman, Boswell & Tintner, Harrisburg, 1971-86, Boswell, Tintner & Piccola, 1986-88, Boswell, Snyder, Tintner & Piccola, 1988-97, Boswell, Tintner, Piccola & Wickersham, 1997—; lectr. Pa. Bar Inst., Am. Soc. C.L.U.s, Pa. Banker's Assn.; bd. dirs. Byers Lumber Co., Inc.Sd Doris M. Lutz, June 9, 1945; children: William D. Jr., Jeffrey R., Nancy Jeanne, Joanne Elizabeth. PhB, Dickinson Coll., 1940, LLB, 1943. Bar: Pa. 1943, U.S. Dist. Ct. (mid. dist.) Pa. 1946, U.S. Dist. Ct. (ea. dist.) Pa. 1965, U.S. Ct. Appeals (3d cir.) 1966, U.S. Ct. Appeals (4th cir.) 1982, U.S. Supreme Ct. 1962. Ptnr. Compton, Handler, Berman & Boswell, Harrisburg, Pa., 1946-71, Berman, Boswell & Tintner, Harrisburg, 1971-86, Boswell, Tintner & Piccola, 1986-88, Boswell, Snyder, Tintner & Piccola, 1988-97, Boswell, Tinther, Piccola & Wickersham, 1997—; lectr. Pa. Bar Inst., Am. Soc. C.L.U.s, Pa. Banker's Assn.; bd. dirs. Byers Lumber Co., Inc. Pres. Tri-County United Way, 1963-64, Tri-County Welfare Council, 1960-61, bd. dirs., Josiah W. and Bessie H. Kline Found., 1979—; v.p. Dauphin County unit Am. Cancer Soc., 1970-72; pres. Children's Home of Harrisburg, Inc., 1965-68, 75—, Estate Planning Council Central Pa., 1970, bd. dirs., solicitor, Harrisburg Symphony Assn., 1986—; solicitor County of Dauphin, 1990-92. Master sgt. AUS, 1942-46. Fellow Am. Coll. Trust and Estate Counsel, mem. ABA, Pa. Bar Assn., Dauphin County Bar Assn. (pres. 1962-63), Am. Judicature Soc., Woolsack Soc. Republican. Presbyterian. Clubs: Executive of Central Pa. (pres. 1978), Masons, K.T., Shriners, Tuesday, Country (pres. 1974-76) (Harrisburg). Pres. Tri-County United Way, 1963-64, Tri-County Welfare Coun., 1960-61; bd. dirs. Josia W. and Bessie H. Kline Found., 1979—; v.p. Dauphin County unit Am. Cancer Soc., 1970-72; pres. Children's Home of Harrisburg, Inc., 1965-68, 75—, Estate Planning Coun. Ctrl. Pa., 1970; bd. dirs., solicitor Harrisburg Symphony Assn., 1986—; solicitor County of Dauphin, 1990-92. Master sgt. AUS, 1942-46. Fellow Am. Coll. Trust and Estate Counsel, mem. ABA, Pa. Bar Assn., Dauphin County Bar Assn. (pres. 1962-63), Am. Judicature Soc., Woolsack Soc., Exec. Club of Ctrl. Pa. (pres. 1978), Masons, K.T., Shriners, Tuesday Club, Harrisburg Country Club (pres. 1974-76). Republican. Presbyterian. General practice, Probate, General corporate. Office: Boswell Tintner Piccola & Wickersham PO Box 741 Harrisburg PA 17108-0741

**BOSWELL, WILLIAM PARET,** lawyer; b. Washington, Oct. 24, 1946; s. Yates Paret and Mary Frances (Hyland) B.; m. Barbara Stelle Schroeder, Sept. 6, 1969; children: Susan Anne, Sarah Mary, Christina Catherine. BA cum laude, Cath. U., 1968; JD, U. Va., 1971. Bar: Va. 1971, D.C. 1972, U.S. Ct. Mil. Appeals 1972, U.S. Supreme Ct. 1975, Pa. 1978. Atty. Peoples Natural Gas Co., Pitts., 1978-82, asst. sec., gen. atty., 1982-85, sec., gen. counsel, 1985-88, 1989—, also bd. dirs.; gen. counsel Hope Gas, Inc., 1998—; dep. gen. counsel Consol. Natural Gas Co., 1999—; bd. dirs., mem. exec. com. United Distbn. Cos.; mem. exec. com. Gas Industry Stds. Bd., 1994-97, bd. dirs., 1997—, vice chmn., 1998—. Pres. Borough Coun., Osborne, Pa., 1984-97, mayor, 1998—; bd. dirs. Mendelssohn Choir Pitts., 1996-98, pres. 1997-98; trustee Laughlin Found., 1995—. Capt. JAGC, USAF, 1971-78, col. USAFR, 1979-98. Decorated Legion of Merit. Mem. ABA (chair gas com. 1992—), Pa. Bar Assn., D.C. Bar Assn., Va. Bar Assn., Am. Gas Assn. (chair regulatory com. 1996-98), Pa. Gas Assn. (chmn. 1989-90), Am. Corp. Counsel Assn. (pres. Pa. chpt. 1991-92, Excellence in Corporate Practice award 1998), Am. Soc. Corp. Secs., Rivers Club, City Club Pitts., Army and Navy Club D.C. Republican. Roman Catholic. Avocations: reading, walking. General corporate, Public utilities, Oil, gas, and mineral. Home: 405 Hare Ln Sewickley PA 15143-2050 Office: CNG Towers 625 Liberty Ave Pittsburgh PA 15222-3110

**BOTELHO, BRUCE MANUEL,** state attorney general, mayor; b. Juneau, Alaska, Oct. 6, 1948; s. Emmett Manuel and Harriet Iowa (Tieszen) B.; m. Guadalupe Alvarez Breton, Sept. 23, 1988; children: Alejandro Manuel, Adriana Regina. Student, U. Heidelberg, Federal Republic of Germany, 1970; BA, Willamette U., 1971, JD, 1976. Bar: Alaska 1976, U.S. Ct. Appeals (9th cir.), U.S. Supreme Ct. Asst. atty. gen. State of Alaska, Juneau, 1976-83, 87-90, dep. commr., acting commr. Dept. of Revenue, 1983-86; mayor City, Borough of Juneau, 1988-91, dep. atty. gen., 1991-94; atty. gen. State of AK, 1994—. Editor: Willamette Law Jour., 1975-76; contbr. articles profl. jours. Assembly mem. City, Borough of Juneau, 1983-86; pres. Juneau Human Rights Commn., 1978-80, Alaska Coun. Am. Youth Hostels, 1979-81, Juneau Arts and Humanities Coun., 1981-83, SE Alaska Area Coun. Boy Scouts Am., 1991-93, coun. commr., 1993—; bd. dirs. Found. for Social Innovations, Alaska, 1990-93, Alaska Econ. Devel. Coun., 1985-87,

Alaska Indsl. Devel. Corp., 1984-86, Juneau World Affairs Coun.; chair adminstrv. law sect. Alaska Bar Assn., 1981-82; chair Alaska Resources Corp., 1984-86, Gov.'s Conf. on Youth and Justice, 1995-96; trustee Alaska Children's Trust, 1996—; mem. exec. com. Conf. of Western Attys. Gen., 1997—; co-chair Alaska Justice Assessment Commn., 1997—, chair Gov. Task Force on Confidentiality of Chldns. Proceedings, 1998—; mem. Commn. for Justice Across the Atlantic, 1999—. Mem. Nat. Assn. Attys. Gen. (exec. com. 1998—). Democrat. Methodist. Avocation: international folk dance. Home: 401 F St Douglas AK 99824-5353 Office: State Alaska Dept Law PO Box 110300 Juneau AK 99811-0300

**BOTTA, FRANK CHARLES,** lawyer; b. Pitts., Aug. 3, 1959; s. Charles Joseph and Rose Patricia (Costanzo) B. BA in Econs., Washington and Jefferson Coll., 1981; JD, Temple U. Bar: Pa., U.S. Dist. Ct. (we. dist.) Pa. Labor cons. Human Resources Mgmt., Inc., Pitts., 1984-86, v.p., 1987-88; assoc. Ogg, Jones, DeSimone & Ignelzi, Pitts., 1988-89; atty. contractor rels. Roadway Package Sys., Inc., Pitts., 1990-92; atty. Caliber Sys. Inc. (formerly Roadway Svcs., Inc.), Akron, Ohio, 1992-96; ptnr. Burns, White & Hickton, Pitts., 1997—. Mem. ABA (labor and employment com., labor arbitration and law of collective bargaining mgmt. com., corp. in-house counsel com., young lawyers divsn.), Am. Corp. Counsel Assn., Pa. Bar Assn. (labor and employment law com., in-house counsel com.), Allegheny County Bar Assn. (labor and employment sect., young lawyers sect.). General civil litigation, Labor, Transportation. Home: 242 Tech Rd Pittsburgh PA 15205-1737 Office: Burns White & Hickton 2400 5th Ave Pl 120 5th Ave Ste 2400 Pittsburgh PA 15222-3011

**BOTTAR, ANTHONY SAMUEL,** lawyer; b. Syracuse, N.Y., July 20, 1950; s. Anthony V. and Lorraine B. (Andrews) B.; m. Nancy A. Hamel, Aug. 17, 1974; 1 child, Michael. BA, U. Rochester, 1972; JD, SUNY, Buffalo, 1976. Bar: N.Y. 1977, U.S. Dist. Ct. (we. dist.) N.Y. 1977, U.S. Dist. Ct. (no. dist.) N.Y. 1978, U.S. Supreme Ct. 1989, U.S. Ct. Claims 1990. Asst. corp. counsel City of Syracuse Dept. Law, 1978-82; assoc. Birnbaum, Manaker & Aquillo, Syracuse, 1982-83; ptnr. Cherundolo, Bottar & McGowan, P.C., Syracuse, 1983—; lectr. SUNY, Buffalo, 1977, 78. Trustee North Syracuse Cen. Sch. Dist. Bd. Edn. (pres. 1989-96), 1988-96; bd. dirs. Onondaga Madison Sch. Bd. Assn., 1994-96; regent SUNY, 1996—. Mem. ABA, Assn. Trial Lawyers Am., N.Y. State Bar Assn., N.Y. State Trial Lawyers Assn., Onondaga County Bar Assn. General civil litigation, Personal injury, Product liability. Home: 4997 Chesapeake Dr Syracuse NY 13212-4409

**BOTTARO, TIMOTHY SHANAHAN,** lawyer, partner; b. Buffalo, Sept. 20, 1958; s. Samuel Domenick and Luetta May Bottaro; m. Kathleen Ann Ballard, Aug. 3, 1960; children: Patrick, Anne. BA, Creighton U., 1981; JD, U. Iowa, 1983. Bar: Iowa 1983, U.S. Dist. Ct. (no. dist.) Iowa 1983, U.S. Ct. Appeals (8th cir.) 1984. Ptnr. Rawlings & Nieland, et al, Sioux City, Iowa, 1983-95, Vriezelaar, Tigges, Edgington, Rossi, Bottaro & Bowen, Sioux City, Iowa, 1995—; chair Woodbury County Jud. Magistrate Nomination Commn., Sioux City, 1992-94. Chair Woodbury County Dem. Party, Sioux City, 1994-98; lay dir., Cathedral of the Epiphany, Sioux City, 1987—; pres., bd. trustees, Sioux City Pub. Libr., 1992-98. Recipient Libr. Pearl award Sioux City Pub. Libr., 1989. Mem. Am. Trial Lawyers Assn., Iowa Trial Lawyers Assn. Democrat. Roman Catholic. Avocations: bicycling, politics. Personal injury, Insurance, General civil litigation. Office: Vriezelaar Tigges et al 421 Nebraska St Sioux City IA 51101-1311

**BOTTITTA, JOSEPH ANTHONY,** lawyer; b. Mar. 9, 1949; s. Anthony S. and Elizabeth (Bellisano) B.; m. Lynda Joan Kloss, Apr. 14, 1979; children: Michelle Emma, Gregory Joseph.; BSBA, Seton Hall U., 1971, JD, 1974. Bar: N.H. 1974, U.S. Dist. Ct. N.J. 1974, U.S. Supreme Ct. 1981. Ptnr. Rusignola & Pugliese, Newark, 1974-78; sr. ptnr. Joseph A. Bottitta, West Orange, N.J., 1979-88, Gilbert, Gilbert, Schlossberg and Bottitta, 1988-89; pvt. practice, 1989-95; with Bottitta and Bascelli, 1995—; chmn. Supreme Ct. Fee Arbitration Com. Dist. V-B., 1984-85; mem. N.J. Uniform Law Commn., 1987-91; mem. N.J. Commn. on Professionalism in Law, 1997—. Fellow Am. Bar Found.; mem. ABA, ATLA, N.J. State Bar Assn. (trustee 1988, sec. 1988-94, treas. 1994-95, v.p. 1995-97, pres.-elect 1997-98, pres. 1998-99), Essex County Bar Assn. (sec. 1983-84, treas. 1984-85, pres.-elect 1985-86, pres. 1986-87). Republican. Roman Catholic. Insurance, Personal injury, Real property. Office: 80 Main St West Orange NJ 07052-5460

**BOUCHER, JOSEPH W(ILLIAM),** lawyer, accountant, educator, writer; b. Menominee, Mich., Oct. 28, 1951; s. Joseph W. and Patricia (Coon) B.; m. Susan M. De Groot, June 4, 1977; children: Elizabeth, Bridget, Joseph William III. BA, St. Norbert Coll., 1973; JD, U. Wis., 1977, MBA in Fin., 1978. Bar: Wis. 1978, U.S. Dist. Ct. (we. dist.) Wis. 1978; CPA, Wis. Adminstrv. aide to Senator Wis. Senate, Madison, 1977; from assoc. to ptnr. Murphy, Stolper et al., Madison, 1977-84; ptnr. Stolper, Koritzinsky, Brewster & Neider, Madison, 1985-94; mng. ptnr. Stolper, Koritzinsky, Brewster, Neider, Madison, 1989-92, Neider & Boucher, S.C., 1995—; lectr. bus. U. Wis., Madison, 1980—; bd. dirs. St. Coletta's E.H.S., 1997—. Co-author: Organizing a Wisconsin Business Corporation, 1995, 99, Wisconsin LLCs and LLPs Handbook, 1996, 1999; contbr. articles to Wis. Bar Assn. Bd. dirs. Jackson Found., 1994-99, West Met. Bus. Assn., 1990-95, Dane County United Way, 1986-89, pres. 1994; bd. dirs. Wis. Chamber Orch., 1990-94, pres., 1993-94; mem. bd. advisors St. Mary's Med. Ctr., Madison, 1989-91; bd. dirs. St. Coletta's, 1997—, Edgewood H.S., 1997—. Named one of Outstanding Young Men of Am., 1979; named Wis. Lawyer Advocate of Yr., SBA, 1983. Mem. ABA, AICPA (mem. bd. examiners, mem. bus. law subcom. 1987-90), Wis. Bar Assn., Wis. State Bar Assn. (mem. corp. com. 1991—, co-chairperson interprofl. com. 1992-95, chair ltd. liability co. subcom.), Dane County Bar Assn., Wis. Inst. CPAs, U. Wis. Bus. Alumni Assn. (bd. dirs. 1980-87). Roman Catholic. Avocations: sports, reading. Contracts commercial, General corporate, Corporate taxation. Office: Neider & Boucher SC 440 Science Dr Madison WI 53711-1064

**BOUDART, MARY CECILE,** lawyer; b. Chester, Pa., Sept. 2, 1951; d. Joseph Albert and Nancy (Dolan) B.; m. Donald W. Callendes Jr., Oct. 16, 1982; children: Samuel D., Joseph B. BA, U. Del., 1973; JD, Temple U., 1976. Bar: Del. 1976, U.S. Dist. Ct. Del. 1976. Asst. city solicitor City of Wilmington, 1976-79; pvt. practice Wilmington, 1979-82; ptnr. Boudart & Houghton, Wilmington, 1982-84, Doroshow & Pasquale, Wilmington, 1984—. Mem. coun. New Castle County Coun., Wilmington, 1983-87; chair Adult Entertainment Commn., State of Del., 1996—. Democrat. Roman Catholic. Avocations: tennis, skiing. Family and matrimonial, General practice. Office: 1202 Kirkwood Hwy Wilmington DE 19805-2120

**BOUDIN, MICHAEL,** federal judge; b. N.Y.C., Nov. 29, 1939; s. Leonard B. and Jean (Roisman) B.; m. Martha A. Field, Sept. 14, 1984. B.A., Harvard Coll., 1961, LL.B., 1964. Bar: N.Y. 1964, D.C. 1967. Law clk. U.S. Ct. Appeals, 2d cir., 1964-65, U.S. Sup. Ct., 1965-66; assoc. firm Covington & Burling, Washington, 1966-72, ptnr., 1972-87; dep. asst. atty. gen. Anti-trust div. Dept. Justice, Washington, 1987-90; judge U.S. Dist. Ct. of D.C., Washington, 1990-92, U.S. Ct. Appeals, Boston, 1992-98; vis. prof. Harvard Law Sch., 1982-83, lectr., 1983-98; lectr. U. Pa. Law Sch., 1984-85. Contbr. revs. to law jours. Mem. ABA, Am. Law Inst. Office: US Ct Appeals 1st Cir 1 Courthouse Way Ste 7710 Boston MA 02210-3009

**BOUDREAUX, GERALD JOSEPH,** lawyer; b. Melrose, Mass., Sept. 28, 1953; s. Roy J. and Dorothy Emma (Steves) B.; m. Ilene Beth Lefkowitz; 1 child, Lauren Rachel. BA in Chemistry, U. Mass., 1977; PhD in Organic Chemistry, Brandeis U., 1982; JD, Widener U., 1992. Bar: Pa. 1993, N.J. 1993, U.S. Dist. Ct. N.J. 1993. Postdoctoral fellow Harvard U., Cambridge, Mass., 1983-86; sr. rsch.scientist E.I. DuPont de Nemours, Wilmington, Del., 1986-89, patent agt., 1989-92; counsel The DuPont Merck Pharm. Co., Wilmington, 1992-93, sr. counsel, 1993-94, asst. gen. counsel, 1995—. Mem. ABA, Am. Chem. Soc., Am. Intellectual Property Lawyers Assn., Phila. Intellectual Property Law Assn. Avocations: biking, reading, travel. Intellectual property, Patent, Contracts commercial. Home: 1717 Gunning Dr Wilmington DE 19803-3933

**BOUGEN, HARRIET SANDRA,** lawyer; b. N.Y.C., Oct. 12, 1939; d. Max David and Pauline (Steinman) Bougen; children: Gideon Orion, Naomi Grace. BA, Bennington Coll., 1960; M in Physics, Columbia U., 1963; MSW, Adelphi U., 1968; JD, Albany Law Sch. of Union U., 1981. Bar: N.Y. 1982, U.S. Dist. Ct. (no. dist.) N.Y. 1983. Ptnr. Oliver and Oliver, Albany, N.Y., 1982-94; sr. atty. N.Y. State Dept. Health, Albany, 1994—. Mem. Nat. Health Lawyers Assn., N.Y. State Bar Assn. Administrative and regulatory, Environmental, Health. Home: 50 Kelton Ct Albany NY 12209-1231 Office: NYS Dept Health Div Legal Affairs Corning Tower Rm 2482 Albany NY 12237-0001

**BOUGH, BRADLEY A.,** lawyer; b. South Bend, Ind., Mar. 25, 1958; s. Max E. and Rebecca (Shedd) B.; 1 child, Taylor Louise. BS, Ind. State U., 1980; JD, Ind. U., Indpls., 1983. Bar: Ind. 1983, U.S. Dist. Ct. (so. dist.) Ind. 1983. Assoc. McGlone Law Office, Terre Haute, Ind., 1983-87; ptnr. McGlone and Bough, Terre Haute, Ind., 1983-90, Modesitt and Bough, Terre Haute, Ind., 1990-98, Modesitt, Bough and Kelly, 1998—. Bd. dirs. Terre Haute Montessori Sch., Inc., pres. 1994-95; bd. dirs. Vigo County Lifeline, 1993—; adv. bd. paralegal studies St. Mary of the Woods Coll., 1995—. Mem. ABA, ATLA, Ind. Trial Lawyers Assn., Terre Haute Bar Assn. (treas. 1989-93). General civil litigation, Personal injury, Insurance. Office: Modesitt Bough & Kelly 321 Ohio St Terre Haute IN 47807-3549

**BOUKIS, KENNETH,** lawyer; b. Cleve., Aug. 28, 1940; s. John and Georgia Boukis; m. Pascalia Mageros, Sept. 8, 1968; children: John Paul, Peter M., Elayna G., Andrew C. BBA, Fenn Coll., Cleve., 1963; JD, Case Western Res. U., 1966; LLM, Cleve. State U., 1976. BAr: Ohio 1966. Ptnr. Strangward, Marshman, Lloyd & Malaga, Cleve., 1966-69, Schaaf, Chalko & Boukis, Cleve., 1970-71, Hohmann, Boukis & Boukis, Cleve., 1971-98, Hohmann, Boukis & Curtis, Cleve., 1998—. Mem. Nat. Lawyers Assn., Ohio Bar Assn., Cleve. Bar Assn., Am. Hellenic Edn. and Progressive Assn. (pres.). Republican. Greek Orthodox. Avocations: Bible study, church work, fishing, health foods, exercise. General civil litigation, Contracts commercial, General practice. Home: 8230 W Ridge Dr Broadview Heights OH 44147-1033 Office: Hohmann Boukis & Curtis 520 Standard Bldg 1370 Ontario St Cleveland OH 44113-1701

**BOULGER, WILLIAM CHARLES,** lawyer; b. Columbus, Ohio, Apr. 2, 1924; s. James Ignatius and Rebecca (Laughlin) B.; m. Ruth J. Schachtele, Dec. 29, 1954; children—Brigid Carolyn, Ruth Mary. A.B., Harvard Coll., 1948; LL.B., Law Sch. Cin., 1951. Bar: Ohio, 1951, U.S. Dist. Ct. (so. dist.) Ohio 1952, U.S. Supreme Ct. 1957. Ptnr. with Thomas A. Boulger, Chillicothe, Ohio, 1951-73; ptnr. Boulger and Boulger, Chillicothe, 1974—. Pres. Ross County Welfare Assn., Chillicothe, 1954-60; mem. Chillicothe. ARC, 1958-84, chmn., 1959-63, 1985—; mem. Democratic Exec. Com., Chillicothe, 1950s. Served as pfc. U.S. Army, 1943-45, ETO. Mem. Ross County Bar Assn. (pres. 1971), Ohio Bar Assn., ABA. Roman Catholic. Clubs: Sunset, Symposiarchs (pres.). Avocations: tennis, golf. Personal injury, Probate, General practice. Home: 31 Club Dr Chillicothe OH 45601-1129 Office: PO Box 204 Chillicothe OH 45601-0204

**BOUMA, JOHN JACOB,** lawyer; b. Ft. Dodge, Iowa, Jan. 13, 1937; s. Jacob and Gladys Glennie (Cooper) B.; m. Bonnie Jeanne Lane, Aug. 15, 1959; children: John Jeffrey, Wendy Sue, Laura Lynne, Jennifer Anne. BA, U. Iowa, 1958, JD, 1960. Bar: Iowa 1960, Wis. 1960, Ariz. 1962, U.S. Ct. Appeals (9th cir.) 1971, U.S. Ct. Appeals (D.C. cir.) 1971, U.S. Supreme Ct. 1975, U.S. Ct. Appeals (10th cir.) 1982, U.S. Tax Ct. 1983. Assoc. Foley, Sammond & Lardner, Milw., 1960; assoc. Snell & Wilmer, Phoenix, 1962-66, ptnr., 1967—, chmn. 1983—. Contbr. articles to profl. jours. Chmn. Phoenix Human Rels. Commn., 1973-75; mem. Phoenix Commn. on LEAP, 1971-72, Phoenix Community Alliance, 1991—; bd. dirs. Phoenix Legal Aid Soc., 1970-76, Ariz. Econ. Coun., 1989-93, Mountain States Legal Found., 1977-95; trustee Ariz. Opera Co. (pres. 1989-91), Phoenix Art Mus., 1994—, pres., 1996-98. Capt. JAGC, U.S. Army, 1960-62. Recipient Walter E. Craig Disting. Svc. award, 1998, Community Legal Svcs. Decade of Dedication award, 1998, Disting. Achievement medal Ariz. State U. Coll. of Law, 1998. Fellow Am. Coll. Trial Lawyers; mem. ABA (Ariz. house of dels. 1989-98, bd. govs. 1998—), Maricopa County Bar Assn. (pres. 1977-78), Nat. Conf. Bar Pres. (exec. coun. 1984-91, pres. 1989-90), Ariz. Bar Assn. (pres. 1983-84), Ariz. Bar Found. (pres. 1987-88), Iowa Bar Assn., Wis. Bar Assn., Phoenix Assn. Def. Counsel (pres. 1972), Attys. Liability Assurance Soc., Ltd. (bd. dirs. 1987—), Iowa Law Sch. Found. (bd. dirs. 1986—), Phoenix C. of C. (bd. dirs. 1988-94), Ariz. State Coll. Law Soc. (bd. dirs., pres. 1997—), Western States Bar Conf. (pres. 1988-89), Ariz Supreme Ct. Spl. Com. on Lawyer Discipline and Profl. Conduct, Order of Coif, Phi Beta Kappa, Phi Eta Signa, Omnicron Delta Kappa. Avocations: fishing, hunting, skiing, travel, golf, tennis. Antitrust, General civil litigation, Professional liability. Home: 800 E Circle Rd Phoenix AZ 85020-4144 Office: Snell & Wilmer One Arizona Ctr Phoenix AZ 85004-2202

**BOUMIL, MARCIA MOBILIA,** legal educator, mediator, writer; b. Boston, Apr. 1958; d. Nicholas J. and Eleanor A. (Fuschetti) M.; m. S. James Boumil, Jr., Aug. 10, 1986; children: S. James III, Gregory M. BS cum laude, Tufts U., 1979, MS in Pub. Health, 1982; JD with honors, U. Conn., 1983; LLM, Columbia U., 1984. Bar: Mass. 1983, U.S. Dist. Ct. Mass. 1985, U.S. Ct. Appeals (1st cir.) 1987. Assoc. clin. prof. family medicine and cmty. health Tufts U. Sch. Medicine, Boston, 1986—; assoc. Herrick & Smith, Boston, 1984-85, Parker, Coulter, Daley & White, Boston, 1985-89; guardian ad litem, ind. ct. investigator Commonwealth of Mass., 1995—; sr. mediator Commonwealth Mediation and Conciliation Inc., Brockton, Mass., 1995—; lectr. in psychology, Boston Coll., 1992—, lectr. in law, 1987-89; instr., grad. program in pub. health, Tufts U., 1984-92; vis. asst. prof. law, 1989-90, 90-91; presenter in field, various lectrs. and seminars. Author: (textbook) Law, Ethics and Reproductive Choice, 1994; co-author: (textbook) Medical Liability: Cases and Materials, 1990, (textbook) Medical Liability: Teachers Manual, 1990, (textbook) Women and the Law, 1992, Sexual Harassment, 1992, Date Rape: The Silent Epidemic, 1993, (textbook) Law and Gender Bias, 1994, (textbook) Medical Liability in a Nutshell, 1995, Betrayal of Trust: Sex and Power in Professional Relationships, 1995, Deadbeat Dads: A National Child Support Scandal, 1996; author (ednl. tng. videotape) Sexual Harassment, 1995; contbr. articles to profl. jours. Vol. Andover (Mass.) Sch. Com., 1993—. Avocation: child care. Home and Office: 243 River Rd Andover MA 01810-3217

**BOURCIER, JOHN PAUL,** state supreme court justice; b. Providence, Mar. 27, 1927; s. Louis J. and Lydia E. (Garceau) B.; m. Norma M. DiLuglio, Aug. 20, 1951; children: Carol Bourcier Fargnoli, Norma J. Bourcier Bucci. BA, Brown U., 1950; LLB, Vanderbilt U., 1953. Bar: U.S. Dist. Ct. R.I. 1955, U.S. Ct. Appeals 1956, U.S. Immigration Svc. 1956, U.S. Ct. Mil. Appeals 1958, U.S. Tax Ct. 1960, U.S. Army Bd. Rev. 1965, U.S. Dist. Ct. Fla. 1965, N.H. 1965, Va. 1965. Trial atty. Bourcier & Bordieri, Providence, 1953-74; assoc. justice R.I. Superior Ct., Providence, 1974-95; justice R.I. Supreme Ct., Providence, 1995—; invited judiciary panelist Rev. of Supreme Ct. Cases, 1987-92; lectr. in field; instr. Roger Williams Coll., 1982-95; guest lectr. Brown U., 1979-95, Bryant Coll., 1990-93, R.I. C.C., 1989-90; lectr. R.I. Fire Marshalls Arson Seminars, 1989—, New Eng. Fire Marshalls Arson Seminars, 1990-95; chmn. Superior Ct. Jury Trial Instrn. Rev. Com., mem. Civil Rules Rev. Com., others. Asst. editor Vanderbilt Law Rev., 1951-53. With USN, 1944-46. Named for life Assoc. Justice R.I. Supreme Ct. by Gov. Lincoln Almond, 1995—. Home and Office: RI Supreme Court 250 Benefit St Providence RI 02903-2719

**BOURGAULT, DENNIS PAUL,** lawyer, entrepreneur; b. Salem, Mass., July 2, 1961; s. George A. and Irene M. (Bourassa) B.; m. Michael O. Suddath. BA, U. Redlands, 1984; JD, Boston Coll., 1987; MALD, Tufts U., 1988. Assoc. Zuckert, Scoutt & Rasenberger, Washington, 1989-90, Lord Day & Lord, Barrett Smith, Washington, 1990-94; pres. Doolittle's Ltd., Washington, 1994—. Vol. Williams for Mayor Campaign, Washington, 1998. Recipient Top Pet Retailer award Pet Product News, 1996, Retailer of Yr. award CHAMPS, 1996. Mem. Greater Washington Dalmation Club (treas. 1989—), Capitol Hill Assn. of Merchants and Profls. (v.p. 1989—). Democrat. Roman Catholic. Fax: 202-544-9712. E-mail: info@doolittles.com. Office: Doolittle's Ltd 224 7th St SE Washington DC 20003-4306

**BOURGOIN, DAVID L.,** lawyer, real estate broker, trade broker, educator, video/television producer; b. Jersey City, Mar. 5, 1946; s. Louis Joseph and Irene Mary Bourgoin. BS, St. Peter's Coll., Jersey City, 1968; MBA, UCLA, 1970; JD, U. San Diego, 1987. Bar: Hawaii 1988, Pa. 1989, U.S. Ct. Appeals (fed. cir.) Hawaii 1988, U.S. Internat. Ct. Appeals, U.S. Ct. Appeals. Tax cons. Calif. and N.J., 1967-69; fin. mgr. Mattel Toys, Hawthorne, Calif., 1969-71; music prodr. Topanga Canyon Records, Redondo Beach, Calif., 1971-76; stock broker Dean Witter, LA, 1976-78; instr. U. Hawaii, Honolulu, 1978-80; trade broker Hawaii chi Trading Co., Honolulu, 1978—; pvt. practice Honolulu, 1988—; real estate broker Realty Offices of D.L.B., Honolulu, 1991—; prof. U. Md., Heidelburg, Germany, 1983-95. Capt. USAR, 1973-85. Mem. Hawaii State Bar, Japanese C. of C., Navy League, K.C. Avocations: culture, music, sports. Private international, General corporate, Real property. Office: 1188 Bishop St Ste 2010 Honolulu HI 96813-3308

**BOUSTANY, ALFRED FREM,** lawyer; b. Lafayette, La., Aug. 4, 1953; s. Antoine Frem and Anne (Morad) B.; m. Patricia Ann Guidry, Apr. 26, 1984; children: Alfred III, Ava, Meredith. BA, U. So. La., 1975; JD, La. State U., 1977. Bar: La. 1977, U.S. Dist. Ct. (we. dist.) La. 1979, U.S. Ct. Appeals (5th cir.) 1980, U.S. Supreme Ct. 1984. Atty. Thompson & Sellers, Abbeville, La., 1977-79; pvt. practice Lafayette, La., 1979—; contract atty. Pub. Defender Office, Lafayette, 1983—; lectr. in field. Treas. Lafayette Criminal Bar, 1989; lectr. U. So. La., Lafayette, 1991, Acadiana High Sch., 1992. Named Pub. Defender of the Yr., 15th Jud. Dist., 1990. Mem. La. State Bar Assn., Lafayette Parish Bar Assn., Lafayette Parish Criminal Bar Assn. (treas. 1989-90). Democrat. Avocations: reading, jogging, basketball, gardening, fatherhood. Criminal, Personal injury, General practice. Home: 504 Beverly Dr Lafayette LA 70503-3114 Office: 421 W Vermilion St Lafayette LA 70501-6729

**BOUTIN, PETER RUCKER,** lawyer; b. San Francisco, Oct. 6, 1950; s. Frank J. and Charlotte (Downey) B.; m. Suzanne Jones, Aug. 31, 1974; children: Jennifer, Lisa, Kevin. AB, Stanford U., 1972; JD magna cum laude, Santa Clara U., 1975. Bar: Calif. 1975, U.S. Dist. Ct. (no., ea., so. and ctrl. dists.) Calif. 1976, U.S. Ct. Appeals (9th cir.) 1977, U.S. Supreme Ct. 1982. Assoc. Keesal, Young & Logan, Long Beach, Calif., 1975-78, ptnr., 1978-84; mng. ptnr. San Francisco office Keesal, Young & Logan, San Francisco, 1984—; arbitrator San Francisco Superior Ct., 1989—, Nat. Assn. Securities Dealers, San Francisco, 1980—; mediator San Francisco Superior Ct., 1989—; early neutral evaluation panel U.S. Dist. Ct., 1993—. Co-author Am. Arbitration Assn. Arbitrator Tng. Materials, 1992. Mem. Bar Assn. San Francisco, Assn. Bus. Trial Lawyers, Securities Industry Assn. Compliance and Legal Divsn., San Francisco Bond Club, Stanford Buck/Cardinal Club. Securities, General civil litigation, Labor. Office: Keesal Young & Logan 4 Embarcadero Ctr Ste 1500 San Francisco CA 94111-4122

**BOUTON, WILLIAM WELLS, III,** lawyer; b. Glen Cove, N.Y., Mar. 14, 1953; s. William Wells Jr. and Joan (Murrans) B. BA, Ohio Wesleyan U., 1976; JD, U. Conn., 1980. Bar: Conn. 1980, U.S. Dist. Ct. Conn. 1980. Assoc. Tyler, Cooper & Alcorn and predecessor firms, Hartford, Conn., 1980-87; ptnr. Tyler, Cooper & Alcorn and predecessor firms, Hartford, 1987—. Chmn. Cromwell (Conn.) Rep. Town Com., 1982-86, Town of Cromwell Planning and Zoning Commn., 1984-90. Mem. ABA, Conn. Bar Assn. (vice chmn. banking, corps. and real estate sects.). Episcopalian. Banking, General corporate, Securities. Office: Tyler Cooper & Alcorn City Pl Hartford CT 06103

**BOUVIER, MARSHALL ANDRE,** lawyer; b. Jacksonville, Fla., Sept. 30, 1923; s. Marshall and Helen Marion B.; m. Zepha Windle, July 11, 1938; children: Michael A., Debra Bouvier Williams, Mark A., Marshall André III, Suzanne, John A. (dec.), Wendy Bouvier Clark, Jennifer Lynn. AB, Emory U., LLB, 1949. Bar: Ga. 1948, Nev. 1960. Commd. USN, 1949; naval aviator, judge advocate; ret., 1959; atty. State of Nevada, 1959-60; pvt. practice, Reno, 1960-82, 88—; dist. atty. County of Storey, Nev., 1982-88, spl. cons. to Nev. Dist. Atty., 1991-95; pres., CEO A.G.E. Corp., 1997—. Mem. Judge Advocates Assn., Am. Bd. Hypnotherapy, Ancient and Honorable Order Quiet Birdmen, Rotary, E Clampus Vitus, Phi Delta Phi, Sigma Chi. State civil litigation, General corporate, Personal injury.

**BOVA, VINCENT ARTHUR, JR.,** lawyer, consultant, photographer; b. Pitts., Apr. 25, 1946; s. Vincent A. and Janie (Pope) B.; m. Breda Murphy, Mar. 20, 1971; 1 child, Kate Murphy Bova. BA in Bus. Adminstrn., Alma (Mich.) Coll., 1968; MPA, Ohio State U., 1972; JD, Oklahoma City U., 1975. Bar: Okla. 1975, N.Mex. 1976, U.S. Dist. Ct. 1976, U.S. Tax Ct., 1976, U.S. Ct. Appeals (10th cir.) 1976, U.S. Supreme Ct. 1979. Mktg. and systems rep., computer systems div. RCA, 1968-70; research analyst Research Atlanta, 1972-73; assoc. Threet, Threet, Glass, King & Maxwell, 1976-78; ptnr. Lill & Bova, P.A., 1978-81; sole practice Albuquerque, 1981—; past pres. Bare Bulls Investment, 1982, Fumilan Investment, 1983, Toastmasters; rsch. analyst urban affairs Ohio Dept. Urban Affairs, Columbus, 1971; panel mem. N.Mex. Med. Rev. Commn., 1981—, N.Mex. Legal/Dental/Osteopathic Podiatry Com., 1981—. Contbr. articles on organizational behavior and mgmt. to profl. jours. Bd. dirs. Rio Grande Nature Ctr.; pres., v.p. spl. projects S.W. Arts and Crafts Festival, Albuquerque, 1986-89; pol. cons. Nov. Group; mem. N.Mex. Estate Planning Coun., 1978—; sec.-treas., vice-chmn. adv. bd. Salvation Army, 1987—; contbr. Ctr. for Home for Prevention of Domestic Violence, 1984-85, Ronald McDonald House, 1984; past chmn. N.Mex. Workers' Compensation Monthly; mem. advt. com. Supreme Ct. Panel; pres. Salvation Army Adv. Bd., Albuquerque; mem. Edn. Forum. With Air N.G., 1969-75. Recipient Pacesetters award Ohio State U., 1972; named one of Outstanding Young Men of Am., 1975, 76. Mem. ATLA (advanced grad. Nat. Coll. Advocacy), Ct. Practice Inst. (advanced diplomate), ABA, N.Mex. Bar Assn. (pres. small firm and solo sect.), State Bar N.Mex. (mem. med. legal panel, med.-dental podiatry legal panel, rep. probate, wills and trusts ann. report), Nat. Def. Lawyers, Assn. (staff chmn. 1986), N.Mex. Trial Lawyers Assn., Internat. Assn. Fin. Planners, Nat. Assn. Social Security Claimants Reps. (past state chmn.), Business Round Table, Albuquerque Bar Assn., N.Mex. Fin. Planning Assn., Sole Practitioners Assn., Internat. Credit Assn. (lectr.), Ohio State U. Alumni Assn. of N.Mex. (pres.), Image Profls. of the S.W. (bd. dirs.), Image Profls. S.W. (photography award), Profl. Photography Assn., Photog. Soc. Am. (pres. chpt.), Toastmasters (past pres., v.p., edn. chmn., Able Toastmaster award), Millionaires Tip Club, Enchanted Lens Camera Club (pres.), Profl. Photographers Am. (merit awards), Albuquerque Knife and Fork (pres., v.p., sec.-treas., bd. dirs.), Phi Alpha Delta, Sigma Tau Gamma. Democrat. Presbyterian. Avocations: flower gardening, photography - video and still, computers, investing, reading. General civil litigation, Probate, Consumer commercial. Office: 5716 Osuna Rd NE Albuquerque NM 87109-2527

**BOVAIRD, BRENDAN PETER,** lawyer; b. N.Y.C., Mar. 9, 1948; s. John Francis and Margaret Mary (Endrizzi) B.; m. Carolyn Warren Boyle, Dec. 18, 1971; children: Anne Warren, Sarah Grant. BA, Fordham U., 1970; JD, U. Va., 1973. Bar: N.Y. 1974, D.C. 1980, Pa. 1983, U.S. Dist. Ct. (so. and ea. dists.) N.Y. 1974, U.S. Ct. Appeals (2d cir.) 1974. Atty., Dewey, Ballantine, Bushby, Palmer & Wood, N.Y.C., 1973-82; asst. gen. counsel Campbell Soup Co., Camden, N.J., 1982-90; sr. v.p., gen. counsel, sec. Orion Pictures Corp., N.Y.C., 1990-91; counsel, mem. exec. com. Wyeth-Ayerst Internat. Inc., St. Davids, Pa., 1992-95; pres. KDH Inc., 1994—; v.p., gen. counsel UGI Corp., Valley Forge, Pa., 1995—; v.p., gen. counsel AmeriGas Propane, Inc., Valley Forge, 1995—; bd. dirs. Motion Picture Export Assn. Am., Inc., 1990-91, United Valley Ins. Co. Member. MPAA (legal com. 1990-91), ABA (corp., bus. law sect., internat. law sect.), Aircraft Owners and Pilots Assn., Phila. Country Club, Phi Delta Phi. Private international, General corporate, Mergers and acquisitions. Office: UGI Corp PO Box 858 Valley Forge PA 19482-0858

**BOVARNICK, PAUL SIMON,** lawyer; b. N.Y.C., Sept. 15, 1952; s. Murray Elliott and Esther (Waters) B.; m. Nan Garner Waller, Aug. 31, 1980; children: Polly Ames, Kate Garner, Samuel Patton. BA, Claremont Men's Coll., 1974; JD, U. Oreg., 1979. Bar: Oreg. 1979, Mont. 1980, U.S. Dist. Ct. Mont. 1980, U.S. Ct. Appeals (9th cir.) 1981, U.S. Dist. Ct. Oreg. 1983, U.S. Dist. Ct. Colo. 1997. Staff atty. Mont. Legal Services, Billings, 1979-80, mng. atty., 1980-82; mng. atty. Oreg. Legal Services, Hillsboro, 1982-83; assoc. Bricker, Zakovics, Portland, Oreg., 1983-85; sole practice Portland, 1992—; ptnr. Rose, Senders & Bovarnick, Portland, 1993—; designated legal counsel Brotherhood of Locomotive Engrs. Chmn., bd. dirs. Forest Park Children's Ctr., Portland, 1986-88, mem., 1985-89; treas. Yellowstone Valley Dem. Club, Billings, 1982; bd. dirs. Oregonians for Individual Rights, Portland, 1984, ACLU, Billings, 1981-82, Rita's Place, 1991-94, Bridlewide Found. Mem. ABA, Oreg. Bar Assn., Mont. Bar Assn., Multnomah County Bar Assn., Assn. Trial Lawyers Am., Oreg. Trial

Lawyers Assn., Acad. Rail Labor Attys. Avocations: fly fishing, skiing, softball. Personal injury, Workers' compensation, Immigration, naturalization, and customs. Home: 2323 SW 64th Ave Portland OR 97221-1338 Office: 1001 SW 5th Ave Ste 1300 Portland OR 97204-1129

**BOVE, EMIL J., JR.,** lawyer; b. Syracuse, N.Y., Aug. 2, 1948; s. Emil J. and Jessie C. Bove; children: Emil J. III, Vincent; m. Lorrilyn Janis Bove, Sept. 26, 1992. BA, Colgate U., 1970; JD, New Eng. Sch. Law, 1973. Bar: N.Y., U.S. Dist. Ct. (no. and we. dists.) N.Y., U.S. Ct. Appeals (2d cir.). Assoc. Zecher and Capacci, Sodus, N.Y., 1974-77, Robert E. Horton, Seneca Falls, N.Y., 1977-79; pvt. practice, Seneca Falls, 1979-95; asst. atty. gen. Office Atty. Gen., Rochester, N.Y., 1995—; spl. svcs. atty., Seneca Falls, 1981-95; acting village justice Village of Seneca Falls, 1994. Trustee Seneca Falls Hist. Soc.; organizer, bd. dirs. Elizabeth Cady Stanton Found.; sec. Seneca County United Way, Seneca County Indsl. Devel. Agy., 1987-95; chmn. Seneca County ARC. Mem. N.Y. State Bar Assn. (del.), Seneca County Bar Assn. (past pres.), Seneca County C. of C. (chmn. 1982), Societie de Mutuo Sucorso, Sons of Am. Legion, Kiwanis. Roman Catholic. Home: 46 State St Seneca Falls NY 13148-1404

**BOVE, MARK STEPHEN,** lawyer, expert witness, consultant; b. N.Y.C., Jan. 15, 1953; s. Dante A. and Julia C. Bove; divorced; children: Ryan N., Aaron J. BA with honors, U. Colo., 1975; JD, U. Denver, 1978. BAr: Colo. 1979, U.S. Dist. Ct. Colo. 1979, U.S. Ct. Appeals (10th cir.) 1980. Civil rights atty. U.S. Dept. HEW, Denver, 1979-80, U.S. Dept. Edn., Denver, 1980-81; ptnr. Bove & Kelley, Denver, 1981-83; sole practitioner Denver, 1983-95; investigative counsel Colo. Supreme Ct., Denver, 1981-98; ptnr. Lafond & Bove, L.L.C., Denver, 1996—; instr. Denver Paralegal Inst., 1983-88; mentor, spkr. in field. Coach, referee Cherry Creek Soccer Assn., Englewood, Colo., 1993-98. Nat. Merit scholar, 1971. Mem. Colo. Trial Lawyers Assn., Plaintiff Employment Law Assn., Faculty of Fed. Advocates. Democrat. Labor, Civil rights, Professional liability. Home: 6504 S Heritage Pl E Englewood CO 80111-4655 Office: Lafond & Bove LLC 1756 Gilpin St Denver CO 80218-1206

**BOWDEN, GEORGE NEWTON,** judge; b. East Orange, N.J., Nov. 21, 1946; s. W. Paul and Catherine A. (Porter) B. BA, Bowdoin Coll., 1971; JD, U. Maine, 1974. Bar: Wash. 1974, Maine 1975, U.S. Dist. Ct. (we. dist.) Wash. 1978, U.S. Ct. Appeals (9th cir.) 1980, U.S. Supreme Ct. 1982. Asst. county atty. Lincoln County, Wiscasset, Maine, 1974; dep. pros. atty. Grays Harbor County, Montesano, Wash., 1974-76, King County, Seattle, 1976, Snohomish County, Everett, Wash., 1976-79; ptnr. Senter & Bowden, Everett, Wash., 1979-97; judge Snohomish County Superior Ct., Everett, Wash., 1997—. Bd. dirs. Everett Symphony Orch. 1993—, pres. 1996-98; v.p. Driftwood Players, Edmonds, Wash., 1978. Sgt. USMC, 1966-68. Mem. ATLA, NADCL, Wash. State Bar Assn. (CLE com., fee arbitration bd., legal aid and pro bono com.), Wash. Assn. Criminal Def. Lawyers (bd. govs., sec. 1993), Wash. State Trial Lawyers Assn., Snohomish County Bar Assn. (pres. 1995), Rotary. Avocations: scuba diving, skiing, bicycling. Office: Snohomish County Courthouse Superior Ct 3000 Rockefeller Ave M/ S502 Everett WA 98201-4046

**BOWDEN, HENRY LUMPKIN, JR.,** lawyer; b. Atlanta, Aug. 2, 1949; s. Henry Lumpkin and Ellen Marian (Fleming) B.; m. Roberta Jeanne Johnson, June 30, 1973; children: Caroline Bruton, Henry Lumpkin III. BA, U. Va., 1971; JD, Emory U., 1974. Bar: Ga. 1974. Law clk. for Hon. Griffin B. Bell U.S. Ct. Appeals (5th cir.), Atlanta, 1974-75; ptnr. King & Spalding, Atlanta, 1975-95; prin. Bowden Law Firm, P.C., Atlanta, 1995—. Trustee Atlanta Ballet, Inc., 1976-85, chmn., 1983-84; trustee Emory U., Atlanta, 1986—; trustee Hist. Oakland Found., Inc., Atlanta, 1987-95, chmn. 1992-95; trustee Westminster Schs., Atlanta, 1995—. Fellow Am. Coll. Trust and Estate Counsel (state chair 1991-96), Am. Bar Found.; mem. ABA, State Bar Ga. (chair fiduciary sect. 1990-91), Atlanta Bar Assn., Lawyers Club Atlanta, Piedmont Driving Club (dir. 1996—), Capital City Club, Nine O'Clocks (pres. 1977-78), Farmington Country Club, Gridiron Secret Soc., Homosassa Fishing Club, The Ten, Phi Beta Kappa, Omicron Delta Kappa, Phi Delta Theta. Methodist. Home: 2542 Habersham Rd NW Atlanta GA 30305-3566 Office: 191 Peachtree St NE Ste 849 Atlanta GA 30303-1741

**BOWE, RICHARD WELBOURN,** lawyer; b. Balt., Nov. 4, 1949; s. Richard Eugene and Virginia Welbourn (Cooley) B.; children: Richard Desmond Welbourn, Hollis Baldwin. AB in Politics, Princeton U., 1971; JD, Am. U., 1976. Bar: Md. 1976, D.C. 1977, U.S. Dist. Ct. D.C. 1977, U.S. Ct. Appeals (D.C. cir.) 1977. Assoc. Howrey & Simon, Washington, 1976-78, Cladouhos & Brashares, Washington, 1978-84; group counsel Md. Cup Corp., Balt., 1984-87; ptnr. Miles & Stockbridge, Washington and Balt., 1987-93; pvt. practice law Washington, 1993—; advisor Dingman Ctr. Entrepreneurship, U. Md., College Park, 1992—; mem. small bus. devel. com. George Mason U., Fairfax, Va., 1992—. Contbr. articles to profl. jours. Active St. Albans Sch. Parent's Assn., 1992—. Mem. ABA, Md. State Bar Assn., D.C. Bar Assn. Episcopal. Avocations: sailing, golf, reading. General corporate, Antitrust, Mergers and acquisitions. Office: 5100 Wisconsin Ave NW Ste 401 Washington DC 20016-4119

**BOWEN, DUDLEY HOLLINGSWORTH, JR.,** federal judge; b. Augusta, Ga., June 25, 1941. AB in Fgn. Lang., U. Ga., 1964, LLB, 1965; profesor invitado (hon.), Universidad Externada de Bogotá, 1987. Bar: Ga. 1965. Pvt. practice law Augusta, 1968-72; bankruptcy judge U.S. Dist. Ct. (so. dist.) Ga., Augusta, 1972-75, judge, 1979-97; chief judge U.S. Dist. Ct. (so. dist.) Ga., 1997—, Augusta, 1997—; ptnr. firm Dye, Miller, Bowen & Tucker, Augusta, 1975-79; bd. dirs. Southeastern Bankruptcy Law Inst., 1976-87; mem. Ct. Security Com. Jud. Conf. U.S., 1987-92. Mem. bd. visitors U. Ga. Sch. Law, 1987-90. Served to 1st lt. inf., U.S. Army, 1966-68. Decorated Commendation medal. Mem. State Bar Ga. (chmn. bankruptcy law sect. 1977), Fed. Judges Assn. (bd. dirs. 1985-90), 11th Cir. Dist. Judges Assn. (sec.-treas. 1988-89, pres. 1991-92, chief judge so. dist. Ga. 1997—). Presbyterian. Office: US Dist Ct PO Box 2106 Augusta GA 30903-2106

**BOWEN, JOHN WESLEY EDWARD, IV,** lawyer; b. Columbus, Ohio, July 11, 1954; s. John Wesley Edward III and Jeanne (Lehar) B. *Great grandfather John W.E. Bowen Sr., an African slave who was purchased out of slavery by his father, Edward Bowen, an ex-African slave, and was educated at Dillard University in New Orleans, Louisiana. He received the degree of Doctor of Philosophy from Boston University in 1887. Dr. Bowen was the first black President of Gammon Theological Seminary in Atlanta, Georgia.* BBA, So. Meth. U., 1976; JD, Columbia U., 1979. Bar: N.Y. 1980, U.S. Ct. Claims 1982, U.S. Supreme Ct. 1983, U.S. Dist. Ct. (so. and ea. dists.) N.Y. 1985, U.S. Ct. Appeals (fed. cir.) 1986. Trial atty. antitrust div. U.S. Dept. Justice, Washington, 1979-85; of counsel Howard & Rhone, N.Y.C., 1985-87; ptnr. Bowen & Bowen, 1989—; dir. N.Y. Bd. of Trade, 1987-89. Contbr. articles to profl. jours. Chmn. Manhattan Jr. Assn. Commerce and Industry, N.Y.C., 1985-87, pres., 1986-87; mem. housing com. N.Y.C. Cmty. Bd. #10. Named one of Outstanding Young Men in Am., U.S. Jaycees, 1981-87. Mem. ABA, Fed. Bar Assn., Nat. Bar Assn., N.Y. County Lawyers Assn., Internat. Platform Assn., Blue Key, Alpha Phi Alpha, French Inst./Alliance Francaise, Columbia U. Club. Methodist. Fax: (614) 418-1873. E-mail: bowenlaw@earthlink.net. Mergers and acquisitions, Municipal (including bonds), Securities. Office: 2720 Airport Dr Columbus OH 43219-2268

**BOWEN, STEPHEN STEWART,** lawyer; b. Peoria, Ill., Aug. 23, 1946; s. Gerald Raymond and Frances Arlene (Stewart) B.; m. Ellen Claire Newcomer, Sept. 23, 1972; children: David, Claire. BA cum laude, Wabash Coll., 1968; JD cum laude, U. Chgo., 1972. Bar: Ill. 1972, U.S. Dist. Ct. (no. dist.) Ill. 1972, U.S. Tax Ct. 1977. Assoc. Kirkland & Ellis, Chgo., 1972-78, ptnr., 1978-84; ptnr. Latham & Watkins, Chgo., 1985—; adj. prof. DePaul U. Masters in Taxation Program, Chgo., 1976-80; lectr. Practicing Law Inst., N.Y.C., Chgo., L.A., 1978-84, N.Y.C., 1986—. Mem. vis. com. U. Chgo. Div. Sch., 1984—, mem. vis. com. Sch. Law, 1991-93; mem. planning com. U. Chgo. Tax Conf., 1985—, chair, 1995-98; trustee Wabash Coll., 1996—. Fellow Am. Coll. Tax Counsel; mem. ABA, Ill. State Bar Assn., Order of Coif, Mich. Shores Club (Wilmette, Ill.), Met. Club (Chgo.), Econ. Club Chgo., Phi Beta Kappa. Corporate taxation. Office: Latham & Watkins Sears Tower Ste 5800 Chicago IL 60606-6306

**BOWER, ALLAN MAXWELL,** lawyer; b. Oak Park, Ill., May 21, 1936; s. David Robert and Frances Emily Bower; m. Deborah Ann Rottmayer, Dec. 28, 1959. BS, U. Iowa, 1962; JD, U. Miami, Fla., 1968. Bar: Calif. 1969, U.S. Supreme Ct. 1979. Internat. aviation law practice L.A., 1969—; ptnr. Kern & Wooley, L.A., 1980-85, Bronson, Bronson & McKinnon, L.A., 1985-90, Lane Powell Spears Lubersky, L.A., 1990-99, Bailey & Marzano, Santa Monica, Calif., 1999—. Contbr. articles to profl. publs. Mem. ABA, L.A. Bar Assn., Lawyer-Pilots Bar Assn., Am. Judicature Soc., Am. Arbitration Assn. (nat. panel arbitrators), Alpha Tau Omega. Republican. Presbyterian. Fax: 310-392-8091. Aviation, Product liability, General civil litigation. Office: Bailey & Marzano 2nd Fl 2828 Donald Douglas Loop N Santa Monica CA 90405-2959

**BOWERS, JAMES WINFIELD,** law educator, legal consultant; b. Billings, Mont., Jan. 9, 1942; s. Charles Winfield and Roberta (Richardson) B.; m. Lucy B. Schow, July 25, 1981; children: Jacob W., Lisa V., Joseph R., Charles Benjamin. BA, Yale U., 1964, LLB, 1967. Bar: Minn. 1967, U.S. Ct. Appeals (8th cir.) 1967. Shareholder, assoc. Briggs & Morgan, St. Paul, 1969-77; lectr. William Mitchell Law Sch., St. Paul, 1974-78; assoc. prof. Tex. Tech. U. Law Sch., Lubbock, 1978-81; from vis. assoc. prof. to prof. La. State U. Law Ctr., Baton Rouge, 1981-98, Byron R. Kentrow prof. law, 1998—; bd. dirs. United Agts. Holdings, Inc., Baton Rouge. Contbr. Encyclopedia of Law and Economics, 1998. Den leader Boy Scouts Am., 1992-96. Capt., USAR, 1967-69, Vietnam. Mem. ABA, Am. Law and Econs. Assn., Yale Alumni Assn. N.W. (bd. dirs. 1972-75, pres. 1975). Avocations: camping, fishing. Home: 5712 Nottaway Dr Baton Rouge LA 70820-5415 Office: La State U Law Center Baton Rouge LA 70803-1000

**BOWERS, MICHAEL JOSEPH,** former state attorney general; b. Jackson County, Ga., Oct. 7, 1941; s. Carl Ernest and Janie Ruth (Bolton) B.; m. Bette Rose Corley, June 8, 1963; children: Carl Wayne, Bruce Edward, Michelle Lisa. BS, U.S. Mil. Acad., 1963; MS, Stanford U., 1965; MBA, U. Utah-Wiesbaden, Germany, 1970; JD, U. Ga., 1974. Bar: Ga. 1974. Sr. asst. atty. gen. State of Ga., Atlanta, 1975-81, atty. gen., 1981-97, candidate for gov., 1998—. Capt. USAF, 1963-70. Mem. Lawyers Club, Kiwanis. Republican. Methodist. Home: 817 Allgood Rd Stone Mountain GA 30083-4803

**BOWERS, WILLIAM CHARLES,** lawyer; b. Washington, Sept. 15, 1946; s. Kenneth Victor and Johnlou (Sweet) B.; children by previous marriage: William Che, Lynn Ann; m. JoAnne Kennedy, July 30, 1988; 1 child, Liam Flynn. AB, Princeton U., 1968; JD, Emory U., 1975. Bar: Ga. 1975, N.Y. 1988. Law clk. to Hon. Griffin Bell, U.S. Ct. Appeals for 5th Circuit, Atlanta, 1975-76; assoc. Sutherland Asbill & Brennan, Atlanta, 1976-82, ptnr., 1982-83; ptnr. Trotter, Smith & Jacobs, Atlanta, 1983-85; counsel Paul, Hastings, Janofsky & Walker, Atlanta, 1985-88; ptnr. Paul, Hastings, Janifsky & Walker, N.Y.C., 1988-90; gen. counsel GPA Capital, Shannon, Ireland, 1990-93; assoc. gen. counsel GE Capital Aviation Svcs., Stamford, Conn., 1993-95; ptnr. Winthrop, Stimson, Putnam & Roberts, N.Y.C., 1995—; bd. dirs. FSC-Disc Tax Assn., N.Y.C., 1997—. Lt. USN, 1968-72. Democrat. Episcopalian. Contracts commercial, Aviation, Corporate taxation. Office: Winthrop Stimson Et Al One Battery Park Pla New York NY 10004

**BOWIE, PETER WENTWORTH,** judge, educator; b. Alexandria, Va., Sept. 27, 1942; s. Beverley Munford and Louise Wentworth (Boynton) B.; m. Sarah Virginia Haught, Mar. 25, 1967; children: Heather, Gavin. BA, Wake Forest Coll., 1964; JD magna cum laude, U. San Diego, 1971. Bar: Calif. 1972, D.C. 1972, U.S. Dist. Ct. D.C. 1972, U.S. Dist. Ct. Md. 1973, U.S. Dist. Ct. (so. dist.) Calif. 1974, U.S. Ct. Appeals (D.C. cir.) 1972, U.S. Ct. Appeals (9th cir.) 1974, U.S. Supreme Ct. 1980. Trial atty. honors program Dept. of Justice, Washington, 1971-74; asst. U.S. Atty. U.S. Atty.'s Office, San Diego, 1974, asst. chief civil div., 1974-82, chief asst. U.S. atty., 1982-88; lawyer rep. U.S. Ct. Appeals (9th cir.) Jud. Conf., 1977-78, 84-87; judge U.S. Bankruptcy Ct., San Diego, 1988—; lectr. at law Calif. Western Sch. Law, 1979-83; exec. com. mem. 9th Cir. Judicial Conf., 1991-94; mem. com. on codes of conduct Jud. Conf. of U.S., 1995—. Bd. dirs. Presidio Little League, San Diego, 1984, coach, 1983-84; mem. alumni adv. bd. Sch. Law U. San Diego, 1998—. Lt. USN, 1964-68, Vietnam. Mem. State Bar Calif. (hearing referee ct. 1982-86, mem. rev. dept. 1986-90), Fed. Bar Assn. (pres. San diego chpt. 1981-82), San Diego County Bar Assn. (chmn. fed. ct. com. 1978-80, 83-85), Assn. Bus. Trial Lawyers (bd. govs.), San Diego Bankruptcy Forum (bd. dirs.), Phi Delta Phi. Republican. Mem. Unitarian Ch. Office: US Bankruptcy Court 325 W F St San Diego CA 92101-6017

**BOWLER, MARIANNE BIANCA,** judge; b. Boston, Feb. 15, 1947; d. Richard A. and Ann C. (Daly) B. BA, Regis Coll., 1967; JD cum laude, Suffolk U., 1976, LLD (hon.), 1994. Bar: Mass. 1978. Rsch. asst. Harvard Med. Sch., Boston, 1967-69; med. editor Mass. Dept. of Pub. Health, Boston, 1969-76; law clk. Mass. Superior Ct., Boston, 1976-77, dep. chief law clk., 1977-78; asst. dist. atty. Middlesex Dist. Atty.'s Office, Cambridge, Mass., 1978; asst. U.S. atty. U.S. Dept. of Justice, Boston, 1978-90, exec. asst. U.S. atty., 1988-89, sr. litigation counsel, 1989-90; magistrate judge U.S. Dist. Ct. Mass., Boston, 1990—; chmn. bd. trustees New England Bapt. Hosp., Boston, 1990-95. Trustee Suffolk U., Boston, 1994—; bd. dirs. The Boston Found., 1995—; dir. South Cove Nursing Facilities Found., Inc., 1995—; co-pres. Boston Coll. Inn of Ct., 1998—. Mem. Jr. League Boston, Suffolk Law Sch. Alumni Assn. (pres. 1979-80), Vincent Club, Isabel O'Neil Found., Save Venice. Democrat. Roman Catholic. Avocations: faux finishing, trompe l'oeil painting. Office: US Dist Ct One Court House Way Ste 8420 Boston MA 02110

**BOWLES, JESSE GROOVER,** lawyer; b. Baconton, Ga., Aug. 24, 1921; s. Jesse Groover Sr. and Bartow (Swann) B.; m. Ruth Florence Bowles, Aug. 31, 1945 (div. 1981); children: Jesse Groover III, Elizabeth Bowles Chastain; m. Jane Parkman, June 26, 1981. JD, U. Ga., 1946. Bar: Ga. 1946, U.S. Dist. Ct. (mid. dist.) Ga. 1946, U.S. Ct. Appeals (5th cir.) 1946, U.S. Supreme Ct. 1960. Justice Ga. Supreme Ct., Atlanta, 1977-81; ptnr. Bowles & Bowles, Cuthbert, Ga., 1981—; pres. Randolph County Fed. Savs. & Loan Assn., 1965-85; mem. State Bd. Bar Examiners, 1972-76. Trustee Andrew Coll., 1997—. Randolph County Hosp. Authority, 1969—. With U.S. Army, 1942-43. Mem. Am. Coll. Trial Lawyers, Pataula Cir. Bar Assn. (pres.), Ga. Bar Assn. (bd. dirs.). Baptist. Avocations: golf, forestry, farming, construction, banking. General civil litigation, Banking, Construction. Office: Bowles & Bowles 201 Court St Cuthbert GA 31740-1453

**BOWLES, MARGO LA JOY,** lawyer; b. Stillwater, Okla., Jan. 26, 1949; d. Joseph Worth and Vivian Alice (Sears) B.; m. Francis E. Jones Jr., Dec. 22, 1987. BS, Okla. State U., 1971; JD, U. Tulsa, 1983. Bar: Okla. 1985, U.S. Dist. Ct. (no. dist.) Okla. Sole practice Tulsa, 1985—; instr. U. Ctr. Tulsa, Langston U., 1988-90, Northeastern State U., 1992—. Precinct officer Tulsa Dem. Party, 1987. Mem. ABA, Okla. Bar Assn., Tulsa County Bar Assn. (pres. solo practice/small firm sect. 1993-94). Methodist. Avocation: travel. Probate, Estate planning. Office: 6363 E 31st St Tulsa OK 74135-5474

**BOWMAN, CATHERINE MCKENZIE,** lawyer; b. Tampa, Fla., Nov. 10, 1962; d. Herbert Alonzo and Joan Bates (Baggs) McKenzie; m. Donald Campbell Bowman, Jr., May 21, 1988; children: Hunter Hall, Sarah McKenzie. BA in Psychology and Sociology, Vanderbilt U., 1984; JD, U. Ga., 1987. Bar: Ga. 1987, U.S. Dist. Ct. (so. dist.) Ga. 1987. Assoc. Ranitz, Mahoney, Forbes & Coolidge, P.C., Savannah, Ga., 1987-91; ptnr. Forbes and Bowman, 1991—. Bd. dirs. Greenbriar Children's Ctr., exec. com. 1995, pres. 1996-98; active Jr. League Savannah; mem. Leadership Savannah, 1994-96. Mem. Am. Employment Law Coun., Ga. Def. Lawyers Assn., Savannah Young Lawyers Assn. (pres. 1996-97), 2000 Club (membership chair 1990-91, pres. 1992), South Atlantic Found. (bd. dirs. 1992). Labor, Insurance, Workers' compensation. Home: 21 Jameswood Ave Savannah GA 31406-5219 Office: Forbes and Bowman PO Box 13929 7505 Waters Ave Ste D-14 Savannah GA 31406-3824

**BOWMAN, DANIEL A.,** lawyer; b. Milw., Apr. 18, 1958; s. George A. and Rosemary B.; m. Tracy A. Ott, Sept. 16, 1962; children: Alex, Mara. BA, Georgetown U., 1979; JD, U. Oreg., 1982; LLM, U. Denver, 1984. Tax atty. Aramco, Dhahran, Saudi Arabia, 1986-91, Freeport-McMoran, New Orleans, 1991-92; sr. v.p. PT Freeport Indonesia, Jakarta, Indonesia, 1992-98; sole practice law Medicine Lodge, Kans., 1998—. Sch. bd. Jakarta Internat. Sch., 1996-98. Mem. ABA (com. on tax of foreigners in U.S.), Oreg. Bar Assn., Colo. Bar Assn., Kans. Bar Assn. Republican. Roman Catholic. Avocation: astronomy. Office: 401 N Walnut St Medicine Lodge KS 67104-1221

**BOWMAN, DAVID WESLEY,** lawyer; b. Mpls., Dec. 14, 1940; s. Burton F. and Eldred (Frudenfeld) B.; m. Patricia L. Schlimme, Nov. 26, 1975; children: Christopher B., Sarah K., David W., Tulley B., Ashley B. B.A., U. Iowa, 1964, J.D., 1967. Bar: Iowa 1967. Asst. counsel Dept. Navy, Washington, 1968-72, Firestone Corp., Akron, Ohio, 1972-77; counsel Harris Corp., Melbourne, Fla., 1977-80, v.p., sec., gen. counsel documation, 1980-81, sector counsel, 1981-83; v.p., sec., gen. counsel Harris Graphics Corp., 1983-87; sr. v.p., gen. counsel, sec. MAPCO Inc., Tulsa, 1987—. Mem. ABA, Fed. Bar Assn., Iowa Bar Assn., Nat. Contract Mgmt. Assn., Nat. Security Indsl. Assn. Episcopalian. Contracts commercial, General corporate, Administrative and regulatory. Home: 3104 S Columbia Cir Tulsa OK 74105-2329 Office: Mapco Inc 1800 S Baltimore Ave PO Box 645 Tulsa OK 74101-0645

**BOWMAN, GEORGE ARTHUR, JR.,** judge; b. Milw., Dec. 1, 1917; s. George Arthur and Edna Oral (Hunter) B.; m. Rose Mary Thorpe, Aug. 8, 1947 (dec. 1980); children: George A. III, Daniel Andrew. Student, U. Wis., 1936-39; JD, Marquette U., 1943. Bar: Wis. 1943, U.S. Supreme Ct. 1943. Asst. dist. atty. Milw. County, 1947-48, children's ct. judge, 1967-72; asst. city atty. City of Milw., 1948-67; adminstrv. law judge Office of Hearing and Appeals Social Security Adminstrn. Dept. HHS, Chgo., 1973-97, adminstrv. law judge emeritus, 1997; pvt. practice, 1997—; appointed Pres.'s Task Force, Law Enforcement Assistance Adminstrn., 1972; former counsel Milw. Police Dept.; advisor Nat. Council of Juvenile Ct. Judges, Nat. Conv., Atlanta; chmn. conv. com. Nat. Council of Juvenile Ct. Judges, Milw., 1972; chmn. State Task Force on Juvenile Delinquency, 1970-71; legis. com. Wis. Bd. Juvenile Ct. Judges, 1970-71; former mem. numerous legis. coms., Milw.; pioneered Legal Defender System in Children's Ct.; lecturer, Marquette U. Co-author: LEAA Uniform Standards for Police Departments, 1973 (Pres.'s citation). Bd. dirs. Am. Indian Info. and Action Group, Inc. "Project Phoenix", Juneau Acad.; chmn. Milw. County Rep. Party, 1961-62; active supporter numerous community juvenile programs, including Milw. Boys' Club, St. Joseph's Home for Children, Mt. Mary Coll. Proglram for Truant and Delinquent Girls, Operation Outreach, others; Social Security judge. With USN, 1943-46. Recipient Continious Svc. award Office of Hearings and Appeals Soc. Security Adminstr., 1991. Mem. Fed. Assn. Adminstrv. Law Judges, Assn. Office of Hearing and Appeals Adminstrv. Law Judges, Wis. State Bar Assn., Milw. Bar. Assn., Nat. Council Juvenile Ct. Judges, Am. Judicature Soc., Nat. Council of Sr. Citizens, Inc., Internat. Juvenile Officers Assn., Am. Legion (former post comdr.), Nat. Probate Judges Assn., New Trier Rep. Orgn., Committeeman's Club, Hawthorne Turf Club, Sigma Alpha Epsilon. Roman Catholic. Home: 2824 Orchard Ln Wilmette IL 60091-2144

**BOWMAN, JUDITH FARRIS,** lawyer, partner; b. Washington, May 5, 1940; d. Frederick Joseph and Mary Louise Farris; m. Thomas Gordon Bever, June 29, 1961 (div. Oct. 1976); children: Frederick Wolfgang Bever, Michael Gordon Bever (dec.); m. Dorian Bowman, Sept. 25, 1977; children: Ariel Justine Bowman, Sarah Katherine Bowman. BA, Radcliffe Coll., 1961; JD, Columbia U., 1974. Bar: N.Y. 1975, Mass. 1977, U.S. Dist. Ct. Mass. 1979, U.S. Ct. Appeals (1st cir.) 1979, U.S. Supreme Ct. 1982. Assoc. appellate counsel Legal Aid Soc., N.Y.C., 1974-77; assoc. Oteri & Weinberg, Boston, 1977-79; ptnr. Bowman & Bowman, Cambridge, Mass., 1979-89; of counsel Gitlin, Emmer & Kaplan, Boston, 1989-92; ptnr. Bowman, Moos & Hilton, Cambridge, 1992—; mem. steering com. probate ct. pilot project Middlesex Multidoor Courthouse, Cambridge, 1997—. Chair awards com., bd. mgmt. Radcliffe Coll. Alumnae Assn., 1995—. Mem. Mass. Bar Assn. (chair ADR subcom. family law sect. 1996-98), Mass. Coun. Family Mediation, Boston Bar Assn. Avocations: family, reading, gardening. Family and matrimonial, Appellate, Real property. Home: 62 Buckingham St Cambridge MA 02138-2229 Office: Bowman Moos & Hilton 222 3d St # 3320 Cambridge MA 02142

**BOWMAN, PASCO MIDDLETON, II,** federal judge; b. Timberville, Va., Dec. 20, 1933; s. Pasco Middleton and Katherine (Lohr) B.; m. Ruth Elaine Bowman, July 12, 1958; children: Ann Katherine, Helen Middleton, Benjamin Garber. BA, Bridgewater Coll., 1955; JD, NYU, 1958; LLM, U. Va., 1986; LLD (hon.), Bridgewater Coll., 1988. Bar: N.Y. 1958, Ga. 1965, Mo. 1980. Assoc. firm Cravath, Swaine & Moore, N.Y.C., 1958-61, 62-64; asst. prof. law U. Ga., 1964-65, assoc. prof., 1965-69, prof., 1969-70; prof. Wake Forest U., 1970-78, dean, 1970-78; vis. prof. U. Va., 1978-79; prof., dean U. Mo., Kansas City, 1979-83; judge U.S. Ct. Appeals (8th cir.), Kansas City, Mo., 1983-98, chief judge, 1998-99. Mng. editor: NYU Law Rev, 1957-58; Reporter, chief draftsman: Georgia Corporation Code, 1965-68. Served to col. USAR, 1959-84. Fulbright scholar London Sch. Econs. and Polit. Sci., 1961-62, Root-Tilden scholar, 1955-58. Mem. N.Y. Bar, Mo. Bar. Office: US Ct Appeals 8th Circuit 10-50 US Courthouse 400 E 9th St Kansas City MO 64106-2607

**BOWMAN, SCOTT MCMAHAN,** lawyer; b. Shaker Heights, Ohio, Mar. 16, 1962; s. George Henry and Patricia (McMahan) B.; children: Chad Marshall, David Chandler, Elizabeth Brooks; stepchildren: Garrett Richard Sevek, Grant Allen Sevek. AA in Bus., Fullerton Coll., 1987; BBA, Calif. State U., Fullerton, 1989; JD, U. Cin., 1992. Pvt. practice Salem, Ohio, 1992—; asst. city solicitor Salem, 1992-94; advisor YWCA Salem, 1994—; advisor Buler Inst. Art, Salem, 1994—; intermediary, counsel Unorganized Militia, 1996—. Author: The Turning Point, 1997. Mem. design review bd. City of Salem (Ohio), 1993-95, v.p., 1995; mem. Salem Planning and Zoning Commn., 1993-95, v.p., 1995; co-founder, trustee Salem Preservation Soc., 1993-95. Mem. ABA, Ohio Bar Assn., Columbiana County Bar Assn. Episcopal. Avocations: camping, hunting, surfing, coaching football, politics. Probate, Estate planning, Real property. Office: PO Box 558 Salem OH 44460-0558

**BOWNES, HUGH HENRY,** federal judge; b. N.Y.C., Mar. 10, 1920; s. Hugh Gray and Margaret (Henry) B.; m. Irja C. Martikainen, Dec. 30, 1944 (dec. Jan. 1991); children: Barbara Anne, David and Ernest (twins); m. Mary Davis, July 12, 1992. B.A., Columbia U., 1941, LL.B., 1948. Bar: N.H. bar 1948. Since practiced in Laconia; ptnr. firm Nighswander, Lord & Bownes, 1951-66; assoc. justice N.H. Superior Ct., 1966-68; judge U.S. Dist. Ct. N.H., Concord, 1968-77; judge U.S. Ct. Appeals (1st cir.), 1977-90, sr. judge, 1990—. Mem. Laconia City Council, 1953-57; chmn. Laconia Democratic Com., 1954-57; mayor, Laconia, 1963-65; mem. Dem. Nat. Com. from N.H., 1963-66; Chmn. Laconia chpt. A.R.C., 1951-52; pres. bd. Laconia Hosp. Assn., 1963-64. Served to maj. USMCR, 1941-46. Decorated Silver Star, Purple Heart. Mem. ABA, N.H. Bar Assn., Belknap County Bar Assn. (pres. 1965-67), Laconia C. of C. (past pres.), Lions Club (past pres. Laconia). Office: US Ct Appeals 1st Cir US Courthouse 1 Courthouse Way Ste 6730 Boston MA 02210-3008

**BOXER, ANDREW CAREY,** lawyer; b. Yonkers, N.Y., May 28, 1969; s. Jeffrey Victor and Joyce Elaine Boxer; m. Anna Maria Cozzaglio, Aug. 16, 1997. AB, Harvard U., 1991; JD, Cornell U., 1994. Bar: Vt. 1995, U.S. Dist. Ct. Vt. 1995. Assoc. Kiel & Ellis, Springfield, Vt., 1994—. Mem. ABA, Vt. Bar Assn., Def. Rsch. Inst. Avocations: snowboarding, hiking, camping, fishing, mountain biking. Insurance, Workers' compensation, Product liability. Office: Kiel & Ellis 20 Park St Box 948 Springfield VT 05156-3023

**BOYAKI, WALTER L.,** lawyer; b. N.Y.C., June 9, 1948; s. Michael J. and Loretta B.; m. Marcia D. Thomas, Oct. 13, 1973; children: Amanda, Natalie, Matthew. BS, U. Houston, 1970, JD, 1972. Bar: Tex., U.S. Dist. Ct. (we. dist.) Tex., U.S. Ct. Appeals (5th cir.). Defense counsel U.S. Army, El Paso, Tex., 1973-75; mng. ptnr. Miranda and Boyaki, El Paso, 1976—. Author, presenter: Suing the Government, 1992—. Capt. U.S. Army, 1973-76. Mem. Am. Trial Lawyers Assn. (life sustaining mem.), Tex. Trial Lawyers Assn. (bd. dirs.). Century Club. Democrat. Roman Catholic. Personal injury. Office: Miranda & Boyaki 4621 Pershing Dr El Paso TX 79903-1017

**BOYANTON, JANET SHAFER,** lawyer; b. Dallas, Dec. 8, 1954; d. Harvey Lee and Helen Louise (Barron) Shafer; m. Robert Earl Boyanton, May 3,

1980; 1 child, Thomas Franklin. BA, Austin Coll., 1976; MBA, Amber U., 1982; JD, Tex. Wesleyan U., 1994. Bar: Tex. 1994, U.S. Dist. Ct. (no. dist.) Tex. 1994; cert. family law mediator. Free lance writer Dallas, 1982-92; legal asst. Law Office of Eddie Vassallo, Dallas, 1992-94; pvt. practice DeSoto, Tex., 1994—. Mem. adv. bd. Tax Advocates for Nursing Home Residents, 1995—; vol. scouting activities Boy Scouts Am., children's choir. Mem. Nat. Acad. Elder Law Attys. Avocations: reading, travel. Probate, Personal injury, Elder. Office: 211 Executive Way De Soto TX 75115-2336

**BOYD, B(EVERLEY) RANDOLPH,** lawyer; b. Richmond, Va., Mar. 8, 1947; s. Henry Armistead and Mary Archer (Randolph) B.; m. Julia Murray Williams, May 14, 1977; children: Peter Armistead Randolph, Alexander Page Monroe. BA, Williams Coll., 1969; JD, U. Va., 1972. Bar: Va. 1973, U.S. Dist. Ct. (ea. and we. dists.) Va. 1974, U.S. Ct. Appeals (4th cir.) 1986. Ptnr. Boyd & Boyd, Richmond, 1973-79, Randolph, Boyd, Cherry & Vaughan, Richmond, 1979—; Commonwealth's atty. Charles City County Va., 1976—. V.p., sec. James River Assn., Richmond, 1984-97, pres. 1998—. Capt. USAR. Mem. Va. Bar Assn., Va. Trial Lawyers Assn. Democrat. Episcopalian. Avocations: hunting, fishing, hiking. Fax: (804) 783-2765. General civil litigation, Personal injury, Real property. Home: 4545 Kimages Wharf Rd Charles City VA 23030-3331 Office: Randolph Boyd Cherry & Vaughan 14 E Main St Richmond VA 23219-2110

**BOYD, DONALD H.,** lawyer; b. Chester, Pa., Aug. 5, 1960; s. Albert Everett and Renee M. (Leveille) B.; m. Amy McCabe Boyd, Oct. 30, 1990; children: Abigail, Caroline. BA, Widener U., Chester, Pa., 1983, JD, 1994. Bar: Pa.

**BOYD, HARRY DALTON,** lawyer, former insurance company executive; b. Huntington Park, Calif., June 13, 1923; s. Randall and Thelma L. (Lewis) B.; m. Margaret Jeanine Gamewell, June 13, 1948; children: Leslie Boyd Cotton, Wayne, Lynn Boyd Denby, Evan, Lance. LLB, U. So. Calif., 1949, LLM, 1960; A degree in Mgmt., Ins. Inst. Am., 1972. Bar: Calif. 1950. Pvt. practice L.A.; assoc. Harvey & Viereck, L.A., 1952-55; assoc. gen. counsel, corp. sec. Farmers Ins. Group, L.A., 1955-77; group v.p., gen. counsel Swett & Crawford Group, L.A., 1977-83; gen. counsel, dir. Harbor Ins. Co., 1983-89; Calif. counsel Continental Ins. Co., 1987-89; of counsel Fidler & Bell, Burbank, Calif., 1990-93, Richard E. Garcia, Atty. at Law, L.A., 1994-96; bd. dirs. FIG Fed. Credit Union, 1958-61, pres., 1960-61; mem. Sherman Oaks Property Owners Assn., 1967—, pres., 1969, 72; mem. Western Ins. Info. Svc., Spkrs. Bur., 1971-77; bd. dirs. Buffalo Reins. Co., 1983-87; expert witness in ins. litigation, 1990—; arbitrator reins., 1990—. Mem. adv. coun. Chandler Elementary Sch., 1970-73, Milliken Jr. H.S., 1973-74. With USAAF, 1943-46. Mem. Calif. Ins. Guarantee Assn. (bd. govs. 1972-77), Los Angeles County Bar Assn. (chmn. exec. com. corp. law depts. sect. 1971-72), Reins. Assn. Am. (legal com. 1979-81), Nat. Assn. Ind. Insurers (chmn. surplus lines com. 1980-82), Calif. Assn. Ins. Cos. (exec. com. 1979-83), Wilshire C. of C. (bd. dirs. 1971-79, pres. 1975), Nat. Assn. Ins. Commrs. (industry adv. com. on reins. regulation 1983-90), Am. Arbitration Assn. (arbitrator). Republican. Lutheran (pres. coun. 1964-65). Insurance, Personal injury. Home: 13711 Weddington St Van Nuys CA 91401-5825

**BOYD, JOSEPH ARTHUR, JR.,** lawyer; b. Hoschton, Ga., Nov. 16, 1916; s. Joseph Arthur and Esther Estelle (Puckett) B.; m. Ann Stripling, June 6, 1938; children: Joanne Louise Boyd Goldman, Betty Jean Boyd Jala, Joseph Robert, James Daniel, Jane N. Ohlin. Student, Piedmont Coll., Demorest, Ga., 1936-38, LLD, 1963; student, Mercer U., Macon, Ga., 1938-39; JD, U. Miami, Coral Gables, Fla., 1948; LLD, Western State U. Coll. Law, San Diego, 1981. Bar: Fla. 1948, U.S. Supreme Ct. 1959, D.C. 1973, N.Y. 1982. Practice law Hialeah, 1948-68, city atty., 1951-58; mem. Dade County Commn., Miami, Fla., 1958-68; chmn. Dade County Commn., 1963; vice mayor Dade County, 1967; justice Fla. Supreme Ct., Tallahassee, 1969-87, chief justice, 1984-86; assoc. Boyd Lindsey & Branch P.A., Tallahassee, 1987—; mem. Hialeah Zoning Bd., 1946-48; juror Freedoms Found., Valley Forge, Pa., 1971, 73. Bd. dirs. Bapt. Hosp., Miami, 1962-66, Miami Coun. Chs., 1960-64; emeritus trustee Piedmont Coll. Recipient Nat. Top Hat award Bus. and Profl. Women in U.S. for advancing status of employed women, 1967. Mem. ABA, Fla. Bar Assn., Hialeah-Miami Springs Bar Assn. (pres. 1955), Tallahassee Bar Assn., Hialeah-Miami Springs C. of C. (pres. 1956), Am. Legion (comdr. Fla. 1953-54), VFW, Shriners, Masons (33 deg.), Lions, Elks, Wig and Robe, Iron Arrow, Phi Alpha Delta, Alpha Kappa Psi. Democrat. Baptist (deacon). Probate, Federal civil litigation. Office: Boyd Lindsey & Branch PA 1407 Piedmont Dr E Tallahassee FL 32312-2943

**BOYD, MARY OLERT,** lawyer, educator, journalist; b. Holland, Mich., Aug. 28, 1930; d. Frederick H. and Sarah (Klooster) Olert; m. Joseph M. Boyd, Jr., Dec. 29, 1953; children: Andrew Martin, David Alexander, Martha Lucile. BA, Hope Coll., 1952; postgrad., Johns Hopkins Med. Sch., 1952-53, Am. U., 1953-54, Sch. Law Vanderbilt U., 1955-56; JD, Memphis State U., 1977. Bar: Tenn. 1977, U.S. Dist. Ct. (we. dist.) Tenn. 1977, U.S. Ct. Appeals (6th cir.) 1982, U.S. Supreme Ct. 1998. Tchr. schs. Nashville, Dyer County, and Dyersburg, Tenn., 1954-61; legal asst. Joseph M. Boyd, Jr. Dyersburg, 1965-74; ptnr. firm Boyd and Boyd, 1977-80; asst. dist. atty. Dyer County (Tenn.), 1980-91; head Child Support Div. for 29th Jud. Cir., Dyer and Lake County (Tenn.); assoc. gen. coun. Tenn. Dept. of Human Svcs., 1993-95; pvt. practice, Nashville, 1996—; instr. bus. law and other paralegal courses, Dyersburg State Community Coll., 1977-90; free-lance writer, Dyersburg, 1961—. 1982-83), Tenn. Jaycettes (pres. 1961-62). Methodist. Club: Dyersburg Woman's (pres. 1964-65). Contbr. photos and articles to Memphis Press-Scimitar and other newspapers; contbr. articles to profl. jours. and popular mags. Chmn. Dyer County Dem. Party, 1979-83; mem. exec. com. Tenn. Dems., 1986-90; legal air officer Tenn. Wing CAP, 1994—; mem. Davidson County Dem. Exec. Com., 1996—, newsletter editor, 1996—. Recipient Labor prize Memphis State Law Sch., 1977. Mem. ABA (family law sect.), Tenn. Bar Assn. (chmn. family law sect. 1985-87), Dyer County Bar Assn. (pres. 1982-83), Tenn. Lawyers Assn. for Women (newsletter editor 1997-98), Lawyers Assn. for Women (newsletter editor 1998-99). Methodist. Club: Dyersburg Woman's (pres. 1964-65). Contbr. photos and articles to Memphis Press-Scimitar and other newspapers; contbr. articles to profl. jours. Family and matrimonial, Pension, profit-sharing, and employee benefits, Probate. Office: 2300 Hillsboro Rd Ste 305 Nashville TN 37212-4927

**BOYD, THOMAS MARSHALL,** lawyer; b. Yorktown, Va., Sept. 10, 1946; s. Laurel Barnett and Mildred Warner Wellford (Marshall) B.; m. Torri Carol Tyler, Oct. 2, 1976; children: Brooke Warner, Tyler Randolph. BA in History, Va. Military Inst., 1968; JD, U. Va., 1971. Bar: Calif. 1973, D.C. 1974. Law clk. to fed. judge U.S. Dist. Ct. (cen. dist.) Calif., Los Angeles, 1973-74; trial atty., atty. advisor U.S. Dept. Justice, Washington, 1974-76; assoc. counsel com. on judiciary U.S. Ho. of Reps., Washington, 1976-86; dep. asst. atty. gen. Dept. Justice Office Legis. Affairs, Washington, 1986-88, asst. atty. gen., 1988-89, dir. office policy devel., 1989-91; dep. gen. counsel Kemper Corp., Washington, 1991-93, v.p. and legis. counsel, 1993-96; v.p. for legis. affairs Investment Co. Inst., Washington, 1996-98; ptnr. Ramsey, Cook, Looper & Kurlander LLP, Washington, 1998-99; sr. counsel Alston & Bird, LLP, Washington, 1999—; house counsel Presdl. Transition Com. on Criminal Justice, Washington, 1980-81; pub. mem. Adminstrv. Conf. U.S., 1992-95. Co-editor U.S. Atty.'s Criminal Trial Manual, 1971, Va. Bar Criminal Law Manual, 1971; contbr. articles to profl. jours. and pub. interest articles to newspapers. Served to capt. USAF, 1968-73. Recipient Nat. Media award Delta Soc., 1985, Edmund J. Randolph award, 1988. Mem. U.S. Supreme Ct. Bar Assn., Calif. Bar Assn., D.C. Bar Assn., Army-Navy Country Club, Leland Country Club. Republican. Episcopalian. Avocations: golf, jogging, writing. Legislative, Constitutional.

**BOYDEN, BRUCE ROBERT,** lawyer; b. Abington, Pa., Apr. 11, 1949; s. Harrison Earl and Lucille Ruth (Nemher) B.; m. Terry Gross, Aug. 20, 1979 (div. Apr. 1983); 1 child, Jennifer Blake; m. Anita Marie Bettinger, Feb. 16, 1985; children: Hillary Marie, Elizabeth Eileen. BA, So. Meth. U., 1971, MTh, 1975; JD, Gonzaga U., 1979. Bar: Wash. 1979, U. S. Dist. Ct. (ea. dist.) Wash. 1979, U. S. Dist. Ct. (no. and we. dist.) Wash. 1983, U.S. Ct. Appeals (9th cir.) 1981. Assoc. Parry & Esposito, Spokane, Wash., 1979-81; law clk. U.S. Bankruptcy Ct., Spokane, 1981-83; ptnr. Woeppel, Hoover & Boyden, Spokane, 1983-93; pvt. practice, 1993—. Mem. Wash. State Bar Assn., Spokane County Bar Assn., Am. Bankruptcy Inst. Bankruptcy. Office: 621 W Mallon Ave Ste 509 Spokane WA 99201-2181

**BOYDSTON, BRIAN D.,** lawyer; b. Leavenworth, Kans., June 12, 1964; s. Bruce John and Jayne Ann B.; m. Michelle Denise, June 17, 1989. BA in Polit. Sci., UCLA, 1986, BA in History, 1986; JD, Loyola Law Sch., L.A., 1991. Bar: Calif. 1991, U.S. Dist. Ct. (ctrl. dist.) Calif. 1992, U.S. Dist. Ct. (no. dist.) Calif. 1994, U.S. Ct. Appeals (9th cir.) 1996. From law clk. to assoc. Law Offices of Alan B. Pick, L.A., 1989-95; ptnr. Pick & Boydston, L.A., 1995—. Coach UCLA Debate Team, 1986-89. Mem. ABA, State Bar Calif. General civil litigation, Insurance, Appellate. Office: Pick & Boydston 523 W 6th St Ste 1134 Los Angeles CA 90014-1219

**BOYER, ANDREW BEN,** lawyer; b. Waukesha, Wis., Dec. 9, 1958; s. Selwyn L. and Gwen B. B. Spl. Studies, Cornell Coll., Mt. Vernon, Iowa, 1981; MA, No. Ill. U., 1982; JD, Valparaiso U., 1985. Bar: Ill. 1986, U.S. Dist. Ct. (no. dist.) Ill. 1985-86. Law clk. for presiding justice Ill. Ct. Appeals (3rd dist.), Pekin, Ill., 1985-86; sole practice Joliet, Ill., 1990—. Mem. ABA, Ill. Bar Assn., Chgo. Bar Assn., Will County Bar Assn. Real property, General corporate, General civil litigation. Office: 57 N Ottawa St Ste 502 Joliet IL 60432-4403

**BOYER, DAVID DYER,** lawyer, judge; b. Peoria, Ill., Oct. 6, 1960; s. John Harold and Sara Haskins Boyer; m. Rosene Marie Glenn, Nov. 22, 1995; stepchildren: Peter H. Monfore, Jennifer L. Monfore. BS, Bowling Green State U., 1982; JD, U. Ala., Tuscaloosa, 1985. Bar: Ala. 1985, U.S. Dist. Ct. (mid. dist.) Ala. 1986, U.S. Ct. Appeals (llth cir.) 1986, Calif. 1989, U.S. Dist. Ct. (ctrl. and so. dists.) Calif. 1990, U.S. Ct. Appeals (9th cir.) 1990. Jud. law clk. to Hon. H. Mark Kennedy, Montgomery, Ala., 1985-86; atty., mgr. Legal Svcs. Corp. Ala., Andalusia, 1986-88; atty., advisor HHS, San Bernardino, Calif., 1988-90; assoc. Kinkle, Rodiger & Spriggs, L.A., 1990-96; sr. assoc., leader litigation team McCormick, Kidman & Behrens, LLP, Costa Mesa, Calif., 1996—; judge pro tem Orange County Superior Ct., Santa Ana, Calif., 1997—. Ex-officio 24th Stat Senate Dist., L.A. Rep. Com., 1994-98; Rep. nominee for Calif. Senate, 1994. With USMC, 1979-81. Frazier Reams fellow Bowling Green State U., 1981, Harold Anderson scholar, 1982. Mem. Bus. Trial Lawyers Assn., Orange County Bar Assn. Roman Catholic. Avocations: writing, tennis, golf, horse training and racing. General civil litigation, Real property, Insurance. Office: McCormick Kidman & Behrens 695 Town Center Dr Ste 1400 Costa Mesa CA 92626-7189

**BOYER, TYRIE ALVIS,** lawyer; b. Williston, Fla., Sept. 10, 1924; s. Alton Gordon and Mary Ethel (Strickland) B.; m. Elizabeth Everett Gale, June 9, 1945; children: Carol, Tyrie, Kennedy, Lee. BA, U. Fla., 1953, LLB, JD, 1954. Bar: Fla. Atty. Crawford, May & Boyer, Jacksonville, Fla., 1954-58, Boyer Law Offices, Jacksonville, 1958-60; judge Civil Ct. of Record, Jacksonville, 1960-63; cir. judge 4th Jud. Cir. of Fla., Jacksonville, 1963-67; atty. Dawson, Galant, Maddox, Boyer, Sulik & Nichols, Jacksonville, 1967-73; appellate judge 1st Dist. Ct. Appeal, Tallahassee, 1973-79; chief judge 1st Dist. Ct. Appeals, Tallahassee, 1975-76; atty. Boyer, Tanzler, Blackburn & Boyer, Jacksonville, 1979-84, Boyer, Tanzler & Boyer, Jacksonville, 1984—; adj. prof. Fla. Coastal Sch. Law, Jacksonville, 1996—, U. North Fla., 1998—; chmn. Supreme Ct. Com. on Standard Conduct Governing Judges, Tallahassee, 1976-79. Contbr. articles to profl. jours. Chmn. Duval County Hosp. Authority, Jacksonville, 1970-73, Jacksonville Bldg. Fin. Authority, 1980-81; pres. Jacksonville Legal Aid Assn., 1954-61; bd. dirs. Jones Coll., Jacksonville, 1978-85; bd. advs. Fla. Coastal Sch. Law, 1996—; adj. prof. U. North Fla., 1998—. With USN, 1942-45, PTO. Mem. ABA, Am. Judicature Soc., Fla. Bar, Amer. Bar Assn., Jacksonville Bar Assn., Fla. Acad. Trial Lawyers, Am. Bd. Trial Advs., SCV (comdr.), Mil. Order Stars and Bars (comdr.), Masons, dir., Safari Club Internat., Fla. Blue Key, Order of Coif, Phi Beta Kappa, Phi Kappa Phi. Methodist. Avocation: big game hunting. Home: 3966 Cordova Ave Jacksonville FL 32207-6019 Office: Boyer Tanzler & Boyer 210 E Forsyth St Jacksonville FL 32202-3320

**BOYETTE, VAN ROY,** lawyer, consultant; b. Alexandria, La., Dec. 20, 1952; s. Van Rex and Virginia (Cook) B. BA, Tulane U., 1974, JD, 1977; LLM, Cambridge (Eng.) U., 1978. Bar: D.C. 1979, La. Legal counsel Sen. Russell Long, Washington, 1978-81; gen. counsel Am. Petroleum Refinery Assn., Washington, 1981-83; ptnr. Nossman Gunther, Washington, 1983-85, Black, Manafort, Stone & Kelly, Washington, 1985-86, Bergner, Boyette, Bockorny & Clough, Washington, 1986-94, Smith, Martin & Boyette, Washington, 1994—. Mem. La. Bar Assn., D.C. Bar Assn., Univ. Club. Democrat. Presbyterian. Avocations: fly fishing, squash. Office: Smith Martin & Boyette 915 15th St NW Ste 800 Washington DC 20005-2311

**BOYKO, CHRISTOPHER ALLAN,** lawyer, judge; b. Cleve., Oct. 10, 1954; s. Andrew and Eva Dorothy (Zepko) B.; m. Roberta Ann Gentile, May 29, 1981; children: Philip, Ashley. B in Polit. Sci. cum laude, Mt. Union Coll., 1976; JD, Cleve. Marshall Coll. Law, 1979. Bar: Ohio 1979, U.S. Dist. Ct. (no. dist.) Ohio 1979, Fla. 1985, U.S. Tax Ct. 1986. Prin. Boyko & Boyko, Parma, Ohio, 1993, 94-95; asst. prosecutor City of Parma, 1981-87, dir. of law, 1987-93; exec. v.p., gen. counsel copy Am., Inc., 1993-94; judge Parma Mcpl. Court, 1993; ptnr. Boyko & Boyko, Attys., Parma, 1994—; judge Ct. Common Pleas, Cuyahoga County, Ohio, 1996—; guardian ad litem Juvenile Ct., 1979-93; legal advisor spl. weapons and tactics divsn. City of Parma Police Dept., 1984-93; chief counsel S.W. Enforcement Bur., 1991-93; mem. faculty Ohio Jud. Coll., Nat. Jud. Coll., lectr. FBI Nat. Acad. Active Citizens League of Greater Cleve., 1985—; trustee Cops & Kids, Inc.; mem. Parma Drug Task Force, 1987—; mem. adv. com. Paradale Children's Svcs., 1991—; mem. St. Anthony's Sch. Commn. Mem. ABA, Fla. Bar Assn., Ohio Bar Assn., Cleve. Bar Assn., Parma Bar Assn. (pres., trustee) Ukrainian Bar Assn., Cuyahoga County Police Chief Assn. (assoc.), Narcotics Law Officers Assn., Cleve. Am. Mid. Eastern Orgn., Mt. Union Coll. Alumni Assn., Cleve. Marshall Law Sch. Alumni Assn., Elks. Byzantine Catholic. Avocations: martial arts, running, weightlifting. General practice, Probate, Municipal (including bonds). Home: 5291 Huntington Reserve Dr Parma OH 44134-6172 Office: Justice Ctr 1200 Ontario St Cleveland OH 44113-1604

**BOYKO, IHOR NESTOR,** lawyer; b. Winnipeg, Man., Can., Nov. 9, 1951; came to U.S. 1966; s. Maksym and Katherina (Huminilowych) B. BA, Ind. U., 1972, JD, 1975; MS, Purdue U., Indpls., 1989. Bar: Ind. 1975, U.S. Dist. Ct. (so. dist.) Ind. 1983. Law clk. Ind. Employment Security Divsn., Indpls., 1975-76; dep. pub. defender State Pub. Defender, Indpls., 1976-82, spl. dep. pub. defender, 1982-85; staff atty. Legal Aid Soc., Indpls., 1983-85; pvt. practice Indpls., 1985-86; atty. Ind. Dept. Environ. Mgmt., Indpls., 1986-92; corp./environ. counsel PWI Environ., Inc., Indpls., 1992-96; legal counsel Divsn. Reclamation, Divsn. Oil and Gas Ind. Dept. Natural Resources, Indpls., 1996—; adj. prof. Sch. Pub. and Environ. Affairs, Ind. U., Indpls., 1990—. Contbr. articles to profl. jours. Sec. Ukrainian-Am. Cultural Soc., Indpls., 1985—, former pres.; Ukrainian and Russian interpreter Internat. Ctr. of Indpls., 1987—. Mem. Com. for Environ. Concerns in Ukraine. Ukrainian Orthodox Ch. Avocations: foreign languages, music. Environmental, Oil, gas, and mineral, Administrative and regulatory. Home: 6224 N Tuxedo St Indianapolis IN 46220-4444 Office: Dept Natural Resources Ind Govt Ctr S W295 Indianapolis IN 46204

**BOYLE, E. THOMAS,** judge; b. Paterson, N.J., Apr. 30, 1939; s. Edwin Thomas Boyle and Anne Aleida Verhagen; m. Mary Lou Kelly, Aug. 28, 1965; children: Mary Laura Anderson, Elizabeth Anne Noll. Diploma, Delbarton Prep. Sch., Mendham, N.J., 1957; BS, Coll. Holy Cross, 1961; student, NYU, 1961-62; LLB, U. Va., 1964. Bar: N.Y. 1965, U.S. Ct. Appeals (2d cir.) 1973, U.S. Dist. Ct. (ea. and so. dists.) N.Y. 1974, U.S. Ct. Appeals (fed. cir.) 1992. Assoc. Mendes & Mount, N.Y.C., 1965-66; from trial atty. to chief asst. criminal div. Legal Aid Soc. Suffolk County, N.Y.C., 1966-71; appellate counsel appeals unit Fed. Defender Svcs., N.Y.C., 1972-75; pvt. practice Smithtown, N.Y., 1976-88; asst. counsel to spkr. N.Y. Assembly, Albany, 1977-78; calendar counsel, asst. counsel N.Y. State Senate, Albany, 1978-80; county atty. Suffolk County, N.Y., 1988-92; ptnr. Boyle, Shea & Nornes, Hauppauge, N.Y., 1992-95; magistrate judge U.S. Dist. Ct., Uniondale, N.Y., 1995—. Contbr. articles to profl. jours. Trustee Village Old Field, 1993-95, chair bd. assessment rev., 1994-95, commr. fire and pub. safety, 1993-95, chair code revision adv. com., 1992-93; bd. dirs. Cmty. Youth Svcs., 1982-86, pres., 1985. Recipient award for pub. svc. in civil rights area NAACP Brookhaven br., 1980. Mem. ABA, N.Y. State Bar Assn., Assn. Bar City N.Y., Suffolk County Bar Assn. (Pres. award 1980), Holy Cross Coll. Club L.I. (bd. dirs. 1985-88), Alexander Hamilton Inn of Ct. Avocations: boating, roller blading, running, traveling. Office: US Dist Ct 2 Uniondale Ave Uniondale NY 11553-1258

**BOYLE, FRANCIS JOSEPH,** retired federal judge; b. 1927; m. M. Delores Roderick; children: Deborah, Carole, Christopher, Mathew, Susan, Patrick, Katherine. Postgrad., Providence Coll., 1949; JD, Boston Coll., 1952. Bar: bar 1952. Assoc. Cornelius C. Moore, 1953-61; ptnr. Moore, Virgadamo, Boyle & Lynch, 1961-77; judge U.S. Dist. Ct. for R.I., Providence, 1977-82, chief judge, 1982-92, now sr. judge, 1992-96. With USN, 1945-46. Mem. Am. Bar Assn., Fed. Bar. Assn., R.I. Bar Assn., Newport County Bar Assn.

**BOYLE, PATRICIA JEAN,** retired state supreme court justice; b. Detroit, Mar. 31, 1937. Student, U. Mich., 1955-57; B.A., Wayne State U., 1963, J.D., 1963. Bar: Mich. Practice law with Kenneth Davies, Detroit, 1963; law clk. to U.S. Dist. judge, 1963-64; asst. U.S. atty., Detroit, 1964-68; asst. pros. atty. Wayne County; dir. research, tng. and appeals Wayne County, Detroit, 1969-74; Recorders Ct. judge City of Detroit, 1976-78; U.S. dist. judge Eastern Dist. Mich., Detroit, 1978-83; assoc. justice Mich. Supreme Ct., Detroit, 1983-98, ret., 1999. Active Women's Rape Crisis Task Force, Vols. of Am. Named Feminist of Year Detroit chpt. NOW, 1978; recipient Outstanding Achievement award Pros. Attys. Assn. Mich., 1978, 98, Mich. Women's Hall of Fame award, 1986, Law Day award ABA, 1998, Champion of Justice award State Bar Mich., 1998. Mem. Women Lawyers Assn. Mich., Fed. Bar Assn., Mich. Bar Assn., Detroit Bar Assn., Wayne State U. Law Alumni Assn. (Disting. Alumni award 1979). Avocation: reading. Address: 15925 Warwick St Detroit MI 48223-1355

**BOYLE, PATRICK OTTO,** lawyer; b. St. Louis, Nov. 15, 1935; s. Otto William and Wilma Louise (Bowers) B.; m. Jane Adeline Roberts, Nov. 22, 1966; children—Laura Jane, Daniel Patrick. B.S.B.A., Washington U., 1957, J.D., 1960. Bar: Mo. 1960, Ill., 1970. Assoc. firm Lucas & Murphy, St. Louis, 1963-67; assoc. csl. Interco Inc., St. Louis, 1967-69; csl. Energy Systems div. Olin Corp., East Alton, Ill., 1969-74; assoc. Winchester Group Csl., 1974-77; asst. sec., 1970-77; partner Boyle & Stillwell, East Alton, 1977-80; sole practice, St. Louis and E. Alton, 1980—. Bd. dirs. Ferguson-Florissant Sch. Bd., 1981-96. Served to comdr. USCGR, 1960-82. Mem. Mo. Bar Assn., Ill. Bar Assn., Madison County Bar Assn., Metro. Bar St. Louis, Beta Gamma Sigma. Mem. United Ch. Christ. Club: Mo. Athletic. Education and schools, Estate planning, General practice. Office: 210 Smith Ave East Alton IL 62024-1156 Home: 3715 Greengrass Dr Florissant MO 63033-6634

**BOYLE, RICHARD EDWARD,** lawyer; b. Westville, Ill., Mar. 27, 1937; s. Kelley George and Florence (Weisert) B.; m. Janet E. Peskar, Nov. 22, 1968; children: Kevin, Douglas, Leslie. BA, U. Ill., 1959, LLB, 1961. Bar: Ill. 1962, Mo. 1985, U.S. Dist. Ct. (so. dist.) Ill. 1962, U.S. Dist. Ct. (cen. dist.) Ill. 1962, U.S. Dist. Ct. (ea. dist.) Mo. 1991, U.S. Ct. Appeals (7th cir.) 1975, U.S. Supreme Ct. 1985. Assoc. Costello, Wiechert, Roberts & Gundlach, 1962-68; ptnr. Gundlach, Lee, Eggmann, Boyle & Roessler, Belleville, Ill., 1968—. With USAFR. Fellow Am. Coll. Trial Lawyers, Am. Bar Found. (mem. Adv. Group Civil Justice Reform Act 1990—); mem. Nat. Assn. R.R. Trial Counsel (pres. 1991-92), St. Clair County Bar Assn. (pres. 1979-80). General civil litigation, Personal injury, Product liability. Home: 13 Oak Knoll Pl Belleville IL 62223-1817 Office: Gundlach Lee Eggmann Boyle & Roessler Box 23560 5000 W Main St Belleville IL 62226-4727

**BOYLE, TERRENCE W.,** federal judge; b. 1945. BA, Brown U., 1967; JD, Am. U., 1970. Minority counsel housing subcom., banking and currence com. U.S. Ho. of Reps., 1970-73; legis. asst. U.S. senator J. Helms, 1973; judge U.S. Dist. Ct. Ea. Dist., N.C., 1984-97; chief judge 1997—. Office: US Dist Ct PO Box 306 Elizabeth City NC 27907-0306

**BOYLE, TIMOTHY EDWARD,** lawyer; b. Cleve., Mar. 11, 1961; s. Robert Jerome and Esther (Sapia) B.; m. Mary Elizabeth Strickland; children: Robert, Andrew. BA with highest honors, Denison U., 1983; JD with honors, Duke U., 1986. Bar: Md. 1986, D.C. 1989, U.S. Dist. Ct. D.C., U.S. Ct. Appeals (D.C. cir.). Assoc. Howrey & Simon, Washington, 1986-95, partner, 1995—. Mem. ABA (antitrust, litig. and pub. utilities sects.), D.C. Bar Assn. Antitrust, General civil litigation. Office: Howrey & Simon 1299 Pennsylvania Ave NW Ste 1 Washington DC 20004-2420

**BOYNTON, FREDERICK GEORGE,** lawyer; b. Yokohama, Japan, May 9, 1948; s. Fred Wenderoth and Buelah Eleanor (Nygaard) B.; m. Nancy Jeanne McLendon, Aug. 3, 1985; children: Emily Margaret, Charlotte Clayton, Susan Jeanne. BA, The Citadel, 1970; JD, Tulane U., 1973. Bar: SC 1973, Ga. 1976, U.S. Dist. Ct. Ga. 1976, U.S. Ct. Appeals (5th and 11th cirs.). Assoc. Smith, Gambrell & Russell, and predecessors, Atlanta, 1976-82, ptnr., 1982-88; sole practice, Atlanta, 1988—. Author: Criminal Defense Techniques, 1976; editor articles Tulane Sch. Law Rev. Mem. exec. com. Southside Progress Assn., Atlanta, 1983-84, Leadership Sandy Springs, 1989-90; bd. dirs. Atlanta Union Mission, 1990—, mem. exec. com., 1991, sec., 1992. Served to capt. JAGC, U.S. Army, 1973-76. Fellow Ga. Bar Found.; mem. ABA, Fed. Bar Assn. (pres. Atlanta chpt. 1981-82, mem. exec. com. 1982—, dep. chmn. adminstrv. law sect. 1986-87, bd. dirs. younger lawyers div. 1981-84, v.p. 11th Cir. 1985-87), State Bar Ga. (chmn. adminstrv. law sect. 1987-88), Lawyers Club of Atlanta, Order of Coif. Republican. Baptist. Administrative and regulatory, Federal civil litigation, State civil litigation. Home: 4860 Northway Dr NE Atlanta GA 30342-2424 Office: Ste 100 6000 Lake Forrest Dr NW Atlanta GA 30328-5902

**BOYNTON, JAMES STEPHEN,** lawyer; b. Stamford, Conn., Apr. 3, 1946; s. Horace William and Lorraine Anne (Nelsen) B.; m. Caroline Foster Cochran, May 9, 1970 (div. Nov. 1996); children: Caroline Lorraine, James Cochran. BA, Williams Coll., 1968; JD, U. Pa., 1971. Bar: N.Y. 1973, U.S. Dist. Ct. (so. dist.) N.Y. 1973. Assoc. Debevoise & Plimpton, N.Y.C., 1971-80; ptnr. Tung, Drabkin & Boynton, N.Y.C., 1980-85, Salans, Hertzfeld, Heilbrown, Christy & Viener, N.Y.C., 1985—. Trustee The Norfolk (Conn.) Land Trust, 1990—, Cushing Acad., 1993—. 1st lt. U.S. Army, 1972. Mem. Norfolk Country Club (pres. 1985-87). Congregationalist. Banking, Mergers and acquisitions, Securities. Home: 626 Winchester Rd Norfolk CT 06058-1365 Office: Salans Hertzfeld Heilbrown Christy & Viener 620 5th Ave New York NY 10020-2402

**BOZZA, MARIO,** lawyer; b. Caserta, Italy, July 10, 1942; s. Fernando and Redenta (Lapalorcia) B.; m. Carmela Varsallona (div. 1972); 1 child, Fernando; m. Barbara Aureli; 1 child, Francesca Romana. JD, U. Naples, Italy, 1969. Bar: Mass. Pvt. practice Boston, 1977—; cons. Consulate Gen. of Italy, Boston, 1985—. Mem. Mass. Bar Assn., Italy-Am. C. of C. (pres. 1996). General practice, Personal injury, Public international. Office: 63 Commercial Wharf Boston MA 02110-3814

**BRACAGLIA, THOMAS PAUL,** lawyer; b. Newark, May 25, 1955; s. John F. and Josephine Bracaglia; m. Wendy J. Bracaglila, Oct. 27, 1984; children: Anne J., Thomas R. BA, Hamilton Coll., 1977; JD, Villanova U., 1980. Bar: N.J. 1980, Pa. 1980, U.S. Dist. Ct. (ea. dist.) Pa. 1980, U.S. Ct. Appeals (3rd cir.) 1980, U.S. Dist. Ct. (mid. dist.) Pa. 1992. Clk. Ct. Common Pleas, Chester County, Pa., 1980; dist. atty. asst. Chester County Dist. Atty., 1981; ptnr. Kelly, McLaughlin & Foster, Plymouth Meeting, Pa., 1982—; mng. ptnr. Kelly, McLaughlin & Foster, Plymouth Meeting, 1997—; fellow Nat. Inst. Trial Advocacy, Hartford, Conn., 1985, Acad. Advocacy, Phila., 1989. Judge pro tem Ct. Common Pleas, Phila., 1998. Mem. ABA, Pa. Bar Assn., N.J. Bar Assn. Avocations: golf, physical fitness. Federal civil litigation, State civil litigation, Personal injury. Office: Kelly McLaughlin & Foster 620 Germantown Ave Plymouth Meeting PA 19462

**BRACETE, JUAN MANUEL,** diplomat, lawyer; b. Mayaguez, P.R., Sept. 10, 1951; s. Manuel and Norma (Mari) B.; m. Maria Elena Poma. BS in Bus. Adminstrn. summa cum laude, Georgetown U., 1971; JD magna cum laude, U. P.R., Rio Piedras, 1976; MBA, Heriot-Watt U., Edinburgh, Scotland, 1996. Bar: P.R. 1976, U.S. Tax Ct. 1978, Fla. 1986, U.S. Ct. Internat. Trade 1988. Mgmt. trainee First Fed. Savs., San Juan, P.R., 1972; pro mgr. CitiBank, N.A., San Juan, 1972-74; law clk. U.S. Dept. Justice, Washington, 1975; atty., advisor Bd. of Immigration Appeals, Washington,

1976-78; assoc. Goldman & Antonetti, San Juan, 1979-84; immigration judge U.S. Dept. Justice, Miami, 1985-89; pvt. practice law Miami, Fla., 1989-92; with Fgn. Svc. U.S., 1993—; U.S. consul Am. Embassy, Caracas, Venezuela, 1993-95, San Salvador, El Salvador, 1995-97; fin. economist Office of Devel. Fin., Dept. of State, 1997—; treas. Am. Immigration Lawyer's Assn. P.R. chpt., 1982-84, chairperson, 1984; adj. prof. law Stetson U. Coll. Law, 1990-92, St. Thomas U. Coll. Law, 1990; coord. Combined Fed. Campaign at Am. Embassy, Caracas, Venezuela, 1995. Contbr. articles to profl. jours. Sec., supr. comm. Dept. Justice Fed. Credit Union, Washington, 1976-78; sec. real estate commn., Alliance Francaise, San Juan, 1980-84; treas. Magdalena 1305 Owners Assn., San Juan, 1983-84; alt. bd. dirs. Harbour Club Villas, Miami, 1986; chmn. citizens adv. com. Miami Sr. Adult Edn. Ctr., 1991-92; chmn. local adv. bd. LNESC Miami Ctr., 1991-92; mem. exec. coun. So. Fla. chpt. Nat. Soc. to Prevent Blindness, 1991-92. Recipient Sustained Achievement award U.S. Dept. Justice, Washington, 1977, Spl. award Fed. Credit Union, Washington, 1979, Superior Honor award U.S. Dept. State, 1995; German-Marshall Fund Immigration fellow, 1987; knight Mil. and Hospitaller Order of St. Lazarus of Jerusalem, Sovereign Mil. Order of Malta, Equestrian Order of the Holy Sepulcher. Mem. ABA (vice chmn. immigration, naturalization and aliens com. 1987-89), P.R. Nat. Bar Assn. (v.p., treas. 1989-90, pres. 1990-92), Fla. Bar Assn., Colegio Abogados de P.R., Nat. Assn. Immigration Judges (sec. 1984-89), Assn. Consular Corps in Venezuela (bd. dirs. 1994-95), Am. Employee Assn. El Salvador (bd. dirs. 1995-96). Republican. Roman Catholic. Avocation: philately. Office: US Dept of State EB/IFD/ODF Rm 3425ms Washington DC 20520-0001

**BRACHT, DAVID LEO,** lawyer; b. West Point, Nebr., Feb. 25, 1960; s. Edward Bernard and Helen Ann (Knievel) B.; m. Susan Geretle Schumacher, Oct. 5, 1984; children: Thomas Edward, Victoria Leigh, Theresa Gerette. BS, U. Nebr., 1982; JD, Georgetown U., 1995. Bar: Minn. 1995, Nebr. 1997. Sales rep. Centennial Internat., Lincoln, 1982-83; analyst First Nat. Bank of Omaha, 1983-85; investment rep. New England Fin. Svcs., Omaha, 1985-87, Comml. Fed. Bank, Omaha, 1987-90; assoc. mgr. U.S. Dept. of Agrl., Washington, 1990-93; dir. mgmt. and fin. Dept. of Agriculture, Nat. Assn. of State, Washington, 1993-95; atty. Dorsey & Whitney LLP, Mpls., 1995-97, Kutak Rock, Omaha, 1997—. Vice-chair Nebr. Fedn. of Young Reps., 1989-90; bd. dirs. Nebr. 4-H Found., 1987-90, 97—, chmn. 1989-90. Recipient Nat. Grand Pres. award Alpha Gamma Rho, 1998. Roman Catholic. Avocations: travel, reading, public policy, youth development, golf. E-mail: david.bracht@kutakrock.com. Finance, Banking, Environmental. Office: Kutak Rock The Omaha Bldg 1650 Farnam St Ste A Omaha NE 68102-2186

**BRACKEN, WILLIAM EARL, JR.,** lawyer; b. Phila., Jan. 25, 1934; s. William Earl and Etholen Alabell (Terry) B.; m. Sarah Lou Graves, May 31, 1958; children: Elizabeth Louise, Terry Suzanne, Sarah Lynn. BBA, Baylor U., 1956, JD, 1958. Bar: Tex. 1958,. Assoc. Bryan-Maxwell, Waco, Tex., 1961-63; 1st asst. city atty. City of Waco, 1963-67, city atty., 1967-96; pvt. practice Waco, 1996—. Trustee Group Benefits Risk Pool Tex. Mcpl. League, Austin, 1979—, chmn., 1979-81; mem. adv. bd. S.W. Legal Found. Mcpl. Legal Ctr., Richardson, Tex., 1994—; bd. dirs. Evangelia Settlement, Waco; pres. Lake Air Meml. Little League, Waco, 1963-67; mem. Tejas Coun. Campfire Bd., 1997; active Bd. Ctrl. Tex. Sr. Ministry, 1997—. Lt. USAF, 1958-61, lt. col. USAFR, 1961-84. Recipient Disting. Svc. award Waco Jaycees. Fellow Tex. Bar Found.; mem. Baylor Law Sch. Alumni Assn. (bd. dirs.), Tex. City Atty. Assn. (hon. life, pres. 1969-71). Baptist. Avocations: family, travel, Texas Rangers baseball, Baylor University sports. Municipal (including bonds). Home: 5000 Ridgeview Dr Waco TX 76710-1727 Office: 5400 Bosque Blvd Ste 466 Waco TX 76710

**BRACKETT, COLQUITT PRATER, JR.,** judge, lawyer; b. Norfolk, Va., Feb. 24, 1946; s. Colquitt Prater Sr. and Antoinette Gladys (Cacace) B.; m. Pamela Susan Colwell, Oct. 11, 1969 (dec. Aug. 1978); 1 child, Susan Elizabeth; m. Frances Sybil Langford, Jan. 1, 1982. BS, U. Ga., 1966, MA, 1968, JD, 1973, LLM, 1976. Bar: Ga. 1973, U.S. Dist. Ct. (so. dist.) Ga. 1974, U.S. Dist. Ct. (mid. dist.) Ga. 1977, U.S. Supreme Ct. 1980, Tenn. 1987. Assoc. Surrett & CoCroft, Augusta, Ga., 1972-74; ptnr. Surrett & Brackett, Augusta, 1974-76; mem. faculty Sch. Law, U. Ga., Athens, 1977-82; mng. ptnr. Brackett, Prince & Neufeld, Athens, 1982-90; adminstrv. law judge Ga. Dept. Med. Assistance, Athens, 1990—; hearing officer Ga. State Bd. Edn., 1979-91; v.p. Mus. Dolls & Gifts, Inc., Pigeon Forge, Tenn., 1983—; pres. Bear Country Lodge and Conf. Ctr., Pigeon Forge, Tenn., 1996—, chmn. bd. Advenutres in Toy Land. Author: Court Administration, 1972. Pres. Athens Clarke Mental Health Assn., 1985; chmn. bd. dirs. N.E. Ga. Mental Health Assn., 1989-90; bd. dirs. Coalition for The Blue Ridge Pkwy., 1994—, Oconee Cultural Arts Found., 1995-97, Blue Ridge Pkwy. Assn., 1997—. Mem. ABA, Ga. State Bar Assn., Ga. Assn. Adminstrv. Law Judges (bd. dirs. 1990-91), Ga. Trial Lawyers Assn., Western Cir. Bar Assn., Internat. Platform Assn., S.E. Tourism Soc., Rotary Internat., Ea. Nat. Parks Assn., Sevier County Bar Assn., Soc. Am. Poets, Soc. Magna Carta Barons. Episcopalian. Avocations: reading, music, golf, cross-country skiing. Home: 636 Middle Creek Rd Ste 4 Sevierville TN 37862-5013 Office: 2884 Parkway Pigeon Forge TN 37863-3316

**BRACKETT, MARTIN LUTHER, JR.,** lawyer; b. Charlotte, N.C., Feb. 23, 1947; s. Martin Luther and Helen Virginia (Smith) B.; m. Lisa Nichol; children—Martin Hunter, Alexander Jones, Amelia Kathleen, Lauren Hart. B.A., Davidson Coll., 1969; J.D., U. N.C., 1972. Bar: N.C. 1972, U.S. Dist. Ct. (we. dist.) N.C. 1973, U.S. Ct. Appeals (4th cir.) 1975. Ptnr. Bailey, Brackett & Brackett, P.A., Charlotte, N.C., 1973-83, Brackett & Sitton, Charlotte, 1983-85, Robinson, Bradshaw & Hinson, P.A., 1985—. Mem. Auditorium-Coliseum-Conv. Ctr. Authority, Charlotte, 1981-87, chmn., 1985-87. Served to capt. U.S. Army, 1972-73. Recipient Van Hecke-Wettach award U. N.C., 1972. Fellow Am. Coll. Trial Lawyers; mem. N.C. Acad. Trial Lawyers (bd. govs. 1980-86, 88-95, v.p. 1984-86). Democrat. Presbyterian. Personal injury, Criminal, Family and matrimonial. Office: 1900 Independence Ctr 101 N Tryon St Charlotte NC 28246-0100

**BRADDOCK, DONALD LAYTON,** lawyer, accountant, investor; b. Jacksonville, Fla., Dec. 14, 1941; s. John Reddon and Harriet (Burgess) B.; children: Stella Helene Knowlton, Leslie Ann Meshad, Donald Layton Jr. BS in Bus. Adminstrn., U. Fla., 1963; JD, 1967. Bar: Fla. 1968, U.S. Dist. Ct. (mid. and no. dists.) Fla. 1968, U.S. Ct. Appeals (5th cir.) 1968, U.S. Ct. Appeals (4th and 11th cirs.) 1968, U.S. Supreme Ct. 1976, U.S. Tax Ct. 1970; CPA; registered real estate broker. Staff acct. Coopers and Lybrand, CPAs, 1964-65, Keith C. Austin, CPA, 1965-67; assoc. Kent, Durden & Kent, attys. at law, 1967-71; sole practice, 1971-73; ptnr. Howell, Kirby, Montgomery, D'Aiuto & Dean, attys. at law, 1974-76; pres., dir. Howell, Liles, Braddock & Milton, attys. at law, Jacksonville, Fla., 1976-88; ret., 1988; bd. dirs., mem. exec. com. Fla. Lawyers Mutual Ins. Co., pres. 1996-97, bd. dirs. 1993, treas. 1993-99; Doctors Lake Marina, Inc.; pres., dir. SafeStop, Inc.; pres., dir. Donald L. Braddock Chartered dba Mandarin Realty, 1970—. Bd. dirs. Jacksonville Vocat. Edn. Authority, 1971-75; mem. Jacksonville Becentennial Commn., 1976; bd. govs. Fla. Bar Found., 1984-86, sec.-treas., 1986-88; sec., dir. Laurel Grove Plantation, Inc., 1988—. Served with Air N.G., 1963-69. Mem. Fla. Bar (bd. govs. young lawyers sec. 1972-77), Fla. Inst. CPAs, Jacksonville C. of C. (com. of 100), Jacksonville Bar Assn. (pres. 1983-84, bd. govs. 1978-84), U. Fla. Alumni Assn. (pres. 1975, bd. dirs. 1968-75), Fla. Blue Key, Friars Club, Phi Delta Phi, Alpha Tau Omega. Republican. Estate taxation, Real property, General corporate. Office: PO Box 57385 Jacksonville FL 32241-7385

**BRADEN, ROGER NEWMAN,** lawyer; b. Providence, Ky., Nov. 17, 1952; s. J. N. and Agnes Lucille Braden; m. Bonnie Braden, May 30, 1971 (div. Nov. 1984); 1 child, Amy; m. Caroline Braden (Busse), Nov. 1, 1987; 1 child, Christopher. AA in Nursing, Henderson C.C., New Jerson, Ky., 1977; BA, No. Ky. U., 1979, JD, 1984. Bar: Ky. 1984, U.S. Dist. Ct. (ea. dist.) Ky. 1986, Ohio 1990, U.S. Dist. Ct. (we. dist.) Ky. 1990, U.S. Ct. Appeals (6th cir.) 1992, U.S. Supreme Ct. 1994. Assoc. Sanders & Assocs., Covington, Ky., 1986-91; ptnr. Greenebaum, Dall & McDonald, Covington, 1991-94; mng. ptnr. Wasson, Braden, Hatere & King, Newport, Ky., 1994-97; lawyer The Lawrence Firm, Covington and Cin., 1997—; spkr. and presenter in field. Contbr. articles to profl. jours. Chair No. Ky. U. Parents Adv. Coun., 1995-96. With USAF, 1971-75. Mem. ABA, ATLA, Ky. Bar Assn., No. Ky. Bar Assn. (chair health law), Ky. Acad. Trial Attys. (bd. govs. 1997—), Cin. Bar Assn., No. Ky. U. Alumni Assn., Chase Alumni Assn. (bd. govs. 1993-98, pres. 1997-98), Salmon P. Chase Am. Inn Ct. Democrat. Personal injury. Home: 3538 Saddlebrook Dr Taylor Mill KY 41015-4415 Office: The Lawrence Firm 2100 Star Bank Bldg 425 Walnut St Cincinnati OH 45202-3923

**BRADFORD, CARL O.,** judge; b. Dallas, Nov. 16, 1932; s. Montie Leroy and Vivian Ila (Milan) B.; m. Claire Solange Chaloux, Jan. 15, 1955 (dec. 1972); children: Timothy, Kathleen, Elizabeth; m. Mary Ellen Sanborn, July 7, 1973; children: Bethany, Michael. Student, U. Detroit, 1956-59; JD, U. Maine, Portland, 1962. Bar: Maine 1963, U.S. Dist. Ct. Maine 1963, U.S. Ct. Appeals (1st cir.) 1963, U.S. supreme Ct. 1978. Asst. atty. gen. State of Maine, Augusta, 1963-64, justice Superior Ct., 1981-98, active-ret. justice Superior Ct., 1998—; bd. dirs. Nat. Ctr. State Cts., 1996—; ptnr. Powers & Bradford, Freeport, Maine, 1964-81; commr. Uniform State Laws, 1972-76; mem. drafting com. Uniform Exemptions Act, 1974-76; bd. dirs. Nat. Ctr. for State Cts., Williamsburg, Va., 1996-99. With USN, 1951-55. Fellow Am. Bar Found., Maine Bar Found.; mem. Maine Bar Assn. (bd. govs. 1970-78, pres. 1977-78), Maine Trial Lawyers Assn. (bd. govs., sec. 1970-81), ABA (ho. of dels. 1978-81, 90-95, state bar del. 1978-81, bd. govs. 1st dist. 1990-93, bd. lisiaon to Nat. Conf. Spl. Ct. Judges 1990-91, liaison to Criminal Justice Sect. 1990-93, liaison to Nat. Conf. State Trial Judges 1991-93, chair subcom. nominations and awards com. 1991-93, bd. govs. program com. 1990-91, mem. oper. com. 1991-93, project 2000 subcom. 1991-93, bd. govs. chair compensation com. 1993, bd. govs. exec. com. 1993, bd. govs. exec. dir. search com. 1990, mem. commn. on multi-disciplinary practice 1998—), Nat. Conf. State Trial Judges (del. 1982-97, jud. immunity com. 1984-97, chair 1991—, conf. vice chair 1993, chair-elect 1994-95, chair 1995-96), Am. Judicature Soc. Home: 225 Sea Meadows Ln Yarmouth ME 04096-5523 Office: Superior Ct PO Box 287 Portland ME 04112-0287

**BRADFORD, DANA GIBSON, II,** lawyer; b. Coral Gables, Fla., Sept. 29, 1948; s. Dana Gibson and Jeanette (Ellis) B.; m. Mary E. Bradford, June 20, 1970 (div. Jan. 1982); 1 child, Jeffrey Dana; m. Donna P. Bradford, Apr. 14, 1984; 1 child, Shannon Claire. BA, U. Fla., 1970; JD, Duke U., 1973. Bar: Fla. 1973, U.S. Middle Dist. Ct. Fla. 1973, U.S. Ct. Appeals (5th cir.) 1974, U.S. Ct. Appeals (11th cir.) 1982, U.S. Supreme Ct. 1977. Lawyer, ptnr. Mahoney, Hadlow & Adams, Jacksonville, Fla., 1973-82, Baumer, Bradford & Walters, Jacksonville, 1982—; mem. Fla. Bd. Bar Examiners, 1989-94, chmn. bd., 1992-93; mem. Fla. Supreme Ct. Commn. on Professionalism, 1996-98; seminar lectr. Contbr. chpt. to book, articles to profl. jours. Mem. Leadership Jacksonville, 1982; spl. counsel Jacksonville Sports Authority. Capt. U.S. Army Res., 1972-80. Mem. ABA, ATLA, Jacksonville Bar Assn. (bd. govs. young lawyers sect. 1976-78, chmn. trial sects. 1989-90), Jacksonville Assn. Def. Counsel (pres. 1978-79). Republican. Methodist. General civil litigation, Federal civil litigation, State civil litigation. Office: Baumer Bradford & Walters 50 N Laura St Ste 2200 Jacksonville FL 32202-3625

**BRADFORD, ELIZABETH,** lawyer; b. Washington, July 20, 1954; d. Saxton Edward and Jean Frances (Phillips) Bradford; m. James C. Francis IV, Aug. 19, 1978; children: Nathaniel, Jeremy. BA, Yale U., 1975; JD, Harvard U., 1979. Bar: N.Y., 1980, U.S. Dist. Ct. (so. and ea. dists.) N.Y. 1980. Law clk. to Hon. Vincent L. Broderick U.S. Dist. Ct. (so. dist.) N.Y., N.Y.C., 1979-80; assoc. Davis Polk & Wardwell, N.Y.C., 1980-83, O'Sullivan, Graev, Karabell & Gross, N.Y.C., 1983-85; asst. atty. gen. N.Y. State Dept. Law, Mineola, 1985-87, asst. atty. gen. in charge Nassau office, 1987-95; v.p., gen. counsel N.Y. Conv. Ctr. Oper. Corp., N.Y.C., 1995—. General civil litigation, Contracts commercial, Labor. Office: NY Conv Ctr Oper Corp 655 W 34th St New York NY 10001-1188

**BRADFORD, J. MICHAEL,** prosecutor; b. Sept. 10, 1952. BS summa cum laude, U. North Tex., 1975; JD, U. Tex., 1978. Bar: Tex. 1978, U.S. Dist. Ct. (ea. dist.) Tex. 1979, U.S. Ct. Appeals (5th cir.) 1980, U.S. Supreme Ct. 1982. Briefing atty. Tex. Ct. Criminal Appeals, 1978-79; ptnr. Mehaffy, Gardia and Bradford, 1979-87; exec. asst. U.S. Atty. for Eastern Dist. Tex., Beaumont, 1983-87; U.S. magistrate Eastern Dist. Tex., Beaumont, 1987-89; dist. judge Tex. 58th Dist. Ct., Jefferson County, 1989-94; U.S. atty. Eastern Dist. Tex., Beaumont, 1994—. Pres. Three Rivers coun. Boy Scouts Am. Recipient Disting. Leadership award Nat. Assn. Cmty. Leadership, 1994, Silver Beaver award Boy Scouts Am., 1994. Mem. Am. Law Inst., Tex. Bar Found., State Bar Tex., Jefferson County Bar Assn., Downtown Rotary Club of Beaumont (pres., Paul Harris fellow 1994). Presbyterian. Office: US Atty Eastern Dist Tex 350 Magnolia St Beaumont TX 77701-2248

**BRADIE, PETER RICHARD,** lawyer, engineer; b. Bklyn., Feb. 19, 1937; s. Alexander Robert and Blanche Isabelle Bradie; m. Anna Barbara Corcoran, Jan. 22, 1960; children: Suzanne J., Barbara L., Michell S. BSME, Fairleigh Dickinson U., 1960; JD, South Tex. Coll. Law, 1978. Bar: Tex. 1978, U.S. Dist. Ct. (so. dist.) Tex. 1981; registered profl. engr., Ala. Performance engr. Pratt & Whitney Aircraft, West Palm Beach, Fla., 1961-63; sr. engr. Hayes Internat. Corp., Huntsville, Ala., 1963-64, Lockheed Missiles and Space, Huntsville, 1964-68; fluidics engr. Double A Products Co., Manchester, Mich., 1968-69; cons. Spectrum Controls, Montvale, N.J., 1969-72; sr. project mgr. Materials Research Corp., Orangebury, N.Y., 1972-74; sr. contracts adminstr. Brown & Root Inc., Houston, 1974-85; sole practice Houston, 1985-91; ptnr. Bradie, Bradie & Bradie, Houston, 1991—; counsel Inverness Forest C.A, Houston, 1978-80; sr. counsel Raymond-Brown & Raymond-Molem, J.V., Houston, 1982-84. Contbr. articles on fluidic controls to mags.; patentee. Dem. committeeman Bergen County, Haworth, N.J., 1959; del. Harris County Reps., Houston, 1984; officer, bd. dirs. Inverness Forest Civic Assn., Houston, 1975-78. Served to 2d lt. USMCR, 1958-61. Mem. Tex. Bar Assn., Houston N.W. Bar Assn. (treas. 1986, bd. dirs. 1988, sec. 1988, pres.-elect 1988-89, pres. 1990-91), Assn. Trial Lawyers Am., Houston Trial Lawyers Assn., Comml. Law League Am., Rotary Club (Montvale bd. dirs. 1973-74), Am. Inn of Ct. Republican. Jewish. Avocations: classical music, history, computers. General civil litigation, Contracts commercial, General practice. Home: 22007 Kenchester Dr Houston TX 77073-1315 Office: 3845 Fm 1960 Rd W Ste 330 Houston TX 77068-3519

**BRADLEY, AMELIA JANE,** lawyer; b. Columbia, S.C., Apr. 18, 1947; d. Hugh Wilson and Amelia Jane (Wylie) B.; m. Richard Bancroft Hovey, Apr. 1, 1977. BA, U. Va., 1968; MA, George Washington U., 1971. Bar: Va. 1976, D.C. 1985. Budget and mgmt. analyst NLRB, Washington, 1968-71, 72; clk. Cohen and Vitt, PC, Alexandria, Va., 1972-76; assoc. Cohen, Vitt & Annand, PC, Alexandria, 1976-80; White House fellow USDA, Washington, 1980-81; White House fellow Office U.S. Trade Rep., Exec. Office of Pres., Washington, 1981, asst. gen. counsel, 1981-82, assoc. gen. counsel, 1982-84; legal advisor to U.S. GATT del. Office U.S. Trade Rep., Exec. Office of Pres., Geneva, 1984-87; prin. dep. gen. counsel Office U.S. Trade Rep., Exec Office of Pres., Washington, 1989-92; asst. U.S. trade rep. for dispute resolution Office U.S. Trade Rep., Exec. Office of Pres., Washington, 1994; assoc. dir. for global environment White House Office on Environ. Policy, Washington, 1994-95; assoc. dir. internat. trade and devel. Coun. on Environ. Quality, Washington, 1995; asst. U.S. trade rep. for monitoring, enforcement Exec. Office of Pres., Washington, 1996—; counsel to U.S. Del. GATT Ministerial Conf., Punta del Este, Uruguay, 1986; chief negotiator U.S. GATT Uruguay Round Dispute Settlement Negotiating Group, 1986-87, 89-93; chmn. Interagy. Sect. 301 Comm., Washington, 1988-92; vis. rsch. assoc. Fletcher Sch. Law and Diplomacy, Tufts U., Medford, Mass., 1987-88; vis. rschr. Harvard U. Law Sch., Cambridge, Mass., 1988. Mem., chmn. Alexandria Human Rights Commn., 1975-80; pres., trustee Alexandria Law Libr., 1978-80; founding mem. Lawyer Referral Svc., Alexandria, 1978. NEH fellow, 1978. Mem. ABA, Va. State Bar (mem., chmn. com. on legal edn. and admission to bar 1977-84), D.C. Bar (chmn. internat. trade com. 1989-90). Episcopalian. Office: Office of US Trade Rep 600 17th St NW Washington DC 20508-0002

**BRADLEY, ANN WALSH,** state supreme court justice. Former judge Marathon County Circuit Ct., Wausau, Wis.; justice Wis. Supreme Ct., Madison, Wis. Office: PO Box 1688 Madison WI 53701-1688 also: 231 E State Capitol Madison WI 53702-0001

**BRADLEY, E. MICHAEL,** lawyer; b. N.Y.C., Apr. 13, 1939; s. Otis Treat Bradley and Marian Booth (Alling) Ward; m. Judith Allen Thompson, June 29, 1962; children: Jennifer Treat, Michael Thompson, Thomas Alcott, Samuel Allen. BA, Yale U., 1961; LLB, U. Va., 1964. Bar: N.Y., 1965. Assoc. Davis, Polk & Wardwell, N.Y.C., 1964-72; assoc. Brown & Wood, N.Y.C., 1972-73, ptnr., 1974-95, mem. policy com., 1981-94, mem. exec. com., 1989-94; ptnr. Jones, Day, Reavis & Poque, N.Y.C., 1995—; lectr. Practicing Law Inst., N.Y.C., 1970-79; 86, Am. Law Inst.-ABA, Phila., 1977-78; arbitrator Am. Arbitration Assn., N.Y.C., 1975—. Contbg. editor: The Use of Experts in Corporate Litigation, 1978, Securites Law Techniques, 1985. Bd. dirs. Bennett Coll. Found., N.Y.C., 1984—; trustee Salisbury (Conn.) Sch., 1987—. Mem. ABA, N.Y. State Bar Assn., Fed. Bar Assn., Assn. of Bar of City of N.Y., River Club, Union Club, Coral Beach Club, Quogue Field Club, Shinnecock Yacht Club, Nat. Golf Links of Am., L.I. Wyandanch Club. Republican. Presbyterian. Federal civil litigation, State civil litigation, Criminal. Home: 200 E 66th St New York NY 10021-6728 Office: Jones Day Reavis & Pogue 599 Lexington Ave Fl C1A New York NY 10022-6030

**BRADLEY, JEAN MARIE,** lawyer; b. Bluffton, Ind., Sept. 16, 1961; d. Louis Francis and Ruth Edna Bradley. BA in Psychology cum laude, St. Mary's of Notre Dame, 1984; JD, U. Houston, 1992. Bar: Tex. 1993, U.S. Dist. Ct. (no., so. and ea. dists.) Tex. 1993, U.S. Ct. Appeals (5th cir.) 1993, U.S. Ct. Appeals (6th cir.) 1997. Dep. bail bond commr. Allen County Superior Ct., Ft. Wayne, Ind., 1985-87; probation officer Dallas County Adult Probation Dept., Dallas, 1987-89; atty. McLeod, Alexander, Powel & Apffel, Galveston and Houston, 1992-94, Sommerman & Moore, P.C., Dallas, 1994-95, Liddell, Sapp, Zively, Hill & LaBoon, L.L.P., Dallas, 1995-98, Nationwide Enterprise, Dallas, 1998—. Mem. Evergreen Gala, Dallas, 1996—; mem. Habitat for Humanity, Dallas, 1998—; mem. Make-A-Wish Found., Dallas, 1998—; bd. dirs. Bridge Breast Ctr., Dallas, 1996—; vol. Housing Crisis Ctr., Dallas, 1996—, Lawyers Mentoring Kids Program, Dallas, 1996; mem. Attys. Serving the Cmty., Dallas, 1996—. Recipient Citizen's Citation award Ft. Wayne Police Dept., 1985, Vol. Atty. award Housing Crisis Ctr., 1997; named to Outstanding Young Women of Am., 1997. Mem. ABA, State Bar Tex., Tex. Young Lawyers Assn., Tex. Women's Lawyers Assn. Avocations: aerobics, skiing, cooking, reading. General civil litigation, Insurance. Office: Nationwide Enterprise Trial Divsn 105 Decker Ct Ste 450 Irving TX 75062-2767

**BRADLEY, LEIGH A.,** government official, lawyer; b. Ft. Benjamin Harrison, Ind., 1956; m. Douglas E. Wade; 1 child, Katie. BA in Polit. Sci. magna cum laude, U. Ala., 1978, JD, 1981. Prosecutor, def. counsel in spl. and gen. courtsmartial Air Force Judge Advocate Gen.'s Dept.; assoc. dep. gen. counsel Dept. of Def., 1987-93; spl. asst. U.S. atty. for mid. dist. Ala. Office of Sec. of Def., 1993-94; prin. dep. gen. counsel USN, 1994-98; gen. counsel Dept. VA, 1998—; legal advisor Def. Adv. Com. on Women in the Svcs. Recipient Sec. of Def. medal for meritorious civilian svc., 1995. Mem. Phi Beta Kappa. Office: VA 810 Vermont Ave NW Washington DC 20420*

**BRADLOW, DANIEL DAVID,** law educator; b. Johannesburg, South Africa, Oct. 23, 1955; s. Basil Arnold and Daphne (Uberstein) B.; m. Karen Joanne Hofman, May 22, 1983; children: Benjamin H., Adam H. BA, U. Witwatersrand, 1977; JD, Northeastern U., 1982; MLIC, Georgetown U., 1985. Bar: N.Y. 1983, D.C. 1984. Rsch. assoc. Internat. Law Inst., Washington, 1983-85; assoc. Reichler & Appelbaum, Washington, 1985-88; asst. prof. Washington Coll. Law/Am. U., Washington, 1989-92, assoc. prof., 1992-95, prof., 1995—, dir. internat. legal studies program, 1996—; vis. prof. Cmty. Law Ctr./U. Western Cape, Cape Town, South Africa, 1996; sr. spl. fellow UN Inst. for Tng. and Rsch., Geneva, 1995-96; cons. UN Inst. for Tng. and Rsch., 1990—. Contbr. articles to profl. jours. Mem. ABA, African Soc. Internat. and Comparative Law, Am. Soc. Internat. Law. Office: Am U Washington Coll Law 4801 Massachusetts Ave NW Washington DC 20016-8196

**BRADSHAW, CARL JOHN,** investor, lawyer, consultant; b. Oelwein, Iowa, Nov. 1, 1930; s. Carl John and Lorraine Lillian (Thiele) B.; m. Katsuko Anno, Nov. 5, 1954; children: Carla K., Arthur Herbert, Vincent Marcus. BS, U. Minn., 1952, JD, 1957; LLM, U. Mich., 1958; MJur, Keio U., Tokyo, 1962. Bar: Minn. 1960, U.S. Supreme Ct., 1981, Calif. 1985,. Assoc. Graham, James & Rolph, Tokyo, 1961-63; assoc. prof. law U. Wash., Seattle, 1963-64; sr. v.p. Oak Industries, Inc., Crystal Lake, Ill., 1964-84, dir. internat. ops., 1964-70, dir. corp. devel., 1970-72, pres. communications group, 1972-78, chief legal officer, 1979-84; counsel Seki & Jarvis, L.A., 1985-87, Bell, Boyd & Lloyd, L.A., 1987; prin. The Pacific Law Group, L.A., Tokyo and Palo Alto, Calif., 1987—, The Asian Mktg. Group, Torrance, Calif., 1992—; participant Japanese-Am. program for cooperation in legal studies, 1957-61. Contbr. articles to legal and bus. jours. Bd. dirs. Japan-Am. Soc., Chgo., 1966-72; bd. dirs., fin. dir. San Diego Symphony Orch. Assn., 1980-81. Served to lt. (j.g.) USN, 1952-55. Fulbright scholar, 1958-59, Ford Found. scholar, 1960-61. Fellow Radio Club Am.; mem. Minn. Bar Assn., Calif. Bar Assn., Am. Soc. Internat. Law, Internat. Fiscal Assn., Regency Club, Order of Coif. Avocation: reading, bible study. Home: 12958 Robleda Cv San Diego CA 92128-1126 Office: Pacific Law Group 12121 Wilshire Blvd Fl 2 Los Angeles CA 90025-1123

**BRADSHAW, JEAN PAUL, II,** lawyer; b. May 12, 1956; married; children: Andrew, Stephanie. BJ, JD, U. Mo., 1981. Bar: Mo. 1981, U.S. Dist. Ct. (we. dist.) Mo. 1982, U.S. Dist. Ct. (so. dist.) Ill. 1988, U.S. Ct. Appeals (8th cir.) 1986, U.S. Supreme Ct. 1987. Assoc. Neale, Newman, Bradshaw & Freeman, Springfield, Mo., 1981-87, ptnr., 1987-89; U.S. atty. we. dist. Mo. U.S. Dept. Justice, Kansas City, 1989-93; of counsel Lathrop & Gage, Kansas City, 1993—; named Spl. Asst. Atty. Gen. State of Mo., 1985-89; mem., chmn. elect U.S. Atty. Gen.'s adv. com., office mgmt. and budget subcom., sentencing guidelines subcom. Chmn. Greene County Rep. cen. com., 1988-89; pres. Mo. Assn. Reps., 1986-87; bd. dirs. Greene County TARGET, 1984-89; mem. com. on resolutions, family and community issues and del. 1988 Rep. Nat. Conv.; mem. platform com. Mo. Reps., 1988; chmn. Greene County campaign McNary for Gov., 1984, co-chmn. congl. dist. Dole for Pres., 1988, regional chmn. Danforth for Senate, 1988, co-chmn. 7th congl. dist. Webster for Atty. Gen., 1988; county chmn. U. Mo.-Columbia Alumni Assn., 1985-87; bd. dirs. Springfield Profl. Baseball Assn., Inc.; past mem. Mo. Adv. Coun. for Comprehensive Psychiat. Svcs., former bd. dirs. Ozarks Coun. Boy Scouts Am.; pres. bd. trustees St. Paul's Episcopal Day Sch., 1997—. Named Outstanding Recent Grad. U. Mo.-Columbia Sch. Law, 1991. Mem. ABA, Mo. Bar Assn., Kansas City Met. Bar Assn., U. Mo.-Columbia Law Sch. Alumni Assn. (v.p. 1988-89, pres. 1990-91), Law Soc. U. Mo.-Columbia Law Sch. Federal civil litigation, Criminal, Labor. Office: 2345 Grand Blvd Ste 2800 Kansas City MO 64108-2612

**BRADSHAW ELLIOTT, KATHY,** judge; b. Beecher, Ill., July 11, 1951; d. Harry A. and Alice Marie (Embry) Bradshaw; m. Roger Charles Elliott; children: Nicholas, Samantha. BS in Speech Edn., So. Ill. U., 1972; MSW, U. Hawaii, 1976; JD, Ill. Inst. Tech., 1984. Bar: Ill. 1995. Tchr. Waipahu (Hawaii) H.S., 1974-75; counselor Hawaii State Prison, Oahu, 1977-78; social worker Ill. Dept. Mental Health, Tinley Park, Ill., 1979-80; asst. state's atty. Kankakee County State's Atty. Office, Kankakee, Ill., 1988-92, 1st asst. state's atty., 1992-97; judge 21st Jud. Circuit Ct., State of Ill., Kankakee, 1997—. Mem. Kankakee Bar Assn. Office: Ill Jud Circuit Ct 450 E Court St Kankakee IL 60901-3917

**BRADY, B(ARBARA) DIANNE,** lawyer; b. Atlanta, July 27, 1947; d. Robert Erle and Alice (Robbins) Downing; m. Edward T. Brady, Oct. 7, 1967; children: Thomas Robert, Ryan Ashley. BA in Psychology, Laverne U., 1978; JD, Campbell U., 1984. Bar: N.C. 1985, U.S. Ct. Appeals (4th cir.) 1986, U.S. Dist. Ct. N.C. 1986, U.S. Supreme Ct. 1989. Ptnr. Brady & Brady, Fayetteville, N.C., 1985—. Troop leader Girl Scouts Am., Fayetteville, N.C., 1987, mem. adv. counsel, 1988. 1st lt. USAR, 1977-79. Mem. ABA, N.C. Bar Assn., N.C. Acad. Trial Lawyers, N.C. Real Estate Commn. (broker), Cumberland County Bar Assn., Phi Alpha Delta. Democrat. Baptist. Personal injury, Family and matrimonial. Office: Brady & Brady 325 Green St Fayetteville NC 28301-5027

**BRADY, LAWRENCE PETER,** lawyer; b. Jersey City, July 26, 1940; s. Lawrence Peter and Evelyn (Mauro) B.; div; children: Deegan, Tara, Kerry, Melissa, James; m. Mary Helen Reynolds, Mar. 28, 1984. BS in Acctg., St. Peters Coll., 1961; JD, Seton Hall U., 1964; LLM, Bklyn. Law Sch., 1966. Bar: N.J. 1964, U.S. Dist. Ct. N.J. 1964, U.S. Supreme Ct. 1969, U.S. Ct. Appeals (3rd cir.) 1972, N.Y. 1991; cert. civil trial atty. State of N.J. 1982; cert. Nat. Bd. Trial Advocacy 1989. Asst. prosecutor Hudson County,

Jersey City, 1964-70; prosecutor Town of Kearny, N.J., 1971-74; sr. ptnr. Doyle & Brady, Kearny, 1974—; dir. and founding incorporator Growth Bank, New Vernon, N.J. Mem. ATLA, Nat. Bd. Trial Advocacy, N.J. State Bar Assn., Hudson County Bar Assn., West Hudson Bar Assn. (sec. 1980, treas. 1981, v.p. 1982, pres. 1983), Am. Trial Lawyers N.J. (bd. govs.), Roxiticus Golf Club (Mendham, N.J.), Sandalfoot Country Club (Boca Raton, Fla.), Ocean Reef Club (Key Largo, Fla.), Ocean Reef Yacht Club. Roman Catholic. Avocations: golf, tennis, travel, fishing, boating. State civil litigation, General civil litigation, Personal injury. Office: Doyle & Brady 377 Kearny Ave Kearny NJ 07032-2600

**BRADY, M. JANE,** state attorney general; b. Wilmington, Del., Jan. 11, 1951; m. Michael Neal. BA, U. Del., 1973; JD, Villanova U., 1976. Dep. atty. gen. Wilmington and Kent County, 1977-87; chief prosecutor Sussex County, 1987-90; solo law practice, 1990-94; atty. gen. State of Del., Wilmington, 1995—. Office: Office of Atty Gen Carvel State Office Bldg 820 N French St Wilmington DE 19801-3509

**BRADY, RUPERT JOSEPH,** lawyer; b. Washington, Jan. 24, 1932; s. John Bernard and Mary Catherine (Rupert) B.; m. Maureen Mary MacIntosh, Apr. 20, 1954; children: Rupert Joseph Jr., Laureen Zegowitz, Kevin, warren, Jeanine Hartnett, Jacqueline Rada, Brian, Barton. BEE, Cath. U. Am., 1953; JD, Georgetown U., 1959. Bar: Md. 1961, U.S. Ct. Appeals (D.C. cir.) 1964, U.S. Patent Trademark Office 1961, D.C. 1962, U.S. Supreme Ct. 1969, U.S. Ct. Appeals (fed. cir.) 1961. Elec. engr. Sperry Gyroscope Co., L.I., 1953-56; patent specifications writer John B. Brady, patent atty., 1956-59; patent agt. B.P. Fishburne, Jr., Washington, 1959-61; pvt. practice patent agt. Washington and Md., 1961; practice Washington, Md. and Va., 1961—; sr. ptnr. Brady, O'Boyle & Gates, Washington & Chevy Chase, Md., 1963-95; of counsel Birth, Stewart, Kolasch & Birch, LLP, Va., 1996—; v.p. Minstr-O-Media Inc. Patentee crane booms, moldboard support assembly. Mem. ABA, Am. Intellectual Property Law Assn., Md. Patent Law Assn., Senator's Alumni Club. Republican. Roman Catholic. Patent, Trademark and copyright, Intellectual property. Home: 7201 Pyle Rd Bethesda MD 20817-5623 Office: 8110 Gatehouse Rd Ste 500E Falls Church VA 22042-1210

**BRADY, STEVEN MICHAEL,** lawyer; b. Norwalk, Conn., June 17, 1962; s. Patrick E. and Gwendolyn (Caskey) B.; m. Jacqueline Nicole, Apr. 8, 1989; 1 child, Patrick Alexander. BS, Fla. State U., 1984; JD, U. Fla., 1987. Bar: Fla. 1988, U.S. Dist. Ct. (so. dist.) Fla. 1999, U.S. Dist. Ct. (mid. dist.) Fla. 1988. Corp. counsel The Travelers Cos., Orlando, Fla., 1987-89; diplomat U.S. Dept. of State, Washington, 1989-94; trial lawyer Floyd Pearson Richman & Greer, Miami, Fla., 1995-96, Richman, Greer, Weil, Brumbaugh, Mirabito & Christensen PA, Miami, Fla., 1994—. Master USCG, 1985—. Mem. Fla. Bar Assn., Phi Delta Phi. Avocation: sailing. Insurance, Product liability, Admiralty. Office: Richman Greer Weil Brumbaugh Mirabito & Christensen PA Miami Ctr 201 S Biscayne Blvd Miami FL 33131-4332

**BRADY, TERRENCE JOSEPH,** judge; b. Chgo., Dec. 24, 1940; s. Harry J. and Othele R. Brady; m. Debra René, Dec. 6, 1969; children: Tara René, Dana Rose. BA cum laude, Coll. St. Thomas, 1963; JD, U. Ill., 1968. Bar: Ill. 1969, U.S. Dist. Ct. (no. dist.) Ill. 1970, U.S. Ct. Appeals (7th cir.) 1971. Pvt. practice Crystal Lake, Ill., 1969-70, Waukegan, Ill., 1970-77; assoc. judge 19th Jud. Cir., Ill. Cir. Ct., Waukegan, 1977—; lectr. Ann. Ill. Assoc. Judge Seminars, Statewide Ill. Traffic Conf., 1982, Lake County Bar Assn. Seminar, 1983, 88, others; faculty Nat. Jud. Coll., Reno, Nev., 1997; presenter, lectr. in field. Contbr. articles to profl. jours. Served with U.S. Army, 1963-64, 68-69. Mem. ISBA (com. on jud. adv. polls 1994—, vice-chair adv. polls 1998, chair jud. adv. polls, 1999), Ill. Judges Assn. (bd. govs.), Ill. Bar Assn. (task force on domestic violence 1988—), Lake County Bar Assn., Libertyville Racquet Club, Am. Inns of Ct. Avocations: tennis, golf, writing, reading. Office: Lake County Courthouse 18 N County St Waukegan IL 60085-4304 *Notable cases include: Adams vs. Adams, 133 Ill. 2d 457 S. Ct., 1989, which involved the Ill. Appellate Ct., in a divided opinion, affirmed, Adams vs. Adams, 174 Ill. App. 3d 595 2d Dist., 1988. The Ill. Supreme Ct. reversed and remanded, holding the issues of paternity and consent must be determined under Fla. law; Agazim vs. Agazim, 176 Ill. App. 3d 225 2d Dist., 1988, which affirmed the trial ct.'s distbn. of marital property requiring the husband to pay off substantial marital debts which he had incurred of his own purposes; Chapman vs. Chapman, 162 Ill. app. 3d 308 2d Dist., 1987; which affirmed trial ct.'s denial of husband's motion to vacate a marital property settlement agreement, without an evidentiary hearing; Peppers vs. FNB of Lake Forest, 151 Ill. App 3d 909 2d Dist., 1987, which affirmed trial ct.'s enjoining the defendant bank, as trustee, from seeking forfeiture of a real estate purchase installment contract; People ex. rel. Foreman vs. Sojourner's Motorcycle Club Ltd.*

**BRADY, THOMAS CARL,** lawyer; b. Malone, N.Y., Sept. 5, 1947; s. Francis Robert and Rosamond Ethel (South) B.; m. Joan Marie Murray, Dec. 4, 1971; children: Erin Marie, Ryan Thomas, Trevor Michael. BA, Niagara U., 1969; JD, SUNY, Buffalo, 1972. Bar: N.Y. 1973, U.S. Dist. Ct. (we. dist.) N.Y. 1973, Fla. 1981. City ct. judge City of Salamanca, N.Y., 1973; atty. County of Cattaraugus, Little Valley, N.Y., 1973-76; ptnr. Eldredge, Brady, Peters & Brooks, Salamanca and Ellicottville, N.Y., 1976-82; sr. ptnr. Brady, Brooks & Smith, Salamanca, N.Y., 1982-96, Brady, Brooks & O'Connell, L.L.P., Salamanca, N.Y., 1996—. Trustee St. Patrick's Roman Cath. Ch., Salamanca, 1991—; mem. N.Y. State Office Parks, Recreation and Hist. Preservation Allegany Region Commn., 1998—, vice chair, 1999; mem. 8th Dist. Atty. Grievance Com., 1994—. Capt. USAR, 1969-76. Mem. ATLA, Nat. Lawyers Assn., Fla. Bar Assn., N.Y. State Trial Lawyers Assn., N.Y. State Bar Assn., Cattaraugus County Bar Assn. (pres. 1984), Kiwanis (pres. Salamanca club 1983-84). Republican. Roman Catholic. Avocations: skiing, golf, swimming, boating. E-Mail: BBOLAW@aol.com. Personal injury, General civil litigation, Municipal (including bonds). Home: 6894 Woodland Dr Great Valley NY 14741-9752 Office: Brady Brooks & O'Connell LLP 41 Main St PO Box 227 Salamanca NY 14779-0227

**BRAFFORD, WILLIAM CHARLES,** lawyer; b. Pike County, Ky., Aug. 7, 1932; s. William Charles and Minnie (Tacket) B.; m. Katherine Jane Prather, Nov. 13, 1954; children—William Charles III, David A. JD, U. Ky., 1957; LLM (fellow), U. Ill., 1958. Bar: Ky. 1957, Ga. 1965, Tax Ct. U.S 1965, Ct. Claims 1965, Ohio 1966, U.S. Ct. Appeals 1966, U.S. Supreme Ct. 1970, Pa. 1973. Trial atty. NLRB, Washington and Cin., 1958-60; atty. Louisville & Nashville R.R. Co., Louisville, 1960-63, So. Bell Telephone Co., Atlanta, 1963-65; asst. gen. counsel NCR Corp., Dayton, Ohio, 1965-72; v.p., sec., gen. counsel Betz Dearborn, inc., Trevose, Pa., 1972-97, ret., 1997; former dir. Betz Process Chems., Inc., Betz, Ltd. U.K., Betz Paper Chem. Inc., Betz Energy Chems., Inc., Betz S.A. France, B.L. Chems., Inc., Betz GmbH, Germany, Betz Entec, Inc., Betz Ges. GmbH, Austria, Betz NV Belgium, Betz Sud S.p.A., Italy, Betz Internat. Inc., Betz Europe Inc., Primex Ltd., Barbados. Served as 1st lt. C.I.C. AUS, 1954-56. Mem. Am. Soc. Corp. Secs., Nat. Assn. Corp. Dirs., Atlantic Legal Found. Republican. Presbyterian.

**BRAGA, STEPHEN LOUIS,** lawyer; b. Newport, R.I., Nov. 29, 1955; s. Manuel Louis and Nancy Rose (Lincourt) B. BA cum laude, Fairfield U., 1978; JD magna cum laude, Georgetown U. Law Ctr., 1981. Bar: D.C. 1982, U.S. Supreme Ct., U.S. Ct. Appeals (D.C., 1st, 2d and 7th cirs.), U.S. Dist. Ct. D.C., U.S. Tax Ct. Law clk. U.S. Dist. Ct. D.C., Washington, 1981-82; atty. Miller, Cassidy, Larroca & Lewin, Washington, 1982—; adj. prof. Georgetown U. Law Ctr., Washington, 1993—. Democrat. Roman Catholic. Avocations: sports. Federal civil litigation, Criminal, Appellate. Office: Miller Cassidy Larroca & Lewin 2555 M St NW Ste 500 Washington DC 20037-1353

**BRAGG, ELLIS MEREDITH, JR.,** lawyer; b. Washington, Jan. 30, 1947; s. Ellis Meredith Sr. and Lucille (Tingstrum) B.; m. Judith Owens, Aug. 18, 1968; children: Michael Andrew, Jennifer Meredith. BA, King Coll., 1969; JD, Wake Forest U., 1973. Bar: N.C. 1973, U.S. Dist. Ct. (we. and mid. dists.) N.C. 1974, U.S. Ct. Appeals (4th cir.) 1980. Assoc. Bailey, Brackett & Brackett, P.A., Charlotte, N.C., 1973-76; ptnr. Howard & Bragg, Charlotte, 1976-77, McConnell, Howard, Johnson, Pruitt, Jenkins & Bragg, Charlotte, 1977-79; sole practice Charlotte, 1979—. Dist. chmn. Mecklenburg County Dems., Charlotte, 1978; coach youth soccer program YMCA, Charlotte, 1982-83; mem. Headstart Policy Council, Charlotte, 1985—. Mem. ABA, N.C. Bar Assn., N.C. Acad. Trial Lawyers. Presbyterian. Avocations: reading, jogging, gardening. General practice, State civil litigation, Family and matrimonial. Home: 6407 Honegger Dr Charlotte NC 28211-4718 Office: 500 E Morehead St Ste 210 Charlotte NC 28202-2694

**BRAGG, J. J.,** lawyer; b. Beaumont, Tex., Mar. 4, 1966; s. Jerry McDaniel and Beverly Gene (Fuller) B. BS in Speech, Lamar U., 1988; JD, Thomas M. Cooley Law Sch., 1994. Bar: Tex. 1994, U.S. Dist. Ct. (ea. dist.) Tex. 1994. Assoc. Tonahill, Hile, Leister & Jacobellis, Beaumont, 1995—. Contbr. articles to profl. publs. Recipient Am. Jurisprudence award. Mem. ABA, ATLA, Jefferson County Bar Assn., Jefferson County Young Lawyers Assn., Thomas M. Cooley So. Law Students Coalition, Delta Theta Phi. Personal injury, Product liability, General civil litigation. Home: 6175 Afton Ln Beaumont TX 77706-6009 Office: Tonahill Bldg 485 Orleans St Beaumont TX 77701-3009

**BRAGG, MICHAEL ELLIS,** lawyer, insurance company executive; b. Holdrege, Nebr., Oct. 6, 1947; s. Lionel C. and Frances E. (Klinginsmith) B.; m. Nancy Jo Aabel, Jan. 19, 1980; children: Brian Michael, Kyle Christopher, Jeffrey Douglas. BA, U. Nebr., 1971, JD, 1975. Bar: Alaska 1976, Nebr. 1976. CLU, ChFC, CPCU. Assoc. White & Jones, Anchorage, 1976-77; field rep. State Farm Ins., Anchorage, 1977-79; atty. corp. law dept. State Farm Ins., Bloomington, Ill., 1979-81, sr. atty., 1981-84, asst. counsel, 1984-86, counsel, 1986-88; asst. v.p., counsel gen. claims dept. State Farm Fire and Casualty Co., Bloomington, 1988-94; v.p., counsel, gen. claims dept. State Farm Ins. Cos., Bloomington, Ill., 1994-97, assoc. gen. counsel corp. law dept., 1997—; lectr., contbr. legal seminars. Contbr. and editor of articles to legal and ins. jours. Pres. McLean County Crime Detection Network, 1988-95. With USNG, 1970-76. Recipient Disting. Legal Svc. award Corp. Legal Times, 1998. Mem. ABA (various offices tort and ins. practices sect. including chmn. ins. coverage litigation com. 1991-92, vice chmn. property ins. law com. 1986-91), Internat. Assn. of Def. Counsel, Am. Corp. Counsel Assn., Def. Rsch. Inst., Fedn. Ins. and Corp. Counsel (chair industry coop. sect. 1995-97), Crestwicke Country Club. Republican. Avocations: golf, tennis. Insurance, General civil litigation, Personal injury. Office: State Farm Ins Cos Assoc Gen Counsel One State Farm Plz E-7 Bloomington IL 61710

**BRAID, FREDERICK DONALD,** lawyer; b. N.Y.C., Aug. 10, 1946; s. Donald Michael and Margaret Anna (Fluty) B.; m. Eleanor Mae Friedman, Oct. 23, 1980; children: Andrew Harris, Roy Leal, Josh Perry, David Barnett, Steven Gabriel. BS in Econs., St. John's U., Jamaica, N.Y., 1968; JD, St. John's U., Bklyn., 1971; LLM, NYU, 1979. Bar: N.Y. 1972, U.S. Dist. Ct. (so. and ea. dists.) N.Y. 1973, U.S. Ct. Appeals (2d cir.) 1973, (D.C. and 4th cirs.) 1997, U.S. Supreme Ct. 1975. Assoc. Rains & Pogrebin, Mineola and N.Y.C., N.Y., 1971-77, ptnr., 1978—; bd. dirs. Rains & Pogrebin, P.C., Mineola and N.Y.C., N.Y.; mem. adv. bd. NYU Sch. Law Ctr. for Labor and Employment Law, 1997—. Mng. editor St. John's Law Rev., 1970-71; contbr. articles to profl. jours. Served to capt. USAR, 1972-80. St. Thomas More scholar, St. John's U. Sch. Law, 1968-71. Mem. ABA, N.Y. Bar Assn., Assn. Trial Lawyers Am., Nassau County Bar Assn., Def. Rsch. Inst., Omicron Delta Epsilon, Delta Mu Delta. Labor, Federal civil litigation, State civil litigation. Home: 17 E 96th St New York NY 10128-0783 Office: Rains & Pogrebin PC 210 Old Country Rd Ste 12 Mineola NY 11501-4288

**BRAISTED, MARY ELIZABETH,** lawyer; b. S.I., N.Y., Oct. 26, 1966; d. Robert John and Aima Lola (Torras) B.; m. Mark W. Weiss, Sept. 28, 1997. BA, Manhattan Ville Coll., 1988; JD, West New Eng. Sch. Law, 1991. Bar: N.Y. 1992, N.J. 1992. Enlisted U.S. Army, 1992—; legal asst. atty. U.S. Army, Judge Advocate Gen. Corp., NYAC, Ft. Hamilton, N.Y., 1992-95; trial counsel U.S. Army, Korean Legal Svcs. Activity, 8th Army, Yongsan, Korea, 1995-96; appellate atty. U.S. Army, U.S. Army Legal Svcs. Agy., Falls Church, Va., 1996—. Vol. Make a Wish Found., 1998. Roman Catholic. Avocations: golf, tennis, running, Spanish. Office: US Army Legal Svcs Agy 5611 Columbia Pike Falls Church VA 22041-5000

**BRAITMAN, BARRY H.,** lawyer; b. Phila., June 7, 1948; s. Jack and Pauline R. (Moskowitz) B.; m. Susan C. Kelly, June 6, 1976; children: Michael, Daniel. BA, U. Wis., 1970, JD, 1974. Bar: Ill., 1974, U.S. Dist. Ct. (no. dist.) Ill. 1974. Ptnr. D'Ancona & Plaum, Chgo., 1983-88, Cherry & Flynn, Chgo., 1988-90; gen. counsel, sr. v.p. The RREEF Funds, Chgo., 1990—. Mem. ABA, Am. Corp. Counsel Assn., Ill. Bar Assn. Republican. Jewish. Pension, profit-sharing, and employee benefits, Real property. Office: The RREEF Funds 875 N Michigan Ave Ste 4100 Chicago IL 60611-1803

**BRAKE, TIMOTHY L.,** lawyer; b. St. Joseph, Mo., Apr. 8, 1948; s. Douglas E. and Ruth E. (Fahling) B.; m. Julia Marie Gerkin, Sept. 3, 1977; children: Jennifer L., Douglas M. BA in English, Regis Coll., 1970; JD, U. Mo., 1973. Bar: Mo. 1973, U.S. Dist. Ct. (we. dist.) Mo. 1973. Assoc. Margolin & Kirwan, Kansas City, 1973-79, ptnr., 1979-80; sole practice Kansas City, 1980—. Bd. dirs. Ozanam Home for Boys, 1990—, Lantz Welch Charitable Found. Fellow U. Mo. Law Found.; mem. Def. Lawyers Assn. (dir. western sect. 1979-80), Assn. Trial Lawyers Am., Mo. Assn. Trial Attys., Mo. Bar Assn., Kansas City Met. Bar Assn., Friends Art, Friends Zoo, Kansas City Athletic Club (dir. 1986-87), Hallbrook Country Club, Homestead Country Club. General civil litigation, Personal injury. Home: 3620 Wyncote Ln Shawnee Mission KS 66205-2739 Office: 1100 Main St Kansas City MO 64105-2105

**BRAMBLE, RONALD LEE,** lawyer, business and legal consultant; b. Pauls Valley, Okla., Sept. 9, 1937; s. Homer Lee and Ethyle Juanita (Stephens) B.; m. Kathryn Louise Seiler, July 2, 1960; children: Julia Dawn, Kristin Lee. AA, San Antonio Coll., 1957; BS, Trinity U., 1959, MS, 1964; JD, St. Mary's U., 1975; DBA, Ind. No. U., 1973; cert. lay spkr. Meth. Ch. Mgr., buyer Fed-Mart, Inc., San Antonio, 1959-61; tchr. bus. San Antonio Ind. Sch. Dist., 1961-65, edn. coordinator, bus. tng. specialist, 1965-67; assoc. prof., chmn. dept. mgmt. San Antonio Coll., 1967-73; prin. Ron Bramble Assocs., San Antonio, 1967-77; pres. Adminstrv. Research Assocs., Inc., 1977-82; v.p. PIA, Inc., 1982-83; v.p. fin. Solar 21 Corp., 1983-84, sr. staff Ausburn, Astoria & Seale (formerly Ausburn, O'Neill & Assocs.), San Antonio, 1984-89; pvt. practice, 1990—; cons., comptr. TEL-STAR Systems, Inc., 1993-95; v.p. MegaTronics Internat. Corp., 1995—; lectr. bus., edn. and ch. groups, 1965—. Cons. editor: Prentice-Hall, Inc., Englewood Cliffs, N.J., 1969-71; contbr. articles to profl. jours. Mem. World Affairs Coun. of San Antonio, diplomat. Served with AUS, 1959. Recipient Wall Street Jour. award Trinity U., 1959, U.S. Law Week award St. Mary's Sch. of Law, 1975. Mem. ABA, San Antonio C. of C., Adminstrv. Mgmt. Soc. (pres. 1966-68, Merit award 1968), Bus. Edn. Tchrs. Assn. (pres. 1964), Sales and Mktg. Execs. San Antonio (bd. dirs. 1967-68, Disting. Salesman award 1967), Internat. Platform Assn., Internat. Assn. Cons. to Bus., Nat. Assn. Bus. Economists, Acad. Mgmt., Christian Legal Soc., Comml. Law League Am., Toastmasters, Phi Delta Phi, Lions. Republican. General corporate, Private international. Home: 127 Palo Duro St San Antonio TX 78232-3026

**BRAME, JOSEPH ROBERT, III,** lawyer; b. Hopkinsville, Ky., Apr. 18, 1942; s. Joseph Robert and Atwood Ruth (Davenport) B.; m. Mary Jane Blake, June 11, 1966; children: Rob, Blake, Virginia, John, Thomas. BA with high honors, Vanderbilt U., 1964; LLB, Yale U., 1967. Bar: Ky. 1968, Va. 1968. Assoc. McGuire, Woods, Battle & Boothe, Richmond, Va., 1967-72; ptnr. McGuire, Woods, Battle & Boothe, Richmond, 1972-97; mem. NLRB, 1997—; lectr. in field. Contbr. articles to profl. jours. Mem. adv. bd. Salvation Army, Richmond, 1980-97, chmn., 1989-91; bd. dirs. Am. Vision, Atlanta; troop com. chmn. Robert E. Lee coun. Boy Scouts Am., 1980-91; chair 10th Amendment Litig. com., Gov.'s Adv. Coun. on Federalism and Self Determination; gen. counsel Rep. Party Va., 1993-96. Mem. Am. Bar Found., Va. State Bar (chmn. sect. A 3d dist. com.), Va. Bar Assn., Phi Beta Kappa. Presbyterian. Antitrust, Constitutional, Labor. Office: NLRB 1099 14th St SE Washington DC 20570-0001

**BRAMER, LISAN HUNG,** lawyer; b. Taipei, Taiwan, Feb. 9, 1969; came to the U.S., 1972; d. Douglas Tu and Vivian F.C. Hung; m. Glenn Joseph Bramer, Oct. 26, 1996. BS, U. Calif., Berkeley, 1991; JD, Santa Clara U., 1994. Bar: Calif. 1994, U.S. Dist. Ct. (no. dist.) Calif. 1994, U.S. Ct. Appeals (9th cir.) 1997. Assoc. Clapp, Moroney, Bellagamba, Davis & Vucinich, Menlo Park, Calif., 1994-95, Lonich & Patton, San Jose, Calif., 1995—; reader gen. bar exam State Bar Calif., San Francisco, 1995—. Contbr. artilce to Santa Clara Computer and High Technology Law Jour., vol. 10. Mem. Asian Pacific Bar Assn. Silicon Valley (bd. mem. 1995-96, sec. 1996—). General civil litigation, Insurance, Contracts commercial. Office: Lonich & Patton 111 W Saint John St Ste 600 San Jose CA 95113-1105

**BRAMLETT, BRENDA SUSAN,** lawyer; b. Oxford, Miss.; d. Julian Chandler and Mary E. Bramlett. BS, Memphis State U., 1976; JD, Nashville U., 1988. Bar: Tenn. 1988, U.S. Dist. Ct. (ea. dist.) Tenn., U.S. Ct. Appeals. Assoc. Norton, Seckler & Bramlett, Shelbyville, Tenn., 1989-92; ptnr. Seckler, Bramlett & Durard, Shelbyville, Tenn., 1992-97, Bramlett & Durard, Shelbyville, Tenn., 1997—. Dir. Tenn. Walking Horse Breeders and Exhibitors Assn., Lewisburg, Tenn., 1998—. Mem. Tenn. Trial Lawyers Assn. Avocation: showing Tennessee Walking Horses. Criminal, Family and matrimonial, Personal injury. Office: Bramlett and Durard PO Box 967 724 N Main St Shelbyville TN 37162

**BRAMLETT, JEFFREY OWEN,** lawyer; b. Detroit, Nov. 13, 1953; s. Melvin C. and Edith H. (Patrick) B.; m. Nancy E. Frakes, May 30, 1981; children: Cynthia, Melissa, Robert, Susanna. BA, U. Md., 1975; JD, U. Tex., 1980. Bar: Tex. 1980, U.S. Ct. Appeals (5th and 11th cirs.) 1980, Ga. 1981, U.S. Dist. Ct. (all dists.) Ga. 1981, U.S. Dist. Ct. (we. dist.) Mich. 1995, U.S. Supreme Ct. 1985. Legis. aide Hon. Robert Eckhardt, U.S. Congress, Washington, 1974-77; law clk. to judge Jerre S. Williams U.S. Ct. Appeals (5th cir.), Austin, Tex., 1980-81; assoc., then ptnr. Bondurant, Mixson & Elmore, Atlanta, 1981—; bd. trustees State Bar Ga. Client Security Fund, Atlanta, 1992-97. Mem. Bar Assn. of Ga. (bd. govs. 1994—), Atlanta Bar Assn. (bd. dirs. 1993—, chmn. litigation sect. 1994-95, pres.-elect 1999—), ACLU, (bd. dirs. 1993-97, pres. Ga. affiliate 1987-89, bd. dirs. 1983-97). General civil litigation, Civil rights, Constitutional. Office: Bondurant Mixson & Elmore 1201 W Peachtree St NW Ste 3900 Atlanta GA 30309-3417

**BRAMLETT, PAUL KENT,** lawyer; b. Tupelo, Miss., May 31, 1944; s. Virgil Preston and McDuff (Goggans) B.; m. Shirley Marie Wilhelm, June 14, 1966; children: Paul Kent II (dec.), Robert Preston. AA with honors, Itawamba Jr. Coll., Fulton, Miss., 1962-64; BA, David Lipscomb Coll., 1966; postgrad., George Peabody Coll., 1966; JD, U. Miss., 1969. Bar: Miss. 1969, Tenn. 1980, U.S. Dist. Ct. (no. dist.) Miss. 1969, U.S. Dist. Ct. (we. dist.) Tenn. 1976, U.S. Dist. Ct. (mid. dist.) Tenn. 1980, U.S. Dist. Ct. (so. dist.) Miss. 1983, U.S. Dist. Ct. (we. dist.) Ky. 1988, U.S. Ct. Appeals (5th cir.) 1974, U.S. Ct. Appeals (6th cir.) 1980, U.S. Ct. Appeals (11th cir.) 1981, U.S. Supreme Ct. 1974. Pvt. practice Tupelo, Miss., 1969-80, Nashville, 1980—; mem. Million Dollar Advs. Forum, 1998. Mem. ABA, ATLA, Miss. Trial Lawyers Assn. (bd. govs. 1976-79), Tenn. Bar Assn., Miss. Bar Assn. (pub. info. com. 1979-81), Nashville Bar Assn. (fed. ct. com. 1980-81), Million Dollar Advocates Forum, Am. Arbitration Assn. (comml. panel), Civitan Club (past gov. and legal counsel no. dist. Miss.). Mem. Ch. of Christ. Avocation: music. Personal injury, General civil litigation, Entertainment. Office: PO Box 150734 2828 Stouffer Tower Nashville TN 37215-0734

**BRAMLETTE, DAVID C., III,** federal judge; b. 1939. BA, Princeton U., 1962; JD, U. Miss., 1965. Assoc., then ptnr. Adams, Forman, Truly, Ward & Bramlette, Natchez, Miss., 1975-91; spl. cir. judge U.S. Dist. Ct. (6th dist.) Miss., 1977, 79; fed. judge U.S. Dist. Ct. (so. dist.) Miss., 1991—. Trustee Miss. Nature Conservancy, 1990—; pres. BBCHA, 1989-90; active Arcole Hunting Camp, Ducks Unlimited, Nat. Wild Turkey Fedn. Office: PO Box 928 Natchez MS 39121-0928

**BRAMLEY, BRUCE C.,** lawyer; b. Poughkeepsie, N.Y., Apr. 17, 1949; m. Cherie M. Bramley, June 18, 1972; children: Erica, Lisa. BA, Union Coll., 1971, JD, 1975. Bar: N.Y. 1976, U.S. Dist. Ct. (no. dist.) N.Y. 1976. Assoc. Pozefsky, Tocci & Pozefsky, Albany, N.Y., 1975-78; ptnr. Pozefsky, Bramley & Murphy, Albany, 1978—. Bd. dirs. Hospice, Upstate N.Y., 1994—. Mem. Mohawk Golf Club. Labor, General practice. Home: 2520 Mcgovern Dr Niskayuna NY 12309-2411 Office: Pozefsky Bramley & Murphy 90 State St Ste 1405 Albany NY 12207-1713

**BRAMMELL, WILLIAM HARTMAN,** lawyer; b. Shelbyville, Ky., Dec. 11, 1955; s. Billy Duard and Helen Combs (Hartman) B.; m. Eleanor Agnes Pesek, Apr. 3, 1982; children: William Hartman Jr., Katherine Elizabeth, Emily Marie. BA, Transylvania U., 1977; JD, U. Louisville, 1980. Bar: Ky. 1980. Atty. pvt. practice, New Castle, Ky., 1980—; city atty. Eminence and Pleasureville, Ky., 1982—; Henry County Planning and Zoning Atty., 1988—; pub. defender Henry and Trimble Counties, Ky., 1983; asst. atty. commr. 12th Jud. Dist., LaGrange, Ky., 1984; trial commr. 12th Jud. Dist., Henry County, 1985—. Sec. Protect Our Children, Inc., Henry County, 1981-82; bd. dirs. Eminence Christian Ch., 1986; pres. Henry County Heart Assn., 1985-86, Henry County Hist. Soc., 1987-89. Mem. Ky. Bar Assn., Carroll County Bar Assn., Ky. Assn. for Gifted Edn. (treas. 1992-95). Avocations: civil war history, fishing, travel. Consumer commercial, Real property, General practice. Home: 118 Tolle Ct Eminence KY 40019-2009 Office: PO Box 629 New Castle KY 40050-0629

**BRAMS, JEFFREY BRENT,** lawyer; b. Ft. Worth, Jan. 24, 1966; s. Samuel David and Barbara Parness B. BS in Fin., Oral Roberts U., 1988; JD, U. Fla., 1992. Bar: Fla. 1993. Assoc. Perry Shapiro Miller & Sarkesy, West Palm Beach, Fla., 1992-94; v.p., gen. counsel Khaki Kamel Exotic Imports, Palm Beach Gardens, Fla., 1993-95; gen. counsel Speedy Sign-A-Rama, West Palm Beach, 1995—; vice-chmn., founder S. Fla. Franchise Bus. Network, Ft. Lauderdale, 1997—. Mentor youth group Covenant Cmty. Ch., Palm Beach Gardens, 1997—; big brother Big Brother/Big Sister program Covenant Cmty. Ch., 1997—. Mem. Internat. Franchise Assn. (mem. corp. counsel com., mem. legal/legis. com., spkr. legal forum). Avocations: travel, golf, tennis, weightlifting. General corporate, Franchising, Private international. Home: 2 Lexington Ln E Apt A Palm Beach Gardens FL 33418-7124

**BRANAN, DEBRA PACE,** lawyer, sales representative; b. Monroe, La., Apr. 15, 1952; d. Wilford Hill and Jerry Katherine Pace; m. Homer Boyd Branan III, Sept. 26, 1975; 1 child, Whitney Frazier; stepchildren—Tucker, Boyd. B.S., U. Miss., 1973, J.D., 1976. Bar: Miss. 1976, Tenn. 1976. Assoc. Garner & Garner, Hernando, Miss., 1976-77; ptnr. Austin & Branan, Hernando, 1977-83; city prosecutor City of Horn Lake, Miss., 1977—, mcpl. ct. judge; city prosecutor City of Southaven, Miss., 1981-82; sole practice, Memphis, 1983-89, ptnr. Branan & Shuttleworth, 1989-93, Austin Law Firm, PA, 1993—; sales rep. West Pub. Co., St. Paul, 1983-89 . Com. chmn. Muscular Dystrophy Telethon, Memphis, 1979—, exec. com., sec.; judge Nat. Collegiate Cheerleader Championships, Dallas, 1983, 84; treas. Mid-South Fair, Memphis, 1984, v.p., 1986, pres. 1990-91, chmn. cert. holders 1996-97, chmn. entertainment, 1998-99, city ct. judge, Memphis, 1991, Horn Lake, Miss., 1985—. Recipient Outstanding Service award City of Horn Lake, 1982-83, Order of Emerald for Outstanding Pub. Svc.; Young Careerist award E. Memphis Bus. and Profl. Women's Club. Mem. Desoto County Bar Assn. (dir.), Miss. State Bar Assn. (bd. commrs. 1996—), Tenn. State Bar Assn., ABA, Miss. Trial Lawyers Assn., Memphis Shelby County Bar Assn., Kappa Delta (nat. officer 1986). Democrat. Presbyterian. Family and matrimonial, Real property, Personal injury. Office: 230 Goodman Rd Southaven MS 38671

**BRANCA, JOHN GREGORY,** lawyer, consultant; b. Bronxville, N.Y., Dec. 11, 1950; s. John Ralph and Barbara (Werle) B. AB in Polit. Sci. cum laude, Occidental Coll., 1972; JD, UCLA, 1975. Bar: Calif. 1975. Assoc. Kindel & Anderson, Los Angeles, 1975-77, Hardee, Barovick, Konecky & Braun, Beverly Hills, Calif., 1977-81; ptnr. Ziffren, Brittenham, Branca & Fischer, L.A., 1981—; cons. N.Y. State Assembly, Mt. Vernon, 1978-82, various music industry orgns., L.A., 1981—. Editor-in-Chief UCLA-Alaska Law Rev., 1974-75; contbr. articles to profl. jours. Cons., bd. trustees UCLA Law Sch. Com., UCLA Athletic Dept., Occidental Coll., Musician's Assistance Program, 1995. Recipient Bancroft-Whitney award; named Entertainment Lawyer of Yr. Am. Lawyer mag., 1981. Mem. ABA (patent trademark and copyright law sect.), Calif. Bar Assn., Beverly Hills Bar Assn. (entertainment law sect.), Phi Alpha Delta, Sigma Tau Sigma. Avocations: art, antiques, music, real estate. Entertainment. Office: Ziffren Brittenham Branca & Fischer 1801 Century Park W Fl 9 Los Angeles CA 90067-6406

**BRANCH, JOHN WELLS (JACK TWIG),** lawyer; b. Rochester, N.Y., May 1, 1912; s. John W. and Luna H. (Howell) B.; m. Caroline Wilbur, May 29, 1937 (dec.); m. Margaret Zutterman, May 25, 1991. BA, Cornell U., 1934; J.S.D., 1937; MA in Econs., U. Rochester, 1937. Bar: N.Y. 1937, U.S. Ct. Appeals (2nd cir.) 1958. Assoc. Mann, Strang, Bodine & Wright, Rochester, N.Y., 1937-42; chief price atty. OPA, Rochester Dist., 1942-44; ptnr. and now of counsel Branch, Wise and Dewart, Rochester, 1945—; pres. Nat. Planning Data Corp., Ithaca, N.Y., 1970-76; co-founder, pres. The Branch-Wilbur Fund, Inc., 1967—, Eldergard Svcs., Inc., 1988-94; co-founder Genesee-Volkhov Connection, Inc., 1994—. Recipient Civic award Rochester, N.Y 1995. Mem. N.Y. State Bar Assn., Monroe County Bar Assn., Estate Planning Coun. Monroe County, Rotary, Phi Beta Kappa. Democrat. Orthodox Christian. Avocations: composing, helping foreign students, reciting light verse. Estate planning, Probate. Home and Office: 34A Larkspur Ct Asheville NC 28805-1368

**BRANCH, TURNER WILLIAMSON,** lawyer; b. Houston, Aug. 22, 1938; s. James Alexander and Juanita (Wilson) B.; m. Margaret Moses; children: Brian Kern, Rebecca Claire. BA, U. N.Mex., 1960; JD, Baylor U., 1965. Bar: N.Mex. 1966; U.S. Dist. Ct. N.Mex. 1968; U.S. Ct. Appeals (10th cir.), U.S. Supreme Ct. 1972; Tex., Colo., U.S. Dist. Ct. (we. and so. dist.) Tex. 1988; U.S. Dist. Ct. Colo. 1988, D.C. 1989, U.S. Ct. Appeals (9th cir.), U.S. Dist. Ct. (no. dist.) Tex. 1992, U.S. Dist. Ct. (ea. dist.) Tex. 1993. Ptnr. The Branch Law Firm, Albuquerque, 1965—; bd. dir. liquor control State of N.Mex., 1966-68; atty. City of Gallup, 1970-72; mem. ho. judiciary com. and ho. corp. and banking com. N.Mex. Ho. of Reps., 1968-74. Author: Branch on Constrn. Pleading and Practice; sect. editor Baylor U. Law Rev., 1964-65; contbr. articles to jours. 1st lt. USMC, 1960-63. Fellow Internat. Acad. Trial Lawyers; mem. ABA (torts vice chmn. ins. practice sect.), Nat. Inst. Trial Advisors, Am. Arbitration Assn. (negligence adv. com.), Am. Soc. Law & Medicine, Am. Judicature Soc., Am. Bd. Trial Advs. (bd. dirs., pres. Albuquerque chpt. 1983-84), N.Mex. Bar Assn. (chmn. fee arbitration com. 1982—, legal med. rev. com.), Albuquerque (chmn. other professions com. 1969), N.Mex. Trial Lawyers Assn. (bd. dirs. 1969-73, 91—), State Bar of Tex., Tex. Trial Lawyers Assn., Colo. Trial Lawyers Assn., Assn. Trial Lawyers Am. (state committeeman 1970-74, sustaining 1978—), Nat. Advance Coll. Trial Advisors (vice chmn. 1984-85, The Best Lawyer in Am.), Nat. Coll. Advocacy (trustee), Pa. and N.Y. Trial Lawyers, Nat. Bd. Trial Advs. (cert.), D.C. Bar Assn., Internat. Acad. Trial Lawyers. Federal civil litigation, State civil litigation. Office: 2025 Rio Grande Blvd NW Albuquerque NM 87104-2525

**BRAND, IRVING,** lawyer; b. Wilkes-Barre, Penn., Oct. 22, 1942; s. Nathan H. and Rose (Mitchneck) B.; m. Marion F. Daitch, Aug. 31, 1967; 1 child, Ross G. BA, Lafayette Col., 1964; LLB, U. Va., 1967. Bar: N.Y. 1968, U.S. Ct. Appeals (2d cir.) 1968, U.S. Dist. Ct. (ea. and so. dists.) N.Y. 1975. Atty. Kelley, Drye & Warren, N.Y.C., 1967-75; labor counsel NBC, Inc., N.Y.C., 1975—. Dir., v.p. Westfield (N.J.) Basketball Assn., 1979-85; alumni admissions rep. Lafayette Coll., 1989—, mem. steering com., 1997—. Named Outstanding Alumni Admissions Rep. Lafayette Col., 1993. Mem. ABA, Assn. Bar of City of N.Y. (labor employment/law com.), Col. Men's Club of Westfield (mem. scholarship com., v.p.). Jewish. Avocations: basketball, tennis. Labor. Home: 214 Lynn Ln Westfield NJ 07090-1811 Office: NBC Inc 30 Rockefeller Plz Fl 2 New York NY 10112-0036

**BRAND, MARK,** lawyer; b. Sauk Centre, Minn., Feb. 1, 1952; s. Milton A. and Margaret (Kay) B.; m. Margrit B. Kuehn, Sept. 4, 1982; children: Peter, Erik, Natalie. BA cum laude, Concordia Coll., 1974; JD, U Notre Dame, 1979. Bar: Wash. 1979, U.S. Dist. Ct. (we. dist.) Wash. 1979, U.S. Ct. Appeals (9th cir.) 1979, Tex. 1981, U.S. Dist. Ct. (so. dist.) Tex. 1981, U.S. Ct. Appeals (5th and 11th cirs.) 1981, Ill. 1988, U.S. Dist. Ct. (no. dist.) Ill. 1988, U.S. Ct. Appeals (7th cir.) 1988, U.S. Dist. Ct. (ea. dist.) Mich. 1992, U.S. Dist. Ct. (cent. dist.) Ill. 1996. Assoc. George, Hull & Porter, Seattle, 1979-80; atty. Gulf Oil Corp., Houston, 1980-85; assoc. Hutcheson & Grundy, LLP, Houston, 1985-87; ptnr. Llkla Pope & John Ltd., Chgo., 1987-93, Brand & Novak Ltd., Chgo., 1993—; spkr., chair various seminars and trial practice, 1986—. Mem. ABA, Chgo. Bar. Assn. General civil litigation, Contracts commercial, Product liability. Office: Brand & Novak Ltd 135 S La Salle St Ste 3700 Chicago IL 60603-4101

**BRAND, STEVE AARON,** lawyer; b. St. Paul, Sept. 5, 1948; s. Allen A. and Shirley Mae (Mintz) B.; m. Gail Idele Greenspoon, Oct. 9, 1977. BA, U. Minn., 1970; JD, U. Chgo., 1973. Bar: Minn. 1973, U.S. Dist. Ct. Minn. 1974, U.S. Supreme Ct. 1977. Assoc. Briggs & Morgan, St. Paul, 1973-78, ptnr. 1978-91; ptnr. Robins, Kaplan, Miller & Ciresi, L.L.P., 1991—. Pres. Jewish Vocat. Svc., 1981-84, Mt. Zion Hebrew Congregation, 1985-87, Sholom Found., 1996—; bd. dirs. Friends of the St. Paul Public Libr., 1997—. Mem. ABA, Minn. Bar Assn. (chmn. probate and trust law sect. 1984-85), Hebrew Union Coll.-Jewish Inst. Religion (bd. overseers 1987—, vice-chmn. 1996—), Am. Coll. Trust and Estate Counsel (Minn. chair 1991-96, regent 1998—), Ramsey County Bar Found. (pres. 1995—), Phi Beta Kappa, B'nai Brith. Democrat. Estate planning, Probate, Estate taxation. Home: 1907 Hampshire Ave Saint Paul MN 55116-2401 Office: Robins Kaplan Miller & Ciresi LLP 2800 LaSalle Plz 800 Lasalle Ave Ste 2800 Minneapolis MN 55402-2015

**BRANDES, JOEL R.,** lawyer; b. Bklyn., Dec. 15, 1943; s. Murray and Evelyn (Levine) B.; children: Bari, Evan. BA, Queens Coll., 1965; JD, Bklyn. Law Sch., 1968; LLM in Corp. Law, NYU, 1974; postgrad., U. Tampa, 1961-62. Bar: N.Y. 1969, U.S. Ct. Appeals (2d cir.) 1969, U.S. Dist. Ct. (so. and ea. dists.) N.Y. 1970, U.S. Supreme Ct. 1972, U.S. Tax Ct. 1974. Assoc. Wallman & Kramer, N.Y.C., 1972-77; pvt. practice Garden City, N.Y., 1977-87; ptnr. Brandes & Stamler, Garden City, 1987-90, Brandes Weidman & Spatz P.C., N.Y.C. and Garden City, 1991-93; prin. The Law Firm of Joel R. Brandes P.C., N.Y.C., Garden City, 1993—; instr. matrimonial law Adelphi U., Garden City, 1976-88; vis. lctr. Sch. Law Hofstra U., Advanced Practice Inst., 1981. Co-author: Digest of Equitable Distribution Cases, 1981, A Practical Guide to the New York Equitable Distribution Law, 1980, Contemporary Matrimonial Law Issues, 1986, Encyclopedia of Matrimonial Practice, 1992, A Comprehensive Analysis of All Reported Equitable Distribution Cases to Date, 1982, Equitable Distribution Case Law, 1983, Law and the Family, New York, 2d edit. (9 vols.), 1986-98, Law and the Family, New York Forms (4 vols.), 1995; contbr. articles to profl. jours; editor: N.Y. Family Law Reporter. Pres. Old Lindenmere Civic Assn., Merrick, N.Y., 1975-80, Community Council Merricks, 1977-80; arbitrator Civil Ct. of City of N.Y. Mem. ABA (family law sect., assoc. editor Family Law Newsletter 1971-78, litigation sect., trial evidence com. 1975-77, exec. mem. child custody com. 1982-83, panel mem. Law in the Fifty States 1986-87), Am. Soc. Writers on Legal Subjects, N.Y. State Bar Assn. (family law sect. 1975—, Family Law Review Editorial Bd. 1975—, sec. com. on legis. 1975-77, com. continuing legal edn. 1980-92, chmn. com. continuing legal edn. 1982-92, fin. officer 1990-92, sec. 1992, mem. com. profl. discipline 1992-93, mem. com. on children and the law 1997—, mem. com. on Cts. of Appellate Jurisdiction 1998—), Nassau County Bar Assn. (com. matrimonial and family law 1975—, mem. newsletter subcommittee 1976, chmn. legis. subcommittee 1978-80, chmn. continuing legal edn. subcommittee 1980-82, chmn. matrimonial and family law 1982-84), Am. Arbitration Assn. (panel mem 1974-82), Internat. Acad. Matrimonial Lawyers, Am. Acad. Matrimonial Lawyers (legal edn. com. 1978, bd. mgrs. 1979-83, bd. examiners 1979-80, chmn. legis. com. 1979-80, com. legal fees in matrimonial matters 1980-81, ad hoc com. on revisions of equitable distribution law 1980-81). Jewish. Family and matrimonial, Juvenile, State civil litigation. *Notable cases include: Tucker v. Tucker, 55 NY 2d 378, which held that equitable distribution law (EDL) was not retroactive and that an action pending prior to the enactment of the N.Y. EDL could not be discontinued to commence a new action under the EDL; Marone v.. Marone 50 NY 2d 481 which held that although N.Y. did not recognize palimony, a meritorious relationship, in and of itself, was not a bar to establishing an oral partnership agreement between a man and woman living together; McSparron v. McSparron, 87 NY 2d 275 which held that a professional (law) license retains its identity as an asset and does not merge into the professional's career or practice.*

**BRANDFASS, ROBERT LEE,** lawyer; b. Pitts., Dec. 3, 1960; s. Charles Robert and Martha Rose (Killeen) B.; m. Paula L. Koenig, Apr. 16, 1988; children: Lara, Allison, Matthew. AB, Ripon Coll., 1983; JD, Case Western Res. U., 1986. Bar: Ohio 1986, W.Va. 1987, U.S. Dist. Ct. (so. dist.) W.Va. 1987, U.S. Dist. Ct. (no. dist.) W.Va. 1992. Atty. Jacobson, Maynard, Tuschman & Kalur, Cleve., 1985-93, Kay, Casto, Chaney, Love & Wise, Charleston, W.Va., 1993-98; gen. counsel W.Va. United Health System, 1998—; pres. Attys. for Integrity, Inc., Charleston, 1996—. Mem. Nat. Health Lawyers Assn., Am. Acad. of Health Care Attys., W.Va. State Bar (mem. law and medicine com. 1992—, mem. jud. improvement com. 1996—), St. Thomas More Cath. Lawyers Soc. Republican. Roman Catholic. Avocations: reading nonfiction and history, hiking, fishing, parenting. General corporate, General civil litigation, Health. Home: 503 Vantage Dr Morgantown WV 26508-2635 Office: WVa United Health System 1000 Technology Dr Ste 2320 Fairmont WV 26554-8834

**BRANDMAN, SCOTT LEWIS,** lawyer; b. Huntington, N.Y., Nov. 22, 1967; s. Jerome S. and Jacquene S. Brandman. BA, SUNY, Albany, 1989; JD, Southwestern U., 1992; LLM in Taxation, Georgetown U., 1993. Bar: N.Y. 1994. Tax assoc. Arthur Andersen LLP, N.Y.C., 1993-95; asst. state tax counsel GE Capital, Stamford, Conn., 1995-96; assoc. Dechert Price & Rhoads, N.Y.C., 1996-98; sr. assoc. Baker & McKenzie, N.Y.C., 1998—; chairperson State Taxation Multinational Conf. Co-author: U.S. Tax of Foreign Controlled Business, 1994; contbr. articles to profl. jours. Dir. N.Am. Youth Hockey Found., Hampton, N.Y., 1993-97. Recipient STAR award Coun. of Internat. Tax Educators, 1997, 98. Mem. ABA, N.Y. State Bar Assn., N.Y.C. Bar Assn. Republican. Jewish. Avocations: golf, skiing, tennis. State and local taxation, Corporate taxation. Office: Baker & McKenzie 805 3rd Ave New York NY 10022-7513

**BRANDON, GEORGE IAN,** lawyer; b. N.Y.C., 1956. BA cum laude, Yale U., 1976; JD magna cum laude, U. Mich., 1980. Ptnr. Milbank, Tweed, Hadley & McCloy, N.Y.C., 1980-96, Steptoe & Johnson LLP, Phoenix, 1996—. Author: Data Processing Contracts, 3d edit., 1990. Lt., Plandome (N.Y.) Fire Dept., 1989-96; pros. atty. Village of Plandome, 1992-96. General civil litigation. Office: 2 Renaissance Sq 40 N Central Ave Ste 2400 Phoenix AZ 85004-4453

**BRANDRUP, DOUGLAS WARREN,** lawyer; b. Mitchel, S.D., July 11, 1940; s. Clair L. and Ruth M. (Wolverton) B.; m. Patricia R. Tuck, Dec. 20, 1986; children: Kendra, Monika, Peter. AB in Econs., Middlebury Coll., 1963; JD, Boston U., 1966. Bar: N.Y. 1969, U.S. Dist. Ct. (so. dist.) N.Y. 1970, U.S. Ct. Appeals (2d cir.) 1970. Assoc. Donovan, Leisure, Newton & Irvine, N.Y.C., 1968-72; ptnr. Griggs, Baldwin & Baldwin, N.Y.C., 1972-80, sr. ptnr., 1980—; chmn. Equity Oil Co.; bd. dirs. Ardshiel, Inc. Mem. Govs. Security Adv. Com., State of N.J., 1975-90. Capt. U.S. Army, 1966-68. Recipient Ellis Island medal of Honor, 1999. Mem. ABA, N.Y. County Bar Assn., N.Y. State Bar Assn., Met. Club (N.Y.C., pres.), Mashomack Preserve Club. Republican. Episcopalian. General corporate, Estate planning, General practice. Office: Griggs Baldwin & Baldwin 27 E 65th St Apt 7D New York NY 10021-6556

**BRANDSDORFER, MARK MICHAEL,** lawyer, accountant; b. Vineland, N.J., Aug. 31, 1968; s. Samuel and Ethel B.; m. Rochelle Lieberman, Nov. 20, 1994. BS with honors, Yeshiva U., N.Y.C., 1990; JD, Georgetown U., 1993. Bar: N.J. 1993, D.C. 1995, Md. 1996, U.S. Dist. Ct. N.J., N.Y. 1994, U.S. Tax Ct. 1994, U.S. Dist. Ct. D.C. 1995, U.S. Ct. Appeals (D.C. cir.) 1995, U.S. Dist. Ct. Md. 1999; CPA. Jr. acct. Karpman & Co. CPAs, N.Y.C., 1988-90; summer assoc. Eisenstat, Gabage et al., Vineland, N.J., 1992; assoc. Feldesman, Tucker et al., Washington, 1994-95; ptnr. Lieberman & Brandsdorfer LLC, Gaithersburg, Md., 1996—; bd. dirs. PelleTech Fuels, Inc., Chaffee, N.Y. Mem. ABA, D.C. Bar, Md. Bar Assn. Intellectual property, General corporate, General practice. Home and Office: 12221 Mcdonald Chapel Dr North Potomac MD 20878-2252

**BRANDT, EDWARD NEWMAN,** lawyer; b. Oklahoma City, Oct. 13, 1960; s. Edward N. Jr. and Patricia (Lawson) B.; m. Janice Faye Nichols, June 19, 1987. BA, St. Edward's U., 1985; JD, Tex. So. U., 1988. Bar: Tex. 1988, Okla. 1989, Va. 1991, Md. 1992, Miss. 1993, Ill. 1994, Ga. 1994, Colo. 1994, N.C. 1994, Fla. 1995, U.S. Ct. Appeals (5th cir.) 1994. Ptnr. Brandt & Brandt, Houston, 1988-93, Law Office of Vaughan de Kirby, Boulder, Colo., 1993-96; pvt. practice Dallas, 1996—. Personal injury, Insurance. Office: 10560 Walnut St Ste 550 Dallas TX 75243-5351

**BRANDT, WILLIAM ARTHUR, JR.,** consulting executive; b. Chgo., Sept. 5, 1949; s. William Arthur and Joan Virginia (Ashworth) B.; m. Patrice Bugelas, Jan. 19, 1980; children: Katherine Ashworth, William George, Joan Patrice, John Peter. BA with honors, St. Louis U., 1971; MA, U. Chgo., 1972, postgrad., 1972-74. Asst. to pres. Pyro Mining Co., Chgo., 1972-74; commentator Sta. WBBM-AM, Chgo., 1977; with Melaniphy & Assocs., Inc., Chgo., 1975-76; pres., cons. Devel. Specialists, Inc., Chgo., 1976—; mem. adv. bd. Sociol. Abstracts, Inc., San Diego, 1979-83. Contbr. articles to profl. jours. Trustee Fenwick H.S., 1991-99, Comml. Law League of Am., Internat. Coun. Shopping Ctrs., Nat. Assn. Bankruptcy Trustees, Ill. Sociol. Assn., Midwest Sociol. Soc., Urban Land Inst. LaVerne Noyes scholar, 1971-74. Mem. Am. Bankruptcy Inst., Am. Sociol. Assn., Amelia Island Plantation Club, Union League Club Chgo., City Club of Miami, sust. fellow of Art Inst. of Chicago, gov. mem. Chicago Symphony, Clinton/Gore '96 Natl. Finance Bd., mnging. trustee Democratic Natl. Comm., maj. trust mem. Democratic Senatorial Campaign Comm., life mem. Zoological Soc. of the Miami Metro Zoo. Democrat. Roman Catholic. Home: 2000 S Bayshore Dr Apt 39 Coconut Grove FL 33133-3251 also: Amelia Island Plantation 6518 Beachwood Rd Amelia Island FL 32034-6512 also: 1134 Sheridan Rd Winnetka IL 60093-1538 also: 23 Sea Colony Dr Santa Monica CA 90405-5321 Office: 3 First Nat Plz Ste 2300 Chicago IL 60602 also: 200 S Biscayne Blvd Ste 900 Miami FL 33131-2310 also: Devonshire House, 60 Goswell Rd, London EC1M 7AD, England also: Wells Fargo Ctr 333 S Grand Ave Ste 2010 Los Angeles CA 90071-1524 also: Two Oliver St 11th Fl Boston MA 02109-4901

**BRANHAM, C. MICHAEL,** lawyer; b. Columbia, S.C., Nov. 6, 1957; s. Mack C. and Jennie Louise (Jones) B.; m. Teresa Barrett; children: Anthony, Mark. BS, Auburn U., Montgomery, Ala., 1979; JD, U. S.C., 1983. Bar: S.C.; cert. tax law specialist; CPA. Acct. Wilson, Price, Barranco & Billingsley, CPAs, Montgomery, 1979-80; law clk. Atty. Gen.'s Office, State of S.C., Columbia, 1981-82; acct. Price, Waterhouse, Columbia, 1983-86; tax lawyer Young, Clement, Rivers & Tisdale, LLP, Charleston, S.C., 1986—, chmn. tax, estate planning and probate group, mem. mgmt. com, 1999—; chmn. taxation law specialization adv. bd. S.C. Supreme Ct., 1995-97; mem., pres. Charleston Tax. Coun., 1993-94; mem. dean's adv. bd. Med. U. S.C. Nursing Sch., Charleston, 1994-97; chmn. MUSC Planned Giving adv. coun., 1993-97; mem. exec. com. Roper Found. Planned Giving Coun., Charleston; S.C. case reporter ABA sect. real property, probate and trust law, 1997—; mem. Bishop Gadsden Estate Planning Adv. Coun., Charleston, 1998—. Soccer coach Hungryneck Internat. Soccer Assn., Mt. Pleasant, S.C., 1989-99; mem. Charleston Estate Planning Coun.; coach James Is. Trident United Soccer Club, 1999—. Recipient Am. Jurisprudence award, 1983. Mem. ABA, AICPA, S.C. Assn. CPAs, S.C. Bar Assn., Charleston Breakfast Rotary. Avocations: soccer coaching, weight lifting. Estate taxation, Probate, Estate planning. Home: 829 Detyens Rd Mount Pleasant SC 29464-5181 Office: Young Clement Rivers & Tisdale LLP 28 Broad St Charleston SC 29401-3070

**BRANHAM, MELANIE J.,** lawyer; b. Kansas City, Mo., Nov. 22, 1960; d. John Francis II and Annette (Bowers) B. BA, U. Kans., 1983, MUP, 1985; JD, We. New Eng. Coll., 1994. Bar: Kans. 1994, Mo. 1995, U.S. Ct. Appeals (10th cir.) 1994, U.S. Ct. Appeals (8th cir.) 1995, U.S. Supreme Ct. 1997. Grad. planner City of Lawrence, Kans., 1984; city planner City of Overland Park, Kans., 1984-85; asst. dir. planning and inspections City of Merriam, Kans., 1985-87; city adminstr. City of Westwood, Kans., 1987-89; town adminstr. Town of Sheffield, Mass., 1989-91; law clk. We. Mass. Legal Svcs., Springfield, Mass., 1992-93; atty./law clk. Kans. Legal Svcs., Olathe, 1993-94; assoc. Johnson County Dist. Atty.'s Office, Olathe, 1994; pvt. practice Olathe, 1994—. Active Nelson-Atkins Mus. of Art, Kansas City, Mo., 1986—; mem. ACLU of Kans. and We. Mo., Kansas City, Mo., 1992—. With CAP Aux., lt. col. USAF, 1972-76. Named to Outstanding Young Women of Am., 1987; recipient Am. Jurisprudence award, 1993. Mem. ABA, Assn. Trial Lawyers Am., Kans. Trial Lawyers Assn., Johnson County Bar Assn., Kans. Bar Assn., Mo. Bar Assn. Unitarian. General civil litigation, Criminal, General practice. Office: 113 S Kansas Ave Olathe KS 66061-4434

**BRANIGAN, THOMAS PATRICK,** lawyer; b. Detroit, Aug. 6, 1963; s. John Thomas and Nancy May (Palmer) B.; m. Carolyn Marie O'Shea, May 27, 1989; 2 children. BA, Wayne State U., 1985; JD cum laude, Detroit Coll. Law, 1988. Bar: Mich. 1988, U.S. Dist. Ct. (ea. dist.) Mich. 1988, U.S. Dist. Ct. (we. dist.) Mich. 1991, U.S. 6th Dist Ct. Appeals, 1996. Assoc. Plunkett & Cooney, Detroit, 1988-91; assoc. Bowman & Brooke, Detroit, 1991-94, ptnr., 1995—; speaker Def. Rsch. Inst. Young Lawyer's Trial Techniques Seminar, 1992, 93. Editor-in-chief Detroit Coll. of Law Rev., 1987-88. Recipient Trial Advocacy award Am. Jurisprudence, 1987, Louis J. Colombo award Detroit Coll. of Law, 1988, Finch Evidence award 1987, Edward Rakow award Detroit Fed. Bar Assn., 1988. Mem. ABA (Automotive Products Subcom.), Def. Rsch. Inst., Detroit Bar Assn., Soc. Automotive Engrs. Roman Catholic. Avocations: family, sailing. E-mail: TBraniga@Bowman-Brooke.com. General civil litigation, Product liability, Contracts commercial. Office: Bowman & Brooke 3011 W Grand Blvd # 3011 Detroit MI 48202-3096

**BRANIGIN, ROGER D., JR.,** lawyer; b. Louisville, Mar. 1, 1931; s. Roger D. and Josephine M. Branigin; m. Marilyn Bechdolt, 1961; children: Elizabeth H. Branigin Cayton, Roger D. III, John F. AB magna cum laude, Dartmouth Coll., 1952; LLB cum laude, Harvard U., 1955. Bar: Ind. 1955. Assoc. Stuart & Branigin, 1957-62, ptnr., 1962—. Trustee Lafayette Sch. Corp., 1963-64, 65-69, pres., 1968-69, United Community Svcs., 1967-68, Capital Funds Found., 1983-84, Tippecanoe County Boys Club, 1976-77; dir. Nat. Homes Corp., 1978-90; chmn. United Way Campaign, 1984; dir. Lafayette Home Hosp., 1978-84, Westminster Village West Lafayette, West Lafayette Econ. Devel. Commn.; dir., North Cen. Health Svcs., 1984—, vice chmn. 1994-96, chmn., 1996—; former trustee Cen. Presbyn. Ch. With U.S. Army, 1955-57, USAR, 1957-59. Fellow Am. Coll. Trust and Estate Counsel, Ind. Bar Found.; mem. ABA, Ind. State Bar Assn., Tippecanoe County Bar Assn. (pres. 1974-75). General corporate, Finance, Probate. Office: PO Box 1010 Lafayette IN 47902-1010

**BRANNEN, JEFFREY RICHARD,** lawyer; b. Tampa, Fla., Aug. 27, 1945; s. Jackson Edward and Tobiah M. (Lovitz) B.; m. Mary Elizabeth Strand, Nov. 24, 1972; 1 child, Samuel Jackson. BA in English, U. N.Mex., 1967, JD, 1970. Bar: N.Mex. 1970, U.S. Dist. Ct. N.Mex. 1970, U.S. Ct. Appeals (10th cir.) 1976, U.S. Supreme Ct. 1978. Law clk. N.Mex. State Supreme Ct., Santa Fe, 1970-71; from assoc. to pres., shareholder Montgomery & Andrews, pa, Santa Fe, 1972-93; pres. Jeffrey R. Brannen, P.A., Santa Fe, 1993—; of counsel Carpenter, Comeau, Maldegan, Nixon & Templeman, Santa Fe, 1995—; faculty Nat. Inst. Trial Advocacy, Hastings Ctr. for Trial & Appellate Advocacy, 1980-93; co-chmn. Pers. Injury Inst., Hastings, 1992. Mem. ABA, Am. Bd. Trial Advocates, Assn. Def. Trial Attys. (state chmn. 1992—), Def. Rsch. Inst. (Exceptional Performance Citation 1989), N.Mex. Def. Lawyers Assn. (pres. 1989). Democrat. Avocations: skiing, soccer, fly fishing, travel. Product liability, Personal injury, General civil litigation. Office: Carpenter Comeau Maldegan Nixon & Templeman 141 E Palace Ave Santa Fe NM 87501-2041

**BRANNEN, JOHN HOWARD,** lawyer; b. Dover, Ohio, July 22, 1949; s. Howard G. and Margaret A. (Shoemaker) B. BA summa cum laude, Ohio U., 1972; JD cum laude, U. Mich., 1975. Bar: Ohio 1975, Fla. 1984, U.S. Dist. Ct. (no. dist.) Ohio 1975, U.S. Ct. Appeals (6th cir.) 1984. Ptnr. Day, Ketterer, Raley, Wright & Rybolt Ltd., Canton, Ohio, 1975—. Trustee Goodwill Industries Rehab. Ctr., Canton, 1979—, Stark County Law Libr., 1987—. Mem. ABA, Ohio Bar Assn., Fla. Bar, Stark County Bar Assn., Rotary Club of Canton, Phi Beta Kappa. Avocations: personal computers, reading, travel, swimming. Securities, Contracts commercial, General corporate. Home: 911 Knollwood Dr NW Canton OH 44708-3424 Office: Day Ketterer Raley Wright & Rybolt Ltd 121 Cleveland Ave SW Ste 800 Canton OH 44702-1914

**BRANNEY, JOSEPH JOHN,** lawyer; b. Casper, Wyo., Aug. 22, 1938; s. John J. and Frances M. (Stanko) B.; m. Sheryl Ann Branney; children: Scott W., John J., Sean W. BA, U. Colo., 1960; JD, U. Denver, 1962. Bar: Colo. 1963, Wyo. 1963. Assoc. Myrick, Criswell & Branney, Englewood, Colo., 1963-69; sole practice Englewood, 1969-72; ptnr. Branney, Hillyard, Ewing & Barnes, Englewood, 1982-85, Branney, Hillyard, Kudla & Lee, Englewood, 1986-95, Branney, Hillyard & Barnhart, Englewood, 1995—; prof. law U. Denver, 1964—. Mem. Wyo. Bar Assn., Arapahoe County Bar Assn., Assn. Trial Lawyers Am., Colo. Trial Lawyers Assn. (pres. 1966-67), Nat. Bd. Trial Advocacy (cert. civil trial adv. 1983), Internat. Soc. of Barristers. Republican. Personal injury, Federal civil litigation, State civil litigation. Home: 1717 E Stanford Ave Englewood CO 80110-6014 Office: Branney Hillyard & Barnhart LLP 7887 E Belleview Ave Ste 1200 Englewood CO 80111-6027

**BRANNON, DAVE LEE,** lawyer; b. Danville, Ill., May 8, 1953; s. Louis Marion and Barbara Jean (Addams) B.; m. Pamela Tarquino, Feb. 21, 1986. BS with honors, USCG Acad., 1975; JD, U. Miami, Coral Gables, Fla., 1980. Bar: Fla. 1980, U.S. Dist. Ct. (so. dist.) Fla. 1982, U.S. Dist. Ct. (mid. dist.) Fla. 1988, U.S. Ct. Appeals (11th cir.) 1986. Commd. ensign USCG, 1975, advanced through grades to lt., 1979; navigator, deck watch officer USCG, Long Beach, Calif., 1975-77; asst. legal officer USCG, Miami, Fla., 1980-84, intelligence officer, 1984-86; resigned USCG, 1986; asst. fed. pub. defender U.S. Dist. Ct. (so. dist.) Fla., West Palm Beach, 1986—; adj. prof. Fla. Atlantic U., Boca Raton, 1990—. Mem. Nat. Mil. Intelligence Assn., U.S. Naval Inst. (life), Craig Barnard Inn of Ct. Office: Fed Pub Defender 400 S Australian Ave Ste 300 West Palm Beach FL 33401-5040

**BRANSON, ALBERT HAROLD (HARRY BRANSON),** judge, educator; b. Chgo., May 20, 1935; s. Fred Brooks and Marie (Vowell) B.; m. Siri-Anne Gudrun Lindberg, Nov. 2, 1963; children: Gunnar John, Gulliver Dean, Hannah Marie, Siri Elizabeth. BA, Northwestern U., 1957; JD, U. Chgo., 1963. Bar: Pa. 1965, Alaska 1972. Atty. Richard McVeigh law offices, Anchorage, 1972-73; ptnr. Jacobs, Branson & Guetschow, Anchorage, 1973-76, Branson & Guetschow, Anchorage, 1976-82; pvt. practice Law Offices of Harry Branson, Anchorage, 1982-84, 85-89; atty. Branson, Bazeley & Chisolm, Anchorage, 1984-85; U.S. magistrate judge U.S. Dist. Ct., Anchorage, 1989—; instr., adj. prof. U. Alaska Justice Ctr., 1980-93; U.S. magistrate, Anchorage, 1975-76. Mem. steering com. Access to Civil Justice Task Force, 1997-98. With U.S. Army, 1957-59. Mem. Alaska Bar Assn. (bd. dirs., v.p. bd. govs. 1977-80, 83-86, pres. bd. govs. 1986, Disting. Svc. award 1992, Spl. Svc. award 1988, editor-in-chief Alaska Bar Rag 1978-86), Anchorage Bar Assn. (bd. dirs., bd. govs. 1982-86), Anchorage Inn of Ct. (pres. 1995). Democrat. Avocations: book collecting, cooking, poetry. Office: US Dist Ct 222 W 7th Ave Unit 33 Anchorage AK 99513-7504

**BRANSON, DEBBIE DUDLEY,** lawyer; b. Jonesboro, Ark., Jan. 17, 1955; d. Robert H. and Sally A. (Wentzell) Dudley; m. Frank L. Branson, July 4, 1986; children: Jennifer, Buck. BS in English, Ark. State U., 1977; JD, U. Ark., 1980; MS, U. Tex., Dallas, 1993. Bar: Ark. 1980, Tex. 1981. Atty. Arnold, Lavender, Rochelle, Barnette & Franks, Texarkana, Ark., 1980-83, Law Offices of Frank L. Branson, Dallas, 1983—; mem. Tex. Jud. Coun., Austin, 1992—; chair Select Com. on Rate and Policy Form Regulation, Austin, 1994; vice chair, bd. trustees Securities Investor Protection Corp., Washington, 1995-98, chair budget com., 1998—. Editor (periodical) Tex. Trial Lawyers Forum, 1991-94; contbr. articles to profl. jours. Mem. Jr. League Dallas; bd. dirs. AIDS Interfaith Network, 1993; bd. dirs. Nat. Com. for Prevention of Child Abuse, 1995, Dallas Women's Found., 1994—, pres.-elect (exec. com.) 1998, pres. 1999, Planned parenthood, 1995—, sec. (exec. com.) 1998; mem. fin. coun. Dallas County Dem. Party; mem. LWV Dallas; Tex. chair Women's Leadership Forum; mng. trustee Dem. Nat. Com., 1992-93, 96-97, bd. dirs. Mem. ABA, Assn. Trial Lawyers Am., Am. Soc. Writers on Legal Subjects, Tex. Jud. Coun., Tex. Trial Lawyers Assn. (comm. com. 1992-93, budget and fin. com. 1993-94, chair 1996, sec./treas. 1996, bd. dirs., pres.-elect 1999), Ark. Trial Lawyers Assn., Ark. Bar Assn., State Bar Tex., Dallas Bar Assn. (publs. com. 1990), Dallas Women Lawyers Assn., Texarkana Bar Assn. (sec./treas. 1981-82), Coll. State Bar Tex., 112th Am. Inn of Ct., DAR (chmn. pub. rels. 1990, 91, corr. sec. 1992-94). Personal injury. Office: Law Offices Frank L Branson Highland Park Pl 4514 Cole Ave Ste 1800 Dallas TX 75205-4185

**BRANSON, FRANK LESLIE, III,** law corporation executive; b. Deport, Tex., Feb. 10, 1945; s. Frank Leslie B. Jr.; m. Debbie Dudley; children: Frank IV, Jennifer. BA, Tex. Christian U., 1967; JD, So. Meth. U., 1969, LLM, 1974. Bar: Tex. 1969. Assoc. Watson & Parkhill, Grand Prairie, Tex., 1969; assoc. Bader, Wilson, Menaker, Cox & Branson, Dallas, 1970-75, ptnr., 1975-77; pvt. practice Dallas, 1978—; lectr. personal injury topics State Bar Tex., Am. Trial Lawyers Assn.; mem. adv. com. Tex. Supreme Ct., 1985-86. Contbr. over 20 articles on personal injury litigation to profl. jours.; four arguments to Million Dollar Argument tapes, (with Matthew Bender) Malpractice video tape series, 1982. Mem. Dallas Dem. Fin. Council, 1985-86; bd. dirs. Garland (Tex.) Community Hosp., 1981, 82-84. Mem. Am. Bd. Trial Advs. (pres. Dallas chpt. 1982), Dallas Trial Lawyers Assn. (pres. 1976-77), Tex. Trial Lawyers Assn. (bd. dirs. 1972-94), Am. Trial Lawyers Coll. Med. Malpractice (dean 1985), Med. Malpractice Com. (chmn. 1974-75, 79), So. Trial Lawyers Assn. (pres. 1988-89), Royal Oaks Country Club, Chapparal Club, 2001 Club, ATLA (bd. govs., 1988—), Lochinvar Country Club. Criminal, State civil litigation, Personal injury. Office: 4514 Cole Ave Ste 1800 Dallas TX 75205-4185

**BRANSON, JOHN R.,** lawyer; b. Jackson, Miss., July 30, 1959; s. James F. and Janet E. Branson; m. Paula K. McConnell, Jan. 7, 1984 (div. Mar. 1996). BBA, U. Miss., 1981, JD, 1984. Bar: Miss. 1984, Tenn. 1984. Assoc. Baker, Donelson, Bearman & Caldwell, Memphis, 1984-91, ptnr., 1991-95; ptnr. Branson & Bearman, Memphis, 1995—. Bd. mem. Goodwill Homes, Inc., Memphis, 1997—. Mem. Tenn. Bar Assn. (mem., chair gen., solo, small firm practice sect. 1997—). Avocations: motorcycling, hiking. General civil litigation, Family and matrimonial, Personal injury. Office: Branson & Bearman 44 N 2nd St Ste 701 Memphis TN 38103-2266

**BRANSTAD, CHRISTINE ELLEN,** lawyer; b. Forest City, Iowa, Nov. 23, 1968; d. Monroe David and Elizabeth Ellen B.; m. David Lee Phillips, June 14, 1997. BS, U. Iowa, 1991; JD, Drake U., 1994. Bar: Iowa 1995, D.C. 1995, U.S. Dist. Ct. (so. dist.) Iowa 1997. Rsch. asst. Drake Law Sch., Des Moines, 1993-94; prosecuting intern Polk County Attys., Des Moines, 1993; law clk. Verne Lawyer & Assocs., Des Moines, 1992-94; asst. county atty. Jasper County, Newton, 1995-97; atty. Hopkins & Huebner, Des Moines, 1997—; spkr. in field. Co-editor: Trial Handbook Supplement, 1993. Mem. ABA, Assn. Trial Lawyers Am. (asst. editor 1992-93, Iowa Bar Assn., Iowa Trial Lawyers Assn., Iowa Sex Crimes Investigators Assn., Jasper County Bar Assn., Blackstone Inn Ct. Avocations: sports, skiing, reading, swimming, scuba diving. Personal injury, Workers' compensation, Criminal. Home: 10993 Lincoln Ave Des Moines IA 50325-7049 Office: Hopkins & Huebner 2700 Grand Ave Ste 111 Des Moines IA 50312-5213

**BRANSTETTER, CECIL DEWEY, SR.,** lawyer; b. Deer Lodge, Tenn., Dec. 15, 1920; s. Miller Henry and Lillie Mae (Adams) B.; m. Charlotte Virginia Coleman, Aug. 5, 1944; children: Kay Frances Johnson, Linda Charlotte Mauk, Kathy Jane Stranch , Cecil Dewey Jr. BA, George Washington U., 1947; JD, Vanderbilt U., 1949. Bar: U.S. Supreme Ct. 1957, U.S. Ct. Appeals (6th cir.) 1963. Ptnr. Branstetter, Kilgore, Stranch & Jennings, Nashville, 1990—; Chmn. Bd. Profl. Responsibility Supreme Ct. Tenn. Contbr. articles to profl. jours. Mem. Gen. Assembly Tenn., Nashville, 1950-53; chmn. Charter Commn. and Charter Revision Commn., Nashville, 1957-62, 78-90; mem. Met. Action Commn., Nashville, 1964-68; pres. Coun. Community Agys. and Tenn. Environ. Coun., Nashville, 1970, 71-73. Sgt. U.S. Army, 1943-46, lt. Res., 1946-52, ETO. Mem. ACLU (bd. dirs.), ABA, Met. Human Rels. Commn., Am. Judicature Soc., Tenn. Conservation League (Carter Patten award), Am. Trial Lawyers Assn., Tenn. Bar Assn., Tenn. Trial Lawyers Assn., Nashville Bar Assn., Davidson County Sportsman Club, Order of Coif. Democrat. Baptist. Avocations: farming, fishing, hunting, raising Angus cattle. Labor, Public utilities, Workers' compensation.

**BRANT, JOHN GETTY,** lawyer; b. Apr. 13, 1946. BBA, U. Okla., 1968; JD, U. Tex., 1972. Bar: Tex. 1972, Colo. 1974, U.S. Dist. Ct. Colo. 1974, U.S. Tax Ct. 1974. Atty. IRS, Houston, 1972-74; ptnr. Bradley, Campbell & Carney, Golden, Colo., 1975-83, Doussard, Brant, Hodel & Markman, Lakewood, Colo., 1983-86; sole practice Wheat Ridge, Colo., 1986—; arbitrator Nat. Assn. Securities Dealers. Bd. dirs. U. Tex. Law Sch. Assn., Austin, 1983-86, Nat. Multiple Sclerosis Soc., Denver, 1975-91. Mem. State Bar of Tex., Colo. Bar Assn., Centennial Estate Planning Coun. (pres. 1976), Denver Estate Planning Coun. Estate taxation, Probate, Estate planning. Office: 4251 Kipling St Unit 390 Wheat Ridge CO 80033-6802

**BRANTLEY, JOHN RANDOLPH,** lawyer; b. Freeport, Tex., Oct. 1, 1951; m. Joan Lawlor, May 17, 1975; children: Brian C., David R., Caroline E. BBA magna cum laude, St. Mary's U., 1974, JD, 1977. Bar: Tex. 1977. Assoc. Bracewell & Patterson LLP, Houston, 1977-83, ptnr., 1983—. Fellow Tex. Bar Foun., Houston Bar Found.; mem. ABA, Tex. Bar Assn., Houston Bar Assn. (coun. antitrust sect. 1989-96, vice chmn. 1993-94, chmn. 1994-95), Phi Delta Phi. Antitrust, Securities, General corporate. Office: Bracewell & Patterson LLP 2900 S Tower Pennzoil Pl Houston TX 77002

**BRANTNER, PAULA ANN,** lawyer; b. St. Louis, Apr. 7, 1967; d. Ronald D. and Phyllis C. B. BA, Mich. State U., 1989; JD, U. Calif., San Francisco, 1992. Bar: Calif. 1992, U.S. Dist. Ct. (no. dist.) Calif. 1992, U.S. Dist. Ct. (ea. dist.) Calif. 1996, U.S. Ct. Appeals (9th cir.) 1992, U.S. Ct. Appeals (5th cir.) 1998, U.S. Ct. Appeals (6th and 10th cirs.) 1999, U.S. Supreme Ct. 1998. Felix Velarde-Munoz fellow Employment Ctr.-Legal Aid Soc., 1992-93; pvt. practice, San Francisco, 1993-94, 95; interim legal dir. Nat. Ctr. Lesbian Rights, San Francisco, 1994; assoc. Siegel & LeWitter, Oakland, Calif., 1995-97; sr. staff atty. Nat. Employment Lawyers Assn., San Francisco, 1997—. Contbr. articles to profl. jours. Bd. dirs. Bay Area Lawyers for Individual Freedom, San Francisco, 1993-95; bd. dirs., co-chair civil rights LIFE Lobby, Sacramento, Calif., 1994-97. Mem. State Bar Calif. (human rights com. 1993-97, chair 1996-97, mem. com. on sexual orientation discrimination 1997—, vice chair 1999—). Labor, Civil rights, Appellate. Office: Nat Employment Lawyers Assn 600 Harrison St Ste 535 San Francisco CA 94107-1370

**BRANTON, JAMES LAVOY,** lawyer; b. Albany, Tex., Apr. 19, 1938; s. George Lyndon Branton and Oletha Imogene (Westerman) Johnson; m. Molly Branton, May 18, 1968; children: Christina, Victoria, Claudia. BA, U. Tex., 1961, LLB, 1962. Bar: Tex., U.S. Dist. Ct. (we., so, ea. and no. dists.) Tex., U.S. Ct. Appeals (5th cir.). Ptnr. Hardberger, Branton & Herrera, Inc., San Antonio, 1974-78, Branton & Mendelsohn, Inc., San Antonio, 1978-83, Branton, Hall, Warncke & Gonzales, P.C., San Antonio, 1983-88, Branton & Hall, P.C., San Antonio, 1988—; bd. dirs. Tex. Lawyers Ins. Exch. Co-author: Trial Lawyer's Series, 1981-91. Capt. USAF, 1962-65. Fellow Am. Coll. Trial Lawyers (state com. 1993-95, chair 1996-98), Internat. Soc. Barristers, Internat. Acad. Trial Lawyers, Tex. Bar Found. (chair 1989-90); mem. Tex. Trial Lawyers Assn. (pres. 1975-76), State Bar Tex. (pres. 1994-95), Am. Bd. Trial Advocates (pres. San Antonio chpt. 1990-91, Tex. Trial Lawyer of Yr. 1994). Avocations: flying, scuba diving. Personal injury, Product liability, Professional liability. Home: 403 Evans Ave San Antonio TX 78209-3725 Office: Branton & Hall PC 711 Navarro St Ste 737 San Antonio TX 78205-1787

**BRAS, ROBERT W.,** lawyer; b. Toronto, Ont., Can., Aug. 1967; s. Robert W. and Kerrie L. Bras; m. Julie A. Matonich, July 1998. BSFS with honors, Georgetown U., 1990; JD magna cum laude, George Washington U., 1994. Bar: Pa. 1994, D.C. 1995, U.S. Ct. of Internat. Trade 1995, U.S. Ct. Appeals (fed. cir.) 1995. Atty. Dorsey & Whitney LLP, Washington, 1994-98, Mpls., 1998—. Mem. Order of Coif. Private international, Federal civil litigation, Administrative and regulatory. Office: Dorsey & Whitney LLP Pillsbury Ctr S 220 S 6th St Ste 2200 Minneapolis MN 55402-1498

**BRASHEAR, JAMES THOMAS,** lawyer; b. Cleve., Dec. 17, 1934; s. Charles O'Niel and Jessi Lee (Drugoo) B.; m. Carol Ann Rowely, Jan. 1, 1956 (div. Sept. 1974); children: Barbara Alice, John Thomas; m. Lori Joan Becker, Mar. 7, 1989. Student, Domiguez Hills El Camino Coll., 1977-78; BA, Calif. State U., Carson, 1980; JD, Loyola U., 1984. Bar: Calif., 1999. Dep. pub. defender John A. Barker, Madera, Calif., 1990-92; supr. atty. Fresno Juvenile Ct. Office John A. Barker, Fresno, Calif., 1992-94, asst. chief def. atty., 1993-96, surperior ct. trial atty., 1994-95, supr. atty. juvenile hall, 1996; chief def. atty. Alt. Def., Fresno, 1997—. Mem. Christian Businessmen's Com., Nat. Rifle Assn. (life), Calif. Bar Assn., Fresno County Bar Assn., Madera County Bar Assn. Republican. Avocations: history, model trains, oil painting, gardening. Office: Alt Def Office 123 N D St Madera CA 93638-3200

**BRASHEAR, WILLIAM RONALD,** lawyer; b. Royal Oak, Mich., Oct. 8, 1932; s. William Wilson and Theresa Elizabeth (Briggi) B.; m. Lydia Mary Rothman Brashear, Jan. 1961 (dec. Apr. 1988); children: Ruth Margot, Lydia Louise. BA, U. Mich., Ann Arbor, 1953, MA, 1956, JD, 1956; MA, Princeton U., N.J., 1958, PhD, 1959. Mich., 1967, U.S. Dist. Ct. (so. dist.) Mich. 1957, U.S. Ct. Appeals (6th cir.) 1973, U.S. Supreme Ct., 1977. Ptnr. Brashear, Tangora & Spence, Livonia, Mich., 1958—; adj. lectr., English Wayne State U., Detroit, 1959-71. Mem. Livonia Rotary Club. General practice, General corporate, Probate.

**BRASSFIELD, EUGENE EVERETT,** lawyer; b. Livingston County, Ill., July 17, 1933; s. Everett Francis and Margaret (Sedory) B.; m. Judith Runge, Aug. 30, 1959 (div. Mar. 1980); m. Betty Patricia Brooks, Jan. 16, 1982; children: Bradley, Jeffry, David, Kenda, Deborah. BA, Valparaiso U., 1959, JD, 1961. Bar: Ill. 1962, U.S. Dist.Ct. (no. and we. dists.) Ill. 1962, U.S. Ct. Appeals (7th cir.) 1974. Prosecuting atty., asst. states atty. Winnebago County, Rockford, Ill., 1962-63; atty. Brassfield, Cowan & Krueger (formerly Maynard & Maynard), 1963—; cons. Woodward Gov. Co., Rockford, 1984—; bd. dirs., State Line found. Co., Roscoe, Ill., 1989-90; mem. Ill. Supreme Ct. commn. adminstrn. justice, 1991-93. Bd. govs. P.A. Peterson Home, Rockford, 1988-93, pres., 1992-94; bd. dirs. Rockford Luth. High Sch., 1964-70; chmn. Our Savior's Luth. Ch., Rockford, 1986-87. With USMC, 1953-56. Recipient Valparaiso U. Alumni Svc. award, 1988. Mem. Ill. State Bar Assn., Winnebago County Bar Assn. Republican. Avocations: golf, hunting, fishing. General corporate, Personal injury. Home: 11 Ridge Rd Streator IL 61364-1427 Office: Brassfield Cowan & Krueger PO Box 590 Rockford IL 61105-0590 also: 203 Armory Ct Streator IL 61364-2768

**BRASWELL, BRUCE WAYNE,** lawyer, educator; b. Amarillo, Tex., June 5, 1955; s. Harvey Leonard and Iva Pearl Braswell; m. Maureen Louise Conklin, June 18, 1988; children: Paul Leonard, Peter Wayne. BA in Math., Eastern Nazarene Coll., Quincy, Mass., 1978, BA in Psychology, 1978; JD, Bklyn. Law Sch., 1983. Bar: N.Y. Sole practitioner Peekskill, N.Y., 1985-88, Poughkeepsie, N.Y., 1988—. Bd. dirs., sec. Ch. of Nazarene, 1988—. Mem. Rotary (newsletter editor 1988—). Conservative. Avocation: chess. Family and matrimonial, General practice, Real property. Home and Office: 30 Manchester Rd Poughkeepsie NY 12603-2412

**BRASWELL, EDWIN MAURICE, JR.,** lawyer; b. Fayetteville, N.C., Mar. 6, 1952; s. Edwin Maurice Sr. and Ruth (Cox) B.; children: Edwin Maurice III, Anna Elizabeth. BSBA, U. N.C., 1973; JD cum laude, N.C. Cen. U., 1978. Bar: N.C. 1978, U.S. Dist. Ct. (ea. dist.) N.C. 1978, U.S. Ct. Appeals (4th cir.) 1985. Law clk. to hon. judge Burley Mitchell N.C. Ct. of Appeals, Raleigh, 1978-79; asst. dist. atty. 8th Prosecuting Dist., Kinston, N.C., 1979-82; ptnr. Wallace, Morris & Barwick, P.A., Kinston, 1982—. Vice pres. legis. affairs com. Lenoir County C. of C., Kinston, 1987-88. Mem. N.C. Assn. Def. Attys., Def. Rsch. Inst., 8th Dist. Bar Assn. (pres. 1988-89), Lenoir County Bar Assn. (pres. 1985). Methodist. Avocations: boating, tennis. State civil litigation, Insurance. Home: 120 Walnut Creek Dr Goldsboro NC 27534-8942 Office: Wallace Morris & Barwick PA PO Box 3557 Kinston NC 28502-3557

**BRASWELL, WALTER E.,** prosecutor; b. Shreveport, La., Apr. 2, 1954. BA, U. Ala., 1976, JD, 1979. Bar: Ala. 1979. Pvt. practice Tuscaloosa, Ala., 1979-86, 93; adminstrv. asst. to Rep. Claude Harris (Dem., Ala.), 1987-93; sr. litigation officer U.S. Dist. Ct. (no. dist.) Ala., Birmingham, 1995—; U.S. atty. Active Birmingham Com. Fgn. Rels. William Randolph Hearst scholar. Mem. Ala. Bar Assn. Methodist. Office: US Attorney for No Dist Ala Federal Bldg 1800 5th Ave N Ste 200 Birmingham AL 35203-2189

**BRASZO, JOHN J.,** lawyer; b. Braddock, Pa., Feb. 22, 1950; s. Clement C. and Helen E. B.; m. Lori A. Braszo, Sept. 15, 1984. BA, W. Va. U., 1972, MA, 1973; JD, Duquesne U., 1981. Bar: Pa., U.S. Dist. Ct. (no. dist.) Pa. Pvt. practice Pitts., 1993—. Workers' compensation, Personal injury, General civil litigation. Office: 1040 5th Ave 8 Pittsburgh PA 15219

**BRATT, HERBERT SIDNEY,** lawyer; b. Milw., Sept. 8, 1931; s. Ishmael and Freda (Nelson) B.; m. Rosalee Bender, Dec. 22, 1957; children: Jay, Annie, Jennifer. BS, U. Wis., 1953; JD, Yale U., 1956. Bar: Wis. 1956, N.Y. 1981. Assoc. M.J. Levin, Milw., 1956-61; ptnr. Bratt & Shapiro, Milw., 1961-64, Zubrensky, Padden, Graf & Bratt, Milw., 1964-80, Laikin, Bratt & Laikin, Milw., 1980-81; pvt. practice Milw., 1981-91; ptnr. Churchill, Duback & Smith, Milw., 1991-94; pvt. practice Milw., 1994—; chpt. 7 panel trustee U.S. Trustee's Office for Ea. Dist. Wis., Milw., 1984-90. Trustee, Congregation Sinai, Milw., 1972-86, pres., 1979-81. Recipient William Gorham Rice Civil Liberties award Wis. Civil Liberties Union, 1968. Mem. ABA, Am. Judicature Soc., State Bar Wis., N.Y. Bar Assn., Milw. Bar Assn. Avocation: running. General corporate, Real property, Probate. Home: 1610 N Prospect Ave Apt 201 Milwaukee WI 53202-2402 Office: 735 N Water St Ste 704 Milwaukee WI 53202-4104

**BRATTAIN, RICHARD HOWARD,** lawyer; b. Toledo, Ohio, May 1, 1955; m. Susan Kay Fong, May 20, 1990. AA, Santa Barbara City Coll., 1978; BA, San Francisco State U., 1980; JD, Golden Gate U., 1985. Bar: Calif. 1987, Nev. 1988, U.S. Ct. Appeals (9th cir.) 1987, U.S. Dist. Ct. (ea. and no. dist.) Calif. 1987, U.S. Dist. Ct. Nev. 1989. Assoc. Law Office of Doan and Vu, San Jose, 1987-88, Law Office of James Sitter, Las Vegas, Nev., 1988-89, Law Office of Leslie Stovall, Las Vegas, Nev., 1989, Law Office of George Bochanis, Las Vegas, Nev., 1989-91; pvt. practice law Las Vegas, Nev., 1991—. Vol. mediator Clark County Neighborhood Justice Ctr., Las Vegas, 1992—. Mem. Assn. Trial Lawyers Am., Nev. Trial Lawyers Assn., Clark County Bar Assn. Personal injury. Office: 1604 Eaton Dr Las Vegas NV 89102-6118

**BRATTON, HOWARD CALVIN,** federal judge; b. Clovis, N.Mex., Feb. 4, 1922; s. Sam Gilbert and Vivian (Rogers) B. BA, U. N.Mex., 1941, LLB, 1971; LLB, Yale U., 1947. Bar: N.Mex. 1948. Law clk. U.S. Cir. Ct. Appeals, 1948; ptnr. Grantham & Bratton, Albuquerque, 1949-52; spl. asst. U.S. atty. charge litigation OPS, 1951-52; assoc., then ptnr. Hervy, Dow & Hinkle, Roswell, N.Mex., 1952-64; judge U.S. Dist. Ct. N.Mex., Albuquerque, 1964-87, chief judge, 1978-87; sr. judge U.S. Dist. Ct. N.Mex., Las Cruces, 1987—; chmn. N.Mex. Jr. Bar Assn., 1952; pres. Chaves County (N.Mex.) Bar Assn., 1962; chmn. pub. lands com. N.Mex. Oil and Gas Assn., 1961-64, Interstate Oil Compact Commn., 1963-64; mem. N.Mex. Commn. Higher Edn., 1962-64, Jud. Conf. of U.S. Com. on Operation of Jury Sys., 1966-72, 79-85, Jud. Conf. U.S. Com. on Ethics, 1987-92; mem. Ad Hoc Com. on Internat. Jud. Rels., 1992-94; 10th cir. rep. Jud. Conf. U.S., 1984-86. Bd. regents U. N.Mex., 1958-68, pres., 1963-64; bd. dirs. Fed. Jud. Ctr., 1983-87. Served to capt. AUS, 1942-45. Mem. Trial Judges Assn. 10th Circuit (pres. 1976-78), Nat. Conf. Fed. Trial Judges (exec. com. 1977-79), Sigma Chi. Office: US Dist Ct 200 E Griggs Ave Las Cruces NM 88001-3523

**BRAUD, RENE S.,** lawyer; b. Cheyenne, Wyo., June 12, 1953. JD, South Tex. Coll. Law, 1990. Bar: Tex. 1991. Chemist Danforth Hosp., Texas City, 1979-81; environ. dir. City of Pasadena, Houston, 1981-85; environ. mgr. Pakhoed Corp., Houston, 1985-89; environ. dir. U.S. Zing, Houston, 1989-90; lawyer Radian Corp., Houston, 1990-93, Harding Lawson, Houston, 1993-96, Exxon, Houston, 1996—. Environmental.

**BRAUDE, JACOB,** lawyer; b. Bklyn., Mar. 23, 1955; s. Max and Edna (Englard) B.; m. Rachel Schachter, Oct. 26, 1984; children: Eliyahu, Chaya, Pinchus, Shifra. Rabbinical Degree, Beth Medrash Govoha Rabbinical Coll., 1983; JD, Hofstra U., 1986. Bar: N.Y., 1986, N.J. 1986; U.S. Dist. Ct. N.J. 1988. Pvt. practice Bklyn., 1986—. Personal injury. Office: 3904 15th Ave Brooklyn NY 11218-4410

**BRAUDRICK, ARTHUR C., JR.,** lawyer; b. Honolulu, Sept. 22, 1941; s. Arthur Carl and Evelyne (Van Horn) B.; m. Marilyn Grace Webb, Dec. 8, 1979; children: Christian, Aaron, Colin, Melody. AB, U. Calif., Berkeley, 1968; JD, U. Calif., Davis, 1971. Bar: Calif. 1971. Dep. dist. atty. Monterey County, Salinas, Calif., 1972-78, dep. pub. defender, 1979-86, asst. dist. atty., 1986-87; dep. pub. defender Los Angeles County, L.A., 1988—. Vol. fireman Carmel (Calif.) Fire Dept., 1972-83. Mem. Calif. State Bar Assn. Democrat. Roman Catholic. Avocations: climbing, fishing, dog training. Office: Los Angeles County Pub Defenders Office 210 W Temple St Fl 19 Los Angeles CA 90012-3210

**BRAULT, LISA J.,** prosecutor; b. L.A., Apr. 2, 1961. BA in Theatre Arts, Calif. State U., Northridge, 1984; JD, Southwestern U., 1991. Bar: Calif. Supreme Ct. 1991, U.S. Dist. Ct. (ctrl. dist.) Calif. 1991, U.S. Ct. Appeals (9th cir.) 1991. Dep. atty. gen. III Calif. Atty. Gen.'s Office, L.A., 1992—. Mem. League Women Prosecutors (bd. mem. 1996-97, events and spkrs. chairperson 1997—). Democrat. Office: Office Calif Atty Gen 300 S Spring St Fl 5 Los Angeles CA 90013-1230

**BRAUN, BRIAN ALAN,** lawyer; b. Chgo., Jan. 21, 1947; s. Jerome and Lillian (Schuster) B.; m. Terre J. Tibbles, Dec. 18, 1980; children: David Joshua, Aaron Jonathan, Max Jacob. BS, U. Ill., 1969; JD, DePaul U., 1975. Bar: Ill. 1975, U.S. Dist. Ct. Ill. 1983, U.S. Ct. Appeals (7th cir.) 1987. Gen. counsel Ill. Assn. Sch. Bds., Springfield, 1977-82; ptnr. Miller, Tracy, Braun & Wilson, Ltd., Monticello, Ill., 1982—; lectr. Ill. State U., 1980-82, St. Xavier Coll., 1981, 85, Ea. Ill. U., 1983, Bradley U., 1980, 85-86, Ea. Ill. U., 1983, U. Ill., 1987-95, So. Ill. U., 1988. Author: Teacher Salaries and Fringe Benefits, 1980, Chicago School Law Survey, 1992, Illinois School Law Survey, 3d edit., 1994; contbr. numerous articles to profl. jours. Mem. ABA, Ill. Bar Assn., Piatt County Bar Assn., Am. Arbitration Assn., Nat. Coun. Sch. Attys. (bd. dirs. 1990-94), Ill. Coun. Sch. Attys. (chmn. bd. dirs. 1991). Jewish. Avocations: gardening, genealogy, running. Home: 1702 Bentbrook Dr Champaign IL 61822-9217 Office: Miller Tracy Braun & Wilson Ltd PO Box 80 Monticello IL 61856-0080

**BRAUN, DAVID LEE,** lawyer; b. Deadwood, S.D., Dec. 19, 1952; s. Edward F. and Mary K. Braun; m. Darlene F. Braun, Dec. 18, 1976; children: Temoe Jo, Amanda Jean. BS, Black Hills State U., 1977; JD, U. S.D., 1981. Bar: S.D. 1981, U.S. Ct. Appeals (8th and fed. cirs.) 1981, U.S. Supreme Ct. 1985,. Law clk. Unified Jud. Sys., Pierre, S.D., 1981-82; ptnr. Gors & Braun, Pierre, 1982-89; asst. atty. gen., legal counsel State of S.D., Pierre, 1989—. Jud. candidate State of S.D., 1998; foster parent, Pierre, 1978-82. With U.S. Army, 1972-76. Mem. Izaac Walton League, N.Am. Hunting Club (life). Republican. Roman Catholic. Avocations: hunting, fishing, collector automobiles. Home: 605 N Taylor Ave Pierre SD 57501-2708 Office: State of SD 700 Govs Dr Kneip Bldg Pierre SD 57501

**BRAUN, JEROME IRWIN,** lawyer; b. St. Joseph, Mo., Dec. 16, 1929; s. Martin H. and Bess (Donsker) B.; children: Aaron, Susan, Daniel; m. Dolores Ferriter, Aug. 16, 1987. AB with distinction, Stanford U., 1951, LLB, 1953. Bar: Mo. 1953, Calif. 1953, U.S. Dist. Ct. (no. dist.) Calif., U.S. Tax Ct., U.S. Ct. Mil. Appeals, U.S. Supreme Ct., U.S. Ct. Appeals (9th cir.). Assoc. Long & Levit, San Francisco, 1957-58, Law Offices of Jefferson Peyser, San Francisco, 1958-62; founding ptnr. Farella, Braun & Martel (formerly Elke, Farella & Braun), San Francisco, 1962—; instr. San Francisco Law Sch., 1958-69; mem. U.S. Dist. Ct. Civil Justice Reform Act Adv. Com., 1991—; spkr. various state bar convs. in Calif., Ill., Nev., Mont.; request moderator/participant continuing edn. of bar pgorams; past chmn. 9th Cir. Sr. Adv. Bd., past chmn. lawyer reps. to 9th Cir. Jud. Conf.; mem. appellate lawyers liaison com. Calif. Ct. Appeals 1st dist.; jud.conf. U.S. Com. Long Range Planning; founder Jon Samuel Abramson Scholarship Endowment Stanford U. Law. Revising editor: Stanford U. Law Rev.; contbr. articles to profl. jours. Mem. Jewish Community Fedn. San Francisco, The Peninsula, Marin and Sonoma Counties, pres., 1979-80; past pres. United Jewish Community Ctrs. 1st lt. JAGC, U.S. Army, 1954-57, U.S. Army Res., 1957-64. Recipient Lloyd W. Dinkelspiel Outstanding Young Leader award Jewish Welfare Fedn., 1967, Professionalism award 9th cir. Am. Inns of Ct., 1999. Fellow Am. Acad. Appellate Lawyers; mem. ABA, Am. Bar Found., Calif. Bar Assn. (chmn. adminstrn. justice com. 1977), Bar Assn. San Francisco (spl. com. on lawyers malpractice and malpractice ins.), San Francisco Bar Found. (past trustee), Calif. Acad. Appellate Lawyers (past pres., mem. U.S. Dist. Ct. Civil Justice Refomr Act adv. com., Calif. Ct. of Appeals 1st Dist. Appellate Lawyers liaison com., jud. conf. of the U.S., com. on long-range planning, panelist 1994), Am. Judicature Soc. (past dir.), Stanford Law Sch. Bd. of Visitors, Am. Coll. Trial Lawyers (teaching trial and appellate advocacy com.), U.S. Dist. Ct. of No. Dist. Calif. Hist. Soc. (past pres., bd. dirs.), 9th Cir. Ct. of Appeals Hist. Soc. (past. pres.), Mex.-Am. Legal Def. Fund (honoree), Order of Coif. Federal civil litigation, General civil litigation, Antitrust.

**BRAUNER, DAVID A.,** lawyer; b. N.Y.C., Mar. 4, 1942; s. Herman M. and Mary (Trachtenberg) B.; m. Amy Jo Kaplan, May 3, 1981; children: Sara Lynne, Jesse Howard. AB, Dickinson Coll., Carlisle, Pa., 1963; JD, Columbia U., 1966. Bar: N.Y. 1968. Vol. VISTA, Denver, 1966-67; staff atty. Mobilization for Youth, N.Y.C., 1967-68; ptnr. Brauner Baron et al, N.Y.C., 1968—; bd. dirs. Helen M. DeMario Found. Bd. dirs. Herman Goldman Found., N.Y.C., 1981—; v.p., dir. The Bridge, Inc., N.Y.C., 1980—. Mem. N.Y. County Lawyers Assn. Democrat. Jewish. Avocations: travel, squash, carpentry. Estate planning, General corporate, Real property. Home: 315 W 106th St New York NY 10025-3445 Office: Brauner Baron et al 61 Broadway New York NY 10006-2701

**BRAUNSDORF, PAUL RAYMOND,** lawyer; b. South Bend, Ind., June 18, 1943; s. Robert Louis and Marjorie (Breitenstein) B.; m. Margaret Buckley, June 18, 1966; children: Christopher, Mark, Douglas, Amy. BA magna cum laude, U. Notre Dame, 1965; LLB, U. Va., 1968. Bar: N.Y. 1968; U.S. Dist. Ct. (we. dist.) N.Y. 1969, U.S. Dist. Ct. (no. dist.) N.Y. 1980; U.S. Ct. Appeals (2d cir.) 1975; U.S. Supreme Ct. 1980. Assoc. Harris, Beach & Wilcox, Rochester, N.Y., 1968-75; ptnr., 1976—; instr. Nat. Inst. for Trial Advocacy, Rochester, 1988. Contbg. author: Antitrust Health Care Handbook II, 1993, Antitrust Law in New York, 1995. Bd. dirs. Mercy Parents' Club, 1989-90, McQuaid Parents' Club, 1984-90, pres. 1986-87, Brighton Baseball, 1987-90. Republican. Roman Catholic. Avocations: tennis, photography, music. Antitrust, Federal civil litigation, State civil litigation. Office: Harris Beach & Wilcox 130 Main St E Rochester NY 14604-1687

**BRAUSE, FRED S., JR.,** lawyer; b. Denver, July 27, 1924; m. Hilda Karsif; children: Pamela, Randolph, Alison, Scott. AB, Muhlenberg Coll., 1947; LLB, Columbia U., 1949, JD, 1949. Bar: N.J. 1952, U.S. Ct. Appeals (3rd cir.), U.S. Supreme Ct. Law clk. Cox & Walberg; from assoc. to ptnr. Ralph Fusco; in house counsel The Hartford Ins. Co.; ptnr. Brause, Callaghan & Coyle (and predecessor firms), Newark; pvt. practice Metuchen, N.J., ret., 1997; of counsel Brause & Brause, Metuchen, 1997—, Galen Booth, Middlesex, N.J., 1997—; of counsel Brause & Brause Esq., Metuchen, N.J., 1997—, Galen Booth Esq., Middlesex, N.J., 1997—. Scoutmaster Allentown Boy Scout Troop, Eagle Scout Troop; mem. adv. bd. to dir. Divsn. of Workers' Compensation; mem. nat. campaign advisor Nat. Rep. Senatorial Com. With USAAF, World War II; with USAF, Korean War. Decorated Disting. Flying Cross, Air medal with 3 oak leaf clusters. Named hon. del. to Republican Conv. 1992. Mem. ABA, VFW, Middlesex County Bar Assn., N.J. State Bar Assn., Am. Legion, DFC Soc. Workers' compensation. Home: 12 Bradford Rd Edison NJ 08820-2643 Office: PO Box 567 276 Main St Metuchen NJ 08840-2453

**BRAUTIGAM, DAVID CLYDE,** lawyer, judge; b. Westfield, N.Y., Nov. 11, 1950; s. Frank C. and Edna M. Brautigam; m. Amy S. Konz, Apr. 30, 1988; children: Sarah, Susanna, Sharon. BA, Houghton Coll., 1972; JD, U. Pitts., 1979. Bar: N.Y. 1980, U.S. Dist. Ct. (we. dist.) N.Y. 1983. Assoc.

Shane & Franz, Olean, N.Y., 1979-84; ptnr. Richardson, Pullen & Brautigam, Fillmore, N.Y., 1984-93; town justice Town of Rushford, N.Y., 1997—; pvt. practice Houghton, N.Y., 1993—. Bd. dirs. So. Tier Legal Svcs., Bath, N.Y., 1981-85, Odosegih Bible Conf., Inc., Mchias, N.Y., 1990-93; chmn., bd. dirs. 1st Bapt. Ch., Rushford, N.Y., 1996-98, deacon, 1988-98. Mem. Nat. Lawyers Assn., Allegany County Bar Assn., Christian Legal Soc., Am. Arbitration (arbitrator). Republican. Baptist. Avocations: hunting, gardening, softball, farming, reading. General practice, Real property, Probate. Office: 9888 County Road 23 Houghton NY 14744-8742

**BRAV, PETER GARY,** lawyer, title insurance company executive; b. N.Y., Mar. 6, 1955; s. Herman Louis and Adele B.; m. Janet M. Latino, Nov. 4, 1984; children: Julia Lynn, Gregory Joseph. BA, Cornell U., 1977; JD, Harvard U., 1980. Bar: Calif. 1980, N.Y. 1981, Pa. 1988. Assoc. Barrett Smith Schapiro Simon & Armstrong, N.Y.C., 1981-82, Colton, Weissberg, Hartwick, Yamin & Sheresky, N.Y.C., 1982-84; pvt. practice, N.Y.C. and L.I., 1984—; pres. Good Deed Abstract Corp., Valley Stream, 1989—. Committee person Nassau County Dem. Party, Westbury, N.Y., 1990-93; vol. Negro League Baseball Players Assn., N.Y.C., 1992. Mem. N.Y. State Land Title Assn., Mortar Bd., Phi Beta Kappa. Jewish. Avocations: writing novels and screenplays, basketball.

**BRAVE, GEORGINE FRANCES,** lawyer; b. Bklyn., Sept. 14, 1940; d. Mannie and Ruth (Baer) Aron; divorced; children: Bradley, Laurence, Elizabeth. BA, Bklyn. Coll., 1960; LLD, U. San Diego, 1983. Bar: Calif. 1983. Pvt. practice San Diego, 1984—. mem. State Bar of Calif., San Diego County Bar Assn. Family and matrimonial, Personal injury, General civil litigation. Address: 1551 4th Ave Ste 801 San Diego CA 92101-3156

**BRAVERMAN, ALAN N.,** lawyer. BA, Brandeis U., 1969; JD, Duquesne U., 1975. Bar: D.C. 1976. Assoc. Wilmer, Cutler & Pickering, 1976-82, ptnr., 1983-93; sr. v.p., gen. counsel ABC, Inc., N.Y.C., 1993—. Office: ABC Inc 77 W 66th St New York NY 10023-6298

**BRAVERMAN, HERBERT LESLIE,** lawyer; b. Buffalo, Apr. 24, 1947; s. David and Miriam P. (Cohen) B.; m. Janet Marx, June 11, 1972; children: Becca Danielle, Benjamin Howard. BS in Econs., U. Pa., 1969; JD, Harvard U., 1972. Bar: Ohio 1972, U.S. Dist. Ct. Ohio 1972, U.S. Supreme Ct. 1975, U.S. Ct. Appeals (6th cir.) 1980, U.S. Ct. Claims 1980. Assoc. Hahn, Loeser, Freedheim, Dean & Wellman, Cleve., 1972-75; sole practice Cleve., 1975-87; ptnr. Porter, Wright, Morris & Arthur, Cleve., 1987-95, Walter & Haverfield, Cleve., 1996—. Councilman Orange Village, Ohio, 1988—, pres., 1998—. Capt. USAR, 1970-82. Fellow Am. Coll. Trust and Estate Counsel; mem. ABA, Ohio Bar Assn., Bar Assn. Greater Cleve. (former chmn. estate planning trust and probate sect.), Suburban East Bar Assn. (pres. 1978-80), Rotary (Cleveland Heights pres. 1980), B'nai Brith (local pres. 1978-84), Wharton Club Cleve. (pres. 1991—), Am. Jewish Congress (Ohio pres. 1992—). Avocations: golf, symphony, reading. Probate, Estate planning, General corporate. Home: 3950 Orangewood Dr Cleveland OH 44122-7406 Office: Walter & Haverfield 1300 Terminal Tower 50 Public Sq Ste 1300 Cleveland OH 44113-2253 also: 23200 Chagrin Blvd Ste 600 Beachwood OH 44122-5402

**BRAWER, MARC HARRIS,** lawyer; b. N.Y.C., June 11, 1946; s. Leonard and Diana R. Brawer; m. Susan L. Brunswick, Nov. 23, 1975; 3 children. BA, Queens Coll., 1967; JD, Bklyn. Law Sch., 1969. Bar: N.Y. 1970, Fla. 1978, U.S. Dist. Ct. (ea. and so. dists.) N.Y. 1974, U.S. Ct. Appeals (2nd cir.) 1974, U.S. Supreme Ct. 1975, U.S. Dist. Ct. (so. dist.) Fla. 1981, U.S. Ct. Appeals (5th cir.) 1980; cert. marital and family lawyer, family mediator. Staff atty. Legal Aid Soc., N.Y.C., 1972-78; ptnr. Meyerson Resnicoff & Brawer, N.Y.C., 1978-83, Meyerson & Brawer, Tamarac, Fla., 1983-84; head firm Marc H. Brawer, Sunrise, Fla., 1984—; of counsel Resnicoff, Samanowitz & Brawer, Great Neck, N.Y., 1985-91; adj. prof. family law St. Thomas Law Sch., 1992; spkr. various orgns. and colls., 1980-96. Contbr. articles to profl. jours., 1970-84. Fellow Am. Acad. Matrimonial Lawyers; mem. Broward County Bar Assn., Queens County Bar Assn. (cert. of svc. 1982-83), Fla. Bar (sec. Family Law Commentator). Avocations: scuba diving, photography, ornamental horticulture. Family and matrimonial. Office: 7771 W Oakland Park Blvd Fort Lauderdale FL 33351-6749

**BRAY, AUSTIN COLEMAN, JR.,** lawyer, investor; b. Dallas, Oct. 25, 1941; s. Austin Coleman and Mary Thelma (Pettigrew) B.; m. Sherrill Ann Farr, Nov. 28, 1964 (div. 1970). Diploma, U. Vienna, Austria, 1962; BA cum laude, Washington and Lee U., 1963; LLB, Columbia U., 1967. Bar: Tex. 1967, U.S. Dist. Ct. (no. dist.) Tex. 1967, U.S. Ct. Appeals (5th cir.) Tex. 1967, U.S. Supreme Ct. 1970, U.S. Dist. Ct. (we. dist.) Tex. 1978, U.S. Ct. Appeals (11th cir.) Tex. 1981. Assoc. Gardere & Wynne, Dallas, 1967-69; asst. atty. gen. State of Tex., Austin, 1969-73; subcom. counsel U.S. Rep. Richard White, Washington, 1973-74; exec. asst. to State Senator Mike McKinnon, Austin, 1974-76; atty. Tex. R.R. Commn., Austin, 1977-78; exec. asst. to State Rep. Bob Close, Austin, 1978-79; sr. staff atty. Tex. Sec. State, Austin, 1979-82, sole practice, 1982-87; asst. gen. counsel Tex. Sec. of State, Austin, 1987-98; pvt. practice Austin, 1998—. Editor-in-chief Columbia Law Sch. News, 1966-67. Mem. ABA, State Bar Tex., English-Speaking Union, Kent Ct., Kappa Alpha Order. Episcopalian. Legislative, Election, Constitutional. Office: Ste 106 1218 Baylor St Austin TX 78703

**BRAY, JOHN MARTIN,** lawyer; b. St. Louis, Feb. 7, 1939; s. Edward Joseph and Rosemary Margaret Bray; m. Joan Maguire, Nov. 24, 1971; children: Kathleen, John P. BS, St. Louis U., 1960, LLB, 1962. Bar: Mo. 1962, D.C. 1968. Atty. U.S. Dept. Justice, Washington, 1962-66, Monsanto Co., St. Louis, 1966-68; assoc. Arent Fox Kintner, Plotkin & Kahn, Washington, 1968-73; ptnr. Arent Fox Kintner Plotkin & Kahn, Washington, 1973-78, Schwalb, Donnenfeld, Bray & Silbert, Washington, 1978-97, King & Spalding, Washington, 1997—. Trustee St. Louis U., 1980-93, 95—. Lt. JAGC, USNR, 1965-70. Fellow Am. Coll. Trial Lawyers; mem. J. Edgar Murdock Am. Inn of Ct. (master of bench). Avocation: Irish history. Federal civil litigation, Criminal, Antitrust. Home: 3202 Cleveland Ave NW Washington DC 20008-3451 Office: King & Spalding Ste 1200 1730 Pennsylvania Ave NW Washington DC 20006-4706

**BRAY, LAURACK DOYLE,** lawyer; b. New Orleans, Nov. 13, 1949; s. Laudrack Doyle Bray and Helen Davis. AA, L.A. City Coll., 1969; BA, Long Beach State U., 1972, MS, 1977, MPA, 1981; JD, Howard U., 1984. Bar: Pa. 1986, D.C. 1986, U.S. Ct. Appeals (D.C. and fed. cirs.) 1987, U.S. Dist. Ct. D.C. 1987, U.S. Ct. Appeals (4th cir.) 1991, Md. 1991, U.S. Supreme Ct. 1992. Cmty. rsch. worker Crenshaw Consortium, L.A., 1977-79; adminstrv. intern City of Lawndale, Calif., 1981; legis. intern U.S. Congress, Washington, 1982; law clk. FDIC, Washington, 1983-84; pvt. practice, Washington, 1987—; mem. moot ct. team Howard U., Washington. Contbr. articles to law jours. Recipient Am. Jurisprudence award, 1982, Best Brief award ABA, 1984. Mem. D.C. Bar Assn., Pi Alpha Alpha, Phi Kappa Phi. Democrat. Avocations: sports, dancing, travel. Federal civil litigation, Criminal, Appellate. Home and Office: 1019 E Santa Clara St Ventura CA 93001-3034

**BRAYER, JANET,** lawyer; b. San Francisco, May 4, 1958; d. Stephen A. and Laurette M. Brayer. BA, BS, St. Mary's Coll., Moraga, Calif., 1980; JD, U. San Francisco, 1984. Bar: Calif., U.S. Dist. Ct. (no. dist.) Calif., U.S. Dist. Ct. (so. dist.) Calif., U.S. Dist. Ct. (ctrl. dist.) Calif., U.S. Ct. Appeals (5th cir.), U.S. Ct. Appeals (9th cir.). Com. chair, antitrust securities litig. Barristers of San Francisco, 1989-91, bd. dirs., sec., 1992-94; ptnr. Low, Ball & Lynch, San Francisco, 1990-92, Vogl & Meredith, San Francisco, 1992-98; of counsel O'Connor, Cohn, Dillon & Barr, San Francisco, 1998—; mem. faculty Hastings Coll. Advocacy, San Francisco, 1997, 98. Mem. San Francisco Trial Lawyers. General civil litigation, Landlord-tenant, Labor. Home: PO Box 954 Moss Beach CA 94038-0954 Office: O'Connor Cohn Dillon & Barr 101 Howard St Fl 5 San Francisco CA 94105-1629

**BRAZELL, IDA HERNANDEZ,** judge; b. Mercedes, Tex., Jan. 28, 1951; d. Guadalupe C. and Juanita (Gamez) Hernandez; children: Patrick Bryan, Andrew Owen. BA, U. Tex., 1973, JD, 1971. Bar: Tex. 1978, U.S. Dist. Ct. (ea. dist.) Tex. 1981, U.S. Dist. Ct. (so. dist.) Tex. 1986. Instr. legal rsch. Lamar U., Beaumont, Tex., 1979-80; briefing clk. Ct. Appeals, 9th Supreme Jud. Dist., Beaumont, Tex., 1978-80; mng. atty. Continental Ins. Cos., Beaumont, Tex., 1980-82; atty. Brazell & Brazell, Corpus Christi, Tex., 1982-85; dir. immigration svcs. Diocese of Corpus Christi, 1984-86; assoc. Calame, Linebarger & Graham, Corpus Christi, 1985-86; atty. pvt. practice, Corpus Christi, 1986-93; mem. commrs. ct. Nueces County Commr., Precinct 3, 1994; judge State of Tex., Office Ct. Adminstrn., 1994—. Mem. Nueces County Cmty. Action Agy., Robstown Econ. Devel. Corp., Vol. Lawyers Project; mem. exec. com. Workforce Devel. Corp. Nueces County; bd. dirs. Vol. Ctr. Fellow, Tex. Bar Found. Mem. Am. Immigration Lawyers Assn. (program chair 1988, sect. co-chair San Antonio sect. 1988-90), Coastal Bend Criminal Defense Lawyers Assn., Coastal Bend Women Lawyers Assn. (v.p. 1993-94, pres. 1994-95), Family Law Assn., Hispanic Women's Network, Latin Am. Coun. Labor Assns., Leadership Western Neuces County, Mexican-Am. Bar Assn. Coastal Bend, Coll. State Bar Tex. Avocations: bicycling, tennis, racquetball. Office: IV-D Ct Master 901 Leopard St Rm 404 Corpus Christi TX 78401-3602

**BRAZIER, JOHN RICHARD,** lawyer, physician; b. Olean, N.Y., Mar. 11, 1940; s. John R. and Edith (Martin) B.; children: Mark, Jennifer. AAS, SUNY, Alfred, 1960; BS in Engring. Physics, U. Colo., 1963, MD, 1969; JD, Santa Clara U., 1989. Bar: Calif., 1989. Intern in surgery Downstate Med. Ctr., Bklyn., 1969-70; resident in surgery U. Colo., Denver, 1970-75; fellowship thoracic and cardiovascular surgery NYU, 1975-77; asst. prof. surgery UCLA, 1977-78; pvt. practice Northridge, 1978-84, Newport News, Va., 1984-86, Sacramento, 1989—. Fellowship NIH, UCLA, 1972-74. Mem. AMA, ACS, Am. Coll. Chest Physicians, Calif. Bar. Avocation: law. State civil litigation, General practice, Personal injury. Home: 1401 36th St Sacramento CA 95816-6606 Office: 915 21st St Sacramento CA 95814-3117

**BRAZIL, WILLIAM CLAY,** lawyer; b. Des Moines, Nov. 23, 1942; s. Clay and Velma (Alford) B.; m. Suzanne Brazil, Aug. 22, 1964; children: Amy Totten, William Clay. BSBA, U. Ark., 1964, JD, 1967. Assoc. Estes & Brazil, Fayetteville, Ark., 1967-68; ptnr. Brazil, Clawson, Adlong, Murphy & Osment, Conway, Ark., 1968—; bd. dirs. Am. Mgmt. Corp., Merrilton, Ark., 1st Nat. Bank, Conway. City atty. Municipality of Conway, 1974-77; prosecuting 20th Jud. Dist., 1977-83. Mem. ABA, Ark. Bar Assn. (ho. of dels. 1988-90, exec. com.), Assn. Trial Lawyers Am., Ark. Trial Lawyers Assn. (various coms.). Banking, Insurance, General practice. Office: Brazil Clawson Adlong Murphy & Osment 913 Oak St Conway AR 72032-4352

**BREACH, DAVID ANDREW,** lawyer; b. Etobicoke, Ont., Can., Oct. 17, 1966; came to the U.S., 1996; s. Arthur William and Eva Marie Breach; m. Cheryl Atkins, Dec. 31, 1990 (div. June 1992); m. Emily Ann Sheley, Oct. 9, 1996. BBA, Ea. Mich. U., 1991; JD, U. Mich., 1994. Atty. Honigman Miller Schwartz & Cohn, Detroit, 1994-98, ptnr., 1998—. Mem. ABA. Securities, General corporate. Office: Honigman Miller Schwartz & Cohn 2290 First National Bldg Detroit MI 48226

**BREARTON, JAMES JOSEPH,** lawyer; b. Troy, N.Y., Aug. 12, 1950; s. James Edward and Lois Marie (Mesnig) B.; m. Margaret Anne Cassidy, Aug. 27, 1977. BA, Coll. Holy Cross, 1972; JD, Albany Law Sch., 1975. Bar: N.Y. 1976, U.S. Dist. Ct. (no. dist.) N.Y. 1976. Assoc. Wager, Taylor, Howd, Brearton & Kessler, Troy, N.Y., 1975-87; sole practice Latham, N.Y., 1987—; mem. bd. arbitrators Nat. Assn. Securities Dealers, Inc., 1992—; mem. Am. Prepaid Legal Svcs. Inst, mem. Monroe Title Ins. Corp., Fidelity Nat. Ins. Co. Exam. Counsel; instr. Am. Inst. Banking, 1994. Co-author: Alternate Dispute Resolution, American Jurisprudence, 2nd rev. edit., 1995. Pres. Alumni Assn. LaSalle Inst., Troy, N.Y., 1997-98, mem., ex-officio, Bd.Trustees, 1998. Mem. ABA, Am. Arbitration Assn., N.Y. State Bar Assn., Rensselaer County Bar Ass., Albany County Bar Assn. (law guardian liaison com. 3d jud. dist. N.Y. 1987—), Mensa. Democrat. Roman Catholic. Personal injury, Probate, Personal income taxation. Office: PO Box 889 6 Century Hill Dr Latham NY 12110-2116

**BREAULT, THEODORE EDWARD,** lawyer; b. N.Y.C., Mar. 7, 1938; m. Gretchen S. Clements, Dec. 10, 1966; children: Victoria Ann, Theodore Edmund, Heidi Sherwin, Edmund Clements. BS, Manhattan Coll., 1960; JD, Cath. U. Am., 1963. Bar: D.C. 1964, Va. 1964, Pa. 1970, U.S. Ct. Appeals (D.C. cir.) 1964, (4th cir.) 1969, U.S. Supreme Ct. 1967. Assoc. Seltzer & Suskind, Washington, 1964-69, Egler & Reinstadtler, Pitts., 1969-77; pvt. practice Fairfax, Va., 1967-69, Pitts., 1977—; lectr. Cath. U. Am. Sch. Nursing, Robert Morris Coll.; mem. Pa. Workmen's Compensation Sect.; spl. master Allegheny County Ct. of Common Pleas; arbitrator U.S. Dist. Ct. Pres. Sewickley (Pa.) Symphony Orch., 1974-75. Fellow Pa. Bar Found. (life); mem. Pa. Bar Assn. (civil litigation sect.), Va. State Bar Assn., D.C. Bar Assn., Allegheny County Bar Assn. (health law sect., workmen's compensation sect.), Am. Soc. Law and Medicine, Pa. Def. Inst., Am. Arbitration Assn. (arbitrator accident and comml. claims), Am. Coll. Legal Medicine (assoc. in law). Workers' compensation, Personal injury, General civil litigation. Home: 108 Claridge Dr Moon Township PA 15108-3204 Office: Breault & Assocs PC 428 Forbes Ave 2200 Lawyers Bldg Pittsburgh PA 15219

**BREAUX, DAWN CROFT,** paralegal; b. Madison, Wis., Sept. 30, 1961; d. Stephen William and Katherine Tsoi Croft; m. Reuben Paul Breaux, Apr. 22, 1989; 1 child, Adam William. BA in Geology, Boston U., 1983; paralegal cert., Tulane U., 1986. Litigation paralegal Christovich & Kearney, New Orleans, 1986-89, Cogswell, Woolley, Nakazawa & Russell, Long Beach, Calif., 1990—; gust spkr. paralegal studies program Tulane U., New Orleans, 1987, 88,. Home: 19252 Congress Cir Huntington Beach CA 92646-1919 Office: Cogswell Woolley Nakazawa & Russell 111 W Ocean Blvd Ste 2000 Long Beach CA 90802-4696

**BREAUX, PAUL JOSEPH,** lawyer, pharmacist; b. Franklin, La., Mar. 11, 1942; s. Sidney J. and Irene (Bodin) B.; m. Marilyn Anne Jones, Aug. 21, 1965; children: Jason E., James P. BS in Pharmacy, Northeast La. U., 1965; JD, La. State U., 1972. Bar: La. 1972, U.S. Supreme Ct. 1975. Pharmacist Belanger's Pharmacy, Morgan City, La., 1965-66, Clinic Pharmacy, Morgan City, La., 1966-69; pvt. practice of law Lafayette, La., 1972-73, 93—; assoc. Allen, Gooch, Bourgeois, Breaux, Robison, Theunissen Attys., Lafayette, 1973-75; ptnr. Allen, Gooch, Bourgeois, Breaux, Robison & Theunissen, Lafayette, 1975-93; sec., bd. dirs. Bank of Lafayette. Bd. dirs. Lafayette Community Health Care Clinic, 1992—, Hvice chmn., 1996—; bd. dirs. Hospice of Acadiana, Inc., 1996—, The Hospice Found., pres. 1998—; mem. Gov.'s Universal Health Care Law Reform Commn., 1992—; active Boy Scouts Am., 1984-92. Mem. ABA, La. Bar Assn., Lafayette Parish Bar Assn., La. Bankers Assn. (mem. bank counsel com. 1983-85, 88-90, La. banking code legislation revision com. 1983), Am. Land Title Assn., Am. Pharm. Assn., La. Pharmacists Assn. (bd. dirs. 1991-99, Pharmacist of Yr. award 1992), Am. Compliane Inst., Nat. Assn. Retail Druggists, Am. Soc. Law and Medicine, Am. Soc. Pharmacy Law, Nat. Health Lawyers Assn., Acad. Hosp. Attys. of Am. Hosp. Assn., Soc. Hosp. Attys. of La. Hosp. Assn., Lafayette C. of C., Kappa Psi, Phi Eta Sigma. Republican. Roman Catholic. Real property, General corporate, Health. Office: 600 Jefferson St Ste 503 Lafayette LA 70501-6998

**BRECHER, ALLISON LEIGH,** lawyer; b. N.Y.C., Apr. 13, 1971; m. Jeffrey Brecher, Aug. 30, 1997. BA, Union Coll., Schenectady, N.Y., 1993; JD, DePaul U., 1996. Bar: Ariz. 1996. Rschr. WNBC-TV, N.Y.C., 1991-92; field reporter WFLD-TV, Chgo., 1993-94; law clk. Cascino & Vaughn, Chgo., 1995; assoc. Horne, Kaplan & Bistrow, Phoenix, 1996-98, Ridenour, Swenson, Cleere & Evans, Phoenix, 1998—. Author: Practicing Before the Registrar of Contractors; contbr. articles to profl. jours. Vol. Florence Crittendon, Phoenix, Modest Means Legal Clinic. Mem. ABA, State Bar Ariz., Ariz. Women Lawyers, Ariz. Contractors Assn. Construction, Intellectual property, General civil litigation. Office: Ridenour Swenson 40 N Central Ave Ste 1400 Phoenix AZ 85004-4457

**BRECHER, ARMIN G.,** lawyer; b. Prague, Czechoslovakia, July 7, 1942; s. Gerhard Otto and Eleanor (Baker) B.; m. Elizabeth Pardue Rountree, July 2, 1966; children: Lindsay Brecher Cobb, Stefan Ryan, Alden Kelsey. BA summa cum laude, Emory U., Atlanta, 1966; LLB, U. Va., 1969. Ptnr., chair exec. com. Powell, Goldstein, Frazer & Murphy, Atlanta, 1969—. Mem. The ESOP Assn. Presbyterian. Administrative and regulatory, General corporate, Pension, profit-sharing, and employee benefits. Office: Powell Goldstein Frazer & Murphy LLP 191 Peachtree St NE Fl 16 Atlanta GA 30303-1740

**BRECHER, HOWARD ARTHUR,** lawyer; b. N.Y.C., Oct. 18, 1953; s. Milton and Dorothy (Zahler) B. AB magna cum laude, Harvard U., 1975, MBA, 1979, JD cum laude, 1979; LLM, NYU, 1984. Bar: N.Y. 1980, U.S. Dist. Ct. (so. dist.) N.Y. 1983, U.S. Tax Ct. 1981. Assoc. Roberts & Holland, N.Y.C., 1979-82, Chadbourne, Parke, Whiteside & Wolff, N.Y.C., 1982-84; atty. legal dept. N.Y. Telephone Co., N.Y.C., 1984-91, counsel, 1991-96; v.p. law Value Line, Inc., 1996—; mem. tax com. N.Y.C. C. of C., 1985-88, 94—. Mem. ABA (tax sect.), N.Y. State Bar Assn. (tax sect., com. taxation of affiliated corps., trusts and estates sect.), Assn. of Bar of City of N.Y., Harvard Bus. Sch. Club of Greater N.Y., N.Y.C. C. of C. (mem. tax com. 1994—). Democrat. Jewish. Clubs: Harvard (N.Y.C. and Boston). Taxation, general, General corporate, Intellectual property. Office: 220 E 42nd St Ste 6000 New York NY 10017-5806

**BRECKBERG, ROBERT LEE,** lawyer; b. Kodiak, Alaska, June 14, 1951; s. Henry and Ruth Lorraine (Davis) B. BA, Amherst Coll., 1974; JD, Lewis and Clark Coll., 1977. Bar: Alaska 1977, U.S. Dist. Ct. Alaska 1978, U.S. Ct. Appeals (9th cir.) 1978, U.S. Ct. Claims 1989. Assoc./ptnr. Robert M. Goldberg, Anchorage, 1978-80; hearing examiner Alaska Transp. Commn., Anchorage, 1980, 81-84; assoc. Lynch, Crosby, Molenda & Sisson, Anchorage, 1985-86, Edgar Paul Boyko, Anchorage, 1986-99; pvt. practice Anchorage, 1999—. Mem. Alaska Bar Assn., Anchorage Bar Assn. Avocations: fishing, biking, skiing, hiking, beachcombing. General practice. Office: 733 W 4th Ave Ste 303 Anchorage AK 99501-2162

**BRECKENRIDGE, FRANKLIN EUGENE,** lawyer; b. Kokomo, Ind., May 8, 1940; s. Frank E. and Emma Jeannette (Artis) B.; m. Cora Lee Smith, June 13, 1964; children: Lejene, Franklin Jr., Emma. BS, Ind. U., 1963, JD, 1968. Bar: Ind. 1968, U.S. Dist. Ct. (no. and so. dists.) Ind. Tchr. Kokomo Pub. Schs., 1963-65; Headstart tchr. Ind. Pre-Sch. Ctrs., Inc., Indpls., 1965-66; asst. adminstr. sales tax Ind. Dept. Revenue, Indpls., 1966-67, supr. corp. income tax sect., 1967-68; pvt. practice, 1968-73; sr. atty., assoc. counsel, asst. sec. Bayer Corp., Elkhart, Ind., 1973-96. Bd. dirs. Ind. U. Bd. Visitors, Indpls.; vice chmn. nat. bd. NAACP, Balt., 1995, nat. bd. mem., 1988—, pres. Ind. state conf., 1978—; elder Cmty. AME Ch., LaPorte, Ind., 1994—, elder, 1996. Recipient William R. Ming Advocacy award for legal svcs. NAACP, 1982, Kelly M. Alexander Sr. Outstanding State Conf. Pres.'s award, 1990. Mem. ABA, Nat. Bar Assn., Ind. State Bar Assn., Elkhart City Bar Assn. Democrat. AME Ch. Avocations: running, reading, travel. General corporate, Antitrust, Contracts commercial. Home: 54653 Briarwood Dr Elkhart IN 46514-4447

**BRECKER, JEFFREY ROSS,** lawyer, educator; b. N.Y.C., June 9, 1953; s. Milton S. and Charlotte (Alpert) B.; m. Phyllis L. Gordon, Oct. 30, 1983. BA in Polit. Sci., NYU, 1975; JD, New Eng. Sch. Law, Boston, 1978. Bar: N.Y. 1979, U.S. Dist. Ct. (so. and ea. dists.) N.Y. 1979, U.S. Supreme Ct. 1982. Atty. Nassau (N.Y.) County Legal Svcs. Commn., 1978-80, Dist. Coun. 37 Legal Svcs., N.Y.C., 1980-82, Wiesner & Shamis, N.Y.C., 1982-85; sr. trial atty., unit supr. Jacobowitz & Lysaght, N.Y.C., 1985-89; mng. atty. Damashak Godosky & Gentile, N.Y.C., 1989-95, Godosky & Gentile, N.Y.C., 1995—; adj. prof. New Coll., Hofstra U., 1981. Personal injury, Product liability, State civil litigation. Office: Godosky & Gentile 61 Broadway 20th Fl New York NY 10006-2701

**BRECZINSKI, MICHAEL JOSEPH,** lawyer; b. El Paso, Tex., Mar. 16, 1953; s. Julius W. and Rosemarie (Kelly) B.; m. Arlene Ann Szafranski, Apr. 20, 1979 (div. Jul. 1999); children: Emily, Nathan, Jacob. AA, Oakland Community Coll., 1973; BA, Mich. State U., 1976; JD, Thomas M. Cooley Law Sch., Lansing, Mich., 1981. Bar: Mich. 1982, Minn. 1983. Sole practice Lansing, 1982-83, Flint, Mich., 1983-85, Mt. Morris, Mich., 1985-87, Burton, Mich., 1987—. Mem. Mich. Bar Assn., Minn. Bar Assn., Genesee County Bar Assn, Assn. Trial Lawyers Am., Cath. Attys. Guild. Republican. Club: Flint Rogues Rugby. Criminal, General practice, Construction. Office: 5005 Lapeer Rd Burton MI 48509-2017

**BREDEHOFT, ELAINE CHARLSON,** lawyer; b. Fergus Falls, Minn., Nov. 22, 1958; d. Curtis Lyle and Marilyn Anne (Nesbitt) Charlson; children: Alexandra Charlson, Michelle Charlson. BA, U. Ariz., 1981; JD, Cath. U. Am., 1984. Bar: Va. 1984, U.S. Ct. Appeals (4th cir.) 1984, U.S. Bankruptcy Ct. (ea. dist.) Va. 1987, D.C. 1994, U.S. Ct. Appeals (D.C. cir.) 1994. Assoc. Walton and Adams, McLean, Va., 1984-88, ptnr., 1988-91; ptnr. Charlson Bredehoft, P.C., Reston, Va., 1991—; spkr. Fairfax Bar Assn., CLE, 1992—, VB Assn., CLE, 1993—, 12th Ann. Multistate Labor and Employment Law Seminar, 1994, Va. CLE Ann. Employment Law Update, 1993-96, Va. Women's Trial Lawyers Assn. Ann. Conf., 1998, Va. Bar Assn. Labor and Employment Conf., 1994-97, 99, Va. Trial Lawyers Assn., 1995, 97, Va. Law Found., 1995—, Va. Assn. Def. Attys., 1996; mem. faculty Va. State Bar Professionalism Courses, 1997—; invitee 4th Circuit Judicial Conf., 1997-99, permanent mem., 1999—, Boyd Groves Conference, 1999; substitute judge 19th Judicial Dist., 1998—; mem. faculty Va. State Bar Professionalism Courses, 1997—, chair Fairfax Bar Assn. Diversity Taskforce, 1998-99 (Pres. Vol. award 1998). Bd. dirs. Va. Commn. on Women and Minorities in the Legal System, 1987-90, sec., 1988-90. Mem. Va. Bar Assn. (mem. exec. com. young lawyers sect., mem. litigation com., mem. nominating com., chmn. model jud. com., spkr. CLE 1993—), Va. Trial Lawyers Assn. (vice chmn. ann. conv. 1996-98, mem. com. on long-range planning 1996-97, spkr. 1995, 97), Minn. State Soc., Fairfax Bar Assn. co-chair subcom. on minorities, Pres.'s Vol. award 1998, 99), George Mason Inns of Ct. (master 1996—). General civil litigation, Personal injury, Civil rights. Office: Charlson Bredehoft PC 11260 Roger Bacon Dr Ste 201 Reston VA 20190-5203

**BREDEHOFT, JOHN MICHAEL,** lawyer; b. N.Y.C., Feb. 22, 1958; s. John William and Viola (Struhar) B.; children: Alexandra Charlson Bredehoft, Michelle Charlson Bredehoft. AB magna cum laude, Harvard Coll., 1980, JD cum laude, 1983. Bar: D.C. 1983, U.S. Dist. Ct. D.C. 1985, U.S. Ct. Appeals (D.C. cir.) 1985, U.S. Ct. Appeals (1st cir.) 1986, U.S. Supreme Ct. 1987, U.S. Ct. Appeals (9th cir. ) 1988, U.S. Ct. Appeals (3d and 5th cir.) 1989, U.S. Tax Ct. 1989, U.S. Ct. Appeals (4th Cir.) 1990, U.S. Dist. Ct. Mont. 1991, Va. 1992, U.S. Dist. Ct. (ea. dist.) Va. 1992. Assoc. Cleary, Gottlieb, Steen & Hamilton, Washington, 1983-91; prin. Charlson & Bredehoft, Fairfax, Va., 1991-98; ptnr. Venable, Baetjer & Howard L.L.P., McLean, Va., 1998—; Contbg. editor Employment Law in Virginia, 1997. Bd. dirs. Falls Brook Assn., Herndon, Va., 1988-91; nat. class 1983 reunion gift chmn. Harvard Law Sch. Fund, Cambridge, 1988, class agt., 1994—; mem. Harvard Debate Centennial Com., 1992. Named Lawyer of Yr., Met. Washington Employment Lawyers Assn., 1996. Mem. ABA (sect. on litigation), Va. Bar Assn. (sect. on labor and employment law), Va. Trial Lawyers Assn. (founding officer, employment law sect.), Fairfax Bar Assn. (sect. on employment law, vice chmn. 1997-98, chmn. 1998-99, nominations com.), Def. Rsch. and Trial Inst. (appellate advocacy com.), Va. Law Found./Va. CLE (employment law com.), Va. Women Attys. Assn. Federal civil litigation, Labor, Civil rights. Office: 2010 Corp Ridge Ste 400 McLean VA 22102-5203

**BREEDING, CARL WAYNE,** lawyer; b. Whitesburg, Ky., Jan. 2, 1954; s. Carl Don and Pearl Marie (Taylor) B.; m. Mary Caufield, Sept. 7, 1974; children: Laura Taylor, Emily Allyn. BA, Transylvania U., 1976; JD, U. Ky., 1979. Bar: Ky. 1979, U.S. Dist. Ct. (ea., we. dists.) Ky. 1982, U.S. Ct. Appeals (6th cir.) 1982, U.S. Supreme Ct. 1984. Atty. Ky. Natural Resources & Environ. Protection Cabinet, Frankfort, 1979-81, dep. gen. counsel, 1981-83, gen. counsel, 1983-87; ptnr. Reece, Lang & Breeding, London, Ky., 1987-93, Breeding, McIntyre & Cunningham, P.S.C., 1993-98; with Greenbaum Doll & McDonald PLLC, Lexington, Ky., 1998—; adj. prof. law No. Ky. U., Highland Heights, 1986. Contbr. to profl. jours. Mem. Gov.'s Ground Water Adv. Com., Frankfort, 1986-87. Mem. ABA, Ky. Bar Assn., Fayette County Bar Assn. Republican. Environmental, General civil litigation, Natural resources. Home: 254 S Ashland Ave Lexington KY 40502-1728 Office: Greenbaum Doll & McDonald PLLC 333 W Vine St Ste 1400 Lexington KY 40507-1622

**BREEN, DAVID HART,** lawyer; b. Ottawa, Ont., Can., Mar. 27, 1960; came to U.S., Aug. 19, 1978; naturalized, 1993; s. Harold John and Margaret

Rae (Hart) B.; m. Pamela Annette Mitchell, Sept. 17, 1988; 1 child, Matthew Mitchell. BA cum laude, U. S.C., 1982, JD, 1986. Bar: S.C., U.S. Dist. Ct. S.C., U.S. Ct. Appeals (4th cir.), U.S. Bankruptcy Ct. S.C. 1987. Law clk. to Hon. Don S. Rushing Cir. Ct. (6th cir.), S.C., 1986-87; sr. ptnr. David H. Breen, P.A., Myrtle Beach, 1988—; C.J.A. panel atty. U.S. Dist. Ct. S.C., 1991-97; mem. family ct. adv. com. 15th Jud. Ct., 1998—. Campaign asst. Joe Clark for Prime Minister, Ottawa, 1975-76. Mem. ABA, S.C. Trial Lawyers Assn., Assn. Trial Lawyers Am., S.C. Bar Assn., Horry County Bar Assn., Am. Bankruptcy Inst., Oshawa Gun Club, Phi Delta Phi. Methodist. Avocations: swimming, computers. General civil litigation, Bankruptcy, Personal injury. Home: Prestwick Country Club 2187 N Berwick Dr Myrtle Beach SC 29575-5835 Office: 4603 Oleander Dr Ste 6 Myrtle Beach SC 29577-5738

**BREEN, KEVIN J.,** lawyer; b. Cleve., Sept. 25, 1958; s. Jack F. and Helen M. Breen; m. Laura M. Marshall, May 26, 1990. BA, Marietta Coll., 1980; JD, 1986. Bar: Ohio 1987, U.S. Dist. Ct. (no. dist.) Ohio 1987. Assoc. Roftzel & Andrews, Akron, Ohio, 1986-89, Thompson, Hane and Flory, Cleve., 1989-94, Forney & Klingsham, Akron, 1994-96; prin. Barren & Co., Akron, 1996—. Bd. dirs. social svcs. adv. bd. Summit County, Akron, 1998—. Mem. ABA, Akron Bar Assn. (chmn. lawyer referral svcs. 1996—). Consumer commercial, General civil litigation. Office: 1 Cascade Plz Ste 1450 Akron OH 44308-1143

**BREEN, NEIL THOMAS,** publishing executive; b. N.Y.C., Oct. 14, 1944; s. Neil G. and Eileen M. Breen; m. Catherine M. Breen, Dec. 2, 1978. BA, Marquette U., 1966; JD, Creighton U., 1970. Bar: Nebr. 1970, U.S. Dist. Ct. Nebr. 1970. Editor-in-chief Shepard's/McGraw Hill, Colorado Springs, Colo., 1979-86, v.p. devel., 1987-89; Thomson Legal Pub., Stamford, Conn.; pres. Callaghan & Co., Deerfield, Ill., 1989-90; v.p., gen. mgr. litigation and fed. products group, 1991-92; v.p. legal divsn. McGraw Hill Ryerson, Whitby, Ont., Can., 1993-95; pres. Law Bull. Pub. Co., Chgo., 1996—. Author: Texas Law Locator, 1973, Illinois Law Locator, 1975. Mem. ABA, Assn. of trial Laywers of Am., Ill. State Bar Assn., Chgo. Bar Assn., Can. Bar Assn. Avocations: skiing, snowshoeing, hiking. Office: Law Bulletin Pub Co 415 N State St Ste 200 Chicago IL 60610-4631

**BREESKIN, MICHAEL WAYNE,** lawyer; b. Washington, Dec. 25, 1947; s. Nathan and Sylvia (Raine) B.; m. Frances Cox Lively, May 29, 1982; children: Molly Louise, Laura Rose. BA cum laude, U. Pitts., 1969; JD, Georgetown U. Law Ctr., 1975. Bar: D.C. 1975, Colo. 1983, U.S. Dist. Ct. D.C. 1977, U.S. Dist. Ct. Colo. 1983, U.S. Ct. Appeals (D.C. cir.) 1978, U.S. Ct. Appeals (10th cir.) 1984, U.S. Supreme Ct. 1995. Mng. atty. Tobin & Covey, Washington, 1977-79; assoc. Donald M. Murtha & Assocs., Washington, 1979-80; counsel NLRB Office Rep. Appeals, Washington, 1980-83; trial atty. NLRB Denver Regional Office, 1983-88; assoc. Wherry & Wherry, Denver, 1989-91; sr. atty. The Legal Ctr. for People with Disabilities and Older People (formerly The Legal Ctr. Serving Persons with Disabilities), Denver, 1991-98; gen. counsel Assn. Cmty. Living Boulder County, Inc., Retarded Citizens), 1998—; pres. Michael W. Breeskin, P.C., Englewood, Colo., 1998—; presenter, lectr. Denver, 1991—. Adv. com. Domestic Violence Initiatives for Women with Disabilities, 1997—. Recipient Outstanding Work for People with Disabilities acknowledgement Very Spl. Arts Colo., 1996; named Profl. of Yr., The Arc of Adams County, 1997; recipient Schenkein award Arc of Denver, Inc., 1997; recipient award Disability Ctr. Ind. Living and Colo. Cross-Disability Coalition, 1999. Mem. ABA (litigation sect.), Colo. Bar Assn. (disability law forum com.), Arapahoe County Bar Assn. Avocations: bicycling, skiing, reading. Civil rights, Labor, Education and schools. Office: PO Box 4392 Englewood CO 80155-4392

**BREGMAN, ARTHUR RANDOLPH,** lawyer, educator; b. Phila., Dec. 9, 1946; s. Nathan and Stella (Husock) B.; m. Patrice Rosalie Gancie, May 30, 1980. BA, Columbia U., 1968; MA, Yale U., 1969; JD, Georgetown U., 1985. Bar: D.C. 1985, U.S. Ct. Appeals (D.C. cir.) 1985, U.S. Dist. Ct. D.C. 1985, U.S. Claims Ct. 1985. Treas. Nat. Coun. for Soviet and E. European Rsch., Washington, 1981-83; law clk. Washington Lawyers' Com. for Civil Rights, 1983-84; assoc. Klores, Feldesman and Tucker, Washington, 1985-86; dir. Soviet and E. European Svcs. APCO, Washington, 1988-91; of counsel Steptoe & Johnson, Washington, Moscow, USSR, 1991-92; ptnr. Steptoe & Johnson, Washington D.C. and Moscow, 1992—; adj. prof. Georgetown U. Law Ctr., Washington, 1986-89; program dir. Internat. Law Inst., Washington, 1986-91; chmn. bd. adv. U.S.-Russia Bus. Law Report, 1990—. Editor: U.S.-Soviet Contract Law, 1987. Recipient Civil Procedure prize Lawyers Coop. Pub. Co., Balt., 1982. Mem. ABA (internat. bar sect.), D.C. Bar. Private international, Public international. Home: 3059 Porter St NW Washington DC 20008-3272 Office: 1330 Connecticut Ave NW Washington DC 20036-1704

**BREGMAN, DOUGLAS M.,** lawyer, educator; b. Ardmore, Pa., Oct. 21, 1949; s. Nathan and Stella Bregman; m. Brenda I. Ladell, June 17, 1973; children: Benjamin, Lauren, Daniel. BA with honors, Colgate U., 1971; JD, Georgetown U., 1974. Bar: Md. 1974, D.C. 1975, U.S. Supreme Ct. 1978. Jud. law clk. to Judge J. Dudley Digges Ct. of Appeals of Md., Annapolis, 1973-75; mem. Duckett, Orem, Christie and Beckett, Hyattsville, Md., 1975-78; instr. U. Md., College Park, 1977-81; mem. Fossett & Brugger Law Firm, Seabrook, Md., 1978; ptnr. Bregman, Berbert & Schwartz, LLP, Bethesda, Md., 1979—; adj. prof. law Georgetown U. Law Ctr., Washington, 1992—. Co-author: Successful Real Estate Negotiations, 1987, 2d edit., 1994, Maryland Landlord/Tenant Law, Practice and Procedure, 1983, 2d edit., 1994; contbr. chpts. to books. Spl. cons., White House intern Office of Consumer Affairs, 1971; mem. Govs.'s Adv. Coun. on Landlord and Tenant Affairs, 1991-95; chmn. Com. to Retain Sitting Judges, 1998. Mem. ABA, Md. State Bar Assn. (exec. com. and bd. govs. 1982-83), Bar Assn. Montgomery County (pres. 1998-99), Prince George's County Bar Assn., D.C. Bar Assn., Montgomery County Bar Found. (treas. 1993-94). Contracts commercial, Real property, Landlord-tenant. Office: Bregman Berbert & Schwartz 7315 Wisconsin Ave Ste 800W Bethesda MD 20814-3244

**BREGMAN, JACQUELINE DE OLIVEIRA,** lawyer; b. Bay Shore, N.Y., July 30, 1961; d. Joseph Armando and Joan Marie (Hunter) De Oliveira; m. Samuel H. Bregman II, Aug. 20, 1989. BA in English, Coll. of the Holy Cross, 1983; JD magna cum laude, Touro Coll., 1988. Bar: N. Mex. 1989, U.S. Dist. Ct. N. Mex. 1989. Acct. exec. Community Mgmt. Svcs., Commack, N.Y., 1984-86; legal asst. Koeppel, Del Casino & Martone, P.C., Mineola, N.Y., 1987-88; adminstrv. legal asst. Bernalillo County Assessor, Albuquerque, 1989; pvt. practice Albuquerque, 1989—; pres., shareholder The Bregman Law Firm, PC, Albuquerque. Mem. com. Groundwater Protection Adv. Com., Albuquerque, 1991—; mem. Nor Este Neighborhood Assn., 1991—; grad. Leadership Albuquerque, 1991. Recipient Community Svc. award Albuquerque Help for Homeless, 1990, dean's merit scholarship Touro Coll., 1988. Mem. N.Mex. Bar Assn., Am. Bus. Women's Assn. (pres. 1991-92, Woman of Yr. 1991, bd. dirs.), N.Mex. Women's Found. Avocation: painting. Family and matrimonial, Real property, General civil litigation. Office: The Bregman Law Firm PC 4901 Chappell Dr NE Albuquerque NM 87107-6825

**BREGMAN, SAM,** lawyer; b. Washington, Aug. 6, 1963; s. Stan Bregman and Sandra Toro; m. Jackie Bregman, Aug. 20, 1989; children: Alexander, Jessica. BA, U. N.Mex., 1985, JD, 1989. Asst. dist. atty. State N.Mex., Albuquerque, 1994-97; ptnr. The Bregman Law Firm, Albuquerque, 1998—. V.p. City Coun., Albuqurque, 1995—, councillor, 1995—; bd. dirs. Anti-Defamation League, Albuquerque Conv. and Visitor Bur.; deouty state auditor State of N.Mex., 1997-98. Mem. N.Mex. Bar Assn., Kiwanis. General civil litigation, Real property, General corporate. Home: 8121 Corona Ave NE Albuquerque NM 87122-2818 Office: The Bregman Law Firm 4901 Chappell Rd NE Albuquerque NM 87107-6825

**BREHL, JAMES WILLIAM,** lawyer. BS engring., U. Notre Dame, 1956; JD, U. Mich., 1959. Bar: Wis. 1989; Minn. and various fed. cts. Lawyer Maun & Simon, St. Paul. Contbr. articles to law jours. Chmn. Minn. builder's adv. coun. Minn. Dept. Commerce, 1991-95; mem. planning commn. City of Afton, 1975-93; dir. Granville House Inc., 1985-95. Recipient Good Neighbor award WCCO, 1968. Mem. ABA, Minn. Bar Assn. (exec. com. 1996-97), Ramsey County Bar Assn. (exec. coun. 1977-80, 87-90, pres. 1993-94), Washington County Bar Assn., St. Paul C. of C. Fax: 612-904-7424. Real property, Labor. Office: Maun & Simon PLC 2000 Midwest Plaza W 801 Nicollet Ave Minneapolis MN 55402-2500

**BREIDENBACH, ROBERT A.,** lawyer. BS in Fin., BA in English, S.W. Mo. State U., 1990; JD, St. Louis U., 1993. Bar: Mo., Ill., U.S. Dist. Ct. (ea. and we. dists.) Mo., U.S. Dist. Ct. (so. dist.) Ill. Spl. asst. atty. gen. Office of Gen. Counsel, Mo. Dept. Revenue, Jefferson City, 1993-97; assoc. Riezman & Blitz, P.C., St. Louis, 1997—. Mem. Am. Bankruptcy Inst., Phi Eta Sigma. Bankruptcy, Consumer commercial, Federal civil litigation. Office: Riezman & Blitz PC 7700 Bonhomme Ave Fl 7 Saint Louis MO 63105-1924

**BREININ, BARTLEY JAMES,** lawyer; b. N.Y.C., Nov. 14, 1957; s. Goodwin Milton and Rose-Helen (Kopelman) B.; m. Rachel Gelin Breinin, Sept. 20, 1986; children: Alexander James, Caroline Rebecca. BA, Yale U., 1979; JD, U. Va., 1983. Bar: N.Y. 1984. Assoc. Simpson Thacher and Bartlett, N.Y.C., 1983-88, Morgan, Lewis and Bockius, N.Y.C., 1988-94; v.p., sr. assoc. counsel Chase Manhattan Bank, NA, N.Y.C., 1994-95; v.p., asst. gen. counsel Cambrian Corp., N.Y.C., 1995-97, sr. v.p., gen. counsel, 1998—. Mem. ABA, Bar Assn. City N.Y., Sunningdale Country Club, Univ. Club Larchmont. General corporate, Mergers and acquisitions, Securities. Office: Cambrian Corp 1114 Ave of Americas New York NY 10036

**BREIT, JEFFREY ARNOLD,** lawyer; b. Norfolk, Va., Apr. 14, 1955; s. Calvin W. and Mildred J. (Jacobs) B.; m. Suzanne Reigel, Aug. 23, 1980. BA, Tulane U., 1977, JD, 1979. Bar: Va. 1979, La. 1979, D.C. 1988, N.Y. 1991, N.C. 1991, U.S. Ct. Appeals (4th, 5th adn 11th cirs.), U.S. Supreme Ct. Ptnr. Breit, Rutter & Montagna, Norfolk, 1979-87, Breit, Drescher & Breit, Norfolk, 1987—. Contbr. articles to profl. jours. Chmn. Virginia Beach. Dem. Party, 1992—, vice chmn., 1995-97; pres. Operation Smile, Norfolk, 1987-90. Mem. ABA, ATLA (bd. govs. 1988—), Va. Trial Lawyers Assn. (pres. elect 1997-98, pres. 1998-99), La. Trial Lawyers Assn., N.C. Trial Lawyers Assn., Maritime Law Assn. U.S., Va. Trial Lawyers Assn. (pres. 1998-99). Jewish. Avocations: tennis, surfing. Admiralty, Personal injury, Civil rights. Home: 608 Linkhorn Dr Virginia Beach VA 23451-3917 Office: Breit Drescher & Breit 1000 Dominion Tower 999 Waterside Dr Ste 1000 Norfolk VA 23510-3304

**BREITENECKER, RUDIGER,** lawyer; b. Balt., July 19, 1965; s. Rudiger and Robin Breitenecker. AB cum laude, Duke U., 1987; JD, Georgetown U., 1992. Bar: N.Y. 1993. Assoc. Marks & Murase, N.Y.C., 1991-94; ptnr. Mason & Breitenecker LLP, N.Y.C., 1995—. Tutor Children's AID Soc., N.Y.C., 1994-96. Mem. U.S.-Australian C. of C., Japan Soc., U. Club, Manhattan Yacht Club. Private international. Office: Mason & Breitenecker LLP 45 Rockefeller Plz New York NY 10111-0100

**BREITENSTEIN, PETER FREDERIC,** lawyer; b. Denver, Mar. 10, 1938; s. Jean Sala and Helen (Thomas) B.; m. Karla Ann Gasser, Jan. 27, 1962; children: Kurt Frederick, Dana Ann, Hugh Thomas. BA in Econs., Amherst Coll., 1960; LLB, U. Calif., Berkeley, 1963. Bar: Colo. 1963. Law clk. to O. Hatfield Chilson U.S. Dist. Ct. for Colo., Denver, 1963-64; assoc. Fairfield and Woods, P.C., Denver, 1964-71, ptnr., 1971—, also bd. dirs. Mem. ABA, Colo. Bar Assn., Denver Bar Assn., Law Club, Denver Country Club, Univ. Club. General civil litigation. Office: Fairfield and Woods PC 1700 Lincoln St Ste 2400 Denver CO 80203-4524

**BREITMAN, LORRAINE RUTH,** lawyer; b. N.Y.C., Apr. 2, 1960; d. Alan M. and Marilyn F. Breitman. BA, George Washington U., 1982; JD, NYU, 1986. Bar: N.J. 1986, N.Y. 1987. Assoc. atty. Pillai, Brick and Roseman, N.Y.C., 1986, Law Office of Robert D. Arenstein, N.Y.C. and Teaneck, N.J., 1987-88, Rose & DeFuccio Esquires, Hackensack, N.J., 1988—. Pro bono atty. Alternatives to Domestic Violence, Hackensack, 1994—; panelist early settlement program Superior Ct. Bergen County, 1992—; vice chair Bergen County family law Com., 1998—; chair Bergen County Mandatory Early Settlement Program. Mem. N.J. Family Inns of Ct. (barrister 1997—), Domestic Violence Working Group Bergen County. Avocations: tennis, reading, cultural events. Family and matrimonial. Office: Rose and DeFuccio 35 Essex St Hackensack NJ 07601-5464

**BREMER, HOWARD WALTER,** consulting patenting and licensing lawyer; b. Milw., July 18, 1923; s. Walter Hugo and Lydia Martha (Schmidt) B.; m. Caryl Marie Faust, May 28, 1948; children: Katharine, William (dec.), Thomas, Timothy, Margaret. BSChemE, U. Wis., 1944, LLB, 1949. Bar: Wis. 1949, U.S. Patent and Trademark Office 1954, U.S. Supreme Ct. 1957, U.S. Ct. Appeals (fed. cir.) 1959, U.S. Dist. Ct. (so. dist.) Ohio 1960. Patent atty. Procter & Gamble Co., Cin., 1949-60; patent counsel Wis. Alumni Rsch. Found., Madison, 1960-88; cons., Madison, 1988—; mem. adv. com. Coun. on Govtl. Rels., Washington, 1975-93; panel mem. Office Tech. Assessment, Washington, 1981-83; mem. Adv. Commn. on Patent Law Reform, Washington, 1991-92. Mem. internat. adv. bd. Industry and Higher Edn. Jour., 1996—; contbr. articles to profl. jours. Pres. Edgewood Campus Sch. PTA, Madison, 1967-69; mem. adv. bd. Edgewood H.S., 1971-80, chmn. adv. bd., 1973-74. With USN, 1944-46. Recipient alumni appreciation award Edgewood H.S., 1990. Mem. ABA (chmn. com. 1993—), Am. Intellectual Property Law Assn. (chmn. com. 1996—), State Bar Wis. (chmn. intellectual property sect. 1967-68, 79-80), Wis. Intellectual Property Law Assn. (pres. 1989-90), Assn. Univ. Tech. Mgrs. (trustee 1977-78, 80-82, pres. 1978-80, com. chmn. 1985-93, mem. editl. bd. jour. 1990—, Birch award 1980). Avocations: building furniture, home maintenance, model railroading, travel, reading. Intellectual property, Patent, Legislative. Home: 1106 Brookwood Rd Madison WI 53711-3116

**BREMER, JOHN M.,** lawyer; b. 1947. BA, Fordham U., 1969; JD, Duke U., 1974. Bar: Wis. 1974. Atty. law dept. Northwestern Mutual Life Ins., Milw., 1974-78, asst. gen. counsel, 1978-90, v.p., gen. counsel and sec., 1990-94, sr. v.p., gen. counsel, sec., 1995-98, exec. v.p., gen. counsel, sec., 1998—. General corporate, Insurance, Real property. Office: Northwestern Mutual Life Ins Co 720 E Wisconsin Ave Milwaukee WI 53202-4703

**BREMER, WILLIAM RICHARD,** lawyer; b. San Francisco, Jan. 5, 1930; m. Margaret H.; children: Mark Richard (dec.), Karen Elizabeth, William Richard Jr. BS in Bus. Adminstrn., Menlo Coll., 1952; JD, U. San Francisco, 1958. Bar: Calif. 1959, U.S. Dist. Ct. (no. dist.) Calif. 1959, U.S. Ct. Appeals (9th cir.) 1959, U.S. Supreme Ct. 1965, U.S. Ct. Mil. Appeals 1973. Pvt. practice San Francisco, 1959—. Bd. dirs. Bay Area USO, Marin County and San Francisco County Ct., arbitrator, 1977—; city councilman City of Tiburon (Calif.), 1966-70, mayor, 1968-69; v.p., bd. dirs. Tiburon Peninsula Found.; regional v.p. no. Calif. Naval War Coll. Found., 1997—. Lt. USMC, 1952-54, Korea; col. USMC Res. (ret.), 1954-82. Mem. Am. ArbitrationAssn. (panel arbitrator 1965—), ATLA, San Francisco Trial Lawyers Assn., san Francisco Bar Assn., San Francisco Lawyers Club, Marin County Bar Assn., Calif. Trial Lawyers Assn., Navy League U.S. (life mem. San Francisco Coun., pres. 1978-80, nat. bd. dirs. 1978-88, no. Calif. state pres. 1981-82, nat. dep. JAG 1997—), Marine Corps Res. Officers Assn. (life), Res. Officers Assn. (life), Naval Order of U.S. (life, San Francisco commandery, comdr. 1982, 83, comdr. gen., nat. pres. 1993-95), Corinthian Yacht (commodore 1986-87), Montgomery St. Motorcycle (pres. 1974-75), Marines Meml. (pres. 1985-86), Kiwanis (bd. dirs. San Francisco chpt. 1981-83), The Tiburon Rotary (bd. dirs. 1997—, chair cmty. svc.). Personal injury, General civil litigation, Criminal. Office: William R Bremer 120 Taylor Rd Tiburon CA 94920-1061

**BREMNER, ANNE MELANI,** lawyer; b. McAlester, Okla., June 4, 1958; d. James Douglas B. BA in History with honors, Stanford U., 1980; JD, U. Puget Sound, 1982. Bar: Wash. 1983, U.S. Dist. Ct. (we. dist.) Wash. 1992, U.S. Ct. Appeals (9th cir.) 1992. Law clerk, bailiff King County Superior Ct., Seattle, 1982; deputy prosecuting attorney King County Prosecutor's Office, Seattle, 1983-88; atty. Stafford Frey Cooper, Seattle, 1988—. Author: Emerging Issues in Civil Rights, 1998. Founding mem. bd. Equal Justice Coalition, Seattle, 1996; treas. Judge Faith Ireland for Supreme Ct., Seattle, 1998; steering com. Norm Maleng for Prosecutor, Seattle, 1998. Grantee Fed. Govt., 1984-86. Mem. Wash. Women Lawyers (dir. media, pub. rels. 1995-96). Republican. Avocations: classical piano, reading. Office: Stafford Frey Cooper 1301 5th Ave Ste 2500 Seattle WA 98101-2621

**BRENDEL, JOHN S.,** lawyer; b. McKeesport, Pa., May 6, 1951. BA with distinction, Cornell U., 1973; JD cum laude, Harvard U., 1976. Bar: Pa. 1977. Atty., v.p., gen. counsel Buchanan Ingersoll Cohen & Brigsby, Pitts., 1977-97; adj. prof. of immigration law, U. Pitts. Sch. of Law., Duquesne U. Sch. Law. Fulbright-DAAD fellow, 1976-77. Mem. Am. Immigration Lawyers Assn. Labor, Immigration, naturalization, and customs. Office: Mastech Corp 1004 Mckee Rd Oakdale PA 15071-1099

**BRENDER, ART,** lawyer; b. Chgo., Feb. 21, 1946; s. Arthur John Sr. and Elenore (McGauley) B.; m. Lynda Gayle Tankersley, Dec. 14, 1968; children: Sarah Blankenship, Erin, John. BA, U. Tex., 1968, JD, 1973. Bar: Tex. 1973, U.S. Dist. Ct. (no. dist.) Tex. 1973, U.S. Dist. Ct. (so. dist.) Tex. 1987, U.S. Dist. Ct. (we. dist.) Tex. 1988, U.S. Dist. Ct. (ea. dist.) Tex. 1989, U.S. Ct. Appeals (5th cir.) 1974, U.S. Ct. Appeals (9th cir.) 1980, U.S. Supreme Ct. 1977; cert. Tex. Bd. Legal Specialization, Criminal Law, Personal Injury Trial Law. Assoc. Law Offices of Don Gladden, Ft. Worth, 1973-77; adj. prof. Tex. Christian U., Ft. Worth, 1976-84; pvt. practice Ft. Worth, 1977—; assoc. Brender, Casey and Colosi, Ft. Worth, 1984-90; advocate Am. Bd. Trial Advocates, 1985—. Contbr. articles to profl. jours. Pres. Humane Soc. North Tex., 1986—; bd. dirs. Tarrant Youth Svcs. Bur., 1973-76; bd. dirs., legal counsel Tarrant County Harvest, Inc., 1991—; parrish coun. St. Ritas Cath. Ch., 1992-93; inner city sch. com. Diocese of Ft. Worth, 1992-95; bd. dirs. S.E. Area Chs., 1978—; basketball coach 6th, 7th, 8th grades St. Rita's Sch., 1985-92; del. state and dist. conv. Tex. Dem. Party, 1974-92; alt. del. Dem. Nat. Conv., Senate Dist. 12, 1988. Lt. USN, 1969-71. Recipient Good Guy award Women's Polit. Caucus, 1985, Fair Employment Practices award Ft. Worth Human Rels. Commn., 1987, award for outstanding svc. in field of civil rights NAACP Tex. br., 1988, Pro Bono award for outstanding contbns. of legal svcs. to low income Texans, 1994. Fellow Tex. Bar Found.; mem. Am. Bd. Trial Advocates, Assn. Trial Lawyers Am., State Bar Tex. (co-chairperson individual ABA rights sect. 1983-84), Tex. Trial Lawyers Assn. (assoc. dir. 1988—), Tarrant County Bar Assn. (dir. 1987-89, law libr. com. 1980-91), Tarrant Count Trial Lawyers Assn. (treas. 1984), Tarrant County Criminal Def. Lawyers Assn. (pres. 1980-81), T Assn. U. Tex., Ex Student Assn. U. Tex. Austin, ACLU (bd. mem. Ft. Worth chpt. 1975-87). Democrat. Roman Catholic. Avocations: organic farming, ranching, gardening, mountain hiking and climbing, fishing, camping. General civil litigation, Labor, Personal injury. Home: 4121 Hampshire Blvd Fort Worth TX 76103-3920 Office: 600 8th Ave Fort Worth TX 76104-2020

**BRENEMAN, DIANE MARIE,** lawyer; b. Wichita, Kans., Apr. 26, 1965; d. Ronald J. and Mary (Niggemann) B.; m. Todd Rohn, Sept. 11, 1998. BS, U. Kans., 1986, JD, 1989. Bar: Kans. 1989, U.S. Dist. Ct. (we. dist.) Kans. 1989, Mo. 1990, U.S. Dist. Ct. Mo. 1990, Tex. 1996. Assoc. Blackwell Sanders Matheny Weary & Lombardi, Overland Park, Kans., 1989-94, Shook Hardy & Bacon, 1994-97, Shaffer Lombardo Shorik, 1997—. Law rev. editor U. Kans. Sch. Law, 1988. Ball chairperson Bacchus Found., Kansas City, Mo., 1992—; advocacy com. mem. Johnson County Coalition Against Child Abuse, Kansas City, 1992—; bd. dirs. Wayside Waters Humane Soc., 1994-96, pres. Mem. Johnson County Bar Assn., Kansas City Met. Bar Assn. Avocations: bicycling, golf, music. Construction, Public utilities, Product liability. Home: 4149 W 124th Ter Leawood KS 66209-2236 Office: Snaffer Lombardo Snurin 4141 Pennsylvania Ave Kansas City MO 64111-3033

**BRENMAN, STEPHEN MORRIS,** lawyer; b. San Francisco, Mar. 25, 1945; s. Irving I. and Vivian H. (Weiss) B.; m. Laura R. Yocum, Aug. 14, 1968; children: Jeremy S., Sara N. BS, Miami U., Oxford, Ohio, 1967; JD with distinction, Valparaiso (Ind.) U., 1970. Bar: Ind. 1970, U.S. Dist. Ct. (no. and so. dist.) Ind. 1970, U.S. Ct. Appeals (7th cir.) 1970, U.S. Supreme Ct. 1973, U.S. Tax Ct. 1973, U.S. Ct. Claims 1973. Assoc. Saul I. Ruman & Assocs., Hammond, Ind., 1970-73; ptnr. Katz & Brenman, Gary and Merrillville, Ind., 1973-78; mng. ptnr. Katz & Brenman, Merrillville, 1978—; lectr. Valparaiso U. Sch. Law, 1970; chief pub. defender Gary City Ct., 1973-78, staff coord., 1973-78; dir. and officer Dunes Volkswagen, Inc., Gary, 1977-80, Len Pollak Buick, Inc., Gary, 1977-83, Merrillville Volkswagen, Porshe-Audi, Inc., Merrillville, 1980-83; lectr. alcoholic beverage laws in Ind., miscellaneous trade orgns., 1980—; temp. probate commr., pro-tem and temp. judge Superior Ct. Lake County, Civil Divsn., East Chicago, Ind., 1980—; lectr. estate planning and right to die Congregation Beth Israel, Inc., Hammond, 1989—, Jewish Fedn., Inc., Highland, Ind., 1989—. Note editor Valparaiso U. Law Rev., 1969-70; contbr. articles to profl. jours. Co-chmn. Ind. Alcoholic Beverage Commn. Study Com., Rules, Regulations and Forms Rev., 1990; election judge and commr. Lake County Election Bd., Crown Point, Ind., 1973-78; dir. Munster (Ind.) Little League, 1980-84, umpire and coach, 1980-84; bd. dirs. Munster Youth Athletic Assn., 1980-84; bd. dirs. Jewish Fedn., Inc., Highland, 1980-85, Congregation Beth Israel, Inc., Hammond, 1980-85; dir. Hoosier Boys Town, Inc., Schererville, Ind., 1990-94, dir. and officer Hoosier Boys Town Found., 1990-94; mem. Munster H.S. Booster Club, 1987—; mem., dir., officer Alpha Epsilon Pi Parents Club, Inc., Bloomington, Ind., 1990-94./. Recipient Disting. Svc. award Jewish Fedn., 1980, 83, 84, Red and White Club, Munster H.S. Booster Club, 1989, Mustang Club, 1989; Valparaiso U. scholar, 1968-70. Mem. ABA (sect. bus. law, adminstrv. law and regulatory practice, real property, probate, trust law sects.), Nat. Assn. Estate Planners and Couns., Nat. Assn. Criminal Def. Attys., Ind. State Bar Assn., Fed. Bar Assn., Assn. Trial Lawyers Am., Ind. Trial Lawyers Assn., Lake County Bar Assn. (chmn. legal forms com.), Am. Judicature Soc. (corp. counsel inst. mem.), Phi Alpha Delta, B'nai B'rith, Miami U. Alumni Assn., Valparaiso U. Sch. Law Alumni Assn., Zeta Beta Tau. Democrat. Avocations: racquetball, tennis, boating, motor vehicle racing. Contracts commercial, Administrative and regulatory, Probate. Office: Katz & Brenman 7895 Broadway Merrillville IN 46410-5529

**BRENNAMAN, SANDRA LEE,** lawyer; b. Charleston, W.Va., Nov. 3, 1970; d. Samuel Lee and Patricia Ruth B. BS in Bus. Adminstrn., Alderson-Broaddus Coll., 1993, BA in Polit. Sci., 1993; JD, W.Va. U., 1996. Bar: W.Va. 1996, U.S. Dist. Ct. (so. dist.) W.Va. 1996. Assoc. Calwell & McCormick, Charleston, W.Va., 1996-97, Hill, Peterson, Carper, Bee & Deitzler, PLLC, Charleston, W.Va., 1997—. Mem. Assn. Trial Lawyers Am., W.Va. Trial Lawyers Assn. Avocations: skiing, scuba diving. Personal injury, Product liability, Insurance. Office: Hill Peterson Carper Bee & Deitzler 500 Tracy Way Charleston WV 25311-1555

**BRENNAN, DANIEL EDWARD, JR.,** state judge; b. Houston, Oct. 2, 1942; s. Daniel E. and Emily (Tabor) B.; m. Ruth Miriam Gonchar, Nov. 16, 1973; children: Danna Julie, Benjamin Tabor. AA, U. State N.Y., 1974, BS, 1976; JD, U. Bridgeport, 1981; IEM, Harvard U., 1974. Bar: Conn. 1981, U.S. Dist. Ct. Conn. 1981, U.S. Supreme Ct. Exec. asst. to pres. Hunter Coll., N.Y.C., 1970-77; pres. S&B Mgmt. Systems, N.Y.C., 1977-80; ptnr. Brennan, McNamara & Baldwin, P.C., Bridgeport, Conn., 1981-96, The Brennan Law Firm, Trumbull, Conn., 1996-99; judge Superior Ct. Conn., 1999—; trial referee Superior Ct., State of Conn.; chief legal advisor Bridgeport Police Dept., 1983-85; chief labor counsel City of Bridgeport, 1981-85, Town of Trumbull, 1982-87. Mem. Conn. Bar Assn. (former chair litigation sect.). Labor, State civil litigation, General practice. Home: 57 Gray Rock Rd Trumbull CT 06611-3307

**BRENNAN, ENDA THOMAS,** lawyer; b. Galway, Connaught, Ireland, Oct. 31, 1955; came to the U.S., 1957; s. Sean Brennan and Philomena Philben. BA, U. Calif., Berkeley, 1976; JD, Harvard U., 1980. Bar: Calif. 1980, U.S. Dist. Ct. (cen. dist.) Cali. 1982, U.S. Dist. Ct. (no. dist.) Calif. 1989. Atty. Manatt, Phelps, Rothenberg & Tunney, L.A., 1980-82; issues dir. Nuc. Freeze Initiative, L.A., 1982; pvt. practice law L.A., 1983-84; dep. county counsel Orange County, Santa Ana, Calif., 1984-85; dep. pub. defender Los Angeles County Pub. Defender, L.A., 1985-88; assoc. Biggam, Christensen & Minsloff, Santa Cruz, Calif., 1988-91; pvt. practice, Santa Cruz, 1992—. Dir. Lawyer's Alliance for Nuc. Arms Control, Boston, 1982-84; treas., mem. Sister Cities Com., Santa Cruz, 1988-98, 99—. Mem. Santa Cruz Criminal Def. Bar. Democrat. Avocations: swimming, skiing, hiking. Criminal, Constitutional, Entertainment. Office: PO Box 475 Santa Cruz CA 95061-0475

**BRENNAN, J. LORRAINE,** lawyer; b. Coral Gables, Fla., June 24, 1964; d. John Lawrence and Eugenie Marie (Warriner) B. BS, Fla. Internat. U., 1986; JD, U. Miami, 1989. Bar: Fla. 1989. Assoc. Womack & Bass, Miami,

1990-96; ptnr. Womack, Appleby and Brennan, Miami, 1996—. Vol. Family Resource Ctr. Crisis Nursing, Miami, 1997—. Republican. Roman Catholic. Avocations: boating, weightlifting, fishing, golf. General civil litigation, Insurance, Personal injury. Office: Womack Appleby and Brennan 7700 N Kendall Dr Ste 705 Miami FL 33156-7591

**BRENNAN, JOHN JOSEPH,** lawyer, legal administrator; b. Troy, N.Y., Nov. 1, 1958; s. James Patrick and Grace Marie (Bartolomeo) B. AAS, Schenectady (N.Y) Community Coll., 1978; BA cum laude, Siena Coll., 1981; JD cum laude, Union U., 1985. Bar: N.Y. 1986, U.S. Dist. Ct. (no. dist.) N.Y. 1986, U.S. Supreme Ct. 1999. Law clk. to Appellate Divsn. Justice 4th Dept., Herkimer, N.Y., 1985-86; assoc. law ck. to justice State Supreme Ct., Herkimer, 1986-90; law clk. to U.S. Magistrate-Judge, Utica, N.Y., 1991-92; assoc. law clk. to justice N.Y. Supreme Ct., Utica, 1992—. Mem. ABA, N.Y. State Bar Assn., Oneida County Bar Assn., Herkimer County Bar Assn. (treas. 1990), KC, Pi Gamma Mu. Roman Catholic. Avocations: running, skiing. General practice. Home: 119 Court St Herkimer NY 13350-1923 Office: Oneida County Ct House Utica NY 13501

**BRENNAN, SIDNEY L.,** lawyer; b. Mpls., Apr. 27, 1951; s. Sidney Louis and Florence (Saladis) B.; m. Carolyn A. Brennan, Apr. 8, 1983; children: Michael, Jennifer, Jason, Andrew. BA, St. Thomas Coll., St. Paul, 1973; JD, William Mitchell Coll. Law, St. Paul, 1977. BAr: Minn. 1977, U.S. Dsit. Ct. Minn. 1978. Atty. Beal Horner DeVaughn & Brennan, Mpls., 1978-80, Brennan, Evans & Sarles, Mpls., 1980-84, Brennan Law Firm, Minnetonka, Minn., 1984—. Mem. Minn. State Bar Assn., Minnetonka County Bar Assn. Roman Catholic. Avocations: hunting, fishing, collecting old cars. General civil litigation, Personal injury, General practice. Office: Brennan Law Firm 1013 Ford Rd Minnetonka MN 55305-1640

**BRENNAN, WILLIAM JOSEPH, III,** lawyer; b. Newark, Apr. 29, 1933; s. William J. Jr. and Marjory (Leonard) B.; m. Georgianna V. Franklin, Sept. 10, 1960; children: William J. IV, Alexandra V. BA, Colgate U., 1955; LLB, Yale U., 1962. Bar: N.Y. 1963, N.J. 1967, U.S. Dist. Ct. (so. and ea. dists.) N.Y. 1964, U.S. Dist. Ct. N.J. 1967, U.S. Ct. Appeals (1st cir.) 1987, U.S. Ct. Appeals (2nd cir.) 1968, U.S. Ct. Appeals (3rd cir.) 1968, U.S. Ct. Appeals (Fed. cir.) 1991, U.S. Supreme Ct. 1967. Assoc. Breed, Abbott & Morgan, N.Y.C., 1962-67; asst. atty. gen in charge of litigation Office of Atty. Gen. of N.J., Trenton, 1967-68; spl. counsel to gov. Office of the Gov. of the State of N.J., Trenton, 1969; ptnr., mng. ptnr. Smith, Stratton, Wise, Heher & Brennan, Princeton, N.J., 1970—. Assoc. editor N.J. Law Jour., 1979—. Trustee St. Peter's Coll., Jersey City, 1988-94. Served to 1st lt. USMC, 1956-59. Recipient Award of Distinction, N.J. State Grand Jurors' Assn., 1969, Alumni Achievement award Newark Acad., 1986, Trial Bar award Trial Attys. N.J., 1994. Fellow Am. Coll. Trial Lawyers (chmn. com. on legal ethics 1987-93, chmn. com. on professionalism 1993-97), Internat. Acad. Trial Lawyers, Am. Acad. Appellate Lawyers, Am. Bar Found. (lie, state chmn. 1990); mem. ABA (mem. com. on legal ethics 1989, 3d cir. mem., com. on fed. judiciary 1989-93, ho. of dels. 1986-95), N.J. State Bar Assn. (pres. 1984-85), Assn. of Fed. Bar of State of N.J. (pres. 1992-94), Assn. of Bar of City of N.Y., Yale Law Sch. Assn. N.J., Am. Law Inst. Avocations: scuba diving, flying. Aviation, General civil litigation, Insurance. Office: Smith Stratton Wise Heher & Brennan 600 College Rd E Princeton NJ 08540-6636

**BRENNECKE, ALLEN EUGENE,** lawyer; b. Marshalltown, Iowa, Jan. 8, 1937; s. Arthur Lynn and Julia Alice (Allen) B; m. Billie Jean Johnstone, June 12, 1958; children: Scott, Stephen, Beth, Gregory, Kristen. BBA, U. Iowa, 1959, JD, 1961. Bar: Iowa 1961. Law clk. U.S. Dist. Judge, Des Moines, 1961-62; assoc. Mote, Wilson & Welp, Marshalltown, Iowa, 1962-66; ptnr. Harrison, Brennecke, Moore, Smaha & McKibben, Marshalltown, 1966—. Contr. articles to profl. jours. Bd. dirs. Marshalltown YMCA, 1966-71; mem. bd. trustees Iowa Law Sch. Found., 1973-86, United Meth. Ch., Marshalltown, 1978-81, 87-89; fin. chmn. Rep. party 4th Congl. Dist., Iowa, 1970-73, Marshall County Rep. Party, Iowa, 1967-70. Fellow ABA (chmn. ho. of dels. 1984-86, bd. govs. 1982-86), Nat. Jud. Coll. (bd. dirs. 1982-88), Am. Coll. Trusts and Estates Counsel, Am. Coll. Tax Counsel, Am. Bar Found., Iowa Bar Assn. (pres. 1990-91, award of merit 1987); mem. Masons, Shriners, Promise Keepers. Republican. Methodist. Avocations: golf; travel; sports. Home: 703 Circle Dr Marshalltown IA 50158-3809 Office: Harrison Brennecke Moore Smaha & McKibben 302 Masonic Temple Marshalltown IA 50158

**BRENNEMAN, GERALD WAYNE,** lawyer; b. Topeka, Kans., Nov. 15, 1959; s. James Christian and Mary Virginia Brenneman; m. Kelly Diana Clark, Aug. 10, 1985; children: Ryan, Sarah. BSBA, Creighton U., 1982; JD, U. Kans., 1985. Bar: Mo. 1985, U.S. Dist. Ct. (we. dist.) Mo. 1985, Kans., U.S. Dist. Ct. Kans. 1988. Assoc. Polsinelli, White, Vardeman & Shalton, Kansas City, Mo., 1985-91, shareholder, 1991—; dir. Brenneco Benefit Adminstrs., Overland Park, Kans., 1988-90. Bd. dirs. Ronald McDonald House Charities, Kansas City, 1997—, Rockhurst H.S. Alumni Bd., Kansas City, 1989—; pres., bd. dirs. Windsor Manor Homes Assn., Overland Park, Kans., 1997—. Mem. Kans. Bar Assn., Mo. Bar Assn., Kansas City Met. Bar Assn. (bus. law com. 1985—, vice chair 1998, chair 1999), Creighton U. Nat. Alumni Assn. (bd. dirs. 1990-93), Order of the Coif. Roman Catholic. Avocations: travel, sports. Mergers and acquisitions, General corporate, Insurance. Office: Polsinelli White Vardeman & Shalton 700 W 47th St Ste 1000 Kansas City MO 64112-1805

**BRENNEMAN, HUGH WARREN, JR.,** judge; b. July 4, 1945; s. Hugh Warren and Irma June (Redman) B.; m. Catherine Sheperd; children: Justin Scott, Ross Edward. BA, Alma Coll., 1967; JD, U. Mich., 1970. Bar: Mich. 1970, D.C. 1975, U.S. Dist. Ct. (we. dist.) Mich. 1974, U.S. Dist. Ct. Md. 1973, U.S. Ct. Mil. Appeals 1971, U.S. Ct. Appeals (6th cir.) 1976, U.S. Ct. Appeals (D.C. cir.) 1981, U.S. Supreme Ct. 1980. Law clk. Mich. 30th Jud. Cir., Lansing, 1970-71; asst. U.S. atty. Dept. Justice, Grand Rapids, Mich., 1974-77; assoc. Bergstrom, Slykhouse & Shaw, P.C., Grand Rapids, 1977-80; U.S. magistrate judge U.S. Dist. Ct. (we. dist.) Mich., Grand Rapids, 1980—; instr. Western Mich. U., Grand Valley State U., 1989-92. Mem. exec. bd. West Michigan Shores coun. Boy Scouts Am., 1984-87, 88-92, adv. coun., 1987-88, 93-95, v.p., 1988-92; mem. Grand Rapids Hist. Commn., 1991-97, pres., 1995-97; dir. Cmty. Reconciliation Ctr., 1991. Capt. JAGC, U.S. Army, 1971-74. Fellow Mich. State Bar Found.; mem. FBA (pres. Western Mich. chpt. 1979-80, nat. del. 1980-84), State Bar Mich. (rep. assembly 1984-90), D.C. Bar Assn., Grand Rapids Bar Assn. (chmn. U.S. Constn. Bicentennial com., co-chmn. Law Day 1991), Fed. Magistrate Judges Assn., Am. Inns of Ct. (master of bench Grand Rapids chpt., pres.), Phi Delta Phi, Omicron Delta Kappa, Peninsular Club, Rotary (past pres., Charities Found. of Grand Rapids v.p., Paul Harris fellow), Econ. Club of Grand Rapids (past bd. dirs.). Office: 580 Fed Bldg Grand Rapids MI 49503

**BRENNENSTUHL, HENRY BRENT,** lawyer. BA, U. Ky., 1985, JD, 1988. Bar: Ky. 1988, U.S. Dist. Ct. (we. dist.) Ky. 1988, U.S. Dist. Ct. (ea. dist.) Ky. 1989, U.S. Ct. Appeals (6th cir.) 1990, U.S. Supreme Ct. 1997; cert. in civil trial advocacy Nat. Bd. Trial Advocacy, 1995. Ptnr. Kerrick, Grise & Stivers, Bowling Green, Ky., 1988—. Co-author: Kentucky Law of Torts, 1996; contbr. articles to profl. jours. Mem. Ky. Bar Assn., Warren County Bar Assn. (pres. 1996). General civil litigation, Insurance, Personal injury. Office: Kerrick Grise & Stivers 1025 State St Bowling Green KY 42101-2652

**BRENNER, ANITA SUSAN,** lawyer; b. Los Angeles, Aug. 18, 1949; d. Morris I. and Lillian F. Brenner; m. Leonard E. Torres, Aug. 19, 1973; children—Andrew Jacob, Rachel Elizabeth. B.A., UCLA, 1970, J.D., 1973. Bar: Calif. 1974, U.S. Dist. Ct. (cen. dist.) Calif. 1974. Atty. Greater Watts Justice Ctr., Los Angeles, 1974-75; sole practice, Los Angeles, 1975; dep. pub. defender Los Angeles County, 1975-84; assoc. Tyre and Kamins, Los Angeles, 1979; ptnr. Torres-Brenner, Pasadena, Calif., 1984—; lectr. criminal law. Mem., assoc. editor UCLA Law Rev., 1971-73. Editor FORUM mag., 1980-83. Contbr. articles to profl. jours. Bd. dirs. One Stop Immigration, 1979-81; vol. Los Angeles Area Council on Child Passenger Safety, 1981; mem. Los Angeles County Med. Assn. joint com. on med.-legal issues, 1983. Mable Wilson Richards scholar, 1971-72. Mem. Calif. Attys. for Criminal Justice (bd. govs. 1980-86), Continuing Edn. of Bar (criminal law sub-com.). State civil litigation, Criminal, Computer. Office: Torres-Brenner 301 E Colorado Blvd Ste 614 Pasadena CA 91101-1918

**BRENNER, EDGAR H.,** legal administrator; b. N.Y.C., Jan. 4, 1930; s. Louis and Bertha B. (Guttman) B.; m. Janet Maybin, Aug. 4, 1979; children from previous marriage—Charles S., David M., Paul R. B.A., Carleton Coll., 1951; J.D., Yale U., 1954. Bar: D.C. 1954, U.S. Ct. Claims 1957, U.S. Supreme Ct. 1957. Mem. 2d Hoover Commn. Legal Task Force Staff, Washington, 1954; trial atty. U.S. Dept. Justice, Washington, 1954-57; assoc. Arnold & Porter, Washington, 1957-62, ptnr., 1962-89; nat. dir. The Behavioral Law Ctr., Washington, 1989—; vis. rsch. prof. law Nat. Law Ctr.; sr. counsel terrorism studies program George Washington U., 1993-99; chmn. conf. com. Alternative Dispute Resolution, 1990-91; dir. Insts. for Behavior Resources, Inc.; co-dir. Inter Univ. Ctr. for Legal Studies, 1999—. Contbr. articles to profl. jours. Commr. Fairfax County Econ. Devel. Corp., Va., 1963-78; pres., bd. dirs. Stella and Charles Guttman Found., N.Y.C., Ams. for Med. Progress, Arlington, Va. Fellow Coll. Problems of Drug Dependency. Mem. ABA (chmn. arbitration com. litigation sect. 1984-87), D.C. Bar Assn., Yale Club, Explorers Club (N.Y.C.). Democrat. Home: 340 Persimmon Ln Washington VA 22747-1845 Office: 4620 Lee Hwy Ste 216 Arlington VA 22207-3400

**BRENNER, JANET MAYBIN WALKER,** lawyer; b. Arkansas City, Kans.; d. D. Arthur and Maybin (Gardner) Walker; children: Margaret Maybin Burns, Theodore Kimball Jonas, Amanda Nash Freeman; m. Edgar H. Brenner, Aug. 4, 1979. AB, U. So. Calif.; JD, George Washington U., 1978. Bar: D.C. 1978; U.S. Dist. Ct. (D.C.). Mem. Brenner Women's Leadership com.; mem. women's com. Corcoran Gallery Art, Washington, 1969—, Pres.'s Cir., Planned Parenthood D.C., 1990—, Found. for Preservation of Historic Georgetown; mem. com. restoration Salon Doré. Mem. D.C. Bar Assn., Sulgrave Club (Washington). Real property. Home: 3325 R St NW Washington DC 20007-2310 also: Shadow Ridge Farm Washington VA 22747

**BRENNER, JOHN FINN,** lawyer; b. Eglin AFB, Fla., Aug. 18, 1956; s. Theodore Engelbert and Maria Theresa (Finn) B.; m. Lydia Snel, Dec. 29, 1979; children: Meredith R., Corinne J., Elise H. BA, Dartmouth Coll., 1977; JD, U. Va., 1980. Bar: N.J. 1980, U.S. Dist. Ct. N.J. 1980, U.S. Ct. Appeals (3d cir.) 1984, N.Y. 1988. Assoc. McCarter & English, LLP, Newark, N.J., 1980-88, ptnr., 1988—. Contbr.: New Jersey Liability Law, 1994. Chmn. planning bd. Borough of Fair Haven, N.J., 1998—. Mem. ABA, Def. Rsch. Inst., N.J. State Bar Assn., Phi Beta Kappa. Product liability, General civil litigation, Appellate. Office: McCarter & English LLP 100 Mulberry St Newark NJ 07102-4096

**BRENNER, LOIS M.,** lawyer, mediator; b. N.Y., Aug. 25, 1944; d. Abraham J. Brenner and Esther Kaufman; m. Robert Stein, Apr. 30, 1989; 1 child, Stephanie. BA, U. Rochester, 1964; JD, Pace U., 1980. Assoc. Sullivan & Cromwell, N.Y.C., 1980-81, Sidamon-Eristoff, Morrison, N.Y.C., 1981-85, Herzfeld & Rubin, N.Y.C., 1985-94; pvt. practice N.Y.C., 1994—. Author: Getting Your Share—Guide to Divorce, 1989. Avocation: music. Office: 135 E 54th St New York NY 10022-4508

**BRENNER, MARSHALL LEIB,** lawyer; b. N.Y.C., Aug. 8, 1933; s. Samuel and Ruth (Novak) B.; m. Gwen A. Krakower, Aug. 9, 1959; children: Scott David, Louri Ann, Robin Lynn. BA, St Lawrence U., Canton, N.Y., 1955; JD, Bklyn. Law Sch., 1959. Bar: N.Y. 1960, U.S. Dist. Ct. (no. and ea. dists.) N.Y. 1960, U.S. Ct. Claims 1964, U.S. Supreme Ct. 1964, U.S. Dist. Ct. (so. dist.) N.Y. 1969. Assoc. Spitz & Levine, Poughkeepsie, N.Y., 1960-62; sr. ptnr. Brenner, Gordon & Lane, Poughkeepsie, 1977—; chief appeals sect. Dutchess County Pub. Defenders Office, Poughkeepsie, 1966-78; tchr. law Marks Realtors/Appraisors, Poughkeepsie and Fishkill, N.Y., 1968-72, Robert-Mark Realtors, Hopewell Junction, N.Y., 1979-92; lectr. Dutchess County Realty Bd. for Sales/Broker Lic. Applicants, 1985—. Contbr. articles to profl. jours. Pres., bd. dirs. Sloper-Willen Community Ambulance, Wappingers Falls, N.Y., 1966-79; bd. dirs. Poughkeepsie Jewish Community Ctr., 1980-82, Dutchess County Assn. for Sr. Citizens, 1988-94, counsel, 1994—, Dutchess County Youth Bd.; mem. adv. bd. Anderson Sch., Staatsburg, N.Y., 1990-95, bd. dirs., 1995—; mem. Town of Poughkeepsie Cablevision Com., Town of Poughkeepsie Ethics in Govt. Com. Capt. U.S. Army, 1956-63. Mem. N.Y. State Bar Assn., Dutchess County Bar Assn., N.Y. State Trial Lawyers Assn. Republican. Jewish. Clubs: Harding (Poughkeepsie) (pres. 1968-69); County Players (Wappingers Falls) (bd. dirs. 1963-74). Lodges: Masons, Rotary (pres. 1973-74, 78-79, Govs. Trophy 1978). Avocations: golf, tennis, swimming, reading, chess. Real property, General practice, Contracts commercial. Home: 30 Robin Rd Poughkeepsie NY 12601-5654 Office: 247 Church St Poughkeepsie NY 12601-4103

**BRENTIN, JOHN OLIN,** lawyer; b. Youngstown, Ohio, Mar. 21, 1953; s. John William and Mary Ann (Ohlin) B.; m. Victoria Jane Barkate, Apr. 19, 1980; children: Steven Alexander, John Gabriel, Benjamin William. BA cum laude, Ohio State U., 1974; JD, U. Houston, 1978. Bar: Tex. 1978; U.S. dist. Ct. (so. dist.) Tex., 1978; U.S. Ct. Appeals (5th cir.) 1979; bd. cert. Estate Planning and Probate Law. Assoc. Sullins and Johnston, Houston, 1978-82, ptnr., 1983-1993; principal John O. Brentin and Assocs., Houston, 1993—; bd. dirs. Planned Giving Coun. of Houston, 1995-98. Author: Basic Drafting of Wills and Trusts in Texas, 1993. Chmn. Econ. Devel. Coun., Bellaire, Tex., 1994-96, Planning and Zoning Bd., Bellaire, Tex., 1991-94. Mem. ABA, Houston Bar Assn., Houston Estate and Fin. Forum, Tex. Acad. Probate and Trust Lawyers, Rotary Club of Houston (pres. 1998—). Republican. Roman Catholic. Avocations: Boy Scouts of Am. Estate planning, General corporate, Estate taxation. Home: 5310 Pine St Bellaire TX 77401-4811 Office: 3700 Buffalo Speedway Ste 560 Houston TX 77098-3707

**BRESLIN, EILEEN MARY,** lawyer; b. N.Y.C.; d. Hugh Edward Breslin Jr. and Eileen Edith Whalen; m. Joseph Amedeo Rocca, Sept. 4, 1983; children: Andrew Amedeo, Adriana Eileen, Stephanie Mary Elizabeth. BA, SUNY, N.Y.C., 1981; JD, Yale U., 1984. Bar: N.Y., U.S. Dist. Ct. (so. dist.) N.Y., U.S. Dist. Ct. (ea. dist.) N.Y. Assoc. corp. and banking dept. Milbank, Tweed, Hadley & McCoy, N.Y.C., 1984-95; ptnr. Greenberger & Forman, N.Y.C., 1995-97, Jaspan Schlesinger & Hoffman, LLP, Garden City, N.Y., 1997—; mem. com. corp. law. Assn. Bar N.Y.C., com. securities regulation Am. Soc. Corp. Secs. Pro Bono work includes social security, VA benefits, domestic violence cases. Avocations: young astronauts program. General corporate, Securities, Mergers and acquisitions. Office: Jaspan Schlesinger et al 300 Garden City Plz Garden City NY 11530-3302

**BRESLIN, ELVIRA MADDEN,** tax lawyer, educator; b. Phila., Oct. 28, 1943; d. Daniel Joseph and Elvira Rose (Leichner) Madden; m. John Anthony Breslin, June 19, 1971; children: Kristen, John A.V. AB in English, Secondary Edn., Chestnut Hill Coll., Phila., 1961-65; MA in High Sch. Adminstrn., Villanova (Pa.) U., 1968; JD, Cath. U. Am., Washington, 1990; LLM in Taxation, Villanova U., 1996. Bar: Pa. 1991, D.C. 1992, U.S. Dist. Ct. D.C. 1992, U.S. Dist. Ct. Pa. 1994, U.S. Ct. Appeals (3rd cir.) 1994, U.S. Tax Ct. 1996. Tchr. Baldwin-Whitehall Pub. Schs./Cheltenham Pub. Schs., Pa., 1965-75; educator counsel duties, prin. cert., legal intern Fairfax County (Va.) Pub. Schs., 1979-94; of counsel, bd. treas., computer and career specialist, guidance and curriculum specialist, tchr. Thomas Jefferson H.S. for Sci. and Tech, Gov.s Sch. for Gifted, Alexandria, Va., 1987-94; computer/paralegal specialist Personnel Pool, Washington, 1987; rsch. assoc. Meade & Assocs., Fairfax, 1988, Akin, Gump, Strauss, Hauer & Feld, Washington, 1988; law clk. Fedn. of Tax Adminstrs., Washington, 1989, Beins, Axelrod, Osborne & Mooney, Washington, 1989-90; pvt. practice Washington and Pa., 1991—; rsch. assoc. Villanova U., 1994-96; legal/computer specialist Nat. Acad. Scis., Smithsonian Instn., Steptoe & Johnson, Akin, Gump, Strauss, Hauer & Feld, Office of Ind. Counsel; legal resource/rsch. specialist Dir. Testing and Evaluation, Walnut Hill Ctr., dir. grad. tax. program. Contbr. articles to profl. jours. Mem. Oakton Glen Homeowners Assn., 1978-97, Neighborhood Watch, 1978-97; mem., religious instr., usher Our Lady of Good Counsel Roman Cath. Ch., Vienna; judge moot ct. competitions Cath. U. Columbus Sch. Law, Washington, 1993-95; exec. treas. Thomas Jefferson H.S. for Sci. and Tech., also investment advisor and counsel computer tchr.; coord. VITA Tax Ctr, Phila., 1997—. Mem. ABA (tax sect. and legal edn. sect.), Fed. Bar Assn. (tax sect.), D.C. Bar Assn. (tax sects.), Pa. Bar Assn. (tax sects., taxation coms., chair edn. com. 1997). Avocations: reading, biking, swimming, gardening, genealogy/family history. Fax: (724) 942-3741. E-mail: taxlaw.sgi.net. Taxation, general, Estate planning, Non-profit and tax-exempt organizations. Office: 306 Doubletree Dr Venetia PA 15367-1434

**BRESLIN, MICHAEL FRANCIS,** lawyer; b. Phila., May 1, 1962; s. Gerard Patrick Breslin and Helen Anne Dougherty; m. Kathleen Mary Higgins, Aug. 8, 1987 (div. May 1993); m. Lori Anne Gardner, Aug. 16, 1997. BS in Acctg. with high distinction, U. Ky., 1984; JD, U. Pa., 1987; LLM in Taxation, Temple U., 1992. Bar: Pa. 1987, N.J. 1988, U.S. Tax Ct. 1991, U.S. Dist. Ct. N.J. 1988, U.S. Dist. Ct. (ea. dist.) Pa. 1988. Tax cons. Deloitte, Haskins & Sells, Phila., 1987-89; assoc. Parker, McCay & Criscuolo P.C., Marlton, N.J., 1989-91, Curtin and Heefner, Morrisville, Pa., 1991-94, Hamburg, Rubin, Mullin, Maxwell & Lupin P.C., Lansdale, Pa., 1994-96, Brett Senior & Assocs., Conshohocken, Pa., 1996-97, Freeman, Rogers & Loev P.C., Blue Bell, Pa., 1997-98; proprietor Law Offices of Michael F. Breslin, King of Prussia, Pa. Treas. Cath. Philopatrian Literary Inst., Phila., 1996—. Mem. Pa. Bar Assn., Montgomery Bar Assn., Bucks County Assn. CPAs, Montgomery County Estate Planning Coun., Brehan Law Soc., Hibernians. Democrat. Roman Catholic. Avocations: golf, softball, basketball, bicycling. General corporate, Probate, Taxation, general. Home: 150 Ridge Pike Apt B-210 Lafayette Hill PA 19444-1929 Office: 1003 W 9th Ave King Of Prussia PA 19406-1210

**BRESLOW, STEPHANIE R.,** lawyer; b. N.Y.C., June 20, 1960; d. Ronald and Esther Breslow. BA cum laude, Harvard U., 1981; JD, Columbia U., 1984. Bar: Ohio 1984, N.Y. 1986. Assoc. Cleary Gottlieb Steen & Hamilton, N.Y.C., 1985-93; ptnr. Schulte Roth & Zabel LLP, N.Y.C., 1993—. Co-author: New York Limited Liability Liability Companies and Partnerships, N.Y. & Del Business Entities: Choice Formation Operation Financing and Acquisitions. Mem. Assn. of the Bar of the City of New York. Securities, General corporate. Office: Schulte Roth & Zabel LLP 900 3rd Ave Fl 19 New York NY 10022-4774

**BRESNAHAN, ARTHUR STEPHEN,** lawyer; b. Chgo., Dec. 26, 1944; s. Arthur Patrick and Margaret Genevieve (Gleason) B.; m. Patricia Margaret Wetz, June 29, 1968; children: Arthur Patrick, Maureen Justina, Brian Michael, Brendan Robert, Sean Matthew. BA in Psychology, Loras Coll., 1967; JD, Ill. Inst. Tech., 1975. Bar: Ill. 1975, U.S. Dist. Ct. (no. dist.) Ill. 1975, U.S. Ct. Appeals (7th cir.) 1978, U.S. Supreme Ct. 1986, U.S Ct. Claims 1986. Assoc. Garbutt, Jacobson & Lee, Chgo., 1975-77; sr. assoc. atty. Purcell & Wardrope, Chgo., 1977-83; ptnr. Bresnahan & Garvey, Chgo., 1983-88, 1988-98; pvt. practice Arthur S. Bresnahan & Assocs., Chgo., 1998—; speaker in field. Asst. scoutmaster Boy Scouts Am., Chgo., 1980—, Webelos Den leader. Capt. USMC, 1967-72. Mem. ABA, ATLA, VFW, Nat. Acad. Elderlaw Attys., Fed. Bar Assn., Ill. Bar Assn., Ill. Trial Lawyers Assn., Fed. Trial Bar Assn., Chgo. Bar Assn., Def. Rsch. Inst., Trial Lawyers Club, Vietnam Vets. Am., Lawyer Pilots Bar Assn., Am. Legion. Democrat. Roman Catholic. Lodges: KC, Moose. Avocations: golf, Girl/Boy Scouts. State civil litigation, Federal civil litigation, Insurance. Home and Office: 4715 N Kenneth Ave Chicago IL 60630-4004

**BRESSAN, PAUL LOUIS,** lawyer; b. Rockville Centre, N.Y., June 15, 1947; s. Louis Charles Bressan and Nance Elizabeth Batteley. BA cum laude, Fordham Coll., 1969; JD, Columbia U., 1975. Bar: N.Y. 1976, Calif. 1987, U.S. Dist. Ct. (so., ea. and no. dists.) N.Y. 1976, U.S. Dist. Ct. (no. and ctrl. dists.) Calif. 1987, U.S. Ct. Appeals (2d cir.) 1980, U.S. Supreme Ct. 1980, U.S. Ct. Appeals (1st and 4th cirs.) 1981, U.S. Ct. Appeals (11th cir.) 1982, U.S. Ct. Appeals (9th cir.) 1987, U.S Ct. Appeals (7th cir.) 1991, U.S. Dist. Ct. (ea. dist.) Calif. 1995; U.S. Dist. Ct. (so. dist.) Calif. 1997. Assoc. Kelley, Drye & Warren, N.Y.C., 1975-84; ptnr. Kelley, Drye & Warren, N.Y.C. and Los Angeles, 1984—. Served to lt. USNR, 1971-72. Named One of Outstanding Coll. Athletes of Am., 1969; Harlan Fiske Stone scholar Columbia Law Sch. Mem. ABA, Calif. Bar Assn., Phi Beta Kappa. Republican. Roman Catholic. Labor, Federal civil litigation, State civil litigation. Office: Kelley Drye & Warren LLP 777 S Figueroa St Ste 2700 Los Angeles CA 90017-5825

**BRESSLER, BARRY E.,** lawyer; b. Phila., Apr. 7, 1947; s. Joseph and Shirley M. (Eiseman) B.; m. Risé Sharon Cohen, June 14, 1970 (dec.); children: Allison Ivy, Michelle Amy. AB, Franklin and Marshall Coll., Lancaster, Pa., 1968; JD, U. Pa., 1971. Bar: Pa. 1971, U.S. Dist. Ct. (ea. dist.) Pa. 1973, U.S. Ct. Appeals (3d cir.) 1977, U.S. Supreme Ct. 1988, U.S. Dist. Ct. (mid. dist.) Pa. 1990. Law clk. to judge Superior Ct. Pa., Phila., 1971-73; assoc. Meltzer & Schiffrin, Phila., 1973-79, ptnr., 1979-86; ptnr. Fox, Rothschild, O'Brien & Frankel, Phila., 1987-88; mem., sr. lawyer real estate litigation & creditors' rights Pelino & Lentz, P.C., Phila., 1988—; coadj. instr. landlord-tenant law Delaware County C.C., Media, Pa., 1985-96, Montgomery County C.C., Blue Bell, Pa., 1987—. V.p. English Ceramic Study Group, Phila.; v.p., sec. Temple Sinai, Dresher, Pa., 1991-97; mem. Leadership, Inc., Phila. Mem. ABA (litigation sect.), Pa. Bar Assn. (corp. banking and bus. sect.), Phila. Bar Assn. (real property sect.), Bankruptcy Conf. Ea. Dist. Pa. (treas.), Am. Arbitration Assn. Republican. Jewish. Avocations: tennis, ceramics, bridge. Bankruptcy, General civil litigation, Landlord-tenant. Office: Pelino & Lentz PC One Liberty Pl 1650 Market St Fl 32 Philadelphia PA 19103-7393

**BRESSLER, H.J.,** lawyer, judge; b. Balt., Dec. 31, 1939; s. Sam Bressler and Rose Cohen; m. Elizabeth Ann Woodward, Dec. 20, 1959; children: Scott, Erika, Jason. Student, U.S. Army Lang. Sch., 1959; BA, Miami U., Oxford, Ohio, 1964; JD, Salmon P. Chase Law Sch., 1968. Regional credit mgr. Procter & Gamble, Cin., 1964-65, U.S. Shoe Co., Cin., 1965-68; ptnr. Holbrock, Jonson, Bressler and Houser, 1972-85, Bressler, Shanks & Gedling Co. L.P.A., Hamilton, Ohio, 1985-96; judge Butler County Ct., Ohio, 1981-96, Butler County Common Pleas Ct., 1997—; lectr. Ohio Jud. Coll., Ohio Bar Assn. Served with U.S. Army, 1958-61. Mem. Ohio Bar Assn., Butler County Bar Assn. (pres. 1981), Am. Acad. Trial Lawyers, Ohio Acad. Trial Lawyers, Greater Hamilton Trial Lawyers Assn. (pres. 1978), Ohio Muni-County Judges Assn. (pres. 1991), Ohio Common Pleas Judges Assn. (trustee 1999—). Republican. Methodist. State civil litigation, Family and matrimonial, Personal injury. Office: Butler County Courthouse 101 High St Hamilton OH 45011-2727

**BREST, PAUL A.,** law educator; b. Jacksonville, Fla., Aug. 9, 1940; s. Alexander and Mia (Deutsch) B.; m. Iris Lang, June 17, 1962; children: Hilary, Jeremy. AB, Swarthmore Coll., 1962; JD, Harvard U., 1965; LLD (hon.), Northeastern U., 1980, Swarthmore Coll., 1991. Bar: N.Y. 1966. Law clk. to Hon. Bailey Aldrich U.S. Ct. Appeals (1st cir.), Boston, 1965-66; atty. NAACP Legal Def. Fund, Jackson, Miss., 1966-68; law clk. Justice John Harlan, U.S. Supreme Ct., 1968-69; prof. law Stanford U., 1969—, Kenneth and Harle Montgomery Prof. pub. interest law, Richard E. Lang prof. and dean, 1987-99. Author: Processes of Constitutional Decisionmaking, 1992. Mem. Am. Acad. Arts and Scis. Home: 814 Tolman Dr Palo Alto CA 94305-1026 Office: Stanford U Sch Law 559 Nathan Abbott Way Stanford CA 94305-8602

**BRETT, STEPHEN M.,** lawyer, entertainment company executive. BS, U. Pa., 1962, JD, 1966. Bar: N.Y. 1966, Colo. 1971. Assoc. Dewey, Ballantine, Bushby, Palmer & Wood, 1966-71; ptnr. Sherman & Howard, 1971-88; exec. v.p. legal, gen. counsel, sec. United Artists Entertainment Co., Denver, 1988-91; gen. counsel, v.p., sec. Tele-Comm., Inc., Englewood, Colo., 1991—, exec. v.p., gen. counsel. General corporate, Securities. Office: Tele-Comm Inc 5619 Dtc Pky Englewood CO 80111-3017

**BRETT, THOMAS RUTHERFORD,** federal judge; b. Oklahoma City, Oct. 2, 1931; s. John A. and Norma (Dougherty) B.; m. Mary Jean James, Aug. 26, 1952; children: Laura Elizabeth Brett Tribble, James Ford, Susan Marie Brett Crump, Maricarolyn Swab. B.B.A., U. Okla., 1953, LL.B., 1957, J.D., 1971. Bar: Okla. 1957. Asst. county atty. Tulsa, 1957; mem. firm Hudson, Hudson, Wheaton, Kyle & Brett, Tulsa, 1958-69, Jones, Givens, Brett, Gotcher, Doyle & Bogan, 1969-79; judge U.S. Dist. Ct. (no. dist.) Okla., Tulsa, 1979—. Bd. regents U. Okla., 1971-78; mem. adv. bd. Salvation Army; trustee Okla. Bar Found. Col. JAG, USAR, 1953-83. Fellow Am. Coll. Trial Lawyers, Am. Bar Found.; mem. Okla. Bar Assn. (pres. 1970), Tulsa County Bar Assn. (pres. 1965), Am. Judicature Soc., U. Okla. Coll. Law Alumni Assn. (bd. dirs.), Order of Coif (hon.), Phi Alpha Delta.

Democrat. Office: US Dist Ct US Courthouse 224 S Boulder Ave Rm 210 Tulsa OK 74103-3026

**BRETT-MAJOR, LIN,** lawyer, mediator, arbitrator, educator, lecturer; b. N.Y.C., Sept. 21, 1943; d. B.L. and Edith H. Brett; children from previous marriage: Dania S., David M. BA, U. Mich., 1965; JD cum laude, Nova Law Ctr., 1978; postgrad., Harvard U., 1993. Bar: Fla. 1978, U.S. Ct. Appeals (5th and 11th cirs.) 1981, U.S. Tax Ct. 1981, U.S. Dist. Ct. (so., mid. and no. dist.) Fla. 1982, U.S. Supreme Ct. 1984, U.S. Dist. Ct. (mid., so. and no. dists.) Fla. 1984, U.S. Ct. Mil. Appeals 1990. Internat. communications asst. Mitsui and Co., Ltd., N.Y.C., 1962; with dept. pub. relations and devel. St. Rita's Hosp., Lima, Ohio, 1965-66; reporter The Lima News, 1969-70; honors intern U.S. Atty.'s Office, Miami, 1977; pvt. practice, Ft. Lauderdale, Fla., 1979-93; alternative dispute resolution mediator Conflict Solutions, Boca Raton, Fla., 1993—; vis. prof. grad. program of dispute resolution Sch. Social and Systemic Studies, Nova Southeastern U., Ft. Lauderdale, 1997-98; participant Gov.'s Conf. on World Trade, Miami and Jacksonville, Fla., 1984, Unidroit Workshop Devel. Pvt. Internat. Comml. Law, 1992; spkr. trial and negotiation trade Bus. Owner's Conf., Hollywood, Fla., 1986, Nova U. Law Ctr., 1988, ABA Nat. Conv., Toronto, 1988, Fla. Atlantic U., 1989, CPA Club, 1992, ABA Sect. Meeting, Bal Harbor, Fla., 1996, Nova U. Sch. Social & Systemic Studies, 1996. Contbr. articles to profl. jours. on internat. anti-trust law. Bd. dirs. Neurol. Rehab. Ctr., Broward Navy Days, 1992-96; mem. Ft. Lauderdale Opera Soc., 1986, Ft. Lauderdale Mus. Art, 1985, Ft. Lauderdale Opera Guild, 1990—; Dept. Def. ESGR Com., 1996—. Recipient Silver Key award ABA, 1977. Mem. ABA, FBA, ATLA, Fla. Bar Assn. (mil. law com. 1989—, chmn. legis. issues subcom. 1990-92, media-law com. 1991-93), U. Mich. Alumni Assn. (Gold Coast pres. 1988-90, S.E. U.S. dist. v.p., sec.-treas. 1992-95, pres. 1995-98, dir. 1998—), U.S. Propeller Club (nat. del. Port Everglades, Fla. 1981). Republican. Avocations: fencing, skeet and trap shooting, tennis, yachting. Office: 1515 N Federal Hwy Ste 418 Boca Raton FL 33432-1954

**BRETTSCHNEIDER, RITA ROBERTA FISCHMAN,** lawyer; b. Bklyn., Nov. 12, 1931; d. Isidore M. and Augusta T. (Singer) Fischman; m. Bertram D. Brettschneider, June 25, 1950 (dec. Nov. 17, 1986); children: Jane King, Joseph Brettschneider; m. Bertram D. Cohn, June 30, 1991. BA, CUNY, 1953; JD, Bklyn. Law Sch., 1956; postgrad., NYU, 1968-69, Nat. Inst. Trial Advocacy, 1976. Bar: N.Y. 1961, U.S. Dist. Ct. N.Y. 1971. Pvt. practice Huntington, N.Y., 1961—; instr. women and the law C.W. Post Coll., Brookville, N.Y., 1969-70; arbitrator med. malpractice arbitration com. Suffolk County (N.Y.), 1974-76; spl. assoc. prof. philosophy and law New Coll. Hofstra U., Hempstead, N.Y., 1974-76; faculty N.Y. Law Jour. Conf. Changing Concepts in Matrimonial Law, 1976; legal advisor Am. Arbitration Assn., 1977-84; arbitrator night small claims ct. Nassau County, 1978-83; of counsel Nassau County Psychol. Assn., 1987—, Suffolk County Psychol. Assn., 1990-95. Contbr. numerous articles to profl. jours. Pres., bd. dirs. For Our Children and Us, 1992—. Mem. Nassau-Suffolk Women's Bar Assn. (chair judiciary com. 1974-80), Nassau County Bar Assn. (demonstrating atty. mock trial contested matrimonial action 1975), Suffolk County Bar Assn. (demonstrating atty. mock trial contested matrimonial action 1976), Am. Arbitration Assn. (legal advisor 1977-84), Nassau-Suffolk Women's Bar Assn. (pres. 1980-81). Family and matrimonial. Home: 2 Crosby Pl Cold Spring Harbor NY 11724-2403 Office: Brettschneider & Brettschneider 83 Prospect St Huntington NY 11743-3306

**BREWER, CHRISTOPHER,** lawyer; b. Waynesburg, Pa., Nov. 8, 1955; s. Donald Johnson and Genevieve Myrtle (Yeager) B.; m. Karen Ruth Mayne, May 14, 1983; children: Lindsey Marie, Jeffrey Morrison. BA summa cum laude, U. Pitts., 1976, JD, 1979. Bar: Pa. 1979, Ohio 1996, U.S. dist. Ct. (we. dist.) Pa. 1979. Assoc. Ruffin, Hazlett law firm, Pitts., 1979-83; assoc. Eckert, Seamans, Cherin & Mellott, Pitts., 1983, Peck, Shaffer & Williams, Cin., 1983-85; ptnr. Peck, Shaffer & Williams, Pitts., 1987-97, Thorp Reed & Armstrong, LLP, Pitts., 1997—; asst. v.p. investment banking Pitts. Nat. Bank, 1985-87. Mem. Nat. Assn. Bond Lawyers, Allegheny County Bar Assn., Pa. Bar Assn. Finance, Personal income taxation. Home: 106 Horizon Dr Venetia PA 15367-1052

**BREWER, DAVID MADISON,** lawyer; b. Bordeaux, Gironde, France, July 8, 1953; s. Herbert L. and Paulyne B. (Ver Benec) B.; m. Andrea M. Bordiga, May 20, 1978; children: James David Madison, Caroline Elizabeth, Geoffrey Andrew. AB summa cum laude, Yale U., 1975, JD, 1978. Bar: N.Y. 1979. Assoc. atty. Cravath Swaine & Moore, N.Y.C., 1978-84; assoc. gen. tax counsel Union Pacific Corp., N.Y.C. and Bethlehem, Pa., 1984-89; pres. Madison Co., Inc., N.Y.C., 1990—; pres. Madison Oil Co., Madison Oil Co. Europe, 1993—. Editor Yale Law Jour., 1977-78. Vice-chmn. Bush/Quayle '92 Fin. Com.; policy asst. Office of the Campaign Mgr., Bush-Quayle campaign, 1988; bd. dirs. Yale U. Law Sch. fund, 1989-93, Yale Alumni Fund, 1989-95; spl. gifts chmn. Yale U. Class of 1975 and Law Sch. Class of 1978, 1985—; nat. vice-chmn. Smithsonian Friends of First Ladies, 1989-92; mem. world bd. USO, 1995—; trustee Pine Ridge Sch. (Vt.), 1998—. Nominated to Bd. Fed. Agrl. Mortgage Corp. by Pres. Bush, 1992. Mem. N.Y. Bar Assn., Phi Beta Kappa. Republican. Episcopalian. Taxation, general. Office: 9400 N Central Expy Ste 1209 Dallas TX 75231-5032

**BREWER, EDWARD CAGE, III,** law educator; b. Clarksdale, Miss., Jan. 20, 1953; s. Edward Cage Brewer Jr. and Elizabeth Blair (Alford) Little; m. Nancy Corr Martin, Dec. 27, 1975 (div. Sept. 1985); children: Katherine Martin, Julia Blair; m. Laurie Carol Alley, June 27, 1993 (div. 1999); 1 child, Caroline Elizabeth McCarty. BA, U. of the South, 1975; JD, Vanderbilt U., 1979. Bar: Ala. 1980, U.S. Ct. Appeals (11th and 5th cirs.) 1981, U.S. Dist. Ct. (so. dist.) Ala. 1981, Ga. 1982, U.S. Dist. Ct. (no. dist.) Ga. 1982, U.S. Ct. Appeals (3d and 8th cirs.) 1983, U.S. Dist. Ct. (mid. dist.) Ga. 1992, U.S. Supreme Ct. 1996. Law clk. to Hon. Virgil Pittman U.S. Dist. Ct. (so. dist.) Ala., Mobile, 1979-81; law clk. to Hon. Albert J. Henderson U.S. Ct. Appeals (11th and 5th cirs.), Atlanta, 1981-82; pvt. practice Atlanta, 1982-96; instr. Coll. of Law Ga. State U., Atlanta, 1992, 94; adj. prof. law Emory U., Atlanta, 1994-96; asst. prof. law No. Ky. U., Highland Heights, 1996—. Co-author: Railway Labor Act of 1926: Legislative History, 1988, Georgia Appellate Practice, 1996; contbr. articles to profl. jours. Mem. Phi Beta Kappa, Omicron Delta Kappa. Episcopalian. Avocations: choral music, guitar, motorcycles, hiking, canoeing. Office: No Ky U Salmon P Chase Coll Law Nunn Dr Highland Heights KY 41099

**BREWER, JOHN BRIAN,** lawyer; b. Phoenix, Jan. 17, 1968; s. Charles Moulton and Ina Lavon Brewer; m. Shannon Eileen Yocum, Sept. 12, 1998. BS in Bus., U. So. Calif., L.A., 1990; M in Internat. Mgmt., Am. Grad. Sch. Internat. Mgmt., 1993; JD, U. San Diego, 1996. Bar: Ariz. 1997. Tchr. Brophy Coll. Preparatory, Phoenix, 1990-92, dir. alumni/devel., 1992; intern Ariz. Ct. Appeals, Phoenix, 1995; atty. Charles M. Brewer, Ltd., Phoenix, 1996—. Named Ariz. Golf Coach of Yr., Jr. PGA Am., 1990. Personal injury, Aviation, General civil litigation. Office: Charles M Brewer Ltd 5500 N 24th St Phoenix AZ 85016-3100

**BREWER, JOHN NELSON,** lawyer; b. San Rafael, Calif., Apr. 22, 1957; s. Robert Roy and Eloise Virginia Brewer; m. Keri Amundsen, Dec. 1, 1990; children: Haylie Eloise, Trenton Robert. BS, U. Minn., 1979; JD, Lewis & Clark Coll., 1984. Bar: Nev. Assoc. Vargas & Bartlett, Las Vegas, Nev., 1984-89, ptnr., 1990-94; ptnr. Kummer Kaempfer Bonner & Renshaw, Las Vegas, 1994—; gen. counsel Nev. Ballet Theatre, Las Vegas, 1994—. Bd. dirs. Nev. Child Seekers, Las Vegas, 1992—. Mem. ABA, Nev. Bar Assn., Clark County Bar Assn. Securities, Mergers and acquisitions, General corporate. Office: Kummer Kaempfer Bonner 3800 Howard Hughes Pkwy Ste 700 Las Vegas NV 89109-0913

**BREWER, LEWIS GORDON,** judge, lawyer, educator; b. New Martinsville, W.Va., Sept. 6, 1946; s. Harvey Lee and Ruth Carolyn (Zimmerman) B; m. Kathryn Anne Yunker, May 25, 1985. B.A., W.Va. U., 1968, J.D., 1971; LL.M., George Washington U., 1979. Bar: W.Va. 1971, Calif. 1978. Commd. 2d lt. USAF, 1968, advanced through grades to Col., 1988; dep. staff judge adv., Travis AFB, Calif., 1976-78, chief civil law San Antonio Air Logistics Center, Kelly AFB, Tex., 1979-83, staff judge adv., MacDill AFB, Fla., 1983-86; chief Air Force Cen. Labor Law Office, Randolph AFB, Tex., 1987-88, dep. staff judge adv. Air Tng. Command, 1988-89; staff judge adv. 7th Air Force, Osan AFB, Korea, 1989-91, 45 Space Wing Patrick AFB, Fla., 1991-93; adminstrv. law judge W.Va. Edn. & State Employee Grievance Bd., Charleston, 1993—, mediator, 1994—; instr. bus. law No. Mich. U., Marquette, 1972, Solano Coll., Suisun City, Calif., 1978; instr. labor law Webster U., Ft. Sam Houston, 1983. Decorated Air Force Commendation medal, Meritorious Service medal, Legion of Merit. Mem. ABA, Nat. Assn. Adminstrv. Law Judges, Soc. Profls. in Dispute Resolution, W.Va. Bar Assn., State Bar Calif., W.Va. U. Alumni Assn., George Washington U. Alumni Assn. Methodist. Home: 528 Sheridan Cir Charleston WV 25314-1063 Office: 808 Greenbrier St Charleston WV 25311-1527

**BREWER, WILLIAM DANE,** lawyer; b. Detroit, Oct. 30, 1961. BA, Yale U., 1983; JD, Harvard U., 1986. Bar: Ill. 1986, N.Y., 1995. Assoc. Kirkland & Ellis, Chgo., 1986-89; assoc. Winston & Strawn, Chgo., 1990-94, ptnr., 1994; ptnr. Winston & Strawn, N.Y.C., 1995—. Mem. ABA, Ill. State Bar Assn., Chgo. Bar Assn, N.Y. State Bar Assn., Assn. Bar City N.Y. Fax: 212 294-4700. Finance, Mergers and acquisitions, Securities. Office: Winston & Strawn 200 Park Ave Fl 41 New York NY 10166-4401

**BREWSTER, CHRISTOPHER RALPH,** lawyer; b. Passaic, N.J., June 6, 1950; s. Ralph Arthur and Ada Barrett Brewster; m. Jane Eldridge, Sept. 29, 1984; children: William Eldridge, Kathryn Barrett. AB, Dartmouth Coll., 1972; JD, U. Va., 1975. Bar: Mo. 1975, D.C. 1988, U.S. Dist. Ct. D.C. 1991. Asst. atty. gen. State of Mo., Jefferson City, 1975-77; legis. asst. U.S. Sen. John C. Danforth, Washington, 1977-82; minority counsel Subcom. on Fed. Spending Practices U.S. Sen. Com. on Govtl. Affairs, Washington, 1979-81, chief counsel/staff dir. Subcom. on Fed. Expenditures, 1981-82; assoc. dir. Bur. Consumer Protection, FTC, Washington, 1982-84; counsel Kaye, Scholer, Fierman, Hays & Handler, Washington, 1984—. Trustee St. John's Child Devel. Ctr., Washington, 1985-91. Republican. Episcopalian. Administrative and regulatory, Legislative, Consumer commercial. Office: Kaye Scholer Fierman Hays & Handler LLP 901 15th St NW Washington DC 20005-2327

**BREWSTER, CLARK OTTO,** lawyer; b. Marlette, Mich., Nov. 5, 1956; s. Charles W. and June V. (Hoff) B.; m. Deborah K. Trowhill, Aug. 3, 1974; m. Cassie Mae, Carson Clark. BA cum laude, Cen. Mich. U., 1977; JD with honor, Tulsa U., 1980. Bar: Okla. 1981, U.S. Dist. Ct. (no. and ea. dists.) Okla. 1982, Tex. 1993. Assoc. Riddle and Assocs., Tulsa, 1981, Braly and McEachin, Tulsa, 1981-82; ptnr. Brewster & Shallcross, Tulsa, 1982—; bd. dirs. Redy Corp., Tulsa, Cottontail Oil Corp., Tulsa; trustee Travis Kerr Magana Trust, Tulsa, 1985—. Mem. ABA, ATLA, Okla. Bar Assn., Okla. Trial Lawyers Assn. (pres. 1998), Tulsa County Bar Assn., Order of Curule chair, Order of Barristers. Avocations: golf, hunting, horseback riding. State civil litigation, Federal civil litigation, Criminal. Home: 2109 E 30th St Tulsa OK 74114-5425 Office: Brewster Shallcross & DeAngelis 2021 S Lewis Ave Ste 675 Tulsa OK 74104-5725

**BREWSTER, FRANCIS ANTHONY,** lawyer; b. Foochow, China, Jan. 28, 1929; s. Francis Thoburn and Eva (Melby) B.; m. Susan Brewster, Apr. 6, 1974; 1 dau., Melissa Leigh; children by previous marriage—Sara, Julia, Anne, Ellen, Rebecca. B.S., U. Wis., 1950, LL.B., 1955. Bar: Wis. 1955. Corporate counsel Scott Paper Co., Phila., 1955-56, labor counsel, 1957; div. personnel mgr. Scott Paper Co. (Detroit div.), 1958-60; corp. counsel RCA, Camden, N.J., 1961; pvt. practice law Madison, Wis., 1961—; dir. Nat. Guardian Life Ins. Co., Stephan & Brady, Inc.; lectr. law U. Wis., 1961—. Contbr. articles to profl. jours. Chmn. personnel bd. City of Madison, 1970-75; bd. dirs. Capitol div. A.R.C., 1965-74, chmn. div., 1973; bd. dirs. Madison Symphony Inc., 1968-75, gen. counsel, 1961-91; gen. counsel Four Lakes council Boy Scouts Am., 1980-94; bd. visitors U. Wis. System, 1972-85, pres., 1976-78; pres. bd. visitors U. Wis.-Madison, 1978-80; mem., gen. counsel Wis. Privacy Coun., 1991-95. Served to capt. USMC, 1950-53, Korea. Recipient Certificate of Merit U. Mich.-Wayne State U., 1959; named Outstanding Madisonian, 1969, Wis. Man of Distinction, 1972. Mem. ABA, Dane County Bar Assn. (past sec. and program chmn.), State Bar of Wis. (chmn. fee arbitration panel 1978—), Wis. Bar Found. (bd. dirs. 1981-87, chmn. investment com.), Interfraternity Alumni Council U. Wis. (pres. 1968-74), Delta Upsilon (pres. Wis. 1965-72, Outstanding Alumnus 1984). Republican. Presbyn. (elder). Club: Kiwanian (Madison) (pres. 1969). General corporate, Labor, Non-profit and tax-exempt organizations. Home: PO Box 55418 Madison WI 53705-9218

**BREWSTER, RUDI MILTON,** judge; b. Sioux Falls, S.D., May 18, 1932; s. Charles Edwin and Wilhemina Therese (Rud) B.; m. Gloria Jane Nanson, June 27, 1954; children: Scot Alan, Lauri Diane (Alan Lee), Julie Lynn Yahnke. AB in Pub. Affairs, Princeton U., 1954; JD, Stanford U., 1960. Bar: Calif. 1960. From assoc. to ptnr. Gray, Cary, Ames & Frye, San Diego, 1960-84; judge U.S. Dist. Ct. (so. dist.) Calif., San Diego, 1994-98, sr. judge, 1998—. Served to capt. USNR, 1954-82 Ret. Fellow Am. Coll. Trial Lawyers; mem. Am. Bd. Trial Advs., Internat. Assn. Ins. Counsel, Am. Inns of Ct. Republican. Lutheran. Avocations: skiing, hunting, gardening. Fax: (619) 702-9927. Office: US Dist Ct Ste 4165 940 Front St San Diego CA 92101-8902

**BREYER, STEPHEN GERALD,** United States supreme court justice; b. San Francisco, Aug. 15, 1938; s. Irving G. and Anne R. B.; m. Joanna Hare, Sept. 4, 1967; children: Chloe, Nell, Michael. A.B., Stanford U., 1959; B.A. (Marshall scholar), Oxford U., 1961; LL.B., Harvard U., 1964; LL.D. (hon.), U. Rochester, 1983. Bar: Calif. 1966, D.C. 1966, Mass. 1971. Law clk. Justice Goldberg, U.S. Supreme Ct., 1964-65; spl. asst. to asst. atty. gen. U.S. Dept. Justice, 1965-67; asst. prof. law Harvard U., 1967-70, prof., 1970-81, lectr., 1981—, prof. govt. J.F. Kennedy Sch., 1978-81; asst. spl. prosecutor Watergate Spl. Prosecution Force, 1973; spl. counsel U.S. Senate Judiciary Com., 1974-75, chief counsel, 1979-81; judge U.S. Ct. Appeals (1st cir.), Boston, 1981-90, chief judge, 1990-94; Oliver Wendell Holmes lectr. Harvard Law Sch., 1992; assoc. justice U.S. Supreme Ct., Washington, 1994—; mem. Judl. Conf. of U.S., 1990-94, U.S. Sentencing commn., 1985-89; vis. lectr. Coll. Law, Sydney, Australia, 1975, Salzburg (Austria) Seminar, 1978, 93; Jud. Conf. rep. to Adminstrv. Conf. U.S., 1981-94; vis. prof. U. Rome, 1993. Author: (with Paul MacAvoy) The Federal Power Commission and the Regulation of Energy, 1974, (with Richard Stewart) Adminstrative Law and Regulatory Policy, 1979, 3rd edit., 1992, Regulation and its Reform, 1982, Breaking the Vicious Circle, 1993; contbr. articles to profl. jours. Trustee U. Mass., 1974-81; bd. overseers Dana Farber Cancer Inst., Boston, 1977—. Mem. ABA, Am. Bar Found., Am. Law Inst., Am. Acad. Arts and Scis., Coun. Fgn. Rels. Office: US Supreme Ct Supreme Ct Bldg 1 1st St NE Washington DC 20543-0001

**BREYFOGLE, EDWIN HOWARD,** lawyer; b. Ann Arbor, Mich., May 16, 1949; s. Ernest Edwin and Dorothy Winefred (Frye) B.; m. Patricia Ann Duncan, Aug. 25, 1973; children—James Edwin, Thomas David. BA, Ohio State U., 1971, JD, 1976; postgrad. Va. Theol. Sem., 1972-74. Bar: Ohio 1976, U.S. Dist. Ct. (no. dist.) Ohio 1976. Sole practice, Massillon, Ohio, 1976—. Sec. Interfaith Campus Ministries, Inc., North Canton, Ohio, 1979-80. Mem. Ohio State Bar Assn. (exec. com. 1993-95, chmn. bankruptcy com. 1996-97), Am. Bankruptcy Inst., Stark County Acad. Trial Lawyers, Stark County Bar Assn., Massillon Lawyers Club (pres. 1980-81). Republican. Bankruptcy, Consumer commercial. Home: 1416 Dunkeith Dr NW Canton OH 44708-1936 Office: 921 Lincoln Way E Massillon OH 44646-6833

**BRIACH, GEORGE GARY,** lawyer, consultant; b. Youngstown, Ohio, Apr. 11, 1954; s. George William and Donna Jean (Phillips) B.; m. Loretta Ann Lepore, May 17, 1985; 1 child, Rachel Renee. BS magna cum laude, Youngstown State U., 1976; JD, U. Akron, Ohio, 1982. Bar: Ohio 1983, Mahoning County, 1983. Assoc. Flask & Policy, Youngstown, 1983-91; asst. atty. gen. State Atty. Gen.'s Office, Youngstown, 1984-90; solicitor Poland (Ohio) Village, 1988-89; cons., dir. Mahoning County (Ohio) Auditor, 1990—; ptnr. White & Briach, Youngstown, 1991—. Fundraiser United Way, Youngstown, 1989-92; bd. dirs., treas. D&E Counseling Ctr., Youngstown, 1992-98; trustee, treas. Children' Challenge Found., Inc., 1998—; bd. dirs. Interfaith Home Maintenance. Mem. Ohio Bar Assn., Mahoning County Bar Assn., Youngstown State U. Alumni Assn., Allegheny Club, Fonderlac Country Club, Tippecanoe Country Club. Avocations: aerobic and weight training, golf, reading, travel. Family and matrimonial, General practice, Probate. Home: 45 Russo Dr Canfield OH 44406-9666 Office: White & Briach 755 Boardman Canfield Rd Youngstown OH 44512-4300

**BRIAN, A(LEXIS) MORGAN, JR.,** lawyer; b. New Orleans, Oct. 4, 1928; s. Alexis Morgan and Evelyn (Thibaut) B.; m. Elizabeth Louise Graham, 1951; children—Robert Morgan, Ellen Graham. B.A., La. State U., 1949, J.D., 1956; M.S., Trinity U., 1954. Bar: La. 1956, U.S. Supreme Ct. 1971. Assoc. Deutsch, Kerrigan & Stiles, New Orleans, 1956-60, ptnr., 1961-79; sr. ptnr. Brian, Simon, Peragine, Smith & Redfearn, New Orleans, 1979-82; sr. ptnr. Fawer, Brian, Hardy & Zatzkis, New Orleans, 1982-86; pvt. practice, New Orleans, 1986—; spl. asst. to La. Atty. Gen., 1982-87; speaker profl. seminars; lectr. Inst. Continuing Legal Edn., La. State U. Law Ctr., 1972—. Local merit badge counselor Boy Scouts Am., 1963—; bd. dirs. Goodwill Industries New Orleans, 1969-84, v.p. and mem. exec. com., 1975-77, mem. adv. bd., 1978, 86—; life deacon, past chmn., trustee, pres., lay preacher, Bible tchr., mem. coms. First Baptist Ch. New Orleans; speaker at convs., confs. So. Bapt. Conv., 1956—, La. Bapt. Conv., 1956—, Am. Platform Assn.; past pres., bd. trustees New Orleans Bapt. Theol. Sem., 1961-74; bd. dirs. New Orleans Bapt. Theol. Sem. Found., 1972-81, Inter-Varsity Christian Fellowship, 1974—, La. State U. Found., 1976-81; mem. nat. legal adv. council Ams. United for Separation of Ch. and State, 1977—. Staff sgt. USAF, 1951-55. Recipient Boss of Yr. award New Orleans Legal Secs. Assn., 1966. Mem. ABA (TIPS fidelity and surety com., forum com. contstrn. industry), La. State Bar Assn. (asst. examiner com. on bar admissions 1968-89, fidelity, surety and constrn. sect. 1991—), New Orleans Bar Assn., Internat. Assn. Def. Counsel (vice chmn. fidelity and surety com. 1978-79, architects, engrs. and constrn. litigation com., advocacy com.), La. Assn. Def. Counsel, Def. Research Inst., Am. Arbitration Assn. (arbitrator 1970—), La. Civil Svc. League, Internat. House, La. State U. Alumni Fedn. (life), Trinity U. Alumni Assn., La. State U. Law Ctr. Alumni Assn. (life), Upper Carrollton Neighborhood Assn. (v.p. 1976), Christian Legal Soc., Theta Xi, Phi Delta Phi. Democrat. Contbr. articles to legal jours. Construction, Government contracts and claims, Insurance. Home: 5216 Pitt St New Orleans LA 70115-4107 Office: 700 Camp St New Orleans LA 70130-3702

**BRICE, ROGER THOMAS,** lawyer; b. Chgo., May 7, 1948; s. William H. and Mary Loretta (Ryan) B.; m. Carol Coleman, Aug. 15, 1970; children: Caitlin, Coleman, Emily. AB, DePaul U., 1970; JD, U. Chgo., 1973. Bar: Ill. 1973, Iowa 1973, U.S. Ct. Appeals (10th, 4th and 7th cirs.) 1975, U.S. Dist. Ct. (no. and ctrl. dists.) Ill. 1977, 1995, U.S. Trial Bar (no. dist.) 1982, U.S. Supreme Ct. 1978. Staff atty. Office of Gen. Counsel NLRB, Washington, 1974-76; assoc. Kirkland & Ellis, Chgo., 1976-79; assoc. Reuben & Proctor, Chgo., 1979-80, ptnr., 1980-86; ptnr. Isham, Lincoln & Beale, Chgo., 1986-88; ptnr. Sonnenschein, Nath & Rosenthal, Chgo., 1988—, legal counsel. Legal counsel, bd. dirs. Boys and Girls Clubs Chgo., 1991—. Roman Catholic. Labor, General civil litigation, Civil rights. Home: 3727 N Harding Ave Chicago IL 60618-4026 Office: Sonnenschein Nath & Rosenthal 233 S Wacker Dr Ste 8000 Chicago IL 60606-6342

**BRICK, BARRETT LEE,** lawyer; b. Middletown, N.Y., Jan. 12, 1954; s. Michael and Barbara Lilian (Rosen) B. BA, Columbia U., 1976, JD, 1979. Bar: N.Y. 1980, U.S. Ct. Appeals (D.C. cir.) 1981, U.S. Supreme Ct. 1984. Atty.-adviser FCC, Washington, 1980—. Contbr. to book, Positively Gay, 1979; book review columnist Washington Blade newspaper, 1982-83; editor National Gay Task Force Action Report, 1975-76. Active Community Bd. Nine, N.Y.C., 1978-80; mem. Gay Men's Chorus, Washington, 1984—; bd. dirs. Congregation Bet Mishpachah, Washington, 1980-84, pres., 1984-85; exec. dir. World Congress Gay and Lesbian Jewish Orgns., Washington, 1987-93. Recipient Advocate 400 award, The Advocate, San Francisco, 1984; named one of Outstanding Young Men of Am. U.S. Jaycees, 1983, 84. Mem. ABA, N.Y. State Bar Assn., Nat. Lesbian and Gay Law Assn. Republican. Jewish. Club: Capital (Washington). Home: 1901 Wyoming Ave NW Washington DC 20009-5079 Office: FCC 445 12th St SW Washington DC 20554-0001

**BRICK, HOWARD ANDREW,** lawyer; b. Boston, Jan. 17, 1961; s. Donald B. and Phyllis M. Brick; m. Jill A. Smilow, Oct. 14, 1990; children: Jenny L., Elijah M. BA, Dartmouth Coll., 1983; JD, Columbia U., 1987. Bar: Mass. 1987, U.S. Dist. Ct. Mass. 1988, U.S. Ct. Appeals (1st cir.) 1988, U.S. Dist. Ct. (so. dist.) N.Y. 1995. Assoc. Hale and Dorr, Boston, 1987-91; asst. atty. gen. Mass. Atty. Gen.'s Office, Boston, 1991-94; assoc. Burns & Levinson, Boston, 1994-97; counsel Donoghue Barrett & Singal, Boston, 1997—. Exec. com. New England region Anti-Defamation League, Boston, 1993—, vice-chair civil rights com. New England region, 1978—; fin. com. Teh Harshbarser, Boston, 1996-98. Democrat. Jewish. Avocations: skiing, tennis, biking, politics, family. Criminal, General civil litigation, Intellectual property. Home: 59 Ward St Lexington MA 02421-4230 Office: Donoghue Barrett & Singal One Bealon St Boston MA 02108

**BRICKEY, JAMES NELSON,** lawyer; b. South Portsmouth, Ky., Mar. 12, 1942; s. Paul Rardin and Geneva (Sturgill) B.; m. Kathleen M. Fitzgerald, Aug. 22, 1969. A.B., Morehead State U., 1966; J.D., U. Ky., 1969; LL.M. in Taxation, Washington U., St. Louis, 1977. Bar: Ohio 1969, Ky. 1969, Mo. 1978, U.S. Dist. Ct. (ea. dist.) Mo. 1978. Assoc. Dolle, O'Donnell, Cash, Fee & Hahn, Cin., 1969-70; dir. fiscal mgmt. Commonwealth Ky., Frankfort, 1970-73; investment banker Halsey Stuart, Inc., Louisville, 1973-74; ptnr. Reed & Brickey, Louisville, 1974-76; assoc. Guilfoil Petzall & Shoemake and predecessor Guilfoil, Symington, Petzall & Shoemake, St. Louis, 1978-81, ptnr., 1981-94; mem. Devereux, Murphy, Striler, Brickey & Sher, L.L.C., 1994—; lectr. in comml. law U. Louisville, 1974-75. Commr., Housing Authority Louisville, 1975. Served with USN, 1960-62. Mem. ABA, Mo. Bar Assn., Met. Bar Assn. St. Louis. Democrat. Corporate taxation, Contracts commercial, Estate planning. Address: Fellowship of Christian Athletes 734 Wesport Plz Ste 216 Saint Louis MO 63146-3000

**BRICKLER, JOHN WEISE,** lawyer; b. Dayton, Ohio, Dec. 29, 1944; s. John Benjamin and Shirley Hilda (Weise) B.; m. Marilyn Louise Kuhlmann, July 2, 1966; children: John, James, Peter, Andrew, Matthew. AB, Washington U., St. Louis, 1966; JD, Washington U., 1968. Bar: Mo. 1968, U.S. Supreme Ct. 1972, U.S. Dist. Ct. (ea. dist.) Mo. 1974, U.S. Ct. Appeals (8th cir.) 1974. Assoc. Peper, Martin, Jensen, Maichel and Hetlage, St. Louis, 1973-77, ptnr., 1978-98; ptnr. Blackwell Sanders Peper Martin LLP, St. Louis, 1998—; chmn. bd. dirs. Concordia Pub. House, St. Louis, 1998—. Bd. dirs. Luth. Family and Children's Svcs. Mo., St. Louis, 1988-93, vice chmn., 1988-89. Capt. JAGC, U.S. Army, 1969-73. Mem. ABA, Nat. Assn. Bond Lawyers, Bar Assn. Met. St. Louis. General corporate, Municipal (including bonds), Securities. Office: Blackwell Sanders Peper Martin LLP 720 Olive St Fl 24 Saint Louis MO 63101-2338

**BRICKLEY, JAMES H.,** state supreme court justice; b. Flint, Mich., Nov. 15, 1928; s. J. Harry and Marie E. (Fischer) B.; 6 children. B.A., U. Detroit, 1951, LL.B., 1954, Ph.D. (hon.), 1977; LL.M., NYU, 1957; Ph.D. (hon.), Spring Arbor Coll., 1975, Detroit Coll. Bus., 1975, Ferris State Coll., Big Rapids, Mich., 1980, Saginaw Valley State Coll., University Center, Mich., 1980, Detroit Coll. Law, 1981. Bar: Mich. 1954. Spl. agent FBI, Washington, 1954-58; sole practice law Detroit, 1959-62; mem. Detroit City Council, 1962-67, pres. pro tem, 1966-67; chief asst. prosecutor Wayne County, Detroit, 1967-69; U.S. atty. U.S. Dist. Ct. (ea. dist.), Detroit, 1969-70; lt. gov. State of Mich., Lansing, 1971-74, 79-82; justice Supreme Ct. of Mich., Lansing, 1982-99; chief justice, 1995-96; pres. Eastern Mich. U., Ypsilanti, 1975-78; lectr., adj. prof. U. Detroit, Wayne State U., U. Mich., Ann Arbor, Cooley Law Sch., 1958-73. Mem. Mich. Bar Assn., ABA, Inst. Jud. Adminstrn. Republican. Roman Catholic. Office: Supreme Ct Mich PO Box 30052 Lansing MI 48909-7552*

**BRICKLIN, DAVID A.,** lawyer; b. Phila., May 8, 1952; s. Albert Louis and Regina Edelman Bricklin; m. Anne Marie Harworth, Aug. 19, 1984; children: Erica, Jennifer, Jacob, Alexander, Laura. BA, Mich. State U., 1974; LLB, Harvard U., 1977. Bar: Wash., U.S. Dist. Ct. (we. dist.) Wash., U.S. Ct. Appeals (9th cir.), U.S. Supreme Ct. Staff atty. FTC, Seattle, 1977-79; assoc. Law Offices of Roger M. Leed, Seattle, 1979-82; prin. Bricklin and Gendler, LLP, Seattle, 1982—. Mem. Legislature's Adv. Com. on State Environ. Policy Act, 1982-83; mem. Municipality of Met. Seattle Toxics Adv. Com., Seattle, 1983; mem. adv. bd. Eckstein Cmty. Ctr., Seattle, 1985-86; co-chair Wash. Conservation Voters, Seattle, 1991-98, bd. dirs., 1987—; founding mem., bd. dirs. 100 Friends of Wash., 1991—; gen. counsel Washington Environ. Coun., Seattle, 1990—, bd. dirs. 1983-90, pres. 1986-90, bd. dirs. Seattle Commons, 1994-96; co-chair Citizens for Balanced Growth,

1990, Citizens Tocis Clean-Up Campaign, Seattle, 1987-88; co-founder, bd. dirs. Environ. Fund Wash., Seattle, 1986-88; pres. Ravenna-Bryant Cmty. Assn., Seattle, 1984-85. Recipient Cert. of Appreciation, Western Pub. Interest Law Conf., 1988. Avocations: bicycling, hiking, kayaking. Office: Bricklin and Gendler LLP 1424 4th Ave Ste 1015 Seattle WA 98101-2217

**BRICKWOOD, SUSAN CALLAGHAN,** lawyer; b. Sydney, NSW, Australia, Dec. 6, 1946; d. Graham Callaghan Brickwood and Nan (Cahaley) Nichols). BA, Swarthmore Coll., 1969; postgrad., Harvard U., 1969-71; JD, U. So. Calif., 1980. Bar: Calif. 1980, U.S. Tax Ct. 1981. Controller Howard Smith, Ltd., Sydney, 1972-74; assoc. Rifkind & Sterling, Beverly Hills, Calif., 1980-81, Armstrong, Hendler & Hirsch, Century City, Calif., 1981-82; pvt. practice L.A., 1982—. Author: Start Over!, 1990. Bankruptcy. Office: 6500 Wilshire Blvd Los Angeles CA 90048-4920

**BRIDENSTINE, LOUIS HENRY, JR.,** lawyer; b. Detroit, Nov. 13, 1940; s. Louis and Mary Ellen (O'Keefe) B.; m. Lucia Elizabeth Pucci, June 18, 1966; 1 child, Lucia McMullin. BS, John Carroll U., 1962; MA, U. Detroit, 1966, JD, 1965. Bar: Mich. 1966, U.S. Dist. Ct. (ea. dist.) Mich. 1966. Trial atty., atty.-advisor FTC, Washington, 1966-72; sr. legal counsel, v.p. dir. comms. Motor Vehicle Mfrs. Assn. U.S., Inc., Detroit, 1972-81; sr. v.p., gen. counsel, sec. Campbell-Ewald Co., Warren, Mich., 1981—; exec. dir. Motorists Info., Inc., Detroit, 1977; legal affairs com. Am. Assn. Advt. Agys., N.Y.C., 1990—. Youth allocations panelist United Way Cmty Svcs., Detroit, 1991-98, chair, 1993-98, fund distbn. panelist, 1994-98; trustee, bd. dirs. Catholic Youth Orgn., Detroit, 1981-97, 99—, chair bd. dirs., 1990-92. Fellow Mich. State Bar Found. (life); mem. Mich. Bar Assn., Am. Corp. Counsel Assn., Alpha Sigma Nu, Blue Key, Detroit Athletic Club. Avocations: travel, reading. Administrative and regulatory, General corporate, Labor. Office: Campbell Ewald Co 30400 Van Dyke Ave Warren MI 48093-2368

**BRIDESTOWE, LORD** See **MOORE, THOMAS RONALD**

**BRIDEWELL, DAVID ALEXANDER,** lawyer; b. Forrest City, Ark., Dec. 8, 1909; s. Alexander Carver and Martha Elizabeth (Hatcher) B.; m. Mary Frances Badger, May 21, 1949; children: Jonathan Lee (dec.), Alexander Hunt. AB, U. South, 1931; MA, Princeton U., 1932; JD, George Washington U., 1938. Bar: Ark. 1933, D.C. 1938, Ill. 1940, U.S. Supreme Ct. 1940. Assoc. Mann & Mann, Forrest City, Ark., 1932; dist. atty. Home Owners Loan Corp., Jonesboro, Ark., 1933-34; atty. and asst. to gen. counsel Fed. Home Loan Bank Bd., Washington, 1935-40; ptnr. Russell & Bridewell, Chgo., 1940-85, Righeimer, Martin, Bridewell & Ciquino, Chgo., 1985-88; counsel Spindell & Kemp, Chgo., 1988-90, Lewis, Overbeck & Furman, Chgo., 1990-93, DeWolfe, Poynton & Stevens, Chgo., 1993-95; pvt. practice Chgo., 1995—; bd. dirs. First Bank & Trust Co., Palatine, Ill., Kankakee (Ill.) Fed. Savs. Bank, No. Ark. Tel. Co., Flippin; rev. atty. Fed. Savings and Loans Ins. Corp., 1936; lectr. John Marshall Law Sch., Northwestern U., 1946-70; arbitrator Cir. Ct. Cook County, 1990—; counsel 1st Fed. Savs and Loan Assn. Chgo., 1960-85, 2d Fed. Savs. and Loan Assn. Chgo., 1945—; sec. Ctrl. Housing Com. Law and Legis. Author: The Legislative History of Federal Home Loan Bank Board and Its Agencies, 1935, Bridewell on Credit Unions, 3d edit., 1945, Bridewell on Bailments, Liens and Pledges, 1945, Credit Unions; editor: Selected Illinois Statutes, 1947; A Lawyer's Guide to Retirement, 3d edit., 1998, Housing Legal Digest; co-editor: Reverse Mortgages and Other Senior Income and Housing Options, 1997. Chancellor Christ Episcopal Ch., Winnetka, Ill., 1960-75. Capt. JAGD, U.S. claims commr. U.S. Army, 1943-46, ETO. Mem. ABA (bus. law sect. 1965—, chmn. savs. and loan comm. 1965-70, coun. 1970-75, sr. lawyer divsn. coun. 1985-93, chmn. bd. editors Experience Mag. 1995), Ill. Bar Assn. (chmn. savs. and loan com. 1980-85), Chgo. Bar Assn. (chmn. sr. lawyer com. 1985-87), Univ. Club Chgo. (chmn. lit. and arts com. 1980-85), Kappa Sigma. Republican. Episcopalian. Avocations: tennis, golf, swimming. Probate, Banking, Estate planning. Home: 789 Burr Ave Winnetka IL 60093-1802 Office: 135 S La Salle St Chicago IL 60603-4159

**BRIDGES, ANDREW PHILLIP,** lawyer; b. Atlanta, Sept. 11, 1954; s. Glenn Jackson and Margaret Eugenia (Raymond) B.; m. J. Rebecca Lyman, July 27, 1985; children: Catherine S. Bridges-Lyman, Thomas A. Bridges-Lyman. AB, Stanford U., 1976; postgrad., Am. Sch. Classical Studies, Athens, Greece, 1977-78; JD, Harvard U., 1983; MA, Oxford (Eng.) U., 1985. Bar: Ga. 1984, Calif. 1986, U.S. Supreme Ct. 1987. Law clk. to hon. Marvin H. Shoob U.S. Dist. Ct., Atlanta, 1983-85; assoc. Farella, Braun & Martel, San Francisco, 1985-91; ptnr., head of trademarks and advt. practices group Wilson, Sonsini, Goodrich & Rosati, Palo Alto, Calif., 1991—; co-chair fed. cts. com. Bar Assn. San Francisco, 1988-90; dir. Hellenic Law Soc. No. Calif., San Francisco, 1990-94; lectr. Practising Law Inst., San Francisco, 1990-97; mem. editl. bd. Intellectual Property Strategist, N.Y.C., 1994—; judge diocesan ct. Episcopal Diocese of Calif., San Francisco, 1995—. Contbr. articles to profl. jours. Sr. warden St. Mark's Episcopal Ch., Berkeley, Calif., 1990-92. Grad. fellow Rotary Found., Athens, 1977-78. Mem. Internat. Trademark Assn., Phi Beta Kappa. Republican. Avocations: Mediterranean history and archaeology, classical philosophy and languages, skiing, tennis. Trademark and copyright, Federal civil litigation, Computer. Office: Wilson Sonsini Goodrich & Rosati 650 Page Mill Rd Palo Alto CA 94304-1050

**BRIDGES, DAVID MANNING,** lawyer; b. Berkeley, Calif., May 22, 1936; s. Robert Lysle and Alice Marion (Rodenberger) B.; m. Carmen Galante de Bridges, Aug. 16, 1973; children: David, Stuart. AB, U. Calif., Berkeley, 1957, JD, 1962. Assoc. Thelen, Marrin, Johnson & Bridges, San Francisco, 1962-70, ptnr., 1970-94; mng. ptnr. Thelen, Marrin, Johnson & Bridges, Houston, 1981-91. Served as lt. (j.g.) USN, 1957-59. Mem. ABA, State Bar of Tex., Tex. Bar Assn., Houston Bar Assn., Internat. Bar Assn., Houston Club, Coronado Club, Pacific-Union Club. Banking, Contracts commercial, Construction. Office: 1111 Bagby St Ste 2450 Houston TX 77002-2555

**BRIDGES, LOUIS EMERSON, III,** lawyer; b. Knoxville, Tenn.; s. Lewis Emerson and Camden Swan Bridges; m. Lisa Jane Herring, Feb. 22, 1992; 1 child, John Louis. BA, Furman U., 1981; JD, Ohio No. U., 1987. Bar: Ga. Lawyer Hyatt & Rhoads, Atlanta, 1987-90, Freeman & Hawkins, Atlanta, 1990-93, Rowe, Foltz & Martin, Atlanta, 1993—. Mem. Atlanta Bar Assn. (bd. dirs. real estate divsn. 1998). Episcopalian. Avocations: golf, tennis. Real property, General corporate, Environmental. Office: Rowe Folte & Martin 5 Piedmont Ctr NE Atlanta GA 30305-1536

**BRIDGMAN, MARY WOOD,** lawyer; b. Jacksonville, Fla., Apr. 16, 1957; d. Joseph Gladstone and Clarice Annette (Thomas) W. BA with high honors, U. Fla., 1978, JD with honors, 1980. Bar: Fla. 1981, U.S. Dist. Ct. (no. and mid. dists.) Fla. 1981, U.S. Dist. Ct. (so. dist.) Fla. 1983, U.S. Ct. Appeals (11th cir.) 1982. Law clk. U.S. Dist. Ct. (mid. dist.) Fla., Jacksonville, 1981-82; assoc. Marks, Gray, Conroy & Gibbs P.A., Jacksonville, 1982-87; asst. gen. counsel Blue Cross & Blue Shield Fla., Inc., Jacksonville, 1987-93, v.p. for corp. compliance, 1994-99, v.p. audit and compliance, 1999—; instr. bus. law Fla. C.C., Jacksonville, 1988-89. Mem. Hendricks Ave. Bapt. Ch., Jacksonville, 1981—, deacon, 1986—, chmn. diaconate, 1995-96; mem. Willing Hands, Inc., Jacksonville, 1985; vol. Legal Aid, Inc., Jacksonville, 1982-95; bd. dirs. Theatre Jacksonville, Inc., 1987-88; nominated for Duval County Ct. Judge, 1991. Named one of Outstanding Young Women of Am., 1985. Mem. Fed. Bar Assn. (pres. Jacksonville chpt. 1986-87), Jacksonville Bar Assn. (bd. govs. young lawyers sect. 1988-93, pres. elect 1991, pres. 1992, bd. govs. 1994-96, editor Jacksonville bar bull, 1993-94), Order of Coif. Democrat. Baptist. Avocations: reading, gardening, entertaining, music. Insurance. Office: Blue Cross Blue Shield Fla Inc 4800 Deerwood Campus Pkwy Jacksonville FL 32246-8273

**BRIEANT, CHARLES LA MONTE,** federal judge; b. Ossining, N.Y., Mar. 13, 1923; s. Charles La Monte and Marjorie (Hall) B.; m. Virginia Elizabeth Warfield, Sept. 10, 1948; children: Cynthia W. Brieant Hendricks, Charles La Monte III, Victoria E. Misuraca, Julia W. Brieant Clavette. B.A., Columbia U., 1947, LL.B., 1949. Bar: N.Y. 1949. Mem. firm Bleakley, Platt, Schmidt & Fritz, White Plains, 1949-71; water commr. Village of Ossining, 1948-51; town justice, 1952-58, town supr., 1960-63; village atty. Briarcliff Manor, N.Y.; also spl. asst. dist. atty. Westchester County, 1958-59; asst. counsel N.Y. State Joint Legis. Com. Fire Ins., 1968; judge U.S. Dist. Ct. (so. dist.) N.Y., N.Y.C., 1971-86, chief judge, 1986-93; judge U.S. Dist Ct. So. Dist. N.Y., White Plains, 1993—; adj. prof. Bklyn. Law Sch.; mem. Jud. Conf. U.S., 1989-95, mem. exec. com., 1991-95. Mem. Westchester County Republican Com., 1957-71; mem. Westchester County Legislature from 2d Dist., 1970-71. Served with AUS, World War II. Mem. ABA, N.Y. State Bar Assn., Westchester County Bar Assn., Ossining Bar Assn. Episcopalian (vestryman). Club: SAR. Office: US Dist Ct US Courthouse 300 Quarropas St White Plains NY 10601-4140

**BRIEDIS, ROBERT A.,** lawyer; b. Ridgewood, N.J., Jan. 6, 1961; s. Ojars A. and Mirdza Briedis. BS, NYU, 1983; JD, George Washington U., 1990. Bar: N.J. 1990, N.Y. 1991, D.C. 1992, U.S. Dist. Ct. N.J. 1990. Atty. Brown Raysman & Millstein, N.Y.C., 1990-93, McCarter & English, Newark, 1993-95, Fischbein Badillo Wagner Harding, N.Y.C., 1996-98, Brown & Wood LLP, N.Y.C., 1998—. Mem. Bergen County Rep. Orgn., 1998—. Mem. Bar Assn. City N.Y., Beta Gamma Sigma. Real property. Office: Brown & Wood LLP One World Trade Ctr New York NY 10048

**BRIEGER, GEORGE,** lawyer; b. Hungary, Apr. 30, 1966; came to the U.S., 1977; s. Jenö and Miriam Brieger. BS in Computer Sci., Bklyn. Coll., 1988; postgrad., Yeshiva U., 1988-90, JD, 1993. Bar: N.Y. 1994, U.S. Dist. Ct. (so. and ea. dists.) N.Y. 1995. Internat. counsel Bacher & Ptnrs. Atty. at Law, Budapest, Hungary, 1996-98; atty. Internat. Trade Litigation U.S. Customs Svc., N.Y.C., 1998—; cons. Fin. Svcs. Vol. Corps, N.Y.C., 1996. Editor New Europe Law Rev. Cardozo Sch. Law, N.Y.C., 1992-93; contbr. chpt. to book. Mem. adv. bd. Budapest-N.Y. Sister City Com., N.Y.C., 1996—. Scholar Revel Grad. Sch., N.Y.C., 1988-90. Mem. N.Y. City Bar Assn. (ctrl. and ea. European law com. 1996-98). Avocations: reading about modern history, philosophy, Tai Chi, swimming. E-mail: george.brieger@customs.treas.gov. Office: US Customs Svc 26 Federal Plz Ste 258 New York NY 10278-0107

**BRIER, BONNIE SUSAN,** lawyer; b. Oct. 19, 1950; d. Jerome W. and Barbara (Srenco) B.; m. Bruce A. Rosenfield, Aug. 15, 1976; children: Rebecca, Elizabeth, Benjamin. AB in Econs. magna cum laude, Cornell U., 1972; JD, Stanford U., 1976. Bar: Pa. 1976, U.S. Dist. Ct. (ea. dist.) Pa., U.S. Tax Ct., U.S. Ct. Appeals (3d cir.), U.S. Supreme Ct. Law clk. to chief judge U.S. Dist. Ct. Pa. (ea. dist.), Phila., 1976-77, asst. U.S. atty. criminal prosecutor, 1977-79; from assoc. to ptnr. Ballard, Spahr, Andrews & Ingersoll, Phila., 1979-90; gen. counsel Children's Hosp. of Phila., Phila., 1990—; legal counsel Womens Way, 1979—; lectr. U. Pa., 1988-95; lectr., speaker various orgns. and seminars. Editor Stanford Law Rev., 1974-76; contbr. articles to profl. jours. Bd. dirs. U.S. Com. for UNICEF, 1994—. Fellow Am. Coll. Tax Counsel; mem. ABA (exempt orgn. com. on tax sect., chair 1991-93, mem. health law sect.), Pa. Bar Assn. (tax sect.), Phila. Bar Assn. (tax sect.), Nat. Health Lawyers Assn., Am. Acad. Healthcare Attys. (bd. dirs. 1991-96), ABA (health law sec. bd. dirs. 1998—). Taxation, general, Health, Education and schools. Home: 132 Fairview Rd Penn Valley PA 19072-1331 Office: Children's Hosp of Pa 34th St and Civic Ctr Blvd Philadelphia PA 19104

**BRIGDEN, ANN SCHWARTZ,** mediator, educator; b. East Aurora, N.Y., Oct. 15, 1932; d. John G. and Mildred (Glaser) Schwartz; m. John Kraig Brigden, June 17, 1953 (div. Nov. 1974); children: Nancy Brigden, Barbara Brigden Victor; m. Steve Nemeth, Dec. 31, 1983 (div. Nov. 1996); children: Kyra Nemeth Akins, Abel Nemeth. *Daughter Nancy Brigden received a BFA from the University of California, Irvine, 1980, and a Master of Oriental Medicine from SAMRA University, 1997. After a career as a dancer, Nancy returned to school and has completed her studies in Acupuncture and Chinese Medicine and is starting her new career. Daughter Barbara Brigden Victor, AA Harbor College, 1984, Registered Nurse, 1984, BS California State University, Long Beach, 1991, Doctor of Medicine Tufts University Medical School, 1996, resident in emergency medicine Loma Linda Hospital, 1996—; she has finally realized her dream, while receiving loving support from her husband, Michael Victor.* BS in Human Ecology, Cornell U., 1954; MA in Behavioral Scis., Calif. State U., Dominguez Hills, 1977, grad. cert. in negotiation/conflict res., 1991, MS in Marriage and Family Counseling, 1993. Cert. mediator, L.A. County. Dist. dir. Girl Scouts of Erie County, Buffalo, N.Y., 1954-55; recreation leader City of Phila., 1955-56; field dir. Angeles Girl Scout Coun., L.A., 1956-58, 69-79; dir. vols. Children's Home Soc. Calif., L.A., 1979-84, dir. Human Maturity Program, 1984-90; counselor-intern Dolores St. Sch., Carson, Calif., 1990-95; developer and dir. Conflict Resolution Programs Dolores and Catskill Schs., Carson, Calif., 1994—; adv. bd. L.A. Unified Sch. Dist. Health Edn., 1985-87; chair Maternal, Child & Adolescent Health Coun. L.A. County West, L.A., 1988-93. Author (textbooks): Maturing as Humanly as Possible, 1986, Becoming a Teenager, 1988; co-author (jr. h.s. curriculum) Curriculum in Human Maturity, 1980, revised 1986, 94. Aux. mem. Children's Hosp. San Diego, 1962-68; Girl Scout leader, bd. mem. Girl Scout Coun. San Diego, 1964-68; com. chair Peninsula Action for Youth, Palos Verdes, Calif., 1971-76; vol. mediator L.A. County, 1992—; bd. dirs. Dispute Resolution Ctr. Calif. State U. Dominguez Hills/L.A. County, 1987—. Grantee Soc. Psychol. Study of Social Issues, 1994-96, L.A. County Dept. Edn., 1996—. Mem. So. Calif,. Mediation Assn., Calif. State U. Dominguez Hills Marriage, Family and Child Counseling Alumni Assn. Avocations: volunteering, piano, family, friends. Home: 3162 Crownview Dr Rancho Palos Verdes CA 90275

**BRIGGS, JOHN MANCEL, III,** lawyer; b. Muskegon, Mich., May 24, 1942; s. John M. II and Margaret Jane (Wren) B.; m. Janice R. Dykema, May 20, 1967; children: Jennifer Anne, Jill Margaret. BS, U. Mich., 1964, JD, 1967. Bar: Mich. 1968, U.S. Dist. Ct. (we. dist.) Mich. 1968, U.S. Ct. Appeals (6th cir.) 1974. Assoc. Parmenter, Forsythe, Rude, Van Epps, Briggs & Fauri and predecessors, Muskegon, 1967-70; ptnr. Parmenter, Forsythe, Rude, Van Epps, Briggs & Fauri and predecessors, 1970-92; shareholder Parmenter O'Toole, Muskegon, Mich., 1992—. Active Muskegon United Appeal, 1968-73; bd. dirs. Big Bros., Muskegon, 1969-74; bd. dirs. Y Family Christian Assn., 1970-80, 81-83, 1st v.p., 1973-76, pres., 1977-78; bd. dirs. Muskegon-Oceana Legal Aid Soc., 1970-73, pres., 1972-73; bd. dirs. Berean Ch., 1985-86, 99, sec., 1988-90, v.p., 1993, pres., 1994, 99. With USAR, 1967-73. Recipient Disting. Svc. award Muskegon Jaycees, 1977. Fellow Mich. State Bar Assn.; mem. ABA, Muskegon County Bar Assn. (sec. 1970-71, v.p. 1974-75, pres. 1975-76), Rotary (bd. dirs. 1981-85, pres.-elect 1982-83, pres. 1983-84, Presdl. Citation). Republican. Real property, Condemnation, Estate planning. Office: Parmenter O'Toole PO Box 786 175 W Apple Ave Muskegon MI 49443-0786

**BRIGGS, M. COURTNEY,** lawyer; b. Phila., Mar. 28, 1960. BA, Wesleyan U., 1982; JD with distinction, U. Okla., 1991. Asst. lit. agt. Curtis Brown Ltd., N.Y.C., 1983-86; fgn. rights assoc. Random House Inc., N.Y.C., 1986-89; assoc. Pringle & Pringle, Oklahoma City, 1991-92; sole practice Oklahoma City, 1993-94; ptnr. Derick & Briggs, Oklahoma City, 1994—. Mem. ABA, Soc. Children's Book Writers, Okla. Bar Assn. (dir. Young Lawyers divsn. 1995-98, chmn. 1997, vice-chair women in law com. 1998-99, mem. AIDS legal resources project panel 1995-99, chairperson disaster legal svcs. com. 1999). Intellectual property, Entertainment. Office: Derrick & Briggs LLP Bank One Ctr 20th FL 100 N Broadway Ave Oklahoma City OK 73102-8606

**BRIGGS, MARJORIE CROWDER,** lawyer; b. Shreveport, La., Mar. 26, 1946; d. Rowland Edmund and Marjorie Ernestine (Biles) Crowder; m. Ronald J. Briggs, July 11, 1970; children: Sarah, Andrew. BA, Carson-Newman Coll., 1968; MA, Ohio State U., 1969, JD, 1975. Bar: Ohio 1975, U.S. Ct. Appeals (6th cir.) 1983, U.S. Ct. Claims 1992. Asst. dean of women Albion Coll., Mich., 1969-70; dir. residence hall Ohio State U., Columbus, 1970-71, acad. counselor, 1971-72; assoc. Porter, Wright, Morris, Arthur, Columbus, 1970-71, ptnr., 1983—; legal aide Community Law Office, Columbus, 1973-74. Contbg. author: Going to Trial, A Step-By-Step Guide to Trial Practice and Procedure, 1989. Trustee, pres. Epilepsy Assn. Central Ohio, Columbus, 1977-84; bd. dirs. Columbus Speech & Hering, 1977-82; mem. allocation com. United Way Franklin County, 1984-88. Fellow Am. Bar Found., Columbus Bar Found. (trustee 1993-95); mem. ABA (litigation sect. 1983—, mem. gavel awards com. 1989-96, gen. practice sect. 1983—, chair litigation com. 1987-89, exec. coun. 1989-93, dir. bus. com. group 1990-91, chair program com. 1991-93, torts and ins. practice sect. 1993—, vice chair health ins. law com. 1993-96, chair-elect alternative dispute resolution com.), Ohio Bar Assn. (Joint Task Force on Gender Fairness 1991-93), Columbus Bar Assn. (com. chmn. 1979-83, docket control task force 1989-91, editor 1981-83), Def. Rsch. Inst., Am. Arbitration Assn., Nat. Assn. Women Lawyers, Women Lawyers Franklin County, Columbus Def. Assn., Capital Club. Federal civil litigation, General civil litigation, Insurance. Home: 4260 Woodhall Rd Columbus OH 43220-4378 Office: Porter Wright Morris & Arthur 41 S High St Ste 2800 Columbus OH 43215-6194

**BRIGGS, RANDY ROBERT,** lawyer; b. Mineola, N.Y., Jan. 23, 1948; s. Robert Oren Briggs and Elizabeth (Pasteur) Keeney; m. Diana Joy Allen; children: Robert Cullen, Allison Elizabeth. BSA, U. Fla., 1970, JD, 1975. Bar: Fla. 1975, U.S. Dist. Ct. (mid. dist.) Fla. 1976; cert. civil trial adv. Nat. Bd. Trial Advocacy, Fla. Bar. Civil Trial Lawyer. With, Maguire, Voorhis & Wells, P.A., Orlando, Fla., 1975-77; ptnr. Ayres, Cluster, Curry, McCall & Briggs, P.A., Ocala, Fla., 1977—. Coach U. Fla. trial team, 1994-97. Served to 1st lt. U.S. Army, 1970-72. Mem. Fla. Bar (bd. govs. young lawyers sect. 1980-83, trial lawyers sect. exec. coun. 1993-96, bd. of cert.), Acad. Fla. Trial Lawyers, Assn. Trial Lawyers Am., Order of Coif, Phi Kappa Phi. Presbyterian. Personal injury, State civil litigation, Federal civil litigation. Home: 3385 SW 17th Ave Ocala FL 34474-3447 Office: Ayres Cluster Curry et al 21 NE First Ave PO Box 1148 Ocala FL 34478-1148

**BRIGGS, TAYLOR RASTRICK,** lawyer; b. Buffalo, June 5, 1933; s. Ernest Rastrick and Althea (Taylor) B.; m. Jane Genske, Sept. 15, 1956; children: Cynthia B. Kittredge, Jennifer B. Braswell, Pamela B. Besnard, Taylor Rastrick. AB, Williams Coll., 1954; LLB, Columbia U., 1957. Bar: N.Y., U.S. Supreme Ct. Assoc. Simpson Thacher & Bartlett, N.Y.C., 1957-59; counsel N.Y. Com. on Govtl. Ops. of City of N.Y., 1959-60; asst. chief counsel N.Y. State Com. of Investigation, Special Unit, 1960-61; ptnr. LeBoeuf, Lamb, Greene & MacRae, N.Y.C., 1961-95, counsel, 1995—; bd. dirs. Nova NET Learning, Inc.; mng. dir. The Berkshires Capital Investors LLP, 1997—. Chmn. Tuxedo Park (N.Y.) Zoning Bd. Appeals, 1972-88; pres. Tuxedo Park Libr., 1971-79; chmn., trustee N.Y. Law Sch., N.Y.C., 1984—; trustee Citizens Budget Commn., 1990-95, Marlboro Sch. Music, Inc., 1992—; trustee Williamstown Art Conservation Ctr., 1997—; mem. adv. coun. Trinity Ctr. for Ethics and Corp. Policy, N.Y.C., 1982-93. Fellow Am. Bar Found., Am. Coll. Trial Lawyers; mem. ABA (ho. of del. 1985-88), Assn. of Bar of City of N.Y., Royal Tennis Club, Mid-Ocean Club, Royal Bermuda Yacht Club, Masons, Phi Delta Phi, Delta Upsilon. Republican. Episcopalian. Antitrust, Federal civil litigation, General corporate. Home: 1425 Main St Williamstown MA 01267-2623 Office: LeBoeuf Lamb Greene & MacRae 125 W 55th St New York NY 10019-5369

**BRIGHAM, MARTIN KENNETH,** lawyer; m. Harriet L. Rubenstein, Dec. 22, 1979; children: Molly, Jacob. BA, Brown U., 1975; JD, Northeastern U., 1979. Bar: Tenn. 1979, Pa. 1981, U.S. Dist. Ct. Pa. 1981, U.S. Ct. Appeals (3d cir.) 1981. Mng. atty., sr. trial counsel Galfand Berger Lurie Brigham et al., Phila., 1981-99; founder, ptnr. Brigham and Trevor, PC, Phila., 1999—. Author: Advanced Issues in Worker's Compensation, 1994, Injured on the Job, 1981, 5th edit., 1996. Avocation: rock climbing. Personal injury, Product liability, Workers' compensation. Office: Brigham and Trevor PC 1818 Market St Ste 3535 Philadelphia PA 19103-3636

**BRIGHAM, SAMUEL TOWNSEND JACK, III,** lawyer; b. Honolulu, Oct. 8, 1939; s. Samuel Townsend Jack, Jr. and Betty Elizabeth (McNeil) B.; m. Judith Catherine Johnson, Sept. 3, 1960; children: Robert Jack, Bradley Lund, Lori Ann, Lisa Katherine. B.S. in Bus. magna cum laude, Menlo Coll., 1963; J.D., U. Utah, 1966. Bar: Calif. 1967. Asso. firm Petty, Andrews, Olsen & Tufts, San Francisco, 1966-67; accounting mgr. Western sales region Hewlett-Packard Co., North Hollywood, Calif., 1967-68; atty. Hewlett-Packard Co., Palo Alto, Calif., 1968-70; asst. gen. counsel Hewlett-Packard Co., 1971-73, gen. atty., asst. sec., 1974-75, sec., gen. counsel, 1975-82, v.p., gen. counsel, 1982-85, v.p. corp. affairs, gen. counsel, mgr./dir. law dept., 1985—, sr. v.p. corp. affairs, gen. counsel, mgr./dir. law dept., 1994—; lectr. law Menlo Coll.; speaker profl. assn. seminars. Bd. dirs. Palo Alto Area YMCA, 1974-81, pres., 1978; bd. govs. Santa Clara County region NCCJ; trustee Menlo Sch. and Coll.; bd. dirs. Just Say No. Served with USMC, 1957-59. Mem. ABA, Calif. Bar Assn., Peninsula Assn. Gen. Counsel, MAPI Law Council, Am. Corp. Counsel Assn. (chmn. 1985, bd. dirs. 1983—), Am. Soc. Corp. Secs. (pres. No. Calif. Chpt. 1983—), Assn. Gen. Counsel (sec.-treas. 1991—). Home: 920 Oxford Dr Los Altos CA 94024-7032 Office: Hewlett-Packard Co 3000 Hanover St Palo Alto CA 94304-1181

**BRIGHT, JAMES STEPHEN,** lawyer; b. Glendale, Calif., Jan. 6, 1949; s. Herbert and Winifred Irene (Hunt) B.; m. Maureen Janet Glick, Aug. 19, 1972; 1 child, McKenzie Elizabeth. BS in Geology, U. So. Calif., 1971; JD, Loyola U., L.A., 1975. Bar: Calif., U.S. Dist. Ct. (no., ctrl., ea., so. dists.) Calif., U.S. Ct. Appeals (9th cir.), U.S. Dist Ct. (no. dist.) Tex. Geologist So. Calif. Edison, Rosemead, Calif., 1971-76; from assoc. to ptnr. Hanna & Morton, L.A., 1976-81; ptnr. Andrews & Kurth, L.A., 1989-90; ptnr. Bright & Brown, L.A., 1981-89, Glendale, 1991—. Fellow Am. Coll. Trial Lawyers. General civil litigation, Oil, gas, and mineral, Environmental. Office: Bright & Brown 550 N Brand Blvd Ste 2100 Glendale CA 91203-3384

**BRIGHT, JOSEPH CONVERSE,** lawyer; b. Richmond, Va., July 28, 1940; s. Joseph Elliott and Marion (Converse) B.; m. Jill Giddens, May 5, 1989; children: Thomas Converse, Elizabeth Chase. BA, U. Va., 1962; LLB, U. Ga., 1965. Bar: Ga. 1964, U.S. Dist. Ct. (so. dist.) Ga. 1965, U.S. Dist. Ct. (mid. dist.) Ga. 1967, U.S. Dist. Ct. (no. dist.) Ga. 1983, U.S. Ct. Appeals (5th cir.) 1965, Fla. 1976, U.S. Dist. Ct. (mid. and no. dist.) Fla. 1982, U.S. Supreme Ct. 1976, U.S. Ct. Appeals (11th cir.) 1981, U.S. Dist. Ct. (no. dist.) Fla. 1998. Assoc. Joseph B. Bergen, Savannah, Ga., 1965-67; sole practice Valdosta, Ga., 1967-69; ptnr. Blackburn & Bright, Valdosta, 1969-91; pvt. practice Valdosta, 1991—; instr. part time Valdosta State U., 1967-81; mem. Ga. Bd. Bar Examiners. Fellow Am. Bd. Criminal Lawyers, Am. Coll. Trial Lawyers; mem. ATLA, Am. Bd. Trial Advocates (advocate), Nat. Assn. Criminal Def. Lawyers, Ga. Trial Lawyers Assn. (v.p.). Avocations: riding, English history, skeet shooting. Personal injury, Criminal, Product liability. Office: PO Box 5889 Valdosta GA 31603-5889

**BRIGHT, MYRON H.,** federal judge, educator; b. Eveleth, Minn., Mar. 5, 1919; s. Morris and Lena A. (Levine) B.; m. Frances Louise Reisler, Dec. 26, 1947; children: Dinah Ann, Joshua Robert. BSL, U. Minn., 1941, JD, 1947. Bar: N.D. 1947, Minn. 1947. Assoc. Wattam, Vogel, Vogel & Bright, Fargo, N.D., 1947, ptnr., 1949-68; judge 8th U.S. Cir. Ct. Appeals, Fargo, 1968-85, sr. judge, 1985—; disting. prof. law St. Louis U., 1985-88, emeritus prof. of law, 1989-95. Capt. AUS, 1942-46, CBI. Recipient Francis Rawle award ALI-ABA, 1996, Lifetime Achievement award U. N.D. Law Sch., 1998. Mem. ABA, N.D. Bar Assn., Met. St. Louis Bar Assn., U.S. Jud. Conf. (com. on adminstrn. of probation sys. 1977-83, adv. com. on appellate rules 1987-90, com. on internat. jud. rels. 1996—). Office: US Ct Appeals 8th Cir 655 1st Ave N Ste 340 Fargo ND 58102-4952

**BRIGHT, THOMAS LYNN,** lawyer; b. Omaha, June 3, 1948. B in Bus., Emporia State U., 1970; JD, Kans. U., 1974; MBA, Tulsa U., 1989. Bar: Okla. 1975, U.S. Ct. Appeals (10th cir.) 1989, U.S. Supreme Ct. 1989. Tax atty. Phillips Petroleum Co., Bartlesville, Okla., 1974-79; assoc. tax counsel Phillips Petroleum Europe/Africa, London, 1979-83, Phillips Petroleum Co., Bartlesville, 1984-87; pvt. practice Tulsa, 1987—; adj. prof. Tulsa U., 1989-92. Mem. ABA, Okla. Bar Assn., Tulsa County Bar Assn. (pres. solo and small practice sect. 1994-95), Tulsa Area Human Resources Assn. Labor, General civil litigation, Pension, profit-sharing, and employee benefits. Office: 406 S Boulder Ave Ste 411 Tulsa OK 74103-3800

**BRIHAMMAR, B. NIKLAS,** lawyer; b. Stockholm, Sweden, Apr. 12, 1964; s. Bengt Axel and Solbritt Linnea Elisabeth (Pettersson) B.; m. Marta Kristina Sjoevall, Dec. 21, 1995. BS in Econs., U. South Ala., Mobile, 1989; JD, U. Miami, 1993. Bar: Fla. 1993, U.S. Dist. Ct. (so. dist.) Fla. 1995. Asst. mgr. Daiwa Securities, Ltd., Stockholm, 1990; assoc. atty. John E. Bigler, P.A., Key West, Fla., 1994, John R. Fiore, P.A., Miami, Fla., 1995, Sheri Smallwood, Chartered, Key West, 1995—. Mem. Gala Task Force, Key West, 1997—. Mem. ABA, Fla. Bar (family law sect.), Monroe County Bar Assn., Swedish-Am. Bar Assn., Swedish-Am. C. of C. Avocations: computers, reading, chess, tennis, film. General civil litigation, Personal injury, Family and matrimonial. Office: Sheri Smallwood Chartered 1016 Eaton St Key West FL 33040-6925

**BRILL, HAYDN J.,** lawyer; b. Luton, U.K., Jan. 1, 1959; came to U.S., 1962; s. Harold and Sheila B.; m. Amy Deborah Hechler, Nov. 10, 1986; children: Chelsea Paige, Jared Michael. Bar: N.Y., N.J., U.S. Dist. Ct. (so. and ea. dists.) N.Y.; U.S. Dist. Ct. N.J. Assoc. Morgan, Melhuish, Monaghan, Arvidson, Abrutyn & Lisowski, Livingston, N.J., 1987-93, N.Y.C., 1987-93; ptnr. Smith Mazure Director Wilkins Young Yagerman & Tarallo PC, N.Y.C., 1993—. Advisor W. Windsor (N.J.) Planning Bd., 1992-93; mem. W. Windsor Site Plan Rev. Adv. Bd., 1992-93. Mem. N.Y. County Lawyers. Federal civil litigation, State civil litigation. Office: Smith Mazure Director Wilkins Young Yagerman & Tarallo PC 111 John St New York NY 10038-3101

**BRILL, NEWTON CLYDE,** lawyer, title and abstract company executive; b. Mountain Grove, Mo., Mar. 10, 1936; s. Newton Clyde and Virginia Marie (Young) B.; m. Margaret Carolyn Saunders, June 10, 1958; children: Julia Elizabeth, Margaret Ann, Joel Newton. AB in Polit. Sci., U. Mo., 1958, JD, 1964. Bar: Mo. 1964, U.S. Ct. Appeals (8th cir.) 1966, U.S. Supreme Ct. 1977. Assoc. Richard D. Moore, West Plains, Mo., 1964-68; ptnr. Moore & Brill, West Plains, 1968-80; ptnr., bd. dirs. Brill, Moore & Wagoner, P.C., West Plains, 1980—; owner, mgr. Kellett-Landis Brill Abstract & Land Title Co., West Plains, 1971—; bd. dirs. Cmty. First Nat. Bank, West Plains. Asst. editor U. Mo. Law Rev., 1964. Chmn. Howell County Rep. Com., 1964-84; commr. Housing Authority West Plains, 1988—. Lt. USMC, 1958-61. Fellow Am. Coll. Trust and Estate Counsel, Am. Coll. Mortgage Attys.; mem. Mo. Bar (bd. govs. 1992-98), Rotary. Baptist. Avocations: gardening, fishing. Real property, Contracts commercial, Probate. Home: 1327 W Broadway St West Plains MO 65775-2315 Office: Brill Moore & Wagoner PC PO Box 527 West Plains MO 65775-0527

**BRILL, STEVEN CHARLES,** financial advisor, lawyer; b. Miami, Fla., Aug. 21, 1953; s. Arthur W. and Joan K. (Caveretta) B. AB, Boston U., 1975; JD, Western New Eng. Coll., 1978; LLM, NYU, 1986. Advanced underwriting cons. Equitable Life Assurance Soc., N.Y.C., 1978-79; sr. advanced underwriting cons. Met. Life Ins. Co., N.Y.C., 1979-85; asst. v.p. personal fin. planning group Dean Witter Reynolds, N.Y.C., 1985-87; v.p., dir. asset allocation group Chase Pvt. Bank, N.Y.C., 1987-98; prin. Spielberger, Dampf, Brill & Levine, LLC, 1998—; dir. Cmty. Housing Innovations, Inc.; past pres., dir. Wychwood Owner's Corp., Great Neck, N.Y., Realty of Bay Terr. Inc., Bayside, N.Y. Contbr. articles to Mature Outlook Mag. Avocations: skiing, tennis, golf. Home: 177 E 75th St Apt 8C New York NY 10021-3232

**BRIM, JEFFERSON KEARNEY, III,** lawyer; b. Sulphur Springs, Tex., July 15, 1945; s. J. Kearney and June Marie (Wester) B.; m. Jeanine Eloise Clymer, July 3, 1971; children: Cari Christen, Brandon Taylor, Jessica Merrill. BA, U. Tex., 1971, JD, 1975. Bar: Tex. 1974, U.S. Dist. Ct. (no. and ea. dists.) Tex. 1976, U.S. Dist. Ct. (we. dist.) Tex. 1978, U.S. Dist. Ct. (so. dist.) Tex. 1981. Ptnr. Carter & Brim, Commerce, Tex., 1974-77; staff atty. Tex. Edn. Agy., Austin, 1977-79; state pres. Tex. Jaycees, Austin, 1979-80; assoc. Davis & Davis, Austin, 1981-83; ptnr. Brim, Tingley & Arnett, Austin, 1983-86; ptnr. Brim & Arnett, Austin, 1986-94, 96-97, Brim, Arnett and Judge, PC, 1994-96; Brim, Arnett & Robinett, P.C., 1997—; mcpl. judge City of Rollingwood, Tex., 1988-96; alderman City of Rollingwood, 1996—; counsel Assn. Tex. Profl. Educators, 1980—. Chmn. Travis County Dem. Com., 1998—. Staff sgt. USAF, 1967-70. Decorated Air medal; recipient Clayton Frost Meml. award U.S. Jaycees, 1979-80. Mem. State Bar Tex. (com. chmn. 1982-84), U.S. Jaycees (nat. v.p. 1980-81), Kappa Delta Pi. Methodist. Administrative and regulatory, Civil rights, Education and schools. Home: 4906 Timberline Dr Austin TX 78746-5535 Office: Brim Arnett & Robinett PC 2525 Wallingwood Dr Bldg 14 Austin TX 78746-6900

**BRIMMER, CLARENCE ADDISON,** federal judge; b. Rawlins, Wyo., July 11, 1922; s. Clarence Addison and Geraldine (Zingsheim) B.; m. Emily O. Docken, Aug. 2, 1953; children: Geraldine Ann, Philip Andrew, Andrew Howard, Elizabeth Ann. BA, U. Mich., 1944, JD, 1947. Bar: Wyo. 1948. Pvt. practice law Rawlins, 1948-71, mcpl. judge, 1948-54; U.S. commr., magistrate, 1963-71; atty. gen. Wyo. Cheyenne, 1971-74; U.S. atty., 1975; chief judge U.S. Dist. Ct. Wyo., Cheyenne, 1975-92, dist. judge, 1975—; mem. panel multi-dist. litigation, 1992—; mem. Jud. Conf. U.S., 1994-97, exec., 1995-97. Sec. Rawlins Bd. Pub. Utilities, 1954-66; Rep. gubernatorial candidate, 1974; trustee Rocky Mountain Mineral Law Found., 1963-75. With USAAF, 1945-46. Mem. ABA, Wyo. Bar Assn., Laramie County Bar Assn., Carbon County Bar Assn., Am. Judicature Soc., Masons, Shriners, Rotary. Episcopalian. Office: US Dist Ct PO Box 985 Cheyenne WY 82003-0985

**BRIND, DAVID HUTCHISON,** lawyer, judge; b. Albany, N.Y., Feb. 4, 1930; s. Charles Albert and Laura Stuart (Hutchison) B.; m. Shirley Jean, Mar. 6, 1954; children: Susan, Charles. AB, Union Coll., 1951; LLB, Albany Law Sch., 1954, JD, 1968. Bar: N.Y. 1954, U.S. Supreme Ct. 1970. Atty. law div. N.Y. State Dep. Edn., Albany, 1954-55; ptnr. Chacchia & Brind, Geneva, N.Y., 1957-64; sole practice, Geneva, 1964-95, ret., 1995; judge Geneva City Ct., 1974-95, ret., 1995; supervising judge, 1986-95, ret., 1995; apptd. jud. hearing officer N.Y. State Supreme Ct., 1995—; hearing officer N.Y. State and Local Ret. Sys., 1997—; counsel real estate N.Y. State Dormitory Authority, 1960-86; gen. counsel Geneva Gen. Hosp., 1966-85; local counsel Conrail. Bd. dirs. Geneva United Way, 1965-89; campaign chmn. United Way of Greater Rochester (N.Y.), 1966-69, pres., 1969-71, bd. dirs., 1979-82; trustee Geneva Gen. Hosp., 1962-73, pres., 1969-71; trustee Geneva Hist. Soc., 1963-90; chmn. Geneva Hist. Commn., 1969-89; mem. exec. bd. Finger Lakes council Boy Scouts Am., 1968-85; bd. dirs. Seven Lakes council Girl Scouts U.S.A., 1966-73; bd. dirs. Geneva Gen. Hosp. Nursing Home, 1969-71; v.p. Geneva Bd. Edn., 1962-67; mem. pres.'s council Eisenhower Coll., 1972-79, Hobart & William Smith Colls., 1967—. Recipient Geneva Community Chest/Red Cross Svc. citation, 1969, named Man of Yr., 1971. Mem. Am. Assn. of Homes for Aging, N.Y. State Sch. Bds. Assn. (law revisions com. and constl. conv. com. 1964-68), Monroe County Judiciary Com., 1976-80, Ontario County Bar Assn., N.Y. State Bar Assn. (mem. jud. coun.), Fedn. N.Y. State Judges, N.Y. Land Title Assn., Am. Arbitration Assn., Am. Hosp. Assn., Soc. Hosp. Attys., N.Y. State Assn. City Ct. Judges (pres. 1989-91), N.Y. State Assn. Jud. Hearing Officers (treas. 1995—), Andrews Soc. Albany, Rotary (pres. 1967-68). Republican. Presbyterian. Probate, Real property. Home: 43 Delancey Dr Geneva NY 14456-2809 Office: PO Box 409 Geneva NY 14456-0409

**BRING, MURRAY H.,** lawyer; b. Denver, Jan. 19, 1935; s. Alfred Alexander and Ida (Molinsky) B.; m. Constance Brooks Evert, Dec. 30, 1963 (div. June 1989); children: Beth, Catherine, Peter; m. Kathleen Delaney, May 19, 1990. BA, U. So. Calif., 1956; LLB, NYU, 1959. Bar: N.Y. 1960, D.C. 1963, U.S. Supreme Ct. 1966. Law clk. to Chief Justice Earl Warren U.S. Supreme Ct., Washington, 1959-61; spl. asst. to asst. atty. gen. civil div. Dept. Justice, Washington, 1961-62; spl. asst. to dep. undersec. state Dept. State, Washington, 1962-63; dir. policy planning anti-trust divsn., 1963-65; ptnr. Arnold & Porter, Washington, 1965-87; sr. v.p., gen. counsel Philip Morris Cos., Inc., N.Y.C., 1988-94, exec. v.p. external affairs and gen. counsel, 1994-97, vice chmn., gen. counsel, 1997—. Editor-in-chief N.Y. Law Rev., 1958-59. Bd. dirs. N.Y.C. Opera, NYU Law Sch. Found.; trustee Whitney Mus. Am. Art. Mem. ABA, Assn. Bar City N.Y., D.C. Bar Assn., Order of Coif, Phi Beta Kappa, Phi Kappa Phi. Avocations: photography; art. General corporate. Office: Philip Morris Cos Inc 120 Park Ave New York NY 10017-5592

**BRINGARDNER, JOHN MICHAEL,** lawyer, clergyman; b. Columbus, Ohio, Nov. 7, 1957; s. John Krepps and Elizabeth (Evans) B.; m. Emily Presley, June 19, 1982; children: John Taylor, Michael Steven, Malee Elizabeth. BA, U. Central Fla., Orlando, 1979; postgrad., Mercer U., 1979; JD, Fla. State U., 1981. Bar: Fla. 1982, Calif. 1994, U.S. Dist. Ct. (mid. dist.) Fla., U.S. Dist. Ct. (no. dist.) Fla., U.S. Ct. Appeals (11th cir.). Assoc. McFarlain, Bobo, Sternstein, Wiley & Cassidy, Tallahassee, Fla., 1982-87, Finley, Kumble Wagner, Tallahassee, 1987; minister Boston Ch. of Christ, 1987-90; evangelist Bankok Christian Ch., 1990-92, Metro Manila Christian Ch., 1992-93; gen. counsel Internat. Chs. of Christ, L.A., 1993—; bd. dirs. Eye Care Corp., Orlando, Fla., Quality Coffee Corp., Tallahassee. Mem. ABA, Fla. Bar Assn. Avocations: football, baseball, triathalons, hiking, music. Non-profit and tax-exempt organizations, General civil litigation, Constitutional. Office: International Churches of Christ 3530 Wilshire Blvd Ste 1750 Los Angeles CA 90010-2238

**BRINGMAN, JOSEPH EDWARD,** lawyer; b. Elmhurst, N.Y., Jan. 31, 1958; s. Joseph Herman and Eileen Marie (Sheehy) B.; m. Laurie Lynn Cunningham, July 11, 1992; children: Joseph Edward Jr., Elizabeth Grace. BA, Yale U., 1980; JD, Stanford U., 1983. Bar: N.Y. 1984, Wash. 1985, U.S. Dist. Ct. (we. dist.) Wash. 1986, U.S. Ct. Appeals (9th cir.) 1986, U.S. Ct. Appeals (fed. cir.) 1988. Acting asst. prof. U. Wash. Law Sch., Seattle, 1983-85; assoc. Perkins Coie, Seattle, 1985-91, of counsel, 1992—; dir. Perkins Coie Cmty. Fellowship, Seattle, 1990-96, chair assoc. tng. com., 1997—. Editor: Stanford Jour. Internat. Law, 1980-83. Mem. Yale Alumni Schs. Com., Seattle, 1983—, Palo Alto, Calif., 1980-83. Nat. Merit scholar, 1976; recipient Pro Bono Publico award Trumbull Coll. (Yale U.), 1980. Mem. ABA, Wash. State Bar Assn., King County Bar Assn. (mem. judicial screening com. 1993-96, chair fair campaign practices com. 1997—). Democrat. Roman Catholic. Federal civil litigation, State civil litigation, Professional liability. Office: Perkins Coie LLP 1201 3rd Ave Fl 48 Seattle WA 98101-3099

**BRINKEMA, LEONIE MILHOMME,** federal judge; b. N.J., June 26, 1944; d. Alexander Juste and Modeste Leonie Milhomme; m. John Robert Brinkema, Dec. 22, 1966; children: Robert Aaron, Eugenie Alexandra. BA with honors, Douglass Coll., 1966; MLS, Rutgers U., 1970; JD with honors, Cornell U., 1976. Bar: D.C. 1976, Va. 1978. Trial atty. U.S. Dept. Justice, Washington, 1976-77, 1983-84; asst. U.S. atty. U.S. Atty's Office Ea. Va., Alexandria, 1977-83; prin. Leonie M. Brinkema Atty., Alexandria, 1984-85; U.S. magistrate judge U.S. Dist. Ct. (ea. dist.) Va., Alexandria, 1985-93, U.S. dist. judge, 1993—; legal lectr. Va. State Bar Professionalism Faculty, 1990-92, No. Va. Criminal Justice Acad., 1984-85; guest lectr. Alexandria Bar Assn., Alexandria Women Attys. Assn., Va. Women Attys. Assn., U.S. Dept. Justice Advocacy Inst., Va. Law Found. Active Fairfax Choral Soc., Alban Chorale. Woodrow Wilson grad. fellow, 1966, Danforth Found. grad. fellow, 1966. Mem. ABA, Va. State Bar, D.C. Bar, Nat. Assn. Women Judges, Va. Women Attys. Assn., George Mason Inn of Ct. (master), Phi Beta Kappa. Avocation: singing. Office: US Dist Ct 401 Courthouse Sq Alexandria VA 22314-5704

**BRINKLEY, JACK THOMAS, JR.,** lawyer; b. Ft. Bragg, N.C., Apr. 27, 1956; s. Jack Thomas and Alma Lois (Kite) B.; m. Stacy Patricia Smith, Jan. 2, 1988; children: Jack Thomas III, Matthew, Victoria, Maryelle, Abbigail, Fredrick. BA summa cum laude, Columbus (Ga.) Coll., 1978; JD cum laude, Mercer U., 1981. Bar: Ga. 1981, U.S. Dist. Ct. (mid. dist.) Ga. 1981, U.S. Ct. Appeals (5th and 11th cirs.) 1981, U.S. Dist. Ct. (no. dist.) Ga. 1986, U.S. Dist. Ct. (ea. dist.) Tenn. 1997. Assoc. Law Offices of Billy E. Moore, Columbus, 1981-83; ptnr. Brinkley, Brinkley & Dugan, Columbus, 1983-85, Brinkley & Brinkley, Columbus, 1986-96; pvt. practice Columbus, 1997—; spkr. in field. Contbr. articles to law jours. Former mem. bd. dirs. March of Dimes, Columbus; campaign chmn. Com. To Elect Rosa Barker, Columbus; leader Cub Scouts Am., Columbus; coach Little League, Columbus. Mem. ATLA, Ga. Trial Lawyers Assn., Columbus Lawyers Club. Avocations: family, gardening, travel, collecting antique furniture and stained glass, attending auctions. Office: PO Box 2016 Columbus GA 31902-2016

**BRINKMAN, DALE THOMAS,** lawyer; b. Columbus, Ohio, Dec. 10, 1952; s. Harry H. and Jean May (Sandel) B.; m. Martha Louise Johnson, Aug. 3, 1974; children: Marin Veronica, Lauren Elizabeth, Kelsey Renee. BA, U. Notre Dame, 1974; JD, Ohio State U., 1977. Bar: Ohio 1977, U.S. Dist. Ct. (so. dist.) Ohio 1979. Assoc. Schwartz, Shapiro, Kelm & Warren, Columbus, 1977-82; asst. tax counsel Am. Elect. Power, Columbus, 1982; gen. counsel Worthington Industries, Inc., Columbus, 1982-99, v.p. adminstrn., gen. counsel, 1999—. Author: Ohio State U. Law Jour.,1975-76, editor, 1976-77. Trustee, officer Friends of Dahlberg Ctr., Columbus, 1980-86; dir., officer Assn. for Developmentally Disabled, Columbus, 1986-94. Mem. ABA, Ohio Bar Assn., Columbus Bar Assn. Republican. Roman Catholic. General corporate, Mergers and acquisitions, Securities. Office: Worthington Industries Inc 1205 Dearborn Dr Columbus OH 43085-4769

**BRINKMANN, ROBERT JOSEPH,** lawyer; b. Cin., Dec. 25, 1950; s. Robert Harry and Helen R. (Streuwing) B.; children: Christopher, Julia. BA, U. Notre Dame, 1972; postgrad., Alliance Française, 1974-75; AM, Brown U., 1977; JD, Loyola U., Los Angeles, 1980. Bar: Calif. 1980, D.C. 1981, U.S. Ct. Appeals (D.C. and 9th cirs.) 1981, U.S. Supreme Ct. 1984, U.S. Ct. Appeals (6th cir.) 1987. Tchr. secondary schs., Los Angeles and Paris, 1974-77; assoc. Hedrick & Lane, Washington, 1980-82; gen. counsel Nat. Newspaper Assn., Washington, 1982-92; exec. dir. Red Tag News Publs. Assn., 1990-92; v.p., postal and regulatory affairs Newspaper Assn. Am., Reston, Va., 1992—; mem. faculty Am. Press. Inst., Reston, Va., 1982-92; adj. faculty U. Md., 1997—. Mem. ABA, Fed. Communications Bar Assn. (former vice chmn. postal affairs com.). Roman Catholic. Administrative and regulatory, Legislative, Communications. Home: 9815 Bristol Square Ln Apt 204 Bethesda MD 20814-5440 Office: Newspaper Assn Am National Press Bldg 529 14th St NW Ste 440 Washington DC 20045-1407

**BRINSMADE, LYON LOUIS,** lawyer; b. Mexico City, Feb. 24, 1924; s. Robert Bruce and Helen (Steenbock) B. (Am. citizens); m. Susannah Tucker, June 9, 1956 (div. 1978); children: Christine Fairchild, Louisa Calvert; m. Carolyn Hartman Lister, Sept. 22, 1979. Student, U. Wis., 1940-43; B.S., Mich. Technol. U., 1944; J.D., Harvard U., 1950. Bar: Tex. 1951. Assoc. Butler, Binion, Rice, Cook & Knapp, Houston, 1950-58, ptnr. in charge internat. dept., 1958-83; ptnr. in charge internat. dept. Porter & Clements, Houston, 1983-91; sr. counsel Porter & Hedges (formerly Porter & Clements), Houston, 1991—. Bd. dirs. Houston br. English-Speaking Union of U.S., 1972-75. Served with AUS, 1946-47. Mem. ABA (chmn. com. internat. investment and devel. of sect. internat. law and practice 1970-76, council 1972-76, 81-82, vice chmn. 1976-79, chmn.-elect 1979-80, chmn. 1980-81, co-chmn. com. Mex. 1982-85), Internat. Bar Assn., Inter-Am. Bar Assn. (co-chmn. sect. oil and gas laws, com. natural resources 1973-76, council 1984-87), Houston Bar Assn., State Bar Tex. (chmn. internat. law com. 1970-74, mem. council sect. internat. law 1975-78), Am. Soc. Internat. Law (exec. council 1984-86), Houston World Trade Assn. (sec., dir. 1967-70), Houston World Trade Assn. (chmn. legis. com. 1967-72), Houston C. of C. (chmn. legis. subcom. internat. bus. com. 1970-72), Houston Com. on Fgn. Relations, SAR, Allegro of Houston, Houston Club, Petroleum Club, Harvard Club (Houston), Sigma Alpha Epsilon. Episcopalian. Private international, General corporate, Contracts commercial. Home: The Beaconsfield 1700 Main St Houston TX 77002-8119 Office: 700 Louisiana St Fl 35 Houston TX 77002-2700

**BRINSON, GAY CRESWELL, JR.,** lawyer; b. Kingsville, Tex., June 13, 1925; s. Gay Creswell and Lelia (Wendelkin) B.; m. Bette Lee Butter, June 17, 1979; children from former marriage: Thomas Wade, Mary Kaye. Student, U. Ill.-Chgo., 1947-48; B.S., U. Houston, 1953, J.D., 1957. Bar: Tex. 1957, U.S. Dist. Ct. (so. dist.) Tex. 1959, U.S. Dist. Ct. (ea. dist.) Tex. 1965, U.S. Dist. Ct. (no. dist.) Tex. 1990, U.S. Ct. Appeals (5th cir.) 1962, U.S. Supreme Ct. 1974; diplomate Am. Bd. Trial Advocates, Am. Bd. Profl. Liability Attys. Spl. agt. FBI, Washington and Salt Lake City, 1957-59; trial atty. Liberty Mut. Ins. Co., Houston, 1959-62; assoc. Horace Brown, Houston, 1962-64; assoc. Vinson & Elkins, Houston, 1964-67, ptnr., 1967-91; of counsel McFall, Sherwood & Sheehy, Houston, 1992—; lectr. U. Houston Coll. Law, 1964-65; mem. staff Tex. Coll. Trial Advocacy, Houston, 1978-86; prosecutor Harris County Grievance Com.-State Bar Tex., Houston, 1965-70. Served with AUS, 1943-46, ETO. Fellow Tex. Bar Found. (life); mem. Tex. Acad. Family Law Specialists (cert.), Tex. Assn. Def. Counsel, Tex. Bd. Legal Specialization (cert.), Fedn. Ins. Counsel, Nat. Bd. Trial Advocacy (cert.), Houston Ctr. Club, Phi Delta Phi. Federal civil litigation, State civil litigation, Personal injury. Home: 3740 Del Monte Dr Houston TX 77019-3018 Office: McFall Sherwood & Sheehy 2500 2 Houston Ctr 909 Fannin St Houston TX 77010-1001

**BRINSON, ROBERT MADDOX,** lawyer; b. Rome, Ga., May 4, 1940; s. Moses Ebenezer and Ruth (Maddox) B.; children: Robert Jr., Ruth E., D. Brooke, Susan Stegall; m. Margaret Dye, May 15, 1982. AB in Law, Emory U., 1962, LLB, 1963. Bar: Ga., 1963. Assoc., then ptnr. Rogers, Magruder and Hoyt, Rome, 1963-75; sr. ptnr. Brinson, Askew, Berry, Seigler, Richardson and Davis, Rome, 1975—; city atty. City of Rome, 1968—. Mem. Ga. Bd. Edn., 1990-96. Fellow Am. Bar Found. (life.), Am. Coll. Trial Lawyers, Internat. Soc. Barristers, Ga. Bar Found. (life trustee, pres. 1992-94); mem. State Bar Ga. (pres. 1986-87), Am. Bd. Trial Advocates (adv.), Beckley Inn of Ct. (master). Presbyterian. Avocations: gardening, travel. General civil litigation, Product liability, Personal injury. Home: 19 Shadow Ln SW Rome GA 30165-8510 Office: Brinson Askew Berry Seigler Richardson & Davis 615 W 1st St Rome GA 30161-3036

**BRIONES, DAVID,** judge; b. 1943. BA, U. Tex., El Paso, 1969; JD, U. Tex., Austin, 1971. Ptnr. Moreno & Briones, 1971-91; judge El Paso County Ct. No. 1, El Paso, 1991-94; dist. judge U.S. DIst. Ct. (we. dist.) Tex., El Paso, 1994—. With U.S. Army, 1964-66. Fellow Tex. Bar Found.; mem. State Bar of Tex., El Paso Bar Assn., Mexican-Am. Bar Assn. Office: US Courthouse Courtroom 2 511 E San Antonio Ave El Paso TX 79901-2401

**BRISCOE, JACK CLAYTON,** lawyer; b. Bradford, Pa., July 23, 1920; s. Park Harry and Elsie Gertrude (Woodward) B.; m. Dorothy Lillian Shaw, Sept. 3, 1949; children: Jacqueline Kamp, Jeffrey S., Joan Ryd. BS in Econs. U. Pa., 1943; LLB Harvard U., 1948. Bar: Pa. 1950. Assoc. Robert C. Duffy, Phila., 1950-66; ptnr. Briscoe, Haggerty & Howard, Phila., 1966-85, Briscoe & Howard, Phila., 1985-89, Briscoe, Carney & Carney, Phila., 1989-91; instr. U. Pa., 1950-56; bd. dirs. Renewal Counseling, Inc., Mark Prodns. Ltd; chmn. bd. dirs. Master's Plan Fin. Svcs., Inc. Dir. Phila. Flag Day Assn., Pa. Bible Soc.; chmn. bd. Community Christian Fellowship Ctr. Inc.; elder United Presbyn. Ch. Manoa; active Fellowship Christian Athletes; bd. dirs. People for People, Inc.; mem. Rep. Presdl. Task Force; bd. dirs. Evang. Community Svcs., Inc. With USAAF, 1943-46. Branch Ricky Assocs. award; Cert Achievement award compulsory arbitration div. Phila. County Ct. Fellow Harry S. Truman Library Inst.; mem. ABA, Pa. Bar Assn., Phila. Bar Assn., Pa. Trial Lawyers Assn., Nat. Fedn. Ind. Bus., Internat. Platform Assn. (Pa Soc.Harvard Law Sch. Assn., Friendly Sons of St. Patrick, Gideons Internat., Missions Unltd. Inc. (bd. dirs.), World Affairs Coun., Chapel of Four Chaplains (legion hon. mem.). Clubs: Harvard, Lawyers (Phila.), Union League. General corporate, Estate planning, Franchising. Office: 4000 Bell Atlantic Tower 1717 Arch St Philadelphia PA 19103-2713

**BRISCOE, JOHN,** lawyer; b. Stockton, Calif., July 1, 1948; s. John Lloyd and Doris (Olsen) B.; divorced; children: John Paul, Katherine. JD, U. San Francisco, 1972. Bar: Calif. 1972, U.S. Dist. Ct. (no., ea. and ctrl. dists.) Calif. 1972, U.S. Supreme Ct. 1978, U.S. Ct. Appeals (9th cir.) 1981. Dep. atty. gen. State of Calif., San Francisco, 1972-80; ptnr. Washburn and Kemp, San Francisco, 1980-88, Washburn, Briscoe & McCarthy, San Francisco, 1988—; bd. dirs. San Francisco Bay Planning coalition, chmn., 1990-93; vis. scholar U. Calif., Berkeley, 1990—; spl. adviser UN Compensation Commn., Geneva, Switzerland, 1998—. Author: Surveying the Courtroom, 1984, Falsework, 1997; editor: Reports of Special Masters, 1991; contbr. articles to profl. and lit. jours. Mem. ABA, San Francisco Bar Assn., Law of the Sea Inst. Roman Catholic. General civil litigation, Land use and zoning (including planning), Real property. Office: Washburn Briscoe & McCarthy 55 Francisco St San Francisco CA 94133-2122

**BRISCOE, MARY BECK,** federal judge; b. 1947. BA, U. Kans., 1969, JD, 1973; LLM, U. Va., 1990. Rsch. asst. Harold L. Haun, Esq., 1973; atty.-examiner fin. divsn. ICC, 1973-74; asst. U.S. atty. for Wichita and Topeka, Kans. Dept. Justice, 1974-84; judge Kans. Ct. Appeals, 1984-95, chief judge, 1990-95; judge U.S. Ct. Appeals (10th cir.), Topeka, 1995—. Fellow Am. Bar Found., Kans. Bar Found.; mem. ABA, Am. Judicature Soc., Nat. Assn. Women Judges, Topeka Bar Assn., Kans. Bar Assn. (Outstanding Svc. award 1992), Women Attys. Assn. Topeka, Kans. Hist. Soc., Washburn Law Sch. Assn. (hon.), U. Kans. Law Soc. Office: US Ct Appeals 10th Cir 645 Massachusetts Ste 400 Lawrence KS 66044-2235

**BRISKIN, BOYD EDWARD,** lawyer; b. Los Angeles, Feb. 9, 1932; s. Paul and Sara (Frankel) B.; m. Sylvia Marilyn Farber, Apr. 3, 1960; children—Randall Kent, Paul Henry. A.A., Riverside Community Coll., 1950; B.A., UCLA, 1952; J.D., U. Calif.-San Francisco, 1955. Bar: Calif. 1955, U.S. Dist. Ct. (so. dist.) Calif. 1955. Sole practice, Riverside, Calif., 1957—; dir. Tel-Law, Inc., Riverside, 1974—, pres., 1978-80. Dir. Inland Area Council Boy Scouts Am., 1960-84; pres. Riverside Temple Beth El, 1977-79. Recipient Silver Beaver award Boy Scouts Am., 1980. Served to 1st lt. JAGC, U.S. Army, 1955-57. Mem. Riverside County Bar Assn. (sec. 1983-84, v.p. 1984-85, pres. 1986-87, Outstanding Leadership award 1978-80), State Bar Calif. Republican. Jewish. Lodge: B'Nai B'rith. Family and matrimonial, Probate, Consumer commercial. Office: PO Box 20402 Riverside CA 92516-0402

**BRISKMAN, LOUIS JACOB,** lawyer. BA, U. Pitts., 1970; JD, Georgetown U., 1973. Bar: Pa. 1973. Chief counsel Westinghouse Electric Corp., 1978-81; v.p., sec., gen. counsel Group W Cable, Inc. divsn. Westinghouse, 1981-83; v.p., sec. Westinghouse Broadcasting Co., 1983-86; assoc. gen. counsel energy and advanced tech. & broadcasting divsn. Westinghouse, 1986-87; dep. gen. counsel Westinghouse Electric, 1987-92; sr. v.p., gen. counsel Westinghouse Electric Corp., 1993-98; exec. v.p., gen. counsel CBS Corp., Pitts., 1998—. General corporate, Communications. Office: CBS Corp 51 West 52nd St New York NY 10019

**BRISTOL, DOUGLAS,** lawyer; b. Chgo., Dec. 24, 1943; s. Charles John and Josephine Eva B.; m. Maureen (dec.); 1 child, Katherine. BS, U. Wis., 1966; JD, U. Ill., 1969. Pvt. practice, Chgo.; lectr. in field. Mem. Am. Immigration Lawyers Assn. (Chgo. chpt. sec. 1987-88, treas. 1988-89, v.p. 1989-90, 1st v.p. 1990-91, pres. 1991-92, co-chmn. liaison to dir. of no. svc. ctr. 1993-94, 96-99, nat. task force 1995, founder, program dir. 1st seminar 1994-95). Immigration, naturalization, and customs, Personal injury. Office: 321 S Plymouth Ct Ste 1525 Chicago IL 60604-3958

**BRISTOW, BILL WAYNE,** lawyer; b. Strawberry, Ark., Dec. 7, 1950; s. Bill and Irene Bristow; m. Mary Rutledge, Aug. 5, 1972; children: Melissa, Benjamin. BA, Ark. Coll., 1972; JD, Harvard U., 1975. Bar: Ark. 1975, U.S. Ct. Appeals (8th cir.) 1977, U.S. Supreme Ct. 1980. Sole practice Jonesboro, Ark., 1975—; examiner Ark. Bar, 1982-87. Federal civil litigation, State civil litigation, Personal injury. Office: 216 E Washington Ave Jonesboro AR 72401-3102

**BRISTOW, WALTER JAMES, JR.,** retired judge; b. Columbia, S.C., Oct. 14, 1924; s. Walter James and Caroline Belser (Melton) B.; m. Katherine Stewart Mullins, Sept. 12, 1952; children: Walter James III, Katherine Mullins (dec.). *Father was a medical doctor specializing in eye, ear, nose and throat, practicing in Columbia. Son Walter III is a medical doctor specializing in gastroenterology, practicing in Columbia. On August 1, 1981, he married Anne Land Jackson of Manning. They have four children: Abbot Land (Abby), Katherine Stewart (Katy), Walter James IV (James), and William Melton II (Melton).* Student, Va. Mil. Inst., 1941-43; AB, U. N.C., 1947; LLB cum laude, U. S.C., 1947-50; LLM, Harvard U., 1950. Mem. Marchant, Bristow & Bates, 1953-76, S.C. Ho. of Reps., 1956-58, S.C. Senate, 1958-76; resident judge 5th Cir. Ct. S.C., 1976-88; ret., 1988; nat. pres. Conf. Ins. Legislators, 1974-75. *Mr. Bristow enlisted in the U.S. Army Reserve on December 1, 1942, and was called to active duty on June 19, 1943. He served as an enlisted man during World War II, serving overseas in the European Theater of Operations as a platoon sergeant of Battery B, 292nd Field Artillery Observation Batallion, receiving battle stars for the battles of Central Europe and Rhineland.* Trustee Elvira Wright Fund for Crippled Children, 1963-76; mem. bd. visitors ex officio The Citadel, Charleston, S.C., 1967-76. Served with AUS, 1943-45; ETO, brig. gen. S.C. Army N.G. Decorated Meritorious Svc. medal. Mem. ABA, Wig and Robe, S.C. Law Inst., S.C. Coun. on Holocaust, Capital City Club, Cotillion Club, Forest Lake Club, Palmetto Club, Columbia Ball Club, Sertoma, Alpha Tau Omega. Democrat. Office: PO Box 1147 Columbia SC 29202-1147

**BRITAIN, JAMES EDWARD,** lawyer; b. Seattle, Jan. 31, 1950; s. Fred Walter and Maryalice (Schneider) B.; m. Carol Elaine Kometz, Dec. 27, 1972 (div. 1977); m. Linda Jeanne Peltier, June 23, 1979 (div. May 1987); m. Patrice Marie Rhoney, Sept. 5, 1987; 1 child, Alex James. BA, Wash. State

U., Pullman, 1972; JD, Duke U., 1975; LLM, Temple U., 1977. Bar: Wash. 1975, Ohio 1983, U.S. Dist. Ct. (so. dist.) Ohio 1984, U.S. Ct. Appeals (6th cir.) 1988. Fellow, instr. law Temple U., Phila., 1975-77; asst. prof. U. Dayton, 1977-79; asst. prof. New Eng. Sch. Law, Boston, 1979-81, assoc. prof., 1981-82; law clk. U.S. Ct. Appeals (6th cir.), Cin., 1982-83; assoc. Taft, Stettinius & Hollister, Cin., 1983-95; adj. prof. U. Cin., 1983, assoc. Atwood, Hager & Anderson, 1995-96; prin. Britain Flynn, P.S., 1996—; participant profl. symposia. Contbr. articles and revs. to profl. publs. Bd. dirs. Youth Opportunities United, 1990-95. Named Best Writer of Yr., Legal Rsch. on Writing Orgn., Duke U. Sch. Law, 1974. Mem. ABA, Wash. State Bar Assn., Whatcom County Bar Assn., Montgomery County ACLU (bd. dirs. 1977-78), Phi Beta Kappa, Phi Kappa Phi. General practice, Personal injury, General civil litigation. Home: 1801 4th St Bellingham WA 98225-7701 Office: 805 Dupont St Ste 4 Bellingham WA 98225-3128

**BRITO, MARIA TERESA,** lawyer, consultant; b. San Antonio, Dec. 12, 1952; d. David Nieto and Maria Christina (Rodriguez) B.; divorced, 1989; 1 child, Teresa Marie. AA, San Antonio Coll., 1973; BA, Southwest Tex. State U., San Marcos, 1975; JD, Tex. Southern U., 1980. Bar: Tex. 1981. Staff atty. Staff Counsel for Inmates, Huntsville, Tex., 1981; spl. investigator Colo. Civil Rights, Denver, 1982; staff atty. Nat. Assn. Govt. Employees, San Antonio, 1983-88; pvt. practice law San Antonio, 1988—. Administrative and regulatory, Personal injury, Workers' compensation. Office: 901 Cincinnati Ave San Antonio TX 78201-6029

**BRITT, W. EARL,** federal judge; b. McDonald, N.C., Dec. 7, 1932; s. Dudley H. and Martha Mae (Hall) B.; m. Judith Moore, Apr. 17, 1976. Student, Campbell Jr. Coll., 1952; BS, Wake Forest U., 1956, JD, 1958. Bar: N.C. 1958. Pvt. practice law Fairmont, N.C., 1959-72, Lumberton, N.C., 1972-80; judge U.S. Dist. Ct. (ea. dist.) N.C., from 1980, chief judge, 1983-90, sr. judge, 1997—; mem. Jud. Conf. Com. on Automation and Tech., 1990-95; 4th cir. dist. judge rep. to Jud. Conf. U.S., 1991-97. Trustee Southeastern Community Coll., 1965-70, Southeastern Gen. Hosp., Lumberton, 1965-69, Pembroke State U., 1967-72; bd. govs. U. N.C. Served with U.S. Army, 1953-55. Mem. N.C. Bar Assn., Fed. Judges Assn. (bd. dirs., v.p., 1993-95, pres. 1995-97). Baptist. Office: US Dist Ct PO Box 27504 Raleigh NC 27611-7504

**BRITTAIN, GREGORY W.,** lawyer; b. Denver, Sept. 1, 1958; s. Frank H. and Judith (Westerman) B.; m. Kayoko Sasamoto, Dec. 31, 1988. BA, U. Calif., Berkeley, 1980, JD, 1984. Bar: Calif. 1984, U.S. Dist. Ct. (cen. dist.) 1990. Lawyer Clayson, Mann, Arand & Yaeger, Corona, Calif., 1984-85, Granowitz & White, San Bernardino, Calif., 1985-96; sole practice law San Bernardino, 1996—. Mem. San Bernardino C. of C., Phi Beta Kappa. Republican. Avocations: skiing, ballroom dancing, Japanese, ultimate frisbee, internet. State civil litigation, Contracts commercial, Real property. Office: 330 N D St Ste 300 San Bernardino CA 92401-1522

**BRITTIGAN, ROBERT LEE,** lawyer; b. Columbus, Ohio, Aug. 24, 1942; s. Virgil Devan and Ruth (Clark) B.; m. Sharon Lynn Amore, Aug. 22, 1964; children: Eric Clark, Robert Lee II. BSBA cum laude, Ohio State U., 1964, JD summa cum laude, 1967. Bar: Ohio 1967, U.S. Ct. Mil. Appeals 1974, U.S. Ct. Claims 1977, U.S. Ct. Appeals (5th cir.) 1978, U.S. Ct. Appeals (6th cir.) 1992, U.S. Supreme Ct. 1974. Commd. 2d lt. U.S. Army, 1968, advanced through grades to maj., 1977; chief mil. justice, Ft. Gordon, Ga., 1972-73; dep. staff judge adv. 5th Inf. Div. (Mech.) and Ft. Polk, Ft. Polk, La., 1974-76; action atty. litigation div. Office of JAG, U.S. Army, Washington, 1976-80; resigned, 1980; gen. counsel Def. Threat Reduction Agy., Washington, 1980—. Col. Res. ret. Decorated Bronze Star medal, Meritorious Svc. medal with oak leaf cluster. Recipient Exceptional Civilian Service medal Def. Nuclear Agy., Meritorious Civilian Svc. medal, Presdl. Rank award, Meritorious Exec. Office: General Counsel Def Threat Reduction Agy 45045 Aviation Dr Sterling VA 20166-7505

**BRITTON, CLAROLD LAWRENCE,** lawyer, consultant; b. Soldier, Iowa, Nov. 1, 1932; s. Arnold Olaf and Florence Ruth (Gardner) B.; m. Joyce Helene Hamlett, Feb. 1, 1958; children: Laura, Eric, Val, Martha. BS in Engring., U. Mich., Ann Arbor, 1958, JD, 1961, postgrad. U. Mich Artificial Intelligence Lab., Elec. Engring. and Computer Sci., 1988-91. Bar: Ill. 1961, U.S. Dist. Ct. (no. dist.) Ill. 1962, U.S. Ct. Appeals (7th cir.) 1963, U.S. Supreme Ct. 1970, Mich. 1989. Assoc., Jenner & Block, Chgo., 1961-70, ptnr., 1970-88; pres. Clarold L. Britton & Assoc., Inc., 1991—. Lectr. DePaul U., 1988. Comdr. USNR, 1952-57. Fellow Am. Coll. Trial Lawyers; mem. Chgo. Bar Assn. (past chmn. fed. civil procedure com., mem. judiciary and computer law coms., civil practice com.), Ill. State Bar Assn. (chmn. Allerton House Conf. 1984, 86, 88, chmn. rule 23 com. 1985-87, chmn. civil practice and procedure coun. 1987-88, antitrust com.), ABA (litigation sect., antitrust com., past regional chmn. discovery com. 1961), 7th Cir. Bar Assn., Def. Rsch. Inst. (com. on aerospace 1984), Mich. Bar Assn., Ill. Soc. Trial Lawyers, Order of Coif, Alpha Phi Mu, Tau Beta Pi, Law Club (Chgo.), Racine Yacht Club (Wis.), Macatawa Yacht Club (Mich), Masons. Republican. Lutheran. Author: Computerized Trial Notebook, 1991; asst. editor Mich. Law Rev., 1960. Antitrust, Federal civil litigation, State civil litigation. Office: 411 E Washington St Ann Arbor MI 48104-2015

**BRITTON, JAMES EDWARD,** lawyer; b. Roswell, N.Mex., June 9, 1946; s. Thomas Warren and Helen Viola (Haynes) B.; m. Sherry Ann Sheehan, May 17, 1969; children: Christa Lynn, Jason Edward. BS, Okla. State U., 1968; postgrad., Iowa State U., 1968, 70-71; JD, U. Okla., 1974. Bar: Okla. 1974, U.S. Dist. Ct. (we., no. and ea. dists.) Okla. 1974, U.S. Ct. Appeals (10th cir.) 1974. Ptnr., sec. McClelland, Collins, Sheehan, Bailey & Bailey, Oklahoma City, 1974-79; v.p., bd. dirs. Hastie and Kirschner, Oklahoma City, 1979-90; pres. Britton, Gray & Hill, Oklahoma City, 1996—; bd. dirs. Guaranty Bank & Trust Co., Oklahoma City; adminstrv. law judge Dept. of Edn., 1978-90. Research editor U. Okla. Law Rev., 1973. Trustee Met. Libr. Endowment Trust, 1995—; bd. dirs. Peaceful Mission, 1998—. Served with U.S. Army, 1968-70, Vietnam. Mem. ABA, Okla. Bar Assn. (ethics com. 1987-89, com. on uniform laws 1990—, chmn. 1994-98), Oklahoma County Bar Assn. (law day chmn. 1978, mem. ethics and grievance com. 1986-89), Order of Coif. Democrat. Methodist. Avocations: running, sailing, tennis, bicycling. Banking, Contracts commercial, Franchising. Home: 1616 Mulholland Dr Edmond OK 73003-4114 Office: Britton Gray & Hill 700 Bank of Oklahoma Plz Oklahoma City OK 93102

**BRITTON, MATTHEW JOSEPH,** lawyer; b. Washington, July 14, 1966; s. Keith and Marjorie Britton; m. Elizabeth Prather Brown, May 30, 1992; children: Katharine, Mary Grace, Elizabeth. BA in Philosophy, BA in Sociology, Boston Coll., 1988; M in Forensic Scis., George Washington U., 1992; JD, Washington U., 1995. Bar: Va. 1995, U.S. Dist. Ct. (ea. dist.) Va. 1996, D.C. 1997, U.S. Dist. Ct. D.C. 1998. Assoc. Odin Feldman & Pittleman, PC, Fairfax, Va., 1995—. Recipient Lewis F. Powell Jr. medal of honor Am. Coll. Trial Lawyers, 1994, Milton F. Napier Excellence in Trial Advocacy award Lawyers Assn. St. Louis, 1995, Judge Samuel L. Breckenridge Practice Ct. prize, 1995; named regional champion, nat. semi-finalist Nat. Mock Trial, 1994. Mem. Am. Acad. Forensic Scis., Nat. Assn. Criminal Def. Lawyers, Va. Trial Lawyers Assn. (co-chmn. criminal CLE sect. 1998—). General civil litigation, Criminal. Office: Odin Feldman & Pittleman PC 9302 Lee Hwy Ste 1100 Fairfax VA 22031-1215

**BRITTON, REBECCA JOHNSON,** lawyer; b. Poughkeepsie, N.Y., Aug. 12, 1963; d. Gustaf Aaron and Muriel Flewelling Johnson; m. John Harold Britton, Aug. 13, 1988; children: Sarah Catherine, Robert Aaron. BA, U. Maine, 1989; JD, Campbell U., 1992. Bar: N.C. 1992, U.S. Dist. Ct. (ea. dist.) N.C. 1992, U.S. Dist. Ct. (mid. dist.) 1995, U.S. Ct. Appeals (4th cir.) 1995, U.S. Supreme Ct. 1998. Paralegal Meiselman, Farber, Poughkeepsie, N.Y., 1982-84; office mgr. Steinberg & Kolb, Poughkeepsie, N.Y., 1984-85; clk. Beaver, Holt, Richardson, Fayetteville, N.C., 1990, assoc., 1992-97, ptnr., 1998—; adj. prof. Campbell U. Sch. Law, Buies Creek, N.C., 1997—. Coach, atty. advisor Westover High Sch. Trial Team, Fayetteville, 1995—. Democrat. Episcopalian. Avocations: vocalist, gardening. E-mail: rjb@bhr-law.com. Personal injury, General civil litigation, Civil rights. Office: Beaver Holt Richardson 230 Green St Fayetteville NC 28301-5026

**BROADBENT, BERNE STEVEN,** lawyer; b. Macon, Ga., Feb. 15, 1955; s. Berne D. and Miriam Sarah (Fullmer) B.; m. Suzanne Claybrook, Oct. 27, 1978; children: David, John, Heidi, Rebecca. BS in Physics cum laude, Brigham Young U., 1979, JD cum laude, 1982. Bar: Utah 1982, U.S. Dist. Ct. Utah 1982, U.S. Patent and Trademark Office 1982. Assoc. Fox, Edwards & Gardiner, Salt Lake City, 1982-84; assoc. Workman, Nydegger & Jensen, Salt Lake City, 1984-87, ptnr., 1987-89; pres., founder, pvt. practice Salt Lake City, 1989—. Bd. mem. Magna Mosquito Abatement Dist., Salt Lake County, Utah, 1987-88; dist. varsity scout chair Boy Scouts Am. Great Salt Lake Coun., Salt Lake City, 1988-89. Mem. ABA, Utah State Bar Assn., Am. Intellectual Property Assn., Copyright Soc. of the U.S.A. (editl. bd. 1986-89). Avocations: hiking, scuba diving. Intellectual property, Patent, Trademark and copyright. Office: 1800 Eagle Gate Tower 60 E South Temple Salt Lake City UT 84111-1004

**BROADDUS, JOHN MORGAN, III,** lawyer; b. El Paso, Tex., June 15, 1953; m. Stacy Shelton, Feb. 1, 1992; children: Shelby, Melissa, John, Andrew. BBA, U. Tex., El Paso, 1975; JD, Tex. Tech U., 1979. Bar: Tex. 1979, U.S. Dist. Ct. (we. dist.) Tex. 1981, U.S. Ct. Appeals (5th cir.) 1982, U.S. Supreme Ct. 1994; cert. in civil appellate law Tex. Bd. Legal Specialization. Briefing atty. 8th Ct. Appeals, El Paso, 1979-80; assoc. Peticolas, Luscombe, Stephens & Windle, El Paso, 1980-83; ptnr. Peticolas, Broaddus & Shapleigh, El Paso, 1983-91; pvt. practice, El Paso, 1992—. Contbr. articles to legal publ. Fellow Tex. Bar Found.; mem. State Bar Coll. Appellate, General civil litigation, General practice. Home: 4906 Love Rd El Paso TX 79922-1745 Office: 619 E Crosby Ave El Paso TX 79902-4316

**BROADUS, CHARLSA DORSANTRES,** lawyer; b. Greer, S.C., Jan. 12, 1968; d. Dorse Gene and Janet Moss Broadus. BA in English, Dartmouth Coll., 1988; JD, Boston U., 1992. Bar: D.C. 1992, U.S. Dist. Ct. D.C. 1995, U.S. Ct. Appeals (4th cir.) 1998. Fellow/supervising atty. Georgetown U. Law Ctr. Criminal Justice Clinic, Washington, 1992-94; assoc. Jenner & Block, Washington, 1994-96, Coale & Van Susteren, Washington, 1996; ptnr. Coale, Cooley, Lietz, McInerny & Broadus, Washington, 1996—. Mem. ABA, ATLA, Nat. Bar Assn. Democrat. Personal injury, General civil litigation, Aviation. Office: Coale Cooley Lietz McInerny & Broadus 818 Connecticut Ave NW Ste 857 Washington DC 20006-2702

**BROADUS, JOSEPH EDWARD,** lawyer, educator; b. Jacksonville, Fla., Sept. 11, 1946; s. Lawrence Franklin and Mary (Lewis) B. BA, Fla. Internat. U., 1978; JD, Fla. State U., 1981; MA, U. Miami, 1984. Bar: Fla. 1986, U.S. Ct. Appeals (11th cir.) 1986. Staff writer Louisville Courier Jour., 1970-71, Miami (Fla.) Herald, 1972-75; sch. and coll. officer Fla. Internat. U., 1977-78; law clk. to judge U.S. Ct. Appeals (11th cir.), Tallahassee, 1981-82; rsch. assoc. Ctr. for Employment Rels. and Law, Tallahassee, 1983-85; analyst/counsel Fla. Ho. of Reps., Tallahassee, 1985-87; asst. prof. law George Mason U., Arlington, Va., 1987—, also advisor Civil Rights Law Jour., American Reporter, Goble Judgments; cons. Fla. Gov.'s Commn. on Quality Incentives, 1984. Author: Supplement, Actions and Remedies, 1989-90, (with others) Law and Economics of Civil Justice Reform. Bd. dirs. Washington chpt. Cath. League for Religious and Civil Rights, Democracy Media Project; mem. acad. bd. advisors Washington Legal Found.; mem. Law Profs. for Bush-Quayle; mem. Citizens Com. to Confirm Clarence Thomas to the Supreme Ct., 1991. With U.S. Army, 1964-67. Fellow Washington Journalism Ctr., 1969. Mem. Federalist Soc. for Law and Pub. Policy, Phi Kappa Phi, Omicron Delta Kappa. Roman Catholic. Civil rights, Labor.

**BROADWIN, JOSEPH LOUIS,** lawyer; b. Nice, France, July 12, 1930; s. Samuel and Lillian Ruth (Messing) B.; m. Maria Antonia Eligio de la Puente, June 1, 1949 (div. 1974); children—David Anthony, Charles Anthony; m. Susan Elizabeth Podufaly, Oct. 24, 1980; children: Elizabeth Antonia, Samuel Edward. A.B., Columbia U., 1949; LL.B., Yale U., 1952. Bar: N.Y. Assoc. Chadbourne Parke Whiteside Wolff & Brophy, N.Y.C., 1954-59; assoc. Proskauer Rose Goetz & Mendelsohn, N.Y.C., 1959-67, ptnr., 1967-70; ptnr. Willkie Farr & Gallagher, N.Y.C., 1970-92; counsel Winick & Rich, P.C., N.Y.C., 1993—. Regent L.I. Coll. Hosp., Bklyn., 1971—, vice chmn. 1985—, chmn. 1991—; bd. dirs. Cobble Hill Nursing Home, Bklyn., 1979—; exec. com. W. Bklyn. Ind. Democrats, 1957-84. Served with U.S. Army, 1952-54. Mem. Assn. Bar City N.Y. Club: Yale (N.Y.C.). Real property. Home: 143 Henry St Brooklyn NY 11201-2501 Office: Winick & Rich PC 919 3rd Ave New York NY 10022-3902

**BROAS, TIMOTHY MICHAEL,** lawyer; b. Detroit, Mar. 21, 1954; s. William Paul and Anita Pauline (St. Germaine) B.; m. Julia Kathleen McAree, Sept. 28, 1985; children: Emily Towles, Allison Bowen, Madeline Hurley. BA, Boston Coll., 1976; JD, Coll. William & Mary, 1979. Bar: N.J. 1979, U.S. Dist. Ct. N.J. 1979, N.Y. 1980, U.S. Dist. Ct. (so. dist.) N.Y. 1981, D.C. 1985. Law clk. to judge N.J. Supreme Ct., Trenton, 1979-80; assoc. Conboy Hewitt O'Brien & Boardman, N.Y.C., 1980-83, Whitman & Ransom, N.Y.C., 1983-85, Clifford & Warnke, Washington, 1985-86; ptnr. Anderson, Hibey & Blair, Washington, 1986-95, Winston & Strawn, Washington, 1995—. Mem. Assn. of Bar of City of N.Y., D.C. Bar Assn., ABA. General civil litigation, Criminal, Health. Office: Winston & Strawn 1400 L St NW Ste 800 Washington DC 20005-3508

**BROBERG, JAMES E.,** judge; b. Mpls., Apr. 29, 1938; s. Elwell E. and Anna S. Broberg; m. Susan Handing Woodard, Dec. 6, 1963 (div. Apr. 1978); children: Stephen M., Richard H.; m. Linda Anne Holland, June 6, 1980. BA, U. Minn., 1963, JD, 1965. Bar: Minn. 1965, U.S. Tax Ct. 1984, U.S. Ct. Appeals (8th cir.) 1968. Asst. city atty. Freeborn County, Albert Lea, Minn., 1965-68, city atty., 1969-80; ptnr. Christian, Peterson PA, Albert Lea, Minn., 1969-97; dist. judge State of Minn. (3d jud. dist.), 1997—. Mem. Albert Lea Good Samaritan Ctr., past bd. dirs.; mem. United Employees Credit Union of Albert Lea, Civic Music Assn. of Albert Lea, Albert Lea Area Quality Coun., United Way of Freeborn County, Albert Lea Cmty. Theater, Harmony Junction Barbershop Chorus, past pres., newsletter editor, chmn. various coms.; mem. Big Island Rendezvous of Albert Lea, bd. dirs., among others. Mem. Miss. City Attys. (pres.), Minn. State Bar Assn. (bd. govs. 1982-85, chmn. conv. com. 1986-88, 10th dist. ethics com., chmn., coach, advisor, and judge in h.s. moot ct. program, rules profl. responsibility com., lawyers advt. com), So. Minn. Regional Legal Svcs. (vol. atty., dist. co-chair for campaign for legal aid, mem. adv. bd.), Freeborn County C. of C. (chmn. edn. com. lakes improvement project com., chmn., participant on various coms. and projects), Lions (pres. Albert Lea club 1992-93, chmn. various projects including cmty. svc. and fundraising for charitable projects, co-chair hearing dog program), Elks (exalted ruler 1990-91, trustee 1991-94, state drug awareness chmn. for state of Minn. 1993-95), Masons, Shriners, KC. Office: 411 S Broadway Ave Albert Lea MN 56007-4505

**BROCK, CHARLES MARQUIS,** lawyer; b. Watseka, Ill., Oct. 8, 1941; s. Glen Westgate and Muriel Lucile (Bubeck) B.; m. Elizabeth Bonilla, Dec. 17, 1966; children: Henry Christopher, Anna Melissa. AB cum laude, Princeton U., 1963; JD, Georgetown U., 1968; MBA, U. Chgo., 1974. Bar: Ill. 1969, U.S. Dist. Ct. (no. dist.) Ill. 1969. Asst. trust counsel Continental Ill. Nat. Bank, Chgo., 1968-74; regional counsel Latin Am. Can. Abbott Labs., Abbott Park, Ill., 1974-77; regional counsel Europe, Africa and Middle East Can. Abbott Labs., Abbott Park, 1977-81, divsn. counsel domestic legal ops., 1981-88, assoc. gen. counsel internat. legal ops., asst. sec., 1989-92, divsnl. v.p., assoc. gen. counsel, asst. sec., 1992—; mem. Coun. Sr. Internat. Legal Officers, The Conf. Bd., N.Y.C. Served with Inter-Am. Def. Coll., U.S. Army, 1964-66. Mem. ABA, Chgo. Bar Assn., Mich. Shores Club, Phi Beta Kappa. Republican. General corporate, Contracts commercial, Private international. Home: 1473 Asbury Ave Winnetka IL 60093-1467 Office: Abbott Labs 100 Abbott Park Rd Abbott Park IL 60064-3502

**BROCK, DAVID ALLEN,** state supreme court chief justice; b. Stoneham, Mass., July 6, 1936; s. Herbert and Margaret B.; m. Sandra Ford, 1960; 6 children. AB, Dartmouth Coll., 1958; LLB, U. Mich., 1963; postgrad., Nat. Jud. Coll., 1977. Bar: N.H. 1963. Assoc. Devine, Millimet, McDonough, Stahl & Branch, Manchester, N.H., 1963-69; U.S. atty. State of N.H., 1969-72; ptnr. Perkins, Douglas & Brock, Concord, N.H., 1972-74, Perkins & Brock, 1974-76; spl. counsel to gov. and exec. coun. N.H., 1974-76, legal counsel to gov. N.H., 1976; assoc. justice N.H. Superior Ct., 1976-78; assoc. justice N.H. Supreme Ct., 1978-86, chief justice, 1986—; chmn. State of N.H. Legal Svcs. Adv. Commn., 1977-79; chmn. dist. ct. reform subcom. Gov.'s Commn. for Ct. System Improvement, 1974-75; chmn. N.H. Commn. Ct. Accreditation, 1986—; mem. Select Commn. on Unified Ct. System, 1980-84, chmn. N.H. Supreme Ct. Com. on Jud. Conduct, 1981-89, rules adv. com., 1985-97; mem. State N.H. Jud. Coun., 1979-87; mem. nat. adv. bd. Leadership Inst. for Jud. Edn., 1989-96, Nat. Jud. Coll. long range planning com., 1990-91; mem. Jud. Edn. and Tech. Assistance Consortium, 1989-97; chmn. Interbranch Coun. on Substance Abuse and the Criminal Justice System, 1991-95; bd. dirs. State Justice Inst., 1992-98, vice-chmn., 1994-95, co-chmn., 1995-98; bd. dirs. Conf. Chief Justices, 1993-94, v.p., 1996-97, pres-elect 1997-98, pres., 1998-99; bd. dirs. Nat. Ctr. for State Cts., 1996—, chmn.-elect, 1997-98, chmn., 1998-99. Bd. dirs. Manchester Cmty. Guidance Ctr., 1966-72, pres., 1969-72; chmn. Manchester Rep. Com., 1967-69; vice chmn. N.H. Rep. State Com., 1968-69; Rep. candidate U.S. Senate, 1972; del. N.H. Constl. Conv., 1974: mem. Gov.'s Commn. for Handicapped, 1978-79. Fellow ABA (mem. edn. com. of appellate judges conf. 1981-97, appellate advocacy com. 1982-84, faculty appellate judges' seminar program 1984-89, del. ho. of dels. 1994-96), N.H. Bar Assn. (chmn. constl. revision com. 1976-77), N.H. Bar Found. (hon.). Office: NH Supreme Ct Noble Dr Concord NH 03301

**BROCK, GLEN PORTER, JR.,** lawyer; b. Mobile, Ala., Nov. 13, 1937; s. Glen Porter Sr. and Esther Alitha (Goodwin) B.; m. Shirley Ann Forbes, Jan. 7, 1961; children: Glen Porter III, Susan Forbes. BS, Auburn U., 1959; JD, U. Ala., 1963; LLM in Taxation, NYU, 1964. Bar: Ala 1963. Assoc. Hand, Arendall, Bedsale, Greaves & Johnston, Mobile, 1964-69, ptnr., 1970-94; mem. Hand Arendall, LLC, 1995—. Served to capt. USAR, 1959-67. Mem. ABA, Ala. Bar Assn. (chmn. tax sect. 1974-75), Mobile Bar Assn. Baptist. Lodge: Lions (pres. 1982-83). Avocations: travel, computers, photography. Taxation, general, Probate, Estate planning. Home: 737 Westmoreland Dr W Mobile AL 36609-6132 Office: Hand Arendall LLC 3000 Am South Bank Bldg 107 Saint Francis St Mobile AL 36602-3334

**BROCK, LINDSEY COOK, III,** lawyer; b. Irvine, Ky., June 14, 1965; s. Lindsey Cook and Billie Lee Brock; m. Carol Stowers, Aug. 1, 1992; children: E. Connor, Caitlin Tara. BA in English, U. Fla., 1987; JD in Law cum laude, Thomas M. Cooley Law Sch., 1991; LLM in Admiralty, Tulane U., 1992. Bar: La. 1992, Fla. 1993, U.S. Dist. Ct. (mid. dist.) Fla. 1993, U.S. Ct. Appeals (11th cir.) 1994, U.S. Dist. Ct. (no. dist.) Fla. 1997, U.S. Dist. Ct. (so. dist.) Fla. 1998. Legal asst., paralegal, law clk., assoc. Rumrell & Johnson, P.A., Jacksonville, Fla., 1987-95; sr. assoc. Rumrell, Costabel & Turk, Jacksonville, 1995-97; sr. atty. Rumrell, Wagner & Costabel LLP, Jacksonville, 1997—, shareholder, 1998—; law clk. Donovan & Lawler, P.A., Metairie, La., 1991-92; rsch. asst. Tulane U. Law Sch., New Orleans, 1992. Active Deermeadows Bapt. Ch., 1992—, Sunday sch. dirs. and tchrs. adult one dept., 1994-98, Sunday sch. tchrs. pre-sch. dept. 5 year old class; pres. Deermeadows Bapt. Choir, 1994. Mem. ABA (spkr.), Maritime Law Assn. (com. on marine fin. 1995, com. on marine ins. and gen. average 1995), Jacksonville Bar Assn., Southeastern Admiralty Law Inst., Propeller Club Jacksonville. Avocations: football fan, softball player, reader, golf, model shipbuilding. E-mail: brock@RumrellLaw.com./thebrocks.jax@worldnet.att.net. Admiralty, general civil litigation, Insurance. Office: Bldg 100 Ste 250 10151 Deerwood Park Blvd Jacksonville FL 32256

**BROCK, MITCHELL,** lawyer; b. Wyncote, Pa., Nov. 10, 1927; s. John W. and Mildred A. (Mitchell) B.; m. Gioia Connell, June 21, 1952; children: Felicity, Marina, Mitchell Hovey, Laura. AB, Princeton U., 1950; LLB, U. Pa., 1953. Bar: N.Y. 1954. Assoc. firm Sullivan & Cromwell, N.Y.C., 1953-59, ptnr., 1960-92; ptnr. Sullivan & Cromwell, Paris, 1965-68; ptnr. in charge Sullivan & Cromwell, Tokyo, 1987-90. Bd. dirs. Frost Valley YMCA, Oliverea, N.Y., 1980-87, 90—, Am. Found. Blind, 1967-87; pres., trustee Helen Keller Internat., N.Y.C., 1970-87, 90-94, chmn., trustee, 1994-96, sec., 1996—. Served with USN, 1945-46. Mem. ABA, Anglers Club, Princeton Club, Ivy Club, Boca Grande Pass Club. Republican. Episcopalian. General corporate, Private international. Home: PO Box 452 Boca Grande FL 33921-0452

**BROCK, P. HUTCHISON, II,** lawyer; b. Dade City, Fla., Apr. 5, 1965; s. Pete Hutchison and Mary Louise (Gasque) B.; m. Natalie Glover, Aug. 5, 1989; children: Carson H., Coleman G., Connor Mack, Ashton G. BSBA, U. Fla., 1987, JD, 1990. Bar: Fla. 1990, U.S. Dist. Ct. (mid. dist.) Fla. 1990. Assoc. Fowler, White, Gillen, Boggs, Villareal & Banker, Tampa, Fla., 1990-94; shareholder Schrader, Johnson, Auvil & Brock, Dade City, 1994—; vis. prof. Pasco-Hernando C.C., 1995-96. Bd. dirs. Leadership Pasco, 1994-95, Downtown Dade City Main St, 1995—, pres. 1999-2000. Mem. ATLA, Acad. Fla. Trial Lawyers (mem. speakers bur.), Pasco County Bar Assn. (pres. 1995-96), Rotary (bd. dirs.). Republican. Methodist. E-mail: hutchxyz@aol.com. Personal injury, General civil litigation, Professional liability. Office: Schrader Johnson Auvil & Brock 37837 Meridian Ave Ste 314 Dade City FL 33525-3802

**BROCKELMAN, KENT,** lawyer; b. Danville, Ill., Mar. 25, 1959; s. Robert E. and Barbara (Perry) B. BA with high honors, U. Notre Dame, 1981; JD, UCLA, 1984. Bar: Ariz. 1984, U.S. Dist. Ct. 1984, U.S. Ct. Appeals (9th cir.) 1985. Assoc. Fennemore Craig, Phoenix, 1984-86; assoc. Daughton, Hawkins & Bacon, Phoenix, 1986-87, Bryan Cave, Phoenix, 1988-92; ptnr. Daughton, Hawkins, Brockelman & Guinan, Phoenix, 1992-96, Brockelman & Brodman, Phoenix, 1996—; mem. Am. Inns of Ct., Phoenix, 1991—, pres. 1997-98; judge pro tempore Ariz. Ct. Appeals, Phoenix, 1994—. Editor-in-chief UCLA Law Rev., 1983-84. Mem., recorder Ariz. Town Hall, Phoenix, 1991—. Mem. ABA, State Bar Ariz., Maricopa County Bar Assn., Ahwatukee Foothills C. of C. (bd. dirs. 1995—). Labor, General civil litigation. Office: Brockelman & Brodman 2 N Central Ave Ste 1750 Phoenix AZ 85004-2395

**BROCKWAY, DAVID HUNT,** lawyer; b. Paterson, N.J., Dec. 18, 1943; s. George Pond and Lucille (Hunt) B.; m. Marilyn Bofshever, July 29, 1979. A.B., Cornell U., 1968; J.D., Harvard U., 1971. Bar: N.Y. 1972, Washington 1990. Assoc. firm Donovan Leisure Newton & Irvine, N.Y.C., 1971-76; legis. atty. Joint Com. on Taxation, U.S. Congress, Washington, 1976, internat. tax counsel, 1978, deputy chief of staff, 1981, chief of staff, 1983-87; ptnr. Dewey Ballantine, Washington, N.Y.C., 1987—, co-chmn. tax dept., 1997—; mem. Am. Law Inst. Project on Sub-chpt. C., 1988—; mem. adv. bd. European Am. Tax Inst., 1989—; cons. Am. Law Inst. Project on Tax Treaties, 1989—; bd. dirs. Nat. Fgn. Trade Coun., 1993—; GE (Bermuda) Ltd., 1993—. With U.S. Army, 1963-66. Recipient Outstanding Achievement award NYU Tax. Soc., 1998—. Mem. N.Y. State Bar Assn. (exec. com. tax sect. 1988-89, 94—). Home: 2829 Woodland Dr NW Washington DC 20008-2743 Office: Dewey Ballantine LLP 1301 Avenue Of The Americas New York NY 10019-6022

**BRODER, ERIC JASON,** lawyer; b. White Plains, N.Y., Mar. 29, 1970; s. Larry and Joan Ellen Broder. BA, Tulane U., 1992; JD, Temple U., 1995. Bar: N.Y., Conn., U.S. Dist. Ct. (so. dist.) N.Y. Assoc. Law Offices of Craig J. Langer, White Plains, 1996-97, Law Offices of Michael G. Berger, N.Y.C., 1997—. Avocations: tennis, music, film, politics. E-mail: ebro19@aol.com. Fax: 212 983 6008. Federal civil litigation, General civil litigation, State civil litigation. Home: 400 E 59th St New York NY 10022-2342 Office: Law Offices Michael G Berger 250 Park Ave Ste 2020 New York NY 10177-2099

**BRODER, JOSEPH ARNOLD,** lawyer; b. Hartford, Conn., Jan. 19, 1939; s. Morris H. and Dora (Levine) B.; m. Andrea L. Goldstein, Feb. 23, 1967; 1 child, Michael. AB, Trinity Coll., 1960; JD, Harvard U., 1963. Bar: Conn. 1963, N.Y. 1964, U.S. Dist. Ct. Conn. 1965, U.S. Military Ct. 1968, U.S. Supreme Ct. 1976. Assoc. Dammann, Blank, Hirsh & Heming, N.Y.C., 1964-65, Broder & Broder, Colchester, Conn., 1965; pvt. practice Colchester, 1966-80; sr. ptnr. Broder & Butts, Colchester, 1981—; dir. Yankee Inst. for Pub. Policy Studies, 1993—; corporator Norwich (Conn.) Savs. Soc., 1982-87; bd. dirs., v.p. Colchester Publs., 1982-88. Mem. Conn. Ho. of Reps., 1981-82; mem. Rep. State Ctrl.Com., 1980-81, 87-93; mem. Glastonbury (Conn.) City Coun., 1993—. Comdr. USNR ret. Mem. ABA, ATLA, Conn. Bar Assn., Nat. Acad. Elder Law Attys., Am. Legion, Rotary Internat. Avocations: tennis, skiing, hunting, fishing, flying. General practice, Estate planning, Personal injury. Home: PO Box 208 East Glastonbury CT 06025-0208 Office: Broder & Butts PO Box 270 188 Norwich Ave Colchester CT 06415-1256

**BRODERICK, DENNIS JOHN,** lawyer, retail company executive. BA, U. Notre Dame, 1970; JD, Georgetown U., 1976. Bar: Ohio 1976. Assoc.

Hahn Loeser Freidheim Dean & Wellman, 1976-81; from staff atty. to asst. gen. counsel Firestone Tire & Rubber Co., 1982-87; counsel for regions, v.p. Federated Dept. Stores, Inc. (formerly Allied Stores Corp.), Cin., 1987-88, v.p., gen. counsel, 1988-90, sr. v.p., gen. counsel, sec., 1990—. Mem. Am. Corp. Counsel Assn. (dir. NE Ohio chpt. 1986). General civil litigation, General practice, Contracts commercial. Office: Federated Dept Stores Inc 7 W 7th St Cincinnati OH 45202-2424*

**BRODERICK, JOHN T., JR.,** state supreme court justice. BA magna cum laude, Coll. Holy Cross, 1969; JD, U. Va., 1972. Atty. Devine, Millimet, Stahl & Branch, Manchester, N.H., 1972-89; shareholder Broderick & Dean (formerly Merrill & Broderick), Manchester, 1989-95; assoc. justice N.H. Supreme Ct., Concord, N.H., 1995—; bd. dirs. Legal Svcs. Corp. Fellow Am. Coll. Trial Lawyers, N.H. Bar Found. (bd. dirs. 1985-91); mem. ABA, Mass. Bar Assn., N.H. Bar Assn. (bd. govs. 1985-91, pres. 1990-91), N.H. Trial Lawyers Assn. (bd. govs. 1977-82, pres. 1982-83). Office: NH Supreme Ct One Noble Dr Concord NH 03301*

**BRODERICK, RAYMOND JOSEPH,** federal judge; b. Phila, May 29, 1914; s. Patrick Joseph and Catharine (Haines) B.; m. Marjorie Beacom, Oct. 2, 1945; children—Patrick J., Timothy B., Tara M., Deidre C., Brian X. A.B. magna cum laude, U. Notre Dame, 1935; J.D., U. Pa., 1938; L.H.D., Pa. Coll. Podiatric Medicine, 1968; LL.D. (hon.), Phila. Coll. Osteo. Medicine, 1969, Allentown Coll. St. Frances De Sales, 1977. Bar: Pa. bar. Civilian agt. U.S. Naval Intelligence, 1941-42; practiced in Phila., 1945-62; sr. partner firm Broderick, Schubert & FitzPatrick, Phila., 1962-71; lt. gov. State of Pa., 1966-71; judge U.S. Dist. Ct. for Eastern Dist. Pa., Phila., 1971-84, sr. judge, 1984—; chmn. Adminstrv. Task Force for Constl. Revision, 1966; mem. Prep. Com. Pa. Constl. Conv., 1967, pres., 1967-68. Chmn. lawyers div. Cath. Charities, Phila.; mem. Phila. Republican Policy Com. Served with USNR, 1942-45. Mem. Am., Pa., Phila. bar assns., Notre Dame Law Assn. Clubs: Constl, Overbrook Farms. Home: 6408 Church Rd Philadelphia PA 19151-2411 Office: US Dist Ct 10613 US Courthouse 601 Market St Philadelphia PA 19106-1713

**BRODERSEN, DANIEL N.,** lawyer; b. Milw., Aug. 17, 1960; s. William Harold and Barbara Ann (Warder) B.; m. Theresa Leigh Jereczek, Mar. 26, 1994 (div. June 1997); 1 child, Zachary Daniel. BA in History, Belmont Abbey Coll., Belmont, N.C., 1983; postgrad., Valparaiso (Ind.) U., 1984; JD, Nova Southeastern Law Sch., 1986. Trial atty. U.S. Dept. Justice, Washington, 1986-89; asst. U.S. atty. U.S. Atty. Office, Orlando, Fla., 1989-91; gen. counsel Seminole County Sheriff, Sanford, Fla., 1991-93; trial atty. Dempsey & Sasso, Orlando, 1993-97, Parker, Burke et al, Orlando, 1998—; legal instr. Rollins Coll., Winter Park, Fla., 1993-96. Fla. Bar (fed. ct. practice com. 1992-94), Orange County Bar Assn., Ctrl. Fla. Criminal Def. Atty.'s Assn. Republican. Roman Catholic. Labor, Federal civil litigation, Criminal. Office: Parker Burke Landerman & Parker 108 Hillcrest St Orlando FL 32801-1210

**BRODHEAD, DAVID CRAWMER,** lawyer; b. Madison, Wis., Sept. 16, 1934; s. Richard Jacob and Irma (Crawmer) B.; m. Nancie Christensen, Aug. 17, 1963; children: Compton, Peter, Christoffer. B.S., U. Wis., 1956, LL.B., 1959. Bar: N.Y. 1960, Wis. 1959, D.C. 1979. Assoc. firm Paul, Weiss, Rifkind, Wharton & Garrison, N.Y.C., 1959-68, ptnr., 1969—; dir. Centennial Industries, Inc., N.Y.C. Editor-in-chief: Wis. Law Rev, 1958-59. Trustee Collegiate Sch., N.Y.C., 1978-85; vestryman Christ and St. Stephen's Episcopal Ch., 1972-82. Mem. N.Y. State Bar, Assn. of Bar of City of N.Y., Wis. Bar. Assn., D.C. Bar Assn., ABA, Westside C. of C. of City of N.Y. (dir. 1970-83), Order of Coif, Delta Theta Phi. Clubs: Washington (Conn.); Holland Soc. of N.Y. General corporate, Contracts commercial, Finance. *Take life one day at a time. Yesterday is gone forever and tomorrow is not here. That leaves only today to deal with.*

**BRODIE, RONALD,** lawyer, author; b. N.Y.C., Sept. 22, 1941; s. S. Robert and Ann Brodie. B.A. in Econs., U. Pa., 1963; S.M. in Mgmt., MIT, 1965; J.D., U. Miami, Fla., 1967, LL.M. in Taxation, 1968. Bar: Fla. 1967, U.S. Tax Ct. 1976, U.S. Ct. Appeals (5th cir.) 1978, U.S. Ct. Appeals (11th cir.) 1981. Sole practice, Miami Beach, 1967—; pres. Taxplan, Inc., 1979—. Author Real Estate Tax Planning Newsletter, 1981-86. Author, editor tax column Jour. of Property Mgmt., 1981—. Contbr. numerous articles on taxation to profl. jours. Lectr. Fla. Bar continuing legal edn. seminars, guest lectr. U Miami Law Sch., 1980-86. Mem., counsel Conservative Caucus of Dade, Inc., Miami; mem. U. Miami Endowment Com., 1969—. Mem. Miami Beach Bar Assn., Real Estate Assn. of Profls. (founder, pres., counsel 1978-80), Fla. Bar (chmn. tax aspects of real property law com. 1979-90, exec. council real property, probate and trust law sect. 1979-90), U Miami Law Alumni Assn., U. Pa. Dade Alumni Club, MIT Club of Miami, U. Miami Alumni Assn., Warton Sch. Club, Turnberry Isle Club, Delta Theta Phi. Republican. Personal income taxation, Corporate taxation, Probate. Home: 951 W 47th Ct Miami Beach FL 33140-2906 Office: 134 Mirasol Internat Ctr 2699 Collins Ave Miami Beach FL 33140-4716

**BRODSKY, DAVID M.,** lawyer; b. Providence, Oct. 16, 1943; s. Irving and Naomi (Richman) B.; m. Stacey J. Moritz; children: Peter, Isabel, Nell. AB cum laude, Brown U., 1964; LLB, Harvard U., 1967. Bar: N.Y. 1968, U.S. Dist. Ct. (so. dist.) N.Y. 1969, U.S. Ct. Appeals (2d cir.) 1974, U.S. Dist. Ct. (ea. dist.) N.Y. 1977, U.S. Supreme Ct. 1977, U.S. Ct. Appeals (D.C. cir.) 1981, U.S. Ct. Appeals (3d cir.) 1984, U.S. Tax Ct. 1984, U.S. Dist. Ct. (no. dist.) Tex. 1986. Law clk. to U.S. Dist. judge U.S. Dist. Ct. (so. dist.) N.Y., 1967-69; asst. U.S. atty. So. Dist. N.Y., 1969-73; assoc. Guggenheimer & Untermyer, N.Y.C., 1973-75, ptnr., 1976-80; ptnr., chmn. litig. dept. Schulte Roth & Zabel, N.Y.C., 1980—; lawyer; b. Providence, Oct. 16, 1943; s. Irving and Naomi (Richman) B.; m. Stacey J. Moritz; children: Peter, Isabel, Nell. AB cum laude, Brown U., 1964; LLB, Harvard U., 1967. Bar: N.Y. 1968, U.S. Dist. Ct. (so. dist.) N.Y. 1969, U.S. Dist. Ct. (ea. dist.) N.Y. 1977, U.S. Dist. Ct. (no. dist.) Tex. 1986, U.S. Ct. Appeals (2d cir.) 1974, U.S. Ct. Appeals (3d cir.) 1984, U.S. Ct. Appeals (D.C. cir.) 1981, U.S. Supreme Ct. 1977, U.S. Tax Ct. 1984. Law clk. to U.S. Dist. judge U.S. Dist. Ct. (so. dist.) N.Y., 1967-69; asst. U.S. atty. So. Dist. N.Y., 1969-73; assoc. Guggenheimer & Untermyer, N.Y.C., 1973-75, ptnr., 1976-80; ptnr., chrmn. litigation dept., Schulte Roth & Zabel, N.Y.C., 1980—, chmn. litig. dept.; lectr. in field. Co-author: Federal Securities Litigation: A Deskbook for the Practitioner, 1997. Chmn., bd. dirs. N.Y. Lawyers for Pub. Interest, Inc., 1991-94, vice chair, 1994-96. Recipient Pathways to Justice award. Fellow Am. Coll. Trial Lawyers; mem. ABA (co-chmn. ann. mtg. 1998, co-chmn. trial practice com. 1990-94, litigation sect. task force on jury sys. 1995—), Assn. of Bar of City of N.Y., Anti-Defamation League (exec. com., legal com. 1994—), Am. Law Inst., N.Y. County Lawyers Assn., Fed. Bar Coun., Harvard Club, Scarsdale Golf Club. Jewish. Co-author: Federal Securities Litigation: A Deskbook for the Practitioner, 1997. Chmn., bd. dirs. N.Y. Lawyers for Pub. Interest, Inc., 1991-94, vice chair, 1994-96. Recipient Pathways to Justice award. Fellow Am. Coll. Trial Lawyers; mem. ABA, (litig. sect., co-chmn. ann. meeting 1998, co-chmn. trial practice com. 1990-94, task force on jury sys. 1995—), Assn. of Bar of City of N.Y., Anti-Defamation League (exec. com., legal com. 1994—), Am. Law Inst., N.Y. County Lawyers Assn., Fed. Bar Coun., Harvard Club, Scarsdale Golf Club. Jewish. General civil litigation, Criminal, Securities.

**BRODSKY, FELICE ADRIENNE,** lawyer; b. Utica, N.Y., July 21, 1952; d. Emile Borden and Harriet Maxine (Berman) Skraly; m. Jeffrey H. Brodsky, Aug. 30, 1981 (div. Dec. 1996). BA, U. Rochester, 1973; MBA, SUNY, Buffalo, 1984, JD, 1993. Bar: N.Y. 1994, Fed. 1994. Claims rep. U.S. Govt./Social Security Adminstrn., Batavia, N.Y., 1976-90; pvt. practice Lockport, N.Y., 1994—; instr. Nat. Coll., Rapid City, S.D., 1973-75, Niagara U., Niagara Falls, N.Y., 1989. Treas. Temple Beth El, Niagara Falls, 1987-93; adv. bd. Salvation Army, Lockport, 1995—; bd. dirs. Niagara County Legal Aid Soc., 1996—, v.p. 1999—. Mem. ABA, N.Y. State Bar Assn., Erie County Bar Assn., Lockport Bar Assn., Women Lawyers of Western N.Y., Nat. Orgn. of social Security Claimants Reps. (sustaining mem.), Phi Delta Phi. Democrat. Jewish. Avocations: travel, reading, civic activities. Pension, profit-sharing, and employee benefits, General practice. Home: 71 Bridlewood Dr PO Box 557 Lockport NY 14095-0557 Office: 556 S Transit St Lockport NY 14094-5933

**BRODSKY, MARK WILLIAM,** lawyer; b. July 14, 1951. BA magna cum laude, Tufts U., 1973; JD, U. Conn., 1977. Bar: Conn. 1977, U.S. Dist. Ct. Conn. 1977. Law clerk Superior Ct., Hartford, Conn., 1977-78; staff attorney Chief Ct. Adminstrs. Office, Hartford, Conn., 1978-80; asst. state's attorney State of Conn. Divsn. Criminal Justice, Hartford, Conn., 1980-90, sr. asst. state's attorney, 1990—. Mem. Nat. Dist. Attorney's Assn. Office: States Attorneys Office 105 Raymond Rd West Hartford CT 06107-2538

**BRODY, ANITA BLUMSTEIN,** judge; b. N.Y.C., May 25, 1935; d. David Theodore and Rita (Sondheim) Blumstein; m. Jerome I. Brody, Oct. 25, 1959; children: Lisa, Marion, Timothy. AB, Wellesley Coll., 1955; JD, Columbia U., 1958. Bar: N.Y. 1959, Fla. 1960, Pa. 1972. With Office of Atty. Gen., State N.Y., 1958-59; dep. asst. atty. gen. State N.Y., 1959; sole practice Ardmore, Pa., 1972-79; ptnr. Brody, Brown & Hepburn, Ardmore, 1979-81; judge Pa. Ct. Common Pleas 38th Jud. Dist., Norristown, 1981-82, U.S. Dist. Ct. (ea. dist.) Pa., Phila., 1992—; lectr. in law U. Pa., Phila., 1978-79. Mem. ABA, Am. Judicature Soc., Nat. Assn. Women Judges, Pa. Bar Assn., Montgomery Bar Assn. (bd. dirs. 1979-81), Temple Am. Inn of Ct. (pres. 1994-95). Republican. Jewish. Office: US Courthouse Philadelphia PA 19106

**BRODY, JAY HOWARD,** lawyer; b. Detroit, Jan. 4, 1953; s. Robert David and Rhea Antoinnette (Orley) B.; m. Helene Cheryl Brodsky, Aug. 11, 1974 (div. Nov. 1998); children: Stuart, Rachel. BA in Anthropology, U. Mich., 1974; JD, Wayne State U., 1976. Bar: Mich. 1977, U.S. Dist. Ct. (ea. dist.) Mich. 1977, U.S. Ct. Appeals (6th cir.) 1977, U.S. Tax Ct. 1979. Acct. Arther Andersen, Detroit, 1977-79; assoc. Raymond & Dillon, Detroit, 1979-80, Rubenstein & Isaacs, Southfield, Mich., 1980-81; atty. pct. practice, Farmington Hills, Mich., 1981—; dir. Thomas Found., Farmington Hills, 1984—. Exec. producer (film) KillZone, 1997. Mem. ABA, AICPAs, State Bar Mich., Mich. Assn. CPAs. Taxation, general, General corporate, Estate planning. Office: 30445 Northwestern Hwy Farmington MI 48334-3158

**BRODY, MORTON AARON,** federal judge; b. Lewiston, Maine, June 12, 1933; s. Henry S. and Pearl (Meltzer) B.; m. Judith Levine, July 3, 1960; children: Ronald, Elizabeth Brody Gluck, John. BA, Bates Coll., Lewiston, 1955; JD, U. Chgo., 1958. Bar: Maine 1959, U.S. Dist. Ct. D.C. 1959, U.S. Ct. Appeals (D.C. cir.) 1959, U.S. Dist. Ct. Maine 1961. Lawyer Washington, 1958-61, Waterville, Maine, 1961-80; justice Superior Ct. of Maine, 1980-85, chief justice, 1985-90; assoc. justice Supreme Judicial Ct. of Maine, Augusta, 1990-91; judge U.S. Dist. Ct., Bangor, Maine, 1991—; city solicitor City of Waterville, 1961-66, 68-70; adj. prof. Colby Coll., 1987-96. Bates Coll. scholar, 1951-55; U. Chgo. Law Sch. scholar, 1955-58; recipient Disting. Citizen of Yr. award, 1981, Elks Citizen of Yr. award, 1984. Mem. Maine Bar Assn., Kennebec County Bar Assn., Waterville Bar Assn., Phi Delta Phi. Jewish. Office: US Dist Ct PO Box 756 Bangor ME 04402-0756

**BRODY, NANCY LOUISE,** lawyer; b. Chgo., Nov. 17, 1954; d. Mitchell and Grace Yaden (Williams) Block; m. Daniel Matthew Brody, Oct. 28, 1979. BA, U. Mich., 1975; JD, Loyola U., Chgo., 1979. Bar: Ill. 1979, Ariz. 1981, Va. 1989. Sec., gen. counsel Block & Co., Inc., 1981—, also bd. dirs. Bd. dirs. Ind. YMCA, 1986-87, Charlottesville YMCA, 1989-90; mem. Jr. League, Charlottesville, rec. sec., 1991-92. Named one of Outstanding Young Women Am., 1983. Fellow Am. Bar Found. (life), Pa. Bar Found. (bd. dirs. 1984-88); mem. ABA (ho. dels. 1986-88, state membership chmn. Pa. 1986-88), Ill. State Bar Assn., Pa. Bar Assn. (bd. govs. 1984-87, treas. 1983-84, chairperson 1985-86 young lawyers div.), Zonta (parliamentarian Ind. chpt. 1985-86, 87-88), Pi Beta Phi (alumnae adv. coun. 1989—). Republican. General corporate.

**BRODY, RICHARD ERIC,** lawyer; b. N.Y.C., Sept. 9, 1947; s. Harold I. and Lillian C. (Albert) B.; m. V. Jane Cohen, May 25, 1974; children: Lauren, Erica. BA, Washington and Jefferson Coll., 1969; JD, Boston U., 1975. Bar: Mass. 1975, U.S. Dist. Ct. Mass. 1975, U.S. Ct. Appeals (1st cir.) 1975, U.S. Supreme Ct. 1987. Law clk. Mass. Superior Ct., Boston, 1975-76, chief law clk., 1976-77; assoc. Sisson, Lee & Bloomenthal, Boston, 1977-78; asst. dist. atty. Atty.'s Office Middlesex County Dist., Cambridge, Mass., 1978-82; assoc. Morrison, Mahoney & Miller, Boston, 1982-85, ptnr., 1985-95; ptnr. Brody, Hardoon, Perkins & Kesten, Boston, 1995—; lectr. Nat. Inst. Trial Advocacy, trial practice series Harvard U., Mass. Continuing Legal Edn., Def. Rsch. Inst.; evaluator Middlesex Multi-Door Courthouse, Cambridge, 1989—; mediator Arbitration Forums, Inc., Tarrytown, N.Y., 1989—, cons. Liability Cons., Inc., Sudbury, 1988—; mem. nat. adv. bd. Govtl. Liability Ins., Richmond, 1985—. Trustee Mass. Civil Liability Ins., Boston, 1983-89. Mem. Mass. Bar Assn. (civil litigation sect. coun.), Mass. Assn. Trial Lawyers, Boston Bar Assn., Def. Rsch. Inst., City Solicitors and Town Counsel Assn. Personal injury, Civil rights, General civil litigation. Office: Brody Hardoon Perkins & Kesten 1 Exeter Plz Fl 12 Boston MA 02116-2848

**BROEKER, JOHN MILTON,** lawyer; b. Berwyn, Ill., May 27, 1940; s. Milton Monroe and Marjorie Grace (Wilson) B.; m. Linda J. Broeker, Dec. 9, 1983; children: Sara Elizabeth, Ross Goddard; stepchildren: Terrance Mercil Jr., Johnny Mercil, Veronica Mercil. BA, Grinnell Coll., 1962; JD cum laude, U. Minn., 1965. BAr: Minn. 1965, Wis. 1982, U.S. Ct. Appeals (8th cir.) 1966, U.S. Dist. Ct. Minn. 1967, U.S. Tax Ct. 1969, U.S. Ct. Appeals (5th cir.) 1971, U.S. Dist. Ct. (we. dist.) Wis. 1982, U.S. Supreme Ct. 1984. Law clk. to presiding judge U.S. Ct. Appeals (8th cir.), 1965-66; ptnr. Gray, Plant, Mooty, Mooty & Bennett, Mpls., 1966-71, Broeker, Geer, Gletcher & LaFond and predecessor firms, Mpls., 1971-91; v.p., gen. counsel NordicTrack, Inc., Mpls., 1991-94; founder Broeker Enterprises, 1992—; pres. Legal Mgmt. Strategies, Inc., Mpls., 1994—; of cousnel Popham, Haik, Schnobrich & Kaufman, Ltd., Mpls., 1995-96, Halleland, Lewis, Nilan, Sipkins & Johnson, Mpls., 1996-97; pvt. practice, 1997—; instr. U Minn. Law Sch., 1967-72; lectr. convs. and seminars, 1969—; lectr. U. Minn. Ctr. for Long Term Care Edn., 1972-77, Gt. Lakes Health Congress, 1972, Sister Kenney Inst., 1972. Contbr. articles to legal jours. Bd. dirs. Minn. Environ. Scis. Found., Inc., 1971-73; bd. dirs. Project Environ. Found., 1977-83, chmn., 1980-82; mem. alumni bd. Grinnell Coll., 1968-71; chmn. MInnetonka Environ. Quality and Natural Resources Commn., 1971-72. Recipient Outstanding Alumni award Grinnell Coll., 1973. Mem. ABA (forum com. on health law 1978-91), Minn. Bar Assn. (chmn. environ. law com. 1970-72), State Bar Wis., Hennepin County Bar Assn. (chmn. environ. law com. 1976-77, legis. com. 1972-76, health law com. 1977-79), Am. Soc. Hosp. Attys., Minn. Soc. Hosp. Attys., Am. Health Care Assn. (legal coordinating com. 1970-75, labor com. 1973-74), Nat. Health Lawyers Assn., Minn. Thoroughbred Assn. (bd. dirs. 1991-92), Minn. Quarterhorse Racing Assn. (bd. dirs. 1994—, pres. 1997-99), Sierra Club (nat. dir. 1974-76, chmn. chpt. 1971-72, regional v.p. 1973-74). Health, Labor, General corporate. Home: 11402 Burr Ridge Ln Eden Prairie MN 55347-4717 Office: 8120 Penn Ave S Ste 151Q Bloomington MN 55431-1326

**BROGAN, JONATHAN WILLIAM,** lawyer; b. Portland, Maine, June 15, 1959; s. Joseph E. and Nancy M. (Lapomarda) B.; m. Elizabeth M. Goett, Oct. 21, 1989; children: Aaron Joseph, Anna Elizabeth. BA, U. San Diego, 1982; JD, U. Maine, 1985. Bar: Maine 1985, U.S. Dist. Ct. Maine 1985. Ptnr. Norman, Hanson & Detroy, Portland, 1985—. Bd. dirs. Cheverus H.S., 1998—. Mem. ATLA, Maine Trial Lawyers Assn., Maine State Bar Assn. (com. of the future of profession 1998—), Cumberland County Bar Assn., Purpodock Club (bd. govs. 1990-93, 96-99, v.p. 1992-93, pres. 1998-99), Pi Sigma Alpha, Phi Alpha Theta, Delta Epsilon Sigma. General civil litigation, Product liability, Personal injury. Home: 42 Stonegate Rd Cape Eliz ME 04107-1637 Office: Norman Hanson & Detroy 415 Congress St Ste 500 Portland ME 04101-3530

**BROGAN, KEVIN HERBERT,** lawyer; b. Pasadena, Calif., Nov. 7, 1953; s. Donald E. and Consuelo Bergere (Mendenhall) B.; m. Nena Jones, Aug. 1, 1981. BS, U. Calif., Berkeley, 1976; JD, U. Calif., San Francisco, 1979. Bar: Calif. 1979, U.S. Dist. Ct. (ce., so., ea. and no. dists.) Calif. 1979, Wis. 1988, U.S. Dist. Ct. (ea. dist.) Wis. 1988, U.S. Claims Ct., U.S. Supreme Ct. Law clk. to judge U.S. Ct. Appeals (10th cir.), Santa Fe, 1979; assoc. Hill, Farrer & Burrill, L.A., 1979-86, ptnr., 1986—; bd. dirs. Nat. Conf., Attys. Ins. Mutual. Bd. dirs. San Marino (Calif.) Community Chest, 1986—. Mem. ABA, Fed. Bar Assn., La. County Bar Assn. (chmn. Eminent Domain and Land Valuation Com. 1992), State Bar of Calif. (real property sect., chmn. inverse condemnation domain subsection), Irish Am. Bar Assn., Beta Theta Pi. Republican. Roman Catholic. Condemnation, General civil litigation, Real property. Office: Hill Farrer & Burrill 300 S Grand Ave Ste 37 Los Angeles CA 90071-3110

**BROGDON, W.M. "ROWE",** lawyer; b. Columbia, S.C., Oct. 14, 1953; s. Wallace M. and Helen (Deloach) B.; m. Cynthia S. Brogdon, Feb. 28, 1987; 1 child, Emily Elizabeth. BS in Biology magna cum laude, Ga. So. U., 1976; JD cum laude, Mercer U., 1982. Bar: Ga. 1982. Law clk. to Hon. B. Avant Edenfield U.S. Dist. Ct. (so. dist.) Ga.; ptnr. Smith & Brogdon Attys., Savannah, Ga., 1983-87, Brannan & Brogdon Attys., Claxton, Ga., 1987-93, Franklin, Taulbee, Rushing & Brogdon, P.C., Statesboro, Ga., 1994—. Contbr. articles to profl. jours. Vice chmn. bd. trustees Bulloch Acad. Sch., Statesboro, 1998—; bd. govs. Mercer U. Law Sch., 1979-81. State of Ga. law scholar, 1980. Mem. ATLA, Ga. Trial Lawyers Assn. (chmn. Amicus com. 1996-98, v.p. mid. cir. 1996-97), Atlantic Cir. Bar Assn. (pres. 1991-92), Ogeechee Cir. Bar Assn. (pres. 1996-97), Nat. Bd. Trial Advocacy (cert.), Rotary (treas. 1992-93), Phi Delta Phi. Methodist. Avocation: fishing. General civil litigation, Personal injury, Product liability. Home: 4599 Country Club Rd Statesboro GA 30458-9007 Office: Franklin Taulbee Rushing & Brogdon 12 Siebald St Statesboro GA 30458-1002

**BROILI, ROBERT HOWARD,** lawyer; b. Reno, Sept. 2, 1942; s. Julius and Verna June (Bradbury) B.; m. Sally Sue M. Atkinson, Jan. 24, 1965; children: Eric Anthony, Susan Heather. AA, Menlo Coll., 1962; BA, U. Nev., 1964; JD, Nev. Sch. Law, 1986. Bar: Nev. 1989, U.S. Dist. Ct. (no. dist.) Nev., 1991. Sales rep. Nev. Machinery & Electric, Reno, 1964-70, ptnr., gen. mgr., 1970-83; paralegal Washoe Legal Svcs., Reno, 1984-86; legal asst. White Law Chartered, Reno, 1986-89; law clk. Douglas County Dist. Ct., Minden, Nev., 1989; chief prosecutor Lander County Office of the Dist. Atty., Battle Mountain, Nev., 1989-91; prin. Robert Broili Law Offices, Reno, 1991—. Mem. State Bar Assn. Nev. (atty. discipline com. 1993-96, fee dispute com. 1991-95), Masons, Lions. Avocations: fishing, hunting, shooting, skiing, biking. Consumer commercial, Probate, Estate planning. Office: 335 W 1st St Reno NV 89503-5301

**BROLLESY, HANY SAYED,** lawyer; b. Benha, Egypt, Jan. 4, 1969; came to U.S., 1970; s. Sayed I. and Lila M. (Abdel-Kawi) B. BA, Rutgers U., 1991; JD, Georgetown U., 1994. Bar: N.J. 1994, N.Y. 1995. Assoc. Hoagland, Longo, Moran, Dunst and Doukas, New Brunswick, N.J., 1994-96, Jamieson, Moore, Peskin & Spicer, Princeton, N.J., 1996-98, Carpenter, Bennett & Morrissey, Newark, 1998-99, Epstein, Becker & Green, PC, N.Y.C., 1999—. Trustee Lawrence Square Village II Assn., Lawrenceville, N.J., 1997-99. Muslim. Avocations: golf, skiing. General civil litigation, Immigration, naturalization, and customs. Office: Epstein Becker & Green PC 250 Park Ave Ste 1200 New York NY 10177-1211

**BROMBERG, ALAN ROBERT,** law educator; b. Dallas, Nov. 24, 1928; s. Alfred L. and Juanita (Kramer) B.; m. Anne Ruggles, July 26, 1959. A.B., Harvard U., 1949; J.D., Yale U., 1952. Bar: Tex. 1952. Assoc. firm Carrington, Gowan, Johnson, Bromberg and Leeds, Dallas, 1952-56; atty. and cons., 1956-76; of counsel firm Jenkens & Gilchrist, P.C., 1976—; asst. prof. law So. Meth. U., 1956-58, assoc. prof., 1958-62, prof., 1962-83, Univ. Disting. prof., 1983—, mem. presdl. search group, 1971-72; faculty adviser Southwestern Law Jour., 1958-65; sr. fellow Yale U. Law Faculty, 1966-67; vis. prof. Stanford U., 1972-73; mem. adv. bd. U. Calif. Securities Regulation Inst., 1973-78, 79-87; counsel Internat. Data Systems, Inc., 1961-65, sec., dir., 1963-65; mem. Tex. Legis. Council Bus. and Commerce Code Adv. Com., 1966-67. Author: Supplementary Materials on Texas Corporations, 3d edit, 1971, Partnership Primer-Problems and Planning, 1961, Materials on Corporate Securities and Finance—A Growing Company's Search for Funds, 2d edit, 1965, Securities Fraud and Commodities Fraud, Vols. 1-7, 1967-93, 2nd edit., 1999, Crane and Bromberg on Partnership, 1968, Bromberg and Ribstein on Partnership, Vols. 1-2, 1988, Vols. 3-4, 1994, Bromberg and Ribstein on Limited Liability Partnerships and the Revised Uniform Partnership Act, 1997; mem. ednl. publs. adv. bd., Matthew Bender & Co., 1977-95, chmn., 1981-94; contbr. articles and revs. to law and bar jours.; adv. editor: Rev. Securities and Commodities Regulation, 1969—, Securities Regulation Law Jour, 1973—, Jour. Corp. Law, 1976—, Derivatives: Tax, Regulation, Finance, 1995-97. Sec., bd. dirs. Community Arts Fund, 1963-73; gen. atty. Dallas Mus. Contemporary Arts, 1956-63; bd. dirs. Dallas Theater Center, 1955-73, sec., 1957-66, fin. com., 1957-65, mem. exec. com., 1957-70, 79-85, life, 1973—, v.p., trustee endowment fund, 1974-85; trustee Found. for the Arts, 1996—; bd. dirs. Found. for the Arts, 1996—. Served as cpl. U.S. Army, 1952-54. Mem. ABA (coms. commodities, partnerships, fed. regulation securities), Dallas Bar Assn. (chmn. com. uniform partnership act 1959-61, libr. com. 1981-83), Tex. Bar Assn. (chmn. sect. corp. banking and bus. law 1967-68, vice chmn. 1965-67, com. corps. 1957—, mem. com. securities 1965—, chmn. 1965-69, mem. com. partnerships 1957—, chmn. 1979-81), Am. Law Inst. (life), Southwestern Legal Found. (co-chmn. securities com. 1982-85), Tex. Bus. Law Found. (bd. dirs. 1988—, co-chmn. legis. com. 1994—). Office: So Meth U Sch Law Dallas TX 75275-0001 also: 1445 Ross Ave Ste 3200 Dallas TX 75202-2785

**BROMBERG, MYRON JAMES,** lawyer; b. Paterson, N.J., Nov. 5, 1934; s. Abraham and Elsie (Baker) B.; m. Lisa Murtha, Nov. 28, 1987; children—Kenneth Karl, Eric Edward, Bruce Abraham. BA, Yale U., 1956; LLB, Columbia U., 1959. Bar: N.J. bar 1960, N.Y. bar 1981. Law asst. to dist. atty. N.Y. County, 1958; law asst. U.S. atty. So. Dist. N.Y., 1958-59; asso. mem. firm Ralph Porzio, Morristown, N.J., 1960-61; ptnr. Porzio, Bromberg & Newman, Morristown, 1962-77, mng. prin., 1980-96; atty. Morris County Bd. Elections, 1963-64; town atty., Town of Morristown, 1965-67; lectr. trial practice Rutgers Inst. CLE, 1965-94. Chmn. fund and membership Morristown chpt. ARC, 1965; chmn. retail div. Community Chest Morris County, 1963; chmn. Keep Morristown Beautiful Com., 1963; mem. Morris Twp. Com., 1970-72; committeeman Morris County Democratic Com., 1962-63, 72-77; lay trustee Delbarton Sch., Morristown, 1972-75; trustee Morris Mus., 1973-79. Fellow Am. Coll. Trial Lawyers (chmn. com. on admission to fellowship 1986-91, com. on complex litigation 1992-98, com. on tchg. of trial and appellate advocacy 1998—), Am. Law Inst. (cons. group product libility), Am. Bar Found. (life); mem. ABA, Internat. Acad. Trial Lawyers (chair N.J. 1997-99, regional chair 3d jud. cir. 1997—), N.J. Bar Assn. (named outstanding young lawyer 1970, chmn. joint conf. com. with N.J. Med. Soc. 1970-72), Morris County Bar Assn., Am. Judicature Soc., Trial Attys. N.J. (pres. 1976-77, Trial Bar award 1989), Internat. Soc. Barristers (N.J. State chmn., bd. govs., sec.-treas. 1996-97, v.p. 1998—), Internat. Assn. Def. Counsel (chair com. on toxic and hazardous substances 1994-96, dir. Def. Counsel Trial Acad. 1996), Andover Alumni Assn. N.Y.C., Columbia U. Law Sch. Assn. of N.J. (bd. dirs. 1986-95), Yale Club (N.Y.C. and ctrl. N.J.), Park Ave. (N.J.) Club, Merchants Club (N.Y.C.), Chi Phi, Phi Delta Phi. Environmental, Product liability, Professional liability. Home: 9 Thompson Ct Morristown NJ 07960-6326 Office: 163 Madison Ave Morristown NJ 07960-7324

**BROMBERGER, ALLEN RICHARD,** legal association administrator; b. Princeton, N.J., May 1, 1955; s. Sylvain and Nancy (Lilienthal) B.; 1 child, Michael Barrows. BA, U. Calif., Berkeley, 1978; JD, U. Calif., San Francisco, 1982. Bar: Calif. 1982, N.Y. 1983. Dir. legal assistance Coun. N.Y. Law Assocs., N.Y.C., 1983-85, assoc. dir., 1985-88, dir. nonprofit law program, 1988-90; exec. dir. Lawyers Alliance for N.Y., N.Y.C., 1990-99; pres. Power of Attorney, N.Y.C., 1999—; bd. dirs. Lawyers Com. Against Violence, N.Y.C., 1996-98, Interlegal USA, N.Y.C., 1994—, Cause Effective, N.Y.C., 1994—, Coalition for the Homeless, N.Y.C., 1994-96; mem. IRS Exempt Orgns. Liaison Com., 1993-99. Editor, author: Getting Organized, 1986, 4th edit., 1995, Advising Nonprofits, 1988, 4th edit., 1995. Mem. ABA, Assn. Bar City N.Y., Nat. Assn. Pro Bono Coords. (exec. com. 1996—), N.Y. State Advisory Task Force on Corps., 1997-99. Office: Power of Attorney 99 Hudson St New York NY 10013-2815

**BROMM, FREDERICK WHITTEMORE,** lawyer; b. Roanoke, Va., Nov. 19, 1953; s. Frederick Thornton and Anne Lee (Cassell) B. BA cum laude, Furman U., 1976; JD cum laude, Washington & Lee U., 1979. Bar: Va. 1979. Assoc. Place, Prillman & Barnett, Roanoke, 1979-81; assoc. Jolly, Place, Fralin & Prillman P.C., Roanoke, 1981-83, ptnr., 1983-86; sole practice Roanoke, 1986—. Treas. Roanoke Reps., 1984-88. Mem. ABA, Va. Bar Assn., Roanoke Bar Assn. (chmn. conflicts com. 1986-87), Legal Aid Soc. Roanoke Valley (bd. dirs. 1990-91), Roanoke Jaycees (bd. dirs. 1980, v.p. 1981, legal counsel 1981, 82). Episcopalian. Bankruptcy, State civil litigation, Contracts commercial. Home: 3071 Poplar Ln SW Roanoke VA 24014-3229 Office: Rt 419 at Ogden Rd Roanoke VA 24014

**BROMM, SUSAN ELIZABETH,** lawyer, government official; b. Miami Beach, Fla., July 6, 1955; d. H. James and Dorothy (Shea) B.; m. Bernard J. Stoll, Jr., Oct. 20, 1984; 1 child, B. Joseph III. BS, SUNY, Albany, 1976; JD, Georgetown U., 1979. Bar: D.C. 1979, U.S. Dist. Ct. D.C. 1980. Atty.-advisor Office Solid Waste, EPA, Washington, 1980-84, sect. chief, 1984-86, dep. dir. permits and state programs divsn., 1986-88, dir. Resource Conservation and Recovery Act enforcement div., 1988-93, dir. chem., cmty. svcs. and mcpl. divsn., 1993-95, dep. dir. Office Site Remediation, 1995—. Mem. Exec. Women in Govt., Am. Law Inst. Avocations: herbalist, nature photography. Office: EPA 401 M St SW # 2271-a Washington DC 20460-0002

**BRONFIN, FRED,** lawyer; b. New Orleans, Nov. 30, 1918; m. Carolyn Pick; children by previous marriage: Daniel R., Kenneth A. BA, Tulane U., 1938, JD, 1941. Bar: La. 1941, U.S. Dist. Ct. (ea. dist.) La. 1941, U.S. Ct. Appeals (5th cir.) 1951, U.S. Supreme Ct. 1973. Assoc. Rittenberg & Rittenberg, New Orleans, 1946-48; ptnr. Rittenberg, Weinstein & Bronfin, New Orleans, 1948-56, Weinstein & Bronfin, New Orleans, 1956-62, Bronfin, Heller, Steinberg & Berins and precessor firms, New Orleans, 1962-91; of counsel Bronfin & Heller, 1991-98, Heller, Draper, Hayden & Horn, 1998—. With USN, 1942-46. Mem. ABA, La. Bar Assn., New Orleans Bar Assn., Order of Coif, Phi Beta Kappa. Estate planning, General corporate, Real property. Office: Heller Draper Hayden Et Al 650 Poydras St Ste 2500 New Orleans LA 70130-6175

**BRONIS, STEPHEN J.,** lawyer; b. Miami, Fla., Feb. 23, 1947; s. Larry and Thelma (Berger) B.; children: Jason Michael, Tyler Adam, Kenneth Lawrence. BSBA, U. Fla., 1969; JD, Duke U., 1972. Bar: Fla. 1972, D.C. 1973, U.S. Dist. Ct. (so. dist.) Fla. 1973, U.S. Ct. Appeals (5th cir.) 1977, U.S. Supreme Ct. 1978, U.S. Ct. Appeals (11th cir.) 1981, U.S. Dist. Ct. (mid. dist.) Fla. 1989, Colo. 1994, U.S. Dist. Ct. Colo. 1996, U.S. Ct. Appeals (10th cir.) 1996, U.S. Tax Ct. 1998. Asst. pub. defender 11th Jud. Cir. Fla., Miami, 1972-75; ptnr. Rosen & Bronis, P.A., Miami, 1975-77, Rosen, Portela, Bronis, et al, Miami, 1977-82, Bronis & Potela, P.A., Miami, 1982-90; pvt. practice Miami, 1990-93; ptnr. Davis, Scott, Weber & Edwards, Miami, 1993-95, Zuckerman, Spaeder, Taylor & Evans, Miami, 1996—; mem. faculty Nat. Inst. of Trial Adv., U. N.C., Yeshiva U, Nova Sch. Law; nominated Fla. Supreme Ct. 1999. Contbr. articles to profl. jours. Recipient Am. Jurisprudence award Bancroft-Whitney Co., 1972, cert. of appreciation Fla. Shorthand Reporters Assn., 1984. Mem. ATLA, Nat. Criminal Def. Attys. Assn., Am. Bd. Criminal Lawyers (v.p. 1981-82), Fla. Criminal Def. Attys. Assn. (Outstanding Svc. award 1981), Calif. Attys. Criminal Justice, Acad. Fla. Trial Lawyers (criminal law sect. dir.). Democrat. Criminal, General corporate, General civil litigation. Home: 3 Grove Isle Dr Apt 1506 Miami FL 33133-4103 Office: 201 S Biscayne Blvd Ste 900 Miami FL 33131-4326

**BRONKESH, NOAH,** lawyer; b. Munich, Nov. 20, 1947; came to U.S., 1951; s. Manasha and Miriam (Kotlan) B.; m. Michele Cotler, June 10, 1979; children: Laura, Elizabeth. BA, Temple U., 1970; JD, NYU, 1973. Bar: N.J. 1973, N.Y. 1985, U.S. Supreme Ct. 1980. Assoc., then ptnr. Okoniewski DiStefano Bronkesh & Daniels, Millville, N.J., 1973-80; ptnr. Sills Cummis Radin Tischman Epstein & Gross, Atlantic City, N.J., 1980—. Chmn. City of Millville Dem. Orgn., 1977-79, Atlantic County (N.J.) Dem. Orgn., 1982-84; mem. N.J. Israel Commn., Trenton, 1990—; trustee So. N.J. Devel. Coun., 1987&, Nat. Conf., 1995—, Congregation Beth Judah, 1994—, Found. Fedn., 1990—; pres. Atlantic Cape May Fedn. Jewish Agys., 1992-94, trustee, 1984—. Recipient Leadership award Fedn. Jewish Agys., 1990. Mem. ABA, State of N.J. Bar Assn., N.J. Assn. Fedns. (treas. 1990-92). Jewish. Avocations: reading, tennis, gardening. Office: Sills Cummis Radin Tischman Epstein & Gross 17 Gordons Aly Atlantic City NJ 08401-7406

**BRONNER, JAMES RUSSELL,** lawyer; b. Chgo., Nov. 14, 1943; s. Maurice Henry and Elaine R. (Rosenberg) B.; m. Barbara Henley, July 3, 1968; children: Michael, Jamie. BA, U. Mich., 1965; JD, Northwestern U., 1968, LLM, 1970. Bar: Ill. 1968, U.S. Dist. Ct. (no. dist.) Ill. 1968, U.S. Ct. Appeals (7th cir.) 1969. Asst. prof. law sch. Northwestern U., Chgo., 1970-72; ptnr. Davis, Miner, Barnhill & Bronner, Chgo., 1972-75; prin. Ct. Club Cir., Chgo., 1975-82; ptnr. Speakers Sport, Inc., Northbrook, Ill., 1976—; lectr. law sch. Northwestern U., 1972-79; vice chmn. Gov.'s Com. on State Salaries, Chgo., 1978. Exec. v.p. Chgo. Shakespeare Repertory Co., 1988-91; masters chmn. U.S. Team for 1989, 93, 97 World Maccabiah Games. Ford Found. fellow, 1968-70. Mem. ABA, Chgo. Bar Assn., Nat. Ct. Club Assn. (pres. 1980). Personal income taxation, Sports. Office: Speakers of Sport Inc 666 Dundee Rd Ste 704 Northbrook IL 60062-2734

**BRONSON, MERIDITH J.,** lawyer; b. N.Y.C., Dec. 4, 1958; d. Ira D. and Carolyn Bronson; children: Logan Alexa, Jordan Alanna. BA, Drew U., 1980; JD, Seton Hall U., 1984. Cert. matrimonial atty. Jud. law clk. Newark, N.J., 1984-85; ptnr. Sternm Steiger Croland, Paramus, 1985-95, Shapiro & Croland, Hackensack, N.J., 1995—; barrister Family Law Inns of Ct., N.J., 1996—. Mem. Phi Beta Kappa. Family and matrimonial. Office: Shapiro & Croland 411 Hackensack Ave Hackensack NJ 07601-6328

**BRONSTEIN, ALVIN J.,** lawyer; b. Bklyn., June 8, 1928. LLD, N.Y. Law Sch., 1951, LLD (hon.), 1990. Bar: N.Y. 1952, Miss. 1967, La. 1971, U.S. Ct. Appeals (D.C., 1st, 2d, 3d, 4th, 5th, 9th, 10th and 11th cirs.), U.S. Supreme Ct. 1961. Ptnr. Bronstein & Bronstein, Bklyn., 1952-63; pvt. practice Elizabethtown, N.Y., 1963-64; chief staff counsel Lawyers Constl. Def. Com., Jackson, Miss., 1964-68; fellow Inst. Politics, Kennedy Sch. Govt. Harvard U., Cambridge, Mass., 1968-69, assoc. dir. Inst. Politics, Kennedy Sch. Govt., 1969-71; ptnr. Elie, Bronstein, Strickler & Dennis, New Orleans, 1971-72; exec. dir. Nat. Prison Project, Nat. Jail Project ACLU Found., Washington, 1972-96; cons. nat. legal dept. ACLU Found., 1996—; cons., trial counsel CORE, NAACP, NAACP Legal Def. Fund, SCLC, SNCC, Miss. Freedom Dem. Party, Black Panther Party, Nat. Inst. for Edn. in Law and Poverty, and others; guest lectr. various law schs., 1964—; cons. various state corrections depts., 1972—; adj. prof. Am. U. Law Sch., 1973; expert witness in various prison litigations, 1978—; appointed mem. Fed. Jud. Ctr. Adv. Com. on Experimentation in the Law, 1978-81. Contbg. author: The Evolution of Criminal Justice, 1978, Prisoners' Rights Sourcebook, Vol. II, 1980, Confinement in Maximum Custody, 1980, Sage Criminal Justice Annual, Vol. 14, 1980, Readings in the Justice Model, 1980, Our Endangered Rights, 1984, Prisoners and the Courts: The American Experience, 1985; author: (with Rudovsky and Koren) The Rights of Prisoners, 1988; author, editor: Representing Prisoners, 1981; editor: Prisoners' Self-Help Litigation Manual, 1977; contbr. articles to profl. jours. MacArthur Found. fellow, 1989; named one of the 100 most influential lawyers in Am., Nat. Law Jour., 1985, 88, 91, 94; recipient Roscoe Pound award Nat. Coun. on Crime and Delinquency, 1981, Karl Menninger award Fortune Soc., 1982, Pa. Prison Soc. award, 1991. Office: Nat Prison Project ACLU Found 1875 Connecticut Ave NW Washington DC 20009-5728

**BRONSTEIN, GLEN MAX,** lawyer; b. N.Y.C., Sept. 14, 1960; s. Melvin and Gloria (Liebman) B. BS, Skidmore Coll., 1982; postgrad., London Sch. Econs., 1982-83; JD, Syracuse U., 1986. Bar: N.Y. 1987, U.S. Dist. Ct. (so. and ea. dists.) N.Y. 1987. Assoc. Williamson and Williamson, N.Y.C., 1986-87, Langan and Levy, N.Y.C., 1987-90, Greenberg, Cantor, Trager & Toplitz, N.Y.C., 1990-93; asst. gen. counsel Fischbach Corp., N.Y.C., 1993—. Mem. Assn. Trial Lawyers Am., Conn. Trial Lawyers Assn., N.Y. Trial Lawyers Assn. (social legis. liaison constrn. law), N.Y. County Lawyers Assn. (com. constrn. law), Assn. Bar City of N.Y., Westchester County Bar Assn., London Sch. Econs. Club. Contracts commercial, Government contracts and claims, Construction. Home: 203 Fox Meadow Rd Scarsdale NY 10583-1643 Office: Fischbach Corp 675 Central Ave New Providence NJ 07974-1560

**BRONSTEIN, RICHARD M.,** lawyer; b. N.Y.C., Feb. 20, 1945; s. Benjamin and Betty Bronstein; m. Ethel Leder; children: Rachel, Susan. BS, Queens Coll., 1965; JD, NYU, 1968. Bar: N.Y. 1969, U.S. Dist. Ct. (so. and ea. dists.) N.Y. 1971. Assoc. N.Y. State Divsn. Human Rights, N.Y.C., 1969-71; asst. dist. atty. Suffolk County Dist. Atty.'s Office, Riverhead, N.Y., 1972-79; assoc. Lustig & Bronstein, Deer Park, N.Y., 1979-94; pvt. practice Central Islia, N.Y., 1994—. Fin. v.p. North Shore Jewish Ctr., Port Jefferson Station, N.Y., 1994-95. Mem. ATLA, N.Y. State Trial Lawyers Assn., Suffolk County Bar Assn. Avocations: golf, tennis, skiing. General civil litigation, Criminal. Office: 84 Wheeler Rd Central Islip NY 11722-2021

**BRONSTEIN, ROBERT,** lawyer; b. East Chicago, Ind., Dec. 8, 1919; s. Phillip and Sarah (Gross) B.; m. Sonia Zeidman, July 4, 1922; children: Eric, Scott. MA in Sociology, U. Chgo., 1948, JD, 1951. Bar: Ill. 1951, Colo. 1961. Dir. mgmt. analysis State of Colo., 1961-64, dir. budget, 1964-70, coordinator environ. problems, 1970-72; sec. Colo. Environ. Commn., 1970-72; project dir. Boulder (Colo.) Area Growth Study, 1972, mgmt. cons., 1973-75; asst. dept. dir. Colo. Dept. Labor and Employment, 1975-76; assoc. dir. Colo. Div. Employment and Tng., 1976-80; pvt. practice Denver, 1981—; part-time faculty U. Denver Grad Sch. Pub. Adminstrn., 1973, U. Colo. Grad. Sch. Pub. Affairs, 1973. Writer screenplays, books. Bd. dirs. Colo. Citizens Com. on Govt., 1975-79, Citizens Inquiry into Colo. Constrn., 1977; mem. arbitration panel Am. Arbitration Assn., Better Bus. Bur., Nat. Assn. Securities Dealers; mediator Ctr. Dispute Resolution. Lt. USAF, 1941-45, lt. col., 1950-57. Mem. ACLU, Common Cause. Alternative dispute resolution. Home: 2457 S Dahlia Ln Denver CO 80222-6119

**BRONSTER, MARGERY S,** state attorney general; b. N.Y., Dec. 12, 1957; married; 1 child. BA in Chinese Lang., Lit. and History, Brown U., 1979; JD, Columbia U., 1982. Assoc. Sherman & Sterling, N.Y., 1982-87; ptnr. Carlsmith, Ball, Wichman, Murray, Case & Ichiki, Honolulu, 1988-94; atty. gen. State of Hawaii, 1994—; co-chair planning com. Citizens Conf. Judicial Selection, 1993. Mem. Am. Judicature Soc. (bd. dirs.; chair gov. com. on crime, VAWA planning com.). Office: Office Attorney General 425 Queen St Honolulu HI 96813-2903*

**BROOKE, EDWARD WILLIAM,** lawyer, former senator; b. Washington, Oct. 26, 1919; s. Edward W. and Helen (Seldon) B. B.S., Howard U., 1940, LL.D., 1967; LL.B. (editor Law Rev.), Boston U., 1948, LL.M., 1949, LL.D., 1968; LL.D., George Washington U., 1967, Skidmore Coll., 1969, U. Mass., 1971, Amherst Coll., 1972; D.Sc., Lowell Tech. Inst., 1967; D.Sc. numerous other hon. degrees. Bar: Mass. 1948, D.C. Ct. Appeals 1979, D.C. Dist. Ct. 1982, U.S. Supreme Ct. 1962. Chmn. Boston Fin. Com., 1961-62; atty. gen. State of Mass., Boston, 1963-66; mem. U.S. Senate from Mass., 1967-79; chmn. Nat. Low-Income Housing Coalition; former ptnr. O'Connor & Hannan, Washington; formrly of counsel Csaplar & Bok, Boston; former pub. mem. Adminstrv. Conf. U.S.; chmn. bd. dirs. Boston Bank Commerce; bd. dirs. Meditrust, Inc., Wellesley, Mass., Grumman Corp., Bethpage, N.Y. Chmn. Boston Opera Co.; former commr. Pres.'s Commns. on Housing and of Wartime Relocation and Internment of Civilians; bd. dirs. Washington Performing Arts Soc. Served as capt. inf. AUS, World War II, ETO. Decorated Bronze Star; recipient Disting. Svc. award Amvets, 1952, Charles Evans Hughes award NCCJ, 1967, Spingarn medal, NAACP, 1967. Fellow Am. Bar Assn., Am. Acad. Arts and Scis. Office: Hanied Brooke 2500 Virginia Ave NW Ste 301-s Washington DC 20037-1901

**BROOKE, WILLIAM WADE,** lawyer; b. Baton Rouge, Apr. 5, 1956; s. Frederick Dixon and Sybil Stringer (Vogtle) B.; m. Margaret Lee Williamson, June 2, 1979; children: William W. Jr., Robert A., Sarah M. BA in Gen. Bus. Mgmt., U. Ala., 1978, JD, 1981. Bar: Ala. 1981. Assoc. Burr & Forman, Birmingham, Ala., 1981-87; mng. ptnr. Wallace, Brooke & Byers, Birmingham, 1987-91; gen. counsel Harbert Corp., Birmingham, 1991-94, COO, 1995—; chmn. Harbert Realty Svcs., Inc., 1998—; trustee Bus. Coun. Alabturt, 1998—. Trustee Discovery 2000 Mus., Birmingham, 1987—; trustee Mountain Brook City Schs. Found., 1993—, pres., 1995-97; trustee Ctrl. Alabturt United Way, 1998—. Mem. ABA, Ala. Bar Assn., Birmingham Bar Assn. (com. chair), Rotary. Republican. Presbyterian. Avocations: sport fishing, golf, tennis. Banking, Contracts commercial, General corporate. Office: Harbert Mgmt Corp 1 Riverchase Pkwy S Birmingham AL 35244-2008

**BROOKER, NORTON WILLIAM, JR.,** lawyer; b. Wilmington, N.C., Jan. 10, 1944; s. Norton William and Mary Stewart (Aycock) B.; m. JoAnne P. Pipes, Aug. 12, 1967; children: William Thomas, Stewart Jefferson. BA, U. Ala., 1966, JD, 1968. Bar: Ala. 1968, U.S. Dist. Ct. (so. dist.) Ala. 1968, U.S. Dist. Ct. (no. dist.) Ala. 1979, U.S. Dist. Ct. (mid. dist.) 1995. Mem. Lyons Pipes & Cook, P.C., Mobile, Ala., 1968—; speaker various oil and gas seminars, 1981—. Active S. Oil Gas Bd. Adv., Tuscaloosa, Ala., 1986—; pres., chmn. Mobile Azalea Trail, 1972-75; vice chmn. Mobile Bay Sailing Sch., 1985—; Ala. rep. Interstate Oil and Gas Compact Commn., 1968—, spl. unitization com., 1999—. Mem. ABA, Ala. Bar Assn. (chmn. continuing edn. com. oil and gas sect. 1987-90), Mobile Bar Assn. (sec. 1975), U.S. Sailing Assn. (sr. race officer 1989—, sr. judge 1991—), Mobile Yacht Club (commodore 1985-87), U.S. Men's Sailing Championship (chmn. 1998—). Avocations: sailing, boating, hunting. Oil, gas, and mineral, Administrative and regulatory, Real property. Home: 313 Shenandoah Rd E Mobile AL 36608-3318 Office: Lyons Pipes & Cook PC PO Box 2727 Mobile AL 36652-2727

**BROOKMAN, ANTHONY RAYMOND,** lawyer; b. Chgo., Mar. 23, 1922; s. Raymond Charles and Marie Clara (Alberg) B.; m. Marilyn Joyce Brookman, June 5, 1982; children: Meribeth Brookman Farmer, Anthony Raymond, Lindsay Logan Christensen. Student, Ripon Coll., 1940-41; BS, Northwestern U., 1947; JD, U. Calif., San Francisco, 1953. Bar: Calif. 1954. Law clk. to presiding justice Calif. Supreme Ct., 1953-54; ptnr. Nichols, Williams, Morgan, Digardi & Brookman, 1954-68; sr. ptnr. Brookman & Talbot, Inc. (formerly Brookman & Hoffman, Inc.), Walnut Creek, Calif., 1969-92, Brookman & Talbot Inc., Sacramento, 1992—. Pres. Young Reps. Calif., San Mateo County, 1953-54. 1st lt. USAF. Mem. ABA, Alameda County Bar Assn., State Bar Calif., Lawyers Club Alameda County, Alameda-Contra Costa County Trial Lawyers Assn., Assn. Trial Lawyers Am., Calif. Trial Lawyers Assn., Athenian Nile Club, Masons, Shriners. Republican. Personal injury, State civil litigation, General civil litigation. Office: 901 H St Ste 200 Sacramento CA 95814-1808 also: 1990 N California Blvd Walnut Creek CA 94596-3742 also: 1746 Grand Canal Blvd Ste 11 Stockton CA 95207-8111

**BROOKS, DAVID EUGENE,** lawyer; b. Chickasha, Okla., Apr. 14, 1953; s. Shirey Sherman and Joyce Faye Brooks; m. Victoria Lynn Ward, Aug. 11, 1973; children: Kristina Kaye, Leah Kathene, Stephen Sherman. BA, Southwestern Okla. State U., 1975; JD, U. Tulsa, 1978. Pvt. practice Chickasha, 1978-81; assoc. dist. judge State of Okla., Mangum, 1981-91; asst. dist. atty. State of Okla., Sayre, 1991-92; pvt. practice Sayre, 1992—. Pres. bd. Beckham County Law Libr., Sayre, 1996—. Mem. Beckham County Bar Assn. (pres. 1993), Kiwanis of Mangum (pres. 1984), Kiwanis of Sayre (pres. 1994), Masons (master). Methodist. Criminal, Family and matrimonial, General practice. Office: Brooks and Israel 119 E Main St Sayre OK 73662-2913

**BROOKS, GENE C.,** lawyer. BA, CUNY, 1971; MBA, NYU, 1975, JD, 1979. Bar: N.Y. 1980. Fin. analyst, regulations specialist Fed. Reserve Bank of N.Y., 1972-80; asst. counsel N.Y. State Banking Dept., 1980-83; assoc. Davis Polk Wardwell, 1983-84; dep. counsel Bank of Tokyo Trust Co.: Bank of Tokyo Ltd., N.Y. Agy., 1984-87; asst. gen. counsel, asst. sec. Anchor Savs. Bank, 1987-88, dep. gen. counsel, 1988-89; 1st sr. v.p., gen. counsel Anchor Savs. Bank, FSB, Hewlett, 1989-95; gen. counsel Dime Savs. Bank N.Y., N.Y.C., 1995-98, sr. legal advisor Office of the Sec., 1998—; also bd. dirs. General corporate, Securities, Finance. Office: Dime Savs Bank NY FSB 589 5th Ave New York NY 10017-1923

**BROOKS, JULIE ANNE,** lawyer; b. Portland, Oreg., Nov. 4, 1945; d. Ralph M. and Jessie (Aukema) B; m. Gerd B. Bode, Dec. 29, 1989. Student, U. Grenoble, France, 1969; BA, U. Wash., 1971; JD, U. Santa Clara, 1974; LLM, Georgetown U., 1981. Bar: Wash., U.S. Dist. Ct. (we. dist.) Wash., U.S. Ct. Claims, U.S. Tax Ct., U.S. Ct. Appeals (9th cir.), U.S. Supreme Ct. Assoc. Lane, Powell et al, Seattle, 1976-81; v.p., gen. counsel, asst. sec. Thousand Trails, Inc., Bellevue, Wash., 1981-86; v.p., gen. counsel, sec. Westmark Internat., Inc., 1986-92; of counsel Buck & Gordon, Seattle, 1992-93; pres. The Gen. Counsel, Inc., Seattle, 1993—. Mem. Leadership Tomorrow, 1989, chmn. screening com., mem. exec. com., bd. dirs., 1991-93; past assoc. council for arts; past mem. annual gifts com. Seattle Symphony; past trustee, past vice chmn. Bus. Vol. for Arts, Seattle; past trustee Seattle Opera Assn.; active Seattle Opera Guild, Jr. League; past trustee, past v.p. Seattle Children's Home, Pike Pl. Market PDA Coun., Seattle; mem. adv. bd. U. Wash. Meany Hall for Performing Arts, 1989—, co-chmn. devel. com., 1993—. Mem. ABA, Am. Corp. Coun. Assn. (mem. internat. law com., sec. law com.), Wash. State Bar Assn., Seattle King County Bar Assn. (exec. com. corp. coun. sect., chair newsletter com.), Wash. Women Lawyers Assn., Am. Soc. Corp. Secs. (securities law com.), Am. Resort and Residential Devel. Assn. (legis com. adv. bd. 1985-86, co-chmn. fed. tax task force 1985-86, others), Seattle Tennis Club, Wash. Athletic Club, City Club, Seattle Club, Rainier Club. General corporate, Securities, Public international. Home: 1630A 30th St # 481 Boulder CO 80301-1014 Office: The Gen Counsel 2802 E Madison St Ste 107 Seattle WA 98112-4841

**BROOKS, KERMITT JEROME,** lawyer; b. Flint, Mich., Mar. 19, 1964; s. Charles E. Sr. and Lillian Pearl Brooks. BA, Mich. State U., 1986; JD, U. Mich., 1989. Bar: N.Y., Conn., U.S. Supreme Ct., U.S. Ct. Appeals (2d cir.), U.S. Dist. Ct. (so. and ea. dists.) N.Y. Assoc. Nixon, Hargrave, Devans & Doyle LLP, N.Y.C., 1989-98; assoc. counsel Met. Life Ins. Co., N.Y.C., 1998—; mem. bd. visitors James Madison Coll., Mich. State U., East Lansing; treas. labor law sect. Nat. Bar Assn., Washington. Fax: 212-251-1530. E-mail: kermittbrooks@msn.com. and kbrooks1@metlife.com. General civil litigation, Contracts commercial, Labor. Office: MetLife One Madison Ave New York NY 10010

**BROOKS, LARRY ROGER,** judge; b. Oklahoma City, Mar. 8, 1949; s. Stanley James and Dorothy Marguerite (Miller) B.; m. Rebecca Jean Nix, June 5, 1971. BS in Agronomy, Okla. State U., 1971, MS in Agronomy, 1973; JD, U. Okla., 1976. Bar: Okla. 1976. Pvt. practice law Idabel, Okla., 1977; asst. dist. atty. Craig County Dist. Attys. Office, Vinita, Okla., 1978, Logan County Dist. Attys. Office, Guthrie, Okla., 1979-94; assoc. judge Dist. Ct., Logan County, Okla., 1995—. Ch. bd. mem. Guthrie (Okla.) Ch. of the Nazarene. mem. Okla. Bar Assn., Guthrie Lions Club (pres. 1991-92), Train Collectors Assn., Nat. Ry. Hist. Soc. Avocations: toy train and railroad memorabilia, railroad history, riding trains. Home: 324 N Capitol St Guthrie OK 73044-3640 Office: Assoc Dist Judge Logan County Courthouse Guthrie OK 73044

**BROOKS, PATRICK WILLIAM,** lawyer; b. Grinnell, Iowa, May 11, 1943; s. Mark Dana and Madge Ellen (Walker) B.; m. Mary Jane Davey, Dec. 17, 1966; children: Carolyn Walker, Mark William. BA, State Coll. Iowa, 1966; JD, U. Iowa, 1971. Bar: Iowa 1971, U.S. Dist. Ct. (so. dist.) Iowa 1972, U.S. dist. ct. (no. dist.) Iowa 1971, U.S. Sup. Ct. 1974, U.S. Ct. Apls. (8th cir.) 1979. Tchr., Waterloo (Iowa) Community Schs., 1966-68; mem. staff Donahue & Brooks, West Union, Iowa, 1971-72; ptnr. Mowry, Irvine, Brooks & Ward, Marshalltown, Iowa, 1972-84, 1992—, Brooks, Ward & Trout, Marshalltown, 1984-92. Mem. Fayette County (Iowa) Republican Central Com., chmn. platform resolutions com., 1971-72; pres. Marshall County (Iowa) Young Reps., 1974; trustee Iowa Law Sch. Found., 1970-71; bd. dirs. Iowa Hist. Found., 1991-96. Mem. Am. Judicature Soc., Iowa Bar Assn., Marshall County Bar Assn. (pres. 1985-86), Iowa Trial Lawyers Assn., Iowa Def. Counsel Assn. Lutheran. Clubs: Buick Am., Elks. Personal injury, Federal civil litigation, Insurance. Office: Box 908 6 W Main St Marshalltown IA 50158-4941

**BROOKS, ROBERT FRANKLIN, SR.,** lawyer; b. Richmond, Va., July 13, 1939; s. Robert Noel Brooks and Annie Mae (Edwards) Miles; m. Patricia Wilson, May 6, 1972; children: Robert Franklin Jr., Thomas Noel, Courtenay M. Brooks Rainey. BA, U. Richmond, 1961, M of Humanities, 1993; JD, 1964. Bar: Va. 1964, N.Y. 1985, U.S. Dist. Ct. (ea. and we. dists.) Va. 1964, U.S. Ct. Appeals (4th cir.) 1965, U.S. Ct. Appeals (5th cir.) 1972, (2d cir.) 1979, (11th cir.) 1981, D.C. 1977, U.S. Supreme Ct. 1979. Assoc. Hunton & Williams, Richmond, 1964-71, ptnr., 1971—; chmn. sect. II 3d Dist. Com., 1983; mem. rules evidence com. Supreme Ct. Va., 1984-85; mem. Fourth Cir. Judicial Conf. Trustee U. Richmond. Fellow ABA, Am. Coll. Trial Lawyers (com. atty.-client relationships 1983-91, chmn. Va. state com. 1993-94), Am. Bar Found., Va. Law Found.; mem. N.Y. Bar Assn., D.C. Bar Assn., Va. State Bar (coun. 1986—, bd. govs. litigation sect. 1984-90, sec. 1985-86, chmn. 1986-87, com. lawyer fin. responsibility 1986-89, nominating com. 1990, spl. com. election methods 1989, chmn. bench-bar rels. com. 1987-88, faculty professionalism course 1988-90, governance com. 1990-91), Richmond Bar Assn. (chmn. judiciary com. 1985-87, chmn. com. on unprofl. conduct 1979-80, com. on improvement of adminstrn. of justice 1981-84), Va. Bar Assn. (profl. responsibility com. 1981-84). Federal civil litigation, State civil litigation. Home: 500 Kilmarnock Dr Richmond VA 23229-8102 Office: Hunton & Williams Riverfront Plz East Tower 951 E Byrd St Ste 200 Richmond VA 23219-4074

**BROOKS, ROY LAVON,** law educator; b. New Haven; s. Freeman and Ruth (Andersen) B.; m. Penny Feller, May 9, 1970; children: Whitney Alison, Courtney Christine. BA, U. Conn., 1972; JD, Yale U., 1975. Bar: Pa. 1976, U.S. Dist. Ct. (ea. dist.) Pa. 1976, U.S. Ct. Appeals (3d cir.) 1976. Law clk. to presiding justice U.S. Dist. Ct. (ea. dist.) Pa., Phila., 1975-77; assoc. Cravath, Swaine & Moore, N.Y.C., 1977-79; prof. law U. San Diego, 1979—. Author law books; contbr. articles to profl. jours. Mem. ABA, Nat. Bar Assn., Fed. BAr Assn., Phi Kappa Phi, Heartland Human Rights Assn. (bd. dirs. 1985-87). Avocations: tennis, chess, reading. Office: U San Diego Alcala Park San Diego CA 92110-2429

**BROOKS, WILBUR CLINTON,** lawyer; b. Wilkes County, Ga., Apr. 9, 1927; s. Joseph Theodoric and Amrentha Josephine (McCurdy) B.; m. Vivian Maxwell, May 7, 1954; children: Wilbur Clinton, Nellie Margaret, Theo Carlton. LLB, U. Ga., 1951. Bar: Ga. 1951, U.S. Dist. Ct. (mid. and so. dists.) Ga. 1951, U.S. Dist. Ct. (no. dist.) Ga. 1972, U.S. Ct. Appeals (11th cir.) 1979, U.S. Supreme Ct. 1979. Adj. instr. Crawford & Co., Raleigh, N.C., 1951-52, Fayetteville, N.C., 1953-57; asst. mgr. Crawford & Co., Phila., 1957-59; mgr. Crawford & Co., Akron, Ohio, 1959-72; assoc. Henning, Chambers, Mabry, Atlanta, 1972-75; ptnr. Chambers, Mabry, McClelland & Brooks, Atlanta, 1975—; chief justice honor ct. U. Ga., Athens, 1950-51; bd. dirs. Ga. Def. Lawyers, 1984-87, sec., treas., 1988, pres., 1990. Bd. dirs. Jr. C. of C., Fayetteville, N.C., 1953, Optimist Club, Fayetteville, 1954; pres. Akron Assn. of Claims Men, 1967, Fairlawn Shrine Club, 1971. Petty officer 3rd class USN, 1945-46. Mem. ABA, DeKalb Bar Assn., Gwinette Bar Assn., Atlanta Bar Assn., Ga. Bar Assn., Masons, Shriners. Republican. Baptist. Product liability, Personal injury. Home: 2927 Bob White Dr Duluth GA 30096-3913 Office: Chambers Mabry McClelland & Brooks 2200 Century Pky NE Fl 10 Atlanta GA 30345-3103

**BROOKSHIRE, JAMES EARL,** lawyer; b. Statesville, N.C., Feb. 16, 1951; s. Earl and Opal (Isenhour) B.; m. Peggy Anne Price, July 31, 1971; children: Jonathan David, Mary Elizabeth. BA in History with honors, N.C. State U., 1973; JD, U. S.C., 1976. Bar: S.C. 1976, D.C. 1979, U.S. Ct. Appeals (4th cir.) 1979, U.S. Ct. Appeals (D.C. cir.) 1980, U.S. Supreme Ct. 1980, U.S. Claims Ct. 1982, U.S. Ct. Appeals (Fed. cir.) 1982. Trial atty. gen. litigation sect. U.S. Dept. Justice Land and Natural Resources Div., Washington, 1976-83, chief, Indian claims sect., 1983-85, dep. chief gen. litigation sect., 1985—; mem. dept. performance standard rev. bd., 1986—, Atty. Gen. Advocacy Inst., 1978-81, jud. conf. planning com. Fed. cir., Washington, 1983—, adv. coun. Claims Ct., Washington, 1983—, vice chmn., 1986—, mem. alternative dispute resolution com., past pres. Claims Ct. Bar Assn., 1988; mem. Claims Ct. Constitution Bicentennial com., 1987—; lectr. Legal Edn. Inst. Contbg. author: The United States Claims Court: A Deskbook for Practitioners, 1987, Claims Court and Federal Circuit Practice Handbook, 1986; co-author: Hospital Franchising Law and Regulation, 1979; editor: Environmental Quality Law, 1976. Councilman Luth Ch. of Abiding Presence, Springfield, Va., 1981-82, coun. chmn., 1982; pres. Interfaith Housing Ministries, 1988-89. Wig and Robe scholar U. S.C., 1975; recipient John Marshall award, 1987. Mem. ABA (nat. resources sect., environ. quality com.), S.C. Bar Assn., D.C. Bar Assn., Fed. Cir. Bar Assn. (constn. com., govt. contract appeals com., Indian claims com.), Ct. of Claims Bar. Club: Orange Hunt (Springfield). Avocations: astronomy, computer applications. Office: US Dept Justice 601 Pennsylvania Ave NW Apt 835 Washington DC 20004-2601

**BROOMAN, DAVID J.,** lawyer; b. Hackensack, N.J., Dec. 25, 1956; s. Bankston T. and Hildegard Brooman; m. Gardenia L. Brooman, July 26, 1958; children: David J., Richard W., Kyle M., Luke A. BA, Rutgers U., 1979; JD, Villanova U., 1982. Bar: Pa., U.S. Dist. Ct. (ea. and mid. dists.) Pa., N.J., U.S. Dist. Ct. N.J., U.S. Ct. Appeals (3d cir.). Ptnr. Cohen Shapiro Polisher Shiekman & Cohen, Phila., 1988-95, Drinker Biddle & Reath, Phila., 1995—. Bd. dirs. Delaware Valley Child Care Coun., Phila., 1986-94; v.p., bd. dirs. Pa. Resources Coun., Media, 1990-98. Named Outstanding Child Adv., Support Ctr. Child Advs., Phila., 1995. Environmental, Land use and zoning (including planning). Home: 71 Shawnee Rd Ardmore PA 19003-1640 Office: Drinker Biddle & Reath 1345 Chestnut St Ste 1300 Philadelphia PA 19107-3496

**BROOME, HENRY GEORGE, JR.,** lawyer; b. Atlantic City, N.J., Mar. 2, 1941; s. Henry George and Edith Gertrude (Shaw) B.; m. Patricia Ann Morrow, June 26, 1976; children: Henry George III, Christopher Shawn. AB, U. N.C., 1963, JD, 1966. Bar: N.J. 1967, D.C. 1978, U.S. Ct. Appeals (D.C. cir. 1967). Assoc. Frank S. Farley, Atlantic City, 1966-68; ptnr. Thomas & Broome, Atlantic City, 1969-73, Broome & Burro, Northfield, N.J., 1973—; asst. prosecutor Atlantic County, N.J., 1968-72; judge City of Pleasantville, N.J., 1975-81, City of Northfield, N.J., 1980—, City of Somers Point, N.J., 1978—, City of Absecon, N.J., 1980—, City of Atlantic, N.J., 1986-88, City of Ventnor, N.J., 1989—, City of Brigantine, N.J., 1991—, City of Longport, N.J., 1992—, Township of Mullica, N.J., 1992—; solicitor Linwood Zoning Bd., 1970—, Atlantic City Zoning Bd., 1970-80, Pleasantville Zoning Bd., 1971-72. Pres., Atlantic Area coun. Boy Scouts Am., 1982-85, mem. nat. coun., 1989; chmn. bd. deacons Margate Community Ch., trustee, 1981-84; pres., bd. dirs. ARC, 1993—; bd. dirs. Salvation Army. Awarded Chapel of Four Chaplains, Phila.; named one of 85 to watch in '85, Atlantic City Mag., 1985, Mainlander of Yr. Mainland C. of C., 1992; recipient Silver Beaver award Boy Scouts Am., 1984, Dist. Citizens award Atlantic Area BSA, 1987, Community Svc. award Salvation Army, award Humanist Soc., 1989; named one of Outstanding Young Men of Am. U.S. Ct. Appeals (D.C. cir.), 1971. Mem. ATLA, Am. Arbitration Assn., N.J. Bar Assn., Atlantic County Bar Assn. (past sec.), Downbeach Jaycees (pres. 1970-71), Delta Sigma Pi. Republican. Club: Atlantic City Exchange Club (pres. mcpl. judges assn. 1982; Golden Deeds award). Lodges: Masons, Shriners (past pres.), Kiwanis (pres.). State civil litigation, Estate planning, Personal injury. Office: PO Box 374 Northfield NJ 08225-0374

**BROOMFIELD, ROBERT CAMERON,** federal judge; b. Detroit, June 18, 1933; s. David Campbell and Mabel Margaret (Van Deventer) B.; m. Cuma Lorena Cecil, Aug. 3, 1958; children: Robert Cameron Jr., Alyson Paige, Scott McKinley. BS, Pa. State U., 1955; LLB, U. Ariz., 1961. Bar: Ariz. 1961, U.S. Dist. Ct. Ariz. 1961. Assoc. Carson, Messinger, Elliot, Laughlin & Ragan, Phoenix, 1962-65, ptnr., 1966-71; judge Ariz. Superior Ct., Phoenix, 1971-85; judge U.S. Dist. Ct. Ariz., Phoenix, 1985—, chief judge, 1994—; faculty Nat. Jud. Coll., Reno, 1975-82. Contbr. articles to profl. jours. Adv. bd. Boy Scouts Am., Phoenix, 1968-75; tng. com. Ariz. Acad., Phoenix, 1980—; pres. Paradise Valley Sch. Bd., Phoenix, 1969-70; bd. dirs. Phoenix Together, 1982—, Crisis Nursery, Phoenix, 1976-81; chmn. 9th Cir. Task Force on Ct. Reporting, 1988—; space and facilities com. U.S. Jud. Conf., 1987-93, chmn., 1989-93, chmn. security, space and facilities com., 1993-95, budget com., 1997—. Recipient Faculty award Nat. Jud. Coll., 1979, Disting. Jurist award Miss. State U., 1986. Mem. ABA (chmn. Nat. Conf. State Trial Judges 1983-84, pres. Nat. Conf. Met. Cts. 1978-79, chmn. bd. dirs. 1980-82, Justice Tom Clark award 1980, bd. dirs. Nat. Ctr. for State Cts. 1980-85, Disting. Svc. award 1986), Ariz. Bar Assn., Maricopa County Bar Assn. (Disting. Pub. Svc. award 1980), Ariz. Judges Assn. (pres. 1981-82), Am. Judicature Soc. (spl. citation 1985), Maricopa County Med. Soc. (Disting. Svc. medal 1979). Lodge: Rotary. Office: US Dist Ct US Courthouse & Fed Bldg 230 N 1st Ave Ste 7025 Phoenix AZ 85025-0008

**BROOTEN, KENNETH EDWARD, JR.,** retired lawyer; b. Kirkland, Wash., Oct. 17, 1942; s. Kenneth Edward Sr. and Sadie Josephine (Assad) B.; m. Patricia Anne Folsom, Aug. 29, 1965 (div. Apr. 1986); children: Michelle Catherine, Justin Kenneth. Diploma Lewis Sch. Hotel, Restaurant and Club Mgmt., Washington, 1963; student, U. Md., 1964-66; AA, Santa Fe C.C., Gainesville, Fla., 1969; BS in Journalism with highest honors, U. Fla., 1971, MA in Journalism and Communications with highest honors, 1972, JD with honors, 1975; law student, U. Idaho, 1972-73; diploma in internat. law, Polish Acad. Scis., Warsaw, 1974; postgrad., Cambridge (Eng.) U., Eng., 1974. Bar: Fla., D.C., U.S. Dist. Ct. (no., mid. and so. dists.) Fla., U.S. Dist. Ct. D.C., U.S. Tax Ct., U.S. Ct. Appeals (5th, 9th, 11th and D.C. circs.), U.S. Supreme Ct., Trial Counsel Her Majesty's Govt. of United Kingdom. Asst. to several congressmen U.S. Ho. of Reps., Washington, 1962-67; adminstrv. asst. VA Cen. Office, Washington, 1967; adminstrv. officer VA Hosp., Gainesville, Fla., 1967-72; ptnr. Carter & Brooten, P.A., Gainesville, Fla., 1975-78, Brooten & Fleisher, Chartered, Washington and Gainesville, Fla., 1978-80; pvt. practice, Washington and Gainesville, 1980-86, Washington, 1987-88, Washington and Orlando, Fla., 1988-91, Washington and Winter Park, Fla., 1991-98; ret., 1998; permanent spl. counsel, acting chief counsel, dir. Select Com. Assassinations U.S. Ho. of Reps., 1976-77; counsel Her Majesty's Govt. of U.K. (in U.S.). Author: Malpractice Guide to Avoidance and Treatment, 1987; episode writher TV series Simon and Simon; nat. columnist Pvt. Practice, 1988-90, Physicians Mgmt., 1991-93; commentator Med. News Network, 1993-94; contbr. more than 200 articles to profl. jours. Served with USCGR, 1960-68. Named one of Outstanding Young Men Am., U.S. Jaycees, 1977. Mem. Fla. Bar Assn., D.C. Bar Assn., Am. Coll. Legal Medicine, Sigma Delta Chi. Roman Catholic. Avocations: writing, marksmanship, dangerous game hunting. Family and matrimonial, Public international, Federal civil litigation. Address: PO Box 390 Marianna FL 32447

**BROPHY, GILBERT THOMAS,** lawyer; b. Southampton, N.Y., July 15, 1926; s. Joseph Lester and Helen Veronica (Scholtz) B.; m. Canora Woodham Brophy, Sept. 3, 1957; m. Isabel Blair Porter; children: Laure Porter Thompson, Erin Brophy Caraballo. BS in Acctg. with high honors, U. Fla., 1949; LLB, George Washington U., 1960; postgrad., U. Miami, 1970-73. Bar: Fla. 1960, U.S. Supreme Ct. 1965, U.S. Dist. Ct. D.C. 1970, D.C. 1974. Title examiner Jesse Phillips Klinge & Kendrick, Arlington, Va., 1959-60; ptnr. Beall, Beall & Brophy, Palm Beach, Fla., 1962-65; asst. city atty. West Palm Beach, Fla., 1965-67; ptnr. Brophy & Skrandel, Palm Beach, 1968-70, Brophy & Aksomitas, Tequesta, Fla., 1974-75, Brophy, Genovese & Sayler, Jupiter, Fla., 1977-78, Brophy & Genovese, 1978-83; town atty. Lantana, Fla., 1967-70; judge ad litem Village of Tequesta, 1970-72; town atty. Jupiter, 1974-75. Bd. dirs., disaster chmn. ARC, Palm Beach; past corr. sec. Palm Beach County Hist. Soc.; del. Fla. Caucus for Presidency, 1979, 87; mem. Rep. Com. Martin County, 1984-87. With AUS, 1944-46, ETO, 1951-54, Japan and Korea. Recipient Dedicated Svc. plaque Town of Jupiter, 1975. Mem. NRA (endowment), Nat. CIC Assn., Assn. Former Intelligence Officers (life), Attys. Title Ins. Fund, Fla. Bar Assn., Palm Beach County Bar Assn., Attys. Bar Assn. Palm Beach County, Rotary Club (pres. 1977-78, dist. 6930 ethics chair-4 way test, Paul Harris fellow), Univ. Club (Washington), Elks, Everglades Rifle and Pistol Club (hon. life), Kappa Sigma Alumni. Family and matrimonial, General practice, Probate. Home: 717 S US Highway 1-504 Jupiter FL 33477-5905 Office: 810 Saturn St Ste 16 Jupiter FL 33477-4398

**BROPHY, THOMAS ANDREW,** lawyer; b. Phila., Apr. 24, 1952; s. Joseph Aloysius and Berenice (Trainor) B.; m. Anne Corr, Oct. 4, 1975; children: Colleen, Patricia, Jessica, Mary Elizabeth, Anne. BA in English, U. Dayton, 1974; JD, Temple U., 1981. Bar: Pa. 1982, U.S. Dist. Ct. (ea. dist.) Pa. 1982, U.S. Ct. Appeals (3d cir.) 1982. Assoc. Marshall, Dennehy, Warner, Coleman & Goggin, Phila., 1982-87, ptnr., 1987—. Author: How to Evaluate and Settle Personal Injury Cases, 1989; contbr. articles to law rev. Athletic coach St. Monica's Track Club, Berwyn, Pa., 1991-92, 92-93. Mem. Phila. Bar Assn., Montgomery Bar Assn. Roman Catholic. Avocations: reading, track and field. Personal injury, Product liability, Professional liability. Home: 265 Keller Rd Berwyn PA 19312-1449 Office: Marshall Dennehy Warner Ste 1002 One Montgomery Pla Norristown PA 19401

**BRORBY, WADE,** federal judge; b. 1934. BS, U. Wyo., 1956, JD with honor, 1958. Bar: Wyo. County and prosecuting atty. Campbell County, Wyo., 1963-70; ptnr. Morgan Brorby Price and Arp, Gillette, Wyo., 1961-88; judge U.S. Ct. Appeals (10th cir.), Cheyenne, Wyo., 1988—. With USAF, 1958-61. Mem. ABA, Campbell County Bar Assn., Am. Judicature Soc., Def. Lawyers Wyo., Wyo Bar Assn. (commr. 1968-70). Office: US Ct Appeals 10th Cir O'Mahoney Fed Bldg Rm 2018 PO Box 1028 Cheyenne WY 82003-1028

**BROSEMAN, GEORGE W.,** lawyer; b. Ridgewood, N.J., July 27, 1965; s. George F. and Ruth A. (Brokaw) B. BS, Susquehanna U., 1987; JD, Villanova U., 1991. Bar: Pa. 1991. Shareholder Fromhold & Jaffe, Rosemont, Pa., 1991—. Mem. Bryn Mawr Rotary (dir., past pres.). Land use and zoning (including planning), Real property. Office: Fromhold & Jaffe 919 Conestoga Rd Bldg 2 Bryn Mawr PA 19010-1352

**BROSKY, JOHN G.,** judge; b. Scott Twp., Pa., Aug. 4, 1920; m. Rose F. Brosky, June 24, 1950; children: John C., Carol Ann, David J. BA, U. Pitts., 1942, LLB, 1949, JD, 1968, D Pub. Svc. (hon.) La Roche Coll., Pa., 1996. Bar: Pa. 1950. Asst. county solicitor, Allegheny County, Pa., 1951-56; judge County Ct. Allegheny County, 1956-61; adminstrv. judge family div. Common Pleas Ct. Allegheny County, 1961-80; judge Superior Ct. Pa., 1980—; mem. faculty Pa. Coll. Judiciary. Chmn. Operation Patrick Henry, Boy Scouts Am.; pres. Scott Twp. Sch. Bd., 1946-56; 1st pres. Chartiers Valley Joint Sch. Dist., Allegheny County, Pa.; pres. Greater Pitts. Guild for Blind. Served with U.S. Army, 1942-46; maj. gen. (ret.) USAF-Pa. Air N.G. Recipient Disting. Jud. Service award Pa., Mason Juvenile Ct. Inst., Man of Yr. award in law Pitts. Jr. C. of C., 1960, Humanitarian award New Light Men's Club, 1960, Loyalty Day award VFW, 1960, Four Chaplains award, 1965; Man of Yr. award Cath. War Vets., 1960, 62; Service award Alliance Coll.; Disting. Citation, Mil. Order World Wars; Humanitarian award Variety Club, 1974; Jimmy Doolittle fellow award Aerospace Edn. Found., 1975; Pa. Meritorious Service medal Pa. N.G., 1976; State Humanitarian award Domestic Relations Assn. Pa., 1978; Man of Yr. award Am. Legion, 1978; Pa. Disting. Service medal; Disting. Service award Pa. N.G. Assn., 1980; Exceptional Service award USAF, 1982; General Ira Eaker fellow, 1981; Brotherhood of Man award Fraternal Socs. of Greater Pitts., 1987; Community Service award Chartiers Valley Commn. on Human Relations, 1988, George Washington Honor medal Freedoms Found., 1990; named Pitts. Polonian of Yr., 1988; recipient St. Thomas More award Allegheny County Bar Assn., 1989, Man of Yr. award Kosciuszko Found., 1991, Vectors/Pitts., 1994, Gen. John G. Brosky Day Pride in Pa. award, 1995. Mem. Am. Judicature Soc., ABA, Pa. Bar Assn. (co-chmn. professionalism com. 1987-88), Assn. Trial Lawyers Am., Inst. Jud. Adminstrn., Inc., Internat. Platform Assn., Air Force Assn. (nat. dir., nat. pres., chmn. bd., presidential citation 1974, 80, 81), Am. Acad. Matrimonial Lawyers, N.G. Assn. of Pa. (pres.), Pa. Conf. State Trial Judges (past pres.), Pa. Joint Family Law Council. Clubs: Press, Variety, Aero (past pres.) (Pitts.). Office: 2703 Grant Bldg Pittsburgh PA 15219-2302

**BROSSEIT, A. KIMBERLY ROCKWELL,** lawyer; b. Atlanta, Mar. 22, 1968; d. Ramon Richard and Alice (Scott) Rockwell; m. Brett Anthony Brosseit, Aug. 17, 1996. BA, Bryn Mawr Coll., 1990; JD with high honors, Fla. State U., 1996. Bar: Fla. 1996, D.C. 1998, Del. 1998. Atty. Treiser Koloza & Volpe, Chartered, Naples, Fla., 1996-97, Duane Morris & Hecksher LLP, Wilmington, Del., 1998—. Mentor Quest for Kids, Naples, 1997; grad. Leadership Del. 1998; pro-bono counsel Ctrl. Del. Habitat for Humanity, 1999—. Land use and zoning (including planning), Real property. Office: Duane Morris & Hecksher LLP 1201 Market St Ste 1500 Wilmington DE 19801-1802

**BROSTRON, JUDITH CURRAN,** lawyer; b. Chgo., Feb. 2, 1950; d. Norman William and Marianne Cecelia (Baron) Curran; m. Kenneth C. Brostron, Nov. 22, 1989. Diploma Nursing, Evanston (Ill.) Hosp., 1971; BA, Nat. Coll. Edn., Evanston, 1981; JD, Chgo.-Kent Coll. Law, 1985; LLM, St. Louis U., 1999. Bar: Mo. 1985, U.S. Dist. Ct. (ea. dist.) Mo. 1985, Ill. 1986. Staff nurse Evanston Hosp., 1971-78, St. Francis Hosp., Evanston, Ill., 1979-81; assoc. Lashly & Baer, P.C., St. Louis, 1985-91, ptnr., 1991—. Mem. ABA, Am. Assn. Nurse Attys., Am. Soc. Law Medicine, Mo. Bar Assn., Ill. Bar Assn. Avocations: running, golf, gardening. Personal injury, Administrative and regulatory, Health. Office: Lashly & Baer P C 714 Locust St Saint Louis MO 63101-1699

**BROTHERS, D. DOUGLAS,** lawyer; b. Princeton, N.J., Mar. 29, 1955; s. Dwight Stanley and Sue (Coker) B.; m. Lynne Marie Rupp, Oct. 1, 1988; children: Dwight Samuel, Robert William. AB, Amherst Coll., 1978; JD, U. Tex., 1981. Bar: Tex. 1981, U.S. Dist. Ct. (we., so. and no. dist.) Tex., U.S. Ct. Appeals (5th cir.). Assoc. Leonard Koehn & Kurt, Dallas, 1981-84; ptnr. Leonard Koehn & Kurt, Austin, 1984-85, Brothers, Reavis & McGinnis, Austin, 1985-92, Brothers & Assocs., Austin, 1992-96, Brothers & Thomas, Austin, 1996—. General civil litigation, Labor, Personal injury. Office: Brothers and Thomas 650 Norwood Twr 114 W 7th St Austin TX 78701-3000

**BROTHERTON, ALLEN C.,** lawyer; b. Gastonia, N.C., Apr. 30, 1960; s. Curtis Gray and Ann McIntosh B.; m. Jody Lynn Haynes, Oct. 19, 1985; children: Haynes Allen, John Gray. BA, U. N.C., 1982, JD, 1985. Bar: N.C. 1985, U.S. Dist. Ct. (we., mid. and ea. dists.) N.C. 1985, U.S. Ct. Appeals (4th cir.) 1985, U.S. Ct. Appeals N.C. 1985, U.S. Supreme Ct. 1985. Ptnr. Knox, Knox, Freeman & Brotherton, Charlotte and Cornelius, N.C., 1985—. Morehead scholar Morehead Found., 1978-82. Mem. N.C. Acad. Trial Lawyers, Phi Eta Sigma. Criminal, Personal injury, General civil litigation. Office: Knox Knox Freeman & Brotherton PO Box 30848 Charlotte NC 28230-0848

**BROTMAN, STANLEY SEYMOUR,** federal judge; b. Vineland, N.J., July 27, 1924; s. Herman Nathaniel and Fanny (Melletz) B.; m. Suzanne M. Simon, Sept. 9, 1951; children: Richard A., Alison B. BA, Yale U., 1947; LLB, Harvard U., 1950. Bar: N.J. 1950, D.C. 1951. Pvt. practice Vineland, 1952-57; ptnr. Shapiro, Brotman, Eisenstat & Capizola, Vineland, 1957-75; judge U.S. Dist. Ct. N.J., Camden, 1975—; acting chief judge Dist. Ct. of V.I., 1989-92; mem. N.J. Bd. Bar Examiners, 1970-74. Chmn. editl. bd. N.J. State Bar Jour, 1969-74; contbr. articles to profl. jours. Trustee Newcomb Hosp., Vineland, 1953-68; v.p. Fed. Judges Assn., 1993-97. With U.S. Army, 1943-45, 51-52. Fellow Am. Bar Found., Jud. Conf. U.S. (space and facilities com. 1987-93); mem. ABA (ho. of dels. 1975-80, state del. 1982-93), Nat. Conf. Fed. Trial Judges (exec. com. 1984-87, chmn.-elect 1986-87, chmn. 1987-88, chmn. standing com. jud. selection, tenure and compensation 1988-92, chmn. steering com. of nominating com. 1992-93, standing com. Fed. Jud. Improvements 1992-96), Am. Judicature Soc. (dir. 1995—), ABA Judicial Immigration Edn. Proj. (chmn. adv. com. 1996—), Fed. Bar Assn., N.J. State Bar Assn. (pres. 1974-75), Cumberland County Bar Assn. (pres. 1969-70), Assn. of Fed. Bar of State of N.J., Harvard U. Law Sch. Assn. N.J. (pres. 1974-75), Fed. Judges Assn. (v.p. 1993-97), Yale U. Alumni Assn., Am. Legion, Jewish War Vets., Yale Club, B'nai B'rith, Masons, Shriners. Office: MH Cohen US Courthouse 1 John F Gerry Plz PO Box 1029 Camden NJ 08101-1029

**BROUDE, MARK ALLEN,** lawyer; b. Skokie, Ill., June 26, 1964; s. Richard F. and Paula G. Broude; m. Susan Zuckerman, Mar. 21, 1992; 1 child, Jacob. BA, Williams Coll., 1986; JD, U. Chgo., 1989. Bar: N.Y. 1990, U.S. Dist. Ct. (so. dist.) N.Y. 1992. Assoc. Shearman & Sterling, N.Y.C., 1989-92; from assoc. to ptnr. Schulte Roth & Zabel LLP, N.Y.C., 1992—. Contbr. articles to profl. jours. Mem. ABA, N.Y. State Bar Assn., Internat. Bar Assn., Assn. Bar City N.Y. Bankruptcy, Banking, Contracts commercial. Office: Schulte Roth & Zabel LLP 900 3d Ave New York NY 10022

**BROUS, THOMAS RICHARD,** lawyer; b. Fulton, Mo., Jan. 7, 1943; s. Richard Pendleton and Augusta (Gilpin) B.; m. Patricia Catlin, Sept. 12, 1964; children: Anna Catlin Brous, Joel Pendleton Brous. BSBA, Northwestern U., 1965; JD cum laude, U. Mich., 1968. Bar: Mo. 1968, U.S. Dist. Ct. (we. dist.) Mo. 1968, U.S. Ct. Mil. Appeals 1968, U.S. Supreme Ct. 1971. Assoc. Watson & Marshall L.C., Kansas City, Mo., 1968-78, ptnr., 1978-96, mng. ptnr., 1992-94; shareholder Stinson, Mag & Fizzell, P.C., Kansas City, Mo., 1996—; mem. steering com. U. Mo. Kansas City Law Sch. Employee Benefits Inst., 1990—, chmn. 1992-93; mid-states key dist. EP/EO coun. IRS, 1997—. Author: Chapter 26, III Missouri Business Organizations, 1998; asst. editor Mich. Law Rev., 1966-68. Mem. vestry St. Andrews Episcopal Ch., Kansas City, 1974-77, Grace & Holy Trinity Cathedral, 1994—, chancellor, 1998—; trustee Mo. Repertory Theatre, Inc., Kansas City, 1990—, pres., 1995-98; v.p., treas. Barstow Sch., Kansas City, 1982-86; dir. Met. Orgn. to Counter Sexual Abuse, Kansas City, 1992-95. Capt. U.S. Army, 1968-72. Mem. ABA, Univ. Club (pres. 1988-89), Greater Kansas City Soc. Hosp. Attys., Kansas City Met. Bar Assn., Heart of Am. Employee Benefit Conf., The Mo. Bar Assn. (vice-chair employee benefits com. 1997—), Mo. Soc. Hosp. Attys., Delta Upsilon, Beta Gamma Sigma. Episcopalian. Avocations: reading, hiking, gardening. Pension, profit-sharing, and employee benefits, Health, General corporate. Office: Stinson Mag & Fizzell PC PO Box 419251 Kansas City MO 64141-6251

**BROUSSARD, PETER O.,** lawyer; b. Houston, Feb. 15, 1961; s. Onesephor P. and Yvonne E. Broussard; m. Roslyn Tene Hubert, Dec. 24, 1985; children: Fallon Tene, Meagon Yvonne. BS in Chemistry, Tex. So. U., 1984; BSChemE, Rice U., 1984; JD, U. Houston, 1993. Bar: Tex. Sr. process engr. Hoechst Celanese Chem. Group, Houston, 1988-92; assoc. gen. counsel Hoechst Celanese Corp., Bridgewater, N.J., 1993-95, Charlotte, N.C., 1995-98; assoc. gen. counsel Celanese, Dallas, 1998—. Dir. Sharonview Fed. Credit Union, Charlotte, 1997-98. Mem. ABA, Dallas Bar Assn. Avocations: golf, reading. Contracts commercial, General corporate, Family and matrimonial. Office: Celanese 1601 Lbj Fwy Dallas TX 75234-6034

**BROVITZ, RICHARD STUART,** lawyer; b. Rochester, N.Y., Aug. 20, 1951; s. Murray H. and Rifka R. (Rotenberg) B.; m. Joan F. Zarkower, Aug. 11, 1974; children—Justin, Jessica. B.S. cum laude with honors in Acctg., Sch. Mgmt., Syracuse U., 1973, M.S., 1973, J.D. cum laude, Coll. Law, 1976. Bar: N.Y. 1977, U.S. Dist. Ct. (we. dist.) N.Y. 1977, U.S. Tax Ct. 1979. Assoc. Wegman, Mayberry, Burgess & Feldstein, Rochester, 1977-79; assoc. Fix Spindelman, Turk, Himelein & Shukoff, Rochester, 1979-81, ptnr., 1982—, mng. principal, 1985—. Pi Mu Epsilon math. scholar Syracuse U. Mem. ABA, N.Y. State Bar Assn., Monroe County Bar Assn. (chmn. Rochester life underwriters com.), Justinian Hon. Law Soc., Beta Gamma Sigma, Beta Alpha Psi, Phi Kappa Phi. Estate planning, Real property, General corporate. Office: Fix Spindelman Brovitz Turk Himelein & Shukoff Two State St Rochester NY 14614

**BROWDY, JOSEPH EUGENE,** lawyer; b. Bklyn., July 23, 1937; s. Philip and Fannie (Asherowitz) B.; m. Anita Sue Rubenstein, June 18, 1958; childrenF: Jennifer, Daniel. BA, Oberlin Coll., 1958; LLB, NYU, 1961. Bar: N.Y. 1962, D.C. 1982. Assoc. Paul, Weiss, Rifkind, Wharton & Garrison, N.Y.C., 1962-71, ptnr., 1972-97, of counsel, 1998—; adj. asst. prof. real estate NYU, 1976-86; lectr. in field. With U.S. Army Res., 1961-62. Mem. Assn. of Bar of City of N.Y. (com. real property law, chmn. subcom. on leasing 1989-92), Am. Coll. Real Estate Lawyers, Order of Coif, Phi Beta Kappa. Real property. Office: Paul Weiss Rifkind Wharton & Garrison 1285 Avenue of the Americas New York NY 10019-6065

**BROWER, DAVID JOHN,** lawyer, urban planner, educator; b. Holland, Mich., Sept. 11, 1930; s. John J. and Helen (Olson) B.; m. Lou Ann Brown, Nov. 26, 1960; children: Timothy Seth, David John, II, Ann Lacey. B.A., U. Mich., 1956, J.D., 1960. Bar: Ill. 1960, Mich. 1961, Ind. 1961, U.S. Supreme Ct. 1971. Asst. dir. div. community planning Ind. U., Bloomington, 1960-70; rsch. prof. dept. city and regional planning U. N.C., Chapel Hill, 1970—, assoc. dir. Ctr. for Urban and Regional Studies, 1970-94; pres. Coastal Resources Collaborative, Ltd., Chapel Hill and Manteo, N.C., 1980—; counsel Robinson & Cole, Hartford, Conn., 1986—; vis. prof., Vt. Law Sch., South Royalton, summers, 1994—. Author: (with others) Constitutional Issues of Growth Management, 1978; Growth Management, 1984, Managing Development in Small Towns, 1984, Special Area Management, 1985, Catastrophic Coastal Storms, 1989, Understanding Growth Management, 1989, Coastal Zone Management: An Evaluation, 1991, An Introduction to Coastal Zone Management, 1994, Natural Hazard Mitication, 1999. Mem. Am. Planning Assn. (bd. dirs. 1982-85, chmn.-founder planning and law div. 1978, co-chmn. substainable devel. group 1995—), Am. Inst. Cert. Planners. Democrat. Episcopalian. Environmental, Land use and zoning (including planning). Home: 612 Shadylawn Rd Chapel Hill NC 27514-2009 Office: U NC CB # 3140 Chapel Hill NC 27599-3140

**BROWER, JOSHUA CHRISTOPHER ALLEN,** lawyer; b. Boston, Oct. 2, 1965; s. Robert Samuel and Donna (Romero) B.; m. Erin Elizabeth Allen, Aug. 1, 1993; 1 child, Owen Samuel. BA, Hampshire Coll., 1988; JD, Seattle U., 1995. Bar: Wash. 1995, U.S. Dist. Ct. (we. dist.) Wash. 1995. Assoc. Law Office of James C. Middlebrooks, Seattle, 1995-96, Preg, O'Donnell, Sargeant & Gillett, Seattle, 1996—. Contbr. articles to profl. jours. Appellate, Real property, Land use and zoning (including planning). Office: Preg O'Donnell Sargeant & Gillett 1215 4th Ave Ste 920 Seattle WA 98161-1008

**BROWN, ALAN CRAWFORD,** lawyer; b. Rockford, Ill., May 12, 1956; s. Gerald Crawford and Jane Ella (Herzberger) B.; m. Dawn Lestrud, Apr. 16, 1998; children: Parker Crawford, Sydney Danielle, Sarah Kate, Drew Kristen. BA magna cum laude, Miami U., Oxford, Ohio, 1978; JD with honors, U. Chgo., 1981. Bar: Ill. 1981, U.S. Dist. Ct. (no. dist.) Ill. 1981, U.S. Tax Ct. 1986. Assoc. Kirkland & Ellis, Chgo., 1981-87; sr. assoc. Coffield Ungaretti Harris & Slavin, Chgo., 1987-89; ptnr. McDermott, Will & Emery, Chgo., 1989—. Deacon Northminster Presbyn. Ch., Evanston, Ill., 1989-92; apiarist Chgo. Botanic Garden, Glencoe, Ill., 1988-97. Mem. Order of Coif, Phi Beta Kappa. Estate planning, Probate, Estate taxation. Office: McDermott Will & Emery 227 W Monroe St Ste 3100 Chicago IL 60606-5096

**BROWN, ANNA L.,** lawyer; b. London; came to the U.S., 1977; d. Edgar A. and Clara J. Brown. BS in Criminology, Fla. State U., 1992; JD, U. Fla., 1995. Bar: Fla. 1995, U.S. Dist. Ct. (mid. dist.) Fla. 1997. Asst. state atty. State Atty., Naples, Fla., 1995-97; in-house counsel IRM, Inc., Naples, 1997-98; pvt. practice law Naples, 1998—; sec. Collier County Womens Bar Assn., Naples; mem. Fla. New Motor Vehicle Arbitration bd., 1999-00. Office: 1100 5th Ave S Ste 201 Naples FL 34102-6407

**BROWN, AVERY R.,** lawyer; b. N.Y.C., Sept. 19, 1964; s. Martin and Danielle D. B. BS in Econ., U. Pa., 1986; JD, UCLA, 1989. Bar: Calif. 1989, U.S. Dist. Ct. (cen. dist.) Calif. 1989, U.S. Ct. Appeals (9th cir.) 1989. Assoc. O'Melveny & Myers, L.A., 1989-97, ptnr., 1998—. Mem. Order of Coif. General corporate, Mergers and acquisitions. Office: O'Melveny & Myers 400 S Hope St Fl 15 Los Angeles CA 90071-2899

**BROWN, BAILEY,** federal judge; b. Memphis, June 16, 1917; s. Joshua Goodlett and Lillian (Pearcy) B.; m. Doris Frances Lawhorn., Dec. 24, 1964; 1 son, Bailey, Jr. A.B., U. Mich., 1939; LL.B., Harvard U., 1942. Bar: Tenn. 1941. Ptnr. Burch, Porter, Johnson & Brown, Memphis, 1946-61; judge U.S. Dist. Ct. (we. dist.) Tenn., Memphis, 1961-79, chief judge, 1966-79; judge (6th cir.) U.S. Ct. Appeals, 1979-98; mem. Jud. Conf. Com. on Ct. Adminstrn., 1969-75, 78-84; past chmn. Subcom. on Judicial Improvements; past mem. ad hoc com. studying Cameras in the Courtroom; guest lectr. Rhodes Coll., Memphis. Pres. Memphis Symphony, 1958-60, Memphis Pub. Affairs Forum, 1955. Lt. USNR, 1942-46. Recipient Charles A. Rond Outstanding Judge of Yr. award Young Lawyers Memphis and Shelby County Bar Assns., 1977. Mem. Memphis Bar Assn. (Lawyer's Lawyer award 1996) Shelby County Bar Assn. (Liberty Bell award 1971, Ann. Dedication and Achievement award Criminal Law Sect. 1979). Episcopalian (vestryman). Home: 115 Morning Side Pl Memphis TN 38104-3037

**BROWN, BAIRD,** lawyer; b. West Chester, Pa., Jan. 9, 1947; s. Charles K. III and Ellen M. Brown; m. Carol Hadley, June 8, 1969; children: Hannah Brown Marzynski, Eliza. AB, SUNY, Buffalo, 1973; JD, U. Pa., 1978. Bar: D.C. 1978, Pa. 1980. Atty. Gen. Counsel Office, Fed. Res. Bd., Washington, 1977-80; assoc. Schnader Harrison Segal & Lewis, Phila., 1980-86, Ballard Spahr Andrews & Ingersoll, Phila., 1986-87; ptnr. Ballard Spahr, Phila., 1987—; rep. Globalaw, 1998; course chmn. ALI-ABA Course on Mcpl. Solid Waste Law, 1987-90. Truste Friends Select Sch., Phila., 1981—, Internat. Visitors Coun., Phila., 1992—; v.p. Fair Hill Burial Ground Corp., Phila., 1993—. Recipient Citizen Diplomat award Internat. Visitors Coun., 1996; participant Leadership, Inc., Phila., 1988-89. Mem. ABA, Internat. Bar Assn., Pa. Bar Assn., Phila. Bar Assn., D.C. Bar Assn., Pyramid Club. Democrat. Quaker. Avocations: gardening, carpentry, economics, rollerblading. Construction, FERC practice, Private international. Office: Ballard Spahr 1735 Market St Fl 51 Philadelphia PA 19103-7501

**BROWN, BARBARA FLETCHER,** lawyer; b. Hartford, Conn., Oct. 20, 1937; d. Irving Abner and Frances Edith Fletcher; m. John Wilson brown, June 7, 1959; children: Alison Hilary, Meredith Leslie. Student, Wells Coll., Aurora, N.Y., 1955-57; BA with honors and distinction, St. Joseph Coll., West Hartford, Conn., 1959; JD, U. San Diego, 1976. Bar: Calif. 1977, U.S. Dist. Ct. (so. dist.) 1977, U.S. Ct. Appeals (9th cir.) 1977. Asst. U.S. atty. U.S. Atty.'s Office-So. Dist. Calif., San diego, 1977-80; assoc. Brennan LaRocque, Rancho Bernardo, Calif., 1980-81; ptnr. LaRocque Brown & Campbell, Rancho Bernardo, 1981-83; sole practitioner La Jolla, Calif., 1983-87; ptnr. Brown & Brown, San Diego, 1988—; judge pro tem San Diego County SuperiorCt., 1986-89, 91-94. Bd. dirs. Legal Aid Soc. San diego, 1978-81. Mem. AAUW, San Diego County Bar Assn. (exec. com. 1986-89, 91-94, rec. sec. 1987-91), State Bar Calif. (mem. com. on fed. cts. 1978-81), Lawyers Club of San Diego (bd. dirs. 1978-80, pres. 1980-81, adv. bd. 1986-88), Calif. Women Lawyers (bd. dirs. and exec. com. 1980-82), San Diego Trial Lawyers Assn., La Jolla Rotary Club. Family and matrimonial. Office: Brown & Brown 4370 La Jolla Village Dr San Diego CA 92122-1249

**BROWN, BONNIE MARYETTA,** lawyer; b. North Plainfield, N.J., Oct. 31, 1953; d. Robert Jeffrey and Diana (Parket) B. AB, Washington U., St. Louis, 1975; JD, U. Louisville, 1978. Bar: Ky. 1978, U.S. Dist. Ct. (we. dist.) Ky. 1979, U.S. Dist. Ct. (ea. dist.) Ky. 1993. Pvt. practice Louisville, 1978—; of counsel Morris, Garlove, Waterman and Johnson PLLC, 1998—; lectr., seminar leader various profl., ednl., govtl. and civic groups; cons. marital rape; registered lobbyist 1994 Ky. Gen. Assembly for Ky. Assn. Marriage and Family Therapy. Editor Ky. Appellate Handbook, 1985; contbr. articles to profl. jours. Vol. legal panel Ky. Civil Liberties Union, Louisville, 1984—; author, chief lobbyist Marital Rape Bill, Ky. Coalition Against Rape and Sexual Assault, 1982—, Sexual Harassment bill, 1996; vol. advisor Louisville RAPE Relief Ctr., 1975—; treas. Family Support Group/ Family Readiness Program. of USAR, 1994-96, 3d Bat., 2nd. bge, 87th divsn., 1996-99, acting coord. 10th bat., 6th bge, 100th divsn. Recipient Cert. Spl. Recognition RAPE Relief Ctr., 1980, Cert. Outstanding Contbn., Louisville YMCA, 1983, Cert. of Appreciation, James Graham Brown Cancer Ctr., 1984, Decade of Svc. award YMCA/Rape Relief Ctr., Outstanding Victim Adv. award Fayette County Govt., 1990, cert. of Recognition Jefferson County Family Ct., 1995. Mem. ABA (family law sect., apptd. to appellate handbook com., jud. adminstrn. divsn. lawyers conf.), Am. Acad. Matrimonial Lawyers, Ky. Bar Assn. (family law sect. vice-chair 1994-95, chair-elect 1995-96, chair 1996-97, seminar spkr., task force solo practitioners and small law firms 1992, chair subcom. on law office automation and networking, solo practitioner and small Law Firm sect. chmn. elect 1998-99, chmn. 1999—, CLE award 1981, 93, 97, 98, 99), Louisville Bar Assn. (liaison to mental health sect., organizer marital rape seminar, chmn. family law sect., mediation com. property divsn., seminar spkr., organizer joint custody child abuse seminars, solo practitioner and small law firm sect., chair 1995, pro bono consortium), Ky. Acad. Trial Attys. (spkr. seminar, editor The Advocate family law sect. 1995-99), Bus. and Profl. Women (pres. River City chpt.), Ky. Fedn. (legis. chair 1986-87, 90-92, legal counsel 1992, 96, 97, 99, lobby corps chair 1993-95), Louisville Internat. Cultural Ctr., Women Lawyers Assn. Jefferson County. Republican. Avocations: basketball fan, classic cars. Family and matrimonial, State civil litigation. Office: Ste 1000 One Riverfront Plz Louisville KY 40202

**BROWN, BRUCE ANDREW,** lawyer; b. Cleve., Oct. 16, 1959; s. Andrew and Ruby Louise (Bishop) B. BA, Brown U., 1981; JD, Columbia U., 1984. Bar: N.Y. 1985, Ohio 1990. Assoc. Moskaver, Rose et al, N.Y.C., 1983-86, Kinley, Kumble, Wagner, et al, N.Y.C., 1986-87; pvt. practice Cleve., 1987—. Mem. NAACP, Urban League (bd. dirs. 1988—), Omega Psi Phi. Democrat. Muslim. Avocation: golf. Office: Willis & Blackwell 310 W Lakeside Ave Ste 595 Cleveland OH 44113-1059

**BROWN, CAROLINE MONTROSE,** lawyer; b. N.Y.C., Mar. 14, 1962; d. Francis Cabell and Nancy Adeline (Leitzow) B.; m. Robert Malley, June 17, 1995; 1 child, Miles. AB, Harvard-Radcliffe U., 1985; JD, Harvard U., 1990. Bar: N.Y. 1993, D.C. 1993. Law. clk. to Hon. Ruth Bader Ginsburg Washington, 1990-91; law clk. to Hon. Sandra Day O'Connor U.S. Supreme Ct., Washington, 1991-92; assoc. Covington & Burling, Washington, 1992—. Trustee Hotchkiss Sch., Lakeville, Conn., 1995—. Office: Covington & Burling 1201 Pennsylvania Ave NW Washington DC 20004-2401

**BROWN, CHARLES DODGSON,** lawyer; b. N.Y.C., Dec. 31, 1928; s. James Dodgson and Leonora Rose (Nichols) B.; m. Martha Lockhart Spindler, Apr. 5, 1963; children: Gregory Spindler, William Howard. BA, NYU, 1949, JD, 1952. Bar: N.Y. 1952, U.S. Dist. Ct. (so. and ea. dists. ) N.Y. 1955, U.S. Supreme Ct. 1958, U.S. Ct. Appeals (2d cir.) 1988. Counsel, former ptnr. Thacher Proffitt & Wood, N.Y.C., 1954—. Co-author: Equipment Leasing, 1995—. Chmn. zoning bd. Asharoken, N.Y., 1965, alt. chmn. environ. bd., 1967, trustee, 1967, village justice, 1980—; chmn. Boy Scout Am., Northport, N.Y., 1989—; elder 1st Presbyn. Ch., Northport. With U.S. Army, 1952-54. Mem. ABA, N.Y. Bar Assn., Maritime Law Assn. U.S. (proctor in Admiralty 1956, chair to marine fin. com. 1996—), N.Y. State Magistrate Assn., Suffolk County Magistrate Assn., Northport Tennis Club. Republican. Avocations: scuba diving, wind surfing, tennis. Admiralty. Office: Thacher Proffitt & Wood 2 World Trade Ctr New York NY 10048-0203

**BROWN, CHARLES R.,** lawyer; b. Twin Falls, Idaho, Aug. 25, 1945. Bar: Utah 1971, U.S. Tax Ct. 1972, U.S. Ct. Claims 1972, U.S. Ct. Appeals (D.C. cir.) 1972, U.S. Dist. Ct. Utah 1976, U.S. Ct. Appeals (10th cir.) 1976, U.S. supreme Ct. 1977. Trial atty. Office Chief Counsel IRS, 1971-76; ptnr. Hunter & Brown, Salt Lake City, 1976—. Mem. ABA (tax. sect., real property, probate and trust law), Utah State Bar Assn. (chmn. tax. sect. 1981-82, Tax Practitioner of Yr. 1995-96, bar commr. 1992-93 94—, chmn. standing com. on solo and small firm practice 1993-94), Salt Lake County Bar Assn. Taxation, general, Mergers and acquisitions, Real property. Office: Hunter & Brown One Utah Ctr 201 S Main St Ste 1300 Salt Lake City UT 84111-2216*

**BROWN, CHRISTOPHER ARTHUR,** partner lawyer, career reserve officer; b. Atlantic City, Aug. 3, 1964; s. Arthur Robert Brown and Shirley May Provost; m. Christine Marie Rhoads, June 20, 1992; children: Matthew Christopher, Daniel Thomas. BA in Polit. Sci., Rutgers Coll., 1987, cert. in criminology, 1987; grad., U.S. Army Infantry Sch., 1988; JD, Widener U., 1991. Bar: N.J. 1992, Pa. 1992. Intern to Hon. L. Anthony Gibson N.J. Superior Ct., 1990-91, clerkship with Hon. Charles R. Previti, 1992-93; assoc. Nugent, Fitzgerald, et. al., Linwood, N.J., 1993-97; asst. solicitor, prosecutor Egg Harbor Twp., N.J., 1996—; ptnr. Brown & Bergman, Atlantic City, 1997—; solicitor Atlantic City Coun., 1997—; solicitor, planning and zoning bd. Estell Manor, N.J., 1997—. Pres., founder Chief Arthur R. Brown, Jr. Meml. Scholarship Found., Atlantic City, 1992—; mem. Atlantic City Zoning Bd. Capt. U.S. Army, 1987-97. Decorated Bronze Star, 82d Airborne Divsn., U.S. Army; D.S.M., N.J. Army N.G., Desert Storm Medal; Nat. Def. Svc. medal, U.S. Army, Army Commendation medal, Army Achievement medal, S.W. Asia Svc. Medal; Saudi Arabian Liberation of Kuwait medal, Govt. Saudi Arabia; Liberation of Kuwait medal, Govt. Kuwait. Mem. N.J. State Bar Assn. (govt. law sect.), N.J. N.G. Assn. (Cantwell award 1995), Atlantic County Mcpl. Prosecutors Assn. (v.p. 1995-96, pres. 1996-98), Atlantic County Bar Assn. (trustee 1998—, co-chmn. com. court orientation program, Rimm award 1997, Haneman-Perskie scholar), Am. Inns of Ct. (early settlement panelist), Chelsea Neighborhood Civil Assn. (sec. 1994-96), Friendly Sons of St. Patrick, Atlantic City Rep. Club, Kiwanis Club, VFW, Am. Legion, Jaycees. Roman Catholic. Avocations: running, traveling, reading, rowing, weightlifting. Insurance, General civil litigation, Land use and zoning (including planning). Office: Brown & Bergman PA 3201 Atlantic Ave Ste 201 Atlantic City NJ 08401-6216

**BROWN, DAVID HURST,** lawyer, partner; b. Houston, May 11, 1950. BS, Northwestern U., 1972; JD, U. Tex., Austin, 1975. Bar: Tex. 1976. Briefing atty. U.S. Dist. Ct. (so. dist.) Tex., Houston, 1975-77; assoc. Vinson & Elkins, Houston, 1977-84, ptnr., 1984—. Mem. Maritime Law Assn. U.S., Tex. Assn. Def. Counsel, Tex. Bar Found., Houston Bar Assn. Episcopalian. Insurance, General civil litigation. Office: Vinson & Elkins LLP 1001 Fannin St Ste 2300 Houston TX 77002-6760

**BROWN, DAVID JAMES,** lawyer; b. Nyack, N.Y., Aug. 10, 1952; m. Liane Davis (dec. Oct. 1995); children: Elia Brown-Davis, Anthony Brown-Davis; m. Mary Klayder. BA in Journalism, U. Ky., 1976; JD, Union U., 1989. Bar: N.Y. 1990, Kans. 1990. Reporter, then asst. editor Rotterdam (N.Y.) Reporter, 1972; truck assembler Walter Motor Truck Co., Voorheesville, N.Y., 1973-75; news editor Corbin (Ky.) Times-Tribune, 1977-79; reporter, copy editor, then weekend regional editor Albany (N.Y.) Times Union, 1979-86; rsch. asst. Union U. Albany Law Sch., 1987-88; rsch. atty. ctrl. staff Kans. Ct. Appeals, Topeka, 1990-91; rsch. atty. for Chief Judge Mary Beck Briscoe, Kans. Ct. Appeals, Topeka, Kans., 1991-92; pvt. practice Lawrence, Kans., 1992—; legal asst. Prisoners' Legal Svcs., Albany, summer 1987; guest lectr. Rockefeller Coll. Pub. Affairs and Policy, SUNY, Albany, 1988. Contbg. author: Practitioner's Guide to Kansas Family Law, 1997. Bd. dirs. Douglas County AIDS Project, 1991-94, vice chmn., 1992-93, sec., 1993-94; vol. mediator Kans. Children's Svc. League, 1991-92; mem. Lawrence City Human Rels. Commn., 1994—. Named Ky. col., 1979. Mem. ABA, Kans. Bar Assn., Douglas County Def. Bar Assn. (joint organizer, pres. 1997—), Deouglas County Bar Assn. (sec.-treas. 1997-98), Judge Hugh Means Am. Inn Ct. (charter, recorder 1997-99). Family and matrimonial, General practice, Probate. Office: 1040 New Hampshire St Ste 14 Lawrence KS 66044-3044

**BROWN, DAVID RONALD,** lawyer; b. Turtle Creek, Pa., Jan. 25, 1939; s. James R. and Mary A. (Barnes) B.; m. Christine Michelle Laquatra, Oct. 9, 1970; children: Michelle, Adrienne, Aaron, Eden, Jeremy. Student, Brown U., 1956-57; BS, U. Pitts., 1960; JD, Duquesne U., 1967. Bar: Penn. 1967, U.S. Dist. Ct. (we. dist.) Penn. 1967, U.S. Ct. Appeals (3d cir. 1972, U.S. Tax Ct. 1986. Rschr. phys. chemistry Mellon Inst., Pitts., 1960-66; real estate lawyer Redevel. Authority of Allegheny County, Pitts., 1966-69; ptnr. Litman, Litman, Harris & Brown, Pitts., 1969—; lectr. Robert Morris Coll., 1978-84. Councilman Borough of Turtle Creek, Penn., 1963-67. Mem. ABA (com. real estate litigation, real property and probate sect., com. title ins., bus. law sect.), Assn. Trial Lawyers Am., Penn. Trial Lawyers Assn., Allegheny County Bar Assn. (com. legal svcs. 1973-74, real property com., probate and trust law com.). Contracts commercial, Real property, Probate. Home: 465 Blackburn Rd Sewickley PA 15143-8398 Office: Litman Litman Harris & Brown 3600 One Oxford Ctr Pittsburgh PA 15219

**BROWN, DOUGLAS COLTON,** lawyer; b. N.Y.C., Sept. 2, 1948; s. Robin Colton and Catherine (Snyder) B. BA, Ohio Wesleyan U., 1970; JD., Calif. Western U., 1973. Bar: Wash. 1973, U.S. Ct. Mil. Appeals 1974, U.S. Supreme Ct. 1978, Calif. 1979, U.S. Dist. Ct. (so. dist.) Calif. 1979, U.S. Ct. Appeals (9th cir.) 1980, U.S. Dist. Ct. (ctrl. dist.) Calif. 1987. Judge adv. gen. Marine Corps, 1973-77; pvt. practice law, 1977—. Capt. USMC, 1973-77. Mem. Nat. Assn. Criminal Def. Attys., Calif. Attys. for Criminal Justice, San Diego Criminal Def. Lawyers Club. Avocation: travel. Criminal, Military. Office: Home Savings Tower 225 Broadway Ste 1210 San Diego CA 92101-5028

**BROWN, ENOLA T.,** lawyer; b. Tampa, Fla., Nov. 30, 1953; d. Fred G. and Enola C. Tobi; m. Edward C. Brown, Oct. 6, 1984. BS, Fla. State U., 1975, MS, 1977; JD, U. Fla., 1984. Environ. scientist Hillsborough County, Tampa, 1978-81; atty. Lawson MCW Hirter Grandoff & Reeves, Tampa, 1984-89, ptnr., 1989-93; ptnr. Annis Mitchell Cockey Edwards & Roehn, Tampa, 1993—; atty. Jr. League Tampa, Inc., 1990-92. Environmental. Office: Annis Mitchell Cockey Edwards & Roehn 201 N Franklin St Ste 2100 Tampa FL 33602-5164

**BROWN, GARRETT EDWARD, JR.,** judge; b. Orange, N.J., Mar. 20, 1943; s. Garrett E. and Josephine L. (Raul) B.; m. Carolyn Powling, Apr. 12, 1985; children: Victoria, Rebecca, Garrett. BA, Lafayette Coll., 1965; JD, Duke U., 1968. Bar: N.J. 1968, D.C. 1972, U.S. Supreme Ct. 1972, N.Y. 1980. Law sec. N.J. Supreme Ct., 1968-69; asst. U.S. atty., Dist. N.J., 1969-73, dep. chief criminal div., 1971-72, exec. asst., 1972-73; assoc. Stryker, Tams & Dill, Newark, 1973-75, ptnr., 1976-81; gen. counsel GPO, Washington, 1981-83; chief counsel Maritime Adminstrn., 1983-85; judge U.S. Dist. Ct., N.J., 1985—; mem. trial advocacy faculty Practising Law Inst., 1979-81; lectr. Inst. Continuing Legal Edn., 1975, 81. Editor, contbr.: Attorneys Fees: Recoverability and Deductability, 1981; Legislative History of Title 44 of the U.S. Code, 1982; issue editor Antitrust Law Jour. Counsel Union County Republican Com., 1981. Active spl. litigation counsel Union County Bd. Chosen Freeholders, 1981. Recipient Atty. Gen.'s Meritorious Service award, 1971, Pub. Printer's Gold medal for Disting. Service, 1983. Mem. ABA, Fed. Bar Assn., N.J. Bar Assn., D.C. Bar Assn. Republican. Office: US Ct House 402 E State St Ste 4050 Trenton NJ 08608-1507*

**BROWN, GEORGE E.,** judge, educator; b. Hammond, Ind., July 27, 1947; s. George E. and Violet M. (Matlon) B.; m. Patricia A. Schneider, June 6, 1970; children: Janet M., Elizabeth A. BS, Ball State U., 1969; JD, DePaul U., 1974; grad., Ind. Jud. Coll., 1996. Bar: Ind. 1974, Ill. 1974, U.S. Dist. Ct. (no. dist.) Ind. 1979, U.S. Supreme Ct. 1977, U.S. Tax Ct. 1977. Pvt. practice LaGrange & Lake Counties, Ind., 1974-84; judge LaGrange County Ct., 1984-87, LaGrange Superior Ct., 1988—; part-time chief dep. prosecutor LaGrange County, 1975-77; adj. faculty Tri-State U., Angola, Ind., 1991—. Vol. Jr. Achievement, 1997—. Mem. ABA, Ind. State Bar Assn. (ho. of dels., com. on written pub.), LaGrange County Bar Assn. (pres. 1978), Ind. Judges Assn., Nat. Conf. State Trial Judges, LaGrange Rotary (past dir., v.p. 1999—). Office: Lagrange Superior Ct Courthouse Lagrange IN 46761

**BROWN, G(LENN) WILLIAM, JR.,** bank executive; b. Waynesville, N.C., June 9, 1955; s. Glenn William and Evelyn Myralyn (Davis) B.; m. Amy Margaret Moss, Apr. 14, 1984; children: Elizabeth Quinn, Lauren Alexandra. BS in Biology, MIT, 1977, BS in Polit. Sci., 1977; JD, Duke U., 1980. Bar: N.Y., 1980. Assoc. Donovan Leisure Newton, N.Y.C., 1980-84; assoc. Sidley & Austin, N.Y.C., 1984-87, ptnr., 1988-89; v.p. Goldman Sachs & Co., N.Y.C., 1990-94; exec. dir. Goldman Sachs Internat. Fin., London, 1994-96; sr. v.p. AIG Internat. Inc., Greenwich, Conn., 1996-97; prin. Morgan Stanley & Co., Inc., N.Y.C., 1997, mng. dir., 1997—. Mem. ABA, Am. Fin. Assn. Presbyterian. Home: 31 Lindsay Dr Greenwich CT 06830-3402 Office: Morgan Stanley Dean Witter & Co 1585 Broadway Frnt 4 New York NY 10036-8200

**BROWN, GREGORY K.,** lawyer; b. Warren, Ohio, Dec. 9, 1951; s. George K. and Dorothy H. (Gaynor) B.; m. Joy M. Feinberg, Apr. 10, 1976. BS in Bus. & Econs., U. Ky., 1973; JD, U. Ill., 1976. Bar: Ill. 1976. Assoc. atty. McDermott, Will & Emery, Chgo., 1976-80, Mayer, Brown & Platt, Chgo., 1980-84; ptnr. Keck, Mahin & Cate, Chgo., 1984-93, Oppenheimer Wolff & Donnelly, Chgo., 1994-97, Seyfarth, Shaw, Fairweather & Geraldson, Chgo., 1997—. Contbg. author: The Handbook of Employee Ownership Plans, 1989, Employee Stock Ownership Plans, 1989. Active Chgo. Coun. Fgn. Rels. Named One of the Top Benefits Lawyers Nat. Law Jour., 1998. Mem. ABA (chair Employee Stock Ownership Plan com. real property, probate and trust law sect., Nat. Ctr. Employee Ownership, Employee Stock Ownership Plan Assn. (chair legis. and regulatory adv. com.), Chgo. Bar Assn. (chmn. employee benefits com. 1988-89). Avocations: basketball, bicycling, golf, opera, theatre. E-mail: browngr@seyfarth.com. Pension, profit-sharing, and employee benefits, Mergers and acquisitions. Office: Seyfarth Shaw Fairweather & Geraldson 55 E Monroe St Ste 4200 Chicago IL 60603-5863

**BROWN, HARRY M.,** lawyer, consultant; b. Oradia-Mare, Romania, Oct. 9, 1947; came to U.S., 1951; s. Bernard and Lydia Brown; m. Perl Keller, Aug. 10, 1969; children: Michael, Elissa, Rochel, Bentzion, Shmuel. BA, Yeshiva Coll., 1969; JD, NYU, 1972. Bar: Ohio 1972. Atty., ptnr. Benesch, Friedlander, Coplan & Aronoff, Cleve., 1972—. Health, Finance. Office: Benesch Friedlander Coplan 200 Public Sq Cleveland OH 44114-2301

**BROWN, HERBERT RUSSELL,** lawyer, writer; b. Columbus, Ohio, Sept. 27, 1931; s. Thomas Newton and Irene (Hankinson) B.; m. Beverly Ann Jenkins, Dec. 2, 1967; children: David Herbert, Andrew Jenkins. BA, Denison U., 1953; JD, U. Mich., 1956. Assoc. Vorys, Sater, Seymour and Pease, Columbus, Ohio, 1956, 60-64, ptnr., 1965-82; treas. Sunday Creek Coal Co., Columbus, 1970-86; assoc. justice Ohio Supreme Ct., Columbus, 1987-93; examiner Ohio Bar, 1967-72, Multi-State Bar, 1971-76, Dist. Ct. Bar, 1968-71; commr. Fed. Lands, Columbus, 1967-68, Lake Lands, Columbus, 1981; bd. dirs. Thurber House, 1992-94, Sunday Creek Coal Co.; adj. prof. Ohio State U. Coll. Law, 1997—; panelist Am. Arbitration Assn., 1993—. Author: (novel) Presumption of Guilt, 1991, Shadows of Doubt, 1994; mem. editl. bd. U. Mich. Law Rev., 1955-56. Bd. dirs. Ctrl. Cmty. House Columbus, 1967-75; deacon, mem. governing bd. 1st Cmty. Ch., 1966-80; trustee Columbus Bar Found., 1993—; candidate Ohio State Legis., 1966. Capt. JAGC, U.S. Army, 1956-57. Fellow Am. Coll. Trial Lawyers; mem. Ohio Bar Assn., Columbus Bar Assn. Democrat. Office: 145 N High St Columbus OH 43215-3006

**BROWN, IFIGENIA THEODORE,** lawyer; b. Syracuse, N.Y., Mar. 14, 1930; d. Gus and Christine Theodore; m. Paul Frederick Brown, Sept. 16, 1956; 1 child, Paul Darrow. BA, Syracuse U., 1951, LLB/JD, 1954. Bar: N.Y. 1965. Acting police justice Village of Ballston Spa, N.Y., 1960-62; sr. ptnr. Brown Brown & Peterson Esqs, Ballston Spa, 1958—; chmn. N.Y. State Bd. Real Property Svcs., Albany, 1996—. Mem. N.Y. State Bar Assn., Saratoga County Bar Assn. (treas. 1983-84, pres. 1984-85). Republican. Greek Orthodox. Avocations: church choir, piano. Family and matrimonial, Probate, Real property. Home: 42 Hyde Blvd Ballston Spa NY 12020-1608 Office: Brown Brown & Peterson One E High St Ballston Spa NY 12020

**BROWN, JACKI CAROL,** lawyer; b. Oakland, Calif., Feb. 2, 1952; d. Ellis Clifford Brown and Joyce Ann Ryberg; m. Peter W. Evans, Aug. 1, 1987 (div. June 1997). BA in History, Mills Coll., 1974; JD, U. San Francisco, 1977. Bar: Calif. 1978; cert. criminal law specialist. Legal editor Matthew Bender Pub., San Francisco, 1979-80; dep. dist. atty. San Mateo Dist. Atty., Redwood City, Calif., 1980-84, Marin County Dist. Atty., San Rafael, Calif., 1984-89; pvt. practice Law Office of Jacki B. Evans, Mill Valley, Calif., 1989-90; sr. rsch. atty. Calif. State Ct. of Appeal, Santa Ana, 1990—; adj. prof. Western State U., Fullerton, Calif., 1994-97. Pres. Angels of the Performing Arts, Saddlebrook Coll., 1994-98, Saddlebrook Master Chorale, 1994-95. Republican. Office: Calif State Ct of Appeal 925 N Spurgeon St Santa Ana CA 92701-3700

**BROWN, JAMES BENTON,** lawyer; b. Pitts., Jan. 18, 1945; s. Sidney J. and Marian R. (Bailiss) B.; m. Susan M. Brenner, Aug. 6, 1967; children: Jessica Lynn, Joshua David. BA, U. Louisville, 1967; JD, Duquesne U., 1971. Bar: Pa. 1971, U.S. Dist. Ct. (we. dist.) Pa. 1971, U.S. Ct. Appeals. (3d cir.) 1974, U.S. Supreme Ct. 1982. Dir., ptnr., v.p. mktg. Cohen & Grigsby, P.C., head employment litigation group; lectr. LaRoche Coll., Pa. Bar Inst.; mediator Justus ADR; arbitrator Am. Arbitration Assn. Mem. ABA, Fed. Bar Assn., Am. Acad. Hosp. Attys., Pa. Bar Assn. (past vice chmn. labor and employment law sect.), Allegheny County Bar Assn., Internat. Assn. Def. Counsel. Democrat. Labor, Federal civil litigation. Home: 6739 Wilkins Ave Pittsburgh PA 15217-1318 Office: 16th fl 11 Stanwix St Ste 15 Pittsburgh PA 15222-1312

**BROWN, JAMES EARLE,** lawyer; b. San Antonio, Aug. 13, 1945; s. Melville Marshall and Hazel Maurine (Bryan) B.; m. Camille Ashby Newsom, June 10, 1967; children: Kristen Bryan, Kasey Margaret. BBA, So. Meth. U., 1968, JD, 1972. Bar: U.S. Dist. Ct. (no. and ea. dists.) Tex. 1972. Assoc. Bean, Francis, Ford, Francis & Wills, Dallas, 1972-74; ptnr. Briggs, Brown & Berkley, Dallas, 1975-86, Baker, Brown & Dixon, Dallas, 1986—. Trustee Presby. Sch. Christian Edn., 1993-97, vice chair, 1996-97; trustee Union Theol. Sem. and Presbyn. Sch. Christian Edn., 1997—, vice chair 1997—; ruling elder Preston Hollow Presbyn. Ch., Dallas, 1981; v.p. Wilcox Endowment, Dallas, 1984. With U.S. Army, 1968-69. Mem. ATLA, Tex. Bar Assn., Dallas Bar Assn., Dallas Trial Lawyers Assn., Tex. Trial Lawyers Assn., Tex. Bd. Legal Specialization (cert.), Nat. Bd. Trial Advocacy (cert.), Coll. State Bar Tex., Dallas Athletic Club. Avocations: golf, snow skiing. Personal injury, Product liability, Insurance. Office: 4315 W Lovers Ln Dallas TX 75209-2803

**BROWN, JAMES JOSEPH,** judge; b. Mineola, N.Y., Mar. 1, 1944; s. Thomas Patrick and Sally (Casey) B.; m. Alice May Manningham, Aug. 3, 1965; children: Thomas P., Scott L., Christine M., Daniel J. BA in History, U. Tex., 1968; JD, Boston Coll., 1971. Bar: Mass. 1971, U.S. Dist. Ct. Mass. 1971, U.S. Dist. Ct. Vt. 1972, U.S. Supreme Ct. 1973, U.S. Ct. Appeals (4th cir.) 1980, U.S. Ct. Appeals (5th cir.) 1983, U.S. Ct Appeals (10th cir.) 1984, Md. 1985, U.S. Dist. Ct. Md. 1985, U.S. Dist. Ct. D.C. 1986. Assoc. Levy & Wimer PC, Greenfield, Mass., 1971-75; trial atty., dep. chief commercial litigation U.S. Dept. Justice, Washington, 1976-85, supervisory trial atty. environ. enforcement sec., 1987-90; supervisory trial atty. Asset Forfeiture Office Criminal div. U.S. Dept. Justice, 1990-95; U.S. adminstrv. law judge Office of Hearings and Appeals, Raleigh, N.C., 1995—; sr. assoc. Weinberg & Green, Balt., 1985-87; lectr., tchr. U.S. Dept. Justice and other govt. agys., Washington, 1978-85. Author: Judgement Enforcement Practice and Litigation, 1994, pocket supplements, 1995-98, 2nd Edition, 1999; editor: Scientific Evidence and Experts Handbook, 1999. Trustee, Manningham Bible Trust, Fond du Lac, Wis., 1984-91; mem. sch. com. Town of Greenfield, 1973-75; bd. elders Forcey Meml. Ch., Silver Spring, Md., 1981-82, mem. missions com. 1980-83, 88-90. With USNR, 1962-64. Recipient Outstanding Performance awards U.S. Dept. Justice, 1980-85, Spl. Achievement award, 1983, Disting. Svc. award, 1985. Mem. Mass. Bar Assn., Md. Bar Assn. Republican. Avocations: skiing, golf, poetry, writing. Office: US Administrative Law Judge Office of Hearings & Appeals 1305 Navaho Dr Raleigh NC 27609-7448

**BROWN, JAMES KNIGHT,** lawyer; b. Rainelle, W.Va., Sept. 25, 1929; s. Hugh Allen and Florence Catherine (Knight) B.; m. Sarah Elizabeth Droste, June 21, 1952; children: Carolyn, Patricia, Julia. BS, W.Va. U., 1951, LLB, 1956. Bar: W.Va. 1956, U.S. Ct. Appeals (4th and 6th cir.), U.S. Supreme Ct. Assoc. Jackson & Kelly, Charleston, W.Va., 1956-62, ptnr., 1962-98; mem. Jackson & Kelly PLLC, Charleston, 1999—; bd. dirs. One Valley Bancorp., Inc., Charleston. 1st lt. USAF, 1951-53. Fellow Am. Bar Found.; mem. ABA, W.Va. State Bar (pres. 1975-76), Order of Coif, Phi Beta Kappa. Democrat. Presbyterian. Avocations: woodworking, golf. General civil litigation, Contracts commercial, Oil, gas, and mineral. Office: Jackson & Kelly PLLC 1600 Laidley Tower Charleston WV 25301-2189

**BROWN, JAMES MARSTON,** lawyer; b. Aberdeen, Wash., Feb. 5, 1950; s. Donald Matthew and Jeanette Marie (Phillips) B.; m. Coleen Tina Chin, July 6, 1974; children: William Lester, Peter James. Student U. Wash., 1968-72, Calif. State U.-Fullerton, 1975-76; BS in Laws, Western State U., Fullerton, 1977, JD, 1978. Bar: Calif. 1979, U.S. Dist. Ct. (no. dist.) Calif. 1979, Wash. 1981, U.S. Dist. Ct. (we. dist.) Wash. 1982. Law clk. Orange County Superior Ct., Santa Ana, Calif., 1977-78; assoc. Gladys Phillips, Aberdeen, 1979-81; ptnr. Phillips & Brown, Aberdeen, 1981-90, mng. ptnr. Phillips, Krause & Brown, 1990—; lectr. Grays Harbor Coll., Aberdeen, 1983—. Bd. dirs. Channel 10 Ministries, Aberdeen, 1980-83; trustee Aberdeen Pub. Libr. Bd., 1979-89; active Aberdeen Sch. Bd., 1991—. Mem. ABA, Wash. Bar Assn. (bar examiner 1982-83, law sch. liason com.), Wash. State Trial Lawyers Assn. (chmn. Grays Harbor round table 1984-85, bd. dirs. 1990—, bd. govs. 1990-92), Assn. Trial Lawyers Am., Grays Harbor Bar Assn. (pres. 1990-91), Christian Legal Soc., Delta Theta Phi. Republican. Baptist. Personal injury, General civil litigation. Home: 527 W 6th St Aberdeen WA 98520-3312 Office: Phillips Krause & Brown 525 Seattle First Nat Bank Aberdeen WA 98520

**BROWN, JAN HOWARD,** lawyer; b. Bklyn., Nov. 13, 1948; s. Monroe and Ruth B.; m. Deborah Lugo, Sept. 28, 1981 (dec. Feb. 26, 1992); children: Richard, Andrew; m. Elizabeth Jo Spaeth, Mar. 3, 1996. BA, Antioch Coll., 1973; JD, Western New Eng. Coll., 1976. Bar: N.Y. 1978, U.S. Dist. Ct. (so. dist. and ea. dist.) N.Y. 1978. Contbg. author: Visa Processing Guide, 1998, 99. Mem. Am. Immigration Lawyers Assn., Assn. of the Bar of the City of N.Y. (immigration com.). Immigration, naturalization, and customs. Office: Jan H Brown PC 250 W 57th St New York NY 10107-0899

**BROWN, JANET LYNN,** lawyer; b. Lafayette, Ind., Nov. 18, 1951; d. William Richard and Florence Patricia (Henderson) B. AA, Cottey Jr. Coll. Women, 1971; BA, Marietta Coll., 1973; JD, Coll. William and Mary, 1976. Bar: U.S. Dist. Ct. (no. dist., so. dist., mid. dist.) Fla. 1977, U.S. Cir. Ct. Appeals (5th cir.) 1977, U.S. Cir. Ct. Appeals (11th cir.) 1981, U.S. Supreme

Ct. 1980; cert. CPCU, cert. civil trial law Fla. Bar, cert. cir. mediator. Contbr. articles to profl. jours.; editor: The Laymen's Guide to Virginia Law, 1977. Del. Am. People Amb. Program, 1995. Mem. ABA (coun. mem. tort and ins. practice sect. 1986-90, del. to ho. dels. tort and ins. practice sect. 1990-92, former vice chair property ins. law com., past chair automobile law com., chair handbook and bylaws com. tort and ins. practice sect. 1996—, mem. tort and ins. practice sect. task force on specialization and certification 1997-98, Andrew C. Hecker Meml. award tort and ins. practice sect. 1997), Am. Arbitration Assn., Fla. Bar Assn. (mem. trial lawyers sect.), Def. Rsch. Inst., Loss Execs. Assn., Internat. Assn. Arson Investigators, Internat. Assn. Def. Counsel, Fedn. Ins. and Corp. Counsel (vice chair property ins. sect. 1994-96, chair property ins. sect. 1996-98, mem. extra contractual sect., mem. external projects com., faculty mem. Fedn. Ins. and Corp. Counsel Litigation Mgmt. Coll. Northwestern U. 1997-98), Property Loss Rsch. Bur. (faculty mem. property loss mgrs. conf. 1985-87, 89, 91-98). Republican. Presbyterian. Avocations: reading, golf, travel. Insurance. Office: Boehm Brown Seacrest Fischer & LeFever PO Box 2593 Orlando FL 32802-2593

**BROWN, JANICE ROGERS,** state supreme court justice. Assoc. justice Calif. Supreme Ct., San Francisco. Office: Calif Supreme Ct 303 2d St South Tower San Francisco CA 94107-3600

**BROWN, JAY W.,** lawyer; b. Beaumont, Tex., Nov. 20, 1959; s. Royce V. and Mary Sue B. BA cum laude, U. Tex., Austin, 1981, JD cum laude, 1984. Bar: Tex. 1984; U.S. Dist Ct. (so. dist.) Tex. 1985, U.S. Dist Ct. (we. dist.) Tex. 1989, U.S. Dist. Ct. (ea. dist.) Tex. 1988, U.S. Ct. Appeals (5th cir.) 1990. Assoc. Fulbright & Jaworski L.L.P., Houston, 1984-87; assoc. Beirne, Maynard & Parsons L.L.P., Houston, 1987-90, ptnr., 1991—; faculty U. Houston Law Found. Houston 1993-97; lect. in the field. Contbr. to profl. jours. Mem. State Bar Tex. (bd. cert. civil trial law 1995, bd. cert. personal injury trial law 1995), Waterford Harbor Yacht Club, Phi Beta Kappa. Avocations: sailing. General civil litigation, Insurance, Personal injury.

**BROWN, JEAN WILLIAMS,** state supreme court justice; b. Birmingham, Ala.; m. E. Terry Brown; 2 children. Grad. with honors, Samford U., 1974; JD, U. Ala., 1977. Bar: Ala. 1977, U.S. Ct. Appeals (11th cir.), U.S. Supreme Ct. Law clerk Tucker, Gray & Thigpen; asst. atty. gen. criminal appeals divsn. Ala. Atty. Gen.'s Office; justice Supreme Ct. Ala., 1999—; chief extradition officer Atty. Gen.'s Office; faculty Ala. Jud. Coll., 1982. Tchr. kindergarten Sunday sch. 1st Bapt. Ch. Mem. Montgomery Jr. League. Office: Ala Supreme Ct 300 Dexter Ave Montgomery AL 36104-3741*

**BROWN, JEFFREY MONET,** lawyer; b. Columbus, Ohio, July 4, 1953; s. Charles Ernest Brown and Barbara (Metzler) Dible; m. Rita Zoia, May 9, 1981; 1 child, Jessica Marie. BA, Wittenberg U., 1975; JD, Ohio State U., 1979. Bar: Ohio 1979; U.S. Dist. Ct. (so. dist.) Ohio 1979. Legal intern Columbus Dept. Law, 1978-79; ptnr. Crabbe, Brown, Jones, Potts & Schmidt, Columbus, 1979—, mng. ptnr., 1991—; mem. devel. commn. City of Columbus, 1990-91; commr. Ohio Supreme Cts. Bd. Commrs. on Grievances and Discipline, 1993-96. Bd. dirs. Rosemont Ctr. for Troubled Youth, Columbus. Mem. ABA, Am. Law Firm Assn., Computer Law Assn., Ohio State Bar Assn., Columbus Bar Assn., U.S. Trademark Assn., Columbus Apt. Assn., Ohio Apt. Assn., Ohio Assn. Civil Trial Attys., Columbus Claims Assn. Avocations: golf, fishing, motorcycling. E-mail address: JBrown@CBJPS.com. Product liability, General civil litigation, Insurance. Office: Crabbe Brown Jones Potts & Schmidt 500 S Front St Ste 1200 Columbus OH 43215-7621

**BROWN, JERROLD STANLEY,** lawyer; b. Little Falls, N.Y., Nov. 8, 1953; s. Stanley Clayton and Ruth Jane Brown; m. Catherine M. Agnello, Aug. 2, 1980. BA, SUNY, Albany, 1975; JD, Union U., 1979. Bar: N.Y. 1980, U.S. Dist. Ct. (no. dist.) N.Y. 1980, U.S. Dist. Ct. (we. dist.) N.Y. 1982, U.S. Ct. Appeals (2nd cir.) 1983, U.S. Supreme Ct. 1989. Law clk. to judge N.Y. Ct. Appeals, Albany, 1979-81; assoc. Hodgson, Russ, Andrews, Woods & Goodyear, Buffalo, 1981-85, ptnr., 1986—; mem. adv. panel N.Y. Clean Air Act, 1996—, bd. dirs., Studio Arena Theatre, 1999—, bd. dirs., Shakespeare in Delaware Park, 1999—. Note and comment editor Albany Law Rev., 1978-79. Trustee Westminster Presbyn. Ch., Buffalo, 1986, pres., 1988, elder, 1992-93, 97—; bd. dirs. Homespace, Inc., 1998—, Shakespeare in Del. Pk., 1999—, Studio Arena Theater, 1999—; ward leader Del. Dist. Rep. Party, 1992; mem. adv. bd. Salvation Army, Buffalo Area, 1999—. Mem. N.Y. State Bar Assn. (task force on commerce and industry 1998—). Federal civil litigation, State civil litigation, Environmental. Office: Hodgson Russ Andrews Woods & Goodyear Ste 2000 One M & T Plz Buffalo NY 14203

**BROWN, JOE BLACKBURN,** judge; b. Louisville, Dec. 9, 1940; s. Knox and Miriam (Blackburn) B.; m. Marilyn McGowen, Aug. 10, 1963; children: Jennifer Knox, Michael McGowen. BA cum laude, Vanderbilt U., 1962, JD, 1965. Bar: Ky. 1965, Tenn. 1972, U.S. Supreme Ct. 1979. Asst. U.S. atty. Dept. Justice, Nashville, 1971-73, 1st asst. U.S. atty., 1974-81, U.S. atty., 1981-91, spl. asst. U.S. trustee, 1991-98; U.S. magistrate judge, U.S. Dist. Ct. (mid. dist.) Tenn., Nashville, 1998—; lectr. law Atty. Gen.'s Advocacy Inst., 1982—; vice chmn. Atty. Gen.'s Adv. Com., 1986-87, chmn. subcom. on sentencing guidelines, mem. subcom. on budget and office mgmt., 1982-91; instr. math. and bus. law Augusta (Ga.) Coll., 1966-69; instr. law Nashville Sch. Law, 1999—. Contbr. articles to legal jours. Bd. dirs. Mid-Cumberland Drug Abuse Coun., Nashville, 1977-86; asst. scoutmastr Boy Scouts Am.; vestryman St. David's Episcopal Ch., sr. warden, 1982, 90; ch. atty. Episcopal Diocese of Tenn., 1995-98; lt. col. CAP, 1996—. Maj. U.S. Army, 1965-71; col. JAGC, USAR ret. Decorated Legion of Merit, Meritorious Svc. medal with 3 oak leaf clusters; recipient Disting. Svc. award Atty. Gen.'s Adv. Com., 1988. Fellow Tenn. Bar Assn., Nashville Bar Found.; mem. FBA (treas. 1978), Nashville Bar Assn. (bd. dirs. 1995-97, exec. com. 1996-97, v.p. 1997), Radio Amateur Transmitting Soc. (pres. 1997-98), Nat. Assn. Flight Instrs., Profl. Assn. Div Instrs., Ky. Bar Assn., NRA (life, Disting. Rifleman award), Harry Phillip Inn of Ct. (master of bench and bar 1994—), Order of Coif, Phi Beta Kappa. Republican. Home: 3427 Woodmont Blvd Nashville TN 37215-1421 Office: US Courthouse 801 Broadway Nashville TN 37203-3816

**BROWN, JOHN ROBERT,** lawyer, priest, philanthropist; b. Muskogee, Okla., Apr. 22, 1948; s. John Robert and Betty Jane (Singleterry) B. BA, MA, Cambridge U., 1972; STB, Gen. Theol. Sem., 1973; STM, Union Theol. Sem., 1978, Harvard U., 1981; MA, STL, U. Louvain, Belgium, 1983; JD, Howard U., 1991. Bar: Ga. 1991, D.C. 1991, U.S. Supreme Ct. 1997; ordained priest Episcopal Ch., 1972. Tchr., headmaster St. John's Sch., Oklahoma City, 1973-77; novice Soc. St. John the Evangelist, Cambridge, Mass., 1979-81; minor canon Pro-Cathedral of Holy Trinity, Brussels, Belgium, 1981-83; assoc. rector St. James Ch., L.A., 1983-87; hon. assisting priest Ch. of the Ascension and St. Agnes, Washington, 1987-91; legis. aide U.S. Ho. of Reps., Washington, 1987-91; hon. asst. priest Ch. of Our Savior, Atlanta, 1991—; staff atty. Ga. Legal Svcs., Atlanta, 1991-1995; asst. gen. counsel State Bar Ga., Atlanta, 1996—; reader Ecumenical Inst. World Coun. Ch., Geneva, 1978, Huntington Libr., San Marino, Calif., 1985-86, Coll. of Preachers, Nat. Cathedral, Washington, 1987, fellow, Center for Ethics in Public Policy and the Professions, Emory U., 1996-98. Contbr. articles to profl. jours. Bd. dirs. S.W. Assn. Episcopal Schs., 1974-77, Anglican Roman Cath. Commn. of Beligum, 1981-83, Cmty. Counseling Svc., L.A., 1983-86, Acad. Performing Arts, L.A., 1984-85, Cape Coast Outreach Found., 1984-86, Coun. Battered Women, Atlanta, 1991-94, AID Atlanta, 1993—, Atlanta Opera, 1993—, ACLU of Ga., 1994—, Fund for So. Cmtys., 1995-98, OUT Fund for Lesbian and Gay Liberation, 1996-99, Funding Exch., 1997—, Cathedral of St. Philip Bookstore, 1998—; vol. NIH. 1987-88. Fed. Charitable Campaign, Washington, 1988-89, Atlanta Project, 1991-96; spiritual adv. com. AIDS Project, L.A., 1984-86; Mayor's Task Force on Family Diversity, 1984-86, Mcpl. Elections Com. L.A., 1984-86; governing bd. Robert Wood Johnson Homeless Care Project, L.A., 1985-87; trustees com. Opera Am., 1994-97; co-trustee Freeman Found., 1994-97; adv. bd. Caring Hands Programs, 1983-87; United Way of Metro Atlanta, 1993-97, Metro Atlanta Cmty. Found., 1994-97; chmn. social justice grants com. Threshold Found., 1994-96; chaplain Most Venerable Order of St. John of Jerusalem, 1996—; capt. The Old Guard of Atlanta, 1998—. Named one of Outstanding Young Men of Am., 1974; Yale U. rsch. fellow, 1983; recipient Mayor's Phoenix award, Atlanta, 1997. Fellow Georgia Bar Found. (life); mem. ABA (vice-chmn. fed. legis. com. gen. practice sect. 1989-91), Nat. Lawyers Guild, Nat. Network Grantmakers, Lambda Legal Def. and Edn. Fund, Lesbian and Gay Victory Fund, Met. Opera Guild, Patrons of the Vatican Mus., United Oxford and Cambridge U. Club (London), Harvard Club (Washington), City Tavern (Washington), Lawyers Club (Atlanta). Administrative and regulatory, Health, General civil litigation. Office: The Hurt Bldg # 800 50 Hurt Plz SE Atlanta GA 30303-2914

**BROWN, JOHN THOMAS,** lawyer; b. Ft. Dix, N.J., Dec. 16, 1948; s. Thomas Maurice and India Olean B.; m. Jerilyn Iris Post, June 24, 1972; children: India Claire, Solon Neville. BA with honors and distinction, Calif. State U., Chico, 1975; JD, U. Calif., San Francisco, 1978; grad. diploma in applied fin., Securities Inst. of Australia, 1999. Bar: Calif. 1978, Guam 1982, No. Mariana Islands 1983, NSW, 1999. Vol. VISTA, Gt. Lakes Region, 1968-69; assoc. Belzer & Jackl, Oakland, Calif., 1978-82; gen. counsel Jones & Guerrero Co., Inc., Agana, Guam, 1982—; v.p. Jones & Guerrero Co. Inc., Sydney, Australia, 1989—; instr. Chabot Jr. Coll., Hayward, Calif., 1980-82; prin. broker Rimpac Realty, Agana, 1987—. Bd. dirs. Job Tng. Partnership Coun., Agana, 1987-89; hon. amb.-at-large for Guam. Fellow Australian Inst. Co. Dirs.; mem. ABA, Calif. Bar Assn., Guam Bar Assn. (ethics com.), Bar Assn. No. Mariana Islands, Lawasia Soc., Guam C. of C. (bd. dirs. 1986-89, chmn. ethics com. 1987-89, chmn. bd. dirs. 1988-89), Sydney Turf Club, Am. Nat. Club, Australia Jockey Club, Law Soc. of NSW. General corporate, Private international, Real property. Office: Jones & Guerrero, GPO Box 3539, Sydney New South Wales 2001, Australia

**BROWN, JOHN WAYNE,** lawyer; b. East Orange, N.J., Nov. 17, 1949; s. John Edison and Margaret Patricia B.; m. Donna Potts, Nov. 18, 1978; children: Savannah Jane, Justin Taylor, Molly Ross. BA cum laude, Meth. Coll., 1971; JD, Wake Forest U., 1974; M in Law and Taxation, William and Mary Coll., 1980. Bar: Va. 1974, U.S. Dist. Ct. (ea. dist.) Va. 1975, U.S. Supreme Ct 1980, U.S. Tax Ct. 1980, U.S. Ct. Appeals (4th cir.) 1981. Pvt. practice Chesapeake, Va., 1974-75; asst. dep. commonwealth atty. Commonwealth Atty's Office, Chesapeake, 1975-80; ptnr. Gordon & Brown, Chesapeake, 1980-86; pvt. practice Chesapeake, 1986—; bd. dirs. Br. Bank and Trust. Co. chmn. Sch. Bond Referendum, Chesapeake. Mem. Va. State Bar Assn., Va. Trial Lawyers Assn., Chesapeake Bar Assn., South Norfolk Ruritan Club, Rotary. Democrat. Methodist. Avocations: sailing, jogging, yard work, fishing, card collecting. State civil litigation, Personal injury, Criminal. Office: The 411 Bldg 411 Cedar Rd Chesapeake VA 23322-5566

**BROWN, JOSEPH WENTLING,** lawyer; b. Norfolk, Va., July 31, 1941; s. Edwin Wallace and Nancy Jack (Wentling) B.; m. Pamela Jones, Aug. 18, 1966; children—Tyree, Palmer, Jeffrey, Hunter. B.A., U. Va., 1965; LL.B., Washington and Lee U., 1968. Bar: Nev. 1969, D.C. 1976, U.S. Dist. Ct. Nev. 1969. Assoc. Laxalt, Bell, Berry, Allison & LeBaron, Las Vegas, Nev., 1969; ptnr. Jones, Jones, Close & Brown, Las Vegas, 1973-97; pres. Jones Vargas, Las Vegas, 1997—; commr. Nev. Dept. of Wildlife, 1979-85; mem. U.S. Fgn. Claims Settlement Commn., 1981-87; bd. dirs. State Justice Inst., 1988-89; mem. Bd. of Litigation, Mountain States Legal Found., 1978-82. Bd. dirs. United Way, Nev. Devel. Authority, Clark County Boys Club, Nev. Catholic Community Services, Voluntary Action Ctr., First Security Bank; dep. counsel Rep. Nat. Conv., 1984. Served with USMCR, 1963-69. Editor Washington and Lee Lawyer, 1967-68. Mem. ABA, ATLA, Nev. Bar Assn., Clark County Bar Assn., Spanish Trail Country Club, Rotary. Republican. Roman Catholic. General practice, General corporate, Administrative and regulatory. Home: 17 Sawgrass Ct Las Vegas NV 89113-1326 Office: Jones Vargas 3773 Howard Hughes Pkwy Suite 300 S Las Vegas NV 89109

**BROWN, JOSEPH WILLIAM,** retired patent agent; b. Evanston, Wyo., Sept. 19, 1919; s. James Jr. and Mary (Duncombe) B. BS, U. Wyo., 1943, JD, 1947. Bar: Wyo. 1947, Patent Bar 1947. Patent agt. Shell Devel., Calif., 1946-54, mgr. polymer divsn., 1954-72; mgr. patents Shell Devel., Houston, 1972-80, ret., 1980. Capt. U.S. Army, 1944-46. Patent, Trademark and copyright. Home: 698 E 2320 N Provo UT 84604-1749

**BROWN, KATHLEEN DOWLING,** lawyer; b. St. Louis, July 18, 1962; d. William Patrick and Rosemary Frances (Schmitz) Dowling; m. Glenn O. Brown, Nov. 19, 1988. BS, Mo. Valley Coll., 1983; JD, St. Louis U., 1987. Bar: Mo. 1987. Legal asst. Farnam Law Firm, St. Louis, 1985-87, assoc., 1987-89; sr. cons. employee benefits svcs. Deloitte & Touche, St. Louis, 1989-90, mgr. employee benefits svc., 1990-91; mgr. employee benefits svc. Price Waterhouse, St. Louis, 1991-95; v.p. adminstrn. Bryant Group, Inc., St. Louis, 1995-97; assoc. atty. Farnam Law Firm, St. Louis, 1997—; spkr. continuing edn. Internat. Soc. Cert. Employee Benefit Specialists, 1994-96. Contbr. articles to profl. jours. Trustee Eugene Field House Found., St. Louis, 1993—. Mem. Mo. Bar, Bar Assn. Met. St. Louis, Employee Benefit Assn. St. Louis, 1987—. Office: Farnam Law Firm 1 Metropolitan Sq Ste 2940 Saint Louis MO 63102-2799

**BROWN, KELLY D.,** lawyer; b. Redding, Calif., June 3, 1959; s. Harlen D. and Patricia A. Brown; m. Celia Ann McBehee, July 10, 1982; children: Andrea, Christopher, Steven. BSChemE, Tex. Tech. U., 1981; JD, South Tex. Coll. Law, 1991. Bar: Tex. 1991, U.S. Dist. Ct. (so. dist.) Tex. 1992. Assoc. McGinnis, Lorhridge & Kilgore, Houston, 1991-94; assoc. Crain, Caton & James, PC, Houston, 1994-96, shareholder, 1996—. Mem. Houston Bar Assn. (treas. environ. sect. 1996-97, vice chair environ. sect. 1997-98, chair-elect environ. sect. 1998—). Environmental, General civil litigation. Office: Crain Caton & James PC 909 Fannin St Ste 3300 Houston TX 77010-1079

**BROWN, KENNETH MACKINNON,** lawyer; b. Honolulu, Oct. 28, 1946; s. Kenneth Stirling and Chandler (Darden) B.; m. Janet Gail Davis, Feb. 3, 1968; children: Jennifer Darden, Matthew Chapin MacKinnon. BA, U. N.H., 1968; JD, Washington U., 1973. Bar: N.H. 1973, U.S. Dist. Ct. N.H. 1973, U.S. Ct. Appeals (1st cir.) 1974. Assoc. Winer, Lynch & Pillsbury, Nashua, N.H., 1973-76; ptnr. Kahn & Brown, Nashua, 1976-95, Sullivan & Gregg, P.A., Nashua, 1995—. Pres. bd. dirs. N.H. Legal Assistance, Concord, 1978-80; chmn. bd. Rivier Coll. Paralegal Adv. Bd., Nashua, 1984—; bd. dirs. N.H. Assn. for Mental Health, Concord, 1978-81, N.H. Soc. Protection of Forests, Concord, 1983-88. Mem. N.H. Bar Assn. (mem. I.O.L.T.A. com. 1984-99, chmn. 1998-99), Assn. Trial Lawyers Am., N.H. Trial Lawyers Assn. Club: Nashua Country (N.H.). Avocations: golf, family. General civil litigation, Personal injury, Product liability. Home: 29 Baxter Rd Hollis NH 03049-5943 Address: Sullivan & Gregg PO Box 888 Nashua NH 03061-0888

**BROWN, LAMAR BEVAN,** lawyer; b. Tooele, Utah, Apr. 26, 1951; s. John B. and Reva M. B.; m. Sherry L. Brown, Aug. 10, 1974; children: Sean La Mar, Kyle Ross, Ian Lawrence. BA, Utah State U., 1974; JD, We. State U., 1980. Bar: Calif. 1980, U.S. Dist. Ct. (so. dist.) Calif. 1980, U.S. Ct. Appeals (9th cir.) 1986, U.S. Dist. Ct. (no. and ctrl. dist.) 1992. Assoc. Law Offices George Andrews, San Diego, 1980-82, Higgs, Fletcher & Mack, San Diego, 1982-90, Law Offices Craig McClellan, San Diego, 1990-95; ptnr. McClellan & Brown, San Diego, 1995—. Democrat. General civil litigation, Personal injury, Product liability. Office: McClellan & Brown 1144 State St San Diego CA 92101-3529

**BROWN, LEWIS NATHAN,** lawyer; b. Miami, Fla., Mar. 12, 1953; s. Edward and Carole (Mendelson) B.; m. Cynthia Lou Katz, Oct. 21, 1978; children: Carly Shaun, Whitney Maris, Chloe Alix. BA cum laude, Harvard U., 1975; JD, U. Miami, 1978. Bar: Fla. 1979, U.S. Dist. Ct. (so. dist.) Fla. 1979, U.S. Ct. Appeals (5th and 11th cirs.) 1979, U.S. Supreme Ct. 1990. Sr. ptnr. Gilbride, Heller & Brown, Miami, Fla., 1981—; chmn. bd. dirs. Exec. Nat. Bank, 1983-86. Vice-chmn. Fla. Philharmonic Orch., 1991-93. Mem. Fla. Bar Assn. (com. mem.), Nat. Found. Advancement in Arts (trustee 1993—, chmn. 1995-97). Federal civil litigation, State civil litigation. Home: 473 Ridge Rd Miami FL 33143-6475 Office: Gilbride Heller & Brown 1 S Biscayne Blvd Ste 1500 Miami FL 33131

**BROWN, LILLIAN ELIZABETH,** publisher, consultant; b. Richmond, Va., Oct. 27, 1954; m. Charles W.K. Gritton, June 18, 1978. BA, U. Va., 1984; JD, Rutgers U., 1988. Bar: N.J. 1988, Pa. 1988, D.C. 1995; U.S. Dist. Ct. N.J., 1988, U.S. Supreme Ct. 1992. Law clk. to presiding justice Supreme Ct. of N.J., Oakhurst, N.J., 1988-89; assoc. Smith, Stratton, Wise, Heher and Brennan, Princeton, N.J., 1989-91; dep. atty. gen. N.J. Divsn. of Law, Trenton, 1991-94; pres. Integritax, Sterling, Va., 1995—; adj. prof. Seton Hall U. Sch. of Law, Newark, N.J., 1991-92. Editor: (newsletter) Responsible Officer Taxes, 1996—. Woman of Yr. nominee, The Leukemia Soc., D.C., 1996. Mem. ABA (chair subcom. on Trust Fund Taxes, chair 6672 Task Force 1997—), Nat. Bar Assn. Office: Integritax 37 Pidgeon Hill Dr # 105 Sterling VA 20165-6102

**BROWN, LORNE JAMES,** lawyer; b. Regina, Sask., Can., Nov. 26, 1937; s. Charles Mervyn and Anne Vera (Frohlick) B.; m. Ursula Theresa Grebe, Sept. 8, 1962; children—Nadine, Matthew. BA, San Jose State U., 1961; LLB, U. Calif.-Hastings, 1964. Bar: Calif. 1965, U.S. Dist. Ct. (cen. dist.) Calif. 1965, U.S. Tax Ct. 1981. Assoc. Holmes, Ross, Woodson, Millard & Ryburn, Pasadena, Calif., 1964-67, ptnr., 1967-72; ptnr. Brown & Reed, Pasadena, 1972-78; pres. Brown & Reed, Inc., Pasadena, 1978-81; ptnr. Brown, Reed, & Gibson, Pasadena, 1981-87; sole practice, 1987-98; ptnr. Brown & Assocs., LLP, 1998—. Treas., dir. Legal Services Program, Pasadena. V.p. La Canada Flintridge Ednl. Found.; dir., treas. Pasadena Tournament of Roses; commr. Calif. Jud. Nominee Evaluation Commn., 1987. Mem. Calif. State Bar, Los Angeles County Bar Assn. (trustee 1987-88), Pasadena Bar Assn. (pres. 1985-86). Clubs: Rotary, Optimists, University (Pasadena). Estate planning, Probate, Estate taxation. Home: 1235 S Orange Grove Blvd Apt 5 Pasadena CA 91105-3348 Office: 600 S Lake Ave Ste 301 Pasadena CA 91106-3955

**BROWN, MABEL WELTON,** lawyer; b. Geneseo, Ill., Dec. 7, 1916; d. Harry E. and Mabel (Welton) B. BA, Oberlin Coll., 1938; JD, U. Chgo., 1941. Bar: Ill. Ptnr. Brown and Brown, Geneseo, 1941-44; sole owner Brown & Brown, Geneseo, 1944-81; sr. ptnr. Brown and Ray, Geneseo, 1981—; atty. Green River Spl. Drainage Dist., Henry and Bureau Counties, Ill.; chmn. Geneseo Planning Commn., 1961-68. Mem. ABA, Ill. Bar Assn., Henry County Bar Assn. (pres. 1973-76). Republican. Methodist. Estate planning, Probate, Real property. Office: Brown and Ray 115 N State St Geneseo IL 61254-1345

**BROWN, MARK CHARLES,** lawyer; b. York, Nebr., Mar. 22, 1952; s. Charles A. and Wanda E. (Nicholas) B.; m. Janice Groff, June 1, 1985. BSBA, U. Nebr., 1975; JD, Pepperdine U., 1979. Bar: Nebr. 1979, U.S. Dist. Ct. Nebr. 1979, U.S. Ct. Appeals (8th cir.) 1988; lic. real estate broker, 1980; cert. real estate law inst., cert. real estate continuing edn. instr. Real estate broker Nebr. Assoc. Law Offices Kenneth Cobb, Lincoln, 1979-80; assoc. Muffly, Lott & Oglesby, Lincoln, 1981-82, ptnr., 1983-85; ptnr. Muffly, Oglesby & Brown, Lincoln, 1985-87, Oglesby, Brown, Thomas, Peterson & Orton, Lincoln, 1987-90, Orton, Brown, Thomas & Peterson, Lincoln, 1990-94, Aksamit and Brown, Lincoln, 1995-96; pvt. practice Lincoln, 1997—; instr. real estate law, S.E. Community Coll., Lincoln, 1985—, Nebr. Sch. Real Estate, 1987-90. Bd. dirs. Near South Neighborhood Assn., 1984-88; chmn. bd. dirs. Neighborhood Watch Assn. Lincoln, 1986-88, Lincoln Goals and Policies Com., 1987-88; bd. elders Christian Ch. Christ, 1998—; mem. exec. com. Lancaster County Rep. Party, leg. dist. 25 chmn.; mem. State GOP State Ctrl. Com.; spl. advisor to bd. dirs. Country Club Neighborhood Assn., 1988-95. Recipient Svc. Appreciation award Lincoln Police Dept. and Neighborhood Watch Assn., 1986. Mem. Nebr. Bar Assn., Lincoln Bar Assn., Christian Legal Soc., Exec. Club (bd. dirs.), Sertoma (bd. dirs. Lincoln 1987—), Phi Alpha Delta. Republican. Avocations: historic preservation, volleyball, antiques. Real property, Probate, General practice. Home: 7121 Framton Rd Lincoln NE 68516-4332 Office: Orton Brown Thomas & Peterson 2935 Pine Lake Rd Ste D Lincoln NE 68516-6009

**BROWN, MEREDITH ELAYNE,** lawyer; b. Houston, Dec. 26, 1961; d. Luther Eli and Mary Helen (Mickens) B.; m. Guy A. Bryant, Sept. 1, 1991. BS, Cornell U., 1984; JD, Boston U., 1988. Bar: Calif. 1989. Law clk. to Magistrate Alexander U.S. Dist. Ct., Boston, 1987; assoc. Lempres & Wulfsberg, Oakland, Calif., 1990-94, Hanson, Bridgett, Marcus, Vlahos & Rudy, San Francisco, 1994—. Mem. San Francisco Bar Assn., Alameda Bar Assn., Charles Houston Bar Assn. Construction. Office: Hanson Bridgett Marcus Vlahos & Rudy 333 Market St Ste 2300 San Francisco CA 94105-2173

**BROWN, MEREDITH M.,** lawyer; b. N.Y.C., Oct. 18, 1940; s. John Mason Brown and Catherine (Screven) Meredith; m. Sylvia Lawrence Barnard, July 17, 1965; 1 child, Mason Barnard. AB, Harvard U., 1962, JD, 1965. Bar: N.Y. 1965, U.S. Ct. Appeals (2d cir.) 1966, U.S. Dist. Ct. (so. dist.) N.Y. 1976. Law clk. to Hon. Leonard P. Moore U.S. Ct. Appeals (2d cir.), N.Y.C., 1965-66; assoc. Debevoise & Plimpton, N.Y.C., 1966-72, ptnr., 1973—, co-chair corp. dept., 1993—. Author: (with others) Takeovers: A Strategist's Manual for Business Combinations, 2d edit., 1993, Global Offerings, 1994, Privatisations, 1994, Mechanics of Global Equity Offerings, 1995, International Mergers and Acquisitions: An Introduction, 1999; contbr. articles to profl. publs. Mem. ABA (fed. regulation of securities com., bus. law sect.), Assn. of Bar of City of N.Y. (chmn. profl. responsibility com. 1987-90), Internat. Bar Assn. (co-chmn. com. on issues and trading of securities, sect. on bus. law 1994-98, co-chmn. capital markets forum, sec. bus. law 1998—). E-mail: mmbrown@debevoise.com. Mergers and acquisitions, Securities, General corporate. Home: 1021 Park Ave New York NY 10028-0959 Office: Debevoise & Plimpton 875 3rd Ave Fl 23 New York NY 10022-6256

**BROWN, MICHAEL DEWAYNE,** lawyer; b. Guymon, Okla., Nov. 11, 1954; s. Wayne E. and R. Eloise (Ferguson) B.; m. Tamara Ann Oxley, July 19, 1973; children: Jared Michael, Amy Aryann. Student, Southeastern State Coll., 1973-75; BA in Polit. Sci. and English, Cen. State U., Edmond, Okla., 1978; JD, Oklahoma City U., 1981. Bar: Okla. 1982, Colo. 1992, U.S. Dist. Ct. (no. and we. dists.) Okla. 1982, U.S. Ct. Appeals (10th cir.) 1982, U.S. Ct. Appeals (D.C. cir.) 1987. Assoc. Long, Ford, Lester & Brown, Enid, Okla., 1982-87; sole practice Enid, 1987—; adj. prof. state and local govt. law legis. Oklahoma City U.; cons. No. Okla. Devel. Assn., Enid, 1983-91; gen. counsel Alpha Oil Co., Duncan, Okla., 1985—, Physicians Mgmt. Svc. Corps., 1985-90, Physicians of Okla., Inc., Physicians Med. Plan Okla., Inc., City Nat. Bank & Trust Co., 1987-88, Stanfield Printing Co., 1987—, Hammell Newspapers, Inc., 1987-90, Dillingham Ins., 1989-91, Suits Rig Corp., Suits Drilling Co., 1989-91; chmn. bd. dirs. Okla. Mcpl. Power Authority, Edmond, 1982-88, judges & stewards commr. Internat. Arabian Horse Assn., 1991—. Councilman City of Edmond, 1981; cons. Okla. Reps., Oklahoma City, 1983; bd. dirs. Okla. Christian Home, Edmond, 1985; Rep. nominee 6th Dist. U.S. Congress, 1988; co-chmn. Nat. Challengers Polit. Coalition, 1989-91; trustee, co-chair fin. com. Theodore Roosevelt Assn., 1994—. Michael D. Brown Hydroelectric Power Plant and Dam named in his honor, Kaw Reservoir, Okla., 1987. Mem. Okla. Bar Assn. (assoc. bar examiner 1984—), MD Physicians Okla., Ariz. and La., MD Physicians of Tulsa. Mem. Christian Ch. (Disciples of Christ). Avocations: travel, photography, reading, wilderness adventures, swimming. Legislative, General corporate, Sports. Home and Office: PO Box 1307 2 Eagle Nest Ln Lyons CO 80540-1307

**BROWN, MICHAEL LANCE,** lawyer; b. Pearsall, Tex., Jan. 3, 1950; s. Alanson Wesley and Ruth (Gillis) B.; m. Nela Laura Thomas, May 12, 1971; 1 child, Robert Allen. BA, U. Tex., 1972, JD, 1975. Bar: Tex. 1975, La. 1981, U.S. Ct. Appeals (5th and 11th cirs.) 1981, U.S. Dist. Ct. (so. dist.) Tex. 1982, U.S. Dist. Ct. (we. dist.) Tex. 1984, U.S. Supreme Ct. 1984, U.S. Dist. Ct. (no. dist.) Tex. 1986, U.S. Dist Ct (es. dist.) Tex. 1987; cert. oil, gas and mineral law Tex. Bd. Legal Specialization, 1987. Lease analyst Exxon Co. U.S.A., Houston, 1975-77; staff atty. land dept. Coastal Corp., Houston, 1977-79, law dept. Getty Oil Co., Houston, 1979-81; ptnr. firm Dohoney & Collier and predecessor firm, Houston, 1981-86; pvt. practice, Houston, 1986-89; ptnr. firm Brown & Adkins, Houston, 1989—. Mem. ABA, Houston Bar Assn., Am. Assn. Petroleum Landmen, Houston Assn. Petroleum Landmen, Downtown Optimist Club (bd. dirs. 1983—), Houston Club, Phi Beta Kappa. Methodist. Oil, gas, and mineral, General corporate, Probate. Home: 150811 Clay Houston TX 77019 Office: 712 Main St Ste 2120 Houston TX 77002-3206

**BROWN, OMER FORREST, II,** lawyer; b. Somerville, N.J., Mar. 4, 1947; s. George Alvin and Frances (Schnitzler) B.; m. Sandra J. Cannon, Apr. 3,

1982. AB, Rutgers U., 1969; JD, Cornell U., 1972. Bar: N.J. 1972, D.C. 1974, U.S. Supreme Ct. 1976. Dept. atty. gen. dept. law and pub. safety State of N.J., Trenton, 1972-75; sr. trial atty. U.S. Dept. Energy, Washington, 1979-83; ptnr. Davis Wright Tremaine, Washington, 1987-96, Harmon & Wilmot, L.L.P., Washington, 1997—; bd. dirs., sec. VideoTakes, Inc., Arlington, Va., 1986—; mem. OECD Contact Group on Nuclear Safety Assistance for Eastern Europe, 1994—; mem. G-7 Joint Task Force on Ukrainian Nuclear Legislation, 1996—. Contbr. numerous articles on energy, enviro. and ins. law to legal jours. Capt. USAR, 1969-75. Recipient Class of 1931 award Rutgers U. Alumni Assn., 1979, Loyal Son of Rutgers award, 1980. Mem. ABA (various offices tort and ins. practice sect. 1981-96, coord. group on energy law 1995-99), Internat. Bar Assn., Internat. Nuclear Law Assn., Fed. Bar Assn., Univ. Club of Washington, D.C. Democrat. Roman Catholic. Public international, Nuclear power, Environmental. Address: PO Box 419 Saint Michaels MD 21663-0419

**BROWN, PATRICIA IRENE,** retired law librarian, lawyer; b. Boston; d. Joseph Raymond and Harriet A. (Taylor) B. BA, Suffolk U., 1955, JD, 1965, MBA, 1970; MST, Gordon Conwell Theol. Sem., 1977. Bar: Mass. 1965. Libr. asst. Suffolk U., Boston, 1951-60, asst. libr., 1960-65, asst. law libr., 1965-85, assoc. law libr., 1985-92; human resources counselor Winthrop (Mass.) Sr. Ctr., 1993—. Dir. Referral/Resource Ctr., Union Congl. Ch., Winthrop, Mass.; vol. health benefits counselor Mass. Dept. Elder Affairs, 1994—. First Woman inducted into Nat. Baseball Hall of Fame, Cooperstown, N.Y., 1988, All- Am. Girls Profl. Baseball League, 1950-51. Mem. Assn. Am. Law Librs., Am. Congl. Assn. (bd. dirs. 1992—), Mass. Bar Assn. Avocations: television and movie history, walking, computers. Home: 1100 Governors Dr Apt 26 Winthrop MA 02152-3254

**BROWN, PATRICIA LEONARD,** lawyer; b. New Brunswick, N.J., Apr. 15, 1950; d. John Francis Xavier and Adella (Florek) Leonard; m. Richard E. Brown, Oct. 1, 1980. BA cum laude, Rosemont Coll., 1972; JD, Union U., Albany, N.Y., 1976; LLM in Taxation, Temple U., 1978. Bar: Pa. 1976, U.S. Dist. Ct. (ea. dist.) Pa. 1978, U.S. Tax Ct. 1978, Nev. 1980, U.S. Dist Ct. Nev 1989. In-house counsel Profl. Assn. Cons. Svcs., Inc., Phila., 1976-79; mgr. pension dept. Longley Assocs., Lewiston, Maine, 1979; assoc. Clark, Greene, Richards & Brown, Las Vegas, Nev., 1980-82; head tax dept. Manos, Cherry & Brown, Las Vegas, 1982-83; pvt. practice law Las Vegas, 1983-87; head tax dept., mem. Beckley, Singleton, DeLanoy, Jemison & List, Chartered, Las Vegas, 1987-91; sole practitioner Las Vegas, 1992—; lectr. SBA, 1982—, CLU seminar on VEBA's, 1983, U. Nev., Las Vegas, 1985—. Contbr. articles to legal jours. Mem. Phila. Coun. Arts, 1978; mem. endowment com. Boulder Dam Area coun. Boy Scouts Am., 1989-91; Nev. co-chmn. White House Conf. on Small Bus., 1986; trustee Las Vegas Symphonic and Chamber Music Soc., 1984-91, United Way Found., 1987-91; legal dir. Small Bus. Coun. Am., Inc., 1984—, sec., 1987—. Recipient Estate Planner of Yr. award U. Nev., Las Vegas, 1986; named Women in Bus. Advisor for Nev., SBA, 1986, 92. Fellow Am. Coll. Trust & Estate Counsel, Am. Coll. Tax Counsel; mem. ABA (tax counsel mem. 1998—, real property, probate and trust sects.), Nev. Bar Assn., Clark County Bar Assn., So. Nev. Estate Planning Coun. (pres. 1985-86), Nev. Tax and Industry Coun., Nat. Assn. Women Bus. Owners (pres. So. Nev. chpt. 1992), Nat. Assn. Estate Planning Couns., Delta Epsilon Sigma. Republican. Roman Catholic. Estate planning, Health, Pension, profit-sharing, and employee benefits. Office: Rose Health Lodge PO Box 80024 Las Vegas NV 89180-0024

**BROWN, PAUL,** publishing executive. MA, Cambridge U., 1976. With Butterworth Group Reed Elsevier, U.K., South Africa, N.Am., 1976-94; v.p., gen. mgr. legal info. svcs. Lexis-Nexis, Dayton, Ohio, 1994-96, COO legal info. svcs., 1996—; pres., CEO Matthew Bender Pub., N.Y.C., 1999—. Office: Lexis-Nexis 9443 Springboro Pike Miamisburg OH 45342

**BROWN, PAUL EDMONDSON,** lawyer; b. Van Buren County, Iowa, Dec. 24, 1915; s. William Allen and Margaret (Edmondson) B.; m. Lorraine Hill, Jan. 9, 1944; 1 child, Scott. BA, U. Iowa, 1938, JD with distinction, 1941. Bar: Iowa 1941, U.S. Supreme Ct. 1966. Ptnr. Mahoney, Brown, Mahoney, Boone, Iowa, 1946-52; v.p., counsel Bankers Life Co. (now Prin. Fin. Group), Des Moines, 1952-80; of counsel Grefe & Sidney, Des Moines, 1980-84, Davis, Hockenberg, Wine, Brown, Koehn, Shors, Des Moines, 1984-91; pvt. practice Des Moines, 1991—; atty. County of Boone, Iowa, 1948-52; pres. Iowa Life Ins. Assn., Des Moines, 1980-85. With U.S. Army, 1942-46, col. USAR, 1946-70. Named Outstanding Young Man of Iowa, Iowa State Jr. C. of C., 1948. Mem. ABA, FBA, Iowa Bar Assn., Polk County Bar Assn., Assn. Life Ins. Counsel, U. Iowa Alumni Assn. (mem. Pres.' Club and various coms.), Civil War Roundtable, World War II State Monument Com., Downtown Des Moines Kiwanis Club (pres. 1961, Hixson fellow 1999). Republican. Congregationalist. Insurance, Legislative, General corporate. Home and Office: 5804 Harwood Dr Des Moines IA 50312-1206

**BROWN, PAUL NEELEY,** federal judge; b. Denison, Tex., Oct. 4, 1926; s. Arthur Chester and Nora Frances (Hunter) B.; m. Frances Morehead, May 8, 1955; children: Paul Gregory, David H. II. JD, U. Tex., 1950. Assoc. Keith & Brown, Sherman, Tex., 1951-53; ptnr. Brown & Brown, Sherman, 1953; asst. U.S. atty. for Ea. Dist. Tex. Texarkana and Tyler, Tex., 1953-59; U.S. atty. Ea. Dist. Tex., Tyler, 1959-61; ptnr. Brown & Brown and Brown Brothers & Perkins, Sherman, 1961-65, Brown and Perkins, Sherman, 1965; sole practice, Sherman, 1965-67; ptnr. Brown & Hill, Sherman, 1967, Brown Kennedy Hill & Minshew, Sherman, 1967-71, Brown & Hill, Sherman, 1971-76, Brown Hill Ellis & Brown, Sherman, 1976-85; U.S. dist. judge U.S. Dist. Ct. (ea. dist.) Tex., Sherman, 1985—. Served with USN, 1944-46, 50-51. Fellow Tex. Bar Found.; mem. Rotary. Presbyterian. Office: US Dist Ct Fed Bldg 101 E Pecan St # 9 Sherman TX 75090-5989

**BROWN, PAUL SHERMAN,** lawyer; b. St. Louis, June 26, 1921; s. Paul Michael and Norma (Sherman) B.; m. Ann Wilson, Feb. 7, 1959; 1 son, Paul S. BS in Commerce, St. Louis U., 1943, JD cum laude, 1951. Bar: Mo. 1951, U.S. Dist. Ct. (ea. dist.) Mo. 1951, U.S. Ct. Appeals (8th cir.) 1951, U.S. Supreme Ct. 1966. Shareholder, Brown & James , P.C., St. Louis, 1980—; instr. St. Louis U. Night Law Sch., 1978—; lectr. in field. Mem. St. Louis Amateur Athletic Assn. (dir. 1974-76, pres. 1976-78); mem. com. on civil pattern jury instructions, Mo. Supreme Ct. Fellow Am. Coll. Trial Lawyers, Internat. Acad. Trial Lawyers, Internat. Soc. Barristers; mem. ABA (vice-chmn. com. consumer products liability 1977-78), Mo. Bar Assn. (bd. govs. 1963-67), Am. Bd. Trial Advocates, Lawyers Assn. St. Louis, Bar Assn. Met. St. Louis (pres. 1970-71), Am. Judicature Soc., Order of Woolsack, Alpha Sigma Nu. Roman Catholic. Contbr. numerous articles to profl. jours. Federal civil litigation, State civil litigation, Insurance. Home: 7331 Kingsbury Blvd Saint Louis MO 63130-4143 Office: Brown & James 705 Olive St Ste 1100 Saint Louis MO 63101-2270

**BROWN, PETER MASON,** lawyer; b. Bklyn., June 13, 1945; s. Hilton Brown and Vera (Mason) Brown Cohn; m. Rita E. Freed, May 25, 1997; children: Emily Ray, Jay Mason. BA, SUNY-Buffalo, 1966; MS, U. Oreg., 1968; JD, Emory U., 1972. Bar: Tenn. 1973, U.S. Dist. Ct. (we. dist.) Tenn. 1973, Mass. 1993, U.S. Dist. Ct. Mass. 1994, U.S. Ct. Appeals (6th cir.) 1975, U.S. Supreme Ct. 1985. Rsch. assoc. Comms. Workers Am., Washington and Atlanta, 1968-70; ptnr. Udelsohn, Turnage & Blaylock, Memphis, 1973-82; assoc. gen. counsel Crump Cos., Inc., Memphis, 1982-85; ptnr. Streibich & Brown, Memphis, 1985-87, Law Offices Peter M. Brown, 1987-94; part-time asst. county atty., 1986-94; adj. assoc. prof. State Tech. Inst. Memphis, 1978-90. Asst. city solicitor City of Somerville, Mass., 1994—. Mem. ABA, Tenn. Bar Assn., Memphis Shelby County Bar Assn., Def. Rsch. Inst., Sertoma Club (pres. Memphis chpt. 1982-85), Rotary (Memphis). General corporate, Contracts commercial, Trademark and copyright. Home: 79 Washington St Newton MA 02458-2248 Office: City Solicitors Office 93 Highland Ave Somerville MA 02143-1740

**BROWN, PETER MEGARGEE,** lawyer, writer, lecturer; b. Cleve., Mar. 15, 1922; s. George Estabrook and Miriam (Megargee) B.; m. Alexandra Johns Stoddard, May 18, 1974; children: Peter, Blair Tillyer, Andree de Rapalyee, Nathaniel Holmes; stepchildren: Alexandra, Brooke Stoddard, Wallace Davis. Student, U. Calif., Berkeley, 1943-44; BA, Yale U., 1945, JD, 1948. Bar: N.Y. 1949. Spl. asst. atty. gen. State N.Y. and asst. counsel N.Y. State Crime Commn., 1951-53; asst. U.S. atty. So. Dist. N.Y., 1953-55, spl. asst., 1956; ptnr. firm Cadwalader, Wickersham & Taft, N.Y.C., 1959-82, head litigation and ethics coms.; ptnr. Brown & Seymour, N.Y.C., 1983-96; counsellor-at-law Peter Megargee Brown, N.Y.C., 1996—; mem. Mayor's Com. on Judiciary, 1965-72, vice chmn., 1972-74. Author: The Art of Questioning: Thirty Maxims of Cross-Examination, 1987, Flights of Memory-Days Before Yesterday, 1989, Rascals: The Selling of the Legal Profession, 1989, One World at a Time: Tales of Murder, Joy and Love, 1991, Village: Where to Live and How to Live, 1997, Riot of the Century (Civil War Draft Riot 1863), 1999; author essays, articles on law profession, life and humor, pub. nationally. Mem. N.Y. County Rep. Com., 1958—; counsel on crime to Nelson Rockefeller, Campaign for Gov. N.Y.S., 1968; bd. dirs. Yale Alumni Fund, 1979-84; bd. dirs., pres. Episcopal Ch. Found., 1989-93; master of ceremonies Yale Class of 1944 50th Reunion, 1994, 55th reunion, 1999; chmn., co-founder Design and Art Soc., Ltd., N.Y.C.; pres. Trustees Riot Relief Fund; bd. regent Cath. St. John Divine; founding mem. Henry Morrison Flagler Mus., Palm Beach, Fla.; mediator, East Side N.Y. gang warfare, 1956-57; counsel Grand Jury Assn. N.Y. County, 1956-79; orientation specialist U.S. Army WWII, 1943-46; editor in ch. Camp Bowie Blade (commendation). Decorated knight Order St. John of Hosp. of Jerusalem, Soc. of Anchor Cross; recipient award for svc. to profession Fed. Bar Assn., N.Y., N.J. and Conn., 1962; recipient Trustees Gold medal for disting. svc., Fed. Bar Coun., 1971; Chmn.'s award Yale Alumni Fund, 1979, Disting. Svc. award Class of 1944, Yale U., 1983, Henry Knox Sherrill medal for outstanding svc. Episcopal Ch. Found., 1993, Speakers prize Browning Sch., Headmaster's medal for pub. svc. St. Andrew's Sch.; Named record scorer U.S. Army Phys. Efficiency Test 1943 (697 out of possible 700 a score still unbroken). Fellow Am. Bar Found., Am. Coll. Trial Lawyers, N.Y. State Bar Found.; mem. ABA, World Assn. Lawyers (founding), Soc. Colonial Wars, New England Soc., Sons of the Revolution, N.Y. State Bar Assn., Assn. of Bar of City of N.Y., Fed. Bar Coun. Found. (trustee, pres. 1961-62, chmn. bd. 1962-64, chmn. judiciary com. 1960-85), chmn. planning and program com. 2d cir. judicial conf. 1976-80), St. Nicholas Soc. (past pres.), Delta Kappa Epsilon (Phi chpt. Yale), Phi Delta Phi (magister Waite Inn 1947, pres. province I 1950-55). Episcopalian (vestryman, sr. warden 1961-77). Clubs: Union (N.Y.C.); Coral Beach (Bermuda). Federal civil litigation, General civil litigation, State civil litigation. Office: 1125 Park Ave Ste 6A New York NY 10128-1243

**BROWN, PETER OGDEN,** lawyer; b. Ithaca, N.Y., Aug. 20, 1940; s. Frederick Shiras and Helen (Ogden) Brown; m. Nancy Tredwell Sunderland, Aug. 25, 1962; children: Jeffrey Scott, Douglas Henderson, Lori MacArthur. BA cum laude, Amherst Coll., 1962; LLD, Duke U., 1965. Assoc. Harter, Secrest & Emery, Rochester, N.Y., 1965-73, ptnr., 1973-80; sr. v.p., mgr. personal banking and trust group Chase Lincoln First Bank N.A., Rochester, 1981-90; exec. v.p., chief operating officer The Glenmede Trust Co., Phila., 1990-92; ptnr. Harter, Secrest & Emery, Rochester, 1993—. Co-author: How to Live and Die with New York Probate, 1975, Proceedings of the 25th Univ. of Miami Institute on Estate Planning, 1991; contbr. articles to profl. jours. Overseer U. Mus. of U. Pa., Phila., 1991-93; trustee Colgate Rochester Div. Sch., 1987-96, Capital Growth Mgmt. Funds, 1993—; mem. Acad. of Music Com., Phila.; mem. endowment com. Phila. Mus. Art, 1990-92; dir. Meml. Art Gallery of U. Rochester, 1992—, pres., chmn., 1980-84; bd. dirs., treas. Rochester Health Care, Inc., 1993-95; dir. Rocester Gen. Hosp., 1981-90, 93—, chmn. Rochester Gen. Hosp/The Genesee Hosp, 1999—; former com. Viahealth, Inc., 1999—; mem. bd. mgrs. Eastman Sch. Music, 1994—; mem. Estate Planning Coun. Rochester; chancellor Episcopal Diocese of Rochester, 1979-90, 98—. Fellow Am. Coll. Trust and Estate Counsel; mem. Am. Bankers Assn. (mem. exec. com. trust divsn., chmn. personal svc. com. 1989-92), N.Y. State Bar Assn. (chmn. com. on taxation of trusts and estates 1988-89), Fla. Bar, Pa. Bar Assn., Genesee Valley Club (treas. 1987-89). Republican. Avocations: archaeology, military history, painting, tennis, golf. Banking, Estate planning, Probate. Office: Harter Secrest & Emery 700 Midtown Tower Rochester NY 14604-2006

**BROWN, RICHARD LAWRENCE,** lawyer; b. Evansville, Ind., Dec. 8, 1932; s. William S. and Mildred (Tenbarge) B.; m. Alice Rae Costello, June 14, 1957; children: Richard, Catherine, Vanessa, Mary, James. AA, Vincennes U., 1953; BA, Ind. State U., 1957; JD, Ind. U., 1960. Bar: Ind., 1960, U.S. dist. ct. (so. dist.) Ind., 1961, U.S. Ct. Apls. (7th cir.), 1972, U.S. Sup. Ct., 1972. Mng. ptnr. Butler, Brown, Hahn and Little, and predecessor firms, Indpls., 1961-85, Butler, Brown and Blythe, Indpls., 1985-92; city atty. City of Beech Grove, Ind., 1967—; pvt. practice Beech Grove, Ind., 1992—; of counsel Blythe & Ost, Indpls., 1994-96, Holwager, Byers & Caughby, Beech Grove, 1996—; sec., treas. Internat. Bus. Inst., Dayton, Ohio, 1987-96, Internat. Pub. Inst., Dayton, 1987-96; bd. dirs. Vincennes U. Found. Editor: Indiana Municipal Lawyers Assn. Newsletter, 1985—. Chmn. bd. zoning appeals small cities and towns Marion County, Ind., 1965-66; gen. counsel Habitat for Humanity Greater Indpls., 1985-95; parish chmn. St. Jude's Ch. With U.S. Army, 1953-55. Fellow Indpls. Bar Assn.; mem. ABA, Ind. Bar Assn., Ind. Mcpls. Lawyers Assn. (co-editor newsletter, bd. dirs., pres. 1987-88), Vincennes U. Alumni Assn. (pres., bd. dirs. 1990-92), KC, Delta Theta Phi. Roman Catholic. Avocation: golf. State civil litigation, Federal civil litigation. Office: 1818 Main St Beech Grove IN 46107-1418

**BROWN, RICHARD RALPH,** lawyer, business law and marketing educator; b. Tiffin, Ohio, Aug. 22, 1941; s. Ralph Clair and Freda Mae (Bacon) B.; m. Carolyn Sue Curlis, Aug. 22, 1964; children: Timothy Richard, Eric Lee. BA, Heidelberg Coll., 1962; MEd, Bowling Green State U., 1964; JD, Cleve. Marshall U., 1968; postgrad. Case Western Res. U., 1967, Ohio State U., 1980. Bar: Ohio 1968. Ptnr. Elyria & Findlay, Upper Sandusky, Ohio, 1968—; atty. Ameritrust (Cleve. Trust Co.), Cleve., 1969-72; sr. real estate atty., analyst Firestone, Akron, Ohio, 1972-75; v.p. trust officer Bancohio, Sandusky, 1975-76; assoc. prof. law Ohio No. U., Ada, 1976-79; adj. prof. Bowling Green State U., Ohio, 1979-82; instr. Marion Tech. Coll., Ohio, 1982—; bd. dirs. privately held corps., Upper Sandusky. Com. mem. Put-Han-Sen council Boy Scouts Am. Mem. Wyandot County Bar Assn., Ohio Bar Assn. Republican. Methodist. Home: 551 S Sandusky Ave Upper Sandusky OH 43351-1631 Office: PO Box 403 114 E Wyandot Ave Upper Sandusky OH 43351-1430

**BROWN, ROBERT CARROLL,** lawyer; b. Ridley Park, Pa., June 24, 1948; s. Robert Carroll Sr. and Marjorie Elizabeth (Nowell) B.; m. Charlene M. Lipp, Oct. 4, 1986; children: Robert Charles, Gregory Scott, Michael Joseph. AB in Polit. Sci., Pa. State U., 1970; JD, Temple U., 1973. Bar: Pa.; U.S. Dist. Ct. (ea. dist.) Pa. 1977, Pa. Supreme Ct. 1973, U.S. Ct. Appeals (3d cir.) 1980. Judicial law clk. Ct. Common Pleas/Northampton County, Easton, Pa., 1973-74; assoc. Fox & Oldt, Easton, 1974-82; ptnr. Fox, Oldt & Brown, Easton, 1982—. Sec. Greater Easton Corp., 1977-82, Two Rivers Area Commerce Coun., Easton, 1983-85; officer Lehigh Valley Flying Club, Allentown, Pa., 1979-99. Mem. Northampton County Bar Assn. (sec. 1983-84), Pa. Bar Assn., Pa. Trial Lawyers Assn., Pa. Def. Inst. Republican. Presbyterian. Avocations: pvt. pilot, sports cars, golf, spectator sports. General civil litigation, Personal injury, Product liability. Home: 420 Wedgewood Dr Easton PA 18045-5753 Office: Fox Oldt & Brown 6 S 3rd St Ste 508 Easton PA 18042-4591

**BROWN, ROBERT G.,** lawyer; b. Boston, Apr. 29, 1956; s. Roger Ellis and Ida Margaret (Roherty) B.; m. Margaret H. Brown Dec. 11, 1991. AA, Cape Cod C.C., 1976; BA, Northeastern U., 1979; JD, Suffolk U., 1982. Counsel Barnstable Conservation Found., Inc., 1983-1990, Hyannis (Mass.) Fire Dist., 1985-93, Cotuit (Mass.) Fire Dist., 1985-88, West Barnstable (Mass.) Fire Dist., 1987—, Old King's Hwy Region Hist. Dist. Com., 1987—, Mass. Dept. Correction, Boston, 1989-95; dir. Barnstable Conservation Found. Inc., 1983-85. Mem. Barnstable Town Meeting, 1975-87, Barnstable Planning Com., Barnstable Charter Com., 1976-77, Barnstable Planning Bd., 1979-85. Mem. Mass. Bar Assn. (small firm mgmt. sect. coun. 1991-93), Mass. Acad. Trial Attys., Barnstable County Bar Assn., Phi Alpha Delta. Probate. Office: 86 Willow St Yarmouth Port MA 02675

**BROWN, ROBERT LAIDLAW,** state supreme court justice; b. Houston, June 30, 1941; s. Robert Raymond and Warwick (Rust) B.; m. Charlotte Banks, June 18, 1966; 1 child, Stuart Laidlaw. BA, U. of the South, 1963; MA in English and Comparative Lit., Columbia U., 1965; JD, U. Va., 1968. Bar: Ark. 1968, U.S. Dist. Ct. (ea. and we. divs.) Ark. 1968. Assoc. Chowning, Mitchell, Hamilton & Burrow, Little Rock, 1968-71; dep. prosecuting atty. 6th Jud. Dist., Prosecuting Atty. Office, Little Rock, 1971-72; legal aide Office Gov. Dale Bumpers, Little Rock, 1972-74; legis. asst. U.S. Senator Dale Bumpers, Washington, 1975-76; adminstrv. asst. Congressman Jim Guy Tucker, Washington, 1977-78; ptnr. Harrison & Brown, P.A., Little Rock, 1978-85; pvt. practice law, 1985-90; assoc. justice Ark. Supreme Ct., Little Rock, 1991—. Contbr. articles to profl. jours. Trustee U. of the South, Sewanee, Tenn., 1983-89, bd. regents, 1989-95. Fellow ABA, Ark. Bar Found (cert. of recognition 1981); mem. Ark. Bar Assn. Episcopalian.

**BROWN, ROBERT WARREN,** prosecutor, educator; b. Corpus Christi, Tex., Mar. 10, 1947; m. Carol; 1 child, Jeanne. BA, Western State U., 1982, JD, 1984; MS, Nat. U., 1985. Bar: Mont. 1986, U.S. Dist. Ct. Mont. 1986, Crow Tribal Ctl 1992, Chippewa-Tree Tribal Ct. 1992, Ft. Belnap Tribal Ct. 1992, Salish-Kootcrai Tribal Ct. 1992. Police officer Costa Mesa, Calif., 1970-85; pvt. practice Bozeman, Mont., 1986-91; asst. atty. gen. Office of Atty. Gen., Helena, Mont., 1991—; asst. prof. criminal law, criminal procedures Montana State U., 1994. Bd. dirs. Dept. Family Svcs., Bozeman, 1993. Sgt. USMC, 1965-69. Mem. Masons. Republican. Christian Reformed. Avocations: horses, backpacking. Home: 2770 Outlaw Ln Belgrade MT 59714-8755

**BROWN, ROBERT WAYNE,** lawyer; b. Allentown, Pa., July 6, 1942; s. P.P. and Rose (Ferrara) B.; m. Rochelle Kaplan, Oct. 23, 1977; m. Shelley Sherman, Mar. 3, 1973; children: Courtney Sherman, Robin Thea, Ryan Palmer; m. Lupe Peance, Nov. 22, 1996. AB, Franklin and Marshall Coll., 1964; JD, Cornell U., 1967. Bar: Ill. 1969, Pa. 1971. VISTA atty. Cmty. Legal Svcs., Detroit, 1967-68; asst. prof. law U. Ill., 1968-70; ct. adminstr., law clk. Lehigh County Ct. Common Pleas, 1971-72; ptnr. Gross & Brown, Allentown, 1972-76; pvt. practice law Allentown, 1976-77; sr. ptnr. Brown & Brown, Allentown, 1977-82, Brown, Brown & Solt, Allentown, 1982-85, Brown, Brown, Solt & Krouse, Allentown, 1985-89, Brown, Brown, Solt & Ferretti, Allentown, 1989—; instr. bus. law Muhlenburg Coll., 1973-76; pub. defender Lehigh County, 1973-74; mem. adv. bd. PNC Bank. Mem. Rape Crisis Coun. Lehigh Valley, 1978-84, Lehigh County Pre-trial Svcs., 1975-82; bd. dirs. Hispanic Am. Orgn., 1982-90, treas., 1983-86; bd. dirs. Lehigh County Sr. Citizens, 1980-88, pres., 1984-86; bd. dirs. Lehigh County Legal Svcs., 1973-77, Boys and Girls Club Allentown, 1994—, pres., 1998—; founding trustee Robert Clemente Charter Sch., 1998—. Recipient Cmty. Svc. award Hispanic Am. Orgn., 1985, Human Rels. Commn. award, Allentown, 1986; Lindback scholar Franklin and Marshall Coll., 1963-64. Mem. ABA, Pa. Bar Assn., Lehigh County Bar Assn., Order of Coif, Rotary (bd. dirs. Allentown 1998—). Democrat. Contracts commercial, Real property, State civil litigation. Home: 225 Parkview Ave Allentown PA 18104-5323 Office: 1425 W Hamilton St Allentown PA 18102-4224

**BROWN, RONALD ERIK,** lawyer; b. Phila., Sept. 26, 1954; s. Ernest Warren and Betty Lee Brown; m. Mary Ellen Jeanette, July 11, 1987; children: Hannah Mackenzie, Sarah Frances (dec.), Meredith Jeanette. BS in Nuclear Engring., Pa. State U., 1975; MS, Rensselaer Poly. Inst., 1980; JD, U. Conn., 1985. Bar: Conn. 1985, U.S. Patent and Trademark Office 1986, U.S. Ct. Appeals (fed. cir.) 1987, U.S. Dist. Ct. Conn. 1987, U.S. Dist. Ct. (so. and ea. dists.) N.Y. 1987, N.Y. 1988, D.C. 1988, U.S. Supreme Ct. 1999. Physicist nuclear engring. dept. Combustion Engring., Windsor, Conn., 1975-80, engr. instrumentation and control engring. dept., 1980-86; assoc. Kane, Dalsimer, Sullivan et al, N.Y.C., 1987-98, ptnr., 1999—. Mem. ABA, IEEE, Conn. Bar Assn., N.Y. Intellectual Property Law Assn., Conn. Patent Law Soc., Mensa. Patent, Intellectual property. Office: Kane Dalsimer Sullivan et al 711 3rd Ave New York NY 10017-4014

**BROWN, RONALD JAMES,** lawyer, political consultant; b. McKeesport, Pa., Nov. 4, 1951; s. James W. and Katherine V. (Amatangelo) B.; children: Claudia Jean, Jocelyn Kaye; m. Kathy E. Brown, July 6, 1996. BA, U. Pitts., 1973, JD, 1976. Bar: Pa. 1976. Assoc. firm Lucchino, Gaitens & Hough, Pitts., 1976-79; asst. dep. contr. Allegheny County Contr.'s Office, Pitts., 1979-86; ptnr. law firm Grogan, Graffam, McGinley & Lucchino, Pitts., 1986—; polit. cons. Brown-Giorgetti Cons., Pitts., 1990—. Candidate for State Senator, Dem. Party, North Hills, Pa., 1986; chmn. Nov. Caucus, Pitts., 1995—; mem. Dem. Forum of We. Pa., Pitts., 1987-91; del. Dem. Nat. Conv., 1978. Recipient Commrs. award citation of merit Allegheny County Bd. Comms., 1984. Mem. Allegheny County Bar Assn. Roman Catholic. Avocations: golf, reading, watching hockey, travel. Finance, Municipal (including bonds), Securities. Office: Grogan Graffam McGinley & Lucchino 3 Gateway Ctr Pittsburgh PA 15222-1000

**BROWN, RONALD LAMING,** lawyer; b. Springfield, Mass., Aug. 26, 1944; s. Douglas Seaton and Elizabeth Ruth (Stover) B.; m. Barbara Jo Roesler Moher, June 13, 1967 (div. Mar., 1987); children: Kimberly Lynn, Kathryn Jo, Karen Elizabeth, Kristine Ann, John Paul; m. Susan Janet Toth, Jan. 2, 1988; 1 child, Megan Christina. Chapman Col., 1968-70; JD, Creighton U., 1972. Bar: Neb. 1973, U.S. Dist. Ct. Neb. 1973, U.S. Ct. Appeals (8th cir.) 1974, U.S. Dist. Ct. Wyo. 1974, U.S. Ct. Appeals (10th cir.) 1976, Colo. 1987, U.S. Dist. Ct. Colo. 1987. 2d v.p., comml. loan counsel Omaha Nat. Bank, Omaha, 1973-74; prosecuting atty. Natrona County Atty., Casper, Wyo., 1974-75; partner Brown, Drew, Apostolos, Massey & Sullivan, Casper, Wyo., 1975-83; shareholder Burke & Brown, Casper, Wyo., 1983-86; pvt. practice Casper, Wyo., 1986-88, Ft. Collins, Colo., 1987—; bd. dirs. Tooke Internat., Inc.; trustee Brown Investment Trust, Ventura, Calif., 1996—; lectr. Casper (Wyo.) Col., 1980. Mem. sch. bd. St. Anthony's Sch., Casper, Wyo., 1979-82, Ft. Collins (Colo.) Connections, 1995—. Sgt. USMC, 1964-68. Mem. Neb. Bar Assn., Wyo. Bar Assn., Colo. Bar Assn. Republican. Avocations: golf, motor cycling, auto restoration, reading, home repair. Federal civil litigation, State civil litigation, General practice. Home: 1400 Wildwood Rd Fort Collins CO 80521-4026 Office: 425 W Mulberry St Ste 105 Fort Collins CO 80521-2864

**BROWN, SANFORD DONALD,** lawyer; b. Neptune, N.J., May 16, 1952; s. Richard B. and Janet (Flint) B.; m. Joan Miller, Sept. 5, 1978; children: Jennifer, Sanford Flint, Edward. BA, Brown U., 1974; JD, Seton Hall U., Newark, 1978. Bar: N.J. 1978, U.S. Dist. Ct. N.J. 1978. Law clk. to Hon. Patrick J. McGann Freehold, N.J., 1978-79; assoc. Dawes & Youssouf, Freehold, 1979-81; ptnr. Dawes & Brown, Freehold, 1981-86, Cerrato, O'Connor, Dawes, Collins et al, Freehold, 1986-89, Cerrato, Dawes, Collins et al, Freehold, 1989—; gen. counsel Manalapan-Englishtown Regional Bd. Edn., N.J., 1979-85, 87—, Monmouth Vocat. Bd. Edn., Colts Neck, N.J., 1979—, Allenhurst Bd. Edn., 1990-98, Interlaken (N.J.) Bd. Adjustment/Planning Bd., 1990—, Manasquan River Regional Sewer Authority, Howell, 1979-91, Pioneer Farm Credit, 1990—, United Meth. Homes N.J., 1992—, Ocean Twp. Bd. Adjustment Spl. Counsel, 1995—; fee arbitrator N.J. Supreme Ct., 1995—, panel chair, 1998—. Chancellor, So. N.J. Ann. Conf., United Meth. Ch., 1995—; coach Ocean Twp. (N.J.) Recreation League, 1986-97, Ocean Twp. Little League, 1992-95; chmn. bd. trustees United Meth. Ch., 1986-91; chmn. county advancement com. Boy Scouts Am., 1989-92, atty., county exec. bd., 1992—, spl. coun., 1995—, dist. chmn., 1996—, nat. rep., 1997—; gen. counsel Monmouth Presbytery Presbyn. Ch. Recipient Monmouth Legal Sec. assn. Employer of the Year award, 1993, Monmouth Coun. Boy Scouts Disting. Adult Eagle Scout award, 1997, Silver Beaver award, 1998, Dist. Award of Merit, 1999. Mem. Monmouth Bar Assn., N.J. Bar Assn., N.J. Sch. Bd. Attys. Assn. (regional v.p. 1991), Brown U. Alumni Assn. (chpt. pres. 1986-89, 95—), Wemrock Profl. Condo Assn. (pres. 1988-96, v.p. 1996—), Nat. Eagle Scout Assn. (life), United Meth. Scouters Assn. (life). Methodist. Avocation: swimming. Education and schools, General civil litigation, Land use and zoning (including planning). Office: Cerrato Dawes Collins 509 Stillwells Corner Rd Freehold NJ 07728-5302

**BROWN, STEPHEN EDWARD,** lawyer; b. Roanoke, Ala., Mar. 10, 1949; s. Edward E. and Jimmie (Dollar) B.; m. Kate Minor Eustis, Sept. 1, 1973; children: William Tucker, Kate Minor, Mary Cox. BA, Dartmouth Coll., 1971; JD, Tulane U., 1974. Bar: Ala, 1974, U.S. Dist. Ct. (no., mid. and so. dist.) Ala. 1974, U.S. Ct. Appeals (11th cir.) 1982, U.S. Supreme Ct. 1975. Ptnr. Bradley, Arant, Rose & White, Birmingham, Ala., 1974-89, Maynard, Cooper & Gale, Birmingham, Ala., 1989—. Co-chmn. Am. Heart Assn., Birmingham, 1987; co-chmn. legal div. United Way Ala., Birmingham, 1986; commr. Mountain Brook Athletics, Birmingham, 1988-91; chmn. Kid's Chance Scholarship Fund, 1994-95. Mem. ABA (labor and employee sect. 1978—), Ala. Bar Assn. (exec. com., chmn. labor and employment law sect. 1981-86, exec. com., chmn. worker's compensation sect. 1991-95), Birmingham Bar Assn. (pres. young lawyers sect. 1982, exec. com. 1982, 88-

90). Labor, Workers' compensation, General civil litigation. Office: Maynard Cooper & Gale 2400 Am South/Harbert Plz 1901 6th Ave N Birmingham AL 35203-2618

**BROWN, STEPHEN SMILEY,** lawyer; b. Little Rock, May 8, 1952; m. Lyda Bunker Hunt, May 28, 1978. BBA in Fin., So. Meth. U., 1974; cert. in Internat. Studies, U. San Diego Internat. Inst., Paris, 1977; JD, So. Meth. U., 1978. Bar: Tex. 1978, U.S. Dist. Ct. (so. dist.) Tex. 1983, U.S. Ct. Appeals (5th cir.) 1984, U.S. Ct. Internat. Trade 1985, U.S. Dist. Ct. (fed. cir.) 1990, U.S. Supreme Ct. 1985. Atty. Hunt Energy Corp., Dallas, 1976, Hunt-Stephens RE Inn, Dallas, 1977, Hughes Tool Co., Houston, 1978-79, U.S. Presdl. Inauguration Com., Washington, 1980-81, U.S. Dept. Energy Internat. Affairs, Washington, 1981, Codus Corp., Washington, 1982-83; sole practice Houston, 1983—. Aide to State Rep. E. Ray Hutchison, 1975; active Reagan Bush campaign, 1980, 84, Bush leadership, 1988, 92, Internat. Coun. Conf. USIA, 1990, White House Conf. on Ea. Ctrl. Europe, 1991; bd. dirs. Very Spl. Arts Tex.; bd. govs. RNLA; state chmn. Rep. Lawyers of Tex. Mem. ABA, Fed. Bar Assn., Tex. Bar Assn., Houston Bar Assn., Assn. Trial Lawyers Am., Coll. of State Bar Tex. Republican. Episcopalian. Avocations: travel, biking, weight lifting. Probate, Estate planning, Real property. Address: 106 Avondale St Houston TX 77006-3314

**BROWN, STEPHEN THOMAS,** judge; b. N.Y.C., Feb. 1, 1947; s. Albert and Ruth Hope (Kaff) B.; m. Yvonne Tobias Brown, Aug. 10, 1968. BS, Fla. State U., 1968; JD, U. Miami, Fla., 1972. Bar: Fla. 1972, U.S. Dist. Ct. (so. dist.) Fla. 1973, U.S. Dist. Ct. (mid. dist.) Fla. 1989, U.S. Ct. Appeals (11th cir.) 1973, U.S. Supreme Ct. 1976. Atty. Preddy, Kutner & Hardy, Miami, Fla., 1972-77; ptnr. Preddy, Kutner & Hardy, 1977-86, Preddy, Kutner, Hardy, Rubinoff, Brown & Thompson, Miami, 1986-91; U.S. magistrate judge U.S. Dist. Ct. (so. dist.) Fla., Miami, 1991—; adj. prof. U. Miami Sch. Law, 1983-84; vice chmn. auto ins. com. Fla. Bar, 1979-80, chmn. grievance com., 1981-84; mem. adv. com. on rules and procedures So. Dist. Fla., 1995—; mem. leadership coun. Fla. State U. Sch. of Arts & Scis. Mem. ABA, Acad. Fla. Trial Lawyers, Dade County Bar Assn., Fla. State U. Alumni Assn. (dist. v.p. 1993—), Seminole Boosters Inc. (bd. dirs. 1988-93), Seminole Club Dade County (pres. 1984-87), U. Miami Law Sch. Alumni Assn. (bd. dirs. 1994—). Avocations: snow skiing, fishing, golf. Office: US Dist Ct 300 NE 1st Ave Miami FL 33132-2126

**BROWN, STEVEN SPENCER,** lawyer; b. Manhattan, Kans., Feb. 26, 1948; s. Gerald James and Buelah Marie (Spencer) B. BBA, U. Mo., 1970, JD, 1973. Bar: Mo. 1973, U.S. Tax Ct. 1974, Ill. 1977, U.S. Dist. (no. dist.) Ill. 1979, U.S. Ct. Appeals (7th cir.) 1980, U.S. Ct. Claims 1986, Calif. 1989, U.S. Ct. Appeals (11th cir.) 1989. Trial atty. IRS Regional Counsel, Chgo., 1973-78; sr. trial atty. IRS Dist. Counsel, Chgo., 1978-79; assoc. Silets & Martin Ltd., Chgo., 1979-85, ptnr., 1985-92; ptnr. Martin, Brown & Sullivan Ltd., Chgo., 1992—; adj. prof. John Marshall, Chgo., 1985—. Republican. Presbyterian. Avocations: golf, tennis. Personal income taxation, Federal civil litigation, Administrative and regulatory. Home: 1340 N Astor St Apt 2903 Chicago IL 60610-8438 Office: Martin Brown & Sullivan Ltd 10th Fl 321 S Plymouth Ct Chicago IL 60604-3912

**BROWN, STUART P.,** lawyer; b. Covington, Ky., July 16, 1970; s. Elbert H. and Frances W. Brown; m. Jane Willis Nall, June 29, 1996. BA, U. Ky., 1992; JD, Salmon P. Chase Coll. of Law, 1997. Bar: Ky. 1997, U.S. Dist. Ct. (ea. dist.) Ky. 1998. Assoc. Bogucki Knoebel & Vice, Florence, Ky., 1995—. Vol. lawyer Northern Ky. Lawyers for the Poor, Covington, Ky., 1997—; mem. Dem. Nat. Com., Washington, 1995-97. Mem. Northern Ky. Bar Assn., (tort and ins. sect., bankruptcy sect., arbitrator 1997—), Sigma Pi (treas. 1991-92). Avocations: golfing, fishing. General civil litigation, Criminal, Bankruptcy. Office: Bogucki Knoebel & Vice 6901 Burlington Pike Ste A Florence KY 41042-1618

**BROWN, SUSAN MCMENAMIN,** lawyer; b. Jacksonville, N.C., July 6, 1967; d. John J. and Annie Winifred McMenamin; m. Richard Scott Browne, June 22, 1991 (div.; m. Mark Nicholas Brown; 1 child, Sydnee Hannah. BA, Ga. State U., 1990, JD, 1997. Assoc. Webb, Stuckey & Lindsey, Peachtree, Ga., 1994—. Pres. Rep. Women in Leadership, Fayette County, 1993-94. Republican. Roman Catholic. Avocations: snow skiing, scuba diving. Office: Webb Stuckey & Lindsey 400 W Park Dr Ste 220 Peachtree City GA 30269-1482

**BROWN, THOMAS CARTMEL, JR.,** lawyer; b. Marion, Va., June 20, 1945; m. Sally Guy Lynch; children: Sarah Preston, Taylor Cardwell. AB, Davidson Coll., 1967; JD, U. Va., 1970. Bar: Va. 1971. Assoc. Boothe, Prichard & Dudley, Alexandria, Va., 1971-76; ptnr. Boothe, Prichard & Dudley, Alexandria, 1976-86, McGuire Woods Battle & Boothe LLP and predecessors, McLean, Va., 1986—; chmn. bd. trustees Dominion Hosp., Falls Church, Va., 1990-93; mem. lawyers com. Nat. Ctr. for State Cts., 1993—; sec., gen. counsel Potomac KnowledgeWay, Inc., 1995—. Mem. Va. Child Day-Care Coun., Richmond, 1987-91, No. Va. Roundtable, 1995—; bd. dirs. Alexandria chpt. ARC, 1982-88. Fellow Am. Bar Found., Va. Law Found. (bd. dirs. 1997—); mem. Va. Bar Assn. (pres. 1992), Va. State Bar (chmn. bus. law sect. 1987-88), Alexandria C. of C. (counsel 1987-89), Omicron Delta Kappa. General corporate, Health. Office: McGuire Woods Battle & Boothe LLP 1750 Tysons Blvd Ste 1800 Mc Lean VA 22102-4215

**BROWN, THOMAS EDWARD,** lawyer; b. Iron Mountain, Mich., Oct. 9, 1946; s. Willard Ernest and Alice Marlburd (Nelson) B.; m. Mary Pat, Aug. 10, 1968; children: Kelly K., Thomas B., Katherine E. BA, Marquette U., 1968, JD, 1970. Bar: Wis. 1970, U.S. Dist. Ct. (ea. dist.) Wis. 1970, U.S. Ct. Mil. Appeals 1970, U.S. Supreme Ct. 1974. Felony pub. defender Wis. Pub. Defender, Milw., 1974-75; asst. U.S. atty. U.S. Justice Dept., Milw., 1975-78; ptnr. Gimbel, Reilly, Guerin & Brown, Milw., 1978—; instr. numerous legal edn. classes. Capt. U.S. Army, 1970-74. Mem. Am. Coll. Trial Attys. (fellow, Best Lawyers in Am. award 1997), Wis. State Bar (chmn. criminal law section 1988-90). Criminal, Federal civil litigation, Product liability. Home: 3907 W Marianna Ct Thiensville WI 53092-5190 Office: Gimbel Reilly Guerin & Brown 111 E Kilbourn Ave Milwaukee WI 53202-6611

**BROWN, THOMAS PHILIP, III,** lawyer; b. Washington, Dec. 18, 1931; s. Raymond T. and Beatrice (Cullen) B.; m. Alicia A. Sexton, July 28, 1955; children: Thomas, Mark, Alicia, Maria, Beatrice. B.S., Georgetown U., 1953, LL.B., 1956. Bar: D.C., Md. Pvt. practice law, 1958—. Author monograph and articles on legal malpractice. Pres. Cath. Youth Orgn. of Washington, 1972. Served to 1st lt. USMCR, 1955-58. Mem. Bar Assn. D.C. (pres. 1986, bd. dirs. 1987), Barristers Club, Columbia Country Club. General practice, Estate planning, Real property. Home: 5210 Norway Dr Chevy Chase MD 20815-6672 Office: 4948 Saint Elmo Ave Bethesda MD 20814-6013

**BROWN, WADE EDWARD,** retired lawyer; b. Blowing Rock, N.C., Nov. 5, 1907; s. Jefferson Davis and Etta Cornelia (Suddreth) B.; m. Gilma Baity (dec.); m. Euzelia Smart (dec.); children: Margaret Rose Johnson, Wade Edward, Sarah Baity Otey. Student Mars Hill Coll., 1928; JD, Wake Forest U., 1931. Bar: N.C. 1930. Pvt. practice, Boone, N.C., 1931—; chmn. N.C. Bd. Paroles, Raleigh, 1967-72; cons. Atty. Gen., N.C. Dept. Justice, 1973; mem. N.C. Senate, 1947-49; mem. N.C. Ho. Reps., 1951-53; mayor Town of Boone, 1961-67; with student legal svcs., Appalachian State U. Chmn., Watauga County Hosp. Author: Wade E. Brown: Recollections and Reflections, 1997. Active Boone Merchants Assn.; mem. gen. bd. Bapt. State Conv. N.C.; trustee Wake Forest U., now trustee emeritus; trustee Appalachian State U., Bapt. Found. N.C. Bapt. State Conv.; founder Watauga County Pub. Libr., 1996—. Probate, Real property. Office: PO Box 1776 Boone NC 28607-1776

**BROWN, WESLEY ERNEST,** federal judge; b. Hutchinson, Kans., June 22, 1907; s. Morrison H. H. and Julia (Wesley) B.; m. Mary A. Miller, Nov. 30, 1934 (dec.); children: Wesley Miller, Loy B. Wiley; m. Thadene N. Moore. Student, Kans. U., 1925-28; LLB, Kansas City Law Sch., 1933. Bar: Kans. 1933, Mo. 1933. Pvt. practice Hutchinson, 1933-58; county atty. Reno County, Kans., 1935-39; referee in bankruptcy U.S. Dist. Ct. Kans., 1958-62, judge, 1962-79, sr. judge, 1979—; apptd. Temporary Emergency Ct. of Appeals of U.S., 1980-93; dir. Nat. Assn. Referees in Bankruptcy, 1959-62; mem. bankruptcy divsn. Jud. Conf., 1963-70; mem. Jud. Conf., U.S., 1976-79. With USN, 1944-46. Mem. ABA, Kans. Bar Assn. (exec. council 1950-62, pres. 1964-65), Reno County Bar Assn. (pres. 1947), Wichita Bar Assn., S.W. Bar Kan., Delta Theta Phi. Office: US Dist Ct 414 US Courthouse 401 N Market St Wichita KS 67202-2089

**BROWN, WILLIAM A.,** lawyer; b. Memphis, Nov. 6, 1957; s. Winn D. Sr. and Annie Ruth (Hurt) B.; m. Mary Lee Walker, Dec. 27, 1980. BBA, U. Miss., 1978, JD, 1981. Bar: Miss. 1981, U.S. Dist. Ct. (no. and so. dists.) Miss. 1981, U.S. Dist. Ct. (we. dist.) Tenn. 1987. Ptnr., pres. Walker, Brown & Brown, P.A., Hernando, Miss., 1981—. Pres. DeSoto Literacy Coun., Hernando, 1988, Am. Cancer Soc., Hernando, 1988, DeSoto County Econ. Devel. Coun., 1995-96; mem. Leadership 2000, 1990-91; vice-chmn. Hernando Preservation Commn., 1997—; chmn. design com. Main Street Project, 1997—; allocations chmn. United Way of Mid-South Desoto County. James O. Eastland scholar, 1978-81; Paul Harris fellow Rotary Internat., 1997. Mem. Miss. Bar Assn. (bd. dirs. young lawyers sect. 1988-89), DeSoto County Bar Assn. (v.p. 1988-89, pres. 1996-98), Rotary (pres. Hernando chpt. 1989-90), Boy Scouts Am., N.W. Miss. (membership chmn. 1990, activities chmn. 1991), Am. Arbitration Assn. Methodist. Avocations: gardening, design and construction projects. Personal injury, Real property, Workers' compensation. Home: PO Box 276 Hernando MS 38632-0276 Office: Walker Brown & Brown PA PO Box 276 Hernando MS 38632-0276

**BROWN, WILLIAM HILL, III,** lawyer; b. Phila., Jan. 19, 1928; s. William H. Jr. and Ethel L. (Washington) B.; m. Sonya Morgan Brown, Aug. 29, 1952 (div. 1975); 1 child, Michele D.; m. D. June Hairston, July 29, 1975; 1 child, Jeanne-Marie. BS, Temple U., 1952; JD, U. Pa., 1955. Bar: Pa. 1956, D.C. 1972, U.S. Ct. Appeals (3d cir.) 1959, U.S. Ct. Appeals (4th cir.) 1978, U.S. Dist. Ct. (ea. dist.) Pa. 1957, U.S. Ct. Appeals (10th cir.) 1986, U.S. Ct. Appeals (5th cir.) 1988, U.S. Dist. Ct. D.C. 1994, U.S. Ct. Appeals (D.C. cir.) 1994, U.S. Ct. Appeals (fed. cir.) 1997. Assoc. Norris, Schmidt, Phila., 1955-62; ptnr. Norris, Brown, Hall, Phila., 1962-68; ptnr. Schnader, Harrison, Segal & Lewis, Phila., 1974—, mem. exec. com., 1983-87; chief of frauds Dist. Atty.'s Office, 1968, dep. dist. atty., 1968; commr. EEOC, Washington, 1968-69; chmn. EEOC, 1969-73; lectr. S.W. Legal Found., Practising Law Inst., Nat. Inst. Trial Advocacy; bd. dirs. United Parcel Svc., Inc., 1983—, Lawyers Com. Civil Rights Under Law; chmn. Phila. Spl. Investigation Commn. MOVE; pres. Nat. Black Child Devel., Inc., 1986-90; bd. dirs. Cmty. Legal Svcs., 1986—; mem. exec. com. Schnader, Harrison, Segal & Lewis, 1983-87; bd. dirs., mem. exec. com. Lawyers Com. Civil Rights Under law, 1977—, co-chair, 1991-93; mem. Commn. on Comml. Operation of U.S. Customs Svc., 1994-98. Contbr. articles to profl. jours. Bd. dirs. Mid. States Colls. and Secondary Schs., 1983-89, Main Line Acad., 1982—, Nat. Sr. Citizens Law Ctr., 1988-94; mem. nat. bd. govs. Am. Heart Assn., 1994-96, mem. audit com., mem. pub. affairs policy com., bd. dirs., 1986-94, mem. audit com., mem. pub. affairs policy com.; mem. adv. com. on appellate ct. rules Supreme Ct. Pa., 1989-95. With USAF, 1946-48. Recipient award of merit Fed. Bar Assn., Columbus, 1971, NAACP award, 1971, Dr. Edward S. Cooper award Am. Heart Assn., 1995, Whitney M. Young Jr. Leadership award Urban League, 1996, Whitney North Seymor award Lawyers Com. for Civil Rights Under Law, 1996, Champions for Social Justice and Equality award Black Law Students Assn. Rutgers-Camden, 1997, Earl G. Harrison Pro Bono award, 1998. Fellow Am. Law Inst.; mem. ABA, Phila. Bar Assn. (Fidelity award 1990), D.C. Bar Assn., Pa. Bar Assn., Fed. Bar Assn., Nat. Bar Assn., Inter-Am. Bar Assn., World Assn. Lawyers (founding mem.), Am. Arbitration Assn. (past bd. dirs.), Barrister's Assn. Phila., Inc. (J. Austin Norris award 1987), Citizens Commn. on Civil Rights, NAACP (bd. dirs. legal def. and ednl. fund), Alpha Phi Alpha (Recognition award 1969). Republican. Episcopalian. Federal civil litigation, Labor, State civil litigation. Office: Schnader Harrison Segal & Lewis 1600 Market St Ste 3600 Philadelphia PA 19103-7240

**BROWNE, AIDAN FRANCIS,** lawyer; b. Dublin, Ireland, Apr. 24, 1955; came to the U.S., 1986; s. Terence J. and Eileen (Dowling) B.; m. Jill Whitney, June 6, 1981; children: Jessica, Sam, Caoimhe. B in Commerce, U. Coll., Dublin, 1979; JD, Suffolk U., 1989. Bar: Ireland, Mass. Ptnr. Hickey Beauchamp Kirwan O'Reilly, Dublin, Dublin, 1981-87; of counsel Sullivan & Worcester, Boston, 1987—; dir. Pacific Internat. Inst., Lewiston, Idaho; trustee Maruzen Coll., Antrim, N.H., 1989-92; bd. dirs. North Atlantic Trade Group, Boston, Univ. Coll. Dublin in N.Am., Boston. Fin. dir. Paul Harold for Congress, Boston, 1992; active Clinton/Gore Campaign, Boston, 1992, Friends of Fianna Fail, Boston, 1990. Mem. Irish Bar Assn., English Bar Assn., Welsh Bar Assn., Asian Pacific Bar Assn., Boston Bar Assn., Royal Dublin Golf Club, Lansdown Rugby Club (sec. 1986). Roman Catholic. Avocations: art, golf, soccer, rugby, snooker. Private international, Real property. Home: 21 Saxony Dr Sudbury MA 01776-2123 Office: Sullivan & Worcester 1 Post Office Sq Ste 2300 Boston MA 02109-2129

**BROWNE, JEFFREY FRANCIS,** lawyer; b. Clare, South Australia, Australia, Mar. 1, 1944; came to U.S., 1975; s. Patrick Joseph and Irene Kathleen (Cormack) B.; m. Deborah Mary Christine West, Aug. 28, 1971; children: Veronique Namur Irene, Jeffrey James, Nicholas Patrick, Sophie Christina, Amy Elizabeth. LLB, Adelaide U., South Australia, 1966; LLM, Sydney U., Australia, 1968, Harvard U., 1976. Bar: South Australia 1969, Australian Capital Territory 1973, N.Y. 1978, Victoria 1982, New South Wales 1983, Western Australia 1983. Assoc. High Ct. Australia, Canberra, Australian Capital Territory, 1967-68; diplomat Dept. Fgn. Affairs, Canberra, 1969; 2d sec. Australian High Commn., London and Malaysia, 1970-71; acting high commr. Australian High Commn., Ghana, 1972; counsel nuclear tests case Internat. Ct. Justice, 1973-74; assoc. Sullivan & Cromwell, N.Y.C., 1976-81, ptnr., 1983—; gen. counsel Alcoa of Australia, Melbourne, 1981-82; bd. dirs. Compinvest Pty. Ltd. Mem. Law Inst. Victoria, Australian Mining and Petroleum Law Assn., Law Coun. Australia (chmn. fin. and securities subcom., internat. trade and bus. law com.), Inst. Dirs. of Australia, Internat. Bar Assn. (sect. on energy and natural resources), Am. C. of C. in Australia (bd. dirs.), Am. Soc. Internat. Law, N.Y. Yacht Club, Melbourne Club. General corporate, Securities, Contracts commercial. Office: Sullivan & Cromwell 125 Broad St Fl 28 New York NY 10004-2489 also: 101 Collins St, Melbourne Victoria 3000, Australia

**BROWNE, RICHARD CULLEN,** lawyer; b. Akron, Ohio, Nov. 21, 1938; s. Francis Cedric and Elizabeth Ann (Cullen) B.; m. Patricia Anne Winkler, Apr. 23, 1962; children: Richard Cullen, Catherine Anne, Paulette Elizabeth, Maureen Frances, Colleen Marie. BS in Econs., Holy Cross Coll., 1960; JD Catholic U. Am., 1963. Bar: Va. 1963, U.S. Ct. Claims 1963, U.S. Ct. Customs and Patent Appeals 1963, D.C. 1964, U.S. Ct. Mil. Appeals, 1963, U.S. Ct. Appeals (D.C. cir.) 1964, U.S. Supreme Ct. 1966, U.S. Ct. Appeals (fed. cir.) 1982, U.S. Ct. Appeals (9th cir.) 1983, U.S. Ct. Appeals (6th cir.) 1991, U.S. Ct. Appeals (7th cir.) 1998. Assoc. Browne, Beveridge, DeGrandi & Kline, Washington, 1963-68, ptnr., 1968-72; ptnr. Shaffert, Miller & Browne, Washington, 1972-74; sr. counsel Office of Enforcement, EPA, Washington, 1974-76; asst. chief hearing counsel U.S. Nuc. Regulatory Commn., Washington, 1976-78; sole practice, Washington, 1978-79; ptnr. Winston & Strawn, and predecessor firms, 1980—; lectr. U. R.I., 1975, Washburn U., 1978, Legal Inst., CSC, 1975-78, Hofstra U., 1987—, Nat. Inst. for Trial Advocacy, 1986—. Del., Montgomery County Civic Fedn., 1970-74; chmn. Citizens Adv. Com. on Rockville Corridor, 1972-77; mem. Montgomery County Potomac River Basin Adv. Com., 1972-74. Served to capt. USAF JAGC, 1963-66, USAFR, 1966-69. Named Disting. Mil. grad. Holy Cross Coll., 1960. Mem. Coll. Holy Cross Alumni Assn. (bd. dirs. 1971-78, 98—, alumni senate 1978-97, mem. nominations and elections com. 1995—), Cath. U. Law Sch. Alumni Soc. (pres. 1992-93, dir. 1991—, bd. visitors 1998—), Cath. U. Gen. Alumni Assn. (bd. govs. 1992—, co-chair Gibbons medal com. 1995—, exec. com. 1995—, chmn. Cath. U. Am. Fund 1996—). Republican. Roman Catholic. Clubs: Holy Cross (pres. Washington 1968-69, 1973-74), Kenwood (Md.), Cosmos Club (Washington), Cripple Creek (Del.). Bd. editors Cath. U. Law Rev., 1962-63. General corporate, Environmental, Trademark and copyright. Home: 7203 Old Stage Rd Rockville MD 20852-4438 Office: Winston & Strawn 1400 L St NW Ste 800 Washington DC 20005-3508

**BROWNER, JULIUS HARVEY,** lawyer; b. N.Y.C., June 14, 1930; s. Irving A. and Anita (Baitcher) B.; m. Barbara Rodney, Oct. 29, 1961; children: Marc Jason. B.A., Bklyn. Coll., 1952; LL.B., Columbia U., 1957. Bar: N.Y. 1959, U.S. Dist. Ct. (so. and ea. dists.) N.Y. 1963, Fla. 1973, U.S. Dist. Ct. (so. dist.) Fla. 1976. Pvt. practice, Bklyn., 1959-73, Margate, Fla., 1973-76, Hollywood, Fla., 1987-94, Ft. Lauderdale, Fla., 1994—; ptnr. Lampert & Browner, Hallandale, Fla., 1976-81, Browner & Militzok, Hallandale, 1981-87. Chmn. Community Dist. Planning Bd. Bklyn., 1972-74; v.p. Assn. Small Claims Arbitrators, Bklyn., 1976; councilman's aide New York City Council, 1973. Served as sgt. U.S. Army, 1952-54. Mem. Bklyn. Bar Assn., Fla. Bar Assn., Broward County Bar Assn. Jewish. Real property, Family and matrimonial, Probate. Home: 4122 NW 29th Way Boca Raton FL 33434-5804 Office: 1915 NE 45th St Ste 210 Fort Lauderdale FL 33308-5100

**BROWNING, DEBORAH LEA,** lawyer; b. Helena, Ark., Aug. 16, 1955; d. William Herman Jr. and Mildred Kate (York) B. BS with honors, U. Ala., 1976; diploma, Oxford U., 1982; JD with honors, U. Tex., 1984. Bar: Tex. 1984, D.C. 1985. Drug abuse counselor Aletheia House, Birmingham, Ala., 1972-76; state parole officer Tex. Bd. Pardons and Parole, Houston, 1978-81; litigation clk. Harris County Dist. Attys. Office, Houston, 1983; appellate clk. Travis County Dist. Attys. Office, Austin, Tex., 1984; litigation assoc. Hogan & Hartson, Washington, 1984-92; pro bono atty. Internat. Human Rights Law Group, Washington, 1984-93, acting legal dir., 1988-89; co-chair Working Group on Human Rights of Women, 1994-98; pro bono atty. Lawyers Com. for Human Rights, 1993, pres. W.E.A.R.E. for Human Rights, 1996—. Author: A Supplemental Report On The Chilean Plebiscite, 1988; co-author: Chile: The Plebiscite and Beyond, 1989, First Steps After Stroessner: An Analysis of the 1989 Paraguayan Elections, 1989; editor Am. Jour. Criminal Law, 1982-84. Vol. atty. Women's Legal Def. Fund., Washington, 1987-88; dir. Chile Election Observor Project and the Paraguay Working Group; crime prevention coord. East End. Civic Assn., Houston, 1979-81. Mem. ABA (vice-chair working group on the internat. criminal ct., co-chair internat. human rights com., sect. internat. law and practice), Women and Internat. Law Interest Group (mem. steering com.), Am. Soc. Internat. Law. Avocation: travel. Federal civil litigation, Public international, Education and schools. Home: 7204 Central Ave Takoma Park MD 20912-6451

**BROWNING, JAMES ROBERT,** federal judge; b. Great Falls, Mont., Oct. 1, 1918; s. Nicholas Henry and Minnie Sally (Foley) B.; m. Marie Rose Chapell. BA, Mont. State U., Missoula, 1938; LLB with honors, U. Mont., 1941, LLD (hon.), 1961, LLD (hon.), Santa Clara U., 1989. Bar: Mont. 1941, D.C. 1950, U.S. Supreme Ct. 1952. Spl. atty. antitrust div. Dept. Justice, 1941-43, spl. atty. gen. litigation sect. antitrust div., 1946-48, chief antitrust dept. N.W. regional office, 1948-49; asst. chief gen. litigation sect. antitrust div. Dept. Justice (N.W. regional office), 1949-51, 1st asst. civil div., 1951-52; exec. asst. to atty. gen. U.S., 1952-53; chief U.S. (Exec. Office for U.S. Attys.), 1953; pvt. practice Washington, 1953-58; lectr. N.Y.U. Sch. Law, 1953, Georgetown U. Law Center, 1957-58; clk. Supreme Ct. U.S., 1958-61; judge U.S. Ct. Appeals 9th Circuit, 1961-76, chief judge, 1976-88, judge, 1988—; mem. Jud. Conf. of U.S., 1976-88, exec. com. of conf., 1978-87, com. on internat. conf. of appellate judges, 1987-90, com. on ct. adminstrn., 1969-71, chmn. subcom. on jud. stats., 1969-71, com. on the budget, 1971-77, adminstrn. office, subom. on budget, 1974-76, com. to study U.S. jud. conf., 1986-88, com. to study the illustrative rules of jud. misconduct, 1985-87, com. on formulation of standard of conduct of fed. judges, 1969, Reed justice com. on cont. edn., tng. and adminstrn., 1967-68; David T. Lewis Disting. Judge-in-residence, U. Utah, 1987; Blankenbaker lectr. U. Mont., 1987, Sibley lectr. U. Ga., 1987, lectr. Human Rights Inst. Santa Clara U. Sch. Law, Strasbourg. Editor-in-chief, Mont. Law Rev. Dir. Western Justice Found.; chmn. 9th Cir. Hist. Soc. 1st lt. U.S. Army, 1943-46. Decorated Bronze Star; named to Order of the Grizzly, U. Mont., 1973; scholar in residence Santa Clara U., 1989, U. Mont., 1991; recipient Devitt Disting. Svc. to Justice award, 1990. Fellow ABA (judge adv. com. to standing com. on Ethics and Profl. Responsibility 1973-75); mem. D.C. Bar Assn., Mont. Bar Assn., Am. Law Inst., Fed. Bar Assn. (bd. dirs 1945-61, Nat. council 1958-62), Inst. Jud. Adminstrn., Am. Judicature Soc. (chmn. com. on fed. judiciary 1973-74, bd. dirs. 1972-75), Herbert Harley award 1984), Am. Soc. Legal History (adv. bd. jour.), Nat Lawyers Club (bd. govs. 1959-63). Office: US Ct Appeals 9th Cir PO Box 193939 San Francisco CA 94119-3939 *Notable cases include: pro bono case Bell vs. U.S., 349 U.S. 81, 1955.*

**BROWNING, WILLIAM DOCKER,** federal judge; b. Tucson, May 19, 1931; s. Horace Benjamin and Mary Louise (Docker) B.; children: Christopher, Logan, Courtenay; m. Zerilda Sinclair, Dec. 17, 1974; 1 child, Benjamin. BBA, U. Ariz., 1954, LLB, 1960. Bar: Ariz. 1960, U.S. Dist. Ct. Ariz. 1960, U.S. Ct. Appeals (9th cir.) 1965, U.S. Supreme Ct. 1967. Pvt. practice Tucson, 1960-84; judge U.S. Dist. Ct., Tucson, 1984—; mem. jud. nominating com. appellate ct. appointments, 1975-79; mem. Commn. on Structural Alternatives, Fed. Ct. Appeals, 1997—; apptd. Commn. on Structural Alternatives for the Fed. Ctrs. of Appeals. Del. 9th Cir. Jud. Conf., 1968-77, 79-82; trustee Inst. for Ct. Mgmt., 1978-84; mem. Ctr. for Pub. Resources Legal Program. 1st lt. USAF, 1954-57, capt. USNG, 1958-61. Recipient Disting. Citizen award U. Ariz., 1995. Fellow Am. Coll. Trial Lawyers, Am. Bar Found.; mem. ABA (spl. com. housing and urban devel. law 1973-76, com. urban problems and human affairs 1978-80), Ariz. Bar Assn. (chmn. merit selection of judges com. 1973-76, bd. gove. 1968-74, pres. 1972-73, Outstanding Mem. 1980), Pima County Bar Assn. (exec. com. 1964-68, med. legal screening panel 1965-75, pres. 1967-68), Am. Bd. Trial Advocates, Am. Judicature Soc. (bd. dirs. 1975-77), Fed. Judges Assn. (bd. dirs.). Office: US Dist Ct US Courthouse Rm 301 55 E Broadway Blvd Tucson AZ 85701-1719

**BROWNLIE, ROBERT WILLIAM,** lawyer; b. Sasebo, Japan, Mar. 5, 1962; s. Robert Philip and Sachiko (Sugita) B.; m. Perla Esteban, Jan. 7, 1989. BA in Economics, U. Calif. San Diego, 1985; JD, U. Calif. Davis, 1988. Bar: Calif. 1988, U.S. Dist. Ct. (so. dist.) Calif. 1988, U.S. Dist. Ct. (ctrl. and no. dists.) Calif. 1991, U.S. Ct. Appeals (9th cir.) 1995. Rsch. asst. U. Calif. Davis Sch. of Law, 1986-87, teaching asst., 1987-88; summer assoc. Gray, Cary, Ames & Frye, San Diego, 1987, assoc., 1988-90; assoc. Milberg, Weiss, Bershad, Specthrie & Lerach, San Diego, 1990-92; assoc. Gray, Cary, Ware & Freidenrich, San Diego, 1992-95, mem., 1995—. Contbr. articles to profl. jours. Pres., v.p., bd. dirs. Asian Bus. Assn., San Diego, 1994-98; bd. dirs. San Diego Mediation Ctr., 1994-95; fin. com. mem. San Diego Automotive Mus., 1993-95. Mem. ABA (mem. class action and derivative litigation com.), Nat. Asian Pacific Am. Bar Assn. (bd. dirs. 1997-99), Calif. Bar Assn., San Diego County Bar Assn. (legis. com. mem. 1988-95), Pan Asian Lawyers Assn. of San Diego (v.p., pres., bd. dirs. 1995-99), Order of Coif, Phi Kappa Phi. Democrat. Avocations: automobile enthusiast, golf, travel, sailing, boating. Securities, General civil litigation, Environmental. Home: 1937 Bordeaux Ter Chula Vista CA 91913-1262 Office: Gray Cary Ware Freidenrich 401 B St Ste 1700 San Diego CA 92101-4240

**BROWNRIGG, JOHN CLINTON,** lawyer; b. Detroit, Aug. 7, 1948; s. John Arthur and Sheila Pauline (Taffe) B.; m. Elizabeth Thurmond, Apr. 30, 1976; children: Brian M., Jennifer A., Katharine T. BA, Rockhurst Coll., 1970; JD cum laude, Creighton U., 1974. Bar: Nebr. 1974, U.S. Dist. Ct. Nebr. 1974, U.S. Tax Ct. 1977, U.S. Ct. Appeals (8th cir.) 1990. Ptnr. Eisenstatt, Higgins, Kinnamon, Okun & Brownrigg, P.C., Omaha, 1974-80, Erickson & Sederstrom, P.C., Omaha, 1980—; lectr. in law trial practice Creighton U. Sch. Law, Omaha, 1978-83; dir. Legal Aid Soc., Inc., Omaha, 1982-88, pres., 1987-88, mem. devel. coun., 1989—; dir. Nebr. Continuing Legal Edn., Inc., Lincoln, 1991-93. Chmn. law sect. Archbishop's Capital Campaign, Omaha, 1991. Sgt. USAR, 1970-76. Fellow Nebr. State Bar Found. (dir. 1991-93); mem. Nebr. State Bar Assn. (pres. 1992-93), Nebr. Assn. Trial Attys., Omaha Bar Assn. (pres. 1990-91). Avocations: golf, bicycling, reading. State civil litigation, Federal civil litigation, Insurance. Office: Erickson & Sederstrom PC Ste 100 10330 Regency Parkway Dr Omaha NE 68114-3761

**BROWNWOOD, DAVID OWEN,** lawyer; b. L.A., May 24, 1935; s. Robert Scott Osgood and Ruth Elizabeth (Bellamy) B.; m. Sigrid Carlson, Mar. 3, 1956 (div. 1972); children: Jeffrey Owen, Kirsten, Scott David, Daniel Stuart; m. Susan Sloane Jannicky, July 4, 1975; 1 child, Mary Ruth Bellamy; stepchildren: Bradbury, Stephanie Ellington. AB with distinction, Stanford U., 1956; LLB magna cum laude, Harvard U., 1964. Bar: Calif. 1965, N.Y. 1969. Law clk. Ropes & Gray, Boston, 1963; assoc. McCutchen, Doyle, Brown & Enersen, San Francisco, 1964-66; lectr. law U. Khartoum, Sudan, 1966-67, Kenya Inst. Adminstrn., Lower Kabete, 1967-68; assoc. Cravath,

Swaine & Moore, N.Y.C., 1968-72, ptnr., 1973—, recruiting ptnr., 1978-82, mng. ptnr. for legal staff, 1983-86; ptnr. in charge London office, 1995—; treas. N.Y. Law Inst., 1978-83, chmn. exec. com., 1983-88, pres., 1988-93. Mem. editorial bd. Harvard U. Law Rev., 1963-64. Dir. Literacy Assistance Ctr., N.Y.C., 1983-94, co-chmn. bd. dirs. 1987-94; trustee Greenwich (Conn.) Country Day Sch., 1985-92, v.p., 1986-88, pres., chmn. bd. trustees, 1988-92; co-chmn. Harvard U. Law Sch. 25th Reunion Gift, 1988-89; nat. chair Harvard U. Law Sch. Fund, 1991-93; N.Y. regional com. campaign for Harvard Law Sch., 1991-95; com. on univ. resources Harvard U., 1991—, mem. Harvard law sch. vis. com., 1995—; keystone regional vice chair centennial campaign Stanford U., 1986-92; exec. com. Stanford U. N.Y. Coun., 1992-95; vice chmn. Stanford U. N.Y. Major Gifts Com., 1993-95; co-chair Stanford U. Ea. Coun., 1993; bd. govs. Stanford Assocs., 1993-95, pres., chmn. bd. govs., 1994-95; bd. advisors Stanford Trust (U.K.), 1995—; mem. nat. adv. bd. Outward Bound USA, 1993-96. 1st lt. USAF, 1956-61, fighter pilot Air Def. Command, capt. USAFR, Mass. Air N.G., 1961-66. Recipient Centennial medallion Stanford U., Stanford Assocs. award. Fellow Am. Bar Found., N.Y. State Bar Found.; mem. ABA, Internat. Bar Assn., N.Y. State Bar Assn., Assn. Bar City N.Y., Round Hill Club (Greenwich), Field Club (Greenwich), Sankaty Head Club (Nantucket), Siasconset Casino Assn. (Nantucket), Harvard Club (N.Y.C.). General corporate, Securities, Banking. Home: 19 Pelham Crescent, London SW7 2NR, England also: 39 Baxter Rd Siasconset MA 02564 Office: Cravath Swaine & Moore, 33 King William St, London EC4R 9DU, England also: Cravath Swaine & Moore 825 8th Ave New York NY 10019-7416

**BRUCE, ROBERT DENTON,** lawyer; b. Houston, Tex., Jan. 29, 1943; s. Simson Kelley and Lucy Jane B.; m. Norma Gene Durant, June 5, 1965; children: Denton, Jennifer, Stuart. BBA, U. Tex., 1966; JD, St. Mary's U., San Antonio, 1972. Bar: Tex. 1972. Pvt. practice Mineola, Tex., 1972—; city atty. Mineola, 1976—, Alba, Tex., 1981—. Trustee sch. bd. Mineola Ind. Sch. Dist., 1976-82; pres. Mineola Indsl. Found., 1980—, adminstrv. bd. Meth. Ch., Mineola, 1978-80. With USNR, 1960-70. Avocations: tennis, reading, hunting. Office: PO Box 266 Mineola TX 75773-0266

**BRUCE, THEODORE ALLEN,** lawyer; b. Pitts., June 5, 1957; s. Theodore and Frances Elaine B.; m. Lori Ames, July 7, 1990; 1 child, Jessica. BS, Murray State U., 1978; JD, St. Louis U., 1981. Bar: Mo. 1981, N.C. 1987, Tenn. 1987. Asst. atty. gen. Mo. Atty. Gen., Jefferson City, 1981-86, unit mgr., 1987-91, dep. chief counsel, 1991—; assoc. atty. gen. N.C. Dept. Justice, Raleigh, 1986-87. Contbr. articles to profl. jours. Named Law Enforcement Instr. of Yr., Mo. Dept. Pub. Safety, 1988. Home: 709 Luper Ln Jefferson City MO 65109-4941 Office: Mo Atty Gen PO Box 899 Jefferson City MO 65102-0899

**BRUCHS, AMY O'BRIEN,** lawyer; b. Portage, Wis., Jan. 19, 1968; d. John Gregory O'Brien and Maxine O'Brien Hibner; m. Michael L. Bruchs, Jan. 1, 1994; children: Tanner, Elizabeth. BA magna cum laude, U. Wis., Green Bay, 1990; JD cum laude, U. Wis., Madison, 1993. Bar: Wis. 1993, U.S. Dist. Ct. (we. and ea. dists.) Wis. 1993, U.S. Ct. Appeals (7th cir.) 1993. Assoc. Michael, Best & Friedrich LLP, Madison, 1993—. Bd. dirs., vol. Badger chpt. ARC, Madison, 1998—. Avocations: fishing, watching sports, basketball, reading, dog training. Labor, Workers' compensation, Federal civil litigation. Office: Michael Best & Friedrich 1 S Pinckney St Madison WI 53703-2892

**BRUCKNER, WILLIAM J.,** lawyer; b. Atlanta, Mar. 28, 1944; s. William Paul and Ruth (Seibert) B.; m. Lucy Clark, June 27, 1970; children: Heather, Christina. BS, The Citadel, 1966; JD, U. Ga., 1969. Bar: Ga. 1970, S.C. 1982, U.S. Dist. Ct. (no. and mid. dists.) Ga., U.S. Ct. Appeals (5th cir.), U.S. Supreme Ct. Asst. solicitor Solicitor's Office County of Fulton, Atlanta, 1971-73; labor solicitor So. Bell, Atlanta, 1973-82; gen. atty. So. Bell, Columbia, S.C., 1982-83, Atlanta, 1983-86; ops. and litigation counsel BellSouth Enterprises, Atlanta, 1986; assoc. gen. counsel Bell South Enterprises, Atlanta, 1990—; gen. atty. human resources divsn. Bell South Corp., Atlanta, 1986-90, assoc. gen. counsel, 1993—. Mem. Atlanta Soc., 1990—; bd. dirs. Ashford-Dunwoody YMCA, Atlanta, 1986-87, Horizon Theater, Atlanta, 1990—. Capt. U.S. Army, 1970-71. Mem. Atlanta Lawyers Club, Greater Atlanta U. Ga. Club (pres. 1990, trustee Ga. Student Ednl. Fund, chmn. ACCA legal office mgmt. com.), Buckhead Club. Roman Catholic. Avocations: photography, sports. General corporate, General civil litigation, Mergers and acquisitions. Home: 11315 Bowen Rd Roswell GA 30075-2238 Office: Bell South Corp 1155 Peachtree St NE Ste 1700 Atlanta GA 30309-3610

**BRUCKNER, ZIVA P.,** lawyer; b. Haifa, Israel, Aug. 27, 1945; came to the U.S., 1967; d. Shlomo and Miriam (Blau) Najari. BA magna cum laude, Bklyn. Coll., 1971; MA, U. Calif., Santa Barbara, 1973, PhD, 1975; JD cum laude, U. S.C., 1986. Bar: Ga. 1986, S.C. 1987. Asst. prof. U. Calif., Santa Barbara, 1973-75; assoc. prof. U. Miami, Fla., 1976-82; ptnr. Capers, Dunbar, Sanders & Bruckner, Augusta, Ga., 1986—. Contbr. chpt. to book and articles to profl. jours. Bd. dirs. YWCA of Augusta, 1983-97, Augusta Opera, 1997—, Adas Teshurun Synagogue, 1997—, Augusta Jewish Fedn., 1994—. Sgt. Israeli Army, 1963-65. Mem. Augusta Bar Assn., Order of the Coif. Jewish. Office: Capers Dunbar Sanders & Bruckner 1500 First Union Bank Bldg Augusta GA 30901

**BRUDNY, PETER J.,** trial lawyer; b. Syracuse, N.Y., Sept. 8, 1952; s. Joseph and Irene Brudny; m. Nita Cario, May 15, 1991; children: Barry Daniel, Ryan Nicole. BBA, Bernard M. Baruch Coll., N.Y.C., 1979; JD, U. Fla., 1989. Bar: Fla. 1989, U.S. Dist. Ct. (mid. dist.) Fla. 1989. Ins. adjuster Safeco Ins. Co., Orlando, Fla., 1981-84, Jack Curley and Assocs., Orlando, 1984-86, Cin. Ins. Co., Palm Harbor, Fla., 1986-87; atty. Prugh and Assocs., P.A., Tampa, Fla., 1990-95; sole practitioner Tampa, 1995—. Mem. ABA, ATLA, Hillsborough County Bar Assn. (pro bono work), Acad. Fla. Trial Lawyers (med.m alpractice task force 1996—), Million Dollar Advs. Forum. Avocations: scuba diving, singing, chess. Personal injury, Insurance, Civil rights. Office: 813 W Kennedy Blvd Tampa FL 33606-1418

**BRUDVIK, JACALYN DEAN,** court commissioner; b. Benton Harbor, Mich., July 25, 1953; d. Charles W. and Carolyn J. Dean; children: Jason W., Kyle R.; m. Jeffrey M. Hamlett, Sept. 22, 1984. BEd, Seattle U., 1975, JD, 1985; M in Special Edn., U. Wash., 1982. Bar: Wash. 1985, U.S. Dist. Ct. (we. dist.) Wash. 1985. Assoc. Law offices of Dan Dubitzky, Seattle, 1985-86, Ferguson, Maynard, Miller & Wolff, Everett, Wash., 1986-88; coord. Soc. Counsel Representing Accused Persons, Seattle, 1988-98; superior ct. commr. Snohomish County Superior Ct., Everett, 1998—; bd. dirs., sec. Wash. Protection and Adv. Sys., 1994-98; spkr. in field. Tutor Edmonds (Wash.) Eve. Acad., 1997—. Avocations: collecting children's books, skiing. Office: Snohomish County Courthouse M/S 502 3000 Rockefeller Ave Everett WA 98201-4046

**BRUEMMER, RUSSELL JOHN,** lawyer; b. Decorah, Iowa, Apr. 23, 1952; s. John William and Marion Jean (Wartinbee) B. BA, Luther Coll., 1974; JD, U. Mich., 1977. Bar: Minn. 1978, D.C. 1980, U.S. Dist. Ct. D.C. 1981. Law clk. to judge U.S. Ct. Appeals (8th cir.), 1977-78; spl. asst. to the dir. FBI, Washington, 1978-80, chief counsel congl. affairs, 1980-81; assoc. Wilmer, Cutler & Pickering, Washington, 1981-84, ptnr., 1985-87, 90—, counsel to dir. of cen. intelligence, 1987-88; gen. counsel CIA, 1988-90; speaker numerous profl. seminars. Editor-in-chief U. Mich. Jour. of Law Rev.; contbr. articles to law and banking jours. Mem. ABA (banking law com. 1982—, subcom. on bank holding cos. and nonbanking activities, chmn. 1985-87, chmn. subcom. on securities activities 1994-96, 98-99, mem. standing com. on law and nat. security 1995-98), Am. Law Inst., Coun. on Fgn. Rels., Order of the Coif (Disting. Intelligence medal 1990). Republican. Lutheran. Banking, Finance, Mergers and acquisitions. Home: 4024 40th St N Arlington VA 22207-4608 Office: Wilmer Cutler & Pickering 2445 M St NW Ste 500 Washington DC 20037-1487

**BRUEN, JAMES A.,** lawyer; b. South Hampton, N.Y., Nov. 29, 1943; s. John Francis and Kathryn Jewell (Arthur) B.; m. Carol Lynn Heller, June 13, 1968; children: Jennifer Lynn, Garrett John. BA cum laude, Claremont Men's Coll., 1965; JD, Stanford U., 1968. Bar: Calif. 1968, U.S. Dist. Ct. (no., ea., so. and cen. dists.) Calif. 1970, U.S. Ct. Claims 1972, U.S. Tax Ct. 1972, U.S. Ct. Appeals (9th cir.) 1972, U.S. Supreme Ct. 1973, Ariz. 1993. Atty. FCC, Washington, 1968-70; asst. U.S. atty. criminal div. Office of US. Atty., San Francisco, 1970-73, asst. U.S. atty. civil div., 1973-75, chief of civil div., 1975-77; ptnr. Landels, Ripley & Diamond, San Francisco, 1977—; mem. faculty Nat. Jud. Coll. ABA; lectr. Am. Law Inst. Am. Bd. Trial Advocates, Practising Law Inst. Def. Rsch. Inst., others. Co-author: Pharmaceutical Products Liability, 1989; contbg. editor: Hazardous Waste and Toxic Torts Law and Strategy, 1987-92; contbr. numerous articles to profl. jours. Mem. ABA (vice chmn. environ. quality com. nat. resources sect. 1989-93, co-chmn. enforment litigation subcom. environ. litigation com. litigation sect. 1990-92), Am. Inn of Ct. (master-at-large), Internat. Soc. for Environ. Epidemiology. Avocations: scuba diving, travel. Environmental, Product liability, Criminal. Office: Landels Ripley & Diamond 350 The Embarcadero San Francisco CA 94105-1250

**BRUENNER, ERIC WILLIAM,** lawyer; b. N.Y.C., Feb. 14, 1949; s. Frederick Herman and Euphemia Bruenner; m. Georgette Kernell, Sept. 9, 1972. BA, U. Va., 1971; JD cum laude, New England Sch. Law, 1975; postgrad., Columbia U., 1976. Bar: N.Y. 1976, U.S. Dist. Ct. (so. and ea. dists.) 1977, N.J. 1993. Assoc. Windels, Marx, Davies & Ives, N.Y.C., 1975-84, ptnr., chmn. banking dept., 1984—; adj. prof. NYU Sch. Bus. and Pub. Adminstrn., N.Y.C., 1983-85; speaker, chmn. numerous panels on various banking issues. Mem. ABA, Sea Cliff (N.Y.) Yacht Club. Banking, Contracts commercial, General corporate. Office: Windels Marx Davies & Ives 156 W 56th St Fl 23 New York NY 10019-3867

**BRUESEKE, HAROLD EDWARD,** magistrate; b. Sandusky, Ohio, Mar. 19, 1943; s. Edward W. and Jolanda (Sommer) B.; m. Bonnie A. Beaver, Aug. 12, 1967; children: Matthew E., Michael A. BA with honors, Elmhurst Coll., 1965; JD, Ind. U., 1968. Bar: Ind., 1968, U.S. Dist. Ct. (no. and so. dists.) 1968, U.S. Supreme Ct. 1978; lic. real estate broker, Ind. Staff atty. Legal Svcs./Legal Edn., South Bend, Ind., 1968-70; pvt. practice South Bend, 1971-92; dep. pros. atty. St. Joseph County, South Bend, 1971-73; juvenile referee St. Joseph Probate Ct., South Bend, 1973-92, judge pro tem, 1993, magistrate, 1993—. Contbg. author: Juvenile Benchbook, 1980-92. Bd. dirs. Eden Theol. Sem., St. Louis, 1989—, various other civic orgns., South Bend, 1968—; bd. dirs., elder Zion United Ch. of Christ, South Bend, 1994-96. Mem. ABA, Ind. State Bar Assn., St. Joseph County Bar Assn., Nat. Coun. Juvenile and Family Ct. Judges, Ind. Coun. Juvenile and Family Ct. Judges (bd. dirs., sec., v.p. pres. 1980—), Judicial Conf. Ind. (dir. 1998—). Avocations: amateur radio, recreational vehicles, computers. Home: 52741 Arbor Dr South Bend IN 46635-1205 Office: Juvenile Justice Ctr 1000 S Michigan St South Bend IN 46601-3426

**BRUFF, HAROLD HASTINGS,** dean; b. 1944. BA in Am. History and Lit., Williams Coll.; JD magna cum laude, Harvard U. Law faculty Ariz. State U., Tempe, 1971-79; sr. atty.-advisor Office of Legal Counsel, U.S. Dept. Justice, 1979-81; cons. to chmn. Pres.'s Commn. on the Accident at Three Mile Island, 1981; law faculty U. Tex., Austin, 1983-85, John S. Redditt prof. law, 1985-92; Donald Rothschild rsch. prof. George Washington U. Law Sch., Washington, 1992-96; dean U. Colo. Sch. Law, Boulder, 1996—. Contbr. articles to profl. jours. Mem. ABA, Phi Beta Kappa. Office: U Colo Boulder Sch Law Boulder CO 80309

**BRUGGER, JOERN-ERIC WALTER,** real estate company executive, lawyer; b. Nuremburg, Fed. Republic Germany, July 11, 1962; came to U.S., 1962; s. Hubert Anton and Gisela Eva (Schruut) B. BS in Biology, UCLA, 1985; JD, Santa Clara U., 1989. Adminstrv. asst. Autohaus Brugger, Redwood City, Calif., 1985-86; v.p. automobile div. Brugger Corp., Redwood City, 1986-87; v.p. BayCity Land Co., Inc., Redwood City, 1987-88, pres., 1989-91; corp. sec. Western AG Systems, Inc., Redwood City, Bankers Indemnity Corp., Redwood City, Brockway Corp., Reno. Republican. Roman Catholic. Avocations: martial arts, writing, skiing. Office: Anderlini Finkelstein & Emerick 400 S El Camino Real Ste 700 San Mateo CA 94402-1744

**BRUMBAUGH, JOHN MOORE,** lawyer; b. Lima, Peru, Aug. 3, 1945; s. John Granville and Annie Lee (Moore) B.; m. Caroline Patterson, Aug. 12, 1967; children: John Patterson, David Elliott, Katherine Anne, Caroline Moore. BA, Wabash Coll., 1967; JD, U. Fla., 1970. Bar: Fla. 1970, U.S. Ct. Appeals (5th and 11th cirs.), U.S. Dist. Ct. (so. dist.) Fla., U.S. Supreme Ct. Law clk. to judge U.S. Dist. Ct. (so. dist.) Fla., Miami, Fla., 1970-72; assoc. Frates, Floyd, Pearson, Miami, 1972-76; ptnr. Richman, Greer, Weil Brumbaugh Mirabito & Christensen, PA, Miami, Fla., 1976—, mng. ptnr., 1990—. Trustee Trinity Episcopal Sch., Miami, 1985-89, chmn. bd. trustees, 1987-90; trustee St. Thomas Episc. Day Sch., 1988-90, Palmer Trinity Sch., 1996—, vice-chmn., 1999—. Fellow Internat. Soc. Barristers; mem. ABA (standing com. on specialization 1997—), Am. Bar Found., Fla. Bar (mem. bd. legal specialization and edn. 1984-85, 87—, chmn. 1993-94, cert. civil trial lawyer), Dade County Bar Assn., Blue Key, Phi Delta Phi. Federal civil litigation, State civil litigation, General civil litigation.

**BRUMM, JAMES EARL,** lawyer, trading company executive; b. San Antonio, Dec. 19, 1942; s. John Edward and Marie Oletha (Gault) B.; m. Alicia Joan Pine, Aug. 17, 1968 (div. Mar. 1991); children: Christopher Kenji, Jennifer Kimiko, Laurie Kiyoko; m. Yuko Tsuchida, Apr. 17, 1991. AB, Calif. State U., Fresno, 1965; LLB, Columbia U., 1968. Bar: N.Y. 1969. Assoc. Reid & Priest, N.Y.C., 1968-72, Logan, Takashima & Nemoto, Tokyo, 1973-76; exec. v.p., gen. counsel, dir. Mitsubishi Internat. Corp., N.Y.C., 1977—; pres. Mitsubishi Internat. Corp. Found., N.Y.C., 1992—; dir. Mitsubishi Corp., Japan, N.Y.C., 1995—; bd. dirs. Brunei LNG, Tembec, Inc. Trustee Spuyten Duyvil Nursery Sch., Bronx, N.Y., 1991-95; mem. lawyers com. for human rights, steering com. Internat. Rule of Law Coun., 1993—; bd. dirs. Jr. Achievement Internat., 1997—, Internat. Sch. Svcs., 1997—; mem. adv. coun. Sanctuary for Families, Ctr. for Battered Women's Legal Svcs., 1997—; bd. vis. Columbia Law Sch., 1998—. Mem. ABA, Assn. Bar City N.Y. (chmn. com. on internat. trade 1990-93, chmn. task force on internat. legal svcs. 1998—), Univ. Club, Nippon Club. General corporate, Private international. Home: 255 W 84th St Apt 6C New York NY 10024-4327 Office: Mitsubishi Internat Corp 520 Madison Ave New York NY 10022-4213

**BRUNAULT-MCGUINNESS, ANDREA LOUISE,** lawyer; b. Holyoke, Mass., June 25, 1963; d. Harold Francis and Paula (Gagliarducci) Brunault; m. Paul McGuiness. BA, Assumption Coll., 1985; JD, Suffolk U., 1988. Bar: Mass. 1988. Assoc. Chartier, Ogan, Brady & Lukakis, Holyoke, 1989-95; chmn. licensing bd. City of Holyoke, 1996—; adj. prof. Our Lady of Elms Coll., Chicopee, Mass., 1992-97. Clk. bd. dirs. Wisteriahurst Mus., Holyoke, 1995-98, Founds., Inc., Holyoke, 1991-96; mem. Bishops Pro-Life Commn., Springfield, Mass., 1996—. Republican. Roman Catholic. Avocations: skiing, cooking, painting. Office: 476 Appleton St Holyoke MA 01040-3236

**BRUNER, PAUL DANIEL,** lawyer; b. San Antonio, Nov. 7, 1952; s. Paul Harold and Doris Elizabeth (Holland) B. BA summa cum laude, Rice U., Houston, 1974; JD magna cum laude, U. Mich., 1981, MPP, 1981. Bar: D.C. 1981. Assoc. Spiegel & McDiarmid, Washington, 1981-89; ptnr. Spiegel & McDiarmid, 1989-95; of counsel Spiegel & McDearind, 1995—; sr. litigation coun. Whitman-Walker Clinic, 1995—. Mem. legal svcs. operating com. Whitman-Walker Clinic (AIDS svcs.), Washington, 1990—, vol., 1987—. Mem. ABA, ACLU, D.C. Bar Assn., Order of Coif. Civil rights, Labor, Insurance. Office: Whitman-Walker Clinic Legal Svcs Dept 1407 S St NW Washington DC 20009-3840

**BRUNER, PHILIP LANE,** lawyer; b. Chgo., Sept. 26, 1939; s. Henry Pfeiffer and Mary Marjorie (Williamson) B.; m. Ellen Carole Germann, Mar. 21, 1964; children: Philip Richard, Stephen Reed, Carolyn Anne. AB, Princeton U., 1961; JD, U. Mich., 1964; MBA, Syracuse U., 1967. Bar: Wis. 1964, Minn. 1968. Mem. Briggs and Morgan P.A., Mpls., St. Paul, 1967-83; founding shareholder Hart, Bruner and O'Brien P.A., Mpls., 1983-90; ptnr., head constrn. law group Faegre & Benson, Mpls., 1991—; adj. prof. William Mitchell Coll. Law, St. Paul, 1970-76; lectr. law seminars, univs., bar assns. and industry; chmn. Supreme Ct. Minn. Bd. Continuing Legal Edn., 1994-98. Contbr. articles to profl. jours. Mem. Bd. Edn., Mahtomedi Ind. Sch. Dist. 832, 1978-86; bd. dirs. Mahtomedi Area Ednl. Found., 1988-94, pres., 1988-91; bd. dirs. Minn. Ch. Found., 1975—, pres., 1989-97; chmn. Constrn. Ind. adv. bd., Fedl. Pub., Inc., 1991—. Capt. USAF, 1964-67. Decorated Air Force Commendation Medal; recipient Disting. Service award St. Paul Jaycees, 1974; named One of Ten Outstanding Young Minnesotans, Minn. Jaycees, 1975. Fellow Am. Coll. Constrn. Lawyers (founding mem., bd. govs.), Nat. Contract Mgmt. Assn., Am. Bar Found.; mem. ABA (chmn. internat. constrn. divsn. forum com. on constrn. industry 1989-91, chmn. fidelity and surety law com. 1994-95, regional chmn. pub. contract law sect. 1990-96), Internat. Bar Assn., Inter-Pacific Bar Assn. (vice chmn. internat. constrn. com. 1995-97), Fed. Bar Assn., Minn. Bar Assn. (vice chmn. litigation sect. 1979-81), Wis. Bar Assn., Hennepin Bar Assn., Internat. Assn. Def. Counsel, Am. Arbitration Assn. (nat. panel arbitrators), Mpls. Club. Presbyterian. Construction, General civil litigation, Government contracts and claims. Home: 8432 80th St N Stillwater MN 55082-9331 Office: Faegre & Benson 2200 Norwest Ctr 90 S 7th St Ste 2200 Minneapolis MN 55402-3901

**BRUNER, STEPHEN C.,** lawyer; b. Chgo., Nov. 11, 1941; s. Henry Pfeiffer and Mary Marjorie (Williamson) B.; m. Elizabeth Erskine Osborn, Apr. 7, 1973; children: Elizabeth, David. B.A. summa cum laude, Yale U., 1963; J.D. cum laude, Harvard U., 1967. Bar: Ill. 1967, U.S. Dist. Ct. (no. dist.) Ill. 1971, U.S. Ct. Appeals (7th cir.) 1983, U.S. Supreme Ct. 1988. Assoc. Winston & Strawn, Chgo., 1971-76, ptnr., 1976—, capital ptnr., 1982—; lectr. Northwestern U. Sch. of Law, 1983-84; cons. Commn. on Govt. Procurement, 1972; mem. Landmarks Commn., Oak Park, Ill., 1978-81; bd. govs. Oak Park-River Forest Community Chest, 1985-90; elected mem. Bd. Edn. Oak Park and River Forest High Sch., 1993—. Served to lt. USN, 1968-71. Recipient Navy Achievement medal; Corning Found. travelling fellow, 1963-64. Mem. ABA (litigation and pub. contracts sects.), Chgo. Bar Assn., Am. Arbitration (panel of arbitrators), Chgo. Coun. on Fgn. Rels., Econ. Club, Univ. Club, Yale Club, Harvard Club (Chgo.). Federal civil litigation, Government contracts and claims. Office: Winston & Strawn 35 W Wacker Dr Ste 4200 Chicago IL 60601-1695

**BRUNER, WILLIAM GWATHMEY, III,** lawyer; b. Gadsden, Ala., Nov. 29, 1951; s. William G. and Nicolette A. (Diprima) B.; m. Eloisa Fernandez, Aug. 7, 1976; children: Nicolette, Virginia, William, Weston. BSE, U. Mich., 1973; JD, U. Va., 1976. Bar: Ind., Pa. Assoc. Bingham, Summers, Indpls., 1976-78; corp. counsel Scott Paper Co., Phila., 1978-86; group counsel Emhart Corp., Farmington, Conn., 1986-89; corp. counsel Black & Decker, Towson, Md., 1989-93, sr. corp. counsel, 1994—. Mem. ABA (EEO com. labor and employment law sect., taxation sect.). Republican. Roman Catholic. Pension, profit-sharing, and employee benefits, Labor, General corporate. Office: Black & Decker Corp 701 E Joppa Rd Baltimore MD 21286-5502

**BRUNETTI, MELVIN T.,** federal judge; b. 1933; m. Gail Dian Buchanan; children: Nancy, Bradley, Melvin Jr. Student, U. Nev.; JD, U. Calif., San Francisco, 1964. Mem. firm Vargas, Bartlett & Dixon, 1964-69, Laxalt, Bell, Allison & Lebaron, 1970-78, Allison, Brunetti, MacKenzie, Hartman, Soumbeniotis & Russell, 1978-85; judge U.S. Ct. Appeals (9th cir.), Reno, 1985—. Mem. Council of Legal Advisors, Rep. Nat. Com., 1982-85. Served with U.S. Army N.G., 1954-56. Mem. ABA, State Bar of Nev. (pres. 1984-85, bd. govs. 1975-84). Office: US Ct Appeals US Courthouse 400 S Virginia St Ste 506 Reno NV 89501-2194

**BRUNNER, JAMES EDWIN,** lawyer; b. Kalamazoo, June 11, 1952; m. Rosemary C. Brunner; children: Matthew, Jacob, Seth. BS in Engring. magna cum laude, U. Mich., 1974, JD cum laude, 1977. Assoc. Consumers Power Co., Jackson, Mich., 1977-93, asst. gen. counsel, 1993—. Mem. ABA. Office: Consumers Power Co 212 W Michigan Ave Jackson MI 49201-2276

**BRUNO, ANTHONY D.,** lawyer; b. Newark, N.J., May 3, 1956; s. Frank and Delores (Fleming) B.; m. Gina Mabey, Aug. 1982; children: Chris, Dan, Will. BA in Polit. Sci., Syracuse U., 1978; JD, George Washington U., 1981. Bar: N.Y. 1981, N.J. 1981. Atty. Shearman & Sterling, N.Y.C., 1981-84; assoc. gen. counsel Warner-Lambert, Morris Plains, N.J., 1984—. Office: 201 Tabor Rd Morris Plains NJ 07950-2614

**BRUNO, FRANK SILVO,** lawyer; b. New Orleans, Sept. 5, 1924; s. Joseph Michael and Francis Marie (Gilberti) B.; m. Marion T. Schexnayder, Aug. 13, 1953; children: Joseph, Frank, Stephen, Robert, Thomas, Christopher. BA, Tulane U., 1947, JD, 1950. Bar: La. 1950, U.S. Dist. Ct. La. 1950, U.S. Ct. Appeals (5th cir.) 1953, U.S. Supreme Ct. Ptnr. Bruno and Bruno, New Orleans, 1950—. With USN, 1942-45. Mem. Assn. Trial Lawyers Am. (past mem. state com.), Assn. Trial Lawyers La. (past pres.), Assn. Trial Lawyers Greater New Orleans (past pres.), KC (past pres.), L'Union Francais (past pres.). Admiralty, Personal injury, Product liability. Office: Bruno & Bruno 825 Baronne St New Orleans LA 70113-1102

**BRUNO, KEVIN ROBERT,** lawyer; b. Newark, June 9, 1953; s. Angelo Joseph and Rita Theresa (Klein) B.; m. Lura Current, Apr. 25, 1981; children: Kevin Robert II, Carrie Elisabeth. BA with honors, Rutgers U., 1975; JD, Union U., 1978. Bar: N.J. 1979, U.S. Dist. Ct. N.J. 1979, N.Y. 1980, N.H. 1980, Vt. 1992, U.S. Dist. Ct. N.H. 1980. Assoc. Freeman & Bass, Newark, 1979, Bennett & Bennett, West Orange, N.J., 1979-80, Office of Luigi J. Castello, Woodsville, N.H., 1980-83; ptnr., officer Castello & Bruno, P.A., Woodsville, 1983-85; sole practice Woodsville, 1985—. Mem. ABA, N.H. Bar Assn., Vt. Bar Assn., Grafton County Bar Assn., Phi Beta Kappa, Pi Sigma Alpha. Democrat. Roman Catholic. Avocations: hiking, camping, skiing, snow shoeing, gardening. General practice, Probate, Real property. Home: 652 Groton Rd Groton VT 05046-9666 Office: 37 S Court St Woodsville NH 03785-1009

**BRUNO, LISA,** law librarian; b. N.Y.C., Apr. 1, 1951; d. Dominic A. and Earline H. (Reed) B. BA, U. South Fla., 1973; MLS, Fla. State U., 1976. Cert. libr., N.Y. Law libr. Carlton, Fields, Ward, Emmanuel, Tampa, Fla., 1986-88; info. specialist Consumers Union, Yonkers, N.Y., 1991; law libr. Libr. of U.S. Cts., 11th Cir., Atlanta, 1992; sales rep. Lawyers Coop. Pub., Rochester, N.Y., 1994-95; cons. Info. Brokers, Atlantic Beach, Fla., 1995—; lectr./guest spkr. in field. Contbr. articles to profl. jours. Avocations: ballet, art appreciation, travel. Office: Information Brokers 377 Plaza St Atlantic Beach FL 32233

**BRUNO, RICHARD THOMAS,** lawyer, financial consultant; b. Summit, N.J., May 31, 1955; s. Anthony Thomas and Violet Henrietta (Andersen) B.; m. Anne Lee Griffiths, Aug. 8, 1981; children: David Thomas, Sarah Anne. AB, Dartmouth Coll., 1977; JD, Vanderbilt U., 1981. Bar: N.Y. 1982, U.S. Dist. Ct. (no. dist.) N.Y. 1982, Ohio 1983, U.S. Tax Ct. 1983. Adminstrv. asst. Dem. Com. of Onondaga County, Syracuse, N.Y., 1977-78; assoc. Davoli, McMahon & Kublick, Syracuse, 1981-83; gen. counsel Pat Bombard Buick, Syracuse, 1983-84; sole practice Fayetteville, N.Y., 1984; assoc. O'Hara & Crough, Syracuse, 1984-87; sole practice Syracuse, 1988—; mem. local rules com. for no. dist. N.Y. U.S. Bankruptcy Ct., Utica, 1985—; legal counsel Fayetteville-Manlius (N.Y.) A Better Chance Program, 1985—. Mem. N.Y. State Dem. Com., Albany, 1982-86, Onondaga County Dem. Com., Syracuse, 1982-86, 88—; dist. enrollment dir. enrollment com. Dartmouth Coll. Alumni Council, 1988, past pres., sec.; enrollment liaison officer Dartmouth Club Cen. N.Y., Syracuse, mem. exec. com., 1981—; agt. Dartmouth Coll. Class of 1977. Mem. ABA (corp., banking and bus. sect., patent, tademark and copyright sect., econs. of law practice sect.), N.Y. State Bar Assn. (corp., banking and bus. sect.), Onondaga County Bar Assn., Dartmouth Lawyers Assn. Roman Catholic. Avocations: downhill skiing, sailing, running, racquetball, nautilus. General corporate, Contracts commercial, Real property. Home: 1900 Grant St Ste 605 Denver CO 80203-4306 Office: 217 Montgomery St Syracuse NY 13202-1937

**BRUSH, KIRKLAND L.,** lawyer; b. Sulphur Springs, Tex., Feb. 18, 1948; s. Robert S. and June R. B.; m. Kathleen M. Nixon, Feb. 24, 1973; children: Melia, Nicole, Veronica. BA, Rice U., 1973; JD, S. Tex. Coll. Law, 1976. Bar: Tex. 1976, Colo. 1986, U.S. Supreme Ct. 1986, U.S. Ct. Appeals (10th and 5th cirs.), U.S. Dist. Ct. (so. dist.) Tex., U.S. Dist. Ct. Colo. Ptnr. Burks & Brush, Houston, 1977-79; asst. criminal dist. atty. Cameron County Tex. Dist. Atty. Office, Brownsville, 1979-86; pvt. practice Ft. Collins, Colo., 1986—; adj. faculty mem. S. Tex. Coll. Law, Houston, 1977-79. Mem. Student Entrepreneur Program Bd., Ft. Collins, 1996-98; chmn. 53rd house dist. Rep. Party, Ft. Collins, 1995—. With U.S. Army, 1969-71. Mem. Tex.

Bar Assn., Colo. Bar Assn., Jud. Performance Commn. Roman Catholic. Criminal, Juvenile, General civil litigation.

**BRUSH, LOUIS FREDERICK,** lawyer; b. Amityville, N.Y., Dec. 7, 1946; s. Frederick and Frances (Annunziata) B.; m. Eileen Forsyth, Aug. 13, 1972; children: Christopher, Brian, Stephen. BS in Acctg. and Bus. Adminstrn., L.I. U., 1971; MBA in Taxation, CCNY, 1975; JD, N.Y. Law Sch., 1980. Bar: N.Y. 1980, U.S. Dist. Ct. (so. and ea. dists.) N.Y. 1980, U.S. Tax Ct. 1980, U.S. Ct. Appeals (2d cir.) 1980. Agt. IRS, Mineola, N.Y., 1971-76; appellate conferee IRS, Carle Place, N.Y., 1976-80; sole practice Mineola, 1980—; lectr. 5th Annual Estate Planning Conf. Am. Inst. CPA's, San Francisco, 1982; dept. chmn. Bramson Tech. Coll., N.Y.C., 1980-81; part-time prof. acctg. and tax law SUNY, Farmingdale, 1974-75, Suffolk County Community Coll., Selden, N.Y., 1975-76, CUNY, Queens, 1980-81. Contbr. articles to profl. jours. Mem. N.Y. State Bar Assn. (award 1980), Nassau County Bar Assn., N.Y. State Trial Laywers Assn., N.Y. County Trial Lawyers Assn. Estate taxation, Personal income taxation, State and local taxation. Office: 101 Front St Mineola NY 11501-4402

**BRUSTAD, ORIN DANIEL,** lawyer; b. Chgo., Nov. 11, 1941; s. Marvin D. and Sylvia Evelyn (Peterson) B.; m. Ilona M. Fox, July 16, 1966; children: Caroline E., Katherine L., Mark D. BA in History, Yale U., 1963, MA, 1964; JD, Harvard U., 1968. Bar: Mich. 1968, U.S. Dist. Ct. (so. dist.) Mich. 1968. Assoc. Miller, Canfield, Paddock and Stone, Detroit, 1968-74, sr. ptnr., 1975—, chmn. employee benefits practice group, 1989-96, dep. chmn. tax dept., 1989-93; bd. dirs. Electrocon Internat., Inc., Ann Arbor, Mich. Mem. editl. adv. bd. Benefits Law Jour.; contbr. articles to profl. jours. Mem. ABA, Mich. Bar Assn., Detroit Bar Assn., Mich. Employee Benefits Conf. Avocations: sailing, skiing, reading, piano. Pension, profit-sharing, and employee benefits, General corporate. Home: 1422 Macgregor Ln Ann Arbor MI 48105-2836 Office: Miller Canfield Paddock & Stone 150 W Jefferson Ave Fl 25th Detroit MI 48226-4432

**BRUTON, CHARLES CLINTON,** lawyer; b. Odessa, Tex., July 3, 1953; s. John Harley and Bonnie Jean (Woodson) B.; m. Janet Grubbs (div.). Student, Ea. N.Mex. U., 1971-73; BA in Polit. Sci. cum laude, Old Dominion U., 1979; JD magna cum laude, Oglethorpe U., 1982. Bar: Ga. 1983, U.S. Dist. Ct. (no. dist.) Ga. 1992, N.Mex. 1993, U.S. Dist. Ct. N.Mex. 1993, U.S. Ct. Appeals (11th cir.) 1993, U.S. Ct. Appeals (10th cir.) 1994. Legal sec. Macey & Zusmann, Atlanta, 1982-83; pvt. practice, Decatur, Ga., 1983-85; title ins. agt. Lincoln County Abstract, Ruidoso, N.Mex., 1985, Alamogordo (N.Mex.) Title Co., 1985-86; in house counsel, owner Otero Land & Title Co., Alamogordo, 1986-92; assoc. The Buck Firm, P.C., Alamogordo, 1992-96; with N.Mex. Pub. Defender, Carlsbad, 1996—; lawyer concerning Indian Child Welfare Act, Cherokee Nation, Tahlequah, Okla., 1992-94; alt. mem. N.Mex. Gov.'s Select Com. on Title Ins. Policy Changes, Santa Fe, 1991. Editor Woodrow Wilson Coll. Law Jour., 1981. Campaign sec. Judith Spear for Treas. Campaign, Alamogordo, 1988; elder Gateway Bapt. Ch., Alamogordo, 1993; mem. Lawyer's Co-op in Real Property and Bankruptcy, 1982. With USN, 1973-76. Mem. ABA, FBA, Lions (sec. Alamogordo 1992-93, tailtwister 1995), Otero County Bar Assn. (v.p. 1995-96, state bar com. on the unauthorized practice of law 1996—), Phi Mu Alpha Sinfonia. Republican. Avocations: computer programming, golf, fishing, role-playing games, music. Native American, Civil rights, General civil litigation. Office: NMex Pub Defenders 211 N Canal St Carlsbad NM 88220-5829

**BRUTON, JAMES ASA, III,** lawyer; b. Ottawa, Ill., Sept. 3, 1949; s. James Asa and Elizabeth (Darling) B.; m. ValAnna Schoeneman, Aug. 23, 1980; children: Jamie Elizabeth, James Asa IV, Anna Leigh. AB in Econs. and Math., U. N.C., 1971; JD, Temple U., 1975; LLM in Taxation, Georgetown U., 1978. Bar: PA. 1975, U.S. Ct. Appeals (6th cir.) 1977, U.S. Supreme Ct. 1978, U.S. Ct. Appeals (3d, 4th and 10th cirs.) 1978, U.S. Ct. Appeals (5th and 9th cirs.) 1979, U.S. Ct. Appeals (1st and 8th cirs.) 1980, D.C. Ct. Appeals 1982, U.S. Dist. Ct. D.C. 1984, U.S. Tax Ct. 1985, U.S. Ct. Appeals (11th cir.) 1985, U.S. Ct. Appeals (2d cir.) 1988, U.S. Ct. Appeals (7th and fed. cirs.) 1993, U.S. Ct. Fed. Claims, U.S. Dist. Ct. (no. dist.) Tex. 1994. Atty. Office of Chief Counsel, IRS, Washington, 1975-77; trial atty. appellate sect. tax divsn. U.S. Dept. of Justice, Washington, 1977-81; assoc. Steptoe & Johnson, Washington, 1981-85, ptnr., 1985-86; ptnr. Williams & Connolly, Washington, 1986-89; dep. asst. atty. gen. tax divsn. U.S. Dept. of Justice, Washington, 1989-92, acting asst. atty. gen., 1992-93; ptnr. Williams & Connolly, Washington, 1993—; bd. visitors Temple U. Law Sch., Phila., 1992—. Assoc. editor Temple Law Quar., 1974-75; editor Money Laundering Law Reporter, 1993—. With U.S. Army, 1971-72. Recipient Commr.'s award Commr. of IRS, 1992, Edmund Randolph award Atty. Gen. of U.S., 1993. Fellow Am. Coll. of Tax Counsel; mem. Fed. Bar Assn., D.C. Bar Assn. (tax sect., tax audits and litigation com. vice chair 1988-89), ABA (tax sect., com. on vicil and criminal tax penalties, subcom. on dept. of justice procedures, com. on spl. projects, com. on stds. of practice, com. on adminstrv. practice). Taxation, general, Criminal, Federal civil litigation. Home: 8390 Sylvan Way Clifton VA 20124-2241 Office: Williams & Connolly 725 12th St NW Washington DC 20005-5901

**BRUZGA, PAUL WHEELER,** lawyer; b. Lawrence, Mass., Oct. 15, 1952; s. Peter Paul and Mary Louise (Wheeler) B. BS, U. Colo., 1974; JD, Franklin Pierce Law Sch., 1978. Bar: N.H. 1978, U.S. Dist. Ct. N.H. 1978. Sole practice Manchester, N.H., 1978—. Mem. ATLA, N.H. Bar Assn. Republican. Roman Catholic. Personal injury, Criminal, General practice. Office: 734 Chestnut St Manchester NH 03104-3001

**BRYAN, ALBERT V., JR.,** federal judge; b. Alexandria, Va., Nov. 8, 1926; m. Marilyn Morgan, Aug. 25, 1950; children: Marie, John, Vickers. Student, Va. Military Inst., 1943-44; grad., Geo. Wash. Univ., 1946; LLB, Univ. Va., 1950. Bar: Va. Practicing atty. Alexandria, Va., 1950-62; circuit judge State of Va., 1962-71; judge U.S. Dist. Ct. (ea. dist.) Va., 1971-91, sr. judge, 1991—. With USMC 1944-46, PTO. Office: US Dist Ct Ea Dist 401 Courthouse Sq Alexandria VA 22314-5704

**BRYAN, BARRY RICHARD,** lawyer; b. Orange, N.J., Sept. 5, 1930; s. Lloyd Thomas and Amy Rufe (Swank) B.; m. Margaret Susannah Elliot, July 24, 1953; children—Elliot Christopher, Peter George (dec.), Susannah Margaret, Sallie Catharine. B.A., Yale U., 1952, J.D. cum laude, 1955; diploma in comparative legal studies, Cambridge U., Eng., 1956. Bar: N.Y. 1959. Legal advisor to gen. counsel Sec. of U.S. Air Force, Washington, 1956-58; assoc. Debevoise & Plimpton, N.Y.C., 1958-62, ptnr., 1963-93, presiding ptnr., 1993-98, of counsel, 1999—. Served to 1st lt. USAF, 1956-58. Fulbright scholar Trinity Coll., Cambridge U., 1956. Mem. ABA, Assn. of Bar of City of N.Y., Union Internationale des Avocats, Country Club of New Canaan, Polo de Paris, Fishers Island Club, Order of Coif, Phi Beta Kappa. Episcopalian. General corporate, Private international, Securities. Home: PO Box 197 Isabella Beach Rd Fishers Island NY 06390 Office: Debevoise & Plimpton 875 3rd Ave Fl 23 New York NY 10022-6256

**BRYAN, CHRISTIAN E.,** lawyer; b. Omaha, Apr. 19, 1957; s. Richard W. and Jean S. (Sprott) Erdenberger; children: Forrest Edward, Walker G. B in Gen. Studies, U. Tex., Dallas, 1980; JD, U. Houston, 1983. Bar: Tex. 1984, U.S. Ct. Appeals (5th cir.) 1988, U.S. Dist. Ct. (no. dist.) Tex. 1988, U.S. Dist. Ct. (ea. dist.) Tex. 1987, U.S. Dist. Ct. (so. dist.) Tex. 1984. Law clk. Law Office of George M. Kuhn, Jr., Houston, 1982-84, assoc., 1984-85; asst. prosecuting atty. Smith County Dist. Atty.'s Office, Tyler, 1985-88; sr. shareholder Cowles & Thompson, P.C., Tyler, 1988—. Mem. First Presbyn. Ch., mem. pers. com., 1996—; campaign vol. Don Kent for State Senate, Dist. 2; bd. dirs. Parent Svc. Ctr., pres., 1994-95, mem. exec. com., 1995-96, mem. policy bd. dirs., 1993-96, mem. adv. coun., 1996—; mem. Smith County Rep. Women's Club, Women's Symphony League, among others. Mem. Am. Bus. Tex. Bar Assn., Am. Bus. Women's Assn., Smith County Bar Assn. (dir. 1996), Smith County Young Lawyers Assn. (dir. 1993), Tex. Assn. Def. Counsel. General civil litigation, Product liability. Office: Cowles & Thompson PC 909 ESE Loop 323 # 777 Tyler TX 75701

**BRYAN, HENRY C(LARK), JR.,** lawyer; b. St. Louis, Dec. 8, 1930; s. Henry Clark and Faith (Young) B.; m. Sarah Ann McCarthy, July 28, 1956; children—Mark Pendleton, Thomas Clark, Sarah Christy Nussbaum. A.B., Washington U., St. Louis, 1952, LL.B., 1956. Bar: Mo. 1956. Law clk. to fed. judge, 1956; assoc. McDonald & Wright, St. Louis, 1956-60; ptnr. McDonald, Bernard, Wright & Timm, St. Louis, 1961-64, McDonald, Wright & Bryan, St. Louis, 1964-81, Wright, Bryan & Walsh, St. Louis, 1981-84; pvt. practice law, 1984-96, ret., 1996; v.p., dir. Harbor Point Boat & Dock Co., St. Charles, Mo., 1966-80, Merrell Ins. Agy., 1966-80. Served to 1st lt. AUS, 1952-54. Mem. ABA, Mo. Bar Assn., St. Louis Bar Assn. (past chmn. probate and trust sect., marriage and div. law com.), Kappa Sigma, Phi Delta Phi. Republican. Episcopalian. Lodge: Elks. Probate, General corporate, Family and matrimonial. Home: 41 Ladue Ter Saint Louis MO 63124-2047

**BRYAN, JUDKINS,** lawyer; b. Montgomery, Ala., Mar. 9, 1956; s. Spede J. and Mary E. Bryan; m. Rebecca Bryan. BA, Davidson Coll., 1978; JD, U. Ala., 1981. Bar: Ala. Ptnr. Hill, Hill, Carter, Montgomery, Ala., 1985-89; v.p., gen. counsel Enstar Speciality Retail, Inc., Montgomery, Ala., 1989-92; ptnr. real property and bus. law sect. Steiner, Crum & Baker, Montgomery, Ala., 1992—. Mem. adv. bd. Storage World, Inc., T.J. Johnson Builders. Capt. U.S. Army, 1981-85. Office: 8 Commerce St Montgomery AL 36104-3520

**BRYAN, NAT,** lawyer; b. Birmingham, Ala., May 8, 1960; s. John Newton and Susan Baarcke B.; m. Ashley Butler Bryan, Dec. 28, 1991; children: Jack & Kate. BA with honors, Auburn U., 1982; JD cum laude, Cumberland Sch. Law, 1985. Bar: U.S. Dist. Ct. (no. dist.) Ala. 1985, U.S. Dist. (middle dist.), Ala. 1991. Atty. Rivers and Peterson, Birmingham, 1985-90, Pittman, Hooks, Birmingham, 1990-97, Marsh, Rickard, Bryan, Birmingham, 1997—. Mem. Birmingham Bar Assn. (scholarship chmn. 1989). Avocations: hunting, golfing, fishing, softball, exercise. Office: Marsh Rickard & Bryan Ste 600 800 Shadow Creek Pkwy Birmingham AL 35209

**BRYAN, ROBERT J.,** federal judge; b. Bremerton, Wash., Oct. 29, 1934; s. James W. and Vena Gladys (Jensen) B.; m. Cathy Ann Welander, June 14, 1958; children: Robert James, Ted Lorin, Ronald Terence. BA, U. Wash., 1956, JD, 1958. Bar: Wash. 1959, U.S. Dist. Ct. (we. dist.) Wash. 1959, U.S. Tax Ct. 1965, U.S. Ct. Appeals (9th cir.) 1985. Assoc., then ptnr. Bryan & Bryan, Bremerton, 1959-67; judge Superior Ct., Port Orchard, Wash., 1967-84; ptnr. Riddell, Williams, Bullitt & Walkinshaw, Seattle, 1984-86; judge U.S. Dist. Ct. (we. dist.) Wash., Tacoma, 1986—; mem. State Jail Comm., Olympia, Wash., 1974-76, Criminal Justice Tng. Com., Olympia, 1978-81, State Bd. on Continuing Legal Edn., Seattle, 1984-86; mem., sec. Jud. Qualifications Commn., Olympia, 1982-83; chair Wash. Fed.-State Jud. Coun., 1997-98. Author: (with others) Washington Pattern Jury Instructions (civil and criminal vols. and supplements), 1970-85, Manual of Model Criminal Jury Instructions for the Ninth Circuit, 1992, Manual of Model Civil Jury Instruction for the Ninth Circuit, 1993. Chmn. 9th Ct. Jury Com., 1991-92. Served to maj. USAR. Mem. 9th Cir. Dist. Judges Assn. (sec.-treas. 1997—). Office: US Dist Ct 1717 Pacific Ave Rm 4427 Tacoma WA 98402-3234

**BRYAN, ROBERT RUSSELL,** lawyer; b. Shelbyville, Tenn., Mar. 14, 1943; s. Russell Duval and Auda Mai (Ellis) B.; m. Nicole Gibier, Apr. 22, 1989; 1 child, Auda Mai. Student U. So. Miss., 1961-62; student Samford U., 1962-63, JD, 1967; student George Washington U., 1964. Bar: Ala. 1967, U.S. Dist. Ct. (no. dist.) Ala. 1967, U.S. Ct. Appeals (5th cir.) 1969, U.S. Supreme Ct., 1971, U.S. Tax Ct. 1972, U.S. Dist. Ct. S.D. 1973, U.S. Ct. Appeals (11th cir.) 1974, U.S. Dist. Ct. (ea. dist.) Wis. 1975, Calif. 1978, U.S. Dist. Ct. (no. dist.) Calif. 1978, U.S. Ct. Appeals (9th cir.) 1979, U.S. Ct. Appeals (4th cir.) 1980, U.S. Ct. Appeals (3d cir.) 1982, N.Y. 1983. Asst. to v.p. DeHavilland Aircraft of Can., Ltd., Toronto, Ont., Can., 1967; ptnr. Lindbergh, Lindbergh, Leach & Bryan, Birmingham, Ala., 1968-73; sr. counsel Law Offices of R.R. Bryan, Birmingham, 1973-75; ptnr. Bryan, Wiggins, Quinn & Appell, Birmingham, 1975-77; sr. ptnr. Law Offices of Robert R. Bryan, San Francisco, 1978—; contbr. articles on capital punishment to profl. jours.; lectr. in field. Chair, mem. exec. bd. Nat. Coalition to Abolish the Death Penalty, Washington, 1984-93; mem. adv. coun. Native Ams. and Death Penalty, 1988-91; bd. dirs. Mill Valley Community Ctr., Calif., 1984-85; co-chmn. No. Calif. Coalition Against Death Penalty, San Francisco, 1988-91. Recipient Metzinger award Mid-West Hypnosis Conv., Chgo., 1990, Presdl. award Assn. to Advance Ethical Hypnosis, Boston, 1984. Fellow Am. Bd. Criminal Lawyers; mem. NAACP, ACLU, Nat. Assn. Criminal Def. Attys., N.Y. Assn. Criminal Def. Lawyers, N.Y. State Defenders Assn., Criminal Trial Lawyers Assn., State Bar of Calif. (criminal law sect.), Nat. Lawyers Guild, Calif. Attys. for Criminal Justice, Internat. Churchhill Soc., Amnesty Internat., Univ. Club of San Francisco. Democrat. Roman Catholic. Criminal. Office: Mchts Exch Bldg 465 California St Ste 210 San Francisco CA 94104-1808

**BRYAN, ROSEMARIE LUISE,** lawyer; b. Erlangen, Germany, May 20, 1951; came to U.S., 1956; d. Rudolf and Elise (Lindner) Schöfer; m. Bates William Bryan Jr., Jan. 6, 1990. BA in English, George Mason U., Fairfax, Va., 1981; JD, U. Va., 1984. Bar: Tenn. 1985, U.S. Dist. Ct. (ea., mid. and we. dists.) Tenn., U.S. Ct. Appeals (6th cir.), U.S. Supreme Ct. Legal liaison and researcher Va. Hwy. Transp. Rsch. Coun., Charlottesville, 1982-84; shareholder, dir. Witt, Gaither & Whitaker, Chattanooga, 1984—. Bd. dirs., sec., treas. Families, Inc., Chattanooga, 1989-94; bd. dirs. Family and Children's Svcs., Inc., Chattanooga, 1986-93, chmn. devel. com., 1988-90; dir., v.p. pers. Girls Inc., 1995-97, pres., 1997—. Fellow Tenn. Bar Found., Chattanooga Bar Found.; mem. Tenn. Bar Assn. (dir. litigation sect. 1987-88), Chattanooga Bar Assn. (dir. 1988-90), Tenn. Assn. Criminal Def. Lawyers (bd. dirs. 1987-89, CLE award 1988), Fed. Pub. Defenders, Inc. (bd. dirs. 1991-93). Mennonite. Avocation: skiing. Fax: 423-266-4138. E-mail: rbryan@wgwlaw.com. Antitrust, General civil litigation, Criminal. Office: Witt Gaither & Whitaker 1100 Suntrust Bank Bldg Chattanooga TN 37402

**BRYAN, SHARON ANN,** lawyer; b. Kansas City, Mo., Dec. 19; d. George William and Dorothy Joan (Henn) Goll; children: Lisa Ann, Holly Renee. BJ, U. Mo., 1963; diploma, Stanford Radio and TV Inst., 1961; postgrad., NYU Sch. Arts and Sci., 1963-64; JD, U. So. Calif., 1989. Cert. specialist in family law; personal fin. plannin profl. designation. Proofreader, copy editor Cadwalader, Wickersham and Taft, N.Y.C., 1963-64; manuscript editor, writer nonsci. sects. N.Y. State Jour. Medicine, Med. Soc. State N.Y., N.Y.C., also mng. editor Staffoscope, 1965-66; manuscript editor Transactions, also editor Perceiver Am. Acad. Ophthalmology and Otolaryngology, Rochester, Minn., 1969-72; hist. writer Am. Acad. Ophthalmology and Otolaryngology, 1972-82; atty. Burkley, Moore, Greenberg & Lyman, Torrance, Calif., 1989-91; with Christopher M. Moore & Assocs., 1991-99, Moore, Bryan & Schroff, 1999—; writer publicity articles Ft. Lee (Va.) Cmty. Theatre. Author: Pioneering Specialists: History of the American Academy of Ophthalmology and Otolaryngology. Mem. vol. honor roll soc. Meml. Sloan-Kettering Cancer Ctr.; active N.Y. Hosp. Women's League, 1965-67; docent Los Angeles County Mus. Natural History; vol. Harriet Buhai Ctr.; pres. Malaga Cove Homeowners Assn., 1999—. Mem. ABA, ATLA, Am. Med. Writers Assn. (editor conv. bull. 1966), N.Y. Acad. Scis., NOW, Women's Lawyers Assn. L.A. (bd. govs. 1991-96, chmn. family law sect.), Los Angeles County Bar Assn. (del. to State Bar Calif., exec. com. 1996-98), South Bay Women Lawyers Assn. (rec. sec. 1994-95, pres. 1996-97), Kappa Tau Alpha, Kappa Alpha Theta (chmn. membership com. N.Y. chpt. 1966). E-mail: Sharon@CMoore.Law.Com. Family and matrimonial. Home: 533 Via Del Monte Palos Verdes Peninsula CA 90274-1205

**BRYANS, RICHARD W.,** lawyer; b. Demver, May 29, 1931; s. William A. and Ruth W. (Waldron) B.; m. Carol Jean, Feb. 17, 1955; children: Richard W., Bridget Ann. BS, Denver U., 1954, JD, 1955. Bar: Colo., U.S. Supreme Ct. 1971. Sole practice Boulder, Colo., 1958-63; ptnr. Kelly, Stansfield & O'Donnell, Denver, 1963-92, Bryans & Bryans, Denver, 1993—. Served to lt. (j.g.) USNR, 1955-58. General corporate, State civil litigation, Condemnation. Office: 1177 Grant St # 308 Denver CO 80203-2362

**BRYANT, ANN LAKE,** lawyer, law educator; b. Springfield, Ohio, June 7, 1949; d. Thomas Allen Bryant and Jane (Lake) Matthews; m. Roy Anson Wyscarver, Nov. 26, 1976; children: Taylor Allan Wyscarver, Meredith Isabel Lake Wyscarver. BA in Govt., Colby Coll., 1971; JD, Cath. U., 1984. Bar: D.C. Assoc. Charles Gordon, P.C., Washington, 1983-88; ptnr. Gordon & Bryant, Washington, 1988-94, owner, 1994—; adj. prof. law Georgetown U. Law Ctr., Washington, 1994—. Contbr. several chpts.: Immigration Law and Procedure. Treas., past pres. AYUDA, Inc., Washington. Recipient Hugh Johnson Jr. Meml. award for contbn. of pro bono svcs., AYUDA, Inc., 1994. Mem. Am. Immigration Lawyers Assn., D.C. Bar Assn. Immigration, naturalization, and customs. Office: Gordon & Bryant 1742 S St NW Washington DC 20009-6145

**BRYANT, DAVID,** lawyer; b. Denison, Tex., Sept. 26, 1951; s. Monroe David and Mavis (Clymer) B.; m. Joy Harper, June 12, 1976; children: Cassie, Joanna, Amy. BA, North Tex. State U., 1972; JD, Harvard U., 1975. Bar: Tex. 1975. Law clk. U.S. Ct. Appeals for 5th Cir., Austin, Tex., 1975-76; assoc. Orrick, Herrington & Sutcliffe, San Francisco, 1976-78; from assoc. to mng. ptnr. Hughes & Luce, Dallas, 1978-90; sr. v.p. Amtech Corp., Dallas, 1990-91; gen. counsel Perot Systems Corp., Dallas, 1991-94, v.p., 1994—. General civil litigation. Office: Perot Systems Corp 12377 Merit Dr Dallas TX 75251-2224

**BRYANT, EVERETT CLAY, JR.,** lawyer; b. Newnan, Ga., Dec. 22, 1946; s. Everett Clay and Mary (Davis) B.; m. Lynn Hawley, Aug. 21, 1968 (div. June 1998); children: Clay Walker, Jennifer Lynn. Student, Vanderbilt U., 1964-66; AB cum laude, U. Ga., 1968, JD cum laude, 1971. Bar: Ga. 1971, U.S. Dist. Ct. (mid. dist.) Ga. 1973, U.S. Ct. Appeals (11th cir.), 1981. Assoc. Erwin, Epting, Gibson, Chilivis, Athens, Ga., 1971-76; ptnr. Erwin, Epting, Gibson & Chilivis, 1976-84, Blasingame, Burch, Garrard, Bryant & Ashley, P.C., Athens, 1984—; bd. dirs. Ga. Nat. Bank, Athens; instr. estate planning U. Ga. Sch. Law, Athens, 1976. Mem. editl. bd. U. Ga. Law Rev., 1968-70. Mem. Clarke County Dem. Com., Athens, 1976-84; bd. dirs. Athens YMCA, 1980-87; chmn. bd. Project Athena, Inc., Athens, 1994-96; mem. bd. visitors U. Ga. Sch. Art, Athens, 1998—. With USAR, Ga. N.G., 1968-74. Mem. State Bar Ga., Western Circuit Bar Assn. (pres. 1985-86), Lawyers Club Atlanta. Avocations: tennis, skin diving, foxhunting. Estate planning, General corporate. Office: Blasingame Burch Et Al PO Box 832 440 College Ave Athens GA 30603

**BRYANT, JACQUELINE SHIM,** lawyer; b. Cross Roads, St. Andrews, Jamaica. BS, Northwestern U., 1985; JD, UCLA, 1989. Bar: Ill. 1990, U.S. Dist. Ct. (no. dist.) Ill. 1990. Assoc. Levin & Funkhouser, Chgo., 1989-91; sole practitioner Chgo., 1991-95; atty. Aronberg Goldgehn Davis & Garmisa, Chgo., 1995-99, D'Ancona & Pflaum LLC, Chgo., 1999—. Contbr. chpt. to book. Trustee Northwestern U., 1993-97. Mem. ABA, Asian-Am. Bar Assn., Women's Edl. Aid Assn. (bd. dirs. 1991—), Northwestern Alumni Assn. (bd. dirs. 1993—), John Evans Club (bd. dirs. 1993—), Jr. League of Chgo., Coun. of 100. General corporate, Real property. Office: D'Ancona & Pflaum LLC 111 E Wacker Dr Ste 2800 Chicago IL 60601-4200

**BRYANT, J(AMES) BRUCE,** lawyer; b. Dettlebach, Fed. Republic Germany, Jan. 23, 1961; came to U.S., 1964; s. John Thomas and Doris Jean (Hazenbuahler) B.; 1 child, James Bruce II. BA, Northwestern State U., Natchitoches, La., 1984; MJ, La. State, 1986; JD, Miss. Coll., 1989. Bar: Miss., Tex. 1995, U.S. Dist. Ct. (no. and so. dists.) Miss., U.S. Ct. Appeals (5th cir.) La. 1991, U.S. Dist. Ct. (we. dist.) La. 1994. With residential life La. State U., Baton Rouge, 1985-86; law libr. worker Miss. Coll. Sch. Law, Jackson, 1986-87; clk. Brunini Law Firm, Jackson, 1987-88; ptnr. Cook & Bryant, Bay St. Louis, Miss., 1989-90; assoc. Cook, Yancey, King & Galloway, Shreveport, La., 1990-93; prof. bus. law La. State U., 1991-92, prof. paralegal sci., 1994-96; staff atty. State of La. Office of Support Enforcement, Shreveport, 1993-95; atty. Storm Operating Co. Inc. of La., 1994—; sr. regional atty. State of La. Dept. Health and Hosps., Shreveport-Bossier City, La., 1995—; prof. comms. law Northwestern State U., 1996—; spl. asst. dist. atty. 1st Jud. Dist., Caddo Parish, La., 1998—; bd. dirs. Extra Mile; cons. Wyman Fed. Credit Union, Geismar, La., 1989-90, Comml. Nat. Bank, Shreveport, 1990—; owner, pres. SHOWBIZZ Entertainment Agys., Shreveport, 1992—; v.p. Godfather Prodns., Inc., Shreveport-Bossier City, La., 1994—; owner La. Ctr. for Law and Justice, 1995—; spl. asst. dist. atty. Caddo Parish, 1998—; owner, pres. Dreamworks Internat., 1999—. Editor, author (with others): Art & Bylaws for Moot Court, 1989. Del. Republican Dist. IV, 1994—; bd. dirs. Shreveport Little Theatre, 1995—, Extra Mile, 1996—. Mem. ABA, Miss. Pro Bono Project, Miss. Bar Assn., Assn. Trial Lawyers Am., La. Trial Lawyers Assn., Hancock County Bar Assn. (social chmn.), Shreveport Bar Assn. (comml. litigation sect., editor newsletter), L.A. Pro Bono Project, TKE Alumni Assn. (pres.), Univ. Club (mem. com. 1994—). Roman Catholic. Avocations: martial arts, weightlifting, skiing, shooting. Contracts commercial, Communications, Entertainment. Home: PO Box 444 Shreveport LA 71162-0444 also: 3012 Pines Rd Shreveport LA 71119-3502 Office: La Ctr for Law and Justice 711 Texas Advocates Bldg Shreveport LA 71120

**BRYANT, KATHY JO,** association executive; b. Salina, Kans., May 1, 1953; d. Archie J. and Jacqueline Ruth (Kaufman) Phillips; 1 child, Shawn Bryant. BBA, U. Iowa, 1977, JD, 1980. Bar: Iowa 1980, Ill. 1983, D.C. 1984. Caucus staff Iowa Senate, Des Moines, 1980-81; legis. atty. AMA, Chgo., 1981-83, Washington, 1983-86; dir. govt. rels. Am. Coll. of Ob-Gyn., Washington, 1986-98; exec. dir. Am. Soc. of Assn. Execs., Alexandria, Va., 1998—. Mem. ABA, Women in Govt. Rels. Office: Am Soc of Association Executives Surgery Assn 700 N Fairfax St Ste 306 Alexandria VA 22314-2040

**BRYANT, RICHARD TODD,** lawyer; b. Kansas City, Mo., Sept. 3, 1952; s. Francis Todd and Marion Audrey (Weum) B.; m. Carol H. Olsen, Mar. 24, 1979. A.A., Longview Community Coll., 1972, A.A.S., 1972; B.B.A., U. Mo.-Kansas City, 1974, M.P.A., 1975, J.D., 1978. Bar: Mo. 1978, D.C. 1995, U.S. Dist. Ct. (we. dist.) Mo. 1978, U.S. Dist. Ct. (ea. dist.) Mo. 1995. Assoc. Harding & Copilevitz P.C., Kansas City, Mo., 1978-85; ptnr. Copilevitz, Bryant, Gray & Jennings, P.C., Kansas City, 1985-95; bailiff ct. Overland Park, Kans., 1974-84; ptnr. Richard T. Bryant & Assocs. PC, Kansas City, 1995-98, mng. shareholder, 1998—. Contbr. articles to legal jours. cons. Westwood & Lenexa (Kans.) Police Dept., 1977-78; adminstrv. hearing officer Housing Authority of Kansas City, 1988—; chmn. ad hoc com. Kansas City (Mo.) City Coun., 1992. Mem. ABA (liaison standing com. assn. standards criminal justice 1978, com. adminstrn. criminal justice 1977-78), Am. Arbitration Assn. (bd. of arbitrators, bd. of mediators), Kansas City (Mo.) Bar Assn. (mcpl. ct. com., vice chmn. 1991-94, chmn. 1994-95), First Amendment Lawyers Assn., Phi Delta Phi, Omicron Delta Kappa, Phi Theta Kappa. Family and matrimonial, Insurance, Constitutional. Office: 804 Bryant Bldg 1102 Grand Blvd Kansas City MO 64106-2316

**BRYANT, WILLIAM B.,** federal judge; b. Wetumpka, Ala., Sept. 18, 1911; s. Benson and Alberta B.; m. Astaire A. Gonzalez, Aug. 25, 1934; children: Astaire, William B. A.B., Howard U., 1932, LL.B., 1936. Asst. U.S. atty. for D.C., 1951-54; partner firm Houston, Bryant & Gardner, 1954-65; sr. U.S. dist. judge U.S. Dist. Ct. Washington, 1965—; prof. law Howard U. Sch. Law, 1965-91. Served with AUS, 1943-47. Mem. ABA. Office: US Dist Ct US Courthouse 333 Constitution Ave NW Washington DC 20001-2802

**BRYCE, TERESA AUDREY,** lawyer; b. Norfolk, Va., July 31, 1959; d. Burie O'Neal and Dorothy Mae (Hicks) Bryce. BA, U. Va., 1981; JD, Columbia U., 1984. Bar: Md. 1985, D.C. 1985. Rsch. asst., Legis. Drafting Rsch. Fund Columbia U. Sch. Law, N.Y.C., 1983-84; law clk. to Chief Justice Robert N. Wilentz N.J. Supreme Ct., Perth Amboy, 1984-85; assoc. Piper & Marbury, Balt., 1985-90; v.p., assoc. gen. counsel The Prudential Ins. Co. of Am., Frederick, Md., 1990-94; v.p., gen. counsel PNC Mortgage Corp. of Am., Vernon Hills, Ill., 1994-97; gen. counsel Nations Banc Mortgage Corp., Charlotte, N.C., 1997—. Bd. dirs. Parks and People Found., Balt., 1993-94, Chesapeake Bay Outward Bound Program adv. bd., Balt., 1988-93; bd. dirs. Total Health Care, Balt., 1988-90, Cmtys. in Schs., Charlotte, 1998—. Mem. ABA (forum on affordable housing and cmty. devel. law, fair housing practice divsn. 1989—, sect. of real property, probate and trust law 1986—, com. on secondary market financing of affordable housing 1995—, mortgages and financing of home ownership com. 1993—), Md. Bar Assn., D.C. Bar Assn., Am. Corp. Counsel Assn., Leary Bar Assn. (treas. 1998—), Alliance of Black Women Attys. (treas. 1987-88), Mortgage Bankers Assn. (legis. com., state legis. and regulatory com. Chair 1996-97, vice chair legal issues com. 1997-98, state issues publ. policy liaison 1996—, mem. RESPA/TILA task force), Delta Sigma Theta. Presbyterian. Avocations: golf, reading, tennis, theatre. Banking, Real property, General corporate. Office: NationsBanc Mortgage Corp 201 N Tryon St Fl 14 Charlotte NC 28202-2146

**BRYCE, WILLIAM DELF,** lawyer; b. Georgetown, Tex., Aug. 7, 1932; s. D. A. Bryce and Frances Maxine (Wilson) Bryce Bakke; m. Sarah Alice Riley, Dec. 20, 1954; children: Douglas Delf, David Dickson. BA, U. Tex., 1955; LLB, Yale U., 1960. Bar: Tex. 1960, U.S. Dist. Ct. (we. dist.) Tex. 1963, U.S. Ct. Claims 1964, U.S. Supreme Ct. 1971. Briefing atty. Tex. Supreme Ct., Austin, 1960-61; sole practice, 1961—; lectr. U. Tex., 1965-66. Editor Tex. Supreme Ct. Jour. Served to 1st lt. USAF, 1955-57. Fellow Tex. Bar Found. (sustaning, life); mem. ABA, Travis County Bar Assn., Williamson County Bar Assn., State Bar Tex., Rotary Internat. (dist. 5870 gov. 1999-2000), Headliners Club (Austin), The Argyle (San Antonio). General corporate, Probate, General practice. Home: 308 E University Ave Georgetown TX 78626-6813 also: 511 S Main St Georgetown TX 78626-5609

**BRYDGER, GORDON CHARLES,** lawyer; b. Miami, Fla., May 30, 1952; s. Lee and Sylvia (Balaban) B.; m. Marjorie Anne Gelber, Aug. 6, 1977; 1 child, Melanie. BS, U. Fla., 1974; JD cum laude, Emory U., 1977. Bar: Fla. 1977, Ga. 1977, Fla. Supreme Ct. 1977, U.S. Dist. Ct. (so. dist.) Fla. 1977, U.S. Ct. Appeals (5th cir.) 1977; bd. cert. marital and family law Fla. Bar. Assoc. Bradford, Williams, McKay, Kimbrell, Hamman & Jennings, PA, Miami, 1977-79, Kaplan, Jaffe & Gates, PA, Hollywood, Fla., 1979-81; ptnr. Brydger & Levitt, PA, Ft. Lauderdale, Fla., 1981-89; pvt. practice Ft. Lauderdale, 1989—; lectr. in field. Contbr. chpt. to book. Fellow Am. Acad. Matrimonial Lawyers (bd. mgrs. 1997—); mem. Fla. Bar Asn. (mem. exec. com. family law sect. 1991-98, family law rules com. 1996—), Broward Bar Assn. (chmn. family law sect. 1992-93), Anti-Defamation League, Phi Beta Kappa. Avocation: wine. Family and matrimonial. Office: Ste 601 600 S Andrews Ave Fort Lauderdale FL 33301-2851

**BRYDGES, JAMES EDWARD,** lawyer; b. Lynchburg, Va., Sept. 7, 1942; s. James Edward Brydges and Helen Virginia Brown; m. Esther Gigliotti, Aug. 10, 1943; children: Jennifer Lynn, Brian James. BA, Duke U., 1964; LLB, U. Va., 1967. Bar: Va. 1967. Assoc. Brydges, Broyles McKenry, Virginia Beach, Va., 1968-72; ptnr. Moore & Brydges, Virginia Beach, 1972-75, Broyles, Gorry, Moore & Brydges, Virginia Beach, 1976-82; shareholder Taylor & Walker P.C., Norfolk, Va., 1982—; substitute judge Gen. Dist. and Juvenile and Domestic Rels. Dist. Ct., Virginia Beach. Mem. Va. Bar Assn., Va. Assn. Def. Attys. (pres. 1998—), Virginia Beach Bar Assn. (pres. 1985), Norfolk Portsmouth Bar Assn. Avocations: golf, tennis, biking. Professional liability, Product liability, Personal injury. Office: Taylor & Walker PO Box 3490 Norfolk VA 23514-3490

**BRYDGES, THOMAS EUGENE,** lawyer; b. Niagara Falls, N.Y., June 1, 1942; s. Earl W. and Eleanor M. (Mahoney) B.; m. Melissa May, May 26, 1990; children: Andrew MacLeod, Elizabeth Hendricks. BA in History, Syracuse U., 1971, JD, 1973. Bar: N.Y. 1974, U.S. Dist. (we. dist.) N.Y. 1974, U.S. Ct. Appeals (2d cir.) 1978. Assoc. Jaeckle, Fleischmann & Mugel, Buffalo, 1973-78, ptnr., 1979—; bd. dirs., sec. Theodore Roosevelt Chroagurve site. Author: (with others) Employment Discrimination Law, 1980—. Trustee Daemen Coll., Amherst, N.Y., 1988—; bd. dirs., v.p. Art Park & Co., Lewiston, N.Y., 1976—. Capt. U.S. Army, 1962-68, Vietnam. Decorated Bronze Star, Air medal, Army Commendation (2). Mem. ABA (labor sect.), Erie County Bar Assn., N.Y. Bar Assn. (labor law com.). Labor. Office: Jaeckle Fleischmann & Mugel 700 Fleet Bldg Buffalo NY 14202

**BRYK, WILLIAM MICHAEL,** lawyer; b. Troy, N.Y., Mar. 12, 1955; s. William Zygmundt and Joy Kathleen (Hart) B.; m. Catherine Leitch Black, Nov. 8, 1990. BS, Manhattan Coll., 1977; JD, Fordham U., 1989. Bar: N.Y. 1990, U.S. Dist. Ct. (so. and ea. dists.) N.Y. 1990, U.S. Supreme Ct. 1993. Adminstrv. asst. N.Y. City Comptroller's Office, N.Y.C., 1977-82; asst. to pres. Manhattan Borough Pres.'s Office, N.Y.C., 1982-85; chief of staff N.Y. City Coun. Mem. W. L. McCaffrey, N.Y.C., 1986-87; spl. asst. to pres., asst. counsel N.Y. City Coun. Pres.'s Office, N.Y.C., 1987-89, 91-93; assoc. Bondy & Schloss, N.Y.C., 1989-90; ct. atty. N.Y. City Civil Ct., N.Y.C., 1990-91; atty. N.Y. City Dept. Social Svcs., N.Y.C., 1994, 95-97; spl. asst., mem. N.Y. City Bd. Edn., Bklyn., 1994-95; pvt. practice, 1997-99; assoc. Spinelli & Assocs., 1999—. Columnist, N.Y. Press. Mem. Manhattan Cmty. Bd. #6, N.Y.C., 1991-82, 89-90. Recipient N.Y. Guard Svc. award, 1984, Long and Faithful Svc. medal Vet. Corps of Arty., 1993, N.Y. State Meritorious Svc. medal, 1998. Mem. N.Y. County Lawyers Assn., Equestrian Order of the Holy Sepulchre of Jerusalem (knight). Roman Catholic. Avocations: reading, writing, model railways, Portugal and the Portuguese. Home and Office: 101 Daniel Low Ter Apt 5C Staten Island NY 10301-1750

**BRYNELSON, FLOYD A.,** lawyer; b. Florence, Wis., May 13, 1914; s. Emil and Hilda Ericka (Hellman) B.; m. Margaret King, Sept. 23, 1944; children: Wade, Paul, Laura, Steven, David, Julia. BA, U. Wis., 1937, LLB, 1940. Bar: Wis. 1940, U.S. Dist. Ct. (we. dist.) Wis. 1940, U.S. Ct. Appeals (7th cir.) 1949. Dir. Hein-Werner Corp., Waukesha, Wis., 1960-88, Bowman Dairy, Inc., Madison, 1975-85, General Telephone of Wis., Madison, 1977-87; dir. Mid-Plains Telephone Inc., 1975-93, pres., gen. counsel, 1981-90; of counsel Axley Brynelson Law Firm, Madison, 1988-95. Pres. Wis. Coun. of Chs., 1963; pres. Wis. Bapt. State Conv., Milw., 1975. Mem. Kiwanis Club. Home: 1022 Seminole Hwy Madison WI 53711-3021

**BRYNER, ALEXANDER O.,** state supreme court justice; b. Tientsin, China; m. Carol Crump; children: Paul, Mara. BA, Stanford U., 1966, JD, 1969. Law clk. to Chief Justice George Boney, Alaska Supreme Ct., 1969-71; legal editor Bancroft Whitney Co., San Francisco, 1971; with Pub. Defender Agy., Anchorage, 1972-74; ptnr. Bookman, Bryner & Shortell, 1974; Alaska dist. ct. judge Anchorage, 1975-77; U.S. atty. Alaska, 1977-80; chief judge Alaska Ct. Appeals, 1980-97; judge Alaska Supreme Ct., Anchorage, 1997—. Office: Alaska Supreme Ct 303 K St Anchorage AK 99501-2013

**BRYSH, PAUL JOHN,** prosecutor; b. New Castle, Pa., Apr. 30, 1949; s. Walter Stanley and Matilda (Gorski) B. B.A., U. Pitts., 1971, J.D., 1974. Bar: Pa. 1974, U.S. Supreme Ct. 1977, U.S. Ct. Appeals (3d cir.) 1981. Law clk. Pa. Supreme Ct., Pitts., 1974-76; atty. U.S. Dept. Justice, Washington, 1976-79; chief appellate sect. western dist. Pa., U.S. Atty.'s Office, Pitts., 1979—. Mem. ABA, Allegheny County Bar Assn. Office: US Atty's Office 633 US Post Office & Courthouse Pittsburgh PA 15219

**BRYSON, ARTHUR JOSEPH,** lawyer; b. Ashland, Ky., Sept. 17, 1946; s. Arthur T. Jr. and Albertina Peña; m. Kathleen Connor May 15, 1971. AB, Ea. Ky. U., 1969; JD, U. Ky., 1972. Accredited estate planner Nat. Assn. Estate Planners and Couns. Trust officer Second Nat. Bank, Lexington, Ky., 1972-80, v.p., 1980-85; v.p. Commerce Nat. Bank, Lexington, 1985-86; prin. Arthur J. Bryson, Lexington, 1986—; of counsel Gess Mattingly & Atchison, Lexington, 1989-91. Bd. dirs. Bluegrass R.R. Mus., Inc., Lexington, 1977-81, So. Rlwy. Hist. Assn., 1994—, sec., 1994—. Mem. Ky. Bar Assn., Lexington Estate Planning Coun., Lexington Employees Benefits Coun. (bd. dirs. 1982-85), Bluegrass Estate Planning Coun. (bd. dirs. 1982-89, sec. 1986, treas. 1987, v.p. 1988, pres. 1989). Avocation: railway history. Estate planning, Probate, Pension, profit-sharing, and employee benefits. Office: 376 S Broadway St Lexington KY 40508-2512

**BRYSON, JEFFREY T.,** lawyer. BS in Bus. Adminstrn., U. N.C.; JD, Cath. U. Reginald Heber Smith fellow Legal Svcs. Corp., Winston-Salem, N.C., staff atty.; pvt. practice, 1983-87; atty. Neighborhood Reinvestment Corp., Washington, 1987-88, dep. gen. counsel, 1988-90, acting gen. counsel, 1990-91, gen. counsel, sec., 1991—; legal svcs. atty. NeighborWorks, bd. dirs., chair loan com. Mem. Am. Corp. Counsel Assn. E-mail: jbryson@nw.org. Office: Neighborhood Reinvestment Corp 1325 G St NW Ste 800 Washington DC 20005-3100*

**BRYSON, WILLIAM CURTIS,** federal judge; b. 1945. B.A. magna cum laude, Harvard Coll., 1969; J.D., U. of Tex. Sch. of Law, 1973. Law clerk to Justice Henry Friendly U.S. Ct. of Appeals, 2nd Circuit, 1973-74; law clerk to Justice Thurgood Marshall U.S. Supreme Ct., 1974-75; atty. Miller, Cassidy, Larroca & Lewin, 1975-78; asst. to the Solicitor General U.S. Dept. of Justice, 1978-79; chief Appellate Section, Criminal Div., 1979-82; special counsel Organized Crime & Racketeering Section, Criminal Div., 1982-86; dep. solicitor gen., 1986-94, dep. assoc. atty. & acting assoc. atty. gen., 1994; circuit judge Federal Circuit, Washington, D.C., 1994—. Office: 717 Madison Pl NW Washington DC 20439-0002*

**BRZOSKA, DENISE JEANNE,** paralegal; b. Wilmington, Del., Mar. 21, 1945; d. Eugene Joseph and Marie Jeanette (Durr) B. Student, U. Del., 1971-84; grad., Citizen's Police Acad., New Castle, Del., 1995. Cert. graphic designer; cert. paralegal. Bookkeeping clk. Del. Div. of Revenue, Wilmington, 1963-66; tech. support personnel dept. physics and astronomy U. Del., Newark, 1966-91; paralegal Wilmington Trust Co./Trust Legal, 1992—; mem. geographic adv. coun. and by-laws com. New Castle County Police, 1996. Artist representing Del. at Colliseum Arts Internat., World Trade Ctr., 1981. Campaign worker Joe Biden for U.S. Senate, Del., 1978, S.B. Woo for Lt. Gov., Del., 1984, S.B. Woo for U.S. Senate, Del., 1988; mem. geographic adv. coun., by-laws com. New Castle County Police Dept., 1996; treas. New Castle County Policy Ctrl. Dist. Adv. Coun., 1996—. Mem. Del. Paralegal Assn., Wilmington Women in Bus., Pa. Horticultural Soc., Del. Art Mus., Nat. Mus. Women in the Arts, Wilmington Garden Day. Roman Catholic. Avocations: painting, gardening, gourmet cooking, theater. Home: 422 Old Airport Rd New Castle DE 19720-1002

**BRZUSTOWICZ, JOHN CINQ-MARS,** lawyer; b. Rochester, N.Y., Feb. 1, 1957; s. Richard J. and Alice (Cinq-Mars) B.; m. Diane Day, Aug. 22, 1981; children: Richard Reed, Megan Day, Emily Day-Hanson. BA, Coll. Wooster, 1979; JD, Case Western Res. U., 1985; cert., Cornell Inst. Labor Rels., 1982. Bar: Pa. 1985, U.S. Dist. Ct. (we. dist.) Pa. 1985, U.S. Ct. Appeals (3d cir.) 1986, U.S. Supreme Ct. 1990. Asst. to dir. Inst. Am. Music U. Rochester, Rochester, 1979-82; assoc. Peacock, Keller, Yohe, Day & Ecker, Washington, Pa., 1985-88, Sable, Makoroff & Libenson, Pitts., 1988-90; pvt. practice Brzustowicz Law Offices, McMurray, Washington, Pa., 1990-94; shareholder Day & Brzustowicz Law Offices, P.C., McMurray, Pa., 1995—; chmn. bd. dirs. Inst. for Am. Music of Eastman Sch. Music, 1997—; bd. dirs. Hanson Inst. Am. Music of Eastman Sch. Music, 1996; chmn. law libr. Washington County ((Pa.) Bar, 1992; mem. com. Jud. Inquiry Bd., Pa., 1991—; dir. Hanson Inst. of Am. Music of the Eastman Sch. of Music, U. Rochester, 1995. Co-author: Pennsylvania School Law, 1992, Pennsylvania Adminstrative Law, 1987; editor: So You Want to Be A Lawyer, 1990; advisor on PBC documentary: Life of Howard Hanson, An American Masterpiece, 1987. V.p. Young Reps., Wooster, Ohio, 1977-79; co-founder, officer Wooster Polo and Hunt Club, 1976-79; bd. dirs. Washington County Found. Recipient Merit award Inst. Am. Music, 1981, Outstanding Scholar award Rotary. Mem. ABA, ATLA, Pa. Bar Assn. (del. 1992), Allegheny County Bar Assn., Washington County Bar Assn., Pa. Young Lawyers for Washington County (state rep. 1988), Peters Twp. C. of C. Roman Catholic. Avocations: reading, woodworking, biology. General corporate, General civil litigation, Bankruptcy. Home: 56 Mckennan Ave Washington PA 15301-3531 Office: 3821 Washington Rd Mc Murray PA 15317-2964

**BUCCI, KATHLEEN ELIZABETH,** lawyer, nurse; b. Malden, Mass., Nov. 1, 1952; d. Harold Edward and Elizabeth Marie (Keefe) B. ASN, Mass. Bay C.C., 1977; BA, U. Mass., 1985; JD, New Eng. Sch. Law, 1985. Bar: Mass. 1989, U.S. Dist. Ct. Mass. 1992, U.S. Ct. Appeals (1st cir.) 1992; cert. hemodialysis nurse. RN staff Nat. Med. Care Inc., Boston, 1977-78; RN ICU St. John's Hosp., Santa Monica, Calif., 1978-79; asst. head nurse UCLA Med. Ctr., Westwood, Calif., 1979-80; nurse coord. P.J. West & Assocs., Inc., Tarzana, Calif., 1980-81; RN mobile acute team Hemodialysis, Inc., Northridge, Calif., 1981-82, Hemostat, Inc., Burbank, Calif., 1982-84; med.-legal cons. Kathleen E. Bucci, RN, Malden, Mass., 1985-92; nurse atty. Ned. C. Lofton, P.C., Wakefield, Mass., 1992-94, Halström Law Offices, P.C., Boston, 1994-96, Kiley & Schlictmann, Andover, Mass., 1996—. Mem. Am. Assn. Nurse Attys. (New Eng. chpt. bd. dirs. 1991-93, pub. rels. chairperson 1989-93), Assn. Trial Lawyers Am., Mass. Bar Assn. Roman Catholic. Avocations: bicycling, ballet en pointe dancer. Personal injury. Office: Kiley & Schlictmann 342 N Main St Andover MA 01810-2611

**BUCCINO, ERNEST JOHN, JR.,** lawyer; b. Phila., Oct. 29, 1945; s. Ernest J. and Rachel (Talarico) B.; m. Martha Mollinedo, Dec. 27, 1968; children: Tasha. BS, Temple U., 1967, MEd, 1969, JD, 1973. Bar: Pa. 1973, U.S. Dist. Ct. (ea. dist.) Pa. 1973, U.S. Ct. Appeals (3d cir.) 1973, N.J. 1974, U.S. Supreme Ct. 1978. Officer, counsel Blue Cross Greater Phila., 1973-74; law clk. Supreme Ct. Pa., Phila., 1974; mem. Gross & Buccino, P.A., Phila., 1975-96; pvt. practice, Phila., 1996-97; prin. Buccino Law Office, Phila., 1997—; lectr. Roscoe Pound, 1986, Trial Advocacy Found. Pa., Phila., 1984; mem. civil procedure rules com. Supreme Ct. Pa., 1994—. Author: The Barrister Vol. XVI, #3, 1985. Chmn. eastern dist. LAWPAC, Harrisburg, Pa., 1983—. Mem. ABA, ATLA, Pa. Bar Assn., Pa. Trial Lawyers Assn. (bd. dirs. 1982—), Phila. Trial Lawyers Assn. (bd. dirs. 1982—, lectr. luncheon series 1986), Justinian Soc. (bd. dirs. 1982—), Phila. Bar Assn. (chmn. econs. of law practice 1983, nominating com. 1982-83), Sons of Italy. Personal injury. Office: 2112 Walnut St Philadelphia PA 19103-4808

**BUCCO, ANTHONY MARK,** lawyer; b. Passaic, N.J., Apr. 12, 1962; s. Anthony Rocco and Helen Bucco; m. Laura Ann Bucco, Apr. 27, 1985; children: Anthony, Lauren, Jenna. BA in Bus. Mgmt./Econs. magna cum laude, Lycoming Coll., 1984; JD cum laude, Seton Hall U., 1987. Bar: N.J. 1987, D.C. 1989. Legal asst. Morris County Prosecutor's Office, Morristown, N.J., 1986; assoc. Villoresi, Edwards & Jansen, Boonton, N.J., 1986-90, Mudge, Rose, Guthrie, Alexander & Ferdon, Parsippany, N.J., 1990-93; ptnr. Jansen, Bucco & DeBona, Boonton, 1994—; mem. adv. bd. DAYTOP at Mendham, N.J., 1992—; dep. commr. Morris County Crime Stoppers, Morristown, 1996—; bd. dirs. Angel Connection Inc., Rockaway, N.J. Active Boonton Fire Dept., 1980—, Boonton Bd. Edn., 1987-93; county com. mem. Boonton Twp. Rep. Com., 1998—; coun. mem. Govs. Coun. on Alcoholism and Drug Abuse, Trenton, N.J., 1998—. Mem. ABA, N.J. State Bar Assn., Morris County Bar Assn., N.J. Inst. for Mcpl. Attys., Boonton Rotary (pres.-elect 1998—). Republican. Roman Catholic. Municipal (including bonds), Land use and zoning (including planning), General practice. Office: Jansen Bucco & DeBona 413 W Main St Boonton NJ 07005-1149

**BUCHAL, JAMES LAURENCE,** lawyer; b. Madison, Wis., Aug. 19, 1959; s. Robert Norman and Anne St. John Buchal; m. Staci Lorell Paley (div.); m. Cathy Lynn Guttormsen, May 20, 1995; children: Christopher, Alethea. AB, Harvard U., 1981; MBA, JD, Yale U., 1985. Bar: N.Y. 1986, Oreg. 1992. Assoc. Cravath, Swaine & Moore, N.Y.C., 1985-91, Heller, Ehrman, White & McAuliffe, Portland, Oreg., 1991-94, Ball Janik LLP, Portland, 1995-98; ptnr. Murphy & Buchal LLP, Portland, 1998—. Author: The Great Salmon Hoax, 1998. Fax: 503-227-1034. E-mail: counsel@buchal.com. Office: Murphy & Buchal LLP 1500 SW 1st Ave Ste 1135 Portland OR 97201-5835

**BUCHANAN, CALVIN D. (BUCK BUCHANAN),** prosecutor; b. Okolona, Miss., Feb. 15, 1958; m. Donna C. BA, U. Miss., 1980, JD, 1983. Bar: Miss. 1983, U.S. Mil. Ct. Rev. 1983, U.S. Dist. Ct. (no. dist.) 1983, U.S. Ct. Appeals (5th cir.) 1991. 1st Lt. MS Army NG, 1980-83; commd. U.S. Army, 1983; advanced through grades to capt., 1990; maj. Individual Ready Res., 1990—; asst. U.S. atty. No. Dist. Miss., 1990-97, U.S. atty., 1997—. Leonard B. Melvin scholar U. Miss. Sch. Law. Mem. Nat. Bar Assn., Miss. Bar Assn., Magnolia Bar Assn., Lafayette County Bar Assn., U. Miss. Alumni Assn. (mem. adv. coun. 1988-97), Inns of Court, Order of Omega, Phi Eta Sigma. Baptist. Office: US Atty No Dist Miss Federal Bldg & USCourthouse PO Box 886 Oxford MS 38655-0886*

**BUCHANAN, GEORGE HOWARD,** lawyer, foundation executive, academic administrator. BA in European History, Purdue U., 1972; JD, Ind. U., 1975; postgrad., Naval Judge Advocate Gen.'s Justice Sch., Newport, R.I., 1975; M in Govt. Adminstrn., Pa. State U., 1985, postgrad., 1990. Law clk. to gen. counsel, rsch. asst. Ind. U., 1972-74; city atty., rsch. asst. City of Louisville, Ky., 1975; sr. legal cousel for sr. mil. exec., govt. prosecutor, def. counsel U.S. Naval Installation, 1975-78; asst. counsel Pa. Pub. Utility Commn., 1983-85, administrv. law judge, 1985-91; mgr. energy policy Union Carbide Found., 1985-91, comml. products issues mgr., 1991-94, pres., mgr. corp. and pub. affairs, 1994—; univ. counsel, vice chancellor legal affairs SUNY, Albany, 1997—. V.p. bd. dirs. Assn. Retarded Citizens Dutchess County. Mem. Pa. Bar Assn. Office: SUNY Univ Counsel & Legal Affairs State Univ Plz Albany NY 12246-0001

**BUCHANAN, J. VINCENT MARINO,** lawyer; b. Ft. Knox, Ky., Feb. 15, 1951; s. Robert Samuel and Jeanice (Moran) B.; children: Thomas Marino, Maria Antonia, Kendra Marina. Student U.S. Mil. Acad., 1969-71; BA, Bowling Green State U., Ohio, 1972; JD, U. Toledo, 1975. Bar: Ohio 1976, U.S. Dist. Ct. (no. dist.) Ohio 1977, U.S. Ct. Appeals (6th cir.), U.S. Tax Ct.; lic. annuity life and health ins. agt. Mng. atty., ptnr. Buchanan & Assocs., Risingsun, Ohio, 1976—; gen. ptnr. Real Estate Diversified, G.P. Bd. dirs. Advs. Basic Legal Equality, Toledo, 1981-88; sec., bd. dirs. Ohio Hispanic Inst., Bowling Green, 1983-86 . Mem ABA (exec. mem. family law div.), Am. Legion, N.W. Ohio Rivers Coun., Elks, Lions. Roman Catholic. Environmental, Criminal, General civil litigation. Home: US 23 N Risingsun OH 43457 Office: Buchanan & Assocs 8500 Us Highway 23 Risingsun OH 43457-9632

**BUCHANAN, JAMES DOUGLAS,** lawyer; b. Modesto, Calif., Aug. 7, 1941; s. James Monroe and Gladys Marian (Crowell) B.; m. Claudia Anne Dukes, May 26, 1963; children: Sarah, Jennifer, Amy, Andrew. BA in Journalism, U. Nev., 1963; JD, U. of the Pacific, 1975. Bar: Calif. 1975, U.S. Dist. Ct. (ea. dist.) Calif. 1976. Dep. dist. atty. Inyo County, Independence, Calif., 1976-77; pub. defender Inyo County, Independence, 1977-78; ptnr. Smith & Buchanan, Bishop, Calif., 1978-86; legal counsel No. Inyo Hosp. Dist., Bishop, 1980—; ptnr. Berger, Buchanan and Berger, 1989-91. Pipe major Loch Ness Scots Pipe Band, Bishop, 1982-99; mem. Selective Svc. Bd. 87, Bishoop, 1982-97; deacon Episc. Ch., 1995. 1st lt. USAR, 1963-65. Mem. Inyo County Bar Assn. (pres. 1980). Office: 459 W Line St Bishop CA 93514-3333

**BUCHANAN, JOHN MACLENNAN,** Canadian provincial official; b. Sydney, N.S., Can., Apr. 22, 1931; s. Murdoch William and Flora Isabel (Campbell) B.; m. Mavis Forsyth, Sept. 1, 1954; children: Murdoch, Travis, Nichola, Natalie, Natasha. BSc, Mt. Allison U., cert. engring., 1954; LLB, Dalhousie U., Halifax, N.S., 1958; DEng (hon.), N.S. Tech. Coll., 1979; LLD (hon.), St. Mary's U., 1982; DCL, Mt. Allison U., 1981; LLD (hon.), St. Francis Xavier U., 1986; D Polit. Sci. (hon.), U. de St. Anne, 1989. Bar: Called to bar, created queen's counsel 1972. Pvt. practice Halifax, 1958-71; mem. N.S. Legislative Assembly, Halifax, from 1967; min. public works, then fisheries; premier of N.S., 1978-90; created Queen's Counsel, 1972; leader Progressive Conservative Party in N.S., from 1971; elected mem. legis. assembly for Halifax-Atlantic provinces gen. election, 1967, 70, 74, 78, 81, 84, 88, apptd. Privy Coun., 1972; apptd. to Senate of Can., 1990, bd. dirs. Legal Aid for N.S. Barristers Assn. Active Boy Scouts Am., pres. exec. oun., chmn. policy bd., 1978-90. Mem. Can. Bar Assn., N.S. Barristers Assn., Can.-U.S. Parliamentary Assn. (bd. dirs.), Royal Can. Legion, Buchanan Soc. of Glasgow, Scotland (bd. dirs.), Halifax Club, City Club, Lions, Masons, Shriners, Odd Fellows. Mem. United Ch. Can. Office: The Senate, Ottawa, ON Canada

**BUCHANAN, ROBERT GRAHAM, JR.,** lawyer; b. Oklahoma City, Nov. 25, 1961. BS, Washington & Lee U., 1984; JD, So. Meth. U., 1987. Bar: Tex. 1987, U.S. Dist. Ct. (no. dist.) Tex. 1988, U.S. Dist. Ct. (we. dist.) Tex. 1991, U.S. Dist. Ct. (ea. dist.) Tex. 1998. Atty. Cowles & Thompson PC, Dallas, 1987—. General corporate, Real property, Contracts commercial. Office: Cowles & Thompson PC 901 Main St Ste 4000 Dallas TX 75202-3793

**BUCHANAN, VIRGINIA MARIE,** lawyer; b. Middletown, Ohio, Oct. 2, 1960; d. Howard and Pat Chandler; m. Samuel Budnyk; 1 child, Samuel R. Budnyk. BA, U. Fla., 1985, JD, 1989. Bar: Fla. 1989. Atty., ptnr. Levin Law Firm, Pensacola, Fla., 1989—. Contbr. articles to profl. jours. Mem. women's life ctr. adv. bd. West Fla. Regional Med. Ctr. Bickel scholar; Scripps-Howard scholar. Mem. ABA, ATLA, Fla. Bar Assn., Santa Rosa Bar Assn., Acad. Fla. Trial Lawyers, Order of Coif. Democrat. Roman Catholic. Avocations: hiking, reading, music, family activities, biking. Insurance, Personal injury, Professional liability. Office: Levin Middlebrooks et al 316 S Baylen St Ste 600 Pensacola FL 32501-5990

**BUCHBINDER, DARRELL BRUCE,** lawyer, b. N.Y.C., Oct. 17, 1946; s. Julian and Bernice (Levy) B.; m. Janet Grey McLean, Jan. 22, 1977; children: Julian Bradford, Andrew Grey, Ian Jeffress. BA in Politics with honors, NYU, 1968, JD, 1971. Bar: N.Y. 1972, U.S. Dist. Ct. (so. and ea. dists.) N.Y. 1973. Sole practice, N.Y.C., 1972-79; atty. Port Authority of N.Y. and N.J., N.Y.C., 1979-83, prin. atty., 1983-86, dep. chief fin. div. Law Dept., 1986-92, chief pub. securities law div. Law Dept., 1992—. Served with USNR, 1968-70. Mem. Nat. Assn. Bond Lawyers, Pi Sigma Alpha. Republican. Club: Larchmont Shore. Office: Port Authority NY and NJ 1 World Trade Ctr Fl 66 New York NY 10048-0202

**BUCHENHORNER, MICHAEL JOSEPH,** lawyer; b. Havana, Cuba, Oct. 16, 1953; came to U.S., 1960; s. Walter Buchenhorner and Margaret Moran; m. Ana Maria Cosculluela, Oct. 15, 1982; children: Carolyn, Michael E. BSEE, U. Miami, 1976, JD, 1981. Bar: Fla., U.S. Dist. Ct. (so. dist.) Fla., U.S. Ct. Appeals (fed. cir.), U.S. Patent and Trademark Office. Atty. Barnett, Alagia et al, Miami, Fla., 1984-86, Fla. Power & Light Co., Miami, 1986-87, Internat. Trade Commn., Washington, 1987-89; IP atty. Motorola, Inc., Ft. Lauderdale, Fla., 1989-92; sr. atty. Internat. Bus. Machines, Boca Raton, Fla., 1992-96; corp. counsel Lucent Techs., Inc., Miami, 1996-97; shareholder Gunster, Yoakley et al, Miami, 1997—; spkr. in field. Patentee in field; contbr. articles to profl. jours. Mem. ABA, Am. Intellectual Property Assn., Am. Electronics Assn. (chmn. internat. com. Fla. chpt.), Fla. Bar Assn. (chmn. computer law com.), Patent Law Assn. Fla. (pres. 1992), Cuban Engrs. Assn., Info. Tech. Forum, Greater Miami C. of C., Eta Kappa Nu. Avocations: bicycling, tennis, astronomy. Fax: 954-523-1722. E-mail: mbuchenhorner@gunster.com. Patent, Trademark and copyright, Intellectual property. Home: 4801 Alhambra Cir Coral Gables FL 33146-1614 Office: 1 Biscayne Tower 2 S Biscayne Blvd Ste 3400 Miami FL 33131-1802

**BUCHENROTH, STEPHEN RICHARD,** lawyer; b. Bellefontaine, Ohio, Feb. 8, 1948; s. Richard G. and Patricia (Muller) B.; m. Vicki Anderson, June 6, 1974; children: Matthew Brian, Sarah Elizabeth. BA, Wittenburg U., Springfield, Ohio, 1970; JD, U. Chgo., 1974. Bar: Ohio 1974, U.S. Dist. Ct. (so. and no. dists.) Ohio 1974, U.S. Ct. Appeals (6th cir.) 1974. Ptnr. Vorys, Sater, Seymour & Pease, Columbus, Ohio, 1974—. Author: Ohio Mortgage Foreclosures, 1986, Ohio Franchising Law, 1990, also chpts. in books. Trustee, v.p. Godman Guild Assn., Columbus, 1977-83; trustee, sec. Neighborhood Homes, Inc., Columbus, 1977-85; mem. bd. rev. Worthington Pers., 1981—; pres. Worthington Alliance for Quality Edn., 1989-91; chmn. bd. advisors paralegal program Capitol U. Law Sch., 1991; pres. bd. trustees Worthington Edn. Found., 1997-98; mem. Ohio Supreme Ct. Commn. on CLE, chmn., 1999; bd. advisors C.H.A.D.D. of Ctrl. Ohio, 1993-97. Recipient Cmty. Svc. award Legal Assts. Ctrl. Ohio, 1987. Mem. ABA (forum com. franchising), Ohio State Bar Assn. (coun. dels., chmn. legal assts. com., bd. govs. real property sect.), Columbus Bar Assn. (bd. govs., pres. 1992-93), Am. Coll. Real Estate Lawyers. Republican. Lutheran. Real property, Contracts commercial, Franchising. Home: 2342 Collins Dr Columbus OH 43085-2810 Office: Vorys Sater Seymore & Pease 52 E Gay St PO Box 1008 Columbus OH 43215-3161

**BUCHER, STEVEN JOHN,** lawyer; b. Sioux Falls, S.D., July 17, 1955; s. Clifford and Eva M. (Scott) B.; married; children: Bert S., Ellen L. BS in Social Sci. and Secondary Edn., Black Hills State Coll., Spearfish, S.D., 1978; JD, U. S.D., 1981. Bar: S.D. 1981. Ptnr. Miller & Bucher Law Offices, Plankinton, S.D., 1982—; bd. dirs. Plankinton Devel. Co. Mem. State Bar S.D., Tri County Bar Assn. Democrat. Methodist/Roman Catholic. Office: Miller & Bucker 109 N Main St Plankinton SD 57368-2013

**BUCHHOLZ, DEBBY,** lawyer. Gen. counsel John F. Kennedy Ctr. Performing Arts, Washington. Office: John F Kennedy Ctr Performing Arts 2700 F St NW Washington DC 20566-0002*

**BUCHMAN, KENNETH WILLIAM,** lawyer; b. Plant City, Fla., Nov. 20, 1956; s. Paul Sidney and Beryle (Solomon) B.; m. MarDee H. Buchman, May 9, 1985; 1 child, Katherine Elizabeth. AA, U. Fla., 1976, BBA, 1978, JD,

1981. Bar: Fla. 1981; U.S. Dist. Ct. (Mid. dist.) Fla. 1981; U.S. Ct. Appeals (11th cir.) 1986; U.S. Supreme Ct. 1988; bd. cert. city, county, local govt. law. Ptnr. Buchman and Buchman, Plant City, 1981-85, Buchman and Buchman, PA, Plant City, 1985-91; pvt. practice Plant City, 1991—; city atty. City of San Antonio, Fla., 1995—; asst. city atty. City of Plant City, 1982-91, city atty., 1991—; mem. exec. coun. city, county and local govt. law sect. Fla. Bar., 1997—. Mem. Fla. Mcpl. Attys. Assn. (steering com. 1999—), Attys. Title Ins. Fund, Plant City Bar Assn., Kiwanis (pres. Plant City club 1986-87), Masons. Jewish. Real property, Municipal (including bonds). Office: 212 N Collins St Plant City FL 33566-3314

**BUCHMAN, M. ABRAHAM,** lawyer; b. Bklyn., Oct. 25, 1916; s. Judah Louis and Augusta Buchman; m. Ann P. Buchman, July 25, 1950; 1 child, Amy. BA cum laude, NYU, 1935; LLB cum laude, St. Lawrence U., 1938, JSD summa cum laude, 1939. Bar: N.Y. 1939, U.S. Dist. Ct. (so. dist.) N.Y. 1946, U.S. Ct. Appeals 1949, Supreme Ct. U.S. 1964. Plant mgr., contr. Atlas Import & Export Co., 1931-39; ptnr. Buchman & O'Brien, N.Y.C., Washington, 1940—, San Francisco; cons. to sec. USAF, 1946-52; cons. to State Dept. at various meetings Coun. of Europe on prep. of conv. for wines and spirits; cons. Am. Wine Assn., 1993—, Vermouth Inst., Inc., 1943-64, Internat. Vermouth Inst., 1964—, Fedn. Italiana Industriali, Produttori ed Esportatori di Vini, Acquavit, Liquori, Sciroppi, Aceti ed Affini, 1962—; Am. Beverage Alcohol Assn., 1963—. Maj. USAF, 1942-46. Fellowship in adminstrv. law named in his honor Columbia U. Law Sch., 1985—. Mem. ABA, FBA (pres. Empire State chpt. 1995-97), Assn. ICC Practitioners, Fed. Bar Coun., Internat. Bar Assn., Phi Beta Kappa. Administrative and regulatory. Home: 5301 Woodlands Blvd Tamarac FL 33319-3025 Office: Buchman & O'Brien 10 E 40th St Rm 2000 New York NY 10016-0285 also: 1331 Pennsylvania Ave NW Washington DC 20004-1710 also: 505 Sansome St San Francisco CA 94111-3106

**BUCHMEYER, JERRY,** federal judge; b. Overton, Tex., Sept. 5, 1933. Student, Kilgore Jr. Coll., 1953; B.A., U. Tex., 1955, LL.B., 1957. Bar: Tex. 1957. Assoc. Thompson, Knight, Simmons & Bullion, Dallas, 1958-63, ptnr., 1963-66, sr. ptnr., 1968-79; judge U.S. Dist. Ct. (no. dist.) Tex., Dallas, 1979-94, chief judge, 1995—. Mem. ABA, Dallas Bar Assn. (pres. 1979), State Bar Tex. (chmn. com. 1978-79, dir. 1982-84, 94-95). Office: US Dist Courthouse 1100 Commerce St Rm 15 D28A Dallas TX 75242-1027

**BUCHWALD, DON DAVID,** lawyer; b. Bklyn., May 10, 1944; m. Naomi Reice, Jan. 19, 1974; children: David, Jennifer. BA, Cornell U., 1965, JD, 1968. Assoc. Marshall, Bratter, Greene, Allison & Tucker, N.Y.C., 1970-73; asst. U.S. atty. So. Dist. of N.Y., N.Y.C., 1973-80; dep. chief criminal So. Dist. of N.Y., 1977-80; ptnr. Buchwald & Kaufman, N.Y.C., 1980-99; pvt. practice N.Y.C., 1999—. Served to sgt. U.S. Army, 1968-70. Mem. ABA, Fed. Bar Council, Assn. of the Bar of the City of N.Y., N.Y. State Bar Assn. Criminal, Federal civil litigation, State civil litigation. Office: 100 Park Ave New York NY 10017-5516

**BUCHWALD, NAOMI REICE,** judge; b. Kingston, N.Y., Feb. 14, 1944. BA cum laude, Brandeis U., 1965; LLB cum laude, Columbia U., 1968. Bar: N.Y. 1968, U.S. Ct. Appeals (2d cir.) 1969, U.S. Dist. Ct. (so. and ea. dists.) N.Y. 1970, U.S. Supreme Ct. 1978. Litigation assoc. Marshall, Bratter, Greene, Allison & Tucker, N.Y.C., 1968-73; asst. U.S. atty. So. Dist. N.Y., 1973-80, dep. chief civil divsn., 1976-79, chief civil divsn., 1979-80; U.S. magistrate judge U.S. Dist. Ct. (so. dist.) N.Y., N.Y.C., 1980—, chief magistrate judge, 1994-96. Editor Columbia Jour. Law and Social Problems, 1967-68. Recipient spl. citation FDA Commrs., 1978, Robert B. Fiske Jr. Assn. William B. Tendy award, Outstanding Pub. Svc. award Seymour Assn., Columbia Law Sch. Class of 1968 Excellence in Pub. Svc. award, 1998. Mem. Fed. Bar Coun. (trustee 1976-82, 97—, v.p. 1982-84), N.Y. State Bar Assn., Assn. of the Bar of the City of N.Y. (trademarks and unfair competition com. 1988-89, mem. long range planning com. 1993-95, litigation com. 1994-96, ad hoc com. on jud. conduct 1996-99), Phi Beta Kappa, Omicron Delta Epsilon. Office: US Ct House 500 Pearl St Rm 2270 New York NY 10007-1316

**BUCK, GURDON HALL,** lawyer, urban planner, real estate broker; b. Hartford, Conn., Apr. 10, 1936; s. Richard Saltonstall ad Aloha Frances (Hall) B.; children: Keith Saltonstall, Frances Josephine, Daniel Winthrop; m. Martha Finder, 1996. BA in English, Lehigh U., 1958; JD, U. Pa., 1965. Bar: Conn. 1965, U.S. Dist. Ct. 1966, U.S. Ct. Appeals (2d cir.) 1966. Assoc. Shipman & Goodwin, Hartford, 1965-67; v.p., counsel R. F. Broderick & Assocs., Hartford, 1968-69; ptnr. Pelgrift, Byrne, Buck & Connolly, Hartford and Farmington, Conn., 1969-75, Byrne, Buck & Steiner and predecessor Byrne & Buck, Farmington, 1975-78; sr. ptnr. real estate and land use sects., chmn. common interest group Robinson & Cole, Farmington and Hartford, 1979—. Author: Condominium Development, Forms with Commentary, 1990, 2d edit., 1992; prin. co-author: The Connecticut Condominium Manual, 1972, Real Estate Brokers Community Associations Handbook, rev. edit., 1982, Connecticut Common Interest Ownership Manual, 1984, The Alaska Common Interest Ownership Manual, 1985, Attorney's and Lenders Guide to Common Interest Communities, 1989, 2nd edit., 1999; contbr. articles on zoning, condominiums, planned unit devels. to profl. jours.; columnist various newspapers. Lt. USCGR, 1958-62. Recipient Disting. Svc. award Glastonbury (Conn.) Jaycees, 1968. Mem. ABA (common interest com. law com., real property and probate, joint editl. bd. real property laws, adv. Uniform Planned Cmty. Act, Model Real Estate Coop. Act, Uniform Common Interest Ownership Act), Am. Law Inst. (advisor, restatement on property 2d servitudes), Am. Coll. Real Estate Lawyers (bd. dirs. 1986-92, common ownership com.), Anglo-Am. Real Property Inst. (bd. dirs. 1994-99), Cmty. Assns. Inst. (nat. trustee 1982-88, pres. Conn. chpt. 1980-83, sec. 1986-89, bd. dirs. 1992-98, pres. rsch. found. 1980-83, Century Club, Byron Hanke Disting. Svc. award, Acad. of Authors), Am. Planning Assn., Am. Inst. Cert. Planners, Internat. Bar Assn. (panelist common ownership consumer protection 1987), Conn. Bar assn. (chmn. com. opinions real estate sect., pro bono com.), Statewide Legal Svcs. (bd. dirs., pres.), Conn. Assn. Realtors (GRI instr.), Hartford County Bar Assn., Conn. Assn. Homebuilders Orgn. (developer's coun.), Hartford Assn. Realtors (gov. rel. com. 1975—). Real property, Environmental, Land use and zoning (including planning). Office: 1 Commercial Plz Hartford CT 06103-3509 *The common interest community is the mutual sharing of resources and lives through the land. It is as old as civilization itself and as modern as the latest marketing techniques.*

**BUCK, THOMAS RANDOLPH,** retired lawyer, financial services executive; b. Washington, Feb. 5, 1930; s. James Charles Francis and Mary Elizabeth (Marshall) B.; m. Alice Armistead James, June 20, 1953; children: Kathryn James, Thomas Randolph, Douglas Marshall, David Andrew; m. Sunny Clark, Sept. 15, 1971; 1 child, Carey Virginia; m. Yvonne Brackett, Nov. 27, 1981. B.A. summa cum laude, Am. U., 1951; JD, U. Va., 1954. Bar: Va. 1954, Ky. 1964, Fla. 1974. Asst. gen. atty. Seaboard Air Line R.R. Co., 1958-63; sec., gen. counsel Am. Comml. Lines. Inc., Houston, 1963-68; asst. gen. counsel Tex. Gas Transmission Corp., 1968-72; sec., gen. counsel Leadership Housing Inc., 1972-77; pres. law firm Buck and Golden, P.A., 1975-92; exec. v.p., gen. counsel Buck Fin. Svcs., Inc., Ft. Lauderdale, Fla., 1992-99; past dir. Computer Resources Inc., Ft. Lauderdale, Fla., So. Aviation Inc., Opa Locka, Fla.; chmn. Hanover Bank of Fla. Bd. dirs. Sheridan House for Youth; trustee Fla. Bapt. Found. Served to capt. USMCR, 1954-58. Mem. Assn. ICC Practitioners (nat. v.p., mem. exec. com.), Maritime Law Assn. U.S., Am. Judicature Soc., Omicron Delta Kappa, Alpha Sigma Phi, Delta Theta Phi. Clubs: Kiwanian, Propeller of U.S. Banking, General corporate, Education and schools. Home: #101 301 N Pine Island Rd Plantation FL 33324

**BUCKAWAY, WILLIAM ALLEN, JR.,** lawyer; b. Bowling Green, Ky., Dec. 3, 1934; s. William Allen and Kathryn Anne (Scoggin) B.; m. Bette Joan Cross, July 27, 1963; 1 child, William Allen III. AB, Centre Coll. of Ky., 1956; JD, U. Louisville, 1961. Bar: Ky. 1961, U.S. Dist Ct. (we. dist.) Ky. 1981, U.S. Dist. Ct. (ea. dist.) Ky. 1986, U.S. Supreme Ct. 1975. Assoc. Tilford, Dobbins, Caye & Alexander, Louisville, 1961-78; ptnr. Tilford, Dobbins, Alexander, Buckaway & Black, Louisville, 1978—; atty. Masonic Homes of Ky., Louisville, 1985—; gen. counsel Kosair Charitites; adj. John Hunt Morgan Camp, 1993-96. Elder 2d Presbyn. Ch., Louisville, 1975; emeritus mem. bd. govs. Lexington (Ky.) unit Shriners Hosp. for Cripled Children, 1986, sec., 1989-94; mem. children's oper. bd. Kosair Children's Hosp., 1986-99; mem. bd. govs. Norton Health Care, Louisville, 1999—. With USNR, 1956-58. Named Disting. Alumnus U. Louisville Sch. Law, 1986, Centre Coll., 1986. Mem. SAR (pres. Ky. soc. 1999-2000), Soc. of the Cin. in State of Va., Sons Confederate Vets., Masons (33 deg., past master Crescent Hill lodge 1967, chmn. jurisprudence and law com. imperial coun. Shrine of N.Am. 1989-91), Kosair Shrine Temple (potentate 1986), Rotary, Soc. Colonial Wars (Ky. coun.), Soc. War of 1812 (pres. Ky. soc. 1998-2000), Sigma Chi, Phi Alpha Delta. Non-profit and tax-exempt organizations, Probate, General corporate. Home: 1761 Sulgrave Rd Louisville KY 40205-1643

**BUCKLES, JOSEPH AARON, II,** lawyer; b. Clay Center, Kans., May 6, 1951; s. Joseph Aaron and Theresa Ruth Buckles; m. Sheri Elaine Daniel; children: Joseph Aaron III, Jacob Alexander. BA, St. Olaf Coll., 1972; JD in Taxation, Oklahoma City U., 1976; LLM, U. Miami, 1980. Bar: Okla. 1976, U.S. Tax Ct. 1980, U.S. Dist. Ct. (fed. dist.) 1983. Chief atty. Legal Aid Western Okla., Oklahoma City, 1976-79; of counsel Andrews Davis Legg Bixler Milsten & Price, Oklahoma City, 1980-94; atty. Joseph A. Buckles II and Assocs., Oklahoma City, 1995—; pro bono atty. Legal Aid Western Okla., 1980—. Mem. ABA, Okla. Bar Assn., Oklahoma City Tax Assn. Taxation, general, Federal civil litigation, Bankruptcy. Home and Office: 6725 NE 63d St Oklahoma City OK 73141

**BUCKLEW, SUSAN CAWTHON,** federal judge; b. 1942. BA, Fla. State U., 1964; MA, U. So. Fla., 1968; JD, Stetson U., 1977; LLD (hon.), Stetson Coll. Law, 1994. Tchr. Plant High Sch., 1964-65, 70-72, Seminole High Sch., 1965-67, Chamberlain High Sch., 1969; instr. Hillsborough C.C., 1974-75; corp. legal counsel Jim Walter Corp., 1978-82; county ct. judge Hillsborough County, 1982-86; circuit ct. judge 13th Jud. Circuit, 1986-93; judge U.S. Dist. Ct. (mid. dist.) Fla., 1993—; mem. Gender Bias Study Commn., 1988-90, Fla. Bar Bench Bar Commn., 1990-92; bd. overseers Stetson Coll. Law, 1994—. Recipient award Disting Svc., Fla. Coun. Crime and Delinquincy, 1990, Disting. Alumnus award Stetson Lawyers Assn., 1994. Mem. ABA, Fla. Gar Assn., Fla. Assn. Women Lawyers, Hillsborough Assn. Women Lawyers (award Outstanding Pub. Svc. ADvancing Status Women 1991), Hillsborough County Bar Assn. (Robert W. Patton Outstanding Jursit award young lawyer's sect. 1990), Fla. State U. Alumni Assn., Am. Inns Ct. (LII, William Glenn Terrell chpt.), Athena Soc., Tampa Club, Delta Delta Delta Alumnae. Office: US Dist Ct 611 N Florida Ave Ste 109 Tampa FL 33602-4509

**BUCKLEY, CHARLES ROBINSON, III,** lawyer; b. Richmond, Va., Oct. 9, 1942; s. Charles Robinson and Eleanor (Small) B.; m. Virginia Lee, Apr. 17, 1971; children: Richard, Rebecca. BS, U. N.C., 1965, JD, 1969. Bar: N.C. 1969, U.S. Supreme Ct. 1979. Asst. city atty. City of Charlotte, N.C., 1969-78; ptnr. Constagny, Goines, Buckley & Boyd, 1978-81, Taylor & Buckley, Charlotte, 1981-85, Buckley McMullen & Buie, P.A., Charlotte, 1994—; town atty. Town of Matthew (N.C.), 1978—; faculty Ctrl. Piedmont C.C., 1970. Bd. dirs. Charlotte City Employees Credit Union, 1974-78; pre. PTA, 1980-82; bd. visitors Luth. Theol. So. Sem., 1989-93. Recipient Cert. of Merit, City of charlotte, 1982. Mem. N.C. Bar Assn., N.C. Assn. Mcpl. Lawyers (bd. dirs. 1979-81, v.p. 1995-96, 1st v.p. 1996-97, pres. 1997-98), Optimist Club (pres. 1982-83), Phi Alpha Delta. Democrat. Lutheran. Consumer commercial, General practice, Municipal (including bonds). Home: 6813 Linda Lake Dr Charlotte NC 28215-4019

**BUCKLEY, EUGENE KENYON,** lawyer; b. St. Louis, Dec. 30, 1928; s. Eugene Patrick and Berenice (Kenyon) B.; m. Rosalie Kohl, Oct. 25, 1952; children: Ann, Daniel, Thomas, Stephen, Martin. AB, St. Louis U., 1952, JD, 1952. Bar: Mo. 1952, U.S. Dist. Ct. (ea. dist.) Mo. 1954, U.S. Supreme Ct. 1956, U.S. Ct. Appeals (8th cir.) 1964. Assoc. Mark D. Eagleton, Atty., St. Louis, 1954-60; assoc. Evans & Dixon, St. Louis, 1960-62, ptnr., 1962-98; of counsel Noce & Buckley, St. Louis, 1998—; mem. 22d Cir. Jud. Commn., St. Louis, 1970-75; co-chmn. fed. practice com. U.S. Dist. Ct. (ea. dist.) Mo., 1983-92; chair CJA adv. group, 1991-95. 1st lt. USAF, 1952-54. Recipient award of Honor, Lawyers Assn. St. Louis, 1989, Disting. Svc. award St. Louis County Bar Assn., 1995, Purcell Professionalism award Mo. Bar Found., 1996. Fellow Am. Coll. Trial Lawyers; mem. Bar. Assn. St. Louis (chmn. trial sect. 1979-80), Assn. Def. Counsel St. Louis (pres. 1971-72), Mo. Orgn. Def. Lawyers (bd. dirs. 1984-90). Roman Catholic. Avocations: fly fishing, travel. Alternative dispute resolution. Office: Noce & Buckley 515 Olive St Ste 800 Saint Louis MO 63101-1834

**BUCKLEY, FREDERICK JEAN,** lawyer; b. Wilmington, Ohio, Nov. 5, 1923; s. William Millard and Martha (Bright) B.; m. Josephine K. Buckley, Dec. 4, 1945; children: Daniel J., Fredrica Buckley Elder, Matthew J. Student, Wilmington Coll., 1941-42, Ohio State U., 1942-43; AB, U. Mich., 1948, LLB, 1949. Bar: Ohio 1950, U.S. Dist. Ct. (so. dist.) Ohio 1952, U.S. Supreme Ct. 1978, U.S. Ct. Appeals (6th cir.) 1981, Fla. 1982, U.S. Dist. Ct. (mid. dist.) Fla. 1991; cert. cir. ct. mediator, Fla. Assoc. G.L. Schilling, Sr., Wilmington, 1951-52; ptnr. Schilling & Buckley, Wilmington, 1953-56; sole practice Wilmington, 1956-62; sr. ptnr. Buckley, Miller & Wright, Wilmington, 1962—; chmn., counsel The Wilmington Savs. Bank, 1971—, also dir.; solicitor City of Wilmington, 1954-63. Contbr. articles in field. With AUS, 1943-46, ETO. Joint program Mich. Inst. Pub. Adminstrn. fellow, 1948. Fellow Am. Coll. Trial Lawyers; mem. ABA, Am. Arbitration Assn. (comml. panel), Fed. Bar Assn., Ohio State Bar Assn., Clinton County Bar Assn., Selden Soc., Fla. Bar, Fla. Acad. Profl. Mediators, Soc. Profls. in Dispute Resolution, Collier County Bar Assn., Ohio State Bar Found. Republican. Methodist. General civil litigation, Alternative dispute resolution, Probate. Office: 145 N South St Wilmington OH 45177-1646

**BUCKLEY, JAMES LANE,** federal judge; b. N.Y.C., Mar. 9, 1923; s. William Frank and Aloise Josephine (Steiner) B.; m. Ann Frances Cooley, May 22, 1953; children: Peter P., James F. W., Priscilla L., William F., David L., Andrew T. BA, Yale U., 1943, LLB, 1949. Bar: Conn. 1950, D.C. 1953. Assoc. Wiggin & Dana, New Haven, 1949-53, Reasoner & Davis, Washington, 1953-57; v.p. Catawba Corp., N.Y.C., 1956-70; mem. U.S. Senate from N.Y. State, 1971-77; with Donaldson, Lufkin & Jenrette, N.Y.C., 1977-78; bus. con., 1978-80; undersec. for security assistance U.S. Dept. State, Washington, 1981-82; pres. Radio Free Europe/Radio Liberty, Munich, 1982-85; cir. judge U.S. Ct. Appeals for D.C. Cir., 1985—, now sr. judge; co-chmn. U.S. del. to UN Conf. on Environ., Nairobi, 1982; chmn. U.S. del. UN Conf. on Population, Mexico City, 1984. Author: If Men Were Angels, 1975. Rep. candidate for U.S. Senate, Conn., 1980. Lt. (j.g.) USNR, 1943-46. Office: US Ct Appeals 333 Constitution Ave NW Washington DC 20001-2866

**BUCKLEY, JOHN JOSEPH, JR.,** lawyer; b. N.Y.C., May 18, 1947; m. Jane Emily Genster, Jan. 12, 1980; children: Emily, Darcy, Claire, Connor. AB, Georgetown U., 1969; JD, U. Chgo., 1972. Bar: N.Y. 1973, D.C. 1977. Law clk. to judge John Minor Wisdom U.S. Ct. Appeals, New Orleans, 1972-73; law clk. to justice Lewis F. Powell Jr. U.S. Supreme Ct., Washington, 1973-74; spl. asst. to atty. gen. U.S. Dept. Justice, Washington, 1975-77; assoc. William & Connolly, Washington, 1977-80, ptnr., 1981—. Mem. ABA, Order of Coif, Phi Beta Kappa. General civil litigation, Criminal. Home: 2955 Newark St NW Washington DC 20008-3339 Office: Williams & Connolly 725 12th St NW Washington DC 20005-5901

**BUCKLEY, MICHAEL FRANCIS,** lawyer; b. Saranac Lake, N.Y., Nov. 1, 1943; s. Francis Edward and Marjorie (Mooney) B.; m. Mary Thornton, June 26, 1965; children: Sean, Kathleen. BA, Dartmouth Coll., 1965; JD, Cornell U., 1968. Bar: N.Y. 1969, Fla. 1982, U.S. Dist. Ct. (we. dist.) N.Y. 1970. Assoc. Harter, Secrest & Emery, Rochester, N.Y., 1968-75, ptnr., 1976—. Contbg. author: Estate Planning and Probate in New York, 1985; co-editor: Administration of New York Estates, 1990. Bd. dirs. Highland Hosp. Found., Rochester, 1981-95, pres., 1984-87; bd. dirs. Highland Hosp., 1987—, pres., 1992-94; bd. dirs. Highland Health Sys., Inc., 1995-97, Strong Ptnrs. Health System, Inc., 1997—, YMCA of Greater Rochester, 1997—, Highland Cmty. Devel. Corp., 1998—, Highland Living Ctr., Inc., 1998—, Rochester Area Cmty. Found., 1999—. Fellow Am. Coll. Trusts and Estates Counsel; mem. ABA, N.Y. State Bar Assn. (exec. com. trusts and estates law sect. 1988-92), Monroe County Bar Assn. (chmn. trusts and estates sect. 1984-85, banking liaison com. 1985-86), Fla. Bar Assn., Estate Planing Coun. Rochester, Internat. Assn. Fin. Planners, Dartmouth Club (Rochester). Roman Catholic. Avocations: racquetball, platform tennis. Estate planning, Probate, Estate taxation. Home: 571 Thomas Ave Rochester NY 14617-1432 Office: Harter Secrest & Emery 700 Midtown Tower Rochester NY 14604-2006

**BUCKLEY, SAMUEL OLLIPHANT, III,** lawyer; b. Union, Miss., May 20, 1947; s. Samuel Olliphant Jr. and Mary Lou (Vance) B.; m. Jennifer Nell Willis, Dec. 31, 1990; children: William Paul, Mary Beth, Samuel Olliphant, Matthew. BS in Chemistry, La. State U., 1969; JD, Loyola U., New Orleans, 1977. Bar: La. 1977, U.S. Dist. Ct. (ea. dist.) La. 1977, U.S. Dist. Ct. (mid. dist.) La. 1978, U.S. Ct. Appeals (5th crct.) 1979, U.S. Ct. Appeals (11th crct.) 1981, U.S. Dist. Ct. (we. dist.) La. 1987, Colo. 1993. Dir. environ. Witco Chem. Corp., Gretna, La., 1970-77; assoc. Jones, Walker, Waechter, Poitevent, Carrere & Denegre, New Orleans, 1977-82, ptnr., 1982-92, of counsel, 1992-97; of counsel Cater & Willis, New Orleans, 1997—; asst. prof. environ. law Loyola U. Law Sch., 1984-87. Lead article editor Loyola U. Law Rev., 1976-77. Mem. Friends of New Orleans Symphony, Friends of Audubon Zoo, New Orleans; vestry mem. Christ Ch. Cathedral, 1997—. Mem. ABA (vice chmn. urban law com. 1980-81, solid and hazardous waste com. 1981-85, biotech. com. 1991-92), La. Bar Assn. (vice chmn. environ. law sect. 1980-82, chmn. 1982-86), New Orleans Bar Assn., Am. Chem. Soc., Loyola U. Law Alumni Assn. (bd. dirs. 1979-80), Nat. Audubon Soc. Democrat. Episcopalian. Avocations: skiing, golf. Environmental, Federal civil litigation, State civil litigation. Home: 319 Fairway Dr New Orleans LA 70124 Office: Cater & Willis 3723 Canel St New Orleans LA 70119

**BUCKLEY, TERRENCE PATRICK,** lawyer; b. N.Y.C., May 7, 1945; s. Cornelius and Catherine (Sheehan) B.; m. Patricia Ann McComb, Oct. 7, 1976; children: Shannondoah, Heather. BA, Iona Coll., 1967; JD, Bklyn. Law Sch., 1972. Bar: N.Y. 1972, U.S. Dist. Ct. (so. and ea. dists.) N.Y. 1977, U.S. Supreme Ct. 1993. Asst. dist. atty. Dist. Atty.'s Office, N.Y.C., 1972-74; law instr. Western State U., Fullerton, Calif., 1975; assoc. McDonald, Pulaski & Harlan, San Diego, 1975-77; atty.-in-charge Nassau-Suffolk Law Svcs., Riverhead, N.Y., 1977-78; spl. asst. atty. gen. N.Y. State Atty. Gen. Office, N.Y.C., 1978-86; trial counsel Pelletreau & Pelletreau, Patchogue, N.Y., 1986-87; pvt. practice Islandia, N.Y., 1988—; instr. health law SUNY, Stony Brook, 1988, 90; adminstrv. law judge Divsn. Parole, L.I. City, N.Y., 1987-88. With U.S. Army, 1969-71. Recipient Excellence award Am. Jurisprudence, 1972. Mem. ATLA, NACDL, Suffolk County Bar Assn., Am. Inns of Ct. (Alexander Hamilton Inn), Brehon Law Soc., Frank Hogan Assocs. Roman Catholic. Avocations: skiing, running, sailing, hiking, kayaking. Criminal, Professional liability, Personal injury. Office: One Suffolk Sq Ste 520 Islandia NY 11722

**BUCKLIN, LEONARD HERBERT,** lawyer; b. Mpls., Apr. 17, 1933; s. Leonard A. and Lilah B. (Norland) B.; m. Charla Lee; children: Karen, Anne, David, Douglas, Lea, Gregory. BS in Law, U. Minn., 1955, JD, 1957. Bar: Minn. 1957, U.S. Dist. Ct. Minn. 1957, N.D. 1960, U.S. Dist. Ct. N.D. 1960, U.S. Ct. Appeals (8th cir.) 1971, U.S. Supreme Ct. 1973, Colo. 1989, U.S. Dist. Ct. Colo. 1989, Tex. 1992, U.S. Dist. Ct. Tex. 1993. Ptnr. Larson, Loevinger, Lindquist, Freeman & Fraser, Mpls., 1957-60, Zuger & Bucklin, Bismark, N.D., 1960-87; gen. counsel Provident Life Ins. Co., 1965-85; pres. Bucklin Trial Lawyers P.C., 1988-95; of counsel Bucklin and Klemine, Bismark, N.D., 1992—, Allison and Huerta, Corpus Christi, 1992-97; owner Bucklin of Counsel Attys., 1997—; lectr. on ins. coverage to various groups, cons. on legal ethics to attys., mem. trial procedures com. N.D. Supreme Ct., 1977-92. Author: Civil Practice of North Dakota, 1975, ann. supplements, 1976-92. Fellow Internat. Acad. Trial Lawyers (bd. dirs.); mem. ABA (ins. coverage and ethics coms., Ctr. Profl. Responsibility), UNOS (patient affairs, ethics, profl. stds. com., bd. dirs.), ATLA, Tex. Trial Lawyers Assn., Winthrop Soc., Joseph Bucklin Soc. (chmn.), Chopin Soc. Tex., Tex. Ctr. for Legal Ethics, Million Dollar Advs. Forum, Rotary (Paul Harris fellow Corpus Christi), Order of Coif, Phi Delta Phi, Delta Sigma Rho. Methodist. Insurance, General civil litigation, Professional liability. Home: 8063 S Michele Ln Tempe AZ 85284-1362

**BUCKNER, MELISSA SPIRT,** lawyer; b. Orange, N.J., Jan. 10, 1969; d. Nathan and Nena Lela (Mih) Spirt; m. David Marc Buckner, Apr. 5, 1997. BA in English and Polit. Sci., Rutgers Coll., 1991, JD, 1994. Bar: Fla. 1994, N.J. 1994, D.C. 1997. Legal intern felony divsn. Dade County Office of Pub. Defender, Miami, Fla., summer 1993; legal intern to Hon. Nicholas H. Politan U.S. Dist. Ct. N.J., Newark, fall 1993; assoc. Stoldt & Horan, Hackensack, N.J., 1994-95; staff atty. King & Spalding, Atlanta, 1995-96; dir. devel. Make-a-Wish of Mid-Atlantic, Inc., Rockville, Md., 1997; atty. U.S. Dept. HHS Office of Gen. Counsel, Washington, 1997-98; assoc. Lash & Goldberg LLP, Miami, Fla., 1998—; mem. student/faculty com. on pub. interest law, chmn. moot ct. bd. Rutgers Law Sch., Newark, 1993-94. Pres. Rutgers Coll. Governing Assn., New Brunswick, N.J., 1990-91, mem. univ. senate, 1989-91; class agt. Rutgers Coll. Class of 1991, New Brunswick, 1991—. Mem. Fla. Bar Assn., Order of Barristers. Home: 12455 SW 93rd Ter # T-206 Miami FL 33186-7125 Office: Lash & Goldberg LLP 100 SE 2d St Ste 1200 Miami FL 33131-2158

**BUCKSTEIN, MARK AARON,** lawyer, educator; b. N.Y.C., July 1, 1939; s. Henry Al and Minnie Sarah (Russ) B.; m. Rochelle Joan Buchman, Sept. 11, 1960; children: Robin Beth, Michael Alan. BS in Math., CCNY, 1960; JD, NYU, 1963. Bar: N.Y. 1963, U.S. Dist. Ct. (so. and ea. dists.) N.Y. 1965, U.S. Supreme Ct. 1981. Assoc. Russ & Weyl, Massapequa, N.Y., 1963-64; assoc. counsel Mut. Life Ins. Co. N.Y., N.Y.C., 1964-65; assoc. Moses & Singer, N.Y.C., 1965-67, Leinwand, Maron & Hendler, N.Y.C., 1967-68; sr. ptnr. Baer Marks & Upham, N.Y.C., 1968-86; sr. v.p. external affairs, gen. counsel TWA, Inc., N.Y.C., 1986-92; exec. v.p. Am. Arbitration Assn., N.Y.C., N.J., 1992-93; exec. v.p., gen. counsel GAF Corp. and Internat. Specialty Products, Wayne, N.J., 1993-96; counsel Greenberg Traurig, Ft. Lauderdale, Fla., 1996-99, Profl. Dispute Resolution, Inc., Boca Raton, Fla., 1999—; spl. prof. law Hofstra U. Law Sch., Hempstead, N.Y., 1981-93; adj. prof. law Rutgers U. Law Sch., Newark, 1994-96; bd. dirs. Bayswater Realty & Capital Corp., N.Y.C., Travel Channel Inc., N.Y.C., TWA; mem. exec. com. Herzfeld & Stern, N.Y.C., 1981-84. Trustee Bronx H.S. Found., 1984—. Mem. ABA, N.Y. Bar Assn., Assn. of Bar of City of N.Y., Soc. for Profls. in Dispute Resolution, KP (past dep. grand chancellor 1978). Democrat. Jewish. Avocations: tennis, music, theater, puzzles. Securities, General corporate, Contracts commercial. Office: Profl Dispute Resolution 1200 N Federal Hwy Boca Raton FL 33432-2803

**BUCKWALTER, RONALD LAWRENCE,** federal judge; b. Lancaster, Pa., Dec. 11, 1936; s. Noah Denlinger and Carolyn Marie (Lawrence) B.; m. Dollie May Fitting, May 9, 1963; children: Stephen Matthew, Wendy Susan. AB, Franklin and Marshall Coll., 1958; JD, Coll. William and Mary, 1962. Prin. Ronald L. Buckwalter, Esquire, Lancaster, 1963-71; ptnr. Shirk, Reist and Buckwalter, Lancaster, 1971-80; dist. atty. Lancaster County, Lancaster, 1978-80; judge 2nd Jud. Dist. Commonwealth Pa., 1980-90, U.S. Dist. Ct., Phila., 1990—. Sec. City Lancaster Authority, 1970; bd. dirs. Am. Cancer Soc., Lancaster, 1982, Boy Scouts Am., Lancaster, 1984, YMCA, Lancaster, 1990. 1st lt. U.S. Army NG, 1962-68. Recipient Pub. Life and Letter award Phi Sigma Alpha, 1990. Mem. Am. Judicature Soc., Fed. Bar Assn., Fed. Judges Assn., Pa. Bar Assn., Lancaster Bar Assn. (pres. 1988). Office: US Dist Ct 14614 US Courthouse 601 Market St Philadelphia PA 19106-1713

**BUDAJ, STEVEN T.,** lawyer; b. Detroit, Dec. 18, 1953; s. Nikolaj and Magda B.; m. Diane B. Budaj, Aug. 27, 1978; 1 child, Evan N. BS, Wayne State U., 1975; JD, Detroit Coll. Law, 1978. Bar: Mich., U.S. Dist. Ct. (ea. and we. dists.) Mich., U.S. Ct. Appeals (6th cir.), U.S. Supreme Ct. Pvt. practice Detroit, 1979-81; pres., atty. Quinn & Budaj, P.C., Detroit, 1981-86, Steven T. Budaj, P.C., Detroit, 1986—. Chmn. woodlands rev. bd. Charter Township W. Bloomfield, Mich., 1986—. Mem. Assn. Trial Lawyers Am., Mich. Trial Lawyers Assn. Personal injury, Constitutional, Federal civil litigation. Office: 2915 Cadillac Tower Detroit MI 48226

**BUDANITSKY, SANDER,** lawyer; b. Riga, Latvia, Feb. 9, 1972; came to the U.S., 1979; s. Grigory and Miriam Budanitsky; m. Kimberly Anne Rudolph, Nov. 16, 1997. BA, Dickinson Coll., 1993; JD, Widener U., 1996. Bar: N.J. 1996, Pa. 1996. Legal intern U.S. Dept. Justice, Office of the U.S.

Trustee, Phila., 1995-96; assoc. Seigel & Mongiardo, P.C., Ridgewood, N.J., 1997-98, Robert C. Diorio, Elizabeth, N.J., 1998—. Avocation: rugby. General civil litigation, General corporate. Office: Law Offices Robert C Diorio 431 Morris Ave Elizabeth NJ 07208-3612

**BUDD, DAVID GLENN,** lawyer; b. Dayton, Ohio, May 19, 1934; s. Glenn E. and Anna Elizabeth (Purdy) B.; m. Barbarann Dumbaugh, Apr. 4, 1964; children: Anne Elizabeth, David Glenn II. AB with honors, Ohio U., 1959; JD with honors, U. Cin., 1962. Bar: Ohio 1962, U.S. Dist. Ct. (so. dist.) Ohio 1963, U.S. Dist. Ct. (no. dist.) Ohio 1967, U.S. Supreme Ct. 1967, Fla. 1980, U.S. Dist. Ct. (mid. dist.) Fla. 1981, U.S. Tax Ct. 1989. Assoc. Young, Pryor, Lynn, Strickland & Falke, Dayton, 1962-65; trial atty. U.S. Dept. Justice, Cleve., 1965-67; chief antitrust sect. Atty. Gen. Ohio, Columbus, Ohio, 1967-69; ptnr., sr. corp. atty. Cox & Brandabur Attys., Xenia, Ohio, 1969-74; asst. v.p., asst. sec. law Jim Walter Corp., Tampa, Fla., 1974-76; sec., gen. counsel, asst. treas. Gardinier Big River, Inc., Gardinier, Inc., Tampa, 1976-80; assoc. Young, Van Assenderp, Varnadoe & Benton, P.A., Naples, Fla., 1981-84; ptnr. Van Koughnet & Budd, Naples, 1984-85; sr. ptnr. Budd, Hines & Thompson, Naples, 1985-88, Budd & Thompson, Naples, 1989-92, Budd, Thompson & Zuccaro, Naples, 1993-95, Budd & Zuccaro, Naples, 1996-97, Budd and Bennett, Naples, 1998—; legal counsel to bd. dirs. of numerous corps. Vol. Legal Aid Soc., Xenia, 1972; active Newcomen Soc. N.Am. With USN, 1952-54. Mem. ABA (bus. law sect.), Fla. Bar Assn., Collier County Bar Assn., Blue Key Club, Omicron Delta Kappa, Pi Gamma Mu, Phi Kappa Tau. Republican. Presbyterian. Avocations: health fitness club, tennis, golf, boating. General corporate, Probate, Real property. Home: 3757 Fountainhead Ln Naples FL 34103-2734 Office: Budd and Bennett 3033 Riviera Dr Ste 201 Naples FL 34103-2750

**BUDD, THOMAS WITBECK,** lawyer; b. Phila., Nov. 1, 1939; s. Reginald Masten and Elizabeth (Charlton) B.; divorced; children—Kelly Lynne, Paige Elizabeth; m. Bernadette Smith Budd, July 4, 1988; stepchildren: Amanda Rose Kronin, Karen Wendy Kronin. B.A., Washington and Lee U., 1961, LL.B., 1964. Bar: Va. 1964, N.Y. 1965, U.S. Supreme Ct. 1982. Assoc., Buell Clifton & Turner, N.Y.C., 1964-69, ptnr., 1969-70; ptnr. Clifton Budd & Burke, N.Y.C., 1970-76, Clifton Budd Burke & Demaria, N.Y.C., 1976-88; ptnr. Clifton, Budd & Demaria, 1988—. Contbg. author, editor to Labor and Employment Law newsletter. Mem. law council Washington and Lee U., 1978-81, 1984-85. Mem. ABA (labor law sect.), N.Y. Bar Assn. (labor law sect.), N.Y.C. Bar Assn. (labor law sect.). Clubs: Princeton (N.Y.C.); St. George's Golf and Country Club (Stony Brook, N.Y.). Labor, Pension, profit-sharing, and employee benefits. Home: 3 Colgate Ct Shoreham NY 11786-1221 Office: Clifton Budd & Demaria 420 Lexington Ave New York NY 10170-0002

**BUDDEN, HARRY EDWARD, JR.,** lawyer; b. Saginaw, Mich., Dec. 28, 1945; s. Harry Edward and Ann Mary (Soskowski) B.; m. Jennie A. Scales, Aug. 3, 1983; 1 child by previous marriage, Priscilla Jean. A.B., Marshall U., 1968; J.D., U. Ky., 1973. Bar: Ky. 1973, U.S. Dist. Ct. Ky., U.S. Ct. Appeals (6th cir.), U.S. Supreme Ct. sole practice,Paris, Ky., 1973—. Served to capt. ACG, U.S. Army, 1969-71; Vietnam. Decorated Bronze star. Mem. Ky. Bar Assn., Acad. Ky. Trial Lawyers, Omicron Delta Kappa, Sigma Alpha Epsilon. Democrat. Episcopalian. Lodge: Masons. Fax: 606-987-7986. General practice, Family and matrimonial, State civil litigation. Home: 1121 Andover Forest Dr Lexington KY 40509-2005 Office: 912 Pleasant St PO Box 410 Paris KY 40362-0410

**BUDMAN, ALAN DAVID,** lawyer, law educator; b. Phila., Feb. 18, 1953; s. Harry and Ida G. B.; m. Susan Arlene Schwartz, Apr. 4, 1981; children: Heather Jana Budman, Traci A. Budman. BS, Penn State U., 1974; JD, Del. Law Sch., 1977. Bar: Pa. 1977, U.S. Dist. Ct. (ea. dist.) Pa. 1977, U.S. Supreme Ct. 1997. Corp. tax atty. Penn Ctrl. Corp., Phila., 1977-79; grad. sch. instr. Villanova U., Phila., 1980; law instr. Penn State U., Abington, 1979—; pvt. practice Phila., Abington, 1979—. Co-author: Comparative Negligence, 1984. Vol. Big Brother, Phila., 1978-84; committeeman Dem. City Com., Phila., 1983-87; v.p. Melrose B'Nai Israel, Cheltenham, Pa., 1985-88; pres. Ctrl. H.S. Alumni Assn., Phila., 1988-91: chmn. Devel. Com. Am. Heart Assn., Phila., 1990-92; bd. dirs. Temple Sinai, Dresher, Pa., 1997—. Mem. Comml. Law League, Pa. Bar Assn., Phila. Bar Assn., Montgomery Bar Assn. Democrat. Jewish. Avocations: skiing, golf, the internet. Bankruptcy, Consumer commercial, General practice. Office: 1150 Old York Rd 2nd Fl Abington PA 19001-3712

**BUDNITZ, ARRON EDWARD,** lawyer, law educator, real estate broker, insurance broker, financial and management consultant; b. Hanover, N.H., Feb. 27, 1949; s. Harry and Frieda Sara (Altschitz) B.; m. Donna F. Stark, May 22, 1994. AB, Dartmouth Coll., 1971; MBA, Boston U., 1973, LLM in Taxation, 1981; JD, Suffolk U., 1979. Bar: Mass. 1979, U.S. Dist. Ct. Mass. 1979, U.S. Tax Ct. 1979, U.S. Ct. Appeals (1st cir.) 1979, Fla. 1979, U.S. Dist. Ct. N.H. 1980, Maine 1987, U.S. Dist. Ct. Maine, 1987; CFP. Pvt. practice, Lexington, 1979—; adj. faculty N.H. Coll., Manchester and Salem, 1984-86. Author Fin. Planning Forum, mem. editorial staff Trowel Mag. Chmn. planned giving com. Masonic Learning Ctrs., Inc., 1995. Mem. Fla. Bar Assn., Mass. Bar Assn., Dartmouth Lawyers Assn., N.H. Estate Planning Coun., Intertel, Mensa, Masons, Shriners, Oriental Band, BunkerHillBillies, Phi Delta Phi. Democrat. Jewish. General practice, General corporate, Estate planning. Home: 65 Williams Rd Lexington MA 02420-3235 Office: PO Box 508 Newport NH 03773-0508

**BUECHEL, WILLIAM BENJAMIN,** lawyer; b. Wichita, Kans., July 27, 1926; s. Donald William and Bonnie S. (Priddy) B.; m. Theresa Marie Girard, Nov. 3, 1955; children: Sarah Ann, Julia Elaine. Student U. Wichita, 1947-49; BS, U. Kans., 1951, LLB, 1954. Bar: Kans., 1954, U.S. dist. ct. (Kans.), 1954. Sole practice, Concordia, Kans., 1954-56; stockholder Paulsen, Buechel, Swenson, Uri & Brewer, Chartered, and predecessors, Concordia, 1971-75, sec.-treas., 1975-77, pres., 1977-92, of counsel, 1993-95; ret.; bd. dirs. County Bank & Trust, Concordia, 1971-92, Cloud County Community Coll. Found., 1983-89, trust and adminstrn. com. Citizens Nat. Bank, 1992—. Mem. ABA, Kan. Bar Assn. (exec. council 1966-68, chmn. adv. sect. profl. ethics com. 1974-76), Cloud County Bar Assn. (pres. 1984-86). Republican. Methodist. Clubs: Concordia Country, Elks, Moose, Rotary (pres. 1969-70). Probate, Estate taxation, Estate planning.

**BUECHNER, JACK W(ILLIAM),** lawyer, government affairs consultant; b. St. Louis, June 4, 1940; s. John Edward and Gertrude Emily (Richardson) B.; children from previous marriage: Patrick John, Terrence J.; m. Nancy Chanitz; 1 child, Charles Chanitz. BA, Benedictine Coll., 1962; JD, St. Louis U., 1965. Bar: Mo. 1965, U.S. Dist. Ct. (ea. dist.) Mo. 1965, U.S. Ct. Appeals (8th cir.) 1965, U.S. Ct. Appeals (D.C. cir.) 1998. Ptnr. Buechner, McCarthy, Leonard, Kaemmerer, Owen & Laderman, Chesterfield, Mo., 1965-93; mem. 100th-102d U.S. Congresses from 2d Mo. dist., 1987-91; dep. minority whip, 1989-90; vice-chmn. Rep. study group, pres. Internat. Rep. Inst., Washington, 1991-93; prin., dir. internat. svcs. The Hawthorn Group, Arlington, Va., 1993-95; ptnr. Manatt Phelps & Phillips, Washington, 1995—; state rep. 94th dist. Mo. Gen. Assembly, 1972-82, minority leader, 1974-78; mem. state adv. com. U.S. Commn. on Civil Rights, 1975-82. Lay advisor St. Louis Med. Soc., 1989-92; Mo. Tourism Commn., 1976, 82-85. Recipient Meritorious Svc. award St. Louis Globe-Democrat, 1973, Legis. Achievement award St. Louis Police Officers, 1982, Pub. Svc. award Women's Polit. Caucus, Mo., Disting. Svc. award Cardinal Glennon Hosp., Mo., 1982, Nat. Security Leadership award Am. Security Coun. Found., 1988, 89, Family and Freedom award, Golden Bulldog award, 1987, 88, Guardian of Small Bus. award Nat. Fedn. Ind. Bus., 1987, 88, 90, 91, Enterprise award U.S. C. of C., 1988, 89, 90, Sound Dollar award, 1988, Eagle of Freedom award Am. Security Coun. Foun., 1990. Mem. Mo. Bar Assn., D.C. Bar Assn., Met. Bar Assn., Mo. Soc. Washington (pres.), Nat. Conf. State Socs. (1st v.p.), Ctr. Nat. Policy (bd. dirs. 1997—), Assn. Former Mems. of Congress (bd. dirs., sec.), John Marshall Club (Outstanding Atty. award 1986), Lions, Phi Delta Phi. Republican. Episcopalian. Avocations: golf, reading, travel. E-mail: jbuechner@manatt.com. Private international, Public international, Legislative. Home: 1303 Altamira Ct Mc Lean VA 22102-2201 Office: Manatt Phelps & Phillips 1501 M St NW Ste 700 Washington DC 20005-1737

**BUECHNER, ROBERT WILLIAM,** lawyer, educator; b. Syracuse, N.Y., Oct. 29, 1947; s. Donald F. and Barbara (Northrup) B.; m. Angela Marian Hoetker, May 28, 1978; children: Julie Marie, Robert William Jr., Leslie Ann, James Bradley. BSE, Princeton U., 1969; JD, U. Mich., 1974. Bar: Ohio, 1974, Fla. 1974, U.S. Dist. Ct. (so. dist.) Ohio 1974, U.S. Tax Ct. 1974. Assoc. Frost & Jacobs, Cin., 1974-79; pres. Buechner, Haffer, O'Connell, Meyers & Healey Co., L.P.A., Cin., 1979—; adj. prof. Salmon P. Chase Coll. Law, No. Ky., 1975-82; instr. Cin. chpt. Chartered Life Underwiters, 1976-96; lectr. Million Dollar Roundtable, Atlanta, 1981. Author: (with others) Why Universal Life, 1982, Prosper Through Tax Planning, 1982, Living Gangbusters, 1986, The 8 Pathways to Financial Success, 1987, 93, 98. Mem. planning divsn. Cin. Cmty. Chest, 1978-84; trustee Cin. Venture Assn., 1994-99, pres., 1997-98; trustee Cin. Country Day Sch., 1979-93, pres., 1990-93. Recipient Alumnus of Yr. award Cin. Country Day Sch., 1985, First winner of John Warrington Cmty. Svc. award, 1997. Mem. Cin. Bar Assn. (chmn. taxation sect. 1984-85), S.W. Ohio Tax Inst. (chmn. 1981-82), Cin. Assn. (trustee 1999—), Gyro Club (sec. 1982-83, v.p. 1999-2000), Princeton Club (pres. 1982-84). Republican. Methodist. Avocations: golf, tennis, bridge. Estate planning, Corporate taxation, Probate. Office: Buechner Haffer O'Connell Meyers Healey Co LPA 105 E 4th St Ste 300 Cincinnati OH 45202-4023

**BUELL, BARBARA HAYES,** lawyer; b. Cambridge, Mass., July 15, 1942; d. James Harvey and Evelyn (McMahon) Hayes; div.; 1 child, Zachary Hayes; m. Paul Langner, Dec. 1, 1990. BA, Brandeis U., 1964; JD, Northeastern U., Boston, 1971. Bar: Mass. 1971, U.S. Dist. Ct. Mass. 1972, U.S. Supreme Ct. 1980, U.S. Ct. Appeals (1st cir.) 1985, R.I. 1996, U.S. Dist. Ct. R.I. 1997. Pvt. practice Boston, 1971-74; ptnr. Bloom & Buell, Boston, 1974—; tax title atty. City of Somerville, Mass., 1971-77; faculty lectr. Boston U., 1974-76; instr. clin. fieldwork Harvard Law Sch., Boston, 1975-78. Trustee Cambridge Sch., Weston, Mass., 1989-96; bd. dirs. Cambridge (Mass.) and Somerville Legal Svcs., 1971-75, Cambridge Family and Children's Svcs., 1980-83. Mem. Mass. Bar Assn., Northeastern U. Alumni (pres. 1984-86). General civil litigation. Office: Bloom & Buell 1340 Soldiers Field Rd Boston MA 02135-1020

**BUELL, EDWARD RICK, II,** lawyer; b. Des Moines, Jan. 28, 1948; s. Edward Rick and Betty-Jo (Heffron) B.; B.S. with high honors, Mich. State U., 1969; J.D. magna cum laude, U. Mich., 1972; children—Erica Colleen, Edward Rick III. Bar: D.C. 1973, Calif. 1975; cert. specialist in taxation law, Calif. Assoc. firm Arent, Fox, Kintner, Plotkin & Kahn, Washington, 1972-74, Brobeck, Phleger & Harrison, San Francisco, 1974-77; ptnr. Winokur, Schoenberg, Maier & Zang, San Francisco, 1977-81; ptnr. Buell & Berner, San Francisco, 1981—. Mem. ABA, San Francisco Bar Assn., Order of Coif. Contbr. articles to legal jours. General civil litigation, Labor. Home: 50 Stewart Dr Belvedere Tiburon CA 94920-1323

**BUELL, MARK PAUL,** lawyer; b. St. Petersburg, Fla., Mar. 9, 1951; s. Harold E. and Jeane Charlotte (Russell) B.; m. Ellen Courtney Rendall, Apr. 28, 1984; children: Mary Ellen, Johnston Rodd, Rendall Jeane. BS, U. Fla., 1973, JD, 1976. Bar: Fla. 1976, U.S. Ct. Appeals (5th and 11th cirs.), U.S. Dist. Ct. (mid., so. and no. dists.) Fla. Assoc. Shackleford, Farrior, Stallings & Evans, P.A., Tampa, Fla., 1976-82, shareholder, 1982-90; shareholder Schropp, Buell & Elligett, P.A., Tampa, 1990—. Contbr. chpt. to Florida Keystone, Lawyer's Desk Library of Practice, 1990, 4th edit., 1994. Mem. Hillsborough County Bar Assn. (pres. young lawyers sect. 1981-82, pres. 1992-93, chmn. eminent domain com. 1993-94), Fla. Bar (young lawyers bd. govs. 1981-87, vice chmn. eminent domain com. 1995-97, bd. govs. 1997—, bd. cert. civil trial lawyer and bus. litigation law). Condemnation, Personal injury, Federal civil litigation. Office: Schropp Buell & Elligett PA 401 E Jackson St Ste 2600 Tampa FL 33602-5232

**BUELL, RODD RUSSELL,** lawyer; b. Pitts., Mar. 31, 1946; s. Harold Ellsworth and Jeanne Charlotte (Russell) B. BS, Fla. State U., 1968; JD, U. Fla., 1970; LLM, U. Miami, 1978. Bar: Fla. 1971, U.S. Dist. Ct. (so., mid. and no. dists.) Fla. 1971, U.S. Ct. Appeals (5th and 11th cirs.) 1971. Gen. ptnr. Blackwell & Walker, P.A., Miami, 1970-95; shareholder Fleming, O'Bryan & Fleming, Ft. Lauderdale, Fla., 1995-97; pvt. practice, Coral Gables, Fla., 1997—. Mem. Dade County Def. Bar Assn. (pres. 1985-86), Def. Trial Attys. Assn. (exec. counsel 1986-88), Maritime Law Assn., Am. Bd. Trial Advs., Internat. Assn. Def. Counsel, Bath Club, Riviera Country Club, Miami Club, Univ. Club. Republican. Methodist. Personal injury, General civil litigation, Admiralty. Home: 4801 Campo Sano Ct Coral Gables FL 33146-1160 Office: 2355 Salzedo St Ste 202 Coral Gables FL 33134-5035

**BUETENS, ERIC D.,** lawyer; b. Rochester, N.Y., Jan. 30, 1953; s. Melvin and Shirley Doris (Gerber) B.; m. Carol Rebecca Osborn, Feb. 7, 1986; children: Rachel Catherine, Sarah Louise. BFA, U. N.Mex., 1976; JD magna cum laude, Syracuse U., 1986. Bar: Fla. 1986. Ptnr. Buetens & Buetens, Hobe Sound, Fla., 1986—. Pres. Friends of the Mid-County Libr., Inc., 1995—; chmn. Sch. Improvement Plan, 1995-96. Mem. Fla. Bar Assn. (vice-chmn. individual rights com. 1988, legis. com. pub. interest sect. 1990-91). Democrat. Real property, Probate, Personal injury. Home: 381 SW Timber Trl Stuart FL 34997-6289 Office: 8965 SE Bridge Rd Hobe Sound FL 33455-5327

**BUFFENSTEIN, ALLAN S.,** lawyer; b. Richmond, Va., Sept. 21, 1940; m. Frona Buffenstein. BA, U. Richmond, 1962, LLB, 1965. Bar: Va. 1965. Ptnr. Mezzullo and McCandlish, Richmond; lectr. Continuing Legal Edn., The Troubled Project, The Troubled Condominium Va. Law Found. Pres., chmn. bd. Richmond Jewish Community Ctr., 1982-84. Mem. ABA, Va. Bar Assn., Am. Bankruptcy Inst., Richmond Bar Assn. Bankruptcy, General corporate, Probate. Office: Mezzullo & McCandlish 1111 E Main St PO Box 796 Richmond VA 23218-0796

**BUFFINGTON, JOHN VICTOR,** lawyer; b. Arlington, Va., July 23, 1947; s. John V. Sr. and Patricia (Messer) B.; m. Cynthia Davis, June 13, 1970. BA, U. Va., 1969, JD, 1972. Bar: D.C. 1973, Va. 1973, U.S. Ct. Appeals (3d cir.) 1976, Pa. 1979. Staff atty. U.S. EPA, Phila., 1973-77; regional counsel U.S. Dept. Energy, Phila., 1977-79; chief counsel Pa. Gov.'s Energy Council, Harrisburg, 1979-82; research fellow U. Del., Newark, 1982-84; sole practice Phila., 1985—; lectr. Del. Humanities Forum, Wilmington, 1984-88; arbitrator Phila. Bd. Common Pleas, 1985—. Contbr. articles to profl. jours. Mem ABA, Phila. Bar Assn. Public utilities, Nuclear power, Real property.

**BUFFORD, SAMUEL LAWRENCE,** federal judge; b. Phoenix, Ariz., Nov. 19, 1943; s. John Samuel and Evelyn Amelia (Rude) B.; m. Julia Marie Metzger, May 13, 1978. BA in Philosophy, Wheaton Coll., 1964; PhD, U. Tex., 1969; JD magna cum laude, U. Mich., 1973. Bar: Calif., N.Y., Ohio. Instr. philosophy La. State U., Baton Rouge, 1967-68; asst. prof. Ea. Mich. U., Ypsilanti, 1968-74; asst. prof. law Ohio State U., Columbus, 1975-77; assoc. Gendel, Raskoff, Shapiro & Quittner, L.A., 1982-85; atty. Paul, Weiss, Rifkind, Wharton & Garrison, N.Y.C., 1974-75, Sullivan Jones & Archer, San Francisco, 1977-79, Musick, Peeler & Garrett, L.A., 1979-81, Rifkind & Sterling, Beverly Hills, Calif., 1981-82, Gendel, Raskoff, Shapiro & Quittner, L.A., 1982-85; U.S. bankruptcy judge Ctrl. Dist. Calif., 1985—; bd. dirs. Fin. Lawyers Conf., L.A., 1987-90, Bankruptcy Forum, L.A., 1986-88; lectr. U.S.-Romanian Jud. Delegation, 1991, Internat. Tng. Ctr. for Bankers, Budapest, 1993, Bankruptcy Technical Legal Assistance Workshop, Romania, 1994, Comml. Law Project for Ukraine, 1995-96, Ea. Europe Enterprise Restructuring and Privitization Project, U.S. AID, 1995-96; cons. Calif. State Bar Bd. Examiners, 1989-90; bd. trustees Endowment for Edn.; bd. dirs. nat. Conf. Bankruptcy Judges, 1994—; mem. San Pedro Enterprise Community, 1997—. Editor-in-chief Am. Bankruptcy Law Jour., 1990-94; contbr. articles to profl. jours.; columnist Norton Bankruptcy Advisor, 1988-90. Younger Humanist fellowship NEH. Mem. ABA, L.A. County Bar Assn. (mem. profl. responsibility and ethics com. 1979—, chair profl. responsibility and ethics com. 1985-86, chair ethics 2000 liaison com. 1997—), Order of Coif. Office: US Bankruptcy Ct 255 E Temple St Ste 1582 Los Angeles CA 90012-3334

**BUFORD, ROBERT PEGRAM,** lawyer; b. Roanoke Rapids, N.C., Sept. 7, 1925; s. Robert Pegram and Edith (Rawlings) B.; m. Anne Bliss Whitehead, June 26, 1948; children: Robert, Bliss, Peyton. LLB, U. Va., 1950. Bar: Va. 1949. sr. counsel Hunton & Williams, Richmond, Va. Bd. visitors U. Va., Charlottesville, 1972-80; chmn. Met. Richmond C. of C., 1973; vice chmn., bd. trustees St. Paul's Coll., Lawrenceville, Va., 1977-85. Lt. (j.g.) USNR, 1943-46. Recipient Disting. Service award Jr. C. of C., 1961, Va. Profl. Assn., 1965, Good Govt. award Richmond First Club, 1967. Fellow Am. Bar Found., Va. Law Found.; mem. ABA, Va. Bar (assoc.), Country Club of Va., Commonwealth Club. Banking, General corporate, Securities. Home: 506 Kilmarnock Dr Richmond VA 23229-8102 Office: Hunton & Williams Riverfront Pla E Tower PO Box 1535 Richmond VA 23218-1535

**BUGBEE, JESSE D.,** lawyer; b. Orlando, Fla., Oct. 15, 1958; s. David D. and Catherine A. B.; m. Dawn D. Martensen, Aug. 8, 1981; children: Laura, Garrett, Erika, Brennan. BA, Castleton State Coll., 1980; JD, Vt. U., 1983. Bar: Vt. 1983, U.S. Dist. Ct. Vt. 1985. Jud. clk. Vt. Supreme Ct., Montpelier, Vt., 1983-84; ptnr. Kissane Assocs., St. Albans, Vt., 1984—. Bd. dirs. Nowthwest Vt. Heart Assn., St. Albans; active Green Mountain Coun. Boy Scouts Am. Mem. Vt. Bar Assn. (bd. dirs. 1992—, Pro Bono award 1994), Vt. Trial Lawyers Assn., Franklin County Bar Assn. Contracts commercial, Estate planning, General civil litigation. Office: Kissane Assocs 2 N Main St Saint Albans VT 05478-1665

**BUHALY IBOLD, CATHERINE,** lawyer; b. S.C., May 28, 1961; d. Albert L. and Elsie K. Buhaly; m. Kenneth R. Ibold, May, 30, 1993; children: Steven, Kaelyn, Parker. BS, BA, U. Fla., Gainesville, 1983; JD cum laude, U. Miami, Coral Gables, 1993. Bar: Fla., Tenn. Pvt. practice Boca Raton/Nashville, Fla./Tenn., 1993-97; atty., editor West Pub., Boca Raton/Nashville, Fla./Tenn., 1994-96; atty. Akerman, Senterfitt & Eidson, Orlando, Fla., 1997-98; atty., CLO Cypress Restaurants, Inc., Cypress Hotel Mgmt. Co., Inc., Signature Realty, Inc., Orlando, Fla., 1999—; exec. counsel Fla. Bar Real Property & Probate, 1998-99. Contbr. articles to profl. jours. Supporter United Way, Orange County, Fla., 1998, 99. Recipient Pro Bono award Dade County Bar, Fla., 1993, First Place award for young lawyers svc. to public Dade County Bar, Fla., 1993. Mem. ABA, Fla. Bar Assn., Tenn. Bar Assn., Ctrl. Fla. Assn. for Women Lawyers. Real property, Contracts commercial, General corporate. Office: Cypress Companies 2250 N Orange Blossom Trl Orlando FL 32804-4801

**BUHLER, LYNN BLEDSOE,** lawyer; b. Memphis, Jan. 23, 1949; d. William Stevenson and Betty (Mullins) Bledsoe; m. Jon Milton Buhler, Jan. 22, 1983. Student, Vanderbilt U., 1967-70; BA, U. Memphis, 1972, MA, 1975, JD, 1980. Bar: Tex. 1980, Tenn. 1983. Assoc. Carrington, Coleman, Sloman & Blumethal, Dallas, 1980-82, Borod & Huggins, Memphis, 1983-85; from assoc. to ptnr. Glankler, Brown, PLLC, Memphis, 1985-99, The Buhler Law Firm, Memphis, 1999—. Bd. dirs. Jr. League Memphis, Inc., 1976, 87-89, Project 1st Offender, Memphis, 1976, Memphis Speech & Hearing Ctr., 1976, Runaway House, Memphis 1976, YWCA, Memphis, 1999—. Mem. ABA (bus. law sect., com. on fed. securities regulation 1993—, subcom. on savs. instns. 1986-88, subcom. on syndications 1990-93, subcom. on investment cos. and investment advisers 1993—), Memphis Bar Assn. (chmn. corp. counsel sect. 1994, dir. securities sect. 1997—, chmn. 1999). Episcopalian. Avocation: horseback riding. General corporate, Securities, Finance. Office: The Buhler Law Firm 50 N Front St Memphis TN 38103-2126

**BUILDER, J. LINDSAY, JR.,** lawyer; b. Miami, Fla., Feb. 6, 1943; s. John Lindsay and Majorie (Merrell) L.; m. Jean Fern, Aug. 3, 1968; children Margaret Merrell, John Lindsay III. BE, Vanderbilt U., 1965, JD, 1970. Bar: Fla. 1970, U.S Dist Ct. (mid. dist.) Fla. 1971, U.S. Supreme Ct. 1976. Assoc., ptnr. Maguire, Voorhis & Wells P.A, Orlando, Fla., 1970-84; ptnr. Godbold, Allen, Brown & Builder P.A., Winter Park, Fla., 1984-88, Allen, Brown & Builder P.A., Winter Park, 1988-90, Honigman Miller Schwartz and Cohn., Detroit, Orlando, 1991-96, Graham, Clark, Jones, Builder, Pratt and Marks, Winter Park, Fla., 1996—. Mem. bd. trust Vanderbilt U., Nashville, 1990-92, Winter Park Mem. Hosp., chmn. 1994-96. Lt. (j.g) USN, 1965-67. Mem. Orange County Bar Assn. (pres. 1983-84), Vanderbilt U. Law Sch. Alumni (bd. dirs. 1985, pres.), Vanderbilt U. Alumni (pres. bd. dirs. 1989-90). Republican. Episcopalian. Avocations: golf, snow skiing, tennis. Office: Graham Clark Jones Builder Pratt and Marks 369 N New York Ave Winter Park FL 32789-3119

**BULDRINI, GEORGE JAMES,** lawyer; b. N.Y.C.; s. Frederick Paul and Emily Geraldine (Bewick) B. BA, St. Johns U., Jamaica, N.Y., 1969; JD, St. Johns U., 1972; LLM, NYU, 1976. Bar: N.Y. 1973, U.S. Dist. Ct. (no. dist.) N.Y. 1975, U.S. Supreme Ct. 1976. Sr. atty. N.Y. State Dept. Health, Albany, 1974—; shop steward Pub. Employees Fedn., 1982—. Mem. ABA, NRA, N.Y. State Bar Assn., Fed. Bar Assn. Republican. Avocations: golf, chess, reading, gardening, photography. Office: NY Dept Health Legal Affairs Empire State Plz Albany NY 12237-0001

**BULKLEY, ROBERT DE GROFF, JR.,** lawyer; b. Toledo, Ohio, June 19, 1943; s. Robert De Groff and Loretta (Coburn) B.; m. Linda Gail Throp, June 20, 1964 (div. May 1982); children: Joanna Eleanor, Katrina Elisabeth; m. Joyce Lorraine MacWilliamson, Feb. 10, 1985. BA, Lewis & Clark Coll., 1964; MA, Princeton U., 1966, PhD, 1971; JD, U. Oreg., 1977. Bar: Oreg. 1977, U.S. Dist. Ct. Oreg. 1978, U.S. Ct. Appeals (9th cir.) 1978, U.S. Supreme Ct. 1990. Instr. history Benedict Coll., Columbia, S.C., 1966-67; asst. prof. history Rocky Mountain Coll., Billings, Mont., 1968-74; law clk. U.S. Ct. Appeals, 9th Cir., Portland, Oreg., 1977-78; asst. atty. gen. Oreg. Dept. Justice, Portland, 1978-83; staff atty. Oreg. Ct. Appeals, Salem, 1983-90, 95—; assoc. Markowitz, Herbold et al, Portland, 1990-92, of counsel, 1992-95. Clk. of session First Presbyn. Ch., Portland, 1986-89, mem. various coms., 1980—; mem. peace and justice com. Presbytery of the Cascades, Portland, 1989-95, mem. higher edn. com., 1998—; mem. cmty. ministries com. Ecumenical Ministries of Oreg., Portland, 1995-97. Woodrow Wilson fellow, 1964. Mem. Oreg. State Bar. Democrat. Avocations: hiking, rail fan, reading. Home: 11585 SW Denfield St Beaverton OR 97005-1580 Office: Oregon Court of Appeals 300 Justice Bldg Salem OR 97310-0001

**BULLINER, P. ALAN,** corporate lawyer. BS, Lehigh U., 1965; AM, Princeton U., 1967, PhD, 1970; JD, U. Pa., 1975. Bar: Pa. 1975. V.p. corp. sec. and counsel Bell Atlantic Corp., Phila., 1992-97; assoc. gen. counsel and sec. Bell Atlantic Corp., N.Y.C., 1997—. Office: Bell Atlantic Corp Rm 3876 1095 Avenue Of The Americas New York NY 10036-6797

**BULLINGTON, DAVID BINGHAM,** lawyer; b. Roanoke, Va., June 3, 1958; s. Frederick Paul and Adrienne L. B.; m. Carolyn Fulcher, May 9, 1992; children: David Frederick, William Merritt. BA, San Francisco State U., 1978; JD with honors, George Washington U., 1987. Bar: Va. 1987, U.S. Ct. Appeals (4th cir.) 1991, U.S. Dist. Ct. (so. and we. dists.) Va. 1989, D.C. 1992. Atty. Jackson & Jessup, Arlington, Va., 1987-88, Katz & Stone, Vienna, Va., 1988-90, David & Hagner, Washington, 1991-94; ptnr. Cranwell, Moore & Bullington, Roanoke, Va., 1995—. Mem. ATLA, Va. State Bar Assn., Va. Trial Lawyers Assn. Avocation: bicycling. General civil litigation, Personal injury, Contracts commercial. Home: 6126 Saint Ives Ct Roanoke VA 24018-3889 Office: Cranwell Moore & Bullington PO Box 11804 Roanoke VA 24022-1804

**BULLOCK, BRUCE STANLEY,** lawyer; b. Kissimmee, Fla., Oct. 29, 1933; s. Arthur Stanley and Athalia (Griffin) B.; m. Lydia Austill, July 8, 1960; children: Bruce Stanley Jr., Margaret Bullock Martin. BA, U. Fla., 1955, LLB, 1962. Bar: Fla. 1962, U.S. Dist. Ct. (mid. and no. dists.), U.S. Supreme Ct., U.S. Ct. Appeals (11th crct.); diplomate Am. Bd. Trial Advocates; cert. crct. ct. mediator. Atty. assoc. Marks Gray Conroy & Gibbs, Jacksonville, Fla., 1962-66, atty., ptnr., 1966-73; atty., pres. Bullock & Alexander, Jacksonville, 1973-74, Bullock, Childs, Pendley & Reed, Jacksonville, 1974-95; ptnr. Bullock, Childs, Pendley, Reed, Herzfeld & Rubin, Jacksonville, 1995—; pres. N.E. Fla. Med. Malpractice Claims Coun. Dir., committeeman, gen. counsel Duval County (Fla.) Rep. Party. Lt. USAF, 1955-59. Mem. Jacksonville Bar Assn., Jacksonville Assn. Def. Counsel (pres.), Fla. Def. Lawyers Assn., Def. Trial Lawyers Assn., Def. Rsch. Inst., U. Fla. Alumni Club (pres.), Rotary Club (v.p. S. Jacksonville chpt.), Am. Bd. Trial Advocates (pres. local chpt. 1999). Republican. Episcopalian. Avocations: fishing, boating, nature. General civil litigation, Personal injury, Product liability. Home: 2510 Hickory Bluff Ln Jacksonville FL 32223-6503 Office: Bullock Childs Pendley Reed Herzfeld & Rubin 233 E Bay St Ste 711 Jacksonville FL 32202-3448

**BULLOCK, FRANK WILLIAM, JR.,** federal judge; b. Oxford, N.C., Nov. 3, 1938; s. Frank William and Wilma Jackson (Long) B.; m. Frances Dockery Haywood, May 5, 1984; 1 child, Frank William III. B.S. in Bus. Adminstrn., U. N.C., 1961, LL.B., 1963. Bar: N.C. 1963. Assoc. Maupin, Taylor & Ellis, Raleigh, N.C., 1964-68; asst. dir. Adminstrv. Office of Cts. of N.C., Raleigh, 1968-73; ptnr. Douglas, Ravenel, Hardy, Crihfield & Bullock, Greensboro, N.C., 1973-82; judge U.S. Dist. Ct. N.C., Greensboro, 1982—, chief judge, 1992—. Mem. bd. editors N.C. Law Rev., 1962-63; contbr. articles to profl. jours. Mem. N.C. Bar Assn., Greensboro Bar Assn., N.C. Soc. of Cin., Fla. Soc. Colonial Wars. Republican. Presbyterian. Clubs: Greensboro Country. Avocations: golf; tennis; running; history. Office: US Dist Ct PO Box 3223 Greensboro NC 27402-3223

**BULLOCK, JAMES N.,** lawyer; b. Sioux City, Iowa, July 29, 1947; s. Joe R. and Margaret M. B.; m. Velma E. Mason, Nov. 20, 1970 (div. Nov. 1981); 1 child, Jonathan L.; m. Betty D. Dukes, July 14, 1986. BA, Miss. Coll., 1970, JD, 1980. Bar: Miss.; U.S. Dist. Ct. (no. and so. dists.) Miss.; U.S. Ct. Appeals (5th cir.). Commd. USAF, advanced through ranks to lt. col.; instr. pilot USAF, Craig AFB/Selma, Ala., 1970-73; pilot, instr. pilot Iowa and Miss. ANG, Des Moines and Meridian, Miss., 1973-92. Lt. Col. USAF, 1970-91. Mem. Miss. Bar Assn., Air Force Assn., Nat. Guard Assn. of U.S. Avocations: sports, aviation. Insurance, Federal civil litigation, Personal injury. Home: 306 Mcdonald Dr Clinton MS 39056-5338 Office: Shell Buford Et Al Ste 920 Trustmark Jackson MS 39205-0157

**BULLOCK, J(AMES) ROBERT,** judge; b. Provo, Utah, Dec. 16, 1916; s. James A. and Norma (Poulton) B.; m. Ethel Hogge, Aug. 29, 1949; children: James Robert Jr., C. Scott, David A., Steven H. BS, Utah State U., 1938; JD with honors, George Washington U., 1942. Bar: U.S. Ct. Appeals (D.C. cir.) 1942, Utah 1946, Colo. 1946, U.S. Supreme Ct. 1969. Ptnr. Aldrich, Bullock & Nelson, Provo, 1950-73; judge 4th Dist. Ct. Utah, 1973-85; sr. judge Dist. Cts. Utah, 1985—, chmn. bd. sr. judges, 1988-92; mem. Utah Jud. Coun., 1973-83, chief judge, 1981-83. Mem. Utah State Ho. of Reps., 1963-67; mem. Utah Constn. Revision Commn., 1969-76, vice chmn., 1974-76. Comdr. USN, 1941-46, ETO, PTO. Mem. ABA, Utah Bar Assn. (pres. 1972-73, Judge of the Yr. 1983), Am. Inns of Ct. (charter), Riverside Country Club, Rotary (pres. 1958-59), Order of Coif, Phi Delta Phi. Avocation: golf. Home and Office: 1584 Willow Ln Provo UT 84604-2802

**BULLOCK, STEPHEN C.,** lawyer; b. Miami, Fla., May 9, 1949. BS, NYU, 1973; JD cum laude, Harvard U., 1989. Bar: Conn. 1989, Pa. 1989. Asst. counsel Pratt & Whitney; staff atty. United Tech. Corp.; asst. gen. counsel Carrier Corp., Syracuse, N.Y.; v.p., counsel Carrier Enterprises, LLC, Syracuse, N.Y. Mem. ABA (mem. business law and antitrust sects.). General corporate, Finance, Mergers and acquisitions. Office: Carrier Corp Carrier Pkwy PO Box 4800 Syracuse NY 13221-4800

**BULLOCK, STEVEN CARL,** lawyer; b. Anderson, Ind., Jan. 19, 1949; s. Carl Pearson and Dorothy Mae (Colle) B.; children: Bradford, Christine. BA, Purdue U., 1971; JD, Detroit Coll., 1985. Bar: Mich. 1985, U.S. Dist. Ct. (ea. dist.) 1985. Pvt. pracitce Inkster, Mich., 1985—. With USAF, 1971-75. Mem. Mich. Bar Assn. (criminal law sect.), Detroit Bar Assn., Detroit Funder's Soc., Recorder's Ct. Bar Assn., Suburban Bar Assn., Criminal Def. Lawyers of Mich. Avocations: golf, travel. Criminal, Family and matrimonial. Office: 2228 Inkster Rd Inkster MI 48141-1811

**BUMBLEBURG, JOSEPH THEODORE,** lawyer; b. Lafayette, Ind., Jan. 5, 1937; s. Theodore Joseph and Elizabeth Mary (Delaney) B.; m. Constance J. Peterson, Dec. 26, 1966; children: Theodore William, Amy Ann. BA, U. Notre Dame, 1958; JD, Ind. U., 1961. Bar: Ind. 1961, U.S. Ct. Mil. Appeals 1962, U.S. Dist. Ct. (no. dist.) Ind. 1964, U.S. Ct. Appeals (7th cir.) 1970, U.S. Supreme Ct. 1970, U.S. Ct. Appeals (fed. cir.) 1985. Capt., judge adv. U.S. Army, Ft. Gordon, Ga., 1961-64; ptnr. Ball, Eggleston, Bumbleburg, McBride, Walkey & Stapleton PC, Lafayette, 1964—. Commr. City of Lafayette Police Civil Svc. Commn., 1971-75, v.p., 1971-72, pres., 1972-75; sec. Tippecanoe County Sheriff's Merit Bd., 1968—; mem. Bd. Zoning Appeals, 1970-71; advisor to registrants SSS, 1967-69, 72-75; mem. pastoral coun. St. Mary's Cathedral, 1968-70, 74-78; mem. nat. bd. govs. ARC, 1975-81; bd. dirs. United Way, Lafayette, 1972-75; mem. cmty. adv. coun. Sch. Nursing, Purdue U., 1979-85; state trustee Ivy Tech. State Coll. (vice chmn. bd.). Recipient Presdl. Cert. Appreciation, SSS, 1972, cert. appreciation Chief Naval Edn., 1978, Gold award United Way, 1978, Pres. U.S. Citation for Community Achievement, 1979, Cert. Appreciation, ARC, 1972, 81, Harriman award for disting. vol. svc. to ARC, 1992. Fellow Ind. Bar Found. (master); mem. Ind. Bar Assn., Greater Lafayette C. of C. (bd. dirs. 1986-91, chmn. 1988-89), Am. Legion (nat. security coun. 1970-83, Legionnaire of Yr. 1982-83), K.C., Phi Theta Kappa. General civil litigation, Land use and zoning (including planning). Home: 726 Owen St Lafayette IN 47905-1878 Office: Ball Eggleston Bumbleburg McBride Walkey & Stapleton PC PO Box 1535 Lafayette IN 47902-1535

**BUMGARDNER, DONNA LEE ARRINGTON,** lawyer; b. Union, S.C., Sept. 29, 1950; d. Quillen Donald and Virgie Lee (Moore) Arrington; m. Thomas Bumgardner, Jr., Sept. 8, 1979; children: Susan Lee Bumgardner Paul-Hus, Christen Lee, Abigail Lee. BSBA, U. S.C., 1984, JD, 1987. Bar: Fla. 1988. Personnel dir. Newberry (S.C.) Mem. Hosp., 1976-80; asst. comptroller Cate-McLaurin Co., Columbia, S.C., 1980-82; ins. coord. Am. Exec. Life Ins., Columbia, 1982-84; sr. law clk. Robert Anderson, Columbia, 1986-87; law clk. Raymond Ray, Ft. Lauderdale, Fla., 1987-88; assoc. Rotella & Boone, Ft. Lauderdale, 1988; sr. lawyer Bumgardner & Assocs., Ft. Lauderdale, 1988—; grant atty. for low income child care. Vol. Broward County Guardian Ad Litem, Ft. Lauderdale, 1987—, Broward County Lawyer's Care, Ft. Lauderdale, 1987—; panel mem. So. Dist. of Fla. Trustee Assn., Ft. Lauderdale, 1989—; chairperson Pastor Parish Com. Mem. Women in the Law, Nat. Assn. Bankruptcy Trustees, Phi Alpha Delta. Republican. Methodist. Bankruptcy, Consumer commercial, Family and matrimonial. Office: Bumgardner & Assocs 7797 N University Dr Tamarac FL 33321-6110

**BUMGARNER, JAMES MCNABB,** judge; b. Peru, Ill., Sept. 13, 1919; s. Joshua Mills and Ethel (McNabb) B.; m. Helen D. Welker, Feb. 7, 1942 (dec. May 1981); children: Barbara Malany, Sally Guth; m. Elizabeth L. Miller, Feb. 12, 1983; step-children: Tad Miller, Brian Miller, Matthew Miller. BS in Psychology with honors, U. Ill., 1941, JD, 1946. Commd. 2nd lt. USAAF, 1942; advanced through grades to col. USAF, 1967, ret., 1974; pvt. practice Rantoul, Ill., 1947, Hannah, Mattoon, Ill.; cir. judge 10th Jud. Cir. of Ill., 1979—. Mem. Rotary Internat., VFW, Am. Legion, Vietnam Vets. Ill., Retired Officers Assn., Retired Judge Advocates Assn., Vietnam Vets. Bar Assn., Ill. Bar Assn., U. Ill. Alumni Assn., Putnam County Bar Assn., Putnam County Hist. Soc., Timber Growers Assn., Judge Advocates Assn., Air War Coll. Alumni Assn., Ill. Coll. Law Deans Club, Phi Alpha Delta. Home: 1010 Market St PO Box 225 Hennepin IL 61327-0225

**BUMPASS, RONALD EUGENE,** lawyer; b. Lubbock, Tex., Jan. 6, 1948; s. Donald E. and Edna (Pricer) B.; children: Bart, Buckley. BS in Pub. Adminstrn., U. Ark., 1970, JD, 1974. Bar: Ark. 1974, U.S. Dist. Ct. (we. dist.) Ark. 1975, U.S. Ct. Appeals (8th cir.) 1986, U.S. Supreme Ct. 1986. Pvt. practice, Fayetteville, Ark.; spl. chief justice Ark. Supreme Ct., Little Rock, 1989; arbitrator Fed. Mediation and Conciliation Svc., U.S. Dept. Labor, Am. Arbitration Assn., U.S. Postal Svc., Am. Postal Workers Union-AFL-CIO arbitration panel, Nat. Health Care Lawyers Arbitration Panel. City coun. mem. Fayetteville, Ark., 1980, chmn. police and fire commn., mem. city hall renovation com., vice mayor, 1984-88. Mem. Ark. Bar Assn. (health law com. 1990-94), Washington and Benton Counties Bar Assn., Nat. Coll. Criminal Def. Lawyers and Pub. Defenders, Nat. Health Care Lawyers, Alpha Kappa Lambda. Avocations: hunting, biking, reading, oil painting, horseback riding. Health, General corporate, General civil litigation. Office: PO Box 4105 Fayetteville AR 72702-4105

**BUNCH, JEFFREY R.,** lawyer; b. Spokane, Wash.. BS in Journalism, East Wash. U., 1988; JD, Gonzaga Sch. Law, 1992. Bar: Wash. 1992, U.S. Dist. Ct. (ea. dist.) Wash. 1992. Asst. atty. gen. Wash. State Atty. Gen., Spokane, 1992-96; atty. Phillabam & Ledlin, Spokane, 1996-97, Leveque & Kirkpatrick, Spokane, 1997-98, Annan & Assoc., Spokane, 1998—; Mem. editl. adv. bd. Wash. State Bar News, 1996-98. Bd. dirs. West Ctrl. C.C., Spokane, 1998—. Mem. ATLA, Wash. State Trial Lawyers Assn., Magnuson Club (v.p./pres.-elect 1997-98). Personal injury, Workers' compensation, Insurance. Office: Annan & Assoc 815 W 7th Ave Spokane WA 99204-2808

**BUNDY, ROBERT CHARLES,** prosecutor; b. Long Beach, Calif., June 26, 1946; s. James Kenneth and Kathleen Ilene (Klosterman) B.; m. Virginia Bonnie Lembo, Feb. 3, 1974; 2 children. BA cum laude, U. So. Calif., L.A., 1968; JD, U. Calif., Berkeley, 1971. Bar: Alaska 1972, Calif. 1972. Supervising atty. Alaska Legal Svcs. Corp., Nome, Alaska, 1972-75; dist. atty. Second Jud. Dist., Nome, 1975-78; asst. dist. atty. Alaska Dept. Law, 1978-80, asst. atty. gen. antitrust sect., 1980-82; chief asst. dist. atty. Alaskan Dept. Law, Anchorage, 1982-84; ptnr. Bogle & Gates, Anchorage, Alaska, 1984-94; now U.S. atty. for Alaska dist. U.S. Dept. Justice, Anchorage, 1994—. Mem. Trout Unlimited, Alaska Flyfishers. Office: Office US Atty for Alaska Rm C-253 222 W 7th Ave Unit 9 Anchorage AK 99513-7504

**BUNN, DOROTHY IRONS,** court reporter; b. Trinidad, Colo., Apr. 30, 1948; d. Russell and Pauline Anna (Langowski) Irons; children: Kristy Lynn, Wade Allen, Russell Ahearn. Student No. Va. C.C., 1970-71, U. Va., Fairfax, 1971-72. Registered profl. reporter; cert. shorthand reporter. Pres., CEO Ahearn Ltd., Springfield, Va., 1970-81, Bunn & Assocs., Glenrock, Wyo., 1981—; cons. Bixby Hereford Co., Glenrock, 1981-89, co-mgr., 1989-97. Del., White House Conf. on Small Bus., Washington, 1986, 95, state chair, 1995; mem. Wyo. adv. coun. Small Bus. Adminstrn., 1994-96. Mem. NAFE, Am. Indian Soc., Nat. Ct. Reporters Assn., Nat. Fedn. Ind. Bus., Wyo. Shorthand Reporters Assn., Nat. Fedn. Ind. Businesses (guardian 1991-96), Nat. Fedn. Bus. and Profl. Women (1st v.p. Casper 1994-95, pres. 1995-96, pub. rels. chair, Choices chair), Assn. for Advancement of CAT Tech. Avocation: photography. Office: Bunn & Assocs 2036 Adobe Ave Douglas WY 82633-3016

**BUNN, G. PETER, III,** lawyer; b. Houston, Apr. 18, 1949; s. George Peter Jr. and Alberta Grace (Jones) B.; m. Catherine Lynn McConnell, July 3, 1971; children: Michael Peter, Julie Catherine. BA, U. Kans., 1971, JD, 1975. Bar: Kans. 1975. Ptnr. Soden, Eisebrandt, Isenhour, Mission, Kans., 1975-80; shareholder Ferree, Bunn & O'Grady, Overland Park, Kans., 1980—. Bd. dirs. Blue Valley Ednl. Found., Overland Park, Kans., 1991—, also past pres.; elder Grace Covenant Presbyn. Ch. Sgt. U.S. Army, 1971-76. Mem. Kans. Bar Assn., Johnson County Bar Assn., Am. Family Conciliation Cts. Avocations: tennis, woodworking, travel. General practice, General corporate, Family and matrimonial. Office: Ferree Bunn & O'Grady 9300 Metcalf Ave Ste 300 Overland Park KS 66212-6319

**BUNN, RANDALL J.,** lawyer; b. Spokane, WA, Feb. 13, 1955; s. Donald K. and Joyce M. (Castro); m. LeeAnne S. Sevy, Aug. 7, 1981; children: Adam, Meghan, Chad. AB, U. Calif., Davis, 1977; JD, Brigham Young U., 1982; LLM, George Washington U. Law Sch., 1996. Bar: Calif. 1983, Utah 1991, U.S. Dist. Ct. (Ea. Dist.) Calif. 1983, U.S. Ct. Appeals Armed Forces 1985, U.S. Dist. Ct., Utah 1991, U.S. Ct. Fed. Claims 1996, U.S. Supreme Ct. 1998. Assoc. atty. Kimble, MacMichael, Jackson & Upton, Fresno, Calif., 1983-84, Kahn, Saores & Conway, Hanford, Calif., 1984-85; dep. staff judge advocate Arnold Engring. Devel. Ctr., Arnold Air Force Base, Tullahoma, Tenn., 1985-87; asst. staff judge advocate Yokota Air Base, Tokyo, Japan, 1987-90, Hill Air Force Base, Ogden, Utah, 1990-92; dep. staff judge advocate Sembach Air Base, Sembach, Germany, 1992-95; fed. trial atty., chief bankrupty br., commercial litigation divsn. Air Force Legal Svcs. Agy., Arlington, Va., 1996-99; procurement counsel Air Force Material Command Law Office Wright-Patterson A.F.B., Dayton, OH, 1999—. Contbr. articles to profl. jours. Docent Ch. Hist. and Art Mus., Salt Lake City, 1990-92, Smithsonian Mus. Am. Hist., Washington, 1998-99; active nat. capital area coun. Boy Scouts Am., 1995-99. Lt. col. U.S. Air Force, 1985-96. Recipient Hist. Citation Dept. Hist. U. Calif. Davis, 1977. Mem. ABA (sect. pub. contract law), Utah Bar Assoc., State Bar Calif., Phi Beta Kappa. Avocations: geneology, history, skiing, scouting. Office: Air Force Material Command Law Office Wright-Patterson AFB Dayton OH 45433

**BUNN, ROBERT BURGESS,** lawyer; b. Boise, Idaho, May 31, 1933; s. Marion Roy and Lois Lucile (Burgess) B.; m. Frances Patten Bull, Sept. 12, 1959; children—Carolyn B., F. Robin, Andrew R., Kathryn B. A.B. cum laude, Harvard U., 1955, LL.B., 1961. Bar: Hawaii 1961, U.S. Dist. Ct. Hawaii 1961, U.S. Ct. Appeals (9th cir.) 1963, U.S. Supreme Ct. 1973. Ptnr., Cades, Schutte, Fleming & Wright, Honolulu, 1961—. Counsel, Honolulu Symphony Soc., 1974-80; counsel Hawaii Opera Theatre, Honolulu, 1980-82, 86—, pres., 1982-86, bd. dirs., 1980— . Served to Lt. USN, 1958-61. Mem. ABA, Am. Coll. Real Estate Lawyers, Hawaii Bar Assn., Pacific Club. Avocations: tennis, wine, investments. Real property, Condemnation, Estate planning. Home: 2493 Makiki Heights Dr Honolulu HI 96822-2547 Office: Cades Schutte Fleming & Wright PO Box 939 Honolulu HI 96808-0939

**BUNNELL, GEORGE ELI,** lawyer; b. Miami, Fla., Apr. 28, 1938; s. George A. and Lillian E. (Hurley) B.; m. Dianne Railton, Dec. 1, 1990; children: Kelley, Courtney. BA, U. Fla., 1960, LLB, 1962. Bar: Fla. 1963, U.S. Dist. Ct. (so. dist.) Fla. 1963, U.S. Ct. Appeals (11th cir.) 1982, U.S. Supreme Ct. 1970. Assoc., Nicholson, Howard & Brawner, Miami, 1963-64; assoc. Dean, Adams, George & Wood, Miami, 1964-67, ptnr., 1968-71; officer, dir. Huebner, Shaw & Bunnell, P.A., Fort Lauderdale, Fla., 1972-77; pres., dir. Bunnell, Woulfe, Kirschbaum, Keller Cohen & McIntyre, P.A., Fort Lauderdale, 1977—. Mem. advance staff White House, 1974-76; mem. City of Fort Lauderdale Marine Adv. Bd., 1974-76, City of Fort Lauderdale Civil Svc. Bd., 1977-79; bd. dirs., sec. Ft. Lauderdale Mus. Art, 1990—. Fellow Am. Coll. Trial Lawyers; mem. Internat. Assn. of Def. Counsel, Am. Bd. Trial Advs. (pres. Ft. Lauderdale chpt. 1992), Def. Rsch. Inst., Fla. Def. Lawyers Assn., Broward County Bar Assn., Fla. Acad. of Hosp. Attys., Am. Health Lawyers Assn., Am. Soc. of Law and Medicine, Fla. Med. Malpractice Claims Coun., Inc. Republican. Clubs: Lago Mar Beach, Lauderdale Yacht (Fort Lauderdale). Personal injury, Insurance, State civil litigation. Office: Bunnell Woulfe Kirschbaum Keller Cohen & McIntyre PA 888 E Las Olas Blvd Fl 4 Fort Lauderdale FL 33301-2272

**BUNNELL, JOHN BLAKE,** lawyer; b. Nashville, Apr. 20, 1958; s. James Crusman Jr. and Virginia Claire (Cross) B.; m. Candace Diane Tucker, Oct. 1, 1982. BS, Austin Peay State U., 1979; MS in Planning, U. Tenn., 1988, JD, 1990. Bar: Tenn. 1991, U.S. Dist. Ct. (mid. dist.) Tenn. 1992, U.S. Dist. Ct. (ea. dist.) Tenn. 1995. Editl. editor, editorialist The All State, Austin Peay State U. Student Newspaper, Clarksville, Tenn., 1975-78; planning intern/adminstrn. Hopkinsville (Ky.)-Christian County Planning Commn., 1978-79; energy tech. analyst Tenn. Energy Authority, Nashville, 1979-80; rsch. asst. U. Tenn. Planning Rsch. Ctr., Knoxville, 1980-83; legal noncommissioned officer 844th Engr. Battalion, Knoxville, 1986-94; asst. dist. atty. gen. Office of Dist. Atty. 21st Dist., Franklin, Tenn., 1991-92; pvt. practice Nashville, 1992; asst. pub. defender Office of Pub. Defender 4th Jud., Newport, Tenn., 1992-96; legal assistance officer U.S. Army Operation Joint Endeavor, Ft. Benning, Ga., 1996-97; sec., dir. Cumberland Cmtys. Commn., Knoxville, 1991-94, 96—; trial def. counsel Team II, 213th Legal Spt. Orgn., Knoxville, 1996—; city atty., Parrottsville, Tenn., 1999—; civil mediator (under Rule 31), Tenn. Supreme Ct., 1999—. Author: The Impact of Industrial Revenue Bonds on Job Creation in Tennessee: A Longitudinal Approach. Exec. com. Cocke County ptnrship., 1998—; pres. Newport/Cocke County C. of C., 1998; mem. Newport Cocke County Econ. Devel. Bd., 1998—. Sgt. U.S. Army, 1990-91. Mem. Tenn. Assn. Criminal Def. Lawyers, Sevier County Bar Assn., Cocke County Bar Assn., Newport (Tenn.) Kiwanis Club (chmn. retention subcom. 1993-94), Nat. Trust for Hist. Preservation, Order Ky. Cols., Phi Kappa Phi, Pi Kappa Alpha. Methodist. Avocations: archaeology, camping, running, swimming. Office: PO Box 286 124 McSween Ave Newport TN 37822

**BUNNER, PATRICIA ANDREA,** lawyer; b. Fairmont, W.Va., Sept. 16, 1953; d. Scott Randolph and Virginia Lenore (Keck) B. AB in History & English magna cum laude, W.Va. U., 1975, JD, 1978; postgrad., Trinity Theol. Sem., 1995—, W.Va. U., 1996—. Bar: W.Va. 1978, N.Y. 1981, D.C. 1981, U.S. Dist. Ct. (so. dist.) W.Va. 1978, U.S. Dist. Ct. (no. dist.) W.Va. 1985, U.S. Ct. Claims 1990, U.S. Supreme Ct. 1989; cert. Christian counselor, 1986—. Mem. staff Dem. Nat. Com., Washington, 1978-79; assoc. Gailor, Elias & Matz, Washington, 1979-81, N.Y. State Bankers Assn., N.Y.C., 1981-83; ptnr. Bunner & Bunner, Fairview, W.Va., 1984-94; exec. dir. N.Y. State Consumer Mortgage Rev. Bd.; chmn. dist. VIII Consumer Mortgage Rev. Com., N.Y.C., 1982-83; cons. atty. Energy Cons. Assocs., Spring Harbor, N.Y., 1981; of counsel Monongahela (W.Va.) Soil Conservation Dist., 1985; vis. scholar Pitts. Theol. Sem., 1997—. Author: How Charley Metheney Broke the Four Minute Mile, 1971, Across the Bennefield Prong, 1973, German Anti-Semitism, Bismarck Through Weimar, 1973, N.Y. State Bankers Assn. Legis. Directory, 1983, Through a Glass Darkly, A Compendium of Film Noir, 1996, The Influence of the Seventeenth Century Scientific Revolution on Anglo-American Law, 1996, Rene Descartes, Phenomenologist, 1996, Psychology of Thomas Aquinas, 1997, John Locke's Influence on Modern Science, 1998, Conceptions of Property in Early America, 1787-1801, 1999; presenter in field. Pres. Monongalia County Dem. Women, 1987-89; sec. Monongalia County Devel. Authority, 1984-91; pres. United Taxpayers Assn., Inc., W.Va., 1985-88; bd. dirs. W.Va. U. Morgantown, 1974-75; active W.Va. State Dem. Exec. Com., 1990, 94. Rilla Moran Woods fellow Nat. Fedn. Dem. Women, Washington, 1978. Mem. ATLA, ABA (vice chmn. legal econs. and new lawyers coms. 1986-87, litigation sect., 1st amendment rights and media law com., gen. practice com., corps. and banking com.), W.Va. Bar Assn. (com. econs. of law practice 1987—, com. corps. and banking 1987—), W.Va. Trial Lawyers Assn., N.Y. State Bar Assn., Monongalia County Bar Assn., Marion County Bar Assn., W.Va. Criminal Def. Lawyers Assn., Women's Info. Ctr. (founding), LWV, NAFE, W.Va. Alliance for Women's Studies (founding), Bus. and Profl. Women (bd. dirs.), Climates, Inc., Monongalia County Hist. Soc., W.Va. Brain Injury Assn., Clay-Battelle Alumni Assn., W.Va. Coll. Law Alumni Assn., Nat. Rifle Assn. (life), Nature Conservancy, Nat. Arbor Day Found., World Wildlife Fund, Am. Farmland Trust, AAUW, Sierra Club, Audobon Soc., Young Dems. Club W.Va. (sec. 1976), Phi Alpha Theta (chpt. pres. 1974-75), Phi Beta Kappa, Zeta Phi Eta, Alpha Rho (chpt. pres. 1974), Phi Kappa Phi. Baptist. Club: Woman's (bd. dirs. Morgantown chpt. 1986—). Avocations: clothing design, cooking, creative writing, piano, swimming. General practice, Personal injury, Environmental. Address: PO Box 86 Fairview WV 26570-0086

**BUNNER, WILLIAM KECK,** lawyer; b. Fairmont, W.Va., Sept. 2, 1949; s. Scott Randolph and Virginia Lenore (Keck) B. BS in Secondary Edn. magna cum laude, W.Va. U., 1970, MA in History, 1973, ABD in History, 1975, JD, 1978, postgrad., 1998—. Bar: W.Va. 1978, U.S. Dist. Ct. (so. dist.) W.Va. 1978, U.S. Dist. Ct. (no. dist.) W.Va. 1985. Tchr. Monongalia County Bd. Edn., Morgantown, W.Va., 1970-78; contract lawyer dept. fin. and adminstrn. State of W.Va., Charleston, 1978-79; pvt. practice law Fairview, W.Va., 1979-84; pres. Farm Home Svc., Inc., 1983—; ptnr. Bunner & Bunner, Morgantown and Fairview, 1984-92; pres. Climates, 1988—; presenter History of Barn Dance in U.S.A., Rush D. Holt History Conf., W. Va. U., 1999. Pres. Monongalia County Young Dems., 1974; parliamentarian Monongalia County Dem. Exec. Com., 1982-94; counsel, parliamentarian Young Dem. Clubs W.Va., 1974-77; bd. dirs., supr. Monongahela Soil Conservation Dist., 1982—; advisor West Run Watershed Improvement Dist., 1983—; mem. W.Va. Commn. on Rural Abandoned Mines, Rural Alliance, Monongalia County Solid Waste Auth., 1989—, also chmn., 1990-92. Mem. ABA, Monongalia County Bar Assn., Assn. Rural Conservation, Soil Conservation Soc. Am., United Taxpayers' Assn. (counsel), Monongalia County Hist. Soc., Marion County Hist. Soc., Marion County Bar Assn., W.Va. Trial Lawyers Assn, Phi Alpha Delta, Phi Alpha Theta. Democrat. Avocations: music, politics, farming, videos, regional history and genealogy. General practice, Environmental, Real property. Home and Office: 109 Lamesa Vlg Morgantown WV 26508-6243

**BUNTON, LUCIUS DESHA, III,** federal judge; b. Del Rio, Tex., Dec. 1, 1924; s. Lucius Desha and Avis Maurine (Fisher) B.; m. Mary Jane Carsey, June 18, 1947; children: Cathryne Avis Bunton Warner, Lucius Desha. Student, U. Chgo., 1943-44; BA, U. Tex., Austin, 1947, JD, 1950. Bar: Tex. 1949. Individual practice law Uvalde, Tex., 1950; assoc. firm H.O. Metcalfe, Marfa, Tex., 1951-54; dist. atty. 83d Jud. Dist. Tex., 1954-59; mem. firm Shafer, Gilliland, Davis, Bunton & McCollum, Odessa, Tex., 1959-79; judge U.S. Dist. Ct. (we. dist.) Tex., Midland, 1979-87, chief judge, 1987-92, sr. judge, 1989—; mem. jud. resources com., 1989-94. Trustee Ector County (Tex.) Ind. Sch. Dist., 1967-76 . With inf. U.S. Army, 1943-46. Mem. Tex. Bar Found. (charter), Am. Bar Assn., Am. Bar Found., Am. Coll. Probate Counsel, Am. Acad. Matrimonial Lawyers, State Bar Tex. (chmn. 1971-72, v.p. 1973-74, pres.-elect 1979), Masons. Baptist.

**BUNT SMITH, HELEN MARGUERITE,** lawyer; b. L.A., Oct. 8, 1942; d. Alan Verbanks and Nettie Virginia (Crandall) Bunt; m. Charles Robert Smith, Jan. 12, 1974; children: John, Sharon. BS, U. Calif., L.A., 1964; JD, Southwestern U., 1972. Bar: Calif. 1972; cert. secondary tchr., Calif. Tchr. L.A. City Schs., 1965-72; pvt. practice Pasadena, Calif., 1973—; Law Day chmn. Pasadena Bar Assn., 1980, sec., 1981. Editor (newsletter) Lawyer's Club, 1984-85. Sunday sch. tchr. Lake Ave. Congrl. Ch., Pasadena; sec. Pasadena Sister Cities Com., 1994-96; Law Day chmn. Pasadena Bar Assn., 1980, sec., 1981. Mem. San Gabriel Bar Assn. (bd. dirs. 1999—). Avocations: jogging, singing, stained glass. Office: 465 E Union St Ste 102 Pasadena CA 91101-1783

**BUNYARD, MELINDA KAY,** lawyer; b. Kansas City, Jan. 31, 1952; d. James Riley and Lily (Shangler) Hunsucker; m. James Patrick Bunyard, Apr. 10, 1971; children: Cali E. Odom, James R. BA, U. Mo., 1975, JD, 1980. Bar: Mo. 1980. Law clk. Jackson County Cir. Ct., Kansas City, 1980-83; asst. prosecuting atty. Jackson County, Kansas City, 1983-86, Cass County, Mo., 1986-87; atty. pvt. practice, Mo., 1987—; dir. Interactive Law, Independence, Mo., 1996—. Dir. Truman Heartland Cmty. Found., Independence, 1996—; v.p. Mo. Mcpl. League-Westgate chpt., 1996-98, Raytown Dem. Assn., 1996—; mem. Bd. Alderman, Raytown, 1994-98, mayor pro tem, 1996-97; chmn. Raytown Coordinated Coun. on Domestic Violence; pres. Mo. Mcpl. League, 1998—; dir. Raytown Emergency Asst. Program, 1998—; liaison Ea. Jackson County Betterment Assn. Named Outstanding Civic Leader in Raytown, 1998; Phi Kappa Phi scholar, 1975. Mem. AAUW, Mo. Bar Assn., Ea. Jackson County Bar Assn., Clay County Bar Assn., Raytown C. of C. Baptist. Avocations: gardening, weight lifting, hollistic health. Office: PO Box 18563 Raytown MO 64133-8563

**BURACK, MICHAEL LEONARD,** lawyer; b. Willimantic, Conn., Oct. 10, 1942; s. Meyer and Rose Ann (Kravitz) B.; m. Maria Gallego, Oct. 20, 1978; children: Victoria Luisa, Cristina Maria. BA summa cum laude, Wesleyan U., Middletown, Conn., 1964; postgrad. in physics, Calif. Inst. Tech., 1965; MS in Applied Physics, Stanford U., 1967, JD, 1970. Bar: Calif. 1971, D.C. 1972. Law clk. to judge U.S. Ct. Appeals for 9th Cir., San Francisco, 1970-71; assoc. Wilmer, Cutler & Pickering, Washington, 1971-77, ptnr., 1978—; mem. staff D.C. Jud. conf. Com. on Adminstrn. of Justice under Emergency Condition, 1972-73; mem. adv. com. govt. applications of ADR of Ctr. for Pub. Resources, 1988; mem. jud. evaluation com. D.C. Bar, 1991-94. Assoc. editor Jour. Pub. Contract Law, 1988-94. Mem. ABA, Order of the Coif, Phi Beta Kappa, Sigma Xi. Office: Wilmer Cutler & Pickering 2445 M St NW Ste 500 Washington DC 20037-1487

**BURAK, H(OWARD) PAUL,** lawyer; b. N.Y.C., July 9, 1934; s. Harry and Bette (Hauer) B.; m. Edna K. Goodman, Oct. 18, 1970; children: Hally Ann., Jason Lewis. BS, Cornell U., 1954; LLB, Columbia U., 1957. Bar: N.Y. 1958, D.C. 1967, U.S. Dist. Ct. (so. and ea. dists.) N.Y. 1967, U.S. Ct. Appeals (2d cir.) 1960, U.S. Supreme Ct. 1964. Assoc. Cadwalader, Wickersham & Taft, N.Y.C., 1957-63; dep. asst., asst. gen. counsel Agy. for Internat. Devel. U.S. State Dept., Washington, 1963-67; assoc. Rosenman Colin Kay Petschek & Freund, N.Y.C., 1967-69; ptnr. Rosenman & Colin, N.Y.C., 1969—; bd. dirs. Sony Corp. Am., N.Y.C., Sony Music Entertainment, Inc., N.Y.C., Sony Pictures Entertainment, Inc., Culver City, Calif., Sony USA Found., N.Y.C. Rev. editor Columbia Law Rev., 1956-57; author pamphlets. Mem. ABA, Assn. of Bar of City of N.Y., Fed. Bar Coun., N.Y. Bar Assn., Internat. Bar Assn., Univ. Club. General corporate, Private international, Mergers and acquisitions. Office: Rosenman & Colin 575 Madison Ave New York NY 10022-2585

**BURBANK, STEPHEN BRADNER,** law educator; b. N.Y.C., Jan. 8, 1947; s. John Howard and Jean (Gedney) B.; m. Ellen Randolph Coolidge, June 13, 1970; 1 child, Peter Jefferson. AB, Harvard U., 1968, JD, 1973. Bar: Mass. 1973, Pa. 1976, U.S. Supreme Ct. 1977. Law clk. Supreme Jud. Ct. of Mass., Boston, 1973-74, Chief Justice Warren Burger, Washington, 1974-75; gen. counsel U. Pa., Phila., 1975-80, asst. prof. law, 1979-83, assoc. prof. law, 1983-86, prof. law, 1986—, Fuller prof. law, 1991-95; Berger prof. law,

1995—; reporter 3d Cir. Jud. Discipline Rules, Phila., 1981-82, 84, 3d Cir. Task Force on Rule 11, Phila., 1987-89; mem. Nat. Commn. on Jud. Discipline and Removal, 1991-93; mediator, arbitrator Ctr. for Pub. Resources, New York, 1986—; cons. Dechert, Price & Rhoads, Phila., 1986—; mem. CPR Arbitration Commn., 1997—. Mem. Com. to Visit Harvard and Radcliffe Coll., Cambridge, Mass., 1979-85; mem. adv. bd. Inst. Contemporary Art, Phila., 1982-99; charter trustee Phillips Acad., Andover, Mass., 1980-97. Mem. Am. Law Inst. (adviser transnational rules of civil procedure 1997-99), Am. Arbitration Assn. (panel of arbitrators 1985—), Century Assn., Am. Jud. Soc. (exec. com., v.p. 1997-99), Phi Beta Kappa. Avocations: swimming, travel, tennis. Office: U Pa Sch Law 3400 Chestnut St Philadelphia PA 19104-6204

**BURCAT, JOEL ROBIN,** lawyer; b. Phila., Oct. 28, 1954; s. David Sidney and Jessie (Goldberg) B.; m. Gail Rene Hartman, May 30, 1982; children: Dina Michelle, Shira Elizabeth. Student, Temple U., 1972-73; BS, Pa. State U., 1976; JD, Vt. Law Sch., 1980. Bar: Pa. 1980, U.S. Dist. Ct. (mid. dist.) Pa. 1980, U.S. Dist. Ct. (we. dist.) Pa. 1988, U.S. Dist. Ct. (ea. dist.) Pa. 1993, U.S. Ct. Appeals (3d cir.) 1981, U.S. Supreme Ct. 1984. Asst. atty. gen. Pa. Dept. Environ. Resources, Harrisburg, 1980-83; assoc. Rhoads & Sinon, Harrisburg, 1983-88; assoc. Kirkpatrick & Lockhart, Harrisburg, 1988-91, ptnr., 1992—; spl. counsel Pa. Senate Com. on Environ. Resources and Energy, Harrisburg, 1986-87; gen. counsel Nat. Wilderness Inst., Washington, 1991-93; mem. rules com. Pa. Environ. Hearing Bd., 1984-88. Author, editor: Pennsylvania Environmental Law and Practice, 1994, 2nd edit., 1999, also supplements; contbr. articles to environ. topics to profl. jours., chpts. to books. Trustee United Jewish Cmty., Harrisburg, 1991-94, v.p., 1996-97; v.p. Yeshiva Acad. Harrisburg, 1986-96, pres., 1996-97; dir. Friends of State of Pa. Mus., 1999—. Recipient Best Publ. award, Assn. Continuing Legal Edn. Mem. ABA (mem. standing com. environ. law 1979-80, law student liaison), Pa. Bar Assn. (sec. environ. mineral and natural resource law sect. 1990-91, vice chmn. 1991-92, chmn. 1992-93, ethics com. 1984-97, Spl. Achievement award 1993, cert. of recognition 1994). Republican. Jewish. Avocations: guitar playing, classical music, jogging, hiking, gardening. Environmental, General civil litigation, Administrative and regulatory. Office: Kirkpatrick & Lockhart 240 N 3d St Harrisburg PA 17101-1503

**BURCH, DONALD VICTOR,** lawyer; b. Niagara Falls, N.Y., Feb. 18, 1944; s. Victor James and Marva (Bogardus) B.; m. Sharron Burch, Aug. 27, 1966; children: Elizabeth Katherine, Craig Donald. BA, Vanderbilt U., 1966; JD, U. Ala., 1969. Bar: Miss. 1970. Assoc. Daniel, Coker, Horton & Bell, Jackson, Miss., 1970-76, ptnr., 1977—; dir. Gulf Coast Law Inst., Gulfport, Miss., 1977-81. Mem. ABA (mem. appellate practice subcom. 1981—), Miss. Bar Assn. (mem. workers compensation com. 1985-87), Hinds County Bar Assn., Def. Research Inst., So. Assn. Workers Compensation Adminstrs. Republican. Episcopalian. Club: Reservoir Area Exchange (Jackson) (pres. 1987-88). Lodge: Optimists. Workers' compensation, Personal injury, General civil litigation. Home: 784 Benwick Dr Brandon MS 39047-8112 Office: Daniel Coker Horton & Bell 111 E Capitol St Ste 600 Jackson MS 39201-2149

**BURCH, FRANCIS BOUCHER, JR.,** lawyer; b. Balt., Feb. 27, 1948; s. Francis Boucher and Mary Patricia (Howe) B.; m. Mary Ann Podesta, June 24, 1972; children: Sara E., Francis B. III, Michael F. Student, U. Fribourg, Switzerland, 1968-69; BA, Georgetown U., 1970; JD with honors, U. Md., 1974. Bar: Md. 1974, U.S. Ct. Appeals (4th cir.) 1975, U.S. Supreme Ct. 1994. Assoc. litigation dept. Piper & Marbury LLP, Balt., 1974-81, ptnr. litigation dept., 1981—, mem. policy and mgmt. com., 1986-93, chmn. litigation dept., 1991-94, chmn., 1994—. Contbr. articles to profl. jours. Bd. dirs. Greater Balt. Com., 1996—, vice-chmn., 1998—, mem. Leadership Program, 1990—, bd. dirs., 1993-98, vice-chmn., 1994-96, chmn., 1996-98, chmn. selection com., 1994-95, mem. pub. policy coun.; trustee Calvert Sch., 1989—, exec. com., 1991—, curriculum and pers. com., 1991—, chmn., 1991-95, sec., 1991-95; trustee Western Md. Coll., 1996—, Johns Hopkins Health Sys. Corp., 1994-96, , Johns Hopkins Hosp., 1994-96, Johns Hopkins Medicine, 1996—, Balt. Mus. Art., 1990-96, 98—, mem. exec. com., 1991-96, chmn. ann. giving com., 1991-93, treas., 1992-94, v.p., 1994-96, co-chmn. devel., 1994-96; bd. visitors U. Md. Sch. Law, Balt., 1993—, U. Md., 1995—; fundraising com. Coll. Bound Found., Balt., 1991; campaign cabinet, chmn. emerging markets United Way Ctrl. Md., 1994; chmn. Leadership Giving, 1999. With U.S. Army N.G., 1970-76. Fellow Am. Bar Found., Am. Coll. Trial Lawyers, Md. Bar Found.; mem. ABA, Am. Law Inst., Md. Bar Assn. (Disting. Svc. award litigation sect. 1981), Balt. City Bar Assn. (chmn. jud. appts. com. 1990-91, exec. coun. 1990-91), 4th Cir. Jud. Conf., Rule Day Club, Lawyers' Round Table Balt., Center Club, Md. Club, Balt. Country Club. Democrat. Roman Catholic. Avocations: skiing, surfing. General civil litigation, Securities, Product liability. Office: Piper & Marbury LLP 36 S Charles St Baltimore MD 21201-3020

**BURCH, JOHN THOMAS, JR.,** lawyer; b. Balt., Feb. 22, 1942; s. John T. and Katheryn Estella (Peregoy) B.; m. Linda Anne Shearer, Nov. 1, 1969; children: John Thomas, Richard James. BA, U. Richmond, 1964, JD, 1966; LLM, George Washington U., 1971. Bar: Va. 1966, U.S. Supreme Ct. 1969, D.C. 1974, Mich. 1983, Md. 1993. Pvt. practice Richmond, 1966, Washington, 1974-77; pres. Burch, Kerns and Klimek, 1977-82, Burch & Bennett, P.C., 1983-85; ptnr. Alagia, Day, Marshall, Mintmire & Chauvin, Washington, 1985-90, Maloney & Burch, Washington, 1990-96; pres. Burch & Cronauer, P.C., Washington, 1995—, Internat. Procurement Cons. Ltd., Washington, 1977-85, Burch & Assocs., Washington, 1982-95; Rep. committeeman, City of Alexandria, Va., 1975-92; aide-de-camp to gov., State of Va., 1976—; alt. del. Rep. Nat. Conv., 1988, 94. Decorated Bronze Star, Meritorious Svc. medal, others; named Ky. Col. Fellow ABA (sec. pub. contract law sect. 1976-77); mem. Fed. Bar Assn. (nat. coun., dep. sec. 1982-83), Am. Arbitration Assn., Am. Legion, VFW (dep. comdr. 1986-87), Spl. Forces Assn., Nat. Vietnam and Gulf War Vets. Coalition (nat. chmn. 1983—), Va. War Meml. Found. (trustee), Va. Soc. SAR (pres. 1975-76, Patriots medal 1978, Good Citizenship award 1970), Sons of Confederate Vets., Soc. of the War of 1812; Cheveliar, Order of St. Constantine Magna, Scabbard and Blade, Phi Alpha Delta, Phi Sigma Alpha. Republican. Episcopalian. Government contracts and claims, State civil litigation, General practice. Home: 1015 N Pelham St Alexandria VA 22304-1905 Office: Burch & Cronauer PC 1200 19th St NW Ste 401 Washington DC 20036-2408

**BURCH, MARY SEELYE QUINN,** law librarian, consultant; b. Worcester, Mass., Oct. 16, 1925; d. James Henry and Mary Seelye (O'Donnell) Quinn; m. Walter Douglas Burch, Aug. 18, 1972; children: Cathi, Andrew, David, John, Joan. BS, Suny, 1976; MLS, Pratt Inst., 1979. Law libr. N.Y. Supreme Ct., Troy, 1969-82; chief law libr. Office Ct. Adminstrn., Albany, N.Y., 1982-86; libr. N.Y. State Libr., 1986-89, ret., 1989; owner Mary S. Burch Law Libr. Svc., 1983—; instr. legal rsch. SUNY, 1981; selected to meet with deans of law schs. in China for improvement of legal reference materials in China. Mem. N.Y. State Bar Assn. (lectr. 1980), Ulster County Bar Assn. (cons. 1980), Am. Assn. Law Librs., Assn. Law Librs. Upstate N.Y. (pres. 1971, v.p. 1981). Roman Catholic. Avocations: pilot, swimming, sewing. Home: 946 Hoosick Rd Troy NY 12180-6635

**BURCH, ROBERT DALE,** lawyer; b. Washington, Jan. 30, 1928; s. Dallas Stockwell and Hepsy (Berry) B.; m. Joann D. Hansen, Dec. 9, 1966; children—Berkeley, Robert Brett, Barrett Bradley. Student, Va. Mil. Inst., 1945-46; B.S., U. Calif. at Berkeley, 1950, J.D., 1953. Bar: Calif. bar 1954. Since practiced in Los Angeles and Beverly Hills; ptnr. Gibson, Dunn & Crutcher, 1961—; lectr. U. So. Calif. Inst. Fed. Taxation, 1960, 62, 65, 75; guest lectr. U. Calif.-L.A. Law Sch., 1959; lectr. C.E.B. seminars U. Calif.; founder Robert D. Burch Ctr. for Tax Policy and Pub. Fin., U. Calif., Berkeley. Author: Federal Tax Procedures for General Practitioners; Contbr. profl. jours., textbooks. Bd. dirs. charitable founds. With AUS, 1945-47. Mem. Beverly Hills Bar Assn. (bd. govs., chmn. probate and trust com.), Law Trust, Tax and Ins. Council (past czar), Los Angeles World Affairs Council. Home: 1301 Delresto Dr Beverly Hills CA 90210-2100 Office: Gibson Dunn & Crutcher 2029 Century Park E Ste 4000 Los Angeles CA 90067-3032 also: 333 S Grand Ave Los Angeles CA 90071-1504

**BURCHAM, RANDALL PARKS,** lawyer, farmer; b. Union City, Tenn., July 20, 1917; s. John Simps and Myrtle Caldwell (Howard) B.; m. Hellon Owens, Sept. 30, 1945; children—Randall Parks Jr., Susan. Student Murray State Coll. (Ky.), 1934-38, U. Miss., 1938-39; LL.B., Cumberland U., Lebanon, Tenn., 1940; J.D., Samford U., Birmingham, 1969. Bar: Tenn. 1941. Sole practice, Union City, 1941; atty. U.S. Govt., Nashville, 1945-49; owner Interstate Oil Co., Fulton, Ky., 1949-53; ptnr. Burcham & Fox, Union City, 1953—. Del., Tenn. Constitutional Conv., Nashville, 1971. Served to comdr. U.S. Navy, 1941-45. Fellow Am. Coll. Probate Counsel; mem. ABA, Tenn. Bar Assn. (bd. govs. 1969-72). Democrat. Methodist. General civil litigation, General corporate, Probate.

**BURCHFIELD, BOBBY ROY,** lawyer; b. Middlesboro, Ky., Oct. 23, 1954; s. Roy and Anna Lee (McCreary) B.; m. Teresa J. Miller, Apr. 6, 1996; 1 child, Taylor Nicole. BA, Wake Forest U., 1976; JD, George Washington U., 1979. Bar: D.C. 1980, U.S. Dist. Ct. D.C. 1982, U.S. Dist. Ct. Md. 1982, U.S. Ct. Appeals (3d cir.) 1981, U.S. Ct. Appeals (D.C. cir.) 1982, U.S. Ct. Appeals (9th cir.) 1985, U.S. Supreme Ct. 1986, U.S. Ct. Appeals (5th cir.) 1989, U.S. Ct. Appeals (6th cir.) 1993. Law clk. to Judge Ruggero J. Aldisert U.S. Ct. Appeals (3d cir.), Pitts., 1979-81; assoc. Covington & Burling, Washington, 1981-87, ptnr., 1987—; gen. counsel Bush-Quayle '92, 1992. Editor in chief George Washington U. Law Rev., 1978-79. Vol. George Bush for Pres., Washington, 1986-88; gen. counsel Rep. Nat. Lawyers Assn., 1991-92; mem. Wake Forest U. Alumni Coun., 1990-93, 97—; chmn. George Washington U. Nat. Law Ctr. Ann Fund, 1990-91. Mem. ABA. Republican. E-mail: BBurchfield@cov.com. Antitrust, General civil litigation, Constitutional. Office: Covington & Burling 1201 Pennsylvania Ave NW PO Box 7566 Washington DC 20044-7566

**BURCHMORE, DAVID WEGNER,** lawyer; b. Evanston, Ill., Mar. 5, 1952; s. Robert Norris and Margaret Rose (Wegner) B.; children: Jonathan, Katherine, Elizabeth. AB, Princeton U., 1973; MA, U. Va., 1975, PhD, 1979, JD, 1986. Bar: Ohio 1986, U.S. Dist. Ct. (no. dist.) Ohio 1986, U.S. Ct. Appeals (6th cir.) 1986. Vis. asst. prof. Calif. Inst. Tech., Pasadena, 1978-81; asst. prof. SUNY, Binghamton, 1981-83; ptnr. Squire, Sanders & Dempsey, Cleve., 1986—; mem. exec. com. Ctr. for Early Renaissance and Med. Studies, Binghamton, 1981-83; sec. med. lit. sect. Philological Assn. Pacific Coast, 1981-82. Editor: Text and Image, 1986; articles editor Va. Law Rev., 1985-86. Princeton U. scholar, 1972-73, Robert D. Saltz Meml. fellow U. Va., 1977, Dillard fellow, 1984-85. Mem. Medieval Acad. Am., Ohio Bar Assn., Cleve. Bar Assn. (exec. coun. environ. law com. 1993-96). Republican. Methodist. Administrative and regulatory, Environmental. Home: 27545 Sherwood Dr Westlake OH 44145-4454 Office: 4900 Key Tower Cleveland OH 44114

**BURCKE, JOSEPH ROBERT,** lawyer; b. St. Louis, Mar. 13, 1951; s. John Bernard and Jane Elizabeth (Wheeler) B. BA cum laude, St. Louis U., 1972; JD, U. Mo., 1975. Bar: Mo. 1975. Assoc. Sachs & Miller, P.C., St. Louis, 1975-76, Rierman & Blitz, St. Louis, 1977-79; shareholder Joseph R. Burcke P.C., St. Louis, 1980-85; ptnr. Beach Burcke Helfers, St. Louis, 1986—. Author: Guide to Wills and Trusts, 1998. Bd. dirs. Juvenile Diabetes Found., 1989-95; mem. Am. Diabetes Assn.; bd. dirs. ITE Sheldered Workshop, St. Louis, 1980-92, fin. com. chmn., 1993—. Recipient Cert. of Appreciation Juvenile Diabetes Found., 1996, Cath. Charities, 1998. Mem. Bar Assn. Metro St. Louis, Mo. Bar Assn. (probate and trust law com. 1996—). Roman Catholic. Estate planning, Probate. Office: Beach Burcke et al 222 S Central Ave Ste 900 Saint Louis MO 63105-3575

**BURDELIK, THOMAS L.,** lawyer; b. Chgo., June 4, 1959; s. Thomas L. and Roberta P. (Raber) B.; m. Mary Kathleen Igyarto; children: Clayton Thomas, Dylan Patrick. BA, North Cen. Coll., 1981; JD, John Marshall Sch. Law, 1984. Bar: Ill. 1984. Assoc. Parrillo, Weiss & Moss, Chgo., 1984-87; sr. assoc. McSherry & Gray, Chgo., 1987, Parillo, Weiss & Moss, Chgo., 1987-89; prin. Thomas L. Burdelik & Assocs., Chgo., 1989—; past guest lectr. on legal argument U. Ill. at Chgo. and St. Xavier Coll., Chgo.; co-mgr. Sheffield Garden Walk, 1997; instr. in fed. trial bar tng. Chgo. Bar Assn. Featured spkr. Chgo. Bar Assn. Seminars on Trial Practice, Cross Exam., Uninsured/Underinsured Motorist Claims, Role of Accident Reconstructionists and Jury Consultants in Trials in Cook County, spkr. sem. spon. by IL Trial Lawyers Assoc on Damages. Mem. Nat. Handgun Control, 1990-95, Nat. Abortion Rights Action League, 1990-95, Internat. CARE, 1991-95; vol. Northwestern Hosp., Chgo., 1991-95; mem. Ranch Triangle Comm. Orgn.; vol. fundraiser Off the Street Club of Chgo., 1991—. Mem. Chgo. Bar Assn. (instr. Fed. Trial Bar Tng. Course), Amnesty Internat., Randolph Athletic Club. Democrat. Roman Catholic. State civil litigation, Personal injury, Insurance. Office: 123 W Madison St Ste 19 Chicago IL 60602-4511

**BURDEN, JAMES EWERS,** lawyer; b. Sacramento, Oct. 24, 1939; s. Herbert Spencer and Ida Elizabeth (Brosemer) B.; m. Kathryn Lee Gardner, Aug. 21, 1965; children: Kara Elizabeth, Justin Gardner. BS, U. Calif., Berkeley, 1961; JD, U. Calif., Hastings, 1964; postgrad., U. So. Calif., 1964-65. Bar: Calif. 1965, Tax Ct. U.S. 1969, U.S. Supreme Ct. 1970. Assoc. Elliott and Aune, Santa Ana, Calif., 1965, White, Harbor, Fort & Schei, Sacramento, 1965-67; assoc. Miller, Starr & Regalia, Oakland, Calif., 1967-69, ptnr., 1969-73; ptnr. Burden, Aiken, Mansuy & Stein, San Francisco, 1973-82, James E. Burden, Inc., San Francisco, 1982—; of counsel, Aiken, Kramer & Cummings, Oakland and San Francisco; bd. dirs. IP Floor Products, Inc., San Leandro, Calif., Denver; underwriting mem. Lloyds of London, 1986-93; instr. U. Calif., Berkeley, 1966-74, Merritt Coll.; prin. Dorset Capital LLC. Contbr. articles to profl. jours. Mem. ABA, Lutine Golf Soc. (London), Claremont Country Club, San Francisco Grid Club, Commonwealth of Calif., The Naval Club (London), Inst. Dirs. (London), The Univ. Club. Real property, Finance, General corporate. Office: One Maritime Plz 4th Fl San Francisco CA 94111-3407

**BURDITT, GEORGE MILLER, JR.,** lawyer; b. Chgo., Sept. 21, 1922; s. George Miller and Flora Winifred (Hardie) B.; m. Barbara Helen Stenger, Feb. 17, 1945; children: Betsey Burditt Blessing, George M., Deborah, Barbara Burditt Perry. BA, Harvard U., 1944, LLB, 1948. Bar: Ill. 1949, D.C. 1981, U.S. Dist. Ct. (no. dist.) Ill. 1952, U.S. Ct. Appeals (7th cir.) 1961, U.S. Ct. Appeals (D.C. cir.) 1962, U.S. Ct. Appeals (4th cir.) 1974, U.S. Supreme Ct. 1974, U.S. Ct. Appeals (2d cir.) 1978, U.S. Ct. Appeals (8th cir.) 1988. With law dept. Swift & Co., Chgo., 1948-54; ptnr. Chadwell & Kayser and predecessors, Chgo., 1955-69, Burditt and Radzius, Chgo., 1969-98, Bell, Boyd and Lloyd, Chgo., 1998—; adj. prof. Northwestern U. Sch. Law, 1967-97; gen. counsel Food and Drug Law Inst.; dir. Gerber Products, 1973-93. Contbr. articles to profl. jours. Mem. Ill. State Ho. of Reps., 1965-72, asst. majority leader, 1971-72; Rep. candidate U.S. Senate, 1974. 2d lt. USAAF, 1943-45. Named Outstanding Legislator, Better Govt. Assn., 1969, 71; recipient Presdl. award Cook County Bar Assn., 1981, Defender of Justice award Nat. Conf. Christians & Jews, 1992. Mem. ABA, Ill. State Bar Assn., D.C. Bar Assn., Chgo. Bar Assn. (pres. 1980-81), N.Y. Bar Assn., Fed. Bar Assn., Met. Bar Leaders Caucus (pres. 1981-82), Harvard Law Sch. Assn. (pres. 1988-90), Harvard Law Soc. Ill. (pres. 1980-81), Union League Club, Econ. Club, Mid-Day Club, Crystal Downs Country Club, Law Club Chgo. (pres. 1980-81). Administrative and regulatory, Federal civil litigation, State civil litigation. Office: Bell Boyd and Lloyd 70 W Madison St Ste 3300 Chicago IL 60602-4284

**BURDMAN, B. RICHARD,** lawyer; b. Youngstown, Ohio; s. Harry and Doris Burdman; m. Babette Feldman, Aug. 21, 1960; children: Pamela S., Linda R. BA, Youngstown State U., 1954; JD, Duke U., 1956. Bar: Ohio 1956. Ptnr. Nadler, Nadler & Burdman and predecessors, Youngstown, 1956—; pres. Burbro Properties, Inc.; bd. dirs. numerous corps. Life mem. bd. visitors Duke U. Sch. Law, Durham, N.C., 1990—. With U.S. Army, 1956-57. Fellow Ohio Bar Found.; mem. ABA, Ohio Bar Assn., Mahoning County Bar Assn., Masons. Jewish. Avocation: golf. Real property, Corporate taxation. Address: 1314 Virginia Trl Youngstown OH 44505-1640 Office: Nadler Nadler & Burdman Co 20 Federal Pla Ste 600 Youngstown OH 44503

**BURG, BRENT LAWRENCE,** lawyer; b. Houston, Mar. 2, 1940; s. Abner Danford and Bess (Levin) B.; m. Patricia S. Petitt, 1980; 1 child, Brook Lawrence. BA, U. Tex., 1962; JD, 1966. Bar: Tex. 1966, U.S. Dist. Ct. (so. dist.) Tex. 1966, U.S. Ct. Appeals (5th cir.) 1966, U.S. Supreme Ct. 1970, U.S. Ct. Appeals (4th cir.) 1976, U.S. Dist. Ct. Md. 1976, U.S. Ct. Appeals (11th cir.) 1981. Dist. judge 309th Dist. Ct., Harris County, Tex., 1981-82; assoc. mcpl. judge City of Piney Point Village, 1990-98, City of Bunker Hill Village, 1991-98; ptnr. Rentz, Burg and Assocs., Houston, 1983-95; pvt. practice Brent Burg, Houston, 1995-97; assoc. judge 312th Dist. Ct., Houston, 1999—; of counsel Fouts & Moore, L.L.P., 1997—. Chairperson Houston Vol. Lawyers Program, Inc., 1988-89, 89-90. Fellow Tex. Bar Found.; mem. Houston Bar Found., State Bar Tex. (grievance com.), Houston Bar Assn. (family law sect. treas. 1978-79, chairperson elect 1980-81, dir. 1982-83, chairperson 1984-85; mem. Supreme Ct. of Tex. child support and visitation guidelines adv. com. 1986-87, 96—), Phi Alpha Delta. Family and matrimonial. Office: 312th District Ct 1115 Congress St Houston TX 77002-1927

**BURG, MICHAEL S.,** lawyer; b. Chgo., Mar. 12, 1950; s. Sydney M. and Phyliss (Shapiro) B.; m. Deborah Ann White, Aug. 17, 1974 (div. Mar. 1984); children: Scott Edward, Stephen Jonathan; m. Kathryn Anne Bush, May 27, 1988. BA, U. Denver, 1972, JD, 1975. Bar: Colo. 1976, U.S. Dist. Ct. Colo. 1976, U.S. Ct. Appeals (10th cir.) 1979, U.S. Supreme Ct. 1990, U.S. Dist. Ct. Ariz. 1993, Nebr. 1996. Assoc. Atler Zall & Hangman P.C., Denver, 1976-77; ptnr. Dunn, Crane, & Burg P.C., Denver, 1977-80; ptnr., pres. Burg & Aspinwall P.C., Denver, 1980-84, Burg & Eldredge P.C., Denver, 1984-98, Burg, Simpson, Eldredge, Hersh & Houliston, P.C., Elglewood, Colo., 1998—; adj. prof. law U. Denver Coll. Law; instr. Metro State Coll., Denver, 1978-82; agt. to profl. athletes, 1988—. Mem. SAG (pres. Denver chpt. 1983-90), Am. Bd. Trial Advocates, Sports Lawyers Assn., Phi Beta Kappa. Jewish. Avocations: acting, lecturing. General civil litigation, Insurance, Personal injury. Office: Burg Simpson Eldredge Hersh & Houliston PC 40 Inverness Dr E Englewood CO 80112-5481 also: 201 3rd St NW Albuquerque NM 87102-3370

**BURGDOERFER, JERRY,** lawyer; b. Jeffersonville, Ind., May 3, 1958; s. Jerry Jack and Barbara Jean (Hofherr) B. BS, Ind. U., 1980, MBA, 1983, JD cum laude, 1983. Bar: Ill. 1984, U.S. Dist. Ct. (no. dist.) Ill. 1984, U.S. Tax Ct. 1984. Assoc. Adams, Fox, Adelstein, Rosen & Bell, Chgo., 1983-88, ptnr., 1988-89; assoc. Jenner & Block, Chgo., 1989-90, ptnr., 1991—; with Mori Sogo Law Offices, Tokyo, 1991-93. Author articles. Vol. United Cerebral Palsy Assn., 1995—, dir., 1999—. Named 2d Benton Nat. Moot Ct. Competition, 1982. Mem. ABA, Internat. Bar Assn., Inter Pacific Bar Assn., Ill. Bar Assn., Chgo. Bar Assn. (chairperson '34 Act Com. 1996-98, reporter, Securities Com. 1997-98, vice chair 1998-99, chair 1999—), Japan Am. Soc. Chgo., Ind. U. Alumni Club Chgo. (vol. 1988-89) , Econ. Club Chgo., Execs. Club Chgo., Chgo. Coun. on Fgn. Rels., Japan-Am. Soc. of Chgo., Phi Eta Sigma, Phi Delta Phi, Phi Delta Theta (sec. chpt. 1977-78, cofounder, steering com. Chgo. alumni club 1988-89). Avocations: bicycling, water skiing, Japanese language. Securities, General corporate, Private international. Office: Jenner & Block 1 E Ibm Plz Fl 4000 Chicago IL 60611-7603

**BURGER, ROBERT THEODORE,** lawyer, partner; b. Coral Gables, Fla., Oct. 20, 1949; s. Eugene Clifford Burger and Dorothy Irene Harrison; m. Janice Marie Colbert, Dec. 14, 1974; children: Melissa Anne, Amy Michelle, Kristin Reneé. BA, U. Fla., 1971, JD, 1974. Bar: Fla. 1974, U.S. Ct. Appeals (11th cir.) 1981, U.S. Dist. Ct. (mid. dist.) Fla. 1977; cert. civil trial lawyer, Fla. Assoc. Collins & Clark, Indian Harbour Beach, Fla., 1974-76; ptnr. Clark & Burger, Indian Harbour Beach, Fla., 1976-86, Burger & Ville, Indian Harbour Beach, Fla., 1986-96, Burger & Paulk, Indian Harbour Beach, Fla., 1996—; founding mem. Am. Inns of Ct., Brevard County Chpt., 1993-96. Pres., dir. Hacienda Girls Ranch, Melbourne, Fla., 1980-95, founder and pres. Community Christian Sch., Melbourne, 1984-88; mem. Brevard County Rep. Party Exec. Com., Melbourne, 1990-91; chmn., dir. Brevard County Jail Chaplain Ministry, Sharpes, Fla., 1994—. Mem. Assn. Trial Lawyers Am., Fla. Acad. Trial Lawyers, Christian Bus. Men's Com. (chmn. 1988-89). Presbyterian. Avocations: boating, horseback riding, fishing, tennis. Personal injury. Office: Burger & Paulk 1901 Hwy A1A Ste 6 Indian Harbor Beach FL 32937-3526

**BURGESS, BRECK KRISTEN,** lawyer; b. Cresco, Iowa, May 21, 1962. BA, Drake U., 1984; JD, Washington U., St. Louis, 1987. Bar: Mo. 1987. Asst. atty. gen. Mo. Atty. Gen.'s Office, Jefferson City, 1987—, head criminal appeals unit, 1994—. Recipient David J. Dixon Appellate Advocacy award Mo. Bar Found., 1997. Mem. Jefferson City Roadrunners. Avocations: running, swimming, hiking. Home: 131 W Circle Dr Jefferson City MO 65109-1228 Office: Atty Gen's Office PO Box 899 Jefferson City MO 65102-0899

**BURGESS, BRYAN SCOTT,** lawyer; b. Gainesville, Fla., June 5, 1954; s. Bernard Ora and Barbara (Bennett) B.; m. Karla Boessmann, Mar. 26, 1983; children: Brenda Nicole, Michelle Marie. BA, Fla. State U., 1976; JD with honors, U. Fla., 1978; MPH, U. South Fla., 1997. Bar: Fla. 1979, U.S. Dist. Ct. (mid. dist.) Fla. 1979, U.S. Ct. Appeals (11th cir.) 1981, U.S. Supreme Ct. 1986. Asst., then assoc. gen. counsel U. South Fla., Tampa, 1979-84, gen. counsel, 1984-93, assoc. v.p. for health scis., legal and instnl. affairs, 1993-95; exec. advisor USF Physicians Group, Tampa, 1995—. Contbg. author: The Responsible Conduct of Research, 1996. Particpant Leadership Tampa, 1984-85. Mem. Am. Health Lawyers Assn., Am. Coll. Healthcare Execs., Med. Group Mgmt. Assn. Democrat. Lutheran. Avocation: golf. Health, General corporate, Education and schools. Home: 4921 Dewey Rose Ct Tampa FL 33624-1070 Office: USF Physicians Group 3500 E Fletcher Ave Tampa FL 33613-4708

**BURGESS, DAVID,** lawyer; b. Detroit, Nov. 30, 1948; s. Roger Edward and Claire Theresa (Sullivan) B.; m. Rebecca Culbertson Stuart, 1985 (dec. Dec. 1988); m. Catherine Mounteer, 1993; children: Jalil Riahi, Leila Riahi, Bryan Valentine, Grace Catherine. BS in Fgn. Svc., Georgetown U., 1970, MS in Fgn. Svc., 1978, JD, 1978. Bar: D.C. 1978, U.S. Dist. Ct. D.C. 1979, U.S. Ct. Appeals (D.C. cir.) 1979, U.S. Ct. Appeals (fed. cir.) 1988, U.S. Ct. Internat. Trade 1988. Rsch. asst. Georgetown U. Sch. Bus. Adminstrn., Washington, 1975, asst. to dean, 1975-76; rsch. assoc., prof. Acad. in the Pub. Svc., Washington, 1976-79; asst. editor Securities Regulation Law Report, Washington; legal editor Internat. Trade Reporter Bur. Nat. Affairs, Washington, 1978-79; atty. Cadwalader, Wickersham & Taft, Washington, 1979-81; mng. editor Bur. Nat. Affairs, Washington, 1981-82; dir. U.S. Peace Corps, Niamey, Niger, 1982-84, Rabat, Morocco, 1984-85; dir. policy planning, mgmt. Peace Corps, Washington, 1985-87; dir. Bur. Human Rights and Humanitarian Affairs U.S. Dept. State, Washington, 1987-92; regional dir. Lawyers for Bush-Quayle Re-Election Campaign, 1992; chief party Rwanda Dem. and Governance Project, 1994, Russia NGO Sector Project, Moscow, 1994; dir. democracy and civil soc. program, sr. advisor World Learning, Washington, 1995 (dir. U.S. Democracy Fellows program, Washington, 1995—); spkr. workshops Minority Legis. Edn. Program, Ind. Assn. Cities and Towns, Georgetown U. Continuing Edn. Program, Comms. Workers Am., Colo. State U., U. Wis. Alumni rep. Internat. Sch. Bangkok, 1972-74. Author: Financing Local Government, 1977, 2d edit., 1978, Preparation of the Local Budget, 2 vols., 1976, 2d edit., 1978, Local Government Accounting Fundamentals, 2d edit., 1977, Understanding Federal Assistance Programs, 2d edit., 1978, The POW/MIA Issue: Perspectives on the National League of Families, 1978; contbr. articles to publs. Adv. com. Arlington County Fiscal Affairs, 1993-94; mem. pres. coun. Mary Washington Coll.; mem. Rep. Nat. Com. With USAF, 1970-74. Mem. D.C. Bar Assn., Washington Fgn. Law Soc., Hoyas Unltd. (pres. 1992-94), Federalist Soc., Georgetown U. Alumni Assn. (bd. govs. 1975—, class rep. 1971-91), Rep. Nat. Lawyers Assn., Pachyderm Club No. Va. (pres. 1992-93), Pres.'s Club. Republican. Roman Catholic. Home: 3115 1st Pl N Arlington VA 22201-1037 Office: 1015 15th St NW Ste 750 Washington DC 20005-2605

**BURGESS, FRANKLIN DOUGLAS,** judge; b. 1935. BS in Engring., Gonzaga U., 1961, JD, 1966. Asst. city atty. City of Tacoma (Wash.), 1967-69; judge pro tem Mcpl. Ct. and Pierce County Dist. Ct., 1971-80; ptnr. Tanner & Burgess, Tacoma, Wash., 1971-76, Tanner, McGavick, Felker, Fleming, Burgess & Lazares, Tacoma, Wash., 1976-79, McGavick, Burgess, Heller & Foister, Tacoma, Wash., 1979-80; regional counsel Dept. Housing and Urban Devel., Seattle, 1980-81; U.S. magistrate judge U.S. Dist. Ct. (we. dist.) Wash., Tacoma, 1981-93, 95—; dist. judge U.S. Ct. Appeals (9th cir.), Tacoma, Wash., 1994-95. Resource person annual Nat. Black History Mo., Shiloh Bapt. Ch.; mem. Tacoma Urban League. Named NCAA All Am., 1961, Gonzaga U. Hall of Fame Basketball, 1989. Mem. Wash. State Bar Assn., Pierce County Bar Assn., Loren Miller Bar Assn., Nat. Conf. U.S. Magistrate Judges, NAACP. Office: US Dist Ct Union Station Courthouse 1717 Pacific Ave Ste 3124 Tacoma WA 98402-3234

**BURGESS, HAYDEN FERN (POKA LAENUI),** lawyer; b. Honolulu, May 5, 1946; s. Ned E. and Nora (Lee) B.; m. Puanani Sonoda, Aug. 28, 1968. B in Polit. Sci., U. Hawaii, JD, 1976. Bar: Hawaii 1976, U.S. Tax Ct., U.S. Ct. Appeals (9th cir.). Pvt. practice Waianae, Hawaii, 1976—; pres. Hawaii Coun. for 1993 and Beyond, Honolulu, 1991—; exec. dir. Waianae Coast Cmty. Mental Health Ctr., 1997—; v.p. World Coun. Indigenous Peoples before UN, 1984-90; human rights adv., writer, speaker in field; pres. Pacific and Asia Coun. Indigenous Peoples; cons. on indigenous affairs, 1984; indigenous expert to ILO Conv.; expert UN seminar on effects of racism and racial discriminations on social and econ. rels. between indigenous peoples and states, 1989—; del. Native Hawaiian Convention. Trustee Office Hawaiian Affairs, Honolulu, 1982-86; mem. Swedish Nat. Commn. on Mus., 1986; leader Hawaiian Independence Movement; mem. Hawaiian Sovereignty Elections Coun. Mem. Law Assn. Asia and Western Pacific (steering com. on human rights 1988), Union of 3d World Journalists. Public international, General practice, Health.

**BURGESS, MYRTLE MARIE,** retired lawyer; b. Brainerd, Minn., May 3, 1921; d. Charles Dana and Mary Elzaida (Thayer) Burgess. BA, San Francisco State U., 1947; JD, Hastings Coll. Law, 1950. Bar: Calif. 1951. Pvt. practice law, San Francisco, 1951-52, Reedley, Calif., 1952—; judge pro tem Fresno County Superior Ct., 1974-77; now owner/operator Hotel Burgess. Bd. dirs. Reedley Indsl. Site Devel. Found., 1970-81; dir., 2d v.p. Kings Canyon unit Calif. Republican Assembly, 1973-75; pres., bd. dirs. Sierra Community Concert Assn., Reedley council Girl Scouts U.S.A., 1955-56, Fresno Cmty. Concert Assn., 1995—; commr. Fresno City-County Commn. Status of Women; bd. dirs., treas. Reedley Downtown Assn., 1983—; bd. dirs. Kinship Program, 1988; bd. dirs., sec. Kings View Found., bd. dirs. Calif. Hotel Motel Assn., 1993—. Recipient award for remodeling and preservation of old bldg. Fresno Hist. Soc., 1975, others. Mem. ABA, Calif. Bar Assn., Fresno County Bar Assn., World Jurist Assn., Am. Trial Lawyers, Reedley C. of C. (bd. dirs. 1958-63, 87-91, Woman of Yr. 1971, Athenian award 1988). Republican. Presbyterian. Clubs: Bus. and Profl. Women's (pres.). Lodge: Order Eastern Star. Office: 1076 N Kady Ave Reedley CA 93654-2319

**BURGESS, TIMOTHY CHRISTOPHER,** lawyer; b. Birmingham, Ala., July 2, 1966; s. John Jackson and Sharon Ann Burgess; m. Vera Denise Davis, Sept. 25, 1991; children: Meredith Elise, Katherine Shelby. BA, Jacksonville State U., 1988; JD, Birmingham Sch. Law, 1993. Bar: Ala. 1993, U.S. Dist. Ct. (no. dist.) Ala. 1993. Atty. Sides Oglesby Held & Dick, Anniston, Ala., 1993-95, Roberts Young Wollstein & Hughes, Anniston, 1995-96, Burnham & Klinefeller, Anniston, 1996—. Democrat. Baptist. Insurance, Workers' compensation. Office: Burnham & Klinefeller PO Box 1618 Anniston AL 36202-1618

**BURGIN, CHARLES EDWARD,** lawyer; b. Marion, N.C., Dec. 16, 1938; m. Ellen Salsbury Burgin; children: Ellen, Lucy. BA, U. N.C., 1961; LLB, Duke U., 1964. Bar: N.C.; U.S. Supreme Ct. Law clk. to Hon. J. Braxton Craven Jr. U.S. Dist. Ct., U.S. Ct. Appeals, 1964-66; prosecuting atty. McDowell County Criminal Ct., 1966-68; sr. ptnr. Dameron, Burgin & Parker, P.A., Marion, N.C., 1968—; bd. dirs. Shadowline, Inc.; lectr. in field. Contbr. articles to profl. jours. Bd. dirs. McDowell County Recreation Commn. 1977-87, First Union Nat. Bank 1975—; McDowell County Mountain Rescue Team 1980—; McDowell Arts and Crafts Assn. 1980—. Fellow Am. Coll. Trial Lawyers (state chmn. 1996-98), Internat. Soc. Barristers, Am. Bar Found.; mem. ABA, N.C. Bar Assn. (pres. 1993-94), Defense Rsch. Inst., Am. Soc. Hosp. Attys., N.C. Assn. Defense Lawyers, U.S. Supreme Ct. Bar Assn. Libel, Personal injury, Insurance. Office: Dameron Burgin & Parker PA PO Drawer 1049 14 W Court St Marion NC 28752-3900

**BURGMAN, DIERDRE ANN,** lawyer; b. Logansport, Ind., Mar. 25, 1948; d. Ferdinand William Jr. and Doreen Yvonne (Walsh) B. BA, Valparaiso U., 1970, JD, 1979; LLM, Yale U., 1985. Bar: Ind. 1979, U.S. Dist. Ct. (so. dist.) Ind. 1979, N.Y. 1982, U.S. Dist. Ct. (so. dist.) N.Y. 1982, U.S. Ct. Appeals (7th cir.) 1982, U.S. Ct. Appeals (D.C. and 2d cirs.) 1984, U.S. Supreme Ct. 1985, D.C. 1988, U.S. Dist. Ct. (ea. dist.) N.Y. 1992. Law clk. to chief judge Ind. Ct. Appeals, Indpls., 1979-80; prof. law Valparaiso (Ind.) U., 1980-81; assoc. Dewey, Ballantine, Bushby, Palmer & Wood, N.Y.C., 1981-84, Cahill Gordon & Reindel, N.Y.C., 1985-92; v.p., gen. counsel N.Y. State Urban Devel. Corp., N.Y.C., 1992-95; dep. insp. gen. State N.Y., 1992-95; of counsel Vandenberg & Felin, N.Y.C., 1995-99; atty. Salans, Hertzfeld, Heilbronn, Christy & Viener, N.Y.C., 1999—. Note editor Valparaiso U. law rev., 1978-79; contbr. articles to law jours. Mem. bd. visitors Valparaiso U. Sch. Law, 1986—, chmn., 1989-92. Ind. Bar Found. scholar, 1978. Mem. ABA (trial evidence com. 1983-86, profl. liability com. 1986-89, ins. coverage litigation com. 1990-92), Assn. Bar City N.Y. (com. profl. responsibility 1988-91, com. profl. and jud. ethics 1991-95, mem. coun. jud. adminstrn. 1997-99), New York County Lawyers Assn. (com. Supreme Ct. 1987-94, chmn. 1990-93, bd. dirs. 1991-97, exec. com. bd. dirs. 1992-95, fin. and pers. com. 1994-95), N.Y. State Bar Assn. (mem. Ho. Dels. 1994-98), Law and humanities Inst., Fed. Bar. Coun., Women's City Club of N.Y. Home: 345 E 56th St Apt 5C New York NY 10022-3744

**BURGWEGER, FRANCIS JOSEPH DEWES, JR.,** lawyer; b. Evanston, Ill., July 5, 1942; s. Francis Dewes and Helen Theodosia (Chancellor) B.; m. Kathleen Marie Wessel, Sept. 3, 1978; children: Lauren Elizabeth, Francis Joseph Dewes III, Sherman Ward Chancellor. BA, Yale U., 1964; JD, U. Pa., 1970. Bar: Calif. 1971, N.Y. 1988, U.S. Ct. Appeals (9th cir.) 1971, U.S. Dist. Ct. (cen. dist.) Calif. 1971. Law clk. to Hon. Shirley M. Hufstedler U.S. Ct. Appeals 9th Cir., L.A., 1970-71; assoc. O'Melveny & Myers, L.A., 1971-78, ptnr., 1978-85; ptnr. O'Melveny & Myers LLP, N.Y.C., 1985-97, sr. counsel, 1997—. Contbr. articles on environ. law. Capt. U.S. Army, 1964-67, Vietnam. Mem. Assn. of Bar of City of N.Y., N.Y. State Bar Assn., L.A. County Bar Assn. (exec. com. R.P. sect.). Avocations: books, wine, agriculture. Real property, Environmental, Finance. Office: O'Melveny & Myers LLP 153 E 53rd St Fl 54 New York NY 10022-4611

**BURHAM, CYNTHIA FAYE,** lawyer; b. Laughlin AFB, Tex.. BA in English, BA in Philosophy, Trinity U., San Antonio, 1991; JD, U. Tex., 1994; LLM in Internat. Law, St. Mary's U., San Antonio, 1997. Bar: Tex. 1994, Nev. 1998, U.S. Dist. Ct. (we. dist.) Tex. 1995, U.S. Dist. Ct. Nev. 1998, U.S. Ct. Appeals (9th cir.) 1999, U.S. Supreme Ct. 1999. Sole practitioner San Antonio, 1995—; mem. Supreme Ct. Tex. Com. Investigating the Unauthorized Practice of Law, San Antonio, 1997. Contbr. articles to profl. jours. Mem. Tex. Ctr. for Legal Ethics and Professionalism, 1995-96. Mem. ABA (mem. planning bd. internat. law sect. 1996-97, bankruptcy law com. 1997—), Fed. Bar Assn. (intellectual property sect.), San Antonio Conservation Soc. Avocation: languages (French, Spanish, Italian). Bankruptcy, Trademark and copyright, Intellectual property. Office: PO Box 169874 San Antonio TX 78280-3474

**BURI, CHARLES EDWARD,** lawyer; b. Lancaster, Pa., Jan. 20, 1950; s. Karl Emerson and Verna Irene (Linville) B.; m. Susan Louise Camou, May 8, 1971; 1 child, Charles David. BS, U. Ariz., 1971, JD, 1973. Bar: Ariz. 1974, U.S. Dist. Ct. Ariz., 1974, U.S. Ct. Appeals (9th cir.) 1977, U.S. Supreme Ct. 1980. Asst. atty Gen. Office Atty. Gen., Phoenix, 1974-83; exec. dir. Ariz. State Lottery, Phoenix, 1983-87; ptnr. Friedl, Richter & Buri, Phoenix, 1987—. Life mem. Fiesta Bown com., Phoenix, 1984—, Luke's Men, Phoenix, 1985—, Gov.'s Cabinet, Phoenix, 1983-87; trustee St. Luke's Hosp., Phoenix, 1990-91. Mem. ABA, Nat. Trial Lawyers Assn., Ariz. Trial Lawyers Assn., Ariz. Bar Assn., Maricopa County Bar Assn., Phoenix-East Rotary. Democrat. Avocations: tennis, skiing, jogging. Personal injury, General civil litigation, Administrative and regulatory. Home: 6002 E Lafayette Blvd Scottsdale AZ 85251-3040 Office: Friedl Richter & Buri 6909 E Greenway Pkwy Ste 200 Scottsdale AZ 85254-2149

**BURI, PHILIP JAMES,** lawyer; b. Spokane, Wash., Dec. 27, 1960; s. Earl James and Bonnie Jean B.; m. Darcie Ann Donegan, May 29, 1993; children: Abraham, Elena, Isabel. AB, Princeton U., 1983; JD, Harvard U., 1987. Bar: Wash. 1988, U.S. Dist. Ct. (we. dist.) Wash. 1998, U.S. Dist. Ct. (ea. dist.) Wash. 1998, U.S. Ct. Appeals (9th cir.) 1998. Law clk. to Hon. Barbara Rothstein U.S. Dist. Ct., Seattle, 1987-89; trial lawyer Antitrust Divsn. U.S. Dept. Justice, Washington, 1989-93; law clk. to Hon. Richard Guy Wash. Supreme Ct., Olympia, 1993-95; ptnr. Brett & Daugert, Bellingham, Wash., 1995—. Bd. dirs. Bellingham Cmty. Food Co-op, 1996—. Mem. Wash. State Bar Assn. (ct. rules com. 1996—). Avocations: bicycling, skiing. Appellate, Land use and zoning (including planning), Contracts commercial. Office: Brett & Daugert 300 N Commercial St Ste 5008 Bellingham WA 98225-4002

**BURISH, MARK DENNIS,** lawyer; b. Menominee, Mich., Apr. 1, 1953; s. Bennie C. and Donna Mae (Willkom) B.; m. Helen Theodore Pappas. June 21, 1980; children: Adam, Nicole. BS, Marquette U., 1975; JD, U. Wis., 1978. Assoc. Aagaard, Nichol & Wyngaard, Madison, 1978-79; ptnr. Aagaard & Burish, Madison, 1979-84; ptnr., pres. Hurley, Burish & Milliken, Madison, 1984—. Mem. ABA, Wis. Bar Assn. Estate planning, Probate, General corporate. Home: 5846 Treeline Dr Madison WI 53711-5829 Office: Hurley Burish & Milliken 301 N Broom St Madison WI 53703-2067

**BURK, ROBERT S.,** lawyer; b. Mpls., Jan. 13, 1937; s. Harvey and Mayme (Cottle) B.; m. Eunice L. Silverman, Mar. 22, 1959; children: Bryan, Pam, Matt. BBA in Indsl. Rels., U. Minn., 1959; LLB, William Mitchell Coll. Law, 1965. Bar: Minn. 1966; qualified neutral under Rule 114 of the Minn. Gen. Rules of Practice, 1995—. Labor rels. cons. St. Paul Employers Assn., 1959-66; labor rels. mgr. Koch Refining Co., St. Paul, 1966-72, mgr. indsl. rels., 1972-75, mgr. indsl. rels., environ. affairs, 1975-77; sr. atty. Popham, Haik, Schnobrich & Kaufman, Ltd., Mpls., 1977-95, pres., CEO, 1986-90; ptnr. Burk & Seaton, P.A., Edina, Minn., 1995—. Chair bd. trustees William Mitchell Coll. Law, St. Paul, 1994-96, sec. 1991. Recipient Hon. Ronald E. Hachey Outstanding Alumnus award William Mitchell Coll. Law Alumni Assn., 1993. Mem. ABA (labor sect.), Minn. Bar Assn. (labor sect.). Labor, Administrative and regulatory. Office: Burk & Seaton PA 7301 Ohms Ln Ste 320 Edina MN 55439-2336 *Credibility is the only trait that marks your existence.*

**BURKE, DENNIS J.,** lawyer; b. Evergreen Park, Ill., July 25, 1949; s. John and Catherine N. (Barrett) B.; m. Carol A. Burke, Nov. 17, 1973; children—Dennis, Kathryn, Mary Ellen. Student Univ. Coll., Dublin, 1969-70; B.A., St. Mary's Coll., Winona, Minn., 1971; J.D., John Marshall Law Sch., 1975. Bar: Ill. 1975, U.S. dist. ct. (no. dist.) Ill. 1975. Mem. firm Burke & Burke, Ltd., Chgo., 1975—; moot ct. judge Loyola Law Sch.; guest lectr. Moraine Valley Jr. Coll., Evang. Sch. Nursing. Fellow Ill. Bar Found.; mem. ABA, Ill. Bar Assn. (sec. 1982-83, vice chmn. civil practice and procedure sect. 1983-85, chmn. 1985-86, bd. of govs. 1986—), Chgo. Bar Assn., Assn. Trial Lawyers Am., Ill. Trial Lawyers Assn. Issue editor Trial Briefs, vol. XXV, No. 5, 1979, vol. XXVII, No. 1, 1981. Personal injury, State civil litigation, Federal civil litigation. Office: Burke & Burke Ltd 20 S Clark St Chicago IL 60603-1802

**BURKE, EDMUND PATRICK, SR.,** lawyer; b. Chgo., Jan. 21, 1943; s. John and Catherine Mary (Barrett) B.; m. Maureen Margaret Sullivan, Dec. 17, 1966; children: Mary Catherine, Edmund Patrick Jr. BA, St. Mary's Coll., Winona, Minn., 1965; JD, U. Chgo., 1969. Bar: Ill. 1969, U.S. Dist. Ct. (no. dist.) Ill. 1969, U.S. Ct. Appeals (7th cir.). Title examiner Chgo. (Ill.) Title & Trust, 1968-70; sr. officer Burke & Burke, Chgo., 1970—. Mem. capital devel. bd. St. Mary's Coll., Chgo., 1994-95. Mem. ABA (banking sect.), Ill. Bar Assn. (comml. and bankruptcy sect.), DuPage Bar Assn., Chgo. Bar Assn. Roman Catholic. Avocations: running, boating, traveling, gardening. Banking, General civil litigation, Contracts commercial. Home: 1111 Mistwood Ln Downers Grove IL 60515-1215 Office: Burke & Burke 20 S Clark St Ste 2200 Chicago IL 60603-1805

**BURKE, HENRY PATRICK,** lawyer; b. Scranton, Pa., May 12, 1942; s. Thomas Joseph and Dorothy Maria (McCloskey) B.; B.S., U. Scranton, 1964; J.D., Villanova U., 1967; m. Alyce Louise McCrone, July 5, 1975; children—Henry Patrick, Daniel. Bar: Pa. 1968. Law clk. Ct. Common Pleas, Lackawanna County, Pa., 1968-69; lectr. bus. law U. Scranton, 1968-69; assoc. Haggerty & McDonnell, Scranton, Pa., 1969-75; assoc. counsel Scranton Redevel. Authority, 1969-70; spl. atty. gen. Pa., 1972-97; sec., gen. counsel Opportunity Products Today, Inc., 1998—; assoc. Burke and Douglass, Scranton, 1975-80. Mem. exec. com. Pa. unit Am. Heart Assn., 1973-74, asst. treas. Keystone chpt., 1972; del. Democratic Nat. Conv., 1972, chmn. econ. com. Dem. Nat. Platform Com., 1972; trustee Lackawanna Jr. Coll., 1977-79, solicitor, 1979-83; mem. alumni bd. govs. U. Scranton, 1969-75, pres. Nat. Alumni Soc., 1983-85; solicitor Catholic Social Services, 1978-95, bd. dirs., 1978-97; pres., owner Scranton-Wilkes Barre Twins, Inc., 1993-94; pres. Atlantic Collegiate Baseball League, 1995-97. Real estate broker, Pa. Mem. ABA, Pa., Lackawanna bar assns., Greater Scranton Bd. Realtors, Pa. Assn. Realtors, Nat. Assn. Realtors, Mensa, Intertel, Internat. Soc. Philos. Enquiry. Democrat. Roman Catholic. Author: The Burke-Duggan Family, From Oppression to Freedom, 1981. General civil litigation, Probate, Real property. Home: 319 Church St Dunmore PA 18512-1911 Office: Connell Bldg Ste 800 Scranton PA 18503

**BURKE, JOHN MICHAEL,** lawyer; b. Chgo., Oct. 9, 1941; s. John and Catherine Mary (Barrett) B.; m. Maureen Kay Fox, Oct. 5, 1968; children: Brian, Timothy, Michael. BBA, Loyola U., 1964, JD, 1965. Bar: Ill. 1965, U.S. Dist. Ct. (no. dist.) Ill. 1965, U.S. Ct. Appeals (7th cir.) 1968, U.S. Dist. Ct. (no.dist.) Ind. 1986. Assoc. Pretzel & Stouffer, Chgo., 1965-69, Shaheen, Lundberg & Callahan, Chgo., 1969-70; ptnr. Burke & Burke, Ltd., Chgo., 1970—. Sgt. U.S. Army, 1965-68. Mem. ABA, Ill. Bar Assn. (chmn. tort council, service award 1984, mem. civil practice com. 1997—), Assn. Trial Lawyers Am., Ill. Trial Lawyers (bd. mgrs. 1988—), Appellate Lawyers Ill. Club: Westmoreland Country (Wilmette, Ill.). Personal injury, State civil litigation, Federal civil litigation. Home: 2241 Kenilworth Ave Wilmette IL 60091-1523 Office: Burke & Burke Ltd 20 S Clark St Ste 2200 Chicago IL 60603-1805

**BURKE, JOHN WILLIAM,** lawyer; b. Willmar, Minn., Feb. 15, 1971; s. Darrel Leon and Bonnie Louise Burke; m. Lisa Marie Capirchio, Oct. 17, 1998. BA, No. State U., Aberdeen, S.D., 1993; JD, U. S.D., 1996. Bar: S.D. 1996, U.S. Dist. Ct. S.D. 1997, Minn. 1998. Jud. law clk. Pierre, S.D., 1996-97; assoc. Schoenbeck Law, Webster, S.D., 1997—; mem. evidence com. State Bar S.D., 1998-99. Firefighter Webster Vol. Fire Dept., 1998-99. Republican. State civil litigation, Personal injury, Federal civil litigation. Office: Schoenbeck Law East Hwy 12 Webster SD 57274

**BURKE, KATHLEEN MARY,** lawyer; b. N.Y.C., Dec. 8, 1950; d. Hubert J. and Catherine (Painting) B. BA magna cum laude, Marymount Manhattan Coll., 1972; JD, U. Va., 1975. Bar: N.Y. 1976, Calif. 1979, U.S. Dist. Ct. (so. and ea. dists.) N.Y. 1977, U.S. Ct. Appeals (2d cir.) 1977, U.S. Ct. Appeals (9th cir.) 1980. Assoc. Donovan Leisure Newton & Irvine, N.Y.C., L.A., 1975-81, Kelley Drye & Warren, N.Y.C., 1981-84; assoc. counsel Soc. N.Y. Hosp., 1984-87; sec. and counsel Soc. N.Y. Hosp., NYC, 1987—; sec., coun. The N.Y. and Presbyn. Hosp. Healthcare Sys., 1991—; joint bd. N.Y. Hosp.-Cornell Med. Ctr.; sec. N.Y. Hosp-Cornell Med. Ctr. Fund, Inc., Soc. N.Y. Hosp. Fund, Inc., Royal Charter Properties, Inc., Royal Charter Properties-East, Inc., Royal Charter Properties-Westchester, Inc., Exec. Registry, Inc., N.Y. Hosp., Queens Med. Ctr., Presbyn. Hosp., N.Y.C., 1996—, N.Y. andPresbyn. Hosp. Health Care Sys., 1996—; faculty Concern for Dying, N.Y.C., 1985-90, NYU Sch. Continuing Edn., 1994-96; lectr. Cornell U. Med. Coll., 1994—. Contbr. articles to profl. jours. Trustee Marymount Manhattan Coll., N.Y.C., 1990—, N.Y. Meth. Hosp., 1995—, Wyckoff Heights Hosp., 1996—. Recipient McKay award, 1997. Mem. ABA, N.Y. State Bar Assn. (health law com. 1989-93), Am. Soc. Corp. Secs., Assn. of Bar of City of N.Y. (children and law com. 1986-89, law and medicine com. 1991-94), Am. Acad. Hosp. Attys. (speaker annual confs. 1987-92), Health Care Exec. Forum, Nat. Health Lawyers, Greater N.Y. Hosp. Assn. Legal Adv. Com. Roman Catholic. Health, General civil litigation. Office: Soc NY Hosp 525 E 68th St # 109 New York NY 10021-4873

**BURKE, MARLIN W.,** lawyer; b. Sioux Falls, S.D.. BA, U. S.D., 1967; JD, U. Denver, 1971. Chief prosecutor City of Lakewood, Colo., 1971-75; pvt. practice Lakewood, Colo., 1975-90, Denver, 1992—; adminstrv. law judge divsn. adminstrv. hearings State of Colo., Denver, 1991. Author: Disability, Civil Rights and Workers' Compensation Law in Colorado, 1993, Workers' Compensation Law and Practice in Colorado, 1991-97. Mem. Art Student's League Denver. Mem. ABA, Colo. Bar Assn. (interprofl. com., grievance policy com.), Denver Bar Assn. (professional com., rule 16 rev. com.), 1st Jud. Bar Assn. (sec.-treas. 1971-89). Avocations: sculpture, painting. Workers' compensation, Labor, Civil rights. Office: Mile High Ctr 1700 Broadway Ste 1800 Denver CO 80290-1801

**BURKE, MICHAEL HENRY,** lawyer; b. Washington, Oct. 28, 1952; s. John Joseph and Mary Catherine (Gaul) B.; m. Ann McFarland, Jan. 31, 1981; children: Allison M., Andrew M. BA magna cum laude, Tufts U., 1974; JD, Georgetown U., 1977. Bar: Mass. 1977, U.S. Dist. Ct. Mass. 1979. Assoc. Bulkley, Richardson and Gelinas L.L.P., Springfield, Mass., 1977-83; ptnr. Bulkley, Richardson and Gelinas L.L.P., 1983—. Pub. adminstr. Commonwealth of Mass., 1980-90. Mem. ABA, Mass. Bar Assn., Hampden County Bar Assn. Roman Catholic. Personal injury, Administrative and regulatory. Home: 50 Meadowbrook Rd Longmeadow MA 01106-1341 Office: Bulkley Richardson and Gelinas LLP 1500 Main St Springfield MA 01115-0001

**BURKE, PATRICK WILLIAM,** lawyer; b. Concord, Calif., Jan. 1, 1965; s. Thomas Edward Burke and Kathryn Henry. BA, Calif. State U., 1992; JD, Empire Sch. Law, 1995. Bar: Calif. 1995, U.S. Dist. Ct. (ea. dist.) 1995. Assoc. James V. Jones-Law Offices, Napa, Calif., 1996—; founding mem. Napa County Family Law Com., 1997-98. Founding mem. Napa Dem. Steering Com., 1994—; mem. Dem. Cen. Com., Napa, 1994—; commr. Cultural Heritage Com., Napa, 1997—. Sgt. U.S. Army, 1983-87; capt. USAR. Mem. ABA, Assn. Army Officers, Native Sons Golden West, Commonwealth Club, 20/30 Active Club. Democrat. Roman Catholic. General practice, Family and matrimonial, Probate. Office: James V Jones-Law Offices 1564 1st St Napa CA 94559-2841

**BURKE, RICHARD JAMES,** lawyer; b. Bronx, N.Y., Jan. 13, 1952; s. Louis E. and Rhoda Burke; m. Evelyn Pleasants, Feb. 18, 1975; children: Matthew Sean, Bryan Richard, Kevin Louis. BA, Hofstra U., 1973, JD, 1982. Bar: N.Y. 1982, U.S. Dist. Ct. (ea. and so. dists.) N.Y. 1983. Lawyer Richard James Burke, Esquire, Melville, N.Y., 1990-94; lawyer, pres. Burke & Burke, Esqs., P.C., Melville, 1994—. Mem. sch. bd. Lindenhurst (N.Y.) Union Free Sch. Dist., 1993—, Plainview (N.Y.)-Old Bethpage Union Free Sch. Dist., 1983-86; assoc. village justice Lindenhurst Village, 1990-91; mem. planning bd. Lindenhurst Village, 1993—; coach Lindenhurst Nat. Little League, 1993—, Lindenhurst Youth Ctr., 1995—; council Lindenhurst Rep. Com., 1995—. Mem. N.Y. State Bar Assn., Suffolk County Bar Assn., Kiwanis of Lindenhurst. Republican. Roman Catholic. Estate planning, Real property, Probate. Home: 420 N Niagara Ave Lindenhurst NY 11757-3513 Office: Burke & Burke PC 510 Broadhollow Rd Ste 304A Melville NY 11747-3606

**BURKE, RICHARD WILLIAM,** lawyer; b. Chgo., Oct. 3, 1933; s. James William and Helen (Creed) B.; m. Maryjeanne Ryan, Feb. 11, 1961; children: Mary, Richard, Sarah, Will. BA cum laude, U. Notre Dame, 1955; JD, U. Chgo., 1958. Bar: Ill. 1959, U.S. Dist. Ct. Ill. 1959, U.S. Ct. Appeals (7th cir.) 1965, U.S. Supreme Ct. 1977. Assoc. William T. Kirby & Assocs., Chgo., 1958-65; assoc. Hubachek, Kelly, Rauch & Kirby, Chgo., 1965-67, ptnr., 1967-80; ptnr. Burke, Griffin, Chomicz & Wienke, Chgo., 1980-88, Burke, Wilson & McIlvaine, Chgo., 1989-92, Burke, Warren & MacKay, P.C., Chgo., 1992-97, Burke, Warren, MacKay & Serritella, PC, Chgo., 1997—; bd. dirs. bank holding co. and various charities. Mem. Ill. Bar Assn., Chgo. Bar Assn. Roman Catholic. Avocations: skiing, reading, travel. Banking, Mergers and acquisitions, Real property. Office: Burke Warren MacKay & Serritella 330 N Wabash Ave Chicago IL 60611-3603

**BURKE, ROBERT BERTRAM,** lawyer, political consultant, lobbyist; b. Cleve., July 9, 1942; s. Max and Eve (Miller) B.; m. Helen Choate Hall, May 5, 1979 (div. Oct. 1983). B.A., UCLA, 1963, J.D., 1966; LL.M., London Sch. Econs., 1967. Bar: D.C. 1972, Calif. 1978, U.S. Supreme Ct. 1977. Exec. dir. Lawyer's Com. Civil Rts. under Law, Washington, 1968-69; ptnr. Fisk, Wolfe & Burke, Paris, 1969-71; assoc. O'Connor & Hannan, Washington, 1972-74; sole practice, Washington, 1974-79, Los Angeles, 1978-93; cons. Commonwealth Pa., Harrisburg, 1973. Chmn. So. Calif. Hollings for Pres., 1984; pres. Bldg. and Appeals Bd. City of Los Angeles; bd. dirs. Vols. of Am.; mem. exec. com. State Bar of Calif. pub. law sect. Mem. ABA, Am. Inst. Architects (profl. affiliate), UCLA Law Alumni Assn. (pres.). Jewish. Administrative and regulatory, Private international. Home: 277 S Irving Blvd Los Angeles CA 90004-3809

**BURKE, THOMAS JOSEPH, JR.,** lawyer; b. Chgo., Oct. 23, 1941; s. Thomas Joseph and Violet (Green) B.; m. Sharon Lynne Forke, Aug. 29, 1964; children: Lisa Lynne, Heather Ann. BA, Elmhurst Coll., 1963; JD, Chgo.-Kent Coll. Law, 1966. Bar: Ill. 1966, U.S. Dist. Ct. (no. dist.) Ill. 1967, U.S. Ct. Appeals (7th cir.) 1972, U.S. Supreme Ct. 1972, U.S. Ct. Appeals (11th cir.) 1994, U.S. Ct. Appeals (6th cir.), 1995. Assoc., Lord, Bissell & Brook, Chgo., 1966-74, ptnr., 1974—. Dir. and pres. Buffalo Prairie Gang Camp. Fellow Am. Coll. Trial Lawyers; mem. ABA, ATLA, Chgo. Bar Assn., Soc. Trial Lawyers, Trial Lawyers Club Chgo., Def. Rsch. Inst., Ill. Assn. Def. Trial Counsel, Product Liability Adv. Coun., Soc. Automotive Engrs., Assn. Advancement Automotive Medicine, Internat. Coun. Motorsport Scis., Mid-Day Club, Pi Kappa Delta, Phi Delta Phi. Republican. Roman Catholic. Product liability, State civil litigation, Federal civil litigation. Office: Lord Bissell & Brook 115 S La Salle St Ste 3200 Chicago IL 60603-3972

**BURKE, THOMAS MICHAEL,** lawyer; b. Summit, N.J., Feb. 10, 1956; s. Robert William and Eleanor Mary (Kelley) B.; m. Nancy Robin Mogab, Sept. 24, 1983; children: Colleen Margaret, Michael Thomas, Brendan Robert. BA, Notre Dame U., 1978; JD, St. Louis U., 1981. Bar: Mo. 1981, Ill. 1982, U.S. Dist. Ct. (ea. dist.) 1981. Assoc. Moser, Marsalek, Carpenter, Cleary & Jaeckel, St. Louis, 1981-86; ptnr. Noonan & Burke, St. Louis, 1986-92; prin. Thomas M. Burke, PC, St. Louis, 1992—; bd. dirs. Legal Svcs. Ea. Mo., 1995-97. Active Vol. Lawyers program, St. Louis, St. Louis Hills Homeowner's Assn., 1984-94. Mem. Mo. Bar Assn., Ill. (bd. govs., 1998—), Bar Assn., Interest On Lawyers' Trust Accounts (bd. dirs. 1997—), Bar Assn. Met. St. Louis (trial sect. asst. chmn. 1987-89, chmn. bylaws and election com. 1989—, treas. 1992-93, sec. 1993-94, v.p. 1994-95, pres.-elect 1995-96, pres. 1996-97), St. Louis Bar Found. (sec. 1993-94, treas. 1995-96), Lawyers Assn. St. Louis (exec. com. 1987-92, sec. 1992-93). Personal injury, Workers' compensation, General civil litigation. Office: 701 Market St Ste 1075 Saint Louis MO 63101-1886

**BURKE, THOMAS RAYMOND,** lawyer; b. Lincoln, Nebr., Apr. 15, 1928; s. Raymond C. and Florine (Kost) B.; children from previous marriage: Thomas R., Timothy J. (dec. 1998), Melanie A., Laura M., Lisa M., Daniel C.; m. Barbara Schafer, Apr. 17, 1993; stepchildren: Robyn, Stephen, Holly, Jamie. JD, Creighton U., 1951. Bar: Nebr. 1951. Assoc. Kennedy, Holland, DeLacy & Svoboda, Omaha, 1956-62, ptnr., 1963—, sr. ptnr., 1970-98; of counsel Lamson Dugan & Murray, 1998—; lectr. Coll. St. Mary, 1960-80. Past pres. adv. bd. Archbishop Bergan Mercy Hosp., former chmn. fin. com.; co-chmn. NCCJ, 1969-77, nat. trustee, 1972-78, bd. dirs., 1969-95, bd. govs., 1995—; mem. Archbishop's Com. for Ednl. Devel., 1975—, chmn., 1975-78, 87-95; founding trustee, pres., gen. counsel Omaha Archdiocesan Ednl. Found.; co-chair Archbishop's $25 Million Campaign for Ednl. Excellence, 1991; mem. adv. bd. Mercy High Sch.; mem. pres.'s coun. U. Nebr., 1979-85, Coll. St. Mary, 1979-85; bd. dirs. Duchesne Acad., 1979-82, trustee, 11982-87, pres., trustee, 1985-87; bd. dirs. Christian Urban Edn. Svc., 1982-97, United Arts Omaha, 1983-98; trustee Nat. Jewish Hosp. (humanitarian award 1983), Denver, 1983; bd. dirs., mem. exec. com., mem. fin. com. United Way of Midlands, 1984-90, ann. campaign chmn., 1986; mem. st. Joseph High Devel. Bd., 1983-88; diocesan rep., trustee Nat. Cath. Ednl. Assn., 1984-87; chmn. bd. dirs. Bergan Mercy Found., 1992-98. Recipient Brotherhood award, 1991, Humanitarian award, 1991; named Citizen of Yr., United Way of Midlands, 1992; named to Aksarben Ct. of Honor, 1998. Fellow Am. Bar Found.; mem. ABA (ho. of dels. 1980-085, state del. 1985-87), Omaha Bar Assn. (pres. 1971), Am. Acad. Hosp. Attys., Am. Hosp. Assn., am. law Inst., Am. Coll. of Trust and Estate Counsel, Nebr. Bar Assn. (pres. 1978-79, exec. coun. 1966-72, 78-87), Omaha Bus. Men's Assn. (pres. 1962, Man of Yr. 1970), Rotary Found. (trustee), Omaha Rotary Club (pres. 1992-93). General corporate, Health, Probate. Office: 10306 Regency Parkway Dr Omaha NE 68114-3708

**BURKE, TIMOTHY MICHAEL,** lawyer, educator; b. Cleve., Feb. 10, 1948; s. Ralph and Frances (Dilley) B.; m. Patricia Kathleen LaGrange, June 6, 1970; children—Nora Frances, Tara Kathleen, Michael Ralph. A.B., Xavier U., Cin., 1970; J.D., U. Cin., 1973. Bar: Ohio 1973, U.S. Dist. Ct. (so. dist.) Ohio 1979, U.S. Ct. Appeals (6th cir.) 1978, U.S. Supreme Ct. 1979. Legis. asst. to council mem. Cin. City Council, 1971-74; spl. asst. to Congressman Tom Luken, Cin., 1974, 76-77; exec. dir. Little Miami, Inc., Cin., 1975-76; prin. Manley, Burke, Lipton and Cook and predecessor, Cin., 1977—; spl. counsel to atty. gen. State of Ohio, 1978-95; law dir. Village of Lockland, Ohio, 1982—; lectr. Xavier U., 1975-78, 81, 82—, adj. asst. prof., 1983—; adj. assoc. prof. U. Cin., 1977-78, 79, dir. law enforcement tech. program, 1977-78. Bd. dirs. Tri State Air Com., 1972-80, chmn., 1976-78; chmn. land use subcom. water quality adv. com. Ohio-Ky.-Ind. Regional Council Govts., 1975-76; bd. dirs. Lower Council of Little Miami, Inc., 1976-82; mem. alumni bd. govs. Xavier U., 1970-76, 78-79, v.p., 1980-81, pres., 1981-82; candidate for U.S. Ho. of Reps. from 1st dist. Ohio, 1978; chmn. legal com. Cin. Zoo, bd. dirs., 1980-91; co-chmn. Zoo Tax Levy Campaign, 1982, 86; commr. Cin. Park Bd., 1991-94; participant Fgn. Policy Conf. for Young Am. Polit. Leaders, U.S. Dept. State, 1980; chmn. Hamilton County Bd. Elections, 1993—; exec. co-chmn. Hamilton County Democratic Party, 1982-86, 88-89, chmn., 1993—; co-chmn. Cin. Dem. Com., 1983-89, chmn., 1989-97; 1st v.p. Ohio Dem. County Chairs Assn., 1995—; internat. supr. bosnia Mcpl. Elections, 1997. Served to 1st lt. U.S. Army, 1974. Recipient service award Ohio River Valley Com. for Occupational Safety and Health, 1983, Leadership award Xavier U., 1984; named Ohio Dem. of Yr. Ohio Dem. Party, 1995. Mem. ABA, Am. Planning Assn. (legal sect.). Roman Catholic. Municipal (including bonds), General civil litigation, Land use and zoning (including planning). Home: 3560 Mcguffey Ave Cincinnati OH 45226-1919

**BURKE, WILLIAM JOSEPH,** lawyer; b. Chgo., Aug. 9, 1949. BS in Acctg., U. Ill., Chgo., 1974; JD, Ill. Inst. Tech., 1978. Bar: Ill. 1978, U.S. Dist. Ct. (no. dist.) Ill. 1978, U.S. Ct. Appeals (7th cir.) 1978, U.S. Supreme Ct. 1993. Ptnr. Demos & Burke, Chgo., 1980—. Personal injury, Product liability, General civil litigation. Office: Demos & Burke 77 W Wacker Dr Ste 600 Chicago IL 60601-1629

**BURKE, WILLIAM MILTON,** lawyer; b. Framingham, Mass., Sept. 26, 1965; s. Dominick F. and Mary E. Burke. BA, Colgate U., 1987; JD, U. Conn., 1991. Bar: Conn. 1991, U.S. Dist. Ct. Conn. 1993. Tchr. Mt. Carmel H.S., Saipan, 1987-88; law clk. City of Hartford, Conn., 1989-90, Town of West Hartford, 1990; atty. Law Offices of D.F. Burke, Fairfield, Conn., 1991—. Sec. Fairfield Zoning Bd. of Appeals, 1997—, Fairfield Dem. Com., 1993—; del. State Dem. Conv., 1994, 96, 98. Mem. ATLA, Conn. Trial Lawyer's Assn., Conn. Bar Assn. General civil litigation, Personal injury, Real property. Office: 1432 Post Rd Fairfield CT 06430-5930

**BURKE, WILLIAM TEMPLE, JR.,** lawyer; b. San Antonio, Oct. 30, 1935; s. William Temple and Adelaide H. (Raba) B.; m. Mary Sue Johnson, June 8, 1957; children: William Patrick, Michael Edmond, Karen Elizabeth. BBA, St. Mary's U., San Antonio, JD, 1961. Bar: Tex. 1961. Practice law Dallas; founder, pres. Burke Wright & Keiffer, P.C., 1985-98; of counsel Hance/Scarborough/Wright, 1998—. Pres., founder Greater Dallas Assn. KC, 1968-69; v.p., co-founder, dir. Tex. Cath. Credit Union, 1966-69, vice-chmn. bd. dirs., 1990-91 (Man of Yr., 1969-70); grand knight, trustee Dallas Coun. City 799 KC, 1964-69; v.p., dir. Dallas Optimists Club, 1965-66 (Mem. of Yr., 1966, Pres.'s award, 1968); dist. exemplar 4th degree KC, 1968-89; pres., dir. Dallas County Small Bus. Devel. Ctr., 1965-66; v.p. Dallas County Hist. Survey Com., 1966; pres. Dallas Mil. Govt. Assn., 1962-63; pres. men's club St. Patrick's Parish Roman Cath. Ch., 1963, prin. jr. H.S. Christian devel. program, 1970, chmn. scout troop com., 1976-78, chmn. fin. com., 1984-87, mem. bldg. com., 1978-87, chmn. bd. consultors, 1978-81; bd. dirs. Dallas County War on Poverty, 1965-66; trustee Montserrat Jesuit Retreat House, 1995—, treas., 1996-97; bd. dirs. The Montserrat Found., 1999—; vice-chmn. Cath. Commn. Appeal Diocese of Dallas, 1993-97. Served to 1st lt. AUS, 1958-60; capt. Res. ret. Fellow Tex. Bar Found., Coll. of State Bar Tex.; mem. ABA, Tex. Bar Assn., Dallas Bar Assn. (chmn. bankruptcy and comml. law sect. 1976-77, 86-87, courthouse liaison com. 1985—, lectr. 1985—), Am. Bankruptcy Inst., Dallas C. of C., Serra Internat. Met. Club (pres. Met. Dallas 1997-98, Outstanding Mem. award 1995), Internat. Order Alhambra (exemplar 1978-95), Phi Delta Phi (life), Tau Delta Sigma. Bankruptcy, Contracts commercial, General corporate. Home: 9751 Larchcrest Dr Dallas TX 75238-2112 Office: 2900 Renaissance Cir Dallas TX 75287-5943

**BURKES, JENNIFER PARKINSON,** lawyer; b. Mendenhall, Miss., Oct. 9, 1963; d. Roy Hubert and Melba (Layton) Parkinson; m. Dennis Jeffery Burkes, Dec. 4, 1993; 1 child, Gentry Isabella. BS, U. So. Miss., 1986; JD, U. Miss., 1992. Bar: Miss. 1992, U.S. Supreme Ct. 1997. Law clk. U.S. Ct. Appeals, 5th Cir., 1992-93; assoc. Scruggs, Millette, Bozeman & Dent, P.A., Pascagoula, Miss., 1993-94, Law Offices of Danny Cupit, Jackson, 1994-95, Scanlon, Sessums, Parker & Dallas, PLLC, Jackson, 1996—; spkr. evidence in trial practice in Miss. Nat. Bus. Inst., Jackson, 1998. Mem. ALTA, Miss. Women Lawyers Assn., Phi Kappa Phi, Kappa Delta Alumni Assn. Methodist. Personal injury, Appellate, General civil litigation. Office: Scanlon Sessums Parker & Dallas 1650 Mirror Lake Plz 2829 Lakeland Dr Jackson MS 39208-9798

**BURKETT, BRADFORD C.,** lawyer; b. Phila., Aug. 29, 1960; s. Frederick R. and Barbara E. Burkett; m. Marcia P. Borggaard, Aug. 17, 1985; children: Gillian, Brady, Kate. BA, Rutgers U., New Brunswick, N.J., 1982; JD, Rutgers U., Camden, N.J., 1985. Bar: N.Y. 1985, N.J. 1985. Assoc. Kaye Scholar Fiarman Hays & Handler, N.Y.C., 1985-94; sr. v.p., gen. counsel The Multicare Cos., Inc., Hackensack, N.J., 1994-97, Telesis Med. Mgmt., Inc., White Plains, N.Y., 1997—. Mem. ABA, Nat. Health Lawyers Assn., Assn. Bar City N.Y. Health, Mergers and acquisitions, Securities. Office: Telesis Med Mgmt Inc 777 Westchester Ave White Plains NY 10604-3520

**BURKETT, GERALD ARTHUR,** lawyer, musician; b. Oklahoma City, Apr. 23, 1939; s. Francis Gerald and Leta Carey (Weaver) B.; m. Carolyn Ruth Hicks, Aug. 7, 1960; 1 child, Debora Lynne Burkett Nutt. BA, David Lipscomb U., 1962; MA, Peabody Coll., 1967; JD, Nashville Sch. of Law, 1974. Bar: Tenn. 1975, U.S. Dist. Ct. (mid. dist.) Tenn., 1976, U.S. Ct. Appeals (6th cir.), 1977, U.S. Tax Ct., 1981, U.S. Supreme Ct. 1993. Leader Fritz's German Band, Nashville, 1972-97; pvt. practice law office Nashville, 1975—; adj. instr. Vol. State Community Coll., Gallatin, Tenn., 1979-93, Nashville State Tech. Inst., 1984-89; band leader Strohaus, 1982 World's Fair, Knoxville, 1982. Conductor of German band for commls. and concerts including Monday Night Football, 1994, Super Bowl, 1995, Oktoberfest Concert, Soldier Field, Chgo., 1995. Accordionist Charlie Rich's Bi-Centennial Album, 1976, film soundtrack Sweet Dreams, 1983. Mem. Nashville Assn. Musicians, Alliance Francaise (treas. 1985-86), Nashville Bar Assn., Tenn. Assn. of Spanish Spkg. Attys., Phi Delta Kappa (treas. 1967-68). Mem. Ch. of Christ. Avocations: travel, foreign languages. Juvenile, Criminal. Office: 211 Union St Ste 610 Nashville TN 37201-1572

**BURKETT, JOE WYLIE,** lawyer, corporate executive; b. Dallas, Aug. 24, 1945; s. Joe Wylie and Marguerite (Barnes) B.; B.A., Vanderbilt U., 1967; J.D., U. Tex., 1971; postgrad. So. Meth. U., 1990-91; MPA Harvard U., 1992, postgrad., 1992-93. Bar: Tex. 1971, D.C. 1977. Legis. aide Tex. Ho. of Reps., 1971; briefing atty. Tex. Ct. Criminal Appeals, 1971-72; law clk. U.S. Dist. Ct. (no. dist.) Tex., 1972-74; trial atty. tax div. U.S. Dept. Justice, 1974-77; with Goins & Underkofler, Dallas, 1977-80; pres., chief exec. officer JJS Inc. and Cord Enterprises, Texarkana (Ark.) and Dallas, 1980—; sec. Wason Ranch Corp., 1988, pres., 1989—. Ford Found. grantee 1970. Mem. ABA, D.C. Bar Assn., Tex. Bar Assn., Assn. Trial Lawyers Am., Tex. Trial Lawyers Assn., Ark. Malt Beverage Assn. (chmn. bd. dirs. 1986-87), Nat. Malt Beverage Wholesalers Assn. (bd. dirs. 1982-90, mem. mgmt. com. 1986-91, sec. 1987, vice chmn. 1988, acting pres. 1989, chmn. bd. dirs. 1989); mem. bd. trustees Creede Repertory Theatre. Federal civil litigation, State civil litigation. Home: 4545 Livingston Ave Dallas TX 75205-2611

**BURKETT, LAWRENCE V.,** insurance company executive. BA, U. Va., 1967, JD, 1973. Bar: Mass. 1974. V.p., assoc. gen. counsel Mass. Mut. Life Ins. Co., Springfield, 1984-88, sr. v.p., assoc. gen. counsel, 1988-92, exec. v.p., gen. counsel, 1993—. Insurance. Office: Mass Mutual Life Ins Co 1295 State St Springfield MA 01111-0002

**BURKETT, LOREEN MARAE,** lawyer; b. Summit, N.J., Jan. 30, 1964; d. Harold Edward and Shirley Adams Burkett; m. James Frank Radakovitz, Apr. 16, 1994; 1 child, Joseph Edward. BA, Albright Coll., 1985; JD, Dickinson Sch. Law, 1988. Bar: Pa. 1988, U.S. Dist. Ct. (mid. dist.) Pa. 1996. Law clk. Ct. Common Pleas, Lebanon County, Pa., 1988-89; staff atty. Ctrl. Pa. Legal Svcs., Lebanon, 1989-91; assoc. Law Office of Robert B. Keys, Esq., Lebanon, 1989-92; ptnr. Keys & Burkett, Lebanon, 1992—. Custody Clinic educator Ctrl. Pa. Legal Svcs., Lebanon, 1996—. Bd. dirs. Domestic Violence Intervention, Lebanon, 1989-95, v.p. bd. dirs., 1996. Mem. Pa. Bar Assn., Lebanon County Bar Assn. (chair young lawyers com.). Democrat. Methodist. Avocations: reading, walking, piano. Criminal, Family and matrimonial, Juvenile. Office: Keys & Burkett 250 S 8th St Lebanon PA 17042-6010

**BURKETT, TERESA MEINDERS,** lawyer; b. Okarche, Okla., Aug. 3, 1959; d. Hadley Clyde and Lois Marie (Schroeder) Meinders; m. Robert Glenn Burkett, Jan. 3, 1993. BSN, U. Okla., 1982, JD, 1985. Atty. Boone Smith Davis Hurst & Dickman, Tulsa, Okla., 1985—; pres. Hillcrest Assocs., Tulsa, Okla., 1996—. pres. Habitat for Humanity, Tulsa, 1993-94; v.p. Leadership Tulsa, 1995-96; bd. dirs. Cmty. Svc. Coun. Met. Tulsa, 1992—; mem. adv. bd. The Nature Conservancy, Okla. chpt., 1998—. Mem. Okla. Health Lawyers Assn. (pres. 1992-93), Okla. Bar Assn. (chmn. health law sect. 1996—), Mental Health Assn. Tulsa (bd. dirs. 1998—). Health, Labor. Office: Boone Smith Davis Hurst & Dickman 500 Oneok Plz 100 W 5th St Ste 500 Tulsa OK 74103-4215

**BURKEY, LEE MELVILLE,** lawyer; b. Beach, N.D., Mar. 21, 1914; s. Levi Melville and Mina Lou (Horner) B.; m. Lorraine Lillian Burghardt, June 11, 1938; 1 child, Lee Melville, III. B.A., U. Ill., 1936, M.A., 1938; J.D. with honor, John Marshall Law Sch., 1943. Bar: Ill., 1944, U.S. Dist. Ct., 1947, U.S. Ct. Appeals, 1954, U.S. Supreme Ct.; 1983; cert. secondary tchr., Ill. Tchr. Princeton Twp. High Sch., Princeton, Ill., 1937-38, Thornton Twp. High Sch., Harvey, Ill., 1938-43; atty. Office of Solicitor, U.S. Dept. Labor, Chgo., 1944-51; ptnr. Asher, Gubbins & Segall and successor firms, Chgo., 1951-94; of counsel, 1995—; lectr. bus. law Roosevelt Coll., 1949-52; chmn. bd. dirs., pres. West Suburban Fin. Corp., 1975-94. Contbr. numerous articles on lie detector evidence. Trustee, Village of La Grange, Ill., 1962-68, mayor, 1968-73, village atty., 1973-87; commr., pres. Northeastern Ill. Planning Commn., Chgo., 1969-73; mem. bd. dirs. United Ch. Christ, Bd. of Homeland Ministries, 1981-87; mem. exec. com. Cook County Coun. Govts., 1968-70; life mem. La Grange Area Hist. Soc.; bd. dirs. Better Bus. Bur. Met. Chgo., Inc., 1975-82, Plymouth Place, Inc., 1973-82; mem. exec. bd., v.p. S.W. Suburban Ctr. on Aging, 1993—. Brevet 2nd Lt. Ill. Nat. Guard, 1932. Recipient Disting. Alumnus award John Marshall Law Sch., 1973, Good Citizenship medal S.A.R., 1973, Patriot medal S.A.R., 1977, meritorious Service award Am. Legion Post 1941, 1974, Honor award LaGrange Area Hist. Soc., 1987; col. Ky., 1989. Fellow Coll. Labor and Employment Lawyers (charter); mem. ABA (coun., sect. labor and employment law 1982-86, governance officer 1986-96), Ill. Bar Assn., Chgo. Bar Assn., SAR (state pres. 1977), S.R., La Grange Country Club, Masons, Order of John Marshall, Theta Delta Chi. Mem. United Ch. of Christ. Labor. Office: 125 S Wacker Dr Chicago IL 60606-4402

**BURKHARDT, DONALD MALCOLM,** lawyer; b. N.Y.C., Jan. 21, 1936; s. Seymour and Ruby Victoria (Brownrigg) B.; m. Gail Lee Burkhardt; children: Susan Lynn McIlhenny, Steven Lee. BA, Dartmouth Coll., 1957; LLB, U. Mich., 1961. Bar: Colo. 1961, U.S. Dist. Ct. Colo. 1961, U.S. Ct. Appeals (10th cir.) 1962, U.S. Supreme Ct. 1988. Assoc. Grant, Shafroth, Toll & McHendrie, Denver, 1961-66; ptnr. Grant McHendrie, P.C., Denver, 1967-93, Inman Flynn & Biesterfeld, P.C., Denver, 1993—. Scoutmaster Boy Scouts Am., Denver, 1962-64; pres. Rangers Club, Young Am. League, Denver, 1972-76; ski patroller Nat. Ski Patrol System, Winter Park, Colo., 1967—. Mem. Colo. Bar Assn., Denver Bar Assn. Republican. Presbyterian. Avocations: sports, outdoors. Consumer commercial, Personal injury, Contracts commercial. Home: 2833 E 8th Ave Denver CO 80206-3827 Office: Inman Flynn & Biesterfeld PC 1660 Lincoln St Ste 1700 Denver CO 80264-1701 *Notable cases include: Burak vs. Gen. Am. Life Ins. Co. 836 F. 2d 1287, 10th cir., 1988; 1st Nat. Bank in Alamosa vs. Ford Motor Credit Co., 748 F Supp. 1464 Colo., 1990.*

**BURKHOLDER, JOHN ALLEN,** lawyer; b. Mansfield, Ohio, Feb. 15, 1949; s. John Herbert and Eleanor (Damoff) B.; m. Patricia Hall Townsend, June 5, 1971 (div. 1978); m. Barbara Ann Pollack, Jan 2, 1984. BA, Yale U., 1971; JD, Am. U., 1978. Bar: D.C. 1978, U.S. Dist. Ct. D.C. 1979, U.S. Ct. Appeals (D.C. cir.) 1979, Calif. 1992, U.S. Dist. (cen. dist.) Calif. 1993. Jud. law clk. D.C. Superior Ct., Washington, 1978-79; assoc. Pitts, Wike, Niklas & Bonner, Washington, 1979-80; staff counsel GSA Bd. Contract Appeals, Washington, 1980-83, dep. chief counsel, 1983-86, chief counsel, 1986-87, adminstrv. judge, 1987-88; pvt. practice, 1989—; of counsel McKenna & Cuneo, LLP, L.A., 1996—; lectr. Legal Edn. Inst. U.S. Dept. Justice, Washington, 1984-88, Fed. Publs. Inc., 1989—. Mem. ABA. Avocations: running, golf. Administrative and regulatory, Government contracts and claims, Contracts commercial. Office: McKenna & Cuneo LLP 444 S Flower St Los Angeles CA 90071-2901

**BURKYBILE, KAREN L.,** lawyer; b. Terre Haute, Ind., July 25, 1956; d. Dean V. and Wilma L. B.; m. Terry L. Hackett, Jan. 12, 1990. BS, Ind. State U., 1978; JD, So. Ill. U., 1983. Bar: Ill. 1983, U.S. Dist. Ct. (so. dist.) Ill. 1983, U.S. Dist. Ct. (ctrl. dist.) Ill. 1984. Atty. Robert L. Douglas Ltd., Robinson, Ill., 1983-84; pub. defender Clark and Edgar Counties, Paris, Marshall, Ill., 1984-91; pvt. practice Paris, Ill., 1984—. Dir. Human Resource Ctr. Paris, Ill., 1984-87; mem. pvt. industry coun. Region 23, Ill., 1988-90; exec. bd. mem. Ill. Fed. Republic Women, 1994-96, 98-99; pres. Edgar County Rep. Women, Paris, 1994-96. Mem. Ill. State Bar Assn., Edgar County Bar Assn. (pres. 1985-86), Clark County Bar Assn. (pres. 1984-85), Am. Legion Auxiliary (v.p. 1993-94, pres. 1994-95). Republican. General practice. Office: 227 West Court St Paris IL 61944-1720

**BURLAND, JAMES S.,** lawyer, lobbyist; b. LaMarque, Tex., Apr. 29, 1955; s. Peter Dennis and Elayne (Kogos) B.; m. Marilyn Rose Richardson, Oct. 12, 1991 (div.); 1 child, Matthew James. BA, La. State U., 1977, JD, 1980. Bar: La. 1981, U.S. Dist. Ct. (ea., we., and mid. dists.) La. 1991. Staff atty. La. Municipal Assn., Baton Rouge, 1979-81; asst. city/parish atty. East Baton Rouge Parish, City of Baton Rouge, 1980-83; prin. owner J.S. Burland & Assocs., Inc., Baton Rouge, 1981—; chief lobbyist, staff atty. La. Assn. Bus. and Industry, Baton Rouge, 1984-90; assoc. Adams & Reese Law Firm, Baton Rouge, 1990-93; prin. owner Polit. Affairs, Inc., 1993—; lectr. Polit. Tng. Inst., Baton Rouge, 1989-92; contract lobbyist Burlington Resources Oil and Gas Co., Riverwood Internat., Plum Creek Timber Co., others. Author: State Pac Fundraising, 1987; contbr. articles to jours. Bd. dirs. Orgn. La. Right-to-Work Com., Baton Rouge, 1984-90, Congressional Contact Network, 1988-90, Fed. Polit. Action Com., 1988-90, Southside Civic Orgn., 1992; asst. dir. La. Polit. Action Com., 1987-90. Mem. La. State Bar Assn., Assn. La. Lobbyists (pres. 1991-92), Baton Rouge Bar Assn., L.A. Assn. Builders and Contractors (dir. govt. rels. 1995-97). Republican. Avocations: sports, sports broadcasts stats. Legislative, Administrative and regulatory, Environmental. Office: Ste 203 343 3d St Baton Rouge LA 70801-1309

**BURLINGAME, JOHN HUNTER,** lawyer; b. Milw., Apr. 27, 1933; s. Leroy James and Mary Janet (Burchard) B.; m. Carolyn Elizabeth Beachley, Aug. 27, 1960 (div. Feb. 1981); children: Carolyn, Janet, Amy, Alexander; m. Dorcas Hodges, June 5, 1982. BS, U. Wis., 1960, LLB, 1963. Bar: Ohio 1964. From assoc. to ptnr. Baker & Hostetler, Cleve., 1963-82, exec. ptnr., 1982-97, ptnr., 1998—; bd. dirs. The E. W. Scripps Co. Lt. USN, 1955-59. Mem. ABA, Cleve. Bar Assn., Union Club, Shoreby Club. Republican. Presbyterian. Avocations: skiing, outdoor life. General corporate, Securities, Administrative and regulatory.

**BURLINGAME, STEPHEN LEE,** lawyer; b. Benton Harbor, Mich., July 25, 1950; s. Ralph Leroy and Ruth Alice (Ross) B.; m. Mary Miller, July 9, 1972; children: Meredith, Christopher, Timothy. BA, Andrews U., 1972; JD, U. Mich., 1976. Bar: Mich. 1977, U.S. Dist. Ct. (we. and ea. dists.) Mich. 1978, U.S. Ct. Appeals (6th cir.) 1978. Assoc. Fraser, Trebilcock, Davis & Foster, P.C., Lansing, Mich., 1977-83, ptnr., 1983—, pres., 1987-90. With U.S. Army, 1972-74. Mem. ABA, Mich. Bar Assn., Ingham County Bar Assn., Rotary. Seventh-day Adventist. Avocations: raquetball, reading, sports. Contracts commercial, Real property, General corporate. Office: Fraser Trebilcock Davis & Foster PC 1000 Michigan Nat Towers Lansing MI 48933

**BURNARD, GEORGE WILLARD,** lawyer; b. Royal Oak, Mich., Sept. 8, 1937; s. Walter Arthur and Carrie Adela (Barnes) B.; m. Constance Ann White, Nov. 24, 1962 (div. July 1971); children: Leslie Karen Rew, Lori Ann (dec.). BA, Western Mich. U., 1960; JD, Wayne State U., 1963. Bar: Mich. 1964, U.S. Supreme Ct. 1969, U.S. Dist Ct. (ea. dist.) Mich. 1990, U.S. Ct. Appeals (6th cir.) 1995. With Dean Fulkerson PC, Troy, Mich., 1981—. Pres. South Oakland Bar Assn., 1972. Mem. Oakland County Bar Assn., Million Dollar Advocates Forum. Avocations: golf, tennis. General civil litigation, Civil rights, Family and matrimonial. Home: 4364 Stonehenge Ct Troy MI 48098-4245 Office: Dean Fulkerson PC 801 W Big Beaver Rd Ste 500 Troy MI 48084-4724

**BURNBAUM, MICHAEL WILLIAM,** lawyer; b. Boston, Sept. 19, 1949; s. Jack Burnbaum. Student, U. Denver, 1967-69; BA in Internat. Studies, U. S.C., 1971; JD, Suffolk U., 1976. Bar: Mass. 1977, U.S. Dist. Ct. Mass. 1977, Fla. 1981, U.S. Ct. Appeals (5th and 11th cir.) 1981, U.S. Dist. Ct. (so. dist.) Fla. 1984, U.S. Ct. Appeals (4th cir.) 1985, U.S. Ct. Appeals (6th cir.) 1986. House counsel Bradford Novelty Co. Inc., Boston, 1976-79; asst. dist. atty. Norfolk County, Mass., 1979-81; asst. U.S. atty. U.S. Dept. Justice, Miami, Fla., 1981-85; ptnr. Bronis & Portela P.A., Miami, 1985-87; sole practice Coral Gables, Fla., 1987—. Creator TV program Eye on the Law, 1976. Pres. Key Colony Phase III Condominium Assn., Miami, 1983-85; chmn. com. to elect Shawn M. Harvey to Boston City Council, 1976. Recipient Letter of Commendation UN Office Spl. Pros. for War Crimes of Former Yugoslavia, 1995. Mem. ABA, Fla. Bar Assn., Fed. Bar Assn., Nat. Assn. Criminal Def. Lawyers, Rotary. Avocations: tennis, travel, golf. Criminal, Federal civil litigation, State civil litigation. Home: 151 Crandon Blvd Miami FL 33149-1573 Office: 240 Crandon Blvd Ste 210 Key Biscayne FL 33149-1543

**BURNETT, ARTHUR LOUIS, SR.,** judge; b. Spotsylvania County, Va., Mar. 15, 1935; s. Robert Louis and Lena Victoria (Bumbry) B.; m. Ann Lloyd, May 14, 1960; children: Darnellena, Arthur Louis II, Darryl, Darlisa, Dionne. B.A. summa cum laude, Howard U., 1957; LL.B., NYU, 1958; grad., Fed. Exec. Inst., 1978. Bar: D.C. 1958, U.S. Dist. Ct. Md. 1963, U.S. Supreme Ct. 1964. Atty. Gen.'s Honor Program atty. fraud sect. criminal div. U.S. Dept. Justice, Washington, 1958; atty. to acting dep. chief gen. crimes sect. U.S. Dept. Justice, 1960-65; spl. asst. U.S. atty., Balt. and East St. Louis, Ill., 1961-63; asst. U.S. atty. D.C., 1965-68; legal adviser, gen. counsel D.C. Dept. Met. Police, 1968-69; U.S. magistrate U.S. Dist. Ct., Washington, 1969-75; asst. gen. counsel legal adv. div. U.S. CSC, 1975-78; assoc. gen. counsel Office of Personnel Mgmt., 1979-80; U.S. magistrate U.S. Dist. Ct. D.C., 1980-87; judge Superior Ct. D.C., 1987-98, sr. judge, 1998—; faculty Fed. Jud. Center, 1970—, Nat. Jud. Coll., 1974—; judge-in-residence Children's Def. Fund, 1998—; program chmn. ann. meeting Nat. Conf. Spl. Ct. Judges, Washington, 1973, chmn. elect, acting chmn., 1974-75, chmn., 1975; program chmn. ann. meeting Nat. Council U.S. Magistrates, Williamsburg, Va., 1974, pres., 1983-84; program participant D.C. Circuit Jud. Conf., 1974, U.S. Ct. Claims Jud. Conf., 1979; adj. prof. Columbus Sch. Law, Cath. U. Am., 1997—, Cath. U., 1997—, Sch. Law Harvard U., 1998—. Mem. NYU Law Rev., 1957-58. Recipient Founders Day award NYU, 1958; Army Commendation medal, 1960; Sustained Superior Performance award U.S. Atty. Gen., 1963; Disting. Service award CSC, 1978; Meritorious Service award U.S. Office of Personnel Mgmt., 1980, Jud. award of excellence Washington Met. Trial Lawyers Assn., 1999, award of excellence Nat. Conf. State Trial Judges, 1999; Outstanding Disting. Service award Fed. Bar Assn., 1983. Mem. ABA (Franklin N. Flashner jud. award as outstanding judge on ct. of spl. jurisdiction 1985, coun. adminstrv. law and regulatory practice sect. 1987-90, liaison rep. of adminstrv. law and regulatory practice sect. to adminstrv. conf. of U.S. 1990-94, mem. JAD task force on improving opportunities for minorities 1988-97, 98—, judge Edward R. Finch Law Day USA speech award 1991, asst. sec. 1991-93, chair civil right and employment discrimination com. 1992-95, sec. adminstrv. law and regulatory practice 1993-95, chair CJS com. on criminal rules and evidence 1993-97, standing com. on substance abuse 1995—, co-chair editl. bd. Criminal Justice Mag.), Fed. Bar Assn. (sect. coord. 1987-88, chmn. fed. litigation sect. 1984-85, chmn. standing com. on U.S. magistrates, dep. chmn. sect. adminstrn. of justice 1983-84, chmn. standing com. on U.S. magistrate, chmn. sect. adminstrn. of justice 1983-84, 95-97, pres. D.C. chpt. 1984-85, chair profl. ethics com. 1991-93, Disting. Svc. award 1978, The Pres.'s award 1994), Washington Bar Assn. (Ollie Mae Cooper award 1997), Nat. Bar Assn. (chair cmty. and youth action com. jud. coun. 1995—, chair profl. ethics com., jud. coun. asst. sec., The Pres.'s award 1996), Bar Assn. D.C., D.C. Unified Bar, Am. Judicature Soc., Am. Judges Assn. (sec-treas. Prettyman-Leventhal Inn of Ct. Washington 1991-92, 1993-94, pres. 1994-95), Phi Beta Kappa, Omega Psi Phi. Office: Superior Ct DC 500 Indiana Ave NW Ste 5520 Washington DC 20001-2131

**BURNETT, E. C., III,** state supreme court justice; b. Spartanburg, S.C., Jan. 26, 1942; s. E.C. Jr. and Lucy (Byars) B.; m. Jami Grant, 1963; children: Curry, Sharon, Jeffrey. AB, Wofford Coll., 1964; JD, U. S.C., 1969. Bar: S.C. 1969. Mem. S.C. Ho. of Reps., 1973-74; probate judge Spartanburg County, 1976-80; judge family ct., 1980-81, Seventh Jud. Cir., 1981-95; assoc. justice S.C. Supreme Ct., 1995—. Elder Mt. Calvary Presbyn. Ch. Mem. ABA, S.C. Bar Assn. Home: 200 Burnett Rd Pauline SC 29374-2610 Office: PO Box 1742 180 Magnolia St Spartanburg SC 29304-1742*

**BURNETT, GARY BOYD,** lawyer, real estate consultant; b. Huntington Park, Calif., Mar. 19, 1954; s. A. Boyd Burnett and Betty J. (Koontz) Wiggins; m. Shelli Green, June 23, 1977 (div. June 1984); 1 child, Justin; m. Lisa D. Parker, May 14, 1988; children: Garrett, Kara. BA, Calif. State U., Fullerton, 1978; JD, Brigham Young U., 1980. Bar: Utah 1990, U.S. Dist. Ct. Utah 1990. Staff atty. Am. Land Devel. Assn., Washington, 1981-83; corp. counsel Preferred Equities Corp., Las Vegas, Nev., 1983-84, Real Corp., Las Vegas, 1984-85; real estate cons. Las Vegas, 1985-86; corp. counsel Ridgeview Pk., Inc., Las Vegas, 1986—; real estate broker Las Vegas, 1986—; corp. counsel S.W. Oasis Constrn., Inc., Las Vegas, 1990—. Contbr. articles to profl. jours. Del. Rep. State Ctrl. Com., Sacramento, Calif., 1976; coach Green Valley Little League, Henderson, Nev., 1992; leader Boy Scouts Am., Henderson, 1992. Mem. ABA, Assn. Trial Lawyers Am. Mem. LDS Ch. Avocations: running, golf, basketball. Real property, General corporate, Construction. Office: 8275 S Eastern Ave Ste 200 Las Vegas NV 89123-2545

**BURNETT, JAMES F.,** lawyer; b. Easton, Pa., Apr. 4, 1941; s. James F. and Helen G. B.; m. Patricia Louise Pease, June 18, 1966; childre: Tracey A., James S., Megan E. BA, East Stroudsburg U., 1966; JD, Georgetown U., 1969. Bar: Del. 1969. Ptnr. Potter, Anderson & Corroon LLP, Wilmington, Del., 1966—. Mem. Wilmington Club, Rodney Square Club. General civil litigation, General corporate, Mergers and acquisitions. Home: Potter Anderson & Corroon LLP PO Box 951 Wilmington DE 19899-0951

**BURNETT, RALPH GEORGE,** lawyer; b. Milw., Apr. 13, 1956; s. Ralph G. and Joan T. Burnett; m. Eileen M. Gallagher, May 31, 1980; children: Christopher, Jessica, Thomas, Sarah, Andrew. BA, Marquette U., 1978; JD, U. Wis., 1981. Bar: Wis. 1981, U.S. Dist. Ct. (ea. and we. dists.) Wis. 1981, U.S. Ct. Appeals (7th cir.) 1981, U.S. Dist. Ct. (we. dist.) Mich. 1997, U.S. Ct. Appeals (6th cir.) 1997. Law clk. U.S. Ct. Appeals 7th Cir., Chgo., 1981-82; lawyer Smith & O'Neil, Milw., 1983-84, Trowbridge, Planert & Schaefer, Green Bay, Wis., 1985-86, Liebmann, Conway, Olejniczak & Jerry, S.C., Green Bay, 1986—; officer Robert J. Parins Inn of Ct., Green Bay, 1997—. Co-author: Wisconsin Trial Practice, 1999. Mem. allocations com. United Way N.E. Wis., Green Bay, 1988-91; bd. mem. paralegal program N.E. Wis. Tech. Coll., Green Bay, 1993—; bd. mem. parish coun. St. Mary's Ch., De Pere, 1997—; bd. mem. Cerebral Palsy, Green Bay, 1989-92; bd. mem. steering com. Notre Dame Sch., De Pere, 1998—. Mem. ABA, State Bar Wis. (bd. dirs., v.p. litigation sect. 1996—), Wis. Acad. Trial Lawyers (bd. dirs. 1995—), Def. Rsch. Inst., Optimist Internat. Avocations: woodworking, athletics. General civil litigation, Personal injury, Product liability. Home: 806 Lawton Pl De Pere WI 54115-2623 Office: Liebmann Conway Olejniczak & Jerry SC 231 S Adams St Green Bay WI 54301-4513

**BURNETTE, HARRY FORBES,** lawyer; b. Chattanooga, Sept. 28, 1947; s. Harry G. and Ruth (Forbes) B.; m. Carolyn G. Gash, Sept. 5, 1970; children: Harry Eric, Chad Forbes, Heather Carolyn. BA, Maryville Coll., 1970; JD, U. Tenn., 1973. Bar: Tenn. 1973, U.S. Dist. Ct. (ea. dist.) Tenn. 1973, U.S. Ct. Appeals (6th cir.) 1977. Assoc., then ptnr. Humphrey, Hutcheson & Mosley, Chattanooga, 1973-78; ptnr. Robinson, Stanley & Burnette, Chattanooga, 1978-83, Burnette Dobson and Hardeman, Chattanooga, 1983—. Mem. ABA, Tenn. Trial Lawyers Assn. (bd. govs. 1989-91), Chattanooga Trial Lawyers Assn. (bd. dirs. 1981-85), Fed. Bar Assn. (pres. Chattanooga chpt. 1979-80), Nat. Employment Lawyers Assn. (Tenn. dir. 1988-89), Assn. Trial Lawyers Am. Democrat. Presbyterian. General civil litigation, Labor, Personal injury. Home: 5117 Mountain Creek Rd Chattanooga TN 37415-1605 Office: Burnette Dobson & Hardeman 713 Cherry St Chattanooga TN 37402-1910

**BURNETTE, JAMES THOMAS,** lawyer; b. Stuart, Va., Apr. 7, 1959; s. Edwin Lee and Marye Joanne (Minter) B.; m. Sarah Katherine Kelly, Dec. 2, 1989; children: Sarah Elizabeth, Thomas Pullen. BS, Campbell U., 1981; JD, Wake Forest U., 1984. Bar: N.C. 1985. Atty. Womble Carlyle Sandridge & Rice, Winston-Salem, N.C., 1985-86; ptnr. Edmundson & Burnette, Oxford, N.C., 1986—; atty. City of Oxford, 1995—; pres. 9th Jud. Dist. Bar Assn., 1998-99. Mem. ATLA, Ninth Jud. Dist. Bar Assn. (pres. 1999), N.C. Acad. Trial Lawyers, N.C. State Bar, N.C. Bar Assn., South Granville Country Club (bd. dirs.), Thorndale Country Club, Capital City Club. Episcopalian. Avocations: golf, traveling, reading. General civil litigation, Criminal, Personal injury. Home: 4129 Salem Farm Rd Oxford NC 27565-9199 Office: Edmundson & Burnette LLp 106 Main St Oxford NC 27565-3319

**BURNETTE, RALPH EDWIN, JR.,** lawyer; b. Lynchburg, Va., Sept. 25, 1953; s. Ralph Edwin and Carlease (Samuels) B. BA, Coll. William & Mary, 1975, JD, 1978. Bar: Va. 1978, U.S. Dist. Ct. (we. dist.) Va., U.S. Ct. Appeals (4th cir.). Assoc. Edmunds & Williams, Lynchburg, 1978-83, ptnr., 1983—; adj. prof. law Coll. William and Mary, 1996—. Deacon Peakland Bapt. Ch., Lynchburg, 1983-86; pres. Kaleidoscope Festival, Lynchburg, 1985, Lynchburg Symphony Orch., 1989-91; bd. dirs. Centra Health, Inc., 1987-97, United Way Cen. Va., 1989-90, Amazement Sq. Children's Mus. Mem. Va. Bar Assn., Va. State Bar (pres. 1993-94, pres. young lawyers conf. 1985, chmn. com. on alternative dispute resolution 1985-89, mem. bar coun., 1986-95, vice chmn. standing com. on legal ethics 1986-88, chmn. com. on long range planning 1988-91, mem. exec. com. 1990-95), Lynchburg Bar Assn. (pres. 1991-92), Va. Trial Lawyers Assn., Va. Assn. Def. Attys., Def. Rsch. Inst. Avocations: golf, music, boating. Federal civil litigation, State civil litigation, Insurance. Home: PO Box 958 Lynchburg VA 24505-0958 Office: Edmunds & Williams 800 Main St Ste 400 Lynchburg VA 24504-1533

**BURNETTE, SARAH KATHERINE,** lawyer; b. Chapel Hill, N.C., May 28, 1959; d. David Lee and Sarah Pullen Kelly; m. James Thomas Burnette, Dec. 2, 1989; children: Sarah Elizabeth, Thomas Pullen. BA, Wake Forest U., 1981, JD, 1984. Bar: N.C. 1984, U.S. Dist. Ct. (ea. and mid. dists.) N.C. 1984, U.S. Ct. Appeals (4th cir.) 1988. Law clk. to hon. Eugene H. Phillips N.C. Ct. Appeals, 1984-85; assoc. Ivey, Ivey & Donahue, Greensboro, N.C., 1985-87, Craige, Brawley, Liipfert & Ross, Winston-Salem, N.C., 1987-91; law clk. to hon. A. Thomas Small U.S. Bank Judge E.D.N.C., 1991-92, 95; assoc. Edmundson & Burnette LLP, Oxford, N.C., 1994—; sec. N.C. State Bd. Elections, 1997—; bd. dirs. Centura Bank, Oxford, N.C. Mem., bd. dirs., Kerr-Vance Acad., Henderson, N.C., 1998. General civil litigation, Family and matrimonial, Bankruptcy. Office: Edmundson & Burnette LLP 106-108 Main St Oxford NC 27565-0428

**BURNETTE, SUSAN LYNN,** lawyer; b. Sylva, N.C., Nov. 20, 1955; d. William M. and Mary (McGrady) B.; m. Mark Howard Morey, June 2, 1984; children: Barbara Elizabeth Morey, Marianne McGrady Morey. Student, Institut d'Etudes Politiques, Paris, 1974-75; BA, U. S.C., 1975, BS, 1976; JD, U. Va., 1979. Bar: Va. 1979, S.C. 1979, Tex. 1980, U.S. Dist. Ct. (no. dist.) Tex. 1980, U.S. Ct. Appeals (5th cir.) 1984, U.S. Tax Ct. 1985; bd. cert. estate planning and probate law Tex. Bd. of Legal Specialization. Ptnr. Whittenburg, Whittenburg & Schachter, Amarillo, Tex., 1983-90; shareholder Conant Whittenburg Whittenburg & Schachter, P.C., Amarillo, 1991-95, Conant Whittenburg French & Schachter, P.S.C., Amarillo, 1995-99, Whittenburg, Whittenburg & Schachter, P.C., Amarillo, 1999—; lectr. in field. Mem. ABA, ATLA, Tex. Bar Assn. (dist. 13A grievance com. pres. 1994-95, coun. sec. 1999—, course dir. Advanced Tax Law Course, 1999), S.C. Bar Assn., Va. Bar Assn., Tex. Acad. Probate and Trust Counsel, Amarillo Bar Assn., Amarillo Area Estate Planing Counsel. Estate planning, Probate, General civil litigation. Home: 2709 Sunlite St Amarillo TX 79106-6113 Office: Conant Whittenburg French & Schachter 1010 S Harrison St Amarillo TX 79101-3426

**BURNHAM, JIM,** lawyer; b. Springfield, Ohio, Dec. 14, 1940; s. Martin Thomas and Virginia Francis Burnham; m. Diane Cecilia DeClerk, May 23, 1970; children: Anne, Amy. BA, U. Dallas, Irving, Tex., 1965; JD, So. Meth. U., 1968. BAr: Tex. 1968, U.S. Dist. Ct. (no., so., ea. and we. dists.) Tex. 1968, U.S. Ct. Appeals (5th cir.) 1975, U.S. Tax Ct. 1989, U.S. Supreme Ct. 1968. Chief felony prosecutor Dallas County Grand Jury, Dallas, 1978-82, Dallas County Dist. Atty.'s Office, Dallas, 1978-85; sole practitioner Dallas, 1985—; bd. dirs. Colonial Bank, Dallas. Pres. St. Thomas More Soc., dallas, 1993; bd. dirs. Big Bros. and Sisters Orgn., Dallas, 1984-85. Fellow Tex. Bar Found.; mem. Dallas Bar Assn. (grants com. 1998, pres. 1996, bd. dirs. 1988-97); Nat. Assn. Criminal Def. Lawyers, Tex. Criminal Def. Lawyers Assn., Salesmanship Club of Dallas, Serra Club of Dallas. Avocations: basketball, history. Criminal. Office: Ste 515 16116 N Central Expy Dallas TX 75206

**BURNISON, BOYD EDWARD,** lawyer; b. Arnolds Park, Iowa, Dec. 12, 1934; s. Boyd William and Lucile (Harnden) B.; m. Mari Amaral; children: Erica Lafore, Alison Katherine. BS, Iowa State U., 1957; JD, U. Calif., Berkeley, 1961. Bar: Calif. 1962, U.S. Supreme Ct. 1971, U.S. Dist. Ct. (no. dist.) Calif. 1962, U.S. Ct. Appeals (9th cir.) 1962, U.S. Dist. Ct. (ea. dist.) Calif. 1970, U.S. Dist. Ct. (ctrl. dist.) Calif., 1992. Dep. counsel Yolo County, Calif., 1962-65; of counsel Davis and Woodland (Calif.) Unified Sch. Dists., 1962-65; assoc. Steel & Arostegui, Marysville, Calif., 1965-66, St. Sure, Moore & Hoyt, Oakland, 1966-70; ptnr. St. Sure, Moore, Hoyt & Sizoo, Oakland and San Francisco, 1970-75; v.p. Crosby, Heafey, Roach & May, P.C., Oakland, 1975—, also bd. dirs. Adviser Berkeley YMCA, 1971—; adviser Yolo County YMCA, 1962-65, bd. dirs. 1965; bd. dirs. Easter Seal Soc. Crippled Children and Adults of Alameda County, Calif., 1972-75, Moot Ct. Bd., U. Calif., 1960-61; trustee, sec., legal counsel Easter Seal Found., Alameda County, 1974-79, hon. trustee, 1979—; bd. dirs. East Bay Conservation Corps, 1997—. Fellow ABA Found. (life); mem. ABA (labor rels. and employment law sect., equal employment law com. 1972—), Nat. Conf. Bar Pres.'s, State Bar Calif. (spl. labor counsel 1981-84, labor and employment law sect. 1982—), Alameda County Bar Assn. (chmn. memberships and directory com. 1973-74, 80, chmn. law office econs. com. 1975-77, assn. dir. 1981-85, pres., 1984, vice chmn. bench bar liaison com. 1983, chmn. 1984, Disting. Svc. award 1987), Alameda County Bar Found. (bd. dirs. 1993-95), Yolo County Bar Assn. (sec. 1965), Yuba Sutter Bar Assn., Bar Assn. San Francisco (labor law sect.), Indsl. Rels. Rsch. Assn., Sproul Assoc. Boalt Hall Law Sch. U. Calif. Berkeley, Iowa State Alumni Assn., Order Knoll, Round Hill Country Club, Rotary (Paul Harris fellow), Pi Kappa Alpha, Phi Delta Phi. Democrat. Labor. Home: PO Box 743 2300 Caballo Ranchero Dr Diablo CA 94528 Office: Crosby Heafey Roach & May 1999 Harrison St Ste 2300 Oakland CA 94612-3520

**BURNS, B. DARREN,** lawyer; b. Balt., Mar. 8, 1964; s. Bruce C. and Barbara (Merson) B.; m. Jennifer Duffy, July 2, 1994; children: Callie Elizabeth, Duffy Patrick. BA in English, Hampden Sydney Coll., 1986; JD, Coll. William & Mary, 1990. Bar: Md. 1991, U.S. Dist. Ct. Md., 1991, U.S. Cir. Ct. (4th cir.) 1992. Law clerk Cir. Ct. Anne Arundel County, Md., 1990-91; assoc. atty. Shapiro and Olander, Balt., Annapolis, Md., 1992-94; staff atty. Anne Arundel County Pub. Schs., Annapolis, 1994—. Class agent Severn Sch., Severna Park, Md., 1983—. Mem. Md. State Bar Assn., Md. Sch. Bd. Attys. Assn., Edn. Law Assn., Anne Arundel Bar Assn., Annapolis Touchdown Club (pres. 1999—). Education and schools, General civil litigation, Construction. Home: 612 Pin Oak Rd Severna Park MD 21146-3607 Office: Anne Arundel County Pub Schs 2644 Riva Rd Annapolis MD 21401-7305

**BURNS, BERNARD JOHN, III,** public defender; b. Alexandria, Va., Apr. 28, 1956; s. Bernard John and Mary Theresa (O'Malley) B.; m. Pamela Sue Endres, June 9, 1990; 1 child, Kristie Keener. BA in Journalism, U. Iowa, 1982, JD, 1984. Bar: Iowa 1985, U.S. Dist. Ct. (so. dist.) Iowa 1987, U.S. Supreme Ct. 1989, U.S. Ct. Appeals (8th cir.) 1992. Asst. appellate defender Iowa Appellate Defender, Des Moines, 1985-94; asst. pub. defender Des Moines Adult Pub. Defender, 1994-99; asst. fed. defender Office of Fed. Defender, Des Moines, 1999—. Bd. mem. Met. Arts Alliance Greater Des Moines, 1996—, pres.-elect, 1999; chmn. Jazz in July Planning Com., Des Moines, 1997; keyboard player Goodnight Dallas. Mem. Iowa Pub. Defenders Assn. (pres. 1991-99), Iowa Criminal and Juvenile Justice Planning Commn., Phi Beta Kappa. Avocations: composer, actor, writer, Tae Kwon Do instructor, musician. Office: Fed Defender 300 Walnut St Ste 295 Des Moines IA 50309-2258

**BURNS, BRIAN DOUGLAS,** lawyer, educator; b. Johnson City, N.Y., Jan. 25, 1963; s. John A. and Barbara Burns; m. Elizabeth Ann Lindell, Aug. 27, 1988; children: Anthony, Kevin, Margaret. BA, Syracuse U., 1985; JD cum laude, Suffolk U., 1991. Bar: N.Y. 1992. Asst. dist. atty. Otsego County Dist. Atty.'s Office, Cooperstown, N.Y., 1992-97, county ct., family ct., and surrogate judge, 1997; pros. City of Oneonta, 1995-97; sch. atty. Otsego No. Catskill Bd. Coop. Edn. Svcs., Stanford, N.Y., 1998—; pvt. practice Oneonta, N.Y., 1992—; adj. prof. Hartwick Coll., Oneonta, N.Y., 1996-97; creator crime victim advocate program, dir. Oneonta City Ct., 1996-97. Contbr. articles to profl. jours. Bd. dirs. YMCA, Oneonta, 1993-98; mem. Otsego County Rep. Com., 1998; coach Oneonta Youth Soccer, 1998; mem. Friends of Pine Lake, 1993—. Recipient Coord.'s award Otsego County Stop DWI, 1997, Cert. of Appreciation Legal Soc. Soc. Mid.-N.Y., 1997, award U.S. Def. Logistics Agy., 1991. Mem. Elks. Education and schools, State civil litigation, Criminal. Office: 6 Ford Ave Oneonta NY 13820-1818

**BURNS, CASSANDRA STROUD,** prosecutor; b. Lynchburg, Va., May 22, 1960; d. James Wesley and Jeanette Lou (Garner) Stroud; m. Stephen Burns; children: Leila Jeanette, India Veronica. BA, U. Va., 1982; JD, N.C. Cen. U., 1985. Bar: Va. 1986, N.J. 1986, U.S. Dist. Ct. (ea. dist.) Va. 1987, U.S. Ct. Appeals (4th cir.) 1987, U.S. Bankruptcy Ct. (ea. dist.) Va. 1987; cert. in criminal law. Law clk. Office Atty. Gen. State of Va., Richmond, summer 1984; law intern Office Dist. Atty. State of N.C., Durham, 1985; staff atty. Tidewater Legal Aid Soc., Chesapeake, Va., 1987-89; asst. atty. Commonwealth of Va., Petersburg, 1989-90; assoc. atty. Bland and Stroud, Petersburg, 1990; asst. pub. defender City of Petersburg, 1990-91; Commonwealth's atty. City of Petersburg, Va., 1991—; founder BED Task Force on Babies Exposed to Drugs, 1991, Buddies of Petersburg Program, 1997. Sec. Chesapeake Task Force Coun. on Youth Svcs., 1987-89; ch. directress and organist; mem. NAACP; chair Petersburg-Dinwiddie Cmty. Criminal Justice Bd. Mem. Va. Bar Assn. (mem. coun. 1993—), Old Dominion Bar Assn., Va. Assn. Commonwealth Attys. (bd. dirs., mem. coun. 1993—), Legal Svcs. Corp. Va. (bd. dirs.), Nat. Bd. Trial Advocacy (cert.), Soutside Va. Legal Aid Soc. (bd. dirs.), Petersburg Bar Assn., Nat. Black Prosecutors Assn. (regional dir.), Petersburg Jaycees, Order Eastern Star, Peterburg C. of C., Kiwanis, Internat., Buddies Club, Phi Alpha Delta, Alpha Kappa Alpha. Democrat. Baptist. Avocations: piano, organ, volleyball, needlework, pets. Home: 326 N Park Dr Petersburg VA 23805-2442 Office: Commonwealth's Atty 39 Bollingbrook St Petersburg VA 23803-4568

**BURNS, DENIS C.,** lawyer; b. St. Louis, Oct. 10, 1944; s. Clement E. and Elenore L. B.; m. Mary Ellen Vournas, Nov. 4, 1972; children: Brian, Daniel. JD, St. Louis U., 1969; BSBA, Marquette U., 1966. Bar: Mo. 1969; U.S. Dist. Ct. (so. dist. Ill.) 1996. Spl. agt. FBI, Mobile, Ala., 1969-72; atty. St. Louis Pub. Def., 1972; ptnr. Godfrey, Vandover and Burns, Inc., St. Louis, 1972—. Recipient Lon O. Hocker Meml. Trial Lawyer award Mo. Bar Found., 1977. Mem. Am. Bd. Trial Advocates, Internat. Assn. Def. Counsel, Mo. State Bar Assn. Fed. Bar Assn. Home: 12403 Cedar Moor Dr Saint Louis MO 63131-3012 Office: Godfrey Vandover and Burns Inc 720 Olive St Saint Louis MO 63101-2338

**BURNS, ELLEN BREE,** federal judge; b. New Haven, Conn., Dec. 13, 1923; d. Vincent Thomas and Mildred Bridget (Bannon) Bree; m. Joseph Patrick Burns, Oct. 8, 1955 (dec.); children: Mary Ellen, Joseph Bree, Kevin James. BA, Albertus Magnus Coll., 1944, LLD (hon.), 1974; LLB, Yale U., 1947; LLD (hon.), U. New Haven, 1981, Sacred Heart U., 1986, Fairfield U., 1991. Bar: Conn. 1947. Dir. legis. legal svcs. State of Conn., 1949-73; judge Conn. Cir. Ct., 1973-74, Conn. Ct. of Common Pleas, 1974-76, Conn. Superior Ct., 1976-78; judge U.S. Dist. Ct. Conn., New Haven, 1978—, chief judge, 1988-92, sr. judge, 1992—. Trustee Fairfield U., 1978-85, Albertus Magnus Coll., 1985—. Recipient John Carroll of Carrollton award John Barry Council K.C., 1973, Judiciary award Conn. Trial Lawyers Assn., 1978, Cross Pro Ecclesia et Pontifice, 1981, Law Rev. award U. Conn. Law Rev., 1987, Judiciary award Conn. Bar Assn., 1987, Raymond E. Baldwin Pub. Svc. award Bridgeport Law Sch., 1992. Mem. ABA, Am. Bar Found., New Haven County Bar Assn. Roman Catholic. Office: US Dist Ct 141 Church St New Haven CT 06510-2030

**BURNS, GEORGE F.,** lawyer; b. Boston, Oct. 4, 1947; s. George (dec.) and BridgetBurns O'Keefe; m. Elizabeth A. Burns; children: Michael, Abigail. BS in Internat. Affairs, Georgetown U., 1969; JD, NYU, 1972. Bar: Maine, N.Y. Assoc. Nixon Hargrave Devans & Doyle, Rochester, N.Y., 1973-78; ptnr. Jensen Baird Gardner & Henry, Portland, Maine, 1978-80, Burns Ray & DeLano, P.A., 1980—; mem. Main Securities Law Revision Com., 1978-81. Contbr. articles to profl. jours. Mem., chmn. Town Coun., Falmouth, Maine, 1981-83; mem. Falmouth Charter Rev. Commn., 1987, 97; bd. dirs. LARK Soc. for Chamber Music, 1980-97, pres., 1993-97; trustee Salt Mag., 1991-93; bd. dirs. Spurwink Inst. and the Spurwink Sch., 1997—; pres. Spurwink Sch., 1997—. Fellow Am. Bar Found.; mem. ABA (sects. on litigation and bus.), Maine State Bar Assn., Cumberland County Bar Assn., Am. Arbitration Assn. (arbitrator, comml. panel). Office: Burns Ray & DeLano PO Box 7486 193 Middle St Portland ME 04112-7486

**BURNS, JAMES B.,** prosecutor; b. Quincy, Ill., Sept. 21, 1945; married; 3 children. BA in History, Northwestern U., 1967, JD, 1971. Former profl. basketball player Chgo. Bulls, Dallas Chaparrals; asst. U.S. atty., then dep. chief and chief criminal litigation divsn. U.S. Dept. Justice, Chgo., 1971-78; assoc. Isham, Lincoln & Beale, Chgo., 1978-80, ptnr., 1980-88; ptnr. Keck, Mahin & Cate, Chgo., 1988-93; U.S. atty. for no. dist. Ill. U.S. Dept. Justice, Chgo., 1993-97; pvt. practice Sibley & Austin, Chgo., 1997—. Bd. trustees Northwestern U., Evanston, Ill., 1981-83; Dem. candidate for lt. gov. State of Ill., 1990. Office: Sibley & Austin 1 First Natl Plz Ste 4700 Chicago IL 60603-2003

**BURNS, JAMES M.,** federal judge; b. Nov. 24, 1924. BA in Bus. Adminstrn., U. Portland, 1947; JD cum laude, Loyola U., Chgo., 1950. Pvt. practice Portland, 1950-52; dist. atty. Harney County, Oreg., 1952-56; assoc. Black, Kendall, Tremaine, Boothe and Higgins, Portland, 1956-60; ptnr. Beason, Whitely McCleanan and Burns, 1960-66; judge Oreg. Cir. Ct., Multnomah County, 1966-72; mem. faculty Nat. Jud. Coll., 1972—; judge U.S. Dist. Ct. Oreg., Portland, 1972-89, chief judge, 1979-84, sr. judge, 1989—; Mem. Oreg. Criminal Law Revision Commn., 1967-72; chmn. continuing legal edn. com. Oreg. State Bar, 1965-66; faculty advisor Nat. Jud. Coll., 1971. Mem. Oreg. Cir. Judges Assn. (pres. 1967-70), U.S. Jud. Conf. (com. on adminstrn. of probation system 1978-87). Address: U S District 807 US Courthouse 1000 SW 3rd Ave Portland OR 97204-2937*

**BURNS, MARK GARDNER,** lawyer; b. Aug. 13, 1952; s. Robert H. and Helen Pauline (Childers) B.; m. Jane Clarke Hobbs, May 18, 1985. BA, U. Vt., 1975; JD, Gonzaga U., 1979. Bar: Mo. 1979, Ill. 1980, U.S. Dist. Ct. (we. dist.) Mo., U.S. Dist. Ct. (ea. dist.) Mo. 1980. Ptnr. Burns, Marshall & Burns, Clayton, Mo., 1979—. Mem. ABA, Mo. Bar Assn. Avocations: flying, skiing, backpacking. Insurance, Personal injury, State civil litigation. Home: 1109 Westmoor Pl Saint Louis MO 63131-1320 Office: Burns Marshall & Burns 7710 Carondelet Ave Saint Louis MO 63105-3312

**BURNS, MARSHALL SHELBY,** arbitrator, lawyer, retired judge; b. Cleve., Jan. 29, 1931; s. Marshall Shelby and Fairybelle (Moses) B.; m. Blanche Marie Coleman, Jan. 28, 1953; children: William M., Brian M. AA, Flint (Mich.) Jr. Coll., 1957; BA, U. Mich., Flint, 1972; JD, Thomas M. Cooley Law Sch., 1979; LLM, Wayne State U., 1984; grad., Nat. Jud. Coll., 1985. Bar; Mich. 1980, U.S. Dist. Ct. (ea. and we. dists.) Mich. 1980, U.S. Tax Ct. 1980, U.S. Supreme Ct. 1980. Tax supr. City of Flint, 1965-69; indsl. recreation adminstr. IMA, Flint, 1969-75; dir. personnel and labor relations Flint Gen. Hosp., 1975-76; asst. dir. personnel dept. pub. health State of Mich., Lansing, 1976-78, judge adminstrv. law, 1978-96; gen. counsel Greater Lansing Urban League, 1983—; arbitrator Fed. Mediation and Conciliation Svc., Washington, 1983—, Better Bus. Bur., 1983—, Am. Arbitration Assn., 1983—; faculty advisor Nat. Jud. Coll., 1986. Mem. exec. bd. Tall Pine Counsel Boy Scouts Am., Flint, 1970-75; bd. dirs. Greater Lansing Urban League, 1982-84, Vol. Action Ctr. of Greater Lansing, 1982-84. Served to pvt. 1st class U.S. Army, 1953-55. Mem. NAACP, Am. Arbitration Assn. (arbitrator), Nat. Bar Assn., Indsl. Rels. Rsch. Assn., Rotary (v.p. East Lansing club 1990-91), Masons, Phi Alpha Delta (justice, treas. 1978-80), Alpha Phi Alpha (chpt. pres. 1989). Office: 417 N Pine St Lansing MI 48933-1025

**BURNS, MARVIN GERALD,** lawyer; b. Los Angeles, July 3, 1930; s. Milton and Belle (Cytron) B.; m. Barbara Irene Fisher, Aug. 23, 1953; children: Scott Douglas, Jody Lynn, Bradley Frederick. BA, U. Ariz., 1951; JD, Harvard U., 1954. Bar: Calif. 1955. Bd. dirs. Inner City Arts for Inner City Children. With AUS, 1955-56. Clubs: Beverly Hills Tennis, Sycamore Park Tennis. General civil litigation, Land use and zoning (including planning), Real property. Home: 10350 Wilshire Blvd Ph 4 Los Angeles CA 90024-4734 Office: 4th Fl 10390 Santa Monica Blvd Los Angeles CA 90025-5058 *I believe that hard work in its time and place, play in its time and place, love, understanding and practice of the golden rule at all times, in all places, a firm belief in truth and honesty and that there is no better land, no better system, no better life than our imperfect, necessary to improve, America, leads to personal fulfillment and a better life for all.*

**BURNS, PAUL EDWARD,** lawyer, educator; b. Bridgeport, Conn., Sept. 9, 1959; s. Anthony Edward and Theresa (Roberti) B.; m. Christine Ann Pennington, June 17, 1989. BS, Boston Coll., 1981, JD, 1984. Bar: Conn. 1984, Mass. 1986, D.C. 1991, N.Y. 1991, U.S. Dist. Ct. Conn. 1984, U.S. Dist. Ct. Mass. 1986, U.S. Ct. Appeals (2d cir.) 1988, U.S. Dist. Ct. (so. dist.) N.Y. 1991, U.S. Supreme Ct. 1990. Assoc. atty. Lovejoy, Hefferan, Rimer & Cuneo, Norwalk, Conn., 1984-85, LeBoeuf, Lamb, Leiby & MacRae, Boston, N.Y.C., 1985-87; prin. Trager & Trager, P.C., Fairfield, Conn., 1987—; adj. inst. law Fairfield U., 1992—, Norwalk (Conn.) Community Coll., 1990—; lectr. in field. Contbr. articles to profl. jours. Recipient Excellence in Torts award Am. Juris prudence, 1982. Mem. ABA, Conn. Bar Assn., Greater Bridgeport Bar Assn. Federal civil litigation, Bankruptcy, Banking. Office: Trager & Trager PC 253 Post Rd W Westport CT 06880-4737

**BURNS, RICHARD GORDON,** retired lawyer, writer, consultant; b. Stockton, Calif., May 15, 1925; s. Earl Gordon and Alberta Viola (Whale) B.; m. Eloise Estelle Beil, June 23, 1951 (div. May 25, 1985); children: Kenneth Charles, Donald Gordon. AA, U. Calif., Berkeley, 1948; AB, Stanford U., 1949, JD, 1951. Atty. Clausen & Burns, San Francisco, 1951-61; pvt. practice Corte Madera, Calif., 1961-86; cons. Wyo. Pacific Oil Co., L.A., 1986—; pub. Good Book Pub., Kihei, Hawaii, 1991—. Author (As Dick B.): New Light on Alcoholism: God, Sam Shoemaker and A.A., 1999, The Akron Genesis of Alcoholics Anonymous, 1998, (with Bill Pittman) Courage To Change, 1998, Anne Smith's Journal, 1998, Dr. Bob and His Library, 1998, The Good Book and The Big Book: AA's Roots in the Bible, 1998, The Oxford Group and Alcoholics Anonymous, 1998, That Amazing Grace, 1996, The Books Early AAs Read for Spiritual Growth, 1998, Good Morning! Quiet Time, Morning Watch, Meditation, and Early A.A., 1998; Turning Point: A History of Early A.A.'s Spiritual Roots and Successes, 1997, Hope!: The Story of Geraldine D., 1998, Utilizing A.A.'s Spiritual Roots for Recovery Today, 1999, The Golden Text of A.A., 1999; case editor Stanford Law Rev., 1950. Dir. Almonte Sanitary Bd., Marin County, Calif., 1962-64; v.p./sec. Lions Club, Corte Madera, 1961-64; pres. Almonte Improvement Club, Mill Valley, Calif., 1960, Cmty. Ch., Mill Valley, 1971, C. of C., Corte Madera, 1972, Corte Madera Ctr. Merchant Co., 1975, Redwoods Retirement Ctr., Mill Valley, 1980. Sgt. U.S. Army, 1943-46. Mem. Am. Hist. Assn., Authors Guild, Maui Writers Guild, Christian Assn. for Psychol. Studies, Phi Beta Kappa. Avocations: travel, Bible study, swimming. Estate planning, General practice, Non-profit and tax-exempt organizations. Office: PO Box 837 Kihei HI 96753-0837

**BURNS, RICHARD OWEN,** lawyer; b. Bklyn., Nov. 16, 1942; s. James I. and Ida (Shore) B.; m. Lynda Gail Birnbaum, Dec. 24, 1967; children: Marc Adam, Lisa Ann, Susan Danielle. BS, Wilkes Coll., 1964; JD, Bklyn. Law Sch., 1967. Bar: N.Y. 1967, U.S. Dist. Ct. (so. dist.) N.Y. 1969, U.S. Dist. Ct. (ea. dist.) N.Y. 1979. Assoc. Clune & O'Brien, Mineola, N.Y., 1967-73, Clune, Burns, White & Nelson, Harrison, N.Y., 1973-78; ptnr. Schurr & Burns, P.C., Spring Valley, N.Y., 1978-98; pvt. practice, 1998—. Bd. dirs. Rockland County unit Am. Cancer Soc., West Nyack, N.Y., 1979-85, 86-92, pres., 1981-83; bd. dirs. Hudson Valley Health System Agy., Sterling Park, N.Y., 1979, Vets. Meml. Assn., Congers, N.Y., 1980-86; mem. Wilkes U. Coun., Wilkes-Barre, Pa., 1995—. Recipient Reese D. Jones award Wilkes Coll. Jr. C. of C., 1964. Mem. Rockland County Bar Assn., N.Y. State Bar Assn., N.Y. State Trial Lawyers Assn. Democrat. Jewish. Personal injury, Labor, State civil litigation. Home: 140 Waters Edge Congers NY 10920-2622 Office: 500 Chestnut Ridge Rd Chestnut Ridge NY 10977-5646

**BURNS, RICHARD RAMSEY,** lawyer; b. Duluth, Minn., May 3, 1946; s. Herbert Morgan and Janet (Strobel) B.; Jennifer, Brian; m. Elizabeth Murphy, June 15, 1984. BA with distinction, U. Mich., 1968, JD magna cum laude, 1971. Bar: Calif. 1972, U.S. Dist. Ct. (no. dist.) Calif. 1972, U.S. Ct. Appeals (9th cir.) 1972, Minn. 1976, U.S. Dist. Ct. Minn. 1976, Wis. 1983, U.S. Tax Ct. 1983. Assoc. Orrick, Herrington, Rowley & Sutcliffe, San Francisco, 1971-76; ptnr. Hanft, Fride, O'Brien, Harries, Swelbar & Burns P.A., Duluth, 1976—; gen. counsel Evening Telegram Co., Superior, Wis., 1982—, Murphy TV Stas., Madison, Wis., 1982—. Chmn. Duluth-Superior Area Cmty. Found., 1988-90; chair United Way of Greater Duluth, Inc., 1998—; bd. dirs. Miller Dwan Found., Duluth Airport Authority. Fellow Am. Coll. Trust and Estate Counsel; mem. Calif. Bar Assn., Wis. Bar Assn., Minn. Bar Assn. (bd. govs., past chmn. probate and trust coun.), 11th Dist. Bar Assn. (past pres., past chmn. ethics com.), Arrowhead Estate Planning Coun. (pres. 1980), Northland Country Club (pres. 1982), Boulders Club, Kitchi Gammi Club, Mpls. Athletic Club. Republican. Avocations: travel, golf, tennis, fishing. Estate planning, Pension, profit-sharing, and employee benefits, Communications. Home: 180 Paine Farm Rd Duluth MN 55804-2609 Office: Hanft Fride O'Brien Harries Swelbar & Burns PA 1000 First Bank Pl 130 W Superior St Ste 1000 Duluth MN 55802-2094

**BURNS, ROBERT EDWARD,** lawyer; b. Bedford, Ohio, June 18, 1953; s. Robert Joseph and Barbara (Charvat) B.; m. Patricia Bosler, Oct. 15, 1983. BA in Polit. Sci. magna cum laude, Marietta Coll., 1975; JD, Ohio State U., 1978. Bar: Ohio 1978. Research asst. Program for Energy Research, Edn. and Pub. Service Ohio State U., Columbus, 1978-80, research assoc. Nat. Regulatory Research Inst., 1980-81, sr. research assoc., 1981-90, sr. rsch. specialist, 1990—. Author, co-author numerous monographs, articles, speeches, presentations, papers and reports to profl. orgns. and journals. Mem. ABA (vice chmn. energy com. 1984—, adminstrv., antitrust and pub. utility law sects.), Nat. Assn. Regulatory Utility Commrs. (subcom. adminstrv. law judges 1985—, subcom. law 1980—, coord. info. conf. 1986-87), Sertoma (pres. University club 1984-85, dist. gov. 1992-94, Internat. Community Svc. award 1984-85, outstanding dist. gov. 1994). Democrat. Methodist. Avocation: reading. Home: 3180 Bowdoin Ct Columbus OH 43204-2167 Office: Ohio State U Nat Regulatory Rsch Inst 1080 Carmack Rd Columbus OH 43210-1002

**BURNS, SANDRA,** lawyer, educator; b. Bryan, Tex., Aug. 9, 1949; d. Clyde W. and Bert (Rychlik) B.; 1 son, Scott. BS, U. Houston, 1970; MA, U. Tex.-

Austin, 1972, PhD, 1975; JD, St. Mary's U., 1978. Bar: Tex. 1978; cert. tchr., adminstr., supr. instrn., Tex. Tchr. Austin (Tex.) Ind. Sch. Dist., 1970-71; prof. child devel./family life and home econs. edn. Coll. Nutrition, Textiles and Human Devel. Tex. Woman's U., Denton, 1974-75; instrnl. devel. asst. Office of Ednl. Resources div. instrnl. devel. U. Tex. Health Sci. San Antonio, 1976-77; legis. aide William T. Moore, Tex. Senate, Austin, fall, 1978, com. clk.-counsel, spring, 1979; legal cons. Colombotti & Assocs., Aberdeen, Scotland, 1980; corp. counsel 1st Internat. Oil and Gas, Inc., 1983; contracted atty. Humble Exploration Co., Inc., Dallas, 1984; assoc. Smith, Underwood, Dallas, 1986-88; pvt. practice, Dallas, 1988—; atty. contracted to Republic Energy Inc., Bryan, Tex., 1981-82, ARCO, Dallas, 1985; vis. lectr. Tex. A&M U., fall 1981, summer, 1981; lectr. home econ. Our Lady of the Lake Coll., San Antonio, fall, 1975. Mem. ABA, State Bar of Tex., Phi Delta Kappa. Contbr. articles on law and edn. to profl. jours. Probate, Personal injury. Office: 8300 Douglas Ave Ste 800 Dallas TX 75225-5826

**BURNS, SUSIE,** lawyer; b. Passaic, N.J., Sept. 18, 1965; d. C.J. and Barbara Ann (Greenwood) Baccarella; m. Bushrod Burns, Aug. 24, 1990. BA, U. Hartford, 1987; JD, Rutgers U., Newark, 1991. Bar: N.J. 1991. Assoc. Baron, Gallagher & Perley, Parsippany, N.J., 1991-98, Genova, Burns & Jennay, Livingston, N.J., 1998—. Republican. Roman Catholic. State civil litigation, Contracts commercial, Labor. Home: 20 Hillside Ave Upper Saddle River NJ 07458-1109 Office: Genova Burns & Jennay Livingston NJ 07054-1315

**BURNS, TERRENCE MICHAEL,** lawyer; b. Evergreen Park, Ill., Mar. 2, 1954; s. Jerome Joseph Burns and Eileen Beatrice (Collins) Neary; m. Therese Porucznik, Mar. 24, 1979; children: David, Steven, Theresa, Daniel. BA, Loyola U., Chgo., 1975; JD, DePaul U., 1978. Bar: Ill. 1978, U.S. Dist. Ct. (no. dist.) Ill. 1978, U.S. Ct. Appeals (7th cir.) 1979, U.S. Supreme Ct. 1985, U.S. Dist. Ct. (no. dist.) Ind. 1989. Asst. state's atty. Cook County, Chgo., 1979-85; ptnr. Rooks, Pitts & Poust, Chgo., 1985—. Commr. inquiry bd. Ill. Supreme Ct. Atty. Registration and Disciplinary Commn., Chgo., 1986-90, commr. hearing bd., 1990—. Mem. ABA, Chgo. Bar Assn. (treas. 1997—, bd. mgrs. 1995-97, chair fin. com. 1997—, criminal law com. 1979-83, jud. candidate evaluation com. 1981-86, 87-95, chmn. investigation divsn. evaluation com. 1991-92, chmn. hearing divsn. evaluation com. 1992-93, gen. chmn. 1993-95, ct. liaison com. 1993-95, tort reform subcom. 1997). Roman Catholic. Personal injury, General civil litigation. Office: Rooks Pitts & Poust 10 S Wacker Dr Ste 2300 Chicago IL 60606-7407

**BURNS, THOMAS DAVID,** lawyer; b. Andover, Mass., Apr. 4, 1921; s. Joseph Lawrence and Catherine (Horne) B.; m. Sylvia Lansing, Sept. 14, 1946 (div. 1982); children—Wendy Tilghman, Lansing, Diane Longley, Lisa; m. Marjorie Andrew Brown, Mar. 12, 1983. Student, Phillips Andover Acad., 1938, Brown U., 1938-41; LLB, Boston U., 1943. Bar: Mass. 1944, U.S. Dist. Ct. 1948, U.S. Ct. Appeals 1951, U.S. Supreme Ct. 1957. Assoc. Friedman, Atherton, King & Turner, Boston, 1946-50, ptnr., 1950-60; sr. and founding ptnr. Burns & Levinson, Boston, 1960—; mem. Jud. Coun. Com. of Mass., 1973-77, mem. Mass. Jud. Nominating Commn., 1979-83; mem. Mass. Spl. Legis. Commn. on Malpractice, 1975—; chmn. Joint Com. Boston and Mass. Bar Com. on Jud. Selection, 1970-75; spl. counsel to Boston City Coun., 1981. Contbr. articles to profl. jours. Chmn. Planning Bd. Appeals, Andover, 1956-57; trustee Stratton Mountain Vt. Civic Assn., Mus. Am. Textile History, 1992—; v.p., bd. dirs. Birch Hill Corp., Stratton, Vt.; chmn. Andover Rep. Fin. Com., 1953-57; trustee, clk. Pike Sch., Andover; mem. alumni coun. and devel. com. Phillips Andover Acad., Boston U. Law Sch.; mem. Mass. Hist. Soc., Western Front Assn.; mem. adv. bd. PBS channel WGBH, Boston. Lt. USNR, 1943-46, PTO, ETO. Fellow Am. Coll. Trial Lawyers, (state chmn. 1968, bd. regents 1970-76, treas. 1974-77), Am. Coll. Trial Lawyers Found. (dir.), Mass. Bar Found (trustee), Mass. Bar Assn. (mem. exec. com.), Am. Bar Found., ABA, Boston Bar Assn. (exec. coun.), Boston Bar Found., Fed. Ins. and Corp. Counsel, Internat. Assn. Def. Counsel, Nat. Assn. R.R. Trial Counsel, Mass. Def. Lawyers Assn. (dir.), Delta Kappa Epsilon, North Andover Country Club, The Country Club (Brookline), Coral Beach Club (Bermuda), Duxbury Yacht Club, Boston City Club, Boston U. Law Sch. (alumni award, Disting. profl. svc. award 1996). Republican. General civil litigation, Personal injury, Insurance. Home: 5 Union Wharf Boston MA 02109-1202 Office: Burns & Levinson 125 Summer St Ste 602 Boston MA 02110-1624

**BURNSIDE, CYNTHIA GRACE,** lawyer; b. Iowa City, Feb. 8, 1969; d. Richard Carlton and Connie Grace Burnside. BA, Smith Coll., 1991; MBA, JD, Tulane U., 1995. Bar: Ala. 1995. Assoc. Balch & Bingham, LLP, Birmingham, Ala., 1995—; parenter in field. Mem. Ala. Def. Lawyers Assn., Birmingham Bar Assn. Avocations: kickboxing, tennis, Habitat for Humanity. Labor, Contracts commercial, Civil rights. Office: Balch & Bingham LLP 1710 6th Ave N Birmingham AL 35203-2015

**BURNSTEIN, DANIEL,** lawyer; b. Hartford, Conn., Oct. 12, 1946; s. Lawrence J. and Margaret (Le Vien) B. AB, U. Calif., Berkeley, 1968; JD cum laude, New Eng. Sch. Law, 1975. Bar: Mass. 1975, U.S. Dist. Ct. Mass. 1976, U.S. Ct. Appeals (1st cir.) 1976. Pres. Beacon Expert Systems, Inc., 1989—; adj. prof. Clark U.; dir. Interactive Video Project Harvard Law Sch., Cambridge, 1985-89, clin. instr.; lectr. Clark U., 1997—; pres. Ctr. for Atomic Radiation Studies, Acton, Mass., 1982—; advisor Am. Mgmt. Assn. for Negotiation Curriculum to Mgrs., 1993; pres. BuzzIT.com, 1999—. Editor: The Digital MBA, 1995. Mem. ABA, Mass. Adv. Coun. on Radiation Protection, The Mgmt. Software. Private international, Computer, Communications. Office: 35 Gardner Rd Brookline MA 02445-4512

**BURR, TIMOTHY FULLER,** lawyer; b. New Bedford, Mass., Oct. 18, 1952; s. John Thayer and Joan (Ames) B.; AB, Harvard U., 1975; JD, U. Miami, 1979; m. Marguerite Conti, Feb. 28, 1981; children: Emily Ames, Lisa Conti, David Thayer. Bar: La. 1979, Tex. 1993, Fla. 1996, U.S. Supreme Ct., U.S. Cir. Ct., U.S. Dist. Ct.; mng. dir. firm Galloway, Johnson, Tompkins & Burr, New Orleans, 1987—, admiralty and litigation atty., 1979—. Past chmn. St. Tammary Parish Zoning Bd. Mem. La. Bar Assn., Tex. Bar Assn., Fla. Bar Assn., Maritime Law Assn. U.S., Tammany Yacht Club, Pensacola Yacht Club. Republican. Admiralty, Personal injury, General civil litigation. Home: 208 Pinetree Dr Gulf Breeze FL 32561-4050 Office: Galloway Johnson Tompkins and Burr 4040 1 Shell Sq Ste 4040 New Orleans LA 70139 also: 55 Bay Bridge Dr Gulf Breeze FL 32561-4468

**BURRELL, GARLAND E., JR.,** federal judge; b. L.A., July 4, 1947. BA in Sociology, Calif. State U., 1972; MSW, Washington U., Mo., 1976; JD, Calif. Wes. Sch. Law, 1976. Bar: Calif. 1976, U.S. Dist. Ct. (ea. dist.) Calif. 1976, U.S. Ct. Appeals (9th cir.) 1981. Dep. dist. atty. Sacramento County, Calif., 1976-78; dep city atty. Sacramento, 1978-79; asst. U.S. atty., dep. chief civil divsn. Office of U.S. Atty. for Ea. Dist. Calif., 1979-85, asst. U.S. atty., chief civil divsn., 1990-92; litigation atty. Stockman Law Corp., Sacramento, Calif., 1985-86; sr. dep. city atty. Office of City Atty., Sacramento, 1986-90; judge U.S. Dist. Ct. (ea. dist.) Calif., Sacramento, 1992—. With USMC, 1966-68. Office: Dist Ct 501 I St Sacramento CA 95814-2322

**BURRIS, DONALD J.,** lawyer; b. Mpls., July 6, 1941; s. Donald S. and Beatrice J. (Jevne) B.; m. Diana L. Lace, July 18, 1965; children: Angela, Robb. BS, Dartmouth Coll., 1963; JD, U. Minn., 1966. Bar: Minn. 1967, Colo. 1976, Ariz. 1984. Pvt. practice Scottsdale, Ariz., 1976—. Author: Protecting Your Assets, 1993, (with others) Stein on Probate, 1976. Estate planning. Office: Ste 180 8777 N Gainey Ctr Dr Scottsdale AZ 85258-2106

**BURRIS, JOHN LEONARD,** lawyer; b. Vallejo, Calif., May 4, 1945; s. Dewitt C. and Imogene (Terrell) B.; m. Ramona Tascoe, Aug. 17, 1983; children: Damon, Monique, Courtney, Jonathan, Justin. BA, Golden Gate U., 1967; MBA, U. Calif., Berkeley, 1970, JD, 1973. Bar: Ill. 1973, Calif. 1976. Assoc. Jenner & Block, Chgo., 1973-74; asst. states atty. States Atty. Office, Cook County, Chgo., 1975-76; dep. dist. atty. Alameda County Dist. Atty.'s Office, Oakland, Calif., 1976-79; ptnr. Alexander, Burris, Millner & McGee, Oakland, 1979-85; owner Law Offices of John L. Burris, Oakland, 1985—; legal analyst for TV and radio. Contbr. articles to profl. jours. Bd. dir. Mentoring Ctr., Oakland. Recipient Outstanding Cmty. Svc. Wiley Manual Law Found, 1996, Civic award Soulbeat TV, 1995, Image award, Morrie Turner, 1996; named Calif. C.C. Alumnus of Yr., 1998. Mem. Calif. Assn. Black Lawyer (pres. 1975), Charles Houston Bar Assn. (pres. 1981-82, O/S Lawyer Civil Advocacy award), Earl Warren Inn Ct. (barrister 1996-97). Avocations: tennis, reading. Civil rights, Criminal. Office: Law Offices of John Burris 1212 Broadway Ste 1200 Oakland CA 94612-1814

**BURRIS, STEVEN MICHAEL,** lawyer; b. L.A., Dec. 30, 1952; s. Michael Victor and Patricia (McNeer) B.; m. Melanie Schultz, Oct. 29, 1983; 1 son by previous marriage, Michael Steven. AB with distinction, Stanford U., 1975; JD with honors, U. So. Calif., 1978. Bar: Nev. 1978, Calif. 1978, Nev. Fed. Dist. Ct. 1978, U.S. Ct. Appeals (9th cir.) 1982. Assoc. firm Rogers, Monsey, Woodbury et al, Las Vegas, Nev., 1978-81; ptnr. Sacco & Burris, Las Vegas, 1981-84; pres. Burris & Thomas, Las Vegas, 1984—; tchr. Clark County Community Coll., Las Vegas, 1979-80. Author: (booklet) Your Personal Injury Case, 1982; co-author: (Manual) Trial Advocacy in Nevada, 1991, Trying the Auto Injury Case in Nevada, 1992. Bd. dirs. Sr. Citizens Mobile Home Park Found., Las Vegas, 1981-84; vice chmn. Council Ministries Fellowship Bapt. Ch., Las Vegas, 1988. Recipient Pres.'s award U.S. Jaycees, 1981; Am. Jurisprudence award Bancroft Whitney' Pubs., 1977. Mem. Nev. Trial Lawyers Assn. (bd. govs., 1992—, pres.-elect 1996), Assn. Trial Lawyers Am., Nev. Bar Assn., Clark County Bar Assn. (Certificate Merit 1987-88), Gideons (pres.). Democrat. Mem. Christian Ch. Personal injury.

**BURRIS, WILLIAM JOSEPH,** judge; b. Bogalusa, La., Nov. 1, 1949; s. Joseph Harold and Gwendolyn Marie (Sylvest) B.; m. Virginia Lynne Pierce, July 17, 1971; children: Jennifer Veillon, Katherine, William H., John Wesley. Student, La. State U., 1967-70, JD, 1973. Bar: La. 1973, U.S. Ct. Appeals (5th cir.), U.S. Supreme Ct. Asst. dist. atty. 15th Jud. Dist., Lafayette, La., 1976-81, 22nd Jud. Dist., Franklinton, La., 1981-96; dist. judge 22nd Jud. Dist., Franklinton, Covington, La., 1997—; pvt. practice Lafayette, La., 1973-81, Franklinton, La., 1981-97. Pres. Washington Parish Fair, Franklinton, 1995, 96; lay leader Centenary Meth. Ch., Franklinton. Mem. Wash. Parish Bar Assn. (pres. 1988, treas. 1981), Masons, Kiwanis (charter pres. 1982). Republican. Avocations: raising Southdown sheep, running. Office: 22nd Jud Dist Ct Washington Parish Ct House Franklinton LA 70438

**BURROWS, CECIL J.,** judge, lawyer; b. Schuyler County, Ill., Mar. 21, 1922; s. Amos R. and Florence M. (Krohe) B.; m. Virginia Pearson, June 27, 1949; children: Sandra, Carol, Deborah. BS, Western Mich. U., 1944; JD, Northwestern U., 1952. Bar: Ill. 1952. City atty. Pittsfield, Ill., 1957-64; state's atty. Pike County, Ill., 1964-70; sole practice, Pittsfield, to 1970; cir. judge 8th cir. Ill., 1970-90. Served as officer USMC, 1943-46. Mem. Ill. Judges Assn., Pike County Bar Assn., Federalist Soc., Masons, Shriners, Jesters. Home: 437 W Washington St Pittsfield IL 62363-1345

**BURROWS, MICHAEL DONALD,** lawyer; b. Oak Park, Ill., May 23, 1944; s. Milford Denton and Helen Jean (Spitali) B.; m. Sandi Miller, Feb. 6, 1982; 1 child, Matthew Denton. BA, Williams Coll., 1967; JD, N.Y. Law Sch., 1973. Bar: N.Y. 1974, U.S. Dist. Ct. (ea. and so. dists.) N.Y. 1974, U.S. Ct. Appeals (2d cir.) 1978, U.S. Supreme Ct. 1981. Assoc. Baker & McKenzie, N.Y.C., 1973-80, ptnr., 1980-95, of counsel, 1995-99, mem. internat. exec. com., 1986-88; of counsel Winston & Strawn, N.Y.C., 1999—. Co-author: The Practice of International Litigation, 1992; co-author monthly column N.Y. Law Jour., 1981-98. Served with USMC, 1968-70. Mem. ABA, Assn. Bar City N.Y. Federal civil litigation, General civil litigation, State civil litigation. Office: Winston & Strawn 200 Park Ave New York NY 10166-0005

**BURROWS, RICHARD HENRY,** lawyer; b. Providence, Aug. 19, 1954; s. Henry Hudson and Olga Marion (Rizzo) B.; m. Jane Marie Santoro, Feb. 17, 1990; children: Lindsay, Christopher. AB, Brown U., 1976; MS with distinction, Ind. U., 1979; JD, Northeastern U., 1990. Bar: R.I. 1990, U.S. Dist. Ct. R.I. 1991, Mass. 1998. Head swimming coach Little Rhody Aquatic Club, Providence, 1979-84; dir. aquatics Providence Coll., 1981-84; head swimming coach, dir. intramurals & recreation Denison U., Granville, Ohio, 1984-87; assoc. Hanson, Curran, Parks & Whitman, Providence, 1990—. Bd. dirs. Brown U. Athletic Hall of Fame, R.I. Aquatic Hall of Fame, R.I. Sports Coun. Inducted into Brown U. Hall of Fame, 1981, R.I. Aquatic Hall of Fame, 1987. Avocations: swimming, biking, weight training. General civil litigation, Insurance, Sports. Office: Hanson Curran Parks Whitman 146 Westminster St Providence RI 02903-2202

**BURROWS, VIRGINIA MOORE,** paralegal; b. Morehead City, N.C., Dec. 5, 1956; d. John Mercer Sr. and Virginia Duncan (Chadwick) Moore. BS in Bus. Edn., East Carolina U., 1978, MEd, 1980; AAS in Paralegal Tech., Pitt Community Coll., 1992. Cert. legal asst. 1993, specialist in real estate 1995; cert. Novell adminstr. 1998. Legal sec. Richard L. Stanley, Beaufort, N.C., 1981; legal sec. Dennis M. Marquardt, Morehead City, 1981-83, paralegal, 1983-85; paralegal Bennett, McConkey, Thompson, Marquardt & Wallace, P.A., Morehead City, 1985-88; legal asst. Ward & Smith, P.A., Greenville, N.C., 1988-93; paralegal Hutson Hughes & Powell, P.A., Durham, 1993—. Mem. Nat. Assn. Legal Assts., N.C. Paralegal Assn. (treas. 1996-98, Nat. Assn. Legal Assts. liaison 1998-99, assoc. news editor 1999—), Durham-Orange Paralegal Assn. (1st v.p. 1994, treas. 1995), N.C. Bar Assn. Legal Assts. Divsn. (treas. 1998-99, vice chair 1999—). Democrat. Methodist. Avocations: reading, cross-stitch. Office: Hutson Hughes & Powell PA PO Box 2252A Durham NC 27702-2173

**BURSLEY, KATHLEEN A.,** lawyer; b. Washington, Mar. 20, 1954; d. G.H. Patrick and Claire (Mulvany) B. BA, Pomona Coll., 1976; JD, Cornell U., 1979. Bar: N.Y. 1980, U.S. Dist. Ct. (ea. and so. dists.) N.Y. 1980, U.S. Ct. Appeals (5th and 11th cirs.) 1981, Fla. 1984, U.S. Dist. Ct. (mid. dist.) Fla. 1984, Tex. 1985, Mass. 1995. Assoc. Haight, Gardner, Poor & Havens, N.Y.C., 1979-81; counsel Harcourt Brace Jovanovich, Inc., N.Y.C. and Orlando, Fla., 1981-85; v.p. and counsel Harcourt Brace Jovanovich, Inc., San Antonio and Orlando, 1985-92; assoc. gen. counsel pub. Harcourt Gen., Inc., Chestnut Hill, Mass., 1992—; gen. counsel Harcourt Brace & Co., Chestnut Hill, Mass., 1992—; v.p. Harcourt Gen., Inc., 1998—. Mem. Maritime Law Assn. (proctor). Intellectual property, Contracts commercial, Trademark and copyright. Office: Harcourt Gen Inc 27 Boylston St Chestnut Hill MA 02467-1719

**BURSON, CHARLES W.,** federal official, former state attorney general; b. Memphis, TN; m. Marion 1971; children: Clare, Kate. BA, U. Mich., 1966; MA, Cambridge U., England, 1968; JD, Harvard U., 1970. Assoc. Burson & Burson and Burson & Walkup, Memphis; ptnr. Wildman, Harrold, Allen, Dixon, & McDonnell, Memphis, 1981-88; atty. gen. State of Tenn., Nashville; counsel to v.p. Office of V.P., Washington, 1993—. Del. Tenn. Constl. Conv., 1977, (chmn. State Spending Limitation Com.). Mem. Nat. Assn. Attys. Gen. (pres. 1994-95, chair FTC working group, mem. exec. com. securities group, chair consumer protection com. 1990-91, vice chair securities working group, Wyman award 1994), Tenn. Bd. Law Examiners (past pres.). Office: Exec Office of VP Old Exec Office Bldg NW Washington DC 20501-0001

**BURSTEIN, ALAN STUART,** lawyer; b. Detroit, Sept. 21, 1940; s. Harry S. and Florence (Rosen) B.; m. Margery E. Gordon, June 23, 1963; children: Mark Albert, Florence Beth, Robert Gordon. BA, U. Mich., 1962, JD, 1965. Assoc. counsel to majority leader N.Y. State Senate, Albany, 1971-73; ptnr. Hiscock & Barclay, Syracuse, N.Y., 1965-85, Scolaro, Shulman, Cohen, Lawler & Burstein, Syracuse, 1985—; bd. dirs. Penfield Mfg. Co., Syracuse; mem. 5th Dist. Grievance Com. Bd. dirs. Pub. Broadcasting Coun., Syracuse, 1977-84; v.p. Temple Adath Yeshurun; past pres. Syracuse Jewish Fedn. Named Outstanding Young Man Syracuse Jaycees, 1976; recipient Community Leadership award Syracuse Jewish Fedn., 1980, Community Svc. award B'nai Brith. Mem. ABA, N.Y. State Bar Assn., Onondaga County Bar Assn. (past bd. dirs.), Century Club, Cavalry Club. Republican. Jewish. Avocations: tennis, boating, fishing, reading. General civil litigation, Environmental, Family and matrimonial. Home: 100 Old Farm Rd Fayetteville NY 13066-2526 Office: 90 Presidential Plz Syracuse NY 13202-2240

**BURSTEIN, BEATRICE S.,** judicial administrator, retired judge; b. Bklyn., May 18, 1915; d. Joseph and Tillie (Star) Sobel; m. Herbert Burstein, June 17, 1937; children: Karen, Patricia, Ellen, Jessica, John, Judd. Bar: N.Y. 1940, U.S. Supreme Ct. 1957. LLB, St. John's U.; LLD (hon.), Hofstra U., 1983. Assoc. Zelby & Burstein, N.Y.C.; ptnr. Burstein & Agata, Mineola, N.Y.; commr. corrections State N.Y., 1956-61; dist. ct. judge, N.Y., 1962-68; family ct. judge, N.Y., 1968-73; justice N.Y. Supreme Ct., Mineola, 1974-92; judicial hearing officer appellate divsn. 2nd judicial dept. N.Y. Supreme Ct., Mineola, 1992—. Mem. N.Y. State Permanent Jud. Commn. on Justice for Children; former bd. dirs. Mental Health Assn. Nassau County, Nassau coun. Girl Scouts U.S.A., NCCJ, Rehab. Inst., Tempo, Health and Welfare Coun. Nassau County, LWV, Nat. Coun. Crime and Delinquency, Nat. Coun. Jewish Women; hon. life mem. Dist. 15 PTA; mem. N.Y. State Commn. on Bicentennial of U.S. Constitution. Named Woman of Yr., Horizon chpt. B'nai B'rith, 1965, Assn. for Help Retarded Children, 1965; recipient Judge Norman Lent award Nassau County Criminal Cts. Bar Assn., 1968, Americanism award Jewish War Vets., 1971, Meritorious Svc. cert. N.E. region Nat. Rehab. Assn., 1972, Human Relations award Am. Jewish Congress, 1973, Outstanding Woman of Year award N.Y. Inst. Tech., 1973, Boss of Year award L.I. chpt. Nat. Secs. Assn., 1975, Myrtle Wreath Achievement award Hadassah, 1975, Disting. Svc. award C.W. Post Ctr. Dept. Criminal Justice, L.I. U., 1979, J.L.E. award Exemplifying the Essence of Justice Women' Bar of State of N.Y., 1987, many others. Mem. ABA, ATLA, Am. Judicature Soc., Internat. Fedn. Women Lawyers (past v.p. for U.S., rep. to UN Social Commn. 1953, 55, 56, 61), Assn. Justices Sup. Ct. State N.Y., Bar Assn. Nassau County (Disting. Svc. medallion 1989), Nat. Assn. Women Judges, Assn. Women Judges of State N.Y., Nassau Women's Bar Assn. (pres., past chmn. legal clinic), Nat. Assn. Women Lawyers, Nat. Conf. State Trial Judges, N.Y. State Permanent Commn. on Juvenile Justice, N.Y. State Bar Assn., Iota Tau Tau. Contbr. articles to profl. lit. Office: NY State Supreme Ct Mineola NY 11501

**BURSTEIN, BERNARDO,** lawyer; b. Havana, Cuba, July 11, 1962; came to U.S., 1967; s. Salomon Burstein and Margarita Cristal; m. Nina Gladstone, Oct. 26, 1991; children: Salomon, Jessica. AB, Columbia Coll., 1984, JD, 1988. Bar: N.Y., Fla., U.S. Dist. Ct. (so. dist.) Fla. Assoc. Cravath, Swaine and Moore, N.Y.C., 1988-92, Greenberg Trarig, Miami, 1992-96; shareholder Akerman Senterfitt & Eidson, P.A., Miami, 1996—. Mem. ABA, N.Y. Bar Assn., Dade County Bar Assn. (chair internat. law sect. 1997-98). Federal civil litigation, State civil litigation, Intellectual property. Office: Akerman Senterfitt & Eidson PA One SE 3rd Ave Miami FL 33131

**BURSTEIN, RICHARD JOEL,** lawyer; b. Detroit, Feb. 9, 1945; s. Harry Seymour and Florence (Rosen) B.; m. Gayle Lee Handmaker, Dec. 21, 1969; children: Stephanie Faith, Melissa Amy. Grad., U. Mich., 1966; JD, Wayne State U., 1969. Bar: Mich. 1969, U.S. Ct. Appeals (ea. dist.) Mich. 1969. Ptnr. Smith Miro Hirsch & Brody, Detroit, 1969-81, Honigman Miller Schwartz & Cohn, Detroit, 1981-96; bd. dirs. Sandy Corp., Troy, Mich.; bd. dirs. Met. Affairs Corp., Detroit; co-chmn. Artrain. Mem. Am. Coll. Real Estate Lawyers. Real property. Office: Honigman Miller Schwartz & Cohn 2290 1st Nat Bldg Detroit MI 48226

**BURSTYN, HAROLD LEWIS,** lawyer; b. Boston, Feb. 26, 1930; s. Julius and Zena (Pezrow) B.; m. Joan Netta Jacobs, Aug. 19, 1958; children: Judith, Gail, Daniel. AB, Harvard Coll., 1951; MS, U. Calif., 1957; PhD in History of Sci., Harvard U., 1964; JD, Rutgers U., 1987. Registered patent atty. Instr. Brandeis Univ., Waltham, Mass., 1962-65; asst., assoc. prof. Carnegie-Mellon U., Pitts., 1966-73; dean, prof. Wm. Paterson Coll., Wayne, N.J., 1973-77; historian U.S. Geol. Survey, Reston, Va., 1976-84; cons. J & H Assocs., Syracuse, N.Y., 1984—; assoc. Melvin & Melvin, Syracuse, 1987-91; ptnr. Morrison Law Firm, Mt. Vernon, N.Y., 1991-95; of counsel McGuire Law Offices, Syracuse, N.Y., 1995-96; patent atty. USAF Rsch. Lab., Rome, N.Y., 1996—; vis. investigator Woods Hole Oceanog. Inst., 1961-76; cons. Coll. Marine Studs, U. Del., 1970; vis. lectr. Rutgers U., Piscataway, N.J., 1977-87; mem. Marine Biol. Lab., Woods Hole, Mass., 1983—; adj. prof. elec. engring. and computer sci., Syracuse U., 1995—. Author, At the Sign of the Quadrant, 1957; assoc. editor Law Practice Mgmt., 1994—; contbr. articles to profl. jours. With USN, USNR, 1952-55. Mem. ABA, Fed. Bar Assn., Am. Assn. Advt. Sci., The Fla. Bar, N.Y. State Bar Assn., Am. Arbitration Assn. (cert.), Computer Law Assn., Am. Intellectual Property Law Assn. Computer, Patent, Trademark and copyright. Home: 216 Bradford Pkwy Syracuse NY 13224-1767 Office: AFRL/IFOJ 26 Electronic Pky Rome NY 13441-4514

**BURT, JACQUELYN JEAN-MARIE,** law school administrator; b. Pompton Plains, N.J., Feb. 17, 1963; d. John Joseph and Phyllis (Boob) B.; m. Frank John Tanzola, July 21, 1991; children: Alexandra, Harrison. AB, Harvard U., 1984; JD, Loyola U. Sch. Law, 1988. Bar: Ohio 1988, U.S. Ct. Appeals (6th cir.) 1988, N.J. 1989. Comml. litigation atty. Columbus, Ohio, 1988-89, Newark, 1989-92; dir. career svcs. Seton Hall U. Law Sch., Newark, 1993—; adj. prof. law Seton Hall U. Law Sch., 1991—; mem. N.J. Supreme Ct. Com. on Women and the Law, 1994—. Co-author: Beyond LA Law, 1997. Class mother Hilltop Country Day Sch. Mem. Nat. Assn. Law Placement, ABA, N.J. Bar Assn., Sussex County Bar Assn. Avocations: movies, dance, swimming, collecting Dept. 56 Dickens houses. Home: 39 Heighwood Trl Sparta NJ 07871-1401 Office: Seton Hall U Sch Law One Newark Pl Newark NJ 07102

**BURT, JEFFREY AMSTERDAM,** lawyer; b. Phila., Apr. 27, 1944; s. Samuel Matthew and Esther (Amsterdam) B.; m. Sandra Cass, Dec. 17, 1967; children: Stephen, Daniel, Jonathan, Andrew. BA, Princeton U., 1966; LLB, Yale U., 1970, MA in Econs., 1970. Bar: Md. 1971, D.C. 1971. Law clk. to judge U.S. Ct. Appeals (4th cir.), Balt., 1970-71; assoc. firm Arnold & Porter, Washington, 1971-77, ptnr., 1978—; adj. prof. law Georgetown U., 1987-95; frequent lectr. Pres., Green Acres, Inc., Ind. Sch., Rockville, Md., 1984-86. Author: (with others) International Joint Ventures, 1986, 2d edit., 1992; co-editor Joint Ventures with Internat. Ptnrs., 1997. Mem. ABA (co-chairperson NIS Law Com. Sect. of Internat. Law and Practice), Russian Am. C. of C. (dir., sec.). Federal civil litigation, Administrative and regulatory, Private international. Office: Arnold & Porter 555 12th St NW Washington DC 20004-1206

**BURTON, CATHERINE MARIE,** lawyer; b. Houston, Sept. 17, 1964; d. Charles Lee and Norma Jean (Welch) B. BA in Polit. Sci., U. Okla., 1987, JD, 1990. Bar: Okla. 1990, U.S. Dist. Ct. (we. dist.) Okla. 1990. Asst. pub. defender Okla. County Pub. Defender, Oklahoma City, 1990-96; ptnr. Coyle & McCoy, Oklahoma City, 1996—. bd. dirs. Okla. Coalition to Abolish Death Penalty, Oklahoma City, 1995; active Amnesty Internat., Oklahoma City, 1996; active ACLU, Oklahoma City, 1997, bd. dirs., 1999. Recipient Cert. of Appreciation, Nat. Assn. Criminal Def. Lawyers, Santa Monica, Calif., 1996. Mem. Okla. Criminal Def. Lawyers (bd. dirs. 1998, 99), Okla. County Bar Assn. (vol. law related edn. 1998). Democrat. Roman Catholic. Avocations: reading, singing, volunteer work, talking, cooking. Criminal. Office: Coyle & McCoy 119 N Robinson Ave Ste 320 Oklahoma City OK 73102-4613

**BURTON, EARL GILLESPIE, III,** lawyer; b. St. Louis, Sept. 20, 1952; s. Earl Gillespie Jr. and Patricia Joan B.; 1 child, Sara Frances. BBA in Fin., U. Mo., 1976, JD, 1980. Bar: Mo. 1980. Legal intern Mo. Atty. Gen., Jefferson City, 1978-80; assoc. gen. counsel Clayton (Mo.) Brokerage Co., 1980-86; pvt. practice Clayton, 1987-97; tax dept. Grace & Co., P.C., St. Louis, 1997—. Trustee Gateway chpt. Leukemia Soc. Am., St. Louis, 1988-89. Mem. Mo. Bar Assn., Order of Barristers. Avocations: fishing, weight-lifting, piano. Corporate taxation, Estate taxation, Estate planning. Home: 7212 Dale Ave # A Saint Louis MO 63117-2321 Office: Grace & Co PC 3117 S Big Bend Blvd Saint Louis MO 63143-3917

**BURTON, HILARY COLEMAN,** lawyer; b. Winston-Salem, N.C., July 26, 1948; s. Hilary June and Lucretia Myrtle (Miller) B.; m. Terri Colwell, Nov. 22, 1969 (div. Apr. 1990); 1 child, Hilary Wade. BA in Am. History, U. Ala., Huntsville, 1970; JD, U. Ala., Tuscaloosa, 1974. Bar: Ala. 1974, U.S. Dist. Ct. (no. dist.) Ala. 1975. Pvt. practice, Huntsville, 1974—. Bd. dirs. Huntsville Amateur Hockey Assn., 1986-90. Mem. ABA, Ala. Criminal Def. Lawyers Assn., Ala. Bar Assn., North South Gun Club (pres. 1990-91). Republican. Baptist. Avocation: skeet shooting. Criminal, Family and matrimonial, Bankruptcy. Office: 107 N Side Sq Huntsville AL 35801-4822

**BURTON, H(UBERT) DICKSON,** lawyer; b. Salt Lake City, Mar. 13, 1958; s. Hubert Criddle and Anna Elaine (Nelson) B.; m. Maria Rona

Erickson, Aug. 10, 1988; children: William Dickson, Michael James, Laura Rose. BA, Brigham Young U., 1980, JD, 1983; student, Utah State U., 1975-76. Bar: Utah 1983, D.C. 1983, U.S. Ct. Appeals (4th cir.), 1984, (10th circle) 1992, (9th circle) 1994, (fed. circle) 1996, U.S. Supreme Ct. 1987. Law clk. to subcom. on constn. U.S. Senate Judicary Com., Washington, 1982; assoc. Ward, Lazarus, Grow & Cihlar, Washington, 1983-87, Watkiss & Campbell (Watkiss & Saperstein), Salt Lake City, 1987-90; mem. Watkiss & Saperstein, Salt Lake City, 1990-92, Woodbury & Kesler, Salt Lake City, 1992-93, Trask, Britt & Rossa, 1993—. Contbtg. editor. Gen. counsel Utah Reps., 1990-95; chmn. Utah Young Reps., 1989-90. Brigham Young U. presdl. scholar, 1979-80. Mem. Utah Bar Assn. (young lawyers exec. com. Salt Lake City chpt. 1989-90), Amer. Bar Assn., Intellectual Property, Litigation, Labor & Employment Sects. Avocations: music, skiing, travel. Labor, General civil litigation. Office: Trask Britt & Rossa 230 S 500 E Ste 300 Salt Lake City UT 84102-2000

**BURTON, JOHN PAUL (JACK BURTON),** lawyer; b. New Orleans, Feb. 26, 1943; s. John Paul and Nancy (Key) B.; m. Anne Ward; children: Jennifer, Susanna, Derek, Catherine. BBA magna cum laude, La. Tech. U., 1965; LLB, Harvard U., 1968. Bar: N.Mex. 1968, U.S. Dist. Ct. N.Mex. 1968, U.S. Ct. Appeals (10th cir.) 1973, U.S. Supreme Ct. 1979. Assoc. Rodey, Dickason, Sloan, Akin & Robb, Albuquerque, 1968-74, dir., 1974—, chmn. comml. dept., 1980-81; mng. dir. Rodey, Dickason, Sloan, Akin & Robb, Santa Fe, 1986-90. Co-author: Boundary Disputes in New Mexico, 1992, Unofficial Update on the Uniform Ltd. Liability Co. Act, 1994. Mem. Nat. Coun. Commrs. on Uniform State Laws, 1989—, drafting com. UCC Article 5, 1990-95, UCC Article 9, 1993-95, Uniform Ltd. Liability Co. Act, 1993-95, Legis. Coun., 1991—, divsn. chair, 1993-95, 99—, chair legis. com., 1995-99, exec. com., 1995-99; liaison for exec. com. to joint editl. bd. Uninc. Bus. Orgns., 1994-95; pres. Brunn Sch., 1987-89. Fellow Am. Coll. Real Estate Lawyers, Lex Mundi Coll. Mediators; mem. ABA, Am. Law Inst. (rep. to UCC Article 5 drafting com. 1992-95), Am. Coll. Mortgage Attys., Am. Arbitration Assn. (mem. panel arbitrators), N.Mex. State Bar Assn. (chmn. comml. litig. and antitrust sect. 1985-86). Contracts commercial, Federal civil litigation, Real property. Office: Rodey Dickason Sloan Akin & Robb PA PO Box 1357 Santa Fe NM 87504-1357

**BURTON, RANDALL JAMES,** lawyer; b. Sacramento, Feb. 4, 1950; s. Edward Jay and Bernice Mae (Overton) B.; children: Kelly Jacquelyn, Andrew Jameson; m. Kimberly D. Rogers, Apr. 29, 1989. BA, Rutgers U., 1972; JD, Southwestern U., 1975. Bar: Calif. 1976, U.S. Dist. Ct. (ea. dist.) Calif. 1976, U.S. Dist. Ct. (no. dist.) Calif., 1990, U.S. Supreme Ct, 1991. Assoc. Brekke & Mathews, Citrus Heights, Calif., 1976; pvt. practice, Sacramento, 1976-93; ptnr. Burton & White, Sacramento, 1993—; judge pro tem Sacramento Small Claims Ct., 1982—. Bd. dirs. North Highlands Recreation and Park Dist., 1978-86, Family Svc. Agy. of Sacramento, 1991-96; active Local Bd. 22, Selective Svc., 1982—, Active 20-30 Club of Sacramento, 1979-90, pres., 1987. Recipient Disting. Citizen award, Golden Empire Council, Boy Scouts Am. Mem. Sacramento Bar Assn., Sacramento Young Lawyers Assn. Presbyterian. Lodge: Rotary (pres. Foothill-Highlands club 1980-81). Personal injury, Probate, Family and matrimonial. Office: 1540 River Park Dr Ste 224 Sacramento CA 95815-4609

**BURTON, RICHARD JAY,** lawyer; b. N.Y.C., May 4, 1949; s. Melvin F. Burton and Shirley (Burton) Silber; m. Truly Demetra Dourdis, June 11, 1972; 1 child, Marc Aaron. BA, George Washington U., 1971; JD, U. Miami, 1974. Bar: Fla. 1974, D.C. 1976, U.S. Supreme Ct. 1979. Adminstrv. aide Fla. Legis., 1973-74; gov. affairs liaison Dade County Fla. Legis., 1974; assoc. Richard H.W. Maloy and Assocs., Coral Gables, Fla., 1974-76; atty., advisor FAA, Washington, 1976-77; assoc. Pompan, Rumizen & Reynolds, Washington, 1978-79, Donald M. Murtha and Assocs., Washington, 1978-79; ptnr. Schoninger, Siegfried, Kipnis, Burton & Sussman PA, Miami, Fla., 1979-82; sole practice Miami, 1982—; gen. counsel Rexall Sundown Inc., 1982-90; guest lectr. U. Miami Sch. of Law, Coral Gables, 1982. Mem. Am. Arbitration Assn. Constr. law panel, 1974—, Builders Assn. S. Fla., legis. com. 1980—, Builder Industry Polit. action com.; fire commr. Met. Dade County, 1988, 92, vice chmn., fire commr., 1989-90. Mem. ABA, D.C. Bar Assn., Fed. Bar Assn., Fla. Bar Assn. (constr. law com.). Democrat. Jewish. Avocations: skiing, scuba diving, tennis. Federal civil litigation, State civil litigation, Construction.

**BURTON, STEPHEN DAVID,** lawyer; b. Oakland, Calif., May 19, 1955; s. David Kerr and Hilde (Scheuer) B.; m. Deborah Ann Hansen, Feb. 14, 1993; children: Sawyer, Olivia. BA in Sociology magna cum laude, U. Calif., San Diego, 1978; JD, Golden Gate U., 1981. Bar: Calif. 1983, U.S. Dist. Ct. (no. dist.) Calif. 1983, Ariz. 1995, U.S. Supreme Ct. 1995, U.S. Dist. Ct. (so., ea. and ctrl. dists.) Calif. 1996, U.S. Ct. Appeals (9th cir.) 1996; lic. pvt. investigator, Calif. Assoc. Kincaid Giannzio et al., Oakland, 1985-87, Larry Klein, Inc., Napa, Calif., 1987-89; pvt. practice, Berkeley, Calif., 1989-96, Tucson, 1996—; lectr. Inst. for Natural Resources, Emeryville, Calif., 1994-96; gen. counsel Arts in Process, San Francisco, 1983-86; panel atty. Bay Area Lawyers for the Arts, San Francisco, 1983-85. Editor: Ethnographic Field Study Manual, 1978; author: Dervish Sema & Spiritual Space, 1978. Vol. docent and propagator U. Calif. Bot. Garden, Berkeley, 1978-85; vol. arbitrator So. Ariz. BBB, Tucson, 1990—; vol. arbitrator and mediator Alameda, Contra Costa, Napa and San Francisco superior cts., Bay Mcpl. Ct., Calif. Mem. ABA, Pima County Bar Assn., Comml. Law League Am., Am. Collector's Assn., Atty. Program. Democrat. Avocations: mountaineering, diving, fishing, skiing, sculpting. Insurance, Contracts commercial, General civil litigation. Office: 5447 E 5th St Ste 201 Tucson AZ 85711-2346

**BURZYNSKI, MARTIN ANDREW,** lawyer; b. Warsaw, Poland, Sept. 10, 1964; came to the U.S., 1971; s. Andrzey Burzynski and Ewa Noble. AB, Bowdoin Coll., 1987; JD, U. Fla., 1993. Asst. state atty. States Atty. Office, Sarasota, Fla., 1994-95; ptnr. Martin A. Burzynski, Esq, PA, Sarasota, 1995—. Mem. Fla. Bar Assn., Sarasota County Bar Assn. Criminal. Office: 1956 Main St Sarasota FL 34236-5915

**BUS, ROGER JAY,** lawyer; b. Kalamazoo, Mich., Oct. 15, 1953; s. Charles J. and Sena (Wolthuis) B.; m. Lida Margaret Sell, Aug. 27, 1977; children: Emily Lynn, Stephen Charles. Student, Calvin Coll., 1971-73; BA, U. Mich., 1975; JD, U. Toledo, 1979. Bar: Mich. 1979, U.S. Dist. Ct. (we. dist.) Mich. 1979. Law clk. to presiding justice Kalamazoo Cir. Ct., 1978; intern Toledo Legal Aid, 1979; staff atty. Legal Aid Bur. SW Mich., Kalamazoo, 1979-81; assoc. Stanley, Davidoff & Gray, Kalamazoo, 1981-83; owner, atty. Debt Relief Law Ctr., Kalamazoo, 1983—. Deacon Ref. Bapt. Ch., Kalamazoo, 1983-85; precinct del. Kalamazoo County Reps., 1986-88; bd. dirs., atty. Kalamazoo Gospel Mission, 1983-86, v.p., 1997—, bd. dirs., 1996—; adult Sunday sch. tchr. Calvary Bible Ch., elder, 1988-91, 92—, elder clk., 1989-91, 97—. Mem. Fed. Bar Assn. (lectr. western dist. Mich. bankruptcy div. 1990-92, 97), Mich. Bar Assn., Kalamazoo County Bar Assn., Nat. Assn. Chpt. 13 Trustees. Avocations: conjuring, golf, reading, religious book collecting. Bankruptcy. Home: 5330 Stoney Brook Rd Kalamazoo MI 49009-3850 Office: Debt Relief Law Ctr 903 E Cork St Kalamazoo MI 49001-4875

**BUSALD, E. ANDRÉ,** lawyer; b. New Albany, Ind., Mar. 24, 1946; s. Edward Albert and Bernadine (Marsh) B.; m. Janis Kathman, July 16, 1966; children: Jacqueline, Andre, Ethan Ashley. BA, Holy Cross Coll., 1968; JD, U. Ky., 1970. Bar: Ky. 1971, Ohio 1989, U.S. Dist. Ct. (ea. and we. dist.) Ky., U.S. Dist. Ct. (so. dist.) Ohio, U.S. Supreme Ct. Trial lawyer Busald, Funk, Zevely, P.S.C., Florence, Ky., 1971—; adj. prof. law Salmon P. Chase Law Sch., Highland Heights, Ky., 1976-86, bd. overseers, 1986—; lectr. in field; spl. justice Ky. Supreme Ct.; spl. judge U.S. Dist. Ct. (ea. dist.) Ky. Mem. Am. Trial Lawyers Assn. (bd.dirs. 1988-94), Ky. Acad. Trial Attys. (bd. dirs. 1972—, pres. 1985), No. Ky. Bar Assn. (pres. 1986, bd. dirs. 1985-97), Salmon P. Chase Inn of Ct. (pres. 1994). Federal civil litigation, General civil litigation, State civil litigation. Office: Busald Funk Zevely 226 Main St PO Box 6910 Florence KY 41022-6910

**BUSBEE, KLINE DANIEL, JR.,** law educator, lawyer, retired; b. Macon, Ga., Mar. 14, 1933; s. Kline Daniel and Bernice (Anderson) B.; children: Rodgers Christopher, Jon Edward. BBA, So. Meth. U., 1961, JD, 1962. Ptnr. Worsham, Forsythe, Sampels & Busbee, Dallas, 1962-70, Locke, Purnell, Rain & Harrell, P.C., Dallas, 1970-98, Gibson, Dunn & Crutcher, Dallas, 1998-99; adj. prof. law So. Meth. U. Sch. Law, 1974-83, 92; adj. prof. pub. internat. law U. Tex. Grad. Sch. Mgmt., Dallas; bd. dirs. Atmos Energy Corp. Mem. ABA, Tex. Bar Assn., Dallas Country Club, Dallas Com. on Fgn. Rels., Snowmass Club, Petroleum Club. Home: 4360 San Carlos St Dallas TX 75205-2052

**BUSH, F. BRAD,** lawyer, mortgage company executive; b. Charlotte, N.C., Feb. 10, 1951; s. Wesley Johnson and Mary Katherine (Bradner) B.; m. Carolyn Little, Jan. 28, 1984; 1 child, Catherine S. Coffey. BA, U. N.C., Charlotte, 1973; JD, South Tex. Coll. Law, 1976. Bar: Tex. 1977, N.C. 1977, U.S. Dist. Ct. (we. dist.) N.C. 1977. Pvt. practice Charlotte, 1977-83; ptnr. Campbell, Morrison and Bush, Charlotte, 1983-85, Casey, Bishop, Murphy, Bush and Chapman, P.A., Charlotte, 1985-89; v.p., counsel Barclays Am./Mortgage Corp., Charlotte, 1989-97; gen. counsel EFC Holdings Corp., EquiFirst Corp., Money Am., Inc., Charlotte, 1997—. Chmn. Cen. Piedmont group Sierra Club, Charlotte, 1982-83. Mem. N.C. Bar Assn. (corp. counsel sect., real property sect.), Mecklenburg County Bar (real property sect.). Avocations: Civil War re-enactments, white-water canoeing, hiking. Real property, Finance, Banking. Home: 4826 Addison Dr Charlotte NC 28211-3060 Office: EFC Holdings Corp. 820 Forest Point Cir Charlotte NC 28273-5601

**BUSH, MICHAEL KEVIN,** lawyer; b. Davenport, Iowa, May 23, 1952; s. Roy Alvin and A. Carmelita (Gilroy) B.; m. Kathleen M. Grace, Nov. 26, 1977; children: Kelly Anne, Daniel Stephen, Brendan Michael. BA, U. Notre Dame, South Bend, Ind., 1974; JD, Valparaiso (Ind.) U., 1977. Bar: Iowa 1977, U.S. Dist. Ct. (no. dist.) Iowa 1980, U.S. Ct. Appeals (7th cir.) 1980, U.S. Dist. Ct. (ctrl. dist.) Ill. 1983, U.S. Ct. Appeals (8th cir.) 1996, U.S. Supreme Ct. 1990. Mem. Wells, McNally & Bowman, Davenport, 1977-80; prosecutor Scott County Atty.'s Office, Davenport, 1980-82; mem. Henninger & Henninger, Davenport, 1979-82; founding ptnr. Walton, Creen & Bush, Davenport, 1982-86; ptnr. Carlin, Hellstrom & Bittner, Davenport, 1987—. Mem. ATLA (sustaining mem.), Am. Bd. Trial Advocates (assoc.), Iowa Assn. Trial Lawyers (bd. govs.), Million Dollar Advocates Forum, Iowa Bar Assn., Scott County Bar Assn. Roman Catholic. Avocation: tennis. Personal injury. Home: 2806 E 42nd Ct Davenport IA 52807-1576 Office: Carlin Hellstrom & Bittner 201 W 2nd St Ste 1000 Davenport IA 52801-1817

**BUSH, RAYMOND GEORGE,** lawyer; b. Phila., Mar. 27, 1952; s. Raymond George and Florence Dorothy (Glassman) B.; children: Katherine Elizabeth, James Crisfield, Margaret Lindsley, Abigail Josephine. BA, Widener U., 1975; MPA, Temple U., 1980, postgrad., 1981-83, JD, 1988. Bar: Pa. 1988, N.J. 1989, U.S. Ct. Appeals (3d cir.) 1988, U.S. Ct. Appeals (fed. cir.) 1989, U.S. Ct. Mil. Appeals 1989, U.S. Dist. Ct. (ea. dist.) Pa. 1989, U.S. Dist. Ct. (mid. dist.) Pa. 1991, U.S. Supreme Ct. 1993, U.S. Dist. Ct. N.J. 1995; cert. estate practitioner. Employee rels. specialist regional office U.S. Dept. Health and Human Svcs., Phila., 1980-83; labor rels. officer U.S. VA, Coatsville, Pa., 1983; paralegal Office Gen. Counsel U.S. Dept. Health and Human Svcs., Phila., 1984; labor rels. specialist Fed. Labor Rels. Authority, Phila., 1984-88; mgmt. rep. U.S. Dept. Navy, Phila., 1988-89; assoc. Duane, Morris and Heckscher, Phila., 1989-90, Tallman, Hudders & Sorentino, Allentown, Pa., 1990-91; pvt. practice Bethlehem, Pa., 1991—; lectr. at profl. meetings and confs.; adj. asst. prof. Widener U., Chester, Pa., 1988-89, instr. paralegal program; adj. faculty Nat. Bus. Inst.; adj. instr. Cedar Crest, Allentown, Pa., 1996-99, Muhlenberg Coll., Easton, Pa., 1999—. Contbr. numerous articles to profl. publs. Bd. dirs. Community Dispute Settlement of Delaware County, Media, Pa., 1988-89; community mediator, bd. dirs. Common Ground, Bethlehem, Pa., 1989-90; personnel com. Cathedral Ch. of Nativity, Bethlehem, 1990, also vestry and solicitor; fundraising capt. Minsi Trail coun. Boy Scouts Am., 1990; active Leadership Lehigh Valley, 1991. Mem. ABA (labor and employment law sect., com. on fed. svc. labor and employment law), Pa. Bar Assn. (labor and employment law sect.), Phila. Bar Assn. (labor com.), Indsl. Rels. Rsch. Assn. (planning com. Phila. chpt. 1986-88, v.p. programming 1991—, mem. adv. bd., past pres. NE chpt.), Soc. Fed. Labor Rels. Profls. (pres. Mid-Atlantic chpt. 1981-88, exec. dir. 1988-89, nat. exec. bd. 1986-87), Northampton County Bar Assn. (chair labor rels. com. 1990-94, mem. pers. com. 1994—), Pi Gamma Mu, Phi Delta Phi. Republican. Episcopalian. Avocations: sailing, cross-country skiing, golf, photography, classical music. Labor, General civil litigation, Estate planning. Home: 226 E Wall St Bethlehem PA 18018-6118 Office: 65 E Elizabeth Ave Ste 901 Bethlehem PA 18018-6516

**BUSH, REX CURTIS,** lawyer; b. Longview, Wash., Oct. 21, 1953; s. Rex Cole Bush and Arline (Quanstrom) Fitzgerald; m. Joy Ann Pallas, July 22, 1977 (div.); children: Alicia, Angela, Carrie; m. Janet Rae Hicks July 2, 1988; children: Jeni, Mykal. BA cum laude, Brigham Young U., 1980; JD, U. Utah, 1983. Bar: Utah 1983, U.S. Dist. Ct. (no. dist.) Utah 1983, U.S. Tax Ct. 1985. Tax atty. Arthur Andersen & Co., Houston, 1983-84; assoc. Mortensen & Neider, Midvale, Utah, 1984-85; in-house counsel Fin. Futures, Salt Lake City, 1985-87; registrar Hollander Cons., Portland, Oreg., 1987-88; in-house counsel Bennett Leasing, Salt Lake City, 1987-88; pres. Bush Law Firm, Sandy, Utah, 1988—; judge pro tempore 3d Cir. Ct., Salt Lake City, 1985-87. Author: (booklet) What To Do in Case of an Automobile Accident, 1994. Mayor University Village, U. Utah, 1981-82; Rep. candidate Utah state senate, 1992; Rep. voting dist. sec., treas., 1992. Recipient Meritorious Leadership award, Nat. Com. for Employer Support of Guard and Reserve, 1990. Mem. ATLA, Utah Trial Lawyers Assn., Utah State Bar (chmn. small firm and solo practitioners com. 1994-96, honored for outstanding svc. to legal profession 1996). Personal injury. Office: Bush Law Firm 9615 S 700 E Sandy UT 84070-3557

**BUSH, ROBERT BRADFORD,** lawyer; b. Indpls., June 13, 1953; s. Robert Leland and Mary Corrine (Burton) B.; m. Denise Marquette, June 14, 1975; children: Christopher, Keith, Matthew. BS, U.S. Naval Acad., 1975; JD, Ind. U., Bloomington, 1983. Bar: Ind. 1983, U.S. Dist. Ct. (no. and so. dists.) Ind. 1983, U.S. Ct. Appeals (7th cir.) 1984, U.S. Dist. Ct. (so. dist.) Ill. 1988. Ptnr. Ice, Miller, Donadio & Ryan, Indpls., 1983—. Contbr. articles to profl. jours. Lt. comdr. USN, 1975-80. Mem. ABA, Ind. Bar Assn., Indpls. Bar Assn., Order of Coif. Republican. Labor, Administrative and regulatory, Civil rights. Office: Ice Miller Donadio & Ryan 1 American Sq Indianapolis IN 46282-0001

**BUSH, ROBERT G., III,** lawyer, state legislator; b. Kansas City, Mo., Jan. 15, 1936; s. Robert G. and Margaret Irene (Woolard) B.; m. Wanda Lou Baker, Jan. 20, 1962; 1 child, Sherry O'Shea Cornell. B.A., Kans. U., 1957; J.D., So. Meth. U., 1963. Bar: Tex. 1963, U.S. Dist. Ct. (ea. dist.) Tex. 1964, U.S. Ct. Appeals (5th cir.) 1974, U.S. Supreme Ct. 1974; sole practice, Sherman, 1967—; Bancroft-Whitney Practice Cons., Right to Die Directives, 1988-94; mem. Tex. Ho. of Reps., 1977-87, majority leader House Democratic Caucus, 1981-85, chmn. judiciary com., 1981-87; instr. Grayson County Jr. Coll., 1968-72. Served with U.S. Army, 1958-59. Fellow Tex. Bar Found. Episcopalian. General civil litigation, Family and matrimonial, Personal injury.

**BUSH, THOMAS NORMAN,** lawyer; b. Lancaster County, Va., Nov. 13, 1947; s. T. Edwin and Willie Ann (Landman) B.; m. Carolyn Sue Brown; children: Jason, Jennifer. BS in Acctg., Va. Tech, 1970; JD, U. Richmond, 1977. Bar: Va.; CPA, Va. Staff acct. KPMG Peat Marwick, Richmond, Va., 1970-71; sr. auditor U.S. Army, Frankfurt, Germany, 1972-74; pvt. practice acctg. Richmond, 1974-77; tax mgr. PricewaterhouseCoopers, Richmond, 1977-81; v.p., tax counsel Fort James Corp., Richmond, 1981—. V.p. James River Found., 1993—; chmn. corp. matching gift U. Richmond Annual Fund steering com., 1996-97; mem. dept. acctg. adv. bd. Va. Tech., 1991—; mem. steering com. Ctr. for Leadership, Govt. and Global Econs., 1995—. Mem. ABA, AICPA, Va. State Bar, Internat. Fiscal Assn., Am. Forest and Paper Assn. (tax com. 1986-94), Tax Execs. Inst. (pres. Va. chpt. 1989-90, regional v.p. 1995-96, bd. dirs. 1993-96, nominating com. 1996-97, vice chair IRS adminstrv. affairs com. 1997-99, mem. IRS customer satisfaction task force 1998-99), Tax Found. (program com. 1996—), Va. Soc. CPAs, Va. Mfrs. Assn. (tax com. 1988—), Civitan (pres. West End Richmond 1982). Methodist. Avocations: coaching, baseball, travel. Corporate taxation, Mergers and acquisitions, Finance. Home: 10007 Ashbridge Pl Richmond VA 23233-5402 Office: Fort James Corp PO Box 2218 6802 Paragon Pl Ste 400 Richmond VA 23230-1655

**BUSH, WENDELL EARL,** lawyer; b. Little Rock, Dec. 10, 1943; s. David J. and Anne (Hampton) B. A.B., Philander South Coll., 1965; postgrad. Atlanta U., 1966; J.D., Emory U., 1969. Bar: Ga. 1971, Ind., Tenn. Atty., Emory U. Law Ctr., Atlanta, 1969-71, Indpls. Legal Aid Soc., 1969-72, EEOC, Memphis, 1973—. Bd. dirs. Boy Scouts Am., Memphis. Hal S. Clark fellow, 1968; Reginald Hebersmitt fellow, 1969-71. Mem. ABA, Nat. Bar Assn., Omega Psi Phi, Phi Alpha Delta (treas.). Methodist. Labor, Federal civil litigation, Administrative and regulatory.

**BUSHINSKI, STEPHEN JOHN,** lawyer; b. Shenandoah, Pa., Apr. 13, 1957; s. Joseph Anthony Bushinski Sr. and Mary Elizabeth Ruth; m. Julie Drumheller, Oct. 18, 1980. AA, Fayetteville State U., 1979; BA, Bloomsburg State Coll., 1980; JD, Widener U., 1994. Bar: Pa. 1994. Law clk. Bur. Workers Compensation, Commonwealth of Pa., Pottsville, 1994-96; judge advocate 213d Area Support Group Pa. Army N.G., Allentown, 1996-98; solicitor New Castle Twp., Arnout's Addition; pvt. practice Ringtown, Pa., 1996—; pub. defender Office of the Pub. Defender, Schuylkill County, Pottsville, 1996—; atty. Schuylkill County Office of Sr. Svcs., Pottsville, 1996—. 1st lt. U.S. Army/Army N.G., 1975-97, ret. Mem. ABA, Nat. Acad. Elder Law Attys., Pa. Bar Assn., Schuylkill County Bar Assn. Republican. Roman Catholic. Office: Masonic Bldg 4 S 2nd St Rm 310 Pottsville PA 17901-3006

**BUSHNELL, GEORGE EDWARD, JR.,** lawyer; b. Detroit, Nov. 15, 1924; s. George E. and Ida Mary (Bland) B.; children: George Edward III, Christopher Gilbert Whelden, Robina McLeod Bushnell Hogan. Mil. student, U. Kans., 1943; BA, Amherst Coll., 1948; LLB, U. Mich., 1951; LLD, Detroit Coll. Law, 1995. Bar: Mich. 1951, D.C. 1980, U.S. Dist. Ct. (ea. dist.) Mich. 1951, U.S. Dist. Ct. (we. dist.) Mich. 1971, U.S. Ct. Appeals (6th cir.) 1955, U.S. Ct. Appeals (fed. cir.) 1995, U.S. Ct. Appeals for the Armed Forces 1995, U.S. Supreme Ct. 1971, U.S. Ct. Internat. Trade 1995. From assoc. to sr. ptnr. Miller, Canfield, Paddock and Stone, Detroit, 1953-77, of counsel, 1989—; sr. ptnr. Bushnell, Gage, Doctoroff & Reizen, Southfield, Mich., 1977-89; commr. Mich. Jud. Tenure Commn., 1969-83, chmn., 1978-80; pres. State Bar Mich., 1975-76; bd. dirs. Nat. Jud. Coll., 1985-89; mem. Mich. Atty. Discipline Bd., 1990-96; lectr. in field. Elder Grosse Pointe Meml. Ch.; moderator Detroit Presbytery, United Presbyn. Ch. U.S.A., 1972, pres. program agy. bd., 1972-76; bd. dirs. Econ. Devel. Corp. of Detroit, 1976—, Econ. Growth Corp. of Detroit, 1978-96, Tax Increment Fin. Authority, Detroit, 1984—, Econ. Devel. Authority, Detroit, 1988-98; bd. trustees New Detroit, Inc., 1972—, chmn., 1974-75. Served with USAR, 1942-56. Decorated Bronze Star, Army Commendation medal. Mem. NAACP (life, co-chmn. fight for freedom fund dinner 1968), ABA (ho. of dels. 1976—, chmn. ho. of dels. 1988-90. pres.-elect 1993-94, pres. 1994-95, past pres. 1995-96, others, Trial Attys. of Am. (pres. 1971-89), State Bar Mich. . bd. of bar commrs. 1970-76, pres. 1975-76, John Hensel award for svcs. to the arts 1990, Roberts P. Hudson award for spl. svcs. to the bar and the people of Mich., 1979, 85, Cooley Law Sch. Louis A. Smith disting. jurist award 1995), Detroit Bar Assn. (bd. dirs. 1958-65, pres. 1964-65, past pres. com. 1980—, bench & bar award for svc. to the judicial sys., the legal profession and the cmty. 1989), Nat. Conf. of Bar Pres. (pres. 1984-85), 6th Jud. Cir. Conf. (life), Am. Law Inst., Am. Arbitration Assn. (bd. dirs. 1970-82), Am. Coll. Trial Lawyers, Am. Bar Found. (life), Am. Judicature Soc. (bd. dirs. 1977-82), Can. Bar Assn. (hon.), Internat. Soc. Barristers, Fed. Bar Assn., Masons (33 deg.), Met. Club (N.Y.C.) Psi Delta Phi, Psi Upsilon. Democrat. Federal civil litigation, State civil litigation, General corporate. Office: Miller Canfield Paddock & Stone 150 W Jefferson Ave Ste 2500 Detroit MI 48226-4416

**BUSHNELL, GEORGE EDWARD, III,** lawyer; b. Detroit, Feb. 18, 1952; s. George Edward Jr. and Elizabeth (Whelden) B.; m. Eileen Mary Maguire, Sept. 16, 1989; children: Ann-Elizabeth, Emily Spears, George Edward. BA, Bucknell U., 1974; JD, Emory U., 1981. Bar: Ga. 1981, D.C. 1983, N.Y. 1986. Vol. U.S. Peace Corps, Burkina Faso, 1974-76, tng. dir., 1976-77; staff asst. to hon. Lucien Nedzi U.S. Ho. of Reps., Washington, 1977-78; assoc. Duncan, Allen and Mitchell, Washington, Ivory Coast, Congo, 1981-85, Shearman & Sterling, N.Y.C., 1985-91; corp. counsel Joseph E. Seagram & Sons, Inc., N.Y.C., 1991—. Mem. ABA, N.Y. State Bar Assn. Mergers and acquisitions, General corporate, Finance. Home: 410 E 57th St New York NY 10022-3059 Office: Joseph E Seagram & Sons Inc 800 3rd Ave New York NY 10022-7604

**BUSHUE, SANDRA KAY,** legal association administrator; b. Paxton, Ill., Sept. 25, 1960; d. Richard Dale and Ruby (Maskal) B. BA, Eureka Coll., 1982; MBA, George Mason U., 1995. Spl. asst. to sec. U.S. Dept. Edn., Washington, U.S. Dept. Transp., Washington; dir. programs White House, Washington; dep. dir. Nat. Commn. Internat. Transp., Washington; cons. Baker, Donelson, Beurman & Caldwell, Washington; mgr. legal affairs Holland & Knight LLP, Washington; mem. Fiscal Affairs Commn. Arlington (Va.) County, 1994—, North Va. Transp. Planning com., Fairfax, 1995—. Candidate House Dels. Rep. 49th dist., Arlington, 1997. Recipient Outstanding Alumni award Eureka Coll., 1991. Mem. Optimist Club, C. of C. Meth. Avocations: reading, jogging. Home: 2902 13th Rd S Arlington VA 22204-4924 Office: Holland & Knight LLP 2100 Pennsylvania Ave NW Washington DC 20037-3295

**BUSICK, DENZEL REX,** lawyer; b. Council Bluffs, Iowa, Oct. 16, 1945; s. Guy Henry and Selma Ardith (Woods) B.; m. Cheryl Ann Callahan, June 17, 1967; children: Elizabeth Colleen, Guy William. BS in Bus. Adminstrn., U. Nebr.-Omaha, 1969; JD, Creighton U., 1971. Bar: Nebr. 1971, U.S. Dist. Ct. Nebr. 1971, U.S. Ct. Appeals (8th cir.) 1975, U.S. Supreme Ct. 1974; Law clk., U.S. Dist. Ct. Nebr., 1970-72; mem. Fraser, Stryker, Veach, Vaughn, Meusey, Olsen & Boyer, Omaha, 1972-78; assoc. Kay & Satterfield, North Platte, Nebr., 1979-80; ptnr. Luebs, Leininger, Smith, Busick & Johnson, Grand Island, Nebr., 1980—. Fellow Am. Coll. Trial Lawyers, Nebr. Bar Found. (bd. dirs.), Am. Coll. Legal Medicine (law); mem. ABA, ATLA, Am. Bd. Trial Advocates (assoc. diplomate), Nat. Bd. Trial Advocacy (civil diplomate), Am. Bd. Profl Liability Attys. (diplomate), Am. Judicature Soc., Nebr. Bar Assn. (past mem. ho. of dels., exec. coun., past chmn. ins. com.), Nebr. Assn. Trial Attys. (bd. dirs., 1991-98), Nebr. Lawyers Trust Account Found. (past pres., bd. dirs.), Nebr. Bar Commn., Grand Island Area C. of C. (past vice-chair, bd. dirs.), Kiwanis (past pres. Grand Island ), Phi Alpha Delta. Republican. Contbr. to publs. in field. State civil litigation, Federal civil litigation, Insurance. Home: 3027 Brentwood Pl Grand Island NE 68801-7222 Office: PO Box 790 Wheeler at 1st St Grand Island NE 68802-0790

**BUSNER, PHILIP H.,** retired lawyer; b. Bklyn., Mar. 26, 1927; s. Joseph and Ray (Grajewer) B.; m. Naomi Marcia Greenfield, June 24, 1951; children: Joan Alexandra, Carey Elizabeth. BA cum laude, NYU, 1949; LLB, Harvard U., 1952. Bar: N.Y. 1953, U.S. Dist. Ct. (so. dist.) N.Y. 1956, U.S. Dist. Ct. (ea. dist.) N.Y. 1958, U.S. Ct. Appeals (2d dir.) 1956, U.S. Supreme Ct. 1974. Assoc. Rein, Mound & Cotton, N.Y.C., 1953, Hess, Mela, Segall, Popkin & Guterman, N.Y.C., 1954-55, Carroad & Carroad, N.Y.C., 1955-72; ptnr. Young, Sonnenfeld & Busner, N.Y.C., 1972-75, Sonnenfeld & Busner, N.Y.C., 1976-78, Sonnenfeld, Busner & Weinstein, N.Y.C., 1978-85; with Sonnenfeld, Busner & Richman, N.Y.C., 1986-88; pvt. practice Great Neck, N.Y., 1989-97; ret., 1998. Trustee Asthmatic Children's Found. N.Y., 1978-87; adminstrv. judge N.Y.C. Dept. Transp., 1989-93; arbitrator N.Y.C. Civil Ct., 1990-92, Nassau County Dist. Co., 1990-95, Suffolk County Dist. Ct., 1990-93. With USAAF, 1945-47. Mem. Am. Arbitration Assn. (arbitrator 1990-92), Phi Beta Kappa. General practice, Federal civil litigation, State civil litigation. Home: One Todd Dr Sands Point NY 11050

**BUSO, EDUARDO L.,** lawyer; b. Boston, Mar. 21, 1951; s. Eduardo and Maria L. Buso; m. Angelika Kroener, Mar. 27, 1986; children: Eduardo Javier, Vanessa Marie. BA, U. Calif., Santa Barbara, 1974; JD, U. Calif., San Francisco, 1977. Bar: P.R. 1978, U.S. Dist. Ct. P.R. 1978, U.S. Ct. Appeals (1st cir.) 1980. Assoc. Quetglas, Subira, Gaztambide & Arrillaga, San Juan, P.R., 1978-80; trial atty. fed. litigation div. Commonwealth of P.R., San Juan, 1980-81, dir. fed. litigation div., 1981-82, asst. sec. justice, 1982-83, undersec. of justice, 1983; assoc. Rivera, Tulla & Ferrer, San Juan, 1983-85; counsel, country exec. GE, P.R., 1985-91; counsel internat. sales GE, Schenectady, N.Y., 1991—; adj. asst. prof. law Cath. U. P.R., Ponce, 1983-84. Mem. ABA (state bar del. 1989—). General corporate, Public international. Office: General Elec Co 1 River Rd Schenectady NY 12305-2500

**BUSTAMANTE, NESTOR,** lawyer; b. Havana, Cuba, Apr. 20, 1960; came to the U.S., 1961; s. Nestor and Clara Rosa (Sanchez) B.; m. Marilyn Gonzalez, Sept. 20, 1986; children: Tiffany Alexandra, Nestor C. AA, U. Fla., 1980, BS in Journalism, 1982, JD, 1985. Bar: Fla. 1986, U.S. Dist. Ct. (so. dist.) Fla. 1989, U.S. Supreme Ct. 1991. Asst. state atty. State Atty.'s Office 11th Cir., Miami, 1986-88; juvenile serious offender prosecutor State Atty.'s Office, Miami, 1987-88, spl. prosecutor, gang prosecutor, 1987-88; asst. divsn. chief State Atty.'s Office-11th Jud. Cir., Miami, 1987-88; of counsel Fernandez-Caubi, Fernandez & Aguilar et al., Miami, 1988-89; atty. Ferencik, Libanoff, Brandt and Bustamante PA, Ft. Lauderdale, Fla., 1989—, ptnr., 1996—; mem. code and rules of evidence com. The Fla. Bar, 1989-90. Contbr. articles to newsletters. Named Hon. mem. Quien es Quien Publs., Inc., N.Y.C., 1990. Mem. ATLA (scoring judge nat. finals student trial advocacy competition 1994, 95), Fed. Bar Assn., Dade County Bar Assn. (mem. juvenile divsn. com. 1988-92, mem. media and pub. rels. com. 1989-91, mem. constrn. law com. 1990-91), Phi Delta Phi, U. Fla. Alumni Assn. Contracts commercial, Construction, Criminal. Office: Ferencik Libanoff Brandt & Bustamante PA 150 S Pine Island Rd Ste 400 Fort Lauderdale FL 33324-2667

**BUTALID, CECILIA ESTORES,** lawyer, real estate company executive; b. Tanza, Cavite, Philippines, Sept. 7, 1936; came to U.S., 1973; d. Crisostomo S. and Carmen (Pulido) Estores; widowed; children: Amando, Zachary. Student, Philippines Secretarial Coll., 1954; BA, Adamson U., Philippines, 1956; LLB, Lycuem Philippines, 1963. Election registrar Commn. on Election, Cavite, Philippines, 1965-67, election supr., 1967-74; sales rep. Roland Land Devel. Co., San Diego, 1974-77; sales mgr. Roland Land Inc., San Diego, 1977-81, dist. mgr., 1981-88, v.p. sales, 1988-97, v.p., gen. mgr., 1997—. Mem. Gloria Macapagal Aroyo Club (organizer 1997—). Home: 2452 Bear Rock Gln Escondido CA 92026-5045 Office: Roland Land Inc 16661 Ventura Blvd PH Encino CA 91436-1919

**BUTCHER, BRUCE CAMERON,** lawyer; b. N.Y.C., Feb. 17, 1947; s. John Richard and Dorothy Helen (Wehner) B.; m. Kathryn Ann Fiddler, Oct. 12, 1979; 1 child, Kristen Ann. BS, Belknap Coll., 1969; JD, St. John's U., N.Y.C., 1972. Bar: N.Y. 1973, U.S. Dist. Ct. (so. dist.) N.Y. 1974, La. 1980, U.S. Dist. Ct. (ea. dist.) La. 1980, U.S. Ct. Appeals (5th and 11th cirs.) 1981, Tex. 1993. Assoc. Laporte and Meyers, N.Y.C., 1972-73; asst. chief contract div. Corp. Counsel's Office City of N.Y., 1973-79; ptnr. Chaffe, McCall, Phillips, Toler & Sarpy, New Orleans, 1980-84; prin. Bruce C. Butcher, P.C., Metairie, La., 1985-93; of counsel Smith Martin & Schneider, New Orleans, 1993-94; gen. coun. The Vulcan Group, Birmingham, Ala., 1994-95, Favalora Constructors, Inc., 1995—; pres., gen. counsel Tailgators Restaurant, LLC, New Orleans, LA, 1994—. Mem. ABA (regional chmn. pub. report 1975, state chmn. pub. contracts sect. 1984-95, cert. of performance 1975), La. Bar Assn., Am. Arbitration Assn., New Orleans Country Club (pres. 1994), New Orleans Squash Club, Crescent Club. Federal civil litigation, General civil litigation, Construction. Home: 344 Homestead Ave Metairie LA 70005-3707 Office: 933 Metairie Rd Metairie LA 70005-4037

**BUTLER, CASS C.,** lawyer; b. Logan, Utah, Feb. 15, 1956; s. Dail Junior and Florence (Griffen) B.; m. Stacia Lynn Taylor, Sept. 2, 1989. BA in Fin., U. Utah, 1980; JD, Brigham Young U., 1983. Bar: Utah 1984, U.S. Dist. Ct. Utah 1986, U.S. Claims Ct. 1984. Law clk to hon. justice Moody T. Tidwell III U.S. Claims Ct., Washington, 1983-84; assoc. solicitor U.S. Dept. Interior, Washington, 1984-87; assoc. Watkiss & Campbell, Salt Lake City, 1987-89; ptnr. Watkiss & Saperstein, Salt Lake City, 1989-92, Ballard Spahr Andrews & Ingersoll, Salt Lake City, 1992-94; shareholder Callister Nebeker & McCullough, Salt Lake City, 1994—. Mem. ABA, Assn. Trial Lawyers Am. General civil litigation, Construction, Insurance. Home: 3925 Prospector Dr Salt Lake City UT 84121-4606 Office: Callister Nebeker et al 10 E South Temple Ste 900 Salt Lake City UT 84133-1115

**BUTLER, CHARLES RANDOLPH, JR.,** federal judge; b. 1940. BA, Washington and Lee U., 1962; LLB, U. Ala., 1966. Assoc. Hamilton Butler Riddick and LaTour, Mobile, Alal., 1966-69; asst. pub. defender Mobile County, 1969-70, dist. atty., 1971-75; ptnr. Butler and Sullivan, Mobile, 1975-84, Hamilton Butler Riddick Tarlton and Sullivan P.C., Mobile, 1984-88; dist. judge U.S. Dist. Ct. (so. dist.) Ala., Mobile, 1988-94, chief dist. judge, 1994—; adj. prof. criminal justice program U. So. Ala., 1972-76. Active UMS Prep. Sch. Alumni Assn. 1st lt. USAR, 1962-64. Named One of Outstanding Young Men of Am., Mobile County Jaycees, 1971. Mem. Ala. Bar Assn., Mobile County Bar Assn. (jud. coun. 11th cir., jud. conf. com. on criminal law, jud. conf. com. 1999—). Office: US Dist Ct 113 Saint Joseph St Mobile AL 36602-3683

**BUTLER, DONALD K.,** lawyer; b. Newport News, Va., Feb. 4, 1944; s. Grover Cleveland Butler and Nettie Louise (Peele) Vince; married Jan. 29, 1965 (div.); 1 child, Robin Player Michelsen; m. Chena Allison, Sept. 15, 1979; children: Allison Peele, Charlotte Louise. BA, U. Richmond, 1966, JD, 1970. Bar: Va. 1970. Assoc., ptnr. Cole, Wells & Bradshaw, Richmond, Va., 1970-78; pvt. practice Richmond, 1978-81; ptnr. Morano, Colan & Butler and predecessor Morano & Butler, Richmond, 1981—; lectr. on family law at seminars and law schs. Contbr. articles to law revs. Mem. Va. State Bar (bd. govs. 1978-82, chmn. family law sect. 1980-81), Va. Trial Lawyers Assn. (chmn. family law sect. 1993), Richmond Bar Assn., Am. Acad. Matrimonial Lawyers (pres. Va. chpt. 1997—). Avocations: golf, cooking. Family and matrimonial. Office: Morano Colan & Butler 526 N Boulevard Richmond VA 23220-3309

**BUTLER, JACK A.,** lawyer; b. Nashville, Oct. 26, 1937. BA, Vanderbilt U., 1959; JD, Nashville Sch. of Law, 1962. Bar: Tenn. 1962. Pvt. practice Nashville, 1962-89; ptnr. Butler & Phillips, Nashville, 1989—; instr. Nashville Law Sch. Moot Ct., 1968—; NITA Faculty U. Tenn., Knoxville, 1978, Vanderbilt U. Law Sch., Nashville, 1988; faculty Nat. Bus. Inst., Inc., 1989-90, 1992-93, Law Seminars Internat., 1990, 91. Contbr. articles to profl. publs. Past pres. Percy Priest P.T.A.; founder former bd. dirs. Brentwood Acad; bd. dirs. March of Dimes 1972-75, Commodore Yacht Club 1972-76 (past pres. 1976), Tenn. Assn. Hosp. Attys. 1977-80, St. Bernard's High Sch. 1977-79, Westside Hosp. 1973-90; mem. Christ Presbyn. Ch.; maj. USAFR, 1954-74. Nashville Bar Found. fellow, 1994—. Mem. ABA (automobile com. 1975-76), Tenn. Bar Assn. (chmn. legal aid referral svc. com. 1967-68), Nashville Bar Assn. (chmn. domestic rels. com., 1968, 69, gen. sessions com. 1968-69, medico-legal dept., 1975-80, medico-legal com., 1972-75, 1983-84; bd. dirs. 1966-70, v.p. 1969, 70), Am. Trial Lawyers Assn., Tenn. Trial Lawyers Assn. (bd. govs. 1973-81, treas. 1977-78), Am. Bd. Trial Advocates (treas. Tenn. chpt. 1985, 89, 90; pres.-elect Tenn. chpt. 1990, pres. Tenn. chpt. 1992), Internat. Soc. Barristers, Inns of Ct., Am. Judicature Soc., Nashville Barrister's Club, Cedar Creek Club (bd. dirs. 1978-81), Scottish Rite Shrine Lodge. Democrat. Avocations: hunting, racquetball. Personal injury, Workers' compensation, Criminal. Office: Butler & Phillips First Am Ctr Ste 2395 315 Deaderick St Nashville TN 37238-0002

**BUTLER, JAMES GLENN, JR.,** lawyer; b. Topeka, Dec. 16, 1943; s. James Glenn and Rubye Louise (Schutter) B.; m. Kathleen M. Harqadon, Sept. 20, 1975 (div. Jan. 1993); children: Jay, Mimi, James Glenn III, Polly, Joe. BS in Acctg., U. Kans., 1965; JD, Washburn U., 1969. Bar: Kans. 1969, U.S. Dist. Ct. Kans. 1969, U.S. Ct. Appeals (10th cir.) 1970, U.S. Tax Ct. 1971, U.S. Dist. Ct. (we. dist.) Mo. 1982. Pvt. practice acctg., Kansas City, Kans., 1965-66; assoc. Wallace Saunders Austin Brown & Enochs, Overland Park, Kans., 1969—, mem. mgmt. com., 1989%; bd. dirs. Berkel & Co. Contractors, Bonner Springs, Kans., 1993—. Pres. Shawnee Mission Med. Ctr. Found., Merriam, Kans., 1985, 86; mem. fin. com. Shawnee Mission Med. Ctr. Mem. Kans. Bar Assn., Mo. Bar Assn., Kansas City Bar Assn. (chmn. mgmt. com. 1990-94), Optimists (pres. Overland Park 1972-73). Avocation: golf. Estate planning, Real property, Banking. Home: 9148 W 116th St Overland Park KS 66210-1911 Office: Wallace & Saunders 10111 W 87th St Overland Park KS 66212-4673

**BUTLER, JOHN EDWARD,** lawyer; b. Teaneck N.J., Dec. 8, 1946; s. John Edward and Alice Mary (Knorr) B.;children: Jennifer, Kathryn, John Michael; m. Elizabeth M. Fair, Mar. 12, 1994. Probate, General practice, Personal injury. Home: 120 E Washington St Ste 825 Syracuse NY 13202-4014

**BUTLER, JOHN THOMAS,** lawyer; b. Coral Gables, Fla., Aug. 6, 1954; s. Donald Hubert and Winifred Empire (Hicks) B.; m. Christina Louise Smith, June 8, 1991. B in Indsl. Engring. with highest honors, Ga. Inst. Tech., 1976; JD cum laude, Harvard U., 1979. Bar: Fla., U.S. Dist. Ct. (so. dist.) Fla., U.S. Ct. Appeals (11th cir.). Student engr. Fla. Power & Light Co., Miami, summer 1973-76; law clk. Bradford, Williams, McKay, Kimbrell, Hamman & Jennings, Miami, summer 1977, Beveridge, Fairbanks & Diamond, Washington, summer 1978; assoc. Steel, Hector & Davis, Miami, 1979-86, ptnr., 1986—. Trustee Miami Mus. of Sci., 1996—; mem. schs. com. Harvard Club of Miami, 1982—. Mem. ABA, Greater Miami C. of C. Democrat. Avocations: bicycle racing, tennis, theater, music. Environmental, Insurance. Home: 5850 SW 85th St South Miami FL 33143-8224 Office: 200 S Biscayne Blvd Ste 4000 Miami FL 33131-2310

**BUTLER, PAUL BASCOMB, JR.,** lawyer; b. Charleston, S.C., Nov. 27, 1947; s. Paul B. and Mary Anna (Tisdale) B.; m. Virginia Eldridge, June 14, 1969; children: Jeffrey Bryan, Robert Paul. BA, Emory U., 1969, MDiv cum laude, 1972, JD with distinction, 1976. Bar: Ga. 1976, Fla. 1977; ordained to ministry United Meth. Ch., 1970. United Meth. Ch., 1970—; Assoc. min. First United Meth. Ch., Phoenix, 1972-73; assoc. Swift, Currie, McGhee and Hiers, Atlanta, 1976-79; ptnr. Butler, Burnette & Pappas, Tampa, Fla., 1979-97, of counsel, 1998—; Chancellor Fla. Ann. Conf. United Meth. Ch., 1997—. Contbr. articles to profl. jours. Chair com. on new church devel. Fla. annual conf. United Meth. Ch., 1996—, chair bd. missions and ch. ext. Tampa dist. Uited Meth. Ch., Inc., 1992-96; pastor Temple Terrace United Meth., Tampa, 1998—. Mem. ABA (chmn. Nat. Inst. sect. of tort and ins. practice 1987-89, ho. of dels. 1993-95, coun. mem. sect. of tort and ins. practice 1990-93, chmn. task force on civil justice reform, chmn. property ins. law com. 1985-86, editor So. Region Annotated Homeowner's Policy), Fedn. of Ins. and Corp. Counsel (dean Litigation Mgmt. Coll. 1996-98, chair litigation mgmt. coll. adv. coun. 1998—), Def. Rsch. Inst. (chmn. ins. law com. 1989-92, chmn. Amcus com. 1994-97, bd. dirs. 1995-98, vice chair law inst. 1998-99, chair law inst. 1999—), Fla. Def. Lawyers Assn., Hillsborough County Bar Assn., Internat. Assn. Def. Counsel (vice chair property ins. com. 1993-96), Assn. Def. Trial Attys. Democrat. Clubs: Temple Terr. (Fla.) Golf and Country. Avocations: golf, tennis. Insurance, Federal civil litigation, State civil litigation. Office: Butler Burnette & Pappas Ste 1100 6200 W Courtney Campbell Cswy Tampa FL 33607-5946

**BUTLER, PETER JOSEPH,** lawyer; b. New Orleans, Oct. 19, 1935; s. Peter Butler and Catherine (Browne) B.; m. Billie Butler, Jan. 30, 1960; children: Peter, Tommy, Julie. BBA, Loyola U., New Orleans, 1957; LLB, Loyola U., 1959. Bar: La., U.S. Supreme Ct., U.S. Ct. Appeals (5th cir.), U.S. Tax Ct., U.S. Ct. Claims, U.S. Dist. Ct. La. Law clk. Orleans Parish Civil Dist. Ct., New Orleans, 1959-60, U.S. Dist. Ct. (ea. dist.) La., New Orleans, 1960-62; assoc./ptnr. Sehrt, Boyle & Wheeler, New Orleans, 1962-70; mng. ptrn. Butler, Heebe & Hirsch, New Orleans, 1970-88; mem. exec. com. Sessions, Fishman, Boisfontaine, Nathan, et al, New Orleans, 1988-90; shareholder Locke Purnell Rain Harrell, Dallas/New Orleans, 1990-95, Deutsch, Kerrigan & Stiles, 1995-96; spl. counsel Breazeale, Sachse & Wilson, LLP, 1997—; mem. faculty, mem. adv. bd. Loyola Law Sch., New Orleans; mem. disciplinary com., mem. civil justice adv. group U.S. Dist. Ct. (ea. dist.) La. Mem. Fed. Bar Assn., ABA, La. State Bar Assn. General civil litigation, Banking, Franchising. Office: 909 Poydras St Ste 1500 New Orleans LA 70112-4016

**BUTLER, RANDALL EDWARD,** lawyer; b. Houston, Sept. 11, 1954; m. Katherine Ann Simmons, Aug. 25, 1973; children: Lauren Elizabeth, Mary Katherine. BA magna cum laude, Houston Bapt. U., 1976; postgrad., Southwestern Bapt. Theol. Sem., 1976-77; JD cum laude, U. Houston, 1980. Bar: Tex. 1980, Fed. Bar 1981. Briefing atty. 14th Ct. of Civil Appeals, Houston, 1980-81; assoc. Fulbright & Jaworski, Houston, 1981-89, ptnr., 1989-91; ptnr. Cook & Wallace PC, 1992, Cook & Butler LLP, 1992-96, Cook Butler & Doyle LLP, Houston, 1996-98; pres. Randall E. Butler P.C., 1992—; instr. Houston Bapt. U., 1980-81; adj. prof. med. malpractice U. Houston Law Ctr. Contbr. articles to profl. jours. Bd. dirs. UBA Ctr. for Counseling, 1989-91, mem. pres.'s coun. Houston Bapt U., 1989-91, bd. trustees, 1990-92. Recipient Pres.'s award Houston Bapt. U., 1976; Riverside scholar, 1976; grantee Houston Bapt. U. Edn. Found. Fellow Houston Bar Found.; mem. ABA, State Bar of Tex. (ADR sect.). Avocations: snow skiing, hiking, history, landscape gardening. Alternative dispute resolution, Personal injury, Product liability. Office: Randall E Butler P C Mediation & Conflict Mgmt 6535 Vanderbilt St Houston TX 77005-3822

**BUTLER, REX LAMONT,** lawyer; b. New Brunswick, N.J., Mar. 24, 1951; s. Ekker and Beatrice (Curry) B.; m. Stephanie Butler; children: Nijel Jaibrun, Vikteria Lamontra, Octavia Reneè Lamontra, Synclaire Lamontra. AA with honors, Fla. Jr. Coll., 1975; BA, U. North Fla., 1977; JD, Howard U., 1983. Bar: Alaska 1983, U.S. Dist. Ct. Alaska 1983, U.S. Ct. Appeals (9th cir.) 1984, U.S. Ct. Appeals (D.C. cir.) 1984, U.S. Supreme Ct. 1996. Assoc. M. Ashley Dickerson, Inc., Anchorage, 1983-84; profl. legis. asst. State of Alaska, Juneau, 1984; asst. atty. gen. State of Alaska, Anchorage, 1984-85; pvt. practice Anchorage, 1985—; adj. prof. law Anchorage C.C., 1985; adj. prof. U. Alaska, Anchorage, 1990—; mem. State Ct. Criminal Pattern Jury Instructions Com., 1997; chmn. lawyer rep. com. Alaska 9th Cir. Judicial Conf., 1997-98. Pres. Alaska Black Caucus, Anchorage, 1986, bd. dirs., 1987-88; gen. counsel NAACP, Anchorage, 1985-87, life mem.; commr. Anchorage Telephone Utility, 1985-87; trustee Anchorage Sr. Ctr., Inc., 1985-87, Shiloh Missionary Bapt. Ch., Anchorage, 1985—; bd. dirs. Ctr. Drug Problems, Anchorage, 1985-86, Alaska Civil Liberties Union, 1987-88; active fin. com. Dem. Cen. Com. Alaska. With USN, 1969-73. Named one of Outstanding Young Men Am., 1984; recipient Cert. Appreciation, African Relief Campaign, 1985. Mem. ABA, Nat. Bar Assn., Nat. Assn. Criminal Defense Lawyers, Alaska Bar Assn., Assn. Trial Lawyers Am., Anchorage Bar Assn., Alaska Trial Lawyers Assn., Lions Internat., Omega Psi Phi (dist. counselor 1995-96, 98—). Democrat. Fax: (907) 276-3306. E-mail: rexb@pobox.alaska.net. Personal injury, Criminal, Juvenile. Home: PO Box 200025 Anchorage AK 99520-0025 Office: 745 W 4th Ave Ste 300 Anchorage AK 99501-2136

**BUTLER, ROBERT ANTHONY,** lawyer; b. Akron, Ohio, Feb. 24, 1932; m. Elva Celli Butler, June 19, 1954 (div. 1976); children: Debra Zahara, Michael C., Dorothy Brundige; m. Carole Cronin Berry, 1976 (div. 1992); 1 child, Beth Ann Butler. JD, Ohio State U., 1955. Bar: Ohio 1956, U.S. Dist. Ct. Ohio, U.S. Ct. Mil. Appeals, 1959; cert. specialist in worker's compensation. Ptnr. William J. Ahern, Columbus, 1960-63; founder, sr. ptnr. Butler, Cincione, DiCuccio & Barnhart, Columbus, 1963—; dir. spl. and continuing legal edn. Capital U. Law Sch.; preceptor Ohio State U. Coll. of Medicine; presenter in field. Contbr. articles to profl. jours. 1st lt. USAF, 1957-60. Mem. Columbus Bar Assn. (former pres., Award of Merit), Franklin County Trial Lawyers Assn. (former pres.). Democrat. Avocations: fiction writing, water colors, calligraphy. Workers' compensation. Office: Butler Cincione DiCuccio & Barnhart 50 W Broad St Ste 700 Columbus OH 43215-3337

**BUTLER, SAMUEL COLES,** lawyer; b. Logansport, Ind., Mar. 10, 1930; s. Melvin Linwood and Jane Lavina (Flynn) B.; m. Sally Eugenia Thackston, June 28, 1952; children: Samuel Coles, Leigh F., Elizabeth J. AB magna cum laude, Harvard U., 1951, LLB magna cum laude, 1954. Bar: D.C. 1954, Ind. 1954, N.Y. 1957. Law clk. to Justice Minton U.S. Supreme Ct., 1954; assoc. Cravath, Swaine & Moore, N.Y.C., 1956-60, ptnr., 1961—; dir. Ashland Inc., Millipore Corp., U.S. Trust Corp. Trustee Vassar Coll., 1969-77, N.Y. Pub. Libr., 1979—, Am. Mus. Natural History, 1989-93, chmn. bd., 1999—; chmn. Harvard Coll. Fund, 1977-85; bd. overseers Harvard U., 1982-88, pres. bd., 1986-88; bd. dirs. Culver Ednl. Found., 1981—. With U.S. Army, 1954-56. Mem. Coun. Fgn. Rels. General corporate, Mergers and acquisitions, Securities. Home: 1220 Park Ave New York NY 10128-1733 Office: Cravath Swaine & Moore 825 8th Ave New York NY 10019-7475

**BUTLER, STEVEN IRWIN,** financial consultant; b. N.Y.C., June 24, 1948; s. Samuel and Isabella (Goodman) B.; m. Barbara Griffin Moss, Aug. 21, 1971 (div. June 1982); children: David, Daniel. BS in Bus. and Econs., Wilmington Coll. of Ohio, 1970; grad. in fin. mgmt., U. Denver, 1982. Asst. br. mgr. Chittenden Trust Co., Burlington, Vt., 1970-74; regional br. mgr. Security Trust Co., Rochester, N.Y., 1974-77; loan officer, asst. treas. Chem. Bank of Syracuse, 1977; v.p. United Bank of Skyline, Denver, 1978-80; pres., dir. Seafirst Indsl. Bank, Denver, 1980-82; sr. v.p. Century Bank, Denver, 1982-84, Dominion Nat. Bank, Denver, 1984-85; pres., dir. Market Nat. Bank, Denver, 1985; dir. of bank cons. Laventhol & Horwath, Washington, 1986-90; v.p. Peterson Cons. Ltd. Partnership, Washington, 1991-94, Tucker Alan, Inc., Washington, 1994-95; ptnr. Altschuler, Melvoin and Glasser LLP, Washington, 1995-98; dir. dispute consulting svcs. Deloitte & Touche, LLP, Washington, 1998—; expert witness in fin.; spkr. in field. Contbr. articles to profl. jours. Mem. Greater Washington Bd. of Trade, Washington, 1996—. Named Nat. Fin. Svcs. Advocate of Yr. Small Bus. Adminstrn., 1985. Mem. ABA, Am. Bankruptcy Inst., D.C. Bar Assn., Greater Washington Soc. of CPAs, Am. Arbitrators. Avocations: biking, tennis, jazz. Fax: 202-955-6592. E-mail: stebutler@dttus.com. Office: Deloitte & Touche LLP Dispute Consulting Svcs 1900 M Street NW Washington DC 20036-3564

**BUTT, EDWARD THOMAS, JR.,** lawyer; b. Chgo., Oct. 27, 1947; s. Edward T. and Helen Kathryn (Guy) B.; m. Leslie Laidlaw Hilton, Oct. 20, 1972; children: Julie Guy, Andrew McNaughton. BA, Lawrence U., 1968; JD, U. Mich., 1971. Bar: Ill. 1971, U.S. Dist. Ct. (no. dist.) Ill. 1971, Wis. 1975, U.S. Dist. Ct. (ea. dist.) Wis. 1978, U.S. Ct. Appeals (7th cir.) 1978, U.S. Ct. Claims 1982, U.S. Ct. Appeals (6th cir.) 1986, U.S. Ct. Appeals (6th cir.) 1987, Mich. 1997. Assoc. Wildman, Harrold, Allen & Dixon, Chgo., 1971-75, 76-78, ptnr., 1979-94; ptnr. Lund & Butt, S.C., Minocqua, Wis., 1975-76; of counsel Swanson, Martin & Bell, Chgo. and Wheaton, Ill., 1994—. Bd. dirs. Constl. Rights Found., Chgo. Mem. ABA, State Bar Wis., 7th Cir. Bar Assn., Def. Rsch. Inst., Crystal Lake Yacht Club, Crystal Downs Country Club. Avocations: distance running, sailing, golf. General civil litigation, Insurance, Product liability. Home: Michabou Shores 1006 Tiba Rd Frankfort MI 49635 also: 3903 Forest Ave Western Springs IL 60558-1049 Office: Swanson Martin & Bell 2100 Manchester Rd Ste 1420 Wheaton IL 60187-4534

**BUTTER, STEPHEN H.,** lawyer, sole practitioner; b. Cambridge, Mass., Nov. 11, 1940; s. Max M. and Ethel (Siletsky) B.; m. Eugenia Butter, June 12, 1994; 1 child, David Jonathan. BBA, U. Miami, 1962, JD, 1965. Bar: Fla. 1965. Sole practitioner Aventura, Fla., 1962—. Author: Legal Rights to Draft Deferrment, 1970, No Fault Divorce in Florida, 1971, Legal Rights of Women in Florida, 1975; contbr. article to Fla. Bar Jour. Mem. Fla. Bar Assn. (com. mem. 1993), Dade County Bar Assn. (com. mem. 1992), North Dade Bar Assn. (com. mem. 1991), Broward Bar Assn. (com. mem. 1990). Jewish. Avocations: golf, tennis. Family and matrimonial. Office: Turnberry Plaza Penthouse 2875 NE 191st St Aventura FL 33180-2801

**BUTTERFIELD, TOBY MICHAEL JOHN,** lawyer; b. London, Dec. 6, 1965; came to U.S., 1989; s. Lord John and Lady Isabel Butterfield. BA with honors, Oxford (Eng.) U., 1988; LLM in Internat. Law, NYU, 1990. Bar: N.Y. 1992, U.S. Dist. Ct. (so. dist.) N.Y. 1992, U.S. Ct. Appeals (2d and 5th cirs.) 1997. Pupil barrister Barristers Chambers, London, 1990-91; assoc. Sullivan & Cromwell, N.Y.C., 1991-94, Kay Collyer & Boose LLP, N.Y.C., 1994—. Hardwicke scholar, 1988; Greenberg scholar, 1989. Mem. ABA (antitrust internat. com. 1993-94), Assn. Bar City N.Y. (chair state cts. superior jurisdiction com. 1997—, cts. subcom.), Lesbian and Gay Law Assn. (bd. dirs. 1995-97, chair membership com. 1997-99). Avocation: squash. General civil litigation, Trademark and copyright, Entertainment. Office: Kay Collyer & Boose LLP One Dag Hammarskjold Plz New York NY 10017-2201

**BUTTERKLEE, NEIL HOWARD,** lawyer; b. Bklyn., Mar. 17, 1958; s. Samuel and Edith (Uday) B.; m. Arlene Marie Eberle, July 5, 1982. BA, SUNY, Stony Brook, 1980, MS, 1982; MBA, Adelphi U., Garden City, N.Y., 1987; JD, N.Y. Law Sch., 1992. Bar: Conn. 1992, N.Y. 1993, D.C. 1994, U.S. Dist. Ct. (ea. and so. dists.) N.Y. 1993, U.S. Ct. Appeals (D.C. cir.) 1997, U.S. Supreme Ct., 1997. Tech. writer Consolidated Edison Co. N.Y. Inc., N.Y.C., 1982-83, analyst, 1983-89, sr. analyst, 1989-93, atty., 1993-95, staff atty., 1995-99, sr. staff atty., 1999—. Editor: Law Review. Recipient Scholarship N.Y. Law Sch., N.Y.C., 1988-92; nationally ranked fencer U.S. Fencing Assn., 1984-88. Mem. ABA, N.Y. State Bar Assn., Conn. Bar Assn., Assn. Bar City N.Y. Avocations: golf, writing. Administrative and regulatory, Contracts commercial, FERC practice. Office: Consolidated Edison Co NY 4 Irving Pl Rm 1815 New York NY 10003-3598

**BUTTERMAN, JAY RONALD,** lawyer; b. N.Y.C., June 15, 1958; s. Louis and Ellen (Schmeltzer) B. BA, Vassar Coll., 1983; JD, Yeshiva U., 1988. Bar: N.J. 1988, N.Y. 1989, U.S. Dist. Ct. (so. dist.) N.Y. 1991, U.S. Dist. Ct. (ea. dist.) N.Y. 1996, U.S. Dist. Ct. N.J. 1988. Assoc. Hoffinger Friedland Dobrish Bernfeld & Hasen, N.Y.C., 1988-91; sole practitioner N.Y.C., 1991-95; mng. ptnr. Law firm of Jay R. Butterman, N.Y.C., 1995—. Recipient Outstanding Acad. Achievement award Acad. Am. Matrimonial Lawyers, 1988. Mem. ABA, N.Y. State Bar Assn., Assn. Bar City N.Y. Democrat. Avocations: Oriental art, antiquarian books. Family and matrimonial, Entertainment, General civil litigation. Office: 425 Park Ave Fl 26 New York NY 10022-3506

**BUTTERS, FREDERICK FRANCIS,** lawyer; b. Albion, Mich., Oct. 8, 1961; s. Frederick Leon and Joyce Kay (Weishar) B. BS in Architecture, Lawrence Tech. U., 1983, BArch, 1984; JD, Wayne State U., 1991. Bar: Mich. 1991, U.S. Dist. Ct. (ea. dist.) Mich. 1991, U.S. Ct. Appeals (6th cir.) 1995, U.S. Ct. Claims 1996, U.S. Supreme Ct. 1996. Asst. prof. architecture Lawrence Tech. U., Southfield, Mich., 1983-84; archtl. detailer Giffels & Assoc., Southfield, 1984-87; project arch. Stucky & Vitale Archs., Royal Oak, Mich., 1987-94; prin. atty. Federlein & Keranen, P.C., Bloomfield Hills, Mich., 1994—. Mem. ABA, AIA, Am. Arbitration Assn. (arbitrator constrn. industry 1994—), State Bar Mich., Lawrence Tech. U. Alumni Assn. (bd. dirs. 1996-97). Construction, Professional liability, General civil litigation. Home: 21738 Fairway Dr Southfield MI 48034-4342 Office: Federlein & Keranen PC 6895 Telegraph Rd Bloomfield Hills MI 48301-3138

**BUTTERWORTH, DAVID GARDNER,** lawyer; b. Bryn Mawr, Pa., Nov. 13, 1957; m. Susan Vinson Cauffman, May 16, 1987; children: D. Gardner, Henry M. BA in Chemistry, Conn. Coll., 1980; MS in Chemistry, Drexel U., 1986; JD, Villanova U., 1989. Bar: Pa., 1989; U.S. Dist. Ct. (ea. dist.) Pa. 1994. Chemist Rohm & Haas, Springhouse, Pa., 1980-86; atty. Morgan Lewis & Bockius, Phila., 1989-97, Miller Dunham & Doering, Phila., 1997-98, Butterworth & Campbell PC, Phila., 1998—. Editor-in-chief Villanova Environmental Law Jour., 1989. Mem. Environmental Profl. Assn. of Phila. Region (sec., treas. 1996—). Environmental, Real property, General civil litigation. Office: Butterworth & Campbell PC 1515 Market St Ste 1801 Philadelphia PA 19102-1918

**BUTTERWORTH, ROBERT A.,** state attorney general; b. Passaic, N.J., Aug. 20, 1942; m. Marta Prado. BA, BS, U. Fla.; JD, U. Miami. Prosecutor Fla., 1970-74; circuit and county judge, 1974-78; sheriff Broward County Sheriff's Office, 1978-82; head Fla. Dept. Hwy. Safety and Motor Vehicles, Tallahassee, 1982-84; mayor City of Sunrise, 1984-87; atty. gen. State of Fla., Tallahassee, 1987—. Office: Capital PL01 Dept Legal Affairs Tallahassee FL 32399-1050

**BUTTS, CYRIL WILLIAM, JR.,** lawyer; b. Galesburg, Ill., June 8, 1954; s. Cyril William Sr. and Anna Rose (Weech) B.; m. Barbara Anne Kraul, Aug. 12, 1978; children: Cyril William III, Anna Kathleen, Brian Daniel. BS, U. Idaho, 1976; JD, St. Louis U., 1979. Bar: Ill. 1979, U.S. Dist. Ct. (cen. dist.) Ill. 1979. Assoc. Nelson, Gustafson & Blake, Galesburg, 1979-81, Peel, Henning, Mathers & McKee, Galesburg, 1981-84, Craig Collins, Chartered, Galesburg, 1984-87; pvt. practice Galesburg, 1987—; spl. asst. atty. gen. State of Ill., Springfield, 1984—; instr. W. Cen. Ill. Police Tng. Unit, Galesburg, 1987—. Active Knox County Dem.; bd. dirs., safety svc. com. mem. Knox County Red Cross; bd. dirs., vice-chmn. Am. Cancer Soc., Knox County chpt.; active Barbershop Quartet. Mem. Ill. State Bar Assn., Knox County Bar Assn., Galesburg Optimist Club, Galesburg Exchange Club, Galesburg Jaycees (bd. dirs.). Roman Catholic. Avocations: swimming, men's chorus, golfing, astronomy, history, theatre. Bankruptcy, Family and matrimonial, Criminal. Home: 1372 N Prairie St Galesburg IL 61401-1884 Office: 119 S Cherry St Galesburg IL 61401-4527

**BUTZBAUGH, ALFRED M.,** lawyer; b. Benton Harbor, Mich., July 25, 1940. AB, U. Mich., 1963, JD, 1966; MBA, U. Chgo., 1983. Bar: Mich. 1967, Tex. 1991. Ptnr. Butzbaugh & Dewane, St. Jospeh, Mich. Mem. ABA, State Bar Mich. (rep. assembly 1973-79, commr. 1992—, treas. 1996-97), State Bar Tex., Berrien County Bar Assn. (pres. 1982-83). E-mail: Al.bdlaw@parrett.net. General civil litigation, Taxation, general. Office: Butzbaugh & Dewane PLC Law and Title Bldg 811 Ship St Saint Joseph MI 49085-1171*

**BUTZBAUGH, ELDEN W., JR.,** lawyer; b. Benton Harbor, Mich., Dec. 2, 1937; s. Elden W. and Lucy Currie (Moore) B.; m. Judith Ann Wise, July 20, 1963; children: Daniel, T.D., Bud, Josh. BA, Western Mich. U., 1961, MBA, 1963; JD, U. Mich., 1968. Bar: Mich. 1968. Pres. Butzbaugh and Ehrenberg, St. Joseph, Mich., 1968—. Author: No-Fault Divorce: Practice and Procedure, 1978. Mem. ABA, State Bar Mich., Berrien County Bar Assn., Assn. Trial Lawyers Am., Mich. Trial Lawyers Assn., Berrien County Trial Lawyers Assn., Benton Harbor-St. Joseph Rotary Club, U. Mich. Alumni Assn., U. Mich. Pres. Club, U. Mich. Victors Club, Western Mich. 300 Club, St. Joseph River Yacht Club, St. Joseph Elks Club. General civil litigation, Personal injury, Product liability. Home: 101 N Pier St Saint Joseph MI 49085-1042 Office: Butzbaugh and Ehrenberg 316 Main St Saint Joseph MI 49085-1298

**BUTZNER, JOHN DECKER, JR.,** federal judge; b. Scranton, Pa., Oct. 2, 1917. B.A., U. Scranton, 1939; LL.B., U. Va., 1941. Bar: Va. bar 1941. Pvt. practice law Fredericksburg, 1941-58; judge 15th and 39th Jud. Cir. of Va., 1958-62; U.S. judge Ea. Dist. Va., 1962-67; cir. judge U.S. Ct. Appeals (4th cir.), Richmond, Va., 1967—; judge for appointment of ind. counsel U.S. Ct. Appeals for D.C. Cir., 1988-98. Served with USAAF, 1942-45.

**BUZAK, EDWARD JOSEPH,** lawyer; b. Jersey City, Apr. 20, 1948; s. Edward and Nellie (Scalone) B.; m. Gail Marie Capizzi, July 24, 1971; children: Craig E., Lindsay T. BA, Union Coll., 1970; JD, Georgetown U., 1973. Bar: N.J. 1973, D.C. 1974. Assoc. Villoresi & Flanagan, Boonton, N.J., 1973-75; ptnr. Villoresi & Buzak, Boonton, N.J., 1976-82; owner Edward J. Buzak, Montville, N.J., 1983—; trustee Housing Partnership of Morris County, Morristown, N.J., 1992—. Contbr. articles to profl. jours. Chmn. affordable housing com., asst. counsel N.J. State League of Municipalities, Trenton, N.J., 1986—; asst. counsel N.J. Planning Ofcls., 1998—. Mem. Assn. Environ. Authorities (legis. com. chair 1986—), N.J. Inst. Mcpl. Attys. (2d v.p.), N.J. State Bar Assn. (local gov. com. chair 1985-87). Roman Catholic. Avocations: running, skiing, music, reading. Municipal (including bonds), Land use and zoning (including planning), Environmental. Office: 150 River Rd Ste N4 Montville NJ 07045-8920

**BUZARD, DAVID ANDREW,** lawyer; b. Evanston, Ill., Dec. 8, 1961; s. Clifford Howard and Mary Louise (Dole) B.; m. Véronique Elisabeth Marie Ravisé-Noël, Nov. 25, 1985; children: Clémentine, Victor. Student, Carleton Coll., 1980-82; BA in Linguistics, Northwestern U., 1984; JD, Tulane U., 1990. Bar: Ill. 1991, Va. 1997, U.S. Ct. Mil. Appeals 1991, U.S. Ct. Appeals (4th cir.) 1991, U.S. Dist. Ct. (ea. dist.) Va. 1997, U.S. Dist. Ct. (no. dist.) Ill. 1998, U.S. Supreme Ct. 1998. Law clk. U.S. Atty.'s Office, New Orleans, 1988-90; judge advocate U.S. Navy, 1990-97; assoc. Glasser & Glasser, PLC, Norfolk, Va., 1997-98, Bennett & Zydron, P.C., Virginia Beach, Va., 1998—; v.p., counsel Alliance Française Chapitre de Grasse, Norfolk, Va., 1996—; judge Jessup Internat. Law Moot Ct. Competition, 1998. Contbr. articles to profl. jours. Lt. USN, 1990-97; lt. comdr. USNR, 1998—. Nat. Merit scholar. Mem. ATLA, Va. Trial Lawyers Assn., Norfolk and Portsmouth Bar Assn. (founder, chair mil. law and lawyers com. 1997—), Judge Advocates Assn., Disabled Am. Vets., Naval Res. Assn. Avocations: helping people, travel. Personal injury, General civil litigation, Military. Office: Bennett & Zydron PC 120 S Lynnhaven Rd Virginia Beach VA 23452-7419

**BUZULENCIA, MICHAEL DOUGLAS,** lawyer; b. Youngstown, Ohio, June 9, 1958; s. George and Emma (McClure) B.; m. Sarah J. Hirt, July 23, 1988; children: Hayley Catherine, Hannah Michelle. BBA, Youngstown State U., 1981; JD, Cleve. Marshall Coll. of Law, 1989. Bar: Ohio 1984, U.S. Dist. Ct. (no. dist.) Ohio 1984, U.S. Ct. Appeals (6th cir.) 1984, Pa. 1994. Lawyer Bennett & Harbarger Co., CPA, Cleve., 1984-86, William J. Urban Jr. Co. CPA, Warren, Ohio, 1986-89; lawyer, owner Michael D. Buzulencia, Atty., Warren, 1989—. Trustee SCOPE Inc. of Trumbull County, Warren, 1989-93, Warren Kiwanis, 1992, 95, Pakard Mus. Assn., Warren, 1989-93, N.E. Ohio Legal Svcs., Big Bros./Big Sisters, 1980-94, Family Svc. Assn.; legal counsel, dir. Warren Area Jaycees; legal counsel Home Builders Assn., Leadership Warren, 1993, Chapt. 7 Bankruptcy Trustee, 1995—, Northeast Ohio Leagal Svcs. bd. mem., 1996—. Avocations: jogging, phys. fitness. Bankruptcy, Contracts commercial, Real property. Office: 106 E Market St Ste 605 Warren OH 44481-1103

**BUZUNIS, CONSTANTINE DINO,** lawyer; b. Winnipeg, Man., Can., Feb. 3, 1958; came to U.S., 1982; s. Peter and Anastasia (Ginakes) B. BA, U. Man., 1980; JD, Thomas M. Cooley Law Sch., 1985. Bar: Mich. 1986, U.S. Dist. Ct. (ea. and we. dists.) Mich. 1986, Calif. 1986, U.S. Dist. Ct. (so. dist.) Calif. 1987, U.S. Supreme Ct. 1993. Assoc. Church, Kritselis, Wyble & Robinson, Lansing, Mich., 1986; assoc. Neil, Dymott, Perkins, Brown & Frank, San Diego, 1987-94, ptnr., 1994—; arbitrator San Diego County Mcpl. and Superior Cts.; judge pro tem San Diego Mcpl. Ct. Sec., treas. Sixty Plus Law Ctr., Lansing, 1985; active Vols. in Parole, San Diego, 1988—; bd. dirs. Hellenic Cultural Soc., 1993-98. Mem. ABA, FBA, ATLA, Mich. Bar Assn., Calif. Bar Assn., San Diego County Bar Assn., Desert Bar Assn., San Diego Trial Lawyers Assn., So. Calif. Def. Coun., State Bar Calif. (gov. 9th dist. young lawyers divsn. 1991-94, 1st v.p. 1993-94, pres. 1994-95, bd. govs. 1995-96) San Diego Barristers Soc. (bd. dirs. 1991-92), Pan Arcadian Fedn., Order of Ahepa (chpt. bd. dirs., v.p. 1995-98), Phi Alpha Delta. State civil litigation, Federal civil litigation, Personal injury. Home: 3419 Overpark Rd San Diego CA 92130-1865 Office: Neil Dymott Perkins Brown & Frank 1010 2nd Ave Ste 2500 San Diego CA 92101-4906

**BUZZARD, STEVEN RAY,** lawyer; b. Centralia, Wash., May 22, 1946; s. Richard James and Phylis Margaret (Bevington) B.; m. Joan Elizabeth Merrow, Nov. 11, 1967; children: Elizabeth Jane, Richard Wolcott, James Merrow. BA, Cen. Wash. State Coll., 1971; postgrad., U. Wash., 1973; JD, U. Puget Sound, 1975. Bar: Wash. 1975, U.S. Dist. Ct. (we. dist.) Wash. 1975, U.S. Supreme Ct. 1979, U.S. Tax Ct. 1983. Assoc. Shires, Kruse, Wallace, Roper & Kamps, Port Orchard, Wash., 1975-77; ptnr. Buzzard & O'Connell, Centralia, 1978-80, Buzzard & Tripp, Centralia, 1980-94, Buzzard & Assoc., Centralia, 1994—; city atty. Mossyrock, Wash., 1979-94, Vader, Wash., 1989-96, Bucoda, Wash., 1989-99; judge Centralia, 1979-80, Winlock, Wash., 1982—; sec. Consolidated Enterprizes Inc., Centralia, 1986-88; judge Clehalis (Wash.) Mcpl. Ct., 1998—. Chmn. bd. dirs. Lewis County Cmty. Svcs., Chehalis, Wash., 1981-84; bd. dirs. Lewis County United Way, 1993-95; mem. adv. bd. Centralia Sch. Dist., 1995—; trustee Dollars for Scholars, Scholarship Found., 1997—. Mem. ABA (rural judges com. 1986), Wash. State Bar Assn. (ct. rules com. 1992—), Lewis County Bar Assn. (past pres.), Assn. Trial Lawyers Am., Wash. State Trial Lawyers Assn., Wash. State Govt. Lawyers Bar Assn. (trustee, dist. and mcpl. rural judges com.), Dist. & Mcpl. Judges Assn. (ct. improvement com., long range planning com.), Kiwanis (pres.-elect 1991, pres. 1992-93, Disting. Past Pres. 1994), Elks (trustee Centralia chpt. 1981—). Avocations: running, boating, hiking, biking, fishing. Fax: (360) 330-2078. Personal injury, State civil litigation, General practice. Office: Buzzard & Assoc 314 Harrison Ave Centralia WA 98531-1326

**BUZZELLO, EILEEN REILLY,** lawyer; b. Lowell, Mass., June 17, 1947; d. Robert Thomas and Regina McKenzie Reilly; m. Edward N. Crofoot, Mar. 27, 1967 (div. Oct. 1974); children: Edward B., Robert M., Nash P.; m. James J. Buzzello, Feb. 28, 1992. AS, U. Nebr., Omaha, 1972, BS, 1988; JD, Creighton U., 1994. Bar: Nebr. 1994, U.S. Dist. Ct. Nebr. 1994, U.S. Ct. Appeals (8th cir.) 1998. Mgr. Union Pacific R.R., Omaha, 1978-93; mgr. quality State Nebr., Omaha, 1994-95; exec. dir. Domestic Violence Coordinating Coun., Omaha, 1995-96; tng. cons. Tng. and Cons. Connection, Omaha, 1996-97; pvt. practice, Omaha, 1994—. Host radio program Ask-A-Lawyer, KIOS-FM, Omaha, 1996—. Mem. ABA, Nebr. Bar Assn. (Pub. Svc. award 1997), Omaha Bar Assn. (chmn. pub. svc. com. 1997—, sec. 1999). Avocations: sculpture, music. Family and matrimonial, General practice. Office: 503 S 36th St Omaha NE 68105-1201

**BYCZYNSKI, EDWARD FRANK,** lawyer, financial executive; b. Chgo., Mar. 17, 1946; s. Edward James and Ann (Ruskey) B.; children—Stefan, Suzanne. B.A., U. Wis., 1968; J.D., U. Ill., 1972; Certificat de Droit, U. Caen, France, 1971. Bar: Ill. 1972, U.S. Dist. Ct. ( no. dist.) Ill. 1972, U.S. Supreme Ct. 1976. Title officer Chgo. Title Ins. Co., 1972-73; asst. regional counsel SBA, Chgo., 1973-76; pres. Alderstreet Investments, Portland, Oreg., 1976-82; pres. Nat. Tenant Network, Portland, 1981—, Bay Venture Corp., Portland, 1984—; ptnr. Haley, Pirok, Byczynski. Chgo., 1973-76. Contbr. articles to profl. jours. Mem. ABA, Ill. Bar Assn. Democrat. Real property, Franchising, Banking. Home: PO Box 2377 Lake Oswego OR 97035-0614 Office: 525 1st St Ste 105 Lake Oswego OR 97034-3100

**BYERS, GARLAND FRANKLIN, JR.,** private investigator, security firm executive; b. Rutherfordton, N.C., Jan. 11, 1968; s. Garland Franklin Sr. and Helen Kathryn (Cannon) B.; m. Heather Kristina Emory, June 5, 1987; children: Amber Dianna, Jonathan Wesley. AAS in Criminal Justice, Isothermal C.C., Spindale, N.C., 1991; BS in Criminal Justice, U. S.C., Spartanburg, 1993; postgrad., N.C. Ctrl. Sch. Law, 1996—. Chief of police Alexander Mills Police Dept., Forest City, N.C., 1988; police officer Rutherfordton Police Dept., 1988-90; cpl., dep. sheriff Rutherfordton County Sheriff's Dept., 1990-91; roving technician The New Cherokee Corp., Spindale, 1992-93; pvt. practice ins./loan agt. Primerica Fin. Svcs., Spindale, 1994-95; criminal justice instr. Isothermal C.C., Spindale, 1994-95; chief investigator N.C. State Dist. Attys. Office 29th Prosecutorial Dist., Rutherfordton, 1995-96; owner, pvt. investigator, counterintelligence specialist Byers Investigations, Hillsborough, N.C., 1997—. Avocations: reading, martial arts, swimming. Office: 1512 S Alston Ave Durham NC 27707-3252

**BYERS, MATTHEW T(ODD),** lawyer, educator; b. Ridley Park, Pa., May 30, 1963; s. Richard Lynn and Joyce Ann (Ralston) B.; m. Lori Byers; children: Amanda Michelle, Amber, Helen, David, Saren, Loren. BA, U. N. Mex., 1985, JD, 1990. Bar: N.Mex. 1990, U.S. Dist. Ct. N.Mex. 1991, U.S. Ct. Appeals (10th cir.) 1991, U.S. Tax Ct. 1991, Pa. 1997. Staff Los Alamos (N.Mex.) Nat. Lab., 1989-90; assoc. Marek, Francis & Byers, P.A., Carlsbad, N.Mex., 1990—; ptnr. Marek, Francis & Byers, P.A., Carlsbad, 1998—; assoc. Forry, Ullman, Ullman & Forry, Reading, Pa., 1997. Assoc. editor N. Mex. U. Law Review, 1990. Bd. dirs. United Way of Carlsbad, 1990-93. Recipient Cert. of Achievement Renaissance Program, Carlsbad, 1991. Mem. ABA, State Bar Assn. N.Mex., Eddy Cty. Bar Assn. (pres. 1993), George L. Reese Jr. Inn of Court, Pa. Bar Assn. Democrat. Baptist. Avocations: softball, music, reading. Bankruptcy, General practice, Probate. Office: Marek Francis & Byers PA 110 W Shaw St Carlsbad NM 88220-5878

**BYERS, RHONDA LEANN,** lawyer; b. Atlanta, Sept. 24, 1962; d. Kenneth Lee and Reecie Lee (Wienke) B. BS, U. Md., 1990; JD, Ga. State U., 1995. Bar: Ga. 1995, U.S. Ct. Appeals Ga. 1995. Rsch. asst. Pros. Atty.'s Coun., Smyrna, Ga., 1992-97; assoc. Law Firm of Mark Kadish, Atlanta, 1995-96; ptnr. Byers & Vignos, P.C., Atlanta, 1996-98; staff atty. UGA Legal Aid Clinic, Athens, Ga., 1998—. Contbr. articles to profl. jours. Mem. ACLU. with USMC, 1982-86. Mem. ABA, Western Cir. of Ga. Bar Assn., Ga. Assn. Criminal Def. Lawyers, Nat. Assn. Criminal Def. Lawyers. Criminal, Appellate, Juvenile. Office: UGA Legal Aid and Defender Clinic 160 E Washington St Athens GA 30602-1518

**BYLER, WILLIAM BRYAN,** lawyer; b. Williamsburg, Va., Dec. 30, 1963; s. M. Elvin and Grace S. Byler; m. Lieke Van Huystee, Mar. 26, 1989; children: Jacqueline S., Katarina A., Elizabeth J., William B. BA in Philosophy, Franklin & Marshall, 1986; JD, Widener U., 1993. Bar: Pa. 1993. Atty. Blakinger Byler & Thomas, Lancaster, Pa., 1993-97; mng. ptnr. Byler Goldman & Goodley P.C., Lancaster, 1997—; lectr. Pa. Real Estate Broker Course Series, Lancaster, 1996—. Mem. Pa. Bar Assn., MEB Sertoma Club (chmn. bd. dirs. 1998—). Real property, Estate planning, Contracts commercial. Office: Byler Goldman Goodley PC 363 W Roseville Rd Lancaster PA 17601-3145

**BYRD, CHRISTINE WATERMAN SWENT,** lawyer; b. Oakland, Calif., Apr. 11, 1951; d. Langan Waterman and Eleanor (Herz) Swent; m. Gary Lee Byrd, June 20, 1981; children: Amy, George. BA, Stanford U., 1972; JD, U. Va., 1975. Bar: Calif. 1976, U.S. Dist. Ct. (ctrl., so. no., ea. dists.) Calif., U.S. Ct. appeals (9th cir.). Law clk. to Hon. William P. Gray, U.S. Dist. Ct., L.A., 1975-76; assoc. Jones, Day, Reavis & Pogue, L.A., 1976-82, ptnr., 1987-96; asst. U.S. atty. criminal divsn. U.S. Atty.'s Office-Cen. Dist. Calif., L.A., 1982-87; ptnr. Irell & Manella, L.A., 1996—; mem. Calif. Law Revision Commn., 1992-97. Author: The Future of the U.S. Multinational Corporation, 1975; contbr. articles to profl. jours. Mem. Calif. State Bar (com. fed. cts. 1985-88), Los Angeles County Bar Assn., Women Lawyers Assn. Los Angeles County, Am. Arbitration Assn. (large and complex case panel 1992—, nat. energy panel 1998—, bd. dirs. 1999—), Stanford Profl. Women Los Angeles County, Stanford U. Alumni Assn., 9th Jud. Cir. Hist. Soc. (bd. dirs. 1986—, pres. 1997—), Assn. Bus. Trial Lawyers (bd. govs. 1996—). Republican. General civil litigation, Criminal. Office: Irell & Manella LLP 1800 Ave Of Stars Ste 900 Los Angeles CA 90067-4276

**BYRD, GARY ELLIS,** lawyer; b. Dothan, Ala., Mar. 8, 1957; m. Emily Marie Reid; children: Elizabeth, Virginia and Victoria (twins). BS in Pre-Law and Am. History summa cum laude, Troy State U., 1979; JD, U. Ala., 1982. Bar: Ga. (no. and middle dists.) 1983, U.S. Dist. Ct. (no. and so. dists), Ga., U.S. Ct. Appeals. Pntr. Bishoff & Byrd, Talbotton, Ga., 1982—; assoc. Bunn & Kirby, Hamilton, Ga., 1993—; ptnr. Bunn & Byrd, Hamilton, Ga., 1996—; city atty. Woodland, Ga., 1986—, Geneva, Ga., 1988—, Shiloh, Ga., 1994—; chmn. bd. dirs. Talbot County Law Libr., Talbotton, 1992-99; bd. dirs. Harris County Law Libr., Hamilton. Contbr. numerous articles to newspapers and profl. jours., chpt. to book; author City of Woodland city code, 1986. Bd. dirs. Chattahoochie-Flint RESA, Americus, Ga., 1986-87, Pine Mountain Regional Arts Coun., Manchester, Ga., 1986-88; pres., chmn. exec. com. Talbot County 2000 Group, Talbotton, 1987-88; coach debate team dept. social studies Manchester (Ga.) H.S., 1982; chmn. appropriations com. Harris County YMCA, Hamilton, 1994, 95, 96, 97, 98, 99, bd. dirs. 1994, 95, 96, 97, 98, 99; mem. budget com. City of Talbotton, 1989-92, councilman, 1985-92, mem. policy adv. com., 1986-92, vol. fireman, 1982-93; ct. apptd. adminstr. City of Geneva, Ga., 1992; mem. adv. com. Am. Security Coun., Washington, 1976-82. Recipient Outstanding Svc. award Talbot County Jaycees, 1983,. Mem. Ga. Bar Assn., Ga. Mcpl. Assn. (atty.'s sect.), Talbot County C. of C. (chmn. membership com. 1992-93, bd. dirs. 1993), Harris County C. of C., Troy State U. Alumni Assn. (membership com. East Ala./West Ctrl. Ga. chpt. 1993-99, Phi Kappa Phi, Phi Alpha Theta (State Hist. Rsch. award 1979). Avocations: model trains, stock car racing, antique car restoration. Probate, General practice, Real property. Home: PO Box 119 Hamilton GA 31811-0119 Office: 103 N College St PO Box 489 Hamilton GA 31811-0489

**BYRD, L(AWRENCE) DEREK,** lawyer; b. Bradenton, Fla., Feb. 5, 1968; s. H. Lawrence and Peggi Jean Byrd; m. Heather Solnoki, Oct. 15, 1996. BS in Criminology, Fla. State U., 1990; JD cum laude, Quinnipiac Coll., 1995. Bar: Fla. 1996, U.S. Dist. Ct. (mid. dist.) Fla. 1997. Assoc. Mark Lipinski, PA, Bradenton, 1996; atty. Pub. Defender's Office, Sarasota, Fla., 1996-98; ptnr. Byrd Law Firm, Sarasota, 1998—. Bd. dirs. YMCA, Sarasota, 1997—. Mem. Fla. Assn. Criminal Def. Lawyers (pres.), Sarasota County Bar Assn., ACLU, Am. Inn of Ct. Avocations: tennis, golf, softball. Criminal, Family and matrimonial, Personal injury. Office: Byrd Law Firm 100 Wallace Ave Ste 250 Sarasota FL 34237-6042

**BYRD, LINWARD TONNETT,** lawyer, rancher; b. Hamburg, Ark., June 25, 1921; s. Charley E. and Arrie (Montgomery) B.; m. Reba Ann Rowe, Dec. 22, 1965; 1 child, Jana Lynn. LLB, U. Tex., 1950. Bar: Tex. 1950, U.S. Dist. Ct. (we. dist.) Tex. 1956, U.S. Ct. Appeals (5th cir.) 1965, U.S. Ct. Appeals (11th cir.) 1981. Sr. ptnr. Byrd, Davis & Eisenberg, Austin, Tex., 1959—. With USN, 1942-43. Fellow Am. Trial Lawyers Found., Tex. Bar Found., Am. Coll. Trial Lawyers; mem. Assn. Trial Lawyers Am., Am. Bd. Trial Advs. (adv.), Tex. Trial Lawyers Assn., State Bar Tex., Travis County Bar Assn. (lifetime disting. achievement award), Travis County Young Lawyers Assn. (lifetime disting. achievement award). Baptist. Personal injury, Aviation, Product liability. Home: 2400 Vista Ln Apt A Austin TX 78703-2344 Office: Byrd Davis & Eisenberg 707 W 34th St Austin TX 78705-1204

**BYRD, PATRICIA,** lawyer; b. Baton Rouge, July 25, 1952; d. Richard E. and Hilda (Cabler) Byrd; m. John B. Camp, 1971 (div. 1986); children: John Robert, Richard Edward. BA, La. State U., 1963; JD, Boston Coll., 1983. Bar: La. 1983. Newspaper editor, writer, comms. and publicity dir. sports writer, sports editor, 1963-83; law clk. La. 19th Jud. Dist. Ct., Baton Rouge, 1983-85; asst. dist. atty. East Baton Rouge dist. Atty., Baton Rouge, 1985—; cons. on domestic violence La. Dist. Attys. Assn., Baton Rouge; pro bono ptnrs. aton Rouge Bar Assn.; mem. East Baton Rouge Domestic Violence Corodinating Coun. Active YWCA, Univ. Bapt. Ch. Mem. Baton Rouge Bar Assn. (publs. com.), Boston Coll. Law Sch. Alumni Assn., La. State U. Alumni Assn. Avocations: sports, travel, reading, word games/puzzles. Address: 222 Saint Louis St Baton Rouge LA 70802-5817

**BYRD, RONALD DICKY,** lawyer; b. Balt., Aug. 19, 1953; s. Charles Merriken and Agnes Marie (Lauriet) B. BA, Bethany Coll., 1975; JD, U. Balt., 1979. Bar: Md. 1980, U.S. Ct. Appeals (4th cir.) 1989. Law clk. to presiding justice Cir. Ct. for Balt. City, Balt., 1979-80; asst. states atty. State of Md., Balt., 1980-82; from litigation atty. to environ. regulatory atty. Balt. Gas and Electric, 1982-97, assoc. gen. counsel litigation, 1997—, assoc. gen. counsel comml., 1999. Mem. Am. Corp. Counsel Assn., Balt. Claimsmens Assn., Balt. Def. Trial Counsel, Balt. Jr. Assn. of Commerce. Republican. Roman Catholic. Avocations: golf, travel. State civil litigation, Personal injury, Construction. Home: 2030 Snapdragon Dr Finksburg MD 21048-2137 Office: Balt Gas And Electric PO Box 1475 Baltimore MD 21203-1475

**BYRD, STEPHEN TIMOTHY,** lawyer; b. Roanoke Rapids, N.C., July 4, 1957; s. William Timothy and Betty Faye (Davis) B.; m. Sandra Jean Sain, May 6, 1989; children: Rachel Leigh, Samuel Davis. BSBA, U. N.C., 1979, JD, 1984. Bar: N.C. 1984; CPA, N.C.; bd. cert. specialist in estate planning and probate law, 1994—. Staff acct. Peat Marwick & Mitchell, Raleigh, N.C., 1980-81; assoc. Petree, Stockton & Robinson, Winston-Salem, N.C., 1984-88, Raleigh, 1988-89; ptnr. Manning, Fulton & Skinner, P.A., Raleigh, 1989—. Contbg. author: Jour. of Partnership Taxation, 1989; author, lectr. partnership & LLC topics for N.C. Bar Found., Nat. Bus. Inst., 1994. Unit chmn. United Way Wake County, Raleigh, 1988, 93, mem. allocation rev. com. 1994-97; mem. adminstrv. coun. Crossroads Fellowship Raleigh, 1995—. Named to Wake County Vol. Lawyers Program Honor Roll. Mem. N.C. Bar Assn. (exec. coun. young layers divsn. 1987-92, dirs. 1990-92, tax sect. newsletter editor 1989-91, coun. 1990-93, 94-97, sec. 1991-92, 97-98, chmn. tax sect. CLE com. 1995-96, legis. com. 1996-98, treas. 1996-97, tax sect. vice chair 1998-99, chair 1999—), N.C. Assn. CPAs, N.C. Forestry Assn., Wake County Estate Planning Coun., Raleigh C. of C. (amb. 1990-93, bd. advisors 1996—), Lincoln Forum. Republican. Avocations: basketball, golf. Taxation, general, Estate planning, Mergers and acquisitions. Office: Manning Fulton & Skinner 500 UCB Plz 3605 Glenwood Ave Raleigh NC 27612-4954

**BYRNE, BRADLEY ROBERTS,** lawyer; b. Mobile, Ala., Feb. 16, 1955; s. Arthur LaCoste and Elizabeth Patricia (Langsdale) B.; m. Rebecca Dow Dukes, May 16, 1981; children: Patrick MacGuire, Kathleen Roberts, Laura Ann, Colin Arthur. BA, Duke U., 1977; JD, U. Ala., 1980. Bar: Ala. 1980, U.S. Dist. Ct. (so. dist.) Ala. 1980, U.S. Ct. Appeals (5th and 11th cirs.) 1981, U.S. Dist. Ct. (mid. dist.) Ala. 1985, U.S. Ct. Appeals (8th cir.) 1985, U.S. Dist. Ct. (no. dist.) Ala. 1986, U.S. Supreme Ct. 1987. Assoc. Miller, Hamilton, Snider & Odom, Mobile, 1980-85, ptnr., 1985-95, ptnr., mem. mgmt. com., 1989-95; mem. Jackson Myrick Chambers & Byrne, Mobile, 1995—. Active Ala. State Bd. of Edn., 1994—; sec. Mobile City Planning Commn., 1990-94. Named one of Outstanding Young Men of Am., 1981, 82. Mem. ABA (litigation sect.), Ala. Bar Assn., Mobile Bar Assn., Mobile Area C. of C. (vice chmn. 1989-91). Episcopalian. Federal civil litigation, State civil litigation, Labor. Office: Jackson Myrick Chambers & Byrne LLC 1100 Regions Bank Bldg Mobile AL 36602

**BYRNE, GREGORY WILLIAM,** lawyer; b. Chgo., Aug. 18, 1939; s. William Daniel and Theresa (Gregory) B.; m. Debra Demert, Oct. 12, 1984; children: Kathleen Minde, Gregory W. Jr., Julianna Rowe, Elizabeth. AB, U. S.C., 1968; JD, Harvard U., 1971. Bar: Oreg. 1971, U.S. Dist. Ct. Oreg. 1971, U.S. Ct. Appeals (9th cir.) 1973, U.S. Supreme Ct. 1990, U.S. Ct. Fed. Claims 1993. Enlisted USMC, 1959, advanced through grades to capt., 1965, resigned, 1967; sole practice Portland, Oreg., 1971—; judge pro tem Multnomah County Cts., Portland, 1983-90; dir. Harvard Legis. Rsch. Bur., 1970-71. Mem. Multnomah Bar Assn. Republican. General civil litigation, Constitutional, Real property. Office: 1001 SW 5th Ave Ste 1300 Portland OR 97204-1129

**BYRNE, KATHARINE CRANE,** lawyer; b. Chgo., Dec. 31, 1958; d. William Patrick and Jane M. (Burke) B.; 1 child, William Byrne Vogt. BA, St. Mary's Coll., Notre Dame, Ind., 1980; JD, Loyola U., 1988. Bar: Ill. 1988, U.S. Dist. Ct. (no. dist.) Ill. 1988, U.S. Ct. Appeals (7th cir.) 1991, Fed. Trial Bar (no. dist.) Ill. 1992. Event planner Gaper's Caterers, Chgo., 1980-84; coord. Jane Byrne Campaign Com., Chgo., 1985-87; law clk. Cooney & Conway, Chgo., 1987-88, atty., 1988—; lectr. Andrews 8th Ann. Asbestos Litigation Conf., 1996, 97. Author: Premises Liability, 1994. Lectr. Ill. Inst. for Continuing Legal Edn., Chgo., 1991; pres. Beautiful Chgo. (Ill.) Commn., 1994. Mem. ATLA, Ill. Trial Lawyers Assn. (lectr. seminar 1995), Celtic Lawyers. Democrat. Roman Catholic. Toxic tort, Personal injury, General civil litigation. Home: 260 E Chestnut St Chicago IL 60611-2401 Office: Cooney & Conway 120 N La Salle St Chicago IL 60602-2412

**BYRNE, ROBERT WILLIAM,** lawyer; b. Frankfurt, Germany, Dec. 12, 1958; s. Robert Patrick and Anne Lise (Brondelsbo) B. BA, Rutgers U., 1981; JD, Seton Hall U., 1984; postgrad., Colo. State U. Bar: N.J. 1984, U.S. Dist. Ct. N.J. 1984, D.C. 1986, U.S. Ct. Appeals (3d cir.) 1987, U.S. Ct. Appeals (D.C. and fed. cirs.) 1988, (11th cir.), 1993, U.S. Dist. Ct. D.C. 1989, U.S. Supreme Ct. 1989, N.Y. 1991, U.S. Dist. Ct. (so. and ea. dists.) N.Y. 1991, Fla. 1992, U.S. Dist. Ct. (no. and mid. dists.) Fla. 1992. Law clk. to presiding judge Superior Ct. Passaic County N.J., 1984-85; asst. prosecutor Bergen County, N.J., 1985-88; assoc. Harwood Lloyd Esqs., Hackensack, N.J., 1988-90, Mudge Rose Guthrie Alexander & Ferdon, N.Y.C., 1990-91; sr. assoc. O'Connor, Reddy & Jensen, N.Y.C., 1991-92; pvt. practice Panama City, Fla., 1992-94; v.p./gen. counsel Bay Bank & Trust Co., Panama City, Fla., 1994—. Contbr. Seton Hall Legislative Jour., 1983-84. Henry Rutgers scholar, 1981. Mem. D.C. Bar, Fla. Bar, Bay County (Fla.) Bar Assn., Assn. Bar City N.Y., St. Andrew Am. Inns Ct. (barrister), Phi Alpha Delta, Pi Sigma Alpha. Democrat. Lutheran. Banking, Consumer commercial, Probate. Home: PO Box 18889 Panama City FL 32417-8889 Office: 509 Harrison Ave Panama City FL 32401-2621

**BYRNE, THOMAS J.,** lawyer; b. Rochester, N.Y., June 17, 1944; m. Brenda C. Byrne, June 4, 1994; children: Thomas, David, Heather. AB, U. Rochester, 1967; JD, U. Denver, 1976. Bar: Colo. 1977, Calif. 1977, U.S. Ct. Appeals (10th cir.) 1977, U.S. Dist. Ct. Colo. 1977, U.S. Dist. Ct. (so. dist.) Tex. 1990, N.Y. 1990, U.S. Ct. Appeals (3d cir.) 1992, U.S. Dist. Ct. (ea. dist.) Pa. 1992, U.S. Dist. Ct. (ea. dist.) Va. 1992, U.S. Ct. Appeals (4th cir.) 1993, U.S. Dist. Ct. (no. dist.) Ill. 1993, U.S. Dist. Ct. Ariz. 1993, U.S. Dist. Ct. Utah 1996, U.S. Dist. Ct. (so. dist.) N.Y. 1997. Law clk. Dist. Ct. Colo., Denver, 1976-77; assoc. Ullstrom Law Offices, Denver, 1978-83; ptnr., Denver mgr. Conklin & Adler, Ltd., Denver and Chgo., 1983-86; mng. ptnr. Byrne, Kiely & White LLP, Denver, 1986—. Mem. fin. com. Citizens for Romer, Denver, 1990—. Capt. USAF, 1967-73. Mem. ABA (tort and ins. practice sect., vice chair aviation and space law com., litigation sect., forum on air and space law), Internat. Bar Assn., Colo. Bar Assn., Denver Bar Assn., State Bar Calif., N.Y. State Bar Assn., Def. Rsch. Inst., Colo. Def. Lawyers Assn., Nat. Bus. Aircraft Assn., Lawyer-Pilot Bar Assn., Aviation Ins. Assn. Avocations: flying, travel, sports. Aviation, Product liability, Insurance. Office: Byrne Kiely & White LLP 1120 Lincoln St Ste 1300 Denver CO 80203-2140

**BYRNE, WALTER ROBBINS, JR.,** lawyer; b. Clarksville, Tenn., May 30, 1947; s. Walter Robbins and Elisabeth (Cross) B.; children: Walter Robbins

III, William Hardwick. BA in English, U. Ky., 1969, MBA, 1974; JD, U. Louisville, 1980. Bar: Ky. 1980. Vice pres. First Nat. Bank of Louisville, 1974-80; ptnr. Stites & Harbison, Lexington, 1980—; bd. dirs. Progressive Nat. Bank, Lexington, People's Exch. Bank, Beattyville, Ky. 1st lt. U.S. Army, 1969-72. Mem. ABA, Ky. Bar Assn., Fayette Bar Assn. Republican. Banking, General corporate. Home: 239 Queensway Dr Lexington KY 40502-1625 Office: Stites and Harbison 250 W Main St Ste 2300 Lexington KY 40507-1758

**BYRNE, WILLIAM MATTHEW, JR.,** federal judge; b. L.A., Sept. 3, 1930; s. William Matthew Sr. and Julia Ann (Lamb) B. BS, U. So. Calif., 1953, LLB, 1956; LLD, Loyola U., 1971. Bar: Calif. 1956. Ptnr. Dryden, Harrington & Schwartz, 1960-67; asst. atty U.S. Dist. Ct. (so. dist.) Calif., 1958-60; atty. U.S. Dist. Ct. (cen. dist.) Calif., Los Angeles, 1967-70, judge, 1971—; now sr. judge U.S. Dist. Ct. (cen. dist.) Calif.; exec. dir. Pres. Nixon's Commn. Campus Unrest, 1970; instr. Loyola Law Sch., Harvard U., Whittier Coll. Served with USAF, 1956-58. Mem. ABA, Fed. Bar Assn., Calif. Bar Assn., Los Angeles County Bar Assn. (vice chmn. human rights sect.), Am. Judicature Soc. Office: US Dist Ct Ste 110 312 N Spring St Los Angeles CA 90012-4703

**BYRNES, WILLIAM JOSEPH,** lawyer; b. Bklyn., Apr. 11, 1940; s. William James and Margaret Mary (English) B.; m. Catherine Belle Rollings, Aug. 15, 1970; children: Jennifer, Suzanne. BS, Fordham U., 1961; JD, Yale U., 1964. Bar: N.Y. 1965, D.C. 1970, Va. 1992. Atty. AEC, Washington, 1964-68; internat. mgr. Comm. Satellite Corp., Washington, 1968-70; ptnr. Haley, Bader & Potts, Arlington, Va., 1970-95; of counsel Irwin Campbell & Tannenwald, Washington, 1995-96; pvt. practice, McLean, Va., 1997—. Author: Telecommunications Regulation: Something Old and Something New in the Communications Act: A Legislative History of the Major Amendments, 1934-1996, 1999; co-author: The Common Carrier Provisions--A Product of Evolutionary Development in A Legislative History of the Communications Act, 1989, Decency Redux: The Curious History of the New FCC Broadcast Indecency Policy, 1989, A New Telecommunications Paradigm, 1993; mem. Great Falls Players, Elden Street Players, Castaways Repertory Theatre, Rockville Little Theatre, Cedar Lane Stage, Sterling Playmakers. Candidate Fairfax County Bd. Suprs., 1995; bd. dirs. McLean Comm. Ctr.; v.p. McLean Citizens Found. Recipient cert. U.S. Atomic Energy Commn., 1967. Mem. Fed. Comms. Bar Assn., Va. State Bar, D.C. Bar Assn., McLean Citizens Assn. (ex-pres.), Fairfax Com. 100. Avocations: acting, videography. Communications, Appellate, Administrative and regulatory. Office: 7921 Old Falls Rd Mc Lean VA 22102-2414

**CABANAS, OSCAR JORGE,** lawyer; b. Havana, Cuba, Dec. 10, 1958; came to U.S., 1959; s. Oscar Jorge and Matilde Carmen (Fors) C.; m. Leonor Diaz, May 1, 1993; children: Oscar Jorge, Olivia Marie. BA in Polit. Sci., Northwestern U., 1981; JD, U. Miami, 1984. Bar: Ill. 1984, U.S. Dist. Ct. (no. dist.) Ill. 1985, U.S. Ct. Appeals (5th cir.) 1985, Fla. 1985, U.S. Dist. Ct. (so. dist.) Fla. 1989. Assoc. Ross and Hardies, Chgo., 1984-85; from assoc. to ptnr. Stephens, Lynn, Klein & McNicholas, Miami, Fla., 1985—. Roman Catholic. Avocations: golf, diving. Personal injury, Product liability, General civil litigation. Office: 9130 S Dadeland Blvd Ph 111 Miami FL 33156-7818

**CABELLO, J. DAVID,** lawyer; b. 1951. BS, Tex. A&M U.; JD, South Tex. Coll. Bar: Tex. 1983. Mng. atty. Compaq Computer Corp, Houston, sr. v.p., v.p., asst. gen. counsel bus. group. Mem. ABA. Intellectual property. Office: Compaq Computer Corp PO Box 123 20555 SH 249 Houston TX 77070*

**CABEZAS-GIL, ROSA M.,** lawyer; b. Santa Cruz Canary Islands, Spain, Oct. 26, 1959; came to U.S., 1973; d. Alejandro and Maria Rosa (Darias) Cabezas; m. Jose D. Gil, July 10, 1982 (div. May 1997); children: Debby F. Gil, Lani Angelina Gil. AA in Humanities with honors, Gavilan Coll., Gilroy, Calif., 1978; BA in Internat. Rels., San Francisco State U., 1980; JD, St. Mary's U., 1987. Bar: Tex. 1987, U.S. Dist. Ct. (we. dist.) Tex. 1989, U.S. Ct. Appeals (5th cir.) 1989, U.S. Supreme Ct. 1991. News anchor, reporter Sta. KDTV-Channel 14, San Francisco, 1980-81; reporter, weather anchor Sta. KWEX-TV Channel 41, San Antonio, 1981-82; atty. Bexar County Legal Aid, San Antonio, 1988-91; pvt. practice San Antonio, 1991—; rep./liaison Canary Islands Govt., San Antonio, 1989-91; spkr. on probate and family law to various orgns., San Antonio. Treas. La Casa de España, San Antonio, 1984—. Nnamed Vol. Beyond Excellence McAulife Mid. Sch., 1994; recipient Cert. of Recognition Leadership, Club Mentor Tafoya Mid. Sch., 1992-93. Fellow San Antonio Bar Found. (bd. dirs. 1996—), State Bar of Tex. Found. 1998—, the College of the State Bar of Tex. 1989—; mem. State Bar Tex. (bd. dirs. women in the law sect. 1995-99, bd. dirs. local bar com. 1994—, bd. dirs. Dist. 10C gr ieveance com. 1996-99), Tex. Women Lawyers (charter bd. dirs., founding mem. 1994—, v.p. 1998), Bexar County Women's Bar Assn. (pres. 1994), San Antonio Mex. Am. Bar A ssn. (pres. 1993), Bexar County Legal Aid Assn. (bd. dirs. 1995—), St. Mary's Univ. Law Sch. Alumni Assn. (bd. dirs. 1992-97); mem. San Antonio Art leag. Mus. (bd. dirs. 1997—). Roman Catholic. Avocations: travel, reading. Family and matrimonial, Personal injury, Probate. Office: 111 Soledad St Ste 1230 San Antonio TX 78205-2296

**CABORN, DAVID ARTHUR,** lawyer; b. Columbus, Ohio, Sept. 28, 1957; s. Loren L. and Hedwig J. C.; m. Leslie Kay Thorpe; children: Joseph L., Lucy A. BA, Ohio State U., 1982; JD, Capital U., 1986. Bar: Ohio 1986. Ptnr. Nemeth, Caborn & Butauski, Columbus, 1986—. Mem. ABA, Ohio State Bar Assn., Columbus Bar Assn. Avocations: reading, auto racing, music, culinary arts. General civil litigation, Construction, Professional liability. Office: Nemeth Caborn & Butauski 21 E Franfort St Columbus OH 43206-1009

**CABOT, STEPHEN JAY,** lawyer; b. Phila., Nov. 21, 1942; s. Charles and Roslyn (Levin) C.; m. Patti D. Gilberg, June 26, 1966 (div. Dec. 1996); children: Michele, Jennifer; m. Anna M. Farmer, Dec. 21, 1996. BS in Econ., Villanova U., 1964; JD, U. Pa., 1967. Bar: Pa. 1967. Field atty. Nat. Labor Rels. Bd., Pitts., 1967-69; labor atty. Obermayer, Rebmann, et al, Phila., 1970-72, Summit Rovens, N.Y.C., Phila., 1990; sr. ptnr., chmn. labor rels. and employment law Pechner, Dorfman et al, Phila., 1973-76, Myerson & Kuhn, N.Y.C., Phila., 1987-89; sr. ptnr., chmn. labor rels. and employment law Harvey, Pennington, Herting & Renneisen, Phila., 1991—, chmn. labor rels. and employment law dept.; cons. Bottom Line Bus., N.Y.C., 1980—; mem. labor rels. com. U.S. C. of C., Washington, 1982-86; lectr. in field. Author: Labor Management Relations Act Manual: A Guide to Effective Labor Relations, 1978, Everybody Wins!, 1986, Labor Relations Guidebook: Practical Techniques for Managing Workplace Issues, 1988; contbg. editor The Developing Labor Law for the ABA, 1980—, Phila. Bus. Jour., 1995—; contbr. numerous articles to profl. publs. Mem. ABA, Fed. Bar Assn., Soc. Human Resource Mgmt., Am. Coll. Health Care Admintrs. (Educator of Yr. 1985), Pa. Bar. Assn., Phila. Bar Assn. Avocations: golf, jogging, hiking, biking, weight lifting. Office: Harvey Pennington et al 1835 Market St Fl 29 Philadelphia PA 19103-2968

**CABRANES, JOSÉ ALBERTO,** federal judge; b. Mayaguez, P.R., Dec. 22, 1940; s. Manuel and Carmen (López) C.; children: Jennifer Ann, Amy Alexandra; m. Kate Stith, Sept. 15, 1984; children: Alejo, Benjamin José. AB, Columbia U., 1961; JD, Yale U., 1965; MLitt in Internat. Law, Cambridge (Eng.) U., 1967; LLD (hon.), Colgate U., 1988. Bar: N.Y. 1968, D.C. 1975, U.S. Dist. Ct. Conn. 1976. Assoc. Casey, Lane & Mittendorf, N.Y.C., 1967-71; assoc. prof. law sch. Rutgers U., Newark, 1971-73; spl. counsel to gov. P.R., head Office Commonwealth P.R., Washington, 1973-75; gen. counsel Yale U., New Haven, 1975-79; judge U.S. Dist. Ct. Conn., New Haven, 1979-94, chief judge, 1992-94; judge U.S. Ct. Appeals for 2d Cir., 1994—; mem. Pres.'s Commn. White House Fellowships, 1993-96, Pres.'s Commn. Mental Health, 1977-78, U.S. del. Conf. Security and Coop. in Europe, Belgrade, 1977-78; mem. James Madison Meml. Fellowship Found., 1995—; founding mem. P.R. Legal Def. and Edn. Fund, 1972, chmn. bd., 1977-80; counsel Internat. League for Human Rights, 1971-77, v.p., 1977-80; cons. to sec. Dept. State, 1978; mem. Fed. Cts. Study Com., 1988-90; instr. history P.R. Colegio San Ignacio de Loyola, Rio Piedras, 1962; supr. in internat. law Queens' Coll., Cambridge U., 1966-67. Author: Citizenship and the American Empire, 1979; co-author: (with Kate Stith) Fear of the Judging: Sentencing Guidelines in the Federal Courts, 1998, (with Kate Stith) Fear of Judging: Sentencing Guidelines in the Federal Courts, 1998; also articles on law and internat. affairs. Trustee Yale U., 1987-99, Yale-New Haven Hosp., 1978-80, 84-87, Colgate U., 1981-90, 20th Century Fund, 1983—, Fed. Jud. Ctr., 1986-90; bd. dirs. Aspira of N.Y. (Puerto Rican edn. agy.), 1970-74, chmn., 1971-73; mem. Coun. on Fgn. Rels. Recipient life achievement award Nat. P.R. Coalition, 1987, John Jay award Columbia Coll., 1991, life achievement award student divsn. Nat. Hispanic Bar Assn., 1991; Kellett rsch. fellow Columbia Coll., Cambridge U., 1965-67. Fellow Am. Bar Found., Mex.-Am. Lawyers Assn. (spl. recognition award 1994); mem. ABA, Conn. Bar Assn., Assn. of Bar of City of N.Y., Am. Law Inst. Roman Catholic. Office: US Ct of Appeals US Courthouse 141 Church St New Haven CT 06510-2030

**CABRASER, ELIZABETH J.,** lawyer; b. Oakland, Calif., June 23, 1952. AB, U. Calif., Berkeley, 1975; JD, U. Calif., 1978. Bar: Calif. 1978, U.S. Dist. Ct. (no., ea., cen. and so. dists.) Calif. 1979, U.S. Ct. Appeals (2d, 3rd, 5th, 6th, 9th, 10th, and 11th cirs.) 1979, U.S. Tax Ct. 1979, U.S. Dist. Ct. Hawaii 1986, U.S. Dist. Ct. Ariz. 1990, U.S. Supreme Ct. 1978. Ptnr. Lieff, Cabraser, Heimann & Bernstein LLP, San Francisco. Contbr. articles to profl. jours. Named one of Top 50 Women Lawyers Nat. Law Jour., 1998. Mem. ABA (tort and ins. practice sect., sect. litig. com. on class action and derivative skills, chair subcom. on mass torts), ATLA, Am. Law Inst., Calif. Constn. Rev. Commn., Nat. Ctr. for State Cts. (mass tort conf. planning com.), Women Trial Lawyer Caucus, Consumer Attys. Calif., Calif. Women Lawyers, Assn. Bus. Trial Lawyers, Nat. Assn. Securities and Comml. Attys., Bay Area Lawyers for Individual Freedom, Bar Assn. San Francisco (v.p. securities litig., bd. dirs.). E-mail: ecabraser@lchb.com. Office: Lieff Cabraser Heimann & Bernstein LLP Embarcadero Ctr W 30th Fl 275 Battery St San Francisco CA 94111-3305*

**CACCESE, MICHAEL STEPHEN,** lawyer; b. Penn Valley, Pa., Nov. 21, 1954; s. Frederick E. and Mary J. Caccese; m. Barbara Mitchel, Jan. 7, 1978; chldren: Stephen M., Michelle L. BA, Pa. State U., 1977; JD, Temple U., 1980. Bar: Pa. 1980, Va. 1993, U.S. Dist. Ct. (we. dist.) Va. 1997. Corp. counsel Federated Ivestors, Inc., 1980-83; sr. v.p., assoc. counsel Frank Russell Co., Tacoma, 1983-93; sr. v.p., gen. counsel, sec. Assn. for Investment Mgmt. and Rsch., Charlottesville, Va., 1993—. Mem. editl. bd. Billanova Jour. Law and Investment Mgmt., 1997—, Jour. for Performance Measurement, 1997—. Mem. ABA, Wash. Soc. Investment Analysts, European Fedn. Analysts. Socs./Permanent Commn. on Performance Mgmt., Assn. for Investment Mgmt. and Rsch. Securities, Non-profit and tax-exempt organizations, General corporate. Home: 2230 Rocky Run Charlottesville VA 22901-9560 Office: AIMR 5 Boars Head Ln Charlottesville VA 22903-4610

**CACCIATORE, RONALD KEITH,** lawyer; b. Donaldsville, Ga., Feb. 5, 1937; s. Angelo D. and Myrtice E. (Williams) C.; children: Rhonda, Donna, Rex. Student, Spring Hill Coll., 1955-56; BA, U. Fla., 1960; JD, 1963. Bar: Fla. 1963, U.S. Supreme Ct. 1969. Asst. state atty. 13th Jud. Cir., 1963-65; pvt. practice Tampa, Fla., 1967; lectr. criminal law; mem. 13th Jud. Cir. Jud. Nominating Commn., 1976-80, chmn., 1980; mem. Fed. Judiciary Adv. Commn. Fla., 1987—. Trustee Hillsborough C.C., 1979-83, chmn., 1982-83. Fellow Am. Coll. Trial Lawyers; mem. Hillsborough County Bar Assn. (pres. 1975-76, chmn. trial lawyers sect. 1983-85), Fla. Bar Assn. (chmn. criminal law sect. 1977-78), Fla. Coun. Bar Pres.'s (chmn. 1979-80), Fed. Bar Assn. (pres. Tampa Bay chpt. 1985-86, fed. jud. nominationcom. Fla. 1999—), Palma Ceia Golf and Country Club, University Club. Criminal.

**CACCIATORE, SAMMY MICHEL,** lawyer; b. Melbourne, Fla., June 18, 1968; s. Carolyn and Sammy C.; m. Joey Lynn Hoffmeier, June 6, 1992; children: Maddison Paige, Claire Ashlynn. BA in Psychology, Stetson U., 1990; MHS in Rehab. Counseling, U. Fla., 1992; JD, Stetson U. Coll. Law, 1995. Bar: Fla. Asst. state's atty. Office of State's Atty. 18th Jud. Cir., Melbourne, 1995-97; assoc. Nance, Cacciatore et al, Melbourne, 1998—. Mem. Fla. Bar Assn. (codes and rules of evidence com.), Brevard County Bar Assn. (sec. 1997—). Avocations: water skiing, fishing. Insurance, Personal injury, Product liability. Home: 523 Rio Casa Dr N Indialantic FL 32903-3703 Office: Nance Cacciatore et al 525 N Harbor City Blvd Melbourne FL 32935-6890

**CACHERIS, JAMES C.,** federal judge; b. Pittsburgh, Pa., Mar. 30, 1933. BS in Econs., U. Pa., 1955; JD cum laude, George Washington U., 1960. Bar: D.C. 1960, Va. 1962. Asst. corp. counsel Washington, 1960-62; assoc. Miller Brown & Gildenhorn, Washington, 1962-64; pvt. practice Washington and Alexandria, Va., 1964-70; ptnr. Howard. Stevens, Lynch, Cake & Cacheris, Alexandria, Va., 1970-71; judge 19th Jud. Cir. Ct. Va., Fairfax, 1971-81; judge U.S. Dist. Ct. (ea. dist.) Va., Alexandria, 1981—, now sr. judge. Mem. Va. Bar Assn., Fairfax County Bar Assn. Office: US Dist Ct 401 Courthouse Sq Alexandria VA 22314-5704

**CADDY, MICHAEL DOUGLAS,** lawyer; b. Long Beach, Calif., Mar. 23, 1938; s. Frank Edward and Tabitha (Miles) C. BS in Fgn. Svc., Georgetown U., 1960; JD, NYU, 1966. Bar: D.C. 1970, Tex. 1979. Practiced in Washington and, Tex.; exec. dir. com. on pub. affairs McGraw-Edison Co., N.Y.C., 1960-61; asst. to lt. gov. State of N.Y., 1962-65; asst. to exec. v.p. NAM, N.Y.C., 1966-67; Washington liaison Gen. Foods Corp., 1968-70; assoc. Gall, Lane, Powell & Kilcullen, 1970-74; legis. counsel Nat. Assn. Realtors, Washington, 1975-76; atty. Office Tex. SEc. of State, 1980-81. Author: The Hundred Million Dollar Payoff, 1974, How They Rig Our Elections, 1975, Understanding Insurance, 1984, Legislative Trends in Insurance Regulation, 1985, Exploring America's Future, 1987. Mem. Rep. County Com., N.Y.C., 1965-66; nat. dir. Young Ams. for Freedom, 1960-62; pres. Conservatives Hall of Fame. Scholar Intercollegiate Studies Inst., 1957-59. Mem. ABA, ATLA, ACLU, FBA, D.C. Bar, Tex. Bar, Houston Bar Assn., Houston Bar Assn. for Human Rights, Federalist Soc., Am. Conservative Union, Am. Judicature Soc., Assn. Former Intelligence Officers, Am. Econ. Assn., Am. Acad. Polit. and Social Sci., Internat. Platform Assn., Nat. Coun. Crime and Delinquency, Supreme Ct. Hist. Soc., People for Am. Way, Nat. Trust for Hist. Preservation. General practice, Bankruptcy, Personal injury. Home: 745 W Creekside Dr Houston TX 77024-3234

**CADE, GREGORY ANDREWS,** legal researcher; b. Tuscaloosa, Ala., Jan. 9, 1968; s. Norman W. and Lillie (Maiden) C. BS in Biology and Chemistry, U. Ala., 1991, MPH in Occupl. Health Safety, 1995. Environ. safety specialist UPS, Birmingham, Ala., 1986-93; environ. legal rsch., occupl. health & safety advisor Environ. Litigation Group, P.C., Birmingham, Ala., 1993—; environ. cons. in field, 1991—. Patent pending for Crash Extinguisher. Com. mem. Nat. Safety Coun., 1995. Recipient stipend U. Ala., 1994-95. Mem. Assn. Trial Lawyers of Am. (toxic tort and environ. law divsn., rschr. 1993—). Baptist. Avocations: hunting, fishing, snorkeling. Office: Environ Litigation Group PC 3529 7th Ave S Birmingham AL 35222-3210

**CADIGAN, RICHARD FOSTER,** lawyer; b. Balt., May 9, 1930; s. Timothy Joseph and Edna (Foster) C.; m. Anne M. Smith, Sept. 5, 1953; children: Anne Cecelia, Richard Foster, Charles Smith, Timothy Joseph, John Arthur. J.D., U. Md., 1957. Bar: Md. 1957. Assoc. Cable & McDaniel, Balt., 1957-59, ptnr., 1959-67; ptnr. Richard F. Cadigan, Towson, Md., 1967-77; sr. ptnr. Beach, Cadigan & Martin, Towson, 1977-95, ret., 1995. Bd. rev. Atty. Grievance Commn., Annapolis, 1976-79, Jud. Nominating Commn., Commn. of Md., 1981—, chmn., 1989—; treas. Com. to Elect Sitting Judges, Baltimore County, Md., 1976, 82. Co-author: Creditor's Rights in Maryland, 1961. Counselor St. Andrew Soc., Balt., 1975—; bd. advisors Villa Julie Coll., Stevenson, Md., 1979—; chmn. Ladies and Gentlemen Jud. Bar Libr. Found., 1990—. Served with USAF, 1951-53. Mem. ABA, Baltimore County Bar Assn. (chmn. 1978-80, chmn. constn. and by-laws com. 1989—), Md. Bar Assn., St. George's Soc., St. Andrew's Soc., Hibernian Soc., St. Thomas More Soc. Democrat. Roman Catholic. Club: Engineering. Construction, Contracts commercial, General corporate.

**CADOGAN, MARJORIE ALISON,** lawyer, public relations specialist; b. N.Y.C., Dec. 11, 1960; d. George and Doreen (Leacock) C. BA, Fordham U., 1982, JD, 1985. Asst. corp. counsel N.Y.C. Dept. Law, 1985-90; gen. counsel N.Y.C. Loft Bd., 1990-91, N.Y.C. Dept. Parks and Recreation, 1991-95; dir. external affairs Primary Care Devel. Corp., N.Y.C., 1995—. Mem. Assn. Black Women Attys. (pres. 1995-97, bd. dirs. 1997—), N.Y. Women's Found. (mem. allocations com. 1997—). Office: Primary Care Devel Corp 291 Broadway Fl 17 New York NY 10007-1814

**CADWELL, DAVID ROBERT,** lawyer; b. Hartford, Conn., June 7, 1934; s. Robert M. and Esther (Pinsky) C.; m. Carolle Cramer, 1964 (div. 1970); children: David, Kimberly; m. Sumiko Hashigiwa, Dec. 28, 1974; children: Kenneth, Daniel. B.A. magna cum laude, U. Minn., 1956; J.D., UCLA, 1959. Bar: Calif. 1960, U.S. Dist. Ct. (cen. and so. dists.) Calif. 1960, U.S. Supreme Ct. 1968. Dep. atty. gen. Calif. Atty. Gen., L.A., 1960-61; pvt. practice, Santa Ana, Calif., 1961-70; adminstr. Jacoby & Meyers, L.A., 1972-74, assoc., 1974-82; sole practice, L.A., 1982-84; mng. ptnr. Cadwell & Glenn, L.A., San Diego, 1984-90, Cadwell & Kohn, L.A., 1990-91; pvt. practice, Beverly Hills, Calif., 1991—; lectr. Practical Law Course, L.A., 1975-80, Ace Seminars, 1995. Author: How to Take a Case to Court, 1975; How to Handle Personal Injury Cases, 1976; How to Evaluate a Personal Injury Case, 1978, 80. Nat. committeeman Calif. Young Democrats, Los Angeles, 1959-60; mem. host com. Dem. Nat. Conv., L.A., 1960, county com. Dem. Party, Orange County, Calif., 1962-64; exec. com. Fox Hills Dem. Club, Los Angeles, 1973-78. Recipient Outstanding Legal Services award NAACP, 1963. Mem. Assn. Trial Lawyers Am. Calif. Trial Lawyers Assn., Los Angeles Trial Lawyers Assn. Jewish. Personal injury, State civil litigation, Private international. Home: 3575 Green Vista Dr Encino CA 91436-4047

**CADY, MARK S.,** state supreme court justice; b. Rapid City, S.D.; married; 2 children. Undergrad. degree, Drake U., JD, 1978. Law clk. 2d Jud. Dist. Ct., 1978-79; asst. Webster County atty.; with law firm Ft. Dodge; dist. assoc. judge, 1983, dist. ct. judge, 1986; judge U.S. Ct. Appeals, 1994, chief judge, 1994; justice Iowa Supreme Ct., 1998—. Chmn. Supreme Ct. Task Force on Ct.'s and Cmty.'s Response to Domestic Abuse. Mem. ABA, Iowa State Bar Assn., Webster County Bar Assn. Office: Iowa Supreme Ct State House Des Moines IA 50319*

**CAFFEE, LORREN DALE,** judge; b. Decatur, Ind., Oct. 22, 1947; s. Howard Dale and Maxine Faye (Smith) C.; m. Mary Katherine Hostetler, May 25, 1968 (div. Apr. 1982); children: Liesl Katherine, Evan Dale, Colin Dale (dec.); m. Mary Jannice Dyer, June 14, 1986. BA, Bluffton Coll., 1969; JD, Georgetown U., 1972. Bar: Ind. 1972, U.S. V.I. 1994, U.S. Dist. Ct. (no. dist.) Ind. 1974. Pvt. practice, Decatur, 1972-73, 74-76; assoc. DeVoss & DeVoss Law Offices, Decatur, 1973-74; judge Adams County Ct., Decatur, 1976-84, Adams Superior Ct., Decatur, 1985-90, Adams Cir. Ct., Decatur, 1991-99; assoc. A.J. Weiss & Assoc. Law Office, 1999—; mem. county ct. com. Ind. Jud. Ctr., 1978-88, chmn., 1983-86; mem. juvenile benchbook com. Jud. Conf. of Ind., 1991-99, bd. dirs., 1995-99. Bd. dirs. Ind. Right to Life, 1974-76; mem. constn. and by-laws com. Ind. Young Reps. Fedn., 1974, of counsel, 1975-76; chmn. Adams County Young Reps., 1973-76. Mem. Ind. State Bar Assn., Adams County Bar Assn. (pres. 1975-76), Ind. Judges' Assn., Am. Judges Assn., Nat. Coun. Juvenile and Family Ct. Judges, Federalist Soc. Lutheran. Avocations: jazz music, aviation, sports cars, art, reading. Home: PO Box 11479 Saint Thomas VI 00801-4479 Office: AJ Weiss and Assoc PO Box 1612 Saint Thomas VI 00804-1612

**CAFFRY, JOHN W.,** lawyer; b. Glens Falls, N.Y., Sept. 17, 1958; s. H. Glen and Jane (Canaday) C.; m. Ellen Marie Nagel, Aug. 11, 1984; 2 children. BA, Middlebury (Vt.) Coll., 1980; JD, U. Pa., 1984. Bar: N.Y 1985, U.S. Dist. Ct. (no. dist.) N.Y. 1985. Assoc. Bartlett, Pontiff, Stewart, Rhodes & Judge, P.C., Glens Falls, 1984-90; ptnr. Noordsy & Caffry, Glens Falls, 1990-92; counsel Lake George (N.Y.) Park Commn., 1987-90; atty. Village of Argyle, N.Y., 1988—. Mem. N.Y. State Bar Assn., Warren County Bar Assn., Adirondack Mt. Club (gov. 1988-91, exec. com. 1989-90, chair conservation com. 1995—). Environmental, State civil litigation, General practice. Office: 100 Bay St Glens Falls NY 12801-3032

**CAGE, CHRISTOPHER ALLEN,** lawyer; b. Anderson, Ind., May 29, 1971; s. Bruce Allen and Dianne Elaine Cage; m. Allison Jane Hughel, Dec. 30, 1994; 1 child, Ryan Christopher. BA, Ball State U., 1993; postgrad., Quinnipiac Coll., 1993-94; JD, Ind. U., 1996. Bar: Ind. 1996, U.S. Dist. Ct. (no. dist.) Ind. 1996, U.S. Dist. Ct. (so. dist.) Ind. 1996. Legis. intern Ind. Ho. of Reps. Dem., Indpls., 1992; intern U.S. Rep. Philip R. Sharp, Washington, 1992-93; restitution officer Unified Cts. Adult Probation, Anderson, Ind., 1993-94; law clk. Hon. Thomas Newman, Jr., Anderson, 1994-96, Cohen & Malad, P.C., Indpls., 1995-96; assoc. Hulse Lacey Hardacre Austin & Shine PC, Anderson, 1996—. Mem. Am. Cancer Soc. (bd. dirs. 1998), Madison County Cmty. Corrections (adv. bd. mem. 1998), Rotary Club Internat. Democrat. Criminal, Family and matrimonial, Appellate. Home: 2123 Ivy Dr Anderson IN 46011-3825 Office: Hulse Lacey Hardacre Austin & Shine PC 911 Meridian Plz PO Box 1448 Anderson IN 46015-1448

**CAGLE, JOE NEAL,** lawyer. BA, Olivet Coll., 1961; JD, Wake Forest U., 1964; MA, Goddard Coll., 1975; LLM, U. Miss., 1980. Bar: N.C. 1964, U.S. Dist. Ct. (we. dist.) N.C. 1965, U.S. Dist. Ct. (mid. dist.) N.C. 1966, U.S. Suprme Ct. 1970, U.S. Ct. Appeals (4th cir.) 1975, U.S. Tax Ct. 1986. Law clk. to Office of Gen. Counsel U.S. Gen. Acctg. Office, Washington, 1962-63; rsch. asst. to Justice Clifton L. Moore N.C. Supreme Ct., 1964-65; pvt. practice Hickory, N.C., 1965—; instr. Am. Inst. Banking, Catawba Valley Cmty. Coll., 1973-89, instr. history, 1990-91; instr. bur. law Caldwell C.C.; dir. paralegal program Gaston Coll., 1993—. Contbr. articles to profl. jours. Past deacon, dir. edn., editor bull., Sunday sch. tchr. Hickory Ch. of Christ; past bd. dirs. Catawba County Libr., chmn. 1979-87. Hon. discharge U.S. Army Res., 1962. Mem. ABA, N.C. Bar Assn., N.C. Bar, N.C. Acad. Trial Lawyers, Catawba County C. of C. (past bd. dirs., past v.p.), Home Builders Assn. Hickory-Catawba Valley, Masons, Srhiners. General civil litigation, General corporate, Real property. Office: PO Box 2050 Hickory NC 28603-2050

**CAGLE, STEPHEN HENDERSON,** lawyer; b. St. Petersburg, Fla., July 24, 1946; s. Henderson and Jean (Horton) C.; m. Pamela A. Cagle, Aug. 17, 1968; children: Barbara, Betsy, Stephen Jr. BS, DePauw U., 1968; JD, U. Cin., 1971. Patent atty. Proctor & Gamble, Cin., 1971-73; assoc. Woodard Weikart Embardt & Naughton, Indpls., 1973-75; assoc. gen. counsel The Mead Corp., Dayton, Ohio, 1975-82; ptnr., shareholder Arnold White & Durkee, Houston, 1982—. Co-author: Patent Law Handbook, 1990-95. Bd. dirs. Nottingham Forest Civic Assn., Houston, 1990-91. Fellow Houston Bar Assn.; mem. ABA, Am. Intellectual Property Law Assn., Lic. Execs. Soc. Intellectual property, Federal civil litigation, State civil litigation. Office: Arnold White & Durkee 750 Bering Dr Houston TX 77057-2149

**CAGNEY, NANETTE HEATH,** lawyer; b. Norfolk, Va., Oct. 3, 1957; d. Thomas Patrick and Phyllis L. (Heath) C. BA in Social Work, Loyola U. of the South, New Orleans, 1976-78; JD, Tulane U., 1982. Bar: La. 1983, U.S. Dist. ct. (we. dist.) La. 1985. Social work asst. VA Psychiat. Hosp., Gulfport, Miss., summer 1977; child care worker Cath. Charities, Metairie, La., 1976-78; elegibility worker family svc. La. Dept. Health and Human Resources, Gretna, 1978-79; landman ARCO Exploration Co., Lafayette, La., 1982-85; staff atty. TXO Prodn. Co., Dallas, 1985-86; pvt. practice Lafayette, 1986-88; ptnr. Beard & Cagney, P.C., Lafayette, 1988-91; law clk. to dist. ct. judge U.S. Dist. Ct., Western Dist. La., Lake Charles, 1992—. Hearing coord. CASA Teen Ct., Lafayette, 1988-90, exec. dir., 1988-90; vice chair Lafayette Bd. Zoning Adjustments, 1988-91; bd. dirs. S.W. La. AIDS Coun., 1993-97, Faith Temple, Sulphur, La., 1995-99; pres. Quota Internat. of Lake Charles, 1996-97, Aglow State Bd., 1996—; state bd. Aglow Internat., 1993-99; steering com. State Bar Assn. Com. on Alcohol and Drug Abuse, 1989—; state ethics com. Bar Assn., 1989-95, ad hoc disciplinary com., 1989-93. Mem. La. Bar Assn., Lafayette County Bar Assn., Acadiana Assn. Women Attys. (community liaison chair 1986-88, pres. 1988-89), Assn. Trial Lawyers Am., Acadiana Assn. Women Bus. Owners (treas. 1986-87, pres. 1987-88), Zeta Tau Alpha (sec. Lake Charles alum 1992—). Democrat. Avocations: sailing, fishing, gardening. Federal civil litigation, Criminal, Constitutional. Office: 511 Broad St Ste 237 Lake Charles LA 70601-4334

**CAHALAN, SCOTT DAVID,** lawyer; b. Des Moines, Apr. 1, 1961; s. Arthur B. and Marge A. Cahalan; m. Erika E. Sybers, Jan. 2, 1962. BS in Constrn. Engring., Iowa State U., 1984; JD cum laude, U. Ga., 1994. Bar: Ga. 1994, U.S. Dist. Ct. (no. dist.) Ga. 1995. Constrn. engr. Green Holdings Inc., Dallas, 1985-91; assoc. Smith Howard & Ajax LLP, Atlanta, 1994-98,

Smith Gambrell & Russell LLP, Atlanta, 1998—. Editor Ga. Jour. Internat. and Comparative Law, 1992-94, Ga. Jour. Intellectual Property Law, 1992-95. Mem. ABA, Atlanta Bar Assn. Construction, General civil litigation, Government contracts and claims. Office: Smith Gambrell & Russell LLP 1230 Peachtree St NE 3100 Promenade II Atlanta GA 30309

**CAHILL, MICHAEL EDWARD,** lawyer, managing director; b. Montreal, Quebec, Can., Feb. 22, 1951; m. Tania de Jong, Aug. 23, 1985. BA, Bishop's U., 1972; LLB, Osgoode Hall, Toronto, 1975; LLM, Harvard U., 1978. Bar: Can. 1977, Calif. 1978, U.S. Dist. Ct. (so. dist.) Calif. 1978, U.S. Supreme Ct. 1983, Ont., Can. 1977. Prin. Shenas & Robbins, San Diego, 1978-83, O'Melveny & Myers, Los Angeles, 1983-89; sr. v.p., gen. counsel Act III Communications, L.A., 1989-91; mng. dir, gen. counsel Trust Co. of the West, L.A., 1991—. Barlow scholarship, 1976. Mem. ABA (com. on fed. regulation of securities), Calif. State Bar Assn. (com. for corp. counsel), Assn. of Corporate Counsel of Am. (bd. dirs.), Constitution Rights Found. (bd. dirs.). Securities, Private international, General corporate. Office: Trust Co of the West 865 S Figueroa St Los Angeles CA 90017-2543

**CAHILL, RICHARD FREDERICK,** lawyer; b. Columbus, Nebr., June 18, 1953; s. Donald Francis and Hazel Fredeline (Garbers) C.; m. Helen Marie Girard, Dec. 4, 1982; children: Jacqueline Michelle, Catherine Elizabeth, Marc Alexander. Student, Worcester Coll., Oxford, 1973; BA with highest honors, UCLA, 1975; JD, U. Notre Dame, 1978. Bar: Calif. 1978, U.S. Dist. Ct. (ea. dist.) Calif. 1978, U.S. Dist. Ct. (cen. dist.) Calif. 1983, U.S. Dist. Ct. (so. dist.) Calif. 1992, U.S. Ct. Appeals (9th cir.) 1992. Dep. dist. atty. Tulare County Dist. Atty., Visalia, Calif., 1978-81; staff atty. Supreme Ct. of Nev., Carson City, 1981-83; assoc. Acret & Perochet, Brentwood, Calif., 1983-84, Thelen, Marrin, Johnson & Bridges, L.A., 1984-89; ptnr. Hammond Zuetel & Cahill, Pasadena, Calif., 1989-98, Pivo, Halbreich, Cahill & Yim, Irvine, Calif., 1999—. Mem. Pasadena Bar Assn., Los Angeles County Bar Assn., Assn. So. Calif. Defense Counsel, Notre Dame Legal Aid and Defender Assn. (assoc. dir.), Phi Beta Kappa, Phi Alpha Delta (charter, v.p. 1977-78), Pi Gamma Mu, Phi Alpha Theta (charter pres. 1973-74), Phi Eta Sigma, Sigma Chi. Republican. Roman Catholic. Avocation: tennis. State civil litigation. Home: 201 Windwood Ln Sierra Madre CA 91024-2677 Office: Pivo Halbreich Cahill & Yim 1920 Main St Ste 800 Irvine CA 92614-7227

**CAHILL, STEVEN JAMES,** lawyer; b. Mpls., May 24, 1948; s. James D. and Helen Kathryn (Stoltman) C.; m. Jeri Lou Smith, Dec. 11, 1981. BA, Winona State U., 1972; JD, William Mitchell Coll. Law, 1976. Bar: Minn. 1976, U.S. Dist. Ct. Minn. 1978, N.D. 1982, U.S. Dist. Ct. N.D. 1984, U.S. Ct. Appeals (8th cir.) 1986, U.S. Supreme Ct. 1979. Assoc. Cahill, Gunhus and Streed, Moorhead, Minn., 1976-79; ptnr. Cahill, Gunhus and Streed, 1979-81, Cahill & Marquart, P.A., Moorhead, 1981—. Mem. Minn. Def. Lawyers Assn. (bd. dirs. 1987—, pres. 1994-95), Clay County Bar Assn., Minn. State Bar, Am. Bd. Trial Advs., Def. Rsch. Inst., Internat. Assn. Def. Counsel, Nat. Bd. Trial Advocacy (cert. civil trial specialist). Republican. Roman Catholic. Avocations: skiing, travel, gardening. Personal injury, Insurance, General civil litigation. Office: Cahill & Marquart 403 Center Ave Moorhead MN 56560-1919

**CAHILL, VIRGINIA ARNOLDY,** lawyer; b. Summit, N.J., Dec. 18, 1942; d. Francis R. and Roberta (Dearing) A.; m. Thomas A. Cahill, June 26, 1965; children: Catherine Frances, Thomas Michael. BS, St. Louis U., 1964; MA, U. Calif., Davis, 1968, JD, 1981. Bar: Calif. 1981, U.S. Dist. Ct. (ea. dist.) Calif. 1981, U.S. Dist. Ct. (no. dist.) Calif. 1984, U.S. Ct. Appeals (9th cir.) 1984, U.S. Supreme Ct. 1995. Law clk. to judge U.S. Dist. Ct. (ea. dist.) Calif., Sacramento, 1981-83; assoc. McDonough, Holland & Allen, Sacramento, 1983-88, ptnr., 1988—; co-chair environ. law sect., 1991—; lectr. water law and water instns. U. Calif., Davis, 1985, 93-96. Mem. ABA, Calif. Bar Assn. (co-chair natural resource subsect. of real property sect. 1995-97), Order of Coif. Real property, General civil litigation, Environmental. Office: McDonough Holland & Allen 555 Capitol Mall Ste 950 Sacramento CA 95814-4692

**CAHN, EDWARD N.,** retired federal judge; b. Allentown, Pa., June 29, 1933; s. Norman A. and Miriam H. C.; m. Alice W.; Dec. 7, 1963; children: Melissa, Jessica. BA magna cum laude, Lehigh U., 1955; LLB, Yale U., 1958. Bar: Pa. 1959. Atty. Cahn & Roberts, 1971-75; judge U.S. Dist. Ct. (ea. dist.) Pa., 1974-98, chief judge, 1993-98; assoc. Blank Rome Comisky & McCauley LLP, Allentown, Pa., 1998—. Corporal USMCR, 1958-64. Mem. Pa. Bar Assn., Lehigh County Bar Assn. Republican. Avocations: golf, tennis, classical guitar. Fax: 610-706-4343; email: cahn@blankrome.com. Office: 1620 Pond Rd Ste 200 Allentown PA 18104-2255

**CAHN, JAMES,** lawyer, martial arts educator; b. Cleve., Apr. 16, 1946; s. Sherman D. and Barbara Cahn; m. Jean A. Johnson, May 20, 1978; children: Rachel, Lucy. BA, U. Pa., 1968; JD, Ohio State U., 1973; 6th Degree Black Belt, Oriental Martial Arts Coll., 1993. Bar: Ohio 1973. Assoc. Calfee, Halter & Griswold, Cleve., 1973-75; pvt. practice Cleve., 1975-77; ptnr. Hermann, Cahn & Schneider, Cleve., 1977—; instr., master Oriental Martial Arts Coll., Cleve. and Columbus, Ohio, 1975—; legal counsel U.S. Taekwondo Union, Colorado Springs, Colo., 1977-81, 85-86; lectr. Ohio Jud. Coll. Fellow Am. Acad. Matrimonial Lawyers (pres. Ohio chpt. 1997-98); mem. ABA, Ohio State Bar Assn., Cuyahoga County Bar Assn. (chair family law sect. 1990-91), Cleve. Bar Assn. (family law sect.), Oakwood Club. Family and matrimonial. Office: Hermann Cahn & Schneider 1301 E 9th St Ste 500 Cleveland OH 44114-1876

**CAHN, JEFFREY BARTON,** lawyer; b. N.Y.C., Jan. 1, 1943; s. Harold Leon and Vivian (Loewy) C.; m. Miriam Epstein, Jan. 22, 1965; children: Lauren Samantha, Vanessa Shari. BA, Ind. U., 1964; JD, Rutgers U., 1967. Bar: N.J. 1967, U.S. Dist. Ct. N.J. 1967, U.S. Ct. Appeals (3d cir.) 1971, U.S. Supreme Ct. 1971, U.S. Tax Ct. 1973, U.S. Ct. Appeals (D.C. cir.), 1979, N.Y. 1980, U.S. Ct. Appeals (9th cir.) 1981, U.S. Claims Ct. 1981, U.S. Dist. Ct. (so. dist.) N.Y. 1992, U.S. Dist. Ct. (ea. dist.) N.Y. 1994, U.S. Ct. Appeals (2nd cir.) 1998. Law clk. to sr. presiding judge Appellate Div. N.J. Superior Ct., Trenton, N.J., 1967-68; assoc. Schapira, Steiner & Walder, Newark, 1968-72; ptnr. Sills, Cummis, Radin, Tischman, Epstein & Gross, Newark, 1972—. Author: (with others) New Jersey Transaction Guide, Vol. 12, 1993, The Use of Another's Trademark: A Review of the Law in The United States, Canada, and Western Europe, 1997; rsch. editor: Rutgers Law Rev., 1966-67; contbr. articles to profl. jours. Mem. ATLA, ABA, N.J. State Bar Assn., Essex County Bar Assn., Internat. Trademark Assn., N.Y. State Bar Assn. (sect. intellectual property), Am. Intellectual Property Law Assn., N.J. Intellectual Property Law Assn., Phi Delta Phi (Outstanding Grad. 1967). Jewish. Federal civil litigation, General civil litigation, Trademark and copyright. Home: 34 Underwood Dr West Orange NJ 07052-1322 Office: Sills Cummis Radin Tischman Epstein & Gross Legal Ctr 1 Riverfront Plz Fl 13 Newark NJ 07102-5401

**CAIN, GEORGE HARVEY,** lawyer, business executive; b. Washington, Aug. 3, 1920; s. J. Harvey and Madeleine (McGettigan) C.; m. Patricia J. Campbell, Apr. 23, 1946 (div.); children: George Harvey, James C., John P., Paul J.; m. Constance S. Collins, Aug. 10, 1985. BS, Georgetown U., 1942; JD, Harvard U., 1948. Bar: N.Y. 1949, Ohio 1972, Conn. 1977, U.S. Supreme Ct. 1995. Practiced law N.Y. State, 1949-71, 73-76; pvt. practice Ohio, 1972-73; sec., gen. counsel Nat. Carloading Corp., 1949-54; mem. firm Spence & Hotchkiss, 1954-55; gen. atty., asst. sec. Cerro Corp., 1955-68, sec., gen. atty., 1968-72; v.p., gen. counsel Pickands Mather Co., Cleve., 1971-73; v.p., sec., gen. counsel Flintkote Co., White Plains, N.Y., 1973-76, Stamford, Conn., 1976-80; spl. counsel Day, Berry & Howard, Hartford and Stamford, Conn., 1980-82; ptnr. Day, Berry & Howard, Stamford, 1983-90, of counsel, 1991—; sec. Cerro Sales Corp., 1955-71; bd. dirs., sec. Leadership Housing Sys., Inc., 1970-71; bd. dirs., gen. counsel Atlantic Cement Co., Inc., 1962-71; bd. dirs. Hajoca Corp., 1975-79, Polymer Bldg. Sys., Inc.; adj. prof. U. Bridgeport Law Sch., 1983-86. Author: Turning Points: New Paths and Second Careers for Lawyers, 1994, Law Firm Partnership: Its Rights and Responsibilities, 1995, 2nd edit., 1999. Served to 1st lt. USAAF, 1942-46; to capt. USAF, 1951-52. Fellow Am. Bar Found.; mem. ABA, N.Y. State Bar Assn., N.Y.C. Bar Assn., Ohio Bar Assn., Conn. Bar Assn., Am. Law Inst., Am. Soc. Corp. Secs., Georgetown U. Alumni Assn. (mem. alumni senate), Harvard Club N.Y., Dutch Treat Club. General corporate, Mergers and acquisitions, Securities. Home: 14 Burnt Hill Rd Farmington CT 06032-2039 Office: Day Berry & Howard City Place I Hartford CT 06103-3499

**CAIN, HOWARD GUESS, JR.,** lawyer; b. Fullerton, Calif., Nov. 15, 1943; s. Howard Guess and Dixie Marie Cain; m. Sharron Sue Jennings, Sept. 22, 1962; children: Destari, Trey, Blakeney. JD, U. Ark., 1972. Bar: Ark., U.S. Dist. Ct. (we. dist.) Ark. Dep. pros. atty. State of Ark., Huntsville, 1972-94; atty. City of Huntsville, 1972—; bd. dirs. Madison Bank and Trust, Huntsville, 1981—; counsel Meadowview Rehab. Ctrs., Huntsville, 1988—. Atty. County of Madison, Ark., 1972-94. Mem. ABA, Ark. Bar Assn., Carroll/Madison Bar Assn., City Attys. Assn. (Appreciation award 1998), Masons. Baptist. Office: Cain Law Office 104 E Main St Huntsville AR 72740

**CAIN, MAY LYDIA,** lawyer; b. Chgo., Feb. 13, 1956; d. William A. and Audrey (Rosin) C.; m. William J. Snihur, Jr. Student, U. Ill., 1973-74; BA, Northwestern U., 1977; postgrad., U. Miami, Coral Gables, Fla., 1979-80; JD, DePaul U., 1980. Bar: Fla. 1980, U.S. Dist. Ct. (so. dist.) Fla. 1980, U.S. Ct. Appeals (5th and 11th cirs.) 1981, U.S. Supreme Ct. 1986. Ptnr. Cain and Cain, North Miami, Fla., 1980-90, Cain and Snihur, North Miami Beach, Fla., 1991—; judge Dade County Ct., 1990-91; adj. prof. Barry U., Miami Shores, Fla., 1986—; atty. Pub. Interest Law Bank, Miami, 1982-83. Editor The Fla. Bar Gen. Practice Sect. newsletter, 1984-86, chmn. editorial bd. Fla. Bar Jour. and News, 1986, 87-90; guest editor The Fla. Bar Jour., Appellate Practice: Setting the Record Straight, 1988; chmn. editorial bd. Fla. Bar Jour. and News, 1989-90; contbr. articles to profl. jours. Mem. North Dade Bar Assn., Fla. Bar Gen. Practice Sect. (exec. council 1984-91), Fla. Assn. Women Lawyers (v.p. 1982-83, pub. relations dir. 1984-85, sec. 1984-86, pres. Dade County chpt. 1983-84, bd. dirs. 1986—), First Am. Family Law Inns of Ct. General practice, State civil litigation, Criminal. Office: Cain and Snihur Ste 304 1550 NE Miami Gardens Dr North Miami Beach FL 33179

**CAIN, PATRICK JOSEPH,** lawyer; b. San Fernando, Calif., Mar. 22, 2957; s. Jack F. Cain and Elizabeth Jo Wartman; m. Margaret Boyle, Aug. 14, 1982; children: Sean, Ryan. BA, Loyola Marymount U., L.A., 1979; JD, UCLA, 1982. Bar: Calif. 1982. Assoc. Overton, Lyman & Prince, L.A., 1982-84, Fried, King & Holmes, L.A., 1984-87, Baker & Hostetler LLP, L.A., 1987—; dir., sec. Inner City Law Ctr., L.A. Mem. Calif. Club, Alumni Assn. Loyola Marymount U. (bd. dirs. 1999—), Calif. Sci. Ctr. Found. (adv. bd. dirs. 1999—). Fax: 213-975-1740. E-mail: pcain@baker-hostetler.com. General civil litigation. Office: Baker & Hostetler LLP 600 Wilshire Blvd Los Angeles CA 90017-3212

**CAIVANO, ANTHONY P.,** lawyer; b. Newark, July 12, 1964; s. Daniel H. and Kathleen Caivano; m. Roxana M. Russo; children: Anthony, Michael Joseph. BA, Rutgers U., 1986; JD, Seton Hall U., 1989. Bar: N.J. 1989. Law sec. Hon. Reginald Stanton, Morristown, N.J., 1989-90; atty. Pitney, Hardin, Kipp et al, Morristown, 1990-94, Nusbaum, Skin, Succasunna, N.J., 1994-97, Bongiovanni, Collins & Warden, Denville, N.J., 1997—. Mem. KC. Democrat. Roman Catholic. Personal injury, Professional liability, Criminal. Home: 16 Tamarack Dr Succasunna NJ 07876-2101 Office: Bongiovanni Collins & Warden 255 Rte 46 E Denville NJ 07834

**CALABRESE, ARNOLD JOSEPH,** lawyer; b. Summit, N.J., Nov. 18, 1960; s. Jack and Valentine (Pannullo) C.; m. Kathryn DeRosa, Aug. 16, 1986. BS in Econs. and Fin., Fairleigh Dickinson U., 1983; JD, U. Bridgeport, 1986. Bar: N.J. 1986, U.S. Dist. Ct. N.J. 1986. Law clk. intern to judge U.S. Dist. Ct. Conn., Hartford, 1985; assoc. Robert J. Hueston (merged with E. Richard Kennedy 1987), Florham Park, Montville, N.J., 1986-88, Rosenberg & Rosenberg, Florham Park, 1988-89; ptnr. Rosenberg, Rosenberg & Calabrese, Florham Park, 1990-96; pvt. practice, 1996—; lectr. N.J. chpt. Community Assn. Inst., Pennington, 1987—. Mem. ABA, N.J. Bar Assn., Morris County Bar Assn., Phi Delta Phi. State civil litigation, Real property, General corporate. Home: 4 Jolen Ct Florham Park NJ 07932-2519 Office: 171 Ridgedale Ave Ste A Florham Park NJ 07932-1764

**CALABRESI, GUIDO,** federal judge, law educator; b. Milan, Oct. 19, 1932; s. Massimo and Bianca Maria (Finzi Contini) C.; m. Anne Gordon Audubon Tyler, May 20, 1961; children: Bianca Finzi Contini, Anne Gordon Audubon, Massimo Franklin Tyler. BS in Analytical Econs., Yale U., 1953, LLB, 1958, MA (hon.), 1962; BA in Politics, Philosophy and Econs., Oxford U., 1955, MA in Politics, Philosophy and Econs., 1959; LLD (hon.), Notre Dame U., 1979, Villanova U., 1984, U. Toronto, 1985, Boston Coll., 1986, Cath. U. Am., 1986, U. Chgo., 1988, Conn. Coll., 1988, Chgo.-Kent-I.T.T., 1989, William Mitchell Coll. Law, 1992, Princeton U., 1992, Detroit Mercy Sch. Law, 1994, Seton Hall U., 1995, Albertus Magnus Coll., 1995, Lewis and Clark Coll., 1996, St. John's U., 1997, Pace U., 1998, Iona Coll., 1998, Roger Williams U., 1999, Hofstra U., 1999, N.Y. Law Sch., 1999; Dott. Ius SD (hon.), U. Turin, Italy, 1982; JD (hon.), U. Pavia, Italy, 1987, U. Stockholm, 1993; PhD (hon.), U. Haifa, Israel, 1988; DPhil, U. Tel Aviv, 1998; LHD (hon.), U. New Haven, 1989, Williams Coll., 1991, Quinnipiac Coll., 1993; DSc in Politics (hon.), U. Padua, Italy, 1990; Dott. Jur. (hon.), U. Bologna, Italy, 1991, U. Milan, 1998. Bar: Conn. 1958. Asst. instr. dept. econs. Yale U., New Haven, Conn., 1955-56; law clk. to Justice Hugo Black U.S. Supreme Ct., Washington, 1958-59; asst. prof. Yale U. Law Sch., 1959-61, assoc. prof., 1961-62, prof., 1962-70, John Thomas Smith prof. law, 1970-78, Sterling prof. law, 1978-95; prof. emeritus, lectr. Yale U., 1995—; dean Yale U. Law Sch., 1985-94; Sterling prof. law emeritus, lectr. Yale U. Law Sch., New Haven, 1995—; judge U.S. Ct. Appeals 2d cir., New Haven, 1994—; fellow Timothy Dwight Coll., 1960—; vis. prof. Harvard U. Law Sch., 1969-70, Japan Am. Studies Seminar, Kyoto-Doshisha Univs., summer 1972, European U. Inst., Florence, Italy, 1979; Arthur L. Goodhart prof. legal sci. Cambridge U., also fellow St. John's Coll., 1980-81. Author: The Costs of Accidents: A Legal and Economic Analysis, 1970; (with P. Bobbitt) Tragic Choices, 1978; A Common Law for the Age of Statutes, 1983 (ABA citation of merit, Order of Coif Triennial Book award); Ideals, Beliefs, Attitudes and the Law: Private Law Perspectives on a Public Law Problem (Silver Gavel award ABA), 1985; contbr. articles to legal jours. Hon. trustee Hopkins Grammar Sch., pres. 1976-80; trustee St. Thomas More Chapel, Yale U.; vice chmn. bd. trustees Carolyn Found., Minn. Rhodes scholar, 1953; named one of Ten Outstanding Young Men Am., U.S. Jaycees, 1962; recipient Laetare Medal, U. Notre Dame, 1985, Marshall-Wythe medal Coll. William and Mary, 1985. Fellow Am. Acad. Arts & Scis., Associazione Italiana di Diritto Comparato, Brit. Acad. (corr.), Royal Swedish Acad. Scis. (fgn.), Accademia Nazionale dei Lincei (fgn.), Accademia delle Scienze di Torino (fgn.); mem. Conn. Bar Assn., Assn. Am. Law Schs. (exec. com. 1986-89), Am. Philos. Soc. Home: 639 Amity Rd Woodbridge CT 06525-1206 Office: US Ct Appeals 2d Cir 157 Church St New Haven CT 06510-2100

**CALAIRO, DONALD ROBERT,** lawyer; b. Trenton, N.J., Aug. 22, 1952; s. Pasquale Thomas and Anna Louise (Hagenlocker) C.; m. Helen M. Goth, June 30, 1996; children: Anthony, Andrea, Nicholas, Michael. BA in History, St. Francis Coll., Laretto, Pa., 1974; LLD, Duquesne U., 1978. Bar: Pa., 1978. Appellate counsel Allegheny County Pub. Defender, Pitts., 1977-81; ptnr. Saldamarco & Calaiaro, Pitts., 1978-86; sole practice Pitts., 1986-89; sr. ptnr. Calairo & Corbett, Inc., 1989—; trustee chpt 7 U.S. Bankruptcy Ct., Pitts., 1975-88, trustee chpt. 13, 1980-86; dir Computer Systems Inst., Pitts., 1977-81; second v.p. Alcobar Fed. Credit Union, Pitts., 1981-85; of counsel Law Offices Edward J. Krug, Pitts., 1986—. Contbr. articles to profl. jours.; lectr. Pa. Bar Inst., 1984-86. Mem. council Allegheny County Comml. Law and Bankruptcy Sect., Pitts., 1983—; Dem. candidate for mayor Dormont, Pa., 1985-86, legal counsel, 1985—, committeeman, 1987-88. Mem. ABA, Pa. Bar Assn., Allegheny County Bar Assn. Roman Catholic. Bankruptcy, Consumer commercial. Office: Calairo & Corbett Inc 1105 Grant Bldg Pittsburgh PA 15219-2301

**CALAMARI, ANDREW M.,** lawyer; b. N.Y.C., Jan. 23, 1918; s. Frank and Caterina Calamari; m. Madeline Redmond, Aug. 1, 1959; children: Andrew, Michael, Joseph, David. BA, CCNY, 1939; JD cum laude, Fordham U., 1942. Bar: N.Y. 1942, U.S. Dist. Ct. (so. dist.) N.Y. 1948, U.S. Dist. Ct. (ea. dist.) N.Y. 1950, U.S. Ct. Appeals (2d cir.) 1964, U.S. Supreme Ct. 1973. Assoc. McLanahan, Merritt & Ingraham, N.Y.C., 1946-59, Buell, Clifton & Turner, N.Y.C., 1959-68; ptnr. Manning, Nakasian & Carey, N.Y.C., 1968-83, Calamari & Calamari, N.Y.C., 1983—. Sgt. U.S. Army, 1943-46. Mem. ABA, N.Y. State Bar Assn., Am. Arbitration Assn. (nat. panel arbitrators 1957—), Fordham Law Rev. Assn. (editorial bd. 1941-42), KC. Democrat. Roman Catholic. General corporate, Federal civil litigation. Office: Calamari & Calamari 2429 Hering Ave Bronx NY 10469-5425

**CALCAGNIE, KEVIN FRANK,** lawyer; b. Glendale, Calif., Feb. 27, 1955; s. Frank Calcagnie Jr. and Margaret Mildred (Bierman) Jones; m. Peggy Melinda Malmberg, Jan. 2, 1982; children: Kelly Shea, Sean Frank. BSBA, Calif. State U., Fullerton, 1977; JD, Western State U., 1983. Bar: Calif. 1983, U.S. dist. Ct. (ea., so. and cen. dists.) Calif. 1983, U.S. Ct. Appeals (9th cir.) 1983, U.S. Supreme Ct. 1987. Ptnr. Robinson, Calcagnie & Robinson, Newport Beach, Calif., 1982—; instr. paralegal studies Fullerton Coll., 1990. Author: (with others) Products Liability Litigation: Product Studies, 1996, A Guide to Toxic Torts, 1987; contbr. articles to profl. jours. Recipient Am. Jurisprudence awards Bancroft Whitney Pub., San Francisco, 1981. Mem. ABA, ATLA, Consumers Attys. of Calif. (bd. govs. 1993-98), Orange County Trial Lawyers Assn. Roman Catholic. General civil litigation, Personal injury, Federal civil litigation. Office: Robinson Calcagnie & Robinson 620 Newport Ctr Dr 7th Fl Newport Beach CA 92660

**CALDARONE, THOMAS J., JR.,** retired state judge; b. Providence, Mar. 7, 1927; s. Thomas J. Caldarone and Margaret Segrella. BS, U. R.I., 1950; LLB, Boston U., 1957. Chief legal svcs. R.I. Dept. Social Welfare, Providence, 1960-63; dep. atty. gen. State of R.I., Providence, 1975-77, dir. dept. bus. regulation, 1977-84; assoc. justice R.I. Superior Ct., Providence, 1984-94; ret., 1994. Nat. Judge Advocate World War II Vets., Washington. With USN. Democrat. Roman Catholic. Home: 129 Forestwood Dr North Providence RI 02904

**CALDERON-HOMS, CARLOS MIGUEL,** lawyer; b. San Juan, Puerto Rico, July 6, 1965; s. Carlos Camilo and Elsie (Homs) C.; m. Diane Frances Weisman Calderon, Sept. 12, 1993; children: Lucas Federico Max, Sara Monserrat. BA in Econ., U. Puerto Rico, San Juan, 1987; JD, U. Conn. Sch. Law, Hartford, 1990. Bar: N.Y., 1991. Asst. dist. atty. Bronx (N.Y.) County Dist. Atty., 1990-95; assoc. Brody & Fabiani, N.Y.C., 1995-96; ptnr. Weisman & Calderon LLP, Mt. Vernon, N.Y., 1996—; lectr. Bronx County Bar Assn., 1998—; mem. exec. com. N.Y. State Bar Assn. Trial Lawyers Divsn., N.Y.C., 1996-98. Mem. Bronx Bar Assn., N.Y. State Bar Assn., N.Y. State Trial Lawyer's Assn., Puerto Rican Bar Assn. Roman Catholic. Avocations: sports, computer science. Office: Weisman & Calderon LLP 6 Gramatan Ave Ste 206 Mount Vernon NY 10550-3209

**CALDERWOOD, JAMES ALBERT,** lawyer; b. Washington, Dec. 4, 1941; s. Charles Howard and Hilda Pauline (Dull) C.; m. Joyce M. Johnson, 1987;. BS, U. Md., 1964; J.D. cum laude, George Washington U., 1970; postgrad., Oxford Ctr. Mgmt. Studies, Oxford, Eng., 1977. Bar: Md. 1970, D.C. 1973, U.S. Supreme Ct. 1974. Trial atty. antitrust div. U.S. Dept. Justice, Washington, 1970-73; spl. asst. U.S. Atty., $, 1973, trial atty. antitrust div., 1973-79; ptnr. Grove, Jaskiewicz, Gilliam & Cobert, Washington, 1979-90, Zuckert, Scoutt, Rasenberger, Washington, 1990—; mem. faculty Transp. Law Inst. U. Denver; adj. prof. Washington Coll. Law, Am. U., 1983, 86; faculty Internat. Law Inst., 1995—; gen. counsel Soc. Fovt. Economists. Contbr. articles to profl. jours. Served to capt. USAF, 1964-68. George Washington U. Law Ctr. scholar, 1969. Mem. ABA (Achievement award 1979), Fed. Bar Assn. (nat. co chmn. council young lawyers 1972-73, chmn. regulated industries com. 1976-79), Fed. Energy Bar Assn. (chmn. antitrust com. 1985-86, 93-95), Transp. Lawyers Assn. (chmn. antitrust com. 1998—); Assn. for Transp. Law, Logistics & Policy (pres. D.C. chpt. 1998—), Md. Bar Assn., D.C. Bar Assn., U. Md. Alumni Assn. (pres. elect 1984-85, pres. 1985-86) Coll. Bus. Alumni Club (pres. 1980-81), Nat. Press Club, Pi Sigma Alpha, Delta Sigma Pi, Delta Theta Phi, English Speaking Union. Episcopalian. Antitrust, Federal civil litigation, FERC practice. Home: 5518 Western Ave Chevy Chase MD 20815-7122 Office: Zuckert Scountt & Rasenberger 888 17th St NW Ste 600 Washington DC 20006-3309

**CALDWELL, COURTNEY LYNN,** lawyer, real estate consultant; b. Washington, Mar. 5, 1948; d. Joseph Morton and Moselle (Smith) C. Student, Duke U., 1966-68, U. Calif., Berkeley, 1967, 1968-69; BA, U. Calif., Santa Barbara, 1970, MA, 1975; JD with highest honors, George Washington U., 1982. Bar: D.C. 1984, Wash. 1986, Calif. 1989. Jud. clk. U.S. Ct. Appeals for 9th Cir., Seattle, 1982-83; assoc. Arnold & Porter, Washington, 1983-85, Perkins Coie, Seattle, 1985-88; dir. western ops. Enl. Real Estate Svcs., Inc., Irvine, Calif., 1988-91, sr. v.p., 1991-98; ind. cons., Orange County, Calif., 1998—. Bd. dirs. Univ. Town Ctr. Assn., 1994; bd. dirs. Habitat for Humanity, Orange County, 1993-94, chair legal com., 1994. Named Nat. Law Ctr. Law Rev. Scholar, 1981-82. Mem. Calif. Bar Assn. Avocation: foreign languages. Real property, Land use and zoning (including planning), Finance. Home and Office: 140 Cabrillo St Apt 15 Costa Mesa CA 92627-3038

**CALDWELL, DOUGLAS CODY,** lawyer; b. Monroe, La., Oct. 7, 1951; s. Jefferson W. Jr. and Marjorie D. (Cody) C.; m. Emily E. May, Aug. 11, 1973; 1 child, Benjamin L. BS in Computer Sci., N.E. La. U., 1972; JD, La. State U., 1976; LLM in Taxation, So. Meth. U., 1978. Law clk. La. 2d Cir. Ct. Appeals, Shreveport, 1976-77; law clk. appellate divsn. IRS, Dallas, 1977-78; assoc. Blackwell Chambliss, West Monroe, La., 1978—. Active numerous civic orgns. Mem. La. State Bar Assn. (bd. cert. tax specialist, bd. cert. estate planning and adminstrn. specialist), West Monroe C. of C. (pres. 1983-84), West Monroe Kiwanis Club (pres. 1983-84). Estate planning, General corporate, Probate. Office: Blackwell Chambliss 2001 N 7th St West Monroe LA 71291-4440

**CALDWELL, JOHN WARWICK,** lawyer; b. Dayton, Ohio, May 19, 1949; s. Curtis Philip and Elizabeth L. (Warwick) C.; m. Janet Hudson, June 14, 1975; children: Philip E., Katherine E., Sarah A. BA, Rice U., 1971; MA, Johns Hopkins U., 1975; JD, Villanova U., 1978. Bar: Pa. 1978, U.S. Dist. Ct. (ea. dist.) Pa. 1978, (mid. dist.) 1990, U.S. Ct. Appeals (3rd cir.) 1980, (fed. cir.) 1983, U.S. Supreme Ct., 1986, U.S. Patent and Trademark. From assoc. to ptnr. Woodcock, Washburn, Kurtz, Mackiewicz & Norris, Phila., 1978—; nat. spkr. in field. Author: The Effects of Gatt Upon Patent Property, 1994, Biotechnology Patents, 1994, Five Ways to Improve the Examination of Biotechnology Patents, 1994, Voo Doo Diligence, 1994, ALI-ABA Videotape: Development in the Law of Copyrights, 1992, Artists' Guide to Copyrights, Patents and Trade Secrets, 1985, 2d edit., 1995; author monograph; contbr. to series Science and the Law, Am. Chem. Soc. Bd. dirs. Phila. Vol. Lawyers for Arts, 1978-80. Robert Welch Found. scholar, 1968-71. Mem. ABA, Internat. Trademark Assn., Licensing Execs.' Soc., Pa. Bar Assn., Phila. Bar Assn. (fed. cts. com.), Phila. Intellectual Property Law Assn. (chmn. antitrust com. 1983-85, moderator ann. rev. of decisions of U.S. Cts. of Appeals 1985—, treas. 1978-80, 95-97, pres.-elect 1998-99, pres. 1999—), Copyright Soc. U.S. (Phila. chpt. co-chair). Republican. Presbyterian. Avocations: sailing, golf. E-mail: Caldwell@Woodcock.com. Patent, Trademark and copyright, Antitrust. Office: Woodcock Washburn Kurtz Mackiewicz & Norris 1 Liberty Place 46th Flr Philadelphia PA 19103

**CALDWELL, RODNEY KENT,** lawyer; b. Washington, Feb. 19, 1937; s. Rodney Huntington and Marion Elisabeth (Sasher) C.; m. Marjorie Lee Zink, Apr. 15, 1965 (div. 1975); children: Dana Kent, Susan Ashley; m. Yolanda Silva, June 22, 1979; 1 child, David Huntington. BChemE, U. Va., 1959; JD, U. Houston, 1969. Bar: Tex. 1969, U.S. Supreme Ct. 1975. With Arnold, White & Durkee, Houston, 1970—. Author: Patent Litigation: Procedure & Tactics, 1978-84. Lt. USAF, 1959-62. Fellow Tex. Bar Found., Houston Bar Found.; mem. ABA, Am. Intellectual Property Law Assn., Internat. Bar Assn., Internat. Intellectual Property Assn., Univ. Club., Army and Navy Club. Methodist. Patent, Trademark and copyright, Federal civil litigation. Home: 4021 Ella Lee Ln Houston TX 77027-3910 Office: Arnold White & Durkee 750 Bering Dr Houston TX 77057-2149

**CALDWELL, WILLIAM WILSON,** federal judge; b. Harrisburg, Pa., Nov. 10, 1925; s. Thomas D. and Martha B. C.; m. Janet W. Garber. A.B., Dickinson Coll., 1948, LL.B., 1951. Ptnr. Caldwell, Fox & Stoner, Harrisburg, 1951-70; 1st asst. dist. Atty. Dauphin County, 1960-62; counsel, chmn. Bd. Arbitration of Claims State of Pa., 1963-70; judge Common Pleas Ct., Dauphin County, 1970-82; judge U.S. Dist. Ct. (mid. dist.) Pa., 1982-94, sr. judge, 1994—. Office: Fed Bldg PO Box 11877 Harrisburg PA 17108-1877

**CALFEE, WILLIAM LEWIS,** lawyer; b. Cleveland Heights, Ohio, July 12, 1917; s. Robert Martin and Alwine (Haas) C.; m. Eleanor Elizabeth Bliss, Dec. 6, 1941; children: William R., Bruce K., Cynthia B. B.A., Harvard Coll., 1939; LL.D., Yale U., 1946. Bar: Ohio 1946. Assoc. Baker & Hostetler, Cleve., 1946-56, ptnr., 1957-90, of counsel, 1990-92. Bd. dirs. Growth Assn. Greater Cleve., 1979-92; trustee Greater Cleve. United Appeal; pres. Health Fund Greater Cleve. Served to lt. col. M.I., U.S. Army, 1941-45. Decorated Legion of Merit; decorated Order of Brit. Empire. Mem. ABA (ho. of dels. 1980-93), Ohio Bar Assn., Bar Assn. Greater Cleve. (trustee 1980-93, pres. 1979-80), Nat. Conf. Bar Pres. (exec. coun. 1982-85), Ohio C. of C. (bd. dirs. 1993), Mayfield Country Club (pres.), Union Club, Pepper Pike Club, Sanctuary Golf Club. Republican. Episcopalian. Home: 21200 Claythorne Rd Shaker Heights OH 44122-1962 Office: Baker & Hostetler 3200 Nat City Ctr 1900 E 9th St Ste 3200 Cleveland OH 44114-3475

**CALHOUN, DONALD EUGENE, JR.,** federal judge; b. Columbus, Ohio, May 15, 1926; s. Donald Eugene and Esther C.; m. Shirley Claggett, Aug. 28, 1948; children: Catherine C., Donald Eugene III, Elizabeth C. BA in Polit. Sci., Ohio State U., 1949, JD, 1951. Bar: Ohio 1951. Pvt. practice, 1951-68; ptnr. Folkerth, Calhoun, Webster, Maurer & O'Brien, 1968-82, Guren, Merritt, Feibel, Sogg & Cohen, 1982-84; of counsel Lane, Alton, Horst, 1984-85; U.S. bankruptcy judge Columbus, 1985—; gen. counsel Ohio Conf. United Ch. of Christ, 1964-85. Chmn. City-wide Citizens Com. for Neighborhood Seminars on Sch. Program and Fin., 1963; mem. Columbus Bd. Edn., 1963-71, pres., 1966, 70. With USNR, 1944-46. Mem. Columbus Bar Assn. (pres. 1967-68, Community Svc. award 1972), Nat. Conf. Bar Pres., Am. Arbitration Assn., Columbus Jaycees (life), Univ. Club, Masons. Congregationalist. Office: US Bankruptcy Ct 170 N High St Columbus OH 43215-2403

**CALHOUN, SCOTT DOUGLAS,** lawyer; b. Aurora, Ill., May 1, 1959; s. Ellsworth L. Calhoun and Mary Louise (Mummert) Wire; m. Gloria Jean Fulvi, Aug. 1, 1987; 1 child, John Daniel. BA cum laude, Knox Coll., 1981; JD, Coll. of William and Mary, 1984. Bar: Ga. 1984, U.S. Dist. Ct. (no. dist.) Ga. 1984, U.S. Ct. Appeals (11th cir.) 1984. Assoc. Swift, Currie, McGhee & Hiers, Atlanta, 1984-90, ptnr., 1990-92; pvt. practice, Atlanta, 1992-94; prin. Byrne, Eldridge, Moore & Davis, P.C., Atlanta, 1994-95; ptnr. Mozley, Finlayson & Loggins, 1996—; seminar spkr. in field, 1995—. Bd. dirs. Atlanta Symphony Assocs., 1991-97, Wildwood Civic Assn., Atlanta, 1991-98; elder Trinity Presbyn. Ch., Atlanta, 1994-97. Mem. Mortar Bd. Avocations: golf, music. General corporate, Estate planning, Contracts commercial. Office: Mozley Finlayson & Loggins 5605 Glenridge Dr NE Ste 900 Atlanta GA 30342-1380

**CALHOUN-SENGHOR, KEITH,** lawyer; b. Richmond, Va., June 14, 1955; s. Clarence Calhoun Jr. and Senegal Senghor; m. Sharon White. AB with honors, Stanford U., 1977; JD, Harvard U., 1981. Bar: D.C. 1981, U.S. Ct. Appeals (4th cir.) 1982. Law clk. to judge U.S. Ct. Appeals for 4th Cir., Richmond, 1981-82; assoc. Gibson, Dunn & Crutcher, L.A. and Washington, 1983-85; fgn. legal fellow Kreuz, Niebler & Mittl, Munich, 1986; v.p., gen. counsel Tech. Applications, Inc., Alexandria, Va., 1986-90; pres. Noma Internat. Enterprises, Inc., Washington, 1990-93; of counsel Wood, Williams, Rafalsky & Harris, Washington, 1991-93; dir. Office of Space Commercialization U.S. Dept. Commerce, Washington, 1993—. Fulbright scholar U. Bonn., 1977-78; German Acad. Exch. Svc. Fgn. fellow, 1985-86. Mem. ABA, D.C. Bar Assn. Office: US Dept Commerce Office Space Commercializtn 15th & Constitution Ave NW Washington DC 20230-0001

**CALISE, NICHOLAS JAMES,** lawyer; b. N.Y.C., Sept. 15, 1941; s. William J. and Adeline (Rota) C.; m. Mary G. Flannery, Nov. 10, 1965; children: James R., Lori K. AB, Middlebury Coll., 1962; MBA, LLB, Columbia U., 1965. Bar: N.Y. 1965, Conn., 1974, Ohio, 1986. Assoc., ptnr. Olvany, Eisner & Donnelly, N.Y.C., 1969-76; corp. staff atty. Richardson-Vicks Inc., Wilton, Conn., 1976-82; div. counsel, dir. planning and bus. devel. home care products div. Richardson-Vicks Inc., Memphis, 1982-84; staff v.p., sec., asst. gen. counsel The B.F. Goodrich Co., Akron, Ohio, 1984-89, v.p., sec., assoc. gen. counsel, 1989—. Mem. Flood and Erosion Control Bd., Darien, Conn., 1976, Rep. Town Meeting, Darien, 1977-78; chmn. Zoning Bd. Appeals, Darien, 1978-82; Justice of the Peace, Darien, 1982. Served to lt. USN, 1965-68, capt. JAGC, USNR, 1984-96, ret. Mem. ABA, Am. Soc. Corp. Secs. (bd. dirs. 1990-93, exec. steering com. 1992-93, chpt. treas. 1988-89, sec. 1989-90, v.p. 1990-91, pres. 1991-92, chmn. nat. conf. com. 1997, chmn. fin. com. 1998—), Am. Corp. Counsel Assn., N.Y. State Bar Assn., Conn. Bar Assn., Ohio Bar Assn., Assn. Bar City of N.Y., U.S. Naval Inst., Navy League (life), Judge Advs. Assn. (life), Naval Res. Assn. (life), Cleve. Bar Assn., Res. Officers Assn. (life), Am. Legion, Country Club of Hudson (bd. trustees 1996-99, sec. 1997-99), Akron City Club, Club Cordillera. Roman Catholic. General corporate, Mergers and acquisitions, Securities. Home: 2731 Stonebridge Ct Hudson OH 44236-2343 Office: B F Goodrich Co 4020 Kinross Lakes Pkwy Richfield OH 44286-9368

**CALISE, WILLIAM JOSEPH, JR.,** lawyer; b. N.Y.C., May 22, 1938; s. William Joseph and Adeline (Rota) C.; m. Elizabeth Mae Gagne, Apr. 16, 1966; children: Kimberly Elizabeth, Andrea Elizabeth. BA, Bucknell U., 1960; MBA, JD, Columbia U., 1963. Bar: N.Y. 1963, D.C. 1981. Assoc. then ptnr. Chadbourne & Parke, N.Y.C., 1967-94; sr. v.p., gen. counsel, sec. Rockwell Internat. Corp., Milw., 1994—. Dir. Henry St. Settlement, N.Y.C., 1977-94; mem. Allendale (N.J.) Sch. Bd., 1977-80. Capt. U.S. Army, 1964-66. Mem. Assn. Bar N.Y.C., Duquesne Club (Pitts.). Roman Catholic. Office: Rockwell Internat Corp 777 E Wisconsin Ave Milwaukee WI 53202

**CALKINS, STEPHEN,** law educator, lawyer; b. Balt., Mar. 20, 1950; s. Evan and Virginia (Brady) C.; m. Joan Wadsworth, Oct. 18, 1981; children: Timothy, Geoffrey, Virginia. BA, Yale U., 1972; JD, Harvard U., 1975. Bar: N.Y. 1976, D.C. 1977, U.S. Dist. Ct. D.C. 1979. Law clk. to FTC commr. S. Nye, Washington, 1975-76; assoc. Covington & Burling, Washington, 1976-83; assoc. law prof. Wayne State U., Detroit, 1983-88, prof., 1988—; gen. counsel FTC, Washington, 1995-97; spl. counsel Covington & Burling, Washington, 1997—; vis. assoc. prof. law U. Mich., Ann Arbor, 1985, U. Pa., Phila., 1987; vis. prof. law U. Utrecht, Netherlands, 1989; chair career devel. Wayne State U., 1990-91. Editor: Antitrust Law Developments, 1984, 86, 88, (legal book revs.) The Antitrust Bulletin, 1986—, (articles) Antitrust, 1991-95. Counsel Ind. Commn. on Admissions Practices in Cranbrook Sch., Detroit, 1984-85; mem. Northville Zoning Bd. Appeals, 1987-95; rep.-at-large Assn. Yale Alumni Assembly, 1989-92; elder First Presbyn. Ch. of Northville, 1989-92. Research fellow Wayne State U., 1984. Mem. ABA (coun. antitrust sect. 1988-91, 97—, counsel to com. on FTC 1988-89, co-chair adjudication com. adminstrv. law sect. 1997—), Am. Law Inst., Am. Assn. Law Schs. (sec. antitrust sect. 1987-91, chair-elect, 1991-93, chair, 1993-95), Harvard Club, Yale Club (Detroit), Northville Swim Club. Avocations: reading, skiing. Antitrust, General corporate, Administrative and regulatory. Home: 317 W Dunlap St Northville MI 48167-1404 Office: Law Sch Wayne State U Detroit MI 48202

**CALKINS, SUSAN W.,** state supreme court justice. Grad., U. Colo.; JD, U. Maine. Staff atty., exec. dir. Pine Tree Legal Assistance; judge Maine Dist. Ct., 1980-90, chief judge, 1990; judge Maine Superior Ct., 1995; justice Maine Supreme Jud. Ct., 1998—. Office: Cumberland County Courthouse PO Box 368 142 Federal St Portland ME 04112-0368*

**CALL, MERLIN WENDELL,** lawyer; b. Long Beach, Calif., Nov. 25, 1931; s. True and Bernice (Johnson) C.; m. Kathryn J. Gage, Dec. 22, 1956 (div.); children: Christopher, Lori. AB, Stanford U., 1951, JD, 1953. Bar: Calif. Assoc. Tuttle & Taylor, L.A., 1955-60, ptnr., 1960—; mem. bd. visitors Stanford Sch. Law, 1987-90. Chmn. bd. trustees Westmont Coll., Santa Barbara, Calif., 1988-94, Fuller Found., Pasadena, Calif., 1987-94, Mission Aviation Fellowship, Redlands, Calif., 1974-78, Gospel Broadcasting Assn., 1967-78; mem. Town Hall Calif., L.A., 1958—; trustee Fuller Theol. Sem., Pasadena, 1963-78, 83—, AirServ Internat., Redlands, 1984-91, 94-96, Fuller Found., 1987—, Westmont Coll., 1984—. 1st lt. U.S. Army, 1953-55. Mem. Calif. Club, Phi Beta Kappa, Order of Coif. General corporate, Probate, Estate taxation. Home: 1660 La Loma Rd Pasadena CA 91105-2158 Office: Tuttle & Taylor 355 S Grand Ave Fl 40 Los Angeles CA 90071-1560

**CALL, SUSAN HOPE,** lawyer; b. Saltville, Va., May 27, 1967; d. Billy Eugene and Carolyn Sue Call. BA cum laude, Emory and Henry Coll., 1989; JD, U. Richmond, 1992. Bar: Va. 1992. Clk. Parker Pollard and Brown, Richmond, 1992, S. Keith Barker, Richmond, 1992-93; assoc. Krumbein & Assocs., Richmond, 1993-94, Affiliated Attys. Inc., Richmond, 1994-97, Framme Law Firm Plc, Richmond, 1997—. Mem. Domestic Rels. Bar. Avocations: animal adoption and rescue. Bankruptcy, Family and matrimonial, General practice. Office: Framme Law Firm PLC 1108 E Main St Fl 11 Richmond VA 23219-3539

**CALLAGHAN, KATHLEEN RICHARD,** lawyer; b. Baton Rouge, Dec. 18, 1949; d. Oscar Gabriel and Billie (Gathright) Richard; m. May 19, 1969 (div. May 1990); children: Maxwell McConnell Magbee, Caitlin Callaghan Magbee; m. John Andrew Broussard, May 31, 1997. BA in Landscape Arch., La. State U., 1985, JD, 1993. Bar: La. 1993. Assoc. Dampf & Edwards, LLP, Baton Rouge, 1993-96; staff rsch. atty. East Baton Rouge Parish Family Ct., Baton Rouge, 1997—. Contbr. article to La. Bar Jour. Vol. hosp. escort Stop Rape Crisis Ctr., Baton Rouge, 1998—; coach Joints in Motion program La. Arthritis Found., 1998—; mem. YWCA. Mem. AAUW, La. Bar Assn., Baton Rouge Bar Assn. (mem. young lawyers sect. coun. 1996, Century Club award 1996), Baton Rouge Assn. Women Attys. (sec. 1997, 98), Dean Henry G. McMahon Am. Inn of Ct. Avocations: long distance running, bicycling. Fax: 225-389-4952. E-mail: kcallagh@communique.net. Office: The Family Ct 222 Saint Louis St Rm 962 Baton Rouge LA 70802-5876

**CALLAHAN, GARY BRENT,** lawyer; b. Ashland, Oreg., Apr. 24, 1942; s. Donald Burr and Joyce Valeri (Powers) C.; m. Nancy Kay King, Feb. 1967 (div. 1978); children: Shawn, Christopher; m. Sally Kornblight, Jan. 18, 1983; 1 child, Zachary. Student, Sacramento State U.; JD, U. of Pacific, 1970. Bar: Calif. 1971, U.S. Dist. Ct. (ea. dist.) Calif. 1971. Assoc. Rust & Mills, Sacramento, Calif., 1971-73, Barrett, Matheny & Newlon, Sacramento, 1973-77; ptnr. Westley & Callahan, Sacramento, 1977-80, Wilcoxen, Callahan, Montgomery & Harbison, Sacramento, 1980-94, Callahan & Deacon, Sacramento, 1994—; instr., lectr. Continuing Edn. Bar, Berkeley, Calif., 1978—; faculty mem. advocacy skills workshop Sch. Law Stanford U., 1994—, Sch. Law U. San Francisco, 1994—. Served with USN, 1960-63. Recipient Outstanding Alumnus award U. The Pacific McGeorge Sch. of Law, 1989. Mem. Calif. Bar Assn., Assn. Trial Lawyers Am. (sustaining), Consumer Attys. Calif., Capitol City Consumer Attys. (pres. 1984-85), Am. Bd. Profl. Liability Attys., Am. Bd. Trial Advs., Nat. Bd. Trial Advs. Democrat. Avocations: lecturing, instructing on trial advocacy, sailing, boating. State civil litigation, Insurance, Personal injury. Office: Callahan & Deacon 77 Cadillac Dr Ste 240 Sacramento CA 95825-8328

**CALLAHAN, JAMES CHRISTOPHER,** lawyer; b. Rutherfordton, N.C., Dec. 17, 1951; s. James Arthur and Janie Evelyn (Gray) C.; m. Donna Hines, June 6, 1985; children: Tristan Elliott, Joshua Grey, James Nicholas. B.A., U. N.C., 1974; J.D., Wake Forest U., 1977. Bar: N.C. 1977, U.S. Dist. Ct. N.C. 1978, U.S. Ct. Appeals (4th cir.) 1979. Ptnr. Arledge-Callahan, Rutherfordton, N.C., 1977-98; pvt. practice, Rutherfordton, 1998—. Mem. N.C. Bar Assn., Rutherford County Bar Assn., 29th Jud. Dist. Bar Assn. Republican. Mem. Charismatic Episcopal Ch. Home: 559 Candy Rock Rd Union Mills NC 28167-8609 Office: Arledge-Callahan 404 Charlotte Rd Rutherfordton NC 28139-2918

**CALLAHAN, JOHN WILLIAM (BILL CALLAHAN),** judge; b. Rockville Centre, N.Y., Feb. 8, 1947; s. Peter Felix and Catherine Lucille (Walbroehl) C. BA, Mich. State U., 1971, JD cum laude, 1974. Atty. Bank of Commonwealth, Detroit, 1974-76; assoc. Hoops & Hudson, P.C., Detroit, 1976-79, Tyler & Canham, P.C., Detroit, 1979-80, Stark & Reagan, P.C., Troy, Mich., 1980-81; pvt. practice Farmington Hills, Mich., 1981-86; mem. Plunkett & Cooney, P.C., Detroit, 1986-96; judge Wayne County Cir. Ct., Detroit, 1996—. Bd. dirs. Vietnam Vets. Am. Chpt. 9, Detroit, 1981-85. With USMC, 1967-69, Vietnam. Mem. ABA, Detroit Bar Assn. Bankruptcy, Federal civil litigation, Banking. Office: 1807 City-County Bldg Detroit MI 48226

**CALLAHAN, KELLEY CHARLES,** lawyer; b. Oklahoma City, Aug. 22, 1952. BA in Religion cum laude, Colgate U., 1974; JD with honors, U. Okla., 1980. Bar: Okla. 1981, U.S. Dist. Ct. (we. dist.) Okla. 1981, Colo. 1993, U.S. Dist. Ct. (ea. dist.) Okla. 1998. Dir., litigation atty. Crowe & Dunlevy, Oklahoma City, 1980—; tchr. bus. law U. Okla., Norman, 1979-80; tchr. pre-trial litigation Oklahoma City U. Law Sch., 1997. Contbr. articles to profl. jours. Active Eagle Ridge Instn. Mem. Okla. Bar Assn. (appellate practice sect.). Appellate, Insurance, Product liability. Office: Crowe & Dunlevy 20 N Broadway Ave Ste 1800 Oklahoma City OK 73102-8273

**CALLAHAN, MICHAEL THOMAS,** lawyer, construction consultant; b. Kansas City, Mo., Oct. 7, 1948; s. Harry Leslie and Venita June (Yohn) C.; m. Stella Sue Paffenbach, Mar. 21, 1970; children: Molly Leigh, Michael Kroh. BA, U. Kans., 1970; JD, U. Mo., 1973, LLM, 1979; postgrad., Temple U., 1976-77. Bar: Kans. 1973, N.J. 1975, Mo. 1977. V.p. T.J. Constrn., Inc., Lenexa, Kans., 1973-74; sr. cons. Wagner-Hohns-Inglis, Inc., Mt. Holly, N.J., 1974-77; v.p. Wagner-Hohns-Inglis, Inc., Kansas City, Mo., 1977-86; exec. v.p. CCL Constrn. Cons., Overland Park, Kans., 1986-88, pres., 1988—; adj. prof. U. Kans., Iowa State U.; arbitrator, lectr. in field, author; chmn. CCL Pacific Corp.; pres. Handcrafted Wines Kans., Inc. Home: 9011 Delmar St Shawnee Mission KS 66207-2343 Office: CCL Constrn Cons 7219 Metcalf Ave Ste 202 Overland Park KS 66204-1974

**CALLAHAN, PATRICK MICHAEL,** lawyer; b. Trenton, N.J., Aug. 1, 1947; s. Aloysius Walter and Doris Beatrice (Schwing) C.; m. Elizabeth R. Cohen, May 6, 1984; children: Andrew Lawrence, Samantha Devon; children by previous marriage: Erin Kathleen, Patrick Michael Jr. AA, Rider Coll., 1977, BA summa cum laude, 1978, MA, 1980; JD, Seton Hall. U., 1984. Bar: N.J. 1984, U.S. Dist. Ct. N.J. 1984; cert. civil trial atty. Supreme Ct. of N.J. bd. on trial atty. cert. Trooper N.J. State Police, 1970-84; assoc. Shanley & Fisher, P.C., Morristown, N.J., 1984-93; ptnr. Tompkins, McGuire & Wachenfeld, Newark, N.J., 1993-98, Tompkins, McGuire, Wachenfeld & Barry, LLP, Newark, 1998—; dir. Appellate Moot Ct., 1983-84; mem. N.J. Supreme Ct. Dist. Ethics Com., Dist. V-A (Newark), 1994-96, chair, 1996-97; master Seton Hall U. Law Sch. Inn of Ct., 1994—. Mem. Somerset County Dem. Com., 1988—. With USNR, 1965-72. Andrew J. Rider scholar, 1976, Oscar W. Rittenhouse scholar, 1982. Mem. ABA, N.J. State Bar Assn. (vice-chmn. malpractice ins. com. 1998-99, chair 1999—), Somerset County Bar Assn. (trustee 1997—), Essex County Bar Assn. (chair civil litigation practice com. 1999—), Trial Attys. of N.J. (trustee 1996—). Unitarian Universalist. Avocation: photography. General civil litigation, Insurance, Product liability. Home: 211 Daval Rd Neshanic Station NJ 08853-3019 Office: Tompkins McGuire Wachenfeld & Barry Four Gateway Ctr 100 Mulberry St Newark NJ 07102-4070

**CALLAHAN, RICHARD PAUL,** lawyer; b. Boston, Oct. 27, 1944; s. William Francis and Ruth (McDonald) C.; m. Cynthia Higdon, Apr. 11, 1970; children: Caroline Higdon, Christopher Richard. BSBA, Georgetown U., 1967; JD, Suffolk U., 1971. Bar: Mass. 1971, N.Y. 1971, U.S. Dist. Ct. Mass. 1971. Assoc. Lyne Woodworth & Evarts, Boston, 1971-77, ptnr., 1978-85; v.p., gen. counsel Oxbow Corp., West Palm Beach, Fla., 1985—. Bd. dirs. Palm Beach (Fla.) Civic Assn., America 3 Found.; bd. advisors Georgetown U., Good Samaritan-St. Mary's Hosp. Served with U.S. Army, 1968-74. Mem. ABA, Mass. Bar Assn. Roman Catholic. Avocation: golf. General corporate, Real property, General practice. Home: 345 Seasray Ave Palm Beach FL 33480 Office: Oxbow Corp 1601 Forum Pl West Palm Beach FL 33401-8101

**CALLAHAN, ROBERT EDWARD,** lawyer; b. N.Y.C., Aug. 17, 1949; s. John Francis and Helen M. (Jones) C.; m. Terry Aune Callahan, Sept. 30, 1989. BA, U. Calif., Santa Barbara, 1971; JD, U. Santa Clara, Calif., 1975. Bar: Calif. 1975, U.S. Dist. Ct. (cen., ea. and so. dists.) Calif. 1976, U.S. Ct. Appeals (9th cir.) 1991. Assoc. Hurwitz and Hurwitz, Orange, Calif., 1976-78; ptnr. Virtue and Scheck, Newport Beach, Calif., 1978-84, Paone, Callahan, McHolm & Winton, Irvine, Calif., 1984—. Pres. U. Calif. Irvine Athletic Found., 1984-86, bd. dirs., 1983-94; bd. dirs. U. Calif. Irvine Found., 1995—; bd. dirs. Orange County Sports Celebrities, 1990—, pres., 1992-95, Orange County Sports Assn., 1991, mem. exec. com., 1993-96. Mem. Newport Harbor Area C. of C., Newport Beach Athletic Club, Ctr. Club, Hoag Hosp. 552 Club (bd. dirs. 1991-97, pres. 1995-96), Commodores Club (exec. com. 1993, pres. 1996-97), Newport Beach Country Club. Family and matrimonial, General civil litigation, Sports. Office: Paone Callahan McHolm & Winton 19100 Von Karman Ave Fl 8 Irvine CA 92612-1539

**CALLAHAN, ROBERT JEREMIAH,** former state supreme court justice; b. Norwalk, Conn., June 3, 1930; s. Jeremiah J. and Elizabeth A. (Connolly) C.; m. Dorothy B. Trudel, Jan. 24, 1959; children: Sheila, Kerry, Denise, Janine, Patrick, Megan, Jane, Robert Jr. BS in History and Govt., Boston Coll., 1952; JD, Fordham U., 1955. Judge Cir. Ct. Conn., 1970-75, Ct. Common Pleas, Conn., 1975-76, Conn. Superior Ct., 1976-85; assoc. justice Conn. Supreme Ct., 1985-96, chief justice, 1996-99; mem. Bd. Pardons, Conn., 1985-87. Served with U.S. Army, 1956-58. Recipient Fordham U. Sch. Law Dean's medal of recognition, 1986, Fordham Law Alumni Assn. medal of excellence, 1997, Fordham Disting. Alumnus award, 1998, U. Conn. Alumni Assn. Disting. Svc. award, 1998. Roman Catholic. Office: Conn Supreme Ct Drawer N Sta A 231 Capitol Ave Hartford CT 06106-1548

**CALLAHAN, ROBERT JOHN, JR.,** lawyer, arbitrator; b. St. Louis, July 3, 1923; s. Robert John and Elizabeth Mae Deck (Gentner) C.; m. Dorothy Foley, Apr. 18, 1958 (dec. Nov. 1980); m. Barbara Kelsall Couture, May 22, 1982. Grad. Chaminade Coll., 1941; B.S. in Bus. Adminstrn., Washington U., 1944; J.D. cum laude, Notre Dame U., 1948. Bar: Mo. 1948, U.S. Ct. Appeals (fed. cir.) 1951, U.S. Supreme Ct. 1955, U.S. Ct. Mil. Appeals. Ptnr. Callahan and Callahan, St. Louis, 1948-56; sole practice, St. Louis, 1956—. Contbr. articles to legal jours. Candidate for judge St. Louis County Cir. Ct., 1960. Coro fellow. Served with FBI and USCGR, 1944-45; former liaison officer USAF Acad. Served to capt. JAGC, USAFR. Mem. ABA, Lawyers Assn. of St. Louis, St. Louis Bar Assn., Am. Assn. Trial Lawyers Notre Dame U. Law Assn., U. Notre Dame Alumni Assn., Nat. Panel Consumer Arbitrators, Ret. Air Force Officers Assn. Phi Delta Theta. Republican. Roman Catholic. Personal injury, Civil rights, Probate. Office: 32 Normandy Dr Lake Saint Louis MO 63367-1502

**CALLAHAN, TENA TOYE,** lawyer; b. Dallas, Dec. 5, 1954; d. Norman Lewis Callahan and Toye Mae Dennis; m. Dennis Bakos, May 27, 1977 (div. Dec., 1982); children: Randall A., Jesse D. BFA, U. Tex., 1977; JD, St. Mary's U., 1991. Bar: Tex. 1992, U.S. Dist. Ct. (no. dist.) Tex. 1992. Lawyer pvt. practice, Dallas, 1992-97; shareholder Callahan & Byrd P.C., Dallas, 1997-98; pvt. practice Tena T. Callahan, P.C., Dallas, 1998—. Named Parent of Yr. Big Brothers and Sisters of Am., Dallas, 1984. Mem. ATLA, Coll. of State Bar of Tex. Avocations: acting, singing, reading. Family and matrimonial, State civil litigation, Juvenile. Office: 4655 Central Expressway Dallas TX 75205

**CALLAHAN, TIMOTHY J.,** lawyer, investment advisor; b. Yokohama, Japan, Jan. 6, 1948; parents Am. citizens; s. Frank T. and Jane A. Callahan; m. Margan Raphael, Aug. 15, 1970; children: Katie E., Zachary P., Carmen C., Elizabeth G. BS in Commerce, U. Va., 1970; JD, Cath. U., 1974. BAr: Va. 1974. Atty./assoc. Simmonds, Coleburn, Towner and Carman, Arlington, Va., 1974-76, Farley, Harrington & Sickels, Fairfax, Va., 1977-79; atty., ptnr. Merrell & Callahan, McLean, Va., 1980-87, Clary, Lawrence, Lickstein and Moore, Falls Church, Va., 1987-91, Tener & Callahan, Vienna, Va., 1992—. Bd. dirs. Joe Gibbs' Youth for Tomorrow, Manassas, Va., 1997, Fresta Valley Christian Sch., Marshall, Va., 1987—; adminstr. I Found It campaign, Washington, 1976. Mem. Nat. Network of Estate Planning Attys., Christian Legal Soc., Internat. Assn. for Fin. Planning, No. Va. Estate Planning Coun. Republican. Evangelical Christian. Estate planning, Estate taxation, Probate. Office: Tener & Callahan PC 8330 Boone Blvd Ste 401 Vienna VA 22182-2624

**CALLEGARI, WILLIAM A., JR.,** lawyer, mediator; b. Baton Rouge, La., Sept. 3, 1961; s. William A. and Ann T. (Roy) C.; m. Denise Bordelon, Dec. 17, 1993; children: Will, Michael, John, Elizabeth. BA, La. State U., 1982; MBA, Emory U., 1985; JD, South Tex. Coll. Law, Houston, 1993. Bar: Tex. 1994. Comml. loan rep. Tex. Commerce Bank, Houston, 1985-86; project mgr. AM-TEX Corp., Houston, 1986-90, project devel. mgr., 1990-94; seconded atty. Vinson & Elkins, LLP, Houston, 1995-96; v.p., sec., gen. counsel S T Environ. Svcs., Houston, 1994-97; sole practitioner Houston, 1997—. Mem. Alpha Tau Omega. General practice, Labor, General corporate. Office: 16350 Park Ten Pl Ste 239 Houston TX 77084-5053

**CALLIES, DAVID LEE,** lawyer, educator; b. Chgo., Apr. 21, 1943; s. Gustav E. and Ann D. Callies; m. Laurie Breeden, Dec. 28, 1996; 1 child, Sarah Anne. AB, DePauw U., 1965; JD, U. Mich., 1968; LLM, U. Nottingham, England, 1969. Bar: Ill. 1969, Hawaii 1978. Spl. asst. states atty. McHenry County, Ill., 1969; assoc. firm Ross, Hardies, O'Keefe, Babcock & Parsons, Chgo., 1969-75; ptnr. Ross, Hardies, O'Keefe, Babcock & Parsons, 1975-78; prof. law Richardson Sch. Law, U. Hawaii, Honolulu, 1978—; Benjamin A. Kudo prof. law U. Hawaii, Honolulu, 1995—; mem. adv. com. on planning and growth mgmt. City and County of Honolulu Coun., 1978-88, mem. citizens adv. com. on State Functional Plan for Conservation Lands, 1979-93. Author: (with Fred P. Bosselman) the Quiet Revolution in Land Use Control, 1971 (with Fred P. Bosselman and John S. Banta) The Taking Issue, 1973, Regulating Paradise: Land Use Controls in Hawaii, 1984, (with Robert Freilich and Tom Roberts) Cases and Materials on Land Use, 1986, 3d edit., 1999, Preserving Paradise: Why Regulation Won't Work, 1994 (in Japanese 1994, in Chinese 1999), Land Use Law in the United States, 1994; editor: After Lucas: Land Use Regulation and the Taking of Property Without Compensation, 1993, Takings! Land Development Conditions and Regulatory Takings: After Dolan and Lucas, 1995, (with Hylton, Mondelker and Franzese) Property Law and the Public Interest, 1998. Life Fell., Clare Hall, Cambridge Univ. Named Best Prof., U. Hawaii Law Sch., 1990-91, 91-92; Mich. Ford Found. fellow U. Nottingham (Eng.), 1969, life fellow Clare Hall, Cambridge U., 1999. Mem. ABA (chmn. com. on land use, planning and zoning 1980-82, coun. sect. on state and local govt. 1981-85, 95—, exec. com. 1986-90, sec. 1986-87, chmn. 1989-90), Am. Law Inst., Am. Inst. Cert. Planners, Am. Planning Assn., Hawaii State Bar Assn. (chair, real property and fin. svc. sect., 1997), Am. Bar Found., Ill. Bar Assn., Internat. Bar Assn. (coun. Asia Pacific Forum 1993-96, co-chair Acads. Forum 1994-96, chair 1996-98), Nat. Trust for Hist. Preservation, Royal Oak Soc., Sierra Club, Lambda Alpha Internat. (pres. Aloha chpt. 1989-90, Internat. Mem. of Yr. 1994). Home: 1532 Kamole St Honolulu HI 96821-1424 Office: U Hawaii Richardson Sch Law 2515 Dole St Honolulu HI 96822-2328

**CALLIS, CLIFFORD LOUIS, JR.,** lawyer; b. Montgomery, Ala., Apr. 25, 1960; s. Clifford Louis Sr. and Lillian Luverne (Rooks) C.; m. Emily Carol Dial, Feb. 3, 1990; children: Cameron, Courtney. BS, Auburn U., 1983; JD, Jones Sch. Law, Montgomery, Ala., 1987. Bar: Ala. 1988, U.S. Dist. Ct. (no. dist.) Ala. 1992, U.S. Dist. Ct. (mid. dist.) Ala. 1996, U.S. Ct. Appeals (11th cir.) 1996, U.S. Supreme Ct. 1998. Asst. dist. atty. Etowah County Office of Dist. Atty., State of Ala., Gadsden, 1989-92; ptnr. Bone & Callis, Gadsden, 1992-93, Simmons, Brunson, Sasser & Callis, Gadsden, 1993-95; sr. ptnr. Simmons, Brunson, Sasser & Callis, 1995—. Mem. ABA (tort and ins. law com.), Am. Trial Lawyers Assn., Nat. Assn. Criminal Def. Lawyers, Ala. Def. Lawyers Assn., Ala. Trial Lawyers Assn., Def. Rsch. Inst. Insurance, Criminal, Family and matrimonial. Home: 218 Bradford Cir Gadsden AL 35901-6427 Office: Callis & Stover PO Box 8090 Gadsden AL 35902-8090

**CALLISON, JAMES W.,** former lawyer, consultant, airline executive; b. Jamestown, N.Y., Sept. 8, 1928; s. J. Waldo and Gladys A. C.; m. Gladys I. Robinson, Oct. 3, 1959; children: Sharon Elizabeth, Maria Judith, Christopher James. AB with honors, U. Mich., 1950, JD with honors (Overbeck award 1952, Jerome S. Freud Meml. award 1953), 1953. Bar: D.C. 1954, Ga. 1960. Atty. Pogue & Neal, Washington, 1953-57; with Delta Air Lines, Inc., Atlanta, 1957-93, v.p. law and regulatory affairs, 1974-78, sr. v.p., gen. counsel, 1978-81, sr. v.p., gen. counsel, corp. sec., 1981-88; sr. v.p. legal and corp. affairs, sec. Delta Air Lines Inc., 1988-90; sr. v.p. corp. and external affairs Delta Air Lines, Inc., 1990-91, sr. v.p. corp. affairs, 1991-93; ret., 1993; cons. Inman Deming Internat., Washington. Contbr. articles to legal jours.; asst. editor: Mich. Law Rev, 1952-53. Bd. dirs. Atlanta Union

Mission, sec. and chmn. pers. com., 1993—, bd. dirs. Atlanta Hist. Soc., St. Joseph's Mercy Found.; adv. bd. mem. Village St. Joseph. Recipient Papal Pro Ecclesia Et Pontifice award, 1966. Mem. ABA (vice chmn. internat. law sect. 1980-81, corp. law depts. com. 1983—), State Bar Ga. (chmn. corp. counsel sect. 1989-90), Atlanta Bar Assn. (life), Atlanta Athletic Club, Order of Coif. General corporate, Legislative, Transportation. Home: 2034 Dunwoody Club Way Dunwoody GA 30338-3024

**CALLISON, JAMES WILLIAM,** lawyer; b. Albemarle County, Va., Dec. 24, 1955; s. James Crofts and Jan (Richelsen) C. AB, Oberlin Coll., 1977; JD, U. Colo., 1982; postgrad., Yale U. Law clk. to judge Dist. Ct. Colo., Boulder, 1982; ptnr. Moye, Giles, O'Keefe, Vermeire & Gorrell, Denver, 1982-96, Faegre & Benson L.L.P., 1997—; lectr. law U. Denver, 1988—; adj. prof. U. Colo. Law Sch., 1997—. Author: Partnership Law and Practice, 1992, Limited Liability Companies, 1994; contbr. articles to profl. jours. Mem. Leadership Denver, 1989-90, Denver Community Leadership Forum, 1991. Mem. ABA (bus. law sect., tax sect.), Colo. Bar Assn. (tax sect., exec. council 1986—, chmn. 1988-89), Denver Bar Assn., Order of Coif. Democrat. Corporate taxation, General corporate, Taxation, general. Home: 4622 S Vine Way Cherry Hl Vlg CO 80110-6045 Office: Faegre & Benson LLP 370 17th St Ste 2500 Denver CO 80202-5665

**CALLISON, RUSSELL JAMES,** lawyer; b. Redding, Calif., Sept. 4, 1954; s. Walter M. and Norma A. (Bruce) C. BA in Polit. Sci., U. of Pacific, 1977, JD cum laude, 1980. Bar: Calif. 1980, U.S. Dist. Ct. (ea. dist.) Calif. 1981, U.S. Dist. Ct. (no. dist.) Calif. 1986, U.S. Ct. Appeals (9th cir.) 1989. Assoc. Memering & DeMers, Sacramento, Calif., 1980-85; pres. DeMers, Callison & Donovan, P.C., Sacramento, 1985-95; ptnr. Lewis, D'Amato, Brisbois & Bisgaard, San Francisco, 1995—; spl. master Calif. State Bar, 1991—; arbitrator, judge pro tem Sacramento County Superior Ct., 1986—. Co-author: Premises Liability in California, 1996. Mem. ABA (litigation sect.), SAR (chpt. pres. 1992-93), Am. Arbitration Assn. (panel of arbitrators), Assn. Def. Counsel No. Calif., Commonwealth Club, Natomas Racquet Club, Order of Coif, Phi Alpha Delta. Republican. Episcopalian. Avocations: golf, hunting, fishing, antique restoration. General civil litigation, Insurance. Home: 3889 20th St San Francisco CA 94114-3018 Office: Lewis D'Amato Brisbois & Bisgaard One Sansome St Ste 1400 San Francisco CA 94104-4431

**CALLNER, BRUCE WARREN,** lawyer; b. Camden, N.J., Sept. 20, 1948; s. Phillip David and Miriam June (Caplan) C.; m. Janet Adams, Apr. 25, 1970 (div. Dec. 1982); children: David, Michelle; m. Kathy Lynne Portnoy, Mar. 9, 1983; 1 child, Samantha. BS in Psychology, Western Mich. U., 1970; JD, U. Notre Dame, 1974. Bar: Ga. 1974, U.S. Dist. Ct. (no. dist.) Ga. 1975, U.S. Ct. Appeals (5th cir.) 1975, U.S. Ct. Appeals (11th cir.) 1981. Ptnr. Nall & Miller, Atlanta, 1974-81, Alembik, Fine & Callner, P.A., Atlanta, 1981—; lectr. law Emory U., Atlanta. Author: Georgia Domestic Relations Casefinder, 1990, 2d edit., 1996. Vol. numerous legal orgns. Mem. ABA (family law and litigation sects.), Ga. Bar Assn. (family law and litigation sects.), Atlanta Bar Assn. (family law, litigation and sects., speaker's bur.); fellow Am. Acad. Matrimonial Lawyers, Nat. Council Family Relations, Southeastern Council Family Relations, NOW, Assn. Family Conciliation Cts. Democrat. Jewish. E-mail: bcallmer@afclaw.com. Family and matrimonial. Home: 956 Heritage Hls Decatur GA 30033-4146 Office: Alembik Fine & Callner PA 4th Fl Marquis One Tower 245 Peachtree Center Ave NE Atlanta GA 30303-1222

**CALLOW, KEITH MCLEAN,** judge; b. Seattle, Jan. 11, 1925; s. Russell Stanley and Dollie (McLean) C.; m. Evelyn Case, July 9, 1949; children: Andrea, Douglas, Kerry. Student, Alfred U., 1943, CCNY, 1944, Biarritz Am. U., 1945; BA, U. Wash., 1949, JD, 1952. Bar: Wash. 1952, D.C. 1974. Asst. atty. gen. Wash., 1952; law clk. to justice Supreme Ct. Wash., 1953; dep. pros. atty. King County, 1954-56; ptnr. Little, LeSourd, Palmer, Scott & Slemmons, Seattle, 1957-62, Barker, Day, Callow & Taylor, 1964-68; judge King County Superior Ct., 1969-71, Ct. of Appeals Wash., Seattle, 1972-84; presiding chief judge Ct. of Appeals Wash., 1985-90; justice State Supreme Ct. Wash., Olympia, 1985-90, chief justice, 1989-90; 2d v.p. Conf. of Chief Justices; Booneville Power Admin. Rate Hearings Officer, 1995-96; lectr. bus. law U. Wash., 1956-62, Shefelman Disting. lectr., 1991; faculty Nat. Jud. Coll., 1980, Seattle U. Environ. Law, 1992, 94-95; co-organizer, sec. Coun. of Chief Judges of Cts. of Appeals; Rep. of Estonia, 1993-96, advisor Nat. Ct. and Ministry of Justice; advisor Kyrgyzstan, Kazakhstan, Georgia, Armenia, 1997; presenter in field. Editor-in-chief Commercial Law Desk Book, 1992-95; editor works in field. Chief Seattle coun. Boy Scouts Am.; adviser Gov. Health Care Commn. State of Washington, 1991-92; pres. Young Men's Rep. Club, 1957. With AUS, 1943-46. Decorated Purple Heart; recipient Brandeis award Wash. State Trial Lawyers Assn., 1981, Douglas award, 1990. Fellow Am. Bar Found.; mem. ABA (chmn. com. on judiciary 1984-90), Wash. State Bar Assn. (mem. exec. com., appellate Judges Conf.), D.C. Bar Assn., Seattle-King County Bar Assn., Estate Planning Coun., Navy League, Rainier Club (sec. 1978, trustee 1989-92), Forty Nine Club (pres. 1972), Masons, Rotary, Psi Upsilon, Phi Delta Phi.

**CALLOW, THOMAS EDWARD,** lawyer; b. Menominee, Mich., Mar. 12, 1954; s. James Kewley and Janet Marie (Drury) C.; m. Kathy Ann Cain, Oct. 26, 1985. BGS, U. Mich., 1976, JD, 1979. Bar: Mich. 1979. Prin. Vestevich, Mallender, DuBois & Dritsas, P.C., Bloomfield Hills, Mich., 1986—. Pres. Beverly Hills (Mich.) Homeowners Assn., 1986. Mem. Mich. Bar Assn., Southeastern Mich. Computer Orgn. (dir. 1988—). Pension, profit-sharing, and employee benefits, Taxation, general, General corporate. Home: 53034 Whitby Way Shelby Township MI 48316-2747 Office: Vestevich Mallender Et Al 800 W Long Lake Rd Ste 200 Bloomfield Hills MI 48302-2058

**CALLOW, WILLIAM GRANT,** retired state supreme court justice; b. Waukesha, Wis., Apr. 9, 1921; s. Curtis Grant and Mildred G. C.; m. Jean A. Zilavy, Apr. 15, 1950; children: William G., Christine S., Katherine H. PhB in Econs, U. Wis., 1943, JD, 1948. Bar: Wis. Asst. city atty. Waukesha, 1948-52; city atty., 1952-60; county judge Waukesha, 1961-77; justice Supreme Ct. Wis., Madison, 1978-92; asst. prof. U. Minn., 1951-52; mem. faculty Wis. Jud. Coll., 1968-75; Wis. commr. Nat. Conf. Commrs. on Uniform State Laws, 1967—; arbitrator Wis. Employment Rel. Commn.; arbitrator-mediator bus. disputes; arbitration and mediation nat. and internat. res. judge, 1992—. With USMC, 1943-45; with USAF, 1951-52, Korea. Recipient Outstanding Alumnus award U. Wis., 1973. Fellow Am. Bar Found.; mem. ABA, Dane County Bar Assn., Waukesha County Bar Assn. Episcopalian.

**CALLOWAY, MARK T.,** prosecutor; married. Grad. in Polit. Sci., N.C. State U., 1980, JD, 1983. Bar: N.C. 1983, U.S. Dist. Ct. (we., mid., ea. dists.) N.C., U.S. Ct. Appeals (4th cir.), U.S. Supreme Ct. Rsch. asst. to Hon. Jack L. Cozort N.C. Ct. Appeals; law clk. to Hon. Robert D. Potter U.S. Dist. Ct. (we. dist.) N.C.; assoc., then ptnr./shareholder James, McElroy & Diehl, P.A., Charlotte, N.C., 1987-94; U.S. atty. for we. dist. N.C. U.S. Dept. Justice, Charlotte, 1994—. Office: US Atty We Dist NC 227 W Trade St Charlotte NC 28202-1675

**CALOGERO, PASCAL FRANK, JR.,** state supreme court chief justice; b. New Orleans, Nov. 9, 1931; s. Pascal Frank and Louise (Moore) C.; children—Deborah Ann Calogero Applebaum, David, Pascal III, Elizabeth, Thomas, Michael, Stephen, Gerald, Katherine, Christine. Student, Loyola U., New Orleans, 1949-51, J.D., 1954; ML in the Jud. Process, U. Va., 1992; DLL (hon.), Loyola U., New Orleans. Bar: La. Ptnr. Landrieu, Calogero & Kronlage, 1958-69, Calogero & Kronlage, 1969-73; gen. counsel La. Stadium and Expn. Dist., 1970-73; assoc. justice Supreme Ct. La., New Orleans, 1973-90, chief justice, 1990—. Mem. La. Democratic State Central Com., 1963-71; mem. subcom. on del. selection La. Dem. Party, 1971; del. Dem. Nat. Conv., 1968. Served to capt. JAGC U.S. Army, 1954-57. Recipient Disting. Jurist award La. Bar Founds., 1991; Judge Bob Jones Meml. award, Am. Judges Assn., 1995. Mem. ABA, La. Bar Assn., New Orleans Bar Assn., Greater New Orleans Trial Lawyers Assn. (v.p. 1967-69), Order of the Coif. Office: Supreme Ct La 301 Loyola Ave New Orleans LA 70112-1814*

**CALVERT, JAY H., JR.,** lawyer; b. Charleston, S.C., Mar. 19, 1945; m. Ann E., June 14, 1969; children: Amanda, Emily, Sarah. BA, Amherst (Mass.) Coll., 1967; JD, U. Va., 1970. Bar: Pa. 1970, U.S. Dist. Ct. (ea. dist.) Pa. 1970, U.S. Ct. Appeals (3d cir.) 1971, U.S. Dist. Ct. (mid. dist.) Pa. 1973, U.S. Ct. Appeals (2d cir.) 1980, U.S. Ct. Appeals (8th cir.) 1987, U.S. Supreme Ct. 1989, U.S. Dist. Ct. Ariz. 1994. Assoc. Morgan, Lewis & Bockius LLP, Phila., 1970-78, ptnr., 1978—, exec. ptnr., 1987-90, mng. ptnr., 1990-94; mgr. litigation sect., firm governing bd. Morgan Lewis & Bockius LLP, Phila., 1990-98, mem. exec. com., 1997-98. Trustee Agnes Irwin Sch., Rosemont, Pa., 1988-94, Leukemia Soc. Am., Phila., 1982—; bd. dirs. St. David's Nursery Sch., Wayne, Pa., 1980-94; chmn. devel. com. Phila. Zool. Soc., 1993-96, chmn. facilities, exhibits and safety com., 1997—, bd. dirs., 1992—, vice-chmn. bd. dirs., 1994-96. Mem. ABA, Pa. Bar Assn., Phila. Bar Assn., Lawyers Club of Phila. Avocations: biking, gardening, hiking, horseback riding, animal husbandry. Fax: 215-963-5299. Antitrust, General civil litigation, Health. Office: Morgan Lewis & Bockius LLP 1701 Market St Philadelphia PA 19103-2903

**CALVERT, MATTHEW JAMES,** lawyer; b. Lynchburg, Va., Apr. 24, 1953; s. George Edward and Helen Owen Calvert; m. Helen Baldwin Saer, Oct. 3, 1981; children: McQueen Saer, Anne Russell, Helen Hardie. BA, Washington & Lee U., 1975, JD, 1979. Bar: Va. 1980, Ga. 1995. Law clk. to hon. John Minor Wisdom 5th Cir. Ct. Appeals, La., 1979-80; assoc. Hunton & Williams, Richmond, Va., 1980-87; ptnr. Hunton & Williams, Richmond and Atlanta, 1987—; chmn. pro bono com. Hunton & Williams, Atlanta, 1995—; chmn. young lawyers sect. Richmond Bar Assn., 1987-88; 6th dist. disciplinary com. Va. State Bar, Richmond, 1993-94. Editor-in-chief Washington & Lee Law Rev., 1978-79. Chmn. workplace com. Metro Coalition on Drugs, Richmond, 1990-93; major gifts com. Woodruff Arts Ctr., Atlanta, 1995—. Recipient Dir.'s award FBI, Richmond, 1993, Charles R. Yates award for fundraising leadership Woodruff Arts Ctr., Atlanta, 1998. Avocations: camping, hunting, golfing. Federal civil litigation, General civil litigation, Product liability. Office: Hunton & Williams 600 Peachtree St NE Ste 4100 Atlanta GA 30308-2214

**CALVEY, BRIAN J.,** lawyer; b. N.Y.C., Jan. 9, 1949; s. William Raymond and Virginia Ann (McElroy) C.; m. Grace Marie Soviero, July 24, 1976; children: Jonathan Reid, Jessica Leigh. BA, U. Notre Dame, 1970; JD, U. Va., 1973. Bar: N.Y. 1974. Assoc. Rogers Hoge & Hills, N.Y.C., 1973-81, ptnr., 1982-86; ptnr. Kelley, Drye & Warren, N.Y.C., 1987—. Mem. ABA, N.Y. State Bar Assn., Assn. of Bar of City of N.Y. Roman Catholic. General corporate, Mergers and acquisitions, Finance. Home: 106 Colony Rd Darien CT 06820-3906 Office: Kelley Drye & Warren 101 Park Ave Fl 30 New York NY 10178-0062

**CALVIN, MARY LOU,** law librarian; b. Cleve., July 7, 1948; d. Fredrick and Mary (Heckman) Wilker; 1 child, Joshua. BA, Ohio U., 1970; MLS, Concordia Coll., Montreal, Que., 1979. Libr. Muskegon (Mich.) Correctional Facility, 1982-87, Warner Norcross & Judd, Grand Rapids, Mich., 1987—; instr. Davenport Coll., Grand Rapids, Mich., 1992. Contbr. articles to profl. jours. Mem. Mich. Assn. Law Librs. (pres. 1994, v.p. bd. dirs. 1993), Grand Rapids Assn. Law Librs. (pres. 1991). Home: 10856 Harkness Rd Belding MI 48809-9749 Office: Warner Norcross & Judd 900 Old Kent Bldg Grand Rapids MI 49503-2487

**CAMBRICE, ROBERT LOUIS,** lawyer; b. Houston, Nov. 23, 1947; s. Eugene and Edna Bertha (Jackson) C.; m. Christine Jackson, Jan. 7, 1972; children: Bryan, Graham. BA cum laude, Tex. So. U., 1969; JD, U. Tex.-Austin, 1972. Bar: Tex. 1973, U.S. Dist. Ct. (so. dist.) Tex. 1975, U.S. Ct. Apls. (5th cir.) 1975, U.S. Ct. Apls. (11th cir.) 1981, U.S. Sup. Ct. 1981. Asst. atty. City of Houston, 1974-76; sole practice, Houston, 1976-81; asst. atty. Harris County, Tex., 1981-85, City of Houston, 1986—; sr. trial atty. City of Houston Legal Dept., 1990-92, chief def. litigation dept., 1992— . Earl Warren fellow, 1969-72. Mem. ABA, NAACP, Nat. Bar Assn., Alpha Kappa Mu. Roman Catholic.

**CAMBRIDGE, WILLIAM G.,** federal judge; b. 1931. BS, U. Nebr., 1953, JD, 1955. With Madgett, Hunter and Cambridge, 1957-63; pvt. practice law Hastings, Nebr., 1964-81; judge 10th Jud. Dist. Nebr., 1981-88; judge U.S. Dist. Ct. Nebr., Omaha, 1988-94, chief judge, 1994—. Hon. trustee Hastings (Nebr.) Coll. 1st lt. U.S. Army, 1955-57, USAR, 1957-65. Mem. ABA, Nebr. Bar Assn., Omaha Bar Assn., 10th Jud. Dist. Bar Assn., Adams County Bar Assn. Office: US Dist Ct PO Box 1076-dts Omaha NE 68101-1076

**CAMBS, DENISE P.,** lawyer; b. Pelham Manor, N.Y., Aug. 16, 1961; s. Henry A. and Josephine T. Pilla; m. Peter J. Cambs, May 10, 1986; children: Peter J. Jr., Morgan Alexandra, Preston Andreas. BA, Fordham U., 1982; JD, Pace U., 1985. Bar: N.Y. 1986. Sr. assoc. trusts and estates Hiscock & Barclay, LLP, Syracuse, N.Y., 1986-94; ptnr. trusts and estates DeLaney & O'Connor, LLP, Syracuse, N.Y., 1994—. Contbr. to legal treatises. Bd. trustees, sec. DeWitt (N.Y.) Cmty. Ch., 1996—; mem. devel. com. Manlius Pebble Hill Sch., DeWitt, N.Y., 1996—, planned giving com., 1997—. Fellow Am. Coll. Trusts and Estates Counsel; mem. N.Y. State Bar Assn. (mem.exec. com. trusts and estates law sect. 1992—, elder law sect. 1994—). Probate, Estate planning, Estate taxation. Home: 1107 Rail Fence Rd Camillus NY 13031-9639 Office: DeLaney & O'Connor LLP One Lincoln Ctr Ste 275 Syracuse NY 13202

**CAMERON, CHRISTIE SPEIR,** lawyer; b. Bethel, N.C., Feb. 12, 1954; d. David Ordway and Betty Maude (Smith) Speir; children: David Craig Price, John Harvey Price. BS, U. N.C., 1976, JD, 1979. Bar: N.C. 1981. Research asst. N.C. Ct. Appeals, Raleigh, 1979-81; asst. reporter appellate div. N.C. Supreme Ct., Raleigh, 1981-84; assoc. Wyrick, Robbins, Yates and Ponton, Raleigh, 1984-91, head real estate sect., 1986-91; clk. of ct. N.C. Supreme Ct., Raleigh, 1991—. Mem. N.C. Bd. Corrections, 1977-84, N.C. Legis. study commn. on neurologically-impaired infants, 1989-91, N.C. legis. study commn. on railroads and pub. transp., 1991—; treas. Wake County Dem. Women, 1985-87, pres., 1987-89; v.p. N.C. Dem. Women, 1984-86; chmn. adv. bd. YWCA, 1988-90; chmn. task force on excellence in secondary edn. Parents Study Panel, 1989-90; treas. Triangle Transit Authority, 1990-91, sec. 1992, vice chair, 1993-94, chair, 1994-95; bd. dirs. N.C. Mus. Natural Scis., 1990-92; bd. dirs. N.C. Child Advocacy Inst., 1991-99, chmn., 1995-97; trustee Edenton St. United Meth. Ch., 1990-95; bd. dirs. Kids Voting of Wake County, 1996-98; Gov.'s Appointee N.C. Rail Coun., 1999. Coun. of States Toll fellow, 1993. Mem. ABA, N.C. Bar Assn., Wake County Bar Assn. Methodist. Real property. Home: 1905 Sturbridge Ct Raleigh NC 27612-4929 Office: NC Supreme Ct PO Box 2170 Raleigh NC 27602-2170

**CAMERON, JOHN CLIFFORD,** lawyer, health science facility administrator; b. Phila., Sept. 17, 1946; m. Eileen Duffy, July 12, 1975; children: Christopher, Meghan. BA, U. Pitts., 1969; MBA, Temple U., 1972; JD, Widener U., 1976; LLM, NYU, 1980. Bar: Pa. 1977, N.J. 1977, Md. 1995. Asst. adminstr. Phila. Psychiatric Ctr., 1972-76; jud. clk. to presiding justice N.J. Superior Ct., Newark, 1976-77; asst. adminstr. St. Elizabeth Hosp., Elizabeth, N.J., 1977; v.p. corp. legal affairs Methodist Hosp., Phila., 1978-94; solicitor, 1988-94; legal cons. North Penn Hosp, Lansdale, Pa., 1994-95; counsel, legal adminstr. Hodes, Ulman, Pessin & Katz, P.A., Towson, Md., 1995-96; asst. to pres. Temple U. Health Sys., Phila., 1996—; asst. sec. Neumann Med. Ctr., Phila., 1997—, Temple U. Children's Med. Ctr., Phila., 1997—, Jeanes Hosp., Phila., 1997—, Northwood Nursing Home, Phila., 1997—, Temple Physicians, Inc., Phila., 1997—, Temple Univ. Hosp., Phila., 1997—, Lower Bucks Hosp., Bristol, Pa., 1997—, Episcopal Hosp., Phila., 1997—, Temple U. Children's Med. Ctr., Phila., 1997—; sec. Suthbrelt Properties, Ltd., Phila., 1981-94, Asbury Corp., Wilmington, Del., 1982-94, Healthmark, Inc., Moorestown, N.J., 1982-94, Meth. Hosp. Nursing Ctr., Phila., 1983-94; asst. sec. various hosps. and nursing homes, 1997—, instr. Grad. Sch. Mgmt., Pa. State U., 1991—; instr. mgmt. dept. Neumann Coll., 1991-96; instr. bus. divsn. Rosemont Coll., 1995-96. Contbr. articles to profl. jours. Mem. campaign United Way, Phila., 1979-94; mem. health and welfare com. United Meth. Eastern Pa. Conf., 1978-94; advisor Explorer Post, Boy Scouts Am., 1988-94; mem. steering com. Golden Cross, Phila., 1984-94; sec. Tredyffrin Twp. Park and Recreation Bd., 1987-95; alumni rep. Widener U.; mem. environ. adv. com. and open space task force Tredyffrin Twp., 1991-95. Fellow Am. Coll. Healthcare Execs. (chmn. bylaws com. 1995-96); mem. ABA, N.J. Bar Assn., Pa. Bar Assn., Phila. Bar Assn., Am. Hosp. Assn., Hosp. Assn. Pa., Swedish Colonial Soc. (bd dirs. 1992—, gov. 1993-95), Sons of Union Vets. of Civil War, SAR. Avocations: swimming, music. Health, General corporate. Home: 1410 Church Rd Malvern PA 19355-9714

**CAMERON, KEN,** lawyer; b. N.Y.C., Oct. 12, 1913; s. Kenneth and Anna (Deane) C.; children: Nancy Faith, Christina, Patricia. BA, Harvard Coll., 1934; MA, U. Calif., Berkeley, 1951. Bar: Calif. 1973, U.S. Dist. Ct. (no., so., cen., ea. and we. dists.) Calif. 1973, U.S. Supreme Ct. 1983, U.S. Ct. Appeals (9th cir.) 1986. Labor commr., supervising dep. Cities of Oakland, L.A., Calif., 1949-62; adminstrv. law judge unemployment ins. appeals bd. City of L.A., 1962-85; pvt. practice Santa Monica, Calif., 1985-98. 1st lt. U.S. Army, 1942-46, PTO. Administrative and regulatory, General civil litigation, Professional liability. Office: 2090 W Alex Bell Rd Dayton OH 45459-1164

**CAMIC, DAVID EDWARD,** lawyer; b. Indpls., June 11, 1954; s. Edward Franklin Camic and Carolyn (Hooker) Camic-Longland. BA, Aurora U., 1982; postgrad., DePaul U., 1982-83; JD cum laude, John Marshall Law Sch., 1987. Bar: Ill. 1987, U.S. Dist. Ct. (no. dist.) Ill. 1990, N.Y. 1996. Ptnr. Camic, Johnson, Wilson & McCulloch P.C., Aurora, Ill., 1987—; mem. faculty, lectr. Aurora U.; lectr. in criminal law Regional Police Tng., Aurora, 1987—. Contbr. articles to profl. jours. Chmn. Rape Def. Seminar, Aurora, 1986. Named Man of Yr. Todays Orgn. Youth, 1987. Mem. ABA, Ill. Bar Assn. (past-chair criminal justice sect.), Kane County Bar Assn. (past chair criminal law com.), Assn. Trial Lawyers Am., Nat. Assn. Criminal Lawyers, Phi Delta Phi. Criminal. Office: Camic Johnson Wilson & McCulloch PC 546 W Galena Blvd Aurora IL 60506-3855

**CAMINERO, RAFAEL,** lawyer; b. Havana, Cuba, Oct. 16, 1927; came to U.S., 1958; s. Jose and Carmen C., June 24, 1960; children: Raphael P., Martha M., Mary Ann. BA, La Salle, Havana, 1949; JD, U. Havana, 1957. Bar: Cuba 1957, Pa. 1976, U.S. Dist. Ct. (we. dist.) Pa. 1976, U.S. Supreme Ct. 1980, U.S. Ct. Appeals (3rd cir.) 1984, U.S. Dist. Ct. (ea. dist.) Pa. 1991. Atty. Nestle S.A., Havana, 1958-59, Stamford, Conn., 1960, Vevey, Switzerland, 1960-62; atty. U.S. Steel Corp., Pitts., 1962-86; ret., 1986-90; assoc. Golin Haefner & Bacher, Lancaster, Pa., 1990—. Hearing commr. Lancaster City Human Rels. Commn., Lancaster, 1995; bd. dirs. ARC, Lancaster, 1995-98. Mem. Pa. Bar Assn., Lancaster Bar Assn. Republican. Roman Catholic. Avocations: tennis, fencing, sailing, golfing. Private international, FERC practice, Contracts commercial. Office: Golin Haefner & Bacher 135 E King St Lancaster PA 17602-2803

**CAMINITI, DONALD ANGELO,** lawyer. BA magna cum laude, Rutgers U., 1973, JD, 1976. Bar: N.J. 1976, D.C. 1977, N.Y. 1980; cert. civil trial atty. N.J. Supreme Ct., cert. trial lawyer Nat. Bd. Trial Advocacy. Ptnr. Breslin & Breslin, P.A., Hackensack, N.J., 1977—; counsel Housing Authority of Bergen County, 1977—; asst. counsel Twp. of River Vale, 1977-80; counsel Housing Devel. Corp. Bergen County, 1978—, North Bergen Rent Leveling Bd., 1980—, North Bergen Housing Authority, 1980-84, Englewood Housing Authority, 1991—, Fort Lee Housing Authority, 1993—; spl. counsel Dept. Housing and Urban Devel., N.J., 1990—; counsel Guttenberg Housing Authority, 1995—; Master Morris Pashman Inns Ct., 1998—; speaker in field. Author: (with others) Products Liability Practice Guide, 1988. With USAF, 1966-70. Mem. ABA, N.J. Bar Assn., D.C. Bar Assn., N.Y. Bar Assn., Bergen County Bar Assn., Assn. Trial Lawyers Am. (bd. govs. N.J. chpt. parliamentarian N.J. chpt. 1984-85, seminar com. chmn. 1984-87, chmn. edn. com. 1990-91, v.p. 1990-91, 2d v.p. 1991-92, 1st v.p. 1992-93, pres.-elect 1993-94, pres. 1994-95), Nat. Bd. Trial Adv., Phi Beta Kappa. Home: 48 Union Ave Saddle River NJ 07458-2020 Office: Breslin and Breslin PA 41 Main St Hackensack NJ 07601-7087

**CAMINO, GEORGE J.,** lawyer; b. Schenectady, N.Y., Aug. 11, 1932; s. Carmin Antonio and Desdemona Nicholina Camino; m. Jeanne Wood Bower, June 2, 1956 (div. July 1972); children: Thomas, Daniel, Stephen, Kim, Lisa, Kathleen, Julie, Robin; m. JoAnn G. Rice, Dec. 9, 1977. BA, Siena Coll., 1958; LLB, JD, Albany Law Sch., 1961. Bar: N.Y. 1962, U.S. Dist. Ct. (no. dist.) N.Y. 1967, U.S. Supreme Ct. 1974. Sole practice Schenectady, 1962-63; ptnr. Nocera and Camino, Schenectady, 1963-83; asst. corp. counsel Schenectady Corp. Counsel, Schenectady, 1970-75; dep. pub. defender Pub. Defender's Office, Schenectady, 1987-95, chief trial counsel, 1995—. Town chmn. Republican Com., Rotterdam, N.Y., 1989-94; chmn. Schenectady County Republican Com., 1994-97. With USN, 1952-53. Mem. ABA, N.Y. State Bar Assn. (arbitrator 1965—; mem. lawyers in classroom), Schenectady County Bar Assn. (mem. lawyers in classroom). Republican. Roman Catholic. Home: 1494 Wendell Ave Schenectady NY 12308-2421

**CAMP, JACK TARPLEY, JR.,** federal judge; b. Newnan, Ga., Oct. 30, 1943; s. Jack Tarpley and Sophia (Stephens) C.; m. Elizabeth Thomas, Apr. 24, 1976; children: Thomas Henry, Sophia Rose. BA, The Citadel, Charleston, S.C., 1965; MA, U. Va., 1967, JD, 1973. Bar: Ala. 1973, Ga. 1975. Atty. Cabaniss, Johnston, Dumas & O'Neal, Birmingham, Ala., 1973-75, Glover & Davis, P.A., Newnan, 1975-88; U.S. dist. judge Atlanta, 1988—; mgr. family timber land holdings. Mem. Newnan Hist. Soc., 1975—, Ga. Trust for Hist. Preservation, Atlanta, 1975—. Capt. U.S. Army, 1967-70, Vietnam. Decorated Bronze Star; Ford Found. fellow, 1965-66. Mem. Ga. State Bar (bd. govs. 1987-89), Newnan-Coweta Bar Assn. (pres. 1978), Fed. Judges Assn., Kiwanis. Presbyterian. Office: US Dist Ct 2142 US Courthouse 75 Spring St SW Atlanta GA 30303-3309

**CAMP, JAMES CARROLL,** lawyer; b. Greenville, S.C., Jan. 7, 1951; s. Willard Alford and Joy (Mills) C. BA, Duke U., 1973; JD, Emory U., 1976. Bar: Ga. 1976, Calif. 1977, U.S. Dist. Ct. (cen. dist.) Calif. 1977, U.S. Tax Ct. 1981. Assoc. Strother, Weiner & Dwyer, Atlanta, 1976; atty. Pacific Lighting Corp., Los Angeles, 1977-78; ptnr. Greenberg, Bernhard, Weiss & Rosin, Los Angeles, 1978-84, Brown, Winfield & Canzoneri, Los Angeles, 1984—; bd. dirs. A-Mark Fin. Corp., Beverly Hills, Calif., 1984-88. Editorial bd. Los Angeles Lawyer, 1984-88, chmn. 1986-87. Mem. ABA (real estate fin. subcom.), Los Angeles County Bar Assn. (chmn. lawyer and arts com. 1982-83), Century City Bar Assn. (chmn. real property com. 1983-84). Avocations: music, travel, wine, food, bicycling. Contracts commercial, General corporate, Real property. Office: Brown Winfield & Canzoneri 300 S Grand Ave Ste 1500 Los Angeles CA 90071-3125

**CAMP, JOHN CLAYTON,** lawyer; b. Arab, Ala., Sept. 23, 1923; s. Roy Hubert and Alice Mellie (Cox) C.; m. Frances Elizabeth Spencer, Nov. 3, 1944; children: John, Elizabeth Camp Bower, Martha Camp Cox, Charles. Student, Birmingham-So. Coll., 1940-42, U. Ala., 1943, Auburn U., 1944; JD, La. State U., 1948. Bar: La. 1948, U.S. Supreme Ct. 1958, D.C. 1974. Assoc. Thomson, Lawes and Cavanaugh, Lake Charles, La., 1948-55; ptnr. Camp, Carmouche, Barsh, Gray, Hoffman & Gill, Lake Charles, 1955-84, Camp, Barsh & Tate, Washington, 1984-94, Patton Boggs LLP, Washington, 1994—. Mem. Presdl. Trade Commn. to People's Republic of China, 1979; trustee Athens (Greece) Coll., 1985-91; mem. exec. com., vice chmn. Meridian House Internat., 1986-96; mem. Med. Ctr. adv. coun. George Washington U. With USAF, 1943-46; bd. advs. Internat. Mgmt. and Devel. Inst., Fowler McCracker Commn. (chmn. policy planning group, 1982-87). Mem. ABA, D.C. Bar Assn., La. State Bar Assn., Southwestern La. Bar Assn., Congl. Country Club. Democrat. Presbyterian. Avocations: golf, photography, reading. Administrative and regulatory. Home: 5450 Whitley Park Ter Apt 510 Bethesda MD 20814-2055 Office: Patton Boggs LLP 2550 M St NW Ste 500 Washington DC 20037-1350

**CAMPANIE, SAMUEL JOHN,** lawyer; b. Oneida, N.Y., May 30, 1952; s. Samuel G. Campanie and Kathryn A. McCarthy Warner, stepson George A. Warner; m. Susan Noyes Garner, June 14, 1975; children: Joseph Warner, Abigail Noyes. AB cum laude, Colgate U., 1974; JD, Albany Law Sch., 1978; postgrad., Syracuse U., 1982—. Bar: N.Y. 1979, U.S. Dist. Ct. (no. and we. dists.) N.Y. 1994. Assoc. Kiley, Feldman, Whalen, Devine & Patane, Oneida, 1977-81; mgr. Mid-east and African divs. Oneida (N.Y.) Ltd. Silversmiths, 1981-83, mgr. export div., 1982-85, mgr. export and mil. divs., 1985; ptnr. Kohn, Moseman, Campanie, Oneida and Remsen, 1986-88; county atty. Madison County, N.Y., 1987—; dir. Kiley, Feldmann, Whalen, Devine & Patane P.C., Oneida, 1988—; accredited rep. Svc. Core of Retired Execs./Active Core Execs., Utica, N.Y., 1979-90; cons. to various firms, 1985-89; pvt. cons. practice Kenwood Assocs. Internat., Oneida, 1986-89. Mem. City of Oneida Planning Commn., 1979-91, chmn. 1990-91; legislator

Madison County Bd. Suprs., Wampsville, N.Y., 1986-87; bd. dirs. Madison County Indsl. Devel. Agy., 1986-90, Oneida-Madison Red Cross, 1979-87, Mansion House Svc. Corp., 1988-98, pres. 1997-98; mem. platform com. N.Y. State Rep. Com., Albany, 1986; mem. exec. com. Madison County Rep. Com., 1979-87; chmn. City of Oneida Rep. Com., 1979-87; mem. N.Y. State Oneida Lake Adv. Com., 1986—, chmn., 1988—. Named one of Outstanding Young Men in Am., 1985. Mem. ABA, N.Y. State Bar Assn., Madison County Bar Assn., N.Y. State County Attys. Assn. (dir. 1988—, pres. 1989-90, treas. 1997—), Oneida Jaycees. Republican. Roman Catholic. Avocations: sailing, biking, skiing, reading, computers. General practice, Private international, Contracts commercial. Home: 209 Kenwood Ave Oneida NY 13421-2809 Office: Kiley Law Firm Oneida Savs Bank Bldg 108 Lenox Ave Oneida NY 13421-1604

**CAMPBELL, BILL,** lawyer, rancher; b. San Angelo, Tex., Aug. 18, 1952; s. Fred R. and Cora E. Campbell; m. Debra Keith, Dec. 31, 1979 (div.); children: Augustus L., John W.; m. Judy M. Wittenborn, June 11, 1994. BS, S.W. Tex. State U., 1974; JD, Tex. Tech. U., 1977. Pvt. practice Eden, Tex., 1977-92; pres., prin. shareholder Concho County Abs. and Title, Eden, Tex., 1982-94; atty. Concho County, Tex., Paint Rock, Tex., 1989—; mem. staff Fred Campbell Ranch, Paint Rock, Tex., 1993-98; owner Bill Campbell Ranch, Paint Rock, Tex., 1998—. Mem. Lions (pres. Eden chpt. 1983). Republican. Baptist. Avocations: equestrian activities, guitar playing, rock masonry. Office: County Atty Concho County PO Box 565 Eden TX 76837-0565

**CAMPBELL, BRUCE IRVING,** lawyer; b. Mason City, Iowa, July 7, 1947; s. E. Riley Jr. and Donna Mae (Andresen) C.; children: Anne, John; m. Beverly J. Evans. BA, Upper Iowa U., 1969; JD, Harvard U., 1973. Bar: Iowa 1973, U.S. Dist. Ct. (so. dist.) Iowa 1973, U.S. Dist. Ct. (no. dist.) Iowa 1974, U.S. Tax Ct. 1976, U.S. Ct. Appeals (8th cir.) 1977, U.S. Ct. Claims 1982. Shareholder Davis, Brown, Koehn, Shors & Roberts, P.C., Des Moines, 1973—; adj. prof. law Drake U., Des Moines, 1974-90. Trustee Upper Iowa U., Fayette, 1978—, chair bd. trustees, 1992—. Mem. ABA, Iowa State Bar Assn., Polk County Bar Assn. Republican. Estate planning, Estate taxation, Taxation, general. Home: 62 Meadowbrook Cir Cumming IA 50061-1014 Office: Davis Brown Koehn Shors & Roberts PC 666 Walnut St Ste 2500 Des Moines IA 50309-3904

**CAMPBELL, CHARLES EDWARD,** lawyer; b. Atlanta, Jan. 12, 1942; s. Borden Burr and Bonnie (McPherson) C.; m. Ann Grovenstein, Apr. 12, 1976; 1 child, Garrett McPherson. Student, Emory U., 1960-61; BA, MA, U. Ga., 1965; JD, Georgetown U., 1971. Bar: Ga. 1972. Legis. asst. to U.S. Sen. Richard B. Russell Washington, 1965-67, exec. sec., 1967-69, adminstrv. asst., 1969-71; assoc. Heyman & Sizemore, Atlanta, 1971-73, ptnr., 1974-77; ptnr. Hicks, Maloof & Campbell, Atlanta, 1977-98, Long, Alridge & Norman, LLP, 1998—. Trustee Richard B. Russell Found., 1978—, mem. exec. com., 1980—, chmn., 1990—. Fellow Am. Coll. Trial Lawyers, Am. Coll. Bankruptcy; mem. Ga. Bar Assn. (mem. legis. com. 1978-79), Southeastern Bankruptcy Law Inst., Inc. (bd. dirs.). Administrative and regulatory, Bankruptcy, General civil litigation. Home: 2485 Dellwood Dr NW Atlanta GA 30305-4075 Office: Long Alridge & Norman LLP 303 Peachtree St NE Ste 5300 Atlanta GA 30308-3264

**CAMPBELL, CLAIR GILLILAND,** lawyer; b. Aberdeen, Md., Nov. 27, 1961; d. Bobby Eugene and Sara Frances (Matkins) G. BA, U. Ala., 1982; JD, Cumberland U., 1985. Bar: N.C. 1985, U.S. Dist. Ct. (we. and mid. dists.) N.C. 1985, S.C. 1986. Ptnr. Karney, Campbell & Karney, Charlotte, N.C., 1985-91; ptnr. Campbell & Taylor, Charlotte, 1991—, Charlotte, N.C., 1996—; instr. Paralegal Inst., Queens, Coll., 1990; participant Wild Dolphin Project. Author: Twas the Night Before the Orange Bowl, 1988. Mem. ABA, ATLA, Mecklenburg County Bar Assn. (program coord. edn. com. 1986-88, panel televised lawyers discussion 1991, mem. speakers forum com. 1992, silent ptnr., law day com. 1996), N.C. Acad. Trial Lawyers, Ducks Unltd., Cumberland Alumni Assn. (reunion com. 1989-90), DAR (vice-regent 1993-94), Nat. Soc. Colonial Dames (sec. 1995—), Nat. Soc. Magna Charta Dames, Alpha Omicron Pi (sec. 1994—). Avocations: private pilot, equestrian, water- and snow-skiing, films, reading. Personal injury. Office: Campbell & Taylor 717 East Blvd Charlotte NC 28203-5113

**CAMPBELL, DARREL LEE,** lawyer; b. Nowata, Okla., Jan. 22, 1951; s. Waldo R. and Beulah A. Campbell; m. Jo Ann Sewell, Aug. 19, 1972; children: Kelly, Ryan, Kari. BA, N.W. Nazarene Coll., Nampa, Idaho, 1973; JD, Drake U., 1976. Bar: Colo. 1977, U.S. Dist. Ct. Colo. 1977, U.S. Supreme Ct. 1996. Atty. Office Adams County Dist. Atty., Brighton, Colo., 1978-80; assoc. Goldstein & Armour, P.C., Denver, 1980-87, Laff Stowe & Assocs., Denver, 1987-88; ptnr. Laff & Campbell PC, Denver, 1988-90, Laff Stein Campbell Tucker & Delaney LLP, Englewood, Colo., 1990—; spkr. Landlord-Tenant Seminar, 1997. Mem. bd. edn. Arvada (Colo.) Covenant Ch., 1985-87; vol. coach Arvada Soccer Assn., 1986-88; mem. bd. elders Trinity Bapt. Ch., Wheat Ridge, Colo., 1993-95. Mem. ATLA, Colo. Bar Assn., Denver Bar Assn. Appellate, General civil litigation, Land use and zoning (including planning). Home: 12423 W 68th Ave Arvada CO 80004-2314 Office: Laff Stein Campbell Et Al 7730 E Belleview Ave Ste 204 Englewood CO 80111-2618

**CAMPBELL, DAVID LEE,** lawyer, educator; b. Dallas, Oct. 4, 1955; s. William Maxwell and Dorothy Lee (Black) C.; m. Sandra Stanley, Aug. 12, 1978; 1 child, Meredith Lee Anne. BS in Edn., Abilene (Tex.) Christian Coll., 1978; MEd, East Tex. State U., 1981; JD, Tex. Tech U., 1985. Bar: Tex., U.S. Dist. Ct. (ea. and we. dists.) Tex., U.S. Ct. Appeals (10th cir.). Assoc. Thompson & Knight, Dallas, 1985-88; mem. Hale, Spencer, Stanley, Pronske & Trust, P.C., Dallas, 1988-94; with McManemin & Smith, P.C., Dallas, 1994-97, Campbell & Cobbe, P.C., Dallas, 1997—. Deacon Highland Oaks Ch. of Christ. Mem. ABA (co-chair workouts, foreclosures and bankruptcy com., subcom. internat. bankruptcy bus. banking com.), Dallas Bar Assn., Mayflower Soc., SAR. Avocations: reading, skiing. Bankruptcy, Contracts commercial. Home: 218 Harris Dr Mesquite TX 75182-9344 Office: Campbell & Cobbe PC 900 Jackson St Ste 120 Dallas TX 75202

**CAMPBELL, DIANA BUTT,** lawyer; b. Ayer, Mass., Nov. 14, 1943; d. Lester A. and Genevieve P. (Ash) Butt; m. James W. Campbell, Feb. 3, 1961; children: James R., Lisa J., Alan D. BS magna cum laude, Suffolk U., 1980; JD, New Eng. Sch. Law, 1984. Bar: Mass. 1984, U.S. Dist. Ct. Mass. 1986, U.S. Supreme Ct. 1988. Editor Danvers (Mass.) State Hosp. Newsletter, 1977, Mass. Press Assn. Bull., 1978-79; mediator, case coordinator Salem (Mass.) Mediation Program, 1979-83; legal adv. Help for Abused Women and Their Children, Salem, 1980-82; pvt. practice law Hamilton, Mass., 1984—. Mem., chair Hamilton Housing Authority, 1975-80; vol. Danvers State Hosp., 1978-92; mem. Cape Ann Area bd. Dept. Social Svc., Beverly, Mass., 1982-84; merit badge counselor Boy Scouts Am., Hamilton, 1984-93; assoc. mem. Hamilton Cable Adv. Bd., 1987-91; bd. dirs. United Way of North Shore, Beverly, 1988-94; mem. adv. bd. of money mgmt. program North Shore Elder Svcs., 1993—. Mem. Nat. Acad. Elder Law Attys., Assn. Trial Lawyers Am., Mass. Acad. Trial Lawyers, Mass. Bar Assn., Soc. Profl. Journalists, Essex County Bar Assn., Salem Bar Assn., North Shore Women Lawyers' Assn., Supreme Ct. Hist. Soc., Kiwanis (pres. 1990-91). Avocations: Volkssporting, photography, travel. Family and matrimonial, Probate, Juvenile. Home: 22 Grant Ave South Hamilton MA 01982-1819 Office: 65 Railroad Ave South Hamilton MA 01982-2218

**CAMPBELL, EDWARD ADOLPH,** judge, electrical engineer; b. Boonville, Ind., Jan. 16, 1936; s.Revis Allen and Sarah Gertrude (Hunsaker) C.; m. Nancy Colleen Keys, July 26, 1957; children: Susan Elizabeth Campbell Frisse, Stephen Edward, Sara Lynne. BEE, U. Evansville, 1959; JD, Ind. U., 1965; grad. Nat. Coll. Dist. Attys., U. Houston, 1972; grad. Nat. Jud. Coll., U. Nev., 1978; grad. Am. Acad. Jud. Edn., U. Va., 1979; grad. Ind. Grad. Program for Judges, Ind. Jud. Ctr., 1999. Bar: Ind. 1965, U.S. Dist. Ct. (so. dist.) Ind. 1965, U.S. Supreme Customs and Patent Appeals 1967, U.S. Supreme Ct. 1973, U.S. Ct. Appeals (fed. cir.) 1982. Patent examiner U.S. Patent Office, Washington, 1959-60; patent adv. U.S. Naval Avionics, Indpls., 1960-65; patent atty. Gen. Elec. Co., Ft. Wayne, Ind., 1965-66; ptnr. Weyerbacher & Campbell, attys., Boonville, Ind., 1966-71; pros. atty. 2nd Jud. Cir., Warrick County, Ind., 1971-77; judge Warrick Superior Ct. No. 1, 1977—. Fellow Ind. Bar Found.; mem. IEEE, Ind.State Bar Assn., Evansville Bar Assn., Warick County Bar Assn., Ind. Judges Assn., Nat. Coun. Juvenile and Family Ct. Judges, Ind. Coun. Juvenile and Family Ct. Judges, Warrick County C. of C. (bd. dirs. 1978-84, 97—), Lions Club, Kiwanis Club, Sigma Pi Sigma, Phi Delta Phi. Democrat. Methodist. Home: 911 Julian Dr Boonville IN 47601-9556 Office: Warrick Superior Ct No 1 PO Box 666 Boonville IN 47601-0666

**CAMPBELL, GEORGE EMERSON,** lawyer; b. Piggott, Ark., Sept. 23, 1932; s. Sid and Mae (Harris) C.; m. Anna Claire Janes, June 22, 1960 (dec. Mar. 1971); children: Dianne, Carole; m. Joan Stafford Rule, Apr. 7, 1973. J.D., U. Ark., Fayetteville, 1955. Bar: Ark. 1955, U.S. Supreme Ct. 1971. Law clk. to judge Ark. Supreme Ct., 1959-60; mem. Rose Law Firm, P.A., Little Rock, 1960—; Del. 7th Ark. Constl. Conv., 1969-70; regional v.p. Nat. Mcpl. League, 1974-86; mem. Ark. Ednl. TV Commn., 1976-92, chmn., 1980-82, 88-91; bd. dirs. Ark. Ednl. TV Found., 1984-92, chmn., 1988-91. Chmn. bd. Pulaski County Law Libr., 1980—; bd. dirs. Ark. Arts Ctr., 1991-95, sec. 1992-93), Ark. Symphony Orch. Soc., 1982-87, Ark. Capital Corp., Ark. Cert. Devel. Corp., Downtown Partnership; bd. dirs. Youth Home Inc., 1986-92, pres., 1991-92. With USNR, 1955-77, ret.. Fellow Am. Bar Found.; mem. ABA, Ark. Bar Assn., Pulaski County Bar Assn., Am. Law Inst., Am. Judicature Soc., Nat. Assn. Bond Lawyers. Municipal (including bonds), General corporate, Real property. Office: Rose Law Firm PA 120 E 4th St Little Rock AR 72201-2893

**CAMPBELL, HUGH BROWN, JR.,** lawyer; b. Charlotte, N.C., Feb. 19, 1937; s. Hugh Brown and Thelma Louise (Welles) C.; m. Mary Irving Carlyle, Nov. 3, 1962; children: Hugh B. III, Irving Carlyle, Thomas Lenoir. AB, Davidson Coll., 1959; JD, Harvard U., 1962. Atty. Craighill, Rendleman, Charlotte, 1964-77, Weinstein & Sturges, Charlotte, 1977-94, Cansler Lockhart Campbell Evans Bryant & Garlitz; chmn. Jury Commn., Mecklenburg County, N.C., 1985-97; exec. com. County Bar Assn., Mecklenburg County, 1989-92, civil cts. com. chair, 1990-92. Rep. N.C. House, Raleigh, 1969-71; legis. liaison Charlotte/Mecklenburg County, Raleigh, 1971-72; state chmn. N.C. Zoo Bond Campaign, 1972; chmn. Carolinas Med. Ctr. Bond Campaign, 1976. Col. JAG U.S. Army, 1962-64, Res., 1964-92. Decorated Legion of Merit, Meritorious Svc. medal (2); Honored Order of Hornet, Mecklenburg County, 1976. Mem. N.C. Bar Coun. (exec. com., chair ethics 1981-90), Planned Parenthood Charlotte (bd. dirs., chmn. 1980-81), YMCA Charlotte (adv. bd. 1992—), Rotary Club E. Charlotte (pres. 1976-77). Democrat. Episcopalian. Avocations: tennis, swimming, hiking, reading, politics. General civil litigation, Alternative dispute resolution, Education and schools. Home: 1428 Scotland Ave Charlotte NC 28207-2561 Office: Cansler Lockhart Campbell Evans Bryant & Garlitz 227 W Trade St Charlotte NC 28202-1675

**CAMPBELL, JAMES, VII,** patent lawyer; b. St. Louis, Oct. 12, 1934; s. James VI and Dorothy Lila (Brown) C.; m. Anne Elizabeth Jaudon, July 19, 1957; children: Elizabeth, Douglas, Kevin, Carolyn. BSEE, U. Colo., 1956; LLB, George Washington U., 1960. Bar: Oreg. 1961, U.S. Dist. Ct. Oreg. 1961, U.S. Ct. Appeals (fed. cir.) 1982, U.S. Ct. Appeals (9th cir.) 1968, U.S. Supreme Ct. 1989. Patent examiner U.S. Patent Office, Washington, 1956-60; patent atty. Klarquist, Sparkman, Campbell, Leigh & Whinston (and predecessor firms), Portland, Oreg., 1960—. Contbr. chpts. to books: Patent Law Essentials, Advising Oregon Businesses. Mem. ABA, IEEE, Oreg. Bar Assn., Am. Intellectual Property Law Assn., Oreg. Patent Assn. (pres.), Kiwanis. Republican. Baptist. Avocations: ocean and river sailing. Fax: 503-228-9446. Intellectual property, Federal civil litigation, Patent. Home: 18460 Ray Ridge Dr Lake Oswego OR 97034-7527 Office: Klarquist Sparkman Campbell Leigh & Whinston 1600 One World Trade Ctr Bl 121 SW Salmon St Ste 1600 Portland OR 97204-2988

**CAMPBELL, JENNIFER KATZE,** lawyer; b. Washington, May 13, 1968; d. Edward and Malissa Ann (Mathews) Katze; m. Thomas Edward Campbell. BA in History, Duke U., 1990; JD, Emory U., 1993. Bar: Ga. 1993, U.S. Dist. Ct. Ga. 1993, U.S. Ct. Appeals (11th cir.) 1995. Assoc. Troutman Sanders, Atlanta, 1993-98; counsel N. Am. Group-Fountain, The Coca-Cola Co., Atlanta, 1998—. Mem. State Bar Ga. Avocations: running, gardening. E-mail: jencampbell@na.ko.com. Trademark and copyright, Personal injury, General civil litigation. Office: The Coca Cola Company PO Box 1734 Atlanta GA 30301-1734

**CAMPBELL, JENNIFER L.,** lawyer; b. Encino, Calif., Sept. 9, 1962; d. Robert Joseph and Margaret Helen Campbell; m. Juan Carlos Cruz, Mar. 20, 1993. BA, Whittier Coll., 1985; JD, U. Calif. Hastings Coll. Law, 1991. Bar: Calif. 1991, U.S. Tax Ct. 1996. Assoc. Pillsbury, Madison & Sutro, San Francisco, 1991-94; assoc. Fenwick & West, Palo Alto, Calif., 1994-96, Rosenfeld, Meyer & Susman, Beverly Hills, Calif., 1996-98, Hoffman, Sabban & Watenmaker, L.A., 1998—. Mem. Jr. League of L.A. (asst. chair rummage sale com. 1997-98), Order of the Coif. Estate planning, Probate, Estate taxation. Office: Hoffman Sabban & Watenmaker 10880 Wilshire Blvd Ste 2200 Los Angeles CA 90024-4123

**CAMPBELL, JOE BILL,** lawyer; b. Bowling Green, Ky., Jan. 28, 1943; s. Charles and Mary Elizabeth (Morrs) C.; children: Ty, Clay, Anne. AB, Western Ky. U., 1965; JD, U. Ky., 1968. Bar: Ky. 1968, U.S. Dist. Ct. (we. and ea. dists.) Ky., U.S. Ct. Appeals (6th cir.), U.S. Supreme Ct. Ptnr. Bell, Orr, Ayers & Moore, Bowling Green, Ky., 1968-76, Campbell & Crandall, Bowling Green, 1977-82, Campbell, Kerrick & Grise, Bowling Green, 1983-95, Stites & Harbison, Lexington, Ky., 1995—; chmn. bd. Lawyers Mut. Ins. Co. Ky., Louisville, 1986—. Chmn. bd., bd. regents Western Ky. U., Bowling Green, 1980-84; chmn. Coun. on Higher Edn., Frankfort, Ky., 1990-91. Mem. Ky. Bar Assn. (bd. govs. 1984-90, v.p. 1990-91, pres.-elect 1991-92, pres. 1992-93, Outstanding Lawyer in Ky. 1988), Ky. Def. Lawyers, Ky. Acad. Trial Attys., Ky. Acad. Hosp. Attys., Am. Coll. Trial Lawyers, Am. Bd. Trial Advs. Democrat. Episcopalian. Avocations: golf, reading. General civil litigation, Insurance, Personal injury. Office: Stites & Harbison 2300 Lexington Fin Ctr 250 W Main St Ste 2300 Lexington KY 40507-1758

**CAMPBELL, JOHN MICHAEL,** lawyer; b. N.Y.C., Nov. 18, 1954; s. John Erin and Margaret Domenica Campbell; m. Karen Sue Ralstin, Mar. 13, 1976; children: Michael Aaron, Matthew Everett, Rebekah Michelle, Benjamin David. BS, U. Notre Dame, 1976; JD, Calif. Western Sch. Law, 1979. Bar: Calif. 1979, U.S. Dist. Ct. (so. dist.) Calif. 1979, U.S. Tax Ct. 1980, Fla. 1986, U.S. Dist. Ct. (mid. dist.) Fla. 1986, U.S. Ct. Mil. Appeals 1980. Asst. counsel U.S. Dept. Def., Orlando, Fla., 1985-87; assoc. gen. counsel Sea World, Inc., Orlando, 1987-92; sr. assoc. Holland & Knight, Orlando, 1992-94; ptnr. Campbell & Heavener, P.A., Casselberry, Fla., 1994—; corp. counsel Sunterra Corp., 1999—. Bd. dirs. Lake Eola Charter Sch., Orlando, 1997-98, Shepherd Care, Orlando, 1990-98. Maj. U.S. Army, 1980-85. Mem. Corp. Counsel Assn. Ctrl. Fla. (v.p. 1991-92). Republican. Baptist. Avocations: photography, scuba diving. General corporate, Intellectual property, Estate planning. Home: 5691 Pond Pine Pt Oviedo FL 32765-9441 Office: Campbell and Heavener PA 1211 Semoran Blvd Ste 171 Casselberry FL 32707-6442

**CAMPBELL, JOHN WILLIAM,** prosecutor; b. Honolulu, Jan. 6, 1955; s. George Willis and Leona Ruth Campbell; m. Lisa Jo Hale, Dec. 31, 1984. BA in Polit. Sci. and History, Washburn U., 1977; JD, U. Kans., 1979, MPA, 1980. Bar: Kans. 1979, U.S. Dist. Ct. Kans. 1979, U.S. Ct. Appeals (10th cir.) 1986, U.S. Supreme Ct. 1986, U.S. Ct. Appeals (D.C. cir.) 1992. Asst. county atty. Ford County Atty.'s Office, Dodge City, Kans., 1979-80; asst. atty. gen. Kans. Atty. Gen.'s Office, Topeka, 1981-86, dep. atty. gen., 1986-95, sr. atty. gen., 1995—. Chmn. Gov.'s Indian Gaming Group, Topeka, 1995; trustee Western Hills Bapt. Ch., Topeka, 1997—. Mem. Kans. Bar Assn., Topeka Bar Assn. Republican. Avocations: motorcycles, reading.

**CAMPBELL, L. COOPER,** lawyer; b. Washington, Feb. 16, 1967; m. F. Hayes Jackson, Sept. 6, 1997. BA, Williams Coll., 1989; JD, Georgetown U., 1994. Bar: N.Y. 1995, Calif. 1996. Asoc. LeBoeuf, Lamb, Greene & MacRae, N.Y.C., 1994-96, Sheppard, Mullin, Richter & Hampton, L.A., 1996-98; counsel Warner Home Video, Burbank, Calif., 1998—. Mem. ABA, Los Angeles County Bar Assn., Women's Law Assn. L.A., Women in Film. Entertainment, Intellectual property, Antitrust. Office: Warner Home Video 4000 Warner Blvd Burbank CA 91522-0001

**CAMPBELL, LEVIN HICKS,** federal judge; b. Summit, N.J., Jan. 2, 1927; s. Worthington and Louise (Hooper) C.; m. Eleanor Saltonstall Lewis, June 1, 1957; children: Eleanor S., Levin H., Sarah H. AB cum laude, Harvard U., 1948, LLB, 1951; postgrad., Nat. Coll. State Judiciary, 1970; LLD (hon.), Suffolk U., 1975. Bar: D.C. 1951, Mass. 1954. Assoc. firm Ropes & Gray, Boston, 1954-64; mem. Mass. Ho. of Reps., 1963-64; asst. atty. gen. State of Mass., 1965-66, spl. asst. atty. gen., 1966-67, 1st asst. atty. gen., 1967-68; assoc. justice Superior Ct. of Mass., 1969-72; judge U.S. Dist. Ct. Mass., Boston, 1972; judge U.S. Ct. Appeals (1st cir.), Boston, 1972—, chief judge, 1983-90, sr. judge, 1992—; fellow Inst. of Politics J.F. Kennedy Sch. Govt. Harvard U., 1968-69, study group leader 1980; faculty chmn. law session Salzburg Seminar in Am. Studies, 1981. Pres. Cambridge 9 Neighborhood Assn., 1960-62; treas. Cambridge Ctr. for Adult Edn., 1961-64; campaign chmn. Cambridge United Fund, 1965; mem. bd. overseers Boston Symphony Orch., 1969-75, 77-80; pres. bd. overseers Shady Hill Sch., 1969-70; mem. vis. com. Harvard U. Press, 1958-64; v.p. Cambridge Community Svcs.; corp. mem. SEA Ednl. Assn., 1982—; trustee Colby Coll., Waterville, Maine 1981-90, 91-99, Asheville (N.C.) Sch.; overseer U.S. Constitution Mus. 1st lt. (j.g.) U.S. Army, 1951-54, Korea. Mem. ABA, Am. Law Inst., Am. Bar Found., Mass. Bar Found., Boston Bar Assn., U.S. Jud. Conf. (ct. adminstrn. com. 1975-83, chmn. subcom. on supporting pers. 1980-83, exec. com. 1985-90, chmn. com. to rev. cir. coun. conduct and disability orders 1989-94, ad hoc com. study jud. conf. 1987, fed. ct. study com. 1988-90, nat. commn. on jud. discipline and removal 1991-93), Mass. Hist. Soc. (coun. 1993-96, v.p. 1996—, long range planning com. 1999—). Office: US Ct of Appeals US Courthouse 1 Courthouse Way Ste 6720 Boston MA 02210-3008

**CAMPBELL, MARGARET SUSAN,** defender; b. Painesville, Ohio, July 15, 1969; d. Alan Maxted and Marlene Sue Campbell. BS, Miami U., 1991; JD, Ohio Northern U., 1994. Bar: Ohio, U.S. Dist. Ct. (no. dist.), U.S. Supreme Ct. Asst. pub. defender Lake County Pub. Defenders, Painesville, Ohio, 1995—; instr. Lake Erie Coll., Painesville, 1997—. Mem. Ohio Bar Assn., Ohio Assn. Criminal Def. Lawyers, Ohio Women's Bar Assn. Avocations: international travel, cooking. Office: Lake County Pub Defenders Office 125 E Erie St Painesville OH 44077-3948

**CAMPBELL, NAOMI SYLVIA,** lawyer; b. Newark, Nov. 17, 1925; d. Isidore and Esther Charner; m. Charles Melton Campbell, Dec. 25, 1947; 1 child, Lori Margaret. BS in Bus. Adminstrn., Upsala Coll., East Orange, N.J., 1947; JD, U. Chgo., 1957. Bar: Ill., N.Y., Hawaii, D.C. Prof. bus. law Fairleigh Dickinson U., 1959-62; ptnr. Sterry, Mah & Campbell, Honolulu, 1966; judge Family Ct., Honolulu, 1966-70; head family support divsn. Dept. of Corp. Counsel, Honolulu, 1971-95; bd. dirs. Legal Aid Soc., Honolulu. Lt. col., legal officer U.S. CAP, Honolulu; chmn. Teen Intervention Program, Honolulu; docent Iolani Palace, Honolulu; chmn. Teen-Age Assembly; mem. adv. com. McKinley High Young Parents Program. Mem. Hawaii State Bar Assn. Avocations: Tai chi, line dancing, yoga, hula dancing. Home: 441 Mananai Pl Apt E Honolulu HI 96818-5345

**CAMPBELL, PAUL, JR.,** lawyer; b. Chattanooga, Dec. 23, 1915; s. Paul and Margaret Douglas (Meriwether) C.; m. Nelson Chambliss Whitaker; children: Nelson Douglas, Paul III, Michael Ross, Douglas Meriwether. BA, Union Coll., 1937; LLB, George Washington U., 1940. Bar: Tenn. 1940, U.S. Dist. Ct. Tenn. 1942, U.S. Ct. Appeals (6th cir.) 1942, U.S. Supreme Ct. 1964. Pvt. practice Chattanooga, 1941-42, 46-96; spl. agt. FBI, Phila. and Buffalo, 1942-44; ptnr. Campbell & Campbell, Chattanooga, 1996—. Served to lt., USNR, 1944-46. Mem. ABA, Tenn. Bar Assn., Am. Judicature Assn., Am. Bed. Trial Advocates, Am. Coll. Trial Lawyers, Chattanooga Bar Assn., Tenn. Bar Found., Fed. Bar Assn., Internat. Assn. Def. Attys., Def. Rsch. Inst., U.S. Sixth Cir. Jud. Conf. (life). Methodist. General civil litigation, Insurance, Product liability. Office: 1200 James Bldg Chattanooga TN 37402

**CAMPBELL, PAUL, III,** lawyer; b. Chattanooga, Feb. 1, 1946; children: Paul IV, Kolter M. BA, Vanderbilt U., 1968; MA, Middlebury Coll., 1972; postgrad., So. Meth. U., 1971-72, Emory U., 1972-73; JD, U. Tenn., 1975. Bar: Tenn. 1976, Ga. 1977. Tchr. English St. Mark's Sch., Dallas, 1968-72; ptnr. Campbell & Campbell, Chattanooga, 1976-98; mem. Witt, Gaither & Whitaker, Chattanooga, 1998—; adj. prof. English, U. Tenn., Chattanooga, 1976, adj. prof. law, 1979-81, adj. prof. pre-trial litigation, Knoxville, 1996; mem. Tenn. Ct. of Judiciary, 1995—; mem. Tenn. Jud. Evaluation Guidelines Commn., 1994-95. Author: Tennessee Admissibility of Evidence in Civil Cases, 1987; co-author: Tennessee Automobile Liability Insurance, 1986, 95, 96, 99; editor-in-chief Tenn. Law Rev., 1975; contbr. articles to profl. jours. Bd. mgrs. YMCA Youth Residential Ctr., 1977-80; mem. McCallie Sch. Alumni Coun., 1987-93, U. Tenn. Dean's Alumni adv. coun. law coll., 1979—; trustee, Harbison Found., 1994-96. Recipient Am. Jurisprudence award U. Tenn., 1974, U. Ten. Coll. Law Pub. Svc. award, 1995; Alumni Achievement award McCallie Sch., 1994. Mem. ABA, Am. Bar Found., Tenn. Bar Assn. (bd. govs. 1985-94, pres. 1992-93), Tenn. Bar Found., Chattanooga Bar Found., Chattanooga Bar Assn. (bd. govs. 1983-85), State Bar Ga., Fed. Bar Assn. (dir. chpt. 1983-88), Fed. Ins. and Corp. Counsel, Def. Rsch. Inst., Internat. Assn. Def. Counsel, Order of Coif, Phi Kappa Phi. Federal civil litigation, Insurance, State civil litigation. Office: Witt Gaither & Whitaker 736 Market St Chattanooga TN 37402-4807

**CAMPBELL, PAUL GARY,** lawyer; b. Lancaster, Pa., Aug. 2, 1965; s. Guy Erb and Daisy Marie (Sellers) C.; m. Melinda Kay Breidenbaugh, May 28, 1988; children: Faith Ann, Gregory Paul, Joy Melinda. BA in Polit. Sci., Millersville U. Pa., 1986; JD, Widener U., 1989. Bar: Pa. 1989. Law clk. to Hon. Richard H. Horn, York County Ct. Common Pleas for 19th Jud. Dist., York, Pa., 1989-90; assoc. Law Offices D. Patrick Zimmerman, Lancaster, 1991-93, Law Offices Michael J. Rostolsky, Lancaster, 1993-96; pvt. practice, Holtwood, Pa., 1997—. Photographer, firefighter, fin. sec. Pequea (Pa.) Vol. Fire Co., 1991—; supr. Martic Twp., Pequea, 1992-98. Mem. Lions (pres. Tucquan, Pa. 1994-95). Republican. Avocations: hunting, sports, woodworking, reading. General corporate, Family and matrimonial, General practice. Home: 168 Pinnacle Rd W Holtwood PA 17532-9673 Office: PO Box 148 Holtwood PA 17532-0148

**CAMPBELL, POLLYANN S.,** lawyer; d. Walter Frederick and and Ann Marie Stuenkel; m. John William Campbell II, Apr. 3, 1970 (div. Oct. 1990); children: Georgia Ann, John William III. BA cum laude, Shorter Coll., 1970; JD magna cum laude, Woodrow Wilson Coll. of Law, 1981. Bar: Ga. 1981, U.S. Dist. Ct. (no. dist.) Ga. 1981. Assoc. Lipshutz, Frankel, Greenblatt, King and Cohen, Atlanta, 1982-85; dist. underwriter, counsel Stewart Title Guaranty Co., Atlanta, 1985-87; state counsel Transamerica Title Ins. Co., Atlanta, 1987-90; appointed div. counsel Commonwealth Land Title Ins. Co. and Transamerica Title Ins. Co., Atlanta, 1990-96; apptd. Ga. State Coun., 1996—, asst. v.p., 1997—; presenter Ga. Real Estate Closing Attys. Assn. seminar, 1991, Commonwealth Land Title Ins. Co. seminar, 1992, other seminars. Editor-in-chief Woodrow Wilson Jour. Law, 1979-81. Mem. coun. Luth. Ch. of Nativity, Austell, Ga., 1982, 89-91, pres., 1990-91; mem. Rudisill Meml. Handbell Choir, 1987-96. Mem. ABA, Ga. Bar Assn., Atlanta Bar Assn., Am. Land Title Assn. (former state ct. mem. of judiciary com.). Real property.

**CAMPBELL, RICHARD BRUCE,** lawyer; b. Phila., Jan. 5, 1947; s. George B. and Edith (Neithammer) C.; m. Patricia Ann James, Mar. 7, 1981; children: Ron Martin, Rebecca Joi. BA, U. S.C., 1968, JD, 1974. Bar: U.S. Dist. Ct. S.C. 1975, U.S. Ct. Appeals (4th cir.) 1976, U.S. Ct. Appeals (5th cir.) 1983, Colo. 1985, U.S. Dist. Ct. Colo. 1986, U.S. Ct. Appeals (fed. cir.) 1989, Fla. 1989, U.S. Dist. Ct. (mid. dist.) Fla., U.S. Ct. Appeals (11th cir.) 1992. Law clk. to presiding justice U.S. Dist. Ct., Columbia, S.C., 1975; ptnr. Henderson & Salley, Aiken, S.C., 1975-80; atty. TVA, Knoxville, 1980-85; ptnr. Wells, Love & Scoby, Boulder, Colo., 1986-89; shareholder Carlton, Fields, Ward, Emmanuel, Smith & Cutler, P.A., Tampa, Fla., 1989—; lectr. in field. Contbr. articles to profl. jours. Served to capt. USAF, 1968-72. Mem. ABA, Am. Arbitration Assn. (panelist), Fla. Bar Assn., Colo. Bar Assn., Hillsborough County Bar Assn. Avocations: travel, skiing, photography. Construction, Government contracts and claims, General civil litigation. Office: Carlton Fields Ward Emmanuel Smith & Cutler PC PO Box 3239 Tampa FL 33601-3239

**CAMPBELL, RICHARD P.,** lawyer; b. Boston, MA, June 17, 1947; s. William Thomas and Mary Patricia (O'Brien) C.; m. Barbara Lydon; children: Rochard, Sean, Lauren. BA, U. Mass, 1970; JD cum laude, Boston Coll., 1974. Bar: N.J. 1974, U.S. Dist. Ct. N.J., 1974, Mass. 1977, U.S. Dist. Ct. R.I. 1979, U.S. Dist. Ct. Maine, U.S. Ct. Appeals (1st cir.) 1980, Fla., 1984, Maine, 1986 , U.S. Supreme Ct. 1991, U.S. Dist. Ct. Conn. 1997, R.I. 1997. Assoc. Shanley & Fisher, Newark, NJ, 1974-77, Nutter McClennen & Fish, Boston, MA, 1979-81, Craig & Macauley, Boston, 1979-81; shareholder, 1981-83; founder Campbell, Campbell & Edwards, Boston, MA, 1983—. Contbr. articles to legal jours. Recipient Founders Medal Boston Coll. Law Sch. for outstanding achievement in the practice of law, 1995. Mem. ABA (chmn. products liability com., tort and ins. practice sect. 1990-91, task force on tort liability systems 1991—, chair, acamedician practitioner task force, 1993-94, chair TIPS ann. meeting 1994, long range planning com. 1995-96, TIPS coun. 1996—, mem. task force autochoice legis. 1997-99, vice chair 1999—), Fed. Bar Assn. (Mass. chpt. pres. 1993-94), Am. Coll. Trial Lawyers, Mass. Bar Assn. (chair white collar crime com. criminal just. sect., co-chair lawyer advt. com. 1993-96, mem. bd. dels. 1993-94, 95-98), Mass. Def. Lawyers Assn. Lwyers for Civil Justice, Def. Rsch. Inst. (prod. liability com. 1984—, amicus curaie com. 1995-97), Assn. for Advancement of Automotive Med. (life), Product Liabilty Adv. Counc. (exec. counc. 1993-97, sustaining), Nat. Assn. Criminal Def. Lawyers, Nat. Bd. Trail Advocacy (cert. civil trial adv.), Internat. Assn. of Def. Couns. (chmn. toxic and hazardous substances litigation com. 1992-94, chair open forum com. 1994-95, exec. com. 1996—, chair CLE bd. 1996-98), Civil Justice Adv. Grp., Boston Coll. Law Sch. Alumni Counc., Notre Dame Acad., Hingham, Mass. (bd. dirs. 1998—), Ireland C of C in US (bd. dirs. 1996), Cath. Charities (bd. dirs.). Algonquin Club, Hawk's Nest Golf Club (Vero Beach, Fla.), Univ. Club, Bay Club Hatherly Country Club. Product liability, Environmental, Criminal. Office: 1 Constitution Plz Boston MA 02129-2025

**CAMPBELL, ROBERT CRAIG, III,** lawyer, educator; b. Drexel Hill, Pa., Dec. 11, 1942; s. Joseph Richardson and Gertrude (Nash) C.; m. Carole Elaine King, Mar. 17, 1979: children: David, Brett, Craig, Nash. BA, Georgetown (Ky.) U., 1964; JD, Samford U., 1967. Bar: Ala. 1967, U.S. Dist. Ct. (so. dist.) Ala. 1970, U.S. Supreme Ct. 1972, U.S. Ct. Appeals (11th and 5th cirs.) 1981. Chief asst. dist. atty. County of Mobile, Ala., 1971-73; sr. ptnr. Sintz, Campbell, Duke, & Taylor, Mobile, 1973—; asst. atty. City of Mobile, 1973-81; atty. Mobile county Sch. Bd., 1977—; instr. pre-law U. So. Ala., Mobile, 1971—; mem. faculty continuing learning edn. Ala. Bar Inst., 1986; spl. asst. atty. gen. State of Ala., Mobile, 1977—; atty. Mobile County Sheriff's Dept.; atty., gen. counsel for Ala. Sch. Math. and Sci. Asst. juvenile judge Mobile County Youth Ctr., 1973-80; v.p. Ala. Coun. Sch. Bd. Attys., 1985-86, pres., 1986-87; pres. Dauphin Island Property Owner's Assn.; bd. dirs. U.S. Sports Acad. Named one of Outstanding Young Men in Am., 1977, 78. Mem. ABA, ATLA, Ala. Bar Assn., Mobile Fed. Bar Assn. (pres.), Ala. Trial Lawyers Assn., Ala. Def. Lawyers Assn., Country Club Mobile, Mirror Lake Racquet Blub (pres. Mobile chpt. 1974, 79), Isle Dauphine (Ala.) Country Club. Avocations: tennis, jogging, photography, golf, reading. Home: 26 Country Club Rd Mobile AL 36608-2357 Office: Sintz Campbell Duke & Taylor 3763 Professional Pky Mobile AL 36609-5414

**CAMPBELL, ROBERT HEDGCOCK,** investment banker, lawyer; b. Ann Arbor, Mich., Jan. 16, 1948; s. Robert Miller and Ruth Adele (Hedgcock) C.; m. Katherine Kettering, June 17, 1972; children: Mollie DuPlan, Katherine Elizabeth, Anne Kettering. BA, U. Wash., 1970, JD, 1973. Bar. Wash. 1973, Wash. State Supreme Ct. 1973, Fed. 1973, U.S. Dist. Ct. (we. dist.) Wash. 1973, Ct. Appeals (9th cir.) 1981. Assoc. Roberts & Shefelman, Seattle, 1973-78, ptnr., 1978-85; sr. v.p. Lehman Bros., Inc., Seattle, 1985-87, mng. dir., 1987—; bd. dirs. Pogo Producing Co.; dir., treas. Nat. Assn. Bd. Lawyers, Hinsdale, Ill., 1982-85; pres., trustee Wash. State Soc. Hosp. Attys., Seattle, 1982-85; mem. econs. dept. vis. com. U. Wash., 1995-97; mem. Law Sch. dean's adv. bd. U. Wash., 1999—. Contbr. articles to profl. jours. Trustee Bellevue (Wash.) Schs. Found., 1988-91, pres., 1989-90; nation chief Bellevue Eastside YMCA Indian Princess Program, 1983-88; trustee Wash. Phikeia Found., 1983-91, Sandy Hook Yacht Club Estates, Inc., 1993-98; mem. Wash. Gov.'s Food Processing Coun., 1990-91. Republican. Avocations: skiing, wind surfing, bike riding, physical fitness, golf. Home: 8604 NE 10th St Medina WA 98039-3915 Office: Lehman Bros Columbia Seafirst Ctr 701 5th Ave Ste 7101 Seattle WA 98104-7016

**CAMPBELL, ROBERT ROE,** ; b. Knoxville, Tenn., Nov. 7, 1930; s. Lacy Roe and Anita Tromp (Wilson) C.; m. Ruth Eleanor VerMeulen, July 7, 1956; children: Robert Roe, Willard B., Cady Ruth. BS, U. Tenn., 1953, JD, 1956. Bar: Tenn. 1956, U.S. Dist. Ct. (ea. dist.) Tenn. 1956, U.S. Ct. Appeals (6th cir.) 1965, U.S. Supreme Ct. 1971. Sole practice Knoxville, 1956-58; assoc. Poore, Cox, Baker & McAuley, 1958-62; assoc. Hodges, Doughty & Carson, 1962-63, ptnr., 1963—. Bd. dirs., vice chmn. Maryville Coll., 1976-82; bd. dirs. Ft. Sanders Hosp., 1969-86; elder 2d Presbyn. Ch., Knoxville, 1960—; active Republican Party. Served with U.S. Army, 1953-55. Mem. ABA, Tenn. Bar Assn., Knoxville Bar Assn., Am. Coll. Trial Lawyers, Tenn. Bar Found., Am. Bar Found., Internat. Assn. Def. Counsel, Am. Bd. Trial Advs., Peninsula Club, LeConte Club, Cherokee Country Club (Knoxville). General corporate, General civil litigation, Alternative dispute resolution. Office: PO Box 869 Knoxville TN 37901-0869

**CAMPBELL, SCOTT ROBERT,** lawyer, former food company executive; b. Burbank, Calif., June 7, 1946; s. Robert Clyde and Jenevieve Anne (Olsen) C.; m. Teresa Melanie Mack, Oct. 23, 1965; 1 son, Donald Steven. BA, Claremont Men's Coll., 1970; JD, Cornell U., 1973. Bar: Ohio 1973, U.S. Dist. Ct. (so. dist.) Ohio 1974, Minn. 1976, Calif. 1989, U.S. Dist. Ct. (no. dist.) Calif. 1989, U.S. Ct. Appeals (9th cir.) 1989, U.S. Dist. Ct. (cen. and so. dists.) Calif. 1990, U.S. Ct. Appeals (5th cir.) 1991, U.S. Tax Ct. 1991. Assoc. Taft, Stettinius & Hollister, Cin., 1973-76; atty. Mpls. Star & Tribune, 1976-77; sr. v.p., gen. counsel, sec. Kellogg Co., Battle Creek, Mich., 1977-89; ptnr. Furth Fahrner Mason, San Francisco, 1989—; U.S. del. ILO Food and Beverage Conf., Geneva, 1984; participant, presenter first U.S.-USSR Legal Seminar, Moscow, 1988; speaker other legal seminars. Mem. ABA, Ohio Bar Assn., Minn. Bar Assn., Calif. Bar. Assn. General corporate, Antitrust, Securities. Office: Furth Fahrner & Mason 1000 Furth Bldg 201 Sansome St San Francisco CA 94104-2303

**CAMPBELL, SELAURA JOY,** lawyer; b. Oklahoma City, Mar. 25, 1944; d. John Moore III and Gyda (Hallum) C. AA, Stephens Coll., 1963; BA, U. Okla., 1965; MEd, Chapel Hill U., 1974; JD, N.C. Cen. U., 1978; postgrad. atty. mediation courses, South Tex. Sch. of Law, Houston, 1991, Atty. Mediators Inst./Dallas, Dallas, 1992. Bar: Ariz 1983; lic. real estate broker, N.C.; cert. tchr. N.C. With flight svc. dept. Pan Am. World Airways, N.Y.C., 1966-91; lawyer Am. Women's Legal Clinic, Phoenix, 1987; charter mem. Sony Corp. Indsl. Mgmt. Seminar, 1981; guest del. Rep. Nat. Conv., Houston, 1992; judge all-law sch. mediation competition for Tex., South Tex. Sch. Law, Houston, 1994. Mem. N.C. Cen. U. Law Rev., 1977-78. People-to-People del. People's Republic of China, 1987; guest del. Rep. Nat. Conv., Houston, 1992. Mem. Ariz. Bar Assn., Humane Soc. U.S., Nat. Wildlife Fedn., People for the Ethical Treatment of Animals, Amnesty Internat., Phi Alpha Delta. Republican. Episcopalian. Avocations: climbed Mt. Kilimanjaro, 1983, also Machu Pichu, Peru, Mt Kenya, Africa, horseback riding, photography. General civil litigation, General practice, Family and matrimonial. Home: 206 Taft Ave Cleveland TX 77327-4539

**CAMPBELL, THOMAS DOUGLAS,** lawyer, consultant; b. N.Y.C., Jan. 5, 1951; s. Edward Thomas and Dorothy Alice (Moore) C.; m. Mary Anne Makin, Dec. 22, 1978; 1 child, Kristen Anne. BA, U. Del., 1972; JD, U. Pa., 1976. Bar: Del. 1977. Law clk. Law Offices Bayard Brill & Handleman, Wilmington, Del., 1974-77; govt. affairs rep. Northeastern U.S. Std. Oil Co. Ind., 1977-78; Washington rep. Std. Oil Co., Ind., 1978-85; pres. Thomas D. Campbell and Assocs., Inc., Alexandria, Va., 1985—; govt. affairs rep. Northeastern U.S., Std. Oil Co. Ind., 1977-78. With U.S. Army, 1968-69, Del. Air N.G., 1969-77. Mem. ABA, Del. Bar Assn., Congl. Awards Found. (chmn. bd. dirs.), Phi Beta Kappa, Phi Kappa Phi, Omicron Delta Epsilon, Omicron Delta Kappa. Republican. Episcopalian. Legislative. Home: 517 Queen St Alexandria VA 22314-2512 also: 300-30 Great Cruz Bay Rd Saint John VI 00830 Office: 517 Queen St Alexandria VA 22314-2512

**CAMPBELL, VINCENT BERNARD,** judge, lawyer; b. Rochester, N.Y., Nov. 1, 1943; s. Paul and Lucy (Tarricone) C.; m. Geraldine Miceli, July 4, 1970; children: Dina, Tracy. BS, Syracuse U., 1965, LLD, 1968. Bar: N.Y. 1969. Lawyer Goldman and Shinder, Rochester, N.Y., 1970-74, Vincent B. Campbell Law Firm, Rochester, N.Y., 1974—; businessman Flower City Builders Supply Corp., Rochester, N.Y., 1974—; real estate developer V.R.J.D. Devel. Inc., 40 West Ave. Properties, Rochester, N.Y., 1970—; judge Town of Greece, N.Y., 1994—. V.p. Monroe County Legislature, Rochester, 1976-88; N.Y. state committeeman Rep. Party, Rochester, 1988-93; town councilman Town of Greece, 1990-94; bd. trustees N.Y. Chiropractic Coll., Seneca Falls, N.Y., 1992; econ. devel. com. Nazareth Coll., Rochester, 1991-93. Recipient Robert Roantree award Syracuse Credit Mfrs. Assn., 1965, Am. Jurisprudence award Lawyers Coop., 1969; named Legislator of the Yr., Monroe County Conservative Party, 1983-84. Mem. ABA, N.Y. State BarAssn., Monroe County Bar Assn., N.Y. State Magistrate's Assn., Rochester Yacht Club. Avocations: sailing, golfing, hunting, winemaking. Office: 1577 Ridge Rd W Ste 203 Rochester NY 14615-2511

**CAMPBELL, WILLIAM J.,** lawyer; b. Grand Junction, Colo., Feb. 10, 1945; s. Timothy Samuel and Narcissa Cooke C.; m. Marsha Logan Campbell, June 16, 1979; children: John Bradford Geiger, Elizabeth Weir Geiger, Anne Wentworth Campbell, Amy Logan Campbell. BA cum laude, Colo. Coll., 1967; JD, U. Colo., 1971. Bar: Colo. 1971, U.S. Dist. Ct. Colo. 1971. Shareholder Bradley, Campbell, Carney & Madsen, P.C., Golden, Colo., 1971-95; ptnr. Faegre & Benson LLP, Denver, 1995—. Mem. U. Colo. Law Rev., 1970-71. Named Outstanding Young Lawyer, First Jud. Dist. Bar Assn., 1982; Boettcher scholar Boettcher Found., 1963-67; Grad. fellow Rotary Found., 1969. Mem. ABA, Colo. Bar Assn., Colo. Assn. Corp. Counsel, Colo. Coll. (bd. trustees), Phi Beta Kappa. Republican. Episcopalian. Avocation: golf. General corporate, Securities, Private international. Home: 3244 Beech Ct Golden CO 80401-1683 Office: Faegre & Benson LLP 2500 Republic Plz 370 17th St Ste 2500 Denver CO 80202-5665

**CAMPBELL, WILLIAM LEE,** lawyer; b. Lamesa, Tex., Apr. 5, 1954; s. Leland Eugene and Bettye L. Campbell; m. Paula Ann Bostick, July 20, 1985; children: Travis Lee, William Ryan. BA, Baylor U., 1975, JD, 1978. Bar: Tex. 1978, U.S. Dist. Ct. (no. dist.) Tex. Assoc. Rudd and Smith Attys., Grand Prairie, Tex., 1978-81; ptnr. Watson Kuvejer Campbell, Grand Prairie, 1981-85; sole practice Arlington, Tex., 1985—; mediator Dispute Resolution Svcs. Tarrant County, Ft. Worth, 1992—; mem. adv. appeals bd. City of Arlington, Tex., 1992-98; mem. jury selection com. State Bar Tex., Austin, 1996—. Mem. ABA, Great S.W. Rotary Club (bd. dirs. 1992—), Arlington Optimist Club. Avocations: running, snow skiing, bird hunting, camping, coaching sports. General practice, General civil litigation, Family and matrimonial. Office: 1101 W Randol Mill Rd Arlington TX 76012-2515

**CAMPION, RENÉE,** lawyer; b. Balt.. BS, U. Md., 1980; JD, U. Balt., 1987. Bar: Md. 1987. Atty. Legal Aid Bur., Inc., Balt., 1988-96; pvt. practice Balt., 1997—. Mem. ABA, Women's Bar Assn., Women's Law Ctr., Balt. County Bar Assn., Bar Assn. Balt. City. Family and matrimonial, Juvenile. Office: 409 Washington Ave Ste 920 Towson MD 21204-4905

**CAMPOS, SANTIAGO E.,** federal judge; b. Santa Rosa, N.Mex., Dec. 25, 1926; s. Ramon and Miquela Campos; m. Patsy Campos, Jan. 27, 1947; children: Theresa, Rebecca, Christina, Miquela Feliz. J.D., U. N.Mex., 1953. Bar: N.Mex. 1953. Asst., 1st asst. atty gen. State of N.Mex., 1955-57; judge 1st Jud. Dist. N.Mex., 1971-78; judge U.S. Dist. Ct. N.Mex., Santa Fe, 1978—, sr. judge, 1992—. Served as seaman USN, 1944-46. Mem. State Bar of N.Mex., First Jud. Dist. Bar Assn. (hon.), Hon. Order of Coif. Office: US Dist Ct PO Box 2244 Santa Fe NM 87504-2244

**CAMPOS, VICTOR MANUEL,** lawyer, probate referee; b. Monterey, Calif., Oct. 18, 1942; s. Manuel and Lupe Campos; children: Tannis Jane, Mark Victor, Victor Manuel, David Miguel. BA, U. Calif., Berkeley, 1964; JD, Monterey Coll of Law, 1987. Adminstrv. asst. trust dept. U.S. Nat. Bank of Oreg., 1965-68; mem. trust dept. ct. and pvt. trust adminstrn. Bank of Am. NT&SA, Salinas and Oakland, Calif., 1968-72; trust officer Bank of Am. NT&SA, Salinas and Oakland, 1982-84; pers. analyst Santa Cruz County, 1975, state inheritance tax referee, 1975-83, Calif. probate referee, 1983—; pvt. practice Santa Cruz, 1989—. Past pres. Chicano Leadership Coun.; co-founder, chmn. bd. dirs. Cypress Found. Cmty. Environ. Ctr., 1975-76; mem. Santa Cruz County Employment Commn., 1976-80, Santa Cruz County Affirmative Action Adv. Com., 1974-75, Santa Cruz Estate Planning Coun., 1972-73; bd. dirs. Santa Cruz chpt. ARC, Dominican Hosp. Found., Santa Cruz Cmty. Found., Barrios Unidos, Santa Cruz; chmn., fin. dir. Camacho for Congress, 1972. Mem. ABA, Calif. State Bar Assn., Santa Cruz County Trial Lawyers, Santa Cruz County Bar Assn., Santa Cruz County Criminal Def. Bar Assn., La Raza Lawyers (co-founder), Nat. Hispanic Bar Assn. Democrat. Avocations: politics, sports. Criminal, General civil litigation, Probate. Office: 916 Soquel Ave Ste A Santa Cruz CA 95062-2101

**CAMPOS-ORREGO, NORA PATRICIA,** lawyer, consultant; b. Lima, Peru, Sept. 3, 1959; came to U.S., 1984; d. Victor M. and Ofelia A. Campos. BA, Cath. U. Peru, 1979, LLB, 1983, Lawyer, 1984; JD magna cum laude, InterAm. U. P.R., San Juan, 1989. Bar: P.R. 1989, Peru, 1984. Legal asst. women's affairs commn. P.R. Gov.'s Office, San Juan, 1988-89, lawyer women's affairs commn., 1989-93; lawyer women's affairs commn. P.R. Gov.'s Office/Immigration Law Practice, Miami, Fla., 1993-94; women's discrimination cons. San Juan, P.R., 1994-95; pvt. practice Miami Beach, 1995—. Co-author: How to Write Public Police and Internal Process to Sexual Harassment Claims, 1989; editor Law Sch. Mag., 1988-89. All Am. scholar U. P.R., 1988-89. Mem. ABA, InterAm. Bar Assn., P.R. Bar Assn., Peru Bar Assn. Roman Catholic. Avocations: sightseeing, reading, dancing, walking. Civil rights, Labor.

**CANADY, MARK HOWARD,** lawyer; b. Lansing, Mich., Mar. 17, 1961; s. Clinton and Hortense (Golden) C.; m. Renèe Lavonne Branch, Aug. 2, 1986; children: Mark Howard (dec.), Marcus Atwater, Alexander Clinton, Wesley Alan. BS in Bus., U. N.C., 1983; JD, U. Mich., 1986. Bar: Mich. 1986, U.S. Dist. Ct. (ea. and we. dists.) Mich. 1986. Assoc. Foster, Swift, Collins, Coey, Lansing, 1986-89, Howard & Howard, Lansing, 1989-91; assoc. Foster, Swift, Collins & Smith, Lansing, 1991-96, ptnr., 1996—. Chmn. Waterfornt Devel. Bd., Lansing, 1986-90, cert. of merit, 1990, City of Lansing Blue Ribbon com. on baseball, 1994; at large mem. Lansing City Coun., 1990-95, v.p., 1991-93, pres., 1993-94; bd. dirs. Lansing Symphony Orch., 1990-94, Camp Highfields, Lansing, 1990-94, Am. Lung Assn., 1991-94, Big Bros./Big Sisters, Lansing, Tri-County Planning Commn., 1990-92, cert. of merit, 1992; mem. transp. bd. Mich. Mcpl. League, 1991-95. Morehead Found. scholar, 1983; named one of Best Politicians in Mid-Mich. Lansing Bus. Mag., 1992, one of 100 Best and Brightest Bus. and Profl. Men Dollars and Sense Mag., 1993. Mem. ABA, Nat. Bar Assn., Ingham County Bar Assn., Inst. for Continuing Legal Edn. (lectr.), U. Mich. Alumni Assn. (v.p., bd. dirs.), Kappa Alpha Psi, Phi Eta Sigma. Democrat. Methodist. Avocations: composing music, golf, sailing. Insurance, General civil litigation, Land use and zoning (including planning). Office: Foster Swift Collins & Smith 313 S Washington Sq Lansing MI 48933-2172

**CANALE, JOHN F.,** lawyer; b. Buffalo, Apr. 29, 1922; s. Jack and Madalene Canale; m. Gladys (Beckett) C.; children: John, Elizabeth, Ann. BS, Norwich (Vt.) U.; BA, U. Rochester, Brockport (N.Y.) U. Bar: N.Y. Resident counsel Liberty Mut. Co., Buffalo, 1948-55; ptnr. Bronnstein & Canale, Buffalo, 1955-71; owner, sr. ptnr. Canale, Madden & Burke, P.C., Buffalo, 1971-92; spl. counsel Bouvier, O'Connor, Buffalo, 1993—. 1st lt. USAAC, 1943-45, ETO. Fellow Am. Coll. Trial Lawyersl; mem. N.Y. State Bar Assn., Erie County Bar Assn. Avocations: reading, travel, grandchildren. State civil litigation, Insurance, Personal injury. Office: Bouvier O'Connor 1400 Main Pl Tower 350 Main St Buffalo NY 14202-3702

**CANAN, MICHAEL JAMES,** lawyer, author; b. Washington, Sept. 28, 1941; s. Robert Harvey and Molly Cornelia (Brown) C.; 1 child, Jennifer Michelle. BA, Stanford U., 1963; JD, U. Calif., Berkeley, 1966; LLM in Taxation, NYU, 1972. Bar: Calif. 1969, Fla. 1972. Assoc. Holland & Knight, Lakeland, Fla., 1972-74; ptnr. Canan & Harris, Lakeland, 1974-76, Canan, Murphy & Clark, Lakeland and Tampa, Fla., 1976-84, Dean Mead Edgeton Bloodworth, Orlando, Fla., 1984-86, Baker & Hostetler, Orlando, 1986, Steel Hector & Davis, Miami, Fla., 1986-93; pvt. practice Law Office Michael J. Canan, Orlando, Fla., 1993-98; atty. Gray, Harris and Robinson, P.A., 1998—. Author: Qualified Retirement plans, 1977, 14th edit., 1999, West's Federal Practice, 1979, part 20, 1992, West's Legal Forms, 1981, ed edit., vol. 8, 1991, 98; (computer software) West's Model Benefit Plans, 1990, Qualified Retirement Plans, 1991, Fringe and Welfare Plans, 1992, Volume Submitter Plans, 1992, IRS Retirement Plan Submittal Package, 1997, Tech Soft Pension Plans, 1998-99; co-author: Employee Fringe and Welfare Benefit Plans, 1990, 10th edit., 1999. Vol. Peace Corps, Venezuela, 1966-67. Capt. USAF, 1967-71. Pension, profit-sharing, and employee benefits, Estate planning.

**CANAN, THOMAS MICHAEL,** lawyer; b. Appleton, Wis., Mar. 22, 1964; s. Michael Edward and Jean Ellen (McLaughlin) C.; m. Elizabeth Jane Levy, Aug. 5, 1989; children: Katherine, William. BA, U. Wis., Eau Claire, 1986; JD, U. Minn., 1989. Bar: Minn. 1989, U.S. Dist. Ct. Minn. 1990. M.J. Murdock fellow Washington Legal Found., 1987; student atty. Civil Practice Clinic, Mpls., 1987-88; summer assoc. Davis & Kuelthau, Milw., 1988; rsch. asst. Minn. Ho. of Rep. Rsch. Dept., Mpls., 1988-89; jud. clk. Olmsted County Dist. Ct., Rochester, Minn., 1989-90; assoc. Streater, Murphy, Gernander, Winona, Minn., 1990-91; asst. city atty. City of Rochester, Minn., 1991-99; pvt. practice Rochester, 1999—; presenter in field. Presenter of various programs including Domestic Abuse Prosecution, Abating Gang Graffiti, Criminal Law Update. Tour guide Olmsted County Hist. Soc., Rochester, 1991-96; vol. Rochester Pk. and Recreation, 1989-93, Woodside Nursing Home, Rochester, 1993-97. Mem. Minn. State Bar Assn., Olmsted County Bar Assn., Kiwanis, Lions. Avocations: bicycling, swimming, sea kayaking. Home: 724 9th St SW Rochester MN 55902-6316 Office: Merchants Exchange Bldg 18 3rd St SW Ste 200 Rochester MN 55902-3022

**CANAS, EDUARDO,** lawyer; b. San Benito, Tex., Dec. 27, 1941. BGS, U. Nebr., Omaha, 1970; JD, Tex. Tech U., 1985. Commd. pvt. U.S. Army, 1959, advanced through grades to maj., 1975, ret., 1979; retail sales exec., 1979-82; pvt. practice Ft. Worth, 1985—. Decorated Bronze Star. Mem. KC. Roman Catholic. Office: 600 N Main St Ste A Fort Worth TX 76106-9416

**CANAVOR, FREDERICK CHARLES, JR.,** lawyer; b. N.Y.C., Mar. 29, 1944; s. Frederick Charles Sr. and Leila (Armstrong) C.; m. Allison Arthur, Nov. 23, 1987; children: Victoria, Rachel Lee, Elaine Elizabeth. BS, Syracuse U., 1965; JD, St. John's U., 1971; LLM, NYU, 1972; MBA, Golden Gate U., 1981. Bar: N.Y. 1972, Calif. 1976, D.C. 1977, Wash. 1978. With Arthur Andersen & Co., N.Y.C., 1971-72; asst. dist. atty. Kings County Dist. Atty., Bklyn., 1972-75; spl. asst. atty. Atty. Gen. State N.Y., N.Y.C., 1975-76; atty. Wettrick, Toulouse, Lirhus & Hove, Seattle, Wash., 1978-86; prosecuting atty. San Juan County, Friday Harbor, Wash., 1986-95; atty. Appel & Glueck, P.C., Seattle, 1995—. Author: Rape One, 1982. With U.S. Army, 1967-69. N.Y. War Svc. scholar N.Y. State, 1969, Regents scholar, 1961. Avocations: travel, writing. General corporate, Criminal. Office: Appel & Glueck PC 2500 Seattle Tower 1218 3rd Ave Ste 2400 Seattle WA 98101-3036

**CANBY, WILLIAM CAMERON, JR.,** federal judge; b. St. Paul, May 22, 1931; s. William Cameron and Margaret Leah (Lewis) C.; m. Jane Adams, June 18, 1954; children—William Nathan, John Adams, Margaret Lewis. A.B., Yale U., 1953; LL.B., U. Minn., 1956. Bar: Minn. 1956, Ariz. 1972. Law clk. U.S. Supreme Ct. Justice Charles E. Whittaker, 1958-59; asso. firm Oppenheimer, Hodgson, Brown, Baer & Wolff, St. Paul, 1959-62; asso., then dep. dir. Peace Corps, Ethiopia, 1962-64; dir. Peace Corps, Uganda, 1964-66; asst. to U.S. Senator Walter Mondale, 1966; asst. to pres. SUNY, 1967; prof. law Ariz. State U., 1967-80; judge U.S. Ct. Appeals (9th cir.), Phoenix, 1980-96, sr. judge, 1996—; chief justice High Ct. of the Trust Ter. of the Pacific Islands, 1993-94; bd. dirs. Ariz. Center Law in Public Interest, 1974-80, Maricopa County Legal Aid Soc., 1972-78, D.N.A.-People's Legal Services, 1978-80; Fulbright prof. Makerere U. Faculty Law, Kampala, Uganda, 1970-71. Author: American Indian Law, 1998; also articles; note editor: Minn. Law Rev, 1955-56. Precinct and state committeeman Democratic Party Ariz., 1972-80; bd. dirs. Central Ariz. Coalition for Right to Choose, 1976-80. Served with USAF, 1956-58. Mem. State Bar Ariz., Minn. Bar Assn., Maricopa County Bar Assn., Phi Beta Kappa, Order of Coif. Office: US Ct Appeals 9th Cir US Courthouse Rm 6445 230 N 1st Ave Phoenix AZ 85025-0230

**CANDITO, JOSEPH,** lawyer; b. Santa Eufemia, Reggio, Italy, Mar. 23, 1954; came to the U.S., 1956; s. Joseph (dec.) and Claudia (Sabina) C.; m. Doris Ann Beutner, Oct. 1, 1983; children: Claudia Christine, Joseph Michael, Jonathan Matthew. AB, Ohio U., 1976, MEd, 1979; JD, U. Dayton, 1986. Bar: Ohio 1986, U.S. Dist. Ct. (so. and we. dist.) Ohio 1986. Staff assoc. Citizens Fed. Savs. and Loan, Dayton, Ohio, 1984-86; mng. atty. Hyatt Legal Svcs., Blue Ash, Ohio, 1986-94; owner Joseph Candito & Assocs., Blue Ash, 1994—. Mem. Cin. Bar Assn. Roman Catholic. Avocations: Christian apologetics, weight lifting, reading, dancing, writing. Family and matrimonial, Probate, Bankruptcy. Address: 9419 Kenwood Rd Cincinnati OH 45242-6811

**CANDLAND, D. STUART,** lawyer; b. Madison, Wis., Sept. 6, 1942; s. Don Charles and Dorothy Jane (Nelson) C.; m. Evelyn McComber, Dec. 3, 1982; children: Ashley, Tara Lynn, Brett. BA with honors, Brigham Young U., 1967; JD, U. Calif., Berkeley, 1970. Bar: Calif. 1971, U.S. Dist. Ct. (no. dist.) Calif. 1971, U.S. Ct. Appeals (9th cir.) 1971. Dep. atty. gen. State of Calif., San Francisco, 1970-73; dep. dist. atty. Solano County Dist. Atty.'s Office, Fairfield, Calif., 1973-75; assoc. Law Offices of M. Craddick, Walnut Creek, Calif., 1976-78; ptnr. Craddick, Candland & Conti, Danville, Calif., 1979—; asst. prof. law Armstrong Sch. Law, Berkeley, 1971-77. Mem. ABA, Assn. Def. Counsel, Contra Costa County Bar Assn. Professional liability, Federal civil litigation, Insurance. Office: Craddick Candland & Conti Ste 260 915 San Ramon Valley Blvd Danville CA 94526-4021

**CANDLER, JAMES NALL, JR.,** lawyer; b. Detroit, Jan. 25, 1943; s. James Nall and Lorna Augusta (Blood) C.; m. Jean Ward McKinnon, Mar. 8, 1974; children: Christine, Elizabeth, Anne. AB, Princeton U., 1965; JD, U. Mich., 1970. Bar: Mich. 1970. Assoc. Dickinson Wright PLLC, Detroit, 1970-77, ptnr., 1977—; adj. prof. real estate planning U. Detroit Sch. of Law, 1975-80. Bd. dirs. Detroit Inst. Ophthalmology Grosse Pointe Park, Mich., 1983—, chmn., 1994—. Lt. USNR, 1965-67. Mem. Internat. Assn. Attys. and Execs. in Corp. Real Estate, State Bar Mich. (chmn. real property law sect. 1998-99), Am. Coll. of Real Estate Lawyers, Grosse Pointe Club (chmn. 1987-89), Country Club of Detroit. Republican. Avocations: sailing, golf, platform tennis. Contracts commercial, Landlord-tenant, Real property. Home: 211 Country Club Dr Grosse Pointe MI 48236-2901 Office: 500 Woodward Ave Ste 4000 Detroit MI 48226-3416

**CANDRIS, LAURA A.,** lawyer; b. Frankfort, Ky., Apr. 5, 1955; d. Charles M. and Dorothy (Jane) Sutton; m. Aris S. Candris, Dec. 22, 1974. AB with distinction in polit. sci., Transylvania Coll., 1975; postgrad., U. Pitts., 1975-77, U. Fla., 1977-78; JD, U. Pitts., 1978. Bar: Fla. 1978, U.S. Dist. Ct. (mid. dist.) Fla. 1978, U.S. Ct. Appeals (4th cir.) 1980, Pa. 1981, U.S. Dist. Ct. (we. dist.) Pa. 1982, U.S. Ct. Appeals (3d cir.) 1983. Assoc. Coffman, Coleman, Andrews & Grogan, Jacksonville, Fla., 1978-80, Manion, Alder & Cohen, Pitts., 1981-85; assoc. Eckert, Seamans, Cherin & Mellott, Pitts., 1985-86, ptnr., 1987-96, vice chmn. labor and employment law dept, mem. practice mgmt. com., mem. strategic planning com.; ptnr. Meyer Unkovic & Scott, LLP, Pitts., 1996—, chair labor, employment law and employee benefits sect.; mem. litigation and transactions depts. Meyer Unkovic & Scott, LLP; counsel Nat. Assn. Women in Constrn. (chpt. 161), Pitts., 1985-86. Contbr. over 30 articles to profl. jours. including Forum Reporter, Pers. Law Update, Employment Law Inst. manuals, and Reference Manual for the 34th Annual Mid-West Labor Law Conf. Coun. mem. O'Hara Twp., 1986-90; mem. O'Hara Twp. Planning Commn., 1990; bd. dirs. Tri-State Employers Assn., 1991-93, Parent and Child Guidance Ctr., 1991—, v.p. exec. com., 1998-99, pres. 1999; treas., mem. exec. com. SMC Bus. Couns., 1993-94, bd. dirs., 1993-96; bd. dirs. Big Bros. & Big Sisters Greater Pitts., 1998—. Nat. Merit Found. scholar 1972-75; named Ky. Col., 1974. Mem. ABA (EEO com. labor sect., labor and employment law com. litigation sect.), Fla. Bar Assn., Pa. Bar Assn. (employment sect.), Allegheny County Bar Assn. (coun. on professionalism, employment and fed. cts. sect., hdqrs. com. and pers. subcom.), Soc. Hosp. Attys. Western Pa., Pitts. Human Resources Assn., Women's Bar Assn. Western Pa. Republican. Avocations: skiing, traveling, bicycling, reading. Federal civil litigation, Labor, Pension, profit-sharing, and employee benefits. Office: Meyer Unkovic & Scott LLP 1300 Oliver Bldg Pittsburgh PA 15222

**CANES, CARMEN DAHLIA,** paralegal, educator; b. Havana, Cuba, Jan. 16, 1952; came to U.S., 1959; d. Rafael and Carmen Canes; m. William Aljure, 1977 (div. 1979). ASD in Paralegal Program, Fla. Nat. Coll., 1987-89. Paralegal, head personal injury dept. Dennison & Dennison, P.A., Miami Lakes, Fla., 1991-93, Gregory A. Moore, P.A., Miami Lakes, Fla., 1993—; bd. govs. Fla. Nat. Coll., 1992—, paralegal program guidance counselor, 1992—. Author: Keep it Light, 1987, (song) Care, 1987. Mem. Rep. Nat. Com., Washington, 1984—; rep. com. mem. Senate Majority Fund, Washington, 1990. Recipient Recognition award Dade County Ednl. Private Program, Miami, 1989. Republican. Roman Catholic. Avocations: bicycle riding, outdoor activities. Home: 6448 W 11th Ln Hialeah FL 33012-6442 Office: Gregory Moore PA 15225 NW 77th Ave Hialeah FL 33014-7804

**CANFIELD, EDWARD FRANCIS,** lawyer, business executive; b. Phila., Apr. 7, 1922; s. Frank James and Eunice C. (Sullivan) C.; m. Janet Powell Trotter, 1952 (div. 1991); children: Andrew Trotter, Janet Powell; m. Margaret Harvey O'Brien, 1993. B.A., St. Joseph's U., 1943; J.D., U. Pa., 1949. Bar: Pa. 1949, D.C. 1972. Practice in Phila., 1949-51; with RCA, 1953-60; with Philco-Ford Corp., 1960-69, corp. dir. govt. planning and mktg., 1961-69; pres. Leisure Time Industries, Inc., 1969; mng. ptnr. Casey, Scott & Canfield, 1971-93; ptnr. Canfield & Smith, Washington, 1993—. Lt. comdr. USNR, ret. Mem. Fed. Bar Assn., D.C. Bar Assn., Phila. Bar Assn., Congl. Country Club (Bethesda, Md.), Overbrook Golf Club (Bryn Mawr, Pa., Atlantic City (N.J.) Country Club. General civil litigation, Contracts commercial, General corporate. Home: 1 Andover Rd Haverford PA 19041-1002 Office: Canfield & Smith Fed Bar Bldg 1815 H St NW Ste 1001 Washington DC 20006-3604 also: 1518 Walnut St Ste 1200 Philadelphia PA 19102-3407

**CANFIELD, ELIZABETH FRANCES,** lawyer; b. Fairport, Mo., Aug. 19, 1913; d. James Arthur and Bertha Mae (Ashley) Foard; m. Robert Roe Canfield, May 7, 1933 (dec. Sept. 1994); children: James Robert, Philip Roe. LLB, LaSalle Law Sch., 1949. Bar: Ill. 1950. Pvt. practice Rockford, Ill., 1950-97; spl. asst. atty. gen. State of Ill., 1974-84; ret. Rockford, Ill., 1997; asst. atty. gen. State Ill., 1974-84; lectr. in field. Women's divsn. chmn. United Fund Dri., Rockford, 1951; bd. trustees Ct. St. United Meth. Ch.; bd. dirs. Family Consultation Svc. Rockford; mem. blue ribbon adv. com. to Mayor of Rockford; elected mem. Dist. 58 Sch. Bd.; bd. dirs. Wesley Willows Retirement Home; bd. trustees North Rockford Convalescent home, Willows Health Ctr. Mem. AAUW, LWV (hon. life, Rockford pres. 1946-48), Winnebago County Bar Assn. (chmn. com. 1950—), Quota Internat. Exec. Women's Svc. (Rockford pres. 1980-82, mem. internat. by-laws and dist. gov.), Philanthropic-Ednl. Orgn. Republican. Methodist. Avocations: writing, reading, swimming, travelling, opera, theater. Office: Canfield Law Offices 202 W State St Ste 1100 Rockford IL 61101-1158

**CANIGLIA, LAWRENCE S.,** lawyer; b. Phila., Oct. 8, 1952; s. Salvatore A. and Laura O. Caniglia; m. Barbara A. Caniglia, July 22, 1978; children: Todd, Craig. BA, Rutgers U., 1974; JD, Okla. City U., 1977. Bar: N.J. 1977, U.S. Dist. Ct. N.J. 1977. Assoc. Ruggeirio & Freeman, Marlton, N.J., 1977-78, Burlington County Welfare, Mt. Holly, N.J., 1978-79, Jones & Lutz, P.A., Cherry Hill, N.J., 1979-84; ptnr. McInerney & Caniglia, Moorestown, N.J., 1984—. Bd. dirs. Networker Assocs. of South Jersey, 1994-98; mem. Mt. Laurel Bd. of Edn. Tactical Adv. Com., 1992. Mem. Cherry Hill Regional C. of C. (bd. dirs. 1998—). Avocation: skiing. General civil litigation, Workers' compensation, Contracts commercial. Office: McInerney & Caniglia 712 E Main St Ste 2A Moorestown NJ 08057-3067

**CANNADY, WALTER JACK,** lawyer; b. Alameda, Calif., July 9, 1942; s. Jack Stephen and Marie E. (Schmalenberger) C.; m. Shirley Padovan, June 26, 1966 (div. June 1980); 1 child, Amber L. BS in Polit. Sci., Calif. State U., Hayward, 1964; JD, Lincoln U., San Francisco, 1969. Bar: Calif. 1970, U.S. Dist. Ct. (no. dist.) Calif. 1970. Pvt. practice Oakland, Calif., 1970-79; ptnr. Cannady & Whitehorn, Oakland, 1979-82; of counsel Moore Clifford Wolfe et al, Oakland, 1982-85; pvt. practice San Leandro, Calif., 1985-96, Emeryville, Calif., 1996—. Office: 2200 Powell St Ste 680 Emeryville CA 94608-1876

**CANNELL, JOHN REDFERNE,** lawyer; b. Cambridge, Mass., Apr. 3, 1937; s. John and Thyra (Larson) C.; m. Elizabeth Ann May, May 28, 1960; children: John R. Jr. (dec.), James C., William H. AB, Princeton U., 1958; LLB, Columbia U., 1961. Bar: N.Y. 1961. Assoc. Simpson Thacher & Bartlett, N.Y.C., 1961-70, ptnr., 1970-95, of counsel, 1996—; gov. Am. Bus. Council, Singapore, 1982-85, vice chmn., 1984-85. Trustee Kessler Inst. for Rehab., West Orange, N.J., 1986-97, vice chmn., 1989-92, chmn., 1992-95; trustee Henry H. Kessler Found., 1992—, chmn., 1996-99; trustee Marcus Ward Home, Maplewood, N.J., 1996—; dir. Kessler Rehab. Corp., 1992—, Kessler Med. Rehab. Rsch. and Edn. Corp., 1997—; bd. dirs. New Alternatives for Children, Inc., 1996—. Mem. ABA, Assn. of Bar of City of N.Y., Montclair Golf Club, Montclair Racquet Club, Univ. Club, Singapore Cricket Club, Tanglin Club. Episcopalian. Avocations: squash, golf. Bankruptcy, General corporate, Finance. Office: Simpson Thacher & Bartlett 425 Lexington Ave Fl 14 New York NY 10017-3903

**CANNELLA, DEWEY V.,** lawyer, food company executive; b. Baton Rouge, La., Oct. 18, 1952; s. Samuel Victor and Mariann Cannella; m. Michaelyn V. Cannella, Aug. 28, 1982; children: Wendy, Sarah, Taneil, Jesse. JD, Rutgers Sch. Law, Camden, N.J., 1989. Bar: N.J., Pa. V.p. labor rels. Lakefern Food Corp., Edison, N.J., 1990—. Mem. ABA, N.J. State Bar Assn. Roman Catholic. Avocation: golf. Labor. Home: 19 Jeri Ann Dr Manahawkin NJ 08050-4255 Office: Wakern Food Corp 33 Northfield Ave Edison NJ 08837-3806

**CANNER, GARY F.,** mediator; b. Bklyn., Apr. 17, 1941; s. Sam and Vivian Canner; m. Joan B. Canner, Aug. 14, 1965; children: Glenn, Michelle C. Sobel. BA, Fla. State U., 1964; JD, U. Miami, 1967. Bar: Fla. 1968, U.S. Dist. Ct. (so. dist.) Fla. 1972; diplomate Fla. Acad. Profl. Mediators; cert. mediator Fla. 1990, U.S. Dist. Ct. U.S. V.I. 1993, 94, U.S. Dist. Ct. (so. dist.) Fla. 1993. Pres. Dade Mediation Assocs., Miami, 1989—; founder, exec. dir. Am. Mediation Inst., St. Thomas, U.S. V.I., 1992-97; pres. Mediation Solutions, Inc., St. Thomas, 1996-97; chair Supreme Ct. of Fla. Mediation Tng. Rev. Bd.; mcpl. ct. judge, 1972-75; spl. master Fla. 11th Jud. Cir., 1993-94; mediation trainer/lectr.; mediator Nat. Assn. Securities Dealers, 1997, panel of neutral hearing officers Nat. Arbitration and Mediation, Great Neck, N.Y., Miami Assn. Realtors, Fla. Divsn. of Land Sales and Condominiums, Resolution Trust Co., Fla. State Ins. Commr., Hurricane andrew Mediation Project; pro-bono instr. conflict resolution techniques Dade County Sch. Tchrs. and Students, 1994. Contbr. articles to profl. jours. Mem. Disput Avoidance and Resolution Task Force of the Constrn. Ind.; bd. dirs. Legal Svcs. of Greater Miami, chair grievance com. Named Outstanding Mediator's Mentor, The Resolution Report, 1996. Fellow Am. Coll. Civil Trial Mediators; mem. ABA, Soc. Profl. Dispute Resolution, Acad. Family Mediators, Am. Mediation Inst. (founder), Dade County Bar Assn., Fla. Assn. Profl. Family Mediators, Am. Arbitration Assn. (arbitrator). Office: Dade Mediation Assocs PO Box 830503 Miami FL 33283-0503

**CANNIZZARO, SAM F.,** lawyer; b. Chgo., Mar. 13, 1959; s. Sam J. and Frances L. (Bandanza) C.; m. Cindy Krueger, Feb. 14, 1987; children: Francesca Rose, Vito Joseph. BBA, Loyola U., Chgo., 1980, JD, 1984. Atty., ptnr. Cannizzaro and Assocs., PC, Chgo., 1984—. Pres. charity orgn. ChiSox Club, Inc., Chgo., 1988—; song leader/cantor Queen of All Saints and St. Mary of Woods parishes, Chgo., 1973—; sec. Sicilian-Am. Cultural Assn., Chgo., 1997—. Mem. Chgo. Bar Assn. (matrimonial law com.), Justinian Soc. Lawyers, Edgebrook/Sauganash C. of C. (pres. 1995-96, 97—, Bus. Leader of Yr. 1997). Roman Catholic. Avocations: music (singing), watching baseball, playing softball, golf, comic book collecting. Family and matrimonial, Personal injury, General civil litigation. Home: 6412 N Leroy Ave Chicago IL 60646-4240 Office: Cannizzaro & Assocs PC 39 S Lasalle St Ste 808 Chicago IL 60603-1603

**CANNON, DEAN HOLLINGSWORTH,** lawyer; b. Jasper, Ala., Mar. 28, 1957; d. Woodrow Wilson and Emma Dean Booker Cannon. BS summa cum laude, U. Ala., Tuscaloosa, 1978; JD cum laude, Georgetown U., 1981. Bar: D.C. 1981, U.S. Dist. Ct. D.C. 1982. Assoc. Beveridge & Diamond, P.C., Washington, 1981-89, dir., 1989—, mng. dir., 1996—. Environmental, General corporate. Office: Beveridge & Diamond PC 1350 I St NW Ste 700 Washington DC 20005-3311

**CANNON, GARY CURTIS,** lawyer, publishing executive; b. Ft. Worth, May 28, 1951; s. Curtis Warfield and Lucile (Curran) C. BA, U.S. Internat. U., 1974; MBA, Nat. U., 1984, JD, 1987. Bar: Calif. 1987, U.S. Dist. Ct. (so. dist.) Calif. 1987, U.S. Dist. Ct. (ctrl. dist.) Calif. 1993, U.S. Ct. Appeals (9th cir.) 1993, U.S. Ct. Internat. Trade 1993, U.S. Supreme Ct. 1993. Pvt. practice San Diego, 1987-89; v.p. Am. Pub., San Diego, 1988-89; pres. Emerald Bay Pub. Inc., San Diego, 1989—; sr. ptnr. Cannon, Potter & Scott, 1989-93, Cannon, Potter & Day, 1993-94; pvt. practice, 1994-95; gen. and corp. counsel Builders Staff Corp., 1995-97, F.Y. Partnership Inc., 1995-97, MUG Corp., 1995-97, Lexo Ins. Brokers Inc., 1995-97; chmn. bd. Fin. Svcs. and Investments Corp., 1994-96; v.p., gen. and corp. counsel Alpha Omega Corp., 1997—; gen. and corp. counsel F-Y Partnership, Inc., Loxo Ins. Brokers, Inc., Mug Corp., 1995-97; adj. prof. bus. law Nat. Univ., 1990—. Mem. ABA, Calif. Bar Assn., San Diego County Bar Assn., San Diego Trial Lawyers Assn. Republican. Presbyterian. General civil litigation, General corporate. Office: 9868 Erma Rd Apt 17 San Diego CA 92131-2416

**CANNON, GAYLE ELIZABETH,** lawyer; b. Dallas, May 12, 1941; d. Harry Feldman and Rosalie Bertha (Fischl) Lack; m. Joe D. Goldstrich, Dec. 23, 1962 (div. July 1977); m. Charles B. Cannon, Oct. 29, 1978; children: Josh, Marc, Jeremy. Student, U. Tex., 1959-60; BA, So. Meth. U., 1961, JD, 1965. Bar: Tex. 1965. Asst. gen. counsel Pizza Inn Inc., Dallas, 1977-88, v.p., sec., gen. counsel, 1986-88; spkr. franchising seminars ABA Forum on Franchising, State Bar of Tex., Dallas Bar, Southwestern Legal Found., Internat. Franchising Assn. Bd. dirs. Shakespeare Festival of Dallas, past pres.; bd. dirs. Children's Cancer Fund. Named in top 200 Dallas Lawyers Best Lawyers in Am., Woodwar/White, Inc., 1998. Mem. ABA, Internat. Bar Assn. Democrat. E-mail: cannong@tklaw.com. General corporate, Franchising.

**CANNON, HUGH,** lawyer; b. Albemarle, N.C., Oct. 11, 1931; s. Hubert Napoleon and Nettie (Harris) C.; m. Jo Anne Weisner, Mar. 21, 1998; AB, Davidson Coll., 1953; BA (Rhodes scholar) Oxford U., 1955, MA, 1960; LLB, Harvard U., 1958; children: John Stuart, Marshall, Martha Janet. Bar: N.C., 1958, D.C., 1978, S.C., 1979; mem. staff U. N.C. Inst. Govt., Chapel Hill, 1959; mem. firm Sanford, Phillips, McCoy & Weaver, Fayetteville, 1960; asst. to Gov. of N.C., Raleigh, 1961; dir. adminstrn. State of N.C., 1962-65, state budget officer, 1963; mem. and mng. ptnr. Sanford, Cannon, Adams & McCullough, Raleigh, 1965-79; pvt. practice, Charleston, S.C., 1979—; mem. Everett, Gaskins, Hancock and Stevens attys., Raleigh, 1990—; v.p. fin. Palmetto Ford, Inc., Charleston, 1979—. Parliamentarian NEA, 1965—; pres. Friends of Coll., Raleigh, 1963; alt. del. Democratic Nat. Conv., 1964; chief parliamentarian, 1976, 80, 84, 88, 92, 96; bd. govs. U. N.C., 1972-81; trustee Davidson Coll., 1966-74, N.C. Sch. Arts, 1963-72. Author: Cannon's Concise Guide to Rules of Order, 1992. Mem. Phi Beta Kappa, Omicron Delta Kappa, Phi Gamma Delta. Democrat. Episcopalian. General corporate, Administrative and regulatory. Home: PO Box 31820 Charleston SC 29417-1820 Office: 1625 Savannah Hwy Charleston SC 29407-2236

**CANNON, JOHN, III,** lawyer; b. Phila., Mar. 19, 1954; s. John and Edythe (Grebe) C. BA, Denison U., 1976; JD, Dickinson Sch. Law, 1983. Bar: Pa. 1983, Hawaii 1986, U.S. Dist. Ct. (ea. dist.) Pa. 1983, U.S. Ct. Appeals (3d cir.) 1985. Account exec. PRO Services, Inc., Flourtown, Pa., 1976-79; br. officer mgr. PRO Services, Inc., Pitts., 1979-80; law clk. Montgomery County Ct. of Common Pleas, Norristown, Pa., 1983-84; assoc. Rawle & Henderson, Phila., 1984-88; comml. litigation counsel CIGNA Corp., Phila., 1988-90; counsel CIGNA Internat. Fin. Svcs. Divsn., Phila., 1990-93; sr. counsel CIGNA Internat., Phila., 1993-95, v.p., sr. counsel, 1995-97, sr. v.p., chief counsel, 1997—; sr. v.p., chief counsel CIGNA Healthcare, Bloomfield, Conn., 1999—, Conn. Gen. Life Ins. Co., Bloomfield, Conn., 1999—; bd. dirs. CIGNA Stu Zychie, Warsaw, Poland, INA Himawari Life Ins. Co. Ltd., Tokyo; v.p. Life Ins. Co. N.Am., 1998—; trustee U.S.-China Legal Coop. Fund, Washington, 1998—. Comments editor Dickinson Internat. Law Ann., 1983. Mem. ABA, Pa. Bar Assn., Hawaii State Bar Assn., Kappa Sigma (pres. 1975-76), Gamma Xi (v.p., trustee 1982-86). Republican. Episcopalian. General civil litigation, Private international, Pension, profit-sharing, and employee benefits. Office: Cigna Cos PO Box 7716 2 Liberty Pl Philadelphia PA 19192

**CANNON, KIM DECKER,** lawyer; b. Salt Lake City, Oct. 15, 1948; s. Morris Nibley Cannon and Bette Jeanne (Decker) Sage; m. Jane B. Howard, June 10, 1972 (div. Sept. 1985); children: Sage, Meredith; m. Susan Margaret Clinch, Sept. 6, 1986; 1 child, Grace. AB, Dartmouth Coll., 1970; JD, U. Colo., 1974. Bar: Wyo. 1974, U.S. Dist. Ct. Wyo. 1974, U.S. Ct. Appeals (10th cir.) 1974. Ptnr. Burgess & Davis, Sheridan, Wyo., 1974-90, Burgess, Davis, Carmichael & Cannon, Sheridan and Cheyenne, Wyo., 1990-94, Davis & Cannon, Sheridan and Cheyenne, 1994—. Pres. Sheridan County Fulmer Pub. Librs., 1980-85, Wyo. Theater, Inc., Sheridan, 1986-91, Wyo. Outdoor Coun., Lander, 1987-91; chmn. Wyo. Environ. Quality Coun., 1992-96; active Commn. on Jud. Conduct and Ethics, 1997—; mem. Rhodes Scholarship selection com., Wyo., 1998—. Mem. Sheridan Bar Assn. (pres. 1982). Avocations: polo, training horses, fly fishing, skiing. General civil litigation, Environmental, Product liability. Home: PO Box 401 Big Horn WY 82833-0401 Office: Davis & Cannon 40 S Main St Sheridan WY 82801-4222

**CANNON, KIMBERLY ANN,** lawyer; b. Jacksonville, Fla., Jan. 22, 1969; d. L. Kinder III and Barbara S. C. BBA, Emory U., 1991; JD, Stetson U., 1994. Bar: Fla., 1995, U.S. Dist. Ct. (mid. dist.) Fla., 1995, U.S. Ct. Appeals (11th cir.), 1996, U.S. Dist. Ct. (so and no. dists.) Fla., 1997. Assoc. Corbin & Duvall, Jacksonville, 1995—. Mem. YESS (Jacksonville Symphony), Up & Cummers (Cummer Mus.); bd. dirs. All Sts. Early Learning & Cmty. Care Ctr., Jacksonville, 1996—, pres., 1999—; bd. dirs. Esprit de Corps, Jacksonville, 1996-98, sec., 1997. Named One of Top Forty Under 40, Jacksonville Bus. Jour., 1996. Mem. ABA (planning bd. labor and employment law com. 1996—), Fla. Bar (liaison for the labor and employment law sect. to the out of state practitioners divsn. 1999—), Jacksonville Women Lawyers Assn. (chmn. spl. events, 1997-98, pres. 1998-99), Jacksonville Bar Assn. (chmn. social com. 1996-98), First Coast Mfrs. Assn. (asst. chairperson cmty. rels. 1999—). Labor. Office: Corbin & Duvall PO Box 41566 Jacksonville FL 32203-1566

**CANNON, WILLIAM E., JR.,** lawyer; b. Albany, Ga., Nov. 22, 1952. AB, Emory U., 1974; JD, U. Ga., 1977. Ptnr. Cannon & Meyer Von Bremen, Albany, Ga.; city att. Leesburg, Ga., 1980—; county atty. Lee County, Ga., 1982-94; Bar: Ga. 1977. Contbr. articles to profl. jours. Fellow Ga. Bar Found.; mem. ABA, ATLA, Ga. State Bar Assn. (bd. govs. 1983-95, chmn. legal econs. sect. 1988-89, pres. 1998-99), Ga. Trial Lawyers Assn., Def. Rsch. Inst., Dougherty Cir. Assn. (pres. 1985-86), FBA (pres. Mid. Ga. chpt. 1993-94), Lawyers Club Atlanta. E-mail: wcannon@cmvb.com. General civil litigation, Product liability, Land use and zoning (including planning). Office: Cannon & Meyer Von Bremen LLP PO Box 70909 2417 Westgate Dr Albany GA 31708-0909*

**CANNON-RYAN, SUSAN KAYE,** lawyer; b. Clarksburg, W.Va., Feb. 27, 1950; d. Michael A. and Vivian (Boylan) Cannon; m. Robert M. Ryan, May 23, 1972; children: Nicholas P., Andrew S. BSJ, W.Va. U., 1972, JD, 1977. Bar: W.Va. 1977, U.S. Dist. Ct. (so. dist.) W.Va. 1977, U.S. Ct. Appeals (4th cir.) 1989, U.S. Dist. Ct. (no. dist.) W.Va. 1987. Law clk. to presiding judge of bankruptcy ct. State of W. Va., Charleston, 1977-78, hearing examiner tax dept., 1978-79; assoc. Denny & Caldwell, Charleston, 1979-81, ptnr., 1981-86; ptnr. Caldwell & Cannon-Ryan, Charleston, 1986-88, Caldwell, Cannon-Ryan & Riffee, Charleston, 1988—. Mem. Charleston Area Businesswomen. Democrat. Avocation: tennis. Bankruptcy, Contracts commercial, Consumer commercial. Home: 1612 Kirklee Rd Charleston WV 25314-2427 Office: Caldwell Cannon-Ryan & Riffee 3818 Maccorkle Ave SE Charleston WV 25304-1528

**CANO, KRISTIN MARIA,** lawyer; b. McKeesport, Pa., Oct. 27, 1951; d. John S. and Sally (Kavic) C. BS in Biochemistry, Pa. State U., 1973; MS in Forensic Sci., George Washington U., 1975; JD, Southwestern U., 1978; LLM in Securities Regulation, Georgetown U., 1984. Bar: Calif. 1978, U.S. Dist. Ct. (cen., no. and so. dists.) Calif. 1984, U.S. Dist. Ct. Ariz., 1988, U.S. Supreme Ct. 1988, U.S. Ct. Appeals (9th cir.) 1992. Assoc. Yusim, Cassidy, Stein & Hanger, Beverly Hills, Calif., 1979-81, Walker and Hartley, Newport Beach, Calif., 1981-82, Milberg, Weiss, Bershad, Spethrie & Lerach, San Diego, 1984; pvt. practice Newport Beach, 1984—. Bd. dirs., v.p. Sandcastle Community Assn., Corona del Mar, Calif., 1987-97; active Leadership Tomorrow Class of 1994. Mem. Orange County Bar Assn., Balboa Bay Club. Democrat. Roman Catholic. Avocations: ballet, ice skating, bicycling, photography, golf. General corporate, Securities, Mergers and acquisitions. Office: 1 Corporate Plaza Dr Ste 110 Newport Beach CA 92660-7924

**CANO, MARIO STEPHEN,** lawyer; b. Miami, Fla., Sept. 2, 1953; s. Mario Arturo Cano and Irene H. Moreno; m. Johanna Marie Van Rossum, Oct. 13, 1979. AA, Miami Dade Jr. Coll., 1973; BA, Fla. Internat. U., 1975; JD, U. Santa Clara, 1978. Bar: Fla. 1979, U.S. Dist. Ct. (so. dist.) Fla. 1979, U.S. Ct. Claims 1979, U.S. Tax Ct. 1979, U.S. Ct. Mil. Appeals 1979, U.S. Ct. Appeals (9th cir.) 1979, U.S. Dist. Ct. (no. and mid. dists.) Fla. 1980, U.S. Dist. Ct. (no. dist.) Calif. 1980, U.S. Ct. Appeals (3d cir.) 1980, U.S. Ct. Internat. Trade 1981, U.S. Ct. Appeals (11th cir.) 1981, U.S. Ct. Appeals (6th and 10th cirs.) 1983, U.S. Supreme Ct. 1983, Nebr. 1984, U.S. Dist. Ct. Nebr. 1984, U.S. Dist. Ct. (no. dist.) Okla. 1984, U.S. Dist. Ct. Hawaii 1984, U.S. Ct. Appeals (2d, 4th, 5th, 7th 8th and D.C. cirs.) 1984, N.Y. 1985, U.S. Dist. Ct. (no., we., ea. and so. dists.) N.Y. 1985, U.S. Ct. Appeals (1st cir.) 1987, U.S. Dist. Ct. (no. and so. dist.) Tex. 1988, U.S. Dist. Ct. (ea. dist.) Wis. 1988, U.S. Dist. Ct. (we. dist.) Pa. 1988, U.S. Dist. Ct. (no. dist.) Ill. 1991, Mass., 1998, U.S. Dist. Ct. Mass. 1999. Assoc. Orta and Assocs., Miami, 1979-80, Law Office of J. Ramirez, Coral Gables, Fla., 1980, Law Office of I.G. Lichter, Miami, 1980-82, Gelb & Spatz, Miami, 1982; pvt. practice Coral Gables, 1982—. Mem. Cuban Am. Bar Assn., Nat. Assn. Criminal Def. Lawyers. Democrat. Fax: (305) 448-2121. Criminal, Immigration, naturalization, and customs, Family and matrimonial. Office: Ste 600 2121 Ponce De Leon Blvd Coral Gables FL 33134-5222

**CANOFF, KAREN HUSTON,** lawyer; b. Medford, Oreg., May 15, 1954; d. Loyd Stanley and Donna Lou (Wall) Huston; m. Lawrence Scott Canoff, May 30, 1981; children: Vincent Jared, Alyssa Rae. BS, U. Oreg., 1977; JD cum laude, Lewis & Clark Coll., 1981. Bar: Oreg. 1981, U.S. Dist. Ct. Oreg. 1982, U.S. Ct. Appeals (9th cir.) 1985, Calif. 1985, U.S. Dist. Ct. (so. dist.) Calif. 1985, U.S. Dist. Ct. (cen. dist.) Calif. 1986, U.S. Ct. Appeals (fed. cir.) 1991. Fin. cons. Stretch & Sew, Inc., Eugene, Oreg., 1975-78; assoc. Margaretta Eakin P.C., Portland, Oreg., 1981-82, 83, Gary M. Bullock, Portland, 1982-83, Markowitz & Herbold, Portland, 1983-86; ptnr. Dorazio, Barnhorst & Bonar, San Diego, 1986-89, shareholder, 1989; ptnr. Hyde & Canoff, San Diego, 1990-96; divsn. counsel Nielsen Dillingham Builders, Inc., San Diego, 1996—; instr. People's Law Sch., Eugene, Oreg., 1978. Author: (with others) Legal Resource Guide, 1983; contbr. articles to profl. jours. Mem. Multnomah County Vol. Lawyers, Portland, Oreg., 1982-83, San Diego Vol. Lawyers Program, 1985-96, Vols. in Parole, San Diego, 1986-87, Charlotte Baker Soc., 1992-93; judge pro tem San Diego County mcpl. Ct., 1988—, San Diego Superior Ct, 1991—, 4th Dist. Ct. Appeals, 1995—; mem. nat. panel comml. arbitrators Am. Arbitration Assn., 1991-96; active Girl Scouts Am. Finalist San Diego Women Who Mean Bus. awards, 1995, 96, 97; recipient Am. Jurisprudence award, 1979. Mem. Calif. State Bar Assn. (bus. law, labor and employment, pub. law and real property sects.), San Diego County Bar Assn., (appellate ct. com. 1987—, editor It's the Law 1987, alternative dispute resolution sec. 1990-95, arbitration com. 1990-96, client rels. com. 1990-96, bus law, comml. law, constrn. law, corp. counsel and labor and employment law sects., editor Bar Briefs 1992, mem. ethics com. 1996), Lawyers Club San Diego (bd. dirs. 1988-91, editor Lawyers Club News 1986-88), Assn. Bus Trial Lawyers, Am. Corp. Counsel Assn., Associated Gen. Contractors (legal issues com.), Constrn. Defect Def. Action Coalition, Nat. Assn. Women Bus. Owners (bd. dirs. 1993-96, sec. 1993-94, chair govt. affairs 1995-96), Mortgage BAnkers Assn. Am. (legal issues com. 1987-89), Phi Beta Kappa. Contracts commercial, Construction, General corporate.

**CANTLON, JAMES DANIEL,** lawyer; b. Niagara Falls, N.Y., Apr. 19, 1962; s. James Daniel and Virginia Lee (Zelinsky) C. BA cum laude, SUNY, Buffalo, 1984; JD, Vt. Law Sch., 1990. Bar: Pa. 1990. Security asst. Sears Roebuck Inc., Niagara Falls, 1984-87; law clk. South Royalton (Vt.) Legal Clinic, 1988-89, student clinician, 1989; law clk. Peggy Reid & Assocs., Niagara Falls, 1990; sr. atty. advisor U.S. Small Bus. Adminstrn., Niagara Falls, 1990—. Gen. mem. The Am. Ireland Fund, Boston, 1992—; supporting mem. U.S. Cycling Team, 1990—. Mem. ABA (young lawyers div., litigation div., Pa. young lawyers div.), Am. Farmland Trust, Niagara Frontier Bicycle Club, Phi Alpha Delta. Avocations: rugby, running, cooking, ice hockey, cycling. Home: 25 Melbourne Pl Buffalo NY 14222-1455 Office: US Small Bus Adminstrn 360 Rainbow Blvd S Ste 3 Niagara Falls NY 14303-1122

**CANTOR, BERNARD JACK,** patent lawyer; b. N.Y.C., Aug. 18, 1927; s. Alexander J. and Tillie (Henzeloff) C.; m. Judith L. Levin, Mar. 25, 1951; children—Glenn H., Cliff A., James E., Ellen B., Mark E. B. Mech. Engring., Cornell, 1949; J.D., George Washington U., Washington, 1952. Bar: D.C. 1952, U.S. Patent Office 1952, Mich. 1953; registered patent atty. U.S., Can. Examiner U.S. Patent Office, Washington, 1949-52; pvt. practice Detroit, 1952-88; ptnr. firm Harness, Dickey & Pierce, Troy, Mich., 1988—; lectr. in field. Contbr. articles on patent law to profl. jours. Mem. exec. council, legal officer Detroit Area Boy Scouts Am., 1972—. Served with U.S. Army, 1944-46. Recipient Ellsworth award patent law George Washington U., 1952, Shofar award Boy Scouts Am., 1975, Silver Beaver award, 1975, Disting. Eagle award, 1985. Fellow Mich. State Bar Found.; mem. ABA, Mich. Bar Assn. (dir. econs. sect., arbitrator State of Mich. grievance com.), Detroit Bar Assn., Oakland Bar Assn., Mich. Patent Law Assn., Am. Arbitration Assn. (arbitrator), Cornell Engring. Soc., Am. Technion Soc. (bd. dirs. Detroit 1970—), Pi Tau Sigma, Phi Delta Phi, Beta Sigma Rho. Patent, Trademark and copyright, Intellectual property. Home: 5685 Forman Dr Bloomfield Hills MI 48301-1154 Office: Harness Dickey & Pierce 5445 Corporate Dr Troy MI 48098-2617

**CANTOR, DARREN R.,** lawyer; b. Denver, Feb. 23, 1961; s. Mel and Elaine Sue (Pozner) C.; m. Cecelia Alyson Fleischner, Aug. 5, 1994. BS in Computer Info. Systems, U. Colo., 1983, JD, 1986. Bar: Colo. 1986, U.S. Dist. Ct. Colo. 1987. Investigator, atty. Pozner, Hutt & Kaplan, Denver, 1986, 87; assoc. Canges & Iwashko, Denver, 1986-87; atty. Colo. State Pub. Defender, Denver, 1987-95; atty., pres. Darren R. Cantor, P.C., Denver, 1995—. Mem. Colo. Criminal Def. Bar, Nat. Assn. Criminal Def. Lawyers. Democrat. Jewish. Avocations: skiing, dogs, exercise. Criminal. Office: Darren R Cantor PC 1675 Larimer St Ste 735 Denver CO 80202-1599

**CANTOR, DONALD JEROME,** lawyer; b. Stamford, Conn., May 11, 1931; s. Albert Adelbert and Lillian (Schoenfield) C.; m. Lois Levin (div.); children: Rachel, Elizabeth, Michael; m. Patricia Kirby, June 19, 1977; children: Jonathan, Stephanie. AB, Harvard Coll., 1953, LLB, 1959. Bar: Conn. 1959. Lawyer Gilman & Marks, Hartford, Conn., 1959-60, Levin & Hultgren, Hartford, 1960-64; ptnr. Levin, Hultgren & Cantor, Hartford, 1964-71, Hyman & Cantor, Hartford, 1971-76, Hyman, Cantor & Seichter, Hartford, 1976-85, Hyman, Cantor, Seichter & Klau, Hartford, 1985-92, Hyman, Cantor & Klau, Hartford, 1992—; corporator Mt. Sinai Hosp., Hartford; lectr. U. Conn. Law Sch., Hartford; founder, first pres. Conn. League Abortion Law Reform; co-founder, counsel Gender Identity Clin. Author: Escape From Marriage, 1971; co-author: Child Custody, 1989; contbr. articles to Am. Jurisprudence Trials, Atlantic Monthly, The Humanist. Founder, 1st pres. Conn. League for Abortion Law Reform; cofounder., counsel Gender Identity Clinic. Mem. Conn. Bar Assn., Hartford County Bar Assn. (chmn. family rels. sect. 1972-73), Tolland County Bar

Assn. Jewish. Avocations: crossword puzzles, travel, reading, softball, children. Family and matrimonial. Home: 49 High Farms Rd West Hartford CT 06107-1544 Office: Hyman Cantor & Klau 21 Oak St Hartford CT 06106-8003

**CANTOR, HERBERT I.,** lawyer; b. N.Y.C., Dec. 10, 1935; s. David and Ethel C.; m. Lynn Hardie, July 8, 1972; children: David, Susan. BA in Chemistry, NYU, 1965; JD, Cath. U. Am., 1970. Bar: Md. 1970, U.S. Dist. Ct. Md. 1970, D.C. 1971, U.S. Dist. Ct. D.C. 1971, U.S. Ct. Appeals (5th, D.C. and fed. cirs.) 1971, U.S. Supreme Ct. 1974, U.S. Ct. Appeals (4th cir.) 1981, U.S. Ct. Claims 1987. Patent examiner U.S. Patent Office, Washington, 1965-67; agt. Jacobi, Davidson & Jacobi, Washington, 1967-68; pvt. practice Washington, 1968-70; with Kraft, Cantor & Singer, Cantor & Lessler, Washington, 1971-85; ptnr. Cantor & Lessler, Washington, 1982-85, Wegner, Cantor, Mueller & Player, Washington, 1985-94; Evenson, McKeown, Edwards & Lenahan, Washington, 1994—; adj. prof. Law Ctr. Georgetown Univ., Washington, 1988-89. Assoc. editor Cath. U. Law Rev., 1969-70. Mem. ABA, Am. Chem. Soc., Fedn. Internat. des Conseils Propriete Industrielle, Am. Intellectual Property Assn. Patent, Trademark and copyright, Intellectual property. Office: Evenson McKeown Edwards & Lenahan 1200 G St NW Ste 700 Washington DC 20005-3814

**CANTOR, IRVIN VICTOR,** lawyer; b. Richmond, Va., June 9, 1953; s. Leo Joseph and Mary Frances (Cohen) C. BS, U. Va., 1975, JD, 1978. Bar: Va. 1978. Law clk. Va. Supreme Ct., Richmond, 1978-79; ptnr. Rilee, Cantor, Arkema, Edmonds (name changed to Cantor, Arkema & Edmonds), Richmond, 1979—; ptnr. World Class, Inc., Richmond, 1983—. Bd. dirs. Richmond Tennis Patrons, Tennis Found. Richmond, Hist. Richmond Found. Zeta Beta Tau Nat. Found. scholar, 1973. Mem. Nat. Head Injury Found., Va. Head Injury Found., Va. Bar Assn., Richmond Bar Assn., Va. Trial Lawyers Assn. (bd. govs. 1992—, legis. chmn. 1993—, v.p. 1997-99), Richmond Trial Lawyers, Am. Bd. Trial Advs., U.S. Tennis Assn., U. Va. Alumni Assn., Westwood Racquet Club. Personal injury, Product liability. Office: Cantor Arkema & Edmonds PO Box 561 Richmond VA 23218-0561

**CANTOR, JAMES ELLIOT,** lawyer; b. Detroit, Mar. 14, 1958; s. Bernard J. and Judith (Levin) C.; m. Susan Elaine Finger, Dec. 26, 1983; children: Tilly Samantha, Brian Alexander. BS in Natural Resources, U. Mich., 1980; JD, Cornell U., 1986. Bar: Alaska 1986. Assoc. Perkins Coie, Anchorage, 1986-91; asst. atty. gen. environ. sect. Alaska, Atty. Gen.'s Office, Anchorage, 1991-98, supervising atty. transp. sect., 1998—. Mem. Eagle River (Alaska) Pk. and Recreation Bd. of Suprs., 1989-95, chmn., 1991-92; dir. Anchorage (Alaska) Trails and Greenways Coalition, 1994-97; commissioner Mcpl. of Anchorage, The Municipality of Anchorage Heritage Land Bank Adv. Commn., 1999—. Mem. Anchorage Inn of Ct. Avocations: dog sled racing. Office: Atty Gen Office 1031 W 4th Ave Ste 200 Anchorage AK 99501-5903

**CANTOR, SAMUEL C.,** lawyer, company executive; b. Phila., Mar. 11, 1919; s. Joseph and Miryl (Ginzberg) C.; m. Dorothy Van Brink, Apr. 9, 1943; children: Judith Ann Stone, Barbara Ann Palm. BSS, CCNY, 1940; JD, Columbia, 1943. Bar: N.Y. 1943, U.S. Dist. Ct. (so. and ea. dists.) N.Y. 1951, U.S. Supreme Ct 1969, D.C. 1971. Asst. dist. atty. N.Y.C., 1943-48; legislative counsel N.Y. State Senate; counsel N.Y.C. Affairs Com. N.Y. State Senate, 1949-59; mem. firm Newcomb, Woolsey & Cantor, Newcomb & Cantor, N.Y.C., 1951-59; 1st dep. supt. ins. State of N.Y., 1959-64, acting supt. ins., 1963-64; 2d v.p., gen. solicitor Mut. Life Ins. Co. N.Y., 1964-66, v.p., gen. counsel, 1967-72, sr. v.p., gen. counsel, 1973-74, sr. v.p. law and external affairs, 1974-75, sr. v.p. law and corp. affairs, 1975-78, exec. v.p. law and corp. affairs, 1978-84; counsel Rogers & Wells, 1984-89; bd. dir. Mut. Life Ins. Co N.Y., Mony Reins. Corp., Monyco, Inc., Key Resources, Inc., Mony Advisors, Inc.; chmn. exec. com. N.Y. Life Ins. Guaranty Corp., 1974-84; mem. spl. com. on ins. holding holding cos. N.Y. Supt. Ins., 1967, N.Y. State select com. pub. employee pensions, 1973. Contbr. articles to Golf and other mags., legal and ins. jours. Fellow Am. Bar Found.; mem. Ins. Fedn. N.Y. (pres. 1967-68), Am. Bar Assn., N.Y. State Bar Assn., Am. Life Conv. (v.p. N.Y. State 1965-70), Am. Coun. Life Ins. (chmn. legal sect. 1977, chmn. legis. com. 1977-78, N.Y. State v.p. 1977-84), Health Ins. Assn. Am. (chmn. govt. rels. com. 1975, chmn. health care com. N.Y. State 1974-80), Assn. Life Ins. Counsel (dir.), Am. Judicature Soc., Bar Assn. City N.Y., N.Y. Law Inst., Nat. Attys. Assn., N.Y. State Dist. Attys. Assn., Union Internationale des Avocats, Columbia U. Law Sch. Alumni Assn. (dir.). Clubs: Mason. (N.Y.C.), University (N.Y.C.); Met., Univ. (Washington); Fort Orange (Albany, N.Y.); Sawgrass Country, Marsh Landing, Ponte Vedra (Fla.); La Costa Country (Carlsbad, Calif.); Confrérie des Chevaliers du Tastevin; Fairview Country (Greenwich, Conn.); Royal Dornoch Golf (Scotland), Am. Seniors Golf Assn., U.S. Golf Assn. (committeeman). Administrative and regulatory, Insurance, Legislative. Home: 10 Audubon Ln Greenwich CT 06831-2501 also: 22 Little Bay Harbor Dr Ponte Vedra Beach FL 32082-3707

**CANTRELL, LUTHER E., JR.,** lawyer; b. Nashville, Aug. 6, 1933; s. Luther E. and Hattie Mai (Cassetty) C.; m. Barbara Ann Richardson, Oct. 4, 1960; children: Luther III, Timothy Richard, Christopher Thomas. BS in fin. and econs., U. Tenn., 1960; LLD, Nashville Sch. Law, 1965. Bar: Tenn., U.S. Dist. Ct. (mid. dist.) Tenn., U.S. Ct. Appeals (6th cir.), U.S. Supreme Ct. Assoc. Smith, Ortale & Smith, Nashville, 1965-70, Taylor, Schlater & Smith, Nashville, 1970-72; ptnr. Smith, Smith & Cantrell, Nashville, 1972-73, Smith, Davies, Smith & Cantrell, Nashville, 1973-84, Davies, Cantrell, Humphreys & McCoy, Nashville, 1984-96; pvt. practice Nashville, 1997—; mem. staff Nashville Sch. of Law, 1966—. Cpl. U.S. Army, 1954-55. Named Disting. Alumni Nashville Sch. Law, 1996. Mem. Tenn. Def. Lawyers Assn., Def. Rsch. Inst., Atlanta Claims Assn., Nashville Bar Assn., Tenn. Bar Assn., U.S. Supreme Ct Historical Soc., U. Tenn. Alumni Assn., Nashville Sch. Law Alumni Assn. (pres. 1971), Shriners, Am. Legion, Masons, Scottish Rite Masons, Optimist Club (pres. 1969, lt. gov. 1970-71, Honor Club 1969), Crime Stoppers Inc. (bd. dirs.). Avocations: music, photography, bowling, reading. General civil litigation, General practice, Personal injury. Home: 2813 Glenoaks Dr Nashville TN 37214-1605 Office: Law Offices Luther E Cantrell Jr 3d Fl Court Square Bldg 300 James Robertson Pkwy Nashville TN 37201-1107

**CANTU, TINA-MARIE,** lawyer; b. Bradford, Pa., Jan. 2, 1956; d. James John and Virginia Ann (Sopko) Pascarella. AAS in Nursing, Jamestown (N.Y.) Community, 1977; BS in Mgmt., Lesley Coll., 1989; MBA, Northeastern U., 1991; JD, Suffolk U. Law Sch., 1997. Bar: Mass. 1997; RN. Unit clk. Bradford (Pa.) Hosp., 1971-72, nurses aide, 1972-73, operating room tech., 1973-77, staff nurse, 1977-78; staff nurse, instr. Emerson Hosp., Concord, Mass., 1978-83, nurse mgr., 1983-94; dir. regulatory and legal affairs RKS Health Ventures Corp., Cambridge, Mass., 1994-97; ptnr. Harbor Law Group, 1997—; chmn. nursing exec. group, Emerson Hosp., 1983-94; ptnr. Harbor Law Group. Mem. ABA, Am. Nurses Assn., Assn. Operating Room Nurses, Mass. Orgn. Nurse Execs., Am. Coll. Sports Medicine, Mass. Middle Mgrs. Assn., Mass. Bar Assn., Nat. Health Lawyer's Assn. Roman Catholic. Avocations: piano, reading. Labor, Sports, Health. Office: 48 Maple Ave Shrewsbury MA 01545-2922

**CANUP, JAMES W.C.,** lawyer, partner; b. Washington; s. William C. and Mireille R. Canup; m. Winnie Perilla, May 30, 1987; children: Elise, William, Ann Charlotte. BA, U. Va., 1980; JD, Washington & Lee U., 1984; LLM, Georgetown U., 1992. Bar: Va. 1984, Md. 1987, D.C. 1987. Sr. atty.-advisor Chief Counsel, IRS, Washington, 1987-93; assoc. Brown & Wood LLP, Washington, 1993-95; ptnr. McGuire, Woods, Battle & Boothe, LLP, Richmond, Va., 1996—. Mem. Nat. Assn. of Real Estate Investment Trusts (govt. rels. com. 1994—), Mortgage-Backed Securities Industry Group. Corporate taxation, Securities, Taxation, general. Office: McGuire Woods Battle & Boothe LLP One James Ctr 901 E Cary St Richmond VA 23219-4057

**CAPANNA, PALOMA A.,** lawyer; b. Newark, N.J., Sept. 26, 1966; d. Donald and Suzanne Genevieve (Mooney) Maddison; m. Nicholas David Capanna, Oct. 26, 1991. BA, Wheaton Coll., 1988; JD, SUNY, Buffalo, 1991. Bar: N.Y., 1992. Ptnr. Nicholas D. Capanna & Paloma A. Capanna, Fairport, N.Y., 1992—. Editor: Women and The Law, 1994; contbg. author: Women and The Law, 1994; contbr. articles to profl. jours. Mem. Monroe County Bar Assn., N.Y. Bar Assn., Phi Beta Kappa. Family and matrimonial, Personal injury, Professional liability. Office: Nicholas D Capanna & Paloma A Capanna 1314 Moseley Rd PO Box 357 Fairport NY 14450-0357

**CAPECELATRO, MARK JOHN,** lawyer; b. New Haven, June 2, 1948; s. Ralph Ettore and Elaine (Scialla) C.; m. Jane Beals, June 19, 1971; children: Christopher Beals, Kate Rowley, Jonathan Mark. BA, Colgate U., 1970; JD, U. Conn., 1973. Bar: Conn. 1973. Assoc. Ells, Quinlan, Eddy & Robinson, Canaan, Conn., 1973-77; ptnr. Ells, Quinlan & Robinson, Canaan, 1977-90, Capecelatro & Nelligan, Canaan, 1991—; bd. advisors Canaan Nat. Bank, 1982—; mortgage counsel People's Bank, Canaan and Hartford, Conn., 1983—; trustee Sharon (Conn.) Hosp., 1984-91, vice chmn., 1990-91, chmn. exec. com., 1990-91; trustee Salisbury Congl. Ch., 1990-98, vice chmn., 1990-93, chmn., 1993-98, fin. com., 1998—. Bd. dirs. Housatonic Homemaker Health Aide, West Cornwall, Conn., 1977-80, Housatonic Day Care Ctr., Inc., Lakeville, Conn., 1981-90, Salisbury Pub. Health Nursing, Lakeville, 1983-85, Salisbury Vol. Ambulance Svcs., Salisbury Winter Sports Assn., 1983-87, Salisbury (Conn.) Congl. Ch., Salisbury Vol. Ambulance Assn., Inc., 1997—; mem. adv. com. Parkside Med. Svcs. Corp., 1988-93. Mem. ABA, Conn. Bar Assn., Litchfield County Bar Assn., Assn. Trial Lawyers Am., Conn. Assn. Trial Lawyers, Nat. Assn. Criminal Def. Lawyers. Republican. Avocations: guitar, fishing, skiing, canoeing, kayaking. General practice, Probate, Real property. Home: 196 Belgo Rd Lakeville CT 06039-1003 Office: Capecelatro & Nelligan 117 Main St Canaan CT 06018-2463

**CAPIZZI, MICHAEL ROBERT,** prosecutor; b. Detroit, Oct. 19, 1939; s. I.A. and Adelaide E. (Jennelle) C.; m. Sandra Jo Jones, June 22, 1963; children: Cori Anne, Pamela Jo. BS in Bus. Adminstrn., Ea. Mich. U., 1961; JD, U. Mich., 1964. Bar: Calif. 1965, U.S. Dist. Ct. (so. dist.) Calif. 1965, U.S. Ct. Appeals (9th cir.) 1970, U.S. Supreme Ct. 1971. Dep. dist. atty. Orange County, Calif., 1965-68; head writs, appeals and spl. assignments sect., 1968-71, asst. dist. atty., dir. spl. ops., 1971-86; legal counsel, mem. exec. bd. Interstate Organized Crime Index, 1971-79; legal counsel, mem. exec. bd. Law Enforcement Intelligence Unit, 1971-95, chief asst. dist. atty., 1986-90, dist. atty., 1990-99; instr. criminal justice Santa Ana Coll., 1967-76, Calif. State U., 1967-86. Commr. City Planning Commn., Fountain Valley, Calif., 1971-80, vice chmn. 1972-73, chmn. 1973-75, 79-80; candidate for Rep. nomination Calif. Atty. Gen., 1998. Fellow Am. Coll. Trial Lawyers; mem. Nat. Dist. Attys. Assn. (bd. dirs. 1995-96, v.p. 1996-99), Calif. Dist. Attys. Assn. (outstanding prosecutor award 1980, v.p. 1995, pres. 1996), Calif. Bar Assn., Orange County Bar Assn. (chmn. cts. com. 1977, chmn. coll. of trial advocacy com. 1978-81, bd. dirs. 1977-81, sec.-treas. 1982, pres. 1984). Office: PO Box 1938 Santa Ana CA 92702-1938

**CAPLAN, ALLEN,** lawyer. AB cum laude, U. Calif., L.A., 1971; JD, Loyola U., L.A., 1974. Bar: Calif. 1974, U.S. Dist. Ct. (cen. dist.) Calif. 1974; U.S. Ct. Appeals (9th cir.) 1976. Apprentice sculptor, sculpture dept. UCLA, 1970; intern U.S. Atty., L.A., 1973, Fed. Trade Commn., L.A., 1973-74; assoc. Gantman & Gantman, Beverly Hills, Calif., 1974-75; pvt. practice L.A., Century City, and Carmel, Calif., 1975-80, 82—; dept. dist. atty. Fresno, Calif., 1980-82; pvt. practice San Diego, L.A., 1982—; Nominated bd. govs. Calif. State Bar, 1977; forensic photographer, 1997—. Photographer (numerous awards); asst. Loyola Law Rev., 1972. Named William Stout scholar U. Calif., L.A., 1969, Calif. State scholar State of Calif., L.A., 1969. Mem. San Diego Bar Assn., L.A. Bar Assn., Fresno County Bar Assn., Assn. of Trial Lawyers of Am., L.A. Trial Lawyers Assn., San Diego Juv. Justice Bar Assn. Juvenile, General corporate, Criminal. Office: 8677 Villa La Jolla Dr Ste 118 La Jolla CA 92037-2354

**CAPLAN, CORINA RUXANDRA,** lawyer; b. Bucharest, Romania, July 29, 1971; came to U.S., 1978; d. Corneliu Dumitru and Maria Teodora Mateescu; m. Bryan Douglas Caplan, June 18, 1994. BA, U. Calif., Berkeley, 1993; JD, Rutgers U., Newark, 1996. Bar: N.J. 1996, N.Y. 1997, D.C. 1998. Assoc. Thacher Proffitt & Wood, N.Y.C., 1996-97, Arter & Hadden LLP, Washington, 1997. Articles editor Rutgers Law Rev. Mem. Order of Coif. Avocation: bicycling. Finance, General corporate. Office: Arter & Hadden LLP 1801 K St NW Washington DC 20006-1301

**CAPLIN, MORTIMER MAXWELL,** lawyer, educator; b. N.Y.C., July 11, 1916; s. Daniel and Lillian (Epstein) C.; m. Ruth Sacks, Oct. 18, 1942; children: Lee Evan, Michael Andrew, Jeremy Owen, Catherine Jean. BS, U. Va., 1937, LLB, 1940; JSD, NYU, 1953; LLD (hon.), St. Michael's Coll., 1964. Bar: Va. 1941, N.Y. 1942, D.C. 1964. Law clk. to Hon. Armistead M. Dobie U.S. Ct. Appeals (4th cir.), Richmond, 1940-41; assoc. Paul, Weiss, Rifkind, Wharton & Garrison, N.Y.C., 1941-42, 45-50; prof. law U. Va., Charlottesville, 1950-61, vis. prof. law, 1965-87; prof. emeritus, 1988—; ptnr. Perkins, Battle & Minor, Charlottesville, 1952-61; U.S. commr. IRS, Washington, 1961-64; sr. ptnr. Caplin & Drysdale, Washington, 1964—; mem. Pres.'s Task Force on Taxation, 1960; bd. dirs. Danaher Corp., Washington, Fairchild Corp., Dulles, Va., Presdl. Realty Corp., White Plains, N.Y.; mem. pub. rev. bd. Arthur Andersen & Co., Chgo., 1980-88; reorgn. trustee Webb & Knapp, Inc., 1965-72. Author: Proxies, Annual Meetings and Corporate Democracy, 1953, Doing Business in Other States, 1959; editor-in-chief Va. Law Rev., 1939-40; contbr. numerous articles on tax and corp. matters to profl. jours. Past chmn. bd. dirs. Nat. Civic Svc. League, Am. Coun. on Internat. Sports; past chmn. nat citizens adv. com. Assn. Am. Med. Colls.; trustee U. Va. Law Sch. Found., Wolf Trap Found. Performing Arts, Shakespeare Theatre, Washington, Peace Through Law Found., Washington; bd. overseers U. V.I.; chmn. adv. bd. Hospitality and Info. Svc., Washington; chmn. Coun. for Arts, U. Va.; past pres. Atlantic Coast Conf.; emeritus trustee George Washington U.; mem. bd. visitors U. Va., 1992-97; pres., bd. dirs. Indigent Civil Litigation Fund. Cited as mem. of initial landing force Normandy Invasion, USN; recipient Va. State Bar and Va. Soc. CPAs award, 1960, Achievement award Tax Soc. of NYU, 1962, Judge Learned Hand Human Rels. award Am. Jewish Com., 1963, 93, Alexander Hamilton award U.S. Treasury Dept., 1964, Disting. Svc. award Tax Execs. Inst., 1964. Fellow Am. Bar Found., Am. Tax Policy Inst., Am. Coll. Tax Counsel; mem. ABA (ho. of dels. 1980-92, mem. fed. jud. com. 1993-96, ALI-ABA com. continuing profl. edn., chair DC Fellows), Am. Law Inst. (life), N.Y. State Bar Assn., Va. Bar Assn., D.C. Bar Assn., D.C. Bar Found. (adv. com.), Univ. Club (N.Y.C., Washington), Fed. City Club (bd. govs.), Colonnade Club (Charlottesville), Order of Coif, Phi Beta Kappa, Phi Beta Kappa Assocs., Omicron Delta Kappa. Democrat. Jewish. Avocations: swimming, tennis, hiking. Taxation, general, Corporate taxation, General corporate. Home: 5610 Wisconsin Ave Apt 18E Chevy Chase MD 20815-4415 Office: One Thomas Circle NW Washington DC 20005-5802

**CAPONE, LUCIEN, III,** lawyer; b. Balt., June 10, 1951; s. Lucien Jr. and Charlotte (Lammers) C.; m. Julia Smith, Oct. 17, 1950; children: William Justice, Margaret Grey. BA, N.C. State U., 1973; JD, Wake Forest U., 1977. Bar: N.C., D.C., U.S. Ct. Appeals (4th cir.), U.S. Ct. Mil. Appeals, U.S. Supreme Ct. Asst. atty. gen. N.C. Dept. Justice, Raleigh, 1977-86, spl. dep. atty. gen., 1986-91; univ. counsel U. N.C. Greensboro, 1991—; bd. dirs. CACREP, Alexandria, Va. Comdr. JAGC, USN, 1982—. Mem. Nat. Assn. Coll. and Univ. Attys., N.C. Bar Assn. Avocation: certified flight instructor. Office: U NC 1000 Spring Garden St Greensboro NC 27412-0001

**CAPORALE, D. NICK,** lawyer; b. Omaha, Sept. 13, 1928; s. Michele and Lucia Caporale; m. Margaret Nilson, Aug. 5, 1950; children: Laura Diane Stevenson, Leland Alan. B.A., U. Nebr.-Omaha, 1949, M.Sc., 1954; J.D. with distinction, U. Nebr.-Lincoln, 1957. Bar: Nebr. 1957, U.S. Dist. Ct. Nebr. 1957, U.S. Ct. Appeals 8th cir. 1958, U.S. Supreme Ct. 1970. Judge Nebr. Dist. Ct., Omaha, 1979-81, Nebr. Supreme Ct., Lincoln, 1982-98; of counsel Baird Holm Law Firm, 1998—; lectr. U. Nebr., Lincoln, 1982-84. Pres. Omaha Community Playhouse, 1976. Served to 1st lt. U.S. Army, 1952-54, Korea. Decorated Bronze Star; recipient Alumni Achievement U. Nebr.-Omaha, 1972. Fellow Am. Coll. Trial Lawyers, Internat. Soc. Barristers; mem. Order of Coif. Office: Baird Holm Law Firm 1500 Woodmen Tower Omaha NE 68102

**CAPOUANO, ALBERT D.,** lawyer; b. Montgomery, Ala., 1945. BS, U. Ala., 1967, JD, 1970; LLM in Taxation, NYU, 1971. Bar: Ala. 1970, Fla. 1973. Mem. Dean, Mead, Egerton, Bloodworth, Capouano & Bozarth P.A., Orlando, Fla. Mem. Fla. Bar (computer law sect. 1984-87), Ala. State Bar. Taxation, general, Mergers and acquisitions, General corporate. Office: Dean Mead Egerton Bloodworth Capouano & Bozarth 800 N Magnolia Ave # 1500 PO Box 2346 Orlando FL 32802-2346

**CAPOZZOLA, THERESA A.,** lawyer; b. Queens, N.Y., Oct. 9, 1963; d. John James and Anna Katherine (Levay) Gregg; m. Peter M. Capozzola, Sept. 8, 1991; children: John G., Christopher M. BS, SUNY, Oneonta, 1985; JD, Union U., 1988. Assoc. Devine, Rutnik, McCarthy, Albany, N.Y., 1988-90, Ferrara Jones, Saratoga, N.Y., 1990-92; pvt. practice Saratoga Springs, N.Y., 1992—. Mem. Saratoga Springs (N.Y.) Zoning Bd. Appeals, 1992-96. Mem. Saratoga County Bar Assn. (exec. com. 1994-96). Avocations: aerobics, biking, jogging, hiking. Probate, Real property, General corporate. Office: 57 Gilbert Rd Saratoga Springs NY 12866-9704

**CAPP, DAVID A.,** prosecutor. Atty. U.S. Atty.'s Office, Dyer, 1985—, criminal divsn. chief, 1988-91, 1st asst. atty., 1991—, interim dir., 1993, 99—. Office: US Attys Office 1001 Main St Ste A Dyer IN 46311-1234

**CAPPELLO, A. BARRY,** lawyer; b. Bklyn., Feb. 21, 1942; s. Gus and Ann (Klukoff) C.; children: Eric Rheinschild, Blythe, Brent. AB, UCLA, 1962, JD, 1965. Bar: Calif. 1966, U.S. Dist. Ct. (cen. dist.) Calif. 1966, U.S. Ct. Appeals (9th cir.) 1974, U.S. Dist. Ct. (no. dist.) Calif. 1981, U.S. Ct. Appeals (7th cir.) 1985, U.S. Supreme Ct. 1985, U.S. Dist. Ct. (ea. dist.) Calif. 1986, U.S. Ct. Appeals (10th cir.) 1986. Dep. atty. gen. State of Calif., L.A., 1965-68; chief trial dep. Santa Barbara County, 1968-70, asst. dist. atty., 1970-71; city atty. Santa Barbara, 1971-77; pvt. practice, mng. ptnr., 1977-85; ptnr. Cappello & McCann, Santa Barbara, 1977—; lectr. complex bus. litigation, lender liability, adv. trial techniques. Author: Lender Liability, 2d edit., 1994, Lender Liability: A Practical Guide, 1987, AmJur Model Trials and Proofs of Facts; contbr. more than 100 articles to profl. legal and bus. jours. Mem. ABA, ATLA, Consumer Attys. Calif. Avocation: triathalons. Banking, General civil litigation, Consumer commercial. Office: Cappello & McCann 831 State St Santa Barbara CA 93101-3227

**CAPPS, JAMES LEIGH, II,** lawyer, reserve military career officer; b. Brunswick, Ga., Dec. 17, 1956; s. Thomas Edwin Sr. and Betty Marie (Greenhill) C.; m. Nancy Ann Fisher, June 25, 1978; children: Bonnie Lynn, James Leigh III. AA, Seminole C.C., Sanford, Fla., 1976; BA in History, U. Cen. Fla., 1981; JD, U. Fla., 1987. Bar: Fla. 1987, U.S. Ct. Mil. Appeals 1988, Colo. 1990, U.S. Ct. Appeals (4th cir.) 1997. Enlisted USAF, 1976, advanced through grades to maj., 1995; med. svc. specialist USAF, MacDill AFB, Fla., 1977-79; air weapons dir. USAF, Germany, 1982-84; claims officer USAF, Homestead AFB, Fla., 1987-88, area def. counsel, 1988-90; dep. staff judge adv. USAF, Onizuka AFB, Calif., 1990-93; atty. office of state atty. 18th Jud. Ct., Sanford, Fla., 1994; assoc. Dominick Salfi Law Offices, Maitland, Fla., 1993-94, of counsel, 1994—; pvt. practice, 1996—; sr. res. judge adv. Moody AFB, Ga., 1996-99; civilian contract officer for Naval Air Warfare Ctr. USN, Orlando, Fla., 1999—; assigned to 16th Air Force Hdqs., Aviano AFB, Italy, Operation Joint Endeavor, 1996; atty. Vietnam Vets. Ctrl. Fla., 1998—; implementation force Dayton Peace Accords UN. Maj. USAFR, 1993—. Recipient McCarthy award for legal svc. Air Combat Command, 1995. Mem. DAV, VFW, Fla. Sheriff's Assn. (hon.). Democrat.

**CAPPY, RALPH JOSEPH,** state supreme court justice; b. Pitts., Aug. 25, 1943; s. Joseph R. and Catherine (Miljus) C.; m. Janet Fry, Apr. 19, 1985; 1 child, Erik. BS in Psychology, U. Pitts., 1965, JD, 1968. Bar: Pa. 1968, U.S. Dist. Ct. (we. dist.) Pa. 1968, U.S. Supreme Ct. 1975. Law clk. to pres. judge Ct. Common Pleas of Allegheny County, Pitts., 1968-70, apptd. judge, 1978-79, assigned family div., 1978-79, elected judge, 1979-85; judge criminal div. Ct. Common Pleas of Allegheny County, Pitts., 1980-85; judge civil div. Allegheny County Ct. Common Pleas of Allegheny County, Pitts., 1985-86, former presiding adminstrv. judge, from 1986; pvt. practice Pitts., 1968-78; now justice Supreme Ct. Pa.; lectr. constl. law U. Pitts., 1970-72; instr. criminal law and trial tactics City of Pitts. Police Acad., Allegheny County Police Acad., 1970-74; trial defender, 1st asst. homicide atty. Office Pub. Defender Allegheny County, Pa., 1970-75; pub. defender Allegheny County, Pa., 1975-78. Mem. Pitts. Health and Welfare Planning Agy., 1984—; mem. jud. ethics com. Pa. Law Jour., 1980-82; trustee U. Pitts., 1992—, bd. visitors, 1992—. Fellow Am. Bar Found.; mem. ABA, Pa. Bar Assn., Allegheny Bar Assn., Pa. Conf. State Trial Judges (legis. and planning com. 1978-83, legis. com., zone rep. 1984—, chmn. edn. com. 1985-88), Pa. Coll. Judiciary (lectr. 1983—, treas. 1987—, sec. 1988—), NACCP (life), Pitts. Athletic Assn. Office: Pa Supreme Ct 1 Oxford Ct Ste 3130 Pittsburgh PA 15219-1407*

**CAPRIOTTI, FRANCO JOHN, III,** lawyer, educator; b. Mpls., Jan. 14, 1950; s. Frank John Jr. and Beatrice Joy (Ahlers) C. BA, Macelester Coll., 1972; JD, Hamline U., 1978. Bar: Minn., U.S. Dist. Ct. Minn., Oreg., U.S. Dist. Ct. Oreg., U.S. Ct. Appeals (8th and 9th cirs.). Of counsel Capriotti & Assocs. Internat. Law, Minnetonka, Minn., 1986—, Portland, Oreg., 1986—; adj. prof. N.W. Sch. of Law, Lewis & Clark Coll., Portland, 1995—. Immigration, naturalization, and customs. Office: PO Box 2792 Portland OR 97208-2792

**CAPRON, ALEXANDER MORGAN,** lawyer, educator; b. Hartford, Conn., Aug. 16, 1944; s. William Mosher and Margaret (Morgan) C.; m. Barbara A. Brown, Nov. 9, 1969 (div. Dec. 1985); m. Kathleen West, Mar. 4, 1989; children: Jared Capron-Brown, Charles Spencer West Capron, Christopher Gordon West Capron, Andrew Morgan West Capron. BA, Swarthmore Coll., 1966; LLB, Yale U., 1969; MA (hon.), U. Pa., 1975. Bar: D.C. 1970, Pa. 1978. Law clk. to presiding judge U.S. Ct. Appeals, Washington, 1969-70; lectr., research assoc. Yale U., 1970-72; asst. prof. law U. Pa., 1972-75, vice dean, 1976, assoc. prof., 1975-78, prof. law and human genetics, 1978-82; exec. dir. Pres.'s Commn. for Study of Ethical Problems in Med. and Biomed. and Behavioral Rsch., Washington, 1980-83; prof. law, ethics and pub. policy Law Ctr. Georgetown U., Washington, 1983-84, inst. fellow Kennedy Inst. Ethics, 1983-84; Topping prof. law, medicine and pub. policy U. So. Calif., L.A., 1985-89, Univ. prof. law and medicine, 1989—, Henry W. Bruce prof. law, 1991—; co-dir. Pacific Ctr. for Health Policy and Ethics, L.A., 1990—; mem. bd. advisors Am. Bd. Internal Medicine, 1985-95, chmn., 1991-95; cons. NIH, mem. recombinant DNA com., 1990-95, mem. subcom. on human gene therapy, 1984-92; chmn. Congrl. Biomed. Ethics Adv. Commn., 1987-91; mem. Joint Commn. on Accreditation of Healthcare Orgns., 1994—, mem. ethics adv. com., 1984-85; mem. Nat. Bioethics Adv. Commn., 1996—. Author: (with Katz) Catastrophic Diseases: Who Decides What?, 1976, (with others) Genetic Counseling: Facts, Values and Norms, 1979, Law, Science and Medicine, 1984, supplements, 1987, 89, 2d edit., 1996, (with others) Treatise on Health Care Law, 1991; contbr. articles to profl. jours. Bd. mgrs. Swarthmore Coll., 1982-85; bd. trustees The Century Found. Fellow AAAS, Am. Coll. Legal Medicine (hon.), Hastings Ctr. (Inst. Society, Ethics and Life Scis., bd. dirs. 1975-98); mem. Inst. Medicine NAS (bd. dirs. 1985-90), AAUP (exec. com. Pa. chpt.), Am. Soc. Law, Medicine and Ethics (pres. 1988-89), Swarthmore Coll. Alumni Soc. (v.p. 1974-77). Office: U So Calif Law Sch University Park Los Angeles CA 90089-0001

**CAPSHAW, TOMMIE DEAN,** judge; b. Oklahoma City, Sept. 20, 1936; m. Dian Shipp; 1 child, Charles W. BS in Bus., Oklahoma City U., 1958; postrad., U. Ark., 1958-59; JD, U. Okla., 1961. Bar: Okla. 1961, Wyo. 1971, Ind. 1975. Assoc. Looney, Watts, Looney, Nichols and Johnson, Oklahoma City, 1961-63, Pierce, Duncan, Couch and Hendrickson, Oklahoma City, 1963-70; trial atty., v.p. Capshaw Well Service Co., Liberty Pipe and Supply Co., Casper, Wyo.; sr. adminstrv. law judge Evansville, Ind., 1973-75, 96-99; hearing office chief adminstrv. law judge Chgo., 1977-78; sr. adminstrv. law judge, 1999—; acting appeals coun. mem., Arlington, Va., 1980, acting chief adminstrv. law judge, 1984; mem. faculty U. Evansville, 1977, Sch. Law Ill. U., 1988—, So. Ind. U., 1990; lectr. in field. Author: A Manual for Continuing Judicial Education, 1981, Practical Aspects of Handling Social Security Disability Claims, 1982, Judicial Practice Handbook, 1990, A Quest for Quality, Speedy Justice, 1991; contbr. numerous articles to profl. jours., chpt. to textbook. Mem. adv. coun. Boy Scouts Am., scoutmaster, den leader, 1969—, Nat. Jud. Coll. U. Nev.; bd. dirs. Casper Symphony, 1972-73, Casper United Fund, 1972-73, Midget Football Assn., Casper, 1972-73, German Twp. Water Dist., 1984-85; pres. Evansville Unitarian Universalist Ch., 1984-86; performer Evansville Philharmonic Orch., 1986-98. Recipient

Kappa Alpha Order Ct. of HOnor award, 1962, Silver Beaver award Boy Scouts Am., 1980, presentation for vol. svc. contbg. betterment of cmty. Office Hearings and Appeals, 1992, presentation outstanding jud. mentor tng. Supreme Ct. Iowa, 1992, presentation dising. mentor tng. Fla. Jud. Coll., 1992. Mem. Okla. Bar Assn., Okla. County Bar Assn. (v.p. 1967), Wyo. Bar Assn., Evansville Bar Assn. (jud. rep. 1986-87, James Bethel Gresham Freedom award 1988), Young Lawyers Assn., Assn. Adminstrv. Law Judges HHS (bd. dirs. 1979-82, presentation dedicated svc. advancing jud. edn. 1992), Oklahoma City U. Alumni Assn. (bd. dirs. 1965). Home: 6105 School Rd # 6 Evansville IN 47720

**CAPUTO, KATHRYN MARY,** paralegal; b. Bklyn., June 29, 1948; d. Fortunato and Agnes (Iovino) Villacci; m. Joseph John Caputo, Apr. 4, 1976. AS in Bus. Adminstrn., Nassau C.C., Garden City, N.Y., 1989. Legal asst. Jacob Jacobson, Oceanside, N.Y., 1973-77; legal asst., office mgr. Joseph Kaldor, P.C., Franklin Square, N.Y., 1978-82, William H. George, Valley Stream, N.Y., 1983-89; exec. legal asst., office adminstr. Katz & Bernstein, Westbury, N.Y., 1990-93; sr. paralegal and office adminstr. Blaustein & Weinick, Garden City, N.Y., 1993—; instr. adult continuing edn. legal sec. procedures Lawrence (N.Y.) H.S., 1992—. Spl. events coord. Bklyn.-Queens Marriage Encounter, 1981, 82, 83, 85, 86; mem. Lynbrook Civic Assn., St. Raymond's R.C. Ch. Pastoral Coun./Renew 2000. Mem. L.I. Paralegal Assn. Avocations: traveling, reading, theatre, gardening. Office: Blaustein & Weinick 1205 Franklin Ave Garden City NY 11530-1629

**CAPUTO, NICHOLAS RAYMOND,** lawyer; b. North Tarrytown, N.Y., Jan. 30, 1968; s. Nicholas Joseph Caputo and Carole Ann Milano. BA, Boston U., 1989; JD magna cum laude, NYU Law Sch., 1993. Bar: N.Y. 1994, N.J. 1993, U.S. Dist. Ct. (so. and ea. dists.) N.Y. 1994. Intern Judge Leisure, U.S. Dist. Ct., N.Y.C., 1992; intern Judge Pratt, U.S. Ct. Appeals, Uniondale, N.Y., 1993; assoc. Mendes & Mount, LLP, N.Y.C., 1993-98, Schekter Rishty Goldstein & Blumenthal P.C., N.Y.C., 1998—. Editor N.Y. Law Sch. Law Rev. Dist. leader Conservative Party, Ossining, N.Y., 1993—; campaign vol. Commn. to Elect Gerald Liebowits, N.Y.C., 1996. Mem. ABA, Assn. Bar City of N.Y. Roman Catholic. Avocations: golf, literature, music, sporting events, camping. Federal civil litigation, General civil litigation, State civil litigation. Office: Schekter Rishty Goldstein & Blumenthal 1500 Broadway New York NY 10036-4015

**CAQUATTO, NORMA MADELINE,** lawyer, mediator, educator; b. Pitts., Oct. 19, 1945; d. Anthony and Madeline (Antonioli) C. BA, Wilson Coll., 1967; MAT, U. Pitts., 1971; JD, Duquesne U., 1979. Bar: Pa., U.S. Dist. Ct. (we. dist.) Pa. Tchr. Pitts. Opportunities Industrialization Ctr., 1969-71; constrn. mgr./legal Pitts. OIC, 1981-86; sr./instr. Pitts. Job Corps, 1971-75; jr. assoc. Weis and Weis, Pitts., 1980-81; sole practitioner southwestern Pa., 1986-92; staff atty. Southwestern Pa. Area Agy. on Aging/Legal Svcs. for Elderly, 1992-99; rschr. Green Internat. Planners, Sewickley, Pa., 1977; grad. asst. Duquesne U. Sch. Edn., 1978; adj. faculty Pa. State U., McKeesport/ New Kensington, 1986—; mediator EEO Commn., 1998—. Mem. scholarship com. Pitts. Job Corps, 1997—; v.p. Women's Polit. Network Allegheny County, 1996—; mem. Consistory, Cmty. of Reconciliation, 1998—. Mem. Pa. Bar Assn., Washington County Bar Assn. (chair Law Day 1997, 98, 99), Women's Bar Assn. Western Pa., Allegheny County Bar Assn. (young lawyers coun. 1989, pub. rels. com. 1995—, elder law com. 1998—). Democrat. Christian. Avocations: dancing, swimming, gardening. Consumer commercial, Family and matrimonial, Probate.

**CARAVASOS, NIALENA,** lawyer; b. Ridley Park, Pa., Oct. 20, 1966. BS in Econs. with honors, U. Pa., 1988; JD, Boston U., 1993. Bar: Mass. 1993, Pa. 1994, U.S. Dist. Ct. (ea. dist.) Pa. 1997, U.S. Ct. Appeals (3rd cir.) 1997, U.S. Supreme Ct. 1997. Law clk. to presiding judge Lisa Aversa Richette Ct. Common Pleas, Phila., 1995-97; assoc. F. Emmett Fitzpatrick, P.C., Phila., 1997—. Edward F. Hennessey scholar. Mem. Pa. Bar Assn., Hellenic Lawyers Assn. Phila., Phila. Bar Assn. (criminal justice sect.), Fed. Bar Assn. (criminal law com.). Criminal. Office: 926 Public Ledger Bldg 610 Chestnut St Philadelphia PA 19106

**CARBARY, JONATHAN LEIGH,** ; b. Elgin, Ill., Nov. 6, 1949; s. Warren Edward and Barbara Jean (Leigh) C.; m. Janice Kay Weingartner, Dec. 29, 1973; children: Nicole, Dana, Jonathan. BA, Knox Coll., 1972; JD, Hamline U., 1978. Bar: Ill. 1978, U.S. Dist. Ct. (no. dist.) Ill. 1979. Assoc. Robert A. Chapski, Ltd., Elgin, 1978-83; ptnr. Roeser, Vucha & Carbary, Elgin, 1984-96; pvt. practice Elgin, 1996—. 1st lt. U.S. Army, 1972-73. Recipient Am. Jurisprudence award Lawyer Co-op Pub. Co., 1978. Mem. Ill. State Bar Assn., Kane County Bar Assn. Republican. State civil litigation, Personal injury, Workers' compensation. Home: 11 N 205 Johnstown Rd Elgin IL 60123 Office: 574 N Mclean Blvd Ste 1B Elgin IL 60123-3259

**CARBAUGH, JOHN EDWARD, JR.,** lawyer; b. Greenville, S.C., Sept. 4, 1945; s. John Edward and Mary Lou (McCarley) C.; m. Mary Middleton Calhoun: children: John, Martha, Leacy, Miller. BA, U. of South, 1967; JD, U. S.C., 1973, postgrad., 1967-69; postgrad., Georgetown U., 1977-79. Bar: S.C. 1973, U.S. Ct. Appeals (4th cir.) 1982, U.S. Supreme Ct. 1982. With White House Staff, Washington, 1969-70; campaign dir. re-elect Thurmond campaign Washington, 1970-73; legis. asst. U.S. Senate, Washington, 1974-82; pvt. practice Washington, 1982—; bd. dirs. Westech. Internat., Inc., Washington Watch, Inc., Splty. Materials and Mfg., Inc., Tech. Holdings, Inc., The Stealth Corp., Inc.; mem. Pres. Commn. on Econ. Justice, Washington, 1985-87. Author: The Revisionists, 1991, We Need Each Other: U.S.-Japan Relations Approach the 21st Century, 1992; co-author: A Program for Military Independence, 1980; contbr. articles to profl. jours. Rep. Nat. Platform Staff, 1976, 80, 84, 88, 92, 96; Presdl. Transition Team, 1980-81. Sgt. USAR, 1969-77. Mem. Met. Club. Republican. Presbyterian. Avocations: tennis, travel, horticulture. Administrative and regulatory, Private international, Legislative. Office: 1300 17th St N Ste 1100 Arlington VA 22209-3873

**CARBERRY, KENNETH ANTHONY,** lawyer, entrepreneur; b. Boston, Sept. 20, 1958; s. Kenneth Richard and Lorayne Anne Carberry; m. Mary Theresa Norton, Apr. 16, 1982; children: Kenneth Thomas, Maura Joyce, Erin Marie. BS, Curry Coll., 1980; JD, New Eng. Sch. Law, 1989. Pub. affairs dir. Carter Broadcasting, WROL, Boston, 1980-84; control rm supr. Boston Red Sox, Fenway Park, Boston, 1978-85; pres. Chart Prodns., Inc., Boston, 1981—; ptnr. Carberry & Morin, Boston, 1997—; legal counsel Carter Broadcasting, Inc., Boston, 1991—; pvt. practice Boston, 1990-97; mem. part-time faculty Curry Coll., Milton, Mass., 1995, Mt. Ida Coll., Newton, Mass., 1996-97. Mem. Radio Round Table, Boston, 1988—; bd. dirs., mem. adv. bd. St. Agatha Sch., Milton, Mass., 1997—. Mem. Mass. Bar Assn. (It's Your Law radio host 1987-94), Cath. Lawyers Guild. Real property, Insurance, Entertainment. Office: Carberry & Morin 20 Park Plz Ste 720 Boston MA 02116-4301

**CARBINE, JAMES EDMOND,** lawyer; b. Scotts Bluff, Nebr., June 3, 1945; s. Edmond Horace Carbine and Mabel (Porterfield) Hukle; m. Marianne Lemly, Aug. 5, 1972; 1 child, Matthew. BA, Mich. State U., 1967; JD, U. Md., 1972. Bar: Md. 1972. Assoc. Weinberg and Green, Balt., 1972-79, ptnr., 1980-96, chmn. litigation dept., 1985-95; pvt. practice Balt., 1996—; panel mem. Nat. Press Club Symposium, 1974. Reporter Govs. Landlord Tenant Commn., Md., 1973-76; mem. Mayor's Bus. Roundtable, Balt., 1983-85; bd. dirs. Greater Homewood Community Corp., Balt., 1980-82; trustee Roland Park Found., 1986-87; bd. dirs. Md. Vol. Lawyers Svc., 1991—. With U.S. Army, 1968-70. Named one of Outstanding Young Men Am., Jaycees, 1977. Mem. ABA (computer litigation com., corp. coun. com., co-chair trial practice com. 1994-97), Md. Bar Assn., Balt. City Bar Assn., Nat. Press Club (panelist 1974). Avocation: outdoor sports. Federal civil litigation, State civil litigation. Office: 111 S Calvert St Ste 2700 Baltimore MD 21202-6143

**CARBONE, EDWARD JOHN,** lawyer; b. Melrose, Mass., Jan. 17, 1970; s. John Anthony and Christine Ann (Neuenhoff) C.; m. Linda Elizabeth Jorge, Apr. 18, 1998. BA cum laude, Boston Coll., 1991, JD, 1994. Bar: Mass. 1995, Fla. 1995, U.S. Dist. Ct. (mid. dist.) Fla. 1996. Jud. law clk. Hon. Arthur Minuskin, Newark, 1994-95; assoc. Solomon and Ginsberg, P.A., Tampa, Fla., 1996-97, Gunn, Ogden & Sullivan, P.A., Tampa, 1997—. Mem. ABA, The Fla. Bar, Hillsborough County Bar Assn. Democrat. Roman Catholic. Avocation: sports. Personal injury, Sports, Appellate. Office: Gunn Ogden & Sullivan PA 100 N Tampa St Ste 2900 Tampa FL 33602-5810

**CARDALENA, PETER PAUL, JR.,** lawyer, educator; b. Bklyn., Dec. 19, 1943; s. Peter Paul and Rose Rita (Femenella) C.; m. Rosalie Brunetti, Sept. 22, 1962; children: Peter Paul III (dec.), Lisa, Kim, Gina, Damian. AAS, St. John's U., Jamaica, N.Y., 1978, BS, 1980; JD, Touro Law Sch., 1984. Bar: N.Y. 1985. Supr. N.Y.C. Transit Authority, 1965—; sole practice law Floral Park, N.Y., 1984—; assoc. prof. law St. John's U., Jamaica, 1985—; lectr. Katharine Gibbs Sch., N.Y.C., 1986—; legal advisor Nassau Co. Shields, 1985—, Sch. Adminstrs. Assn., Albany, N.Y., 1986—. Editor periodical Call Box, 1985; contbr. articles to profl. jours. Named Mem. of the Yr. Nassau Co. Shields, 1986. Mem. ABA, Nassau County Bar Assn., Bklyn. Bar Assn., Columbian Lawyers Assn. (Serafin Calabrese award 1984), N.Y.C. Transit Police Dept., Lt.'s Benevolent Assn. (counsel 1987—, exec. sec. 1987—), Nassau County Shields (counsel 1985—, Mem. of Yr. 1986). Roman Catholic. General practice, Labor. Home and Office: 37 Fern St Floral Park NY 11001-3207

**CARDAMONE, RICHARD J.,** federal judge; b. Utica, N.Y., Oct. 10, 1925; s. Joseph J. and Josephine (Scala) C.; m. Catherine Baker Clarke, Aug. 28, 1946; 10 children. BA, Harvard U., 1948; LLB, Syracuse U., 1952. Bar: N.Y. 1952. Pvt. practice law Utica, 1952-62; judge N.Y. State Supreme Ct., 1963-71, Appelate div. 4th Dept. N.Y. State Supreme Ct., 1971-81, U.S. Ct. Appeals (2d cir.), Utica, 1981—. Lt. (j.g.) USNR, 1943-46. Mem. Am. Law Inst., N.Y. State Bar Assn., Oneida County Bar Assn. Roman Catholic. Office: US Ct Appeals 10 Broad St Utica NY 13501-1233

**CARDILLO, JOHN POLLARA,** lawyer; b. Ft. Lee, N.J., July 1, 1942; s. John E. and Margaret (Pollara) C.; m. Linda Bentey, Sept. 25, 1976; children: John Thomas, Joseph Pollara, Margaret Celia, Mark Luigi. BA, Furman U., 1964; postgrad., W.Va. U., 1965; JD, U. S.C., 1968. Bar: S.C. 1968, N.Y. 1970, Fla. 1972, U.S. Ct. Appeals (2d cir., 4th cir. 5th cir. 11th cir.) 1972, U.S. Dist. Ct. (ea. and so. dists.) N.Y. 1972, U.S. Dist. Ct. S.C. 1968, U.S. Dist. Ct. (so. and mid. dists.) Fla. 1974, U.S. Tax Ct. 1972, U.S. Supreme Ct. 1984. Assoc. Cardillo & Corbett, N.Y.C., 1968-71, Mays & McLellan, Columbia, S.C., 1971-72, Sorokoty, Monaco & Cervelli, Naples, Fla., 1972-75; ptnr. Monaco, Cardillo & Keith, P.A., Naples, 1975-96, Cardillo, Keith & Bonaquist, P.A., 1997—. Mem. Furman U. Alumni Bd. Dirs., 1984-89; active Environ. Adv. Coun., Collier County, Fla., 1983-87, past chmn.; past pres. Pine Ridge Civic Assn.; bd. dirs. YMCA Collier County, past pres., 1978-80, United Arts Coun. of Collier County, pres., 1991-92, bd. dirs. Big Bros., 1974-76; past pres. Naples Leadership Sch., 1987-88; mem. Leadership Collier, 1992; mem. Gov.'s Task Force on Drug Abuse, 1985; bd. advisors Gene and Mary Sarazen FDN, 1997—; bd. trustees Edison C.C., 1998-99. Mem. ATLA, ABA, Am. Arbitration Assn. (arbitrator), Acad. Fla. Trial Lawyers, Fla. Bar (20th jud. cir., bd. govs. 1992—), Fla. Criminal Def. Attys., Collier County Bar Assn. (past pres.), S.C. Bar Assn., Assn. Bar City N.Y., Maritime Law Assn., Naples Area C. of C. (bd. dirs. 1990-95, pres. 1994-95). General civil litigation, Criminal, Personal injury. Home: 395 Ridge Dr Naples FL 34108-2933 Office: Cardillo Keith & Bonaquist PA 3550 Tamiami Trl E Naples FL 34112-4999

**CARDINALE, PHILIP JOHN,** lawyer, educator; b. Bklyn., Dec. 14, 1948; s. Alerio A. and Louise D. Cardinale; m. Susan Marie Porreco, Aug. 19, 1972; children: Philip Jr., Cristina, Joseph. AB, Georgetown U., 1970, MA, 1971, JD, 1973. Bar: N.Y., U.S. Dist. Ct. (ea. dist.) N.Y. 1974. Asst. dist. atty. Suffolk County (N.Y.) Dist. Atty.'s Office, Riverhead, 1973-80; ptnr. Cardinale & Cardinale, Jamesport, N.Y., 1980—; assoc. adj. prof. Suffolk County C.C., Selden, N.Y., 1978—. Councilman Town of Riverhead, 1997—; trustee Riverhead Lib., 1996—. Mem. Rotary. Roman Catholic. Real property, Probate, Municipal (including bonds). Home: 785 Peconic Bay Blvd Riverhead NY 11901-5906 Office: Cardinale & Cardinale 1451 Main Rd Jamesport NY 11947

**CARDON, LAWRENCE MARC,** lawyer; b. Bklyn., Apr. 3, 1943; s. Leon and Selma (Bennett) C.; m. Lucy Ann Proto, June 27, 1970; children: David Aaron, Rebecca Lynn. BS in Commerce, U. Va., 1965; JD, U. Richmond, 1973. Ptnr. Decker, Cardon, Thomas, Norfolk, Va. Mem. Norfolk Portsmouth Bar Assn., Virginia Beach Bar Assn. Home: 446 Discovery Rd Virginia Beach VA 23451-2158 Office: Decker Cardon Thomas 201 E Plume St Norfolk VA 23510-1706

**CARDONI, HORACE ROBERT,** retired lawyer; b. Jessup, Pa., July 24, 1916; s. Louis and Maria (Saldi) C.; m. Florence D'Arienzo, July 2, 1945; children: Mary Clare, Ann, Louise, Robert L., Joseph W., John G. B.A., U. Scranton, 1938; LL.B., U. Pa., 1941. Bar: Pa. 1941, U.S. Dist. Ct. (mid. dist.) Pa. 1941. Pvt. practice Scranton, 1941-42; area rent atty. Office Housing Expediter, OPA, Scranton, 1946-51; with Daystrom, Inc. (name changed to Weston Instruments, Inc. 1964), Newark, 1953-76, sec., 1962-76, gen. counsel, 1963-76; assoc. counsel Schlumberger Ltd., 1976-81, asst. sec., 1977-81, ret., 1981; sec., bd. dirs. Cryodynamics Inc., Mountainside, N.J., 1984-90; pres., bd. dirs. N.J. Bd. Profl. Engrs. and Land Surveyors, 1978, mem., 1975-80; bd. dirs. N.J. Health Enterprises, Inc. Mem. Nat. Def. Exec. Res., U.S. Dept. Commerce, 1956-83; treas. cub pack Boy Scouts Am., Mountainside, N.J., 1964-66; active Mountainside Little League, 1965-66; treas., trustee Community Access Unlimited, Elizabeth, N.J., 1981-92, United Way of Mountainside, 1979—; mem. planning bd. Borough of Mountainside, 1982—, Ethics com., 1992—; dist. committeeman Democratic Com., 1967—, mcpl. chmn., 1969-74; counselor Vols. in Probation, Union County, N.J., 1981-85; mem. Union County Child Placement Adv. Bd., 1985-88; lay trustee Our Lady Lourdes Roman Cath. Ch., Mountainside, 1965—. Served with USNR, 1942-45, 51-52. Mem. ABA, UNICO Internat. (Springfield/Mountainside chpt.), Pa. Bar Assn., Lackawanna County Bar Assn. Home: 326 Short Dr Mountainside NJ 07092-2001

**CARELLAS, THEODORE T.,** lawyer; b. Savannah, Ga., Aug. 14, 1959; s. Tykie Basil and Sonya (Petropoulos) C. ABJ magna cum laude, U. Ga., 1981, JD, 1984. Bar: Ga., U.S. Ct. Appeals Ga., U.S. Dist. Ct. (so. dist.) Ga. 1984. Teaching asst. U. Ga., Athens, 1983-84; assoc. Hunter, Maclean, Ekley & Dunn, P.C., Savannah, 1984—. Sec. parish council St. Paul' Greek Orthodox Ch.; profl. div. mem. United Way of Savannah, 1984—. Mem. Ga. Assn. Def. Lawyers, Def. Research Inst., Nat. Assn. R.R. Trial Counsel, Phi Beta Kappa, Phi Kappa Phi, Phi Delta Theta. Democrat. Greek Orthodox. Avocations. running, reading, investing. General civil litigation, Personal injury, Real property. Office: Godlove & Carellas LLP Hwy 21 272 Columbia Ave Rincon GA 31326-9026

**CARESS, TIMOTHY CHARLES,** lawyer; b. Indpls., June 30, 1969; s. John Hugh and Marianna (Milani) C.; m. Megan Theresa Ryan, Dec. 31, 1994. BA in Journalism, Ind. U., 1991, JD summa cum laude, 1994. Bar: Ind. 1994, U.S. Dist. Ct. (no. and so. dists.) Ind. 1994. Legal writing instr. Sch. of Law Ind. U., Indpls., 1995-96; assoc. Yosha Ladendorf Krahulik & Weddle, Indpls., 1994-96, Cline Farrell Christie & Lee, Indpls., 1996—; mem. sect. Inadequate Security Litig. Group, Mpls., 1995—, Attys. Info. Exch. Group, 1998—, Elec. Accident Group, 1998—. Editor Ind. Law Rev., 1993-94; contbr. (civil summaries) The Ind. Lawyer, 1995—. Chmn. annual fund drive Chatard H.S., Indpls., 1995—; moot ct. judge Sch. of Law Ind. U., Indpls., 1994—. Named Forrest E. Jump scholar Howard County Bar Assn., 1992-94. Mem. ABA, ATLA, Ind. Trial Lawyers Assn., Ind. State Bar Assn. General civil litigation, Personal injury, Product liability. Office: Cline Farrell Christie & Lee 342 Massachusetts Ave Indianapolis IN 46204-2132

**CAREY, ELEANOR MACKEY,** lawyer; b. Providence, Jan. 31, 1942; d. Joseph A. and Margaret D. Mackey; m. Anthony M. Carey, Oct. 7, 1967. LLB, Wellesley Coll., 1963; JD, U. Md., 1973. Bar: Md. 1973, U.S. Supreme Ct. 1980. Dep. atty. gen. Atty. Gen. Office of Md., Balt., 1979-87; on air legal reporter WJZ-TV Channel 13, Balt., 1987-88; pres. Multi Media Ednl. Tech., 1988-91; pvt. practice Balt., 1988-95; spl. counsel Gov. State of R.I., Providence, 1991-93; ptnr. Brand Lowell & Ryan, Washington, 1995-96; sr. counselor Gov. of Md., Annapolis, 1996-98; pres. Govs. Workforce Investment Bd., 1998—. candidate for Atty. Gen. of Md., 1986, 94. Address: 15 W Barre St Baltimore MD 21201-2465

**CAREY, JOHN LEO,** lawyer; b. Morris, Ill., Oct. 1, 1920; s. John Leo and Loretta (Conley) C.; m. Rhea M. White, July 15, 1950; children: John Leo III, Daniel Hobart, Deborah M. BS, St. Ambrose Coll., Davenport, Ia., 1941; JD, Georgetown U., 1947, LLM, 1949. Bar: Ind. 1954. Legislative asst. Sen. Scott W. Lucas, 1945-47; spl. atty. IRS, Washington, 1947-54; since practiced in South Bend; ptnr. Barnes & Thornburg, 1954—, now of counsel; law prof. taxation Notre Dame Law Sch., 1968-90. Trustee LaLumire Prep. Sch., Laporte, Ind. Served with USAAF, World War II; to lt. col. USAF, Korean War. Decorated D.F.C., Air medal. Mem. ABA (bd. govs. 1986-89, treas. 1990-93), Ind. Bar Assn. (pres. 1976-77), St. Joseph County Bar Assn., Signal Point Country Club. General corporate, Corporate taxation. Home: H H 28 Ocean Reef Club Key Largo FL 33037 Office: 600 1st Source Bank Ctr 100 N Michigan St South Bend IN 46601-1630

**CAREY, RAYMOND J.,** lawyer; b. Plainfield, N.J., Oct. 13, 1953; s. Albert Daniel and Eileen Veronica (Patterson) C.; m. Mary Ellen, Aug. 7, 1981; children: Meghan Grace, Kathryn Elizabeth. AB, U. Notre Dame, 1975, JD, 1981. Bar: Mich., U.S. Dist. Ct. (ea., we. dists.) Mich., U.S. Ct. Appeals (6th cir.). Shareholder Butzel Long, Detroit. Mem. ABA, ATLA, Mich. Bar Assn., Fed. Bar Assn., Detroit Bar Assn., Detroit Barristers Assn., Soc. Irish-Am. Lawyers, Mich. Soc. Hosp. Attys. Civil rights, General civil litigation, Labor. Home: 460 Lakeland St Grosse Pointe MI 48230-1655

**CAREY, WAYNE JOHN,** lawyer; b. Phila., Jan. 27, 1948; s. James Burton and Marguerite (Frantz) C.; m. Jane H. Carey, Apr. 1, 1972; 1 child, Michael Steven. BS, Union Coll., Barbourville, Ky., 1970; JD, Widener U., 1981. Bar: Del. 1982, U.S. Dist. Ct. Del. 1982, U.S. Ct. Appeals (3d cir.) 1982. Acct. Vita Food Products, Phila., 1970-73; bus. analyst, acct. DuPont Co., Wilmington, Del., 1973-80; law clk. Del. Supreme Ct., Wilmington, 1981-82; assoc. Prickett Jones Elliott, Wilmington, 1982-87; ptnr. Prickett Jones Elliott Kristol & Schnee, Wilmington, 1987—. Co-author: Delaware LLC's, 1995. Mem. ABA, MLA, Del. State Bar Assn. Avocation: golf. Contracts commercial, General corporate, State civil litigation. Office: Prickett Jones et al 1310 King St Wilmington DE 19801-3220

**CARGERMAN, ALAN WILLIAM,** lawyer; b. Chgo., Jan. 17, 1945; s. Harry and Bertha (Snider) C.; m. Linda Swanson Leifheit, July 28, 1990; children from previous marriage: Jack Marshall, Jill Faith. Student, U. Ill., 1961-64; LLB, DePaul U., 1970. Bar: Ill. 1970. Editorial writer Commerce Clearing House, Inc., Chgo., 1969-70; asst. state's atty. Ogle County, Oregon, Ill., 1970-72; assoc. judge 15th Jud. Cir. Ill., Oregon, 1972-90; with Fearer, Nye, Ahlberg & Chadwick, Oregon, 1991-96, of counsel, 1996—; lectr. Ill. Jud. Conf., 1981—, Nat. Jud. Coll., 1982; vice chmn. Northwest Ill. Criminal Justice Commn., 1971. Author Ill. Judges Assn. Manual History of the Illinois Judicial System, 1984. Mem. Ill. Commn. on Am. Constn. Bicentennial, 1985-87; chmn. Ogle County Commn. on Bicentennial, Oreg., 1987-91; mem. spl. com. on courtroom standards Ill. Supreme Ct., 1991-93. Fellow Ill. Bar Found.; mem. ABA, Ill. State Bar Assn. (sec. criminal law sect. 1971), Ogle County Bar Assn. (sec. 1971), Am. Judicature Soc., Ill. Judges Assn. (dir. Chgo. 1977-83, 86-89, jud. selection and retention com. 1981-84, spl. task force on dispute resolution 1985-87, publs. com. 1988-90, pub. affairs com. 1988-90), Ill. Jud. Conf. (chmn. study com.), Conf. Chief Cir. Judges (rules com. Chgo. 1981-87, chmn. 1988-90). General practice, Criminal, Constitutional. Office: Fearer Nye Ahlberg & Chadwick 209 S 5th St Oregon IL 61061-1806

**CARGILL, ROBERT MASON,** lawyer; b. Atlanta, Nov. 15, 1948; s. George Slade Jr., and Emma Elizabeth (Matthews) C.; m. Sharon McEver, June 12, 1971; children: Ansley Lauren, Kristin Lucille. BS summa cum laude, Ga. Inst. Tech., 1970; JD magna cum laude, Harvard U., 1973. Bar: Ga. 1973, D.C. 1975. Assoc. atty. Hansell & Post, Atlanta, 1976-81, ptnr., 1981-89; ptnr. Jones, Day, Reavis & Pogue, Atlanta, 1989—. Lt. USNR 1973-76. Mem. Swedish Am. C. of C. Atlanta (chmn. bd. dirs.), Japan Am. Soc. of Ga. (bd. dirs.), Swiss Am. C. of C. (Atlanta chpt. bd. dirs.), World Trade Ctr. Atlanta (bd. dirs.), Cherokee Town Country Club. Methodist. Avocations: tennis, travel. Private international, General corporate, Contracts commercial. Home: 230 Colewood Way NW Atlanta GA 30328-2923 Office: Jones Day Reavis & Pogue 303 Peachtree St NE Ste 3500 Atlanta GA 30308-3242

**CARGO, DAVID FRANCIS,** lawyer; b. Dowagiac, Mich., Jan. 13, 1929; s. Francis Clair and Mary E. (Harton) C.; children: Veronica Ann, David Joseph, Patrick Michael, Maria Elena Christina, Eamon Francis. AB, U. Mich., 1951, M of Pub. Adminstrn., 1953, JD, 1957. Bar: Mich. 1957, N.Mex. 1957, Oreg. 1974. Practice in Albuquerque, 1957, asst. dist. atty., 1958-59; mem. N.Mex. Ho. of Reps., 1962; gov. N.Mex., 1967-71; practice law Santa Fe, 1970-73, Portland, Oreg., 1973-83. Chmn. Four Corners Regional Commn., 1967-71, Oil and Gas Conservation Commn.; chmn. N.Mex. Young Reps., 1959-61, Clackamas County Rep. Ctrl. Com.; mem. Israel Bond Com.; former mem. bd. govs. St. John Coll.; bd. dirs. Albuquerque Tech. Vocat. Sch.; chmn. governing bd. Albuquerque Tv.I. C.C.; mem. Albuquerque City Pers. Bd.; adv. bd. mem. N.Mex. State Fair; exec. bd. Found. for Open Govt. With AUS, 1953-55. Named Man of Yr. Albuquerque Jr. C. of C., 1964; recipient Outstanding Conservationist award N.Mex. Wildlife Assn., 1969, 70. Mem. Mich. Bar Assn., Oreg. Bar Assn., N.Mex. Bar Assn., Albuquerque Bar Assn., Isaac Walton League (past v.p. N.Mex.), World Affairs Coun. Oreg. (pres.), Interstate Oil and Gas Compact, Isaak Walton League Oreg., Hispano C. of C., Am. Leadership Conf. (bd. dirs.), Nat. Fedn. Blind. Personal injury, Workers' compensation, Family and matrimonial. Home: 6422 Concordia Rd NE Albuquerque NM 87111-1228 Office: 400 Gold Ave SW Albuquerque NM 87102-3283

**CARLBERG, JAMES EDWIN,** lawyer; b. Jeffersonville, Ind., May 3, 1950; s. Dale Levan and Nanette (Prendergast) C.; m. Donna S. Funk, Oct. 28, 1950; children: Jason, Lindsay, Kelly. BS highest distinction, Ind U., 1972, JD cum laude, 1974. Bar: Ind. 1974, U.S. Dist. Ct. (no. and so. dists.) Ind. 1974. Ptnr. Klineman, Rose, Wolf & Wallack, Indpls., 1974-94, Bose, McKinner & Evans, Indpls., 1994—. Author: (with others) Indiana Continuing Legal Education Forum. Mem. ABA (secured creditors' sub com. of bankruptcy com., bus. and banking sect.), Ind. State Bar Assn., Indpls. Bar Assn. Bankruptcy, Contracts commercial, General corporate. Office: Bose McKinney & Evans 2700 1st Indiana Pla Indianapolis IN 46204

**CARLEN, LEON C.,** lawyer; b. N.Y.C., Oct. 22, 1915; s. Eisig and Fanny (Lazarus) C.; m. Esta Seligman, June 27, 1948; children—Elliott Cardozo, Frances A. B.A., Bklyn. Coll., 1936, LL.B., 1939. Bar: N.Y. 1940, U.S. Dist. Ct. (so. dist.) N.Y. 1948, U.S. Dist. Ct. (ea. dist.) N.Y. 1957, U.S. Supreme Ct. 1960, U.S. Ct. Appeals (2d cir.) 1966. Assoc. Fuchsberg & Fuchsberg, N.Y.C., 1950-54; ptnr. Jaffe, Carlen & Stern, Mineola, N.Y., 1972-82. Served with USAF, 1942-45; CBI. Mem. Nassau County Bar Assn., N.Y. State Bar Assn., Bklyn. Coll. Law Assn. Democrat. Jewish. State civil litigation, Personal injury. Home: 2 Caffrey Ave Bethpage NY 11714-1404

**CARLENO, HARRY EUGENE,** lawyer; b. Denver, Mar. 3, 1928; s. Benjamin Edward and Elizabeth Bess (De Rose) C.; m. Ann Marie Kraft, Sept. 14, 1957; children: Gregory S., Paul C., Jennifer A., Machelle L. BBA, U. Denver, 1951, LLB, 1955, JD, 1970. Bar: Colo. 1955, U.S. Dist. Ct. Colo. 1955, U.S. Ct. Appeals (10th cir.) 1959, U.S. Supreme Ct. 1959. Pres., atty. H.E. Carleno & Assoc., P.C., Englewood, Colo., 1955-79, Littleton, Colo., 1979—; mcpl. judge City of Wheat Ridge, Colo., 1971-78; dep. dist. atty. Arapahoe County, Littleton, 1958-68. Chmn. Dem. Com., Arapahoe County, 1964-65; chmn. Career Service Commn., Englewood, 1961-64; pres. Inter Faith Task Force Found., Englewood, 1986-88. Col. USAF, 1947-53. Recipient St. George award Denver Area council Boy Scouts Am., 1980. Mem. ABA (life), Colo. Bar Assn., Arapahoe County Bar Assn. (trustee 1968-70), Res. Officers Assn. of U.S. (life), Ret. Officers Assn. (life), Fraternal Order of Eagles (life). Roman Catholic. Lodge: Kiwanis (local pres. 1966-67). Probate, Family and matrimonial, State civil litigation. Home and Office: 5471 S Sherman St Littleton CO 80121-1253

**CARLEY, DONALD MARTIN,** lawyer; b. Mpls., Feb. 28, 1968; s. Harold Edwin and Mary Elizabeth Carley. BS, Coll. William and Mary, 1990; JD, Temple U., 1995. Bar: Calif. 1995, U.S. Dist. Ct. (no. dist.) Calif. 1995, U.S. Ct. Appeals (9th cir.) 1995, U.S. Dist. Ct. (ea. dist.) Calif. 1996, U.S. Dist. Ct. (ctrl. dist.) Calif. 1997; CPCU. Environ. claims rep. The PMA Group,

Phila., 1990-92, CIGNA Property and Casualty, Phila., 1992-95; assoc. Gordon & Rees, LLP, San Francisco, 1995-97, Luce Forward Hamilton & Scripps LLP, San Francisco, 1997-98, Sonnenschein Nath & Rosenthal, San Francisco, 1998—. Contbr. articles to profl. jours. Mem. ABA, CPCU Soc. (mem. Golden Gate chpt. 1995—, exec. com. mem. Golden Gate chpt. 1998—, bd. dirs. 1999—), Calif. Bar Assn., San Francisco Bar Assn., Barristers Club San Francisco (vice chair bridging the gap com. 1996, chair bridging the gap com. 1997, 98), Alpha Lambda Delta, Phi Eta Sigma. Avocations: cycling, travel, fly fishing, photography. E-mail: d3c@sonnenschein.com. Fax: 415-543-5472. Office: Sonnenschein Nath & Rosenthal 685 Market St Fl 6 San Francisco CA 94105-4200

**CARLEY, GEORGE H.,** state supreme court justice; b. Jackson, Miss., Sept. 24, 1938; s. George L. Jr. and Dorothy (Holmes) C.; m. Sandra M. Lineberger, 1960; 1 child, George H. Jr. AB, U. Ga., 1960, LLB, 1962. Bar: Ga. 1961. Pvt. practice Atlanta and Decatur, Ga., 1961-71; ptnr. McCurdy & Candler, Decatur, Ga., 1971-79; also spl. asst. atty. gen. Office. Atty. Gen.; judge Ct. Appeals Ga., 1979-89, chief judge, 1989-91, presiding judge, 1991-93; justice Supreme Ct. Ga., Atlanta, 1993—; chmn. bd. visitors U. Ga. Law Sch., 1995-96. Bd. Visitors U. Ga. Law Sch.; past pres. U. Ga. Law Sch. Assn. Coun., 1989-90, active, 1986-91; trustee Ga. Legal History Found., Inc.; active Holy Trinity Episc. Ch., Decatur. Mem. ABA, State Bar Ga., Ga. Bar Found., Lawyers Club Atlanta, Old Warhorse Lawyers Club (pres. 1997-98), Joseph Henry Lumpkin Am. Inn of Ct. (pres. 1994-95), Pythagoras Lodge, Scottish Rite. Office: Supreme Court 504 State Judicial Bldg Atlanta GA 30334-9007*

**CARLEY, JOHN HALLIDAY,** lawyer; b. N.Y.C.; s. John T. and Edna May (Halliday) C.; children: Melinda S., Caroline H. BA, Rutgers Coll., 1962; LLB, Yale U., 1968. Bar: N.Y. 1969. Assoc. Mudge Rose Guthrie & Alexander, N.Y.C., 1968-72; assoc., ptnr. Rogers & Wells, N.Y.C., 1972-81; gen. counsel FTC, Washington, 1981-85, Office Mgmt. & Budget, The White House, Washington, 1985-87; ptnr. Donovan Leisure Newton & Irvine, N.Y.C., 1987-94; spl. coun. to deputy mayor N.Y.C., 1994-95; deputy atty. gen. Pub. Advocacy N.Y. State, 1995-96; exec. v.p., gen. counsel Avis, Inc., Garden City, N.Y., 1997-98; sr. v.p. law & regulatory affairs Cendant Corp., N.Y.C., N.J., 1998—. 1st lt. U.S. Army, 1963-65. Mem. Assn. Bar of City of N.Y. Fax: 212-413-1922. General civil litigation. Office: Cendant Corp 9 W 57th St New York NY 10019-2701

**CARLILE, ROBERT TOY,** lawyer; b. Phila., July 27, 1926; s. Robert and Eva (MacQueen) C.; m. Gill S. Carlile; children: Robert A., Regan J. BBA, U. Miami, 1949; JD, U. Fla., 1958. Bar: Fla. 1958. Assoc., Grimditch & Smith, Deerfield Beach, Fla., 1958-60; sole practice, Deerfield Beach, 1960-65, 73-91, Boca Raton, Fla., 1991—; ptnr. Carlile & Pulskamp, Deerfield Beach, 1965-69, Carlile, Pulskamp & Fletcher, 1969-72, Carlile & Fletcher, 1972-73; city atty., Deerfield Beach, 1963-68, 88-91; mcpl. judge, 1971-77. With U.S. Army, 1944-46, USAF, 1951-53. Mem. Fla. Bar Assn., North Broward County Bar Assn. (pres. 1966), Broward County Bar Assn., Broward County Mcpl. Judges Assn. (v.p. 1975), Deerfield Beach C. of C. (pres. 1966), Phi Alpha Delta. Democrat. Clubs: Kiwanis (pres.), Billiken (pres.), Mahi Temple Shriners, Jesters (dir.). Probate, Real property. Office: 1200 N Federal Hwy Boca Raton FL 33432-2803

**CARLIN, CLAIR MYRON,** lawyer; b. Sharon, Pa., Apr. 20, 1947; s. Charles William and Carolyn L. (Vukasich) C.; children: Eric Richard, Elizabeth Marie, Alexander Myron. BS in Econs., Ohio State U., 1969, JD, 1972. Bar: Ohio 1973, Pa. 1973, U.S. Dist. Ct. (so. dist.) Ohio 1973, U.S. Dist. Ct. (no. dist.) Ohio 1975, U.S. Supreme Ct. 1976, U.S. Ct. Claims, 1983, U.S. Tax Ct. 1985. Staff atty. Ohio Dept. Taxation, Columbus, 1972-73; asst. atty. City of Warren, Ohio, 1973-75; assoc. McLaughlin, DiBlasio & Harshman, Youngstown, Ohio, 1975-80; ptnr. McLaughlin, McNally & Carlin, Youngstown, 1980-98, Carlin & Vasvari, LLC, Poland, Ohio, 1998—. Mem. editl. bd. Ohio Trial mag. Mem. Trumbull County Bicentennial Commn., Ohio, 1976; v.p. Svcs. for the Aging, Trumbull County, 1976-77; mem. Pres.' Club Ohio State U. With Ohio NG, 1972-82. Mem. ATLA (bd. govs. 1996—, trustee PAC 1996-98), ABA, Ohio State Bar Assn. (negligence law com. 1991—), Ohio State Bar Coll., Mahoning County Bar Assn. (chmn. legal edn. com. 1985-86, counsel 1986-87), Ohio Acad. Trial Lawyers (trustee 1988-92, polit. action com. chmn. 1991, exec. com. 1991-97, treas. 1992-93, sec. 1993-94, pres.-elect 1994-95, pres. 1995-96), Mahoning-Trumbull Acad. Trial Lawyers (pres. 1991), Ohio State U. Alumni Assn. (pres. Trumbull County chpt. 1985—), Cath. War Vets. (Ohio state commdr., Vet. of Yr. 1988), Rotary. Democrat. Roman Catholic. Professional liability, Product liability, Personal injury. Home: 3524 Hunters Hl Poland OH 44514-5303 Office: Carlin & Vasvari LLC PO Box 5369 Youngstown OH 44514-0369

**CARLIN, KEVIN FRANCIS CHRISTOPHER,** lawyer; b. Phila., July 16, 1952; s. Frank J. and Louise T. (Vitretti) C. BA, Temple U., 1974; MPA, NYU, 1976; JD, Temple U., 1979. Bar: Pa. 1982. Law clk. to Hon. Eugene Clarke Ct. of Common Pleas, Phila., 1979-82; atty., advisor HUD, Phila., 1982—; spl. asst. U.S. atty. U.S. Dept. of Justice, Phila., 1991—. Mem. steering com. Gray Panthers, Phila., 1974—. Mem. Fed. Bar Assn., Phila. Bar Assn., Tau Epsilon Rho. Home: 9014 Cargill Ln Philadelphia PA 19115-4021 Office: Office Asst Gen Coun for the Mid-Atlantic 100 Penn Sq E Philadelphia PA 19107-3322

**CARLIN, PAUL VICTOR,** legal association executive; b. McKeesport, Pa., Nov. 11, 1945. BA, Grove City Coll., 1967; JD, Dickinson Law Sch., 1970. Bar: Pa. 1971, D.C. 1978, U.S. Dist. Ct. (we. dist.) Pa. 1971, U.S. Dist. Ct. D.C. 1978, U.S. Supreme Ct. 1979. Exec. dir. Balt. City Bar Assn., 1981-84, Conn. Bar Assn., Rocky Hill, 1984-85, Md. State Bar Assn., Balt., 1985—; exec. v.p. Pro Bono Resource Ctr., 1990—; asst. sec. treas. Md. Bar Found. Mem. Am. Soc. Assn. Execs. (mem. devel. com. 1995-97, legal sect. coun. 1997—), Legal Mut. Liability Soc. Md. (charter, bd. dirs. 1986—), Phila. Bar Assn. (dir. legal svcs. 1975-77), ABA (standing com. lawyer referral 1977-80, standing com. delivery of legal svcs. com. 1987-89, standing com. assn. com. 1992-96, standing com. on legal assts. 1996-99), Nat. Assn. Bar Execs. (state del. 1987-89, treas. 1989-91, v.p. 1991, pres. elect 1992, pres. 1993, Bolton award for profl. excellence). Office: Md State Bar Assn Inc 520 W Fayette St Baltimore MD 21201-1781

**CARLING, FRANCIS,** lawyer; b. N.Y.C., Nov. 2, 1945; s. James Andrew and Mary Amelia (Lorenzo) C.; m. Elisabeth Morse Kelley, Aug. 30, 1969 (div. Apr. 1979); 1 child, Duncan Campbell; m. Christina Ellen Black, Sept. 28, 1991; children: Graham Black, Gillian Kirova. AB, Fordham U., 1967; JD, Yale U., 1970. Bar: Conn. 1970, U.S. Dist. Ct. Conn. 1971, N.Y. 1972, U.S. Dist. Ct. (so. and ea. dists.) N.Y. 1972, U.S. Ct. Appeals (2nd cir.) 1972, U.S. Supreme Ct. 1973, U.S. Dist. Ct. (no. dist.) Ohio 1978, U.S. Ct. Appeals (3d cir.) 1980, U.S. Dist. Ct. (we. dist.) N.Y. 1981, U.S. Ct. Appeals (6th cir.) 1986, U.S. Ct. Appeals (4th cir.) 1990. Staff atty. New Haven Legal Assistance Assn., 1970-72; assoc. Sullivan & Cromwell, N.Y.C., 1972-80; assoc. Winthrop, Stimson, Putnam & Roberts, N.Y.C., 1980-82, ptnr., 1982-97; ptnr. Collazo Carling & Mish LLP, N.Y.C., 1997—. Author: Move Over: Students, Politics, Religion, 1969. Bd. dirs. Big Bros., Inc. N.Y., N.Y.C., 1974—, pres., 1993-95; v.p. Friends of Afghanistan, Inc., N.Y.C., 1985-90; bd. dirs. Vol. Cons. Group, Inc., N.Y.C., 1988-97. Mem. ABA, N.Y. State Bar Assn., Assn. Bar City N.Y., Union Club. Democrat. Episcopalian. Avocation: music. General civil litigation, Labor, Pension, profit-sharing, and employee benefits. Home: 205 E 69th St New York NY 10021-5402 Office: Collazo Carling & Mish LLP 747 3rd Ave New York NY 10017-2803

**CARLINSKY, MICHAEL BARRY,** lawyer; b. Bklyn., Mar. 7, 1965; s. Herbert and Lucille (Wittman) C.; m. Denise Anne Lindenauer, May 1, 1994; 1 child, Dillon Joseph. BA, Susquehanna U., Selinsgrove, Pa., 1986; JD, Hofstra U., 1989. With Weil Gotshal & Manges, N.Y.C., 1989-93; ptnr. Orrick Herrington & Sutcliffe, N.Y.C., 1993—. Mem. ABA, N.Y. State Bar Assn. General civil litigation, Intellectual property, Securities. Office: Orrick Herrington & Sutcliffe 666 5th Ave Rm 203 New York NY 10103-1798

**CARLIS, BRIAN ALEXANDER,** lawyer; b. Melbourne, Fla., Oct. 2, 1963; s. Bernard Carlis and Nancy McGinley; m. Catherine Ann Costantino, May 13, 1995. BA in Govt. and Politics, U. Md., 1985; JD, Widener U., 1989, LLM in Corp. Law and Fin., 1990. Bar: N.J. 1990, Pa. 1990, U.S. Dist. Ct. N.J. 1990, U.S. Supreme Ct. 1996, U.S. Dist. Ct. (ea. dist.) Pa. 1998, U.S. Ct. Appeals (3d cir.) 1998. Atty. Stark & Stark P.C., Princeton, N.J., 1990—; bd. arbitrators N.Y. Stock Exch., 1998—; panel of arbitrators Am. Arbitration Assn., Somerset, N.J., 1992—. Bd. dirs. Jewish Family and Children's Svcs., Princeton, N.J., 1992—; bd. trustees Jr. Achievement, Princeton, 1991—, cons. project bus. program, 1991—. Avocation: golfing. Securities, General corporate, Non-profit and tax-exempt organizations. Office: Stark & Stark PC PO Box 5315 Princeton NJ 08543-5315

**CARLOCK, GEORGE READ,** lawyer; b. Globe, Ariz., Mar. 10, 1922; s. Frank Hubbard and Judith (Kavanaugh) C.; m. Wanda Drane, Apr. 30, 1950; children: Robert, John, James, Judith. LLB, U. Ariz., 1948. Bar: Ariz. 1948, U.S. Dist. Ct. Ariz. 1948, U.S. Ct.Appeals (9th cir.) 1960, U.S. Supreme Ct. 1966. Ptnr. Ryley, Carlock & Applewhite, Phoenix, 1948—. Served with U.S. Army, 1942-46, USAR, 1946-82. Fellow Am. Coll. Trusts and Estates Counsel, Am. Judicature Soc., Am. Bar Found.; mem. ABA, State Bar Ariz., Ariz. Club (Phoenix), Univ. Club (Phoenix). Republican. Avocation: blacksmithing. Natural resources, Antitrust, General civil litigation. Home: 103 E Palm Ln Unit C Phoenix AZ 85004-1558 Office: Ryley Carlock & Applewhite 101 N 1st Ave Ste 2600 Phoenix AZ 85003-1973

**CARLOCK, MAHLON WALDO, II (STEVE CARLOCK),** lawyer; b. Indpls., June 3, 1955; s. Mahlon Waldo and Betty Lou (Dobbs) C.; m. Robin Elaine Wall Carlock, Dec. 1, 1984; children: Caleb Michael, Hannah Mary. AB, Ind. U., Bloomington, 1977; JD, Ind. U., Indpls., 1981. Bar: Ind. 1981. Dir. Student Asst. Commn., Indpls., 1977-81; atty. pvt. practice, Indpls., 1981-84; v.p., corp. counsel U.S.A. Group, Inc., Indpls., 1985-94; atty. pvt. practice, Indpls., 1994—; mem., 1982-86, pres., 1986 Warren Twp Sch. Bd., Indpls. Author: The Reindeer Rule, 1997, Is Christianity Relevant?, 1998. Elder Trinity Luth. Ch., Indpls., 1997—. Named Hon. Father God and Wife, Indpls., 1987, 91. Mem. Ind. Bar Assn., Indpls. Bar Assn., Am. Corp. Counsel Assn. Republican. Avocations: family, golf, God. Estate planning, Probate, Estate taxation. Office: 8140 Krue Rd Ste 107 Indianapolis IN 46250

**CARLOTTI, STEPHEN JON,** lawyer; b. Providence, Apr. 28, 1942; s. Albert Edward and Rose C.; m. Nancy Ann Arnold, Sept. 16, 1961; children: Stephen J., Cristina C. AB, Dartmouth Coll., 1963; LLB, Yale U., 1966. Bar: R.I. 1966, U.S. Ct. Mil. Appeals 1967, U.S. Ct. Appeals (9th cir.) 1969, U.S. Dist. Ct. R.I. 1970, U.S. Supreme Ct. 1972. Assoc. Hinckley, Allen, Salisbury & Parsons, Providence, 1966, 70-72; ptnr. Hinckley, Allen, & Snyder, Providence, 1972-89, 91, mng. ptnr., 1986-89, 92-96; with The Mut. Benefit Life Ins. Co., Newark, 1989-91; bd. dirs. Fleet Nat. Bank., Accessories Assoc., Inc., W.P.I. Group, Inc. Chmn. Town Com., 1975-76; trustee Roger Williams U., 1978-93, Health Provider Svcs., R.I. Pub. Expenditures Coun. Capt. JAGC, U.S. Army, 1967-70. Mem. ABA, R.I. Bar Assn., R.I. Country Club, Univ. Club. Republican. Roman Catholic. Avocations: golf, tennis, sailing. General corporate, Securities, Real property. Office: Hinckley Allen & Snyder 1500 Fleet Ctr Providence RI 02903-2319

**CARLSON, CHARLES DAVID,** lawyer; b. Washington, June 7, 1954; S. Charles and Louise (Bloom) C.; 1 child: Katherine Anne. BA in History with distinction, Pa. State U., 1975; attended, U. Exeter, Eng., 1975; JD, U. Oreg., 1979. Bar: Oreg. 1980, U.S. Dist. Ct. Oreg. 1980, U.S. Ct. Appeals (9th cir.) 1983, U.S. Ct. Claims 1988, U.S. Supreme Ct. 1993. Rsch. atty. Flinn Brown & Roseta, Eugene, Oreg., 1980; assoc. Flinn Brown & Roseta, Eugene, 1981-86, ptnr., 1987-89; dep. dist. atty. Lane County Dist. Atty.'s Office, Eugene, 1980-81; ptnr. Brown Roseta Long McConville Kilenken & Carlson, Eugene, 1989—; bd. dirs. County View Estate Water System, 1989-91, v.p., 1991-95, pres. 1996-97; judge pro tem Lane County Dist. Ct. and Cir., Eugene, 1991—; adj. instr. Sch. of Law, U. Oreg., Eugene, 1992. Mem. Lane County Bar Assn. (bd. dirs. 1989-91, sec.-treas. 1991-92, pres. 1993-94), Roland Rodman Inns of Ct. (barrister). Republican. Personal injury, Product liability, Insurance. Office: Brown Roseta Long McConville Kilaken & Carlson 44 Club Rd Ste 210 Eugene OR 97401-2460

**CARLSON, CRAIG W.,** lawyer; b. Omaha, Nov. 3, 1963; m. Vicki Carlson. BA in Polit. Sci., U. Nebr., 1986, JD, 1989. Bar: Nebr. 1994, Tex., U.S. Dist. Ct. (we. dist.) Tex., U.S. Dist. Ct. Nebr., U.S. Ct. Mil. Appeals, U.S. Army Ct. Mil. Rev. Assoc. Law Offices Ted Smith, Killeen, Tex.; ptnr. Smith & Carlson, Killeen. With U.S. Army. Mem. ABA, ATLA, Nebr. State Bar Assn., State Bar Tex., Tex. Trial Lawyers Assn., Tex. Young Lawyers Assn., Bell County Young Lawyers Assn., Bell-Lampasas-Mills County Bar Assn. Insurance, Military, General civil litigation. Office: Smith & Carlson PC PO Box 10520 Killeen TX 76547-0520

**CARLSON, DALE LYNN,** lawyer; b. Buffalo, Feb. 21, 1946; s. Andrew Eugene and Edna Lucille (Atwell) C.; m. Virginia Ann Kesler, June 2, 1996. BSChemE, SUNY, Buffalo, 1968, MBA, 1969; JD, Syracuse U., 1975; LLM, NYU, 1979. Bar: N.Y. 1976, D.C. 1978, U.S. Supreme Ct. 1978, U.S. Ct. Appeals (fed. cir.) 1982, Conn. 1988. Mem. legal dept. Union Carbide Corp., N.Y.C. and Danbury, Conn., 1976-86; assoc. patent counsel Olin Corp., 1986-88, counsel, 1988-92, sr. counsel, 1992-93; counsel, Wiggin & Dana, New Haven, Conn., 1993-96, ptnr. Wiggin & Dana, 1997—; lectr. N.Y. Patent, Trademark and Copyright Law Assn., 1978, 87, 90, 96, 97. Editor Syracuse Journal of International Law & Commerce, 1974-75; contbr. articles to profl. jours. Obtained state hist. designation Millplain Community Ch. of Danbury, 1983. Mem. ABA, Am. Intellectual Property Law Assn., Fed. Cir. Bar Assn., Conn. Patent Law Assn., Internat. Intellectual Property Assn., N.Y. Intellectual Property Law Assn. (chmn. continuing legal edn. com. 1985-88, bd. dirs. nominating com. 1986-87, 1991-92, bd. dirs. 1988-91, chmn. lic. to practice requirements com. 1991-94, mem. com. profl. ethics and grievances 1994-97), Internat. Legion of Intelligence, Licensing Execs. Soc., Mensa, Phi Alpha Delta. Patent, Trademark and copyright. Home: 126 Aunt Hack Rd Danbury CT 06811-2724 Office: Wiggin & Dana One Century Twr New Haven CT 06508-1832

**CARLSON, DAVID RUSCO,** lawyer; b. San Antonio, Apr. 17, 1961; s. Robert Dalner C. and Penelope Rusco; m. Kay Marie Lethlean, Apr. 28, 1983; children: Josiah, Erica, Lauren, Noah. BA in English, Portland State U., 1986; JD, Ariz. State U., 1989. Bar: Idaho 1990, Oreg. 1990, U.S. Dist. Ct. Oreg. 1990, U.S. Dist. Ct. Idaho 1990, Ariz. 1994. Prosecutor Malheur County Dist. Atty., Vale, Oreg., 1990-93; county atty. Malheur County, Vale, Oreg., 1993-96; atty. pvt. practice, Vale, Oreg., 1993—; instr. Treasure Valley C.C., Ontario, Oreg., 1990-94, mem. budget bd., 1991-97, vice chair, 1997—, bd. dirs.; mem. Malheur County Commn. Juvenile Drug Ct. Policies and Implementation; lectr. theory and practice of "domestic violence" cases. Scout leader Boy Scouts Am., 1983—. Mem. Nat. Assn. Criminal Defense Lawyers, Oreg. Criminal Defense Lawyers Assn. (bd. dirs. 1995—). Republican. Mem. LDS Ch. Avocations: travel, current events, family, reading. Criminal. Office: 449 Washington St E Vale OR 97918-1254

**CARLSON, EDWARD D.,** lawyer; b. Paterson, N.J., Oct. 6, 1942. BA, U. S. Fla., 1964; JD, U. Fla., 1966. Bar: Fla. 1967. Ptnr. Carlson & Meissner, Clearwater, Fla., 1971—; gen. counsel toups Tech. Inc., St. Petersburg, Fla., 1998. Avocations: water sports, boating, travel. Personal injury, Workers' compensation, General civil litigation. Office: Carlson & Meissner 250 N Belcher Rd Ste 102 Clearwater FL 33765-2600

**CARLSON, J(OHN) PHILIP,** lawyer; b. Shickley, Nebr., Apr. 16, 1915; s. Christopher Theodore and Klara Louise (Blomquist) C.; m. Maryjo Suverkrup, Oct. 14, 1950. AB, Wayne State Coll., 1935; MA, Columbia U., 1967; JD, Georgetown U., 1951. Bar: D.C. 1952, U.S. Dist. Ct. D.C. 1952, U.S. Ct. Appeals D.C. cir. 1952, U.S. Supreme Ct. 1957, U.S. Ct. Mil. Appeals 1970, D.C. Ct. Appeals 1972. Tchr., athletic coach high schs. of Bristow, Nebr., 1935-37, Carroll, Nebr., 1937-38, Ashland, Nebr., 1938-42; vets. rels. advisor OPA, Washington, 1946-47; tng. specialist Dept. Navy, 1947-56; minority counsel House Com. on Govt. Ops., 1956-80; pvt. practice, Washington, 1980-93. Bd. dirs. Fellowship Sq. Found., Reston, Va., 1961-86, Peter Muehlenberg Meml. Assn., 1972-86. Capt. USAAF, 1942-45; ETO. Congl. Staff fellow Am. Polit. Sci. Assn., 1964-65, 66-67; Decorated D.F.C., Air medal with oak leaf cluster; recipient Meritorious Svc. award Am. Nat. Standards Inst., 1984, Meritorious Svc. award Fellowship Square Found., 1986. Mem. ABA, Fed. Bar Assn., D.C. Bar Assn., Am. Judicature Soc., Am. Econ. Assn., Air Force Assn., Res. Officers Assn., Metropolitan Club, Capitol Hill Club, George Town Club, Nat. Econs. Club, Belle Haven Country Club. Republican. Lutheran. Home: 2206 Belle Haven Rd Alexandria VA 22307-1100

**CARLSON, JON GORDON,** lawyer; b. Wakefield, Mich., June 25, 1943; s. John Edwin and Irene Anne (Erickson) C.; m. Jane McCann, June 17, 1965; children: Christine, Eric, Susan. BA, U. Ill., 1965, JD, 1967. Bar: Ill. 1967, Mo. 1990. Assoc. Edward F. O'Malley, East St. Louis, Ill., 1967-68, Kassly, Weihl & Bone, Belleville, Ill., 1968-70; ptnr. Kassly, Weihl, Bone, Becker & Carlson, Belleville, 1970-78, Chapman & Carlson, Ill., 1978-84, Talbert, Carlson & Mallon, Ill., 1985-86, Carlson & Alfeld, Edwardsville, Ill., 1986-87; prin. Jon G. Carlson & Assocs., P.C., Edwardsville, Ill., 1987-94; prin. Carlson, Wendler & Assocs., P.C., Edwardsville, Ill., 1994-99, St. Louis, 1996-99; prin. Carlson & Carlson, P.C., 1999—. Mem. Ill. Trial Lawyers Assn. (pres. 1987-88). Democrat. Avocations: flying (multi-engine instrument rated pilot), walking, hiking. Labor, Personal injury, Product liability. Office: 90 Edwardsville Profl Park PO Box 527 Edwardsville IL 62025-0527

**CARLSON, KATHLEEN BUSSART,** law librarian; b. Charlotte, N.C., June 25, 1956; d. Dean Allyn and Joan (Parlette) Bussart; m. Gerald Mark Carlson, Aug. 15, 1987. BA in Polit. Sci., Ohio State U., 1977; JD, Capital U., 1980; MA in Libr. and Info. Sci., U. Iowa, 1986. Bar: Ohio 1980 (inactive). Editor Lawyers Coop. Pub. Co., Rochester, N.Y., 1980-83; asst. state law libr. State of Wyo., Cheyenne, 1987-88, state law libr., 1988—. 2d v.p., bd. dirs. Wyo. coun. Girl Scouts U.S., Casper, 1990-92, 1st v.p., bd. dirs., 1993-96. Mem. Am. Assn. Law Librs. (sec.-treas., state, ct. and county SIS 1992-95, SCCLL edn. com. 1991-92, chair grants com. 1997-98, nominating com. 1998-99, indexing legal periodical lit. adv. com. 1993-96, chair 1994-96, scholarship com. 1996-98, citation format com. 1998—), Western Pacific Assn. Law Librs. (pres. 1996-97), Wyo. Libr. Assn. (sec. acad. and spl. librs. sect. 1990-92, pres. 1994-95), Bibliog. Ctr. for Rsch. (trustee 1991-95), Kappa Delta, Beta Phi Mu, Zonta Internat. Avocations: arts and crafts, baking. Home: 911 E 18th St Cheyenne WY 82001-4722 Office: State Law Libr 2301 Capitol Ave Cheyenne WY 82002-0001

**CARLSON, RAYMOND HOWARD,** naval officer, lawyer; b. Evergreen Park, Ill., June 19, 1951; s. Howard E. and Elizabeth J. (Lee) C. BSChE, Purdue U., 1973; JD summa cum laude, Ind. U., 1981; LLM, U. Va., 1988; MA in Nat. Security and Strategy, USN War Coll., 1997. Bar: Ind. 1981, Fla. 1993. Commd. ensign USN, 1973, advanced through grades to comdr., 1990; Naval Legal Office, Seattle, 1981-84, Naval Sta., Rota, Spain, 1984-88, Navy Legal Office, Subic Bay, Philippines, 1988-91; prin. legal advisor to comdr. Naval Base, Jacksonville, Fla., 1991-95; prof. jt. mil. ops., internat. law Naval War Coll., Newport, R.I., 1995-97. Mem. ABA, Fed. Bar Assn., Judge Advocates' Assn. Office: Naval Legal Svc Office SE Detachment PO Box 280017 Jacksonville FL 32228-0017

**CARLSON, ROBERT EDWIN,** lawyer; b. Bklyn., Oct. 11, 1930; s. Harry Victor and Lenore Marie (Hanrahan) C.; m. Maureen Eleanor Donnelly, Aug. 24, 1963; children: John T., Katherine L., Elizabeth A., Robert E. Jr. BS, U. Oreg., 1953; JD, U. Calif., San Francisco, 1958; LLM, Harvard U., 1963. Bar: Calif. 1959, U.S. Dist. Ct. (ctrl. dist.) Calif. 1959, U.S. Ct. Appeals (9th cir.) 1959. Assoc. Kindel & Anderson, L.A., 1958-63, ptnr., 1963-67; ptnr. Agnew, Miller & Carlson, L.A., 1967-80, Hufstedler, Miller, Carlson & Beardsley, L.A., 1980-88, Paul, Hastings, Janofsky & Walker, L.A., 1988—; pres. Constl. Rights Found., L.A., 1978-80, L.A. County Bar Found., 1988-89; mem. exec. com. bus. sect. L.A. Bar Assn., 1982-89; bd. dirs. Legal Aid Found., L.A. Bd. dirs. Westridge Sch. for Girls, Pasadena, Calif., 1985-91, Trust for Pub. Land, San Francisco, 1987—; chair bd. Skid Row Housing Trust, L.A., 1989—; bd. visitors Santa Clara Law Sch., 1986-92. With U.S. Army, 1953-55. Recipient Griffin Bell award Dispute Resolution Svcs., Inc., 1992, Katherine Krause award Inner City Law Ctr., 1996. Mem. ABA (mem. securities com., co-chair com. devel. investment svcs., mem. task force to prepare guidebook for dirs. mut. funds 1995, chairperson youth edn. for citizenship, Chgo. 1982-85), Calif. State Bar (mem. corp. com. 1990—), Valley Hunt Club, Chancery Club, Calif. Club. Democrat. Avocations: hiking, tennis, reading, skiing. General corporate, Securities, Finance. Office: Paul Hastings Janofsky & Walker 555 S Flower St Fl 23 Los Angeles CA 90071-2300

**CARLSON, SUSAN MARIE,** lawyer; b. Seattle, June 8, 1956; d. Donald Graham and Etta Joyce (Davis) Lomax; m. Stanley Jon Carlson, Mar. 10; 1 child, Cody Jon. ATA, South Puget Sound C.C., 1975; BA in Polit. Sci., Wash. State U., 1978; JD, U. Wash., 1981. Bar: Wash. 1981. Dep. prosecuting atty. Chelan County Prosecutor's Office, Wenatchee, Wash., 1982-89; chief criminal dep. asst. atty. gen. Atty. Gen.'s Office, Olympia, Wash., 1989-90; staff counsel to law and justice com. Wash. State Senate, Olympia, 1990-96, dep. sec. of senate, 1996—. Recipient S. Towne Stevenson scholar award Wash. State U., 1978. Avocation: Equestrian drill team, gardening, sewing. Home: 2818 Madrona Beach Rd NW Olympia WA 98502-8865 Office: Wash State Senate 306 Legislative Bldg Olympia WA 98502

**CARLTON, ALFRED PERSHING, JR.,** lawyer; b. Raleigh, N.C., Aug. 27, 1947; s. Alfred P. and Katherine (Singleton) C.; children: Mary Elizabeth, Troy Eugene. BSBA, U. N.C., 1969, JD, 1975; MPA, U. Dayton, 1973. Bar: N.C. 1975, U.S. Dist. Ct. (ea. dist.) N.C. 1975, U.S. Ct. Appeals (4th cir.) 1976, U.S. Supreme Ct. 1993. Pvt. practice Raleigh, 1975-77; counsel N.C. Bankers Assn., Raleigh, 1977-79; sec., gen. counsel Bancshares N.C., Inc., Raleigh, 1979-82; adj. prof. law Campbell U., Buies Creek, N.C., 1979-82; ptnr. Sanford, Adams, McCullough & Beard, Raleigh, 1983-89; shareholder McNair & Sanford, Raleigh, 1990-95; ptnr. The Sanford Holshouser Law Firm, Raleigh, 1995—. Mem. City of Raleigh Hist. Properties and Hist. Dists. Commn., 1978-82; mem. exec. bd. Occoneechee coun. Boy Scouts Am., 1983-84; trustee U. N.C. at Wilmington, 1997—. Served to 1st lt. Med. Svc. Corps, USAF, 1970-73. Fellow Am. Bar Found.; mem. ABA (ho. of dels. 1987—, chair of the house 1996-98, bd. govs. 1996-98), N.C. Bar Assn. (bd. govs. 1981-82, 92-95), Am. Law Inst., N.C. Legis. Rsch. Commn. (study com. on pub. financing 1985-88). Democrat. Episcopalian. Avocations: tennis, gardening. Securities, Banking, Municipal (including bonds). Office: The Sanford Holshouser Law Firm PO Box 2447 Raleigh NC 27602-2447

**CARLUCCI, PAUL PASQUALE,** lawyer; b. N.Y.C., Sept. 26, 1949; s. Nicholas Carlucci and Anastasia Di Vincenzo; m. Marie A. McNamee, Aug. 18, 1973; children: Christine Marie Anastasia, Patricia Ann Rebecca. BS, Fordham U., 1971, JD, 1974. Bar: N.Y. 1975, D.C. 1975, U.S. Dist. Ct. (so. and ea. dists.) N.Y. 1975, U.S. Supreme Ct. 1982. Staff atty. Legal Aid Soc., N.Y.C., 1975; atty. of record Liberty Mutual Ins., Scarsdale, N.Y., 1975-88; atty. Belkin, Natale & Oxman, Hawthorne, N.Y., 1988-90; prin. law sec. hon. Harold L. Wood N.Y. State Supreme Ct., White Plains, 1990-95; mng. atty. Nat. Grange Mutual Ins. Co., N.Y.C., 1995-99. Contbr. articles to profl. jours. Chmn. Cons. Bd., New Castle, N.Y., 1987-88, Environ. Rev. Bd., New Castle, 1988-90; councilman Town Bd., New Castle, 1990-95. Regents scholar, Nat. Merit scholar. Mem. N.Y. State Bar Assn. (civil practice com., surrogate decision making com.). Avocations: legal writing, camping, reading. State civil litigation, Personal injury, Insurance. Home: 3916 Appletree Dr Valrico FL 33594

**CARMACK, AMIE FLOWERS,** lawyer; b. Sanford, N.C., June 18, 1969; s. Louis Eskal and Betty Catherine (Halees) Flowers; m. Kenneth L. Carmack, II, Apr. 25, 1992. BA, Wake Forest U., 1991, JD, 1995. Law clk. to Hon. William L. Osteen U.S. Dist. Ct., Greensboro, N.C., 1995-96; assoc. atty. Fisher, Gayle, Clinard, Craig & Lackey, P.A., High Point, N.C., 1996-98, Smith Helms Mulliss & Moore L.L.P., Greensboro, 1998—; adj. prof. High Point U., 1997—. Editor-in-chief Wake Forest Law Rev., 1994-95. Mem. ABA, Greensboro Bar Assn., Guilford Inn of Ct. Avocations: painting, drawing and design; cycling; water sports. Appellate, Federal civil litigation, State civil litigation. Office: Smith Helms Mulliss & Moore 300 N Greene St Greensboro NC 27401-2167

**CARMAN, ERNEST DAY,** lawyer; b. Mpls.; s. Ernest Clarke and Juanita Howland (Day) C.; children Eric, Brooke (dec.), Christiane, Dayna. BA, U. So. Calif.; MA, Stanford U.; Dr. ès Sci. Pol., U. Geneva, Switzerland; JD, U. San Francisco. Bar: Calif. 1957, U.S. Supreme Ct. 1973. Ptnr. Adams, Carman, Mansfield, Ball and Wenzel, Carman and Mansfield, 1965-70; judge protem Santa Clara County Superior Ct., Orange County Superior Ct.; dir.

various corps. Contbr. articles to profl. jours. Past chmn. Santa Clara County Dem. Cen. Com. Maj. USMCR. Mem. ABA, Calif. Trial Lawyers Assn., Calif. Employment Lawyers Assn. Civil rights, General civil litigation, General practice. Office: 250 Newport Center Dr Ste 102 Newport Beach CA 92660-7517

**CARMAN, GREGORY WRIGHT,** federal judge; b. Farmingdale, N.Y., Jan. 31, 1937; s. Willis B. and Marjorie (Sosa) C. Exch. student, U. Paris, 1956-57; BA, St. Lawrence U., 1958; JD, St. John's U., 1961; Judge Adv. Gen. honors grad., U. Va. Law Sch., 1962. Bar: N.Y. 1961. Atty. Carman, Callahan & Sabino, Farmingdale, N.Y., 1964-83; councilman Town of Oyster Bay, N.Y., 1972-81; mem. 97th Congress from 3d Dist. N.Y., 1981-82; U.S. Congl. del. I.M.F. Cong., 1982; judge U.S. Ct. Internat. Trade, N.Y.C., 1983—, acting chief judge, 1991, now chief judge; statutory mem. Jud. Conf. U.S., 1991. Capt. AUS, 1962-64. Fellow Am. Bar Found.; mem. ABA, N.Y. State Bar Assn. (cts. and cmty. com.), N.Y. State Defs. Assn., Criminal Cts. Bar Assn., Nassau County Bar Assn., Nassau Lawyers Assn., St. John's Law Rev. Republican. Episcopalian. Office: US Ct Internat Trade 1 Federal Plz New York NY 10278-0001

**CARMAN, LAURA JUNGE,** lawyer; b. New Orleans, Mar. 23, 1952; d. Lester Ernest and Bernice D. Junge; m. Allen Solari Carman Jr., Feb. 23, 1986; 1 child, Richard Junge Carman. BA magna cum laude, Vanderbilt U., 1974; JD, Tulane U., 1977. Bar: La. 1977, U.S. Dist. Ct. (ea. dist.) La. 1978. Pvt. practice New Orleans, 1978—; assoc. adj. prof. Tulane U., New Orleans, 1983-87, fellow, Amer. Coll. of Trust and Estate Couns. Author: Louisiana Succession Pleadings: A Systems Approach, 1986, Louisiana Successions (2d edit., 1998), 1991. Recipient Tchr. Recognition award Tulane U., 1986-87. Mem. New Orleans Bar Assn. (past chairperson com. on probate trusts and estate planning), La. Bar Assn. (past pres. sect. on immovable property, probate and estate trusts). E-mail: ljcaplc@aol.com. Estate planning, Probate, Estate taxation. Office: 25 Crane St New Orleans LA 70124-4309

**CARMAN, STEVEN F.,** lawyer; b. Evanston, Ill., July 25, 1959; s. Bruce P. and Barbara J. Carman; m. Alice E. Blondin, June 30, 1984. BA, Hamilton Coll., 1981; JD, MBA, U. Pa., 1985. Bar: N.Y. 1985, Mo. 1989. Assoc. Cadwalader, Wickersham & Taft, N.Y.C., 1985-88, Morrison & Hecker, Kansas City, Mo., 1988-95; ptnr. Blackwell Sanders Matheny Weary & Lombardi LLP, Kansas City, Mo., 1995—. Mem. Prairie Village (Kans.) City Coun., 1991—; bd. dirs. United Cmty. Svcs. of Johnson County, Enterprise Ctr. Johnson County. Mem. Mo. Bar Assn., Alumni Coun. Hamilton Coll. Securities, General corporate, Real property. Office: Blackwell Sanders Peper Martin LLP 2300 Main St Fl 11 Kansas City MO 64108-2415

**CARMICHAEL, JAMES EDWARD,** lawyer; b. Marshalltown, Iowa, Feb. 18, 1954; s. V. Edward Carmichael and Mary Francis McCaffrey; m. Cindy L. Carmichael, Nov. 28, 1980 (dec. Nov. 1987); m. Karen L. Carmichael, Oct. 24, 1992; children: Richard, Ryan, Christopher. BA, Truman State U., 1976; JD, Washington U., St. Louis, 1979. Bar: Mo., U.S. Dist. Ct. (ea. dist.) Mo. Founding ptnr. Carmichael & Burlison, O'Fallon, Mo., 1980-85; ptnr. Kennedy & Carmichael, St. Charles, Mo., 1985-86, Rollings, Gernardt, St. Charles, 1987-96, Niedner, Bodeux, Carmichael Huff & Lenox, St. Charles, 1997—. Contbr. articles to profl. jours. Mem. St. Charles County Bar Assn. (pres. 1990), Mo. Assn. of Trail Attys. (bd. govs. 1998—), Kiwanis (bd. dirs. 1988-92). Southern Baptist. Avocations: snow skiing, coaching boys sports. Personal injury, Criminal. Office: Niedner Bodeux Carmichael Huff & Lenox 131 Jefferson St Saint Charles MO 63301-2819

**CARMODY, ARTHUR RODERICK, JR.,** lawyer; b. Shreveport, La., Feb. 19, 1928; s. Arthur R. and Caroline (Gaughan) C.; m. Renee Aubry, Jan. 26, 1952 (div. 1980); children: Helen Bragg, Renee, Arthur Roderick, Patrick, Timothy, Mary, Virginia, Joseph; m. Mary Wells, Sept. 1, 1990. Grad. with honors, N.Mex. Mil. Inst.; BS, Fordham U., 1949; LLB, La. State U., 1952. Bar: La. 1952, U.S. Supreme Ct. 1971. Mem. firm Wilkinson, Carmody & Gilliam and its predecessors, Shreveport, 1952—; bd. dirs. Kansas City So. Transport Co., Kansas City, Shreveport and Gulf Terminal Co., Shreveport Braves Baseball Club (Tex. League), Sta. KDAQ-FM Pub. Radio, pres., 1991, chmn., 1992, RED River Pub. Radio Newtwork; mem. Shreveport Steamer (World Football League) Partnership; pres. Touchdown Club of Shreveport, 1960. Author: Legal Problems in the Development and Mining of Lignite, 1976; legal history columnist Shreveport Bar Review, 1995—; La. adv. editor The Insurance Bar, 1961—. Chmn. Met. Shreveport Zoning Bd. Appeals, 1959-72; pres. bd. trustees Jesuit H.S., 1976-82; chmn. bd. govs. Loyola Found. Shreveport, 1991-94; trustee Schumpert Med. Ctr., 1965-85; bd. dirs. La. State U. Found., Baton Rouge, Agnew Day Sch., Shreveport, 1970-82, Ridgewood Montessori Sch.; nat. bd. dirs. N.Mex. Mil. Inst., Roswell, 1967-68 (named to Alumni Hall of Fame 1994); adv. coun. La. State U., Shreveport, 1982-86; govs. ad hoc com. for preparation rules and regulations for mining and reclamation of lignite in the State of La., Dept. Conservation, 1978-79; select com. mem. for rev. stds. jud. conducts Supreme Ct. of La., 1994-98. 1st lt. USAR, 1948-50. Recipient Alumni Achievement award Fordham U., 1995; named Hon. Alumnus, elected to Ring of Honor Loyola Coll. Prep., 1993. Master Am. Inns of Ct.; fellow Am. Coll. Trial Lawyers, La. Bar Assn. (mem. com. on lawyer and judicial conduct 1996-98); mem. ABA, Fed. Bar Assn., Shreveport Bar Assn., U.S. Supreme Ct. Hist. Soc., Fifth Fed. Cir. Bar Assn., Federalist Soc., North La. Hist. Soc., La. Hist. Assn., Confederate Meml. Lit. Soc., Nat. Soc. SAR (pres. Galvez chpt. 1997), Scribes Soc., Supreme Ct. of La. Hist. Soc., Univ. Assocs. of La. State U., Am. Judicature Soc., La. Law Inst., Trial Attys. Am., Nat. Assn. R.R. Trial Counsel, Internat. Assn. Def. Counsel, La. Assn. Def. Counsel, Nat. Acad. Law and Medicine, Am. Arbitration Assn. (panel arbitrators), Mid-Continent Oil and Gas Assn. (exec. com. 1984—), La. R.R. Assn. (exec. com. 1992—), Tarshar Soc., La. Assn. Bus. and Industry, Nat. Legal Ctr. for the Pub. Interest, Pub. Affairs Rsch. Coun., Shreveport C. of C. (dir. 1968-70), Kansas City So. Hist. Soc., Railway and Locomoitve Hist. Soc., Soc. Hosp. Counsel, La. Civil Svc. League, La. State U. Found., Res. Officers Assn., North La. Civil War Round Table, U.S. Horse Cavalry Assn., Soc. for Mil. History, Soc. for Civil War History, Federalist Soc., Sovereign Mil. Order of Malta, Phi Delta Phi, Kappa Alpha. General civil litigation, Labor, Transportation. Home: 255 Forest Ave Shreveport LA 71104-4506 Office: Wilkinson Carmody & Gilliam 1700 Beck Bldg 400 Travis St Shreveport LA 71101-3108

**CARMODY, JAMES ALBERT,** lawyer; b. St. Louis, Nov. 21, 1945; m. Helen Tippy Valin, mar. 22, 1969; children: Paul Valin, Leigh Christin. BA, Vanderbilt U., 1967; JD, U. Ark., 1973. Bar: Tex. 1974, U.S. Dist. Ct. (so. dist.) Tex. 1974, U.S. Ct. Appeals (5th, 9th and 10th cirs.) 1975, U.S. Supreme Ct., 1996. Assoc. Mabry & Gunn, Texas City, Tex., 1974-75; mcpl. ct. judge Texas City, Tex., 1975; assoc. Chamberlain & Hrdlicka, Houston, 1975-78, ptnr., 1978-89; ptnr. Keck Mahin & Cate, Houston, 1989-94, Carmody & Yokubaitis, L.L.P., Houston, 1995—. Assoc. editor U. Ark. Law Rev., 1973. Incorporator, Gulf Coast Big Bros. and Sisters, Inc., Galveston County, Tex., 1975; mem. St. Maximillian Cath. Community Bldg. Com., Houston, 1985-88. Served to lt. USN, 1967-71. Mem. Galveston County Jr. Bar Assn. (pres. 1975, Outstanding Young Lawyer award 1975), Harris County Bar Assn. (arbitrator fee dispute com. 1997—), Entrepreneurship Inst. Houston (chmn. 1991-94), Greater Houston Partnership (Mex. and Ams. com.), Delta Theta Phi (master insp. 1983-85, dean Houston alumni senate 1988, bd. dirs. Found.). Republican. Roman Catholic. Avocations: ham radio, international travel, satellite communications. E-mail: carmody@lawyer.com. General civil litigation, Contracts commercial, Private international. Home: 15910 Congo Ln Houston TX 77040-2120

**CARMODY, RICHARD PATRICK,** lawyer; b. Chgo., June 2, 1942; s. Thomas Francis and Margaret (Tully) C.; m. Alison Pierce Cutter, Dec. 27, 1968; children: Elizabeth Hall Carmody, Emily Pierce Carmody. BA, U. Ill., 1964; JD, Vanderbilt U., 1975. Bar: Ala. 1975, U.S. Dist. Ct. (no., mid. and so. dists.) Ala. 1975, U.S. Ct. Appeals (11th cir.) 1985, U.S. Supreme Ct. 1988. Assoc. Lange, Simpson, Robinson & Somerville, Birmingham, Ala., 1975-81, ptnr., 1981—; chmn. exec. com. Lange, Simpson Robinson & Somerville, Birmingham, Ala., 1987-93; mem. Am. Bankruptcy Inst., Washington, 1985—, c-chair ethics com. 1999—; bd. dirs. Coun. of Cert. Bankruptcy Specialists, 1993—; bd. cert. Bus. Bankruptcy Am. Bd. of Cert. Bd. dirs. Birmingham coun. Campfire Boys and Girls Inc., 1978-90, pres., 1983-85; mem. exec. com. Ala. region NCCJ, 1995—, chair fin. com. Fellow Am. Coll. Bankruptcy, 1999—. Mem. Ala. Bar Assn. (chmn. bankruptcy and comml. law sect. 1985, mem. exec. com. 1986-93), Greystone Golf Club, Kiwanis. Roman Catholic. Avocations: golf, sports. Banking, Bankruptcy, Contracts commercial.

**CARNAHAN, ROBERT NARVELL,** lawyer; b. Littlefield, Tex., Nov. 22, 1928; s. C.D. and Wilma L. (Hartness) C.; children from previous marriage: Cynthia, Michael, Christopher; m. Natalie Kay Kowalik, May 8, 1993. BBA, Tex. Tech. Coll., 1950; JD with honors, U. Tex.-Austin, 1957. Bar: Tex. 1956. Asst. county atty. Potter County, Tex., Amarillo; ptnr. Stokes, Carnahan & Fields, Amarillo; sole practice Corpus Christi, Tex. Contbr. articles to profl. jours. 1st lt. USAF, 1954. Named one of top ten young lawyers in Am., Nat. Jaycees, 1967. Mem. State Bar Tex., Nueces County Bar Assn., Tex. Trial Lawyers Assn., Tex. Assn. Criminal Def. Lawyers, Am. Judicature Assn. Personal injury, Labor, Product liability. Office: 730 Wilson Plz Corpus Christi TX 78476

**CARNES, EDWARD E.,** federal judge; b. 1950. BS, U. Ala., Tuscaloosa, 1972; JD, Harvard U., 1975. Asst. Ala. atty. gen. Office Atty. Gen., 1975-92; cir. judge U.S. Ct. Appeals (11th cir.), Montgomery, Ala., 1992—. Office: Frank M Johnson Jr Fed Bldg US Courthouse 15 Lee St Ste 410 Montgomery AL 36104-4055*

**CARNES, JULIE ELIZABETH,** federal judge; b. Atlanta, Oct. 31, 1950; m. Stephen S. Cowen. AB summa cum laude, U. Ga., 1972, JD magna cum laude, 1975. Bar: Ga. 1975. Law clk. to Hon. Lewis R. Morgan U.S. Ct. Appeals (5th cir.), 1975-77; spl. counsel U.S. Sentencing Commn., 1989, commr., 1990-96; asst. U.S. Atty. U.S. Dist. Ct. (no. dist.) Ga., Atlanta, 1978-90, judge, 1992—. Office: US Courthouse 75 Spring St SW Ste 2167 Atlanta GA 30303-3309

**CARNES, THOMAS MASON,** lawyer; b. Buffalo, Apr. 9, 1931; s. Ernest S. and Mary (Bowes) C.; m. Alice Ann Carnes, Aug. 28, 1955; children: Juliana, Christine, Dell. BA, St. John's Coll., Annapolis, Md., 1952; LLB, U. Mich., 1958. Bar: Calif. 1959, U.S. Dist. Ct. (no. dist.) Calif. 1959. Assoc. Pillsbury Madison & Sutro, San Francisco, 1958-59, Partridge, O'Connel Patrridge & Fall, San Francisco, 1959-64; sole practitioner San Francisco, 1965—. Mem. bd. visitors and govs. St. John's Coll., 1979-98. Cpl. U.S. Army, 1953-56. Mem. Bar Assn. San Francisco (bd. dirs. 1985-87), Am. Bd. Trial Advocates. Avocation: yachting. Professional liability, Personal injury, Insurance. Office: 50 Francisco St Ste 420 San Francisco CA 94133-2114

**CARNESI, KENNETH BRIAN,** lawyer; b. N.Y.C., May 29, 1953; s. Frank and Angela (Dinardo) C.; m. Daria Mary Chmil, July 22, 1978; children: Kenneth Brian Jr., Katherine Elizabeth. BA, Bklyn. Coll., 1975; MPS, L.I. U., 1977; JD, N.Y. Law Sch., 1982. Bar: N.Y. 1983. Bank officer Chemical Bank, N.Y.C., 1978-82, counsel, 1982-84; ptnr. Carnesi & Assocs., Garden City, N.Y., 1984—; pres. Banfinanz Internat., Inc., N.Y.C., 1996—; bd. dirs. The Prime Mint, Inc., N.Y.C., FAS Fragrances, Inc., N.Y.C., Granite State Mint, Inc., Amherst, N.H.. Contbr. articles to profl. jours. Recipient Elsberg award N.Y. Law Sch., N.Y.C., 1982, Human Rights Jour. award N.Y. Law Sch., 1982. Mem. Nassau County Bar Assn., ABA, Am. Mgmt. Assn. Republican. Roman Catholic. Private international, Public international, Real property. Office: EAB Plaza W Tower Fl 6 Uniondale NY 11556-0001

**CARNESOLTAS, ANA-MARIA,** lawyer; b. Havana, Cuba, Feb. 9, 1948; came to U.S., 1962; d. Manuel Ramon and Zenaida de las Mercedes (Enriquez) C.; 1 child, Caroline. BA, U. Calif., Santa Barbara, 1970; JD, Loyola U., L.A., 1978. Bar: Calif. 1978, Fla. 1979. Dep probation officer Probation Dept., Santa Barbara, Calif., 1970-73; personnel analyst Dept. Personnel, L.A., 1973-77; dep. dist. atty. Dist. Atty.'s Office, L.A., 1978-80; asst. U.S. atty. U.S. Atty.'s Office, Miami, Fla., 1980-82; pvt. practice law, Miami, 1982-83, Coral Gables, Fla., 1985-89; asst. city atty. City Atty.'s Office, Miami, 1983-85; judge Dade (Fla.) County Ct., 1989-93; pvt. practice, 1993—; lectr. YMCA, Miami, 1983-89; adj. prof. Fla. Internat. U.; prof. Miami-Dade C.C., 1989-92; hearing officer Dade County Pub. Schs., Miami, 1985-89; legal commentator Sta. WCMQ, Miami, 1993—. Bd. dirs. Am. Heart Assn., Miami, 1983-86, YWCA, 1985-89, Alzheimer's Disease and Related Disorders Assn., 1987. Named Disting. Advocate, Loyola Law Sch., 1978. Mem. Nat. Assn. Women Judges (outreach com., task force on minority concerns, internat. community outreach com.), Conf. County Ct. Judges (edn. com., small claims com., civic proc. rules com.), Calif. Probation Parole and Corrections Assn. (v.p. 1972-73), Cuban Am. Attys. Council (sec. 1979-80), Cuban Am. Bar Assn. (dir. 1983, 88, sec. 1984), Dade County Bar Assn., ABA, Fla. Assn. Women Lawyers, Assn. Trial Lawyers Am., Fed. Bar Assn., Latin Bus. and Profl. Women's Club (pres. 1984-85, v.p.), Cuban Women's Club. Republican. Roman Catholic. General civil litigation, Criminal, Family and matrimonial. Office: 7800 SW 57th Ave Ste 220A South Miami FL 33143

**CARNEY, DEBORAH LEAH TURNER,** lawyer; b. Great Bend, Kans., Aug. 19, 1952; d. Harold Lee and Elizabeth Lura (Dillon) Turner; m. Thomas J.T. Carney, Mar. 20, 1976; children: Amber Blythe, Sonia Briana, Ross Dillon. BA in Human Biology, Stanford U., 1974; JD, U. Denver, 1976. Bar: Kans. 1977, U.S. Dist. Ct. Kans. 1977, U.S. Ct. Appeals (10th cir.) 1982, Colo. 1984, U.S. Dist. Ct. Colo. 1984, U.S. Supreme Ct. 1989, U.S. Claims Ct. 1990. With Turner & Boisseau, Great Bend, 1976-84, of counsel, 1984-93; assoc. Lutz & Oliver, Arvada, Colo., 1984-85; prin. Deborah Turner Carney, P.C., Golden and Lakewood, Colo., 1985-92; shareholder Carney Law Office, Golden, Colo., 1992-95; owner Carney Law Office, 1995—. Author (newsletter) Profl. Solutions, 1984, (chpt.) Courtroom Handbook; editor Apple Law newsletter, 1984-86; contbr. articles to profl. jours. Pres. Canyon Area Residents for the Environment (C.A.R.E.), 1998. Mem. Colo. Trial Lawyers Assn., 1st Jud. Dist. Bar Assn. (Colo.), Genesee Daytime Bookclub (co-chair 1997-98), Kiwanis (bd. dirs. Denver club 1988-90, trustee 1990-92, sec. 1992-93). Republican. Avocations: horses, dancing, computers. E-mail: deb@carneylaw.net. Personal injury, Federal civil litigation, State civil litigation. Office: 21789 Cabrini Blvd Golden CO 80401-9488

**CARNEY, DONALD FRANCIS, JR.,** lawyer; b. Detroit, July 30, 1948; s. Donald F. and Kathryn (Lucas) C.; m. Jacqueline Anne Miller, Aug. 28, 1971; children: Jennifer Suzanne, Julianne, Rebecca Ann. BA, Mich. State U., 1970; JD, Detroit Coll. Law, 1976. Assoc. Dinan & Schenden, P.C., Troy, Mich., 1977-79, Joslyn & Keydel, Detroit, 1979-83; ptnr. Joslyn, Keydel, Wallace & Joslyn, Detroit, 1983-88, Joslyn Keydel Wallace & Carney, Detroit, 1988-93; shareholder Kemp, Klein, Humphrey & Endelman, Detroit, 1993—. Mem. ABA, Oakland County Bar Assn., Detroit Bar Assn., Fin. and Estate Planning Council Detroit, Quarton Lake Neighborhood Assn. (pres. 1989-96), Sigma Chi Alumni Assn. (pres. 1984), Gamma Psi Alumni House Corp. (bd. dirs. 1970-86, pres. 1975-76). Roman Catholic. Clubs: Detroit Athletic, Orchard Lake Country. Probate, Estate planning, State civil litigation.

**CARNEY, GERARD BARRY,** lawyer; b. Brockton, Mass., Aug. 9, 1949; s. John T. and Helen G. (Butler) C.; m. Cynthia A. Jones, June 25, 1976; children: Brendan Gerard, Meredith Patricia. BS, Boston Coll., 1971; JD, Suffolk U., 1980. Bar: Mass. 1980, U.S. Ct. Appeals (1st cir.) 1980, U.S. Dist. Ct. R.I. 1981, U.S. Supreme Ct. 1984. Asst. dist. atty. Bristol County, Mass., 1980; ptnr. Ashcraft & Gerel, Boston and Washington, 1980-86, Wynn & Wynn P.C., Raynham, Mass., 1986-90, Hislop, Carney & Troupe, Boston, 1990-98, Carney & Troupe, Boston, 1999—. Fides patron Boston Coll. Alumni Assn., Chestnut Hill, Mass., 1991—. Mem. ATLA, ABA, Mass. Acad. Trial Attys. (co-chair worker's compensation sect. 1998—), Mass. Bar Assn., Sports Lawyers Assn. Avocations: outdoor sports, jogging, student pilot. Workers' compensation, Personal injury, Sports. Office: Carney & Troupe 5th Fl 10 High St Ste 5 Boston MA 02110-1605

**CARNEY, JOSEPH BUCKINGHAM,** lawyer; b. Greensburg, Ind., July 8, 1928; s. Edward O. and Grace Rebecca (Buckingham) C.; m. Constance J. Caylor, July 8, 1950; children: Elizabeth, Joseph Buckingham Jr., Julia, Sarah. AB, DePauw U., 1950; LLB, Harvard U., 1953. Bar: D.C. 1953, Ind. 1953, U.S. Dist. Ct. (so. dist.) Ind. 1953, U.S. Supreme Ct. 1957, U.S. Ct. Appeals (7th cir.) 1961; ind. cert. mediator. Assoc. Hogg, Peters & Leonard, Ft. Wayne, Ind., 1953-54; assoc. Baker & Daniels, Indpls., 1957-62, ptnr., 1962-95, mem. mgmt. com., 1993-94, sec., 1994, of counsel, 1996—; mem. lawyers com. Nat. Ctr. State Cts., Williamsburg, Va., 1985—; assoc. Environ. Law Inst., Washington. Chmn. bd. dirs. Parkinson Awareness Assn. Ctrl. Ind., Inc.; past pres. Interfaith Homes, Inc., Indpls.; past chmn., elder Northwood Christian Ch., Indpls. 1st lt. U.S. Army, 1954-57. Recipient Disting. Alumni award DePauw U., 1984. Mem. ABA, Ind. Bar Assn., Indpls. Bar Assn., Am. Judicature Soc., 7th Cir. Bar Assn. (pres. 1983-84), Univ. Club, Indpls. Athletic Club, Columbia Club, Contemporary, Lawyers Club Indpls. (past pres.), Phi Eta Sigma, Phi Gamma Delta (bd. dirs. 1974-78, sec. 1976-78, pres. 1980-82), Phi Gamma Delta Ednl. Found. (bd. dirs., pres. 1996-98). Avocations: scuba diving, travel, photography. Environmental, Administrative and regulatory, General civil litigation. Office: Baker & Daniels 300 N Meridian St Ste 2700 Indianapolis IN 46204-1782

**CARNEY, T. J,** lawyer; b. Denver, July 18, 1952; s. Thomas Joseph Carney and Patricia (Amack) Carney Calkins; m. Deborah Leah Turner, Mar. 20, 1976; children: Amber Blythe, Sonia Briana, Ross Dillon. BA in Econs., U. Notre Dame, Ind., 1974; JD, U. Denver, 1976. Bar: Colo. 1977, Kans. 1977, U.S. Dist. Ct. Colo. 1977, U.S. Dist. Ct. Kans. 1977, U.S. Dist. Ct. Ariz. 1995, U.S. Ct. Appeals (10th cir.) 1983. Legal asst. Turner & Hensley, Chartered, Great Bend, Kans., 1977; atty.-shareholder Turner and Boisseau, Chartered, Great Bend, 1977-84; atty., shareholder Bradley, Campbell, Carney & Madsen, Golden, Colo., 1984-92, 95-97; atty.-shareholder Deborah & T.J. Carney, P.C., Lakewood and Golden, 1992-95; atty. officer Carney Law Office, 1997-99; spl. counsel Oliver & Kirven, P.C., Arvada, Colo., 1999; shareholder Oliver and Carney, P.C., 1999—; CLE instr. Nat. Inst. Trial Advocacy, 1st Jud. Bar Assn., Colo. Inc.; cons. Vocat. Econs., Inc., 1998, others. Precinct com. Rep. Party, Jefferson County, Colo., 1988-94, area capt., 1994-96. Mem. Colo. Bar Assn., Colo. Trial Lawyers Assn. (CLE), Kansas Bar Assn., Kans. Trial Lawyers Assn., 1st Jud. Dist. Bar Assn. (trustee 1990-94), Phi Delta Phi (Province Grad. of Yr. 1977). Avocations: flying, martial arts, skiing, lacrosse, ballroom dancing. Fax: 303-424-3629. Fax: (978) 334-5992. E-mail: tjc@carneylaw.net. Real property, General civil litigation, Contracts commercial. Office: Oliver and Carney PC 7903 Ralston Rd Arvada CO 80002-2435

**CAROL, JOAN,** mediator, consultant; b. Hershey, Pa., Aug. 25, 1947; 1 child, Byron T. Hogan. BS, Shippensburg U., 1968; postgrad. studies, Calif. State U., L.A., 1970-71; JD, Southwestern U., L.A., 1975; postgrad., U. Tex., 1997. Bar: Calif. 1975, Tex. 1993; ordained interfaith minister Congregational Ch. of Practical Theology, Springield, La.; Reiki master; cert. instr. Nat. Guild Hypnotists. Tchr. Lower Paxton Sch. Dist., Harrisburg, Pa., Pasadena (Calif.) Sch. Dist.; adminstrv. asst., comml. paper buyer Transam. Investment Mgmt. Co., L.A., Calif.; law clk. Am. Civil Liberties Union, L.A., 1974-75; pvt. practice law Beverly Hills, Calif., 1976-93; conflict resolution mediator, 1987—; pvt. practice law Brenham, Tex., 1993-98. Author: (poetry) Journey of Many Sojourns, 1993; (book) Practice Guide: Protect Your Rights to Health, Healing, Hypnotherapy, 1994; contbr. poems to anthologies of Nat. Libr. Poetry. Bd. dirs. Tex. Assn. Against Sexual Assault, Austin, 1997-98, Felicity House for Women in Recovery, L.A., 1987-89; organizer, chair Parents on Patrol Program, Brenham (Tex.) Ind. Sch. Dist., 1993-94; vol. political campaigns, pro bono legal counseling and mediation; vol. women's prison project Calif. Inst. for Women, Chino through Loyola U., L.A. Office: PO Box 60418 Colorado Springs CO 80960-0418

**CAROME, PATRICK JOSEPH,** lawyer; b. Cleve., Nov. 20, 1957; s. Edward Francis and Jeanne Marie (Carrabine) C.; m. Elsie Elizabeth Orr, Oct. 7, 1989. BA, Boston Coll., Chestnut Hill, Mass., 1980; JD, Harvard U., 1983. Bar: Mass. 1984, D.C. 1985, U.S. Dist. Ct. D.C. 1985, U.S. Ct. Appeals (D.C. cir.) 1987, U.S. Supreme Ct. 1988, U.S. Ct. Appeals (4th cir.) 1989, U.S. Ct. Appeals (9th cir.) 1993, U.S. Ct. Appeals (10th cir.) 1999. Law clk. to Judge Milton Pollack, U.S. Dist. Ct. for So. Dist. N.Y., N.Y.C., 1983-84; staff atty. Washington Post, 1984-86; staff counsel select com. to investigate covert arms trans. U.S. Ho. of Reps., Washington, 1987; assoc. Wilmer, Cutler & Pickering, Washington, 1986-87, 88-90, ptnr., 1991—. Mem. ABA (vice chmn. com. on govt. info. and right to privacy com. adminstrv. law sect. 1988-90, chmn. 1990-94). General civil litigation, Communications, Libel. Office: Wilmer Cutler & Pickering 2445 M St NW Ste 500 Washington DC 20037-1487

**CARON, WILFRED RENE,** lawyer; b. N.Y.C., July 23, 1931; s. Joseph Wilfred and Eva Caron; m. Anne Theresa Flanagan, AUg. 2, 1958. JD, St. John's U., 1956. Bar: N.Y. 1956, D.C. 1977, U.S. Dist. Ct. D.C. 1977, U.S. Dist. Ct. (no. dist.) N.Y. 1957, U.S. Dist. Ct. (so. and ea. dists.) N.Y. 1961, U.S. Ct. Appeals (2d cir.) 1965, U.S. Ct. Appeals (3d cir.) 1973, U.S. Ct. Appeals (5th cir.) 1977, U.S. Ct. Appeals (6th cir.) 1973, U.S. Ct. Appeals (8th cir.) 1975, U.S. Ct. Appeals (9th cir.) 1976, U.S. Ct. Appeals (D.C. cir.) 1975, U.S. Supreme Ct. 1961. Law clk. to chief judge N.Y. State Ct. Appeals, 1956-59; spl. asst. atty. gen. N.Y., 1959-60; assoc. Goldman & Drazen, 1960-64, Corner, Finn, Cuomo & Charles, N.Y.C., 1964-69; asst. gen. counsel Ronson Corp., Woodbridge, N.J., 1969-71; assoc. gen. counsel Securities Investor Protection Corp., Washington, 1972-80; gen. counsel U.S. Cath. Conf., Inc., Washington, 1980-87, Nat. Conf. Cath. Bishops, 1980-87, Cath. Telecom. Network Am., Inc., N.Y.C., 1981-88; ptnr. O'Connor & Hannan, Washington, 1987-88; sr. advisor Office of Policy Devel., U.S. Dept. of Justice, Washington, 1988-90; appellate counsel Travelers Ins. Co., 1990-92. Contbr. articles to profl. jours. ADv. bd. St. Thomas More Inst. Legal Rsch., St. John's U. Sch. Law, N.Y.C., 1981-92; exec. bd. Ctr. for Ch.-State Studies, DePaul U. Law Coll., Chgo., 1982—. Served to 1st lt. U.S. Army, 1952-54, Korea. Mem. ABA, D.C. Bar Assn., N.Y. Bar Assn., VFW, Am. Legion. Roman Catholic. Home: 44 Old Main Rd Little Compton RI 02837-1321

**CARPENETI, WALTER L.,** state supreme court justice; b. San Francisco, 1945; m. Anne Dose, 1969; children: Christian, Marianna, Lia, Bianca. AB in History with distinction, Stanford U., 1967; JD, U. Calif., Berkeley, 1970. Law clk. Justice John H. Dimond Alaska Supreme Ct., 1970-71; pvt. practice San Francisco, 1972-74; pub. defender Juneau, Alaska, 1974-78; with William T. Council, 1978-81; judge Alaska Supreme Ct., Juneau, 1981-98, justice, 1998—. Office: Alaska Supreme Ct 303 K St Anchorage AK 99501-2083*

**CARPENTER, CHARLES ELFORD, JR.,** lawyer; b. Greenville, S.C., Nov. 3, 1944; s. Charles Elford and Mary Charlotte (Campbell) C.; m. Nancy Townsend, June 8, 1968; children: Charlotte Elizabeth, John Morrison. BA, Furman U., 1966; JD, U. Va., 1969; MPA, U. S.C., 1976. Bar: Va. 1969, S.C. 1972, U.S. Dist. Ct. S.C. 1974, U.S. Ct. Appeals (4th cir.) 1978, U.S. Ct. Appeals (11th cir.) 1984, U.S. Supreme Ct. 1983. Assoc. Leatherwood, Walker, Todd & Mann, Greenville, 1969, Richardson, Plowden, Grier & Howser, Columbia, S.C., 1974-78; ptnr. Richardson, Plowden, Carpenter & Robinson, P.A., Columbia, S.C., 1978—; mem. com. on grievances and discipline S.C. Supreme Ct., 1986-89, 1996; spkr. Law Seminars, Inc., Columbia, 1987, Outline for Post-Trial Practice, 1988, 89, 90; mem. S.C. Supreme Ct. Bd. Law Examiners. Editor Appeal and Error, S.C. Jurisprudence; contbr. articles to legal jours. Mem. bd. visitors Presbyn. Coll., Clinton, S.C., 1983-87; trustee James H. Hammond Sch., Columbia, 1986-89, Trinity Presbytery; pres. A.C. Flora PTO; elder Eastminster Presbyn. Ch. Capt. U.S. Army, 1969-72. Fellow Am. Acad. Appellate Lawyers; mem. ABA (speaker appellate process program 1990, editor Appellate Practice Jour. 1989—, co-chair oral arguement subcom. litigation sect., mem. task force on unreported opinions 1996—), S.C. Bar Assn. (mem. Richland County fee dispute com. 1984-88, speaker 1987, appellate practice, panel mem. proposed rules of appellate practicefor S.C. Bar ann. meeting 1989, mem. practice and procedure com., health and hosp. law subcom., appellate rules subcom., chmn. merit selection of judges subcom., alternative dispute resolution com. 1993—), Richland County Bar Assn., S.C. Def. Trial Attys. (chmn. amicus curiae com. 1981-85), Forest Lake Club, St. Andrews Soc., Tarantella Club, Columbia Ball Club, Torch Club (pres.). Avocations: reading, hunting, tennis, fishing. General civil litigation, Insurance, Administrative and regulatory. Office: Richardson Plowden Carpenter & Robinson PA 1600 Marion St # 7788 Columbia SC 29201-2913

**CARPENTER, CHARLES FRANCIS,** lawyer; b. Raleigh, N.C., Apr. 3, 1957; s. William Lester and Mattie Frances (Wallace) C.; m. Heidi Ann Athanas, June 14, 1980. BA with honors, U. N.C., 1979, JD, 1982. Bar: N.C. 1982, U.S. Dist. Ct. (mid. dist.) N.C. 1982, U.S. Dist. Ct. (ea. dist.) N.C. 1986, U.S. Ct. Appeals (4th cir.) 1986, U.S. Dist. Ct. (we. dist.) N.C. 1988. Assoc. Newsom, Graham, Hedrick, Murray, Bryson & Kennon, Durham, N.C., 1982-87; ptnr. Newsom, Graham, Hedrick, Bryson & Kennon, Durham, 1988-93; pvt. practice, Charles F. Carpenter, P.A., Durham, 1993-98; ptnr. Pulley, Watson, King & Lischer, P.A., Durham, 1998—. Trustee N.C. Conf. United Meth. Ch., 1993—; mem. exec. bd. Occoneechee Coun. Boy Scouts Am., 1988—. Mem. ABA, N.C. State Bar, N.C. Bar Assn., Durham County Bar Assn. (medico-legal com. 1994—, bd. dirs.), Order of the Old Well, Honorable Order of Ky. Colonels, Phi Beta Kappa. Democrat. Avocations: karate, golf, softball, jogging, skiing, soccer. Bankruptcy, General civil litigation, Consumer commercial. Home: 1325 Arnette Ave Durham NC 27707-1601 Office: 905 W Main St Ste 21 F Durham NC 27701-2076

**CARPENTER, DAVID ALLAN,** lawyer; b. Cambridge, Mass., May 16, 1951; s. David Lawrence and Jane (Boucher) C.; m. Nancy Joan Surdyka, Apr. 29, 1973. BS in Bus. Adminstrn., Bucknell U., Lewisburg, Pa., 1972; MBA in Fin., Temple U., Phila., 1975; JD, Rutgers U., 1981. Banking officer Girard Bank, Phila., 1972-77, mng. ptnr., 1983-85, mng. ptnr. Mid Atlantic region, 1985-89, mng. ptnr. Atlantic region, 1989-92; nat. dir. litigation and claims svcs. Coopers & Lybrand, Phila., 1987-92; nat. dir. fin. adv. svcs. Coopers & Lybrand, Boston, 1992-94; founding ptnr. Ptnrs. for Mkt. Leadership, Inc., Atlanta, 1995—. Co-editor: Proving and Pricing Construction Claims, 1990, Environmental Dispute Handbook, 1991; contbr. articles to profl. jours., chpts. to books. Mem. Inst. Mgmt. Consultants, Turnaround Mgmt. Assn., Beta Gamma Sigma. General civil litigation, Bankruptcy, Banking. Address: PO Box 903 Great Barrington MA 01230-0903 Office: Ptnrs for Mkt Leadership Inc 100 Galleria Pkwy SE Ste 400 Atlanta GA 30339-3122

**CARPENTER, RANDLE BURT,** lawyer; b. Raleigh, N.C., Oct. 19, 1939; s. Randle Burt and Adonis (Watson) C.; m. Suzanne Gronemeyer, Aug. 21, 1965; children: Randle III, Christine. BA in Internat. Rels., Duke U., 1962, LLB, 1965; LLM in Fgn. Law, NYU, 1969. Bar: N.Y. 1967, N.C. 1965, U.S. Supreme Ct., U.S. Ct. Appeals (2d cir.), U.S. Dist. Ct., U.S. Ct. Internat. Trade. Official asst. First Nat. City Bank, N.Y.C., 1965-67; with Exxon Internat. Inc., N.Y.C., 1967-68; gen. counsel Occidental Crude Sales Inc., N.Y.C., 1968-75; v.p. law Wesco Internat. Inc., N.Y.C., 1975-76; gen. counsel A. Johnson & Co., Inc., N.Y.C., 1976-81; ptnr. Davidson Dawson & Clark, N.Y.C., 1981-84, Schoeman, Marsh & Updike, N.Y.C., 1984-97, Jackson & Nash, N.Y.C., 1997—; adj. prof. law Pace U., White Plains, N.Y., 1984—. Contbr. articles to profl. jours. Angier B. Duke scholar Duke U., 1958. Mem. Am. Arbitration Assn., Assn. of Bar of City of N.Y. (inter-Am. affairs com.), Maritime Law Assn., Church Club N.Y., Colonial Order of the Acorn (companion). Private international, Environmental, Bankruptcy. Home: 29 Hazel Ln Larchmont NY 10538-4007 Office: Jackson & Nash 330 Madison Ave Rm 1800 New York NY 10017-5095

**CARPENTER, RANDY ALAN,** engineer, lawyer; b. Savannah, Ga., July 27, 1957; s. Roy Talton and Lula Louise (Carter) C. BCE, So. Tech. Inst., 1982; MS in Engring./Environ. Mgmt., Air Force Inst. of Tech., 1992; M of Studies in Environ. Law, Vt. Law Sch., 1996, JD, 1996. Bar: N.C. 1997; registered profl. engr., land surveyor. Environtl. engr. Delta Rsch. Corp., Niceville, Fla., 1992-93; planning cons. Royalton Planning Commn., South Royalton, Vt., 1993-96; pvt. practice Newland, N.C., 1997—. Capt. USAF, 1982-92. Mem. ABA, N.C. Soc. of Surveryors, N.C. Bar Assn. Avocations: mountain biking, white water kayaking. Office: 1751B Three Mile Hwy Newland NC 28657-8581

**CARPENTER, RICHARD NORRIS,** lawyer; b. Cortland, N.Y., Feb. 14, 1937; s. Robert P. and Sylvia (Norris) C.; m. Elizabeth Bigbee, Aug. 1961 (div. June 1975); 1 child, Andrew Norris; m. Leslie Nordby, July, 1991. BA magna cum laude, Syracuse U., 1958; LLB, Yale U., 1962. Bar: N.Y. 1962, N.Mex. 1963, U.S. Dist. Ct. (no. dist.) N.Y., U.S. Dist. Ct. N.Mex., U.S. Ct. Appeals (D.C. and 10th cirs.), U.S. Supreme Ct. Assoc. Breed, Abbott & Morgan, N.Y.C., 1962-63, Bigbee Law Firm, Santa Fe, 1963-78; ptnr. Carpenter Law Firm, Santa Fe, 1978-97, Carpenter & Nixon L.L.P., Santa Fe, 1997—; spl. asst. atty. gen., State of N.Mex., 1963-74, 90-96; sec. Bokum Corp., Miami, Fla., 1969-70. Mem. adv. bd. Interstate Mining Compact, N.Mex., 1981-88; elder 1st Presbyn. Ch., Santa Fe, 1978-80, 86-89, trustee, 1975-77, pres., 1977; bd. dirs. Santa Fe Community Coun., 1965-67, St. Vincent Hosp. Found., Santa Fe, 1980-84; trustee Santa Fe Prep. Sch., 1981-84, pres., 1982-84; trustee St. Vincent Hosp., 1980-86, 87—, chmn. 1985-86, 90-93, 98—; bd. dirs. Santa Fe YMCA, 1964-69, pres., 1969; trustee Santa Fe Prep. Permanent Endowment Fund., 1987-90. Rotary Found. fellow, Panjab U., Pakistan, 1959-60. Mem. ABA, N.Mex. Bar Assn., 1st Jud. Bar Assn., N.Y. State Bar Assn., The Best Lawyers of Am., Phi Beta Kappa, Pi Sigma Alpha, Phi Beta Phi. Public utilities, Legislative, Natural resources. Home: 1048 Bishops Lodge Rd Santa Fe NM 87501-1009 Office: PO Box 1837 Santa Fe NM 87504-1837

**CARPENTER, ROBERT BRENT,** lawyer; b. Newton, Mass., Feb. 9, 1949; s. Edward N. and Charlotte F. (Grant) C.; m. L. Deborah Gorchov, Mar. 25, 1978; children: Stephen Michael, Matthew Jeremy, Meredith Anne. AB, Bowdoin Coll., 1971; JD, Boston Coll., 1975; LLM, Temple U., 1977. Bar: Mass. 1975, U.S. Dist. Ct. Mass. 1977, U.S. Ct. Appeals (1st cir.) 1977, U.S. Supreme Ct. 1980. Teaching fellow, lectr. Temple U., Phila., 1975-77; shareholder, dir. Goldstein & Manello, P.C., Boston, 1977—. Contbr. articles to profl. jours. Mem. ABA, Mass. Bar Assn., Boston Bar Assn. Federal civil litigation, State civil litigation, General civil litigation. Home: 1 Commonwealth Park Wellesley MA 02481-3213 Office: Goldstein & Manello PC 265 Franklin St Ste 2000 Boston MA 02110-3192

**CARPENTER, SCOTT ROCKWELL,** lawyer; b. Newport Beach, Calif., Mar. 7, 1962; s. Dennis Eugene Carpenter and Frances Hereford; m. Gina Angela Garrett, Mar. 24, 1990; children: Catherine Anne, Benton Rockwell. AB in Internat. Rels., Stanford U., 1985; JD, UCLA, 1989. Bar: U.S. Dist. Ct. (cen. dist.) Calif., U.S. Ct. Appeals (9th cir.). Mktg. assoc. RNG Mortgage, Santa Ana, Calif., 1985-86; assoc. Palmieri, Tyler, Wiener, Wilhelm & Waldron, Irvine, Calif., 1989-97, ptnr., 1998—. Author numerous poems. Seminar leader, Bible study leader and occasional preacher Grace Fellowship Ch., Costa Mesa, Calif., 1997—. Postgrad. scholar NCAA, 1984. Mem. ABA, Calif. State Bar, Orange County Bar Assn. Republican. Avocations: poetry, theology. General civil litigation, Real property. Office: Palmieri Tyler Wiener Wilhelm & Waldron 2603 Main St Ste 1300 Irvine CA 92614-4281

**CARPENTER, SUSAN KAREN,** public defender; b. New Orleans, May 6, 1951; d. Donald Jack and Elise Ann (Diehl) C. BA magna cum laude with honors in English, Smith Coll., 1973; JD, Ind. U., 1976. Bar: Ind. 1976. Dep. pub. defender of Ind. State of Ind., Indpls., 1976-81, pub. defender of Ind., 1981—; chief pub. defender Wayne County, Richmond, Ind., 1981; bd. dirs. Ind. Pub. Defender Coun., Indpls., 1981—; Ind. Lawyers Comm., Indpls., 1984-89; trustee Ind. Criminal Justice Inst., INdpls., 1983—. Mem. Criminal Code Study Commn., Indpls., 1981—, Supreme Ct. Records Mgmt. Com., Indpls., 1983—. Mem. Ind. State Bar Assn. (criminal justice sect.), Nat. Legal Aid and Defender Assn., Nat. Assn. Defense Lawyers, Phi Beta Kappa.

**CARPEY, STUART A.,** lawyer; b. Phila., Feb. 17, 1961; s. Aldrich and Estelle Carpey; m. Laura C. Carpey, Dec. 12, 1987; children: Benjamin, Julia, Emily. BA, U. Md., 1983; JD, Villanova U., 1987. Assoc. Kreithen, Baron & Assocs., Phila., 1987-89; assoc. Kreithen, Baron, Villari & Golomb, Phila., 1989-95, shareholder, 1995-96; shareholder Kreithen, Baron & Carpey, P.C., Phila., 1996—; spkr. Pa. Bar Inst., Phila. Trial Lawyers Assn. on ins. law issues. Mem. ATLA, Pa. Bar Assn., Pa. Trial Lawyers Assn., Phila. Bar Assn., Phila. Trial Lawyers Assn. Personal injury, General civil litigation. Home: 120 Hollyhock Dr Lafayette Hill PA 19444-2106 Office: Kreithen Baron & Carpey PC 1201 Chestnut St Fl 10 Philadelphia PA 19107-4123

**CARR, ADAM E.,** lawyer; b. Cleve., Sept. 22, 1968; m. Valerie Wax Carr, May 28, 1995. BA, Rice U., 1990; JD, Cleve. State U., 1993. Bar: Ohio, 1993; U.S. Dist. Ct. (no. dist.) Ohio, 1994. Fellow Law & Pub. Policy Clinic/Cleve. State U., 1992; law clk. Cleveland Heights Mcpl. Ct., Ohio, 1992-93; gen. counsel Cleve. Orthopedic and Spine Ctr., Inc., 1993-95; assoc. Williams, Sennett & Scully Co. LPA, Cleve., 1995—. Recipient Appellate Practice award Am. Jurisprudence, 1993, William H. Thomas Found. award Cleve. State U., 1993, Law and Pub. Policy fellowship, 1992. Insurance, Personal injury, General civil litigation. Office: Williams Sennett & Scully Co LPA 2241 Pinnacle Pkwy Twinsburg OH 44087-2367

**CARR, CHRISTOPHER C.,** lawyer; b. Bryn Mawr, Pa., Feb. 11, 1950; s. Herman E. Jr. and Iris (Constantine) C.; m. Wynne Alys Wilking, Aug. 23, 1996; children: Ethan F., Wellesley H., Spencer C. Student, Boston U., 1969-70; BA magna cum laude, Ripon Coll., 1973; JD, MBA in Fin., Ohio State U., 1981. Bar: Ohio 1981, Pa. 1986, U.S. Dist. Ct. (ea. dist.) Pa. 1988. Fin. analyst NCR Corp., Dayton, Ohio, 1980-84; pvt. practice Phila., 1985-91; corp. counsel, sec. Sanchez Computer Assocs., Inc., Malvern, Pa., 1991—. Mem. ABA, Computer Law Assn., Phila. Bar Assn., Beta Gamma Sigma, Phi Beta Kappa. Democrat. Computer, Intellectual property, Private international. Home: 6 Sycamore Ct Paoli PA 19301-1048 Office: Sanchez Computer Assocs 40 Valley Stream Pky Malvern PA 19355-1482

**CARR, CYNTHIA,** lawyer; b. San Antonio, Nov. 4, 1953; d. Robert Claude Carr and Alta Mae (Bletsch) Holmes; m. Marc Allan Wallman; children: Lydia Michael, Aidan Holmes. BA, Austin Coll., 1975; JD, Harvard U., 1984; LLM, NYU, 1990. Bar: N.Y. 1985, Conn. 1988. Coord. Cambodian sect. Internat. Rescue Com., Bangkok, Thailand, 1980-81; legal intern Mental Health Legal Advisers Com., Boston, 1982-83; assoc. White & Case, N.Y.C., 1984-87; assoc. gen. counsel, exec. dir. planned giving Yale U., New Haven, 1988—; vis. lectr. Yale U. Law Sch., New Haven, 1988-90. Vol. Peace Corps, West Africa, 1975-77, 79-80; bd. dirs. Yale Law Sch. Early Learning Ctr., 1990-95; trustee Yale U. Hong Kong Charitable Trust, Oak Leaf Endowment Trust for Yale. Mem. ABA, Conn. Bar Assn. (mem. charitable giving exempt orgns. subcom.), Trusts and Estates Mag. (charitable giving mini bd. mem. 1996-99), Jewish Found. New Hampton (tax and law com). Estate planning, Taxation, general. Home: 30 Hawley Rd Hamden CT 06517-2128 Office: Yale U PO Box 2038 265 Church St New Haven CT 06510-7013

**CARR, DAVID J.,** lawyer; m. Sandra S. Carr; children: Jacob, Angela, Alex. BA summa cum laude, DePauw U., 1981; JD, Georgetown U., 1984. Bar: Ind., U.S. Dist. Ct. (so. dist.) Ind. 1984, U.S. Ct. Appeals (7th cir.) 1987, U.S. Supreme Ct. 1989. Assoc. Bingham Summers Welsh & Spilman, Indpls., 1984-90; assoc. Johnson Smith LLP, Indpls., 1990-92, ptnr., 1992—. Contbr. articles to profl. publs. Coun. mem. Zionsville Town Coun., 1998—; bd. dirs. Zionsville Parks and Recreation Bd., 1996-98. Mem. ABA, Ind. State Bar Assn., Indpls. Bar Assn., Christian Legal Soc., Federalist Soc., Ct. Practice Inst. (diplomate), Delta Chi, Phi Beta Kappa. E-mail: dcarr@jsplaw.com. Labor, Entertainment, General civil litigation. Office: Johnson Smith LLP 1 Indiana Sq Ste 1800 Indianapolis IN 46204-2007

**CARR, DAVIS HADEN,** lawyer; b. Richmond, Va., July 21, 1940; s. Frederick Clifton Jr. and Bernice (Haden) C.; m. Judith A. Guerry, Aug. 1959 (div. Apr. 1979); children: Wendy Carr Conners, Julia Carr Stewart; m. Martha Cash, Feb. 12, 1983. BEE, U. Va., 1961; JD, Vanderbilt U., 1970. Bar: Tenn. 1970, Ky. 1989. Assoc. Boult, Cummings, Conners & Berry PLC, Nashville, 1970-74; ptnr. Boult, Cummings, Conners & Berry PLC, 1974—; mng. ptnr. Boult, Cummings, Conners & Berry, 1984-94, chmn., 1995—. Active Leadership Nashville, 1977-78, chmn. alumni assn., 1978-79, bd. trustees 1997—; pres. Cumberland Museums, Nashville, 1978-80; bd. dirs. Greater Nashville Arts Found., 1991-97; bd. dirs. Jr. Achievement Mid. Tenn., 1991-, chmn., 1995-97; trustee Vol. State Horesemen's Found., 1988-; mem. bd. trustees, exec. com. Fisk U., 1996—; bd. dirs. Nashville Downtown Partnership, 1994—, chmn., 1994-95, exec. com., 1994—. Mem. ABA, Tenn. Bar Found., Tenn. Bar Assn., Nashville Bar Found., Nashville Bar Assn., Vanderbilt U. Law Alumni Assn. (bd. dirs.), Cumberland Club (pres. 1986-87), Nashville City Club, Belle Meade Country Club, Nashville Area C. of C. (gen. counsel, mem. exec. com. 1992-96, bd. govs.). General corporate, Finance, Mergers and acquisitions. Home: Martlesham Heath 1344 Carnton Ln Franklin TN 37064-3258 Office: Boult Cummings Conners & Berry PO Box 198062 Nashville TN 37219-8062

**CARR, EDWARD A.,** lawyer; b. Borger, Tex., July 31, 1962. AB with honors and distinction, Stanford U., 1984; JD, UCLA, 1987. Bar: Tex. 1988, D.C. 1989, U.S. Dist. Ct. (so. dist.) Tex. 1989, U.S. Ct. Appeals (5th cir.) 1989, U.S. Ct. Appeals (fed. cir.) 1989. Assoc. Vinson & Elkins, Houston, 1988-97, ptnr., 1997—; lectr. in field. Contbr. articles to profl. jours., contbg. author: (6-vol. book set) Business and Commercial Litigation in Federal Courts, 1998, mem. editl. bd. UCLA Law Review, 1986-87. Fellow Tex. Bar Found. (life); Mem. ABA (sects. antitrust law, litigation), Am. Judicature Soc. (life), Coll. State Bar Tex., D.C. Bar, Fed. Bar Assn. (sect. fed. litigation), State Bar Tex., Houston Bar Assn., Tex. Ctr. Legal Ethics and Professionalism. Federal civil litigation, State civil litigation. Address: Vinson & Elkins LLP 2300 First City Tower 1001 Fannin St Houston TX 77002-6706

**CARR, GARY THOMAS,** lawyer; b. El Reno, Okla., July 25, 1946; s. Thomas Clay and Bobbye Jean (Page) C.; m. Ann Elizabeth Smith, Jan. 5, 1985. AB, Washington U., St. Louis, 1968, BSCE, 1972, JD, 1975. Bar: Mo. 1975, U.S. Dist. Ct. (ea. and we. dists.) Mo. 1975, U.S. Ct. Appeals (8th cir.) 1977, U.S. Ct. Appeals (fed. cir.) 1980, U.S. Ct. Appeals (5th cir.) 1991. Jr. ptnr. Bryan, Cave, McPheeters & McRoberts, St. Louis, 1975-83, ptnr., 1984—; lectr. law Washington U., 1978-82, adj. prof., 1982-85; sec., dir. Bruton-Stroube Studios, Inc., 1978—, bd. dirs. Trustee Parkview Subdiv. Assn., St. Louis, 1982-90. 1st lt. U.S. Army, 1968-71, Vietnam. Mem. ABA, Mo. Bar Assn., St. Louis Bar Assn., Order of Coif. Club: Mo. Athletic (St. Louis). Avocations: racquet sports, woodworking, hunting, fishing, scuba. Government contracts and claims, Federal civil litigation, State civil litigation. Office: Bryan Cave 1 Metropolitan Sq 211 N Broadway Saint Louis MO 63102-2733

**CARR, JAMES FRANCIS,** lawyer; b. Buffalo, May 7, 1946; s. Maurice Kilner and Cecelia Francis (Harmon) C.; children: James Robert, Marguerite Louise. BS, USAF Acad., 1968; JD, George Washington U., 1971. Bar: D.C. 1972, Mich. 1972, Pa. 1972, U.S. Dist. Ct. D.C. 1972, U.S. Ct. Appeals (D.C. cir.) 1972, U.S. Supreme Ct. 1975, Colo. 1979, U.S. Dist. Ct. Colo. 1979, U.S. Ct. Appeals (10th cir.) 1979. Atty. Unity Ctr., Meadville, Pa., 1971-73; asst. pros. atty. Genesee County, Flint, Mich., 1973-79; sr. asst. atty. gen. State of Colo., Denver, 1979-82, 85—; assoc. Sumners, Miller & Clark, Denver, 1982-83, Miles & McManus, Denver, 1983-85; mem. Colo. Bd. Law Examiners, 1992—. Contbr. articles to profl. jours. Mem. Mich. Pub. Consultation Panel of Internat. Joint Commn., 1976-78; treas. Denver South High Sch. PTSA, 1988-91, pres., 1991-93; athletic dir. Most Precious Blood Sch., 1988-90; bd. dirs. Pioneer Jr. Hockey Assn., 1988-90. Mem. ABA (house of dels. 1997—, chair commn. on mental & physical disability law, 1998—, commn. on mental and phys. disability law 1995—, chmn. 1998—, tort and ins. practice sect., chmn. environ. law com. 1978-81, liaison jud. adminstrn. divsn. 1987-90, chmn. govt. liability com. 1988-89, 92-93, chmn. emerging issues com. 1996-97, sect. sec. 1997-99, mem. TIPS coun. 1999—, mem. coun. govt. and pub. sector lawyers divsn. 1991-97, editor-in-chief The Brief 1981-87, spkr. ann. meeting 1991-94), ATLA, Denver Bar Assn. (chmn. pub. legal ednl. com. 1989-91, del. 1997—), Colo. Bar Assn. (spkr. ann. meetings 1991-95, chmn. health law sect. 1993-94, chmn. law edn. com. 1993-96, coun. licensure, enforcement and regulation, spkr. ann. meetings 1992-97, chmn. profl. discipline com. 1992-93, 98-99, program chmn. ann. meeting 1993-94, chair publs. com. 1995-97), Colo. Bd. Law Examiners. Democrat. Roman Catholic. Home: 10406 W Glasgow Ave Littleton CO 80127-3468 Office: Atty Gen Office 1525 Sherman St Fl 5 Denver CO 80203-1760

**CARR, JAMES GRAY,** judge; b. Boston, Nov. 14, 1940; s. Edmund Albert and Anna Frances C.; m. Eileen Margaret Glynn, Dec. 17, 1966; children: Maureen M., Megan A., Darrah E., Caitlin E. AB, Kenyon Coll., 1962; LLB, Harvard U., 1966. Bar: Ill. 1966, Ohio 1972, U.S. Dist. Ct. (no. dist.) Ill. 1966, U.S. Dist. Ct. (no. dist.) Ohio 1970, U.S. Supreme Ct. 1980. Assoc. Gardner & Carton, et al., Chgo., 1966-68; staff atty. Cook County Legal Asst. Found., Evanston, Ill., 1968-70; prof. U. Toledo Law Sch., 1970-79; U.S. magistrate judge U.S. Dist. Ct., Toledo, 1979-94, U.S. dist. judge, 1994—; adj. prof. law Chgo. Kent Law Sch., 1969, Loyola U., Chgo., 1970; reporter, juvenile rules com. Ohio Supreme Ct., Columbus, 1971-72; reporter, mem. nat. wiretap com. U.S. Congress, Washington, 1976-77. Contbr. articles to profl. law jours. Founder, bd. dirs. Child Abuse Ctr., Toledo, 1970-84; active Lucas County Mental Health Bd., Toledo, 1984-89, Lucas County Children Svcs. Bd., Toledo, 1989-94. Fulbright fellow, 1977-78. Mem. ABA (reporter, elec. survey stds. 1979-80, mem. task force on tech. and law enforcement 1995—, mem. task force on jury initiatives 1995—), Toledo Bar Assn. (bd. dirs.), Phi Beta Kappa. Roman Catholic. Office: US Dist Ct 203 US Courthouse 1716 Spielbusch Ave Toledo OH 43624-1363

**CARR, JAMES PATRICK,** lawyer; b. Cheverly, Md., Apr. 13, 1950; s. Lawrence Edward Jr. and agnes (Dyer) C.; m. Mona L. Kyle, May 28, 1986; children: James P. Jr., Kristin, Kevin, Sean. BA, U. Notre Dame, 1972, JD, 1976. Bar: Md. 1976, Calif. 1977, U.S. Dist. Ct. (cen. dist.) Calif. 1977, U.S. Dist. Ct. (so. dist.) Calif. 1986. Assoc. Carr, Jordan et al, Washington, 1976-77; ptnr. Breidenbach, Swainston et al, L.A., 1977-84, Harney, Wolfe, Shaller & Carr, L.A., 1984-88, Carr & Shaller, L.A., 1988-89; pvt. practice law L.A., 1989—. Mem. Am. Bd. Trial Advs., Assn. Trial Lawyers Am., Consumer Attys. Calif., Consumer Attys. Assn. L.A. Democrat. Roman Catholic. Personal injury. Office: 11755 Wilshire Blvd Ste 1170 Los Angeles CA 90025-1539

**CARR, LAWRENCE EDWARD, JR.,** lawyer; b. Colorado Springs, Colo., Aug. 10, 1923; s. Lawrence Edward and Lelah R. (Rubert) C.; m. Agnes Isabel Dyer, Dec. 26, 1946; children—Mary Lee, James Patrick, Lawrence Edward III, Eileen Louise, Thomas Vincent. B.S., U. Notre Dame, 1948, LL.B., 1949; LL.M., George Washington U., 1954. Bar: Colo. 1949, D.C. 1952, Md. 1961. With Travelers Ins. Co., 1949-51; practiced in Washington, 1952—; sr. ptnr. Carr Goodson Warner, P.C., Washington, 1984—. Mem. adv. coun. U. Notre Dame Coll. Law, 1985—. With USMCR, 1943-46, 51-52; col. Res.; ret. Fellow Am. Bar Found.; mem. ABA (ho. of dels. 1973-75), Bar Assn. D.C. (dir. 1969-71, pres. 1974-75), Internat. Assn. Ins. Counsel, D.C. Def. lawyers Assn. (pres. 1978-79), Bar Assn. D.C. Rsch. Found. (pres. 1985-86). E-mail: lec@cgu-law.com. Federal civil litigation, Insurance, Environmental. Home: 111 Storm Haven Ct Stevensville MD 21666-3707 Office: Carr Goodson Warner PC 400 East Tower 1301 K St NW Ste 400E Washington DC 20005-3317

**CARR, OSCAR CLARK, III,** lawyer; b. Memphis, Apr. 9, 1951; s. Oscar Clark Carr Jr. and Billie (Fisher) Carr Houghton; m. Mary Leatherman, Aug. 4, 1973; children: Camilla Fisher, Oscar Clark V. BA in English with distinction, U. Va., 1973; JD with distinction, Emory U., 1976. Bar: Tenn. 1976, U.S. Dist. Ct. (we. dist.) Tenn. 1977, U.S. Dist. Ct. (no. dist.) Miss. 1977, U.S. Ct. Appeals (6th cir.) 1985, U.S. Ct. Appeals (5th cir.) 1995; cert. mediator, Tenn. Assoc. firm Glankler Brown, PLLC (formerly Glankler, Brown, Gilliland, Chase, Robinson & Raines), Memphis, 1976-82, chief mgr. Glankler Brown PLLC, 1998—, ptnr., 1982—, chief mgr., 1998—. Bd. dirs. Memphis Ballet Soc., 1980, Memphis-Shelby County Unit Am. Cancer Soc., 1985—, Memphis Oral Sch. for Deaf, 1988-91; treas., vestryman St. John's Episcopal Ch., Memphis, 1988-91, sr. warden, 1991; mem. Commn. on Ministry Diocese of West Tenn., 1987-90, King of Carnival Memphis, 1994; pres., dir. Juvenile Diabetes Found. Memphis chpt., 1998; bd. dirs. Carnival Memphis. Mem. ABA, Tenn. Bar Assn.(western dist. coun. environ. law 1992—), Memphis and Shelby County Bar Assn. (bd. dirs. 1985-87), bd. dirs. Carnival Memphis, 1997—, atty. Memphis Country Club, 1998—, U. Va. Alumni Assn. Federal civil litigation, State civil litigation, Environmental. Office: Glankler Brown PLLC 1700 One Commerce Sq Memphis TN 38103

**CARR, STEPHEN KERRY,** lawyer; b. L.A., Apr. 30, 1930; s. Richard Bruce and Katherine Ward C.; m. Vivian Manno. BA, U. Toronto, Can., 1951; JD, Georgetown U., 1954. Bar: N.Y. 1957, P.A. 1995, U.S. Dist. Ct. N.Y., U.S. Dist. Ct. Pa., U.S. Dist. Ct. Conn., U.S. Dist. Ct. Ga., U.S. Ct. Appeals (2nd, 3d, 4th and 11th cirs.), U.S. Supreme Ct. Assoc. Haight, Gardner, Poor & Havens, N.Y.C., 1957-68, ptnr., 1969-95; pvt. practice Pipersville, Pa., 1996—. With Counter Intelligence Corps, U.S. Army, 1954-56. Fellow Am. Coll. Trial Lawyers; mem. Maritime Law Assn., Bucks County Bar Assn. Democrat. Roman Catholic. Avocations: sailing, rowing, tennis, mentoring. Admiralty, Federal civil litigation, Personal injury. Home: 6057 Schlentz Hill Rd Pipersville PA 18947-1318

**CARR, THOMAS ELDRIDGE,** lawyer; b. Austin, Tex., Aug. 16, 1953; s. Peter Gordon and Margaret (Johnson) C.; children: Christopher Allen, Austin Thomas. BA, Tex. Tech U., 1975, JD, 1977. Bar: Tex. 1978, U.S. Dist. Ct. (no. and we. dist.) Tex. 1978, U.S. Ct. Appeals (5th cir.) 1981, U.S. Supreme Ct. 1982. Assoc. Morgan, Gambill & Owen, Ft. Worth, 1978-81; ptnr. Morgan, Owen, & Carr, Ft. Worth, 1981-85; ptnr. Quillin, Owen & Thompson, Ft. Worth, 1985-87; ptnr. Owen, Wilson & Carr, Ft. Worth, 1987-91; ptnr. Owen & Carr, Ft. Worth, 1991-94; ptnr. Lane, Ray, Wilson, Carr & Steves, Ft. Worth, 1994—. Co-author: Of Counsel to Classrooms: A Resource Guide to Assist Attorneys and Teachers in Law Focused Education. Active Benbrook City Council, Tex., 1984-86, Benbrook Park and Recreation Bd., 1981-84; mem. exec. bd. Longhorn coun. Boy Scouts Am., 1983-86; mem. Home Rule Charter Commn., Benbrook, 1983. Selected Outstanding Young Lawyer of Tarrant County, 1990. Mem. ABA (chmn. com), Ft. Worth Tarrant County Young Lawyers Assn. (pres. 1983), State Bar Tex. (chmn. sch. law sect. 1991, bd. dirs. 1998—, treas., sec. 1988), Tex. Young Lawyers Assn. (bd. dirs. 1984-86), Ridglea Country Club. Education and schools, General corporate, Probate. Office: 6115 Camp Bowie Blvd Ste 200 Fort Worth TX 76116-5500

**CARR, WILLARD ZELLER, JR.,** lawyer; b. Richmond, Ind., Dec. 18, 1927; s. Willard Zeller and Susan (Brownell) C.; m. Margaret Paterson, Feb. 15, 1952; children: Clayton Paterson, Jeffrey Westcott. BS, Purdue U., 1948; JD, Ind. U., 1951. Bar: Calif. 1951, U.S. Supreme Ct. 1963. Ptnr. Gibson, Dunn & Crutcher, Los Angeles, 1952—; mem. nat. panel arbitrators Am. Arbitration Assn.; former labor relations cons. State of Alaska; lectr. bd. visitors Southwestern U. Law Sch.; mem. adv. council Southwestern Legal Found., Internat. and Comparative Law Ctr. Trustee Calif. Adminstrv. Law Coll.; bd. dirs. Employers' Group, Calif. State Pks. Found., Los Angeles coun. Boy Scouts Am.; mem. Mayor's Econ. Devel. Policies Com.; past chmn. Pacific Legal Found.; past chmn. men's adv. com. Los Angeles County-USC Med. Ctr. Aux. for Recruitment, Edn. and Service; past chmn. bd. Wilshire Republican Club; past mem. Rep. State Central Com.; past mem. pres.'s coun. Calif. Mus. Sci. and Industry; mem. Nat. Def. Exec. Res., Los Angeles World Affairs Coun.; bd. dirs., sec. Los Angeles Police Meml. Found.; past chmn. Los Angeles sect. United Way; mem. adv. com. Los Angeles County Human Rels. Commn., commr., Calif. State World Trade Commn.; Los Angeles chpt. ARC. Fellow Am. Bar Found.; mem. ABA (past chmn. com. benefits to unemployed persons, econ. and resources controls com. of corp., banking and bus. law sect.; internat. labor rels. law com. of labor and employment law sect., also com. devel. of law under Nat. Labor Rels. Act), Internat. Bar. Assn. (past chmn. labor law com. of bus. law sect.), chmn. Labor Employment Com., The Federalist Soc., Calif. Bar Assn., L.A. County Bar Assn., L.A. C. of C. (past chmn. 1991), Calif. C. of C. Administrative and regulatory, Labor. Home: 2185 Century Hl Los Angeles CA 90067-3516 Office: Gibson Dunn & Crutcher 333 S Grand Ave Ste 4400 Los Angeles CA 90071-3197

**CARRAHER, JOHN BERNARD,** lawyer; b. Denver, Feb. 13, 1934; s. Thomas Peter and Mary Agnes (Carroll) C.; m. Carol J. Steffens Carraher, June 28, 1958; children: Steven, Constance, Lee Anne, Patti. BS, Regis Coll., Denver, 1956; LLB, Denver U., 1958. Bar: Colo., U.S. Dist. Ct. 1959. Pvt. practice pvt. practice, Denver, 1958-80; lawyer, shareholder, dir. Feder, Morris, Tamblyn & Goldstein, Denver, 1980-96; of counsel Michael R. Dice & Co. LLC, Denver, 1996-97, Bryant and Van Nest LLC, Denver, 1997-99, Van Nest LLC, Englewood, 1999—; lectr. advanced estate planning symposium U. Denver, 1993, Guardianship Symposium, 1997. Contbr. articles to profl. jours. Coord. Risen Christ Parish Edn. Program, Denver, 1968-71; mem. jud. adv. coun. Colo. Supreme Ct., 1987-93; lectr. Nat. Bus. Inst., Eau Claire, Wis., 1992, 94. Named Presidency Colo. Mcpl. Judges Assn., 1984-85; mem. Nat. Hon. Soc., 1992. Fellow Am. Acad. Forensic

Scis. (lectr. Cin. 1990, L.A. 1991, New Orleans 1992, Boston 1993, Seattle 1995, co-chair edn. jurisprudence sect. 1996, 97); mem. Denver Probate Ct. Vis. program, Greenwood Village Ct. Mediation Program, Greenwood Village Ct. Jud. Intern Program Colo. Bar Assn. (bd. govs. 1984-85), Colo. Trial Lawyers Assn. (lectr. 1989), Am. Colo. Denver Arapahoe Bar Assn., Elder Law Adv. Coun. U. Denver Inst. for Advanced Legal Studies (coun. co-chair 1995-97). Avocations: skiing, reading. Estate planning, Probate, Estate taxation. Office: Van Nest LLC PO Box 9276 4660 S Yosemite St Englewood CO 80127-1227

**CARREL, MARC LOUIS,** lawyer, policy advisor; b. Buffalo, Aug. 31, 1967; s. Jerome D. and Judith E. (Fish) C. BA with distinction, U. Mich., 1988; JD, U. Pa., 1993. Bar: Calif., 1993, D.C., 1995. Staff asst. U.S. Senate Com. Agriculture, Nutrition, and Forestry, Washington, 1989, calender clk., 1989-90; assoc. cons. Office of Calif. State Assemblyman Richard Polanco, Sacramento, 1994; legis. cons. Office of Calif. State Senator Richard Polanco, Sacramento, 1994-96; counsel Calif. State Senate Dem. Caucus, Sacramento, 1995-96; legis. policy cons. to Calif. Assembly Spkr. Cruz M Bustamante, Sacramento, 1997, counsel, 1997-98; dep. issues dir. Jane Harman for Gov., 1998; sr. cons. Office of Assemblymem. Cruz M. Bustamante, 1998; policy dir. Cruz M. Bustamante for Lt. Gov., 1998; transition dir. Office of Lt. Gov.-Elect, 1998-99, sr. advisor to Lt. Gov., 1999—; mem. Legis. Task Force Land Use, Sacramento, 1995, L.A. Fiscal Crisis Working Group, Sacramento, 1995, Calif. Organized Investment Network Econ. Devel. Com., 1996; co-chair Ins. Reinvestment Task Force, Sacramento, 1995; staff Gov.-Elect's Agr. Water Transition Task Force, 1998; mem. rural devel. strategic plan steering com. USDA; coord. Gov.'s Emergency Freeze Assistance Task Force, 1999; mem. designee State Job Tng. Coord. Coun., 1999—. Sec. Pa. Law Equal Justice Found., Phila., 1990-92; comm. dir. Arlo Smith for Atty. Gen. '94, San Francisco, 1993; co-chair Young Leadership Divsn., Sacramento, 1996-97; trustee Jewish Fedn. Sacramento Region, 1996-97; mem. Jewish Cmty. Rels. Coun., Sacramento, 1997—, vice-chair, 1998-99, chair, 1999—; cofounder, sec. Jewish Civic Action Network, 1997-99; mem. Sacramento Police Adv. Com., 1999—; commr. Human Rights/Fair Housing Commn., Sacramento, 1999—. Recipient U.S. Atty.'s Office Spl. Achievement award, Buffalo, 1991; William J. Branstrom Freshman prize, 1986. Mem. Am. Polit. Items Collectors, State Bar Calif., D.C. Bar, Sacramento Bar Assn., U. Mich. Alumni Assn., U. Pa. Law Alumni Soc. Avocation: collector of political paraphernalia. Office: Office of Lt Gov State Capitol Rm 1114 Sacramento CA 95814-4906

**CARRELL, DANIEL ALLAN,** lawyer; b. Louisville, Jan. 2, 1941; s. Elmer N. and Mary F. (Pfingst) C.; m. Janis M. Wilhelm, July 3, 1976; children: Mary Monroe, Courtney Adele. AB, Davidson Coll., 1963; BA, Oxford U., 1965, MA, 1969; JD, Stanford U., 1968. Bar: Va. 1972, U.S. Dist. Ct. (ea. dist.) Va. 1972, U.S. Ct. Appeals (4th cir.) 1975, U.S. Dist. Ct. (we. dist.) Va. 1985. Asst. prof. U.S. Mil. Acad., West Point, N.Y., 1968-71; assoc. Hunton & Williams, Richmond, Va., 1971-79, ptnr., 1979-95; prin. Carrell & Rice, Richmond, Va., 1996—. Active Richmond Rep. Com., 1974—; co-counsel Dalton for Gov. campaign, Richmond, 1977; counsel Obenshain for Senate campaign, Richmond, 1978; treas. Va. Victory '92; state fin. chmn., mem. fin. com., state ctrl. com. and budget com. Rep. Party Va., 1993-96; bd. dirs. Southampton Citizens Assn., v.p., 1985-94; pres. Davidson Coll. Alumni Assn., 1987-88; trustee Davidson Coll., 1987-88; bd. dirs. Needles Eye Ministries, 1986-90, mem. adv. bd., 1990—; elder, trustee Stony Point Reformed Presbyn. Ch., 1993—; moderator James River Presbytery Presbyn. Ch. Am., 1998. Rhodes scholar, 1962; recipient Award of Merit Sports Illustrated Mag., 1963. Mem. ABA (chmn. exemption and Noerr Doctrine com. 1986-87, antitrust sect.), Va. Bar Assn. (chmn. young lawyers joint law-related edn. com. 1978-79, young lawyers fellow award 1980), Va. State Bar (chmn. com. on legal edn. and admission to bar 1984-91, bd. govs. sect. edn. lawyers 1992-99), Richmond Bar Assn., Christian Legal Soc., Westwood Club. Avocations: tennis, basketball, theatre, concerts. General civil litigation, Antitrust, General corporate. Home: 3724 Custis Rd Richmond VA 23225-1102 Office: Carrell & Rice 7275 Glen Forest Dr Richmond VA 23226-3772

**CARRERA, VICTOR MANUEL,** lawyer; b. Rio Grande City, Tex., Nov. 20, 1954; s. Eladio and Ines Olivia (Guerra) C. BS, U. Tex., 1975, BA with honors, 1976, JD, 1979. Bar: Tex. 1979, U.S. Dist. Ct. (so. dist.) Tex. 1980, U.S. Dist. Ct. (we. dist.) Tex. 1996, U.S. Ct. Appeals (5th cir.) 1986; cert. civil trial law, personal injury trial law, civil appellate law, Tex. Assoc. Cardenas & Whitis, McAllen, Tex., 1979-80; briefing atty. U.S. Dist. Ct. (so. dist.) Tex., Brownsville, 1980-81; assoc. Keys, Russell & Seaman, Corpus Christi, Tex., 1981-84; assoc. Wood, Boykin, Wolter & Keys, Corpus Christi, 1984-86, ptnr., 1987-88; participating mem. Law Offices of Ramon Garcia, P.C., Edinburg, Tex., 1988-90; ptnr. Munoz, Hockema & Reed, McAllen, Tex., 1990-96, Reed & Carrera, Edinburg, Tex., 1997, Reed, Carrera & McLain, Edinburg, TX, 1997—; lectr. South Tex. Coll. Law, Houston, 1987, U. Houston, 1989-90, 96-99, State Bar Tex., 1992. Mng. editor Tex. Internat. Law Jour., 1978-79. Recipient Outstanding Individual Contbn. Award Vol. Lawyers of Coastal Bend, 1985. Mem. Tex. Bar Assn., Tex. Trial Lawyers Assn. (dir. 1991-96, lectr. 1993-94), Hidalgo County Bar Assn. Democrat. Avocations: history, archaeology. General civil litigation, Private international, Personal injury. Home: 1208 Xanthisma Ave McAllen TX 78504-3520 Office: Reed Carrera & McLain PO Box 9702 Mcallen TX 78502-9702 also: Reed Carrera & McLain Bldg 101 1 Paseo del Prado Edinburg TX 78539

**CARRERE, CHARLES SCOTT,** law educator, judge; b. Dublin, Ga., Sept. 26, 1937; 1 son, Daniel Austin. B.A., U. Ga., 1959; LL.B., Stetson U., 1961. Bar: Fla. 1961, Ga. 1960. Law clk. U.S. Dist. Judge, Orlando, Fla., 1962-63; asst. U.S. atty. Middle Dist. Fla., 1963-66, 68-69, chief trial atty., 1965-66, 68-69; ptnr. Harrison, Greene, Mann, Rowe & Stanton, 1970-80; judge Pinellas County, Fla., 1980-96; vis. prof. law Stetson Coll. Law, 1997-98, Cumberland Law Sch., 1998-99. Recipient Jud. Appreciation award St. Petersburg Bar Assn., 1996, Alumnus of Yr. award Stetson Student Bar Assn., 1998. Mem. State Bar Ga., Fla. Bar, Phi Beta Kappa. Presbyterian. Address: PO Box 22034 Gateway Mall Sta Saint Petersburg FL 33742

**CARREY, NEIL,** lawyer, educator; b. Bronx, N.Y., Nov. 19, 1942; s. David L. and Betty (Kurtzburg) C.; m. Karen Krysher, Apr. 9, 1980; children: Jana, Christopher; children by previous marriage: Scott, Douglas, Dana. BS in Econs., U. Pa., 1964; JD, Stanford U., 1967. Bar: Calif. 1968. Mem. firm, v.p. corp. DeCastro, West, Chodorow, Inc., L.A., 1967-97; of counsel Jenkens & Gilchrist, L.A., 1997—; instr. program legal paraprofls., U. So. Calif., 1977-89; lectr. U. So. Calif. Dental Sch., 1987—, Employee Benefits Inst., Kansas City, Mo., 1996; legal cons. 33rd Dist. Calif. PTA, 1997—. Author: Nonqualified Defered Compensation Plans-The Wave of the Future, 1985. Officer Vista Del Mar Child Care Ctr., L.A., 1968-84; treas. Nat. Little League Santa Monica, Calif., 1984-85, pres., 1985-86, coach, 1990-95; coach Bobby Sox Softball Team, Santa Monica, 1986-88, bd. dirs., 1988, umpire in chief, 1988; referee, coach Am. Soccer Youth Orgn., 1989-95; curriculum com. Santa Monica-Malibu Sch. Dist., 1983-84 comm. health adv. com., 1988-95, chmn., 1989-95, sports and phys. edb adv. com., 1991—, chmn., 1991—, dist. com. for sch. based health ctr., 1991-94, title IX/gender equity com., chmn. 1992—, athletic study com., chmn., 1989-91, fin. adv. com., 1994, ad hoc com. dist. facilities chmn., 1998; dir. The Santa Monica Youth Athletic Found., 1995— (exec. comm. 1997-98, v.p. 1998—); dir. The Small Bus. Coun. of Am. 1995—, dir. Santa Monica H.S. Booster Club, 1995-97, dir. Santa Monica Bay Rep. Club, 1995-96, Santa Monica Police Activities League, 1995-97, v.p. fin., 1997-98, pres.-elect, 1998—; pres. Gail Dorin Music Found., 1994—; v.p. Sneaker Sisters, 1996—; pres. Santa Monical Jr. Rowing, 1997—; legal cons. 33d Dist. Calif. PTA, 1997—; recreation and parks commr. City of Santa Monica, 1999—; sec. Santa Monica Leaders Club, 1999—. Mem. LWV (dir. 1997—), U. Pa. Alumni Soc. (pres. 1971-79, dir. 1979-87), Mountaingate Tennis Club, Alpha Kappa Psi (life). Jewish. Pension, profit-sharing, and employee benefits, General corporate, Health. Home: 616 23rd St Santa Monica CA 90402-3130 Office: 12100 Wilshire Blvd Fl 15 Los Angeles CA 90025-7120

**CARRICK, PAULA STRECKER,** lawyer, nurse; b. Phila., Feb. 29, 1944; d. Joseph Warren Carrick and Agnes Dorothea Strecker. Diploma, St. Francis Hosp. Sch. Nursing, 1965; BS, Troy State U., 1979; cert., Air Command and Staff Coll., 1978; JD, Walter F. George Sch. Law, 1982. Bar: S.C., Ga.; RN, Del., S.C. Quality assurance/risk mgmt. coord. Med. U. S.C., Charleston, 1983-85; sr. risk mgmt. cons. Va. Ins. Reciprocal, Richmond, 1985-88, sr. cons., 1988-90; sr. atty Beverly Enterprises, Ft. Smith, Ark., 1990-91; sr. counsel Beverly Enterprises, Ft. Smith, 1991-98, chief counsel, 1998—; cons. AACCN, Charleston; cons. to chief Nurse Corps, USAF; cons. to surgeon gen. USAF; mem. adj. faculty Shenandoah U., Winchester, Va.; lectr. on health care law and risk mgmt. Contbr. articles to profl. publs. Ret. col. USAFR, 1993. Mem. ABA, ANA, Am. Soc. Healthcare Risk Mgmt., Am. Soc. Law, Medicine and Ethics, Aerospace Med. Assn., Assn. Mil. Surgeons U.S., Nat. Health Lawyers Assn., Res. Officers Assn., Phi Delta Phi. Administrative and regulatory, Health, Personal injury. Home: 4105 Colton Dr Fort Smith AR 72903-6353 Office: Beverly Enterprises Inc PO Box 3324 Fort Smith AR 72919-3324

**CARRICO, HARRY LEE,** state supreme court chief justice; b. Washington, Sept. 4, 1916; s. William Temple and Nellie Nadalia (Willett) C.; m. Betty Lou Peck, May 18, 1940 (dec. 1987); 1 child, Lucretia Ann; m. Lynn Brackenridge, July 1, 1994. Jr. cert., George Washington U., 1938, JD, 1942, LLD, 1987; LLD, U. Richmond, 1973, Coll. William & Mary, 1993. Bar: Va. 1941. With Rust & Rust, Fairfax, Va., 1941-43; trial justice Fairfax, Va., 1943-51, pvt. practice, 1951-56; judge 16th Jud. Cir., Va., 1956-61; justice Va. Supreme Ct., Richmond, 1961-81, chief justice, 1981—; chmn. bd dirs. Nat. Ctr. for State Cts., 1989-90. With USNR, 1945-46. Recipient Alumni Profl. Achievement award George Washington U., 1981. Mem. McNeill Law Soc., Conf. Chief Justices (bd. dirs. 1985-91, 1st v.p. 1987, pres.-elect. 1988, pres. 1989-90, co-chmn. nat. jud. coun. 1991-97), Order of Coif, Phi Delta Phi, Omicron Delta Kappa. Episcopalian. Office: Va Supreme Ct 101 N 9th St Fl 4 Richmond VA 23219-2307*

**CARRICO, LUCRETIA A.,** lawyer; b. Alexandria, Va., May 17, 1942; d. Harry L. and Betty Lou C.; m. Robert Langston Irby, Nov. 28, 1961 (div. 1975); children: Ann Temple Irby Roberts, Robert Lee Irby; m. Wallace Lafayette Cliborne, Dec. 11, 1990. BA, U. Richmond, 1976, JD, 1978. Bar: Va. Asst. gen. counsel The Life Ins. Co. Va., Richmond, 1978-83; asst. corp. sec. Blue Cross Blue Shield Va., Richmond, 1983-84; pvt. practice Cumberland, Va., 1985-87; lawyer Hayes & Carrico, P.C., Powhatan, Va., 1987—. Comments editor U. Richmond Law Rev., 1977-78. Pres., dir. Neighbor to Neighbor Literacy Counsel, Powhatan, 1990-96, Goochland Powhatan Cmty. Svcs. Bd., 1991-95; dir. Children at Risk Today, Chesterfield, Va., 1996—. Mem. Powhatan Bar Assn., Powhatan C. of C. (pres., dir.), Powhatan Breakfast Lions Club. Episcopalian. Avocations: restoring old houses and decorating, gardening, reading, antiques. Fax: 804-598-7058. E-mail: LA-Carrico@aol.com. Home: 2510 Mill Rd Powhatan VA 23139-5203 Office: Hayes & Carrico PC 3891 Old Buckingham Rd Powhatan VA 23139-7020

**CARRICO, MICHAEL LAYNE,** lawyer; b. Danville, Ill., Apr. 2, 1963; s. Leeon and Diane Beverly Carrico; m. Susan Elaine Sutton, July 30, 1994; children: Emily, Maggie. BSEE, U. Ill., 1985; JD, U. Ky., 1991. Bar: N.Mex. 1991, U.S. Dist. Ct. N.Mex. 1991, U.S. Ct. Appeals (10th cir.) 1991, U.S. Supreme Ct. 1996. Elec. engr. Fairchild Semiconductor Corp., Costa Mesa, Calif., 1985-87, Nat. Semiconductor Corp., Tustin, Calif., 1987-88; lawyer Modrall, Sperling, Roehl, Harris & Sisk, Albuquerque, 1991—. Big brother Big Bros./Big Sisters Program, Albuquerque, 1992—. Mem. ABA, N.Mex. Bar Assn., Albuquerque Bar Assn., U. Ill. Alumni Assn. (pres. 1996—). Education and schools, General civil litigation, Toxic tort. Office: Modrall Sperling Roehl Harris & Sisk 500 4th St Albuquerque NM 87103-2168

**CARRIERE, EDWARD E., JR.,** judge; b. Bklyn., Dec. 7, 1941; s. Edward E. Sr. and Ursula Marie (Myers) C.; m. Jane Eloise Rohrabaugh, Feb. 27, 1981; children: Elizabeth Howell, Edward E. III. BA, Loyola U., New Orleans, 1965, JD, 1967. Staff atty. Dept. HUD, Atlanta, 1969-71; asst. dist. atty. Stone Mountain Jud. Cir., Decatur, Ga., 1971-73; sole practitioner Decatur, 1973-98; judge Mcpl. Ct., City of Decatur, 1986-98; assoc. judge Recorders Ct. of DeKalb County, Ga., 1989-98; trial judge State Ct. of DeKalb County, 1998—; chair governing com. DeKalb Pub. Defender's Office, 1989—, chair, 1993-98. Mem. State Bar Ga. (exec. com. 1997—, bd. govs. 1992—). Office: State Ct DeKalb County 210 The Callaway Bldg 120 W Trinity Pl Decatur GA 30030-3304

**CARRIGAN, JIM R.,** arbitrator, mediator, retired federal judge; b. Mobridge, S.D., Aug. 24, 1929; s. Leo Michael and Mildred Ione (Jaycox) C.; m. Beverly Jean Halpin, June 2, 1956. Ph.B., J.D., U. N.D., 1953; LL.M. in Taxation, NYU, 1956; LLD (hon.), U. Colo., 1989, Suffolk U., 1991, U. N.D., 1997. Bar: N.D. 1953, Colo. 1956. Asst. prof. law U. Denver, 1956-59; vis. assoc. prof. NYU Law Sch., 1958, U. Wash. Law Sch., 1959-60; Colo. jud. adminstr., 1960-61; prof. law U. Colo., 1961-67; partner firm Carrigan & Bragg (and predecessors), 1967-76; justice Colo. Supreme Ct., 1976-79; judge U.S. Dist. Ct. Colo., 1979-95; mem. Colo. Bd. Bar Examiners, 1969-71; lectr. Nat. Coll. State Judiciary, 1964-77, 95; bd. dirs. Nat. Inst. Trial Advocacy, 1971-73, 78—, chmn. bd. 1986-88, also mem. faculty, 1972—; adj. prof. law U. Colo, 1984, 1991—; bd. dirs. Denver Broncos Stadium Dist., 1996—. Editor-in-chief: N.D. Law Rev., 1952-53, Internat. Soc. Barristers Quar., 1972-79; editor: DICTA, 1957-59; contbr. articles to profl. jours. Bd. regents U. Colo., 1975-76; bd. visitors U. N.D. Coll. Law, 1983-85. Recipient Disting. Svc. award Nat. Coll. State Judiciary, 1969, Outstanding Alumnus award U. N.D., 1973, Regent Emeritus award U. Colo., 1977, B'nai Brith Civil Rights award, 1986, Thomas More Outstanding Lawyer award Cath. Lawyers Guild, 1988, Oliphant Disting. Svc. award Nat. Inst. Trial Advocacy, 1993, Constl. Rights award Nat. Assn. Blacks in Criminal Justice (Colo. chpt.), 1992, Disting. Svc. award Colo. Bar Assn., 1994, Amicus Curiae award ATLA, 1995. Fellow Colo. Bar Found., Boulder County Bar Found.; mem. ABA (action com. on tort system improvement 1985-87, TIPS sect. long range planning com., 1986-97; coun. 1987-91, task force on initiatives and referenda 1990-92, size of civil juries task force 1988-90, class actions task force 1995-97), Colo. Bar Assn., Boulder County Bar Assn., Denver Bar Assn., Cath. Lawyers Guild, Inns. of Ct., Internat. Soc. Barristers, Internat. Acad. Trial Lawyers (bd. dirs. 1995—), Fed. Judges Assn. (bd. dirs. 1985-89), Am. Judicature Soc. (bd. dirs. 1985-89), Tenth Circuit Dist. Judges Assn. (sec. 1991-92, v.p. 1992-93, pres. 1994-95), Order of Coif, Phi Beta Kappa. Roman Catholic. Office: Judicial Arbiter Group 1601 Blake St Ste 400 Denver CO 80202-1328

**CARRO, JORGE LUIS,** law educator, consultant; b. Havana, Cuba, Nov. 27, 1924; came to U.S., 1967, naturalized, 1973; s. Luis and Maria G. (Gonzalez) C.; m. Edy Jimenez; 1 dau., Edy C. B.A., Havana Inst., 1945; J.D., U. Havana, 1950; M.L.S., Kans. State Tchrs. Coll., 1969. Bar: Havana, Cuba 1950. Practice, Havana, 1950-67; legal cons. Swiss embassy, Havana and legal adv. Apostolic Nuncio, Havana, 1963-67; asst. libr. U. Wis.-Milw., 1969; asst. libr., instr. U. Wis.-Whitewater, 1969-72; libr., asst. prof. Ohio No. U., 1972-75, assoc. prof., 1975-76; assoc. prof. law, libr. U. Cin., 1976-78, acting dean, 1978-79, prof., libr., 1979-86, prof., 1986—. Mem. ABA, Cin. Bar Assn. Republican. Roman Catholic. Author: Government Regulation of Business Ethics, 3 vols., 1981-82; contbr. articles, books revs. to profl. jours. Office: U Cin Coll Law Cincinnati OH 45221-0001

**CARROLL, DIANE C.,** lawyer; b. Mineola, N.Y., Apr. 15, 1960; d. Manuel Niceto and Irene Louisa (Mandra) Lopez; m. Paul J. Antico, May 10, 1992; children: Bryan Paul, Jared Joseph. BA, Hofstra U., 1982; JD, Bklyn. Law Sch., 1985. Bar: N.Y. 1986, U.S. Dist. Ct. (ea. dist.) N.Y. 1986, U.S. Ct. Mil. Appeals 1991, U.S. Ct. Claims 1991, U.S. Ct. Appeals (fed. cir.) 1991, U.S. Supreme Ct. 1991. Assoc. Ansell & Weiss, Huntington, N.Y., 1986-90; litigating atty. Alan Paul Ansell, Huntington, 1990-91; pvt. practice Melville, N.Y., 1991—; mem. Suffolk County Matrimonial Com., Commack, N.Y., 1988—; arbitrator Suffolk County Small Claims Ct., Hauppauge, N.Y., 1989—; matrimonial arbitrator, 1996—. Mem. Nassau/Suffolk Womens Bar Assn. (fee dispute com. 1993—), N.Y. State Bar Assn., Suffolk County Bar Assn. Avocations: reading, gardening, raising Rottweiler dogs. Family and matrimonial, General practice, Bankruptcy. Office: 900 Walt Whitman Rd Melville NY 11747-2293

**CARROLL, DOUGLAS JAMES,** lawyer; b. Milw., Jan. 23, 1949; s. John Edmund and Madeline Vera Carroll; m. Christine Lee Rudolph, May 13, 1972; children: Douglas Jr., Michael, Daniel, Thomas. Student, Northwestern U., Evanston, Ill., 1967-68; BA, U. Wis., 1972, JD, 1975. Bar: Wis., U.S. Dist. Ct. (ea. dist.) Wis. 1975, U.S. Ct. Appeals (7th cir.) 1978, U.S. Supreme Ct. 1978, U.S. Dist. Ct. (we. dist.) Wis. 1989. Assoc. Arnold, Murray, O'Neill & Schimmel, Milw., 1975-89; shareholder O'Neill, Schimmel, Quirk & Carroll, S.C., Milw., 1989—. Mem. ABA (tort and ins. practice sect., litigation sect., appellate advocacy, ins. coverage, automobile law, fidelity and surety law, products and gen. liability, trial techniques coms. 1975—), State Bar Wis. (litigation sect., ins. law com., bus. law sect. 1990—), Milw. County Bar Assn. (civil bench-bar com. 1995—, chmn. judicial efficiency subcom. 1997—, membership com. 1996—), Def. Rsch. Inst., Phi Beta Kappa. Avocations: fishing, camping, golf, baseball. General civil litigation, Insurance, Product liability. Office: O'Neill Schimmel Quirk & Carroll 312 E Wisconsin Ave Ste 616 Milwaukee WI 53202-4368

**CARROLL, EARL HAMBLIN,** federal judge; b. Tucson, Mar. 26, 1925; s. John Vernon and Ruby (Wood) C.; m. Louise Rowlands, Nov. 1, 1952; children—Katherine Carroll Pearson, Margaret Anne. BSBA, U. Ariz., 1948, LLB, 1951. Bar: Ariz., U.S. Ct. Appeals (9th and 10th cirs.), U.S. Ct. of Claims, U.S. Supreme Ct. Law clk. Ariz. Supreme Ct., Phoenix, 1951-52; assoc. Evans, Kitchel & Jenckes, Phoenix, 1952-56, ptnr., 1956-80; judge U.S. Dist. Ct. Ariz., Phoenix, 1980—, sr. judge, 1994—; spl. counsel City of Tombstone, Ariz., 1962-65, Maricopa County, Phoenix, 1968-75, City of Tucson, 1974, City of Phoenix, 1979; designated mem. U.S. Fgn. Intelligence Surveillance Court by Chief Justice U.S. Supreme Ct., 1993-99; chief judge Alien Terrorist Removal Ct., 1996-01. Mem. City of Phoenix Bd. of Adjustment, 1955-58; trustee Phoenix Elem. Sch. Bd., 1961-72; mem. Gov.'s Council on Intergovtl. Relations, Phoenix, 1970-73; mem. Ariz. Bd. Regents, 1978-80. Served with USNR, 1943-46; PTO. Recipient Nat. Service awards Campfire, 1973, 75, Alumni Service award U. Ariz., 1980, Disting. Citizen award No. Ariz. U., Flagstaff, 1983, Bicentenial award Georgetown U., 1988, Disting. Citizen award U. Ariz., 1990. Fellow Am. Coll. Trial Lawyers, Am. Bar Found.; mem. ABA, Ariz. Bar Assn., U. Ariz. Law Coll. Assn. (pres. 1975), Phoenix Country Club, Sigma Chi (Significant Sig award 1991), Phi Delta Phi. Democrat. Office: US Dist Ct US Courthouse & Fed Bldg 230 N 1st Ave Ste 6000 Phoenix AZ 85025-0005

**CARROLL, FRANK JAMES,** lawyer, educator; b. Albuquerque, Feb. 10, 1947; s. Francis J. and Dorothy (Bloom) C.; m. Marilyn Blume, Aug. 9, 1969; children: Christine, Kathleen, Emily. BS in Acctg., St. Louis U., 1969; JD, U. Ill., 1973. Bar: Iowa 1973, U.S. Dist. Ct. Iowa, U.S. Tax Ct., U.S. Ct. Appeals (8th cir.); CPA, Mo., Iowa. Acct. Arthur Young & Co., St. Louis, 1969-70; shareholder Davis, Brown, Koehn, Shors & Roberts, P.C., Des Moines, 1973—; lectr. law Drake U. Law Sch., Des Moines, 1976-86, lectr. Sch. of Bus., 1988-92; bd. dirs. Newton Mfg. Co., Pella Plastics, Inc. Mem. commr.'s adv. group IRS, Washington, 1989; mem. grad. tax adv. bd. U. Mo. Kansas City Sch. Law, 1995. Mem. ABA, Iowa Bar Assn. (chair bus. law sect. 1995-98), Polk County Bar Assn., Des Moines C. of C., Wakonda Club, Des Moines Variety Club (bd. dirs. 1998), Beta Gamma Sigma. Corporate taxation, General corporate. Home: 5725 Harwood Dr Des Moines IA 50312-1203 Office: Davis Brown Koehn Shors Roberts PC 666 Walnut St Ste 2500 Des Moines IA 50309-3904

**CARROLL, JAMES EDWARD,** lawyer; b. Milford, Mass., July 9, 1952; s. James William and Anna (Bertoni) C.; m. Nancy Louise Baker, Oct. 12, 1974; children: Jonathan Patrick, Benjamin James, Jeremy David. BS, Fairfield U., 1974; MA, U. R.I., 1977; JD cum laude, Suffolk U., 1983. Bar: Mass. 1983, U.S. Dist. Ct. Mass. 1984, U.S. Ct. Appeals (1st cir.) 1984, U.S. Tax Ct. 1989, U.S. Supreme Ct. 1995. Tchr. Prout Meml. High Sch., Wakefield, R.I., 1974-76, Walpole (Mass.) High Sch., 1976-83; assoc. Gaston Snow & Ely Bartlett, Boston, 1983-86; trial atty. U.S. Dept. Justice, Washington, 1986-88; assoc. Hale & Dorr, Boston, 1988; ptnr. Peabody & Arnold, Boston, 1988-95; founding ptnr. Cetrulo & Capone, LLP, Boston, 1995—; mem. criminal justice panel, U.S. Dist. Ct. Mass., 1993—. Contbr. articles to law rev. Bd. dirs. Am. Cancer Soc. Mem. ABA, Mass. Bar Assn. (speaker 1991-92), Boston Bar Assn., Nat. Assn. Criminal Def. Attys., Supreme Jud. Ct. Hist. Soc., Phi Delta Phi. Roman Catholic. Avocations: running, baseball, football, children's soccer. Criminal, Federal civil litigation, General civil litigation. Home: 139 Lawndale Rd Mansfield MA 02048-1621 Office: Cetrulo & Capone 53 State St Boston MA 02109-2804

**CARROLL, MARK THOMAS,** lawyer; b. Queens, N.Y., May 12, 1956; s. Bernard James and Thalia (Antypas) C.; m. Joanne Mary Grinnell, Aug. 4, 1979; children: Stephen, Thomas. BA, Columbia U., 1977; JD, Harvard U., 1980. Bar: Pa. 1980, U.S. Ct. Appeals (3d cir.) 1980, U.S. Dist. Ct. (ea. dist.) Pa. 1980. Assoc. Duane, Morris & Heckscher, Phila., 1980-82; asst. dir. ALI-ABA, Phila., 1982-85, dir. office of publs., 1985—. Bd. dirs. Bradford Glen Homeowners Assn., 1988-90; active Boy Scouts Am.; founding mem. Joseph's People Com. Mem. ABA, Assn. for Continuing Legal Edn. (dir.-at-large). Republican. Roman Catholic. Home: 1402 Ashcom Dr Downingtown PA 19335-3566 Office: ALI-ABA 4025 Chestnut St Ste 500 Philadelphia PA 19104-3099

**CARROLL, MICHAEL DENNIS,** lawyer; b. Grosse Pointe, Mich., May 14, 1970; s. Edward Joseph and Patricia Anne (Lynch) C. BA in English, U. Mich., 1992, JD, 1995. Bar: Mich. 1995, U.S. Dist. Ct. (ea. dist.) Mich. 1995, U.S. Dist. Ct. (we. dist.) Mich. 1997. Assoc. Kerr, Russell & Weber, PLC, Detroit, 1995—. Mem. Irish-Am. Assn. Lawyers. Roman Catholic. Avocation: hockey. Construction, Contracts commercial. Home: 1851 Lancaster St Grosse Pointe MI 48236-1608 Office: Kerr Russell & Weber 500 Woodward Ave Ste 2500 Detroit MI 48226-3427

**CARROLL, THOMAS COLAS,** lawyer, educator; b. Phila., Jan. 5, 1943; s. George Colas and Mary F. (Dempsey) C.; m. Peg Kelly, June 19, 1966; children: Kevin, Beth Ann. BS, St. Joseph's U., 1964; JD, Villanova U., 1967. Bar: Pa. 1967, U.S. Ct. Appeals (3d cir.) 1967, U.S. Ct. Appeals (D.C. cir.) 1988, U.S. Ct. Appeals (11th cir.) 1990, U.S. Supreme Ct. 1975. Assoc. Wolf, Block, Schorr & Solis-Cohen, Phila., 1967-69; staff atty., chief of family div., asst. chief fed. div. Defender Assn. of Phila., 1969-75; ptnr. Carroll Creamer Carroll & Duffy, Phila., 1975-80, Carroll & Carroll, Phila., 1980-89; sole practitioner Phila., 1989-93; ptnr. Carroll & Cedrone, Phila., 1993—; adj. prof. law Villanova (Pa.) U., 1972—; lectr. Pa. Trial Lawyers Assn., Pa. Criminal Def. Lawyers Assn.; chmn. criminal justice act selection com. for ea. dist. Pa., 1980-89. Assoc. editor Law Review. Mem. Am. Arbitration Assn. (arbitrator), U. Pa. Am. Inn of Ct., Order of the Coif. Avocation: sailing. Criminal, Federal civil litigation. Office: Pub Ledger Bldg Ste94 150 S Independence Mall W Philadelphia PA 19106-3413

**CARRUTH, PAUL,** lawyer; b. Raleigh, N.C., July 30, 1948; s. Paul and Roberta (Fields) C.; m. Carolyn Skipwith, May 19, 1973; children: Rebecca Anne, Allison Elaine, James Scott. BA, Duke U., 1970; JD, U. N.C., 1973. Bar: N.C. 1974. Assoc. Poyner, Geraghty & Hartsfield, Raleigh, 1974-77; pvt. practice Raleigh, 1977-88; ptnr. McNamara, Pipkin, Knott & Carruth, Raleigh, 1989-91; sole practitioner Raleigh, 1991—. Mem. ABA, N.C. Bar Assn., Wake County Bar Assn. Republican. Methodist. Real property, Probate, General corporate. Office: 5834 Faringdon Pl Raleigh NC 27609-3930

**CARSON, ROBERT WILLIAM,** lawyer; b. Port Huron, Mich., Nov. 26, 1948; s. Robert Y. and Cecilia E. (DeMars) C.; m. Pamela Jean French, May 3, 1974; children: Shayna, Keeley, Robbie. AA, St. Clair County Community Coll., 1968; BA, U. Mich., 1970; JD, U. Detroit, 1973. Bar: Mich. 1973. Assoc. Raymond L. Krell, Detroit, 1973-74, McIntosh, McColl, Carson, McName & Strickler (predecessor), Port Huron, 1975-77; ptnr. McIntosh, McColl, Allen, Carson, McNamee & Strickler and predecessor firms, Port Huron, 1977-79, sr. ptnr., 1979—; bd. dirs. Guaranteed Tires, Inc., Port Huron. Campaign dir. St. Clair County March Dimes, Port Huron, 1978-80, chmn., 1980-82, bd. dirs. 1982—, legal liaison, 1984-85. Republican. Roman Catholic. Club: Port Huron Golf. Avocations: golf, basketball. Personal injury, Workers' compensation, Federal civil litigation. Office: McIntosh McColl Carson McNamee & Strickler 3024 Commerce Dr Fort Gratiot MI 48059-3819

**CARSON, WALLACE PRESTON, JR.,** state supreme court justice; b. Salem, Oreg., June 10, 1934; s. Wallace Preston and Edith (Bragg) C.; m. Gloria Stolk, June 24, 1956; children: Scott, Carol, Steven (dec. 1981). BA in Politics, Stanford U., 1956; JD, Willamette U., 1962. Bar: Oreg. 1962, U.S. Dist. Ct. Oreg. 1963, U.S. Ct. Appeals (9th cir.) 1968, U.S. Supreme Ct. 1971, U.S. Ct. Mil. Appeals 1977; lic. comml. pilot FAA. Pvt. practice law Salem, Oreg., 1962-77; judge Marion County Cir. Ct., Salem, 1977-82; assoc.

justice Oreg. Supreme Ct., Salem, 1982-92, chief justice, 1992—. Mem. Oreg. Ho. of Reps., 1967-71, maj. leader, 1969-71; mem. Oreg. State Senate, 1971-77, minority floor leader, 1971-77; dir. Salem Area Community Council, 1967-70, pres., 1969-70; mem. Salem Planning Commn., 1966-72, pres., 1970-71; co-chmn. Marion County Mental Health Planning Com., 1965-69; mem. Salem Community Goals Com., 1965; Republican precinct committeeman, 1963-66; mem. Marion County Rep. Central Exec. Com., 1963-66; com. predinct edn. Oreg. Rep. Central Com., 1965; vestryman, acolyte, Sunday Sch. tchr., youth coach St. Paul's Episcopal Ch., 1935—; task force on cts. Oreg. Council Crime and Delinquency, 1968-69; trustee Willamette U., 1970—; adv. bd. Cath. Ctr. Community Services, 1976-77; mem. comporehensive planning com. Mid-Willamette Valley Council of Govts., 1970-71; adv. com. Oreg. Coll. Edn. Tchr. Edn., 1971-75; pres. Willamette regional Oreg. Lung Assn., 1974-75, state dir., exec. com., 1975-77; pub. relations com. Williamette council Campfire Girls, 1976-77; criminal justice adv. bd. Chemeketa Community Coll., 1977-79; mem. Oreg. Mental Health Com., 1979-80; mem. subcom. Gov's Task Force Mental Health, 1980; you and govt. adv. com. Oreg. YMCA, 1981—. Served to col. USAFR, 1956-59. Recipient Salem Disting. Svc. award, 1968; recipient Good Fellow award Marion County Fire Svc., 1974, Minuteman award Oreg. N.G. Assn., 1980; fellow Eagleton Inst. Politics, Rutgers U., 1971. Mem. Marion County Bar Assn. (sec.-treas. 1965-67, dir. 1968-70), Oreg. Bar Assn., ABA, Willamette U. Coll. Law Alumni Assn. (v.p. 1968-70), Salem Art Assn., Oreg. Hist. Soc., Marion County Hist. Soc., Stanford U. Club (pres. Salem chpt. 1963-64), Delta Theta Phi. Office: Oregon Supreme Ct Supreme Ct Bldg 1163 State St Salem OR 97310-1331*

**CARSTARPHEN, EDWARD MORGAN, III,** lawyer; b. Ancon, Panama Canal Zone, Oct. 25, 1957; s. Edward Morgan and Norlavine (Carson) C.; m. Celia LaRae Rawlings Buchalski, June 3, 1979 (div. Apr. 1990); 1 child, Lucy Catherine; m. Darleen Colton, Aug. 29, 1991; 1 child, Desirae Dixon Peters. BA cum laude, Vanderbilt U., 1979; JD, U. Tex., 1982. Bar: Tex. 1982, U.S. Dist. Ct. (so. dist.) Tex. 1983, U.S. Ct. Appeals (5th cir.) 1984; cert. in civil trial law Tex. Bd. Legal Specialization. Assoc. Holtzman & Urquhart, Houston, 1982-84; briefing atty. to chief justice Tex. State Ct. Appeals for 6th Dist., Texarkana, 1984-85; ptnr. Brockway & Carstarphen, Houston, 1985-86, Powers & Carstarphen, Houston, 1987; of counsel Woodard, Hall & Primm, P.C., Houston, 1988-91, ptnr., 1991—. Contbr. articles to profl. publs., chpt. to book. Fellow Tex. Bar Found.; mem. State Bar Tex., Phi Delta Phi. General civil litigation, Toxic tort, Product liability. Office: Woodard Hall & Primm PC 7100 Texas Commerce Tower Houston TX 77002

**CARTEN, FRANCIS NOEL,** lawyer; b. Bryn Mawr, Pa., Dec. 25, 1935; s. Francis Patrick and Louise Cathleen (Leach) C. BS, U. Notre Dame, 1960; JD, Villanova U., 1964. Bar: Pa. 1967, N.Y. 1967, Conn. 1976. Assoc. Eyre, Mann & Lucas, N.Y.C., 1966-74; pvt. practice law, Danbury and Stamford, Conn., 1975-78; patent counsel TIE/communications, Inc., Shelton, Conn., 1978-79, Automation Industries, Inc., Greenwich, 1979-85; pvt. practice law, Stamford, 1985-88; pntr. Wyatt, Gerber, Meller & O'Rourke, L.L.P., 1988—. With U.S. Army, 1954-56. Mem. Am. Intellectual Property Law Assn., N.Y. State Bar Assn., N.Y. Intellectual Property Law Assn., Conn. Patent Law Assn., Seawanhaka Corinthian Yacht Club (Oyster Bay, N.Y.). Republican. Patent, Trademark and copyright, Intellectual property. Office: 1177 High Ridge Rd Stamford CT 06905-1211

**CARTER, BARRY EDWARD,** lawyer, educator, administrator; b. L.A., Oct. 14, 1942; s. Byron Edward and Ethel Catherine (Turner) C.; m. Kathleen Anne Ambrose, May 17, 1987; children: Gregory Ambrose, Meghan Elisabeth. A.B. with great distinction, Stanford U., 1964; M.P.A., Princeton U., 1966; J.D., Yale U., 1969. Bar: Calif. 1970, D.C. 1972. Program analyst Office of Sec. Def., Washington, 1969-70; mem. staff NSC, Washington, 1970-72; rsch. fellow Kennedy Sch., Harvard U., Cambridge, Mass., 1972; internat. affairs fellow Coun. on Fgn. Rels., 1972; assoc. Wilmer, Cutler & Pickering, Washington, 1973-75; sr. counsel Select Com. on Intelligence Activities, U.S. Senate, Washington, 1975; assoc. Morrison & Foerster, San Francisco, 1976-79; assoc. prof. law Georgetown U. Law Ctr., Washington, 1979-89, prof., 1989-93, 96—; exec. dir. Am. Soc. Internat. Law, Washington, 1992-93; acting undersec. for export adminstrn. U.S. Dept. Commerce, Washington, 1993-94, deputy undersec., 1994-96; vis. prof. law Stanford U. Law Sch., 1990; bd. dirs. Nukem, Inc., 1998—; chmn. adv. bd. Def. Budget Project, 1990-93; mem. UN Assn. Soviet-Am. Parallel Studies Project, 1976-87. Author: International Economic Sanctions: Improving the Haphazard U.S. Legal Regime, 1988 (Am. Soc. Internat. Law Cert. of Merit 1989); co-author: International Law, 3d edit., 1999; contbr. articles to profl. jours. With U.S. Army, 1969-71. Mem. ABA, Calif. Bar Assn., D.C. Bar Assn., Coun. on Fgn. Rels., Am. Soc. Internat. Law (hon. v.p. 1993-99, counselor, 1999—), Phi Beta Kappa. Democrat. Roman Catholic. Home: 2922 45th St NW Washington DC 20016-3559 Office: Georgetown U Law Ctr 600 New Jersey Ave NW Washington DC 20001-2075

**CARTER, BRET ROBERT,** lawyer; b. Muscatine, Iowa, Oct. 8, 1959; s. Burt Eugene and Mary Esther Carter; m. Hazel Mary Williams, Oct. 5, 1991. BS, Iowa State U., 1982; JD, Pepperdine U., 1987. Bar: Calif. 1987, U.S. Dist. Ct. (so. dist.) Calif., 1987, U.S. Dist. Ct. (cen., no. dists.) Calif., 1988, U.S. Dist. Ct. (ea. dist.) Calif., 1990, U.S. Ct. Appeals (9th cir.), 1993. Atty. Booth Mitchell & Strange, L.A., 1986-88, John T. Heaney, A Law Corp., L.A., 1988-93, Hart & Watters, L.A., 1993—. Contbr. articles to profl. jours. Mem. ARC, Santa Monica, Calif., City Hope-Bus. L.A. Recipient Young Lawyer award Achievement ABA, 1990. Mem. L.A. Venture Assn., Beverly Hills Bar Assn. (v.p. bd. govs. 1990-92), L.A. Bus. Property Coun. Avocations: hiking, biking. General corporate, Estate planning, Real property. Office: Hart & Watters 12400 Wilshire Blvd Ste 500 Los Angeles CA 90025-1055

**CARTER, CANDY LORRAINE,** lawyer; b. N.Y.C., Aug. 9, 1961; d. Ralph Bellamy and Lola Marie Whitaker; m. Arthur Herbert Carter Jr., June 20, 1979; children: Kevin Arthur, Andrew David. AA, Anne Arundel C.C., 1992; BA, U. Balt., 1994, JD, 1996. Vol., paralegal Anne Arundel County Bar Found., Annapolis, Md., 1991-92; paralegal Legal Aid, Annapolis, Md., 1992-93; law intern Hon. Warren B. Duckett Jr., Annapolis, Md., 1995; law clk. Howard County State's Atty., Elliott City, Md., 1996; teaching asst. U. Balt., 1995-96; law clk. Daniel H. Green, Eldersburg, Md., 1996, assoc., 1996-97; atty. pvt. practice, Hanover, Md., 1996—; student atty. Howard County State's Atty., 1995-96. Asst. leader Cub Scouts, Hanover, Md., 1990-93; coun. v.p. Christ the Servant Luth. Ch., Severn, Md., 1996, coun. mem., 1995-96. Mem. ABA, Md. State Bar Assn., Women's Bar Assn., Heuisler Honor Soc., Phi Theta Kappa. Avocations: reading, arts & crafts. Bankruptcy, Family and matrimonial, General practice. Office: PO Box 664 Hanover MD 21076-0664

**CARTER, CHRISTOPHER O'HARA,** lawyer, public defender; b. Adak, Alaska, Feb. 6, 1961; s. Frank and Jane Carter; m. Karen Ann Garrett, July 1, 1989; children: Scott-Christopher, Eric, Cameron. AA in Secondary Edn., Montgomery Coll., Germantown, Md., 1980; BA in History, St. Mary's Coll., St. Mary's City, Md., 1982; JD, U. Ark., 1988. Bar: Ark. 1988, Mo. 1989, D.C. 1990. Pvt. practice, Flippin, Ark., 1988-97; trial pub. defender Ark. 14th Jud. Dist. Pub. Defender's Office, Mt. Home, Ark., 1998—. Chmn. Marion County Rep. Com., Yellville, Ark., 1992-93. Mem. Ark. Bar Assn., Mo. Bar Assn., Nat. Geog. Soc. (life). Roman Catholic. Home: PO Box 369 Flippin AR 72634-0369 Office: 14th Jud Dist Pub Defender's Office 1 Courthouse Sq Mountain Home AR 72653

**CARTER, DANIEL PAUL,** lawyer, educator; b. Massillon, Ohio, Mar. 22, 1948; s. Harry A. and Anna Jean (Steiner) C.; m. Regina Ranieri, July 9, 1983; children: Emily Hedges, Daniel Paul Jr., Anne Baldwin, Elizabeth Regina. BS, St. Joseph's Coll., Phila., 1971; JD, Villanova U., 1974. Bar: Pa. 1974, U.S. Dist. Ct. (ea. dist.) Pa. 1980, U.S. Ct. Appeals (3d cir.) 1981, U.S. Dist. Ct. (mid. dist.) Pa. 1985, U.S. Ct. Claims 1986, U.S. Dist. Ct. (we. dist.) Pa. 1989, U.S. Supreme Ct. 1991, U.S. Ct. Appeals (1st cir.) 1995, U.S. Dist. Ct. (no. dist.) Ohio 1996. Asst. prof. of law, dir. admissions Widener U., Wilmington, Del., 1974-79; ptnr. LaBrum & Doak, Phila., 1979-86, Shaffer, Palma, Dougherty & Carter, West Chester, Pa., 1986-87, Murphy & O'Connor, Phila., 1988-90; founding ptnr. Timby Brown & Timby, Phila., 1990-96; ptnr., head environ. dept. Buckley King & Bluso, Cleve., 1996—; counsel jury study Delaware County, Media, Pa., 1976; adj. prof. law Widener U., 1984—. legal counsel Pa. Young Reps., 1977-78; regional legal counsel Young Rep. Nat. Fedn., 1978-79. Named One of Outstanding Young Men of Am., Jaycees, 1979. Mem. ABA, Del. County Bar Assn., Chester County Bar Assn., Phila. Bar Assn., Pa. Bar Assn. (vice chmn. law sch. liaison 1981-82). Republican. Presbyterian. State civil litigation, Insurance, Environmental. Home: 30651 Brookwood Dr Pepper Pike OH 44124-5422 Office: Buckley King & Bluso 1400 Bank One Bldg Cleveland OH 44114-2652

**CARTER, DANIEL ROLAND,** lawyer; b. Shreveport, La., Aug. 6, 1956; s. Jerry Glen and Sandra Jane (Roland) Griffith; m. Lauri Ann Witek, Nov. 13, 1993. BA in Polit. Sci., La. Tech. U., 1979, BSChemE, 1983; JD, South Tex. Coll. Law, 1991. Bar: Tex. 1991, U.S. Dist. Ct. (so., no., ea. and we. dists.) Tex. Prodn. engr. Transco Exploration & Prodn. Co., Houston, 1982-83; transmission engr. Transcontinental Gas Pipe Line Corp., Houston, 1984-87, environ. engr., 1987-88, sr. environ. engr., 1988-91, atty., 1991-95; sr. assoc. Phillips & Akers, Houston, 1995-98; chief legal officer NATCO Group Inc., Houston, 1998—. Mem. Tex. Bar Assn., Houston Bar Assn., Tex. Soc. Profl. Engrs., La. Tech. Alumni Assn. (bd. dirs.), Phi Delta Phi, Tau Beta Pi, Phi Alpha Theta, Order of the Lytae. Republican. Baptist. Avocations: running, reading, wines, travel, cooking. General corporate. Home: 1706 Lofty Maple Trl Kingwood TX 77345-1936 Office: NATCO Group Inc 2950 North Loop W Houston TX 77092-8839

**CARTER, GENE,** federal judge; b. Milbridge, Maine, Nov. 1, 1935; s. K.W. and S. Loreta (Beal) C.; m. Judith Ann Kittredge, June 24, 1961; children: Matthew G., Mark G. BA, U. Maine, 1958, LLD (hon.), 1985; LLB, NYU, 1961. Bar: Maine 1962. Ptnr. Rudman, Winchell, Carter & Buckley (and predecessors), Bangor, Maine, 1965-80; assoc. justice Maine Supreme Jud. Ct., 1980-83; judge U.S. Dist. Ct. Maine, 1983-89, chief judge, 1989-96; chmn. adv. com. on rules of civil procedure Maine Supreme Jud. Ct., 1976-80. Chmn. Bangor Housing Authority, 1970-77; trustee Unity (Maine) Coll. Mem. Am. Trial Lawyers Assn., Internat. Soc. Barristers, Am. Coll. Trial Lawyers. Office: US Dist Ct 156 Federal St Portland ME 04101-4152

**CARTER, GLENN THOMAS,** lawyer, clergyman; b. Beaumont, Tex., July 20, 1934; s. Glenmore Rust and Sarah Elizabeth (Woods) C.; m. Janette Lucile Mullikin, Aug. 1, 1954; children: Penny Lucile Loucks, Sylvia Lee De Vries. BA, Union Coll., 1956; JD, Emory U., 1967. Bar: Ga. 1968, Tex. 1969, D.C. 1976, Md. 1976, U.S. Dist. Ct. (no. dist.) Tex. 1981, Calif. 1984; ordained to ministry Seventh-day Adventist Chs., 1960. Pastor chs. in Tex., Wyo., Ga., 1956-65; spl. legal advisor Cumberland Conf. Seventh-day Adventists, Decatur, 1968-69; dir. trust svcs. and pub. affairs Texico and Tex. Conf. Seventh-day Adventists, Amarillo and Ft. Worth, Tex., 1969-76; assoc. dir. trust svcs. Gen. Conf. Seventh-day Adventists, Washington, 1976-80; dir. pub. affairs, assoc. dir. trust svcs. Southwestern Union Conf. Seventh-day Adventists, Burleson, Tex., 1980-82; bd. dir. trust svcs. Pacific Union Conf. Seventh-day Adventists, Westlake Village, Calif., 1982-85; dir. Trust Svcs. Gen. Conf. of Seventh-day Adventists, Washington, 1985—. Contbr. articles to ch. pubs. Recipient Am. Jurisprudence prize for litigation Lawyers Co-op, 1967. Mem. Rotary (Paul Harris fellow). Estate planning, Civil rights. Office: 12501 Old Columbia Pike Silver Spring MD 20904-6601

**CARTER, J. DENISE,** lawyer; b. Kansas City, Mo., Mar. 21, 1963; d. Ronald Ira and Sharon Kay (Williams) C. AA, Longview C.C., 1986; BA, U. Mo., Kansas City, 1989, JD, 1992. Bar: Mo. 1992. Pvt. practice Kansas City, 1993—. Republican. Avocations: golf, tennis, scuba diving. Bankruptcy, Criminal, General practice. Office: 4218 Roanoke Rd Ste 300 Kansas City MO 64111-4735

**CARTER, JAMES ALFRED,** lawyer; b. Shelbyville, Tenn., June 29, 1941; s. Granville Thomas and Elaine (Thrasher) C.; m. Kathleen Shaughness, Oct. 6, 1967; children: James Byrne, Stephen Thomas. BBA, U. Tex., Arlington, 1962; JD, U. Tex., 1967. Bar: U.S. Dist. Ct. (no. dist.) Tex. 1969, U.S. Tax Ct. 1970, U.S. Ct. Claims 1977, U.S. Supreme Ct. 1980, U.S. Ct. Appeals (5th cir.) 1985; CPA, Tex. Acct. Price Waterhouse, Ft. Worth, 1967; assoc. Smith, Carter, Rose & Finley, San Angelo, Tex., 1969-71; ptnr. Smith, Carter, Rose, Finley & Griffis, San Angelo, Tex., 1971-97; pvt. practice James A. Carter & Assocs., San Angelo, 1997—; chmn. estate planning, probate and tax law Tex. Bd. Legal Specialization, Austin, Tex., 1980-84. Chmn. March of Dimes, San Angelo, 1971; pres. West Tex. Boys Ranch, San Angelo, 1980-84; mem. St. John's Hosp. Yr. 2000, San Angelo, 1980-84, Century Club YMCA, San Angelo; bd. dirs. Rio Concho Manor, San Angelo, 1980-90; trustee San Angelo Ind. Sch. Dist., 1992-98, pres., 1997-98. Capt. U.S. Army, 1968-69. Fellow Tex. Bar Found.; mem. ABA, AICPA (chmn. regional trial bd.), Tex. Bar Assn. (cert. in tax law, estate planning, probate bd. legal specialization, chmn. tax specialization, estate planning and probate specialization coms., revision bd. Tex. guardianship statute, com. inheritance and state tax), Tex. State Soc. CPA's (chmn. by-laws com.), Kiwanis (pres. 1978-79). Republican. Mem. Ch. Christ. Avocations: handball, farming. Estate planning, Probate, State and local taxation. Home: 915 Montecito Dr San Angelo TX 76901-4555 Office: 515 W Harris Ave Ste 100 San Angelo TX 76903-6362

**CARTER, JAMES EDWARD,** judge; b. Phoenix, Apr. 9, 1935; s. Charles Albert Carter and Edna Ruth (Edwards) Woehler; m. Virginia N. Jenkins, Mar. 7, 1958; children: Tonya Elise Carter Zeien, Tiffany Jaye Carter, Heath. BS, Grand Canyon Coll., 1957; MA in Edn., Ariz. State U., 1960; JD, U. Ariz., 1964. Bar: Ariz. 1964, U.S. Dist. Ct. Ariz. 1965, U.S. Ct. Appeals (9th cir.) 1986. Tchr., coach Sunnyslope H.S., Phoenix, 1957-61; assoc. Cox and Hedberg, Phoenix, 1964-65; asst. city prosecutor City of Phoenix, 1965-72, city prosecutor, 1972-74, asst. city atty. (civil), 1974-86; assoc. DeConcini McDonald et al, Phoenix, 1986-88; ptnr. Heron Burchette et al, Phoenix, 1988-90; pvt. practice Phoenix, 1990-91; city mcpl. judge City of Phoenix, 1991—; mem. faculty for new judge orientation Supreme Ct. Jud. Coll., 1994—; mentor New Judges Ltd. Jurisdiction, 1994—, mentor chmn., 1997; vice chmn. Ltd. Jurisdiction Judges, 1997, chmn., 1998-99. Bd. dirs. Bapt. Hosp. and Health Sys., Phoenix, Phoenix Bapt. Hosp., 1965—; trustee Grand Canyon U., Phoenix. Mem. State Bar Ariz., Maricopa County Bar Assn. Republican. Baptist. Avocations: basketball, softball, skiing, fishing. Office: Phoenix Mcpl Ct Divsn 12 400 N 7th St Phoenix AZ 85006-3386

**CARTER, JAMES H.,** state supreme court justice; b. Waverly, Iowa, Jan. 18, 1935; s. Harvey J. and Althea (Dominick) C.; m. Jeanne E. Carter, Mar. 1959; children: Carol, James. B.A., U. Iowa, 1956, J.D., 1960. Law clk. to judge U.S. Dist. Ct., 1960-62; assoc. Shuttleworth & Ingersoll, Cedar Rapids, Iowa, 1962-73; judge 6th Jud. Dist., 1973-76, Iowa Ct. Appeals, 1976-82; justice Iowa Supreme Ct., Des Moines, 1982—. Office: Iowa Supreme Ct State House Des Moines IA 50319-0001*

**CARTER, JAMES HAL, JR.,** lawyer; b. Ames, Iowa, Sept. 25, 1943; s. James H. Sr. and Louise (Benge) C.; m. Sara N. Meeker, July 27, 1974; children: Janet, Faith, Katherine. BA, Yale U., 1965, LLB, 1969. Bar: N.Y. 1971, U.S. Dist. Ct. (so. dist.) N.Y. 1972, U.S. Dist. Ct. (ea. dist.) N.Y. 1975, U.S. Dist. Ct. (no. dist.) N.Y. 1992, U.S. Dist. Ct. (west. dist.) Mich. 1992, U.S. Dist. Ct. Conn. 1981, U.S. Ct. Internat. Trade 1980, U.S. Ct. Appeals (2nd cir.) 1971, U.S. Supreme Ct. 1976, U.S. Ct. Appeals (1st and 5th cirs.) 1984, U.S. Ct. Appeals (fed. cir.) 1988, U.S. Ct. Appeals (3rd cir.) 1990. Fulbright scholar Cambridge U., Eng., 1965-66; law clk. U.S. Ct. Appeals (2d cir.), 1969-70; with Sullivan & Cromwell, N.Y.C., 1970, ptnr., 1977; lectr. internat. comml. arbitration Practicing Law Inst.; bd. dirs. Am. Arbitration Assn., Am. Assn. for Internat. Com. of Jurists, Am. Bar Found. Corr. editor: Internat. Legal Materials; contbr. articles to profl. jours. Mem. adv. bd. Southwestern Legal Found. Internat. and Comparative Law Ctr., Inst. for Transnational Arbitration. Mem. ABA (past chair internat. law and practice sect., former co-chmn. internat. comml. arbitration com.), U.S. Coun. Internat. Bus. (com. on arbitration), Am. Soc. Internat. Law (v.p.), Am. Law Inst., N.Y. State Bar Assn. (former chmn. internat. dispute resolution com.), Assn. of Bar of City of N.Y. (chmn. internat. affairs coun.), Coun. on Fgn. Rels. Private international, Federal civil litigation. Office: Sullivan & Cromwell 125 Broad St Fl 28 New York NY 10004-2489

**CARTER, JEANNE WILMOT,** lawyer, publisher; b. Iowa City, Iowa, Oct. 25, 1950; d. John Robert and Adelaide Wilmot (Briggs) Carter; m. Daniel Halpern, Dec. 31, 1982; 1 child, Lily Wilmot. BA cum laude, Barnard Coll., N.Y.C., 1973; MFA, Columbia U., 1977; JD, Yeshiva U., N.Y.C., 1986. Bar: N.Y. 1987. Assoc. Raoul Lionel Felder, P.C., N.Y.C., 1986—; pres., co-owner, dir. Ecco Press, Hopewell, N.J., 1992—. Author: Dirt Angel, 1997, Tales from the Rain Forest, 1997; editor: On Music, 1994; contbr. articles to profl. jours. and books including Reading the Fights, N.Am. Rev., O'Henry Prize Stories 1986, Antaeus, Antioch Rev., Arts and Entertainment Law Jour., Ont. Rev., Denver Quar., Jour. Blacks in Higher Edn., others. Bd. dirs. Nat. Poetry Series, 1981—, AIDS Helping Hand, N.Y.C., 1987-95, Planned Parenthood of Mercer County, 1998—; vol. litigator Womanspace, Princeton, N.J., 1994; mem. Jr. League of N.Y.C., 1980-91. N.Y. Found. of the Arts fellow, 1989. Mem. ABA, N.Y. State Bar Assn. Family and matrimonial. Home: 60 Pheasant Hill Rd Princeton NJ 08540-7502

**CARTER, JOHN LOYD,** lawyer; b. Clayton, N.Mex., Oct. 2, 1948; s. John Allen and Ruth (Laughlin) C.; m. Dorel Susan Payne, Sept. 20, 1975; children: Matthew, Caroline, Susan. BA, So. Meth. U., 1970, JD cum laude, 1973. Bar: Tex. 1973, U.S. Ct. Appeals (5th and 11th cirs.) 1975, U.S. Supreme Ct. 1976, U.S. Dist. Ct. (so. dist.) Tex. 1974, U.S. Dist. Ct. (no. dist.) Tex. 1978, U.S. Dist. Ct. (ea. dist.) Tex. 1985. Assoc. Vinson & Elkins, Houston, 1973-80, ptnr., 1980—. Fellow Am. Coll. Trial Lawyers, Tex. Bar Found., Houston Bar Found. General civil litigation, Antitrust, Securities. Office: Vinson & Elkins 2300 First City Tower Houston TX 77002-6760

**CARTER, PAMELA LYNN,** former state attorney general; b. South Haven, Mich., Aug. 20, 1949; d. Roscoe Hollis and Dorothy Elizabeth (Hadley) Fanning; m. Michael Anthony Carter, Aug. 26, 1971; children: Michael Anthony Jr., Marcya Alicia. BA cum laude, U. Detroit, 1971; MSW, U. Mich., 1973; JD, Ind. U., 1984. Bar: Ind. 1984, U.S. Dist. Ct. (no. dist.) Ind. 1984, U.S. Dist. Ct. (so. dist.) Ind. 1984. Rsch. analyst, treatment dir. U. Mich. Sch. Pub. Health and UAW, Detroit, 1973-75; exec. dir. Mental Health Ctr. for Women and Children, Detroit, 1975-77; consumer litigation atty. UAW-Gen. Motors Legal Svcs., Indpls., 1983-87; securities atty. Sec. of State, Indpls., 1987-89; Gov.'s exec. asst. for health and human svcs. Gov.'s Office, Indpls., 1989-91, dep. chief of staff to Gov., 1991-92; with firm Baker & Daniels, 1992-93; atty. gen. State of Ind., Indpls., 1993-96; partner Johnson & Smith, 1996-97; v.p., gen. counsel and sec. Cummins Engine Co., Inc., Columbus, Ind., 1998—. Author poems. mem. Cath. Social Svcs., Indpls., Jr. League, Indpls., Dem. Precinct, Indpls. Recipient Outstanding Svc. award Indiana Perinatal Assn., 1991, Community Svc. Coun. Ctrl. Ind., 1991, non-profl. healthcare award Family Health Conf. Bd. Dirs., 1991, award for excellence Women of the Rainbow, 1991; named Outstanding Young Woman of America, 1977, Breakthrough Woman of the Year, 1989. Mem. Nat. Bar Assn., Ind. Bar Assn., Coalition of 100 Black Women. Democrat. First African-American woman to hold title of Atty. Gen. in the nation, first woman atty. gen. in Ind. Avocations: gardening, hiking, traveling, reading. Office: Cummins Engine Co Inc Mail Code 60903 500 Jackson St Columbus IN 47201-6258

**CARTER, RICHARD DENNIS,** lawyer, educator; b. Newburgh, N.Y., Feb. 17, 1949; s. Edward Francis and Catherine Florence (Harding) C. BA, Pace U., 1977; JD, George Washington U., 1980. Bar: D.C. 1980, Va. 1991, Md. 1991, U.S. Dist. Ct. D.C. 1981, U.S. Dist. Ct. Md. 1990, U.S. Dist. Ct. (ea. dist.) Wis. 1994, U.S. Dist. Ct. Ariz. 1994, U.S. Ct. Appeals (4th cir.) 1991, U.S. Supreme Ct. 1987. Supervising atty., adj. prof. law D.C. Law Students in Ct., Washington, 1980-90, dep. dir., 1981-85, exec. dir., 1985-90; adj. prof. trial advocacy Georgetown U., Washington, 1982—; ptnr. Cunningham and Hudgins, Alexandria, Va., 1990, Hudgins, Carter & Coleman, Alexandria, 1990-98, Carter & Coleman, Alexandria, 1998—. Contbr. articles to profl. jours. Mem. ABA, D.C. Bar Assn., Washington Bar Assn., Alexandria Bar Assn., Am. Inns of Ct. Episcopalian. Avocation: motor sports. Federal civil litigation, State civil litigation, Health. Home: 3416 Sharon Chapel Rd Alexandria VA 22310-2311 Office: Carter & Coleman 602 Cameron St Alexandria VA 22314

**CARTER, ROBERT LEE,** federal judge; b. Caryville, Fla., Mar. 11, 1917; s. Robert and Annie (Martin) C.; m. Gloria Spencer, Dec. 4, 1946 (dec. Nov. 1971); children: John Walton, David Christopher. A.B. magna cum laude, Lincoln U., 1937, D.C.L., 1964; LL.B. magna cum laude, Howard U., 1940; LL.M., Columbia U., 1941; LLD, Northeastern U., 1988, Coll. Holy Cross, 1994, Howard U., 1995. Bar: N.Y. 1945. Asst. spl. counsel NAACP, N.Y.C., 1944-56; gen. counsel NAACP, 1956-68; mem. firm Poletti, Freidin, Prashker, Feldman & Gartner, N.Y.C., 1969-72; judge U.S. Dist. Ct. So. Dist. N.Y., N.Y.C., 1972-87, sr. judge, 1987—; adj. prof. Law Sch. NYU, 1965-70, Yale U., 1975-77, U. Mich., 1977; apl. asst. U.S. atty. So. Dist. N.Y., 1968; mem. N.Y.C. Mayor's Jud. Com., 1968-72. Contbr. articles to profl. jours. Pres. Nat. Com. Against Discrimination in Housing, 1966-72; mem. N.Y. State Spl. Commn. on Attica, N.Y. State Temp. Commn. on Ct. Reform, 1970-72, Am. del. UN Third World Conf. on Crime and the Treatment of Offenders, Stockholm, 1965; bd. dirs. Northside Ctr. Child Devel., New Sch. for Social Rsch.; chmn. Pub. Svc. Awards Program, City of N.Y., 1982-83. 2d lt. USAAF, 1941-44. Rosenwald fellow, 1940-41, Shikes fellow Harvard U., 1990; Columbia Urban Center fellow, 1968-69; recipient Howard U. Disting. Alumni award, 1980, Emory Bucknor award Fed. Bar Coun., 1995. Mem. Nat. Conf. Black Lawyers (co-chmn. 1968-82). Office: US Dist Ct So Dist NY US Courthouse 500 Pearl St Rm 2220 New York NY 10007-1316*

**CARTER, ROBERT PHILIP, SR.,** lawyer; b. Lexington, Ky., Sept. 4, 1946; s. George Philip and Alice Joy (Scott) C.; m. Carol Sharon Hall, Aug. 23, 1969 (div. Feb. 1976); 1 child, Robert Philip Jr.; m. Sandra Collins, Mar. 24, 1995. BS, Morehead State U., 1971; JD, Emory U., 1973. Bar: Ky. 1974, W.Va. 1986, U.S. Dist. Ct. (ea. dist.) Ky. 1975, U.S. Dist. Ct. (so. dist.) W.Va. 1986. Pvt. practice law Louisa, Ky., 1974-75; gen. counsel Black Diamond Coal Co., Lexington, 1975-76, Ky. Mortgage Co., Lexington, 1976-78; pvt. practice law Louisa, 1978—; approved atty. Chgo. Title Ins. Co., 1976—, Commonwealth Land Title Ins. Co., Louisville, 1974—, Title Ins. Co. Minn., 1976—; cons. Louisa Med. Ctr., Inc., 1974—. Mem. Mensa, Phi Delta Phi. Democrat. General practice, Criminal, Family and matrimonial. Office: PO Box 336 108 Lady Washington St Louisa KY 41230

**CARTER, STEPHEN EDWARD,** lawyer; b. Louisa, Ky., Feb. 11, 1954; s. Edward Carter and Ima Jean (Workman) Heraldson; m. Roxanne Swank, May 4, 1973; 1 child, McKenzie. BA, Ohio State U., 1975; JD, Capital U., 1980. Bar: Ohio 1980, U.S. Dist. Ct. (so. dist.) Ohio 1982, U.S. Ct. Appeals (6th cir.) 1985, U.S. Supreme Ct. 1985, S.C. 1989, U.S. Dist. Ct. S.C. 1990. Assoc. Federico, Myers & Enz, Columbus, Ohio, 1980; pvt. practice law Circleville, Ohio, 1981-84; ptnr. Dumm & Carter, Circleville, 1984-87, Farthing, Carter & Dumm, Circleville, 1987-89, McNair Law Firm, Hilton Head Island, S.C., 1990-92, Bethea, Jordan & Griffin, P.A., Hilton Head Island, 1992—. Mem. ABA (litigation sect.), Ohio Bar Assn., Assn. Trial Lawyers Am., Ohio Acad. Trial Lawyers, Leadership Hilton Head. Personal injury, General civil litigation, Federal civil litigation. Office: Bethea Jordan & Griffin PA 23 Shelter Cove Ln Ste 400 Hilton Head Island SC 29928-3542

**CARTER, T(HOMAS) BARTON,** law educator; b. Dallas, Aug. 6, 1949; s. Sydney Hobart and Josephine (Wren) C.; m. Eleonore Dorothy Alexander, June 3, 1978 (div. 1988); 1 child, Richard Alexander. BA in Psychology, Yale U., 1971; JD, U. Pa., 1974; MS in Mass Communication, Boston U., 1978. Bar: Mass. 1974, U.S. Dist. Ct. Mass. 1975, U.S. Ct. Appeals (1st cir.) 1975. Asst. prof. law Boston U., 1979-85, assoc. prof., 1985-96, prof., 1996—; pvt. practice Boston, 1974—; pres. Tanist Broadcasting Corp., Boston, 1981—. Co-author: The First Amendment and the Fourth Estate, 1985, 7th edit., 1997, The First Amendment and the Fifth Estate, 1986, 5th edit., 1999, Mass Communications Law in a Nutshell, 1988, 4th edit., 1994. Mem. ABA, Assn. for Edn. in Journalism and Mass Comm. (chk. 1981-82, asst. head 1982-83, head 1983-84), Broadcast Edn. Assn. (chair law and policy divsn. 1989-90, Fed. Comm. Bar Assn., Univ. Club. Avocation: bridge. Home: 109 Commonwealth Ave Apt 6 Boston MA 02116-2345 Office: Boston U 640 Commonwealth Ave Boston MA 02215-2422

**CARTER, W. LEE, III,** lawyer, legal staffing company executive; b. Dallas, Sept. 10, 1944; s. William L. Jr. and Dorothy Marie Carter; m. Martha Gravely, June 3, 1967; children: Carita, Grant, Gravely. BBA, So. Meth. U., 1966, JD, 1971; MBA, U. Pa., 1968. Bar: Tex. 1971. Account exec.

Alexander & Alexander, Dallas, 1967-84, dir. R&D, 1989-96; exec. dir. Dallas City Ctr. Assn., 1996-97; mng. dir. Ad Hoc Legal Resources, 1997—. Treas., Eastern Seals of Dallas, 1997—. Mem. Salesmanship Club (Dallas). Republican. Methodist. Office: Ad Hoc Legal Resources 600 Founders Sq 900 Jackson St Dallas TX 75202-4436

**CARTER, WILLIAM JOSEPH,** lawyer; b. Balt., Sept. 1, 1949; s. Henry Merle and Florence (Rogan) C.; m. Monica Anne Urlock, July 17, 1976. BS in Psychology, Va. Poly. Inst., 1971; JD, Coll. William and Mary, 1974. Bar: Va. 1974, Pa. 1974, Md. 1980, U.S. Dist. Ct. D.C. 1981, U.S. Dist. Ct. Md. 1983, U.S. Dist. Ct. (ea. dist.) Va. 1985, U.S. Ct. Claims 1977, U.S. Tax Ct. 1977, U.S. Ct. Mil. Appeals 1975, U.S. Ct. Appeals (D.C. and 4th cirs.) 1979, U.S. Ct. Appeals (fed. cir.) 1982, D.C. 1980, U.S. Supreme Ct. 1977, U.S. Ct. Appeals (6th cir.) 1988, U.S. Ct. Appeals (3d and 5th cirs.) 1992. Commd. 2d lt. U.S. Army, 1971, advanced through grades to capt., 1974, served with JAGC, 1971-79, resigned, 1979; assoc. Carr, Jordan, Coyne & Savits, Washington, 1979-84; shareholder Carr, Goodson & Lee, P.C., 1984-95, Carr Goodson Lee & Warner Profl. Corp., Washington, 1996-98, Carr Goodson Warner Profl. Corp., Washington, 1999—; exec. com. deans adv. roundtable Coll. Arts and Scis., Va. Poly. Inst. Author: Appellate Practice Handbook for Maryland, Virginia and District of Columbia, 1996; editor: Appellate Practice Manual for the District of Columbia Court of Appeals, 1992. Mem. ABA, Md. Bar Assn., Bar Assn. D.C., Counsellors, D.C. Bar Assn. (cts. and adminstrn. of justice sect., ct. rules com., chair 1999—). Episcopalian. Avocations: ice hockey, tennis, music, scuba diving, skiing. General civil litigation, Insurance, Personal injury. Office: Carr Goodson Warner East Tower 1301 K St NW Ste 400 Washington DC 20005-3317

**CARTER, ZACHARY W.,** prosecutor. BA, Cornell U., 1972; JD, NYU, 1975. Bar: N.Y., U.S. Dist Ct. (ea. dist.) N.Y., U.S. Dist. Ct. (so. dist.) N.Y., U.S. Ct. Appeals (2d cir.), U.S. Supreme Ct. Asst. U.S. atty. U.S. Dist. Ct. (ea. dist.) N.Y., 1975-80; mem. Patterson, Belknap, Webb & Tyler, 1980-81; exec. asst. dist. atty. King County Dist. Atty's. Office, Bklyn., 1982-87; exec. asst. to dep. chief adminstrv. judge N.Y. City Cts., 1987; judge criminal ct. City of N.Y., 1987-91; U.S. magistrate judge E.D.N.Y., 1991-93; U.S. atty. ea. dist. N.Y. U.S. Dept. Justice, Bklyn., 1993-99; ptnr. Dorsey & Whitney, N.Y.C., 1999—. Mem. N.Y. Bar Assn. (mem. exec. com. criminal law sect.), Assn. Bar of the City of N.Y. (mem. com. to encourage judicial svc.). Office: Dorsey & Whitney LLP 250 Park Ave New York NY 10177*

**CARTER-WHITE, KATHY JEAN,** lawyer; b. Tahlequah, Okla., Feb. 14, 1957; d. Eugene Clenten and Bertie Jean (Kirk) Carter; m. Daniel E. White, June 21, 1974 (div. 1976); 1 child, Justin Eugene; m. David Winbray, Dec. 31, 1982 (div. 19186); 1 child, Katy Simone; m. Ronald Dean Thompson, May 22, 1990; children: Sommer Rose, Ry Lee. BA, U. Okla., 1980; JD, Tulsa U., 1983. Assoc. Strout Law Office, Tahlequah, Okla., 1983-85; ptnr. Barksdale Carter-White, Tahlequah, Okla., 1985-86, Carter-White Law Office, Tahlequah, Okla., 1986—; atty. ecoLaw Inst., Inc., Tahlequah, Okla., 1990—. Author children's book: Gentle Folks' Book, 1987, A Family History, 1995; editor anthology Crystal Sundial, 1977. Bd. dirs., co-founder reCycle, Inc., Tahlequah, 1988—; bd. dirs. Save the Ill. River, Inc., Tahlequah, 1989—; bd. dirs. CMH Montessori Sch., 1990—; spl. master Cherokee Tribal Ct. Recipient Paddle award, Save the Ill. River, 1990; AAUW scholar, 1992. Mem. AAUW (bd. dirs. 1985—, bioregional coord. environ. network 1991—), Sierra Club (congl. dist. coord. 1989—). Democrat. Avocation: permaculture. Environmental, Natural resources, Native American. Office: ecoLaw Inst Inc PO Box 36 Welling OK 74471-0036

**CARTISANO, LINDA ANN,** lawyer; b. Phila., Dec. 11, 1953; d. S. James and Anna M. (Morley) C. BA cum laude, Widener U., 1974; JD, Temple U., 1978. Bar: Pa. 1978, U.S. Dist. Ct. (ea. dist.) Pa. 1979. Pvt. practice law Chester, Pa., 1978—; asst. city solicitor City of Chester, 1982—; solicitor Chester Devel. Office, 1985-90, Darby Creek Joint Authority, Springfield, Pa., 1987—, Borough Of Upland, Upland, Pa., 1988—; counsel Chester Redevel. Authority, Chester, 1986-92; acting exec. dir. Chester Redevel. Authority, 1989; custody conciliator Del. County Ct. Common Pleas, Media, Pa., 1996—; solicitor City of Chester, Pa., 1996—. Mem. Widener-PMC Alumni Assn., Chester, 1978, v.p. 1996—; mem. Chester City Health Assn., 1981-91, Chester-Widener Community Commn. Mem. Pa. Bar Assn., Delaware County Bar Assn., Chester Coun. Republican Women. Roman Catholic. Municipal (including bonds). Office: 513 Welsh St Chester PA 19013-4520

**CARTMELL, THOMAS PHILIP,** lawyer; b. Kansas City, Mo., July 8, 1968; s. Philip Martin and Eugenia (Francis) C.;m. Shelley Elizabeth Atkinson, June 4, 1994; 1 child, Philip Trent. BBA, U. Kans., 1991, JD, 1994. Bar: Mo. 1994, Kans. 1995, U.S. Dist. Ct. Mo. Assoc. Blackwell Sanders, Kansas City, Mo., 1994-97; ptnr. Wagstaff & Cartmell, Kansas City, 1997—. Note and comment editor Kans. Law Rev., 1993. Coach, Gt. Am. Basketball League, Kansas City, 1995—. Mem. ABA, Kans. Bar Assn., Johnson County Bar Assn., Mo. Bar Assn., Mercury Club. Presbyterian. Avocations: family activities, sports, travel, reading. General civil litigation, Personal injury, Product liability. Office: Wagstaff & Cartmell 4520 Main St Ste 124C Kansas City MO 64111-1816

**CARTO, DAVID DRAFFAN,** lawyer; b. St. Paul, Jan. 10, 1956; s. David Lawrence and Frances Eleanor (Draffan) C.; m. Carolyn Elizabeth Malkis, Sept. 6, 1981; children; David Willis, Anne Donnelly. BA, Ohio Wesleyan U., 1978; JD, Case Western Res. U., 1981. Bar: Ohio 1981, U.S. Dist. Ct. (no. dist.) Ohio 1981. Assoc. Weldon, Huston & Keyser, Mansfield, Ohio, 1981-86, ptnr., 1986—. Bd. govs. Discovery Sch., 1987-97; bd. dirs. Richland County Heart Assn., Mansfield, 1983-84, Mansfield Art Ctr., 1986-96, Kingwood Ctr., 1997—. Mem. ABA, Ohio Bar Assn., Richland County Bar Assn. Republican. Congregationalist. Clubs: University, Our (Mansfield). Lodge: Kiwanis (bd. dirs. Mansfield club, 1983-87, v.p. 1988-89, pres., 1989-90). Avocations: skiing, tennis, hunting, golf. State civil litigation, Personal injury, Criminal. Office: Weldon Huston & Keyser 28 Park Ave W Mansfield OH 44902-1648

**CARTY, PAUL VERNON,** lawyer; b. Uchitomari, Okinawa, Aug. 2, 1954; s. Leo Sylvester and Dolores Iola (Inniss) C.; m. Kimberly Ann Fickett, Jan. 23, 1982; children: Rachel Lee, Paul Jr., Trevor Dudley. BA, Wesleyan U., Middletown, Conn., 1977; JD, U. Conn., 1985. Bar: Conn. 1985, U.S. Dist. Ct. (Conn.) 1992, Mashantucket Pequot Tribal Ct. 1995. Claims adjustor Liberty Mut. Ins. Co., Bklyn., 1977-80; sr. claims rep. Cigna Corp., Farmington, Conn., 1980-85; assoc. Farren & King, New Haven, 1985-97; solo practitioner New Haven, 1997—. Chmn. West Haven (Conn.) Bd. Ethics, 1987-90. Mem. ABA, Conn. Bar Assn., Conn. Trial Lawyers Assn., Conn. Criminal Def. Lawyers Assn., New Haven County Bar Assn., West Haven Bar Assn., George Crawford Law Assn. Episcopalian. Avocations: karate, photography. General civil litigation, Criminal, Personal injury. Home: 20 Swampscott St West Haven CT 06516-1424 Office: 506 Whalley Ave PO Box 3192 New Haven CT 06515-0292

**CARUSO, MARK JOHN,** lawyer; b. L.A., Apr. 27, 1957; s. John Mondella and Joyce Dorothy C.; m. Judy F. Velarde, Aug. 15, 1987. BS cum laude, Pepperdine U., 1979, JD, 1982. Bar: Calif. 1982, N.Mex. 1987, U.S. Dist. Ct. (ctrl. dist.) Calif. 1982, U.S. Dist. Ct. N.Mex. 1987, U.S. Dist. Ct. (no. and so. dists.) Calif. 1995, U.S. Ct. Appeals (9th cir.) 1983, U.S. Ct. Appeals (10th cir.) 1987. Pvt. practice, Burbank, Calif., 1982—, Albuquerque, 1987—; mem. House labor com., House consumer and pub. affairs com., House workers compensation oversight interim com., House ct. correction and justice interim com.; mem. N.Mex. Ho. of Reps., 1990-94, mem. jud. com., labor com., workers compensation oversight com., 1990-94; lobbyist Nat. Right to Work Com., 1984-86. Col., aide de camp to gov. State of N. Mex., 1987; chmn. N. Mex. Mcpl. Boundary Commn., 1988—; del. Rep. Nat. Conv., 1988, 92; lectr. breast implant litigation, Fen Phen diet drug litigation; Sandoval county chmn. George Bush for Pres., 1988. Recipient platinum award N.Mex. Free Enterprise Adv., 1986. Mem. ATLA, Breast Implant Litigation Group, Consumer Attys. of Calif., Albuquerque Hispano C. of C., Greater Albuquerque C. of C. Fax: 505-883-5012. Personal injury, Product liability, General civil litigation. Office: 4302 Carlisle Blvd NE Albuquerque NM 87107-4811

**CARUTHERS, DENNIS MICHAEL,** lawyer; b. Tacoma, June 3, 1945; s. Clyde Dean and Millicent Florence Caruthers; m. Katherine Mendenhall, Feb. 10, 1981 (div. June 1991); m. Sharon Marie Moore, Dec. 25, 1995; children: Anthony, Todd, Brian, Matthew, Adam. BS in Bus. and Polit. Sci., Portland State U., 1966; JD, Lincoln U., 1977. Atty. Boccardo, Loll, Nidand & Bell, San Francisco, 1977-79, Kinkle, Rodger & Griggs, Riverside, Calif., 1979-81, McLaughlin, Burford & Arias, San Bernardino, Calif., 1981-85, Law Offices Barry Regar, Palm Springs, Calif., 1985-88; sole practice Law Offices D. Michael Caruthers, Palm Springs, Calif., 1988—. Mem. ATLA, Calif. Trial Lawyers Assn., Calif. Consumer Attys., Riverside County Bar Assn., Calif. Applicant Atty. Assn. Democrat. Baptist. Avocations: tennis, hiking, gardening. State civil litigation, Personal injury, Workers' compensation. Office: 500 S Palm Canyon Dr Ste 215 Palm Springs CA 92264-7454

**CARVAJAL, ARTHUR GONZALEZ,** editor, lawyer; b. San Antonio, Dec. 14, 1962; s. Arthur Carrillo Carvajal and Maria Antonia Gonzalez Berumen. BA, St. Mary's U., San Antonio, 1985; JD, U. Notre Dame, 1988. Bar: Ill. 1989, Tex. 1998. Assoc. Kralovec, Marquard, Doyle & Gibbons, Chartered, Chgo., 1989-93, Robert S. Fritzshall & Assocs., Chgo., 1995-96; legal editor Dearborn Fin. Pub., Inc., Chgo., 1997—. Pro bono counsel Chgo. Vol. Legal Svcs., 1990. Mem. Tex. Bar Assn., Chgo. Bar Assn., Lambda Chi Alpha. Roman Catholic. Fax: 312-836-1201. E-mail: carvajal@dearborn.com. Office: Dearborn Fin Pub Inc 155 N Wacker Dr 9th Fl Chicago IL 60606-1719

**CARVER, GEORGE ALLEN, JR.,** lawyer; b. Washington, Nov. 8, 1940; s. George Allen and Barbara Ellen (Bristol) C.; m. Joan Page, Dec. 13, 1964; children: George Allen III, Robert William. BS, U.S. Mil. Acad., 1964; JD, U. Va., 1972. Bar: Va. 1972, D.C. 1978, U.S. Dist. Ct. (D.C. cir.) 1979, U.S. Ct. Appeals (9th cir.) 1986, U.S. Ct. Appeals (4th cir.) 1988. Trial atty. gen. crimes sect. Criminal divsn. U.S. Dept. Justice, Washington, 1972-76, trial atty. pub. integrity sect., 1976-81, dir. conflicts of interest crimes br., pub. integrity sect., 1981-88, dep. chief fraud sect., 1988-92, prin. dep. chief fraud sect., 1992-95, sr. counsel to chief asset forfeiture/money laundering sect., 1995-96, dep. chief, sr. counsel to the chief, 1996—. Capt. inf. U.S. Army, 1964-69. Decorated Silver Star, Bronze Star, Purple Heart. Avocations: photography, fishing, boating, walking, reading. Home: 6049 Makely Dr Fairfax Station VA 22039-1324 Office: US Dept Justice Criminal Div/Asset Forfeit/Money Launder 1400 New York Ave NE Washington DC 20002-1722

**CARVER, TERESA ANN,** lawyer; b. La Grange, Tex., Oct. 21, 1966; d. Clarence G. and Dorris V. Chovanec; m. William Matthew Carver, Mar. 6, 1993; 1 child, Keleigh Ann. BBA, S.W. Tex. State U., 1988; JD, South Tex. Coll. Law, 1992. Bar: Tex. 1992, U.S. Dist. Ct. (so. and ea. dists.) Tex. 1995. Sr. assoc. Lorance & Thompson, P.C., Houston, 1992—. Mem. Am. Law Firm Assn. (retail practice group), Def. Rsch. Inst., Tex. Assn. Def. Counsel, Houston Bar Assn. Avocations: hunting, fishing, travel, family activities. Insurance, Personal injury, Appellate. Office: Lorance & Thompson PC 2900 North Loop W Ste 500 Houston TX 77092-8826

**CARVER, TODD B.,** corporate lawyer, law professor; b. Dayton, Ohio, Oct. 25, 1958; s. Ellis B. and Patricia L. (Boggs) C.; m. Deborah K. Tucker, June 21, 1980; children: Edwin, Brittany. BA in Polit. Sci. cum laude, Wright State U., 1987; JD magna cum laude, U. Dayton Sch. Law, 1991. Investigator Smith & Schnacke Attys., Dayton, 1978-81, paralegal, 1981-84; litigation paralegal NCR Corp., Dayton, 1984-91, atty., 1991-92; sr. atty. NCR Corp. (AT&T-GIS), Dayton, 1992-98; prof. law U. Dayton Sch. Law, 1996-98; sr. atty. U.S. West, Inc., Denver, 1998—; legal, civic lectr., hist. researcher. Editor U. Dayton Law Rev., 1990-91; contbr. articles to profl. jours. including Harvard Bus. Rev. Mem. Community Adv. Coun., Bank One of Dayton, 1986-92; various positions Boy Scouts Am., Dayton, 1970—; chmn. local bd. Selective Svc. Commn., Dayton, 1982—; pres. St. Anne's Hill Hist. Soc., Dayton, 1983-84, Dayton Area Coun. Hist. Neighborhoods, 1985-87; pres. Preservation Dayton, Inc., 1987-89, trustee, 1991-98; mem. exec. com. Dayton Neighborhood Leadership Inst., 1991-98, preservation com. Montgomery County Hist. Soc., 1990-98, U. Dayton Sch. Law (bd. mem. 1994—). Named one of Outstanding Young Men Am., U.S. Jaycees, 1982, Moot Ct. Top Oralist, Law Rev., 1989-90; recipient Vigil honor Order of the Arrow, Boy Scouts Am., 1977, Founder's awrd, 1984, Community Svc. award City of Dayton, 1987, Community Preservation award, 1985, 5 awards Am. Jurisprudence Soc., 1989-91, 2 awards of excellecne Judge Walter Rice Moot Ct. Competition, Lawyers' Lawyer award U. Dayton Sch. Law, 1991. Mem. Optimists (bd. dirs. 1984-86). Republican. Methodist. Avocations: historic architecture preservation, civic activities, outdoorsmanship, golf. Home: 5851 Northwood Dr Evergreen CO 80439-5519 Office: US West Inc Dept Law 1801 California St Ste 5100 Denver CO 80202-2610

**CARWIE, ANNETTE MCDERMOTT,** lawyer; b. Mobile, Ala., Oct. 5, 1963; d. William Henry and Catherine (O'Brien) McD.; m. John Gregory Carwie, Aug. 19, 1989; children: Catherine Amelia, Anna Elizabeth, John Gregory Jr. JD, U. Ala., Tuscaloosa, 1989, BS, 1986. Bar: Ala. 1989, U.S. Dist. Ct. (so. dist.) Ala. 1997. Atty. Sirote & Permutt P.C., Mobile, 1989-93, Pierce Carr Alford, Mobile, 1995-96, Carr Alford Clausen & McDonald, Mobile, 1996—. Mem. Woman Lawyers Assn. (v.p. Mobile chpt. 1998), Mobile Bar Assn. (treas. 1993). Product liability. Home: 312 Ridgelawn Dr W Mobile AL 36608-2422 Office: Carr Alford Clausen & McDonald LLC PO Box C Ste 5000 Mobile AL 36601-0020

**CARY, FREDERICK ALBERT,** lawyer; b. Trieste, Italy, Apr. 6, 1950; came to U.S., 1966; s. Frederick W. and Lydia (Tozzini) C.; 1 child, Amelia Rose. JD, Thomas Jefferson U., 1984. Bar: Calif., D.C., U.S. Ct. Appeals (2nd, 4th, 6th, 9th, and 11th). Pvt. practice Ft. Lauderdale, San Diego. Antitrust, Federal civil litigation, Civil rights. Office: The Cary Law Firm PO Box 273 Rancho Santa Fe CA 92067-0273

**CARYL, MICHAEL R.,** lawyer; b. Syracuse, N.Y., Apr. 20, 1947; s. Robert S. and Elizabeth J. (Kirby) C.; m. Claire Cordon, Oct. 25, 1983; children: Courtney, Hillary, Galen. AB, St. Lawrence U., Canton, N.Y., 1969; JD, Georgetown U., 1972; LLM, George Washington U., 1977. Staff atty. U.S. Army JAG Corps, 1972-76; contract lawyer McDonald Hoague Bayless, Seattle, 1977-78; assoc. Edwards, Weatherall & Barbieri, Seattle, 1978; pvt. practice Seattle, 1978-80, 84-90, 1993-94; ptnr. Duvall & Caryl, Seattle, 1980-84; of counsel Mikkelborg Broz Wells & Fryer, Seattle, 1990-93; pvt. practice Michael R. Caryl, P.S., Seattle, 1993—. Dist. conv. del. presdl. primary Wash. State Dem. Party, Seattle, 1984. Capt. U.S. Army, 1969-76. Named Toastmaster of Yr., Seattle Profl. Toastmasters, 1984. Mem. Wash. State Bar Assn., Wash. State Trial Lawyers Assn. (Eagle mem.). Avocations: mountaineering, golf, coaching soccer. Personal injury, Federal civil litigation, State civil litigation. Office: 720 Olive Way Ste 1300 Seattle WA 98101-1855

**CASANOVA, LORENZO,** lawyer; b. Manati, P.R., Sept. 5, 1933; s. Rafael Casanova and Altagracia Peraza; m. Ana R. Casanova, Feb. 7, 1957; children: Dianna, Marc Antonio. BA in Edn., U. P.R., Rio Piedras, 1962; JD, NYU, 1968. Bar: U.S. Dist. Ct. (so. and ea. dists.) 1970, U.S. Ct. Appeals (2nd cir.) 1970. Chief counsel Bronx Legal Svcs., N.Y.C., 1970-73; asst. to the mayor City of N.Y., 1973-75; dep. police commr. N.Y.C. Police Dept., 1975-77; gen. counsel U.S. Dept. Hwys., Washington, 1977-80, assoc. adminstr. for hwy. safety and motor carriers, 1982-85; pvt. practice law N.Y.C., 1985—. Trustee Yonkers (N.Y.) Bd. Edn., 1991-96. Cpl. USMC, 1952-56, ETO. Mem. P.R. Bar Assn., Queens Bar Assn. Contracts commercial, Family and matrimonial, State civil litigation. Office: 78-27 37th Ave Jackson Heights NY 11372

**CASARONA, ROBERT B.,** lawyer; b. Ohio, Nov. 13, 1960; s. Frank Joseph and Shirley May Casarona; m. Melanie Marie Mason, Oct. 6, 1990; children: Robert B., Lauren, Joseph. BS in Econs., Ariz. State U., 1983; JD, U. Cin., 1986. Prin. Climaco, Lefkowitz & Garofoli Co., LPA, Cleve., 1986—. Contbr. chpt. to book. Chmn. charity golf tourney Ronald McDonald House, Cleve., 1996; mem. children's Oncology Svcs. of Ohio, Cleve.; mem. Dads' Club, Chagrin Falls (Ohio) Schs., 1997—. Mem. ABA, Ohio State Bar Assn., Cuyahoga County Bar Assn. (chmn. environ. law com. 1990-92), Cleve. Bar Assn. (sect. on natural resources, energy, environ. law 1989—). Environmental, General civil litigation, Criminal. Home: 314 Whitetail Dr Chagrin Falls OH 44022-4133 Office: Climako Lefkowit et al 1228 Euclid Ave Ste 900 Cleveland OH 44115-1845

**CASBY, ROBERT WILLIAM,** lawyer; b. Norwood, Mass., Aug. 18, 1951; s. William M. Casby and Charlotte Rita (Rice) Warnock; m. Patricia Alice Myers, Jan. 6, 1979; children: James Myers, Michael Robert. BA magna cum laude, Boston Coll., 1975; JD, Suffolk U., 1982. Bar: Mass. 1982, U.S. Dist. Ct. Mass. 1983, U.S. Ct. Appeals (1st cir.) 1993, U.S. Supreme Ct. 1993. Assoc. Sugarman & Sugarman, P.C., Boston, 1982-87, ptnr., 1987—; lectr. in field. Editor, bd. dirs. Suffolk Law Rev., 1981-82. With USMC, 1969-71. Fellow Mass. Bar Found.; mem. Mass. Bar Assn. (lectr. 1987—), Mass. Acad. Trial Attys. (lectr. 1987—), Am. Bd. Trial Advocates, Suffolk Law Alumni Assn. (bd. dirs. 1992—). General civil litigation, Personal injury, Product liability. Office: Sugarman & Sugarman PC One Beacon St Boston MA 02108

**CASCINO, ANTHONY ELMO, JR.,** lawyer, insurance executive; b. South Bend, Ind., Aug. 21, 1948; s. Anthony E. and Lorayne (Allegretti) C.; m. Mary Anne Dory, July 28, 1973; children: Anthony Elmo, III, Christine Anne, Caroline Stephanie. B.A., Loyola U., Chgo., 1970; J.D., Ill. Inst. Tech., 1974; MMgt. Northwestern U., 1987. Bar: Ill. 1974, U.S. Dist. Ct. (no. dist.) Ill. 1974, U.S. Supreme Ct. 1986. Div. counsel CF Industries Inc., Long Grove, Ill., 1974-79; sec., gen. counsel Energy Coop., Inc., Rosemont, Ill., 1979-83; v.p., gen. counsel GHR Energy Corp., Good Hope, La., 1983; dep. gen. counsel AM Internat., Inc., Chgo., 1983-86; v.p. bus. devel. Multigraphics div. AM Internat., Mt. Prospect, Ill., 1986-88; exec. v.p., sec., gen. counsel, bd. dirs. United Fin. Group Inc. of Ill., Oak Brook, 1988-96; bd. dirs. Oak Brook Property and Casualty Ins. Co., First Oak Brook Corp. Syndicate, United Comml. Affiliated, Inc., Combined Adjustment Co., Inc., Central States Ins. Cons., Inc.; ptnr., exec. v.p. Tait Adv. Svcs., 1997; mem. inquiry bd. Atty. Registration and Disciplinary Commn., 1992-96; alt. trustee Ill. Ins. Exchange, 1988-97; arbitrator Cook County Mandatory Arbitration Program; lectr. Ill. Inst. Continuing Edn., 1986; mem. adv. com. on postgrad. programs, Ill. Inst. Tech., 1987-88. Hon. chmn. Tony C. and Carole Segal Patient Assistance Fund. Contbg. author: Commercial Damage, 1984. Mem. ABA, Fed. Energy Bar Assn., Ill. State Bar Assn., Chgo. Bar Assn., DuPage County Bar Assn., Art Inst. Chgo., Lyric Opera of Chgo. (Glencoe chpt.), Bar and Gavel Soc., DuPage Club, Union League Club (Chgo.), Club Internat. (Chgo.), Bob O' Link Golf Club. Democrat. Roman Catholic. General corporate, Bankruptcy, Insurance. Home: 385 Lincoln Ave Glencoe IL 60022-1521 Office: Tait Adv Svcs LLC 1 S Wacker Dr Ste 2700 Chicago IL 60606-4698

**CASE, BASIL TIMOTHY,** lawyer; b. Florence, Ala., May 26, 1966; s. Basil Harvey and Virginia Nell Case. BA, U. No. Ala., 1987; JD, Samford U., 1992. Bar: U.S. Dist. Ct. (no. dist.) Ala. 1993. General civil litigation, Criminal. Office: 412 S Court St Ste 303 Florence AL 35630-5648

**CASE, DAVID LEON,** lawyer; b. Lansing, Mich., Sept. 22, 1948; s. Harlow Hoyt and Barbara Jean (Denman) C.; m. Cynthia Lou Rhinehart, Jan. 28, 1968; children: Beau, Ryan, Kimberly, Darren, Stephanie. BS with distinction, Ariz. State U., 1970, JD cum laude, 1973. Bar: Calif. 1973, U.S. Dist. Ct. (cen. dist.) Calif. 1973, U.S. Tax Ct. 1974, Ariz. 1976, U.S. Supreme Ct. 1997. Assoc. Willis, Butler & Scheifly, Los Angeles, 1973-75; from assoc. to mem. Ryley, Carlock & Applewhite, Phoenix, 1975—. Fellow Ariz. Bar Found.; mem. ABA (tax sect., corp. sect., probate and trust sect.), Ariz. Bar Assn., Ctrl. Ariz. Estate Planning Coun. (bd. dirs., pres. 1988-89), Beta Gamma Sigma. Republican. Presbyterian. Avocations: running, guitar, sports. Taxation, general, Estate planning, General corporate. Office: Ryley Carlock & Applewhite PO Box 634 Phoenix AZ 85001-0634

**CASE, DOUGLAS MANNING,** lawyer; b. Cleve., Jan. 3, 1947; s. Manning Eugene and Ernestine (Bryan) C.; m. Marilyn Cooper, Aug. 23, 1969. BA, U. Pa., 1969; JD, MBA, Columbia U., 1973. Bar: N.Y. 1974, N.J. 1975, Calif. 1980, Ohio 1991. Assoc. Brown & Wood, N.Y.C., 1973-77; corp. counsel PepsiCo Inc., Purchase, N.Y. and Irvine, Calif., 1977-83, Nabisco Brands Inc., N.Y.C., East Hanover, N.J. and London, 1983-89; asst. gen. counsel Chiquita Brands Internat., Inc., Cin., 1989-92; prin. Douglas M. Case Law Offices Inc., Cin., 1993—; lectr. numerous seminars. Contbr. articles to profl. jours. Chmn. Olde Colonial Dist.; active Morris-Susssex Area Coun. Boy Scouts Am., 1986-88; sec., trustee Marble Scholarship Com., N.Y.C., 1983-88; bd. dirs. Cin. Opera Guild, 1994—, pres. 1997-98, chmn., 1998—. Mem. ABA, Internat. Bar Assn., Ohio State Bar Assn. (mem. internat. com. 1993—), Cin. Bar Assn. (chair solo and small firm practitioners com. 1995-97, continuing legal edn. chair internat. law com. 1994-96, sec. 1996-97, vice chair 1997-98, chair 1998—), Quality in Law (chmn. 1996-98), Munich Sister City Assn. of Greater Cin. (chmn. econ. devel. com. 1995-96), Greater Cin. Venture Assn., The Lawyers Club of Cin. (exec. com. 1995—, treas. 1996, sec. 1997, 2d v.p. 1998, 1st v.p. 1999), Morris County Golf Club, Columbia Bus. Sch. Club (N.Y.C., pres., bd. dirs. 1974-79), Kenwood Country Club, Cin. Opera Assn. (bd. dirs., exec. com. 1997-98). Avocation: golf. Private international, Contracts commercial, General corporate. Office: 8700 Old Indian Hill Rd Cincinnati OH 45243-3724

**CASE, FORREST N., JR.,** lawyer; b. Albany, N.Y., July 14, 1932; s. Forrest N. and Helen (Reed) C.; m. Frances Watkins, June 4, 1988; children: Marjorie, Joanne, Kenneth. AB, Union Coll., 1954; LLB, Albany Law Sch., 1957. Bar: N.Y. 1957, U.S. Dist. Ct. (no. dist.) N.Y. 1957. Ptnr. Carter, Conboy & Case, Albany, 1961—; treas. Northeastern N.Y. Def. Rsch. Inst., Albany, 1972-74. Fellow Am. Coll. Trial Lawyers; mem. ABA, N.Y. State Bar Assn., Albany County Bar Assn., Am. Bd. Trial Advocates (adv.), N.Y. State Trial Lawyers Assn., Def. Rsch. Inst. General civil litigation, Personal injury, Product liability. Office: Carter Conboy & Case 20 Corporate Woods Dr Albany NY 12211-2500

**CASE, KAREN ANN,** lawyer; b. Milw., Apr. 7, 1944; d. Alfred F. and Hilda M. (Tomich) Case. BS, Marquette U., 1963, JD 1966; LLM, NYU, 1973. Bar: Wis. 1966, U.S. Ct. Claims, 1973, U.S. Tax Ct. 1973. Ptnr. Meldman, Case & Weine, Milw., 1973-85, Meldman, Case & Weine div. Mulcahy & Wherry, S.C., 1985-87; Sec. of Revenue State of Wis., 1987-88; ptnr. Case & Drinka, S.C., Milw., 1989-91, Case, Drinka & Diel, S.C., Milw., 1991-97, CoVac, 1997—; lectr. U. Wis., Milw., 1974-78; guest lectr. Marquette U. Law Sch., 1975-78; dir. WBBC, 1998—. Mem. gov.'s Commn. on Taliesin, 1988, gov.'s Econ. Adv. Commn., 1989-91, pres.'s coun. Alverno Coll., 1988-94, nat. coun., 1998—; bd. dirs. WBCC, 1998—. Fellow Wis. Bar Found. (dir. 1977-90, treas. 1980-90); mem. ABA, Milw. Assn. Women Lawyers (founding mem., bd. dirs. 1975-78, 81-82), Milw. Bar Assn. (bd. dirs. 1985-87, law office mgmt. chair 1992-93), State Bar Wis. (bd. govs. 1981-85, 87-90, dir. taxation sect. 1981-87, vice chmn. 1986-87, 90-91, chmn. 1991-92), Am. Acad. Matrimonial Lawyers (bd. dirs. 1988-90), Nat. Assn. Women Lawyers (Wis. del. 1982-83), Milw. Rose Soc. (pres. 1981, dir. 1981-83), Friends of Boerner Bot. Gardens (founding mem., pres. 1984-90), Profl. Dimensions Club (dir. 1985-87), Tempo Club (sec. 1984-85). Contbr. articles to legal jours. Corporate taxation, Personal income taxation, Probate. Home: 2212 Harbour Ct Longboat Key FL 34228-4174 Office: CoVac 9803 W Meadow Park Dr Hales Corners WI 53130-2261 *Delegate tasks for responsibility and accountability, then spend the resulting freed time nourishing your soul. Resign yourself to the fact that the tasks will not be completed as you would have, but they will be done, sometimes with more creativity. Give credit and praise away.*

**CASE, ROSEMARY PODREBARAC,** lawyer; b. Kansas City, Mo., Sept. 15, 1961; d. Eugene George and Mary Josephine (Musick) Podrebarac; m. Kevin Dudley Case, Apr. 30, 1994. BA in Math. and French, U. Kans., 1983; JD, Washington U., St. Louis, 1986. Bar: Kans. 1986, U.S. Dist. Ct. Kans. 1986, Mo. 1987, U.S. Dist. Ct. (we. dist.) Mo. 1987. Assoc. McAnany, Van Cleave & Phillips, P.A., Kansas City, Kans., 1986-90, shareholder, 1991—. Contbr. chpts. to legal handbooks. Bd. dirs. Caritas Clinics, Inc., Kansas City, 1995—. Mem. Mo. Bar, Kans. Bar Assn., Wyandotte County Bar Assn. (treas. 1990-92), Wyandotte County Bar Found. (bd. dirs., treas. 1993—). Non-profit and tax-exempt organizations, Real property, Probate. Office: McAnany Van Cleave & Phillips PA 707 Minnesota Ave 4th Fl PO Box 171300 Kansas City KS 66117-0300

**CASE, THOMAS LOUIS,** lawyer; b. Dallas, June 14, 1947; s. Donald L. and Ellen (Hanson) C.; m. Bonnie Nally, July 8, 1972. BA, Vanderbilt U., 1969, JD, 1972; cert. civil trial law, Tex. Bd. Legal Specialization. Bar: Tex. 1972, U.S. Dist. Ct. (no. dist.) Tex. 1973, U.S. Dist. Ct. (we. and ea. dists.) Tex. 1978, U.S. Dist. Ct. (so. dist.) Tex. 1979, U.S. Dist. Ct. (ea. dist.) Ark. 1981, U.S. Ct. Appeals (5th cir.) 1977, U.S. Supreme Ct. 1978, U.S. Ct. Appeals (8th cir.) 1984, U.S. Ct. Appeals (11th cir.) 1981. Assoc. Johnson, Bromberg, Leeds & Riggs, Dallas, 1972-77; ptnr. Bickel & Case, Dallas, 1977-84, St. Claire & Case, Dallas, 1984-93, Thomas L. Case & Assocs., P.C., Dallas, 1993—. Mem. ABA, Tex. Bar Assn., Tex. Assn. Def. Coun., Dallas Assn. of Def. Counsel, Dallas Bar Assn. Federal civil litigation, General civil litigation, Labor. Office: Thomas L Case & Assocs PC 5910 N Central Expy Ste 1450 Dallas TX 75206-5146

**CASELLA, PETER F(IORE),** patent and licensing executive; b. June 5, 1922; s. Fiore Peter and Lucy (Grimaldi) C.; m. Marjorie Eloise Enos, March 9, 1946 (dec. Aug. 1989); children: William Peter, Susan Elaine, Richard Mark. BChE, Poly. Inst., Bklyn., 1943; student in chemistry, St. John's U., N.Y.C., 1940. Registered to practice by the U.S. Patent and Trademark Office, Can. Patent and Trademark Offices. Head patent sect. Hooker Electrochem. Co., Niagara Falls, N.Y., 1943-54; mgr. patent dept. Occidental Chem. Corp. (formerly Hooker Chem. Corp.), Niagara Falls, N.Y., 1954-64, dir. patents and licensing, 1964-81, asst. sec., 1966-81, ret., 1981; pres. TFA Products, Inc., Houston, Intra Gene Internat., Inc., Lewiston, N.Y., 1981-92; chmn. bd. In Vitro Internat., Inc., Linthicum, Md., 1983-86; cons. patents and licensing, Lewiston, N.Y., 1981—; Dept. Commerce del. on patents and licensing exchange, USSR, 1973, 90, Poland and German Dem. Rep., 1976. Editor: Drafting the Patent Application, 1957. Mem. Lewiston Bd. Edn., 1968-70. With AUS, 1944-46. Recipient Centennial citation Poly. Inst. Bklyn., 1955, Golden Jubilee Soc., 1993. Mem. ACS, AIChE, Assn. Corp. Patent Counsel (emeritus, exec. com. 1974-77, charter mem.), N.Y. Intellectual Property Law Assn. (Niagara Frontier chpt. pres. 1973-74, founder award 1974), Licensing Execs. Soc. (v.p. 1976-77, Trustees award 1977), Chartered Inst. Patent Agts. Gt. Britain (emeritus), Patent and Trademark Inst. Can., Internat. Patent and Trademark Assn. (emeritus), U.S. Trademark Assn., Nat. Assn. Mfrs. (patent com.), Mfg. Chemists Assn., Pacific Indsl. Property Assn., U.S. Patent Office Soc. (assoc.), U.S. Trademark Office Soc. (assoc.), Chemists Club (emeritus N.Y.C. chpt.), Niagara Club (Niagara Falls pres. 1973-74).

**CASELLA, RALPH PHILIP,** lawyer; b. N.Y.C., Feb. 11, 1943; s. Ralph E. and Olympia G. Casella; m. Beverly B. Peters, June 18, 1966; children: Ralph P. Jr., Christopher, Traci, Keith. BA in English Lit., Fordham U., 1964; LLB, JD, Bklyn. Law Sch., 1967. Bar: N.Y. 1968, U.S. Dist. Ct. (so. dist.) N.Y. 1978, U.S. Dist. Ct. (ea. dist.) N.Y. 1975, U.S. Dist. Ct. (no. dist.) N.Y. 1993, U.S. Ct. Appeals (2d cir.) 1993, U.S. Supreme Ct. 1980. Mng. atty. Ralph P. Casella & Assocs. PC, S.I., N.Y., 1970—. Avocations: golf, fishing. Labor, Family and matrimonial, General civil litigation. Office: 14 1st St Staten Island NY 10306-2202

**CASELLAS, SALVADOR E.,** judge; b. 1935. BS in Fgn. Svc. cum laude, Georgetown U., 1957; LLB magna cum laude, U. P.R., 1960; LLM, Harvard U., 1961. Ptnr. Fiddler, Gonzalez & Rodriguez, 1962-72, 77-94; judge U.S. Dist. Ct. P.R., San Juan, 1994—; mem. P.R. Acad. Jurisprudence, P.R. Commn. on Bicentennial of U.S. Constn., 1987-89; aide to Sec. of U.S. Army, 1985-89, emeritus, 1990—. Dir. Alliance for Drug Free P.R., 1993-94. 1st lt. U.S. Army, 1961-62, Res., JAGC, 1963-67. Recipient Comdrs. medal Second U.S. Army, 1990, P.R. Nat. Guard medal, 1990. Mem. ABA, Am. Bar Found., P.R. Bar Assn., P.R. Bar Assn. Found., Caparra Country Club, Banker's Club. Office: US Dist Ct PR US Courthouse 150 Ave Carlos Chardon # 111 San Juan PR 00918-1703

**CASEY, BERNARD J.,** lawyer; b. Pawtucket, R.I., June 4, 1942; s. Andrew J. and Theresa (Lennon) C.; m. Kathleen A. Wall; children: Brendan, B. John. A.B., Providence Coll., 1964; J.D., Catholic U., 1967. Bar: R.I. Supreme Ct. 1967, D.C. 1971, U.S. Supreme Ct. 1972, U.S. Cir. Ct. (D.C. cir., 4th cir., 6th cir.). Assoc., Gall, Lane & Powell, Washington, 1971-76, ptnr., 1976; ptnr. Reed Smith Shaw & McClay, Washington, 1976—, mem. exec. com. 1982-87, litigation group chief D.C., 1987-98. Bd. dirs. Cath. Charities, 1994—, chmn., 1997-98. Served to capt. AUS, 1967-71. Decorated Bronze Star medal. Mem. ABA (mem. litigation com.), D.C. Bar Assn., Barristers, Lawyers Club, Univ. Club (bd. govs. 1989-97, pres. 1990-92), Chevy Chase Country Club. Roman Catholic. Labor, Product liability, General civil litigation. Home: 3257 Worthington St NW Washington DC 20015-2354 Office: Reed Smith Shaw & McClay East Tower 1301 K St NW Ste 1100 Washington DC 20005-3317

**CASEY, DAVID ROBERT,** lawyer; b. Wichita Falls, Tex., Dec. 1, 1945; s. Robert Joseph and Betty Lou (Baily) C.; m. Sue C. Hartness; children: Kristen Boenicke, Ryan B. BBA, North Tex. State U., 1968; JD, Tex. Tech., Lubbock, 1971. Bar: Tex. 1971, U.S. Dist. Ct. (no. dist.) Tex. 1972. Assoc. King & Massey, Ft. Worth, 1972-78; ptnr. Naler & Casey, Hurst, Tex., 1978-80; prin. Law Office David R. Casey, Hurst, Tex., 1980—. Mcpl. judge City of North Richland Hills, Tex., 1980-85, judge teen ct., 1992—. Mem. ABA, Tex. Assn. Bank Counsel, Tex. Bar Assn., Tarrant County Bar Assn. Banking, Consumer commercial, State civil litigation. Office: 1840 Norwood Plaza Ct Ste 102 Hurst TX 76054-3749

**CASEY, JOHN FREDERICK,** lawyer; b. Martinsville, Ohio, May 19, 1939; s. Raymond J. and Esther E. (Read) C.; m. Karen S. Bollenbacher, Sept. 2, 1978. BS, Ohio State U., 1961, JD, 1965. Bar: Ohio, 1965, U.S. Dist. Ct. (so. dist.) Ohio 1967, D.C. 1981, U.S. Tax Ct. 1967. Ptnr. Means, Bichimer & Burkholder, Columbus, Ohio, 1965-70, Chamblin, Snyder & Casey, Columbus, 1971-75; pvt. practice Columbus, 1976-83, 91-93; ptnr., shareholder Wiles, Doucher, Van Buren, Boyle & Casey, Columbus, 1984-85; ptnr. Thompson, Hine & Flory, Columbus, 1986-88, Casey & Christensen, Columbus, 1989, Casey, McFadden & Winner, Columbus, 1990, Harris, McClellan, Binau & Cox, Columbus, 1994; prin. John F. Casey, A Legal Profl. Assn., 1994—; adv. coun. mem. U.S. Small Bus. Adminstrn., Columbus, 1985-93. Mem. gov.'s Ohio Farmland Preservation Task Force, 1996-97. Mem. Ohio State Bar Assn. (bd. govs. 1990-99, estate planning, trust, and probate law sect.), Internat. Assn. Fin. Planning, Columbus Bar Found., Ohio State U. Coll. Law (nat. coun.), Greater Columbus C. of C. Avocations: gardening, golf. General practice, General corporate, Estate planning. Home: 207 E Whittier St Columbus OH 43206-2638 Office: Lucas Predergast Albright Gibson & Newman 600 S High St Columbus OH 43215-5622

**CASEY, NAN ELIZABETH,** lawyer; b. Petoskey, Mich., Aug. 16, 1954; d. Glenn H. and Jessie M. C.; m. James F. Dunn, Nov. 24, 1986; children: Jamie, Casey, Danny Patrick, Joseph. BS, Ctrl. Mich. U., Mt. Pleasant, 1976; JD, T.M. Cooley, Lansing, Mich., 1980. Gen. counsel Cata, Lansing, Mich., 1980-82; ptnr. Reid & Reid, Lansing, Mich., 1982-90; counsel Bernick & Omer, E. Lansing, Mich., 1990-92; ptnr. Reynolds, Guyselman & Easex, E. Lansing, Mich., 1992-96, Casey & Boog, E. Lansing, Mich., 1996—; bar bench adv. bd. Ingham County Lawyers, Lansing, Mich., 1994—; spl. asst. atty. gen. State of Mich., Lansing, 1995—; bd. mem. Bar Assn., Lansing, Mich., 1995-97; arbitrator Cath. Diocese, Lansing, Mich., 1998. Contbr. articles tor profl. jours. Bd. mem. Ele's Place, Lansing, Mich., 1996—, Liturgical Commn., Lansing, Mich., 1997—; bd. mem., legal counsel Child Abuse Prevention Svcs., Lansing, Mich., 1993—, Capitol Nat. Bank, 1996—; bd. mem., pres., sec. Cath. Lawyers, 1990-96. Avocations: sports, reading. Family and matrimonial, Transportation, Health. Office: 321 W Lake Lansing Rd East Lansing MI 48823-1437

**CASEY, PATRICK ANTHONY,** lawyer; b. Apr. 20, 1944; s. Ivanhoe and Eutimia (Casados) C.; m. Gail Marie Johns, Aug. 1, 1970; children: Christopher Gaelen, Matthew Colin. BA, N.Mex. State U., 1970; JD, U. Ariz., 1973. Bar: N.Mex. 1973, U.S. Ct. Appeals (10th cir.) 1979, U.S. Supreme Ct. 1980. Assoc. Bachicha & Casey, Santa Fe, 1973-76; pvt. practice Santa Fe, 1976—. Bd. dirs. Santa Fe Sch. Arts and Crafts, 1974, Santa Fe Animal Shelter, 1975-81, Cath. Charities of Santa Fe, 1979-82, Old Santa Fe Assn., 1979-88, Santa Fe Fiesta Coun., 1982—; bd. dirs. United Way, 1986-89, N.Mex. State U. Found., 1985-93. With USN, 1961-67. Mem. ATLA (state del. 1988-89, bd. govs. 1990-91, 93-95), ABA, Western Trial Lawyers Assn. (bd. dirs. 1988-91, parliamentarian 1990-91, gov. 1987-90, treas. 1991-95, sec. 1991-92, pres.-elect 1995-96, pres. 1996-97), N.Mex. Trial Lawyers Assn. (dir. 1977-79, 85—, treas. 1979-83, pres. 1983-84), Bar Assn. 1st Jud. Dist. (pres. 1980), Hispanic Bar Assn., Am. Legion, Vietnam Vets. of Am., VFW, Elks. General civil litigation, Personal injury, Product liability. Office: 1421 Luisa St Ste P Santa Fe NM 87505-4073

**CASEY, PAULA JEAN,** prosecutor; b. Charleston, Ark., Feb. 16, 1951; d. Arthur Clinton and Mildred Aleene (Underwood) C.; m. Gilbert Louis Glover II, Mar. 13, 1981. BA, Ea. Cen. (Okla.) U., 1973; JD, U. Ark., 1977. Staff atty. Ctrl. Ark. Legal Services, Hot Springs, Ark., 1977-79; dep. pub. defender 6th Jud. Dist. Pub. Defender, Little Rock, 1979; clinic supr. U. Ark. at Little Rock Law Sch., 1979-81, asst. prof., 1981-84, assoc. prof., 1984-92, prof., 1992-93, assoc. dean, 1986-90; legis. dir., chief counsel U.S. Senator Dale Bumpers, 1990-92; lobbyist Ark. Bar Assn., 1993; U.S. atty. Ea. Dist. Ark., 1993—; cons. for juvenile affairs 6th Jud. Dist. Judges, Ark., 1987. Author, editor: Poverty Law Practice Manual, 1985. Sec. Pulaski County Dem. Com., Little Rock, 1984-89; mem. Ark. Dem. Com., 1984-89; mem. Juvenile Adv. Group, Little Rock, 1985-89; mem. Gov.'s Task Force on Juvenile Cts., Ark., 1987; chmn. Ark. Dem. Jud. Com., 1987; bd. dirs. Ctrl. Ark. Legal Svcs., Little Rock, 1986-89. Named One of Top 100 Women in Ark., Ark. Bus. Pubs., 1996, 98, 99; recipient Gale Pettus Pontz award U. Ark.-Fayetteville Law Sch. Women Students Assn., 1994, award of merit Organized Crime Drug Enforcement Task Force, 1997. Fellow Ark. Bar Found. (bd. dirs.); mem. Ark. Bar Assn. (del. 1986-90), Am. Inns Ct., Overton Am. Inns of Ct. Democrat. Office: US Attys Office PO Box 1229 # P Little Rock AR 72203-1229

**CASEY, PAULA KIDD,** lawyer; b. Wellington, Kans., Feb. 16, 1953; d. Paul Lee and Patricia (Brown) Packard; m. Roger C. Kidd, May 2, 1981 (div. Oct. 1985); 1 child, Skylar Kidd; m. Michael A. Casey, Aug. 6, 1988; 1 child, Connor Austin Casey. B of Social Welfare, U. Kans., 1975; JD, Washburn U., 1979. Bar: Kans. 1979; U.S. Dist. Ct. (10th dist.) Fed. 1979, U.S. Supreme Ct. 1997. Assoc. Joehem, Sargent & Blaes, Wichita, Kans., 1979-80; bankruptcy analyst U.S. Trustee Office, Wichita, Kans., 1980-81; pvt. practice Wichita, Kans., 1981-86; ptnr. Alexander, Floodman & Casey, Wichita, Kans., 1986—; presenter in field. Presenter in field. Bd. trustees Coll. Hill United Meth. Ch., Wichita, 1992-95; pres. Homeless Task Force, Wichita, 1994-97; traffic com. chair Coll. Hill Neighborhood Assn., Wichita, 1996-97. Mem. Wichita Bar Assn. (Family Law chair 1996—), Kans. Bar Assn. (family law chair 1996-97), Am. Family and Conciliatory Cts. (exec. com. 1996-97). Republican. Family and matrimonial. Office: Alexander Floodman & Casey PO Box 2955 Wichita KS 67201-2955

**CASEY, RICHARD W.,** lawyer; b. Berkeley, Calif., Sept. 3, 1953; s. Edward Francis and Jeanne (Bjork) C.; married; children: Andrew, Alysan Jeanne, Eric Thomas. BA, U. Calif., Davis, 1975; JD, U. Calif., Berkeley, 1978. Bar: Utah 1979, Calif. 1979, Fla. 1980, U.S. t. Appeals (9th, 10th and 11th cirs.) 1980. Ptnr. Giague, Crockett, Bendinger & Peterson, Salt Lake City, 1979—. Bd. dirs. Adoption Exch., Salt Lake City, 1996-98, Salt Lake Acting Co., 1992-95, Big Bros./Big Sisters, Salt Lake City, 1988-89. Mem. Am. Inns of Ct. (master of bench). Avocations: SCUBA diving, skiing. Office: Giague Crockett Bendinger & Peterson 170 S Main St Ste 400 Salt Lake City UT 84101-3636

**CASEY, SUSAN ANNE,** lawyer; b. Passaic, N.J., Jan. 4, 1952; d. John Joseph Bieber and Rose Panico; m. G. Scott Giebink, July 22, 1989. BA, Douglass Coll., 1974; JD, U. Minn., St. Paul, 1994. Bar: Minn. 1994. Dir. comm. N.J. Dental Assn., New Brunswick, 1975-80; dir. pub. affairs Am. Assn. Oral and Maxillofacial Surgeons, Chgo., 1980-84, Am. Acad. Pediatrics, Chgo., 1984-88; dir. mktg. U. Minn., Mpls., 1988-91; asst. atty gen. State of Minn., Office of Atty. Gen., St. Paul, 1994—. Office: State of Minn Office of Atty Gen 525 Park St Ste 500 Saint Paul MN 55103-2122

**CASH, ARTHUR LEE, JR.,** lawyer, editor; b. Winston-Salem, N.C.. AB, Wash. U., 1989, JD, 1994. Bar: Ill. 1994, D.C. 1995. Sr. atty. editor West Group, Deerfield, Ill., 1995—. Mem. ABA, Chgo. Bar Assn. Office: West Group 155 Pfingsten Rd Deerfield IL 60015

**CASH, MICHELLE HOOGENDAM,** lawyer; b. Houston, Apr. 20, 1964; d. Cornelis and Helen Marie (Rigamonti) Hoogendam; m. Warren P. Cash III, Nov. 30, 1991. Student, St. Andrews (Scotland) U., 1984-85; BA in Econs. and Polit. Sci., Tulane U., 1985; JD, U. Tex., 1989. Bar: Tex. 1989, U.S. Dist. Ct. (so. dist.) Tex. 1990, U.S. Dist. Ct. (we. dist.) Tex. 1991, U.S. Ct. Appeals (5th cir.) 1990; cert. labor & employment lawyer. Assoc. Bracewell & Patterson LLP, Houston, 1989—. Mem. editl. bd. Houston Lawyer, 1994-96; contbr. articles to profl. jours. Vol. Soc. for the Prevention of Cruelty to Animals, Houston, 1994-96. Mem. Tex. Bar Assn. (com.), Houston Bar Assn. (com. chair), Tex. Young Lawyers Assn. General civil litigation, Labor.

**CASHMAN, GIDEON,** lawyer; b. N.Y.C., Sept. 10, 1929; s. Abba Morris and Rachel (Cashman) C.; m. Ruth Lucinda Parker, Sept. 8, 1956 (div.); married Kathryn Batchelder, 1985; children—Adam Parker, Lindsey Avril. A.B., NYU, 1951; J.D., Columbia U., 1954. Bar: D.C. 1954, N.Y. 1954. Asst. counsel Waterfront Commn. of N.Y., 1954-55; asst. U.S. atty. criminal div. U.S. Dist. Ct. So. Dist. N.Y., 1958-61, chief criminal apls., 1959-61; assoc. Christy Perkins & Christy, N.Y.C., 1961-63; ptnr. Pryor Cashman Sherman & Flynn, N.Y.C., 1963-82, sr. ptnr., 1973—; lectr. trial tactics Practicing Law Inst. Bd. dirs. Irvington House Inst. for Med. Research, 1982—; trustee Friars Found., Heart Research Found., Eugene O'Neill Theatre Ctr. Mem. ABA, N.Y. State Bar Assn., Assn. Bar City N.Y., N.Y. County Lawyers Assn. Jewish. Club: Friars (N.Y.C.). Federal civil litigation, State civil litigation, General corporate. Home: 812 Park Ave New York NY 10021-2759 Office: 410 Park Ave New York NY 10022-4407

**CASHORE, AMY C.,** lawyer; b. Cin., Sept. 21, 1970; d. William J. and Pauline M. Cashore. BA in Govt., U. Notre Dame, 1992; JD, Boston Coll., 1995. Bar: Mass. 1995, Maine 1998, U.S. Dist. Ct. Mass. 1996, Maine 1998, U.S. Ct. Appeals (1st cir.) 1998, U.S. Dist. Ct. Maine 1999. Assoc. Ardiff & Morse, P.C., Danvers, Mass., 1995-98, Campbell Campbell & Edwards, P.C., Boston, 1998—. Mem. ABA, Mass. Bar Assn., Boston Bar Assn. Avocations: skiing, travel, reading. Product liability, Labor, General civil litigation. Office: Campbell Campbell & Edwards PC One Constitution Plz Boston MA 02129

**CASILLAS, MARK,** lawyer; b. Santa Monica, Calif., July 8, 1953; s. Rudolph and Elvia C.; m. Natalia Settembrini, June 2, 1984. BA in History, Loyola U., L.A., 1976; JD, Harvard U., 1979. Bar: N.Y. 1982, Calif. 1983. Clk. to chief judge U.S. Ct. Appeals (10th cir.), Santa Fe, 1979-80; assoc. Breed, Abbott & Morgan, N.Y.C., 1980-82; counsel Bank of Am. Nat. Trust and Savs. Assn., San Francisco, 1982-84; assoc. Lillick & Charles, San Francisco, 1984-87, ptnr., 1988-95; ptnr. Russin & Vecchi LLP, San Francisco, 1995-96; of counsel LeBoeuf, Lamb, Greene & MacRae, LLP, San Francisco, 1997—; counsel Internat. Bankers Assn. in Calif., L.A., 1984-89, 94-97. Co-author: California Limited Liability Company: Forms and Practice Manual, 1994; mng. editor Harvard Civil Rights-Civil Liberties Law Rev., 1978-79. Mem. ABA (apptd. mem. airfin. subcom. 1991—), N.Y. Bar Assn., Calif. Bar Assn. (vice-chmn. fin. instn. com. 1987-88), Internat. Bar Assn., The Japan Soc., Bankers Club (bd. dirs. 1996—). Avocations: skiing, travel. Banking, Finance, Securities. Office: LeBoeuf Lamb Et Al One Embarcadero Ctr San Francisco CA 94111-2919

**CASPER, DENISE JEFFERSON,** lawyer; b. East Patchogue, N.Y., Jan. 9, 1968; d. Eugene and Marcia Jefferson; m. Marc N. Casper, Aug. 20, 1994. BA, Wesleyan U., 1990; JD, Harvard, 1994. Bar: Mass. 1994, N.Y. 1995; U.S. Dist. Ct. Mass. 1995, U.S. Ct. Appeals (1st. cir.) 1996. Law clk. to Hon. Justice Edith Fine and Hon. Justice J. Harold Flannery Mass. Appeals Ct., Boston, 1994-95; assoc. Bingham Dana L.L.P., Boston, 1995-98; asst. U.S. atty. U.S. Atty's Office, Boston, 1999—; bd. dirs. Vol. Lawyer's Project Boston, 1998—. Chair, bd. dirs. People Making a Difference Through Community Svc. Inc. Boston 1995-99. Mem. Mass. Black Women's Atty's Assn. (exec. bd. mem. 1998—), Delta Sigma Theta. Office: US Atty's Office US Courthouse 1 Courthouse Way Ste 9200 Boston MA 02210-3011

**CASPER, ERIC MICHAEL,** lawyer; b. Long Branch, N.J., Feb. 27, 1959; s. Walter Jr. and Lois Ann (Countryman) C. BS in Polit. Sci. with high honors, U. Iowa, 1980, MBA, JD with high honors, 1984. Bar: Ariz. 1985, U.S. Dist. Ct. Ariz. 1985, U.S. Tax Ct. 1986, U.S. Ct. Appeals (9th cir.) 1997. Assoc. Snell & Wilmer, Phoenix, 1984-91; trial atty. civil tax litigation Dept. Justice, Washington, 1991-95; pvt. practice Phoenix, 1995—; ptnr., mem. mgmt. com. Walker Ryan, PLC, Phoenix. Contbr. articles to profl. publs. Tchr. Jr. Achievement, various Phoenix area jr. high and high schs., 1986-91; tutor Dept. Labor TEAM Project; vol. Phoenix chpt. Am. Cancer Soc., 1987-91. Mem. ABA (former com. on tax-exempt financing, com. ct. practice and procedure), Ariz. Bar Assn., Mensa, Kiwanis (dir. Camelback). Methodist. Avocations: basketball, volleyball, science fiction. Home: 5778 W Corrine Dr Glendale AZ 85304-1890 Office: Walker Ryan PLC 3101 N Central Ave Ste 1500 Phoenix AZ 85012-2644

**CASPER, STEWART MICHAEL,** lawyer; b. Fitchburg, Mass., Jan. 12, 1953; s. Irwin Stanley and Dorothy (Cohen) C.; children: Stacey Lynn, Allison Rose. BA, U. Mass., 1975; JD, Hofstra U., 1978. Bar: Conn. 1978, U.S. Dist. Ct. Conn. 1978, N.Y. 1985, U.S. Dist. Ct. (so. dist.) N.Y. 1987, U.S. Ct. Appeals (2d cir.) 1987, U.S. Supreme Ct. 1987. Assoc. McAnerney & Millar, Darien, Conn., 1978-80, Glazer Seelig & Glazer, Stamford, Conn., 1980-82, Arnold H. Rutkin PC, Westport, Conn., 1982-86; ptnr. Wynn Casper & de Toledo, Stamford, 1986-88, Casper & de Toledo LLC, Stamford, 1988—. Trustee Temple Beth El, Stamford, 1987-92. Mem. ATLA (state del. 1999—), Conn. Trial Lawyers Assn. (bd. govs. 1984-85, 87—, exec. com. 1990—, legis. com. 1990—, parliamentarian 1991-92, sec. 1992-93, treas. 1993-94, v.p. 1994-95, pres.-elect 1995-96, pres. 1996-97, immediate past pres. 1997-98), Conn. Bar Assn., Regional Bar Assn. Democrat. Jewish. Avocations: golf, photography. General civil litigation, Personal injury, Workers' compensation. Office: Casper & de Toledo LLC 1111 Summer St Stamford CT 06905-5511

**CASS, NEIL EARL,** lawyer; b. Carthage, Ill., Jan. 8, 1952; s. Earl and Katheryn Louise (Lovell) C.; m. Marilyn Kay Schell, Nov. 14, 1970; children: Brian, Sara, Amy. BBA with honors, U. Puget Sound, 1974; MBA, U. Iowa, JD with high distinction, 1977; LLM in Estate Planning, U. Miami, 1980. Bar: Iowa 1977, Wis. 1977, Ill. 1980; CPA Ill. Tax staff. Touche Ross, Milw., 1977, Den, Hartog & Hogan, Waterloo, Iowa, 1977-78; assoc. Strand & Anderson, Decorah, Iowa, 1978-79; assoc. Kirkland & Ellis, Chgo., 1980-85, ptnr., 1985-87; ptnr. Coffield, Ungaretti, Harris & Slavin, 1987-89; ptnr. Jenner & Block, Chgo., 1989—, chmn. estate planning and probate dept., 1995—; former bd. trustee Flossmoor, Ill. and Baccalaureate Trust Authority State Ill.; spkr. in the field of Estate Planning, Fin. Planning, Ownership Succession and Tax Issues. Author: A Primer On Estate Planning; contbr. to profl. journals. Served to staff sgt. USAF, 1970-74. Mem. ABA, Ill. Bar Assn., Iowa Bar Assn., Wis. Bar Assn., Chgo. Estate Planning Council, Fox Valley Estate Planning Council. Republican. Estate taxation, Estate planning, General corporate. Office: Jenner & Block One IBM Plz Chicago IL 60611

**CASS, ROBERT MICHAEL,** lawyer, consultant; b. Carlisle, Pa., July 5, 1945; s. Robert Lau and Norma Jean (McCaleb) C.; m. Patricia Ann Garber, Aug. 12, 1967 (dec. Jan. 1999); children: Charles McCaleb, David Lau. BA, Pa. State U., 1967; JD, Temple U., 1971. Bar: N.Y. 1974; cert. arbitrator Aida Reins. and Ins. Arbitration Soc. Benefit examiner Social Security Adminstrn., Phila., 1967-68; mktg. rep. Employers Comml. Union Ins. Co., Phila., 1968-70; asst. sec. Nat. Reins. Corp., N.Y.C., 1970-77; asst. v.p. Skandia Am. Reins. Corp., N.Y.C., 1977-80; mgr. Allstate Reins. div., South Barrington, Ill., 1980-86, R.K. Carvill, Inc., Chgo., 1986-87; pres. R. M. Cass Assocs., Barrington, 1987—; v.p. Assurance Alliance, Inc., Crystal Lake, Ill., 1989; lectr. Ins. Sch. Chgo., Coll. of Ins. N.Y., U. Wis., Am. Inst. for Chartered Property Casualty Underwriters; bd. dirs. Legion Indemnity Co., Phila. Author: (with others) Reinsurance Contract Wording, Reinsurance Practices, 2d edit.; editor, reviewer: (with others) The Legal Environment of Insurance, 4th edit. Mem. ABA (tort and ins. practice sect., past chair com. on excess, surplus lines and reins. law, standing com. on professionalism, chmn. com. internat. tort and ins. law, liaison to ABA Ctrl. & East European Law Initiative, dispute resolution sect., past chair com. large complex case arbitration), Soc. CPCUs (past chair risk mgmt. sect. com., mem. excess, surplus and splty. lines sect. com., v.p., bd. dirs. Chgo. N.W. suburban chpt.), Am. Arbitration Assn. (panel arbitrators), Assn. Ind. Reins. Cons. (pres.), Internat. Assn. Ins. Receivers (publs. com., past chair membership com.), N.Y. State Bar Assn., Assn. Internat. de Droit des Assurances, Ill. Captive and Alternative Risk Funding Ins. Assn. (pres. bd. dirs.), Coalition Alternative Risk Funding Mechanisms (bd. dirs.), Assn. Internat. de Droit des Assurances. Insurance, Alternative dispute resolution, Private international. Home: 325 Old Mill Rd Barrington IL 60010-4734 Office: PO Box 1362 Barrington IL 60011-1362

**CASS, RONALD ANDREW,** dean; b. Washington, Aug. 12, 1949; s. Millard and Ruth Claire (Marx) C.; m. Valerie Christina Swanson, Aug. 24, 1969; children: Laura Rebecca, Alexander Stephan. BA with high distinction, U. Va., 1970; JD with honors, U. Chgo., 1973. Bar: Md. 1973, D.C. 1974, U.S. Dist. Ct. D.C. 1974, U.S. Ct. Appeals (D.C. cir.) 1974, U.S. Supreme Ct. 1977, Va. 1979. Law clk. to chief judge U.S. Ct. Appeals (3d cir.), Wilmington, Del., 1973-74; assoc. Arent, Fox, Kintner, Plotkin & Kahn, Washington, 1974-76; asst. prof. law U. Va. Sch. Law, Charlottesville, 1976-81; assoc. prof. law Boston U., 1981-83, prof., 1983-95; dean Boston U. Law Sch., 1990—; Melville Madison Bigelow prof. Boston U., 1995—; legal advisor Office Plans and Policy, FCC, Washington, 1987-88; mem. U.S. Internat. Trade Commn., Washington, 1988-90, vice chmn., 1989-90; cons. comm. program Aspen (Colo.) Inst., 1977-78, Adminstrv. Conf. U.S., Washington, 1980-87, Helsell, Fetterman, Martin, Todd & Hokanson, Seattle, 1984-85, Assn. Trial Lawyers Am., Phila., 1985-87, UN Conf. Trade and Devel., Geneva, 1991, U.S. Dept. Justice, 1998, Microsoft Corp., 1998-99; spl. cons. Nat. Econ. Rsch. Assn., Cambridge, Mass., 1990-94; adj. scholar Am. Enterprise Inst., Washington, 1993—; sr. fellow Internat. Ctr. Econ. Rsch., Turin, 1996-97, 1999—; sesquicentennial assoc. Ctr. Advanced Studies U. Va. Law Sch., 1980-81; mem. nat. adv. bd. Case Western Res. U. Sch. of Law, 1996-97; disting. lectr. U. Francisco Marroquin, Guatemala City, 1996. Author: Revolution in the Wasteland: Value and Diversity in Television, 1981, (with Colin S. Diver) Administrative Law: Cases and Materials, 1987, (with Colin S. Diver and Jack M. Beermann) Administrative Law: Cases and Materials, 2nd edit., 1994, 3rd edit., 1998, (with John R. Haring) International Trade in Telecommunications, 1998; contbr. articles and essays to profl. jours., also chpts. to books. Bd. dirs. Northwestern Va. Health Systems Agy., Culpeper, 1980, New Eng. Coun., 1995—; bd. govs. Sightsavers Internat., Washington, 1989-91; bd. dirs. Telecomm. Policy Rsch. Conf., Washington, 1989-92, sec.-treas. 1989-90, vice chmn., 1991-92; bd. dirs. New Eng. Legal Found., 1994—, New Eng. Coun., 1995—; bd. overseers Boston Bar Found., 1992-94, Supreme Jud. Ct. Hist. Soc., 1997—; sr. Europe Discussion Group, Ctr. for Strategic and Internat. Studies, 1989-96; bd. advisors George Mason U. Law Sch. Law & Econs. Ctr., 1996—, Inst. Dem. Comm., Boston, 1991-92, Fundación de la Commn. Social, Madrid, 1995—. Sr. fellow Internat. Ctr. Econ. Rsch., Turin, 1996-97. Fellow Am. Bar Found.; mem. ABA (adminstrv. law and regulatory practice sect., coun. 1993-95, chair 1998-99, legal edn. and admission bar sect., review commn. 1994-95), Am. Law Inst., Am. Law Deans Assn. (bd. dirs. 1995—, pres. 1995-97), Mont Pelerin Soc., Boston Bar Assn. (coun. 1992-95), Adminstrv. Conf. U.S. (pub. mem. 1990-95, govt. mem. 1988-90), Transatlantic Policy Network (U.S. Working Group), Spring Valley C. C., Order of Coif, Phi Beta Kappa, Bay Club. Republican. Jewish. Home: 36 Forest St Wellesley Hills MA 02181 Office: Boston U Sch Law 765 Commonwealth Ave Boston MA 02215-1401

**CASSEL, DOUGLASS WATTS, JR.,** lawyer, educator, journalist; b. Balt., Aug. 29, 1948; s. Douglass Watts and Vivian Elizabeth (Keller) C.; m. Joan Ellen Steinman, June 1, 1974 (div. 1986); children: Jennifer Lynn, Amanda Hilary; m. Beatriz Cervantes, Sept. 10, 1988; 1 child, Magdalena Maria. BA, Yale Coll., 1969; JD, Harvard Law Sch., 1972. Bar: Md. 1972, D.C. 1973, Ill. 1976. Writer, rschr. Ralph Nader's Congress Project, Washington, 1972; lawyer USNR, Great Lakes Naval Base, Ill., 1973-76; from atty. to gen. counsel BPI, Chgo., 1976-91; journalist Chgo. Reader, 1989; exec. dir. DePaul U. Coll. Law Internat. Human Rights Law Inst., Chgo., 1990-98; dir. Northwestern U. Sch. Law Ctr. for Internat. Human Rights, Chgo., 1998—; legal advisor UN Truth Commn. for El Salvador, N.Y.C., 1992-93; human rights cons. U.S. Dept. State, Washington, 1997—; commentator

WBEZ, Chgo., 1994—. Mem. ABA, Am. Soc. Internat. Law. Democrat. Roman Catholic. Avocation: swimming. Office: Northwestern U Sch Law 357 E Chicago Ave Chicago IL 60611-3059

**CASSEL, MARWIN SHEPARD,** lawyer; b. N.Y.C., July 4, 1925; s. Irwin M. and Mana-Zucca Cassel; children by a previous marriage: Bradley William, James Scott, Thomas Drew; m. Leslie Stein, Nov. 24, 1983; 1 child, Michael Alan. JD, U. Fla., 1949. Bar: Fla. 1949, D.C. 1980. Sr. ptnr. Broad and Cassel, Miami, Fla., 1985—; chmn. bd., pres. Internat. Savs. and Loan Assn., Miami, 1980-83. Vice chmn. Miami Beach Redevel. Authority, 1978-82; mem. nat. jud. council Dem. Nat. Com., 1976-80; mem. State Fla. Hosp. Cost Containment Bd., 1986-88; bd. dirs., v.p. corp. affairs Friends of the Art, Lowe Gallery, Coral Gables, Fla., 1985-87, chmn. bd. trustees, 1990-91; pres., dir. Downtown Miami Bus. Assn., 1988-91; active Downtown Devel. Authority, 1991-94, City of Miami Heritage Conservation Bd. 1988-90, Met. Dade County Citizen's Transp. Adv. Com., 1995-97; pres. Greater Miami Technion Soc., 1988-90, Swan lake Owners Assn., 1994-96; mem. zoning bd. Village of Pinecrest, 1997-98. Served with USAAF, 1943-45. Named Outstanding Alumni U. Fla., 1979. Mem. ABA, Fla. Bar (Fla. realtor com. 1994—). Jewish. Real property, Probate, General corporate. Office: 201 S Biscayne Blvd Ste 3000 Miami FL 33131-4330

**CASSELL, RICHARD EMMETT,** lawyer; b. N.Y.C., Jan. 3, 1949; s. Max and Sylvia (Cohen) Cassell; m. Madeline Gail Erdman, June 13, 1970; children: Lori Faith, Marc Joshua. BA cum laude, SUNY, Buffalo, 1971; JD, Georgetown U., 1974. Bar: D.C. 1974, Va. 1974, Md. 1985. Assoc. Ira Lechner, Washington, 1974-75, Benson, Stien & Braunstien, Washington, 1975-85; sole practice Alexandria, Va., 1986—; Mem. Landlord-Tenant Commn., Arlington, 1974-76. Committeeperson Arlington Dems., 1973-76, Arlingtonians for Better County, 1973-76. Mem. ABA, Va. Bar Assn., D.C. Bar Assn., Md. Bar Assn. Personal injury, Workers' compensation, Family and matrimonial. Home: 7497 Covent Wood Ct Annandale VA 22003-5731 Office: 1513 King St Alexandria VA 22314-2716

**CASSIDAY, BENJAMIN BUCKLES, III,** lawyer; b. Honolulu, Sept. 6, 1950; s. Benjamin B. Jr. and Barbara (Dennison) C.; m. Maile Burgundy, May 8, 1996. BS, Stanford U., 1973; JD, Boston Coll., 1977. Bar: Colo. 1977, Hawaii 1980, U.S. Ct. Appeals (9th cir.) 1982. State pub. defender Pub. Defender's Office, Littleton, Colo., 1977-80; pvt. practice Honolulu, 1981-82, 88—; 1st dep. Fed. Pub. Defender's Office, Honolulu, 1982-87; lawyer rep. 9th Cir. Boston Coll., 1993-95. Mem. Am. Bd. Criminal Lawyers, Hawaii Assns. Criminal Def. Lawyers (bd. dirs.). Avocations: poker, pool. Criminal, Federal civil litigation, Private international. Home: 5699 Kalanianaole Hwy Honolulu HI 96821-2303 Office: Law Office of Ben Cassiday 841 Bishop St Ste 2201 Honolulu HI 96813-3921

**CASSIDY, DAVID MICHAEL,** lawyer; b. Amityville, N.Y., May 31, 1954; s. Paul Francis and Theresa Alice (Britts) C.; m. Janet Patricia Johnson, Aug. 26, 1978; children: Daniel B., Caitlin E. BA, SUNY, Stony Brook, 1981; JD, St. John's U., Jamaica, N.Y., 1985. Bar: N.Y. 1986. Assoc. Rivkin, Radler & Kremer, Uniondale, N.Y., 1985-92, ptnr., 1992—. Mem. Suffolk County Bar Assn., L.I. Assn. Insurance, General civil litigation. Office: Rivkin Radler & Kremer Eab Plz Uniondale NY 11556-0001

**CASSIDY, EDWARD Q.,** lawyer; b. Pekin, Ill., July 15, 1951; s. Clement James and Patricia Quinn Cassidy; m. Michele A. Cohn, Oct. 30, 1982. JD, Hamline U., 1981. Ptnr. Felhaber, Larson, Fenlor & Vogt, St. Paul, 1994—. Workers' compensation, Labor. Office: Felhaber Larson Fenlon & Vogt 2100 World Trade Ctr Saint Paul MN 55105

**CASSIDY, ELIZABETH KANDRAVY,** lawyer; b. Passaic, N.J., Dec. 14, 1965; d. John and Alice Elizabeth (Sullivan) Kandravy; m. Joseph Patrick Cassidy, May 9, 1998. BA, Wesleyan U., 1988; JD summa cum laude, Am. U., 1992. Bar: N.J., 1992, N.Y., 1993, D.C., 1994. Jud. clerk Hon. William G. Bassler U.S. Dist. Ct., Newark, 1992-93; jud. clerk Hon. Richard K. Nygaard U.S. Ct. Appeals (3d cir.), Erie, Pa., 1993-94; assoc. Akin, Gump, Strauss, Hauer, Feld, Washington, 1994-98; cons. Legal Assistance Ctr., Windhoek, Namibia, 1998—; lectr. Faculty Law U. Namibia, Windhoek, 1999—. Editor: Am. U. Law Rev., 1991-92. Office: US Embassy Windhoek Dept State 1333 New Hampshire Ave NW Washington DC 20521-2540

**CASSIDY, M. SHARON,** lawyer; b. Latrobe, Pa., Nov. 1, 1946; d. Raymond and Helen (Ankney) C.; children: Matthew, Ryan. BS, Wheeling Jesuit U., 1968; JD, U. Pitts. Sch. Law, 1974. Bar: Pa., N.Y. Lawyer, gen. atty. USX Corp., Pitts., 1974-90; gen. counsel U.S. Steel & Carnegie Pension Fund, N.Y.C., 1990—; adv. Pension Benefit Guaranty Corp., Washington, 1994—. Mem. ABA. Finance, Pension, profit-sharing, and employee benefits, Securities.

**CASSIMATIS, EMANUEL ANDREW,** judge; b. Pottsville, Pa., Dec. 2, 1926; s. Andrew Emanuel and Mary H. (Calopedis) C.; m. Thecla Karambelas, June 2, 1952; children: Mary Ann Maza, John E., Gregory E. BA, Dickinson Coll., 1949, LLB, 1951, LLD (hon.) York Coll., 1991. Bar: Pa. 1951. Sole practice law, York, Pa., 1951-53, 55-57; assoc. Kain, Kain & Kain, York, Pa., 1953-55; ptnr. Stock & Leader, York, 1957-78; judge Ct. Common Pleas, York, Pa., 1978-96, sr. judge, 1996—; solicitor Springettsbury Twp., York, Pa., 1960-66, Sewer Authority, 1965-66; solicitor Wrightsville Borough, Pa., 1966-71, Mcpl. Authority, 1968-78, York Suburban Sch. Dist., 1970-77; faculty Pa. Coll. Judiciary, 1981, 82, 83; pres. Pa. Conf. State Trial Judges, 1989-90, chmn. spl. projects com., 1980-82, ann. meeting com., 1984-85, pres. Juvenile Ct. sect., 1988-89; mem. juvenile adv. com. Pa. Commn. Crime and Deliquency, 1996—; mem. Juvenile Ct. Judges' Commn. 1989-98, chmn., 1990-94; mem. Pa. three-judge breast implant coord. panel, 1993—. Pres. United Way of York County, 1964-65; co-chmn. steering com. York Community Audit for Human Rights, 1959; pres. Children's Growth and Devel. Clinic, 1974; trustee Meml. Osteopathic Hosp., 1963-80; bd. dirs. Capital Blue Cross, Harrisburg, Pa., 1970-79, Historic York, 1977-82. Served with U.S. Army, 1945-46. Named Young Man of Yr., York Jr. C. of C., 1960; Vol. of Yr., Pilot Club, 1965; Mem. Hall of Fame, William Penn Sr. High Sch., York, 1981; Nat. Juvenile Ct. Judge of Yr., CASA, 1995. Greek Orthodox. Lodges: Masons (hon. mem. supreme council). Home: 176 Rathton Rd York PA 17403-3720

**CASSON, RICHARD FREDERICK,** lawyer, travel bureau executive; b. Boston, Apr. 11, 1939; s. Louis H. and Beatrix S. C. AB, Colby Coll., 1960; JD, U. Chgo., 1963. Bar: Ill. 1963, Mass. 1964. Ptnr. Casson & Casson, Boston, 1967-68; assoc. counsel, corporate sec. Bankers Leasing Corp., 1968-75; asst. gen. counsel, corp. sec. Commonwealth Planning Corp., 1975-76; assoc. gen. counsel, asst. sec. Prudential Capital Corp., 1976-92; pres. Autumn Crest Corp., 1991-98; v.p. Casseden Corp.; career advisor Vt. Assocs. Capt. JAGC U.S. Army, 1964-67. Decorated Bronze Star. Jewish. Contracts commercial, General corporate, Nuclear power. Home and Office: PO Box 233 Randolph Center VT 05061-0233

**CASTAGNA, WILLIAM JOHN,** federal judge. Student, U. Pa., 1941-43; LLB, JD, U. Fla., 1949. Bar: Fla. 1949. Ptnr. MacKenzie, Castagna, Bennison & Gardner, 1970-79; judge U.S. Dist. Judge (mid. dist.) Fla., 1979—, now sr. judge. Democrat.

**CASTAGNOLA, GEORGE JOSEPH, JR.,** lawyer, mediator, secondary education educator; b. Scotia, Calif., July 6, 1950; s. George Joseph and Olga Esther Castagnola; m. Sandra Annette Castagnola, June 7, 1975; children: George Joseph III, Laura, Joseph. Grad., U. San Francisco, 1974; JD, N.W. Calif. U., Sacramento, 1990, D Juridical Sci., 1992. BAr: Calif. 1990. Tchr. El Molino H.S., Forestville, Calif., 1977—; charter boat capt. Castagnola Fishing, Petaluma, Calif., 1971—; prof. law N.W. Calif. U., 1990—; atty., mediator Law and Mediation Office of George Castagnola, Petaluma, Calif., 1990—. Cpl. USMCR, 1968-74. Mem. ABA (family law sect.), Calif. Bar Assn., Sonoma County Bar Assn., Calif. Tchrs. Assn., Golden Gate Sport Fishing Assn. Roman Catholic. Avocations: weightlifting, fishing. Home and Office: 802 Wine Ct Petaluma CA 94954-7420

**CASTANO, GREGORY JOSEPH,** lawyer; b. Kearny, N.J., Feb. 17, 1929; s. Nicholas and Marianna (Prestinaci) C.; m. June Dwyer, Oct. 15, 1966; children: Gregory, Christopher, John, Timothy. BS, Seton Hall U., 1950; JD, Fordham U., 1953; LLM, NYU, 1956. Bar: N.J. 1956, U.S. Ct. Appeals (3d cir.) 1957, U.S. Supreme Ct. 1959, U.S. Tax Ct. 1974, N.Y. 1985. Sports writer Newark Star-Ledger, 1946-53; pvt. practice Harrison, N.J., 1959-78; atty. Bd. Adjustment, Harrison, 1978; judge Superior Ct. N.J., Jersey City, 1978-85; ptnr. Tompkins, McGuire & Wachenfeld, Newark, 1985-88, Waters, McPherson & McNeill, Secaucus, N.J., 1988—; asst. atty. Town of Harrison, 1959-64; asst. prosecutor County of Hudson, N.J., 1963-71; atty. Town of West New York, N.J., 1977-78, Town of Kearny, N.J., 1999; adj. prof. Seton Hall U. Sch. Law, Newark, 1988—; master com. to computerize criminal cts. Essex County; mediator U.S. Dist. Ct., Superior Ct. Mem. editorial bd., The Cath. Adv., 1976-78. Tax assessor Town of Harrison, 1964-78; del. N.J. Constl. Conv., 1964; mem. juvenile conf. com. Twp. West Caldwell, N.J., 1977-78; trustee Caldwell (N.J.) Coll., 1985-91, chmn. acad. affairs com. bd. trustees, 1987-91; chmn. County Govt. Transition Com., Hudson County, 1987-88; mem. Hudson County Community Coll. Blue Ribbon Task Force, 1992-93. With U.S. Army, 1953-55. Named Man of Yr., Kearny Jaycees, 1963, Alumnus of Yr., Dorf Feature Service, 1987. Fellow Am. Bar Found.; mem. ABA, N.J. Bar Assn., Hudson County Bar Assn. (Justice medallion 1985), Essex County Bar Assn., West Hudson Bar Assn. (pres. 1977-78), Assn. Fed. Bar N.J., Essex Fells Country Club. General civil litigation, General corporate, General practice. Home: 19 Sunset Rd West Caldwell NJ 07006-6540 Office: Waters McPherson & McNeill 300 Lighting Way PO Box 1560 Secaucus NJ 07096-1560

**CASTELLANI, EDWARD JOSEPH,** lawyer; b. Lansing, Mich., Oct. 16, 1952; s. Arthur M. and Dorena Castellani; m. Robin Carboni, Oct. 7, 1988; children: Michael, Christopher. BBA, U. Mich., 1976; JD, Detroit Coll. Law, 1979. Bar: Mich. 1979, U.S. Tax Ct. 1996; CPA, Mich. CPA Deloitte & Touche, Lansing, 1980-82; atty. Willingham & Coté, P.C., East Lansing, 1982—; spkr. in field of taxation and assn. law. Contbr. articles to profl. jours. Mem. East Lansing Kiwanis Club, 1990—. Fellow Mich. State Bar Assn.; mem. Mich. Assn. CPA (state and local tax com. 1998, govt. adv. com. 1994), Mich. Soc. Assn. Execs. (svcs. com. 1996—), Mich. C. of C. (tax com. 1996—). Avocations: golf, chess, music. General corporate, Taxation, general, Non-profit and tax-exempt organizations. Office: Willingham and Coté PC 333 Albert Ave Ste 500 East Lansing MI 48823-4394

**CASTELLANOS, RICHARD HENRY,** lawyer; b. San Ysidro, Calif., Oct. 8, 1965; s. Roberto and Rachel (Garcia) C. BA in Polit. Sci./Sociology, U. Calif., San Diego, 1987; JD, U. Calif., Berkeley, 1990. Bar: Calif. 1990, U.S. Dist. Ct. (ctrl. dist.) Calif. 1990. Assoc. atty. Wyman Bautzer Kuchel & Silbert, Century City, Calif., 1990-91, Nossaman Guthner Knox & Elliott, L.A., 1991-93; legal advisor, of counsel Gangs for Peace, 1993-94; discrimination atty. AIDS Project L.A., 1993-94; atty. San Diego County Pub. Defender's Office, 1994—; instr. role model program L.A. County Sch. Dist., L.A., 1990—. Active Rebuild L.A. Task Force, L.A., Ptnrs. for Success, Legal Los Padrinos Program, Vols. in Parole, 1997—. Alba 80 Soc. scholar ALBA 80 Soc., 1987-90. Mem. ABA, Mex.-Am. Bar Assn., Hispanic Profl. Roundtable, Calif. Pub. Defenders Assn., La Kaza Lawyers Assn., San Diego County Bar Assn., L.A. County Bar Assn., Beverly Hills Bar Assn., Juvenile Justice Com., Nat. Moot Ct. Com., Children's Rights Com. Federal civil litigation, General civil litigation, State civil litigation. Home: 129 Olive Dr San Diego CA 92173 Office: Office of Pub Defender 233 A St Ste 300 San Diego CA 92101-4008

**CASTELLITTO, MARIO,** lawyer; b. Bronx, N.Y., May 9, 1967; s. Giuseppe and Nunziatina Castellitto; m. Kathleen E. Gill, Oct. 25, 1997. BS, Fordham U., 1989; JD cum laude, Pace U., 1993. Bar: N.Y. 1994, U.S. Dist. Ct. (so. and ea. dists.) N.Y. 1994. Assoc. Polstein Ferrara Dwyer and Speed PC, N.Y.C., 1993—. Mem. ABA, Assn. Criminal Advocacy Com., N.Y. State Bar Assn., Assn. of Bar of City of N.Y. (sec. criminal cts. com. 1994-96). Democrat. Roman Catholic. Avocations: riding, skiing. Criminal, Insurance, General civil litigation. Home: 40 Green Pl New Rochelle NY 10801-3618 Office: Polstein Ferrara Dwyer & Speed PC 2 Park Ave Rm 1516 New York NY 10016-5783

**CASTELLO, DAVID A.,** lawyer; b. Sacramento, Calif., Oct. 21, 1958; s. Hector A. and Vivian (Christo) C.; m. Lorna S. Castello, June 6, 1981; children: Jennifer, Dominic, Dylan. BA, Grinnell Coll., 1981; JD, George Washington U., 1985. Bar: Nebr. 1985. Lawyer Katskee, Henatsch 7 Suing, Omaha, 1985—. Author: Law & the Martial Arts, 1993. With USAR, 1977-83. Black belt Tae Kwon Do 2d degree. Mem. Phi Beta Kappa. Personal injury, Workers' compensation, Entertainment. Office: Katskee Henatsch & Suing 10404 Essex Ct Ste 100 Omaha NE 68114-3746

**CASTELLO, JOE, JR.,** lawyer; b. Coronado, Calif., Feb. 1, 1943; s. Joseph William Sr. and Fern (Noel) C.; m. Kathie Means, Sept. 11, 1981; 1 child, Matthew Noel; 1 stepchild, Heather Jo Means. BA, U. Fla., 1965; JD, Stetson U., 1971. Bar: Fla. 1971, U.S. Dist. Ct. (mid. dist.) Fla. 1971. Assoc. Trenam, Simmons, Kemker, Scharf, Frye & O'Neill, Tampa, Fla., 1969-79; assoc., ptnr. Holland & Knight, Lakeland, Tampa, Fla., 1979-81; pvt. practice Tampa, 1981—. Alternative dispute resolution, General civil litigation, Real property. Office: PO Box 290589 Tampa FL 33687-0589

**CASTELLO, RAYMOND VINCENT,** lawyer; b. San Jose, Calif., Apr. 25, 1939; s. Joseph V. and Josephine M. (Gallina) C.; m. W. Karla Grusonik, July 29, 1963; children: Joseph W., Julie A. BS, Calif. State U., San Jose, 1961; JD, Stanford U., 1964. Bar: Calif. 1965, U.S. Dist. Ct. (no. dist.) Calif. 1965, U.S. Ct. Appeals (9th cir.) 1965, U.S. Supreme Ct. 1976. Sole practice Campbell, Calif., 1965-68; ptnr. Finch, Castello & Tennant, Campbell, 1968-78, Castello, Daily & Gerbino, Campbell, 1978—; gen. ptnr. Castello, Marino & Orr, Tracy, Calif., 1963—, Castello Farms, Tracy, 1963—, Castello Properties, San Jose, 1975—, Teresi & Castello, San Jose, 1985—. Coach Police Athletic League, San Jose, 1973-83; pres. Dry Creek Community Assn., San Jose, 1975—. Mem. Calif. Bar Assn., Santa Clara County Bar Assn. (trustee 1973-80), West Valley Bar Assn. (pres. 1973), Am. Arbitrary Assn., Phi Alpha Delta. Club: Civic of Santa Clara County (San Jose) (pres. 1982-84). Lodge: Rotary (bd. dirs. Campbell club 1966-74). State civil litigation, Personal injury, Probate. Office: Law Office of Raymond V Castello 1790 Winchester Blvd Ste 1 Campbell CA 95008-1150

**CASTELNOVO, ANNIE TERESA,** legal nurse consultant; b. Salzburg, Austria, Feb. 9, 1957; d. Frank Peter and Mary Louise Castelnovo. BS in Natural Resources, U. R.I., 1979; BSN magna cum laude, Boston U., 1983. RN R.I. Hosp., Providence, 1984-88; legal nurse cons. Wistow & Barylick, Inc., Providence, 1988—. Mem. R.I. Assn. Legal Nurse Cons. Avocations: birdwatching, travel, outdoor activities. Office: Wistow & Barylick Inc 61 Weybosset St Providence RI 02903-2824

**CASTIGLIONE, VINCENT ALFRED,** lawyer; b. N.Y.C., July 28, 1964. B of Mech. Engring., Ga. Inst. Tech., 1986; JD, Emory U., 1989. Bar: Conn. 1989, N.Y. 1990, U.S. Patent Office 1990. Assoc. Morgan & Finnegan, N.Y.C., 1989-94; patent atty. Becton Dickson & Co., Franklin Lakes, N.J., 1994-97; sr. atty. patents and trademarks C.R. Bard, Inc., Murray Hill, N.J., 1997—. E-mail: vincent.castiglione@crbard.com. Intellectual property. Office: CR Bard Inc 730 Central Ave New Providence NJ 07974-1199

**CASTILLE, RONALD D.,** state supreme court justice; b. Miami, Mar. 16, 1944; s. Henry and Marie Nash Castille. BS in Econs., Auburn U., 1966; JD, U. Va., 1971. Dep. dist. atty. Pre-Trial Divsn. Phila., 1971-85; chief Career Criminal Unit, 1971-85; asst. dist. atty. Phila. Dist. Atty.'s Office, 1971-85; dist. atty. Phila., 1986-91; with litigation dept. Reed Smith Shaw & McClay, Phila., 1991-93; justice Supreme Ct. Pa., 1993—. Exec. bd. dirs. Criminal Justice Coordinating Commn., 1986-91; bd. dirs. Urban Coalition, 1988-91; co-chmn. Pa. Anti-Crime Coalition for George Bush for Pres., 1988, 92; commr. Pres.'s Commn. on Model State Drug Laws, 1992. Lt. USMC, 1966-68. Decorated Bronze Star with Combat V, Purple Heart (2); recipient Disting. Pub. Svc. award Pa. County and State Detectives Assn., 1987, Layman award Pa. Chiefs of Police Assn., 1987, Spirit of Am. award Inst. for Study of Am. Wars, 1988, Pres.'s award for Outstanding Svc., Nat. Dist. Attys. Assn., 1991; named Man of Yr., Fraternal Order of Police Lodge #5, 1988, Outstanding Disabled Vet. of Yr., Nat. Disabled Am. Vets., 1988. Mem. Nat. Dist. Attys. Assn. (v.p. 1986-91), Pa. Dist. Attys. Assn. (legis. chmn. 1986-91). Office: 1818 Market St Ste 3730 Philadelphia PA 19103-3639*

**CASTILLO, ANGEL, JR.,** lawyer; b. Havana, Cuba, Nov. 29, 1946; came to U.S., 1960; s. Angel and Graciela (Blanco) C. m. Stormie G. Stafford, Dec. 16, 1977; children: Arielle Caridad, Angel Marti. BA, Stetson U., 1968; JD with high honors, U. Fla., 1978; LLM, Yale U., 1980. Bar: Fla. 1979, U.S. Supreme Ct. 1982. Various positions in pub. and journalism, 1968-80; legal affairs reporter The N.Y. Times, N.Y.C., 1980-81; assoc. Shutts & Bowen, Miami, Fla., 1981-83; sr. assoc. Morgan, Lewis & Bockius, Miami, 1983-86; ptnr. Soto & Castillo, Miami, 1987-89, Castillo, Stafford & Wald, Miami, 1989-99; of counsel Morgan, Lewis & Bockius LLP, Miami, 1999—; exec. asst. to chmn. Ways and Means Com., Fla. Senate, Tallahassee, 1978-79; mem. jud. nominating com. Fla.Dist. Ct. Appeal (3d dist.), 1992-95. Exec. editor U. Fla. Law Rev., 1978. Del. Creative Crime Control Conf., Fla., 1982. Mem. ABA, Dade County Bar Assn. (chmn. internat. law com.), Cuban-Am. Bar Assn., Hispanic Nat. Bar Assn., Inter-Am. Bar Assn., Order of Coif, Phi Kappa Phi. Fax: (305) 579-0321. E-mail: casstawal@aol.com. Trademark and copyright, General civil litigation, Private international. Office: Morgan Lewis & Bockius LLP 200 S Biscayne Blvd Ste 5300 Miami FL 33131-2339

**CASTILLO, DANIEL L.,** lawyer; b. Tampa, Fla., July 15, 1961; s. Daniel and Yara Elizabeth Catillo; m. Michelle Andrea Garcia, May 30, 1987; children: Andrea, Mary Elizabeth, Selena, Laura, Sarah, Daniel L. Jr. BA, U. South Fla., 1988; JD, Stetson U., 1991. Bar: Fla. 1991, U.S. Dist. Ct. (mid. dist.) Fla. 1991, U.S. Ct. Appeals (11th cir.) 1991, U.S. Ct. Appeals (3rd, 4th, 5th, 6th 7th 8th 9th and 10th cirs.) 1997, U.S. Supreme Ct. 1995. Police officer City of Tampa, Police Dept., 1985-90; pvt. practice Tampa, 1991—; civil traffic magistrate, hearing officer Hillsborough County, 13th Jud. Cir., Tampa, 1997—. Mem. Tampa Cath. Lawyers Guild, KC (dep. grand knight 1997-98). Criminal, Appellate, Probate. Office: 3900 N Boulevard Tampa FL 33603-4628

**CASTILLO, RUBEN,** judge; b. 1954. BA, Loyola U., 1976; JD, Northwestern U., 1979. Pvt. practice Chgo., 1979-84, Kirkland & Ellis, Chgo., 1991-93; dist. judge U.S. Dist. Ct. (no. dist.) Ill., 1994—; adj. prof. Northwestern U., 1988—. Mem. ABA, Latin Am. Bar Assn., Chgo. Bar Found., Chgo. Coun. of Lawyers (v.p. 1991-93). Office: U S Courthouse 2378 Dirksen Bldg 219 S Dearborn St Chicago IL 60604-1702

**CASTLEBERRY, JAMES NEWTON, JR.,** retired law educator, dean; b. Chatom, Ala., Dec. 28, 1921; s. James Newton and Nellie (Robbins) C.; m. Mary Ann Blocker, Feb. 12, 1944 (dec.); children: Jean, Nancy, James III (dec.), Elizabeth, Cynthia, Robert, Mary Ann. JD magna cum laude, St. Mary's U., 1952; diploma, Nat. U. Mex., 1960; diploma in teaching of comparative law, Strasburg, 1963. Bar: Tex. 1952. Asst. atty. gen. State of Tex., 1953-55; prof. law St. Mary's U., San Antonio, 1955-92, dean, 1978-89, dean emeritus, 1989—, ret., 1992; dir. St. Mary's U. Summer Program in Internat. and Comparative Law, Innsbruck, Austria, 1986-89; exec. dir. Tex. Ctr. for Legal Ethics and Professionalism, 1990-92; lectr. comparative law fgn. legal study tours Corp. for Profl. Confs., 1990—. Co-author: Water & Water Rights, 1970; contbr. articles to law jours. Bd. dirs. Preservation Tex.; trustee Tex. Supreme Ct. Hist. Soc. Mem. ABA, Am. Bar Found., San Antonio Bar Assn., Tex. Bar Found., San Antonio Bar Found., Tex. State Bar, Phi Delta Phi (internat. pres. 1977-79). Home: 7727 Woodridge Dr San Antonio TX 78209-2223

**CASTLEBERRY, RONALD LEROY,** judge; b. Tacoma, Wash., Aug. 10, 1944; s. Loren Philip and Lonitia Margeret Castleberry; m. Mary Jo Ann McFadden, June 4, 1966; children: Elizabeth Ann, David Andrew. BA, U. Portland, 1966; JD, U. Wash., 1969. Dir., atty. Snohomish County Pub. Defender, Everett, Wash., 1973-77; ptnr. Williams Novack Hansen, P.S., Everett, 1977-86, Newton Kight Adams & Castleberry, Everett, 1986-91; superior ct. judge Snohomish County Superior Ct., Everett, 1992—. Bd. dirs. Evergreen Legal Svcs., Everett, 1986, Snohomish Soccer Assn., 1993. Capt. U.S. Army, 1969-73. Mem. Snohomish County Bar Assn. (bd. dirs. 1989), Snohomish County Pub. Defenders (bd. dirs. 1986), Rotary (Paul Harris award 1998). Roman Catholic. Avocations: golf, soccer. Office: Snohomish County Superior Ct 3000 Rockefeller Ave Everett WA 98201-4046

**CASTNER, CHARLES FREDERICK,** lawyer; b. Lexington, Ky., Sept. 15, 1957; s. John Paul and Martha Anne Castner; m. Kimberly Brewer, Oct. 10, 1981; 1 child, Killian Patrick. BA, Ctr. Coll. of Ky., 1979; MBA, Wake forest U., 1989; JD, Washington 7 Lee U., 1994. Bar: S.C., N.C., U.S. Ct. Appeals (4th cir.), U.S. Dist. Ct. S.C., U.S. Dist. Ct. N.C. Plant contract supr. So. Bell Telephone, Lincolnton, N.C., 1979-80, asst. mgr., 1980-84; facility engr. So. Bell Telephone, Newton, N.C., 1984-85; staff mgr. So. Bell Telephone, Charlotte, N.C., 1985-89, BellSouth, Atlanta, 1989-91; assoc. Ogletree, Deakins, Nash, Smoak & Stewart, Charleston, 1994—. Mem. ABA (labor and employment law sect. 1994-98), S.C. Bar Assn. (labor and employment law sect. 1994-98), N.C. Bar Assn. (labor and employment law sect. 1994-98), Charleston County Bar Assn., Charleston C. of C. (bus.-expo task force 1998—, legis. agenda adv. com. 1997-98). Avocations: sailing, camping. Home: 29 Brisbane Dr Charleston SC 29407-3418 Office: Ogletree Deakins Nash Smoak 177 Meeting St Ste 310 Charleston SC 29401-3160

**CASTO, JEFFREY JOSEPH,** lawyer; b. Akron, Ohio, Oct. 22, 1954; s. Richard Casto; m. Valerie Jean Casto, June 30, 1955; children: Scott, Erin, Lauren. BA in Biology, Ohio State U., 1976; JD, Case Western Res. U., 1981. Assoc. Roetzel & Andress, Akron, 1981-88, ptnr., 1988—, adminstrv. ptnr., 1996—. Office: Roetzel & Andress 222 S Main St Akron OH 44308-1533

**CASTRATARO, BARBARA ANN,** lawyer; b. Bethpage, N.Y., Apr. 25, 1958; d. Vincent James and Theresa (Chiarini) C. BA in Music, L.I. U., 1984; JD, N.Y. Law Sch., 1989. Bar: N.Y. 1990, U.S. Dist. Ct. (so. dist.) N.Y. 1990. Music dir. CBS Network, N.Y.C., 1979-81, exec. officer ops., 1984-88; music dir. NBC Network/Score Prodns., N.Y.C. and L.A., 1983-84, Score Prodns./ABC Network, N.Y.C. and L.A., 1980-84; assoc. Donald Frank Esq., N.Y.C., 1989-93, Law Offices of Joel C. Bender, White Plains, N.Y., 1993-99, Bender, Jenson, Silverstein & Castrataro, LLP, White Plains, 1999—; lectr. on divorce and separation; founder Castrataro Artist Mgmt., 1997-99; adj. faculty mem. Berkeley Coll., White Plains, N.Y. Recipient 3 Emmy nominations N.Y. Acad. TV Arts and Sci., 1979, 82-83. Mem. N.Y. State Bar Assn., Womens Bar Assn. Avocations: sailing, gourmet cooking, gardening. Family and matrimonial, Entertainment. Office: 140 Grand St White Plains NY 10601-4831

**CASTRO, LEONARD EDWARD,** lawyer; b. L.A., Mar. 18, 1934; s. Emil Galvez and Lily (Meyers) C.; 1 son, Stephen Paul. A.B., UCLA, 1959, J.D., 1962. Bar: Calif. 1963, U.S. Supreme Ct. 1970. Assoc. Musick, Peeler & Garrett, Los Angeles, 1962-68, ptnr., 1968—. Mem. ABA, Internat. Bar Assn., Los Angeles County Bar Assn. General corporate, Private international, Securities. Office: Musick Peeler & Garrett 1 Wilshire Blvd Ste 2000 Los Angeles CA 90017-3876

**CASTRO, SONIA MENDEZ,** lawyer; b. N.Y.C., Apr. 2, 1967; d. Efrain and Maria Mendez (Gonzalez) Mendez; m. Edward Castro, June 20, 1992. BA, Baruch Coll., 1989; JD, St. Johns U., 1993. Bar: N.Y. 1994, U.S. Dist. Ct. (ea. and so. dist.) 1996. Sr. atty. Advocates for Children of N.Y., Bklyn., 1994—; dir. mobilization for equity sch. reform project Advocates for Children, 1995—. Mem. Assn. of the Bar of the City of N.Y. (mem. edn. law com. 1995—), Puerto Rican Bar Assn. Avocation: English. Education and schools, Non-profit and tax-exempt organizations. Office: Advocates for Children of NY 105 Court St Brooklyn NY 11201-5645

**CATALDO, ALEXANDER LAWRENCE,** lawyer; b. Boston, Jan. 25, 1957; s. Alan L. Cataldo and Janet M. (White) Glancy. BA magna cum laude, Northeastern U., 1980; JD, Syracuse U., 1986. Bar: Mass. 1986, U.S. Dist. Ct. Mass. 1987, U.S. Ct. Appeals (1st cir.) 1990; bd. cert. specialist comml. and consumer bankruptcy. Assoc. Aronson & Goldstein, P.A., Boston, 1986-88; pvt. practice Law Office of Alexander L. Cataldo, Boston, 1988-89; assoc. Cuddy Bixby, Boston, 1989-92, ptnr., 1993—; lectr. in field. Contbr. articles to profl. jours. Bd. trustees Dockside Pl. Condominium Assn., Boston, 1994-95. Mem. Boston Bar Assn. (bankruptcy law com., vol. lawyers project), Comml. Law League Am. (bankruptcy and insolvency sect.). Republican. Roman Catholic. Avocations: offshore power boat racing, art, antiques. Bankruptcy, Contracts commercial. Office: Cuddy Bixby 125 Summer St Boston MA 02110-1616

**CATALFO, ALFRED, JR. (ALFIO CATALFO),** lawyer; b. Lawrence, Mass., Jan. 31, 1920; s. Alfio and Vincenza (Amato) C.; m. Caroline Joanne Mosca (dec. Apr. 1968); children: Alfred Thomas, Carol Joanne, Gina Marie; m. Gail Varney, 1988. BA, U. N.H., 1945, MA in History, 1952; LLB, Boston U., 1947, JD (hon.), 1969; postgrad., Suffolk U. Sch. Law, 1955-56, Am. Law Inst., N.Y.C., 1959. Bar: N.H. 1947, U.S. Dist. Ct. 1948, U.S. Ct. Appeals 1978, U.S. Supreme Ct. 1979. Pvt. practice Dover, N.H., 1948—; ptnr. Catalfo Law Firm, Dover, 1980—; county atty. Strafford County, Dover, N.H., 1949-50, 55-56; bd. immigration appeals U.S. Dept. Justice, 1953—; football coach Berwick Acad., South Berwick, Maine, 1944, Mission Catholic H.S., Roxbury, Mass., 1945-46. Author: Laws of Divorces, Marriages, and Separations in New Hampshire, 1962, History of the Town of Rollinsford, 1623-1973, 1973. Pres. Young Dems. of Dover, 1953-55; 1st vice-chmn. Young Dems., N.H., 1954-56; mem. Strafford County Dem. Com., 1948-75; vice-chmn. N.H. Dem. Com., 1954-56, 1st chmn., 1956-58, chmn. spl. activities, 1958-60; del. Dem. Nat. Conv., 1956-60, 76; chmn. N.H. Dem. Conv., 1958, conv. dir., 1960; mem. Dem. state exec. com., 1960-70; Dem. nominee for U.S. Senate, 1962; vice-chmn. Dover Cath. Sch. Com., 1969-71; mem. Dover Bd. Adjustment, 1960-65; apptd. lt. commdr. N.H. Govs. Mil. Staff. Pilot U.S. Naval Air Corp., lt. commdr. USNR, 1942-44. Recipient keys to cities of Dover, Somersworth, Concord, Berlin, Manchester and Rochester N.H., 6 nat. plaques DAV, 3 disting. svc. awards Am. Legion, Am. Legion Life Membership award, spl. recognition award Berwick Acad., 1985. Mem. ABA, N.H. Bar Assn., Strafford County Bar Assn. (v.p. 1966-67, pres. 1968-69), Assn. Trial Lawyers Am., N.Y. State Trial Lawyers Assn., Mass. Trial Lawyers Assn., N.H. Trial Lawyers Assn., Tex. Trial Lawyers Assn., Nat. Assn. Criminal Def. Lawyers, N.H. Assn. Criminal Def. Lawyers, Am. Judicature Soc., Phi Delta Phi, DAV (judge adv. N.H. dept. 1950-68, 72—; comdr. chpt. 1953-54, comdr. N.H. 1956-57), Am. Legion (life, chmn. state conv. 1967, 77, 84), Navy League, N.H. Hist. Soc., Dover Hist. Soc., Rollinsford Hist. Soc., Eagles Club, Sons of Italy, Lions, Elks, K.C. (grand knight 1975-77), Moose, Lebanese Club. Clubs: Eagles (Somersworth, N.H.), Sons of Italy (Portsmouth, N.H.). Lodges: Lions, Elks, K.C. (grand knight 1975-77), Moose, Lebanese (Dover). Criminal, General civil litigation, Family and matrimonial. Home: 20 Arch St Dover NH 03820-3602 Office: 450 Central Ave Dover NH 03820-3451

**CATANIA, FRANCIS JAMES,** lawyer, retired judge; b. Woodlyn, Pa., Mar. 26, 1920; s. James V. and Mary E. Catania; m. Elizabeth Frandsen, July 29, 1950; children: Francis Jr., Beth Anne Leighton, Nancy Gremminger, Mary Louise Esten, Chris Catania, Amy Kulper. Pre-law degree, Temple U., 1941, JD, 1949. Bar: Pa., U.S. Dist. Ct., U.S. Supreme Ct. Coroner Delaware County Coroner's Office, Media, Pa., 1958-62; dep. atty. gen. Pa. Dept. Revenue, Harrisburg, Pa., 1962-63; adminstrv. judge Ct. Common Pleas, Media, 1971-76, pres. judge, 1976-91; pres. Pa. Trial Judges State of Pa., Harrisburg, 1987-88; atty., of counsel Sprague and Sprague, Media; solicitor Sheriff of Delaware County, Media, 1951-55, Chester Township Eddystone Folcroft and Brookhaven Boroughs, 1951-63, contr. Delaward County, Media, 1957-61. Capt. U.S. Air Corps, 1943-45. Mem. ABA, Delaware County Bar Assn., Pa. Bar Assn. Office: Sprague & Sprague Ste 114 1400 N Providence Rd Media PA 19063-2043

**CATANZANO, RAYMOND AUGUSTINE,** lawyer; b. Bklyn., Sept. 16, 1946; s. Raymond E. and Ruth M. (Powers) C.; m. Lucille M. Rotondo, Mar. 29, 1970; children—Kimberly, Tara. BS, St. Johns U., 1968, JD, 1973; LLM, London Sch. Econs., 1985. Bar: N.Y. 1974, U.S. Dist. Ct. (ea. dist.) N.Y. 1974, U.S. Ct. Appeals (2d cir.) 1975, U.S. Supreme Ct. 1978. Prof. law Nassau Community Coll., Garden City, N.Y., 1973—; pvt. practice, Elmont, N.Y., 1974—. Dir. real estate studies Nassau Community Coll., 1981—; referee Med. Malpractice Panel Supreme Ct. N.Y., 1983; judge moot ct., 1984—; del. to U.S./Japan Bilateral Session: A New Era in Legal and Econ. Relations, 1988; bd. dirs. Nat. Coalition Family Justice, 1997; com. mem. Elmont North Rep. Club. Author: Student Course Mastery Guide, 1984. Recipient Holt Rinehart and Winston Honorarium award, 1979; named to Men of Achievement, Cambridge, Eng., 1986, Internat. Hall of Leaders, Cambridge, 1988. Mem. ABA, N.Y. State Bar Assn., Bar Assn. Nassau County, Am. Arbitration Assn. (arbitrator 1989-95). Roman Catholic. Contracts commercial, General corporate, Real property. Office: 220 Litchfield Ave Floral Park NY 11003-2718

**CATANZARO, MICHAEL A.,** lawyer, judge; b. Springfield, Ohio, Nov. 22, 1949; s. Anthony Joseph Catanzaro and Eva Lyle Merritt-Catanzaro; m. Catherine Catanzaro, Aug. 16, 1975 (div. Nov. 1988); m. Susanne Renee Copas, Feb. 26, 1992; children: Claire, Anne. BS, U. Dayton, 1972; postgrad., Ohio State U., 1972-73; JD cum laude, Capital U., 1976. Bar: Ohio, U.S. Dist. Ct. (we. dist.) Ohio, U.S. Supreme Ct. Asst. atty. gen. Ohio Atty. Gen., Columbus, Ohio, 1976-77, spl. counsel, 1977-95; practicing atty. Pavlatos, Catanzaro & Lancaster Co. LPA, Springfield, 1977—; acting judge Mcpl. Ct., Springfield, 1985—; mem. jud. corrections adv. bd. Multicounty Bd., Springfield, 1998. Mem. Ohio Trial Lawyers, Rotary, Masons, Order of Curia. Roman Catholic. General civil litigation, Construction, Family and matrimonial. Office: Pavlatos Catanzaro & Lancaster Co LPA 700 E High St Springfield OH 45505-1086

**CATE, FRED HARRISON,** law educator, lawyer; b. McRae, Ga., May 20, 1963; s. Robert L. and Dorothy W. (Wright) C.; m. Beth E. Orlowsky. AB, Stanford (Calif.) U., 1984, JD, 1987. Bar: Calif. 1987, U.S. Dist. Ct. Calif. 1987, U.S. Ct. Appeals (9th cirs.) 1987, D.C. 1988, D.C. Ct. Appeals 1998, Ind. 1998. Assoc. Debevoise & Plimpton, Washington, 1987-90; assoc. prof. Sch. of Law Ind. U., Bloomington, 1990-96, prof., 1996—; sr. fellow Annenberg Washington Program in Comm. Policy Studies, Washington, 1990-96; of counsel Fields & Dir., Washington, 1990-94; dir. Inst. on Info. and Comml. Law, Ind. U., 1997—; sr. counsel Ice, Miller, Donadio & Ryan, 1997—. Author: (with others) Death and Organ Donation, 1991, Privacy in the Information Age, 1997, The Internet and the First Amendment, 1998; faculty advisor Fed. Comm. Law Jour., 1993—; contbr. articles to profl. jours. Bd. dirs. Nat. History Day, 1989—. Mem. Phi Beta Kappa Assocs. Home: 2928 Olcott Blvd Bloomington IN 47401-2400 Office: Ind U School of Law 211 S Indiana Ave Bloomington IN 47405-7001

**CATHCART, ROBERT JAMES,** lawyer; b. Palo Alto, Calif., Sept. 28, 1945; s. Arthur James and Martelle Leeper Cathcart; m. Joan Anglin Kirkland, Mar. 29, 1969; children: Benjamin Patrick, Barbara Wynne, Kara Anglin. AB, Stanford U., 1968; JD, U. Wash., 1972. Bar: Calif. 1972, Wash. 1973, U.S. Dist. Ct. Calif. 1973, U.S. Ct. Appeals (9th cir.) 1973. Law clk. to Judge David Soukup, Superior Ct., Seattle, 1972-73; assoc. McCutchen, Doyle, Brown & Enersen, San Francisco, 1973-75; assoc., ptnr. Severson, Werson, Berke & Melchior, San Francisco, 1975-82; ptnr. Allen, Matkins, Leck, Gamble & Mallory, L.A., 1982—; adv. bd. Inst. Corp., L.A., 1996—; panelist EDUC panels CEB, 1990—; mem. State Bar Com. on AD Justice, L.A. and San Francisco, 1979-83; temp. judge L.A. Superior and Mcpl. Cts., 1982—. Mem. Assn. Bus. Trial Lawyers. Avocations: golf, swimming, hiking, sailing, reading. General civil litigation, Construction, Real property. Office: Allen Matkins Leck Et Al 515 S Figueroa St Fl 8 Los Angeles CA 90071-3301

**CATHELL, DALE ROBERTS,** judge; b. Berlin, Md., July 30, 1937; s. Dale Parsons Cathell and Charlotte Robert (Hocker) Terrell; m. Charlotte M. Keabin; children: Kelly Ann, Dale Kerbin, William Howard. Student, U. Md., 1962-64; LLB, U. Balt., 1967; cert., Nat. Jud. Coll., 1983. Bar: Md. 1967. Atty. City of Ocean City, Md., 1970-76; assoc. judge Md. Dist. Ct., Worcester County, 1980-81; judge Md. Cir. Ct., Worchester City, 1981-89, Ct. Spl. Appeals, 1st Appellate Cir., 1989—; mem. family and domestic rels. law com. Md. Jud. Conf., 1995-97, past mem. exec. com.; instr. WOR-WIC C.C., 1973, Salisbury State U., 1978. Mem. Pub. Service Commn. Adv. Panel, Md., 1970, charity revision com. Mayor City Council, Ocean City, 1970; mem. Worchester County Shoreline Com., Md., 1971; mem. charter revision com. City of Ocean City, 1973, mem. utility consumer adv. panel, 1978; creator Alt. Com. Service Program, Md., 1980—; organizer Legal Intern Program Pub. Schs., Worchester County, 1981—. Served with USAF, 1955-59. Mem. Md. Bar Assn. (jud. appointment com. 1970), Worchester County Bar Assn. (pres. 1970), Balt. City Bar Assn. Democrat. Episcopalian. Office: Ct Appeals Md Robert C Murphy Cts Apl Bld 361 Rowe Blvd Annapolis MD 21401*

**CATHERWOOD, KATHRYN M.S.,** lawyer; b. Madison, Wis., July 14, 1959; d. Vernon Charles and Gertrude (Mueller) Struck; m. Daryl Frederick Catherwood, June 8, 1991; chldren: Caitlin Nicole, Ian Frederick. BS in Zoology, U. Wis., 1979, BSN, 1982, JD, 1990. Bar: Wis. 1990, Calif. 1990, U.S. Dist. Ct. (all dists.) Calif., U.S. Ct. Appeals (9th cir.); RN. Nurse Kapiolani Women's and Children's Med. Ctr., Honolulu, 1982-87; atty. Luce Forward Hamilton & Scripps LLP, San Diego, 1990—; bd. dirs., pres. Women's Insolvency Network, San Diego, 1994-98; bd. dirs., officer San Diego Bankruptcy Forum, 1997—; bd. dirs. Calif. Bankruptcy Forum, 1998—. Bd. dirs. Share a Vision Found., San Diego, 1995—. Recipient Wiley W. Manuel award for pro bono legal svcs., 1993, 94. Mem. Receivers Forum, Coronado Yacht Club. Avocations: travel, music, gardening, cooking. E-mail: kcatherwood@luce.com. Bankruptcy, Consumer commercial, Contracts commercial. Office: Luce Forward et al 600 W Broadway Ste 2600 San Diego CA 92101-3311

**CATHEY, M. ELIZABETH,** lawyer; b. Syracuse, N.Y., Dec. 19, 1946; d. Phil Franklin Blub and Helen Marie (Yarwood) Drew; children: Denise Anne Beving Richtmeier, Cynthia Marie Beving; m. Robert Heaton Cathey, July 21, 1988. BA cum laude (Nat. Merit scholar), U. No. Iowa, 1973; postgrad., Schoitz Hosop. Sch. Med. Tech., 1973-74; JD (rsch. scholar), Washburn U., 1981. Bar: Kans., 1981, U.S. Dist. Ct. Kans. 1981. Quality supr. U.S. Gypsum Co., Ft. Dodge, Iowa, 1974-75; employment supr., 1975-77; realtor assoc. Toothaker Real Estate Agy., Manhattan, 1978-79; law clk. Kans. Corp. Commn., Topeka, 1980-81; pvt. practice law Manhattan, Kans., 1981-83; mgr. pres. K-State Union, Manhattan, Kans., 1983-89; atty. Myers & Pottroff, Manhattan, Kans., 1983-89; civilian atty. U.S. Army, Ft. Riley, Kans., 1989-92; trust officer 1st Manhattan Trust Co., 1993; v.p. Trust Co. of Manhattan, 1993-94; adminstr. Advanced Dermatology P.A., 1994-98; ret., 1998; asst. counselor Riley County, Kans., 1983-89; mem. univ. staff devel. task force, 1981-83, mem. univ. appeal and rev. com., 1982-83. Active LWV, 1977-80; mem. adv. bd. 4-H Club, 1981-84, chmn., 1983-84; solicitor United Way, 1981, 82, bd. dirs., 1984-89, v.p., 1987, pres., 1988, allocations chair, 1986, 87; mem. Local Fed. Coordinating Com., 1990-92; solicitor Cancer Crusade, 1975; active with Leadership Kans., 1994. Mem. ABA (sec. on corps., bus., banking, real property, probate, trust, taxation, econs.), Kans. Bar Assn. (coms. on legal malpractice prevention, continuing legal edn., sects. on corp., bus., banking, real estate, probate, trust, tax), Riley County Bar Assn. (chmn. Law Day 1984, pres. 1987), Am. Trial Lawyers Assn., Kans. Trial Lawyers Assn., North Ctrl. Iowa Pers. Assn. (sec. 1976-77), Manhattan Pers. Assn., Bus. and Profl. Women, Washburn Women's Legal Forum (v.p. and pres. 1979-80), Manhattan C. of C. (various coms., Leadership award 1983), Manhattan Arts Coun., Am. Legion Aux., Phi Delta Phi. Republican. Methodist. Home: 203 Bobcat Bend San Antonio TX 78231-1437

**CATINA, JANET K.,** lawyer; b. East Stroudsburg, Pa., Apr. 7, 1962; d. James R. and Helen J. Marsh; m. Gerard W. Catina, Dec. 24, 1992; children: James J., Kathryn F. BA in Polit. Sci. and Acctg., Muhlenberg Coll., 1984; JD, Dickinson U., 1987. Bar: Pa. 1987, U.S. Dist. Ct. (mid. dist.) Pa. 1989, U.S. Ct. Appeals (3rd cir.) 1989, U.S. Dist. Ct. (ea. dist.) Pa. 1994, U.S. Supreme Ct. 1998. Assoc. James F. Marsh Law Offices, Stroudsburg, 1987-88; asst. dist. atty. Monroe County, Stroudsburg, 1988-90; assoc. Hanna, Young, Upright & Pazuhanich, Stroudsburg, 1988-94; ptnr. Hanna, Young, Upright & Catina, Stroudsburg, 1995—; solicitor Paradise Twp. Planning Commn., Cresco, Pa., 1991-93. V.p. Am. Heart Assn., 1992-94, bd. dirs. Monroe County div.; chmn. daffodil days Am. Cancer Soc., 1993-94, bd. dirs. Monroe unit, 1994-95, chmn. spkrs. bur., 1996—; chmn. profl. div. United Way Monroe County, 1998—; tchr. Sunday sch. Christ Hamilton United Luth. Ch.; youth soccer coach YMCA. Mem. ATLA, NACDL, Pa. Bar Assn., Pa. Trial Lawyers Assn., Monroe County Bar Assn., Pocono Mountains C. of C. (chair legis. com. 1997-99, chair employment com. 1999—, bd. dirs.), Pi Sigma Alpha, Omicron Delta Epsilon. Federal civil litigation, State civil litigation, Criminal. Office: Hanna Young Upright & Catina LLP 800 Main St Stroudsburg PA 18360-1602

**CATLIN, CATHERINE M.,** lawyer; b. Coral Gables, Fla., July 3, 1961; d. H. James and Betty (Mershon) C. BA, U. Miami, 1982, JD cum laude, 1987. Bar: Fla. 1987, U.S. Dist. (mid. dist.) Fla. 1988. Assoc. Catlin, Saxon, Tuttle and Evans, P.A., Miami, Fla., 1987-88, Muga & Real, P.A., Tampa, Fla., 1988-89, Garcia & Fields, P.A., Tampa, 1989-90; shareholder Langford, Hill, Trybus & Whalen, P.A., Tampa, 1990—; lectr. on family law topics for C.L.E. credits. Contbr. articles to legal jours. Mem. ABA, Fla. Bar Assn., Hillsborough County Bar Assn. (exec. coun. family law sect.). Democrat. Baptist. Avocations: weightlifting, movies, bowling, all kinds of sporting events. Family and matrimonial. Office: Langford Hill Trybus & Whalen PA 316 S Macdill Ave Tampa FL 33609-3142

**CATRON, STEPHEN BARNARD,** lawyer; b. Bowling Green, Ky., Feb. 4, 1949; s. Eugene and Gladys (Bell) C.; m. Deborah Faye Grigsby, Nov. 28, 1981. BA, Western Ky. U., Bowling Green, 1971; JD, U. Miss., 1974. Bar: Ky. 1974, Miss. 1974, Tenn. 1988, U.S. Dist. Ct. (we. dist.) Ky, 1974, U.S. Dist. Ct. (no. dist.) Miss. 1974, U.S. Ct. Appeals (6th cir.) 1983. Atty. Ky. Dept. Human Resources, Bowling Green, Ky., 1974-75; atty., ptnr. Reynolds, Catron, Johnson & Hinton, Bowling Green, Ky., 1975, Lewis, King, Krieg, Waldrop and Catron, P.C., Bowling Green, Ky., 1975—; pres. Bowling Green-Warren County Bar, 1989-90; chair., bd. trustees Ky. IOLTA Fund, Frankfort, Ky., 1990-94; bd. trustees Ky. Bar Found., Frankfort, Ky., 1990-94; bd. dirs. Nat. Assn. IOLTA Programs, Chgo., 1991-92. Author: Kentucky Corporations Law, 1989. Bd. dirs. Bowling Green (Ky.) Human Rights Commn., 1976-78; vice chair Ky. Ednl. TV Auth., Lexington, Ky., 1988-92; bd. regents Western Ky. U., Bowling Green., 1991-92; chairperson Bowling Green-Warren County Indsl. Authority; trustee Western Ky. U. Found. Fellow Am. Bar Found.; mem. Rotary Club, Bowling Green C. of C. Democrat. Presbyterian. Avocations: reading, jogging, golf, computers. E-mail: scatron@lkkwc.com. Banking, Contracts commercial, General corporate. Home: 146 Ridgewood Dr Bowling Green KY 42103-1331 Office: Lewis King Krieg Waldrop and Catron PC PO Box 1220 Bowling Green KY 42102-1220

**CATTANI, MARYELLEN B.,** lawyer; b. Bakersfield, Calif., Dec. 1, 1943; d. Arnold Theodore and Corinne Marilyn (Kovacevich) C.; m. Frank C. Herringer; children: Sarah, Julia. AB, Vassar Coll., Poughkeepsie, N.Y., 1965; JD, U. Calif. (Boalt Hall), 1968. Assoc. Davis Polk & Wardwell, N.Y.C., 1968-69; assoc. Orrick, Herrington & Sutcliffe, San Francisco, 1970-74, ptnr., 1975-81; v.p., gen. counsel Transamerica Corp., San Francisco, 1981-83, sr. v.p., gen. counsel, 1983-89; ptnr. Morrison & Foerster, San Francisco, 1989-91; sr. v.p. gen. counsel APL Ltd., Oakland, Calif., 1991-95, exec. v.p., gen. counsel, 1995-97; bd. dirs. Golden West Fin. Corp., World Savs. & Loan Assn., ABM Industries Inc. Author: Calif. Corp. Practice Guide, 1977, Corp. Counselors, 1982. Regent St. Mary's Coll., Morega, Calif., 1986—, pres., 1990-92, trustee, 1990-99, chmn., 1993-95; trustee Vassar Coll., 1985-93, The Head-Royce Sch., 1993—, Mills Coll., 1999—, The Benilde Religious & Charitable Trust, 1999—, Alameda County Med. Ctr. Hosp. Authority, 1998—; bd. dirs. The Exploratorium, 1988-93. Mem. ABA, State Bar Calif. (chmn. bus. law sect. 1980-81), Bar Assn. San Francisco (co-chair com. on women 1989-91), Calif. Women Lawyers, San Francisco C. of C. (bd. dirs. 1987-91, gen. counsel 1990-91), Am. Corp. Counsel Assn. (bd. dirs. 1982-87), Women's Forum West (bd. dirs. 1984-87). Democrat. Roman Catholic. Club: Women's Forum West. General corporate, Securities, Mergers and acquisitions.

**CAULFIELD, SHARON ELIZABETH,** lawyer; b. Santa Rosa, Calif., Jan. 16, 1956; d. Edward Nelson Caulfield and Alicelee (Freeman) Ewan; m. Edmund Daniel Andrews, Dec 28, 1976; children: Daniel Graham, Caroline Elizabeth. Student, U. Calif., Berkeley, 1974-76; BA in Anthropology, U. Colo., 1979, JD, 1982. Bar: Colo. 1982, U.S. Dist. Ct. Colo. 1982, U.S. Ct. Appeals (10th cir.) 1982. Legal writing instr. U. Colo. Sch. Law, Boulder, 1981-82; assoc. Davis Graham & Stubbs, Denver, 1982-88, ptnr., 1988-93, practice leader health care group, 1991-93; mem. Caplan & Earnest, L.L.C., Boulder, 1993—. Mem. Leadership Denver, 1989. Mem. ABA, Am. Health Lawyers Assn., Healthcare Fin. Mgmt. Assn., Colo. Bar Assn., Denver Bar Assn., Colo. U. Boulder Alumni Assn. (pres. 1991-92, bd. dirs. 1985-93). Democrat. Episcopalian. Avocations: mountaineering, traveling, cooking. Labor, Health. Office: Caplan & Earnest 2595 Canyon Blvd Ste 400 Boulder CO 80302-6737

**CAULK, GLEN PAUL,** lawyer, associate; b. Columbia, S.C., Nov. 29, 1966; s. Robert Glen Caulk and Ila Miles Morris; m. Carol Lea Caulk, Mar. 7, 1998; 1 child, Devin. BS, U. S.C., 1989, JD, 1994. Bar: S.C. 1995, U.S. Dist. Ct. S.C. 1995. Br. mgr. C & S Nat. Bank, Columbia, 1989-92; comml. loan officer Nationsbank, Columbia, 1992; atty. Rogers Towensend & Thomas, Columbia, 1994—. Chmn. Family Friends of Scouting, cubmaster, Boy Scouts Am., Columbia, 1998; vol. Salvation Army, Lexington, S.C., 1998; active First Bapt. Ch. Mem. S.C. Homebuilders Assn., S.C. Mortgage Bankers Assn., Rotary. Contracts commercial, Real property, Land use and zoning (including planning). Office: Rogers Townsend & Thomas PO Box 1 Columbia SC 29202-0001

**CAULKINS, CHARLES S.,** lawyer; b. Great Bend, Kans., Sept. 22, 1949; s. Daniel P. Caulkins and Martha Taylor; m. Kelley D. Harris, Nov. 27, 1973; children: Kipp, Sloane, Sydney. BA, Monmouth Coll., 1971; JD, Creighton U., 1976; LLM in Labor Law, NYU, 1977. Bar: Kans. 1977, S.C. 1978, U.S. Dist. Ct. S.C. 1978, U.S. Ct. Appeals (4th and 10th cirs.) 1979, Fla. 1985, U.S. Dist. Ct. (so. dist.) Fla. 1985, U.S. Ct. Appeals (11th cir.) 1985, U.S. Supreme Ct. 1985. Ptnr. Thompson, Mann & Hutson, Greenville, S.C., 1977-84; mng. ptnr. Fisher & Phillips, Ft. Lauderdale, Fla., 1984—. Author: Florida Bar Journal, 1991. Labor, Pension, profit-sharing, and employee benefits, Immigration, naturalization, and customs. Office: Fisher & Phillips 1 Financial Plz Ste 2300 Fort Lauderdale FL 33394-0001

**CAUMMISAR, ROBERT LEE,** lawyer; b. Louisville, Mar. 5, 1939; s. Frank T. C. Jr.; m. Laura Lee Koellner, June 6, 1964; children: June, Jeanne, Robert M. BA in History, Bellarmine-Ursuline Coll., Louisville, 1964; JD, U. Ky., 1967. Exec. dir. N.E. Ky. Legal Svcs., Inc., Grayson, 1967-70, 72-75; exec. dir. Citizens Commn. on Consumer Protection, Frankfort, Ky., 1970-72; pvt. practice Grayson, 1975—; mem. Atty. Gen. Consumer Adv. Coun., Frankfort, 1993—;. Bd. dirs. Pathways, Inc., Ashland, Ky. (pres. 1987-89, 97-99); corp. sec. Grayson Area C. of C., 1987—. Mem. Ky. Bar Assn., Carter County Bar Assn. (sec.-treas. 1978—). Democrat. Roman Catholic. General practice, Family and matrimonial, Consumer commercial. Home: 121 Jane Ln Grayson KY 41143-7167 Office: 301 W Main St Grayson KY 41143-1246

**CAUTHRON, ROBIN J.,** federal judge; b. Edmond, Okla., July 14, 1950; d. Austin W. and Mary Louise (Adamson) Johnson. BA, U. Okla., 1970, JD, 1977; MEd, Cen. State U., Edmond, Okla., 1974. Bar: Okla. 1977. Law clk to Hon. Ralph G. Thompson U.S. Dist. Ct. (we. dist.) Okla., 1977-81; staff atty. Legal Svcs. Ea. Okla., 1981-82; pvt. practice law, 1982-83; spl. judge 17th Jud. Dist. State Okla., 1983-86; magistrate U.S. Dist. Ct. (we. dist.) Okla., Oklahoma City, 1986-91, judge, 1991—. Editor Okla. Law Rev. Bd. dirs. Juvenile Diabetes Found. Internat., 1989—; mem. nominating com. Frontier Coun. Boy Scouts Am., 1987, Edmond Ednl. Endowment; trustee, sec. First United Meth. Ch., 1988-90. Mem. ABA, Okla. Bar Assn. (vice chmn. 1990), Okla. County Bar Assn. (bd. dirs. 1990— bench and bar com.), McCurtain County Bar Assn. (pres. 1986), Am. Judicature Soc., Nat. Assn. Women Judges, Fed. Bar Assn., Okla Assn. Women Lawyers, Nat. Coun. Women Magistrates (bd. dirs. 1990-91), Okla. Jud. Conf. (v.p. 1985), Am. Inns of Ct. (pres. elect 1990-91), Order of Coif, Phi Delta Phi. Office: US Courthouse 200 NW 4th St Ste 3108 Oklahoma City OK 73102-3029

**CAVALARIS, NICHOLAS CURTIS,** lawyer; b. Phila., Oct. 14, 1966; s. Constantine John and Lynda (Curtis) C. BA, Miami U., Oxford, Ohio, 1988; JD, Loyola U., Chgo., 1993. Asst. city prosecutor City Atty.'s Office, Columbus, Ohio, 1994-95; assoc. atty. Lane, Alton & Horst, Columbus, 1996-98, Schottenstein, Zox & Dunn, Columbus, 1998—; lectr. Ohio Mcpl. League, Columbus, 1998—. Serves with USN, 1984-85. General civil litigation. Home: 1481 Westwood Ave Columbus OH 43212-2768 Office: Schottenstein Zox & Dunn 41 S High St Columbus OH 43215-6101

**CAVALIERE, FRANK JOSEPH,** lawyer, educator; b. N.Y.C., Dec. 29, 1949; s. Alfred and Margaret Joan Cavaliere. BA in Econs., Bklyn. Coll., 1970; BBA in Acctg., Lamar U., 1976; JD, U. Tex., 1979. Bar: Tex. 1979. Atty. Coke & Coke, Dallas, 1979-81, Weller, Wheelus & Green, Beaumont, Tex., 1981-84; pvt. practice law Beaumont, 1985—; from asst. to full prof. bus. law Lamar U., Beaumont, 1985—; editl. adv. bd. mem. CPA Internet Connection, Harcourt Brace Co., 1997—; tech. advisor Am. Law Inst.-ABA, 1998—. Author (column) Web-Wise Lawyer, The Practical Lawyer, 1996—; contbr. articles to profl. jours. Advisor Pi Kappa Alpha Fraternity, Beaumont, 1987-90, Delta Sigma Pi Fraternity, Beaumont, 1994-97. Lt. USNR, 1970-75. Mem. ABA, Tex. Bar Assn., Coll. of the State Bar Tex., Jefferson County Bar Assn., Phi Beta Kappa. Estate planning, Computer, General corporate. Office: 148 S Dowlen Rd # 683 Beaumont TX 77707-1755

**CAVALLINI, DONNA FRANCESCA,** law librarian; b. St. Louis, Nov. 3, 1962; d. Giovanni Iader and Yolanda Marie (Boveri) Cavallini; m. Jeffrey Alan Mills, Jan. 13, 1986 (div. Nov. 1991). BA, Washington U., St. Louis, 1983; JD, St. Louis U., 1990. Ref. libr. Huey, Guilday, Kuersteiner & Tucker, P.A., Tallahassee, 1988-91; libr. program adminstr. Office of the Atty. Gen., Tallahassee, 1991-96; ref. libr. Kilpatrick Stockton, LLP, Atlanta, 1996—. Fla. State Ct. and County Law Librs. scholar, 1992; recipient Davis Productivity award Fla. Taxwatch Inc., 1994. Mem. Am. Assn. Law Librs., Tallahassee Assn. Law Librs. (acting pres. 1993-96). Home: 446 Cumberland Sq SE Smyrna GA 30080-7758

**CAVALLO, FRANK P., JR.,** lawyer; b. Camden, N.J., Dec. 26, 1960; s. Frank P. Cavallo Sr. and Pearl A. Buxton; m. Donna M. Remick, May 22, 1985; children: Christina M., Giana M. BA in Polit. Sci., Widener U., 1983; JD, Rutgers U., 1986. Bar: N.J. 1986, Pa. 1986. Law clk. Camden, N.J., 1986-87; assoc. Parker, McCay & Criscoulo, Marlton, N.J., 1987-89; of counsel Parker, McCay & Criscoulo, Marlton, 1995—; assoc. Slimm, Dash & Goldborg, Westmont, N.J., 1989-91, Jacobs, Bruso & Barbone, Atlantic City, N.J., 1991-92; pvt. practice Moorestown, N.J., 1992-95. Me. Camden County Bar Assn., Burlington County Bar Assn., Winslow Twp. Rep. Club. Republican. Roman Catholic. Education and schools, Municipal (including bonds), Criminal. Office: Parker McCay & Criscoulo 3 Greentree Ctr Ste 401 Marlton NJ 08053-3292

**CAVANAGH, ELIZABETH ANNE,** lawyer; b. Bklyn., May 21, 1970; d. John Thomas and Maureen Lillian (Mallon) C.; m. Jon Sharp Wilkins, Jr., Dec. 17, 1994. BA summa cum laude, Dartmouth Coll., 1992; JD, Yale U., 1995. Bar: Md. 1998, D.C. 1998. Jud. law clk. U.S. Dist. Ct., Washington, 1995-96; assoc. Jenner & Block, Washington, 1996-97, 98—; jud. law clk. U.S. Supreme Ct., Washington, 1997-98.

**CAVANAGH, MICHAEL FRANCIS,** state supreme court justice; b. Detroit, Oct. 21, 1940; s. Sylvester J. and Mary Irene (Timmins) C.; m. Patricia E. Ferriss, Apr. 30, 1966; children: Jane Elizabeth, Michael F., Megan Kathleen. BA, U. Detroit, 1962, JD, 1966. Bar: Mich. 1966. Law clk. to judge Ct. Appeals, Detroit, 1966-67; atty. City of Lansing, Mich., 1967-69; ptnr. Farhat, Story, et al., Lansing, Mich., 1969-73; judge 54-A Dist. Ct., Lansing, 1973-75, Mich. Ct. Appeals, Lansing, 1975-82; justice Supreme Ct., Lansing, 1983—, chief justice, 1991-94; Supreme Ct. liaison Mich. Indian Tribal Cts./Mich. State Cts.; supervising justice Sentencing Guidelines Com., Lansing, 1983-94, Mich. Jud. Inst., Lansing, 1986-94; bd. dirs. Thomas M. Cooley Law Sch., 1979-88; chair Mich. Justice Project, 1994-95, Nat. Interbranch Conf., Mpls., 1994-95. Bd. dirs. Am. Heart Assn. Mich., 1982—, chmn. bd. Am. Heart Assn. Mich., Lathrup Village, 1984-85; bd. dirs. YMCA, Lansing, 1978. Mem. ABA, Fed. Bar Assn., Ingham County Bar Assn., Inst. Jud. Adminstrn. (hon.), Inc. Soc. of Irish/Am. Lawyers (pres. 1987-88). Democrat. Roman Catholic. Avocations: jogging, racquetball, fishing. Office: Mich Supreme Ct 525 W Ottawa St Lansing MI 48933-1067

**CAVANAUGH, JOHN JOSEPH, JR.,** lawyer; b. Albany, N.Y., June 14, 1936; s. John J. Sr. and Jane A. (McKeon) C.; m. Judith A. Myers, Sept. 5, 1964. BA cum laude, Siena Coll., 1958; JD, Albany U., 1961. Bar: N.Y. 1961, U.S. Dist. Ct. (no. dist.) N.Y. 1961, U.S. Supreme Ct. 1967. Assoc.

Donohue & Bohl, Albany, 1961-64, Arthur J. Harvey, Albany, 1964-67; pvt. practice Albany, 1967—; ind. counsel Rosenblum & Sarachan, Albany, 1978-87. Assoc. editor Albany Law Rev., 1961. Cpl. U.S. Army, 1956-63. Mem. N.Y. State Bar Assn., Albany County Bar Assn., Capital Dist. Trial Lawyers Assn., Am. Arbitration Assn. (arbitrator), Am. Legion, K.C. Avocations: reading, tennis, travel, coin collector. Family and matrimonial, General practice, Personal injury. Home: 135 Homestead Ave Albany NY 12203-1937 Office: 264 Delaware Ave Delmar NY 12054-1123

**CAVANAUGH, MICHAEL EVERETT,** lawyer, arbitrator, mediator; b. Seattle, Dec. 23, 1946; s. Wilbur R. Cavanaugh and Gladys E. (Herring) Barber; m. Susan P. Heckman, Sept. 7, 1968. AB, U. Calif., Berkeley, 1973; JD, U. Wash., 1976. Bar: Wash. 1976, U.S. Dist. Ct. (we. dist.) Wash. 1977, U.S. Ct. Appeals (9th cir.) 1977, U.S. Dist. Ct. (ea. dist.) Wash. 1978. Staff atty. U.S. Ct. of Appeals (9th crct.) Calif., San Francisco, 1976-77; from assoc. to ptnr. Preston & Thorgrimson, Seattle, 1981-85; ptnr. Bogle & Gates, Seattle, 1985-97, assoc., 1977-81, ptnr., 1985-97; propr. Michael E. Cavanaugh, J.D., Arbitration and Mediation, Seattle, 1997—. Contbg. author: Employment Discrimination Law, 3d edit., 1995. Avocations: sailing, creative writing, music. Labor, Alternative dispute resolution. Office: 1420 5th Ave Ste 2200 Seattle WA 98101-1346

**CAVENAGH, TIMOTHY JOSEPH,** lawyer; b. Oak Park, Ill., Feb. 19, 1959; s. John Baird and Madeline (Kessler) C.; m. Janet Marie Schmitz; children: Timothy Jr., Catherine, Margaret, John. BA, U. Ill., 1983; JD, DePaul U., 1986. Bar: Ill. 1986, U.S. Dist. Ct. (no. dist.) Ill. 1986, U.S. Ct. Appeals (7th cir.) 1987, U.S. Supreme Ct. 1989. Asst. atty. gen. Ill. Atty Gen.'s Office, Chgo., 1986-89; staff counsel Traveler's Ins. Co., Chgo., 1989-92, Hartford Ins. Co., Chgo., 1992-96; pvt. practice Chgo., 1996—. Mem. ATLA, Ill. Trial Lawyers Assn. Personal injury, Product liability, Professional liability. Office: 77 W Washington St Ste 1313 Chicago IL 60602-2901

**CAVIN, CLARK,** lawyer; b. Bunch, Okla., Aug. 17, 1939; s. Champ Clark and Ruby Madeline (Mitchell) c. BA, U. Wash., 1961; postgrad., U. Calif., Irvine, 1972-73; JD, U. Calif., San Francisco, 1976. Bar: Calif. 1976, Wash. 1977, U.S. Dist. Ct. (no. dist.) Calif. 1976, U.S. Dist. Ct. (we. dist.) Wash. 1977. Pvt. practice Seattle, 1977—; magistrate pro tem. Mpcl. Ct., Seattle, 1981, judge pro tem., 1987-91. With USMC, 1961-72. Mem. Tchrs. Assn. Can., Royal Scottish Country Dance Soc. (Seattle br., cert. tchr.). Avocations: fiddling, geneology. Estate planning, General practice, Probate. Office: 4800 Stone Way N Seattle WA 98103-6740

**CAVIN, KRISTINE SMITH,** lawyer; b. Decatur, Ga., Mar. 26, 1969; d. Richard Theodore and Sherri (Nash) Smith; m. James Michael Cavin, May 13, 1995. BA, Furman U., 1991; JD, Calif. Western Sch. Law, 1995. Bar: Ga. 1995. Legal asst. Smith & Jenkins, P.C., Atlanta, 1991-92; intern child abuse and domestic violence unit San Diego City Atty.'s Office, 1995; assoc. Smith, Ronick & Corbin, L.L.C., Atlanta, 1995—. Mem. ABA, Nat. Assn. Women Lawyers, Assn. Profl. Mortgage Women, Mortgage Bankers Assn. (assoc.), Ga. Bar Assn., Ga. Assn. for Women Lawyers, Ga. Real Estate Closing Attys. Assn. (sec. 1997—), Atlanta Bar Assn. Avocations: gourmet cooking, wine, gardening. Real property, General practice. Office: Smith Ronick & Corbin LLC 750 Hammond Dr NE Bldg 11 Atlanta GA 30328-5532

**CAWLEY, JOHN ARNOLD, JR.,** lawyer; b. Elkhart, Ind., July 14, 1943; s. John Arnold Cawley and Willa Reiber (Mueller) Compton; m. Janis M. Edson, June 12, 1971 (div. Apr. 1980); 1 child, John Arnold III; m. Janet D. Ianello, Aug. 14, 1982 (div. Dec. 1993). AB, Duke U., 1965; JD, Ind. U., 1968. Bar: Ind. 1968, U.S. Dist. Ct. (no. and so. dists.) Ind. 1968. Assoc. Church, Meteiver & Weaver, Elkhart, 1968-71; trust officer Midwest Commerce Banking Co., Elkhart, 1971-72; pvt. practice law Elkhart, 1973-75, 79—; ptnr. Virgil, Cawley & Platt, 1976-78. Bd. dirs., past pres. United Cancer Svcs.; bd. dirs. past pres. Elkhart Symphony Soc. Mem. Elkhart Golf Assn (bd. dirs., pres.), Elks (trustee, past chmn. Elkhart, Elk of Yr. 1988). General corporate, Probate, Real property. Office: PO Box 2646 Elkhart IN 46515-2646

**CAYEA, DONALD JOSEPH,** lawyer; b. Bklyn., Mar. 3, 1948; s. Glendon Vernon and Marie Nicola (Gesualdo) C.; m. Elizabeth Mary Peck, Jan. 27, 1973 (div. Sept. 1975); m. Yvonne Karen Kemeny, Sept. 11, 1983 (div. Sept. 1989). BA, L.I. U., 1969; JD, Western New Eng. Coll., 1975. Bar: N.Y. 1976, U.S. Dist. Ct. (so. and ea. dists.) N.Y. 1978, D.C. 1979, U.S. Supreme Ct. 1979. Prin. Donald J. Cayea & Assoc., N.Y.C., 1976—; ptnr. Kroll & Tract, N.Y.C., 1988-90, Levitan, Frieland & Cayea, N.Y.C., 1990-94, Klepner & Cayea, N.Y.C., 1994-98, Brand, Cayea & Brand, LLC, N.Y.C., 1998—, Brand, Cayea & Brand LLC, 1998—; gen. counsel Entertainment USA, 1990—; lectr. Paralegal Inst., NYU, 1984—, adult edn. program Nassau County Bar Assn., Mineola, N.Y., 1978-79; panelist trial advocacy program Cardozo Law Sch., Yeshiva U., N.Y.C., 1984—; spkr. Ft. Lauderdale (Fla.) Film Festival, 1989, 90, Coun. on Mgmt. Worker's Compensation Update, N.Y.C., 1995, 96; guest panelist Property Loss Rsch. Bur., Washington, 1989, Chgo., 1991; spkr. coun. edn. mgmt., N.Y.C., 1995. Prodr.: (video) Dahmer, the Secret Life, 1993, (off Broadway) West Side Stories, Theatre Airelle, N.Y.C., 1993, Conversations with My Daughter; exec. prodr. (film) The Hunt for CM24; assoc. prodr. (film) Prague Duet; prodr. (theatre) The Remarkable Thing About Star Dust. Pres. Seascape Condominium, Westhampton Beach, N.Y., 1986-92; sponsor Richmond Roller Hocker Assn., Staten Island, N.Y., 1984-89; mem. Pres.'s Coun., L.I. Univ. Served in U.S. Army, 1970-71. Mem. ABA (editor TIPS publ. editorial bd. 1990-93), Assn. Trial Lawyers Am., N.Y. State Bar Assn., Internat. Bar Assn., Assn. of Bar of City of N.Y., New York County Lawyers Assn., Phi Epsilon Pi. Federal civil litigation, Insurance, Libel. Office: 720 5th Ave Fl 14 New York NY 10019-4107

**CAYLEY, SUSAN NICOLE,** lawyer; b. Ozark, Ala.. BS in Polit. Sci., UCLA, 1990; JD, Loyola U., L.A., 1993. Bar: Calif. 1993. Assoc. Brobeck, Phleger & Harrison, Newport Beach, Calif., 1993-97; gen. counsel Xylan Corp., Calabasas, Calif., 1997-98; v.p., gen. counsel ACT Networks, Inc., Camarillo, Calif., 1998—. Securities, Mergers and acquisitions, Finance. Office: ACT Networks 188 Camino Ruiz Camarillo CA 93012-6700

**CAYLOR, JOHN WILL,** lawyer, prosecutor; b. Knoxville, Tenn., Oct. 3, 1941; s. Glen Edison and Martha Ellen C.; m. Mary Jane Smith, Nov. 17, 1966; 1 child, Anastasia. BS, Athens Coll., 1966; JD, Samford U., 1970. Bar: Ala., 1976. From uniformed patrol officer to detective Police Dept., Huntsville, Ala., 1963-67; juvenile probation and parole officer 23d Circuit Ct., Huntsville, 1968 summer; exec. asst. to commn., acting chief examiner Ala. Securites Commn., Montgomery; chief courts planner Ala. Law Enforcement Planning (gov.'s office), Montgomery; chief planner Ala. Atty. Gen.'s Office, Montgomery; chief adminstr. legis. act No. 488 23rd Judicial Circuit Ct., Huntsville, Ala., 1976-78; lawyer Atty. Gen.'s Office, Huntsville, Ala., 1991-95; dep. atty. gen. Atty. Gen.'s Office, Huntsville, 1995—; instr. N.E. Ala. C.C., Rainsville; instr. Troy State U., Montgomery, Athens State Coll., U. Ala., Huntsville. Author: (monograph) Police Immunity and Liability, 1988; co-author Courts Master Plan, State of Ala., 1974. With USAF. Mem. ABA, ATLA, Huntsville-Madison County Bar Assn., Fraternal Order of Police, Phi Alpha Delta. Democrat. Baptist. Home: 2345 County Road 67 Scottsboro AL 35769-3015 Office: NE Ala CC PO Box 159 Rainsville AL 35986-0159

**CAYTAS, IVO GEORGE,** lawyer; b. Plovdiv, Bulgaria, Feb. 3, 1958; s. George I. and Hilda (Plankl) Kaitasow. MA in Diplomacy, U. St Gallen, Switzerland, 1982, PhD in Law, 1984, PhD in Fin., 1986; LLM, Yale U., 1986. Bar: D.C. 1997, U.S. Ct. Internat. Trade, U.S. Claims Ct., U.S. Tax Ct., U.S. Dist. Ct. (so. and ea. dists.) N.Y. 1992, (no. and ctrl. dists.) Calif. 1992, U.S. Ct. Appeals (1st-11th cirs., fed. and D.C. cir.), U.S. Supreme Ct. 1996. Asst. to chmn. IMAG Corp., Vienna, Austria, 1979-80; ptnr. Caytas & Cie, St. Gallen, 1984-89, CCCC, St. Gallen, 1989-91; mng. dir. Swissconsult Corp., N.Y.C., 1990-91; pres., gen. counsel Swiss Am. Group Inc., N.Y.C., 1991-95; ptnr. Caytas & Assocs., 1996—; bd. dirs. The London Ct. of Internat. Abritration. Author: Investment Banking, 1988, Global Political Risk, Modern Financial Instruments, 1992, Transnational Legal Practice, 1992; contbr. articles to profl. publs. Fellow Swiss Nat. Sci. Found., 1985, 88, Max Planck Inst., 1987; recipient Walther-Hug Found. award, 1984. Mem. ABA (sect. of internat. law and practice, internat. investment com., internat. taxation com.), Assn. of Bar of City of N.Y. (com. on govt. ethics), Calif. Bar Assn. (internat. law com., task force on internat. legal svcs.), Yale Club. Roman Catholic. Banking, Finance, Securities. Office: 146 W 57th St New York NY 10019-3301

**CAZALAS, MARY REBECCA WILLIAMS,** lawyer, nurse; b. Atlanta, Nov. 11, 1927; d. George Edgar and Mary Annie (Slappey) Williams; m. Albert Joseph Cazalas (dec.). *Her great-great-grandfather, General John Coffee, fought in the Battle of New Orleans. His wife, Mary Donelson, was niece of Mrs. Andrew Jackson. Their son, Major John A. Coffee, served in the Civil War. His daughter, Mary Stevens Coffee, married Dr. John George Slappey, prominent physician at Jeffersonville, Georgia. His grandfather was Hans (John) George Slappey, who fought in the Revolution, and his father was Robert Rutherford Slappey. His daughter, Mary Annie Slappey, married George Edgar Wiliams. His mother was Sarah Cobb of Kosiesco, Mississippi. He graduated from Mercer University and was Chief Dispatcher of Central of Georgia Railroad.* BS in Pre-medicine, Oglethorpe U., Atlanta, 1954; MS in Anatomy, Emory U., 1960; JD, Loyola U., 1967, Loyola U., New Orleans, 1967. RN, Ga. Gen. duty nurse, 1948-68; instr. maternity nursing St. Josephs Infirmary Sch. Nursing, Atlanta, 1954-59; med. rschr. in urology Tulane U. Sch. Medicine, New Orleans, 1961-65; legal rschr. for presiding judge La. Ct. Appeals (4th cir.), New Orleans, 1965-71; pvt. practice New Orleans, 1967-71, asst. U.S. atty., 1971-79; sr. trial atty. EEOC, New Orleans, 1979-84; owner Cazalas Apts., New Orleans, 1962—; lectr. in field. Contbr. articles to profl. jours. Bd. advisors Loyola U. Sch. Law, New Orleans, 1974, v.p. adv. bd., 1975; active New Orleans Drug Abuse Adv. Com., 1976-80; task force Area Agy. on Aging, 1976-80, pres. coun. Loyola U., 1978—; adv. bd. Odyssey House, Inc., New Orleans, 1973; chmn. womens com. Fed. Exec. Bd., 1974; bd. dirs. Bethlehem House of Bread, 1975-79. Named Hon. La. State Senator, 1974; recipient Superior Performance award U.S. Dept. Justice, 1974, Cert. Appreciation Fed. Exec. Bd., 1975-78, Rev. E.A. Doyle award, 1976, Commendation for tchg. Guam Legislature, 1977, Career Achievement award Mt. de Sales Acad., 1995. Mem. Am. Judicature Soc., La. Sate Bar Assn., Fed. Bus. Assn. (v.p. 1976—, pres. 1976-78, bd. dirs. 1972-75), Fed. Bar Assn. (1st v.p. 1973, pres. New Orleans chpt. 1974-75, nat. coun. 1974-79), Assn. Women Lawyers, Nat. Health Lawyers Assn., DAR, Bus. and Profl. Womens Club, Am. Heart Assn., Emory Alumni Assn., Oglethorpe U. Alumni Assn., Loyola U. Alumni Assn. (bd. dirs. 1974-75, 77, v.p. 1976), Jefferson Parish Hist. Soc., Sierra Club, Zonta, Leconte Hon. Sci. Soc., Phi Delta Delta (merged with Phi Alpha Delta pres. 1970-72, bd. dirs., vice justice 1974-75), Alpha Epsilon Delta, Phi Sigma. Democrat. Real property, Health.

**CAZARES, JORGE V.,** lawyer; b. Chgo., Oct. 2, 1963; s. Ricardo and Aida C.; m. Patricia Herrera, May 24, 1994; 1 child, Jorge A. Jr. BS, Yale U., 1985; JD, Loyola U., 1990. Bar; Ill. 1990, U.S. Dist. Ct. (no. dist.) Ill. 1990, U.S. Ct. Appeals (7th cir.) 1992, U.S. Dist. Ct. (cen. dist.) Ill. 1993, U.S. Supreme Ct. 1993. Assoc. Altheimer & Gray, Chgo., 1990-92; assoc. Pugh Jones & Johnson, Chgo., 1992-97, ptnr., shareholder, 1998—; chair, arbitrator Cool County Mandatory Arbitration Program, 1995—. Contbr. articles to profl. jours. Mem. ABA, Ill. State Bar Assn., Latin Am. Bar Assn. Avocations: golf, tennis, basketball. General civil litigation, Libel, Education and schools. Office: Pugh Jones & Johnson 180 N Lasalle St Ste 2910 Chicago IL 60601-2700

**CAZDEN, ELIZABETH,** lawyer; b. Ann Arbor, Mich., Feb. 6, 1950; d. Norman and Courtney (Borden) C.; m. Richard B. Kleinschmidt, May 25, 1980; children: David C., Sarah C. BA, Oberlin Coll., 1971; JD, Harvard U., 1978; MA, Andover Newton Theol. Sch., 1997. Bar: N.H. 1978, U.S. Dist. Ct. N.H. 1978, U.S. Ct. Appeals (1st cir.) 1981, U.S. Spreme Ct. 1990. Law clk. N.H. Supreme Ct., Concord, 1978-79; assoc. O'Neill, Backus & Spielman, Manchester, N.H., 1979-82; pvt. practice Manchester, 1982—; lectr. U. N.H., 1985, 87. Author: Antoinette Brown Blackwell, 1983; co-editor handbook on appellate advocacy, 1984. Presiding clk. New England Yearly Meeting of Friends (Quaker), 1990-94. Mem. ABA, N.H Bar (chair citizens rights com. 1988-90, econ. of law practice com., computer subcom. 1987-89, AIDS Task Force 1990-94). Avocations: cello, hiking, computers. Appellate. Office: 118 Walnut St Manchester NH 03104-4223

**CEARLEY, ROBERT M., JR.,** lawyer. JD, U. Ark., 1969. Pvt. practice Little Rock. Co-editor: Domestic Relations Handbook, chair editl. bd. Vol. II, 1996. Fellow Am. Coll. Trial Lawyers; mem. ABA, ATLA, Ark. Bar Assn. (pres. 1998-99), Ark. Trial Lawyers Assn., Am. Bd. Trial Advocates, Pulaski County Bar Assn. Personal injury, Product liability, Contracts commercial. Office: Ark State Bar Assn 400 W Markham St Little Rock AR 72201-1520

**CEBALLOS, M(ICHAEL) ALAN,** lawyer; b. Jacksonville, Fla., Sept. 1, 1955; s. Michael and Rose Marie (Johnson) C.; m. Kay Frances Peavy, July 16, 1977 (div.); m. Robyn Carole Dickson, May 21, 1994; children: Michael Brandon, Michael Dylan. BA, U. North Fla., Jacksonville, 1977; JD, Georgetown U., 1980. Bar: Va. 1981, D.C. 1981, Fla. 1982. Assoc. firm Cadeaux & Taglieri, Washington, 1980-83; asst. U.S. atty. U.S. Dept. Justice, Jacksonville, 1983-88; ptnr. Harris Guid Rosner Ceballos & Daze, Jacksonville, 1988-92; sr. ptnr., pres. firm Ceballos Shorstein & Kelly, Jacksonville, 1992-96; sole practitioner Jacksonville, 1996—. Mem. various polit. fin. coms., Jacksonville, 1992-94; sponsor Little League teams, 1991-94. Mem. ABA, ATLA, Fla. Acad. Trial Lawyers, Fed. Bar Assn. (v.p. 1991-94), Jacksonville Bar Assn. (mem. criminal law sect.), Jacksonville C. of C. Democrat. Baptist. Avocations: reading, exercise, travel. Criminal, Federal civil litigation, Personal injury. Office: 200 E Forsyth St Jacksonville FL 32202-3320

**CECI, LOUIS J.,** former state supreme court justice; b. N.Y.C., Sept. 10, 1927; s. Louis and Filomena C.; m. Shirley; children—Joseph, Geraldine, David; children by previous marriage: Kristin, Remy, Louis. Ph.B., Marquette U., 1951, J.D., 1954. Bar: Wis. 1954, U.S. Dist. Ct. (ea. dist.) Wis. 1954, U.S. Dist. Ct. (we. dist.) Wis. 1987; cert. mediator-arbitrator. Sole practice Milw., 1954-58, 63-68; asst. city atty. City of Milw., 1958-63; mem. Wis. Assembly, Madison, 1965-66; judge Milw. County Ct., 1968-73, Milw. Circuit Ct., 1973-82; justice Wis. Supreme Ct., Madison, 1982-93, retired, 1993; res. judge State of Wis., 1993—; lectr. Wis. Jud. Confs., 1970-79. Lectr. Badger Boys State, Ripon, Wis., 1961, 1982-84; asst. dist. commr. Boy Scouts Am., 1962. Recipient Wis. Civic Recognition PLAV, Milw., 1970; recipient Community Improvement Pompeii Men's Club, Milw., 1971, Good Govt. Milw Jaycees, 1973, Community-Judiciary Pompeii Men's Club, 1982. Mem. ABA, Wis. Bar Assn., Dane County Bar Assn., Milw. County Bar Assn., Waukesha County Bar Assn., Am. Legion (comdr. 1962-63).

**CEDARBAUM, MIRIAM GOLDMAN,** federal judge; b. N.Y.C., Sept. 16, 1929; d. Louis Albert and Sarah (Shapiro) Goldman; m. Bernard Cedarbaum, Aug. 25, 1957; children: Daniel Goldman C., Jonathan Goldman C. BA, Barnard Coll., 1950; LLB, Columbia U., 1953. Bar: N.Y. 1954, U.S. Dist. Ct. (so. dist.) N.Y. 1956 U.S. Ct. Appeals (2d cir.) 1956, U.S. Ct. Claims 1958, U.S. Supreme Ct. 1958, U.S. Dist. Ct. (ea. dist.) N.Y. 1980, U.S. Ct. Appeals (5th and 11th cirs.) 1981. Law clk. to judge Edward Jordan Dimock U.S. Dist. Ct. (so. dist.) N.Y., 1953-54, asst. U.S. atty., 1954-57; atty. Dept. Justice, Washington, 1958-59; part-time cons. to law firms in litigation matters, 1959-62; 1st asst. counsel N.Y. State Moreland Act Commn., 1963-64; assoc. counsel Mus. Modern Art, N.Y.C., 1965-79; assoc. litigation dept. Davis, Polk & Wardwell, N.Y.C., 1979-83, sr. atty., 1983-86; acting justice Village of Scarsdale, N.Y., 1978-82, justice, 1982-86; judge U.S. Dist. Ct. (so. dist.) N.Y., 1986-98, sr. judge, 1998—; mem. com. defender svcs. Jud. Conf. U.S., 1993—; bd. vis. Columbia Law Sch.; trustee Barnard Coll.; co-counsel Scarsdale Open Soc. Assn., 1968-86. Mem. adv. com. on labor rels. Scarsdale Bd. Edn., 1976-77; mem. Scarsdale Bd. Archtl. Rev., 1977-78. Recipient Medal of Distinction Barnard Coll., 1991. Mem. Am. Law Inst., ABA (chmn. com. on pictorial graphic sculptural and choreographic works 1979-81, copyright com. fed. practice and procedure, 1983-84), N.Y. State Bar Assn. (chmn. com. on fed. legislation 1978-80, com. on dist., city, village and town cts., 1983-84), Assn. of Bar of City of N.Y. (com. on copyright and literary property, 1982-84, com. on the Bicentennial 1988-92), Fed. Bar Coun., Copyright Soc. U.S.A. (trustee, mem. exec. com. 1979-82), Supreme Ct. Hist. Soc. Jewish. Office: US Dist Ct US Courthouse 500 Pearl St Rm 1330 New York NY 10007-1316

**CEDEROTH, RICHARD ALAN,** lawyer; b. Peoria, Ill., May 17, 1958. BSEE, Bradley U., 1980; JD, U. Ill., 1983. Bar: Ill. 1983, U.S. Dist. Ct. (no. dist.) Ill. 1984. Assoc. Cook Wetzel & Egan, Chgo., 1983-85; ptnr. Newman Williams, Chgo., 1985-91, William Brinks Hofer Gibson & Lione, Chgo., 1991-96, Sidley & Austin, Chgo., 1996—. Mem. ABA, IEEE, Am. Intellectual Property Law Assn. Intellectual property, Federal civil litigation, Patent. Office: Sidley & Austin One First National Pla Chicago IL 60603

**CEDILLOS, STEVE H.,** lawyer, actor; b. L.A., Oct. 17, 1951; s. Henry and Velia (Espalin) C.; 1 child, Andrea Haunani. BA, U. Hawaii, 1974, JD, 1980. Bar: Hawaii, U.S. Ct. Appeals (9th cir.) Sole practitioner Honolulu, 1980—. Mem. SAG. Avocations: sports, writing, reading, travel. Criminal, Bankruptcy, Family and matrimonial. Office: 1088 Bishop St Ste 810 Honolulu HI 96813-3117

**CEKALA, CHESTER,** lawyer; b. Attleboro, Mass., May 18, 1959; s. Chester and Eileen (Polefka) C.; m. Suzanne Collette Cloutier, June 21, 1981 (div. May 1989); 1 child, Allison Rene; m. Carol Lee Raleigh, Oct. 7, 1990; 1 child, Samuel Chester. BS, Worcester Poly. Inst., 1982; JD, Suffolk U., 1987. Bar: Ohio 1987, Mass. 1996, U.S. Ct. Appeals (fed. cir.) 1989, U.S. Patent and Trademark Office 1988, U.S. Supreme Ct. 1996. Chem. engr. Moleculon Biotech, Cambridge, Mass., 1981-87; patent atty. Procter & Gamble, Cin., 1987-90, W.R. Grace & Co., Lexington, Mass., 1990-91, The Gillette Co., Boston, 1991—. Mem. ABA, Am. Intellectual Property Assn., Boston Patent Law Assn., Cin. Intellectual Property Assn. (sec. 1987-88). Avocations: sailing, bicycling, skiing. Patent, Intellectual property, General corporate. Office: The Gillette Co Prudential Tower Bldg Boston MA 02199

**CELANO, PETER J., JR.,** lawyer; b. Camden, N.J., Apr. 2, 1956; s. Peter J. and Dorothy (Lopez) C.; m. Mary Beth Kramer, Mar. 31, 1984; children: Peter III, William. BS, Villanova U., Pa., 1978, JD, 1981. N.J. 1981, Pa. 1981, U.S. Dist. Ct. (ea. dist.) Pa., U.S. Dist. Ct. N.J., U.S. Ct. Appeals (3d cir.). Sr. assoc. Law Office of Joel Feldscher, Cherry Hill, N.J., 1984-87; ptnr. Law Office Celano & Kramer, Woodbury, N.J., 1987—. Mem. Gloucester Cty. Bar Assn., Assn. Trial Lawyers Am., Woodbury Country Club. Avocations: golf, swimming, scuba diving, boating, skiing. General civil litigation, Personal injury, Real property. Office: Celano & Kramer 903 N Broad St Ste 2 Woodbury NJ 08096-3598

**CELENTANO, LESLIE ZYTO,** lawyer; b. N.Y.C., Aug. 12, 1954; d. Marcel Wolf and Muriel (Mankoff) Zyto; m. Domenick Anthony Celentano, Apr. 4, 1976. BS, Montclair State Coll., 1975; JD, N.Y. Law Sch., 1980. Bar: N.J. 1981, Fla. 1981, N.Y. 1988. Treas. Celentano, Inc., Verona, N.J., 1980—; assoc. Slavitt et al, West Orange, N.J., 1981-83; asst. prosecutor Essex County Prosecutor's Office, Newark, 1984-85; of counsel Gulkin, Hock & Lehr, Livingston, N.J., 1985—; commr. Police Tng. Commn., Livingston, N.J., 1986-95. Committeewoman Bedminster Twp. com., 1993-95; chair N.J. State Commn. Investigation, 1995—. Mem. Fla. Bar Assn., N.J. Bar Assn. Office: 354 Eisenhower Pkwy Livingston NJ 07039-1022

**CELLA, CARL EDWARD,** lawyer; b. New Haven, Apr. 2, 1941; s. Louis J. and Helen (Beale) C.; m. Mauriann L. Parmelee; children: Carl Jr., David, Lynn Jean. AB in Govt., Georgetown U., 1963; JD, U. Conn., 1966. Bar: Conn. 1966, U.S. Dist. Ct. 1967, U.S. Ct. Appeals (2d cir.) 1976, U.S. Supreme Ct. 1976. Assoc. DeLaney, Mantzaris & Cella, Wallingford, Conn., 1967-70; ptnr. Loughlin, Kraemer, Noonan & Cella, Wallingford, 1970-76; sr. ptnr. Cella-McKeon, P.C., North Haven, Conn., 1976-89, Cella, McKeon & Williams P.C., North Haven, 1989—; law clk. to justice Supreme Ct. of Conn., Hartford, 1966-67; sec. Jud. Coun., State of Conn., Hartford, 1975-80; spl. master Fed. Ct. Dist. Conn., 1990—; fact finder Conn. Superior Ct., 1992—, spl. arbitrator, 1992—. Chmn. planning and zoning com. North Haven Ct., 1973-76, elderly housing com., North Haven, Conn., 1976-80; pres. Columbus Club KC, Wallingford, Conn., 1969-70; mem. state cen. com. Conn. Rep. Party, 1975-85. Mem. ABA, Assn. Trial Lawyers Am., Def. Rsch. Inst., Conn. Bar Assn., Quinnipiac C. of C. (bd. dirs. 1989-92), Wallingford Country Club. Roman Catholic. Avocations: skiing, golf, salt water fishing, boating. Personal injury, Alternative dispute resolution, General civil litigation. Home: 17 Mulligan Dr Wallingford CT 06492-5456 Office: Cella McKeon & Williams PO Box 221 21 Washington Ave North Haven CT 06473-2310

**CEMBER, M. NATHAN,** lawyer, speaker; b. N.Y.C., July 18, 1928; s. Arthur and Lilly (Shuster) C.; m. Esther Weissman, June 29, 1952; children—Richard, Mark, William. LL.B., Bklyn. Law Sch., 1950, LL.M., 1955. Bar: N.Y. 1951, U.S. Dist. Ct. (so. dist.) N.Y. 1960, U.S. Supreme Ct., 1967. House counsel Tenax, Inc., N.Y.C., 1953-66; Cember & Cember PC, Nyack, N.Y., 1966—. Chmn. Rockland County Com. for Soviet Jewry, N.Y., 1975; pres. Congregation Sons of Israel, Nyack, 1964-65. Served with U.S. Army, 1950-52, Korea. Mem. N.Y. State Bar Assn., Rockland County Bar Assn., Comml. Law League. Democrat. Lodges: B'nai B'rith (v.p. dist. 1, 1982-85 pres. dist. 1, 1985-86). Contracts commercial, Real property. Office: Cember & Cember PC 10 S Broadway Nyack NY 10960-3119

**CENATIEMPO, MICHAEL J.,** lawyer; b. Houston, June 16, 1946; s. Benedict S. and Mary E. C.; m. Mary Lou Rickel, May 31, 1970; children: Diana F., R. Matthew, Carla A. AB, St. Louis U., 1968; JD, U. Houston, 1971. Bar: Tex. 1971; cert. estate planning and probate specialist. Briefing atty. to Hon. Ruel C. Walker Supreme Ct. Tex., 1971-72; with Butler, Binion, Rice, Cook & Knapp (now Butler & Binion), Houston, 1972-78, Wyckoff, Russell, Frazier & Cenatiempo, Houston, 1978-85; ptnr. Cenatiempo & Ditta, Houston, 1985—; Mem. Supreme Ct. Tex. Task Force on Jud. Appointments, 1991-93; presenter in field. Contbr. articles to profl. jours. Dir. St. Thomas H.S. Found., Houston, 1980-92, sec.-treas., 1989-92. Fellow Am. Coll. Trust and Estate Counsel (mem. state membership com. 1991-95, mem. estate and gift tax com. 1993, 97, mem. fiduciary litig. com. 1993—), Houston Bar Found. (dir. 1989, 90), State Bar Tex. Found.; mem. Houston Bar Assn. (chmn. probate, estates and trust law sect. 1983-84, media rep. on guardianship and mental health issues 1992—), State Bar Tex. (mem. real property, probate and trusts sect., mem. probate code subcom. 1995, mem. Tex. trust code com., statutory probate cts. liaison com.), Disability and Elder Law Attys. Assn., Houston Estate and Fin. Forum, Houston Bus. and Estate Planning Coun. Roman Catholic. Avocations: cycling, gardening, fly fishing, hunting, literature. Fax: 713-655-9635. Probate, Estate taxation, Estate planning. Office: Cenatiempo & Ditta 1550 Two Houston Ctr 909 Fannin St Houston TX 77010-1001

**CENSOR, MARTIN A.,** lawyer; b. N.Y.C., Oct. 6, 1959. BA in Econs., CUNY, 1981; JD, Hofstra U., 1984. Bar: N.Y. Assoc. Warren, Gorham & Lamont, N.Y.C. Consumer commercial, General practice. Office: Rsch Inst Am 395 Hudson St New York NY 10014-3669

**CENTER, CHARLES R.,** lawyer, educator, military officer; b. Campton, Ky., Aug. 8, 1958; s. Charles A. and Bonnie Mae (Haney) C.; m. Anne Catherine Evavold, July 2, 1983; children: Chad, Andrew. BA, Eastern Wash. U., 1982; JD, U. Ga., 1986. Bar: Ga. 1986. Commd. 2d lt. USAF, 1986, advanced through grades to maj., 1987, asst. staff judge advocate, 1986-87, area def. counsel, 1987-89, dep. staff judge adv., 1989-91; from asst. to assoc. prof. USAF Acad., 1991—; prof. Golden Gate U., Holloman AFB, 1987-89, Park Coll., 1987-89, U. So. Colo, U. No. Colo., 1992—. Mem. ABA, ATLA, Ga. Bar Assn., Nat. Assn. Criminal Def. Lawyers, Phi Alpha Delta. Avocations: golf, scuba diving. Office: USAF Academy/DFL Dept Law U S A F Academy CO 80840 *Notable cases include: U.S. vs. Roe, murder acquittal; U.S. vs. Fayne, appellate relief.*

**CENTNER, CHARLES WILLIAM,** lawyer, educator; b. Battle Creek, Mich., July 4, 1915; s. Charles William and Lucy Irene (Patterson) C.; m. Evi Rohr, Dec. 22, 1956; children: Charles Patterson, David William, Geoffrey Christopher. AB, U. Chgo., 1936, AM, 1938, 39, PhD, 1941; JD, Detroit Coll. Law, 1970; LLB, LaSalle Extension U., 1965. Bar: Mich. 1970. Asst. prof. U. N.D., 1940-41, Tulane U., New Orleans, 194-142; liaison officer for Latin Am., Lend-Lease Adminstrn., 1942; assoc. dir. Western Hemisphere divsn. Nat. Fgn. Trade Coun., N.Y., 1946-52; exec. Ford Motor Co., Detroit, 1952-57, Chrysler Corp. and Chrysler Internat. S.A., Detroit and Geneva, Switzerland, 1957-70; adj. prof. Wayne State U., U. Detroit,

Wayne County C.C., 1970—. Author: Great Britian and Chile, 1810-1914, 1941. Lt. comdr. USNR, 1942-45. Mem. ABA, State Bar Mich., Oakland County Bar Assn., Masons. Republican. Episcopalian. Home: 936 Harcourt Rd Grosse Pointe Park MI 48230

**CERAUL, DAVID JAMES,** lawyer; b. Easton, Pa., Dec. 8, 1955; s. David A. Ceraul and Josephine (Ruggiero) Barczynski; m. Jacqueline A. Onjack, May 17, 1986. BS in Polit. Sci., U. Scranton, 1977; JD, U. Pitts., 1980. Bar: Pa. 1980. Law clk. to presiding justice Ct. of Common Pleas, Stroudsburg, Pa., 1980-81; pvt. practice Bangor, Pa., 1981—; solicitor Wind Gap (Pa.) Borough, 1981-85, State Belt Mcpl. Assn., Bangor, 1981—. Bd. dirs. Unico Nat., Roseto, Pa., 1983-84, United Way, Lehigh Valley, Pa., 1985-86; solicitor zoning and hearing bd. Upper Mt. Bethel Twp., 1988-91, Bangor Borough, 1990—; solicitor Washington Twp. 1993—, zoning and hearing bd., 1989-92, Roseto Zoning and Hearing Bd., 1988—. Mem. Northampton County Bar Assn., Monroe County Bar Assn., KC Lodge, Bangor Lions, Elks. Democrat. Roman Catholic. Real property, General practice, Municipal (including bonds). Office: 22 Market St Bangor PA 18013-1902

**CEREZO, CARMEN CONSUELO,** federal judge; b. 1940. BA, U. P.R., 1963, LLB, 1966. Pvt. practice, 1966-67; law clk. U.S. Dist. Ct., San Juan, 1967-72; judge Superior Ct., P.R., 1972-76, Ct. Intermediate Appeals, 1976-80; judge U.S. Dist. Ct., P.R., 1980-93, chief judge, 1993—. Office: Federico Degetau Fed Bldg Rm CH-131 150 Carlos Chardon Ave Hato Rey PR 00918-1761

**CERIANI, GARY JAMES,** lawyer; b. Kremmling, Colo., Oct. 1, 1947; s. Ernest G. and Bernetha M. (Anderson) C.; m. Marianne L. Wormley, June 29, 1974; children: Kelly, Barbara. BA, Colo. Coll., 1968; postgrad., U. Edinborough, 1968-69; JD, U. Colo., 1972. Bar: Colo. 1972, U.S. Dist. Ct. Colo. 1972, U.S. Ct. Appeals (10th cir.) 1972, U.S. Ct. Claims 1989. Assoc. Helmick, Conover & Burkhardt, Denver, 1972-76; pvt. practice Denver, 1976-78; ptnr. Davis & Ceriani P.C., Denver, 1979—. Editor: U. Colo. Law Review, 1970-72. Mem. ATLA, ABA, Colo. Bar Assn., Denver Bar Assn., Colo. Trial Lawyers Assn. Avocations: hunting, fishing, golf, skiing. Securities, General civil litigation. Office: Davis & Ceriani 1350 17th St Ste 400 Denver CO 80202-1575

**CERMINARA, LAURA MARY,** lawyer; b. Green Bay, Wis., Feb. 1, 1970; d. Daniel Emanuel and Priscilla Mary Cerminara. Student, St. Norbert Coll., 1987-88; BA, U. Wis., 1991; JD, Thomas M. Cooley Law Sch., 1995. Bar: Wis. 1996, Mich. 1997. Assoc. Roels, Keidatz & Parent, De Pere, Wis., 1996-99; ptnr. Roels, Keidatz, Parent & Cerminara, LLP, De Pere, Wis., 1999—; guardian ad litem Brown County, Green Bay, Wis., 1997—; mem. bd. advisors Team Security, Inc., Green Bay, 1998—. Com. and panel mem. fund distbn. United Way Brown County, Green Bay, 1997—; bd. dirs. United Way, 1999—. Mem. State Bar Wis., State Bar Mich., Brown County Bar Assn. Republican. Roman Catholic. Avocations: waterskiing, traveling, volleyball, softball, reading. State civil litigation, General practice, Personal injury. Office: Roels Keidatz Parent & Cerminara LLP PO Box 5065 515 George St De Pere WI 54115-2713

**CERNICKY, ANN HARDMAN,** lawyer; b. Davis-Monthan AFB, Ariz., June 8, 1967; d. Richard Wayne and Louise Ann (Hanten) Hardman; m. Mark Allen Cernicky, Dec. 19, 1992; 1 child: Andrew Mark Cernicky. BSBA in Econs., U. Ctrl. Fla., 1990; JD, Vanderbilt U., 1993; LLM in Taxation, U. Fla., 1994. Bar: S.D. 1993, D.C. 1995. Assoc. Davis & Harman, Washington, 1994—. Mem. ABA, S.D. Bar Assn., D.C. Bar Assn. Avocations: horseback riding, dog obedience training, classical music. Legislative, Personal injury, Probate. Office: Davis & Harman Ste 1200 1455 Pennsylvania Ave NW Washington DC 20004-1034

**CERUTTI, PATRICK BERNARD,** lawyer; b. Chgo., Jan. 31, 1945; s. Bernard C. and Kathleen A. (O'Connell) C.; m. Dee A. Leoni, Jan. 15, 1968; children: Susan M., Gina M. BA, Gonzaga U., 1967, JD, 1971. Asst. corp. counsel City of Spokane, Wash., 1968-72; ptnr. Underwood, Campbell, Brock & Cerutti, P.S., Spokane, 1972-95, Lukins & Annis, P.S., Spokane, 1995—. General corporate, Contracts commercial. Home: 5225 S Madelia St Spokane WA 99223-8134 Office: Lukis Annis PS 1600 Washington Trust Fin Ctr 701 W Sprague Ave Spokane WA 99201-3915

**CERVONE, ANTHONY LOUIS,** lawyer; b. Providence, Nov. 19, 1962; s. Anthony and Mary Gloria (Borrelli) C.; m. Joy D'Amico, Dec. 31, 1995. BA, R.I. Coll., 1984; JD, U. Bridgeport, 1988; Cert. Program Instrn. Lawyers, Harvard U., 1996. Bar: R.I. 1989, U.S. Dist. Ct. R. I. 1990, U.S. Ct. Appeals (1st cir.) 1991, U.S. Supreme Ct. 1996. Founder, prin. Cervone Law Firm, Cranston, R.I., 1989—; spl. coun. to The City of Providence, 1991-92; mem. bench-bar com. R.I. Superior Ct., R.I. Family Ct., R.I. Dist. Ct.; affiliate atty. Am. Ctr. for Law and Justice, The Rutherford Inst. Mem. ABA, ATLA, R.I. Bar Assn., R.I. Trial Lawyers Assn., Supreme Ct. Hist. Soc., Smithsonian Instn., Library of Congress. Avocations: snowboarding, rollerhockey, golf, surfing, cycling, triathlons. Entertainment, Personal injury, Sports. Home: 68 White Birch Ln Hope RI 02831-1106 Office: Renaissance Park 37 Sockanosset Crossroad Cranston RI 02920

**CESARANO, MICHAEL CHAPMAN,** lawyer; b. Miami, Fla., July 29, 1944; s. Patrick J. and Beryl L. (Chapman) C.; m. Marilyn J. Wisner, Sept. 2, 1974 (div. June 1984); children: Patrick Chapman, Ashley Joy; m. Sheila Marie Burnstin, Oct. 10, 1987; 1 child, Michelle Patrice. BEE, U. Va., 1967; JD cum laude, U. Puget Sound, 1974; LLM, London Sch. Econs., 1976. Bar: Wash. 1975, U.S. Dist. Ct. (we. dist.) Wash. 1975, Fla. 1980, U.S. Dist. Ct. (so. dist.) Fla. 1980, U.S. Ct. Appeals (5th cir.) 1980, U.S. Ct. Appeals (11th cir.) 1981, U.S. Patent and Trademark Office 1985, Pa. 1988, U.S. Dist. Ct. (mid. dist.) Fla. 1988, U.S. Dist. Ct. (ea. dist. Pa. 1989), U.S. Ct. Appeals (3d, 4th & Fed. cirs.) 1989, U.S. Ct. Appeals (6th cir.) 1990. Law clk., atty. div. II, Wash. State Ct. Appeals, Tacoma, 1976-77; assoc. Law Office Robert C. Keating, Seattle, 1977-78, Helsell, Fetterman, Martin, Todd and Hokanson, Seattle, 1978-79, Mershon, Sawyer, Johnston, Dunwody and Cole, Miami, 1980-83; patent atty. David L. Garrison & Assocs., Seattle, 1985, Boeing Co., Seattle, 1985-86, Law Office John Cyril Malloy, Miami, 1987, Steele, Gould & Fried, Miami, 1988-90; patent atty., ptnr. Cesarano & Kain, P.A., Miami, 1990-96, Bienstock & Clark, Miami, 1996—; adj. prof. law U. Puget Sound, Tacoma, 1978-79, St. Thomas Law Sch., 1993-94. Organizer, speaker Crime Watch Dade County, Miami, 1981-82; bd. dirs. South Fla. chpt. March of Dimes, Miami, 1983; pres. Family Svcs. Found., Miami, 1992. Capt. USMC, 1967-72, Vietnam. Decorated Air medal with two stars. Mem. ABA, Fed. Bar Assn., Fla. Bar (bd. cert. civil trial lawyer, designated field of patents, trademarks and copyrights), Dade County Bar Assn. (chmn. computer law com. 1988-89), Am. Intellectual Property Law Assn., U. Puget Sound Law Alumni Soc. (exec. bd. 1977-78). Avocations: aviation, snow skiing, computers. General civil litigation, Patent, Trademark and copyright. Home: 815 E Dilido Dr Miami Beach FL 33139-1241

**CHABAN, LAWRENCE RICHARD,** lawyer; b. Pitts., Apr. 8, 1955; s. Donald W. and June H. (Klee) C.; children: Matthew A., Mich R. BA, U. Pitts., 1977, JD, 1980. Bar: Pa. 1980, U.S. Dist. Ct. (we. dist.) Pa. 1980, U.S. Ct. Appeals (3rd cir.) 1981, U.S. Ct. Appeals (4th cir.) 1984. Compensation atty. Dist. 5 United Mine Workers Am., Pitts., 1980-81; with Yablonski, Costello & Leckie, P.C., Washington, Pa., 1980—. Mem. ABA, Pa. Bar Assn., Allegheny County Bar Assn., Order of Coif. Democrat. Jewish. Avocations: miniature gaming, golf. Fax: 724-225-9203. E-mail: Larrychab@aol.com. Labor, Pension, profit-sharing, and employee benefits, Workers' compensation. Home: 111 Overlook Dr Pittsburgh PA 15216-1434 Office: Yablonski Costello & Leckie PC 505 Washington Trust Washington PA 15301

**CHABOT, ELLIOT CHARLES,** lawyer; b. Anniston, Ala., Mar. 29, 1955; s. Herbert L. and Aleen (Kerwin) C.; m. Christine H. Swan, July 3, 1998. BA with honors, U. Md., 1977; JD, George Washington U., 1980. Bar: D.C. 1980, U.S. Dist. Ct. D.C. 1981, U.S. Ct. Fed. Claims 1981, U.S. Ct. Internat. Trade 1981, U.S. Tax Ct. 1981, U.S. Ct. Appeals Armed Forces 1981, U.S. Temporary Emergency Ct. Appeals 1981, U.S. Ct. Appeals (D.C. cir.) 1981, U.S. Ct. Appeals (4th, 5th, 8th, 9th, 10th, 11th, fed. cirs.) 1982, U.S. Ct. Appeals (7th cir.) 1983. Applications analyst, atty., House Info. Systems U.S. Congress, Washington, 1980-81; project leader integrated law revision and retrieval project U.S. Congress, Washington, 1981-89; legal support project leader House Info. Systems U.S. Congress, Washington, 1989-95; webmaster internet law libr. U.S. Congress, Washington, 1994-99, legal sys. team leader House Info. Resources, 1995-99, legis. applications sustainment project leader, 1999—; bd. dirs. Am. Revenue Assn., Rockford, Iowa, 1983-87, Threshold Services, Inc., Silver Spring, Md., 1984-89; v.p. Banor Housing Inc., Kensington, Md., 1987-88, 90—, dir. 1987—. Columnist Aspen Hill Gazette, 1987-96. Pres. Aspen Hill (Md.) Civic Assn., 1985-95, dir. 1995—; pres. Parkland Community Sch. Coun., Aspen Hill, 1983-87, 94-96, v.p., 1971-73, mem. coun. 1970-74, 82-96; chmn. community svcs. com. Greater Wheaton (Md.) Citizens Adv. Bd., 1986-92; chmn. Ga. Ave. Men's Shelter Adv. Bd., Aspen Hill, 1989-96, Community Edn. Devel. subcom. of Citizens Adv. com. to the Interagency Coordinating Bd. for Community Use of Ednl. Facilities and Svcs. , 1985-88; dist. 3 v.p. Montgomery County Civic Fedn., 1990-91; exec. com. Robert E. Peary High Sch. PTA, Aspen Hill, 1972-73; Montgomery County Coun. com. on re-use of Peary High Sch., 1986, task force to examine the regional dist. act, 1991; corr. sec. Area 2 adv. coun. Montgomery County Pub. Schs, 1972-74, adv. com. spl. edn. programs, 1974; commr. Gov.'s Commn. on Student Affairs, Md., 1976-77; adv. com. Aspen Hill Libr., 1972, 1986—; sec. Friends Aspen Hill Libr., 1994-96, dir., 1996—; rec. sec. Dist. 19 Dem. Club, Montgomery County, 1983-86, 2d v.p., 1986-89, 1st v.p., 1989-92; legal and acctg. div. steering com. Washington Israel Bonds, 1984-86; mem. exec. com. Allied Civic Group, Silver Spring, 1987-89, corr. sec., 1992-94; chmn. Kensington/Wheaton Human Svcs. Area Plan Adv. Group, 1988; mem. Sta. 21 com. Kensington Vol. Fire Dept., 1989; mem. Greater Layhill Community Night Com., 1989, Aspen Hill Master Plan Citizens Adv. com., 1990-94; sec. Montgomery County Dem. Party, 1994—, chmn. rules com., 1994—, chmn. Internet Svcs. com., 1995-99, mem. ballot questions adv. com., 1988, 90, 98, vice chmn. precint orgn. com. of the party opers. task force, 1991-92; area coord. Dist. 19, 1992-94, chmn. Precinct 13-43, 1987-92, treas. Precinct 13-45, 1978-85; mem. Wheaton Action Group, 1990-95; campaign chmn. Dist. 19 Democratic Team, 1989-90; chmn. Wheaton Woods Recreation Ctr. Adv. Com., 1990; dir. dist. 3 Montgomery Citizens Polit. Action Com., 1991-92; mem. Bauer Drive Community Ctr. Adv. Com., 1992—; vice chmn. homeless com. Temple Shalom, Chevy Chase, Md., 1992-93; sec. Montgomery County United Democrats, 1997-99; mem. Md. State Dem. Ctrl. Com., 1994—. Recipient George Washington award, George Washington U., 1980, Donald R. Spivak award Montgomery County Interagency Coordinating Bd. Community Use of Edn. Facilities and Services, 1987, Total Quality Team award Chief Adminstrv. Office of U.S. Ho. of Reps., 1996; named One of Outstanding Young Men, U.S. C. of C., 1982, Ky. Col. Hon. Order Ky. Cols., 1967, Citizen of Yr. Greater Wheaton Citizen's Adv. Bd., 1990, One of the Federal 100 Federal Computer Week, 1994. Mem. ABA, Fed. Bar Assn., D.C. Bar Assn., George Washington U. Law Alumni Assn. (pres. Capitol Hill chpt. 1987-89, sec. 1985-87), Phi Alpha Delta (clk. Jay chpt. 1979-80), Omicron Delta Kappa. Home: 12929 Magellan Ave Rockville MD 20853-3037 Office: US Congress House Info Resources H2-641 Ford Ho Office Bldg Washington DC 20515-6165

**CHABOT, HERBERT L.,** judge; b. N.Y.C., July 17, 1931; s. Meyer and Esther (Mogilansky) C.; m. Aleen Carol Kerwin, Jun. 16, 1951; children: Elliot C., Donald J., Lewis A., Nancy Jo. BA, CCNY, 1952; LLB, Columbia U., 1957; LLM, Georgetown U., 1964. Bar: N.Y. 1958. Staff counsel Am. Jewish Congress, 1957-60; law clk. U.S. Tax Ct., Washington, 1961-65, judge, 1978—; atty. Joint Congl. Com. Taxation, 1965-78. Del. Md. Constl. Conv., 1967-68. With U.S. Army, 1953-55. Mem. ABA, Fed. Bar Assn. Office: US Tax Ct 400 2nd St NW Washington DC 20217-0002

**CHABOT, PHILIP LOUIS, JR.,** lawyer; b. Coaldale, Pa., Mar. 23, 1951; s. Philip Louis and Dorothy Louise (Casselberry) C.; m. Karen Sue Pirko, June 6, 1970 (div. 1981); m. Lynne Marx, Nov. 23, 1985; children: Alexander, Elizabeth, Patrick. BA with high honors, U. Va., 1973, JD, 1976. BAr: Va. 1976, D.C. 1976, U.S. Ct. Claims 1978, U.S. Dist. Ct. D.C. 1976, U.S. Dist. Ct. (ea. dist.) Va. 1984, U.S. Ct. Appeals (1st, 2d, 4th, 5th, 6th, 8th, 9th and 10th cirs.), U.S. Ct. Appeals (D.C. cir.) 1976, U.S. Ct. Internat. Trade 1996, U.S. Supreme Ct. 1979. Assoc. Northcutt Ely, Washington, 1976-77; prin. Duncan, Weinberg & Miller, P.C., Washington, 1978-84; pres. Philip Chabot, Chartered, 1984-92; of counsel Brickfield, Burchette & Ritts, Washignton, 1992-96; ptnr. Wilkinson Barker Knauer & Quinn, 1996—; aide U.S. Senator John V. Tunney, 1973, U.S. Senator William V. Roth, 1974-75; adj. prof. law Am. U., Washington, 1977-81; asst. to dir. com. on tech., transfer and utilization Nat. Acad. Engring., Washington, 1973-74; bd. dirs. Route One Corridor Housing, Inc., 1985-89. Editor newsletter Stateline, 1983-85. Dem. candidate Va. Ho. of Dels, 44th House Dist., 1983; state coord. Va. Youth Coalition for Muskie, 1972; mem. Mt. Vernon Dem. Com., 1982-89, 92-93; mem. Fairfax County Dem. Com., 1982-89, 92-93; trustee Va. Outdoors Found., 1982-86; trustee, vice chmn. Fairfax County Uniform Retirement Sys. Bd., 1982-86; nat. vice chief Order of Arrow, Boy Scouts Am., 1968-70; pres. Sherwood Estates Citizens Assn., 1988-89; pres. Fairfax County Citizens Assembly, 1990-91. Recipient Eagle Scout award Boy Scouts Am., 1964. Mem. ABA, Internat. Bar Assn., Fed. Energy Bar Assn., Va. State Bar Assn., D.C. BAr Assn., Am. Ry. Devel. Assn., Indsl. Devel. Rsch. Coun. (assoc.), Phi Beta Kappa. Avocation: sailing. Federal civil litigation, Natural resources, Legislative. Office: 2300 N St NW Ste 700 Washington DC 20037-1122

**CHABROW, PENN BENJAMIN,** lawyer; b. Phila., Feb. 16, 1939; s. Benjamin Penn and Annette (Shapiro) C.; m. Sheila Sue Steinberg, June 18, 1961; children: Michael Penn, Carolyn Debra, Frederick Penn. BS, Muhlenberg Coll., Allentown, Pa., 1959; JD, George Washington U., 1962, LLM in Taxation, 1968; postgrad. in econs. Harvard U. Bar: Va. 1963, D.C. 1964, U.S. Ct. Appeals (D.C. cir.) 1964, U.S. Tax Ct. 1964, U.S. Supreme Ct. 1966, Fla. 1972, U.S. Ct. Claims 1974, U.S. Ct. Appeals (5th and 11th cirs.) 1981; bd. cert. tax atty., Fla. Tax law specialist IRS, Washington, 1961-67; tax counsel C. of C. U.S., Washington, 1967-74; pvt. practice, Miami, Fla., 1974—; shareholder Wampler, Buchanan & Breen, P.A., Miami, 1993—; pres. Forum Realty Co., Phila., Pure Poultry Enterprises, Inc., Miami, Heartland Farms of Fla., Inc.; lectr. fed. taxation Barry U. Grad. Sch. of Bus., 1977-81. Founding dir. The Dan Marino Found., Inc., The Melissa Inst. for Violence Prevention and Treatment, Inc. Fellow Am. Coll. Tax Counsel; mem. ABA, Fla. Bar Assn., Fed. Bar Assn., Va. Bar Assn., D.C. Bar Assn., Greater Miami Estate Planning Coun., Muhlenberg Coll. Internat. Vis. Com., Phi Alpha Delta, Phi Sigma Tau. Contbr. articles profl. jours. Taxation, general, General corporate, Estate planning. Office: 777 Brickell Ave Ste 900 Miami FL 33131-2807

**CHACKES, KENNETH MICHAEL,** lawyer, legal educator; b. St. Louis, Sept. 12, 1949; s. Alex and Shirlee (Radloff) C.; m. Carole Gail Breen, June 14, 1970; children: Laura Michelle, Andrew Scott, Brian Carl. BA in Psychology, Tulane U., 1971; JD cum laude, St. Louis U., 1976. Bar: Mo. 1976, U.S. Dist. Ct. (ea. and we. dists.) Mo. 1976, U.S. Ct. Appeals (8th cir.) 1976, U.S. Ct. Appeals (D.C. cir.) 1976, U.S. Ct. Appeals (7th cir.) 1981. Ptnr. Chackes & Hoare, St. Louis, 1976-84; vis. asst. prof. law Washington U., St. Louis, 1984-87; atty. Mo. Protection & Advocacy Svcs., St. Louis and Jefferson City, 1988-90, mng. atty., 1990-92; pvt. practice, of counsel Vines, Frankel, Rubin, Bond & Dubin, P.C., St. Louis, 1992-96; ptnr. Van Amburg, Chackes, Carlson & Spritzer, LLP, St. Louis, 1996—; adj. prof. law Washington U., 1982-83, 88, supr. clin. students, 1981-84, 88-89, 91—; lectr. various orgns.; appearances on TV shows Law Talk, 1985-86, Special People, Special Needs, 1989-90; judge Fed. Practice Tng. Inst., St. Louis, 1983, judge trial tng. program, 1986, 89, instr., 1984-85, 92; mem. fed. practice com. U.S. Dist. Ct. for Ea. Dist. Mo., chmn. subcom. on appointment of counsel in civil rights cases; mem. discovery abuse and civil jury instrns. subcom. Mem. editorial bd. St. Louis U. Law Jour. Mem. exec. com. Access Resources of Mo., 1991—; mem. adv. com. on disabilities issues, HUD, 1990-91; mem. Coalition of Citizens with Disabilities of Greater St. Louis, 1989—, Mo. Coalition for Homeless, 1989—; steering com. St. Louis Lawyers' Project on Homelessness and Inadequate Housing, 1987-92. Recipient Legal Advocate award Mo. Assn. for Social Welfare, 1992, Equal Justice award Legal Svcs. of Ea. Mo., 1993. Mem. ABA (individual rights and responsibilities, labor and employment law and litigation sects.), Mo. Bar Assn. (lectr. at seminars and ann. meetings), Nat. Employment Lawyers Assn. (pres. St. Louis chpt. 1995-98). Alternative dispute resolution, Education and schools, Labor. Home: 8100 Gannon Ave Saint Louis MO 63130-3731 Office: 8420 Delmar Blvd Ste 406 Saint Louis MO 63124-2179

**CHACON, GERALD GILBERT,** lawyer; b. San Jose, Calif., Oct. 28, 1966; s. Gerald Gilbert and Barbara Kaye C. BS, Stanford U., 1988; JD, U. Calif., Davis, 1991; LLM, Boston U., 1995. Lawyer Hopkins & Carley, San Jose, 1991-94, Rosenblum Parish & Isaacs, San Jose, 1995—; adj. lectr. Golden Gate U. Sch. Taxation, San Francisco, 1998—. Sr. campaign staff Tom Campbell for Congress, San Jose, 1995. Republican. Roman Catholic. Taxation, general, Contracts commercial, Mergers and acquisitions. Office: Rosenblum Parish & Isaacs 160 W Santa Clara St # 15th fl San Jose CA 95113-1701

**CHADWICK, ROBERT,** lawyer, judge; b. Jackson, Miss., Apr. 5, 1924; s. Hudson and Annie (Eley) C.; m. Helen Faye Josey, Apr. 5, 1953; children: Robert Hudson, Celia, Dan, Lea Ann, Robin. BA, Auburn U., 1950; JD, Miss. Coll., 1957; postgrad., U. So. Calif., 1973, 75-76. Bar: Miss. 1963, U.S. Supreme Ct. 1970, U.S. Ct. Mil. Appeals 1975, Ky. 1980, U.S. Dist Ct. (ea. dist.) Ky. 1987. Chief regulation staff div. pesticide regulation USDA, Washington, 1965-70; atty., ecologist div. enforcement EPA, Washington, 1970-75, chmn. com. pesticide misuse rev., 1975-79; asst. gen. counsel Presdl. Clemency Bd. White House Dept. Justice, Washington, 1975; pvt. practice law Frankfort, Ky., 1980-82, 83—; law judge parole bd. Corrections Cabinet, Frankfort, 1982-83; asst. dir. div. hazardous materials Ky. Dept. Natural Resources and Environ. Protection, Frankfort, 1983—; chmn. bd. Exis, Inc.; staff atty., gen. counsel Ky. Cabinet for Human Resources, 1989-90. Pres. PTA Oxon Hill (Md.) Jr. High Sch., 1974, Frankfort Audubon Soc., 1981-83. Cpl. U.S. Army, 1943-45. Mem. ABA, Nat. Assn. Adminstrv. Law Judges, Miss. State Bar Assn., Ky. State Bar Assn., Franklin County Bar Assn., VFW, Masons. Environmental, Criminal, General practice. Home and Office: 16 Ryswick Ln Frankfort KY 40601-3848

**CHADWICK, VERNON HENRY,** lawyer; b. Woodville, Miss., May 4, 1941; s. Carl A. and Elvena P. Chadwick; m. Julia B. Chadwick, Aug. 31, 1963; children: Price Conerly, Swayze Amelia. BS, Miss. Coll., 1978, LLB, 1966. Bar: Miss. 1966, U.S. Dist. Ct. (so. dist.) Miss. 1969. Ptnr. Chadwick & Chadwick, Natchez, Miss., 1966-71, Chadwick & McAllister, Jackson, Miss., 1973-85; pvt. practice Jackson, Miss., 1985—; adj. prof. Miss. Coll., Clinton, 1980-90. Chmn. March of Dimes, Natchez, 1967; charter mem. Friends of the Jackson Zoo, 1977; active St. Andrew's Cathedral, Jackson, 1971—. With U.S. Army, 1959-62. Mem. ABA, Miss. Bar Assn., Hinds County Bar Assn. (chmn. libr. com. 1994-96), Adams County Bar Assn. (sec.-treas. 1968), Sigma Delta Kappa. Avocations: reading, writing, hiking, fishing. General practice, Real property, Probate. Home: 920 Meadowbrook Rd Jackson MS 39206-5944 Office: 1640 Lelia Dr Ste 210 Jackson MS 39216-4832

**CHAE, DON B.,** judge, educator, lawyer; b. Kwangju, Korea, Aug. 27, 1937; came to U.S., 1960; s. He Byong and Woo Ae (Park) C.; m. Yoon Jung Lee, Aug. 14, 1950; children: Donald, Sue, Sarah, Michael. BA, Chonnam Nat. U., 1959; MA, U. Pa., 1962; PhD, U. Tex., 1972; JD, So. Meth. U. Law Sch., 1980. Bar: Tex. 1980, U.S. Dist. Cts., U.S. Tax Ct., Immigration Ct. From asst. prof. to assoc. prof. Chonnam Nat. U., Kwangju, 1962-69; instr. Tarrant County Jr. Coll., Ft. Worth, 1975-80; pvt. practice law Dallas, 1980-94; judge Dallas Mcpl. Ct., 1995—; bd. dirs. Dallas Dispute Mediation Svc., 1994—; immigration and nationality com. State Bar Tex., Austin, 1993—; adminstr. Am. Studies Inst., Kwangju, 1966-72. Chmn. human rights commn. Fedn. of Korean-Am. Assocs. in U.S.A., 1993—; chmn. Korean-Am. Scholarship, Inc., Dallas, 1993—, Korean-Am. Fedn. Southwest, 1991—; mem. Overseas Korean Leadership Conf., 1996—. Mem. ABA, Am. Immigration Lawyers, Asian-Am. Bar Assn. Dallas (bd. dirs. 1992—), Asian-Am. C. of C. Dallas, Korean Assn. Ft. Worth (pres. 1978-80), Korean Assn. Dallas (chmn. 1996—). Office: Chae & Assocs PC 2828 Forest Ln Ste 1100 Dallas TX 75234-7500

**CHAFETZ, MARC EDWARD,** lawyer; b. Boston, Apr. 21, 1953; s. Morris Edward and Marion (Donovan) C.; m. Andrea Laurie Barkan, Aug. 20, 1977; children: Drew Edward, Maria Caitlin. BA, Oberlin Coll., 1975; JD, U. Va., 1979. Bar: D.C. Ct. Appeals 1980, U.S. Dist. Ct. D.C. 1980, U.S. Ct. Appeals (D.C. cir.) 1982. Law clk. to presiding justice U.S. Dist. Ct., Bryan, Va., 1979-80; assoc. Fulbright & Jaworski, Washington, 1980-82; sr. counsel SEC, Washington, 1982-84; gen. counsel Health Communications Inc., Washington, 1984—, also bd. dirs.; assoc. Ballard, Spahr, Andrews & Ingersoll, Washington, 1984-87; pres. Health Comms., Inc., Washington, 1987-94; COO The Tech. Group, Balt., 1996-97; of counsel Tighe, Patton, Tabackman & Babbin, Washington, 1996; CEO Train, Inc., Washington, 1995—; mng. dir. Bozman Ptnrs., LLC, Washington, 1997—; sr. v.p., gen. counsel In Touch Techs. Ltd., Washington, 1998—. Contbr. articles to profl. jours. Trustee Health Edn. Found., 1979—, Nat. Child Rsch. Ctr., 1989-91; bd. dirs. Foodfit.com., Washington, 1998—. Mem. ABA, Fed. Bar Assn., D.C. Bar Assn. Federal civil litigation, Securities, Criminal. Home and Office: 5105 Chevy Chase Pky NW Washington DC 20008-2920

**CHAFETZ, SAMUEL DAVID,** lawyer; b. Memphis, Mar. 6, 1945; m. Patricia S. Shandel, Aug. 20, 1967. BA, U. Mich., 1967; JD, Harvard U., 1970. Bar: N.Y. 1971, Tenn. 1973. Assoc. Wachtell Lipton Rosen & Katz, N.Y.C., 1970-73; from assoc. to ptnr. Ireland Gibson Reams Henderson & Chafetz, Memphis, 1973-77; ptnr. Waring Cox PLC, Memphis, 1977—. Mem. Memphis Shelby County Bar Assn. (chmn. securities sect. 1998-99). Securities, Mergers and acquisitions, Health. Office: Waring Cox PLC 50 N Front St Ste 1300 Memphis TN 38103-1113

**CHAFFIN, WILLIAM MICHAEL,** lawyer; b. Memphis, Jan. 27, 1947; s. William Emmett and Mary (DeWeese) C.; m. Paula Gayle Young, Apr. 5, 1969; children: Katherine Young, Courtney DeWeese. BBA, U. Miss., 1969, JD, 1972. Bar: Miss. 1972, U.S. Dist. Ct. (no. and so. dists.) Miss. 1972, U.S. Dist. Ct. Ark. 1992. Assoc. Maynard, Fitzgerald & Bradley, Clarksdale, Miss., 1972-73; ptnr. Maynard, Fitzgerald, Bradley & Chaffin, Clarksdale, 1973-74; assoc. Holcomb, Dunbar, Connell, Merkel & Tollison, Clarksdale, 1975-78; ptnr. Holcomb, Dunbar, Connell, Chaffin & Willard, Clarksdale, 1978—; counsel to bd. dirs. United So. Bank, Clarksdale, 1982-90, N.W. Miss. Regional Med. Ctr., Clarksdale, 1988—; former chmn. Commn. Continuing Legal Edn. for State of Miss. Mem. Dem. exec. com. Coahoma County, Miss., 1976-84; counsel to Coahoma County Bd. Suprs., 1984-94. Fellow Miss. Bar Found.; mem. ABA, Miss. Bar Found., Miss. Defense Lawyers Assn., Assn. County Bd. Attys., Miss. State Bar. Episcopalian. Avocations: hunting, scuba diving, golf. Insurance, Real property, Banking. Home: 111 Cypress Ave Clarksdale MS 38614-2603 Office: Holcomb Dunbar Connell Chaffin & Willard 152 Delta Ave Clarksdale MS 38614-4212

**CHAGARIS, ARTHUR N.,** lawyer; b. Jersey City, N.J., Oct. 30, 1948; s. John S. and Helen A. Chagaris; m. Lia Chagaris, June 18, 1988; children: John, Alexis Christina. BA in Econs., Boston U., 1970; JD, American U., 1974. Bar: D.C. 1975, N.J. 1975; cert. civil trial atty., N.J. Supreme Ct., Trenton, 1991. Law clk. D.C. Ct. of Appeals, Washington, 1974-75; assoc. Law Office Robert Ables, Washington, 1975-76, Goodman, Stoat & Nonan, Hackensack, N.J., 1976-78; sole practitioner Hackensack, N.J., 1978-80; ptnr. Chagaris & SaFro, Hackensack, N.J., 1980-91; sole practitioner Hackensack, N.J., 1991—. Editor-in-chief American U. Law Rev., 1974, contbr., 1973. Pres. parish coun. St. John the Theologian, Tenafly, N.J., 1992; pres., bd. dirs. Shenbrooke Co-op, Hackensack, 1990. With U.S. Army Res., 1970-76. Dean's fellow American U. Law Sch., Washington, 1974. Mem. N.J. Bar Assn., D.C. Bar Assn., Bergen County Bar Assn. Avocations: skiing, golf. General civil litigation, Environmental, Insurance. Office: 829 Main St Hackensack NJ 07601-4812

**CHAIKIN, BONNIE PATRICIA,** lawyer; b. N.Y.C., Apr. 4, 1953; d. Max and Paula (Blechman) Chaikin. Student, Cornell U., 1970-73; BA, Hofstra U., 1974; JD, St. John's U., 1977. Bar: N.Y. 1978, Fla. 1979, U.S. Customs Ct. 1979, U.S. Tax Ct. 1979, U.S. Dist. Ct. (ea. and so. dists.) N.Y. 1979, U.S. Ct. Customs and Patent Appeals 1979, U.S. Supreme Ct. 1986. Law asst. firm Weingold & Berman, N.Y.C., 1977-78; assoc. Dollinger, Gonski and Grossman, Carle Place, N.Y., 1978-79; mng. atty. firm Marsha Edelman, N.Y.C., 1979-80; individual practice law Oceanside, N.Y., 1980—; dep. county atty. Nassau County, 1982—, dep. bur. chief, Mcpl. Affairs, 1986—; profl. fashion model Other Dimensions, N.Y.C., 1980-82. Bd. dirs., counsel South Shore Planning Coun., 1982-85, v.p. Yashar. Mem. Fla. Bar Assn., N.Y. State Bar Assn., Am. Immigration Lawyers, Nassau County Bar

Assn. Labor, Municipal (including bonds), Immigration, naturalization, and customs. Office: 1 West St Mineola NY 11501-4813

**CHAITMAN, HELEN DAVIS,** lawyer; b. N.Y.C., July 5, 1941; d. Philip and Miriam (Pfeffer) D.; m. Edmund Chaitman, Feb. 29, 1964 (div. 1978); children: Jennifer, Alison; m. George B. Gelman, Oct. 21, 1979. AB cum laude, Bryn Mawr Coll., 1963; JD, Rutgers U., 1976. Bar: N.Y. 1976, N.J., U.S. Dist. Ct. N.Y., U.S. Dist. Ct. N.J., U.S. Ct. Appeals (3d cir.), U.S. Supreme Ct. Assoc. Paul, Weiss, Rifkind, Wharton & Garrison, N.Y.C., 1977-82; ptnr. Wilentz, Goldman & Spitzer, Woodbridge, N.J., 1983-87, Ross & Hardies, Somerset, N.J., 1987-99, Wolf Haldenstein Adler Freeman & Herz LLP, N.Y.C., 1999—. Author: The Law of Lender Liability, 1990; contbg. author: Commercial Damages, 1985; editor Emerging Theories of Lender Liability, 1985-87. Mem. ABA (chmn. comml. fin. svcs. com. 1994-97, sect. bus. law), Am. Law Inst. (sustaining mem. 1992-99), Pub. Law Inst. Bankruptcy, Contracts commercial. Home: The Farm 115 Fairview Rd Frenchtown NJ 08825-3013 Office: Wolf Haldenstein Adler Freeman & Herz LLP 270 Madison Ave New York NY 10016-0601 also: Wolf Haldenstein Adler Freeman & Herz LLP 580 Howard Ave Somerset NJ 08873-1136

**CHALFANT, WILLIAM YOUNG,** lawyer, author, historian; b. Hutchinson, Kans., Oct. 3, 1928; s. Claude Edward and Junia Maurine (Young) C.; m. Martha Ann Wallbillich, June 30, 1956; children: William David, Kristin. AB, U. Kans., 1950; JD, U. Mich., 1956. Bar: Kans. 1956, U.S. Ct. Appeals (10th cir.), U.S. Supreme Ct. Ptnr. Branine, Chalfant & Hill, Hutchinson, 1956—; bd. dir. First Nat. Bank, Hutchinson. Author: Cheyennes and Horse Soliders, 1989, Dangerous Passage, 1993, Without Quarter, 1991, Cheyennes at Dark Water Creek, 1997. Drive chmn. Reno County Cmty. Chest, Hutchinson, 1957-58l bd. dirs. Reno County Red Cross, Hutchinson, 1960-64; dist. commr. Boy Scouts Am., 1965-75. Capt. USMC, 1950-53. Recipient Gold award Santa Fe Nat. Hist. Trail/Nat. Park Svc., 1995. Mem. ABA, Kans. Bar Assn., Santa Fe Trail Assn. (bd. dirs., award of merit 1995), Western History Assn. (chmn. fin. com.). Avocations: history, writing. Contracts commercial, Constitutional, General practice. Home: 1007 W 95th Ave Hutchinson KS 67502-8325 Office: Branine Chalfant & Hill 418 First Nat Ctr Hutchinson KS 67501

**CHALKER, RONALD FRANKLIN,** lawyer, educator; b. Atlanta, Oct. 18, 1957; s. Nolan Franklin and Beverly Jean (Granger) C.; m. Brenda Elise Wright, June 13, 1981; children: Jessica Elise, Hannah Nichole, Jordan Annette. BS, Ga. So. U., 1979; JD, Woodrow Wilson Coll. Law, 1982. Bar: Ga. 1982, U.S. Dist. Ct. (no. dist.) Ga. 1982, U.S. Ct. Appeals (11th cir.) 1989. Assoc. Brooks & Brock, Marietta, Ga., 1983-85; ptnr. Hogan, Casey, Chalker & Cooper, Marietta, 1985-87, Robert A. Falanga, P.C., Atlanta, 1988-90, Falanga, Barrow & Chalker, Atlanta, 1991-94; Falanga & Chalker, Atlanta, 1995—; adj. prof. law So. Poly. U., Marietta, 1989—. Contbr. articles to profl. jours. mem. ABA, ATLA, Ga. Trial Lawyers Assn., Atlanta Bar Assn., Cobb County Bar Assn., Kiwanis (pres. Marietta Club 1992-93, Pres.'s award 1989). Republican. Avocations: golf, skiing. Personal injury, Insurance, Workers' compensation. Office: Falanga & Chalker 1820 The Exchange NW Ste 400 Atlanta GA 30339-2018

**CHAMBERLAIN, DENISE KAY,** lawyer, banking counsel; b. Steubenville, Ohio, Oct. 19, 1956. BA cum laude, Bethany (W.Va.) Coll., 1978; JD, W.Va. U., 1984. Bar: W.Va. 1984, Pa. 1986, U.S. Dist. Ct. (no. and so. dists.) W.Va. 1984, U.S. Dist. Ct. (we. dist.) Pa. 1986, U.S. Ct. Appeals (3d cir.) 1991; registered environ. profl. Atty. Recht & Johnson, Wheeling, W.Va., 1984-86, Buchanan Ingersoll, P.C., Pitts., 1986-88, Manion McDonough & Lucas, Pitts., 1988-90; assoc. counsel Mellon Bank, N.A., Pitts., 1990—; bd. advs. Lender's Legal Alert pub., 1995—. Contbg. author: Lender's Guide to Environmental Liability, 1992, Environmental Issues for Real Estate, 1992; contbr. articles to profl. jours. Advisor Pa. Chamber Bus. and Industry Superfund and Old Indsl. Site Rev. Com., 1993—, Allegheny County Planning Commn. Indsl. Site Reuse Com., 1993, S.W. Growth Alliance Indsl. Site Reuse Com., 1993, Pa. gov. Tom Ridge on the Great Lake Gov.s Coun., 1996—. Mem. ABA (chmn. environ. aspects lenser liab. comm.), Am. Bankers Assn. (environ. task force 1994), Pa. Banker Assn. (chmn. environ. liability task force 1992—), Environ. Bankers Assn. (cofounder 1994), W.Va. U. Coll. Law Alumni Assn. (pres. 1995). Environmental, Bankruptcy, Banking. Office: Mellon Bank NA One Mellon Bank Ctr Pittsburgh PA 15258

**CHAMBERLAIN, DOUGLAS REGINALD,** lawyer; b. Burlington, Vt., Sept. 8, 1951; s. Reginald B. and Ethelda B. (Towle) C.; m. Linda J. Canfield, Sept. 11, 1982; children: Samuel Douglas, Sarah Riley. AB, Harvard Coll., 1973; JD, Columbia U., 1976. Bar: N.H. 1976, U.S. Dist. Ct. N.H. 1976. Assoc. Wiggin & Nourie, Manchester, N.H., 1976-81, ptnr., 1982-91, chmn. corp. dept., 1987-93, shareholder Wiggin & Nourie, P.A., 1992—. N.H. Minimum CLE (bd. mem. 1992—, chmn. 1997—). Bd. dirs. N.H. Performing Arts Ctr., Manchester, 1981-89; mem. Mayor's Child Care Com., 1988-92 . Mem. N.H. Employee Benefits Council (pres. 1983-84), N.H. Bar Assn. (com. on ethics 1981-86, chmn., 1986-88, chmn. group ins. pension plan com. 1984-85, continuing legal edn. com. 1988-98, legislation com. 1996—, lawyer dispute resolution com. 1988-90, tax sect., bus. law sect., intellectual property sect.), ABA (employee benefits com. 1982—, taxation sect.). Republican. General corporate, Pension, profit-sharing, and employee benefits, Corporate taxation. Office: Wiggin & Nourie PA PO Box 808 Manchester NH 03105-0808

**CHAMBERLIN, HARVEY H.,** lawyer; b. Seattle, Nov. 13, 1947; s. Charles R. and R. Marian (Rose) C.; m. Anna Basich, Febr. 14, 1978 (div. Oct. 1986); 1 child, Nicole Ann. BA, U. Wash., 1970; attended, Willamette Coll. Law, 1970-71; JD, U. Wash., 1974. Bar: U.S. Dist. Ct. (we. dist.) Wash., 1974, U.S. Ct. Appeals (9th cir.) 1978. Assoc. Franco, Asia, Bensussen, Coe & Finegold, Seattle, 1978-80; trial atty. Snohomish County Pub. Defender, Everett, Wash., 1987-91; sole practitioner 6th Amendment Samurai, Everett, 1991—; instr. U. Wash., Seattle, 1977-83, Seattle U., 1974-76. Author: (books) Strategies and Techniques in Criminal Defense, 1978, Criminal Defense and the Appellate Court, 1980. With U.S. Marine Corps., 1969. Avocations: boxing, kickboxing, music (string bass), self-defense instructor. Criminal. Office: 3221 Oakes Ave Everett WA 98201-4407

**CHAMBERS, JULIUS LEVONNE,** academic administrator, lawyer; b. Montgomery County, N.C., Oct. 6, 1936. BA, N.C. Central U., 1958; MA, U. Mich., 1959; LLB, U. N.C., 1962; LLM, Columbia U., 1963. Bar: N.C. 1962, N.Y. 1986. Ptnr. Chambers, Ferguson, Watt, Wallas, Adkins, & Fuller, Charlotte, N.C., 1964-84; dir., counsel NAACP Legal Def. and Ednl. Fund, N.Y.C, 1984-92; chancellor N.C. Ctrl. U., Durham, N.C., 1993—; bd. dirs. RJR Nabisco Holdings. Trustee N.J. State Bd. of Higher Edn.; bd. visitors Harvard U., Columbia Law Sch.; trustee U. Pa., mem. bd. overseers Law Sch.; bd. dirs. Children's Def. Fund, Legal Aid Soc. N.Y. Mem. ABA (bd. editors ABA jour.), N.C. Bar Assn., Mecklenburg County Bar Assn., N.Y. State Bar Assn., Assn. of Bar of City of N.Y., Nat. Bar Assn., Assn. Black Lawyers N.C., Order of Coif, Order of Golden Fleece, Phi Alpha Theta. Office: NC Ctrl U 1801 Fayetteville St Durham NC 27707-3129

**CHAMBERS, MARGARET WARNER,** lawyer; b. West Chester, Pa., Oct. 12, 1959; d. Samuel Lippincott and Margaret Ewing (Warner) C.; m. Bruce Wayne Nifong, June 21, 1986. BS in Edn., Pa. State U., 1980; JD, Suffolk U., 1983. Bar: Mass. 1983. Staff atty. pub. records div. Mass. Sec. of State's Office, Boston, 1983-84, staff atty. securities div., 1984-86; assoc. Ropes & Gray, Boston, 1986-96; v.p., asst. gen. counsel Loomis, Sayles & Co., L.P., Boston, 1996—. Mem. ABA (state regulation of securities com., investment advisers/investment co. subcom., sec. state regulation of securities com. 1991-95, vice chair 1995—), Mass. Bar Assn. (sect. coun. bus. law sect. 1990-92, mem. securities law com.), Boston Bar Assn. (securities com.). Mem. Soc. of Friends. Securities, General corporate. Office: Loomis Sayles & Co LP One Financial Ctr Boston MA 02111

**CHAMBLESS, RICKY THOMAS,** lawyer; b. Birmingham, Ala., Jan. 29, 1971; s. Ricky Gene and Jane Anita C.; m. Krista Beth Spradley, Aug. 5, 1995; 1 child, Wilson Thomas. BS, David Lipscomb U., 1993; JD, U. Ala., 1996. Bar: Ala. 1996; U.S. Dist. Ct. (no. dist. Ala.) 1998. Clk., intern Tenn. State Atty. Gen., Nashville, 1993; clk. Gene Ch. & Assocs. Attys., Haleyville, Ala., 1993-95; legal cons. So. Energy Homes, Inc., Addison, Ala., 1995; atty. W. Allen Grocholski, Fayette, Ala., 1996—. Mem. ABA, Ala. Bar Assn., Fayette County Bar Assn. (sec. 1998—), Ala. Trial Lawyers Assn., Am. Assn. Criminal Def. Attys., Tuscaloosa County Rep. Party. Republican. Ch. of Christ. Avocations: golf, racquetball, music, gardening, collegiate football. General civil litigation, General practice, Real property. Home: 909 Princeton Pl Northport AL 35473-2665 Office: 201 Temple Ave S Fayette AL 35555-2713

**CHAMPAGNE, DEBRA,** judge; b. Houston, Jan. 13, 1957; m. Terry L. Champagne, Aug. 15, 1981; 1 child, Morgan Lee-Ann. BA in Psychology, U. North Tex., 1979; JD, Tex. So. U., 1988. Bar: Tex. Asst. city atty. City of Houston, 1989-93, mcpl. ct. judge, 1993—. Candidate state dist. ct. judge, Ft. Bend County, Tex., 1998; cell dir. U-Woman in the Now Houston, 1994—. Recipient Alex award NAACP, Houston br., 1997, Nat. Achiever award Nat. Women of Achievement, Houston, 1998. Mem. State Bar of Tex., Ft. Bend C. of C. Office: Municipal Court 901 Bagby St Fl 4 Houston TX 77002-2526

**CHAN, DANIEL CHUNG-YIN,** lawyer; b. Kowloon, Hong Kong, June 5, 1948; came to U.S., 1969; s. David Chi-Kwong and Betty Wai-Lan (Kwok) C.; m. Mary Ching-Fay Wong, June 11, 1977; children: Pamila Wai-Sum (dec.), Derrick Ming-Deh. BA cum laude, Azusa Pacific U., 1972; postgrad., Calif. State U., L.A., 1973-75; JD, U. West L.A., 1983. Bar: Calif. 1984, U.S. Dist. Ct. (cen. dist.) Calif. 1984, U.S. Ct. Appeals (9th cir.) 1984, U.S. Dist. Ct. (so. dist.) Calif. 1985, U.S. Dist. Ct. (no. dist.) Calif. 1986. Mgr. Elegant Sewing Co., L.A., 1977; legal asst. Otto Frank Swanson Law Office, Marina Del Ray, Calif., 1978-84, assoc., 1984-87; pvt. practice, Pasadena, Calif., 1987—; legal counsel Chinese Grace Missions Internat., Inc., Duarte, Calif., 1984—, Diao Jiou Chinese Christian Ch. L.A., Highland Park, Calif., 1988—, Ruth Hitchcock Found. Mem. ABA, Assn. Trial Lawyers Am., So. Calif. Chinese Lawyers Assn., Am. Immigration Lawyers Assn., Delta Epsilon Chi, Alpha Chi. Private international, Family and matrimonial, Immigration, naturalization, and customs. Office: 283 S Lake Ave Ste 219 Pasadena CA 91101-4818

**CHAN, DAVID RONALD,** tax specialist, lawyer; b. L.A., Aug. 3, 1948; s. David Yew and Anna May (Wong) C.; m. Mary Anne Chan, July 21, 1980; children: Eric, Christina. AB in Econs., UCLA, 1969, MS in Bus. Adminstrn., 1970, JD, 1973. Bar: Calif. 1973, U.S. Tax Ct. 1974, U.S. Ct. Appeals (9th cir.) 1974, U.S. Dist. Ct. (ctrl. dist.) Calif. 1980. Acct. Oxnard Celery Distbrs., L.A., 1968-73, Touche Ross & Co., L.A., 1970; tax prin. Kenneth Leventhal & Co. (name now E&Y Kenneth Leventhal Real Estate Group), L.A., 1973—. Contbr. chpts. to books and articles to profl. jours. Founder, dir. Chinese Hist. Soc. So. Calif., L.A., 1975—; mem. spkrs. bur. L.A. 200 Bicentennial, L.A., 1981; spkr. Project Follow Through, L.A., 1981, EY Tax Forum, UCLA Real Estate Forecast, Merril Lynch Symposium, Calif. CPA Soc. Recipient Forbes Gold medal Calif. Soc. CPAs, L.A., 1970, Elijah Watt Sells cert. AICPA, L.A., 1970, cert. recognition Chinese Hist. Soc. So. Calif., L.A., 1985. Mem. So. Calif. Chinese Lawyers Assn., L.A. County Bar Assn., Chinese Am. CPAs So. Calif., Asian Bus. League, Chinese For Affirmative Action. Republican. Avocations: Chinese cuisine, sports memorabilia, philately. Office: E&Y Kenneth Leventhal Real Estate Group 2049 Century Park E Ste 1700 Los Angeles CA 90067-3119

**CHAN, LAI LEE,** lawyer; b. Jan. 18, 1969. BA, NYU, 1991, JD, 1994. Bar: N.Y. 1997, U.S. Dist. Ct. (so. and ea. dists.) N.Y. 1997. Assoc. Law Offices Richard S. Missan, N.Y.C., 1994-97; pvt. practice N.Y.C., 1997—. Labor, Civil rights, Federal civil litigation. Office: 805 3rd Ave New York NY 10022-7513

**CHAN, THOMAS TAK-WAH,** lawyer; b. Kowloon, Hong Kong, June 5, 1950. BA magna cum laude, U. Wis., Whitewater, 1973; JD, U. Wis., 1979. Bar: Wis. 1979, U.S. Dist. Ct. (ea. dist.) Wis. 1979, Minn. 1983, Calif. 1987. Judicial intern Wis. Supreme Ct., 1978; atty. Wausau (Wis.) Ins., 1979-82; staff atty. CPT Corp., Eden Prairie, Minn., 1982-84; gen. counsel Lee Data Corp., Eden Prairie, 1984-85; dep. gen. counsel Ashton-Tate Corp., Torrance, Calif., 1985-87; pres. Chan Law Group LC, L.A., 1989—; mem. adv. bd. SBA Export Devel. Ctr., 1992—; founder Bus. Software Alliance, Washington, 1987; U.S. trade rep., mem. adv. com. industry sector U.S. Dept. Commerce, 1988-91; founder Asian Pacific Am. Coord. Com., 1996. Mem. Asian Pacific Am. Bar Assn. (founder, dir. 1998—), Wis. Bar Assn., Calif. Bar Assn. (lectr. 1988) Computer Law Assn., So. Calif. Chinese Lawyers Assn. (gov. 1990-92) Export Mgrs. Assn. So. Calif. (dir. 1990-92), S.Bay Chinese Am. C. of C. (founder, dir. 1997—), S.Bay Chinese Culture Ctr. (dir. 1998—), Cause (dir. 1994-97, chmn. 1995-96), Phi Kappa Phi. Avocations: skiing, hiking. Computer, Private international, Intellectual property. Office: Chan Law Group 911 Wilshire Blvd Ste 2288 Los Angeles CA 90017-3451

**CHANDER, ANUPAM,** lawyer; b. Hoshiarpur, India, Apr. 15, 1967; s. Harish and Yash (Garg) C. AB, Harvard U., 1989; JD, Yale U., 1992. Bar: N.Y. 1993. Clk. to Judge W. Norris U.S. Ct. Appeals (9th cir.), L.A., 1992-93; clk. to Chief Judge Newman U.S. Ct. Appeals (2d cir.), Hartford, Conn., 1993-94; assoc. Cleary, Gottlieb, Steen & Hamilton, N.Y.C., 1994-99; assoc. prof. law Ariz. State U., Tempe, 1999—. Contbg. author: UNHCR Human Rights Manual, 1998. Co-dir. South Asian Youth Action, N.Y.C., 1998-99. Mem. Assn. Bar City N.Y. (human rights com. 1997-99). Avocation: reading. Private international, Securities, Finance. Office: Arizona State University Coll of Law PO Box 877906 Tempe AZ 85287-7906

**CHANDLER, ALBERT BENJAMIN III,** attorney general; m. Jennifer Chandler; children: Lucie Brasher, Albert Benjamin IV, Russell Branham. BA in History with distinction, U. Ky., JD, 1986. Bar: Ky. 1986. Assoc. Brown, Todd & Heyburn, Lexington, Ky., Reeves & Graddy, Versailles, Ky.; state auditor, atty. gen. Office of Atty. Gen., Ky. Recipient Achievement of the Yr. award Assn. Govt. Accts., 1993-94. Mem. ABA, Ky. Bar Assn. (named Outstanding Young Lawyer 1993), Woodford County Bar Assn. Office: Office of Atty Gen Ste 118 Capitol Bldg Frankfort KY 40601-2831

**CHANDLER, BURTON,** lawyer; b. Fitchburg, Mass., Apr. 12, 1934; s. Samuel O. and Eunice B. (Silverman) C.; m. Harriet Levy, July 12, 1959; children: Frank L., Victoria J., Edward L. BA, Harvard U., 1956, LLB, 1959. Bar: Mass. 1959, U.S. Tax Ct. 1965, U.S. Ct. Appeals (1st cir.) 1973. Assoc. Seder & Chandler, Worcester, Mass., 1959-75, ptnr., 1975—. Mem. ABA (litigation sect.), Mass. Bar Assn. (past chmn. pre-paid legal ins. com.). General civil litigation, General corporate, Estate planning. Home: 7 Brook Hill Dr Worcester MA 01609-1314 Office: Seder & Chandler 339 Main St Ste 300 Worcester MA 01608-1585

**CHANDLER, EVERETT ALFRED,** lawyer; b. Columbus, Ohio, Sept. 21, 1926; s. Everett P. and Mary C. (Turner) C.; children: Wayne B., Brian E., V. Rhette; m. Mittie Rene Olion, Mar. 20, 1987 (div. Sept. 1991); 1 child, Mae Evette. BEd, Ohio State U., 1955; JD, Howard U., 1958. Bar: Ohio 1958, U.S. Dist. Ct. (no. dist.) Ohio 1962, U.S. Ct. Appeals (6th cir.) 1991, U.S. Tax Ct. 1967. Asst. county pros. Cuyahoga County, 1968-71; chief pros. City of Cleve., 1971-75; prin. Everett A. Chandler, Atty., Cleve. Author book rev. Cleve. State Law Jour., 1974. Chair bd. dirs. Cmty. Action Against Addiction, Cleve., 1975—, Crisis Intervention Team, Cleve., 1976-91; trustee Legal Aid Soc., Cleve., 1982-84, Boys Club Cleve., 1969-72; Dem. candidate for judge, Cuyahoga County, 1994. With USN, 1945-53. Mem. Norman S. Minor Bar Assn., Kappa Alpha Psi (past pres. 1980-83, 76-80, chmn. bd.). Democrat. Baptist. Avocations: golfing, traveling. Criminal, General civil litigation, General practice. Home: 16010 Talford Ave Cleveland OH 44128-1237 Office: PO Box 28459 Cleveland OH 44128-0459

**CHANDLER, GEORGE FRANCIS, III,** lawyer, naval architect; b. Winthrop, Mass., Dec. 15, 1940; s. George Francis Jr. and Phyllis (McKay) C.; children: Heather Suzanne, George Francis IV. BSME, Va. Poly. Inst., 1963; JD, Suffolk U., 1972. Bar: Mass. 1972, N.Y. 1973, N.J. 1978, U.S. Dist. Ct. Mass. 1972, U.S. Dist. Ct. (so. dist.) N.Y. 1973, U.S. Dist. Ct. (ea. dist.) N.Y. 1977, U.S. Dist. Ct. (so. dist.) Tex. 1990), U.S. Dist. Ct. N.J. 1977, U.S. Ct. Appeals (2d cir.) 1973, U.S. Supreme Ct. 1977, U.S. Ct. Appeals (4th cir.) 1978, U.S. Ct. Appeals (11th cir.) 1983, U.S. Ct. Appeals (1st cir.) 1984, U.S. Ct. Appeals (5th cir.) 1992 ; profl. engr., Mass. Naval architect Dept. BuShips USN, Boston, 1958-63, 67-72; assoc. Bigham, Englar, Jones & Houston, N.Y.C., 1972-78; ptnr. Hill, Rivkins & Hayden LLP (and predecessor firm), N.Y.C., 1978—; U.S. rep. to UNCITRAL for Electronic Commerce, 1991-96; mem. joint work group UNCITRAL/CMI, 1995-96; del. Comitè Maritime Internat., 1990, 98, CMI subcom. on H/V Rules, 1995-99, CMI steering commn. on transport law, 1997—; titulary mem. CMI Subcom. on Electronic B/L. Contbr. articles to profl. jours. Pres., founder Spl. Edn. PTA, Maplewood, N.J., 1984-87. Lt. USNR, 1963-67. Mem. ABA, Soc. Naval Archs. (chmn. N.Y. sect. 1986-87), Maritime Law Assn. (proctor, bd. dirs. 1993-96, chmn. com. on carriage of goods 1991-95, chmn. subcom. on electronic contracts of carriage 1990-91, chmn. electronic comm. com. 1995-99), Houston Maritime Arbitrators Assn. (founder, pres., bd. dirs. 1998—). Admiralty, Contracts commercial, Private international. Office: Hill Rivkins & Hayden LLP Ste 1515 712 Main St Houston TX 77002-3209

**CHANDLER, KENT, JR.,** lawyer; b. Chgo., Jan. 10, 1920; s. Kent and Grace Emeret (Tuttle) C.; m. Frances Robertson, June 19, 1948; children: Gail, Robertson Kent. BA, Yale U., 1942; JD, U. Mich., 1949. Bar: Ill. 1949, U.S. Dist. Ct. (no. dist.) Ill. 1949, U.S. Ct. Appeals (7th cir.) 1955, U.S. Ct. Claims 1958. Assoc. Wilson & McIlvaine, Chgo., 1949-56, ptnr., 1957-94, spl. counsel to firm, 1994-98; of counsel Bell, Jones, Quinlisk & Palmer, Chgo., 1998—; bd. dirs. Internat. Crane Found., 1988—. Mem. zoning bd. appeals City of Lake Forest, Ill., 1953-63, chmn., 1963-67, mem. plan commn., 1955-69, chmn., 19690-70, pres. bd. local improvements, 1970-73, mayor, 1970-73, mem. bd. fire and police commn., 1975-82, chmn., 1982-84. Served to maj. USMCR, 1941-46. Mem. ABA, Ill. State Bar Assn., Chgo. Bar Assn., Lake County Bar Assn., Legal Club Chgo., Law Club (pres. 1985-86), Univ. Club, Onwentsia Club (Lake Forest), Old Elm Club (Highland Park, Ill.). Republican. Presbyterian. Estate planning, Pension, profit-sharing, and employee benefits, Personal income taxation. Office: 200 W Adams St Ste 2620 Chicago IL 60606-5233

**CHANDLER, KIMBERLEY ANN,** lawyer; b. Providence, Sept. 17, 1952; d. Jerome Thomas and Anne Louise (Sheary) Bieter; m. Christopher L. Chandler; 1 child, Allison Marie Duran. BA, Cornell U., 1974; JD, U. Colo., 1981. Bar: Colo. 1982, U.S. Dist. Ct. Colo. 1982, U.S. Ct. Appeals (10th cir.) 1985. Atty. C. James Cooper Jr., Denver, 1982-83, Duran & Duran, Denver, 1983-89; Atty. pvt. practice, Denver, 1989-90, Rothgerber, Appel, Powers & Johnson, Denver, 1990—; lectr. in field. Mem. Am. Immigration Lawyers Assn. (co-chmn. improved adjudications task force 1991-92, v.p. Colo. chpt. 1993—), Colo. Bar Assn., Colo. Women's Bar Assn., Denver Bar Assn. Immigration, naturalization, and customs. Office: Rothgerber Appel Powers & Johnson 1200 17th St Ste 3000 Denver CO 80202-5855

**CHANDLER, LAWRENCE BRADFORD, JR.,** lawyer; b. New Bedford, Mass., June 20, 1942; s. Lawrence Bradford and Anne (Crane) C.; m. Madeleine Bibeau, Sept. 7, 1963 (div. June 1984); children: Dawn, Colleen, Brad. BS in Bus. Adminstrn., Boston Coll., 1963; LLB, U. Va., 1966, JD, 1970. Bar: Mass. 1966, U.S. Supreme Ct. 1967, Va. 1970, W.Va. 1993; diplomate Nat. Bd. Trial Advocacy; advocate Am. Bd. Trial Advocates. Ptnr. Chandler, Franklin & O'Bryan, Charlottesville, Va., 1971—. Pres. Western Va. Chpt., 1992-93. Capt. U.S. Army, 1967-71. Mem. ABA, ATLA (chair state dels. 1993-94, exec. com. 1993-94, bd. govs. 1995—), Va. Trial Lawyers Assn. (pres. 1985-86), Am. Bd. Trial Advs. (pres. Va. chpt.), Nat. Bd. of Trial Advocacy (bd. examiners), Charlottesville Bar Assn., Assn. U.S. Army (pres. 1971-73), Am. Coll. Legal Medicine, Am. Soc. on Law, Medicine and Ethics, Am. Assn. Profl. Liability Attys. Roman Catholic. Personal injury. Home: 1445 Old Ballard Rd Charlottesville VA 22901-9469 Office: Chandler Franklin & O'Bryan PO Box 6747 Charlottesville VA 22906-6747

**CHANDLER, RONALD JAY,** lawyer; b. Springfield, Mo., Jan. 15, 1949; s. Jack Dempsey and Esta Lee (Cravens) C.; m. Patricia Ann Meyer, June 17, 1973; 1 child, Mary Coday. BA, Mo. So. State Coll., 1975; JD, U. Tulsa, 1979. Bar: Okla. 1979, U.S. Dist. Ct. (no. dist.) Okla. 1980, U.S. Ct. Appeals (10th cir.) 1981. Asst. dist. atty. Office of Dist. Atty., Tulsa, 1979-80; ptnr. Chandler & Cantrell, Tulsa, 1980; atty. Cities Svc. Co., Tulsa, 1980-82; assoc. Prichard, Norman & Wohlgemuth, Tulsa, 1982-84; ptnr. Norman, Wohlgemuth & Thompson, Tulsa, 1984-89, Norman Wohlgemuth Chandler & Dowdell, Tulsa, 1989—; instr. Tulsa Jr. Coll., 1980-83, 86; vis. asst. prof. Univ. Ctr., U. Okla., Tulsa, 1990-97. With U.S. Army, 1968-70. Mem. ABA, Okla. Bar Assn., Tulsa County Bar Assn., Summit Club, Tulsa So. Tennis Club, Phi Alpha Delta. Republican. Episcopalian. Avocations: sailing, tennis, reading. General corporate, Contracts commercial, Real property. Office: Norman Wohlgemuth Chandler & Dowdell 2900 Mid-Continent Tower Tulsa OK 74103

**CHANELES, STEVEN BENNETT,** lawyer; b. New Haven, Oct. 3, 1960. BS in Bus. Adminstrn. cum laude, U. Conn., 1983; JD cum laude, U. Richmond, 1991. Tax sr. acct. Arthur Andersen & Co., Stamford, Conn., 1984-87; atty. Williams, Mullen, Christian & Dobbins, Richmond, Va., 1991-92, Silver & Garvett PA, Coconut Grove, Fla., 1992-94, Buchanan Ingersoll, PA, Aventura, Fla., 1994-95; pvt. practice Aventura, 1995-97; dir. bus. affairs SportsLine USA, Inc., Ft. Lauderdale, Fla., 1997—. Bd. dirs. Cmtys. in Schs. Miami (Fla.) Inc., 1996-97. Mem. Sigma Phi Epsilon (alumni bd. 1997—). Office: SportsLine USA Inc 6340 NW 5th Way Fort Lauderdale FL 33309-6130

**CHANEN, STEVEN ROBERT,** lawyer; b. Phoenix, May 15, 1953; s. Herman and Lois Marion (Boshes) C. Student, UCLA, 1971-73; BS in Mass Communications, Ariz. State U., 1975, JD, 1979. Bar: Ariz. 1980, U.S. Dist. Ct. Ariz. 1980, U.S. Ct. Appeals (9th cir.) 1980, Calif. 1981, U.S. Dist. Ct. (no. dist.) Calif. 1982. Ptnr. Wentworth & Lundin, Phoenix, 1980-86, of counsel, 1986-87; pres. Chanen Constrn. Co., Inc., 1987—; appointed bd. dirs. Ariz. Gov.'s Commn. on Motion Pictures and TV, 1986, chmn., 1990; appointed bd. dirs., exec. v.p. Chanen Corp.; fin. intermediary, chmn. bd. dirs. S.R. Chanen and Co, Inc.; pres. Chanen Constrn. Co., Inc. Bd. dirs. Anytown, Am., Phoenix, 1986—, COMPAS, Inc., Phoenix, 1986—, Ariz. Mus. Sci. and Tech., Phoenix, 1987—, Mus. Theater Ariz., Phoenix, 1988-89, Temple Beth Isreal, Ariz. Politically Interested Citizens, Jewish Fedn.; v.p. bd. dirs. Community Forum, Phoenix, Phoenix Children's Hosp., Nat. Conf. (dir.) Maricopa County C.C. Dist. Found. (pres.). Recipient J. Leonard Amdur Man of the Year award; Leader of Distinction award Anti-Defamation League. Mem. ABA (forum com. entertainment and sports industries 1981—), Ariz. Bar Assn., Calif. Bar Assn., Maricopa County Bar Assn., Assn. Trial Lawyers Am. Republican. Jewish. General corporate, Securities, Administrative and regulatory. Office: 3300 N 3rd Ave Phoenix AZ 85013-4304

**CHANG, DEBORAH,** lawyer, educator; b. Man, W.Va., Feb. 15, 1960; d. C.H. Joseph and Chung Sook (Chun) C. BA, Kans. U., 1983; JD with honors, Drake U., 1986. Bar: Conn. 1986, Ariz. 1991, U.S. Dist. Ct. Conn., 1987, U.S. Dist. Ct. Ariz. 1991, U.S. Dist. Tex. 1992. Law clk. to judge Conn. Appellate Ct., Hartford, 1986-87; assoc. Day, Berry & Howard, Hartford, 1987-91, Snell & Wilmer, Phoenix, 1991—, 1991—; instr. Law Sch. U. Conn., Hartford, 1988-91. Contbr. articles to profl. jours. Counsel Ariz. Kids Project, McKinney Scholarship Fund, Fairfield, 1989-91; speaker, adv. AIDS Project Hartford & Discrimination Forums, 1988—, vol., 1989. Named one of 20 Young Lawyers Whose Work Makes a Difference ABA Young Lawyers' div., 1990; recipient Women of Distinction award Soroptimist Internat. of the Ams., 1990. Mem. ABA (young lawyer's divsn. award 1990), State Bar of Ariz., Conn. Bar Assn. (young lawyers sect., mem. legal aid com., mem. human rights com.), Maricopa County Bar Assn. (AIDS assistance com. young lawyers divsn.). Avocations: reading, writing. General civil litigation, Personal injury, Product liability.

**CHANG, JANICE MAY,** lawyer, administrator, notary public; b. Loma Linda, Calif., May 24, 1970; d. Belden Shiu-Wah (dec.) and Sylvia (Tan) C. BA, Calif. State U, San Bernardino, 1990, cert. paralegal studies, 1990, cert. creative writing, 1991; JD, LaSalle U., 1993; D in Naturopathy, Clayton Sch. Natural Healing, 1993; MS in Psychology, Calif. Coast U., 1997; PhD in Bus. Adminstrn., Columbia State U., 1997; postgrad., Calif. Coast U., 1999. Notary pub., Calif. Victim/witness contact clk.-paralegal Dist. Atty.'s Office Victim/Witness Assistance Program, San Bernardino, Calif., 1990; gen. counsel JMC Enterprises, Inc., Loma Linda, Calif., 1993-98; law prof. LaSalle U., Mandeville, La., 1994-97; corp. counsel, CFO, JDS Assocs., Inc., Loma Linda, 1998-99; corp. counsel, CFO DJS, L.P., Loma Linda, 1998-99; with trust mgmt.-legal dept./trust svcs. Southeastern Calif. Assn. Seventh-Day Adventists, Riverside, 1998—; spkr. Internat. U. Graduation Ceremony/Conv., Las Vegas, 1998; sponsor La Sierra U. Student Employment Recognition Banquet, Riverside, Calif., 1999, La Sierra U. Path of the Just Tree Project, 1998, vol. La Sierra U., Riverside, Ca. Health Fair Expo, 1988, 89, Am. Red Cross First Aid & CPR classes, 1994—. Contbr. poetry to anthologies, including Am. Poetry Anthology, 1987-90, The Pacific Rev., 1991, The Piquant, 1991, River of Dreams, 1994, Reflections of Light, 1994, Musings, 1994 (Honorable Mention award 1994), Best Poems of 1995 (Celebrating Excellence award 1995, Inspirations award 1995), Am. Poetry Annual, 1996, Best New Poems of 1996, Interludes, 1996, Meditations, 1996, Perspectives, 1996 (Honorable Mention award 1996), Keepsakes, 1997 (Honorable Mention award 1997), Best Poems of 1997, Poetic Voices of America, 1997, The Isle of View, 1997, The Other Side of Midnight, 1997, Treasures, 1998, Best Poems of 1998, Writingscapes: Insights & Approaches to Creative Writing, 1998. Vol. Health Fair Expo., La Sierra U., Riverside, 1988, 89, ARC first aid and CPR, 1998, 99; donor Loma Linda Indonesian SDA Ch. Belden S. Chang Meml. Fund-Bldg. Annex, 1998, 99. Recipient Poet of Merit award Am. Poetry Assn., San Francisco, 1989, Golden Poet award World of Poetry, Washington, 1989, Publisher's Choice award Watermark Press, 1990, Editor's Choice award The Nat. Libr. of Poetry, 1990-97, Pres.'s award for lit. excellence Iliad Press, 1995-97. Mem. APA, Nat. Notary Assn. Republican. Seventh-Day Adventist. Avocations: poetry writing, music, drama, lit., numismatics. Estate planning, Landlord-tenant, General corporate. Home: 11466 Richmont Rd Loma Linda CA 92354-3523 Office: Southeastern Calif Assn 7th-Day Adventists PO Box 8050 11330 Pierce St Riverside CA 92515-8050

**CHANG, LEE-LEE,** lawyer; b. Taipei, Taiwan, May 26, 1954; came to U.S., 1986; parents: T.S. and B.H. (Ong) C. LLB, Nat. Chung Hsing U., Taipei, 1976; JD, CUNY, 1990. Bar: N.Y. 1990. Chinese law specialist Stephen S. Lee & Assocs., Taipei, 1981-86; tchg. asst. CUNY Law Sch., Flushing, 1989-90; assoc. Wise, Lerman & Katz, P.C., N.Y.C., 1990-93; pvt. practice Flushing, 1994—; cons. Dorcas & Kalam Co., Hicksville, N.Y., 1994—; adv. bd. mem. Chgo. Title Ins. Co., Garden City, N.Y., 1996—. Co-author: A Practical Usage Guide to Commercial Papers in R.O.C., 1983, Chinese Businessman's Guide to American Law-Business Practice-Taxation, 1993. Mem. Christian Legal Soc. Avocations: tennis, golf, traveling, swimming, reading. Real property, Probate, Contracts commercial. Office: 13621 Roosevelt Ave 3d Fl Flushing NY 11354-5507

**CHANG, PETER ASHA, JR.,** lawyer; b. Honolulu, Feb. 1, 1937; s. Peter Asha and Helen (Lee) C.; m. Maybelle Ching, Sept. 3, 1955 (div. Aug. 1982); children: Catherine, Peter III, Christopher. AB, Stanford U., 1958, JD, 1961. Bar: Calif. 1962, U.S. Dist. Ct. (no. and cen. dists.) Calif. 1962, U.S. Ct. Appeals (9th cir.) 1962, U.S. Supreme Ct. 1964. Asst. dist. atty. Monterey, Calif., 1961-66, chief asst. dist. atty., 1966-75; dist. atty. Santa Cruz County, Washington, 1975; pvt. practice Santa Cruz, 1975—; instr., cons. Calif. Dist. Atty.'s Assn., Sacramento, 1967-74, Nat. Coll. Dist. Attys., 1968-72, Stanford Law Sch., Palo Alto, Calif., 1969-71; faculty mem. Nat. Criminal Def. Coll., Macon, Ga., 1990—; lectr. in field. Recipient Pros. of Yr. award Calif. Dist. Atty.'s Assn., 1972. Fellow Am. Bd. Criminal Lawyers; mem. ABA, Nat. Assn. Criminal Def. Lawyers (bd. dirs. 1991-96), Calif. Atty. for Criminal Justice. Democrat. Criminal, Personal injury. Office: 331 Soquel Ave Santa Cruz CA 95062-2323

**CHANG, TA-TUNG JACOB,** diplomat; b. Chia-Yi, Taiwan, Republic of China, May 28, 1951; s. Chenp-Ping C. and Shu-Chen Chin; m. Holen Helen, Jan. 21, 1984; children: Sandra K., Maria K. LLB, Nat. Taiwan U., Republic of China, 1973; LLM, Ind. U., 1978; SJD, George Washington U., 1988. Bar: N.Y. 1991. Exec. dir. Chinese Am. Soc., Washington, 1986-88; staff cons. Coord. Coun. N. Am. Affairs, Washington, 1988-94; sect. chief, sr. specialist, asst. dir. gen. Min. Fgn. Affairs, Taipei, China, 1994-97; deputy dir. Taipei Econ. & Cultural Rep. Office in U.S., Washington, 1997-99, dir., 1999—. Assoc. editor Chinese Yearbook of International Law and Affairs, 1993—. 2d lt. Republic of China Army, 1973-75. Mem. ABA, Am. Soc. Internat. Law, N.Y. State Bar Assn., Internat. LAw Assn., Chinese Soc. Internat. Law, Ind. U. Alumni Assn., George Washington U. Alumni Assn. Roman Catholic. Avocations: reading, Chinese opera, music. Office: TECRO in US 4201 Wisconsin Ave NW Washington DC 20016-2146

**CHANIN, BERNARD,** lawyer; b. Phila., Oct. 12, 1932; s. Benjamin and Irene (Holutin) C.; children—Heidi, Susan, Gary, Eve; m. Eileen Levy. B.A., U. PA., 1962, LL.B. cum laude, 1965. Bar: Pa. 1965, U.S. Supreme Ct. 1976. Law clk. Assoc. Justice Supreme Ct. Pa., Phila., 1965-66; ptnr. Wolf, Block, Schorr, & Solis-Cohen, Phila., 1966—. Served with USMC, 1951-54, Korea. Mem. ABA, Pa. Bar Assn., Phila. Bar Assn., Order of the Coif. Federal civil litigation, General civil litigation. Office: Wolf Block Schorr & Solis-Cohen 15th & Chestnut Sts 1650 Arch St Fl 21 Philadelphia PA 19103-2097

**CHANIN, MICHAEL HENRY,** lawyer; b. Atlanta, Nov. 11, 1943; s. Henry and Herma Irene (Blumenthal) C.; m. Margaret L. Jennings, June 15, 1968; children: Herma Louise, Richard Henry, Patrick Jennings. A.B., U. N.C., 1965; J.D., Emory U., 1968. Bar: Ga. 1968, D.C. 1981. Dir. So. Ctr. for Studies in Pub. Policy, Atlanta, 1968-69; asst. and acting legal officer 1st Coast Guard Dist., Boston, 1969-72; atty. Powell, Goldstein Frazer & Murphy, Atlanta, 1972-77; spl. asst. to sec. U.S. Dept. Commerce, Washington, 1977-78; dep. asst. to pres. The White House, Washington, 1978-81; ptnr. Powell, Goldstein, Frazer & Murphy, Washington, 1981—. Served to lt. USCGR, 1969-72. Mem. ABA, D.C. Bar Assn., State Bar Ga. Democrat. General corporate, Finance, Private international. Office: Powell Goldstein Frazer & Murphy 1001 Pennsylvania Ave NW Fl 6 Washington DC 20004-2505

**CHAO, CEDRIC C.,** lawyer; b. Cambridge, Mass., Apr. 9, 1950. BA, Stanford U., 1972; JD, Harvard U., 1977. Bar: Calif. 1977, U.S. Dist. Ct. (no. dist.) Calif. 1977, U.S. Ct. Appeals (9th cir.) 1979, U.S. Supreme Ct. 1988. Law clk.to Hon. William H. Orrick U.S. Dist. Ct. (no. dist.) Calif., San Francisco, 1977-78; asst. U.S. atty. U.S. Atty.'s Office, San Francisco, 1978-81; assoc. Morrison & Foerster, San Francisco, 1981-83, ptnr., 1983—; lawyer del. 9th cir. judicial conf., 1990-92; chair magistrate judge selection com. No. Dist. Calif., 1996. Author: Creating Your Discovery Plan, 1997. Named One of Calif.'s Top 25 Lawyers Under Age 45, Calif. Law Bus., 1994. Fellow Am. Bar Found.; mem. ABA (standing com. fed. judiciary, 1991-94), State Bar Calif. (com. profl. responsibility and conduct 1980-84, exec. com. litigation sect. 1986-91, vice chair 1989-90, chair 1990-91), San Francisco Bar Assn. (bd. dirs. 1988-90), Am. Law Inst., Asian Am. Bar Assn. Greater Bay Area (bd. dirs. 1977-82, pres. 1982), San Francisco C. of C. (bd. dirs. 1996—), World Affairs Coun. No. Calif. (trustee 1994—), Commonwealth Club Calif. (quar. chair 1989). General civil litigation, Criminal, Private international. Office: Morrison & Foerster 425 Market St Ste 3100 San Francisco CA 94105-2482

**CHAPIN, BARRY W.,** lawyer, consultant; b. Rochester, N.Y., Mar. 16, 1967; s. Harrison Lyon and Vera (Berry) C.; m. Clarise M. Chapin, Dec. 30, 1995; 1 child, Brittany Anne. BS in Computer Sci., SUNY, Potsdam, 1989; student, Boston U., 1990-93; JD, Suffolk U., 1997. Bar: Mass. 1997, U.S. Patent Office 1995. Software engr. GTE Govt. Systems, Needham, Mass., 1989-93; computer network engr. MIT/Draper Lab., Cambridge, Mass., 1993-95; registered patent agt. Wolf, Greenfield & Sacks, P.C., Boston, 1995-97; patent atty. Hamilton, Brook, Smith & Reynolds, P.C., Lexington, Mass., 1997—; pres. Intellectual Property Law Students Assn., Suffolk U., 1995, 96;. Author and editor computer and software related patents filed with U.S. Patent Office, 1995—. Weekend cook Homeless Food Shelter, Cambridge, 1995—. Mem. Boston Patent Lawyers Assn. (co.-chmn. law com. 1996, 97, 98), Am. Intellectual Property Lawyers Assn., IEEE Entrepreneurs Network, USENIX Orgn., Porsche Club of Am. Unitarian. Avocations: landscaping, skiing, reading, computers, auto mechanics. Patent, Intellectual property, Computer. Home: 3 Reed Ave Westborough MA 01581-3643

**CHAPIN, MARY Q.,** arbitrator, mediator, writer, perfoming artist; b. Shepherdstown, W.VA., May 5, 1933; d. Guy Estil and Anne Mildred (Jones) Quisenberry; m. Edward John Chapin Jr.; children: John Edward, Susan Q. (dec.). SUNY Regent's Degree, 1985; AAS, SUNY, Binghamton, BS, 1991. Pers. adminstr. Mohawk Valley Psychiatric Ctr., Utica, N.Y., 1976-89; arbitrator Am. Arbitration Assn., N.Y.C., 1989-99; pres. Dispute Resolution Internat., New Hartford, N.Y., 1993—; neutral chair NYSDOL Office of Labor Mgmt., Albany, N.Y., 1993—; mem. adv. coun. on safety and security in N.Y. State schs. N.Y. State Dept. Edn., Albany, 1995-97; founder, mem., bd. dirs. Forum on Conflict and Concensus, 1993-94l chiar Mohawk Valley Women's History Project, 1998—. Author: Woman's Suffrage: A Dream of Full Citizenship; author, performer An Afternoon with Susan B. Anthony; contbr. articles to profl. jours. Pres. Utica/Rome Metro League of Women Voters, 1992-97; coord. Com. on Met. Orgn., 1995-97; coord. of multicultural commn. League of Women Voters Edn. Fund, 1997; trustee Mohawk Valley Cmty. Coll., 1996—; mem. edn. com. Assn. Bd. of Trustees of C.C., 1997—; Utica C. of C., 1995-98. Recipient Found. award The Found. of SUNY at Binghamton, 1992, Recognition award NYS League of Women Voters, 1995, 97, Recognition award U.S. LWV Edn. Fund, 1998, Labor Mgmt. award Office of Mental Health, 1988. Mem. AAUW (v.p.), Central N.Y. Futurist, Bd. Neighborhood Ctr. Avocations: medical herbalist, human rights and women's rights. Home and Office: 56 Woodbrooke Rd New Hartford NY 13413-4805

**CHAPIN, MELVILLE,** lawyer; b. Boston, Dec. 14, 1918; s. Edward Barton and Jeannette (Thomas) C.; m. Elizabeth Ann Parker, Sept. 6, 1940; children: Allan M., Elizabeth M. B.A., Yale U., 1940; J.D., Harvard U., 1943. Bar: Mass. 1943. Of counsel Warner & Stackpole LLP now Kirkpatrick & Lockhart LLP, Boston, 1954—; chmn. bd. dirs. H.B. Smith Co., Inc.; pres., trustee emeritus Phillips Acad.; chmn. emeritus, trustee Mass. Eye and Ear Infirmary and Found. Bd. dirs. Chewonki Found. Inc.; chmn. Yale U. Planned Giving, Coun. Mass. Hist. Soc.; trustee Sturbridge Village; mem. adv. com. Salvation Army; bd. dirs. dir. Bostonian Soc.; mem. leadership coun. New Bedford Whaling Mus.; mem. state adv. com. Salvation Army; v.p. Polly Hill Found. Fellow Am. Bar Found., Mass. Bar Found.; mem. ABA, Boston Bar Assn., Mass. Bar Assn., Internat. Bar Assn., Edgartown Yacht Club (trustee). Estate planning, Probate, Estate taxation. Home: 15 Traill St Cambridge MA 02138-4738 Office: 75 State St Fl 6 Boston MA 02109-1807

**CHAPLIN, ANSEL BURT,** lawyer; b. Deerfield, Ill., June 12, 1931; s. Robert Tappan and Ruth (Burt) C.; m. Maud Denise Hazeltine, 1959 (div. 1993); children: Rawson, Margaret, Jane; m. Anne Carol Kenney, 1995. BA magna cum laude, Princeton U., 1953; postgrad., Inst. Polit. Sci., Paris, U. Algiers; JD, Harvard U., 1959. Bar: Mass. 1959. Law clk. to chief justice Mass. Supreme Ct., 1959-60; ptnr. Chaplin & Chaplin, Boston; practice Boston, 1960-99, Cape Cod, Mass., 1981—; owner Cape Cod Fishnet Industries, North Truro, Mass., 1980-96; chmn. com. legal edn. Mass. Supreme Ct., 1979-90, mem. com. lawyer advt., 1979-82; vice chmn. commn. on legal profession and the economy of New Eng., New Eng. Bd. Higher Edn., 1991; mem. U.S. Dist. Ct. Ad. Practice Com., 1981-85; chmn. vis. com. So. New England Sch. Law, 1992-93. Author papers in field. Pres. Truro Neighborhood Assn., 1979-83; mem. corp. Perkins Sch. for Blind, Watertown, Mass., 1973—, Winsor Sch., Boston, 1980-83; sec., adminstrv. trustee Truro Conservation Trust, 1981—, trustee Payomet Performing Arts Charitable Trust, 1998—, Dexter Deezer CMty. Fund, 1998—; pres. Compact of Cape Cod Conservation Trusts, 1986—; pres. Friends of the Pamet, Inc., 1994-96; mem. bd. dirs. Mass. Appleseed Ctr. for Law and Justice, 1994-96. With AUS, 1954-56. Recipient Thoreau award Cape Cod Mus. Natural History, 1987; Fulbright fellow, 1953-54. Fellow Am. Bar Found., Mass. Bar Found.; Mem. ABA, Am. Law Inst., Mass. Bar Assn. (chmn. law practice sect. 1978-80), Boston Bar Assn. (co-chair peer support com. 1997—), Harvard Law Sch. Assn. Mass. (pub. interest coord. 1994—), Harvard Law Sch. Assn. (mem. coun. 1997—), Wellesley Boat Club. Democrat. Unitarian. Club: Harvard (Boston). General civil litigation, Environmental, General practice. Office: 203 S Orleans Rd Orleans MA 02653-4009

**CHAPLIN, DOLCEY ELIZABETH,** lawyer; b. Mt. Vernon, N.Y., Apr. 20, 1949; d. John Michael and Angelina Claire (Campanile) De Giacomo; m. James E. Chaplin III, June 24, 1972 (div. Apr. 1987); children: Tara Marie, James E. IV. BA, Ladycliff Coll., Highland Falls, 1971; MA, Wright State U., 1976; JD, Seton Hall U., 1984. Bar: N.J. 1985; cert. tchr., Ohio, N.J., N.Y. Tchr. Dayton (Ohio) Pub. Schs., 1972-75; contracts atty. ITT Avionics, Nutley, N.J., 1985-87; gen. counsel GEC Aerospace Inc., Whippany, N.J., 1988-92; contracts cons. ISSC(IBM), White Plains, N.Y., 1993; atty. Amex TRS, N.Y.C., 1994; pvt. practice Ridgewood, N.J., 1994—; adj. prof. William Paterson U., Wayne, N.J., 1996—; dir. N.J. Inst. Tech., Newark, 1994—; dir. Def. Procurement Ctr., State of N.J., Newark, 1994—. Pro bono work Blessed Sacrament Re-Employment Ctr., Franklin Lakes, N.J., 1993—. N.Y. State Regents scholar, 1967. Mem. Nat. Contract Mgmt. Assn. (cert., nat. dir., chpt. v.p. 1994—), N.J. Assn. Women Bus. Owners (state chair 1996—). Avocation: biking. Government contracts and claims, Administrative and regulatory. Home: 448 Fairfield Ave Ridgewood NJ 07450-1838 Office: New Jersey Inst Tech DPTAC 240 Martin Luther King Blvd Newark NJ 07102

**CHAPMAN, CONRAD DANIEL,** lawyer; b. Detroit, July 31, 1933; s. Conrad F. and Alexandrine C. (Baranski) C.; m. Carol Lynn DeBash, Sept. 1, 1956; children: Stephen Daniel, Richard Thomas, Suzanne Marie. BA, U. Detroit, 1954, JD summa cum laude, 1957; LLM in Taxation, Wayne State U., 1964. Bar: Mich. 1957, U.S. Dist. Ct. (so. dist.) Mich. 1957. Pres., chmn. bd. dirs. Powers, Chapman, DeAgostino, Meyers & Milia and predecessor firms, Troy, Mich., 1964—. Mem. ABA, Detroit Bar Assn., Oakland Bar Assn., Am. Arbitration Assn., Detroit Estate Planning Coun., Oakland Estate Planning Coun., Nat. Assn. Estate Planning Counc., Detroit Athletic Club, Detroit Golf Club, Elks. Estate planning, General corporate, Corporate taxation. Office: Powers Chapman DeAgostino Meyers & Milia 3001 W Big Beaver Rd Ste 704 Troy MI 48084-3193

**CHAPMAN, EDMUND WHYTE,** lawyer; b. Boston; s. Richard Blair; married; 2 children. BS, Norwich U.; JD, Suffolk U. Bar: Mass., U.S. Ct. Internat. Trade, U.S. Ct. Appeals (fed. cir.), U.S. Ct. Fed. Claims. Atty. U.S. Justice Dept., Washington, Mobil Oil Corp., Fairfax, Va. Federal civil litigation, Environmental, General corporate. Office: Mobil Oil Corp 3225 Gallows Rd Fairfax VA 22037-0002

**CHAPMAN, GERALD FREDERICK,** lawyer, banker; b. Jackson, Mich., Apr. 27, 1948; s. C. Joseph and Vera Ann Chapman; m. Mary Daugherty; children: Anne, Erin, John, Lindsay, Caroline. BA, Mich. State U., 1972; JD, U. Balt., 1978. Bar: Md., D.C., U.S. Dist. Ct. D.C., U.S. Dist. Ct. Md. Dep. dir. enforcement Fed. Home Loan Bank Bd., Washington, 1978-85; pres. Vista Fed. Savs. Bank, Reston, Va., 1985-92, City Nat. Bank, Washington, 1992-93; ptnr. Cooter, Mangold, Tompert & Chapman, Washington, 1993-97; prin. Gerald F. Chapman, LLC, Bethesda, Md., 1997—. Treas. Young Pres. Orgn., 1989-92. With U.S. Army, 1967-70. Mem. ABA. Democrat. Roman Catholic. Contracts commercial, Banking, General civil litigation. Office: 6917 Arlington Rd Ste 350 Bethesda MD 20814-5289

**CHAPMAN, JOHN WHITAKER,** lawyer, educator; b. Charleston, S.C., Sept. 28, 1953; s. John Greely and Marcia W. Chapman; m. Kim S. Chapman, June 20, 1993; children: Lindsey, Adam. BA, Bowdoin Coll., 1975; JD, U. So. Maine, 1980. Bar: Maine, U.S. Dist. Ct. Maine, U.S. Ct. Appeals (1st cir.), U.S. Supreme Ct. Law clk. Maine Superior Ct., Augusta, 1980-81; assoc. Richardson, Tyler & Troubh, Portland, Maine, 1981-88; dir. Richardson & Troubh, Portland, 1988-95, Kelly & Chapman, P.A., Portland, 1995—; critical incident counsel Maine State Troopers, Augusta, 1992—; bd. dirs. Sportsman Alliance, Augusta. Mem. ABA, NRA, Maine Trial Lawyers Assn., Maine State Bar. Avocations: archery, fishing, computer, firearms, off and on road bicycling. Workers' compensation, Labor, Criminal. Office: Kelly & Chapman PA 97A Exchange St Portland ME 04101-5016

**CHAPMAN, PATRICIA GAYLE,** lawyer; b. Ft. Worth, Feb. 18, 1955; d. James Edwin Harris and Virginia Faye (Watson) Adams; m. Philip Craig Chapman, June 25, 1977. BS, Tex. Women's U., 1977; JD, U. Houston, 1982; LLM in Environ. Law & Natural Resources, Lewis & Clark Coll., 1997. Bar: Tex., U.S. Dist. Ct. (no., so. & ea. dists.) Tex. Assoc. Ferebee & Ferebee, Houston, 1982-85; assoc. gen. counsel WNS, Inc., Houston, 1985-87; sr. assoc. Brucewell & Patterson, Houston, 1987-94; sr. counsel Law Office of Martin Dies, Orange, Tex., 1995-96; pvt. practice Houston, 1997—. Mem. steering com. Com. to Elect Judge L. Millard, Houston, 1993-94, 97—. Republican. Avocations: aerobics, weight-lifting, music, art. Environmental, General civil litigation, Personal injury. Office: 40 Fm 1960 Rd W Ste 225 Houston TX 77090-3530

**CHAPMAN, PHILIP LAN RENCE,** lawyer; b. Jersey City, Apr. 24, 1935; s. Norman and Gertrude Chapman; m. Vera Friedman, June 14, 1959; 1 child, Avery S. BA in History, Princeton U., 1957; LLB, Harvard U., 1966. Bar: N.J., 1961. Assoc. Hellring, Lindeman & Landau, Newark, 1961-68; assoc. Hannoch Weisman, Newark, 1968-70, ptnr., 1970-80; ptnr. Klein Chapman, Clifton, N.J., 1981-93, Chapman, Henkoff, Kessler, Peduto & Saffer, Clifton and Roseland, N.J., 1993—; mem. 3 person com. to revise N.J.'s non-profit corp. law, 1979-83. Lectr. Inst. Continuing Legal Edn., New Brunswick, N.J., 1983—. With U.S. Army, 1960-61. Mem. N.J. State Bar Assn. (trustee corp. and bus. law sect. 1979—), Preakness Hills Country Coub. Democrat. Jewish. Avocations: golf, reading. General corporate, Real property. Office: Chapman Henkoff Kessler Peduto and Saffer 425 Eagle Rock Ave Roseland NJ 07068-1720

**CHAPMAN, RALPH E.,** lawyer; b. Memphis, Dec. 30, 1950; s. Edwin Volney and Mary Ruth Chapman; m. Lisa Harlow, Sept. 10, 1977; children: William Brennan, Elizabeth Camille. BA, Miss. State U., 1972; JD, U. Miss., 1974. Bar: Miss. 1974, U.S. Dist. Ct. (no. and so. dists.) Miss. 1974, U.S. Dist. Ct. (no. dist.) N.Y. 1974, U.S. Dist. Ct. (we. dist.) Tenn. 1974, U.S. Dist. Ct. (ea. dist.) Ark. 1974, U.S. Ct. Appeals (5th and 6th cir.) 1977, U.S. Supreme Ct. 1977. Pres. U. Miss. Sch. Law, 1974; mem. Miss. Jud. Nominating Com., 1984. Capt. USAR. Mem. ATLA, ABA, Miss. State Bar (mem. by-laws study com. 1979-80), Coahoma County Bar Assn., Miss. Trial Lawyers Assn. (bd. govs.), Civil Justice Found., Nat. Assn. Criminal Def. Attys., Million Dollar Advs. Forum, Omicron Delta Kappa, Phi Delta Phi, Lamar Order, Scabbard and Blade. Episcopalian. Avocations: outdoor recreation, hunting, fishing. Fax: 662-627-4171. Personal injury, Product liability. Office: Chapman Lewis & Swan PO Box 428 501 1st St Clarksdale MS 38614-4409

**CHAPMAN, ROBERT FOSTER,** federal judge; b. Inman, S.C., Apr. 24, 1926; s. James Alfred and Martha (Marshall) C.; m. Mary Winston Gwathmey, Dec. 21, 1951; children: Edward, Foster, Winston. BS, U. S.C., 1945, LLB, 1949, LLD (hon.), 1986. Bar: S.C. 1949. Assoc. firm Butler & Moore, Spartanburg, 1949-51; partner firm Butler, Chapman & Morgan, Spartanburg, 1953-71; U.S. dist. judge for S.C., 1971-81, U.S. cir. judge, 1981—. Chmn. S.C. Republican Party, 1961-63. Served to lt. USNR, 1943-46, 51-53. Recipient Nat. Patriot's award Congl. Medal of Honor Soc., 1985. Fellow Am. Coll. Trial Lawyers. Presbyn. (ruling elder). Home: PO Box 1043 Camden SC 29020-1043 Office: US Ct Appeals 4th Ct PO Box 7097 Columbia SC 29202-7097

**CHAPNICK, ELLEN P.,** lawyer, law school administrator; b. N.Y.C., July 3, 1947; d. Irving and Bess (Ferst) C.; m. William E. Schleicher, Apr. 15, 1983; stepchldren: Eric V., David N. BA, Cornell U., 1969; JD, Georgetown U., 1973. Bar: D.C. N.Y., N.Y., U.S. Dist. Ct. (so. dist.) N.Y. 1981, U.S. Supreme Ct. Legal intern United Mine Workers Am. Internat., Washington, 1972-74, assoc. gen. counsel, 1974-77; assoc. gen. counsel Airline Pilots Assn. Internat., Washington, 1977-78; dist. counsel AFSCME, N.Y.C., 1979; staff atty. P.R. Legal Project, San Juan, 1979-80; sr. assoc. gen. counsel Com. of Interns and Residents, N.Y.C., 1980-81; sr. assoc. Wolf Popper Ross Wolf & Jones, N.Y.C., 1981-86, ptnr., 1987-93, founding chair environ./toxic torts dept., 1990-93; dir. pub. interest programs Columbia Sch. Law, N.Y.C., 1993, asst. dean, dir. Ctr. for Pub. Interest Law, 1994—; co-pres. Ctr. for Constitutional Rights, N.Y.C., 1997—, 2d cir. task force on race, gender & ethnic fairness in the cts., 1994-97; mem. task force on pro bono and pub. svc. opportunities Assn. Am. Law Schs., 1998. Recipient Pro Bono award Legal Aid Soc. N.Y., 1998; honoree Nat. Lawyers Guild, 1996. Mem. Assn. Bar City N.Y. (mem. fed. cts. com. 1993-96, mem. com. on provision of legal svcs. to the poor 1997—). Office: Columbia Law Sch Ctr for Pub Interest Law 435 W 116th St New York NY 10027-7297

**CHAPOTON, JOHN EDGAR,** lawyer, government official; b. Galveston, Tex., May 18, 1936; s. Otis Byron and Grace Donaldson (Wayman) C.; m. Sarah Eastham, Jan. 5, 1963; children: John Edgar, Clare Eastham. Student, Washington and Lee U., 1954-55; BBA with honors, U. Tex., 1958, LLB with honors, 1960. Bar: Tex. 1960, D.C. 1985. Assoc. Andrews, Kurth, Campbell & Jones, Houston, 1961-69; with Dept. Treasury, Washington, 1969-72, 81-84; tax legis. counsel Dept. Treasury, 1970-72, asst. sec. for tax policy, 1981-84; ptnr. Vinson & Elkins, Houston, 1972-81; mng. ptnr. Vinson & Elkins, Washington, 1984—. Chmn. law firms div. United Way Capital Area, Washington, 1988-90; bd. dirs. Boys and Girls Clubs Greater Washington, 1990—. Recipient Achievement award Tax Soc. NYU, 1984. Fellow Am. Coll. Tax Counsel (vice-chmn.); mem. ABA (sect. taxation), Tex. State Bar Assn., D.C. Bar Assn., Am. Law Inst. Republican. Episcopalian. Avocations: golf. Corporate taxation, Taxation, general, Personal income taxation. Office: Vinson & Elkins LLP 1455 Pennsylvania Ave NW Washington DC 20004-1008

**CHAPPARS, TIMOTHY STEPHEN,** lawyer; b. Cin., July 23, 1952; s. Gregory S. and Helen (Maragos) C.; m. Laurie A. Kress, Dec. 24, 1986 (div. Sept. 1987); m. Laurie A. Kress, Apr. 18, 1990; children: Alexander T., Jake A. BS, Duke U., 1974; JD, U. Cin., 1978. Assoc. Cox & Chappars, Xenia, Ohio, 1978-94, Bryant Law Office, Wilmington, Ohio, 1981—; trial atty. Pub. Defender's Office, Clinton County, Wilmington, 1978-88; lectr. So. State Jr. Coll., Wilmington, 1982. Mem. Ohio Bar Assn., Am. Trial Lawyers Acad., Ohio Acad. Trial Lawyers. Methodist. Avocations: tennis, piano, hiking, cycling, skiing. Personal injury, Criminal. Home: 2025 Winding Brook Way Xenia OH 45385-9382 Office: PO Box 280 Xenia OH 45385-0280

**CHAPPELEAR, STEPHEN ERIC,** lawyer; b. Columbus, Ohio, Dec. 25, 1952; s. Thornton White and Phyllis Evelyn (Williams) C.; m. Sharon Sue Starr, June 8, 1974; children: Katherine Sue, Christopher Charles. BA, Ohio State U., 1974, JD, 1977. Bar: Ohio 1977, U.S. Dist. Ct. (so. dist.) Ohio, U.S. Dist. Ct. (no. dist.) Ohio, U.S. Dist. Ct. (ea. dist.) Wis., U.S. Tax Ct., U.S. Ct. Appeals (6th cir.). Assoc. Emens, Hurd, Kegler & Ritter, Columbus, 1977-82, prin., 1983—; prin. Kegler Brown Hill & Ritter, Columbus; mem. exec. coun. Nat. Conf. Bar Pres., 1997-2000, Met. Bar Caucus, 1996—. Author: The Complete Book of Jury Verdicts II, Franklin County, Ohio, 1985-91, The Complete Book of Franklin County Jury Verdicts, 1990, So What's Your Case Reaaly Worth?: A Decade of Jury Trial Verdicts, 1995; editor jour. Bar Briefs, 1986-88. Mem. ABA (litig. sect., trial practice com., torts and ins. practice sects. com. on sports law, trial techniques and comml. torts sects.), Ohio State Bar Assn. (bd. govs., coun. dels., former chair fed. cts. and practice com., litigatin sect.), Columbus Bar Found., Columbus Bar Assn. (bd. govs., pres. 1995-96), Am. Inns of Ct. (Franklin chpt. pres. 1994-95), Million Dollar Adv. Forum, Lawyers Club of Columbus, New Albany Country Club. Avocations: sports, movies, theater, writing. General civil litigation, Appellate, Personal injury. Office: Kegler Brown Hill & Ritter 65 E State St Ste 1800 Columbus OH 43215-4295

**CHAPPELL, CLOVIS GILLHAM, JR.,** lawyer; b. Waverly, Tenn., Sept. 13, 1911; s. Clovis Gillham and Cecil (Hart) C.; m. Pauline Mikell LaRoche, Oct. 28, 1938; children: Carolyn (Mrs. D.W. Light III), Polly (Mrs. F. Ferrell Davis), Marian (Mrs. David Scott Miles). Student, Rhodes Coll., 1929-30; B.A., So. Methodist U., 1934, LL.B., 1936. Bar: Tex. 1936. Landman Humble Oil & Refining Co., 1938-44; atty. Baker & Botts, Houston, 1944-50; ptnr. Stubbeman, McRae, Sealy & Laughlin, Midland, 1950-59; ptnr. Lynch, Chappell & Alsup, Midland, 1959-90, of counsel, 1991—; Past sec., dir. Tex. Am. Oil Corp., Midland. Contbr. articles to profl. jours. Past mem. bd. visitors So. Meth. U. Law Sch.; former trustee 1st United Meth. Ch., Midland, Tex. Fellow Am. Coll. Probate Counsel; mem. Am., Tex., Midland County bar assns., Pi Kappa Alpha. Methodist. Oil, gas, and mineral, Real property. Home: 1605 Bedford Dr Midland TX

79701-5704 Office: Lynch Chappell & Alsup 300 N Marienfeld St Midland TX 79701-4345

**CHAPPELL, DAVID FRANKLIN,** lawyer; b. St. Louis, Apr. 18, 1943; married; children: Libbey Paige, Wade Garrett. BA in Polit. Sci., U. Tex., 1964, JD with honors, 1968. Bar: Tex., U.S. Ct. Appeals (5th, 9th, and 11th cirs.); cert. civil trial law, Tex. Bd. Legal Specialization, 1978. Ptnr. Chappell & Handy, P.C., FT. Worth, Tex.; appointed to Tarrant County CSC, 1975, task force on delay Supreme Ct. Tex., 1985, spl. master U.S. Dist. Ct. (no. dist.) Tex., Ft. Worth. Editorial bd. The Texas Lawyer, 1985-86. V.p., gen. counsel Tarrant County Arts Council, 1980-86; vice chmn. City of Ft. Worth Human Relations Com.; mem. Ft. Worth City Coun., 1989-93; chair nat. adv. coun. U.S. Small Bus. Adminstrn., 1998-99; chair Area Ambulance Authority, 1994-98. Named Outstanding Young Man, Ft. Worth Jaycees, 1975. Fellow Tex. Bar Found. (program coordinator symposium on solicitation and legal advt. 1985, sec. bd. trustees 1985-86, chmn. bd. trustees 1987-88); mem. Am. Bar Found., Tex. Bar Assn. (bd. dirs. 1982-86, chmn. bd. 1984-85, health law sect. 1985-86, spl. com. to revise grievance process), ABA (editor Practice TIPS 1980, sec., exec. council of tort and ins. practice sect. 1983-87, chmn. young lawyers div. 1978), Am. Judicature Soc. (exec. com, bd. dirs. 1979), Tex. Young Lawyers Assn. (sec. 1976), Ft. Worth and Tarrant County Young Lawyers Assn. (pres. 1974, Outstanding Young Lawyer award 1979), Am. Arbitration Assn. (arbitrator). Federal civil litigation, State civil litigation, Personal injury. Office: Chappell Armalee Johnson & Hill 1800 City Center Tower II 301 Commerce St Fort Worth TX 76102-4140

**CHAPPELL, MILTON LEROY,** lawyer; b. Accra, Ghana, Mar. 25, 1951; (parents Am. citizens); s. Derwood Lee and Helen Jean (Freeman) C.; m. Margot Cecelia Shields, Dec. 18, 1972; children: Marton Gerald, Monet Louise. BA summa cum laude, Columbia Union Coll., 1973; JD, Cath. U., 1976; diploma, Nat. Inst. Trial Advocacy, Boulder, Colo., 1978; cert., U. Miami, 1982. Bar: Md. 1976, D.C. 1977, U.S. Ct. Appeals (4th, 5th, 9th and D.C. cirs.) 1977, U.S. Dist. Ct. D.C. 1978, U.S. Ct. Appeals (6th cir.) 1979, U.S. Supreme Ct. 1980, U.S. Ct. Appeals (11th cir.) 1981, U.S. Dist. Ct. Md. 1982, U.S. Ct. Appeals (7th cir.) 1988, U.S. Dist. Ct. (no. dist.) Calif., 1990. Sole practice Silver Spring, Md., 1976—; staff atty. Nat. Right to Work Legal Def. Found., Springfield, Va., 1976—; lectr. Columbia Union Coll., Takoma Park, Md., 1976-77; legal cons. JNA Elem. Sch., Takoma Park, 1980-83; gen. counsel Playgrounds Unltd., Inc., 1988—. Internat. Play Equipment Mfrs. Assn., Inc., 1995—; participant play settings subcom. recreation access adv. com. U.S. Archtl. and Transp. Barriers Compliance Bd., 1993-94. Contbr. to Ohio No. U. Law Rev., Govt. Union Rev. Mem. Hillandale Civic Assn., Silver Spring, 1980—; legal cons., bd. dirs. Silver Spring Seventh-day Adventist Ch., 1976-84, Takoma Park.; participant U.S. Arch. and Trans. Barriers Compliance Bd., Recreation Access Adv. Com., Play Settings subcom., 1993-94. Mem. ABA, Md. Bar Assn. D.C. Bar assn. (assoc.). Labor, Federal civil litigation, General practice. Home: 10321 Royal Rd Silver Spring MD 20903-1616 Office: Nat Right to Work Legal Def Found 8001 Braddock Rd # 600 Springfield VA 22151-2110

**CHAR, VERNON FOOK LEONG,** lawyer; b. Honolulu, Dec. 15, 1934; s. Charles A. and Annie (Ching) C.; m. Evelyn Lau, June 14, 1958; children: Richard, Daniel, Douglas, Charles, Elizabeth. BA, U. Hawaii, 1956; LLB, Harvard U., 1959. Bar: Hawaii 1959. Dep. atty. gen. Office of Atty. Gen., Honolulu, 1959-60, 62-65; ptnr. Damon Key Char & Bocken, Honolulu, 1965-89, Char, Sakamoto, Ishii, Lum & Ching, Honolulu, 1989—. Chmn. Hawaii Ethics Commn., Honolulu, 1968-75, Hawaii Bicentennial Com., 1986-91, 1st Hawaii Jud. Conf., 1985. Mem. ABA (bd. govs. 1991-94), Hawaii Bar Assn. (pres. 1985), U. Hawaii Alumni Assn. (pres. 1989-90). Antitrust, Aviation, General corporate. Home: 351 Anonia St Honolulu HI 96821-2052 Office: Char Sakamoto Ishii Lum & Ching Davies Pacific Ctr 841 Bishop St Ste 850 Honolulu HI 96813-3957

**CHARLA, LEONARD FRANCIS,** lawyer; b. New Rochelle, N.Y., May 4, 1940; s. Leonard A. and Mary L. Charla; m. Kathleen Gerace, Feb. 3, 1968 (div. Dec. 1988); children: Larisa, Christopher; m. Elizabeth A. Du Mouchelle, Aug. 27, 1993. BA, Iona Coll., 1962; JD, Cath. U., 1965; LLM, George Washington U., 1971. Bar: D.C. 1967, N.J. 1970, Mich. 1971. Tech. writer IRS, Washington, 1966-67; atty. adv. ICC, Washington, 1967, atty., 1968-69; mgmt. intern HEW, Washington, 1967-68; atty. Bowes & Millner, Transp. Cons., Newark, 1969-71; atty. legal staff GM, Detroit, 1971-85, sr. counsel, 1985-87, asst. gen. counsel, 1987-89; sr. v.p. Clean Sites Inc., Alexandria, Va., 1989-90; shareholder Butzel Long, Detroit and Birmingham, Mich., 1990—; mem. faculty Ctr. for Creative Studies, Coll. Art and Design, Detroit, 1978-89, adj. asst. prof., 1982-89; faculty art U. Mich., 1980, 84-89, adj. asst. prof. 1988-89. Author: Never Cooked Before/Gotta Cook Now!, 1999. Bd. dirs. Gt. Lakes Performing Artists Assocs., 1983-85; bd. dirs. Mich. Assn. Cmty. Arts Agys., 1983-89, 92-93, vice-chair, 1986-88, chair, 1988-89; bd. govs. Cath. U. Am. Alumni, 1982, v.p., 1993—; active Info. Network Superfund Settlements, 1988—; bd. regents Cath. U. Am., 1992—, Birmingham Bloomfield Art Assn., 1987-88, 94-95; bd. dirs. Friends of Modern Art, Detroit Inst. Arts, 1996—, v.p., 1998—. Fellow N.Y. State Regents, 1962; scholar Cath. U. Law Sch., 1962-65. Mem. ABA, Mich. State Bar Assn. (chmn. arts sect. 1980-81, arts comm. entertainment and sports sect. coun. 1979-88, 92—). Environmental, Art. Office: Butzel Long 1500 W Jefferson Ave Ste 900 Detroit MI 48216

**CHARLES, ROBERT BRUCE,** lawyer; b. Portsmouth, Va., Aug. 23, 1960; s. Roland Wilbur Charles Jr. and Doris Anne (Hassell) Barbineau; m. Marina Timasheff, Oct. 16, 1988; 1 child, Nicholas Westcote. AB, Dartmouth Coll., 1982; MA, Oxford U., 1984; JD, Columbia U., 1987. Bar: N.Y. 1989, Conn. 1989, Maine 1990. Law clk. to judge U.S. Ct. Appeals (9th cir.), Seattle, 1987-88; assoc. Kramer, Levin, Nessen, Kamin & Frankel, N.Y.C., 1988-91; assoc. Weil, Gotshal & Manges, N.Y.C., 1991-92, Washington, 1993-95; dep. assoc. dir. office of policy devel The White House, Washington, 1992-93; chief staff, chief counsel nat. security, internat. affairs and criminal justice subcommittee U.S. Ho. of Reps., Washington, 1995-99; prof. govt. and cyberlaw Harvard U. Extension Sch., 1998-99; pres. Direct Impact, L.L.C., 1999—; summer assoc. The White House, Washington, 1982-84, Supreme Ct. India, 1985. Contbr. articles to profl. jours., chpts. to books. Active Coun. on Fgn. Rels. Theodore Roosevelt Assn. Officer USNR, 1998—. Keasbey Scholar, Phila. 1982, Tony Patino Fellow Columbia, 1984. Republican. Avocations: distance running, cycling, hiking, writing. Criminal, General civil litigation, Government contracts and claims. Office: US Ho Com on Govt Reform US Congress Rayburn Hob Rm B-373 Washington DC 20515-0001

**CHARME, STEPHEN MARK,** lawyer; b. Dayton, Ohio, June 10, 1947; s. Samuel Lewis and Miriam C.; m. Ronnie Yellin, Aug. 3, 1975; children: Lauren Jennifer, David Barrett. BA, Rutgers Coll., 1969; JD, Columbia U., 1975. Bar: N.Y., N.J.; U.S. Ct. Appeals (2nd and 3rd cirs.), U.S. Dist. Ct. (so., ea. and no. dists.) N.Y., U.S. Dist. Ct. N.J. Assoc. Parker, Chapin, N.Y.C., 1975-78, Robinson, Silverman, N.Y.C., 1978-85; ptnr. Liebman & Charme, N.Y.C., 1985-94, Holtzman, Wise & Shepard, N.Y.C., 1994-96, Witman, Stadtmaner & Michaels, Florham Park, N.J., 1996—. Mem. ABA, N.J. Bar Assn., N.Y. Bar Assn. Avocations: skiing, tennis, hiking, boating. Federal civil litigation, State civil litigation. Office: Witman Stadtmauer & Michaels 26 Columbia Tpke Florham Park NJ 07932-2213

**CHASANOW, DEBORAH K.,** federal judge; b. 1948. BA, RUtgers U., 1970; JD, Stanford U., 1973. Pvt. practice atty. COle & Groner, Washington, 1975; asst. atty. gen. State of Md., 1975-79; chief criminal appeals divsn. Md. Atty. Gen.'s Office, 1979-87; U.S. magistrate judge U.S. Dist. Ct. Md., 1987-93, dist. judge, 1993—; instr. law schs. U. Balt., U. Md., 1978-84. Mem. Fed. Magistrate Judges Assn., Md. Bar Assn., Prince George's County Bar Assn., Montgomery County Bar Assn., Women's Bar Assn., Marlborough Am. Inn. Ct. (pres. 1988-90), Wrangler's Law Club, Phi Beta Kappa. Office: US Courthouse 6500 Cherrywood Ln Rm 465A Greenbelt MD 20770-1249

**CHASANOW, HOWARD STUART,** judge, lecturer; b. Washington, Apr. 3, 1937; 1 child from previous marriage, Andrea; m. Deborah Hovis Koss, May 15, 1983. BA, U. Md., 1959, JD, 1961; LLM, Harvard U., 1962. Bar: Md. 1961, U.S. Supreme Ct. 1965. Asst. states atty. Prince George County, Upper Marlboro, Md., 1963-64, dep. states atty., 1964-68; judge Dist. Ct., Upper Marlboro, 1971-77, 7th Jud. Cir., 1977-90; judge Ct. Appeals of Md., 1990—; lectr. Sch. Law U. Md., Balt., 1973—, Nat. Jud. Coll., Reno, 1980—, Am. Acad. Jud. Edn., 1984—; founder Prince George's County Drinking Driving Sch.; chmn. adv. bd. Sentencing Guidelines, Md., 1982-90, chmn. jud. adminstrn. sect., 1982-84; mem. Md. Commn. on Criminal Sentencing Policy, 1996—; mem. standing com. on rules of practice and procedure Ct. Appeals, 1985-90; mem. govs. task force to Revise Criminal Code, 1992—. Contbr. law rev. articles. Served with USAF, 1968-69. Office: Ct Appeals Md Prince George County Courthouse PO Box 399 Upper Marlboro MD 20773-0399

**CHASE, DANIEL E.,** partner; b. Trenton, N.J., Dec. 2, 1953; s. Daniel Anthony and Doris Marie (Keller) C.; m. Maryann Chase, Oct. 2, 1982; children: Andrew, Nathaniel. AA, Mercer County Community Coll., Trenton, 1974; BA, Drew U., 1976; JD, Union U., Albany, N.J., 1979. Bar: N.J., U.S. Dist. Ct. N.J. Assoc. McKaughlin & Cooper, Trenton, 1980-88; ptnr. Teich, Groh & Frost, Trenton, 1988-95, Hartrough, Kenny & Chase, Trenton, 1995—. Mem. ABA, ATLA, N.J. State Bar Assn., Mercer County Bar Asssn. (bench bar com. 1990—). Personal injury, Insurance, Product liability. Office: Hartrough Kenny & Chase 3812 Quakerbridge Rd Hamilton NJ 08619-1003

**CHASE, EDWARD THORNTON,** lawyer; b. Palo Alto, Calif., June 25, 1942; s. Edward Tinsley Chase and Cathalene (Crane) Widdoes; m. Joan Gregory Chase, Dec. 4, 1982; children: Lila Gregory, Edward Browning. BA, Harvard U., 1964; LLB, U. Pa., 1967. Bar: N.Y. 1969, U.S. Dist. Ct. (so. and ea. dists.) N.Y. 1970, U.S. Supreme Ct. 1981. Assoc. Botein, Hays, Sklar & Herzberg, N.Y.C., 1968-70, Legal Aid Soc., N.Y.C., 1970-78; pvt. practice N.Y.C., 1978—; ptnr. Chase & Greenberg, N.Y.C., 1980-82; trial techniques instr. Nat. Inst. for Trial Advocacy, N.Y.C., 1978-81; arbitrator Civil Ct., City of N.Y., 1981; mem. Mayor's Adv. Coun. on Juvenile Facilities and Programs, N.Y.C., 1973-74. Mem. ATLA, Assn. of the Bar of the City of N.Y., N.Y. State Trial Lawyers Assn. Personal injury, Product liability. Office: Ste 4500 60 E 42nd St Rm 4500 New York NY 10165-4599

**CHASE, ERIC LEWIS,** lawyer; b. Princeton, N.J., Sept. 21, 1946; s. Harold William and Bernice Mae (Fadden) C.; m. Jamie Campbell, Dec. 29, 1979; children: Eric Campbell, Kathryn Dianne, John Harold. BA, Princeton U., 1968; JD cum laude, U. Minn., 1974. Bar: N.J. 1974, D.C. 1975, U.S. Ct. Appeals (3d cir.) 1979, U.S. Supreme Ct. 1981, U.S. Claims Ct. 1982, U.S. Tax Ct. 1982, N.Y. 1983. Trial atty. FCC, 1974-78; asst. U.S. atty. Dist. N.J., Newark, 1978-80; ptnr. Margolis Chase, Verona, N.J., 1980-90, Hannoch Weisman, Roseland, N.J., 1990-93, Bressler, Amery & Ross, Florham Park, N.J., 1993—; prof. law of war Marine Corps Command and Staff Coll., Quantico, Va., 1990—. Author: Automobile Dealers and the Law, 1994, 6th edit., 1999; contbr. articles on law and mil. to profl. publs., including N.Y. Times, Washington Post, Newsweek mag. With USMC, 1968-71; col. Res., ret. Mem. ABA (mem. task force on internat. criminal ct.), N.J. State Bar Assn. (franchise com 1997—, co-chair franchise com. 1999-00). General civil litigation, Franchising, Communications. Office: Bressler Amery & Ross 325 Columbia Tpke Ste 8 Florham Park NJ 07932-1212

**CHASE, NORMA,** lawyer; b. Evergreen Park, Ill., Dec. 30, 1952; d. Harry and Joan (Sirutis) C.;. AB, U. Pitts., 1972; JD, Duquesne U., 1978. Bar: Pa. 1978, U.S. Dist. Ct. (fed. dist.) 1978, U.S. Ct. Appeals (3rd cir.) 1983, U.S. Supreme Ct. 1984. Pvt. practice Pitts., 1978—. Contbr. articles to Word Perfect for the Law Office, 1995. Mem. Pa. Bar Assn. (atty. discipline study com. 1991-97, client security fund study com. 1991-94, vice chair latter com. 1991-93, chmn. 1993-94, mem. plain English com. 1998—, mem. coun. of solo and small firm practice sect. 1998—). Democrat. Avocations: reading, writing, computing, hiking. Family and matrimonial. Office: 220 Grant St Pittsburgh PA 15219-2123

**CHASE, ROBERT L.,** lawyer; b. Newport, R.I., Apr. 29, 1942; s. Wanton G. and Caroline L. Chase; m. Marla S. Moes Novia, Oct. 20, 1962 (div. June 1980); children: Bradley E., Douglas P.; m. Mary R. Sforza, Oct. 11, 1980. BA, U. N.H., 1063; JD, St. John's U., Jamaica, N.Y., 1966; LLM in Taxation, George Washington U., 1970. Bar: N.Y. 1966, U.S. Supreme Ct. 1970, Conn. 1971, U.S. Dist. Ct. Conn. 1971. Ptnr. Gager & Peterson, Waterbury, Conn., 1971-78, Elliott & Chase, Waterbury, 1978-83, Feeley Nichols Chase McDermott & Pellett, P.C., Waterbury, 1983—; pres., treas., bd. dirs. Waterbury Title Co., 1978-86, Transatlantic Securities Co. Hartford, Inc., Wilmington, Del., 1986-97. Capt. UAGC, U.S. Army, 1967-71. Recipient Disting. Svc. award Greater Waterbury YMCA, 1986. Mem. ABA, Conn. Bar Assn., Waterbury Bar Assn., Lions (pres. Woodbury, Conn. 1985-86). Avocations: commercial pilot and flight instructor, offshore sailing, scuba diving, tennis, skiing. General corporate, Real property, Estate planning. Office: Feeley Nichols Et Al 37 Leavenworth St Waterbury CT 06702-2130

**CHASE, STEVEN ALAN,** lawyer; b. Pasadena, Calif., Aug. 24, 1946; s. Norman Charles and Do-re Ruth (Small) C.; m. Gayle Donsky, Dec. 28, 1968; m. Sheila Gail Earnest, Sept. 26, 1980; children: Samuel Tillman, Susanna Ruth. BA, U. Calif., Berkeley, 1968; JD, U. Calif., San Francisco, 1971. Bar: Calif. 1972, U.S. Dist. Ct. Calif. 1972. Assoc. Long and Long, San Bruno, Calif., 1972; ptnr. Chase and Long, San Bruno, 1972-73; assoc. Barrick and Chase, San Bruno, 1973-80; ptnr. Chase and Winslow, Millbrae, Calif., 1980-84; pvt. practice Millbrae, 1984-90, Burlingame, Calif., 1990—; prof. Skyline Coll., San Bruno, 1974-77. Mem. North San Mateo County Bar Assn. (pres. 1989-90, past v.p., past sec., past treas.). Democrat. Jewish. Avocations: photography, woodworking, car restoration. Criminal, Personal injury. Office: 1818 Gilbreth Rd # 100 Burlingame CA 94010-1217

**CHASE, THOMAS CHARLES,** lawyer; b. Portsmouth, N.H., May 26, 1943; s. Lester Charles and Geraldine Frances (Foster) C.; m. Paula Marie Reddy, June 5, 1965; children: John Charles, Emily Anne. AB, Bowdoin Coll., 1965; LLB, Harvard U., 1968. Bar: Mass. 1968, U.S. Dist. Ct. Mass. 1969. Atty. Gaston & Snow, Boston, 1968-86, 90-91; v.p. adminstrn., gen. counsel Stellar Computer Inc., Newton, Mass., 1986-90; ptnr. Hill & Barlow, P.C., Boston, 1991—. Mem. Zoning Bd. Appeals, Reading, Mass., 1974-76, Fin. Com., Reading, 1977-78. Mem. ABA, Mass. Bar Assn., Boston Bar Assn., Salem Country Club. General corporate, Securities. Office: Hill & Barlow PC One International Pl Boston MA 02110-2607

**CHASEY, JACQUELINE,** lawyer. Bar: N.J. 1983, N.Y. 1984. Formerly counsel Bertelsmann, Inc.; sr. counsel Bertelsman, Inc., 1990-93; v.p., legal affairs, 1994—. General corporate. Office: Bertelsmann Inc 1540 Broadway New York NY 10036-4039

**CHASIN, KEITH A.,** lawyer; b. N.Y.C., Dec. 11, 1957; s. Edwin Seymour and Lila Natalie C.; m. Diane Chasin, Aug. 31, 1980; children: Jessica, Nicole, Danielle. JD, U. Miami, Fla., 1982. Bar: Fla., U.S. Dist. Ct. Fla. Atty. pvt. practice, 1982-85. Bd. dirs. YMCA, 1998—. Democrat. Jewish. Personal injury. Office: Ste 1515 9130 S Dadeland Blvd Miami FL 33156-7851

**CHASNIS, JOHN ALEX,** lawyer; b. Saginaw, Mich., July 15, 1948; s. John Joseph and Mary Lu (Collison) C.; m. Priscilla Lynn Martin, June 20, 1970; children: Alexander, Benjamin, John J. II, Charles. BS, Western Mich. U., 1970; JD, Wayne State U., 1973. Bar: Mich. 1973, U.S. Dist. Ct. (ea. dist.) Mich. 1974. Assoc. Collison & Fordney, P.C., Saginaw, 1973-76, ptnr., 1976-78; ptnr. Collison, Chasnis & Dogger, Saginaw, 1978-88, Chasnis, Dogger & Grierson, Saginaw, 1988—; arbitrator, mediator mid-Mich., 1985—. Mem. ABA, Mich. Bar Assn., Mich. Trial Atty. Assn., Def. Trial Counsel Mich., Saginaw Bar Assn. Insurance, Personal injury, Product liability. Office: Chasnis Dogger & Grierson 155 Plymouth Rd Saginaw MI 48603-7136

**CHASNOFF, JULES,** lawyer; b. St. Louis, July 15, 1927; s. Jacob and Julia Linenthal C.; m. Martha Slay, Aug. 21, 1949; children: David M., Paul E., Richard A. AB, Washington U., St. Louis, 1949; LLB, Havard U., 1952. Bar: Mo. 1952, U.S. Dist. Ct. (ea. dist.) Mo. 1953, U.S. Ct. Claims 1960. Assoc. Tucker & Chasnoff, St. Louis, 1952-54, Grand, Peper, Martin & Roudebush and predecessors, St. Louis, 1954-59; assoc. Lowenhaupt, Chasnoff, Armstrong & Mellitz, St. Louis, 1959-63, ptnr., 1963—. Mem. ABA, Mo. Bar Assn., Met. St. Louis Bar Assn., Am. Judicature Soc. Jewish. Probate, Real property, General corporate. Office: Lowenhaupt & Chasnoff LLC 10 S Broadway Ste 600 Saint Louis MO 63102-1733

**CHASTAIN, ROBERT LEE,** educational psychologist; b. Olean, N.Y., Aug. 5, 1950; m. Floyd Paul and Patricia Louise (Burroughs) C.; m. Marica Denise Means, July 7, 1973 (div. Sept. 1989); children: Robert Jr., Christy, Michael; m. Susan Lee Frank, Oct. 3, 1992. BA in Religion, Houghton Coll., 1980; MS in Ednl. Psychology, Tex. A&M U., 1983; PhD, Stanford U., 1992, JD, 1997. Bar: Calif. 1997, Nebr. 1998. Diplomate Am. Bd. Psychological Specialties. Inspector Harrison Radiator, Lockport, N.Y., 1968-77, first line supr., 1977-78, inspector, 1978-83; test supr. MCAT, Iowa, 1982-84; grad. asst., research asst. Tex. A&M U., College Station, 1982-83; staff research asst. Behavioral Research Program, College Station, 1983-85; research asst. Stanford U., 1985-89; dir. test devel. Wonderlic Personnel Test, 1991-92; law clerk McCutchen Doyle Brown & Enersen, 1996-97; assoc. Wilson Sonsini Goodrich & Rosati, 1997; pres., CEO Chastain Rsch. Group, Inc., 1983—. Contbr. articles to profl. jours. Served with USMC, 1969-72, Vietnam. N.Y. Regents scholar, 1968, Freshman D scholar, 1973. Mem. ABA, Am. Ednl. Research Assn., Am. Psychol. Assn., Am. Statis. Assn., Internat. Assn. Statis. Computing, Nat. Council on Measurement in Edn., Psychometric Soc., Santa Clara County Bar Assn. Democrat. Avocations: chess, golf, computer programming, writing. Office: Chastain Research Group Inc 310 Ballymore Cir San Jose CA 95136-3932

**CHATHAM, LLOYD REEVE,** lawyer; b. Jackson, Miss., Aug. 16, 1958; s. Archie Reeves Chatham and Anna C. Smith; m. Louise Lucas, July 2, 1983; 1 child, Christopher Lloyd. Student, Hinds Jr. Coll., Raymond, Miss., 1977-78; BS, Miss. State U., 1981; JD, Miss. Coll. Sch. Law, Clinton, 1996. Bar: Miss. Supreme Ct. 1996, U.S. Dist. Ct. (no. and so. dist.) Miss. 1996, U.S. Ct. Appeals (5th cir.) 1996. Mgr. Miss. State U. Food Svcs., Starkville, 1981-83; gen. mgr. Dobbs Houses, Inc., Jackson, 1983-92; lawyer Waller & Waller, Jackson, 1996-99; pvt. practice Chatham Law Office, Brandon, Miss., 1999—; dir. Miss. Restaurant Assn., Jackson, 1989-92; v.p. Jackson Restaurant Assn., 1990, pres., 1991. Choir mem. St. Peters By-The-Lake, Brandon, Miss., 1997, Miss. Chorus, Brandon, 1998. Named Miss. Restaurant Mgr. of Yr., Miss. Restaurant Assn., Jackson, 1992. Mem. ATLA, ABA, Miss. Bar Assn., Hinds County Bar Assn., Jackson Young Lawyers, Christian Legal Soc., Federalist Soc., Phi Delta Phi, Alpha Phi Omega (v.p., pres.). Avocations: antique collecting, traveling, music. Administrative and regulatory, Personal injury, Family and matrimonial. Home: 1201 Martin Dr Brandon MS 39047-6448 Office: PO Box 4041 Brandon MS 39047-4001

**CHATIGNY, ROBERT NEIL,** judge; b. 1951. AB, Brown U., 1973; JD, Georgetown U., 1978. Atty. Williams & Connolly, Washington, 1981-83; ptnr. Chatigny and Palmer, Hartford, Conn., 1984-86, Chatigny & Cowdery, Hartford, 1991-94; pvt. practice Hartford, 1986-90; dist. judge U.S. Dist. Ct., Hartford, Conn., 1994—. Office: 450 Main St Hartford CT 06103-3022

**CHATOFF, MICHAEL ALAN,** lawyer; b. N.Y.C., Aug. 18, 1946; s. Alexander Zelig and Leona Rhoda (Weiss) C. BA, CUNY, 1967; JD, Bklyn. Law Sch., 1971; LLM, NYU, 1978. Bar: N.Y. 1971, U.S. Dist. Ct. (so. and ea. dists.) N.Y. 1978, U.S. Ct. Appeals (2d cir.) 1980, U.S. Supreme Ct. 1980. Reader Chgo. Title Ins. Co., N.Y.C., 1972; chief U.S. Code Congl. and Adminstrv. News West Pub. Co., Westbury, N.Y., 1972-97; cons. N.Y. Sch. for Deaf, N.Y.C. Mayor's Office for Disabled, Westchester County Legis.; lectr. N.Y. State Dept. of Edn. Vocat. Ednl. Svcs. for Individuals with Disabilities, N.Y. Sch. Deaf, Lexington Sch. for Deaf, Parents for Deaf Awareness, Am. Profl. Soc. for Deaf, N.Y. Ctr. for Law and the Deaf, Coun. on Jewish Deaf Edn. and Rehab., Nat. Coun. on Deaf People and Deafness, NYU. Assoc. law editor Ency. on Deaf People and Deafness; contbr. articles to Nat. Law Jour., N.Y. Law Jour., Able Adv., Communication Outlook, Deaf Spectrum. Bd. dirs. Westchester Cmty. Svcs. for Hearing Impaired; counsel Conn. African-Am. Deaf Advocate; mem. Supreme Ct. Hist. Soc.; del. nominee Dem. Nat. Conv., 1992. Mem. ABA, Queens County Bar Assn., Assn. of Bar of City of N.Y., Nat. Assn. Deaf, Am. Contract Bridge League. Avocations: bridge, jogging, weight-lifting. Civil rights, Education and schools, Legislative. Home: 26909T Grand Central Pkwy Floral Park NY 11005-1010

**CHATROO, ARTHUR JAY,** lawyer; b. N.Y.C., July 1, 1946; s. George and Lillian (Leibowitz) C.; m. Christina Daly, Aug. 6, 1994; 1 child, Alexander. *Wife Christina Daly Chatroo practices anesthesia at the VAMC San Diego, is an ACLS instructor, Sigma Theta Tau Honor Society member, enjoys yoga, playing bridge, growing orchids, and genealogy. She has been a student at the College of New Rochelle, American College in Paris, France, New York Medical College Graduate School, and Case Western Reserve University. Her parents are Dr. Charles and June Daly. She has two brothers, Owen Grant and Douglas Patrick, and a sister, Deborah June.* BChemE, CCNY, 1968; JD cum laude, New York Law Sch., 1979; MBA with distinction, NYU, 1982. Bar: N.Y. 1980, Ohio 1992, Calif. 1993, U.S. Patent Office 1998. Process engr. Std. Oil Co. of Ohio, various locations, 1968-73; process specialist BP Oil, Inc., Marcus Hook, Pa., 1974-75; sr. process engr. Sci. Design Co., Inc., N.Y.C., 1975-78; mgr. spl. projects The Halcon SD Group, N.Y.C., 1978-82; corp. counsel, tax and fin. The Lubrizol Corp., Wickliffe, Ohio, 1982-85; sr. counsel spl. investment projects The Lubrizol Corp., Wickliffe, 1989-90; gen. counsel Lubrizol Enterprises, Inc., Wickliffe, 1985-89; chmn. Correlation Genetics Corp., San Jose, Calif., 1990-91; gen. counsel Agrigenetics Co., Eastlake, Ohio, 1990-92; gen. counsel, dir. comml. contracting Agrigenetics, L.P., San Diego, 1992-93; counsel Agrigenetics, Inc. dba Mycogen Seeds, Mycogen Corp., San Diego, 1994-97; dir. legal affairs Mycogen Corp., San Diego, 1997-98; exec. v.p. bus. devel., legal and regulatory affairs Global Agro, Inc., Encinitas, Calif., 1998-99; exec. v.p., gen. counsel Akkadix Corp., San Diego, 1999—. Mem. Met. Parks Adv. com., Allen County, Ohio, 1973. Mem. ABA, AIChE, Am. Chem. Soc., N.Y. State Bar Assn., San Diego County Bar Assn., Am. Corp. Counsel Assn., Jaycees (personnel dir. Lima, Ohio chpt. 1972-73), Licensing Execs. Soc., Toastmasters, Omega Chi Epsilon, Beta Gamma Sigma. Club: Toastmasters. Avocations: sailing, photography, skiing. General corporate, Intellectual property, Private international. Home: 3525 Del Mar Hts Rd # 285 San Diego CA 92130-2122 Office: Global Agro Inc 12626 High Bluff Dr Ste 250 San Diego CA 92130-2072

**CHAUNCEY, TOM WEBSTER, II,** lawyer; b. Phoenix, May 30, 1947; s. Tom Webster and Kathryn (Geare) C.; m. Mary Kathleen LaCroix, Dec. 28, 1972. BA in Sociology with departmental honors, Northwestern U., 1970; JD, Ariz. State U., 1973. Bar: Ariz. 1973, U.S. Dist. Ct. Ariz. 1973. Ptnr. Gust Rosenfeld, Phoenix; exec. v.p., counsel KOOL Radio-TV, Inc., Phoenix, 1972-82; gen. counsel, sta. mgr. KOOL-AM-FM, Phoenix, 1982-86; chmn. Cameras in the Courtroom Com., 1979-86; mem. bd. CBS Radio Network Affiliates, 1984-86. Founding bd. dirs., v.p. 1st Amendment Coalition, 1981-83, pres., 1984-85; bd. dirs. Park Found. of Phoenix, 1980-84, NCCJ, 1978—, rep. nat. exec. bd. 1986-92; bd. dirs. Ariz. Bus.-Industry-Edn. Coun., Inc., 1979-83, Friendly House, 1983-84, Ariz. Community Found., 1981-85; mem. fin. com. YMCA Phoenix and Valley of Sun, 1974-80, mem. camp com., 1978-80; bd. dirs., mem. Project Pool It, Valley Forward Assn., 1977-83; mem. media adv. bd. Traffic Accident Reduction Task Force, 1980; bd. dirs. Meml. Hosp. Found., 1978-83, planning com., 1980-83, community rels. com., 1982-83; bd. dirs. Barrow Neurol. Found., 1979-89, mem. exec. com., 1980-89, v.p., 1983-85, pres., 1985-89, mem. investment com. 1985-89; bd. dirs. Ariz. Hist. Soc., 1982-84, mem. bldg. com., 1983, bylaws com., 1983; bd. dirs. Cen. Ariz. Mus. chpt., 1979-84, St. Joseph's Meml. Hosp., 1989-91; mem. fin. com., 1989-91, mem. strategic planning com., 1990-91, Found. for Blind Children, 1990-91, 95—, fin. com., 1990-91,, mem. pers. com., 1990-91, treas., 1996—; mem. Crisis Nursery, 1988-90; mem. Walter Cronkite Found. for Journalism and Telecommunications, Ariz. State U., 1992—, mem. fundraising com., 1986—, nominating com., 1986—; mem. task force on productivity Ariz. Supreme Ct. Commn. on Cts., 1988-89; mem. Maricopa County voter awareness com. 1986-88. Fellow Ariz. State Bar Found.; mem. ABA, Ariz. Bar Assn. (pub. rels. com. 1975-86, fee arbitration com. 1976-86), FCC Bar Assn., Lawyer-Pilots Bar Assn., Maricopa County Bar Assn. (past dir. Young Lawyers sect.), Ariz. Trial Lawyers Assn., Phoenix Assn. Def. Counsel, Orme Sch. Alumni Assn., Northwestern

U. Alumni Assn. Phoenix (pres. 1975-76), Ariz. State U. Law Alumni Assn., Phoenix Press Club, Nat. Assn. Broadcasters, Ariz. Broadcasters Assn. (bd. dirs. 1985-86), Met. Phoenix Broadcasters (bd. dirs. 1976-86, v.p. 1984-85, pres. 1985-86), Phi Delta Phi, Sigma Delta Chi, Phi Gamma Delta. Libel, General corporate, Real property. Office: Gust Rosenfeld 201 N Central Ave Ste 3300 Phoenix AZ 85073-3300

**CHAUVIN, LEONARD STANLEY, JR.,** lawyer; b. Franklin, Ky., Feb. 13, 1935; s. Leonard Stanley Sr. C.; m. Cecilia McKay; children: Leonard Stanley III, Jacqueline, McKay. Grad., Castle Heights Mil. Acad., 1953; AB in Polit. Sci., U. Ky., 1957; JD, U. Louisville, 1961, LLD (hon.), 1990; LLD (hon.), Ohio No. U., 1990. Bar: Ky. 1961, U.S. Dist. Ct. (we. dist.) Ky. 1962, U.S. Ct. Appeals (6th cir.) 1964, U.S. Ct. Mil. Appeals 1966, U.S. Ct. Claims 1966, U.S. Supreme Ct. 1966, N.Y. 1983, Ind. 1983, Tenn. 1983, D.C. 1983, U.S. Dist. Ct. (so. and na. dists.) Ind. 1983, U.S. Dist. Ct. D.C. 1983, U.S. Ct. Appeals (7th, D.C. and Fed. cirs.) 1983, U.S. Tax Ct. 1983, U.S. Ct. Internat. Trade 1983, Wis. 1984, U.S. Dist. Ct. (so.and ea. dist.) 1984, U.S. Ct. Appeals (2d cir.) 1984, Fla. 1985, Nebr. 1985, Minn. 1985, Mass. 1986, W.Va. 1986. Assoc. Daniel B. Boone, Louisville, 1962-63, Laurence E. Higgins, Louisville, 1963-68; ptnr. Brown & Chauvin, Louisville, 1968-78, Carroll, Chauvin, Miller & Conliffe, Louisville, 1978-82; sole practice Louisville, 1982-83; ptnr. Barnett & Alagia, Louisville, 1983-92, Chauvin & White, Louisville, 1992-93, Chauvin & Chauvin, 1993—; asst. Commonwealth atty. Jefferson County Commonwealth Attys. Office, Louisville, 1962-63; asst. gen. counsel dept. hwys. Commonwealth of Ky., Louisville; judge pro tem Louisville Police Ct.; master commr. Jefferson Cir. Ct., Louisville, 1992—; asst. county atty. of Jefferson County, 1978-87. Chmn. Registry of Election Fin.; mem. Ky. jud. retirement form system Old Ky. Home Boy Scouts, Frankfort, Ky. Fellow Am. Bar Found. (chmn.); mem. ABA (chmn. ho. of dels. 1982-84, pres. 1989-90), Am. Coll. Tax Counsel, Ky. Bar Assn. (Lawyer of Yr. award), Nat. Jud. Coll., Am. Judicature Soc. (pres. 1986-88, Harley award), Am. Coll. Trust and Estate Counsel. Federal civil litigation, State civil litigation, Probate. Home: 1648 Cherokee Rd Louisville KY 40205-1369 Office: 1228 Starks Bldg Louisville KY 40202

**CHAVERS, DANE CARROLL,** lawyer; b. Cleve., Mar. 20, 1956; s. Clarence Louis and Lee Myrtle (Simpson) C.; m. Christine Kumer, Sept. 21, 1991; stepchildren: Mary Elizabeth Curtin, Laura Louise Curtin. BA, Hiram Coll., 1978; JD, Ohio State U., 1981. Bar: U.S. Dist. Ct. (so. dist.) Ohio 1981. Staff atty. common pleas unit Franklin County Pub. Defender, Columbus, Ohio, 1980—; lectr. Ohio Assn. Criminal Def. Attys., Columbus, 1997—. Bd. dirs. Friends of Homeless, Columbus, Summit United Meth. Ch., Columbus. Democrat. Avocations: reading, tennis, church choir. Office: Franklin County Pub Defender 373 S High St Columbus OH 43215-4591

**CHAVEZ, JOHN ANTHONY,** lawyer; b. Auburn, Calif., Oct. 5, 1955; s. Marco Antonio and Barbara Ann (Lawrence) Chavez-Rivas. BA, U. Calif., Santa Barbara, 1977; JD, Stanford U., 1981. Bar: Calif. 1981, Tex. 1982, U.S. Dist. Ct. (so. and no. dists.) Calif. 1982, (cen. dist.) Calif. 1983, U.S. Dist. Ct. (so. dist.) Tex. 1982, (we. dist.) Tex. 1983, (no. dist.) Tex. 1991, N.Y. 1986, U.S. Dist. Ct. (ea. and so. dists.) N.Y. 1986, U.S. Supreme Ct. 1986. With legal dept. Exxon Co. U.S.A., Houston, 1981-85, N.Y.C., 1985-86; assoc. gen. counsel Sybron Corp., Saddlebrook, N.J., 1986-88, Crown Equipment Corp., New Bremen, Ohio, 1989-90; trial atty. Exxon Co. U.S.A., Houston, 1990-92; counsel complex litigation Exxon Chem. Co., Houston, 1992-95; counsel internat. oil and gas exploration Exxon Exploration Co., Houston, 1995-96; counsel antitrust, mergers and acquisitions Exxon Chem. Co., Houston, 1996—; presenter numerous legal edn. seminars and programs. Contbr. articles to profl. jours. Mentor Ft. Bend Ind. Sch. Dist., 1998, Houston Bar Assn., 1998. Chancellor's scholar U. Calif., 1976; Univ. Svc. award for dist. svc. to campus cmty. U. Calif., Santa Barbara, 1977. Mem. ABA (antitrust, bus. law, criminal justice and litigation sects., joint venture agreements task force of the negotiated acquisitions com. 1998, white collar crime com., criminal litigation com., Sherman Act Sect. 1 com., vice chair corp. counseling com. 1998—), Houston Bar Assn. (chair antitrust and trade regulation sect., 1997-98, vice-chair 1996-97, sec.-treas. 1995-96, coun. 1993-95), Coll. State Bar Tex., Wong Sun Soc.; fellow Houston Bar Found. Republican. Avocations: hiking, theatre, travel. E-mail: anthony.chavez@exxon.com. Antitrust, Federal civil litigation, Trade. Home: 7767 Cambridge St Houston TX 77054-2011 Office: Exxon Chem Co PO Box 3272 Houston TX 77253-3272

**CHAZIN, SETH PAUL,** lawyer; b. Lackawanna, N.Y.. BS in Broadcasting, U. Fla., 1979; JD, Golden Gate U., 1984. Bar: Mass. 1987, Calif. 1988. Criminal, Appellate, Juvenile. Office: 1164 Solano Ave Ste 205 Albany CA 94706-1639

**CHECK, MELVIN ANTHONY,** lawyer; b. Milw., Nov. 12, 1951; s. Mathew N. and Lorraine L. (Michels) C.; m. LuAnn E. Mueller, July 10, 1976. BBA, U. Wis.-Milw., 1976; JD, Marquette U., 1979. Assoc. atty. Miller Law Office, Jefferson, Wis., 1979-81; atty. Check Law Office, Port Washington, Wis., 1981-82, 85—; corp. counsel Mutual Savs. and Loan Assn., Milw., 1982-85; owner Coldwell Banker N. Suburban Realty, Port Washington, Wis., 1994—; instr. Wis. Realtors Assn., Madison, 1991—, Milw. Area Tech. Coll., 1985-91. Bd. dirs. Econ. Devel. for Grafton Enhancement, Inc., Grafton, 1990-93. With U.S. Army, 1971-73. Recipient Outstanding Svc. by an Individual Atty. Milw. Young Lawyers Assn. Vol. Lawyers Project, 1987. Mem. Ozaukee Realtors Assn. (Affiliate of Yr. 1990, Realtor of the Yr. 1995), Wis. Realtors Assn., Nat. Assn. of Realtors (Instr. of Yr. 1995), Ozaukee County Bar Assn., State Bar of Wis., Grafton Area C. of C. (pres. 1990-92), Beta Gamma Sigma. Avocations: softball, bowling, woodworking. Real property, Probate. Office: 429 W Grand Ave Port Washington WI 53074-2143

**CHECKMAN, NEIL BRUCE,** lawyer; b. N.Y.C., Mar. 26, 1947; s. Joseph and Berenice Dorothy (Price) C.; children: Alexandra Josephine, Joseph Jacob. AB, Herbert Lehman Coll., 1968; JD, Bklyn. Law Sch., 1971. Bar: N.Y. 1971, U.S. Ct. Appeals (2d cir.) 1973, U.S. Dist. Ct. (so. and ea. dists.) N.Y. 1975. Assoc. atty. criminal def. divsn. Legal Aid Soc., N.Y.C., 1971-83; spl. asst. atty. gen. Office of Spl. Prosecutor for Medicaid Fraud Control, N.Y.C., 1983-90; pvt. practice N.Y.C., 1990—. Mem. Assn. of Bar of City of N.Y., N.Y. County Lawyers Assn., N.Y.C. Criminal Bar Assn., N.Y. State Assn. Criminal Def. Lawyers, Nat. Assn. Criminal Def. Lawyers. Criminal. Office: 170 Broadway Rm 500 New York NY 10038-4154

**CHEEK, LEWIS ALEXANDER,** lawyer; b. Phila., May 9, 1951; s. John Merritt and Margaret Lincoln (Harris) C.; m. Bonnie McFarlane Rhoads, Aug. 19, 1973; children: John Lewis, Jeffrey Edwards. BA in History, Wake Forest U., 1973, JD, 1976. Bar: N.C. 1976, U.S. Dist. Ct. (ctrl. dist.) N.C. 1977, U.S. Dist. Ct. (ea. dist.) N.C. 1980, U.S. Ct. Appeals (4th cir.) 1983, U.S. Supreme Ct. 1996. Atty. Newsom, Graham, Strayhorn, Hedrick, Murray, Bryson & Kennon, Durham, N.C., 1976-94, Moore and Van Allen, Durham, N.C., 1994—; advisor Durham Tech. C.C., 1977—, Durham Acad., 1990—, Nat. Humanities Ctr., Research Triangle Park, N.C., 1980—, Raleigh-Durham Airport Authority, 1985—. Arbitrator 14th Judicial Dist. N.C., Durham, 1990—; various alumni activities Wake Forest U., Winston-Salem, N.C., 1976—; cons. Vol. Ctr. Durham, 1987—. Mem. ABA, Internat. Assn. Def. Counsel, N.C. Bar Assn., N.C. Assn. Def. Counsel, Am. Bd. Trial Advocates. Democrat. Baptist. Avocations: golf, tennis, skiing, basketball, children's sports. General civil litigation, Personal injury. Home: 5 Roswell Ct Durham NC 27707-5070

**CHEEK, MICHAEL CARROLL,** lawyer; b. Fostoria, Ohio, Aug. 28, 1948; s. Carroll Wright and Mabel A. (Smith) C. BA, Hanover Coll., 1970; JD, U. Cin., 1974. Bar: Ohio 1974, Fla. 1974, U.S. Dist. Ct. (mid. dist.) Fla. 1975. Pub. defender Clearwater, Fla., 1974-77, lawyer sole practice, 1977—; vice chmn. bar grievance Clearwater, 1990-94; trustee Pinellas County Law Libr., Clearwater, 1977-92; chmn. Ct. Law Libr., 1982-89. Pres. 1st Step Corp., Clearwater, 1986-93; vice chmn. Long Ctr. Found., Clearwater, 1994-95. Mem. Nat. Assn. Criminal Def. Lawyers, Pinellas Criminal Def. Assn. (v.p. 1987), Am. Inn of Ct. Criminal. Office: 814 Chestnut St Clearwater FL 33756-5642

**CHEELEY, ROBERT DAVID,** lawyer; b. Buford, Ga., July 13, 1957; s. Joseph E. Jr. and Selma (Medlock) C.; m. Lisa Ackerman, July 24, 1982; children: David, Amelia, Harrison. BA, U. Ga., 1978, JD, 1982. Bar: Ga. 1982, U.S. Dist. Ct. (no. dist.) Ga. 1982, U.S. Supreme Ct. 1990, U.S. Ct. Appeals (11th cir.) 1992. Assoc. Cheeley & Chandler, Buford, 1982-88; ptnr. Butler, Wooten, Overby & Cheeley, Atlanta, 1988—; bd. dirs. Attys. Info. Exch. Group, Birmingham, Ala.; mem. faculty Nat. Inst. Trial Advocacy, Athens, Ga., 1992. Contbr. articles to profl. publs. Mem. Gov. Zell Miller's Roundtable, State of Ga., Atlanta, 1992; sustaining mem. Dem. Party Ga., Atlanta, 1988—. Mem. ABA, Assn. Trial Lawyers Am. (v.p.), Ga. Trial Lawyers Assn., Atlanta Bar Assn., Gwinnett Bar Assn., Kiwanis (Buford chpt.). Avocations: bicycling, tennis, water and snow skiing. Personal injury, Product liability, General civil litigation. Office: Butler Wooten Overby & Cheeley 2719 Buford Hwy NE Atlanta GA 30324-5420

**CHELEOTIS, TASSOS GEORGE,** lawyer; b. Miami, May 18, 1956; s. George T. and Marie (Hoffman) C.; m. Deborah Hollie Presner, Apr. 26, 1987; children: Courtney A., Alyssa R. AA in Computer Systems, Miami Dade C.C., 1977; BA in Econs., Fla. Internat. U., 1980; JD, Nova Law Ctr., 1983. Bar: Fla. 1983, U.S. Tax Ct. 1984, U.S. Dist. Ct. (so. dist.) Fla. 1984, U.S. Ct. Appeals (11th cir.) 1984, U.S. Dist. Ct. (mid. dist.) Fla. 1994. Assoc. Lyons & Farrar P.A., Miami, 1983-84; sr. atty. 3rd Dist. Ct. of Appeals, Miami, 1984-90; clk. of ct. U.S. Dist. Ct. (so. dist.), Fla., 1990-94, spl. asst. ct. adminstr., 1994—; mem. jud. evaluation com. Fla. Bar, 1989-90; mem. civil justice reform act com. U.S. Dist. Ct. (so. dist.) Fla., 1991-96, mem. criminal justice act com., 1993—, mem. mediation com. 1993—, mem. local rules com., 1994—; guest lectr. Fla. Bar on Fed. Practice Rev., 1992-96, U. Miami Alternative Legal Careers, 1993, U.S. State Dept. Bahamian Islands Modernization Project, 1994, 95, 96, 97. Mem. Fed. Bar Assn. (mem. exec. bd. S. Fla. chpt. 1993-96, 2d v.p. 1996—), Am. Soc. for Quality Control (Fla. State Gov's. Sterling Coun. Examiner, 1995—). Avocations: hiking, target pistol shooting. Office: US Dist Ct So Dist Fla 301 N Miami Ave Rm 321 Miami FL 33128-7702

**CHEMA, SUSAN RUSSELL,** lawyer; b. Dayton, Ohio, June 2, 1956; d. Thomas F. and Marjorie Bess (Wilson) Russell; m. J. Richard Chema, Aug. 7, 1982; children: Alexis K., Caroline K. BA, U. Dayton, 1977; JD, Ohio State U., 1982. Assoc. Smith & Schnacke, LLP, Dayton, 1982-83; lt. comdr. JAGC USN, various locations, 1983-91; lawyer Navy Gen. Counsel, Washington, 1991-95; sr. atty. NCR Corp., Dayton, 1995—. General civil litigation, Alternative dispute resolution, Public international. Office: NCR Corp 101 W Schantz Ave Dayton OH 45409-2260

**CHEMERS, ROBERT MARC,** lawyer; b. Chgo., July 24, 1951; s. Donald and Florence (Weinberg) C.; m. Lenore Ziemann, Aug. 16, 1975; children: Brandon J., Derek M. BA, U. So. Calif., 1973; JD, Ind. U.-Indpls., 1976. Bar: Ind. 1976, Ill. 1976, U.S. Dist. Ct. (so. dist.) Ind. 1976, U.S. Dist. Ct. (no. and so. dists.) Ill. 1977, U.S. Ct. Appeals 7th cir.) 1977, U.S. Ct. Appeals (5th cir.) 1985. Assoc. Pretzel & Stouffer, Chgo., 1976-79, officer, 1979-81, dir., 1981—. Author: IICLE - Civil Practice, 1978, rev. edit. 1982, 87; IICLE Settlements, 1984. Mem. ABA, Ill. State Bar Assn., Chgo. Bar Assn., Def. Rsch. Inst., Ill. Def. Counsel, Appellate Lawyers Assn. State civil litigation, Federal civil litigation, Insurance. Office: Pretzel & Stouffer One S Wacker Dr Chicago IL 60606

**CHEN, WESLEY,** lawyer; b. N.Y.C., Nov. 29, 1954; s. Tom Y.M. and Mary (Don) C.; m. Vivien Wong, Dec. 10, 1983; 2 children: Marissa, Jocelyn. BA, N.Y. U., 1976, JD, 1980. Bar: N.Y. 1981, U.S. Dist. Ct. (so. and ea. dists.) N.Y. 1981. Lawyer Meissner, Tisch & Kleinberg, N.Y.C., 1980-81; pvt. practice N.Y.C., 1982-85, 89, 91—; of counsel Serchuk, Wolfe & Zelermyer, White Plains, N.Y., 1985-88; ptnr. Cantwell & Chen, N.Y.C., 1988, Kimmelman, Sexter, Warmflash & Leitner, N.Y.C., 1990-91, Krasner & Chen, N.Y.C., 1992-94, Serchuk & Zelermyer, N.Y.C., 1995—; bd. dirs. United Orient Bank, N.Y.C., 1982-92, MFY Legal Svcs., Inc., 1993-96; mem. N.Y. State Banking Bd., 1992—. Mem. ABA, N.Y. State Bar Assn. (mem. banking law com.), N.Y.County Lawyers Assn. (mem. banking law com.), Asian-Am. Bar Assn. of N.Y., Chinese C. of C. (legal adviser 1982—). Contracts commercial, Real property, Banking. Office: 641 Lexington Ave Fl 20 New York NY 10022-4503

**CHENAL, THOMAS KEVIN,** lawyer; b. Cin., Nov. 9, 1953; s. Robert C. and Marion K. Chenal; m. Carmen A. Amador, Dec. 30, 1978; children: Robert, Cristina, Grace. Cert. d'honneur, U. Catholique de l'Ouest, Angers, France, 1974; BA cum laude, U. Notre Dame, 1976; JD, U. Ariz., 1979. Bar: Ariz. 1979, U.S. Dist. Ct. Ariz. 1979, U.S. Ct. Appeals (9th cir.) 1979. Ptnr. Mohr, Hackett, Pederson, Blakley & Randolph, P.C., Phoenix, 1979—. Councilman Carefree (Ariz.) Town Coun., 1996-99. Mem. ABA (bus. law, trial practice internat. sect. 1998-99), Ariz. State Bar Assn. (bankruptcy sect., chair internat. sect.), Ariz. Assn. Def. Counsel, Ariz. Trial Lawyers Assn. Avocations: private piloting, travel. General civil litigation, Private international, Bankruptcy. Office: Mohr Hackett et al 2800 N Central Ave Ste 1100 Phoenix AZ 85004-1043

**CHENAULT, JAMES STOUFFER,** judge; b. Richmond, Ky., May 1, 1923; s. Joe Prewitt and Russell (Stouffer) C.; m. Dorothy Neff, Apr. 21, 1960; children: Jean Russell. AB, Ea. Ky. U., 1949, LLD (hon.), 1975; LLB, U. Ky., 1949. Bar: Ky. 1949, U.S. Ct. Mil. Appeals 1956, U.S. Supreme Ct. 1960. Prosecuting atty. City of Richmond, Ky., 1950-57; commonwealth's atty. 25th Jud. Ct. of Ky., Clark, Jessamine and Madison Counties, 1964-66, cir. judge, 1966-80; chief cir. judge 25th Jud. Ct. of Ky., Clark and Madison Counties, 1980-93; chief regional judge Bluegrass Region of Ky., 1978-93; spl. judge Ky. Ct. of Appeals, 1973, Ky. Supreme Ct., 1984; Ky. rep. Nat. Ctr. State Cts., 1972-78; mem. Ky. Commn. on Corrections and Community Svc., 1973-77, Ky. Crime Commn. Cts. Sect., 1972-80, chmn., 1976-80, Task Force on Office for Pub. Advocacy, 1981-82, Gov.'s Jud. Adv. Coun., 1972-75, Ky. Jud. Coun., 1977-81, State and Fed. Jud. Coun., 1979-84; vol. faculty intensive trial seminar U. Ky., 1983, 85, 87, 90; lectr. So. Police Inst., 1970-80, Nat. Conf. Appellate Ctr. Clks., 1985, Nat. Conf. U.S. Dist. Ct. Clks., 1988, Nat. Conf. on Tech. and the Cts., Chgo., 1984, Denver, 1988, 3rd Fed. Jud. Cone, 1987, Ala. Appellate Judges Conf., 1990; adj. faculty Sch. Law Enforcement Ea. Ky. U., 1967-73; lectr. numerous state jud. confs.; presenter 1st Nat. Jud. State of the Art Conf., Phoenix, 1987. Councilman City of Richmond, 1949-50. Lt. (j.g.) USN, 1943-46, PTO. Recipient Outstanding Contbn. award Ky. Coun. Crime and Delinquency, 1974, Outstanding Contbn. award City of Richmond, 1977, Disting. Svc. award Dept. Mass Comm. Ea. Ky. U., 1993, Outstanding Trial Judge award Ky. Acad. Trial Attys., 1993, Ky. Chief Justice Spl. award, 1994; named Outstanding Alumnus Ea. Ky. U., Richmond, 1982. Mem. ABA (lectr., presenter ann. meeting San Francisco chpt. 1987), Am. Judicature Soc., Internat. Acad. Trial Judges, Ky. Bar Assn. (pres. younger lawyers conf. 1956-57), Ky. Assn. Cir. Judges (pres. 1970-75, editor newsletter 1976-93, Outstanding Contbn. award 1978), Ky. Commonwealth's Attys. Assn. (pres. 1965-66), Richmond C. of C. (Outstanding Svc. award 1983, Outstanding Achievement award 1989), Exch. Club (pres. Richmond chpt. 1955), Elks. Avocations: Ky. history, home gardening. Home and Office: 302 High St Richmond KY 40475-1344

**CHENEVERT, DONALD JAMES, JR.,** lawyer; b. New Orleans, June 8, 1967; s. Donald James Sr. and Elly Nae Chenevert; m. Elizabeth Boyd, June 1, 1991; children: Donald James III, Sarah Elizabeth. BA in History, Miss. Coll., 1989; JD, Emory U., 1993. Bar: Ga. 1993, U.S. Dist. Ct. (no. dist.) Ga. 1993, U.S. Dist. Ct. (so. dist.) Ga. 1996, U.S. Ct. Appeals (11th cir.) 1996. Sr. assoc. Lord, Bissell & Brook, Atlanta, 1993—; mem. legal com., co-dir. Environ. Clinic, Upper Chattahoochee Riverkeeper Fund., Inc., Atlanta; coun. mem. Emory Law Alumni Coun., Atlanta; chair employers' duties and problems com. State Bar Ga., Atlanta, 1995-97. Coun. mem. Young Law Alumni Coun. Emory U., Atlanta, 1994-96; chair Commerce Soc. of the Commerce Club, Atlanta, 1995-97. Mem. Miss. Coll. Alumni Assn.-Ga. (pres. 1993—), Miss. Coll. Nat. Alumni Assn. (bd. mem. 1995—). Avocations: backpacking, camping, canoeing, kayaking, reading. E-mail: dcheneve@lordbissell.com. Fax: 404-872-5547. General civil litigation, Labor, Consumer commercial. Office: Lord Bissell & Brook 1201 W Peachtree St NW Ste 3700 Atlanta GA 30309-3462

**CHENG, ANDREW YUAN-SUNG,** lawyer; b. Ann Arbor, Mich., Mar. 20, 1967; s. chu-yuan and Alice (Hua) C.; m. Yvonne Chan, Jan. 5, 1967; 1 child, Samuel. BA, Columbia U., 1989; JD, Yale U., 1992. Bar: Calif. 1993, U.S. Dist. Ct. (no. dist.) Calif. 1993, U.S. Ct. Appeals (9th cir.) 1993, U.S. Dist. Ct. (ea. dist.) Calif. 1995. Assoc. atty. Pillsbury Madison Sutro, San Francisco, 1992-93; jud. law clk. Hon. Sarah Evans Barker, Indpls., 1993-95; assoc. Steinhart & Falconer, San Francisco, 1995-97; dep. city atty. San Francisco City Atty.'s Office, 1997—; lectr. Boalt Hall Law Sch., U. Calif., 1996-97. Contbr. articles to profl. jours. Elder Old First Presbyn. Ch., San Francisco, 1997—. Mem. Asian Am. Bar Assn., Bar Assn. of San Francisco. Avocations: piano, literature, scrabble, tennis, theology. E-mail: andrewúcheng@ci.sf.ca.us. Home: 1750 Sutter St Apt 206 San Francisco CA 94115-3232 Office: San Francisco City Attys Office 1390 Market St Ste 6 San Francisco CA 94102-5402

**CHENOWETH, JENNY K.,** lawyer; b. Elkhart, Ind., Jan. 14, 1964. BS, Ind. U., 1988; JD, Calif. Western Sch. Law, San Diego, 1991. Bar: Calif., U.S. Dist. Ct. (so. dist.) Calif. Regional dir. Bar/BRI Bar Rev., San Diego, 1992-94; sole practitioner San Diego, 1994-97; assoc. English & Gloven, APC, San Diego, 1997—; cons. Bar/BRI Bar Rev., 1995-96. Vol., Helen Woodward Animal Ctr., Rancho Santa Fe, 1993—. Mem. San Diego County Bar Assn., Ind. U. Alumni Club (pres.). Avocations: waterskiing, dog training, sports, gourmet cooking, gardening. Federal civil litigation, State civil litigation. Office: English & Gloven PC 501 W Broadway Ste 1875 San Diego CA 92101-8567

**CHERCHIGLIA, DEAN KENNETH,** lawyer; b. Cold Springs, N.Y., Apr. 11, 1956; s. Patrick Joseph and Bella (Feld) C.; m. Susan Elaine Sonkin, July 5, 1980; children: Brian Alden, Evan James. BBA cum laude, Ohio U., 1977; JD, Case Western Res. U., 1984. Bar: Ohio 1984. Contract specialist NASA Lewis Rsch. Ctr., Cleve., 1980; atty. Hermann, Cahn & Schneider, Cleve., 1984-85; assoc. Schwarzwald, Robiner, Wolf & Rock, Cleve., 1985; asst. counsel HealthAm. Corp., Cleve., 1986-87; atty. TransOhio Savs. Bank, Cleve., 1987-91; asst. v.p., counsel Chase Fin. Corp., Cleve., 1991-97; of counsel Benesch, Friedlander, Coplan & Aronoff, Cleve., 1997-99; counsel CompliSource, LLC, 1999—. Mem. Case Western Res. U. Law. Rev., 1982-84. Mem. Ohio State Bar Assn., Cleve. Bar Assn., Amnesty Internat. Avocations: photography, scuba diving, weightlifting. General corporate, Consumer commercial, Contracts commercial. Home: 3620 Stoer Rd Shaker Heights OH 44122-5116

**CHEREWKA, MICHAEL,** lawyer; b. Taylor, Pa., July 3, 1955; s. Michael Jr. and Anne (Regan) C.; m. Michele Mary Robinson, Aug. 2, 1980; children: Michael Colin, Matthew Bryan, Meaghan Kelly. Student, U. Bristol, Eng., 1976-77; BSBA cum laude, Bucknell U., 1978; JD cum laude, Dickinson Sch. Law, 1981. Bar: Pa. 1981, U.S. Dist. Ct. (mid. dist.) Pa. 1983, U.S. Tax Ct. 1983, U.S. Ct. Appeals (3d cir.) 1983, U.S. Supreme Ct. 1985. Sr. mem. tax staff Ernst & Whinney, Harrisburg, Pa., 1981-83; assoc. Ball, Skelly, Murren & Connell (formerly Ball & Skelly), Harrisburg, 1983-89; pvt. practice Harrisburg, 1989-96; mng. ptnr. Cherewka & Radcliff, LLP, 1996—. Co-author: Pennsylvania Tax Service, 1987; contbg. editor (legal column) Cen. Penn Bus. Jour., 1985-88; advisor Dauphin County Law Explorers Post, 1982-88. Mem. Country Club Park Civic Assn., 1983-98, pres., 1987-88; mem. Hist. Harrisburg Assn., 1982-84; active Tri-County United Way, 1985-90, cons. planning giving, mem. adv. com., 1988-90; bd. dirs. Capital divsn. Am. Heart Assn., chmn. 1989-91, bd. dirs. Pa. affiliate, 1989-98 , exec. com., 1989-90, 93, treas., 1994-95, incoming chmn. bd., 1995-96, chmn. 1996-97; chmn., bd. dirs. Concertante Chamber Ensemble, 1996-97; mem. planned giving com. Keystone Svc. Sys. Found., 1995—; mem. adv. bd. Found. Caths. United in Svc., Cath. Diocese of Harrisburg, 1991-97. Named Outstanding Young Man Am., U.S. Jaycees, 1983. Mem. Pa. Bar Assn. (tax sect. 1981—, real estate, probate and trust law sect. 1981—, com. state taxation 1984—, chmn. subcom. on compromise tax 1986-97), Dauphin County Bar Assn. (interprofl. rels. com. 1984-89, estate planning sect. 1992—), Estate Planning Coun. Cen. Pa. (chmn. CPA subcom. 1982-83, bd. dirs. 1988-96, treas. 1989-90, v.p. 1990-91, pres. 1991-92), Polit. Info. Com. CPAs Pa. (treas. 1982-83), Greater Harrisburg C. of C. (bus. liaison com. 1984-87, econ. devel. com. 1988-89, 93-94, reaccreditation task force 1996), Nat. Assn. Estate Planners (charter 1988—), Pa. Chamber Bus. and Industry (bus. subcom. 1989), Greater West Shore Area C. of C. (comml.-indsl. devel. com. 1987-89), Alzheimer's Assn. of So. Ctrl. Pa. (bd. dirs. 1998—), Delta Mu Delta, Omicron Delta Kappa. Republican. Orthodox Greek Catholic. Avocations: coin collecting, golf, basketball. General corporate, Estate planning, Taxation, general. Home: 125 Pelham Rd Camp Hill PA 17011-1353 Office: 624 N Front St Wormleysburg PA 17043-1022

**CHERNESKY, RICHARD JOHN,** lawyer; b. Scranton, Pa., July 27, 1939; s. Frank Peter and Mary (Stialect) C.; m. Alice Faye Nyfenger, Aug. 1, 1959; children: Christopher John, Joshua James. BA, Ohio St. U., 1963, JD, 1966. Bar: Ohio 1966. Ptnr. Smith & Schnacke, Dayton, Ohio, 1966-88; mng. ptnr. Chernesky, Heyman & Kress P.L.L., Dayton, 1988—; bd. dirs. Am. Indoor Soccer Assn., Inc., 1992-96; pres. Ohio Sports Ctr., Miamisburg, Ohio, 1991—; trustee Hipple Cancer Rsch. Ctr., Kettering, Ohio, 1994-96, Dayton Internat. Aviation Corp., Inc., 1990-92; sec. Iams Co., 1997—. Bd. dirs. Miami Valley Hosp. Found., Dayton, 1987-88, Chapel of the Air, Wheaton, Ill., 1985-91, 94-95, Mike-sell's, Inc., 1994—, Dolly Inc., Tipp City, Ohio, 1989-93; trustee The Luth. Sch. of Dayton, 1988-91, The Waynesville Area Friends of the Parks, 1992—; mem. Luth. Social Svcs. Devel. Com., Dayton, 1987-93; chmn. Wayne Twp. Zoning Bd., Waynesville, 1987-95; bd. dirs. U.S. Soccer Fedn. Found., Inc., 1996—. Mem. Ohio State Bar Assn., Dayton Bar Assn., Dayton Better Bus. Bur. (bd. dirs. 1989-94). Contracts commercial, General corporate, Public utilities. Home: 8027 New Burlington Rd Waynesville OH 45068-9705 Office: Chernesky Heyman & Kress PLL PO Box 3808 Ste 1100 10 Courthouse Plz SW Dayton OH 45401-3808

**CHERNEY, ANDREW KNOX,** lawyer; b. Hamilton, Ohio, June 6, 1947; s. Andrew William and Florence Emily (McKee) C. BA, U. South, 1970; JD summa cum laude, Ohio State U., 1973. Bar: Ohio 1973. Assoc. Smith & Schnacke, Dayton, 1973-79; ptnr. Smith & Schnacke, 1979-89, Chernesky, Heyman & Kress, Dayton, 1989—. Mem. ABA, Ohio Bar Assn., Dayton Bar Assn. (chmn. bus. law com. 1986-88). Republican. Episcopalian. Avocations: sports, travel. Mergers and acquisitions, Finance, Banking.

**CHERNEY, JAMES ALAN,** lawyer; b. Boston, Mar. 19, 1948; s. Alvin George and Janice (Elaine) Cherney; m. Linda Bienenfeld. BA, Tufts U., 1969; JD, Columbia U., 1973. Bar: Ill. 1973, U.S. Supreme Ct. 1977, U.S. Ct. Appeals (7th cir.) 1979, U.S. Ct. Appeals (3d cir.) 1982, U.S. Ct. Appeals (10th cir.) 1984, U.S. Ct. Appeals (8th and 9th cirs.) 1987. Assoc. Kirkland & Ellis, Chgo., 1973-76; assoc. Hedlund, Hunter & Lynch, Chgo., 1976-79, ptnr., 1979-82; ptnr. Latham & Watkins, Chgo., 1982—. Mem. ABA, Chgo. Bar Assn., Saddle and Cycle Club (sec. 1989, v.p. 1991-92, pres. 1992-94). Federal civil litigation, State civil litigation, Health. Office: Latham & Watkins Sears Tower Ste 5800 Chicago IL 60606-6306

**CHERNIN, RUSSELL SCOTT,** lawyer; b. Bklyn., Feb. 5, 1957; s. Julius and Sara Sidne (Fuchsman) C.; m. Diane M. Clay, Sept. 27, 1986. AB, Clark U., 1978; JD, George Washington U., 1981. Bar: Mass. 1981, U.S. Dist. Ct. Mass. 1983, U.S. Ct. Appeals (1st cir.) 1985. Law clk. FERC, Washington, 1979-81; assoc. Labovitz & Assocs., Worcester, Mass., 1982-83; pvt. practice Worcester, 1983—; instr. bus. law Becker Jr. Coll., Leicester, Mass., 1985-89. Co-author handbook: Sex and the Law, 1979; contbr. to profl. publs. Mem. Legal panel Civil Liberties Union Mass., 1988. Mem. Mass. Bar Assn., Worcester County Bar Assn., Am. Arbitration Assn., Clark U. Alumni Assn. Avocations: scuba diving, skiing. Contracts commercial, Bankruptcy, Construction. Office: 390 Main St Worcester MA 01608-2583

**CHERNOW, JEFFREY SCOTT,** lawyer, educator, author; b. Phila., Mar. 8, 1951; s. William and Sylvia Ann (Rosenberg) C.; m. Debra Sharon Shapiro, Dec. 29, 1974; children: William Ross, Stephanie Lynne. BS, Pa. State U., 1972; JD, U. Balt., 1976. Bar: Md. 1976, U.S. Dist. Ct. Md. 1977, U.S. Supreme Ct. 1980, U.S. Ct. Claims 1991. Assoc. Goodman, Meagher & Enoch, Balt., 1977-79; asst. atty. gen. State of Md., Balt., 1980-85; assoc. Cardin & Cardin, P.A., Balt., 1985-86; pvt. practice law Balt., 1986-89; ptnr. Kandel, Klitenic & Chernow, Owings Mills, Md., 1990—; asst. prof. Towson (Md.) State U., 1978-83, assoc. prof., 1983-86; panel chmn. Md. Health Claims Arbitration Office, 1983-84; lectr. Md. Inst. for Continuing Profl. Edn. of Lawyers, Inc., 1986; dir. Altex Industries, Inc., 1989. Contbr. chpt. to book. Sec., trustee Basic Cancer Rsch. Found., Inc., 1986—; chmn. bldg.

com. Congregation Adat Chaim, 1985-86, trustee, 1986-90. Mem. ABA, Md. Bar Assn., Bar Assn. Balt. City, N.Am. Securities Adminstrs. Assn. (mem. various coms. 1980-85, chmn. franchise and bus. opportunities com. 1984-85), Md. State Bar Assn. (sec. bus. law, franchise law com. 1991). Securities, General corporate, Franchising. Home: 214 Berry Vine Dr Owings Mills MD 21117-4500 Office: Kandel Klitenic & Chernow LLP 1838 Greene Tree Rd Ste 370 Baltimore MD 21208-7102

**CHERNY, DAVID EDWARD,** lawyer; b. Brookline, Mass., Jan. 21, 1957; s. Jacob and Anne (Gray) C.; m. Elise Joan Sallen, June 4, 1978; children: Michael Aaron, Allyson Jill. BSBA cum laude, Boston U., 1978; JD cum laude, Suffolk U., 1981. Bar: Mass. 1981, U.S. Dist. Ct. Mass. 1982, U.S. Tax Ct. 1982, U.S. Ct. Appeals (1st cir.) 1982, U.S. Supreme Ct. 1985, Tex. 1990. Assoc. Atwood & Wright, Boston, 1981-84, Jacob M. Atwood P.C., Boston, 1984-86; ptnr. Atwood & Cherny, Boston, 1986—; prin. Algonquin Assocs., Boston, 1986—; pres. Geneva/Roth Holdings Ltd., 1989—. Fellow Am. Acad. Matrimonial Lawyers, Internat. Acad. Matrimonial Lawyers; mem. ABA, Mass. Bar Assn., Boston Bar Assn., Assn. Trial Lawyers Am., Mass. Acad. Trial Attys. (lectr. family law), Blue Hill Country Club, Algonquin Club, Phi Delta Phi. Family and matrimonial, Probate. Office: Atwood & Cherny 393 Commonwealth Ave Boston MA 02115-1802

**CHERRY, PAUL STEPHEN,** lawyer; b. Phila., Oct. 6, 1943; s. Herbert Isdor and Toby (Ring) C.; m. Hilary Kirwan, Apr. 8, 1972. BA, Temple U., 1966; JD, Widener U., 1982. Pa. 1983, U.S. Dist. Ct. (ea. dist.) Pa. 1983, U.S. Ct. Appeals (3d and fed. cirs.) 1983, U.S. Ct. Internat. Trade 1983, U.S. Ct. Claims 1983, U.S. Tax Ct. 1983, U.S. Supreme Ct. 1986, U.S. Ct. Vets. Appeals 1995, U.S. Ct. Appeals (11th cir.) 1996, Fla. 1997; registered sanitarian. Sci. tchr. Cen. High Sch., Phila., 1966-67; instr. physiology Regional Sch. Nursing, Owen Sound, Ont., Can., 1967-68; tchr. natural sci. Sir Sanford Fleming Coll., Peterborough, Ont., 1968-69; sanitarian Dept. Pub. Health, Phila., 1972-73, Chester County Health Dept., West Chester, Pa., 1974-79; pvt. practice law Wayne, Pa., 1983-95; asst. pub. defender 20th Jud. Cir., Fla., 1998—. Operating engr. Sound and Light Show at Independence Hall, Phila., 1961-82; bd. dirs. Hist. Soc. of U.S., Dist. Ct. (ea. dist.) Pa., Phila., 1985-95; mem. traffic com. Tredyffrin Twp., Berwyn, Pa., 1991. Recipient Annual recognition Women Against Abuse, Phila., 1986. Fellow Lawyers in Mensa (main line coord. 1985-95); mem. Pa. Bar Assn., B'nai B'rith (pres. Freedom Valley Lodge, Valley Forge, Pa. 1992-95). Democrat. Jewish. Avocations: classical music, acoustics, computers, pipe organ constrn. Criminal, General practice, Contracts commercial. Home: 6625 Taeda Dr Sarasota FL 34241-9149 Office: PO Box 510304 Punta Gorda FL 33951-0304

**CHERUNDOLO, JOHN CHARLES,** lawyer; b. Pitts., Nov. 24, 1948; s. John Charles and Margaret E. (Whitehead) C.; m. Elizabeth Flack, July 26, 1980; children: Allison Belle, Leane Elizabeth, James Charles. BA in Polit. Sci., Syracuse U., 1970, M Pub Adminstrn., 1972, JD, 1973. Bar: Ill. 1974, N.Y. 1974, U.S. Dist. Ct. (ea. dist.) Ill. 1974. Asst. gen. atty. Roper Corp., Kankakee, Ill., 1974-75; assoc. Hancock Law Firm, Syracuse, N.Y., 1975-80, Banbaum & Manaker, Syracuse, 1980-83; sr. ptnr. Cherundolo, Bottar & McGowan, P.C., Syracuse, 1983—. Bd. dirs. Syracuse Friends of Amateur Boxing, 1980—; fin. chmn. Congressman James Walsh; mem. fin. and chmn.'s com. Onondaga County Republican Party. Named All-Am. UPI, AP, Syracuse, 1970, Acad. All-Am., U.S. Coaches, Syracuse, 1970. Mem. ABA, Assn. Trial Lawyers Am. (state del.), N.Y. State Trial Lawyers (bd. dirs., v.p.), Upstate Trial Lawyers (past pres.), Trial Lawyers for Pub. Justice (state coord.), Onondaga County Bar Assn., Syracuse U. Varsity Club (bd. dirs. 1976—), Order of Coif. Roman Catholic. Avocation: sports. State civil litigation, Federal civil litigation, Personal injury. Home: 4443 Dolomite Dr Syracuse NY 13215-1500 Office: Cherundolo Bottar & McGowan, PC 1 Lincoln Ctr Ste 1180 Syracuse NY 13202-1324

**CHERVITZ, DAVID HOWARD,** lawyer; b. St. Louis, Dec. 30, 1958; m. Robin B. Blinder, June 14, 1981; children: Zachary, Mandi, Jordi. BSEE, Washington U., St. Louis, 1981; JD, U. Mo., 1986. Bar: Mo. 1986, U.S. Patent Office 1988, U.S. Dist. Ct. (ea. dist.) Mo. 1989, U.S. Ct. Appeals (fed. dist.) 1990. Product engr. United Techs. Communications, St. Louis, 1981-83; assoc. Rogers, Howell, Moore & HaferKamp, St. Louis, 1986-88, Senniger, Powers, Leavitt, & Roedel, St. Louis, 1988-89; ptnr. Haverstock, Garrett & Roberts, St. Louis, 1990—. Bd. dirs. Alexandra Ballet Co., St. Louis, 1987-91. Mem. ABA. Patent, Trademark and copyright, Computer. Office: Haverstock Garrett & Roberts 611 Olive St Ste 1610 Saint Louis MO 63101-1711

**CHERWIN, JOEL IRA,** lawyer; b. Winthrop, Mass., Apr. 29, 1942; s. Melvin Arthur and Martha C.; m. Sherry Lenore Cherwin, July 5, 1970; children: Alison, Matthew, Joshua. BS in Econs., U. Pa., 1963; JD, Boston U., 1966. Bar: Mass. 1966, U.S.. Dist. Ct. Mass. 1968, U.S. Tax Ct. 1969. Ptnr. Cherwin & Glazier, Boston, 1967-77, Cherwin & Glickman, Boston, 1977-96, Cherwin, Glickman & Theise LLP, Boston, 1996—. Mem. ABA, Mass. Bar Assn. Democrat. Jewish. General corporate, Banking. Office: Cherwin Glickman & Theise LLP One International Pl Boston MA 02110

**CHESHIRE, LUCIUS MCGEHEE,** lawyer; b. Raleigh, N.C., Mar. 29, 1925; s. James Webb and Anne Ludlow (McGehee) C.; m. Nellie David, Nov. 16, 1946; children—Lucius McGehee, Carl Davis. Student U. N.C., 1946, cert. in law, 1965. Bar: N.C. Sup. Ct. 1965, U.S. dist. ct. (mid. dist.) N.C. 1969, U.S. Sup. Ct. 1971. Assoc., Graham and Levings, Hillsborough, N.C., 1965; ptnr. Graham, Levings & Cheshire, 1966-67; ptnr. Graham & Cheshire, 1967-81; sr. ptnr. Cheshire & Parker, 1981—; pres. 15 Jud. Dist. Bar, 1971-72, chmn. Dist. 15 B Bar Candidate Com. Active Hist. Hillsborough Commn.; trustee N.C. State Employees Retirement System. Served with USMC, 1943-46. Mem. N.C. State Bar, N.C. Bar Assn., N.C. Acad. Trial Lawyers, Orange County Bar Assn. (pres. 1969-70). Democrat. Anglican Orthodox. Club: Sphinx (Raleigh). Contbr. article to legal review. State civil litigation, General practice. Home: Barracks Rd Hillsborough NC 27278 Office: PO Box 100 Hillsborough NC 27278-0100

**CHESLER, STANLEY RICHARD,** federal judge; b. Bklyn., June 15, 1947; s. Rubin and Beatrice (Horowitz) C.; m. Francine Richer, June 29, 1969; 1 child, Elizabeth. BA, SUNY, Binghamton, 1968; JD magna cum laude, St. John's U., 1974. Bar: N.Y. 1975, N.J. 1985, U.S. Dist. Ct. (ea. dist., so. dist.) N.Y. 1975, U.S. Dist. Ct. N.J. 1985, U.S. Ct. Appeals (2d cir.) 1975. Asst. dist. atty. Bronx County, N.Y., 1974-80; dep. chief investigations bur. Bronx County, 1976-78, chief investigations bur., 1978-79, chief rackets, narcotics bur., 1979-80; trial atty. U.S. Dept. Justice Organized Crime Strike Force, Newark, 1980-84, deputy chief, 1984-86; asst. U.S. atty. Dist. of N.J., Newark, 1987; U.S. magistrate judge U.S. Dist. Ct. N.J., Newark, 1987—. Fellow Am. Bar Found.; mem. Assn. Fed. Bar State of N.J. (bd. advisors), John J. Gibbons Am. Inn of Ct. (master). Avocations: cross country skiing, biking. Office: US Dist Ct NJ US PO Office & Courthouse Bldg Newark NJ 07101

**CHESLEY, PATRICK J.,** lawyer, educator; b. Jersey City, Jan. 11, 1951; s. Ray F. and Catherine G. (Veitenheirmer) C.; children: Kevin Christopher, Sean Phillip. BA, U. Okla., 1973, JD, 1977. Bar: Okla. 1977, U.S. Dist. Ct. (no. and ea. dists.) Okla., U.S. Ct. Appeals (10th cir.), U.S. Supreme Ct. Tenant counsel U. Okla., Norman, 1978-79, criminal def. counsel, 1991-93; corp. counsel Celtek Inc., Norman, 1980-84; pvt. practice Chesley Law Office, Norman, 1985—; prof. law Okla. City U. Coll. Law, 1995—. Bd. dirs. Bethesda Child Abuse Counseling Ctr., Norman, 1988-92. Served with USAR, 1969-70. Mem. ATLA, Okla. Trial Lawyers Assn. Personal injury, Criminal, Juvenile. Home: 1513 Magnolia St Norman OK 73072-6829 Office: 628 24th Ave NW Norman OK 73069-6312

**CHESLEY, STANLEY MORRIS,** lawyer; b. Cin., Mar. 26, 1936; s. Frank and Rachel (Kinsburg) C.; children: Richard A., Lauren B. BA, U. Cin., 1958, LLB, 1960. Bar: Ohio 1960, Ky. 1978, W.Va., Tex., Nev. 1981. Ptnr. Waite, Schneider, Bayless & Chesley Co., Cin., 1960; Contbr. articles to profl. jours. Past chmn. bd. commrs. on grievances and discipline Supreme Ct. Ohio; past pres. Jewish Fedn. Cin.; nat. vice chair, bd. govs., trustee, joint distbn. com. United Jewish Appeal; exec. bd., nat. bd. govs. Am.Jewish Com.; nat. bd. govs. Hebrew Union Coll.; exec. com. U.S. Holocaust Meml. Mus. Mem. ABA, ATLA, Am. Judicature Soc., Fed. Bar Assn., Melvin M. Belli Soc., Ohio Bar Assn., Ky. Bar Assn., W.Va. Bar Assn., Tex. Bar Assn., Nev. Bar Assn., Cin. Bar Assn. Personal injury, General civil litigation, Product liability. Office: Waite Schneider Bayless & Chesley 1513 Central Trust Towers Cincinnati OH 45202

**CHESLEY, STEPHEN ROBERT,** lawyer; b. N.Y.C., Apr. 5, 1956; s. Jack and Edith C.; m. Caren Greenberg, Sept. 20, 1987; children: Jonathan, Daniel. BA, SUNY, Buffalo, 1978; JD, Pace U., 1981. Bar: N.Y. 1982, U.S. Dist. Ct. (ea. and so. dist.) 1982. Mem. Krause & Krause, N.Y.C., 1982, Chasine Levine & Ross, N.Y.C., 1982-85; ptnr. Reitz & Chesley, Bklyn., 1985—. Mgr. Merrick Little League, N.Y. Mem. Assn. Trial Lawyers Am., N.Y. State Trial Lawyers Assn., Brooklyn Bar Assn., Delta Theta Phi. Avocations: sports, camping, hiking. Personal injury, Real property, Product liability. Office: Reitz & Chesley 16 Court St Ste 2506 Brooklyn NY 11241-2501

**CHESLEY-LAHM, DIANE,** lawyer; b. Norwood, Mass., Sept. 27, 1942; d. Casimir Peter and Christine (Zabelle) Chesley; m. Wen-hsien Wu, Dec. 26, 1964 (div. July 1973); children: Wendi Ann, Lisa Marie; m. Gunther Karl Lahm, Dec. 14, 1973 (div. Feb. 1993); children: Michael Christopher, Gregory Andrew. AB, Trinity Coll., 1964; postgrad., Temple U., 1973-74; JD, Capital U., 1976. Bar: Ind. 1976, U.S. Dist Ct. (so. dist.) Ind. 1976, Ohio 1977. Pvt. practice Richmond, Ind., 1976, Columbus, Ohio, 1977; asst. atty. gen. Office Atty. Gen. Ohio, Columbus, 1977; counsel, exec. Ohio Dental Assn., Columbus, 1977-79; dir. Continuing Legal Edn. Capital U. Law Sch., Columbus, 1980-88; sec. to commn. on Continuing Legal Edn. Columbus, 1988—. Leader Green Circle Program, Phila. Human Rels. Com., 1969-71; Brownie leader Girl Scouts U.S., Morgantown (W.Va.) Pub. Schs., 1972-73; leader study group PTA, Morgantown, 1973; panelist Ohio State U. Continuing Edn. Forum, Columbus, 1976; team cons. Ohio Mock Trial Program, Columbus, 1985-86, judge for competition, 1988-93. Mem. ABA, Ohio State Bar Assn., Columbus Bar Assn., Orgn. of Regulatory Adminstrs. for Continuing Legal Edn. Lutheran. Avocations: quilting, cooking, gardening, singing, reading. Office: Supreme Ct Commn Continuing Legal Edn 30 E Broad St Columbus OH 43215-3414

**CHESNEY, BRENT JACKSON,** lawyer; b. Corpus Christi, Tex., Mar. 26, 1963; s. Alfred Jackson and Lois Byrd C. BS in Journalism, Tex. Christian U., 1985; JD, S. Tex. Coll. Law, 1996. Legis. liaison Atty. Gen. Dan Morales, Austin and Houston, Tex., 1995; atty., lobbyist Hunters & Handel P.C., Corpus Christi and Austin, 1996-99; pvt. practice Corpus Christi, 1999—; mng. ptnr. Christina Holdings, Corpus Christi, 1991—. Pres. Corpus Christi Food Bank, 1992-93; commr., chmn. Spl. Olympics, Corpus Christi, 1992, 93, 97, 98; chmn. Leadership Corpus Christi, 1993-94; mem. Nueces County Citizens Adv. Bd., 1998; deacon Christian Ch. (Disciples of Christ). Mem. Travis County Bar Assn., Corpus Christi Bar Assn., Travis County Young Lawyers, Corpus Christi Young Lawyers, TCU Nat. Alumni Bd., Corpus Christi Planning Commn. (vice-chmn. 1997—). Avocations: basketball, tennis, running, weightlifting, theater. Family and matrimonial, Criminal, State civil litigation. Home: 4600 Ocean Dr Apt 404 Corpus Christi TX 78412-2542 Office: 870 Tower II 555 N Carancahua St Corpus Christi TX 78478-0002

**CHESNEY, MAXINE M.,** judge; b. 1942. BA, U. Calif., Berkeley, 1964, JD, 1967. Trial atty. Office Dist. Atty., San Francisco, 1968-69, sr. trial atty., 1969-71, prin. trial atty., 1971-76, head atty., 1976, asst. chief dep., 1976-79; judge San Francisco Mcpl. Ct., 1979-83, San Francisco Superior Ct., 1983-95, U.S. Dist. Ct. (no. dist.) Calif., San Francisco, 1995—. Bd. dirs. San Francisco Child Abuse Coun., 1976-79, Hosp. Audiences, 1978-81. Mem. Fed. Judges Assn., Nat. Assn. Women Judges, Edward J. McFetridge Am. Inn of Ct., U.S. Assn. Constl. Law, Queen's Bench, Ninth Jud. Cir. Hist. Soc. Office: US Dist Ct No Dist Calif PO Box 36060 450 Golden Gate Ave San Francisco CA 94102-3661

**CHESNIK, CONSTANCE MARY,** lawyer; b. West Bend, Wis., July 28, 1958; d. Ronald William and Susan Claire Hron; m. Kevin Chesnik, Sept. 25, 1982; children: Kelly Susan, Hayley Kathryn, Valerie Margaret. BA, U. Wis., 1981, JD, 1986. Bar: Wis. 1986, U.S. Dist. Ct. (we. dist.) Wis. 1986. Legal counsel Wis. Dept. Workforce Devel., Madison, 1986—. Contbr. articles to profl. jours. Mem. Wis. Child Support Enforcement Assn., Wis. State Bar, N.H. Child Support Enforcement Assn., Dane County Bar Assn., Wis. Jr. Women's Club. Democrat. Roman Catholic. Avocations: volunteer service work, fundraising, local theatre, interior decorating. Home: 3301 Nottingham Way Madison WI 53713-3461 Office: Dept Workforce Devel 201 E Washington Ave Madison WI 53702-0006

**CHESNUT, CAROL FITTING,** lawyer; b. Pecos, Tex., June 17, 1937; d. Ralph Ulf and Carol (Lowe) Fitting; m. Dwayne A. Chesnut, Dec. 27, 1955; children: Carol Marie, Stephanie Michelle, Mark Steven. BA magna cum laude, U. Colo., 1971; JD, U. Calif., San Francisco, 1994. Rsch. asst. U. Colo., 1972; head quality controller Mathematics, Inc., Denver, 1973-74; cons. Mincome Man., Winnipeg, Can., 1974; cons. economist Energy Cons. Assocs. Inc., Denver, 1974-79; exec. v.p. tng. ECA Intercomp, 1980-81; gen. ptnr. Chestnut Consortium, S.F., 1981—; sec., bd. dirs. Critical Resources, Inc., 1981-83. Rep. Lakehurst Civic Assn., 1968; staff aide Senator Gary Hart, 1978; Dem. precinct capt., 1982-88. Mem. ABA, ACLU, AAUW (1st v.p. 1989-90), Soc. Petroleum Engrs., Am. Nuc. Soc. (chmn. conv. space activities 1989, chair of spouse activities 1989), Am. Geophys. Union, Assn. Women Geoscientists (treas. Denver 1983-85), Associated Students of Hastings (rep. 1994), Calif. State Bar, Nev. State Bar, Nev. Trial Lawyers Assn., Nat. Acad. Elder Law Attys., Canyon Ranch Homeowners Assn. (ssec. bd. dirs. 1994-97), Phi Beta Kappa, Phi Chi Theta, Phi Delta Phi. Uniterian. Estate planning, Probate, Elder. Office: 2921 N Tenaya Way Ste 201 Las Vegas NV 89128-0454

**CHESNUTT, MARCUS WILKES,** lawyer; b. Lumberton, N.C., Aug. 31, 1953; s. James Moseley and Ruth (Wilkes) C.; m. Alice Armstrong Holman, July 25, 1981; children: Parker Bryant, Marcus Holman. BA, U. N.C., 1975; JD, Cumberland U., 1978. Bar: N.C. 1978. Sr. law clk. Fed. Cts., Trenton, N.C., 1978; atty. Stubbs, Perdue, Chesnutt & Wheeler, PA, New Bern, N.C., 1979-95, Chesnutt, Clemmons & Thomas, P.A., New Bern, 1995—. Mem. Craven County Bar Assn., 3d Dist. Bar, N.C. Acad. Trial Lawyers. Criminal, Personal injury.

**CHESS, FAYE ROSALIND,** lawyer; b. Laurel, Miss., Dec. 5, 1962; d. Robert Hubert Chess and Gloria Faye Thompson Chess-Hanley. BA, Purdue U., 1984; JD, U. Cin., 1988. Bar: Wash. 1989, U.S. Dist. Ct. (we. dist.) Wash. 1990. Legal intern Cin. Legal Aid Soc., 1987; legal extern Hamilton County Prosecutors Office, Cin., 1988; staff atty. Seattle-King County Pub. Defenders Office, Seattle, 1988—. vice chairperson bd. dirs. Victim-Offender Reconciliation Program, Seattle, 1992—. Mem. ABA, Assn. Trial Lawyers Am., Wash. Bar Assn., Wash. Defenders Assn., Delta Sigma Theta (rec. sec. 1983—). Avocations: reading, travel, piano. Address: Chess -Prentice 180207 154th Pl SE Renton WA 98058-9667

**CHESSON, CALVIN WHITE,** lawyer, educator; b. Williamston, N.C., July 23, 1936; s. Bruce Cecil Chesson and Debby Beatrice White; m. Ann Cooke; children: Courtney Ann Haas, Stephanie Lynn. BA in Bus. Adminstrn., East Carolina U., 1958; JD, U. N.C., 1962. Bar: N.C. 1962, U.S. Dist. Ct. (ea., we. and mid. dists.) N.C. 1995, U.S. Ct. Appeals (4th cir.) 1998. Assoc. Lassiter, Moore & Van Allen, Charlotte, N.C., 1962-65; dist. atty. for Mecklenburg County N.C. Superior Ct., Charlotte, 1965-68; sr. ptnr. Cole & Chesson, Charlotte, 1968-80, Curtis, Millsaps & Chesson, Charlotte, 1980-85; pvt. practice law Charlotte, 1985—. Dir., chmn. Voluntary Action Ctr.-United Way, Charlotte, 1983-86; pres. Lions Club, Charlotte, 1984-85, 92-93; commr. Mecklenburg County Pk. and Recreation Commn., Charlotte, 1986-88; dir. Family Support Ctr., Charlotte, 1989-90, Hope Springs, Charlotte, 1991-93. Pvt. USAR, 1959-65. Mem. ABA, N.C. Bar Assn., N.C. State Bar, Mecklenburg County Bar Assn. Democrat. Methodist. Avocation: tennis. General civil litigation, Contracts commercial, General corporate. Office: PO Box 34514 Charlotte NC 28234-4514

**CHESTER, ROBERT SIMON GEORGE,** lawyer; b. Chelmsford, Essex, England, Feb. 11, 1949; arrived in Can., 1971.; s. Robert John and Elizabeth Poyitt (Forteath) C.; m. Anna Tharyan, Sept. 18, 1975; 1 child, Rahael Elizabeth Anna. BA, Oxford U., England, 1971, MA, 1979; postgrad., Osgoode Hall Law Sch., Toronto, 1971-72. Bar: Ontario 1982, England and Wales 1988. Vis. lectr. Osgoode Hall Law Sch., Toronto, 1972-74; rsch. staff Ontario Law Reform Commn., Toronto, 1974-77; exec. counsel Dep. Atty. Gen. Ontario, Toronto, 1977-82; counsel policy devel. Ministry Atty. Gen., Ontario, 1982-85; dir. rsch. McMillan Binch, Toronto, 1985—, ptnr., 1988—; counsel Study on Access to Legal Svcs. by Disabled, Ontario, 1982-83; cons. Royal Commn. on Employment Equity, 1983-84, Royal Commn. on Electoral Reform, 1990-91, Royal Commn. on Aboriginal Peoples, 1992. Author: (with others) Environmental Rights in Canada, 1981, Barristers and Solicitors in Practice, 1998; co-editor: Winning with Computers, 1991, 2d vol., 1993; contbr. articles to profl. jours. Can. Rhodes Found. scholar, 1972; trustee and fellow Coll. Law Practice Mgmt. Mem. ABA (chmn. New Media and Internet bd., chmn. edn. bd. law practi mgmt. sect. 1994-96, chmn. Techshow 1992-93), Can. Bar Assn. (com. legal opinions 1992—). Anglican. General corporate, Libel, Computer. Home: 41 Walmsley Blvd, Toronto, ON Canada M4V 1X7 Office: McMillan Binch, Royal Bank Plz PO Box 38, Toronto, ON Canada M5J 2J7

**CHESTER, STEPHANIE ANN,** lawyer, banker; b. Oct. 8, 1951; d. Alden Runge and Nina Lavina (Hanson) C.; divorced. BA magna cum laude, Augustana Coll., 1973; JD, U. S.d., 1977; postgrad. C.F.S.C., ABA Nat. Grad. Trust Sch., Evanston, Ill., 1984. Bar: S.D. 1977, Minn. 1979. Asst. counselor Minnehaha County Juvenile Ct. Ctr., Sioux Falls, S.D., 1972-73; child care worker Project Threshold, Sioux Falls, 1973-74; legal intern Davenport, Evans, Hurwitz & Smith, Sioux Falls, 1976; law clk. S.D. Supreme Ct., Pierre, 1977-78; originations dept. buyer Dain Bosworth, Inc., Mpls., 1978-79; v.p., trust officer 1st Bank of S.D., N.A., Sioux Falls, 1979-86; v.p. First Trust Co., Inc., St. Paul, 1986-93; lawyer Westby, Chester & Lees, P.A., 1994-96; pres. Sioux Falls Estate Planning Coun., 1983-85. Projects and rsch. editor S.d. Law Rev., 1977; author law rev. comment. Mem. fund raising coms. S.D. Symphony, Sioux Falls Cmty. Playhouse, Augustana Coll., 1982-83; mem. S.D. divsn. Nat. Women's Polit. Caucus; mem. events com. Augustana Coll. Fellows, Sioux Falls, 1984; bd. dirs. YWCA, Sioux Falls, 1984, Sioux Falls Arena/Coliseum, 1985; mem. Sioux Falls Jr. Svc. League, 1984. Augustana Coll. scholar, 1969-73; Augustana Coll. Bd. Regents scholar, 1973. Mem. ABA, S.D. Bar Assn., Minn. Bar Assn., 2d S.D. Jud. Cir. Bar Assn., Nat. Assn. Bank Women (state conv. com. 1983-85), Mensa, Network Club, Portia Club, Phi Delta Phi, Chi Epsilon. Probate, Family and matrimonial, General corporate. Home: 25 N 4th St # 502 Minneapolis MN 55401-1719

**CHESTNUT, JOHN WILLIAM,** lawyer; b. Berwyn, Ill., July 3, 1940; s. James Edward and Alice Mary (Cotter) C.; m. Margaret Barbara Angland, Aug. 8, 1964; children: Edward, Nancy. BS cum laude, U. Notre Dame, 1962; JD cum laude, Northwestern U., 1965. Bar: Ill. 1965, U.S. Dist. Ct. (no. dist.) Ill. 1965, U.S. Supreme Ct. 1978, U.S. Ct. Appeals (fed. cir.) 1982. Assoc. Dawson, Tilton, Fallon & Lungmus, Chgo., 1965-68; ptnr. Tilton, Fallon, Lungmus & Chestnut, Chgo., 1968-94. Mem. editorial bd. The Trademark Reporter, N.Y.C., 1975—. Mem. ABA, Am. Intellectual Property Law Assn., Ill. State Bar Assn., Intellectual Property Law Assn. Chgo., Patent Law Assn. Chgo. (bd. govs. 1979-81). Patent, Federal civil litigation, Intellectual property. Office: Tilton Fallon Lungum & Chestnut 100 S Wacker Dr Ste 960 Chicago IL 60606-4002

**CHESTNUT, KATHI LYNNE,** lawyer; b. Springfield, Mo., Nov. 7, 1959; d. Stanley Carl and Onita Faye (Weir) C. BA in Polit. Sci. summa cum laude, William Woods Coll., 1980; JD, Washington U., St. Louis, 1983. Bar: Mo. 1983, U.S. Dist. Ct. (ea. dist.) Mo. 1983, Ill. 1984, (so. dist.) Ill. 1991, U.S. Ct. Appeals (8th cir.) 1984, U.S. Supreme Ct., 1991. Assoc. Evans and Dixon, St. Louis, 1983-89, ptnr., 1990-96; prin. Kathi L. Chestnut, P.C., St. Louis, 1996-99; officer Greensfelder, Hember & Gale, PC, St. Louis, 1999—; reviewer Mo. Jud. Edn. Com., Jud. Desk Book, Civil Procedure. Mem. Mo. Bar Assn. (contbg. author Mo. Civil Procedure publ. 1988, 90, 95, 98), Ill. Bar Assn., Met. Bar Assn. St. Louis, Order of Coif, Alpha Chi Omega (Sigma Sigma Psi chpt. sec. 1985-86). Republican. Presbyterian. Avocations: choir, piano. E-mail:klc@greensfelder.com. Insurance, Labor, Civil rights. Home: 5318 N Kenrick Parke Dr Saint Louis MO 63119-5047 Office: Greensfelder Hember & Gale PC Ste 2000 10 S Broadway Saint Louis MO 63102

**CHESTON, SHEILA CAROL,** lawyer; b. Washington, Nov. 5, 1958; d. Theodore C. and Gabrielle Joan (Hellings) C. BA, Dartmouth Coll., 1980; JD, Columbia U., 1984. Bar: N.Y. 1986, D.C. 1986, U.S. Dist. Ct. D.C. 1987, U.S. Ct. Appeals (D.C. cir.) 1987, U.S. Dist. Ct. (so. and ea. dists.) N.Y. 1989, U.S. Ct. Appeals (2d cir.), U.S. Supreme Ct. 1989. Law clk. to judge U.S. Ct. Appeals for 9th Cir., L.A., 1984-85; assoc. Wilmer, Cutler & Pickering, Washington, 1985-92, ptnr., 1992-93; gen. counsel Def. Base Closure and Realignment Commn., 1993; spl. assoc. counsel to Pres. of U.S., 1994; dep. gen. counsel Dept. Air Force, 1993-95, gen. counsel, 1995-98; ptnr. Wilmer, Cutler & Pickering, Washington, 1998—; adj. prof. in internat. litigation Georgetown Law Sch., 1991—. Mem. ABA, D.C. Bar Assn., Women's Bar Assn., Am. Soc. Internat. Law. Democrat. Episcopalian. Federal civil litigation, Private international, Election. Office: Wilmer Cutler & Pickering 2445 M St NW Ste 500 Washington DC 20037-1487

**CHETTLE, A(LVIN) B(ASIL), JR.,** lawyer, educator; b. Hollywood, Calif., Apr. 13, 1937; s. Alvin Basil Sr. and Evelyn Teresa (Olsen) C. BS, Georgetown U., 1959, JD, 1962, LLM, 1964. Bar: Va. 1962, D.C. 1962, U.S. Ct. Mil. Appeals 1962, U.S. Ct. Appeals (D.C. cir.) 1962, U.S. Ct. Claims 1963, U.S. Tax Ct. 1963, U.S. Ct. Appeals (9th cir.) 1964, Calif. 1965, U.S. Dist. Ct. (cen. dist.) Calif. 1965, U.S. Supreme Ct. 1975, U.S. Dist. Ct. (so. dist.) Calif. 1977. Adminstrv. asst. to dir. claims div. Nat. Canners Assn. (now Nat. Food Processors Assn.), Washington, 1962-64; assoc. Keel & Pressman, Hawthorne, Calif., 1964; ptnr. Keel & Chettle, Hawthorne, Calif., 1965, Keel, Chettle & Valentine, Hawthorne, Calif., 1966-71; city prosecutor City of Hawthorne, 1965-69; sr. ptnr. Chettle & Valentine, Manhattan Beach, Calif., 1971-92; pvt. practice Manhattan Beach, 1971—; lectr. Food Processors Inst., Washington, Massey U., New Zealand, 1983; spl. counsel City of Inglewood, Calif., 1971, City of Hawthorne, Calif., 1977-84, City of Torrance, Calif., 1979—; arbitrator South Bay Mcpl. Ct., Torrance and L.A. Superior Ct.; judge pro tem L.A. Jud. Dist., 1982—, South Bay Jud. Dist., Torrance, 1985—, L.A. County Superior Ct., 1990—; hearing officer City of Garden Grove, 1989-92, City of Hawthorne, 1992-94. Active L.A. chpt. ARC, 1966-96, ARC Blood and Tissue Svcs., 1966-96; 1st chair emeritus bd. dirs. ARC Blood Svcs.-So. Calif. Region, 1997—; bd. dirs. Coalition of Food Industry Counsel; mem. bd. advisors Cath. Distance U., 1983-98. Recipient Life Time Achievements award Nat. Food Processors Assn. Mem. Am. Judicature Soc., D.C. Bar Assn., Calif. Bar Assn. (del. conf. of dels. 1969), Va. Bar Assn., Assn. So. Calif. Def. Counsel, Def. Rsch. Isnt., Inglewood Dist. Bar Assn. (trustee 1967, 70, treas. 1967, nominating com. 1966, 75, 76, 77, v.p. 1968, pres. 1969), L.A. County Bar Assn. (conf. affiliated bar pres. 1969, parking lot com. 1969, 70). Office: PO Box 7 Manhattan Beach CA 90267-0007

**CHEVIS, CHERYL ANN,** lawyer; b. Ann Arbor, Mich., Nov. 9, 1947; d. Peter Paul and Antoinette (Slapinski) C.; m. Edwin Mahaffey Gerow, Nov. 18, 1976. BA, U. Wash., 1969, MA, 1974; postgrad. in Sanskrit, U. Chgo., 1974-77, JD, 1980. Bar: Ill. 1980, U.S. Dist. Ct. (no. dist.) Ill. 1980, U.S. Ct. Appeals (7th cir.) 1982, U.S. Tax Ct. 1982, Oreg. 1986. Tax assoc. Sidley and Austin, Chgo., 1979-80, Mayer Brown and Platt, Chgo., 1981-85; sr. tax atty. Perkins Coie, Portland, 1985-87, tax ptnr., 1987—; mem. faculty Ill. Continuing Legal Edn., Chgo., 1982; vis. lectr. U. B.C., Vancouver, Can., 1983; lectr. Chgo. Tax Club, 1983, Oreg. Securities Lawyers Bar, Bend, 1986, Internat. Employers Seminar, Portland, 1991. Contbr. articles to Jour. Taxation. Vol. atty. Com. Civil Rights Under Law, Chgo., 1982-85. Smithsonian Inst. grantee, 1981. Mem. ABA (tax sect., com. capital recovery and leasing), Oreg. State Bar (sister-bar com. with Lithuanian Lawyers Assn. 1997—). Avocations: music, theater, outdoor sports. Corporate taxation, State and local taxation, Real property. Home: 4260 SW Council Crest Dr Portland OR 97201-1531 Office: Perkins Coie LLP 1211 SW 5th Ave Portland OR 97204-3713

**CHEWNING, MARTHA FRANCES MACMILLAN,** lawyer; b. Orlando, Fla., Oct. 11, 1951; d. James Francis and Frances Sybil (Es'Dorn) MacMillan; m. John Quinton Chewning, June 3, 1978. BA in Social Work magna cum laude, LaGrange Coll., 1972; JD, Mercer U., 1979. Bar: Ga. Pvt.

practice Hamilton, Pine Mountain, Ga., 1979-85; judge probate ct., traffic ct., supt. of elections Harris County, Hamilton, Ga., 1985-98; pvt. practice Hamilton, Ga., 1985—; bd. dirs. First Union Nat. Bank, Pine Mountain. Mem. State Bar Assn. Ga., Pine Mountain C. of C. (pres. 1985), Harris County C. of C. (pres. 1998). Methodist. Avocations: SCUBA diving, motorcycles. Office: PO Box 354 Hamilton GA 31811-0354

**CHIACCHIERE, MARK DOMINIC,** lawyer; b. Phila., Dec. 10, 1966; s. Dominic Joseph and Diana (Alosi) C. BSBA, Georgetown U., 1989; JD, Villanova U., 1992. Bar: Pa. 1992, N.J. 1992, U.S. Dist. Ct. (ea. dist.) Pa. 1993, U.S. Ct. Appeals (3d cir.) 1993, U.S. Dist. Ct. N.J. 1992. Assoc. O'Brien & Ryan, Plymouth Meeting, Pa., 1992-94, White & Williams, Phila., 1994-97. Facilitator Parish Coun., Phila., 1996-97. Mem. ABA, Phila. Bar Assn., Savoy Co. (bd. dirs.), Alpha Phi Omega (Mu Alpha alumni sec. 1991-97, bd. dirs. 1995—). Personal injury, General civil litigation, General corporate. Office: 1500 Locust St Apt 3507 Philadelphia PA 19102-4324

**CHIANG, YUNG FRANK,** law educator; b. Taichung, Taiwan, Jan. 2, 1936; came to U.S., 1961; s. Ruey-ting and Yueh-yin (Ho) C.; m. Quay-yin Lin, Nov. 1, 1969; children: Amy P., David H. LLB, Nat. Taiwan U., 1958; LLM, Northwestern U., 1962; JD, U. Chgo., 1965. Bar: Taiwan 1960, N.Y. 1974. Assoc. Yen & Lai Law Office, Taipei, Taiwan, 1960-61; editor The Lawyers Co-op Pub. Co., Rochester, N.Y., 1965; rsch. assoc. in law Harvard Law Sch., Cambridge, Mass., 1965-67; asst. prof. law U. Ga. Sch. Law, Athens, 1967-72; assoc. prof. law Fordham U. Sch. Law, N.Y.C., 1972-76, prof. law, 1976—; legal cons., vice chmn. Asia Bank, N.A., Flushing, N.Y., 1983-88; leader N.Y. judge and lawyers del. to China and Hong Kong, People to People Internat., 1994; organizer, moderator 5 Russian delegations to U.S., People to People Amb. Program, 1994-95. *One of the articles published by Professor Chiang titled, The characterization of a vessel as a common private carrier, was cited in Gilmore and Black, the Law Admiralty, and by three federal courts to support their judgements in the following cases: Alamo Chemical Transport Co. v. M/V Overseas Valdea, 469 F.Supp. 203 (EDNY 1985), Larsen v. A.C. Carpenter Inc., 620 F.Supp. 1084, 2 UCC Rep. Serv.2d 433 (EDNY 1985), Shell Oil Co. v. M/T/ Gilda, 790 F.2d 1209 (5th Cir., (La.) 1986). The article was also cited in "Admiralty-International Uniform Law and the Carriage of Goods by Sea," by David M. Collins in 60 Tulane Law Review. His recent publication is Payment By Mistake in English Law.* Contbr. articles to law jours. Organizer, bd. dirs. The Taiwan Mcht. Assn. N.Y., Flushing, 1976-96, pres., 1980-84; pres. N.Y. chpt. Formosan Assn. for Pub. Affairs, Washington, 1991, 92. Mem. N.Y. State Bar Assn., N.Am. Taiwanese Profs. Assn. (bd. dirs. 1994-96, 1997—, v.p. 1997-98, pres. 1998-99), Nat. Assn. of Securities Dealers (arbitrator 1976-98), Order of Coif. Avocations: reading, skiing, archery, swimming. Office: Fordham U Sch Law 140 W 62nd St New York NY 10023-7407

**CHIDNESE, PATRICK N.,** lawyer; b. Neptune, N.J., May 26, 1940; s. Louis and Helen C.; 1 child, Krista; m. Kathy J. Chidnese, Feb. 16, 1985; children: Patrick, Nicole. B.A., U. Miami, 1964, J.D., 1968. Assoc. Sinclair, Louis & Huttoe, Miami, 1968-69; assoc. Stephens, Demos, Magil & Thornton, Miami, 1969-70; assoc. Howell, Kirby, Montgomery, D'Aiuto, Dean & Hallowes, Fort Lauderdale, Fla., 1970-71; sole practice, Fort Lauderdale, 1971—; county atty. Broward County Juvenile Ct., 1971-72. Mem. Fla. Bar Assn. (chmn. auto ins. com. 1977-78, chmn. 17th jud. circuit legis. com. 1977-80), Broward County Bar Assn., Acad. Fla. Trial Lawyers, Broward County Trial Lawyers Assn. (bd. dirs. 1974-80). Insurance, Personal injury, Workers' compensation. Home: PO Box 18419 Asheville NC 28814-0419

**CHIECHI, CAROLYN PHYLLIS,** federal judge; b. Newark, Dec. 6, 1943. BS magna cum laude, Georgetown U., 1965, JD, 1969, LLM in Taxation, 1971. Bar: D.C. 1969, U.S. Dist. Ct. D.C., U.S. Ct. Fed. Claims, U.S. Tax Ct., U.S. Ct. Appeals (5th, 6th, 9th, D.C. and fed. cirs.), U.S. Supreme Ct. Atty., advisor to Judge Leo H. Irwin U.S. Tax Ct., Washington, 1969-71; assoc. Sutherland, Asbill & Brennan, Washington, 1971-76, ptnr., 1976-92; judge U.S. Tax Ct., 1992—; mem. bd. regents Georgetown U., Washington, 1988-94, 95—, mem. nat. law alumni bd., 1986-93; bd. dirs. Stuart Stiller Meml. Found., Washington, 1986—; prin. Coun. for Excellence in Govt., Washington, 1990-92. Dept. editor Jour. of Taxation, 1986-92; contbr. articles to profl. jours. Fellow Am. Bar Found., Am. Coll. Tax Counsel; mem. ABA, FBA, D.C. Bar Assn., Women's Bar Assn., Am. Judicature Soc., Georgetown U. Alumni Assn. (bd. govs. 1994—, Alumni award 1994, Alumnae award 1998). Office: US Tax Ct 400 2nd St NW Washington DC 20217-0002

**CHIERICHELLA, JOHN W.,** lawyer; b. N.Y.C., Mar. 26, 1947; s. Pasquale Joseph and Ruth Cecilia (White) C. AB, Cornell U., 1969; JD, Columbia U., 1972. Bar: N.Y. 1973, D.C., 1975, U.S Dist. Ct. Columbia, 1976, U.S. Claims Ct., 1976, U.S. Ct. Appeals (D.C. cir. 1976, Fed. cir. 1980), U.S. Supreme Ct., 1980. Assoc., Cravath, Swaine & Moore, N.Y.C. 1972-73; assoc., then ptnr. Jones, Day, Reavis & Pogue, Washington, 1975-79, 87-93; ptnr. Crowell & Moring, Washington, 1979-84, Gibson, Dunn & Crutcher, Washington, 1984-87; ptnr. Fried, Frank, Harris, Shriver & Jacobson, 1993—. Contbr. articles to profl. jours. Served to capt. USAF, 1973-75. Harlan Fiske Stone scholar, 1971, James Kent scholar, 1972. Mem. ABA (past chmn. contracts com., contracts clauses and forms com., pub. contracts law sect.), Nat. Contract. Mgmt. Assn., Nat. Security Indsl. Assn. Roman Catholic. Avocation: athletics. Government contracts and claims, Administrative and regulatory, General civil litigation. Office: Fried Frank Harris Shriver & Jacobson Ste #800 1001 Pennsylvania Ave NW Washington DC 20004-2505

**CHILCOTE, LEE A.,** lawyer; b. Cleve., May 5, 1942. BA, Dartmouth Coll., 1964; BE, Thayer Sch. Engring., 1965; JD, U. Calif., San Francisco, 1972. Bar: Ohio 1972. With Arter & Hadden, Cleve.; bd. dirs., The Chilcote Co., sec., 1972—. Trustee Hough Housing Corp. 1972-88; bd. dirs. Cleve. Warehouse Dist. Local Devel. Corp., 1986—. Mem. ABA (real property and corp. sects.), Am. Coll. Real Estate Lawyers, Cleve. Bar Assn., Order of Coif, Thurston Soc. Real property, Finance, Banking. Office: Arter & Hadden 1100 Huntington Bldg 925 Euclid Ave Ste 1100 Cleveland OH 44115-1475

**CHILDERS, JOHN AARON,** lawyer; b. Chgo., June 9, 1955; s. John A. and Lorna R. Childers; m. Charene M. Alessi, Aug. 25, 1979; children: John, Joey, Caitlin. BA, Northwestern U., 1977, JD, 1980. Bar: Ill. 1980, U.S. Dist. Ct. (no. dist.) Ill. 1980. Law clk. Johnson & Bell, Ltd., Chgo., 1979-80, assoc. atty., 1980-86, shareholder, 1986—. League counsel Elgin (Ill.) Youth Football League, 1980-98; v.p. Elgin Classic Little League, 1988-92, pres. 1992-94. Mem. ABA, Ill. State Bar Assn., Trial Lawyers Club of Chgo. (trustee 1986-93), Def. Rsch. Inst. (steering com. mass tort sub-group 1986—). Avocations: golfing, coaching. Insurance, Personal injury, General civil litigation. Home: 10n872 York Ln Elgin IL 60123-6752

**CHILDERS, JOHN CHARLES,** lawyer, engineer; b. Gallipolis, Ohio, Oct. 27, 1950; s. Frank W. and Bernice E. (Ziler) C.; m. Judith Marie Hughes, Jan. 1, 1976; children: Rachel Grace, Benjamin Hughes. BS in Civil Engring. cum laude, Ohio U., 1972; JD cum laude, Capital U., 1978. Bar: Ohio 1978, U.S. Supreme Ct. 1987. Pvt. practice Carrollton, Ohio, 1978—; asst. pros. atty. County of Carroll, Carrollton, Ohio, 1981-89; ptnr. Childers and Smith, Attys., Carrollton, 1982—. Mem. Ohio Bar Assn. (coun. of dels. 1988—), Carroll County Bar Assn. (pres. 1984—). General practice, Real property, Probate. Office: Childers and Smith 70 Public Sq # 252 Carrollton OH 44615-1403

**CHILDRESS, STEVEN ALAN,** law educator; b. Mobile, Ala., Feb. 9, 1959; s. Roy and Mary Helen (Gillion) C.; children: Ani, Steven. BA, U. Ala., 1979; JD, Harvard U., 1982; PhD in Jurisprudence and Social Policy, U. Calif., Berkeley, 1995. Bar: Calif. 1983, U.S. Ct. Appeals (5th cir.) 1984, D.C. 1986, U.S. Ct. Appeals (9th cir.) 1986, U.S. Supreme Ct. 1987. Law clk. to judge U.S. Ct. Appeals (5th cir.), Shreveport, La., 1982-83; assoc. Morrison & Foerster, San Francisco, 1983-84; adj. lectr. law Golden Gate U. Sch. Law, San Francisco, 1984-86; grad. instr. U. Calif., Berkeley, 1985-86; assoc. Brobeck, Phleger & Harrison, San Francisco, 1987-88; assoc. prof. law Tulane U. Law Sch., New Orleans, 1988-96, prof. law, 1996—. Co-author: Federal Standards of Review, 1986, 2d edit., 1992; contbr. articles to profl. jours. Regents fellow U. Calif. at Berkeley, 1985. Mem. Law and Soc. Assn., Phi Beta Kappa. Office: Tulane U School of Law New Orleans LA 70118

**CHILES, STEPHEN MICHAEL,** lawyer; b. Chillicothe, Ohio, July 15, 1942; s. Daniel Duncan and Helen Virginia (Hayes) C.; m. Deborah E. Nash, June 13, 1964; children: Stephen, Abigail. BA, Davidson Coll., 1964; JD, Duke U., 1967. Bar: N.Y. 1970, Pa. 1978, Wis. 1981, U.S. Supreme Ct. 1978, U.S. Ct. Appeals (3d cir.) 1978, U.S. Dist. Ct. (ea. dist.) Pa. 1978, U.S. Tax Ct. 1978, Ill. 1986. Officer trust dept. Irving Trust Co., N.Y.C., 1970-75, v.p., 1975-77; assoc. atty. Stassen Kostos & Mason, Phila., 1978-79, mem., shareholder, 1979-85; ptnr. McDermott, Will & Emery, Chgo., 1986—. Contbr. articles to profl. jours. Served to capt. U.S. Army, 1967-69. Decorated Bronze Star, Army Commendation medal. Mem. ABA, State Bar Wis., Exmoor Country Club (Highland Park, Ill.). Republican. Episcopalian. Estate planning, Estate taxation. Office: McDermott Will & Emery 227 W Monroe St Ste 3100 Chicago IL 60606-5096

**CHILIVIS, NICKOLAS PETER,** lawyer; b. Athens, Ga., Jan. 12, 1931; s. Peter Nickolas and Wessie Mae (Tanner) C.; m. Patricia Kay Tumlin, June 3, 1967; children—Taryn Tumlin, Nicole Tumlin, Nickolas Peter Tumlin. LL.B., U. Ga., Athens, 1953; LL.M., Atlanta Law Sch., Ga., 1955. Bar: Ga. 1952, U.S. Supreme Ct. 1965. Ptnr. Lester & Chilivis, Athens, Ga., 1953-58; ptnr. Erwin, Epting, Gibson & Chilivis, Athens, Ga., 1958-75; commr. of revenue State of Ga., Atlanta, 1975-77; ptnr. Powell, Goldstein, Frazer & Murphy, Atlanta, 1977-84, Chilivis & Grindler, Atlanta, 1984-95, Chilivis, Cochran, Larkins & Bever, Atlanta, 1995—; adj. prof. U. Ga. Sch. Law, Athens, 1965-75. Author: Termination Settlement, 1955. Contbr. chpts. to books, articles to profl. jours. Bd. visitors U. Ga., Athens, 1983-85; trustee Skandalakis Found., Atlanta, 1984, Found. of the Holy Apostles; former trustee U. Ga. Found.; former mem. U. Ga. Rsch. Found. Bd.; pres. and sr. warden Ch. of Apostles. With USAFR, 1953-55. Recipient Archdiocesan medal Archbishop of North and South Am., 1980. Fellow Am. Coll. Trial Lawyers, Am. Acad. Appellate Lawyers; mem. Am. Inns. of Ct. (emeritus, master), Old War Horse Lawyers Club, Lawyers Club Atlanta, Commerce Club, Heritage Club, (Atlanta), Pres.'s Club (U. Ga.), Elks. Avocations: Handball; tennis; writing; lecturing. General civil litigation, Criminal. Home: 855 W Paces Ferry Rd NW Atlanta GA 30327-2655 Office: Chilivis Cochran Larkins & Bever Chilivis Bldg 3127 Maple Dr NE Atlanta GA 30305-2503

**CHILSTROM, ROBERT MEADE,** lawyer; b. San Diego, July 1, 1945; s. Arne Oswald and Margaret Myra (Kippax) C.; m. Buena Lelia Hamlin, Aug. 24, 1968; children: Per Benjamin, Mikaela Lynn. BA, Princeton U., 1967; MA, Columbia U., 1969; JD, Yale U., 1973. Bar: N.Y. State 1975, U.S. Dist. Ct. (so. dist., ea. dist.) N.Y. 1975, U.S. Ct. Appeals (2d cir.) 1975. Assoc. Cravath, Swaine & Moore, N.Y.C., Paris, London, 1973-85; assoc. Skadden, Arps, Slate, Meagher & Flom LLP, N.Y.C., 1985-87, ptnr., 1987—. General corporate, Finance, Private international. Office: Skadden Arps Slate Meagher & Flom LLP 919 3rd Ave New York NY 10022-3902

**CHIMPLES, GEORGE,** lawyer; b. Canton, Ohio, Oct. 8, 1924; s. Mark and Katherine (Hines) C.; m. Margaret Joanna Cavalaris, July 31, 1949; children: Alicia Candace, Mark II, John Hines, Katherine Hines. AB, Princeton U., 1951; LLB, Harvard Coll., 1954. Bar: Pa. 1955, U.S. Dist. Ct. (ea. dist.) Pa. 1955, U.S. Ct. Appeals (3d cir.) 1955, U.S. Ct. Claims, 1965, U.S. Tax Ct., 1965. Assoc. Stradley, Ronon, Stevens & Young, Phila., 1954-61, gen. ptnr., 1961-92; pvt. practice Wayne, Pa., 1993—; adj. prof. law U. Pa., Drexel U. Grad. Sch. Bus.; co-authored establishment of overseas infrastructure for securities mktg. in Europe and the Antilles. Trustee Christ Ch. Preservation Trust; permament assoc. Phila. Mus. Art. Capt. USAAF, 1942-46, ETO. Decorated D.F.C., Air medal with four oak leaf clusters, Air Force Commendation medal, Victory medal, four Battle Stars; recipient Royal Air Force plaque, 1994. Mem. ABA (chmn. subcom. regulated investment cos.), Phila. Bar Assn. (tax sect.), Internat. Bar Assn., Internat. Fiscal Assn. (tax treaty sect.), Mid-Atlantic Coun., Commanderie de Bordeaux aux Etats-Unis d'Amerique (archivist), Newcomen Soc. U.S. (com. chmn., nat. trustee, life mem.) Army and Navy Club (Washington chpt.), Penn Club (life, bd. dirs., historian) Athenaeum of Phila. (life), Libr. Co. of Phila. (life), Phila. Mus. Art (permanent assoc.), Phila. Club, Princeton Club N.Y., Cannon Club (Princeton chpt.), Merion Cricket Club. General corporate, Estate planning, Taxation, general. Home: 1179 Lafayette Rd Wayne PA 19087-2110 Office: 1522 Overington St Philadelphia PA 19124-5808

**CHIN, DAVIS,** lawyer; b. Evansville, Ind., Dec. 13, 1947; s. Frank S. M. and Mamie (Shu) C.; m. Pauline C., Aug. 3, 1974; 1 child, Davis M. BS, Rose-Hulman Inst. Tech., Terre Haute, Ind., 1969; JD, U. Balt., 1974; LLM in Taxation, John Marshall Law Sch., 1981. Bar: Ill. 1974, U.S. Dist. Ct. (no. dist.) 1974, U.S. Ct. Appeals (7th cir.) 1974, U.S. Patent and Trademark Office 1974, U.S. Claims Ct. 1977, U. S. Tax Ct. 1977, U.S. Supreme Ct. 1977, U.S. Ct. Appeals (fed. cir.) 1982. Staff atty. CTS Corp., Elkhart, Ind., 1974; assoc. Petherbridge, Lindgren & Gilhooly, Chtd., Chgo., 1974-78; staff atty. Borg-Warner Corp., Chgo., 1978-80, Container Corp. Am., Chgo., 1980-84; pvt. practice Chgo., 1984—; instr. Prairie State Coll., Chgo. Heights, 1987-90, 94, South Suburban Coll., South Holland, Ill., 1989-91, Roosevelt U., Olympia Fields, Ill., 1990-93. Elder United Presbyn. Ch., South Holland, 1986—; panel program atty. Chgo. Vol. Legal Svcs., 1988—. Mem. Am. Intellectual Property Law Assn., Chgo. Bar Assn., Intellectual Property Law Assn. Chgo., Patent Law Assn. Chgo. (bd. mgrs. 1985-87, 94-96). Avocations: tennis, golf, travel. Intellectual property, Taxation, general, General practice. Home: 11428 Plattner Dr Mokena IL 60448-9228 Office: 111 W Washington St Ste 1025 Chicago IL 60602-2745

**CHIN, DENNY,** judge; b. 1954. BA magna cum laude, Princeton U., 1975; JD, Fordham U., 1978. Law clerk Hon. Henry F. Werker, 1978-80; with Davis, Polk & Wardwell, N.Y., 1980-82, Campbell, Patrick & Chin, N.Y., 1986-90, Vladeck, Waldman, Elias & Engelhard, N.Y., 1990-94; dist. judge U.S. Dist. Ct. (so. dist.), N.Y., 1994—; adj. prof. Fordham Law Sch. Mem. ABA, Asian Am. Bar Assn. N.Y. (pres. 1992-94), Assn. Bar of N.Y.C., Fordham Law Review Alumni Assn., N.Y. County Lawyers Assn. Office: U S Dist Ct 500 Pearl St New York NY 10007-1316

**CHIN, KELVIN HENRY,** legal association executive, mediator, consultant; b. Boston, Jan. 7, 1951; s. Henry W.F. and King (Lee) C.; m. Peggy Abbott, July 26, 1987; children: Jesse, Samantha. Student, U. Strasbourg, France, 1971; AB cum laude, high distinction in French, Dartmouth Coll., 1973; MA, Yale U., 1974; JD, Boston Coll., 1983. Dir. in East Asia, Found. for Creative Intelligence, Hong Kong, 1974-78; co-founder Microtex Corp., Cambridge, Mass., 1978-83; life ins. agent Sun Life of Canada, Wellesley, Mass., 1979-81; law clerk Bingham, Dana & Gould, Boston, 1980-83; summer assoc. to assoc. Choate, Hall & Stewart, Boston, 1982-84; employee benefits cons. Hicks Pension Svcs., Lexington, Mass., 1984-86; pres. Bus. Consulting Assocs., Boston, San Diego, 1986-92; dir. mediation ctr. for Mediation, Am. Arbitration Assn., San Diego, 1992-93; regional v.p. Am. Arbitration Assn., Las Vegas, Nev., 1993-96, L.A., 1996—; mem. nat. adv. bd. Ctr. for Med. Ethics and Mediation, San Diego, 1992—; cons. Continuing Edn. of the Bar, Calif. 1992—. Editor: International Law Dictionary, 1983. Ombudsman Calif. Dept. on Aging, San Diego, 1991-93; com. mem. Waldorf Sch. of San Diego PTA, 1992-93; vol. mediator Ctr. for Mcpl. Dispute Resolution City Atty.'s Office, San Diego, 1990-93; v.p. bd. advs. exec. com. U. W.L.A., 1996-97. Rufus Choate scholar Dartmouth Coll., 1971-73; Nat. Def. Fgn. Language fellow U.S. Dept. Edn., 1973-74. Mem. ABA (dispute resolution sect.), Am. Arbitration Assn. (blue ribbon mediator panel 1992—), San Diego County Bar Assn. (treas. alternative dispute resolution sect. 1991-93), Soc. Profls. in Dispute Resolution, So. Calif. Mediation Assn., The Ombudsman Assn., Nat. Panel of Mediators, Nat. Assn. Securities Dealers, Asian Bus. League, Turnaround Mgmt. Assn. Avocations: basketball, philosophy. Office: Am Arbitration Assn 3055 Wilshire Blvd Los Angeles CA 90010-1108

**CHIN, LLEWELLYN PHILIP,** lawyer; b. Saigon-Cholon, Vietnam, 1957; s. Thomas and Kim C. AA, Glendale (Calif.) Coll., 1980; BS, U. So. Calif., L.A., 1982; JD, Columbia U., 1986. Bar: Calif. 1988, U.S. Dist. Ct. (cen. dist.) Calif. 1988, U.S. Ct. Appeals (9th cir.) 1988. Sr. counsel Calif. Assn. of Realtors, L.A., 1989—; polit. cons. Robert Kwan for Alhambra Sch. Bd., Monterey Park, Calif., 1988; bus. cons. Larry L. Berg, Inc., L.A., 1986-88; legal advisor L.A. chpt. Chinese Consol. Benevolent Assn., Elderly Indo-Chinese Assn.; adj. prof. Southwestern U. Sch. Law, summer 1995, Loyola Law Sch., 1996; speaker in field. Columnist L.A. County Bar Real Property Newsletter; contbr. articles to profl. jours. Bd. dirs. Chinese-Am. Polit. Action Com., Alhambra, 1986-93, Golden Tours, Alhambra, 1993; candidate Alhambra City Coun., 1992; pres. Chinese Am. Edn. Assn., Monterey Park, 1994-95; bd. dirs. San Gabriel Valley YMCA, 1995-97; planning commr. City of Alhambra, 1995-99; commr. L.A. County Local Govtl. Svcs., 1995-97; commr. State Bd. Dental Examiners, 1998—. Beren Found. scholar, 1983-86, Harlan Fisk Stone scholar, 1986. Mem. ABA (chair home improvements, constrn. and purchase and sale of residential real estate subcom. 1992—, vice chair real estate brokerage subcom. 1998—), L.A. County Bar Assn. (disaster relief com., corp. counsel, elderline, continuing edn. com., gen. real property subsect. steering com.), Calif. Trial Lawyers Assn., So. Calif. Chinese Lawyers Assn., Calif. State Bar (co-chair sales and brokerage subsect. real property sect., 1993-96, 98—, cons. real property sect. 1993-96, continuing edn. of the bar com. 1992-95), Chinese Am. Real Estate Profls. So. Calif. (bd. dirs.), Alhambra C. of C. (legis. com., chair anti-graffiti task force 1993—). Avocations: reading, stamp and coin collecting, organizing political events, hiking. Environmental, Private international, Real property. Office: Calif Assn Realtors 525 S Virgil Ave Los Angeles CA 90020-1403

**CHIN, MING,** state supreme court justice; b. Klamath Falls, Oreg., Aug. 31, 1942; m. Carol Lynn Joe, Dec. 19, 1971; children: Jennifer, Jason. BA in Polit. Sci., U. San Francisco, 1964, JD, 1967. Bar: Calif., 1970, U.S. Fed. Ct., U.S. Tax Ct. Assoc., head trial dept. Aiken, Kramer & Cummings, Oakland, Calif., 1973-76, prin., 1976-88; dep. dist. atty. Alameda County, Calif., 1970-72; judge Alameda County Superior Ct., 1988-90; assoc. justice divsn. 3 Ct. Appeal 1st Dist., 1990-94; presiding justice 1st Dist. Ct. Appeal Divsn. 3, San Francisco, 1994-96; assoc. justice Calif. Supreme Ct., San Francisco, 1996—. Capt. U.S. Army, 1967-69, Vietnam, USAR, 1969-71. Mem. ABA, Calif. Judges Assn., State Bar Calif., Alameda County Bar Assn., San Francisco Dist. Atty.'s Commn. Hate Crimes, Commonwealth Club of Calif. (pres. 1998), Asian Am. Bar Assn., Alpha Sigma Nu. Office: Supreme Court Calif 350 Mcallister St Fl 1st San Francisco CA 94102-4783

**CHIN, STEPHANIE ANNE,** lawyer; b. San Francisco, Oct. 21, 1965. BSBA, U. Calif., Berkeley, 1987; JD, U. Calif., San Francisco, 1991. Bar: Hawaii 1991, U.S. Dist. Ct. Hawaii 1991. Ptnr. Torkildson, Katz, Fonseca, Jaffe, Moore, Hetherington, Honolulu, 1991—. Editor, mem. Hastings Law Jour., 1989-91. Recipient Am. Jurisprudence award Lawyer's Cool. Pub. Co., 1989. Mem. ABA, Nat. Assn. Pacific Am. Bar Assn., Hawaii Women Lawyers, Hawaii State Bar Assn., Arbitrator-Ct. Annexed Arbitration Program. General civil litigation, Contracts commercial. Office: Torkildson Katz Fonseca 700 Bishop St Fl 15 Honolulu HI 96813-4187

**CHING, LOUIS MICHAEL,** lawyer; b. New Orleans, June 26, 1956. BS, Tulane U., 1979; JD, Willamette U., 1985. Bar: Oreg. 1986, Hawaii, 1986, U.S. Dist. Ct. Hawaii 1986, U.S. Ct. Appeals (9th cir.) 1989, U.S. Supreme Ct. 1990. Pvt. practice law Honolulu, 1986-87, 90—; arbitrator, 1999. Mem. Hawaii Assn. Crimimal Def. Lawyers, Phi Beta Kappa. Avocations: tennis, online Internet short-term stock trading. Criminal.

**CHINN, MARK ALLAN,** lawyer; b. Jackson, Miss., June 9, 1953; s. Rollin J. and Ann M. (Heiberg) C.; m. Cathy Hawkinson, Aug. 6, 1978; children: Courtney, Casey, Carly, Conley. BA in Polit. Sci., Iowa State U., 1975; JD, U. Miss., 1978. Bar: U.S. Dist. Ct. (no. dist.) Miss. 1978, U.S. Dist. Ct. (so. dist.) Miss. 1980; U.S. Ct. Appeals (5th and 11th cirs.) 1981; U.S. Supreme Ct. 1980; cert. civil trial expert Nat. Bd. Trial Advocacy. Staff atty. Miss. Senate, Jackson, 1978-79; spl. asst. Atty. Gen. Office, Jackson, 1979-80; assoc. Louis Baine, Jackson, 1980-82, Law Office William Latham, Jackson, 1982-88; atty. pvt. practice, Jackson, 1988—; adj. prof. law Miss. Coll. Sch. Law. Bd. dirs. Arts Alliance, Jackson, 1990-97, Miss. Children's Home, Jackson, 1990-95; pres. Jackson Urban League Bd., 1995-99; bd. dirs. Jubilee Jam Found., 1995-97, chmn. Jubilee! Jam '96. Recipient Award of Merit, Miss. Bar Assn., 1996, Lamar Order, Miss. Bar Found. Mem. ABA, Lamar Order, Miss. Bar Assn. (chmn. family law sect. 1995-96, chmn. small firm practice com. 1995-96, Award of Merit 1996), Miss. Trial Lawyers Assn., Hinds County Bar Assn. (dir. 1994-95, pres. 1998—), Am. Inn of Ct. (master Charles Clark), Rotary, Jackson C. of C., Miss. Bar Found. (supreme ct. gender fairness task force). Avocations: golf, physical fitness, Karate, Tae Kwan Do (Black Belt), flying. E-mail: divorce@meta3.net. Family and matrimonial, Personal injury, Administrative and regulatory. Office: Chinn & Assocs 4316 Old Canton Rd Ste 200 Jackson MS 39211

**CHIPMAN, MARION WALTER,** judge; b. Penokee, Kans., May 5, 1920; s. James Edwin and May Maude (Hatcher) C.; m. Thelma Nadine Clark, Nov. 1, 1941 (div. 1965); m. Nancy Jo Payne, May 28, 1983; children: Clark D., Jill Ellen. AB in Social Sci., Ft. Hays (Kans.) State U., 1942; JD, Washburn U., 1948. Bar: Kans. 1948, U.S. Dist. Ct. Kans. 1948, U.S. Ct. Appeals 1970, U.S. Supreme Ct. 1970. Supt. Prairieview (Kans.) Sch., 1942; atty. County of Graham, Hill City, Kans., 1949-53; counselor County of Johnson, Olathe, Kans., 1967-68; judge 10th Jud. Dist. Kans. Dist. Ct., Olathe, 1980-91, sr. judge, 1996—. Sgt. USAAF, 1942-46. Mem. ABA (life), Johnson County Bar Assn. (life), Kans. Bar Assn. (life), Am. Judicature, Am. Judge's Assn., Am. Arbitration Assn., Am. Legion, Masons, Shriners, Elks. Methodist. Home: 1012 S Stratford Rd Olathe KS 66062-2117 Office: Kans Dist Ct 10 Jud Dist Johnson County Courthouse Olathe KS 66061

**CHISHOLM, TOMMY,** lawyer, utility company executive; b. Baldwyn, Miss., Apr. 14, 1941; s. Thomas Vaniver and Rubel (Duncan) C.; m. Janice McClanahan, June 20, 1964; children: Mark Alan (dec.), Andrea, Stephen Thomas, Patrick Ervin. BSCE, Tenn. Tech. U., 1963; JD, Samford U., 1969; MBA, Ga. State U., 1984. Registered profl. engr., Ala., Ark., Del., Ga., Fla., Ky., La., N.H., Miss., N.C., Pa., Tenn., S.C., Va., W.Va. Civil engr. TVA, Knoxville, Tenn., 1963-64; design engr. So. Co. Svcs., Birmingham, Ala., 1964-69; coord. spl. projects So. Co. Svcs., Atlanta, 1969-73; sec., house counsel So. Co. Svcs., 1977-82, v.p., sec., house counsel, 1982—; asst. to pres. So. Co., Atlanta, 1973-75; sec., asst. treas. So. Co., 1977—; mgr. adminstrv. svcs. Gulf Power Co., Pensacola, Fla., 1975-77; sec. So. Energy, Inc., Atlanta, 1981-82; v.p., sec. So. Energy Resources Inc., Atlanta, 1982—; sec. So. Co. Energy Solutions Inc., 1985—, So. Energy N.Am. Inc., 1993—, So. Electric R.R. Co., 1993—; Birchwood Devel. Corp., 1992—, SEI Birchwood, Inc., 1992—, So. Energy Inc., 1993—, So. Electric Bahamas Holdings, Ltd., 1993—, So. Electric Bahamas, Ltd., 1993—; asst. sec. Freeport Power Co. Ltd., 1993—. Mem. Am. Bar Assn., State Bar Ala., Am. Soc. Corp. Secs., Am. Corp. Counsel Assn., Phi Alpha Delta, Beta Gamma Sigma. General corporate. Office: The Southern Co 270 Peachtree St Ste 2200 Atlanta GA 30303

**CHISNELL, JANICE HOFFMAN,** lawyer; b. Pitts., Oct. 11, 1960; d. Jack Edward and Mary Lou (Hazeltine) Hoffman; m. Dennis William Chisnell, Dec. 11, 1982. BA, Grove City Coll., 1982; JD, U. Pitts., 1988. Bar: Pa. 1988, U.S. Dist. Ct. (we. dist.) Pa. 1988. Legal asst. Buchanan Ingersoll, P.C., Pitts., 1982-85; law clk. Brennan Robins & Daley, Pitts., 1986-88; trust adminstr. Equibank, Pitts., 1989-90; lawyer sole practice, Pitts., 1990—. Recipient David Bookstaver award U. Pitts. Sch. Law, 1988, Robert Sisler Meml. award Grove City Coll., 1982. Avocations: photography, riding horses, sewing. Probate, Estate taxation, Personal income taxation. Home: 140 Golden Gate Dr Verona PA 15147-2606

**CHO, TAI YONG,** lawyer; b. Seoul, Republic of Korea, May 27, 1943; came to U.S., 1966; s. Nam Suck and Sun Yeo (Yoon) C; m. Hea Sun Cho, July 14, 1973; children: Robert, Richard, Susan. BS, Seoul U., 1965; MS, Cooper Union, 1971; CE, Columbia U., 1971; JD, Fordham U., 1981. Bar: N.Y., 1982; registered profl. engr., N.Y., 1973. Engr. Ministry of Constrn., Seoul, 1965-66, Andrews & Clark, N.Y.C., 1967-68, Parsons, Brinckerhoff, Quade & Douglas, N.Y.C., 1969-71; v.p. John R. McCarthy Corp., N.Y.C., 1972-80. Mem. ASCE, ABA, N.Y. State Bar Assn., Am. Arbitration Assn. (panel of arbitrators), Am.-Korean Lawyers Assn. of N.Y. (pres. 1988), Korean TV Broadcasters Assn., Am. (pres. 1990), Internat. Korean Lawyers Assn. (v.p. 1991). Contracts commercial, General corporate, Private international. Home: 56 Tuttle Rd Briarcliff Manor NY 10510-2233 Office: 309 5th Ave New York NY 10016-6509

**CHOATE, EDWARD LEE,** lawyer, educator; b. Carbondale, Ill., Jan. 8, 1951; s. Loree and Geraldine Louise (Minton) C.; m. Lenetta Kay Blackburn, Sept. 10, 1983. BA with honors in History, So. Ill. U., 1972; JD, U. Notre Dame, 1975. Bar: Ill. 1975, U.S. Dist. Ct. (so. dist.) Ill. 1981, U.S. Ct. Appeals (7th cir.) 1981, Conn. 1996. Sole practice Carterville, Ill., 1975-92; assoc. to v.p. student and univ. affairs So. Conn. State U., New Haven, 1992—; asst. state's atty. Williamson County, Ill., 1982-84; asst. vis. prof. aviation law Sch. Tech. Careers, So. Ill. U., Carbondale, 1981, 82. Precinct committeeman Carterville Rep. Com., 1982-92. Named one of Outstanding Young Men in Am., 1985; So. Ill. U. Pres.'s scholar. Mem. ABA, Phi Alpha Theta. Baptist. Clubs: Masons (32 degree, numerous offices in various local and state divsns.), Shriners, KT (past comdr.), Order Eastern Star (past pastron). Education and schools, Labor, General practice. Home: 68 Nutmeg Hill Rd Hamden CT 06514-1163 Office: 501 Crescent St 144 Engleman Hall New Haven CT 06515

**CHOATE, JOHN,** lawyer, consultant. BA, U. Okla., 1966; JD, Yale U., 1969; grad., Air War Coll., Montgomery, Ala., 1984. Bar: Calif. 1971, D.C. 1973, Okla. 1976, N.Y. 1992, Conn. 1996; admitted to practice Am. Samoa. Registered rep., account exec. NYSE, 1969-71; with USAFR, 1963-95, ret., 1995; pvt. practice, 1979-87; guest speaker, patentee Keyboarding and Software Devel., 1992—, Finger Relief, 1993; chmn. sect. on taxation Am. Assn. Law Schs., 1977. Writer, producer, editor indsl. tng. videos Evidence, NTSB Trial; prin. Sta. KGCT-TV Tulsa, 1979-87. Mem. Okla. Jaycees, Calif. Jaycees, 1971-80; mem. exec. com. Yale Law Sch., 1988-90. Recipient Legal Writing award Ark. Bar Found., 1977. Mem. Judge Adv. Assn., Phi Delta Phi, Delta Upsilon. Mem. LDS Ch. Computer, Public international, General civil litigation. Office: Finger Relief PO Box 65 Seminole OK 74818-0065

**CHOBOT, JOHN CHARLES,** lawyer; b. N.Y.C., Feb. 14, 1948; s. Arthur E. and Eleanore L. (Lotito) C.; m. Catherine Anne Moran, Aug. 24, 1974; children: Christine, Keith. BA, Cornell U., 1969; MS in Edn., CCNY, 1971; JD, Fordham U., 1975. Bar: N.Y. 1976, U.S. Dist. Ct. (we. dist.) N.Y. 1976, N.J. 1985, U.S. Dist. Ct. N.J. 1985. Assoc. Phillips, Lytle, Hitchcock, Blaine & Huber, Buffalo, 1975-85; The CIT Group/Sales Financing, Inc., Livingston, N.J., 1985-90; v.p., gen. counsel, sec. AT&T Capital Corp., Morristown, N.J., 1990-98, sr. v.p., chief counsel bus. fin. divsn., 1993-98; v.p. law, asst. gen. counsel Newcourt Credit Group Inc., Parsippany, N.J., 1998—. Contbr. articles on equipment leasing, bankruptcy and secured transactions to legal jours. Mem. ABA, N.Y. State Bar Assn., Am. Bankruptcy Inst., Comml. Law League, Equipment Leasing Assn. of Am., Kappa Alpha Soc. Fax: 973-355-7057. E-mail: johnchobot@newcourt.com. Bankruptcy, Contracts commercial, General corporate. Home: 23 Laurel Hill Dr Randolph NJ 07869-4632 Office: Newcourt Credit Group Inc 2 Gatehall Dr Parsippany NJ 07054-4513

**CHOI, JAY JUNEKUN,** lawyer; b. Seoul, Korea, Oct. 19, 1956; came to U.S., 1972; s. Lim and Ok Lim C.; m. Grace Hyesook Kim, Dec. 21, 1982; children: Aretha, Jessica. BA, U. No. Colo., 1976; MBA, Regis U., 1982; JD, U. Denver, 1988. Bar: Colo. 1989, D.C. 1990; CPA. Ptnr. Law Office Jay Choi, Englewood, Colo., 1989-97; dir. Cohen Brame & Smith, Denver, 1997-98, Burns Figa and Will P.C., 1999—; commr. Jud. Performance Commn., Aurora, Colo., 1994-98; mem. Multicultural Commn. Colo. Supreme Ct., 1995-97, U.S.-- Korea Com. Bus. Coop., 1996—. Staff editor: Asia Pacific Lawyers Assn. Jour., 1988. With USN. Recipient World Friendship award Martin Luther King Commn., 1996, Cmty. Activist award Asian Pacific Devel. Ctr., 1996. Fellow Colo. Bar. General corporate, Private international, Real property. Office: Burns Figa & Will PC Ste 1030 6400 S Fiddlers Green Cir Englewood CO 80111-4957

**CHOKEY, JAMES A.,** lawyer; b. Pitts., Sept. 2, 1943. AB, U. Pitts., 1965; JD, Duquesne U., 1969. Bar: Pa. 1969, U.S. Dist. Ct. (we. dist.) Pa., Wis. 1973. Atty. Westinghouse Electric Corp., 1972-73; v.p., gen. counsel, sec. Joy Mfg., 1973-87, RTE Corp., 1987-88, A.O. Smith Corp., 1989-91; v.p., gen. counsel Cooper Industries Inc., Houston, 1991—; v.p. corp. affairs, gen. counsel Beloit (Wis.) Corp.; exec. v.p., sec. and gen. counsel Harnischfeger Industries Inc., Milw. and St. Francis, Wis., 1997—. Mem. ABA, Am. Corp. Counsel Assn. (pres. we. Pa. chpt. 1985-86). E-mail: jchokey@HI-I.com. Office: Harnischfeger Industries Inc PO Box 554 Milwaukee WI 53201-0554

**CHONG, STEPHEN CHU LING,** lawyer; b. Lakewood, Ohio, Aug. 1, 1957; s. Richard Seng Hoon C. and Betty J. (Chong) Wamego; m. Sheryl Kay Horton, Nov. 23, 1984; children: Evan M. G., Erin M.L., Elena M.L., Eric M.K., Ethan M.L. BA, Calvin Coll., 1979; JD, Ohio State U., 1982. Bar: Fla. 1982, U.S. Dist. Ct. (mid. dist.) Fla. 1983, U.S. Ct. Appeals (11th cir.) 1982, U.S. Tax Ct. 1985; bd. cert. real estate lawyer Fla. Bar Bd. Legal Specialization and Edn. Assoc. Caudill, Drage, de Beaubien, Orlando, Fla., 1982-83; shareholder Caudill, Chong & Migliaccio, Winter Garden, Fla., 1983-84; assoc. Thomas R. Rogers & Assocs., Longwood, Fla., 1984-90; of counsel Litchford, Christopher, Orlando, 1990-92; pres., shareholder Marks & Chong, Orlando, 1992—; mem. nominating bd. City of Orlando, 1993-98, chmn. 1996-97; mem. area bus. com. Naval Tng. Ctr. Reuse Com., Orlando, 1994-95; bd. trustees Minority/Women Bus. Enterprise Alliance, Orlando, 1994—; chair Realtor Rels. Com., Orlando, 1992-93; presenter in field. Contbr. articles to profl. jours. Mem. cultural diversity com. Orlando Sci. Ctr., 1993—; mem. cmty. adv. bd. WMFE-TV/FM, Orlando, 1994-95; mem. adv. bd. Ctrl. Fla. Family, Orlando, 1994—; pres. Asian Am. C. of C., Orlando, 1993-94; trustee Calvin Coll., Grant Rapids, Mich. Recipient Vision award-Small Bus. Downtown Orlando Partnership, 1994. Mem. ABA, Fla. Bar Assn., ORange County Bar Assn., Christian Legal Soc. Presbyterian. General corporate, Franchising, Real property. Office: Marks & Chong 605 E Robinson St Ste 510 Orlando FL 32801-2045

**CHONG-SPIEGEL, GINGER GEROMA,** lawyer; b. N.Mex., Oct. 30, 1963; d. Vincent Yung Yet and Shirley Jane Chong; 1 child: Sean Ikaika O'pohaku; m. Steven Barry Spiegel, Dec. 27, 1996. Bar: Hawaii, U.S. Ct. Appeals (9th cir.). Assoc. Law Office Richard Turbin, Honolulu, 1991-94; pvt. practice Honolulu, 1994—; dealer, distbr. motorcycles. Mem. Hawaii State Bar Assn. Avocations: playing poker, writing short stories. Insurance, Contracts commercial, Landlord-tenant.

**CHONIN, NEIL HARVEY,** lawyer; b. Bklyn., Dec. 30, 1936; s. Morris Joseph and Shirley (Goldberg) C.; m. Lynn Barbara Weinstein (div.); children: Mitchell, David, Loree; m. Patricia Lane Perrin, Aug. 13, 1972; children: Tiffany, Jason. BA in Govt., U. Fla., 1958, LLD, 1961. Bar: Fla. 1963, U.S. Dist. Ct. (so., mid. and no. dists.) Fla. 1963, U.S. Supreme Ct. 1975, U.S. Ct. Appeals (11th cir.) 1981. Assoc. Dermer Rosen & Mofsky, Miami Beach, Fla., 1961-63; ptnr. Rosen & Chonin, Miami Beach, Fla., 1963-66, Goldstein, Franklin & Chonin, Miami Beach, Fla., 1966-72, Chonin & Sher, P.A., Coral Gables, Fla., 1972-92, Chonin, Sher & Nauvarette, Coral Gables, Fla., 1992—; lectr. on trial advocacy. Contbr. articles to profl. jours. Pres. Legal Svcs. Greater Miami, 1974-76; chmn. 3d DCA Jud. Nominating Com., Miami, 1983-87. Named Man of Yr., ACLU, 1993, 94; recipient Tobias Simon Pro Bono award, 1984. Fellow Am. Acad. Matrimonial Lawyers (bd. mgrs. 1992), Am. Bd. Civil Trial Advs.; mem. ATLA, Acad. Fla. Trial Lawyers, Family Inns of Ct. Federal civil litigation, Family and matrimonial, State civil litigation. Office: Chonin Sher & Navarrete 95 Merrick Way Ste 100 Coral Gables FL 33134-5308

**CHOPIN, SUSAN GARDINER,** lawyer; b. Miami, Fla., Feb. 23, 1947; d. Maurice and Judith (Warden) Gardiner; m. M.S. Rukeyser, Jr. Mar. 10, 1997; children: Philip, Alexandra, Christopher. BBA, Loyola U., New Orleans, 1966; JD cum laude, U. Miami, 1972; MLitt (Law), Oxford U., Eng., 1983. Bar: Fla. 1972, Iowa 1979. Sr. law clk. to judge U.S. Dist. Ct. (so. dist.) Fla., Miami, 1972-73; ptnr. Chopin & Chopin, Miami, 1973-77; assoc. prof. law sch. Drake U., Des Moines, 1979-80; pvt. practice law Palm Beach, Fla., 1981—; ptnr. Chopin & Chopin, 1999—. Mem. editorial bd. Fla. Bar Jour., 1975—; contbr. articles to profl. jours., legal revs. Trustee Preservation Found. of Palm Beach, 1986-89. Mem. ABA, Fla. Bar Assn., Iowa Bar Assn., Fed. Bar Assn., Internat. Bar Assn., Fla. Assn. Women Lawyers, Soc. Wig and Robe, Palm Beach County Bar Assn., English Speaking Union, Phi Kappa Phi, Phi Alpha Delta. State civil litigation, Family and matrimonial, General practice. Office: Esperante Bldg 222 Lakeview Ave Ste 1150 West Palm Beach FL 33401-6148

**CHOSLOVSKY, WILLIAM,** lawyer; b. Gary, Ind., Sept. 18, 1968; s. Sydney and Binnie Choslovsky. BS in Acctg., U. Ill., 1990; JD, Harvard U., 1994. Bar: Ill. 1994, Alaska 1995, Colo. 1997. Law clk. Justice Jay A. Rabinowitz Alaska Supreme Ct., Juneau, 1994-95; jud. law clk Judge Wiley Y. Daniel U.S. Dist. Ct., Denver, 1995-96; assoc. Grippo & Elden, Chgo., 1996-98; gen. counsel, CFO Certificate Clearing Corp., Chgo., 1998—. Contbr. articles to profl. jours. General civil litigation, Sports, Bankruptcy.

**CHOTAS, ELIAS NICHOLAS,** lawyer; b. Washington, Feb. 8, 1947; s. Nicholas Eli and Georgia (Angel) C.; m. Carla Townsend, Apr. 15, 1984; children: Carl Nicholas Townsend, William Elias Townsend. BS, Duke U., 1969; MS, Ohio State U., 1972; JD, U. Fla., 1976. Bar: Fla. 1976. Ptnr. Carlton, Fields, Ward, Emmanuel, Smith & Cutler, P.A., Tampa, Fla., 1976-84, Dean, Mead, Egerton, Bloodworth, Capouano & Bozarth, P.A., Orlando, Fla., 1984—. Bd. trustees Fla. TaxWatch, Inc., Tallahassee, 1990—; mem. East Ctrl. Fla. Regional Planning Coun., Orlando, 1992—, Econ. Devel. Coun. of Mid-Fla., Orlando, 1988—. Mem. ABA, Fla. Bar Assn. (environ. and land use law sect., real property sect.), Tiger Bay Club of Orlando. Democrat. Presbyterian. Environmental, Land use and zoning (including planning), Real property. Home: 1205 Windsong Rd Orlando FL 32809-3034 Office: Dean Mead Egerton Bloodworth Capouano & Bozarth 800 N Magnolia Ave Ste 1500 Orlando FL 32803-3276

**CHOU, YUNG-MING,** lawyer; b. Tainan, Taiwan, Jan. 29, 1959; came to U.S., 1985; s. Ming-Chien and Hong-Hsi Chou; m. Chueh Wang; 1 child, Hsueh-Ting. LLB, Fu Jen Cath. U., Taipei, Taiwan, 1981; M of Criminal Justice Adminstrn., Oklahoma City U., 1986, JD, 1993. Bar: Calif. 1994, N.Y. 1994, U.S. Dist. (no. dist.) Calif. 1995, U.S. Dist. Ct. (ctrl. dist.) Calif. 1996, U.S. Tax Ct. 1998. In-house legal counsel, claim adjuster The First Ins. Co., Ltd., Taipei, 1983-85; lectr. Taiwan Police Coll., Taipei, 1988-89; claims mgr. Ins. Co. N.Am., Taipei, 1987-91; copr. counsel Aces Rsch., Inc., Fremont, Calif., 1994-96; pvt. practice Yung-Ming Chou, Atty. at Law, Fremont, Calif., 1995—. Recipient Dr. Sun Yat Sen scholarship Kuomintang, Taipei, 1991-93; named Amb. at Large, Oklahoma City Mayor, 1986, Hon. Citizen, Oklahoma City Mayor, 1986. Mem. Alameda County Bar Assn. General corporate, Contracts commercial, General civil litigation. Office: 39111 Paseo Padre Pkwy Ste 207 Fremont CA 94538-1695

**CHOUKAS-BRADLEY, JAMES RICHARD,** lawyer; b. Hartford, Conn., Sept. 11, 1950; s. William Lee and Paula Ann (Elliott) Bradley; m. Melanie Rose Choukas, June 21, 1975; children: Sophia Crane, Jesse Elliott. BA cum laude, U. Vt., 1974; JD cum laude, Georgetown U., 1980. Bar: D.C. 1980, U.S. Ct. Appeals (D.C. cir.) 1981, U.S. Ct. Appeals (11th cir.) 1984, U.S. Ct. Appeals (10th cir.) 1985, U.S. Ct. Appeals (4th cir.) 1990. Reporter, editor The Berlin (N.H.) Reporter, 1974; editor, pub., creative dir. Ad Lib, Gorham, N.H., 1974-75; asst. to city mgr. City of Berlin, 1975-77; legal intern Congl. Budget Office, Washington, 1978; rsch. assoc. Schlossberg-Cassidy & Assocs., Washington, 1978-80; assoc. Miller, Balis & O'Neil, P.C., Washington, 1980-84, mem., v.p., 1985—, mem. exec. com., 1993-97; legal advisor, first v.p. Sugarloaf Citizens Assn., Barnesville, Md., 1987—, Mcpl. Gas Authority of Miss., Natural Gas Acquisition Corp. of City of Clarksville, TN; legal advisor, first v.p. S.E. Ala. gas dist. Mcpl. Gas Authority of Miss.; gen. counsel Tenn. Energy Acquisition Corp.; spkr. in field. Author: The Early Days, 1975. Pres. D.C. Dukes Athletic Club, Washington, 1978-81, Montgomery Dukes, 1987-92; com. chmn. Berlin Bicentennial Commn., Berlin, 1975-76. Regents scholar State of N.Y., 1968. Mem. Fed. Energy Bar Assn., Phi Beta Kappa, Randolph Mountain Club, For a Rural Montgomery. Avocations: softball, guitar, songwriting, hiking, travel. FERC practice, Contracts commercial, Municipal (including bonds).

**CHOVANES, EUGENE,** lawyer; b. Hazleton, Penn., Jan. 1, 1926; s. Michael and Anna (Watro) C.; m. Claire Amelia Puhak, Mar. 27, 1952; children: Michael, George, Nicholas, Joseph, John. BS Engring., Lehigh U., 1950; JD, Villanova U., 1960. Bar: Pa. 1961. Assoc. William Steell Jackson & Sons, Phila., 1957-63; ptnr. Jackson & Chovanes, Phila. and Bala-Cynwyd, Pa., 1963—; lectr. in patent law Villanova U., 1957-80. Served to sgt. U.S. Army, 1943-46, to 1st lt. Ordnance Corps, 1951-52. Mem. ABA, Phila. Intellectual Property Law Assn., Phila. Bar Assn., Soc. Registered Profl. Engrs., Am. Intellectual Property Law Assn. Patent, Trademark and copyright. Office: 1 Bala Plz Ste 319 Bala Cynwyd PA 19004-1403

**CHOVANES, JOSEPH EUGENE,** lawyer; b. Abington, Pa., Oct. 29, 1960; s. Eugene and Claire Amelia (Puhar) C.; m. Martha Satterfield Baskett, Feb. 13, 1988; children: Kathryn, Anna, Alexander. BA, Villanova U., 1983, BS in Biology, BS in Gen. Sci., 1984, JD, 1987. Bar: Pa. 1987, U.S. Dist. Ct. (ea. dist.) Pa. 1987, U.S. Patent and Trademark Office 1988. Assoc. Paul & Paul, Phila., 1987-95; pvt. practice Phila., 1995—; adj. prof. Sch. Law Villanova U., 1995, 97. Author: Computer Technology and IP Law, 1999, The Law of Digital, 1999; contbr. articles to profl. jours. Patentee in field. Bd. dirs., v.p. Ctr. for Law and Info. Policy, Villanova, 1995-97. Mem. ABA, Benjamin Franklin Inn of Ct. (bd. dirs. 1995-97), Intellectual Property Owners Assn. Intellectual property, Trademark and copyright, Patent. Office: 2047 Locust St Philadelphia PA 19103-5613

**CHOW, STEPHEN Y(EE),** lawyer; b. Cleve., Miss., Sept. 8, 1952; s. Chester H. and June (Eng) C.; children: Astrid Crockett, Augustus Stephen. AB cum laude, SM in Applied Physics, Harvard U., 1975; JD, Columbia U., 1979. Bar: N.Y. 1980, Mass. 1983, U.S. Supreme Ct. 1983, U.S. Patent Office 1984. Assoc. Donovan Leisure Newton & Irvine, N.Y.C., 1979-82, Gaston Snow & Ely Bartlett, Boston, 1982-85, Cesari and McKenna, Boston, 1985-88; ptnr. Nutter, McClennen & Fish, Boston, 1988-90, Cesari and McKenna, Boston, 1990-93, Perkins, Smith & Cohen, Boston, 1993—; adj. faculty Suffolk U. Law Sch., 1995—; mem. Nat. Conf. Mass. Commn. on Uniform State Laws, 1994—; Nat. Conf. Drafting Com. Uniform Comml. Code, 1995—, Drafting Com. Uniform Electronic Transactions Act, 1996—; mem. study com. on taxation of electronic commerce. Bd. editors Mass. Law Rev., 1991-98. Trustee Hawthorne Pl. Condominium Trust, Boston, 1985-92; spl. asst. dist. atty. N.Y. County, 1980-82. Mem. ABA, IEEE, Am. Intellectual Property Law Assn. (chmn. uniform comml. code com. 1997—), Am. Law Inst. (elected), Mass. Bar Assn. (chmn. uniform comml. code project 1990-98, chmn. banking and comml. law com. 1998—), Licensing Execs. Soc. (chmn. uniform comml. code com. 1991-93), Boston Bar Assn. (chmn. intellectual property com. 1991-95, mem. governing coun. 1994-96), N.Y.C. Bar Assn., Boston Patent Law Assn. (chmn. trade secrets law com. 1996—), Assn. Computing Machinery (chmn. ad hoc com. on software patenting 1991-93), Asian Am. Law Assn. Mass. (dir.), Boston Racquet Club. Republican. Avocations: painting, squash, sculling. Patent, Computer, Private international. Home: 9 Hawthorne Pl Boston MA 02114-2344 Office: Perkins Smith & Cohen LLP One Beacon St Boston MA 02108

**CHOY, HERBERT YOUNG CHO,** federal judge; b. Makaweli, Hawaii, Jan. 6, 1916; s. Doo Wook and Helen (Nahm) C.; m. Dorothy Helen Shular, June 16, 1945. BA, U. Hawaii, 1938; JD, Harvard U., 1941. Bar: Hawaii 1941. Law clk. City and County of Honolulu, 1941; assoc. Fong & Miho, 1947-48; ptnr. Fong, Miho and Choy, 1948-57; atty. gen. Territory of Hawaii, 1957-58; ptnr. Fong, Miho, Choy & Robinson, Honolulu, 1958-71; sr. judge U.S. Ct. Appeals (9th cir.), Honolulu, 1971—; adv. com. on constrn. judiciary bldgs. Chief Justice Hawaii, 1970-71; compilation commn. to compile Revised Laws of Hawaii, 1955, 1953-57; com. to draft Hawaii rules of criminal procedure Supreme Ct., 1958-59; com. on pacific ocean territories Jud. Conf. the U.S., 1976-79. Dir. Legal Aid Soc. Hawaii, 1959-61; trustee Hawaii Loa Coll., 1963-79. Capt. U.S. Army, 1941-46, lt. col. Res. Recipient Order of Civil Merit award Republic of Korea, 1973. Fellow Am. Bar Found.; mem. ABA, Hawaii Bar Assn. (exec. com. 1953, 57, 61, legal ethics and unauthorized practices com. 1953, com. on legis. 1959). Office: US Ct Appeals 300 Ala Moana Blvd Rm C305 Honolulu HI 96850-0305

**CHRESTMAN, DON MARSHALL,** lawyer; b. Sinton, Tex., July 5, 1942; s. John Marshall and Nancy Marjorie (Baker) C.; m. Melinda June Dean, Jan. 25, 1969; children: Shelley Gae, Dean Marshall, Laura Elizabeth. BBA, Baylor U., 1965, JD, 1970. Bar: Tex. 1970, U.S. Ct. Appeals 1992, U.S. Claims Ct. 1992, U.S. Ct. Internat. Trade, 1992, U.S. Ct. Military Appeals 1992. Mgmt. trainee Cen. Power and Light Co., Corpus Christi, Tex., 1965-68; sole practice Taft, Tex., 1970-72; ptnr. Nicolas and Morris, Corpus Christi, 1972-73; atty. Lone Star Gas Co., Dallas, 1973-74, Dept. of Energy, Dallas, 1974-75; sr. atty. United Gas Pipeline Co., Houston, 1975-76; corporate counsel Southland Royalty Co., Ft. Worth, 1976-80; sole practice Weatherford, Tex., 1980-84; ptnr. Vick Chrestman Carney LLP, Weatherford, Tex., 1984—; dir. Power Service Products, Inc., Weatherford, 1985—. Pres. Parker County United Way, Weatherford, 1986; councilman Weatherford City Council, 1981-87; rep. North Cen. Tex. Council of Govts., Weatherford, 1986-87; past chmn. Bd. of Deacons 1st Baptist Ch., Weatherford, 1983-84; trustee Baylor Bear Found., dir. Weatherford/Packer Co. Econ. Devel. Corp., 1991-99; trustee Weatherford Coll., 1998—. Mem. Tex. Bar Found. (life), Am. Trial Lawyers Assn., Tex. Trial Lawyers Assn., Parker County Bar (pres. 1983). Republican. Baptist. Lodges: Lions (dir. 1982-85), Rotary (v.p. 1971-72). Avocations: reading, golf, travel. Home: 2146 Lakeforest Dr Weatherford TX 76087-3703 Office: Vick Chrestman Carney & Smith 111 York Ave Weatherford TX 76086-3250

**CHRISANT, ROSEMARIE KATHRYN,** law library administrator; b. Chgo., Oct. 9, 1946; d. Theodore and Angeline Frances (Pawlik) Layne; m. William C. Chrisant, Mar. 16, 1973; 1 child, Paula Ellen Marie. BS in Edn., No. Ill. U., 1967; MLS, Rosary Coll., 1971. High sch. English tchr. Chgo. Sch. System, 1967-70; asst. libr. Akron (Ohio) Law Libr. Assn., 1971-76, libr. dir., 1976—; cons. law firms, Akron. Contbr. articles to profl. jours. Mem. ABA, Am. Assn. Law Librs., Ohio Regional Assn. Law Librs. (Outstanding Svc. award 1986), Spl. Libr. Assn., Ohio Libr. Assn. E-mail: allarkc@en.com. Office: Akron Law Libr Assn Summit County Courthouse 209 S High St Rm 4 Akron OH 44308-1625

**CHRISMAN, JAMES PAUL,** lawyer; b. Omaha, Jan. 4, 1958; s. Robert Thomas and Patti Lou (Wolff) C.; m. Consuelo E. Emerson, May 27, 1990. BA, U. Nebr., 1981, JD, 1985. Bar: Nev. 1985, U.S. Dist. Ct. (no. and so. dists. Nev. 1985, U.S. Ct. Appeals (9th cir.) 1985, U.S. Supreme Ct. 1995. Dep. prosecutor Lancaster County Attys., Lincoln, Nebr., 1984; litigator Barker, Brown, Busby Chrisman & Thomas, Las Vegas, 1986—. Exec. editor: Nebraska Law Review vol. 63, 1984. Mem. ABA, Nev. Bar Assn., Am. Inns Ct. (barrister), Clark County Bar Assn., Sierra Club, Phi Delta Phi. Avocations: sports fan, softball, hiking, camping, boating. Alternative dispute resolution, General civil litigation, Construction. Office: Barker Brown et al 300 S 4th St Ste 800 Las Vegas NV 89101-6018

**CHRISS, TIMOTHY D. A.,** lawyer; b. Balt., Oct. 26, 1950; s. Evan Alevizatos and Ceres (Rogokos) C.; m. Karin Elizabeth Jones, Feb. 25, 1978; children: Alexander Wilhelm Alevizatos, Caroline Elizabeth. BA, Washington and Lee U., 1972; JD, Cath. U. Am., 1976. Bar: Md. 1976, U.S. Dist. Ct. Md. 1976. Assoc. Gordon, Feinblatt, Rothman, Hoffberger & Hollander, Balt., 1976-83, ptnr., 1983—; mem. com. on character Ct. Appeals Md., 1991—. Bd. dirs. Citizens Planning and Housing Assn., Balt.,1978-80, Devel. Credit Fund, inc., 1996—, Union Meml. Hosp. Found., 1996—, Greater Homewood Comty. Corp., 1997—; trustee Gilman Sch., 1988-92, Maryvale Prep. Sch., 1997—. Fellow Md. Bar Found.; mem. ABA, Am. Coll. Real Estate Lawyers, Md. Bar Assn. (coun. real property sect. 1988—, sec. 1992-94, chmn.-elect 1994-96, chmn. 1996-98, chmn. real property code revision com. 1988-92), Bar Assn. Balt. City (exec. coun. 1988-90), Balt. City C. of C. (bd. dirs. 1993—), Balt. Country Club, Ctr. Club, Md. Club. Republican. Greek Orthodox. Real property. Office: Gordon Feinblatt Rothman Hoffberger & Hollander 233 E Redwood St Baltimore MD 21202-3332

**CHRIST, CHRIS STEVE,** lawyer; b. Canonsburg, Pa., Jan. 3, 1936; s. Michael C. and Katina (Hantzigorgis) C.; m. Lula Koutroulakis, Dec. 31, 1942; 1 child, Gina Reneé. BBA, U. Pitts., 1957; JD, Samford U., 1968. Bar: Ala., U.S. Dist. Ct. (no. dist.) Ala., U.S. Ct. Appeals (5th and 11th dists.), U.S. Supreme Ct. Sales rep. Mennen Cos., Morris Plains, N.J., 1960-62, Beecham Cos., Atlanta, 1965-66; sales rep. Beecham Cos., Atlanta, 1965-66; councilman City of Vestavia Hills, 1972-76; pvt. practice, Birmingham, Ala., 1968—; ptnr. Christ & McCary, Birmingham, 1988—. Pres., Jeff, Blount, St. Clair Mental Health/Mental Retardation Auth., 1981-83. Served to 1st lt. USAF, 1958-60. Mem. Ala. State Bar Assn., Birmingham Bar Assn., Nat. Assn. Criminal Defense Lawyers, Ala. Trial Lawyers Assn., Vestavia C. of C., Poinsetta's Men's Club, Masons, Shriners, Pinetree Country Club, Summit Club, The Club, Phi Alpha Delta (pres. Alumni Club 1982-88). Greek Orthodox. Criminal, Consumer commercial, General civil litigation. Office: 205 20th St N Ste 730 Birmingham AL 35203-4709

**CHRIST, EARLE L.,** lawyer; b. Racine, Wis., Aug. 8, 1915; s. Thomas Christ and Martha Peterson; m. Agnes Barabra Meurer, Dec. 4, 1943; children: Joellyn K. Keleske, Thomas E. LLB, JD, Marquette U., 1998. Pvt. practic Racine. Maj. USAFR, 1942-64. Mem. Wis. State Bar Assn., Racine County Bar Assn. Republican. Roman Catholic. Avocations: cmaping, flying. General corporate, Estate planning, Probate. Home and Office: 17920 Gulf Blvd Apt 1906 Redington Shores FL 33708-1100

**CHRISTENBURY, EDWARD SAMUEL,** lawyer; b. Boone, N.C., May 22, 1941; s. Edward S. Sr. and Frances (Timme) C.; m. Suzanne Bernfeld, Dec. 27, 1971. BS, U. Tenn., 1963, JD, 1965. Bar: Tenn. 1965, U.S. Ct. Appeals (D.C. cir.) 1972, U.S. Ct. Appeals (6th cir.) 1987, U.S. Supreme Ct. 1970. Trial atty., dep. chief edn. sect. civil rights div. Dept. of Justice, Washington, 1968-71, dep. chief appellate and civil litigation sect. internal security div., 1971-73, chief spl. civil litigation unit criminal div., 1973-77, trial atty. civil div., 1977-79; asst. gen. counsel Nuclear Regulatory Commn., Washington, 1979-87; sr. v.p., gen. counsel TVA, Knoxville, 1987—. Lt. U.S. Army, 1966-67. Mem. Tenn. Bar Assn., Knoxville Bar Assn. Presbyterian. Avocation: reading. Office: TVA ET 11A 400 W Summit Hill Dr Knoxville TN 37999-0002

**CHRISTENFELD, ALAN M.,** lawyer; b. N.Y.C., Apr. 19, 1951; s. Paul and Renee Christenfeld. BA, Bowdoin Coll., 1974; JD, Cornell U., 1976; LLM in Taxation, NYU, 1978. Bar: N.Y. 1977, U.S. Dist. Ct. (ea. and so. dists.) 1978, U.S. Dist. Ct. Ariz. 1994, U.S. Dist. Ct. D.C. 1998, U.S. Ct. Appeals (2d cir.) 1978). Assoc. Rathheim, Hoffman, Kassel & Silverman, N.Y.C., 1978-83, ptnr., 1984-86; ptnr. Sidley & Austin, N.Y.C., 1987-90, Rosenman & Colin, N.Y.C., 1991-93, Rogers & Wells LLP, N.Y.C., 1994—. Co-author bi-monthly column N.Y. Law Jour., 1996—; contbr. chpt. to book, articles to profl. jours. Mem. adv. bd. Comml. Fin. Assn. Edn. Found., N.Y.C., 1992—; mem. exec. bd. Assn. Comml. fin. Attys., N.Y.C., 1992—. Fellow Am. Coll. Comml. Fin. Lawyers. Avocations: American history, classical music, ice hockey. Banking, Bankruptcy, Contracts commercial. Office: Rogers & Wells LLP 200 Park Ave Fl 8E New York NY 10166-0800

**CHRISTENSEN, CHARLES BROPHY,** lawyer; b. Altadena, Calif., July 3, 1948; s. Charles Warren and Barbara Louise (Kruger) C.; m. Susan Marie Stricklin, Aug. 22, 1970; children: Charles Brophy, Michelle K., Courtney Marie, Timothy Patrick. BA in Biology, Claremont Men's Coll., Calif., 1970; JD, U. San Diego, 1973. Bar: Calif. 1973, U.S. Dist. Ct. (so. dist.) Calif. 1973, U.S. Dist. Ct. (cen. dist.) Calif. 1994, U.S. Ct. Appeals (9th cir.) 1995, U.S. Supreme Ct. 1997. Assoc. Biafora & Weiner, Reseda, Calif., 1974-76; ptnr. Biafora, Weiner & Christensen, Reseda, 1977-78; gen. counsel Charles W. Christensen & Assocs., San Diego, 1978-90; ptnr. Detisch, Christensen & Wood, San Diego, 1983-95, Detisch & Christensen, San Diego, 1995—; bd. dirs. Fairbanks-Sturdivant Co., L.A. Mem. ABA, San Diego County Bar Assn. Republican. Roman Catholic. Avocations: golf, tennis. State civil litigation, Insurance. Home: 2684 Jonquil Dr San Diego CA 92106-1135 Office: Detisch & Christensen 444 W C St Ste 200 San Diego CA 92101-3582

**CHRISTENSEN, DARIN S.,** lawyer; b. Provo, Utah, May 23, 1967; s. Paul E. and Janet D. Christensen; m. Elizabeth Mathewsen, May 23, 1994; 1 child, George Douglas. BS in Bus. Mgmt., Brigham Young U., 1991, JD, 1996; LLM from Taxation, U. Fla., 1997. Bar: Oreg. 1997, U.S. Tax Ct. 1998, U.S. Ct. Appeals (9th cir.) 1998. Assoc. Wetzel DeFrang & Sandor, Portland, Oreg., 1997—. Articles editor Jour. Pub. Law, 1995-96. With Utah N.G., 1989-96. Trustee scholar Brigham Young U., 1991-95, Edwin S. Hinckley scholar, 1993-96. Mem. Phi Delta Phi. Taxation, general, Estate planning, Personal income taxation. Home: 12010 SW Summer Crest Dr Tigard OR 97223-3241 Office: Wetzel DeFrang & Sandor 838 SW 1st Ave Ste 300 Portland OR 97204-3374

**CHRISTENSEN, HENRY, III,** lawyer; b. Jersey City, Nov. 8, 1944; s. Henry Jr. and M. Louise (Brooke) C.; m. Constance L. Cumpton, July 1, 1967; children: Alexander, Gustavus, Elizabeth, Katherine. BA, Yale U., 1966; JD, Harvard U., 1969. Bar: N.Y. 1970, U.S. Tax Ct. 1973, U.S. Ct. Appeals (2d. cir.) 1973, U.S. Supreme Ct. 1975. Assoc. Sullivan & Cromwell, N.Y.C., 1969-77, ptnr., 1977—; adj. assoc. prof. NYU, N.Y.C., 1985-88, U. of Miami Law Sch., 1997—. Author: International Estate Planning, 1999; contbr. articles to profl. jours. Chmn. Prospect Park Alliance, Bklyn., 1985—; trustee, 1st vice chmn. Peddie Sch., Hightstown, N.J., 1986—; trustee Am. Fund for the Tate Gallery, 1987—, Bklyn. Acad. Music, 1992—, Vincent Astor Found., 1993—; dir., sec. Freedom Inst., N.Y.C., 1980—, The Friends of Jiangnan U., 1987—; dir., v.p. Am. Friends of Whitechapel Art Gallery Found., 1991—; trustee, mem. exec. com. Am. Ctr. Oriental Rsch. in Amman, 1993—. Fellow Am. Coll. Trust and Estate Counsel; mem. N.Y. State Bar Assn. (chmn. estate and gift tax com. 1983-84, chmn. exempt orgn. com. 1986, chmn. income taxation of trusts com. 1984-85, 87-89, exec. com. tax sect. 1983-89), Internat. Acad. Estate and Trust Law (academician). Probate, Estate taxation, Personal income taxation. Home: 35 Prospect Park W Apt 8/9B Brooklyn NY 11215-2370 Office: Sullivan & Cromwell 125 Broad St Fl 28 New York NY 10004-2489

**CHRISTENSEN, KAREN KAY,** lawyer; b. Ann Arbor, Mich., Mar. 9, 1947; d. Jack Edward and Evangeline (Pitsch) C.; m. Kenneth Robert Kay, Sept. 2, 1977; children: Jeffrey Smithson, Braden, Bergen. BS, U. Mich., 1969; JD, U. Denver, 1975. Bar: Colo. 1975, D.C. 1976, U.S. Supreme Ct. 1979. Atty., advisor office of dep. atty. gen. U.S. Dept. of Justice, Washington, 1975-76, trial atty. civil rights div., 1976-79; legis. counsel ACLU, Washington, 1979-80; staff atty. D.C. Pub. Defender Service, Washington, 1980-85; asst. gen. counsel Nat. Pub. Radio, Washington, 1985-93; gen. counsel Nat. Endowment Arts, Washington, 1993-98, acting dep. chmn. for grants and partnership, 1997-98, dep. chmn. grants and awards, 1998—; mem. D.C. Bd. Profl. Responsibility, 1990-98, chair, 1996-98. Mem. D.C. Bar Assn., NCA/ACLU (exec. bd. 1986-93, chair 1993), Phi Beta Kappa. Communications, Civil rights, Criminal. Office: 1100 Pennsylvania Ave NW Washington DC 20004-2501

**CHRISTENSEN, PATRICIA ANNE WATKINS,** lawyer; b. Corpus Christi, Tex., June 24, 1947; d. Owen Milton Jr. and Margaret (McFarland) Watkins; m. Steven Ray Christensen, May 28, 1977 (dec. 1985); children: Geoffrey Holland, Jeremy Ladd. BS, U. North Tex., 1971; JD, U. Houston, 1977. Bar: Utah 1977, Tex. 1977, U.S. Dist. Ct. Utah 1977, U.S. Ct. Appeals (10th cir.) 1977, U.S. Supreme Ct. 1990. Assoc. Berman & Giauque, Salt Lake City, 1977-80; ptnr. Parr, Waddoups, Brown, Gee & Loveless, Salt Lake City, 1980—, pres., 1991-93; adj. prof. law U. Utah Law Sch., Salt Lake City, 1979-81; judge pro tem Third Dist. Ct., 1995—. Legis. asst. U.S. Senate, 1970-74; bd. dirs. Comml. Law Affiliate, 1997—; co-chair litigation sect., trustee Rowland Hall St. Mark's Sch., chair devel. com., 1987-90; mem. steering com., comprehensive capital campaign U. Utah Sch. Nursing; mem. steering com. Am. Election Law Project. Named Utah Woman Lawyer of Yr., 1992. Mem. ABA, Utah State Bar (Dorothy Merrill Brothers award 1996), State Bar of Tex., Salt Lake County Bar Assn. (exec. com. 1979-87, author editor Utah Lawyers Practice Manual 1986), Women Lawyers Utah (pres. 1988-89, bd. dirs. 1987-90), Phi Delta Phi, Delta Gamma, Alpha Lambda Delta. Avocations: hiking, mountain biking, writing, travel, languages.E-mail: pac@prolaw.com. Federal civil litigation, State civil litigation. Office: Parr Waddoups Brown Gee & Loveless 185 S State St Ste 1300 Salt Lake City UT 84111-1537

**CHRISTENSEN, ROBERT PAUL,** lawyer; b. Mpls., June 26, 1949; s. Otto and Cora Alice C.; m. Cindy G. Christensen, July 15, 1972; children: Nicholas, Lindsey, Callie. BA, U. Minn., 1971, JD cum laude, 1974. Ptnr. Carlsen, Gneiner & Law, Mpls., 1974-86, Dunkley, Bennett & Christensen, Mpls., 1986—. Mem. Minn. Trial Lawyers Assn. (bd. dirs. 1986-96), Creative Dispute Resolution Assn. (bd. dirs. 1995-97, pres. 1998—). General civil litigation, Personal injury, Product liability. Office: Dunkley Bennett & Christensen 701 4th Ave S Ste 700 Minneapolis MN 55415-1812

**CHRISTENSON, GORDON A.,** law educator; b. Salt Lake City, June 22, 1932; s. Gordon B. and Ruth Arzella (Anderson) C.; m. Katherine Joy deMik, Nov. 2, 1951 (div. 1977); children: Gordon Scott, Marjorie Lynne, Ruth Ann, Nanette; m. Fabienne Fadeley, Sept. 16, 1979. BS in Law, U. Utah, 1955, JD, 1956; SJD, George Washington U., 1961. Bar: Utah 1956, U.S. Supreme Ct. 1971, D.C. 1978. Law clk. to chief justice Utah Supreme Ct., 1956-57; assoc. firm Christenson & Callister, Salt Lake City, 1956-58; atty. Dept. of Army, Nat. Guard Bur., Washington, 1957-58; atty., acting asst. legal adviser Office of Legal Adviser, U.S. Dept. State, Washington, 1958-62; asst. gen. counsel for sci. and tech. U.S. Dept. Commerce, 1962-67, spl. asst. to undersec. of commerce, 1967, counsel to commerce tech. adv. bd., 1962-67, chmn. task force on telecommunications missions and orgn., 1967, counsel to panel on engring. and commodity standards, tech. adv. bd., 1963-65; assoc. prof. law U. Okla., Norman, 1967-70; exec. asst. to pres. U. Okla., 1967-70; univ. dean for ednl. devel., central adminstrn. State U. N.Y., Albany, 1970-71; prof. law Am. U. Law Sch., Washington, 1971-79; dean Am. U. Law Sch., 1971-77; on leave, 1977-79; Charles H. Stockton prof. internat. law U.S. Naval War Coll., Newport, R.I., 1977-79; dean, Nippert prof. law U. Cin. Coll. Law, 1979-85, univ. prof. law, 1985—; assoc. professorial lectr. in internat. affairs George Washington U., 1961-67; vis. scholar Harvard U. Law Sch., 1977-78, Yale Law Sch., 1985-86, Law Sch. U. Maine, Portland, 1997; Wallace S. Fujiyama vis. disting. prof. law Univ. Hawaii Law Sch., 1997; participant summer confs. on internat. law Cornell Law Sch., Ithaca, N.Y., 1962, 64; cons. in internat. law U.S. Naval War Coll., Newport, R.I., 1969; faculty mem., reporter seminars for experienced fed. dist. judges Fed. Jud. Center, Washington, 1972-77. Author: (with Richard B. Lillich) International Claims: Their Preparation and Presentation, 1962, The Future of the University, 1969; Contbr. articles to legal jours. Cons. to Center for Policy Alternatives Mass. Inst. Tech., Cambridge, 1970-81; mem. intergovtl. com. on Internat. Policy on Weather Modification, 1967; Vice pres. Procedural Aspects of Internat. Law Inst., N.Y.C., 1962—. Served with intelligence sect. USAF, 1951-52, Japan. Recipient Silver Medal award Dept. Commerce, 1967; fellow Grad. Sch. U. Cin. Mem. Am. Soc. Internat. Law (mem. panel on state responsibility), Utah Bar Assn., Cin. Bar Assn., Order of Coif, Phi Delta Phi, Kappa Sigma. Clubs: Literary (Cin.); Cosmos (Washington). Home: 3465 Principio Ave Cincinnati OH 45208-4242 Office: U Cin Coll Law 2600 Clifton Ave Cincinnati OH 45221-0001

**CHRISTIAN, GARY IRVIN,** lawyer; b. Albany, Ga., July 7, 1951; s. Rupert Irvin and Alice Amelia (Smith) C.; 1 child, Amy Margaret. BA in History, Polit. Sci., David Lipscomb Coll., 1973; MPA, U. Tenn., 1974; JD, Vanderbilt U., 1979. Bar: Fla. 1979, U.S. Dist. Ct. (no. and mid. dists.) Fla 1979. Rsch. dir. Ala. League of Mcpls., Montgomery, 1974-76; instr. in pub. adminstrn. David Lipscomb Coll., Nashville, 1977-79; assoc. Rogers, Towers, Bailey, Jones & Gay, Jacksonville, Fla., 1979-83, Foley & Lardner, Jacksonville, 1983-86; ptnr. Christian, Prom, Korn & Zehmer, Jacksonville, 1986-92, Rumph, Stoddard & Christian, Jacksonville, 1992—. Editor-in-chief Vanderbilt Jour. of Transnational Law, 1978-79. Bd. dirs. PACE Ctr. for Girls, Inc., Jacksonville, 1984—, pres., 1984-86; mem. leadership Jacksonville, 1986-87; chmn. site selection com. St. Johns County Sch. Bd., 1993-95; mem. site selection com., St. Johns County Sch. Bd., 1989-91. Mem. ABA (condominiums and planned devels. com.), Jacksonville Bar Assn. (coord. continuing edn. 1984-85, vice chmn. real property sect. 1986-87, chmn. 1987-88, chmn. corps., banking & bus. sect. 1991-92), Wavemasters Soc. (pres. 1986-87), Jacksonville C. of C. (com. 100 1986-94), Southpoint Bus. Assn. (bd. dirs. 1990—, pres. 1991-93), Oak Bridge Country Club, Seminole Club, Salt Creek Homeowners Assn. (bd. dirs. 1993—, pres. 1994-96). Republican. Mem. Ch. of Christ. Avocations: golf, fishing, racquetball, stamp collecting. Real property, Contracts commercial, Banking. Home: PO Box 550620 Jacksonville FL 32255-0620 Office: Rumph Stoddard & Christian 3100 University Blvd S Ste 101 Jacksonville FL 32216-2777

**CHRISTIAN, JOHN CATLETT, JR.,** lawyer; b. Springfield, Mo., Sept. 12, 1929; s. John Catlett and Alice Odelle (Milling) C.; m. Peggy Jeanne Cain, Apr. 12, 1953; children: Cathleen Marie, John Catlett, Alice Cain. AB, Drury Coll., 1951; LLB, Tulane U., 1956. Bar: La. 1956, Mo. 1956, U.S. Supreme Ct. 1975. Assoc. Porter & Stewart, Lake Charles, La., 1956-58; assoc. Wilkinson, Lewis, Wilkinson & Madison, Shreveport, La., 1958-62, ptnr., 1962-64; ptnr. Milling, Benson, Woodward, Hillyer, Pierson & Miller, New Orleans, 1964-92, of counsel, 1993-94; pres. Sherburne Land Co., 1974-83, Pointe-Martin Mgmt., Inc., 1983—; dir. Emerald Land Corp. Pres. Kathleen Elizabeth O'Brien Found., 1963—. Served with USMCR, 1951-53. Fellow Am. Coll. Trial Lawyers; mem. ABA, Fed. Bar Assn., Am. Judicature Soc., Mo. Bar Assn., La. Bar Assn., La. Landowners Assn. (bd.dris. 1983—), Boston Club, Beau Chene Country Club, Kappa Alpha Order, Omicron Delta Kappa, Phi Delta Phi. Home: 807 Tete Lours Dr Mandeville LA 70471-1774 Office: Whitney Bank Bldg PO Box 1317 Mandeville LA 70470-1317

**CHRISTIAN, WARREN HAROLD, JR.,** lawyer; b. Greenville, S.C., June 11, 1949; s. Warren Harold Sr. and Doris Marie (Hopkins) C.; m. Connie Sue Collett, June 19, 1971; children: Matthew, Joshua, Jill. BA, Carson Newman Coll., 1971; JD, U. S.C., 1975. Bar: S.C. 1975, U.S. Dist. Ct. S.C. 1977, U.S. Ct. Appeals (4th cir.) 1982. Assoc. Law Offices of John Bolt Culbertson, Greenville, 1975-80; ptnr. Christian & Davis, Greenville, 1980—; vis. instr. paralegal program Greenville Tech. Edn. Ctr. Coach youth soccer teams YMCA; v.p. Dem. precinct, 1978; mem. sch. bd. Shannon Forest Christian Sch., 1990-97, chmn., 1995-97. Named one of Outstanding Young Men of Am., U.S. Jaycees, 1978. Mem. S.C. Trial Lawyers Assn. (sustaining mem.), ATLA (sustaining mem.), S.C. Bar Assn. (spkr. S.C. Workers Compensation Seminar 1984, 87), Greenville County Bar Assn. Baptist. Avocations: basketball, tennis. Workers' compensation, Personal injury. Home: 33 Bateswood Dr Greer SC 29651-7681 Office: Christian & Davis PO Box 332 1007 E Washington St Greenville SC 29601-3128

**CHRISTIANSEN, ERIC ROBERT,** lawyer; b. Milw., Dec. 29, 1953. Student, Williams Coll., 1972-74, Conn. Coll., 1974; student in speech, Northwestern U., 1974-75, Hartman Theatre Conservatory, 1975-77; BA in Philosophy, Marquette U., 1979; JD, U. Wis., 1982. Bar: Wis. 1982, U.S. Dist. Ct. (ea. dist.) Wis. 1982, Mich. 1983. Assoc. Michael, Best & Friedrich, Milw., 1982-87; pres., chief exec. officer Great Lakes Capital Mgmt. Corp., Milw., 1988-89; shareholder Whyte Hirschboeck & Dudek, S.C., Milw., 1989-96; shareholder firm of Eric R. Christiansen S.C., Milw., 1996—. AFS Internat. Scholarship, Belgium, 1971-72. Securities, General corporate.

**CHRISTIANSEN, MARK D.,** lawyer; b. Olney, Tex., June 10, 1955; s. Leon H. and Doris J. (Jennings) C.; m. Jane M. Evenson, Mar. 5, 1988. BA, U. Okla., 1977, JD, 1980. Bar: U.S. Dist. Ct. (we. dist.) Okla. 1984, U.S. Dist. Ct. (ea. dist.) Okla. 1993, U.S. Ct. Appeals (10th cir.) 1987. Assoc. Crowe & Dunlevy, Oklahoma City, 1980-85, mem., 1986—. Editor: The Oil and Gas Reporter. Mem. ABA (vice chmn. publs. oil and natural gas exploration and prodn. com. 1985—), Oklahoma City Mineral Lawyers Soc. (pres. 1989-90), Okla. Bar Assn. Oil, gas, and mineral, General civil litigation. Home: 7202 Waverly Ave Oklahoma City OK 73120-1214 Office: Crowe & Dunlevy 1800 Mid America Tower 20 N Broadway Ave Ste 1800 Oklahoma City OK 73102-8273

**CHRISTIANSEN, PATRICK T.,** lawyer; b. Mpls., 1947. BSEE summa cum laude, U. Notre Dame, 1969; JD, Harvard U., 1972. Bar: Fla. 1972, Minn. 1974, U.S. Tax Ct. 1977, U.S. Supreme Ct. 1980. Mem. Akerman, Senterfitt & Eidson P.A., Orlando, Fla. Chmn. bd. Orlando Mus. Art; mem., bd. dirs. The Greater Orlando C. of C., Jobs and Edn. Partnership; chmn. Orange County Transp. Roundtable; mem. Orange County Blue Ribbon Commn., steering com., chmn. transp. com.; bd. dirs. United Arts Cen. Fla., Orlando Downtown Devel. Bd. Mem. ABA (sects. on bus. law, taxation, real property), Fla. Bar (trial lawyers sect., co-chmn. land trust com. real property, probate and trust law sect. 1978-82, dir. real property divsn. 1982-84, vice chmn. 1984-85, chmn. 1985-86, vice-chmn. UCC subcom. corp., banking and bus. law sect. 1979-84, bd. govs. young lawyers sect. 1981-83), Am. Coll. Real Estate Lawyers, Minn. State Bar Assn., Orange County Bar Assn. Banking, Consumer commercial, Real property. Office: Akerman Senterfitt & Eidson PA 17th Fl Citrus Ctr PO Box 231 255 S Orange Ave Orlando FL 32801-3445

**CHRISTIANSEN, ROY HVIDKAER,** lawyer; b. Detroit, Dec. 24, 1932; s. Rasmus H. and Gudrun (Lohmann-Sorensen) C.; m. Barbara L. Stauffer, June 9, 1956; children: Kathryn G. Hardy, Patricia L. Kalbfleich, Kai H., Karl H. BA, U. Mich., 1954, JD, 1957. Bar: Mich. 1957, U.S. Dist. Ct. (ea. dist.) Mich. 1957, U.S. Supreme Ct. 1962, U.S. Ct. Appeals (6th cir.) 1966, U.S. Dist. Ct. (we. dist.) Mich. 1989. Assoc. Erickson, Dyll, Marentay & Van Alsburg, Detroit, 1958-59; gen. counsel Transam. Freight Lines, Inc., Detroit, 1959-71; of counsel Kerr, Russell and Weber, Detroit, 1972-98. Judge City of Huntington Mcpl. Ct., Huntington Woods, Mich., 1969-76, City of Detroit Recorders Ct., 1971-73; past mayor, councilman City of Huntington Woods. Fielding H. Yost scholar. Fellow Am. Coll. Trial Lawyers, Mich. State Bar Found.; mem. ABA, Mich. Bar Assn., Detroit Bar Assn., Oakland County Bar Assn. Republican. Presbyterian. Avocations: travel, fishing, music, gardening, sports observing. Federal civil litigation, General civil litigation, State civil litigation. Office: Kerr Russell and Weber 500 Woodward Ave Ste 2500 Detroit MI 48226-3427

**CHRISTIANSON, CHARLES ANTHONY PATRICK,** lawyer; b. N.Y.C., Oct. 29, 1965; s. Charles Linden and Mary Catherine C. BA, Dickinson Coll., 1987; JD cum laude, U. Md., 1991. Bar: Md. 1991, U.S. Dist. Ct. Md. 1992, U.S. Ct. Appeals (4th cir.) 1995. Law intern, clk. U.S. Dist. Ct., Balt., 1989; assoc. Niles, Barton & Wilmer, Balt., 1990-92; atty. Adelberg Rudden, Dorf, Hendler & Sameth, Balt., 1992—. Mem. ABA, Am. Trial Lawyers Assn., Md. Trial Lawyers Assn. Democrat. Roman Catholic. Avocations: guitar, photography, travel, theater. Product liability, Personal injury, General civil litigation. Office: Adelbert Rudon Dorf Hendler & Sameth 2 Hopkins Plz Ste 600 Baltimore MD 21201-2908

**CHRISTIANSSEN, KENNETH GORDON,** lawyer; b. Chgo., Aug. 5, 1931; s. Einar Christianssen and Ida R. (Skromme) Edisen; m. Carol Jean Bauman, June 13, 1959; children: Curt Alan, Carl Dean, Keith Eric, Karen Jean. Student, Moody Bible Inst., 1949-50; AB, Wheaton (Ill.) Coll., 1954; JD, U. Mich., 1959. Bar: Colo. 1960, U.S. Dist. Ct. Colo. 1960. Asst. trust officer Denver U.S. Nat. Bank, 1959-64; ptnr. Gorsuch Kirgis LLP, Denver, 1964—; mem. com. on probate rules and forms colo. Supreme Ct., 1974-76; lectr. legal seminars and profl. meetings on estate planning, probate and tax subjects. Author: (with others) Colorado Estate Planning, 1985; contbr. articles to legal publs. Trustee Bear Creek Evangelical Presby. Ch., Lakewood, Colo., 1972-75, chmn., 1974-75, treas., 1973-75, elder, 1973-75, 81-84, 87-89. With U.S. Army, 1954-56. Mem. Colo. Bar Assn. (past chmn. estate and trust adminstrn. com., statutory revisions com., probate coun., bd. govs.), Denver Bar Assn. (econs. of law practice com., past chmn. adv. and planning com.), Am. Coll. Probate Counsel, Denver Estate Planning Coun., Gideons Internat. (bd. dirs., treas. Lakewood chpt. 1974-77), Kiwanis. Republican. Estate planning, Probate, Estate taxation. Home: 5429 S Iris St Littleton CO 80123-7415 Office: Gorsuch Kirgis LLP 1515 Arapahoe St Denver CO 80202-3150

**CHRISTISON, WILLIAM HENRY, III,** lawyer; b. Moline, Ill., Aug. 30, 1936; s. William Henry and Gladys Evelyn (Matherly) C.; m. Mary Proctor Stone, Sept. 16, 1958; children: William Henry IV, Elizabeth S., Caroline S. BA, Northwestern U., 1958; LLB, U. Iowa, 1961. Bar: Ill., Iowa 1961. Ptnr. Baymiller, Christison & Radley, Peoria, Ill., 1961-93; panel trustee in bankruptcy U.S. Bankruptcy Ct., Cen. Dist. Ill., Peoria, 1967-96; counsel Husch & Eppenberger, Peoria, 1993—; v.p. W.H.C., Inc., Moline, 1958-86, pres., 1987-95; mem. exec. com., trustee investment com. 1st Nat. Bank, Peoria, 1967-92. Mem. Peoria Sesquicentennial Commn., 1968, Peoria Downtown Redevel. Commn., 1993-95; bd. dirs. John C. Proctor Endowment, 1964-96, pres., 1972-96; bd. dirs. Ill. Masonic Youth Found., 1976-82, Meth. Med. Ctr. Found., chmn. bd. 1987-90; bd. dirs. Meth. Med. Ctr. Ill., 1984-97, chmn., 1990-92; bd. dirs. Meth. Health Svcs. Corp., 1985-97, chmn., 1990-92; dir. Great Peoria Family YMCA, 1992-96. Mem. ABA, Ill. Bar Assn. (dist. sec. 1966), Iowa Bar Assn., Peoria Bar Assn. (dir. 1968-69), Greater Peoria Legal Aid Soc. (dir. 1971-74), Peoria Hist. Soc., Peoria Country Club (bd. dirs., sec. 1992-96), Masons (master 1970), Shriners (potentate 1984), Jesters, Rotary (pres. 1979), Phi Gamma Delta, Phi Delta Phi. Home: 7103 N Willow Bend Pt Peoria IL 61614-1190 Office: 800 Central Bldg 101 SW Adams Peoria IL 61602

**CHRISTMAN, BRUCE LEE,** lawyer; b. Bethlehem, Pa., Apr. 1, 1955; s. Raymond J. Jr. and Irene May (Bowman) C.; m. Lynn Eloise Brodt, Oct. 11, 1980; children: Jennifer Lynn, Amy Nicole. BA, Coll. William and Mary, 1977; JD, U. Pa., 1980. Bar: Va. 1980, U.S. Ct. Appeals (4th cir.) 1980, U.S. Dist. Ct. (ea. dist.) Va. 1980. Assoc. Hunton & Williams, Richmond, Va., 1980-84; prin., ptnr. Hazel & Thomas, P.C., Fairfax, Va., 1984—; adj. prof. George Mason Sch. Law; vice-chmn. bd. dirs. Luth. Social Svcs. Officer ch. coun., mem. exec. com., trustee St. Andrew Luth. Ch., Centreville, Va., 1988; mem. Leadership Fairfax Class of 1993, bd. dirs. 1997. Mem. Va. State Bar Assn., Phi Beta Kappa, Omicron Delta Kappa, Kappa Sigma. Democrat. Avocations: tennis, basketball, swimming, bicycling, camping. Real property, Banking, Finance. Home: 13610 Flintwood Pl Herndon VA 20171-3331 Office: Hazel & Thomas PC 3110 Fairview Park Dr Falls Church VA 22042-4503

**CHRISTODOULO, GEORGE EVANS,** lawyer; b. Manchester, N.H., Dec. 22, 1948; s. Pedro George and Sophie (Kyriacos) C.; m. Pamela Caragianes, May 29, 1976; children—Peter George, Thayer Sybil. A.B. cum laude, Harvard U., 1971, J.D., 1975, M.B.A., 1975. Bar: Mass. 1975. Assoc. Burns & Levinson, Boston, 1975-80; ptnr. Posternak, Blankstein & Lund, Boston, 1980-92, Burns & Levinson, 1992-97, Lawson & Weitzen, LLP, 1998—. Bd dirs. Harvard Student Agys., Cambridge, Mass., 1980—. Mem. Harvard Bus. Sch. Assn. of Boston (bd. dirs., counsel 1978—), NCCJ (bd. dirs. 1994—). Democrat. Greek Orthodox. Clubs: Harvard (Boston); Winchester Country (Mass.), Belmont Hill (Mass.). General corporate, Securities, Real property. Office: Lawson & Weitzen LLP 425 Summer St Boston MA 02210-1736

**CHRISTOF, JOSEPH S. D., II,** lawyer; b. Pitts., Apr. 7, 1948; s. Joseph S. D. and Sarah Christof; m. Martha Elizabeth Kaufman, May 3, 1975; children: Joseph III, Bradley, Peter, Laura. BA, Holy Cross U., 1970; JD, Vanderbilt U., 1974. Bar: Pa., W.Va. Law clk. to Judge H. Sorg U.S. Dist. Ct. (we. dist.) Pa., Pitts., 1974-75; lawyer Dickie, McCamey & Chilcote PC, Pitts., 1975—, shareholder, 1980—, also bd. dirs. Chmn. bd. Leetsdale (Pa.) Mcpl. Authority, 1995-96. Mem. ABA, Internat. Assn. Def. Counsel, Pa. Bar Assn., Pa. Def. Rsch. Inst. Republican. Roman Catholic. Avocations: golf, skiing, reading. Federal civil litigation. Home: 461 Maple Ln Sewickley PA 15143-1075 Office: Dickie McCamey & Chilcote 2 Ppg Pl Ste 400 Pittsburgh PA 15222-5491

**CHRISTOPHER, DANIEL ROY,** lawyer; b. Denver, Apr. 10, 1947; s. Gordon Lawrence and Rita Marie (Gaulick) C.; m. Pamela Kay Frangos, Jan. 10, 1970; children: Peter Daniel, Stacy A. BS, U. Colo., 1969; MBA, Idaho State U., 1971; JD, U. Denver, 1974. Bar: Colo. 1974, U.S. Dist. Ct. Colo. 1974, U.S. Ct. Appeals (10th cir.) 1978, U.S. Supreme Ct. 1979. Law clk. Denver Dist. Ct., 1972-73; dep. dist. atty. Office of Dist. Atty., Denver, 1974-79; spl. pros. on police corruption Alamosa, Colo., 1979; asst. U.S. atty. Denver, 1979-81; ptnr. Kennedy & Christopher, P.C., Denver, 1981—; spl. asst. atty. gen. State of Colo., 1991-99; asst. clin. prof. legal medicine U. Colo. Health Scis. Ctr., 1991—, Faculty Fed. Advs. Contbg. editor Dist. Atty. Evidence Manual, 1976; author: Risk Management for Health Care Professionals, 1992. Vol. Rep. party worker Arapahoe County Ct., 1980—; bd. dirs. U. Colo. at Denver, 1986—, Holy Ghost Ch. Foodline for the Homeless, 1997—. Recipient Am. Jurisprudence awrad 1974. Mem. ABA, Colo. Bar Assn., Colo. Def. Lawyers Assn. (pres. 1995), Denver Bar Assn., Def. Rsch. Inst., Cath. Lawyers Guild, Am. Health Lawyer's Assn., U. Colo. Alumni Assn. (bd. dirs. 1989—), Faculty Fed. Advocates. Roman Catholic. Administrative and regulatory, Federal civil litigation, General civil litigation. Home: 5670 Big Canon Dr Greenwood Village CO 80111-3512 Office: Kennedy & Christopher PC 1660 Wynkoop St Ste 900 Denver CO 80202-1197

**CHRISTOPHER, JOHN ANTHONY,** lawyer; b. Everett, Mass., Jan. 10, 1947; s. Anthony Domenic and Madeline Catherine (Kehoe) C.; m. Lynne Christie Olsen, June 28, 1980; children: Alyson Madeline, Loren Elizabeth. BA in Math., U. Maine, 1970; JD cum laude, Suffolk U., 1976. Bar: Mass. 1977, U.S. Dist. Ct. 1977. Pub. defender Essex Defenders, Lynn, Mass., 1977-78; asst. dist. atty. Essex Dist. Atty. Office, Salem, Mass., 1978-79; assoc. Ankeles, Harmon & Bonfanti, Peabody, Mass., 1979-83; sole practice Peabody, Mass., 1984-86; ptnr. Decoulos & Spitzer, Peabody, Mass., 1986-87, Spitzer, Christopher, Gelineau & Arvanites, Salem, Mass., 1987-94, Spitzer, Christopher & Arvanites, Danvers, Mass., 1994—. Chmn. Danvers (Mass.) Hist. Dist. Commn., 1987—, Groveland (Mass.) Zoning Bd. Appeals, 1991—. Fellow Mass. Bar Found.; mem. Mass. Bar Assn. Avocations: jogging, skiing. General civil litigation, Criminal, Municipal (including bonds). Home: 17 Coleman Rd Groveland MA 01834-1000 Office: Spitzer Christopher & Arvanites 1990 Rosewood Dr Ste 350 Danvers MA 01923-1388

**CHRISTOPHER, THOMAS VAN,** lawyer; b. Portsmouth, Va., Feb. 17, 1970; s. A.D. and Sue (Estes) C. BA, U. Calif., Riverside, 1993; JD, U. Calif., Berkeley, 1996. Bar: Calif. 1996. Assoc. Skadden, Arps, Slate Meagher & Flom, San Francisco, 1996—. Vol. San Francisco Opera, 1993-96. General civil litigation, Securities. Office: Skadden Arps Slate et al 4 Embarcadero Ctr San Francisco CA 94111-4106

**CHRISTOPHER, TRACY ELIZABETH KEE,** judge; b. Kansas City, Mo., July 17, 1956; d. James Jefferson and Ruth Anne (Brunton) Kee; m. C. Vance Christopher, May 30, 1981; children: Sarah, Julia, Jeffrey. BA in Econs. with honors, U. Notre Dame, 1978; JD with honors, U. Tex., 1981. Bar: Tex. 1981, U.S. Ct. Appeals (5th cir.) 1982, U.S. Dist. Ct. (so. dist.) Tex. 1992; cert. in civil trial law and personal injury trial law Tex. Bd. Legal Specialization. Assoc. Vinson & Elkins, Houston, 1981-86; of counsel Susman Godfrey, Houston, 1986-94; judge 295th Dist. Ct., Houston, 1994—. Contbr. articles to legal jours. Leader Girl Scouts U.s., Houston, 1990-93, 94—. Fellow Tex. Bar Found., Houston Bar Found.; mem. Coll. of State Bar Tex., Tex. Assn. Civil Trial and Appellate Specialists. Republican. Roman Catholic. Office: 295th Dist Ct 301 Fannin St Houston TX 77002-2066

**CHRISTOPHER, WILLIAM GARTH,** lawyer; b. Beaumont, Tex., Oct. 14, 1940; s. Garth Daugherty and Ollye Mittie (Harkness) C.; m. Kathleen S. Christopher; children: John William, David Noah, Michael O'Hara. BS in Engring., U.S. Mil. Acad., 1962; JD, U. Va., 1970. Bar: Va. 1970, D.C. 1970, U.S. Supreme Ct. 1975, Mich. 1977, Fla. 1988, Tex. 1989. Assoc. Steptoe & Johnson, Washington, 1970-77; ptnr. Honigman Miller Schwartz & Cohn, Detroit, 1977-94, Holland & Knight, Tampa, Fla., 1994-95, Brown Clark, P.A., Sarasota, Fla., 1995—. Contbr. articles to legal publ. Pres. Birmingham (Mich.) Hockey Assn., 1982-84; mem. Episc. Diocese of Mich. Commn. on Ministry, 1983-88, co-chmn. 1987-88, standing com., 1988. Capt. C.E. U.S. Army, 1962-67. Mem. ABA, Va. Bar, D.C. Bar, Fla. Bar (cert. bus. litigation law), Tex. Bar, Sarasota County Bar Assn., Raven Soc., Nat. Bd. of Trial Advocacy (cert. civil trail advocacy), Order of Coif, Phi Delta Phi. Episcopalian. General civil litigation, Contracts commercial, Construction. Office: Brown Clark PA 1819 Main St Ste 1100 Sarasota FL 34236-5999

**CHRISTOPHERSON, JAMES A.,** lawyer; b. Petoskey, Mich., July 22, 1956; s. Arthur Jacob and Ruth Doris Christophenson; m. Lauri M. Christophenson, Aug. 24, 1984; children: Matthew Richard, Alison Ruth. BA magna cum laude, Mich. State U., 1977; JD cum laude, Wayne State U., 1980. Bar: Mich., U.S. Dist. Ct. (we. dist.) Mich., U.S. Ct. Appeals (6th cir.). Atty. Dingeman, Dancer & Christopherson, Traverse City, Mich. Mem. County Treas. Sec. Assn. (pres. 1991). Health. Office: Dingeman Dancer and Christopherson 100 Park St Traverse City MI 49684-2511

**CHRISTOPHILLIS, CONSTANTINE S.,** lawyer; b. Greenville, S.C., Nov. 27, 1953; s. Gus and Fofo (Stamati) C.; m. Catherine Lynn Carr, May 14, 1978; children: Tina, Cory, Anna Kate. BA, Wofford Coll., 1975; JD, U. S.C., 1977. Bar: S.C. 1978, U.S. Dist. Ct. S.C. 1978, U.S. Ct. Appeals (4th cir.) 1981. Ptnr. Christophillis Law Offices, Greenville, 1978-88; shareholder Culbertson & Christophillis, Greenville, 1988—. Mem. ABA, S.C. Bar Assn., Greenville County Bar Assn., S.C. Trial Lawyers Assn., Nat. Orgn. Social Security Claimants Reps., Assn. S.C. Claimant Attys. for Workers Compensation, Rotary (bd. dirs. Greenville, Paul Harris fellow 1996). General civil litigation, Personal injury, Workers' compensation. Office:

Culbertson & Christophillis 1615 Wade Hampton Blvd Greenville SC 29609-5049

**CHRISTOVICH, ALVIN RICHARD, JR.,** lawyer, partner; b. New Orleans, Mar. 30, 1921; s. Alvin Richard Christovich and Elyria Kearney; m. Jane Elizabeth Pope, Dec. 7, 1943; children: Richard, David. BA, Tulane U., 1942, LLB, 1947. Ptnr. Christovich & Kearney, New Orleans, 1947—. 1st lt. U.S. Army Air Corps, 1943-45, Eng. Mem. Internat. Assn. Def. Counsel (former exec. com.), Def. Rsch. Inst. (former v.p., adminstrn.), La. State Bar Assn. (former bd. govs.), New Orleans Bar Assn. (former pres.), New Orleans Country Club, Pickwick Club. Roman Catholic. Avocation: second home in Jackson, Wyoming. Personal injury, General civil litigation, Product liability. Office: Christovich & Kearney 601 Poydras St Ste 2300 New Orleans LA 70130-6078

**CHRISTY, CYNTHIA ULLEM,** lawyer; b. Des Moines, July 9, 1969; d. Benjamin Brandon and Martha (Sands) Ullem; m. Geoffrey Robert Christy, Aug. 27, 1994. BA, DePauw U., Greencastle, Ind., 1991; JD, Drake U., 1997. Bar: Colo. 1997. Legis. aide U.S. Senator Charles E. Grassley, Washington, 1991-94; assoc. Holland & Hart LLP, Denver, 1997—. Mem. com. Campaign Drake--The Law Sch., Des Moines, 1997—; tutor Denver Pub. Schs., 1997—. Mem. Colo. Bar Assn., Denver Bar Assn., Colo. Women's Bar Assn. General corporate, Real property. Office: Holland & Hart LLP 555 17th St Ste 3200 Denver CO 80202-3950

**CHU, HAROLD,** lawyer; b. Pine Bluff, Ark., Dec. 12, 1947; s. Yen and Lum (Ying) C.; m. Faye Watanabe, Aug. 27, 1972 (div. 1981); 1 child, Laura Yukiko. BA in Psychology with honors, Stanford U., 1971; JD, Northwestern U., 1974. Bar: Hawaii 1975, U.S. Ct. Appeals (9th cir.) 1975, U.S. Supreme Ct. 1979; lic. real estate broker. Assoc. Law Offices of Kenneth S. Robbins, Honolulu, 1975-78; ptnr. Robbins, Chu & Reilly, Honolulu, 1978-80; pvt. practice Honolulu, 1980—; lectr. Kapioluni Community Coll. Paralegal Program, Honolulu, 1980—; mem. Ct. Arbitration Program, Honolulu, 1987-90. Mem. rules com. Dem. party, Honlulu, 1990; mem. Hawaii State Disciplinary Coun., Honolulu, 1988-90; mem. Com. for Unauthorized Practice Law, Honolulu, 1977-79; del. State Jud. Coun., Honolulu, 1989-90. Mem. ABA (litigation sect., real property, probate and trust law sect.), Nat. Assn. Realtors, Hawaii Assn. Realtors, Hawaii State Bar Assn. (publs. com. 1980-82). Avocations: photography, tennis, reading, theater. E-mail: HaroldC@worldnet.att.net. Real property, General civil litigation, Contracts commercial. Office: Pacific Tower 1001 Bishop St Ste 1570 Honolulu HI 96813-3407

**CHUBB, JANET L.,** lawyer; b. Bremerton, Wash., Feb. 27, 1943; m. Gary Silverman; children: David, Aaron, Noah, Leah. BA, La Sierra Coll., 1964; JD, Loyola U., L.A., 1967. Bar: Calif. 1968; U.S. Dist. Ct. (cen. and no. dists.) Calif.; U.S. Dist. Ct. Nev. 1980, U.S. Ct. Appeals (9th cir.) 1975; cert. in consumer and bus. law Am. Bd. of Cert. Law clk. L.A. County Superior Ct., L.A., 1968-71; dep. atty. gen. State of Calif., 1971-74; city atty. Winnemucca, Nev., 1974-75; ptnr. Chubb & Silverman, Reno, 1975-82, Janet L. Chubb & Assocs., Reno, 1982-89, Jones Vargas (formerly Jones, Jones, Close & Brown), Reno, 1989—; lawyer rep. 9th Cir. Conf., San Francisco, 1990-93; expert witness various state cts.; settlement judge Nev. Supreme Ct., 1997—. Contbr. articles to profl. jours. Pres. Sparks (Nev.) YMCA, 1979-80; law adv. counsel Old Coll., 1981-86; bd. dirs. Boys and Girls Club of Truckee Meadows, 1993-98. Named one of Best Lawyers in Am., 1992. Fellow Am. Bar Found.; mem. ABA, No. Nev. Women Laywers (pres. 1990-91), Reno Bd. Realtors, State Bar of Nev. (bd. govs. 1979-91, chair bankruptcy sect. 1995-97), ), Nev. Law Fedn. (trustee 1982-90), Washoe County Bar Assn., Am. Bankruptcy Inst., No. Nev. Bankruptcy Bar Assn. (pres. 1995-99), others. Bankruptcy, Consumer commercial. Home: 2225 Thomas Jefferson Dr Reno NV 89509-3056 Office: Jones Vargas PO Box 281 100 W Liberty St # 12 Reno NV 89504-0281 also: Jones Jones Close & Brown Chartered 3773 Howard Hughes Pkwy Fl 3 Las Vegas NV 89109-0949

**CHUCK, WALTER G(OONSUN),** lawyer; b. Wailuku, Maui, Hawaii, Sept. 10, 1920; s. Hong Yee and Aoe (Ting) C.; m. Marian Chun, Sept. 11, 1943; children: Jamie Allison, Walter Gregory, Meredith Jayne. Ed.B., U. Hawaii, 1941; J.D., Harvard U., 1948. Bar: Hawaii 1948. Navy auditor Pearl Harbor, 1941; field agt. Social Security Bd., 1942; labor law insp. Terr. Dept. Labor, 1943; law clk. firm Ropes, Gray, Best, Coolidge & Rugg, 1948; asst. pub. prosecutor City and County of Honolulu, 1949; with Fong, Miho & Choy, 1950-53; ptnr. Fong, Miho, Choy & Chuck, 1953-58; pvt. practice law Honolulu, 1958-65, 78-80; ptnr. Chuck & Fujiyama, Honolulu, 1965-74; ptnr. firm Chuck, Wong & Tonaki, Honolulu, 1974-76, Chuck & Pai, Honolulu, 1976-78; pres. Walter G. Chuck Law Corp., Honolulu, 1980-94; pvt. practice Honolulu, 1994—; dist. magistrate Dist. Ct. Honolulu, 1956-63; gen. ptnr. M & W Assocs., Kapalama Investment Co.; bd. dirs. Aloha Airlines, Inc., Honolulu Painting Co., Ltd. Chmn. Hawaii Employment Rels. Bd., 1955-59; bd. dirs. Nat. Assn. State Labor Rels. Bds., 1957-58, Honolulu Theatre for Youth, 1977-80; chief clk. Hawaii Ho. of Reps., 1951, 53, Hawaii Senate, 1959-61; govt. appeal agt. SSS, 1953-72; former mem. jud. coun. State of Hawaii; mem. exec. com. Hawaiian Open; former dir. Friends of Judiciary History Ctr. Inc., 1983-94; former mem. bd. dirs. YMCA. Capt. inf. Hawaii Terr. Guard. Recipient Ha'Aheo award for cmty. svc. Hawaii chpt. Am. Bd. Trial Advocates, 1995. Fellow Internat. Acad. Trial Lawyers (founder, dean, bd. dirs., state rep.), Am. Coll. Trial Lawyers; mem. ABA (former chmn. Hawaii sr. lawyers divsn., former mem. ho. of dels.), Hawaii Bar Assn. (pres. 1963), ATLA (former editor), U. Hawaii Alumni Assn. (Disting. Svc. award 1967, former dir., bd. govs.), Law Sci. Inst., Assoc. Students U. Hawaii (pres.), Am. Judicature Soc., Internat. Soc. Barristers, Am. Inst. Banking, Chinese C. of C., U. Hawaii Founders Alumni Assn. (v.p., bd. dirs., Lifetime Achievement award 1994), Harvard Club of Hawaii, Waialae Country Club (pres. 1975), Oahu Country Club. Republican. Federal civil litigation, State civil litigation, General practice. Home: 2691 Aaliamanu Pl Honolulu HI 96813-1216 Office: Pacific Tower 1001 Bishop St Ste 2750 Honolulu HI 96813-3410

**CHUDLEIGH, G. STEPHEN,** lawyer; b. Houston, Dec. 15, 1951; s. James Painter and Mary Lillian Chudleigh; m. Anna Marie Saldana, Oct. 29, 1977; children: Sky, Sabina, Dylan, Alexis. BA, U. Tex., 1973; JD, U. Houston, 1988. Bar: Tex. 1988, U.S. Dist. Ct. (so. dist.) Tex. 1989. Real estate broker Temple, Tex., 1980-85; pvt. practice law Friendswood, Tex., 1988-93, Pasadena, Tex., 1993-97, League City, Tex., 1997—. Founding mem. League City C. of C. and Bus. Assn., 1997. Mem. ATLA, Tex. Bar Assn., Tex. Real Estate Commn. Roman Catholic. Avocation: soccer coach. General civil litigation, Family and matrimonial, Real property. Home: 2002 Sunny Bay Ct League City TX 77573-6964 Office: 608A W Main St League City TX 77573-3760

**CHUDZINSKI, MARK ADAM,** lawyer; b. Chgo., Oct. 13, 1956; s. Brunon and Maria (Chmielinski) C.; m. Barbara Podkul, July 31, 1993; 1 child, Anna. BA, Northwestern U., 1977, MBA, 1981, JD, 1981; Diplome d'Etudes Approfondies, U. Paris, 1982. Bar: N.Y. 1982, Ill. 1990, U.S. Supreme Ct. 1994. Assoc. Coudert Bros., N.Y.C., 1982-85, London, 1985-88, Sydney, Australia, 1988-89; sr. assoc. Winston & Strawn, Chgo., 1990-95, ptnr., 1995-96; gen. counsel Ameritech Internat., 1996—. Articles editor Northwestern Jour. Internat. Law and Bus., 1981. Trustee Window To The World Comm., Inc. (Stas. WTTW-TV and WFMT-FM), Chgo.; mem. adv. bd. Sta. WBEZ-FM, Chgo.; bd. dirs. Chgo. Legal Clinic, Inc., Polish Mus. Am., 1991-98, Polish Am. Congress, 1992-96. Austin scholar 1978; fellow Leadership Greater Chgo., 1990; U.S. Champ Jessup Moot Ct., 1979. Mem. ABA, N.Y. State Bar Assn., Am. Soc. Internat. Law, French-Am. C. of C., German-Am. C. of C., U.S.-Poland C. of C. (founder, chmn. 1991-95). Roman Catholic. General corporate, Private international, Communications. Home: 6005 N Oconto Ave Chicago IL 60631-3620 Office: Ameritech Internat 225 W Randolph St Fl 18 Chicago IL 60606-1824

**CHUMAN, FRANK FUJIO,** lawyer; b. Montecito, Calif., Apr. 29, 1917; s. Hitsuji Henry and Kiyo (Yamamoto) C.; m. Ruby Ryoko Dewa, June 22, 1948 (div. Oct. 1968); children: Daniel Christopher, Paul Randolph; m. Donna Daungvipar Karschamroon, Apr. 17, 1983; children Diana, Daniel, Paul. BA in Polit. Sci., UCLA, 1938; postgrad., U. So. Calif., 1940-42, U. Toledo, 1943-44; JD, U. Md., 1945. Bar: Md. 1945, Calif. 1947. Clk. with probation dept. County of Los Angeles, 1939-42; adminstr. Base Hosp., Manzanar, Calif., 1942-43; acct. Goodyear Tire and Rubber Co., Balt., 1945; sole practice Los Angeles, 1947—; ptnr. Chuman and McKibbin, L.A., 1950-68; judge pro tem L.A. Mcpl. Ct., 1968-83; arbitrator Los Angeles County Superior Ct., 1968-83; judge pro tem Los Angeles Dist. Mcpl. Ct., 1968-83; gen. ptnr. Japanese Village Plaza Shopping Ctr., Los Angeles, 1976-85; chmn. Founders Savs. and Loan; pres., CEO Chuman Internat. Author: "Bamboo People" Law and Japanese Americans, 1976. Mem. Japanese Am. Citizens League (nat. pres. 1960-62); bd. dirs. Chuman Found. Recipient Bishop's Merit award Episc. Diocese of Los Angeles, 1963, Disting. Svc. award UCLA Alumni Assn., 1963, Eagle Scout award Boy Scouts Am. 1939, Silver Beavers award, 1974, Disting. Svc. award Govt. Japan, 1977, Disting. Eagle Scout award, 1979. Mem. ABA, Japanese Am. Bar Assn., Assn. Immigration Lawyers (chmn. Los Angeles chpt. 1958-59). Avocations: golf, music. Immigration, naturalization, and customs, General corporate.

**CHUNG, ERIC C.,** lawyer, associate; b. Toronto, Ont., Can., Dec. 23, 1971; s. Yin Ho and Gina Chung. BA in Adminstrv. and Comml. Studies, U. We. Ont., London, 1993; JD, Vanderbilt U., 1996. Bar: Mo. Assoc. Bryan Cave LLP, St. Louis, 1996—. Mem. ABA, Bar Assn. Met. St. Louis, Metropolis St. Louis. Avocations: running, weight lifting, martial arts, kick boxing, motorcycles. Real property, Construction. Office: Bryan Cave LLP 211 N Broadway Ste 3600 Saint Louis MO 63102-2733

**CHURCH, GLENN J.,** lawyer; b. Grand Island, Nebr., Aug. 20, 1932; s. Glenn Jennings and Rachel Frances (Cochran) C.; m. Mary L. Church; children: Susan Jo, Zackary William. AB, U. Ill., 1954, JD, 1959. Bar: Ill. 1959, U.S. Dist. Ct. (cen. dist.) Ill. 1960, U.S. Ct Appeals (7th cir.) 1967, U.S. Supreme Ct. 1971, Ohio 1983. Assoc. Kavanaugh, Bond, Scully, Sudow & White, Peoria, Ill., 1959-62; ptnr. Smith & Church, Peoria, 1962-64, Smith, Whitney & Church, Peoria, 1964-65; pvt. practice Peoria, 1965-88, Columbus, Ohio, 1988—; spl. asst. atty. gen. water pollution div. State of Ill., 1960-61; hearing officer Am. Arbitration Assn., Chgo., 1966—; mem. Ill. Fair Employment Practice Commn., 1974-79. Liasion officer Air Force Acad., Colorado Springs, Colo., 1968-82; bd. dirs. W.D. Boyce council Boy Scouts Am., 1970-86, Heart of Ill. Fair and Exposition Gardens, Peoria, 1978-84; exec. bd. chmn. eagle rev. com. Boy Scouts Am. , Peoria, 1977-86. Served to lt. col. USAF, 1954-82. Mem. Ill. Bar Assn., Ohio Bar Assn., Peoria Bar Assn., Assn. Trial Lawyers Am., Phi Alpha Delta. Republican. Methodist. Lodge: Sertoma. Personal injury, Workers' compensation, Family and matrimonial. Home and Office: 665 Heather Stone Dr Merritt Island FL 32953-4341

**CHURCH, RANDOLPH WARNER, JR.,** lawyer; b. Richmond, Va., Nov. 6, 1934; s. Randolph Warner and Elizabeth Lewis (Gochnauer) C.; m. Lucy Ann Canary, July 4, 1970; children: Leslie R. Pennell, L. Weeks Kerr. BA with honors, U. Va., 1957, LLB, 1960. Bar: Va. 1960, U.S. Dist. Ct. (ea. dist.) Va. 1962, U.S. Ct. Appeals (4th cir.) 1981. Assoc. McCandlish, Lillard & Marsh, Fairfax, Va., 1960-63; ptnr. McCandlish, Lillard, Rust & Church, Fairfax, 1963-75; city atty. Fairfax, 1968-72; mng. ptnr. McCandlish, Lillard, Rust & Church, Fairfax, 1975-83; mng. ptnr. Hunton & Williams, Fairfax, 1984—, mem. exec. com., 1988-94; bd. dirs. George Mason Bank, George Mason Bankshares, Inc., George Mason Mortgage Co., 1991-98, Va. Found. for Rsch. and Econ. Edn., Inc., 1994—. Author: Appellate Civil Litigation, 1984; panelist: Lawyer Professionalism: Is Change in Order? 1988, Marketing Legal Services: What's Hot and What's Not, 1990. Active Fairfax Com. of 100, 1988—, bd. dirs., 1989-92; bd. visitors George Mason U., Fairfax, 1982-90, rector, 1983-86; bd. dirs. George Mason Fund for Arts, 1987-96, Fairfax Symphony, 1991—, gen. counsel, exec. com., 1996—; bd. dirs. Va. Found. for Humanities and Pub. Policy, 1999; vice pres., exec. com. Va. Found. for Rsch. and Econ. Edn., 1996—; lectr., author Va. Continuing Edn. Program Appellate Litigation, 1985, Equity Practice, 1987-90; panelist Va. Continuing Edn. Programs; trustee George Mason U. Edn. Found., 1986-95, trustee emeritus, 1995—. Fellow Va. Law Found., Am. Bar Found.; mem. ABA, Am. Judicature Soc., Va. Bar Assn. (v.p. 1975), Tower Club, Country Club Fairfax County, U. Va. Club, Phi Beta Kappa. Episcopalian. General corporate, State civil litigation. Home: 5114 Forsgate Pl Fairfax VA 22030-4507 Office: Hunton & Williams 1751 Pinnacle Dr Ste 1700 Mc Lean VA 22102-3836

**CHURCH, SANFORD ALLAN,** lawyer; b. Albion, N.Y., June 18, 1958; s. Sanford L. and Joyce E. Church; m. Diane Katz. BA in History, Wake Forest U., 1980; JD, Duke U., 1984. Asst. dist. atty. Orleans County, Albion, 1985, 89-97, pub. defender, 1997—; ptnr. Church & Church, Albion, 1989—. Mem. Orleans County Bar Assn. (pres. 1997—), Rotary Club of Albion (pres. 1997-98). Family and matrimonial, Criminal, Real property. Office: Church & Church 3 E Bank St Albion NY 14411-1209

**CHURCHILL, ALLEN DELOS,** lawyer; b. Sioux Falls, S.D., June 5, 1921; s. Edward Delos and Iva Edna (Allen) C.; m. Melva Fein, Jan. 16, 1925; 1 child, Victoria Ann. BA, Washington U., St. Louis, 1948, JD, 1950. Bar: Mo. 1950, U.S. Dist. Ct. (ea. dist.) Mo. 1950, Ill. 1965, U.S. Dist. Ct. (so. and cen. dists.) Ill. 1965, U.S. Ct. Appeals (7th cir.) 1974. Trial atty. Mo. Pacific R.R., St. Louis, 1950-62; solo practice, St. Louis, 1962-65, Belleville, Ill., 1965-77; ptnr. Dunham, Boman, Leskera & Churchill, Belleville, 1967-77, Churchill, Nester & McDonnell, Belleville, 1977-85, Churchill & McDonnell, 1985-90, Churchill, McDonnell & Hatch, 1990-97, Brown & Assocs., Belleville, 1997—. Served with U.S. Army AC, 1942-45. Fellow Internat. Soc. Barristers, Am. Coll. Trial Lawyers, Ill. Bar Found., Am. Bd. Trial Advs. (adv.); mem. Ill. State Bar Assn., Mo. Bar Assn., St. Louis Met. Bar Assn., St. Clair (Ill.) County Bar Assn. (pres. 1974-75), Media Club. Federal civil litigation, General civil litigation, State civil litigation. Office: 5520 W Main St Belleville IL 62226-4736

**CHURCHILL, JAMES PAUL,** federal judge; b. Imlay City, Mich., Apr. 10, 1924; s. Howard and Faye (Shurte) C.; m. Ann Muir, Aug. 30, 1950; children: Nancy Ann Churchill Nyquist, David James, Sally Jo. BA, U. Mich., 1947, JD, 1950. Bar: Mich. Pvt. practice law Vassar, Mich., 1950-65; judge 40th Jud. Cir. Mich., 1965-74, U.S. Dist. Ct. (ea. dist.) Mich., Detroit, 1974—; now sr. judge; ct. commr. Tuscola County Cir., 1963-65; adj. prof. Detroit Coll. Law, 1980-81. Served with U.S. Army, 1943-46. Mem. Fed. Judges Assn., Fed. Bar Assn., 40th Jud. Cir. Bar Assn. Office: PO Box 913 Bay City MI 48707

**CHURCHILL, SALLY JO,** lawyer; b. Saginaw, Mich., Oct. 29, 1955; d. James P. and Annabel I. (Muir) C.; m. Edward L. Kulka, Jan. 14, 1989. B of Gen. Studies, U. Mich., 1977; MA, Tufts U., 1980; JD, U. Mich., 1987. Bar: Mich. 1987. Resource specialist Ecological Rsch. Svcs. Inc., Iron River, Mich., 1980-82; rsch. specialist Mich. United Conservation Clubs, Lansing, Mich., 1986; asst. atty. gen. Office of Atty. Gen., Lansing, Mich., 1987-91; atty. Rosi, Olson & Levine, Traverse City, Mich., 1991-92; land protection specialist Little Traverse Conservancy, Harbor Springs, Mich., 1992-93; assoc. Honigman, Miller, Schwartz & Cohn, 1993-94; ptnr. Honigman Miller Schwartz & Cohn, Detroit, 1994-96; univ. atty. U. Mich., Ann Arbor, 1996—; spkr. in field. Mem. State Bar of Mich. (mem. environ. law sect., chair environ. law sect. 1996-97). Office: U Mich Office of Gen Counsel 4010 Fleming Adminstrn Bldg Ann Arbor MI 48109-1340

**CIACCIO, KARIN MCLAUGHLIN,** lawyer; b. Galesburg, Ill., Feb. 9, 1947; d. Cleo Edward and Kathryn Louise (Payton) McLaughlin; m. Frederick Steven Ciaccio, May 4, 1968; children: John, Jennifer. BS, So. Ill. U., 1969; postgrad., Temple U. Law Sch., 1971-72; JD, DePaul U., 1975. Bar: Ill. 1975, U.S. Dist. Ct. (no. dist.) Ill. 1975. Tchr. French Sherrard (Ill.) High Sch., 1969-70; prof. law U. Wis., Racine, 1975, Coll. DuPage, Glen Ellyn, Ill., 1976; sole practice Chgo. and Lombard, Ill., 1975-80, Galesburg and Woodhull, Ill., 1980-90, 96-98; internat. rels. Galesburg and Woodhull, 1990-93; deputy city attorney City of Moline, Ill., 1993-96; real estate attorney U.S. Army Corps. of Engrs., Rock Island, Ill., 1998—; lectr. on consumer law, various orgns., 1976—; city atty. Woodhull, 1983—. Ofcl. Lombard Zoning Bd., 1978-80; mem. Alpha (Ill.) Cemetary Bd., 1980—, St. John's Cemetery Bd., Woodhull, 1983—; legis. chmn. Rep. Women Henry County, 1981-83; bd. dirs. Alwood Bus. Assn., 1984-86, People to People and Japanese Internat. bd. rels., Japan, 1990-92; v.p. AlWood Music Boosters, 1987—. Mem. ABA, Ill. Bar Assn., Henry County Bar Assn., Ninth Jud. Circuit Women's Bar Assn., Phi Alpha Delta. Lodge: Altrusa. Avocation: photography. General practice, Probate, Real property. Office: 147 S Division St Woodhull IL 61490-9329

**CIAMPA, JEFFREY NELSON,** lawyer; b. Detroit, June 7, 1967; s. Nelson Joseph Ciampa and Dolores Mary Heilig. BA in Internat. Bus., U. Mich., 1989; JD cum laude, Wayne State U., 1992; LLM in Corp. Law and Fin., NYU, 1995. Bar: Mich. 1992, N.Y. 1995. Atty. in pvt. practice Mich. and N.Y., 1992-97; corp. counsel Compuware Corp., Farmington Hills, Mich., 1997—. Mergers and acquisitions, General corporate, Contracts commercial. Home: 32005 W 12 Mile Rd Unit 311 Farmington Hills MI 48334-3647 Office: Compuware Corp 31440 Northwestern Hwy Farmington Hills MI 48334-2564

**CICALA, CONTE CARMELO,** lawyer; b. Washington, Sept. 6, 1968; s. Carmelo Orazio Cicala and Nancy Gunther Snyder; m. Angele Kieran Taormino, June 27, 1998. BA in English, Yale U., 1990; JD, Tulane U., 1994. Bar: Calif. 1994, U.S. Dist. Ct. (no. dist.) Calif., 1994, U.S. Dist. Ct. Hawaii 1995, U.S. Ct. Appeals (9th cir.) 1996, U.S. Dist. Ct. (ctrl. dist.) Calif. 1998. Assoc. Flynn, Delich & Wise, San Francisco, 1995—. Capt. USAR, 1990—. Recipient Svc. award Disabled Am. Vets., Conn., 1990. Mem. Bar Assn. San Francisco. Admiralty, General civil litigation, Transportation. Office: Flynn Delich & Wise 1 California St Ste 350 San Francisco CA 94111-5405

**CICCARELLO, ARTHUR T.,** lawyer; b. Charleston, W. Va., June 7, 1930; s. Joseph Daniel and Carmen Marie (Pacilio) C.; m. Doris Rozala Pauley, Dec. 25, 1951; children: Beverly, Julia, Joseph III. Student, U. Va., 1947-50; LLB, W. Va. U., 1955. Bar: W. Va. Lawyer Legal Aid Soc., Charleston, W. Va., 1955-56; ins. com. counsel State of W. Va., Charleston, 1961; asst. prosecuting atty. Kanawa County, Charelston, 1961-63. 1st lt. USAF, 1951-53. Democrat. Roman Catholic. Criminal, Personal injury, General civil litigation. Office: Cicarello Del Guidice & La Fan 1219 Virginia St E Charleston WV 25301-2912

**CICCHETTI, TAMMY DESOTO,** lawyer. BA in English Lit., Fla. State U., Tallahassee, 1988, JD, 1991. Bar: Fla. 1991, U.S. Dist. Ct. (no. dist.) Fla. Assoc. Callahan, Dobbins & Derr, Tallahassee, 1991-94; ptnr. Callahan & Cicchetti, P.A., Tallahassee, 1994-97; founder Cicchetti Law Firm, Tallahassee, 1997—. Bd. dirs. Big Bros. and Big Sisters of the Big Bend, Tiger Shark's Charities of the Tallahassee Tiger Sharks Hockey Club. Mem. ABA, Tallahassee Bar Assn., Fla. Bar, Tallahassee Women Lawyers Assn., Def. Rsch. and Trial Lawyer Assn., Fla. Def. Lawyers Assn., Nat. Assn. for Women in Constrn., Tallahassee Builders Assn., Tallahassee Zonta Club, Gold Key, Phi Eta Sigma. Construction. Office: 1435 Piedmont Dr E Ste 210 Tallahassee FL 32312-2938

**CICCONI, CHRISTOPHER M.,** lawyer; b. Anaheim, Calif., Aug. 19, 1949; s. Samuel A. and Ercilia (Silva) C.; m. Cynthia Anne June 20, 1981; children: Christina Michelle, Kelly Melissa. BA in Comm. Arts, U. Notre Dame, 1971; JD, Villanova U., 1974; LLM in Taxation, Temple U., 1978. Bar: Pa., U.S. Dist. Ct. (ea. and mid. dists.) Pa., U.S. Ct. Appeals (3d dist.), U.S. Tax Ct., U.S. Supreme Ct. Assoc. Rocap, Rocap & Guinta, Media, Pa., 1974-77; 1st asst. pub. defender Pub. Defender's Office of Delaware County, Media, 1977-78; ptnr. Hepford Zimmerman & Swartz, Harrisburg, Pa., 1978-90; mng. ptnr. Hepford Zimmerman & Swartz, Harrisburg, 1985-90; atty., mem. Eckert Seamans Cherin & Mellott, Harrisburg, 1990—; chairperson corp. dept., 1999—; bd. dirs. York Saw & Knife Co., Inc., dBi Labs., Inc., Harrisburg, Ollie's Bargain Outlets, Inc., Harrisburg; instr. Coll. Med., Pa. State U., 1992-98.$dtr. Coll. Med., Pa. State U., 1992-98. Author, editor: Buying and Selling a Business, 1998. Mem., chair Zoning Hearing Bd., Derry Twp., Pa., 1984-89; mem. Preservation of Hershey Com., Derry Twp., 1987-88. Recipient Cmty. Achievement award Derry Twp., 1989, award of yr. Notre Dame Alumni Assn., 1995. Mem. Pa. Bar Assn. (chair legal affairs of older persons com. 1986-88, arbitrator dispute resolution com. 1988—), Dauphin County Bar Assn., Estate Planning Coun. Ctrl. Pa., Sorin Soc. of U. Notre Dame. Avocations: playing piano, wine collecting, travel, golf. Mergers and acquisitions, Finance, Estate planning. Home: 1045 Fairdell Dr Hummelstown PA 17036-8710 Office: Eckert Seamans et al 213 Market St Harrisburg PA 17101-2132

**CICCONI, JAMES WILLIAM,** lawyer; b. Elmira, N.Y., June 8, 1952; s. Raymond Joseph and Doris Arlene (Strong) C.; m. Patricia Olivia Burgess, Aug. 10, 1974; children: Jill, Sara, Rachel. BA, U. Tex., 1974, JD, 1977. Bar: Tex. 1977, D.C. 1985. Issues dir. Jim Baker for Atty. Gen. campaign, Austin, Tex., 1977-78; adminstrv. asst. to the gov. State of Tex., Austin, 1979-80, gen. counsel to the sec. of state, 1980-81; spl. asst. to the pres., to the chief of staff The White House, Washington, 1981-85; sr. issues advisor Bush-Quayle '88 campaign, Washington, 1987-88; asst. to the pres., dep. to the chief of staff The White House, Washington, 1989-90; atty. Akin Gump Strauss Hauer & Feld, Washington, 1985-88, 91—, ptnr., 1991—; gen. counsel, exec. v.p. law and govt. affairs AT&T, N.Y.C., 1998—; bd. dirs. Found. for Nat. Archives, Washington, Tex. Pub. Policy Found., San Antonio; issues dir. Bush-Quayle '92 Campaign; dep. dir. strategy Dole-Kemp '96 Campaign; dir. El Paso Electric Co., Am. Coun. Germany; cons. U.S. State Dept. V.p. George Bush Presdl. Libr. Found., College Station, Tex., 1991—; legal adv. bd. Defenders of Property Rights, Washington; del. Conf. Security Cooperation Europe (CSCE); mem. Adminstrv. Conf. U.S., U.S. Reform Observation Panel for UNESCO. Mem. D.C. Bar Assn., State Bar Tex. Republican. Roman Catholic. Avocations: baseball, tennis. Administrative and regulatory. Office: AT&T 32 Ave of the Americas New York NY 10013*

**CICET, DONALD JAMES,** lawyer; b. New Orleans, May 24, 1940; s. Arthur Alphonse and Myrtle (Ress) C.; m. Iona Perry. BA, Nicholls State U., 1963; JD, Loyola U., New Orleans, 1969. Bar: La. 1969, U.S. Dist. Ct. (ea. dist.) La. 1972, U.S. Dist. Ct. (mid. dist.) La. 1978, U.S. Dist. Ct. (we. dist.) La. 1979, U.S. Ct. Appeals (5th cir.) 1972, U.S. Supreme Ct. 1972. Pvt. practice Reserve, La., 1969-88, LaPlace, La., 1988—; staff atty. La. Legis. Coun., 1972-73; legal counsel Nicholls State U. Alumni Fedn., 1974-76, 78-80; spl. counsel Pontchartrain Levee Dist., 1976—; adminstrv. law judge La. Dept. Civil Svc., 1981—. Mem. St. John the Bapt. Parish Emergency Planning Com., 1987—; pres. Boys' State of La. Inc., 1990-92, bd. dirs., 1988—. With AUS, 1964, USNG, 1964-70. Recipient Am. Jurisprudence award Loyola U., 1968. Fellow La. Bar Found.; mem. ABA, La. Bar Assn. (ho. dels. 1973-77, 79-85), 40th Jud. Dist. Bar Assn. (pres. 1985-87). ATLA, La. Trial Lawyers Assn., Nicholls State U. Alumni Fedn. (exec. coun. 1972-76, 77-85, pres. 1982, James Lynn Powell award 1980), Am. Legion (post cmdr. 1976-77, dist. judge adv. 1975-95, judge adv. La. dept. 1990-92, 93-96, mem. La. dept. commn. on nat. security and govtl. affairs 1974-89, chmn. 1977-78, 79-81, 85-89, M.C. Gehr blue cap award 1983). Roman Catholic. Administrative and regulatory, Juvenile. Home: 116 Dave St Reserve LA 70084-6611 Office: 197 Belle Terre Blvd PO Box 461 La Place LA 70069-0461

**CICIO, ANTHONY LEE,** lawyer; b. Birmingham, Ala., July 8, 1926; s. Joseph and Rosa (Tombrello) C.; m. Yvonne Antonio, Nov. 4, 1959; children: Valerie, Anthony Jr., Mark. BS, Samford U., 1951; LLB, Birmingham Sch. Law, 1955. Bar: Ala. 1956, U.S. Dist. Ct. Ala. 1956, U.S. Supreme Ct. 1961, U.S. Ct. Appeals (11th cir.) 1968. Ptnr. Cicio & Cicio, Birmingham, 1976—. Served as Spl. asst. Atty. Gen. State of Ala., 1980; served Brimingham-Jefferson County Transit Authority, 1962; appt. Birmingham-Jefferson County regional planning com., 1999—. Served with USAF, 1944-46, PTO. Mem. ABA, Ala. Bar Assn. (chmn. pub. relations com.), Birmingham Bar Assn. (ethics com., ch. com. on media and pub. relations), Trial Lawyers Assn. Am., Ala. Trial Lawyers Assn. (exec. com. 1983—), State Indsl. Revenue Bond (adv. coun.), The Club, Vestavia Country Club (Birmingham). Democrat. Roman Catholic. Personal injury, Probate, General practice. Home: 3128 N Woodridge Rd Birmingham AL 35223-2750 Office: Cicio & Cicio PC 2153 14th Ave S Birmingham AL 35205-3921

**CIHON, CHRISTOPHER MICHAEL,** lawyer; b. Carlisle, Pa., Dec. 7, 1971; s. Patrick J. and Nancy A.W. Cihon. BA, Williams Coll., 1993; JD cum laude, Tulane U., 1996. Bar: Md. 1996, D.C. 1997, U.S. Dist. Ct. Md. 1997, U.S. Dist. Ct. D.C. 1997, U.S. Ct. Appeals (4th cir.) 1997. Assoc. Jackson & Campbell, P.C., Washington, 1996-98, Nixon, Hargrave, Devans & Doyle, LLP, Washington, 1998-99, Nixon Peabody LLP, Washington, 1999—. Editor-in-chief Tulane Environ. Law Jour., 1995-96. Mem. ABA. E-mail: ccihon@nhdd.com. General civil litigation, Alternative dispute resolution, Constitutional. Office: Nixon Peabody LLP 1 Thomas Cir NW Ste 700 Washington DC 20005-5802

**CILZ, DOUGLAS ARTHUR,** lawyer; b. Rugby, N.D., Feb. 22, 1949; s. Fred W. and Arliene (Nelson) C.; m. Kathy Ann Walker, June 10, 1972; children: Jennifer, Nicholas. BS, Dickinson State U., 1976; JD, U. N.D., Grand Forks, 1980. Bar: N.D. 1980, U.S. Dist. Ct. N.D. 1980, Minn. 1981, U.S. Tax Ct. 1981, U.S. Claims Ct. 1981. Atty. Qualley Larson & Jones, Fargo, N.D., 1980-81, Pearson & Christensen, Grand Forks, N.D., 1981-87; ptnr. Juntunen, Cilz & Hagen, Grand Forks, 1987-98; atty. N.D. Dept. Transp., Grand Forks, 1998—; instr. East Grand Forks (Minn.) Tech. Coll., 1989-92; apptd. spl. asst. atty. gen. Bank N.D., 1993—; apptd. temporary adminstrv. law judge N.D. Office Adminstrv. Hearings, 1995—. Sgt. USAF, 1968-71. Mem. ABA, Minn. Bar Assn., N.D. Bar Assn., Am. Trial Lawyers Assn., Grand Forks C. of C. Lutheran. Avocations: golf, tennis, skiing, hunting, fishing. Estate planning, General civil litigation, Taxation, general. Office: ND Dept Transportation 1951 N Washington St Grand Forks ND 58201

**CIMINI, JOSEPH FEDELE,** law educator, lawyer, former magistrate; b. Scranton, Pa., Sept. 8, 1948; s. Frank Anthony and Dorothy Theresa (Musso) C. AB in German and Polit. Sci., U. Scranton, 1970; JD Columbus Sch. Law, Cath. U. Am., 1973. Bar: Pa. 1973, U.S. Dist. Ct. (mid. dist.) Pa. 1973, D.C. 1976, U.S. Ct. Appeals (3d cir.) 1978, U.S. Supreme Ct. 1978. Law clk. to judge Ct. Common Pleas Lackawanna County (Pa.), 1973-75; asst. U.S. atty. Middle Dist. Pa., Pa. Dept. Justice, 1975-80; spl. asst. to U.S. Atty. Middle Dist. Pa., 1980-81; asst. prof. sociology/criminal justice U. Scranton, 1980-94, assoc. prof., 1994—; U.S. magistrate judge U.S. Dist. Ct. (mid. dist.) Pa., 1981-92; spl. trial master Lackawanna County Ct. Common Pleas, 1995—. Past pres. Lackawanna Hist. Soc.; v.p. adv. bd. Holy Family Residence, Scranton, Pa., 1997—; v.p. pastoral coun. St. Francis Ch., 1994-96. Recipient Meritorious award Dept. Justice; German Acad. Exchange Service fgn. study travel grantee, W.Ger., 1981. Mem. ABA, Fed. Bar Assn. (past v.p. mid. dist. Pa. chpt.), Am. Judges Assn., Fed. Magistrate Judges Assn., Acad. Criminal Justice Scis., Pa. Bar Assn., Northeastern Assn. Criminal Scis. (pres. 1987-88), Lackawanna Bar Assn., Pa. Sociol. Soc. (treas.), U. Scranton Alumni (nat. sec. 1997-99), Cath. U. Law Alumni, Purple Club, Victor Alfieri Lit. Soc., UNICO Nat. Republican. Roman Catholic. Address: Univ Scranton Dept Sociology/Criminal Justice Scranton PA 18510-4605

**CIMINO, RICHARD DENNIS,** lawyer; b. Omaha, Nebr., June 6, 1947; s. Lewis Raymond and Louise (Monaco) C.; m. Mary Scott Reins, Feb. 12, 1977; children: John Damon, Mary Drusilla, Robert Andrew, Ann Marie. BBA, U. Notre Dame, 1969; JD, St. Louis U., 1974. Bar: Nebr. 1975, U.S. Dist. Ct. Nebr. 1975, Kans. 1989, U.S. Dist. Ct. Kans. 1989, Fla. 1995. Assoc. Kutak, Rock & Campbell, Omaha, 1975-78, ptnr., 1979; v.p., gen. counsel Silvey Refrigerated Carriers, Omaha, 1980-86, pres., 1987; ptnr. Dwyer, Pohren, Wood, Heavey & Grimm, Omaha, 1988-89; sole practice St. Marys, Kans., 1989-93; ptnr. Treadwell, Cimino & McElrath, Naples, Fla., 1993—. Editor St. Louis U. Law Jour., 1972-74. Bd. dirs. Bergan Mercy Hosp. Found., Omaha, 1986-87. With U.S. Army, 1969-71, Vietnam. Mem. Fla. Bar Assn., Kans. Bar Assn., Nebr. Bar Assn., Notre Dame Alumni Club (pres. Omaha chpt. 1980), Alpha Sigma Nu. Republican. Roman Catholic. Avocations: golf, family activities. General practice, State civil litigation, Estate planning. Office: 3838 Tamiami Trl N Naples FL 34103-3556

**CIOFFI, MICHAEL LAWRENCE,** lawyer; b. Cin., Feb. 2, 1953; s. Patrick Anthony and Patricia (Schroeder) C.; children: Michael A., David P., Gina M. BA magna cum laude, U. Notre Dame, 1975; JD, U. Cin., 1979. Bar: Ohio 1979, U.S. Dist. Ct. (so. dist.) Ohio 1980, U.S. Dist. Ct. (no. dist.) Ohio 1983, U.S. Ct. Appeals (6th cir.) 1985. Asst. atty. gen. Ohio Atty. Gen., Columbus, 1979-81; from assoc. to ptnr. Frost & Jacobs, Cin., 1981-87; staff v.p., asst. gen. counsel Penn Cen. Corp., Cin., 1988-93; v.p., asst. gen. counsel Am. Fin. Group, Cin., 1993—; adj. prof. law U. Cin. Coll. Law, 1983—. Author: Ohio Pretrial Litigation, 1991; co-author: Sixth Circuit Federal Practice Manual, 1993. Bd. dirs. Charter Com. of Greater Cin., 1985-88. Recipient Goldman Prize for Tchg. Excellence U. Cin. Coll. Law, 1995, Nicholas Longworth Disting. Alumni award, 1996. Mem. ABA, Fed. Bar Assn. (mem. exec. com., pres.1994), Ohio Bar Assn., Cin. Bar Assn. Avocations: tennis, travel. General civil litigation, Federal civil litigation, Environmental. Office: Am Fin Group 1 E 4th St Cincinnati OH 45202-3717

**CION, JUDITH ANN,** lawyer; b. N.Y.C., June 27, 1943. AB, Pomona Coll., 1965; LLB, Harvard U., 1968. Bar: N.Y. 1968, U.S. Dist. Ct. (so. dist.) N.Y. 1973, U.S. Dist. Ct. (ea. dist.) N.Y. 1974, U.S. Ct. Appeals (2d cir.) 1974. Assoc. Poletti, Freidin, Prashker, Feldman & Gartner, N.Y.C., 1968-71; assoc. Lovejoy, Wasson, Lundgren & Ashton, N.Y.C., 1971-75, ptnr., 1976-80; fin. and securities counsel The Coca-Cola Co., Atlanta, 1980-84; mng. counsel Mellon Bank, N.A., Pitts., 1984-87; sr. v.p., gen. counsel, sec. Hibernia Nat. Bank, New Orleans, 1988-93; gen. counsel, sec. Hibernia Corp., New Orleans, 1988-93. Bd. dirs. New Orleans Ballet Assn., 1992—, Women's Profl. Coun., New Orleans, 1991—. Mem. Am. Soc. Corp. Secs. (sec. 1986-89, dir. 1989-94, chmn.-elect 1991-92, chmn. 1992-93). Banking, General corporate, Securities.

**CIOTOLI, EUGENE L.,** lawyer; b. Endicott, N.Y., Nov. 15, 1952; s. Eugene E. and M. Jeanette C.; m. Kathryn Marie Jackson, Aug. 4, 1984; children: Christina, Victoria, Dominic. BS, Fla. State U., 1973, JD with hons., 1982. Assoc. McFarlain, Bobo, et al., Tallahassee, Fla., 1982-85; ptnr. Bobo, Spicer & Ciotoli, W. Palm Beach, Fla., 1985—; mng. ptnr. Bobo, Spicer, Ciotoli Fulford, Bacchino, DeBevoise, Le Clainche, W. Palm Beach, Orlando, 1995—; Cert. civil trial lawyer Fla. Bar Bd. Legal Specialization & Edn. Treas., chmn. fin. com. St. Mark's Episcopal Sch., Palm Beach Gardens, Fla., 1991-98, mem. fin. and nominating coms., 1998—. Mem. Fla. Defense Lawyers Assn, Defense Rsch. Inst. General civil litigation, Professional liability, Personal injury. Home: 10 Alnwick Rd Palm Beach Gardens FL 33418-6834 Office: Bobo Spicer Ciotoli Fulford et al 222 Lakeview Ave Fl 6 West Palm Beach FL 33401-6147

**CIPARICK, CARMEN BEAUCHAMP,** state judge; b. N.Y.C., 1942. Grad., Hunter Coll., 1963; JD, St. John's U., 1967; LLD (hon.), CUNY, Queens Coll., 1994. Staff atty. Legal Aid Soc., N.Y.C.; asst. counsel Office of the Judicial Conf., 1969-72; chief law asst. N.Y.C. Criminal Ct., 1972-74; counsel Office of N.Y.C. Adminstrv. Judge, 1974-78; judge N.Y.C. Criminal Ct., 1978-82, N.Y. Supreme Ct. 1982-94; assoc. judge N.Y. State Ct. Appeals, N.Y.C., 1994—; former mem. N.Y. State Commn. Judicial Conduct. Trustee Boricua Coll.; bd. dirs. St. John's U. Sch. of Law Alumni Assn. Named to Hunter Coll. Hall of Fame, 1991. Office: 122 E 42nd St New York NY 10168-0002*

**CIPOLETTA, JAMES JOSEPH,** lawyer; b. Winthrop, Mass., May 29, 1952; s. James and Eleanor M. (Carroll) C. AB, Suffolk U., 1974; JD, New Eng. Sch. Law, 1978; M Liberal Arts in Govt., Harvard U., 1995. Bar: Mass. 1978, U.S. Dist. Ct. Mass. 1979, U.S. Ct. Appeals (1st cir.) 1980, U.S. Supreme Ct. 1982, U.S. Dist. Ct. Md. 1990. Pvt. practice, Revere, Mass., 1978-83; ptnr. Cipoletta & Ogus, Revere, 1983—; bd. trustee Savio Prep H.S., Boston, 1996—; tchg. asst. Harvard Univ., 1996-97. Co-author: Medical Records, 1996. Spl. counsel Town of Wintrhop, Mass., 1996—, mem. fin. com., 1989-92, chmn. bd. appeals, 1992—. Mem. Mass. Bar Inst. (faculty mem. 1996-97, panel mem. 1993-95), Nat. Assn. Criminal Def. Lawyers, Mass., Assn. Criminal Def. Lawyers, Harvard Club Boston. Republican. Avocations: sailing, raquetball. Criminal, Land use and zoning (including planning), Municipal (including bonds). Home: 217 Cliff Ave Winthrop MA 02152-1062 Office: Cipoletta & Ogus 385 Broadway Revere MA 02151-3033

**CIPOLLA, CARL JOSEPH,** lawyer; b. Chgo., Sept. 19, 1922; s. Settimo and Maria (Latino) C.; m. JoAnn B. Nutley, June 7, 1952; children—Cara, Carl, Marisa, Christopher, Michael, Gia, Lisa, Lara. A.B., U. Ill., 1947; J.D., DePaul U., 1949. Bar: Ill. 1949, U.S. Dist. Ct. (no. dist.) Ill. 1951, U.S. Supreme Ct. 1959, U.S. Ct. Mil. Appeals 1959. Sole practice, Chgo., 1949-85; judge Cir. Ct. Cook County, Chgo., 1985—. Trustee Village of Glenview, Ill., 1963-65; pres. 43d Ward Citizen's Com., Chgo., 1949-55, Bel-Air Community Assn., 1958-59, Waller Community Council, Chgo., 1951-55; co-founder Joint Civic Com. of Italian-Americans, Chgo., 1952; mem. Mayor's Com. for Cleaner Chgo., 1951-54. Served to 1st lt. U.S. Army, 1943-46, PTO. Mem. Ill. Bar Assn., Ill. Bar Found., Ill. Judge's Assn. (bd. dirs. 1995—). Federal civil litigation, State civil litigation, Personal injury. Home: 505 N Lake Shore Dr Apt 2404 Chicago IL 60611-6416 Office: Room 1303 Daley Ctr Chicago IL 60602

**CIPOLLONE, ANTHONY DOMINIC,** judge; b. N.Y.C., Mar. 15, 1939; s. Domenico and Caterina (Brancazio) C.; m. Eileen Mary Patricia Kelly, Sept. 14, 1963; children: Catherine Mary, Kelly Ann, Mary Rose. BA, CCNY, 1961, MA, 1968; JD, Seton Hall U., 1978. Bar: N.J. 1978, Pa. 1978, U.S. Patent Office 1978, Fla. 1980, N.Y. 1984, D.C. 1985, Mass. 1988; cert. civil trial atty. N.J., 1987. Chemist Am. Chicle Co., Long Island City, N.Y., 1961-65; research chemist Denver Chem. Mfg. Co., Stamford, Conn., 1965-66; chem. sales engr. GAF Corp., N.Y.C., 1966-68; nat. acct. rep. Stauffer Chem., N.Y.C., 1968-72; sales mgr. Rhone-Poulenc Inc., South Brunswick, N.J., 1972-78; prosecutor Town of Elmwood Park, N.J., 1981-85, Town of Paramus, N.J., 1982-85; mcpl. ct. judge Town of Paramus (N.J.), 1985-90, Town of Little Ferry (N.J.), 1986-89; atty. planning bd. Twp. Saddle Brook, 1986-87; mcpl. ct. judge Town of Elmwood Park (N.J.), 1991, Town of Saddle Brook (N.J.), 1991-94; atty. Twp. Saddle Brook, 1987-90; adj. faculty MBA program for chmn. and pharm. mgrs. Fairleigh Dickinson U.; atty. Zoning Bd., City of Hackensack, N.J., 1989-90, atty. Planning Bd., 1991—. Served to sgt. USMC, 1961-66. Mem. ABA, Bergen Bar Assn., N.J. Bar Assn., Pa. Bar Assn., N.Y. Bar Assn., D.C. Bar Assn., Fla. Bar Assn., Mass. Bar Assn., Am. Chem. Soc., Am. Mensa. Roman Catholic. Home: 535 E Ridgewood Ave Apt 4 Ridgewood NJ 07450-3347 Office: 1 Essex St Hackensack NJ 07601-5414

**CIPPARONE, ROCCO C., JR.,** lawyer; b. Phila.. BA, St. Joseph's U., Phila., 1984; JD, U. Pa., 1987. Bar: N.J. 1987, Pa. 1987, U.S. Dist. Ct. (ea. dist.) Pa., U.S. Dist. Ct. N.J. 1987, U.S. Dist. Ct. (ea. dist.) Mich.; cert. criminal trial atty., N.J. Law clk. to Hon. Anthony J. Scirica U.S. Ct. Appeals, 3d Cir., Phila., 1987-88; asst. U.S. atty., criminal divsn. U.S. Dept. Justice, Camden, N.J., 1988-92; atty. in pvt. practice, Phila., also Haddon Hts., N.J., 1992—; adj. faculty Rutgers U. Law Sch., Camden, 1991—; lectr. N.J. Inst. for Continuing Legal Edn. Contbr. articles to profl. jours. Recipient Spl. Achievement award U.S. Atty. Gen., 1992, others. Mem. Camden County Bar Assn. Criminal, Personal injury, Family and matrimonial. Office: 205 Black Horse Pike Haddon Heights NJ 08035-1009

**CIPRIANO, GENE RALPH,** lawyer; b. New Haven, Aug. 10, 1959; s. Gene Ralph and Sandela Cipriano. AA, St. Petersburg Jr. Coll., 1983; BA, Stetson U., 1985, JD, 1987. Asst. state atty. Dade County State Atty.'s Office, Miami, Fla., 1988-91; litigation atty. Law Office Kevin F. Jursinski, Ft. Meyers, Fla., 1991-93; pvt. practice Ft. Meyers, 1993—. Bd. dirs. Soc. Prevent Blindness, A Place Called Home, 1996-97, South Gulf Basketball Ofcls. Assn., 1996-98. Avocations: sports officiating, tennis, racquetball, reading. General civil litigation, Criminal, Probate. Office: PO Box 611 Fort Myers FL 33902-0611

**CIRANDO, JOHN ANTHONY,** lawyer; b. Syracuse, N.Y., June 25, 1942; s. Daniel John and Anne Marie (Farone) C.; m. Carolyn Joyce Lace, Sept. 17, 1966; children: Lisa Marie, Julie Lynn, Jennifer Mary. BA in History, St. Bonaventure (N.Y.) U., 1963; JD, SUNY, Buffalo, 1966. Bar: N.Y. 1966, U.S. Dist. Ct. (no. dist.) N.Y. 1966, U.S. Dist. Ct. (we. dist.) N.Y. 1994, U.S. Claims Ct. 1991, U.S. Ct. Mil. Appeals 1967, U.S. Ct. Appeals (2d cir.) 1985, U.S. Supreme Ct. 1974. Chief asst. dist. atty. Onondaga County Dist. Atty.'s Office, Syracuse, N.Y., 1971-87; atty. D.J. & J.A. Cirando, Syracuse, 1966—; treas. N.Y. State Dist. Atty.'s Office, 1977-87; chair Govs. Jud. Screening Com. 4th Jud. Dept., 1997—. Pres. bd. dirs. Vera House, Shelter for Women and Children in Crisis, Syracuse, 1988-90; bd. trustees Leukemia Soc. Am., 1995—, asst. sec., 1995-96, sec., 1996—. Capt. JAG, U.S. Army, 1967-71. Mem. N.Y. State Bar Assn. (chair com. on county cts. 1975-78, chair com. on pub. rels. 1979-83), Onondaga County Bar Assn. (bd. dirs. 1974-77, sec. 1979). Appellate, Probate, Real property. Office: DJ & JA Cirando 101 S Salina St Ste 1010 Syracuse NY 13202-4303

**CIRESI, MICHAEL VINCENT,** lawyer; b. St. Paul, Apr. 18, 1946; s. Samuel Vincent and Selena Marie (Bloom) C.; m. Ann Ciresi; children: Dominic, Adam. BBA, U. St. Thomas; JD, U. Minn. Bar: Minn. 1971, U.S. Dist. Ct. Minn. 1974, U.S. Ct. Appeals (8th cir.) 1971, U.S. Supreme Ct. 1981, U.S. Ct. Appeals (2d cir.) 1986, U.S. Ct. Appeals (9th cir.) 1987, U.S. Ct. Appeals (10th cir.) 1990, N.Y. 1995, fed. cir., 1998, U.S. Ct. Appeals (5th cir.) 1999. Assoc. Robins, Kaplan, Miller & Ciresi, Mpls., 1971-78, ptnr., 1978—, exec. bd., 1983—, chmn. exec. bd., 1995—; adv. bd. Ctr. Advanced Litigation, Nottingham (Eng.) Law Sch. Trustee U. St. Thomas. Named Product Liability Lawyer of Yr., Australian Nat. Consumer Law Assn., 1989, Trial Lawyer of Yr. Trial Lawyers for Public Justice Found., 1998. Mem. ABA, Minn. State Bar Assn., Hennepin County Bar Assn., Ramsey County Bar Assn., Assn. Trial Lawyers Am., Am. Bd. Trial Advocates, Internat. Bar. Assn., Inner Circle of Advocates, Trial Lawyers for Pub. Justice (bd. dirs.). Roman Catholic. Avocation: sports, U.S. history. Federal civil litigation, State civil litigation. Home: 1247 Culligan Ln Saint Paul MN 55118-4151 Office: Robins Kaplan Miller & Ciresi 2800 Lasalle Plz Minneapolis MN 55402

**CIRIACO, ANTHONY CHARLES,** lawyer; b. Jersey City, N.J., Apr. 26, 1958; s. Andrew Samuel and Julia Louise C.; m. Martha Ann Hammonds, Oct. 15, 1983; children: Nicholas, Andrea. BS in Commerce, U. Va., 1980; JD, U. N.C., 1983. Bar: Ohio 1983, U.S. Dist. Ct. (so. dist.) Ohio, 1983. Assoc. Vorys, Sater, Seymour and Pease, Columbus, Ohio, 1983-90, 1990—; bd. trustees Gladden Cmty. House, Columbus, Ohio, Buckeye Ranch, Columbus. Recipient Merit award Ohio Legal Ctr. Inst., 1992. Fellow Ohio State Bar Assn.; mem. Columbus Bar Assn. Republican. Roman Catholic. Avocations: sports, reading. Pension, profit-sharing, and employee benefits. Home: 4915 Brand Rd Dublin OH 43017-8514 Office: Vorys Sater Seymour Pease 52 E Gay St Columbus OH 43215-3161

**CIRINA, ANGELA MARIE,** lawyer; b. Enid, Okla., Mar. 3, 1970; d. Lawrence Joseph and Rosemarie Theresa Cirina. BA, Fairfield U., 1992; JD, MBA, Widener U., 1995. Bar: Ga. 1995, Tenn. 1996, D.C. 1996. Assoc. Luther-Anderson, Chattanooga, 1996-98; mgr., staff atty. Permanent Gen. Cos., Chattanooga, 1998—. Paul Harris fellow Rotary Internat., 1998. Mem. ABA (vice chair ins. law divsn. 1998—), CBA (bd. govs.), Ga. Bar Assn., Tenn. Bar Assn., D.C. Bar Assn., Southeastern Tenn. Lawyers Assn. for Women (pres. elect 1999). Republican. Roman Catholic. Avocations: skin diving, travel. Insurance, General civil litigation, Personal injury. Home: 1103 E Dallas Rd Apt 24 Chattanooga TN 37405-2336 Office: Permanent Gen cos Inc 606 Georgia Ave Ste 201 Chattanooga TN 37402-1408

**CISSELL, JAMES CHARLES,** lawyer; b. Cleve., May 29, 1940; s. Robert Francis and Helen Cecelia (Freeman) C.; children: Denise, Helene-Marie, Suzanne, James. Student, Sophia U., Tokyo, 1961; AB, Xavier U., 1962; JD, U. Cin., 1966; postgrad., Ohio State U., 1973-74; D. Tech. Letters, Cin. Tech. Coll., 1979. Bar: Ohio 1966, U.S. Dist. Ct. (so. dist.) Ohio 1967, U.S. Ct. Appeals (6th cir.) 1978, U.S. Supreme Ct. 1980, U.S. Dist. Ct. (ea. dist.) Ky. 1981. Pvt. practice law, 1966-78, 82—; asst. atty. gen. State of Ohio, 1971-74; first v.p. Cin. Bd. Park Commrs., 1973-74; vice mayor City of Cin., 1976-77; U.S. atty. So. Dist. Ohio, Cin., 1978-82; adj. instr. law No. Ky. U., 1982-86; sec. Nat. Assn. Former U.S. attys., 1998-99. Author: Oil and Gas Law in Ohio, 1964, Federal Criminal Trials, 4th edit., 1996; editor; Proving Federal Crimes. Gen. chmn. amateur pub. links championship U.S. Golf Assn., 1987; mem. coun. City of Cin., 1974-78, 85-87, 89-92; clk of cts., Hamilton County, 1992—, commr. Recreation Bd. Cin., 1974, Planning Bd. Cin., 1977; pres. Ohio Clk. of Cts. Assn., 1998; mem. Ohio Bicentennial Commn., 1998—; mem. Ohio Cts. Futures Commn., 1998—. Ford Found. fellow Ohio State U., 1973-74. Mem. Ohio Bar Assn., Cin. Bar Assn., Fed. Bar Assn., Former U.S. Attys. Assn. (v.p. 1999—). Avocations: golf, jogging. Federal civil litigation, Probate, Criminal. Home: 201B Belvedere 3900 Rose Hl Cincinnati OH 45229 Office: 602 Main St Ste 320 Cincinnati OH 45202-2521

**CITRON, BEATRICE SALLY,** law librarian, lawyer, educator; b. Phila., May 19, 1929; d. Morris Meyer and Frances (Teplitsky) Levinson; m. Joel P. Citron, Aug. 7, 1955 (dec. Sept. 1977); children: Deborah Ann, Victor Ephraim. BA in Econs. with honors, U. Pa., 1950; MLS, Our Lady of the Lake U., 1978; JD, U. Tex., 1984. Bar: Tex. 1985; cert. all-level sch. libr., secondary level tchr., Tex. Claims examiner Social Security Adminstrn., Pa., Fla. and N.C., 1951-59; head libr. St. Mary's Hall, San Antonio, 1979-80; media, reference and rare book libr., asst. and assoc. prof. St. Mary's U. Law Libr., San Antonio, 1984-89; asst. dir. St. Thomas U. Law Libr., Miami, Fla., 1989-96, assoc. dir./head pub. svc., 1996-99, acting dir., 1997-98. Mem. ABA, Am. Assn. Law Librs. (publs. com. 1987-88, com. on rels. with info. vendors 1991-93, bylaws com. 1994-96), S.W. Assn. Law Librs. (continuing edn. com. 1986-88, chmn. local arrangements 1987-88), S.E. Assn. Law Librs. (newsletter, program and edn. coms. 1991-98), South Fla. Assn. Law Librs. (treas. 1992-94, v.p. 1994-95, pres. 1995-96). Office: St Thomas U Law Libr 16400 NW 32nd Ave Opa Locka FL 33054-6498

**CLABAUGH, ELMER EUGENE, JR.,** lawyer; b. Anaheim, Calif., Sept. 18, 1927; s. Elmer Eugene and Eleanor Margaret (Heitshusen) C.; m. Donna Marie Organ, Dec. 19, 1960 (div.); children: Christopher C., Matthew M. BBA cum laude, Woodbury U.; BA summa cum laude, Claremont McKenna Coll., 1958; JD, Stanford U., 1961. Bar: Calif. 1961, U.S. Dist. Ct. (cen. dist.) Calif., U.S. Ct. Appeals (9th cir.) 1961, U.S. Supreme Ct. 1971. With fgn. svc. U.S. Dept. State, Jerusalem and Tel Aviv, 1951-53, Pub. Adminstrn. Svc., El Salvador, Ethiopia, U.S., 1953-57; dep. dist. atty. Ventura County, Calif., 1961-62; pvt. practice, Ventura, Calif., 1962-97; mem. Hathaway, Clabaugh, Perrett and Webster and predecessors, 1962-79, Clabaugh & Perloff, Ventura, 1979-97; state inheritance tax referee, 1968-78, ret. Bd. dirs. San Antonio Water Conservation Dist., Ventura Community Meml. Hosp., 1964-80; trustee Ojai Unified Sch. Dist., 1974-79; bd. dirs. Ventura County Found. for Parks and Harbors, 1982-96, Ventura County Maritime Mus., 1982-94. With USCGR, 1944-46, USMCR, 1946-48. Mem. NRA, Calif. Bar Assn., Safari Club Internat., Mason, Shriners, Phi Alpha Delta. Republican. Probate, Real property, Contracts commercial.

**CLAGETT, BRICE MCADOO,** lawyer, writer; b. Washington, July 6, 1933; s. Brice and Sarah Fleming (McAdoo) C.; m. Virginia Lawrence Parker, Sept. 18, 1965; children: John Brice, Ann Calvert Brooke; m. Diana Wharton Sinkler Knop, July 26, 1987. AB summa cum laude, Princeton U., 1954; postgrad. U. Allahabad (India), 1954-55; JD magna cum laude, Harvard U., 1958. Bar: D.C. 1958, U.S. Supreme Ct. 1962. Assoc., Covington & Burling, Washington, 1958-67, ptnr., 1967—; jud. counsellor Cambodian delegation to Internat. Ct. Justice, 1960-62; legal adviser Transition Team U.S. Dept. State, 1980-81; mem. nat. steering com. U.S. Iran Claimants Com., 1982—; adv. bd. Inst. for Transnat. Arbitration, 1989—; mem. lawyers com. Ctr. Individual Rights, 1992—; mem. records preservation access com. Fedn. Geneal. Socs., 1993-97. Bd. advisors Nat. Trust for Hist. Preservation 1978-81; Clagett family com. Chesapeake Bay Found., 1982—; trustee Md. Hist. Trust, 1971-78, chmn., 1972-78, Md. State House Trust, 1972-76, Md. Environ. Trust, 1978—, vice chmn., 1981-85, chmn. 1985-89; mem. Internat. Human Rights Law Group del. to Romania, 1990; bd. dirs. Chester-Sassafras Found., 1985-89; trustee New Eng. Hist. Geneal. Soc., 1989-92, 1995-98, Tudor Place Found., 1992-96; counsellor to the Pres. Gen., Soc. of the Cin., 1988-98, solicitor, 1998—; mem. adv. coun. Accokeek Found., 1989-91, trustee, 1991-94; mem. arbitration com. U.S. Coun. Internat. Bus., 1989—. Commdr. Royal Order Cambodia, 1962. Recipient Cert. Disting. Citizens State of Md., 1978. Mem. Am. Soc. Internat. Law, Am. Law Inst., Am. Arbitration Assn. (panel of arbitrators 1990—, large complex case panel arbitrators 1993—, internat. panel arbitrators 1997—), Internat. Law Assn., Washington Inst. Fgn. Affairs, Federalist Soc., Sons Confederate Vets., Mil. Order Stars and Bars, So. Md. Soc., Phi Beta Kappa. Republican. Episcopalian. Clubs: Met., City Tavern, Harvard (N.Y.C.), Soc. Cin. Md., Marlborough Hunt (Upper Marlboro, Md.), Radnor (Pa.) Hunt. Co-author: The Valuation of Property in International Law, vol. 4, 1987, An Illustrated History of St. Albans School, 1981; bd. editors: Harvard Law Review, 1956-58; contbr. numerous articles to legal, geneal. and hist. jours. Federal civil litigation, Private international, Public international. Home: Holly Hill PO Box 86 Friendship MD 20758-0086 also: 3331 O St NW Washington DC 20007-2814 Office: Covington & Burling PO Box 7566 1201 Pennsylvania Ave NW Washington DC 20044

**CLANCY BOLES, SUSAN,** lawyer; b. Winfield, Ill., Apr. 9, 1965; d. Wendell White and Kay Ellen Clancy; m. Robert Irl Boles, Jr., Sept. 9, 1988; children: Brogan, Cassie, Timothy. Student, Vanderbilt U., 1983-87; JD, Valparaiso U., 1990. Bar: Ill. 1990, U.S. Dist. Ct. (no. dist.) Ill., U.S. Ct. Appeals (7th cir.). Assoc. Rooks, Pitts & Poust, Chgo., 1990-93, Clancy, Higgins & Clancy, St. Charles, Ill., 1993—. General civil litigation, Personal injury, Product liability. Office: Clancy Higgins & Clancy 7 S 2nd Ave Saint Charles IL 60174-1921

**CLAPMAN, PETER CARLYLE,** lawyer, insurance company executive; b. N.Y.C., Mar. 11, 1936; s. Jack and Evelyn (Clapman); m. Barbara Posen, May 8, 1966; children: Leah, Alice. AB, Princeton U., 1957; JD, Harvard U., 1960. Bar: N.Y. 1961, Conn. 1972. Assoc. Sage, Gray, Todd & Sims, N.Y.C., 1961-63; asst. counsel Stichman Commn., N.Y.C., 1964; legal cons. OEO, Washington, 1965; assoc. counsel Equitable Life, N.Y.C., 1965-72; sr. v.p., chief counsel investments Tchrs. Ins. and Annuity of Am., Coll. Ret. Equities Fund, N.Y.C., 1972—. Author: Fiduciary Responsibilities of Institutional Managers on Proxy Issues, Iowa Law Jour., 1994, SEC Market 2000 Report; co-author: Notre Dame U. Law Rev., 1981. Mem. ABA, Assn. Bar City N.Y. (com. on securities regulation special com. on mergers), Am. Law Inst., Assn. Life Ins. Counsel (bd. govs., chmn. investment sect.), Am. Coll. Investment Counsel (trustee), Am. Coun. Life Ins. (chmn. securities investment commn.). Contracts commercial, Private international, Administrative and regulatory. Home: 3 Valley Rd Scarsdale NY 10583-1123 Office: Tchrs Ins & Annuity Assn Am 730 3rd Ave New York NY 10017-3206

**CLAPP, RICHARD ALLEN,** lawyer; b. Cin., Mar. 20, 1948; s. Hubert Dickason and Eletha May (Armstrong) C.;m. Sonja Petkovic, Mar. 16, 1968 (div. Apr. 1982); children: Shawn, Christian; m. Lori Plaisted, Sept. 8, 1990 (div. 1998). Student, Hamline U., 1966-68, U. Minn., 1968; BA, U. N.D., 1972, JD with distinction, 1976. Bar: N.D. 1976, U.S. Dist. Ct. N.D. 1976, U.S. Ct. Appeals (8th cir.) 1976, Minn. 1982, U.S. Dist. Ct. Minn. 1989. Atty. Haughland & Heustis, Devils Lake, N.D., 1976-79; ptnr. Letness Marshall Fiedler & Clapp Ltd., Grand Forks, N.D., 1979-95, Pearson, Christensen, Clapp, Fiedler & Fisher, Grand Forks, N.D., 1995—; instr. bus. law Lake Region Jr. Coll., Devils Lake, 1977-79; adj. prof. trial advocacy U. N.D. Sch. Law, Grand Forks, 1985-87. Mem. ABA, Am. Bd. Trial Advocates (advocate, nat. bd. dirs.), Def. Rsch. Inst., State Bar Assn. N.D. (inquiry com. east 1977-80), Minn. State Bar Assn. (cert. civil trial specialist), Phi Delta Phi, Grand Forks Country Club. Republican. Presbyterian. Avocations: travel, golf, literature, fishing, theater. General civil litigation, Product liability, Insurance. Home: 201 Plain Hills Dr Grand Forks ND 58201-7941 Office: Pearson Christensen Clapp Fielder & Fisher PO Box 5758 Grand Forks ND 58206-5758

**CLAPPER, JEFFREY CURTIS,** lawyer; b. Aberdeen, S.D., June 11, 1967; s. William Harlan Clapper and Mary Lue McAtee; m. Cathryn Ann Schuchard, Aug. 7, 1993; children: Bevin Victoria, Vincent Jeffrey. BSBA, Creighton U., 1989; JD, U. S.D., Vermillion, 1993. Atty. Moore Rasmussen Kading & Kunstle, Sioux Falls, S.D., 1993-99, Boyce Murphy McDowell & Greenfield, LLP, Sioux Falls, 1999—. Administrative and regulatory, Personal injury, General civil litigation. Office: Boyce Murphy McDowell & Greenfield LLP 101 N Phillips Ave Sioux Falls SD 57104-6714

**CLARDY, THELMA SANDERS,** lawyer; b. Okemah, Okla., Jan. 11, 1955; d. Hobart Curtis and Maurine Yvonne (Lee) Sanders; m. James E. Clardy, June 28, 1980; 1 child, Michelle Elizabeth. BS cum laude, Tenn. State U., 1976; JD, Tex. So. U., 1979. Bar: Tex. Staff atty. U.S. Dept. Edn., Dallas, 1979-87; assoc. Law Offices Earl Luna, Dallas, 1987-88; staff atty. Legal Svcs. North Tex., Dallas, 1988-91; assoc. Robinson & West, P.C., Dallas, 1992-94; pvt. practice Dallas, 1995—. Pres. Oak Tree Colony Neighborhood Assn., Dallas, 1984-85, North Meadows Community Improvement Assn., DeSoto, Tex., 1992-94; bd. dirs. Women's Ctr. Dallas, Child Care Partnership, Dallas; with Nat. Assn. Negro Bus. and Profl. Women, Dallas, 1984-86. Recipient Juanita Craft award NAACP, Dallas, 1985; named Member of

Yr. United for Action, Dallas, 1982. Fellow Tex. Bar Found.; mem. State Bar Tex. (bd. dirs.), Dallas Bar Assn. (sec.-treas. 1991), Dallas Assn. Black Women Attys. (founder, 1st pres. 1982-84), Vis. Nurse Assn. Tex. (bd. dirs. 1989-94), Alpha Kappa Alpha. Baptist. Avocations: education, health care, reading, tennis. Family and matrimonial, Probate, General civil litigation. Home: 1117 Bluffview Dr De Soto TX 75115-3519 Office: Ste # 950 1845 Woodall Fwy Ste 1200 Dallas TX 75201

**CLARK, BRUCE ARLINGTON, JR.,** lawyer; b. Hopewell, Va., Nov. 17, 1951; s. Bruce Arlington Sr. and Thelma (Givens) C.; m. Catherine Mary Lambert, Aug. 11, 1973; children: Andrew, David, Caryn. BA, Coll. William and Mary, 1973; JD, U. Richmond, 1979. Bar: Va. 1979, U.S. Dist. Ct. (ea. dist.) Va. 1979, U.S. Ct. Appeals (4th cir.) 1979. Law clk. to presiding justice U.S. Bankruptcy Ct., Richmond, Va., 1979-80; assoc. Marks, Stokes & Harrison, Hopewell, 1980-82; sole practice Hopewell, 1982—; asst. commonwealth atty. City of Hopewell, 1986—. Pres. PTO, Hopewell, 1985; chmn. Hopewell chpt. Am. Heart Soc., 1986—; mem. Hopewell chpt. Am. Cancer Soc., 1985—; bd. dirs. Hopewell Youth Soccer League, 1984. Served with U.S. Army, 1973-77. Mem. ABA, Va. Bar Assn., Hopewell Bar Assn. (pres. 1986—), Va. Trial Lawyers Assn., Hopewell-Prince George C. of C. (vice chmn. 1986—, chmn. bd. dirs. 1987—, pres. 1987), Ducks Unltd. (chmn. 1986—). Methodist. Avocations: golf, fishing, youth soccer. Bankruptcy, General practice. Home: 2703 Princess Anne Ave Hopewell VA 23860-1929 Office: 105 N 2nd Ave Hopewell VA 23860-2701

**CLARK, CELIA RUE,** lawyer; b. N.Y.C., Aug. 16, 1951; d. Edward Frank and Rosemary (Reddick) Clark, Jr.; m. Edgar Crawford Gentry, Jr., Aug. 11, 1979; children: Diana Marron, Carl Edgar. B.A. with distinction, U. Wis., 1974; J.D., U. Chgo., 1979, LLM, NYU, 1988. Bar: N.Y. 1980. Mng. editor Heldref Publs., Washington, 1974-78; assoc. Rogers & Wells, N.Y.C., 1979-84; adj. asst. prof. law Yeshiva U., 1985; assoc. Weitzner, Levine & Hamburg, N.Y.C., 1988-92; counsel Pirro, Collier, Cohen, Crystal & Block, White Plains, N.Y., 1992-96; ptnr. Smith, Buss & Jacobs, L.L.P., Yonkers, N.Y., 1996—. Contbg. author: Asset-Based Financing, 1984, Jour. Taxation, 1998. Mem. ABA, Westchester County Bar Assn. Democrat. Taxation, general, Estate planning, General corporate. Office: Smith Buss & Jacobs LLP 733 Yonkers Ave Yonkers NY 10704-2635

**CLARK, CHARLES EDWARD,** arbitrator; b. Cleve., Feb. 27, 1921; s. Douglas James and Mae (Egermayer) C.; m. Nancy Jane Hilt, Mar. 11, 1942; children: Annette S. (Mrs. Paul Gernhardt), Charles Edward, John A., Nancy P. Gonzalez, Paul R., Stephen C., David G. Student, Berea Coll., 1939-40, King Coll., 1945; JD, U. Tex., 1948. Bar: Tex. 1948, Mass. 1956, U.S. Supreme Ct. 1959. Sole practice San Antonio, 1948-55; writer legal articles, editor NACCA Law Jour., Boston, 1955-58; legal asst. to vice chmn., chief voting sect. U.S. Commn. on Civil Rights, Washington, 1958-61; spl. counsel Pres.'s Com. on Equal Employment Opportunity, Washington, 1961-65; sr. compliance officer Office Fed. Contract Compliance, Washington, 1965-66; regional dir. Equal Employment Opportunity Commn., Kansas City, Mo., 1966-79, arbitrator, 1979—; prof. law, asst. dean St. Mary's U. Sch. Law, 1948-55; lectr. Rockhurst Coll., 1980-91, Longview Coll., 1988—. Contbr. articles to legal jours. Active Boy Scouts Am. Served with AUS, 1943-44. Mem. VFW, Soc. Profls. in Dispute Resolution, State Bar Tex., Tex. Law Rev. Assn., Am. GI Forum (D.C. vice chmn. 1962-63), Soc. Fed. Labor Rels. Profls., Indsl. Rels. Rsch. Assn. (exec. bd. Kansas City 1976-91, pres. chpt. 1986), Phi Delta Phi (province pres. 1951-55). Home and Office: 6418 Washington St Kansas City MO 64113-1732

**CLARK, DANIEL,** law researcher; b. Riverside, Calif., May 26, 1953; s. Robert R. and Virginia (Muscato) C.; m. Jan. 23, 1971; children: Danell, Tricia. AAS, Lee Coll., 1982; student, Sam Houston State U., 1982-84. Pvt. practice legal researcher Richardson, Tex., 1974—; advisor Valetti Corp., Richardson, 1985—. Leading authority in U.S. on criminal courtroom demeanor and defendent self representation. With USAF, 1972-73. Office: Valetti Corp 808 Sherbrook Dr Richardson TX 75080-3014

**CLARK, DAVID LEWIS,** lawyer; b. Forest Grove, Oreg., Mar. 11, 1946; s. Virgil James and Lovina (Culbertson) C.; divorced; children: Emily Janis, Bradley David. BS in Sociology, U. Oreg., 1968, JD, 1975. Bar: Oreg. 1975, U.S. Dist. Ct. Oreg. 1976. Ptnr. Nicholson & Clark, Florence, 1978-86; sole practice Florence, 1986—; atty. City of Florence, 1975-81, Port of Siuslaw, Florence, 1975—. Bd. dirs. Western Ln. County Found., Florence, 1982-89; justice of peace, Florence, 1983-90. Served with USAF, 1968-72. Mem. U. Oreg. Law Sch. Alumni Assn. (bd. dirs. 1982-83). Roman Catholic. Lodges: Rotary (pres., bd. dirs. 1982-89), Elks (justice 1976—). Avocations: family activities, reading. General practice. Office: PO Box 146 Florence OR 97439-0005

**CLARK, DAVID MCKENZIE,** lawyer; b. Greenville, N.C., Sept. 1, 1929; s. David McKenzie and Myrtle Estelle (Brogdon) C.; m. Martha McKellar Early; children: David, Martha Dockery, Marietta Brogdon, Carolyn Elizabeth; m. Susan Summers Mullally; 1 child, McKenzie Lawrence. BA, Wake Forest Coll., 1951; LLD, NYU, 1957. Law clerk Chambers of Justice Black U.S. Supreme Court, Washington, D.C., 1957-59; assoc. Smith, Moore, Smith, Schell & Hunter, Greensboro, N.C., 1959-63; ptnr. Stern Rendleman & Clark, Greensboro, N.C., 1964-68, Clark & Wharton, Greensboro, N.C., 1968-98, Clark Bloss & McIver, Greensboro, 1999—. Mem. bd. dirs. Legal Svcs. of N.C., Raleigh, 1976-82; pres. Summit Rotary Club, Greensboro, 1967; mem. bd. trustees W. Market Street Methodist Ch., Greensboro; chmn., co-founder Greensboro Legal Aid Found., 1965-68. Mem. ABA, Am. Trial Lawyers Assn., Am. Bd. Trial Advocates, N.C. Bar Assn. (bd. govs. 1982-85), N.C. Acad. Trial Lawyers, Greensboro Bar Assn. (bd. dirs.). Avocations: golf, tennis. General civil litigation, Securities, Personal injury. Home: 328 E Greenway Dr N Greensboro NC 27403-1560 Office: Clark & Wharton 125 S Elm St Ste 600 Greensboro NC 27401-2644

**CLARK, DAVID ROBERT,** lawyer; b. Streator, Ill., May 28, 1953; s. Robert Allen and Marcia Grace (Hile) C.; m. Patricia Kathleen Bostock, Sept. 26, 1982; 1 child, Ryan Michael. BA, Purdue U., 1975; JD, U. So. Calif., 1978. Bar: Calif. 1978, U.S. Dist. Ct. (so. dist.) Calif. 1978, U.S. Tax Ct. 1979, U.S. Ct. Appeals (9th cir.) 1979, U.S. Supreme Ct. 1982. Assoc. Higgs, Fletcher & Mack, San Diego, 1978-81; ptnr. Aylward, Kintz & Stiska, San Diego, 1981-87, Jenkins & Perry, San Diego, 1987-90, Musick, Peeler & Garrett, San Diego, 1990-91, Higgs, Fletcher & Mack, San Diego, 1991—; bd. dirs. Defenders Program of San Diego, 1984-87. Mem. ABA, Calif. Bar Assn., San Diego County Bar Assn., PGA West Golf Club, Phi Beta Kappa, Phi Kappa Phi. Avocation: golf. General civil litigation, Real property, Federal civil litigation. Office: Higgs Fletcher & Mack 401 W A St Ste 2600 San Diego CA 92101-7913

**CLARK, DAVID WRIGHT,** lawyer; b. West Point, Miss., May 19, 1948; s. Douglas Earl and Sarah Evelyn (Wright) C.; m. Victoria Baugher, Oct. 16, 1976; children: Alexander, Nicholas, Peter. BA with high honors, Millsaps Coll., 1970; MA, Harvard U., 1971; JD, U. Mich., 1974. Bar: Ill. 1974, Miss. 1978, U.S. Dist. Ct. (no. dist.) Ill. 1974, U.S. Ct. Appeals (7th cir.) 1974, U.S. Dist. Ct. (so. and no. dists.) Miss. 1978, U.S. Ct. Appeals (5th cir.) 1978. Adj. prof. Miss. Coll. Sch. Law, Jackson, 1978-82; assoc. Wildman, Harrold, Allen & Dixon, Chgo., Friedman & Koven, Chgo., 1974-78; shareholder Wise Carter Child & Caraway, P.A., Jackson, 1978-96; ptnr. Lake Tindall, LLP, Jackson, 1996—; bd. dirs. Ctrl. Miss. Legal Svcs., Jackson, 1989-97; pres. Miss. Bar Rev., 1979—. Mem. Miss. Constitution Study Commn., Jackson, 1985-87; bd. dirs. Miss. First, Inc., Jackson, 1983-87; pres. U.S.A. Internat. Ballet Competition, Jackson, 1990-98; mem. Leadership Jackson, 1989-90. Mem. ABA (dir. sect. litigation divsn., com. chmn. and task force chmn. 1987-95, chmn. gun violence coord. com. 1998—), Miss. Bar Assn. (chmn. litigation sect. 1994-95), Am. Law Inst., Charles Clark Am. Inn of Ct. Avocations: musicals, opera. E-mail: dlark@laketindall.com. Federal civil litigation, General corporate, State civil litigation. Home: 110 Olympia Fields Jackson MS 39211-2509 Office: Lake Tindall LLP One Jackson Pl Ste 450 Jackson MS 39201

**CLARK, DONALD H.,** lawyer; b. Washington, Jan. 29, 1937. BS, U.S. Naval Acad., 1959; JD, George Washington U., 1968. Bar: Va. 1968, U.S. Dist. Ct. (ea. dist.) Va. 1969, U.S. Ct. Appeals (4th cir.) 1974, U.S. Supreme Ct. 1974, U.S. Ct. Fed. Claims 1998. Engr. Naval Elec. Sys., Washington, 1965-68; assoc. Kellam & Kellam, Norfolk, 1968-72; ptnr. Clark & Stant, Virginia Beach, Va., 1972-99; pres., chief ops. officer Williams, Mullen, Clark & Dobbins, Virginia Beach, 1999—; appointed to Va. State Bar disciplinary bd., 1982-86, med. malpractice rev. panel, 1978-85, 2d dist. ethics com. 1975-77, vice chmn. 1976, chmn. 1977; lecr. continuing legal edn. Co-author: Virginia Construction Law. Vice chmn., chmn.-elect bd. dirs. Sentara Health Sys., 1998—; chmn. bd. dirs., mem. exec. com. Tidewater Health Care Inc., 1993-98; chmn. bd. dirs. Virginia Beach Gen. Hosp., 1988-91; chmn. mayor's com. for reapportionment; mem. vestry Eastern Shore Chapel, 1971-74, sr. warden, 1974. Lt. USN, 1959-65. Mem. ABA (litigation and law practice mgmt. sects.), Va. State Bar Assn. (litigation and constrn. law sects., bd. govs. constrn. law sect. 1983-86), Virginia Beach Bar Assn. (pres. 1982), Am. Inns of Ct. James Kent Inn (master 1995—). Federal civil litigation, General civil litigation, State civil litigation. Office: Williams Mullen Clark & Dobbins One Columbus Ctr Virginia Beach VA 23462

**CLARK, DONALD OTIS,** lawyer; b. Charlotte, N.C., May 30, 1934; s. Otis and Ruby Lee (Church) C.; m. Jo Ann Hager, June 15, 1957 (div. 1980); children: Deborah Elise, Stephen Merritt; m. Anja Maria Smith, Nov. 5, 1983. AB, U. S.C., 1956, JD cum laude, 1963; MA, U. Ill., 1957. Bar: S.C. 1963, Ga. 1964, D.C., 1999. Practice law Atlanta, 1963-83; mem. Candler, Cox, McClain & Andrews, 1968-70, McClain, Mellen, Bowling & Hickman, 1970-75; ptnr. King & Spalding, 1975-78; sr. ptnr. Hurt, Richardson, Garner, Todd & Cadenhead, 1978-83; ptnr. Bishop, Liberman, Cook, Purcell & Reynolds, Washington, 1983-86, Kaplan Russin & Vecchi, Washington, 1986-92, Whitman & Ranson (merged with Breed Abbot & Morgan 1993), Washington, 1992-93; sr. ptnr. Whitman Breed Abbott & Morgan, Washington, 1993-95; ptnr. Keck, Mahin & Cate, Washington, 1995-97, Reed Smith Shaw & McClay, Washington, 1997—; mem. dist. export council U.S. Dept Commerce, 1974—; adj. prof. law Emory U., 1970—, U.S.C., 1974; lectr. Ga. State U., 1972; lectr. numerous internat. trade seminars and workshops. Author: German govt. study on doing bus. in Southeastern U.S., 1974; editor-in-chief: S.C. Law Rev., 1963; contbr. articles to profl. jours. Served to capt. USAF, 1957-60. Decorated knight Order St. John of Jerusalem, Knights of Malta, knight and minister of justice Order of New Aragon, Sungrye medal Korea; recipient Nat. Leadership medal Air Force Assn., 1956, Coll. award Am. Legion, Outstanding Sr. award U. S.C., 1956, hon. consul Republic of Korea, 1972—. Mem. Atlanta Bar Assn., ABA, S.C. Bar Assn., Ga. Bar Assn., D.C. Bar Assn., Lawyers Club Atlanta, Am. Judicature Soc., Am. Soc. Internat. Law, Atlanta C. of C., Ga. C. of C. (exec. com. Internat. Councils), Inst. Internat. Edn. (chmn. Southeastern regional adv. bd. 1974—, nat. trustee), So. Consortium Internat. Edn. Inc. (dir.), Wig & Robe, Sigma Chi (pres. 1956 Province Balfour award), Omicron Delta Kappa, Kappa Sigma Kappa, Phi Delta Phi (pres. 1963 Province Grad. of Yr. award). Private international, Public international, Taxation, general.

**CLARK, GARY CARL,** lawyer; b. Flippin, Ark., Mar. 4, 1947; m. Jane W. Clark; children: Ross, Lauren. BS in Agrl. Edn., Okla. State U., 1969, MS, 1972; JD with honors, U. Tex., 1975. Bar: Okla. 1975, U.S. Dist. Ct. (no. dist.) Okla. 1975, U.S. Ct. Appeals (10th cir.) 1979. Tchr. Laverne H.S., Okla., 1969-70; assoc. Conner, Winters, Ballaine, Barry & McGowen, 1975-81, ptnr., 1981; ptnr. Baker & Hoster, Tulsa, 1981-97; dir. Crowe & Dunlevy, PC, Tulsa, 1997—; lawyer-staffed Panel of Ct. Appeals, 1991; speaker in field. Vol. Legal Svcs. Ea. Okla., 1993—; trustee Okla. State Univ., Tulsa, 1999—; mem. bd. regents Okla. State Univ. and A&M Colls., 1993—, chmn., 1997-98; past v.p. Jane Addams Elem. Sch. PTA, sch. vol.; chair site adv. Recipient Silver Beaver award Boy Scouts Am., 1996. Fellow Am. Bar Found., Okla. Bar Found.; mem. Okla. Bar Assn. (bd. govs. 1997-99, chair estate planning and probate sect. 1988-89, vice chair probate code com. 1991, bd. dirs. young lawyers divsn., mem. real property sect.), Tulsa County Bar Assn. (pres. 1993-94, Golden Rule award 1993, Outstanding Sr. Lawyer 1996), Tulsa County Bar Found. (pres. 1994-95, treas. 1995-99, charter fellow), Tulsa Title and Probate Lawyers Assn. (pres. 1989-90), Okla. State U. Alumni Assn. (life), FFA Alumni Assn. (life), Order of Coif, Alpha Gamma Rho Alumni Assn. (Okla. chpt. dir., past pres.), Phi Delta Phi. Estate planning, Probate, Bankruptcy. Home: 5505 S 97th West Ave Sand Springs OK 74063-4726 Office: Crowe & Dunlevy 500 Kennedy Bldg Tulsa OK 74103

**CLARK, GLEN EDWARD,** judge; b. Cedar Rapids, Iowa, Nov. 23, 1943; s. Robert M. and Georgia L. (Welch) C.; m. Deanna D. Thomas, July 16, 1966; children: Andrew Curtis, Carissa Jane. BA, U. Iowa, 1966; JD, U. Utah, 1971. Bar: Utah 1971, U.S. Dist. Ct. Utah 1971, U.S. Ct. Appeals (10th cir.) 1972. Assoc. Fabian & Clendenin, 1971-74, ptnr., 1975-81, dir., chmn. banking and comml. law sect., 1981-82; judge U.S. Bankruptcy Ct. Dist. Utah, Salt Lake City, 1982-86, chief judge, 1986—; bd. govs. nat. Conf. Bankruptcy Judges, 1988-94; mem. com. on bankruptcy edn. Fed. Jud. Ctr., 1989-92; vis. prof. U. Utah, Salt Lake City, 1977-79, 83; pres. Nat. Conf. Bankruptcy Judges, 1992-93; chair bd. trustees Nat. Conf. Bankruptcy Judges Endowment for Edn., 1990-92. vis. assoc. prof. law Univ. Utah; instr. adv. bus. law Univ. Utah. Articles editor: Utah Law Review. With U.S. Army, 1966-68. Finkbine fellow U. Iowa. Fellow Am. Coll. Bankruptcy (charter, mem. bd. regents 1995—); mem. Jud. Conf. U.S. (mem. com. jud. br. 1992—, 10th cir. bankruptcy appellate panel 1996—), Utah Bar Assn., Order of Coif. Presbyterian. Office: 365 US Courthouse 350 S Main St Salt Lake City UT 84101-2106

**CLARK, GRANT LAWRENCE,** corporate lawyer; b. Syracuse, N.Y., Apr. 15, 1954; s. Robert William and Linda (Grant) C.; m. Diana Christine Baker, Aug. 5, 1983. BA, Framingham State Coll., 1979; JD, Suffolk U., 1983. Bar: Mass. 1983, Calif. 1992, U.S. Dist. Ct. Mass. 1983, U.S. Dist. Ct. (so. dist.) Calif. 1992, U.S. Ct. Appeals (D.C. cir.) 1995, U.S. Ct. Claims 1995, U.S. Ct. Mil. Appeals 1984. Staff judge advocate USAF, Washington, 1983-87; asst. gen. counsel GSA, Washington, 1987-88; assoc. Rivkin, Radler, Dunne & Bayh, Washington, 1988-91; assoc./ptnr. McKenna & Cuneo, Washington, 1991-94; asst. gen. counsel Sci. Applications Internat. Corp., San Diego, 1994—; instr. Fed. Publs., Inc., Washington, 1991—. Mem. pres.'s coun. Scripps Rsch. Found., LaJolla, Calif., 1998-99; mem. Founder's Soc., Morris Animal Found., Englewood, Colo., 1998-99. Capt., USAF, 1983-87. Mem. ABA, Fed. Bar Assn., Nat. Contracts Mgmt. Assn. Avocations: mountain biking, Latin dance, medieval history. Government contracts and claims, Contracts commercial, General civil litigation. Home: 2260 Del Mar Scenic Pkwy Del Mar CA 92014-3616 Office: Sci Applications Internat Corp 10260 Campus Point Dr F-3 San Diego CA 92121-1522

**CLARK, J. DAVID, JR.,** lawyer, financial planner. BS, Old Dominion U., 1985; JD with spl. distinction, Miss. Coll., 1990. CFP; ChFC. Pvt. practice Madison, Miss., 1996—; pres. Medallion Fin. Svcs., P.A., Madison, 1998—. Recipient Robert E. Hauberg award FBA, Jackson, 1989; Miss. Bar Found. scholar, Jackson, 1989. Mem. Inst. CFPs, Leadership Madison County Alumni. Fax: 601-853-9845. E-mail: Dclarkmfs@aol.com. Office: 317 Beacon Hill Dr Allen TX 75013-3401

**CLARK, JAMES CLYDE,** lawyer, judge; b. Alexandria, Va., July 18, 1950; s. Henry Masten and Elizabeth Henrietta Clark; m. Mary Alice Bohanan, May 11, 1990; children: Alice Lloyd, James Travers. BA, Bridgewater Coll., 1972; JD, U. Richmond, 1976. Bar: Va. 1976, U.S. Dist. Ct. (ea. dist.) Va. 1978, U.S. Ct. Appeals (4th cir.) 1978. Asst. commonwealth's lawyer City of Alexandria, 1976-78; lawyer Land, Clark, Carroll, Mendelson & Blair P.C., Alexandria, 1978; substitute judge 18th Jud. Cir., Alexandria, 1990—; faculty mem. Va. Bar Professionalism Course, Va., 1997—, Va. Bar, 1976. Mem. adv. com. Alexandria Sch. Bd., 1998—; youth coach Alexandria Soccer and Baseball, 1976—. Mem. Alexandria Bar Assn. Avocations: running, fishing, working with children. Office: Land Clark Carroll Mendelson & Blair PC 112 S Alfred St Alexandria VA 22314-3061

**CLARK, JAMES E.,** lawyer; b. Strong, Ark., Feb. 10, 1929; s. Carey Eugene Clark and Mary (Braswell) Matthews; m. Susie Erskine (dec.); children: Christopher G., David D., Jeffrey F. BBA, La. Tech U., 1952; JD, La. State U., 1957. Bar: La. 1957, U.S. Dist. Ct. (we. dist.) La. 1957, U.S. Ct. Appeals (5th cir.) 1957. Sr. ptnr. Cook, Clark, Egan, Yancey and King, Shreveport, La., 1957-72; dist. judge State of La. 1st Jud. Dist., Shreveport, La., 1972-90; pvt. practice arbitration and mediation Shreveport, La., 1991—; pres. La. Dist. Judges Assn., 1982-83; mem. State-Fed. Jud. Coun., 1983-90. Mem. Caddo Parish Dem. Exec. Com., Shreveport, 1964-72, La. State Dem. Exec. Com., 1964-72; del. Dem. Nat. Conv., 1964, 68. Capt. USAFR, 1952-64; corp. USMC, 1946-48. Recipient Communication award Shreveport Toastmaster Internat., 1987. Mem. ABA, La. State Bar Assn. (del. 1968-72), Shreveport Bar Assn., Mason, Scottish Rite, Shriner, Elks Lodge #122, Rotary Club of Shreveport (pres. 1990-91). Democrat. Episcopalian. Avocation: reading. Personal injury, General civil litigation, Alternative dispute resolution. Office: 416 Travis St Ste 1105 Shreveport LA 71101-5504

**CLARK, JAMES KENDALL,** lawyer; b. Miami, Feb. 4, 1948; s. William Rourk and Martha Elizabeth (Johnson) C.; m. Linda Faith Forbes, Mar. 18, 1971; children: Matthew Forbes, Christopher James. BA, U. Fla., 1970, JD, 1973. Bar: Fla. 1973, U.S. Dist. Ct. (so. dist.) Fla. 1973, U.S. Dist. Ct. (mid. dist) Fla. 1992, U.S. Ct. Appeals (11th cir.) 1990. Assoc. Talburt, Kubicki & Bradley, Miami, 1973-80, Dickman & Barnett, Coral Gables, Fla., 1981-82; ptnr. Barnett & Clark, Coral Gables, 1982-88, Barnett, Clark & Barnard, Miami, 1988-92, Clark, Sparkman, Robb and Nelson, Miami, 1992-95; mng. atty. James K. Clark & Assocs., Miami, 1995—; mem. ad hoc trial practices com. 11th Jud. Cir. of Fla., 1989-95. Mem. ABA, Am. Arbitration Assn. (arbitrator), Fla. Bar Assn. (designated by bar assn. in field of appellate practice), Dade County Bar Assn. Federal civil litigation, State civil litigation, Personal injury. Office: James K Clark & Assocs Suntrust Internat Ctr #1800 One SE 3d Ave Miami FL 33131

**CLARK, JEFFREY A.,** lawyer; b. Knightstown, Ind., Mar. 17, 1965; s. Terry Lee and Judith Ann Clark; m. Wendy Sue Clark, June 15, 1991; children: Megan, Sarah, Cara. BA, Ind. U., Bloomington, 1987; JD, Ind. U., Indpls., 1995. Bar: Ind., U.S. Dist. Ct. (so. and no. dists.) Ind. Atty., law clk. Allen Superior Ct., Ft. Wayne, Ind., 1995-96; atty. Burt Blee Dixon & Sutton, Ft. Wayne, 1996—. General civil litigation, Consumer commercial, Contracts commercial. Office: Burt Blee Dixon & Sutton 1000 Standard Federal Plz Fort Wayne IN 46802

**CLARK, JEFFREY BOSSERT,** lawyer; b. Phila., Apr. 17, 1967; s. Thomas Joseph and Betty Anne (Bossert) C.; m. Eun Ha Hwang; 1 child, Jeffrey Bossert Jr. AB, Harvard U., 1989; MA, U. Del., 1992; JD, Georgetown U., 1995. Bar: D.C. 1997, U.S. Dsit. Ct. D.C. 1998, U.S. Ct. Appeals (D.C. cir.) 1998. Tax policy analyst Dept. Fin. State of Del., Wilmington, 1989-92; law clk. Hon. Danny J. Boggs U.S. Ct. Appeals (6th cir.), Louisville, 1995-96; assoc. Kirkland & Ellis, Washington, 1996—. Co-author: 1997 Annual Review of Antitrust Law Developments, 1998. Mem. Federalist Soc. (vice chmn. for publs., environ. law, and property rights 1998—). Republican. Roman Catholic. Avocations: tennis, reading history, wargaming, Internet. Appellate, Administrative and regulatory, Constitutional. Home: 7107 Rock Ridge Ln Apt A Alexandria VA 22315-5140 Office: Kirkland & Ellis 655 15th St NW Fl 12 Washington DC 20005-5793

**CLARK, JENNIFER BABBIN,** lawyer; b. N.Y.C., June 1, 1961; d. Malcolm J. and Fredlyn (Goodman) Babbin; m. William M. Clark, May 5, 1991; 1 child, Benjamin Frederic. BA, Brandeis U., 1983; JD, Boston U., 1986. Bar: N.Y. 1987, Mass. 1988. Assoc. Weil, Gotshal & Manges, N.Y.C., 1986-88; assoc. Sullivan & Worcester LLP, Boston, 1988-94, ptnr., 1994—. Finance, Real property. Office: Sullivan & Worcester LLP One Post Office Sq Boston MA 02109

**CLARK, JOHN A., JR.,** lawyer; b. Pitts., Apr. 3, 1953. BA in History, Lincoln (Pa.) U., 1976; JD, Tex. So. U., Houston, 1982. Bar: Tex. 1982. Atty. Irvin & Clark, Houston, 1983—. Gen. counsel Antioch Bapt. Ch., Houston, 1990—; scout leader Boy Scouts Am., Houston, 1994—; vol. Houston Zoning Commn., 1992-93. Avocations: skiing, boxing. Contracts commercial, General corporate. Office: Irvin & Clark 440 Louisiana St Ste 400 Houston TX 77002-1634

**CLARK, JOHN GRAHAM, III,** lawyer; b. Greenville, N.C., Dec. 28, 1950; s. John Graham Jr. and Ariane (Downarowicz) C. BA, U. N.C., 1973; MA, E. Carolina U., 1977; JD, Campbell U., 1984. Bar: N.C. 1984, U.S. Dist. Ct. N.C. 1988, U.S. Supreme Ct. 1988; cert. specialist criminal law N.C. State Bar. Assoc. Nelson Taylor, III, Morehead City, N.C., 1985; asst. dist. atty. State of N.C., 1985-87; ptnr. Clark & James law firm, Greenville, 1987—. Named to Internat. Law Moot Ct. Assn. Student Internat. Law Socs., 1983. Mem. N.C. Bar Assn., N.C. Acad. Trial Lawyers, Phi Alpha Delta, Pi Sigma Alpha, Phi Alpha Theta. Avocations: golf, travel, tennis. Criminal, Family and matrimonial, Personal injury. Office: 315 S Evans St Greenville NC 27858-1845

**CLARK, JOHN H., JR.,** lawyer; b. Chester, Pa., June 6, 1928; s. John H. and Emma E. (Higler) C.; m. Esther F. Giaccio, June 12, 1954; 1 child, Jacqueline Ann. B.A. with honors, U.Pa., 1948, J.D. cum laude, 1951. Bar: Pa. 1951. Pvt. practice Ridley Park, Pa., 1973—; chmn. hearing com. Pa. Supreme Ct. Disciplinary Bd., 1980-86. Pres. Historic Delaware County, Inc., 1972; del. Democratic Nat. Conv., 1960; solicitor Tinicum Twp., 1960-64, Folcroft Borough Sch. Dist., 1959-63, Norwood Borough, 1972-76, Folcroft Borough, 1973-74. Served with USAF, 1952-53; to maj. Res. Mem. ABA, Pa. Bar Assn. (ho. of dels. 1972-82), Delaware County Bar Assn., Delaware County Hist. Soc. (pres. 1989-92), Rotary (pres. Chester Pike club 1973-74). Roman Catholic. Home: 207 Knoll Rd Wallingford PA 19086-6009 Office: PO Box 152 204 E Chester Pike Ridley Park PA 19078-1730

**CLARK, JOHN HOLLEY, III,** retired lawyer; b. N.Y.C., May 31, 1918; s. John Holley, Jr. and Mary (Angus) C.; m. Eleanor Jackson, June 4, 1964; children: Benjamin Hayden, Christopher Angus. BA with high honors, Princeton U., 1939; JD, Columbia U., 1942; MA, NYU, 1965. Bar: N.Y. 1942, U.S. Dist. Ct. (so. dist.) N.Y. 1949, U.S. Ct. Appeals (2d cir.) 1952, U.S. Ct. Mil. Appeals 1986. Assoc. Cahill, Gordon, Reindel & Ohl, N.Y.C., 1946-54; atty. Antitrust div. U.S. Dept. Justice, N.Y.C., 1954-95. V.p. N.Y. Young Republican Club, 1953-54; mem. sch. com. Cathedral Ch. St. John the Divine, N.Y.C., 1979-81. Served with USAAF, 1942-46, PTO. Democrat. Episcopalian. Home: 375 Riverside Dr Apt 9C New York NY 10025-2138

**CLARK, JONATHAN MONTGOMERY,** retired lawyer; b. Bklyn., Oct. 20, 1937; s. Russell Inslee and Lillian (Longmore) C.; m. Priscilla M. Jorgensen, Sept. 24, 1960; children: Jonathan M. Jr., Christopher D. BA, Yale U., 1959; LLB, U. Va., 1964. Bar: N.Y. 1965. Assoc. Davis Polk & Wardwell, N.Y.C., 1964-71, ptnr., 1971-93; gen. counsel, mng. dir. Morgan Stanley & Co., Inc., N.Y.C., 1993-97. advisor mission to Poland, Fin. Svcs. Vol. Corps, 1990, 92; cons. Warren Commn., Washington, 1965; bd. dirs. Greenwich Hosp. Assn., 1990-98, Prentice Cup Com. 1st lt. USMC, 1959-61. Mem. ABA, N.Y. State Bar Assn., Assn. Bar City N.Y., Securities Industry Assn. (bd. dirs., 1995-96), N.Y. Stock Exchange Legal Adv. Com. Republican. Episcopalian. Avocations: golf, fly fishing, birding.

**CLARK, JOSEPH FRANCIS, JR.,** lawyer; b. Tulsa, Okla., Jan. 20, 1949; s. Joseph F. and Betty Sue C.; m. Carol J. Coleman, Nov. 2, 1974 (div. 1981); m. Cathy A. Baker, Jan. 6, 1989; children: Joseph F. Clark III, Thomas S. Clark, Joshua B. Baker. BA, Villanova U., 1971; JD, Tulsa U., 1973. Bar: Okla. 1974. Atty. Gibbon, Gladd, Clark et al, Tulsa, 1974-78; pvt. practice Tulsa, 1979-80; atty. Williams, Clark et al, Tulsa, 1980-90; ptnr. Clark & Stainer, Tulsa, 1990-94, Layon, Cronin, Clark & Kaiser, P.L.L.C., Tulsa, 1994-99; pvt. practice Tulsa, 1999—. Mem. Am. Inns of Ct. (term master), Tulsa County Bar Assn. (fee dispute com. 1998—). Democrat. Roman Catholic. Insurance, General civil litigation, Appellate. Home: 2922 E 39th St Tulsa OK 74105-3704 Office: 1605 S Denver Ave Tulsa OK 74119-4232

**CLARK, LEIF MICHAEL,** federal judge; b. Washington, Nov. 12, 1947; s. Charles G. and Gertrude Lyda (Zimmer) C. BA cum laude, U. Md., 1968; MDiv, Trinity Luth. Sem., Columbus, Ohio, 1972; JD cum laude, U. Houston, 1980. Bar: Tex. 1980, U.S. Dist. Ct. (we. dist.) Tex. 1981, U.S. Dist. Ct. (so. dist.) Tex. 1983, U.S. Ct. Appeals (5th cir.). 1984. Dir. Housing for Exceptional People, Detroit, 1974-75; ptnr. Cox & Smith, Inc., San Antonio, 1980-87; judge for western dist. Tex. U.S. Bankruptcy Ct., San Antonio, 1987—; prof. McGeorge Internat. Law Program, Salzburg, Austria, 1989-99; mem. adv. group U.S. Del. Working Group UNCITRAL, 1995-96; mem. adv. bd. ALI-ABA Cross Border Insolvency Project, 1995-96, USAID Jud. Tng. Project, 1995-98. Adv. bd. Insol Internat. Project, 1995. Mem.

ABA, Am. Coll. Bankruptcy, Am. Bankruptcy Inst. (dir. 1991—, exec. com. 1995—, v.p. rsch. 1998—), Nat. Conf. Bankruptcy Judges (planning com. 1992 ann. meeting), Comml. Law League, State Bar Tex. Lutheran. Avocations: photography, choral singing, running, traveling. Office: PO Box 2676 San Antonio TX 78299-2676

**CLARK, MARCIA RACHEL,** prosecutor; b. Berkeley, Calif., 1954; d. Abraham I. Kleks; m. Gabriel Horowitz, 1976 (div. 1980); m. Gordon Clark (div. 1994); 2 children. BA in Polit. Sci., UCLA, 1974; JD, Southwestern U., 1979. Atty. Brodey and Price, L.A., 1979-81, L.A. County Dist. Attys. Office, 1981-97. Author (with Teresa Carpenter) Without a Doubt, 1997. Office: William Morris Agy 151 S El Camino Dr Beverly Hills CA 90212-2704

**CLARK, MARK ADRIAN,** lawyer; b. Austin, Tex., May 11, 1956; s. Fred Ray and Marion Anita Clark; m. Kelly Lee Gibson, Feb. 11, 1984; 1 child, Rachel Lynn. BA in Polit. Sci., U. Tex., 1978; JD, St. Mary's Coll. Law, San Antonio, 1981. Bar: Tex. Atty. in pvt. practice, New Braunfels, Tex., 1981—. Pres., Mental Health Mental Retardation, New Braunfels, 1998; bd. dirs. New Braunfels Pub. Libr. Found., 1995—; pres. Comal County Rep. Men's Club, 1995, 96. Mem. Comal County Bar Assn. (pres.), New Braunfels Rotary, Lake Breeze Ski Lodge, San Antonio Zoo. Avocations: golf, water skiing, skiing. Family and matrimonial, Criminal, Personal injury. Office: 260 N Castell Ave New Braunfels TX 78130-5020

**CLARK, MARK JEFFREY,** paralegal, researcher; b. Alton, Ill., Nov. 2, 1953; s. William Alfred and Winifred May (Young) C.; m. Patricia Ann Newell, July 29, 1989; children: Jason William, Brandi Leigh. AS in Bus. Adminstrn., Lewis & Clark Coll., 1978; cert. paralegal, Paralegal Inst., Atlanta, 1994, diploma in civil lit. and bus. law, 1994. Commd. spl. officer Lake Ozark (Mo.) Police Dept., 1975-78; ind. paralegal J & B Enterprises, Woodriver, Ill., 1994—; criminal rschr. Pinkerton Svcs. Group, Charlotte, N.C., 1998—; cons., rschr. Nationwide Corps., 1994—. With USN, 1972-75, Vietnam. Mem. Nat. Paralegal Assn., KC (4th degree), Am. Legion. Democrat. Roman Catholic. Avocations: scuba diving, golf, bowling. Home: Rt # 71 Box 272 Camdenton MO 65020

**CLARK, MARK LEE,** lawyer; b. Muskegon, Mich., July 13, 1953; s. Alva Lee and Esther Luella (Bellinger) C.; m. Jane Ellen Lyons, Sept. 3, 1983; children: Zachary, Caitlin. BA with high honors, Mich. State U., 1975; JD with honors, Wayne State U., 1978. Bar: Mich. 1978, U.S. Dist. Ct. (ea. dist.) Mich. 1982. Assoc. McLean & Mijak, Romeo, Mich., 1978-82; ptnr. McLean, Mijak & Clark, P.C., Romeo, 1982—; mcpl. atty. Village of Romeo, 1985—. Pres. bd. trustees, bd. dirs. Romeo Dist. Library, 1981-85. Mem. ATLA, Mich. Bar Assn., Macomb County Bar Assn. Avocations: running, golf. General practice, State civil litigation, Municipal (including bonds). Home: 268 W Saint Clair St Romeo MI 48065-4662 Office: McLean Mijak & Clark P C 137 W Saint Clair St Romeo MI 48065-4657

**CLARK, MICHAEL PATRICK,** lawyer; b. Chgo., Aug. 4, 1958; s. Richard Leroy and Lillian Lois Clark; m. Sharon Lynn Winterhoff, Aug. 9, 1980; children: Ryan William, Megan Feeney. BA, U. No. Iowa, 1980; JD, Valparaiso U., 1983. Bar: Calif. 1983, U.S. Dist. Ct. (no. dist.) Calif. 1984. Assoc. Walkup, Shelby et al, San Francisco, 1984-87; ptnr. Hinton & Alfert, Walnut Creek, Calif., 1987-98. Mem. No. Calif. Mediation Assn., Soc. Profls. in Dispute Resolution, Alameda County Bar Assn., Contra Costa County Bar Assn., Alameda/Contra Costa Trial Lawyers Assn. (treas. 1998, bd. govs. 1987—). Avocations: sports, automobiles, reading, computers. Alternative dispute resolution, Personal injury, General civil litigation. Home: 928 Cochise Ct Walnut Creek CA 94598-4426

**CLARK, MORTON HUTCHINSON,** lawyer; b. Norfolk, Va., Apr. 21, 1933; s. David Henderson and Catharine Angelica (Hutchinson) C.; m. Lynn Harrison Adams, Aug. 12, 1961; children: Allison Adams, David Henderson, Susan West, Julia Dixon. BA in English, U. Va., 1954, LLB, 1960. Bar: Va. 1960, U.S. Dist. Ct. (ea. dist.) Va. 1960, U.S. Ct. Appeals (4th cir.) 1976, U.S. Ct. Appeals (1st cir.) 1993, U.S. Supreme Ct. 1993. Assoc. Vandeventer Black LLP, Norfolk, 1960-65, ptnr., 1965—. Co-editor: The Virginia Lawyer, 1991-93. Chmn. Va. Commn. for Children and Youth, Richmond. Fellow Am. Coll. Trial Lawyers, Va. Law Found.; mem. Maritime Law Assn. (exec. com. 1984-87), Hoffman I'Anson Am. Inns of Ct. (exec. com. 1993-95), The Harbor Club (pres.), Town Point Club, Princess Anne Country Club, Farmington Country Club. Episcopalian. Avocations: off shore racing, cruising. Admiralty, Federal civil litigation. Home: 103 Rivers Edge Kingsmill Williamsburg VA 23185-8930 Office: Vandeventer Black LLP 500 World Trade Ctr Norfolk VA 23510-1679

**CLARK, NANNETTE,** lawyer; b. Marshall, Tex., June 29, 1964; d. Jessie and Tommie (Lee) Uselton; m. Brett Clark; 1 child, Colleen. BBA, Belmont U., Nashville, 1986; student, Calif. Sch. Law, San Diego, 1989; JD, Nashville Sch. Law, 1993. Bar: Tenn. 1993. Atty. sole practitioner, Nashville, 1994—; ct.-apptd. spl. advocate CASA; mem. juvenile ct. bd. Mem. ABA, Nashville Bar Assn., Tenn. Trial Lawyers. Juvenile. Office: PO Box 22436 Nashville TN 37202-2436

**CLARK, PAUL THOMAS,** lawyer; b. Long Beach, Calif., Oct. 10, 1954; s. Thomas Joseph and Lois (Olney) C.; m. Deborah Elaine Myers, May 18, 1991. AB in History, U. Calif., 1976, JD, 1980. Bar: D.C. 1980. Legis. asst. Congressman Mark W. Hannaford, Washington, 1976-77; assoc. Williams & Jensen, P.C., Washington, 1980-84; assoc. Seward & Kissel, Washington, 1984-87, legis. counsel, 1987-88, ptnr., 1989—; bd. dirs. Bank 2000, N.A., 1985-91. Pres. Calif. State Soc., Washington, 1986; bd. dirs. Washington Chamber Symphony, 1996—. Mem. ABA, D.C. Bar Assn., Internat. Bar Assn., Berkeley Alumni Club (v.p.). Avocation: tennis, golf. Banking, Legislative, Securities. Office: Seward & Kissel 1200 G St NW Ste 350 Washington DC 20005-3881

**CLARK, R. THOMAS,** lawyer; b. Milw., Dec. 22, 1951; s. Al T. and Sophie A. (Rakowski) C.; m. Mary Coldagelli, July 1, 1978; children: Rachael Mary, Elizabeth Mary. BS cum laude, Marquette U., 1975; JD, William Mitchell Coll. Law, 1979. Bar: Minn. 1979, U.S. Dist. Ct. Minn. 1980, U.S. Ct. Appeals (8th cir.) 1980, U.S. Mil. Ct. 1981, U.S. Mil. Ct. Appeals 1983, U.S. Supreme Ct. 1983, Conn. 1985, U.S. Dist. Ct. Conn. 1985, U.S. Ct. Appeals (2d cir.) 1985. Regional mgr. Security Schs., Inc., Mpls., 1979-81; instr. law Mohegan Community Coll., Norwich, Conn., 1983—; pvt. practice law New London, Conn., 1985—; instr. Acad. of Accountancy, Mpls., 1979; assoc. faculty Mitchell Coll., New London, 1984-92; asst. prof. Eastern Conn. State U., Willimantic, 1985—; adj. faculty U. New Haven, Groton, Conn., 1987—, Teikyo Post U., 1990—; jud. hearing officer Ea. Conn. State U., 1990-98, lectr. bus. ethics dept. bus., 1998—; asst. dir. student affairs for jud. programs and comty. rels. Plymouth (N.H.) State Coll., 1998—; jud. hearing officer Dept. Edn. State Conn., 1997—; mediator Ctr. for Dispute Resolution Svcs., 1990-98, exec. dir., 1994-98; impartial hearing bd. State Bd. of Edn., State of Conn., 1997—. Co-author: Legal Assistance Guide for Members of Armed Forces in Connecticut, 1984; contbr. articles to mil. newspaper. Bd. dirs. Covenant Shelter of New London, Inc., 1991-93; bd. dirs. Martin House, Inc., 1992—, pres. bd. dirs., 1995-97; bd. dirs. Thames River Community Svc., Inc ., 1992—, pres. bd. dirs., 1995-97; bd. dirs. Associated Resource Mgmt. Svcs., 1994—. Lt. USNR, 1981-85. Mem. Am. Bus. Law Assn., Assn. for Student Jud. Affairs, Conn. Bar Assn. (chair G.A. 10 Ct. Visitation Program 1992-97), Nat. Assn. Student Pers. Adminstrs., Nat. Assn. Mediation in End., Nat. Inst. Dispute Resolution, New London County Bar Assn., Guild Cath. Lawyers, Alpha Sigma Nu, Beta Gamma Sigma. Roman Catholic. Avocations: sports, travel, reading. Contracts commercial, Constitutional, Family and matrimonial. Office: PO Box 141 Plymouth NH 03264-0141

**CLARK, ROBERT CHARLES,** law educator, dean; b. New Orleans, Feb. 26, 1944; s. William Vernon and Edwina Ellen (Nuessly) C.; m. Kathleen Margaret Tighe, June 1, 1968; children—Alexander Ian, Matthew Tighe. BA, Maryknoll Sem., 1966; PhD, Columbia U., 1971; JD, Harvard U., 1972. Bar: Mass. 1972. Assoc. firm Ropes & Gray, Boston, 1972-74; asst. prof. Yale U. Law Sch., New Haven, 1974-76, assoc. prof., 1976-77, prof., 1977-78; prof. law Harvard U., Cambridge, Mass., 1978—, dean of Law Sch., 1989—. Contbr. articles to profl. jours. Mem. Am. Bar Assn. Office: Harvard Law Sch Office of Dean 200 Griswold Hall 1525 Massachusetts Ave Cambridge MA 02138-2903*

**CLARK, ROBERT MUREL, JR.,** lawyer; b. Dallas, Mar. 7, 1948; s. Robert M. Sr. and Dorrace Helen (Schaerdel) C.; m. Kimberly Ann Kerss, Oct. 25, 1986; 1 child, Ashley Pendleton. BBA, U. Tex., 1972; MBA, So. Meth. U., 1978; JD, Oklahoma City U., 1982. Bar: Tex. 1982, U.S. Dist. Ct. (no. dist.) Tex. 1982, U.S. Ct. Appeals (5th cir.) 1982, U.S. Supreme Ct. 1988; cert. in civil trial law Tex. Bd. Legal Specialization; cert. trial specialist Nat. Bd. Trial Advocacy. Ptnr. Eddleman, Clark & Rosen, Dallas, 1989—. Contbr. articles to profl. jours. Del. state conv. Tex. Rep. Party, 1970, 72, 74, 82, 90; bd. dirs. Haile Selassie Fund for Ethiopian Children in Need; sec., bd. dirs. Dallas Goethe Ctr. Decorated grand officer Order of Ethiopian Lion, hon. knight Order of Vitez (Hungary), knight Order of St. John (Brandenburg). Fellow Tex. Bar Found. (life), Soc. Antiquaries (Scotland); mem. State Bar Tex., Am. Bd. Trial Advs. (Dallas chpt.), Oak Cliff Bar Assn. (pres. 1990), Am. Soc. Legal History, Soc. of the Cin., Aztec Club, Sons Republic of Tex., Founders and Patriots Am., Nat. Huguenot Soc. (former coun. gen. and 3d v.p. gen.), St. Nicholas Soc., Johanniterorden-Bailiwick of Brandenburg, Johanniter Hilfsgemeinschaften (bd. dirs., Washington), Army and Navy Club (Washington), City Tavern Club (Washington), Phi Delta Phi, Phi Delta Theta. Episcopalian. General civil litigation, Contracts commercial. Office: 4627 N Central Expy Dallas TX 75205-4022

**CLARK, ROBERT STOKES,** lawyer; b. Bogota, Colombia, Aug. 6, 1954; came to U.S., 1956; s. Robert Sevy and Verna (Stokes) C.; m. Wendy K. Williams, July 9, 1976; children: Robert, Joseph, Christopher, Kathleen, Callie, Margaret, Rebecca. BS, Brigham Young U., 1977, JD magna cum laude, 1980. Bar: Calif. 1980, Utah 1983, U.S. Supreme Ct. 1987. Assoc. O'Melveny & Myers, L.A., 1980-83; shareholder Parr, Waddoups, Brown, Gee, & Loveless, Salt Lake City, 1983—. Editor Brigham Young U. Law Rev., 1979-80. Joseph Fielding Smith scholar Brigham Young U., 1972-77, J. Reuben Clark scholar, 1980. Federal civil litigation, General civil litigation. Office: Parr Waddoups Brown Gee & Loveless Ste 1300 185 S State St Salt Lake City UT 84111-1537

**CLARK, ROSS BERT, II,** lawyer; b. Lafayette, Ind., Dec. 23, 1932; s. Ross Bert and Pauline Frances (Wilkinson) C.; m. Madge Logan, Dec. 27, 1959; 1 stepchild, George W. Johnson III. BA in History, U. of the South, 1954; JD, U. Tenn., 1960. Bar: Tenn. 1961, U.S. Dist. Ct. (we. dist.) Tenn. 1961, U.S. Dist. Ct. (no. dist.) Miss. 1981, U.S. Dist. Ct. (ea. dist.) Ark. 1996, U.S. Ct. Appeals (6th cir.) 1962. Law clk. to presiding judge U.S. Dist. Ct. (we. dist.) Tenn., Memphis, 1961-62; assoc. Rupert & Ewing, Memphis, 1962-64, Laughlin, Watson, Garthright & Halle, Memphis, 1964-68; ptnr. Laughlin, Halle, Clark, Gibson, McBride, Memphis, 1968-84, McKnight, Hudson, Lewis, Henderson & Clark, Memphis, 1985-91, Apperson, Crump, Duzane & Maxwell, Memphis, 1991-96, Armstrong, Allen, Prewitt, Gentry, Johnston & Holmes, Memphis, 1996—; instr. med. and dental jurisprudence U. Tenn., Memphis, 1963-72; asst. city atty. City of Memphis, 1972-78. Chmn. bd. dirs. Memphis Heart Assn., 1971-72; mem. U. Tenn. Law Sch. Adv. Coun., 1983-90, chmn., 1986-88; trustee U. of The South, 1992-95, 97-2000. Fellow Am. Bar Found., Tenn. Bar Found. (trustee 1989-98, chmn. 1996-97); mem. ABA, Nat. Conf. Commr. on Uniform State Laws, Tenn. Bar Assn. (ho. of dels. 1986-88, bd. govs. 1988-94), Memphis Bar Assn. (treas. 1981, sec. 1982, v.p. 1983, pres. 1984), Rotary (sec. 1988, bd. dirs. 1988-90). Republican. Episcopalian. Federal civil litigation, Labor. Office: Armstrong Allen Prewitt Gentry Johnston & Holmes LLP Brinkley Plz Ste 700 80 Monroe Ave Memphis TN 38103-2481

**CLARK, R(UFUS) BRADBURY,** lawyer; b. Des Moines, May 11, 1924; s. Rufus Bradbury and Gertrude Martha (Burns) C.; m. Polly Ann King, Sept. 6, 1949; children: Cynthia Clark Maxwell, Rufus Bradbury, John Atherton. BA, Harvard U., 1948, JD, 1951; diploma in law, Oxford U., Eng., 1952; D.H.L., Ch. Div. Sch. Pacific, San Francisco, 1983. Bar: Calif. 1952. Assoc. O'Melveny & Myers, L.A., 1952-62, sr. ptnr., 1961-93; mem. mgmt. com., 1983-90; of counsel O'Melveny & Myers LLP, L.A., 1993—; bd. dirs. Econ. Resources Corp., Brown Internat. Corp., Brown Citrus Sys., Inc., Avoco Internat. Corp., John Tracy Clinic, also pres. 1982-88, Tracy Family Hearing Ctrs. Editor: California Corporation Laws, 6 vols, 1976—. Chancellor Prot. Episcopal Ch. in the Diocese of L.A., 1967—, hon. canon, 1983—. Capt. U.S. Army, 1943-46. Decorated Bronze Star with oak leaf cluster, Purple Heart with oak leaf cluster; Fulbright grantee, 1952. Mem. ABA (com. law and acctg., task force on audit letters 1976-93, com. on opinions 1988-92), State Bar Calif. (chmn. drafting com. on gen. corp. law 1973-81, drafting com. on nonprofit corp. law 1980-84, mem. exec. com. bus. law sect. 1977-78, 84-87, sec. 1986-87, mem. com. nonprofit orgns. 1991—), L.A. County Bar Assn., Harvard Club, Chancery Club, Alamitos Bay Yacht Club (Long Beach, Calif.). Republican. General corporate, Public utilities, Banking. Office: O'Melveny & Myers LLP 400 S Hope St Los Angeles CA 90071-2899

**CLARK, RUSSELL GENTRY,** federal judge; b. Myrtle, Mo., July 27, 1925; s. William B. and Grace Frances (Jenkins) C.; m. Jerry Elaine Burrows, Apr. 30, 1959; children: Vincent A., Viki F. LLB, U. Mo., 1952. Bar: Mo. 1952. Mem. firm Woolsey, Fisher, Clark, Whiteaker & Stenger, Springfield, Mo., 1952-77; judge U.S. Dist. Ct. (we. dist.) Mo., Kansas City, 1977-91, sr. judge, 1991—. 2d lt. U.S. Army, 1944-46. Fellow Am. Bar Found.; mem. ABA, Internat. Platform Soc., Mo. Bar Assn. (continuing legal edn. com. 1969), Greene County Bar Assn. (dir. 1968-71), Kiwanis (past pres. Springfield chpt.). Democrat. Methodist. Club: Kiwanis (past pres. Springfield chpt.). Office: US Dist Ct 3100 US Courthouse 222 N John Q Hammons Pkwy Springfield MO 65806-2541 *Notable cases include: Jenkins vs. State of Mo., which involved the desegregation of the Kansas City, Mo. Schs.; Bauer vs. Kincaid, et al, which resolved whether news media were entitled to S.W. Mo. State's criminal activity reports; U.S. vs. Nepacco, which established liability for cost of cleaning up toxic waste.*

**CLARK, SHERRY WALKER,** lawyer, consultant; b. L.A., Dec. 25, 1954; d. Sherman and Sylvia (Bennett) Walker; m. Walter Clark, June 3, 1990; 1 child, Chandler O. BA, UCLA, 1976; JD, U. Calif., San Francisco, 1979. Bar: Calif. 1980, U.S. Dist. Ct. (no. dist.) Calif., U.S. Supreme Ct. City atty. City of San Jose, Calif., 1980-85; legal counsel Kaiser Found. Health Plan, Oakland, Calif., 1985-91; cons. State Bar Calif., San Francisco, 1993-95; gen. counsel Western Med. Svcs., Walnut Creek, Calif., 1995—; mem. adv. bd. Charles Houston Bar Assn., Oakland; bd. dirs. Wiley Manuel Law Found., Oakland. Mem. ABA, State Bar Calif., Charles Houston Bar Assn. Health, General corporate, Labor. Office: Western Med Svcs Inc 220 N Wright Ln Walnut Creek CA 94598

**CLARK, STEVEN A.,** lawyer; b. Limestone, Maine, Jan. 14, 1963. BA in Pub. Adminstrn., U. Maine, 1985; JD, Franklin Pierce Law Ctr., 1995. Town adminstr. Town of Hinsdale, N.H., 1986-88, Town of Seabrook, N.H., 1988-92; atty. Boutin and Solomon, Londonderry, N.H., 1995-97, Boutin & Assocs., Londonderry, 1997—. Mem. ABA, N.H. Bar Assn., Maine Bar Assn. Home: 403B High St Hampton NH 03842-2339 Office: Boutin & Assocs 1 Buttrick Rd PO Box 1107 Londonderry NH 03053-1107

**CLARK, THOMAS ALONZO,** federal judge; b. Atlanta, Dec. 20, 1920; s. Fred and Prudence (Sprayberry) C.; m. Betty Medlock, July 16, 1978; children: Thomas Alonzo, Christopher S., Julia M.; stepchildren: Allen L. Carter, Rosalyn Lackey Howell. BS, Washington and Lee U., 1942; LLB, U. Ga., 1949. Pvt. practice law Bainbridge, Ga., 1949-55; ptnr. Dykes, Marshall & Clark, Americus, Ga., 1955-57, Fowler, White et al, Tampa, Fla., 1957-61; sr. ptnr. Carlton, Fields, et al, Tampa, 1961-79; judge U.S. Ct. Appeals (5th cir.), 1979-81; judge U.S. Ct. of Appeals (11th cir.), Atlanta, 1981-99, sr. judge, 1991-99; ret., 1999. Mem. Ga. Ho. of Reps., 1951-52; pres. Fla. Assn. for Retarded Citizens, 1974-75, Served to lt. comdr. USN, 1942-46. Fellow Am. Coll. Trial Lawyers; mem. ABA, Ga. Bar Assn., Fla. Bar Assn.

**CLARK, WENDELL W.,** lawyer; b. Tulsa, Okla., June 10, 1944; s. Wesley D. and M. Janice (Ford) C.; children from previous marriage: Lanette C., Ashley A.; m. Kimberly G. Finch, Dec. 2, 1978; stepchildren: James W., Amanda G. Simmons. BA in History and Polit. Sci., U. Tulsa, 1966, JD, 1968. Assoc. VanCleave, Thomas, Liebler & Gresham, Tulsa, 1968-73, Gresham, Bivens, Clark and Bennett, Tulsa, 1973-74; ptnr. Wendell W. Clark & Assoc., Tulsa, 1974-77, Clark & Williams, Tulsa, 1977—. Pres. Minshall Park Homeowners, Tulsa, 1996-98; pub. defender, Tulsa, 1969-70; pres. Philcrest Hills Tennis Club, 1991. Capt. Okla. Air N.G., 1971-78. Mem. Okla. Bar Assn., Tulsa County Bar Assn. (sec. 1984, bd. dirs. 1985-86, Meritorious Svc. award 1984, 86, chmn. fee arbitration 1982-83), Tulsa Apartment Assn., Bldg. Owners and Mgrs. Assn. (bd. dirs. 1999), City of Tulsa Sales Tax Overview Com., pres., Philcrest Hills Tennis Club, 1991. Democrat. Methodist. Real property, Family and matrimonial, General civil litigation. Office: 5416 S Yale Ave Ste 600 Tulsa OK 74135-6244

**CLARK, WILLIAM FREDERICK,** lawyer; b. Denver, Aug. 2, 1941. Student, Am. Univ., 1960, U. Colo., 1963; JD, San Francisco Law Sch., 1967. Bar: Calif. 1969, U.S. Supreme Ct. 1975. Mng. ptnr. William Clark and Assocs., San Jose, 1979-97; sr. dep. city atty. City San Jose, 1997—; judge pro-tem Worker's Compensation Appeals Bd., 1982—; lectr. Continuing Edn. of Bar Def. Attys. Assn., 1988—, Indsl. Claims Assn., 1988—. Mem. ABA, Calif. Bar Assn., Santa Clara County Bar Assn. (worker's compensation com.). Workers' compensation, Insurance, Personal injury. Office: City Attys Office City San Jose 151 W Mission St San Jose CA 95110-1710

**CLARK, WILLIAM H., JR.,** lawyer; b. Phila., Apr. 10, 1951; s. William H. and Alice Kimes (Metts) C.; m. Cristine D. Merkel, Aug. 18, 1973; children: Matthew, Alison, Daniel. BA summa cum laude, Amherst Coll., 1973; MA in Religion, Westminster Sem., 1979; JD magna cum laude, Temple U., 1983. Bar: Pa. 1983. Assoc. Morgan, Lewis & Bockius, Phila., 1983-89; ptnr. Klett Lieber Rooney & Schorling, Pitts., 1989-98, Phila., 1998-99; ptnr. Drinker Biddle & Reath LLP, Phila., 1999—; chmn. corp. bur. advisory com. Pa. Dept of State, 1991—; cons. rules disciplinary bd. Supreme Ct. Pa., Harrisburg, 1983—. Fellow Am. Bar Found.; mem. ABA (com. on corp. laws, com. on bus. courts), Pa. Bar Assn. (draftsman, lobbyist, corp. law com. 1984—, coun. sect. corp. banking and bus. law 1989-93, officer 1993—), Allegheny County Bar Assn. (coun. sect. corp. banking and bus. law 1991-97, officer 1997-98), Phila. Bar Assn. (coun. bus. law sect. 1998—), Am. Law Inst., Phi Beta Kappa. Republican. Presbyterian. General corporate, Mergers and acquisitions, Securities. Office: Drinker Biddle & Reath LLP One Logan Sq Philadelphia PA 19103

**CLARK, WILLIAM J.,** lawyer; b. N.Y.C., May 21, 1957; s. William Joseph and Joan R. (Upton) C. BS in Govt. and Politics, St. John's U., 1979, JD, 1983. Bar: N.Y., N.J. Ct. atty. Kings County N.Y.C. Criminal Ct., 1984-85, law clrk to admin. judge, 1985-92, chief ct. atty., 1992—. Co-author, editor: Procedure Manual for Judges, 1993, 94, 97, 99. Office: NYC Criminal Ct 100 Centre St New York NY 10013-4308

**CLARKE, ALAN WILLIAM,** lawyer; b. Arlington, Va., Aug. 19, 1949; s. William Garland and Josephine Sessions (Cornell) C.; 1 child, Benjamin Alan; m. Laurie Anne Whitt, Oct. 22, 1994. BA, William and Mary Coll., 1972, JD, 1975; LLM, Queen's U., Kingston, Ont., Can. Bar: Va. 1975, Mich. Assoc., Clarke & Johnston, P.C., Lively, Va., 1975-83; ptnr. Clarke & Clarke, Kilmarnock, VA., 1983—; sole practitioner, Chassell, Mich.; cons.; dir. Rappahanock Legal Svcs. Corp., Fredricksburg, Va.; asst. prof. Ferris State U., Big Rapids, Mich. Contbr. articles to legal jours. Fireman, Upper Lancaster Fire Dept.; bd. dirs. York chpt. Chesapeake Bay Found., 1974, No. Neck Audubon Soc., Kilmarnock, Va., 1982. Recipient Spl. Recognition award Lancaster County br. NAACP, 1993, Cert. of Recognition for pub. svc. Coll. William and Mary, 1993, Cert. of Appreciation, Va. State Bar, 1993. Mem. ABA, ATLA, Va. Bar Assn., Va. Trial Lawyers Assn., Lancaster Jaycees (sec. 1977). Democrat. Episcopalian. Club: Upper Lancaster Ruritan (pres. 1982-83). Federal civil litigation, State civil litigation, Criminal. Home: 1804 N State St Big Rapids MI 49307-9073

**CLARKE, ANNE-MARIE,** family court commissioner; b. St. Louis; d. Thomas P. and Mary Ann (Vincent) C.; m. Richard K. Gaines. Student, Forest Park Community Coll.; BA in Polit. Sci., N.W.M.O. State U.; JD, St. Louis U. Bar: Mo. Past rschr. Arthur D. Little, Inc., Cambridge, Mass.; past asst. corp. sec. N.E. Utilities, Hartford, Conn.; past staff counsel Bi-State Devel. Agy., St. Louis; pvt. practice St. Louis; hearing officer St. Louis City Juvenile Ct., 1986-98; bd. mem. The Bar Plan, St. Louis, 1985-98. Bd. mem. St. Louis Office for Mentally Retarded and Developmentally Disabled, St. Louis, 1984-91, pres., 1989-91; bd. dirs. Family and Personal Support Ctrs. Greater St. Louis, 1987-89; mem. mems.' bd. Mo. Bot. Gardens, 1991-94, The Bar Plan, 1985-98, Police Commnrs., 1993-98 (pres. 1994-98); mem. St. Louis Bd. Police Commrs., 1993-98, pres. 1994-98. Mem. Mo. Bar (bd. govs. 1986-90, 91-95), Mound City Bar Assn. (pres. 1981-83). Avocations: traveling, phys. fitness. Home: 3439 Longfellow Blvd Saint Louis MO 63104-1630 Office: Family Ct Juvenile Divn 920 N Vandeventer Ave Saint Louis MO 63108-3530

**CLARKE, DAVID ALAN,** lawyer; b. Hillsboro, Ohio, Apr. 15, 1950; s. Thomas C. and Dorothea S. Clarke; m. Marilee Ann Miller, Dec. 27, 1980; children: Douglas, Kevin. BA, Claremont McKenna Coll., 1972; JD, Stanford U., 1975. Bar: Ariz. 1975, U.S. Dist. Ct. Ariz. 1976. Assoc. Rawlins, Ellis, Burrus & Kiewit, Phoenix, 1975-81; asst. corp. counsel Greyhound Capital Corp., Phoenix, 1981-86; assoc. corp. counsel Bell Atlantic Sys. Leasing Internat., Inc., Phoenix, 1986-93; corp. counsel BHFC Fin. Svcs., Inc., Phoenix, 1994—. Mem. Maricopa County Bar Assn. Democrat. Methodist. Avocations: golf, biography. Consumer commercial, Contracts commercial, General corporate. Office: BHFC Financial Svcs Inc 3320 W Cheryl Dr # B-120 Phoenix AZ 85051-9594

**CLARKE, DAVID GORDON,** lawyer; b. Norwalk, Conn., Jan. 6, 1967; s. Phelps A. and Alice J. Clarke; m. Elizabeth A. Mullaney, Aug. 7, 1994. BS in Acctg. magna cum laude, U. Conn., 1990; JD cum laude, Quinnipiac Coll., 1994; LLM with honors distinction, Georgetown U., 1996. Bar: Mass. 1995, Conn. 1996, Va. 1996. Revenue examiner Conn. Dept. Labor, Bridgeport, 1992-95; corp. tax counsel Mass. Mutual Life Ins. Co., Springfield, 1996—. Corporate taxation, Personal income taxation, Taxation, general. Office: Mass Mutual Life Ins Co 1295 State St Springfield MA 01111-0002

**CLARKE, J. CALVITT, JR.,** federal judge; b. Harrisburg, Pa., Aug. 9, 1920; s. Joseph Calvitt and Helen Caroline (Mattson) C.; m. Mary Jane Cromer, Feb. 1, 1943 (dec.1985); children: Joseph Calvitt III, Martha Tiffany; m. Betty Ann Holladay, May 29, 1986. BS in Commerce, U. Va., 1945, JD, 1945. Bar: Va. 1944. Practiced in Richmond, Va., 1944-74; partner firm Bowles, Anderson, Boyd, Clarke & Herod, 1944-60; firm Sands Anderson, Marks and Clarke, 1960-74; judge U.S. Dist. Ct. (ea. dist.) Va., 1975-91, sr. judge, 1991—; mem. 4th Circuit Judicial Conf., 1963; hon. consul for Republic of Bolivia, 1959-75. Chmn. Citizen's Advisory Com. on Joint Water System for Henrico and Hanover counties, Va., 1968-69; mem. Mayor's Freedom Train Com., 1948-50; del. Young Republican Nat. Conv., Salt Lake City, 1949, Boston, 1951; chmn. Richmond (Va.) Republican Com., 1952-54; candidate for Congress, 1954; chmn. Va. 3d Dist. Rep. Com., 1955-58, 74-75, Va. State Rep. Conv., 1958—; co-founder Young Rep. Fedn. of Va., 1950, nat. committeeman, 1950-54, chmn., 1955; chmn. 3d dist. Speakers Bur., Nixon-Lodge campaign, 1960, mem. fin. com., 1960-74; chmn. Henrico County Republican Com., 1956-58; fin. chmn. 1956; pres. Couples Sunday Sch. class Second Presbyn. Ch., Richmond, Va., 1948-50, mem. bd. deacons, 1948-61, elder, 1964—; bd. dirs. Family Service Children's Aid Soc., 1948-61, Gambles Hill Community Center, 1950-60, Christian Children's Fund, Inc., 1960-67, Children, Inc., 1967-75, Norfolk Forum, 1978-83; mem. bd. of chancellors Internat. Consular Acad., 1965-75; trustee Henrico County Pub. Library, chmn., 1971-73. Fellow Va. Law Found.; mem. Va. State Bar (mem. 3rd dist. com. 1967-70, chmn. 1969-70), Richmond Bar Assn., Norfolk-Portsmouth Bar Assn., Va. Bar Assn., Thomas Jefferson Soc. of Alumni U. Va. Lile Law Soc., McGuires U. Sch. Alumni (pres. 1995-96), Am. Judicature Soc., ABA, Va. Bar Assn. (vice chmn. com. on cooperation with fgn. bars 1960-61), Richmond Jr. C. of C. (dir. 1946-50), Windmill Point Yacht Club, Westwood Racquet Club (pres. 1961-62), Commonwealth Club, Delta Theta Phi. Office: US Dist Ct 420 US Courthouse 600 Granby St Norfolk VA 23510-1915

**CLARKE, JOHN O'BRIEN, JR.,** lawyer; b. Bklyn., Aug. 23, 1943; s. John O'Brien and Gertrude Helena (Graszynski) C.; m. Sharon Lynn McKenna,

May 23, 1947; children—John O'Brien, Timothy McKenna, Emily Kathleen. B.S. in Acctg., Mt. St. Mary's Coll., Emmitsburg, Md., 1965; J.D., Georgetown U., 1968; LL.M. in Criminal Law, Northwestern U., 1975. Bar: Ill. 1968, U.S. Dist. Ct. (no. dist.) Ill. 1968, N.Y. 1969, D.C. 1969, U.S. Dist. Ct. D.C. 1969, U.S. Ct. Appeals (D.C. cir.) 1969, Va. 1979, U.S. Dist. Ct. (ea. dist.) Va. 1979, U.S. Ct. Appeals (2d cir.) 1977, U.S. Ct. Appeals (3d cir.) 1980, U.S. Ct. Appeals (4th cir.) 1975, U.S. Ct. Appeals (5th cir.) 1978, U.S. Ct. Appeals (6th cir.) 1977, U.S. Ct. Appeals (7th cir.) 1980, U.S. Ct. Appeals (8th cir.) 1982, U.S. Ct. Appeals (9th cir.) 1984, U.S. Ct. Appeals (10th cir.) 1981, U.S. Supreme Ct. 1973, U.S. Ct. Appeals (1st cir.) 1986. Asst. states atty. Cook County (Ill.), 1968-69; asst. U.S. atty., Washington, 1969-74, spl. asst. U.S. atty., 1974-75; assoc. Highsaw & Mahoney, Washington, 1974-78, ptnr., 1978—; lectr. in field. Recipient Spl. Achievement award U.S. Dept. Justice, 1974. Mem. ABA. Roman Catholic. Federal civil litigation, Labor, Transportation. Office: 1050 17th St NW Suite 210 Washington DC 20036

**CLARKE, JUDY,** lawyer; b. Asheville, N.C., 1953. B in Psychology, Furman U., 1974; JD, U. S.C., 1977. Trial atty. Fed. Defenders San Diego, Inc., exec. dir.; pvt. practice, 1991-92; pub. defender Fed. Pub. Defender's Office, Spokane, Wash., 1992—; mem. faculty Nat. Criminal Def. Coll., Macon, Ga., bd. regents, 1985—. Author: Federal Sentencing Manual; contbr. articles to profl. jours. Mem. NADCL (pres. 1996-97). Office: Fed Pub Defenders Office 10 N Post St Ste 700 Spokane WA 99201-0705*

**CLARKE, MILTON CHARLES,** lawyer; b. Chgo., Jan. 31, 1929; s. Gordon Robert and Senoria Josephine (Carlisa) C.; m. Dorothy Jane Brodie, Feb. 19, 1955; children: Laura, Virginia, Senoria K. BS, Northwestern U., 1950, JD, 1953. Bar: Ill. 1953, Mo. 1956, U.S. Dist. Ct. (we. dist.) Mo. 1961, U.S. Ct. Appeals (8th cir.) 1961. Assoc. Swanson, Midgley, Gangwere, Clarke & Kitchin, Kansas City, Mo., 1955-61, ptnr., 1961-91; of counsel Olsen & Talpers, P.C., Kansas City, 1994—. Served with U.S. Army, 1953-55. Mem. Rotary. Federal civil litigation, State civil litigation, Probate. Office: Olsen and Talpers PC 1500 City Center Square 1100 Main St Ste 1500 Kansas City MO 64105-2125

**CLARKE, SHAUN G.,** lawyer; b. Oyster Bay, N.Y., Feb. 19, 1960; s. William Anthony Jr. and Eileen Sheila (Walsh) C.; m. Catherine Rightor McCall, Oct. 10, 1987; children: John Lavin, Christian McCall, Caitlin Walsh. BA, Brown U., 1982; JD, Yale U., 1987. Bar: Calif. 1987, La. 1996. Law clk. to judge D. Lowell Sensen U.S. Dist. Ct., San Francisco, 1987-88; dep. city atty. City and County of San Francisco, 1988-92; asst. U.S. atty. U.S. Dept. of Justice, New Orleans, 1992-96; ptnr. Liskow & Lewis, LLP, New Orleans, 1996—. Dir. Young Leadership Coun., New Orleans, 1995-98; chmn. cmty. adv. bd. Teach for Am., New Orleans, 1997-99. Recipient Chief Postal Inspector's award U.S. Postal Svc., 1993, Fed. Women's Appreciation award Fed. Exec. Bd., 1994. General civil litigation, Criminal. Home: 43 Yellowstone Dr New Orleans LA 70131-8617 Office: Liskow & Lewis 50th Fl One Shell Square New Orleans LA 70139

**CLARKE, THOMAS LEE, JR.,** lawyer; b. Thomasville, Ga., Mar. 6, 1937; s. Thomas Lee Sr. and Pauline (Eaton) C.; m. Mary Ann Benedict, Dec. 20, 1959; children: Melinda Cay, Virginia Ann, Mary Elizabeth. BS in Bus., Fla. State U., 1959; LLB, U. Fla., 1963; U. Bar: Fla. 1964, U.S. Dist. Ct. (so. and mid. dists.) Fla. 1965, U.S. Ct. Appeals (11th cir.) 1966, U.S. Supreme Ct. 1972. Ptnr. Lane, Trohn, Clarke, Bertrand & Williams, P.A., Lakeland, Fla., 1964-80, 84-96; cir. ct. judge 10th Jud. Cir. of Fla., 1980-84; pres. Sunshine Mediation Co., Lakeland, 1996—. Chmn. Polk County Code Enforcement Bd., 1985-86. With Army N.G., 1959-65. Mem. Lakeland Bar Assn. (Merit award 1984, pres. 1972-73). Republican. Episcopalian. Avocation: fishing. Alternative dispute resolution. Office: Sunshine Mediation Co PO Box 2431 Lakeland FL 33806-2431

**CLARKE, WILLIAM,** lawyer; b. Bat Cave, N.C., Jan. 30, 1956; s. James McClure and Elspeth McClure Clarke; m. Sinclair Berden; 1 child, Phelps; m. Cynthia Williams, Sept. 21, 1996; children: Winslow, Durban, Ambrose. BA, Princeton U., 1979; JD, U. N.C., 1982. Atty., now shareholder Roberts & Stevens, Asheville, N.C., 1982—; sect. coun. mem. natural resources and environment sect. N.C. Bar Assn., 1989-95; presenter in field. Active local legal svc. programs. Democrat. Office: Roberts & Stevens BB&T Bldg One Weset Pack Sq Asheville NC 28802

**CLARKE, WM. A. LEE, III,** lawyer; b. Balt., May 7, 1949; s. William Anthony Jr. and Eileen Shiela (Walsh) C.; m. Dara Ford, May 8, 1994. Student, John Carroll U., 1969-72; JD magna cum laude, U. Balt., 1975. Bar: Md. 1975, U.S. Dist. Ct. Md. 1975, U.S. Supreme Ct. 1979, U.S. Ct. Appeals (4th cir.) 1981. Trial atty. Tenn. Valley Authority, Knoxville, 1975-76; pvt. practice Salisbury, Md., 1977—; vis. lectr. criminal law U. Md. Eastern Shore, Princess Anne, 1989. Pres. Wicomico County Dems., Salisbury, 1981-83; commr. Md. Human Rels. Commn., Balt., 1983-85. Served to cpl. USMC, 1967-69, Vietnam. Mem. Md. Criminal Def. Attys. Assn. (bd. dirs. 1984-93), Salisbury Jaycees (legal counsel 1977-79), Nat. Bd. Trial Adv. (cert. criminal trial advocate 1987—). E-mail: walc@attymail.com. Criminal, State civil litigation, Federal civil litigation. Office: 30644 Brandywine Ct Salisbury MD 21804-2558

**CLARKIN, E. THOMAS,** lawyer; b. St. Louis, July 29, 1942; s. Edward Joseph and Eileen C. (Brennan) C.; m. Janice M. Alcott, June 10, 1972; 1 child, Kelly E. BA, So. Ill. U., 1967; JD, U. Mo., 1972. Assoc. Gray & Stewart, Clayton, Mo., 1972-77; ptnr. Gray, Stewart & Clarkin, Clayton, 1977-91, pvt. practice, 1991—; asst. city atty. City of Woodson Terrace, Mo., 1974-88; mcpl. judge City of Woodson Terrace, 1992—; ptnr. Gray, Stewart & Clarkin, 1977-91; adj. instr. Webster U., Webster Groves, Mo., 1976-78. Sgt. U.S. Army, 1970. Mem. Mo. Bar Assn., St. Louis County Bar Assn., Mo. Mcpl. Judges Assn., St. Louis Elks. General civil litigation, Insurance, Personal injury. Office: 8230 Forsyth Blvd Ste 100 Clayton MO 63105-1692

**CLARY, BRADLEY G.,** lawyer, educator; b. Richmond, Va., Sept. 7, 1950; s. Sidney G. and Jean B. Clary; m. Mary-Louise Hunt, July 31, 1982; children: Benjamin, Samuel. BA magna cum laude, Carleton Coll., 1972; JD cum laude, U. Minn., 1975. Bar: Minn. 1975, U.S. Dist. Ct. Minn. 1975, U.S. Ct. Appeals (10th cir.) 1977, U.S. Ct. Appeals (8th cir.) 1979, U.S. Ct. Appeals (6th cir.) 1980, U.S. Ct. Appeals (7th cir.) 1981, U.S. Supreme Ct. 1986, U.S. Ct. Appeals (4th cir.) 1989, U.S. Ct. Appeals (9th cir.) 1991. Assoc. Oppenheimer Wolff & Donnelly, St. Paul, 1975-81, ptnr., 1982—; legal writing dir. Law Sch. U. Minn., 1999—; adj. prof. Law Sch. U. Minn., Mpls., 1985-99; adj. instr. William Mitchell Coll. Law, St. Paul, 1995-96, 98, adj. prof., 1997, 99. Author: Primer on the Analysis and Presentation of Legal Argument, 1992. Vestryman St. John Evangelist Ch., St. Paul, 1978-81, 98—, pledge drive co-chmn. 1989-90; mem. alumni bd. Breck Sch., Mpls., 1981-85, 89-96, exec. com., 1991-96, dir. emeritus, 1996—; mem. adv. bd. Glass Theatre Co., West St. Paul, Minn., 1982-87; mem. antitrust adv. panel dept. health State of Minn., 1992-93. Mem. ABA (adv. group antitrust sect. 1987-89, corp. counseling com.), Minn. Bar Assn. (program chmn. antitrust sect. 1986-87, treas. 1987-88, vice-chmn. 1989-90, co-chmn. 1990-92), Phi Beta Kappa. Avocations: tennis, sailing. Antitrust, General civil litigation. Office: U Minn Law Sch 229 19th Ave S Rm 444 Minneapolis MN 55455-0400

**CLARY, RICHARD WAYLAND,** lawyer; b. Tarboro, N.C., Oct. 10, 1953; s. S. Grayson and Jean (Beazley) C.; m. Suzanne Clerkin, July 21, 1991; children: Grayson Edward, Taryn Fenner. BA magna cum laude, Amherst Coll., 1975; JD magna cum laude, Harvard U., 1978. Bar: N.Y. 1981, U.S. Dist. Ct. (so. and ea. dists.) N.Y. 1981, U.S. Dist. Ct. (no. dist.) Calif., 1982, U.S. Ct. Appeals (9th cir.) 1983, U.S. Supreme Ct. 1989, U.S. Ct. Appeals (3d cir.) 1990, U.S. Ct. Appeals (2d cir.) 1994, U.S. Ct. Appeals (fed. cir.) 1995. Law clk. to judge U.S. Ct. Appeals (2d cir.), N.Y.C., 1978-79; law clk. to Justice Thurgood Marshall U.S. Supreme Ct., Washington, 1979-80; assoc. Cravath, Swaine & Moore, N.Y.C., 1980-85, ptnr., 1985—, mng. ptnr. litigation, 1997—. Bd. dirs. Legal Aid Soc., 1998—. John Woodruff Simpson fellow Amherst Coll., 1975-76. Mem. ABA, Fed. Bar Found. (bd. dirs. 1998—), N.Y. State Bar Assn., Assn. Bar City N.Y., Fed. Bar Coun., Phi Beta Kappa. Episcopalian. Intellectual property, Federal civil litigation, Antitrust. Office: Cravath Swaine & Moore Worldwide Pla 825 8th Ave New York NY 10019-7475

**CLAWATER, WAYNE,** lawyer; b. Tyler, Tex., Sept. 14, 1954; s. Earl William and Jean (Shaw) C.; m. Hollee Susann Hedge, July 18, 1981; children: Jean Rose, Rebekah Grace. BBA in Fin., U. Tex., 1977; JD summa cum laude, South Tex. Coll. Law, Houston, 1980. Bar: Tex., U.S. Dist. Ct. (so. and ea. dists.) Tex.; U.S. Ct. Appeals (5th cir.)Tex. Briefing atty. Supreme Ct. Tex., Austin, 1981-82; from assoc. atty. to ptnr. Andrews & Kurth, Houston, 1982-91; shareholder McFall & Sartwelle, P.C., Houston, 1991—. Mem. vestry Christ Ch. Cathedral, Houston, 1991—, every mem. canvass chmn., 1991. Mem. Houston Bar Assn. (chair law internship com. 1991—, chmn. Harris County Grievance Com. 1988—). Episcopalian. Avocations: reading, hunting, fishing, U. Tex. football. State civil litigation, Personal injury, Product liability. Home: 6630 Wakeforest St Houston TX 77005-3956 Office: McFall & Sartwelle 2500 Two Houston Ctr 909 Fannin St Houston TX 77010-1001

**CLAWSON, JAMES F., JR.,** judge, mediator, arbitrator; b. Coryell County, Tex., Aug. 31, 1923; s. James F. and Julia Josephine (Doolittle) C.; m. Mary Louise Forester, May 4, 1945; children: Marylou Bowen, Cathy Jo Young. JD, Baylor U., 1948. Bar: Tex. 1948, U.S. Dist. Ct. (so. dist.) Tex. 1995. Atty. Clawson, Jennings & Clawson, Houston, 1948-59; banker, trust officer First Nat. Bank of Temple, Tex., 1959-67; county judge Bell County, Belton, Tex., 1967-69; presiding judge 3d Adminstrv. Jud. Region of Tex., Belton, 1985-90; dist. judge 169th Jud. Dist. of Tex., Belton, 1969-85, sr. judge, 1985—; chmn. Bd. Regional Judges of Tex., 1985-90; chmn. Ctrl. Tex. Coun. Govts., belton, 1985-90. Served to capt. USAF, 1942-46, 51-53. Named Outstanding Citizen of Yr., Temple (Tex.) Jaycees, 1966. Fellow Tex Bar Found.; mem. State Bar Tex. (mem. exec. com. jud. sect. 1972-82, chmn. jud. sect. 1982-83). Home: 1211 N Pea Ridge Rd Temple TX 76502-4917

**CLAY, ERIC L.,** judge; b. Durham, N.C., Jan. 18, 1948. BA, U. N.C., 1969; JD, Yale U., 1972. Bar: Mich. 1972, U.S. Dist. Ct. (ea. dist.) Mich. 1972, U.S. Supreme Ct. 1977, U.S. Ct. Appeals (6th cir.) 1978, U.S. Dist. Ct. (we. dist.) Mich. 1987, U.S. Ct. Appeals (D.C. cir.) 1994. Law clk. to Judge Damon J. Keith U.S. Dist. Ct. (ea. dist.) Mich., 1973-97; shareholder, dir. Lewis, White & Clay, P.C., Detroit, 1997; now judge U.S. Ct. Appeals (6th cir.), Detroit, 1997—. John Hay Whitney fellow Yale U. Mem. ABA, Nat. Bar Assn., Nat. Assn. Railroad Trial Counsel, U.S. Sixth Jud. Conf. (life), Detroit Bar Assn., Wolverine Bar Assn., Phi Beta Kappa. Office: US Courthouse 231 W Lafayette Blvd Detroit MI 48226-2700

**CLAY, JAMES FRANKLIN,** lawyer; b. Danville, Ky., Nov. 6, 1911; s. Sanders Eaves and Katherine A. (Curry) C.; m. Martha Bisset, Jan. 23, 1933 (div.); children: Martha Ann, James Franklin, Thomas E., J. Richard, Elisabeth L. AB, Ctr. Coll. of Ky., 1932; LLB, U. Mich., 1936. Bar: Ky. 1936, U.S. Dist. Ct. (ea. dist.) Ky. 1939, U.S. Dist. Ct. (we. dist.) Ky. 1943, U.S. Ct. Appeals (6th cir.) 1962, U.S. Supreme Ct. 1978. Referee Ky. Workmen's Compensation Bd., 1938-43; commonwealth atty. 13th Jud. Dist. Ky., 1943-58; ptnr. Clay, Hudson & Shewmaker, Danville, 1977-79, Clay & Shewmaker, Danville, 1979-80, Clay & Clay, 1969-79, 80—. Mem. ABA, Ky. Bar Assn., Boyle County Bar Assn. Democrat. Episcopalian. General practice, State civil litigation, Personal injury. Office: PO Box 1256 319 Main St Danville KY 40422

**CLAY, RICHARD H.C.,** lawyer; b. Huntington, W.Va., July 24, 1951. AB, Davidson Coll., 1973; postgrad., Yale U., 1974; JD, U. Ky., 1977. Bar: Ky. 1977. Ptnr. Woodward, Hobson & Fulton, Louisville; adj. prof. law, ins. U. Louisville, 1978-83. Mng. editor Ky. Law Jour., 1976-77; contbr. articles to profl. jours. Trsutee Presbyn. Ch. (U.S.A.) Found.; trustee, counsel The Norton Found., Inc. Mem. ABA, Ky. Def. Counsel (pres. 1989-90), Ky. Bar Found., Ky. Bar Assn. (chmn. ann. conv. 1991, bd. govs. 1992-96, v.p. 1996-97, pres.-elect 1997-98, pres. 1998-99), Louisville Bar Assn. (treas. 1982, bd. dirs. 1992—), Omicron Delta Kappa, Omicron Delta Epsilon. E-mail: rclay@whf-law.com. General civil litigation, Product liability, Appellate. Office: Woodward Hobson & Fulton 2500 Nat City Tower 101 S 5th St Ste 2500 Louisville KY 40202-3175*

**CLAYCOMB, HUGH MURRAY,** lawyer, author; b. Joplin, Mo., May 19, 1931; s. Hugh and Fern (Murray) C.; m. Jeanne Cavin, May 6, 1956; children: Stephen H., Scott C. BS in Bus., U. Mo., 1953, JD, 1955; LLM, U. Miss., 1969. Bar: Mo. 1955, Ark. 1957, U.S. Tax Ct. 1956, U.S. Dist. Ct. (ea. dist.) Ark. 1957, U.S. Supreme Ct. 1979. Asst. staff judge advocate USAF, 1955-57; law clerk Ark. Supreme Ct., Little Rock, 1957-58; ptnr. Gregory & Claycomb, Pine Bluff, Ark., 1958-69; partner Haley, Claycomb, Roper & Anderson, Warren, Ark., 1969—; dir. Strong Systems, Inc., Pine Bluff, Ark., 1967—. Author: Arkansas Corporations, 1967, 82, 92. Pres. Jefferson County Bar Assn., Pine Bluff, 1969, Warren YMCA, 1973-75, S.E. Ark. Legal Inst., 1980-81, Ctrl. Ark. Estate Planning Coun., 1963-64; trustee Bradley County YMCA Found.; spl. assoc. justice Ark. Supreme Ct., 1978, 87. Lt. USAF, 1955-57. Recipient Pres.'s award Ark. Trial Lawyers Assn., 1985. Mem. Ark. Bar Found. (pres. 1990), Ark. Bar Assn. (sec.-treas. 1998—, C.E. Ransick award 1996), Warren Rotary (pres. 1972). Episcopalian. General corporate, Estate planning, Probate. Home: 619 E Cedar St Warren AR 71671-3001

**CLAY-CONTI, DONNA PAULETTE,** lawyer; b. Houston, Jan. 2, 1950; d. Donald Eugene and Tommie Senior (Shackelford) C.; m. Drake Conti; 1 child, Kirstin. B.A., UCLA, 1971; M.Ed., U. Nev.-Las Vegas, 1973; J.D., U. Calif.-Berkeley, 1980. Bar: Calif. 1980; cert. elem. edn., Calif. Elem. tchr. Oakland Unified Sch. Dist. (Calif.), 1973-76, resource instr., 1976-77; assoc. Pettit & Martin, San Francisco, 1980-82, Kornblum, Kelly & Herlihy, San Francisco, 1982-86, Kelly & Herlihy, San Francisco, 1986-87, Law Offices of Michael D. Michel, Walnut Creek, Ca., 1987— ; mem. Sch. Instructional Strategy Council, Oakland, 1976-77; participant Hastings Coll. Advocacy, San Francisco, 1983. Assoc. editor Calif. Law Rev., 1978-80. Recipient Am. Jurisprudence award, 1978. Mem. ABA, Nat. Bar Assn., Charles Houston Bar Assn. (v.p. 1983-85), Assn. Trial Lawyers Am., Assn. Def. Counsel, Alpha Kappa (grammateus Los Angeles 1969-70). Democrat. Office: Law Offices of Michael D Michel 925 Ygnacio Valley Rd Walnut Creek CA 94596-3875

**CLAYTON, CLAUDE F., JR.,** lawyer; b. Tupelo, Miss., June 15, 1948; s. Claude F. and Bronson (Munday) C.; children from a previous marriage: Frances, Claude III; m. Tacey Clark, July 25, 1997. Student, Stanton Mil. Acad., 1966; BA, Tulane U., 1971; JD, U. Miss., 1973. Bar: Miss. 1973. Mem. judiciary com. U.S. Senate, Washington, 1968; ptnr. Mitchell, Voge, Clayton and Beasley, Tupelo, 1973-85, Mitchell, McNutt, Threadgill, Smith & Sams, Tupelo, 1985—; mem. complaints tribunal Supreme Ct. Miss., 1990-93; speaker Miss. Jud. Coll., also various trial practice and ethics seminars. Mem. ABA (young lawyers div., chmn. justice dept. liaison com. 1978-79), Miss. State Bar (pres. fellows of young lawyers 1990-91, vice chmn. specialization com. 1990-92, chmn., 1980-82, lawyer econs. com. 1988-89, ethics com. 1982-85, vice chmn. continuing legal edn. com. 1980-81, law jour.-law sch. liaison com. 1974-76, various coms. young lawyers sect. 1985-90, bd. dirs. 1975-80), Miss. Def. Lawyers Assn. (bd. dirs. 1992-95), Def. Rsch. Inst., Internat. Assn. Def. Counsel. General civil litigation, Personal injury, Product liability. Office: Mitchell McNutt Threadgill Smith & Sams 105 S Front St Tupelo MS 38804-4869

**CLAYTON, DANIEL LOUIS,** lawyer; b. Chgo., Mar. 11, 1963; s. James D. and Betty (Brisendine) C.; m. Stacy Elizabeth Johnson, June 29, 1985; children: Amy Brooke, Hannah Margaret, Kay Ellen. BA, David Lipscomb Coll., Nashville, 1984; JD, U. Tenn., 1987. Bar: Tenn. 1987, U.S. Dist. Ct. (mid. and we. dists.) Tenn. 1987, U.S. Ct. Appeals (6th cir.) 1991. Ptnr. Kinnard & Clayton, Nashville, 1987—; mem. faculty Law Seminars Internat., Seattle, 1991. Elected mem. Franklin Spl. Sch. Dist. Bd. Edn., 1994—. Recipient Lewis F. Powell, Jr. medal for excellence in advocacy. Mem. Tenn. Bar Assn., Tenn. Trial Lawyers Assn., Nashville Bar Assn. Republican. Mem. Ch. of Christ. Avocations: golf, tennis. Personal injury, Workers' compensation, General civil litigation. Office: The Woodlawn 127 Woodmont Blvd Nashville TN 37205-2240

**CLAYTOR, WILLIAM MIMMS,** lawyer; b. Nashville, Mar. 31, 1941; s. George White and Dorothy (Mimms) C.; m. Anne Edwards, June 1, 1968; children: Justin H., Graham F. BA in Econs. and Math., Northeast Mo. State U., 1963; MA in Econs. and Math., Memphis State U., 1964, JD, 1969. Estate tax atty. IRS, Charlotte, 1970-72; ptnr. Baucom, Claytor, Benton, Morgan & Wood, Charlotte, 1973—. Bd. trustees Ctrl. Piedmont C.C., 1977-93, chmn. 1982-93; past bd. dirs. Goodwill Industries of So. Piedmont Inc., mem. exec. com.; past chmn., bd. deacons St. John's Bapt. Ch.; bd. dirs. Met. YMCA; bd. dirs. Habitat for Humanity of Charlotte, mem. constrn. crew; bd. dirs. Alzheimer's Assn. Mem. N.C. Bar Assn., 26th Jud. Bar Assn., Mecklenburg Bar Assn., Mecklenburg County Bar Assn., (pres. 1996-97), Mecklenburg Bar Found. (vice chmn. 1992), Mecklenburg County Bar Found. (chmn. capital funds drive 1990), Charlotte C. of C., Omicron Delta Kappa. Estate planning, General corporate, Elder. Office: Baucom Claytor Benton Morgan & Wood PO Box 35246 Charlotte NC 28235-5246

**CLEAR, JOHN MICHAEL,** lawyer; b. St. Louis, Dec. 16, 1948; s. Raymond H. and Marian (Clark) C.; m. Isabel Marie Bone, May 10, 1980. BA summa cum laude, Washington U., St. Louis, 1971; JD with honors, U. Chgo., 1974. Bar: Mo. 1974, D.C. 1975, U.S. Ct. Appeals (5th and D.C. cirs.) 1975, U.S. Supreme Ct. 1977, U.S. Ct. Appeals (3d cir.) 1978, U.S. Ct. Appeals (8th cir.) 1980, U.S. Ct. Appeals (9th cir.) 1990, U.S. Dist. Ct. (so. dist.) Ill. 1995, U.S. Ct. Appeals (7th cir.) 1997. Law clk. to judge U.S. Ct. Appeals (5th cir.), Atlanta, 1974-75; assoc. Covington & Burling, Washington, 1975-80; jr. ptnr. Bryan, Cave, McPheeters & McRoberts, St. Louis, 1980-81, ptnr., 1982—. Mem. ABA, Mo. Bar Assn., D.C. Bar Assn., St. Louis Met. Bar Assn., Am. Law Inst., Order of Coif., Racquet Club, Noonday Club, Fox Run Golf Club, Phi Beta Kappa. Antitrust, Federal civil litigation, Securities. Office: Bryan Cave LLP One Metropolitan Sq Saint Louis MO 63102-2750

**CLEAVER, WILLIAM LEHN,** lawyer; b. Harrisburg, Pa., Dec. 7, 1949; s. Gene Franklin and Goldie Jean (Haldeman) C.; children: Benjamin Neville, Valerie Anne. BA, Augustana Coll., 1971; JD, U. Iowa, 1974. Bar: Iowa 1974, Ill. 1975, U.S. Dist. Ct. (so. dist.) Iowa 1975, U.S. Dist. Ct. (so. dist.) Ill. 1975. Ptnr. Bozeman, Neighbour, Patton & Noe, Moline, Ill., 1991—; chmn. bd. govs. BBB Ctrl. Ea. Iowa. Mem. adv. coun. Luth. Social Svcs. of Ill. Adult Day Care Ctr., Rock Island; v.p., bd. dirs. United Way of Quad Cities, Rock Island; pres. adv. coun. Ret. Sr. Vol. Program, Moline; bd. govs. Rock Island Cmty. Found.; commr., chmn. Rock Island Preservation Commn.; mem. Citizen's Adv. Com.; bd. dirs. Quad Cities chpt. ARC; mem. Rock Island/Milan Dist. 41 Sch. Bd. Col. USAR. Mem. ABA, Ill. State Bar Assn., Iowa State Bar Assn., Rock Island County Bar Assn., Scott County Bar Assn. Lutheran. Lodge: Kiwanis (pres. 1983-84, bd. dirs. 1984-85). Avocations: fine arts, racquet sports. Contracts commercial, Consumer commercial, Real property. Home: 8806 Ridgewood Rd Rock Island IL 61201-7655 Office: Bozeman Neighbour Patton & Noe 1630 5th Ave Moline IL 61265-7910

**CLEEK, ROBERT JOSEPH,** lawyer; b. San Francisco, July 5, 1949; s. Robert Allen and Margaret (O'Donoghue) C.; m. Therese Anne Menzel, Dec. 22, 1972 (div. July 1991); m. Catherine Anne Elin, Jan. 6, 1994; 1 child, Elizabeth Therese. BA, U. San Francisco, 1970; postgrad., St. Joseph's Coll., 1967-68; JD, Golden Gate U., 1978. Bar: Calif. 1978, U.S. Dist. Ct. (no. dist.) Calif. 1978, U.S. Supreme Ct. 1984, U.S. Ct. Appeals (9th cir.) 1986, U.S. Dist. Ct. (so. dist.) Calif. 1990. Correctional officer Calif. Dept. Corrections, San Quentin, 1971-73, correctional counselor, 1973-80; assoc. Bornstein Law Offices, Fairfax, Calif., 1980-81; ptnr. Donovan and Cleek, San Rafael, Calif., 1981-83; pvt. practice, San Rafael, 1983-90, Novato, Calif., 1990-94; ptnr. Whitener Cleek and Elin, Novato, 1994-96, Cleek and Elin, Novato, 1996—; discovery referee, settlement judge pro tem Marin Superior Ct., San Rafael, 1993—, mem. drafting com. for local rules of ct., 1994. Mem. Marin County Bar Assn. (com. mem. 1982-83), San Rafael Yacht Club (dir. 1986, 95-97), North Marin Breakfast Club. Democrat. Roman Catholic. Avocations: classic sailing yachts, maritime history, wooden boat building. Family and matrimonial, Appellate, Pension, profit-sharing, and employee benefits. Office: Cleek & Elin 7665 Redwood Blvd Ste 200 Novato CA 94945-1405

**CLEGG, TREVOR CLEMENT,** lawyer; b. Fresno, Calif., Aug. 9, 1947; s. Reed Kenneth and Irene Lockwood Clegg. AB in Govt., U. Calif., Santa Cruz, 1969; JD, Stanford U., 1973. Bar: Calif. 1974, U.S. Dist. Ct. (ea. dist.) Calif. 1974, U.S. Ct. Appeals (9th cir.) 1979, U.S. Dist. Ct. (no. dist.) Calif. 1983, U.S. Dist. Ct. (so. dist.) Calif. 1989, U.S. Dist. Ct. Ariz. 1991. Pvt. practice law Fresno, Calif., 1974-76, 97—; assoc. Wild, Carter & Tipton, Fresno, 1976-79, shareholder, 1979-92; of counsel Frampton, Hoppe, Williams & Boehm, Fresno, 1992-97; judge pro tem Fresno County Cts., 1993—; lectr. continuing edn. programs Nat. Bus. Inst., Fresno, 1993—. Author: (program booklets) Successful Judgment Collections in California, 1993-97, Fundamentals of Bankruptcy Law, 1998. Founder, prin. contbr. Clegg Meml. Scholarship Fund, U. Utah, Salt Lake City, 1997—. Mem. State Bar Calif., Fresno County Bar Assn. General civil litigation, Bankruptcy, Appellate. Office: 2090 N Winery Ave Fresno CA 93703-2831

**CLELAND, EDWARD GORDON,** lawyer; b. Montreal, Que., Can., Aug. 16, 1949; came to U.S. 1979; s. Edward Samuel and Diana Elizabeth (McLennan) C.; m. Thelma Alicia Chen, Jan. 2, 1992. BCommerce, McGill U., 1970; LLB, York U., 1974; LLM in Taxation, NYU, 1980. Bar: Ont. 1976, Conn. 1987, N.Y. 1987, U.S. Tax Ct. 1990. Adv. counsel Dept. Justice, Ottawa, Ont., Can., 1976-79; mgr. Coopers & Lybrand, N.Y.C., 1979-86; pvt. practice N.Y.C., 1987—. Treas. Alden Owners, Inc., N.Y.C., 1987-88. Mem. ABA, N.Y. State Bar Assn., Law Soc. Upper Can. Republican. Episcopalian. Clubs: Can Soc. N.Y., St. Andrews Soc. (N.Y.C.). Lodge: Loyal Orange. Personal income taxation, Corporate taxation, General corporate. Home: 225 Central Park W Apt 1405 New York NY 10024-6051 Office: 29 Broadway Ste 1000 New York NY 10006-3101

**CLELAND, ROBERT HARDY,** federal judge; b. 1947. BA, Mich. State U., 1969; JD, U. N.C., 1972. Pvt. practice Port Huron, Mich., 1972-75; chief trial atty. County Prosecuting Atty's. Office, Port Huron, 1975-80; prosecuting atty. St. Clair County, 1981-90; judge U.S. Dist. Ct. (ea. dist.) Mich., Bay City, 1990—. Positions with Port Huron Hosp., 1989-91, United Way of St. Clair County, 1988-90, Civic Theater of Port Huron, Blue Water YMCA, First Congl. Ch. of Port Huron, MADD, St. Clair Rep. Party. Mem. ABA, Mich. Bar Assn., St. Clair County Bar Assn., Prosecuting Atty's. Assn. Mich. (pres. 1988-89). Office: US Dist Ct 214 US Courthouse Bay City MI 48708-5749

**CLEMEN, JOHN DOUGLAS,** lawyer; b. Mineola, N.Y., Dec. 18, 1944; s. John Douglas and Amy Gertrude (Ackerson) C.; m. Judith Anne Davis, June 3, 1967; children: Elizabeth, Jennifer. BA, Hobart Coll., 1966; JD, Seton Hall U., 1974. Bar: N.J. 1974, U.S. Dist. Ct. N.J. 1974, U.S. Ct. Appeals (3d cir.) 1980, U.S. Supreme Ct. 1982, N.Y. 1984, U.S. Dist. Ct. (so. dist.) N.Y. 1985, U.S. Dist. Ct. (ea. dist.) N.Y. 1989, U.S. Ct. Appeals (2d cir.) 1989. Law sec. to assoc. justice N.J. Supreme Ct., Trenton, 1974-75; assoc. Shanley & Fisher, P.C., Newark, 1975-83, ptnr., 1983—; arbitrator U.S. Dist. Ct. N.J., 1985—, N.J. Superior Ct., Morristown, 1986—; guest lectr. Acad. Medicine N.J., 1980-82. Contbg. editor Seton Hall Law Rev., 1973-74. Bd. dirs. Acad. Decathalon of N.J., 1997—; mem. Mass Disaster Response Team, ARC, 1997—. Capt. USAF, 1966-71, Vietnam. Decorated Air medal. Mem. ABA, N.J. Bar Assn. (chmn. aviation sect. 1992-94), N.Y. State Bar Assn., Trial Attys. N.J., Bergen County Bar Assn., Morris County Bar Assn. (chmn. continuing legal edn.), Commerce & Industry Assn. N.J. (bd. dirs., counsel 1988-92), Morristown Club. Insurance, Aviation, General civil litigation. Home: 574 Colonial Rd River Vale NJ 07675-6107 Office: Shanley & Fisher PC 89th Fl One World Trade Ctr New York NY 10048

**CLEMENT, CLAYTON EMERSON,** lawyer; b. Oakland, Calif., Dec. 3, 1943; s. Robert Emerson and Dorothy Winslow (Deacon) C.; m. Barbara Jonas, Sept. 4, 1965 (div. Aug. 1984); children: Robert, Jason; m. Kimberly Anderson, Nov. 30, 1991. BA with honors, U. Pacific, 1965; JD, U. Calif., Berkeley, 1968. Bar: Calif. 1969, U.S. Dist. Ct. (no. dist.) Calif. 1969, U.S. Ct. Appeals (9th cir.) 1969, U.S. Supreme Ct. 1972. Assoc. Cox & Cummins, Martinez, Calif., 1968-71; ptnr. Arata, Misuraca & Clement, Santa Rosa, Calif., 1972-75; pvt. practice Santa Rosa, 1976-78; ptnr. Clement, Fitzpatrick & Kenworthy, Santa Rosa, 1978—; instr. Santa Rosa Jr. Coll., 1977-85; assoc. prof. law Kennedy U., Martinez, Calif., 1969-72. Dir. Sonoma County Family YMCA, Santa Rosa, 1985-91; treas. BOSCO for Congress Com., Santa Rosa, 1982-90. Fellow Am. Coll. Trial Lawyers; mem. ABA, Assn. Bus. Trial Lawyers, Am. Bd. Trial Advocates. Democrat. Avocations: flying, fishing. General civil litigation, Condemnation, Real property. Home: 4199 Pine Rock Pl Santa Rosa CA 95409-4014 Office: Clement Fitzpatrick & Kenworthy 3333 Mendocino Ave Ste 200 Santa Rosa CA 95403-2233

**CLEMENT, DANIEL EVAN,** lawyer; b. N.Y.C., Mar. 15, 1961; s. Stanton J. and Lorraine Clement; m. Michelle Sue Schwartz, Oct. 24, 1998. BA, SUNY, Albany, 1983; JD, Bklyn. Law Sch., 1986. Bar: N.J. 1986, N.Y. 1987, U.S. Dist. Ct. N.J. 1986, U.S. Dist. Ct. (so. and ea. dists.) N.Y. 1987, U.S. Ct. Appeals (2d cir.) 1991. Sole practitioner N.Y.C., 1996—; of counsel Wallman Greenberg Gasman & McKnight, LLP, N.Y.C., 1996—; arbitrator N.Y.C. Small Claims Ct. Mem. Assn. Bar City N.Y. E-mail: dclement@clementlaw.com. Family and matrimonial, General civil litigation, Contracts commercial. Office: 350 5th Ave Ste 3000 New York NY 10118-3022

**CLEMENT, EDITH BROWN,** federal judge; b. Birmingham, Ala., Apr. 29, 1948; d. Erskine John and Edith (Burrus) Brown; m. Rutledge Carter Clement Jr., Sept. 3, 1972; children: Rutledge Carter III, Catherine Lanier. BA, U. Ala., 1969; JD, Tulane U., 1972. Bar: La. 1973. Law clk. to Hon. Herbert W. Christenberry U.S. Dist. Ct., New Orleans, 1973-75; ptnr. Jones, Walker, Waechter, Poitevent, Carrere & Denegre, New Orleans, 1975-91; judge U.S. Dist. Ct. (ea. dist.) La., New Orleans, 1991—. Fellow La. Bar Found. (life); mem. Am. Law Inst., La. Bar Assn., Federalist Soc., Maritime Law Assn. U.S., Fed. Bar Assn. Office: US Dist Ct 500 Camp St Rm C-455 New Orleans LA 70130-3313

**CLEMENT, FRANCES ROBERTS,** lawyer, mediator, nurse, consultant; b. Columbia, S.C., Oct. 1, 1945; d. Ralph Winfred and Frances Lucille (Harter) Roberts; m. Tom F. Clement; children: Everett Hudson Smith, Armenta Harter Smith. BS in Biology, U. Ala., 1967; MS in Counseling, Fla. State U., 1970; AA in Nursing, Victoria Coll., Tex., 1978; JD with honors, Jones Sch. Law, Montgomery, Ala., 1986. Bar: Ala. 1987, U.S. Supreme Ct. 1997. Staff nurse Citizen's Meml. Hosp., Victoria, Tex., 1978-81, DeTar Hosp., Victoria, Tex., 1981, Bapt. Med. Ctr., Montgomery, 1982-84; adminstr sch. nurse Bloomington (Tex.) Sch. Dist., Montgomery, 1981-82; supr. Humana Hosp., Montgomery, 1985; legal asst. Kaufman, Rothfeder & Blitz, Montgomery, 1985-87; assoc. Powers & Willis, Montgomery, 1987-88; pvt. practice Montgomery, 1988-90, with Office of Atty. Gen., 1990—; adj. prof. U. Houston, Victoria, 1980, Auburn U., Montgomery, 1988-90, facilitator, mediator, 1999—. Mem. Montgomery County Bar Assn. Methodist. Avocation: computers. Home: 3502 Bankhead Ave Montgomery AL 36111-2018 Office: Criminal Appeals Divsn 11 S Union St Montgomery AL 36130-2103

**CLEMENT, LESLIE JOSEPH, JR.,** lawyer; b. Thibodaux, La., June 26, 1948; s. Leslie Joseph and Shirley Marie (Picou) C.; m. Sandra Ann Rome, June 18, 1971; children: Paul, Philip, Rebecca. BA, Nicholls State Coll., 1970; JD, La. State U., 1974. Assoc. Porteous, Toledano, Hainkel & Johnson, Thibodaux, 1974-76; ptnr. Boudreaux & Clement, Thibodaux, 1976-78; sole practice Thibodaux, 1978—. Served to 1st lt. La. N.G., 1970-76. Mem. ABA, La. Bar Assn., Lafourche Parish Bar Assn., La. Trial Lawyers Assn. Democrat. Roman Catholic. State civil litigation, Family and matrimonial, General practice. Office: 409 Canal Blvd Thibodaux LA 70301-3413

**CLEMENT, ROBERT LEBBY, JR.,** lawyer; b. Charleston, S.C., Dec. 14, 1928; s. Robert Lebby and Julia Axson (Thayer) C.; m. Helen Mathilda Lewis, Nov. 26, 1954; children: Jeanne Marie, Robert Lebby III, Thomas L.T. AB, The Citadel, 1948; JD, Duke U., 1951. Bar: N.C. 1951, S.C. 1954. Practiced in Charlotte N.C., 1951-53; ptnr. Cornish, Clement & Horlbeck, Charleston, 1955-60, Hagood, Rivers & Young, 1960-65; ptnr. Young, Clement, Rivers & Tisdale, LLP, 1965-93, of counsel, 1994—; pres. Charleston Automotive Parts, Inc., 1969-84, Charleston Mus., 1980-83; mem. adv. bd. NationsBank, 1960—; asst. city atty., Charleston, 1960; judge Mcpl. Ct., Charleston, 1961-63. Mem. Charleston County Coun., 1983-86, chmn., 1985-86. With JAGC, USAF, 1953-55. Mem. ABA, N.C. Bar Assn., S.C. Bar Assn., Charleston County Bar Assn. (pres. 1990-91), Rotary. Presbyterian. Mergers and acquisitions, General corporate, General practice. Office: Young Clement Rivers & Tisdale PO Box 993 Charleston SC 29402-0993

**CLEMENT, WILLIAM SCOTT,** lawyer; b. Bellingham, Wash., June 8, 1958; s. Alfred William and Dorothy Jane Clement; 1 child, Haley Marie. BA in Polit. Sci., Western Wash. U., 1983; JD, U. Puget Sound, 1986. Bar: Wash. 1986, U.S. Dist. Ct. (we. and ea. dists.) Wash. 1986, U.S. Ct. Appeals (9th cir.) 1986. Assoc. Lee Smart Cook Martin & Patterson PS Inc., Seattle, 1986-95, shareholder, 1995-96; ptnr. Gardner Bond Trabolsi St. Louis & Clement PLLC, Seattle, 1997—. Mem. citizen adv. group Bothell (Wash.) Planning Commn., 1997; mem. City of Bothell Pks. Bd., 1999—. Mem. ABA, Wash. Def. Trial Lawyers, Seattle-King County Bar Assn. Avocations: racketball, skiing, running, biking, hiking. Product liability, Construction, Personal injury. Office: Gardner Bond Trabolsi St Louis & Clement 2200 6th Ave Ste 600 Seattle WA 98121-1849

**CLEMENTE, MARK ANDREW,** lawyer; b. Newark, Nov. 12, 1951; s. Celestino and Marie (Strangio) C. BS, Cornell U., 1974, MPS in Hotel Adminstrn., 1977; JD cum laude, Seton Hall U., 1981. Bar: N.J. 1981, U.S. Dist. Ct. N.J. 1981, U.S. Ct. Appeals (3d cir.) 1991. Law sec. to Hon. Paul B. Thompson Judge Superior Ct., Newark, 1981-82; assoc. Lum, Biunno & Tompkins (Tompkins, McGuire & Wachenfeld), Newark, 1982-84; trial atty. Law Offices of Robert W. McAndrew, Roseland, N.J., 1984-85; mng. trial atty. CNA Ins. Cos., Roseland, Fairfield, N.J., 1986-89; pvt. practice Catania and Harrington, 1989-90; mng. atty. Clemente & Gesicki (Royal Ins.), 1990—. em. N.J. State Bar Assn., Cornell Soc. Hotelmen, Delta Upsilon. Republican. Roman Catholic. General civil litigation, Insurance, Personal injury. Home: 366 Ridgewood Ave Glen Ridge NJ 07028-1513 Office: 75 Eisenhower Pkwy Roseland NJ 07068-1600

**CLEMENTE, ROBERT STEPHEN,** lawyer; b. Bklyn., May 5, 1956; s. Hugo and Mildred (Wilinsky) C.; m. Mary Martin, June 8, 1985. AA, St. John's U., 1976; BFA, NYU, 1978; JD, Southwestern U., 1981. Bar: N.Y. 1982, U.S. Dist. Ct. (ea. and so. dists.) N.Y. 1982, U.S. Supreme Ct. 1988, Calif. 1997, U.S. Dist. Ct. (ctrl. dist.) Calif. 1997. Counsel Composto & Longo, Bklyn., 1981-86; arbitration counsel N.Y. Stock Exch., N.Y.C., 1986-88, mgr. arbitration, 1988-91, dir. arbitration, 1991—; arbitrator N.Y.C. Civil Ct., 1988—; adj. prof. securities arbitration NYU, 1999—. Mem. ABA, Am. Arbitration Assn., Am. Judges Assn., N.Y. Bar Assn., Assn. of Arbitrators, Phi Alpha Delta. Avocations: reading, exercising, golf. Securities, Finance, Alternative dispute resolution. Office: NY Stock Exch Inc 20 Broad St Fl 5 New York NY 10005-2601

**CLEMENTS, ALLEN, JR.,** lawyer; b. Macon, Ga., Jan. 15, 1924; s. Allen C. and Mamie F. (Vinson) C.; children: Mary, Jill, Byng, Allen. BBA, U. Miami, 1948, JD cum laude, 1951. Bar: Fla. 1951, U.S. Tax Ct. 1951, U.S. Dist. Ct. (so. dist.) Fla. 1951, U.S. Ct. Appeals (5th cir.) 1952, U.S. Ct. Appeals (11th cir.) 1981. Sr. assoc. Claude Pepper Law Offices, Miami Beach, Fla., 1953-72; ptnr. Pepper, Clements, Hopkins & Weaver, Miami Beach, 1972-79; of counsel Tew, Critchlow, Sonberg, Traum & Friedbauer, Miami, Fla., 1979-82, Finley, Kumble, Wagner, Heinz, Underberg & Casey, Miami, 1982-87; pros. atty. City of West Miami, Fla., 1954-56, city atty., 1956-83; legal advisor Dade County Coun. Mayors, 1964-72; cons. atty. Dade County League of Cities, 1966-77; city atty. City of South Miami, 1969-72; atty. Miami Beach Tourist Devel. Authority, 1970-78, Village of Biscayne Park, 1972-75. Mem. West Miami Town Coun., 1952-53; bd. dirs. Claude Pepper Found., Tallahassee, 1992—, sec., 1994—. Served with U.S. Army, 1943-45. Decorated Bronze Star. Mem. ABA, Lake County Bar Assn., Dade County Bar Assn. (bd. dirs. 1984-86, grievance com., ethics com.). Democrat. Methodist. Fax: 352-753-7785. Home and Office: 1004 Aloha Way Lady Lake FL 32159-1304

**CLEMENTS, ROBERT W.,** lawyer; b. Lake Charles, La., Oct. 2, 1934; s. Arthur Joseph and Ruth (Lewis) C.; m. Gay Nell McDonnold, Apr. 14, 1960; children: Robert Scott, Shannon Ruth, Jennifer Gay. BBA, LLB, Tulane U., 1959. Bar: La. 1959, U.S. Dist. Ct. (we. dist.) La. 1959, U.S. Ct. Appeals (5th cir.) 1967, U.S. Dist. Ct. (ea. dist.) La. 1977, U.S. Dist. Ct. (mid. dist.) La. 1984, U.S. Ct. Appeals (11th cir.) 1987, U.S. Dist. Ct. (ea. dist.) Tex. 1992. Law clk. to Hon. E.F. Hunter, Jr., U.S. Dist. Ct. for Western Dist. La., Lake Charles, 1962; assoc. Stockwell, Sievert, Viccellio, Clements & Shaddock, Lake Charles, 1963-66, ptnr., then sr. ptnr., 1967—. Pres., bd. dirs. Lake Charles YMCA, 1973-74. 1st lt. U.S. Army, 1960-61. Mem. ABA, S.W. La. Bar Assn. (pres. 1985), La. Assn. Def. Counsel (bd. dirs. 1973), La. Assn. Hosp. Attys. (pres. 1989), Maritime Law Assn. U.S. Democrat. Presbyterian. Avocations: golf, hunting, photography. Health, Admiralty, Personal injury. Home: 2301 Barbe Ct Lake Charles LA 70601-9015 Office: Stockwell Sievert Viccellio Clements & Shaddock One Lakeside Plz Ste 400 Lake Charles LA 70601

**CLEMON, U. W.,** federal judge; b. Birmingham, Ala., Apr. 9, 1943; m. Barbara Lang; children: Herman Issac, Addine Michele. Bar: Ala. Ptnr. Adams and Clemon and predecessor, Birmingham, 1969-80; fed. judge U.S. Dist. Ct. (no. dist.) Ala., Birmingham, 1980—. Mem. Ala. Senate, 1974-80. Recipient Law and Justice award SCLC, 1980. Mem. ABA (exec. coun. 1976-79, C. Francis Stratford award 1986), Alpha Phi Alpha. Office: US Dist Ct US Courthouse 1729 5th Ave N Ste 519 Birmingham AL 35203-2049

**CLEMONS, JOHN ROBERT,** lawyer; b. Oak Park, Ill., June 9, 1948; s. Robert N. and Arline (Flatland) C.; m. Susan Morrison, June 19, 1971; children: Jason, David, Joseph. BA, U. Iowa, 1970; JD, DePaul U., 1975. Bar: Ill. 1975, U.S. Dist. Ct. (so. dist.) Ill. 1978, U.S. Ct. Appeals (7th cir.) 1989, U.S. Supreme Ct. 1989. Asst. village mgr. Village of Riverside, Ill., 1970-72; co-dir. dist. 208 Youth Ctr., Riverside, 1970-73; area dir. S.W. area Cook County OEO, 1972-73; clk., legal researcher Klein, Thorpe & Jenkins, attys., Chgo., 1974-75; asst. state's atty. Jackson County, Murphysboro, Ill., 1975-80, state's atty., 1980-88; asst. prof. So. Ill. U., Carbondale, 1977-79, lectr., 1987—; pvt. practice law, Carbondale, 1988-91; ptnr. Clemons & Hood, Carbondale, 1991—. Mem. Jackson County Youth Svc. Program, Carbondale, 1975-78, chmn., 1978-80; mem. Criminal Justice Standards Project, So. Ill., 1978; mem. Suspected Child Abuse and Neglect Team, Carbondale, 1978-88, Gov.'s Task Force on Detention Standards, 1986-87, State Coordinated Systems Response Project for Child Abuse, 1987-90, Atty. Gen.'s Task Force on Domestic Violence, 1989; bd. dirs. Good Samaritan House, 1989-94; pres. Jackson County Dem. Booster Club; chair pub. rels. Covenant Christian Sch. Mem. Jackson County Bar Assn. Democrat. Lutheran. Criminal, Juvenile. Home: 375 Mount Joy Rd Murphysboro IL 62966-4464 Office: 813 W Main St Carbondale IL 62901-2537

**CLENDENEN, WILLIAM HERBERT, JR.,** lawyer; b. New London, Conn., Dec. 2, 1942; s. William H. and Ethel L. (Clifford) C.; children: William, Patrick, Allison, Derek, Luke; m. Corinna P. Smith. BA, Providence Coll., 1964; JD, Cath. U. Am., 1967. Bar: Conn. 1967, U.S. Dist. Ct. Conn. 1971, U.S. Dist. Ct. (so. dist.) N.Y. 1977, U.S. Dist. Ct. R.I. 1977, U.S. Ct. Clms. 1977, U.S. Ct. Appeals. (2d cir.) 1971, U.S. Sup. Ct. 1976. Reginald Heber Smith Cmty. Lawyer fellow U. Pa. 1967-68; staff atty. New Haven Legal Assistance Assn., Inc., 1968-73; prin. William H. Clendenen Jr., P.C., New Haven, 1973—; supervising atty. Yale Law Sch., 1981; alt. pub. mem. Conn. State Bd. Mediation and Arbitration, 1976-78; co-chmn. U.S. Dist. Ct. Conn. Spcl. Masters Com., New Haven, 1985-89. Fellow Am. Coll. Trial Lawyers, Conn. Bar Found. (life, dir. 1991—, treas. 1992—); mem. ABA, ATLA, Conn. Bar Assn. (chmn. consumer law sect. 1974-78, chmn. lawyer referral com. 1987-89, jud. independence task force 1998—), New Haven County Bar Assn. (sec. 1986-87, treas. 1987-88, v.p. 1988-89, pres. 1989-90), Conn. Trial Lawyers Assn., New Haven County Bar Found. (dir. 1993—). Federal civil litigation, State civil litigation, Consumer commercial. Home: 102 River Edge Farms Rd Madison CT 06443-2756

**CLENNAN, JOHN JOSEPH,** lawyer; b. St. Paul, Feb. 10, 1951; s. Mary Grace (Walsh) Clennan. BS, U. Wis., River Falls, 1976; JD, South Tex. Coll., 1979. Bar: Tex. 1980, U.S. Ct. of Appeals (5th cir.) 1981, U.S. Dist. Ct. (so. dist.) Tex. 1987. Assoc. Jonathan Brook and Assocs., Houston, 1980-82; prin. John J. Clennan, P.C., Houston, 1982-94; ptnr. Tucker & Clennan PLLC, Sugar Land, Tex., 1994—. Mem. ABA. Roman Catholic. Avocations: tennis, golf. Oil, gas, and mineral, Real property, Appellate. Home: 311 Bay Bridge Dr Sugar Land TX 77478-4738 Office: Tucker & Clennan PLLC 101 Southwestern Blvd Ste 145 Sugar Land TX 77478-3649

**CLERMONT, KEVIN MICHAEL,** law educator; b. N.Y.C., Oct. 25, 1945; s. William Theodore and Rita Ruth (Healy) C.; 1 child, Adrienne Shaine. AB summa cum laude, Princeton U., 1967; postgrad., U. Nancy, France, 1967-68; JD magna cum laude, Harvard U., 1971. Bar: Mass. 1971, N.Y. 1974, U.S. Dist. Ct. (so. and ea. dists.) N.Y. 1974, U.S. Ct. Appeals (2d cir.) 1974. Law clk. to judge U.S. Dist. Ct. (so. dist.) N.Y., 1971-72; assoc. Cleary, Gottlieb, Steen & Hamilton, N.Y.C., 1972-74; asst. prof. Sch. Law Cornell U., Ithaca, N.Y., 1974-77; assoc. prof. Cornell U., Ithaca, 1977-80, prof., 1980-89, Flanagan prof. law, 1989—; vis. prof. Sch. Law Harvard U., Cambridge, 1991. Author: Civil Procedure: Territorial Jurisdiction and Venue, 1999, (with others) Materials for a Basic Course in Civil Procedure, 7th edit., 1997, Civil Procedure, 5th editor., 1999, (with others) Law: Its Nature, Functions, and Limits, 3d edit., 1986; editor Harvard Law Rev., 1969-71. Fulbright scholar, 1967-68. Mem. ABA, Assn. Am. Law Schs., Order of Coif, Phi Beta Kappa, Sigma Xi. Home: 100 Iroquois Rd Ithaca NY 14850-2223 Office: Cornell U Sch Law Myron Taylor Hall Ithaca NY 14853

**CLEVELAND, BLAIR KNOX,** lawyer; b. Macon, Ga., Dec. 1, 1969; s. Robert Joseph and Nancy (Standard) C. BBA, U. Ga., 1992, JD cum laude, 1995. Bar: Ga. 1995, U.S. Dist. Ct. (mid. dist.) Ga. 1995. Assoc. Martin, Snow, Grant & Napier, Macon, 1995—. Trustee Middle Ga. Hist. Soc., 1996—; fundraiser United Way, 1998, Am. Heart Assn., 1995, Muscular Dystrophy, Macon, 1996, 97, 98. Mem. Bons Hommes (treas. 1996, v.p. 1997). Episcopalian. Insurance, General civil litigation. Office: Martin Snow Grant & Napier 240 3d St Macon GA 31202

**CLEVELAND, JOSEPH F., JR.,** lawyer; b. Ft. Worth; s. Joe F. and Jessika W. Cleveland; m. Mary M. Kratochvil, Dec. 30, 1988; 1 child, Hudson Baines. BA, Tex. Christian U., 1987; JD, Miss. Coll., 1990. Bar: Tex. 1990. Law clk. to Hon. Eldon B. Mahon, sr. judge U.S. Dist. Ct. (no. dist.) Tex., Ft. Worth, 1990-92; assoc. McLean & Sanders, Ft. Worth, 1992-96, shareholder, 1997—. Bd. dirs., v.p. Greater Ft. Worth Youth Orch., 1995—. Mem. ABA, Tex. Bar Assn., Tarrant County Bar Assn. (chmn. spkers com. 1993—), Tarrant County Young Lawyers Assn. (sec.-treas. 1990—). Republican. Methodist. Avocation: violin. General civil litigation, Personal injury, Product liability. Home: 3800 Winifred Dr Fort Worth TX 76133-2004 Office: McLean & Sanders PC 100 Main St Ste 400 Fort Worth TX 76102-3090

**CLEVENGER, RAYMOND C., III,** federal judge; b. Topeka, Kans., Aug. 27, 1937; s. Raymond C. and Mary Margaret (Ramsey) C.; m. Celia Faulkner, Sept. 9, 1961 (div. Mar. 1987); children: Winthrop, Peter. BA, Yale U., 1959, LLB, 1966. Ptnr. Wilmer Cutler & Pickering, Washington, 1975-90; judge U.S. Ct. Appeals (Fed. Cir.), Washington, 1990—. Mem. ABA, D.C. Bar Assn. Office: Fed Cir Ct 717 Madison Pl NW Washington DC 20439-0002*

**CLICK, DAVID FORREST,** lawyer; b. Miami Beach, Fla., Dec. 17, 1947; s. David Gorman and Helen Margaret (McPhail) C.; m. Helaine London, June 2, 1974; children: Kenneth Randall, Adam Elliott. BA, Yale U., 1969, JD, 1973, MA, 1974. Bar: Conn. 1973, Md. 1983, U.S. Supreme Ct. 1983, Fla. 1984, Maine 1984. Asst. prof. Western New England Sch. Law, Springfield, Mass., 1974-77; assoc. prof. Ind. U., 1977-78, U. Md., Balt., 1978-84; assoc. Nixon, Hargrave, Devans and Doyle, Jupiter, Fla., 1984-86; sole practice Jupiter, 1986—; pres., dir. Click Farms, Inc., Clewiston, Fla.; vice chmn. adv. com. Palm Beach County Coop. Ext. Svc. Contbr. articles to profl. jours. Mem. Christmas Cove (Maine) Improvement Assn., Palm Beach-Martin County Estate Planning Coun., pres. 1988-89; participant Leadership Palm Beach County, 1991-92. Mem. ABA, Fla. Bar Assn., Palm Beach County Bar Assn. (cultural activities award 1992), Nat. Soc. Arts and Letters, Yale Club of the Palm Beaches (pres.), Kiwanis. Presbyterian. Estate planning, Probate, Real property. Home: 19216 Pinetree Dr Jupiter FL 33469-2002 Office: 810 Saturn St Ste 15 Jupiter FL 33477-4456

**CLIFF, WALTER CONWAY,** lawyer; b. Detroit, Jan. 2, 1932; s. Frank V. and Virginia L. (Conway) C.; m. Ursula McHugh, Nov. 5, 1960; children: Walter C., Mary F., Catherine C. B.S., U. Detroit, 1955, LL.B., 1955; LL.M., NYU, 1956. Bar: Mich. 1956, N.Y. 1958. Assoc. firm Cahill Gordon & Reindel, N.Y.C., 1958-66, ptnr., 1966—; pres. Walter C. Cliff, P.C., N.Y.C., 1982—. Bd. dirs. Florence Gould Found., N.Y.C., 1983—; bd. dirs. Austen Riggs Center, Stockbridge, Mass., 1983-89, Geoffrey Hughes Found., 1992—; mem. Collections com. Harvard U. Art Mus., 1992—. Served with U.S. Army, 1956-58. J.K. Lasser fellow NYU, 1955-56. Mem. ABA, Assn. of Bar of City of N.Y., N.Y. Bar Assn. Democrat. Roman Catholic. Clubs: Down Town, Stockbridge Golf. Corporate taxation. Office: Cahill Gordon & Reindel 80 Pine St Fl 17 New York NY 10005-1790

**CLIFFORD, EUGENE THOMAS,** lawyer; b. Utica, N.Y., July 15, 1941; s. James Anthony and Mary Margaret (Ellard) C.; m. Joyce Victoria Siwinski, Sept. 4, 1965; children: Michael Sean, Elizabeth Joyce, Thomas More. BA, Boston Coll., 1963, LLB, 1966. Bar: N.Y. 1967, U.S. Dist. Ct. (we. dist.) N.Y. 1967. Assoc. Chamberlain, D'Amanda, Bauman, Chatman & Oppenheimer, Rochester, N.Y., 1967-72, Lamb, Webster, Walz, Telesca & Donovan, Rochester, 1972-76; ptnr. Webster, Sullivan, Santoro & Clifford, Rochester, 1976-86, Fulreader, Rosenthal, Sullivan, Clifford, Santoro & Kaul, Rochester, 1986—. Bd. dirs. N.Y. state divsn. Am. Cancer Soc., Syracuse, 1972-78, 82-88, 90-97, chmn. bd. dirs., 1982-83, nat. bd. dirs., 1991-97; bd. dirs. Urban League of Rochester, 1988-91. Recipient Nat. Bronze award N.Y. state divsn. Am. Cancer Soc., 1984, Hope award Monroe County unit, 1983. Estate planning, Probate, Real property. Office: 1350 Midtown Tower Rochester NY 14604-2010

**CLIFFORD, JOHN A.,** lawyer; b. Detroit, Dec. 22, 1956. BS in Physics, Creighton U., 1978, JD, 1981. Bar: Minn. 1981, U.S. Patent and Trademark Office 1981. Ptnr. Merchant & Gould P.C., Mpls., 1981—. Filing corr. over 1000 U.S. trademark applications. Intellectual property. Office: Merchant & Gould PC 3100 Norwest Ctr 90 S 7th St Ste 3100 Minneapolis MN 55402-4131

**CLIFFORD, PETER,** lawyer; b. Danbury, Conn., July 30, 1964; s. Paul J. and Ann (Malloy) C.; m. Stephanie Perkins, Sept. 12, 1992; 1 child, Meghan. BS, Boston Coll., 1986; JD cum laude, U. Maine, 1991. Bar: Maine 1991, Mass. 1991, U.S. Dist. Ct. Maine 1991, U.S. Ct. Appeals (1st cir.) 1992, U.S. Dist. Ct. Mass. 1992, U.S. Supreme Ct. 1994. Fin. analyst Raytheon Co., Lexington, Mass., 1986-88; assoc. Monaghan Leahy Hochadel & Libby, Portland, Maine, 1991-92; pvt. practice Kennebunk, Maine, 1992—; lectr. in field. Bd. dirs. KIDS, Inc., Kennebunk, 1994-95. Mem. Maine State Bar Assn., Maine trial Lawyers Assn., York County Bar Assn., Kennebunk C. of C. (bd. dirs. 1994-95), Kennebunk Rotary. Avocations: sailing, tennis. Criminal, General civil litigation. Office: PO Box 1069 62 Portland Rd Kennebunk ME 04043-6658

**CLIFFORD, ROBERT WILLIAM,** state supreme court justice; b. Lewiston, Maine, May 2, 1937; s. William H. and Alice (Sughrue) C.; m. Clementina Radillo, Jan. 18, 1964; children: Laurence M., Matthew P. BA, Bowdoin Coll., 1959; LLB, Boston Coll., 1962; LLM in Jud. Process, U. Va., 1998. Bar: Maine 1962, U.S. Dist. Ct. Maine 1965. Ptnr. Clifford & Clifford, Lewiston, 1964-79; justice Maine Superior Ct., Auburn, 1979-83, chief justice, 1984-86; assoc. justice Maine Supreme Jud. Ct., Auburn, 1986—. Mem. Lewiston City Coun., 1968-70, mayor, 1971-72; mem. Maine State Senate, 1973-76; chmn. Lewiston Charter Commn., 1978-79; mem. Maine Probate Law Revision Commn., 1973-79. Mem. Maine Bar Assn., Androscoggin County Bar Assn., Am. Judicature Soc. Roman Catholic. Home: 14 Nelke Pl Lewiston ME 04240-5318 Office: Maine Supreme Jud Ct PO Box 3488 Auburn ME 04212-3488

**CLIFFORD, SIDNEY, JR.,** lawyer, judge; b. Providence, Jan. 3, 1937; s. Sidney Sr. and Mary Elizabeth (Freeman) C.; m. Irene Kulpa, Sept. 23, 1989. BA, Marlboro (Vt.) Coll., 1959; JD, U. Va., 1962. Bar: R.I. 1962, U.S. Dist. Ct. R.I. 1963, Mass. 1985. Law clk. to assoc. justice Supreme Ct. R.I., Providence, 1963-64; chief examiner div. taxation State of R.I., Providence, 1964-66; ptnr. Quinn & Quinn, 1966-70; chief dep. clk. U.S. Dist. Ct. R.I., 1970-74; atty. legal dept. Commonwealth Land Title Ins. Co., 1980-84; title atty., head title dept. Old Colony Coop. Bank, 1980-82; assoc. Rustigian, Rosenfield, Portnoy & Nasif, 1984-85; legal counsel real estate R.I. Dept. Transp., 1985—; probate judge Little Compton, R.I., 1978—. Pres. Episcopal Charities R.I., 1989-91; bd. dirs., 1980-91; bd. dirs., sec. Legal Aid Soc., 1985-95; dep. Nat. Episc. Convention, 1994. Mem. ABA (exec. coun. young lawyers sect. 1987-89), SAR (v.p. R.I. soc. 1991-93, pres. 1993-95, trustee 1997—), Colonial Wars R.I. Soc. (dep. gov. 1996—), Providence Charitable Fuel Soc. (bd. dirs. 1985-95), Legal Aid Soc. R.I. (bd. dirs., sec. 1985-95), Marlboro Coll. Alumni Assn. (pres., trustee 1969-71), Moses Brown Sch. Alumni Assn. (bd. dirs. 1979—), Warrens Point Beach Club (treas. 1969-74, sec. 1973—), Agawam Hunt and Hope Club, Univ. Club, Providence Art Club, Sakonnet Golf Club, Masons (grand marshall 1981-82). Republican. Episcopalian. Avocations: travel, tennis, swimming. Home: 22 Taylors Ln S Little Compton RI 02837-1115 Office: RI Dept Transp Office Chief Counsel 2 Capitol Hl Rm 251 Providence RI 02903-1111

**CLIMACO, MICHAEL LOUIS,** lawyer; b. Cleve., Apr. 30, 1946; s. John and Isabel (Mazzeo) C.; m. Karen Lee Freitag, Mar. 14, 1981; children: Christina Diane, Catherine Lee. BA in Polit. Sci., Ashland U., mem, 1969; JD, Cleve. State U., 1972. Bar: Ohio 1973, U.S. Dist. Ct. (no. dist.) Ohio 1973. Atty., mng. ptnr., pres., dir. Climaco, Climaco, Lefkowitz & Garofoli Co., LPA, Cleve., 1972—; vis. com. Cleveland-Marshall Coll. Law, Cleve. State U.; bd. trustees Freedom House. Vice chmn. Cuyahoga County Dem. Party, 1972-78; mem. Cleve. City Coun., 1972-76Leadership Cleve; trustee Juvenile Diabetes Assn. Cleve., 1989-92; mem. bd. trustees Cleve. State U.; active Assn. for Retarded Citizens-Cuyahoga County, Parents' Vol. Assn. for Retarded Children and Adults, Alzheimer's Assn.; pres. ch. coun. St. Rocco's Ch. Recipient Columbian award Fedn. of Italian-Am. Socs. No. Ohio, 1992, Pres.'s award Cleveland Marshall Law Alumni Assn., 1993, Alumni of Yr. award Cleveland Marshall Coll. of Law, 1995. Mem. Justinian Forum. Roman Catholic. State civil litigation, Personal injury, Municipal (including bonds). Office: Climaco Climaco et al 1228 Euclid Ave Ste 900 Cleveland OH 44115-1891

**CLINE, ANDREW HALEY,** lawyer; b. Fountain Hill, Pa., Nov. 30, 1951; s. William Matthew and Eleanor Mary (Bosich) C.; m. Eileen Louise Feher, Mar. 2., 1986; children: Haley Andrea, Catherine Anne. BA, Guilford Coll., 1973; JD, U. Ala., 1978. Bar: Pa. 1978, U.S. Dist. Ct. (mid. dist.) Pa. 1982, U.S. Dist. Ct. (ea. dist.) 1989, U.S. Ct. Appeals (3rd cir.) 1988, U.S. Supreme Ct. 1990. Law clk. Commonwealth Ct. Pa., Harrisburg, 1978-80; asst. counsel Dept. Transportation, Harrisburg, 1980-86; assoc. dep. gen. counsel Gov's. Office, Harrisburg, 1986-87, dep. gen. counsel, 1987-89; with Kirkpatrick & Lockhart, LLP, Harrisburg, 1989—. Editor-in-chief Ala. Law Rev., 1978. Named one of Outstanding Young Men Am. Jaycees, 1978. Mem. Fed. Bar Assn. (pres. Ctrl. Pa. chpt. 1994-95, nat. del. 1995-97), Pa. Bar Assn., Dauphin County Bar Assn. (chmn. continuing legal edn. com. 1992-95, bd. dirs. 1993-95, chmn. govt. law sect. 1994, sec. 1996), Bench and Bar Soc., Am. Inns of Ct. (master emeritus J.S. Bowman chpt.), St. Thomas More Soc. (bd. dirs. 1997-98), Omicron Delta Kappa. Avocation: photography. Administrative and regulatory, General civil litigation, Government contracts and claims. Office: Kirkpatrick & Lockhart 240 N 3rd St Harrisburg PA 17101-1521

**CLINE, CRISTEN LYNNE,** lawyer; b. Hobart, Okla., Dec. 16, 1966; d. Richard M. and Myrna (Hall) C.; m. Stephen C. Ash, Sept. 4, 1993. BA in Polit. Sci. with honors, Tex. A&M U., 1988; JD, Baylor U., 1991. Bar: Tex. 1991. Assoc. Vinson & Elkins L.L.P., Houston, 1991-96; assoc. gen. counsel Keystone Internat., Inc., Houston, 1996-97; gen. counsel, corp. sec. The York Group, Inc., Houston, 1997—. Mem. Jr. League of Houston, 1993—; vol. Lawyers in Public Schs., Houston, 1992—. Mem. Houston Young Lawyers Assn., Houston Bar Assn., Tex. State Bar Assn. Office: The York Group Inc 8554 Katy Fwy Ste 200 Houston TX 77024-1851

**CLINE, LANCE DOUGLAS,** lawyer; b. Columbus, Ind., Oct. 8, 1951; s. Leon Dale and Jo Ann Alice (Fauser) C.; m. Mary Margaret Nagle, Oct. 8,

1977; children—Rachel Ann, Natalie Brooke, Kathleen Nagle. B.A., Ind. U., 1973, J.D., 1980. Bar: Ind. 1980, U.S. Dist. Ct. (so. dist.) Ind. 1980. Ptnr. Cline, Farrell, Christie & Lee, Indpls., 1980—. Contbr. articles to profl. jours. Mem. Ind. Trial Lawyers Assn. (bd. dirs. 1984—), Am. Trial Lawyers Assn., ABA, Ind. State Bar Assn., Indpls. Bar Assn., Phi Beta Kappa. Personal injury. Home: 8645 Bay Colony Dr Indianapolis IN 46234-2912 Office: Cline Farrell Christie & Lee 342 Massachusetts Ave Indianapolis IN 46204-2132

**CLINE, LEE WILLIAMSON,** lawyer; b. Ft. Sill, Okla., June 19, 1944; s. Harvey V. Jr. and Virginia Jo (McCarter) Marmon; m. Betty Gail Browning; children: Christopher, Meghan. AB in Polit. Economy, Wabash Coll., 1966; JD, Miss. Coll., 1979. Bar: La. 1985. Of counsel Chandeleur, Ltd., Laurel, Miss., 1989—; pvt. practice Laurel, 1985—; cons. Utility Mgmt. Corp., Jackson, Miss., 1991, Commerce Energy, Inc., New Orleans. Mem. ABA, La. Bar Assn., Ind. Petroleum Assn. Am., New Orleans Natural Gas Assn., Laurel C. of C. Republican. Episcopalian. Administrative and regulatory, FERC practice, Environmental. Office: 137 Jeff Byrd Rd Laurel MS 39443-6136

**CLINE, MICHAEL ROBERT,** lawyer; b. Parkersburg, W.Va., Oct. 13, 1949; s. Robert Rader and Hazel Mae (Boice) C.; m. Carole R. Davis, Aug. 28, 1972. A.B., Morris Harvey Coll., 1972; J.D., Wake Forest U., 1975. Project coordinator Gov.'s Office Fed.-State Relations, Charleston, W.Va., 1970-72; spl. asst. W.Va. Office Econ. Opportunity, 1973; spl. asst. W.Va.-Dept. Labor, Charleston, 1974; staff asst., hearing officer, 1975-77; sole practice, Charleston, 1977—. Mem. ABA, Assn. Trial Lawyers Am., Comml. Law League Am., So. Mems. Assn. (bd. dirs.), Nat. Assn. Criminal Defense Lawyers, W.Va. Trial Lawyers Assn. (bd. dirs. 1982—, treas. 1984, v.p. 1985-86, Outstanding Mem. 1983), W.Va. State Bar (chmn. com. on econs. of law practice 1986, 91-92), Pi Kappa Delta, Phi Alpha Delta. Republican. Methodist. Lodge: Elks, Rotary. Consumer commercial, Personal injury, Criminal. Home: 1531 Dixie St Charleston WV 25311-1903 Office: 323 Morrison Bldg Charleston WV 25301

**CLINE, RICHARD ALLEN,** lawyer; b. Columbus, Ohio, Oct. 1, 1955; s. Ralph S. and Myrtle O. (Harrison) C.; m. Nora Jean Arth, Oct. 2. 1982; children: Caitlin, Patrick. BA in Polit. Sci., Kent State U., 1977, BS in Criminal Justice, 1977; JD, Ohio State U., 1981. Bar: Ohio 1981, U.S. Dist. Ct. (so. dist.) Ohio 1981, U.S. Ct. Appeals (6th cir.) 1983, U.S. Supreme Ct. 1985. Assoc. David Riebel, Columbus, 1981-84; ptnr. Riebel & Cline, Columbus, 1984-85; ptnr., pres. Durkin, Cline and Co. L.P.A., Columbus, 1985-88; pres. Richard Cline & Co. L.P.A., Columbus, 1988-92; mem. Mitchell Allen Catalano & Boda Co. LPA, Columbus, 1992—, ptnr., 1996—; prosecutor City of Whitehall, Ohio, 1980-81, Village of Powell, Ohio, 1983-85, Powell Village Coun., 1996—; instr. Ohio Peace Officers Tng. Counsel, Columbus, 1985. Bd. dirs. Woodbridge Village Assn., Columbus, 1983-86. Served with JAGC, Ohio Nat. Guard, 1983—. Mem. Ohio Bar Assn., Jaycees (named one of Outstanding Young Men of Am., 1979), Phi Alpha Delta, Omicron Delta Kappa. Republican. Baptist. Avocations: martial arts, military history. Criminal, State civil litigation, General practice. Home: 290 Weatherburn Ct Powell OH 43065-9103 Office: Mitchell Allen Catalano & Boda 490 S High St Columbus OH 43215-5603

**CLINE, TODD WAKEFIELD,** lawyer; b. Greenville, S.C., Apr. 28, 1964; s. Terry Gene and Shirley Ann (Smith) C. BA in Econs. magna cum laude, Wofford Coll., 1986; JD, U. S.C., 1989. Bar: S.C. 1989, Ga. 1990, N.C. 1993. Assoc. Constangy, Brooks and Smith, Atlanta, 1989-93, Smith, Helms, Mulliss & Moore, Greensboro, N.C., 1993—, Donaldson & Black, Greensboro. Contbg. editor: Developing Labor Law, 1990. Mem. NELA, ATLA (litigation, employment law com.), Blue Key, Pi Kappa Alpha. Republican. Baptist. Avocations: basketball, baseball, travel, reading. Labor, General civil litigation, Entertainment. Office: Donaldson & Black 208 W Wendover Ave Greensboro NC 27401-1307

**CLINE, WILSON ETTASON,** retired judge; b. Newkirk, Okla., Aug. 26, 1914; s. William Sherman and Etta Blanche (Roach) C.; m. G. Barbara Verne Pentecost, Nov. 1, 1939 (div. Nov. 1960); children: William, Catherine Cline MacDonald, Thomas; m. Gina Lana Ludwig, Oct. 5, 1969; children: David Ludwig, Kenneth Ludwig. Student, U. Ill., 1932-33; A.B., U. Okla., 1935, B.S. in Bus. Adminstrn., 1936; J.D., U. Calif., Berkeley, 1939; LL.M., Harvard U., 1941. Bar: Calif. 1940, U.S. Ct. Appeals (9th cir.) 1941, U.S. Dist. Ct. (no. dist.) Calif. 1943, U.S. Supreme Ct. 1953. Atty. Kaiser Richmond Shipyards, 1941-44; pvt. practice Oakland, 1945-49; prof., asst. dean, dean Eastbay Div. Lincoln U. Law Sch., Oakland, 1946-50; atty., hearing officer, asst. chief adminstrv. law judge, acting chief adminstrv. law judge Calif. Pub. Utilities Commn., San Francisco, 1949-80, ret. administrative law judge, 1981, dir. gen. welfare Calif. State Employees Assn., 1966-67, chmn. retirement com., 1965-66, mem. member benefit com., 1980-81, mem. ret. employees div. council dist., 1981-82; executor estate of Warren A. Cline. Past trustee Cline Ranch Trust, various family trusts. Mem. ABA, State Bar Calif., Conf. Calif. Pub. Utility Counsel (steering com. 1967-71), Am. Judicature Soc., Boalt Hall Alumni Assn., Harvard Club of San Francisco, Commonwealth Club San Francisco, Sleepy Hollow Swim and Tennis Club (Orinda, Calif.), Masons (Orinda lodge # 494 sec. 1951-55, past Master 1949), Sirs (Peralta chpt. 12), Phi Beta Kappa (pres. No. Calif. assn. 1969-70), Beta Gamma Sigma, Delta Sigma Pi (Key award 1936), Phi Kappa Psi, Phi Delta Phi, Pi Sigma Alpha. Democrat. Mem. United Ch. Christ. Home: 110 Saint Albans Rd Kensington CA 94708-1035 Office: 3750 Harrison St Unit 304 PO Box 11120 Oakland CA 94611-0120

**CLINTON, EDWARD XAVIER,** lawyer; b. Chgo., July 13, 1930; s. Michael Xavier and Mary Agnes (Joyce) C.; m. Margaret Mary Clinton, May 1, 1965 (div. Oct. 1978); 1 child, Edward Xavier Jr. Student, DePaul U., 1949-50; JD, John Marshall U., 1953. Bar: Ill. 1953, U.S. Dist. Ct. (no. dist.) Ill. 1955, U.S. Ct. Appeals (7th cir.) 1955. Assoc. Schultz & Biro, Chgo., 1955-56; with securities dept. Ill. State Dept., Springfield, 1956-57; assoc. Hough, Young & Coale, Chgo., 1957-65, Keck, Mahin & Cate, Chgo., 1965-92; pvt. practice Chgo., 1992—; spl. counsel Bullrinkel Ptnrs., Ltd.; instr. John Marshall Law Sch., Chgo., 1965-74; arbitrator N.Y. Stock Exch. Contbr. articles to profl. jours.; speaker in field. Bd. dirs. Chgo. Opera Theatre, 1983-88, Children's Care Found., Records Mgmt. Svcs., 1966-97; pastoral coun. Holy Name Cathedral, 1989-94; mem. adv. bd. Steppenwolf Theatre, Chgo., 1988-89. With U.S. Army, 1953-55. Postgrad. scholar John Marshall Law Sch., 1953, John Jewell scholar, 1953. Mem. ABA, Ill. Bar Assn., Chgo. Bar Assn., Bar. Assn. of 7th Cir., Rotary, Law Club, Union League Club, Execs. Club of Chgo. (bd. dirs. 1985-95), Evanston Golf Club, Am. Legion. Roman Catholic. Avocations: golf, prisoner appeals (pro bono). General corporate, Securities, Real property. Home: 990 N Lake Shore Dr Chicago IL 60611-1366 Office: 19 S La Salle St Ste 1300 Chicago IL 60603-1406

**CLINTON, MICHAEL W.,** lawyer; b. Phila., Aug. 15, 1958. BA in Social Sci. magna cum laude, Muhlenberg Coll., 1980; JD, Temple U., 1983. Pa. 1983, U.S. Dist. Ct. (ea. dist.) Pa. 1983, U.S. Ct. Appeals (3rd cir.) 1983. Ptnr. Kessler & Cohen, Phila., 1984-98, Clinton & McKain, Phila., 1998—. Mem. ATLA, ABA, Pa. Bar Assn., Phila. Bar Assn. (mem. state civil jud. procedures com.), Phila. Trial Lawyers Assn. E-mail: clintonmw@lawguys.com. Personal injury, Construction, Product liability. Office: Clinton & McKain Ste 528 111 S Independence Mall E Philadelphia PA 19106-2515

**CLINTON, SAM HOUSTON,** retired judge; b. Waco, Tex., Sept. 17, 1923; s. Samuel Houston and Faye (Ramsey) C.; m. Hazel Anne Lindsay, 1970; children: Carol, Sam, Scot, Lindsay. JD, Baylor U., 1949. Bar: Tex. 1949, U.S. Dist. Ct. (ea., we., so., no. dists.) Tex., U.S. Ct. Appeals (5th cir.), U.S. Supreme Ct. 1966. retired judge; b. Waco, Tex., Sept. 17, 1923; s. Samuel Houston and Faye (Ramsey) C.; m. Hazel Anne Lindsay, 1970; children: Carol, Sam, Scot, Lindsay. JD, Baylor U., 1949. Bar: Tex. 1949, U.S. Supreme Ct. 1966, U.S. Ct. Appeals (5th cir.), U.S. Dist. Ct. (ea., we., so., no. dists.) Tex. Aide, Congressman W.R. Poage, Washington, 1949-50; atty. Mullinax & Wells, Dallas, 1952-55; sole practice, Austin, Tex., 1955-69; ptnr. Clinton & Richards, Austin, 1969-78; judge Tex. Ct. of Criminal Appeals, Austin, 1979-96; lectr. in field. Contbr. articles to profl. jours. Mem. Austin Hist. Landmark Commn., 1977-79. Served with USN, 1943-45. Recipient Humanitarian award Native Am. Ch. of Navajoland, 1968; Best Law Rev. Article, Tex. Bar Found., 1981. Mem. Tex. Bar Assn. (Outstanding Criminal Jurisprudence Jurist criminal law sect. 1985-86), Travis County Bar Assn., Save Our Streams. Democrat.

**CLITHERO, MONTE PAUL,** lawyer; b. Vandalia, Mo., Dec. 18, 1953; s. Paul L. and Patsy S. (Bland) CL.; m. Marilyn V. Easterly, Nov. 1, 1980; children: Ryan P., Lauren A. BA, Culver Stockton Coll., Canton, Mo., 1975; JD, U. Mo., 1978. Bar: Mo. 1978, U.S. Dist. Ct. (we. dist.) Mo. 1978, U.S. Ct. Appeals (8th cir.) 1993. Assoc. Taylor, Stafford et al, Springfield, Mo., 1978-82; ptnr. Taylor, Stafford, Woody, Clithero & FitzGerald LLP, 1983—. Mem. ABA, Mo. Bar Assn., Internat. Assn. Def. Counsel, Def. Rsch. Inst. General civil litigation, Insurance, Personal injury. Home: 1478 S Summer Pl Springfield MO 65809-2246 Office: Taylor Stafford et al 3315 E Ridgeview St Ste 1000 Springfield MO 65804-4083

**CLODFELTER, DANIEL GRAY,** lawyer; b. Thomasville, N.C., June 2, 1950; s. Billy G. and Marie Lorene (Wells) C.; m. Elizabeth Kay Bevan, Aug. 20, 1974; children: Julia Elizabeth, Catherine Gray. BA, Davidson Coll., 1972; AB, MA, Oxford U., Eng., 1974; JD, Yale U., 1977. Bar: N.C. 1977, U.S. Dist. Ct. (we. dist.) N.C. 1977, U.S. Dist. Ct. (ea. dist.) N.C. 1979, U.S. Ct. Appeals (4th cir.) 1984, U.S. Dist. Ct. (mid. dist.) N.C. 1985. Law clk. to presiding judge U.S. Dist. Ct., Charlotte, N.C., 1977-78; assoc. Moore & Van Allen, Charlotte, 1978-82, ptnr., 1983—; mem. N.C. Senate, 1999—. Mem. Charlotte City Coun., 1987-93, Charlotte-Mecklenburg Planning Commn., 1984-87, chmn., 1986-87; state sec. Rhodes Scholarship Trust, N.C., 1986-97; trustee Z. Smith Reynolds Found., Inc., Winston-Salem, N.C., 1983—; bd. dirs. N.C. Ctr. for Pub. Policy Rsch., 1994-96. Rhodes scholar, 1972. Mem. N.C. Bar Assn. (antitrust law com., bankruptcy sect. coun.). Bankruptcy, Environmental, Antitrust. Office: Moore & Van Allen 100 N Tryon St Fl 47 Charlotte NC 28202-4000

**CLOSE, DAVID PALMER,** lawyer; b. N.Y.C., Mar. 16, 1915; s. Walter Harvey and Louise De Arango (Palmer) C.; m. Margaret Howell Gordon, June 26, 1954 (dec. July 1992); children: Louise, Peter, Katharine, Barbara. B.A., Williams Coll., 1938; JD, Columbia U., 1942; LHD, Mount Vernon Coll., 1998. Bar: N.Y. State bar 1942. Practice law Washington, 1946—; ptnr. Dahlgren & Close. Mem. adv. council Nat. Capital area Boy Scouts Am., 1961—; bd. dirs. Nat. Soc. Prevention Blindness, 1961-63, Internat. Eye Found., 1965—, chmn., 1985-89; bd. dirs. D.C. Soc. Prevention of Blindness, 1957-63, pres., 1961-63; bd. dirs. Internat. Humanities, Inc., 1960—, pres., 1989—; bd. dirs. Marjorie Merriweather Post Found., 1974—, sec.-treas., 1974-76, sec., 1991—; trustee Williams Coll., 1963-68; trustee Hill Sch., 1965-85, chmn., 1973-85 ; trustee Mount Vernon Coll., 1963-75 , pres., 1971-74; mem. Am. coun. UN U., 1980—. Served with O.N.I., USN, 1942-46. Mem. ABA, Inter-Am. Bar Assn., D.C. Bar Assn., Assn. Bar City of N.Y., Assn. Trial Lawyers Am., World Jurist Assn. of World Peace Through Law Ctr., Pilgrims, Order of St. John, Chevy Chase (Md.) Club, Fauquier Springs Country Club (Warrenton, Va.), Univ. Club (Washington). General practice, Administrative and regulatory, Probate. Home: 40 Hungry Run Farm Ln Amissville VA 20106-4017 Office: Dahlgren & Close 1000 Connecticut Ave NW Ste 204 Washington DC 20036-5395

**CLOSSON, WALTER FRANKLIN,** prosecutor; b. Phila., Dec. 24, 1944; s. David Mayard Jr. and Florence Louise (Anderson) C.; m. Irene Veronica Jones, Aug. 10, 1968; children: Forrest Troy, Carey-Walter Franklin. BS in Music Edn., West Chester U., 1967; JD, Potomac Sch. Law, Washington, 1981. Bar: Ga. 1983, Md. 1985. Tchr. music D.C. Pub. Schs., Washington, 1967-77; tchr. woodwinds D.C. Youth Orch. Program, Washington, 1969-71; dist. ct. commr. Dist. Ct. of Md., Ellicott City, 1978-89; supervising dist. ct. commr. Dist. Ct. of Howard County, Ellicott City, 1984-89; asst. state's atty. State's Atty.'s Office, Ellicott City, 1989-99; chief child support divn. State's Atty.'s Office, 1999—. Mem.. Howard County Bar Assn., Waring-Mitchell Law Soc. (pres. 1992-94, Man of Yr. 1990), Masons (sr. deacon 1996-97, sr. warden 1997-98, worshipful master, 1998-99), Delta Theta Phi (v.p. 1979-80). Office: Howard County States Atty 3565 A-1 Ellicott Mills Dr Ellicott City MD 21043

**CLOUDT, JIM B.,** lawyer; b. San Angelo, Tex., Aug. 22, 1949. BBA, So. Meth. U., 1971, MBA, 1972, JD, 1976. Bar: Tex. 1976, U.S. Dist. Ct. (we. dist.) Tex. 1987, U.S. Dist. Ct. (so. dist.) Tex. 1991, U.S. Dist. Ct. (no. dist.) Tex. 1992, U.S. Ct. Appeals (5th cir.) 1992. Lawyer Austin, Tex. Administrative and regulatory, Appellate, Taxation, general. Office: PO Box 49856 Austin TX 78765-0856

**CLOUES, EDWARD BLANCHARD, II,** lawyer; b. Concord, N.H., Dec. 28, 1947; s. Alfred Samuel and H. Jeannette (Callas) C.; m. Mary Anne Matthews, Aug. 21, 1971; children: E. Matthew, M. Elizabeth. BA, Harvard U., 1969; JD, NYU, 1972. Bar: Pa. 1972, U.S. Dist. Ct. (ea. dist.) Pa. 1973. Law clk. to hon. judge James Hunter III U.S. Ct. Appeals (3d cir.), Phila. and Camden, N.J., 1972-73; assoc. Morgan, Lewis & Bockius, LLP, Phila., 1973-79, ptnr., 1979-98; chmn., CEO K-Tron Internat., Inc., Pitman, N.J., 1998—; bd. dirs. K-Tron Internat., Pitman, N.J., vice chmn. bd., 1987-94; bd. dirs. Amrep Corp., chmn., 1995—; bd. dirs. AmeriQuest Tech., Inc. Republican. Lutheran. Avocations: travel, reading. Mergers and acquisitions, General corporate, Bankruptcy. Office: K-Tron Internat Inc PO Box 888 Rtes 55 & 553 Pitman NJ 08071

**CLOUSE, JOHN DANIEL,** lawyer; b. Evansville, Ind., Sept. 4, 1925; s. Frank Paul and Anna Lucille (Frank) C.; m. Georgia L. Ross, Dec. 7, 1978; 1 child, George Chauncey. AB, U. Evansville, 1950; JD, Ind. U., 1952. Bar: Ind. 1952, U.S. Supreme Ct. 1962, U.S. Ct. Appeals (7th cir.) 1965. Assoc. Firm of James D. Lopp, Evansville, 1952-56; pvt. practice law James D. Lopp, Evansville, 1956—; guest editorialist Viewpoint, Evansville Courier, 1978-86, Evansville Press, 1986-98, Focus, Radio Sta. WGBF, 1978-84; 2d asst. city atty. Evansville, 1954-55; mem. appellate rules sub-com. Ind. Supreme Ct. Com. on Rules of Practice and Procedure, 1980.. Pres. Civil Svc. Commn. Evansville Police Dept., 1961-62, v.p., 1988; pres. Ind. War Memls. Com., 1963-69; mem. jud. nominating com. Vanderburgh County, Ind., 1976-80; dir. Ind. Fed. Cmty. Defender Project, Inc., 1993-98. With inf. U.S. Army, 1943-46. Decorated Bronze Star; named one of World's Most travelled Man Guinness Book of Records, 1993, Most Travelled Man, 1995-99. Fellow Ind. Bar Found.; mem. Evansville Bar Assn. (v.p. 1972, James Bethel Gresham Freedom award 1997), Ind. Bar Assn. (chmn. com. on civil rights 1991-92), Travelers Century Club (L.A.), Pi Gamma Mu. Republican. Methodist. Criminal, Family and matrimonial, State civil litigation. Office: 123 NW 4th St Ste 317 Evansville IN 47708-1712

**CLOUTIER, MONIQUE LEGENDRE,** lawyer; b. New Orleans, Sept. 29, 1965; d. Byron Peter Legendre and Barbara Ann Escoffier; m. Jude Anthony Cloutier, Aug. 6, 1993; 1 child, Charles Pierre. Degree in computer info. processing, Loyola U., New Orleans, 1987; JD, So. U., 1992. Bar: La. 1992, U.S. Dist. Ct. (ea., we. and mid. dists.) La. 1992. Law clk. 15th Jud. Dist. Ct., Abbeville, La., 1992-95; atty. Pub. Defender Office, Lafayette, La., 1995—. Mem. La. State Bar Assn., Lafayette Young Lawyers Assn. (ann. meeting chairperson 1997—), Lafayette C. of C. Democrat. Roman Catholic. Home: 319 Live Oak Dr Lafayette LA 70503-3903 Office: 15th Jud Dist Pub Defender 207 W Main St Lafayette LA 70501-6843

**CLOUTMAN, EDWARD BRADBURY, III,** lawyer; b. Lake Charles, La., Dec. 8, 1945; s. Edward Bradbury Jr. and Evelyn (Daniel) C.; m. Kathryn Sue Robinson, Aug., 1967 (div. 1974); children: Michael Edward, Chad Edward; m. Elizabeth Katherine Julian, June 11, 1976; 1 child, Edward Bradbury IV. JD, La. State U., 1969. Bar: La. 1969, U.S. Dist. Ct. (we. dist.) La., U.S. Ct. Appeals (5th cir.) 1970, Tex. 1971, U.S. Dist. Ct. (no., we., and ea. dists.) Tex., U.S. Supreme Ct. 1973, U.S. Ct. Appeals (10th cir.) 1974, U.S. Ct. Appeals (6th cir.) 1980, U.S. Ct. Appeals (11th cir.) 1982. Reginald Heber Smith fellow CENLA Legal Aid Soc., Alexandria, La., 1969-70, Dallas Legal Svcs. Found., 1970-71; ptnr. Johnston, Polk, Larson, Cloutman & Dixon, Dallas, 1971-73; assoc. Mullinax, Wells, Mauzy and Baab, Inc., Dallas, 1973-74; ptnr. Mullinax, Wells, Baab and Cloutman, P.C., Dallas, 1975-90; pvt. practice Dallas, 1990—; adj. prof. So. Meth. U. Sch. Law, 1990—. Mem. ABA, Inns of Ct. (master 1990—). Democrat. Civil rights, Labor. Office: 3301 Elm St Dallas TX 75226-1637

**CLUKEY, LAURA LYNN,** lawyer; b. Albany, N.Y., Nov. 15, 1963; d. James Edward and Virgie Ann (Klein) C.; m. Michael J. Gosling, Oct. 28, 1996; 1 child, Melissa Ann. BA, North Ctrl. Coll., Naperville, Ill., 1985; JD, John Marshall Law Sch., Chgo., 1989. Lawyer KPMG Peat Marwick, Chgo., 1989-90, Hopkins & Sutter, Chgo., 1990-93, Rubenstein & Rubenstein, Chgo., 1994-97, Michael A. Babiarz & Assocs., Palatine, Ill., 1997—. Mem. ABA (dep. editor). Office: Michael A Babiarz & Assocs 579 N 1st Bank Dr Ste 220 Palatine IL 60067-8126

**CLYMER, JOHN HOWARD,** lawyer; b. Boston, Nov. 19, 1939; s. Russell Sturgis and Eileen Newell (Williams) C.; m. Diana Payne Walker, Aug. 22, 1964; children: Sarah Payne, Amy Newell. BA, Princeton U., 1962; JD, Harvard U., 1965. Bar: Mass. 1965. Assoc. Hutchins & Wheeler, Boston, 1965-71; ptnr. Hutchins Wheeler & Dittmar, Boston, 1972—; trustee Hyams Found., Family Service Assn. of Greater Boston. Contbr. articles to profl. jours. Mem. Concord Planning Bd., Mass., 1972-77, concord Bd. Selectmen, 1988-94; trustee, treas. Walter E. Fernald State Sch., Waltham, Mass., 1975-82; bd. dirs., clk. Anatolia Coll., Boston, 1984—; trustee clk. Sofia Am. Schs., Boston, 1985—. Mem. Am. Bar Assn. (bus. law section, com. chmn. health law 1987, real propr., probate and trust law sect., com. chmn. exempt orgn. 1996—), Mass. Bar Assn., Boston Bar Assn., Am. Coll. Trust and Estate Coun., Union Club (Boston), Concord Country Club. Unitarian. Avocations: photography, travel. Estate planning, Non-profit and tax-exempt organizations, Probate. Office: Hutchins Wheeler & Dittmar 101 Federal St Boston MA 02110-1817

**COATES, FREDERICK ROSS,** lawyer; b. Madison, Va., June 27, 1933; s. Fred Icer and Sarah (Hale) C.; m. Rebecca White, Nov. 25, 1959; children: Stephanie Renee Piper, Susan C. McCoy. BA, U. Richmond, 1954, JD, 1959. Bar: Va., U.S. Dist. Ct. (we. dist.) Va. 1959. Vice chmn. Madison County Rep. party, 1968-88; mem. Rescue Squad Madison County, Madison County Planning com.; commr. accounts Madison County; asst. commn. accounts Greene County, Va. Served with U.S. Army, 1954-57. Recipient Key Man award Madison Jaycees, 1962-64. Mem. ABA, Va. State Bar. Assn., Madison-Greene Bar Assn., Red Land Club, Greene Hills Club, Masons, Boosters Club, Lions, Shriners. Baptist. Avocation: golf. Probate, Estate planning, Real property. Home and Office: PO Box 328 Madison VA 22727-0328

**COATES, GLENN RICHARD,** lawyer; b. Thorp, Wis., June 8, 1923; s. Richard and Alma (Borck) C.; m. Dolores Milburn, June 24, 1944; children—Richard Ward, Cristie Joan. Student, Milw. State Tchrs. Coll., 1940-42, N.M.A. and M.A., 1943-44; LL.B., U. Wis., 1949, S.J.D., 1953. Bar: Wis. 1949. Atty. Mil. Sea Transp. Service, Dept. Navy, 1951-52; pvt. practice law Racine, Wis., 1952—; of counsel Dye, Foley, Krohn, Shannon, S.E.; sec., gen. counsel Racine Federated Inc.; lectr. U. Wis. Law Sch., 1955-56. Author: Chattel Secured Farm Credit, 1953; contbr. articles to profl. publs. Chmn. bd. St. Luke's Meml. Hosp., 1973-76, bd. dirs., 1990-91; pres. Racine Area United Way, 1979-81; bd. curators State Hist. Soc. Wis., 1986—, pres., 1995-97; bd. dirs. Racine County Area Found., 1983-89; bd. dirs. Wis. History Found., Inc., 1983-99, Hist. Sites Found., Inc., 1987-89, St. Luke's Hosp./St. Mary's Med. Ctr. Healthcare Found., 1992-96. With U.S. Army, 1943-46. Fellow Am. Bar Found. (life); mem. ABA, State Bar Wis. (bd. govs. 1969-74, chmn. bd. 1973-74), Wis. Jud. Coun. (chmn. 1969-72), Am. Law Inst. (life), Order of Coif. Methodist (chmn. fin. com. 1961-67). Club: Racine Country. Lodge: Masons. General corporate, Estate planning, Mergers and acquisitions. Home: 2830 Michigan Blvd Racine WI 53402-4254 Office: 1300 S Green Bay Rd Racine WI 53406-4469

**COATES, MELANIE DIANA,** lawyer; b. Marietta, Ga., May 16, 1970; d. Clyde Joseph and Ingeborg Mueller Jones; m. Robert J. Coates III, Nov. 11, 1995. AB, Duke U., 1991; JD, U. Richmond, 1995. Bar: Va. 1995, U.S. Dist. Ct. Va., Md. 1996, U.S. Dist. Ct. Md., D.C. 1997, U.S. Dist. Ct. D.C. Assoc. McGuire, Woods, Battle & Boothe LLP, McLean, Va., 1995-99, Wilmer, Cutler & Pickering, Washington, 1999—. Mem. Fairfax Bar Assn. (pro bono vol. 1997—, bd. dirs. young lawyers sect. 1997, pres. young lawyers sect. 1998). Avocations: antiques, dogs, travel. State civil litigation, Federal civil litigation. Office: Wilmer Cutler & Pickering 2445 M St NW Ste 500 Washington DC 20037-1487

**COATES, WINSLOW SHELBY, JR.,** lawyer; b. Bayville, N.Y., Mar. 4, 1929; s. Winslow Shelby and Jane (Brush) C.; m. Frances Ward White, Feb. 16, 1959;children: Susan F. White, Trevor D. BA, Yale U., New Haven, Conn., 1952; LLB, U. Va., Charlottesville, 1959. Bar: N.Y. 1961, U.S. Dist. Ct. (so. dist.) N.Y. 1962. Assoc. Dow & Stonebridge, N.Y.C., 1961-67; pvt. practice N.Y.C., 1967-77; ptnr. Miller, Montgomery, Sogi, Brady & Taft, N.Y.C., 1977-80; shipping exec. Oceanic Fleet Carriers S.A., N.Y.C., 1980-86; pvt. practice Oyster Bay, N.Y., 1986—; founder Trident Maritime Svcs., Ld., Oyster Bay, 1994—. Author: Maritime Product Liability, 1979; contbr. articles to local newspapers. Co-founder Friends of the Bay, 1988; active Bd. Zoning Appeals, Matinecock, N.Y. Lt. USN, 1953-56. Mem. Maritime Law Assn. of the U.S., Piping Rock Club, Army and Navy Club. Republican. Roman Catholic. Avocations: chess, tennis, reading literature on history, travel, yachts. Admiralty, Private international. Home: 200 Piping Rock Rd Locust Valley NY 11560-2509 Office: 115 South St Oyster Bay NY 11771-2291

**COATS, ANDREW MONTGOMERY,** lawyer, former mayor, dean; b. Oklahoma City, Okla., Jan. 19, 1935; s. Sanford Clarence and Mary Ola (Young) C.; m. Linda M. Zimmerman; children—Andrew, Michael, Jennifer, Sanford. B.A., U. Okla., 1957, J.D., 1963. Assoc. Crowe and Dunlevy, Oklahoma City, Okla., 1963-67, ptnr., 1967-76, sr. trial ptnr., 1980—; dist. atty. Oklahoma County, Oklahoma City, Okla., 1976-80; mayor City of Oklahoma City, 1983-87; dean U. Okla. Coll. Law; vis. prof. law U. Okla., 1969-71; pres. Okla. Young Lawyers Conf., 1968-69; dir. Meml. Bank, N.A., Oklahoma City, Federal Bank. Democratic nominee U.S. Senate, 1980; pres. Oklahoma County Legal Aid Soc., 1972-73 Served to lt. USN, 1960-63. Named Outstanding Lawyer in Okla., Oklahoma City U., 1977. Fellow Am. Coll. Trial Lawyers (pres. 1996-97, pres.-elect 1995-96), Am. Bd. Trial Advocates (charter pres. Okla. 1986); mem. ABA, Okla. Bar Assn. (pres. 1992-93), Oklahoma County Bar Assn. (pres. 1976-77), Order of Coif, Oklahoma City Golf and Country Club (bd. dirs. 1977-80, 93-96), Beacon Club, Petroleum Club (pres. 1995), Phi Beta Kappa (pres. 1975), Pi Kappa Alpha (pres. 1956), Phi Delta Phi (pres. 1962). Democrat. Episcopalian. Clubs: Oklahoma City Golf and Country (bd. dirs. 1977-80), Beacon, Petroleum. Avocations: music; golf. General civil litigation, Product liability. Office: Crowe and Dunlevy 1800 Mid-Am Tower 20 N Broadway Ave Ste 1800 Oklahoma City OK 73102-8273

**COATS, CHRISTOPHER DALE,** judge; m. Allison Cathey, May 3, 1985. BA, Vanderbilt U., 1980; JD, Nashville Sch. Law, 1989. Bar: Tenn. 1989; approved mediator, Tenn. Analyst Nissan Motor Mfg. Corp., Smyrna, Tenn., 1984—; judge Smyrna Mcpl. Ct., 1993—. Mem. Am. Judges Assn., Tenn. Gen. Sessions Judges' Conf. (com. mem. Future of the Cts.), Sam Davis Meml. Assn. (bd. dirs. 1992-97). Office: Smyrna Mcpl Judge 315 S Lowry St Smyrna TN 37167-3416

**COATS, DAVID STEBBINS,** lawyer; b. New Orleans, Feb. 20, 1962; s. John Bussey Coats and Mary Elizabeth Brunson; m. Nancy Elizabeth Schoelkopf, Dec. 28, 1985; 1 child, Celia Valentina. BS, Guilford Coll., 1984; JD, Wake Forest U., 1988. Bar: N.C. 1988, U.S. Dist. Ct. (4th cir.) 1990, U.S. Dist. Ct. (ea. dist.) N.C. 1989. Law clk. Judge Phillips N.C. Ct. Appeals, Raleigh, 1988-89; from assoc. to ptnr. Bailey & Dixon LLP, Raleigh, 1989—; counsel bd. dirs. N.C. Rails Trails, Inc., Durham, N.C., 1994—. Nat. platform com. Dem. Party, Washington, 1992. Mem. Rotary. Methodist. Avocations: tennis, golf, scuba diving. Insurance, Construction. Office: Bailey & Dixon LLP PO Box 1351 Raleigh NC 27602-1351

**COATS, WILLIAM SLOAN, III,** lawyer; b. Fresno, Calif., Mar. 31, 1950; s. William Sloan Jr. and Willa (Macdonell) C.; m. Sherri Lee Young, Aug. 3, 1980; children: Devin Roseanne, Allyn Elizabeth. AB, U. San Francisco, 1972; JD, U. Calif., San Francisco, 1980. Bar: Calif. 1980, U.S. Dist. Ct. (no. dist.) Calif. 1980, U.S. Dist. Ct. (cen. and so. dists.) Calif. 1982. Assoc. Bancroft, Avery & McAlister, San Francisco, 1980-82, Hopkins, Mitchell & Carley, San Jose, Calif., 1982-84, Gibson, Dunn & Crutcher, San Francisco, 1984-93; ptnr. Brown & Bain, Palo Alto, Calif., 1993-96, Howrey & Simon,

Menlo Park, Calif., 1996—. Nat. Merit scholar, 1968. Mem. ABA (vice chair program com., sect. on sci. and tech.), Calif. Bar Assn. (co-chair copyright com. intellectual property sect., co-chair edn. com.), Green and Gold Club, Univ. Club. Republican. Roman Catholic. Computer, Intellectual property, General civil litigation. Office: Howrey & Simon 301 Ravenswood Ave Menlo Park CA 94025

**COATY, THOMAS JEROME,** lawyer, partner; b. Marshfield, Wis., Aug. 14, 1957; s. Jerome Clarence and Mary Ellen Coaty. BA, U. Wis., Milw., 1980, MA, 1983; JD, John Marshall Law Sch., 1992. Bar: Wis. 1992. Sole practitioner Madison, Wis., 1992-97; ptnr., sr. litigator Coaty & Stangl, S.C., Madison, Wis., 1998—; lectr. U. Wis. Law Sch., Madison, 1995-97; mem. Criminal Justice Act com., U.S. Dist. Ct., Madison, 1994—. Sr. Rep. party field dir. Wis., 1988; mem. Gov.'s Commn. on Devel., Madison, 1987; legal counsel Rep. party of Dane County, Madison, 1993; bd. visitors U. Wis., Milw., 1979. Mem. Fed. Soc. (sec. 1994), KC (3d degree; Outstanding Young Man award 1986). Federal civil litigation, Criminal, General civil litigation. Office: Coaty & Stawgh SC Ste 245 6515 Grand Teton Plz Madison WI 53719-1060

**COBAU, JOHN REED,** lawyer; b. New Castle, Pa., Aug. 28, 1934; s. William D. and Sarah M. (Weinschenk) C.; m. Arlene L. Gilbert, June 22, 1960; children: William, Joseph, Thomas, John. BA, Princeton U., 1956; LLB, Harvard U., 1960. Bar: D.C. 1960, Ohio 1961, Mich. 1966. Assoc. Kyte, Conlan, Wulsin & Vogeler, Cin., 1960-66, Freud, Markus, Slavin & Mountain, Detroit, 1966-73; pvt. practice Grosse Pointe Woods, Mich., 1974—. Mem. ABA, Mich. Bar Assn., Detroit Bar Assn., Grosse Pointe Hunt Club (bd. dirs. 1976-78), Rotary (pres., bd. dirs. Grosse Pointe). General corporate, Probate, Real property. Office: 20233 Mack Ave Grosse Pointe MI 48236-1769

**COBB, BRUCE WAYNE,** lawyer; b. San Antonio, Jan. 15, 1954; s. James Leonard and Rebecca Ashby C.; m. Charlene Hays, Dec. 2, 1992; 1 stepchild, Michael Loucus. AD, N.Mex. Mil. Inst., 1974; BA in History, Trinity U., 1976; JD, St. Mary's U., 1984. Bar: Tex. 1984, U.S. Ct. Appeals (5th cir.) 1984, U.S. Dist. Ct. (eas. dist.) Tex. 1986, U.S. Dist. Ct. (so. dist.) Tex. 1993, U.S. Supreme Ct. 1991. Atty. Tex. Ct. Appeals (9th cir.), Beaumont, 1985-86; asst. dist. atty. Jefferson County, Beaumont, 1986; atty. pvt. practice, Beaumont, 1987-88, 95—; asst. city atty. City of Beaumont, 1989-93, City of Galveston (Tex.), 1993; assoc. Flores Law Firm, Beaumont, 1993-95. Scoutmaster Boy Scouts Am., Beaumont, 1998. Mem. State Bar Tex. (appellate practice sect., appellate practice sect., appellate pro bono com.). Lutheran. Appellate, General civil litigation, Municipal (including bonds). Office: 595 Orleans St Ste 528 Beaumont TX 77701-3203

**COBB, DAVID RANDALL,** lawyer; b. Iraan, Tex., Feb. 6, 1948; s. Cleveland Ira Jr. and Geraldine (Taylor) C.; m. Jana Ree Mahon, Jan. 2, 1971; 1 child, Shannon Brooke. BA, Tex. Tech. U., 1970, JD, 1974. Bar: Tex. 1974, U.S. Dist. Ct. (no. dist.) Tex. 1975, U.S. Ct. Appeals (5th cir.) 1993. Clk. to judge U.S. Dist. Ct. (no. dist.) Tex., Lubbock, 1974-75; assoc. Crenshaw, Dupree & Milam, Lubbock, 1975-78, Whitten & Sprain, Abilene, Tex., 1978-79; ptnr. Whitten, Haag, Cobb & Halker, Abilene, 1979-82, McMahon, Smart, Surovik, Suttle, Abilene, 1982-88; shareholder McMahon, Surovik, Suttle, Buhrmann & Cobb, Abilene, 1988-95, Crenshaw, Dupree & Milan, Lubbock, 1995—. Named one of Outstanding Young Men Am., 1983. Fellow Am. Coll. Trial Lawyers, Tex. Bar Found. (life), Tex. Assn. Def. Counsel (bd. dirs. 1985-88), Internat. Assn. Def. Counsel, Tex. State Bar Assn. (chair grievance com. 1988-94). Personal injury, Product liability, General civil litigation. Office: Crenshaw Dupree & Milan 1500 Broadway St Ste 1000 Lubbock TX 79401-3188

**COBB, HOWELL,** federal judge; b. Atlanta, Dec. 7, 1922; s. Howell and Dorothy (Hart) C.; m. Torrance Chalmers (dec. 1963); children: Catherine Cobb Cook, Howell III, Mary Ann Cobb Walton; m. Amelie Suberbielle, July 3, 1965; children: Caroline Cobb Ervin, Thomas H., John L. Student, St. John's Coll., Annapolis, Md., 1940-42; LLB, U. Va., 1948. Assoc. Kelley & Ryan, Houston, 1949-51, Fountain, Cox & Gaines, Houston, 1951-54; assoc. Orgain, Bell & Tucker, Beaumont, 1954-57, ptnr., 1957-85; judge U.S. Dist. Ct. (ea. dist.) Tex., Beaumont, 1985—; mem. jud. coun. U.S. Ct. Appeals (5th cir.), 1994-97; mem. adv. com. East Tex. Legal Svcs., Beaumont. Pres. Beaumont Art Mus., 1969, bd. dirs., 1967-68; mem. vestry St. Stephens Episcopal Ch., Beaumont, 1973; mem. bd. adjustment City of Beaumont, 1972-82; trustee All Saints Episcopal Sch., Beaumont, 1972-76. 1st lt. USMC, 1942-45, PTO. Mem. ABA, State Bar Tex. (grievance com. 1970-72, chmn. 1972, admissions com. 1974—, bd. dirs. 1993-94, adv. mem.), Jefferson County Bar Assn. (sec. 1960, bd. dirs. 1960-61, 67-68), Am. Judicature Soc., Am. Bd. Trial Advs., Maritime Law Assn. U.S., Beaumont Country Club. Office: US Dist Ct 118 US Courthouse PO Box 632 Beaumont TX 77704-0632

**COBB, JAMES ABERNETHY, JR.,** assistant prosecutor; b. Rock Hill, S.C., July 10, 1951; s. James Abernethy Sr. and Helen (Smith) C.; m. Mariza DeGuzman, June 4, 1994. BA, U. N.C., 1974; JD, U. Toledo, 1989. Bar: Fla., 1989, U.S. Dist. Ct. (so. dist.) Fla., 1997; cert. criminal trial law. Asst. state atty. Dade State Atty. (11th cir.), Miami, Fla., 1989-96; asst. statewide atty. Fla. Office Statewide Prosecution, Ft. Lauderdale, 1996-98, dep. chief statewide prosecutor, 1999—. Recipient award Honor MADD, Miami, 1994, 1995. Mem. Broward County Bar Assn. Democrat. Office: Statewide Prosecution 110 SE 6th St Fort Lauderdale FL 33301-5000

**COBB, KAY B.,** state supreme court justice, former state senator, lawyer; m. Larry Cobb; children: Barbara Cobb Murphy, Elizabeth Cobb DeBusk. BS, Miss. U. Women; JD, U. Miss. Former spl. asst. atty. gen. North Miss.; atty. Oxford, Miss.; assoc. justice Miss. Supreme Ct. Mem. Nat. Alliance/Model State Drug Laws, Vets. Aux., C. of C. Republican. Baptist. E-mail: jcobb@mssc.state.ms.us. Office: Miss Supreme St PO Box 117 450 High St Jackson MS 39205*

**COBB, STEPHEN A.,** lawyer; b. Moline, Ill., Jan. 27, 1944; s. Archibald William and Lucile Bates C.; m. Nancy L. Hendrix, Dec. 18, 1972. AB cum laude, Harvard U., 1966; MA in Sociology, Vanderbilt U., 1968, PhD in Sociology, 1971, JD, 1977. Bar: Tenn. 1978, U.S. Dist. Ct. (mid. dist.) Tenn. 1978. Asst. prof. Tenn. State U., Nashville, 1970-74, dept. head, 1972-74; mem., chair edn. oversight com. Tenn. Ho. Reps., Nashville, 1974-86; pvt. practice law Nashville, 1978-86; with Waller Lansden Dortch & Davis, Nashville, 1986-90, ptnr., 1990—; Fullbright Jr. lectr. U. Caen, France, 1977-78; lectr. dept. sociology Fisk U., 1981-86. Former pres. Sister Cities of Nashville, Inc.; former vice chmn. commn. ednl. quality So. Regional Edn. Bd. Recipient Paul Simon Internat. award, 1990, Edwin Cudeki Internat. Bus. award, 1992; fellow NDEA, NIMH, 1966-70; officer l'Ordre des Palmes Academiques, Govt. France. Mem. ABA, Am. Immigration Lawyers Assn., Am. Sociol. Assn., So. Sociol. Soc., Tenn. Bar Assn., Tenn Fgn. Lang. Inst., Nashville Bar Assn., Fedn. Alliances Francaises (former pres.), Order of Coif. Family and matrimonial, Immigration, naturalization, and customs, Government contracts and claims. Home: 1929 Castleman Dr Nashville TN 37215-3901 Office: 511 Union St Ste 2100 Nashville TN 37219-1760

**COBB, TY,** lawyer; b. Great Bend, Kans., Aug. 25, 1950; s. Grover Cowling and Elizabeth Anne (McCleary) C.; m. Leigh Elliott Stevenson, Aug. 21, 1976; children: Chance Wyatt, Chelsea Leigh, Brady Elliott, Chloe Elizabeth. AB, Harvard U., 1972; JD, Georgetown U., 1978. Bar: D.C. 1979, U.S. Dist. Ct. D.C. 1979, U.S. Dist. Ct. Md. 1979, U.S. Ct. Appeals (4th and D.C. cirs.) 1979, U.S. Ct. Internat. Trade 1980, U.S. Ct. Appeals (3d cir.) 1987, U.S. Supreme Ct. 1986, Md. 1987, Colo. 1998. Legis. adminstrv. asst. U.S. Ho. of Reps., Washington, 1974-75; law clk. to fed. judge U.S. Dist. Ct., Balt., 1978-79; assoc. Collier, Shannon, Rill & Scott, Washington, 1979-81; asst. U.S. atty. Office of U.S. Atty., Balt., 1981-86; chief criminal cases Office U.S. Attorney, Balt., 1984-86; ptnr. Hogan & Hartson LLP, Washington and Balt., 1988-98; mng. ptnr. Hogan & Hartson LLP, Denver, 1998—; mid-atlantic regional coord. Organized Crime Drug Enforcement Task Force, U.S. Dept. Justice, Balt., 1985-86, spl. trial counsel Office of Ind. Counsel HUD, 1994-95; instr. U.S. Atty. Gen.'s Adv. Inst., U.S. Dept. Justice, 1983-86; mem. Jud. Conf. of U.S. Ct. Appeals (4th cir.). Contbr. articles to ABA Complex Crimes Jour. Chmn. Md. lawyers Dole for Pres., 1986-87; counsel Forest Glen Park Civic Assn., Montgomery County, Md., 1981-84. Fellow Am. Coll. Trial Lawyers; mem. ABA, Harvard Alumni Assn. (bd. dirs. 1990-92). Republican. Criminal, Federal civil litigation. Office: Hogan & Hartson LLP 555 13th St NW Ste 800 E Washington DC 20004-1161 also: Hogan & Hartson 1200 17th St Ste 1500 Denver CO 80202-5835

**COBB, WILLIAM DOWELL, JR.,** lawyer; b. Dallas, Oct. 3, 1958; s. William Dowell and Gail Palmer Cobb; m. Stacy Lee Brainin, May 4, 1985; children: Claire, Will. BA, U. Denver, 1981; JD, U. Tex., 1984. Bar: Tex. 1984, U.S. Dist. Ct. (no. dist.) Tex. 1985, U.S. Ct. Appeals (5th cir.) 1987, U.S. Dist. Ct. (we. dist.) Tex. 1989, U.S. Dist. Ct. (ea. dist.) Tex. 1992, U.S. Dist. Ct. (so. dist.) Tex. 1998. Shareholder Cowles & Thompson P.C., Dallas, 1984—. Co-author: Texas Torts Handbook, 1998. Mem. ABA (litigation sect., tort and ins. practice sect., comml. torts com., profls.', officers' and dirs. liability law com., ins. coverage com., profl. liability com.), Assn. Profl. Responsibility Lawyers, Def. Rsch. Inst., Tex. Assn. Def. Counsel, Dallas Bar Assn. (legal ethics com.), Dallas Assn. Def. Counsel. General civil litigation, Insurance, Professional liability. Office: Cowles & Thompson PC 901 Main St Ste 4000 Dallas TX 75202-3793

**COBBS, NICHOLAS HAMMER,** lawyer; b. N.Y.C., June 28, 1946; s. John Lewis and Phyllis Cobbs; m. Louise Bertram Stolman, Mar. 26, 1983; children: Robert White, Rebecca Ann. AB cum laude, Amherst (Mass.) Coll., 1968; JD, U. Pa., 1974. Bar: N.Y. 1975, D.C. 1982, Md. 1984, Va. 1990, U.S. Dist. Ct. (so. dist.) N.Y. 1975, U.S. Dist. Ct. D.C. 1982, U.S. Dist. Ct. (ea. dist.) Va. 1990, U.S. Dist. Ct. (we. dist.) Va. 1990, U.S. Dist. Ct. Md. 1989, U.S. Supreme Ct. 1984. Assoc. Burlingham Underwood & Lord, N.Y.C., 1974-77, Haight, Gardner, Poor & Havens, N.Y.C., 1977-83; ptnr., of counsel Tigert & Roberts, Washington, 1984-89; ptnr. Law Offices of Nicholas H. Cobbs, Washington, 1989—; of counsel Harris Beach & Wilcox, LLP, N.Y.C. and Rochester, 1995—. Contbr. articles to profl. jours. Arbitrator, mediator D.C. Superior Ct., Washington, 1990—; instr. D.C. Bar Continuing Legal Edn., 1993—. Lt. USNR, 1969-73. Mem. ABA, Fed. Bar Assn., Lawyer-Pilot's Bar Assn., Maritime Law Assn. of the U.S. Episcopalian. Admiralty, Administrative and regulatory, Aviation. Office: 1776 K St NW Ste 300 Washington DC 20006-2304

**COBERLY, JENNIFER RAE,** lawyer; b. Lawrence, Kans., May 19, 1963; d. R.L. and Lucille Coberly. BA, Fla. State U., 1984; JD, Yale U., 1989. Bar: Fla. 1992, Tex. 1990, U.S. Dist. Ct. (so. dist.) Fla. 1992, U.S. Ct. Appeals (5th cir.) 1992, U.S. Dist. Ct. (we. dist.) Tex. 1991. Trial cons., 1986; assoc. Gage & Tucker, summer 1989, Graves, Dougherty, Hearon and Moody, Austin, 1990-91, Zuckerman, Spaeder, Taylor & Evans, LLP, Miami, Fla., 1991—. Assoc. dir. Fla. State U. Women's Ctr., Tallahassee, 1983-84. Mem. Fla. Assn. Women Lawyers (v.p. Dade chpt. 1994, pres.-elect Fla. chpt. 1996, pres. Fla. chpt. 1997, newsletter editor 1995). Federal civil litigation, Contracts commercial, General practice. Office: Zuckerman Spaeder Taylor & Evans LLP 201 S Biscayne Blvd Ste 900 Miami FL 33131-4394

**COBEY, CHRISTOPHER EARLE,** lawyer; b. Merced, Calif., Mar. 18, 1949; s. James and Virginia Cobey; m. Elizabeth Jordan Rantz, Aug. 26, 1972; children: Sarah Elizabeth, Carolyn Branum. Student, Pomona Coll., 1967-69; BA with distinction and honors, Stanford U., 1971; JD, U. Calif., Davis, 1974. Bar: Calif. 1974, U.S. Dist. Ct. (no. dist.) Calif. 1981, U.S. Supreme Ct. 1983, U.S. Ct. Appeals (9th cir.) 1984, U.S. Dist. Ct. (ea. dist.) Calif. 1985. Dep. dist. atty. Los Angeles County, 1974-75, San Mateo County, Redwood City, Calif., 1975-77; assoc. ptnr. Hession & Creedon, San Mateo, Calif., 1979-85; of counsel Jackson, Lewis, Schnitzler & Krupman, San Francisco, 1985-88; ptnr. Seyfarth, Shaw, Fairweather & Geraldson, 1988-93, Ferrari, Alvarez, Olsen & Ottoboni, San Jose, 1993-96, Schachter, Kristoff, Orenstein & Berkowitz, Menlo Park, 1996-99; sr. counsel Littler Mendelson, San Jose, 1999—; lawyer; b. Merced, Calif., Mar. 18, 1949; s. James and Virginia Cobey; m. Elizabeth Jordan Rantz, Aug. 26, 1972; children—Sarah Elizabeth, Carolyn Branum. Student Pomona Coll., 1967-69; B.A. with distinction and honors, Stanford U., 1971; J.D., U. Calif.-Davis, 1974. Bar: Calif. 1974, U.S. Dist. Ct. (no. dist.) Calif. 1981, U.S. Supreme Ct. 1983, U.S. Ct. Appeals (9th cir.) 1984, U.S. Dist. Ct. (ea. dist.) Calif. 1985. Dep. dist. atty. Los Angeles County, 1974-75, San Mateo County, Redwood City, Calif., 1975-77; assoc. ptnr. Hession & Creedon, San Mateo, Calif., 1979-85; of counsel, Jackson, Lewis, Schnitzler & Krupman, San Francisco, 1985-88; ptnr. Seyfarth, Shaw, Fairweather & Geraldson, 1988-93; ptnr. Ferrari, Alvarez, Olsen & Ottoboni, San Jose, 1993—. Mem. San Mateo County Dem. Cen. Com., 1975-84, Calif. Dem. State Cen. Com., 1978-80; chmn. Town of Atherton Planning Commn, 1985-86; mem. Atherton Town Council, 1986-94, mayor, 1990-92; bd. dirs. Calif. Common Cause, 1980-81. Mem. ABA, San Mateo County Bar Assn. (bd. dirs. 1982-86; chmn. conf. of dels. delegation 1987), State Bar Calif. (resolutions com., conf. of dels. 1980-85, chmn. 1985),. Mem. San Mateo County Dem. Cen. Com., 1975-84, Calif. Dem. State Cen. Com., 1978-80; chmn. Town of Atherton Planning Commn., 1985-86; mem. Atherton Town Council, 1986-94, mayor, 1990-92; bd. dirs. Calif. Common Cause, 1980-81. Mem. ABA, San Mateo County Bar Assn. (bd. dirs. 1982-86, chmn. conf. on dels. delegation 1987), State Bar Calif. (resolutions com., conf. of dels. 1980-85, chmn. 1985), Stanford Alumni Assn. Presbyterian. Labor, State civil litigation, Federal civil litigation. Office: Littler Mendelson 50 W San Fernando St Ste 1400 San Jose CA 95113-2431

**COBEY, JOHN GEOFFREY,** lawyer; b. Cleve., Aug. 16, 1943; s. Herbert Todd and Phyllis Jean (Weston) C.; m. Jan M. Frankel, 1983; children: Max Todd, David William. BS, Cornell U., 1966; postgrad. U. de Deusto, Balboa, Spain, 1968, Exeter U. (Eng.), 1969; JD, U. Cin., 1969. Bar: Ohio 1969, U.S. Dist. Ct. (so. dist.) Ohio 1969, U.S. Ct. Appeals (6th cir.) 1970, Ky. 1978, U.S. Dist. Ct. (no. dist.) Ky. 1978. Mem. Cohen, Todd, Kite and Stanford LLC, 1969—; bd. dirs. 1st Nat. Bank No. Ky., C&W Equipment Repair, Armstrong Coffee Co.; sec. bd. dirs. Elegant Fare; bd. dirs., sec. Apt. Assn. Title Co.; bd. dirs. Real Time Sys., Inc.; counsel coop. housing City of Cin. Founder, pres. Young Men's Wing, Mercantile Library, 1971; regional amb. Cornell U., 1998, 99; trustee Ohio chpt. Nature Conservancy, 1974-82, Hillel of Cin., 1980-86, Women's Def. Fund, 1977, Holmes House, 1978-80; sec. Arts Consortium, Cin., 1975-77, trustee, 1975-78; mem. exec. com. Cin. chpt. Am. Jewish Com., 1981—; trustee Hillel House, Better Housing League; chmn. bd. Friends Cin. Parks, 1982-84, pres., 1977-79; chmn. bd. dirs. Washington Park Housing Co., 1997—; bd. dirs. Greater Cin./No. Ky. apt. Assn., 1975-94, Chinese Music Festival, 1996-98, United Jewish Cemetary, 1999, Opn. Smile, 1998. Mem. Ohio State Bar Assn., Ky. Bar Assn., Cin. Bar Assn., No. Ky. Bar Assn., Fed. Bar Assn., Lawyers Club, Cornell U. Coll. Life Scis. and Agr. Alumni Assn. (dist. dir.), Ohio Apt. Assn. (bd. dirs.), Cin. Apt. Assn. (bd. dirs., v.p. 1986-87), U. Cin. Law Sch. Alumni Assn. (bd. dirs 1973-76). General corporate, Real property. Home: 231 Oliver Rd Cincinnati OH 45215-2638 Office: Cohen Todd Kite and Stanford 525 Vine St Ste 16 Cincinnati OH 45202-3121

**COBRIN, JILL ALLYSON,** lawyer; b. N.Y.C., Jan. 22, 1953; d. Benjamin and Eleanor (Reiner) C.; m. Edward Joseph Brailey, June 8, 1980; children: Erica Cobrin Brailey, David Laurence Brailey. BA with honors, U. Mich., 1974; JD, Emory U., 1977. Bar: N.Y., Ga., D.C. Atty. City of N.Y.C., 1978-79; v.p. ins. Planned Parenthood Fedn. Am., Inc., N.Y.C., 1979—. Co-author: Fertility Control, 1994. Mem. ABA, Nat. Health Lawyers. Avocations: reading, travel, skiing. Office: Planned Parenthood Fedn Am 810 7th Ave New York NY 10019-5818

**COCCA, ANTHONY,** lawyer; b. Orange, N.J., Aug. 6, 1966; s. Giovanni and Filomera Cocca; m. Susan A. Dragone, June 20, 1998. BA, U. Ariz., 1988; JD, Thomas M. Cooley Law Sch., 1994. Bar: N.J., U.S. Dist. Ct. Legal intern Gov. Ergler, Lansing, Mich., 1993-94; law clk. to Hon. Donald R. Roenston Superior Ct. Judge, Pederson, N.J., 1994-95; assoc. atty. Ressler & Caserton, Pederson, 1995-97, Giblin & Combs, Morristown, N.J., 1997-98. Personal injury, Health, Criminal. Office: Giblin & Combs 10 Madison Ave Morristown NJ 07960-7303

**COCHRAN, ERIC L.,** lawyer; b. Norwalk, Conn., 1960. BA, Williams Coll., 1982; MS, NYU, 1984, JD, 1986. Bar: N.Y. 1987. Mem. firm Skadden, Arps, Slate, Meagher & Flom LLP, N.Y.C. Office: Skadden Arps Slate Meagher & Flom LLP 919 3rd Ave New York NY 10022-3902

**COCHRAN, GEORGE MOFFETT,** retired judge; b. Staunton, Va., Apr. 20, 1912; s. Peyton and Susie (Robertson) C.; m. Marion Lee Stuart, May 1, 1948; children—George Moffett, Harry Carter Stuart. BA, U. Va., 1934, LLB, 1936; LLD (hon.), James Madison U., 1991. Bar: Va. 1935, Md. 1936. Asso. law firm Balt., 1936-38; partner firm Peyton Cochran and George M. Cochran, Staunton, 1938-64, Cochran, Lotz & Black, Staunton, 1964-69; justice Supreme Ct., Richmond, Va., 1969-87; Pres. Planters Bank & Trust Co., Staunton, 1963-69. Chmn. Woodrow Wilson Centennial Commn. Va., 1952-58, Va. Cultural Devel. Study Commn., 1966-68, Frontier Culture Mus. Va., 1986-98; mem. Va. Commn. Constl. Revisi on, 1968-69, Jud. Coun. Va., 1963-69, Va. Ho. Dels., 1948-66, Va. Senate, 1966-68; chmn. bd. dirs. Stuart Hall, 1971-86; mem. bd. visitors Va. Poly. Inst., 1960-68; trustee Mary Baldwin Coll., 1967-81, U. Va. Law Sch. Found., 1975-89, Woodrow Wilson Birthplace Found., 1955-93. Lt. comdr. USNR, 1942-46. Recipient Algernon Sydney Sullivan award Mary Baldwin Coll., 1981. Mem. ABA, Va. Bar Assn. (pres. 1965-66), Raven Soc., Soc. of Cin., Phi Beta Kappa, Phi Delta Phi, Beta Theta Pi. Episcopalian.

**COCHRAN, JOHNNIE L., JR.,** lawyer; b. Shreveport, La., Oct. 2, 1937. BS, UCLA, 1959; JD, Loyola U., 1962; postgrad., U. So. Calif. Bar: Calif. 1963, U.S. Dist. Ct. (we. dist.) Tex. 1966, U.S. Supreme Ct. 1968. Dep. city atty. criminal divsn. City of L.A., 1963-65; asst. dist. atty. L.A. County, 1978-82; now pvt. practice atty. L.A.; former adj. prof. law UCLA Sch. Law, Loyola U. Sch. Law; lawyer rep. U.S. Dist Ct. (ctrl. dist.) Calif., 1990, U.S. Ct. Appeals (9th cir.) Judicial Conf., 1990; bd. dirs. L.A. Family Housing Corp., Lawyers Mut. Ins. Co. Spl. counsel, chmn. rules com. Dem. Nat. Convention, 1984; spl. counsel com. on standard ofcl. conduct, ethics com. 99th congress U.S. Ho. Reps.; bd. dirs. L.A. Urban League, Oscar Joel Bryant Found., 28th St. YMCA, ACLU Found. So. Calif. Fellow Am. Bar Found.; mem. Am. Coll. Trial Lawyers, State Bar Calif. (co-chair bd. legal svc. corps 1993), L.A. African Am. C. of C. (bd. dirs.), Airport Commrs. City of L.A., Black Bus. Assn. L.A. (pres. 1989). Office: 4929 Wilshire Blvd Ste 1010 Los Angeles CA 90010-3825

**COCHRAN, STEPHEN GREY,** lawyer; b. N.Y.C., Aug. 7, 1947; s. John M. and Madeline (Grey) C.; m. Irene Gomberg, Oct. 10, 1975 (div.); m. Ruth Swart, Jan. 8, 1982; children: Stephanie Alice, Michael Edward. BA, William and Mary Coll., 1969; JD, Am. U., Washington, 1972. Bar: Va., U.S. Supreme Ct. 1972, U.S. Ct. Appeals (4th cir.) 1978, U.S. Tax Ct. 1980. Assoc. Furniss, Davis & Sachs, Norfolk, Va., 1972-74; ptnr. Bennett, Goram & Cochran, Vienna, Va., 1974-79, Gattsek, McConnel & Cochran, Annandale, Va., 1979-80, Clary & Pijor, Springfield, Va., 1980-85, Cochran & Pijor, McLean, Va., Peterson, Pesner, Cochran & Basha, P.C., Vienna, Va., 1991-92, Cochran & Rathbun, P.C., McLean, 1992-97, The Jefferson Law Firm PLC, Vienna, 1997—. Mem. Assn. Trial Lawyers Am., Va. Trial Lawyers Assn. (chmn. comml. litigation sect.), Fairfax Bar Assn. (chmn. civil litigation sect. 1984—, law day com. 1982-84). General civil litigation, Family and matrimonial, Personal injury. Home: 6155 Farver Rd Mc Lean VA 22101-3239 Office: The Jefferson Law Firm PLC 6862 Elm St Ste 740 Mc Lean VA 22101-3833

**COCKE, JOHN HARTWELL,** lawyer; b. Clarksdale, Miss., Oct. 9, 1947; s. Cary H. Cocke and Mary Edmonds Gustis; m. Robin Page, Nov. 20, 1971; 1 child, David B. BA in Econs., U. Va., 1969, JD, 1975. Bar: Miss. 1975, Tenn. 1992. Ptnr. Hollomb Dunbar, Clarksdale, Miss., 1975-82; founding ptnr. Merkel & Cocke, Clarksdale, 1982—. With U.S. Army, 1969-72. Mem. ABA (co-chair med. malpractice sub com. 1997-98), Miss. Trial Lawyers Assn. (bd. govs. 1992-98), Rotary Club. Episcopalian. Avocations: fishing, skiing, scuba, tennis. Personal injury, Professional liability, Federal civil litigation. Home: 1700 Riverside Ave Clarksdale MS 38614-2614 Office: Merkel & Cocke PA PO Box 1388 Clarksdale MS 38614-1388

**COCKRELL, RICHARD CARTER,** retired lawyer; b. Denver, Oct. 9, 1925; s. Harold Arthur Sweet and Mary Lynne Cockrell. AB, U. Denver, 1949, JD cum laude, 1950. Bar: Colo. 1950, U.S. Supreme Ct. 1954. Supr. real estate, tax and claims Standard Oil, Denver, 1950-52; from assoc. to ptnr. Cockrell, Quinn & Creighton and predecessor firms, Denver, 1952-91; of counsel Cockrell, Quinn & Creighton, Denver, 1992-99, ret., 1999. Mem. law com. Colo. State Bd. Law Examiners, Denver, 1958-79; mem. bd. mgrs. Nat. Conf. Bar Examiners, Chgo., 1965-69. With U.S. Army, 1943-46, USAR, 1946-51, maj. USAFR, 1951-67, ret. 1985. Mem. Denver Bar Assn., Colo. Bar Assn., Denver Law Club (pres. 1963-64, Svc. to Bar and Cmty. Lifetime Achievement award 1996), University Club (bd. dirs. 1982-88), Phi Beta Kappa, Beta Theta Pi, Phi Delta Phi. Episcopalian. Home: 1155 Ash St Apt 1504 Denver CO 80220-3727

**COCO, MARK STEVEN,** lawyer; b. Alliance, Ohio, Nov. 1, 1952; s. John Robert and Mabel Ann (Paletti) C.; children: Steven, Matthew. BA cum laude, Ohio State U., 1974, JD summa cum laude, 1977. Bar: Ohio 1977, U.S. Dist. Ct. (no. and so. dists.) Ohio 1977. Assoc. Schwartz, Kelm, Warren & Rubenstein, Columbus, Ohio, 1977-80, Jones, Day, Reavis & Pogue, Columbus, Ohio, 1980-87; ptnr. Minton, Leslie & Coco, Columbus, Ohio, 1987-89, Jones, Troyan, Coco, Pappas & Perkins, Columbus, 1989-94, Harris, McClellan, Binau & Cox, Columbus, 1994—. Mem. ABA (litigation sect.), Ohio Bar Assn. (labor and litigation sect.), Columbus Bar Assn., Ohio State U. Alumni Assn., Order of Coif. Federal civil litigation, Labor, State civil litigation. Home: 8622 Gairloch Ct Dublin OH 43017-9754

**CODDINGTON, CLINTON HAYS,** lawyer; b. Honolulu, July 8, 1939; s. L. Clinton and Patricia Carolyn (Richer) C.; m. Martha Ann Stevens, June 20, 1970; children: Clinton Stevens, Catherine Hadley. BSCE, U.S. Mil. Acad., 1961; JD, U. Calif., Berkeley, 1968. Bar: Calif. 1969, U.S. Ct. Appeals (2nd, 5th, 7th, 8th and 9th cirs.), U.S. Supreme Ct. 1974. Assoc. Bronson, Bronson & McKinnon, San Francisco, 1969-70, Rogers Majeski Kohn Bentley Wagner & Kane, Redwood City, Calif., 1970-77, Tucker & Coddington, Palo Alto, Calif., 1977-78; ptnr., pres. Coddington, Hicks & Danforth, Redwood City, 1978—. Contbr. articles to profl. jours. Chmn. Easter Seals; vestryman, sr. warden, chancellor various Episcopal chs.; pres. Chinquapin Homeowners Assn., Lake Tahoe, Calif., 1991-92, Stanford Hills Homeowners Assn., Palo Alto, Calif. Capt. U.S. Army, 1961-64. Mem. ABA, Assn. Def. Counsel of No. Calif., Lawyer/Pilot Bar Assn., Internat. Assn. Def. Counsel, San Mateo County Bar Assn., Calif. Bar Assn., Def. Rsch. Inst., Am. Bd. Trial Advocates. Republican. Avocations: tennis, aviation, boating, reading. Aviation, Federal civil litigation, State civil litigation. Office: Coddington Hicks & Danforth 555 Twin Dolphin Dr Ste 300 Redwood City CA 94065-2133

**CODON, DENNIS P.,** lawyer. V.p., gen. counsel, corp. sec. Unocal Corp., L.A. Office: Unocal Corp 2141 Rosecrans Ave Ste 4000 El Segundo CA 90245-4746

**CODY, DANIEL SCHAFFNER,** lawyer; b. Columbus, Ohio, Nov. 21, 1948; s. Ralph Eugene and Grace (Schaffner) C.; m. Susan Ragsdale, Mar. 27, 1992; 1 child, Sean. Student, Kent State U., 1977; BA, Ohio State U., 1970, BSEd, 1973; JD, U. Akron, 1990. Bar: Ohio 1990, U.S. Dist. Ct. (no. dist.) Ohio 1990, U.S. Ct. Appeals (6th cir.) 1990, U.S. Ct. Appeals (4th cir.) 1992. Tchg. Archbishop Hoban H.S., Akron, Ohio, 1973-88, athletic dir., 1980-84; rsch. asst. Hon. Arthur Goldberg (ret.) U.S. Supreme Ct., U. Akron, 1989, staff intern Appellate Rev. Office, 1990-91; jud. clk. Ohio Ct. Appeals (9th dist.), Akron, 1990-91; assoc. Jacobson, Maynard, Tuschman & Kalur, Cleve., 1991-93; pvt. practice Akron, 1993—. Trustee U. Akron Law Alumni Assn., 1992—, Archbishop Hoban H.S., 1995—. Mem. Ohio State Bar Assn., Akron Bar Assn. Democrat. Roman Catholic. Personal injury, Criminal. Office: 17 S Main St Ste 201 Akron OH 44308-1803

**CODY, THOMAS GERALD,** lawyer; b. N.Y.C., Nov. 4, 1941; s. Thomas J. Cody and Esther Mary Courtney; m. Mary Ellen Palmer, Nov. 26, 1966; children: Thomas Jr., Mark, Amy, Anne. BA in Philosophy, Maryknoll Coll., 1963; JD, St. John's U., 1967; LLD (hon.), Cen. State U., Wilberforce, Ohio, 1985. Bar: N.Y. 1967. Assoc. Simpson Thacher & Bartlett, N.Y., 1967-72; asst. prof. law sch. St. John's U., N.Y., 1972-76; sr. v.p., gen. counsel, sec. Pan Am. Airways, N.Y., 1976-82; sr. v.p. law and pub. affairs Federated Dept. Stores, Cin., 1982-88, exec. v.p. legal & human resources, 1989—. Trustee Xavier U., Cin., Children's Hosp. Med. Ctr., Cin. Mem. ABA, Bankers Club, Queen City Club, Hyde Park Country Club, Commonwealth Club of Cin. Roman Catholic. Office: Federated Dept Stores Inc 7 W 7th St Cincinnati OH 45202-2424

**COE, ILSE G.,** retired lawyer; b. Koenigsberg, Germany, May 28, 1911; came to U.S., 1938, naturalized, 1946. Referendar, U. Koenigsberg, 1935, JSD, 1936; LLB, JD, Bklyn. Law Sch., 1946. Bar: N.Y. 1946. Dir. econ. research Internat. Gen. Electric Co., Berlin, 1936-38; asst. to sales promotion and advt. mgr. Ralph C. Coxhead Corp., N.Y.C., 1940-44; law clk. Mendes & Mount, N.Y.C., 1944-46; assoc. Hill, Rivkins & Middleton, N.Y.C., 1946-50, McNutt, Longcope & Proctor, N.Y.C., 1950-52, Chadbourne, Hunt, Jaeckel & Brown, N.Y.C., 1952-54; asst. v.p., asst. trust officer Schroder Trust Co. and J. Henry Schroder Banking Corp., N.Y.C., 1954-76; dir., sec., editor Fgn. Tax Law Assn., Inc., L.I., 1945-55; tchr. Drakes Bus. Sch., N.Y.C., 1946-49; lectr. on estate planning to ch., women's and bar assn. groups; tutor literacy vols., 1977-79; lectr. wills, trusts, estates, investment counseling and photography Pace U., St. Francis Coll. Mem. exec. bd. Pace Adult Resource Ctr. (formerly Pace Active Retirement Ctr.), Pace U., 1977-79, v.p., 1980-81, pres., 1982-85, life mem. exec. bd., 1986—; Rep. county com. woman, 1948-50; former deacon, past ruling elder, chmn. investment com. 1st Presbyn. Ch., Bklyn.; v.p., chair house com. Florence Ct. Corp. Coop., 1986-89; bd. dirs. 130 Hicks St. Apts. Corp. Coop., 1991-93. Recipient Human Relations award NCCJ, 1979. Mem. Bklyn. Women's Bar Assn. (past treas., sec., bd. dirs. 1960-92, 93-94), Protestant Lawyers Assn. of N.Y. Inc. (sec. 1960-75, 1st v.p. 1976-77, pres. 1978-88, lifetime pres. emeritus 1988—, bd. dirs. 1988—), Internat. Fedn. Women Lawyers, Bklyn. Heights Assn., Bklyn. Hist. Soc. (former mem. investment com.), N.Y. Color Slide Club (by-laws chmn. 1983—, bd. dirs. 1973-74), Bklyn. Mus., Bklyn. Botanic Garden, others. Estate planning, Probate. Home: Miller Bldg #A001 1925 W Turner St Allentown PA 18104-5551

**COE, RICHARD THOMAS,** lawyer, psychotherapist; b. Detroit, May 10, 1932; s. Thomas Richard and Olive Ethel (Westcott) C.; m. M. Joan Smith, July 27, 1957 (div. 1992); 1 child, Paul Richard; m. Dolores Panebianco, Dec. 28, 1994. BA, Wheaton Coll., 1953; MDiv, Northern Sem., Chgo., 1957; JD, U. Detroit, 1965; MA, Oakland U., 1984. Bar: Mich. 1966, U.S. Dist. Ct. (ea. dist.) Mich. 1966, U.S. Ct. Appeals (6th cir.) 1967. Sr. pastor First Hebrew Christian Ch., Detroit, 1957-65; ins. agt. Tom Coe Ins. Agy., Detroit, 1965-84; pvt. practice law Troy, Mich., 1966—; psychotherapist Friends of the Family, Inc., Troy, Mich., 1988—, New Life Clinic, 1998—. Bd. dirs. Detroit Metro Youth for Christ, 1970-82, Christian Conciliation Svc., Detroit, 1980—. Clarence M. Burton Meml. scholar Detroit Coll. Law, 1961. Mem. Am. Contract Bridge League, Delta Theta Phi (sec. 1960-63). Avocations: contract bridge, theatre, music, sailing, bowling. Family and matrimonial, General practice, Probate. Office: 1721 Crooks Rd Ste 108 Troy MI 48084-5392

**COEY, DAVID CONRAD,** lawyer; b. Chgo., Oct. 20, 1930; s. David R. and Marion E. (Sullivan) C.; children from previous marriage: David R., Kurt T.; m. Barbara Stephenson, Aug. 24, 1972; 1 child, Deborah. BS, Mich. State U., 1956; JD, U. Mich., 1959. Bar: Mich. 1959, U.S. Dist. Ct. (ea. and we. dists.) M ich. 1960, U.S. Ct. Appeals (6th cir.) 1965. Ptnr. Foster, Swift, Collins & Coey, P.C., Lansing, Mich., 1966-89, Howard & Howard P.C., Lansing, 1990-97, Dickinson, Wright, Lansing, 1997—; lectr. Mich. State U. Med. Sch., U. Mich. Inst. Continuing Legal Edn.; past chmn. workers' disability compensation sect. State Bar Mich.; lectr., adv. Am. Bd. of Trial Advocates. With USN, 1950-54. Recipient Outstanding Lawyer of the Yr. award Ingham County Bar, 1995, Excellence in Def. award Mich. Def. Trial Counsel, 1995. Fellow Am. Coll. Trial Lawyers; mem. ABA, Am. Bd. Trial Advs., Mich. Trial Lawyers Assn., Mich. Def. Trial Counsel Assn., Univ. Club (East Lansing, Mich.), Mich. Bar Found., Am. Bar Found. Personal injury, Federal civil litigation, State civil litigation. Home: 988 Lantern Hill Dr East Lansing MI 48823-2832 Office: 215 S Washington Sq Ste 200 Lansing MI 48933-1888

**COFFEE, BRETT BLAIR,** lawyer; b. Chgo., Oct. 27, 1971; s. William Noel and Coena Blossom (Blair) C. BA, U. Ill., 1993; JD, Fordham U., 1996. Bar: N.Y. 1996. Assoc. Sierchio & Albert, P.C., N.Y.C., 1996-97, Gilbert, Segall and Young LLP, N.Y.C., 1997-98, Curtis, Mallet-Prevost, Colt & Mosle, N.Y.C., 1998—. Mem. ABA, Assn. Bar City N.Y., N.Y. Alumni Club/U. Ill. (pres. 1995-96, mem. steering com. 1995—). Republican. Home: 789 9th Ave Apt 4C New York NY 10019-5641 Office: Curtis Mallet-Prevost et al 101 Park Ave Fl 34 New York NY 10178-0061

**COFFEY, JAMES FRANCIS,** lawyer; b. Lewiston, Maine, Aug. 8, 1962; s. Thomas Francis and Mary Ann (Amnott) C.; m. Christina Beau Coursen, June 17, 1995; children: Bridget Catherine, Caroline Claire. BA, Providence Coll., 1984; JD, New Eng. Sch. Law, Boston, 1988; LLM, NYU, 1989. Bar: Mass. 1988, U.S. Dist. Ct. Mass. 1990, U.S. Ct. Appeals (1st cir.) 1990, D.C. 1991. Assoc. Boroff & Assocs., Boston, 1989-93; ptnr. Coffey & Shea, Boston, 1993-97, Curran, Coffey & Tavenner, LLP, Boston, 1997-99, Curran, Coffey & Moran, LLP, Boston, 1999—; lectr., panel chair Mass. Continuing Legal Edn., Inc., Boston, 1992—; lectr. Mass. Bar Assn., Boston, 1993—. Vol. NYU Soup Kitchen, N.Y.C., 1988-89. Recipient Gerald L. Wallace Scholarship NYU, N.Y.C., 1988. Mem. ABA (bus. law divsn., bankruptcy law subcom. 1989—), D.C. Bar, Mass. Bar Assn. (bus. law sect. 1989—), Boston Bar Assn. (bankruptcy law com. 1989—), Boston Racquet Club. Roman Catholic. Avocations: travel, history, golf, squash, skiing. Bankruptcy, General civil litigation, General corporate. Office: Curran Coffey & Moran LLP 85 Merrimac St Boston MA 02114-4728

**COFFEY, JOHN LOUIS,** federal judge; b. Milw., Apr. 15, 1922; s. William Leo and Elizabeth Ann (Walsh) C.; m. Marion Kunzelmann, Feb. 3, 1951; children: Peter, Elizabeth Mary Coffey Robbins. BA, Marquette U., 1943, JD, 1948; MBA (hon.), Spencerian Coll., 1964. Bar: Wis. 1948, U.S. Dist. Ct. 1948, U.S. Supreme Ct. 1980. Asst. city atty. City of Milw., 1949-54; judge Civil Ct., Milw. County, 1954-60, Milw. County Mcpl. Ct., 1960-62; judge criminal divsn. Cir. Ct., Milw. County, 1962-72, sr. judge criminal divsn., 1972-75, chief presiding judge criminal divsn., 1976, judge civil divsn., 1976-78; justice Wis. Supreme Ct., Madison, 1978-82; cir. judge U.S. Ct. Appeals (7th cir.), Chgo., 1982—; mem. Wis. Bd. Criminal Ct. Judges, 1960-78, Wis. Bd. Circuit Ct. Judges, 1962-78. Chmn. adv. bd. St. Joseph's Home for Children, 1958-65; mem. adv. bd. St. Mary's Hosp., 1964-70; past bd. dirs., mem. exec. bd. Milw.-Waukesha chpt. ARC; past mem. Milwaukee County council Boy Scouts Am.; chmn. St. Eugene's Sch. Bd., 1967-70; pres. St. Eugene's Ch. Coun., 1974; mem. vol. svcs. adv. com. Milwaukee County Dept. Pub. Welfare. Served with USNR, 1943-46. Named Outstanding Man of Yr., Milw. Jr. C. of C., 1951, One of 5 Outstanding Men in the State, 1957, Outstanding Law Alumnus of Yr., Marquette U., 1980. Fellow Am. Bar Found.; mem. Wis. Bar Assn., 7th Cir. Bar Assn., Ill. State Bar Assn., Nat. Lawyers Club, Am. Legion (Disting. Svc. award 1973), Marquette U. Law Alumni Assn. (Disting. Profl. Achievement Merit award 1985), Marquette U. M Club (former dir.), Alpha Sigma Nu, Phi Alpha Delta (hon.). Roman Catholic. *I have tried to the best of my ability to render justice to all and remember that "We are a country of laws, not of men" and while protecting the individual's rights I have not lost sight of the common good of all mankind and cautioned each and every one who appeared before me that with every right there is a corresponding obligation.*

**COFFEY, KENDALL BRINDLEY,** lawyer; b. Merced, Calif., Dec. 5, 1952; s. John Brindley and Valerie Althea (Kendall) C.; m. Joni Beth Armstrong, Jan. 28, 1984; 1 child, Meredith Armstrong. BS in Broadcasting, U. Fla., 1975, JD, 1978. Bar: Fla. 1978, U.S. Ct. Appeals (9th and 11th cirs.) 1982. Law clk. U.S. Ct. Appeals (5th cir.), Newnan, Ga., 1978; assoc., bd. dirs. Greenberg, Traurig, Askew, Hoffman, Lipoff, Rosen & Quentel, P.A., Miami, Fla., 1978-88; ptnr. Coffey, Aragon, Martin & Burlington, P.A., Miami, 1988-93, also bd. dirs.; U.S. atty. U.S. Dept. of Justice, Miami, Fla., 1993-96; ptnr. Coffey, Diaz & O'Naghten, Miami, 1996—; lectr. in field. Contbr. articles to profl. jours. Named Outstanding Young Dem. in Fla., Fla. Dem. Women's Clubs, 1975. Mem. Dade County Bar Assn. (pres. 1990), U. Fla. Law Rev. Alumni Assn. (pres. 1986-88, Most Productive Young Lawyer in Fla.). Banking, State civil litigation, Contracts commercial. Home: 1639 S Bayshore Dr Miami FL 33133-4213 Office: Coffey Diaz & O'Naghten LLP 2665 S Bayshore Dr Miami FL 33133-5448*

**COFFEY, LARRY B(RUCE),** lawyer. BA, Wabash Coll., Crawfordsville, Ind., 1962; JD with honors, Ind. U., 1965; M of Comparative Law, U. Chgo., 1967. Bar: Ind. 1965, U.S. Dist. Ct. (so. dist.) Ind. 1965, N.Y. 1975, N.C. 1989, U.S. Dist. Ct. (we. dist.) N.C., 1989. Atty. European Cmty. Commn., Brussels, 1967; assoc. Dewey Ballantine, N.Y.C. and Brussels, 1968-71; atty. GM, N.Y.C. and London, 1971-78; v.p. Revlon, Europe, Mid. East and Africa, Paris, 1978-83; pvt. practice Paris, 1983-89; counsel Womble, Carlyle, Sandridge & Rice, Charlotte, N.C., 1989-91; pvt. practice, 1991—. Editor: The Common Market and Common Law, 1967. Wabash Coll. scholar 1958-62, Ind. U. Law Sch. fellow, 1962-65, U. Chgo. Law Sch. fellow, 1965-67. Mem. ABA, N.Y. State Bar Assn., N.C. Bar Assn. Contracts commercial, Mergers and acquisitions, Private international. Office: 2449 Ardmore Manor Winston Salem NC 27103-4866

**COFFEY, THOMAS WILLIAM,** lawyer; b. Cin., Jan. 19, 1959; s. Joseph Paul and Doris June (Adams) C.; m. Shirley Ann Strode, July 24, 1982. MusB, U. Cin., 1981, JD, 1987. Bar: Pa. 1987, U.S. Dist. Ct. (we. dist.) Pa. 1987, U.S. Ct. Appeals (3d cir.) 1988, Ohio 1990, U.S. Dist. Ct. (so. dist.) Ohio 1990, U.S. Ct. Appeals (6th cir.) 1990. Dir. band Ea. Local Sch., Brown County, Ohio, 1981-83, Goshen (Ohio) High Sch., 1983-84; assoc. Buchanan Ingersoll, P.C., Pitts., 1987-90; chmn. bankruptcy group Cors & Bassett, Cin., 1990—. Mem. ABA, Ohio Bar Assn., Cin. Bar Assn., Am. Fedn. Musicians, Masons, Shriners. Avocations: symphonic and Dixieland jazz. Bankruptcy, Banking, Contracts commercial. Home: 933 Monastery St Cincinnati OH 45202-1510 Office: Cors & Bassett 537 E Pete Rose Way Ste 400 Cincinnati OH 45202-3578

**COFFIELD, CONRAD EUGENE,** lawyer; b. Hot Springs, S.D., Nov. 26, 1930; s. Eugene M. and Alice (Hotvet) C.; children: Conrad Eugene, Michael, Megan, Edward, Philip; m. Mona L. Enfield, May 2, 1992. Student S.D. Sch. Mines and Tech., 1948-49; BBA, Washington U., St. Louis, 1952; LLB, U. Tex., 1959. Bar: Tex. 1959, N.Mex. 1959. Mem. Hervey, Dow & Hinkle, Roswell, N.Mex., 1959-64; gen. ptnr. Hinkle, Cox, Eaton, Coffield & Hensley, Roswell, 1964-66, resident ptnr., Midland, 1966-94, resident ptnr., Santa Fe, N.Mex., 1994—. Trustee Petroleum Mus., Library and Hall of Fame; bd. govs. Midland Community Theatre; bd. dirs. Santa Fe Pro Musica. Served with USCGR, 1952-56. Fellow Tex. Bar Found.; mem. ABA, Tex. Bar Assn., N.Mex. Bar Assn. (mem. bd. dirs. sr. lawyers), Santa Fe County Bar Assn., N.Mex. Oil and Gas Assn. Episcopalian. Oil, gas, and mineral, Administrative and regulatory, General practice. Office: Hinkle Cox Eaton Coffield Hensley 218 Montezuma Ave Santa Fe NM 87501-2625

**COFFIN, FRANK MOREY,** federal judge; b. Lewiston, Maine, July 11, 1919; s. Herbert Rice and Ruth (Morey) C.; m. Ruth Ulrich, Dec. 19, 1942; children: Nancy, Douglas, Meredith, Susan. A.B., Bates Coll., 1940, LL.D., 1959; postgrad. indsl. adminstrn., Harvard U., 1943, LL.B., 1947; LL.D., Bates Coll., 1959, U. Maine, 1967, Bowdoin Coll., 1969; degree (hon.), Colby Coll., 1975. Bar: Maine 1947. Law clk. to fed. judge Dist. of Maine, 1947-49; engaged in practice Lewiston, 1947-52; Verrill, Dana, Walker, Philbrick & Whitehouse, Portland, Maine, 1952-56; mem. 85th-86th Congresses from 2d Dist. Maine, House Com. Fgn. Affairs; mng. dir. Devel. Loan Fund, Dept. State, Washington, 1961; dep. adminstr. AID, 1961-64; U.S. rep. devel. assistance com. Orgn. Econ. Coop. and Devel., 1964-65; judge 1st circuit U.S. Ct. Appeals, 1965—, chief judge, 1972-83, sr. judge, 1989—; chmn. com. jud. br. U.S. Jud. Conf., 1984-90; adj. prof. U. Maine Sch. Law, 1986-89. Author: Witness for Aid, 1964, The Ways of a Judge-Reflections from the Federal Appellate Bench, 1980, A Lexicon of Oral Advocacy, 1984, On Appeal, 1994. 25798620emeritus Bates Coll.; dir. The Governance Inst., 1987—; mem. emeritus The Examiner; chair Maine Justice Action Group, 1996—. Lt. USNR, 1943-46. Mem. Am. Acad. Arts and Scis. Office: US Ct Appeals 156 Federal St Portland ME 04101-4152

**COFFIN, RICHARD KEITH,** lawyer; b. St. Louis, Apr. 6, 1940; s. Kenneth and Agnes (Ryan) C.; m. June Springmeyer, Apr. 8, 1972; children: Jennifer, Joanna. B.S., U. Notre Dame, 1962; MBA, St. Louis U., 1967, JD, 1971. Engr., Nooter Corp., St. Louis, 1962-72; spl. prosecutor U.S. Dept. Justice, St. Louis, 1972-74; ptnr. Coffin & Torrence, P.C., St. Louis; gen. counsel Southwestern Linen & Indsl. Supply Assn., St. Louis; gen. counsel Mission Industries, Las Vegas, Nev., 1996. Mem. Citizens Adv. Com., Parkway Sch. Bd., Chesterfield, Mo., 1980-82; treas. PSO Com., Parkway Sch., 1982-83. Mem. ABA, Mo. Bar Assn., Met. Bar Assn. St. Louis, Assn. Trial Lawyers Am., Mo. Assn. Trial Attys., Phi Alpha Delta. Roman Catholic. Club: Optimist (sec. 1981). General corporate, Real property, General practice. Home: 1748 Orchard Hill Dr Chesterfield MO 63017-5127

**COFFINAS, ELENI,** lawyer; b. Bklyn., Jan. 12, 1961. BA, Bklyn. Coll., 1982, JD, 1985. BAr: N.Y. 1985. Assoc. Sullivan & Liapakis, P.C., N.Y.C., 1986-93; ptnr. Sullivan, Papain, Block, McGrath & Cannavo, N.Y.C., 1993—, ptnr., supr. med. malpractice dept., 1994—. Mem. ATLA, Assn. Bar City N.Y. (med. malpractice com. 1996—), N.Y. State Trial Lawyers Assn. (bd. dirs. 1997—). Greek Orthodox. Personal injury. Home: 9425 Shore Rd Brooklyn NY 11209-7259 Office: Sullivan Papain Block McGrath & Cannavo PC 120 Broadway New York NY 10271-0002

**COFFINAS, MARIA,** lawyer; b. Bklyn., Jan. 4, 1940; d. Nicholas and Dolly (Zanetakos) C.; m. Clifford Lazzaro, June 8, 1986. BA, Bklyn. Coll., 1981, JD, 1984. Bar: N.Y. Assoc. atty. Louis R. Rosenthal, Esq., Bklyn., 1984—. Assoc. editor jour. Barrister, 1986—. Mem. Bklyn. Bar Assn., N.Y. State Bar Assn., ABA, Bklyn. Law Sch. Alumni Assn. (bd. dirs., sec. 1987—). Republican. Greek Orthodox. Office: Coffinas & Lusthaus PC 16 Court St Brooklyn NY 11241-0102

**COFFMAN, JENNIFER B.,** federal judge; b. 1948. BA, U. Ky., 1969, MA, 1971, JD, 1978. Ref. libr. Newport News (Va.) Pub. Libr., 1972-74, U. Ky., 1974-76; atty. Law Offices Arthur L. Brooks., Lexington, Ky., 1978-82; ptnr. Brooks, Coffman and Fitzpatrick, Lexington, 1982-92, Newberry, Hargrove & Rambicure, Lexington, 1992-93; judge U.S. Dist. Ct. (ea. dist. and we. dist.) Ky., London, 1993—; adj. prof. Coll. Law, U. Ky., 1979-81. Bd. dirs. YWCA Lexington, 1986-92; elder Second Presbyn. Ch., 1993. Mem. Ky. Bar Assn., Fayette County Bar Assn., U. Ky. Law Sch. Alumni Assn. Office: 207 US Courthouse 300 S Main St London KY 40741-1924

**COFFMAN, PENELOPE DALTON,** judge; b. Pulaski, Va., Apr. 16, 1938; d. Gomez and Hazel (Davis) Dalton; m. Aldine J. Coffman, Mar. 27, 1965; children: D'Maris, Derek. AB, Randolph-Macon Women's Coll., 1958; JD, Coll. William and Mary, 1965. Bar: Va. 1966, Utah 1977, Colo. 1984. Law clk. Va. Supreme Ct., Richmond, 1966-68; asst. commonwealth atty. Commonwealth Atty.'s Office, Virginia Beach, va., 1970-73; ptnr. Coffman & Coffman, Virginia Beach, 1968-75, Moab, Utah, 1975-88; ptnr. Dodd, Scott, Stockton & Coffman, Lakewood, Colo., 1990-94; substitute judge Cherry Hills Village and Greenwood Village, Colo., 1992—. Articles editor William and Mary Law Rev., 1964-66; book reviewer. Bd. dirs. Four County Travel Coun., Grand County, Utah, 1978-82, Health Coun., Grand County, 1978-82, Mental Health, Grand County, 1978-82, Va. Coun. Ednl. TV, 1970-72. Mem. Denver Women's Press Club (bd. dirs.). Republican. Episcopalian. Avocations: competitive bridge, chess. Office: 6 Cherry Lane Dr Englewood CO 80110-4210

**COGAN, JOHN P.,** lawyer; b. Baton Rouge, La., Jan. 14, 1944; s. John P. and Stell E. (Greene) C.; m. Jean M. Wilson, May 2, 1970; children: John, Malcolm, Elizabeth, James, Victoria, Charles. BA, U. Tex., 1965, LLB, 1968. Bar: Tex. 1969. Assoc. Baker & Botts, L.L.P., Houston, 1969-76, ptnr., 1977-94, sr. ptnr., 1995-97; ptnr. Baker & McKenzie, Houston, 1997—. Contbr. numerous articles to profl. jours. Pres. parish coun. St. Anne Ch., 1984-85, mem. fin. com., 1986-87; mem. sch. bd. St. Anne Sch., 1983-87; mem. Mayor's Com. for a Houston World Trade Ctr., 1985; bd. dirs., mem. exec. com. HoustonWrold Trade Assn., 1983—, pres., 1980-82; intermediate league coord. Inner S.W. Youth Baseball Assn., 1984; adv. dir. Inst. for Transnat. Arbitration; adv. dir., chmn. fin. com. Duchesne Acad. of Sacred Heart, 1975-82, bd. dirs., 1988-95, corp. sec., 1990-95; mem. N.Y. adv. bd. Coun. of the Ams.; chmn. bd. trustees Broadacres Civic Assn., 1983-85, chmn. deed restrictions com., 1985—; adv. dir. Asia Soc., 1988—. Lt. JAG, USNR, 1971-77, with Tex. N.G., 1968. Fellow Tex. Bar Found., Houston Bar Found.; mem. ABA, State Bar Tex. (mem. coun. internat. law sect. 1986-89, chmn. internat. banking and fin. com. 1988-89), Houston Bar Assn. (sec. internat. law com. 1969), Am. Soc. Internat. Law. Private international, Oil, gas, and mineral, Contracts commercial. Office: Baker & McKenzie 1200 Smith St Ste 1200 Houston TX 77002-4592

**COGAN, MARY JO GLEBER,** lawyer; b. Wilmington, Del., Aug. 13, 1954; d. Jacob Adam and Marilyn Roberta (Fox) Gleber; m. Julian N. Cogan; children: Caitlin, Amanda. BA in Polit. Sci., U. Del., 1978; JD, U. San Diego, 1981. Bar: Calif. 1982. Assoc. Stebleton, Waters & May, El Cajon, Calif., 1982-83; ptnr. George & Allred, El Cajon, 1983-84; assoc. O'Dorisio, Wedell & Wade, San Diego, 1984-85; sole practice, San Diego, 1985—. Lillian Kratter Women's scholar U. San Diego, Law Sch., 1980-81. Mem. Calif. State Bar Assn., San Diego County Bar Assn., U. San Diego Law Sch. Alumni Assn. Democrat. Home: 11145 Calle Dario San Diego CA 92126-1714

**COGAN, SARAH EDWARDS,** lawyer; b. N.Y.C., May 12, 1956; d. James R. and Arrial S. (Seelye) C.; m. Douglas H. Evans, May 28, 1983; children: Anne Morrill, Thomas Taylor Seelye, Elizabeth Hayward. BA, Yale U., 1978; JD, Georgetown U., 1981. Bar: N.Y. 1982. Assoc. Simpson Thacher & Bartlett, N.Y.C., 1981-88, ptnr., 1989—. Mem. ABA, Assn. of the Bar of the City of N.Y. Securities, General corporate, Mergers and acquisitions. Office: Simpson Thacher & Bartlett 425 Lexington Ave New York NY 10017-3954

**COGBURN, MAX OLIVER,** lawyer; b. Canton, N.C., Mar. 21, 1927; s. Chester Amberg and Ruby Elizabeth (Davis) C.; m. Mary Heidt, Oct. 15, 1949; children: Max O. Jr., Michael David, Steven Douglas, Cynthia Diane. AB, U. N.C., 1948, LLB, 1950; LLM, Harvard U., 1951. Bar; N.C. 1950, U.S. Dist. Ct. (we. dist.) N.C. 1953, U.S. Ct. Appeals (4th cir.) 1984. Asst. dir. Inst. Govt., Chapel-Hill, N.C., 1951-52; staff mem. Atty. Gen. N.C., Raleigh, 1952-54; adminstr. asst. Chief Justice N.C., Raleigh, 1954-55; judge Gen. County Ct. Buncombe County, Asheville, N.C., 1968-70; sole practice Canton, Asheville, N.C., 1968, 1971—; ptnr. Roberts, Stevens & Cogburn, P.A., Asheville, 1986-95, Cogburn, Cogburn, Goosmann & Brazil, P.A., Ashville, 1995—. Chmn. Buncombe County Dem. Exec. Com., Asheville, 1974-76; mem. State Dem. Exec. Com., Raleigh, 1974-76. Mem. ABA, N.C. State Bar Assn., N.C. Bar Assn. (Gen. Practice Hall of Fame 1997), 28th Jud. Dist. Bar State of N.C., Buncombe County Bar Assn. (past pres.). Roman Catholic. Federal civil litigation, State civil litigation, General practice. Home: RR 1 Candler NC 28715-9801 Office: 77 Central Ave Ste H Asheville NC 28801-2451

**COGGINS, PAUL EDWARD, JR.,** prosecutor; b. Hugo, Okla., May 21, 1951; s. Paul E. and Rebecca (Cates) C.; m. Regina T. Montoya, June 12, 1976; 1 child, Jessica Chandler. BA in Polit. Sci. summa cum laude, Yale U., 1973; BA with honors, Oxford U., 1975; JD cum laude, Harvard U., 1978. Bar: Tex. 1978. Tchr. Project New Gate N.Mex. State Penitentiary, 1973; law clk. Mass. Ct. Appeals, 1978-79; fed. prosecutor U.S. Attys. Office, Dallas, 1980-83; assoc. Johnson & Swanson, Dallas, 1979-80, ptnr., 1983-86; ptnr. Meadows, Owens, Collier, Reed & Coggins, Dallas, 1986-93; U.S. atty. U.S. Dept. of Justice, Dallas, 1993—; mem. adv. com. Magnet Sch. in Dallas, 1984—. Author: The Lady is the Tiger, 1987; co-author: Out of Bounds, 1992. Pres. bd. dirs. Dem. Forum, Dallas, 1985—. Rhodes scholar, 1973-76. Mem. ABA, Dallas Bar Assn. (mem. pro bono panel), Harvard Club (v.p. 1987—), Yale Club. Office: US Attys Office Earle Cabell Federal Bldg 1100 Commerce St Fl 3 Dallas TX 75242-1027

**COGGIO, BRIAN D.,** lawyer, educator; b. Yonkers, N.Y., Apr. 25, 1949; s. Joseph G. and Catherine T. Coggio; m. Nancy L. Sourbeck, Aug. 17, 1974; children: Jennifer, Brian Jr. BChemE, Manhattan Coll., 1971; JD, Fordham U. cum laude, 1974; LLM in Trade Regulations, NYU, 1980. Bar: N.Y., U.S. Ct. Appeals (2d cir.), U.S. Ct. Appeals (fed. cir.), U.S. Patent and Trademarks. Assoc. Pennie & Edmonds LLP, N.Y.C., 1974-82, ptrn., 1982-93, sr. ptnr., 1994—; adj. prof. law N.Y. Law Sch., 1996-98, Fordham U. Sch. of Law, 1999; mem. bd. editors Intellectual Property Litigator, 1995—. Contbr. articles to profl. jours. Avocation: piano. Patent. Home: 34 Moore Rd Bronxville NY 10708-5410 Office: Pennie & Edmonds LLP 1155 Avenue Of The Americas New York NY 10036-2711

**COGHILL, WILLIAM THOMAS, JR.,** lawyer; b. St. Louis, July 20, 1927; s. William Thomas and Mildred Mary (Crenshaw) C.; m. Patricia Lee Hughes, Aug. 7, 1948; children: James Prentiss, Victoria Lynn, Cathryn Anne. JD, U. Mo., 1950, undergrad., 1944-45, 46-47. Bar: Mo. 1950, Ill. 1958. Pvt. practice Farmington, Mo., 1950-51; spl. agt. FBI, 1951-52; ptnr. Smith, Smith & Coghill, Farmington, 1952-57; assoc. Coburn & Croft, St. Louis, 1957-58; ptnr. Thompson Coburn (formerly Thompson & Mitchell and predecessor firm), Belleville, Ill., 1958—. Co-author: Illinois Products Liability, 1991, Cavaliers, 1999. With USN, 1945-46. Fellow Am. Coll. Trial Lawyers; mem. ABA, Ill. State Bar Assn., Mo. State Bar Assn., Trial Attys. Am., Product Liability Adv. Coun. (sustaining mem.), Def. Rsch. Inst., Inc., Ill. Assn. Def. Counsel, Nat. Assn. R.R. Trial Counsel, Media Club, Elks. Federal civil litigation, State civil litigation, Insurance. Home: 715 W Moon Valley Dr Phoenix AZ 85023-6234 Office: Thompson Coburn 525 W Main St Belleville IL 62220-1534

**COGHLAN, CAROL LYNN,** lawyer; b. Jackson, Miss., Oct. 21, 1955; d. Charles O. Coghlan and Billie J. (Peebles) Steiner. BA, U. Ala., Tuscaloosa, 1979; JD, U. Kans., 1987. Bar: Ariz. 1987. Pvt. practice Phoenix, 1987—. Mem. ABA, State Bar of Ariz. (juvenile practice com.), Maricopa County Bar Assn., Aircraft Owners & Pilots Assn. Democrat. Avocation: pvt. pilot. Juvenile, Family and matrimonial, General practice. Office: 4025 E Chandler Blvd Ste 70-f5 Phoenix AZ 85048-8829

**COHAN, JOHN ROBERT,** retired lawyer; b. Arnhem, Netherlands, Feb. 10, 1931; came to U.S., 1940, naturalized, 1945; s. Max and Ann (deWinter) C.; m. Joan B. Gollob, Sept. 6, 1954; children: Deborah Joyce, Steven Mark, Judson Seth; m. Patricia S. Cohan, Nov. 8, 1970; m. Roberta Cohan, Nov. 23, 1980; 1 child, Alexis Marissa Muffin. B.S. in Bus. Adminstrn, U. Ariz., 1952; LL.B., Stanford U., 1955. Bar: Calif. 1956; cert. specialist in taxation. Assoc. firm Irell & Manella, Los Angeles, 1955-61, ptnr., 1961-95; ret., 1995; adj. prof. U. Miami Sch. Law, 1975-85, Ventura/Santa Barbara Coll. Law, 1996—; lectr. fed. income taxation U. So. Calif. Sch. Law, 1961-63; lectr., writer Calif. Continuing Edn. Bar Program, 1959, Practicing Law Inst., 1968—, also various tax and probate insts. Editor: Drafting California Revocable Trusts, 1972, 2d edit., 1984, Drafting California Irrevocable Trusts, 1973, 3d edit., 1997, Inter Vivos Trusts, Shephard's Citations, 1975; mem. supervisory bd. Thesaurus of World Tax Data, 1987—; contbr. articles on tax, estate planning, probate law to profl. jours. Pres. Portals House, Inc., 1966-69; chmn. Jewish Big Bros., Los Angeles, 1963-65; trustee Hope for Hearing Research Found., 1979-81, pres., 1972-75; chmn. charitable founds. com. Big Bros. Big Sisters Am., 1965-67, chmn. internat. expansion, 1967—, pres. western region, 1977-78, also bd. dirs.; bd. dirs. Jewish Community Found., 1979—, v.p., chmn. legal com., 1978—; mem. planning com. U. So. Calif. Tax Inst., 1969—, chmn., 1983—; mem. planning com. U. Miami Estate Planning Inst., 1971-86; bd. dirs. Los Angeles Campus Hebrew Union Coll., 1974-77; mem. Mayor's Commn. on Ethics in Charitable Giving, L.A., 1991-93. Fellow Am. Coll. Probate Counsel (mem. planning com. 1986—); mem. ABA (chmn. com. on estate planning for closely held bus. 1979-80, vice chmn. estate and gift tax com. of sect. on taxation), Los Angeles Bar Assn. (com. on fed. and Calif. death and gift taxation 1965-67, co-chmn. com. on bioethics 1979-80, Outstanding Tax Lawyers of the Year Dana Latham award 1987), Beverly Hills Bar Assn. (past chmn., lawyer placement com. and probate com.), Calif. State Bar (probate and trust com. 1971-74), Internat. Acad. Probate and Trust Law (exec. com.), Town Hall of Los Angeles (exec. com., past pres. Western div.), Beta Gamma Sigma, Alpha Kappa Psi, Phi Alpha Delta. Estate planning, Probate, Estate taxation. Home: 79 Daily Dr # 199 Camarillo CA 93010-5807 Office: Irell & Manella 1800 Avenue Of The Stars Los Angeles CA 90067-4276 *I have tried to make my life a quest for excellence, not only in my career, but in serving others through charitable and educational organizations.*

**COHAN, MICHAEL CHARLES,** lawyer; b. Nov. 7, 1952; s. Gerard Francis and Helen (Dewhirst) C.; m. Sarah E. Barker, May 5, 1979; children: Lucy Elizabeth, Hanna Dooley, Cary Michael, Grace Margaret. AB in Polit. Sci., Boston Coll., 1974; JD, Loyola U., New Orleans, 1977. Bar: Ohio 1977, U.S. Dist. Ct. (no. dist.) Ohio 1977, U.S. Ct. Appeals (6th cir.) 1979. Assoc. Cavitch, Familio & Durkin, Cleve., 1977-85, ptnr., 1985—. Asst.

editor: Ohio Transaction Guide, 1978—, Ohio Taxation, 1985-90. Mem. ABA (labor and employment sect., litigation sect.), Ohio State Bar Assn. Federal civil litigation, State civil litigation, Construction. Home: 1106 W Forest Rd Cleveland OH 44107-1041 Office: Cavitch Familo & Durkin Co LPA 14th Fl 1401 E Ohio Bldg Cleveland OH 44114

**COHAN, MICHAEL JOSEPH,** lawyer; b. Washington, Jan. 9, 1965. BSBA, The Citadel, 1986; JD, Samford U., 1993. Bar: Ala. 1993, U.S. Dist. Ct. (no., mid., and so. dists.) Ala. 1993, U.S. Ct. Appeals (11th cir.) 1993, U.S. Dist. Ct. (no. dist.) Ga. 1997. Lawyer Starnes and Atchison, Birmingham, Ala., 1993-95, Janecky Newell Potts Wells & Wilson, Birmingham, 1995—; claims adjuster Mut. Assurance, Birmingham, 1986-90. Mem. ABA, Ala. Bar Assn., Ala. Def. Lawyers Assn., Ga. Bar Assn., Birmingham Bar Assn., Birmingham Inn of Ct., Def. Rsch. Inst. Baptist. Insurance, General civil litigation, General practice. Office: Janecky Newell Potts Wells & Wilson 505 20th St N Ste 1475 Birmingham AL 35203-4636

**COHEN, ANITA MARILYN,** lawyer; b. Pitts., Dec. 4, 1945; d. Rosalie (Agger) C. BA, U. Pitts., 1967; JD, Duquesne U., 1970. Bar: Pa. 1970, U.S. Dist. Ct. (ea. dist.) Pa. 1978, U.S. Dist. Ct. (we. dist.) Pa. 1970. Law clk., asst. pub. defender Appellate divsn. Office Pub. Defender of Allegheny County, 1968-71; asst. dist. atty. trial divsn. Office of Dist. Atty. of Philadelphia County, 1971-78; pvt. practice Phila., 1978—; lectr. in field; counsel Phila. Boosters Assn., 1982-86. Contbr. articles to profl. jours. Bd. dirs. Girls Coalition of Southeastern Pa., 1981-85, cousel, 1983-86; bd. dirs. Planned Parenthood Southeastern Pa., 1981-85. Mem. ABA, Pa. Bar Assn. (legal ethics and profl. responsibility com. 1985-95), Am. Judicature Soc., Nat. Dist. Atty. Assn., Shomrim Club, F.O.P. Criminal, Family and matrimonial, State civil litigation.

**COHEN, ANNE ELIZABETH,** lawyer; b. Cin., Aug. 18, 1954; d. Samuel Nathan and Fredericka Susan (Barnet) C. AB, Smith Coll., 1976; MSL, Yale U., 1982; JD, Columbia U., 1985. Bar: N.Y. 1986, U.S. Dist. Ct. (so. and ea. dists.) N.Y. 1986, U.S. Ct. Appeals (6th cir.) 1987, U.S. Supreme Ct. 1993. Reporter The Cin. Post, 1977-83; law clk. Hon. Richard S. Arnold U.S. Ct. Appeals (8th cir.), Little Rock, 1985-86; assoc. Debevoise & Plimpton, N.Y.C., 1986-93, ptnr., 1993—; mem. faculty ALI/ABA Civil Practice seminars, 1993—. Mem. ABA, Fed. Bar Coun. (program com., co-chair 1999—), Assn. of Bar of City of N.Y., Columbia Law Sch. Assn. (bd. dirs. 1993-97). Product liability, General civil litigation, Federal civil litigation. Home: 300 Central Park W New York NY 10024-1513 Office: Debevoise & Plimpton 875 3rd Ave Fl 23 New York NY 10022-6256

**COHEN, BARRY DAVID,** lawyer; b. Vineland, N.J., Apr. 21, 1952; s. Joseph and Doris Marian (Maier) C.; m. Ronnie Kesterbaum, June 15, 1975; children: Joshua Aaron, Noah Avram, Talia Aviva. BA summa cum laude, Rutgers U., 1974; JD, Cath. U., 1979. Bar: N.J. 1979, U.S. Dist. Ct. N.J. 1979, U.S. Supreme Ct. 1985. Assoc. Cooper, Perskie, April, Niedelman, Wagenheim & Levenson, Atlantic City, N.J., 1979-84, ptnr., 1984-98, co-chmn. personal injury sect., 1991-98; founding ptnr. Petro Cohen PC, 1998—; v.p. N.J. Def. Rsch. Inst., 1987-89. Contbr. articles to profl. jours. Mem. exec. com. Nat. Jewish Community Rels. Adv. Coun., N.Y., 1990-95, 99—; v.p. Fedn. Jewish/Atlantic County, 1990-96, Congregation Beth Judah, Ventnor, N.J., 1995—; chmn. Jewish Community Rels., 1985-92. Recipient Vol. award Atlantic County Vol. Assn., 1995, Humanitarian award Nat. Conf. Christians and Jews, 1993. Mem. ABA, Atlantic County Bar Assn. (Community Svc. award 1989), N.J. Bar Assn., Am. Trial Lawyers Assn., N.J. Am. Trial Lawyers Assn. (bd. trustees 1995—, mem. civil practice sect. 1995), Phi Beta Kappa. Avocations: political science, history, song writing. Personal injury, Product liability, State civil litigation. Office: Petro Cohen PC 2111 New Rd Ste 202 Northfield NJ 08225-1512

**COHEN, BARTON POLLOCK,** lawyer; b. Kansas City, Kans., Dec. 11, 1930; s. Joseph Cohen and Margaret Pollock; m. Mary Davidson, Dec. 30, 1989; children: Thomas M., Margo, John. BA, Yale U., 1952; JD, Harvard U., 1955. Bar: Kans. 1955, U.S. Dist. Ct. Kans., U.S. Supreme Ct., U.S. Ct. Appeals (10th cir.). Assoc., ptnr. Cohen, Schnider, Shamberg, Kansas City, Kans., 1957-66; ptnr. Cohen, Benjamin, Comer, Overland Park, Kans., 1966-88, Blackwell Sanders Mathery Weary Lombardi, Overland Park, 1988-96; of counsel Blackwell Sanders Peper Martin LLP, Overland Park, 1997—; pres. Metcalf BancShares Inc., Overland Park, 1980—; dir., vice-chmn. Metcalf Bank, Overland Park, 1968—, dir. Rosedale Bank, Kansas City, Kans., 1958-80. Councilman City of Prairie Village, Kans., 1964-69; bd. chmn. Johnson County Mental Health Ctr., Johnson County, 1974. With U.S. Army, 1955-57. Fellow Johnson County Bar Found. (treas.); mem. Am. Arbitration Assn. (arbitrator), Nat. Assn. Security Dealers, Kans. State Hist. Soc. (bd. dirs.). Republican. Jewish. Avocations: golfing, traveling. Fax: (913-696-7070. Estate planning, Contracts commercial, Banking. Home: 12617 Briar Dr Leawood KS 66209-3169 Office: Blackwell Sanders Peper Martin LLP 9401 Indian Creek Pkwy Ste 1200 Overland Park KS 66210-2020

**COHEN, CYNTHIA MARYLYN,** lawyer; b. Bklyn., Sept. 5, 1945. AB, Cornell U., 1967; JD cum laude, NYU, 1970. Bar: N.Y. 1971, U.S. Ct. Appeals (2nd cir.) 1972, U.S. Dist. Ct. (so. and ea. dists.) N.Y. 1972, U.S. Supreme Ct. 1975, U.S. Dist. Ct. (cen. and no. dists.) Calif. 1980, U.S. Ct. Appeals (9th cir.) 1980, U.S. Dist. Ct. (so. dist.) Calif. 1981, U.S. Dist. Ct. (ea. dist.) Calif. 1986. Assoc. Simpson Thacher & Bartlett, N.Y.C., 1970-76, Kaye, Scholer, Fierman, Hayes & Handler, N.Y.C., 1976-80; assoc. Stutman, Treister & Glatt, P.C., L.A., 1980-81, ptnr., 1981-87; ptnr. Hughes Hubbard & Reed, N.Y.C. and L.A., 1987-93, Morgan, Lewis & Bockius, LLP, L.A., Phila., N.Y.C., 1993-98, Jeffer, Mangels, Butler & Marmaro LLP, L.A. and San Francisco, 1998—. Bd. dirs. N.Y. chpt. Am. Cancer Soc., 1977-80. Recipient Am. Jurisprudence award for evidence, torts and legal instns., 1968-69; John Norton Pomeroy scholar NYU, 1968-70, Founders Day Cert., 1969. Mem. ABA, Assn. Bar City N.Y. (trade regulation com. 1976-79), Assn. Bus. Trial Lawyers, Fin. Lawyers Conf., N.Y. State Bar Assn. (chmn. class-action com. 1979), State Bar Calif., Los Angeles County Bar Assn., Order of Coif, Delta Gamma. Avocations: tennis, bridge, rare books, wines. Antitrust, Bankruptcy, General civil litigation. Home: 4531 Dundee Dr Los Angeles CA 90027-1213 Office: Jeffer Mangels Butler Marmaro LLP 2121 Ave Of Stars Fl 10 Los Angeles CA 90067-5010

**COHEN, DAVID LOUIS,** lawyer; b. N.Y.C., Apr. 11, 1955; s. Arthur Stanley and Barbara (Cohen) C.; m. Rhonda Resnick, Aug. 14, 1977; children: Benjamin Jeffrey, Joshua Scott. BA, Swarthmore Coll., 1977; JD summa cum laude, U. Pa., 1981; LLD (hon.), Drexel U., 1997. Bar: Pa. 1981, U.S. Dist. Ct. (ea. dist.) Pa. 1982, U.S. Ct. Appeals (3rd cir.) 1982, U.S. Supreme Ct. 1983. Press sec. U.S. Rep. James H. Scheuer, Washington, 1976, adminstrv. asst./chief of staff, 1977-78; law clk. to Hon. Joseph S. Lord III U.S. Dist. Ct., Phila., 1981-82; from assoc. to ptnr. Ballard Spahr Andrews & Ingersoll, LLP., Phila., 1982-92; ptnr. Ballard Spahr Andrews & Ingersoll, Phila., 1997—, chmn., 1998—. Co-author: Continuing Care Retirement Communities: An Empirical, Financial and Legal Analysis, 1984; contbr. articles to profl. jours. Dir. comms. Rendell for Mayor, Phila., 1987, campaign mgr., 1991; chief of staff Hon. Edward G. Rendell, Mayor, Phila., 1992-97; bd. dirs. Wistar Inst., Phila., 1994—, Stratford Friends Sch., Phila., 1993—, Regional Performing Arts Ctr., 1997—, United Way of Southeastern Pa., Phila., 1993—, first vice chair, 1997-98, chair 1998—; bd. dirs. Greater Phila. C. of C., 1998—; bd. dirs., exec. com. Port Wardens of the Ind. Seaport Mus., 1998—; trustee Phila. Bar Found., 1999—, Hosp. U. Pa., 1999, Overseers Sch. Medicine U. Pa., 1999; mem. health sys. trustee bd. U. Pa., 1999; co-chair Phila. 2000, 1998. Recipient Hatikvah award Jewish Nat. Fund, 1993, Americanism award Anti-Defamation League, 1993, Cmty. Leader of Yr. award Arthritis Found., 1994, Citizen of the Yr. award March of Dimes, 1994, ARC, 1999, Outstanding Young Leader award Jaycees, 1995, Jerusalem Covenant award State of Israel Bonds, 1996, Clarence Farmer Service award Phila. Commn. Human Rels., 1997, Phila. Bar medal, 1997, Champions award Cmty. Legal Svcs., 1997, Cora Svcs. award, 1997, Cmty. Svc. award Episcopal Hosp., 1997, Golden Heart Humanitarian award Variety Club, 1998, Cmty. Svcs. Recognition award Phila. Tribune Charities, 1998, Success award March of Dimes Found., 1999, Cmty. Svc. award Operation Understanding, 1999, Vision for Phila. award Phila. Hospitality, 1999, Dr. John Kearsley award, 1999. Mem. ABA, Pa. Bar Assn., Phila. Bar Assn. Dem. General practice, Antitrust, General corporate. Home: 7 W Sunset Ave Philadelphia PA 19118-3621 Office: Ballard Spahr Andrews & Ingersoll LLP 1735 Market St Ste 5100 Philadelphia PA 19103-7599

**COHEN, DAVID R.,** lawyer; b. Pitts., May 7, 1959; s. Robert A. and Frances S. (Steiner) C.; m. Meredith Mileti, Jan. 5, 1991; children: Stephanie, Amanda, Mark. BA summa cum laude, Kenyon Coll., 1980; JD cum laude, Harvard U., 1983. Bar: Pa. 1983, U.S. Dist. Ct. (we. dist.) Pa. 1983, U.S. Ct. Appeals (3d cir.) 1983, U.S. Ct. Appeals (fed. cir.) 1997. Ptnr. Kirkpatrick & Lockhart, Pitts., 1983—; bd. dirs., sec. The Extended Court House, Inc., 1997—. Co-author: Arbitration Practice and Procedure, 1988. Bd. trustees, chair Torah ctr. adv. bd. Temple Emanuel South Hills, 1996-99. Fellow NSF, 1979. Mem. ABA, Pa. Bar Assn. (statewide computerization com.), Harvard Law Sch. Assn. Western Pa. (v.p. 1996—), Phi Beta Kappa, Sigma Xi. Democrat. Avocation: magician. Federal civil litigation, General civil litigation, Insurance. Home: 226 Lynn Haven Dr Pittsburgh PA 15228-1821 Office: Kirkpatrick & Lockhart LLP 1500 Oliver Building Bldg Pittsburgh PA 15222-2312

**COHEN, DAVID SACKS,** lawyer, educator; b. Warwick, N.Y., Dec. 1, 1968; s. Jerry I. and Patricia B. C.; m. Karla Valladares. BS in Agr., U. Fla., 1989; JD, Fla. State U., 1992. Bar: Fla. 1993, U.S. Dist. Ct. (mid. dist.) Fla. 1993, Ga. 1994. Atty. Bush & Derr, P.A., Orlando, Fla., 1992-93, Korshak & Beaulieu, Orlando, 1993—; adj. prof. Fla. Met. U., Orlando, 1996—. Mem. Orange County Bar Assn., Winderlakes Homeowners Assn. Real property, State civil litigation, General practice. Office: Korshak & Beaulieu 2345 Sand Lake Rd Ste 120 Orlando FL 32809-9120

**COHEN, DAVID SAUL,** lawyer, consultant; b. Chgo., Dec. 7, 1945; s. Samuel Theodore and Sara (Wineberg) C.; m. Jane Copie, July 25, 1969; children: Rachel Melissa, Jonah Avriel. BA, Am. U., 1967; JD, Ill. Inst. Tech., 1974. Bar: N.Mex. 1974, U.S. Dist. Ct. N.Mex. 1974, U.S. Claims Ct. 1980. Vol. U.S. Peace Corps, Turkey, 1967-69; ednl. cons. AVCO Corp., Washington, 1970; atty. N.Mex. Dept. Health and Social Svcs., Santa Fe, 1974-76; chief atty. N.Mex. Pub. Svc. Commn., Santa Fe, 1976-82, chmn., 1982-84; sole practice Santa Fe, 1985-89; ptnr. Cohen & Throne, Santa Fe, 1989-94; shareholder Cohen & Cohen, P.A., Santa Fe, 1994—. Contbr. articles to law revs. Mem. ABA, N.Mex. Bar Assn., Regulatory Commrs. Emeriti (pres. 1991-92). Democrat. Jewish. Avocations: reading, travel. Public utilities, Administrative and regulatory, General civil litigation. Office: Cohen & Cohen PA 121 Sandoval St Ste 300 Santa Fe NM 87501-2161

**COHEN, DIANE BERKOWITZ,** lawyer; b. Vineland, N.J., June 11, 1938; d. Myer and Ida Mae (Subin) Berkowitz; children: Ronald Jay, Stuart Daniel, Amy Suzanne; m. Samuel Gerstein, Aug. 5, 1984. AA magna cum laude, Fairleigh Dickinson U., 1958; BA summa cum laude, Glassboro State Coll., 1976; JD, Temple U., 1979. Bar: Pa. 1979, N.J. 1979, U.S. Ct. Appeals (3d cir.) 1981, U.S. Dist. Ct. N.J., 1981, U.S. Dist. Ct. (ea. dist.) Pa., 1979, U.S. Supreme Ct., 1991. Assoc. Lewis Katz, Cherry Hill, N.J., 1979-81, Steven D. Weinstein, Cherry Hill, 1981-83; sole practice Collingswood, N.J., 1983-85; ptnr. Gerstein, Cohen & Grayson, P.A., Haddonfield, N.J., 1985—; mem. com. on women in the cts. N.J. Supreme Ct., 1994-96. Vice chmn. Allied Jewish Appeal, Cherry Hill, 1968-72; v.p. Nat. Council Jewish Women, Haddonfield, 1969-71; bd. dirs. Planned Parenthood Assn. Camden County, N.J., 1982—. Fellow Camden County Bar Found. (life); mem. ABA (family law custody com. 1994-95, family law bankruptcy com. 1994-95, family law ethical practice and procedure 1994-95)), ATLA, N.J. Bar Assn., (del. to gen. coun. 1989—, women's rights section 1990-96, judicial and prosecutorial appointment com. 1990-96, chmn. 1996-97; profl. responsibility com. 1991-92, judicial adminstrn. com. 1993—, meetings and travel com. 1993—), Camden County Bar Assn. (family law com. 1984—, chmn. women lawyers com. 1984-87, mem. jud. appt. com. 1991-92, budget and fin. com., trustee 1986-89, sec. 1988-89, treas. 1989-90, 1st v.p. 1991-92, pres. 1993-94, N.J. Supreme Ct. Michels commn. on ethics 1991-93, mem. nominating com. 1996-97, program com. 1996-97), N.J. Trial Lawyers Assn., Women's Am. Technion (founding mem.), Nat. Assn. Women Lawyers. General practice, Family and matrimonial. Office: Gerstein Cohen & Grayson PA 20 Kings Hwy W Haddonfield NJ 08033-2116

**COHEN, DONALD N.,** lawyer; b. N.Y.C., Oct. 28, 1958. BA, U. Pa., 1980; JD, Harvard U., 1983. Bar: N.Y. 1983. Assoc. Wachtell, Lipton, Rosen & Katz, N.Y.C., 1983-88, Gaston & Snow, N.Y.C., 1988-91, Loeb & Loeb, N.Y.C., 1991-94; assoc. gen. counsel Gruntal & Co., L.L.C., N.Y.C., 1994—. Alternative dispute resolution, General civil litigation, Securities. Office: Gruntal & Co LLC One Liberty Plaza New York NY 10006

**COHEN, EARL HARDING,** lawyer; b. St. Paul, Mar. 24, 1948; s. Samuel W. and Sylvia S. (Peters) C.; m. Phyllis S. Bruzonsky; children: Melissa Anne, Amy Beth. BS with distinction, U. Minn., 1970, JD, 1973. Bar: Minn. 1973, D.C. 1980, U.S. Tax Ct. 1981. Trust officer Norwest Bank Mpls., 1973-76; atty. Halpern & Halpern, Mpls., 1976-77; prin. Halpern & Cohen, Mpls., 1977-80, Cohen & Bialick, Mpls., 1980-84, Cohen & Cohen, Mpls., 1984-90; pres. Kensington Properties, Inc., Mpls., 1978-90; of counsel Mansfield & Tanick, Mpls., 1990-92; CEO, dir. Mansfield, Tanick & Cohen, P.A., Mpls., 1992—; counsel, bd. cons. No. Computer Sys., Inc., Mpls., 1987-92; dir. United Sys. Techn., Inc., 1995—. Bd. trustees Torah Acad. of Mpls., St. Louis Park, Minn., 1973-91, Talmud Torah of Mpls., 1988. Mem. ABA, Minn. State Bar Assn., Am. Bankruptcy Inst., St. Pauls Boys and Girls Club. Avocations: skiing, golf, travel. E-mail: cohene@mainsfieldtanick.com. Bankruptcy, Real property, Estate planning. Home: 6700 Field Way Minneapolis MN 55436-1719 Office: Mansfield Tanick & Cohen PA 900 2nd Ave S Ste 1560 Minneapolis MN 55402-3383

**COHEN, EDWARD,** lawyer; b Hamilton, Ohio, Dec. 20, 1954; s. Alfred Sylvan and Marilyn (Melnikoff) C.; m. Dee Anne Bryll; children: Daniel, Briana L. BA, U. Cin., 1976; MA, Ind. U., 1982; JD, U. Cin., 1982. Bar: Ohio 1982, U.S. Dist. Ct. (so. dist.) Ohio 1982, U.S. Ct. Appeals (6th cir.) 1982. Doctoral fellow U. Cin., 1978-79, instr. coll. law, 1982-83; assoc. Goodman & Goodman Co., Cin., 1982-84, Kondritzer, Gold & Frank Co., Cin., 1984-88; ptnr. Clements, Mahin & Cohen, LLP, Cin., 1988—. Mem. ABA, ASCAP, Ohio Acad. Trial Lawyers, Ohio Bar Assn., Cin. Bar Assn. (sec. workers compensation com. 1990-91, chmn. 1992—), Order of Barristers, Ohio Cmty. Theatre Assn. (bd. dirs. 1995-98). Workers' compensation, Personal injury, General civil litigation. Office: Clements Mahin & Cohen 708 Walnut St Ste 600 Cincinnati OH 45202-2022

**COHEN, EDWARD ARTHUR,** lawyer; b. Newark, Feb. 6, 1936; s. Harry G. and Helen (Lifland) C.; m. Judith Berman, Apr. 9, 1961; children: Stephen D., Harris M. BA, Rutgers U., 1958, LLB, 1961. Bar: N.J. 1962, U.S. Dist. Ct. N.J. 1962, U.S. Ct. Appeals (3d cir.) 1963, U.S. Supreme Ct. 1966, U.S. Ct. Appeals (2d cir.) 1986. Law clk. U.S. Ct. Appeals (3d cir.), Newark, 1961-62; assoc. Friedland & Schneider, Jersey City, 1962-65, Beckerman & Franzblau, Newark, 1965-68; ptnr. Beckerman, Franzblau & Cohen, Newark, 1968-75, Schneider, Cohen & Solomon, Jersey City, 1975-86, Schneider, Cohen, Solomon, Leder and Montalbano, Cranford, N.J., 1986-92, Schneider, Goldberger, Cohen, Finn, Solomon, Leder & Montalbano, P.C., Cranford, N.J., 1992—; lectr. labor econs., Fairleigh Dickinson U., Teaneck, N.j., 1970, 71; lectr. numerous orgns. Mem. ABA (labor mgmt. sect.), N.J. State Bar Assn. (labor sect.). Labor, Pension, profit-sharing, and employee benefits, General civil litigation. Office: Schneider Goldberger Cohen Finn Solomon Leder & Montalbano 1700 Galloping Hill Rd Kenilworth NJ 07033-1303

**COHEN, EDWARD HERSCHEL,** lawyer; b. Lewistown, Pa., Sept. 30, 1938; s. Saul Allen and Barbara (Getz) C.; m. Arlene Greenbaum, Aug. 12, 1962; children: Fredrick, James, Paul. AB, U. Mich., 1960; JD, Harvard U., 1963. Bar: N.Y. 1964. Assoc. Rosenman and Colin, N.Y.C., 1963-72, ptnr., 1972-86, 88—, counsel, 1987; v.p., gen. counsel, sec. Phillips-Van Heusen Corp., N.Y.C., 1987. Republican. Jewish. Club: Fenway Golf (Scarsdale, N.Y.). Avocations: golf, travel. General corporate, Securities. Home: 21 Sycamore Rd Scarsdale NY 10583-7322 Office: Rosenman & Colin 575 Madison Ave Fl 26 New York NY 10022-2585

**COHEN, EDWIN LOUIS,** lawyer; b. Louisville, May 7, 1930; s. Abe and Belle (Bass) C.; m. Helen Lois Kasdan, July 23, 1967; children—Deborah, Jennifer, Joseph. A.B., U. Louisville, 1955; LL.B., 1958. Bar: Ky. 1958, U.S. Dist. Ct. (we. dist.) Ky. 1960, U.S. Ct. Appeals (6th cir.) 1980, U.S. Supreme Ct. 1981. Ptnr., Cohen & Cohen, Louisville, 1958—. Served to staff sgt. USAF, 1951-55, Korea. Mem. Ky. Bar Assn. Democrat. Jewish. Condemnation, Construction, Federal civil litigation. Office: Cohen & Cohen 3415 Bardstown Rd Ste 306 Louisville KY 40218-4605

**COHEN, EDWIN SAMUEL,** lawyer, educator; b. Richmond, Va., Sept. 27, 1914; s. LeRoy S. and Miriam (Rosenheim) C.; m. Carlyn Labenberg, June 27, 1936 (dec. 1942); m. Helen Herz, Aug. 31, 1944; children: Edwin C., Roger, Wendy. B.A., U. Richmond, 1933; J.D., U. Va., 1936. Bar: Va. 1935, N.Y. 1937, D.C. 1973. Assoc. firm Sullivan & Cromwell, N.Y.C., 1936-49; ptnr. Root, Barrett, Cohen, Knapp & Smith (and predecessor firm), N.Y.C., 1949-65; counsel Root, Barrett, Cohen, Knapp & Smith, 1965-69; prof. law U. Va., Charlottesville, 1965-68, Joseph M. Hartfield prof., 1968-69, 73-85, prof. emeritus, 1985—, Professorial Lectr. in Law, 1994—; asst. sec. treasury for tax policy, 1969-72, under sec. treasury, 1972-73; of counsel Covington & Burling, Washington, 1973-77, ptnr., 1977-86, sr. counsel, 1986—; vis. prof. Benjamin N. Cardozo Sch. Law, Yeshiva U., 1987-92, U. Miami Law Sch., 1993, 95, 99, chmn. grad. program in taxation and estate planning, 1995-98; mem., counsel adv. group on corp. taxes ways and means com. U.S. Ho. of Reps., 1956-58; spl. cons. on corps. fed. income tax project Am. Law Inst., 1949-54; mem. adv. group Fed. Estate and Gift Tax Project, 1964-68; mem. Va. Income Tax Conformity Study Commn., 1970-71; cons. Va. Income Tax Conformity Study Commn., 1966-68; mem. adv. group to commr. IRS, 1967-68. Author: A Lawyer's Life Deep in the Heart of Texas, 1994. Recipient Alexander Hamilton award Treasury Dept. Mem. Am. Judicature Soc., ABA (chmn. com. on corporate stockholder relationships 1956-58, mem. council 1958-61, chmn. spl. com. on substantive tax reform 1962-63, chmn. spl. com. on formation tax policy 1977-80, Disting. Svc. award taxation sect. 1997), Va. Bar Assn., D.C. Bar Assn., N.Y. State Bar Assn., Va. Tax Conf. (planning com. 1965-68, 85-95, trustee emeritus 1995—), C. of C. of U.S. (bd. dirs., chmn. taxation com. 1979-84), Assn. Bar City N.Y., N.Y. County Lawyers Assn., Am. Law Inst., Am. Coll. Tax Counsel, Order Coif, Raven Soc., Colonnade Club, Boar's Head Club, Farmington Club, City Club, Phi Beta Kappa, Omicron Delta Kappa, Pi Delta Epsilon, Phi Epsilon Pi (Nat. Achievement award). Corporate taxation, Personal income taxation, Legislative. Home: 104 Stuart Pl Ednam Forest Charlottesville VA 22903

**COHEN, ERIC MARTIN,** lawyer; b. Mineola, N.Y., May 22, 1955; s. Emanuel and Irene (Kushner) C. BA, SUNY, Albany, 1977; JD, U. Miami, Fla., 1981. Bar: Fla. 1981, U.S. Dist. Ct. (so. dist.) Fla. 1982, (mid. dist.) Fla. 1989, U.S. Ct. Appeals (11th cir.) 1981, (1st cir.) 1988, (9th cir.) 1993, U.S. Supreme Ct. 1991. Jr. ptnr. Blumenfeld & Cohen, Coral Gables, Fla., 1981-87; pvt. practice, Coral Gables, 1988—. Mem. Nat. Assn. Criminal Def. Lawyers, Fla. Assn. Criminal Def. Lawyers, Soc. Wig and Robe. Democrat. Avocation: running. Criminal. Home: 12710 SW 119th St Miami FL 33186-4502 Office: 9130 S Dadeland Blvd Ste 1504 Miami FL 33156-7850

**COHEN, EZRA HARRY,** lawyer; b. Macon, Ga., Mar. 13, 1942; s. Harry M. and Rena C. Cohen; m. Bonnie E. Cohen, Feb. 1, 1969 (div. Mar. 1988); children: Aaron M., Eileen R.; m. Katherine C. Meyers, June 18, 1989. BA, Columbia U., 1964; JD, Emory U., 1969. Bar: Ga. 1969. Ptnr. Troutman, Sanders, Lockerman & Ashmore, Atlanta, 1969-76, 79—; judge U.S. Bankruptcy Ct., U.S. Dist. Ct. (no. dist.) Ga., Atlanta, 1976-79; dir. S.E. Bankruptcy Law Inst., Atlanta. Contbg. author: Cowan's Bankruptcy Laws & Practices, 1979. Mem. Emory U. Law Sch. Coun., Atlanta, 1988—. With U.S. Army, 1964-66, ETO. Fellow Am. Coll. Bankruptcy; mem. Ga. Bar Assn. (chmn. bankruptcy law sect.), Assn. Former Bankruptcy Judges (bd. dirs.), Nat. Assn. Bank Judges (assoc.), Atlanta Bar Assn. (bd. dirs. 1988-90), Lawyers Club of Atlanta. Bankruptcy. Home: 546 W Wesley Rd Atlanta GA 30305-3534 Office: Troutman Sanders 600 Peachtree St NE Ste 5200 Atlanta GA 30308-2231

**COHEN, FRED HOWARD,** lawyer, investment company executive; b. Pitts., Mar. 22, 1948; s. Morris and Sylvia (Kalickman) C.; m. Katherine Jane Litman, July 12, 1970; children: Julia Jackson, Joseph Litman. BA, Stanford U., 1970; MA, York U., Toronto, Can., 1971; postgrad., Princeton U., 1971-72; JD, Harvard U., 1976. Bar: Calif. 1976. Assoc. Latham & Watkins, L.A., 1976-82; ptnr. Latham & Watkins, 1983-85; v.p. Salomon Bros. Inc., N.Y.C., 1985-86; dir. Salomon Bros. Inc., 1986-88; v.p. Goldman Sachs & Co., N.Y.C., 1988-89; ptnr. Shearman & Sterling, N.Y.C., 1989-94; mng. dir. Salomon Bros. Inc., N.Y.C., 1994—. Mem. Phi Beta Kappa. Bankruptcy, Mergers and acquisitions, Securities. Home: 86 Kellogg Hill Rd Weston CT 06883-2640

**COHEN, GAIL EHRLICH,** lawyer, banker; b. Jersey City, Mar. 7, 1956; d. Alex and Florence (Levine) Ehrlich; m. Ofer Cohen, Oct. 5, 1980; children: Daniel, Michelle, Michael; 1 stepchild, Jaime. BA, Mt. Holyoke Coll., 1978; JD summa cum laude, Bklyn. Law Sch., 1985. Bar: N.J., 1986, N.Y. 1986. Paralegal Law Office of E.S. Schlesinger, N.Y.C., 1978-85, assoc., 1985-88; assoc. Debevoise & Plimpton, N.Y.C., 1988-94; sr. v.p., chief trust counsel Fiduciary Trust Internat., N.Y.C., 1994—. Mem. trust and estates com. UJA Fedn., N.Y.C., 1998—; mem. trusts and estates adv. bd. N.Y.C. Ballet, 1997—; mem. planned giving com. Anti-Defamation League, N.Y.C., 1998—; mem. steering com. profl. network City of Hope, N.Y.C., 1997—; bd. dirs. Yemenite Jewish Fedn. of Am., N.Y.C., 1993—. Martha Prince scholar Bklyn. Law Sch., 1984, 85. Mem. Assn. Bar City N.Y. (chmn. com. on estate and gift tax 1998—, com. on trusts, estates and surrogate cts. 1992-95), N.Y. State Bar Assn. Office: Fiduciary Trust Internat 2 World Trade Ctr Fl 97 New York NY 10048-0772

**COHEN, GARY,** lawyer; b. Bklyn., June 26, 1948; s. Irving and Henrietta Elizabeth (Weinkofsky) C.; 1 child, Celeste. BS in Physics, Cooper Union, 1969; JD, Bklyn. Law Sch., 1977. Bar: N.Y. 1978, U.S. Patent Office 1979. Patent atty. Western Electric Corp., N.Y.C., 1978; patent atty. Striker & Stenby, N.Y.C., 1979-82; sole practitioner Bklyn., 1983—. Mem. Bklyn. Bar Assn. (past chmn. com. on patents, trademark & copyright), Ind. Order Odd Fellows. Home: 141 Joralemon St Brooklyn NY 11201-4071 Office: PO Box 020618 Brooklyn NY 11202

**COHEN, H. ADAM,** lawyer, partner; b. Detroit, May 7, 1967; s. I. William and Recia H. Cohen; m. Lauren G. Grumet, Aug. 22, 1992; children: Aaron Benjamin, Lily Beth. BA in History, Tulane U., 1989; JD, George Washington U., 1992. Bar: Mich. 1992, U.S. Dist. Ct. (ea. dist.) Mich. 1992, U.S. Ct. Appeals (6th cir.) 1994. Atty. Mason, Steinhardt, Jacobs & Perlman, P.C., Southfield, Mich., 1992—. Mem. exec. com. Mich. region Anti-Defamation League, Southfield/Detroit, 1997—. Mem. ABA, State Bar of Mich., Oakland County Bar Assn. Jewish. Condemnation, General civil litigation. Office: 4000 Town Ctr Ste 1500 Southfield MI 48075-1588

**COHEN, HAROLD,** lawyer; b. Boston, Aug. 10; s. Samuel Cohen and Matilda Richards; m. Rae Silverman, March 14; 1 child, Leslie. JD, Suffolk U., 1955. Commd. ensign USN, 1942, advanced through grades to lt. commdr., ret., 1955. Dir. New England Sinai Hosp., Staughton, Mass., 1979—; chmn., trustee Norfolk County Agrl. High Sch., Welpole, Mass., 1981—. Paul Harris fellow Freboro Rotary Club, 1985. General civil litigation, Personal injury, Criminal. Office: Cohen & Sherwood PC 38 Mechanic St Foxboro MA 02035-4006

**COHEN, HENRY RODGIN,** lawyer; b. Charleston, W.Va, May 7, 1944; s. Louis W. and Bertie (Rodgin) C.; m. Barbara Latz, Aug. 31, 1969; children: Sarah Abigail, Jonathan David. BA, Harvard U., 1965, LLB, 1968. Bar: W.Va. 1968, N.Y. 1970. Assoc. Sullivan & Cromwell, N.Y.C., 1970-77, ptnr., 1977—. Contbg. editor Fin. Svcs. Regulation Newsletter, 1985; bd. advisors Banking Law Rev.; mem. editorial adv. bd. Banking Expansion Reporter; mem. nat. bd. contbrs. Am. Lawyers Newspaper Group. Served with U.S. Army, 1968-70. Banking. Office: Sullivan & Cromwell 125 Broad St Fl 28 New York NY 10004-2489

**COHEN, HOLLACE T.,** lawyer; b. Bklyn., May 10, 1948; d. Benjamin Carl and Esther (Abramowitz) Topol; m. Steven L. Cohen, June 22, 1969; children: Harlan Grant, Lauren Cecily. BA, CCNY, 1969; JD, NYU, 1972. Bar: N.Y. 1973. Assoc. Whitman & Ransom, N.Y.C., 1972-81, ptnr.,

1981—. Mem. ABA, Am. Bankruptcy Inst., N.Y. State Bar Assn., Assn. Bar City N.Y., Sky Club. Bankruptcy, General corporate, Securities. Office: Whitman Breed Abbott Morgan 200 Park Ave New York NY 10166-0005

**COHEN, HOWARD MARVIN,** lawyer; b. Bklyn., Mar. 22, 1926; s. A. Louis and Claire (Bisgier) C.; m. Judith Rothstein, July 6, 1952 (div. Apr. 1967); children: Jonathan David, Tamara Beth; m. Marjory Hexter, Oct. 12, 1969; children: Theresa Abrams, John Abrams. Student, Yale U., 1945; AB cum laude, Columbia U., 1947; JD magna cum laude, Harvard U., 1949. Bar: N.Y. 1949. Ptnr. Kaye Scholar Fierman, Hays & Handler, N.Y.C., 1963-65; v.p., gen. counsel Revlon Inc., N.Y.C., 1966-71; ptnr. Finley, Kumble, Underberg, Persky & Roth, N.Y.C., 1971-72, Poletti, Freidin, Prashker, Feldman & Gartner, N.Y.C., 1973-78, Warshaw, Burstein, Cohen, Schlesinger & Kuh, N.Y.C., 1978—. Past editor Harvard Law Rev. Trustee Assoc. YM-YWHA, N.Y.C., 1972-90. With U.S. Army, 1943-45. Mem. ABA, Bar of Assn. of City of N.Y., Phi Beta Kappa, Harvard Club. Jewish. Avocations: skiing, tennis, computers, reading, travel. General corporate, Mergers and acquisitions, Private international. Home: 16 Sutton Pl Apt 16A New York NY 10022-3057 Office: Warshaw Burstein Cohen 555 5th Ave Fl 12 New York NY 10017-2456

**COHEN, HYMAN K.,** lawyer; b. Balt., July 26, 1925; s. Jacob and Tillie Cohen; m. Eileen Ruth Manko, Nov. 7, 1954; children: Jill Leslie, Brent Paul (dec.). AB, U. N.C., 1948; JD, U. Balt., 1954. Bar: Md. 1954, U.S. Dist. Ct. Md. 1955, U. S. Supreme Ct. 1959, D.C. 1979. Pvt. practice Balt., 1954—; adj. asst. prof. U. Md., Catonsville, 1983—; bd. dirs. Fgn. Motors Ltd., Koren Furniture House, Inc.; bd. dirs. 7800, Ltd. pres. Liberty Rd. Recreation and Parks Council, Randallstown, Md., 1977-81; pres. Reserve Officers Assn. Balt. Naval Chpt., 1963-67, treas. 1967—; bd. dirs. Cockpit in Ct., Essex Community Coll., Balt. 1983—; vol. Jewish Big Brother League. Named Big Brother of Yr. Jewish Big Brother League, 1983, Vol. of Yr. Liberty Rd. Recreation and Parks Council, 1984. Mem. Md. State Bar Assn. Democrat. Jewish. Avocations: theater, reading, community activities. General practice, Personal injury, Family and matrimonial. Home: 9013 Bruno Rd Randallstown MD 21133-3613 Office: 514 Saint Paul St Baltimore MD 21202-2209

**COHEN, JAMES E.,** lawyer; b. New Haven, Conn., Dec. 29, 1946; s. David B. and Jane C. (Cotter) C.; 1 child, Matthew. BA, U. Pa., 1968; JD, U. Conn., 1971. Bar: Conn. 1971, U.S. Dist. Ct. Conn. 1971, U.S. Supreme Ct. 1975. Ptnr. Cohen & Thomas, Derby, Conn., 1971—; dir. Birmingham Utilities, Inc., 1982—. Mem. corp. coun. City of Derby, 1973-80, 92-94; justice of peace State of Conn., 1970—. Mem. Conn. Bar Assn., Naugatuck Valley Bar Assn., New Haven County Bar Assn. Real property, Land use and zoning (including planning), Probate. Home: 280 Loughlin Rd Oxford CT 06478-1794 Office: Cohen & Thomas 315 Main St Derby CT 06418-1938

**COHEN, JAMES HILSON,** lawyer; b. Cambridge, Mass., BA with honors, Cornell U., 1964; JD with honors, U. Mich., 1967. Bar: Minn., N.Mex., D.C., Conn., U.S. Supreme Ct. Law faculty asst. Tuebingen (Germany) U., 1967-68; assoc. Covington and Burling, 1968-73; dep. asst. dir. FTC, 1973-75; internat. lectr. U.S. Dept. of State, 1975-78; dir., sr. legislator, mgr. Sierra Club Legal Def. Fund, Inc., Washington, 1978-80; founder, CEO Environ. Task Force, Inc., 1980-87; CEO Phoenix Environ. Techs., Inc., Washington, 1987-89; mng. ptnr. Cohen Law Office, P.A., Mpls., 1989—; adj. prof. law sch. NYU, U. Mich.; gen. coun. D.C. Citizens' Com. for a Better Pub. Edn.; mgr. alternative dispute resolution Environ. Common Sense. Mem. U. Mich. Law Rev.; contbr. articles to profl. jours. Candidate from Conn. for U.S. Ho. of Reps. Ford Found. fellow. Office: Cohen Law Offices PA 301 4th Ave S Ste 376 Minneapolis MN 55415-1033

**COHEN, JAY I.,** lawyer; b. N.J., Feb. 4, 1948; s. Paul and Frieda Cohen. AB in Internat. Rels., U. So. Calif., 1970, JD, 1973. Bar: N.J. 1973, Calif. 1974, Fla. 1976, Tex. 1977, U.S. Dist. Ct. (so. dist.) Tex. 1977. Trial atty. Pub. Defender's Office, Elizabeth, N.J., 1974-76; ptnr. Jay I. Cohen & Assoc., P.C., Houston, 1977—. Mem. Cmty. Assns. Inst., Houston, 1990—. Real property, General corporate, General civil litigation. Office: Jay I Cohen and Assocs PC 10370 Richmond Ave Ste 850 Houston TX 77042-4138

**COHEN, JEFFREY MICHAEL,** lawyer; b. Dayton, Ohio, Nov. 13, 1940; s. H. Mort and Evelyn (Friedlob) C.; m. Betsy Z. Zimmerman, July 3, 1966; children: Meredith Sue, Seth Alan. AB, Colgate U., 1962; JD, Columbia U., 1965. Bar: Fla. 1965, U.S. Supreme Ct. 1969; cert. civil trial lawyer Fla. Bar Bd. Cert., diplomate Nat. Bd. Trial Advocacy. Asst. pub. defender Dade County (Fla.), 1968-70, asst. state's atty., 1970-72, spl. asst. state's atty., 1973; ptnr. Fromberg Fromberg Gross Cohen Shore & Berke, P.A., 1972-84, Cohen, Berke, Bernstein, Brodie & Kondell, P.A., Miami, Fla., 1984—; adj. prof. litigation skills U. Miami Sch. Law, 1989—, chmn. Fla. bar com. on civil trial cert. Mem. ABA, Dade County Bar Assn. (bd. dirs.), Acad. Fla. Trial Lawyers, Assn. Trial Lawyers Am., Am. Judicature Soc., Nat. Inst. Trial Advocacy (chair and faculty mem.), Fla. Criminal Def. Attys. Assn. Personal injury, Federal civil litigation, State civil litigation. Home: 3628 Saint Gaudens Rd Miami FL 33133-6533 Office: Cohen Berke Bernstein Brodie & Kondell PA 2601 S Bayshore Dr Fl 19 Miami FL 33133-5419

**COHEN, JEREMY V.,** lawyer; b. Rochester, N.Y., Apr. 25, 1936; s. Jacob H. and Clara S. Cohen; m. Peggy U. Cohen, Nov. 27, 1962; children: Michael H., Lauren R., Diana L. BA, Oberlin Coll., 1957; JD, Albany Law Sch., 1961. Bar: N.Y. 1961. Pres. Flaherty, Cohen, Grande, Randazzo & Doren, P.C., Buffalo, 1966-97; ptnr. Bond, schoeneck & King, LLP, Buffalo, 1997—. Served with U.S. Army. Mem. ABA, N.Y. State Bar Assn., Erie County Bar Assn. (labor law com.), Am. Arbitration Assn. (Whitney North Seymour Sr. award), Buffalo Club. Jewish. Labor. Home: 71 Stonybrook Ln Williamsville NY 14221-1837 Office: Bond Schoeneck & King 135 Delaware Ave Ste 210 Buffalo NY 14202-2410

**COHEN, JONATHAN MORLEY,** lawyer; b. Phila., July 24, 1968; m. Sabrina June Sacks, June 6, 1998. BA, George Washington U., 1990; JD, Temple U., 1993. Assoc. Kline & Specter, P.C., Phila., 1998—. Personal injury, Product liability, Civil rights. Office: Kline & Specter PC 1525 Locust St Philadelphia PA 19102-3732

**COHEN, JOSHUA ROBERT,** lawyer; b. East Patchogue, N.Y., Aug. 20, 1963; s. Abraham Cohen and Elizabeth Joan Caufield; m. Robin Renee Conlon, Feb. 28, 1967. BA, Hartwick Coll., 1985; JD, Fordham U., 1991. Bar: Conn. 1991, N.Y. 1992, U.S. Dist. Ct. (so. and ea. dists.) N.Y., 1992. Sr. assoc. Belair & Evans LLP, N.Y.C., 1991-99; ptnr. Garson, Gerspach, De Corato & Cohen, LLP, N.Y.C., 1999—. Personal injury, Insurance, Health. Office: Garson Gerspach De Corato & Cohen LLP One Whitehall St New York NY 10004

**COHEN, KAREN BETH,** lawyer; b. N.Y.C.; d. Irwin Melvin and Phyllis (Friedlander) Drucker. JD, Touro Coll., 1990. Bar: N.Y. 1991, Fla. 1992, U.S. Dist. Ct. (ea. dist.) N.Y. 1992, U.S. Dist. Ct. (so. dist.) N.Y. 1994, U.S. Dist. Ct. (so. dist.) Fla. 1996, U.S. Supreme Ct. 1999. Atty. Rivkin, Radler & Kremer, Uniondale, N.Y., 1990-93, Green, Kahn & Piotrkowski, P.A., Miami Beach, Fla., 1993—. Recipient Am. Jurisprudence Legal Writing award, 1987, Lawyers Co-op. Pub. Legal Writing award, 1987. Mem. ATLA. Admiralty, Personal injury, Toxic tort. Office: Green Kahn & Piottkowski 317 71st St Miami Beach FL 33141-3013

**COHEN, LAURA,** lawyer; b. Pitts., Feb. 26, 1958; d. Alfred and Rita K. Cohen; (div.); children: Sarah Hackney, Beth Hackney. BA in Polit. Sci. with honors, Chatham Coll., 1993; JD, U. Pitts., 1996. Bar: Pa. 1996, U.S. Dist. Ct. (we. dist.) Pa. 1996. Lawyer, owner Family Legal Ctr., Monroeville, Pa., 1996—. Mem. ABA, Pa. Bar Assn., Allegheny County Bar Assn., Greater Pitts. Bus. Connection (v.p. 1997—). Family and matrimonial, Probate, Juvenile. Office: Family Legal Ctr 3825 Northern Pike Monroeville PA 15146-2133

**COHEN, LISA C.,** lawyer; b. Bklyn., June 20, 1962; d. Joseph and Judith May Wiles Cohen; m. Win Thin, June 30, 1991; children: Anna Mae Cohen Thin, Daniel Ilan Cohen Thin. BA summa cum laude, Brandeis U., 1984; JD, Columbia U., 1987. Bar: N.Y. 1988, U.S. Dist. Ct. (so. and ea. dists.) N.Y. 1988, U.S. Dist. Ct 1989. Law clk. to Hon. Irving R. Kaufman U.S. Ct. of Appeals (2d cir.), N.Y.C., 1987-88; assoc. Patterson, Belknap Webb & Tyler, N.Y.C., 1988-96; founding ptnr. Schindler Cohen & Hochman LLP, N.Y.C., 1997—. Bd. dirs. Families First, Bklyn., 1996-98. Mem. ABA, N.Y. State Bar Assn., N.Y.C. Bar Assn., Phi Beta Kappa. Intellectual property, General civil litigation. Office: Schindler Cohen & Hochman LLP 1 Liberty Plz Fl 35 New York NY 10006-1404

**COHEN, LOUIS RICHARD,** lawyer; b. Washington, Nov. 28, 1940; s. Milton Howard and Rowna (Chaffetz) C.; m. Bonnie Rubenstein, Aug. 29, 1965; children: Amanda Carroll, Eli Augustus. AB, Harvard U., 1962, LLB, 1966; student, Wadham Coll., Oxford, Eng., 1962-63. Bar: D.C. Law clk. to Hon. John M. Harlan U.S. Supreme Ct., Washington, 1967-68; assoc. Wilmer, Cutler & Pickering, Washington, 1968-74, ptnr., 1974-86, 88—; dep. solicitor gen. U.S. Dept. Justice, Washington, 1986-88; ptnr. Wilmer, Cutler & Pickering, Wash., 1988—; vis. prof. Stanford (Calif.) Law Sch., 1981; lectr. law Harvard Law Sch., Cambridge, Mass., 1986. Author: Book Review Michigan Law Review, 1993. Chair Harvard Law Sch. Fund, 1993-96; mem. overseers com. to Visit Harvard Law Sch., 1986-92; bd. dirs. Woolly Mammoth Theatre Co., Washington, 1988-91, 96—. Mem. Supreme Ct. Hist. Soc., Am. Acad. Appellate Lawyers, The Met. Club (Washington). Jewish. Avocation: hiking. Federal civil litigation, General corporate, Securities. Office: Wilmer Cutler & Pickering 2445 M St NW Ste 500 Washington DC 20037-1487

**COHEN, MARY ANN,** judge; b. Albuquerque, July 16, 1943; d. Gus R. and Mary Carolyn (Avriette) C. BS, UCLA, 1964; JD, U. So. Calif., 1967. Bar: Calif. 1967. Ptnr. Abbott & Cohen, P.C. and predecessors, Los Angeles, 1967-82; judge U.S. Tax Ct., Washington 1982—, chief judge 1996—. Mem. ABA (sect. taxation), Legion Lex. Republican. Office: US Tax Ct 400 2nd St NW Washington DC 20217-0002

**COHEN, MELANIE ROVNER,** lawyer; b. Chgo., Aug. 9, 1944; d. Millard Jack and Sheila (Fox) Rovner; m. Arthur Wieber Cohen, Feb. 17, 1968; children: Mitchell Jay, Jennifer Sue. AB, Brandeis U., 1965; JD, DePaul U., 1977. Bar: Ill. 1977, U.S. Dist. Ct. (no. dist.) Ill., U.S. Ct. Appeals (7th cir.). Law clk. to Justice F.J. Hertz U.S. Bankruptcy Ct., 1976-77; ptnr. Altheimer & Gray, Chgo., 1977-89, 89—, Antonow & Fink, Chgo., 1977-89; mem. Supreme Ct. of Ill. Atty. Registration and Disciplinary Commn. Inquiry Bd., 1982-86, hearing bd., 1986-94; instr. secured and consumer transactions creditor-debtor law DePaul U., Chgo., 1980-90; bd. dirs. Bankruptcy Arbitration and Mediation Svcs., 1994—; instr. real estate and bankruptcy law John Marshall Law Sch., Chgo., 1996-98. Contbr. articles to profl. jours. Panelist, spkr., bd. dirs., v.p., fellow Brandeis U. Nat. Alumni Assn., 1981—; life mem. Nat. Women's Com., 1975—, pres. Chgo. chpt., 1975-82; mem. Glencoe (Ill.) Caucus, 1977-80; chair lawyers com. Ravinia Festival, 1990-91, chmn. sustaining com., 1991—, chair sustaining fund subcom., 1992—. Mem. ABA (co-chair com. on enforcement of creditors' rights and bankruptcy), Ill. State Bar Assn., Chgo. Bar Assn. (chmn. bankruptcy reorganization com. 1983-85), Comml. Law League, Ill. Trial Lawyers Assn., Comml. Fin. Assn. Edn. Found. (bd. govs.), Turnaround Mgmt. Assn. (pres. Chgo./midwest chpt. 1990-92, nat. bd. dirs. 1990—, mem. mgmt. com. 1995—, pres. nat. bd. dirs. 1999—). Banking, Bankruptcy, Contracts commercial. Home: 167 Park Ave Glencoe IL 60022-1351 Office: Altheimer & Gray 10 S Wacker Dr Ste 4000 Chicago IL 60606-7407

**COHEN, MYRON,** lawyer, educator; b. Paterson, N.J., Feb. 4, 1927; s. Jacob B. and Rose (Stone) C.; m. Nancy Kamin, Nov. 4, 1951 (div. 1960); m. Barbara Levitov, May 12, 1963; children: Peter Fredric, Lee Susan. BEE, Cornell U., 1948; LLB, Columbia U., 1951. Bar: N.Y. 1951, U.S. Dist. Ct. (so., ea. dists.) N.Y. 1955, U.S. Ct. Appeals (2nd cir.) 1960, U.S. Ct. Appeals (Fed. cir.) 1984, U.S. Supreme Ct. 1974. Staff atty. Union Switch and Signal, Swissvale, Pa., 1952-54; assoc. Levisohn, Niner & Cohen, N.Y.C., 1954-56; sr. ptnr. Hubbell, Cohen, Stiefel & Gross, N.Y.C., 1956-85, Cohen, Pontani, Lieberman & Pavane, N.Y.C., 1985—; adj. prof. N.Y. Law Sch., 1970—; bd. dirs. Tri Magna Corp.; sec. Medallion Funding Corp., N.Y.C., 1979-86, 86-96. Author: U.S. Patent Law and Practice, 1976, Recent Developments in U.S. Law of Intellectual Property, 1985. Chmn. Mayor's Subway Watchdog Commn., N.Y.C., 1974-76. Lt. j.g. USNR, 1944-57. Mem. ABA, N.Y. State Bar Assn., Assn. Bar City N.Y., N.Y. Intellectual Property Law Assn., Internat. Trademark Assn. Democrat. Jewish. Avocation: skiing. Patent, Trademark and copyright, Intellectual property. Home: Two Fifth Ave New York NY 10011 Office: Cohen Pontani Lieberman & Pavane 551 5th Ave Rm 1210 New York NY 10176-0091

**COHEN, NANCY MAHONEY,** lawyer; b. Boston, July 14, 1941; d. Gerald Murray and Margaret (Callahan) Mahoney; m. William Cohen, Aug. 8, 1976; 1 child, Margaret Emily. AB, Emmanuel Coll., 1963; JD, Stanford U., 1975. Bar: Calif. 1975. Asst. gen. counsel Bendix Forest Products Corp., San Francisco, 1976-81; assoc. Brown & Bain, Phoenix, Ariz., 1981; counsel Syntex Corp., Palo Alto, Calif., 1982-86; sr. counsel Syntex Corp., Palo Alto, 1986-88, asst. dir. comml. law, 1988-95; gen. counsel Dendreon Corp., Palo Alto, 1995-97; v.p. legal affairs Roche, Palo Alto, 1997—; bd. dirs. Syntex Fed. Credit Union, Palo Alto. Chmn. Rental Housing Mediation Task Force, Palo Alto, 1972-74; mem. All Saints Vestry, Palo Alto, 1985-88, 93-95, 97—. Mem. ABA, Calif. Bar Assn., Am. Corp. Counsel Assn. General corporate, Antitrust, Environmental. Office: Roche 3401 Hillview Ave Palo Alto CA 94304-1347

**COHEN, NELSON CRAIG,** lawyer; b. Harrisburg, Pa., Nov. 8, 1947; s. Raymond and Rhea (Jaschik) C. BS in Acctg., Pa. State U., 1969; JD, George Washington U., 1973. Bar: Md. 1973, D.C. 1974. Assoc., ptnr. Levitan Ezrin West & Kerxton, Bethesda, Md., 1973-84; ptnr. Kerxton & Cohen Chartered, Bethesda, 1984-87, Zuckerman, Spaeder, Goldstein, Taylor & Kolker, Washington, 1987—; speaker on bankruptcy matters. Mem. ABA (bus. banking sec.), Bankruptcy Bar Assn. Md., Montgomery County Bar Assn., Md. State Bar Assn. Republican. Jewish. Avocation: golf. Bankruptcy, Consumer commercial. Office: Zuckerman Spaeder et al 1201 Connecticut Ave NW Washington DC 20036-2605

**COHEN, PHILIP MEYER,** lawyer; b. L.A., Oct. 28, 1947; s. Norman R. and Freyda (Manheim) C.; m. Laura Dee Fink, May 23, 1976; children: Megan, Justin, Sydney. BA, San Diego State U., 1969; JD, UCLA, 1972. Bar: Calif. 1972. Staff atty. Defenders Program of San Diego Inc., 1973-78; pvt. practice San Diego, 1978—. Mem. Calif. Trial Lawyers Assn., Calif. Applicant's Atty.'s Assn., San Diego Trial Lawyers Assn., San Diego County Bar Assn. Avocation: tennis. Personal injury, Workers' compensation, Consumer commercial. Office: Philip M Cohen APL 1550 Hotel Cir N Ste 170 San Diego CA 92108-2907

**COHEN, RICHARD PAUL,** lawyer; b. Bklyn., Nov. 18, 1945; s. Morris T. and Ida (Tepletsky) C.; m. Laura Diane Keller, July 4, 1968; 1 child, Adam Morris. BME, CCNY, 1968; JD, Fordham U., 1973. Bar: N.Y. 1974, W.Va. 1979, U.S. Ct. Appeals (2d cir.) 1974, U.S. Dist. Ct. (so. dist.) N.Y. 1974, U.S. Dist. Ct. (so. and no. dists.) W.Va. 1979, U.S. Ct. Appeals (fed. cir.) 1994, U.S. Supreme Ct. 1977, U.S. Ct. Vets Appeals 1993. Asst. counsel Waterfront Commn. N.Y. Harbor, N.Y.C., 1973-78; asst. atty. Westchester County Atty's. Office, White Plains, N.Y., 1977-78; asst. prosecutor Wetzel County Atty's. Office, New Martinsville, W.Va., 1980-82; pvt. practice law Hundred and Fairmont, W.Va., 1979-83; ptnr. Cohen, Abate & Cohen, L.C., Fairmont, W.Va., 1984—. Named One of Oustanding Young Men of Am., Outstanding Young Men of Am., 1981; recipient Meritorious Svc. award Am. Assn. Mental Dificiency, 1987. Mem. ABA, Nat. Assn. Soc. Sect. Claimants Rep, Nat. Assn. Vets. Advocates, W.Va. State Bar Assn. Pension, profit-sharing, and employee benefits, Consumer commercial, Workers' compensation. Home: 116 Lincoln Ave Morgantown WV 26501-6512 Office: Cohen Abate & Cohen LC Security Bank Bldg PO Box 846 Fairmont WV 26555-0846

**COHEN, ROBERT,** medical device manufacturing marketing executive, lawyer; b. Glen Cove, N.Y., Sept. 23, 1957; s. Alan and Selma (Grossman) C.; m. Nancy A. Arey, Jan. 17, 1981. BA, Bates Coll., 1979; JD, U. Maine, 1982. Bar: N.Y. 1983, U.S. Dist. Ct. (so. and ea.) N.Y. 1983. Atty. Pfizer Inc., N.Y.C., 1982-86; asst. corp. counsel, asst. sec. Pfizer Hosp. Products Group, Inc., N.Y.C., 1986-88; v.p. bus. devel., dir. for med. device mfr. and marketer Deknatel Inc., Fall River, Mass., 1988-92; pres., CEO GCI Med., Braintree, Mass., 1992-93; v.p. bus. devel. Sulzermedica USA, Inc., Angleton, Tex., 1993-94, group v.p., 1994-98; v.p. bus. & tech. devel. St. Jude Med., Inc., St. Paul, Minn., 1998—; dir. Horizon Med. Products, Inc., Atlanta, 1998—, CardioFocus, Inc., Atlanta, Mass., 1999—; bd. dirs. Horizon Med. Products, Inc., CardioFocus, Inc. Author: 19th Century Maine Authors, 1978. Mem. ABA, Am. Corp. Counsel Assn., Licensing Execs. Soc. Republican. Private international, Contracts commercial, Mergers and acquisitions. Home: 18683 Bearpath Trl Eden Prairie MN 55347-3476 Office: St Jude Med Inc One Lillehei Plz Saint Paul MN 55117

**COHEN, ROBERT (AVRAM),** lawyer; b. Pitts., July 23, 1929; s. Max R. and Mollie (Segal) C.; m. Frances H. Steiner, Dec. 24, 1951 (div. Feb. 1974); children: Deborah E., David R.; m. Mary E. Connors, Mar. 11, 1974; children: Deborah A., Charles E., Chrisann (dec.). AB magna cum laude, Harvard U., 1951, JD, 1954. Bar: Pa. 1955, Fla. 1974, U.S. Dist. Ct. (we. dist.) Pa. 1955, U.S. Dist. Ct. (so. dist.) Fla. 1974, U.S. Tax Ct. 1983, U.S. Ct. Appeals (3d cir.) 1961, U.S. Supreme Ct. 1962. Assoc. Goldstock, Schwartz, Teitelbaum & Schwartz, Pitts., 1955-60; ptnr. Goldstock, Schwartz, Cohen & Schwartz, Pitts., 1960-67, Fine, Perlow, Stone & Cohen, Pitts., 1967-70, Cohen & Goldstock, Pitts., 1970-73; assoc. Herring, Evans & Fulton, West Palm Beach, Fla., 1974; from assoc. to ptnr. Rothman, Gordon, Foreman and Groudine, P.A., Pitts., 1974-86; pvt. practice Pitts., 1986—. Trustee Western Allegheny Cmty. Libr., 1989-91, pres., 1991-98; pres. County Libr. Assn. Serving the People, 1993-94; mem. Zoning Bd. Borough of Oakdale, 1991—. Mem. ABA, Assn. Trial Lawyers Am. (pres. western Pa. chpt. 1972-73), Am. Judicature Soc., Pa. Bar Assn. (com. on ethics and profl. responsibility 1988—, com. on professionalism 1990-94, civil rights com. 1995-97), Acad. Trial Lawyers Allegheny County, Pa. Trial Lawyers Assn., Allegheny County Bar Assn. (civil litigation coun. 1988-90, continuing legal edn. 1977—, profl. ethics com. 1996—), Golden Triangle Lodge (v.p. 1966-69), B'nai B'rith. Democrat. Jewish. Personal injury, Federal civil litigation, State civil litigation. Home: 205 Oak Heights Dr Oakdale PA 15071-1137 Office: 819 Frick Bldg Pittsburgh PA 15219

**COHEN, ROBERT F.,** lawyer, journalist; b. N.Y.C., Feb. 19, 1951; s. Abraham and Ruth Hope Cohen. BA, SUNY, Stony Brook, 1975; BS in Law, Glendale U., 1990, JD, 1992. Bar: Calif. 1992, U.S. Dist. Ct. (cen. dist.) Calif. 1992, U.S. Dist. Ct. (no. dist.) Calif. 1993. Radio news anchor, news dir. various radio stas., 1972-79; radio news reporter Sta. WCBS, N.Y.C., 1979-80; broadcast bus. journalist Wall St. Jour., Bus. Week, UPI, N.Y.C., 1980-86; systems supr. Dern, Mason & Floum, L.A., 1988-89; paralegal Perkins Coie, L.A., 1989-92; pvt. practice Law Office of Robert F. Cohen, Santa Monica, Calif., 1992—. Editor-in-chief Glendale Law Rev., 1991-92. Vol. fundraiser AIDS Project L.A., 1989—, vol. atty., 1993—; col. 1992 Voter Registration Drive, L.A.; vol. atty. Disaster Emergency Ctr., 1994. Mem. AFTRA, ACLU, State Bar Calif., Santa Monica Bar Assn., L.A. County Bar Assn., Lawyers for Human Rights. Democrat. Avocations: computer programming, photography, hiking, scuba diving, traveling. Office: 9024 W Olympic Blvd Beverly Hills CA 90211-3564

**COHEN, ROBERT STEPHAN,** lawyer; b. N.Y.C., Jan. 14, 1939; s. Abraham and Florence C.; children: Christopher, Ian, Nicholas. BA, Alfred U., 1959; LLB, Fordham U., 1962. Bar: N.Y. 1963, U.S. Dist. Ct. (so. and ea. dists.) N.Y 1964, U.S. Ct. Appeals (2nd cir.) 1965. Assoc. Saxe, Bacon & O'Shea, N.Y.C., 1963-68; mng. ptnr. Morrison, Cohen, Singer & Weinstein and predecessor firms, N.Y.C., 1968—; lectr. in field; mem. faculty Am Acad. Psychiatry and the Law, 1984—. Bd. dirs. N.Y. Pops, 1983—. 1st lt. JAG, USAR, 1965-67. Fellow Am. Coll. Family Trial Lawyers; mem. ABA, FBA, ATLA, N.Y. State Bar Assn., N.Y.C. Bar Assn., N.Y. Acad. Matrimonial Lawyers, Univ. Club (N.Y.C.). Contbr. articles to legal jours. Federal civil litigation, State civil litigation, Family and matrimonial. Home: 920 5th Ave New York NY 10021-4160 Office: 750 Lexington Ave New York NY 10022-1200

**COHEN, RONALD J.,** lawyer; b. Englewood, N.J., Dec. 16, 1950; s. Irwin and Shirley (Kushel) C.; m. Jeanne K. Houser, June 22, 1981; children: Shay, Emily. BA, U. Fla., 1973; JD, U. Miami, 1976. Asst. city atty. City of Miami, 1979-83; assoc. Paul, Landy, Beiley & Harper, Miami, 1983-87; ptnr. Klausner & Cohen, PA, Hollywood, Fla., 1987-97, Ronald J. Cohen, PA, Miami, 1997—. Civil rights, Labor, Pension, profit-sharing, and employee benefits. Office: Brickell Bayview Ctr 80 SW 8th St Ste 1910 Miami FL 33130-3047

**COHEN, RONALD JAY,** lawyer; b. Des Moines, Mar. 2, 1948; s. Maurice Marvin and Edith (Levitt) C.; m. Ruthie Eisenberg, Dec. 19, 1984; children: Daniel, Brad. BA, U. Wis., 1970; JD, U. Minn., 1972. Bar: Ariz. 1972. Assoc. Streich Lang, Phoenix, 1972-76; ptnr. Streich, Lang, Weeks & Cardon, Phoenix, 1977-91; dir., ptnr. Cohen & Cotton, P.C., Phoenix, 1991—; vis. prof. Ind. U., 1976; adj. prof. Ariz. State U., 1980; appointed judge pro tempore Maricopa County Superior Ct., 1983-91. Contbr. articles to profl. jours. Mem. ABA (program chair litigation sect., 1992, chair nat. inst., 1992-93), Maricopa County Bar Assn. (Robert E. Mills Mem. of Yr. award 1986). Federal civil litigation, State civil litigation. Office: Cohen & Cotton PC 400 E Van Buren St Ste 440 Phoenix AZ 85004-2223

**COHEN, SEYMOUR,** lawyer; b. Chgo., Sept. 27, 1917; s. Sol and Sophie (Norinsky) C.; m. Marcia Meltzer, Aug. 10, 1952; children: Susan Ruth, James Burton. BS, Ind. U., 1939, JD, 1941. Bar: Ind. 1941, Ill. 1948, U.S. Supreme Ct. 1971. Atty. NLRB, Washington, 1946-47; practice law Chgo., 1947—; mem. firm Dorfman, Cohen, Laner & Muchin, Ltd. (and predecessor), 1953-86. Mem. Northbrook (Ill.) Library Bd., 1963-69, pres., 1965-67. Served to lt. comdr. USNR, 1941-45. Mem. ABA, Chgo. Bar Assn. (chmn. com. labor law 1961-63). Labor, Pension, profit-sharing, and employee benefits. *A belief in one's own abilities is not enough. There must be a need by others for what those abilities can provide. The utilization of those abilities then will produce rewards both for the provider and the receiver.*

**COHEN, SHELDON IRWIN,** lawyer; b. Newark, July 25, 1937. BS in Ceramic Engring., Rutgers U., 1959, AB in Humanities, 1959; LLB, Georgetown U., 1964. Bar: Va. 1964, D.C. 1964, U.S. Ct. Appeals (D.C. and 4th cirs.) 1964, U.S. Supreme Ct. 1967. Assoc. Chapman, Disalle & Friedman, Washington, 1964-70; pvt. practice law Washington, Arlington, Va., 1970—. Author: Security Clearances and the Protection of National Security Information, Law and Procedure, 1999. Vice chmn. Arlington Dem. Com., 1968-70; mem. Va. Dem. Cen. Com., 1969-70. Capt. USAR, 1959-67. Mem. ABA (chmn. govt. pers. com. 1986-89, chmn. nat. security interests com. 1990-95), D.C. Bar Assn. (chmn. civil svc. law com. 1984-86). Democrat. Labor, Administrative and regulatory, Military. Office: 2009 14th St N Ste 708 Arlington VA 22201-2514

**COHEN, STEPHEN M(ARTIN),** judge; b. West Palm Beach, Fla., Oct. 15, 1957; s. Joseph R. and Marilyn F. Cohen. BA, U. S.C., 1978; J.D., John Marshall Law Sch., 1981. Bar: Fla. 1981, U.S. Dist. Ct. (mid. and so. dists.) Fla. 1985. Asst. state atty. Office of the State Atty., West Palm Beach, 1981-83; assoc. Alley, Maass, Rogers, Lindsay & Chauncey, P.A., Palm Beach, Fla., 1984-88; ptnr. Alley, Maass, Rogers, Lindsay, P.A., Palm Beach, 1989-92; county ct. judge 15th Jud. Cir. Ct., Palm Beach County, Fla., 1993—; dep. adminstrv. judge, criminal div. 15th Jud. Cir. Ct., Palm Beach County, 1999—; program atty. Guardian ad Litem, West Palm Beach, 1984-86. Contbr. articles to prof. jours. Trustee Temple Israel, West Palm Beach, 1985-86; chmn. Soviet Jewry Legal Adv. Ctr., 1990-92; del. CSCE Meeting of Helsinki Commn., Paris, 1989, Copenhagen, 1990, Moscow, 1991; bd. dirs. Union Couns. for Soviet Jews, Washington, 1989-93; dir. Palm Beach Orthodox Synagogue, 1996-98. Mem. ABA, Palm Beach County Bar Assn. Avocations: tennis, golf, travel. Office: Palm Beach County Courthouse 205 N Dixie Hwy West Palm Beach FL 33401-4599

**COHEN-GALLET, BONNIE ROBIN,** lawyer; b. N.Y.C., Oct. 3, 1954; d. Nathan and Sylvia Cohen; m. Jeffry H. Gallet, Nov. 10, 1996. BA cum laude, Boston U., 1975; JD, SUNY, Albany, 1978. Bar: N.Y. 1979, U.S. Dist. Ct. (so. and ea. dists.) N.Y. 1984. Asst. dist. atty. Office of Dist. Atty. Queens County, N.Y.C., 1978-82; law clk. Hon. Bernard Dubin N.Y. State Supreme Ct., N.Y.C., 1982-83; asst. counsel dep. minority leader Emanuel Gold N.Y. State Senate, 1988-92; assoc. atty. Garfunkel, Wild & Travis, N.Y.C., 1993; counsel N.Y.C. Councilmember Karen Koslowitz, 1994; pvt. practice law, 1984-94; prin. law clk. N.Y. State Supreme Ct., Queens,

1995—. Mem. N.Y. State Bar Assn., Network of Bar Leaders, Assn. Bar City of New York, Queens County Bar Assn., Queens County Women's Bar Assn. (pres. 1989-90), Queens County Criminal Ct. Bar Assn. (treas. 1993-95), N.Y. County Women's Bar Assn. Avocation: horseback riding.

**COHILL, MAURICE BLANCHARD, JR.,** federal judge; b. Pitts., Pa., Nov. 26, 1929; s. Maurice Blanchard and Florence (Clarke) C.; m. Suzanne Miller, June 27, 1952 (dec. May 1986); children: Cynthia Cohill Plattner, Jonathan, Jennifer, Victoria Cohill Rifai. AB, Princeton U., 1951; LLB, U. Pitts., 1956. Bar: Pa. 1957. Judge family div. Common Pleas Ct., Allegheny County, Pitts., 1965-76; judge U.S. Dist. Ct. Pa. (we. dist.), 1976-94, chief judge, 1985-92, sr. judge, 1994—; bd. dirs. Pa. George Jr. Republic, Grove City; bd. visitors Grad. Sch. Social Work, U. Pitts.; chmn. bd. fellows Nat. Center for Juvenile Justice. Served to capt. USMCR, 1951-53. Mem. Am., Pa., Allegheny County bar assns., Nat. Council Juvenile Ct. Judges (v.p.), Pa. Council Juvenile Ct. Judges (past pres.), Pa. Conf. State Trial Judges, Phi Delta Phi. Republican. Presbyterian. Office: US Dist Ct US Courthouse 8th Fl Rm 3 7th and Grant Sts Pittsburgh PA 15219

**COHN, ANDREW HOWARD,** lawyer; b. N.Y.C., Jan. 17, 1945; s. Maurice John and Margaret Ethel (Gordon) C.; m. Marcia Bliss Leavitt, July 10, 1977; children: Marisa Leavitt, David Herman. BA, U. Pa., 1966; AM, Harvard U., 1970, PhD, 1972; JD, Yale U., 1975. Bar: Mass. 1975, U.S. Dist. Ct. Mass. 1976, U.S. Ct. Appeals (1st cir.) 1976. Law clk. to presiding justice U.S. Ct. Appeals (1st cir.), Providence and Boston, 1975-76; assoc. Hill & Barlow, Boston, 1976-80; sr. ptnr. Hale and Dorr, Boston, 1980—; chmn. exec. com. Hale and Dorr, 1990-91, real estate dept., 1991-97, energy group, 1992—; cons. for juvenile justice standards project ABA and Inst. for Judicial Adminstrn., N.Y.C., 1973-74; rsch. fellow MIT-Harvard U. Joint Ctr. for Urban Studies, Cambridge, Mass., 1969-71, Univ. Coll., Nairobi, Kenya, 1968. Contbr. articles to profl. jours.; note and project editor Yale Law Jour., New Haven, 1974-75. Advisor Newton (Mass.) Community SChs. Found., 1987-88. Named Law and Social Sci. fellow Russell Sage Found., 1972-74. Mem. ABA (environ.controls com., bus. law sect.), Am. Coll. Real Estate Lawyers, Boston Bar Assn. (chmn. real estate sect. 95-97), Yale Law Sch. Assn. Mass. (treas. 1985-87). Democrat. Jewish. Real property, Environmental, Finance. Office: Hale and Dorr 60 State St Ste 25 Boston MA 02109-1816

**COHN, AVERN LEVIN,** federal judge; b. Detroit, July 23, 1924; s. Irwin I. and Sadie (Levin) C.; m. Joyce Hochman, Dec. 30, 1954 (dec. Dec. 1989); m. Lois Pincus Cohn, June 1992; children: Sheldon, Leslie Cohn Magy, Thomas. Student, John Tarleton Agrl. Coll., 1943, Stanford U., 1944; J.D., U. Mich., 1949. Bar: Mich. 1949. Practiced in Detroit, 1949-79; mem. firm Honigman Miller Schwartz & Cohn, Detroit, 1961-79; U.S. dist. judge, 1979—. Mem. Mich. Civil Rights Commn., 1972-75, chmn., 1974-75; Mem. Detroit Bd. Police Commrs., 1975-79, chmn., 1979; bd. govs. Jewish Welfare Fedn., Detroit, 1972—. Served with AUS, 1943-46. Mem. ABA, Mich. Bar Assn., Am. Law Inst.

**COHN, BRADLEY M.,** lawyer; b. Chgo., July 5, 1953; s. Charles M. and Marian Cohn C.; m. Janet M. Minow, Mar. 25, 1995; 1 child, Robert M. BA, U. Iowa, 1975; JD, U. Miami, 1978. Assoc. Hanson & Shire, P.C., Chgo., 1978-88; ptnr. Thrun, Tallman & Cohn, Ltd., Mt. Prospect, Ill., 1988—. Dir., officer Ctr. for Enriched Living, Deerfield, Ill., 1989—. General corporate, Real property. Office: Thrun Tallman & Cohn Ltd 111 E Busse Ave Ste 504 Mount Prospect IL 60056-3248

**COHN, MARJORIE F.,** law educator, legal analyst; b. Pomona, Calif., Nov. 1, 1948; d. Leonard L. and Florence Cohn; m. Pedro López children: Victor, Nicolas; m. Jerome P. Wallingford. BA, Stanford U., 1970; JD, Santa Clara U., 1975. Bar: Calif. 1975, U.S. Dist. Ct. (so. dist.) Calif. 1982, U.S. Dist. Ct. (no. dist.) Calif. 1983. Staff atty. Nat. Lawyers Guild, San Francisco, 1975-76, Agrl. Labor Rels. Bd., Sacramento, 1976-78, Appellate Defenders, Inc., San Diego, 1987-91; dep. pub. defender Fresno County Pub. Defender's Office, Fresno, Calif., 1978-80; pvt. practice Monterey and San Diego Counties, San Diego, 1981-87; prof. law Thomas Jefferson Sch. Law, San Diego, 1991—; legal analyst on TV, radio and in print media. Co-author: Cameras in the Courtroom: Television and the Pursuit of Justice, 1998; editor-in-chief Guild Practitioner, 1994—. Mem. adv. bd. Support Com. for Maquiladora Workers, 1996—. Recipient Golden Apple award Student Bar Assn., Thomas Jefferson Sch. Law, 1995-98. Mem. Nat. Lawyers Guild (nat. exec. com. 1996—), Calif. Attys. for Criminal Justice, Phi Alpha Delta. Office: Thomas Jefferson Sch Law 2121 San Diego Ave San Diego CA 92110-2928

**COHN, MARK BARRY,** lawyer; b. Cleve., Dec. 28, 1947; s. David J. and Dorothy (Camin) C.; m. Marlene Sherman, Dec. 27, 1969; children: Mindy D., Laurie A., Jill R. BS, Ohio State U., 1969, JD, 1973. Bar: Ohio 1974, Fla. 1976. Assoc. Jones, Day, Reavis & Pogue, Cleve., 1973-76, Trenam, Simmons, Kemkar et al, Tampa, Fla., 1976-79, Kadish & Krantz, Cleve., 1979-82; pvt. practice, Cleve., 1982-87; Prin. McCarthy, Lebit, Crystal & Haiman Co., L.P.A., Cleve., 1987—. Author: Smith's Review of Civil Procedure, 1985. Mem. ABA, Cleve. Bar Assn., Ohio Bar Assn., Fla. Bar Assn., Nat. Trial Lawyers Assn., Order of Coif. Democrat. Jewish. General civil litigation, Taxation, general, Personal injury. Home: 31349 Gates Mills Blvd Cleveland OH 44124-4352 Office: McCarthy Lebit Crystal & Haiman 101 W Prospect Ave Ste 1800 Cleveland OH 44115-1027

**COHN, MELVIN E.,** judge; b. San Francisco, Jan. 23, 1917; s. Benjamin and Henrietta Cohn; m. Nita Waxman, Mar. 2, 1947; children: Lawrence, Catherine Gilley, Janet Borg. AB, U. Calif., Berkeley, 1937, JD, 1940. Bar: Calif. 1941, U.S. Dist. Ct. (no. dist.) Calif. 1947, U.S. Dist. Ct. Hawaii 1984, U.S. Ct. Appeals (9th cir.) 1952. Atty. Social Security Bd., Washington, San Francisco, 1940-42, 46; ptnr. Aaronson, Cohn & Dickerson, San Carlos, Calif., 1947-63; city atty. City of San Carlos, Calif., 1956-63; mcpl. judge San Mateo County, Redwood City, Calif., 1963-64, supr. ct. judge, 1964-83; pvt. judge, arbitrator San Carlos, Calif., 1983—. Contbr. articles to profl. jours. Master sgt. U.S. Army, 1942-46, PTO. Recipient Trial Judge of Yr. award Calif. Trial Lawyers Assn., 1981. Mem. Calif. Bar Assn., Calif. Coun. for Criminal Justice (vice chmn. 1975-83), Assn. Family Cts. (pres. 1971-72), Calif. Jud. Coun. (court mgmt. com. 1973-77), San Mateo County Bar Assn. (pres. 1959), Bay Meadows Found., Kiwanis (pres. San Carlos chpt. 1953). Democrat. Office: Aaronson Dickerson Cohn & Lanzone 939 Laurel St # 1065 San Carlos CA 94070-3943

**COHN, NATHAN,** lawyer; b. Charleston, S.C., Jan. 20, 1918; s. Samuel and Rose (Baron) C.; 1 child, Norman; m. Carolyn Venturini, May 18, 1970. JD, San Francisco Law Sch., 1947. BAr: Calif. 1947, U.S. Supreme Ct. 1957. Pvt. practice law San Francisco, 1947—, 1947—; judge pro tem Mcpl. Ct., Superior Ct. Columnist, San Francisco Progress, 1982-86; contr. and author seminars in field. Mem. Calif. State Recreation Commn., 1965-68; former mem. Dem. State Ctrl. Com. Served to 1st lt. USAF, 1950-55. Fellow Am. Bd. Criminal Lawyers (founder, past pres.), Am. Bd. Trial Advs. (diplomate; chpt. pres. 1984), Internat. Acad. Law and Sci., San Francisco Trial Lawyers (past pres.), Criminal Trial Lawyers Assn. No. Calif., Irish-Israeli-Italian Soc. (co-founder, co-pres.), Internat. Footprinters Assn., Regular Vets. Assn., Calamari Club, Goldfather Club, Press Club (life), Lawyers Club San Francisco, Masons (32 deg.), Shriners, South of Market Boys, Ancient Order Hibernians Am. (hon. life). Jewish. Criminal, General practice, Personal injury. Office: 2107 Van Ness Ave Ste 200 San Francisco CA 94109-2572

**COKER, HOWARD C.,** lawyer; b. Jacksonville, Fla., Apr. 30, 1947. B in Journalism, U. Fla., 1969, JD, 1971. Bar: Fla. 1972. Asst. state atty. Fourth Jud. Cir., 1972; assoc. Howell, Kirby, Montgomery, D'Aiuto & Dean, P.A., 1973-76; pres., dir. Coker, Meyers, Schickel, Sorenson & Higginbotham, Jacksonville, Fla., 1976—; guest lectr. more than 40 CLE seminars on litig. and trial matters throughout Fla., for Fla. Bar Assn., Acad. Fla. Trial Lawyers; advisor mock trial team U. Fla. Law Sch., 1991—; adj. prof. U. North Fla. Chair ednl. adv. coun. U. North Fla., 1992-94, chair adv. bd. for paralegals, 1990-92. Fellow Am. Bar Found.; mem. ABA, ATLA, Am. Arbitration Assn. (panel arbitrators 1983—), Fla. Bar Assn. (pres.-elect 1997-98, bd. govs. 1994—, exec. com. 1995-97, all bar fconf. del. 1990-92, 94, 96, 97, budget com. 1995-97, bd. rev. coml. on profl. ethics chair 1995-96, disciplinary rev. com. 1994-95, jud. qualification screen com. 1994-95, legis. com. 1994-95, profl. retreat chair 1996, program evaluation com. chair 1996-97, 4th jud. cir. grievance com. reviewer 1994-97, com. sects. 1991-94, chair 1993-94, sect. leadership conf. chair 1995, trial lawyers sect. exec. coun. 1987-94, bd. govs. liaison 1996, chair 1992-93, exec. co. 1989-93, legis. com. 1988-93), Am. Bd. Trial Advocates (pres. Jacksonville chpt. 1988—, media rep. 1988, exec. com. 1988—, diplomate), Am. Judicature Soc., Chester Bedell Meml. Found. (trustee 1996—), First Coast Trial Lawyers Assn., Fla. Acad. Trial Lawyres (bd. dirs. 1995—, Eagle sponsor 1990—), Fla. Lawyers Assn. for Maintenance of Excellence (bd. dirs. 1995-97), Fla. Supreme Ct. Hist. Soc., Jacksonville Bar Assn., Roscoe Pound Found., U.S. Supreme Ct. Hist. Soc., Fla. Conservation Assn. (pres. 1993-94), Fla. Ducks Unltd. (Sportsman of Yr. 1994), Fla. Wildlife Fedn., Seminole Club (bd. dirs. 1988, pres., 1989), U. Fla. Nat. Alumni Assn. (pres.'s coun. 1992-97), Sigma Alpha Epsilon, Phi Delta Phi. E-mail: Cokermyers@aol.com. Personal injury, General civil litigation, Consumer commercial. Office: PO Box 1860 136 E Bay St Jacksonville FL 32201

**COLAGIOVANNI, JOSEPH ALFRED, JR.,** lawyer; b. Providence, Dec. 26, 1956; s. Joseph Alfred Sr. and Rosemarie (Giordano) C.; m. Mary Jo Gagliardo, Aug. 9, 1980. AB in Polit. Sci. and Philosophy, Brown U., 1979; JD, Boston U., 1982. Bar: Mo. 1982, U.S. Dist. Ct. (ea. and we. dists.) Mo. 1982, U.S. Ct. Appeals (7th cir.) 1992. Asst. atty. gen. State of Mo., Jefferson City, 1982-84; ptnr., co-leader constrn. group Bryan, Cave, St. Louis, 1984—; adj. prof. of law Wash. U. Sch. of Law, 1997—; hon. vice consul to Italy, 1997—. Mem. ABA, Mo. Bar Assn., Noonday Club. Avocations: tennis, music, collecting matchbooks. Construction. Office: Bryan Cave 211 N Broadway Ste 3600 Saint Louis MO 63102-2733

**COLAMARINO, KATRIN BELENKY,** lawyer; b. N.Y.C., Apr. 29, 1951; d. Allen Abram and Selma (Burwasser) Belenky Lang; m. Leonard J. Colamarino, Mar. 20, 1982; m. Barry E. Brenner, June 1, 1974 (div. June 1979); 1 child, Rachel Erin. BA, Vassar Coll., 1972; JD, U. Richmond, 1976. Bar: Ohio 1976, U.S. Ct. Apls. (Fed. cir.), 1982. Staff atty. AM Internat. Inc., Cleve., 1977-79; atty. Lipkowitz & Plaut, N.Y.C., 1980-81; atty. Docutel Olivetti Corp., Tarrytown, N.Y., 1981-84; atty. NYNEX Bus. Info. Systems, White Plains, N.Y., 1984-85; corp. counsel, sec. Logica Data Architects, Inc., N.Y.C., 1986-90; corp. counsel SEER Technologies, Inc., N.Y.C., 1990-91; v.p. chief tech. counsel global relationship bank Citibank N.A., N.Y.C., 1991-97; v.p., asst. gen. counsel The Chase Manhattan Bank, N.Y.C., 1997—; lectr. continuing legal edn. Computer Law Assn., Cyberspace Camp Conf., San Jose, Ca., 1997. Class agt. Fieldston Sch., N.Y.C., 1980—, exec. bd. Ethical Fieldston Alumni Assn., 1980-90, 92-95, v.p. 1987-90; alumnae coun. rep. Vassar Coll., 1982-86, class corr. Vassar Quar., 1992-97, mem. Alumni/Alumnae fund adv. bd., 1997—. Mem. ABA (com. on cyberspace law), Assn. Bar City N.Y., Computer Law Assn. General corporate, Intellectual property, Computer. Office: Chase Manhattan Bank 1 Chase Manhattan Plz Fl 25 New York NY 10081-0001

**COLAPIETRO, BRUNO,** lawyer, educator; b. Endicott, N.Y., Aug. 11, 1935; s. Felice and Vincenza (Ricci) C.; m. Jane Larson, Aug. 22, 1959; children: Jennifer, Karen, Christopher. BA, Hamilton Coll., 1957; JD, Cornell U., 1960. Bar: N.Y. 1960. Trial atty. U.S. Dept. Justice, Washington, 1960-61; ptnr. Chernin & Gold, Binghamton, N.Y., 1962—; adj. prof. law Cornell U., Ithaca, N.Y., 1970—, SUNY, Binghamton, 1980-90; hearing referee N.Y. State Commn. on Jud. Conduct, Albany, 1983—. Author: Law & the Family, 1988. Chmn. Broome County Ethics Com., Binghamton, 1975-85. Named one of Best Lawyers in Am. in field of domestic relations Seaview Putnam Pub., 1983. Fellow Am. Acad. Matrimonial Lawyers; mem. ABA, N.Y. State Bar Assn. (exec. com., family law sect. 1980—), Broome County Bar Assn. (pres. 1977-78). Lodge: Rotary (pres. Endwell, N.Y. club 1965-90). Avocations: tennis, hockey, collecting stamps, computers. Family and matrimonial. Home: 2723 Hamilton Dr Endicott NY 13760-2307 Office: Chernin & Gold 71 State St # 1563 Binghamton NY 13901-3318

**COLAPINTO, DAVID KEITH,** lawyer; b. Springfield, Mass., Dec. 4, 1958; s. Daniel Peter and Dorothy Madeline (Hood) C. BA, Boston U., 1984; JD, Antioch U., 1987. Bar: D.C. 1988, Mass. 1989, U.S. Dist. Ct. D.C. 1989, U.S. Ct. Appeals (fed. cir.) 1994, U.S. Ct. Appeals (D.C. cir.) 1998. Ptnr. Kohn, Kohn & Colapinto, PC, Washington, 1988—; founder Nat. Whistleblower Ctr., Washington, 1988; dir. Nat. Whistleblower Legal Def. and Edn. Fund, Washington, 1996—; gen. counsel Forensic Justice Project, Washington, 1998—. Legal editor: (newsletter) Whistleblower News, 1995—. Mem. Nat. Lawyers Guild, Nat. Assn. Criminal Def. Lawyers. Democrat. Roman Catholic. Civil rights, Labor. Office: Kohn Kohn & Colapinto PC 3233 P St NW Washington DC 20007-2756

**COLAW, THIERRY PATRICK,** judge; b. Kansas City, Mo., Jan. 9, 1947; s. Albert E. and Josette Colaw; m. Jeri Williams, Oct. 11, 1980; children: Case, Clayton. BA cum laude, UCLA, 1974; JD, U. Santa Clara, Calif., 1977. Bar: Calif. Assoc. Smith & Brissenden, Santa Ana, Calif., 1978-79, Vernon W. Hunt, Inc., Santa Ana, 1979-84; ptnr. Hunt, Colaw & Roe, Inc., Santa Ana, 1984-89, Hunt, Colaw & Adams, Inc., Santa Ana, 1989-97; judge Calif. Superior Ct., Santa Ana, 1997—. With USN, 1968-72. Mem. Orange County Bar Assn. (bd. dirs. 1983-96), Orange County Trial Lawyers Assn. (pres. 1989), Orange County Barristers (pres. 1983). Roman Catholic. Avocations: photography, classical music. Office: Orange County Superior Ct 700 Civic Center Dr W Santa Ana CA 92701-4045

**COLBECK, J. RICHARD,** lawyer; b. Detroit, Sept. 25, 1939; s. John Harle and Virginia (Glance) C.; m. Judith Ann Kish, Nov. 25, 1961 (div. June 13, 1974); m. Christine Lynn Wallace, June 4, 1981; children: Craig, Brian, Kevin, Timothy, Julia. Student, St. Joseph's Coll., 1957-58; Coll. of St. Thomas, 1958-61; JD, U. Detroit, 1966. Bar: Mich. 1967, U.S. Dist. Ct. (ea. and we. dists.) Mich. 1967, U.S. Ct. Appeals (6th cir.) 1980. Assoc. Brasher, Mies & Duggan, Livonia, Mich., 1967-69; atty. sole practice Allen Park, Mich., 1969-73; prosecuting atty. Branch County, Coldwater, Mich., 1973-76; assoc. Gibbons & Nye, Hillsdale, Mich., 1978-79; atty. sole practice Richard Colbeck, Coldwater, 1978-88; ptnr. Colbeck, McAlhaney & Stewart, Coldwater, 1988—; pres. Coldwater Sch. Bd., 1998—; instr. Kellogg Community Coll., Battle Creek, Mich., 1979—, Glen Oaks Community Coll., Sturgis, Mich., 1980—. Trustee Tibbits Opera Found., Coldwater, 1989. Mem. State Bar of Mich. (del. 1997—), Frat. Order of Elks. Avocations: performing arts, directing TV, radio commls., golf. Personal injury, Criminal, Family and matrimonial. Office: Colbeck McAlhany & Stewart 53 E Chicago St Coldwater MI 49036-1644

**COLBERT, DIA TERESA,** legal assistant; b. N.Y.C., July 10, 1963; d. Mack and Sarah (St. John) C. BS in Gen. Mgmt., Boston Coll., 1985; paralegal cert., Katharine Gibbs, 1988; MBA in Mgmt., Barry U., 1995; law student, Nova Southea. U. Legal asst. Legal Assistants Corp., N.Y.C., 1988-89; litigation asst. Sullivan and Cromwell, N.Y.C., 1989-91; legal asst. Mandler & Silver, Miami, 1991-92, Jenner & Block, Miami, 1992-95, Gallway Gillman et al, Miami, 1995-96, Stearns Weaver et al, Miami, 1996—. Alumni admission vol., county chairperson Boston Coll., 1993-98, Broward County, Fla., 1991—. Democrat. Roman Catholic. Avocations: tennis, travel, daily fitness program. Office: 150 W Flagler St Miami FL 33130-1536

**COLBERT, DOUGLAS MARC,** lawyer; b. N.Y.C., Feb. 8, 1948; s. Leonard M. and Estelle (Ginsberg) C.; m. Amy Jo Guryan, May 1, 1976 (div. 1977); m. Angel Mendez, Dec. 28, 1986. Student, Hunter Coll., N.Y.C., 1964-67; BBA cum laude, Bernard Baruch Coll., N.Y.C., 1969; JD, Bklyn. Law Sch., 1972. Bar: N.Y. 1974. Honor law intern N.Y. County Dist. Atty., N.Y.C., 1971; law asst. N.Y.C. Corp. Counsel, 1972-74; arbitrator N.Y.C. Civil Ct., 1979—; atty. Hauser & Rosenbaum Esq., N.Y.C., 1974-76; pvt. practice law N.Y.C., 1974—. Vol. atty. Vol. Lawyers for the Arts, N.Y.C., 1979-85; spl. investigator N.Y. State Bd. Elections, N.Y.C., 1981-84. Mem. N.Y. State Trial Lawyers Assn., N.Y. County Lawyers Assn., USCG Aux., Moot Ct., Sigma Alpha Mu (founder). Avocations: scuba, health & fitness, travel, boating. Personal injury, Family and matrimonial, Real property. Office: 350 5th Ave Ste 7220 New York NY 10118-7299

**COLBERT, KATHRYN HENDON,** lawyer; b. Englewood, N.J., Aug. 26, 1947; d. Charles R. and Rosemary F. (Schrafft) C. AB, Vassar Coll., 1969; JD, Tulane U., 1972. Bar: La. 1972, D.C. 1975, U.S. Supreme Ct. 1977, Miss. 1989, Tex. 1994. Atty. SBA, Harrisburg, Pa., 1972-73; staff mem. for rep. Leonor K. Sullivan Ho. of Reps., Washington, 1973-74; sole practice New Orleans, 1975; atty. office of hearings and appeals Social Security Adminstrn., HHS, New Orleans, 1976-87; sr. trial atty. EEOC, New Orleans, 1987-92; pvt. practice New Orleans and Dallas, 1993-94; sr. regional atty. Advocacy, Inc., Dallas, 1994-98. Democrat. Presbyterian. E-mail: k.colbert@worldnet.att.net. Home: 4037 N O'Connor Rd Irving TX 75062-7649

**COLBURN, JAMES ALLAN,** lawyer; b. Huntington, W.Va., July 5, 1942; s. Ray S. and Edith Abigail (Blood) C.; m. Virginia Ann Carter, June 19, 1965; children: Heather Lara, Sarah Carter. AB, Davidson (N.C.) Coll., 1964; JD, Rutgers U., 1967; postgrad. Marshall U., Austin Peay State U. Bar: W.Va. 1970, U.S. Dist. Ct. (no. and so. dists.) W.Va. 1970, U.S. Ct. Appeals (4th cir.) 1973, U.S. Dist. Ct. (ea. dist.) Ky. 1975, U.S. Tax Ct. 1982, U.S. Supreme Ct. 1983, U.S. Ct. Appeals (6th cir.) 1985. Assoc., Levy & Patton, 1970-72; sole practice, Huntington, W.Va., 1973-75; ptnr. Baer, Napier & Colburn, Huntington, 1975-81; ptnr., pres. Baer and Colburn, L.C., Huntington, 1981—; instr. legal asst. program Marshall U., 1978-82; lectr. in field. Asst. pros. atty. Cabell County, 1977-79, spl. prosecuting atty. 1986-87; Nicholas County, 1985-87, Wayne County, 1987—, Mingo County, 1986-88. Served with U.S. Army, 1968-70. Mem. W.Va. Bar Assn., ABA, Assn. Trial Lawyers Am., West. Va. Trial Lawyers Assn. (bd. govs.), Union Internat. des-Advocats, Cabell County Bar Assn. (pres. 1980), Nat. Assn. Dist. Attys., Am. Arbitration Assn. (panel comml. arbitrators). Democrat. Presbyterian. Personal injury, General practice, General corporate. Office: 731 5th Ave Huntington WV 25701-2010

**COLBURN, STUART DALE,** lawyer; b. Houston, July 3, 1969; s. Roy Dale and Sonda Gail (Peacock) C. BA cum laude, Southwestern U., 1991; JD, U. Tex., 1994. Bar: Tex. 1994. Mgr. hearings sect. Harris & Harris, Austin, 1994—. Recipient John Engalitcheff Jr. Outstanding Young Am. award Inst. Comparative Polit. and Econ. Sys., Georgetown U., 1989. Mem. Austin Young Lawyers Assn. (chmn. law related edn. for children com. 1996-98). Avocations: boating, golfing. Workers' compensation, Administrative and regulatory, State civil litigation. Office: Harris & Harris 8701 N Mopac Ste 400 Austin TX 78759

**COLBY, WILLIAM MICHAEL,** lawyer; b. Pontiac, Mich., Jan. 24, 1942; s. Orville Edgar and Jeannette (Nadon) C.; m. Brenda Schneckenburger, Nov. 28, 1964; children: Kathleen C. Scott, Thomas Brownell. AB, U. Mich., 1963, JD, 1966. Bar: N.Y. 1966, U.S. Tax Ct. 1969, U.S. Supreme Ct. 1972, Fla. 1982. Assoc. Harter, Secrest & Emery, Rochester, N.Y., 1966-74, ptnr., 1975—; cons. various tax pubs.; mem. N.Y. adv. panels on bus. tax studies and tax appeals tribunal. Contbr. articles to profl. jours.; editor various tax publs. Bd. dirs. Rochester Mus. and Sci. Ctr.; v.p. Sojourner House. Fellow Am. Bar Found.; mem. ABA, Monroe County Bar Assn. (treas., trustee 1974-76), N.Y. State Bar Assn. (exec. com. tax sect. 1972-93, continuing legal edn. com. 1983—), Monroe County Bar Found. (pres. 1980-81), Oak Hill Country Club. Avocations: golf, tennis, wine tasting, collecting ancient Greek coins, traveling. Taxation, general, Estate planning, Pension, profit-sharing, and employee benefits. Home: 194 Dorchester Rd Rochester NY 14610-1327 Office: Harter Secrest & Emery 700 Midtown Tower Rochester NY 14604-2006

**COLE, BETTY LOU MCDONEL SHELTON (MRS. DEWEY G. COLE, JR.),** judge; b. Elwood, Ind., June 5, 1926; d. Bernard Miller and Vee Marie (Robertson) McDonel; m. Elbert Shelton, Dec. 13, 1944; children: Steven Elbert, Jeanette Louise; m. 2d, Dewey G. Cole, Jr., Dec. 24, 1975. Student, Ind. U., 1947-50, LLB, 1969; student, Ball State U., 1964-65. Bar: Ind. 1969, Fed. Cts., 1969; cert. sr. judge. Pvt. practice, Muncie, Ind., 1969—, Betty L. Shelton Law Office, 1970-78; sr. ptnr. firm Dunnuck, Cole, Rankin and Wyrick, Muncie, 1978-80; judge Delaware County Superior Ct., 1980-95, ret., 1995. Mem. ABA, Ind. Bar Assn., Muncie Bar Assn., Ind. Judges Assn., Am. Trial Lawyers, Ind. U. Law Alumni Assn., Nat. Assn. Women Judges, LWV (league pres. 1963-64), Riley-Jones Club, Columbia Club; recipient State of Ind. Sagamore of the Wabash award, 1998.

**COLE, CHARLES DEWEY, JR.,** lawyer; b. Lower Merion Twp., Pa., Aug. 12, 1952; s. Charles Dewey and Margaret Ann (Leach) C. AB, Columbia U., 1974; JD, St. John's U., Jamaica, N.Y., 1979; ML Info. Sci., U. Tex., 1982; LLM, NYU, 1988; LLM in Environ. Law, Pace U., 1993; LLM in Trial Advocacy, Temple U., 1999. Bar: N.Y. 1980, Tex. 1980, N.J. 1986, D.C. 1988, U.S. Dist. Ct. (we. and ea. dists.) Tex. 1980, U.S. Dist. Ct. (so. and ea. dists.) N.Y. 1980, U.S. Dist. Ct. (no. dist.) Tex. 1982, U.S. Dist. Ct. (no. dist.) N.Y. 1983, U.S. Dist. Ct. (we. dist.) N.Y. 1984, U.S. Dist. Ct. N.J. 1986, U.S. Dist. Ct. D.C. 1994, U.S. Ct. Internat. Trade 1980, U.S. Tax Ct. 1984, U.S. Ct. Appeals (5th and 11th cirs.) 1981, U.S. Ct. Appeals (Fed. cir.) 1982, U.S. Ct. Appeals (2d cir.) 1984, U.S. Ct. Appeals (D.C. cir.) 1987, U.S. Ct. Appeals (3d cir.) 1993, U.S. Supreme Ct. 1984; solicitor, Eng. and Wales, 1995. Law clk. to chief judge U.S. Dist. Ct. (ea. dist.), Beaumont, Tex., 1979-80, U.S. Ct. Appeals (5th cir.), Austin, Tex., 1981-82; assoc. Moore, Berson, Lifflander & Mewhinney, Garden City and N.Y.C., N.Y., 1982-85; assoc. and ptnr. Newman Schlau Fitch & Burns P.C., N.Y.C. and Mineola, N.Y., 1985-88; assoc. Meyer, Suozzi, English & Klein, P.C., Mineola and N.Y.C., 1988-95; of counsel Newman Fitch Altheim Myers, P.C., N.Y.C. and Newark, 1995—. Author: Law Books as a Charitable Contribution, 1975, The EPA Lender Liability Regulations: EPA's Questionable Authority to Promulgate the Regulations as Part of the National Contingency Plan, 1993; contbr. book revs. to profl. publs. Mem. The Law Soc., N.Y. State Bar Assn., N.J. State Bar Assn., D.C. Bar, N.Y. County Lawyers Assn. (com. on fed. cts.), Maritime Law Assn. U.S. (proctor), Bar Assn. 5th Fed. Cir., Am. Assn. Law Librs., Law Libr. Assn. Greater N.Y., Brit. and Irish Assn. Law Librs., Osgoode Soc., Am. Soc. for Legal History, Soc. Advanced Legal Studies, Supreme Ct. Hist. Soc., Selden Soc., Federalist Soc. for Law and Pub. Policy, Scribes (chair brief-writing competition com.), Clarity. Republican. Federal civil litigation, State civil litigation. Home: 16 94th St Apt 3B Brooklyn NY 11209-6643 Office: Newman Fitch Altheim Myers PC 14 Wall St New York NY 10005-2101

**COLE, CHARLES EDWARD,** lawyer, former state attorney general; b. Yakima, Wash., Oct. 10, 1927; married; 3 children. BA, Stanford U., 1950, LLB, 1953. Law clk. Territory of Alaska, Juneau, 1954, Territorial Atty. Gen.'s Office, Fairbanks, Alaska, 1955-56, U.S. Dist. Ct. Alaska, Fairbanks, 1955-56; city magistrate City of Fairbanks, 1957-58; pvt. practice law, 1957-90; atty. gen. State of Alaska, 1990-94; pvt. law comml. litigation, 1995—; profl. baseball player, Stockton, Calif. and Twin Falls, Idaho, summers of 1950, 51, 53. With U.S. Army, 1946-47. Mem. Calif. State Bar, Washington State Bar Assn., Alaska Bar Assn. Office: Law Dept State of AK Office of Atty Gen PO Box 110300 Juneau AK 99811-0300 also: Law Offices of Charles E Cole 406 Cushman St Fairbanks AK 99701-4632

**COLE, DANA KEITH,** lawyer; b. Dayton, Ohio, May 16, 1956. BA, U. Cin., 1980; JD magna cum laude, U. Dayton, 1986. Bar: Ohio 1986, U.S. Dist. Ct. (so. dist.) Ohio 1986. Assoc. Smith & Schacke, Dayton, 1986-89, Crew Buchanan & Lowe, Dayton, 1990—; staff atty. Artemis House, Dayton, 1987—; adj. prof. U. Dayton Sch. Law, 1990—; mem. faculty Gerry Spence's Trial Lawyers Coll., Jackson, Wyo., 1996. Mem. Mongomery Dem. Ctrl. Com., Mongomery Dem. Screening Com., Mongomery Dem. Exec. Com., 1994—. Recipient Am. Jurisprudence award Lawyers Coop. Pub. Co. and Bancroft-Whitney Co. Avocations: motorcycles, photography, sky diving. Personal injury, Criminal. Office: Crew Buchanan & Lowe 2580 Kettering Tower Dayton OH 45423-1005

**COLE, GEORGE STUART,** lawyer; b. Mpls., Sept. 22, 1955; s. John Peck and Carol Dubois (Thayer) C.; m. Elena Lyn Reese, Aug. 28, 1988. AB in Internat. Rels., Stanford U., 1978; JD, U. Mich., 1981; MS in Computer Sci., Stanford U., 1987. Bar: Calif. 1981, N.D. 1981, U.S. Patent Bar, 1997. Assoc. Cooper White & Cooper, San Francisco, 1981-82; pvt. practice Palo Alto, Calif., 1982-84; teaching fellow Stanford (Calif.) U., 1987; pvt. practice Menlo Park, Calif., 1987—; rsch. asst. Xerox PARC, Palo Alto, 1985-87. Contbr. articles to profl. jours. Unitarian-Universalist. Avocation: history. Patent, Computer, Intellectual property. Home and Office: 495 Seaport Ct Ste 101 Redwood City CA 94063-2785

**COLE, JAMES OTIS,** lawyer; b. Florence, Ala., Feb. 6, 1941; s. Calloway and Eula (Reynolds) C.; m. Ada Dolores Cole, Dec. 16, 1961; children: James Otis Jr., Lerone Barrington. BA, Talladega Coll., 1963; JD, Harvard U., 1971. Bar: Ill. 1971, U.S. Dist. Ct. (no. dist.) Ill. 1971, Calif. 1977, U.S. Supreme Ct. 1981. Assoc. Kirkland & Ellis, Chgo., 1971-73; div. counsel The Clorox Co., Oakland, Calif., 1973—; now sr. v.p., gen. counsel, sec. AutoNation, Inc., Ft. Lauderdale; arbitrator Contra Costa County Superior Ct., Martinez, Calif., 1980—. Counsel East Oakland Youth Devel. Ctr.; bd. dirs. Oakland Ballet, Bay Area Urban League, Oakland; bd. dirs. Black Filmmakers Hall of Fame, Oakland, pres. 1980-83. Mem. ABA, Nat. Bar Assn. (bd. govs. 1981—), Calif. Assn. Black Lawyers (pres.-elect 1986—), Charles Houston Bar Assn. (pres. 1985—), Calif. Bar Jud. Nominees Evaluation Commn. (commr. 1985—). Clubs: Oakland Athletic, Lakeview (Oakland). General corporate. Home: 10 Nurmi Dr Fort Lauderdale FL 33301-1403 Office: AutoNation Inc AutoNation Tower 110 SE 6th St Fort Lauderdale FL 33301*

**COLE, JAMES YEAGER,** legal services associate, sentencing advocate; b. Cleve., Sept. 20, 1957; s. Charles and Nancy C. JD, Blackstone Sch. Law, Dallas, 1980, Elysion Coll., 1980; MA, M.C.I., London, 1981; PhD, N.W. London U., 1981. CEO Cole Corp., Tallahassee, 1979-81; judge Inst. Advanced Law Study, Las Vegas, 1981-84; cons., sentencing advocate Cullowhee, N.C., 1984—. Recipient Presdl. medal of Merit Pres. Ronald Reagan, Washington, 1980; Knight Comdr. Royal Knights of Justice, London, 1981; Venerable Order of the Knights of Michael the Archangel Knight Chevalier, Disting. Leadership award ABA Jud. Divsn., 1997; lifetime dep. gov. Am. Biog. Rsch. Inst. Mem. Am. Judges Assn., World Judges Assn., Nat. Judges Assn., Internat. Bar Assn., Human Rights Inst., Island Found., Am. Fedn. of Police, Heirs, Inc., Nat. Sheriff's Assn., N.C. Sheriff's Assn., Haywood County C. of C., Maggic Valley C. of C., Internat. Platform Assn., So. Legal Found. Avocations: swimming, snow/water skiing, volleyball, tennis, cinema. Home and Office: PO Box 25 Chestnut Walk Waynesville NC 28786-0025

**COLE, JANICE MCKENZIE,** prosecutor; b. Feb. 16, 1947; m. James Carlton Cole. BA summa cum laude, John Jay Coll Criminal Justice, 1975, MPA, 1978; JD, Fordham U., 1979. Bar: N.Y. 1980, N.C. 1983. Asst. U.S. atty. Eastern Dist. N.Y., 1979-83; sole practitioner, 1983-89; with firm Cole & Cole, 1989-90; dist. ct. judge First Jud. Dist. N.C., 1990-94; U.S. atty. N.C. Eastern Dist., 1994—. Office: US Attys Office 310 New Bern Ave Rm 800 Raleigh NC 27601-1441

**COLE, JEANNIE BENNETT,** lawyer; b. Huntsville, Ala., June 23, 1963; d. George William and Linda (Strong) Bennett; m. Trevor Ian Cole, Apr. 18, 1992. BA, Birmingham-Southern Coll., 1984; JD, Cumberland Sch. Law, 1987. Bar: Ala. 1987, Tenn. 1988, U.S. Dist. Ct. Ala. 1989. Assoc. Watson, Gammon & Fees, Huntsville, 1987-90; asst. dist. atty. Madison County, Huntsville, 1990—. Mem. Jr. League. Republican. Presbyterian. Office: Madison County DA's Office 100 N Side Sq Huntsville AL 35801-4800

**COLE, JEFFREY,** lawyer; b. Chgo., Sept. 22, 1942; s. David S. and Perle J. C.; m. Jillian (div. May 1988); m. Jill, Nov. 1992. BS, U.Ill., 1965; JD, DePaul U., 1968. Assoc. Mayer, Brown & platt, Chgo., 1972-75; U.S. atty. Chgo., 1969-72; ptnr. Cole & States, Ltd., Chgo., 1975—; adj. prof. law Chgo.-Kent Coll. Law, 1975-87; lectr. John Marshall Coll. Law, 1974; spkr. in field. Contbr. articles to profl. jours. Capt. U.S. Army Res., 1969-75. Mem. ABA (assoc. editor litigation mag. 1988—). Avocation: reading. Federal civil litigation, State civil litigation, Criminal. Home: 680 N Lake Shore Dr Apt 1024 Chicago IL 60611-3076 Office: Cole & States 321 S Plymouth Ct Chicago IL 60604-3912

**COLE, JOHN PRINCE,** lawyer, university official; b. Carrollton, Ga., Mar. 18, 1963; m. Mary Stewart Donovan. AB, Harvard U., 1985; JD magna cum laude, Mercer Law Sch., 1991. Bar: Ga. 1991, U.S. Dist. Ct. (no., mid. dist.) Ga. 1991, U.S. Ct. Appeals (11th cir.) 1991. Law clerk Mitchell, Coppedge, Wester, Bisson & Miller, Dalton, Ga., 1989, Ga. Atty. Gen., Atlanta, 1990; assoc. Anderson, Walker & Reichert, Macon, Ga., 1991-94; gen. asst. to pres. Mercer U., Macon, Ga., 1994—. Trustee First Bapt. Ch., Macon, 1993-97, Ga. Children's Home, 1996—; funds allocation com. United Way Ctrl. Ga., 1992-94. Capt. Ga. Army NG. Mem. ABA, Nat. Assn. Coll. and Univ. Attys., Macon Bar Assn. (treas. 1997-98, sec. 1998-99, pres. elect 1999—), Phi Kappa Phi. Democrat. Avocations: hiking, music, golf. General civil litigation, General corporate, General practice. Office: Mercer U 1400 Coleman Ave Macon GA 31207-0003

**COLE, LEIGH POLK,** lawyer; b. Boston, Dec. 14, 1963; d. P. William and Nancy Cooley Polk; m. Christopher J. Cole, July 30, 1988; children: Robert P., Bradley W. Grad., Phillips Exeter (N.H.) Acad., 1981; BA, Cornell U., 1985; JD, Albany Law Sch. Union U., 1991. Bar: N.Y. 1992, U.S. Dist. Ct. (no. dist.) N.Y. 1992, Vt. 1994, U.S. Dist. Ct. Vt. 1994, U.S. Ct. Appeals (D.C. cir.) 1997. Legis. policy analyst N.Y. State Legis., Albany, N.Y., 1986-88; assoc. atty. O'Connell & Aronowitz, P.C., Albany, 1991-96, Gravel and Shea, P.C., Burlington, Vt., 1996—; solicitor atty. div. United Way, Burlington, 1998. Editor-in-Chief Albany Law Rev., 1990-91. Mem. South Hero (Vt.) Bd. Adjustment, 1996-98; co-founder, dir. South Hero Land Trust, 1997-98; mem. bylaws revision com. South Hero Congl. Ch., 1997—; mem. class 1998 Leadership Champlain, Burlington, 1997-98. Mem. ABA, Am. Immigration Lawyers Assn., Vt. Bar Assn., 525 Found. (dir., sec.). Avocations: horses, skiing, boating, golfing, backpacking. General corporate, Contracts commercial, Immigration, naturalization, and customs. Office: Gravel and Shea PO Box 369 Burlington VT 05402-0369

**COLE, PHILLIP ALLEN,** lawyer; b. Washington, D.C., Mar. 3, 1940; s. Gordon Harding and Dorothy Barbara (Jugel) C.; m. Mary Jo Ruff, July 2, 1994; children: Jennifer Leigh, Christopher Harding, Catherine Anne. BA, U. Maryland, 1961; JD, Georgetown U., 1964. Bar: Md. 1964, Minn. 1968, U.S. Supreme Ct. 1967, U.S. Ct. Appeals (8th cir.) 1968, U.S. Dist. Ct. Minn. 1965, U.S. Ct. Military Appeals 1965; cert. civil trial specialist. Assoc. Beatty & McNamee, Hyattville, Md., 1968; founder, sr. mem. Lommen, Nelson, Cole & Stageberg, Mpls., 1969—; special counsel Md. House of Dels., 1968. Contbr. articles to profl. jours. Capt. USMC, 1965-67. Mem. Minn. Def. Lawyers, Am. Bd. Profl. Liability Attys., Internat. Assn. Def. Counsel. Avocations: golf, reading. General civil litigation, Securities, Professional liability. Office: Lommen Nelson Cole & Stageberg 1800 IDS Ctr Minneapolis MN 55402

**COLE, RANSEY GUY, JR.,** judge; b. Birmingham, Ala., May 23, 1951; s. Ransey Guy and Sarah Nell (Coker) C.; m. Kathleine Kelley, Nov. 26, 1983; children: Justin Robert Jefferson, Jordan Paul, Alexandra Sarah. BA, Tufts U., 1972; JD, Yale U., 1975. Bar: Ohio 1975, D.C. 1982. Assoc. Vorys, Sater, Seymour and Pease, Columbus, Ohio, 1975-78, ptnr., 1980-87, 93—; trial atty. U.S. Dept. Justice, Washington, 1978-80; judge U.S. Bankruptcy Ct., Columbus, 1987-93; circuit judge U.S. Ct. Appeals (6th cir.) Ohio, Cinn., 1996—. Mem. ABA, Nat. Bar Assn., Columbus Bar Assn. Office: US Courthouse 85 Marconi Blvd Columbus OH 43215-2823

**COLE, ROBERT THEODORE,** lawyer; b. Bklyn., Mar. 16, 1932; s. Harold I. and Bella (Weisman) C.; m. C. Margaret Hall, Oct. 25, 1959; children: Elizabeth, Tanya, Judith Amy. BS, U. Pa., 1953; LLB magna cum laude, Harvard U., 1956; diploma in law, London Sch. Econs., 1958. Bar: N.Y. 1956, D.C. 1972. Assoc. Law Office Frank Boas, Brussels, 1960-62, Nixon Mudge Rose et al, N.Y.C., 1962-67; atty. U.S. Treasury Dept., Washington, 1967-73, internat. tax counsel, 1971-73; ptnr. Cole Corette & Abrutyn, Washington, 1973-96, Alston & Bird LLP, Washington, 1997—; lectr. on internat. tax. Contbr. articles on internat. taxes to legal jours. Capt. USAF, 1957-59. Recipient exceptional svc. award U.S. Treasury Dept., 1973. Fellow Am. Coll. Tax Counsel; mem. N.Y. State Bar Assn., Assn. Bar City N.Y., Nat. Fgn. Trade Coun. (vice-chair tax com. 1989-95), Harvard Club (N.Y.C.). Avocations: hiking, theatre. Corporate taxation, Private international, Public international. Home: 4000 Chancery Ct NW Washington DC 20007-2140 Office: Alston & Bird LLP 601 Pennsylvania Ave NW Washington DC 20004-2601

**COLE, ROLAND JAY,** lawyer; b. Seattle, Dec. 15, 1948; s. Robert J. and Josephine F. C.; m. Elsa Kircher, Aug. 16, 1975; children: Isabel Ashley, Madeline Aldis. AB in Econs. magna cum laude, Harvard U., 1970, M in Pub. Policy, 1972, PhD in Pub. Policy, JD, 1975. Bar: Wash. 1975, U.S. Supreme Ct. 1980, U.S. Dist. Ct. (we. dist.) Wash. 1984, Mich. 1989. Rsch. scientist Battelle Human Affairs Rsch. Ctrs., Seattle, 1975-83; assoc. Appel and Glueck, P.C., Seattle, 1984-89; gen. counsel Indsl. Tech. Inst., Ann Arbor, Mich., 1990-94; founder, exec. dir. Software Patent Inst., Overland Park, Kans., 1994—; of counsel Shughart Thomson & Kilroy PC, Overland Park, 1997—; founder, dir. MIS; bd. dirs. Cobro Pub., Inc., Lynnwood, Wash., 1984-90. Co-author: Government Requirements of Small Business, 1980, The Containment of Organized Crime, 1984; co-programmer Quadrant I software program, 1983. HUD fellow, 1970-71. Mem. Assn. Personal Computer User Groups (dir., founding pres. 1986), Wash. Athletic Club. Congregationalist. Avocations: squash, racquetball, volleyball, music. Computer, Non-profit and tax-exempt organizations, Trademark and copyright. Office: 9225 Indian Creek Pkwy Ste 1100 Overland Park KS 66210-2029

**COLE, RONALD CLARK,** lawyer; b. Balt., June 6, 1951; s. Alfred Joseph and Roselda (Katz) C.; m. Sharon Love, June 8, 1974; children: Ryan Scott, Heather Love. BA, Am. U., Washington, 1972; JD, U. Balt., 1975. Bar: Md. 1976. Law clk., atty. Pub. Defender's Office, Glen Burnie, Md., 1976-97; ptnr., founder Scherr Cole & Murphy, Glen Burnie, 1976—; instr. divorce course Anne Arundel C.C., Arnold, Md., 1982-87; panelist weekly radio show Sta-WCBM, Balt., 1997—. Mgr. Little League baseball team, Pikesville (Md.) Recreation, 1984-86, head coach basketball team, 1985-87. Mem. U.S. Tennis Assn. (vol. 1996), Booster Club (vol. 1997). Personal injury, Family and matrimonial, Criminal. Home: 1 Woodholme Village Ct Pikesville MD 21208-1409 Office: Scherr Cole & Murphy 791 Aquahart Rd Ste 120 Glen Burnie MD 21061-3981

**COLEMAN, BRYAN DOUGLAS,** lawyer, educator, arbitrator, mediator; b. Texarkana, Tex., Aug. 16, 1948; s. William Bryan and Nona Armeda (Crawford) C.; children: Douglas Patrick, Sarah Elizabeth. AS, Texarkana Coll., 1968; BSBA, Stephen F. Austin U., 1970; postgrad. Rice U., 1971-73; JD, South Tex. Coll. Law, 1973; grad. JAG Sch., U.S. Army, 1978, Atty. Mediators Inst., 1991, Am. Arbitration Assn. Mediation Sch., 1991, A.A. White Dispute Resolution Ctr., 1992, SMU Mediation Sch., 1992. Am. Acad. Atty. Mediators, 1993. Bar: Tex. 1973, U.S. Dist. Ct. (ea., no., so. and we. dists.) Tex. 1974, U.S. Tax Ct., 1987, U.S. Ct. Appeals (11th cir.) 1982, U.S. Ct. Appeals (5th cir.) 1975, U.S. Supreme Ct., 1992; cert. Fellow Life Mgmt. Inst. Quality control insp. Lone Star Ammunition Plant, Texarkana, 1966-68; law clk. Fulbright & Jaworski, Houston, 1970-71, Boswell, O'Toole, Davis & Pickering, Houston, 1971-72, Helm, Pletcher & Hogan, Houston, 1972-73; assoc. Law Office Gus Zgourides, Houston, 1973-76, Ray & Coleman, P.C., Houston, 1976-97; gen. counsel Great Southwest Life Ins. Co., 1982-90, United Internat. Life Ins. Co., 1987-90; pres., dir. Conflict Analysis and Resolution, Inc., 1997—; v.p., bd. dirs. Med. Assurance Group, Houston; of counsel Alliance Tex. Life and Health Agts.; instr. U. Houston, 1979-81; v.p. U.S.A. Svc. Corp.; reg. head Neutral Resolute Sys., Inc., 1997—, Jud. Arbitration and Mediation Svc. Endispute, Inc., 1996-97. Served to comdr. Army ROTC, 1972-73, to 1st lt. U.S. Army, 1973-79. Recipient E.E. Townes award, Am. Jurisprudence award South Tex. Coll. Law, 1973. Fellow Houston Bar Found. (life), Assn. Atty.-Mediators, Tex. Bar Found.; mem. ABA, State Bar Tex. (founder law student div. 1973, chmn. grievance com. 1979-81), Am. Arbitration Assn. (panel of arbitrators 1991, meditation instr. 1992), Am. Judicature Soc., Am. Legion, Am. Soc. Law and Medicine, Tex. Assn. Mediators, Houston Trial Lawyers Assn., Soc. Profls. in Dispute Resolution, Rep. Lawyers of Tex. (pres. elect), Rep. Nat. Lawyers Assn., Rep. Presdl. Task Force, Hearthstone Country Club, Alpha Kappa Psi (sec. 1969-70), Alpha Phi Omega (pledge trainer 1970), Delta Theta Phi. State civil litigation, Insurance, Personal injury. Home: 18223 Harrow Hill Dr Houston TX 77084-3228 Office: Conflict Analysis & Resolution Inc 550 Westcott St Ste 300 Houston TX 77007-5043

**COLEMAN, GEORGE JOSEPH, III (JAY COLEMAN),** lawyer; b. Plainfield, N.J., Aug. 25, 1958; s. George Joseph and Alice Burke (McHugh) C. BA in Philosophy, U. Notre Dame, 1980, JD, 1983. Bar: Conn. 1984, Ariz. 1984, U.S. Dist. Ct. Ariz. 1984, U.S. Ct. Appeals (9th cir.) 1985, N.Y. 1993. Law clk. Hon. William E. Eubank, Ariz. Ct. Appeals, Phoenix, 1983-84; assoc. Snell & Wilmer, Phoenix, 1984-90, ptnr., 1991—. Mem. Men's Arts Coun. of Phoenix Art Mus., 1991—. Mem. ABA (sect. of litigation). Democrat. Roman Catholic. Federal civil litigation, State civil litigation, Professional liability. Home: 111 E Alvarado Rd Phoenix AZ 85004-1413 Office: Snell & Wilmer One Arizona Ctr Phoenix AZ 85004

**COLEMAN, GREGORY FREDERIC,** lawyer; b. Ellijay, Ga., Nov. 23, 1963; s. Billy Burch Coleman and Mary Beth (Welch) Mothershed; m. Stephanie Marsengill, June 14, 1986; children: Danielle, Morgan. BA, Jacksonville State U., 1986; JD, U. Tenn., 1989. Bar: Tenn. 1990, U.S. Dist. Ct. Tenn. 1990, U.S. Ct. Appeals (6th cir.) 1993. Cert. civil trial splst., rule 31 mediator Tenn. Commn. on Legal Edn. and Specialization. Assoc. Jenkins & Jenkins, Knoxville, Tenn., 1989-95; mng. ptnr. Dunn, MacDonald & Coleman P.C., Knoxville, 1995—. Bd. dirs. Bapt. Hosp. of East Tenn., Knoxville, 1992—. Mem. Gideons Internat., Nat. Order of Barristers, Nat. Bd. Trial Advocacy. Republican. Baptist. Avocations: golf, reading, church music. General civil litigation, Insurance. Office: Dunn MacDonald & Coleman PC 1221 1st Tenn Plz Knoxville TN 37929

**COLEMAN, JAMES H., JR.,** state supreme court justice; b. Lawrenceville, N.J., May 4, 1933; s. James H. Sr. and Neda (Rivers) C.; m. Sophia Coleman, May 12, 1962; 2 children. BA cum laude, Va. State U., 1956; JD, Howard U., 1959. Bar: N.J. 1960, U.S. Dist. Ct. N.J. 1960, U.S. Supreme Ct. 1963. Asst. and/or cons. various N.J. commns. and divs., 1960-64; pvt. practice law Elizabeth and Roselle, N.J., 1960-70; judge N.J. Workers' Compensation Ct., 1964-73, Union County Ct., 1973-78, Law div. N.J. Superior Ct., 1978-81; mem. spl. three-judge resentencing panel N.J. Superior Ct., 1979-81; judge Appellate div. N.J. Superior Ct., 1981-87, presiding judge, 1987-94; assoc. justice Supreme Ct. of N.J., Springfield, 1994—; Mem. various Supreme Ct. coms.; lectr. in field. Chmn. Elizabeth Good Neighbor Coun.; mem. Elizabeth Adv. Bd. on Urban Renewal; incorporator, bd. dirs. Union County Legal Svcs., Elizabeth Anti-Poverty Program; v.p., bd. dirs., counsel to Urban League of Union County; counsel to Elizabeth NAACP; v.p. Scotch Plains-Fanwood Human Rights Coun.; Mem. N.J. Com. on Hiring the Handicapped; mem. Union County Coordinating and Adv. Com. on Higher Edn.;mem. Essex County Coll. Equal Edn. Opportunity Fund Bd., others. Fellow ABA; mem. Nat. Bar Assn. (judicial coun.), N.J. Bar Assn., Union County Bar Assn., Am. Law Inst., Am. Judicature Soc., Garden State Bar Assn., Omega Psi Phi. Baptist. Avocations: tennis, gardening. Office: Supreme Ct of NJ 99 Mount Bethel Rd Warren NJ 07059-5126

**COLEMAN, JAMES JULIAN, JR.,** lawyer, industrialist, real estate executive; b. New Orleans, May 7, 1941; s. James Julian Sr. and Dorothy Louise (Jurisich) C.; m. Carol Campbell Owen, Dec. 19, 1970 (dec. Sept. 1979); 1 child, James Owen; m. Mary Olivia Cochrane Cushing, Oct. 12, 1985. BA, Princeton U., 1963; postgrad. in law, Oxford (Eng.) U., 1963-65; JD, Tulane U., 1968. Bar: La. 1969, U.S. Supreme Ct. 1969. Chmn. Internat.-Matex Tank Terminals, New Orleans, 1969—; pres. Coleman Devel. Co., New Orleans, 1969—, IMTT, Quebec, 1993—, Nfld. Transhipment Terminal Inc.; ptnr. Coleman, Johnson & Artigues, New Orleans, 1972—; chmn. DownTown Parking Service, New Orleans, 1978—; pres. City Ctr. Properties, New Orleans, 1980—; chmn. East Jersey R.R. and Terminal Co., 1993; trustee Loving Found., New Orleans, R.L. Blaffer Found., Houston; dir. U.S. Coast Guard Found. Author: Gilbert Antoine de St. Maxent: The Spanish Frenchman of New Orleans, 1975. Mem. Princeton U. History Coun., 1982—; mem. N.J. Commn. on Sci. and Tech., 1992—; bd. dirs. N.J. Mfg. Extension Program, 1998—. Named H.M. Hon. Brit. Consul for La., Brit. Consulate, New Orleans, 1975—, to Order of Brit. Empire, Queen Elizabeth II, London, 1986. Mem. ABA, La. Bar Assn., N.Y. Yacht Club, N.Y. Racquet Club, Newport Reading Room, So. Yacht Club, New Orleans Lawn Tennis Club, USN League (bd. dirs. New Orleans). Republican. Mem. Ch. of Christ Scientists. General corporate, Environmental, Real property. Office: Coleman Johnson & Artigues 321 St Charles Ave 10th Fl New Orleans LA 70130-3145

**COLEMAN, JEFFREY PETERS,** lawyer; b. Providence, Nov. 21, 1959; s. Gerard Giles and Molly Claire (Armbrecht) C.; m. Vonnie Lynn Hendrickson, July 11, 1981; children: Chelsea Adelle, Rebecca Rose, Martin Daniel, Angelyn Marie. BA in Psychology, Davidson (N.C.) Coll., 1981; postgrad., Exeter (Eng.) U., 1984; JD, Coll. of William and Mary, 1985. Bar: Fla. 1985, U.S. Dist. Ct. (mid. dist.) Fla. 1986. Assoc. Harris, Barrett, Mann & Dew, St. Petersburg, Fla., 1985-86; ptnr. Bonner, Hogan & Coleman, P.A., Clearwater, Fla., 1986-97; pres. Coleman Law Firm, 1997—. Counsel Pineallas County (Fla.) Habitat for Humanity, 1989, Boy Scouts Am. Pinellas County. Mem. Fla. Bar Assn., Clearwater Bar Assn. (pres. young lawyers div., coord. pub. rels. com. 1989-90), Publ. Investors Arbitration Bar Assn. Republican. Episcopalian. Avocations: scuba diving, golf, camping, boating. E-mail: Colmnlaw@ix.netcom.com. Fax: (727) 461-7476. General civil litigation, Contracts commercial, Real property. Office: Coleman Law Firm 619 Cleveland St Clearwater FL 33755-4104

**COLEMAN, JEROME P.,** lawyer; b. Washington, July 3, 1948; s. Francis Thomas and Helen Theresa (Hile) C. AB, Princeton U., 1970; JD, Georgetown U., 1973. Bar: D.C. 1973, N.Y. 1976, U.S. Dist. Ct. (so. and ea. dists.) N.Y. 1976, U.S. Ct. Appeals (2d cir.) 1976, U.S. Ct. Appeals (3d cir.) 1978, U.S. Supreme Ct. 1988. Atty., advisor Nat. Labor Rels. Bd., Washington, 1973-74; assoc. Townley & Updike, N.Y.C., 1974-81, ptnr., 1982-95; ptnr. Nixon, Hargrave, Devans & Doyle, N.Y.C., 1995—. Steering com. Inner-City Schs. Laywers Com., N.Y.C., 1993—; mem. exec. com. Princeton Class of 1970, 1991-95, chmn. bd. govs., 1995—. Mem. ABA, Federal Bar Assn. (chair labor law com. 1978-82), N.Y. State Bar Assn.(chmn. labor arbitration com. 1983-86), Univ. Club (governing coun. 1991-95, sec. 1996, chmn. nominating com. 1996). Federal civil litigation, Labor. Home: 124 E 84th St Apt 8B New York NY 10028-0917 Office: Nixon Hargrave Devans & Doyle 437 Madison Ave New York NY 10022-7001

**COLEMAN, JOHN EDWARD,** lawyer; b. Dayton, Ohio, May 28, 1907; s. George Leidigh and Verrell (Chaffin) C.; m. Jean MacMicken, May 16, 1931 (dec. 1985); children: George L., Chase Coleman Davies; m. Julia Gilliam, 1995. BA with honors in Econs., Cornell U., 1929; JD, 1932. Bar: Ohio 1932. Sole practice Dayton, 1932-86. Bd. dirs. Ohio chpt. Nature Conservatory, 1959—, pres. 1060; bd. dirs., treas., chmn. Boonshoft Mus. Discovery, 1959—. Col. U.S. Army. Mem. ABA, Ohio Bar Assn., Dayton Bar Assn., Res. Officers Assn. U.S. (nat. pres. 1951-52), Army and Navy (DC), Dayton Racquet, Engrs. of Dayton, Masons (master 1955, trustee 1962-83).

**COLEMAN, JOHN JAMES, III,** lawyer, educator; b. Birmingham, Ala., Apr. 10, 1956; s. John James Jr. and Yonceil Oden (Foster) C.; m. Lizabeth Gaines, Aug. 24, 1985; 1 child, John J. IV. AB in History and Econs. magna cum laude, Duke U., 1978, JD, 1981. Bar: Ala., U.S. Dist. Ct. (no. and mid. dists.) Ala., U.S. Ct. Appeals (4th and 11th cirs.), U.S. Supreme Ct. Law clerk Judge Donald Russell, U.S. Ct. Appeals 4th cir., Richmond, Va., 1981-82; assoc. Balch & Bingham, Birmingham, 1982-88, ptnr., 1989—; adj. instr. Cumberland Sch. Law, Birmingham, 1990—, Birmingham Sch. Law, 1994—; v.p. Indsl. Rels. Rsch. Assn., Birmingham, 1990-91; bd. dirs. Indsl. Health Coun. of Ala., Inc., Birmingham, 1991-96. Author: Disability Discrimination in Employment, Employment Discrimination in Alabama, Supplement to Employment Discrimination in Alabama; co-author: (guide publ.) Workers Compensation Practice, 1994; contbr. articles to profl. jours. Ballot security atty. Rep. Party, Ala., 1988, 92, 94; co-chmn. Kidschance Scholarship, Birmingham, 1992. Mem. ABA (labor and employment law sect. OSHA com.), Am. Arbitration Assn. (mem. panel arbitrators), Ala. State Bar (exec. com. labor and employment sect. treas. 1995-96, com. chmn. workers compensation law sect. 1991-93, vice chmn. 1996-97), Shades Mountain Sunrise Rotary Club (treas. 1994-96), Redstone Club. Republican. Roman Catholic. Avocations: tennis, cycling, riding, writing. Labor, Civil rights, Workers' compensation. Home: 10 Peachtree St Birmingham AL 35213-3018 Office: Balch & Bingham 1710 6th Ave N Birmingham AL 35203-2015

**COLEMAN, JOHN MICHAEL,** lawyer, consumer products executive; b. Boston, Dec. 28, 1949; s. John Royston Coleman and Mary Norrington Irwin; m. Susan Lee Lavine, Oct. 29, 1978; children: William L., Anne H. L. BA, Haverford (Pa.) Coll., 1975; JD, U. Chgo., 1978. Bar: N.Y. 1978, Pa. 1979, U.S. Ct. Appeals (3rd and 4th cirs.) 1979, U.S. Dist. Ct. (ea. dist.) Pa. 1979, U.S. Dist. Ct. (so. dist.) N.Y. 1981, U.S. Supreme Ct., 1982, N.J. 1988. Law clk. to judge U.S. Ct. Appeals, Richmond, Va., 1978-79; law clk. to chief justice Warren Burger U.S. Supreme Ct., Washington, 1980-81; assoc. Dechert Price & Rhoads, Phila., 1981-86, ptnr., 1986-89; v.p., gen. counsel Campbell Soup Co., Camden, N.J., 1989-90, sr. v.p. law and pub. affairs, 1990-97; sr. v.p., gen. counsel The Gillette Co., Boston, 1998-99; adj. prof. law U. Pa., Phila., 1985-88; bd. dirs. CDI Corp. Contbr. articles to profl. jours. Chmn. bd. trustees Campbell Soup Found., 1990-97; trustee N.J. State Aquarium, 1991-94, Food and Drug Law Inst., 1991-98, Inst. for Law and Econs., 1993-97, Am. Judicature Soc., 1995—; mem. vis. com. U. Chgo. Law Sch., 1993-95; mem. corp. Haverford Coll., 1994—. Mem. Am. Law Inst., Order of the Coif, Phi Beta Kappa. Mem. Religious Soc. of Friends. General corporate.

**COLEMAN, LESTER L.,** corporate lawyer. Gen. counsel, exec. v.p. Halliburton Co., Dallas. Office: Halliburton Co 3600 Lincoln Plz 500 N Akard St Ste 3600 Dallas TX 75201-3391

**COLEMAN, LOUIS KRESS,** prosecutor; b. Balt., Mar. 8, 1947; s. Edward Lee and Bernice Edith (Kress) C.; m. Laura Lee Vulgaris, May 14, 1980; 1 child, John M. K. BA, Washington & Lee, 1969; JD, U. Md., 1973; LLM in Taxation, U. Balt., 1996. Bar: U.S. Ct. Appeals Md. 1973, U.S. Dist. Ct. Md. 1974. Assoc. Lichter, Coleman, Pezzula & Rogers, Balt., 1973-75; asst. state's atty. Baltimore City, 1975—. Bd. dirs. Beth Am Synagogue, Balt., 1993-95; pres. parents assn. Norbel Sch., Balt., 1992-94; hon. mem. N.W. Citizens Patrol, Balt., 1992. Home: 2508 Guilford Ave Baltimore MD 21218-4618 Office: Office of State's Atty 110 N Calvert St Baltimore MD 21202-1745

**COLEMAN, MALINA,** law educator; b. Akron, Ohio, Sept. 23, 1954; d. Dorlan Oliver and Virginia (Dove) C. BS, Cen. State, 1980; JD, Yale U., 1985. Bar: Pa. 1987. Asst. prof. Sch. Law U. Akron, 1989-96, assoc. dean, assoc. prof. of law, 1996—. Bd. dirs. Planned Parenthood, Summit County, Ohio, 1992-94, Western Reserve Girl Scouts, Akron, 1991-94. Mem. ABA, Akron Barristers' Assn., Nat. Bar Assn. Office: U Akron Sch Law Akron OH 44325-0001

**COLEMAN, REXFORD LEE,** lawyer, educator; b. Hollywood, Calif., June 2, 1930; s. Henry Eugene and Antoinette Christine (Dobry) C.; m. Aiko Takahashi, Aug. 28, 1953 (dec.); children: Christine Eugenie, Douglass Craig; m. Sucha Park, June 15, 1978. Student, Claremont McKenna Coll., 1947-49; A.B., Stanford U., 1951, J.D., 1955; M. in Jurisprudence, Tokyo U., 1960. Bar: Calif. 1955, Mass. 1969. Mem. faculty Harvard U., 1959-69; mem. firm Baker & McKenzie, 1969-83, income ptnr., 1971-73, capital ptnr., 1973-83, mng. ptnr. Tokyo office, 1971-78; sr. ptnr. The Pacific Law Group, L.A., 1983—; adj. prof. McGeorge Sch. Law, U. Pacific, 1989—; lectr. Gray's Inn, The Inns of Ct. Sch. Law, London, 1989; cons. U.S. Treasury Dept., 1961-70; counselor Japanese-Am. Soc. for Legal Studies, 1964—; guest lectr. Ford Seminar on Comparative History, MIT, 1968; lectr. Legal Tng. and Research Inst., Supreme Ct., Japan, 1970-73; guest lectr. Colloguium Scholars, Calif. Luth. U., 1989; chmn. fgn. bus. customs consultative com. Bur. Customs, Ministry of Fin., Govt. of Japan, 1971-72; chmn. fgn. bus. consulatative commn. Japanese Ministry of Internat. Trade and Industry, 1973-76; mem. U.S. Del., U.S.-Japan Income Tax Treaty Negotiations, 1961, internat. bd. advisors, McGeorge Sch. Law, U. Pacific, 1989—. Author: Am. Index to Japanese Law, 1961, Standard Citation of Japanese Legal Materials, 1963, The Legal Aspects Under Japanese Law of an Accident Involving a Nuclear Installation in Japan, 1963, An Index to Japanese Law, 1975; editor: Taxation in Japan, World Tax Series, 1959-70; founding chmn. bd. editors: Law in Japan: An Ann., 1964-67; mem. bd. editors Stanford Law Rev., 1954-55, Japan Ann. Internat. Law, 1970-92; mem. Internat. Adv. Bd., The Transnational Lawyer, 1988—; contbr. articles to profl. jours. Participant in Japanese-Am. Program for Cooperation in Legal Studies, 1956-60; co-chmn. Conf. on Internat. Legal Protection Computer Software, Stanford Law Sch., 1986, Tokyo, Japan, 1987. Served to 1st lt., Inf. AUS, 1951-53; lt. col. Ret. Ford Found. grantee, 1956-60. Mem. ABA,

State Bar Calif., Mass. Bar Assn., Japanese-Am. Soc. for Legal Studies, Internat. Fiscal Assn. Japan, Res. Officers Assn. (v.p. army dept. Far East 1974-75), Ret. Officers Assn., Internat. House Japan (Tokyo), Stanford U. Alumni Assn., Gakushi Kai (grads. of former Japanese Imperial Univs. Assn.), Internat. Law Assn. Japan, Japan-Western Assn., Pacific Basin Econ. Council, (U.S. exec. com. 1985-87), Nihon Shihō Gakkai, Nihon Kokusai Hō Gakkai, Nihon Kokusai Shihō Gakkai, Sozei Hō Gakkai, Phi Alpha Delta. Episcopalian (vestryman 1966-69, del. Conv. Episcopal Diocese Mass. 1968, Conv. Episcopal Diocese L.A., 1989-91, Bishop's com. 1983-87, 91-93). Clubs: Tokyo Am; Harvard (N.Y.C.), North Ranch Country. Corporate taxation, Private international. Home: 32314 Blue Rock Rdg Westlake Vlg CA 91361-3912 Office: The Pacific Law Group 12121 Wilshire Blvd Ste 205 Los Angeles CA 90025-1164

**COLEMAN, RICHARD MICHAEL,** lawyer; b. Bklyn., Sept. 16, 1935; s. Frank T. and Eileen (Cafferty) C.; m. Bonnie S. Mathews, May 30, 1980; 1 child, Matthew Stephen. A.B. summa cum laude, Georgetown U., 1957; J.D. Harvard U., 1960; LLM, Georgetown U., 1961; postgrad., U. So. Calif., 1968-70; postgrad. Pepperdine U., 1996—. Bar: D.C. 1960, Calif. 1967, U.S. Supreme Ct. 1964; U.S. Ct. Appeals (dist. Columbia, 1960) (9th cir., 1973, 3rd Cir. 1990). Asst. U.S. atty., spl. atty. in organized crime racketeering sect. Dept. Justice, Washington, 1961-64; chief organized crime sect. U.S. Atty.'s Office, Washington, 1964-66, chief spl. fed. prosecutor So. and Cen. Divs. Calif., 1966-67; assoc. McKenna & Fitting, Los Angeles, 1967-68, ptnr., 1969-70; ptnr. Coleman & Richards and predecessor, Los Angeles, 1971—; officer JASOP L.A. Superior Ct. 1995—; host Law Forum, Sta. KSCI-TV, 1982-83, Sta. KWHY, 1985-86; lectr. Loyola U., Los Angeles, 1971-74, 76, 79-85; spkr. mediation workshop Pepperdine U. Strauss Inst. Dispute Resolution, 1997, UCLA Extension, 1998; bd. advisors Coll. Arts & Scis. Georgetown U., 1990-93; bd. vis. Pepperdine U. Sch. Law, 1995—; adv. group Ctr. Dist. Calif. Civil Justice Reform Act, 1990-94. Charter mem. Fraternity of Friends of the Music Ctr.; nat. co-chmn. Lawyers for Reagan/Bush, 1984. E. Prettyman Trial Advocacy fellow Georgetown U., 1960-61; recipient Daniel O'Connell award Irish Am. Bar Assn., 1997, John Corroll award Georgetown U., 1983. Fellow Am. Bar Found., Am. Coll. Trial Lawyers, 1992; mem. ABA (pres. nat. caucus of met. bar leaders 1982-83, exec. council 1981, exec. coun. nat. conf. bar pres. 1985-88), Calif. Bar Assn. (commn. jud. nominees evaluation 1986-89), Los Angeles County Bar Assn. (pres. 1981-82, trustee 1978-80, cert. Dispute Resolution 1997), Century City Bar Assn. (pres. 1977-78, bd. govs. 1973-86, Outstanding Achievement award 1975, 77, 79, outstanding svc. award 1989), Los Angeles Trial Lawyers Assn. (pres.' award 1981, 82), Assn. Bus. Trial Lawyers (bd. govs. 1976-78), Century City C. of C. (bd. dirs. 1977-89, sec. 1978-79, v.p. 1979-80), Georgetown U. Alumni Assn. (past pres., So. Calif. dir., nat. bd. govs., recip. John Carroll award 1983), So. Calif. Mediation Assn. Alternative dispute resolution, General civil litigation, Appellate. Office: 1801 Avenue Of The Stars Los Angeles CA 90067-5801

**COLEMAN, RICHARD WILLIAM,** lawyer; b. Brookline, Mass., Dec. 9, 1935; s. Michael John and Mary Ellen (Motherway) C.; m. Mary M. Kilcommins, June 3, 1961; children: Lauren, Christopher. BS, Boston Coll., Newton, Mass., 1957; JD, Boston Coll., Brighton, Mass., 1960. Bar: Mass. 1960, U.S. Dist. Ct. Mass. 1961, U.S. Ct. Appeals (1st cir.) 1981. Field atty. NLRB, Newark, 1960-61; assoc. Segal & Flamm, Boston, 1961-69; labor rels. advisor Scott Paper Co., Phila., 1969-70; labor rels. mgr. Harvard U., Cambridge, Mass., 1970-72; ptnr. Segal, Roitman & Coleman, Boston, 1972-93; pres. Richard W. Coleman, P.C., Needham, 1994—. Contbg. editor Development of Law Under National Labor Relations Act, 1988. Recipient Cushing award Cath. Labor Guild Boston, 1976. Mem. ABA, Am. Prepaid Legal Svcs. Inst. (bd. dirs. 1997—), Indsl. Rels. Rsch. Assn., Mass. Bar Assn., Boston Bar Assn., AFL-CIO Lawyers Coord. Com. Democrat. Roman Catholic. Avocations: golf, reading, choir singing. Labor, Pension, profit-sharing, and employee benefits. Office: 214 Garden St Needham MA 02492-2330

**COLEMAN, ROBERT J.,** lawyer; b. Phila., Dec. 24, 1936; s. Francis Eugene and Mary Veronica (McCullough) C.; m. Mary Patricia Coleman, June 26, 1955; children: Debra, Robert P., Linda, Martin S. AB, Villanova U., 1959; JD, Temple U., 1964. Bar: Pa., U.S. Dist. Ct. (ea. dist.) Pa., U.S. Ct. Appeals (3d cir.), U.S. Supreme Ct. With First Pa. Bank, Phila., 1955-57; underwriter Employer's Mut. Co., Phila., 1957-59; claim adjuster Safeco Ins. Co., Phila., 1959-62; claim supr. Gen. Accident Ins., Phila., 1962-64; assoc. Rappaport & Lagakos, Phila., 1964; trial atty. Allstate Ins. Co., Phila., 1964-67; chmn., CEO Marshall, Dennehey, Warner, Coleman & Goggin, Phila., 1967—; bd. dirs. Jeff Banks Inc., Phila., ; hearing com. chmn. Pa. Disciplinary Bd., Phila., 1986-94. Assoc. editor Phila. County Reporter, 1984-96; contbr. articles to legal publs. Bd. dirs. Ins. Soc. Phila.; dir. HERO Scholarship Fund Delaware County; bd. visitors Temple U. Law Sch.; mem. State Bd. Law Examiners. With USAR, 1954-62. Mem. ABA, Pa. Bar Assn., Phila. Bar Assn., Phila. Bar Found. (trustee), Pa. Def. Inst., Internat. Assn. Def. Lawyers, Def. Rsch. Inst. Republican. Roman Catholic. Avocations: tennis, boating, travel. Personal injury, Product liability. Home: 908 Penn Valley Rd Media PA 19063-1652 Office: Marshall Dennehey Warner Coleman & Goggin 1845 Walnut St Philadelphia PA 19103-4708

**COLEMAN, ROBERT LEE,** retired lawyer; b. Kansas City, June 14, 1929; s. William Houston and Edna Fay (Smith) C. BMus in Edn., Drake U., 1951; LLB, U. Mo., 1959. Bar: Mo. 1959, Fla. 1973. Law clk. to judge U.S. Dist. Ct. (we. dist.) Mo., Kansas City, 1959-60; assoc. Watson, Ess, Marshall & Enggas, Kansas City, 1960-66; asst. gen. counsel Gas Svc. Co., Kansas City, 1966-74; v.p., corp. counsel H & R Block, Inc., Kansas City, 1974-94; retired, 1994. With U.S. Army, 1955-57. Mem. ABA. General corporate.

**COLEMAN, ROBERT WINSTON,** lawyer; b. Oklahoma City, Mar. 1, 1942; s. Clint Sheridan and Genevieve (Ross) C.; m. Judith Moore, Sept. 7, 1963; children: Robert Winston, Jr., Claire Elizabeth. BA, Abilene Christian Coll., 1964; JD with hons., U. Tex., 1968. Bar: Tex. 1968, Ga. 1970. Law clk. to presiding justice U.S. Ct. Appeals (5th cir.), Montgomery, Ala., 1968-69; assoc. Kilpatrick, Cody, Rogers, McClatchey & Regenstein, Atlanta, 1969-75, Stalcup, Johnson, Meyers & Miller, Dallas, 1975-77; ptnr. Meyers, Miller, Middleton, Weiner & Warren, Dallas, 1977-80, Jones, Day, Reavis & Pogue, Dallas, 1981-85; dir. Geary, Glast and Middleton, P.C., Dallas, 1985-92; ptnr. Vial, Hamilton, Koch & Knox, LLP, Dallas, 1992—. Mem. exec. com. Dallas County Dem. Com., 1980-87. Mem. ABA, Dallas Bar Found., Dallas Bar Assn., Tex. Bar Assn., Ga. Bar Assn., Am. Judicature Soc. Federal civil litigation, State civil litigation, Professional liability. Office: Vial Hamilton Koch & Knox 4400 Bank One Ctr 1717 Main St Dallas TX 75201-7388

**COLEMAN, RODERICK FLYNN,** lawyer; b. Washington, Pa., Sept. 20, 1958; s. Harry Sullivan and Marlyn Hope (McAninch) C.; m. Gale Faith Zeisel, July 28, 1984; children:, Tara, Lindsey. BA, Oglethorpe U., 1980; JD, Stetson U., 1983. Bar: Fla. 1983, U.S. Dist. Ct. (so. dist.) Fla. 1984, U.S. Ct. Appeals (11th cir.) 1984, U.S. Dist. Ct. (mid. dist.) Fla. 1988. Assoc. Law Offices of Richard Ralph, Miami, Fla., 1983-85, Schwartz and Assocs., Miami, 1986-87; ptnr. Marlow, Connell, Valerius, Abrams, Lowe & Adler, Miami, 1988-96, Stettin & Coleman, P.A., Miami, 1996-97; spl. counsel Coleman & Assocs., P.A., Coral Gables, 1997—. Mem. ABA, Fla. Bar, Dade County Bar Assn., Fla. Trial Lawyers Assn., Am. Judicature Soc., Riviera Country Club, Kiwanis Club. Republican. Avocations: golf, sailing. General civil litigation, State civil litigation, Professional liability. Home: 1470 Mendavia Ave Coral Gables FL 33146-1608 Office: 2151 LeJeune Rd Mezzanine Coral Gables FL 33134

**COLEMAN, RUSSELL FORESTER,** lawyer; b. El Paso, Tex., Apr. 2, 1960; s. Barry Organ and Barbara Forester C.; m. Martha Crandall, Aug. 17, 1985. BSCE, Rice U., 1982; JD, U. Tex., 1985. Bar: Tex. 1985. Assoc. Locke Purnell Rain Harrell, Dallas, 1985-92, shareholder, 1993—. Dir. Ctrl. Dallas Assn., 1998—, Southwest Higher Edn. Authority, Inc., Dallas, 1997—; mem. Am. Coun. Germany, N.Y.C., 1992. Mem. Dallas Bar Assn. (securities sect. 1995—, corp. counsel sect. 1998—). Presbyterian. General corporate, Finance, Securities. Office: Locke Liddell & Sapp 2200 Ross Ave Ste 2200 Dallas TX 75201-2748

**COLEMAN, SEAN JOSEPH,** lawyer; b. Washington, Sept. 22, 1968; s. Francis Thomas and Joann Mary Coleman. AB, Princeton U., 1991; JD, U. Va., 1995. Bar: Ga. 1995, U.S. Dist. Ct. (no. dist.) Ga. 1994. Legal asst. Patton Boggs LLP, Washington, 1991-92; dir. Princeton Club of Ga., Washington, 1991-92; assoc. Troutman Sanders LLP, Atlanta, 1995—. Leader for new mems. Christ the King Ch., Atlanta, 1996—. Mem. ABA, State Bar Ga., Atlanta Bar Assn., Princeton Club of Ga. (v.p. 1996-98). Republican. Roman Catholic. Avocations: basketball, tennis, marathon running, skiing, golf. General corporate, Mergers and acquisitions, Entertainment. Home: 984 Northcliffe Dr NW Atlanta GA 30318-1661 Office: Troutman Sanders LLP 600 Peachtree St NE Atlanta GA 30308-2265

**COLEMAN, THOMAS,** federal lawyer; b. Rochester, N.Y., May 12, 1950; s. Thomas James and Amy Desmond Coleman. BA, U. Kans., 1972, JD, 1976; MS, Johns Hopkins U., 1999. Dir. energy project Kans. Legal Svcs., Topeka, 1977-82; asst. atty. gen. State of Kans., Topeka, 1982-84; atty.-advisor U.S. Dept. of Housing and Urban Devel., Kansas City, Mo., 1984-86; asst. gen. counsel U.S. Dept. of Housing and Urban Devel., Kansas City, 1996—; assoc. field counsel U.S. Dept. of Housing and Urban Devel., Denver, 1986-89, chief counsel, 1989-96. Avocations: music, flyfishing, canoeing, marital arts. Fax: 913-551-5857. E-mail: ThomasúJ.úColeman@hud.gov. Home: 1217 W 71st Ter Kansas City MO 64114-1237 Office: US Dept of Housing and Urban Devel 400 State Ave Fl 5 Kansas City KS 66101-2402

**COLEMAN, VERONICA FREEMAN,** prosecutor. U.S. atty. We. Dist. Tenn., U.S. Dept. Justice, Memphis, 1993—. Office: US Attys Office 800 Federal Office Bldg 167 N Main St Memphis TN 38103-1816

**COLEMAN, WILLIAM THADDEUS, III,** federal official. BA cum laude, Williams Coll., 1970; JD, Yale U., 1973. Civil rights atty. Hill, Jones & Farrington, Savannah, Ga.; law clk. Hon. Edward T. Gignoux, U.S. Dist. Ct. Maine; assoc. Pepper, Hamilton & Sheetz, Phila., 1975; assoc. Pepper, Hamilton & Sheetz, Detroit, ptnr.; gen. counsel U.S. Army, Washington, 1994—; founder's group mem. Wayne County Devel. Bank; author, lectr. and panelist on employment, affirmative action, defense, ethical and litigation issues; del. 6th Cir. Jud. Conf. Bd. dirs. Wayne County Neighborhood Legal Svcs. Mem. ABA (conf. on minority ptnrs. in majority law firms), U.S. Ct. Fed. Claims, Am. Law Inst., Detroit Bar Assn. (chmn. pub. adv. com. for evaluation of qualifications of Mich. Supreme Ct. jud. candidates, mem. com. on minority and female involvement), Fed. Bar Assn. (exec. bd. for ea. dist. Mich.). Office: Dept of the Army General Counsel 104 Army Pentagon 2E722 Washington DC 20310-0104

**COLEN, FREDERICK HAAS,** lawyer; b. Pitts., May 16, 1947; married, 1972. BSChemE, Tufts U., 1969; JD, Emory U., 1975. Bar: Pa. 1975, Ga. 1975, U.S. Patent Office 1976, U.S. Dist. Ct. (we. dist.) Pa. 1975, U.S. Dist. Ct. (no. dist.) Ga. 1975, U.S. Ct. Appeals (fed. and 3d cirs.) 1975, U.S. Supreme Ct. 1980. Chem. engr. Shell Oil Co., New Orleans, 1969-71; san. engr. USPHS, Morgantown, W.Va., 1971-73; patent atty. Mobay Chem. Corp., Pitts., 1975-79; assoc. Reed Smith Shaw & McClay, Pitts., 1979-86, ptnr., 1986—. Contbr. articles to profl. jours. Mem. ABA, Allegheny County Bar Assn., Pa. Bar Assn., Ga. Bar Assn., Am. Intellectual Property Law Assn. Patent, Trademark and copyright, Computer. Home: 4940 Ellsworth Ave Pittsburgh PA 15213-2807 Office: Reed Smith Shaw & McClay 435 6th Ave Ste 2 Pittsburgh PA 15219-1886

**COLESON, RICHARD EUGENE,** lawyer, minister; b. Bulsar, India, Feb. 6, 1951; came to U.S., 1952; s. Ralph James and Olive Leone Coleson; m. Linda Sue McCrory, Aug. 19, 1972; children: Nathan Edward, Heather Anne, Jason Andrew. BA, Ind. Wesleyan U., 1973; MA in Religion, Asbury Theol. Sem., Wilmore, Ky., 1975; JD, Ind. U., 1987. Bar: Ind. 1987, U.S. Dist. Ct. (so. and no. dists.) Ind. 1987, U.S. Ct. Appeals (7th cir.) 1994, U.S. Ct. Appeals (5th cir.), 1991, U.S. Ct. Appeals (4th cir.) 1995, U.S. Supreme Ct. 1990. Pastor Wyoming (Mich.) Wesleyan Ch., 1975-78; prof. Bartlesville (Okla.) Wesleyan Coll., 1978-82; pastor Blue River Wesleyan Ch., Arlington, Ind., 1983-87, Oak Hill & Riley (Ind.) United Meth. Chs., 1990—; assoc. Brames, Bopp, Abel & Oldham, Terre Haute, Ind., 1987-92; staff counsel Nat. Legal Ctr. for the Medically Dependent and Disabled, Terre Haute, Ind., 1992-99; sr. assoc. Bopp, Coleson & Bostrom, Terre Haute, Ind., 1992—. Contbr. articles to profl. jours. Mem. Vigo County Election Bd., Terre Haute, 1993-97; precinct committeeman Vigo County Rep. Party, 1997—. Recipient Outstanding Achievement award Ind. Wesleyan U. Alumni Assn., 1997. Constitutional, Federal civil litigation, Appellate. Office: Bopp Coleson & Bostrom 1 South 6th St Terre Haute IN 47807-3510

**COLESSIDES, NICK JOHN,** lawyer; b. Kavala, Greece, Jan. 14, 1938; came to U.S., 1958; s. John T. and Maroula (Karakas) C.; m. Sophia Simons Symeonidis, Oct. 5, 1970. BS in Polit. Sci., U. Utah, 1963, MS Polit. Sci., 1967, JD, 1970. Bar: Utah 1970, U.S. Dist. Ct. Utah 1970, U.S. Ct. Appeals (10th cir.) 1970, U.S. Dist. Ct. (so. dist.) Ohio 1975, U.S. Ct. Appeals (9th cir.) 1976. Chief deputy county atty. Salt Lake County (Utah) Atty.'s Office, 1970-74; city atty. West Jordan (Utah) City Atty.'s Office, 1971-78, Park City (Utah) Atty.'s Office, 1976-80; atty. pvt. practice, Salt Lake City, 1970—; bd. dirs. Merrill Lynch Bank, U.S.A., Salt Lake City Utah. Bd. trustees Greek Orthodox Ch., SaltLake City, 1976, 77, 87, 88, 98, 99. Mem. Assn. Trial Lawyers Am., Utah Trial Lawyers Assn., U. Utah Coll. of Law Alumni Assn. (trustee 1995-98), Utah State Bar Assn., Salt Lake County Bar Assn., Am. Inn of Ct. VII (master of the bench, pres. 1997, 98). Greek Orthodox. Avocations: gardening, cooking, reading. Real property, Federal civil litigation, State civil litigation. Home: 32 Haxton Pl Salt Lake City UT 84102-1410 Office: 466 S 400 E Ste 100 Salt Lake City UT 84111-3325

**COLETTA, RALPH JOHN,** lawyer; b. Chillicothe, Ill., Dec. 13, 1921; s. Joseph and Assunta Maria (Aromatario) C.; m. Ethel Mary Meyers, Nov. 19, 1949; children: Jean, Marianne, Suzanne, Joseph, Robert, Michele, Renee. BS, Bradley U., 1943; JD, U. Chgo., 1949. Bar: Ill. 1949. Practice law Peoria, Ill., 1949—; pres. White Star Corp., Mark Tidd, Inc.; asst. state's atty. Peoria County. Chmn. United Fund. Served to 1st lt. AUS, 1943-46. Mem. ABA, Peoria County Bar Assn., Chgo. Bar Assn., Ill. State Bar Assn., Creve Coeur Club, Mt. Hawley Country Club, K.C., Union League Club. Republican. Roman Catholic. Real property, Probate, Estate planning. Home: 301 W Crestwood Dr Peoria IL 61614-7328 Office: 1st Financial Plaza Ste 1714 Peoria IL 61602

**COLETTI, JOHN ANTHONY,** lawyer, furniture and realty company executive; b. Cherry Point, N.C., Sept. 22, 1952; s. Joseph Nicholas and Gloria Lucy (Fusco) C.; m. Barbara Nancy Carlotti, July 20, 1975; children: Lisa M., Kristen B. Student, Biscayne Coll., 1970-72; BA summa cum laude, Boston Coll., 1974, JD, 1977. Bar: R.I. 1977, U.S. Dist. Ct. R.I. 1977. Assoc. Resmini, Fornaro, Colagiovanni & Angell, Providence, 1979-81; ptnr. Coletti & Tente, Cranston, R.I., 1981—; pres. Coletti's Furniture, Inc., Johnston R.I., 1983-95, Coletti's Realty, Inc., Johnston, 1983-96. Legal counsel Cranston Housing Authority, 1988—; interviewer alumni admissions coun. Boston Coll., 1980—. Mem. ABA, R.I. Bar Assn., R.I. Conveyancers Assn., Nat. Assn. Retail Collection Attys., Phi Beta Kappa. Roman Catholic. Avocations: horseback riding, golf, figure skating. Consumer commercial, Real property, General practice. Office: Coletti & Tente 311 Doric Ave Cranston RI 02910-2903

**COLETTI, JULIE A.,** lawyer; b. Pitts., Jan. 13, 1968. BA cum laude, Rutgers U., 1989; JD, U. Pitts., 1993. Bar: Pa. 1993, U.S. Ct. Appeals (fed. cir.) 1997, U.S. Ct. Claims, U.S. Ct. Internat. Trade 1996, U.S. Supreme Ct. 1997. Assoc. Babst, Calland, Clements & Zomnir, P.C., Pitts., 1993-96; atty. LeBoeuf, Lamb, Green & MacRae, LLP, Pitts., 1996—. Bd. dirs. Friends United for Need, Pitts., 1996—. Mem. Allegheny County Bar Assn. General civil litigation, Construction, Contracts commercial.

**COLEY, F(RANKLIN) LUKE, JR.,** lawyer; b. Monroeville, Ala., Apr. 17, 1958; s. Franklin Luke and Margaret Boyce (Green) C. BA in History, U. Ala., 1980, JD, 1983. Bar: Ala. 1985, U.S. Dist. Ct. (so. dist.) Ala. 1987, U.S. Ct. Appeals (11th cir.) 1990. Law clk. Robert S. Edington, Mobile, Ala., 1983-85; pvt. practice Mobile, 1985—. Active Mobile County Dem. Exec. Com., 1986-98; bd. dirs. United Methodist Children's Home, 1999—. Mem. ABA, Mobile Bar Assn., Kiwanis (sec. local chpt. 1987-89, v.p. 1989-91, pres. 1991-92). Methodist. General practice, Criminal, General civil litigation. Home: 5906 Reams Dr N Mobile AL 36608-3658 Office: Ste 512 Two Office Pk Mobile AL 36609-1957

**COLFIN, BRUCE ELLIOTT,** lawyer, video producer; b. Bklyn., June 9, 1951; s. Abraham and Sylvia (Laykin) C.; m. Virginia Mary Faszczewski, Sept. 27, 1981. BA, CUNY, 1977; JD, N.Y. Law Sch., 1980. Bar: N.Y. 1982, U.S. Dist. Ct. (so., ea. dists.) N.Y., 1987, U.S. Ct. Internat. Trade, 1990. Audio engr. Snowball Sound Systems, N. Bergen, N.J., 1974-77; producer, dir. cable TV program What's On, N.Y.C., 1976-84; stage mgr. Peter Tosh U.S. tour Rolling Stones Records, 1978; v.p., producer Upswing Artists Mgmt., N.Y.C., 1979-86; pres., producer, dir. LegalVision, Inc., N.Y.C., 1982-87; ptnr. Jacobson & Colfin, N.Y.C. and Washington, 1985-90; mem. Jacobson & Colfin, P.C., N.Y.C. and Washington, 1990—; pres. Fifth Ave. Media, Ltd., N.Y.C., 1996—; spkr. Discovery Ctr., N.Y., 1st Ann. Musicians Seminar, L.I., N.Y. Law Sch. Media Law Soc., 1986; vis. lectr. SUNY, Oneonta, 1988—; panelist New Eng. Music Orgn. Conf., 1998, Emerging Artists and Talent in Music, 1999. Assoc. producer music video Blues Alive, 1982; exec. producer, dir. video series Entertainment Law Video Primer, 1984; monthly columnist Ind. Music Producers Soc. Jour., NARAS N.Y. chpt. newsletter; contbr. articles to profl. jours.; columnist: Replication News, 1998. Mem. ABA (com. on entertainment sports law, subcom. chmn. patent, trademark and copyright com. 1989, subcom. chmn. internat. law and practice, internat. intellectual property rights com., spl. subcom. on multimedia 1994—, editl. advisor pubs. com. internat. law sect. 1990-92, exec. com. entertainment law cir. 1989-91), NATAS (N.Y. chpt.), N.Y. State Bar Assn. (entertainment, arts and sports law sect., com. on talent agys. and talent mgmt., com. on rights of publicity 1994—), Nassau County Bar Assn., Speaker's Bureau (entertainment and sports law comm.), Copyright Soc. U.S.A. (editl. bd. 1986-88), Nat. Acad. of Recording Arts and Scis. (N.Y. chpt.). Jewish. Avocations: traveling, writing, stamp collecting, hockey. E-mail: BRUCE@Thefirm.com. Entertainment, Trademark and copyright, General civil litigation. Office: Jacobson & Colfin PC 156 5th Ave Ste 434 New York NY 10010-7002

**COLIVER, NORMAN,** lawyer; b. Balt., June 19, 1918; divorced; children: Susan, Lillian Sandra. BS in Philosophy, U. Va., 1939; postgrad., Harvard U., 1946-47; JD, Stanford U., 1951. Bar: Calif. 1952. With Dinkelspiel & Dinkelspiel Attys., San Francisco, 1952-90, Cooper, White & Cooper, San Francisco, 1990-96; labor relations cons. Italian Govt., Rome, 1951. Past bd. dirs. Hunters Point Boys Club, United Bay Area Crusade, ARC, San Francisco, Presidio Heights Assn. Neighbors, Jewish Com. Ctr., Jewish Family Svc. Agy., J.L. Magnes Mus. of Berkeley; v.p., past bd. dirs. San Francisco Mental Health Assn., Congregation Emanu-El, Vol. Bur. of San Francisco, Internat. Inst. San Francisco; past pres., bd. dirs. San Francisco Sponsors; co-founder, past bd. dirs. San Francisco Home Health Svc. Major U.S. Army, 1941-46, PTO. Decorated Three Bronze Stars, 1943-44, Philippine Liberation Ribbon with Battle Star, 1944. Fellow Am. Coll. Probate Counsel; mem. Am. Bar Assn., Calif. Bar Assn., San Francisco Bar Assn. (chmn. internat. & comparative law com. 1965, chmn. ethics com., 1973, chmn. probate & trust law sect., 1982), Attys. Probate Coun. (bd. dirs.). Avocations: history, geneology, great books.

**COLL, JOHN PETER, JR.,** lawyer; b. Pitts., Oct. 5, 1943; s. John Peter and Lelia (Nicolussi) C.; m. Nancy Kaye Swan; children: John Peter, Alexis S. AB in Polit. Sci., Duke U., 1965; JD, Georgetown U., 1968. Bar: N.Y. 1969, U.S. Dist. Ct. (so. dist.) N.Y. 1970, U.S. Dist. Ct. (ea. dist.) N.Y. 1974, U.S. Ct. Appeals (2d cir.) 1972, U.S. Supreme Ct. 1974, U.S. Ct. Appeals (5th cir.) 1981, U.S. Ct. Appeals (11th cir.) 1981, U.S. Ct. Appeals (8th cir.) 1980, U.S. Ct. Appeals (6th cir.) 1991, U.S. Ct. Appeals (1st cir.) 1993, U.S. Ct. Appeals (3d cir.) 1994, U.S. Ct. Appeals (9th cir.) 1994, U.S. Dist. Ct. (no. dist.) Calif. 1983, U.S. Dist. Ct. (no. dist.) N.Y. 1984, U.S. Dist. Ct. (we. dist.) N.Y. 1988, U.S. Tax Ct. 1990, U.S. Ct. Appeals (fed. cir.) 1999. Assoc. Donovan Leisure Newton & Irvine LLP, N.Y.C., 1968-76, ptnr., 1976-98, chmn. exec. com., 1989-98; ptnr. Orrick, Herington & Sutcliffe LLP, N.Y.C., 1998—; bd. advisors product safety and liability rep. BNA, 1991—; mem. litigation steering com. Def. Rsch. Inst., 1991—. Contbg. author: Preparing for and Trying the Civil Law Suit, 1987, Supplement, 1997, Commercial Litigation in New York State Courts, 1995, Products Liability in New York, Strategy and Practice, 1997. Mem. ABA (litigation sect. 1983—), Fed. Bar Coun., N.Y. State Bar Assn., Assn. of Bar of City of N.Y., N.Y. Coun. Law Assocs. (mem. steering com. 1971-72), Lawrence Beach Club (bd. govs.), Cherry Valley Club, Univ. Club. Democrat. Roman Catholic. General civil litigation, Federal civil litigation, State civil litigation. Home: 385 Stewart Ave Garden City NY 11530-4615 Office: Orrick Herrington and Sutcliffe LLP 666 5th Ave Rm 203 New York NY 10103-1798

**COLL, NORMAN ALAN,** lawyer; b. East Grand Rapids, Mich., Sept. 24, 1940; s. Harry H. and Elizabeth (Kelley) C.; m. Mona Fondren, July 23, 1977; children: Kevin M., Kelley S., Patrick P. BSME, U. Mich., 1962; LLB, U. Fla., 1965. Bar: Fla. 1965, U.S. Dist. Ct. (so. dist.) Fla. 1965, U.S. Supreme Ct. 1970, D.C. 1979, U.S. Ct. Appeals (D.C. cir.) 1979, U.S. Ct. Appeals (11th cir.) 1981. Assoc. Scott McCarthy Preston & Steel, Miami, Fla., 1965-69; ptnr. Steel Hector & Davis, Miami, 1969-87; officer, shareholder Coll Davidson et al., Miami, 1987—. Mem. Coral Reef Yacht Club, Riviera Country Club, Miami City Club, Sigma Alpha Epsilon. General civil litigation, Environmental, Product liability. Office: Coll Davidson et al 3200 Miami Ctr 201 S Biscayne Blvd Miami FL 33131-4310

**COLLARD, STACEY LEE,** lawyer; b. Chicopee Falls, Mass., June 30, 1971; d. Robert Liles Collard Jr. and Barbara Ellen Collard. BA summa cum laude, U. Ctrl. Fla., 1993; JD, Duke U., 1996. Bar: Fla. 1996, U.S. Dist. Ct. (mid. dist.) Fla. 1997. Atty. Lowndes, Drosdick, Doster, Kantor & Reed, Orlando, Fla., 1996—. Mem. St. James Cathedral Choir, Orlando, 1998. Mem. ABA, Ctrl. Fla. Assn. Women Lawyers, Orange County Bar Assn., Duke Alumni Club (bd. dirs. 1997—), Duke Alumni Assn. (admissions adv. com. 1998), U. Ctrl. Fla. Alumni Assn. Avocations: golf, theatre, classical singing. Securities, Mergers and acquisitions, Municipal (including bonds). Office: Lowndes Drosdick Doster Kantor & Reed 215 N Eola Dr Orlando FL 32801-2095

**COLLAS, JUAN GARDUÑO, JR.,** lawyer; b. Manila, Apr. 25, 1932; s. Juan D. and Soledad (Garduño) C.; m. Maria L. Moreira, Aug. 1, 1959; children: Juan Jose, Elias Lopes, Cristina Maria, Daniel Benjamin. LLB, U. of Philippines, Quezon City, 1955; LLM, Yale U., 1958, JSD, 1959. Bar: Philippines 1956, Ill. 1960, Calif. 1971, U.S. Supreme Ct. 1967. Assoc., Sy Cip, Salazar & Assocs., Manila, 1956-57; atty. N.Y., N.H. & H. R.R., New Haven, 1959-60; assoc. Baker & McKenzie, Chgo., 1960-63, ptnr., Manila, 1963-70, San Francisco, 1970-95, Manila, 1995—. Contbr. articles to profl. jours. Trustee, sec. Friends of U. of Philippines Found. in Am., San Francisco, 1982—; co-chmn. San Francisco Lawyers for Better Govt., 1982—; chmn. San Francisco-Manila Sister City Com., 1986-92. Recipient Outstanding Filipino Overseas in Law award, Philippine Ministry Tourism Philippines Jaycees, 1979. Mem. ABA, Am. Arbitration Assn. (panelist), Ill. State Bar Assn., State Bar Calif., Integrated Bar of Philippines, Filipino-Am. C. of C. (bd. dirs. 1974-91, 94-96, pres. 1985-87, chmn. bd. dirs. 1987-89, 95-96). Republican. Roman Catholic. Clubs: World Trade, Villa Taverna (San Francisco). Private international, General corporate, Contracts commercial. Office: Baker & McKenzie 2 Embarcadero Ctr Ste 2400 San Francisco CA 94111-3909

**COLLEN, JOHN,** lawyer; b. Chgo., Dec. 26, 1954; s. Sheldon and Ann Collen; m. Lauren Kay Smulyan, Sept. 20, 1986; children: Joshua, Benjamin, Sarah, Joel. AB summa cum laude, Dartmouth Coll., 1977; JD, Georgetown U., 1980. Bar: Ill. 1980, U.S. Dist. Ct. (no. dist.) Ill. 1980, Trial 1982, U.S. Ct. Appeals (7th cir.) 1984, U.S. Supreme Ct. 1990. Ptnr. Peterson and Ross, Chgo.; mem. editl. adv. bd. Journal of Bankruptcy Law & Practice. Author: Buying and Selling Real Estate in Bankruptcy, 1997; contbr. articles to profl. jours.; lectr. in field. Mem. ABA, Chgo. Bar Assn., Phi Beta Kappa. Avocations: scuba diving, biographies. Fax: 312-565-0832. E-mail: jcollen@petersonross.com. Bankruptcy, Real property. Office: Peterson & Ross 200 E Randolph Dr Ste 7300 Chicago IL 60601

**COLLERAN, KEVIN,** lawyer; b. Spalding, Nebr., July 16, 1941; s. James Edward and Helen Marcella (Vybiral) C.; m. Karen Ann Rooney, Aug. 1, 1964; children: Mary Jane, Patrick. BS, U. Nebr., 1964, JD with distinction,

1968. Bar: Nebr. 1968, U.S. Dist. Ct. Nebr. 1968, U.S. Dist. Ct. (we. dist.) La. 1975, U.S. Dist. Ct. (no. dist.) Tex. 1978, U.S. Supreme Ct. 1980, U.S. Ct. Appeals (8th cir.) 1981. Law clk. U.S. Dist. Ct. Nebr., 1968-69; assoc. Cline, Williams, Wright, Johnson & Oldfather, Lincoln, Nebr., 1969-74; ptnr., 1975—, mng. ptnr., 1985-89, 96—. Bd. dirs. Lancaster County unit Am. Cancer Soc., 1972-83, pres., 1979. Fellow Am. Coll. Trial Lawyers; mem. ABA, Am. Bd. Trial Advocates, Nebr. Bar Assn. (chmn. worker's compensation com. 1980-82), Internat. Assn. Def. Counsel, Nat. Assn. Trial Attys., Order of Coif. Democrat. Federal civil litigation, State civil litigation, Environmental. Office: Cline Williams Wright Johnson & Oldfather First Tier Bank Bldg Lincoln NE 68508

**COLLERAN, ROBERT T.,** lawyer; b. 1945. BA, Manhattan Coll., 1966; JD, Cath. U., 1969; LLM, NYU, 1977. Bar: N.Y. 1969. Sr. v.p., assoc. gen. counsel Chase Manhattan Bank, N.Y.C. Mem. ABA, Assn. of the Bar of the City of N.Y. General corporate, Insurance, Banking. Office: Chase Manhattan Bank 1 Chase Manhattan Plz New York NY 10081-0001*

**COLLETTA, ANTHONY J.,** lawyer; b. Flushing, N.Y., 1963. BA, Fordham U., 1985; JD, St. John's U., 1988. Bar: N.Y. 1988. Ptnr. Sullivan & Cromwell, N.Y.C. Office: Sullivan & Cromwell 125 Broad St New York NY 10004-2489

**COLLETTE, CHARLES T. (CHIP COLLETTE),** lawyer; b. Lima, Ohio, Nov. 8, 1944; s. Charles Herman Collett and Roma Kathleen (Runyan) Wickenden; m. M.A. Taff Zaebst, May 5, 1973; children: Daniel McKay, Kelly Cardinal Bayless, Kira Kathleen. Student, Ohio No. U., 1963-66; BA, U. Fla., 1967, JD, 1970. Bar: Fla. 1970, Ohio 1971, D.C. 1971, U.S. Dist. Ct. (no. dist.) Ohio 1973, (so. dist.) Ohio 1976, (no. dist.) Fla. 1977, (mid. dist.) Fla. 1980, (so. dist.) Fla. 1983, U.S. Ct. Appeals (5th cir.) 1978, (6th cir.) 1976, (11th cir.) 1981, U.S. Tax Ct. 1972, U.S. Supreme Ct. 1979. Asst. atty. gen. Atty. Gen. of Ohio, Columbus, 1971-76; staff atty. Fla. Dept. Bus. Regulation, Tallahassee, 1976-77; asst. gen. counsel Fla. Dept. Health and Rehab. Svcs., Tallahassee, 1977-82; assoc. Mang & Stowell, Tallahassee, 1982-86; prin., ptnr. Mang, Rett & Collette, Tallahassee, 1986-93; sr. atty. Fla. Dept. Environ. Protection, Tallahassee, 1994—; lawyer rep. U.S. 11th Cir. Jud. Conf., 1993—. Contbr. articles to legal jours.; contbr. poetry to mags. Bd. dirs. Refuge House, 1992—, Tallahassee Alzheimer's Project, 1993—; sec., parliamentarian Leon County Rep. Exec. Com., 1992—. With USAFR, 1963-69. Mem. ABA, Fla. Bar Assn. (vice-chmn. jud. adminstrn., selection and tenure com. 1982-84, 91-92, chmn. 1984-85, chmn. N.D. Fla. subcom., fed. ct. practice com. 1993—), Tallahassee Bar Assn. (treas. 1991-92), Fla. Govt. Lawyers Bar Assn., Fed. Bar Assn., Advocates Assn. Nat. Inst. Trial Advocacy, Fla. Supreme Ct. Hist. Soc. (trustee 1990—), Tallahassee Family YMCA (bd. mgmt. 1992—), Masons, Kappa Delta Pi, Phi Alpha Theta, Pi Sigma Alpha, Delta Theta Phi. Republican. Methodist. Avocations: jogging, camping, sci. fiction, current sci., current affairs. Constitutional, Labor, Federal civil litigation. Home: 108 Winn Cay Dr Tallahassee FL 32312-2747 Office: Fla Dept Environ Protection PO Box 10161 Tallahassee FL 32302-2161

**COLLIE, KATHRYN KAYE,** lawyer; b. Orlando, Fla., Mar. 5, 1952; d. Robert Lee and Marie (Shealy) C. BS in Edn., U. Fla., 1974, JD, 1978. Bar: Fla. 1978, U.S. Dist. Ct. (mid. dist.) Fla. 1979, U.S. Ct. Appeals (11th cir.) 1987. Tchr. Orange County Pub. Schs., Orlando, 1974-76; asst. state atty. 9th Jud. Cir., Orlando, 1978; assoc. Fishback, Davis, Dominick & Bennett, Orlando, 1979-81; asst. county atty. Orange County, Orlando, 1981—. Mem. Nat. Women's Polit. Caucus, Washington, Met. Orlando Women's Polit. Caucus. Mem. ABA, Fla. Bar Assn., Fla. Assn. Women Lawyers (bd. dirs. 1981-82), Cen. Fla. Assn. Women Lawyers (pres. 1981-82), Orange County Bar Assn. Avocations: skiing, bowling. Civil rights, General civil litigation. Office: Orange County Atty's Office 315 E Robinson St Ste 650 Orlando FL 32801-4342

**COLLIER, JAMES BRUCE,** lawyer; b. Ironton, Ohio, Sept. 25, 1920; s. James W. and Faye L. (Clark) C.; m. Bette E. Fawcett, Mar. 24, 1943; children: James B. Jr., Gretchen J. Randall. Student, Miami U., Oxford, Ohio, 1938-41; LLB, State U. Iowa, 1949. Bar: Iowa 1949, Ohio 1949, U.S. Dist. Ct. (so. dist.) Ohio 1950, U.S. Supreme Ct. 1960, U.S. Dist. Ct. (so. dist.) Ohio 1961, U.S. Ct. Appeals (6th cir.) 1961. Pvt. practice Ironton, 1949—. Chmn. Lawrence County Rep. Ctrl. Com., Ironton, 1955-85; mem., pres. Ironton City Sch. Bd., 1962-66. Capt. USAAF, 1941-46. Mem. Ohio Bar Assn., Lawrence County Bar Assn. Episcopalian. Avocations: fishing, boating, competitive pistol shooting. Probate, General civil litigation. Home: 1111 Mastin Ave Ironton OH 45638-2223 Office: Collier & Collier 411 Center St Ironton OH 45638-1506

**COLLIER, LACEY ALEXANDER,** federal judge; b. Demopolis, Ala., June 23, 1935; s. James Porter and Virginia Slade (Lacey) C.; m. Beverly Anne Brady, Sept. 1, 1956; children: Lorrie Collier Berry, Teri Collier Siebert, Frank. Student, U. Ala., 1953-55; BA in Govt. and Internat. Rels., U.S. Naval Postgrad. Sch., 1970; MA in Polit. Sci., U. West Fla., 1972, BA in Acctg., 1975; JD with honors, Fla. State Sch. Law, 1977. Bar: Fla. 1978, U.S. Dist. Ct. (no. dist.) Fla. 1978, U.S. CT. Appeals (5th cir.) 1978, U.S. Ct. Appeals (11th cir.) 1981. Commd. USN, 1955, advanced through grades to lt. comdr., ret., 1975; asst. state atty. Office of State Atty. 1st. Jud. Cir. of Fla., 1977-84; cir. judge 1st Jud. Cir., 1984-91; U.S. dist. judge U.S. Dist. Ct. (no. dist.) Fla., 1991—; adj. prof. polit. sci. U. West Fla., 1973; adv. grand juries 1st Jud. Cir., 1978-84; lectr. La. Judges Conf., 1986, Robert A. Taft Inst. Govt., 1989—; faculty Fla. New Judges' Coll., 1989-92. Pres. St. Paul's Cath. Ch. Men's Club, 1972; chmn. leadership in action program Pensacola Jaycees, 1971-72; divsn. leader CFC/United Way, 1973; mem. public safety task force Action '76, 1974; vice chmn. Escambia County charter com., 1978-79; bd. dirs. Fla. State Law Sch. Alumni Assn., 1980-81; pres. city-county Drug Abuse Commn., 1982-83; chmn. City Pensacola Revenue Study Com., 1985-86; official adv. Escambia Govtl. Study Commn., 1986-87; mem. Presdl. Search Com. U. W. Fla., 1987; chmn. Edn. Conf. subcom. Fla. Conf. Crct. Judges, 1987-89; trustee, pres.U. W. Fla. Found., 1988—; mem. adv. bd. students in free enterprise U. W. Fla., 1989—; trustee Pensacola Little Theater/Cultural Ctr., 1989—; lectr., mem. adv. bd., chmn. Nativity Cath. Ch., 1990—; chmn. Pensacola com. Nat. Mus. Naval Aviation Found., 1990—; bd. dirs. Big Brother/Big Sister of NW Fla., sec., 1990-92; mem. adv. bd. African-Am. Heritage Soc., 1990—; mem. adv. bd. Sacred Heart Hosp., 1991—. Recipient 11 air medals; named Disting. Alumni U. W. Fla., 1988, Pensacola BIP Profl. Leader of Yr., 1989. Mem. ABA, Fla. Bar (standard jury instrns. com. civil 1989—), Okalossa-Walton Bar Assn., Escambia-Santa Rosa Bar Assn., Am. Inns of Court (exec. bd. Pensacola chpt., founding mem.), Assn. Naval Aviation, Gulf Coast Econs. Club (v.p. 1990-92, pres. 1993—), Fla. State Law Sch. Alumni Assn. (bd. dirs. 1981-81), Fla. Conf. Cir. Judges, C. of C. (chmn. Com. 100 1987-89, task force on port/airport devel., chmn. bldg. and sites task force 1989—). Office: US Courthouse 100 N Palafox St Pensacola FL 32501-4839

**COLLIN, THOMAS JAMES,** lawyer; b. Windom, Minn., Jan. 6, 1949; s. Everett Earl and Genevieve May (Wilson) C.; m. Victoria Gatov, Oct. 11, 1985; children: Arielle, Elise, Sarah. BA, U. Minn., 1970, AM, Harvard U., 1972; JD, Georgetown U., 1974. Bar: Ohio 1975, U.S. Dist. Ct. (no. dist.) Ohio 1975, U.S. Ct. Appeals (10th cir.) 1977, U.S. Supreme Ct. 1980, U.S. Ct. Appeals (6th cir.) 1981, U.S. Ct. Appeals (8th cir.) 1982, U.S. Ct. Appeals (7th cir.) 1997, U.S. Ct. Appeals (11th cir.) 1999. Law clk. to Judge Myron Bright U.S. Ct. Appeals, 8th Cir., St. Louis, Mo., 1974-75; assoc. Thompson, Hine & Flory, LLP, Cleve., 1975-82, ptnr., 1982--. Author: Ohio Business Competition Law, 1994, (with others) Criminal Antitrust Litigation Manual, 1983; editor: Punitive Damages and Business Torts: A Practitioner's Handbook, 1998; contbr. articles to profl. jours. Active Citizens League, Cleve., 1987—, bd. trustees, 1994—, v.p., 1995-97, pres. 1997-99. Mem. ABA (chair bus. torts and unfair competition com., antitrust sect. 1995-98), Ohio State Bar Assn. (bd. govs. antitrust sect. 1988-98). Republican. Avocations: book collecting, music. Antitrust, Federal civil litigation, Intellectual property. Home: 7879 Oakhurst Dr Cleveland OH 44141-1123 Office: Thompson Hine & Flory LLP 127 Public Sq Cleveland OH 44114-1216

**COLLINGS, ROBERT L.,** lawyer; b. May 22, 1950. AB, Harvard U., 1972; JD, Boston Coll., 1977. Bar: Pa. 1977, U.S. Ct. Appeals (3d and D.C. cirs.), U.S. Dist. Ct. (ea. and mid. dists.) Pa. Atty. U.S. EPA, 1977-84, sect. chief, 1979-81, br. chief, 1981-84; ptnr., co-chair environ. practice group Schnader, Harrison, Segal & Lewis LLP, Phila. Editor: Environmental Spill Reporting Handbook; contbr. Municipal Solicitors Handbook, 1994, Brownfields: A Comprehensive Guide, 1997. Mem. Phila. Bar Assn. (chair environ. law com. 1986), Pa. Bar Assn. (nominating com. environ. mineral and natural resources law sect. 1992), Water Resources Assn. (sec. exec. com. 1990—), Am. Soc. Testing and Materials. Administrative and regulatory, Environmental, Personal injury. Office: Schnader Harrison Segal & Lewis LLP 1600 Market St Ste 3600 Philadelphia PA 19103-7240

**COLLINS, ADRIAN ANTHONY,** lawyer, accountant, educator; b. Los Angeles, June 23, 1937; s. Oscar P. and Beverly Francis (Moushey) C.; m. Marian Burke, Aug. 16, 1958; children—Elizabeth, Edmond. BA, U. Rochester, 1958; JD, Georgetown U., 1961, MBA, 1964, DBA, 1967. Bar: Va. 1961, D.C. 1963, N.Y. 1968; C.P.A., Va., N.Y. Assoc., Phillips, Kendrick, Gearheardt & Aylor, Arlington, Va., 1961-62; tax atty. Gosnell & Durkin, Washington, 1962-65; sr. tax acct. Price Waterhouse & Co., N.Y.C., 1965-67; tax counsel Exxon Corp., 1967-71, sr. tax counsel, 1971-82; sole practice, N.Y.C., 1982—; pres., gen. counsel Mortenson Benefits Group, P.C., Cranford, N.J., 1989-93; adj. prof. Mgmt. Inst. NYU, 1981-82, adj. prof. continuing legal edn. Farileigh Dickinson U., 1988-90; active N.Y. Better Bus. Bureau; acct. rep. Met. Life; mem. legal and legis. com. Profit Sharing Coun. Am.; lectr. in field. Mem. ABA, N.Y. State Bar Assn., Am. Inst. CPAs, N.Y. State Soc. CPAs, Am. Assn. Atty.-CPAs, Va. State Bar, N.J. C. of C. Roman Catholic. Author: Federal Income Taxation of Employee Benefits; contbr. articles to profl. jours. Corporate taxation, Personal income taxation, Pension, profit-sharing, and employee benefits. Office: Film Ctr Bldg 630 9th Ave Ste 405 New York NY 10036-3708 also: Primerila Financial Services Solution Representative 630 9th Ave Ste 405 New York NY 10036-3708

**COLLINS, AUDREY B.,** judge; b. 1945. BA, Howard U., 1967; MA, Am. U., 1969; JD, UCLA, 1977. Asst. atty. Legal Aid Found. L.A., 1977-78; with Office L.A. County Dist. Atty., 1978-94, dept. dist. atty., 1978-94, head dep. Torrance br. office, 1987-88, asst. dir. burs. ctrl. ops. and spl. ops., 1988-92, asst. dir. atty., 1992-94; judge. U.S. Dist. Ct. (Ctrl. Dist.) Calif., 1994—; dep. gen. counsel Office Spl. Acad. scholar Howard U.; named Lawyer of Yr., Langston Bar Assn., 1988; honoree Howard U. Alumni Club So. Calif., 1989; recipient Profl. Achievement award UCLA Alumni Assn., 1997. Mem. FBA, Nat. Assn. Women Judges, Nat. Bar Assn. (life ), State Bar Calif. (com. bar examiners, chmn. subcom. on moral character 1992-93, co-chmn. 1993-94), Los Angeles County Bar Assn. (exec. com. litigation sect.), Assn. Los Angeles County Dist. Attys. (pres. 1983), Black Women Lawyers Los Angeles County, Women Lawyers L.A. (life), Los Angeles County Bar Assn. Inn of Ct., Order of Coif, Phi Beta Kappa. Office: US Dist Ct Edward R Roybal Fed Bldg 255 E Temple St Ste 680 Los Angeles CA 90012-3334

**COLLINS, CHARLES EDWARD, JR.,** lawyer, retired policeman; b. Washington, Sept. 28, 1950; s. Charles Edward Sr. and Marguerite Ellen (Burns) C.; m. Kathleen Alice Barry, June 22, 1974; children: Tiffanie Amber, David Barry, Christopher Charles. BS cum laude, Am. U., Washington, 1974, MS with distinction, 1981; JD, George Mason Sch. Law, 1988. Bar: Va. 1998. Police comdr. Washington, D.C. Met. Police Dept., 1969-94; pvt. practice Law Office of Charles E. Collins, Jr., Fairfax, Va., 1995—. Co-author: A Police Officer's Guide to Firearm Detection, Recovery and Enforcement Techniques, 1998. Election ofcl. Commonwealth of Va., Bancroft-Whitney Co., Fairfax, 1996-98. Recipient Am. Jurisprudence award Lawyers Coop. Pub. Co., 1988. Mem. ABA, Va. Coll. Criminal Def. Attys., Fairfax Bar Assn. (co-chair lawyers referral svc. 1997-98). Republican. Roman Catholic. Avocation: coaching soccer. Criminal, Juvenile. Office: Law Office of Charles E Collins Jr 4120 Leonard Dr Fairfax VA 22030-5118

**COLLINS, DANIEL FRANCIS,** lawyer; b. N.Y.C., Mar. 5, 1942; s. Daniel Joseph and Madeline Elizabeth (Berger) C.; m. Margaret Mary Heyden, Jan. 15, 1966; children: Matthew C., Elizabeth C. BA in History and Polit. Sci., Hofstra U., 1964; JD, Am. U., 1967. Bar: D.C. 1968. Law clk. to E. Barrett Prettyman, U.S. Ct. Appeals, Washington, 1967-68; assoc. Ross, Marsh & Foster, Washington, 1970-74, mem., 1974-78; ptnr. Brackett & Collins, P.C., Washington, 1978-87; v.p. regulatory law, The Coastal Corp., 1987—. Administrative and regulatory, FERC practice, Public utilities. Office: Coastal Corp 2000 M St NW Washington DC 20036-3307

**COLLINS, DEBORAH ELAINE,** lawyer; b. N.Y.C., Nov. 21, 1950; d. William A. and Sarah J. Brown. BA, NYU, 1972; MA, NYU, Madrid, 1973; JD, Rutgers U., Newark, 1983. Bar: N.Y. 1986, U.S. Dist. Ct. (so. dist.) N.Y. 1987, U.S. Ct. Appeals (2nd cir.) 1989. Atty. Sipser, Weinstock, Harper, Dorn, N.Y.C., 1983-86, Davidoff & Malito, N.Y.C., 1986-87; spl. counsel, litigator N.Y.C. Transit Authority, N.Y.C., 1987-91; mgr. employment law Time Inc., N.Y.C., 1991-94; employment lawyer human resources J.P. Morgan & Co., N.Y.C., 1994—. Martin Luther King scholar NYU, N.Y.C., 1968-72; Martin Luther King Jr. fellow NYU, N.Y.C., 1972-73. Mem. Assn. of the Bar of the City of N.Y., Com. Minority Labor Attys., Bibliophiles Lit. Group (historian). Avocations: tennis, poetry, chess.

**COLLINS, DONNELL JAWAN,** lawyer; b. Nov. 13, 1970; s. Artis Lee and Ruby Collins; m. Tonia Yvette Holloway, Nov. 28, 1998; 1 child, Demi Arnell. BA summa cum laude, Morehouse Coll., 1993; JD, Emory U., 1996. Bar: Ga. 1996, Supreme Ct. Ga. 1998, U.S. Dist. Ct. (no. dist.) Ga. 1998, U.S. Ct. Appeals (11th cir.) 1998. Atty. King & Spalding, Atlanta, 1996-97; assoc. Zirkle and Hoffman, Atlanta, 1997-99, sr. assoc., 1999—. Recipient Nat. Trio Achiever award Nat. Coun. for Ednl. Opportunity Assns., 1998. Mem. ATLA, ABA, Atlanta Bar Assn., Ga. State Bar Assn., Phi Beta Kappa, Phi Delta Phi. Avocations: geography, travel, philosophy. State civil litigation, General civil litigation, Insurance. Office: Zirkle and Hoffman 5 Concourse Pkwy NE Ste 2900 Atlanta GA 30328-6104

**COLLINS, G. BRYAN, JR.,** lawyer; b. North Wilkesboro, N.C., Sept. 13, 1960; s. George B. and Ida Maude (Black) C.; m. Donna Jarvis, Feb. 15, 1992; children: Kristy, Katie. AB cum laude, Davidson Coll., 1982; JD, U. N.C., Chapel Hill, 1985. Bar: N.C. 1985, U.S. Dist. Ct. (ea. dist.) N.C. 1985, U.S. Ct. Appeals (4th cir.) 1986. Assoc. Tharrington, Smith & Hargrove, Raleigh, N.C., 1985-89; pvt. practice Raleigh, 1989—; instr. Meredith Coll., Raleigh, 1989. Bd. dirs. Wake County Criminal Justice Partnership; mem. Gov.'s Task Force on Driving While Impaired, 1995, Raleigh Jaycees, 1990, Wake Dem. Men's Club, Raleigh, 1990, Raleigh YMCA, 1985—. Mem. N.C. Bar Assn. (exec. coun. young lawyers div. 1986), Wake County Bar Assn. (bd. dirs. 1991-92), Wake County Young Lawyers (pres. 1992), Wake County Acad. Criminal Trial Lawyers (pres. 1991). Democrat. Methodist. Criminal. Home: 8601 Bensley Ct Raleigh NC 27615-3702 Office: Bryan Collins Law Offices 16 W Martin St Ste 501 Raleigh NC 27601-2931

**COLLINS, GEORGE VINCENT, III,** lawyer; b. Albany, N.Y., Sept. 27, 1965; s. George Vincent Collins Jr. and Dolores Elizabeth Hart. BA, Siena Coll., 1987; JD, Albany Law Sch., 1990. Bar: N.Y., 1991, U.S. Dist. Ct. (no. dist.) N.Y., 1991. Assoc. Harris & Bixby, Albany, 1990-92; pvt. practice Albany, 1992—. Mem. ABA, N.Y. State Bar Assn., N.Y. State Defenders Assn., Capital Dist. Bankruptcy Bar Assn., Albany County Bar Assn., Rensselaer County Bar Assn. Avocation: Golf. Criminal, Family and matrimonial, Personal injury. Office: 311 State St Albany NY 12210-2001

**COLLINS, GLENN,** lawyer; b. Chgo., June 3, 1962; s. Joyce A. Collins. BA, Brown U., 1985; JD, Boston Coll., 1989. Bar: Ill. 1989. Assoc. atty. Katten Muchin & Zavis, Chgo., 1991-94; sole prctitioner Chgo., 1994—. Bd. dirs. USO, Chgo., 1995—. Capt. U.S. Army, 1990-91. Mem. Ill. Bar Assn., Chgo. Bar Assn., Assn. Aircraft Accident Investigators. Aviation, General civil litigation, General corporate. Office: 20 S Clark St Ste 2210 Chicago IL 60603-1805

**COLLINS, J. BARCLAY, II,** lawyer, oil company executive; b. Gettysburg, Pa., Oct. 21, 1944; s. Jennings Barclay and Golda Olevia (Hook) C.; m. Janna Claire Fall, June 25, 1966; children: J. Barclay III, L. Christian. AB magna cum laude, Harvard U., 1966; JD magna cum laude, Columbia U., 1969. Bar: N.Y. 1969. Law clk. to presiding judge U.S. Ct. Appeals (2d cir.), N.Y.C., 1969-70; assoc. Cravath, Swaine and Moore, N.Y.C., 1970-78; v.p., asst. gen. counsel City Investing Co., N.Y.C., 1978-84; exec. v.p., gen. counsel Amerada Hess Corp., N.Y.C., 1984—, also bd. dirs.; bd. dirs. Dime Bancorp Inc. Trustee Bklyn. Hosp.-Caledonian Hosp., Plymouth Ch. of the Pilgrims, Bklyn.; bd. dirs. United Hosp. Fund N.Y., John Milton Soc. for Blind; past gov. Bklyn. Heights Assn. Mem. ABA, N.Y. Bar Assn., N.Y.C. Yacht Club. Clubs: Heights Casino (Bklyn.); Harvard N.Y.C. Office: Amerada Hess Corp Ste 810 1185 Avenue Of The Americas Fl 800 New York NY 10036-2601

**COLLINS, JAMES FRANCIS,** lawyer, financial consultant; b. Evanston, Ill., July 31, 1943; s. James Francis Jr. and Jeanne (Moss) C.; m. Ann Peake Rogers, Apr. 5, 1983. BSc in Mktg., U. Louisville, 1969, JD, 1977; JD, Xavier U., 1971; MEd in Bus. Adminstrn. Bar: Ky. 1977, Ill. 1977, Fla. 1978, U.S. Dist. Ct. (we. dist.) Ky. 1978, U.S. Mil. Ct. Appeals 1978, U.S. Tax Ct. 1978, U.S. Customs Ct. 1978, U.S. Ct. Appeals (6th cir.) 1980, U.S. Supreme Ct. 1980, U.S. Dist. Ct. (so. dist.) Ind. 1981, U.S. Dist. Ct. (mid. dist.) Fla. 1982, Wis. 1989 (inactive status), Ind. 1989; cert. secondary tchr., Ill., Ky. Br. mgr., mcht. rep. Household Fin. Corp., Chgo., 1962-66; tchr. bus. Jefferson County Bd. Edn., Louisville, 1968-77; pvt. practice Louisville, 1977-82; criminal def. trial lawyer Pub. Defender, Sanford, Fla., 1982-83; pvt. practice Schaumburg, Ill., 1984-96, Louisville, 1997—; arbitrator, chairperson Cir. Ct. Cook. County, Mandatory Ct. Annexed Arbitration, 1990—; part-time instr. in comml. and internat. law Watterson Coll., Louisville, 1974-75. Dist. ct. judge candidate Jefferson County, Ky., 1981; cir. ct. judge candidate Dem. Primary, Chgo., 1986, 88, 92, 96; appellate ct. judge candidate, Chgo., 1990, Dem. Primary, Chgo., 1994; Dem. cir. ct. judge candidate, 1996; mem. S.E. Side Community Orgn.; legal counsel election day Dem. Party of Proviso Twp., 1985-90, 37th Ward of Chgo., 1991-94, 27th Ward of Chgo., 1991-94, election day legal counsel to Sen. Rickey Hendon, 1989—; mem. Berkeley (Ill.) Citizens Party, 1987; life mem. United Helenic Voters Asn., 1996—; life mem. Gary Marinaros Reg. Dem. Orgn., Proviso Twp., Ill., Sen. Rickey Hendon's 27th Ward of Chgo. Progressive Dem. Orgn.; mem. Maine Twp. (Ill.) Dem. Com., 1996—; mem. peoples assembly of Congressman Danny K. Davis of 7th Congl. Dist. Chgo.; mem. Alderman Percy Giles 37th Ward Dem. Orgn., Chgo., Alderman Madeline Haithcock 2d Ward Regular Dem. Orgn.; mem. or polit. cons. Polit. Action Com. Jean Kohn and Rev. Melvin Dlep, Chgo.; mem. Jean Soliz for Congress, Dem. Orgn. Chgo.; mem. Donald and Karen Marie Smith S.W. Side Chgo. 12th Ward and 23d Ward Polit.. Cons. Orgn. for Regular Dems.; mem. Robert Bachs Dep. Committeeman of West Provciso Dem. Orgn., Melrose Prk, Ill.; assoc. Alderman Richard Mell 33d Ward Dem. Orgn., Chgo.; mem. Ill. State Senator Robert Mulano Regular Dem. Orgn., Committeeman Andy Prysbo Maine Twp. of Cook County Regular Dem. Orgn.; mem. Rep. Nat. Com., chmn. cons. nonpartisan com. Recipient ICLE 32 Hour Bankruptcy Course award, 1985, Recognition award Berkeley (Ill.) Citizens party, 1986, Continuing Legal Edn. Recognition award Ky. Bar Assn., 1987, 91, 92, 93, 94, 95, 96, 97, 98, Recognition awards Westside Chgo. Black Polit. Leaders Assn., 1990, 92, Recognition award Cook County Dem. Party Fair Coalition, 1992, Continuing Legal Edn. Recognition award Ky. Bar Assn., 1996; named Disting. Citizen of Louisville, Ky. by Mayor Harvey Stone, 1976, Hon. Cpt. Belle Louisville by County Judge Exec. Todd Hollenbach, 1974, Hon. Ky. Col. by Gov. Wenden Ford, Lt. Gov. Thelma Stoval, 1974. Mem. Ky. Bar Assn. (Clie award 1998), Louisville Bar Assn., Internat. Platform Assn., Chgo. Bar Assn. (Ill. indsl. commn. worker's compensation com., adminstrv. law com.), U. Louisville Bus. Sch. Alumni Assn., Xavier U. Alumni Assn., U. Louisville Law Sch. Alumni Assn., United Hellenic Voters of Am. (life), Sigma Delta Kappa. Avocation: politics. Consumer commercial, General corporate, Finance.

**COLLINS, JAMES SLADE, II,** lawyer; b. St. Louis, June 9, 1937; s. James Slade and Dolma Ruby (Neilsen) C.; m. Neva Frances Guinn, June 27, 1959; children: Shari, Camala Ann. BSBA, Washington U., 1958, JD, 1961. Bar: Mo. 1961, U.S. Supreme Ct. 1969, U.S. Dist. Ct. (ea. dist.) Mo. 1972, U.S. Ct. Appeals (8th cir.) 1972. Assoc., Whalen, O'Connor, Grauel & Sarkisian, St. Louis, 1961-70, ptnr., 1970-72, Whalen, O'Connor, Collins & Danis, St. Louis, 1972-75; assoc. Hullverson, Hullverson & Frank, Inc., St. Louis, 1975-78; pvt. practice, St. Louis, 1979—. Trustee, Village of Hanley Hills, Mo., 1966-69, mayor, 1967, mcpl. judge, 1967-68, 1969-70. Mem. ABA, Bar Assn. Met. St. Louis, Lawyers Assn., St. Louis Am. Trial Lawyers Assn., Mo. Trial Lawyers Assn., Phi Delta Phi. Republican. Baptist. Federal civil litigation, State civil litigation, Personal injury. Home: 916 Parkwatch Dr Ballwin MO 63011-3640 Office: 1015 Locust St Ste 428 Saint Louis MO 63101-1333

**COLLINS, JOSEPH BERNARD,** lawyer; b. Bennington, Vt., Feb. 11, 1953; s. James Bernard and Mary Agnes (O'Neil) C.; m. Denise Claire Banville, June 11, 1977. AA, Holyoke Community Coll., Mass., 1973; AB, Boston Coll., 1975; JD, Suffolk U., Boston, 1978. Bar: Mass. 1978. Assoc. Kamberg, Berman & Hendel, P.C., Springfield, Mass., 1978-82; ptnr. Hendel & Collins P.C., Springfield, 1982—; adj. prof. law Western New Eng. Coll., Springfield, 1982-93. Fin. com. Town of Wilbraham, Mass., 1982-84. Mem. Comml. League Am. (New Eng. regional chmn. 1989-90, vice chmn. 1988-89), Hampden County Bar Assn. (chmn. young lawyers div. 1982-83). Roman Catholic. Avocations: scuba diving, skiing. Bankruptcy. Office: Hendel & Collins PC 101 State St Ste 525 Springfield MA 01103-2020

**COLLINS, MARY ELIZABETH,** lawyer; b. White Plains, N.Y., Aug. 24, 1953; d. Gerard P. and Mary E. (Fleming) C.; m. Samuel D. Ellis, May 11, 1983; children: Megan Elizabeth, Katherine Anne, Anne Caroline. BA in Art History, Stanford U., 1975; JD with honors, U. San Francisco, 1978. Bar: Calif. 1978, U.S. Dist. Ct. (no. dist.) Calif. 1978. Assoc. Orrick, Herrington & Sutcliffe, San Francisco, 1978-82; asst. gen. counsel Transam. Corp., San Francisco, 1982-84, asst. sec., 1984, asst. treas., 1984-85; ptnr. Law Offices Ellis & Collins, San Luis Obispo, Calif., 1985—. Editor-in-chief: U. San Francisco Law Review, 1977-78. Bd. dirs. Hospice of San Luis Obispo County, 1996—, sec., 1997-99, 2d v.p., 1999—. Mem. Calif. Bar Assn. (corps. com. bus. law sect. 1983-84), San Luis Obispo County Bar Assn., San Luis Obispo County Women Lawyers Assn. (sec. 1987-88). Avocations: reading, travel, ballet. General corporate, Mergers and acquisitions, Finance. Office: Ellis & Collins 1150 Osos St Ste 203 San Luis Obispo CA 93401-3693

**COLLINS, MOSELEY,** lawyer; four children. BA in History, U. Fla., 1969, MA in Psychology, 1979; postgrad., Ga. State U., 1972; JD, LaSalle U., 1980. Bar: Calif. 1980. Pvt. practice El Dorado Hills, Calif., 1980—. Founding pres. Santa Clara County (Calif.) chpt. Mothers Against Drunk Drivers; vol. dep. dist. atty. for Santa Cruz County, Santa Clara County and Sacramento County; past youth soccer coach, softball coach. Mem. ATLA, Calif. State Bar Assn., Consumer Attys. of Calif., San Diego County Bar Assn. Personal injury. Office: 980 9th St Fl 16 Sacramento CA 95814-2736 also: PO Box 5500 El Dorado Hls CA 95762-0009

**COLLINS, PATRICIA LYNNE,** judge; b. Buffalo, Apr. 23, 1953; d. William Joseph and Fedora Marie C. Student, Canisius Coll., 1971-72; BA summa cum laude, SUNY, Buffalo, 1975; JD cum laude, Georgetown U., 1979. Bar: Calif., 1979, U.S. Dist. Ct. (cen. dist.) Calif., 1979, U.S. Dist. Ct. (so., no. dists.) Calif., 1981, U.S. Ct. Appeals (9th cir.), 1982. Assoc. Adams Duque & Hazeltine, L.A., 1979-82; asst. U.S. atty. U.S. Atty. Cen. Dist., L.A., 1982-88; judge L.A. Mcpl. Ct., 1988-92, L.A. Superior Ct., 1992—; mem. adv. bd. Civil Trial Manual Bur. Nat. Affairs, 1984-88. Mem. Adv. Com. Correctional Edn., Sacramento, 1988-90; referee AYSO, Pacific Palisades, Calif., 1995—; asst. leader Girls Scouts U.S., Pacific Palisades, 1997. Recipient Appellate Adv. award Internat. Assn. Trial Lawyers, 1979. Mem. Nat. Assn. Women Judges, Calif. Judges Assn., Women Lawyers Assn. L.A. Office: LA Superior Ct 1725 Main St Dept Q Santa Monica CA 90401-3261

**COLLINS, PHILIP REILLY,** lawyer, educator; b. New Orleans, July 26, 1921; s. James Mark and Katherine (Gallaher) C.; m. Mary Catherine O'Leary, Feb. 9, 1946. BA, Loyola U., New Orleans, 1939, JD, 1942; MA in Govt. and Internat. Law and Rels., Georgetown U., 1948, PhD, 1950; LLM, George Washington U., 1952. Bar: La. 1942, Mass. 1948, D.C. 1953, Md. 1983, Va. 1986. Atty. Bur. Land Mgmt., Dept. Interior, Washington, 1946-47; asst. legis. counsel Office of Solicitor, P.O. Dept., 1947-48; pvt. practice Washington, 1954-77, 79—; ptnr. MacCracken, Collins & Hawes, 1960-69; chief counsel, staff dir. com. on rules U.S. Ho. of Reps., 1977-78; spl. counsel Fed. Home Loan Bank Bd., 1961-69, Ky. Savs. and Loan

League, 1967-68, State of Alaska, 1967-68; vis. prof., spl. asst. to pres. for labor rels. Queens Coll., 1969-70; lectr. pub. adminstrn. Sch. Social Scis. Cath. U. Am., 1954-56, lectr. Sch. Law, 1954-60. Mem. adv. com. on wills, trusts and other bequests Loyola U., New Orleans, 1966-69, charter mem. bd. visitors Law Sch., 1968-85, mem. pres.'s coun., 1976-85. Capt USAAF, 1942-46, PTO; maj. USAF, Korea; col. Res., ret. Mem. ABA, La. Bar Assn., Mass. Bar Assn., D.C. Bar Assn., Assn. of Bar of City of N.Y., Md. Bar Assn., Va. State Bar, KC, Mil. Order of Carabao, Univ. Club (Washington), Delta Theta Phi, Phi Alpha Theta. Democrat. Roman Catholic. Probate, Legislative, Federal civil litigation. Home: 1300 Crystal Dr Apt 209 Arlington VA 22202-3234

**COLLINS, SAMUEL W., JR.,** judge; b. Caribou, Maine, Sept. 17, 1923; s. Samuel Wilson Collins & Elizabeth Black C; m. Dorothy Small, 1952; children: Edward, Elizabeth, Diane. BA, U. Maine; JD, Harvard U. Lawyer Rockland, Maine, 1947—; justice Supreme Jud. Ct., Portland, Maine. Trustee Rockland Sch. Dist, 1949-61; Maine State Senate Dist. 21, 1975-84, Majority Leader, 1981-82, Minority Leader, 1983-84. Recipient Disting. Svc. award Jaycees, 1978. Mem. Maine Bar Assn., Rotary, Phi Beta Kappa, Phi Kappa Phi, Delta Tau Delta. Unitarian Universalist. Republican. Office: Knox County Courthouse 62 Union St Rockland ME 04841-2836

**COLLINS, STEVEN M.,** lawyer; b. Atlanta, Oct. 22, 1952; s. E.B. and Judith (Morse) C.; divorced; 1 child, Erin M.; m. Anne Frances Garland, Oct. 31, 1987; 1 child, Timothy G. AB, Harvard U., 1974, JD, 1977. Bar: Ga. 1977, U.S. Dist. Ct. (no. dist.) Ga. 1977, U.S. Ct. Appeals (5th cir.) 1977, U.S. Ct. Appeals (11th cir.) 1981, U.S. Dist. Ct. (mid. dist.) Ga. 1982, U.S. Tax Ct. 1984, U.S. Ct. Appeals (4th cir.) 1986, U.S. Supreme Ct. 1994. Assoc. Alston & Bird, Atlanta, 1977-83, ptnr., 1983—; editor-in-chief Ga. State Bar Journal, Atlanta, 1982-84. Mem. ABA, State Bar Ga., Atlanta Bar Assn. General civil litigation, Banking, Securities. Office: Alston & Bird One Atlantic Ctr 1201 W Peachtree St NW Atlanta GA 30309-3424

**COLLINS, SUSAN E.,** lawyer; b. Mobridge, S.D., Oct. 20, 1950; d. Frank X. and Muriel (Culp) Sonnek; children: Elizabeth, John. BA, U. S.D., 1973, JD, 1976. In-house counsel, trust officer Toy Nat. Bank, Sioux City, Iowa, 1976-78; trust officer Rainier Nat. Bank, Seattle, 1978-80; assoc. Finley, Kumble, Wagner, Heine, Underberg & Casey, Washington, 1980-81, Liddell, Sapp, Zivley, Hill & La Boon, Houston, 1981-87; v.p., assoc. gen. counsel Chase Bank of Tex., Houston, 1991—. Mem. State Bar Tex. (bus. law sect., UCC com., bd. cert. estate planning and probate). Episcopal. Contracts commercial, Estate planning, Probate. Office: Chase Bank Tex PO Box 2558 Houston TX 77252-2558

**COLLINS, THEODORE JOHN,** lawyer; b. Walla Walla, Wash., Oct. 2, 1936; s. Robert Bonfield and Catherine Roselle (Snyder) C.; m. Patricia Spengler Pasieka, May 11, 1968; children: Jonathan, Caitlin, Matthew, Patrick, Flannary. BA, U. Notre Dame, 1958; postgrad., U. Bonn, Fed. Republic Germany, 1959; LLB, Harvard U., 1962. Bar: Wash. 1962, U.S. Supreme Ct. 1982, U.S. Ct. Appeals (fed. cir.) 1982, U.S. Dist. Ct. (ea. dist.) Wash. 1965, U.S. Dist. Ct. (we. dist.) Wash. 1962. Ptnr. Perkins Coie Law Firm, Seattle, 1962-86; v.p., gen. counsel The Boeing Co., Seattle, 1986-98, sr. v.p., gen. counsel, 1998—. Mem. ABA, Boeing Mgmt. Assn., Wash. State Bar Assn., King County Bar Assn., Wash. Athletic Club. General corporate, General civil litigation, Government contracts and claims. Office: Boeing Co PO Box 3707 MS 13-08 Seattle WA 98124-2207*

**COLLINS, TODD STOWE,** lawyer; b. Chgo., Oct. 18, 1952; s. Thomas Hightower and Beulah Stowe Collins; m. Susan Faith Burt, June 19, 1982; children: Rachel, Katherine, Leila. BA, U. Pa., 1973, JD, 1978. Bar: Pa. 1979, Del. 1979, U.S. Dist. Ct. (ea. dist.) Pa. 1979, U.S. Dist. Ct. Del. 1979, U.S. Ct. Appeals (llth cir.) 1989, U.S. Ct. Appeals (9th cir.) 1996. Assoc. Potter Anderson & Carroon, Wilmington, Del., 1978-80, Braemer & Kessler, Phila., 1980-82; assoc. Berger & Montague, PC, Phila., 1982-85, shareholder, 1986-98, mem. planning (or exec.) com., 1998—. Bd. dirs. Phila. Sr. Ctr., 1994—. Mem. Phila. Bar Assn. Episcopalian. Avocations: child-raising, tennis, biking, gardening, military history. Email: tscgbm.net. Securities, Federal civil litigation. Office: Berger & Montague PC 1622 Locust St Philadelphia PA 19103-6305

**COLLINS, WHITFIELD JAMES,** lawyer; b. Dallas, Aug. 26, 1918; s. Jasper and Gertrude (James) C.; m. Beth Cooper, June 5, 1951 (dec. Aug. 1980); children: Whitfield James Jr., Kay, Cooper R. AA, Kemper Mil. Sch., 1936; BA, U. Tex., 1938, JD, 1940; LLM, Harvard U., 1941. Bar: Tex. 1940, U.S. Dist. Ct. (no. dist.) Tex. 1950, U.S. Ct. Claims 1978, U.S. Tax Ct. 1949, U.S. Ct. Appeals (5th cir.) 1981. Atty. Office Gen. Counsel Treasury Dept., Washington, 1941-42, Office Chief Counsel, IRS, Washington and N.Y.C., 1946-48; assoc. Cantey, Hanger, Johnson, Scarborough & Gooch, Ft. Worth, 1949-54; ptnr. Cantey & Hanger and predecessor firms, Ft. Worth, 1954-96, of counsel, 1996—; sec., bd. dirs. Vol. Purchasing Groups, Inc., Bonham, Tex., 1968-95; pres. Fifth Ave. Found. and C.J. Wrightsman Ednl. Fund, 1980—; bd. dirs., sec.-treas. T.J. Brown and C.A. Lupton Found., Ft. Worth; former chmn. bd. Intercultura, Inc., Ft. Worth. Contbr. articles in field to profl. jours. Bd. dirs., past pres. Moncrief Radiation Ctr., Ft. Worth, Ft. Worth Art Assn., Arts Council Ft. Worth and Tarrant County, Ft. Worth Art Commn.; bd. dirs. Van Cliburn Found., Ft. Worth Opera Assn. Served to lt. commdr. USNR, 1942-46. Fellow ABA (life), State Bar Tex. (chmn. taxation sect. 1964-65); mem. Tarrant County Bar Assn. (Blackstone award 1995). Episcopalian. General corporate, Estate planning, Probate. Home: 6732 Brants Ln Fort Worth TX 76116-7202 Office: Cantey & Hanger 801 Cherry St Ste 2100 Fort Worth TX 76102-6898

**COLLINS, WILLIAM COLDWELL,** lawyer; b. El Paso, June 19, 1921; s. William Reuben and Julia (Coldwell) C.; m. Marian Bainbridge (dec. May 1977; children: Nancy, Cynthia, Marian; m. Betty Wing. BS, U. Tex., El Paso, 1943; LLB, U. Tex., Austin, 1949; JD, U. S.C., 1959. Bar: Tex. 1949. Pvt. practice El Paso. Bd. dirs. El Paso chpt. Girl Scouts U.S., 1960-61; bd. dirs. El Paso chpt. ARC, 1960-75, pres., 1975-77; v.p. El Paso Hist. soc., 1974-75. Mem. El Paso Bar Assn. (bd. dirs. 1961-64, pres. 1978-79), El Paso C.C., Rotary (pres., bd. dirs. 1969-76). Avocations: railroads, philately. Appellate, General civil litigation, Family and matrimonial. Home: 5817 Mira Serena Dr El Paso TX 79912-2013 Office: 5738 N Mesa St El Paso TX 79912-5427

**COLLINSON, DALE STANLEY,** lawyer; b. Tulsa, Okla., Sept. 1, 1938; s. Harold Everett and Charlotte Elizabeth (Bonds) C.; m. Susan Waring Smith, June 7, 1969; children—Stuart, Eleanor. A.B. summa cum laude in Politics and Econs., Yale U., 1960; LL.B., Columbia U., 1963. Bar: N.Y. 1963, U.S. Tax Ct. 1977. Law clk. U.S. Ct. Appeals (2d cir.), N.Y.C., 1963-64; law clk. to Justice Byron R. White, U.S. Supreme Ct., Washington, 1964-66; asst. prof. Stanford (Calif.) Law Sch., 1966-68, assoc. prof., 1968-72; atty.-advisor Office of Tax Policy, U.S. Dept. Treasury, Washington, 1972-73, assoc. tax legis. counsel, 1973-74, dep. tax legis. counsel, 1974-75, tax legis. counsel, 1975-76; now tax ptnr. Willkie Farr & Gallagher, N.Y.C.; panel mem. Practising Law Inst. programs, 1981, 82, 84, 86, 88, Am. Law Inst.-ABA program, 1984, Investment Co. Inst. programs, 1992, 94. Fellow Am. Coll. of Tax Counsel; Mem. ABA, N.Y. State Bar (chmn. tax sect. 1985), Assn. of Bar of City of N.Y. (tax coun. 1990-93, vice chmn. taxation of corps. com. 1990-93), Nat. Assn. Bond Lawyers. Republican. Contbr. articles to legal jours. Corporate taxation, Taxation, general, Municipal (including bonds). Home: 320 King St Chappaqua NY 10514-2729 Office: Willkie Farr & Gallagher 787 7th Ave New York NY 10019-6099 *Our country is becoming dangerously dependent on computers. Not that using a computer is bad, but that we are more and more lacking the human resources (in computer hardware and software technicians) to keep them working. To be self reliant in the future, one must be able to keep his own computer working.*

**COLLYER, MICHAEL,** lawyer; b. N.Y.C., Feb. 5, 1942; s. Clayton Johnson and Heloise (Green) C.; m. Karen Machon, Nov. 4, 1963 (div. July 1979); m. Sandra Karen Schaum, July 28 1979; children: Sophie Marie; stepdaughter Shelley Malia. BA, Williams Coll., 1963; LLB, Columbia U., 1966. Bar: N.Y. 1966, Assoc., Becker & London, N.Y.C., 1966-70; ptnr. Kay Collyer & Boose and predecessors, N.Y.C., 1970—; legal adviser NATAS, N.Y.C., 1978—, trustee, 1982—, nat. officer, 1982—, chmn., 1990—; instr. bus. law Columbia U., N.Y.C., 1966-69; speaker conv. Practicing Law Inst., 1977, mem. chpt. motion pictures and TV under new copyright statute, 1978. Trustee George Heller Meml. Scholarship Fund; active N.Y.C. Mayor's Adv. Coun. Film and Broadcasting, 1993. With U.S. Army, 1966-71. Mem. Assn. of Bar of City of N.Y. (com. Entertainment Law 1992—), N.Y. Bar Assn. (author TV sect. entertainment law 1995), Internat. Radio and TV Soc., Internat. Coun. Nat. Acad. Arts and Scis. (bd. dirs.), N.Y. Yacht Club. Entertainment. Home: 25 Chester Ct Cortlandt Mnr NY 10567-6361 Office: Kay Collyer & Boose LLP One Dag Hammarskjold Pla New York NY 10017-2299

**COLMAN, RICHARD THOMAS,** lawyer; b. Boston, Sept. 22, 1935; s. Albert Vincent and Marie Catherine (Henehan) C.; m. Marilyn Flavin, Dec. 1, 1962; children: Elizabeth B., Catherine B., Richard T. Jr., Patrick B. AB magna cum laude, U. Notre Dame, 1957; LLB cum laude, Boston Coll., 1962. Bar: Mass. 1962, D.C. 1966. Trial atty. Antitrust Div. U.S. Dept. Justice, Washington, 1962-66; ptnr. Howrey & Simon, Washington, 1970—. Trustee Indian Mountain Sch., Lakeville, Conn., 1992-98; regional del. Boston Coll. Law Sch. Alumni Assn., 1992-99. Mem. ABA, Internat. Bar Assn., Fed. Bar Assn., D.C. Bar Assn., Wianno Club, Beach Club. Democrat. Roman Catholic. Administrative and regulatory, Antitrust, Federal civil litigation. Office: Howrey & Simon 1299 Pennsylvania Ave NW Ste 1 Washington DC 20004-2420

**COLMANT, ANDREW ROBERT,** lawyer; b. Bklyn., Oct. 10, 1931; s. Edward J. and Mary Elizabeth (Byrne) C.; children: Stephen, Robert, Elizabeth, Carolyn. BBA, St. Johns U., Jamaica, N.Y., 1957, LLB, 1959. Bar: N.Y. 1959, U.S. Dist. Ct. (so. and ea. dists.) N.Y. 1961, U.S. Ct. Appeals (2nd cir.) 1969, U.S. Ct. Appeals (4th cir.) 1977, U.S. Supreme Ct. 1991. Assoc. Hill, Rivkins, Carey, Loesberg, O'Brien & Mulroy and predecessor firms, 1959-73, ptnr., 1973-87; of counsel Jerrold E. Hyams, 1988-91, Peter F. Broderick, 1992; proctor in admiralty; active USMC amphibious reconnaissance Army Gen. Intelligence Sch. Author: Outline of General Average. Cpl. USMC, 1952-54. Mem. ABA, Assn. Trial Lawyers of Am., N.Y. State Bar Assn., N.Y. County Lawyers Assn., Maritime Law Assn. (life), Asia Pacific Law Assn., Pacific Rim Maritime Law Assn., Assn. Internat. de Droit des Assurances. Admiralty, Insurance, Private international. Home: Bethany Manor 500 Broad St Apt 11Y Keyport NJ 07735-1640

**COLOGNE, GORDON BENNETT,** lawyer; b. Long Beach, Calif., Aug. 24, 1924; s. Knox M. Cologne; m. Patricia Cologne; children: Steven J., Ann Maureen Meyer. BS, U. So. Calif., 1948; LLB cum laude, Southwestern U. Sch. of Law, L.A., 1951. Bar: Calif. 1951, U.S. Supreme Ct. 1961. Trial atty. U.S. Dept. of Justice, Jacksonville, Fla., 1951-52; pvt. practice Indio, Calif., 1952-61; mayor Indio City Coun., 1954; mem. state assembly Calif. Legis., Sacramento, 1961-65; mem. senate Calif. State Senate, Sacramento, 1965-72; justice Ct. of Appeal, San Diego, 1972-84; govt. rels. atty. Sacramento, 1984-99. With USN, 1944-46. Named one of Outstanding Young Men of Calif., Calif. Jr. C. of C., 1961; recipient Freedom Found. award, 1965.

**COLOMA, MARIA LOURDES CLARIS,** lawyer; b. Quezon City, The Philippines, Aug. 14, 1966; came to U.S., 1981; d. Rogelio Baligad and Adelaida Claris C. BA, Coll. St. Benedict, 1989; JD, William Mitchell Coll. Law, 1994. Bar: Minn. 1994. Asst. pub. defender Hennepin County Pub. Defender's Office, Mpls., 1995—. Mem. ABA, Nat. Asian Bar Assn. (sec. 1996-97, bd. dirs.). Office: Hennepin County Pub Defender 317 2d Ave S Ste 200 Minneapolis MN 55401

**COLOMBIK, RICHARD MICHAEL,** lawyer; b. Chgo., July 10, 1953; s. S. Robert and Rose Y. (Ziegler) C.; m. Colleen Colombik; children: Jeremy Paul, Justin Franklin, Samantha Brooke. BS, U. Colo., 1975; CPA, U. Ill., Champaign, 1977; JD with distinction, John Marshall Law Sch., Chgo., 1980. Bar: Ill. 1980, U.S. Dist. Ct. (no. dist.) Ill. 1980, U.S. Tax Ct. 1980. Tax acct. Henry Crown and Co., Chgo., 1977-78, Schur, Yormark & Rabyne, Northfield, Ill., 1978-80; tax mgr. Touche Ross and Co., Chgo., 1980-82; ptnr. Colombik & Bell P.C., Palatine, Ill., 1982-87, Richard M. Colombik & Assocs. P.C., Schaumburg, Park Ridge, Ill., 1987—; gen. ptnr. United Holsteins, Owosso, Mich., 1982-87; regional dir. Amtax Mgmt., N.Y.C., 1985-86; chief exec. officer Sports Communication Agy., 1987. Trustee Rep. Presdl. Task Force, 1985—. Named to Order of John Marshall. Mem. Am. Assn. Attys.-CPAs, Ill. State Bar Assn. (fed. taxation sect. coun.), N.W. Suburban Bar Assn. (estate and tax com.), Ill. CPA Soc., Gavel Soc., Beta Alpha Psi. Republican. Club: Meadows (Rolling Meadows, Ill.). Estate planning, Personal income taxation, Real property. Office: Richard M Colombik & Assocs PC 1111 N Plaza Dr Ste 430 Schaumburg IL 60173-4970

**COLTEN, RICHARD J.,** lawyer; b. N.Y.C., Sept. 21, 1943; s. Oscar Aaron and Zina (Radin) C.; m. Susanne Swett Carey, July 14, 1965 (div. Oct. 1982); children: Tamara Colten Stevens, Bradley P.; m. Elizabeth S. Johns, Feb. 24, 1984. BS, Am. U., 1965; JD with honors, George Washington U., 1972. Bar: Va. 1972, U.S. Supreme Ct. 1976. Counselor, supr. Juvenile and Domestic Rels. Dist. Ct., Fairfax, Va., 1965-72; asst. commonwealth's atty. Office of Commonwealth Atty. of Fairfax County, Fairfax, 1972-74; prin. Surovell, Jackson, Colten & Dugan, P.C., Fairfax, 1974—; commr. in chancery Cir. Ct. of Fairfax County, 1972—, concilator and neutral case evaluator for equitable distbn. cases, 1995—; bd. dirs. Legal Svcs. No. Va. Inc., 1996—; substitute judge Gen. Dist. and Juvenile and Domestic Rels. Dist. Cts. of Fairfax County, 1976-88; bd. dirs. Legal Aid Soc. Fairfax County, 1976-79. Mem. ABA, ATLA, Va. State Bar (disciplinary bd. 1998—, bar coun. 1989-95, standing com. on lawyer discipline 1995-97, grievance com. 1985-88), Fairfax County Bar Assn. (jud. screening com., family law com. 1980—, pub. svc. com. 1996—, bd. dirs. 1981-94), Va. Trial Lawyers Assn. Family and matrimonial. Office: Surovell Jackson et al 4010 University Dr Ste 200 Fairfax VA 22030-6805

**COLTON, ROBERTA ANN,** lawyer; b. N.Y.C., July 22, 1957; d. John Adam Colton and Roberta (Phillips) Russell. BS in Commerce, U. Va., 1979; JD, William & Mary Coll., 1982. Bar: Fla. 1983, U.S. Dist. Ct. (mid., so. and no. dists.) Fla. 1983, U.S. Ct. Appeals (11th cir.) 1983. Law clk. to Hon. James C. Hill U.S. Ct. Appeals (11th cir.), Atlanta, 1982-83; assoc. Trenam, Kemker et al, Tampa, Fla., 1983-87; ptnr. Trenam, Simmons, Kemker et al, Tampa, Fla., 1988—; v.p., bd. dirs. Playmakers, Inc., Tampa, 1986-92. Author: Workout Strategies and Risks, 1988, Fraudulent Transfers and Preferences in Bankruptcy, 1988, Litigating Commerical Cases in Bankruptcy Court, 1989, Buying and Selling Assets in Bankruptcy, 1990, Contract Disputes in Bankruptcy, 1991. Collections lt. Heart Assn., Tampa, 1988; coach Brandon High Sch. Legal Studies Program, Brandon, Fla., 1986-88; pres.'s counsel Fla. Orch.; bd. dirs. Bay Area Aids Consortion, Inc., 1990-93. Mem. ABA, Am. Bankruptcy Inst., Fla. Bar Assn. (bankruptcy sect. 1986-92, vice chmn. bankruptcy/UCC com. 1991-92, chmn. bankruptcy/UCC com. 1992-93, exec. counsel bus. law sect. 1988-99, chair 1997-98, CLE com. 1988-91), Fla. Assn. Woman Lawyers, Fed. Bar Assn. (bd. dirs.), Tampa Bay Bankruptcy Bar Assn., So. Dist. Bankruptcy Bar Assn., Hillsborough County Bar Assn. Democrat. Roman Catholic. Bankruptcy, General civil litigation, Contracts commercial. Office: Trenam Kemker Scharf Barkin Frye O'Neill & Mullins Barkin Frye & O'Neill 101 E Kennedy Blvd Tampa FL 33602-5179

**COLTON, STERLING DON,** lawyer, business executive, missionary; b. Vernal, Utah, Apr. 28, 1929; s. Hugh Wilkins and Marguerite (Maughan) C.; m. Eleanor Ricks, Aug. 6, 1954; children: Sterling David, Carolyn, Bradley Hugh, Steven Ricks. BS in Banking and Fin., U. Utah, 1951; JD, Stanford U., 1954. Bar: Calif. 1954, Utah 1954, D.C. 1967. Ptnr. Van Cott, Bagley, Cornwall & McCarthy, Salt Lake City, 1957-66; vice chair, sr. v.p., gen. counsel, bd. dirs. Marriott Corp. and Marriott Internat., 1954-95; former pres. Can. Vancouver Mission Ch. of Jesus Christ of Latter Day Saints, 1995-98, also bd. dirs.; pres. Washignton Temple, Ch. of Jesus Christ of Latter Day Saints, 1999—; v.p. Colton Ranch Corp., Vernal, 1987—; former bd. dirs. Megaherz Corp. and Dyncorp; former chmn. bd. dirs. Nat. Chamber Litigation Ctr. Former bd. dirs. Polynesian Cultural Ctr.; former chmn. nat. adv. coun. U. Utah, Ballet West, nat. adv. coun.; mem. adv. coun. The Nat. Conservancy. Maj. JAG, U.S. Army, 1954-57. Mem. ABA, Calif. Bar Assn., Utah Bar Assn., D.C. Bar Assn., Washington Met. Corp. Counsel Assn. (former pres., dir.), Sigma Chi. Republican. Mem. LDS Ch. General corporate, Finance, Real property.

**COLUSSY, SUSAN EILEEN HILLICK,** lawyer; b. Fulton, N.Y., Aug. 5, 1945; d. W. Kenneth and Helen MacLaughlan (Forbes) Hillick; m. Alan Robert Colussy; children: Tait Katharine, Alan R. II. BA in Religion and Philsophy, Davis and Elkins Coll., 1967; JD, Ga. State U., 1986. Bar: Ga. 1986, U.S. Dist. Ct. (no. dist.) Ga. 1987. Dir. Christian edn. Covenant Presbyn. Ch., Atlanta, 1968-72, 77-80; dir., tchr. Peachtree Internat. Pre-Sch., Atlanta, 1973-75; staff Presbyn. Pub. House, Atlanta, 1980-82; atty., program dir. Cath. Social Svcs., Atlanta, 1986—. Gov.'s Task Force on Tchr. Cert., State of Ga., Atlanta, 1979; bd. mem. Morningside/Lenox Park Assn., Atlanta, 1980-82, Jubilee Ptnrs., Comer, Ga., 1989-95; elder Covenant Presbyn. Ch., Atlanta. Named Disting. Alumna, Coll. of Law, Ga. State U., Atlanta, 1988. Mem. Am. Immigration Lawyers Assn. (Asylum liaison Atlanta chpt. 1990-95, nat. Asylum task force 1994). Democrat. Avocations: music, politics. Immigration, naturalization, and customs. Office: Cath Social Svcs Inc 680 W Peachtree St NW Atlanta GA 30308-1931

**COLVILLE, ROBERT E.,** judge; b. Pitts., May 23, 1935; s. John and Mary M. (Goldbronn) C.; children: Michael C., Robert J., Molly. B.A. Duquesne U., 1963, J.D., 1969. Bar: Pa. 1969, U.S. Dist. Ct. (we. dist.) Pa. 1969. Tchr., coach North Catholic High Sch., Pitts., 1959-64; patrolman, detective Bur. of Police, Dept. Pub. Safety, Pitts., 1964-68, police legal adviser, 1969-70, asst. dir. Dept. Pub. Safety, 1970-71, supt. Bur. of Police, Pitts., 1971-75; clk., detective Dist. Atty.'s Office of Allegheny County, Pitts., 1968-69, dist. atty., 1976-97; judge Allegheny County Ct. Common Pleas, 1998—; adj. prof. law Duquesne U. Sch. of Law, Pitts., 1976-78; instr. in labor law LaRoche Coll., Pitts., 1983-84. Contbr. articles to profl. jours. Past chmn. Joint Allegheny County Narcotics Task Force; chmn. Allegheny County Drug Initiative; mem. Pa. Democratic Com. Served with USMC, 1953-56; foremr trustee Community Coll. of Allegheny County. Recipient Dapper Dan award Pitts. Post Gazette, 1963, Disting. Service award County Detectives Assn., 1977, Service Recognition award Pitts. Community Crime Prevention Coalition, 1980; Law Enforcement award Dep. Sheriff's Assn. of Pa., 1983; Outstanding Grad., Duquesne U., 1969; Jr. C. of C. Man of Yr. in Law, 1973; Phi Alpha Delta Law Alumni of Yr., 1976; Outstanding Grad., Duquesne U. Century Club, 1978; Outstanding Law Alumnus Duquesne U. Law Alumni Assn., 1985. Office: 436 Grant St Pittsburgh PA 15219-2400

**COLVIN, JOHN O.,** federal judge; b. 1946. AB, U. Mo., 1968; JD, Georgetown U., 1971, LLM in Taxation, 1978. Tax counsel Office of Sen. Bob Packwood, 1975-84; senate fin. com. chief counsel, 1985-87; chief minority counsel U.S. Senate, 1987-88; judge U.S. Tax Ct., Washington, 1988—; adj. prof. law Georgetown U. Law Ctr., 1987—. Served with USCG, 1971-75. Mem. Fed. Bar Assn. Office: US Tax Ct 400 2nd St NW Washington DC 20217-0002

**COMBS, W(ILLIAM) HENRY, III,** lawyer; b. Casper, Wyo., Mar. 18, 1949; s. William Henry and Ruth M. (Wooster) C.; divorced; 1 child, J. Bradley. Student, Northwestern U., 1967-70; BS, U. Wyo., 1972, JD, 1975. Bar: Wyo. 1975, U.S. Dist. Ct. Wyo. 1975, U.S. Ct. Appeals (10th cir.) 1990, U.S. Supreme Ct. 1990. Assoc. Murane & Bostwick, Casper, 1975-77, ptnr., 1978—. Mem. com. on resolution of fee disputes, 1988-92. Mem. ABA (tort and ins. practice, law office mgmt. sects.), NRA, Natrona County Bar Assn., Def. Rsch. Inst., Am. Judicature Soc., Def. Lawyers Assn. of Wyo., Assn. Ski Def. Attys., Nat. Bd. Trial Advocacy (cert.), U.S. Handball Assn., Waterski USA, Casper Boat Club, Casper Petroleum Club, Porsche Club Am., BMW Club Am. Republican. Episcopalian. Avocations: handball, waterskiing, snow skiing, climbing, driving. Federal civil litigation, State civil litigation, Personal injury. Office: Murane & Bostwick 201 N Wolcott St Casper WY 82601-1922

**COMEAU, MICHAEL GERARD,** lawyer; b. Balt., July 13, 1956; s. Joseph Gerard and Irma (Cullison) C.; m. Penny Lee Derrickson, Apr. 14, 1984; children: Joseph Gerard, Nicole Lee. BA, Randolph-Macon Coll., 1978; JD, U. Balt., 1981; postgrad., George Washington U., 1982-83, U.S. Army Judge Advocate Gen.'s Basic Course, 1992; Advanced Course, 1994. Bar: Md. 1981, U.S. Dist Ct. Md. 1982, U.S. Ct. Mil. Appeals 1982, U.S. Ct. Appeals (4th and D.C. cirs.) 1982, D.C. 1984, U.S. Dist Ct. D.C. 1984, U.S. Supreme Ct. 1985. Law clk. Balt. County Solicitor's Office, Towson, Md., 1980-81; assoc. county atty. Prince George's County, Upper Marlboro, Md., 1981-84, 86-89; assoc. Knight, Manzi, Brennan & Ostrom, Upper Marlboro, 1984-86; chief dep. clk. Ct. Spl. Appeals, Annapolis, Md., 1986; asst. atty. gen. State of Md., Towson, 1989-94; chief of litigation, asst. county atty. Balt. County Atty.'s Office, Towson, Md., 1994—; mem. adv. com. Loyola Coll. Bar Rev., Balt., 1982; mem. gen. assembly's task force on gaming laws in Prince George's County, 1987. Mem. ch. coun. All Saints Luth. Ch., Bowie, Md., 1986-88, pres., 1987-88; mem. Dem. State Ctrl. Com. for Harford County, 1995-98; mem. procurement adv. coun. State of Md., 1995-98, Gubernatorial Transition Team, 1994-95; mem. judiciary com. Md. Ho. of Dels., Harford County, 1997-99. Maj. Md. Army N.G., 1991—. Recipient Exceptional Svc. award, Md. Atty. Gens.'s Office, 1991. Mem. Md. Bar Assn., Harford County Bar Assn., Baltimore County Bar Assn., Prince George's County Bar Assn. (bd. dirs. 1988-90), Kappa Alpha. Democrat. Avocations: baseball card collecting, softball. Home: 3509 Glen Oak Dr Jarrettsville MD 21084-1837 Office: Old Court House 400 Washington Ave Fl 2 Towson MD 21204-4606

**COMER, JEROME EDWARD,** lawyer; b. Richmond, Va., Aug. 18, 1948. BA, Am. U., 1979; JD, Ind. U., 1986; grad., Nat. Inst. Trial Advocacy, 1991. Bar: Ind. 1986, Ill. 1995, U.S. Dist. Ct. (no. and so. dists.) Ind., U.S. Tax Ct. V.p., program coord. Profl. Edn. Corp., Indpls., 1984-95; legal intern Indpls. Life Ins. Co., 1985-86; retirement plan adminstr. Kaufman's Fin. Corp., Indpls., 1985-86; pvt. practice Indpls., 1986—; investment adviser Weaver & Weaver Assocs., Indpls., 1986-88; ptnr., prin. Kashani & Comer, Indpls., 1990-91; assoc. Randall & Katz, P.C., Indpls., 1993-94; investment broker Anderson & Standwick, Inc., Indpls., 1983-84; investigative sgt. Henrico County Police Dept., Richmond, 1972-80; engring. draftsman Va. Dept. Hwys., Richmond, 1966-67; lectr. Nat. Bus. Inst., Inc., 1994, Profl. Edn. Corp., Indpls., 1993-94. Mem. vol. staff Sci. Mus. Va., Richmond, 1983-84. Sgt. USMC, 1967-71, Vietnam. Mem. ABA (sect. on taxation), Ind. Bar Assn. (sects. on taxation, real property and probate), Ill. Bar Assn., Rotary (Indpls. Airport club). Avocations: chess, woodworking, hiking. Estate planning, Taxation, general, General corporate. Home and Office: 9498 Bridgewater Cir Indianapolis IN 46250-3412

**COMFORT, ROBERT DENNIS,** lawyer; b. Camden, N.J., Nov. 22, 1950; s. Joseph Albert Sr. and Elizabeth (Rogers) C.; m. Loretta Masullo, Aug. 24, 1974; 1 child, Adam. AB summa cum laude, Princeton U., 1973; JD magna cum laude, Harvard U., 1976. Bar: Pa. 1976, N.J. 1977, U.S. Dist. Ct. N.J. 1977, U.S. Dist. Ct. (ea. dist.) Pa. 1977, U.S. Ct. Appeals (3d cir.) 1977, U.S. Tax Ct. 1978, U.S. Claims Ct. 1983. Law clk. to Hon. James Hunter III U.S. Ct. Appeals 3d Cir., Phila., 1976-77; law clk. to Lewis F. Powell Jr. U.S. Supreme Ct., Washington, 1977-78; assoc. Morgan, Lewis & Bockius, Phila., 1978-82; ptnr. Morgan, Lewis & Bockius, 1982—; adj. prof. U. Pa. Law Sch., Rutgers-Camden Law Sch. Mem. ABA, Phila. Bar Assn. (vice chair tax sect. 1990-92, chair 1993-94). Avocations: golf, camping, music, history, fishing. Corporate taxation, Taxation, general, Personal income taxation. Office: Morgan Lewis & Bockius 1701 Market St Philadelphia PA 19103-2903

**COMISKY, IAN MICHAEL,** lawyer; b. Phila., Feb. 5, 1950; s. Marvin and Goldye (Elving) C. BS magna cum laude, U. Pa., 1971, JD, 1974; LLM in Taxation, U. Miami, 1984. Bar: Pa. 1974, Fla. 1976, D.C. 1976, U.S. Ct. Appeals (3rd and 11th cirs.), U.S. Ct. Claims, U.S. Tax Ct., U.S. Supreme Ct., U.S. Dist. Ct. (ea. dist.) Pa., U.S. Dist. Ct. (so. dist.) Fla., U.S. Dist. Ct. (mid. dist.) Fla. Law clk. to Hon. Alfred Luongo Jr. U.S. Dist. Ct. Pa., Phila., 1974-75; asst. dist. atty. Office of Dist. Atty., Philadelphia County, Phila., 1975-78; asst. U.S. atty. So. Dist. Fla., 1978-80; spl. asst. Office of Dist. Atty., So. Dist. Fla., 1980; ptnr. tax dept. Blank Rome Comisky & McCauley, Phila., 1980—; presenter various profl. confs. seminars, 1981—; guest TV and radio programs, 1990. Co-author: Tax Fraud and Evasion (2 vols.); contbr. articles to profl. publs. Sec. Mann Music Ctr.; participant Fedn. Jewish Agys. Mem. ABA (past chmn. civil and criminal tax penalties com. tax sect., mem. CLE com. tax sect., cogs spl. projects, mem. various coms. criminal justice and litig. sect.), ATLA, Am. Law Inst., Am. Coll. Tax Counsel, Fed. Bar Assn., Pa. Bar Assn., Fla. Bar Assn. (bd. govs. 1998), D.C. Bar Assn., Phila. Bar Assn., Assn. Fellows and Legal Scholars or Ctr. for Internat. Legal Studies (hon.). Avocations: sailing, gardening, karate, jogging. Criminal, Taxation, general, Federal civil litigation. Office: Blank Rome Comisky & McCauley 1200 N Fed Hwy Ste 309 Boca Raton FL 33432

**COMISKY, MARVIN,** retired lawyer; b. Phila., June 5, 1918; m. Goldie Elving; children: Ian M., Hope A., Matthew J. B.S.C. summa cum laude, Temple U., 1938; LL.B., U. Pa., 1941; LL.D., Dickinson Sch. Law, 1970. Bar: Pa. 1942. Law clk. Pa. Superior Ct., 1941-42; law clk. to presiding justice Pa. Supreme Ct., 1946; assoc. Lemuel B. Schofield, Phila., 1946-54; ptnr. Brumbelow & Comisky, 1954-59; ptnr. Blank, Rome, Comisky & McCauley LLP, Phila., 1959-68, mng. ptnr., 1968-88; chmn. Blank, Rome, Comisky & McCauley, Phila., 1988-90, chmn. emeritus, 1991-99, ret., 1993; mem. Pa. Bd. Law Examiners, 1974-75; former dir. Midlantic Bank. Co-author: Judicial Selection, Compensation, Ethics and Discipline, 1986. Gen. counsel Pa. Constl. Conv., 1967. Fellow Am. Bar Found., Am. Coll. Trial Lawyers, Internat. Acad. Trial Lawyers; mem. ABA (del. 1965, 70), Phila. Bar Assn. (chancellor 1965), Pa. Bar Assn. (past pres.), Order of Coif, Beta Gamma Sigma. Office: Blank Rome Comisky & McCauley LLP One Logan Square Philadelphia PA 19103

**COMITO, FRANK JOSEPH,** lawyer; b. Des Moines, Sept. 8, 1954; s. William J. and Joanne E. (Porto) C.; m. Margaret Katherine Beiter, Aug. 23, 1975. B.S., Iowa State U., 1976; J.D., Georgetown U., 1979. Bar: Iowa 1979, U.S. Dist. Ct. (no. and so. dists) Iowa 1980, U.S. Tax Ct. 1984. Clk. to presiding justice Md. Ct. of Appeals, Annapolis, 1978-80; sole practice Carroll, Iowa, 1980—; asst. county atty. Carroll County, 1981-83, magistrate, 1983—. Pres. Carroll Arts Council, 1982. Mem. ABA, Iowa State Bar Assn., Carroll County Bar Assn. (pres. 1984—). Democrat. Roman Catholic. Office: Neu Minnich Comito & Hall PC 721 N Main St Carroll IA 51401-2327

**COMPARETTO, ANTHONY J.,** lawyer; b. Tampa, Fla.. BA in Polit. Sci., U. South Fla., 1986; JD, Stetson Coll. Law, 1988. Spl. master Pinellas Value Adjustment Bd., Clearwater, Fla., 1991—, Hillsborough Value Adjustment Bd., Tampa, 1992—; spl. master pub. transp. com. City of Tampa, 1994—, Value Adjustment Bd., Manatee, Fla., 1998—; hearing officer City of Pinellas Park, 1993, City of Clearwater, 1996—. Office: 5340 Central Ave Saint Petersburg FL 33707-6130

**COMPTON, ALLEN T.,** state supreme court justice; b. Kansas City, Mo., Feb. 25, 1938; m. Sue Ellen Tatter; 3 children. B.A., U. Kans., 1960; LL.B., U. Colo., 1963. Pvt. practice Colorado Springs, 1963-68; staff atty. Legal Svcs. Office, Colorado Springs, 1968-69, dir., 1969-71; supervising atty. Alaska Legal Svcs., Juneau, Alaska, 1971-73; pvt. practice Juneau, 1973-76; judge Superior Ct., Alaska, 1976-80; justice Alaska Supreme Ct., Anchorage, 1980-98, chief justice, 1995-97, ret., 1998. Mem. 4 bar assns. including Juneau Bar Assn. (past pres.). Office: Alaska Supreme Ct 303 K St Anchorage AK 99501-2013

**COMPTON, ASBURY CHRISTIAN,** state supreme court justice; b. Portsmouth, Va., Oct. 24, 1929. BA, Washington and Lee U., 1950, LLB, 1953, LLD, 1975. Bar: Va. 1957. Mem. firm May, Garrett, Miller, Newman & Compton, Richmond, 1957-66; judge Law and Equity Ct., City of Richmond, 1966-74; justice Supreme Ct. Va., Richmond, 1974—. Trustee Collegiate Schs., Richmond, 1972-89, chmn. bd., 1978-80; former chmn. adminstrv. bd. Ginter Park United Meth. Ch., Richmond; former mem. adminstrv. bd. Trinity United Meth. Ch., Richmond; trustee Washington and Lee U., 1978-90. With USN, 1953-56, USNR, 1956-62. Decorated Letter of Commendation. Mem. Va. Bar Assn., Va. State Bar, Bar Assn. City Richmond, Washington and Lee U. Alumni Assn. (past pres., dir.), Omicron Delta Kappa, Phi Kappa Sigma, Phi Alpha Delta. Club: Country of Va. Office: Va Supreme Ct 100 N 9th St Richmond VA 23219-2335

**COMPTON, CARNIS EUGENE,** lawyer; b. Grundy, Va., June 20, 1948; s. Virginia (Compton) Hughart; m. Dollie McGlothlin, Aug. 24, 1966; children: Wade Trent, Nicholas Brian. BA, U. Va.-Clinch Valley, Wise, 1976; JD, Campbell Coll., 1979. Bar: Va. 1979, Fla. 1982, U.S. Dist. Ct. (we. dist.) Va. 1979, U.S. Supreme Ct. 1982, U.S. Ct. Appeals (4th cir.) 1984. Assoc. John L. Bagwell, P.C., Grundy, 1979; ptnr. Bagwell & Compton, P.C., Grundy, 1980-82, Watts & Compton, Deland, Fla., 1982; pvt. practice Honaker, Va., 1982-86; ptnr. Compton & Jessee, P.C., Abingdon, Va., 1986-87; pvt. practice Honaker, 1987-88, Lebanon, Va., 1988—. Sec. Buchanan County Republican Party, Grundy, 1980; chmn. Reagan/Bush Com.-Buchanan County, Grundy, 1980; Republican candidate 40th State Senatorial Dist., Va., 1983; mem. Young Republicans of CVC, Wise, 1975. With USAF, 1967-73, Vietnam. Mem. ABA, ATLA, Va. Bar Assn., VA. Trial Lawyers Assn. (com. mem., dist. gov. 1995-96), Russell County Bar Assn. (pres. 1989), Fla. State Bar, Am. Legion. Avocations: bird dog field trials, reading history, horse back riding. General civil litigation, Criminal, Family and matrimonial. Home: Rte 614 PO Box 1090 Lebanon VA 24266 Office: PO Box 1000 Lebanon VA 24266-1000

**COMROE, EUGENE W.,** lawyer, pilot; b. Cambridge, Mass., Nov. 16, 1942; m. Bliss Comroe; children: Courtney, Carly. BS in Bus. Adminstrn., UCLA, 1966, MBA in Fin., 1966, JD, 1969. Bar: Calif. 1970, Tex. 1973; lic. airline transport pilot. Pvt. practice Woodland Hills, Calif.; arbitrator, settlement officer, mem. fast track and sanctions com. L.A. Superior Ct.; lectr. U. San Fernando Valley Col. Law, 1977; chair and spkr. numerous profl. meetings. Contbg. editor L.A. Trial Lawyers Assn. Advocate. Mem. ATLA, L.A. Trial Lawyers Assn. (big brother program, 1982-85, arbitration com. 1975-82, ct. congestion com. 1982-83, compensation for victims com., 1984, med. malpractice com., 1985, pub. rels. com., 1985, liaison so. Calif. def. com. 1985-86, membership drive), Calif. Trial Lawyers Assn. (Chpt. Pres. of Yr. award, 1991, bd. govs. 1987-92, 94, various coms.), Am. Bd. Trial Advocates, Lawyer Pilots Bar Assn., L.A. County Bar Assn. (superior cts. com. 1983, ct. improvements com. 1983-85), Am. Arbitration Assn., Calif. Trial Lawyer Pol. Action Com. Avocations: scuba diving, marathon running, aviation piloting. Personal injury, Product liability, General civil litigation. Office: 20750 Ventura Blvd Ste 220 Woodland Hills CA 91364-6235

**COMSTOCK, BRIAN LLOYD,** lawyer; b. Omaha, Sept. 23, 1932; s. Lloyd Russell and Leila Adele (Logan) C.; m. Karen Wells, Feb. 14, 1960; children: Michael B., John L., Pamela J. Tobinson. AB magna cum laude, U. Wash., 1954; LLB, Harvard U., 1959. Bar: Wash. 1959, U.S. Dist. Ct. (we. dist.) Wash. 1959, U.S. Ct. Appeals (9th cir.) 1961. Ptnr. Roberts & Shefelman, Seattle, 1959-88, Foster, Pepper & Shefelman, Seattle, 1988-90, Short, Cressman & Burgess PLLC, Seattle, 1990—. Contbr. articles to profl. jours. Mem., officer Mcpl. League, Seattle, 1960-85. 1st lt. U.S. Army, 1954-56. Mem. King County Bar Assn. (trustee 1975-78), The Rainier Club, The Harbor Club, Seattle Tennis Club, Mercer Island Country Club, Rotary. Lutheran. Avocation: competetive tennis. Mergers and acquisitions, Securities, General corporate. Home: 8375 E Mercer Way Mercer Island WA 98040-5622 Office: Short Cressman & Burgess 999 3rd Ave Ste 3000 Seattle WA 98104-4088

**CONABOY, RICHARD PAUL,** federal judge; b. Scranton, Pa., June 12, 1925; m. Marion Hartnett; children: Mary Ann, Richard, Judith, Conan, Michele, Kathryn, Patrick, William, Margaret, Janet, John, Nancy. BA, U. Scranton, 1945; LLB, Cath. U. Am., 1950. Bar: Pa. 1951. Ptnr. firm Powell & Conaboy, Scranton, 1951-54; dep. atty. gen., 1953-62; assoc. firm Kennedy O'Brien & O'Brien, 1954-62; judge Pa. Ct. Common Pleas, 1962-79, pres. judge, 1978-79; judge U.S. Dist. Ct. (mid. dist.) Pa., Scranton, 1980—, chief judge, 1989-93, now sr. judge; pres. Pa. Joint Council on Criminal Justice System, 1971-79; mem. Nat. Conf. Juvenile Justice, Nat. Conf. Corrections. Contbr. articles to legal jours. Bd. dirs. Marywood Coll., U. Scranton; apptd. chmn. U.S. States Sentencing Commn., 1994. Mem. Pa. Conf. State Trial Judges (pres. 1976-77, v.p. 1973-76, sec. 1968-73), ABA, Pa. Bar Assn., Am. Judicature Soc. Office: US Dist Courthouse & Post Office Bldg PO Box 189 Scranton PA 18501-0189

**CONANT, ALLAH B., JR.,** lawyer; b. Waco, Tex., July 24, 1939; s. Allah B. and Frances Louise (James) C.; m. Sheila Conant; children: Heather Lee Arsham, Lisa Lynn, Leslie Marie; stepchild, Thomas R. Bone II. B.A., N. Tex. State Coll., Denton, 1961; J.D. cum laude, Baylor U., 1963. Bar: Tex. 1963, U.S. Ct. Dist. (no. dist.) Tex. 1964, U.S. Dist. Ct. (so. dist.) Tex. 1969, U.S. Dist. Ct. (ea. dist.) Tex. 1986, U.S. Dist. Ct. (we. dist.) Tex. 1986, U.S. Ct. Appeals (5th cir.) 1970, U.S. Ct. Appeals (8th cir.) 1975, U.S. Ct. Appeals (4th and 7th cirs.)1978, U.S. Ct. Appeals (3d and 11th cirs.) 1981, U.S. Ct. Appeals (10th cir.) 1987, U.S. Tax Ct. 1963, U.S. Supreme Ct. 1971. Since practiced in Dallas; ptnr. Shank, Irwin, Conant, Lipshy & Casterline, 1964-90; owner ABC Ranch, 1981-89; of counsel Whittenburg Whittenburg and Schachter, 1990; mem. Conant Whittenburg French & Schachter, Dallas, 1991-99; ptner. Conant French & Chaney, LLP, Dallas, 1999—. Contbr. to legal jours. Trustee St. John's Episcopal Sch., 1987-90. Fellow Am. Bar Found. (life), Tex. Bar Found. (life), Dallas Bar Found. (life); mem. ABA (coun. gen. practice sect. 1977-80, chmn. 1982-83, del. 1983-86), Dallas Bar Assn., State Bar Tex., Trial Attys. Am., Baylor Law Sch. Counsellors, Baylor Law Alumni Assn. (dir. 1979-82), Baylor Law Rev. Ex-Editors Assn., N.Tex. State U. Alumni Assn. (dir., v.p.), Sigma Phi Epsilon, Omicron Delta Kappa, Phi Delta Phi (historian 1962). Clubs: Petroleum (Dallas). Avocations: swimming, reading, travel, boating. Federal civil litigation, General civil litigation, State civil litigation. Home: 8247 Forest Hills Blvd Dallas TX 75218-4410 Office: Conant French & Chaney LLP 1717 Main St Ste 3880 Dallas TX 75201

**CONBOY, KENNETH,** lawyer, former federal judge; b. 1938. AB, Fordham Coll., 1961; JD, U. Va., 1964; MA in History, Columbia U., 1980. Asst. dist. atty., exec. asst. dist. atty. Manhattan Dist. Atty.'s Office, 1966-77; dep. commr., gen. counsel N.Y. Police, 1978-83; criminal justice dir. N.Y.C., 1984-86; N.Y.C. commr. of investigation, 1986-87; judge U.S. Dist. Ct. (so. dist.) N.Y, 1987-93; sr. litigation ptnr. Mudge, Rose, Guthrie, Alexander & Ferdon, N.Y.C., 1994-95; ptnr. Latham & Watkins, N.Y.C., 1995—; summer faculty Cornell Law Sch.; adj. prof. of law Fordham Law Sch. Author: Grand Jury Examination of the Recalcitrant Witness, 1977; contbr. articles to profl. jours. Mem. N.Y. State Crime Control Planning Bd., N.Y. Sovern Commn. Capt. U.S. Army, 1964-66. Mem. Am. Soc. Legal History, N.Y. State Bar Assn., Assn. of Bar of City of N.Y., Fed. Bar Coun. General civil litigation, Constitutional, Securities. Office: Latham & Watkins 885 3rd Ave Ste 1000 New York NY 10022-4834

**CONBOY, MARTIN JAMES,** lawyer, prosecutor; b. Omaha, Mar. 22, 1955; s. Martin J. and JoAnn L. (Koopman) C.; m. Cheryl Diana Mancuso, Nov. 17, 1971; children: Erin, Marty, Joseph, Matthew. BA, Creighton U., 1977, JD, 1980. Bar: Nebr., U.S. Dist. Ct. Nebr. Legal clk. Douglas County (Nebr.) Dist. Ct., Omaha, 1978-81; city prosecutor City of Omaha, 1981—, acting city atty., 1997-98; instr. U. Nebr., Omaha, 1992—. Sec. Project Xtra mile, 1997-98; mem. Safety and Health Coun. of Greater Omaha, 1994-98. Mem. Omaha Bar Assn., Nebr. League of Cities. Democrat. Roman Catholic. Office: City Prosecutor Office 2 W Hall Of Justice Omaha NE 68183-0001

**CONCANNON, ANDREW DONNELLY,** lawyer; b. Willoughby, Ohio, May 1, 1967. BA in History, Mich. State U., 1990; JD, U. Detroit, 1993. Bar: Mich. 1994, U.S. Dist. Ct. (ea. dist.) Mich. 1994. Sr. assoc. Kitch, Drutchas, Wagner & Kenney, Lansing, Mich., 1995-97; assoc. Smith, Bovill, Fisher, Meyer & Borchard, P.C., Saginaw, Mich., 1997—. Mem. ABA, State Bar Mich., Saginaw Bar Assn., Am. Judicature Soc. Avocations: tennis, golf. Personal injury, Professional liability, General civil litigation. Office: Smith Bovill et al 200 Saint Andrews Rd Saginaw MI 48603-5938

**CONCANNON, JAMES M.,** law educator, university dean; b. Columbus, Ga., Oct. 2, 1947; s. James M. Jr. and Mary Jane (Crow) C.; m. Melissa P. Masoner, June 9, 1988. BS, U. Kans., 1968, JD, 1971. Law clk. Kans. Ins. Commn., Topeka, 1971; rsch. atty. Kans. Supreme Ct., Topeka, 1971-73; asst. prof. law Washburn U., Topeka, 1973-75, assoc. prof. law, 1976-81, prof., 1981—, dean, 1988—; vis. prof. law Washington U., St. Louis, 1979; active Kans. Commn. on Pub. Understanding of Law, 1983-89, Task Force on Law Enforcement Consolidation, Topeka, 1991-92; mem. Nat. Conf. Commrs. on Uniform State Laws, 1998—. Co-author: Kans. Appellate Practice Manual, 1978, Kansas Statutes of Limitations, 1988; sr. contbn. editor: Evidence in America-Federal Rules in the States, 1987. Coord. Citizens to Keep Politics Out of Our Courts, Topeka, 1984; co-reporter Citizens Justice Initiative, 1997—. chmn. legal com. Concerned Citizens Topeka, 1995—; bd. dirs. United Funds, Inc., 1997—. Master Topeka Am. Inn of Ct.; fellow Am. Bar Found., Kans. Bar Found.; mem. Kans. Bar Assn. (CLE com. 1976—, Outstanding Svc. award 1982), Assn. Am. Law Schs. (com. on bar admission, lawyer performance 1994-97), Washburn Law Sch. Alumni Assn. (life), Order of Coif. Office: Washburn U Law Sch 1700 SW College Ave Topeka KS 66621-0001

**CONDENI, JOSEPH ANTHONY,** lawyer; b. Cleve., Nov. 21, 1956; s. Joseph George and Marie Dorothy Condeni; m. Maritza Acevedo, Aug. 29, 1987. BLS, Bowling Green U., 1979; JD, Cleve. State U., 1982. Bar: Ohio 1982, U.S. Dist. Ct. (no. dist.) Ohio 1983, U.S. Ct. Appeals (6th cir.) 1990. Assoc. Jerome and Smith, Cleve., 1982-88; ptnr. Jerome, Smith and Condeni, Cleve., 1988-92; prin. Smith, Condeni & Abel Co., Lic. P.A., Cleve., 1992—. Editor Cleveland State Law Rev., 1980-81, mng. editor, 1981-82. Mem. ATLA, Nat. Employment Lawyers Assn., Cleve. Bar Assn., Cuyahoga County Bar Assn., Cleve. Acad. Trial Lawyers, Cleve. Acad. Employment Lawyers. Avocations: snow skiing, golf. Personal injury, Product liability, Insurance. Office: Smith & Condeni Co LPA 1801 E 9th St Ste 900 Cleveland OH 44114-3103

**CONDO, JAMES ROBERT,** lawyer; b. Somerville, N.J., Mar. 2, 1952; s. Ralph Vincent and Betty Louise (MacQuaide) C.; m. Rhonda H. King, June 7, 1997. BS in Bus. and Econs., Lehigh U., 1974; JD, Boston Coll., 1979. Bar: Ariz. 1979, U.S. Dist. Ct. Ariz. 1979, U.S. Ct. Appeals (9th cir.) 1982, U.S. Ct. Appeals (D.C. cir.) 1989, U.S. Ct. Appeals (10th cir.) 1989, U.S. Supreme Ct. 1983, U.S. Ct. Appeals (6th cir.) 1991, U.S. Ct. Appeals (4th cir.) 1994. Assoc. Snell & Wilmer, Phoenix, 1979-84, ptnr., 1985—; judge pro tem Ariz. Ct. Appeals. Bd. dirs. Ariz. Town Hall. Fellow Ariz. Bar Found.; mem. ABA, State Bar Ariz., Maricopa County Bar Found. E-mail: jcondo@swlaw.com. Federal civil litigation, General civil litigation, Product liability. Office: Snell & Wilmer One Arizona Ctr Phoenix AZ 85004

**CONDON, CHARLES MOLONY,** state attorney general; b. Charleston, S.C., May 2, 1953; s. James Joseph and Harriet (Molony) C.; m. Emily Yarbrough, June 21, 1980; children: Charles Molony Jr., Patrick Monaghan, Doreen Yarbrough, Emily Elliot. Student, Saltzburg (Austria) Summer Sch., 1972, U. Innsbruck, Austria, 1972-73; BA, U. Notre Dame, 1975; JD, Duke U., 1978. Bar: S.C. 1978, U.S. Dist. Ct. S.C. 1978, U.S. Ct. Appeals (4th cir.) 1987, U.S. Supreme Ct. 1988. Assoc. Nexsen, Pruet, Jacobs & Pollard, Columbus, S.C., 1978-79; asst. solicitor S.C. 9th Jud. Cir., Charleston, 1979-80, solicitor, 1980-92; atty. gen. State of S.C., Columbia, 1992—; lectr. Med. U. S.C., 1982, U. S.C., 1983, Coll. Charleston, 1986, various confs.; bd. visitors com., Charleston, 1992—; panel mem. Nat. Inst. for Drug Abuse, Washington; prosecuter City of Isle Palms, S.C., 1993—; cons. Nat. Consortium for Justice Info. and Stats. profl. rep. So. Environ. Network, 1990-91. profl. rep. So. Envion. Network., 1990-91. Mem. com. Charleston County Criminal Justice Task Force; sect. chmn. govtl. divsn. United Way; bd. dirs. com. for drug free soc. Charleston County Sch. Dist., 1989, Children's Ctr., Charleston, S.C., 1990-91, S.C. Commn. on Presecution Coord., 1991-92; ex-officio mem. Friends of Charleston County Courthouse. Mem. ABA, S.C. Bar Assn., Richland County Bar Assn., Charleston Lawyers Club, S.C. Cir. Solicitors Assn. (v.p. 1987-88, pres. 1988-89), S.C. Law Enforcement Assn., Notre Dame Club, Silver Elephant Club. Republican. Home: 835 Middle St Sullivans Island SC 29482-8728 Office: Office of Attorney General PO Box 11549 Columbia SC 29211-1549*

**CONDON, DAVID BRUCE,** lawyer; b. Tacoma, May 20, 1949; s. Lester Milo and Ruby Elizabeth (Elson) C.; m. Constance Lynn Montgomery, Aug. 27, 1971; children: Amy M., Anne E. BA, U. Wash., 1971; JD cum laude, Gonzaga U., 1974. Bar: Wash. 1974, U.S. Dist. Ct. (we. dist.) Wash. 1974, U.S. Ct. Appeals (9th cir.) 1976, U.S. Dist. Ct. (ea. dist.) Wash. 1989. Assoc. Griffin & Enslow, Tacoma, 1974-78; ptnr. Welch & Condon, Tacoma, 1978—; examiner Wash. State Higher Edn. Pers. Bd., 1979-95. Bd. dirs. Bldg. A. Scholastic Heritage, pres., 1991-92; bd. dirs. Tacoma Art Mus., 1993-94. law. ABA, Wash. State Bar Assn., Tacoma-Pierce County Bar Assn., Assn. Trial Lawyers Am., Wash. Trial Lawyers Assn., Nat. Assn. Social Security Claimants Reps. Avocations: running, swimming. Workers' compensation, Personal injury, Labor. Office: Welch & Condon PO Box 1318 Tacoma WA 98401-1318

**CONDRA, ALLEN LEE,** lawyer, state official; b. Middlesboro, Ky., Apr. 11, 1950; s. Allen and Dorothy Dell (Douglas) C. BA, Western Ky. U., 1972; JD, No. Ky. U., 1978. Bar: Ky. 1979, U.S. Dist. Ct. (we. dist.) Ky. 1980. Staff atty. West Ky. Legal Services, Madisonville, 1979-81; dist. atty. Dept. Transp. Commonwealth of Ky., Madisonville, 1981—. Mem. Ky. Bar Assn., Hopkins County Bar Assn., Phi Alpha Delta. Democrat. Methodist. Lodge: Elks, Masons, K.T.

**CONDRELL, WILLIAM KENNETH,** lawyer; b. Buffalo, N.Y., Sept. 19, 1926; s. Paul Kenneth and Celia Olga (Schinas) C.; m. Stacie J. Oliver, June 9, 1991; children: Paul, William, Alexander. B.S., Yale U., 1946; S.M., MIT, 1947; JD, Harvard U., 1950. Bar: N.Y. 1951, D.C. 1964, U.S. Ct. Appeals (4th cir.) 1974, U.S. Ct. Appeals (Fed. cir.) 1982, U.S. Ct. Appeals (D.C. cir.) 1984, U.S. Supreme Ct. 1965. Assoc. econ. adv. Exec. Office Pres., D.C., 1951-54; mgmt. cons. McKinsey and Co., Chgo., 1954-55; mgr. budgets Hotpoint div. Gen. Electric Co., Chgo., 1955-59; sole practice, 1959-68; ptnr. Steptoe & Johnson, Washington, D.C., 1968-90; of counsel Steptoe & Johnson, Washington, 1990—. Lt. (j.g.) USNR, 1944-46. Mem. ABA (adv. com. judicial edn. and tng.). Club: Congressional Country (Bethesda, Md.). Environmental, Taxation, general. Home: 2510 Virginia Ave NW # 502 Washington DC 20037-1904 Office: 1330 Connecticut Ave NW Washington DC 20036-1704

**CONERLY, CHARLES SAMUEL,** lawyer, associate; b. Carrollton, Ga., Dec. 8, 1969; s. Milt Seymour and Patricia (Mitchell) C.; m. Michelle Leigh Miller, July 24, 1993; 1 child, Caroline Leigh. BA in English and Polit. Sci. cum laude, State U. West Ga., 1992; JD magna cum laude, Vt. Law Sch., 1996, MSEL magna cum laude, 1996. Bar: Ga. 1997, U.S. Dist. Ct. (no. dist.) Ga. 1998. Law clk., Judge R. Butler U.S. Dist. Ct. (so. dist.) Ala., Mobile, 1996-97; assoc. Alston & Bird, LLP, Atlanta, 1997—. Contbr. articles to Ga. Bar Jour. Avocations: sports, reading, politics. Office: Alston & Bird LLP 1201 W Peachtree St NW Ste 4200 Atlanta GA 30309-3424

**CONETTA, TAMI FOLEY,** lawyer; b. Akron, Ohio, Aug. 29, 1965; d. Charles David and Roxanne (Onyett) Foley; m. Anthony Joseph Conetta, July 29, 1989; 1 child, Emory Elizabeth Conetta. BA in Polit. Sci., Furman U., 1987; JD with honors, U. Fla., 1990. Bar: Fla. 1991; bd. cert. estates, trusts and wills Fla. Bar Bd. Legal Specialization. Ptnr. Gassman & Conetta, PA, Clearwater, Fla., 1990-98, Ruden, McClosky, Smith, Schuster & Russell, PA, Sarasota, Fla., 1998—. Contbr. articles to profl. jours. Recipient Am. Jurisprudence awards in Estate Planning and Taxation of Gratuitous Transfers, 1990. Mem. Am. Bus. Womens Assn., Sarasota County Bar Assn., Clearwater Bar Assn. (chair law week 1994, Pres.'s award 1994), Clearwater Bar Probate Com. (chair 1996-98), Southwest Fla. Estate Planning Coun. Avocations: golf, reading. Probate, Estate taxation, Estate planning. Office: Ruden McClosky Smith Schuster & Russell PA 1549 Ringling Blvd Ste 600 Sarasota FL 34236-6772 also: PO Box 49017 Sarasota FL 34230-6017

**CONGALTON, CHRISTOPHER WILLIAM,** lawyer; b. N.Y.C., Apr. 8, 1946; s. William Alexander and Jacqueline Rose (Ryan) C.; m. Susan Tichenor, May 29, 1971. AB, Fairfield (Conn.) U., 1968; JD, Georgetown U., 1971. Bar: N.Y. 1972, U.S. Dist. Ct. (so. dist.) N.Y. 1974, U.S. Ct. Appeals (2d cir.) 1974, U.S. Supreme Ct. 1976, Ill. 1988, Colo. 1990. Assoc. Dunnington, Bartholow & Miller, N.Y.C., 1971-78; asst. gen. counsel Diamond Internat. Corp., N.Y.C., 1978-82; gen. counsel, v.p. Children's TV Workshop, N.Y.C., 1987-88; chmn. and ceo Moffitt Co., Schiller Park, Ill., 1988—. Mem. ABA, (corp. banking & bus. sect.), Am. Corp. Counsel Assn., N.Y. State Bar Assn., Assn. of Bar of City of N.Y., Chgo. Bar Assn., Eagle Springs Golf Club. General corporate, Securities. Home: 1500 N Lake Shore Dr Chicago IL 60610-6657 Office: Moffitt Co 9347 Seymour Ave Schiller Park IL 60176-2206

**CONINO, JOSEPH ALOYSIUS,** lawyer; b. Hammond, La., Aug. 17, 1920; s. Dominic and Catherine (Tamborella) C.; m. Mae Evelyn Moragas, Feb. 27, 1943; children: Joseph Aloysius Jr., Robert Carl. BBA, Tulane U., 1950; JD, Loyola U., 1961; MBA, U. Pa., 1951. Bar: La. 1961, U.S. Dist. Ct. (ea. dist.) La. 1961, U.S. Ct. Appeals (5th cir.) 1972, U.S. Supreme Ct. 1989. Pvt. practice Jefferson, La., 1961—; county judge State of La. Parish, Jefferson, 1970; del. State of La. Constl. Conv., Baton Rouge, 1973-74; asst. atty. Parish of Jefferson, 1977—. With USN, 1942-45. Mem. La. Bar Assn. (ho. of dels. 1963-92, bd. dirs. 1981-83, 96—), Jefferson Bar Assn. (pres.), New Orleans C. of C. (bd. dirs. 1974-77), Kiwanis (pres. Metairie, La. chpt.). Avocations: golf, swimming, tennis. Construction, Probate, Personal injury. Office: 1920 Jefferson Hwy Jefferson LA 70121-3816

**CONKEL, ROBERT DALE,** lawyer, pension consultant; b. Martins Ferry, Ohio, Oct. 13, 1936; s. Chester William and Marian Matilda (Ashton) C.; m. Elizabeth A. Cargill, June 15, 1958; children: Debra Lynn Conkel McGlone, Dale William, Douglas Alan; m. Brenda Jo Myers, Aug. 2, 1980; 1 child, Chelsea Ashton. BA, Mt. Union Coll., 1958; JD cum laude, Cleve. Marshall Law Sch., 1965; LLM, Case Western Res. U., 1972. Bar: Ohio 1965, U.S. Tax Ct. 1974, U.S. Supreme Ct. 1974, Tex. 1978, U.S. Ct. Appeals (5th cir.) 1979. Supr., Social Security Adminstrn., Cleve., 1958-65; trust officer Harter Bank & Trust Co., Canton, Ohio, 1965-70; exec. v.p. Am. Actuaries, Inc., Grand Rapids, Mich., 1970-73, pension cons., southwest regional dir., Dallas, 1974-88; mgr. plans and rsch. A.S. Hansen, Inc., Dallas, 1973-74; pvt. practice, Dallas, 1973—; sr. cons., Coopers & Lybrand, Dallas, 1989; pres. Robert D. Conkel, Inc., 1989—; mem. devel. bd. Met. Nat. Bank, Richardson, Tex.; instr. Am. Mgmt. Assn., 1975, Am. Coll. Advanced Pension Planning, 1975-76. Sustaining mem. Rep. Nat. Com., 1980-88. Enrolled actuary, Joint Bd. Enrollment U.S. Depts. Labor and Treasury. Mem. ABA (employee benefit com. sect. taxation), Ohio State Bar Assn., Tex. Bar Assn., Dallas Bar Assn., Am. Soc. Pension Actuaries (dir. 1973-81), Am. Acad. Actuaries. Contbr. articles to legal publs.; mem. editl. adv. bd. Jour. Pension Planning and Compliance, 1974-83. Pension, profit-sharing, and employee benefits, Estate planning, Personal income taxation. Office: 100 N Central Expy # 519 Richardson TX 75080-5332

**CONKLIN, HOWARD LAWRENCE,** lawyer; b. N.Y.C., Apr. 16, 1943; s. Weldon F. and Gladys (Meyer) C.; m. Barbara Ann Janas, Aug. 1, 1982. BS, Fairleigh Dickinson U., 1961; MBA, Syracuse U., 1969; JD, Fordham U., 1974. Bar: Fla. 1974, U.S. Dist. Ct. (so. dist.) 1976, U.S. Supreme Ct. 1978, U.S. Dist. Ct. (mid. dist.) Fla. 1980. Mktg. planning specialist Trans World Airlines, N.Y.C., 1969-71; sr. transp. analyst Paine Webber, N.Y.C., 1971-74; ptnr. Tripp, Scott, Conklin & Smith, Ft. Lauderdale, Fla., 1974-97; v.p. govt. and airport rels. Alamo Rent-a-Car, Inc., Ft. Lauderdale, 1997; exec. dir. govt. rels. AutoNation, Inc., Ft. Lauderdale, 1997—. Col. USAF, 1964-68, Vietnam, mem. Res. Decorated Bronze Star, Legion of Merit. Mem. ABA, Broward County Bar Assn., Am. League of Lobbyists, Air Force Assn., Res. Officers Assn., Army Navy Club (Washington), Pelican Yacht Club, Sons of Norway. Avocation: flying. Government contracts and claims, Legislative, Trade. Office: AutoNation Inc 110 SE 6th St Fort Lauderdale FL 33301-5000

**CONLEY, CHARLES SWINGER,** lawyer; b. Montgomery, Ala., Dec. 8, 1921; s. Prine E. and Fannie (Thompson) C.; m. Ellen Johnson. BS, Ala. State U., 1942; AM in Edn., U. Mich., 1947, AM in History, 1948; JD, NYU, 1955. Assoc. prof. law Fla. A&M U., Tallahassee, 1956-60; judge Ala. Dist. Ct., Tuskegee, 1975; atty. So. Leadership Conf., 1976-85; county lawyer Macon County, Tuskegee, 1988-89; pvt. practice Montgomery, 1989—; counsel Ala. S.W. Farmer's Coop., 1967-79, Ala. Legal Def. Com., Montgomery, 1968-80; juvenile ct. judge, 1970-74. Cpl. USAF, 1943-46. Mem. ABA, Nat. Bar Assn. (regional dir.). Democrat. Civil rights, Real property, Public utilities. Home: 3321 Rosa Parks Ave Montgomery AL 36104 Office: 315 S Bainbridge St Montgomery AL 36104-4315

**CONLEY, MARTHA RICHARDS,** lawyer; b. Pitts., Jan. 12, 1947; d. Writt Adam Richards and Mary Jane (Brunges) Jennings; m. Charles Donald Conley, Jan. 20, 1978; children: David, Daniel. BA, Waynesburg Coll., 1968; JD, U. Pittsburgh, 1971. Bar: Pa. 1972, U.S. Dist. Ct. (we. dist.) Pa. 1972, U.S. Supreme Ct. 1977. Asst. solicitor Sch. Dist. of Pitts., 1972-73; ptnr. Brown & Cotton, Pitts., 1973-74; staff asst. U.S. Steel Corp., Pitts., 1974-76, asst. mgr. arbitration, 1976-84, asst. mgr. compliance, 1984-85, mgr. compliance, 1985-87, atty., 1987-94; gen. atty., 1994—; hazard commn. com. mem. Am. Iron and Steel Inst., Washington, 1984-87. Mem. resource devel. com. YWCA, Pitts., 1984-86. Mem. Nat. Bar Assn. (life), Allegheny County Bar Assn., Aurora Reading Club (pres. 1983-84). Democrat. Presbyterian. Avocations: gardening, reading, writing. Administrative and regulatory, Workers' compensation. Home: 6439 Navarro St Pittsburgh PA 15206-1813 Office: 600 Grant St Ste 1500 Pittsburgh PA 15219-2702

**CONLEY, WILLIAM VANCE,** lawyer; b. Phila., Dec. 2, 1952; s. Charles Edmond and Anna May Conley; m. Janet Lee Pagnanelli, June 22, 1974; children: Katherine, Stephanie, Michael. BA, Ind. (Pa.) U., 1974; JD magna cum laude, U. Pitts., 1981. Bar: Pa. 1981, U.S. Dist. Ct. (we. dist.) Pa. 1981. Asst. dist. atty. Allegheny County Dist. Atty.'s Office, Pitts., 1981-84; dep. atty. gen. Pa. Atty. Gen.'s Office, Pitts., 1984-87; asst. U.S. atty. U.S. Atty.'s Office, Pitts., 1987-91; shareholder Babst Calland Clements & Zomnir, Pitts., 1991-95, 97-98; dir. criminal law divsn. Pa. Atty. Gen.'s Office, Harrisburg, 1996-97; of counsel LeBoeuf Lamb Greene & MacRae, Pitts., 1998—. Bd. dirs. Dollar Energy Fund, Pitts., 1994—. Maj. USMC, 1974-78. Mem. Am. Inns of Ct., Pa. Bar Assn., Allegheny County Bar Assn. Avocation: golf. Criminal, Federal civil litigation, State civil litigation. Office: LeBoeuf Lamb Greene & MacRae 420 Fort Duquesne Blvd # 1600 Pittsburgh PA 15222-1435

**CONLIN, ROXANNE BARTON,** lawyer; b. Huron, S.D., June 30, 1944; d. Marion William and Alyce Muraine (Madden) Barton; m. James Clyde Conlin, Mar. 21, 1964; children: Jacalyn Rae, James Barton, Deborah Ann, Douglas Benton. BA, Drake U., 1964, JD, 1966, MPA, 1979; LLD (hon.), U. Dubuque, 1975. Bar: Iowa 1966. Assoc. Davis, Huebner, Johnson & Burt, Des Moines, 1966-67; dep. indsl. commr. State of Iowa, 1967-68, asst. atty. gen., 1969-76; U.S. atty. So. Dist. Iowa, 1977-81; ptnr. Conlin, P.C., Des Moines, 1983—; adj. prof. law U. Iowa, 1977-79; chmn. Iowa Women's Polit. Caucus, 1973-75, del. nat. steering com., 1973-77; cons. U.S. Commn. on Internat. Women's Year, 1976-77; gen. counsel NOW Legal Def. and Edn. Fund, 1985-88, pres., 1986-88; lectr. in field. Contbr. articles to profl. jours. Nat. committeewoman Iowa Young Dems.; pres. Polk County Young Dems., 1965-66; del. Iowa Presdl. Conv., 1972; Dem. candidate for gov. of Iowa, 1982; bd. dirs. Riverhills Day Care Ctr., YWCA; chmn. Drake U. Law Sch. Endowment Trust, 1985-86; bd. counselors Drake U., 1982-86; pres. Civil Justice Found., 1986-88, Roscoe Pound Found., 1994-97; chair Iowa Dem. Party, 1998—. Recipient award Iowa ACLU, 1974, Iowa Citizen's Action Network, 1987, Alumnus of Yr. award Drake U. Law Sch., 1989, ann. award Young Women's Resource Ctr., 1989, Verne Lawyer award as Outstanding Mem. Iowa Trial Lawyers Assn., 1994, Rosalie Wahl award Minn. Women Lawyers, 1998; named one of Top Ten Litigators Nat. Law Jour., 1989, 100 Most Influential Attys., 1991, 50 Most Powerful Women Attys. Nat. Law Jour., 1998; scholar Reader's Digest, 1963-64, Fishcher Found., 1965-66. Mem. NOW (bd. dirs. 1986-88), ABA, ATLA (chmn. consumer and victims coalition com. 1985-87, chmn. edn. dept. 1987-88, parliamentarian 1988-89, sec. 1989-90, v.p. 1990-91, pres.-elect 1991-92, pres. 1992-93), Iowa Bar Assn., Assn. Trial Lawyers Iowa (bd. dirs.), Internat. Acad. Trial Lawyers, Iowa Acad. Trial Lawyers, Higher Edn. Commn. Iowa (co-chmn. 1988-90), Inner Circle of Advocates, Phi Beta Kappa, Alpha Lambda Delta, Chi Omega (Social Svc. award). General civil litigation, Civil rights, Personal injury. Office: 300 Walnut St Ste 5 Des Moines IA 50309-2258

**CONLON, RAYMOND JOSEPH,** lawyer; b. Butler, Pa., Aug. 21, 1962; s. Hugh L. and Frances J. (Augustine) C.; m. Nance Lee Hirsch, Mar. 21, 1992. BA, Duquesne U., 1984; JD, Dickinson Sch. Law, 1987. Bar: Pa. 1987, U.S. Dist. Ct. (we. dist.) Pa. 1987. Assoc. Myer Darragh, Pitts., 1987-88; shareholder Zimmer Kunz, Pitts., 1988—. Mem. bd. editors Dickinson Law Rev., 1986-87. Active Big Bros., Pitts., 1990-91; bd. dirs. Butler County chpt. Big Bros., 1996—. Named Lord Mayor, Dublin, Ireland by George the Earl of Stewart. Mem. ABA, Pa. Bar Assn., Allegheny County Bar Assn., Maritime Law Assn., Assn. Transp. Lawyers, Am. Arbitration Assn. (arbitrator), Moose. Republican. Roman Catholic. Personal injury, General civil litigation. Office: Zimmer Kunz 3300 Usx Towers Pittsburgh PA 15219

**CONLON, STEVEN DENIS,** lawyer; b. Evanston, Ill., Aug. 17, 1957; s. Denis J. and Carolyn J. (Buck) C. BBA, Loyola U., Chgo., 1982, JD, 1986. CPA, Ill. Tax acct. Arthur Young & Co., Chgo., 1982-86; assoc., ptnr. Chapman and Cutler, Chgo., 1986-95; ptnr. Baker & McKenzie, Chgo., 1995-99, Katten, Muchin & Zavis, Chgo., 1999—; adj. prof. law Kent Coll. Law, Chgo., 1988—; mem. adv. bd. Derivatives mag., N.Y.C., 1994—. Co-author: Principles of Financial Derivatives: U.S. and International Taxation, 1999; co-editor: Tax-Exempt Derivatives—A Guide to Legal Considerations for Lawyers, Finance Professionals and Municipal Issuers, 1994; co-author (chpt.) The Handbook of Derivatives and Synthetics, 1994; contbr. more than 20 articles to profl. jours. Mem. ABA (tax sect., chair fin. transactions com. 1994-95), Chgo. Bar Assn. (chair fed. tax com. 1997-98), Nat. Assn. Bond Lawyers (Bond Attys. Workshop steering com. 1993-95), Chgo. Fed. Tax Forum. Avocations: music, poetry, opera, karate. Banking, Taxation, general, Securities. Office: Katten Muchin & Zavis 525 W Monroe St Ste 1500 Chicago IL 60661-3693

**CONLON, SUZANNE B.,** federal judge; b. 1939. AB, Mundelein Coll., 1963; JD, Loyola U., Chgo., 1968; postgrad., U. London, 1971. Law clk. to judge U.S. Dist. Ct. (no. dist.) Ill., 1968-71; assoc. Pattishall, McAuliffe & Hostetter, 1972-73, Schiff Hardin & Waite, 1973-75; asst. U.S. atty. U.S. Dist. Ct. (no. dist.) Ill., 1976-77, 82-86, U.S. Dist. Ct. (cen. dist.) Calif., 1978-82; exec. dir. U.S. Sentencing Commn., 1986-88; spl. counsel to assoc. atty. gen., 1988; judge U.S. Dist. Ct. (no. dist.) Ill., 1988—; asst. prof. law De Paul U., Chgo., 1972-73, lectr., 1973-75; adj. prof. Northwestern U. Sch. Law, 1991-95; vice chmn. Chgo. Bar Assn. Internat. Inst., 1993—; vis. com. U. Chgo. Harris Grad. Sch. Pub. Policy, 1997—. Mem. ABA, FBA, Fed. Judges Assn., Nat. Assn. Women Judges, Am. Judicature Soc., Internat. Bar Assn. Judges Forum, Chgo. Bar Assn., Law Club Chgo., Legal Club Chgo. (pres. 1996-97). Office: US Dist Ct No Dist Everett McKinley Dirksen Bldg 219 S Dearborn St Ste 2356 Chicago IL 60604-1878*

**CONMY, PATRICK A.,** federal judge; b. 1934. BA, Harvard U., 1955; JD, Georgetown U., 1959. Bar: Va. 1959, N.D. 1959. Ptnr. Lundberg, Conmy et al, Bismarck, N.D., 1959-85; mem. Bismarck City Commn., 1968-76; state rep. N.D. House Reps., Bismarck, 1976-85; judge U.S. Dist. Ct. N.D., Bismarck, 1985—. Office: US Dist Ct Fed Bldg 220 E Rosser Ave Rm 411 PO Box 1578 Bismarck ND 58502-1578

**CONN, DEANNA,** lawyer; b. Albuquerque, July 29, 1964; d. Donald N. and Margot A. Conn.; m. Steven Robert Brodersen, May 21, 1997; 1 child, Sedona Elise. BA, Pomona Coll., Claremont, Calif., 1986; JD, Columbia U., 1993. Bar: D.C. 1995, Ariz. 1995, U.S. Dist. Ct. (so. dist.) Ariz. 1997. Supr. McMaster-Carr Supply Co., Santa Fe Springs, Calif., 1987-90; law clk. U.S. Dist. Ct. (ctrl. dist.) Calif., Santa Ana, 1993-94; atty. assoc. Covington & Burling, Washington, 1994-97, Streich Lang, P.A., Tucson, 1997—; mem. Wellness City of Tucson, 1997. Vol., Vol. Lawyers Program, Tucson, 1998, Streich Force Children's Village, Tucson, 1997, KUAT Pub. TV, 1997. Harlan Fiske Stone scholar, 1990-93. Mem. FBA, Pima County Bar Assn., Info. Tech. Assn. So. Ariz. (intellectual property law sect.), Exec. Women's Golf Assn., Phi Beta Kappa. Democrat. Avocations: skiing, rollerblading, golf. Intellectual property, Federal civil litigation, Computer. Office: Streich Lang 1 S Church Ave Ste 1700 Tucson AZ 85701-1630

**CONNELL, JAMES BERNARD,** lawyer; b. Milw., June 21, 1948; s. Bernard Joseph and mary Susan C.; m. Teresa Mary Seelman Connell, June 15, 1974; children: Elizabeth, Ann, Matthew, Mary, Thomas, Margaret. BA, Regis Coll., Denver, 1970; JD, Marquette U., Milw., 1974. Atty. Crooks, Low & Connell, Wausau, Wis., 1974—; mem. Wis. Bar Assn., Madison, 1974—, Wis. Assn. Criminal Def. Lawyers, Madison, 1985—, Marathon County Bar Assn., Wausau, Wis., 1974—. Dir., officer United Cerebral Palsy of No. Ctrl. Wis., Wausau, 1975-80; mem. Task Force on the Legal Sys. and Refuge Population, Wausau, 1990-92. Mem. Wausau Area Softball Assn., Wausau Curling Club, Alpha Delta Gamma, Phi Alpha Delta. Roman Catholic. General practice, Criminal, General civil litigation. Office: Crooks Low & Connell 531 Washington St Wausau WI 54403-5438

**CONNELL, JANICE T.,** lawyer, author, arbitrator, business executive. BS in Fgn. Service, Georgetown U., 1961; M in Polit. and Internat. Adminstrn., U. Pitts., 1976; JD, Duquesne U., 1979. Bar: U.S. Dist. Ct. (we. dist.) Pa. 1979, U.S. Ct. Appeals (3d cir.) 1979, U.S. Supreme Ct. 1983. Pres. Regency Advertising, Jacksonville, Fla. and Pitts., 1968-74, Connell Leasing of Fla., Jacksonville and Pitts., 1970-80; v.p., sec. Nat. Motor Leasing Inc., Pitts., 1980-86; ptnr. Connell & Connell, Pitts., 1980-1986; arbitrator N.Y. Stock Exchange, 1981—, Am. Arbitration Assn., 1985—, Nat. Assn. Securities Dealers, 1983—. Author: Queen of the Cosmos, 1990, Visions of the Children, 1992, The Triumph, 1993, Angel Power, 1995, Meetings with Mary, 1996, Praying with Mary, 1997, Prayer Power, 1998, Queen of Angels, 1999. Founder Pitts. Ctr. for Peace, Inc., 1988—, Marion Ctr. World Peace, 1990—, Ctr. for Peace Ams., 1991; bd. dirs. Assn. Jr. Leagues Am., Wheeling, W.Va., Pitts., 1964—, Salvation Army, Wheeling, 1967-68, United Way, Jacksonville, 1971, YMCA, Jacksonville, 1992, Legal Aid Soc., Pitts., 1985—; bd. dirs. women's adv. bd. Duquesne U., Pitts., 1980—; founding dir. Inst. for World Concern, 1981—. Mem. ABA (real property sect.), Pa. Bar Assn., Allegheny County Bar Assn., Epiphany Assn. Estate planning, Securities, Probate. Office: 2 Gateway Ctr Ste 620 Pittsburgh PA 15222-1425

**CONNELL, WILLIAM D.,** lawyer; b. Palo Alto, Calif., Apr. 1, 1955; s. Robert Charles and Audrey Elizabeth (Steele) C.; m. Kathy Lynn Mleko, Aug. 13, 1977; children: Hilary Anne, Andrew James. BA in Polit Sci. with honors, Stanford U., 1976; JD cum laude, Harvard U., 1979. Bar: Calif. 1979, U.S. Dist. Ct. (cen., no. and ea. dists.) Calif. 1979, U.S. Ct. Appeals (9th cir.) 1979. Assoc. Gibson, Dunn & Crutcher, L.A., 1979-80; assoc. Gibson, Dunn & Crutcher, San Jose, Calif., 1980-87, ptnr., 1988-97; ptnr. Gen. Counsel Assocs. LLP, 1997—. Mem. Christian Legal Soc. Mem. Stanford Alumni Assn. (life), Commonwealth Club Calif., The Churchill Club, Sports Car Club Am., The Federalist Soc., Phi Beta Kappa. Republican. Avocation: photography. General civil litigation, Environmental, Product liability.

**CONNELLY, COLIN CHARLES,** lawyer; b. Hopewell, Va., Nov. 1, 1956; s. Charles Bernell and Doris Louise (Beasley) C.; m. Stephanie Paige Lowder, May 9, 1981. AA, Richard Bland Coll., 1977; BA, Va. Commonwealth U., 1979; JD, U. Richmond, 1983. Bar: Va. 1983, U.S. Ct. Appeals (4th cir.) 1983. Assoc. Tuck, Freasier, & Herbig, Richmond, Va., 1984-87; ptnr. Tuck & Connelly Profl. Assocs., Inc., Richmond, Va., 1988-95, Connelly & Assocs., P.C., Chester, Va., 1996—; bd. dirs., v.p. Cen. Title Ins. Agy., Richmond, 1988—; agt. Chgo. Title Ins. Corp., Richmond, 1988—. Mem., assoc./counsel Home Builders Assn. South Side Va. Mem. ABA, Va. Bar Assn., Richmond Bar Assn., Southside Bd. Realtors (affiliate), Chester Jaycees, Omicron Delta Kappa, Phi Kappa Phi, Phi Alpha Delta (justice 1983-86). Baptist. Avocations: biking, racquetball, basketball. Real property, Construction. Home: 14206 Masada Ct Chesterfield VA 23838-8725 Office: Connelly & Assocs 4830 W Hundred Rd Chester VA 23831-1746

**CONNELLY, JAMES P.,** prosecutor; b. Hartford, Conn., Apr. 15, 1947. BA, Marquette U., 1969; JD, Georgetown U., 1972. Bar: Wis. 1972. Spl. asst. to Sec. of Treasury, 1975-76; ptnr. Foley & Lardner, Milw.; U.S. atty. U.S. Dist. Ct. (ea. dist.) Wash., Spokane, 1994—. Editor-in-chief Georgetown Law Jour., 1971-72. Mem. State Bar Wis., Phi Alpha Delta. Office: US Atty Office US Courthouse PO Box 1494 920 W Riverside Ave Spokane WA 99210-1494*

**CONNELLY, MARY JO,** lawyer; b. Chgo., May 19, 1949; d. Joseph Anthony and Veronica Colette (Casey) C. BSN, Coll. St. Teresa, 1971; JD, DePaul U., 1980. Bar: Ill. 1980, U.S. Dist. Ct. (no. dist.) Ill. 1980, U.S. Dist. Ct. (ctrl. dist., no. dist.) Ill. 1990. Head nurse neurosurgery St. Mary's Hosp., Rochester, Minn., 1971-73; head nurse ambulatory care U. Calif., San Francisco, 1973-77; ptnr. Sweeney & Riman Ltd., Chgo., 1980-98. Mem. ABA, Women's Bar Assn. Ill., Ill. Bar Assn., Chgo. Bar Assn. (investigator hearing, bd. dirs. jud. evaluation com. 1984-89). General civil litigation, Personal injury. Home: 340 W Diversey Pky Apt 618 Chicago IL 60657-6242

**CONNELLY, THOMAS JOSEPH,** lawyer; b. Kansas City, Kans., Jan. 31, 1940; s. Edward J. and Mary (McCallum) C.; m. Barbara Helen Marciniak, Aug. 1, 1964; children: Catherine, Jennifer. AB, U. Detroit, 1963, JD, 1968. Bar: Mich. 1969, U.S. Dist. Ct. (so. and ea. dists.) Mich. 1969, U.S. Ct. Appeals (6th cir.) 1969. Sr. ptnr. Connelly, Crowley, Groth & Seglund, Walled Lake, Mich., 1975—. Exec. bd. dirs. Oakland County (Mich.) Reps., 1979-82. Mem. Mich. Bar Assn. (rep. assembly 1978—), Oakland County Bar Assn., Internat. Arabian Horse Assn. (pres.), Mich. Arabian Horse Assn. (pres. 1986—). Roman Catholic. Personal injury, Real property. Home: 1635 S Garner Rd Milford MI 48380-4127 Office: Connelly Crowley Groth & Seglund 2410 S Commerce Rd Walled Lake MI 48390-2129

**CONNER, ERNEST LEE, JR.,** lawyer; b. Jasper, Ala., Dec. 17, 1955; s. Ernest Lee and Sara Lynette (Maroney) C.; m. Lisa Ann Doig, Dec. 14, 1980; children: Melissa Ann, Jessica Lee. BS in Polit. Sci., E. Carolina U., 1984; JD, U. N.C., 1987. Bar: N.C. 1987, U.S. Dist. Ct. (ea. dist.) N.C. 1991. Ptnr. Dixon, Doub & Conner, Greenville, N.C., 1987—. Editor Hawaii Army Weekly newspaper, 1977. Bd. dirs. New Directions Family Violence Ctr., Greenville, 1989-91. Staff sgt. U.S. Army, 1974-81. Mem. N.C. Bar Assn. (chair criminal justice sect. 1997-98), N.C. Acad. Trial Lawyers, Pitt County Bar Assn. (treas. 1992—), Kiwanis. Democrat. Episcopalian. Avocations: jogging, water skiing, chess. Family and matrimonial, Criminal. Office: Dixon Doub & Conner 110 Arlington Blvd Greenville NC 27835

**CONNER, FRED L.,** lawyer; b. Hutchinson, Kans., Nov. 30, 1909; s. Hugh and Ida (Guldner) C.; m. Helen Opie, Sept. 15, 1940; 1 child, Brian. JD, U. Kans., 1934. Bar: Kans. 1934. Assoc. Andrew F. Schoeppel, Ness City, Kans., 1934-37; sole practice Gt. Bend, Kans., 1937-38; ptnr. Conner & Opie and predecessor firms, Gt. Bend, 1938—; dir. Insured Titles, Inc.; mem. faculty Philmont Scout Ranch, 1956; mem. Kans. Jud. Council Com. to Redistrict Dist. Cts. of Kans., 1968. Served to lt. comdr. USN, 1942-45. Fellow Am. Coll. Trust and Estate Counsel (chmn. Kans. sect. 1974-78), Probate Attys. Assn. (rsch. and editl. bd. 1959-62); mem. ABA (admissions com. 1951-58), Kans. Bar Assn. (program com. chmn. 1955-56, profl. ethics chmn. 1962-69, nominating com. chmn. 1969-70, Outstanding Svc. award 1970-71, 78-79, pres. 1980-81), S.W. Kans. Bar Assn., Kans. Bar Found. (trustee 1958-61), Barton County Bar Assn. (pres. 1946), Rotary (pres. Gt. Bend 1948), Masons, Am. Legion, Phi Delta Phi. Republican. Methodist. Probate, Real property. Home and Office: PO Box 763 Salina KS 67402-0763

**CONNER, JAMES LEON, II,** lawyer, mediator; b. Roanoke, Va., June 29, 1956; s. James Leon and Avis Christine (Craig) C.; m. Lorraine Joyce McNamara, Aug. 11, 1979 (div. 1987); children: Patrick James, Daniel Silas; m. Kathy Lynelle Watson, July 28, 1996; children: Benjamin Micah, Caleb Thomas. AB, Duke U., 1978; JD, U. N.C. Bar: N.C. 1983, U.S. Dist. Ct. (mid. dist.) N.C. 1984; U.S. Ct. Appeals (4th cir.). Vis. law instr. U. Ill. Coll. Law, Champaign, 1983-84; assoc. editor Environ. Law Inst., Washington, 1984-85; ptnr. Abernathy, Roberson & Conner, Graham, N.C., 1985-88; recycling dir. Alamance County, Burlington, N.C., 1988-89; assoc. atty. Brooks Pierce Mclendon Humphrey & Leonard, Greensboro, N.C., 1989-93; lead environ. atty. Kennedy Covington Lobdell & Hickman, Charlotte, N.C., 1993-95; prin. atty. J. Conner & Assocs., Durham, N.C., 1995—; mem. coun. environ. and natural resources law sect. N.C. Bar Assn., 1987-91. Contbr. articles to profl. jours. Mem. Durham (N.C.) City and County Environ. Affairs Bd., 1995—, vice chair 1997-98, chmn. 1998—; bd. dirs. Piedmont Land Conservancy, Greensboro, 1992-93; elder Presbyn. Ch.; founder U. N.C. chpt. Equal Justice Found., 1982; bd. dirs. North State Legal Svcs., 1986-89. Recipient Chpt. Svc. award N.C. Sierra Club, 1990, Am. Jurisprudence award. Avocations: hiking, canoeing, golf. Environmental, General civil litigation, Toxic tort. Office: J Conner & Assocs 311 E Main St Durham NC 27701-3717

**CONNER, JOHN SHULL,** lawyer; b. Sioux City, Iowa, Jan. 9, 1954; s. Raymond Dudley and Sally Elizabeth (Shull) C.; m. Mary Ziemba, Aug. 16, 1980; children: Courtney, John, Margaret. BSBA, U. Nebr., 1976; JD, Drake U., 1979. Bar: Mo. 1979, U.S. Dist. Ct. (we. dist.) Mo. 1979,U.S. Dist. Ct. (no. dist.) Calif. 1984, U.S. Supreme Ct. 1988, U.S. Dist. Ct. Ariz. 1992, U.S. Ct. Appeals (10th cir.) 1992, U.S. Dist. Ct. Kans. 1998. Assoc. Shughart Thomson & Kilroy, P.C., Kansas City, Mo., 1979-83, dir., 1984—. Co-author: Kansas and Missouri Law for Design Professionals, 1997, Missouri Civil Actions, Vol. 1, 1989; contbr. articles to various publs. Coord. United Way, Kansas City, 1984—, loaned exec., 1998—; bd. dirs., pres. Pinehurst Estate, Overland Park, Kans., 1992-94; bd. dirs. Gillis Ctr., Kansas City, 1996—; com. mem. Valley View United Meth. Ch., Overland Park, 1998. Mem. ABA (constrn. forum), Mo. Bar Assn., Kansas City Bar Assn., Kansas City Club. General civil litigation, Construction, Insurance. Office: Shughart Thomson & Kilroy 120 W 12th St Ste 1500 Kansas City MO 64105-1929

**CONNER, LESLIE LYNN, JR.,** lawyer; b. Oklahoma City, July 15, 1939; s. Leslie Lynn and Grace Dorothy (Hartnell) C.; m. Nancy Newblock, Sept. 9, 1960; children: Deborah Lynn, Lauren Elaine, Thomas Hartnell. BA, Okla. U., 1961, LLB, 1963. Bar: Okla. 1963, U.S. Dist. Ct. (we. dist.) Okla. 1963, U.S. Ct. Appeals (10th cir.) 1963, U.S. Dist. Ct. (no. dist.) Okla. 1967, U.S. Supreme Ct. Sole practice P.C. Oklahoma City, 1992—; ptnr. Conner & Little, Oklahoma City, 1966-92; bd. dirs. First State Bank, Jones, Okla.; hearing examiner Okla. Ins. Dept., 1995—. Trustee Heritage Hall Sch., Oklahoma City, 1977-83, sec. bd. trustees, 1977-78, pres. bd. trustees, 1979-82; trustee, chmn. various coms., mem. choir, lay leader United Meth. Ch., Nichols Hills, Okla., 1963—; bd. dirs. Ctrl. Okla. United Meth. Retirement Facility, 1990-96. Served to capt. USAF, 1963-66, lt. col. res. ret. Fellow Am. Coll. Probate Council; mem. ABA (ho. of dels. 1978-81), Okla. Bar Assn. (bd. of govs. 1977-81, pres. 1980, chmn. various coms.), Am. Arbitration Assn. (bd. dirs. 1991-98, comml. arbitrator 1968—, mediator 1985—), Okla. Trial Lawyers Assn., Okla. County Bar Assn. (Outstanding Service award 1974). Democrat. Methodist. Avocations: reading fiction, woodworking. General practice, Probate, Alternative dispute resolution. Home: 5812 Chestnut Ct Edmond OK 73003-2513 Office: Ste 205 6801 N Broadway Oklahoma City OK 73116-9037

**CONNER, LEWIS HOMER, JR.,** lawyer; b. Chattanooga, Mar. 21, 1938; s. Lewis H. Sr. and Cleo (Johnson) C.; m. Ashley Whitsitt, June 1, 1960; children: Holland Ashley, Lewis Forrest. BA, Vanderbilt U., 1960, JD, 1963. Bar: Tenn. 1963, U.S. Dist. Ct. (all dists.) Tenn. 1963, U.S. Ct. Appeals (6th cir.) 1963, U.S. Ct. Mil. Appeals 1964, U.S. Supreme Ct. 1990; cert. mediator, Tenn. Founding ptnr., atty. Dearborn & Ewing, Nashville, 1972-80; judge Ct. Appeals Middle Dist., Nashville, 1980-84; sr. ptnr., atty. Waller Lansden Dortch & Davis, Nashville, 1985-89, Boult, Cummings, Conners & Berry, Nashville, 1989-96; of counsel Stokes & Bartholomew, Nashville, 1997—; chmn. Willis Coroon, Tenn., 1996—; spl. chief justice Supreme Ct. Tenn., 1980-81; lectr. law Vanderbilt U. Sch. Law, Nashville, 1984-93; life del. Sixth Cir. Ct. Appeals Jud. Conf. Mng. editor Vanderbilt Law Rev. Elder Westminster Presbyn. Ch.; bd. dirs. Tenn. Golf Assn., Nashville, 1965—, pres., 1985, chmn. 1994-95, 98—; fin. co-chmn. Alexander for Gov., 1974-78; chmn. Tenn. Rep. Fin. Com., 1975, Tenn. Corrections Overcrowding Commn., 1985-86; bd. dirs. Boys & Girls Club Middle Tenn., 1980—, pres., 1991-92; bd. govs. Tenn. State Mus., 1987—, vice chmn. bd., 1988-89, chmn. bd., 1990-91; mem. nat. fin. com. Bush for Pres., 1988, 92; bd. dirs., exec. com. Nashville Sports Coun., 1994—; bd. dirs. BellSouth Sr. Classic, Nashville, 1994—; nat. fin. co-chmn. Lamar Alexander for Pres., Inc., Nashville, 1995-96, 1999-2000. Fellow Am. Acad. Matrimonial Lawyers, Am. Bar Found., Tenn. Bar Found., Nashville Bar Found.; mem. ABA, Am. Arbitration Assn. (bd. dirs. 1990—, chmn. Tenn. large complex case panel 1992—, panel of arbitrators 1995, panel of mediators 1995—), Tenn. Bar Assn., Tenn. Jud. Conf., Nashville Bar Assn. (pres. 1986-87, bd. dirs., 1984-87), Commn. on the Future of the Cts. in Tenn., Order of the Coif, PGA of Am. (hon. Tenn. sect.), The Golf Club Tenn. (founder, exec. com. 1991-97), Richland Country Club (bd. dirs. 1976-79, pres. 1978-79), Belle Meade Country Club, The Honors Course, Quail West Golf Club, Nashville City Club, Nashville Cumberland Club, Nashville Stadium Club, Tenn. Golf Assn. (amateur player of yr., 1973). Republican. Avocations: golf, basketball, softball, politics. Alternative dispute resolution, General civil litigation, Family and matrimonial. Home: 163 Charleston Park Nashville TN 37205-4703 Office: Stokes & Bartholomew 424 Church St Ste 2800 Nashville TN 37219-2386

**CONNER, MICHAEL TIMOTHY,** lawyer; b. Berkeley Heights, N.J., Oct. 6, 1947; s. Joseph H. and Marion C.; m. Carol Ann Mann, July 4, 1981; children: Kelly, Lindsay, David. BA in Polit. Sci., Am. U., 1969, JD, 1976. Bar: D.C. 1977, U.S. Ct. of Appeals (D.C. cir.) 1979, U.S. Ct. of Appeals (1st cir.) 1986, U.S. Ct. of Appeals (4th cir.) 1983. Staff atty. Nat. Oceanic & Atmospheric Adminstrn., Washington, 1977-81; staff atty. U.S. Dept of Commerce, Washington, 1981-85, chief, gen. litig. divsn., 1985—. Named Atty. of the Year, Dept. Commerce Gen. Coun., 1989. Home: 12588 Cross Hollow Ct Herndon VA 20170-5741 Office: US Dept Commerce Office Gen Counsel Rm 5890 Washington DC 20230-0001

**CONNER, TIMOTHY JAMES,** lawyer; b. Panama City, Fla., Jan. 7, 1954; s. James F. Conner and Margie (Scott) Roberts; divorced; children: Jessica, Harris, Monica. BA in Polit. Sci., Fla. Tech. U., 1977; JD, U. Fla., 1980. Bar: Fla. 1981, U.S. Dist. Ct. (mid. dist.) Fla. 1982. Law clk. David M. Lipman, Miami, Fla., 1980-82; staff atty. Cen. Fla. Legal Services, Palatka, 1982-83, mng. atty., 1983-86; ptnr. Berns & Conner, Palm Coast, Fla., 1986-95; shareholder Timothy J. Conner & Assocs., P.A., Palm Coast, 1995-97, Timothy J. Conner, P.A., Palm Coast, 1997—. Pres. Fla. Low Income Housing Coalition, Inc., Tallahassee, 1982-86; mem. adv. bd. Flagler County Legal Apprenticeship Program, Flagler Teen Ct. Adv. Bd., Vol. Lawyers Project. Mem. ABA, Fla. Trial Lawyers Assn., Flagler County Bar Assn. (sec. 1989, v.p. 1991, pres. 1992-93, sec./treas. 1994—), Assn. Trial Lawyers Am. Democrat. Avocations: electronics, boating, motorcycles, woodworking. General corporate, General practice, Real property. Home: PO Box 354191 Palm Coast FL 32135-4191 Office: Timothy J Conner PA 1 Florida Park Dr N Ste 110 Palm Coast FL 32137-3844

**CONNER, TONYA SUE,** lawyer; b. Frankfort, Ky., May 28, 1969; d. Dudley Jefferson and Betty Sue C. BA, Transylvania U., 1991; JD, U. Ky., 1994; LLM, Loyola U., Chgo., 1996. Bar: Ky. 1994, U.S. Dist. Ct. (ea. dist.) Ky. 1997. Law clk. Spl. Fund--Labor Cabinet, Frankfort, 1992-93; law clk. Savage, Garmer & Elliott, Lexington, Ky., 1993-94, Motherway & Glenn, Chgo., 1994-95; staff atty. Ky. Ct. of Appeals, Bowling Green, 1995-97, Ky. Ct. Appeals, Versailles, 1997; assoc. McCoy & West, Lexington, 1997—. Mem. ABA, Ky. Bar Assn., Fayette County Bar Assn., Bowling Green Bar Assn. Appellate, General civil litigation, Criminal. Office: McCoy & West PO Box 1660 Lexington KY 40588-1660

**CONNER, WARREN WESLEY,** lawyer; b. Cat Spring, Tex., Aug. 14, 1932; s. George William and Frieda Johanna (Kollatschny) C.; m. Suzanne Rosser, Oct. 29, 1955; children: Connie Suzanne, Cathy Lorrane; m. Sharon Ann Welch, July 28, 1978. BBA, So. Meth. U., 1959, JD, 1963. Bar: Tex. 1963, U.S. Dist. Ct. (so. dist.) Tex. 1971. Ptnr. Sheehan & Conner, Friona, Tex., 1963-65; founder, ptnr. Conner & Clover, P.C., Sealy, Tex., 1965-95; with Conner, Cantey & Clover, Sealy & Brenham, Tex., 1995, ret., 1996; bd. dirs. Citizens State Bank, Sealy, Industry Telephone Co.; past pres. Austin County (Tex.) chpt. Am. Cancer Soc.; past v.p. Sealy Area Hist. Soc. Served with U.S. Army, 1953-55. Mem. State Bar Tex., Austin County Bar Assn. (past pres.), Masons, Shriners (past pres.), Rotary (past pres.), LIons (past pres. New Ulm chpt.). Presbyterian. Banking, Family and matrimonial, Probate. Office: RR 1 Box 68-f Cat Spring TX 78933-9604

**CONNER, WILLIAM CURTIS,** judge; b. Wichita Falls, Tex., Mar. 27, 1920; s. D.H. and Mae (Weeks) C.; m. Janice Files, Mar. 22, 1944; children: William Curtis, Stephen, Christopher, Molly. B.B.A., U. Tex., 1941, LL.B., 1942; postgrad., Harvard, 1942-43, Mass. Inst. Tech., 1943. Bar: Tex. bar 1942, N.Y. State bar 1949. Asso., mem. firm Curtis, Morris & Safford (and predecessor firm), N.Y.C., 1946-73; judge U.S. Dist. Ct. (so. dist.) N.Y., White Plains, 1973—, now sr. judge. Editor Tex. Law Rev. Served to lt. USNR, 1942-45, PTO. Recipient Jefferson medal N.J. Patent Law Assn. Mem. Am. Judicature Soc., N.Y. Patent Law Assn. (pres. 1972-73). Presbyterian (elder). Club: St. Andrews Golf. Office: US Dist Ct US Courthouse 300 Quarropas St White Plains NY 10601-4140

**CONNEY, CARL M.,** attorney general; b. St. Paul, Minn., Feb. 2, 1940; s. Frank P. and Alvina Conney. BA, U. St. Thomas, 1962; JD, U. Minn., 1965; MA in Internat. Mgmt., Am. Grad. Sch. Internat. Mgmt., 1972. Bar: Minn. 1966, Calif. 1974, U.S. Dist. Ct. Minn. 1967. Asst. county atty. Ramsey County Attys. Office, St. Paul, 1966-70; asst. to v.p., treas. Econs. Lab. for Internat. Ltd., St. Paul, 1972-74; pvt. practice St. Paul, 1974-77; asst. atty. gen. Minn. Atty. Gen.'s Office, St. Paul, 1977—. Mem. Calif. State Bar Assn., Minn. State Bar Assn. Office: Minn Atty Gens Office 445 Minnesota St Saint Paul MN 55101-2190

**CONNOLLY, CARLA GARCIA,** lawyer; b. San Antonio, Jan. 12, 1953; d. Gus C. Garcia and Eleanor (Rodriguez) McCusker; m. James M. Connolly, Nov. 1, 1985; children: Erin C., Cara A. BA, Tex. A&I U., 1974; JD, U. Tex., 1980. Bar: Tex. 1980, U.S. Dist. Ct. (we. dist.) Tex. 1991. Asst. dist. atty. Travis County Dist. Atty.'s Office, Austin, 1980-89; shareholder Wright & Greenhill, P.C., Austin, 1989-98; ptnr. Black & Connolly LLP, Austin, 1998—. Mem. Tex. Assn. Def. Counsel, Travis County Bar Assn. General civil litigation, Personal injury, Labor. Office: Black & Connolly LLP 115 E 5th St Ste 100 Austin TX 78701-3601

**CONNOLLY, K. THOMAS,** lawyer; b. Spokane, Wash., Jan. 23, 1940; s. Lawrence Francis and Kathleen Dorothea (Hallahan) C.; m. Laurie Samuel, June 24, 1967; children: Kevin, Megan, Amy, Matthew. BBA, Gonzaga U., Spokane, Wash., 1962; JD, Gonzaga U., 1966; LLM in Taxation, NYU, 1972. Bar: Wash. 1966, U.S. Ct. Mil. Appeals 1967, U.S. Tax Ct. 1983. Assoc. Witherspoon, Kelley, Davenport & Toole, Spokane, 1972-77; ptnr./prin. Witherspoon, Kelley, Davenport & Toole, 1977—; assoc. prof. law Gonzaga Sch. Law, 1973-77. Bd. overseers Gonzaga Prep. Sch., Spokane, 1988-89; bd. trustees Spokane Guild Sch. for the Handicapped, 1975-78, Wash. State U. Found. Bd., 1992-97, Whitman Coll. Planned Giving Coun., 1994—. Capt. U.S. Army, 1966-70. Recipient Wall St. Jur. award, 1962; decorated Bronze Star medal. Mem. Wash. State Bar Assn. (founder, chmn. health law sect. 1989-92, health law coun. 1989-94, pres. tax sect. 1987-88, mem. tax coun. 1984—), ABA (chmn. health care subcom. 1990-94). Republican. Avocations: tennis, astronomy. Health, Pension, profit-sharing, and employee benefits, Corporate taxation. Office: Witherspoon Kelley Davenport & Toole 1100 Old National Bldg Spokane WA 99201

**CONNOLLY, KEVIN JUDE,** lawyer; b. N.Y.C., May 25, 1954; s. John William and Beatrice Joan (Fallon) C.; m. Audrey Mason, May 25, 1995; children: Shea Alexander, Ciaran Jude. BA cum laude, Fordham Coll., 1976; JD, Fordham U., 1985. Bar: N.Y. 1990. Assoc. Stroock & Stroock & Lavan, N.Y.C., 1985-89, Shapiro & Byrne, P.C., Mineola, N.Y., 1989-92; counsel Schreiber, Simmons, MacKnight & Tweedy, N.Y.C., 1992-94, Eaton & Van Winkle, N.Y.C., 1994-97; assoc. Robinson, Silverman, Pearce, Aronsohn & Berman LLP, N.Y.C., 1998—; vis. lectr. Sch. Visual Arts, N.Y.C., 1996—; dir. Internet Soc., N.Y.C. chpt., 1997—; outside counsel Internet Policy Adv. Body, Geneva, Switzerland, 1997—, Internet Coun. Registrars, Geneva, 1997-98, Hatewatch, Inc., 1998—. Tactical field trainer U.S. Mil. Acad., West Point, 1989—. Avocations: antiques, paintball. E-mail: jawz@cybersharque.com. Computer, Construction, Intellectual property. Home: 205 Blackheath Rd Lido Beach NY 11561-4838 Office: Robinson Silverman Pearce Aronsohn & Berman 1290 Ave of Amers New York NY 10104

**CONNOLLY, L. WILLIAM,** lawyer; b. Gary, Ind., June 14, 1923; s. Leo W. and Lauretta E. (Feely) C.; m. Suzanne M. Irving, Sept. 2, 1950; children—Thomas A., Charles D., Alicia M., James J., Charlene Susan, John J., Robert P. Student, Miss. State U., CUNY; Ph.B., Marquette U., 1948, J.D., 1951. Bar: Wis. 1952, U.S. Supreme Ct. 1967. With Am. Automobile Ins. Co., Milw., 1951-52; mem. Rummel & Connolly, Milw., 1952-55, Spence, Rummel & Connolly, Milw., 1955-59, Spence & Connolly, Milw., 1959-64; practice law Spence & Connolly, 1964—. Trustee Village of Thiensville, Wis., 1957-61. Served with AUS, 1943-46. Fellow Internat. Acad. Lex et Scienta; mem. ABA, Wis. Bar Assn., Milw. Bar Assn., Am. Arbitration Assn. (nat. panel arbitrator 1973—), Am. Judicature Soc., Delta Theta Phi. State civil litigation, Criminal. Home: 830 Wood Dr Oconomowoc WI 53066-3930 Office: 3106 N 80th St Milwaukee WI 53222-3802

**CONNOLLY, THOMAS EDWARD,** judge; b. Boston, Nov. 7, 1942; s. Thomas Francis and Catherine Elizabeth (Skehill) C. AB, St. John's Sem., Brighton, Mass., 1964; JD, Boston Coll., 1969. Bar: Mass., 1969. Assoc. Schneider & Reilly, Boston, 1969-73; ptnr. Schneider, Reilly, Zabin, Connolly & Costello, P.C., Boston, 1973-85, Connolly Leavis & Rest, Boston, 1986-90; judge Mass. Superior Ct., Boston, 1990—; instr. law Northeastern Law Sch., Boston, 1975-76. Mem. governing coun. Boston Coll. Law Sch. Alumni Coun., 1980—. Mem. ABA (vice chmn. products liability sect. 1978—), Trial Lawyers Assn. Am. (nat. gov. 1977-80), Mass. Acad. Trial Lawyers (gov. 1976—), Am. Coll. Trial Lawyers, Univ. Club (Boston), Algonquin Club (Boston). Democrat. Roman Catholic. Home: 253 Marlborough St # 4 Boston MA 02116-1731 Office: The Superior Ct Boston MA 02108

**CONNOLLY, THOMAS JOSEPH,** lawyer; b. Boston, Sept. 25, 1957; s. William Joseph and Jacquline (Wetzel) C. BA in History, Bates Coll., 1979; JD, U. Maine, 1982. Bar: Maine 1982, Mass. 1982, U.S. Dist. Ct. Maine 1982, U.S. Ct. Appeals (1st cir.) 1986, U.S. Supreme Ct. 1986. Pvt. practice, Portland, Maine, 1982—. Co-author: Fuel for Thought: The Case Against Energy Independence, 1977, Traders in Our Midst: The Case Against Trade Reform, 1978. Recipient Faculty Advocacy award U. Maine, 1982. Mem. ABA, Maine Bar Assn., Mass. Bar Assn., Assn. Trial Lawyers Am., Maine Trial Lawyers Assn. Democrat. Roman Catholic. Avocations: Civil War history, Grateful Dead, W.B. Yeates, bible studies, Arnold's 1775 March Que. *. Criminal, Civil rights, Personal injury. Office: PO Box 7563 Portland ME 04112-7563

**CONNOLLY, WILLIAM M.,** state supreme court justice. Former judge Nebr. Ct. of Appeals, Lincoln; assoc. justice Nebr. Supreme Ct., Lincoln. Office: Nebr Supreme Ct PO Box 98910 2413 State Capitol Bldg Lincoln NE 68509*

**CONNOR, JOHN THOMAS, JR.,** lawyer; b. N.Y.C., June 16, 1941; s. John Thomas and Mary (O'Boyle) C.; m. Susan Scholle, Dec. 18, 1965; children: Seanna, Marin, John. BA cum laude, Williams Coll., 1963; JD, Harvard U., 1967. Bar: N.Y. 1968, D.C. 1980. Assoc. Cravath, Swaine & Moore, N.Y.C., 1967-71; dep. dir. Office Econ. Policy and Case Analysis, Pay Bd., Washington, 1971-72, Bur. East-West Trade, U.S. Dept. Commerce, Washington, 1972-73; sr. v.p. U.S.-USSR Trade and Econ. Coun., Moscow, 1973-76; assoc. Milbank, Tweed, Hadley & McCloy, N.Y.C., 1976-79; ptnr. Curtis, Mallet-Prevost, Colt and Mosle, Washington, 1980-82; v.p., gen. counsel, sec. PHH Corp., 1982-88; v.p., asst. gen. counsel Prudential Ins. Co. Am., Newark, 1988-90; ptnr. Sills Cummis, Newark, 1990-94; counsel Chadbourne & Parke, N.Y.C., 1994-96, Patterson, Belknap, Webb & Tyler, LLP, 1996-98; chmn. Great Am. Life Corp., 1993—, ROSGAL Group Fin Cos., Moscow, 1993—; portfolio mgr., chmn. Third Millennium Funds, 1998—; of counsel Curtis, Mallet-Prevost, Colt and Mosle, Washington, 1999—. Exec. dir. Dem. Party N.J., 1969-70; pres., trustee Newark Boys Chorus Sch.; Fulbright tutor Ferguson Coll., Poona, India, 1963-64; chmn. Coun. on Econ. Priorities. Mem. N.Y. State Bar Assn., D.C. Bar Assn., Coun. Fgn. Rels., Am. Law Inst., Baltusrol Club N.J., Met. Club (Washington), Union Club (N.Y.C.), Chevy Chase Club (Md.), Wianno Club (Cape Cod), Mountain Lake Club (Fla.), Phi Beta Kappa. General corporate, Private international, Securities. Home: PO Box 832 Lake Woler FL 33859-0832 Office: Third Millennium Funds 32d Fl 1185 Ave of the Americas New York NY 10022

**CONNOR, JOSEPH PATRICK, III,** lawyer; b. Phila., Apr. 15, 1953; s. Joseph Patrick Jr. and Wanda Delores (Filipkowski) C.; m. Mary Margaret Kazanicka, Aug. 13, 1977; children: Cathleen Marie, Christopher Joseph, Christine Anne. BA in Polit. Sci., Villanova U., 1974; JD, St. Mary's U., San Antonio, 1974. Bar: Pa. 1977, U.S. Dist. Ct. (ea. dist.) Pa. 1977, U.S. Dist. Ct. (mid. dist.) Pa. 1997, U.S. Ct. Appeals (3d cir.) 1977, U.S Supreme Ct. 1982. Assoc. ptnr. Gibbons, Buckley, Smith, Palmer & Proud, Media, Pa., 1977-82; pres. Connor & Weber, P.C., Phila., Paoli, 1982—. Mem. ABA (tort & litigation sects.), Pa. Bar Assn., Pa. Def. Inst., Def. Research Inst., Pa. Trial Lawyers Assn., Chester County Bar Assn. Republican. Roman Catholic. Club: Overbrook County (Bryn Mawr). Avocations: flying, golf, swimming, traveling. Insurance, Personal injury, General civil litigation. Office: Connor & Weber PC 2401 Pennsylvania Ave Philadelphia PA 19130-3061

**CONNOR, KENNETH LUKE,** lawyer; b. Atlanta, Apr. 24, 1947; s. Kenneth B. and Fay C.; m. Amy Reddoch, Mar. 20, 1971; children: Kathryn Lynn, Amy Elizabeth, Christopher Caleb, Joshua Lee. AA, Chipola Jr. Coll., 1967; BA, Fla. State U., 1969, JD cum laude, 1972. Bar: Fla. 1972, U.S. Dist. Ct. (mid. dist.) Fla. 1973, U.S. Ct. Appeals (11th cir.) 1973, U.S. Supreme Ct. 1984, U.S. Dist. Ct. (no. dist.) Fla. 1986, Fla. Bar Bd. Cert. Trial Lawyers 1984. Ptnr. Gibson, Connor, Lilly & Dodson, Lake Wales, Fla., 1973-85, Connor & Martinez, Tallahassee, 1986-88, Connor & Assocs., Tallahassee, 1989-95, Connor & Gwartney, Tallahassee, 1996-98; of counsel Wilkes & McHugh, P.A., 1998—; frequent lectr. various bar assns.; adj. prof. Fla. State U. Coll. Law, 1983, 86, 87. Mem. Coun. Nat. Policy, 1993-97, Fla. State Commn. on Ethics, 1984-86 (chmn. 1985-86); Gov.'s Constituency for Children, 1988-90, Fed. Jud. Adv. Comsn. Fla., 1989-92; bd. dirs. Fla. Right to Life, 1986-92, Ams. United for Life, 1990-93; internat. bd. dirs. Christian Action Coun., 1988-92; chmn. Care Net, 1996—; spl. counsel The Justice Task Force, 1988-89; gen. counsel Rep. Party of Fla., 1989-90; mem. Gov.'s Partnership for Adoption, 1996—, Fla. Constn. Rev. Commn., 1997—. With USAR 1971-79. Mem. Am. Bd. Trial Advocates, Acad. Fla. Trial Lawyers, Assn. Trial Lawyers Am. General civil litigation, Personal injury, Product liability. Office: Connor & Gwartney PO Box 11187 Tallahassee FL 32302-3187

**CONNOR, TED ALLAN,** lawyer; b. Joliet, Ill., Feb. 21, 1962; s. Charles Patrick and Alice Jean Connor. BA in Govt. Studies, U. Notre Dame, 1984; JD, U. San Diego, 1987. Bar: Calif. 1987, Ill. 1998, U.S. Dist. Ct. (so. and ctrl. dists.) Calif. 1987. Assoc. Fisch, Spiegler, Ginsburg and Ladner, San Diego, 1987-88; ind. contract atty., 1990-91; assoc. atty. Law Offices of Maurile C. Tremblay, La Jolla, Calif., 1988-90, 91-95; sr. assoc., br. mng. atty. Kolod, Wager & Gordon, LLP, Santa Ana, Calif., 1995—. Vol. atty. Vols. in Parole of San Diego, 1989-96. Mem. Alternative dispute resolution, Insurance, Construction. Office: The Bentall Ctr 1551 N Tustin Ave Ste 195 Santa Ana CA 92705-8666

**CONNORS, DONALD LOUIS,** lawyer, land use planner; b. Boston, Mar. 25, 1936; s. Edward Joseph and Rosella (Adams) C.; m. Margaret Sheffield, June 15, 1957; children: Joan F., Brian E., Thomas M., Christopher Sean. BS cum laude, Boston Coll., 1957; JD, Suffolk U., 1967. Bar: Mass., U.S. Dist. Ct. Mass., U.S. Ct. Appeals (1st cir.). Legis. counsel Greater Boston C. of C., 1963-68; counsel pub. affairs New Eng. Telephone, Boston, 1968-71; prin., pres. Tyler & Reynolds, Boston, 1971-81; ptnr., chmn. land use and environ. law group Choate, Hall & Stewart, Boston, 1981-93; of counsel Foley, Hoag & Eliot, Boston and Washington, 1993-95; pirn. Connors & Bliss P.C., 1996—; lectr. Grad. Sch. Design, Harvard U., 1978-89; adj. lectr. in regional planning U. Mass., Amherst, 1984-89; counsel Cape Cod and Martha's Vineyard Commns.; counsel, bd. dirs. Environ. League Mass., Inc., Boston, 1989—, Cape Cod Ctr. for Environ. and Sustainable Devel., 1991—; chair counsel The Growth Mgmt. Inst., Washington, 1992—; founder, chair, dir. Environ. Bus. Coun. N.E., Boston, pres., 1993—; chmn. environ. law curriculum adv. com. Mass. Continuing Edn. Inc., 1990-94; chmn. Internat. Environ. Bus. and Tech. Inst., Inc., 1993; mem. Environ. Bus. Practice Group; founder Pres. Environ. Bus. Coun. U.S., Inc., Internat. Environ. Bus. Tech. Inst., Inc.; chair adv. com. Southeastern Mass. Vision 2020, 1997—. Co-author: The Public Trust Doctrine, 1991; author, editor: State and Regional Planning, 1991; contbr. numerous articles to profl. jours. Mem. bd. advisors Sea Grant Coll., MIT, Cambridge, 1972—; chair, bd. dirs. Conservation Law Found. New Eng., Boston, 1976-79; chair com. adv. bd. Sta. WGBH Pub. Broadcasting, Boston, 1976-79; co-chair marine sci. policy adv. bd. U. Mass., Boston, 1991. Capt. U.S. Army, 1957-62; mem. environ. technol. trade adv. com. U.S. Dept. Commerce, Washington, 1994-96. Recipient award Assn. for Preservation Cape Cod, 1990, Pres. award for Environ. Leadership The Conte Inst., Mass., 1993, Environ. merit award U.S. EPA Region One, 1995. Mem. ABA, Mass. Bar Assn., Boston Bar Assn., AICP (cert.), Urban Land Inst. (co-chmn. policy forum on state and regional planning 1989-92), Cross and Crown Soc., Beta Gamma Sigma, Alpha Sigma Nu. Democrat. Roman Catholic. Avocations: hiking, canoeing, bicycling, travelling. Environmental, Land use and zoning (including planning), General corporate. Office: Connors & Bliss PC 420 Boylston St Boston MA 02116-4002

**CONNORS, FRANK JOSEPH,** lawyer; b. N.Y.C., Oct. 8, 1944; s. Frank Joseph and Nina Florence (Kirk) C.; m. Evelyn Noreen Mills, Oct. 14, 1983. BA, UCLA, 1965; MA, Columbia U., 1966; JD, Harvard U., 1969. Bar: N.Y. 1970, Fla. 1982, Mass. 1986, U.S. Supreme Ct. 1973. Assoc. Dewey, Ballantine, Bushby, Palmer & Wood, N.Y.C., 1969-75; asst. atty. gen. N.Y. State Spl. Prosecutor, N.Y.C., 1975-77; gen. atty. Am. Broadcasting Cos., Inc., N.Y.C., 1977-85; atty. Harvard U., Cambridge, Mass., 1985—; acting gen. counsel, 1992; arbitrator N.Y.C. Civil Ct., 1980-85; comml. arbitrator Am. Arbitration Assn., N.Y.C., 1984-85. Bd. dirs. World Teach, Inc., 1992—. Mem. Am. Judicature Soc., N.Y. State Bar Assn. (copyright com. 1981-85), Assn. of Bar of City of N.Y. (profl. discipline com. 1983-85). Republican. Methodist. General corporate, Taxation, general. Office: Harvard U 1350 Massachusetts Ave Cambridge MA 02138-3846

**CONNORS, JAMES PATRICK,** lawyer; b. N.Y.C., May 28, 1952; s. Joseph Patrick Connors and Edna Theresa Fitzgerald; m. Gloria Ann Ciccarelli, Jan. 12, 1974; children: Nicholas, Patrick, Jamie Cathleen. BA, Herbert H. Lehman Coll., 1974; JD, N.Y. Law Sch., 1977; LLM, NYU, 1985. Bar: N.Y. 1978, U.S. Dist. Ct. (so. and ea. dists.) N.Y. 1978. Assoc. Bower & Gardner, N.Y.C., 1978-80, Joseph W. Conklin, N.Y.C., 1980-82; ptnr. Jones, Hirsch, Connors & Bull, N.Y.C., 1982—; lectr. NYU Sch. Medicine, 1983, N.Y. Law Jour., 1984, Bellevue Hosp., 1984, Hillcrest Gen. Hosp., 1984, Mt. Sinai Hosp., 1985, Am. Coll. Ophthalmologists, 1986-88. Contbr. articles to profl. jours. Recipient Am. Jurisprudence award Lawyers Pub. Coop., 1977. Mem. ABA, N.Y. State Bar Assn., N.Y. County Bar Assn., Def. Assn. of N.Y. State civil litigation, Personal injury, Insurance. Home: 85 Mayflower Dr Yonkers NY 10710-3801

**CONNORS, JOSEPH ALOYSIUS, III,** lawyer; b. Washington, June 24, 1946; s. Joseph Aloysius Jr. and Charlotte Rita (Fox) C.; m. Mary Louise Bucklin, June 14, 1969. BBA, U. Southwestern La., 1970; JD, U. Tex., 1973. Bar: Tex. 1973, U.S. Dist. Ct. (so. dist.) Tex. 1975, U.S. Supreme Ct. 1976, U.S. Ct. Appeals (5th cir.) 1976, U.S. Dist. Ct. (ea., we. and no. dists.) Tex. 1981, U.S. Ct. Appeals (11th cir.) 1981, U.S. Ct. Appeals (3d, 4th, 6th, 7th, 8th, 9th, 10th and D.C. cirs.) 1986. Law clk. to assoc. justice Tex. Ct. Civil Appeals, Amarillo, 1973-74; assoc. Rankin & Kern, McAllen, Tex., 1974-76; asst. criminal dist. atty. Hidalgo County, Tex., 1976-78; pvt. practice, McAllen, 1978—; faculty Criminal Trial Advocacy Inst., Huntsville, Tex., 1981-84; speaker seminars State Bar Tex., 1980-81, 84; adj. prof. Reynaldo G. Garza Sch. Law, Edinburg, Tex., 1988-89. Contbg. editor Criminal Trial Manual, Tex., 1984-95; contbr. articles to profl. jours. Bd. dirs. Tex. Rural Legal Aid, 1991—, pres. bd. dirs., 1994-96. With USMCR, 1966-71. Mem. NACDL, State Bar Tex. (grievance com. 12B 1984-91, chmn. com. 1989-90, profl. enhancement program, 1997—), Tex. Assn. Criminal Def. Lawyers (bd. dirs. 1982-89, Excellence award 1983, medal of honor 1987), Hidalgo County Bar Assn. (bd. dirs. 1981-83), Am. Soc. Writers on Legal Subjects, Hidalgo County Criminal Def. Lawyers Assn. (bd. dirs. 1991-98). Democrat. Roman Catholic. Criminal. Office: PO Box 5838 McAllen TX 78502-5838

**CONNORS, JOSEPH CONLIN,** lawyer; b. Mineola, N.Y., Sept. 9, 1948; s. Gerard Edward and Mary Helen (Conlin) C.; m. Mary Napolitano, May 29, 1971; children: J.C., Ryan. BA, SUNY-Oneonta, 1970; JD, Fordham U., 1973. Bar: N.Y. 1974, Tenn. 1985. Confidential law sec. to judge N.Y. Supreme Ct., Cortland, 1973-75; atty. Chevron Corp., Perth Amboy, N.J., 1975-76, Schering-Plough Corp., Kenilworth, N.J., 1976-82; assoc. gen. counsel Schering-Plough Corp., Memphis, 1982-87; staff v.p., planning and bus. devel. Schering-Plough Corp., Madison, N.J., 1987, dep. gen. counsel, 1987-91, v.p., gen. counsel, 1991-92, sr. v.p., gen. counsel, 1992-96, exec. v.p. and gen. counsel, 1996—; mem. adv. com. Met. Corp. Counsel; sr. advisor N.J. Corp. Counsel Assn. Mem. ABA (com. of corp. gen. counsel), N.Y. Bar Assn., Tenn. Bar Assn. (former chmn. corp. sect.), Assn. Nat. Advertisers (bd. dirs. 1987-90), N.J. Legal Aid andDefender Assn. (corp. adv. com.), N.J. Corp. Counsel Assn. (sr. advisor), N.J. Panel of the CPR Inst. for Dispute Resolution (bd. dirs.), Food and Drug Inst. (trustee, editl. adv. bd.), Pharm. Rsch. and Mfrs. Am. (exec. com. law sect. 1998). Roman Catholic. Avocations: travel, golf. General corporate, Antitrust. Office: Schering Plough Corp 1 Giralda Farms Madison NJ 07940-1010

**CONNORS, KEVIN CHARLES,** lawyer; b. New Haven, Jan. 1, 1954; s. Charles Joseph Jr. and Frances (Brown) C.; m. Janet Dorothy Manchester, Oct. 27, 1979; 1 child, Timothy. BA magna cum laude, U. Conn., 1974; JD, U. Conn., Hartford, 1979. Bar: Conn. 1979, U.S. Dist. Ct. Conn. 1983. Dep. asst. pub. defender State of Conn., Hartford, 1979-81, asst. pub. defender, 1981-83; sole practitioner East Hartford, Conn., 1983-86, Hebron, Conn., 1986-88; assoc. Treiber & Guarnaccia, Willimantic, Conn., 1988-97; ptnr. Treiber, Guarnaccia & Connors, Willimantic, 1997—. Judge of probate Probate Ct., Hebron, 1996—; mem. Bd. of Selectmen, Hebron, 1985-87, 89-95; trustee Douglas Libr. of Hebron, 1997—. Mem. Conn. Bar Assn., Windham County Bar Assn., Phi Beta Kappa, Phi Kappa Phi. General civil litigation, Probate, General practice.

**CONNORS, RICHARD F.,** judge; b. N.Y.C., Mar. 20, 1930; s. Patrick Francis and Marie (Goss) C.; m. Jacqueline M., June 16, 1956; children: Maureen, Patricia C., Richard F. Jr. BA, St. Peter's Coll., 1951; JD, Seton Hall U., 1956. Trial atty. Sam Lieberman, Newark, 1957-59; ptnr. Lieberman, Gorrin, Connors, Newark, 1959-71, Gorrin, Connors & Ironson, 1971-73; judge Hudson County Ct., Jersey City, N.J., 1973-78, Superior County Ct., Jersey City, N.J., 1978—. With USN, 1948-53. Mem. ABA, Am. Trial Attys. Assn., N.J. Bar Assn., Essex County Bar Assn., Trial Attys. N.J. Office: Superior Ct NJ 583 Newark Ave Jersey City NJ 07306-2301

**CONNORS, SUSAN ANN,** lawyer; b. Middletown, Conn., Feb. 20, 1966; d. Donald Edward Connors and Patricia (Maltese) Byrne; m. Robert M. Zadroga, Apr. 7, 1995. BS, U. Conn., 1988, JD, 1991. Bar: Conn. 1991, U.S. Dist. Ct. Conn. 1991. Assoc. Schatz & Schatz, Ribicoff & Kofkin, Hartford, Conn., 1991-95; ptnr. Krevolin, Roth & Connors L.L.C., West Hartford, Conn., 1995—. Mem. ABA, ATLA, Conn. Trial Lawyers Assn., Conn. Bar Assn., Hartford County Bar Assn., Hartford Assn. Women Attys. (v.p. 1995—). Democrat. Roman Catholic. General civil litigation, Personal injury, Family and matrimonial. Office: Krevlin Roth & Connors LLC 433 S Main St Ste 403 West Hartford CT 06110-1670

**CONNOT, MARK JEFFREY,** lawyer; b. Winner, S.D., Mar. 25, 1963; s. Lawrence Joseph and Delores Jeanne (Holden) C.; m. Crystal Lori Gronewold, June 1, 1991; children: Robert, Laramie. BS, S.D. State U., 1989; MBA, U. S.D., 1992, JD with honors, 1992. Bar: S.D. 1993, Nebr. 1994, N.D. 1994, Wyo. 1996, U.S. Dist. Ct. S.D. 1994, Oglala Sioux Tribal Ct. 1995, Rosebud Tribal Ct., 1995. Legal intern Tobin Law Offices, P.C., Winner, 1990-92; fed. dist. ct. law clerk Hon. John B. Jones, Chief Judge, Sioux Falls, S.D., 1992-94; atty. Gunderson, Palmer, Goodsell and Nelson, LLP, Rapid City, S.D., 1994—; mem. negligence and tort law com. S.D. Bar Assn. Spkr. on citizenship in our schs. S.D. Young Lawyers, 1992-95, cir. coord. 1995-96. Mem. ABA (litigation sect., pretrial practice and discovery com. 1993—, trial evidence com. 1993—, trial practice com. 1993—, coord. atty.-client privilege and work product subcom.), Am. Trial Lawyers Assn., S.D. Trial Lawyers Assn., Order of Barristers, Omicron Delta Epsilon. Avocations: hunting, hiking, carpentry. General civil litigation, Insurance, Personal injury. Office: Gunderson Palmer Goodsell & Nelson PO Box 8045 440 Mount Rushmore Rd Rapid City SD 57709

**CONNUCK, ERIC S.,** lawyer; b. Bklyn., Nov. 14, 1965; m. Wendy E. DiMarco, Aug. 23, 1991; children: Marc, David. BS, SUNY, Binghampton, 1986; JD, NYU, 1991. Bar: Conn. 1991, N.Y. 1992, U.S. Dist. Ct. (ea. and so. dists.) N.Y. 1992, U.S. Dist. Ct. (no. dist.) N.Y. 1998, U.S. Dist. Ct. Colo. 1998. Assoc. Rogers & Wells, N.Y.C., 1991-94, McCarrick, Finnerty & Mayer, N.Y.C., 1994-96, Piper & Marbury, N.Y.C., 1996—. Insurance, General civil litigation. Office: Piper & Marbury LLP 1251 Ave of Americas New York NY 10020

**CONOM, TOM PETER,** lawyer; b. Seattle, Jan. 2, 1949; s. Peter T. and Madeline (Barbas) C.; m. Ann H. Earsley, Jan. 28, 1978; children: Lisa, Tracy, Derek. BA in Journalism, U. Wash., 1971, JD, 1974. Bar: Wash. 1974, U.S. Dist. Ct. (we. dist.) Wash. 1974, U.S. Ct. Appeals (9th cir.) 1984, U.S. Supreme Ct. 1984. Pvt. practice Seattle, Lynnwood, Edmonds, Wash., 1974—. Dem. state del. King, Snohomish County, 1972—. Mem. Wash. Assn. Criminal Def. Attys. (founder, bd. dirs. 1987-89, columnist jour. 1987—), Wash. State Trial Lawyers Assn. (bd. dirs. 1982-86, chmn. criminal law sect. 1986-88, contbr. articles to jour.), Nat. Assn. Criminal Def. Lawyers (life), Assn. Trial Lawyers Am. Snohomish County Bar Assn., Seattle-King County Bar Assn. Constitutional, Criminal, Personal injury. Office: 51 W Dayton St Ste 206 Edmonds WA 98020-4111

**CONOUR, WILLIAM FREDERICK,** lawyer; b. Indpls., June 21, 1947; s. William E. and Marian L. (Smith) C.; m. Jennifer Hentges; children: Tonja, Andrea, Erin, Rachel, Tyler. AB in History, Ind. U., 1970, JD cum laude, 1974. Bar: Ind. 1974, U.S. Dist. Ct. (so. dist.) Ind. 1974, U.S. Dist. Ct. (no. dist.) Ind. 1996, U.S. Ct. Appeals (7th cir.) 1975, U.S. Supreme Ct., 1982; cert. mediator Ind. Supreme Ct., 1992—. Dir. training Ind. Pros. Attys. Council, Indpls., 1974-82; ptnr. Conour & Davis, Indpls., 1974-86; pvt. practice Indpls., 1986-88; ptnr. Conour Doehrman, 1988—; assoc. prof., adjunct faculty Ind. U. Purdue U. Indpls., 1974—; lectr. Ind. Law Enforcement Acad.; rsch. analyst Ind. Criminal Law Study Commn., 1973-74. Contbg. author Indiana Criminal Procedure Sourcebook, 1974, Indiana Prosecuting Attorney's Deskbook; editor profl. bulletins; contbr. articles to profl. jours. Guarantor Butler U. Clowes Hall; patron Ind. Repertory Theatre, Indpls. Symphony Orch.; mem. Gov.'s club Ind. Dems., Conner Prairie Pioneer Settlement, Nat. Safety Coun., Hoosier Safety Coun. Recipient commendation Drug Enforcement Adminstrn. U.S. Dept. Justice, 1977, Commendation award Hoosier Safety Coun., 1989, Commendation award Ind. State Bar Assn. Criminal Justice Sect., 1990. Fellow Roscoe Pound Found. (life), Found. Am. Bd. Trial Advocates (sr. life), Indpls. Bar Found. (life); mem. ABA (litigation sect.), Am. Bd. Trial Advocates (pres. Ind. chpt.), Am. Soc. Safety, Ind. Bar Assn. (sec. litigation 1981-82, ad hoc com. on legal cert., mem. litigation sect., criminal justice sect., sec. 1977-78, treas. 1981-82), Indpls. Bar Assn. (grievance com. 1983-91, litigation sect.), Assn. Trial Lawyers Am. (cert. Nat. Coll. Advocacy 1979, Advanced Coll. Advocacy 1981, cons. site litigation group, M Club, lectr.), Coll. of Legal Medicine, Am. Coll. of Legal Medicine, Ind. Trial Lawyers Assn. (sustaining mem., bd. dirs., lectr., amicus curie com., rule of evidence com.), Ind. Lawyers Commn. (ad hoc com. on criminal justice standards and goals 1976-80), Am. Bd. Trial Advs., Trial Lawyers for Pub. Justice (sustaining founder), Woodburn Guild (life), Ind. U. Alumni Assn. (life), Aquatic Injury Safety Assn., Indpls. Law Club, Indpls. Athletic Club, US Equestrian Team (contbg. mem.), US Dressage Fedn. Ind. Dressage Soc. (dir.), Indpls. Mus. Art, Phi Delta Phi (hon.). Democrat. Clubs: Inpls. Athletic; Ind. Soc. Chgo., Atla "M". Personal injury, Federal civil litigation, General civil litigation. Home: 10858 Sedgemoor Cir Carmel IN 46032-9189 Office: 10333 N Meridian St Ste 100 Indianapolis IN 46290-1074

**CONOVER, RICHARD CORRILL,** lawyer; b. Bridgeport, Nebr., Jan. 12, 1942; s. John Cedric and Mildred (Dunn) C.; m. Cathy Harlan, Dec. 19, 1970; children—William Cedric, Theodore Cyril. B.S., U. Nebr., Lincoln, 1965, M.S., 1966; J.D., Cornell U., 1969. Bar: N.Y. 1970, Mont. 1982, U.S. Dist. Ct. (so. and ea. dists.) N.Y. 1971, U.S. Supreme Ct. 1977, U.S. Ct. Customs and Patent Appeals 1979, U.S. Ct. Claims 1980, U.S. Dist. Ct. Mont. 1984, U.S. Tax Ct. 1986. Assoc. Brumbaugh, Graves, Donohue & Raymond, N.Y.C., 1969-73; assoc. Townley, Updike, Carter & Rodgers, N.Y.C., 1974-75; assoc. gen. csl. legal office Automatic Data Processing,

Inc., Clifton, N.J., 1975-77; assoc. Nims, Howes, Collison & Isner, N.Y.C., 1977-81; sole practice, Mont., 1981—; lectr. indsl. and mech. engring. dept. Mont. State U., 1981-97. Mem. Mont. Gov.'s Bd. Sci. and Tech., 1985-87. Mem. ABA, Assn. Bar City N.Y., Mont. Bar Assn., Am. Pat. Law Assn. Patent, Trademark and copyright, General civil litigation. Home: PO Box 1329 Bozeman MT 59771-1329 Office: 104 E Main St Ste 404 Bozeman MT 59715-4787

**CONRAD, CHARLES THOMAS,** lawyer; b. Milw., Aug. 8, 1949; s. Robert Joseph and Monica Mary (Farrell) C.; m. Georgeana Jane Shoemaker, Feb. 24, 1973; children: Charles, Michael. BA cum laude, Gonzaga U., 1972, JD, 1977. Bar: U.S. Dist. Ct. (ea. dist.) Wash. 1977, U.S. Ct. Appeals (9th cir.) 1980. Atty. Schimanski, Leeds & Conrad, Spokane, Wash., 1977-93; sole practice law Spokane, 1993—; arbitrator NASD, San Francisco, 1989—, Nat. Futures Assn., Chgo., 1996—. Mem. Wash. State Bar assn., Wash. State Trial Lawyers Assn., Spokane County Bar Assn. Avocations: skiing, scuba diving. Personal injury, Labor, Pension, profit-sharing, and employee benefits. Home: 6605 S Westchester Dr Spokane WA 99223-6221 Office: 9011 E Valleyway Ave Spokane WA 99212-2835

**CONRAD, DAVID WILLIAMS,** lawyer; b. St. Louis, Jan. 10, 1930; s. Lawrence Henry and Roberta (Williams) C.; m. Marilyn Russo, Sept. 26, 1959; children: Roberta Lucy, Philip Lloyd, Angela Beth. AB, Colgate U., 1951; JD, Harvard U., 1954. Bar: N.J. 1954, U.S. Supreme Ct. 1973. Assoc. McCarter & English, Newark, 1956-59; ptnr. Conrad & Jones, Montclair, N.J., 1964-71; pvt. practice Montclair, 1959-64, 71-93; ptnr. Conrad & Boutillier, Montclair, 1993—; counsel Montclair State U. Found., 1959—, Homes of Montclair Ecumenical Corp., 1988—. Legis. candidate N.J. State Assembly, 1971; pres. N.J. Chamber Music Soc., Montclair, 1984-86, Union Congl. Ch., Montclair, 1988-91. With U.S. Army, 1954-56. Mem. N.J. State Bar Assn., Montclair-West Essex Bar Assn., Essex County Bar Assn. Democrat. Congregationalist. Avocations: piano, music composition, travel. Probate, Real property, Land use and zoning (including planning). Home: 23 Hyde Rd Bloomfield NJ 07003-3018 Office: 31 S Fullerton Ave Montclair NJ 07042-3358

**CONRAD, FREDERICK LARUE, JR.,** lawyer; b. Carlisle, Pa., June 26, 1958; s. Frederick Larue and Patricia McBath Conrad; m. Louise Patterson Stites, June 13, 1981; children: Louise Patterson, Frederick Larue III, John Stites. BA, Duke U., 1980; JD, U. Tenn., 1983. Bar: Tenn. 1985, U.S. Dist. Ct. (ea. dist.) Tenn. 1985, U.S. Ct. Appeals (6th cir.) 1998. Law clk. Bo Edwards, Nashville, 1981, Ambrose, Wilson, Grimm & Durand, Knoxville, Tenn., 1982-83; life ins. agt. Fidelity Union Life, Auburn, Ala., 1983-85; assoc. Ambrose, Wilson, Grimm & Durand, Knoxville, 1985-88, ptnr., 1988-99; pvt. practice Knoxville, 1999—; faculty Nat. Bus. Inst. Coach YMCA Youth Basketball, Knoxville, 1993-98, Cedar Springs Baseball, Knoxville, 1996-98, Cedar Bluff Youth Basketball, 1998-99. Mem. ABA, Comml. Law League Am. (cert. creditor's rights specialist), Tenn. Bar Assn., Knoxville Bar Assn. Avocations: reading, tennis, stamps, fossil collecting, parenting. Consumer commercial, General civil litigation, General practice. Home: 8509 Cartwright Ln Knoxville TN 37923-5554 Office: PO Box 30192 Knoxville TN 37930-0192

**CONRAD, JOHN REGIS,** lawyer, engineering executive; b. Bloomington, Ind., Feb. 23, 1955; s. John Francis and Patricia Ann (English) C.; m. Paula Jane Vessels, July 4, 1980; children: William Celestine Vessels, John Paul Vessels, M. Alexander Vessels, David Thomas Kelamalamalamanokeakua Vessels, Rachel Elizabeth Ho'ouluolaikealoha Vessels. AB cum laude, Harvard U., 1977; MBA, JD, Ind. U., 1981. Bar: Hawaii 1981, Fla. 1994, Tex. 1994, N.C. 1995, U.S. Dist. Ct. Hawaii 1981, U.S. Ct. Appeals (9th cir.) 1981, U.S. Ct. Claims 1981, U.S. Tax Ct. 1981. Assoc. Cades, Schutte, Fleming & Wright, Honolulu, 1981-85, 89-90, Thompson & Chan, Honolulu, 1985-89; ptnr. Cades Schutte Fleming & Wright, Honolulu, 1991-94; regional bus. mgr. Kimley-Horn and Assocs., Inc., West Palm Beach, Fla., 1994-96, regional prodn. mgr., 1996-98; regional bus. mgr. Kimley-Horn and Assocs., Inc., Phoenix, 1999—; lectr. law Kapiolani C.C., Honolulu, 1984-86; adj. prof. Richardson Sch. Law, U. Hawaii, 1989-90. Author: A Conrad Genealogy, 1979, Hawaii Probate Sourcebook, 1985, rev. 1986, rev. 1992; co-author: Beyond the Basics: Hawaii Estate Planning & Probate, 1985, Hawaii Wills & Trusts Sourcebook, 1986, Hawaii Guardianship Sourcebook, 1988; editor HICLE Fin. and Estate Planning Manual, vol. II, 1989, vol. I, 1990. Planned giving com. Hawaii Heart Assn., Honolulu, 1983-86; arbitrator Hawaii Ct. Annexec Arbitration Program, 1989-94; sch. bd. Star of the Sea Sch., Honolulu, 1992-94, pres., 1993-94, chair Carnival, 1992; chair Cub Scout Pack Aloha Coun. Boy Scouts Am., den leader Cub Scout Pack, Gulf Stream Coun.; lector Good Shepherd of the Hills Ch., Cave Creek, Ariz. Fellow Am. Coll. Trust and Estate Coun.; mem. ABA, Am. Arbitration Assn., Hawaii Bar Assn. (chmn. estate and gift tax com. 1984-85, CFO probate and estate planning sect. 1989-90), Hawaii Bar Found. (bd. dirs. 1985-92, v.p. 1989, pres. 1989-91), Hawaii Estate Planning Coun. (bd. dirs. 1991-94, sec. 1993). Roman Catholic. Avocations: running, genealogy, coin collecting, scouting. Home: 33214 N 61st St Cave Creek AZ 85331-5206 Office: Kimley-Horn and Assocs Inc 7600 N 15th St Ste 250 Phoenix AZ 85020-4335

**CONRAN, JOSEPH PALMER,** lawyer; b. St. Louis, Oct. 4, 1945; s. Palmer and Theresa (Bussmann) C.; m. Daria D. Conran, June 8, 1968; children: Andrew, Lisabeth, Theresa. BA, St. Louis U., 1967, JD with honors, 1970. Bar: Mo. 1970, U.S. Ct. Mil. Appeals 1971, U.S. Ct. Appeals (8th cir.) 1974. Assoc. Husch and Eppenberger, St. Louis, 1974-78, ptnr., 1978—, chmn. litigation dept., 1980-95, chmn. mgmt. com. 1995—; mem. faculty Trial Practice Inst. Capt., JAGC, USAF, 1970-74. Mem. Bar Assn. Met. St. Louis (Merit award 1976,77), Mo. Bar Assn. (bd. govs. 1987-92), Mo. Athletic (pres. 1986-87), Norwood Hills Country Club. Roman Catholic. Federal civil litigation, State civil litigation, Securities. Home: 53 Hawthorne Est Saint Louis MO 63131-3035 Office: Husch & Eppenberger 100 N Broadway Ste 1300 Saint Louis MO 63102-2789

**CONROY, KEVIN THOMAS,** lawyer; b. Flint, Mich., Sept. 1, 1965; s. Joe and Mary Ann Conroy; m. Sheila Marie Brennan, Aug. 17, 1996; 1 child, Meghan. BSEE, Mich. State U., 1988, JD. Assoc. Dykema Gossett, Grand Rapids, Mich., 1991-92, McDermott Will Emery, Chgo., 1992-96; ptnr. Pattishall McAuliffe Newbury Hilliard & Geraldson, Chgo., 1996—. Mem. ABA, Chgo. Bar Assn., Internat. Trademark Assn., Am. Intellectual Property Law Assn. Office: Pattishall McAuliffe Newberry Hilliards & Geraldson 311 S Wacker Dr Chicago IL 60606-6627

**CONROY, ROBERT JOHN,** lawyer; b. Newark, Feb. 17, 1953; s. Michael John and Frances (Goncalves) C.; m. Mary Catherine McGuire, June 7, 1975; children: Caitlin Michaela, Michael Colin. BS, St. Peter's Coll., 1977; M in Pub. Adminstrn., CUNY, 1981; JD, N.Y. Law Sch., 1981; MPH, Harvard U., 1985. Bar: N.Y. 1981, N.J. 1981, U.S. Dist. N.J. 1981, Calif. 1982, U.S. Dist. Ct. (so. and ea. dists.) N.Y. 1982, U.S. Dist. Ct. (we. dist.) Calif. 1990, U.S. Ct. Appeals (2d, 3d and 11th cirs.) 1982, Fla. 1984, D.C. 1984, U.S. Supreme Ct. 1984. Asst. corp. counsel City of N.Y., 1981-83, dep. chief med. malpractice unit, 1983, chief med. malpractice unit, 1984; assoc. Jones, Hirsch, Connors & Bull, N.Y.C., 1985-88; counsel Kern & Augustine, P.A., Morristown, N.J., 1988-90; prin. Kern Augustine Conroy & Schoppmann, P.C., Bridgewater, N.J. and Lake Success, N.Y., 1990—; spl. counsel pro bono med. malpractice rsch. project, N.Y.C., 1985-88. Solomon scholar, N.Y. Law Sch., 1979. Fellow Coll. Law Practice Mgmt.; mem. ABA (chmn. govt. mgmt. com. 1984-86, mgr. products media bd. 1985-92, chmn. document retrieval com. 1985-86, vice chmn. ins. and malpractice com. 1986-88, co-chmn. glass ceiling task force 1992-95, vice chmn. law practice mgmt. phb. bd. 1992-95, coun. mem. 1989-95, co-chmn. law practice mgmt. pub. bd. 1995-98), N.J. Bar Assn. (dir., chmn. health hosp. sect. 1993-95, mem. com. health law litigation, mem. subcom. profl. licensing 1997—, del. gen. coun. adminstrn. sect. 1995-97), Soc. Health Care Risk Mgmt. N.J. (chmn. legis. com. 1987-96), Westfield Sr. Citizens Housing Corp., Inc. (trustee 1994—, v.p. 1996-98, pres. 1998—), Cmty. Health Law Project N.J., Inc. (trustee 1988-91), Assn. of Bar of City of N.Y., N.Y. Bar Assn. (mem. health law sect. 1996—), Harvard Club, Phi Alpha Alpha. Health, Administrative and regulatory, General civil litigation. Home: 905 Pennsylvania Ave Westfield NJ 07090-3433 Office: Kern Augustine Conroy & Schoppmann PC 1120 Rt 22 Bridgewater NJ 08807

**CONSOLE, DALE ELIZABETH,** lawyer; b. N.Y.C., Aug. 9, 1952. BA, Kirkland Coll., Clinton, N.Y., 1974; JD, Rutgers U., Camden, N.J., 1985. Bar: N.J. 1985, Penn. 1985, U.S. Dist. Ct. N.J. 1985. Cert. matrimonial law atty., N.J. Law clk. to Hon. Virginia Long Appellate divsn. Superior Ctr., Trenton, N.J., 1985-86; assoc. Jamieson, Moore et al, Princeton, N.J., 1986-87, Szaferman, Lakind et al, Lawrenceville, N.J., 1987-88; ptnr. Ulrichsen, Amarel & Eory, Rocky Hill, N.J., 1988—; sec. The N.J. Lawyer Newspaper, 1995—. Fellow Am. Acad. Matrimonial Lawyers, N.J. State Bar Assn. (exec. com. family law sect. 1998—, appellate practice com. 1996—). Family and matrimonial, Appellate. Office: Ulrichsen Amarel & Eory PO Box 547 Rocky Hill NJ 08553-0547

**CONSTANT, TERRY LYNN,** lawyer; b. Decatur, Ill., Dec. 16, 1942; s. Mathew Jacob and Virginia Florence C.; div.; children: Nicole L., Brett A., Amber K. BS, U. Wis., 1965; JD, Marquette U., 1968. Bar: 1968, U.S. Dist. Ct. (ea. dist.) Wis. 1968. Asst. city atty. City of Kenosha, Wis., 1970-75; atty. Baumgartner & Anderson, Kenosha, 1976-77; pvt. practice Kenosha, 1975-76, 77—; tchr. law Gateway Tech. Inst., Kenosha, 1975-80. Bd. dirs. United Way of Kenosha Inc., Salvation Army, Kenosha, 1982; svc. mem. Kenosha Family Counseling, 1975-81. Mem. ATLA, Wis. Assn. Trial Lawyers, Kenosha County Bar Assn., Kenosha Golf Assn. (treas. 1987—). Avocations: golf, travel, reading. Fax: (414) 654-8696. Personal injury, Criminal, Family and matrimonial. Office: 5712 6th Ave Kenosha WI 53140-4104

**CONSTANTINO, JAMES PETER,** lawyer, tax and business consultant; b. Poughkeepsie, N.Y., July 17, 1953; s. Dominick Peter and Adeline (Troiano) C.; m. Evelyn Suzan Panichi, Oct. 15, 1988; children: Emil Dominick, Matthew William, Elisabeth Emily. BS, Syracuse U., 1975; MS, SUNY, Albany, 1977; JD, Tulane U., 1979; LLM, NYU, 1984. Bar: N.Y. 1980, U.S. Dist. Ct. (so. dist.) N.Y. 1986, U.S. Tax Ct. 1986; CPA, N.Y. Mgr. Deloitte, Haskins & Sells, N.Y.C., 1979-86; pvt. practice Poughkeepsie, 1986-89; ptnr. Teahan & Constantino, Poughkeepsie, 1989—. Mem. AICPA, N.Y. State Bar Assn. (mem. tax aspects of internat. trade and investment com., fgn. activities of U.S. taxpayers com., tax acctg. matters com.), N.Y. State Soc. CPAs (mem. N.Y. state, mcpl. and local taxation com.), Assn. of Bar of City of N.Y., Dutchess County Bar Assn., Rotary. Taxation, general, Contracts commercial. Office: Teahan & Constantino PO Box 1969 Poughkeepsie NY 12601-0969

**CONTE, ANTHONY R.,** lawyer; b. Mass., 1948. BA, Boston U., 1970, JD, 1973. Pvt. practice Medford/Revere, Mass., 1974-82; regional solicitor U.S. Dept. of Interior, Newton, Mass., 1982—. City councilor City of Revere, 1978-87. Office: Office of Regional Solicitor 1 Gateway Ctr Ste 612 Newton MA 02458-2881

**CONTI, JOY FLOWERS,** lawyer; b. Kane, Pa., Dec. 7, 1948; d. Bernard A. Flowers and Elizabeth (Tingley) Rodgers; m. Anthony T. Conti, Jan. 16, 1971; children: Andrew, Michael, Gregory. BA, Duquesne U., 1970, JD summa cum laude, 1973. Bar: Pa. 1973, U.S. Dist. Ct. (we. dist.) Pa. 1973, U.S. Ct. Appeals (3rd cir.) 1976, U.S. Supreme Ct. 1993. Law clk. Supreme Ct. Pa., Monessen, 1973-74; assoc. Kirkpatrick & Lockhart, Pitts., 1974-76, 82-83, ptnr., 1983-96; shareholder Buchanan, Ingersoll, P.C., Pitts., 1996—; prof. law Duquesne U., Pitts., 1976-82; hearing examiner Pa. Dept. State, Bur. Profl. Occupation and Affairs, 1978-82; chairperson search com. for judge U.S. Bankruptcy Ct. (we. dist.) Pa., 1987, 95; active Pa. Futures Commn. on Justice in 21st Century, 1995-97. Contbr. articles to profl. jours. Mem. disciplinary hearing com. Supreme Ct. Pa., 1982-88; v.p. Com. for Justice Edn., Pitts., 1983-84; mem. Leadership Pitts., 1987-88. Named One of Ten Outstanding Young Women in Am., 1981. Fellow Am. Bar Found. (Pa. state chair 1991-97); mem. ABA (ho. of dels. 1980-86, 91-97), Am. Law Inst., Am. Coll. Bankruptcy, Pa. Bar Assn. (gov. 1993-95, ho. of dels. 1978—, corp. banking and bus. law sect. coun. 1983-89, treas. 1991-93, v.p. 1993-95, chair-elect 1995-97, chmn. 1997-99, chmn. commn. comml. law 1990-93, co-chair 1995—, chairperson civil rights and responsibilities com. 1986-89, Achievement award 1982, 87, 99, Anne X. Alpern award 1995), Nat. Conf. Bar Pres. (exec. coun. 1993-96), Allegheny County Bar Assn. (adminstrv. v.p. 1984-86, 90, chairperson corp. banking and bus. law sect. 1987-89, treas. 1988-90, gov. 1991, pres.-elect 1992, pres. 1993), Internat. Women's Insolvency and Restructuring Confedn. (chair Tri-State Network 1996), Pa. Bar Inst. (dir. 1991-97), Duquesne Club, Treesdale Country Club. Roman Catholic. General corporate, Bankruptcy, Health. Home: 3469 Palomino Dr Gibsonia PA 15044-8965 Office: Buchanan Ingersoll PC 301 Grant St Fl 20 Pittsburgh PA 15219-1410

**CONTI, LOUIS THOMAS MOORE,** lawyer; b. Phila., Aug. 31, 1949; s. Alexander and Yolanda (DiLorenzo) C.; m. Christina M.S. Moore, May 1, 1982; children: Charles Alexander, Whitney Caroline. BS, LaSalle Coll., 1971; MBA, Drexel U., 1972; JD, Creighton U., 1975; LLM, Temple U., 1981. Bar: U.S. Claims Ct. 1975, U.S. Tax Ct. 1975, Pa. 1975, U.S. Dist. Ct. (ea. dist.) Pa. 1978, U.S. Ct. Appeals (3d cir.) 1979, U.S. Supreme Ct. 1981, Fla. 1982, U.S. Dist. Ct. (mid. dist.) Fla. 1988. Tax atty. Office Chief Counsel IRS, Washington and Phila., 1975-81; tax mgr. Touche Ross & Co., Phila., 1981-84; assoc. Saul, Ewing, Remick & Saul, Phila., 1984-87; shareholder Swann & Haddock, P.A., Orlando, Fla., 1987-89; ptnr., chmn. corp. tax and securities dept. Holland & Knight, Orlando, 1989—. Mem. fin. com. S.E. Pa. chpt. ARC, Phila., 1984-87; advisor Vol. Lawyers for Arts, Phila., 1984-87; bd. dirs. Fla. Hosp. Found., 1989—, Ctrl. Fla. Planned Giving Coun., 1989-97, Cmty. Found. Ctrl. Fla. Inc., 1993—, World Trade Ctr., Orlando, 1992-95; mem. internat. bus. adv. bd. Metro Orlando; grad. Leadership Orlando, 1994, Leadership Fla., 1996; chair recruiting com. East Ctrl. Region of Leadership Fla., 1997, bd. dirs. Orlando Performing Arts & Edn. Ctr., Inc., 1998—. Mem. ABA (tax and bus. law sect., chmn. task force on drafting prototype ltd. liability co. operating agreements 1998—, chmn. Fla. Bar drafting com. 1999), Fla. Bar Assn. (tax and bus. law sect., chmn. drafting com. ltd. liability co. act 1998—, chair corps. and securities com., bus. law sect. 1999—, chair long-range planning com. tax sect. 1999—), Orange County Bar Assn. (chmn. tax sect. 1990-91), Seminole County C. of C. (bd. dirs. 1994-97), Racquet Club, Alaqua Country Club, Citrus Club. Republican. Avocations: traveling, skiing, golfing, tennis, theatre. Corporate taxation, General corporate, Mergers and acquisitions. Home: 3003 Timpana Pt Longwood FL 32779-3108 Office: Holland & Knight PO Box 1526 Orlando FL 32802-1526

**CONTI, SAMUEL,** federal judge; b. L.A., July 16, 1922; s. Fred and Katie C.; m. Dolores Crosby, July 12, 1952; children: Richard, Robert, Cynthia. BS, U. Santa Clara, 1945; LLB, Stanford U., 1948, JD. Bar: Calif. 1948. Pvt. practice, San Francisco and Contra Costa County, 1948-60; city atty. City of Concord, Calif., 1960-69; judge Superior Ct. Contra Costa County, 1968-70; judge U.S. Dist. Ct. (no. dist.) Calif., San Francisco, 1970-88, sr. judge, 1988—. Mem. Central Contra Costa Bar Assn. (pres.), Concord C. of C. (pres.), Alpha Sigma Nu. Office: US Dist Ct PO Box 36060 San Francisco CA 94102*

**CONTIE, LEROY JOHN, JR.,** federal judge; b. Canton, Ohio, Apr. 2, 1920; s. Leroy John and Mary M. (DeSantis) C.; m. Janice M. Zollars, Nov. 28, 1953; children: Ann L., Leroy John III. BA, U. Mich., 1941, JD, 1948; JD (hon.), U. Akron, 1993. Bar: Ohio 1948, U.S. Dist. Ct. (no. dist.) Ohio, 1953, U.S Supreme Ct. 1959. Law dir. City of Canton, 1952-60; chmn. Canton City Charter Commn., 1963; mem. Stark County Bd. Elections, Canton, 1964-69; judge Common Pleas Ct., Stark County, 1969-71, U.S. Dist. Ct., No. Dist. Ohio, Cleve., 1971-82, U.S. Ct. Appeals (6th cir.), Cin., 1982—; now senior judge U.S. Ct. Appeals (6th cir.). Trustee Stark County Legal Aid Soc., Canton chpt. ARC; mem. adv. bd. Walsh U., Canton, U. Akron Law Coll. With AUS, 1942-46. Mem. Am., Ohio, Stark County, Summit County, Cuyahoga County, Akron bar assns., Am. Judicature Soc., U.S. Jr. C. of C. (internat. senator), Canton Jr. C. of C. (trustee), Stark County Hist. Soc., Stark County Wilderness Soc., Am. Legion, Sigma Phi Epsilon (Nat. citation award), Phi Alpha Delta., Omicron Delta Kappa, K.C. Club (4 deg.), Elks Club. Roman Catholic. Office: US Ct Appeals 365 US Courthouse 2 S Main St Akron OH 44308-1813

**CONTINO, RICHARD MARTIN,** lawyer, leasing executive, consultant; b. Richmond, Va., Mar. 31, 1940; s. Samuel and Theresa Contino. B in Aero. Engring., Rensselaer Poly. Inst., 1962; JD, U Md., 1965; LLM, NYU, 1972. Bar: Md. 1965, D.C. 1965, N.Y. 1969. Assoc. Winthrop, Stimson, Putnam & Roberts, N.Y.C., 1969-72, Fried, Frank, Harris, Shriver & Jacobson, N.Y.C., 1972-74; eastern regional counsel Gatx Leasing Corp., N.Y.C., 1974-76, v.p. mktg., 1976-78; ptnr. Contino Ross & Benedict, N.Y.C., 1978-86, Contino & Ptnrs., White Plains, N.Y., 1986—; cons. equipment lease bus.; lectr. in field, 1987—; chmn., founder ELM Corp. 1986—; with Liberty Credit Corp., Rye, N.Y.; with First Street Credit Corp., Islandia, N.Y., 1993—. Author: Legal and Financial ASpects of Equipment Leasing Transactions, 1979, Business Emotions, 1988, Handbook for Equipment Leasing--The Deal Maker's Guide, 1989, 2d edit., 1996, The Complete Book of Equipment Leasing Agreements, Worksheets and Checklists, 1997, Trust Your Gut, 1997. Capt. USAF, 1966-68. Mem. ABA, N.Y. State Bar Assn., Assn. Bar City N.Y. Finance, Contracts commercial, General corporate.

**CONVERY, SAMUEL VINCENT, JR.,** lawyer; b. Perth Amboy, N.J., Jan. 16, 1939; s. Samuel V. and Kathryn Ann Convery; m. Elaine M. Hack, June 23, 1962; children: Sam, David, Michael, Mary, Ann. AB, Franklin & Marshall Coll., 1961; MS, Rutgers U., 1963; JD, Seton Hall U., 1969. Bar: N.J. 1969, N.Y. 1969, U.S. Dist. Ct. N.J. 1969, U.S. Dist. Ct. (ea. and so. dists.) N.Y. 1969, U.S. Supreme Ct. 1969. Chemistr tchr. Woodbridge Twp., N.J., 1963-65; corp. lawyer NL Industries, Inc., N.J., 1969-71; sole practitioner Metuchen, N.J., 1971—; mayor Twp. of Edison, N.J., 1991-93; mem. N.J. State Coun. on Local Mandates; past mem. Supreme Ct. N.J. com. on character; former atty. City of Perth Amboy zoning, planning, and libr. bds., and housing authority; former atty. Edison zoning bd. of adjustment. Candidate 18th dist. N.J. State Senate, 1993; trustee JFK Med. Ctr.; pres. Cath. Lawyers Guild of Diocese of Metuchen, 1985-86; past atty. United Way of Ctrl. Jersey; chmn. Edison Dem. Orgn., 1991-92; vice chmn. Champaign 2000, Metuchen YMCA; trustee Flame of Charity Found., Metuchen; mem. bishops com. of 100, Diocese of Metuchen, mem. planned gifts exec. com.; past chmn., adv. bd. Cath. H.S. Devel. Com., Mt. St. Mary's Acad.; trustee Middlesex County Coll. Found. Mm. N.J. State Bar Assn., Metuchen C. of C., Rotary (past officer and dir.), Menlo Oaks Dem. Club, Edison Dem. Assn., Clara Barton Dem. Club. Land use and zoning (including planning), Real property, General corporate. Office: 1 Highland Ave Metuchen NJ 08840-1956

**CONWARD, CYNTHIA MAE,** law educator, lawyer; b. Acushnet, Mass., May 12, 1951; d. Benjamin F. and Mary (Delgado) Oliver; m. Walter Alan, May 18, 1974; children: Kelli Janiel, Corey Alan. BA in Sociology/Edn., U. Mass., Dartmouth, 1973; MA in Rehab. Counseling, Assumption Coll., 1980; JD, New Eng. Sch. Law, 1990. Tchr. New Bedford (Mass.) Pub. Schs.; instr. Newberry Coll., New Bedford, Mass.; asst. reg. counsel Dept. Social Svcs., Brockton, Mass.; adj. prof. So. New Eng. Sch. Law, Dartmouth, asst. prof.; pvt. practice law, Bristol County, Mass. Pro bono atty. NAACP Legal Redress Com., New Bedford. Mem. NAACP (youth advisor 1983-86), Mass. Bar Assn., Black Profl. Assn. (sec. 1990-93), New Bedford Hist. Soc. (v.p. 1997—). Office: So New Eng Sch Law 333 Faunce Corner Rd North Dartmouth MA 02747-1252

**CONWAY, ANNE CALLAGHAN,** federal judge; b. Cleve., July 30, 1950. AB, John Carroll U., 1972; JD, U. Fla., 1975. Bar: Fla. 1975, U.S. Supreme Ct. 1981, U.S. Ct. Appeals (5th and 11th cirs.), U.S. Dist. Ct. (mid., no. and so. dists.) Fla. Law clk. to justice U.S. Dist. Ct., Orlando, Fla., 1975-77; from assoc. to ptnr. Wells, Gattis & Hallowes, Orlando, 1978-81; assoc. Carlton, Fields, Ward, Emmanuel, Smith & Cutler, P.A., Orlando, 1982-85, ptnr., 1985-91; judge U.S. Dist. (Mid. Dist.) Fla., Orlando, 1991—; mem. adv. com. on local rules U.S. Dist. Ct., Orlando, 1990-91, grievance com. Orlando div., mid. dist., 1986-91. Bd. dirs. So. Ballet Theatre, Winter Park, Fla., 1985-89, adv. bd., 1985-89; bd. dirs. Greater Orlando Area Legal Svcs., 1978-85. Mem. ABA, Orange County Bar Assn. (chairperson state and fed. trial practice com. 1989-90). Office: US Courthouse 80 N Hughey Ave Rm 646 Orlando FL 32801-2231

**CONWAY, BERRY LESLIE, II,** lawyer; b. Morganfield, Ky., Apr. 14, 1956; m. Darlene Conway; children: Michael, John, Nicole. BA with high distinction, U. Ky., 1979, JD, 1986. Bar: Va. 1987, U.S. Dist. Ct. (we. dist.) Va. 1987. Sr. assoc. Penn, Stuart, Eskridge, Abingdon, Va., 1987-93; ptnr. Conway & Conway, L.L.C., Abingdon, 1993—. Mem. Phi Beta Kappa. Avocations: breeding standardbred horses. E-mail: conway-horacy@nexs.com. Personal injury, Criminal, General civil litigation. Office: Conway & Conway LLC 165 W Main St Abingdon VA 24210-2837

**CONWAY, FRENCH HOGE,** lawyer; b. Danville, Va., June 11, 1918; s. Lysander Broadus and Mildred (Hoge) C.; BS, U. Va., 1942, JD, 1946; m. Louise Throckmorton, Feb. 3, 1961; children—French Hoge, William Chenery, Helen (Mrs. Carlton Bedsole), Donna (Mrs. Michael Henderson). Starnes. Bar: Va. 1942. sole practice, Danville, 1942—; mem. firm Clement, Conway & Winston, 1950-60. Sec., Danville City Bd. Rev., 1985—; v.p. Va. Election Bd. Assn., 1974. Served with USNR, 1942-46. Mem. Am., Va., Danville (pres. 1985-86) bar assns., Am. Trial Lawyers Assn., Va. Trial Lawyers Assn., Soc. Cincinnati in State of Va., Ret. Officers Assn., Boat Owners Assn. U.S. Lodges:Kiwanis, Masons. General practice, Personal injury, Probate. Home: 912 Main St Danville VA 24541-1810 Office: 105 S Union St Danville VA 24541-1113

**CONWAY, JOHN E.,** federal judge; b. 1934. BS, U.S. Naval Acad., 1956; LLB magna cum laude, Washburn U., 1963. Assoc. Matias A Zamora, Santa Fe, 1963-64; ptnr. Wilkinson, Durrett & Conway, Alamogordo, N.Mex., 1964-67, Durrett, Conway & Jordon, Alamogordo, 1967-80, Montgomery & Andrews, P.A., Albuquerque, 1980-86; city atty. Alamogordo, 1966-72; mem. N.Mex. State Senate, 1970-80, minority leader, 1972-80; chief fed. judge U.S. Dist. Ct. N.Mex., Albuquerque, 1986—. 1st lt. USAF, 1956-60. Mem. Nat. Commrs. on Uniform State Laws, Fed. Judges' Assn. (bd. dirs.), 10th Cir. Dist. Judges' Assn. (pres.), N.Mex. Bar Assn., N.Mex. Jud. Coun. (vice chmn. 1973, chmn. 1973-75, disciplinary bd. of Supreme Ct. of N.Mex. vice chmn. 1980, chmn. 1981-84), Albuquerque Lawyers Club. Office: US Dist Ct 333 Lomas Blvd NW Ste 770 Albuquerque NM 87102-2277

**CONWAY, JOHN K.,** lawyer. Gen. counsel Kemper Ins. Co., Long Grove, Ill. Office: Lumbermens Mutual Casualty Co 1 Kemper Dr Long Grove IL 60049-0001

**CONWAY, MARK ALLYN,** lawyer; b. Dayton, Ohio, Dec. 13, 1957; s. Allyn Walter and Doris Jean (Wright) C.; m. Dawn Elizabeth Manning, July 31, 1982; children: Ashley Wright, Alexandra Mills. BA, Denison U., 1980; JD, Calif. Western Sch. of Law, 1983; LLM in Taxation, Georgetown U., 1984. Bar: D.C. 1983, U.S. Tax Ct. 1983, Calif. 1988, Ohio 1991. Ptnr. Thompson, Hine & Flory LLD, Dayton, 1990—. Mem. ABA (real property, probate and trust law sect.), D.C. Bar Assn. (taxation sect. Washington chpt.), Calif. Bar Assn. (real property, probate and trust law sect. 1988—), Dayton Racquet Club. Republican. Presbyterian. Avocations: tennis, skiing, sailing. Estate planning, Estate taxation, Probate. Home: 5712 Price Hill Pl Dayton OH 45459-1428 Office: Thompson Hine & Flory LLD 2000 Courthouse Plz NE Dayton OH 45402

**CONWAY, NEIL JAMES, III,** title company executive, lawyer, writer; b. Cleve., Feb. 15, 1950; s. Neil J. and Jeanne Louise (Gensert) C.; m. Maureen Dolan; children: Seanna, Neil James IV, Declan, Liam. BSBA, John Carroll U., 1972; MBA, Suffolk U., 1974; JD, Antioch Sch. Law (named change to The U. of D.C.), 1983. Bar: Ohio, 1983, U.S. Dist. Ct. (no. dist.) Ohio, 1983, U.S. Supreme Ct., 1987, D.C., 1988. Auditor U.S. Dept. Interior, Arlington, 1974-77; systems acct. Mil. Dist. Washington, 1978-79; legal intern Govt. Accountability Project, Washington, 1980-81; jud. intern presiding judge U.S. Dist. (no. dist.) Ct. Ohio, 1982; legal asst. Spiegel & McDiarmid, Washington, 1982-83; pvt. practice Painesville, Ohio, 1983—; from title examiner to pres. Conway Land Title Co., Painesville, 1983—; adj. prof. legal studies Lake Erie Coll., Painesville, Ohio. Editor in chief Antioch Law Jour., 1982-83; pub. The Ohio Irish Times, 1993—; contbr. articles to profl. jours. Mem. Lake County Econ. Devel. Coun.; mem. Lawyers Com. for Human Rights, N.Y.C. Capt. USAR, 1972-81. Mem. ABA, Am. Soc. Internat. Law (Dean Rusk award 1980), Ohio Bar Assn., Lake County Bar Assn. (co-author real estate symposium 1989), Brehon Law Soc. N.Y., Ohio Land Title Assn., Lake County Bd. Realtors (Affiliate of Yr. 1986), Painesville Title Assn. (pres. 1985-86), Irish Am. Cultural Inst. (Editl. citation Ohio Irish Bull. 1990), Amnesty Internat. Democrat. Roman Catholic.

Avocations: racquetball, youth hockey. Home: 10930 Bradley Ct Concord OH 44077-2443

**CONWAY, REBECCA ANN KOPPES,** lawyer; b. Colorado Springs, Colo., May 18, 1952; d. Virgil Lee and Betty J. Koppes; children: Kelley, Kathrine; m. Sean P. Conway, Nov. 26, 1994. BA, U. Colo., 1975, JD, 1978. Bar: Colo. 1978, U.S. Dist. Ct. Colo. 1978. Atty. EEOC, Denver, 1978-79, Dist. Atty.'s Office, Adams County, Brighton, Colo., 1979-80; ptnr. Gutierrez & Koppes, Greeley, Colo., 1980-92; pvt. practice Law Office of Rebecca Koppes Conway, Greeley, 1992—; mem. Colo. Pub. Defenders Commn., 1985-95, chair, 1990-95. Chmn. Placement Alternatives Commn., Weld County, Colo., 1987-89; mem. Our Saviors Luth. Ch., Greeley, 1985—, exec. dir., 1987-89; chmn. bd. dirs. Colo. Rural Legal Svcs., Denver, 1983-86, 93-96; vice-chair Weld Child Care Network, 1988. Fellow ABA Found., Colo. Bar Found. (dir. 1998—, bd. dirs. 1999—); mem. ABA (house of dels. 1994-97), Colo. Bar Assn. (com. mem., exec. coun. 1986-90, bd. govs. 1983-90, 94—, pres.-elect. 1996-97, pres. 1997-98, chair young lawyers divsn. 1988-89, Outstanding Young Lawyer 1988, v.p. 1989-90), Weld County Bar Assn. (pres. 1992-93, dem. state exec. com. 1998-99, state ctrl. com. 1993—, Weld County exec. com. 1993—). Avocation: reading. Workers' compensation, Personal injury. Home: 2595 56th Ave Greeley CO 80634-4503 Office: 912 8th Ave Greeley CO 80631-1112

**CONWAY, ROBERT GEORGE, JR.,** lawyer; b. Albany, N.Y., Apr. 26, 1951; s. Robert George Sr. and Kathryn Ann (Kelly) C.; m. Lynda Rae Christenson, Dec. 15, 1979; 1 child, Phillip Christopher. AB, Dartmouth Coll., 1973; JD, Union U., 1976; diploma, U.S. Army JAGC Sch., 1986. Bar: Pa. 1978, U.S. Ct. Mil. Appeals 1978, N.C. 1983, U.S. Dist. Ct. (ea. dist.) N.C. 1983, U.S. Dist. Ct. (no. dist.) N.Y. 1998, U.S. Army Ct. Mil. Rev. 1986, U.S. Supreme Ct. 1986, U.S. Ct. Appeals (4th and fed. cirs.) 1987, N.Y. 1998; cert. USMC judge advocate. Commd. 2d lt. USMC, 1975, advanced through grades to maj., 1983; gen. staff sec. USMC, Camp Lejeune, N.C., 1982-83, chief rev. officer, 1983-84, spl. asst. U.S. atty., 1984-85; dir. joint law ctr. air sta. USMC, Cherry Point, N.C., 1986-88, chief rsch. officer air sta., 1988; dep. asst. staff judge adv. to comdt. USMC, Washington, 1989; mil. justice officer Marine Corps Base, Quantico, Va., 1990-91; assoc. counsel for land use law Ea. Area Counsel Office USMC Dept. of Navy Office of Gen. Counsel, Camp Lejeune, N.C., 1991-96; ret. USMC, 1996; counsel N.Y. State Divsn. Mil. and Naval Affairs, Latham, 1996—; adj. faculty mem. Ga. Inst. Tech., 1993, Webster U., 1994-96; spkr. in field. Trustee Cath. student ctr. Aquinas House, Dartmouth Coll., Hanover, N.H., 1973-89, sec. Dartmouth class of 1973, 1994—. Recipient Legion of Merit, 1996. Mem. ABA, Pa. Bar Assn., N.C. Bar Assn., N.Y. Bar Assn., Fed. Bar Assn. (contbg. author assn. news and jour. 1990), Dartmouth Lawyers Assn., Am. Legion, U.S. Naval Inst., Marine Corps Assn., KC (adv. 1984-85), Rotary, Dartmouth Club Ea. N.Y. (v.p. 1998—). Roman Catholic. Home: 27 Manor Dr Glenmont NY 12077-3326 Office: NY State Divsn Mil and Naval Affairs Attn MNLA 330 Old Niskayuna Rd Latham NY 12110-3514

**CONWAY, RONALD ANTHONY,** lawyer; b. Oceanside, Calif., Nov. 30, 1958; s. Edward Burton and Nancy Lorraine (Harrow) C.; m. m. Julianna Marie Harmon, Sept. 17, 1988; children: William Edward, Benjamin Anthony. BS, S.W. Mo. State U., 1981; JD, U. Mo., 1984. Bar: Mo. 1984, U.S. Dist. Ct. (we. dist.) Mo. 1988, U.S. Ct. Appeals (8th cir.) 1989, U.S. Supreme Ct. 1998. Law clk. Mo. Ct. Appeals, So. Dist., Springfield, Mo., 1984-85; asst. pub. defender Mo. Pub. Defender System, Springfield, 1985-88; assoc. Jerry L. Reynolds & Assocs., Springfield, 1988-91; ptnr. Reynolds & Conway, Springfield, 1991—. Mem. Greene County Bar Assn. General civil litigation, Criminal, Personal injury. Home: PO Box 50293 Springfield MO 65805-0293 Office: Reynolds & Conway 318 Park Central E Ste 406 Springfield MO 65806-2216

**CONWAY, SHARON ELIZABETH,** lawyer; b. Abilene, Tex., Oct. 10, 1964; d. Harold E. and Clara H. Conway. BA magna cum laude, Tex. Tech. U., 1986, JD, 1989. Bar: Tex. 1989, U.S. Dist. Ct. (so. dist.) Tex. 1990. Atty. Caperton, Rodgers & Miller, P.C., Bryan, Tex., 1989-90; assoc. atty. Dishongh & Thompson, A.P.C., Houston, 1990-93; asst. gen. counsel/asst. disciplinary counsel State Bar of Tex., Houston, 1993-94; pvt. practice Houston, 1994-96, 97—; counsel Evans, Kosut, Kasprzak & Benson, Houston, 1996-97; atty. Mediators Inst., Houston, 1997—. Com. mem. Adopt-an-Angel, 1998. Mem. Tex. Young Lawyers Assn., State Bar Assn. Tex., Houston Young Lawyers Assn., Houston Bar Assn. (mem. profl. rels./media com. 1995-96, mem. professionalism com. 1995-96), Tex. Tech U. Law Sch. Found. Professional liability, General civil litigation. Office: Atty at Law and Mediator Paragon Center One 450 Gears Rd Ste 625 Houston TX 77067-4532

**CONWELL, JOHN FREDRICK,** lawyer; b. Oklahoma City, Nov. 4, 1966; s. Fred Ern and Linda Louise (Wells) C. BA in Polit. Sci., U. Okla., 1989; JD, Villanova U., 1993. Bar: Md. 1994, Pa. 1994, U.S. Dist. Ct. Md. 1996, U.S. Ct. Appeals (4th cir.) 1998. Assoc. Davis & Assocs. Law Offices, Towson, Md., 1993-97, 99—; FCC, 1997-98. Mem. staff Villanova Environ. Law Jour. Mem. Md. State Bar Assn. (law practice mgmt. sect., tech. com. 1995-97), Balt. County Cir. Ct. Bar Assn. Avocations: photography, running, softball, computers. Communications, Administrative and regulatory, Public utilities. Office: Davis & Assocs 409 Washington Ave Ste 909 Towson MD 21204-4905

**COOCH, EDWARD W(EBB), JR.,** lawyer; b. Wilmington, Del., Mar. 22, 1920; s. Edward Webb and Eleanor Bedford (Wilkins) C.;m. Sarah Rodney, June 12, 1946; children: Richard Rodney Cooch, Anne Bedford Cooch Doran. BA, U. Del., 1941; LLB, U. Va., 1948. Bar: Del. 1948, U.S. Dist. Ct. Del. 1949, U.S. Ct. Appeals (3d cir.) 1949, U.S. Supreme Ct. 1965. Law clk. to Hon. John Biggs Jr. chief judge U.S. Ct. Appeals (3d cir.), Wilmington, 1948-49; pvt. practice Wilmington, 1949-60; ptnr. Cooch and Taylor, Attys. at Law, Wilmington, 1960-81; pres. Cooch and Taylor, PA, Wilmington, 1981-94; of counsel, 1994—. Bd. dirs., past pres. Del. Wild Lands, Inc. Wilmington, 1962-95; trustee U. Del. Libr. Assocs., Newark, 1986-99; pres. Christina Conservancy, Inc., Wilmington, 1991-99; bd. dirs. Wilmington Trust Co., 1974-93. Maj. Coast arty. U.S. Army, 1941-46. Mem. ABA, Del. State Bar Assn. (sec. 1952-53, cmty. svc. award 1991), Wilmington Club. Democrat. Episcopalian. Avocations: farming, conservation, historical study. Estate planning, Probate. Office: Cooch and Taylor 824 Market St Ste 1000 Wilmington DE 19801-3027

**COOK, AUGUST JOSEPH,** lawyer, accountant; b. Devine, Tex., Sept. 25, 1926; s. August E. and Mary H. (Schmidt) C.; m. Matie M. Brangan, July 12, 1952; children: Lisa Ann, Mary Beth, John J. BS, Trinity U., 1949; BBA, U. Tex., 1954; JD, St. Mary's U., 1960. Bar: Tex. 1960, Tenn. 1975. Bus. mgr., corp. sec. Life Enterprises, Inc. and affiliated cos., San Antonio, 1950-58, also dir.; mgr. Ernst and Whinney, San Antonio, 1960-69, ptnr. Memphis, 1970-84; ptnr. McDonnel Boyd, Memphis, 1984-91; counsel Harris, Shelton, Dunlap and Cobb, Memphis, 1991-97; counsel Pietrangelo Cook, Memphis, 1997—. Author newspaper column A.J.'s T ax Fables, 1983—. Author: A.J. $ Tax Court, 1987; contbr. articles to profl. jours. Alderman City of Castle Hills, Tex., 1961-63, mayor, 1963-69; chmn. Bexar County Coun. Mayors, 1967-69; v.p. Tex Mcpl. League, 1968-69; bd. dirs. San Antonio Met. YMCA. With U.S. Army, 1945-46, PTO. Mem. AICPA, Tex. Soc. CPAs, Tex. Bar Assn., Estate Planning Coun. San Antonio (pres. 1967), Tenn. Soc. CPAs, Tenn. Bar Assn. (chmn. tax, probate and trust sect., 1993-95), Estate Planning Coun. Memphis (pres. 1983-84), Toastmasters (pres. 1963), Delta Theta Phi, Kappa Pi Sigma. Roman Catholic. Clubs: University (Memphis); Canyon Creek Country (San Antonio) (bd. dirs.); Chickasaw Country. Lodges: Optimists (bd. dirs.), Rotary (treas. 1978, bd. dirs. 1986-87, 1997-98). Estate planning, Corporate taxation, Personal income taxation. Home: 6785 Slash Pine Cv Memphis TN 38119-5617 Office: Pietrangelo Cook PLC 6410 Poplar Ave Ste 190 Memphis TN 38119-4841

**COOK, BRYSON LEITCH,** lawyer; b. Balt., Apr. 17, 1948; s. A. Samuel C. B.A. magna cum laude, Princeton U., 1970; J.D. cum laude, U. Pa., 1973, M.B.A., 1973. Bar: Md. 1974, U.S. Dist. Ct. Md. 1976, U.S. Tax Ct. 1977. Assoc. Alex Brown & Sons, Balt., 1973-75, Venable, Baetjer & Howard, Balt., 1975-81, ptnr., 1981; adj. prof. U. Md. Law Sch., Balt., 1981, Loyola U. Bus. Sch., Balt., 1980-82. Contbr. articles to legal jours.; author tax mgmt. portfolios. Trustee, Balt. Ballet, 1980-83, Keswick Home for the Incurables, Balt., 1983—; bd. dirs. Balt. City Jail, 1980-82; counsel Md. Hist. Soc., Balt., 1981—. Recipient Gordon A. Block award U. Pa. Law Sch., 1973. Mem. Bar Assn. Balt. City, Md. State Bar Assn., ABA, Internat. Fiscal Assn., Order of Coif. Republican. Methodist. Club: Elkridge (Balt.). Corporate taxation, Estate taxation, General corporate. Home: 201 Woodbrook Ln Baltimore MD 21212-1037 Office: Venable Baetjer & Howard LLP 1800 Mercantile Bank & Trust Bldg 2 Hopkins Plz Ste 2100 Baltimore MD 21201-2982

**COOK, DEANNA DWORAKOWSKI,** lawyer; b. Dayton, Ohio, June 22, 1966; m. Richard D. Cook, Sept. 3, 1993; 1 child, Spencer Lane. BA, U. Richmond, 1988, JD, 1991. Bar: Va. 1991. Ptnr. Bremner, Janus & Cook, Richmond, Va., 1991—. Mem. Metro Women's Bar Assn., Metro Family Law Bar Assn., Richmond Bar Assn. Family and matrimonial. Office: Bremner Janus & Cook 701 E Franklin St Ste 1500 Richmond VA 23219-2510

**COOK, DEBORAH L.,** state supreme court justice. BA in English, U. Akron, 1974, JD, 1978, LLD (hon.), 1996. Ptnr. Roderick, Myers & Linton, Akron, 1976-91; judge 9th dist. Ohio Ct. Appeals, 1991-94; justice Ohio Supreme Ct., 1995—. Bd. trustees Summit County United Way, Vol. Ctr., Stan Hywet Hall and Gardens, Akron Sch. Law; bd. dirs. Women's Network; vol. Mobile Meals, Safe Landing Shelter. Named Woman of Yr., Women's Network, 1991. Fellow Am. Bar Found.; mem. Omicron Delta Kappa, Delta Gamma (pres., Nat. Shield award). Office: Ohio Supreme Ct 30 E Broad St Fl 3 Columbus OH 43266*

**COOK, EUGENE AUGUSTUS,** lawyer; b. Houston, May 2, 1938; s. Eugene A. and Estelle Mary (Stiner) C.; m. Sondra Attaway, Aug. 27, 1968; children: Laurie Ann, Eugene A. BBA, U. Houston, 1961, JD, 1966; LLM, U. Va., 1992. Bar: Tex. 1966, U.S. Dist. Ct. (so. dist.) Tex. 1967, U.S. Ct. Appeals (5th cir.) 1969, U.S. Supreme Ct. 1971, U.S. Ct. Claims 1972, U.S. Tax Ct. 1974, U.S. Ct. Appeals (11th cir.) 1982, U.S. Dist. Ct. (no., we. and ea. dists.) Tex. 1983. Ptnr. Butler & Binion, Houston, 1966-85; founding ptnr. Cook, Davis & McFall, 1985-88; justice Tex. Supreme Ct., Austin, 1988-93, chmn. jud. edn. exec. com., chmn. professionalism com., 1988-92; sr. ptnr. Bracewell & Patterson, Houston, 1993—; adj. asst. prof. law U. Houston, 1971-72, 74. Editor in chief, contbg. author: Creditors Rights in Texas, 2d edit., 1981; bd. dirs. U. Houston Law Rev., 1978-79; contbr. articles to profl. jours. Vice-chmn. bd. YMCA, 1977; bd. dirs. Spl. Olympics, Tex., 1989-95, chmn. bd. dirs., 1994. Recipient Disting. Alumnus award U. Houston Law Ctr., 1990, Am. Inns of Ct.-Lewis F. Powell Jr. award, 1992. Fellow Am. Coll. Trial Lawyers, Am. Acad. Matrimonial Lawyers, Internat. Acad. Matrimonial Lawyers, Am. Bar Found., Tex. Bar Found. (Outstanding Pub. Svc. award 1990); mem. ABA, Am. Inns of Ct. (pres. Austin Inn 1990-91), Tex. Bar Assn. (chmn. grievance com. 1971-72, vice chmn. consumer law sect. 1976-77, chmn. consumer law sect. 1979-80, Presdl. Citation 1979, dir. family law sect. 1984-88, Presdl. Cert. Merit, 1983, 84, 86, Pres.'s award as most outstanding lawyer in Tex., 1989, chmn. pubs. com. 1981-82, Achievement award 1982, chmn. litigation sect. 1982-84, chmn. CLE, 1988-89), Houston Bar Assn. (seminar com. 1976-77, Chmn. of Yr. award, 1976-77, chmn. insts. com. 1977-78, Outstanding Svc. award 1977-78, chmn. CLE com. 1978-79, Pres.'s award, 1978-79, 96-97; chmn. consumer law sect. 1978-79, vice-chmn. family law sect. 1981-82, chmn. family law sect. 1982-83, Officers award 1983, chmn. staff and staffing com. 1985-86, chmn. Spl. Olympics Com. 1987-88, chmn. long range planning and devel. com. 1988-89, dir. 1984-86, 2d v.p. 1986-87, 1st v.p. 1987-88, pres. elect 1988-89, pres. 1989-90, chmn. profl. com. 1996-97), Texas Bd. Legal Specialization (cert.), Civil Trial and Family Law, Nat. Bd. Trial Advocacy (bd. cert. civil trial law), Tex. Assn. Cert. Civil Trial Law Lawyers, Gulf Coast Family Law Specialists Assn., Tex. Acad. Family Law Specialists, ABA, State Bar Tex., Phi Kappa Phi, Phi Theta Kappa (chmn. bd. dirs. 1966-71, 87-88, Most Disting. Alumnus in Nat. award, 1988), Omicron Chi Epsilon, Omicron Delta Kappa, Phi Rho Pi, U. Houston Alumni Assn. (bd. dirs. 1996—). State civil litigation, Family and matrimonial. Office: Bracewell & Patterson LLP S Tower Pennzoil Pl 711 Louisiana St Ste 2900 Houston TX 77002-2781

**COOK, GAVIN A.,** lawyer, administrative law judge; b. Phila., Nov. 26, 1953. BA, Rowan U., 1983, MA, 1983; JD, Seton Hall U., 1988. Staff atty. Prisoners Legal Svcs., Albany, N.Y., 1988-89; adminstrv. law judge N.Y. State Office of Temp. and Disability Assistance, N.Y.C., 1998—. Civil rights. Home: YMWCA 600 Broad St Newark NJ 07102-4504 Office: NY State Office Temporary and Disability Assistance Social Svcs Dept Albany NY 12208-2070

**COOK, HAROLD DALE,** federal judge; b. Guthrie, Okla., Apr. 14, 1924; s. Harold Payton and Mildred Arvesta (Swanson) C.; children: Harold Dale II, Caren Irene, Randall Swanson; m. Kristen Elizabeth Ward; stepchildren: Kimberley Ward, Stephanie Ward, Erica Ward. BS in Bus., U. Okla., 1950, LLB, 1950, JD, 1970. Bar: Okla. 1950. Pvt. practice law Guthrie, Okla., 1950; county atty. Logan County, Okla., 1951-54; asst. U.S. atty. Oklahoma City, 1954-58; assoc. Butler, Rinehart and Morrison, Oklahoma City, 1958-61; ptnr. Rinehart, Morrison and Cook, 1961-63; legal counsel and adviser to Gov. State of Okla., 1963-65; ptnr. Cook & Ming, Oklahoma City, 1965, Cook, O'Toole, Ming & Tourtellotte, Oklahoma City, 1966-68, Cook, O'Toole & Tourtellotte, 1969-70, Cook & O'Toole, 1971; gen. counsel Shepherd Mall State Bank, Oklahoma City, 1967-71; pres. Shepherd Mall State Bank, 1969-71, chmn. bd., 1969-71; dir. Bur. of Hearings and Appeals, Social Security Adminstrn., HEW, 1971-74; judge U.S. Dist. Ct., Tulsa, 1974-79; chief judge U.S. Dist. Ct. (no. dist.) Okla., Tulsa, 1979-91, sr. judge, 1992; mem. legal adv. coun. Okla. Hwy. Patrol, 1969-70; mem. magistrates com. Jud. Conf. U.S., 1980-88; mem. indsl. adv. coun. Bur. Bus. and Econ.Rsch., U. Okla., 1970-71. First v.p. PTA, Sunset Elementary Sch., 1959-60; v.p. Parent-Tchrs. & Students Assn., John Marshall High Sch., Oklahoma City, 1970-71, pres., 1971; mem. Econ. Opportunity Com., Okla., 1963-65; tchr. Sunday sch. classes for coll., high sch. and adult ages Village Methodist Ch., Oklahoma City, 1959-65; mem. bd. of stewards First Meth. Ch., Guthrie, Okla., 1951-54. Served with USAAF, 1943-45. Recipient Secretary's Spl. Citation HEW, 1973. Fellow Am. Bar Found.; mem. ABA, Fed. Bar Assn., Okla. Bar Assn. (del. to state bar convs.), Oklahoma City C. of C. Republican. Clubs: So. Hills Country, Shriners, Masons, Tulsa, Order Eastern Star (past worthy patron Okla.). Office: Tulsa Fed Bldg Ste 241 224 S Boulder Ave Tulsa OK 74103-3026

**COOK, JULIAN ABELE, JR.,** federal judge; b. Washington, June 22, 1930; s. Julian Abele and Ruth Elizabeth (McNeill) C.; m. Carol Annette Dibble, Dec. 22, 1957; children: Julian Abele III, Peter Dibble, Susan Annette. BA, Pa. State U., 1952; JD, Georgetown U., 1957, LLD (hon.), 1992; LLM, U. Va., 1988; LLD (hon.), U. Detroit, 1996, Wayne State U., 1997. Bar: Mich. 1957. Law clk. to judge Pontiac, Mich., 1957-58; pvt. practice Detroit, 1958-78; judge U.S. Dist. Ct. (ea. dist.) Mich., Detroit, 1978, chief judge, 1989-96, sr. judge, 1996—; spl. asst. atty. gen. State of Mich., 1968-78; adj. prof. U. Detroit Sch. Law, 1971-74; gen. counsel pub. TV Sta. WTVS, 1973-78; labor arbitrator Am. Arbitration Assn. and Mich. Employment Rels. Commn., 1975-78; mem. Mich. State Bd. Ethics, 1977-78; instr. trial advocacy workshop Harvard U., 1988—, trial advocacy program U.S. Dept. Justice, 1989-90; com. on fin. disclosure Jud. Conf. U.S., 1988-93, chmn., 1990-93; screening panel NYU Root-Tilden-Snow Scholarship Program, 1991, 96—; mem. U.S. Sentencing Commn. Judicial Adv. Group, 1996—; mem. nat. bd. trustees Am. Inn Ct., 1996—; mem. adv. com. Nat. Publs., 1994-96, chmn. nat. nominations and election com., 1994-95; pres. chpt. XI, Master of Bench, 1984-95. Contbr. articles to profl. jours. Exec. bd. dirs., past pres. Child and Family Svcs. Mich.; bd. dirs. Am. Heart Assn. Mich., 1984-89, Hutzel Hosp., 1984-95; chmn. Mich. Civil Rights Commn., 1968-71; co-chair exec. com. Walter P. Reuther Libr. Labor and Urban Affairs, Wayne State U.; mem. bd. visitors Georgetown U. Law Ctr., 1992—. With Signal Corps, U.S. Army, 1952-54. Recipient Merit citation Pontiac Area Urban League, 1971, Pathfinders award Oakland U., 1977, Svc. award Todd-Phillips Home, Inc., 1978, Disting. Alumnus award Pa. State U., 1987, Georgetown U., 1989, Focus and Impact award Oakland U., 1985; resolution Mich. Ho. of Reps., 1971, Outstanding Community Svc. award Va. Park Community Investment Assocs., 1992, 1st Ann. Trailblazers award D. Augustus Straker Bar Assn., 1993, Renowned Jurist award Friends of African Art, 1993, Brotherhood award Jewish War Vets. U.S., 1994, Paul R. Dean award Georgetown U. Law Sch., 1997; named Boss of Yr., Oakland County Legal Secs. Assn., 1974, one of Mich. Most Respected Judges, Mich. Law Weekly, 1990-91; named one of the Best Judges, Detroit Monthly, 1991; named Disting. Citizen of Yr., NAACP Oakland County, Mich., 1970. Fellow Am. Bar Found., Mich. Bar Found. (vice-chmn. 1992-93, chmn. 1993—); mem. NAACP (mem. state constl. revision and legal redress com. 1963, Disting. Citizen of Yr. 1970, Presdl. award North Oakland County, Mich. chpt. 1987), ABA, Fed. Bar Assn. (fed.-state ct. seminar lectr. Detroit chpt. 1981—), Am. Law Inst., Mich. Bar Assn. (chmn. constl. law com. 1969, vice-chmn. civil liberties com. 1970, co-chmn. profl. devel. task force 1984-87, U.S. cts. com. 1988-95, com. on professionalism 1991—, Champion of Justice 1994), Mich. Tribunal Assn. (bd. dirs. 3rd cir. 1992—), Detroit Bar Assn. (Bench-Bar award 1987), Oakland County Bar Assn. (chmn. continuing legal edn. com. 1968-69, jud. liaison Dist. Ct. com. 1977, unauthorized practice law com. 1977), Wolverine Bar Assn. (Bench-Bar award 1987, D. Augustus Straker award 1988), Mich. Assn. Black Judges, Am. Inn of Ct. (founder Met. Detroit chpt., pres., master of bench, chmn. 6th cir. com. on standard jury instructions 1986—), Am. Law Inst., Union Black Episcopalians (Detroit chpt., Absalom Jones award 1988), Justice Frank Murphy Honor Soc.

**COOK, LEANN CECILIA,** paralegal; b. Wheeling, W.Va., Oct. 14, 1950; d. Leo Elbin Cook and Phyllis Marie (Bargiel) Cook-Allen. Cert. in computers and computer programming, Contemporary Inst., Pitts., 1971; student, Ohio U., 1979-81; Paralegal Cert., Am. Inst. Paralegal Studies, Inc., North Canton, Ohio, 1986. Computer operator Riechart's Furniture Co., Wheeling, 1971-72, Wheeling Machine Products Co., 1972-74; data technician Belmont Tech. Coll., St. Clairsville, Ohio, 1974-76; adminstrv. asst. Belmont County Treas. Office, St. Clairsville, 1977-87; paralegal specialist Office of Dist. Counsel VA, Lexington, Ohio, 1987-88; fin. litigation agt. U.S. Atty.'s Office, Columbus, 1988-90; office mgr. Streski Reporting Svc., Martins Ferry, 1990; paralegal practice St. Clairsville, Ohio, 1990-95; with Nat. Tech. Transfer Ctr., St. Clairsville, Ohio, 1995-97; paralegal Office of Law Enforcement Tech. Commercialization, Wheeling, W.Va., 1997—; data processing instr. adult edn. Belmont Joint Vocat. Sch., St. Clairsville, 1974-79; seminar speaker Profl. Edn. Svcs., Inc., 1993, others; cons. Paralegal Cons. Assn. N.Y.C., 1993-94; mem. Akron region U.S. Postal Consumer Adv. Coun.; personal injury paralegal faculty mem. P.E.S.I., Eau Claire, Wis., 1993. Author compilation Personal Injury Paralegal manual, 1993. Mem. pub. rels. com., Tri-County Task Force for Sexual Abuse, St. Clairsville, 1985-86; mem. Women's Crisis Ctr., St. Clairsville, 1986, St. Clairsville's Bus. and Profl. Women, 1986-87; coord. fed. women's program So. Dist. Ohio, Columbus, 1989; vol. amb. Chinese Imperial Arts Program, Columbus, 1989; bd. dirs. Am. Cancer Soc., 1995-96, A Spl. Wish Found.; vol. State of Ohio Women's Policy and Rsch. Orgn., 1988; mem. Nat. Ctr. for Missing and Exploited Children's Poster Network; mem. stewardship com. Wheeling Jesuit U., mem. adult edn. and grad. adv. bd., 1995, mem. univ. employee picnic com.; mem. internal security com. NTTC bldg. on campus. Mem. St. Clairsville Law Libr. Assn., Ohio State Bar Assn. (assoc.). Orthodox. Avocations: baseball, helping people. Home and Office: PO Box 156 Saint Clairsville OH 43950-0156

**COOK, MICHAEL LEWIS,** lawyer; b. Rochester, N.H., Mar. 5, 1944; s. Israel J. and Molly L. Cook; m. Roberta Tross, Feb. 25, 1995; children: Jonathan, Alexander. AB, Columbia U., 1965; JD, NYU, 1968. Bar: N.Y. 1968. Assoc. Weil, Gotshal & Manges, N.Y.C., 1970-75, ptnr., 1975-80; ptnr. Skadden, Arps, Slate, Meagher & Flom, LLP, N.Y.C., 1980—; adj. prof. law NYU Sch. Law, 1975—. Co-author: A Practical Guide to the Bankruptcy Reform Act, 1979, Creditors' Rights, Debtors' Protection and Bankruptcy, 1985, rev. edit., 1997; contbr.: Collier on Bankruptcy, 1979, rev. edit., 1998, Collier Bankruptcy Practice Guide, 1998; editor and contbg. author: Bankruptcy Litigation Manual, rev. edit., 1998. Bd. dirs. Goddard Riverside Cmty. Ctr.; bd. dirs., chair Lawyers Alliance for N.Y. Fellow Am. Coll. Bankruptcy; mem. ABA, Assn. of Bar of City of N.Y., Practicing Law Inst. (mem. bankruptcy law adv. com.), Columbia Coll. Alumni Assn. (bd. dirs., v.p.), Soc. of Columbia Grads. (bd. dirs.). Bankruptcy, Federal civil litigation. Home: 45 E 89th St New York NY 10128-1251 Office: Skadden Arps Slate Meagher & Flom LLP 919 3rd Ave New York NY 10022-3902

**COOK, PHILIP CARTER,** lawyer; b. Atlanta, Nov. 4, 1946. BS, Ga. Inst. Tech., 1968; JD cum laude, Harvard U., 1971. Bar: Ga. 1972. Law clk. to Hon. Lewis R. Morgan U.S. Ct. Appeals (5th cir.), 1971-72; mem. Alston & Bird, Atlanta. Pres. Harvard Journal of Legislation 1970-71. Fellow Am. Coll. Tax Counsel; mem. ABA (chmn. sect. taxation, com. on banking and savs. instns. 1995), D.C. Bar, State Bar Ga. (chmn. taxation sect.), Am. Law Inst., Atlanta Tax Forum (trustee 1986-91, pres. 1991), Phi Kappa Phi, Omicron Delta Kappa. Taxation, general, Corporate taxation. Office: Alston & Bird 1 Atlantic Ctr 1201 W Peachtree St NW Ste 4200 Atlanta GA 30309-3424

**COOK, QUENTIN LAMAR,** lawyer, healthcare executive, church leader; b. Sept. 8, 1940; s. J. Vernon and Bernice (Kimball) C.; m. Mary Gaddie, Nov. 30, 1962; children: Kathryn Cook Knight, Quentin Laurance, Joseph Vernon III. BS, Utah State U., 1963; JD, Stanford U., 1966. Bar: Calif. 1966. Assoc. Carr, McClellan, Ingersoll, Thompson & Horn, Burlingame, Calif., 1966-69, ptnr., 1969-93; interim pres., CEO Calif. Healthcare Sys., San Francisco, 1993-94, pres., CEO, 1994-95; vice chmn. Sutter Health/Calif. Healthcare Sys., San Francisco, 1996; gen. authority LDS Ch., 1996—. City atty. Town of Hillsborough, Calif., 1982-93; mem. adv. bd. Utah State U., Logan, 1985-95; mem. bd. visitors Brigham Young U. Law Sch., Provo, 1994-96.

**COOK, RALPH D.,** state supreme court justice. Former judge Ala. Cir. Ct. (10th jud. dist.), Ala. Dist. Ct.; assoc. justice Ala. Supreme Ct., Montgomery. Office: 300 Dexter Ave Montgomery AL 36104-3741*

**COOK, RUSSELL AUSTIN,** lawyer; b. Oklahoma City; s. Jim A. and Loretta A. Cook. BA, U. Okla., 1979; JD with distinction, Oklahoma City U., 1982. Atty. Linn & Neville, Oklahoma City, 1982—. General civil litigation. Office: Linn & Neville PC 201 Robert S Kerr Ave Ste 1200 Oklahoma City OK 73102-4204

**COOK, THOMAS ALFRED ASHLEY,** lawyer; b. Merriam, Kans., Oct. 24, 1964; s. Alfred Harrison and Donna Rebecca Cook; m. Lisa Ann Kehr, Dec. 9, 1983; children: Ashley Alizabeth, Mackenzie Ann. BS in Acct. and Bus. Adminstrn., U. Kans., 1985, MBA, 1987, JD, 1989. Bar: Mo. 1989, Ill. 1990. Assoc. Peper, Martin, Jensen, Maichel & Hetlage, St. Louis, 1989-97; ptnr. Peper, Martin Jensen, Maichel & Hetlage, St. Louis, 1997-98, Blackwell, Sanders, Peper, Martin, St. Louis, 1998—. Mergers and acquisitions, Contracts commercial, General corporate. Office: Blackwell Sanders Et Al 720 Olive St Fl 24 Saint Louis MO 63101-2338

**COOK, THOMAS S.,** lawyer, educator; b. Middletown, Conn., Jan. 22, 1952. BA, Antioch Coll., 1975; JD, SUNY, Buffalo, 1978. Bar: Pa. 1978. Dir. Pa. Bur. Workers Compensation, Harrisburg, 1987-91; atty. Cook and Niven, Harrisburg, 1991—. Workers' compensation. Office: Cook & Niven 1323 N Front St Harrisburg PA 17102-2609

**COOK, WILLIAM LESLIE, JR.,** lawyer; b. July 1, 1949; s. William Leslie and Mary Elizabeth (Roberts) C.; m. Mary Jo Dorr, July 17, 1976; children: Leslie Patton, William Roberts, Maribeth Dorr. BA, U. Miss., 1971, JD, 1974. Bar: Miss. 1974, U.S. Dist. Ct. (no. dist.) Miss. 1974, U.S. Dist. Ct. (we. dist.) Tenn. 1986. Assoc. Bailey & Trusty, Batesville, Miss., 1974-79; ptnr. Bailey, Trusty & Cook, Batesville, Miss., 1980-90, Bailey & Cook, Batesville, Miss., 1990-92, Bailey, Cook & Womble, Batesville, Miss., 1992—; Chmn., Miss. Coll. Rep. Clubs, 1973, Panola County March of Dimes, Batesville, 1976-78; Miss. chmn. Nat. Orgn. Social Security Claimants Reps., 1981-82; rep. Honor Coun., U. Miss. Sch. Law, 1974. Paul Harris fellow 1998—. Mem. ABA (torts and ins. practice sect. 1979—, vice chmn. com. on delivery of legal svcs. tothe disabled young lawyers divsn. 1983-85, gen. practice sect. 1985-86), ATLA, Miss. State Bar (state bd. bar admissions 1978-79, mem. ethics com. 1980-83, bd. dirs. Young Lawyers sect. 1980-83, chmn. com. on unauthorized practice of law 1983-86, workers compensation sect., mem. com. on Kid's Second Chance 1992), Panola County Bar Assn. (pres. 1979-80), Miss. Trial Lawyers Assn. (membership com. 1983-84), Ct. Practice Inst. (diplomate), Lawyer-Pilots Bar Assn.,

Lamar Soc. Internat. Law, Batesville Jaycees (legal counsel 1975-77), Masons, Shriners, Rotary (pres. 1991-92, 96-97, asst. dist. gov. 1997—, dist. gov. nominee 1999—, Paul Harris fellow), Omicron Delta Kappa, Pi Sigma Alpha, Delta Theta Pi. Methodist. Personal injury, Workers' compensation. Home: 110 Shagbark Dr Batesville MS 38606-8470 Office: Panola Plz 118 Highway 6 W Batesville MS 38606-2507

**COOKE, ALEXANDER HAMILTON,** lawyer; b. Louisville, Ky., Jan. 25, 1941; s. Henry Thurston and Elizabeth Hamilton (Davis) C.; m. Genie Ray Watson, Aug. 8, 1964; children: Henry Thurston II, Katherine Watson. AB, Davidson (N.C.) Coll., 1963; JD, Vanderbilt U., 1968. Bar: Fla. 1968, U.S. Dist. Ct. (mid dist.) Fla. 1969; cert. wills, trusts and estates. Assoc. Mahoney, Hadlow, Chambers & Adams, Jacksonville, Fla., 1968-71, Adams & Adams, Jacksonville, 1972-74; sole practice Jacksonville, 1974; ptnr. Alexander, Spraker, Cooke & Hand, Jacksonville, 1975-78; ptnr., pres. Cooke, Hand, Carithers, Showalter & Mercier, Jacksonville, 1979-88; ptnr. Ulmer, Murchison, Ashby & Taylor, Jacksonville, 1988-92; ptrn., pres. A. Hamilton Cooke, P.A., Jacksonville, 1993—. Chmn. Jacksonville Community Rels. Commn., 1979; bd. dirs. Luth. Social Svcs., Inc., 1984-90, Presbytery of St. Augustine, 1989—. 1st lt. U.S. Army, 1963-65. Mem. Fla. Bar Assn. (bd. govs. 1987-91, exec. coun. cir. rep. real property, probate and trust law sect. 1981-97), Jacksonville Bar Assn. (pres. 1982-83), Fla. Bar Found. (bd. dirs. 1991—, pres.-elect 1999-2000). Democrat. Presbyterian. Avocations: golf, camping, canoeing, traveling. Estate planning, Probate, Real property. Office: A Hamilton Cooke PA 1301 Riverplace Blvd Ste 2254 Jacksonville FL 32207-9036

**COOKE, HUGH SHANNON,** lawyer; b. Ft. Pierce, Fla., Aug. 26, 1967; s. Hugh Edwin and Carole Buskell C. BA, King Coll., 1988; JD, U. Va., 1991. Bar: Va. 1991, U.S. Ct. Appeals (4th cir.) 1991, U.S. Bankruptcy Ct. (we. dist.) Va. 1993. Assoc. Street, Street, Street, Scott & Bowman, Grundy, Va., 1991-92; pvt. practice Cedar Bluff, Va., 1992—; asst. commonwealth atty. Buchanan County, Grundy, 1998—. Mem. editl. bd. Va. Tax Rev., 1990-91. Bd. dirs. Southwest Va. Human Rights Bd., 1992—; bd. dirs., vice-chmn. Tazewell (Va.) County Airport Authority, 1994-97. Mem. ABA, Va. Trial Lawyers Assn. Avocations: travelling, SCUBA diving. Office: 3111 West Cedar Valley Dr Cedar Bluff VA 24609

**COOKE, MORRIS DAWES, JR.,** lawyer; b. Beaufort, S.C., July 20, 1954; s. Morris Dawes and Georgianna (McTeer) C.; m. Helen Cecilia Haffey, May 16, 1961; children: Morris Dawes III, George Henry, Ellen Cecilia. BA with distinction, U. Va., 1976; JD cum laude, U. S.C., 1979; LLD (hon.), The Citadel. Bar: S.C. 1979, U.S. Dist. Ct. S.C. 1979, U.S. Ct. Appeals (4th cir.) 1980, U.S. Supreme Ct. 1986. Law clk. to presiding judge U.S. Dist. Ct. S.C., Charleston, 1979-80; assoc. Barnwell, Whaley, Patterson & Helms, Charleston, 1980-82, ptnr., 1982—. Mem. Charleston County Bar Assn. (pres. 1999-2000), S.C. Bar Assn., Am. Bd. Trial Advocates, Am. Judicature Soc., Nat. Assn. Coll. and Univ. Attys., Am. Soc. Law and Medicine, Southeastern Admiralty Law Inst, Def. Rsch. Inst. Republican. Episcopalian. General civil litigation, General corporate, Insurance. Home: 113 Bennett St Mount Pleasant SC 29464-4301 Office: Barnwell Whaley Patterson & Helms LLC 134 Meeting St Ste 300 Charleston SC 29401-2240

**COOKE, WILLIAM L.,** lawyer; b. Aulander, N.C., May 19, 1925; s. Willie A. Cooke and Nina Parker; m. Betty Butler; 1 child, Elizabeth Leigh. AB, U. N.C., 1948, LLB, 1950. Bar: N.C. 1950, U.S. Dist. Ct. N.C., U.S. Supreme Ct. Assoc. J.A. Pritchett, Windsor, N.C., 1950; ptnr. Pritchett & Cooke, Windsor, 1951-97. Lt. USNR, 1945-65. Mem. N.C. Bar Assn., Bertie County County and Dist. Bar Assn., Rotary (pres. 1958). Democrat. Baptist.

**COOL, DWIGHT I.,** lawyer; b. Balt., Jan. 18, 1955; s. Argel L. and Alberta L. C.; m. Edith Ann Lawson; children: Jerry, Laura. BS, Fla. State U., 1976; JD, U. Fla., 1979. Bar: Fla. 1979. Assoc. Gunster, Yoakley et al, Palm Beach, Fla., 1979-83, Swann & Haddock, Orlando, Fla., 1983-87; ptnr. Lefkowitz, Miner & Cool, Orlando, Fla., 1987-88; assoc. Graham, Clark et al, Winter Park, Fla., 1988-93; ptnr. Pohl & Short, Winter Park, Fla., 1993—. Mem. ABA, Fla. Bar, Orange County Bar Assn., Kiwanis. Real property, Landlord-tenant, Land use and zoning (including planning). Office: Pohl & Short 280 W Canton Ave Ste 410 Winter Park FL 32789-3168

**COOLEY, RICHARD EUGENE,** lawyer; b. Flint, Mich., Apr. 28, 1935; s. Eugene J. and Helen Frances (Lumbert) C.; m. Wanda Lee Ford, Feb. 20, 1965; children: Scott Richard, Courtney Cooley Breaugh. AB, Albion Coll., 1957; JD, Duke U., 1960. Bar: Mich. 1960, U.S. Supreme Ct. 1970. Asst. pros. atty. Genesee County, Mich., 1962-64; ptnr. Bellairs, Dean, Cooley, Siler, Moulton & Smith, Flint, 1964—; spl. asst. atty. gen. State of Mich., 1975-81; city atty. City of Linden, Mich., 1964-89; twp. atty. Fenton (Mich.) Twp., 1970—; village atty. Village of Gaines, Mich., 1989-96; mediation panel mem. Genesee County Cir. Ct., 1978—. Past bd. dirs. Tall Pines coun. Boy Scouts Am., Fairwinds coun. Girl Scouts U.S.A.; past pres. and bd. dirs. Child and Family Svcs. Mich., Flint. Mem. ABA, State Bar Mich. Genesee County Bar Assn. (bd. dirs. 1973-76, v.p. 1976-77, pres. 1977-78), Flint Estate Planning Coun. (bd. dirs. 1994—, pres. 1999-2000), Rotary, Masons. Republican. Presbyterian. Avocations: skiing, sailing, travel. Estate planning, Family and matrimonial, Municipal (including bonds). Home: 8292 Butternut Ct Grand Blanc MI 48439-2080 Office: Bellairs Dean Cooley Siler Moulton & Smith 412 S Saginaw St Ste 300 Flint MI 48502-1810

**COOLIDGE, DANIEL SCOTT,** lawyer; b. Portland, Maine, Sept. 20, 1948; s. John Walter and Mary Louise (Arnold) C.; m. Carolyn Stiles, Nov. 23, 1984; children: Lillian Mae, Lydia Stiles. BS summa cum laude, U. Bridgeport, 1976; JD, Harvard U., 1980. Bar: Conn. 1980, N.H. 1982, U.S. Ct. Appeals (1st cir.) 1983, U.S. Supreme Ct. 1985. Assoc. Cummings & Lockwood, Stamford, Conn., 1980-82; assoc. Sheehan, Phinney, Bass & Green PA, Manchester, N.H., 1982-87, ptnr., 1987—; chmn. juvenile diversion com. Pittsfield (N.H.) Dist. Ct., 1982-85. Author: Survival Guide for Road Warriors, 1996; mem. editl. bd. Law Office Tech. Solutions; columnist Law Office Computing, 1997—; patentee tel. test equipment. Chmn. Bradford Constitution Bicentennial Com.; mem. Pittsfield Planning Bd., 1984-85; treas., trustee First Congl. Ch., Pittsfield, 1984-85, First Bapt. Ch. Bradford; pres. Pittsfield Arts Coun., 1985; del. N.H. Constl. Conv., Concord, 1984-94; founding bd. dirs., officer U.S. Found. for Inspiration and Recognition of Sci. and Tech. Mem. ABA (environ. law sect., intellectual property law sect., acting chmn., chmn. computer and tech. divsn., vice-chmn. sys. and tools law practice mgmt. sect. 1994—, governing coun. 1996—, advisor UCC article 2B drafting com. 1995-99), N.H. Bar Assn. (vice-chmn. tech. sect. 1993-96, chmn. lex mundi intellectual property sect. 1992-93), Manchester Bar Assn. Avocations: computers, physics, fly fishing, hiking, motorcycling. Computer, Environmental, Intellectual property. Home: 106 Bible Hill Rd Warner NH 03278-3701 Office: Sheehan Phinney Bass & Green PA 1000 Elm St Ste 1801 Manchester NH 03101-1792

**COOLLEY, RONALD B.,** lawyer; b. Manchester, N.H., Feb. 15, 1946; s. Mace A. and Ruth A. C. BS, Iowa State U., 1969; MBA, U. Iowa, 1972, JD, 1972. Bar: Ill. 1974, Tex. 1987. Assoc. Mason, Kolehmainen, Chgo., 1973-87, Arnold, White & Durkee, Chgo., 1987—. Contbr. articles to profl. jours. Recipient Gerald Rose award John Marshall Law Sch., 1985, Rossman award, Patent and Trademark Office Soc., 1985. Mem. ABA (bd. dirs. 1988-90), Patent Law Assn. Chgo. (pres.1988-89). Patent, Trademark and copyright. Office: Arnold White & Durkee 321 N Clark St Chicago IL 60610-4714

**COON, ROBERT MORELL, JR.,** lawyer; b. Bronxville, N.Y., Nov. 17, 1930; s. Robert Morell Coon and Pearl Edna Weekley; m. Aileen Blanche Edwards, June 10, 1961 (div. Mar. 1978); 1 child, Charles Nicholas; m. Jean Hall Tuttle, Oct. 8, 1983. AB magna cum laude, Harvard U., 1952, JD, 1958. Bar: N.Y. 1958, U.S. Tax Ct. 1963. Assoc. Carter, Ledyard & Milburn, N.Y.C., 1958-65, O'Connor & Farber, N.Y.C., 1965-66, Putney, Twombley, Hall & Skidmore, N.Y.C., 1966-69; ptnr. O'Connor & Farber, N.Y.C., 1969-70; assoc. Fulton, Walter & Duncombe, N.Y.C., 1970-71, ptnr., 1971-77; ptnr. Fulton, Duncombe & Rowe, N.Y.C., 1977-81, Farber & Childs, N.Y.C., 1981-86; pvt. practice Bronxville, 1986-93; ptnr. Fulton, Duncombe & Rowe, N.Y.C., 1994-96, Fulton, Rowe, Hart & Coon, N.Y.C., 1997—; dir. Nat. Com. to Preserve Social Security and Medicare, Washington, 1987-97. Mem. Bronxville Rep. Com., 1966-73, chmn., 1971-73. Sgt. U.S. Army, 1952-55, Germany. Mem. N.Y. State Bar Assn., Assn. of Bar of City of N.Y., Bronxville Field Club., Phi Beta Kappa. Republican. Reformed. Probate, Estate taxation, Estate planning. Home: 844 Gramatan Ave Mount Vernon NY 10552-1048 Office: Fulton Rowe Hart & Coon 1 Rockefeller Plz Ste 301 New York NY 10020-2002

**COONER, DAVID JAMES,** lawyer; b. Bklyn., July 19, 1963. BA, Villanova U., 1985; JD, Seton Hall U., 1989. Bar: N.J. 1989, Pa. 1989. Jud. clk. U.S. Dist. Ct., Trenton, N.J., 1989-90; atty. McCarter & English, Newark, 1990—. Product liability, Personal injury. Office: McCarter & English 4 Gateway Ctr Ste 1200 Newark NJ 07102-4096

**COONEY, CHARLES HAYES,** lawyer; b. Nashville, Apr. 25, 1937; s. Robert G. and Annie Lee (Hayes) C.; m. Patsy M. Cooney, Dec. 25, 1986; children: Susan, Hayes Jr. BA, Vanderbilt U., 1959, JD, 1963. Bar: Tenn. 1963. Pvt. practice Cornelius & Collins, Nashville, 1963-67; chief def. atty. gen. State of Tenn., Nashville, 1967-80; ptnr. Watkins, McGugin, McNeilly & Rowan, 1980—. Staff mem. Vanderbilt U. Law Review, 1961-62. Capt. U.S. Army, 1959. Mem. ABA, Rotary, Tenn. Bar Assn. (pres. young lawyers sect., 1961), Nashville Bar Assn. (bd. dirs. 1985-87). Presbyterian. Avocations: golf, tennis, travel. General civil litigation, Personal injury, Workers' compensation. Office: Watkins McGugin McNeilly & Rowan 214 2nd Ave N Ste 300 Nashville TN 37201-1638

**COONEY, JAMES PATRICK,** lawyer; b. Texarkana, Ark., Feb. 22, 1944; s. James Raphael and Kathlyn Mary (Price) C.; m. Pamela Joy Pagano, July 15, 1967; children: Elena Valentine, Kathlyn Mary, Erin Joy, James Brennan. AB cum laude, U. Notre Dame, 1966, JD, 1969. Bar: Tex. 1969, U.S. Dist. Ct. (ea. dist.) Tex. 1969, U.S. Dist. Ct. (so. dist.) Tex. 1974, U.S. Ct. Appeals (5th cir.) 1971, U.S. Supreme Ct. 1976. Law clk. Hon. Lewis R. Mangan U.S. Ct. Appeals (5th cir.), Newnan, Ga., 1969-71; assoc. Powell, Goldstein, Frazen & Murphy, Atlanta, 1971-74; assoc. Royston, Rayzor, Vickery & Williams, Houston, 1974-77, ptnr., 1977—; chmn. Southeastern Admiralty Inst., 1992-93. Editorial assoc. Notre Dame Lawyer, 1968-69. Bd. dirs. Houston Internat. Seafarers Ctr., 1992—; pres. Westheimer Ecumenical Social Ministry, 1994-96. Mem. Maritime Law Assn. U.S. (proctor), Notre Dame Club Houston (pres. 1990-92). Roman Catholic. Admiralty, Personal injury, General civil litigation. Office: Royston Rayzor Vickery & Williams 2200 Texas Commerce Tower Houston TX 77002

**COONEY, JOHN GORDON,** lawyer; b. Bklyn., Jan. 21, 1930; s. John Philip and Josephine (Gordon) C.; m. Patricia Ruth McEwen, June 8, 1957; 1 child, J. Gordon Jr. AB, St. John's U., 1951, JD, 1953. Bar: N.Y. 1953, Pa. 1962, D.C. 1970. Asso. Patterson, Belknap & Webb, N.Y.C., 1953-55; staff counsel U.S. Industries, N.Y., 1956-57; atty. SEC, Washington, 1957-59, FTC, 1959-61; ptnr. Schnader, Harrison, Segal & Lewis, Phila., 1962-97; bd. dirs. PH II, Inc.; arbitrator Am. Arbitration Assn., 1964—; public mem. nat. com. on arbitration Nat. Assn. Securities Dealers, 1977-83; dir. Attys. Liability Assurance Soc., 1979-85. Dir., pres. Strafford Village Assn., 1969-70; bd. govs. N.Y.C. Young Republican Club, 1957. Recipient Superior Service award FTC, 1961. Fellow Am. Bar Found.; mem. ABA (coun. sect. corp. banking and bus. law 1980-84, 93-97), Am. Law Inst. (life mem., adviser project on corp. governance: analysis and recommendations 1980-92), D.C. Bar Assn., N.Y. State Bar Assn., Pa. State Bar Assn., Phila. Bar Assn., Union League Club, Overbrook Golf Club, Merion Cricket Club. Roman Catholic. Securities, Mergers and acquisitions, Finance. Home: 320 Gatcombe Ln Bryn Mawr PA 19010-3628 Office: Schnader Harrison Segal & Lewis 1600 Market St Ste 3600 Philadelphia PA 19103-7240 *Deceased.*

**COONEY, J(OHN) GORDON, JR.,** lawyer; b. Alexandria, Va., Mar. 22, 1959; s. John Gordon Sr. and Patricia Ruth (McEwen) C.; m. Gretchen Smith Millspaugh, July 17, 1999. BA, Wesleyan U., 1981; JD magna cum laude, Villanova U., 1984. Bar: Pa. 1984, U.S. Dist. Ct. (ea. dist.) Pa. 1986, U.S. Ct. Appeals (3d cir.) 1988. Law clk. to hon. judge J. William Ditter Jr. U.S. Dist. Ct. (ea. dist.) Pa., Phila., 1984-86; assoc. Morgan, Lewis & Bockius, LLP, Phila., 1986-92, ptnr., 1992—; adj. lectr. Villanova U. Sch. of Law, 1993—, master Inn of Ct., 1999—; barrister U. Pa. Law Sch. Inn of Ct., 1994-96. Editor-in-chief Villanova U. Law Rev., 1983-84; mem. lawyer's editl. bd. The Legal Intelligencer, 1997—. Trustee Rosemont Sch. of the Holy Child, 1997—; alumni bd. mgrs. Episcopal Acad., 1996—. Mem. ABA (com. on class actions and derivative suits), Pa. Bar Assn., Phila. Bar Assn. (profl. guidance com., fed. cts. com.), Union League Phila., Merion Cricket Club, Pyramid Club, Wesleyan U. Alumni Assn. (pres. Phila. area 1993-96), Arthritis Found. (bd. dirs Ea. Pa. chpt. 1993-96), Order of Coif. Republican. Roman Catholic. Federal civil litigation, General civil litigation, State civil litigation. Office: Morgan Lewis & Bockius LLP 1701 Market St Philadelphia PA 19103-2903

**COONEY, WILLIAM J.,** lawyer; b. Augusta, Ga., July 31, 1929; s. John F. and Ellen (Joy) C.; m. Martha L. Whaley, May 1, 1971; children: William J. IV, Sarah C. BS, U. Notre Dame, 1951; JD, Georgetown U., 1954, LLM, 1955. Bar: Ga. 1963, Calif. 1961, D.C. 1954. Law clk. U.S. Ct. Appeals, Washington, 1954, U.S. Claims Ct., Washington, 1955; asst. U.S. atty. Washington, 1958-60, San Francisco, 1960-63; sole practice Augusta, 1963—. Capt. JAGC, U.S. Army, 1955-58. Mem. State Bar Ga., Spl. Master State Bar Ga., Augusta Bar Assn. (mem. exec. com., arbitrator), Am. Arbitration Assn. (arbitrator). Roman Catholic. Federal civil litigation, Probate, Franchising. Office: 1 Habersham Sq 3602 Wheeler Rd Augusta GA 30909-1826

**COOPER, BRAD,** lawyer; b. Phila., June 1, 1955; s. Stanton and Diane Cooper; m. Sharon Cooper, July 16, 1983; children: Kate, Sam, Ben. BS, St. Joseph's Coll., 1977; JD, Temple U., 1980. Bar: Pa. 1980, U.S. Dist. Ct. (ea. dist.) Pa. 1980. Jud. law clk. Phila. Ct. Common Pleas, 1980-81; assoc. Boardman & Schermer, Phila., 1981-85; ptnr. Schermer & Cooper, Phila., 1985—. Mem. ABA, Am. Trial Lawyers, Pa. Trial Lawyers, Phila. Bar Assn., Phila. Lawyers Club. General civil litigation, Insurance, Family and matrimonial. Office: Schermer and Cooper 1818 Market St Fl 37 Philadelphia PA 19103-3639

**COOPER, CANDACE DECAROL,** judge; b. .Los Angeles, Nov. 23, 1948; d. Cornelius M. and Eunice (Farris) C. B.A., U. So. Calif., 1970, JD, 1973. Bar: Calif. 1984. Assoc. Gibson Dunn & Crutcher, L.A., 1974-80; judge L.A. Mcpl. Ct., 1980-87, L.A. Superior Ct., 1987—. Bd. dirs. Watts Boys and Girls Club, L.A., 1981-87. Exceptional Children's Found., L.A., 1982-87. Mem. Nat. Bar Assn., Nat. Assn. Women Judges, Calif. Judges Assn. (pres. 1988-89), Calif. Assn. Black Lawyers (pres.-jud. 1983-84), Langston Bar Assn. (jud. convenor 1983-84), Calif. Women Lawyers. Office: 111 N Hill St Los Angeles CA 90012-3117

**COOPER, CECILIA MARIE,** lawyer, judge; b. Erie, Pa., Apr. 22, 1966; d. Ronald C. and Mary Anne Cooper. BA, Washington & Jefferson Coll., 1988; JD, Emory U., 1991. Bar: Ga. 1992, U.S. Dist. Ct. (mid. dist.) Ga. 1996. Law clk. Southwestern Jud. Cir., Americus, Ga., 1991-93; pvt. practice law Americus, 1993—; mcpl. ct. judge City of Richland, Ga., 1997—; mediator 3rd Adminstrv. Jud. Dist., Columbus, Ga., 1996—. Coach mock trial team Sumter County H.S., Americus, 1997—. Mem. Ga. Assn. Criminal Def. Attys., Exch. Club Americus (pres. 1997). Democrat. Roman Catholic. Avocations: guitar, reading. Criminal, Family and matrimonial, Probate. Office: 416 W Lamar St Americus GA 31709-3496

**COOPER, CLARENCE,** federal judge; b. 1942. BA, Clark Coll., 1964; JD, Emory U., 1967; MA, Harvard U., 1978. Atty. Atlanta Legal Aid Soc., 1967; asst. dist. atty. Fulton County, 1968-75; judge City of Atlanta Mcpl. Ct., 1975-80, Fulton County Superior Ct., 1980-90, Ga. Ct. Appeals, 1990-93; dist. judge U.S. Dist. Ct. (no. dist.) Ga., Atlanta, 1994—; co-chair Supreme Ct. Commn. Racial & Ethnic Bias in Ct. Sys. Mem. adv. com. Internat. Friendship Force; active Butler St. YMCA, Atlanta Conv. and Visitors Bur., 100 Black Men of Atlanta, Ga. Health Decisions. With U.S. Army, 1968-70. Decorated Bronze Star; recipient Al Thompson Award for Cmty. Svc., Thurgood Marshall award, Outstanding Jurist, 1974. Mem. ABA, NAACP, Nat. Bar Assn., State Bar Ga., Atlanta Bar Assn., Fed. Bar Assn., Gate City Bar Assn., Omega Phi Psi (Omega Man of Yr. award 1991), Kappa Boule, Lawyers Club Atlanta, Old Warhorse Lawyer's Club. Office: Richard B Russell Fed Bldg 1721 US Courthouse 75 Spring St SW Atlanta GA 30303-3309

**COOPER, CLEMENT THEODORE,** lawyer; b. Miami, Fla., Oct. 26, 1930; s. Benjamin Leon and Louise (Bethel) C.; m. Nan Coles Cooper; children: Patricia, Karen, Stephanie, Bridgette, Jessica (dec.), Stacy. AB, Lincoln U., 1952; student, Boston U., 1954-55; JD, Howard U., 1958; PhD in Bus. Adminstrn. honoris causa, Colo. Christian Coll. Bar: D.C. 1960, Mich. 1960, U.S. Supreme Ct. 1963. Sole practice Washington, 1960—; adj. prof. Strayer U., Washington; legal cons. No. Calif. Mining Assn. Author: Sealed Verdict, 1964; contbr. articles to legal jours. Mem. adv. coun. D.C. Dept. Welfare, 1963-66; mem. adv. bd. Com. on Irish Ethnicity, N.Y.C. Mem. ABA, ATLA, D.C. Bar Assn., Nat. Bar Assn., ACLU, Am. Judicature Soc., Rocky Mountain Mining Law Found., Internat. Platform Assn., Nat. Assn. Securities Dealers (arbitrator), Alpha Phi Alpha. Real property, Appellate, General civil litigation. Home: 728 Dahlia St NW Washington DC 20012-1844 Office: PO Box 76135 Washington DC 20013-6135

**COOPER, CORINNE,** law educator; b. Albuquerque, July 12, 1952; d. David D. and Martha Lucille (Rosenblum) C. BA magna cum laude, U. Ariz., 1975, JD summa cum laude, 1978. Bar: Ariz. 1978, U.S. Dist. Ct. Ariz. 1978, Mo. 1985. Assoc. Streich, Lang, Weeks & Cardon, Phoenix, 1978-82; asst. prof. U. Mo., Kansas City, 1982-86, assoc. prof., 1986-94, prof., 1994—; vis. prof. U. Wis., Madison, 1985, 91, U. Pa., Phila., 1988, U. Ariz., 1993, U. Colo., 1994. Author: (with Bruce Meyerson) A Drafter's Guide to Alternative Dispute Resolution, 1991; editor: The Portable UCC, 1993, 2d edit., 1996, Getting Graphic I and II, 1993, 94; editor in chief Bus. Law Today, 1995-97; contbr. articles to profl. jours., chpts. to books. Legal counsel Mo. for Hart campaign, 1984; dir. issues Goddard for Gov. campaign, 1990; bd. dirs. Com. for County Progress, Kansas City, 1985—. Mem. ABA (mem. coun. bus. sect. 1992-96, uniform comml. code com., chmn. membership com. 1992-94, editl. bd. Bus. Law Today, 1991-97, sect. of bus. law pubs. 1998—, jour. editorial bd. 1999—), Am. Assn. Law Schs. (comml. law 1982—, chair 1992-93, alternative dispute resolution com.), Am. Arbitration Assn. (arbitrator, mediator, mem. large complex case panel 1991-96), Mo. Bar Assn. (comml. law com.), Order of Coif, Phi Beta Kappa, Phi Kappa Phi. Democrat. Jewish. Office: U Mo Sch Law 5100 Rockhill Rd Kansas City MO 64110-2446

**COOPER, ELLEN SCHIFF,** lawyer; b. N.Y.C., Sept. 16, 1948; d. Nathan Schiff and Florence Goldstein; m. David Stephen Cooper, Aug. 23, 1970; children: Jonathan Micah, Ethan Alexander, Susanna Elizabeth. BA, Goucher Coll., 1969; MA, NYU, 1970; JD, Washington U., St. Louis, 1976; LLM, Harvard U., 1977. Bar: Mass. 1977, Md. 1985, U.S. Dist. Ct. Mass. 1977, U.S. Ct. Appeals (1st cir.), 1978, U.S. Dist. Ct. Md. 1987, U.S. Ct. Appeals (4th and 9th cirs.) 1990, U.S. Supreme Ct. 1992. Tchr. secondary sch. English, Avon (Mass.) Pub. Schs., 1970-73; law clk. to justices Superior Ct. Mass., Boston, 1977-78; assoc. Parker, Coulter, Daley & White, Boston, 1978-85; asst. atty. gen. Office Atty. Gen. Md., Balt., 1985-89, dep. chief antitrust divsn., 1989-92, chief antitrust divsn., 1992—. Contbg. author: (monograph) Antitrust Federalism: The Role of State Law, 1988; contbr. articles to law jours. Vol. Balt. Hebrew Congregation, Balt., 1987—; trustee Profs. Oncology Trust Fund, Md. chpt. Am. Cancer Soc., Balt., 1987—; com. mem., chmn. subcom. Goucher Coll. Alumnae and Alumni Fund, Towson, Md., 1993—. Mem. ABA, Nat. Assn. Attys. Gen. (chmn. health care working group 1990—, vice chmn. for amicus matters 1990-95, 98—, vice chmn. for legis. and policy 1995, Marvin award 1993), Md. Women's Bar Assn. Office: Office Atty Gen Antitrust Divsn 200 Saint Paul Pl Baltimore MD 21202-2004

**COOPER, EMILY K.,** lawyer; b. St. Paul, Nov. 14, 1969. BA cum laude, Macalester Coll., 1991; JD cum laude, U. Minn., 1996. Bar: Ohio 1996, Mich. 1997, U.S. Dist. Ct. (no. dist.) Ohio 1997, U.S. Dist. Ct. (ea. dist.) Mich. 1997, U.S. Ct. Appeals (6th cir.) 1997. Atty. Shumaker, Loop & Kendrick, Toledo, 1996—. Editor Jour. Law and Inequality, 1994-95. Bd. mem. South Toledo YMCA, 1997—, Maumee Valley Girl Scouts, Toledo, 1998—, Warren Sherman Area Coun., Toledo, 1998—. Mem. ABA, Ohio State Bar Assn., Toledo Bar Assn., Toledo Womens Bar Assn., Thurgood Marshall Bar Assn. (pres. 1999). Avocations: golf, martial arts. General civil litigation, Environmental, Family and matrimonial. Office: Shumaker Loop & Kendrick LLP 1000 Jackson St Toledo OH 43624-1573

**COOPER, GARY ALLAN,** lawyer; b. Bristol, Va., Feb. 3, 1947; s. Earl Clarence and Reba Evelyn (Jenkins) C.; m. Lynn Ellen Weir, Feb. 17, 1973; chidlren: Drew Kelsey, Gavin Morgan. BS in Journalism, U. Tenn., 1969, JD, 1972. Bar: Tenn. 1972, U.S. Dist. Ct. (ea. dist.) Tenn. 1972, U.S. Supreme Ct. 1979, Fla. 1981. Assoc. Luther, Anderson & Ruth, Chattanooga, 1972-76; ptnr. Luther, Anderson, Cleary, Luhowiak & Cooper, Chattanooga, 1976-79, Luther, Anderson, Cleary & Cooper, Chattanooga, 1979-80, Anderson, Cleary & Cooper, Chattanooga, 1981, Fleissner & Cooper, Chattanooga, 1982, Fleissner, Cooper & Marcus, Chattanooga, 1983-88, Fleissner Cooper Marcus & Steger, Chattanooga, 1988-89, Fleissner Cooper Marcus & Quinn, Chattanooga, 1990-97, Franklin, Cooper & Marcus, PLLC, Chattanooga, 1998—. Author: Tennessee Forms for Trial Practice, 1977, 4th edit., 1994, Tennessee Law Office Adminstration, 1977, Tenesee Forms for Trial Practice-Damages, 1997. With USAR, 1972-79. Recipient Herman Hickman Postgrad. scholarship for Athletes U. Tenn., 1969. Mem. ABA, Chattanooga Bar Assn. (bd. dirs. 1984-86), Fla. Bar Assn. (mem. out-of-state practitioners com. 1983-86), Tenn. Bar Assn., Tenn. Def. Lawyers Assn. (chmn. amicus curiae com. 1987-89), Phi Delta Phi, Signal Mt. Golf and Country Club. Republican. Methodist. Avocations: golf, reading. State civil litigation, Insurance, Federal civil litigation. Home: 55 Carriage Hl Signal Mountain TN 37377-2331 Office: Franklin Cooper & Marcus PLLC 837 Fortwood St Chattanooga TN 37403-2313

**COOPER, JAMES RUSSELL,** retired law educator; b. New Kensinston, Pa., July 21, 1928; s. John Edward and Isabella Bird (Bowen) C.; m. Carolyn Hocker, Sept. 21, 1953 (div. Dec. 1975); children: L. Rachel, Julia Anderoni, Evan Lloyd, Jennifer Meyer; m. Leigh Ann Brian, Feb. 25, 1995. BS in Econs., U. Pa., 1952, JD, 1955. Bar: D.C., 1955, U.S. Supreme Ct., 1964. Pres., chmn. Radio WKPA-AM, WYDD-FM, New Kensington, 1959-64; urban renewal dir. Redevelopment Authority, New Kensington, 1964-68; assoc. prof. U. Ill., Champaign-Urbana, 1968-74; prof. legal studies Ga. State U., Atlanta, 1974-94, emeritus prof., 1994—. Author: Twilights Last Gleaming, 1992, Real Estate Investments, 3d edit. 1982. Sgt. U.S. Army, 1946-48. Mem. Fed. Bar Assn., D.C. Bar Assn., Am. Real Estate Soc. (founder, dir.). Home: Two West Wesley Rd #4NW Atlanta GA 30305-3500

**COOPER, JAY LESLIE,** lawyer; b. Chgo., Jan. 15, 1929; s. Julius Jerome and Grayce (Wolkenheim) C.; m. Darice Richman, July 30, 1970; children: Todd, Leslie, Keith. J.D., De Paul U., 1951. Bar: Ill. 1951, Calif. 1953, U.S. Supreme Ct. 1965, N.Y. 1987. Ptnr. Cooper, Epstein & Hurewitz (and predecessors), Beverly Hills, Calif., 1955-93; ptnr. Manatt, Phelps & Phillips, L.A., 1993—; guest lectr. Advanced Profl. Program Legal Aspects of Music and Rec. Industry, U. So. Calif., 1968, 70, 75, Entertainment Industry Conf., 1971, Harvard Law Sch., 1985-98; guest lectr. Calif. Copyright Conf., 1967, 71, 73, 75, 77, 97, v.p., 1975, pres., 1976-77; co-chmn. ann. program The Rec. Contract, UCLA, 1977—; lectr. Midem, 1977-95, 96-97; adj. prof. entertainment law Loyola U. Law Sch., Los Angeles, 1978-80; moderator UCLA Seminar, 1994. Profl. musician with, Les Brown, Charlie Barnet, Frank Sinatra, Los Angeles Philharm. others, 1945-55; editor: (with Irwin O. Spiegel) Record and Music Publishing Forms of Agreement in Current Use, 1971, Annual Program on Legal Aspects of Entertainment Industry, Syllabus, 1966-70; contbr. (with Irwin O. Spiegel) articles to profl. jours. Named Entertainment Lawyer of Yr. Billboard mag., 1975. Mem. ABA (chmn. forum com. on entertainment and sports industries 1983-86), NARAS (chpt. pres. 1973-75, nat. pres. 1975-77), Beverly Hills Bar Assn. (co-chmn. entertainment law com. 1972-75), Calif. Copyright Soc. (pres. 1976), Los Angeles County Bar Assn., Calif. Bar Assn., Ill. Bar Assn., L.A. Copyright Soc., Internat. Assn. Entertainment Lawyers (exec. com.), French-Am. C. of C. Entertainment. Office: Manatt Phelps & Phillips 11355 W Olympic Blvd Los Angeles CA 90064-1614

**COOPER, LAWRENCE ALLEN,** lawyer; b. San Antonio, Feb. 1, 1948; s. Elmer E. and Sally (Tempkin) C.; 1 child, Jonathan Alexander. BA, Tulane

U., 1970; JD, St. Mary's U., San Antonio, 1974; LLM, Emory U., 1980. Bar: Ga. 1975, Tex. 1975. Ptnr. Cohen & Cohen, Atlanta, 1979-88; pvt. practice Atlanta, 1989—; arbitrator Fulton Superior Ct.; mem. Ga. Bar fee dispute com. Mem. ABA, ATLA, Atlanta Bar Assn., Ga. Trial Lawyers Assn., Tex. Bar Assn. E-mail: lacooperaty@mindspring.com. Personal injury, Family and matrimonial, Product liability. Home: 2460 Peachtree Rd NW Apt 1704 Atlanta GA 30305-4159 Office: 1770 Resurgens Plaza 945 E Paces Ferry Rd NE Atlanta GA 30326-1125

**COOPER, LINDA DAWN,** lawyer; b. Cleve., April 30, 1953; d. Robert Boyd and Catherine S. (Powell) C. B.S. in Psychology with honors, Eastern Ky. U., 1975; J.D., Cleve.-Marshall Law Sch., 1977. Bar: Ohio 1978, U.S. Dist. Ct. (no. dist.) Ohio 1980. Law clk. Vanik, Monroe, Zucco and Klein, Cleve., 1976-78; legal intern Cleve.-Marshall Legal Clinic, 1977; assoc. Vanik, Monroe, Zucco, Klein & Scanlon, Cleve. and Chesterland, Ohio, 1978-79; sr. staff atty. Lake County Pub. Defender, Painesville, Ohio, 1979-80; ptnr. Heffernan & Cooper, Painesville, Cleve., 1980-83; sole practice Painesville, 1983-94, ptnr. Cooper & Forbes, Painesville, Ohio, 1994— ; lectr. criminal justice seminar, Painesville, 1981, family law seminar, 1994, 99. Speaker, adv., counselor Cleve. Rape Crisis Center, 1976; appointee Congressman Eckart's Com. on Health, Environment and Energy, Mentor, Ohio, 1983; chmn. juvenile justice com. LWV, Painesville, 1983; councilwoman Willoughby (Ohio) City Council,1984; grand jury forewoman, Lake County, 1986. Mem. Assn. Trial Lawyers Am., ABA, Ohio Bar Assn., Lake County Bar Assn. (treas. 1999). Democrat. Episcopalian. General practice, Estate planning, Family and matrimonial. Home: 5534 Wrens Ln # D Willoughby OH 44094-3253 Office: 166 Main St Painesville OH 44077-3403

**COOPER, MARGARET LESLIE,** lawyer; b. Geneva, N.Y., Apr. 13, 1950; d. Jack Frederick and Barbara Ann (Hitchings) C. BA in Math., Rollins Coll., 1972; JD, Mercer U., 1976. Bar: Fla. 1976, U.S. Dist. Ct. (so. dist.) Fla. 1977, U.S. Ct. Appeals (5th cir.) 1977, U.S. Ct. Appeals (11th cir.) 1981; bd. cert. civil litigation and bus. litigation. Assoc. Jones, Foster, Johnston & Stubbs, PA, West Palm Beach, Fla., 1976-81, ptnr., 1981—; assoc. prof. Palm Beach Jr. Coll., West Palm Beach, 1985-86. Pres. Young People's Pres.'s Coun., Norton Gallery Art, West Palm Beach, 1982-84; chmn. campaign Lou Frey for Gov., Palm Beach County, 1986; bd. dirs. Planned Parenthood of Palm Beach; bd. trustees Ann Norton Sculpture Gardens. Named to Sports Hall Fame, Rollins Coll., 1986, 88, Winter Park H.S. Sports Hall of Fame, 1998. Fellow Am. Bar Found.; mem. Palm Beach County Bar Assn., Exec. Women Palm Beach, Palm Beach Jr. League, Women's Internat. Tennis Assn. (disciplinary rev. bd. 1985), Adult Tennis Coun., U.S. Tennis Assn. (pres.-elect Fla. sect., vice chair grievance com.), The Beach Club. Republican. Avocations: tennis, snow skiing. Contracts commercial, Consumer commercial. Home: 2121 S Flagler Dr West Palm Beach FL 33401-8005 Office: Jones Foster Johnston & Stubbs PA PO Box 3475 West Palm Beach FL 33402-3475

**COOPER, MARY LITTLE,** federal judge, former banking commissioner; b. Fond du Lac, Wis., Aug. 13, 1946; d. Ashley Jewell and Gertrude (McCoy) Little; m. John Francis Parell, May 28, 1972 (div. 1990); children: Christie, Morgan, Shawn, John Brady; m. John F. Cooper, Dec. 26, 1997. AB in Polit. Sci. cum laude, Bryn Mawr Coll., 1968; JD, Villanova U., 1972; LLD (hon.), Georgian Ct. Coll., 1987. Bar. N.J. 1972. Assoc. McCarter & English, Newark, 1972-80, ptnr., 1980-84; commr. N.J. Dept. Banking, Trenton, 1984-90; assoc. gen. counsel Prudential Property & Casualty Ins. Co., Holmdel, N.J., 1991-92; judge U.S. Dist. Ct. N.J., 1992—; chmn. bd. Pinelands Devel. Credt Bank. Bd. trustees Exec. Commn. Ethical Standards, Trenton, 1984-90, Corp. Bus. Assistance, Trenton, 1984-91, N.J. Housing & Mortgage Fin. Agy., Trenton, 1984-90, N.J. Cemetery Bd. Assn., 1984-90, N.J. Hist. Soc., 1976-79., YMCA of Greater Newark, 1973-76, Diocesan Investment; mem. Supreme Ct. N.J. Civil Practice Com., 1982-84, Supreme Ct. N.J. Dist. Ethics Com., 1982-84; lay assesor Ecclesiastical Ct. Episc. Diocese Newark, 1980-84. Fellow Am. Bar Found.; mem. ABA, N.J. Bar Assn., Princeton Bar Assn., John J. Gibbons Am. Inn of Ct. Office: US Courthouse 402 E State St Ste 5000 Trenton NJ 08608-1507

**COOPER, MICHAEL ANTHONY,** lawyer; b. Passaic, N.J., Mar. 29, 1936. B.A., Harvard U., 1957, LL.B., 1960. Bar: N.Y. State 1961, U.S. Supreme Ct. 1969. With firm Sullivan & Cromwell, N.Y.C., 1960—; ptnr. Sullivan & Cromwell, 1968—; pres. Legal Aid Soc., 1981-83; bd. fellows Inst. Jud. Adminstrn. Co-chair Lawyers Com. for Civil Rights Under Law, 1993-95; bd. dirs. Fund for Modern Cts., Vols. of Legal Svcs. Fellow Am. Coll. Trial Lawyers; mem. ABA, N.Y. State Bar Assn., Assn. Bar City N.Y. (chmn. exec. com. 1996-97, v.p. 1997-98, pres. 1998-99), Fed. Bar Coun. (trustee ), Am. Law Inst., Am. Judicature Soc. Federal civil litigation, Antitrust, Securities. Office: Sullivan & Cromwell 125 Broad St Fl 28 New York NY 10004-2489

**COOPER, MICHAEL LEE,** lawyer; b. Roseburg, Oreg., July 9, 1958; s. Leroy Everett Cooper and Mattie Verline Orrell. BS with honors, U. Oreg., 1979, JD, 1984. Bar: Oreg. 1984, U.S. Dist. Ct. Oreg. 1986, U.S. Ct. Appeals (9th cir.) 1988, U.S. Supreme Ct. 1988. Pvt. practice Eugene, Oreg., 1984—. Speaker seminar Clergy and the Law, 1992-93. Deacon 1st Landmark Missionary Bapt. Ch., Springfield, Oreg., 1984—, treas. 1997—; trustee Union Roque Bapt. Camp, Springfield, 1985-98; tchr. Bapt. history Springfield Sch. of Bible, 1992-96, tchr. ancient history, 1984-96. Mem. Oreg. State Bar. General practice, Estate planning, Personal injury. Home: 1465 Cottonwood Ave Springfield OR 97477-7661 Office: 895 Country Club Rd Ste C175 Eugene OR 97401-6006

**COOPER, N. LEE,** lawyer; m. Joy Clark; children: Clark, Catherine. BS, U. Ala., 1963, LLB, 1964. Pvt. practice Birmingham, Ala., 1966—; founder Maynard, Cooper & Gale, P.C., Birmingham. Articles and Notes editor Ala. Law Rev., 1962-64. Nat. bd. dirs. U. Ala.; trustee Ala. Law Sch. Found. 1st lt. U.S. Army, 1964-66, capt. USAR. Fellow Am. Bar Found.; mem. ABA (chair, litig. sect. 1985-86, sec. litig. sect. 1976-78, Birmingham bar del. to ho. of deps. 1979-80, Ala. del. to ho. of dels. 1980-89, chair ho. of dels. drafting com. on model rules of profl. conduct 1982-84, mem. commn. on professionalism 1985-87, chair select com. on ho. of dels. 1989-90, chair ho. of dels. 1990-92, pres.-elect 1995-96, pres. 1996-97), Am. Judicature Soc. (dir.), Am. Bar Endowment (dir.), Am. Law Inst. (council, advisor project on restatement of law governing lawyers), Ala. Bar Assn. (pres. young lawyers sect. 1974-75, Merit award 1976), Birmingham Bar Assn. (sec.-treas. 1972, vice chair congl. commn. on structural alts. for the fed. cts. of appeals, dir. lawyers com. for civil rights). Office: AmSouth Harbert Plz 1901 6th Ave N Ste 2400 Birmingham AL 35203-4604

**COOPER, NEIL A.,** lawyer; b. Haverford, Pa., Feb. 25, 1969; s. Lawrence B. and Marilyn M. Cooper; m. Susan Hass, Aug. 6, 1995; 1 child, Matthew A. AB, Harvard U., 1991; JD, Columbia U., 1995. Bar: Pa. 1995, N.J. 1995. Assoc. Morgan, Lewis & Bockius LLP, Phila., 1995—. Office: Morgan Lewis & Bockius 1701 Market St Philadelphia PA 19103-2903

**COOPER, RANDALL F.,** lawyer; b. Rochester, N.H., Nov. 28, 1946. Grad., Phillips Exeter Acad.; AB, Dartmouth Coll., 1969; JD, Boston U., 1976. Bar: N.H. 1976, Maine 1987. Ptnr. Cooper, Deans & Cargill, North Conway, N.H. Chmn. N.H. Bd. Probation, 1979-83. Comdr. USN, 1969-73, USNR, 1973-94, ret. Mem. ABA, ATLA, N.H. Trial Lawyers Assn., N.H. Bar Assn. (bd. govs. 1985-89, v.p. 1996-97, pres. 1998-99), Carroll County Bar Assn., New Eng. Bar Assn.. Maine State Bar Assn. Personal injury, General civil litigation, Municipal (including bonds). Office: Cooper Deans & Cargill PA PO Box 450 92 Pine St North Conway NH 03860-5210*

**COOPER, RICHARD CASEY,** lawyer; b. Tulsa, Jan. 20, 1942; s. Winston Churchill and Frances Margaret (Coppinger) C.; m. Ireen Lysbeth Evans, Nov. 24, 1965; children: Christopher Casey, Kimberly Ireen. BSBA, U. Tulsa, 1965, JD, 1967. Bar: Okla. 1967, U.S. Dist. Ct. (no., ea. and we. dists.) Okla. 1967, U.S. Ct. Mil. Appeals 1967, U.S. Ct. Appeals (10th cir.) 1972. Assoc. Boesche, McDermott & Eskridge, Tulsa, 1972-76, ptnr., 1977-92, mng. ptnr., 1990—. Editor in chief: Tulsa Law Jour., 1967. Counsel Tulsa Philharm. Orch., 1990-92; trustee Mervin Bovaird Found., Tulsa, 1991—, pres., 1995—; trustee The Philbrook Mus. Art, 1997—. Lt. USNR, 1967-71, mil. judge JAGC, 1970-71. Villard Martin scholar U. Tulsa, 1967, recipient Order of the Curule Chair, 1967. Mem. ABA, Okla. Bar Assn., Tulsa County Bar Assn., So. Hills Country Club. Republican. Avocations: family activities, fly fishing, travel. General civil litigation, General corporate, Environmental. Home: 2923 E 58th St Tulsa OK 74105-7453 Office: Boesche McDermott Eskridge 100 W 5th St Ste 800 Tulsa OK 74103-4291

**COOPER, RICHARD MELVYN,** lawyer; b. Phila., Nov. 13, 1942; s. Arthur Martin and Sophia Phyllis (Gottlieb) C.; m. Sabina Abbe Karp, June 12, 1965 (div. 1978); children: Alexander, Stephanie; m. Judith Carole Areen, Feb. 17, 1979; children: Benjamin, Jonathan. BA summa cum laude, Haverford Coll., 1964; BA 1st class, Oxford U., 1966, MA, 1970; JD summa cum laude, Harvard U., 1969. Bar: D.C. 1970, U.S. Ct. Appeals (5th, 6th and 9th cirs.) 1988, U.S. Ct. Appeals (10th cir.) 1982, U.S. Ct. Appeals (11th cir.) 1984, U.S. Ct. Appeals (fed. cir.) 1985, U.S. Ct. Appeals (4th cir.) 1997, U.S. Supreme Ct. 1973. Law clk. to Justice William J. Brennan, Jr. U.S. Supreme Ct., Washington, 1969-70; sr. lectr. Law Devel. Ctr., Kampala, Uganda, 1970-71; assoc. Williams, Connolly & Califano, Washington, 1971-77; chief counsel FDA, Rockville, Md., 1977-79; ptnr. Williams & Connolly, Washington, 1980—, mem. exec. com., 1983-84, 89-92; sr. mem. Office Energy Policy and Planning, Exec. Office of Pres., Washington, 1977; adj. prof. Georgetown U. Law Ctr., Washington, 1987-92, 96; mem. Adminstrv. Conf. U.S., 1978-79, Jud. Conf. D.C., Washington, 1979; mem. Adv. Panel on Strategies for Med. Tech. Assessment, Washington, 1980-81; mem. coms. NAS, 1980-83, 87-90. Editor: Food and Drug Law, 1991; co-editor: Fundamentals of Law and Regulation, 1997; contbr. articles to profl. jours. Chief counsel credentials com. Dem. Nat. Conv., Washington and N.Y.C., 1976; bd. mgrs. Haverford Coll., 1997—. Rhodes Trust scholar 1964; recipient FDA Award of Merit, 1979. Jewish. Office: Williams & Connolly 725 12th St NW Washington DC 20005-5901

**COOPER, ROBERT ELBERT,** state supreme court justice; b. Chattanooga, Oct. 14, 1920; s. John Thurman and Susie Inez (Hollingsworth) C.; m. Catherine Pauline Kelly, Nov. 24, 1949; children: Susan Florence Cooper Hodges, Bobbie Cooper Martin, Kelly Ann Smith, Robert Elbert Jr. B.A., U. N.C., 1946; J.D., Vanderbilt U., 1949. Bar: Tenn. 1948. Asso. Kolwyck and Clark, 1949-51; partner Cooper and Barger, 1951-53; asst. atty. gen. 6th Jud. Ct. Tenn., 1951-53; judge 6th Jud. Circuit Tenn., 1953-60; judge Tenn. Ct. Appeals, 1960-70, presiding judge Eastern div., 1970-74; justice Tenn. Supreme Ct., 1974-90, chief justice, 1976-77, 84-85; chmn. Tenn. Jud. Coun., 1967-90; chmn. Tenn. Code Commn., 1976-77, 84-85; mem. Tenn. Jud. Standards Commn., 1971-77. Mem. exec. bd. Cherokee council Boy Scouts Am., 1960-64; bd. dirs. Met. YMCA, 1956-65, St. Barnabas Nursing Home and Apts. for Aged, 1966-69. With USNR, 1941-46. Recipient Nat. Heritage award Downtown Sertoma Club, Chattanooga, 1989. Mem. Am., Tenn., Chattanooga bar assns., Conf. Chief Justices, Phi Beta Kappa, Order of Coif, Kappa Sigma, Phi Alpha Delta. Democrat. Presbyterian. Clubs: Signal Mountain Golf and Country, Masons (33 deg.), Shriners. Home and Office: 196 Woodcliff Cir Signal Mountain TN 37377-3147

**COOPER, ROBERT GORDON,** lawyer; b. Roanoke, Va., July 2, 1953; s. Arthur Darrah and C. Jane (Redman) C.; m. Ruth K. Cathcart, June 7, 1975; 1 child, Kimberly Anne. BBA, Furman U., 1974; JD, U. S.C., 1977. Bar: S.C. 1977, U.S. Dist. Ct. S.C. 1977, U.S. Ct. Appeals (4th cir.) 1980, U.S. Supreme Ct. 1982. Assoc. Robinson, McFadden, Moore & Pope, Columbia, S.C., 1977-80; asst. city atty. City of Columbia, 1980-82; pvt. practice Columbia, 1982-98; asst. city atty. City of Columbia, 1998—. Advisor, lectr. City of Columbia Police Dept.; elder Grace Fellowship Ch., Columbia. Mem. S.C. Bar Assn., Richland County Bar Assn. State civil litigation, Consumer commercial, Personal injury. Home: 104 Old Ridge Ct Columbia SC 29212-1355 Office: PO Box 147 Columbia SC 29217-0001

**COOPER, R(OBERT) MAURICE,** lawyer, accountant; b. Spokane, Wash., Sept. 27, 1915; s. Robert and Fenella (Christianson) C.; m. Margaret E. Millgard, Dec. 1, 1941 (div. 1976); children: Robert M., Theodore J., Maureen E. Cooper Everett; m. Donna Southern, June 13, 1996. LLM, Gonzaga U., 1941, LLD (hon.), 1967; MCS, Kinman Edn., 1946. Bar: Wash. 1941; CPA, Wash. Regional sales mgr. Remington Rand, Inc., Seattle, 1940-43; regional acctg. supr. Office Price Adminstrn., Spokane, 1943-46; pvt. practice law Spokane, 1946-97; ptnr. Cooper & Roberts, Spokane, 1970-81; lectr., atty. Wash. Assn. Realtors, Spokane, 1968-83. Pres. Spokane Interstate Fair, 1946. Named One of Outstanding Young Men of Wash., Jr. C. of C., 1946, 47; recipient Eddy award Wash. Real Estate Found., 1977. Mem. ABA, Wash. State Bar Assn. (chmn. legis. com., arbitratgion com.), Spokane County Bar Assn. (bd. dirs. 1946), Spokane Estate Planning Coun. (charter, pres. 1964), Moose (internat. pres. 1976-77), Lions (dist. gov. 1978-79), Manito, Shriners. Episcopalian. Avocations: hunting, fishing, golf, sports. Family and matrimonial, Probate, Real property. Home: 17611 N Saddle Hill Rd Colbert WA 99005-9635 Office: 515 W Francis Ave Ste 5 Spokane WA 99205-6413

**COOPER, SONJA JEAN MULLER,** lawyer; b. N.Y.C., Oct. 23, 1942; d. William Otto and Bertha Ella (Moos) Muller; m. Glenn Roy Cooper, Aug. 12, 1972; 1 child, Gregory Ross. BS, Syracuse U., 1964, MS, 1968; EdD, Columbia U., 1975; JD, Yeshiva U., 1986. Bar: N.Y. Tchr. Syracuse (N.Y.) City Schs., 1964-66, North Syracuse (N.Y.) Ctrl. Schs., 1966-72; assoc. prof. Coll. of New Rochelle, N.Y., 1975-84; assoc. Glenn Roy Cooper, P.C., N.Y.C., 1987—; fair hearing officer N.Y. State Dept. Edn., 1990—. Contbr. to book Souls in Extremis, 1972. Bd. dirs. Westchester Holocaust Commn., recording sec., Louise and Arde Bulova Fund, 1995—; mem. legal panel N.Y. State Commn. on Quality of Care for the Mentally Disabled, 1992—; pres. Joseph Bulova Found., N.Y.C., 1993-98, Tanglewood Acres Adult Home, Inc., 1993—, NOW, Onondonga County, N.Y., 1971-72, Westchester County, N.Y., 1993—. Grantee U.S. Dept. Health, Edn. and Welfare, Columbia U., 1972-73. Mem. N.Y. State Bar Assn. (com. on issues affecting persons with disabilities), Bar Assn. City of N.Y. Avocations: reading, walking. Personal injury, Constitutional, Pension, profit-sharing, and employee benefits. Office: 405 Lexington Ave New York NY 10174-0002

**COOPER, STEPHANIE R.,** lawyer; b. Phila., Sept. 8, 1944; d. Eli Louis and Dvora (Wolinsky) C.; 1 child, Joshua Cooper Olesker. BA, Sarah Lawrence Coll., 1965, MFA, 1976; JD, Yeshiva U., 1986. Bar: Conn. 1987, N.Y. 1988, U.S. Dist. Ct. (so. and ea. dists.) N.Y. 1988. Assoc. Edwards & Angell, N.Y.C., 1986-88, Burrows, Poster & Franzblau, N.Y.C., 1988-90, Janvey Gordon, N.Y.C., 1990-95; of counsel Moses & Singer LLP, N.Y.C., 1995—. Author: Get Your Back in Shape, 1984. Mem. ABA, Assn. of Bar of City of N.Y. Avocations: chamber music, fiction and non-fiction writing, painting. Intellectual property, Entertainment, General practice. Office: Moses & Singer LLP 1301 Avenue of The Americas New York NY 10019-6022

**COOPER, STEPHEN HERBERT,** lawyer; b. N.Y.C., Mar. 29, 1939; s. Walter S. and Selma (Herbert) C.; m. Linda Cohen, Aug. 29, 1965 (dec.); m. Karen Gross, Sept. 6, 1981; 1 child, Zachary Noel. A.B., Columbia U., 1960, J.D. cum laude, 1965. Bar: N.Y. 1965. Assoc. Breed, Abbott & Morgan, N.Y.C., 1965-66; assoc. Weil, Gotshal & Manges, N.Y.C., 1966-73, ptnr., 1973—; lectr. Nat. Inst. Securities Regulation U. Colo., Boulder, 1985, Practicing Law Inst. 25th Annual Nat. Inst. Securities Regulation, N.Y.C., 1993, Law Jours. Seminars, 1997, 98. Served to lt. USNR, 1960-62. Fellow Am. Bar Found.; mem. ABA (com. fed. regulation securities, subcom. internat. securities matters, co-chmn. 1990—). Securities, General corporate, Private international. Home: 1125 Park Ave New York NY 10128-1243 Office: Weil Gotshal & Manges LLP 767 5th Ave Fl Concl New York NY 10153-0119

**COOPER, STEVEN MARK,** law educator; b. N.Y.C., Apr. 9, 1947; s. Fred Morris and Martha (Tieger) C.; divorced. BA, NYU, 1970; MS, N.Mex. Highlands U., 1973; MA, U. Calif., Santa Barbara, 1978; JD with honors, Rutgers U., 1985; LLM, Harvard U., 1990. Bar: N.J. 1985, U.S. Dist. Ct. N.J. 1985, N.Y. 1986. Pres., chief exec. officer RT, Inc., Bronx, N.Y., 1978-86; adj. prof. law sch. We. State U., San Diego, 1986-87, Nat. U., San Diego, 1988-89; assoc. prof. Tex. Wesleyan U. Sch. Law, Irving, Tex., 1990-97, Appalachian Sch. Law, Grundy, Va., 1997—; corp. assoc. Paul, Weiss, Rifkind, Wharton and Garrison, N.Y.C., 1985-86. Articles editor Rutgers Computer & Tech., 1984-85; sr. editor Harvard Jour. Law and Pub. Policy, 1984-85. Sustaining mem. Rep. Nat. Com. Mem. ABA, Federalist Soc. (founder, pres. Rutgers chpt., 1984). Avocations: computers, walking. Home and Office: 2350 Ballycastle Dr Dallas TX 75228-2920

**COOPER, THOMAS RANDOLPH,** lawyer; b. Bath, Maine, July 8, 1953; s. Tommy Gene and Cecile Sunshine (Butler) C.; m. Twila Ann Pirkle, Sept. 15, 1984; 1 child, Kimberly Nicole. BS, U. Houston, 1975; JD, South Tex. Coll. Law, Houston, 1978. Bar: Tex. 1978, U.S. Dist. Ct. (so., no., ea. and we. dists.) Tex. 1987, U.S. Ct. Appeals (5th cir.) 1991. Gen. counsel Umm Al-Qaiwain Oil Consortium, United Arab Emirates, 1978-80; assoc. Hill & Spochansky, Dubai, United Arab Emirates, 1979-81; gen. counsel, v.p. Unigulf Petroleum, Inc., Dubai, 1981; legal cons. Azusa Internat., Ltd., Sharjah, United Arab Emirates, 1982; assoc. Shoemake & Selwyn, Houston, 1982-85, Law Offices of David N. Williams, Houston, 1987-92; sole practitioner Houston, 1985-87, 92—; bd. dirs. Hazard Assessment Leaders, Inc., Houston. Columnist What's On Mag., 1981-82. Sigma Nu ednl. grantee, 1975. Mem. Coll. of State Bar of Tex., Nat. Assn. Eagle Scouts, Masons, Omicron Delta Kappa. Republican. Methodist. Avocations: woodworking, photography. General practice, Construction, General corporate. Home: 1158 Chantilly Ln Houston TX 77018-3240 Office: 119 E 20th St Houston TX 77008-2563

**COOPER, WENDY FEIN,** lawyer; b. Irvington, N.J., May 10, 1946; d. Jacob and Rose (Rothman) Fein; m. James C. Faltot, Apr. 4, 1971 (div. 1982); m. Leonard J. Cooper, June 19, 1983; children: Jennifer Regan, Ian Joshua. AB cum laude, Bryn Mawr Coll., 1968; JD, Temple U., 1973, LLM in Taxation, 1983. Assoc. Beitch & Block, Phila., 1973-76, ptnr., 1976-80; assoc. Narin & Chait, Phila., 1980-83, ptnr., 1983-85; assoc. Griffith & Burr P.C., Phila., 1985-87; shareholder Dolchin, Slotkin & Todd, P.C., Phila., 1987—. Bd. dirs., sec. Phila. Festival Theatre for New Plays, 1981-97. Mem. ABA, N.J. Bar Assn., Phila. Bar Assn. Taxation, general, Probate, General corporate. Home: 1603 Harris Rd Laverock PA 19038-7206 Office: Dolchin Slotkin & Todd PC 2005 Market St Fl 24 Philadelphia PA 19103-7042

**COOPER, WILLIAM S.,** state supreme court justice. BA, U. Ky., 1963, JD with high distinction, 1970. Justice Ky. Supreme Ct., Frankfort, 1996—. Capt. USAF, 1963-67. Office: Supreme Ct Ky 2825 Ring Rd Elizabethtown KY 42701*

**COOTER, DALE A.,** lawyer; b. Syracuse, N.Y., Aug. 28, 1948; s. Charles Henry and Mavis Elizabeth (Wagner) C.; m. Mary Kathryn Nolan, Oct. 8, 1977; children: John Andrew, Jessica Averie. BA cum laude, SUNY, Fredonia, 1970; JD, Georgetown U., 1975. Bar: Md. 1975, D.C. 1976, Va. 1984, U.S. Dist. Ct. Md. 1976, U.S. Dist. Ct. D.C. 1976, U.S. Ct. Appeals (4th and D.C. cirs.) 1976, U.S. Supreme Ct. 1979. Ptnr. Cooter, Mangold, Tompert & Wayson, P.L.L.C., Washington, 1976—; adj. prof. law Georgetown U., Washington, 1985—. Editor Georgetown U. Law Jour., 1973-75. Served with N.G. Mem. ABA, Va. Bar Assn., Md. Bar Assn., D.C. Bar Assn. Federal civil litigation, State civil litigation. Home: 4675 Kenmore Dr NW Washington DC 20007-1914 Office: Cooter Mangold Tompert & Wayson PLLC 5301 Wisconsin Ave NW Ste 500 Washington DC 20015-2015

**COOVER, ANN E.,** lawyer; b. Sparta, Wis., Aug. 23, 1948; d. Orlin H. Runde and Kathleen Ann Dwyer; m. David M. Coover, July 22, 1972; 1 child, D. Marshall. BS, U. Wis., 1971; JD magna cum laude, U. Houston, 1975. Bd. cert. family law Tex. Bd. Legal Specialization. Sr. law clk. to dist. judge U.S. Dist. Ct., Corpus Christi, Tex., 1976-78; ptnr. Coover & Coover, Corpus Christi, 1978—. Chair Am. Cancer Soc. Cattlemen's Ball, Corpus Christi, 1998; chair Auction for Art Mus. Gala, Corpus Christi, 1997. Avocations: gardening, antiques, bridge. Environmental, Alternative dispute resolution. Office: Coover & Coover 921 N Chaparral St Corpus Christi TX 78401-2008

**COPANI, ANTHONY FRANK,** lawyer; b. Syracuse, N.Y., Mar. 13, 1957; s. Salvatore and Virginia C.; m. Kathleen P. Fornito, Apr. 1, 1978; children: Anthony S., Marc J., Elizabeth K. BA, Syracuse U., 1981, JD, 1983. Bar: N.Y. 1984, U.S. Dist. Ct. (no. dist.) N.Y. 1984. Law clk.Dept. Social Svcs. Onondaga County, Syracuse, 1983-84, dep. county atty. dept. law, 1985-89; pvt. practice, ptnr. Mannion & Copani, 1989—; bd. dirs., gen. counsel Just For Babies, Inc. Campaign worker Rep., Syracuse, 1985, 87. Recipient cert. of appreciation March of Dimes, 1986; named One of Outstanding Young Men of Am., 1987. Mem. N.Y. State Bar Assn. Avocations: golf, basketball, reading. General civil litigation, Personal injury, Federal civil litigation. Home: 7592 Winterhaven Dr Liverpool NY 13088-3624 Office: Mannion Copani Alderman & Brown 306 Syracuse Bldg 224 Harrison St Syracuse NY 13202-3039

**COPE, JOHN R(OBERT),** lawyer; b. San Angelo, Tex., May 30, 1942; s. Robert Lloyd and Meta (Young) C.; m. Jeannette L. Naylor; 1 child, Lloyd Chapman. BBA, U. Tex., 1964, JD, 1966. Bar: Tex. 1966, D.C. 1976. Ptnr. Bracewell & Patterson, Attys., Houston, 1966-76; ptnr. Bracewell & Patterson, Attys., Washington, 1976—, mem. adv. mgmt. com., 1987-90; sr. ptnr., 1994—; vice chmn. bd. dirs., gen. counsel Century Nat. Bank, Washington, 1982—; bd. dirs., gen. counsel Columbia Nat. Bank, Washington, 1987-90; bd. dirs., v.p., gen. counsel Century Bancshares, Washington, 1985—; mem. fed. savs. and loan adv. coun. Fed. Home Loan Bank Bd., Washington, 1980-81; chmn., lectr. Practicing Law Inst. Seminars on Energy Litigation, Washington, 1980, 81; chief judge Wake Island Ct., Wake Island, North Pacific Ocean, 1989. Bd. govs. Wesley Theol. Sem., Washington, 1997—; mem. devel. bd. Lon Morris Coll., Lake Jackson, Tex., 1974-76; mem. Southwest U. Spl. Edn. Found., San Marcos, Tex., 1973-76; v.p., dir. Harris County Easter Seal Soc., Houston, 1972-76; bd. dirs., sec. Nemours Wildlife Found., Yemassee, S.C., 1993—; treas. Dem. Party Harris County, Houston, 1976-77; mem. nat. fin. coun. Dem. Nat. Com., Washington, 1976-80; cert. lay spkr. United Meth. Ch., dist. dir. lay speaking dist. Washington-Columbia. Mem. ABA (mem. litigation sect.), D.C. Bar Assn. (mem. litigation and govt. contracts sect.), Tex. Bar Assn. (mem. litigation sect.), Houston Bar Assn. (mem. gen. litigation sect.), Orton Soc. Republican. General civil litigation, Government contracts and claims, Banking. Office: Bracewell & Patterson 2000 K St NW Ste 500 Washington DC 20006-1872

**COPE, JOSEPH ADAMS,** lawyer; b. Summit, N.J., Jan. 15, 1945; s. Joseph H. and Eunice (Adams) Cope; m. Michele Zeleny, Sept. 25, 1982. BA, U. Colo., 1967, JD, 1976. Bar: Colo. 1976, U.S. Dist. Ct. Colo. 1976, U.S. Ct. Appeals (10th cir.) 1977, U.S. Claims Ct. 1984, U.S. Supreme Ct. 1984, Calif. 1985. Assoc. Vranesh & Musick, Boulder, Colo., 1976-78; ptnr. Musick and Cope, Boulder, Colo., 1978-91; of counsel Frascona, Joiner and Goodman, P.C., Boulder, 1991—. Served to lt. USN, 1967-73. Mem. ABA, Colo. Bar Assn., Boulder County Bar Assn., State Bar Calif., Lawyer-Pilots Bar Assn., Order of Coif. Avocation: raising shire draft horses. General civil litigation, Natural resources. Home: 8595 N 95th St Longmont CO 80504-7768 Office: Frascona Joiner & Goodman 4750 Table Mesa Dr Boulder CO 80303-5500

**COPE, THOM K.,** lawyer; b. Bremen, Fed. Republic Germany, Feb. 26, 1948; came to U.S., 1960; s. Ray and Gabriele E. (Meyer) C.; m. Melba D. Van Hemert, Nov. 8, 1980. BA with honors, Syracuse U., 1969; JD, U. Nebr., 1972. Bar: Nebr. 1972, U.S. Dist. Ct. Nebr. 1972, U.S. Ct. Appeals (8th cir.) 1972, Calif. 1976, U.S. Dist. Ct. (no. dist.) Calif. 1976, U.S. Ct. Appeals (9th cir.) 1976, U.S. Supreme Ct. 1987, U.S. Claims Ct. 1988, U.S. Ct. Appeals (D.C. cir.) 1990. Agy. legal counsel Nebr. Workers' Compensation Ct., Lincoln, 1972-73; assoc. counsel Fireman's Fund Ins. Co., San Francisco, 1973-76; asst. gen. counsel Argonaut Ins. Co., Menlo Park, Calif., 1976-78; assoc. counsel Ins. Svcs. Office, N.Y.C., 1978-82; assoc. atty. Tate & Assocs., Nebr., 1982-83, Bailey, Polsky, Cada & Todd, Nebr., 1983-84; ptnr. Bailey, Polsky, Cope & Knapp, Lincoln, 1984-97, Polsky Cope Shiffermiller & Coe, Lincoln, 1997—; judge Nebr. Commn. of Indsl. Rels., 1986-91; mem. Nebr. Supreme Ct. Gender Bias Task Force; mem. Nebr. Motor Vehicle Industry Licensing Bd.; mem. Fed. Practice Adv. Com.; lectr. in field; bd. dirs. Nat. Org. Women. Author: Executive Guide to Employment Practices, 1985, 3d edit., 1999. Bd. dirs. Friends of Elderly Found., Lincoln, 1986-90, Capital Humane Soc., Planned Parenthood Lincoln, 1997—, v.p., 1998, pres. 1999-00; bd. dirs. Child Advocacy Ctr., 1995-97; bd. trustees Lincoln Bar Assn. Fellow Coll. Employment and Labor Law; mem. Nat. Employ & Lawyers Assn., Nebr. Bar Assn. (labor and employment sect., exec. com., sec.), Nebr. Trial Lawyers Assn. Avocation: golf. Fax: (402) 484-7714. Labor, State civil litigation, Civil rights. Home: 2244 Heritage Pines Ct Lincoln NE 68506-2874 Office: Polsky Cope Shiffermiller and Coe 3901 Normal Blvd Ste 102 Lincoln NE 68506-5200

**COPE-GIBBS, AMY MICHELLE,** paralegal; b. Jerseyville, Ill., Apr. 28, 1972; d. Robert Jerry Cope Jr. (dec.) and Cynthia Lea (Mayhall) Hayes; stepfather Steven Duane Hayes; m. Jon Michael Gibbs, Aug. 13, 1994. Student, Culver-Stockton Coll., 1990-91; AAS in Legal Asst., St. Louis (Mo.) C.C., 1994. Paralegal, legal sec. Strang & Barron Law Firm, Jerseyville, Ill., 1993-94; temporary paralegal Panhandle Ea. Corp., Houston, 1994; paralegal, legal sec. Sanes & Stanford, Houston, 1995-96; paralegal Law Office of Stewart K. Smith, Houston, 1996—. Mem. ATLA. Avocations: Longaberger consultant, reading, volunteering. Office: 4828 Loop Central Dr Ste 710 Houston TX 77081-2219

**COPELAND, CHARLENE CAROLE,** lawyer; b. Gloversville, N.Y., July 22; d. Joseph Frank and Marion (Dye) Born; m. E. Allen Copeland, June 18; children: Christopher, Todd, Tiffani. BS in Polit Sci., Lamar U.; JD, John Marshall U. Bar: Ill. 1991, U.S. Dist. Ct. (no. dist.) Ill. 1991, U.S. Ct. Appeals (7th cir.) 1993, Fed. Trial Bar, 1993. Assoc. Brenner, Mavrias & Alm, New Lenox, Ill., 1992-96; assoc. civil divsn. Will County State's Attys. Office, Joliet, Ill., 1997—. Mem. Will County Pro Bono Project; pres. Jaycettes, Port Authur, Tex., 1970-71; fin. chmn. League of Women Voters, 1971, pres. Joliet Region, 1979-81; area capt. March of Dimes Mothers' March, 1971; day chmn. George Bush for Senate Campaign, 1970; mem. Village of Shorewood Ad Hoc Com. on Ordinances, 1975, Fin. Com., 1976-78; pres. United Meth. Women of Grace Meth. Ch., 1980-81; crusade chmn. Shorewood Residential Cancer Crusade, 1982. Named Outstanding Pro Bono Vol., 1995. Mem. ATLA, Ill. State Bar Assn., Will County Bar Assn., Will County Arbitration Panel, Will County Women's Bar Assn. Environmental, General civil litigation. Home: 516 Ca Crest Dr Shorewood IL 60431-9729 Office: Will County States Atty 54 N Ottawa St Joliet IL 60432-4345

**COPELAND, DENISE A.,** lawyer; b. Birmingham, Ala., Oct. 25, 1962; d. William E. and Jacqueline T. Copeland. BS in Edn., Emporia State U., 1984; JD, U. Ala., Tuscaloosa, 1989. Bar: Ala., U.S. Dist. Ct. (no., mid. and so. dists.) Ala., U.S. Ct. Appeals (11th cir.). Atty. Legal Svcs. Corp. Ala., Dothan, 1990-93, Legal Svcs. of Metro Birmingham, Ala., 1993-94, Office of Hearings and Appeals, Social Security Adminstrn., Birmingham, 1996—; assoc. Christopher P. Turner, P.C., Abbeville, Ala., 1994-96. Vol. Birmingham AIDS Outreach, 1998. Mem. ABA, Ala. State Bar Assn. (mem. com. for access to legal svcs. 1995), Birmingham Bar Assn. (mem. com. for CLE 1997, mem. com. for vol. lawyer project 1997). Democrat. Home: 144 Chase Creek Cir Pelham AL 35124-1766 Office: Social Security Adminstrn Office Hearings & Appeals 1910 3d Ave N Ste 100 Birmingham AL 35203

**COPELAND, FLOYD DEAN,** lawyer; b. Jackson, Miss., Apr. 11, 1939; s. Clyde Xenephon and Dorothy Russell (Dean) C.; m. Linda Gail Langston, Dec. 22, 1965; children: Albion Ehlers, Russell Braden. BA, U. Miss., 1961, U. Oxford, Eng., 1963; LLB, Yale U., 1965. Bar: Ga. 1967, Tenn. 1998. Assoc. Alston, Miller & Gaines, Atlanta, 1967-71; ptnr. Alston & Bird, Atlanta, 1972-97; exec. v.p., gen. coun. Provident Cos., Inc., Chattanooga, 1997—. Bd. dirs. Atlanta Metro Boys and Girls Clubs, 1986-97; sec. State and Dist. Rhodes Scholarship Selection Coms., Atlanta, 1976-97. Capt. U.S. Army, 1965-67. Rhodes scholar, 1961, Carrier scholar, 1957. Mem. Am. Law Inst. Presbyterian. Avocations: racquetball, reading, travel. Insurance, Mergers and acquisitions, Securities. Home: 214 Camden Rd NE Atlanta GA 30309-1512 Office: Provident Cos Inc One Fountain Sq Chattanooga TN 37402

**COPELAND, JOHN DEWAYNE,** law educator; b. Wichita Falls, Tex., Apr. 9, 1950; s. Howard R. and Lorene (Sharp) C.; m. Vannette Sue Thomas, July 2, 1970; children: Aaron, Seth, Sarah. BA, U. Tex., Arlington, 1971; JD, So. Meth. U., 1974; LLM, U. Ark., 1986, EdD, 1997. Bar: Tex. 1974, Ark. 1986, U.S. Dist. Ct. (no. dist.) Tex. 1974, U.S. Dist. Ct. (ea. and we. dists.) Ark. 1986, U.S. Ct. Appeals (5th cir.) 1975, U.S. Ct. Appeals (8th cir.) 1987, U.S. Supreme Ct. 1979. Ptnr. Short & Copeland, Wichita Falls, 1974-76, Helton, Copeland & Southard, Wichita Falls, 1976-78, Oldham, Copeland & Barnard, Wichita Falls, 1978-81; mem. Russell, Tate & Gowan, Wichita Falls, 1981-84; assoc. Roy & Lambert, Springdale, Ark., 1985-88; vis. asst. prof. U. Ark. Sch. Law, Fayetteville, Ark., 1988-89; dir. and rsch. prof. law Nat. Ctr. for Agrl. Law Rsch. and Info., Fayetteville, Ark., 1989-98; exec. v.p. for ethics, food safety and environ. compliance Tyson Foods, Springdale, Ark., 1998—; cons. environ. com. Nat. Pork Producers Coun., Des Moines, 1991-98, Am. Meat Inst., Washington, 1994-98, mem. environ. compliance com. Dairy Quality Assurance Bd. Author: Understanding the Farmers Comprehensive Personal Liability Policy, 1992, Recreational Access to Private Land: Liability Issues and Solutions, 1995; author book chpts.; contbr. articles to profl. jours. Legal advisor City Charter Revision Commn., Wichita Falls, 1976-77; bd. dirs. Wichita County Bar Assn., Wichita Falls, 1976-78, treas., 1978-79, dir. lawyer referral, 1982-84. Recipient grad. fellowship U. Ark. Sch. Law, 1984. Mem. ABA (vice chair agrl. law com. 1990-91), Am. Agrl. Law Assn. (bd. dirs. 1997—, Excellence in Profl. Scholarship award 1996, Dissertation of Yr. award, U. Ark., 1998). Baptist. Home: 5059 Tall Pine Cir Springdale AR 72762-2577 Office: Univ Ark Leflar Law Ctr Fayetteville AR 72701

**COPELAND, ROY WILSON,** lawyer; b. Ft. Knox, Ky., Jan. 2, 1957; s. George Wilson and Mary Lou Copeland; m. Cheryl LaFayne Smith, June 17, 1989; children: Roy II, Rachelle, Kelleigh, Kameron. AB, U. So. Calif., L.A., 1979; JD, U. Ga., 1983. Bar: Ga. 1984, U.S. Dist. Ct. (mid. dist.) Ga. 1984, U.S. Ct. Appeals (11th cir.) 1984. With Drew, Eckl & Farnham, Atlanta, 1983-84, Copeland & Haugabrook, Valdosta, Ga., 1985—. Contbr. articles to UCLA Black Law Rev., Howard Law Jour. Counsel NAACP, Valdosta, 1988-94; chmn. of bd. Georgians United, Atlanta, 1994-96; bd. dirs. Valdosta State Coll. Found., 1992-94; pres., bd. dirs. 100 Black Men of Valdosta, 1994-96; v.p. Ga. Legal Svcs., Atlanta, 1996-98. Recipient Comty. Svc. award NAACP, 1993, Outstanding Svc. award 100 Black Men of Valdosta, 1997. Mem. Nat. Bar Assn., Ga. Assn. of African Am. Attys., State Bar Ga., Valdosta Bar Assn. General civil litigation, Personal injury. Office: Copeland & Haugabrook 102 E Adair St Valdosta GA 31601-4506

**COPENBARGER, LLOYD GAYLORD,** lawyer; b. Geary, Okla., Feb. 25, 1941; s. Lloyd G. and Audrey G. C.; m. Laura M. Drinnon, Mar. 6, 1943; children: Gwendolyn Ann, Larry G. BS, U. Okla., 1968, JD, 1971, LLM, 1988. Bar: Okla. 1971, Ohio 1976, Calif. 1979. Ptnr. Copenbarger & Welch, Norman, Okla., 1971-76; gen. counsel Rex Humbard Found., Akron, Ohio, 1976-79; prin. Lloyd, Copenberger & Assoc. (formerly Copenbarger & Copenbarger), Irvine, Calif., 1979—. Non-profit and tax-exempt organizations, Estate planning, Probate. Office: 4675 Macarthur Ct Ste 700 Newport Beach CA 92660-1842

**COPENHAVER, JOHN THOMAS, JR.,** federal judge; b. Charleston, W.Va., Sept. 29, 1925; s. John Thomas and Ruth Cherrington (Roberts) C.; m. Camille Ruth Smith, Oct. 7, 1950; children: John Thomas III, James Smith, Brent Paul. A.B., W.Va. U., 1947, LL.B., 1950. Bar: W.Va., 1950. Law clerk to presiding judge U.S. Dist. Ct. (so. dist.) W.Va., 1950-51; mem. firm Copenhaver & Copenhaver, Charleston, 1951-58; U.S. bankruptcy judge So. Dist. W.Va. Charleston, 1958-76; U.S. dist. judge, 1976—; adj. prof. law W.Va. U. Coll. Law, 1970-76; mem. faculty Fed. Jud. Center, 1972-76; Pres. Legal Aid. Soc. Charleston, 1954; Chmn. Mcpl. Planning Commn. City of Charleston, 1964; chmn., pres. W.Va. Housing Devel. Fund, 1969-72; chmn. vis. com. W.Va. U. Coll. Law, 1980-83; mem. adv. com. on bankruptcy rules Jud. Conf. U.S., 1978-84. Contbr.: articles in fields of bankruptcy and comml. law to Bus. Lawyer, Am. Bankruptcy Law Jour., Personal Fin. Law Quar., W. Va. Law Rev., others. Served with U.S. Army, 1944-46. Recipient Gavel award W.Va. U. Coll. Law, 1971, Outstanding Judge award W. Va. Trial Lawyers Assn., 1983. Fellow Am. Bar Found.; mem. ABA, W.Va. Bar Assn., Kanawha County Bar Assn., Nat. Bankruptcy Conf., Nat. Conf. Bankruptcy Judges (past pres.), Phi Delta Phi, Beta Theta Pi. Republican. Presbyterian. Office: US Courthouse PO Box 2546 Charleston WV 25329-2546

**COPLEY, ROCKY K.,** lawyer; b. Rabat, Morocco, Feb. 1, 1955; s. Melvin C. and Joyce E. Copley; m. Patricia Ann Cantwell, July 14, 1979; children: Patrick, Catlin, Erin. BBA in Mgmt., Coll. William & Mary, 1979; JD, U. Pacific, 1981. Bar: Calif. 1981, U.S. Dist. Ct. (so., ea., ctrl. dists.) Calif., 1981. Assoc. Borton, Petrini & Conron L.L.P., Bakersfield, Calif., 1981-84; non-capital ptnr., mng. ptnr. Borton, Petrini & Conron L.L.P., Santa Maria, Calif., 1983-86; non-capital ptnr., mgn. ptnr. Borton, Petrini & Conron L.L.P., San Diego, 1986-89, capital ptnr., mng. ptnr., 1989—. Columnist Judicial Notice, Calif. DEf. Mag., 1986—. Vol. basketball coach YMCA, La Jolla, 1994—. Mem. Def. Rsch. Inst. (mem. agrl. constrn. mining & indsl. subcommittee 1992—), Calif. Bar Assn., San Diego Def. Counsel Assn. Republican. Avocations: basketball, scuba diving, fishing. E-mail: bpcúrcopley@bpclaw.com. Product liability, Contracts commercial, Personal injury. Office: Borton Petrini & Conron LLP 402 W Broadway Ste 880 San Diego CA 92101-8506

**COPPAGE, JAMES ROBERT,** lawyer; b. Miami, Fla., Jan. 3, 1963. BBA in Acctg., West Ga. U., Carrollton, 1987; JD, Mercer U., 1991. Bar: Ga. 1991, Fla. 1992. Jud. law clk. Judge Tuten, Brunswick, Ga., 1991-92; asst. dist. atty. Dist. Attys. Office, Brunswick, 1992-94; pvt. practice Darien, Ga., 1994—. Capt. Ga. Army Nat. Guard, 1994—. Personal injury, Criminal, General practice. Home and Office: PO Box 2120 Darien GA 31305-2120

**COPPEL, LAWRENCE DAVID,** lawyer; b. Washington, July 3, 1944; s. Albert and Anne (Gold) C.; m. Arlene Cohen, Aug. 10, 1968; children: Jennifer, Allison. BA, U. Md., 1966, JD, 1969. Bar: Md. 1969, U.S. Dist. Ct. Md. 1971, U.S. Ct. Appeals (4th cir.) 1976, U.S. Ct. Appeals (3d cir.) 1983. Law clk. Md. Ct. Appeals, Annapolis, 1969-70; assoc. Gordon, Feinblatt, Rothman, Hoffberger & Hollander, LLC, Balt., 1970-77, mem., 1977—. Fellow Am. Coll. Bankruptcy; mem. ABA, Md. State Bar Assn., Bankruptcy Bar Assn. Dist. Md. (pres. 1988-89), Balt. City Bar Assn. Jewish. Bankruptcy. Office: Gordon Feinblatt Rothman Hoffberger & Hollander LLC 233 E Redwood St Baltimore MD 21202-3332

**COPPERSMITH, SAM,** lawyer; b. Johnstown, Pa., May 22, 1955; m. Beth Schermer, Aug. 28, 1983; children: Sarah, Benjamin, Louis. AB in Econs. magna cum laude, Harvard U., 1976; JD, Yale Law Sch., 1982. Fgn. svc. officer U.S. Dept. State, Port of Spain, Trinidad, 1977-79; law clk. to Judge William C. Canby Jr. U.S. Ct. Appeals (9th cir.), Phoenix, 1982-83; atty. Sacks, Tierney & Kasen, P.A., Phoenix, 1983-86; asst. to Mayor Terry Goddard City of Phoenix, 1984; atty. Jones, Jury, Short & Mast P.C., Phoenix, 1986-88, Bonnett, Fairbourn & Friedman P.C., Phoenix, 1988-92; mem. 103d Congress from 1st Ariz. Dist., 1993-95; atty. Coppersmith Gordon Schermer Owens & Nelson PLC, 1995—. Former dir., pres. Planned Parenthood Ctrl. and No. Ariz.; former chair City of Phoenix Bd. of Adjustment; former dir. Ariz. Cmty. Svc. Legal Assistance Found., 1986-89; chair Ariz. Dem. Party, 1995-97; trustee Devereux Found., 1997—. Mem. ABA, State Bar of Ariz., State Bar of Calif., Maricopa County Bar Assn. Democrat. Contracts commercial, General corporate, Real property. Office: Coppersmith Gordon Schermer Owens & Nelson PLC 2633 E Indian School Rd Ste 300 Phoenix AZ 85016-6765

**COPPLE, WILLIAM PERRY,** federal judge; b. Holtville, Calif., Oct. 3, 1916; s. Perry and Euphie (Williams) C.; m. Nancy Matson, May 30, 1981; children by previous marriage—Virginia (Mrs. Richard Schilke), Leonard W., Steven D. A.B., U. Calif. at Berkeley, 1949, LL.B., 1951. Bar: Ariz. 1952. Various positions with U.S. Govt., also pvt. employers, 1936-48; practice in Yuma, Ariz., 1952-65; U.S. dist. atty. Dist. Ariz., Phoenix, 1965-66; judge U.S. Dist. Ct. Dist. Ariz., 1966—, now sr. judge; Mem. Ariz. Hwy. Commn., 1955-58, Gov. Ariz. Com Fourteen for Colo. River, 1963-65; chmn. Yuma County Democratic Central Com., 1953-54, 59-60. Mem. Am. Bar Assn. Office: US Dist Ct US Courthouse & Fed Bldg 230 N 1st Ave Ste 3007 Phoenix AZ 85025-0230

**COPSETTA, NORMAN GEORGE,** real estate executive; b. Pennsauken, N.J., Mar. 11, 1932; s. Joseph J. and Mary P. (DeMello) C.; m. Patricia Fitzpatrick, Mar. 5, 1971; children: Gregory, Margaret, Andrew, Norman G. Jr.; stepchildren: Samuel Sassano, James Sassano. Cert. real estate, Rutgers U. Extension, Camden, N.J., 1952; AA, Internat. Accts. Soc. Schl. Acctg., Chgo., 1968. Lic. title insurance agent, N.J. Settlement clk. Market Street Title Abstract Co., Camden, 1949-53; settlement administrator West Jersey Title & Guaranty Co., Camden, 1953; title examiner, abstract adminstr. Realty Abstract Co., Cherry Hill, N.J., 1954-64; mcpl. treas., tax collector Borough of Somerdale, N.J., 1961-65; title examiner, legal adminstr. Davis, Reberkenny & Abramowitz, Cherry Hill, 1974-97; pres., title officer Cooper Abstract Co., Cherry Hill, 1974—; N.J. fgn. commr. of deeds in and for Pa., 1959—; mem. faculty Title Acad. N.J. Custodian of funds Somerdale Bd. Edn., 1960-64. Mem. ABA (assoc.), N.J. Title Ins. Agts. Assn., Haddonfield (N.J.) Hist. Soc., Camden County Hist. Soc. Avocation: local history. Office: Cooper Abstract Co 401 Cooper Landing Rd Ste C6 Cherry Hill NJ 08002-2598

**COQUILLETTE, DANIEL ROBERT,** lawyer, educator; b. Boston, May 23, 1944; s. Robert McTavish and Dagmar Alvida (Bistrup) C.; m. Judith Courtney Rogers, July 5, 1969; children: Anna, Sophia, Julia. A.B., Williams Coll., 1966; M.A. Juris., Univ. Coll., Oxford U., Eng., 1969; J.D., Harvard U., 1971. Bar: Mass. 1974, U.S. Dist. Ct. Mass. 1974, U.S. Ct. Appeals (1st cir.) 1974. Law clk. Mass. Supreme Ct., 1971-72; to Warren E. Burger, chief justice U.S. Supreme Ct., 1972-73; assoc. Palmer & Dodge, Boston, 1973-75, ptnr., 1980-85; assoc. prof. law Boston U., 1975-78; dean, prof. Boston Coll. Law, 1985-93, prof., 1993-96, J. Donald Monan univ. prof. law, 1996—; vis. assoc. prof. law Cornell U., Ithaca, N.Y., 1977-78, 84; vis. prof. law Harvard U., 1978-79, 84-85, 94-95, 95-96, 96-97, 97-98, mem. overseers com.; reporter com. rules and procedures Jud. Conf. U.S.; mem. task force on rules of atty. conduct Supreme Jud. Ct. of Mass., 1996-97. Author: The Civilian Writers of Doctors Commons, London, 1988, Francis Bacon, 1993, Lawyers and Fundamental Moral Responsibility, 1995, Working Papers on Rules Governing Attorney Conduct, 1997, (with Basile, Beston, Donahue) Lex Mercatoria and Legal Pluralism, 1999, The Anglo-American Legal Heritage, 1999; editor: Law in Colonial Massachusetts, 1985, Moore's Federal Practice, 3d edit., 1997; bd. dirs. New Eng. Quar., 1986—; contbr. articles to legal jours. Trustee, sec.-treas. Ames Found; bd. overseers vis. com. Harvard Law Sch.; treas. Byron Meml. Fund; propr., trustee Boston Athenaeum. Recipient Kaufman prize in English Williams Coll., 1966; recipient Sentinel of the Republic prize in polit. sci. Williams Coll., 1965; Hutchins scholar, 1966-67; Fulbright scholar, 1966-68. Mem. ABA (com. on profl. ethics 1990-93), Am. Law Inst., Mass. Bar Assn. (task force on model rules of profl. conduct), Boston Bar Assn., Am. Soc. Legal History (bd. dirs. 1985-89), Mass. Soc. Continuing Legal Edn. (bd. dirs. 1985-89), Selden Soc. (state corr.), Colonial Soc. Mass. (v.p., mem. coun.), Anglo-Am. Cathedral Soc. (bd. dirs.), Mass. Hist. Soc., Am. Antiquarian Soc., Phi Beta Kappa. Democrat. Quaker. Home: 12 Rutland St Cambridge MA 02138-2503 Office: Boston Coll Sch Law 885 Centre St Newton MA 02459-1154

**CORASH, RICHARD,** lawyer; b. N.Y.C., Mar. 31, 1938; s. Paul and Mildred (Spanier) C.; m. Carol A. McKevitt, Dec. 11, 1966; children: Richard Jr., Sharon, Peter, Amy. BA, Harpur Coll., SUNY, Binghampton, 1959; MA, Bklyn. Law Sch., 1966; JD, Rutgers U., 1963. Bar: N.Y. 1964, U.S. Dist. Ct. D.C. 1964, U.S. Sup. Ct. 1972. Pvt. practice, N.Y.C., 1964-77; pres. Corash & Hollender, P.C., N.Y.C., 1977—; pres. Kobe Trading Co., N.Y.C.; chmn. North Eastern Fiscal Mgmt. Co., N.Y.C.; pres. North Eastern Abstract Assn.; counsel Caywood Homeowners Assn. Mem. N.Y. State Bar Assn. (real estate sect., guest panelist grievance procedures 1989), N.Y. Bankruptcy Bar Assn. (chmn. grievance com.), Richmond County Bar Assn. Democrat. General corporate, Real property, Estate planning. Address: 81 Roxiticus Rd Far Hills NJ 07931-2225

**CORBETT, PATRICK JAMES,** lawyer; b. N.Y.C., May 20, 1955; s. James Joseph and Marilyn Virginia Corbett; m. Joy M. Kelly. BS, Iona Coll., 1983; JD, Pace U., 1987. Bar: N.Y. 1988, U.S. Dist. Ct. (so. and ea. dists.) N.Y. 1989. Firefighter City of Yonkers, N.Y., 1979-90; assoc. atty. Eltman, Eltman & Cooper, White Plains, N.Y., 1989-93; assoc. atty. Bigham Englar Jones & Houston, N.Y.C., 1993-98, ptnr., 1998—; lectr. Recovery Forum, N.Y.C., 1996—. Mem. Internat. Assn. Firefighters, Maritime Law Assn., Brehon Law Soc. Avocation: sailing. Insurance, Personal injury, Transportation. Office: Bigham Englar Jones & Houston 40 Wall St New York NY 10005-2301

**CORBETT, THOMAS WINGETT, JR.,** lawyer; b. Phila., June 17, 1949; s. Thomas Wingett and Mary Bernadine (Diskin) C.; m. Susan Jean Manbeck, Dec. 16, 1972; children: Thomas Wingett III, Katherine. BA, Lebanon Valley Coll., 1971; JD, St. Mary's U., 1975. Bar: Pa. 1976, U.S. Dist. Ct. (we. dist.) Pa. 1976, U.S. Ct. Mil. Appeals 1979, U.S. Supreme Ct. 1984. Asst. dist. atty. Allegheny County, Pitts., 1976-80; asst. U.S. atty. Office U.S. Atty. for Western Dist. Pa., Pitts., 1980-83; assoc. Rose, Schmidt, Hasley & DiSalle, Pitts., 1983-86, former ptnr., from 1986; U.S. atty. We. Dist. Pa., Pitts., mem. U.S. atty. gen.'s adv. com., 1991—, chmn., 1993; Atty. Gen. State of Pa., Harrisburg, 1995-97; ptnr. Thorp, Reed & Armstrong, Pitts., 1993-95, 97-98; ast. gen. counsel for govt. affairs Waste Mgmt. Inc., Pitts., 1998—. Pres. St. Mary's Parent-Tchr. Guild, Glenshaw, Pa., 1983-85; mem. Allegheny County Republican Com., 1985-89; mem. Shaler Twp. Bd. Commrs., 1988-89. Mem. ABA, Pa. Bar Assn., Allegheny County Bar Assn. (judiciary com.). Roman Catholic. Avocations: skiing, golf, reading. Criminal, General civil litigation. Office: Waste Mgmt Inc 2000 Cliffmine Rd Pittsburgh PA 15275-1008

**CORBIN, DONALD L.,** state supreme court justice; b. Hot Springs, Ark., Mar. 29, 1938. BA, U. Ark., 1964, JD, 1966. Bar: Ark. 1966, U.S. Dist. Ct. (we. dist.) Ark. 1966. Lawyer Lewisville and Stamps, 1967-80; judge Ark. Ct. Appeals, 1981-87, chief judge, 1987-90; assoc. justice Ark. Supreme Ct., Little Rock, 1991—; state rep. Ark. Gen. Assembly, 1971-80. Served with USMC, 1955-59. Mem. ABA, Ark. Bar Assn., SW Ark. Bar Assn., Sigma Alpha Epsilon. Democrat. Avocation: duck hunting. Office: Supreme Ct Justice Bldg 625 Marshall St Little Rock AR 72201-1054*

**CORBIN, SOL NEIL,** lawyer; b. N.Y.C., Apr. 16, 1927; s. Nathan I. and Sarah (Kaiser) C.; m. Tanya Jacobs, Aug. 7, 1963; 1 son, David J. BS, Columbia U., 1948; JD cum laude, Harvard U., 1951. Bar: N.Y. 1952. Practiced N.Y.C., 1952—; law clk. Judge Charles D. Breitel, 1954-56; counsel Gov. of N.Y., 1962-65; ptnr. Corbin, Silverman & Sanseverino LLP, N.Y.C., 1970-96, sr. counsel, 1997—; mem. N.Y. State Banking Bd., 1969-76; Chmn. N.Y. State Commn. Constl. Conv., 1966-67; mem. N.Y. State Commn. Local Govt. Powers, 1971-73; chmn. N.Y. State Crime Control Planning Bd., 1974-75; mem. Chief Judge's Com. to Recruit State Ct. Adminstr., 1973; trustee in bankruptcy Franklin N.Y. Corp., 1974-90; spl. counsel v.p. U.S., 1975. Trustee N.Y. Pub. Libr., 1977—; mem. Chief Judge's com. on Availability of Legal Svcs., 1988-90. With USNR, 1945-46. Mem. ABA, N.Y. State Bar Assn., Assn. Br. City N.Y., New York County Bar Assn., Am. Law Inst., Lotos Club. Banking, General corporate, Securities. Home: 1100 Park Ave New York NY 10128-1202 Office: 805 3rd Ave New York NY 10022-7513

**CORCHIN, MARK ALAN,** lawyer; b. Phila., Nov. 3, 1947; s. Jerome and Jean Edith (Mayerson) C.; m. Randi Beth Levy, June 4, 1978; children: Carolyn, Max, Daniel. BSBA, Villanova U., 1969; JD, N.Y. Law Sch., 1973; LLM in Trial Advocacy, Temple U., 1994. Bar: Pa. 1973, U.S. Dist. Ct. (ea. dist.) Pa. 1973, U.S. Ct. Appeals (3d cir.) 1981, U.S. Supreme Ct. 1982. Pvt. practice, Blue Bell, Pa., 1973-80; ptnr. Malis, Tolson, Meltzer & Corchin, Phila., 1980-83, Merirov, Gelman, Jaffe, Cramer & Jamieson, Phila., 1983-91, Mayerson, Munsing, Corchin & Rosato, Norristown, Pa., 1991-95, Corchin, Graham, Rosato & Mauer, Valley Forge, Pa., 1995—, Corchin & Rosato, P.C., Valley Forge; fed. arbitrator U.S. Dist. Ct. for Ea. Dist. Pa., 1976-95, fed. mediator, 1991-93. Author: Medical Malpractice in Pennsylvania, 1991, Proving Damages in Pennsylvania, 1991; editor Lawyer-Pilots Bar Assn., 1975. Counsel Barren Hill Vol. Fire Co., Lafayette Hill, Pa., 1990. Recipient cert. of appreciation U.S. Dist. Ct. for Ea. Dist. Pa., 1982. Avocations: fishing, flying, football. Aviation, Personal injury, General civil litigation. Home: 4103 Fields Dr Lafayette Hl PA 19444-1531 Office: Corchin & Rosato PC PO Box 987-23 Ste 7 Valley Forge PA 19482

**CORCORAN, ANDREW PATRICK, JR.,** lawyer; b. Fredrick, Md., Nov. 20, 1948; s. Andrew Patrick and Beatrice Josephine (Poletti) C.; m. Margaret Cecila Boyle, July 3, 1971; children: Maureen Meredith, Andrew Patrick III. BA, Villanova U., 1970; JD, Seton Hall U., 1973. Bar: Pa. 1973, U.S Dist. Ct. (ea. dist.) Pa. 1974, U.S. Ct. Appeals (7th cir.) 1976, U.S. Ct. Appeals (3d cir.) 1977, U.S. Supreme Ct. 1982. Atty. Pa. Cen. Transp. Co., Phila., 1973-75, sr. atty., 1975-79; asst. gen. atty. Consol. Rail Corp., Phila., 1979-82, gen. atty., 1982-85, sr. gen. atty., 1985-92, assoc. gen. counsel, 1992-99; gen. atty. Norfolk (Va.) So. Corp., 1999—. Mem. Conf. of Rwy. and Airline Labor Lawyers, Assn. of Am. R.R.'s (legal affairs com.). Republican. Roman Catholic. Administrative and regulatory, Federal civil litigation, Transportation. Home: 2433 Haversham Close Virginia Beach VA 23454 Office: Norfolk So Corp Three Commercial Pl Norfolk VA 23510-9241

**CORCORAN, CHRISTOPHER HOLMES,** lawyer; b. Rochester, N.Y., Jan. 24, 1951; s. Victor F. and Merrill (Holmes) C.; m. Mary P. Fritschler, Aug. 1, 1992. AB, Princeton U., 1973; JD, Union U., 1976. Bar: N.Y. 1977, U.S. Dist. Ct. N.Y. (so. dist.) 1977. Atty. Dunnington Bartholow & Miller, N.Y.C., 1976-78, Shearman & Sterling, N.Y.C., 1978-79, Harris Beach & Wilcox, Rochester, 1979-82; ptnr. Wiedman Vazzana & Corcoran, Rochester, 1982—. Mem. Country Club Rochester. Avocations: golf, aviation, reading. Estate planning, Probate, Real property. Office: Wiedman Vazzana & Corcoran 5 Fitzhugh St S Rochester NY 14614-1413

**CORCORAN, CLEMENT TIMOTHY, III,** judge; b. Kansas City, Mo., Dec. 18, 1945; s. Clement T. and Bette Lou (Hohl) C. BA, U. N.C., 1967; JD, U. Va., 1973. Bar: Fla. 1973, U.S. Dist. Ct. (mid. dist.) Fla. 1973, D.C. 1974, U.S. Dist. Ct. (no. and so. dists.) Fla. 1975, U.S. Supreme Ct. 1979, U.S. Ct. Appeals (11th cir.) 1981. Law clk. U.S. Dist. Ct., Tampa, Fla., 1973-75; assoc. Carlton, Fields, Ward, Emmanuel, Smith & Cutler, P.A., Tampa, 1975-78, ptnr., 1978-89; judge Bankruptcy Ct. (mid. dist.) Fla., Orlando, 1989-93, Tampa, 1993—; dir. Bay Area Legal Svcs., Inc., Tampa, 1983-89, v.p., 1987, pres., 1988; bd. dirs. Fla. Coun. Bar Pres., 1982-88, pres., 1986-87; arbitrator Ct. Annexed Arbitration Program, U.S. Dist. Ct. (mid. dist.) Fla., 1984-89; counselor U. Tampa, 1981-86, fellow, 1986-89. Co-author: Conflicts of Interest, 1984; contbr. articles to legal jours. Lt. USNR, 1967-70. Mem. ABA (litigation sect., coun. mem. 1999—, co-chair comm. com. 1990-92, chair book pub. bd. 1992-98, assoc. editor Litigation News 1982-87, mng. editor 1987, editor-in-chief 1988-90, Nat. Conf. of Lawyers and Reps. of Media 1992-95, mem. adv. com. on nominations 1994-95, chair media-law roundtable 1994, chair sect. officers conf. com. on non-dues revenue 1995-96, mem. working group on ABA bus. plan for pub. 1995-96, standing com. on pub. oversight 1996—), Fla. Bar (chmn. voluntary bar liaison com. 1985-86, chmn. grievance com. 13-D 1986-88, chmn. legal edn. com. 1981-82, Most Productive Young Lawyer award 1981), Am. Judicature Soc., Hillsborough County Bar Assn. (Red McEwen award 1980, pres. 1982-83), Am. Inns of Ct. (Master of the Bench 1990-93, 96—). Roman Catholic. Office: Sam M Gibbons US Courthouse 801 N Florida Ave Tampa FL 33602-3849

**CORCORAN, ROBERT THOMAS,** lawyer; b. Jersey City, N.J., July 3, 1951; m. Susan Corcoran; children: Sara, Chelsea. BS cum laude, Fairleigh Dickinson U., 1974; JD, Ohio No. U., 1977. Bar: N.J. 1977, U.S. Dist. Ct. N.J. 1977, N.Y. 1986, U.S. Dist. Ct. N.Y. (so. dist.) 1988, U.S. Ct. Appeals (3d cir.) 1988, U.S. Supreme Ct. 1991; cert. mediator Am. Acad. Matrimonial Lawyers, 1997. prof. bus. law Fairleigh Dickinson U., 1978-83; lectr. Law Edn. Inst. Bur. Nat. Affairs, Bergen County Bar Assn., N.J. Inst. for Continuing Legal Edn., Assn. Trial Lawyers (fam. law sect.), Am. Acad. Matrimonial Lawyers (N.J. chpt.), orientation seminar for newly-apptd. judges, 1998. T.V. appearances: NBC News, CBS News, MSNBC News, TCI Cable, Justice Jour.; contbr. articles to profl. jours. Fellow Am. Acad. of Matrimonial Lawyers (econ. law com. 1996-97, bd. mgrs. N.J. chpt. 1996-98, continuing legal edn. com. 1998-99) mem. ABA (family law sect.), Assn. Trial Lawyers Am. (family law sect.), Assn. Trial Attys. Am. (N.J. affiliate), Trial Attys. N.J., Bergen County Bar Assn. (co-chmn. fam. law com. 1995-97, chmn. 1998-99, matrimonial early settlement panel, bench bar liason com.), N.J. State Bar Assn. (exec. com. family law sect. 1995-98, mem. com., subcom. mem: Keeping Child Support in Family Ct., early settlement panel study), Supreme St. N.J. (bd. atty. cert., matrimonial law com. 1996-98). Family and matrimonial. Office: 401 Hackensack Ave Hackensack NJ 07601-6411

**CORDAY, LANE ALLAN,** lawyer; b. Chgo., Mar. 20, 1954; s. Jack S. and Louise Corday; m. Jann Corday, June 29, 1980; children: Frank, Lauren, Brandon. BS, U. Ill., 1976, JD, 1980. Bar: Ill. 1980, U.S. Dist. Ct. (no. dist.) Ill. 1980. Atty. Murges & Bowman Ltd., Chgo., 1980-85; ptnr.

Murges Bowman & Corday Ltd., Chgo., 1985-91, Bowman & Corday Ltd., Chgo., 1991—. Avocations: golf, basketball, coaching youth sports. Workers' compensation, Pension, profit-sharing, and employee benefits, Personal injury. Office: Bowman & Corday Ltd 20 N Clark St Ste 500 Chicago IL 60602-4111

**CORDOVA, ADOLFO ENRIQUE,** lawyer; b. Harlingen, Tex., May 10, 1967; s. Adolfo Enrique and Laura (Rodriguez) C.; m. Teresa Stella Marroquin, Aug. 21, 1993; 1 child, Camilla. BA in Govt., U. Tex., 1990; JD, U. Houston, 1993. Bar: Tex. 1993. Law clk. Umphrey, Williams & Bailey, Houston, 1991-93; assoc. Law Offices of Randall D. Crane, San Benito, Tex., 1993-94; ptnr. Law Offices of Crane & Cordova, San Benito, Tex., 1994—. Mem. San Benito C. of C. (bd. dirs. 1994-95). Avocations: hunting, fishing. Personal injury, Product liability, General practice. Home: PO Box 1584 San Benito TX 78586-1584 Office: Law Offices of Crane & Cordova 201 S Sam Houston Blvd San Benito TX 78586-3866

**CORDOVA, RON,** lawyer; b. L.A., Aug. 18, 1946; s. Reuben and Lya (Gruber) C.; m. Mariann Pehrson, June 2, 1970; children: Danielle, Andrea. AB, Dartmouth Coll., 1967; postgrad., Trinity Coll., Dublin, Ireland, 1966; JD, U. So. Calif., 1972. Bar: U.S. Dist. Ct. (ctrl. dist.) Calif., 1979, U.S. Dist. Ct. (so. dist.) Calif., 1989, U.S. Dist. Ct. (no. dist.) Calif., 1995, U.S. Dist. Ct. (we. dist.) Tex., 1996, Ariz., 1994, U.S. Dist. Ct. (ea. dist.) Mich., 1995, U.S. Dist. Ct. Colo., 1999. Dep. dist. atty. Orange County Dist. Atty., Santa Ana, Calif., 1973-76; legis. Calif. State Assembly, Sacramento, 1976-78; trial lawyer Newport Beach, Calif., 1979—; adj. prof. U. Calif., Irvine, 1975-77, 81-84. Author: Orange County Bar Journal, 1975. Recipient Outstanding Young Men. Am. Jaycees, 1977, 78. Mem. Lincoln Club. Republican. Jewish. Avocations: travel, languages, photography. State civil litigation, Criminal, Family and matrimonial. Office: 130 Newport Center Dr Newport Beach CA 92660-6922

**COREIL, C. BRENT,** lawyer; b. Ville Platte, La., Apr. 23, 1949; s. Armand B. and Juanita (Smith) C.; m. Linda Veillon, Apr. 19, 1969; children: Christopher, Virginia, Kathryn. BS, U. So. La., 1971; JD, La. State U., 1974. Bar: La., U.S. Dist. Ct. (we. dist.) La., U.S. Ct. Appeals (5th cir.) La. Sole practice Ville Platte, 1974-78; pros. atty. City of Ville Platte, 1975-97; city atty. Village of Turkey Creek, La., 1978-90; ptnr. Fusilier, Pucheu, et al, Ville Platte, 1978-81, Soileau & Coreil, Ville Platte, 1981-90, Coreil & Deshotel, Ville Platte, 1990-98; dist. atty. 13th Jud. Dist., 1997—. Mem. ABA, La. Bar Assn., La. Trial Lawyers Assn. (bd. gov.'s 1983-84), Evangeline Parish Bar Assn., Fed. Bar Assn. Lodge: Rotary (pres. Ville Platte club 1980). Personal injury, Probate, Consumer commercial. Home: 1810 Chicot Park Rd Ville Platte LA 70586-1906 Office: C Brent Coreil Ltd PO Box 450 Ville Platte LA 70586-0450

**CORESON, LATRICIA KADENE,** lawyer, eduactor; b. Portland, Oreg., June 10, 1970; d. Richard Lyle and Peggy Noreen Coreson. BA, U. Oreg., 1992; JD, Willamette U., 1996. Assoc. Bertoni & Todd, Portland, Oreg., 1995-98, Meyer & Wyse, LLP, Portland, Oreg., 1998—; adj. prof. Portland State U., 1997-98. Mem. City Club. Democrat. General civil litigation, Real property. Office: Meyer & Wyse LLP 900 SW 5th Ave Ste 1900 Portland OR 97204-1228

**COREY, BARRY MARTIN,** lawyer; b. Louisville, Apr. 15, 1942; s. Joseph and Ann (Friedman) C.; m. Arlene Corey; children: David, Pamela; stepchildren: Vanessa Rivera, Sarah Rivera, Esther Rivera. BA, U. Colo., 1963; JD, Georgetown U., 1966. Bar: Ariz. 1967, U.S. Dist. Ct. D.C. 1967, U.S. Ct. Appeals (9th cir.) 1973, U.S. Supreme Ct. 1990. Law clk. to chief judge U.S. Dist. Ct. Ariz., Tucson, 1966-7; assoc. Schorr & Karp, P.C., Tucson, 1967-69; asst. city atty. Tucson, 1969-71; ptnr. Schorr, Karp & Corey, Tucson, 1971-73; pvt. practice Tucson, 1974-78; shareholder Corey Farrell Kime & Bromiel P.C., Tucson, 1978—. Pres., co-founder Cmty. Food Bank, Inc., Tucson, 1980, bd. dirs. 1975—; bd. dirs. United Way Tucson, 1982-95, chmn. bd., 1990-91. Fellow Ariz. Bar Found.; mem. ABA, ATLA, Am. Judicature Soc., Ariz. Trial Lawyers Assn., State Bar Ariz. (chmn. pub. rels. com. 1987-89), Pima County Bar Assn. (bd. dirs. 1978-85, pres. 1983-84). Democrat. Jewish. Avocations: reading, hiking, music, golf. Personal injury, Education and schools, Administrative and regulatory. Office: Corey Farrell Kime & Bromiel PC 830 Norwest Tower 1 S Church Ave Tucson AZ 85701-1612

**CORIDEN, MICHAEL WARNER,** lawyer; b. Sioux City, Iowa, June 3, 1948; s. Thomas Lou and Patricia (Warner) C.; m. Karen Baldrige, Oct. 12, 1974; children: Courtney Anne, Torrey Erin, Shannon Marielle. B of Gen. Studies, U. Iowa, 1971; postgrad., Inst. Internat. & Compar. Law, Paris, 1973; JD, Creighton U., 1974; MBA, U. Denver, 1983. Bar: Iowa 1974, Nebr. 1974, U.S. Tax Ct. 1974, U.S. Ct. Claims 1976, U.S. Internat. Trade 1976, Colo. 1980, U.S. Supreme Ct. 1980. Atty. Land of Lincoln Legal Assistance Found., Champaign, Ill., 1974-75; asst. atty. gen. State of Iowa, Des Moines, 1975-77; atty. Peter Kiewit Sons' Inc., Omaha, 1977-79; counsel La. Land and Exploration Co., Lakewood, Colo., 1979-83; gen. counsel Tenneco Minerals Co., Lakewood, 1983-85; pvt. practice Denver, 1985-88; gen. counsel, sec. CF&I Steel Corp., Pueblo, Colo., 1988-93; gen. counsel CF&I Steel, L.P., Pueblo, 1993—; of counsel LeBouef, Lamb, Greene & MacRae, Denver, 1993-95; pvt. practice Denver, 1995—; bd. dirs. Pueblo Diversified Industries, Inc., Aspen Lane Ltd., Ctr. Hearing, Speech & Lang.; instr. Denver Paralegal Inst., 1988. Mem. Colo. Bar Assn., Colo. Assn. Corp. Counsel. General corporate, Private international, Environmental. Office: 2289 S Hiwan Dr Evergreen CO 80439-8927

**CORK, ROBERT LANDER,** lawyer; b. Central, S.C., Oct. 27, 1927; s. James Walter and Lila (Mitchell) C.; m. Anne McNeill Ward, Oct. 11, 1952; children: Leah, Robert Jr. (dec.), Travis, Patrick. AB, U. Ga., 1952, LLB, 1953. Bar: Ga. 1951, Fla. 1958, S.C. 1989, U.S. Dist. Ct. (mid. dist.) Ga. 1951, U.S. Ct. Appeals (11th cir.) 1981, U.S. Dist. Ct. (mid. dist.) Fla. 1983. Ptnr. Cork & Gaines, Athens, Ga., 1951-53; pvt. practice law Valdosta, Ga., 1954-83; ptnr. Cork & Cork, Valdosta, 1983—; gen. counsel Warrior Cattle Co., Sylvester, Ga., 1964-70; legal draftsman charter and mcpl. code Town of Dasher, Ga., 1967; gen. counsel Edwards Aircraft, Inc., Dover, Del., 1978-87; counsel Firstline Corp., Valdosta, Ga., 1996-98, Truman Arnold Co., Texarkana, Ark., 1995—, Internat. Petroleum, Inc., Jacksonville, Fla., 1990—, Strasburg and Assocs. (Petroleum), Waco, Tex., 1996—. County co-chmn. campaign Goldwater for Pres., Valdosta, 1964, county chmn. campaign Wallace for Pres., Valdosta, 1968; precinct chmn., del. to state Rep. Conv., Valdosta, 1983, 84, 87-88, 89, 91, 92, 94, 96, 98, 99. With AUS, 1953-54. Mem. Am. Legion, Shriners, Masons, St. John the Baptist, Lions, Delta Theta Phi. Republican. Methodist. Real property, Probate, General practice. Home: Sunnyside Lake Francis Lake Park GA 31634 Office: Cork & Cork 700 N Patterson St Valdosta GA 31601-4527

**CORLETO, RAYMOND ANTHONY,** lawyer; b. Bklyn., Nov. 27, 1931; s. Sal A. and Ida (Cianci) C.; m. Annette Grasso, Aug. 30, 1958; children: Anthony, Brian, Suzann, Todd. BA, Bklyn. Coll., 1953; LLB, Bklyn. Law Sch., 1959. Bar: N.Y. 1960, U.S. Ct. Appeals (2d cir.) 1991, U.S. Claims Ct. 1991, U.S. Supreme Ct. 1991. Assoc. Morris, Duffy, Ivone & Jensen, N.Y.C., 1976-82; ptnr. Schiavetti, Begos & Nicholson, N.Y.C., 1982-88, Rossano, Mosé, Corleto & Andron PC, Garden City, N.Y., 1988—; mem. med. malpractice panels Supreme Ct. Nassau County, 1982-91. Cpl. U.S. Army, 1953-55, Germany. Mem. Nassau County Bar Assn., Nassau Suffolk Trial Lawyers, Def. Rsch. Inst., Def. Assn. N.Y., Columbian Lawyers Nassau. Republican. Roman Catholic. Avocations: golf, chorus. Insurance, Personal injury, State civil litigation. Office: Rossano Mose Corleto & Andron PC 595 Stewart Ave Ste 700 Garden City NY 11530-4736

**CORLETT, EDWARD STANLEY, III,** lawyer; b. Miami, Fla., May 28, 1924; s. Edward Stanley, Jr., and Marjorie (Cook) C.; m. Jeanne Sherouse, Mar. 27, 1948; children—Karen Marie Corlett McCammon, Edward S. A.A., U. Fla., 1946, LL.B., 1949. Bar: Fla. 1949, U.S. Dist. Ct. (so. dist.) Fla. 1949, U.S. Ct. Appeals (5th cir.) 1949, U.S. Ct. Appeals (11th cir.) 1981. Sole practice, 1949-58; sr. ptnr. Sherouse and Corlett, and successor Corlett, Killian, Hardeman, McIntosh and Levi, P.A., Miami, 1958—. Fellow Am. Coll. Trial Lawyers; chmn. bd. Internat. Oceanographic Found.; pres. Miami Met. Fishing Tournament, 1973-80. mem. Fed. Jud. Nominating Panel. Served with USN, 1942-44. Recipient Henry Hyman trophy, 1974. Fellow Am. Coll. Trial Lawyers; mem. ABA, Fla. Bar Assn., Dade County Bar Assn., Fedn. Ins. Counsel (pres. 1978-79, testimonial award 1979), Fla. Def. Lawyers Assn. (pres. 1970), Def. Research Inst. (dir. 1978-79, testimonial award 1979), Internat. Assn. Ins. Counsel. Republican. Presbyterian. Clubs: Miami Rod and Reel, Riviera Country, Bankers. Insurance, Personal injury, State civil litigation. Office: PO Box 188 Blowing Rock NC 28605-0188

**CORLEW, JOHN GORDON,** lawyer; b. Dyersburg, Tenn., July 13, 1943; s. Emmett Atkins and Margaret Elizabeth (Swann) C.; m. Elizabeth Lee Scott, July 8, 1967; children: John Scott, William Heath, Carey Elizabeth. BA, U. Miss., 1965; JD, Vanderbilt U., 1968. Bar: Miss. 1968. Clk. to judge U.S. Dist. Ct. (so. dist.) Miss., 1968-69; assoc., then ptnr. Megehee, Brown, Williams & Corlew, Pascagoula, Miss., 1969-74; sole practice Pascagoula, 1975-78; ptnr. Corlew, Krebs & Hammond, Pascagoula, 1978-84, Watkins & Eager, Jackson, Miss., 1984. Mem. Miss. State Senate, 1974-80, chmn. appropriations com., 1979, chmn. constn. com., 1975-79, chmn. legis. audit com., 1978; chmn. Miss. State Bd. Pub. Welfare, 1980-84. Mem. ABA, Miss. Bar Assn., Hinds County Bar Assn., Miss. Bar Found., Order of Coit, Phi Delta Phi. Democrat. Methodist. Product liability, General corporate, General civil litigation. Home: 2124 Eastover Dr Jackson MS 39211-6719 Office: Emporium Bldg 400 E Capitol St Jackson MS 39201-2610

**CORMAN, JAMES C.,** lawyer; b. Galena, Kans., Oct. 20, 1920; s. Ransford Darwin and Edna Vivia (Love) C.; m. Virginia Little, June 22, 1946 (dec. May 1966); children: Mary Anne Avendano, James Charles Corman; m. Nancy Lee Malone, Jan. 1, 1978; children: Adam Ransford, Brian Christopher. BA, UCLA, 1942; JD, U. So. Calif., 1948; LLD (hon.), San Fernando U., 1968. Mem. L.A. City Coun., 1957-61, U.S. Ho. Reps., L.A., 1961-81; ptnr. Manatt, Phelps & Rothenberg, Washington, 1981-82; prin. Corman Law Offices, Washington, 1982-91; ptnr. Silverstein & Mullen, PLLC, Washington, 1991-93, of counsel, 1993—. Mem. Pres.'s Adv. Bd. Civil Disorders, Washington, 1967-68. Legislative. Office: Silverstein and Mullens PLLC 1776 K St NW Ste 800 Washington DC 20006-2333

**CORN, STEPHEN LESLIE,** lawyer; b. Danville, Ill., June 12, 1944; s. Clyde C. and Minnie Kathryn (Collins) C.; m. Judith Rae Petkas, June 11, 1966; children: Stephanie Lynn, Suzanne Michelle. BA, U. Ill., 1966, JD, 1969. Bar: Ill. 1969, U.S. Dist. Ct. (so. and cen. dists.) Ill. 1971, U.S. Ct. Appeals (7th cir.) 1976, U.S. Supreme Ct. 1976. Ptnr. Craig & Craig, Mattoon, Ill., 1969—. Bd. dirs. Mattoon Area YMCA, 1981-88, pres., 1987-88; bd. dirs. Harlan E. Moore Heart Rsch. Found., Champaign, Ill., 1982—, Lawyers Trust Fund of Ill., 1991-97. Mem. Ill. Bar Assn., Coles Cumberland Bar Assn. (pres. 1987-88), Ill. Assn. Def. Trial Counsel (pres. 1991-92), Ill. Bar Found., Am. Coll. Trial Lawyers. Episcopalian. General civil litigation, Personal injury, Workers' compensation. Office: Craig & Craig 1807 Broadway Ave Mattoon IL 61938-3800

**CORNABY, KAY STERLING,** lawyer, former state senator; b. Spanish Fork, Utah, Jan. 14, 1936; s. Sterling A. and Hilda G. Cornaby; m. Linda Rasmussen, July 23, 1965; children: Alyse, Derek, Tara, Heather, Brandon. AB, Brigham Young U., 1960; postgrad. law, Heidelberg, Germany, 1961-63; JD, Harvard U., 1966. Bar: N.Y. 1967, Utah 1969, U.S. Patent and Trademark Office 1967. Assoc. Brumbaugh, Graves, Donahue & Raymond, N.Y.C., 1966-69; ptnr. Mallinckrodt & Cornaby, Salt Lake City, 1969-72; sole practice Salt Lake City, 1972-85; mem. Utah State Senate, 1977-91, majority leader, 1983-84; shareholder Jones, Waldo, Holbrook & McDonough, Salt Lake City, 1985—. Mem. Nat. Commn. on Uniform State Laws, 1988-93; mem. adv. bd. U. Mich. Ctr. for Study of Youth Policy,1990-93; mem. Utah State Jud. Conduct Commn., 1983-91, chmn., 1984-85; bd. dirs. KUED-KUER Pub. TV and Radio, 1982-88; bd. dirs. Salt Lake Conv. and Visitors Bur., 1985—. Mem. N.Y. Bar Assn., Utah Bar Assn., Utah Harvard Alumni Assn. (pres. 1977-79), Harvard U. Law Sch. Alumni Assn. (pres. 1995—). Patent, Trademark and copyright, Real property. Office: Jones Waldo Holbrook & McDonough 1500 Wells Fargo Bank Plz 170 S Main St Salt Lake City UT 84101-1644

**CORNEJO, GONZALO MIGUEL,** lawyer; b. Lima, Peru, Nov. 26, 1959; s. Lino and Nelida (Arestegui) C.; m. Cecilia Esparza, July 25, 1987; 1 child, Blas Miguel. LLB, Cath. U., Lima, 1989; LLM, NYU, 1994. Bar: N.Y. 1995. Ptnr. Estudio Grau, Lima, 1990-91; cons. Sterling Winthrop, N.Y.C., 1991-95; counsel SmithKline Beecham, Phila., 1995—. Private international. Office: SmithKline Beecham One Franklin Plz Philadelphia PA 19101

**CORNELIUS, JAMES RUSSELL,** lawyer; b. Houston, Feb. 18, 1953; s. William Ralph and Betty Jean (Singley) C. BBA, Sam Houston State U., 1980; JD, S. Tex. Coll., 1984. Bar: Tex. 1985, U.S. Ct. Appeals (5th cir.) 1986, U.S. Dist. Co. (so. dist.) Tex. 1986, U.S. Dist. Ct. (ea. dist.) Tex. 1988, U.S. Tax Ct. 1986. Mgmt. Proven Products Co., Inc., Houston, 1976-83, W.W. Marine Sales & Svcs., Inc., Houston, 1983-85; assoc. Franklin, Kelly, Graham & Killough, Houston, 1985-88; ptnr. Cornelius and Salhab, Houston, 1988—. Mem. ABA, Houston Bar Assn., Delta Theta Phi, Pi Kappa Alpha. Roman Catholic. Avocation: fishing. General practice. Home: 1901 Ebony Ln Houston TX 77018-5022 Office: Cornelius Salhab and Spjut 2028 Buffalo Ter Houston TX 77019-2408

**CORNELIUS, O. RAY,** lawyer; b. Killeen, Tex., Nov. 25, 1953; s. Bert Lee and Imogene Cornelius; m. Gloria Jane Brumfield, Aug. 7, 1976; children: Brian Ray, Emily Jane, Timothy Jordan. BA, U. Ark., 1976, JD, 1979. Bar: Ark. 1979, La. 1981. Corp. atty. Wal-Mart Stores, Inc., Bentonville, Ark., 1979-80; assoc. Foley, Judell, Beck, Bewley & Martin, New Orleans, 1980-84; ptnr. Foley, Judell, Beck, Bewley, Martin & Hicks, New Orleans, 1984-93; mng. ptnr. Foley & Judell, LLP, New Orleans, 1993—. Municipal (including bonds). Office: Foley & Judell LLP 365 Canal St Ste 2600 New Orleans LA 70130-1138

**CORNELIUS, WALTER FELIX,** lawyer; b. Homewood, Ala., Apr. 20, 1922; s. William Felix and Nancy Ann (Cross) C.; m. Virginia Holliman, Jan. 30, 1942, (div. Feb. 1973); children: Nancy Carol, Susan Elaine; m. Lenora Black, May 4, 1974; 1 stepchild, Kristy Ann Wells. AB, Birmingham So. U., 1949; JD, U. Ala., 1953. Bar: Ala. 1953, U.S. Dist. Ct. (no. dist.) Ala. 1953, U.S. Tax Ct. 1954. Sole practice Birmingham, Ala., 1953—; bd. dirs. numerous corps., Birmingham. Elder, teacher Presbyn. Ch., Birmingham, 1963—; chmn. bd. dirs. Brother Bryan Mission, Birmingham, 1981—; pres. bd. trustees Cahaba Valley Fire and Medical Res. Dist., Shelby County, Ala., 1984—; mem. Horizon 280 Assn., Birmingham, 1985—. Served to cpl. USAAF, 1943-46, PTO. Recipient Pacific Theater Victory Med. award, Army Air Corps, Saipan and Iwo Jima, 1946. Mem. ABA, Ala. Bar Assn., Birmingham Bar Assn., Farrah Order Jurisprudence. Avocations: guitar, hunting, hiking, fishing, bird watching. General practice, Contracts commercial, Real property. Home and Office: 1101 Dunnavant Valley Rd Birmingham AL 35242-6725

**CORNELL, G(EORGE) WARE, JR.,** lawyer; b. Miami, Fla., Apr. 20, 1950; s. George Ware and Ann (Newton) C.; m. Karen H. Curtis, Nov. 10, 1978; children: Laurel Elizabeth, Jaime Rodriguez. BA, Emory U., 1972; JD, U. Ga., 1975. Bar: Ga. 1975, Fla. 1975, U.S. Dist. Ct. (so. and mid. dists.) Fla. 1975, U.S. Ct. Appeals (11th cir.) 1975, U.S. Supreme Ct. 1986. Assoc. Knight, Peters, Hoeveler, Pickle, Niemoller & Flynn, Miami, 1975-76, Bradford, Williams, McKay, Kimbrell, Hamann & Jennings, Miami, 1976-77; sr. law clk. to judge U.S. Dist. Ct. (So. Dist.), Miami, 1977-78; assoc. McCune, Hiaasen, Crum, Ferris & Gardner, Ft. Lauderdale, Fla., 1978-83, ptnr., 1984-88; pvt. practice, Ft. Lauderdale, 1988—; del. 11th Cir. Jud. Conf., 1984-89. Author: Going to Trial: A Step By Step Guide to Trial Practice. Mem. ABA, Fed. Bar Assn. (pres. Broward County chpt. 1984-85, v.p. 11th cir. 1986-90, Outstanding Cir. Officer 1987), Broward County Bar Assn. General civil litigation, Civil rights, Labor. Home: 6444 Allison Rd Miami FL 33141-4540 Office: 1401 E Broward Blvd Fort Lauderdale FL 33301-2118

**CORNELL, HELEN LOFTIN,** lawyer, educator; b. Nashville, Sept. 27, 1935; d. George Payne and Ruth Blalock Loftin; m. Donald Ray Cornell, Dec. 28, 1957 (Feb. 1964); 1 child, Ruth Anne Cornell Lowry. MusB, George Peabody Coll., 1956; MA, U. Louisville, 1971; PhD, Ohio State U., 1973; JD, Nashville U., 1983. Bar: Tenn. 1987, U.S. Dist. Ct. (mid. dist.) Tenn. 1987. Piano tchr., music educator, 1956—; instr. music George Peabody Coll., Nashville, 1976-79; rschr., writer Lewis Laska Legal Publs., Nashville, 1983-87; law libr. Nashville Sch. Law, 1987-91; pvt. practice Law Office of Helen Loftin Cornell, 1987—; libr. asst. Tenn. Supreme Ct. Libr., Nashville, 1989. Composer numerous pieces for piano, voice, choir and chamber instruments; contbr. articles to profl. jours. Mem. Nashville Choral Soc., 1950-56, Nashville Pro Musica, 1973-79. Mem. ABA, Tenn. Bar Assn., Nashville Bar Assn. (pro bono atty. 1987—). Democrat. Avocations: music, dancing, walking, swimming, fishing. General civil litigation, Probate, Appellate. Home and Office: 3635 Woodmont Blvd Nashville TN 37215-1837

**CORNELL, KENNETH LEE,** lawyer; b. Palo Alto, Calif., Feb. 23, 1945; s. Clinton Burdette and Mildred Lucy (Sheafer) C.; m. Barbara J. Smith, June 26, 1966; children: Melinda Lee, Geoffery Mark. BBA, BA in Social Sci., Pacific Union Coll., 1966; JD, U. Wash., 1971. Bar: Wash. 1971, U.S. Dist. Ct. (we. dist.) Wash. 1971, U.S. Supreme Ct. 1974. Ptnr. Keller & Rohrback, Seattle, 1971-75, Richard, Rossano & Cornell, Seattle, 1975-77, Moren, Lageschulte (now Cornell, Hansen, Bugni & McConnell), Seattle, 1978-87, Cornell, Hansen, Bugni & McConnell PS (firm name change), 1995-98; pvt. practice Seattle, 1998—; cons. atty. Town of Clyde Hill, Wash. 1980-87. Editor Wash. U. Law Rev., 1970-71. Bd. dirs. Kirkland (Wash.) Seventh Day Adventist Sch., 1972-78, Auburn (Wash.) Acad., 1974-80, Western Wash. Corp. Seventh Day Adventists, Bothell, 1974-80. Mem. Assn. Trial Lawyers Am., Wash. State Bar Assn., Wash. State Trial Lawyers Assn., Order of Coif. Democrat. Avocations: skiing, reading, gardening. State civil litigation, Real property, Personal injury. Office: 11320 Roosevelt Way NE Seattle WA 98125-6228

**CORNELL, RICHARD FARNHAM,** lawyer; b. Pitts., June 9, 1952; s. Paul Watson and Margaret Lucy (Boose) C.; m. Denise Vandevelde, May 24, 1975; children: Jonathan Watson, Julie Elizabeth, Benjamin Dunlap. BA in Polit Sci. and Econs., U. Calif., Irvine, 1974; JD, U. San Francisco, 1977. Bar: Calif. 1977, U.S. Dist. Ct. (no. dist.) Calif. 1977, Nev. 1979, U.S. Dist. Ct. Nev. 1979, U.S. Ct. Appeals (9th cir.) 1981. Law clk. to chief judge U.S. Dist. Ct. Nev., Las Vegas, 1978-80; dep. dist. atty. Washoe County Dist. Atty., Reno, 1980-81; assoc. Raggio, Wooster & Lindell, Reno, 1981-86; sole practice Reno, 1986—; pro-tem judge Reno Justice Ct., 1992—. Co-editor Nevada Civil Practice Manual, 1985-86. Bd. dirs. Drunk Drivers Inc. d/b/a Call-a-Ride, Reno, 1984-85, Assn. Excellence in Edn., Reno, 1986. Mem. Nev. Bar Assn. (criminal practice and procedures com. 1986, fee dispute com. 1998—). Club: Toastmasters (Reno). Appellate, Criminal, Family and matrimonial. Office: 150 Ridge St Reno NV 89501-1938

**CORNETT, BRADLEY WILLIAMS,** lawyer; b. Maryville, Tenn., Apr. 15, 1970; s. Billy Kenneth and Wilda Cornett; m. Wendy Leigh Love, Apr. 27, 1996. BS, U. Tenn., 1991; JD, U. N.C., 1995. Bar: Ala. 1995, U.S. Dist. Ct. (no. dist.) Ala. 1996. Atty. Ford & Howard P.C., Gadsden, Ala., 1996—. Mem. ABA, Ala. Def. Lawyers Assn., Def. Rsch. Inst. General civil litigation, Insurance, Product liability. Office: Ford & Howard PC PO Box 388 Gadsden AL 35902-0388

**CORNETT, PAUL MICHAEL, SR.,** lawyer; b. Chgo., Jan. 24, 1949; s. Paul Elvon and Phyllis (Pedone) C.; m. Marianne Elizabeth Hofer, Aug. 14, 1971; children: Paul Michael Jr., Matthew Charles, Nicholas Robert. BBA, Western Mich. U., Kalamazoo, 1971; JD, Marquette U., Milw., 1974. Bar: Supreme Ct. Wis., 1974. Officer, capt. legal asst. USAR, Green Bay, Wis., 1974-87; assoc. atty. Mazza Law Offices, New Berlin, Wis., 1974-75; pvt. practice Shawano, Wis., 1975-77; asst. dist. atty. Shawano County, Menominee County, Wis., 1977-78; dist. atty. Shawano and Menominee County, Wis., 1978-82; assoc. Direnzo and Bomier, Neenah, Wis., 1982-84; ptnr. Van Hoof, Van Hoof and Cornett Law Offices, Little Chute, Wis., 1984-93, 1993—; pro bono atty. Legal Svcs. N.E. Wis., Appleton, 1990—; atty. Village of Combined Locks (Wis.) 1984—, Darboy (Wis.) Sanitary Dist., 1984—, Town of Buchanan, Wis., 1984—; mentor to juvenile offender Outagamie County Juvenile Offender Program, Appleton, Wis., 1995—; lawyers in the classroom State Bar of Wis., 1974—; judge Mock Trial Competition, Appleton, Wis., 1993—. Bd. dirs., 1989—, chmn. bd., 1995-96, Heart of Valley C. of C., Kaukauna, Wis.; pres. Little Chute (Wis.) Businessman's Assn., 1994-95, bd. dirs., 1989—; pal to 13 yr. old boy Outagamie County PAL Program, Appleton, Wis., 1994—; bd. mem., chmn. bd., big brother Big Bros. and Big Sisters of Shawano County, Wis., 1976-82; mentor Little Chute Elem. Sch., 1998—. 2nd lt. U.S. Army, 1974. Recipient Dedication award Shawano and Menominee Counties, Wis., 1982, Army Commendation medal, 1987, Army Achievement medal, 1985, USAR, Washington. Mem. KC, State Bar of Wis., Outagamie County Bar Assn., Optimist Internat. Republican. Roman Catholic. Avocations: fishing, travel, camping, woodworking. General practice, Criminal, Municipal (including bonds). Home: 2963 W Creek Valley Ln Appleton WI 54914-1557 Office: Van Hoof Van Hoof & Cornett Law Offices 200 E Main St Little Chute WI 54140-1834

**CORNETT, WENDY LOVE,** lawyer; b. Ft Walton Beach, Fla., Oct. 24, 1970; d. James D. and Patricia A. Love; m. Bradley Williams Cornett, Apr. 27, 1996. BS in Comml. and Bus. Adminstrn., U. Ala., Tuscaloosa, 1992; JD, U. N.C., 1995. Bar: Ala. 1995. Assoc. Burr & Forman, LLP, Birmingham, Ala., 1995—. Contracts commercial, Landlord-tenant, Real property. Office: Burr & Forman LLP 420 20th St N Birmingham AL 35203-5200

**CORNING, NICHOLAS F.,** lawyer; b. Seattle, Nov. 8, 1945; s. Frank C. and Jessie D. (Weeks) C.; m. Patricia A. Tomlinson, Dec. 14, 1968; children: Kristen Marie, Lauren Margaret. BCS cum laude, Seattle U., 1968; JD, U. Wash., 1972. Bar: Wash. 1972, U.S. Ct. Appeals (9th cir.) 1972, U.S. Dist. Ct. (we. dist.) Wash. 1973, U.S. Supreme Ct. 1976, U.S. Ct. Claims 1981. Assoc. Jennings P. Felix, Seattle, 1972-75; ptnr. Lagerquist, McConnell & Corning, Seattle, 1975-77; pres., ptnr. Treece, Richdale, Malone, Corning & Abbott, Inc., P.S., Seattle, 1977-99; atty. Corning Law Firm, Seattle, 1999—; pres. Windermere Corp., Seattle, 1988, also bd. dirs. Recipient Am. Jurisprudence award in Criminal Law U. Wash., 1971. Mem. Assn. Trial Lawyers Am., Nat. Inst. Trial Advocacy, Wash. State Bar Assn., Wash. State Trial Lawyers Assn. (pres. 1994-95, bd. dirs.), King County Bar Assn. (spkrs. bur. 1983-85, chmn. pub. info. com. 1985-87), Ballard C. of C. (bd. dirs., pres. 1989-92), Beta Gamma Sigma (Key award 1968). Federal civil litigation, State civil litigation, Personal injury. Home: 5640 NE 55th St Seattle WA 98105-2835 Office: The Corning Law Firm 5301 Ballard Ave NW Seattle WA 98107-4061

**CORNISH, JEANNETTE CARTER,** lawyer; b. Steelton, Pa., Sept. 17, 1946; d. Ellis Pollard and Anna Elizabeth (Stannard) C.; m. Harry L. Cornish; children: Lee Jason, Geoffrey Charles. BA, Howard U., 1968, JD, 1971. Bar: N.J. 1976, U.S. Dist. Ct. N.J. 1976. Atty. Newark-Essex Law Reform, 1971-72; technician EEOC, Newark, 1972-73; atty., asst. sec. Inmont Corp., N.Y.C., 1974-82; sr. atty., asst. sec. Inmont Corp., Clifton, N.J., 1982-85; sr. atty. BASF Corp., Mt. Olive, N.J., 1986-99; speaker on diversity in bus. Past mem., bd. dirs. YWCA, Paterson, N.J.; trustee Barnert Hosp., Paterson; bd. dirs. Lenni-Lenape coun. Girl Scouts Am. Mem. ABA (commn. on opportunities for minorities in the profession, minority in-house counsel group, diversity vice chair gen. practice sect. corp. counsel com.), Nat. Bar Assn., Assn. Black Women Lawyers, Am. Corp. Counsel Assn., Internat. Trademark Assn. (past mem. editorial bd. The Trademark Reporter, mem. exec. commn. com., mem. meetings com., program quality and evaluation subcom.). Contracts commercial, General corporate, Trademark and copyright.

**CORNISH, RICHARD POOL,** lawyer; b. Evanston, Ill., Sept. 9, 1942; s. William A. and Rita (Pool) C.; children: William Darby, Richard Gordon. B.S., Okla. State U., 1964; LL.B., U. Okla., 1966. Bar: Okla. 1966, U.S. Dist. Ct. (ea. dist.) Okla. 1969, U.S. Supreme Ct. 1979. Ptnr., Baumert & Cornish, McAlester, Okla., 1967-71, Cornish & Cornish, Inc., McAlester, Okla., 1971-77; magistrate U.S. Dist. Ct. Eastern Dist. Okla., 1976—; prin. Richard P. Cornish, Inc., McAlester, Okla., 1977—. Bd. dirs. McAlester Boys Club, 1970-80, pres., 1974. Served to capt. JAGC, USAR, 1966-78. Mem. Okla. Bar Assn. (mem. legal aid to servicemen com., legal specialization com.), Pittsburg County Bar Assn., McAlester C. of C. (dir. 1973-75). Roman Catholic. Probate, General practice. Home: 611 E Creek Ave Mcalester OK 74501-6929 Office: PO Box 1106 Mcalester OK 74502-1106

**CORNWELL, DONALD LEE,** lawyer; b. Denver, Dec. 16, 1952; s. Donald E. and Rosemary N. Cornwell; m. Pamela J. Pleasants, May 31, 1986. BBA summa cum laude, U. Ga., 1975; JD, U. Va., 1978. Bar: Calif. 1978, U.S. Dist. (ctrl, no., so. and ea. dists.) Calif. 1978, U.S. Ct. Appeals (9th cir.) 1978, U.S. Ct. Appeals (fed. cir.) 1995. Assoc. Latham & Watkins, L.A., 1978-82; assoc., then of counsel Jones, Day, Reavis & Pogue, L.A., 1982-88; of counsel Orrick, Herrington & Sutcliffe, L.A., 1988-91; pvt. practice, L.A., 1991—. Co-author: Alternative Dispute Resolution in the Construction Industry, 1991; editor Va. Law Rev., 1976-78, Calif. Employment Law Newsletter, 1994—. Mem. Los Angeles County Bar Assn., Order of Coif. Avocation: wine. General civil litigation, Labor, Trademark and copyright. Office: 12100 Wilshire Blvd Ste 1900 Los Angeles CA 90025-7107

**CORNWELL, WILLIAM JOHN,** lawyer; b. Wheeling, W.Va., Nov. 9, 1959; s. James Miller Cornwell and Judith (Shock) Clark; m. Leslie Glickstein, May 23, 1987. BBA, Ga. State U., 1982, JD, 1985. Bar: Ga. 1985, U.S. Dist. Ct. (no. and mid. dists.) Ga. 1985, U.S. Ct. Appeals (11th cir.) 1985, Fla. 1988. Gov.'s intern Coun. for Maternal and Infant Health, Atlanta, 1982; adminstrv. asst. Coun. Juvenile Ct. Judges, Atlanta, 1983; law clk. HHS, Atlanta, 1984; legal intern Office Fulton County Dist. Atty., Atlanta, 1984-85; ptnr. Pope, McGlamry, Kilpatrick & Morrison, Atlanta, 1985-97; active Cuban Detainee Assistance Program, 1985-87. Mem. Ga. Bar Assn. (moot ct. com. 1987), Atlanta Bar Assn. (pub. rels. com. 1988), Fla. Bar Assn., Assn. Trial Lawyers Am., Ga. Trial Lawyers Assn., Ga. State U. Law Alumni Assn., Phi Alpha Delta. Democrat. Methodist. Avocations: water skiing, tennis, softball, history. Fax: 561-218-3552. General civil litigation, Personal injury, Banking. Office: Pope McGlamry Kilpatrick & Morrison 83 Walton St NW Ste 400 Atlanta GA 30303-2123

**CORNYN, JOHN,** state attorney general; b. Feb. 2, 1952; married; 2 children. BA, Trinity U., 1973; JD, St. Mary's U., 1977; postgrad., U. Va. Cert. personal injury trial law Tex. Bd. Legal Specialization. Assoc., ptnr. Groce, Locke & Hebdon, San Antonio, 1977-84; judge 37th Dist. Ct., Bexer County, 1985-90; presiding judge 4th Adminstrv. Jud. Region, 1989-92; justice Supreme Ct. Tex., Austin, 1991-98; atty. Thompson & Knight; atty. gen. State of Tex., Austin, 1999—; Tex. Supreme Ct. liaison Bd. LAw Examiners, 1991—, Gender Bias Task Force, 1993-95; lectr. CLE programs. Bd. vis. Trinity U., Pepperdine U. Sch. Law. Fellow Tex. Bar Found., San Antonio Bar Found.; mem. Am. Law Inst., William Sessions Inn of Ct. (master bencher 1988-90, pres. 1989-90), Robert W. Calvent Inn of Ct. (pres. 1994-95). Office: Office of Atty Gen PO Box 12548 Austin TX 78711-2548*

**CORONADO, SANTIAGO SYBERT (JIM CORONADO),** judge; b. Laredo, Tex., Nov. 12, 1951; s. Bill Gee and Lucía (Coronado) Sybert; m. Dawn Dittman, Apr. 27, 1996. BA cum laude, U. Tex., 1974, JD, 1978. Bar: Tex. 1978. Pvt. practice Austin, Tex., 1979-89; mcpl. judge City of Austin, 1989-91, City of Kyle, Tex., 1989-91; magistrate judge Travis County Dist. Ct., 1991—. Bd. dirs. Am. Heart Assn., Austin, 1990; state pres. Mex. Am. Bar Assn., Tex., 1988-89; pres. Capital Area Mex. Am. Lawyers, Austin, 1986-87. Recipient Lifetime Achievement award Hispanic Issues Sect. State Bar of Tex., 1995, Presdl. citation for disting. svc., 1999. Mem. Hispanic Nat. Bar Assn. (regional pres. 1989-90, nat. v.p. 1991-92), Travis County Bar Assn. (dir. 1995—, treas. 1999). Democrat. Home: 5602 Palisade Ct Austin TX 78731-4508 Office: Travis County Ct House Austin TX 78701

**CORPUZ, MARCELO NAVARRO, III,** lawyer; b. Quezon City, The Philippines, May 22, 1968; came to U.S., 1969; s. Marcelo Barrios and Amy (Navarro) C. BA, Georgetown U., 1990; MPH, George Washington U., 1995, JD, 1995. Bar: Ohio 1995, D.C. 1997, Ill. 1998. Rsch. asst. Ctr. Health Policy Rsch., Washington, 1993; law clk. Horty, Springer, & Mattern, Pitts., 1994; assoc. Bricker & Eckler, LLP, Columbus, Ohio, 1995-97, Ross & Hardies, Chgo., 1998—. Bd. dirs. Asian Am. Profls. Columbus, Asian Am. Cmty. Svcs. Columbus; logistics com. mem. Christmas in April, Columbus, 1996-97. Mem. ABA (health law com. planning bd. mem.), Am. Health Lawyers Assn., Asian Am. Bar Assn., Columbus Bar Assn. (immersion com.), Chgo. Bar Assn. Roman Catholic. Avocations: golf, skiing. Fax: 312-920-7230. Health. Office: Ross & Hardies 150 N Michigan Ste 2500 Chicago IL 60601-7567

**CORR, MARTIN JOSEPH,** lawyer; b. Phila., Jan. 29, 1937; s. John A. and Helen (Fallon) C.; m. Mary Lee Rothwell, Oct. 14, 1961; children: Sean M., Marguerite M., Mary Helen, Elizabeth Ann. AB, St. Joseph's U., 1958; JD, Temple U., 1961, LLM, 1994. Bar: Pa. 1961, U.S. Dist. Ct. (ea. dist.) Pa. 1962, U.S. Ct. Appeals (3rd cir.) 1966, U.S. Supreme Ct. 1979. Assoc. Law Offices Joseph R. Thompson, Phila., 1965-66, Liebert, Harvey, Bechtle, Herting & Short, Phila., 1966-71; assoc., then ptnr. Connolly, McAndrews, Kihm & Stevens, Warminster, Pa., 1971-78; ptnr. Connolly, McAndrews, Stevens, Drexler & Corr, Warminster, 1979-83, Corr, Stevens & Fenningham, Warminster and Trevose, Pa., 1983—. Committeeman Bucks County Rep. Com., Doylestown, Pa., 1973-75, exec. committeeman, 1976-80; mem., pres. State St. Players, Doylestown, 1978—. Capt. JAGC, USAF, 1962-65. Mem. ABA, Pa. Bar Assn., Phila. Bar Assn., Bucks County Bar Assn. (pres. 1989-90), Assn. Trial Lawyers Am., Phi Delta Phi (chancellor Conwell chpt. 1960-61). Republican. Roman Catholic. Avocations: fishing, hunting, boating, jogging. General civil litigation, Insurance, Personal injury. Office: Corr Stevens & Fenningham 1035 W Bristol Rd Warminster PA 18974-1009

**CORRADA DEL RIO, BALTASAR,** supreme court justice; b. Morovis, P.R., Apr. 10, 1935; s. Romulo and Ana Maria (del Rio) Corrada del R.; m. Beatrice Betances, Dec. 24, 1959; children: Ana Isabel, Francisco Javier, Juan Carlos, Jose Baltasar. BA in Social Scis., U. P.R., 1956, JD, 1959. Bar: P.R., 1959. Ptnr. McConnell Valdes Sifre & Ruiz Suria, San Juan, 1959-75; atty., chmn. Civil Right Commn., P.R., 1970-72; mem., resident commr. from P.R. 95th-98th Congress; mayor City of San Juan, P.R., 1985-89; atty. Baltasar Corrada Law Office, 1989-92; sec. of state Govt. of P.R., 1993-95; Puerto Rico assoc. justice Supreme Ct., P.R., 1995—; pres. New Progressive Party, 1986-89. Pres. editorial bd. P.R. Human Rights Rev., 1971-72. Bd. dirs. P.R. Teleradial Inst. Ethics. Recipient Great Cross of Civil Merit of Spain King Juan Carlos I, 1987. Mem. ABA, Fed. Bar Assn., P.R. Bar Assn. Roman Catholic. Club: Exchange, San Juan Rotary. Office: P R Supreme Ct PO Box 9022392 San Juan PR 00902-2392

**CORREALE, ROBERT D.,** lawyer; b. Morristown, N.J., Jan. 30, 1955; s. Salvatore Gerald and Edith Jean Correale; m. Margaret Alice Correale, Nov. 16, 1985; children: Catherine, Mary. BS, Trenton State Coll., 1977; JD, Ohio No. U., 1982. Bar: N.J. 1982, U.S. Dist. Ct. N.J. 1981, U.S. Ct. Appeals (3d cir.) 1989. Asst. pros. Somerset County Pros.'s Office, Somerville, N.J., 1981-84; assoc. Cohen & Kron, Succasunna, N.J., 1984-88; ptnr. Kron & Correale, Succasunna, N.J., 1988—. Mem. ABA, ATLA, Morris County BAr Assn., Nat. Dist. Atty.'s Assn., Morris County Mcpl. Pros.'s Assn., KC. Republican. Roman Catholic. Avocations: tennis, traveling, history. State civil litigation, Criminal, General practice. Office: Kron & Correale PO Box 362 Succasunna NJ 07876-0362

**CORREIRA, DAVID J.,** lawyer; m. Ann M. Correira; children: Eric, Jonathan. BA, Bridgewater State Coll., 1980; MPA, U. R.I., 1984; JD, New Eng. Sch. Law, 1989; postgrad., Harvard U., 1993. Bar: Mass. 1989, R.I. 1990, U.S. Dist. Ct. Mass. 1990. Counsel Eastern Utilities Assocs. and Subs., Boston, 1982-89; individual practice law Swansea, Mass., 1989—; lectr. in field. Contbr. articles to profl. jours. Mem. Southeastern Mass. div. bd. dirs. Am. Cancer Soc.; vol. United Way of Southeaster New Eng.; town moderator Somerset, 1996—; active Boy Scouts Am., PTO. Mem. ABA (law practice sect., utility sect., energy litigation sect.), R.I. Bar Assn., Boston Bar Assn., Bristol County (Mass.) Bar Assn., Nat. Acad. Elder Law Attys., Am. Soc. for Pub. Adm,instrn., Polit. Sci. Acad., Ea. Comm. Assn., New Eng. C. of C. Execs., No. R.I. C. of C., No. R.I. Pvt. Industry Coun., others. Home: 8 Lynch Ave Somerset MA 02726-4037 Office: Law Office Swansea Profl Pk 1010 GAR Hwy Swansea MA 02777

**CORRELL, JOANNA RAE,** lawyer; b. Indpls., Apr. 17, 1948; d. Philip Ray Correll and Dorothy Jane (Morris) Aslaner; m. Bruce Harold Sheetz, June 15, 1968 (div. 1978); m. Christopher Miles Althof, June 29, 1985; children: Tanya, Dustin, Kurt, Korine, Kiri, Kara. BS in Edn., Ind. U., 1970; JD, Western State U., San Diego, 1978. Bar: Calif. 1979, U.S. Dist. Ct. (no. dist.) Calif. 1981, U.S. Dist. Ct. (ea. dist.) Calif. 1979. Tchr. Laredo (Tex.) Unified Sch. Dist., 1970; subs. tchr. Napa (Calif.) Unified Sch. Dist., 1970-72; investigator Hughes Atty. Svcs., San Diego, 1976-78; assoc. Wagner, Pistole & Correll, Napa, 1978-82; ptnr. Childers & Correll, Weaverville, Calif., 1982-86; pvt. practice Weaverville, 1987—; patient's rights adv. State of Calif., Sacramento, 1984—. Dancer Studio 5, Weaverville, 1982—; actress/dancer Trinity Players, Weaverville, 1982-84. Mem. Ca. State Bar Assn., Bus. and Profl. Women (v.p. 1983-84). Democrat. Avocations: running long distance, skiing, backpacking. General civil litigation, Criminal. Office: PO Box 1329 248 Main Weaverville CA 96093-0631

**CORRIGAN, ANN PHILLIPS,** lawyer; b. Des Moines, May 20, 1963; d. Lawrence Marvin and Jo Ann S. Phillips; m. William M. Corrigan Jr., Aug. 20, 1988; children: Kathleen, Maura. BJ, U. Mo., 1985; JD, U. Wis., 1988. Bar: Wis. 1988, Mo. 1988, Ill. 1989, U.S. Dist. Ct. (ea. dist.) Mo. 1988. Assoc. Thompson & Mitchell, St. Louis, 1988-91; staff atty. ITT Comml. Fin., Clayton, Mo., 1991-94; assoc. Descher & Schultz, Clayton, 1995-99, Schultz & Little, LLC, Clayton, 1999—. General civil litigation, Trademark and copyright. Office: Schultz & Little LLC 7700 Bonhomme Ave Ste 325 Saint Louis MO 63105-1995

**CORRIGAN, MAURA DENISE,** judge; b. Cleve., June 14, 1948; d. Peter James and Mae Ardell (McCrone) C.; m. Joseph Dante Grano, July 11, 1976; children: Megan Elizabeth, Daniel Corrigan. BA with honors, Marygrove Coll., 1969; JD with honors, U. Detroit, 1973; LLD (hon.), No. Mich. U., 1999. Bar: Mich. 1974. Jud. clk. Mich. Ct. Appeals, Detroit, 1973-74; asst. prosecutor Wayne County, Detroit, 1974-79, asst. U.S. atty., 1979-89, chief appellate divsn., 1979-86; chief asst. U.S. Atty. Wayne County, 1986-89; ptnr. Plunkett & Cooney PC, Detroit, 1989-92; judge Mich. Ct. Appeals, 1992-98, chief judge, 1997-98; justice Mich. Supreme Ct., 1999—; vice chmn. Mich. Com. to formulate Rules of Criminal Procedure, Mich. Supreme Ct., 1982-89; mem. Mich. Law Revision Commn., 1991-98; mem. com. on standard jury instrns., State Bar Mich., 1978-82; lectr. Mich. Jud. Inst., Sixth cir. Jud. Workshop, Inst. CLE, ABA-Cin. Bar Litigation Sects., Dept. Justice Advocacy Inst. Contbr. chpt. to book, articles to legal revs. Vice chmn. Project Transition, Detroit, 1976-92; mem. citizens Adv. Coun. Lafayette Clinic, Detroit, 1979-87; bd. dirs. Detroit Wayne County Criminal Advocacy Program, 1983-86; pres. Rep. Women's Bus. and Profl. Forum, 1993—, bd. dirs., 1990-91. Recipient award of merit Detroit Commn. on Human Rels., 1974, Dir.'s award Dept. Justice, 1985, Outstanding Practitioner of Criminal Law award Fed. Bar Assn., 1989, award Mich. Women's Commn., 1998. Mem. Mich. Bar Assn., Detroit Bar Assn., Fed. Bar Assn. (pres. Detroit chpt. 1990-91), Inc. Soc. Irish Am. Lawyers (pres. 1991-92), Federalist Soc. (Mich. chpt.). Office: Mich Supreme Ct 500 Woodward Ave Fl 20 Detroit MI 48226-5498

**CORRY, ROBERT EMMETT,** lawyer; b. Mobile, Ala., Dec. 22, 1935; s. Robert Emmett and Rachel Christine C.; m. Anne Yound; children: Robert, Megan, Peter. AB, U. Ala., 1957; JD with honors, George Washington U., 1964. Bar; Ga. 1964, U.S. Dist. Ct. Ga. 1964, U.S. Ct. Appeals (5th and 11th cirs.) 1964. Ptnr. Nall, Miller, Cadenhead & Dennis, Atlanta, 1964-70, Dennis & Fain, Atlanta, 1970-75, Dennis, Corry, Webb & Carlock, Atlanta, 1975-85, Dennis, Corry & Porter, Atlanta, 1985—; adj. prof. law Emory U. Law Sch., Atlanta, 1970-73. Co-author, co-editor: Motor Carrier Laibility, 1998; contbr. articles to profl. jours. Capt. USAF, 1957-60. Mem. Ga. Def. Lawyers Assn., Internat. Assn. Def. Counsel, Trucking Industry Def. Assn. (Ann. Svc. award 1996). Avocations: reading, gardening, cooking, hiking. Insurance, Personal injury, General civil litigation. Home: 2 W Wesley Rd NW Atlanta GA 30305-3500 Office: Dennis Corry & Porter 3300 Atlanta Plz Atlanta GA 30326

**CORSO, FRANK MITCHELL,** lawyer; b. N.Y.C., July 28, 1928; s. Joseph and Jane (DeBenedetto) C.; m. Dorothy G. McVeety, Apr. 7, 1951; children: Frank, Elaine, Patricia, Dorothy. LLB, St. John's U., 1952. Bar: N.Y. 1954, D.C. 1981, U.S. Ct. Mil. Appeals 1954, U.S. Sup. Ct. 1960. Ptnr. Corso & Fertig, 1957-61, Corso & Petito, 1966-69, Corso & Landa, Jericho, N.Y., 1971-73, Corso & Engelberg, 1973-82; sr. ptnr., Mitchell Corso, P.C., Westbury, N.Y., 1982—. Appointed bd. dirs. UN Devel. Corp. by N.Y. Gov., N.Y. Mcpl. Bond Bank Agy.; lectr. St. John's U. Sch. of Law; U.S. congl. candidate, N.Y.; trustee WLIW pub. TV channel. With U.S. Army 1951-53. Named Man of Yr., Am.-Itals of L.I., 1966. Mem. ABA, N.Y. State Bar Assn., Nassau Bar Assn., Assn. Trial Lawyers Am., Internat. Bar Assn., World Assn. Lawyers (founding mem.), Vatican Knight of Holy Sepulchre. Contbr. articles to legal jours.; TV commentator legal topics. State civil litigation, Personal injury, General corporate. Home: 1 Southdown Ct Huntington NY 11743-2548 Office: 350 Jericho Tpke Jericho NY 11753-1317

**CORSO, VICTOR PAUL,** lawyer; b. Freeport, N.Y., Aug. 2, 1961; s. Victor Anthony and Hope (Rostron) C.; m. Maureen Gerette Duffy, Aug. 19, 1988; children: Kathryn Mary, Rachel Victoria, Olivia Gerette. BS, SUNY Maritime Coll., Ft. Schuyler, 1983; JD, Bklyn. Law Sch., 1990. Bar: N.Y., U.S. Dist. Ct. (so. & ea. dists.) N.Y. Average adjuster, ins. broker Alexander & Alexander of N.Y., Inc., N.Y.C., 1984-87; law clk. Healy & Baillie, N.Y.C., 1988-89, Walker & Corsa, N.Y.C., 1989-90; atty. Kirlin, Campbell & Keating, N.Y.C., 1991-96; mgr. claims dept. CNA/MOAC Ins. Co., N.Y.C., 1997—. Lic. 3d mate U.S. Merchant Marine. Eagle Scout, Boy Scouts Am. Mem. ABA, ATLA, Maritime Law Assn. U.S., Average Adjusters Assn. U.S., N.Y. County Lawyers Bar Assn., Propeller Club Port of N.Y. Admiralty, Insurance, Private international. Home: 18 Greenhill Ln Huntington NY 11743-5819 Office: CNA/MOAC 180 Maiden Ln New York NY 10038-4925

**CORSON, KIMBALL JAY,** lawyer; b. Mexico City, Sept. 17, 1941; came to U.S., 1942; s. Harland Jerry and Arleen Elizabeth (Jones) C.; m. Ann Dudley Wood, May 25, 1963 (div. Apr. 1978); 1 child, Claudia Ring; m. Joy Lorann Sligh, June 16, 1979; children: Bryce Manning, Jody Darlene. BA, Wayne State U., 1966; MA, U. Chgo., 1968, JD, 1971. Bar: Ariz. 1972, U.S. Dist. Ct. 1971, U.S. Supreme Ct. 1991. Assoc. Lewis & Roca, Phoenix, 1971-74, ptnr., 1974-90; ptnr. Horne Kaplan & Bistrow, Phoenix, 1990-99; of counsel Shields and Andersen, 1999—. Co-author: Document Control: Organization, Management and Production, 1988; co-author: Litigation Support Using Personal Computers, 1989. Co-founder Desert Hills Improvement Assn., Phoenix, 1988—. With U.S. Army, 1961-64. Fellow Woodrow Wilson Found., 1966-67. Mem. ABA (civil practice and procedures com. antitrust sect. 1988—), Ariz. Bar Assn. (spkr. 1991—), Maricopa County Bar Assn., Internat. Trademark Assn. (editl. bd. The Trademark Reporter 1993-94, 99—, mem. publs. com. 1995-96, INTA Speaker, Am. Sailing Assn., Phi Beta Kappa. Avocations: music, computers, sailing, photography, first century history. Federal civil litigation, State civil litigation, Intellectual property. Home: Summit Ranch 35808 N 15th Ave Phoenix AZ 85086-7228 Office: Shields and Andersen 7830 N 23rd Ave Phoenix AZ 85021-6808

**CORTES, WILLIAM PATRICK,** lawyer, telecommunications executive; b. Ellenville, N.Y., Apr. 23, 1955; s. Robert Paul and Joan Helen (Whitstock) C. AB, Stanford U., 1977; MBA, U. Wash., 1983, JD, 1984. Bar: Wash. 1984; CPA, Wash. Fin. instr. Sch. Bus. Adminstrn. U. Wash., Seattle, 1980-83; strategic planning analyst Burlington No., Inc., Seattle, 1982, 83; sr. cons. Ernst & Young Telecommunications Group, Tacoma, 1985-86; fin. mgr. spec. projects U S WEST NewVector Group Inc., Bellevue, Wash., 1986-88, dir. investor rels. and bus. analysis, 1988-90; dir. investor rels. U S WEST, Inc., Englewood, Colo., 1990; dir. bus. devel. U S WEST Internat. Inc., Paris, 1990-92; U S WEST Internat. Inc., London, 1992-93; dir. new opportunity devel. US West Comm., Denver, 1993-95, exec. dir. product devel. wireless group, 1995-96; exec. dir. bus. devel. American Portable Telecom, Chgo., 1996—. Mem. ABA, AICPAs, Wash. State Bar Assn., Fed. Comms. Bar Assn., Wash. Soc. CPAs. Democrat. Roman Catholic. Avocations: mountain climbing, squash. Communications, Mergers and acquisitions, Private international. Office: American Portable Telecom 8410 W Bryn Mawr Ave Ste 1100 Chicago IL 60631-3422

**CORTESE, ALFRED WILLIAM, JR.,** lawyer, consultant; b. Phila., Apr. 2, 1937; s. Alfred William and Marie Ann (Coccio) C.; m. Rosanna S. Zimmerman, Aug. 18, 1962 (div. Aug. 1981); children: Aline Elizabeth, Alfred William II, Christina Nicole. BA cum laude, Temple U., 1959; JD, U. Pa., 1962. Bar: Pa. 1963, U.S. Supreme Ct. 1972, D.C. 1977. Assoc., ptnr. Pepper, Hamilton & Scheetz, Phila., 1962-71; asst. exec. dir. FTC, Washington, 1972-73; assoc. Dechert, Price & Rhoads, Phila., 1974-76; ptnr. Clifford & Warnke, Washington, 1977-81; chmn., chief exec. officer Cortese & Loughran Inc., Washington, 1982-84; ptnr. Kirkland & Ellis, Washington, 1985-94, Pepper Hamilton, LLP, Washington, 1994-98; mng. mem. Cortese PLLC, Washington, 1999—; cons. Gen. Motors Corp., Detroit, 1985—. Lt. U.S. Army, 1959-60. Mem. ABA, Am. Law Inst., Pa. Bar, D.C. Bar Assn., Def. Rsch. Inst., Lawyers for Civil Justice (mem. exec. com., bd. dirs.), Racquet Club (Phila.), Univ. Club, Capitol Hill Club. Avocations: vintage automobile racing and restoration, art & antique collecting, cooking. Fax: 202-637-9797. Legislative, Federal civil litigation, Administrative and regulatory. Home: 113 3rd St NE Washington DC 20002-7313 Office: Cortese PLLC 600 Hamilton Sq 600 14th St NW Washington DC 20005

**CORTESE, JOSEPH SAMUEL, II,** lawyer; b. Des Moines, Aug. 17, 1955; s. Joseph Anthony and Kathryn Mary (Marasco) C.; m. Diane Caniglia, Aug. 5, 1978; children: Joseph III, James David, Kathryn Elizabeth. BA, Ind. U., 1977; JD with honors, Drake U., 1980. Bar: Iowa 1981, U.S. Dist. Ct. (no. and so. dists.) Iowa 1981, U.S. Ct. Appeals (8th cir.) 1984. Assoc. Jones, Hoffman & Huber, Des Moines, 1981-85; ptnr. Huber, Book, Cortese, Happe & Brown, P.L.C., Des Moines, 1985—. Mem. ABA, ATLA, Iowa State Bar Assn., Polk County Bar Assn., Def. Research Inst., Iowa Trial Lawyers Assn. Roman Catholic. E-mail: jcortese@desmoineslaw.com. Fax: 515-243-5481. Personal injury, Workers' compensation, Product liability. Home: 2915 Sherry Ln Urbandale IA 50322-6813 Office: Huber Book Cortese Happe & Brown PLC 317 6th Ave Ste 200 Des Moines IA 50309-4127

**CORTEZ, HERNAN GLENN,** lawyer; b. Harlingen, Tex., Nov. 12, 1934; s. Hernan and Laura (Howell) C.; m. Carole Elaine DuBois, Jan. 29, 1958 (div. Aug. 1976); children: Vicky Foss, Marta Stephens, Jill Hubach, Ingrid Standard, H. Glenn Jr.; m.Carole Jean Simms, Dec. 31, 1976; 1 child, Troy Dillinger. BA, U. Tex., 1956, JD, 1962. Bar: Tex. 1962, U.S. Dist. Ct. (we. dist.) Tex. 1970, U.S. Ct. Appeals (5th cir.) 1981; bd. cert. pers. injury trial law Tex. Bd. Legal Specialization. Asst. atty. City of Austin, Tex., 1962-69; assoc. atty. City of Austin, 1969, atty., 1969-70; sole practice Austin, 1971—; atty. City of Manor, Tex., 1972-90, City of Rollingwood, Tex., 1972-86, City of Pflugerville, Tex., 1974-93, City of Sunset Valley, Tex., 1980-86, City of Granite Shoals, Tex., 1983-86. Served as capt. U.S. Army, 1957-59, USAR. Mem. Tex. Bar Assn., Travis County Bar Assn. Personal injury, Public utilities, Administrative and regulatory. Home: 4701 Fieldstone Dr Austin TX 78735-6309 Office: 1411 West Ave Ste 200 Austin TX 78701-1537

**CORUM, JESSE MAXWELL, IV,** lawyer; b. Richmond, Va., Dec. 19, 1950; s. Jesse Maxwell and Joy (MacKubbin) C.; m. Lynn Hummel, Aug. 12, 1972; children—Jesse Maxwell V, Scott William. B.A., Guilford Coll., 1973; J.D., Vt. Law Sch., 1977. Bar: Vt. 1977, U.S. Dist. Ct. Vt. 1978. Dep. state's atty. Windham County State's Atty.'s Office, Brattleboro, Vt., 1977-81; assoc. Gale, Gale & Barile, Brattleboro, 1981-82; ptnr. Gale, Gale, Barile & Corum, Brattleboro, 1982-86; ptnr. Gale, Gale & Corum, Brattleboro, 1987-94, Gale, Corum & Stern, Brattleboro, 1995-98, Gale & Corum, 1998—. pres. Windham County Law Library, Brattleboro, 1981-85. Sec.-clk. Youth Services Windham County, Brattleboro, 1981-85, pres., 1985—; mem. Brattleboro Planning Commn., Vt., 1981-85, chmn., 1984-85. Mem. Vt. Bar Assn., Windham County Bar Assn. (sec. 1978), Assn. Trial Lawyers Am., Vt. Trial Lawyers Assn. Club: Optimists Investment (Brattleboro, Vt.) (pres. 1982-83, 97-98). Lodge: Rotary (sec. 1984-86, v.p. 1986-87, pres. 1987-88). Criminal, State civil litigation, Family and matrimonial. Home: 116 Oak St Brattleboro VT 05301-2999 Office: PO Box 1171 42 Park Pl Brattleboro VT 05301-2882

**CORWIN, GREGG MARLOWE,** lawyer; b. Mpls., May 4, 1947; s. Gerald Sidney Corwin and Shirley Mae (Nathenson) Nadler; m. Frances Gail Shapiro, mar. 21, 1971; children: Mitchell, David. BA summa cum laude, U. Minn., 1969, JD cum laude, 1972. Bar: Minn. 1972, U.S. Dist. Ct. Minn. 1972, U.S. Ct. Appeals (8th cir.) 1976, U.S. Supreme Ct. 1977. Assoc. Fred Burstein Law Firm, Mpls., 1972-77; ptnr. Cortlen Cloutier, Mpls., 1977-78; pvt. practice, Mpls., 1978—. Capt. USAF. Mem. ABA, Minn. Bar Assn., Hennepin County Bar Assn., Phi Beta Kappa. Democrat. Jewish. Avocations: reading, music, sports. Labor, Civil rights. Office: 1660 Hwy 100 Ste 508 E Minneapolis MN 55416-1534

**CORWIN, MELANIE S.,** lawyer; b. Cin., July 9, 1962. BA, Ea. Ky. U., 1984; JD, No. Ky. U., 1984. Bar: Ohio 1990, U.S. Dist. Ct. (so. dist.) Ohio 1991, U.S. Ct. Appeals (6th cir.) 1992. Paralegal Brown, Cummins & Brown Co., CPAs, Cin., 1984-90, assoc., 1990-97, ptnr., 1998—. Mem. ABA, Ohio Bar Assn. Office: Brown Cummins & Brown Co 3500 Carew Tower Cincinatti OH 45202

**CORYELL, FRANK,** lawyer; b. Louisville, Mar. 16, 1939; s. Cornelius Edwin and Mary Louise Coryell; m. Linda Louise Coryell, May 6, 1960; children: Cornelius Edwin Coryell, Renette Coryell Jones. BS, U. Louisville, 1963, JD, 1967. Bar: Ky. 1967, U.S. Supreme Ct. 1973. Dep. commr. Jefferson Cir. Ct., Louisville, 1968-70; asst. commonwealths atty. Jefferson Commonwealth, Louisville, 1970-76; sole practice Louisville, 1967—. Author: The Legend of Redbird—A History of Zit-Kala Sha Lodge, 1995. Active Boy Scouts Am., Louisville, 1947—. Mem. Suburban Masonic Lodge (master 1974). Republican. Baptist. Avocations: camping, bicycling. General practice, Family and matrimonial, Probate.

**CORZINE, DARRELL W.,** lawyer; b. Odessa, Tex., Nov. 5, 1967; s. Danny C. and Glyndel M. Corzine; m. Dawn Cherie Corzine, Jan. 2, 1993. BBA, Baylor U., 1991; JD, Tex. Tech. U., 1994. Bar: Tex. 1994, U.S. Dist. Ct. (we. dist.) Tex. 1998. Atty. McMahon, Tidwell, Hansen, Atkins & Peacock, PC, Odessa, 1994—. Trustee Odessa Chamber Leadership, 1998; bd. dirs. Presdl. Mus., Odessa, 1997-98; adv. coun. Jr. Achievement, Odessa, 1997-98. Mem. Tex. Assn. Def. Counsel, Tex. Young Lawyers Assn. (needs of sr. citizens com. 1996-98), Ector County Young Lawyers Assn., Def. Rsch. Inst. Baptist. Insurance, Real property, General practice. Office: McMahon Tidwell Hansen Atkins & Peacock PC Ste 200 4001 E 42d Odessa TX 79761

**COSENTINO, ROBERT J(OHN),** lawyer; b. Providence, Jan. 28, 1954; s. John R. and Lena (Aloia) C. BA, Holy Cross Coll., 1976; JD, U. Bridgeport, 1980. Bar: R.I. 1980, U.S. Dist. Ct. R.I. 1980, U.S. Supreme Ct. 1987. Pvt. practice Providence, 1980—. Mem. Italo-Am. Club R.I. (pres. 1988-90), Alpine Country Club (pres. 1998-99). Personal injury, Workers' compensation, Real property. Office: 950 Smith St Providence RI 02908-2717

**COSGROVE, JOSEPH MATTHIAS,** lawyer; b. Pittston, Pa., Feb. 1, 1957; s. Richard Bernard and Mary Elizabeth Cosgrove. BA in Govt., U. Notre Dame, 1979, MA in Theology, 1982, JD, 1982; MA in Studio Art, Marywood Coll., 1993. Bar: Pa. 1982, U.S. Dist. Ct. (ea. dist.) Pa. 1982, U.S. Dist. Ct. (mid. dist.) Pa. 1983, U.S. Ct. Appeals (3d cir.) 1983, U.S. Supreme Ct. 1988. Atty. Wilkes Barre, Pa., 1982—; asst. dean King's Coll., Wilkes Barre, 1983-85; law clk. Pa. Superior Ct., Wilkes Barre, 1985; lectr. King's Coll., Wilkes Barre, 1988—. Appeared in film The Maid, 1990; exec. prodr.: (pub. svc. announcement) Domestic Violence, 1989; (documentary film) Children of the Lie, 1991. Dir. Pittston Area Sch. Bd., 1985-89. Democrat. Roman Catholic. Avocation: ceramic art. Criminal, Constitutional, Civil rights. Office: Conflict Coun Pub Def 1460 Wyoming Ave Forty Fort PA 18704

**COSMAN, MARIN,** lawyer; b. N.Y.C., Oct. 24, 1961; d. Bard and Madeleine (Pelner) C. BA, Yale U., 1984; MusM, Manhattan Sch. Music, 1988; JD, U. Chgo., 1995. Bar: Calif. 1997. Opera singer N.Y.C., 1984-90; med. practice broker Med. Equity, Inc., Tenafly, N.J., 1989-95; atty. Mitchell & Skola, San Diego, 1995—. Co-author: (chpts.) Encyclopedia of Matrimonial Law Practice, 1991; contbr. articles to profl. jours. Bd. dirs. Congregation Beth El, La Jolla, Calif., 1996—. Avocations: singing, scuba diving, hiking. Office: Mitchell & Skola 11545 W Bernardo Ct Ste 302 San Diego CA 92127-1632

**COSNER, ALAN G.,** lawyer; b. Bklyn., Apr. 26, 1945; s. Irving and Lillian C.; m. Jacqueline, June 27, 1970; children: Staci, Stephanie. BSBA, Bucknell

U., 1966; JD, Seton Hall U., 1970; LLM, NYU, 1974. Bar: N.J. 1970, U.S. Dist. Ct. (3d dist.) N.Y. 1970. Agt. IRS, N.Y.C., 1968-70; sole practice law East Brunswick, N.Y., 1970—. Served in U.S. Army. Banking, Family and matrimonial, Personal injury. Office: 214 Route 18 East Brunswick NJ 08816-1910

**COSTA, CAROL ANN,** lawyer; b. Canton, Ohio, Nov. 30, 1961; d. Charles Barnard and Velma Frances (Crouse) C. BA, Mt. Union Coll., Alliance, Ohio, 1984; JD cum laude, U. Akron, 1990. Bar: Ohio 1990; U.S. Dist. Ct. (no. dist.) Ohio, 1990; U.S. Ct. Appeals (6th cir.), 1990. Assoc. Baker Meekison & Dublikar, Canton, 1990-95, Buckingham Doolittle & Burroughs, Canton, 1995—. Mem. ABA, Ohio Bar Assn. (chair Amicus Curiae com. 1997-98), Stark County Bar Assn., (mem. grievance com., chair soc. com. 1997—), Ohio Assn. Civil Trial Attys. Avocations: theater, travel. Family and matrimonial, General civil litigation. Office: Buckingham Doolittle & Burroughs 4518 Fulton Dr NW Canton OH 44718-2332

**COSTA, MICHAEL R.,** lawyer; b. Providence, July 15, 1970. BS, Roger Williams U., 1992; JD, Suffolk U., 1997; postgrad., Boston U. Bar: Mass. 1998, U.S. Dist. Ct. Mass. 1998. Assoc. Gargiulo, Rudnick & Gargiulo, Boston, 1998—. Author Suffolk Transnat. Law Rev., 1997. Health, State civil litigation, Federal civil litigation. Office: Gargiulo Rudnick & Gargiulo 66 Long Wharf Boston MA 02110-3605

**COSTALES, MARCO DANIEL,** lawyer; b. L.A., Dec. 14, 1962; s. Armando Aguilar and Sharon Rose (Cooper) C.; m. Virginia Louise Childs, Aug. 7, 1988; children: Michelle Louise, Kevin Daniel. BA in Internat. Rels., Stanford U., 1984; JD, MBA, U. Calif., Berkeley, 1988. Bar: Calif. 1988. Atty. Loeb & Loeb LLP, L.A., 1989—. Active La Canada First Presbyn. Ch., 1997—. Avocations: music, scuba diving. General corporate, Mergers and acquisitions, Non-profit and tax-exempt organizations. Office: Loeb & Loeb LLP 1000 Wilshire Blvd Ste 1800 Los Angeles CA 90017-2475

**COSTELLO, DANIEL BRIAN,** lawyer, consultant; b. Arlington, Va., Apr. 23, 1950; s. James Russell and Hazel Virginia (Caudle) C.; m. Margaret Ruth Dow, June 13, 1970; children: James Brian, Rebecca Ruth, Kathleen Marie. BA, U. Va., 1972; JD, Coll. of William and Mary, 1975. Bar: Va. 1975, U.S. Dist. Ct. (ea. dist.) Va. 1979, U.S. Ct. Appeals (4th cir.) 1979, U.S. Bankruptcy Ct. (ea. dist.) Va. 1979, D.C. 1984. Reporter Globe Newspapers, Vienna, Va., 1965-68; freelance journalist Williamsburg, Va., 1972-73; news dir. Sta. WMBG, WBCI-FM, Williamsburg, 1973-76; spl. asst. atty. gen. Commonwealth of Va., Suffolk, Va., 1976-78; asst. atty. gen. Commonwealth of Va., Richmond, Va., 1978-80; ptnr. Dameron, Costello & Hubacher, Alexandria, Va., 1980-89, Costello & Hubacher, Alexandria, 1989-99; pvt. practice Alexandria, 1999—; corp. sec., gen. counsel Olivares U.S.A., Inc., Fairfax, Va., 1999—; press rels. cons. Va. Bar Assn., No. Va. Dem. Combined Campaign; spl. commr. in chancery Alexandria Cir. Ct. Author: Land Use Planning and Eminent Domain, 1997, Foreclosure in Virginia, 1991; co-editor, co-author The Layman's Guide to Virginia Law, 1977; editor night news Sta. WINA, 1969-72; contbr. articles to profl. jours. Mem. Va. State Bar, Alexandria Bar Assn., D.C. Bar, Soc. Alumni Coll. of William and Mary, U. Va. Alumni Soc., Rolling Hills Club. Presbyterian. Avocations: hunting, fishing, coin collecting. General civil litigation, Real property, General practice. Office: D. Brian Costello 429 N Saint Asaph St Alexandria VA 22314-2317

**COSTELLO, DON OWEN,** lawyer; b. Berkeley, Calif., Oct. 17, 1948; s. Howard Wesley and Marjorie (Hughes) C.; m. Charlene Groskopf; children: Ian Miles, Eryn Carolina; m. Denissia Withers, Oct. 12, 1995. AB in Anthropology, U. Calif., Berkeley, 1970; JD, Lewis and Clark Coll., 1976. Bar: Oreg. 1977, U.S. Dist. Ct. Oreg. 1977. Tchr. phys. edn., coach crew team U. Oreg., Eugene, 1971-72; pvt. practice Portland, Oreg., 1977-78; ptnr. Costello and Goodwin, Sisters, Oreg., 1978-88; pvt. practice Redmond, Oreg., 1991-92; ptnr. Smith, McCabe and Costello, Bend, Oreg., 1993-96; pvt. practice, arbitrator, mediator, Bend, Oreg., 1996—; founder, coach Sta. L. Rowing Club and rowing programs Lewis and Clark Coll. and Reed Coll., Portland, 1972-78; chief judge Tribal Ct., Burns Paiute Colony, 1984-86, Confederated Tribes Warm Springs Reservation Oreg., 1988-92, Coquille Indian Tribe, North Bend, Oreg., 1997—; instr. social sci. dept. Ctrl. Oreg. C.C., Bend; arbitrator Arbitration Svc. Portland, Oreg., 1992—; mem. arbitration adv. bd and arbitration anel 11th Jud. Dist., 1994—; mem. arbitration panel 22d Jud. Dist.; mem. roster of mediators alternative dispute resolution program Oreg. Dept. Transp.; judge Redmond Mcpl. Ct., 1984-93; juvenile ct. referee Deschutes County Circuit Ct., 1986-88; judge workers' compensation program Ct. Appeals, Confederated Tribes Warm Springs Reservation Oreg., 1988-92; trainer Nat. Indian Justice Ctr., 1989-92; prodr., trainer juvenile justice and alternative dispute resolution confs. Warm Springs Tribal Ct., 1988-92; former instr. cmty. edn. dept. Ctrl. Oreg. C.C., Sisters Ctr., also Warm Springs Ctr., 1990-91; guest spkr. U. Calif. Boalt Sch. Law, 1991. Mem. budget bd. Ctrl. Oreg. C.C., 1981-86, mem. coll. found. bd., 1984-88, planning commr., 1981-83. Mem. Oreg. State Bar (law-related edn. com. 1986-88, local profl. responsibility com. 1988-91, fee dispute arbitration panel 1988—, com. for balancing personal life, family and career 1998—, exec. com. Indian law sect. 1998—). Fax: 541-330-5093. E-mail: donc.@bendnet.com. General civil litigation, Native American, Alternative dispute resolution. Office: 377 SW Century Dr Ste B Bend OR 97702-1112

**COSTELLO, EDWARD J., JR.,** arbitrator, mediator, lawyer; b. N.Y.C., Apr. 18, 1939; m. Karin Bergstrom, Aug. 21, 1981; 1 child, Catharine A. AB, Fordham U., 1961; JD, NYU, 1964. Bar: Fla. 1965, N.Y. 1967, Calif. 1969, U.S. Supreme Ct. 1973. Assoc. Donovan, Leisure, Newton & Irvine, N.Y.C., 1962-64; spl. agt. FBI, Washington, 1964-67; assoc. O'Melveny & Myers, Los Angeles, 1963, 68-72; ptnr. Costello & Walcher, Los Angeles, 1972-85, Proskauer, Rose, Goetz & Mendelsohn, Los Angeles, 1985-89; professional neutral Santa Monica, Calif., 1989—; adj. assoc. prof. law, evidence and criminal procedure Southwestern U. Sch. Law, Los Angeles, 1970-73, internat. bus. trans. U. So. Calif. Law Ctr., Los Angeles, 1973-75; judge pro tem Los Angeles Mcpl. Ct., 1971—; pres. The Compass Orgn. Inc., Los Angeles, 1985—; chmn. bd. dirs. Year Labs. Inc., Los Angeles; bd. dirs. Nat. Exchange Inc., McLean, Va.; instructor arbitration/mediation Loyola Law Sch.; dispute resolution lectr. Am. Arbitration Assn., ABA, Calif. Continuing Ed. of the Bar, Ctr. for Profl. Edn., U. Calif. Editorial bd. mem. NYU Law Review; author: Controlling Conflict: Alternative Dispute Resolution for Business, 1996; author: (with others) Dispute Resolution Alternatives 1994, Insurance Alternative Dispute Resolution Manual, 1994. Chmn., trustee Brentwood Sch., Los Angeles, 1986-87. Root-Tilden scholar NYU. Mem. ABA (litigation, internat. law and antitrust law sects.), Calif. Bar Assn. (bar examiners com.), N.Y. State Bar Assn., Fla. Bar Assn., Los Angeles County Bar Assn. (past mem. juvenile ct. and judiciary coms., trial lawyer sect.), Assn. Bus. Trial Lawyers, Western Assn. Venture Capitalists, Am. Arbitration Assn. (mem. large complex case panel, specialty panels in construction, employment, healthcare, intellectual property). Office: 620 E Channel Rd Santa Monica CA 90402-1316

**COSTELLO, JAMES PAUL,** lawyer; b. Elgin, Ill., Nov. 12, 1953; s. John Desmond and Helena (Brennan) C.; m. Kathryn Charlotte Schafer, June 16, 1979; children: James Albert, Robert Francis, Paul Desmond, Philip Schafer Costello. BA, U. Ill., 1975; JD, DePaul U., 1978. Bar: Ill. 1978, U.S. Dist. Ct. (no. dist.) Ill. 1978. Assoc. J. Thomas Demos & Assocs., Chgo., 1978-83; ptnr. James Paul Costello Ltd., Chgo., Ill., 1983—. Contbg. author: Law Enforcement Legal Defense Manual, 1977-78; editor: Jail Law Bulletin, Police Plaintiff, Law Enforcement Employment Digest, 1977-78. Mem. Ill. Bar Assn., Assn. Trial Lawyers Am., Ill. Trial Lawyers Assn. (amicus curiae com. 1981—), Chgo. Bar Assn. (judicial evaluation com.). Democrat. Roman Catholic. Personal injury, Product liability, Professional liability. Home: 1202 E Clarendon St Arlington Heights IL 60004-5050 Office: 150 N Wacker Dr Ste 3050 Chicago IL 60606-1660

**COSTENBADER, CHARLES MICHAEL,** lawyer; b. Jersey City, Dec. 9, 1935; s. Edward William and Marie Veronica (Danaher) C.; m. Barbara Ann Wilson, Aug. 1, 1959; children: Charles Michael Jr., William E., Mary E. BS in Acctg., Mt. St. Mary's Coll., 1957; JD, Seton Hall U., 1960; LLM in Taxation, NYU, 1968. Bar: N.J 1960; U.S. Tax Ct. 1961, U.S. Ct. Appeals (3d cir.) 1973, U.S. Supreme Ct. 1983. Trial atty. office regional counsel IRS, N.Y.C., 1961-69; tax assoc. Shanley & Fisher, Newark, 1969-76; tax ptnr. Stryker, Tams & Dill, Newark, 1976-98; spl. counsel McCarter & English, Newark, 1998—. Mem. N.J. State and Local Expenditure and Revenue Commn., 1985-88. Mem. ABA, N.J. Bar Assn. (chmn. taxation sect. 1984-85), N.J. State C. of C. (chmn. cost of govt. com. 1988—), Am. Coll. Tax Counsel. Republican. Roman Catholic. Avocations: gardening, reading, sports. Taxation, general, State and local taxation. Home: 8 Neptune Pl Colonia NJ 07067-2502 Office: McCarter & English Gateway Four Ctr 100 Mulberry St Newark NJ 07101-4096

**COSTIKYAN, EDWARD N.,** lawyer; b. Weehawken, N.J., Sept. 14, 1924; s. Mihran Nazar and Berthe (Muller) C.; m. Frances Holmgren, 1950 (div. 1975); chldren: Gregory, Emilie; m. Barbara Heine, Mar. 6, 1977. AB, Columbia U., 1947, LLB, 1949. Bar: N.Y. 1949, U.S. Dist. Ct. (so. dist.) N.Y. 1950, U.S. Ct. Appeals (2d cir.) 1950, U.S. Supreme Ct. 1964. Law sec. to judge Harold R. Medina U.S. Dist. Ct., N.Y.C., 1949-51; ptnr. Paul, Weiss, Rifkind, Wharton & Garrison, N.Y.C., 1960-93, of counsel, 1994—; spl. advisor to mayor on sch. and borough governance City of N.Y., 1994-96, chairperson mayor's investigative commn. on sch. safety, 1995-96; mem. Commn. on Integrity in Govt., N.Y.C., 1986, mem. joint com. on jud. adminstrn., 1985-92; adj. fellow Ctr. for Edn. Innovation, 1997—. Author: Behind Closed Doors: Politics in the Public Interest, 1966, How to Win Votes: The Politics of 1980, 1980; co-author: Re-Structuring the Government of New York City, 1972, New Strategies for Regional Cooperation, 1973; rsch. editor Columbia Law Rev.; mem. editl. bd. City Jour., 1992—; mem. bd. editors N.Y. Law Jour., 1976—; contbr. articles on legal and polit. subjects to profl. publs. Chmn. N.Y. State Task Force on N.Y.C. Juristiction and Structure, 1971-72; vice chmn. State Charter Revision for N.Y.C., 1972-77; county leader New York County Dem. Com., 1962-64; Dem. presdl. elector, 1964, 88; trustee, mem. exec. com., chmn. alumni adv. bd. Columbia U., 1981-93, trustee emeritus, 1993—; bd. dirs., mem. coun. Mcpl. Art Soc., 1993-98; chmn. bd. dirs. N.Y. Found. for Sr. Citizens, 1993—. 1st lt. inf. U.S. Army, 1943-46. Recipient William J. Brennan Jr. award for Outstanding Cont. to Pub. Discourse, 1997. Fellow Am. Coll. Trial Lawyers; mem. Assn. of Bar of City of N.Y. (mem. exec. com. 1986-90), Century Club. Unitarian. General practice, State civil litigation. Home: 50 Sutton Pl S New York NY 10022-4167 Office: Paul Weiss Rifkind Wharton & Garrison Ste 3910 1285 Avenue Of The Americas Fl 21 New York NY 10019-6065

**COTCHETT, JOSEPH WINTERS,** lawyer, author; b. Chgo., Jan. 6, 1939; s. Joseph Winters and Jean (Renaud) C.; children—Leslie F., Charles P., Rachael E., Quinn Carlyle, Camilla E. B.S. in Engring., Calif. Poly. Coll., 1960; LL.B., U. Calif. Hastings Coll. Law, 1964. Bar: Calif. 1965, D.C. 1980. Ptnr. Cotchett, Pitre & Simon, Burlingame, Calif., 1965—; mem. Calif. Jud. Coun., 1975-77, Calif. Commn. on Jud. Performance, 1985-89, Commn. 2020 Jud. Coun., 1991-94; select com. on jud. retirement, 1992—. Author: (with R. Cartwright) California Products Liability Actions, 1970, (with F. Haight) California Courtroom Evidence, 1972, (with A. Elkind) Federal Courtroom Evidence, 1976, (with Frank Rothman) Persuasive Opening Statements and Closing Arguments, 1988, (with Stephen Pizzo) The Ethics Gap, 1991, (with Gerald Uelmen) California Courtroom Evidence Foundations, 1993; contbr. articles to profl. jours. Chmn. San Mateo County Heart Assn., 1967; pres. San Mateo Boys and Girls Club, 1971; bd. dirs. U. Calif. Hastings Law Sch., 1981-93. With Intelligence Corps, U.S. Army, 1960-61; col. JAGC, USAR, ret. Fellow Am. Bar Found., Am. Bd. Trial Advs., Am. Coll. Trial Lawyers, Internat. Acad. Trial Lawyers, Internat. Soc. of Barristers, Nat. Bd. Trial Advs. (diplomate civil trial adv.), State Bar Calif. (gov. 1972-75). Clubs: Commonwealth, Press (San Francisco). Federal civil litigation, State civil litigation. Office: 840 Malcolm Rd Burlingame CA 94010-1401 also: 12100 Wilshire Blvd Ste 1100 Los Angeles CA 90025-7124

**COTE, JENNIFER WANTY,** lawyer; b. Ann Arbor, Mich., Sept. 7, 1954. BGS, U. Mich., Ann Arbor, 1977; JD, Detroit Coll., 1980. Bar: Mich. 1981, U.S. Dist. Ct. (ea. dist.) Mich. 1981. Pvt. practice Grosse Pointe, Mich., 1981-89, Brighton, Mich., 1989—; prof. Madonna U., Livonia, Mich., 1982—; chair legal asst. dept. Madonna Coll., Livonia, 1985—. Den leader Cub Scouts Am., Grosse Pointe, Mich., 1989, Brighton, Mich., 1990-95; educator Grosse Pointe Bd. Realtors, 1987. Mem. ABA (approval com. 1987—), Am. Assn. Paralegal Edn., Nat. Assn. Legal Assts. (cert.), Mich. Bar Assn., Legal Assts. Assn. Mich. Real property, Estate planning. Office: Madonna U 36600 Schoolcraft Rd Livonia MI 48150-1176

**COTE, THOMAS JACQUES,** lawyer; b. Ste-Foy, Quebec, Can., Oct. 26, 1951; came to U.S., 1970; s. Andre and Virginia (Aponovich) C.; m. Josee L. Bourbeau, Aug. 29, 1987; children: Christine J., Julie M. BA, Suffolk U., 1972, JD, 1975. Bar: N.H. 1975. Pvt. practice Gorham, N.H., 1976—; faculty Sch. for Life Long Learning, Berlin. Pres. United Way, Berlin. Mem. Berlin Arts Assn. (pres.), Berlin C. of C. (bd. dirs.). Avocations: skiing, hockey, piano, tennis, hiking. E-mail: cotetj@ncia.net. Personal injury, Bankruptcy, Family and matrimonial. Office: 74 Main St Gorham NH 03581-1632

**COTTER, EDWARD FRANCIS, JR.,** lawyer; b. Long Beach, Calif., Sept. 24, 1951; s. Edward F. and Ann M. Cotter; m. Susan van Hart, Jan. 8, 1977; children: Edward F. III, Elizabeth G. BS, U.S. Naval Acad., 1973; JD, U. Calif., San Francisco, 1980; LLM, George Washington U., 1988. Bar: Calif. Commd. ensign USN, 1973, advanced through grades to comdr., 1990, ret., 1993; counsel Kaiser Permanente, Oakland, Calif., 1993—. Bd. dirs. St. Luke's Episcopal Ch., San Francisco, 1988-91. Decorated Meritorious Svc. medal USN, 1993. Mem. U.S. Naval Acad. Alumni Assn. (pres. San Francisco Bay 1997-99). Avocations: sailing, mountain sports. Administrative and regulatory, Health, Legislative. Office: Kaiser Found Health Plan Inc 19th Fl One Kaiser Plaza Oakland CA 94612

**COTTER, JAMES MICHAEL,** lawyer; b. Providence, May 12, 1942; s. James Henry and Marguerite Louise (Clark) C.; m. Melinda Irene Tighe, Feb. 6, 1971; children; Elizabeth, Heather, Kathryn. AB, Fairfield U., 1964; LLB, U. Va., 1967. Bar: N.Y. 1967. Assoc. Simpson Thacher & Bartlett, N.Y.C., 1967-75, ptnr., 1975—. Trustee Fairfield U., 1995—; bd. dirs. M.G.A. Found., 1990—, chmn., 1990-92. Mem. ABA, N.Y. State Bar Assn., N.Y. Law Inst. (bd. dirs. 1984—, chmn. exec. com. 1993-98, pres. 1997—), Met. Golf Assn. (bd. dirs. 1974—, pres. 1990-92), Greenwich Conn. Country Club, Hudson Nat. Golf Club. General corporate, Securities, Mergers and acquisitions. Office: Simpson Thacher & Bartlett 425 Lexington Ave Fl 15 New York NY 10017-3954

**COTTER, RICHARD TIMOTHY,** lawyer; b. Chgo., Sept. 2, 1948; s. Edward Timothy and Julia Maria C.; m. Janet M. Sorrentino, Dec. 3, 1977 (div. Jan. 1993); children: Mary Julia, Carol Ann; m. Kimberly A. Morris, Sept. 11, 1993; children: Kathleen, Julia Ann. Bar: Fla. 1975, Ill. 1976, U.S. Supreme Ct. 1982. Ptnr. Echols & Cotter, Ft. Myers Beach, Fla., 1978-85, Echols, Cotter & Shenko, Ft. Myers Beach, Fla., 1985-95, Echols & Cotter, Ft. Myers Beach, 1995—; prof. Internat. Coll. Paralegal Instrn., Ft. Myers, 1992. Contbr. articles to profl. jours.; newspaper columnist Legal Eagle, 1995—. Pres. Cmty. Assn. Inst., South Gulf Coast chpt., Ft. Myers, 1984; dir. United Way of Lee County, Inc., Ft. Myers, 1990-92; dir. Chamber of S.W. Fla., Ft. Myers, 1989-91, vice-chmn. legal affairs, 1990-94; del. Fla. Democratic State Conv., 1995. Mem. Ill. Bar Assn., Fla. Bar (condo. and planned devel. com. 1993—, real property professionalism com. 1993—), Lee County Bar Assn., Fla. Assn. Realtors (local bd. attys. com. 1986-94), Ft. Myers Beach Lodge 362, Araba Shrine Temple, U.S. C. of C. (coun. mem. small bus. coun. 1994—, mem. social security com. 1995—). Avocations: golf, flying. General practice, Probate, Real property. Office: Richard T Cotter PA 6100 Estero Blvd Fort Myers Beach FL 33931-4347

**COTTON, JAMES ALEXENDRE,** lawyer; b. Ft. Riley, Kans., Nov. 22, 1939; s. James and Myrtle (Lallis) C.; m. Margaret A. Davis, Aug. 15, 1965 (div. Dec. 1978); children: Lallis A., Allison M.; m. Marjorie Evangeline Keene, Mar. 15, 1980; 1 child, William J.K. AA, Mesa Coll., 1961; BA, Colo. Coll., 1963; JD, U. Colo., 1970. Bar: N.Y., U.S. Dist. Ct. (so. dist.) N.Y. 1970. Atty. IBM Corp., Armonk, N.Y., 1970-73; staff atty. IBM Corp., Poughkeepsie, N.Y., 1973-75, Boulder, Colo., 1975-78; area counsel IBM Corp., Tucson, 1978-81; sr. atty. IBM Corp., Armonk, 1981-92, corp. staff counsel, 1992-96; prof. law Tex. So. U., Houston, 1996—; vis. prof. Thurgood Marshall Sch. Law, Houston, 1981-82, adj. prof., 1982—. Bd. dirs. Nat. Urban League, Tucson, 1978-79, chmn. 1979-80; capt. dist. Yorktown (N.Y.) Dems., 1982—. Served to capt. U.S. Army, 1963-67. Mem. ABA. Democrat. Baptist. Avocations: chess, tennis. Securities, Antitrust, General corporate. Office: Tex So U 3100 Cleburne St Houston TX 77004-4501

**COTTONGAME, W. BRICE,** lawyer; b. Ft. Worth, June 4, 1958; s. William Robert and Nelda Ree Cottongame; m. Elizabeth Cramer, Jan. 9, 1992; children: Kate, Will. BA in Polit. Sci., U. Tex., 1980; JD, S. Tex. Coll. Law, 1984. Bar: Tex., 1984, U.S. Dist. Ct. (no. and so. dists.) Tex., U.S. Ct. Appeals (5th cir.), U.S. Supreme Ct.; bd. cert. personal injury trial law Tex. Bd. Legal Specialization. Atty. Wallace Craig & Assocs., Ft. Worth, 1980-95, Henderson Haksell & Cottongame, Ft. Worth, 1995-98, Law Office W. Brice Cottongame & Assocs., Ft. Worth, 1998—. Fellow State Bar Tex., Tarrant County Bar Found.; Mem. Tex. Trial Lawyers Assn. (assoc. dir. 1986-90, dir. 1990-95), Tarrant County Trial Lawyers Assn. (dir. 1989-93, pres. 1994), Tarrant County Bar Assn. Democrat. Methodist. Personal injury, General civil litigation, Insurance. Office: Law Office W Brice Cottongame PC 414 E Bluff St Ste 200 Fort Worth TX 76102-2216

**COTTRELL, FRANK STEWART,** lawyer, manufacturing executive; b. Boulder, Colo., July 11, 1942; s. Frank Stewart Sr. and Dorris Mary (Payne) C.; m. Janet Anne Goode, Jan. 8, 1966; children: Kristin, Jeffrey, Steven. AB, Knox Coll., 1964; JD, U. Chgo., 1967. Bar: Ill. 1967. Atty. Deere & Co., Moline, Ill., 1967-77, internat. atty., 1977-80, sr. atty., 1980-82, asst. gen. counsel, 1982-87, assoc. gen. counsel, corp. sec., 1987-91, gen. counsel, sec., 1991-93, v.p., gen. counsel, sec., 1993-98, sr. v.p., gen. counsel, sec., 1998—. Mem. adv. bd. Butterworth Trust; trustee Knox Coll. Mem. ABA, Ill. Bar Assn., Assn. Gen. Counsel. Office: Deere & Co One John Deere Pl Moline IL 61265-8098

**COUCH, LESLIE FRANKLIN,** lawyer; b. Albany, N.Y., July 22, 1930; s. Leslie S. and Mary J. (Owens) C.; m. Joan Dunham, Dec. 29, 1951; children—Sharon DeBonis, Lawrence, Mark, Todd. LL.B., Union U., 1955, J.D., 1968. Bar: N.Y. 1955, U.S. Dist. Ct. (no. dist.) N.Y. 1955, U.S. Ct. Claims 1963, U.S. Ct. Appeals (2d cir.) 1962, U.S. Dist. Ct. (so. dist.) N.Y. 1979, U.S. Supreme Ct. 1979, U.S. Dist. Ct. Vt. 1987, U.S. Dist. Ct. D.C. 1997. Pvt. practice law, Albany, 1955-62; ptnr. Medwin & Couch, Albany, 1962-65, DiFabio & Couch, P.C., Albany, 1965-79, Couch & Howard, P.C., Albany, 1979-88, Couch, White, Brenner, Howard & Feigenbaum, 1988—; lectr. Am. Arbitration Assn., N.Y. State Bar Assn., others. Mem. North Colonie Sch. Dist., 1975-78. Mem. ABA, Am. Arbitration Assn. (nat. panel), Albany County Bar Assn. (com. on continuing legal edn. 1983—), N.Y. Bar Assn. (com. unlawful practice 1960-63, com. pub. info. 1969-72, com. media awards 1970-76, chmn. constrn. and surety law div. 1988-90), Capital Dist. Trial Lawyers Assn. Clubs: Fort Orange (Albany); Schuyler Meadows (Loudonville, N.Y.). General civil litigation, Construction, Government contracts and claims. Home: 20 Loudonwood E Loudonville NY 12211-1465 Office: PO Box 22222 540 Broadway Albany NY 12207-2705

**COUCH, MARK WOODWORTH,** lawyer; b. Albany, N.Y., Sept. 5, 1956; s. Leslie Franklin and Joan Teresa (Dunham) C.; m. Mary Jane Bendon, Oct. 25, 1985; children: Braden Bendon, Dylan Bendon. BA, Worcester State Coll., 1982; JD, Union U., 1985. Bar: N.Y. 1986, U.S. Dist. Ct. (no. dist.) N.Y. 1986, U.S. Dist. Ct. (we. dist.) N.Y. 1995. Prin. Couch & Howard, Albany, 1986-88; atty. Couch, White, Brenner, Howard & Feigenbaum, Albany, 1988-89; prin. Breakell & Couch, Albany, 1989—. Bd. dirs. Downtown Day Care Ctr. Inc., Albany, 1991-96. Mem. ABA, N.Y. State Bar Assn., Albany County Bar Assn., Schuyler Meadows Club. Construction, Labor, General civil litigation. Home: 8 Dyke Rd Latham NY 12110-1204 Office: Breakell & Couch 11 N Pearl St Ste 1200 Albany NY 12207-2789

**COUCH, STEVE EARL,** lawyer; b. Akron, Ohio, June 10, 1963; s. Charles Earl and Wilma Jean (Duncan) C.; m. Cynthia Piro, Sept. 26, 1992. BS in Polit. Sci., U. Houston, 1986; JD, S. Tex. Coll. of Law, 1989. Bar: Tex. 1990, U.S. Dist. Ct. (so. dist.) Tex. 1990, U.S. Ct. Appeals (5th cir.) 1991, U.S. Dist. Ct. (ea. dist.) Tex. 1993. Law clk. John O'Quinn & Assocs., Houston, 1987-88, Helm, Pletcher, Hogan, Bowen & Saunders, Houston, 1988-89; assoc. Griggs & Harrison, Houston, 1989-93, Kelly, Sutter, Mount & Kendrick, Houston, 1993—. Contbr. articles to publs. in field, 1988—. Mem. Houston Bar Assn. (mem. editl. bd. Houston Lawyer, Best Legal Article of Yr. 1990, 1991), Tex. Bar Assn., Omicron Delta Kappa. Achievements include acting as lead counsel in landmark case FDIC v. Dawson, 5th cir., 1993. Avocations: tennis, golf, poetry, jogging. State civil litigation, Insurance, Personal injury. Office: Kelly Sutter Mount & Kendrick PC 1600 Smith St Ste 3200 Houston TX 77002-7362

**COUGHENOUR, JOHN CLARE,** federal judge; b. Pittsburg, Kans., July 27, 1941; s. Owen M. and Margaret E. (Widner) C.; m. Gwendolyn A. Kieffaber, June 1, 1963; children: Jeffrey, Douglas, Marta. B.S., Kans. State Coll., 1963; J.D., U. Iowa, 1966. Bar: Iowa 1966, D.C. 1963, U.S. Dist. Ct. (we. dist.) Wash. 1966. Ptnr. Bogle & Gates, Seattle, 1966-81; vis. asst. prof. law U. Washington, Seattle, 1970-73; judge U.S. Dist. Ct. (we. dist.) Wash., Seattle, 1981-97, chief judge, 1997—. Mem. Iowa State Bar Assn., Wash. State Bar Assn. Office: US Dist Ct US Courthouse 1010 5th Ave Ste 609 Seattle WA 98104-1130

**COUGHLIN, THOMAS A.,** lawyer; b. Boston, Dec. 8, 1945; s. Thomas A. and Eva Marie Coughlin; m. Nancy Lee Rueckert, Jan. 3, 1976; children: Rebecca, Lisa, Susan, Karen. Student, Hiram Coll., 1963-65; BA, Brandeis U., 1967; JD, Boston Coll., 1970. Bar: Mass. 1970, D.C. 1979, Md. 1991, Va. 1993. Claims atty. Fidelity and Deposit Co. of Md., Balt., 1971-73; atty. advisor Dept. HUD, Washington, 1973-76; dep. staff counsel Nat. Trust for Hist. Preservation, Washington, 1976, chief counsel real estate, 1977-80, asst. gen. counsel, 1980-85; ptnr. Bodsberg & Norton, Washington, 1985-91; prin. Law Offices of Thomas A. Coughlin, Washington, 1992—. Co-author: Appraising Easements for Land Conservation and Historic Preservation, 1994, 2d edit., 1990, Historic Preservation Law and Taxation, 1986. Mem. Estate Planning Coun. Washington, Estate Planning Coun. No. Va. Estate planning, Estate taxation, Non-profit and tax-exempt organizations. Office: Law Offices of Thomas A Coughlin 1750 K St NW Ste 1200 Washington DC 20006-2303

**COUKOS, STEPHEN JOHN,** lawyer; b. Boston, July 23, 1959; s. John Stephen and Agnes (Liakos) C.; m. Jody Isselbacher, June 23, 1985; children: Jennifer Ashley, Andrew Jay; m. Marie J. Buttarazzi, Sept. 17, 1994; 1 child, Allison Marie. AB, Trinity Coll., Hartford, Conn., 1981; postgrad., Harvard U., 1985-86; JD, Stanford U., 1986. Assoc. Sullivan & Worcester, Boston, 1986-88; assoc. Bingham, Dana & Gould, Boston, 1988-94, ptnr., 1994-95; ptnr. Sullivan & Worcester, Boston, 1995—. Mem. ABA (banking law com., subcom. bank holding co. activities; bank and bank holding company acquisitions and dispositions), Mass. Bar Assn. (banking law com.), Boston Bar Assn. (banking law com.). Avocations: sports, physical fitness. Banking, General corporate, Mergers and acquisitions. Home: 819 Watertown St Newton MA 02465-2127 Office: Sullivan & Worcester 1 Post Office Sq Ste 2300 Boston MA 02109-2129

**COULSON, ROBERT,** retired association executive, arbitrator, author; b. New Rochelle, N.Y., July 24, 1924; s. Robert Earl and Abby (Stewart) C.; m. Cynthia Cunningham, Oct. 16, 1961; children: Cotton Richard, Dierdre, Crocker, Robert Cromwell, Christopher. BA, Yale U., 1949; LLB, Harvard U., 1953; DSc in Bus. Adminstrn. (hon.), Bryant U., 1985; LLD (hon.), Hofstra U., 1987. Bar: N.Y. 1954, Mass. 1954. Assoc. Whitman, Ransom & Coulson, N.Y.C., 1954-61; ptnr. Littlefield, Miller & Cleaves, N.Y.C., 1961-63; exec. v.p. Am. Arbitration Assn., N.Y.C., 1963-71; pres. Am. Arbitration Assn., 1971-94; ret., 1994; Cons. N.Y. State Div. Youth, 1961-63; pres. Youth Consultation Service of N.Y., 1970. Author: How to Stay Out of Court, 1968, Labor Arbitration: What You Need to Know, 1973, Business Arbitration: What You Need to Know, 1980, The Termination Handbook, 1981, Fighting Fair, 1983, Arbitration in Schools, 1985, Business Mediation, 1987, Alcohol and Drugs in Arbitration, 1988, Empowered at Forty, 1990, Police Under Pressure, 1993, ADR in America, 1994, Family Mediation, 1996; editor: Racing at Sea, 1958; contbr. articles to profl. jours. Bd. dirs. Fedn. Protestant Welfare Agys., pres., 1982-84, chmn. 1985-87; adv. com. Internat. Coun. for Comml. Arbitration. Mem. N.Y. Yacht Club, Cruising Club Am., Riverside Yacht Club. Avocations: sailing, travel, writing. Home: 9 Reginald St Riverside CT 06878-2522

**COULSON, WILLIAM ROY,** lawyer; b. Waukegan, Ill., Oct. 5, 1949; s. Robert E. and Rose (Stone) C.; m. Elizabeth A. Shafernich, Feb. 14, 1986. AB, Dartmouth Coll., 1969; JD, U. Ill., 1972. Bar: Ill. 1972, U.S. Dist. Ct. (no. dist.) Ill. 1974, U.S. Supreme Ct. 1976. Law clk. to judge U.S. Dist. Ct., East St. Louis, Ill., 1972-74, Chgo., 1975; asst. U.S. atty. U.S. Dept. Justice, Chgo., 1975-88, supr. criminal div., 1980-88; mng. ptnr. Cherry & Flynn, Chgo., 1988-99, Gold, Rosenfeld & Coulson, 1999—; faculty Atty. Gens. Adv. Inst., Washington, 1980-88, Ill. Inst. for Continuing Legal Edn., Springfield, 1983-88, Fed. Law Enforcement Tng. Ctr., Glynco, Ga., 1983-86; co-chmn. U.S. Magistrate Merit Selection Panel, 1989-91. Author: Federal Juvenile Law, 1980; contbg. author Animation mag., 1993—. Served to 2d lt. Ill. N.G., 1965-66. Finalist U.S. Senate Jud. Selection Panel, 1996. Mem. ABA, Chgo. Bar Assn. (jud. evaluation com. 1987-89, vice chair 1990-91), Fed. Bar Assn. (pres. 1991-92), Dartmouth Club. Federal civil litigation, Criminal. Office: 30 N La Salle St Chicago IL 60602-2590

**COULTER, CHARLES ROY,** lawyer; b. Webster City, Iowa, June 10, 1940; s. Harold L. Coulter and Eloise (Wheeler) Harrison; m. Elizabeth Bean, Dec. 16, 1961; 1 child, Anne Elizabeth. BA in Journalism, U. Iowa, 1962, JD, 1965. Bar: Iowa 1965. Assoc. Stanley, Bloom, Mealy & Lande, Muscatine, Iowa, 1965-68; v.p. Stanley, Lande & Hunter, Muscatine, 1969—, also bd. dirs. County fin. chmn. Leach for Congress, 1980-96; county coord. George Bush for Pres. , 1980, 88, Reagan-Bush Campaign, 1984. Fellow Coll. of Law Practice Mgmt., Am. Bar Found., Iowa State Bar Found., Am. Coll. Trust and Estate Counsel; mem. ABA (mem. coun. law practice mgmt. sect. 1984-88, sec. 1988-89, vice chair 1989-90, chair 1991-92, chair coord. commn. legal tech. 1994-97, mem. standing com. on tech. and info. sys. 1997-98), Iowa Bar Assn., Muscatine County Bar Assn., Thirty-Three Club (pres. 1981), Rotary, Order of Coif. Episcopalian. Avocation: tennis. Real property, Probate, General corporate. Office: Stanley Lande & Hunter 301 Iowa Ave Ste 400 Muscatine IA 52761-3881

**COULTER, JEAN WALPOLE,** lawyer; b. Oklahoma City, Apr. 10, 1953; d. George C. and Frances Helen (Covelle) Walpole; m. Patrick William Coulter, Apr. 20, 1987; children: Jay Thomas, Courtney Covelle. BS, U. Tulsa, 1975, JD, 1981. Bar: Okla. 1981, U.S. Dist. Ct. (no. dist.) N.C. 1981, U.S. Dist. Ct. Okla. 1981, U.S. Tax Ct. 1981. Assoc. Waddel & Buzzard, Tulsa, 1981-84; shareholder Jean C. Walpole & Assoc., Inc., Tulsa, 1984-89, Pray, Walker, Williamson & Marlar, P.C., Tulsa, 1989-95, Jean Walpole Coulter & Assocs., Inc., Tulsa, 1995—; tax instr. PDI, Denton, Tex., 1984-89. Trustee Univ. of Tulsa, 1990-91; dir. Big Bros./Big Sisters, Tulsa, 1983-89, Univ. Tulsa Alumni Assn., 1984-92, U. Tulsa Golden Hurrican Club, 1989-92. Mem. ABA (tax sect., labor sect.), Tulsa Employee Benefits Group. Episcopalian. Fax: 918-583-6398. Pension, profit-sharing, and employee benefits, Civil rights, Health. Office: 1638 S Carson Ave Ste 1107 Tulsa OK 74119-4261

**COUNARD, ALLEN JOSEPH,** lawyer; b. Green Bay, Wis., Dec. 5, 1937; s. Clifford Paul and Yvonne Mary C.; m. Valerie Ann Vorderlandwehr, Sept. 10, 1960; children: Catherine, Craig, Cara. BA, Mich. State U., 1965; JD, Wayne State U., 1969. Bar: Mich., U.S. Dist. Ct. (ea. and we. dists.) Mich., U.S. Ct. Appeals (6th cir.). Pvt. practice Southfield, Wyandotte and Trenton, Mich., 1969—. With U.S. Army, 1956-59. Mem. ATLA, Mich. Trial Lawyers Assn., Downriver Bar Assn., Rotary Club (pres. Gross Isle Mich. 1982-83), Gross Isle Yacht Club (past commodore, bd. chmn. 1982-83). Avocations: fly fishing, canoeing, boating, tennis. Personal injury, General civil litigation, Insurance. Office: 2320 W Jefferson Ave Trenton MI 48183-2706

**COUNCIL, PAULINE CARTER,** lawyer; b. Camilla, Ga., Apr. 26, 1950; d. Willie Frank D. Sr. and Bernice (Brown) Carter; m. James F. Council, Jr., Jan. 26, 1980; children: Dawn Nichole, Kimberly Michelle, Ashley Monique, James F., III. BA, Morris Brown Coll., 1972; JD, U. Fla., 1994. Asst. planner S.W. Ga. Area Planning and Devel. Commn., Camilla, 1972-73, rev. coordinator, 1973-74, sr. planner, 1974-75; area agy. on aging coordinator S. Ga. Area Planning and Devel. Commn., Valdosta, 1975-77, area agy. on aging dir., 1977-85; dir. Quitman/Brooks CDC, 1987-89; worker adjustment specialist, 1989-91; atty. pvt. practice, 1995—. Chmn. Foster Grandparents, Valdosta, 1982-85, Dist. 8. Social Svcs. Adv. Coun. Valdosta/Albany Area, 1985—; mem. Ga. Coalition of Black Women, Minority Affairs Com. Moody AFB, Valdosta, 1975-78, Nat. Congress Community Econ. Devel., Citizens For Better Valdosta/Lowndes County, Lowndes County Community Ptnrs. in Edn.; local rep. Martin Luther King, Jr. Ctr. for Non-Violent Social Change, Atlanta, 1984-85; Brownie troop leader Flint River Council Girl Scouts U.S.A., Valdosta, 1982; asst. leader Girl Scouts of Am., 1996—; mem. bd. dirs. Area Agy. on Aging, 1996—; mem., asst. dir. youth dept. Macedonia First Bapt. Ch.; chairperson Westside Neighborhood Assn., 1994-96; chairperson LMS Adv. Com., 1994-95. Com. for Humanities grantee, 1977, 79; Ga. Dept. Human Resources grantee, 1977-85. Mem. Ga. Bar Assn., Lowndes County Bar Assn., Nat. Council on Aging, Nat. Assn. AAAs, Ga. Assn. AAAs. Democrat. Pentecostal. Administrative and regulatory, Bankruptcy, Family and matrimonial. Home: 2410 Patrick Pl Valdosta GA 31601-7936

**COUNTISS, RICHARD NEIL,** lawyer; b. Midland, Tex., July 1, 1936; s. Floyd Curnutte and Lakie Ida (Wilson) C.; m. Karen Kay Hopkins, Aug. 9, 1958; children: Richard Jeffrey, William Michael, Julie Ann. BS, McMurry Coll., 1958; JD, So. Meth. U., 1961. Bar: Tex. 1961. Appellate atty. U.S. Dept. Justice, Washington, 1962-65; assoc. Linn & Helms, Spearman, Tex., 1965-68; ptnr. Linn, Helms & Countiss, Spearman, 1968-69, Countiss & Blackburn, Spearman, 1969-74; dist. atty., then dist. judge 84th Jud. Dist., Spearman, 1973-79; justice U.S. Ct. Appeals (7th cir.), Amarillo, Tex., 1979-88; bd. dirs. Windle Turley P.C., Dallas, 1988-90; of counsel Burrow & Williams, Houston, 1990-92; ptnr. Burrow, Countiss & Barrie, Houston, 1992-93; pvt. practice, 1993—; of counsel Williams & Bailey, Houston, 1995—; adj. prof. sch. law So. Meth. U., 1988-90, U. Houston, 1990—. Mem. Tex. Bar Assn. (bd. dirs. 1987-88), Tex. Bar Found. (trustee 1987-88), 5th Cir. Bar Assn., Houston Bar Assn., Amarillo West Rotary (pres. 1984-85), Spearman C. o fC. (pres. 1968-69). Democrat. Methodist. Avocations: gardening, fishing. General civil litigation, Personal injury. Home: 204 Travis St Apt 7E Houston TX 77002-1724 Office: Williams & Bailey 8441 Gulf Fwy # 6000 Houston TX 77017-5000

**COUNTRYMAN, THOMAS ARTHUR,** lawyer; b. Cleve., Mar. 14, 1957; s. Ralph Lyon Jr. and Dorothy Jean (Doherty) C.; m. Jean Millard Judson, June 7, 1980; children: Matthew Judson, Rachel Marie, Stephen Anthony. BS in Criminal Justice summa cum laude, Tex. Christian U., 1979; JD, Baylor U., 1982. Bar: Tex. 1982, U.S. Ct. Appeals (5th cir.) 1983, U.S. Dist. Ct. (we., so. and ea. dists.) Tex. Assoc. Cox & Smith, Inc., San Antonio, 1982-88, shareholder, v.p., 1989-91; asst. gen. counsel Chuska Energy Co., 1991-92; of counsel Fulbright & Jaworski L.L.P., 1992-98, sr. counsel, 1999—; spkr. San Antonio Legal Secs. Assn., San Antonio, 1984-86, U. Tex. Sch. Law. Annual Sch. Law Conf., 1998. Founder, dir., producer Univ. Players Drama Guild, San Antonio, 1983-99; chmn. coun. on ministries U. United Meth. Ch., San Antonio, 1987-88; mem. bd. mgmt. YMCA, 1995-97. Named Vol. of Yr. YMCA, 1996. Mem. ABA, State Bar Tex. (moot ct. com. 1990), 5th Cir. Bar Assn., Def. Counsel San Antonio (sec. 1992), San Antonio Young Lawyers Assn. (mock trial com. 1986), Nat. and Tex. Assns. Sch. Bd. Attys. Republican. Avocations: drama, running, tennis, golf, softball. General civil litigation, Health, Personal injury. Home: 114 Fawn Dr San Antonio TX 78231-1515

**COUPE, JAMES WARNICK,** lawyer; b. Utica, N.Y., Mar. 3, 1949; s. J. Leo and Helen Carbery (Brennan) C.; m. Andrea Jean Schaaf, Nov. 26, 1983; children: Helen Shriver, Benjamin Warnick, Charlotte Fitzgerald. AB, Hamilton Coll., 1971; JD, Vanderbilt U., 1974. Bar: N.Y. 1975, Calif. 1981, Tenn. 1995, U.S. Dist. Ct. (so. and ea. dists. ) N.Y. 1975, U.S. Ct. Appeals (2d cir.) 1975. Law clk. to judge U.S. Dist. Ct. (so. dist.) N.Y., N.Y.C., 1974-75; assoc. Donovan, Leisure, Newton & Irvine, N.Y.C., 1975-79, Phillips, Nizer, Benjamin, Krim & Ballon, N.Y.C., 1979-81; sr. atty. Atlantic Richfield Co., L.A., 1981-86; chief counsel Beverly Enterprises, Inc., Pasadena, Calif., 1986-88; gen. counsel Completion Bond Co., Inc., Century City, Calif., 1988-93; exec. Sullivan & Curtis Ins. Brokers, Pasadena, Calif., 1993-95; v.p. bus. & legal affairs Cinema Completions Internat., L.A., 1995-97, sr. v.p. bus. and legal affairs, 1997—. Mem. L.A. County Bar Assn., State Bar Calif. Republican. Roman Catholic. Entertainment, Finance, General corporate. Office: Cinema Completions Internat Ste 2800 Universal City Plz Universal City CA 91608

**COURINGTON, KAYE NEWTON,** lawyer; b. Cherry Point, N.C., Nov. 18, 1958; m. Lance Read Rydberg, Apr. 28, 1990; children: Read, Kathryn. BA, Newcomb Coll., 1980; MEd, Tulane U., 1982, JD cum laude, 1987. Bar: La. 1988, U.S. Dist. Ct. (ea., we. and mid. dists.) La. 1988, Tex. 1994. Assoc. Phelps Dunbar, New Orleans, 1987-89, Ellefson, Pulver & Staines, New Orleans, 1989-93, Woodley, Williams & Fenet, New Orleans, 1993-95; ptnr. Duncan & Courington, Ltd., New Orleans, 1995—. Author: Dining and Dieting: A Calorie Counter's Guide to New Orleans Restaurants, 1983. Mem. ABA, Women in Bus., Women in Shipping, New Orleans Bar Assn., La. Bar Assn. Episcopalian. E-mail: KCourington@Duncour.com. Toxic tort, Product liability, Insurance. Home: 579 Broadway St New Orleans LA 70118-3560 Office: Duncan & Courington 322 Lafayette St New Orleans LA 70130-3244

**COURSEN, CHRISTOPHER DENNISON,** lawyer; b. Mpls., Dec. 6, 1948; s. Richard Dennison and Helen Wilson (Stevens) C.; m. Pamela Elizabeth Lynch, June 3, 1978; children: Cameron Dennison, Matthew Ashbolt, Madeline Messurier. BA, Washington & Lee U., 1970; JD, George Washington U., 1975. Bar: D.C. 1975, U.S. Dist. Ct. D.C., 1976, U.S. Ct. Appeals (D.C. Cir.) 1976, U.S. Ct. Mil. Appeals 1976, U.S. Supreme Ct. 1978. Sole practice Washington, 1975-78; assoc. Dempsey & Koplovitz, Washington, 1978-80; majority communications counsel U.S. Senate Com. Commerce, Sci., and Transp., Washington, 1980-83; ptnr. O'Connor & Hannan, Washington, 1983-87; pres. The Status Group, Washington, 1988-90, The Coursen Group, Washington, 1990—; adj. prof. law The George Washington U., Washington, 1983. Team mem. Pres.-Elect Reagan's Transition Team, Washington, 1980; atty. adv. Reagan-Bush 1984, Washington; telecomms. advisor Bush/Quayle presdl. campaign, 1988; mem. Pres.' Adv. Bd. for Cuba Broadcasting, 1991, chmn., 1998—; mem. nat. fin. com. Bush-Quayle 1992; mem. adv. bd. Blue Ribbon Commn. on Reconstruction of Cuba; mem. bd. Children's Hosp. Found. Mem. D.C. Bar Assn., Chevy Chase Club, Chatham Beach and Tennis Club. Roman Catholic. Communications, Legislative, Administrative and regulatory. Home: 5006 Nahant St Bethesda MD 20816-2463 Office: The Coursen Group 1133 Connecticut Ave NW Ste 900 Washington DC 20036-4356

**COURT, LEONARD,** lawyer, educator; b. Ardmore, Okla., Jan. 11, 1947; s. Leonard and Margaret Janet (Harvey) C.; m. JoAnn Dilleshaw, Sept. 2, 1967; children: Chris, Todd, Brooke. BA, Okla. State U., 1969; JD, Harvard U., 1972. Bar: Okla. 1973, U.S. Dist. Ct. (we. dist.) Okla. 1973, U.S. Dist. Ct. (no. dist.) Okla., 1978, U.S. Dist. Ct. (ea. dist.) Okla. 1983, U.S. Ct. Appeals (10th cir.) 1980, U.S. Ct. Mil. Appeals 1973. Assoc. Crowe & Dunlevy, Oklahoma City, Okla., 1977-81, shareholder, dir., 1981—; adj. prof. Okla. U. Law Sch., Norman, 1984-85, 88-89, 99, Okla. City U. Law Sch., 1998-2000; planning com. Ann. Inst. Labor Law, S.W. Legal Found., Dallas, 1984—. Contbg. author: (supplement book) The Developing Labor Law, 1978, Corporate Counsel's Annual, 1974, Labor Law Developments, 1993, Employment Discrimination Law, 1998 Supplement. Chmn. bd. elders Meml. Christian Ch., Oklahoma City, 1980, 98-2000; cubmaster Last Frontier coun. Boy Scouts Am., 1984, co-chmn. sustaining fund raising drive Oklahoma City Downtown YMCA, 1989, mem. bd. mgmt., 1994-96; participant Leadership Oklahoma City, 1987-88, bd. govs. Okla. State U. Found., 1990—; Oklahoma City Ronald McDonald House, 1990-93, mem. exec. com. 1991-93; co-chmn. ann. teleparty fundraising drive Am. Heart Assn., Okla. City, 1996-98, bd. dirs., 1996-98. Capt. USAF, 1973-77. Fellow Am. Coll. Labor and Employment Lawyer; mem. Am. Employment Law Coun., U.S. C. of C. (mem. labor rels. com. 1997—), Okla. State U. Bar Assn. (bd. dirs. 1980—), Oklahoma City C. of C. (mem. sports and recreation com. 1982-85, indsl. devel. com. 1986), Okla. State U., Okla. State U. Alumni Assn. (nat. bd. dirs. 1989—, nat. exec. com., 1992-97, pres. 1995-96, chmn. alumni ctr. task force 1998—, Disting. Alumni award 1998), Okla. County Alumni Assn. (bd. sec. 1987-88, treas. 1988-89, v.p. 1989-90, pres. 1990-91), Harvard Law Sch. Assn., ABA (labor and employment law sect. com. on devel. of law under Nat. Labor Rels. Act, com. on EEO law, subcom. on substantive devels. involving sex under Title VII, and subcom. of EEOC process Title VII coverage and multiple forums, lititgation sect./employment and labor rels. law com.), Okla. Bar Assn. (labor and employment law sect. coun. 1978-83, 85-87, chmn. 1986), Okla. County Bar Assn., Fed. Bar Assn., U.S. Tennis Assn. (life). Labor, Civil rights. Office: Crowe & Dunlevy Mid America Tower 20 N Broadway Ave Ste 1800 Oklahoma City OK 73102-8273

**COURTEAU, GIRARD ROBERT,** prosecutor; b. St. Paul, Aug. 21, 1942; s. Robert William and Laura Florence Courteau; m. Mary Linda Lucas, Apr. 3, 1964 (div. May 1997); m. Susan Frances DeBaca, Aug. 8, 1997; children: Steven, Girard, Devin, Heather. AA, Coll. Marin, 1965; BA, U. Calif., Berkeley, 1967; JD, U. Calif., 1970. Bar: Calif. 1971, U.S. Dist. Ct. (ctrl. dist.) Calif. 1971, U.S. Dist. Ct. (no. dist.) Calif. 1983. Dep. dist. atty. Monterey County, Calif., 1971, Marin County, San Rafael, Calif., 1972—. Assoc. editor Hasting's Law Jour., 1970; editor (monthly newsletter) Marin Law Enforcement Newsletter, 1974-89. Named Prosecutor of the Yr., Marin County Dist. Attys. Office, San Rafael, Calif., 1987. Mem. Calif. Dist. Attys. Assn., Marin County Bar Assn., Order of the Coif, Thurston Soc. Roman Catholic. Avocations: gardening, reading. Home: 516 Julliard Park Dr Santa Rosa CA 95401-6312 Office: Marin Dist Attys Office Rm 130 Hall of Justice San Rafael CA 94903

**COURTNEY, ANN M.,** lawyer; b. 1951. BA, Bridgewater State Coll.; JD, Western New Eng. Coll. Bar: Maine 1989. Pvt. practice Portland, Maine. Mem. ABA, Maine State Bar Assn. (pres.). Office: 75 Pearl St Portland ME 04101-4101*

**COURTNEY WESTFALL, CONSTANCE,** lawyer; b. Plainview, Tex., Nov. 29, 1960; d. M.H. and Carolyn Courtney; m. Monte Jay Westfall, Jan. 3, 1998; 1 child, William Henry Westfall. BS, U. Tex., 1982, JD, 1985. Bar: Tex., U.S. Dist. Ct. (we. and no. dists.) Tex., U.S. Dist. Ct. (we. and ea. dists.) Ark., U.S. Dist. Ct. (we. dist.) Okla., U.S. Ct. Appeals (5th and 8th cirs.) Tex. Com. clk. Natural Resources Com., Tex. Ho. of Rep., 1979; legis. staff to hon. Buck Florence Tex. Ho. of Rep., 1980-82; law clk. to hon. Jerre Williams U.S. Ct. Appeals (5th cir.), 1985-86; assoc. Thompson & Knight, Dallas, 1986-92, Brown McCarroll, Dallas, 1992-94; ptnr. Hutcheson & Grundy, Dallas, 1994-98, Strasburger & Price, Dallas, 1998—. Contbr. articles to profl. jours. Moderator So. Meth. U. Sch. Law Environ. Career Seminar, 1989—. Mem. ABA, State Bar Tex. (coll., chair outreach com. environ. sect. 1989-92, mem. law sch. com. 1988-97, chair law sch. com. 1997—, State Bar Coll., 1995—). Environmental, Administrative and regulatory. Office: Strasburger & Price 901 Main St Ste 4300 Dallas TX 75202-3714

**COUSINS, WILLIAM, JR.,** judge; b. Swiftown, Miss., Oct. 6, 1927; s. William and Drusilla (Harris) C.; m. Hiroko Ogawa, May 12, 1953; children: Cheryl Akiko, Noel William, Yul Vincent, Gail Yoshiko. BA, U. Ill., 1948; LLB, Harvard U., 1951. Bar: Ill. 1953, U.S. Dist. Ct. (no. dist.) Ill. 1961, U.S. Supreme Ct. 1975. Title examiner Chgo. Title & Trust Co., 1953-57; asst. state's atty. Cook County, Ill., 1957-61; sole practice, Chgo., 1961-76; judge Circuit Ct. Cook County, Chgo., 1976-92; justice Ill. Appellate Ct., 1992—; chair exec. com. 1st Dist. Appellate Ct., 1997—; lectr. De Paul Law Sch., Chgo., 1981-84; bd. dirs. Nat. Ctr. State Cts., 1996—; faculty advisor Nat. Jud. Coll., 1987; mem. exec. com. Ill. Jud. Conf., 1983—, former chmn. exec. com.; liaison assoc. judges coordinating com.; former chmn. Ill. Jud. Council. Bd. dirs. Ind. Voters Ill., 1964-67, Ams. for Democratic Action, 1968, Operation PUSH, 1971-76, Nat. Ctr. for State Cts.; mem. Chgo. City Coun., 1967-76; del. Democratic Nat. Conv., 1972; asst. moderator United Ch. of Christ, N.Y.C., 1981. Served with U.S. Army, 1951-53. Decorated Army Commendation medal; named Judge of Yr., John Marshall Law Sch., Chgo., 1980; recipient Thurgood Marshall award Kent Law Sch., 1985, Kenneth E. Wilson award Ill. Judicial Coun., 1992, Earl Burris Dickerson award, 1998. Mem. ABA, Nat. Bar Assn. (bd. dirs. 1992-93, chair NBA jud. conf. 1995-96, Hall of Fame 1994), Ill. Bar Assn., Cook County Bar Assn. (former bd. dirs., Edward N. Wright award 1968, William R. Ming award 1974, Hall of Fame 1997), Chgo. Bar Assn., Kappa Alpha Psi, Alpha Kappa Alpha (Monarch award for Statesmanship 1995), Sigma Pi Phi. Home: 1745 E 83rd Pl Chicago IL 60617-1714 Office: Ill Appellate Ct 160 N La Salle St Rm 1905 Chicago IL 60601-3103

**COUSINS, WILLIAM JOSEPH,** lawyer, litigation consultant; b. New Haven, Conn., Sept. 28, 1917; s. Salvatore Colombieri and Mary (Arpaia) C.; m. Betty Jean Collins, June 25, 1954; children: Mimi Causey, Anna Maria, William J. Jr. BA, Yale U., 1940, LLB, 1943. Bar: Conn., U.S. Dist. Ct. Conn., U.S. Ct. Appeals (2d cir.) 1946. Law clk. New Haven (Conn.) Superior Ct., 1946-48; pvt. practice New Haven, 1946-52; ptnr. Arpaia & Cousins, New Haven, 1952-56; sr. ptnr. Cousins, Dooley & Barnston, Conn., 1956-68, Cousins, Ritter & Silverstone, New Haven, 1968-81, Carmody & Torrance, New Haven, 1981-87; dir. William J. Cousins & Assoc., Woodbridge, Conn., 1987; ret., 1987; apptd. spl. master and parajud. officer U.S. Dist. Ct. Conn.; sr. ptnr. conflict resolution svc. Cousins and Cooper; prosecutor Woodbridge Town Ct., 1948-60, town counsel Town of Woodbridge, 1948-76, chmn. Citizens Action Commn., 1952-55. Chmn. New Haven County Reps., 1960-64; chmn. Cath. Interracial Council, 1952-56. Served as sgt. USAAF 1943-46, PTO. Mem. ABA (lawyers conf. of jud. adminstrn. divsn.), Fed. Bar Assn., Am. Judicature Soc., Soc. Profl. Dispute Resolution, Nat. Inst. for Dispute Resolution (assoc.), Law and Soc. Assn. Republican. Roman Catholic. Clubs: Yale, Mory's, The Graduate. General civil litigation, Workers' compensation. Home and Office: 24 Barberry Ln Woodbridge CT 06525-1326

**COUVILLION, DAVID IRVIN,** federal judge; b. Simmesport, La., Oct. 27, 1934; s. J. Forest Couvillion and Leontine Rabalais. BS, La. State U., 1956, JD, 1959; LLM, Georgetown U., 1973. Bar: La. 1959. Pvt. practice Marksville, La., 1959-67; adminstrv. asst. U.S. Congressman Speedy O. Long, Washington, 1967-72; assoc. McCollister, McCleary, Fazio and Holliday, Baton Rouge, 1974-85; spl. trial judge U.S. Tax Ct., Washington, 1985—. Mem. ABA, La. State Bar Assn. Office: US Tax Ct 400 2nd St NW Washington DC 20217-0002

**COVELL, KENNETH,** lawyer; b. N.Y.C., Mar. 4, 1955; married. JD, U. Alaska, 1983. Bar: Alaska. Pvt. practice Fairbanks, Alaska, 1986—. Mem. Tanana Valley Bar Assn. (pres. 1996-97). Criminal, General civil litigation, Labor. Office: 712 8th Ave Fairbanks AK 99701-4402

**COVELL, ROBERT MARTIN,** lawyer; b. West Chester, Pa., Dec. 4, 1957; s. Ralph Joseph and Helen A. (Goworowsky) C.; m. Cynthia Garland Croft, Apr. 19, 1986; children: Joseph Edward, Margaret Cristina. BSBA, Pa. State U., 1980; JD, Dickinson Sch. Law, 1983. Bar: Pa. 1983, U.S. Dist. Ct. (mid. dist.) Pa. 1986. Law clk. Newton C. Taylor, Huntington, Pa., 1984-85; pvt. practice Huntington, 1985—; mem. adv. bd. Huntington County Children and Adult Devel. Corp. Inc., 1990—. Avocations: sports, home repair. Bankruptcy, Family and matrimonial, Real property. Office: 206 Penn St Huntingdon PA 16652-1444

**COVIELLO, FRANK JOSEPH,** lawyer; b. Washington, Dec. 27, 1940; s. Francis George and Mary Louise (Martini) C. BA, Western Car. U., 1966; LLB, U. Balt., 1969. Bar: Md. 1971, U.S. Dist. Ct. (4th cir.) 1971, U.S. Dist. Ct. D.C. 1985, U.S. Ct. Appeals (4th cir.) 1985. Law clk. Circuit Ct. for Montgomery County, Rockville, Md., 1969-71; asst. state's atty. Montgomery County, Rockville, 1971-73; pvt. practice, 1974-84; ptnr. Bivona & Cohen, Rockville, 1984-89, Gilberg & Kurent, Gaithersburg, 1989-90; pvt. practice Gaithersburg, 1990—. With U.S. Army, 1961-64. Mem. Montgomery County Bar Assn., D.C. Bar Assn. Roman Catholic. Avocations: tennis, skiing, scuba diving. General civil litigation, Personal injury, Product liability.

**COVINGTON, ANN K.,** state supreme court justice; b. Fairmont, W.Va., Mar. 5, 1942; d. James R. and Elizabeth Ann (Hornor) Kettering; m. James E. Waddell, Aug. 17, 1963 (div. Aug. 1976); children: Mary Elizabeth Waddell, Paul Kettering Waddell; m. Joe E. Covington, May 14, 1977. BA, Duke U., 1963; JD, U. Mo., 1977. Bar: Mo. 1977, U.S. Dist. Ct. (we. dist.) Mo. 1977. Asst. atty. gen. State of Mo., Jefferson City, 1977-79; ptnr. Covington & Maier, Columbia, Mo., 1979-81, Butcher, Cline, Mallory & Covington, Columbia, Mo., 1981-87; justice Mo. Ct. Appeals (we. dist.), Kansas City, 1987-89; justice Mo. Supreme Ct., 1989-93, chief justice, 1993-95; now judge, 1995—; bd. dirs. Mid Mo. Legal Services Corp., Columbia, 1983-87; chmn. Juvenile Justice Adv. Bd., Columbia, 1984-87. Bd. dirs. Ellis Fischel State Cancer Hosp., Columbia, 1982-83, Nat. Ctr. for State Cts., 1998—; chmn. Columbia Indsl. Revenue Bond Authority, 1984-87; trustee United Meth. Ch., Columbia, 1983-86, Am. Law Inst., 1998—; bd. dirs. Nat. Ctr. State Cts., 1998—. Recipient Citation of Merit, U. Mo. Law Sch., 1993, Faculty-Alumni award U. Mo., 1993; Coun. of State Govt. Toll fellow, 1988. Fellow Am. Bar Found.; mem. ABA (jud. adminstrv. divsn., mem. adv. com. on Evidence Rules, U.S. Cts.), Mo. Bar Assn., Boone County Bar Assn. (sec. 1981-82), Am. Law Inst., Acad. Mo. Squires, Order of Coif (hon.), Mortar Bd. (hon.), Phi Alpha Delta, Kappa Kappa Gamma. Home: 1201 Torrey Pines Dr Columbia MO 65203-4825 Office: Mo Supreme Ct 101 High St Jefferson City MO 65102-0150

**COVINGTON, GEORGE MORSE,** lawyer; b. Lake Forest, Ill., Oct. 4, 1942; s. William Slaughter and Elizabeth (Morse) C.; m. Shelagh Tait Hickey, Dec.28, 1966 (div. May 1995); children: Karen Morse, Jean Tait, Sarah Ingersoll Covington; m. Barbara Schilling Trentham, Dec. 19, 1998. AB, Yale U., 1964; JD, U. Chgo., 1967. Assoc. Gardner, Carton & Douglas, Chgo., 1970-75, ptnr., 1976-95; atty. pvt. practice, Lake Forest, Ill., 1995—; lectr. in field. Contbr. articles to profl. jours. active Grant Hosp. of Chgo., 1974-95, chmn. of bd. 1990-95; bd. dirs. Grant Healthcare Found., 1995—; trustee Chgo. Acad. Sci., 1974-85, pres., 1980-82; trustee, chmn. Ill. chpt. Nature Conservancy, Chgo., 1974-88; bd. dirs. Latin Sch Chgo., 1979-80, Open Lands Project, Chgo., 1972-86, Chgo. Farmers, 1994-96; bd. dirs., sec. Lake Forest Open Lands Assn., 1984—; bd. dirs., sec., treas. Les Cheneaux Found., 1978—; bd. dirs. Student Conservation Assn., 1996—, Little Traverse Conservancy, 1998—; mem. Bd. Fire and Police Commrs., Village of Lake Bluff, Ill., 1991—. With U.S. Army, 1967-69. Mem. ABA, Ill. Bar Assn., Lake County Bar Assn., Chgo. Bar Assn., Univ. Club (bd. dirs. 1985-88), Commonwealth Club, Legal Club, Shoreacres (Lake Bluff, Ill.), Les Cheneaux Club (Cedarville, Mich.), Lambda Alpha. Real property, Land use and zoning (including planning). Office: 500 N Western Ave Ste 204 Lake Forest IL 60045-1955

**COVINGTON, MARLOW STANLEY,** retired lawyer; b. Langhorne, Pa., Apr. 25, 1937; s. Marlow O. and Madalyn L. (Johnson) C.; m. Laura Aline Wallace, Aug. 28, 1965; children: Lisa M., Scott, Eric (dec.). BS, Bloomsburg U., 1959; postgrad., Rutgers U., 1960; JD, Howard U., 1965. Bar: D.C. 1971, U.S. Dist. Ct. D.C. 1971, U.S. Supreme Ct. 1975, U.S. Dist. Ct. Md. 1981, Md. 1985. Tchr. Pub. Schs., Long Branch, N.J., 1959-62; referee N.J. Dept. Labor, Newark, 1965-66; claim examiner Allstate's Ins. Co., Verona, N.J., 1966-71; house counsel Allstate's Ins. Co., Washington, Greenbelt, Md., 1971-97; sr. trial atty. Allstate Ins. Co., Greenbelt, Md., 1989-96; ret., 1996; mem. adv. bd. Inverness Custom Plastics, Inc., Barrington, Ill., 1990—. Recipient cert. of recognition Balt.-Washington area Fellowship Christian Athletes, 1981. Mem. ABA (com. ins. negligence and compensation sect.), Md. Bar Assn., Montgomery County Bar Assn., D.C. Bar Assn. (com. ins. and compensation sect.), Nat. Bar Assn., Prince George's County Md. Bar Assn., Bloomsburg U. Alumni Assn. (bd. dirs. 1977-80), Sigma Delta Tau, Gamma Theta Upsilon. Avocation: collecting antique pocket knives. Fax: 301-421-4329. E-mail: SCoving104@aol.com. Insurance, Personal injury, General corporate. Home: 16001 Amina Dr Burtonsville MD 20866-1039

**COVNER, ELLEN B.,** lawyer; b. New Haven, Conn., Apr. 2, 1947; d. Bernard and Thelma (Crockin) C.; children: Jamie Beth, Seth Lawrence. BA, Goucher Coll., 1969; postgrad., Suffolk U., 1972-73; JD, Boston Coll., 1975. Bar: Mass. 1975, Pa. 1988, U.S. Dist. Ct. Mass. 1976, U.S. Ct. Appeals (1st cir.) 1976, U.S. Ct. Appeals (3d cir.) 1989. Assoc. Chayet & Sonnenreich, Boston, 1975-77; ptnr. Elder, Moses & Weiss, Boston, 1977-79; gen. counsel The Children's Hosp., Boston, 1979-86; assoc. exec. dir. legal affairs Hosp. of the U. Pa., Phila., 1986-90; assoc. v.p. legal affairs U. Pa. Med. Ctr., Phila., 1990-92; atty., cons. Health Law and Risk Mgmt., Wayne, Pa., 1993; assoc. Karafin Gruenstein & Dubrow, P.C., Bala Cynwyd, Pa., 1999—; treas. Pa. Soc. of Healthcare Attys.; adj. assoc. prof. legal studies psychiatry U. Pa. Sch. Medicine. Author: Legal Aspects of

Infection Control, 1989; co-author: (with others) The Role of Hospital Ethics Committees in Decisions to Terminate Treatment, 1987. Mem. ABA (vice chmn. com. on medicine and law 1989-92). Fax: 610-664-9449. E-mail: mail@kgdlaw.com. Health, Personal injury. Office: Karafin Gruenstein & Dubrow PC 401 E City Ave Ste 200 Bala Cynwyd PA 19004-1117

**COWAN, CASPAR FRANK,** lawyer; b. Calais, Maine, May 7, 1915; s. Frank Irving and Helen Anna (Caspar) C.; m. Nancy Hopkinson Linnell, Oct. 19, 1946; children—Joanna Cowan Allen, Seth W., June Cowan Roelle. A.B., Bowdoin Coll., 1936; J.D. Harvard U., 1940. Bar: Maine 1940, U.S. Dist. Ct. Maine 1941, U.S. Ct. Appeals (1st cir.) 1946. Assoc. Cowan and Cowan, Portland, Maine, 1940-48; assoc. Perkins, Thompson, Hinckley and Keddy, Portland, 1948-51, ptnr. 1951-91. Author: Maine Real Estate Law and Practice. Chmn. Portland Renewal Authority, 1952-64; chmn, Portland Housing Authority, 1958-59. Served to lt. U.S. Army, 1942-46. Decorated Bronze Star. Mem. ABA, Maine State Bar Assn. (econs. practice law com., title standards com.), Cumberland County Bar Assn., Am. Coll. Real Estate Lawyers, 10th Mt. Div. Alumni Assn., Maine Charitable Mechanics Assn. Clubs: Woodfords, Junto. Lodge: Masons (32d degree). Real property, Probate, Personal income taxation. Home and Office: 99 Vannah Ave Portland ME 04103-4510

**COWAN, DOUGLAS LEO,** lawyer; b. L.A., May 22, 1943; s. Douglas L. and Mildred R. (Zimmerman) C.; m. Bettina VanDeCamp, Sept. 12, 1964 (div. Jan. 1972); 1 child, Kristina; m. Corinne Ellen Crawley, July 21, 1973; children: John, Greg. BA, Wash. State U., 1965; JD, U. Wash., 1968. Bar: Wash. 1968, U.S. Dist. Ct. (we. dist.) Wash. 1969. Ptnr. Schafer, Mitchell & Cowan, Seattle, 1969-74, Kinzel, Cowan & Allen, Bellevue, Wash., 1978-87; pros. atty. City of Bellevue, 1974-78; ptnr. Cowan Hayne & Fox, Bellevue, 1988-98; founder The Cowan Law Firm, Bellevue, 1998—; pres. Wash. Found. for Criminal Justice, Bellevue, 1987—. Mem. Nat. Coll. for Driving Under Influence Def. (founder, dean 1996-97), Wash. Assn. Criminal Def. Lawyers (bd. govs. 1987-88), East King County Bar Assn. (pres. 1979). State civil litigation. Office: 3805 108th Ave NE Ste 204 Bellevue WA 98004-7613

**COWAN, FREDERIC JOSEPH,** lawyer; b. N.Y.C., Oct. 11, 1945; s. Frederic Joseph Sr. and Mary Virginia (Wesley) C.; m. Linda Marshall Scholle, Apr. 28, 1974; children: Elizabeth, Caroline, Allison. AB, Dartmouth Coll., 1967; JD, Harvard U., 1978. Bar: Ky. 1978, U.S. Dist. Ct. (we. dist.) Ky. 1979, U.S. Ct. Appeals (6th cir.) 1984, U.S. Supreme Ct. 1989. Vol. Peace Corps, Ethiopia, 1967-69; assoc. Brown, Todd & Heyburn, Louisville, 1979-83; ptnr. Rice, Porter, Seiller & Price, Louisville, 1983-87; atty. gen. Commonwealth of Ky., 1988-92; counsel Lynch, Cox, Gilman & Manan, 1992—; Ky. State Rep., 32d legis. dist., 1982-87; chair Ky. Child Support Enforcement Commn., 1988-91, Ky. Sexual Abuse and Exploitation Prevention Bd., 1988-91; bd. dirs. Ky. Job Tng. Coordinating Council, Frankfort, Louisville Bar Found., 1986. Vice chmn. judiciary criminal com. Ky. Ho. of Reps., 1985-87; chmn. budget com. on justice Judiciary and Corrections Ky. Ho. of Reps., 1985-87, Leadership Ky., 1985; U.S. del. election mission to Namibia Nat. Dem. Inst. for Internat. Affairs, 1989; U.S. del. dem. instns. seminar Nat. Dem. Inst. for Internat. Affairs, Slovenia, 1992; electoral supr. Orgn. for Security and Cooperation in Europe, Bosnia and Herzogovina, 1996. Mem. ABA, Ky. Bar Assn., Louisville Bar Assn., Ky. Acad. Trial Attys. Methodist. General civil litigation, Communications, Administrative and regulatory. Home: 1747 Sulgrave Rd Louisville KY 40205-1643 Office: 500 Meidinger Tower Louisville KY 40202

**COWAN, JOHN JOSEPH,** lawyer; b. Chester, Pa., Nov. 14, 1932; s. John Joseph and Helen Marie (Frame) C.; m. Hilary Ann Gregory, Dec. 29, 1960; children—Daniel, Patrick, Meg, Jennifer. A.B., LaSalle Coll., 1954; J.D. cum laude, U. Pa., 1959. Bar: D.C. 1960, Ohio 1964, W.Va. 1968, U.S. Supreme Ct. 1971. Teaching fellow Stanford U., Palo Alto, Calif., 1959-60; trial atty. civil div. U.S. Dept. Justice, Washington, 1960-63; assoc. Taft, Stettinius & Hollister, Cin., 1963-67; gen. atty. Chesapeake & Potomac Telephone Co. of W.Va., Charleston, 1968-79; ptnr. Sullivan & Cowan, Charleston, 1979-82; sole practice, Charleston, 1982—. Served to 1st lt. AUS, 1954-56. Mem. ABA. Sr. adv. editor U. Pa. Law Rev., 1958-59. State civil litigation, Federal civil litigation, Criminal. Home and Office: 2326 Windham Rd Charleston WV 25303-3021

**COWAN, STUART MARSHALL,** lawyer; b. Irvington, N.J., Mar. 20, 1932; s. Bernard Howard and Blanche (Hertz) C.; m. Marilyn R.C. Toepfer, Apr., 1961 (div. 1968); m. Eleanor Schmerel, June, 1953 (dec.); m. Jane Alison Averill, Feb. 24, 1974 (div. 1989); children: Fran Lori, Catherine R.L., Erika R.L., Bronwen P.; m. Victoria Yi, Nov. 11, 1989. BS in Econs., U. Pa., 1952; LLB, Rutgers U., 1955. Bar: N.J. 1957, Hawaii 1962, U.S. Supreme Ct. 1966. Atty. Greenstein & Cowan, Honolulu, 1961-70, Cowan & Fewy, Honolulu, 1970-89; pvt. practice, 1989—; of counsel Price Okomoto Himeno & Lum, 1993—; arbitrator Fed. Mediation & Conciliation Svc., Honolulu, 1972—, Am. Arbitration Assn., Honolulu, 1968—, Hawaii Pub. Employee Rels. Bd., 1972—. Pres. Hawaii Epilepsy Soc., 1984-86; acquisition chair Hawaii Family Support Ctr., 1995-97. Lt. USN, 1955-61. Mem. ABA, Hawaii Bar Assn., Am. Judicature Soc., Assn. Trial Lawyers Am. (state committeeman for hawii 1965-69, bd. govs. 1972-75), Consumer Lawyers Hawaii, Hawaii Trial Lawyers Assn. (v.p. 1972-78), Japan-Hawaii Lawyers Assn., Soc. Profls. in Dispute Resolution, Inter Pacific Bar Assn., Honolulu Symphony Soc. (bd. dirs. 1989-99), Hawaii Epilepsy soc. (pres. 1984-86), Royal Order of Kamehameha, Order of St. Stanislas, Waikiki Yacht Club, St. Francis Yacht Club, Hawaii Yacht Club, Plaza Club, Honolulu Club, Hawaii Scottish Assn. (chieftain 1983-88), St. Andrews Soc., Caledonian Soc. (vice chieftain 1983-85), Honolulu Pipes and Drums (sec.-treas. 1985-90), New Zealand Police Pipe Band, Masons (York Rite, Scottish Rite no. and so. jurisdictions, Grand Lodge Hawaii, grand orator 1992, sr. grand steward 1993, jr. grand warden 1994, sr. grand warden 1995, grand master 1997), Red Cross of Constantine, Royal Order Scotland, Pearl Harbor (master 1971, chaplain 1992-96), Masada (#51 N.J.), USS Missouri Meml. Assn., Hawaiian Koolau, Elks, Chinese Acacia Club, Royal Hawaiian Ocean Racing Club. Jewish. Home: 47-339 Mapumapu Rd Kaneohe HI 96744-4922 Office: 707 Richards St Honolulu HI 96813-4616 also: 47-653 Kamehameha Hwy # 202 Kaneohe HI 96744-4965

**COWAN, WALLACE EDGAR,** lawyer; b. Jersey City, Jan. 28, 1924; s. Benjamin and Dorothy (Zunz) C.; m. Ruth Daitzman, June 8, 1947; children: Laurie, Paul, Judith. BS magna cum laude, NYU, 1947; JD cum laude, Harvard U., 1950. Ptnr. Stroock, Stroock & Lavan, N.Y.C., 1950-93, of counsel, 1994—; dir. Ametek, Inc., Paoli, Pa., 1982-93, sec., 1969-93, sec. H.S. Stuttman, Inc., Westport, Conn., to 1996. Mem. Teaneck (N.J.) Adv. Bd. on Parks, Playgrounds and Recreation, 1966—, chmn., 1974—; pres. No. Valley Commuters Assn.; past pres., life trustee Congregation Beth Sholom, Teaneck; mem. Forum adv. bd. Sch.-Based Youth Svcs. Project, 1998—. 1st lt. USAF, 1942-45, ETO. Decorated Air medal with silver cluster; recipient Vol. in the Parks award Bergen County, N.J., 1993, Disting. Svc. award, 1994. Mem. Beta Gamma Sigma. General corporate, Securities, Contracts commercial. Home: 499 Emerson Ave Teaneck NJ 07666-1927 Office: Stroock Stroock & Lavan 180 Maiden Ln New York NY 10038-4925

**COWART, T(HOMAS) DAVID,** lawyer; b. San Benito, Tex., June 12, 1953; s. Thomas W. Jr. and Glenda Claire (Miller) C.; children: Thomas Kevin, Lauren Michelle, Megan Leigh; m. Greta E. Gerberding, Aug. 12, 1995. BBA, U. Miss., 1975, JD, 1978; LLM in Taxation, NYU, 1979. Bar: Miss. 1978, Tex. 1979; CPA Tex., Miss. Assoc. Dossett, Magruder & Montgomery, Jackson, Miss., 1978, Strasburger & Price, Dallas, 1979-87; ptnr., assoc., shareholder Johnson & Gibbs, Dallas, 1988-90; shareholder Jenkens & Gilchrist, Dallas, 1991—; adj. prof. law So. Meth. U. Sch. Law, 1988; mem. key dist. adv. com. IRA, Dallas, 1989-95, chmn., 1990-93; mem. Coll. State Bar Tex.; lectr. in field. Mem. editl. bd. Flexible Benefits, 1993—, 401k Advisor, 1994—, COBRA Adv., 1996—. Mem. adv. com. Goals for Dallas, 1984-85; vol. Children's Med. Ctr., 1992-96. Mem. ABA (sect. taxation, employee benefits com., vice-chmn. 1995-97, chmn. elect 1997-98, chmn. 1998-99, sect. 83 issues task force, chmn. health plan designs issues subcom. 1992-95, health care task force 1991-98, chmn.-designate joint com. on employee benefits 1997-99, chmn. joint com. employee benefits 1999—), State Bar Tex. (sect. taxation, com. compensation and employee benefits, fed. legislation, regulations and revenue rulings subcom. 1986-87, chmn. fiduciary stds. for trustees subcom. 1987-88), Dallas Bar Assn. (lectr. 1985—, coun. mem. employee benefits sect. 1989-92, treas. 1992, sec. 1993, v.p. 1994, pres. 1995), S.W. Benefits Assn. (bd. dirs. 1994-97), Dallas Benefits Soc. (co-moderator 1991-92, bd. dirs. 1991-93), Omicron Delta Kappa, Beta Alpha Psi, Phi Alpha Phi. Pension, profit-sharing, and employee benefits. Office: Jenkens & Gilchrist 1445 Ross Ave Ste 3200 Dallas TX 75202-2799

**COWDEN, JOHN WILLIAM,** lawyer; b. Springfield, Mo., June 3, 1945; s. John Marshall and Laura Alice (Lemmon) C.; m. Carol Jean Avery, Jan. 27, 1968; children: Jennifer, John. BA, Southwest Mo. State U., 1967; JD, U. Mo., 1970. Bar: Mo. 1970, U.S. Dist. Ct. (we. dist.) Mo. 1971, U.S. Ct. Appeals (8th cir.) 1980, U.S. Supreme Ct. 1982. Asst. atty. gen. State of Mo., Jefferson City, 1970-71; assoc. Morrison, Hecker, Curtis, Kuder & Parrish, Kansas City, Mo., 1971-76; ptnr. Morrison, Hecker, Curtis, Kuder & Parrish, Kansas City, 1976-89, Baker, Sterchi & Cowden, Kansas City, 1989—. Co-author: Missouri Evidence Restated. Chmn. human devel. bd. YMCA, Kansas City; bd. dirs. Gt. Am. Basketball League, Johnson City, Kans., 1986-88. Mem. ABA, Mo. Bar Assn., Kansas City Bar Assn., Lawyers Assn. Kansas City, Am. Bd. Trial Advs., Am. Coll. Trial Lawyers, Internat. Assn. Def. Counsel, Def. Rsch. Inst., U. Mo. Law Soc., Indian Hills Country Club, Univ. Club. Avocations: golf, travel. Federal civil litigation, General civil litigation, State civil litigation. Home: 6827 Linden St Shawnee Mission KS 66208-1427 Office: 2100 Commerce Towers Kansas City MO 64199

**COWDERY, ALLEN CRAIG,** lawyer; b. Bartlesville, Okla., July 1, 1943; s. Herman Charles and Jane (Sparr) C.; m. Jane Reed, May 31, 1969; children—Elizabeth, Owen. B.A., Okla. U., 1965, J.D., 1968. Bar: Okla. 1968, Kans. 1973, Tex. 1976. Staff atty. Koch Industries, Inc., Wichita, Kans., 1968-74; sr. assoc. counsel Mitchell Energy & Devel. Corp., Houston, 1974-81; v.p., gen. counsel, sec. Tex. Internat. Petroleum Corp., Oklahoma City, 1981-83; gen. counsel, v.p. Samson Resources Co., Tulsa, 1983-86; sole practice, 1986—. Mem. ABA, Okla. Bar Assn., Kans. Bar Assn., Tex. Bar Assn., Tulsa Bar Assn., Oklahoma City Bar Assn. Republican. Episcopalian. General practice, State civil litigation, Probate. Home: 6816 E 105th St Tulsa OK 74133-6757 Office: PO Box 701583 Tulsa OK 74170-1583

**COWELL, MARION AUBREY, JR.,** lawyer; b. Wilmington, N.C., Dec. 25, 1934; s. Marion Aubrey and Alice Saunders (Hargett) C.; m. Norma Hearne; children: Lindsay G., Mark P., Kathryn Huffman, Graham Shannonhouse, Elizabeth Shannonhouse, Mary Robbins Whisnant. BSBA, U. N.C., 1958, LLB, 1964. Bar: N.C. 1964. Pvt. practice law Durham, N.C., 1964-72; assoc. Bryant, Lipton, Bryant and Battle, 1964-69, ptnr., 1971-72; pvt. practice law Durham, 1969-70; gen. counsel Cameron Brown Co., Raleigh, N.C., 1972-78; exec. v.p., gen. counsel, sec. First Union Corp., Charlotte, N.C., 1978—. Office: First Union Corp 1 First Union Ctr Charlotte NC 28288-0013

**COWEN, EDWARD S.,** lawyer; b. N.Y.C., Mar. 3, 1936; s. Michael and Edith (Cohen) C.; m. Lesley J. Hoffman, Nov. 16, 1958; children: Adriene, Justine. BS, Syracuse U., 1957; JD, NYU, 1961. Bar: N.Y. 1962, U.S. Dist. Ct. (so. dist.) N.Y. 1965, U.S. Ct. Appeals (2d cir.) 1965, U.S. Supreme Ct. 1967, U.S. Dist. Ct. (ea. dist.) N.Y. 1979. Law clk. to judge U.S. Dist. Ct. (so. dist.) N.Y., 1961-62; ptnr. Seligson & Morris, N.Y.C., 1963-69, Robinson, Silverman, Pearce, Aronsohn & Berman, N.Y.C., 1975-90, Kirkland & Ellis, N.Y.C., 1991-96; counsel Winthrop, Stimson, Putnam & Roberts, N.Y.C., 1996—; mem. faculty Practicing Law Inst. Author: Bankruptcy in Joint Venture Partnerships, Practicing Law Institute, 1985, Enforcing Liens Postpetition, Bankruptcy Strategist, 1998. With USAF, 1958. Recipient Honoree of Yr. awad UJA Fed. N.Y. Lawyers Divsn. Mem. ABA, N.Y. State Bar Assn., Assn. Bar City N.Y. (chmn. bankruptcy and corp. reorgn.), Harmonie Club. Bankruptcy, General corporate, Contracts commercial. Home: 993 Park Ave New York NY 10028-0809 Office: Winthrop Stimson Putnam & Roberts 34th Fl One Battery Park Plaza New York NY 10004

**COWEN, MICHAEL RAPHAEL,** lawyer; b. Brownsville, Tex., June 26, 1970; s. Louis Raphael Thomas and Susan Grace Cowen. BA, Tex. A&M U., 1991; JD, U. Tex., 1995. Bar: Tex. 1996, N.Y. 1996, U.S. Dist. Ct. (so. dist.) Tex., U.S. Dist. Ct. (so. and ea. dists.) N.Y., U.S. Ct. Appeals (5th cir.). Law clk. Hon. Reynaldo Garza, Brownsville, 1995-96; assoc. Cadwalader, Wickersham & Taft, N.Y.C., 1996-97, Law Office of Ed Stapleton, Brownsville, 1997; ptnr. Stapleton, Livesay & Cowen, Brownsville, 1998—; instr. bus. law U. Tex., Brownsville, 1996, vice chmn. legal asst. program adv. bd., 1998. Mem. Order of the Coif. Roman Catholic. Personal injury, Product liability, General civil litigation. Office: Cowen & Livesay 1325 Palm Blvd Brownsville TX 78520-7268

**COWEN, ROBERT E.,** federal judge; b. Newark, N.J., Sept. 4, 1930; s. Saul and Lillie (Selzer) C.; m. Toby Cowen, Dec. 21, 1973; children: Shulie, Eve. BS, Drake U., 1952; LLB, Rutgers U., 1958. Assoc. Schreiber, Lancaster & Demos, Newark, 1959-61; asst. prosecutor Essex County, N.J., 1969-70; dep. atty. gen. organized crime Criminal Justice Dept., N.J., 1970-72, dir. Div. Ethics and Profl. Svcs., 1972-78; magistrate U.S. Dist. Ct. N.J., Newark, 1978-85; judge U.S. Dist. Ct. N.J., Trenton, 1985-87; from judge to sr. judge U.S. Ct. Appeals (3d cir.), Trenton, 1987—; pvt. practice, Newark, 1961-69. Office: US Ct Appeals 3d Cir US Courthouse Rm 700 402 E State St Trenton NJ 08608-1507*

**COWEN, WILSON,** federal judge; b. nr. Clifton, Tex., Dec. 20, 1905; s. John Rentz and Florence Juno (McFadden) C.; m. Florence Elizabeth Walker, Apr. 18, 1930; children: W. Walker, John E. LL.B., U. Tex., 1928. Bar: Tex. 1928. Pvt. practice Dalhart, Tex., 1928-34; judge Dallam County, Tex., 1935-38; Tex. dir. Farm Security Adminstrn., 1938-40, regional dir., 1940-42; commr. U.S. Ct. Claims, Washington, 1942-43, 45-59, chief commr., 1959-64, chief judge, 1964-77, sr. judge, 1977-82; sr. judge fed. cir. U.S. Ct. Appeals, Washington, 1982—; asst. adminstr. War Food Adminstrn., 1943-45; spl. asst. to sec. agr., 1945; mem. Jud. Conf. U.S., 1964-77. Mem. ABA, State Bar Tex., Fed. Bar Assn., Order of Coif, Cosmos Club (Washington), Delta Theta Phi. Presbyterian. Home: 2512 Q St NW Apt 205 Washington DC 20007-4310 Office: US Ct Appeal Federal Circuit 717 Madison Pl NW Washington DC 20439-0002

**COWLES, FREDERICK OLIVER,** lawyer; b. Steubenville, Ohio, Oct. 18, 1937; s. Oliver Howard and Cornelia Blanche (Regal) C.; m. Christina Monica Muller, Sept. 9, 1961; children: Randall, Eric, Gregory, Cornelius. AB magna cum laude, Yale U., 1959; JD, Harvard U., 1962. Bar: R.I. 1963, Mich. 1967, Ill. 1969, N.Y. 1998, Conn. 1998. Assoc. Hinckley, Allen, Salisbury & Parsons, Providence, 1962-67; internat. atty. Upjohn Co., Kalamazoo, Mich., 1967-69; chief internat. atty. Am. Hosp. Supply Crp., Evanston, Ill., 1969-71; internat. atty. Kendall Co., Boston, 1971-73; chief internat. counsel Colgate Palmolive Co., N.Y.C., 1973-86, assoc. gen. counsel, asst. sec., 1986-90, assoc. gen. counsel, asst. sec., v.p. legal ops., 1990-94, sr. assoc. gen. coun., asst. sec., v.p. legal ops., 1994-97, multinat. estate planning, 1997—; dir. various cos. Deacon South Salem Presbyn. Ch.; mem. com. Lewisboro Boy Scouts; co-founder Internat. House R.I. Inc.; group leader Operation Crossroads Africa, Gambia. Mem. ABA, Am. Corp. Coun. Assn., Internat. Bar Assn., Westchester Fairfield Corp. Csl. Assn., Yale Alumni Assn., Internat. Lawyers Assn., Phi Beta Kappa. E-mail: focowles@bestweb.net. FAX: 914-276-7853. Estate planning, Immigration, naturalization, and customs, Private international. Home: 111 Oscaleta Rd South Salem NY 10590-1003 Office: Multinational Estate Planning PLLC 358 Route 202 Somers NY 10589-3207

**COWLES, JOHN EMERSON,** lawyer; b. Kansas City, Mo., Mar. 29, 1957; s. Gordon Tracy and Jean Elizabeth Cowles; m. Gloria Darlene Quick, May 1, 1993; children: Morgan Tracy, Michelle Irene. BA in Polit. Sci., Tex. Christian U., 1979; JD, Kans. U., 1983. Bar: Kans. 1983, U.S. Dist. Ct. Kans. 1983, U.S. Ct. Appeals (10th cir.) 1983, U.S. Supreme Ct. 1991. Atty. Fleeson Gooding Coulson & Kitch, Wichita, Kans., 1983-87; asst. dist. atty. Sedgwick County Dist. Atty.'s Office, Wichita, 1987-89; atty. McDonald, Tinker et al, Wichita, 1989-93, Law Office of John Cowles, Wichita, 1993-96; asst. dist. atty. Johnson County Dist. Atty. Office, Olathe, Kans., 1996—. Mem. Johnson County Bar Assn., Sedgwick County Bar Assn., Kans.-Mo. High Tech. Crime Investigators Assn. (pres. 1997). Office: Johnson County Dist Atty's Office 100 N Kansas Ave Olathe KS 66061-3273

**COWLES, ROBERT LAWRENCE,** lawyer; b. Jacksonville, Fla., Feb. 5, 1942; m. Barbara Bearden; children: Robert L., Kelli R. McMullin. BS, U. N.C., 1964; JD, Emory U. Law Sch., 1969. Bar: Fla. 1969, Ga. 1969. Claims adjuster, supr. Travelers Ins. Co., Jacksonville, Atlanta,, N.Y.C., 1964-68; assoc. Neely, Freeman & Hawkins, Atlanta, 1968-69, Swift, Currie, McGhee & Hiers, Atlanta, 1969-71; dir. Howell, Kirby, Montgomery, D'Aiuto, Dean & Hallowes PA, Jacksonville, 1971-76; pres. Cowles, Coker & Myers, Jacksonville, 1976-83, Cowles, Coker, Myers, Schickel & Pierce PA, Atlanta, 1982-83, Cowles, Hayden, Facciolo, McMorrow & Barfield PA, Atlanta, 1984-87; judge Fourth Judicial Cir. Ct., Atlanta, 1987-90; comdr. Legler, Werber, Dawes, Sadler & Howell PA, Jacksonville, 1990-91; pvt. practice Law Offices of Robert L. Cowles, 1991-93; ptnr. Cowles & Shaughnessy PA, Jacksonville, 1993—. Bd. dirs. Boys Home of Jacksonville, 1989—. Mem. Am. Bd. Trial Advocacy, Fla. Bar Assn. (chmn. civil trial lawyers com. 1998-99), State Bar Ga. Avocations: golfing, gardening, travel. State civil litigation, Product liability, Professional liability. Office: Cowles & Shaughnessy PA Blackstone Bldg 233 E Bay St Ste 901 Jacksonville FL 32202-3456

**COWLEY, MICHAEL C.,** lawyer; b. Scranton, Pa., Feb. 13, 1953; s. Patrick Joseph and Dorothy (Fagan) C.; m. Margaret McGrath, Oct. 3, 1980; children: Maura, Maggie, Patrick, Caroline. BS, Marywood Coll., 1975; JD, Del. Law Sch., 1978. Bar: Pa., 1978; U.S. Dist. Ct. (mid. dist.) Pa. 1978; U.S. Supreme Ct., 1988. Law clk. to chief justice Pa. Supreme Ct., Phila., 1978-79; ptnr. Foley, Cognetti & Cowley, Scranton, 1979-92; owner Cowley Law Offices, Scranton, 1992-94; ptnr. Cowley & McGrath, Scranton, 1994—. Bd. dirs. United Cerebral Palsy of N.E. Pa., Scranton, Lackawanna County Redevel. Authority, Scranton; treas., bd. dirs. Ecologia, Harford, Pa.; bd. dirs. Scranton C. of C., 1990-93. Mem. Am. Trial Lawyers Assn., Pa. Trial Lawyers Assn., Lackawanna Bar Assn. (pres. young lawyers divsn. 1979-80, bd. dirs. 1992—), Pa. Bar Assn. Personal injury, Real property, General civil litigation. Office: Cowley & McGrath 436 Spruce St Ste 200 Scranton PA 18503-1835

**COWNIE, WILLIAN GARRY,** lawyer; b. Sioux City, Iowa, Oct. 4, 1958; s. William Garry and Marie Francis (Hanna) C.; m. Louanne Marie Junck, Dec. 16, 1978; children: Amanda, Abigail, Ashley. BA, Morningside Coll., 1980; JD, U. Mo., 1982. Bar: Mo. 1982, Kans. 1992, U.S. Dist. Ct. Mo. 1982. Assoc. Neiwald, Waldeck & Brown, Kansas City, 1982-84; claims atty. Amoco Corp., Kansas City, 1984-92; atty. pvt. practice, Lees Junction, Mo., 1992—. Mem. Kansas City Met. Bar Assn. Avocations: exercising, reading, reading, travel. Personal injury. Office: 401 SW Oldham Pkwy Ste 101 Lees Summit MO 64081-2700

**COWSER, DANNY LEE,** lawyer, mental health specialist; b. Peoria, Ill., July 7, 1948; s. Albert Paul Cowser and Shirley Mae (Donaldson) Chatten; m. Nancy Lynn Hatch, Nov. 11, 1976; children: Kimberly Catherine Hatch Cowser, Dustin Paul Hatch Cowser. BA, No. Ill. U., 1972, MS, 1975; JD, DePaul U., 1980. Bar: Ill. 1980, Wis. 1981, U.S. Dist. Ct. (no. dist.) Ill. 1981, U.S. Ct. Appeals (7th cir.) 1983, U.S. Dist. Ct. (ea. and we. dists.) Wis. 1984, U.S. Supreme Ct. 1984, Ariz. 1985, U.S. Ct. Appeals (9th cir.) 1987, U.S. Dist. Ct. Ariz. 1989, U.S. Tax Ct. 1990, U.S. Ct. Claims 1990. Adminstr. Ill. Dept. Mental Health, Elgin, 1972-76, psychotherapist, 1976-79; assoc. Slaby, Deda & Henderson, Phillips, Wis., 1982-83; ptnr. Slaby, Deda & Cowser, Phillips, 1983-86; asst. atty. City of Flagstaff, Ariz., 1986-88; pub. defender Coconino County, Flagstaff, 1988-89; pvt. practice Flagstaff, 1989-97; atty. City Park Falls, Wis., 1983-86; spl. dep. Mohave County capital def., 1989-90; instr. speech comms. No. Ariz. U., 1992-93; adminstrv. law judge Ariz. Dept. Econ. Security, 1997—. Bd. dirs. DeKalb County (Ill.) Drug Coun., 1973-75, Counseling and Personal Devel., Phillips, 1985-86, Northland YM-WYCA, 1990-91. Reginald Heber Smith fellow, 1980-81; C.J.S. legal scholar, 1979. Mem. ABA, Ariz. Bar Assn., State Bar Ariz. (cert. specialist in criminal law 1993-98), State Bar Wis., Ill. Bar Assn. Democrat. Avocations: skiing, photography, bicycling. Criminal, Bankruptcy, Family and matrimonial. Office: PO Box 22329 Flagstaff AZ 86002-2329

**COX, BARBARA LYNNE,** lawyer; b. Frankfurt, Germany, Feb. 16, 1951; d. Albert Wesley and Lillian (Burnley) C.; m. D. Alan Bitker, Aug. 8, 1981; 2 children. BA with highest dictinction, Pa. State U., 1974; JD, U. Conn., 1982. Bar: Conn. 1982, U.S. Dist. Ct. Conn. 1983, U.S. Ct. Appeals (2d cir.) 1988. Law clk. Hon. Ralph K. Winter U.S. Ct. Appeals (2d cir.), New Haven, Conn., 1982-83; assoc. Garvey & Walsh, P.C., New Haven, Conn., 1983-87, Dennis N. Garvey, P.C., New Haven, Conn., 1987-91, Gallagher Gallagher & Calistro, New Haven, Conn., 1991-99, Gallagher & Calistro, New Haven, 1999—. Bd. dirs. Leila Day Nursery, New Haven, 1990-92. Mem. ABA, Conn. Bar Assn., Conn. Trial Lawyers Assn., New Haven County Bar Assn. Appellate, Federal civil litigation, State civil litigation. Office: Gallagher & Calistro PO Box 1925 1377 Ella T Grasso Blvd New Haven CT 06509-1925

**COX, DALLAS WENDELL, JR.,** lawyer; b. Mar. 10, 1943; s. Dallas Wendell Sr. Cox and Fern (Maurer) Heidbreder; m. Lynn Barbre, Aug. 2, 1969 (div. Oct. 1982); children: Dallas Barbre, Ryan Ralph. BA, U. Ill., Champaign, 1964; JD, U. Mo., 1967; MLA, Washington U., 1991, MA, 1994. Bar: U.S. Supreme Ct. 1967, Mo. 1967, U.S. Dist. Ct. Mo. 1967. Ptnr. Cox, Moffitt & Cox, St. Louis, 1967-78; pvt. practice law St. Louis, 1978—; attendee global forum UN Conf. on Environ. and Devel., Rio de Janeiro, 1992. Editor Jour. Mo. Bar., Mo. Conservationist; contbr. articles to profl. jours. Asst. scoutmaster St. Louis area Boy Scouts Am., 1984-94; advocate Mo. Prairie Found., bd. dirs., 1993—; alderman City of Town and County, Mo., 1995-continue commn. chmn., 1995-99. Lt. (j.g.) USNR, 1971. Mem. ATLA, Mo. Assn. Trial Lawyers (bd. govs. 1990-93), Lawyers Assn. St. Louis, Eagle Scouts Assn. (bd. dirs. 1988-91, vol. award of merit 1992), Greater Yellowstone Coalition, Windstar Found., Wilderness Soc., Nature Conservancy, Sigma Chi. Avocations: conservation, backpacking. Personal injury. Office: 111 Westport Plz Ste 610 Saint Louis MO 63146-3015

**COX, EMMETT RIPLEY,** federal judge; b. Cottonwood, Ala., Feb. 13, 1935; s. Emmett M. Cox, Jr. and Myra E. (Ripley) Stewart; m. Ann MacKay Haas, May 16, 1964; children: John Haas, Catherine MacKay. BA, U. Ala., 1957, JD, 1959. Bar: Ala. 1959, U.S. Ct. Appeal (5th, 8th and 11th cirs.), U.S. Supreme Ct. Assoc. Mead, Norman & Fitzpatrick, Birmingham, Ala., 1959-64; assoc. then ptnr. Gaillard, Wilkins, Smith & Cox, Mobile, Ala., 1964-69; ptnr. Nettles, Cox & Barker, 1969-81; judge U.S. Dist. Ct. (so. dist.) Ala., Mobile, 1981-88, U.S. Ct. Appeals (11th cir.), Mobile, 1988—; mem. def. svcs. com. Jud. Conf. U.S. Mem. Ala. Bar Assn., Mobile Bar Assn., Fed. Bar Assn., Maritime Law Assn. of the U.S., Omicron Delta Kappa, Phi Delta Phi, Alpha Tau Omega (past pres.). Office: US Courthouse 11th Circuit 113 Saint Joseph St Ste 433 Mobile AL 36602-3624

**COX, GILBERT W., JR.,** lawyer; b. Stoneham, Mass.; s. Gilbert W. and Verna O. (Linscott) C.; m. Helen Pillsbury, June 6, 1959; children: Gilbert, David, Carol, Elizabeth. BA, Northeastern U., 1955; JD, Boston U., 1962. Pvt. practice law Needham, Mass., 1962—. Elected legislator, Mass., 1968-76. Comdr. USN. Estate planning, Probate. Home: 60 Dedham Ave Needham MA 02492-3061

**COX, HERBERT DAVID,** lawyer; b. Lynchburg, Va., Apr. 1, 1970; s. Herbert Bartle and Evelyn (King) C.; m. Alison Nyhof, June 27, 1998. BA in Comms., Va. Tech. Inst., 1992; JD, U. Richmond, 1995. Bar: Va. 1995, U.S. Bankruptcy Ct. (we. dist.) Va. 1996. Law clk. 12th Jud. Cir., Chesterfield, Va., 1995-96; assoc. Davies & Davies, Lynchburg, Va., 1996-98; jud. law clk. U.S. Bankruptcy Ct. (we. dist.) Va., Lynchburg, 1998—. Mem. editl. bd. Bankruptcy Law News, 1998. Bd. dirs. New Vistas Sch., Lynchburg, 1997—, Robert E. Lee Soil and Water Conservation Dist., Lynchburg, 1997; mem. com. Lynch's Landing, Lynchburg, 1997—. Mem. Lynchburg Bar Assn., Lynchburg Bankruptcy Bar, Lynchburg Jr. Bar (sec.-treas. 1997—), Omicron Delta Kappa (Va. Tech. chpt.). Office: US Bankruptcy Ct West Dist Va PO Box 442 Lynchburg VA 24505-0442

**COX, JACK SCHRAMM,** lawyer; b. Jacksonville, Fla., May 14, 1951; s. John Francis Schramm and Frances Shaw Cox; m. Mary Anne Golonka, Nov. 10, 1985; children: Michael Joseph, Kaitlin Alyce. AA, Palm Beach Jr. Coll., 1971; BS, Fla. State U., 1973; JD, Cumberland Sch. Law, 1978. Bar:

Fla. 1978, U.S. Ct. Appeals (11 cir.) 1982, U.S. Dist. Ct. (so. dist.) Fla. 1983, U.S. Bankruptcy Ct. 1994. Tchr. Palm Beach County Sch. Dist., West Palm Beach, Fla., 1973-75; assoc. atty. Levy Plisco Perry et al., Palm Beach, Fla., 1978-81; ptnr. Perry McCarthy & Cox, West Palm Beach, 1981-84, Merola McCarthy & Cox, Palm Beach Gardens, Fla., 1984-94, Jack Schramm Cox P.A., Palm Beach Gardens, 1994—. Leader Boy Scouts Am., Wellington, Fla., 1993-97; dir. Hobe Sound (Fla.) Citizens Alliance Inc., 1998. Mem. Palm Beach County Bar Assn., Palm Beach County Trial Lawyers Assn., Am. Inn of Ct. (bd. dirs. 1996—). Roman Catholic. Avocations: hunting, fishing, boating. Construction, Appellate, Real property. Office: 4400 Pga Blvd Ste 201 Palm Bch Gdns FL 33410-6554

**COX, JAMES CLIFTON,** lawyer, consultant. BA summa cum laude, Stetson U., Deland, Fla., 1979; JD, Vanderbilt U., 1982; LLM in Taxation, U. Fla., 1987. Bar: Fla. 1982, U.S. Dist. Ct. (so. dist.) Fla. 1983, U.S. Ct. Appeals (11th cir.) 1983, U.S. Tax Ct. 1986; bd. cert. tax lawyer, Fla. Assoc. McCune, Hiaasen, Crum, Ferris & Gardner, P.A., Ft. Lauderdale, Fla., 1982-85, Buck & Golden, P.A., Ft. Lauderdale, 1985-86; ptnr. Cox & Reynolds, Ft. Lauderdale, 1988—. Contbr. articles to profl. jours. Estate planning, Estate taxation, Labor. Office: Cox & Reynolds 4875 N Federal Hwy Fl 10 Fort Lauderdale FL 33308-4610

**COX, JOHN NEEDHAM,** lawyer; b. Mount Olive, N.C., Aug. 17, 1954; s. Zach Davis and Mary Gwin (Olive) C.; m. Clare Kay Johnston, Apr. 25, 1981. BSChE, N.C. State U., Raleigh, 1980; JD, U. Pitts., 1992. Bar: Pa., W.Va., N.C., U.S.-PTO. Chemical engr. Tenn. Valley Authority, Paradise, Ky., 1980-88; process engr. Kaiser Engrs., Homer City, Pa., 1988-89; assoc. Dickie, McCamey & Chilcote, Pitts., 1991-98, Sweeney, Metz, et al, Charlotte, 1988—. Contbr. articles to profl. jours. Sgt. U.S. Army, 1975-78. Recipient Henderson scholarship Henderson Trust, 1972. Mem. AICE. Democrat. Methodist. Avocations: hiking, photography. Office: Sweeney, Metz, et al 11 Stanwix St Pittsburgh PA 15222-1312

**COX, JOHN THOMAS, JR.,** lawyer; b. Shreveport, La., Feb. 9, 1943; s. John Thomas and Gladys Virginia (Canterbury) C.; m. Tracey L. Tanquary, Aug. 27, 1966; children: John Thomas, III, Stephen Lewis. BS, La. State U., 1965; JD, 1968. Bar: La. 1968, U.S. Dist. Ct. (we., mid. and ea. dist.) La., U.S. Dist. Ct. (ea. dist.) Tex., U.S. Ct. Appeals (5th and 8th cir.), U.S. Tax Ct., U.S. Supreme Ct. Assoc. Sanders, Miller, Downing & Keene, Baton Rouge, 1968-70, Blanchard, Walker, O'Quin & Roberts, Shreveport, La., 1970-71; ptnr., 1971—; tchr. bus. law Centenary Coll. La. Served to lt. USAR, 1963-69. Lt. USAR, 1963-69. Recipient George Washington Honor medal Valley Forge Freedoms Found. Mem. ABA, La. Bar Assn., Caddo parish Bar Assn., Am. Assn. Def. Counsel, La. Assn. Def. Counsel, Shreveport Club. Presbyterian. Labor, Banking, General corporate. Address: 555 Dunmoreland Dr Shreveport LA 71106-6124

**COX, JOSEPH LAWRENCE,** judge; b. Trenton, Mo., Dec. 7, 1932; s. Forrest Curtis and Lillian Judson (Ritzenthaler) C.; m. Lois Marie Hubble, May 20, 1956; children: Margaret Marie Cox Jarvis, Martha Mae Cox Anderson. BA, U. Mo., Kansas City, 1961, JD, 1965. Bar: Kans. 1965, U.S. Supreme Ct. 1970. Ptnr. Cox, Anderson & Covell, Mission, Kans., 1965-70; pvt. practice, Tonganoxie, Kans., 1968-90; city atty. of Tonganoxie, 1967-73, Linwood, Kans., 1972-78; mcpl. judge, Mission, 1969-80, Tonganoxie, 1983-90, Topeka, 1990—. With USAF, 1952-54. Mem. Kans. Bar Assn., Kans. Mcpl. Judges Assn. (bd. dirs. 1975-79, pres. 1977-78), Topeka Bar Assn., Masons, Shriners, Sertoma (pres. 1973-76, gov. Kans. dist. 1998-99), Topeka Evening Sertoma (pres. 1995-96). Avocations: photography, boating, travel. Home: 910 SE 43rd St Topeka KS 66609-1620 Office: 214 E 8th St Topeka KS 66603

**COX, KENNETH ALLEN,** lawyer, communications consultant; b. Topeka, Dec. 7, 1916; s. Seth Leroy and Jean (Sears) C.; m. Nona Beth Fumerton, Jan. 1, 1943; children—Gregory Allen, Jeffrey Neal, Douglas Randall. B.A., U. Wash., 1938, LL.B., 1940; LL.M., U. Mich., 1941; LL.D., Chgo. Theol. Sem., 1969. Bar: Wash. bar 1941. Law clk. Wash. Supreme Ct., 1941-42; asst. prof. U. Mich. Law Sch., 1946-48; with firm Little, Palmer, Scott & Slemmons (and predecessor), Seattle, 1948-61; partner Little, Palmer, Scott & Slemmons (and predecessor), 1953-61; spl. counsel com. interstate and fgn. commerce charge TV inquiry U.S. Senate, 1956-57; chief broadcast bur. FCC, Washington, 1961-63; commr. FCC, 1963-70; counsel to communications law firm Haley, Bader & Potts, 1970—; sr. v.p., dir. MCI Communications Corp., 1970-87; cons. MCI, 1987—; lectr. U. Washington Law Sch., part-time 1954, 60; adj. prof. Georgetown U. Law Center, 1971, 72. Vice pres. Municipal League Seattle and King County, 1960, Seattle World Affairs Council, 1960; pres. Seattle chpt. Am. Assn. UN, 1957; chmn. one of five citizen subcoms. Legis. Interim Com. Edn., 1960; Bd. dirs. Nat. Pub. Radio, 1971-80; bd. dirs. Nat. Advt. Rev. Bd., 1971-74, chmn. bd., 1976-96. Served to capt. Q.M.C. AUS, 1943-46, 51-52. Recipient Alfred I. duPont award in broadcast journalism Columbia U., 1970. Mem. Am., Fed. Communications, Wash. State, D.C. bar assns., Order of Coif, Phi Beta Kappa, Phi Delta Phi. Democrat. Conglist. Communications, Administrative and regulatory. Home: 5836 Marbury Rd Bethesda MD 20817-6076 Office: MCI Comm Corp 1801 Pennsylvania Ave NW Washington DC 20006-3606

**COX, MELVIN MONROE,** lawyer; b. Omaha, Jan. 31, 1947; s. Monroe M. Cox and Wilma Grace (Prickett) McPherson. BA with high honors, U. Wyo., 1969; JD, Harvard U., 1972. Bar: Pa. 1972, U.S. Dist. Ct. (we. dist.) Pa. 1972, N.J. 1987, U.S. Dist. Ct. (N.J.) 1987. Assoc. Rose, Schmidt & Dixon, Pitts., 1972-78; atty. Chgo. Pneumatic Tool Co., N.Y.C., 1978-81, asst. sec., 1981-88; asst. gen. counsel Sun Chem. Corp., Ft. Lee, N.J., 1989-93, asst. gen. counsel and asst. sec., 1993-97, v.p., gen. counsel, sec., 1997—; adj. prof. engring. law The Cooper Union, N.Y.C., 1984-91; asst. sec. DIC Ams., Inc., Ft. Lee, 1993-97; mng. dir. Sun Chem. B.V., Soest, The Netherlands; bd. dirs. Polychrome Corp., Ft. Lee, Kemtek Imaging Sys. Ltd., Johannesburg, South Africa; bd. visitors U. Wyoming, Coll. Arts and Scis., 1997—, vice chmn., 1998—. Bd. dirs. Good Shepherd Cmty. Svcs., Inc., Ft. Lee, 1999—. Mem. ABA, Am. Corp. Counsel Assn., Phi Beta Kappa, Phi Kappa Phi. General corporate, Private international, Mergers and acquisitions. Office: Sun Chem Corp 222 Bridge Plz S Fort Lee NJ 07024-5703

**COX, REED ELBREDGE,** lawyer; b. Lauderdale County, Ala., July 4, 1934. BA, U. No. Ala., 1956; MBA, Ga. Coll., 1970; JD, John Marshall U., 1979. Bar: Ga. 1979. Pvt. practice Marietta, Ga., 1979—. With U.S. Army, 1956-76. Mem. Ga. Bar Assn., Cobb County Bar Assn., Officers Club, Indian Hills Country Club. Republican. Avocation: tennis. Criminal, Workers' compensation. Office: 591 Lawrence St NE Marietta GA 30060-2172

**COX, SANFORD CURTIS, JR.,** lawyer; b. El Paso, Tex., July 31, 1929; s. Sanford Curtis Sr. and Iva M. (Richardson) C.; m. Helen A. Thurston, Sept. 27, 1958; children: Sanford Curtis III, Christopher Thurston. *Sanford Cox is a member of the ninth generation from Robert Cox of Massachusetts, born 1670. His great-grandfather, Reverend Leonard Cox, moved from Massachusetts to Charlotte Courthouse, Virginia, where grandfather, Edwin Peter Cox, and father were born. Wife Holly (Helen), a 3rd generation El Paso artist recognized for her research of early El Paso artists, is the granddaughter of artist Fern Thurston and daughter of artist Eugene B. Thurston. Son, Christopher Thurston Cox, JD 1993, is practicing law with his father. Elder son, S. Curtis Cox, III, JD 1996, is practicing law in Tacoma, Washington.* BA, Tex. Western Coll., 1951, MA, 1952; LLB, U. Tex., 1957. Bar: Tex. 1957, U.S. Dist. Ct. (we. dist.) Tex. 1960, U.S. Ct. Appeals (5th cir.) 1964, U.S. Ct. Appeals (D.C. cir.) 1975. Assoc. Andress, Lipscomb, Peticolas & Fisk, El Paso, 1957-61; ptnr. Lipscomb, Fisk & Cox, El Paso, 1961-74, Fisk & Cox, El Paso, 1974-79; sole practice El Paso, 1979-81; pres./shareholder Sanford C. Cox Jr. P.C., El Paso, 1981-93, mem., 1993—. Mem. bd. editors U. Tex. Law Rev. Mem. adv. bd. Booth Meml. Home, 1963-79, Pleasant View Home, 1979-91. Served with U.S. Army, 1952-54. Mem. ABA, Tex. Bar Assn. (admissions com. 17th dist. 1976), El Paso Bar Assn. (ethics com. 1965-69, fee arbitration com. 1973-75), Order of Coif, Phi Delta Phi. Republican. Episcopalian. Probate, General civil litigation, Real property. Office: Coronado Tower Bldg Ste 220 6006 N Mesa El Paso TX 79912

**COX, STANLEY BRIAN,** lawyer; b. Boonville, Mo., Dec. 26, 1949; s. Ulysses Grant and Mary Virginia (Toler) C.; m. Kristeen Kay Richardson, June 8, 1954; children: Adam Brian, Sarah Kristeen. BS in Polit. Sci., Cen. Mo. State U., 1971; JD, U. Mo., 1976. Bar: Mo. 1976. Pvt. practice, Sedalia, Mo., 1976—; pros. atty. Pettis County, Sedalia, 1979-82. Chmn. Pettis County Rep. Com., 1982—; west ctrl. coord. Ashbroft for Gov., 1984, 88; chmn. Mo. Housing Devel. Commn., 1987; vice-chmn. Mo. Vets. Commn., 1989-91, Ctrl. Mo. State U. Bd. Regents, 1993-97, pres., 1994, 96; bd. dirs. Pettis County Fire Protection Dist., 1992—. Capt. U.S. Army, 1971-73, Korea. Recipient Tough Tusk award Pettis County Pachyderm Club, 1991. Mem. Nat. Dist. Attys. Assn., Nat. Lawyers Assn., Knife and Fork Club (pres. Sedalia 1981), Rotary (sec. Sedalia 1978-81, bd. dirs. 1999—, Paul Harris fellow 1990). Methodist. Home: 1700 Hickory Ln Sedalia MO 65301-8923 Office: 202 W 4th St Sedalia MO 65301-4243

**COX, STEVEN ST. LEGER,** lawyer; b. Akron, Ohio, July 17, 1966; s. David St. Leger and Judith Ann (Mace) C. BA in Econs., Ohio State U., 1989; JD, U. Akron, 1994, M in Tax., 1995. Bar: Ohio 1994, U.S. Ct. Appeals (6th cir.) 1994, U.S. Tax Cts. 1994, U.S. Dist. Ct. (no. dist.) Ohio 1995. Ind. assoc. Briggs & Pry, Akron, 1994-97; assoc. Amer Cunningham Brennan Co., Akron, 1997—. Mem. ABA, Ohio State Bar Assn., Akron Bar Assn., Alpha Tau Omega. General corporate, Taxation, general, Non-profit and tax-exempt organizations. Office: Amer Cunningham Brenna Co LPA 6th Fl Key Bldg 159 S Main St Akron OH 44308-1317

**COX, WALTER CLAY JR.,** lawyer, real estate broker; b. Danville, Ky., Nov. 9, 1922; s. Walter Clay Cox and Blanche Marie Phillips; m. Mary Lee Engle, Dec. 20, 1943 (div. Dec. 1975); children: Mary Eugenia Cox Wakefield, Rebecca Lee Cox Woods; m. Pam G. Collis, July 3, 1988; 1 child, Walter Clay III. JD, U. Ky., 1948. Bar: Ky., U.S. Supreme Ct., U.S. Dist. Ct. Ky., U.S. Ct. Appeals, Korea Supreme Ct. Police judge City of Lancaster, 1949-52; ptnr. Walker & Cox, Lancaster, Ky., 1948-52, Fowler, Measle & Bell, Lexington, Ky., 1953-88; of counsel Fowler, Measle & Bell, Lexington, 1988—; assoc. broker Ky. Real Estate, Lexington, 1961-97; broker Realty Depot, Lexington, 1997—. Author: Commercial Collections, 1986. Capt. inf. U.S. Army, 1943-46, ETO, judge advocate, 1951-52, Korea. Mem. Ky. Bar Assn. (sr. counselor 1997), Bluegrass Sportsmans Club (bd. dirs. 1993-94), Lexington Country Club (v.p. 1993-96). Republican. Baptist. Avocation: golf. General civil litigation, Bankruptcy, Consumer commercial. Home: 4830 Wyndhurst Rd Lexington KY 40515-1251 Office: Fowler Measle & Bell 300 W Vine St Ste 600 Lexington KY 40507-1621

**COX, WALTER THOMPSON, III,** federal judge; b. Anderson, S.C., Aug. 13, 1942; s. Walter Thompson and Mary (Johnson) C.; m. Victoria Grubbs, Feb. 8, 1963; children: Lisa, Walter. BS, Clemson U., 1964; JD, U. S.C., 1967. Bar: S.C., 1967, U.S. Dist. Ct. S.C., 1967, U.S. Ct. Appeals (4th cir.), 1976, U.S. Ct. Appeals for Armed Forces, 1984, U.S. Supreme Ct., 1987. Commn. capt. U.S. Army, 1964, atty., 1964-73; ptnr. Jones, McIntosh, Threlkeld, Newman & Cox, Anderson, S.C., 1973-78; trial judge 10th cir. State S.C., Anderson, 1978-84; chief judge U.S. Ct. Appeal for Armed Forces, Washington, 1984—. Mem. ABA, FBA, Judge Advocate's Assn., S.C. Bar Assn. (del.), Army Navy Club, Wild Dune Golf & Racquet Club. Episcopalian. Office: US Ct Appeals Armed Forces Office of Chief Judge 450 E St NW Washington DC 20442-0001

**COX, WILLIAM DONALD, JR.,** lawyer; b. Haverhill, Mass., Nov. 26, 1957; s. William Donald Sr. and Beatrice Mary (Denzin) C. BA, Bradford Coll., 1979; postgrad., Am. U., 1979-80; JD, New Eng. Sch. of Law, 1987. Bar: Mass. 1987, U.S. Dist. Ct. Mass. 1989, Maine 1990. Pers. dir. City of Haverhill, 1984-88; asst. dist. atty. Dist. Atty.'s Office County of Essex, Salem, Mass., 1988; pvt. practice Haverhill, 1988—; asst. city solicitor City of Haverhill, 1994—. Treas. WD 3 Dem. Com., Haverhill, 1984—. Mem. ABA, Mass. Bar Assn., Boston Bar Assn., Essex County Bar Assn. Avocation: politics. General practice, Family and matrimonial, Probate. Home: 8 Richmond St Haverhill MA 01830-6010 Address: 145 S Main St Bradford MA 01835-7438

**COX, WILLIAM MARTIN,** lawyer, educator; b. Bernardsville, N.J., Dec. 26, 1922; s. Martin John and Nellie (Fotens) C.; m. Julia Sebastian, June 14, 1952; children: Janice Cox Trautman, William Martin, Joann Cox Cahoon, Julieann Cox Allen. *Mr. Cox is a decendant of an English family which includes Sir Richard, Bishop of Ely (1559-1581). Isaac came to Elizabethtown NJ in 1690 following Whig predominance commencing in 1688, after which the Tories were eclipsed until the time of George III. Ancestors were essentially Tory and Anti-Federalist. Family seat has been Sussey Co. NJ since the early 18th century. Notwithstanding Tory sympathies during the Revolutionary War, John Cox served in the NJ General Assembly as early as 1810.* AB, Syracuse U., 1947; JD, Cornell U., 1950. Bar: N.J., U.S. Dist. Ct. Mem. Dolan & Dolan, Newton, N.J., 1950—; mem. faculty, tchr. zoning admintrn. Rutgers U.; gen. counsel emeritus N.J. Planning Ofcls., bd. dirs. Newton Cemetary Assn., pres. N.J. Inst. Mcpl. Attys., 1982-84, mem. Land Use Law Drafting Com., 1970— (chmn. 1993-98), dir., sec. Equip, Inc., Marion, N.C. Author: Zoning and Land Use Administration in New Jersey, 18th edit., 1999. With U.S. Army, 1943-45. Recipient Resolution of Appreciation award N.J. Senate and Gen. Assembly, 1994,Pres.'s Disting. Svc. award N.J. League Municipalities, 1999. Mem. ABA, N.J. Bar Assn., Sussex County Bar Assn., Am. Planning Assn., Monarchist League, Rotary (Vocat. award 1996), Am. Legion, VFW. Baptist. Land use and zoning (including planning). Office: 1 Legal Ln Newton NJ 07860-1827

**COX, WILLIAM VAUGHAN,** lawyer; b. Jersey City, N.J., Nov. 12, 1936; s. Walter Miles and Emily (McNenney); divorced; children: Millicent S., Jennifer V. BA, Princeton U., 1958; LLB, Yale U., 1964. Bar: Colo. 1965, Conn. 1972, N.Y. 1974. Law clk. Holland & Hart, Denver, 1963; atty. Conoco Inc., Denver, 1966-72; asst. to v.p., gen. counsel Conoco Inc., Stamford, Conn., 1972-73; v.p., gen. counsel Stromberg-Carlson Corp., Rochester, N.Y., 1974-78; mng. ptnr. Bader & Cox, Denver, 1979-86, of counsel, 1986-88; pres. William V. Cox, P.C., Denver, 1988—, also bd. dirs.; project and planning dir. Interwest Comm. Corp., 1995-97; pres., bd. dirs. New West Indies Trading Co., Denver, 1984—; pres. Coll. Football Ltd., Denver, 1990—. Sportswriter/editor: Colorado Springs (Colo.) Free Press, 1960-61. Football coach Cheyenne Mountain H.S., Colorado Springs, 1961; founder, bd. dirs., v.p., com. chmn., editor Colo. chpt. Nat. Football Found., 1992—; mem. adv. bd. Downtown Denver Dist., 1991-93; bd. dirs., com. chmn. Downtown Denver Residents, 1990-93; pres., bd. dirs. Barclay Towers Condominiums, Denver, 1990-92, sec., bd. dirs., 1998—; dist. capt. Rep. Party, Cherry Hills, Colo., 1980-85; bd. dirs. Monroe County Humane Soc., Rochester, 1975-78. Mem. Colo. Bar Assn., Denver Bar Assn., Denver Lower Downtown Bar Assn. (v.p. 1992-94), Am. Legion, Lincoln Club, Univ. Club Denver (bd. dirs.), Rocky Mountain Princeton Club (com. chmn. 1972), Law Club Denver (com. chmn. 1971), Corbey Ct., Phi Delta Phi. Roman Catholic. Avocations: running, politics, college football history, military history, animal rights. Alternative dispute resolution, State civil litigation, Contracts commercial. Office: 1625 Larimer St Ste 2707 Denver CO 80202-1538

**COYLE, DENNIS PATRICK,** lawyer; b. Detroit, Aug. 29, 1938; s. Myron Patrick and Vernice Beatrice (Smith) C.; children: Ian Patrick, Sean Patrick. B.A., Dartmouth Coll., 1960; J.D., Columbia U., 1964. Bar: N.Y. 1965, Fla. 1971. Assoc. Breed, Abbott & Morgan, N.Y.C., 1964-70; assoc. Courshon & Courshon, Miami Beach, Fla., 1970-74; mng. trustee First Mortgage Investors, Miami Beach, 1974-79; ptnr. Steel Hector & Davis, Miami, Fla., 1979-89; gen. counsel FPL Group, Inc., Fla. Power & Light Co., 1989—, dir. Fla. Power and Light Co., 1991—, Adelphia Comms. Corp., 1995—. Mem. ABA, Miami Beach C. of C. (hon. lifetime trustee). Contracts commercial, General corporate, Securities. Home: 405 Eagleton Cove Way Palm Beach Gardens FL 33418-8464 Office: FPL Group Inc PO Box 14000 700 Universe Blvd North Palm Beach FL 33408-2657

**COYLE, MARTIN ADOLPHUS, JR.,** lawyer; b. Hamilton, Ohio, June 3, 1941; s. Martin Adolphus and Lucille (Baird) C.; m. Sharon Sullivan, Mar. 29, 1969 (div. Dec. 1991); children: Cynthia Ann, David Martin, Jennifer Ann; m. Linda J. O'Brien, July 31, 1993 (div. July 1996); m. Sandra C. Lund, July 1998. BA, Ohio Wesleyan U., 1963; JD summa cum laude, Ohio State U., 1966. Bar: N.Y. 1967. Assoc. Cravath, Swaine & Moore, N.Y.C., 1966-72; chief counsel securities and fin. TRW Inc., Cleve., 1972-73, sr. counsel, asst. sec., 1973-75, asst. gen. counsel, asst. sec., 1976, asst. gen. counsel, sec., 1976-80, v.p., gen. counsel, sec., 1980-89, exec. v.p., gen. counsel, sec., 1989-97, exec. v.p., 1997-99; sec. TRW Found., Cleve., 1975-80, trustee, 1980-88; sec. TRW Found., 1975-80, trustee, 1980—. Co-inventor voting machine. Pres. Judson Retirement Cmty., 1986-88, trustee, 1986-90; chmn., sec. Martin A. Coyle Found.; trustee Berea Coll. 1989—, Chautauqua Inst., 1990—; trustee Fairhill Inst. for the Elderly, 1990—, Ohioesleyan U., 1992—. Mem. ABA, Am. Soc. Corp. Secs. (pres. Ohio regional group 1978-80, nat. dir. 1981-87, nat. chmn. 1985-86), Assn. Gen. Counsel (exec. com. 1992—, pres. 1995-97), Ohio Bar Assn., Bar Assn. Greater Cleve., Shoreby Club, Union Club. General corporate. Home: 5051 Overlook Ave Bemus Point NY 14712-9777 Office: TRW Inc 1900 Richmond Rd Cleveland OH 44124-3760

**COYLE, MICHAEL LEE,** lawyer; b. Mechanicsburg, Pa., Oct. 2, 1944; s. Patrick G. and Bertha M. (Wix) C.; m. Kathleen J. West, July 15, 1967; children: Patrick M., Darren W. BS in Acctg., Utica Coll., 1966; JD, Syracuse U., 1971; LLM in Taxation, Georgetown U., 1975. Bar: N.Y. 1972, Conn. 1975, U.S. Tax Ct. 1975. Acct. Peat, Marwick, Mitchell & Co., Syracuse, N.Y., 1966, tax acct., 1969-71; atty., adviser interpretive div. Office Chief Counsel IRS, Washington, 1971-73; atty. adviser to judge U.S. Tax Ct., Washington, 1973-75; mem. firm Reid & Riege, P.C., Hartford, Conn., 1975—; trustee U. Hartford Tax Inst., 1982-86; bd. dirs. adv. coun. Nat. Inst. State & Local Taxation, Old Lyme, Conn., 1987—. Mem., v.p., pres. St. Paul's Luth. Ch. Coun., Wethersfield, Conn., 1976-82, 87-92; bd. dirs. Children's Home Cromwell, Inc., Conn., 1980-88; mem. leadership Greater Hartford, 1978, Conn. Task Force Corp. Taxation; pres. Wethersfield Bus. & Civic Assn., 1978-80. With U.S. Army, 1966-68. Mem. ABA (chmn. sales and fin. transaction com., tax sect. 1983-85), Conn. Bar Assn. (tax exec. com., ltd. liability subcom. 1991—), Conn. Bus. & Industry Assn. (tax com. 1987—), Hartford Tax Study Group, Tax Club Hartford (pres.). Avocations: tennis, reading. Corporate taxation, State and local taxation, General corporate. Home: 6 Silo Dr Wethersfield CT 06109-2715 Office: Reid & Riege PC 1 State St Ste 16 Hartford CT 06103-3185

**COYLE, ROBERT EVERETT,** federal judge; b. Fresno, Calif., May 6, 1930; s. Everett LaJoya and Virginia Chandler C.; m. Faye Turnbaugh, June 11, 1953; children—Robert Allen, Richard Lee, Barbara Jean. BA, Fresno State Coll., 1953; JD, U. Calif., 1956. Bar: Calif. Ptnr. McCormick, Barstow, Sheppard, Coyle & Wayte, 1958-82; chief judge U.S. Dist. Ct. (ea. dist.) Calif., 1990-96, sr. judge, 1996—; former chair 9th Cir. Conf. of Chief Dist. Judges, chair 9th Cir. space and security com., mem. com. on state and fed. cts. Mem. Calif. Bar Assn. (exec. com. 1974-79, bd. govs. 1979-82, v.p. 1981), Fresno County Bar Assn. (pres. 1972). Office: US Dist Ct 5116 US Courthouse 1130 O St Fresno CA 93721-2201

**COYNE, CHARLES COLE,** lawyer; b. Abington, Pa., Dec. 3, 1948; s. James Kitchenman Jr. and Pearl (Black) C.; m. Paula J. Latta, May 15, 1976; 1 child, Anna Elizabeth. BS in Econs., U. Pa., 1970; JD, Temple U., 1973. Bar: Pa. 1973, U.S. Supreme Ct. 1982, N.J. 1985. Of counsel Hepburn, Willcox, Hamilton & Putnam, 1994—; dir., sec., chmn. fin. com. George S. Coyne Chem. Co., Inc., Croydon, Pa. Assoc. editor Temple Law Quar., 1972-73; columnist "Life In the Country", Ledger Newspaper Group, 1993—. Chester County (Pa.) rep. Delaware Valley Regional Planning Commn., 1982—; mem. Chester County Health and Edn. Facilities Authority, 1982—, chmn., 1996—; bd. suprs. East Fallowfield Twp., Chester County, 1982-83; mem. Panel of U.S. Bankruptcy Trustees, 1991-93; Chester County Pk. and Recreation Bd., 1998—. Mem. racing com. Pa. Hunt Cup, 1992—. AIESEC Exch. fellow, U. Melbourne, 1968; recipient Disting. Young Rep. award Greater Phila. Young Reps., 1976. Mem. ABA, Pa. Bar Assn., Phila. Bar Assn., Temple Law Sch. Alumni Assn. (chmn. 10th reunion com.), U. Pa. Gen. Alumni Soc. (exec. bd. organized classes, pres. Class of 1970). Clubs: Union League (Phila.), Capitol Hill Club (Washington), Lawyer's Club of Phila., Nat. Steeplechase Assn., Hartefeld Nat. Golf Club, Quaker City Farmers Club, Pa. Soc., Masons (master 1982), Kappa Alpha Soc. E-mail: cccoyne@aol.com. General corporate, Contracts commercial, Environmental. Home: Sycamore Run Farm PO Box 155 Unionville PA 19375-0155 Office: Hepburn Willcox Hamilton & Putnam 1100 One Penn Ctr 1617 John F Kennedy Blvd Philadelphia PA 19103-1979

**COYNE, DENNIS MICHAEL,** lawyer; b. Mpls., Feb. 13, 1944; s. Edward Joseph Coyne and Marcia Marie Dagenhardt Pizinger; m. Hendella Meinster, July 9, 1972; children: Amanda L., Jessica L. BA, U. Minn., 1966; JD, Villanova U., 1969. Bar: Minn. 1980, Pa. 1970, U.S. Dist. Ct. Minn., U.S. Dist. Ct. (ea. dist.) Pa., U.S. Ct. Appeals (3d and 8th cirs.). Sr. litigator Pa. Dept. Environ. Resources, Phila., 1972-80; spl. asst. atty. gen. representing Minn. Pollution Control State of Minn., St. Paul, 1980-87; shareholder Hart, Bruner & O'Brien, Mpls., 1987-90, Fredrikson & Byron, P.A., Mpls., 1990—; mediator Minn. State Ct. Neutrals List, 1996-97. Mem. ABA (litigation sect., sect. natural resources, energy and environ. law), Minn. State Bar Assn. (governing coun. environ. and natural resources sect.), Hennepin County Bar Assn. (co-chair governing coun. environ. law com.). Environmental, Administrative and regulatory, General civil litigation. Office: Fredrikson & Byron PA 1100 Internat ctr 900 2nd Ave S # D Minneapolis MN 55402-3314

**COYNE, MARY JEANNE,** retired state supreme court justice; b. Mpls., Dec. 7, 1926; d. Vincent Mathias and Mae Lucille (Steinmetz) C. BS in Law, U. Minn., 1955, JD, 1957. Bar: Minn. 1957, U.S. Dist. Ct. Minn. 1957, U.S. Ct. Appeals (8th cir.) 1958, U.S. Supreme Ct. 1964. Law clk. Minn. Supreme Ct., St. Paul, 1956-57; assoc. Meagher, Geer, Markham & Anderson, Mpls., 1957-70, ptnr., 1970-82; assoc. justice Minn. Supreme Ct., St. Paul, 1982-98; ret.; mem. Am. Arbitration Assn., 1967-82; mem. bd. conciliation Archdiocese St. Paul and Mpls., 1981-82; instr. U. Minn. Law Sch., Mpls., 1964-68; mem. Lawyers Profl. Responsibility Bd., St. Paul, 1982; chmn. adv. com. rules of civil appellate procedure Minn. Supreme Ct., St. Paul, 1982—, chair adv. com. rules of civil procedure, 1984—. Editor: Women Lawyers Jour., 1971-72. Mem. ABA, Minn. State Bar Assn., Nat. Assn. Women Lawyers, Nat. Assn. Women Judges, Minn. Women Lawyers Assn., U. Minn. Law Alumni Assn. Home: 1156 Fairmount Ave Saint Paul MN 55105-2741*

**COYNE, ROBERT PATRICK,** lawyer; b. Providence, R.I., Nov. 25, 1961; s. Thomas Joseph and Roberta Claire (Connolly) C. BA, Boston Coll., 1983, JD, 1986. Bar: Mass. 1986, N.Y. 1987, Colo. 1999. Assoc. Mudge Rose Guthrie Alexander & Ferdon, N.Y.C., 1986-95, Nixon, Hargrave, Devans & Doyle, LLP, N.Y.C., 1995-98; spl. counsel Brownstein Hyatt & Farber, P.C., Denver, 1998—. Mem. ABA, Nat. Assn. Bond Lawyers, Assn. of Bar of City of N.Y., Mass. Bar Assn. Democrat. Roman Catholic. Avocations: running, golf, rugby, Irish history, skiing. Municipal (including bonds). Office: Brownstein Hyatt & Farber PC 410 17th St Fl 22 Denver CO 80202-4402

**COZAD, JOHN CONDON,** lawyer; b. Portland, Maine, Dec. 18, 1944; s. Francis E. and Arlyn Odell (Condon) C.; m. Linda Hickerson, Feb. 18, 1978. B.A. in Polit. Sci., Westminster Coll., Fulton, Mo., 1966; J.D., U. Mo.-Columbia, 1972. Bar: Mo. 1972. Assoc. & ptnr. Field, Gentry, Benjamin, & Robertson, Kansas City, Mo., 1972-83; ptnr. Morrison & Hecker, Kansas City, Mo., 1983—; chmn. Mo. Rep State Party, 1995-99. Chmn. Mo. Hwy. and Transp. Commn., 1985-91; mem. desegregation monitoring com. U.S. Dist. Ct. (we. dist.) Mo., 1989-91; bd. curators U. Mo. Sys., 1991-96; bd. trustees U. Kansas City, 1991—; mem. Rep. Nat. Com., 1995-99. Lt. USNR, 1967-69, Vietnam. Decorated Bronze Star. Navy Commendation medals, Presdl. Unit Citation. Mem. Mo. Bar Assn., Kansas City Bar Assn., Carriage Club. Republican. Mem. Disciples of Christ Ch. Avocations: politics, pheasant hunting, reading. Insurance, Administrative and regulatory. Home: RR 2 Box 140 Platte City MO 64079-9805

**CRABB, BARBARA BRANDRIFF,** federal judge; b. Green Bay, Wis., Mar. 17, 1939; d. Charles Edward and Mary (Forrest) Brandriff; m. Theodore E. Crabb, Jr., Aug. 29, 1959; children: Julia Forrest, Philip Elliott. A.B., U. Wis., 1960, J.D., 1962. Bar: Wis. 1963. Assoc. Roberts, Boardman, Suhr and Curry, Madison, Wis., 1962-64; legal rschr. Sch. Law, U. Wis., 1968-70, Am. Bar Assn., Madison, 1970-71; U.S. magistrate Madison, 1971-79; judge U.S. Dist. Ct. (we. dist.) Wis., Madison, 1979—, chief judge, 1980-96, sr. judge, 1996—; mem. Gov. Wis. Task Force Prison Reform, 1971-73. Membership chmn., v.p. Milw. LWV, 1966-68; mem. Milw. Jr. League,

1967-68. Mem. ABA, Nat. Assn. Women Judges, State Bar Wis., Dane County Bar Assn., U. Wis. Law Alumni Assn. Office: US Dist Ct PO Box 591 120 N Henry St Madison WI 53701-0591

**CRABTREE, JOHN GRANVILLE,** lawyer; b. Sarasota, Fla., Apr. 30, 1964; s. Granville Hayward Crabtree Jr. and Patricia Paulette Vitrier Schindler; m. Erin Kathleen Dunaway, May 10, 1991. Cert., The Sorbonne, Paris, 1985-86; BA in English, U. Fla., 1987, JD, 1990. Bar: Fla. 1991, Colo. 1993, D.C. 1994, U.S. Dist. Ct. (mid. dist.) Fla. 1992, U.S. Dist. Ct. (no. dist.) Fla. 1993, U.S. Dist. Ct. Ariz. 1994, U.S. Dist. Ct. (so. dist.) Fla. 1997, U.S. Ct. Appeals (11th cir.) 1993, U.S. Ct. Appeals (9th cir.) 1995, U.S. Supreme Ct. 1995, U.S. Ct. Appeals (5th cir.), 1996, U.S. Dist. Ct. (so. dist.) Fla. 1997. Postgrad. rsch. asst. U. Fla. Coll. Law Appellate Advocacy Dept., Gainesville, summer 1991; assoc./ptnr. Pflaum & Crabtree, Gainesville, 1991-92; assoc. Messer, Vickers et al, Tallahassee, Fla., 1992-95, Greenberg Traurig, Miami, Fla., 1995-97; ptnr. MacQuarrie & Crabtree, P.A., Ocala, Fla., 1997—. Named Outstanding Mem., U. Fla. Coll. Law Justice Campbell Thornall Nat. Moot Ct. Bd., 1990; U. Fla. Coll. Law teaching fellow, 1989. Mem. ABA (brief judge nat. appellate advocacy competition 1993, litigation sect. appellate practice com. 1992—, fed. appellate rules subcom. 1994—), Fla. Bar (appellate rules com. 1996—, amicus curaie com. 1995—, exec. coun. appellate practice and advocacy sect. 1997—, civil appellate practice com. 1994—, chmn. amicus curiae subcom. 1994-96, com. 1995—). Republican. Roman Catholic. Avocations: golf, fitness, politics, travel. Federal civil litigation, Appellate, Product liability. Office: MacQuarrie & Crabtree PA 409 SE Fort King St PO Box 1088 Ocala FL 34478-1088

**CRADDOCK, STEPHEN JAMES,** lawyer; b. Barre, Vt., Sept. 20, 1951; s. James Spear and Barbara (Lawliss) C.; m. Debra Prescott, Sept. 28, 1985; 1 child, Corey. BA, Harvard U., 1973; JD, Vt. Law Sch., 1984. Bar: Vt. 1985. Law clk. Vt. Atty. Gen., Montpelier, 1984-85; dep. states atty. Rutland (Vt.) County States Atty., 1985-86; pvt. practice Barre, 1986—. Lt. USN, 1975-80. Mem. ABA, Vt. Bar Assn., Vt. Trial Lawyers Assn., Elks. Avocation: golf. Personal injury, General civil litigation, Criminal. Home: 325 Culver Hill Rd Middlesex VT 05602-9266 Office: 1413 Paine Tpke N Berlin VT 05602-9151

**CRAFT, JOHN CHARLES,** lawyer; b. Nov. 28, 1938; m. Karen J. Winfrey; children: Gretchen, Elizabeth. AB, U. Nebr., 1961; JD, Northwestern U., 1965. Bar: Mo. 1965. Ptnr. Craft Fridkin & Rhyne, Kansas City, Mo., 1988—. Avocations: golf, tennis. Administrative and regulatory, Government contracts and claims, Insurance. Office: Craft Fridkin & Rhyne 304 E High St Jefferson City MO 65101-3213

**CRAFT, ROBERT HOMAN, JR.,** lawyer; b. N.Y.C., Sept. 24, 1939; s. Robert Homan and Janet Marie (Sullivan) C.; m. Margaret Jamison Ford, Feb. 6, 1971; children: Robert H. III, Gerard Ford. AB, Princeton U., 1961; BA, Oxford U., 1963; LLB, Harvard U., 1966. Bar: N.Y. 1973, U.S. Dist. Ct. (so. and ea. dists.) N.Y. 1977, U.S. Ct. Appeals (D.C. cir.) 1977, U.S. Dist. Ct. D.C. 1978, U.S. Ct. Appeals (2nd cir.) 1974, U.S. Supreme Ct. 1977. Assoc. Sullivan & Cromwell, N.Y.C., 1966-74; spl. asst. to under sec. of state for security assistance U.S. Dept. State, Washington, 1974-76; exec. asst. to chmn. SEC, Washington, 1976; ptnr. Sullivan & Cromwell, Washington, 1977—. Bd. trustees Washington Opera, 1978—, pres. 1998—; dir. Coun. for Excellence in Govt., 1989—. Mem. ABA, D.C. Bar Assn., N.Y. State Bar Assn., Assn. Bar City of N.Y., Am. Soc. Internat. Law, Met. Club (Washington), Chevy Chase (Md.) Club. Securities, General corporate. Home: 5010 Millwood Ln NW Washington DC 20016-2620 Office: Sullivan & Cromwell 1701 Pennsylvania Ave NW Washington DC 20006-5866

**CRAIG, GREGORY BESTOR,** lawyer, government official; b. Norfolk, Va., Mar. 4, 1945; s. William Gregory and Lois (Bestor) C.; m. Margaret Davenport Noyes, July 27, 1974; children: William Eliot, Eliza Noyes, Margaret Bestor, Mary Duncan, James Gregory. AB magna cum laude, Harvard Coll., 1967; diploma in historical studies, Cambridge U., 1968; JD, Yale U., 1972. Bar: D.C. 1972, U.S. Ct. Appeals (D.C., 2d, 3d, 4th, 6th and 7th cirs.), U.S. Supreme Ct. Assoc. Williams Connolly & Califano, Washington, 1972-74; asst. fed. pub. defender U.S. Dist. Ct. Conn., 1974-76; assoc. Williams & Connolly, Washington, 1977-78, ptnr., 1979-84; sr. advisor on fgn. policy and def. Sen. Edward M. Kennedy, Washington, 1984-88; ptnr. Williams & Connolly, Washington, 1989—; dir. Office of the Policy and Planning staff, Dept. of State, 1997—; chmn. Internat. Human Rights Law Group, 1992-96; tchr. trial practice Yale Law Sch., 1975-76; mem. Mex. Am. Legal Def. and Edn. Fund, 1995—; chmn. Internat. Human Rights Law Group, 1989-96. Trustee Overseas Devel. Coun., 1993-96, Carnegie Endowment for Internat. Peace, 1990-97, Robert F. Kennedy Meml. Found., 1989-97, Fgn. Student Svc. Coun., 1990-96, Mexican-Am. Legal Def. and Edn. Fund, 1995-97. John Harvard scholar, 1967. Mem. ABA, Phi Beta Kappa. Avocations: mountain climbing, hiking. Criminal, Private international, General civil litigation. Office: Policy Planning Staff 2201 C St NW Washington DC 20520-0001

**CRAIG, LAURIE BAKER,** lawyer; b. Helena, Ark., Feb. 1, 1944; s. Laurie Moreland Craig and Mary Baker; m. Pamela Kay Redd, July 22, 1972; children: Mary Rebecca, Stephen Marshall, Nancy Kay, Katheryne Ann, Austin Michael, Angela Jane. BA, Brigham Young U., 1967; JD, U. Utah, 1972. Bar: Ariz. 1972, U.S. Dist. Ct. Ariz. 1972. Ptnr. Streich, Lang, Weeks & Cardon, Phoenix, 1976-90, Benns, Gilbert & Morrill, Phoenix, 1990-97, Bens, Gilbert & Devitt, Phoenix, 1998—. With U.S. Army, 1969-71. Mem. LDS Ch. Avocations: jogging, boating, skiing. Banking, Real property. Office: Bens Gilbert & Devitt 3200 N Central Ave Ste 1000 Phoenix AZ 85012-2430

**CRAIG, ROBERT MARK, III,** lawyer, educator; b. Mpls., Sept. 21, 1948; s. Robert Mark Jr. and Shirley A. (Collier) C.; m. Suzanne Bartlett, Aug. 22, 1970; children: Shannon Michelle, Scott Collier. BA in Journalism, Tex. Christian U., 1970; JD, U. Va., 1973. Bar: Va. 1973, U.S. Ct. Mil. Appeals 1974, Tex. 1975, U.S. Dist. Ct. (no. dist.) Tex. 1976, U.S. Dist. Ct. (so. dist.) Tex. 1980, U.S. Dist. Ct. (we. dist.) 1985, U.S. Ct. Appeals (5th and 11th cirs.) 1981, U.S. Supreme Ct. 1981, U.S. Ct. Appeals (9th and 10th cir.) 1984. Assoc. Judin, Ellis & Barron, McAllen, Tex., 1979-80, ptnr., 1980-81; sr. atty. Tenneco Oil Co., Houston, 1981-88; sr. v.p., assoc. gen. counsel First City, Tex., Houston, 1988-93; assoc. gen. counsel Am. Gen. Corp., Houston, 1993—; staff atty. Presdl. Clemency Bd., Washington, 1975; mem. faculty Vernon Regional Jr. Coll., Sheppard AFB, 1975-76; instr. paralegal tng., Houston, 1982-85; instr. USAF Acad., 1976-77, asst. prof. law, 1977-79; councilman City of Oak Ridge North, Tex., 1988-94, also mayor pro tem; dir. Oak Ridge Mcpl. Utility Dist., 1994-96; pres. Oak Ridge Econ. Devel. Corp., 1994-96. Vice pres. Upper Rio Grande Valley Heart Assn., McAllen, 1980-81; ruling elder Timber Ridge Presbyn. Ch., 1983-88; pres. Montgomery County Assn. for Gifted and Talented, Conroe, Tex., 1985; chmn. Permanent Jud. Commn., New Covenant Presbytery, 1986-92; legal counsel Tex. Jaycees, 1981-82. Capt. USAF, 1973-79. Mem. ABA (co-chair subcom. on counsel retention com. on corp. counsel litigation sect.), Va. Bar Assn. (assoc.), Tex. Bar Assn. (coun. mem. antitrust and bus. litigation sect.), McAllen Jaycees (sec., bd. dirs. 1979-81). Republican. Avocations: youth coaching, golf, racquetball, softball. Federal civil litigation, State civil litigation, General corporate. Home: 27122 Wells Ln Oak Ridge North TX 77385-9080 Office: Am Gen Corp Legal Div WT3-04 2727 Allen Pkwy Houston TX 77019-2115

**CRAIG, STEPHEN WRIGHT,** lawyer; b. N.Y.C., Aug. 28, 1932; s. Herbert Stanley and Dorothy (Simmons) C.; m. Margaret M. Baker, June 10, 1958 (div. 1984); children: Amelia Audrey, Janet Elizabeth, Peter Baker; m. Bette Piller, 1984. AB, Harvard U., 1954, JD, 1959. Bar: Maine 1959, Calif. 1960, Ariz. 1963. Reporter Daily Kennebec Jour., Augusta, Maine, 1956; with pub. rels. staff Am. Savoyards, 1957; atty. IRS, San Francisco, 1959-61; atty.-adviser U.S. Tax Ct., 1961-63; ptnr. Snell & Wilmer, Phoenix, 1963-78, Winston & Strawn (formerly Craig, Greenfield & Irwin), Phoenix, 1978-87; investment banker Myers, Craig, Vallone, Francois, 1987-89; ptnr. Brown & Bain, Phoenix and Palo Alto, Calif., 1989-97; guest lectr. Amos Tuck Sch. Bus., Dartmouth U., 1962; lectr. Ariz. and N.Mex. Tax Insts., 1966-67; guest lectr. sch. law Ariz. State U., 1984, adj. prof. law, 1985-87. Chmn. Jane Wayland Child Guidance Ctr., 1968-70; mem. Maricopa County Health Planning Coun., chmn. mental health task force; bd. dirs. Combined Met. Phoenix Arts, 1968, adv. bd., 1968-69; adv. bd. Ariz. State U. Tax Insts., 1968-70; bd. dirs. Phoenix Cmty. Coun., Phoenix Cmty. Alliance, Arizona Acad.

**CRAIG, VICKI RENE,** lawyer; b. Selma, Ala., Sept. 14, 1957. BS, U. Ala., 1979; JD, Howard U., 1987; LLM in Taxation, Georgetown U., 1991, cert. in employee benefits law, 1992. Bar: Pa. 1989, D.C. 1989, U.S. Dist. Ct. D.C. 1991, U.S. Claims Ct. 1991, U.S. Tax Ct. 1991, U.S. Ct. Appeals (D.C. and fed. cirs.) 1991, U.S. Supreme Ct. 1992. Tax atty. IRS, Washington, 1987—; rsch. asst Am. Jour. Tax Policy, Tuscaloosa, Ala., summer 1986. Contbr. articles to profl. publs. Mem. Smithsonian Assocs., Washington, 1989, NAACP, Washington, 1989; founder, dir. English tutorial program Shiloh Bapt. Ch., Washington. Mem. ABA, Nat. Bar Assn. (Greater Washington Area chpt., women lawyers' divsn.), Fed. Bar Assn., D.C. Bar Assn., Nat. Polit. Congress of Black Women, Pa. Bar Assn., Assn. Trial Lawyers Am., Alpha Kappa Alpha, Delta Theta Phi.

**CRAIG, WILLIAM EMERSON,** lawyer; b. Springfield, Mass., July 6, 1942; s. W. Emerson and Vera L. (Platt) C.; m. Susan Hart Ryan; children: Lathrop B., Linsley G. BA, Dartmouth Coll., 1964; LLB, Yale U., 1967. Assoc. Wiggin & Dana, New Haven, 1967-73, ptnr., 1974-97, sr. counsel, 1997—; sec. HGT Fund, Inc., New Haven, 1972-90, pres., bd. dirs. 1990-93; sec. Pomperaug Woods, Inc., Southbury, Conn., 1986-91; sec. bd. dirs. Fairbank Corp., New Haven, 1975—. Mem. New Haven Rep. Town Com., 1969-75, New Haven Bd. Fin., 1976-81, New Haven Environ. Adv. Coun., 1988-91; bd. dirs., treas. Planned Parenthood Coun., 1988-93, Planned Parenthood Conn. Found., 1991-95. Fellow Conn. Bar Found. (bd. dirs. 1987-97, treas. 1987-91); mem. ABA, Conn. Bar Assn. (exec. com. of real property and banking law sects.), New Haven County Bar Assn., Quinniplack Club, The Quechee Club (Vt.). Congregationalist. Avocations: skiing, tennis, squash, bicycling. Banking, Finance, Real property. Home: PO Box 411 Quechee VT 05059-0411 Office: Wiggin & Dana One Century Tower New Haven CT 06508-1832

**CRAIGIE, ALEX WILLIAM,** lawyer, writer; b. Hollywood, Calif., Sept. 19, 1966; s. Donald Alexander and Mary Louise C.; m. Patricia Task, Oct. 16, 1994 (div. Mar. 1997). BA in Philosophy, U. Calif., San Diego, 1990, BA in Lit. and Writing, 1990; JD, Loyola U., L.A., 1993. Bar: Calif. 1993. Assoc. atty. Hill, Genson, Even, Crandall & Wade, L.A., 1993-94, Grace, Genson, Cosgrove & Schirm, L.A., 1994—. Mem. Def. Rsch. Inst., Assn. So. Calif. Def. Counsel. Avocations: skiing, golf, raquetball, tennis. Product liability, Construction, General civil litigation. Office: Grace Genson Cosgrove & Schirm 444 S Flower St Fl 11 Los Angeles CA 90071-2901

**CRAIN, ANNETTE BRASHIER,** lawyer; b. Detroit, Mar. 12, 1965; d. R.B. and Mary E. (Hunter) Brashier; m. B. Darin Crain, Dec. 31, 1988; children: B. Darin II, Lauren A. BA, Jacksonville State U., 1985; JD, U. Ala., Tuscaloosa, 1988. Bar: Ala. 1988, U.S. Dist. Ct. (no. dist.) Ala. 1988, U.S. Ct. Appeals (11th cir.) 1991. Assoc. Margie Tyler Searcy, 1988-90; ptnr. Davis & Crain, Tuscaloosa, 1990—. Mem. Tuscaloosa County Bar Assn. (pres. young lawyers sect. 1995-96, sec.-treas. bankruptcy sect. 1996-97, entertainment com. 1995-97). General civil litigation, Bankruptcy. Office: Davis and Crain 1320 22nd Ave Tuscaloosa AL 35401-2938

**CRAIN, CHRISTINA MELTON,** lawyer; b. Dallas, Mar. 18, 1966; d. William Allen Sr. and Sandra (Hays) Melton. BA in Govt., U. Tex., 1988; JD, Oklahoma City U., 1991. Bar: Tex. 1992, U.S. Dist. Ct. (no. dist.) Tex. 1992, U.S. Ct. Appeals (5th cir.) 1992, U.S. Dist. Ct. (ea. dist.) Tex. 1993, U.S. Dist. Ct. (so. and we. dists.) Tex. 1994. From law clk. to assoc. Nichols, Jackson, Dillard, Hager & Smith, LLP, Dallas, 1990-93; ptnr. Kirk, Griffin & Melton, LLP, Dallas, 1994-96; pres. Christina Melton Crain PC, Dallas, 1996—; sr. v.p., gen. counsel Shop On Line. Chmn. Tex. Young Reps. Fedn., 1993-95; pres., 1st v.p., 3rd v.p. Pub. Affairs Luncheon Club, Dallas, 1993—; patient navigator Bridge Breast Ctr., Dallas, 1994-95; vol. Twice Blessed House, 1995—; mem. Leadership Dallas, 1998. Recipient U.S. Congl. Silver Medal of Honor, U.S. Congress, 1987; named 40 Under 40, The Dalls (Tex.) Bus. Jour., 1993, Outstanding Young Rep. Woman of Yr., Tex. Young Reps. Fedn., 1994, 95, Oustanding Young Lawyer Dallas, 1997-98. Mem. Dallas Bar Assn. (chair memls. history com.), Dallas Assn. Young Lawyers (bd. dirs., co-chair legal aid to elderly com., Outstanding Com. Chair award 1997). Baptist. Avocations: singing, reading, traveling, politics. Estate planning, Probate, General corporate. Office: 5521 Greenville Ave # 104-944 Dallas TX 75206-2925

**CRAIN, GAYLA CAMPBELL,** lawyer; b. Cleburne, Tex., June 13, 1950; d. R. C. and Marilyn Ruth (McFadyen) Campbell; m. Howard Leo Crain, May 27, 1978; 1 child, Robert Leo. BA, Baylor U., 1972, JD, 1974. Bar: Tex. 1974, U.S. Dist. Ct. (no., ea., we., and so. dists.) Tex., U.S. Ct. Appeals (5th cir.) 1988, U.S. Ct. Appeals (10th cir.) 1994, U.S. Supreme Ct. 1999, U.S. Supreme Ct. 1999. Asst. counsel Trailways, Inc., Dallas, 1975-79; counsel Schering Plough, Inc., Kenilworth, N.J., 1979-80, sr. counsel, 1980-81; assoc. Epstein Becker & Green, P.C., Ft. Worth, 1985-86; ptnr. Epstein Becker & Green, P.C., Dallas, 1986—. Contbg. author: State by State Guide to Human Resources Law, 1990, 91; editl. adv. bd. Employee Rels. Law Jour., Tex. Employment Law, 1998. Trustee Dallas Bapt. U., 1989-97, 98—. Labor, General civil litigation. Office: Epstein Becker & Green PC 12750 Merit Dr Ste 1320 Dallas TX 75251

**CRAMER, ALLAN P.,** lawyer; b. Norwich, Conn., Mar. 8, 1937; s. E.L. and Dorothy N. (Pasnik) C.; children—Peter Alden, Alison Jane. B.A. cum laude, U. Pa., 1958; J.D., U. Conn., 1964. Bar: Conn. 1964, U.S. Dist. Ct. Conn. 1965, U.S. Ct. Appeals (2d cir.) 1965. Atty. HEW, Washington, 1964-65; ptnr. Cramer & Ahern, Westport, Conn., 1966—. Chmn. Westport Democratic Town Com., 1972-73; J.P., Town of Westport, 1973-77; bd. dirs. Westport Pub. Library, 1975-82; mem. Westport Zoning Bd. Appeals, 1984-88 . Mem. Conn. Bar Assn., Westport Bar Assn. Real property, Personal injury, General practice. Home: Yankee Hill Rd Westport CT 06880 Office: Cramer & Ahern 38 Post Rd W Westport CT 06880-4207

**CRAMER, HAROLD,** lawyer; b. Phila., June 16, 1927; s. Aaron Harry and Blanche (Greenberg) C.; m. Geraldine Hassuk, July 14, 1957; 1 dau., Patricia Gail. AB, Temple U., 1948; LLB cum laude, U. Pa., 1951. Bar: Pa. 1951. Law clk. to judge Common Pleas Ct. No. 2, 1953; mem. law faculty U. Pa., 1954; assoc. firm Shapiro, Rosenfeld, Stalberg & Cook, 1955-56, ptnr., 1956-67; ptnr. Meslrov, Gelman, Jaffe & Levin, 1967-74, Mesirov, Gelman, Jaffe & Cramer, Phila., 1974-77; ptnr. Mesirov, Gelman, Jaffe, Cramer & Jamieson, Phila., 1977-89, of counsel, 1996—; CEO Grad. Health System, Phila., 1989-96; instr. Nat. Inst. Trial Advocacy, 1970—; pres. Jewish Exponent, 1987-89, Times., 1987-89. Co-author: Trial Advocacy, 1968; contbr. articles to profl. jours. Chmn. bd. Eastern Pa. Psychiat. Hosp., 1974-81, Grad. Hosp., 1975-91; trustee Fedn. Jewish Agys., Jewish Publ. Soc., pres., 1996-98. 1st lt. U.S. Army, 1951-53. Decorated Bronze Star. Fellow Am. Bar Found.; mem. ABA, Am. Law Inst., Pa. Bar Assn. (ho. of dels. 1966-75, 78—, bd. govs. 1975-78), Phila. Bar Found. (pres. 1988, trustee, pres. elect), Phila. Bar Assn. (bd. govs. 1967-69, chmn. 1969, vice chancellor 1970, chancellor 1972, editor The Shingle 1970-72), U. Pa. Law Alumni Soc. (bd. mgrs. 1959-64, pres. 1968-70), Order of Coif (past chpt. pres., nat. exec. com. 1973-76), Tau Epsilon Rho (chancellor Phila. grad. chpt. 1960-62), Philmont Country Club, Pyramid Club. Federal civil litigation, General corporate, Health. Home: 728 Pine St Philadelphia PA 19106-4005 Office: Mesirov Gelman Jaffe Cramer & Jamieson 1735 Market St Ste 38 Philadelphia PA 19103-7501

**CRAMER, JEFFREY ALLEN,** lawyer; b. Kansas City, Mo., Mar. 16, 1951; s. Robert Donald and Betty Jane (Leventhal) C.; m. Melinda Gail Segal, Nov. 18, 1993; 1 child, Margaret Elizabeth. BA, Vanderbilt U., 1972; JD, U. Fla., 1974. Bar: Fla. 1975, U.S. Dist. Ct. (no. dist.) 1975, U.S. Dist. Ct. (so. dist.) Fla. 1980, U.S. Dist. Ct. (mid. dist.) Fla. 1981, U.S. Ct. Appeals (5th cir.) 1975, U.S. Ct. Appeals (11th cir.) 1981. Assoc. Levin, Warfield, Middlebrooks, Graff, Mabie & Rosenbloum, Pensacola, Fla., 1975-76; mem. Carlton, Fields, Ward, Emmanuel, Smith & Cutler, Pensacola and Tampa, Fla., 1976-84; prin. Law Offices of Jeffrey A. Cramer, P.A., Pensacola, 1984-93; with The Cramer Law Firm, Jacksonville, FL, 1993—. Mem. Leadership Pensacola, 1985-86; pres. Five Flags Sertoma, Pensacola, 1985-86; dist. gov., Gulf Coast Dist. Sertoma Internat., 1986-87; bd. dirs. Speech-Hearing Bd. Bapt. Health Care Found., Pensacola, 1987. Mem. Fla. Bar Assn., Am. Bd. Trial Advocates (N.W. Fla. chpt. sec. 1990, v.p. 1991, pres. 1992, nat. bd. dirs. 1993-94), Escambia-Santa Rosa Bar Assn. (treas. 1988-89, v.p. 1989-90, pres.1990-91), Fla. Bar (cert. civil trial lawyer, workers' compensation lawyer, cir. ct. mediator). Labor, Personal injury, Workers' compensation. Office: 1 Independent Dr Ste 3300 Jacksonville FL 32202-5027

**CRAMER, JENNIFER GOLDENSON,** lawyer; b. Utica, N.Y., Nov. 3, 1967; d. David Bernard and Sharon Lee Goldenson; m. Jeffrey H. Cramer, Oct. 2, 1993; 1 child, Mollie Elisabeth. BA, Cornell U., 1989; JD, U. Pa., 1992. Bar: Pa. 1993, U.S. Dist. Ct. (ea. dist.) Pa. 1993, N.Y., U.S. Dist. Ct. (so. and ea. dists.) N.Y. 1994, D.C. 1995, Mass. 1997, U.S. Ct. Appeals (1st cir.) 1998. Assoc. Ballard, Spahr, Andrews & Ingersoll, Phila., 1992-93, Sutherland, Asbill & Brennan, N.Y.C., 1993-95, Graham & James, N.Y.C., 1996-97, Bromberg & Sunstein, Boston, 1997—. Mem. ABA, Mass. Bar Assn., Boston Bar Assn., Phi Beta Kappa. Avocations: biking, hiking, theater. General civil litigation, Intellectual property, Trademark and copyright. Office: Bromberg & Sunstein 125 Summer St Ste 1100 Boston MA 02110-1618

**CRAMER, MARK KENLEY,** lawyer; b. Syracuse, N.Y., May 24, 1960; s. Kenley Dale Cramer and Mildred Pauline Glaser; m. Jane Volk, Oct. 17, 1987; children: Kyle, Colin. BA magna cum laude, SUNY, Albany, 1982; JD, SUNY, Buffalo, 1986. Bar: N.Y. 1987, U.S. Dist. Ct. (we. dist.) N.Y. 1987. Atty. Moot & Sprague, Buffalo, 1986-88; ptnr. Block & Colucci P.C., Buffalo, 1988-95, Falk & Siemer LLC, Buffalo, 1995-98, Hiscock & Barclay, LLP, Buffalo, 1998—. Officer, bd. dirs. Kelly for Kids Found., Buffalo, 1991-98; chmn. Horizon Human Svcs., Buffalo, 1995-98; of counsel Hunter's Hope Found., Buffalo, 1998—. Mem. Am. Acad. Healthcare Attys., Nat. Health Lawyers Assn., N.Y. State Bar Assn. (lectr. CLE courses 1990—), Erie County Bar Assn. (lectr. CLE courses 1990—), Phi Beta Kappa. Presbyterian. Avocations: skiing, golfing, Rosarian, painting. Contracts commercial, General corporate, Mergers and acquisitions. Home: 149 Leicester Rd Buffalo NY 14217-2113 Office: Hiscock & Barclay LLP Key Bank Towers 50 Fountain Plz Ste 301 Buffalo NY 14202-2291

**CRAMPTON, REBEKAH JEAN,** judge, educator; b. New Marlborough, Mass., Mar. 26, 1938; d. John and Marion Caroline (Jones) Somes; m. Harold W. Crampton Jr., July 9, 1966; children: Kate, Gregory, Stephen. BS cum laude, U. Mass., 1959; JD magna cum laude, Western New Eng. coll., 1978. adj. prof. Western New Eng. Coll. Sch. Law, Springfield, 1980-85; spl. asst. atty. gen. sect. lead poisoning prevention Dept. Pub. Health, Commonwealth of Mass., 1981-84. Tchr. Apponequet High Sch., East Freetown, 1959-61, 65-66; dean, tchr. Amrikan Kiz Koleji, Izmir, Turkey, 1961-65; tchr. West Springfield (Mass.) H.S., 1966-67; assoc. Walder & Pepyne, Greenfield, Mass., 1978-81; ptnr. Crampton, Dion & Johnston, PC, Springfield, 1979-86; assoc. justice Trial Ct. Juvenile Dept., Springfield, 1986-98; first justice Hampden County (Mass.) Juvenile Ct., 1998—; adj. prof. Western New Eng. Coll. Sch. law, Springfield, 1980-85; spl. asst. atty. gen. sect. lead poisoning prevention Dept. Pub. Health, Commonwealth of Mass., 1981-84. Bd. dirs Springfield Mentoring Partnership, 1999; Open Pantry Inc., Springfield, 1982—, CASA of Springfield, 1988-95 (Vol. appreciation award 1994), Hampden County Civil Liberties Union, Springfield, 1983-85, Cmty. United Way, 1995—, Mass. Judge's Conf., 1994— (mem. 1986—). Recipient Mass. Judge's Conf. 1999 Jud. Excellence award, Cmty. Svc. award Child and Family Svcs., 1993, Appreciation award Dispute Resolution Svcs., 1999, Alumni of Yr. Dept. Consumer Svcs. U. Mass., 1996. Mem. ABA, Nat. Women Judges Assn. (regional dir. 1990-91), Hampden Young Lawyers Assn. (treas. 1981-82, asst. chmn. 1982-83, chmn. 1983-84), Mass. Bar Assn., Hampden Bar Assn. (exec. bd. 1983-84). Home: 215 Maynard Rd Wilbraham MA 01095-1212 Office: Hampden County Juvenile Ct 80 State St PO Box 559 Springfield MA 01102-0559

**CRAMTON, ROGER CONANT,** law educator, lawyer; b. Pittsfield, Mass., May 18, 1929; s. Edward Allen and Dorothy Stewart (Conant) C.; m. Harriet Cutter Haseltine, June 29, 1952; children: Ann, Charles, Peter, Cutter. AB, Harvard U., 1950; JD, U. Chgo., 1955; LLD, Nova U., 1980; MA (hon.), Oxford U., 1987. Bar: Vt. 1956, Mich. 1964, N.Y. State 1979. Law clk. to Hon. S.R. Waterman U.S. Ct. of Appeals (2d cir.), 1955-56; law clk. to assoc. justice Harold H. Burton U.S. Supreme Ct., 1956-57; asst. prof. U. Chgo., 1957-61; assoc. prof. U. Mich. Law Sch., 1961-64, prof., 1964-70; chmn. Adminstrv. Conf. of U.S., 1970-72; asst. atty. gen. Justice Dept., 1972-73; dean Cornell U. Law Sch., Ithaca, N.Y., 1973-80, Robert S. Stevens prof., 1982—; mem. U.S. Commn. on Revision Fed. Ct. Appellate Sys., 1973-75; bd. dirs. U.S. Legal Svcs. Corp., 1975-79, chmn. bd., 1975-78; mem. U.S. Commn. on Jud. Discipline and Removal, 1991-93. Co-author: Conflict of Laws, 5th rev. edition, 1993, Law and Ethics of Lawyering, 2d rev. edit., 1994; editor Jour. Legal Edn., 1981-87; contbr. articles to profl. jours. Guggenheim fellow, 1987-88. Mem. ABA, Am. Law Inst. (council mem.), Assn. Am. Law Schs. (pres. 1985), Am. Acad. Arts and Scis., Order of Coif, Phi Beta Kappa. Congregationalist. Home: 49 Highgate Cir Ithaca NY 14850-1486 Office: Cornell Law Sch Myron Taylor Hall Ithaca NY 14853-4901

**CRANDALL, NELSON DAVID, III,** lawyer; b. Auburn, Calif., Aug. 8, 1954; s. Nelson David and Alice (Reimer) C.; m. Elizabeth L. Donovan, Aug. 25, 1984; children: Darren J., Colin M. Student, U. Calif., Irvine, 1974-76; AB with high honors, U. Calif., Berkeley, 1976; JD, U. Calif., Davis, 1979. Bar: Calif. 1979, U.S. Dist. Ct. (no. dist.) Calif. 1979, U.S. Dist. Ct. (ea. dist.) Calif. 1980. Ptnr. Hopkins & Carley Law Corp., San Jose, Calif., 1979-94; prin. Enterprise Law Group, Inc., Menlo Park, Calif., 1994—. Contbr. articles to profl. jours. Mediator, arbitrator Santa Clara County Neighborhood Small Claims Project, San Jose, 1980-92; bd. dirs. Ctrl. Calif. region ARC Blood Svcs., 1992-94, sec., 1992-94; active Santa Clara Valley chpt. ARC, San Jose, 1986-92, sec., 1987-90; trustee Jr. Statesman Found., 1987—; bd. dirs. Hope Rehab. Svcs., San Jose, 1985-88. Mem. ABA, Calif. Bar Assn., Santa Clara County Bar Assn., Phi Beta Kappa. Republican. Avocations: travel, photography, backpacking, reading. General corporate, Securities, Banking. Office: Enterprise Law Group Inc 4400 Bohannon Dr Ste 280 Menlo Park CA 94025-1071

**CRANE, KATHLEEN D.,** lawyer; b. Ridgewood, N.J., Jan. 17, 1954; m. Milan D. Smith, Jr., 1996. BA, Boston Coll., 1975; JD, Emory U., 1980; LLM, George Washington U., 1984. Bar: Ga. 1980, S.C. 1981, D.C. 1982, Ohio 1985, Calif. 1987, U.S. Dist. Ct. S.C., U.S. Ct. Claims. Assoc. Sinkler, Gibbs, Simons, Charleston, S.C., 1980-82; tchg. fellow George Washington U., Washington, 1982-84; assoc. Smith & Schnacke, Dayton, Ohio, 1984-86; ptnr. Smith, Crane, Robinson & Parker, Torrance, Calif., 1986—. Mem. adv. bd. YWCA, Torrance, 1992-97, Calif. State U., Domingues Hills, 1993-98; bd. dirs. Torrance Meml. Med. Ctr., 1988-97, chairwoman, 1994-97; pres. South Bay Estate Planning Coun., 1995-96. Avocations: skiing, activities with children. Taxation, general, Estate planning, General corporate. Office: Smith Crane Robinson & Parker 21515 Hawthorne Blvd Ste 500 Torrance CA 90503-6568

**CRANE, ROGER RYAN, JR.,** lawyer; b. Washington, Mar. 28, 1946; s. Roger Ryan Crane and Jeanette (Hurlbut) Rosar. AB, Coll. of Holy Cross, 1968; JD, Fordham U., 1973; LLM, NYU, 1980. Bar: N.Y. 1974; U.S. Dist. Ct. (so. and ea. dist.) N.Y. 1974; U.S. Ct. Appeals (2nd cir.) 1974, (1st cir.) 1994. Assoc. Dunnington Bartholow & Miller, N.Y.C., 1973-79, Trubin Sillcocks Edelman, N.Y.C., 1979-81; ptnr. Trubin Sillcocks Edelman, N.Y.C., 1981-84; ptnr., head litig. dept. Bachner Tally Polevoy & Misher, N.Y.C., 1984—. Contbr. articles to profl. jours. Mem. N.Y.C. Bar Assn. (prof. discipline com. 1996—), Univ. Club N.Y., Tuxedo Club. Avocations: golf, tennis, fly fishing, riding. General civil litigation, Securities, Intellectual property. Office: Bachner Tally Polevoy & Misher 380 Madison Ave New York NY 10017-2513

**CRANE, WILLIAM GRACE,** lawyer; b. N.Y.C., Mar. 25, 1932; s. Thomas Francis and Rose (Illions) C.; m. Catherine A. Polsenski, Aug. 21, 1958; children: William Jr., Matthew, Genevieve, Bridget, James. BA, Manhattan Coll., 1953; JD, St. John's U., Bklyn., 1958. Bar: N.Y. Law clk. Ct. of Appeals N.Y., Albany, 1958-60; assoc. Gilbert & Segall, N.Y.C., 1960-61; law asst. 2d dept. Appellate Divsn., Bklyn., 1961-64; law clk. N.Y. Supreme Ct., White Plains, 1964-69; ptnr. Rosen, Crane & Wolfson, Poughkeepsie, N.Y., 1969-86, Crane Wolfson & Roberts, Poughkeepsie, 1986-91; prin. ct. atty. Surrogate's Ct. Dutchess county, Poughkeepsie, 1993-98; sole practitioner Poughkeepsie, 1991—; lar clk. Family Ct. Dutchess County, Poughkeepsie, 1973-93. Served with U.S. Army, 1955. Republican. Roman Catholic. Office: 11 Market St Ste 204 Poughkeepsie NY 12601-3215

**CRANFORD, JAMES MICHAEL,** lawyer; b. Washington, Jan. 26, 1946; s. Jack and Wanda C.; m. Teresa, July 23, 1994; children: William Bodie, James Michael, Heather, Christopher. BA, Mercer U., 1978; JD, Woodrow Wilson U., 1984. Atty. pvt. practice, Macon, Ga., 1985—. Mem. city coun. Macon, 1996—. Mem. Ga. Bar Assn., Ga. Trial Lawyers Assn., Ga. Assn. Criminal Defense Lawyers, Macon Bar Assn., Macon Assn. Criminal Justuce Lawyers, Middle Ga. Trial Lawyers Assn. Episcopalian. Avocations: family, motorcycle racing, scuba diving, boxing, fishing. General civil litigation, Criminal, Personal injury. Home: 1842 Williamson Rd Macon GA 31206-3342 Office: 913 Washington Ave Macon GA 31201-6720

**CRANMER, THOMAS WILLIAM,** lawyer; b. Detroit, Jan. 13, 1951; s. William Eugene and Betty Lee (Orphal) C.; m. Judy Kay Henson, Apr. 19, 1986; children: Jacqueline, Taylor, Chase. BA, U. Mich., 1972; JD, Ohio No. U., 1975. Bar: Mich. 1975, U.S. Dist. Ct. (ea. dist.) Mich. 1978, U.S. Ct. Appeals (6th cir.) 1978, U.S. Supreme Ct. 1982, U.S. Tax Ct. 1986. Asst. pros. atty. Oakland County, Mich., 1975-78; asst. atty. U.S. Dist. Ct. (ea. dist.) Mich., 1978-80, asst. chief criminal div., 1980-82; assoc. Miro, Miro & Weiner, Bloomfield Hills, Mich., 1982-84, ptnr., 1984—; mem. faculty Atty. Gen.'s Adv. Inst., Washington, 1980-82, Nat. Inst. Trial Adv., Northwestern Chicago, Ill., 1987—, trial adv. workshop Inst. Continuing Legal Edn., 1988—, local rules adv. com. U.S. Dist. Ct. (ea. dist.) Mich., 1989-92; hearing panelist Atty. Discipline Bd., 1987—. Fellow Oakland Bar-Adams Pratt Found. (charter, trustee 1994—), Mich. State Bar Found.; mem. ABA (chair litigation sect., Detroit graphic subcom. of com. on complex crimes litigation 1990), FBA (exec. bd. dirs. Detroit chpt. 1988—, pres. 1995—, Leonard R. Gilman award 1995), Am. Arbitration Assn. (mem. hearing panel 1990), Mich. Bar Assn. (rep. assembly 1986-92, mem. grievance com. 1990—, chair 1993-97, bd. commrs. 1998—), Oakland County Bar Assn. (chair CLE com. 1992, bd. dirs. 1994—, Disting. Svc. award 1996, chair membership com. 1997). Republican. Presbyterian. Criminal, General civil litigation, Labor. Home: 4249 Cherry Hill Dr Orchard Lake MI 48323-1607 Office: Miro Weiner & Kramer PC 500 N Woodward Ave Ste 100 Bloomfield Hills MI 48304-2962

**CRANNEY, MARILYN KANREK,** lawyer; b. Bklyn., June 18, 1949; d. Sidney Paul and Aurelia (Valice) Kanrek; m. John William Cranney, Jan. 22, 1970 (div. June 1975); 1 child, David Julian. BA, Brandeis U., 1970; MA in History, Brigham Young U., 1975; JD, U. Utah, 1979; LLM in Tax Law, NYU, 1984. Bar: N.Y. 1980, U.S. Dist. Ct. (so. and ea. dists.) N.Y. 1992. Assoc. Cravath Swaine & Moore, N.Y.C., 1979-81; 1st v.p., asst. gen. counsel Morgan Stanley Dean Witter Advisors Inc., N.Y.C., 1981—. Mem. Order of the Coif. Democrat. Jewish. Avocations: travel, reading. Securities, General corporate. Home: 1830 E 23rd St Brooklyn NY 11229-1529 Office: Morgan Stanley Dean Witter Advisors Inc 2 World Trade Ctr New York NY 10048-0203

**CRARY, MINER DUNHAM, JR.,** lawyer; b. Warren, Pa., Sept. 8, 1920; s. Miner D. and Edith (Ingraham) C.; m. Mary Chapman, Jan. 23, 1943; children: Edith Crary Howe, James G., Laura Crary Hall, Harriet Crary, Miner A. BA, Amherst Coll., 1942; MA, Harvard U., 1943, LLB, 1948. Bar: N.Y. 1949. Assoc. Curtis, Mallet-Prevost, 1949-61, ptnr., 1961-1996, coun., 1996—. Trustee Am. U. in Cairo, 1959—; trustee Heckscher Art Mus., Huntington, N.Y., 1968—; trustee Sterling and Francine Clark Art Inst., Williamstown, Mass., 1974—; bd. dirs. Robert Sterling Clark Found., N.Y.C., 1972—; chmn. exec. com. alumni coun. Amherst Coll., 1961-68; chmn. Huntington Bd. Edn. and Central Sch. Dist. 2, 1961-67; dep. village justice, Village of Asharoken, Northport, N.Y, 1987—. Lt. USNR, 1942-45. Mem. ABA (real property and probate com.), N.Y. State Bar Assn. (taxation and estate com. 1973), Assn. of Bar of City of N.Y. (surrogate ct. com. 1969-73). Clubs: Union League, Century Assn. (N.Y.C.); Huntington Country. Probate, Estate taxation, Estate planning. Office: Curtis Mallet-Prevost Colt 101 Park Ave Fl 34 New York NY 10178-0061

**CRASSWELLER, ROBERT DOELL,** retired lawyer, writer; b. Duluth, Minn., Sept. 17, 1915; s. Arthur Hallifax and Mary Elizabeth (Doell) C.; m. Mildred Elizabeth Clarke, Mar. 21, 1942; children: Peter, Karen Farbman, Pamela Baldino. BA, Carleton Coll., 1937; LLB, Harvard U., 1941. Bar: Minn. 1941, N.Y. 1960. Pvt. practice Duluth, Minn., 1942-43; econ. warfare posts U.S. Dept. State, Washington, 1943-45; ptnr. McCabe, Gruber, Clure, Donovan & Crassweller, Duluth, Minn., 1946-51; mining exec. West Indies Mining Corp., San Juan, P.R., 1951-53; counsel Pan Am. Airways, N.Y.C., 1954-67; vis. fellow Coun. Fgn. Rels., N.Y.C., 1967-70; vis. prof. Bklyn. Coll., Sarah Lawrence, N.Y.C., 1969-70; staff atty. ITT, N.Y.C., 1970-74, gen. coun. Lat. Am., 1975-81. Author: Trujillo: Life and Times of a Caribbean Dictator, 1966, The Caribbean Community, 1972, Perón and the Enigmas of Argentina, 1986; reviewer (books) for Fgn. Affairs, 1968-81. Dir. Forum for World Affairs, Stamford, Conn., 1986-87. Mem. Internat. Assn. Torch Clubs (Chapel Hill Club v.p. 1994-95), Soc. Automotive Historians. Republican. Avocations: gardening, travel, reading, writing, antique cars. Estate planning, Probate, General practice. Home: 101 York Pl Chapel Hill NC 27514-6521

**CRAVEN, JAMES BRAXTON, III,** lawyer, priest; b. Portsmouth, Va., Dec. 8, 1942; s. James Braxton and Mary Wilson (Kistler) C.; m. Sara Ann Harris, Aug. 22, 1964; children: James, Joseph, William. Midshipman, U.S. Naval Acad., 1960-61; A.B., U. N.C., 1964; J.D., Duke U., 1967, M.Div., 1981. Bar: N.C. 1967; ordained priest Episcopal Ch. Law clk. U.S. Dist. Ct., Alexandria, Va., 1967-68; trial atty. Civil Rights Divns. Dept. Justice, 1968-69; ptnr. Everett, Everett, Creech & Craven, Durham, N.C., 1969-80; sole practice Durham, 1980—; vis. prof. U. N.C., Chapel Hill, 1971-81; clin. assoc. in law Duke U., 1973-85. Contbr. articles to legal jours. Served to LCDR, JAGC, USNR (ret.). Mem. ABA, N.C. State Bar, N.C. Bar Assn., Am. Law Inst. (life), Jud. Conf. 4th Cir. (permanent mem.). Democrat. Bankruptcy, Federal civil litigation, Criminal. Home: 1015 Watts St Durham NC 27701-1534 Office: PO Box 1366 Durham NC 27702-1366

**CRAVEN, ROBERT EMMETT,** lawyer, educator; b. Providence, R.I., Nov. 19, 1955; s. Richard and Rose Mary Craven; m. Dianne B. Connors, Aug. 30, 1981 (div. Dec. 1988); m. Susan Mary Restivo, Jan. 5, 1968; children: Robert E. Jr., Joseph Edmond. BA, U. R.I., 1978; JD, 1983. Bar: R.I., U.S. Dist. Ct. R.I. Law clk. R.I. Supreme Ct., Providence, 1983; asst. att. gen. R.I. Atty. Gen.'s Office, Providence, 1984-93; atty., ptnr. Craven, Vieira & DiGianflippo, Providence, 1993—; prof. law C.C. R.I., Warwick, 1984—; legal counsel R.I. State Bd. Elections, Providence, 1995—. Pres. Ctr. for Non-Violence, Providence, 1992-95; counselman Town of North Kingstown, R.I., 1994-96. Mem. U. R.I. Alumni Assn. (v.p. 1992-94). Roman Catholic. Avocations: running, golf, coaching soccer. General civil litigation, Criminal, Personal injury.

**CRAVEN, TERRY MARIE,** lawyer; b. Boston, Jan. 17, 1952; s. James J. Jr. and Olivia M. (Bartels) C. BA in Psychology, Westfield State Coll., 1973; JD, New England Sch. of Law, Boston, 1987. Bar: Mass. Fed. Dist. Ct., U.S. Supreme Ct.; lic. real estate broker, social worker. Tchr. City of Boston Sch. Dept.; juvenile probation officer Herrick Ctr. for Girls Boston Juvenile Ct., 1976-88; sole practice family law, juvenile law, family crisis intervention, 1988—; lectr. Westfield State Coll., Boston Coll. Mem. ABA, Bd. Dirs. Juvenile Bar Assn. Mass. (founding mem. 1992—), Westfield State Coll. Alumni Assn. (past pres.), Ky. Colonel (com. 1990—), New England Sch. Law Alumni Assn. Juvenile, Native American, Family and matrimonial. Home: 670 E 6th St Boston MA 02127-3132

**CRAWFORD, B(URNETT) HAYDEN,** lawyer; b. Tulsa, June 29, 1922; s. Burnett Hayden and Margaret Sara (Stevenson) C.; m. Carolyn McCann, June 5, 1946 (div.); m. Virginia Baker, July 23, 1970 (dec. June 1994); m. Melanie Crowley, Dec. 24, 1994; children: Margaret Louise Crawford Brucks, Robert Hayden. BA, U. Mich., 1944, JD, 1949. Bar: Okla. 1949, U.S. Dist. Ct. (no. dist.) Okla. 1949, U.S. Supreme Ct. 1954, U.S. Ct. Appeals (10th cir.) 1954, U.S. Dist. Ct. (so. dist.) Ill. 1959, U.S. Ct. Mil. Appeals 1959, U.S. Ct. Appeals (fed. cir.) 1959, U.S. Dist. Ct. (we. and ea. dists.) Okla. 1960, U.S. Tax Ct. 1967. Law clk. to chief judge U.S. Dist. Ct. (no. dist.) Okla., 1950-51; asst. city prosecutor City of Tulsa, 1951-52, alt. mcpl. judge, 1952-54; U.S. atty. No. Dist. Okla., 1954-58; asst. dep. atty. gen. U.S. Dept. Justice, 1958-60; sole practice Tulsa, 1960-77; sr. ptnr. Crawford Crowne and Bainbridge, Tulsa, 1981-96, The Law Office of B. Hayden Crawford, Tulsa, 1996—; lectr. in field. Rep. nominee U.S. Senate from Okla., 1960, 62; Okla. mem. adv. com. U.S. Ct. of Appeals (10th circuit); active civic and mil. orgns. Served to Rear Adm. USNR, 1942-78. Decorated Legion of Merit, Purple Heart, Disting. Pub. Svc. medal, Dept. Def. Disting. Svc. award; recipient Okla. Minute Man award 1974. Fellow Am. Assn. Matrimonial Lawyers; mem. ABA, Okla. Bar Assn., Tulsa County Bar Assn., Assn. Trial Lawyers Am., Okla. Trial Lawyers Assn., U.S. Res. Officers Assn. (nat. pres. 1973-74), Phi Delta Theta, Phi Delta Phi, Tula Summit Club, Army and Navy Club (Washington), Garden of Gods Club (Colorado Springs, Colo.), So. Hills Country Club (Tulsa), Masons, Kiwanis (pres. 1969). Presbyterian. General civil litigation, Appellate, Estate planning. Home: 2300 Riverside Dr Tulsa OK 74114-2400 Office: 240 Mid-Continent Tower 401 S Boston Ave Tulsa OK 74103-4016

**CRAWFORD, DEWEY BYERS,** lawyer; b. Saginaw, Mich., Dec. 22, 1941; s. Edward Owen and Ruth (Wentworth) C.; m. Nancy Elizabeth Eck, Mar. 24, 1974. AB in Econs., Dartmouth Coll., 1963; JD with distinction, U. Mich., 1966. Bar: Ill. 1967, U.S. Dist. Ct. (no. dist.) Ill. 1969. Assoc. Gardner, Carton & Douglas, Chgo., 1969-74, ptnr., 1975—; adj. prof. law, ITT, Kent Sch. Law, 1992—. Contbr. articles to profl. jours. Chmn. Winnetka (Ill.) Caucus Coun., 1988-89. With U.S. Army, 1966-68, Vietnam. Mem. ABA, Chgo. Bar Assn., Am. Coll. Investment Counsel, Law Club Chgo., Legal Club Chgo. Republican. Congregationalist. Avocations: running, reading, music. Securities, Finance, Mergers and acquisitions. Office: Gardner Carton & Douglas 321 N Clark St Ste 3000 Chicago IL 60610-4762

**CRAWFORD, GERALD MARCUS,** lawyer; b. Arcadia, Wis., May 23, 1940; s. Marcus Gerard and Margaret Alvina (Dascher) C.; m. Kathleen Jonna Brown, May 11, 1968; children: Kelly, Laurie, Sharon, Marcus. Student, Dominican Coll., 1958-60; BA in History, Marquette U., 1962; LLB, Marquett U., 1964. Bar: Wis. 1964, U.S. Dist. Ct. (ea. and we. dists.) Wis. 1964. Asst. dist. atty. Racine County, Racine, Wis., 1965-69, City of Racine, 1969; ptnr. Stewart, Peyton, Crawford, Crawford & Stutt, Racine, 1969—. Sec. Racine YMCA, 1975-77; pres. Big Bros. of Greater Racine, 1979, St. Rita Sch. Bd., Racine, 1978-84. Fellow Am. Acad. Matrimonial Lawyers; mem. ABA, Racine Bar Assn. (pres. 1986-87), State of Wis. Bar Assn. Avocation: college basketball. Family and matrimonial, Probate. Office: 840 Lake Ave Ste 200 Racine WI 53403-1566

**CRAWFORD, HOMER,** retired lawyer, paper company executive; b. St. Louis, Nov. 28, 1916; s. Raymond S. and Mary (Homer) C.; m. Esther Wilkinson, Oct. 4, 1944 (div. 1949); 1 dau., Candace C.; m. Sara E. Twigg, May 3, 1952; children: Georgiana, William Twigg. A.B., Amherst Coll., 1938; LL.B., U. Va., 1941. Bar: N.Y. 1942. Assoc. firm LeBoeuf, Lamb, Leiby & MacRae, 1942-54, partner, 1954-56, v.p., sec. St. Regis Paper Co., 1956-82, gen. counsel, 1981, now ret. Mem. Am., N.Y. State bar assns., Am. Soc. Corp. Secs. (dir. 1965-68), Theta Delta Chi. Republican. Presbyterian. General corporate. Home: 11 Laurel Heights 87 Maple St Scarsdale NY 10583-5428

**CRAWFORD, JENNIFER CHAPMAN,** editor. Editor N.C. State Bar Quar., Raleigh. Office: NC State Bar PO Box 25908 Raleigh NC 27611-5908

**CRAWFORD, JOHN RICHARD,** lawyer; b. St. Petersburg, Fla., Sept. 18, 1951; s. Robert Ray and Mary Lorraine (Allen) C.; m. Barbara S. Dula, June 9, 1973 (div. Nov. 1997); children: Daniel E., Neil P. BA, U. Fla., 1973, JD, 1975. Bar: Fla. 1976, U.S. Dist. Ct. (mid. dist.) Fla. 1976, U.S. Tax Ct. 1979, Ga. 1995. Atty. Jennings, Watts, Clarke & Hamilton, Jacksonville, Fla., 1976-78, Kent, Watts & Durden, Jacksonville, Fla., 1978-86; mng. atty. Kent, Crawford & Gooding, Jacksonville, Fla., 1986—. Mem. Estate Planning Coun. N.E. Fla., Planned Giving Coun. N.E. Fla. Republican. Roman Catholic. E-mail: jrc@FirstCoastLaw.com. Office: Kent Crawford & Gooding 225 Water St Ste 900 Jacksonville FL 32202-5142

**CRAWFORD, KAREN SHICHMAN,** lawyer; b. N.Y.C., Dec. 27, 1955; d. David and Rita (Doobin) Shichman; children: Ryan Samuel, Jacob Stevenson. BA, Boston U., 1977; JD, Calif. Western Sch. Law, San Diego, 1980. Bar: Calif. 1980, Pa. 1991. Trial atty. civil div. torts br. U.S. Dept. Justice, Washington, 1980-83; asst. U.S. atty. civil div. U.S. Atty.'s Office for So. Dist. Calif., San Diego, 1984-91; shareholder Buchanan Ingersoll P.C., Pitts., 1991—; instr. Advocacy Inst., Dept. Justice, Washington, 1985-90; trustee Am. Inn of Ct. Found., 1994—, sec. 1996—. Recipient Atty. Gen.'s Spl. Achievement award Dept. Justice, 1982, Dir.'s award for superior performance, 1988. Recipient A. Sherman Christenson award Am. Inns of Ct. Found., 1998. Mem. Am. Inns of Ct. (pres. Pitts. chpt. 1992-95, counselor emeritus 1995—, hon. master U. Pitts. 1996—, A. Sherman Christneson award 1998). General civil litigation, Personal injury, Contracts commercial. Office: Buchanan Ingersoll PC One Oxford Centre 301 Grant St Fl 20 Pittsburgh PA 15219-1410

**CRAWFORD, LINDA SIBERY,** lawyer, educator; b. Ann Arbor, Mich., Apr. 27, 1947; d. Donald Eugene and Verla Lillian (Schenck) Sibery; m. Leland Allardice Crawford, Apr. 4, 1970; children: Christina, Lillian, Leland. Student, Keele U., 1969; BA, U. Mich., 1969; postgrad., SUNY, Potsdam, 1971; JD, U. Maine, 1977. Bar: Maine 1977, U.S. Dist. Ct. Maine 1982, U.S. Ct. Appeals (1st cir.) 1983. Tchr. Pub. Sch., Tupper Lake, N.Y., 1970-71; asst. dist. atty. State of Maine, Farmington, 1977-79; asst. atty. gen. State of Maine, Augusta, Maine, 1979-95; prin. Litigation Consulting Firm, N.Y.C & Hallowell, Maine, 1986—, Linda Crawford and Assoc. Law Firm, Hallowell, Maine, 1995—; legal adv. U. Maine, Farmington, 1975; legal counsel Fire Marshall's Office, Maine, 1980-83, Warden Svc., Maine, 1981-83, Dept. Mental Health, 1983-90, litigation divsn. 1990-95; mem. tchg. team trial advocacy Law Sch., Harvard U., 1987—; lectr. Sch. Medicine Harvard U., 1991; counsel to Bd. of Registration in Medicine, 1994-95; chmn. editl. bd. Mental and Physical Disability Law Reporter, 1993-95; arbitrator Am. Arbitration Assn., 1995—; facilitator Nat. Constrn. Task Force, St. Louis, 1995. Contbg. editor Med. Malpractice Law and Strategy, 1997—. Mem. Natural Resources Coun., Maine, 1985-90; bd. dirs. Diocesan Human Rels. Coun., Maine, 1977-78, Arthritis Found., Maine, 1983-88; atty. expert commn. experts UN War Crime Investigation in the former Yugoslavia, 1994. Named one of Outstanding Young Women of Yr. Jaycees, 1981. Mem. ATLA, ABA (com. on disability 1992-95), Maine Bar Assn., Kennebec County Bar Assn., Nat. Assn. State Mental Health Attys. (treas. 1984-86, vice chmn. 1987-89, chmn. 1989-91), Nat. Health Lawyers Assn. Health, State civil litigation, Personal injury. Home: 25 Winthrop St Hallowell ME 04347-1150 Office: PO Box 268 Hallowell ME 04347-0268 also: 45 Rockefeller Plz Fl 20 New York NY 10111-2099

**CRAWFORD, MURIEL LAURA,** lawyer, author, educator; d. Mason Leland and Pauline Marie (DesIlets) Henderson; m. Barrett Matson Crawford, May 10, 1959; children: Laura Joanne, Janet Muriel, Barbara Elizabeth. BA with honors, U. Ill., 1973; JD with honors, Ill. Inst. Tech., 1977; cert. employee benefit splst., U. Pa., 1989. Bar: Ill. 1977, Calif. 1991, U.S. Dist. Ct. (no. dist.) Ill. 1977, U.S. Dist. Ct. (no. dist.) Calif. 1991, U.S. Ct. Appeals (7th cir.) 1977, U.S. Ct. Appeals (9th cir.) 1991; CLU; chartered fin. cons. Atty. Washington Nat. Ins. Co., Evanston, Ill., 1977-80; sr. atty., 1980-81, asst. counsel, 1982-83, asst. gen. counsel, 1984-87, assoc. gen. counsel, sec., 1987-89, cons. employee benefit splst., 1989-91; assoc. Hancock, Rothert & Bushoft, San Francisco, 1991-92. Author: (with Beadles) Law and the Life Insurance Contract, 1989, (sole author) 7th edit., 1994, Life and Health Insurance Law, 8th edit., 1998; co-author: Legal Aspects of AIDS, 1990; contbr. articles to profl. jours. Recipient Am. Jurisprudence award Lawyer's Coop. Pub. Co., 1975, 2nd prize Internat. LeTourneau Student Med.-Legal Article Contest, 1976. Fellow Live Mgmt. Inst.; mem. Ill. Inst. Tech./Chgo.-Kent Alumni Assn. (bd. dirs. 1983-89, Bar and Gavel Soc. award 1977). Democrat. Conregationalist.

**CRAWFORD, SUSAN JEAN,** federal judge; b. Pitts., Apr. 22, 1947; d. William Elmer Jr. and Joan Ruth (Bielau) C.; m. Roger W. Higgins; 1 child, Kelley S. BA, Bucknell U., 1969; JD, New Eng. Sch. Law, 1977. Bar: Md. 1977, D.C. 1980, U.S. Ct. Appeals for Armed Forces 1985, U.S. Supreme Ct. 1993. Tchr. history, coach Radnor (Pa.) H.S., 1969-74; assoc. Burnett & Eiswert, Oakland, Md., 1977-79; ptnr. Burnett, Eiswert and Crawford, Oakland, 1979-81; prin. dep. gen. counsel U.S. Dept. Army, Washington, 1981-83, gen. counsel, 1983-89; insp. gen. U.S. Dept. Def., Arlington, Va., 1989-91; judge U.S. Ct. Appeals for the Armed Forces, Washington, 1991-99, chief judge, 1999—; asst. states atty. Garrett County, Md., 1978-79; instr. Garrett County C.C., 1979-81. Del. Md. Forestry Adv. Commn., Garrett County, 1978-81, Md. Commn. for Women, Garrett County, 1980-83; chair Rep. State Cen. Com., Garrett County, 1978-81; trustee Bucknell U., 1988—, New England Sch. Law, 1989—. Mem. FBA, Md. Bar Assn., D.C. Bar Assn., Edward Bennett Williams Am. Inn of Ct. Presbyterian. Office: US Ct Appeals Armed Forces 450 E St NW Washington DC 20442-0001

**CRAWFORD, TIMOTHY PATRICK,** lawyer, accountant; b. Racine, Wis., Aug. 23, 1948; s. Marcus Gerald and Margaret Alvina (Dascher) C.; m. Jeanne Drager, May 27, 1972; children: Amy, Ryan. BS, Marquette U., 1970, JD, 1972. Bar: Wis. 1972, U.S. Dist. Ct. (ea. and we. dists.) Wis. 1972; cert. elder law atty. 1995; CPA, 1975. Ptnr. Demark Kolbe Brodek & Crawford, Racine, Wis., 1972-81, Stewart, Peyton, Crawford, Crawford & Stut, Racine, 1981—. pres. Racine Jaycees, 1979-80. Mem. Rotary (Paul Harris fellow 1988). Avocation: travel. Real property, Estate planning, General corporate. Office: 840 Lake Ave Ste 200 Racine WI 53403-1566

**CRAWFORD, WILLIAM MATTERSON,** lawyer; b. Bremerton, Wash., June 12, 1945; s. Harold Pritchard and Elsie Henrietta (Graber) C.; m. Marilyn Yvonne Mikkola; children: Matthew Alexander, Elizabeth Anne. BA in Polit. Sci., Wash. State U., 1967; JD, U. Wash., 1972. Bar: Wash. 1972, U.S. Dist. Ct. (we. dist.) Wash. 1973, U.S. Dist. Ct. (ea. dist.) Wash. 1979, U.S. Ct. Appeals (9th cir.) 1980, U.S. Supreme Ct. 1980. Assoc. James Munro, Atty. at Law, Bremerton, 1972-79; ptnr. Kimbrough, Everett & Crawford, Grandview, Wash., 1979-80, Crawford, McGilliard, Peterson, Yelish & Dixon, Port Orchard, Wash., 1980—; bd. mem. Kitsap County Pro Bono Bd., Bremerton, 1990-94; co-chair Leadership Conf., Wash. State Bar Assn., 1994. Mem. Kitsap County Coun. Alcoholism, Bremerton, 1982-88; mem. budget com. South Kitsap Sch. Dist., Port Orchard, 1989-93, mem. facilities rev. com., 1992. With USN, 1970-72. Recipient Merit award Kitsap County Vol. Atty. Svc., Bremerton, 1990-94. Mem. Kitsap County Bar Assn. (pres. 1993-94). Lutheran. Avocations: sailboat racing, reading, woodworking, skiing. General civil litigation, Criminal, Family and matrimonial. Office: Crawford McGilliard Peterson Yelish & Dixon 623 Dwight St Port Orchard WA 98366-4619

**CRAWFORD, WILLIAM WALSH,** retired consumer products company executive; b. Clearwater, Fla., Oct. 7, 1927; s. Francis Marion and Frances Marie (Walsh) C. B.S., Georgetown U., 1950; LL.B., Harvard, 1954. Bar: N.Y. 1955, Ill. 1972. Assoc. Sullivan & Cromwell, N.Y.C., 1954-58; counsel Esso Standard Oil, N.Y.C., 1958-60; ptnr. Alexander & Green, N.Y.C., 1960-71; v.p., gen. counsel Internat. Harvester Co., Chgo., 1971-76; v.p., gen. counsel, sec. Internat. Harvester Co., 1976-80; sr. v.p. gen. counsel Kraft, Inc., Glenview, Ill., 1980-81; sr. v.p., gen. counsel, sec. Dart & Kraft, Inc., 1981-86; sr. v.p., gen. counsel, sec. Kraft, Inc., 1986-88, sr. v.p., sec., 1988-89, ret., 1989. Mem. ABA, Ill. Bar Assn., Assn. Bar City N.Y., Am. Judicature Soc., Am. Law Inst., Assn. Gen. Counsel, Chgo. Club, River Club (N.Y.C.), Beach Club, Everglades Club, Old Guard Soc. Palm Beach Golfers.

**CRAWSHAW, DONALD R.,** lawyer; b. Hamilton, Ont., Can., 1957. BA, U. Toronto, Ont., 1979, LLB, 1982; LLM, Columbia U., 1983. Bar: N.Y. 1984. Ptnr. Sullivan & Cromwell, N.Y.C. General corporate, Finance, Mergers and acquisitions. Office: Sullivan & Cromwell 125 Broad St Fl 28 New York NY 10004-2489

**CRAWSON, SUSAN SMITH,** lawyer; b. San Antonio, June 17, 1967; d. Bernard Harold Jr. and Barbara Ann (Seremet) Smith; m. Robbie Lee Crawson, July 5, 1997. Student, Vassar Coll., 1985-86; BA, Hampshire Coll., 1989; student, Trinity Coll., Dublin, Ireland, 1992; JD, Suffolk U., 1993. Bar: Mass. 1993, D.C. 1995. Assoc. M.O.S.E.S., Boston, 1994-97; labor rels. rep. Mass. Bd. Trial Advocates, Boston, 1997—. Trustee Lawyers Alliance for Justice in Ireland, Denville, N.J., 1993-97, regional coord., 1997—; observer Peacewatch Ireland, Jamaica Plain, Mass., 1995. Mem. Mass. Bar Assn., Therapy Dog Internat. Office: MBTA Labor Rels 10 Park Plz Ste 1 Boston MA 02116-3975

**CREAGAN, DAVID JOHN,** federal official; b. Lorain, Ohio, Jan. 12, 1954; s. James Malcolm and Mareta Catherine (Traxler) C.; m. Janet Lynne Haight, Dec. 6, 1980; children: Arielle Denise, Rachel Aileen. BA, U. Notre Dame, 1974; MA, U. Chgo., 1981. Vice-consul U.S. Embassy Dept. of State, Santo Domingo, Dominican Republic, 1982-83, econ. officer U.S. Embassy, 1983-84; polit. officer U.S. Embassy Dept. of State, Budapest, Hungary, 1984-86; ops. officer Exec. Secretariat Dept. of State, Washington, 1986-87, staff officer Exec. Secretariat, 1987-88; spl. asst. The Sec. State, Washington, 1988-89; dep. sect. chief Office of Security and Polit. Affairs, Bur. European Affairs, U.S. Dept. of State, Washington, 1989—. Mem. Am. Fgn. Svc. Assn. Roman Catholic. Avocations: fly fishing, skiing, sailing. Office: Harkins Cunningham 2800 One Commerce Sq Philadelphia PA 19103

**CREASMAN, WILLIAM PAUL,** lawyer; b. Washington, Dec. 6, 1952; s. Paul and Esther B. (Tucker) C.; m. S. Teresa Deese, Aug. 18, 1973; 3 children. BA, Johns Hopkins U., 1974; JD, Wake Forest U., 1977. Bar: N.C. 1977, U.S. Dist. Ct. (mid. dist.) N.C. 1978, Ark. 1992. Asst. trust officer First Citizen's Bank & Trust Co., Raleigh, N.C., 1977-78; atty. Wrangler div. Blue Bell Inc., Greensboro, N.C. and Brussels, Belgium, 1978-83; sr. corp. atty. Hardee's div. Imasco USA Inc., Rocky Mount, N.C., 1983-84; asst. gen. counsel Imasco USA Inc., Rocky Mount, N.C., 1985-87; gen. counsel Church's Fried Chicken, San Antonio, 1984-85; sr. v.p., gen. counsel TCBY Enterprises, Inc., Little Rock, Ark., 1987—; panelist Am. Arbitration Assn., Dallas, 1988—; adj. prof. U. Ark. Sch. Law, Little Rock, . Mem. N.C. Bar Assn., Ark. Bar Assn. Antitrust, Contracts commercial, Labor. Home: 12 Barber Dr Maumelle AR 72113-6481 Office: TCBY Enterprises Inc 1200 TCBY Tower Capitol And Broadway Little Rock AR 72201

**CREATURA, MARK A.,** lawyer; b. Conn., 1959. AB, Harvard U., 1980; JD, U. Calif., Berkeley, 1985. Bar: Calif. 1985. Atty. Troy & Gould, L.A., 1985-93; v.p., gen. counsel Urethane Technologies, Inc., Santa Ana, Calif., 1993-96; sr. v.p., gen. counsel Consumer Portfolio Svcs., Inc., Irvine, Calif., 1996—. Finance, Securities. Office: Consumer Portfolio Svcs Inc 16355 Laguna Canyon Rd Irvine CA 92618-3801

**CREBBIN, ANTHONY MICEK,** lawyer, retired military officer; b. Columbus, Neb., Sept. 10, 1952; s. Harry and Donna Mae (Micek) C. BA, Rockhurst Coll., 1974; JD, St Louis U., 1977; LLM, JAG's Sch., 1989. Bar: Mo. 1977, U.S. Ct. Mil. Appeals 1980, Hawaii 1987, U.S. Supreme Court 1989. Commd. 2d lt. USMC, 1978, advanced through grades to maj., 1986; trial counsel USMC, Cherry Point, N.C., 1979, officer legal assistance, def. counsel, 1980, chief trial counsel, 1982; chief def. counsel USMC, Kaneohe Bay, Hawaii, 1986-87, chief legal assistance, 1987-88, staff judge adv. marine amphibious unit, 1980-81, 84-85; mil. judge USMC, Camp Pendleton, Calif., 1989-92, Saudi Arabia, 1991; dep. staff judge adv. Camp Pendleton, Calif., 1992-95; judge adv. 3d Marine Air Wing, Miramar, Calif., 1995-97; ret. Mem. ABA, Mo. Bar Assn., Hawaii Bar Assn., Assn. Trial Lawyers Am., Phi Alpha Delta. Democrat. Roman Catholic. Avocations: marathoning, scuba diving, snow skiing. Criminal, Military.

**CREECH, JAY HEYWARD,** lawyer; b. Richmond, Va., Nov. 26, 1956; s. Cecil Knight and Eleanor Longard (Tinkham) C.; m. Laura Mattausch Bosseler, Apr. 30, 1988. BS, U. Md., 1979, JD, 1982. Bar: Md. 1982, U.S. Dist. Ct. Md. 1983, U.S. Ct. Appeals (4th cir.) 1985, U.S. Supreme Ct. 1986. Law clk. to presiding justice Md. Cir. Ct. (7th cir.), Upper Marlboro, 1982-83; asst. state's atty. Prince George's County, Upper Marlboro, 1983-90, assoc. county atty., 1990—. Mem. ABA, Md. Bar Assn., Prince George's County Bar Assn., Nat. Dist. Atty.'s Assn., Md. State's Atty.'s Assn. Democrat. Methodist. Avocations: computers, skiing, tennis, camping, photography. Office: Prince Georges County Office Law County Adminstrn Bldg Ste 5121 Upper Marlboro MD 20772

**CREED, CHRISTIAN CARL,** lawyer, investigator; b. Alexandria, La., Oct. 31, 1963; s. George Alton and Mickey (Svebek) C.; m. Catherine Campbell, Aug. 12, 1995. BA, La. State U., 1985; JD, Loyola U., New Orleans, 1995. Bar: La. 1995, U.S. Dist. Ct. (we., mid., and ea. dists.) La. 1995, U.S. Dist. Ct. (no. and so. dists.) Miss. 1998, U.S. Ct. Appeals (5th cir.) 1995. Assoc. Boles, Boles & Ryan, Monroe, La., 1995-98; mng. ptnr. Creed & Creed, Monroe, La., 1998—. Author, contbg. editor (newsletter) Young Lawyers Newsletter, 1997-98. Mem. adv. bd. Salvation Army, Monroe, 1997—; mem. cabinet United Way, Monroe, 1998-99. Mem. ABA, La. Bar Assn., 4th Jud. Dist. Ct. Bar Assn. (exec. com.), Baton Rouge Bar Assn., La. Trial Lawyers Assn. (bd. govs.), Am. Inns of Ct. (Fred Fudickar chpt. 1995—), Rotary, Phi Delta Phi (life mem.). E-mail: law@creedlaw.com. Personal injury, Real property, Family and matrimonial. Office: Creed & Creed 1811 Tower Dr Ste C Monroe LA 71201-4964

**CREEKMORE, DAVID DICKASON,** lawyer, educator; b. Knoxville, Tenn., Aug. 8, 1942; s. Frank Benson and Betsey (Beeler) C.; 1 child, Walton N.; m. Betty Jo Huffaker, May 1998; stepchildren: Seth Huffaker, Zach Hufaker, Christy White. LLB, U. Tenn., 1965, JD, 1966; grad., Judge Adv. Gen.'s Sch., 1979, Army Command Gen. Staff Sch., 1985. Bar: Tenn. 1966, U.S. Supreme Ct. 1970, U.S. Ct. Mil. Appeals 1985. Law clk. Gen. Session Ct. Knox County, Knoxville, Tenn., 1963-66; judge divsn. II, Gen. Sessions Ct. Knox County, Knoxville, 1972-86; asst. county atty. Knox County, Knoxville, 1966-70; ptnr. Creekmore, Thomson & Hollow, Knoxville, 1966-72, Walter, Regan & Creekmore, Knoxville, 1993-97; pvt. practice Knoxville, 1986-93, 97-98; dep. law dir. Knox County, Knoxville, 1998—; instr. criminal law and evidence Walters State Coll., Morristown, Tenn., 1974-80, U. Tenn., 1982-89. Committeeman Knox County Rep. Com., 1970—; active Tenn. Hist. Assn., Blount Mansion Assn. Lt. Col. JAGC, USAR, 1997. Mem. ABA, FBA, Tenn. Bar Assn., Tenn. Judges Conf. (v.p. 1976-78), Knox Bar Assn., Res. Officers Assn. (pres. 1989-91), Am. Legion (post judge adv. 1984-87), Studebaker Drivers Assn. (pres. 1992-97), Masons, Shriners, Elks, Eagles, Lions. Home: 11530 Midhurst Dr Knoxville TN 37922-4768 Office: Knox County Law Dept 612 City-County Bldg 400 W Main St Knoxville TN 37902-2405

**CREENAN, KATHERINE HERAS,** lawyer; b. Elizabeth, N.J., Oct. 7, 1945; d. Victor Joseph and Katherine Regina (Lederer) Petervary; m. Edward James Creenan; 1 child, David Heras. BA, Newark State Coll., 1968; JD, Rutgers U., 1984. Bar: N.J. 1984, Maine, 1996, U.S. Dist. Ct. N.J. 1984, U.S. Ct. Appeals (3d cir.), 1998. Various teaching positions including, Union and Stanhope, N.J., 1968-81; law clk. to presiding judge Superior Ct. of N.J. Appellate Div., Newark, 1984-85; assoc. Lowenstein, Sandler, Kohl, Fisher & Boylan, Roseland, N.J., 1985-88, Kirsten, Simon, Friedman, Allen, Cherin & Linken, Newark, 1988-89, Whitman & Ranson, Newark, 1989-93; sr. atty. Whitman Breed Abbott & Morgan LLP, Newark, 1993-99; assoc. Skadden, Arps, Slate, Meagher & Flom LLP, Newark. Mem. ABA, N.J. State Bar Assn., Union County Bar Assn., Essex County Bar Assn. General civil litigation, General corporate. Office: Skadden Arps Slate Meaghar & Flom LLP 1 Newark Ctr Newark NJ 07102-5297

**CREHAN, JOSEPH EDWARD,** lawyer; b. Detroit, Dec. 8, 1938; s. Owen Thomas and Marguerite (Dunn) C.; m. Sheila Anderson, Nov. 6, 1965; children: Kerry Marie, Christa Ellen. A.B., Wayne State U., Detroit, 1961; J.D., Ind. U., 1965. Bar: Ind. 1965, Mich. 1966, U.S. Supreme Ct. 1984. Pvt. practice Detroit, 1966-68; assoc. Louisell & Barris (P.C.), 1968-72; ptnr. Fenton, Nederlander, Dodge, Barris & Crehan (P.C.), 1972-74, Barris & Crehan (P.C.), 1975-88; pvt. practice Bloomfield Hills, Mich. and Naples, Fla., 1977—. Mem. Am. Trial Lawyers Assn. Roman Catholic. Personal injury, Federal civil litigation, General practice. Home and Office: 827 Bentwood Dr Naples FL 34108-8204

**CREHORE, CHARLES AARON,** lawyer; b. Lorain, Ohio, Sept. 15, 1946; s. Charles Case and Catherine Elizabeth Crehore; 1 child, Charles Case II. BA, Wittenberg U., 1968; postgrad., U. Mich., 1968-69, Cleve. State U., 1972-73; JD, U. Akron, 1976; diploma mgmt. mgrs. program, Pa. State U., 1983. Bar: U.S. Patent Office 1975, Ohio 1976, U.S. Dist. Ct. (no. dist.) Ohio 1976, U.S. Ct. Appeals (6th cir.) 1976, U.S. Ct. Appeals (D.C. cir.) 1977, U.S. Tax Ct. 1977, U.S. Supreme Ct. 1980, U.S. Ct. Appeals (fed. cir.) 1982. Assoc. chemist B.F. Goodrich Co., Akron, 1969-70, chemist, 1970-72, sr. chemist, 1972, patent atty. trainee, 1972-74, sr. patent atty. trainee, 1974-75, patent assoc., 1975-76, patent atty., 1976-79; atty. regulatory affairs The Lubrizol Corp., Wickliffe, Ohio, 1979-81; corp. counsel environment, health and safety The Lubrizol Corp., Wickliffe, 1981-85, sr. corp. counsel, 1985-94, counsel, 1994—; guest lectr., moot ct. judge Case Western Res. U., 1983—; spkr. environ. regulations in Ohio seminar Calif. Inst. Bus. Law, 1991; adv. bd. applied environ. mgmt. program Lake Erie Coll., 1991-94. Kennedy Found. grantee, 1968-69; Delta Sigma Phi Found. scholar, 1968-69. Mem. ABA, Cleve. Internat. Law Assn., Environ. Law Inst., Industry Coun. on Environ., Safety and Health (adv. panel 1987-95), Phi Alpha Delta. Trademark and copyright, General corporate, Environmental. Home: PO Box 466 Wickliffe OH 44092-0466 Office: 29400 Lakeland Blvd Wickliffe OH 44092-2201

**CREIM, JERRY ALAN,** lawyer; b. Chattanooga, Oct. 20, 1956; s. James Mond and Claire Sylvia Creim; m. Sarah McNeel Hrobsky, Mar. 25, 1983; children: Daniel, Elizabeth. BA, Emory U., 1978; JD cum laude, U. Puget Sound, Tacoma, 1981. Bar: Wash. 1981, U.S. Dist. Ct. Wash. 1984, U.S. Ct. Appeals (9th cir.) 1984. Law clk. to chief judge Wash. State Ct. Appeals, Seattle, 1981-83; assoc. Williams, Kastner & Gibbs PLLC, Seattle, 1983-89, ptnr., 1990—. Fellow Am. Coll. Mortgage Attys.; mem. Bldg. Owners and Mgrs. Assn. (assoc.; course instr. 1993-95). Avocations: fly fishing, fly tying, golf. Real property, General corporate, Mergers and acquisitions. Office: Williams Kastner & Gibbs PLLC 601 Union St Ste 4100 Seattle WA 98101-1368

**CREITZ, DANIEL DALE,** lawyer; b. Iola, Kans., Feb. 13, 1959; s. Daniel Edward and Jeannene Ann (Brazil) C.; m. Shaila Jean Marcy, Aug. 6, 1983; children: Daniel, Aubrey. AA, Allen County Coll., 1979; BS, Emporia State U., 1982; JD, Washburn U., 1985. Bar: Kans. 1985, U.S. Dist. Ct. Kans. 1985. Legal intern Shawnee County Dist. Atty., Topeka, 1984-85; atty. Hines, Ahlquist, Creitz P.A., Erie, Kans., 1985—; city atty. Erie, 1990—. Pres. Beantown Boosters, Erie, 1993-94. Mem. Nat. Assn. Criminal Def. Lawyers, Kans. Assn. Criminal Def. Lawyers. Methodist. Avocations: golf, coaching children in sports, travel. Office: Hines Ahlquist Creitz PA 301 S Main St Erie KS 66733-1438

**CREMER, LEON EARL,** federal agent, lawyer; b. Cin., Dec. 30, 1945; s. Walter H. and Beatrice (Campbell) C. BS, Calif. State U., 1973; MA, George Washington U., 1976; JD, Rutgers U., 1982. Bar: Pa. 1982. Officer U.S. Secret Svc., Washington, 1975-77; spl. agt. U.S. Bur. Alcohol Tobacco and Firearms, U.S. Dept. Treasury, Phila., 1977-83, FBI, U.S. Dept. Justice, N.Y.C., 1983—. With U.S. Army, 1968-69. Mem. ABA, FBI Agts. Assn., Phila. Bar Assn., Pa. Bar Assn., Am. Trial Lawyers Assn., Internat. Platform Assn., Am. Mensa Soc. Avocations: yachting, aviation, skiing, tennis, long-distance running. Office: FBI 26 Federal Plz New York NY 10278-0127

**CREMER, RICHARD ANTHONY,** lawyer; b. Portland, Oreg., Aug. 3, 1950; s. Cornelius Vincent and Madeleine Josephine (Avena) C.; m. Teresa Ann Headrick, Oct. 1, 1988. BS, Portland State U., 1972; JD cum laude, Lewis & Clark Coll., 1975. Bar: Oreg. 1975, U.S. Dist. Ct. Oreg. 1979. Law clk. Judge Phillip Roth, Portland, Oreg., 1976; staff Pub. Defender's Office, Roseburg, Oreg., 1976-94; pvt. practice Roseburg, 1995—; bd. dirs. Dist. 6 Manpower, Roseburg, 1975. Commr., pres. City of Roseburg Planning Commn., 1977-87; mem. Eagle Scout Bd. of Rev., Roseburg, 1980—; referee Douglas County Football Officials, Roseburg, 1990—. Mem. Nat. Assn. Criminal Defense Lawyers (bd. dirs.), Oregon Criminal Defense Lawyers (pres. 1988-89). Avocations: skiing, bicycling, mountain climbing, hiking. Criminal, Family and matrimonial. Office: 727 SE Cass Ave # 400 Roseburg OR 97470-4982

**CREMINS, WILLIAM CARROLL,** lawyer; b. Virginia Beach, Va., Nov. 13, 1957; s. James Smyth and Mary Louise (Gallagher) C.; m. Kelly Robin Knapp, July 6, 1985; children: William Carroll Jr., Robert Gallagher. BA, BJ, U. Mo., 1980; JD, St. John's U., 1984. Bar: Tenn. 1984, N.Y. 1985, U.S. Dist. Ct. (ea. dist.) Tenn., U.S. Ct. Appeals (6th cir.). Assoc. Law Offices of J.D. Lee, Knoxville, Tenn., 1984-85; pvt. practice, Knoxville, 1986—. Dep. nat. organizer Ancient Order of Hibernians in Am., Inc., Tenn., 1985, pres. James Dardis divsn., 1997, 98; bd. dirs. Florence Crittenton Agy. of Knoxville, Inc., 1989-96, pres., 1995; Little League baseball coach, 1993-97, football coach, 1987, 1993-94, soccer coach, 1992, 1995. Recipient Pro Bono award Knoxville Bar Assn. Vol. Legal Assistance Program, 1992. Mem. ATLA (Advocate recognition 1994), ABA, Tenn. Bar Assn., Knoxville Bar Assn., Tenn. Trial Lawyers Assn. Roman Catholic. Fax: (865) 546-1394. Personal injury, Family and matrimonial, General civil litigation. Home: 710 Saint John Ct Knoxville TN 37922-1556 Office: 810 Henley St Knoxville TN 37902-2901

**CRENSHAW, MARVA LOUISE,** lawyer; b. DeFuniak Springs, Fla., Sept. 21, 1951; d. Lewis and Helen (Anderson) Crenshaw; m. Norman P. Campbell, Dec. 30, 1977; children: Kalinda I., Kamaria A. BS in Polit. Sci. with honors, Tuskegee Inst., Ala., 1973; JD, U. Fla., Gainesville, 1975. Bar: U.S. Dist. Ct. (mid. dist.) Fla., 1978, U.S. Ct. Appeals (11th cir.) 1978. Asst. state's atty. Dade County State's Atty. (Fla.), Miami, 1976-78; mng. atty. Bay Area Legal Services, Tampa, Fla., 1978-84, dep. dir., 1984-89; cons. tng. adv. com. Fla. Legal Service, Tallahassee, 1982-84; judge Hillsborough County Ct., 1989—. Vice pres. bd. dirs. Suicide and Crises Ctr., Tampa, 1983-84, pres., 1984-85, also mem. aux.; tutor Literacy Volunteers of Am. Mem. ABA, Hillsborough County Bar Assn. (chmn. county ct. civil rules com. 1984-85, mem. mock trial com. 1987-88, bulletin com. 1988-89, law week com. 1990, gender and ethnic bias implementation com. 1991—), Fla. Bar Assn., George Edgecomb Bar Assn., Nat. Inst. Trial Advocacy, Hillsborough Assn. for Women Lawyers (bd. dirs. 1991-92, 96-98), William Glenn Terrell Inns of Ct. (pres. 1995-96), Athena Soc. (bd. dirs. 1997—), Fla. Bar Found. (mem. LAP com. 1991-92, bd. dirs. 1995—), Acad. Holy Names (mem. bd. trustees, 1995—), Tuskegee Alumni Club (v.p. 1997—), Athena Soc. (bd. dirs. 1997-98), Delta Sigma Theta (legal advisor local chpt. 1988-89). Democrat. Baptist. Home: 14522 Wessex St Tampa FL 33625-6619

**CREPEAU, DEWEY LEE,** lawyer, educator; b. Richmond Heights, Mo., June 3, 1956; s. Dewey Lee and Floy Evelyn (Lacefield) Crapo; m. Susan Jane Stonner, July 15, 1978; children: Elizabeth, Courtney. AB, U. Mo., 1977, JD, 1980. Bar: Mo. 1980, U.S. Dist. Ct. (we. dist.) Mo. 1980, U.S. Ct. Appeals (8th cir.) 1984. Assoc. William Johnson, P.C., Versailles, Mo., 1980-81; asst. prosecutor Morgan County, Mo., 1980; legal aid atty. Mid-Mo. Legal Services Corp., Columbia, 1981; pvt. practice Columbia, 1982—; adj. prof. criminal justice Columbia Coll., 1983-84; adj. prof. bus. law U. Mo., 1988-90. Active Christian Fellowship of Columbia. Mem. Mo. Bar Assn., Boone County Bar Assn., Nat. Orgn. Social Security Claimants' Reps., Order Barristers. Workers' compensation, Pension, profit-sharing, and employee benefits. Home: 212 Bright Star Dr Columbia MO 65203-0279 Office: 2501 W Ash St Columbia MO 65203-4609

**CRESCENZI, ARMANDO A.,** lawyer, real estate broker; b. N.Y.C., June 28, 1962; s. Gene and Nelly-Theresa (Brandt) C.; m. Virginia Felix, Nov. 17, 1990; children: Armando, Uziel, Amarissa. BA, Lehman Coll./CUNY, Bronx, 1991; JD, Pace U., White Plains, N.Y., 1994. Bar: N.Y. 1994. Sole practitioner Bronx, 1994—. 2d lt. U.S. Army, 1985-91. Real property. Office: 660 E Fordham Rd Bronx NY 10458-5020

**CRESSEY, BRYAN CHARLES,** venture capitalist; b. Seattle, Sept. 28, 1949; s. Charles Ovington and Alice Lorraine (Serry) C.; m. Christina Irene Petersen, Aug. 19, 1972; children: Monique Joy, Charlotte Lorraine, Alicia Lin. BA, U. Wash., 1972; MBA, Harvard U., 1976, JD, 1976. Bar: Wash. 1976, Ill. 1977. Sr. investment mgr. First Chgo. Investment Corp., Chgo., 1976-80; prin. Golder, Thoma, Cressey, Fauner, Inc., Chgo., 1980—; prnt. Thoma, Cressey Equity Ptnrs., 1998—; chmn., bd. dirs. Cable Design Techs., Inc.; bd. dirs. Paging Network, Inc., Am. Habilitation, Inc., Houston, Assistive Tech., Ill., Clarion tech., Ill., Select Med., Harrisburg, Pa., Boston. Author: (theatrical play) Explosions. Bd. dirs. Infant Welfare Soc., Chgo., 1984—, Jr. Achievement, Chgo. Home: 500 W County Line Rd Barrington IL 60010-9629 Office: Thoma Cressey Equity Partners 4400 Sears Tower Chicago IL 60606

**CREW, WILLIAM LUNSFORD,** lawyer; b. Pleasant Hill, N.C., Oct. 29, 1917; s. James Winfield and Texas S. Crew; m. Nancy H. Crew, Nov. 14, 1940 (divorced); m. Dorothy Salter. BA, U. N.C., 1939, LLB, 1941. Pvt. practice Roanoke Rapids, N.C., 1941—; atty. Halifax (N.C.) County Dept. Social Svcs., 1972—, City of Roanoke Rapids, 1977-97. State senator State of N.C., 1953-65. Lt. USN, 1943-46. Mem. ABA, N.C. Acad. Trial Lawyers, N.C. Bar Assn. Democrat. Avocations: hunting, fishing. General practice. Office: W Lunsford Crew PO Box 160 Roanoke Rapids NC 27870-0160

**CREWS, GLENNA ENGLAND,** lawyer; b. Abilene, Tex., Apr. 14, 1949; d. Rudolph and Imo D. England; m. Delbert Lester Bruns, Aug. 24, 1968 (div. Sept. 1983); children: Victoria Elyse Bruns Tackett, Travis Byron Bruns; m. Dennis Keith Crews, Oct. 3, 1992; 1 child, Emily Kate. BS in Math/Spanish Secondary Edn., U. Houston, 1970, JD, 1992. Bar: Tex. 1992, U.S. Ct. Appeals (5th, 6th cirs.), U.S. Dist. Ct. (no., so. dists.) Tex. Tchr. Klein Ind. Sch. Dist., Houston, 1971-91; assoc. Weil, Gotshal & Manges, Houston, 1992-95, Broocks, Baker & Lange, Houston, 1995, Verner, Liipfert, Bernhard, McPherson & Hand, Houston, 1996—. Contbr. articles to profl. jours. Mem. Houston Bar Assn., Fifth Cir. Bar Assn., Houston Law Rev. Alumni Assn. (bd. dirs. 1999—). Avocations: painting, outdoor activities. Bankruptcy, Appellate, Contracts commercial. Office: Verner Liipfert Bernhard McPherson & Hand 1111 Bagby St Ste 4700 Houston TX 77002-2543

**CREWS, GRASTY, II,** lawyer; b. Richmond, Va., Jan. 22, 1927; s. John Grasty and Susie Boyd (Roberts) C.; m. Pauline Elizabeth Heermance, June 3, 1952; children John Grasty, Peter Thornton. Student, Stevens Inst. Tech., 1946-49; LLB, U.Va., 1952. Bar: Va. 1952, U.S. Dist. Ct. (we. dist.) Va. 1954, U.S. Ct. Appeals (D.C. cir.) 1952, U.S. Supreme Ct. 1971, U.S. Ct. Appeals (fed. cir.) 1980, U.S. Dist. Ct. (ea. dist.) Va. 1989. Pvt. practice N.Y., D.C. and Va., 1952-56, Falls Church, Va., 1979—; mem. Office Legisl. Counsel, U.S. House of Reps., 1958-70, Legal Div. Bd. Govs. Fed. Reserve System, 1971; gen counsel Spl. Action Office for Drug Abuse Prevention, Exec. Office of the Pres., 1972-75; counsel Com. on Banking, Fin. and Urban Affairs, U.S. House of Reps., 1975-79. Editorial Bd. Va. Law Review. Mem. Va. State Bar. Probate, General practice. Home: 4762 26th St N Arlington VA 22207-2653 Office: 210 E Broad St Falls Church VA 22046-4505

**CREWS, WILLIAM EDWIN,** lawyer; b. Cin., Oct. 29, 1944; s. Donald Luther and Mary Ruth (Gardiner) C. BA, Miami U., Oxford, Ohio, 1966; JD with honors, George Washington U., 1969. Bar: Ohio 1971, Ga. 1978, U.S. Dist. Ct. (no. dist.) Ga. 1978, U.S. Ct. Appeals (11th cir.) 1978. Assoc. Hausser & Atkinson, Marietta, Ohio, 1971-74; asst. counsel Union CommerceBank, Cleve., 1974-76; asst. corp. counsel Trust Co. Ga., Trust Co. Bank Atlanta, 1976-84; assoc. corp.counsel Trust Co. Ga., Trust Co. Bank, Atlanta, 1984-94; sr. atty. SunTrust Banks, Inc., Atlanta, 1994—. Mem. ABA, State Bar Ga. Banking, Contracts commercial, Finance. Home: 2460 Peachtree Rd NW Apt 1411 Atlanta GA 30305-4158 Office: SunTrust Banks Inc 25 Park Pl NE Atlanta GA 30303-2900

**CRIBARI, ARNOLD DAVID,** lawyer; b. Mt. Vernon, N.Y., Nov. 20, 1951; s. Arnold David and Idaehla Short Cribari; m. Shawn Kennedy, Aug. 5, 1978; children: Maria Kennedy, David Joseph. BA, Columbia Coll., 1973; JD, Union U., 1976. Bar: N.Y. 1977, U.S. Dist. Ct. (ea. and so. dists.) N.Y. 1978. Assoc. Kahn & Goldman, Esq., White Plains, N.Y., 1976-77; pvt. practice White Plains, 1977-85, 91-97; ptnr. Cribari & Fletcher, Esq., White Plains, 1985-91, Goldman & Cribari, P.C., White Plains, 1997—. Mem. N.Y. State Bar Assn., Yorktown Bar Assn. (bd. dirs. 1981-85, 94-97, treas. 1991-92, pres. 1992-93), Westchester County Bar Assn. (mem. profl. econs. com. 1993—), Atty. Client Fee Dispute Com. Avocations: model railroading, songwriting, playing and coaching basketball. Family and matrimonial. Home: 2611 Darnley Pl Yorktown Heights NY 10598-2921 Office: Goldman and Cribari PC 175 Main St White Plains NY 10601-3105

**CRIEGO, FRANZ ANDRE-MARIE,** defender; b. L.A., May 31, 1950; s. John Erskin Criego-Surrindjur and Atinal Nadija C. BA, Calif. State U., L.A., 1973; MSW, Calif. State U., Sacramento, 1975; JD, Northrop U., 1980. Bar: Calif. 1981, U.S. Tax Ct. 1981; cert. specialist criminal law Calif. State Bar, 1989. Client rights advocate Regional Ctr. Orange County, Calif., 1971-81; pvt. practice L.A., 1982-83; mng. atty. Jacoby & Meyers, Inglewood, Calif., 1983-84; dept. pub. defender Merced (Calif.) Pub. Defender's Office, 1984-89; def. counsel Fresno (Calif.) Pub. Defender's Office, 1989-92, sr. dept., 1992—. Avocations: horseback riding. Office: Fresno County Pub Def 2220 Tulare St Fresno CA 93721-2106

**CRIGLER, B. WAUGH,** federal judge; b. Charlottesville, Va., July 17, 1948; s. Bernard Weaver and Jayne (Waugh) C.; m. Anne Kendall, June 20, 1970; children: C. Kendall, Jason C., Anne Stuart. BA in History, Washington & Lee U., 1970; JD, U. Tenn., 1973. Bar: Tenn. 1973, U.S. Dist. Ct. (ea. dist.) Tenn. 1973, Va. 1974, D.C. 1974, U.S. Dist. Ct. (we. and ea. dists.) Va. 1975, U.S. Ct. Appeals (4th cir.) 1978, U.S. Supreme Ct. 1979. Law clk. to presiding judge U.S. Dist. Ct. Tenn., Knoxville, 1973-74; ptnr. Lea & Crigler, Culpeper, Va., 1974-75, Lea, Davies, Crigler & Barrell, Culpeper, 1975-79, Davies, Crigler, Barrell & Will, PC, Culpeper, 1979-81; magistrate judge U.S. Dist. Ct., Charlottesville, 1981—; instr. trial practice Sch. Law, U. Va., 1986—; mem. criminal rules adv. com. Jud. Conf. U.S., 1992-97; mem. Fed.-State Jud. Coun., Va., 1992—. Mem. ABA (criminal law com. young lawyers divsn. 1974-80), Thomas Jefferson Inn of Ct. (pres. 1991-92), Va. State Bar (standing com. on professionalism 1997—), Va. Bar Assn. (chmn. criminal law corrections young lawyers divsn. 1979-80), Tenn. Bar Assn., Order of Coif, Phi Kappa Phi. Avocations: landscaping, swimming, Biblical studies. Home: 100 Peterson Pl Charlottesvle VA 22901-3175 Office: US Magistrate Judge 255 W Main St Rm 328 Charlottesville VA 22902-5058

**CRILLINE, JOHN FRANCIS,** lawyer; b. Providence, Aug. 7, 1938; s. John B. and Lucy S. Crilline; m. Sabra Peskin, Dec. 5, 1956; children: John, Roberta, David, Susan, Stephanie. BA, Providence Coll., 1960; LLB, Suffolk U., 1964. Bar: R.I., U.S. Dist. Ct. R.I., U.S. Ct. Appeals (1st cir.). Rsch. dir. Legis. Coun., R.I., 1960-64; adminstrv. asst. to mayor City of Providence, 1964-68; pvt. practice, Providence, 1968—; instr. R.I. Jr. Coll., 1983-93. Criminal. Home: 54 Palm Beach Ave Narragansett RI 02882-4439 Office: 381 Atwells Ave Providence RI 02909-1026

**CRINION, GREGORY PAUL,** lawyer; b. Eau Claire, Wis., Feb. 19, 1959; s. Harlan D. and Shirley P. (Paff) C. BBA cum laude, U. Wis., Eau Claire, 1981; MBA, U. Minn., 1982; JD cum laude, U. Wis., 1985. Bar: Wis. 1985, Tex. 1985, D.C. 1987, Colo. 1994, U.S. Dist. Ct. (we. dist.) Wis. 1985, U.S. Dist. Ct. (so. dist.) Tex. 1985, U.S. Ct. Appeals (5th cir.) 1985, U.S. Dist. Ct. (ea. dist.) Tex. 1986, U.S. Ct. Appeals (7th cir.) 1986, U.S. Dist. Ct. (we. dist.) Tex. 1989, U.S. Dist. Ct. (no. dist.) Tex. 1990, U.S. Supreme Ct. 1989. Atty. Exxon Co., U.S.A., Houston, 1985-87, Exxon Corp., N.Y.C., 1987; assoc. Dotson, Babcock & Scofield, Houston, 1987-89; assoc. Jackson & Walker, Houston, 1990-93, ptnr., 1993-97; ptnr. Citti & Crinion, L.L.P., Houston, 1997-99; shareholder Ashby & Whitmire, P.C., Houston, 1999—. Cons. Jr. Achievement, Houston, 1988. Recipient Scroll of Appreciation U.S. Army, Fed. Republic of Germany, 1984. Mem. ABA, Houston Bar Assn., San Antonio Bar Assn., Profl. Ski Instrs. Avocations: profl. ski instr., bicycling. Federal civil litigation, Environmental, State civil litigation. Office: Ashby & Whitmire PC 1002 Gemini Ste 116 Houston TX 77058

**CRISLIP, STEPHEN RAY,** lawyer; b. Oak Hill, W.Va., Apr. 23, 1948; s. Raymond Brooks and Virginia Lucille Crislip; m. Melinda Lee White, Mar. 6, 1976; children: Brooks H., Seth M. BA in Polit. Sci., W.Va. U., 1970, JD, 1973. Bar: W.Va. 1973, U.S. Dist. (no. and so. dists.) W.Va. 1973, U.S. Dist. Ct. (ea. dist.) Ky. 1974, U.S. Ct. Appeals (4th cir.) 1987. Assoc. Jackson, Kelly, Holt & O'Farrell, Charleston, W.Va., 1973-80; ptnr. Jackson & Kelly, Charleston, 1980—; mem. vis. com. W.Va. Coll. Law, 1997—. Bd. dirs. Greater Kanawha Valley Found., Charleston, 1996—; chmn. bd. dirs. YMCA, Charleston, 1997-98. Mem. ABA, Assn. Def. Trial Attys. (exec. coun. 1992-95, nat. membership chair 1998—), Def. Trial Attys. W.Va. (pres. 1997), W.Va. Bar Assn., Kanawha County Bar Assn., Def. Rsch. Inst. Republican. Methodist. General civil litigation, Personal injury, Professional liability. Office: Jackson & Kelly 1600 Laidley Tower Charleston WV 25301-2189

**CRISPI, MICHELE MARIE,** lawyer; b. Neptune, N.J., Mar. 10, 1962; d. Michael and Mary (Vaccaro) C.; m. Lawrence J. Moloney. BS in Accountancy magna cum laude, Villanova U., 1984, JD, 1987, LLM in Taxation, 1989. Bar: N.J. 1988, U.S. Dist. Ct. N.J. 1988, D.C. 1989, U.S. Tax Ct. 1989. Assoc. Lampf, Lipkind, Prupis & Petigrow, West Orange, N.J., 1987-88, Lautman, Henderson & Wight, Manasquan, N.J., 1990-97; pvt. practice Sea Girt, N.J., 1997—. Mem. ABA (bus. law, real property, probate and trust law, taxation and gen. practice sects., solo and small firm and law practice mgmt. sects.), N.J. State Bar Assn. (corp. and bus. law, real property, probate and trust law, elder law, taxation and gen. practice sects.), D.C. Bar Assn. (taxation sect.), Monmouth County Bar Assn., Phi Kappa Phi, Beta Gamma Sigma, Gamma Phi. Republican. Roman Catholic. Avocations: tennis, swimming. Estate planning, General practice, Real property. Home: 32 Hunters Pointe Rd Middletown NJ 07748-5148 Office: 2164 Hwy 35 Bldg C Ste 8 PO Box 424 Sea Girt NJ 08750-0424

**CRISTE, VIRGINIA SPIEGEL,** lawyer; b. Chgo., Feb. 7, 1944; d. Gerhard and Hilde (Fabian) S.; m. Michael A. Criste, Feb. 7, 1970 (div. Dec. 1995); children: Michael J., Julia. BA, Mt. Holyoke Coll., 1966; JD, George Washington U., 1969. Bar: Calif. 1977, D.C. 1969, Md. 1971, Pa. 1976, U.S. Dist. Ct. (mid. dist.) Pa., U.S. Dist. Ct. Md., U.S. Dist. Ct. (ctrl. dist.) Calif., U.S. Ct. Appeals (D.C. and 9th cirs.). Atty. Neighborhood Legal Svcs., Washington, 1969-71; assoc. county atty. Prince George's County, Md., 1971-74; sr. atty. Ctrl. Pa. Legal Svcs., Lancaster, 1974-79, Inland Counties Legal Svcs., Indio, Calif., 1979-81; assoc. Robert Stewart Law Corp., Palm Desert, Calif., 1981-84; ptnr. Mack, Kahn, Criste, Palm Springs, Calif., 1984-86, Criste Criste & Pippin, Palm Desert, 1991-94; sole practitioner Palm Desert, 1982-84, Rancho Mirage, Calif., 1986-91, 94—. Mem. Parks and Recreation Commn., Palm Desert, 1994-97. Mem. ABA, Desert Bar Assn. (trustee to pres. 1990-97). Avocations: historical research, musical theater. Family and matrimonial. Home: 44047 Erie Ct Indian Wells CA 92210-7200 Office: 45-200 Club Dr # B Indian Wells CA 92910

**CRISTOL, A. JAY,** federal judge; b. Fountain Hill, Pa., Feb. 25, 1929; s. Samuel and Mae (Stein) C.; m. Eleanor Rubin; children: Stephen Michael, David Alan. BA, U. Miami, 1958, LLB, 1959, PhD, 1997. Bar: Fla. 1959. Spl. asst. to Atty. Gen. of Fla. Tallahassee, 1959-65; sr. ptnr. Cristol, Mishan, Sloto, Miami, 1959-85; judge U.S. Bankruptcy Ct., Miami, 1985-93; chief judge, 1994-99; trustee U.S. Bankruptcy Ct., Miami, 1982-84; adj. prof. U. Miami Law Sch.; bd. govs. 11th cir. Nat. Conf. Bankruptcy Judges; bankruptcy rules adv. com. Jud. Conf. of U.S., 1995; bankruptcy com. U.S. Ct. Appeals (11th cir.), 1996-98; tchr. bankruptcy law to judges in Czech Republic, Slovenia, Thailand, Russia, India, Malaysia, Hong Kong, South Africa. Bd. trustees U. Miami, 1988-90, Coral Gables; bd. dirs. ARC, Miami, 1989-97. Capt. USNR, 1951-89. Fellow Am. Coll. Bankruptcy; mem. ABA, Am. Bankruptcy Inst., Nat. Conf. Bankruptcy Judges, Fla. Bar Assn., Dade County Bar Assn. Avocations: water skiing, windsurfing, flying, reading. Office: US Bankruptcy Ct 1412 Fed Bldg 51 SW 1st Ave Miami FL 33130-1669

**CRITCHLOW, RICHARD H.,** lawyer; b. Pitts., Mar. 28, 1947; s. John Park and Ruth Lauderbaugh C.; m. Deirdre Lynn Flower, Feb. 18, 1979; children: Courtney Leigh, Caitlin Anne. BA in Polit. Sci., Union Coll., 1969; JD, U. Miami, 1973. Bar: Fla., 1973, U.S. Supreme Ct., 1976, U.S. Tax Ct., 1978, U.S. Dist. Ct. (ea. dist.) La. 1980, U.S. Dist. Ct. (so. dist.) Fla. 1973, U.S. Dist. Ct. (mid. dist.) Fla. 1978, U.S. Ct. Appeals (5th and 11th cirs.) 1973. Assoc. Tew, Tew, Rosen & Murray, Miami, Fla., 1973-76; ptnr. Tew & Tew, Miami, Fla., 1976-77, Tew, Critchlow, Sonberg, et al, Miami, Fla., 1977-82, Finley, Kumble, Wagner, Underberg, Manley & Casey, Miami, Fla., 1982-88; mng. ptnr. McDermott, Will & Emery, Miami, Fla., 1988-91; ptnr. Kenny, Nachwalter, Seymour, Arnold & Critchow, Miami, Fla., 1991—; arbitrator Nat. Assn. Securities Dealers, Miami, 1988—. Active United Way of Miami, 1991. Mem. ABA (vice-chmn. TIPS 1985-87), Fla. Bar Assn. (chmn. grievance com. 1987-90). Republican.

Congregational. General civil litigation, State civil litigation, Securities. Office: Kenny Nachwalter Seymour Arnold & Critchow 201 S Biscayne Blvd Miami FL 33131-4332

**CRITELLI, CHRISTOPHER WILLIAM,** lawyer; b. Lake Success, N.Y., June 28, 1959; s. Louis and Rosemarie (Tusa) C.; m. Roseanne Perrotta, Sept. 1, 1985; children: Jacqueline Rose, Christopher Louis,. BA, Adelphi U., 1981; JD, Bklyn. Law Sch., 1985. Bar: N.Y. 1986, U.S. Dist. Ct. (ea. dist.) 1987. Pvt. practice Garden City, N.Y., 1987—; gen. counsel for estate planning Benjamin Securities, Hicksville, N.Y., 1989—, Harbourview Ctr., Inc., Syosset, N.Y., 1991-92; adj. prof. Court Reporting Inst., Hicksville, 1990-91. Guest lectr. churches and sr. citizen groups. Mem. Nat. Acad. Elder Attys., N.Y. State Bar Assn. (elder law sect. and matrimonial law sect.), Nassau County Bar Assn. (mem. trusts and estate com. 1990—, matrimonial com. 1990—). Republican. Roman Catholic. Avocations: golf, bicycling. Estate planning, Family and matrimonial, Entertainment. Office: 999 Franklin Ave Garden City NY 11530-2913

**CRITELLI, MICHAEL J.,** lawyer, manufacturing executive; b. 1948. BA, U. Wis., 1970; JD, Harvard U., 1974. Bar: Ill. 1974, N.Y. 1982. Assoc. Ross & Hardies, Chgo., 1974-76, Schwartz & Freeman, Chgo., 1976-79; counsel Pitney Bowes, Inc., 1979-83, sr. counsel, 1983-84, asst. gen. counsel, 1984-86, assoc. gen. counsel, 1986-88, v.p., sec., gen. counsel, 1988, chief personnel officer, 1990-94, vice chmn., 1994—, chmn., CEO, 1996—. Antitrust, General corporate, Private international. Office: Pitney Bowes Inc World Hdqrs Location 5001 1 Elmcroft Rd Stamford CT 06926-0700

**CRITES, RICHARD DON,** lawyer; b. Ft. Worth, Sept. 3, 1943; s. Ewell Barnett Crites and Frances Loretta (Prichard) Castro; m. Annabel Lee Sheilds, June 17, 1964 (div. 1975); children—Amy Lee, Jonathon Peter; m. Judith Jean Gildig, May 30, 1976 (div. 1996); children—Kimberly Ann, Kevin John. B.S., Ariz. State U., 1965; J.D., U. Ariz., 1968. Bar: Ariz. Assoc., Knez & Glatz, Tucson, 1968-73; ptnr. Knez, Glatz & Crites, Tucson, 1973-78; chief counsel City Utilities, Springfield, Mo., 1978-79; sole practice, Springfield, 1979—; referee Pima County Juvenile Ct., Tucson, 1972-76. Contbr. articles to law revs. Recipient Excellence in Ins. Law award Bancroft-Whitney Co., 1967, Excellence in Criminal Law award, 1968. Mem. Greene County Bar Assn., Mo. Bar Assn., ABA. Republican. Presbyterian. Lodges: Elks, Shriners, Optomists, Royal Order of Jesters. Personal injury, Workers' compensation, Labor. Home and Office: 1909 E Bennett St Springfield MO 65804-1419

**CRIVELLI, FRANK MICHAEL,** lawyer; b. Trenton, N.J., July 19, 1969; s. James Vincent and Josephine C.; m. Annamaria Arpaia Crivelli, Sept. 14, 1996; children: Giancarlo, Rafaielle. BA, Washington Coll., 1991; JD, CUNY, 1994. Bar: Ga. 1994, N.J. 1994, Pa. 1994, U.S. Dist. Ct. N.J. 1994, U.S. Mil. Ct. 1995. Atty. Brotman & Graziano P.C., Trenton, 1998—; instr. U.S. Naval Acad., Annapolis, Md., 1995; prof. Ctrl. Tex. Coll., Camp Pendleton, Calif., 1995-97. Capt. USMCR, 1991—, judge advocate, 1995-98. Home: 1 Jared Dr Robbinsville NJ 08691-2525 Office: Brotman & Graziano PC 3685 Quakerbridge Rd Trenton NJ 08619-1207

**CRIZER, CELESTE LISANNE,** lawyer; b. Gary, Ind., June 26, 1964; d. Donald Oliver Crizer Jr. and Vahona Joan (Fryar) Walta. BA in Psychology and Sports Medicine, Denver U., 1986, JD, 1990. Bar: Colo. 1990, U.S. Dist. Ct. Colo. 1992. Figure skating instr. Denver U., North Jefferson County Ice Arena, Denver, 1984-88; intern Storage Tech. Corp., Louisville, Colo., 1989, Colo. Atty. Gen.'s Office, Denver, 1989, Arapahoe County Pub. Defender, Denver, 1990; law clk. Grant, McHendrie, Haines & Crouse, Denver, 1988-90; law clk. to Hon. Alan Sternberg, Chief Judge Colo. Ct. Appeals, Denver, 1990-91; assoc. Cooper & Kelley, P.C., Denver, 1991-92; jr. ptnr. J. Gregory Walta, P.C., Colorado Springs, Colo., 1992-95, ptnr., 1995—. Coord. Legal-Med. Substance Use Prevention Program, Colorado Springs, 1993—. Recipient Hoffman Cup (champion trial moot ct. competition) Denver U., 1989. Mem. Colo. Bar Assn. (young lawyers exec. coun. 1994—), El Paso County Bar Assn. (chair young lawyers 1994-95, women lawyers 1992—, treas. 1996—, Bryan S. Gardner Outstanding Young Lawyer award 1995), Psi Chi, Delta Gamma. Episcopalian. Avocations: cross-country and downhill skiing, bicycling, mountain climbing, roller blading, (was competitive figure skater 10 yrs.). Personal injury, Criminal, General civil litigation. Home: 2032 N Cleveland Ave Chicago IL 60614-4503 Office: J Gregory Walta PC 620 S Cascade Ave Ste 101 Colorado Springs CO 80903-4050

**CROAK, FRANCIS R.,** lawyer; b. Janesville, Wis., Feb. 19, 1929; s. Francis Joseph and Virginia (Blakey) C.; m. Susan Nolte, Aug. 15, 1953 (dec.); m. 2d, Judith Torbenson, Apr. 30, 1976; children: Carolyn, Martha, Daniel, David, Joseph. BS, U. Wis., 1950, JD, 1953. Bar: Wis. 1953, U.S. Ct. Appeals (7th cir.) 1960, U.S. Supreme Ct. 1980. First asst. dist. atty. Milwaukee County, Wis., 1956-60; ptnr. Cook & Franke S.C., Milw., 1960—; lectr. in law Marquette U., 1972-74, U. Wis., 1973-78. Mem. Wis. Jud. Coun., 1971-82. Pres. Greater Milw. Open, 1995—. Served to 1st lt. U.S. Army, 1953-56; to col. USAR, 1956-80. Fellow Am. Coll. Trial Lawyers; mem. Am. Law Inst. Democrat. Clubs: Milwaukee Athletic, Westmoor Country. Federal civil litigation, Environmental. Home: 12555 W Grove Ter Elm Grove WI 53122-1974 Office: 660 E Mason St Milwaukee WI 53202-3830

**CROAKE, PAUL ALLEN,** lawyer; b. Janesville, Wis., Sept. 1, 1947; s. Willard m. and Dorothy R. Croake; children: Katherine, John Paul, Patrick. BA, Lawrence U., 1969; JD, U. Wis., 1972. Bar: Wis. 1972, U.S. Dist. Ct. (we. dist.) Wis. 1972, U.S. Tax Ct. 1982. Lawyer DeWitt Ross & Stevens S.C., Madison, Wis., 1972-99. Capt. U.S. Army, 1969-80. Mem. ABA, Madison Club. Roman Catholic. Avocations: tennis, golf. Contracts commercial, Taxation, general, Insurance. Office: 2 E Mifflin St Ste 600 Madison WI 53703-2865

**CROCKER, CHARLES ALLAN,** lawyer; b. Waco, Tex., May 26, 1940; s. Wiley Vernon and Edith Mae Crocker; m. Mary Ann Herndon, Sept. 1, 1962; children: Cathryn Ann, Amy Lynn. BBA, Tex. Tech. U., 1962; LLB, U. Tex., 1965. Bar: Tex. 1965, U.S. Tax Ct. 1979, U.S. Dist. Ct. (so. dist.) Tex. 1980, U.S. Ct. of Appeals (fed. cir.) 1984, U.S. Claims Ct. 1981; cert. estate planning and probate. Estate tax examiner IRS, Houston, 1965-72; acct. Peat, Marwick, Mitchell, Houston, 1972-74; atty. Baker & Botts, Houston, 1974-86, Hendricks Mgmt. Co., Houston, 1986-87; pvt. practice Houston, 1987—; dir. Houston Estate and Fin. Forum, 1976-80, Pinnacle Mgmt. and Trust Co., Houston, 1996—. Mem. Winedale (Tex.) Adv. Coun., 1997—. Mem. ABA, Houston Bar Assn. (probate sect.). Avocations: golf, skiing. Estate planning, Probate, Estate taxation. Office: 2001 Kirby Dr Ste 1100 Houston TX 77019-6081

**CROCKER, MICHAEL PUE,** lawyer; b. Bel Air, Md., July 23, 1918; s. Henry Trew and Berthenia Stansbury (Pue) C.; m. Rosa Tucker Fletcher, June 11, 1945; children: Forest Fletcher, Berthenia Stansbury, Rosa Tucker. BA cum laude, Washington and Lee U., 1940; LLB, U. Va., 1947. Bar: Md. 1947, U.S. Dist. Ct. Md. 1948, U.S. Ct. Appeals (4th cir.) 1951, U.S. Supreme Ct. 1967, D.C. 1982. Assoc. Marbury, Miller & Evans, Balt., 1947-55; ptnr. Piper & Marbury, Balt., 1955-83; sole practice, Bel Air, Md., 1983—. Trustee Md. Children's Aid and Family Svc. Soc., 1967-77. Served with USMC, 1942-45, PTO; to maj. USMCR, 1945-57. Decorated Purple Heart, three battle stars (Bougainville, Guam, Iwo Jima). Mem. Maritime Law Assn. U.S., Jud. Conf. U.S., (4th Jud. Cir., permanent mem.), Balt. City Bar Assn., Md. State Bar Assn., Bar Assn. D.C., Harford County Bar Assn., ABA, ATLA, Phi Beta Kappa, Phi Delta Phi. Episcopalian. General civil litigation, Condemnation, Insurance. Home and Office: 1326 Somerville Rd Bel Air MD 21015-5817

**CROCKER, MYRON DONOVAN,** federal judge; b. Pasadena, Calif., Sept. 4, 1915; s. Myron William and Ethel (Shoemaker) C.; m. Elaine Jensen, Apr. 26, 1941; children—Glenn, Holly. A.B., Fresno State Coll., 1937; LL.B., U. Calif. at Berkeley, 1940. Bar: Calif. bar 1940. Spl. agt. FBI, 1940-46; practiced law Chowchilla, Calif., 1946-58; asst. dist. atty. Madera County, Calif., 1946-51; judge Chowchilla Justice Ct., 1952-58, Superior Ct. Madera County, 1958-59; U.S. judge Eastern Dist. Calif., Sacramento, 1959—, now sr. judge. Mem. Madera County Republican Central Com., 1950—. Named Outstanding Citizen Chowchilla, 1960. Mem. Chowchilla C. of C. (sec.). Lutheran. Club: Lion. Office: US Dist Courthouse 1130 O St Rm 5007 Fresno CA 93721-2201

**CROCKER, PATRICK DAVID,** lawyer, consultant; b. Kalamazoo, Sept. 21, 1964; s. David Gene and Doris Marie Crocker; m. Krista Kathleen Grabowski, Dec. 2, 1995; 1 child, David James. BA, U. Mich., 1986; JD, U. Detroit, 1989. Bar: Mich. 1989. Ptnr. Early, Lennon, Peters & Crocker, Kalamazoo, 1989—. Mem. Telecom. Resellers Assn., Kalamazoo Country Club. Communications. Office: Early Lennon Peters Et Al 900 Comerica Bldg Kalamazoo MI 49007-4719

**CROFT, TERRENCE LEE,** lawyer; b. St. Louis, Apr. 13, 1940; s. Thomas L. and Anita Belle (Brown) C.; m. Merry Patton, July 9, 1977; children: Michael, Shannon, Kimberly, Kristin, BethAnn, Katherine. AB, Yale U., 1962; JD with distinction, U. Mich., 1965. Bar: Mo. 1965, U.S. Dist. Ct. (ea. dist.) Mo. 1965, Ga. 1970, Fla. 1970, U.S. Dist. Ct. (no. dist.) Ga. 1970, U.S. Ct. Appeals (5th, 8th and 11th cirs.) 1970, U.S. Supreme Ct. Assoc. Coburn, Croft & Kohn, St. Louis, 1965-69, Hansell, Post, Brandon & Dorsey, Atlanta, 1969-73; ptnr. Huie, Sterne & Ide, Atlanta, 1973-78, Kutak, Rock & Huie, Atlanta, 1978-83; shareholder Griffin, Cochrane & Marshall, Atlanta, 1983-93; ptnr. King & Croft LLP, Atlanta, 1994—. Mem. ABA (ho. of dels. 1994—), ATLA, Atlanta Bar Assn. (pres., sec., treas. bd. dirs. 1986—, chmn., bd. dirs. litigation sect. 1982-86, pres. Alt. Dispute Resolution Lawyers sect. 1996-97), Atlanta Bar Found. (pres. 1998—), Ga. Trial Lawyers Assn., Lawyers Club Atlanta. Episcopalian. Avocations: hiking, shooting, motorcycling, reading. E-mail: tlc@king-croft.com. Fax: 404-577-8401. General civil litigation, Construction, Alternative dispute resolution. Home: 2580 Westminster Heath NW Atlanta GA 30327-1449 Office: King & Croft LLP 707 The Candler Bldg 127 Peachtree St NE Atlanta GA 30303-1810

**CROLAND, BARRY I.,** lawyer; b. Paterson, N.J., Jan. 11, 1938; s. Louis L. and Rae R. (Levine) C.; m. Joan Kohlreiter, Dec. 20, 1958; children: Richard, Heidi, Lizabeth, Jennifer. BA, Middlebury Coll., 1959; JD, Rutgers U., Newark, 1961. Bar: N.J. 1962, N.Y. 1983, U.S. Ct. Appeals (3d cir.) 1973. Law clk. to Hon. John Grimshaw N.J. Superior Ct., 1961, law clk. to Hon. Morris Pashman, 1961-62; assoc. Cole, Berman & Garth, Paterson, 1962-63, Shavick, Thevos, Stern, Schotz & Steiger, Paterson, 1963-68; ptnr. Shavick, Stern, Schotz, Steiger & Croland, Paterson, 1968-79, Stern, Steiger, Croland, Tanenbaum & Schielke, Paterson, 1979-95, Shapiro & Croland, Hackensack, N.J., 1995—; asst. bar examiner State of N.J., 1965-68; mem. Fed. Ethics Com., Dist. of N.J., 1975—; lectr. Inst. for Continuing Legal Edn., Trial Advocacy and Family Law, 1975—. Mem. bd. editors Rutgers Law Rev., 1959-61, case editor, 1960-61; sr. editor N.J. Family Lawyer. Fellow Am. Acad. Matrimonial Lawyers; mem. ABA (family law sect.), Am. Coll. Family Trial Lawyers (diplomate 1994—), Am. Inns of Ct. (master Morris Pashman 1990-95, pres.-master N.J. family law 1995—), N.J. State Bar Assn. (mem. exec. com. family law sect. 1981-95), Bergen County Bar Assn. (chmn. jud. and prosecutorial appts. com. 1983-95). Family and matrimonial. Home: 243 Myrtle St Haworth NJ 07641-1137 Office: Shapiro & Croland 411 Hackensack Ave Hackensack NJ 07601-6328

**CROLLETT, RICHARD JACQUES,** lawyer; b. Albuquerque, Oct. 13, 1944; s. Fred Robert and Prudence Ann C.; m. Florence Dolores Crollett, Nov. 14, 1964; children: Roxane, Ronda, Deborah. BA, U. N.Mex., 1971, JD, 1974. Bar: N.Mex. 1976, U.S. Dist. Ct. Atty. Albuquerque, 1976—; dir.-at-large Workers' Compensation Assn., Albuquerque, 1998;. Eucharistic minister, 1993—; sec. Serra Club for Religious Vocations, 1991—, 100 Club for Religious Vocations, 1993—. Sgt. USAF, 1963-67. Recipient HEROICS award (Helping Everyone Reach Out in Cmty. Svc.) Coronado Ctr., Albuquerque, 1997. Democrat. Avocations: church activities, hunting, fishing. Workers' compensation, Personal injury, State civil litigation. Home and Office: 12600 Elyse Pl SE Albuquerque NM 87123-3808

**CROMARTIE, ERIC ROSS,** lawyer; b. Washington, Jan. 14, 1955; s. William Adrian and Dorothy Jane (Cann) C.; m. Lynn Prendergast, Sept. 12, 1981; children: William Ross, Morgan Nicole. BA, Amherst (Mass.) Coll., 1977; JD, Harvard U., 1980. Bar: Tex. 1980, U.S. Dist. Ct. (no. and ea. dists.) Tex. 1980, U.S. Tax. Ct. 1983, U.S. Ct. Appeals (5th and 11th cirs.) 1980, U.S. Ct. Appeals (8th and 10th cirs.) 1984, U.S. Supreme Ct. 1985. Assoc. Hughes and Luce, Dallas, 1980-85, ptnr., 1985-97. Mem. ABA, Dallas Bar Assn., Am. Law Inst. General civil litigation. Home: 6724 Avalon Ave Dallas TX 75214-3703

**CROMER, CHARLES LEMUEL,** lawyer, state legislator; b. High Point, N.C., Jan. 27, 1939; s. Charles Norman and Wilma (Duggins) C.; m. Sheila Whitlow, Oct. 8, 1966; children: Tonja Dawn, Ashley Nicole. AA, Sandhills Community Coll., Pinehurst, N.C., 1973; BA with hons., U. N.C., 1973; JD cum laude, Wake Forest U., 1975. Bar: N.C. 1975, U.S. Ct. Appeals (4th cir. 1977). Tchr. law Davidson County Community Coll., Lexington, N.C., 1975-84; prin. Charles L. Cromer, Atty. at Law, Thomasville, N.C., 1975-90; elected mem. N.C. House Reps., 1984-90; legis. counsel Gov. Jim Martin, 1990-94; mem. various legis. study commns., 1985—; Rep. Whip Ho. ofReps., 1989—, del. Rep. Nat. Conv., 1988. Exec. mem. Republican Party, N.C., 1982—. Served with U.S. Army, 1962-65. Mem. N.C. Acad. Trial Lawyers, High Point Assn. Retarded Citizens (Legislator of Yr. 1985, Parent of Yr. 1987). Methodist. Avocation: reading. State civil litigation, Legislative, Criminal. Home and Office: 503 Center Pointe Dr Cary NC 27513-5731

**CROMLEY, BRENT REED,** lawyer, legal association administrator; b. Great Falls, Mont., June 12, 1941; s. Arthur and Louise Lilian (Hiebert) C.; m. Dorothea Mae Zamborini, Sept. 9, 1967; children: Brent Reed Jr., Giano Lorenzo, Taya Rose. AB in Math., Dartmouth Coll., 1963; JD with honors, U. Mont., 1968. Bar: Mont. 1968, U.S. Dist. Ct. Mont. 1968, U.S. Ct. Appeals (9th cir.) 1968, U.S. Supreme Ct. 1978, U.S. Ct. Claims 1988, U.S. Ct. Appeals (D.C. cir.) 1988. Law clk. to presiding justice U.S. Dist. Ct. Mont., Billings, 1968-69; assoc. Hutton & Sheehy and predecessor firms, Billings, 1969-77, ptnr., 1977-78; ptnr. Moulton, Bellingham, Longo & Mather, P.C., Billings, 1979—, also bd. dirs.; mem. Montana Ho. Reps., 1991-92; pres. State Bar Mont., 1998-99. Contbr. articles to profl. jours. Mem. Yellowstone Bd. Health, Billings, 1972—; chmn. Mont. Bd. Pers. Appeals, 1974-80. Mem. ABA (appellate practice com.), ACLU, Internat. Assn. Def. Counsel, State Bar Mont. (chmn. bd. trustees 1995-97, trustee 1991—, pres. 1998-99), Yellowstone County Bar Assn. (various offices), Internat. Assn. Defense Counsel, Christian Legal Soc., Internat. Brotherhood of Magicians, Kiwanis. Avocations: running, magic, pub. speaking. E=mail: Cromley@moultonlawfirm.com. General civil litigation, General practice. Home: 235 Parkhill Dr Billings MT 59101-0660 Office: Moulton Bellingham Longo & Mather PC 27 N 27th St Ste 1900 Billings MT 59101-2343 also: State Bar Montana PO Box 577 Helena MT 59624-0577

**CROMLEY, JON LOWELL,** lawyer; b. Riverton, Ill., May 23, 1934; s. John Donald and Naomi M. (Mathews) C. BS, U. Ill., 1958; JD, John Marshall Law Sch., 1966. Bar: Ill. 1966. Real estate title examiner Chgo. Title & Trust Co., 1966-70; pvt. practice, Genoa, Ill., 1970—; mem. firm O'Grady & Cromley, Genoa, 1970-96; bd. dirs. Citizen's First Nat. Bank, 1984-92, Kingston Mut. Ins. Co., Genoa Main St., Inc. Mem. ABA, Am. Judicature Soc., Am., Ill. State Bar Assn., Chgo. Bar Assn., DeKalb County Bar Assn. Probate, Real property, General practice. Home: 130 Homewood Dr Genoa IL 60135-1260

**CROMWELL, JAMES JULIAN,** lawyer; b. Washington, Feb. 19, 1935; s. Stephen Clusky Cromwell and Phyllis Elaine Spooner; m. Barbara Lawrence Betts, Dec. 8, 1962 (dec. Nov. 1995); children: Elisabeth, James Jr., David C.; m. Louise Mathews, Dec. 13, 1997. BA, U. Va., 1956, LLB, 1959. Prin. Miles & Stockbridge, Rockville, Md., 1992—; chmn. Potomac Valley Bank, Gaithersburg, Md. Chmn. Nat. Rehab. Hosp., Washington, 1995-97. Fellow Am. Coll. Trial Lawyers (state chair 1993-94), Am. Coll. Estate and Trust Coun., Am. Law Insts. Avocation: golf. General civil litigation, Estate planning. Home: 8301 Hectic Hill Ln Rockville MD 20854-2602 Office: Miles & Stockbridge PC 22 W Jefferson St Rockville MD 20850-4215

**CRONAN, WILLIAM PATRICK,** lawyer; b. Columbia, Mo., Nov. 19, 1946; s. Patrick Daniel and Jean Wilma (Dearing) C.; m. Sara Frances Russell, June 8, 1974; 1 child, Sara Kathlene. BA, So. Meth. U., 1968; JD, U. Mo., 1978. Bar: Mo. 1973, U.S. Dist. Ct. (we. dist.) Mo. 1973. Ptnr. Cronan & Robinson, Columbia & Fayette, Mo., 1973—; prosecuting atty. Howard County, Mo., 1975-78; state and local govt. specialist U. Mo., Columbia, 1986-92. Mem. editorial staff Mo. Law Rev., 1973; contbr. numerous articles to legal newsletters in Mo. City atty. numerous Mo. cities. With U.S. Army,, 1969-71. Mem. Mo. Bar Assn., Am. Planning Assn., Pub Risk Mgmt. Assn., Order of Coif. Democrat. United Methodist. Avocation: flying. Home: 13750 W Highway Bb Rocheport MO 65279-9757 Office: Cronan & Robinson 306 N College Ave Columbia MO 65201-4973

**CRONIN, KEVIN BRIAN,** lawyer; b. Worcester, Mass., Sept. 2, 1943; s. Jeremiah Joseph and Julia Elizabeth (Alavosius) C.; m. Patti Adrienne Wright, May 1, 1971; 1 child, Kevin Brian. AB, U. Pa., 1965; JD, U. Wis., 1970, MA in Am. History, 1983, MA in Pub. Policy and Adminstrn., 1994. Bar: Wis. 1971, U.S. Dist. Ct. (we. dist.) Wis. 1971, U.S. Tax Ct. 1975, U.S. Dist. Ct. (ea. dist.) Wis. 1975, Hawaii 1979, U.S. Dist. Ct. Hawaii 1979, U.S. Ct. Appeals (9th cir.) 1980, U.S. Ct. Appeals (7th cir.) 1981. Vol. U.S. Peace Corps, Turkey, 1965-67; asst. dist. atty. Rock County, Beloit, Wis., 1970-73; pvt. practice Janesville & Hartford, Wis., 1974-78; trust officer First Hawaiian Bank, Honolulu, 1978-79; pvt. practice Honolulu, 1980; legal counsel Beloit Coll., 1981-83, Wis. Elections Bd., Madison, 1983-87; chief counsel Wis. dept. Employee Trust Funds, Madison, 1987-89; counsel Wis. Dept. Revenue, Madison, 1989-97; chief counsel elec. divsn. Pub. Svc. Commn. Wis., Madison, 1997—; trustee in bankruptcy U.S. Dist. Ct., We. Dist., 1974-77; rsch. asst. U. Wis., Madison, 1980; founder, chmn. bd. dirs., pres. Cronin Constrn. Co., Inc., Middleton, Wis., 1986—; mem. unemployment compensation adv. coun. Wis. Dept. Industry, Labor and Human Rels., Madison, 1992-94; counsel Implement Wis. State Interagy. Land Use Coun. Report, Madison, 1996-97; selectee, tax policy advisor U.S. Treasury Dept. to Min. of Fin. Republic of Armenia, 1997. Mem. Mayor's Com. on Crime Prevention, Hartford, 1977; bd. dirs. Hartford Area Day Care Ctr., 1977. Recipient Cert. of Commendation, Hartford City Coun., 1977. Mem. State Bar of Wis. (interim bd. dirs. energy and telecom. sect. 1998-99, sect. bd. dirs. 1999—), Hawaii Bar Assn., Hartford Area C. of C. (bd. dirs. 1977). Home: 1215 Boundary Rd Middleton WI 53562-3862 Office: Pub Svc Commn Wis PO Box 7854 Madison WI 53707-7854

**CROOK, CHARLES SAMUEL, III,** lawyer; b. Des Moines, Iowa, Oct. 24, 1944; s. Charles S. Jr. and Gertrude A. (Nichols) C.; children—Donald, Michael, Brian, Nicole. B.A., Drake U., 1969, J.D., 1971. Bar: Iowa 1971. Law clk. to chief dist. judge U.S. Dist. Ct. (so. dist.) Iowa, 1971-73; pros. atty. Polk County Atty.'s Office, Des Moines, 1973-76; ptnr. Beving, Swanson & Forrest, P.C., Des Moines, 1976-83; sole practice, 1983—; lectr. Des Moines Area Community Coll., 1979; assoc. prof. med. jurisprudence U. Osteo. Health Scis. Leader Cub Scouts Am., Des Moines. Served with U.S. Army, 1963-66. Mem. ABA, Iowa Bar Assn., Nat. Dist. Atty's. Assn., Polk County Bar Assn., Nat. Bd. Trial Advocacy (cert.). Democrat. Roman Catholic. Contbr. articles to profl. jours. General civil litigation, Workers' compensation, Administrative and regulatory. Home: PO Box 721 Des Moines IA 50303-0721 Office: Fleming Bldg 218 6th Ave Ste 1100 Des Moines IA 50309-4005

**CROOK, DONALD MARTIN,** lawyer; b. Wichita, Kans., Dec. 18, 1947; s. Leroy R. and Audrey E. (Mattiason). BA in History with honors, U. Kans., 1970; JD, U. Chgo., 1973. Bar: N.Y. 1974, Tex. 1982. Assoc. Kramer, Levin, Nessen, Kamin & Frankel, N.Y.C., 1973-75, Layton & Sherman, N.Y.C., 1975-80; counsel LTV Corp., Dallas, 1980-85; chief counsel corp. affairs Kimberly-Clark Corp., Dallas, 1985—, v.p., sec., 1986—. Mem. ABA, Dallas Bar Assn. (chmn. corp. counsel sect. 1986-87), Am. Soc. Corp. Secs. (securities law com.). Banking, General corporate, Mergers and acquisitions.

**CROOK, JENNIFER MARIE,** lawyer; b. Akron, Ohio, July 19, 1967; d. David J. and Carolyn M. Crook. BA, U. Mich., 1989; JD, Mich. State U., 1996; postgrad., NYU, 1998—. Bar: N.Y. 1997, U.S. Dist. Ct. (so. and ea. dists.) N.Y. 1997, D.C. 1998, U.S. Ct. Appeals (2nd and 5th cirs.) 1998. Assoc. Clifton, Budd & DeMaria, LLP, N.Y.C., 1996—. Mem. ABA (labor and employment sect. 1996-98), N.Y. State Bar Assn. (labor and employment sect. 1996-98). Labor. Office: Clifton Budd & DeMaria 420 Lexington Ave New York NY 10170-0089

**CROOK, RONALD R.,** lawyer; b. Butler, Calif., Oct. 26, 1946; s. Purvis L. and Neva B. C.; m. Carole S. Jones, Jan. 10, 1976 (div. Apr. 1986). BS, U. Ga., 1968; BS in Med. Technology, Med. Coll. Ga., 1969; M in Med. Sci., Emory U., 1975; JD, Cumberland Sch. Law, Birmingham, Ala., 1985. Bar: Ala. 1985, U.S. Dist. Ct. (no. dist.) Ala. 1985, U.S. Dist. Ct. (mid. dist.) Ala. 1990, U.S. Dist. Ct. (no. dist.) Miss. 1989; cert. med. technologist. Med. technologist Ga. Bapt. Hosp., Atlanta, 1971-76; tech. dir. USA Med. Ctr., Mobile, Ala., 1976-78; asst. prof. U. South Ala., Mobile, 1978-82; lawyer Hogan, Smith & Alspaugh, Birmingham, 1985—. Mem. ATLA, Ala. Trial Lawyers Assn. (bd. govs. 1990-98). Democrat. Unitarian. Personal injury, Product liability, General civil litigation. Office: Hogan Smith & Alspaugh 2323 2d Ave N Birmingham AL 35203

**CROOKS, N(EIL) PATRICK,** state supreme court justice; b. Green Bay, Wis., May 16, 1938; s. George Merrill and Aurelia Ellen (O'Neill) C.; m. Kristin Marie Madson, Feb. 15, 1964; children: Michael, Molly, Kevin, Kathleen, Peggy, Eileen. BA magna cum laude, St. Norbert Coll., 1960; JD, U. Notre Dame, 1963. Bar: Wis. 1963, U.S. Supreme Ct. 1969. Assoc. Cohen and Parins, Green Bay, 1963; ptnr. Cohen, Grant, Crooks and Parins, Green Bay, 1966-70; sr. ptnr. Crooks, Jerry, Norman and Dilweg, Green Bay, 1970-77; judge Brown County (Wis.) Ct., 1977-78, Brown County (Wis.) Cir. Ct., 1978-96; justice Wis. Supreme Ct., Madison, 1996—; instr. bus. law U. Wis., Green Bay, 1970-72; mem. faculty Wis. Jud. Coll., 1982. Editor Law Rev. Notre Dame, 1962-63. Pres. Brown County United Way, 1976-78; chmn. Brown County Legal Aid, 1971-73; mem. Northeast Criminal Justice Coord. Coun., 1973-85; pres. St. Joseph Acad. Sch. Bd., 1987-89. Capt. U.S. Army, 1963-66. Recipient Human Rights award Baha'i Community of Green Bay, 1971, Disting. Achievement award in Social Sci. St. Norbert Coll., 1977 award of Yr. U. Notre Dame, 1978, Brown County Vandalism Prevention Assn. award, 1982, W. Heraly MacDonald award Brown County United Way, 1983, Community Svc. award St. Joseph Acad., 1989, Alma Mater award St. Norbert Coll., 1992; named Wis. Trial Judge of the Year Wis. Chpt. Am. Bd. of Trial Advocates, 1994. Mem. ABA, FBA, State Bar Wis., Brown County Bar Assn. (pres. 1977), Wis. Acad. Trial Lawyers, Wis. Law Found. (bd. dirs., mem. exec. com.), Nat. Conf. of Appellate Ct. Judges, Assn. of Women Lawyers for Brown County, Dane County Bar Assn., James E. Doyle Am. Inn of Ct., Wis. Jud. Coun. Roman Catholic. Home: 5329 Lighthouse Bay Dr Madison WI 53704-1113 Office: PO Box 1688 231 East State Capitol Madison WI 53701

**CROONE, ERIC,** lawyer; b. Cleve., June 17, 1968; s. Arthur Wells and Mary Delores Croone. BA, Emory U., 1990; JD, U. Va., 1993. Bar: Ga. Assoc. Powell Goldstein Frazer & Murphy, Atlanta, 1993-95; sr. dir. bus. and legal affairs LaFace Records, Atlanta, 1995—. Vol. Big Bros. & Big Sisters, Atlanta, 1997—. Mem. ABA, Black Entertainment and Sports Lawyers Assn., Ga. Bar Assn., Omega Psi Phi. Entertainment. Office: LaFace Records 3350 Peachtree Rd NE Ste 1500 Atlanta GA 30326-1425

**CROSBY, ROBERT BERKEY,** lawyer; b. North Platte, Nebr., Mar. 26, 1911; s. Mainard E. and Cora M. (Berkey) C.; m. Elizabeth D. Ehler, Nov. 29, 1934; children—Robert M., Susan M. Smith, Mary Bolin, Michael, James Timothy, Frederick; m. 2d, LaVon K. Kehoe Stuart, May 22, 1971. B.A., U. Minn., 1931; LL.B., Harvard U., 1935. Bar: Nebr. 1935, U.S. Dist. Ct. Nebr. 1935, U.S. Ct. Appeals (8th cir.) 1970, U.S. Supreme Ct. 1970. Ptnr. Henry J. Beal, Omaha, 1936; ptnr. Crosby & Baskins, North Platte, Nebr., 1937-47, Crosby & Crosby, North Platte, 1948-54; sr. ptnr. Crosby, Guenzel, Davis, Kessner & Kuester, Lincoln, Nebr., 1955—; bd. dirs. Landmark Legal Found.; speaker State of Nebr. Legislature, 1943; lt. gov. State of Nebr., 1947-49, gov., 1953-55. Acting state chmn. Nebr. Republican Com., 1948, chmn. fin. com., 1972-73; chmn. bd. dirs. Nebr. Heart Assn., 1958-59. Served to lt. USNR, 1944-46. Mem. Am. Coll. Trial Lawyers, Nebr. Abr Assn., Lincoln Bar Assn., Am. Legion. Roman Catholic. Club:

Kiwanis. General corporate, Legislative, General practice. Home: 3440 Hillside St Lincoln NE 68506-5737 Office: Crosby Guenzel Davis Kessner & Kuester 400 Lincoln Benefit Bldg Lincoln NE 68508

**CROSBY, WILLIAM DUNCAN, JR.,** lawyer; b. Louisville, Sept. 1, 1943; s. William Duncan and Lucille (Edwards) C.; m. Constance Elaine Frederick, June 2, 1973; children: William Duncan III, Lelia Margaret. BA, Yale U., 1965; JD, Columbia U., 1968. Bar: Ky. 1968, U.S. Dist. Ct. D.C. 1971, U.S. Supreme Ct. 1977. Minority chief counsel Com. on Rules U.S. Ho. of Reps., Washington, 1972-94, chief counsel Com. on Rules, 1995-99; v.p., COO The Solomon Group, Washington, 1999—. Chmn. Dranesville Dist., Fairfax County (Va.) Rep. Party, 1987-89; mem. Fairfax County Rep. Com., 1981—. Lt. (j.g.) USNR, 1968-71. Mem. ABA, FBA, Ky. Bar Assn., D.C. Bar, Columbia Law Sch. Alumni Assn. of Washington (pres. 1987-89). Baptist. Avocation: swimming. Home: 920 Mackall Ave Mc Lean VA 22101-1618 Office: The Solomon Group 801 Pennsylvania Ave NW Ste 750 Washington DC 20004-2670

**CROSS, CHESTER JOSEPH,** lawyer, accountant; b. June 16, 1931; s. Chester Walter and Stephanie (Nowaczyk) Krzyzaniak. Student, Northwestern U., 1950-56, DePaul U., 1958-59; LLB, U. Ill., 1962. Bar: Ill. 1963, U.S. Dist. Ct. (no. dist.) Ill. 1963; CPA, Ill. 1957. Sr. acct. S.D. Leidesdorf & Co., Chgo., 1954-57, Hall, Penny, Jackson & Co., Chgo., 1957-58; contr. Comml. Discount Corp., Chgo., 1958-59; pvt. practice Oak Park and Chgo., Ill., 1963—; corp. dir. The Protectoseal Co. Mem. AICPA, Ill. State Bar Assn., Chgo. Bar Assn. (probate practice com., real property law com.), Ill. CPA Soc., East Bank Club (Al Lipman Black Shoe award 1989). Probate, Estate taxation, General corporate. Home: River's Edge at Sauganash 5320 N Lowell # 301 Chicago IL 60630 Office: PO Box 30339 Chicago IL 60630

**CROSS, DANIEL ALBERT,** lawyer; b. Moorhead, Minn., Jan. 30, 1965; s. Earl Stanley and Mary Theresa Cross; m. Michele Catherine Rini, June 6, 1992; 1 child, Siena Caterina. BA, Reed Coll., 1989; JD, Lewis and Clark Coll., 1993. Bar: Oreg. 1993. Talk show host KFXX Radio, Portland, Oreg., 1991-93; legal intern Saxon, Marquoit & Bertoni, Portland, Oreg., 1992-93; atty. Bertoni & Todd, Portland, Oreg., 1993—; judge mock trial competition Northwestern Sch. Law, Lewis and Clark Coll., 1994-97, mentor, 1997—. Mem., v.p. Order of Sons of Italy in Am., Beaverton, Oreg., 1997—. Mem. Oreg. State Bar, Oreg. Criminal Def. Lawyers Assn., Multnomah Bar Assn. Avocations: wine, literature (1st editions), blues music, gourmet food. Criminal, Juvenile, Appellate. Office: Bertoni and Todd 520 SW Yamhill St Ste 430 Portland OR 97204-1327

**CROSS, DAVID MARTIN,** lawyer; b. Albany, N.Y., Aug. 20, 1957; s. Perry Martin and Winnie Miller C.; m. Jennifer Hoover, Aug. 29, 1987; children: Terron Mae, Lora Marie Martin Hooven. AB, We. Ky. U., 1981; JD, U. Louisville, 1984. Bar: Ky. 1984, U.S. Dist. Ct. (we. dist.) 1984. Assoc. Wilson & Smith Attys., Jamestown, Ky., 1984-85; pvt. practice Albany, 1986—; domestic rels. commr. 40th Jud. Dist., Albany, 1995—; master commr. Clinton Cir. Ct., 1995—. Mem. exec. com. Clinton County Rep. Party, 1980-82, 86-88; pres. Albany Little League, 1997-98. General practice. Home: 508 W Wood St Albany KY 42602-1530

**CROSS, MILTON H.,** lawyer; b. Phila., July 28, 1942; s. Sidney B. and Edythe Cross; m. Joyce Volchok, June 4, 1966; children: Brian, Jonathon. BS, U. San Francisco, 1965; JD, Villanova U., 1968. Bar: Pa. 1968. Corp. counsel AEL, Inc., Phila., 1968-75; assoc. Cohen, Verlin, Sherzer & Porter, Phila., 1975-78; pvt. practice Phila., 1978-79; ptnr. Monteverde & Hemphill, Phila., 1980-96, Spector, Gadon & Rosen, Phila., 1996—; adj. prof. Phila. Coll. Textiles and Sci., 1970-73. Chmn. Cheltenham Twp. Sch. Bd. Authority. Mem. ABA (sect. corp., banking and bus. law), Pa. Bar Assn., Phila. Bar Assn. General corporate, Contracts commercial, Real property. Home: 251 Ironwood Cir Elkins Park PA 19027-1315 Office: Spector Gadon & Rosen 7 Penn Ctr 7th Fl Philadelphia PA 19103

**CROSS, THOMAS ROBERT,** lawyer; b. Flint, Mich., Apr. 12, 1942; s. Robert Henry and Ora Leone (Adams) C.; m. Patricia Ann Witham, July 31, 1970; children: Scott, Stephanie, Timothy. BA, U. Mich., 1965, JD, 1968. Bar: Colo. 1971, U.S. Dist. Ct. Colo. 1971. Mgmt. trainee Met. Life, Colorado Springs, Colo., 1968-71; pvt. practice, Colorado Springs, 1971-76; ptnr. Cross, Gaddis, Kin & Quicksall, P.C., Colorado Springs, 1976-96; pvt. practice Colorado Springs, 1996—. Mem. Colo. Supreme Ct. Nominating Commn., Denver, 1982-88. Chmn. El Paso County Dem. Party, Colorado Springs, 1974-76; bd. dirs. NAACP, 1981-82. Fellow Am. Bar Found., Colo. Bar Found.; mem. ABA, Colo. Bar Assn. (sr. v.p. 1986-87, pres. 1991-92), El Paso County Bar Assn. (pres. 1982-83), Colo. Trial Lawyers Assn., Colorado Springs C. of C. (bd. dirs. 1977-78). Democrat. Roman Catholic. Family and matrimonial. Office: 118 S Wahsatch Ave Colorado Springs CO 80903-3677

**CROSS, WILLIAM DENNIS,** lawyer; b. Tulsa, Nov. 7, 1940; s. John Howell and Virginia Grace (Ferrell) C.; m. Peggy Ruth Plapp, Jan. 30, 1982; children: William Dennis Jr., John Frederick. BS, U.S. Naval Acad., 1962; JD, NYU, 1969. Bar: N.Y. 1970, U.S. Dist. Ct. (so. and ea. dists.) N.Y. 1970, U.S. Ct. Appeals (2d cir.) 1970, U.S. Supreme Ct. 1974, Calif. 1977, U.S. Dist. Ct. (ctrl. dist.) Calif. 1977, U.S. Ct. Appeals (9th cir.) 1977, U.S. Ct. Appeals (5th, 10th and 11th cirs.) 1981, Mo. 1982, U.S. Dist. Ct. (we. dist.) Mo. 1982, U.S. Ct. Appeals (8th cir.) 1989, U.S. Ct. Appeals (fed. cir.) 1992, U.S. Dist. Ct. Ariz. 1997, U.S. Dist. Ct. Colo. 1997, U.S. Dist. Ct. Kans. 1998. Commd. ensign USN, 1962, advanced through ranks to lt., 1965, resigned, 1966; assoc. Cravath, Swaine & Moore, N.Y.C., 1969-76, Lillick, McHose & Charles, L.A., 1976-77; asst. gen. counsel FTC, Washington, 1977-82; of counsel Morrison & Hecker, Kansas City, Mo., 1982-83; ptnr. Morrison & Hecker, 1983—. Staff mem. NYU Law Rev., 1967-69, editor, 1968-69. Mem. ABA (vice-chair sports, labor and entertainment com., antitrust sect.), Calif. Bar Assn., Mo. Bar Assn., Assn. Bar City N.Y., Kansas City Bar Assn., Lawyers Assn. Kansas City. Federal civil litigation, Antitrust, Administrative and regulatory. Home: 1223 Huntington Rd Kansas City MO 64113-1347 Office: Morrison & Hecker 2600 Grand Blvd Kansas City MO 64108-4606

**CROTTY, ROBERT BELL,** lawyer; b. Dallas, Aug. 16, 1951; s. Willard and Betty (Bell) C.; m. Sarah Smith, Mar. 8, 1980; children: Robert Edwin, Rebecca Bell. BA, Va. Mil. Inst, 1973; JD, U. Tex., 1976. Bar: Tex. 1976, U.S. Dist. Ct. (no. dist.) Tex. 1977, U.S. Ct. Appeals (5th cir.) 1978. Assoc. Akin, Gump, Strauss, Hauer & Feld, Dallas, 1976-82, ptnr., 1983-92, hiring ptnr., 1988-91; prin. McKool Smith, P.C., Dallas, 1992-94; ptnr. Crotty & Johansen, L.L.P., Dallas, 1995—; bd. visitors Va. Mil. Inst., 1995-99. Mem. Leadership Dallas, 1981; dir. Salesmanship Club, 1989-90, 94-95, Va. Mil. Inst. Alumni Assn., 1991-95, Highland Park Ind. Sch. Dist. Edn. Found., 1991-97, pres. 1997—; chmn. GTE Byron Nelson Classic, 1995; pres. Dallas Bus. League, 1983, Big Bros./Big Sisters Met. Dallas, 1987-88; deacon North Dallas Bible Ch., 1989-95. 1st lt. U.S. Army, 1976, USAR, 1973-81. Fellow Tex. Bar Found. (life), Dallas Bar Found.; mem. Dallas Bar Assn., Tex. Law Rev. Assn. (life), State Bar Tex. Avocations: golf, reading, rock climbing, hiking. General civil litigation. Office: Crotty & Johansen LLP 2311 Cedar Springs Rd Ste 250 Dallas TX 75201-7810

**CROUCH, ROBERT P., JR.,** prosecutor; b. Mar. 28, 1948; s. Robert and Rosa Crouch; m. Clara Johnson Sept. 2, 1973; 1 child, Emily. BA, U. Md., 1971; MPA, U. N.C., 1982; JD, U. Va., 1988. Bar: Va. 1988. Aide to William B. Spong U.S. Senate, 1971-73; asst. mgr. employee benefits Fieldcrest Mills, 1973-75; adminstrv. asst. Patrick Henry Comm. Coll., 1975; adj. prof. Ferrum Coll., 1984-85; clerk circ. ct., 1976-85; assoc. McGuire, Woods, Battle & Boothe, 1988-89, Young, Haskins, Mann & Gregory, 1989-93; atty. U.S. Dept. Justice, Roanoke, Va., 1993—. Mem. bd. trustees Va. Mus. Nat. History, 1989-95, pres. bd. dirs., 1990-93; mem. edn. found. Patrick Henry C.C., 1984-93; mem. bd. visitors George Mason U., 1983-91; vice chmn. Dem. Party Va., 1989-93, state party sec., 1985-89, 5th dist. com. chmn., 1981-85; chmn. statewide Wilder-Beyer-Terry Campaign Com., 1989. Mem. Va. Bar Assn., Va. Trial Lawyers Assn. Democrat. Presbyterian. Office: Thomas B Mason Bldg 105 Franklin Rd SW Ste 1 Roanoke VA 24011-2305*

**CROUCHLEY, DANIEL GERARD,** lawyer; b. Wiesbaden, Germany, Nov. 1, 1950; came to U.S., 1952; s. Edward Alfred and Mary Elizabeth (Stafford) C.; m. Maureen Therese Shanahan, Dec. 27, 1975; children: Mary Esther, Anne Maureen. BA, Creighton U., Omaha, 1973, JD cum laude, 1976. Bar: Nebr. 1976, U.S. Dist. Ct. Nebr. 1976, U.S. Ct. Appeals (8th cir.) 1980. Adminstrv. asst. Douglas County Commn., Omaha, 1976-78; dep. Douglas County atty. Omaha, 1978-81; assoc. Dwyer, O'Leary & Martin, attys., Omaha, 1981-83; atty. law dept. Met. Utilities Dist., Omaha, 1983-93, asst. gen. counsel, 1993—. Bd. dirs. Greater Omaha Cmty. Action, 1979-82; adult leader Boy Scouts Am., Omaha, 1993—. Mem. Nebr. Bar Assn. (exec. com. corp. counsel sect. 1995-97), Omaha Bar Assn. Democrat. Roman Catholic. Avocations: music, history, astronomy. Home: 4211 William St Omaha NE 68105-1749 Office: Met Utilities Dist 1723 Harney St Omaha NE 68102-1907

**CROUSE, FARRELL R.,** lawyer; b. Portsmouth, Va., Dec. 23, 1963; s. Farrell Rondall and Grace Alice (Kenworthy) C. BA in History and Sociology, Bucknell U., Lewisburg, Pa., 1986; JD, Widener U., Wilmington, Del., 1989, LLM in Taxation, 1992. Bar: N.J. 1989, Pa. 1989, U.S. Dist. Ct. N.J. 1989. Assoc. Law Offices John William Neef, Carneys Point, N.J., 1990-91; pvt. practice Woodstown, N.J., 1991—. Mem. ABA, N.J. Bar Assn., Pa. Bar Assn. Avocations: auto racing, travel, collecting auto racing books and memorabilia. Family and matrimonial, General practice, Personal injury. Home and Office: 317 Auburn Rd # A Pilesgrove Township NJ 08098-2608

**CROUSE, REBECCA ANN,** lawyer, academic administrator; b. Balt., June 13, 1971; d. Harry Thomas Crouse and Barbara Jean Young. BA in Polit. Sci. with honors, Goucher Coll., 1993; JD, U. Cin., 1997. Bar: Ohio 1997. Tchr. acad. and h.s. God's Bible Sch. and Coll., Cin., 1993-94, dir. instnl. law, 1994-97, dir. devel., 1997-99; dir. devel. Urban League of Greater Cin., 1998—. Author (monthly column) God's Revivalist & Bible Advocate, 1997, 98. Trustee Goucher Coll., Towson, Md., 1993-96; bd. dirs., sec. Burlington (Ky.) Bible Method, 1994-97; vol. Tenant Info. Project, 1994-95, Vol. Income Tax Asst., Cin., 1995; pres. Mt. Auburn Cmty. Coun., Cin., 1996-98. Mem. Ohio State Bar Assn., Cin. Bar Assn. Avocations: piano, reading, writing. Non-profit and tax-exempt organizations, Estate taxation, Estate planning. Home: 830 Sunderland Dr Cincinnati OH 45255-4519 Office: Urban League Greater Cin 3458 Reading Rd Cincinnati OH 45229-3128

**CROUT, DANIEL WESLEY,** lawyer; b. Covington, Ky., Jan. 26, 1937; s. Charles Wesley and Mary Margaret (Meier) C.; m. Nancy Ann Keys, July 20, 1968; children: Amy Marie, Steven Wesley. BA, Villa Madonna Coll., 1959; JD, Chase Law Sch., 1975. Bar: Ky. 1975, Ohio 1976, U.S. Dist. Ct. (ea. dist.) Ky. 1976, U.S. Ct. Appeals (6th cir.) 1977, U.S. Supreme Ct. 1982. Surg. tech. Children's Hosp. Rsch. Found., Cin.; spl. agt. Ky. Dept. Alcoholic Beverage Control, Frankfort, 1968-77; pvt. practice Covington, 1975—; rsch. asst. Christ Hosp. Inst. Med. Rsch., Cin., 1959—; salesman Gene Snyder Realty, Erlanger, Ky., Austin Mann Realty, Erlanger, 1972. Active Kenton County (Ky.) Bd. Adjustment, 1992—; candidate dist. judge, Kenton County, 1977, 87. Mem. Ky. Bar Assn., Kenton County Bar Assn. (Cert. of Merit 1984), Kenton County Fraternal Order Police. Avocations: flower gardening, photography. General practice, General civil litigation, Criminal. Office: 121 E 4th St Covington KY 41011-1752

**CROW, NANCY REBECCA,** lawyer; b. Ridgecrest, Calif., Nov. 3, 1948; d. Edwin Louis and Eleanor Elizabeth (Gish) C.; 1 child, Rebecca Ann Carr; m. Mark A.A. Skrotzki, Apr. 4, 1987. BA, Antioch Coll., 1970; JD, U. Colo., 1974; LLM in Taxation, NYU, 1977. Bars: Colo. 1974, Calif. 1977. Atty., advisor IRS, N.Y.C., 1975-77; assoc. Brawerman & Kopple, Los Angeles, 1977-80; prof. Sch. Law, U. Denver, 1980-81; of counsel Krendl & Netzorg, Denver, 1981-84; shareholder Krendl & Krendl, Denver, 1984-92, Pendleton, Friedberg, Wilson & Hennessey, P.C., Denver, 1992—. Editor estate and trust forum Colorado Lawyer, 1992-93, bd. editors, 1993—; contbr. chpts. to books. Bd. dirs. Centennial Philharm. Orch., 1998—. Mem. ABA (chmn. Welfare Benefits subcom. of personal svcs. orgns. com. com., tax sect. 1987-92), Colo. Bar Assn. (exec. coun. tax sect. 1990-93, sec. tax sect. 1993-94, chair-elect 1994-95, chair 1995-96, bd. govs. 1996-98), Colo. Women's Bar Assn. (chair pub. policy com. 1982-83), Denver Bar Assn., Denver Tax Assn., Denver Tax Inst. Planning Com., Alliance of Profl. Women, Women's Estate Planning Coun. (bd. dirs. 1996-98), U.S.-Mex. C. of C. (bd. dirs. Rocky Mountain chpt., sec. 1998—), Sierra Club. Democrat. Unitarian. Avocations: skiing, backpacking, cello, running. Taxation, general, Estate planning, Pension, profit-sharing, and employee benefits. Home: 1031 Marion St Denver CO 80218-3016 Office: Pendleton Friedberg Wilson & Hennessey PC 303 E 17th Ave Ste 1000 Denver CO 80203-1263

**CROW, SAM ALFRED,** federal judge; b. Topeka, May 5, 1926; s. Samuel Wheadon and Phyllis K. (Brown) C.; m. Ruth M. Rush, Jan. 30, 1948; children: Sam A., Dan W. BA, U. Kans., 1949; JD, Washburn U., 1952. Ptnr. Rooney, Dickinson, Prager & Crow, Topeka, 1953-63, Dickinson, Crow, Skoog & Honeyman, Topeka, 1963-70; sr. ptnr. Crow & Skoog, Topeka, 1971-75; part-time U.S. magistrate, 1973-75, U.S. magistrate, 1975-81; judge U.S. Dist. Ct. Kans., Wichita, 1981-92; sr. judge U.S. Dist. Ct. Kans., Topeka, 1992—; lectr. Washburn U. Sch. Law; participant adv. com. on criminal rules Jud. Conf., 1990-96; mem. 10th Cir. Jud. Coun., 1987-88; pres., 1992-94; criminal rules adv. com.'s liaison Ct. Adminstrn. and Case Mgmt. Com.'s Subcom. on Criminal Case Mgmt., 1994-96; bd. dirs. Riverside Hosp., Wichita, 1986-92; mem. The Honorable Sam A. Crow Am. Inn of Ct.; lectr. in field. Bd. rev. Boy Scouts Am., 1960-70, cubmaster, 1957-60; mem. vestry Grace Episcopal Ch., Topeka, 1960-65; chmn. Kans. March of Dimes, 1959, bd. dirs. 1960-65; bd. dirs. Topeka Council Chs., 1960-70; mem. Kans. Hist. Soc., 1960—; pres., v.p. PTA.; bd. govs. Washburn Law Sch. Alumni Assn., 1993—. Col. JAGC, USAR, ret. Fellow Kans. Bar Found.; mem. ABA (del. Nat. Conf. Spl. Ct. Judges 1978, 19), Kans. Bar Assn. (trustee 1970-76, chmn. mil. law sect. 1965, 67, 70, 72, 74, 75), Kans. Trial Lawyers Assn. (sec. 1959-60, pres. 1960-61), Nat. Assn. U.S. Magistrates (com. discovery abuse), Topeka Bar Assn. (chmn. jud. reform com., chmn. bench and bar com., chmn. criminal law com.), Wichita Bar Assn., Topeka Lawyers Club (sec. 1964-65, pres. 1965-66), Am. Legion, Shawnee Country Club, Delta Theta Phi, Sigma Alpha Epsilon. Office: US Dist Ct 444 SE Quincy St Topeka KS 66683

**CROWDER, BARBARA LYNN,** judge; b. Mattoon, Ill., Feb. 3, 1956; d. Robert Dale and Martha Elizabeth (Harrison) C.; m. Lawrence Owen Taliana, Apr. 17, 1982; children: Paul Joseph, Robert Lawrence, Benjamin Owen. BA, U. Ill., 1978, JD, 1981. Bar: Ill. 1981. Assoc. Louis E. Olivero, Peru, Ill., 1981-82; asst. state's atty. Madison County, Edwardsville, Ill., 1982-84; ptnr. Robbins & Crowder, Edwardsville, 1985-87, Robbins, Crowder & Bader, Edwardsville, 1987-88, Crowder, Taliana, Rubin & Buckley, 1988-98; assoc. judge 3d Jud. Cir. of Madison County, Ill., 1999—; spkr. Continuing Legal Edn. Seminars Family Law Update, 1993-99. Co-editor ISBA Family Law Newsletter, 1993; co-author chpts. in ISBA Family Law Handbook, 1995, Maintenance Chapter Ill. Family Law, 1998; contbr. articles to profl. jours. Chmn. City of Edwardsville Zoning Bd. Appeals, 1986-87; committee woman Edwardsville De, Precinct 15, 1986-98; mem. City of Edwardsville Planning Commn., 1985-87; bd. dirs. Madison-Bond County Workforce Devel. Bd., 1995-96, 96-97. Named Best Oral Advocate, Moot Ct. Bd., 1979, Outstanding Young Career Woman, Dist. XIV, Ill. Bus. and Profl. Women, 1986; recipient Alice Paul award Alton-Edwardsville NOW, 1987, Outstanding Working Woman of Ill. Ill. Fed. of Bus. and Profl. Women, 1988-89, Woman of Achievement YWCA, 1996; recipient Athena award Edwardsville/Glen Carbon C. of C., 1991. Fellow Am. Acad. Matrimonial Lawyers; mem. ABA, Ill. Bar Assn. (family law coun. sect. 1990-99, chair 1997-98, co-editor family law newsletter 1993, vice chair 1996-97), Ill. Fedn. Bus. and Profl. Women (parliamentaria dist. XIV 1991-92), Women Lawyers Assn. Met. East (pres. 1986), Edwardsville Bus. and Profl Women's Club (pres. 1988-89, 95-96, treas. 1989-90, Woman of Achievement award 1985, Jr. Svc. award 1987), Ul Ill. Alumni Assn. (v.p. met.-east club 1994-95, bd. dirs. 1995-97). Democrat. Office: Madison County Courthouse 155 N Main St Edwardsville IL 62025-1955

**CROWE, DANIEL WALSTON,** lawyer; b. Visalia, Calif., July 1, 1940; s. J. Thomas and Wanda (Walston) C.; m. Nancy V. Berard, May 10, 1969; children: Daniel W., Karyn Louise, Thomas Dwight. BA, U. Santa Clara, 1962; JD, U. Calif. Hastings Coll. Law, 1965. Bar: Calif. 1966, U.S. Dist. Ct. (ea. dist.) Calif. 1969, U.S. Dist. Ct. (cen. dist.) Calif. 1973, U.S. Ct. Appeals (9th cir.) 1973, U.S. Supreme Ct. 1973. Assoc. Crowe, Mitchell & Crowe, and predecessors, Visalia, Calif., 1968-74, ptnr., 1974-83; ptnr. Crowe, Williams, Jordan and Richey and predecessor firm Crowe & Williams, 1975-90, The Crowe Law Offices, 1991—; sec., treas., dir. The Exeter Devel. Co., 1969-84, Willson Ranch Co., 1983—. Founding mem., dir. Visalia Balloon Assn., Inc. Served to capt. U.S. Army, 1965-68. Decorated Bronze Star, Air medal, Purple Heart, Nat. Def. Service medal. Mem. ABA, Calif. Bar Assn., Tulare County Bar Assn., NRA, Rotary, Elks, Moose, Am. Radio Relay League, DAV. Real property, State civil litigation, Probate. Address: PO Box 1110 Visalia CA 93279-1110

**CROWE, JAMES JOSEPH,** lawyer; b. New Castle, Pa., June 9, 1935; s. William J. and Anna M. (Dickson) C.; m. Joan D. Verba, Dec. 26, 1959. BA, Youngstown State U., 1958; JD, Georgetown U., 1963. Bar: Va. 1963, Ohio 1966. Atty. SEC, Washington, 1964-65, Gen. Tire & Rubber Co., Akron, Ohio, 1965-68; sr. atty. Eaton Corp., Cleve., 1968-72; sec., gen. counsel U.S. Shoe Corp., Cin., 1972-95, v.p., 1975-95; ptnr. Kepley, Gilligan & Eyrich, Cin., 1996—. Chmn. divsn. Fine Arts Fund, 1976; trustee Springer Ednl. Found., 1978-84, Cin. Music Festival Assn., 1980-86, 96—; group chmn. United Appeal, 1980; mem. pres.'s coun. Coll. Mt. St. Joseph, 1985-88; trustee Tennis for Charity Inc., 1986—, Playhouse in the Park, 1990-96, Greater Cin. Ctr. for Econ. Edn., 1992-96, Leadership Cin., Class 1990-91; trustee Cin. Nature Ctr., 1993—, chmn. 1996-98; bd. visitors U. Cin. Coll. Law, 1993—; trustee Invest in Neighborhoods, 1982-89, pres. 1984-86; trustee Cin. Hort. Soc., 1996—. 2d lt. U.S. Army, 1958-59. Mem. Ohio Bar Assn., Va. Bar, Cin. Bar Assn., Am. Soc. Corp. Secs., Cin. Country Club, Queen City Club, Cin. Tennis Club, Met. Club. General corporate.

**CROWE, JOHN T.,** lawyer; b. Cabin Cove, Calif., Aug. 14, 1938; s. J. Thomas and Wanda (Walston) C.; m. Marina Protopapa, Dec. 28, 1968; 1 child, Erin Aleka. BA, U. Santa Clara, 1960, JD, 1962. Bar: Calif. 1962, U.S. Dist. Ct. (ea. dist.) Calif. 1967. Lawyer Visalia, Calif., 1964—; ptnr. Crowe, Mitchell & Crowe, 1971-85; bd. dirs. World Parts Industries, Willson Ranch Co., pres. 1997—; referee State Bar Ct., 1976-82; gen. counsel Sierra Wine, 1986—. Bd. dirs. Mt. Whitney Area Coun. Boys Scouts Am., 1966-85, pres., 1971, 72; bd. dirs. Visalia Associated In-Group Donors (AID), 1973-81, pres., 1978-79, Tulare County Libr. Found.; mem. Visalia Airport Commn., 1982-90. 1st lt. U.S. Army, 1962-64; mem. Army Res. Forces Policy Com., 1995-99, chmn., 1997-99. Decorated D.S.M. with Oak Leaf Cluster, Legion of Merit with oak leaf cluster, Meritorious Svc. Medal with 3 oak leaf clusters, Army Commendation Medal; named Young Man of Yr., Visalia, 1973; Senator Jr. Chamber Internat., 1970; recipient Silver Beaver awrd Boy Scouts Am., 1983, Rudder medal Assn. U.S. Army, 1999. Mem. ABA, Tulare County Bar Assn., Nat. Assn. R.R. Trial Counsel, State Bar Calif., Visalia C. of C. (pres. 1979-80), Rotary (pres. 1980-81). Republican. Roman Catholic. General corporate, General practice. Home: 3939 W School Ave Visalia CA 93291-5514

**CROWE, PATRICIA MARY,** family court commissioner; b. Albany, N.Y., May 6, 1946; d. James Gordon and Helen (Trenor) C.; 1 child, Adam Thimmig. MusB, U. Mo., Columbia, 1969; MusM, U. Ill., Champaign, 1971; JD, U. Wis., Madison, 1978. Bar: Wis. Assoc., shareholder Wheeler, Van Sickle, Madison, Wis., 1979-96; family ct. commr. Dane County, Madison, Wis., 1996—. Pres. bd. Madison Boychoir, 1997-98, Downtown Madison Optimist Club, 1996-97. Avocations: singing, martial arts. Office: Rm 104 210 Martin Luther King Jr Blvd 104 Madison WI 53709-0001

**CROWE, THOMAS LEONARD,** lawyer; b. Amsterdam, N.Y., Aug. 3, 1944; s. Leonard Hoctor and Grace Agnes (O'Malley) C.; m. Barbara Ann Hauck, Aug. 2, 1969; children: Patrick, Brendan. AB, Georgetown U., 1966, JD, 1969. Law clk. to chief judge U.S. Dist. Ct. (no. dist.), Elkins, W.Va., 1969-70; trial atty. U.S. Dept. Justice, Washington, 1970-72; asst. U.S. atty. Balt., 1973-78; chief of criminal div. U.S. Atty.'s Office, Balt., 1977-78; ptnr. Cable, McDaniel, Bowie & Bond, Balt., 1979-91, McGuire, Woods, Battle & Boothe, Balt., 1991-95; of counsel Monshower & Miller, LLP, Columbia, Md., 1996-98; pvt. practice Balt., 1998—; mem. jud. conf. U.S. Ct. Appeals for 4th Cir. Fellow Md. Bar Found.; mem. Fed. Bar Assn. (pres. Balt. chpt. 1981-82), Md. Bar Assn., Barristers Club (pres. 1990-91),. Democrat. Roman Catholic. Federal civil litigation, State civil litigation, Criminal. Home: 11 Osborne Ave Baltimore MD 21228-4935 Office: Law Offices of Thomas L Crowe 1622 The World Trade Ctr 401 E Pratt St Baltimore MD 21202-3117

**CROWELL, GEORGE BRADFORD,** lawyer; b. Columbia, Mo., Mar. 22, 1964; s. Hillis D. and Jane (Vandenberg) C. BA, Westminster Coll., 1986; JD, U. Mo., 1990; LLM, U. Wash., 1991. Bar: Mo. 1991. Asst. prosecuting atty. Iron County Prosecuting Atty., Ironton, Mo., 1992-95, prosecuting atty., 1995—; assoc. Sen. Marvin L. Dinger, Ironton, 1992—; mem. exec. adv. bd. Law Enforcement Acad., Park Hills, Mo., 1992—; chmn. Iron Co. Child Fatality Rev. Bd., Ironton, 1992—. Mem. Elks. Avocations: scuba diving, sailing, martial arts. Criminal, General civil litigation. Office: Sen Marvin L Dinger PO Box 185 21 E Jackson Rd Webster Groves MO 63119-3817

**CROWELL, ROBERT LAMSON,** lawyer; b. Tonopah, Nev., Nov. 28, 1945; s. William Jefferson and Harriet (Lamson) C.; m. Susan Asbury, Dec. 18, 1971; children: Caroline, Brad, David, Todd. AB in Econs., Stanford U., 1967; JD, U. Calif., 1973. Bar: Nev. 1973, U.S. Ct. Appeals (9th cir.) 1973, U.S. Supreme Ct. 1995. Ptnr. Crowell, Crowell & Crowell, Carson City, Nev., 1973-77; dep. atty. gen. State of Nev., Carson City, 1974-77; ptnr. Crowell, Susich, Owen & Tackes, Carson City, 1977—. Mem. Colo. River Commn., Nev., 1988-96, chmn., 1992, 94; chmn. Nev. Continuing Legal Edn. Bd., 1992-94; mem. bd. govs. State of Nev., 1990-97; trustee Carson City Sch. Bd., 1997—. Mem. State Bar nev. (pres. 1996-97), Masons, Rotary. Democrat. Administrative and regulatory, General corporate, Probate. Office: Crowell Susich Owen & Tackes 510 W 4th St Carson City NV 89703-4254

**CROWLEY, DALE ALAN,** prosecutor; b. Saginaw, Mich., May 29, 1951; s. Lester Robert and Esther Irene C.; m. Deanne Kay Westendorp, Dec. 30, 1983; children: Jessica Erin, Leslie Ann, Kelsey Jo. BA in Econs. with honors, Mich. State U., 1973; JD, Wayne State U., 1976. Bar: Mich. 1976, U.S. Dist. Ct. (we. dist.) Mich. 1981. Counsel trust dept. Security Nat. Bank, Battle Creek, Mich., 1976-78; counsel claims dept. Transamerica Ins. Group, Battle Creek, 1978-80; asst. pros. atty Barry County, Mich., 1980; chief asst. pros. atty. Barry County, 1980-88, pros. atty., 1989—; vice chmn. Barry County Cmty. Corrections Bd.; legal advisor Barry County E-911 Central Dispatch Bd.; served as spl. pros. atty. in Allegan, Kalamazoo and Eaton Counties. Recipient Profl. Excellence citation Mich. State Police, 1989, 92. Mem. Nat. Dist. Attys. Assn., Pros. Attys. Assn. Mich., Barry County Bar Assn. (past pres., vice pres., treas., sect.), Kiwanis Club, Exchange Club (treas.). Republican. Lutheran. Avocations: sports, reading, computers, bicycling. Office: Barry County Pros Atty 220 W Court St Ste 201 Hastings MI 49058-1857

**CROWLEY, DAVID JAMES,** lawyer; b. Medford, Mass., Feb. 16, 1942. BS, U.S. Mcht. Marine Acad., 1964; MS, MIT, 1969; JD, South Tex. Coll. Law, 1987. Bar: Tex. 1987, U.S. Dist. Ct. (so. dist.) Tex. 1988. Marine engr. U.S. Lines, N.Y.C., 1964-67; econ. analyst Humble Oil/Exxon Corp., Houston, 1969-73; ops. mgr. Acad. Tankers, Inc., Houston, 1973-77, Nova Contract Carriers, Houston, 1977-79; dispatch mgr. Zapata Tankships, inc., Houston, 1979-81; gen. mgr. Titan Nav., Inc., Houston, 1981-84; pvt. practice Houston, 1988—. Co-author, editor: Governmental Causes of Action, 1987. Mem. Houston Bar Assn., Harris County Bar Assn., Masons, Shriners, Elks. Personal injury, Family and matrimonial, General civil litigation. Office: 11307 Chimney Rock Rd Houston TX 77035-2901

**CROWLEY, JAMES WORTHINGTON,** retired lawyer, business consultant, investor; b. Cookville, Tenn., Feb. 18, 1930; s. Worth and Jessie (Officer) C.; m. Laura June Bauserman, Jan. 27, 1951; children: James Kenneth, Laura Cynthia; m. Joyce A. Goode, Jan. 15, 1966; children: John Worthington, Noelle Virginia; m. Carol Golden, Sept. 4, 1981. BA, George Washington U., 1950, LLB, 1953. Bar: D.C. 1954. Underwriter, spl. agt. Am. Surety Co. of N.Y., Washington, 1953-56; adminstrv. asst., contract adminstr. Atlantic Rsch. Corp., Alexandria, Va., 1956-59; mgr. legal dept., asst. sec., counsel Atlantic Rsch. Corp., 1959-65, sec., legal mgr., counsel, 1965-67; sec., legal mgr., counsel Susquehanna Corp. (merger with Atlantic Rsch. Corp.), 1967-70; pres., dir. Gen. Communication Co., Boston, 1962-70; v.p., gen. counsel E-Systems, Inc., 1970-95, sec., 1976-95; ret., 1995; ind. cons. bus. and fin., investor Dallas, 1995—; v.p., asst. sec., dir. Cemco, Inc.; v.p., dir. TAI, Inc., Serv-air, Inc., Greenville, Tex., Engrng. Rsch. Assocs., Inc., Vienna, Va., HRB Systems, Inc., State Coll., Pa.; mem. adv. bd. sec. Internat. and Comparative Law Ctr.; v.p., sec., dir. Advanced Video Products, 1992-95; v.p., sec., gen. counsel E-Systems Med. Electronics, Inc., 1992-95. Mem. Am. Soc. Corp. Secs. (pres. Dallas regional group 1988-89, nat. dir. 1989-92), Inf. Mus. Assn., Nat. Security Indsl. Assn., Mfrs.' Alliance for Productivity and Innovation (mem. law coun.), Omicron Delta Kappa, Alpha Chi Sigma, Phi Sigma Kappa. Republican. Baptist. General corporate, Government contracts and claims, Pension, profit-sharing, and employee benefits. Home and Office: 16203 Spring Creek Rd Dallas TX 75248-3116

**CROWN, NANCY ELIZABETH,** lawyer; b. Bronx, N.Y., Mar. 27, 1955; d. Paul and Joanne Barbara (Newman) C.; children: Rebecca, Adam. BA, Barnard Coll., 1977, MA, 1978; MEd, Columbia U., 1983; JD cum laude, Nova Law Sch., 1992. Cert. tchr.; Bar: Fla. 1992. Tchr. Sachem Sch. Dist., Holbrook, N.Y., 1978-82; v.p. mail order dept. Haber-Klein, Inc., Hicksville, N.Y., 1984-88; mgr. mdse., dir. ops. Sure Card Inc., Pompano Beach, Fla., 1988-89; legal intern Office U.S. Trustee/Dept. Justice, 1992; assoc. John T. Kinsey, P.A., Boca Raton, Fla., 1993-95; pvt. practice Nancy E. Crown, P.A., Boca Raton, Fla., 1995—. Recipient West Pub. award for acad. achievement, 1992. Mem. NAFE, Fla. Bar Assn., South Palm Beach County Women's Exec. Club, Phi Alpha Delta. Democrat. Jewish. Avocations: theatre, walking, reading, jazz. Bankruptcy, Real property, General corporate.

**CROWSON, DAVID LEE,** lawyer, educator; b. San Juan, Tex., Jan. 15, 1954; s. Charles Felton and Vivian (Cates) C.; m. Jane Ann Whitley, Dec. 13, 1980; children: Luke, Drew, Cara. BBA in Acctg., Baylor U., 1976, JD, 1979. Bar: Tex. 1979. Assoc. Smead & Anderson, Longview, Tex., 1979-81; ptnr. Smead Anderson & Crowson, Longview, 1981-84; assoc. Kenley Boyland & Coghlan, Longview, 1984-86; ptnr. Coghlan Crowson, Longview, 1986—; adj. prof. LeTourneau U., Longview, 1980—. Chmn. of deacons First Bapt. Ch., Longview, 1993; chmn. east Tex. chpt. ARC, Longview, 1995; sec. United Way, Longview, 1998. Southern Baptist. Estate planning, Probate, Oil, gas, and mineral. Office: Coghlan Crowson 1127 Judson Rd Ste 211 Longview TX 75601-5193

**CROWSON, JAMES LAWRENCE,** lawyer, financial company executive, academic administrator; b. Duncan, Okla., Aug. 3, 1938; s. George L. and Emry Elifair (McKee) C.; children from previous marriage: James Lawrence Jr., Jason, Donna Kristan Nickel; m. Linda Sue Crowson, Mar. 2, 1986; stepchildren: Chadwick Lanier Johnson, Kim Johnson Osborn. BA in English Lit., U. Okla., 1960; LLB, So. Meth. U., 1963. Bar: Tex. 1963. Legis. counsel Tex. Legis. Coun., Austin, 1966-67; dir. hearings Tex. Water Quality Bd., Austin, 1967-68, chief legal officer, 1967-68, dir. hearings and enforcement, 1969-70; adminstrv. asst. Office of Gov., Austin, 1968-69; univ. atty. U. Tex. System, Austin, 1970; asst. to pres. U. Tex., Austin, 1970-71; asst. to pres. U. Tex., Dallas, 1971-74, v.p., 1974-77, exec. v.p., 1977-80; vice chancellor, gen. counsel U. Tex. System, Austin, 1980-87; sr. v.p., gen. counsel Lomas Fin. Group, Dallas, 1987-94, exec. v.p., 1994-95; pvt. investment practice Dallas, 1995-96; dep. chancellor Tex. Tech. Univ. System, Austin, 1996—; sec. Tex. Higher Edn. Found., 1988—, Higher Edn. Legis. Polit. Action Com., 1987—; vice chmn. HCB Enterprises Inc., 1995—; bd. dirs. KOHM Pub. Radio Sta., Market Lubbock, Inc., 1997—, v.p. 1999. Trustee Alliance for Higher Edn., 1991-96, Dallas Edn. Ctr., 1995-96. Capt. U.S. Army, 1963-66. Mem. Mortgage Bankers Assn. Am. (mem. legal issues com., mem. legis. com.), U.S. C. of C. (mem. edn. employment and tng. com., mem. labor rels. com., mem. S.W. pub. affairs task force). General corporate, Bankruptcy, Legislative. Office: PO Box 42013 Lubbock TX 79409-2013

**CRUDEN, JOHN CHARLES,** lawyer; b. Topeka, Feb. 23, 1946; s. George Harry and Agnes (Telban) C.; m. Sharon Lynn Holland, June 15, 1968; children: Kristen, Heather. BS, U.S. Mil. Acad., 1968; JD, U. Santa Clara, 1974; MA, U. Va., 1975; grad. Gen. Staff Coll., 1982; fellow Army War Coll., 1988. Bar: Calif. 1975, D.C. 1979, U.S. Supreme Ct. 1979. Commd. 2d lt. U.S. Army, 1968; advanced through grades to col., 1987; with airborne, ranger, spl. forces, Fed. Republic Germany and Republic of Vietnam, 1968-71; clk. Calif. Supreme Ct., 1974; prosecutor Fed. Republic Germany, 1975-76; chief litigation br. Hdqrs. Europe, 1976-78; sr. trial atty. comml. br. Litigation div. Dept. Army, 1978-79, 80-81; gen. counsel Def. Nuclear Agy., 1979-80; prof., chief Adminstrv. and Civil Law div. Judge Adv. Gen.'s Sch., Charlottesville, Va., 1982-85; staff Judge Adv., Europe, 1985-87; spl. counsel to asst. atty. gen. civil div. Dept. Justice, 1987-88; chief legis. counsel Dept. Army, 1988-91; chief environ. enforcement sect. Environ. & Natural Resource divsn. U.S. Dept. Justice, Washington, 1991-95, dep. asst. atty. gen., 1995—. Contbr. articles to profl. jours. Mem. Fed. Bar Assn. (chpt. pres. 1984-85, Younger Fed. Lawyers award 1981), JAG Sch. Alumni Assn. (pres. 1982-85), D.C. Bar Assn., Calif. Bar Assn., ABA (vice chmn. adminstrv. law and gen. practice sect. 1985-88, vice chmn. fed. legis. com. 1989-92, adv. com., standing com. on law and nat. security, 1988-94). E-mail: john.cruden@usdoj.gov. Office: US Dept Justice 950 Pennsylvania Ave NW Rm 2734 Washington DC 20530-0001

**CRUM, HENRY HAYNE,** lawyer; b. Denmark, S.C., Oct. 1, 1914; s. J. Wesley Jr. and Priscilla (Hart) C.; m. Mary Bass, July 27, 1946; children: Elizabeth, J. Wesley III, H. Hayne III. AB, Wofford Coll., 1935; LLB, U. S.C., 1939. Bar: S.C. 1939, U.S. Ct. Appeals (4th cir.) 1953, U.S. Dist. Ct. S.C. 1959, U.S. Tax Ct. 1963, U.S. Supreme Ct. 1953. Ptnr. Crum & Crum Attys., Denmark, 1939-40, 45—; mem. S.C. Supreme Ct. Grievance and Discipline Com., 1978-81, S.C. Supreme Ct. Specialization Adv. Bd. for Taxation, 1982-84, S.C. Bar Resolution of Fee Disputation Bd., 1983-84; city atty. City of Denmark, 1946-76. With AUS, 1940-45, ETO, Col. USAR ret. Decorated Bronze Star, ETO Ribbon with 5 Campaign Stars, Bronze Arrowhead. Democrat. Methodist. Avocations: golf, tennis, reading. Home: 277 N Palmetto Ave Denmark SC 29042-1107 Office: Crum & Crum Attys PO Box 12B Denmark SC 29042-0012

**CRUMBLEY, R. ALEX,** lawyer; b. McDonough, Ga., Jan. 31, 1942; s. Reuben Alexander and Lucy Margaret (Turner) C.; m. Claire Herd, Nov. 11, 1967; 1 son, Alexander Herd. B.A. in Journalism, U. Ga., 1964, J.D., 1966; student Am. Acad. Jud. Adminstrn., 1980. Bar: Ga. 1965, U.S. Dist. Ct. (no. dist.) Ga. 1970, U.S. Supreme Ct. 1976. Asst. atty. gen. State of Ga., 1967-70; ptnr. Weltner, Kidd, Crumbley & Tate, Atlanta, 1970-76; pub. defender Flint Jud. Cir., 1976-77; judge Flint Jud. Circuit Superior Ct., 1978-83; ptnr. Crumbley & Crumbley, McDonough, Ga., 1983—; senator 17th dist. Ga. Senate, 1987-89; mem. bd. gov. state bar Ga., 1992-94; prof. Woodrow Wilson Coll. Law, Atlanta, 1971-75; counsel to com. on judiciary Ga. State Senate, 1970. Served with Ga. N.G., 1966-72. Mem. ABA, Henry County Bar Assn., State Bar Ga. (mem. disciplinary bd. 1985-87). Lawyers Club Atlanta, Henry County Kiwanis (hon.), Rotary. Democrat. Presbyterian. Contbr. articles to profl. jours. State civil litigation, Alternative dispute resolution, Family and matrimonial. Office: PO Box 775 Mcdonough GA 30253-0775

**CRUMLEY, JOHN WALTER,** lawyer; b. Ft. Worth, July 20, 1944; s. Frank E. and Mary Cecilia (Gaudin) C.; m. Paulette Gavin, July 25, 1970; children: John Gavin, Brian Christopher. BS, Springhill Coll., 1967; JD, So. Meth. U., 1970, M of Comparative Law, 1973. Bar: Tex. 1970, U.S. Dist. Ct. (no. dist.) Tex. 1976, U.S. Ct. Appeals (5th cir.) 1981, U.S. Tax Ct. 1988. Assoc. McBryde & Bogle, Ft. Worth, 1973-75; ptnr. Crumley, Murphy & Shrull, Inc., Ft. Worth, 1975-85, Tracy, Crumley & Holland, Ft. Worth, 1985-92; prin. John W. Crumley, P.C., Ft. Worth, 1992—; mem. bd. dirs. Goodrich Ctr. for the Deaf, 1995—; vice chair Bingo Advisor Com., 1995-96. Mem. steering com. Tarrant County Vol. Guardianship, Ft. Worth, 1986-87; bd. dirs. Camp Fire, Ft. Worth, 1985-87, Cath. Social Svcs., Ft. Worth, 1985-86. Capt. U.S. Army, 1970-72. Mem. State Bar Tex., Tarrant County Bar Assn., Tex. Assn. Def. Counsel, Tex. Assn. Diocesan Attys., U.S. Conf. Diocesan Attys. Assn., Serra Club (pres. Ft. Worth club 1985-86), KC (state adv. 1986-91, 95-96). State civil litigation, Probate, Construction. Office: 316 University Ctr 1300 S University Dr Fort Worth TX 76107-5737

**CRUMP, FRANCIS JEFFERSON, III,** lawyer; b. Alexandria, Va., Dec. 4, 1942; s. Ross Gault and Pauline (DeVore) C.; BS in Math., Va. Mil. Inst., 1964; JD, Ind. U., 1967; m. Nancy Jo Burkle, Aug. 20, 1966; children: Tom, Laura, Elizabeth. Admitted to Ind. bar, 1967, U.S. Dist. Ct. (so. dist.) Ind. 1967; gen. ptnr. firm Jewell, Crump & Angermeier, Columbus, Ind., 1971—; pres. First Nat. Corp.; lectr. on estate planning and legal aspects of child abuse and neglect; bd. dirs., sec., treas. Hawpatch Corp.; past pres., bd. dirs. Columbus Boys' Club; past pres., bd. dirs., v.p., treas. Found. Youth, Inc., Babe Ruth Baseball, Inc., sr. v.p. 1983-88; past deacon, elder 1st United Presbyn. Ch. of Columbus, 1972-75, 1977-80; bd. dirs. Ecumenical Assn. Barth County Chs., Inc. Mem. Ind. State Bar Assn., Bartholomew County Bar Assn. (pres. 1983), Rotary, Phi Alpha Delta. Republican. Estate planning, Probate, Real property. Home and Office: PO Box 1061 Columbus IN 47202-1061

**CRUMP, GERALD FRANKLIN,** retired lawyer; b. Sacramento, Feb. 16, 1935; s. John Laurin and Ida May (Banta) C.; m. Glenda Roberts Glass, Nov. 21, 1959; children: Sara Elizabeth, Juliane Kathryn, Joseph Stephen. AB, U. Calif., Berkeley, 1956; JD, U. Calif., 1959; MA, Baylor U., 1966. Bar: Calif. 1960. Dep. county counsel L.A. County, 1963-73, legis. rep., 1970-73, chief pub. works div., 1973-84, sr. asst. county counsel, 1984-85, chief asst. county counsel, 1985-97; ret., 1997; lectr. Pepperdine U., 1978, U. Calif., 1982. Former v.p. San Fernando Valley Girl Scout Coun. Served to capt. USAF, 1960-63; to maj. gen. USAFR, 1963-95, ret.; mobilization asst. to the JAG. Mem. ABA, Am. Judicature Soc., Am. Acad. Polit. and Social Sci., State Bar Calif., L.A. County Bar Assn. (past chmn. trustee govtl. law sect., past mem.exec. com. litig. sect.), Air Force Assn., Res. Officers Assn., Phi Alpha Delta, Delta Sigma Phi. Municipal (including bonds), Military, Government contracts and claims. Home: 4020 Camino De La Cumbre Sherman Oaks CA 91423-4522

**CRUMP, RONALD CORDELL,** lawyer; b. Washington, Nov. 2, 1951; s. Robert Callwell and Marie Evangeline (Greene) C. BS, U. Ariz., 1974; JD, U. Notre Dame, 1979. Bar: D.C. 1980, U.S. Dist Ct. D.C. 1980, U.S. Ct. Appeals 1980, U.S. Ct. Claims 1980, U.S. Tax Ct. 1980, U.S. Ct. Mil. Appeals 1980, U.S. Ct. Appeals (4th cir.) 1981, U.S. Supreme Ct. 1984. Intern Law Revision Counsel U.S. Ho. of Reps., Washington, 1978; law clk. to assoc. judge D.C. Ct. Appeals, Washington, 1979-80; gen atty. VA, Washington, 1980-86; asst. atty. Office of U.S. Atty., Washington, 1986-90; atty. com. on stds. ofcl. conduct U.S. Ho. of Reps., Washington, 1990-93, atty. com. on internat. rels., 1995—; pvt. practice, 1993-95. Mem. FBA (bd. dirs. 1984—), Washington Bar Assn. (pres. 1995-97), D.C. Bar Assn., Notre Dame Club, Sigma Delta Tau. Republican. Roman Catholic. Home: 3819 Kansas Ave NW Washington DC 20011-5709

**CRUMPLER, JOAN GALE,** lawyer, associate; b. Clinton, N.C., Nov. 30, 1961; d. Rueben S. and Joyce P. Crumpler. BS, U. N.C., 1984; JD, Mercer U., 1988. Bar: Ga. 1988, U.S. Dist. Ct. (so. dist.) Ga. 1988, U.S. Dist. Ct. (no. dist.) Ga. 1990, U.S. Ct. Appeals (11th cir.) 1990. Assoc. Dickey, Whelchel, Brown & Readdick, Brunswick, Ga., 1988-90; staff atty. UAW-GM Legal Svcs. Plan, Atlanta, 1990-98; assoc. Chambers, Mabry, McClelland & Brooks, Atlanta, 1998—. Contbr. articles to profl. jours. Mem. HRC, Atlanta, 1990-98. Mem. ABA, DeKalb County Bar Assn., Atlanta Bar Assn. Avocations: marathon running, tennis. General civil litigation, Insurance, Product liability. Home: 629 Sherwood Rd NE Atlanta GA 30324-5226 Office: Chambers Mabry McClelland & Brooks 2200 Century Pkwy NE Ste 10 Atlanta GA 30345-3103

**CRUMPTON, CHARLES WHITMARSH,** lawyer; b. Shreveport, La., May 29, 1946; s. Charles W. and Frances M. (McInnis) C.; m. Thu-Huong T. Cong-Huyen, Sept. 17, 1971; children: Francesca, Ian. BA, Carleton Coll., 1968; MA, U. Hawaii, 1974, JD, 1978. Bar: Hawaii 1978, U.S. Dist. Ct. Hawaii 1978, U.S. Ct. Appeals (9th cir.) 1982. Tchr. dept. edn. State of Hawaii, Honolulu, 1972-73, 75-77; Fulbright prof. U. Can Tho, Vietnam, 1973-75; assoc. John S. Edmunds, Honolulu, 1978-80, Ashford & Wriston, Honolulu, 1980-85, David W. Hall, Honolulu, 1985-88; dir. Hall & Crumpton, Honolulu, 1988-93; dir., shareholder Stanton Clay Chapman Crumpton & Iwamura, Honolulu, 1993—; pres./dir. Internat. Law Found., 1996—; barrister Am. Inn of Ct. IV, Honolulu, 1985-87; arbitrator Court-Annexed Arbitration program 1st Cir. Ct. State of Hawaii, 1987—; arbitrator, mediator Am. Arbitration Assn., 1988—, Arbitration Forums, 1990—, Mediation Specialists, 1994—, Dispute Prevention & Resolution, 1995—; mem. com. on lawyer professionalism Hawaii State Jud. Conf., 1988-89; arbitrator/mediator com. fee disputes Hawaii Bar Assn., 1990—, mem. com. jud. adminstrn., 1990—, mem. com. jud. performance, 1992-94, chair sect. on alternative dispute resolution, 1997—; prof. Hawaii Pacific U., 1995—; faculty/spkr. on ins. law, employment law, alternative dispute resolution, civil litigation, 1993—. Asst. dir. youth vols. Am. Cancer Soc., Honolulu, 1972-73. Fulbright grantee U.S. Dept. State, 1973-75. Mem. ATLA, ABA (torts and ins. practice sect., litigation sect., alt. dispute resolution sec.), Hawaii Bar Assn., Inter-Pacific Bar Assn. Avocations: sports, guitar. E-mail: crumpton@paclawteam.com. Personal injury, Alternative dispute resolution, Insurance. Home: 47-538 Hui Iwa St Kaneohe HI 96744-4658 Office: Stanton Clay Chapman Crumpton & Iwamura 700 Bishop St Ste 2100 Honolulu HI 96813-4120

**CRUSE, REX BEACH, JR.,** lawyer; b. Sherman, Tex., July 2, 1941; s. Rex Beach and Mary Ellen (Sim) C.; m. Maebeth Ann Brock, Mar. 19, 1958 (div. 1975); 1 child, Vicki Ann.; m. Carol A. Schaller, July 14, 1977 (div. 1983). BBA highest honors, U. Tex., 1962, PhD in Bus. Adminstrn., 1973; JD, St. Mary's U., San Antonio, 1988. Bar: Tex. 1989, N.Y. 1989, D.C. 1991, U.S. Dist. Ct. (we. dist.) Tex. 1990, U.S. Tax Ct. 1990, U.S. Bankruptcy Ct. 1990, U.S. Ct. Internat. Trade 1993, U.S. Ct. Fed. Claims 1996; CFP; CPA. Various Am. Inst. CPA's, N.Y., 1964-75, mng. dir., 1976-83; dean Sch. Accountancy U. Hawaii, Honolulu, 1983-84; pvt. practice acctg. San Antonio, 1985-89, pvt. practice law, 1989-96; assoc. Duncan, Ulman, Weakley & Bressler, Inc., San Antonio, 1996—. Pres. San Antonio Coun. on Alcohol and Drug Abuse, 1994-96; bd. dirs. Unicorn Ctrs., Inc., 1994-96. Mem. ABA, AICPA (cert. spl. merit 1992), Am. Health Lawyers Assn., State Bar Tex. (The Coll. of the State of Bar of Tex.), Barra de Abogados de Mex. y Tex., Tex. Soc. CPAs (Outstanding com. chmn. 1993-94), San Antonio Bar Assn. Democrat. Methodist. Avocation: aerobics. Taxation, general, Health, Administrative and regulatory. Home: # 106 8401 N New Braunfels Ave San Antonio TX 78209-1110 Office: Duncan Ulman Weakley & Bressler 603 Navarro St Ste 1000 San Antonio TX 78205-1838

**CRUZ, BENJAMIN JOSEPH FRANQUEZ,** territory supreme court justice; b. Agana, Guam, Mar. 3, 1951; s. Juan Quenga Cruz and Antonia (Franquez) Guerrero. BA, Claremont Men's Coll., 1972; JD, U. Santa Clara, 1975. Asst. consumer counsel Office Atty. Gen., Agana, 1975; gov.'s legal counsel Gov. of Guam, Agana, 1975-79; sole practice law Agana, 1979-82; minority legal counsel Guam Legis., Agana, 1979-82; dir. Guam/Wash. Liaison Office, Washington, 1983-84; judge Superior Ct. Guam, Agana, 1984—; assoc. justice Guam Supreme Ct., Guam, 1997—. Pres. Am. Cancer Soc., 1978-80; committeeman Dem. Nat. Com., Washington, 1984; treas. Guam Nat. Olympic Com., 1987-88, v.p., 1988—; exec. dir. Dem. Party Guam, Agana, 1979-83. Mem. Nat. Judges Assn., Nat. Assn. Juvenile and Family Ct. Judges. Avocations: aerobics, weightlifting. Home: PO Box 3326 Agana GU 96932-3326 also: 123 Manga St Piti GU 96925-4503 Office: Superior Ct of Guam Jud Bldg 120 W O'Brien Dr Agana GU 96910*

**CRYNE, ROBERT FRANCIS,** lawyer, educator; b. Bklyn., Feb. 29, 1952; s. Michael Joseph Sr. and Camillus Catherine (Donnelly) C.; m. Ann L. Wright, May 21, 1978; children: Julia, Patrick. BA, Stockton State Coll., 1974; JD, Creighton U., 1978. Bar: Nebr. 1978, U.S. Dist. Ct. Nebr. 1978, U.S. Army Ct. Review 1985, U.S. Ct. Appeals Armed Forces 1979, Supreme Ct. 1982. Pvt. practice Omaha, 1978-79, 82-87; capt., judge advocate U.S. Army, Wuerzburg, Germany, 1979-82; deputy county attorney Douglas County Attorney's Office, Omaha, 1987-95, deputy in charge narcotics divsn., 1995—; adj. prof. Metropolitan Cmty. Coll., Omaha, 1990—. Den Leader Cub Scouts of Am., Omaha, 1993—. Capt. U.S. Army, 1979-82. Recipient Inspector Generals award U.S. Dept. Housing Urban Devel., Omaha, 1997, Meritorious Svc. award Organized Crime Enforcement Task Force, West Ctrl. Region, 1997. Mem. Nebr. County Attorney Assn., Inns of Court (master of bench 1997—), Am. Legion. Office: Douglas County Attorneys Office 428 Hall Of Justice Omaha NE 68183-0001

**CUBA, BENJAMIN JAMES,** lawyer; b. San Antonio, Dec. 12, 1936; s. Ben and Patricia (Machalek) C.; m. Bernadette Theresa Haney, Sept. 4, 1964; children: Benjamin Courtney, Tristan Konrad. AA, Temple Coll., 1957; BBA, U. Tex., 1959; JD, Baylor U., 1963. Bar: Tex. 1964, U.S. Dist. Ct. (we. dist.) Tex. 1970, U.S. Ct. Appeals (5th and 11th cirs.) 1981, U.S. Supreme Ct. 1978. Assoc. Law Offices of Jarrard Secrest, Temple, Tex., 1964-66; ptnr. Secrest & Cuba, Temple, 1966-68; sr. ptnr. Cuba & Cuba and predecessor firms, Temple, 1968—; dir. Founding trustee, atty. Inst. for Humanities at Salado, Tex., 1980—, founding trustee, legal counsel First House, Inc., Temple, 1981-86; legal counsel, mem. cmty. adv. bd. Jr. League of Temple, Inc. (and predecessor orgn. Svc. League of Temple, Inc.), 1976—; v.p. Temple Indsl. Devel. Corp., 1984-89. Fellow Tex. Bar Found. (life); mem. Bell-Lampasas-Mills Counties Bar Assn. (pres. 1973-74), State Bar Tex., Tex. Assn. Defense Counsel, Tex. Assn. Bank Counsel, U. Tex. Ex Students Assn., Baylor Law Alumni Assn., Quarterback Club (dir. 1984, 85), Phi Delta Phi. Lutheran. General civil litigation, General corporate, Real property. Office: Cuba & Cuba PLC 18 S Main St Ste 802 Temple TX 76501-7608

**CUBIT, WILLIAM ALOYSIUS,** lawyer; b. Phila., Aug. 7, 1930; s. William C. and Sophie (Kelly) Cubit Levey; m. Loretta E. Brooks, Feb. 12, 1952; children: William, Mark John, Dennis, Phyllis, Christine, Thomas. BSBA, St. Joseph's U., 1959; JD, Widener Law Sch., 1988. Bar: N.J. 1989, U.S. Supreme Ct. 1989, U.S. Dist. Ct. (ea. and we. dists.) Pa. 1989, U.S. Ct. Appeals (D.C. dir.) 1990, Fla. 1993, U.S. Dist. Ct. (so. dist.) Fla. 1993. Claims adjuster Home Ins., Phila., 1957-63, Wilmington, Del., 1957-63; claims adjuster Nationwire Ins., Phila., 1963-69, claims mgr., 1969-77; claims mgr. Nationwire Ins., Wilkes Barr, 1969-77; claims negotiator Chubb Ins. Group, Phila., 1977-89, atty., 1989—. Pres. S.E. Delco Sch. Bd., Folcroft, Pa., 1972-74; v.p. Sharon Hill (Pa.) Sch. Bd., 1968-70. Staff sgt. USMC, 1948-52, Korea. Mem. ABA, CPCU, Pa. Trial Lawyers Assn. Republican. Roman Catholic. General civil litigation, Insurance, Personal injury. Home: 1301 Woodland Ave Sharon Hill PA 19079-2121 Office: 727 NE 3rd Ave Fort Lauderdale FL 33304-2646

**CUCCI, GARDENIA PAOLA,** lawyer; b. N.Y.C., July 15, 1969; d. Cesare Eleuterio and Gilda Morillo Cucci; m. Christopher De Turk Galiardo, Oct. 3, 1998. BA, Franklin & Marshall Coll., 1990; JD, NYU, 1994. Atty. Am. Internat. Group, Inc., N.Y.C., 1994-96, asst. gen. counsel, 1996-98; assoc. Lord, Bissell & Brook, N.Y.C., 1998—. Insurance. Home: 136 E 36th St New York NY 10016-3521 Office: Lord Bissell & Brook 1 Penn Plz Ste 1926 New York NY 10119-1926

**CUDAHY, RICHARD D.,** federal judge; b. Milwaukee, Wisc., Feb. 2, 1926; s. Michael F. and Alice (Dickson) C.; m. Ann Featherson, July 14, 1956 (dec. 1974); m. Janet Stuart, July 17, 1976; children: Richard D., Norma K., Theresa E., Daniel M., Michaela A., Marguerite L., Patrick G. BS, U.S. Mil. Acad., 1948; JD, Yale U., 1955; LLD (hon.), Ripon Coll., 1981, DePaul U., 1995, Wabash Coll., 1996, Stetson U., 1998. Bar: Conn. 1955, D.C. 1957, Ill. 1957, Wis. 1961. Commd. 2d. lt. U.S. Army, 1948, advanced through grades to 1st lt., 1950; law clk. to presiding judge U.S. Ct. Appeals (2d cir.), 1955-56; asst. to legal adv. Dept. State, 1956-57; assoc. firm Isham, Lincoln & Beale, Chgo., 1957-60; pres. Patrick Cudahy, Inc., Wis., 1961-71, Patrick Cudahy Family Co., 1968-75; ptnr. firm Godfrey & Kahn, Milw., 1972; commr., chmn. Wis. Pub. Service Commn., 1972-75; ptnr. Isham, Lincoln & Beale, Chgo., 1976-79; judge U.S. Ct Appeals (7th cir.), Chgo., 1979-94, sr. judge, 1994—; lectr. law Marquette U. Law Sch., 1961-66; vis. prof. law U. Wis., 1966-67; prof. lectr. law George Washington U., Washington, D.C., 1978-79, DePaul U. Coll. Law, 1996-99; adj. prof. DePaul U., 1996-99. Commr. Milw. Harbor, 1964-66; pres. Milw. Urban League, 1965-66; trustee Environ. Def. Fund, 1976-79; chmn. DePaul Human Rights Law Inst., 1990-98; chmn. Wis. Dem. party, 1967-68; Dem. candidate for Wis. atty. gen., 1968. Mem. ABA (spl. com. on Energy Law 1978-84, 90-96, pub. utility/sect. coun. group), Am. Law Inst., Wis. Bar Assn., Milw. Bar Assn., Chgo. Bar Assn., Fed. Judges' Assn. (bd. dirs.), Am. Inst. for Pub. Svc. (bd. selectors), Cath. Theol. Union (trustee), Law Club Chgo. (pres. 1992-93, spl. divsn. D.C. cir. for appt. ind. counsel 1998—). Roman Catholic. Office: US Ct Appeals 219 S Dearborn St Chicago IL 60604-1702

**CUDDIGAN, TIMOTHY JOHN,** lawyer; b. Mpls., Aug. 1, 1949; s. Jerome Charles and Florence Elizabeth (Downing) C.; m. Janet Elizabeth Gilbert, Aug. 2, 1974; children: Patrick, Maureen, Sean. BA, Creighton U., 1971, JD, 1974. Bar: Nebr. 1975. Assoc. atty. Marks & Clare, Omaha, 1975-79, ptnr., 1979-93; ptnr. Brodkey and Cuddigan, Omaha, 1994—. Bd. dirs. Creighton U. Alumni Assn., Omaha, 1986-88, Nebr. Civil Liberties Union, Lincoln, 1986-87; advisor Greater Omaha Assn. of Retarded Citizens, 1988—. Mem. Nebr. Assn. Trial Attys. (bd. dirs. 1991—). Democrat. Roman Catholic. Personal injury, Product liability, Workers' compensation. Office: Brodkey and Cuddigan 444 Regency Parkway Dr Ste 200 Omaha NE 68114-3779

**CUELLAR, NORBERT,** lawyer; b. Mpls., Nov. 26, 1963; s. Norberto and Oralia (Galvan) C. BA in Polit. Sci. and Art History, U. Minn., 1990; JD, William Mitchell Law Sch., 1994. Bar: Minn., U.S. Dist. Ct. Minn. Assoc. Moeller Law Office, Mpls., 1995-97; pvt. practice Mpls., 1997—. Mem. Minn. Bar Assn., Minn. Trial Lawyers Assn. Avocations: golf, fishing. Fax: 612-333-3161. Workers' compensation, Personal injury. Office: 800 Washington Ave N Ste 502 Minneapolis MN 55401-1184

**CUIFFO, FRANK WAYNE,** lawyer; b. Houston, Oct. 13, 1943; s. Richard and Helen (Giaco) C.; m. Barbara Joyce Streeter, Nov. 26, 1966; children: Karen, Deborah, Richard, Steven. BS, U. Notre Dame, 1964; JD, Fordham U., 1967. Bar: N.Y. 1967. Assoc. Pennie & Edmonds (formerly Pennie, Edmonds, Morton, Taylor & Adams), N.Y.C., 1967-69; sr. assoc. Emmet, Marvin, & Martin, N.Y.C., 1969-74, Golenbock & Barell, N.Y.C., 1974-78; mng. ptnr. Carro, Spanbock, Kaster & Cuiffo, N.Y.C., 1978-93; chmn. real estate dept., exec. com. Donovan, Leisure, Newton & Irvine, N.Y.C., 1993-98; ptnr. McDermott, Will & Emery, N.Y.C., 1998—. Mem. ABA, U.S. Patent Bar, N.Y. State Bar, Siwanoy Country Club, South Seas Club. Real property. Office: McDermott Will & Emery 50 Rockefeller Plz Fl 12 New York NY 10020-1605

**CULBERT, PETER VAN HORN,** lawyer; b. San Antonio, July 27, 1944; s. Robert William and Dorothy Fairfax (Kift) C.; m. Elizabeth Tamara Spagnola, July 12, 1980; children: Michael, Daniel, Robert, David, William. BA, Cornell U., 1966; MA, SUNY, Buffalo, 1969; JD, U. N.Mex., 1977. Bar: N.Mex. 1977, U.S. Dist. Ct. N.Mex. 1977, U.S. Ct. Appeals (10th cir.) 1977. Law clk. to Hon. Mack Easley N.Mex. Supreme Ct., Santa Fe, 1977-78; sr. ptnr. Jones, Snead, Wertheim, Wentworth & Jaramillo, Santa Fe, 1978-98; pvt. practice Santa Fe, 1998—. Mem. adv. bd., legal counsel Desert Chorale, Santa Fe, 1991—, bd. dirs., 1986-91. Recipient hon. cert. Strathmore Registry Bus. Leaders, 1995-97. Mem. ABA, ATLA, N.Mex. Trial Lawyers Assn., Canyon Assn., Alpha Delta Phi (life). Avocations: flamenco guitarist, bicycling, horticulture, camping. E-mail: pvculbert@law-sf.com. Personal injury, Insurance, General civil litigation. Office: 911 Old Pecos Trl Santa Fe NM 87501-4566

**CULBRETH, JAMES HAROLD, JR.,** lawyer; b. Durham, N.C., Nov. 12, 1953; s. James Harold and Florence Rittenhouse C.; m. Kate Dickson Banks, Oct. 24, 1981; children: Julia Fairbairn, Duncan Banks. BA in Psychology, Wake Forest U., 1977; JD, George Washington U., 1980. Bar: D.C. 1981, Va. 1982, N.C. 1984. Assoc. Baylinson Kudysh & Greenberg, Washington, 1981-84; trust officer, asst. v.p. Ctrl. Carolina Bank & Trust Co., Durham, 1984-90; assoc. McGuire Woods Battle & Boothe, Richmond, Va., 1990-93, Wishart Norris Henninger & Pittman, Burlington, N.C., 1993-95; ptnr. Smith Helms Mulliss & Moore LLP, Charlotte, N.C., 1995—; lectr. employee benefits Am. Bankers Assn. Nat. Trust Sch., 1987—. Chair stewardship com. University City United Meth., Charlotte, 1998—. Democrat. Avocations: tennis, bicycling, camping, writing. Pension, profit-sharing, and employee benefits, Mergers and acquisitions, General corporate. Office: Smith Helms Mulliss & Moore LLP 201 N Tryon St Charlotte NC 28202-2146

**CULHANE, JOHN LANGDON,** lawyer; b. Washington, Jan. 4, 1952; s. John Langdon and Callie (Doorley) C.; m. Carol Fern Simonson, Apr. 10, 1982; children: James Nelson, Andrew Davis. BA, U. Notre Dame, 1973; JD, U. Va., 1978. Bar: Va. 1978, U.S. Ct. Appeals (4th cir.) 1978, U.S. Dist. Ct. (ea. dist.) Va. 1980, U.S. Supreme Ct. 1981, Calif. 1983, U.S. Dist. Ct. (no. dist.) Calif. 1983, U.S. Ct. Appeals (9th cir.) 1983, Pa. 1988, U.S. Dist. CT. (ea. dist.) Pa. 1989. Sr. atty., sect. chief Nat. Credit Union Adminstrn., Washington, 1978-82; assoc. counsel Bank of Am. Nat. Trust & Savings Assn., San Francisco, 1982-84, Mellon Bank, Phila., 1985-88; assoc. Wolf Block Schorr & Solis-Cohen, Phila., 1989-92, ptnr., 1993-94; ptnr. Ballard Spahr Andrews & Ingersoll, Phila., 1995—; mem. bd. advisors CFI Compliance News, Portland, 1990—; mem. adv. bd. The Bank Atty., Washington, 1993-94. Mem. adv. panel: Truth in Lending Compliance Manual, 1981; reviewer: Family Legal Guide, 1994; editor Collection of Jour. Articles Annual Survey of Legal Devels., 1986-89; contbr. articles to profl. jours. Chair Sch. House Lane Neighbors, Phila., 1990—; advisor Friends of Queen Lane Station, Phila., 1994—. Recipient Vol. Svc. award City of Phila., Pa., 1993, 94. Mem. ABA (sect. on adminstrv. law, sect. on real property, probate and trust law, sect. on bus. law com. on credit unions, com. on consumer fin. svcs., chair task force on lender liability limitation amendments to state statutes of frauds 1989-90, vice chair subcom. on access to svcs. 1989-92, chair subcom. on access to svcs. 1993), Pa. Bar Assn. (sect. on bus. law), Phila. Bar Assn. (com. on banking law, com. on consumer fin. svcs.), Am. Coll. Consumer Fin. Svcs. Attys. (charter mem.). Consumer commercial, Real property, Computer. Home: 438 W School House Ln Philadelphia PA 19144-4506 Office: Ballard Spahr Andrews & Ingersoll 1735 Market St Fl 51 Philadelphia PA 19103-7501

**CULLEN, JACK JOSEPH,** lawyer; b. Sept. 20, 1951; s. Ray Brandes (stepfather) and Helen Cullen; m. Deborah L. Vick, Oct. 28, 1978; children: Cameron, Katherine. BA, Western Wash. State Coll., 1973; JD, U. Puget Sound, 1976. Bar: Wash. 1977, U.S. Dist. Ct. (we. dist.) Wash. 1977, U.S. Dist. Ct. (ea. dist.) Wash. 1977, U.S. Tax Ct. 1984, U.S. Ct. Appeals (9th cir.) 1980. Staff atty. Wash. State Bar Assn., Seattle, 1977-79; assoc. Hatch & Leslie, Seattle, 1979-85, mng. ptnr., 1985-91; ptnr. Foster Pepper & Shefelman, Seattle, 1991-96, mng. ptnr., 1996—, mng. chair, 1991—; spkr. in field. Co-author: Prejudgment Attachment, 1986. Active Frank Lloyd Wright Bldg. Conservancy, 1989—. Mem. ABA (bus. law sect.), Am. Bankruptcy Inst., Wash. State Bar Assn. (creditor-debtor sect., chair exec. 1982-90, spl. dist. counsel 1988—, hearing officer 1990), Seattle-King County Bar Assn. (bankruptcy rules subcom. 1988-90), Vancouver-Seattle Involvency Group (charter mem. 1990—), U.S. Sport Parachuting Team (nat. and world champions 1976, instrument rated pilot), Wash. Athletic Club. Avocations: skiing, bicycling. Bankruptcy, Contracts commercial, Real property. Office: Foster Pepper & Shefelman PLLC 1111 3rd Ave Ste 3400 Seattle WA 98101-3299

**CULLEN, JAMES D.,** lawyer; b. St. Louis, May 18, 1925; s. James and Frances C. Cullen; m. Joyce Marie Jackson, Aug. 19, 1950; children: Mary Lynn Cullen Walsh, James D., Michael Parnell, Carol Cullen Bernstein. LLD, St. Louis, 1948. Bar: Mo. 1948. Assoc. Spalding & Cullen, St. Louis, 1950-99; pvt. practice law St. Louis. Bd. dirs. Marygrove, Gen. Protestant Children's Home; counsel Dismas House of St. Louis, Richard Greene Co. 1st lt. USAF, 1943-45. Mem. ABA, Mo. Bar Assn., St. Louis Bar Assn., Lawyers Assn. St. Louis, MAC Club. Roman Catholic. General corporate, Real property, Probate. Home: 16 Berkshire Dr Saint Louis MO 63117-1030

**CULLEN, KATHLEEN JOY,** lawyer; b. Albany, N.Y., Dec. 21, 1957; d. Bruce L. and Gloria Joy Pehl; m. Bryan P. Cullen, Jan. 28, 1995; stepchildren: Brendan, Maura. BA cum laude, Mt. Holyoke Coll., 1979; JD, Union U., Albany, N.Y., 1982. Bar: N.Y. 1983. Assoc. Tate, Bishko & Assocs., Albany, 1983-93; hearing examiner Washington-Schenectady County Family Cts., 4th Jud. Dist., Office Ct. Adminstrn., N.Y. State, Ft. Edward, 1993—. Committeewoman Albany County Dem. Com., 1993. Mem. ABA, N.Y. State Bar Assn. Office: Washington County Family Ct Broadway Fort Edward NY 12828

**CULLEN, KIM MICHAEL,** lawyer; b. San Diego, June 27, 1966; s. Phillip Dean and Paula Barnhill C.; m. Margaret Louise Cummings, Aug. 4, 1990; children: John William, Michael Burns. BS in Bus. Adminstrn., U. Fla., 1988; JD, Mercer U., 1993. Bar: Fla. 1993, U.S. Dist. Ct. (mid. dist.) Fla. 1993. Assoc. Troutman, Williams, et al, P.A., Winter Park, Fla., 1993-98, W. Riley Allen, P.A., Orlando, Fla., 1998—. Mem. ABA, Assn. Trial Lawyers Am., Acad. Fla. Trial Lawyers. Democrat. Episcopalian. Personal injury, State civil litigation. Office: W Riley Allen PA 228 Annie St Orlando FL 32806-1208

**CULLEN, MARK KENNETH,** lawyer; b. Springfield, Ill., Sept. 27, 1962; s. Richard W. and Ann (Orr) Carlson; m. Marica L. Heagy, Aug. 5, 1989; 1 child, Kristin Anne. BA with honors, Northwestern U., 1984; MBA/JD, U. Ill., Urbana-Champaign, 1988. Bar: Ill. 1988, U.S. Dist. Ct. (no. dist.) Ill. 1988, U.S. Dist. Ct. (ctrl. dist.) Ill. 1991. Rsch. analyst Fed. Res. Bank Chgo., Chgo., 1983-84; tchg. and rsch. asst. U. Ill., Urbana-Champaign, 1984-88; atty., asst. cashier The First Nat. Bank Chgo., Chgo., 1988-91; shareholder, dir. Sorling Northrup Hanna Cullen and Cochran Ltd., Springfield, Ill., 1991—. Vice-chmn., trustee First United Meth. Ch., Springfield, 1991-95; v.p. Boy Scouts Am., Springfield, 1994—. Mem. Springfield Lions Club (pres. 1996-97). Avocations: golf, scouting, computers, basketball, collectibles. General corporate, Securities, Mergers and acquisitions. Office: Sorling Northrup Hanna Cullen & Cochran Ltd PO Box 5131 607 E Adams St Ste 800 Springfield IL 62701-1623

**CULLEN, RAYMOND T.,** lawyer; b. June 26, 1937. AB, LaSalle Coll., 1959; JD, Temple U., 1969. Bar: Pa. 1969; U.S. Supreme Ct. 1977. Mem. Morgan, Lewis & Bockius, Phila. General civil litigation, Intellectual property, Product liability. Office: Morgan Lewis & Bockius 1701 Market St Philadelphia PA 19103-2903

**CULLEN, RICHARD,** lawyer, former state attorney general; b. N.Y.C., Mar. 10, 1948; m. Agnes Tullidge; children: Thomas, Anne Gray, Elizabeth, Richard. BS, Furman U., 1971; JD, U. Richmond, 1977. Bar: Va. Ptnr. McGuire, Woods, Battle and Boothe, Richmond, 1977-97, 98—; atty. gen. Commonwealth of Va., 1997-98; spl. counsel Senate Iran-Contra Investigation, 1987; U.S. atty. for ea. dist. Va., 1991-93. Editor-in-chief U. Richmond Law Rev., 1976-77. Mem. Juvenile Criminal Commn.; mem. Va. Criminal Sentencing Commn.; co-chmn. Gov.'s Commn. on Parole Abolition and Sentencing Reform. Office: McGuire, Woods, Battle & Boothe One James Ctr 901 E Cary St Richmond VA 23219-4057

**CULLEN, WILLIAM ZACHARY,** lawyer; b. Stamford, Conn., Feb. 15, 1955; s. John Cornelius and Ann D. (Woytowicz) C. BA, U. Conn., 1977; JD, New Eng. Sch. Law, 1980. Bar: Ala. 1989, U.S. Dist. Ct. (no. dist.) Ala. 1989, U.S. Ct. Appeals (11th cir.) 1989. Legal asst. Birmingham (Ala.) Legal Svcs., 1980-82; legal asst. Cooper, Mitch, Crawford, Kuykendall & Whatley, Birmingham, 1983-89, atty., 1989-98; atty. Sexton, Cullen & Jones P.C., Birmingham, 1998—. Workers' compensation, Pension, profit-sharing, and employee benefits. Office: Sexton Cullen and Jones PC 3021 Lorna Rd Ste 310 Birmingham AL 35216-4500

**CULLEY, PETER WILLIAM,** lawyer; b. Dover-Foxcroft, Maine, Oct. 17, 1943; s. William Redfern and Kathryn (Boyle) C.; children: Courtney Little, Jonathan Redfern. BA, U. Maine, 1965; JD, Boston U., 1968. Bar: Maine 1969, U.S. Dist. Ct. Maine 1969. Asst. atty. gen. Dept. of Atty. Gen. State of Maine, 1969-72, chief, criminal div., 1971-72; ptnr. Hewes, Culley and Beals, Portland, Maine, 1972-85, Pierce Atwood, Portland, 1985—. Chmn. Falmouth (Maine) Town Coun., 1986-87. Fellow Am. Coll. Trial Lawyers (state chmn. 1990-92); mem. ABA, Maine State Bar Assn., Internat. Assn. Def. Counsel, Def. Rsch. Inst. (state chmn. 1978-87), No. New England Def. Counsel (pres. 1985-86), Am. Bd. Trial Advocates. Federal civil litigation, General civil litigation, Product liability. Home: 406 Chandlers Wharf Portland ME 04101-4653 Office: Pierce Atwood One Monument Sq Portland ME 04101

**CULLIGAN, KEVIN JAMES,** lawyer; b. Monticello, N.Y., Sept. 11, 1954; s. James Robert and Ann Audrey Culligan; m. Nancy Jean Segal, Aug. 10, 1980; children: Ryan James, Katherine Lynn, Casey Ann. AB in Biology, Colgate U., 1976; JD, Cornell U., 1980. Bar: N.Y. 1981, U.S. Dist. Ct. (so. and ea. dists.) N.Y. 1981, U.S. Ct. Appeals (fed. cir.), U.S. Dist. Ct. (we. dist.) N.Y. 1988, U.S. Supreme Ct. 1998. Mem. ABA, N.Y. Intellectual Property Law Assn., Assn. of the Bar of the City of N.Y. Intellectual property, Patent, Trademark and copyright. Home: 41 Kent Dr Cortlandt Manor NY 10567-6232 Office: Fish & Neave 1251 Avenue Of The Americas New York NY 10020-1104

**CULLINA, WILLIAM MICHAEL,** lawyer; b. Hartford, Conn., July 22, 1921; s. Michael Stephen and Margaret (Carroll) C.; m. Gertrude Evelyn Blasig, Apr. 29, 1961; children: William Gregory, Kevin Michael, John Stephen, Susan Margaret. AB, Catholic U. Am., 1942; LLB, Yale U., 1948. Bar: Conn. bar 1948. Assoc. Murtha, Cullina, Richter & Pinney, Hartford, 1948—, ptnr., 1952-91, of counsel, 1992—. Bd. dirs. St. Francis Hosp. and Med. Ctr.; trustee St. Joseph Coll., 1986-98, trustee emeritus, 1998—; bd. govs. The Hartford Club, 1984-89, chair, 1987-88. Served with USNR, 1942-46. Fellow Am. Bar Found.; mem. ABA, Conn. Bar Assn., Hartford County Bar Assn., Hartford Tennis Club, Country Club of Farmington, Knight of St. Gregory, Phi Beta Kappa. Roman Catholic. Labor, Pension, profit-sharing, and employee benefits, General corporate. Office: Murtha Cullina Richter & Pinney City Pl 185 Asylum St Ste 29 Hartford CT 06103-3469

**CULP, CHARLES WILLIAM,** lawyer; b. Louisville, Nov. 13, 1931; s. Charles Cantrell and Carolyn Marticia (O'Bannon) C.; m. Elisabeth Martha Stoker, Sept. 22, 1962; children: Charles Cantrell, Virginia Sheldon. BA, Yale U., 1953; JD, Harvard U., 1958. Bar: Ind. 1958. Ptnr., Cadick, Burns Duck & Peterson, Indpls., 1958-81, Shortridge & Culp, Indpls., 1981-88; pvt. practice, 1988—. Mem. Lawyers Club, Traders Point Hunt Club, University Club, Dramatic Club. Pension, profit-sharing, and employee benefits, Estate planning, General corporate. Home: 9251 Spring Forest Dr Indianapolis IN 46260-1267

**CULP, DONALD ALLEN,** lawyer; b. Atchison, Kans., June 13, 1938; s. Roy Allen and Audrey Mae (Moyer) C.; m. Judy Wayne Smith, Sept. 10, 1966; children: Brian David, Matthew Allen, Lindsey Beth. Bar: Kans. 1965, Mo. 1987. Ptnr. Culp & Sheppard, Overland Park, Kans., 1969-79; gen. counsel Electronic Realty Assn., Overland Park, Kans., 1979-87; v.p., gen. counsel Signature Foods, Inc., Kansas City, Mo., 1987-89; ptnr. Shughart, Thomson & Kilroy, Overland Park, 1989-97, Blackwell, Sanders, Pepper, Martin, Kansas City, Mo., 1997—. Pres. Am. Cancer Soc., Overland Park, 1970-73, hon. life mem., 1981—; elder Rolling Hills Presbyn. Ch., Overland Park, 1972-80; pres., bd. dirs. Shawnee Mission Bd. Edn., Overland Park, 1975-83; bd. dirs. Overland Park C. of C., 1978-81. Mem. ABA, Kans. Bar Assn., Mo. Bar Assn., Johnson County Bar Assn. Republican. Presbyterian. Avocations: marathon running, race walking. Franchising, Family and matrimonial. Home: 9609 W 104th St Shawnee Mission KS 66212-5606 Office: Blackwell Sanders Peper Martin PO Box 419777 2300 Main St Ste 1100 Kansas City MO 64108-2416

**CULP, NATHAN CRAIG,** lawyer; b. Camden, Ark., 1965; s. Harold Lloyd and Carole Culp; m. Clara M. Graves, 1995. BA, La. Tech. U., 1988; JD, U. Ark., 1991. Bar: Ark. 1991, U.S. Dist. Ct. Ark. 1992. Law clk. Walker, Roaf, Campbell, Ivory and Dunkin, Little Rock, 1989-91, assoc., 1991-94; staff atty. Pub. Employee Claims divsn. Ark. Dept. Ins., Little Rock, 1994-99, Ark. Hwy. and Transp. Dept., 1999—. Mem. Ark. Bar Assn. Methodist. Avocations: computers, reading. Office: Ark Hwy and Transp Dept Pub Employee Claims Divsn PO Box 2261 Little Rock AR 72203-2261

**CULPEPPER, DAVID CHARLES,** lawyer; b. Quantico, Va., Mar. 15, 1946; s. Carlton Milburn and Eleanor Louise (Hart) C.; m. Marie T. Francher, June 21, 1969; children: Larissa, Danielle. BA, Santa Clara (Calif.) U., 1968; JD, U. Oreg., 1974. Bar: Oreg. 1974, U.S. Dist. Ct. Oreg. 1974, U.S. Tax Ct. 1974, U.S. Ct. Appeals (9th cir.) 1974. Ptnr. Miller, Nash, Wiener, Hager & Carlsen, Portland, Oreg., 1974—. Contbg. author: Advising Oregon Businesses, 1986, 89; contbr. articles to profl. jours. Mem. ABA (partnership com. taxation sect. 1983), Oreg. Bar Assn. (chair exec. com. tax sect. 1992-93), Portland Tax Forum (bd. dirs., co-chair tax force on ltd. liability co. legis.). Taxation, general, Corporate taxation, General corporate. Office: Miller Nash Wiener Hager & Carlsen 111 SW 5th Ave Ste 3500 Portland OR 97204-3699

**CUMBERLAND, WILLIAM EDWIN,** lawyer; b. Washington, Sept. 11, 1938; m. Clare Hogan, Aug. 17, 1973; children: Lisa, Joseph, Kara. AB, Georgetown U., 1960; LLB, Harvard U., 1963. Bar: D.C. 1963, Va. 1963. Law clk. to judge U.S. Dist. Ct. D.C., Washington, 1963-64; from assoc. to ptnr. Cefaratti & Cumberland, Washington, 1964-71; atty. HUD, Washington, 1971-72; counsel Mortgage Bankers Assn. Am., Washington, 1972—, gen. counsel, sr. v.p., 1988—. Banking, Finance, Real property. Office: Mortgage Bankers Assn Am 1125 15th St NW Ste 700 Washington DC 20005-2707

**CUMBEY, CONSTANCE ELIZABETH,** lawyer, author, lecturer; b. Ft. Wayne, Ind., Feb. 29, 1944; d. John Merrill and Margaret Elizabeth (Kutsch) Butler; m. Alan Fletcher Cumbey, Oct. 7, 1962 (div. Aug. 1969); 1 child, Stephen Alan; m. Barry Drennan MacIntosh, Nov. 23, 1974. Student, Wayne State U., 1966-71, Mich. State U., 1969-70; JD, Detroit Coll. Law, 1975. Bar: Mich. 1975. Legis. analyst, aide to speaker Mich. Ho. of Reps., Lansing, 1969-70; exec. asst. to mayor City of Highland Park, Mich., 1970-72; pvt. practice Detroit, 1975-90, Bloomfield Hills, Mich., 1990—; moderator Law Talk Radio, Detroit. Author: The Hidden Dangers of the Rainbow, 1983 (transl. into German, Norwegian , Finnish and Dutch), A Planned Deception, 1986; editor newsletter New Age Monitor, 1986-92. Bd. dirs. N.W. Community Orgn., Detroit, 1968-70, Mich. Cancer Found., Detroit, 1972-80. Mem. ABA (chmn. family law subcom. gen. practice sect. 1981), State Bar Mich., Oakland County Bar Assn., N.W. Bar Assn. (sec. 1979-81), Nat. Assn. Women Lawyers (corr. sec. 1979-81). Avocations: piano, reading. Constitutional. Home: 3675 Hi Crest Dr Lake Orion MI 48360-2413 Office: 2525 S Telegraph Rd Ste 306 Bloomfield Hills MI 48302-0289

**CUMMINGS, FRANK,** lawyer; b. N.Y.C., Dec. 11, 1929; s. Louis and Florence (Levine) C.; m. Jill Schwartz, July 6, 1958; children: Peter Ian, Margaret Anne. BA, Hobart Coll., 1951; MA, Columbia U., 1955, LLB, 1958. Bar: N.Y. 1959, D.C. 1963. Adminstrv. asst. to U.S. Senator Javits, 1969-71; minority counsel com. labor and pub. welfare U.S. Senate, 1965-67, 71-72; assoc. Cravath, Swaine & Moore, N.Y.C., 1958-63, Gall, Lane & Powell, Washington, 1967-68; ptnr. Gall, Lane & Powell, Washington, 1972-75, Marshall, Bratter, Greene, Allison & Tucker, Washington, 1976-82, Nossaman, Krueger & Knox, 1982-83, Cummings & Cummings, P.C. and predecessor firm (Cummings & Kershaw, P.C.), 1983-86, LeBoeuf, Lamb, Greene & MacRae, L.L.P., Washington, 1986—; lectr. law Columbia U. Law Sch., 1970-74; adj. prof. Georgetown U. Law Sch., 1983-86; chmn. Am. Law Inst.-ABA Ann. Course Employee Benefits Litigation, 1989—, Employment and Labor Rels. Law for Corp. Coun. and Gen. Practitioner, 1978—; mem. pub. adv. coun. employee welfare and pension benefit plans Dept. Labor, 1972-74; mem. adv. bd. Pension Reporter Bur. Nat. Affairs. Author: Capitol Hill Manual, 1976, 2nd edit., 1984, Pension Plan Terminations-Single Employer Plans, 2nd edit., 1994, Multiemployer Plans, 2nd edit., 1986; articles editor Columbia U. Law Rev., 1957-58. Mem. ABA (chmn. com. pension, welfare and related plans 1976-79), Am. Law Inst.; Bar Assn. D.C. (chmn. com. labor rels. law 1972-73), Cosmos Club, Phi Beta Kappa. Articles editor Columbia U. Law Rev., 1957-58. Federal civil litigation, Insurance, Pension, profit-sharing, and employee benefits. Home: 4305 Bradley Ln Chevy Chase MD 20815-5232 Office: LeBoeuf Lamb Greene & MacRae LLP 1875 Connecticut Ave NW Washington DC 20009-5728

**CUMMINGS, FREDERIC ALAN,** lawyer; b. Mobile, Ala., Sept. 5, 1944; s. J.V. and Alice Cummings; m. Elise Bell Pichard, Dec. 18, 1993; children from previous marriage: Christian Gordon, Sara Elise, Alice Kate Griffith. BS in Econs., Auburn U., 1967; JD, Fla. State U., 1975. Bar: U.S. Ct. Appeals (11th cir.), U.S. Dist. Ct. (mid. and no. dists.) Fla. Ptnr. Holland & Knight, Tallahassee, Fla., 1975-86, Cummings, Lawrence & Vezina P.A., Tallahassee, 1986—. Construction, Contracts commercial, Administrative and regulatory. Office: Cummings Lawrence & Vezina PO Box 589 Tallahassee FL 32302-0589

**CUMMINGS, FREDERICK MICHAEL,** lawyer; b. Tucson, June 22, 1958; s. Frank Carrillo and Jacqueline (Day) C.; m. Karin Jean Nelson, Aug. 13, 1983; children: Brett Michael, Caroline Elena, Christina Ingrid. BSFS, Georgetown U., 1980, JD, 1984. Bar: Va. 1984, D.C. 1984, Ariz. 1986, U.S. Dist. Ct. (ea. dist.) Va. 1984, U.S. Dist. Ct. Ariz. 1986, U.S. Ct. Appeals (4th cir.) 1985, U.S. Ct. Appeals (9th cir.) 1987, U.S. Claims Ct. 1992. Assoc. Lewis Mitchell & Moore, Washington, 1984-85; assoc. Jennings Strouss & Salmon, Phoenix, 1986-92, ptnr., 1992-95; shareholder White Cummings & Longino, Phoenix, 1995—. Judge pro tem Maricopa County, Ariz., 1996—. Mem. Ariz. Assn. Def. Counsel. Democrat. Roman Catholic. Professional liability, Product liability, State civil litigation. Office: White Cummings & Longino 2920 E Camelback Rd Ste 150 Phoenix AZ 85016-4499

**CUMMINGS, JOHN PATRICK,** lawyer; b. Westfield, Mass., June 28, 1933; s. Daniel Thoams and Nora (Brick) C.; m. Dorothy June D'Ingianni, Dec. 27, 1957 (div. May 1978); children: John Patrick, Mary Catherine, Michael Brick, Kevin Andrew, Colleen Elise, Erin Christine, Christopher Gerald; m. Marilyn Ann Welch, May 23, 1980. BS, St. Michael's Coll., 1955; PhD, U. Tex., 1969; JD, U. Toledo, 1973, MCE, 1977. Bar: Ohio 1973, U.S. Mil. Appeals 1974, U.S. Dist. Ct. (no. dist.) Ohio 1979. Mgr. Hamilton Mgmt., Inc., Austin, Tex., 1962-68; scientist Owens Ill., Toledo, 1968-73, risk mgr., 1974-76, staff atty., 1977-80, mgr. legis. affairs, 1981-84; pres. Hansa World Cargo Svc., Inc., Oakland, Calif., 1984-86; in-house counsel Brown Vence & Assocs., San Francisco, 1987-88; gen. counsel Pacific Mgmt. Co., Sacramento, 1986-88; pres. John P. Cummings & Assoc., Fremont, Calif., 1988—; cons. Glass Packaging Inst., Washington, 1970-83, EPA, Washington, 1970-74. Contbr. articles to profl. jours.; patentee in field. With USAF, 1955-62, 68-69, 75-76, 84-85, col. Res. ret. 1986. USPHS fellow, 1963-66. Fellow Royal Chem. Soc.; mem. ABA, VFW, Am. Chem. Soc., ASTM (chmn. 1979), Am. Ceramic Soc. (chpt. chmn. 1973), Res. Officers Assn. (legis. chmn. 1979-85), Am. Legion, KC (4th degree). Roman Catholic. Avocations: reading, travel, coin and stamp collecting. Environmental, Private international, Immigration, naturalization, and customs. Home: 843 Barcelona Dr Fremont CA 94536-2607 Office: PO Box 2847 Fremont CA 94536-0847

**CUMMINGS, RICHARD M.,** law educator; b. N.Y.C., Mar. 23, 1938; s. Albert Martin and Betty (Benjamin) Cohen; m. Mary Araminta Johnson, Aug. 3, 1965; children: Benjamin, Orson. AB, Princeton U., 1959; JD, Columbia U., 1962; MLitt, Cambridge (Eng.) U., 1964, PhD, 1989. Bar: N.Y. 1964, U.S. Dist. Ct. (so. dist.) N.Y. 1970. Assoc. Breed, Abbott & Morgan, N.Y., 1964-65; atty. adv. Agy. for Internat. Devel., 1965-66; asst. prof. U. Louisville Sch. Law, 1966-70; ptnr. Ross & Cummings, Southampton, N.Y., 1971-73; lectr. law U. W.I., Barbados, 1973-74; assoc. prof. SUNY, Stony Brook, 1974-77; legis. counsel N.Y. State Assembly, Albany, 1978-80; dir. natural resources Town of East Hampton, N.Y., 1981-82; ptnr. Richard Cummings, Sanford Katz, Ira Kornbluth, Attys.-at-Law, East Hampton, 1982—; of counsel Beatie & Osborn, N.Y.C.; vis. asst. prof. Haile Sellassie I U, Addis Ababa, Ethiopia, 1967-69; vis. assoc. prof. Southampton (N.Y.) Coll., 1970-71; adj. prof. Duke U., Durham, N.C., 1977—; polit. cons. Richard Cummings Comm., Bridgehampton, 1979—; prof. law Pace U., White Plains, N.Y., 1987-95. Author: Proposition 14, 1980; The Pied Piper, 1985; editor: Nine Scorpions in a Bottle, 1995; contbr. articles to law jours.; polit. columnist East Hampton (N.Y.) Star, 1971-77. Committeeman Town Dem. Com., Southampton, 1971-73; del. Dem. Nat. Conv., Miami, Fla., 1972; chmn., N.Y. State campaign Terry Sanford for Pres., 1976; candidate for U.S. Congress, Suffolk County, N.Y., 1980. Recipient Buchanan Prize in politics Princeton U., 1959; grantee Albert and Bessie Warner Fund, Bridgehampton, 1974-82, N.Y. Coun. for Humanities, 1974-77; James Kent scholar Columbia U., 1962. Fellow Nat. Assn. Trial Lawyers (hon.); mem. Authors Guild, Am. Soc. Journalists and Authors, , PEN Am. Ctr., Overseas Press Club, Princeton Club (N.Y.C.). Real property, Environmental, Private international. Home and Office: PO Box 349 Bridgehampton NY 11932-0349

**CUMMINGS, SAM R.,** federal judge; b. 1944. BBA with high honors, Tex. Tech. U., 1967; JD cum laude, Baylor U., 1970. With Culton, Morgan, Britain & White, Amarillo, Tex., 1970-87; dist. judge No. Dist. Tex., Lubbock, 1987—. Com. chmn. Troop 86, Boy Scouts Am., Amarillo; trustee Presbyn. Children's Home, Amarillo, Howard Payne U., Brownwood, Tex. Recipient Wall St. Jour. award, Am. Jurisprudence award; Judge Hunter D. Barrow Meml. scholar Baylor U. Sch. Law. Mem. Kiwanis (v.p. South Amarillo club). Office: US Dist Ct 1205 Texas Ave Rm 210C Lubbock TX 79401

**CUMMINGS, STACEY L.,** lawyer; b. Kingston, N.Y.; d. Edward A. and Karen A. Jabs; m. John G. Cummings, July 8, 1989; 1 child, Elise McKernon. AS, Ulster County C.C., 1987; BA, Union Coll., 1989; JD, Widener U., 1993. Bar: Del. 1993, U.S. Dist. Ct. Del. 1995, Pa. 1995. Intern Chancery Ct. Del., Wilmington, 1993; judicial clk. Superior Ct. Del., Wilmington, 1993-95; assoc. Casarino Christman & Shalk, Wilmington, 1995—; invited spkr., judge Widener U., 1993—. V.p. Mendenhall Village Homeowners Assn., Hockessin, Del., 1996, pres., 1997. Mem. Del. State Bar Assn. (women in law sect.), Del. Trial Lawyers Assn., Def. Counsel Del. Avocations: playing with daughter, scrapbooks. Personal injury, Product liability, Contracts commercial. Office: Casarino Christman & Shalk 222 Delaware Ave Ste 1220 Wilmington DE 19801-1611

**CUMMINS, CHARLES FITCH, JR.,** lawyer; b. Lansing, Mich., Aug. 19, 1939; s. Charles F. Sr. and Ruth M. Cummins; m. Anne Warner, Feb. 11, 1961; children: Michael, John, Mark. AB in Econs., U. Mich., 1961; LLB, U. Calif., Hastings, 1966. Bar: Calif. 1966, Mich. 1976. Assoc. Hall, Henry, Oliver & McReavy, San Francisco, 1966-70, ptnr., 1971-75; ptnr. Cummins & Cummins, Lansing, Mich., 1976-82, Pitto & Ubhaus, San Jose, Calif., 1982-85; prin. Law Offices Charles F. Cummins Jr., San Jose, 1985-87; ptnr. Cummins & Chandler, San Jose, 1987-92; prin. Law Offices of Charles F. Cummins, Jr., San Jose, 1992—. Bd. dirs., officer various civic orgns., chs. and pvt. shcs. Lt. (j.g.) USNR, 1961-63. Mem. Kiwanis. Alternative dispute resolution, General civil litigation, Estate planning. Office: 4 N 2nd St Ste 1230 San Jose CA 95113-1307

**CUMMINS, HOWARD WALLACE,** lawyer; b. Portland, Oreg., May 4, 1937; s. Robert Vinton and Lenore Ethel (Lindholm) C.; m. Susan Roberta Smith, Dec. 21, 1969 (div. Apr. 1982); children: Mark, Jason. BA, Stanford U., 1959; JD, Golden Gate U., 1964; MA, U. Oreg., 1968, PhD, 1972. Asst. prof. U. Alta., Edmonton, 1969-74, assoc. prof., 1974-78; legis. liaison Bd. Commrs., Lane County, Oreg., 1979; adminstrv. asst. Congressman Jim Weaver 4th Dist. Oreg., 1984-86; CEO, rsch. dir. Profiles Northwest, Portland, 1980-92; rsch. dir., adj. rsch. dir. Portland State U., 1987—; dir. Radlaw, Washington, 1992-95; mng. ptnr. Cummins & Brown, Washington, 1995-99; pres. Cummins & Assoc., Washington, 1999—; pres., CEO Environ. Svcs. Group Internat., Inc., Washington, 1999—; host, commentator Radio Noon Show, CBC/Radio Can., Edmonton, 1972-76, freelance interviewer pub. affairs divsn., 1970-73; guest commentator CTV and ITV TV Networks, Edmonton, 1971-73; v.p. Garneau Cmty. League, 1974-75; jour. referee Sage Profl. Papers in Internat. Studies, 1974, Gonzaga Law Rev., 1995; mem. panel Can. Inst. Internat. Affairs, Edmonton, 1970; spkr. Christian Fellowship Conf., Edmonton, 1970, Hinton Citizens Conf., Edmonton, 1970, Can. Inst. Internat. Affairs, Calgary, 1972, U. Alta., Edmonton, 1972, Hinton Citzens Edn. Coun., 1971, U. Alta., 1972; dir. Western Regional Symposium on Instrnl. Simulations, Edmonton, 1971; mem. planning commn. Athabasca U., Edmonton, 1972, mem. seminar on human cmty. studies program, 1972; chmn. panel Western Polit. Sci. Assn., L.A., 1978; keynote spkr. Nat. Assn. Radiation Survival Nat. conf., Seattle, 1991, Nat. Assn. Atomic Vets. Nat. conf., Orlando, Fla., 1991, Hanford Concerns of Wash. conf., Spokane, 1992, Healing Global Wounds conf., Las Vegas, Nev., 1992; mem. univ. coll. health phsyics adv. bd. U. Md., 1992—. Contbr. articles to profl. jours. Bd. dirs. Centennial Montessori Sch., 1973-76; treas. Oregonians for McCarthy, 1968-69. Capt. U.S. Army, 1962-66. Mem. ABA (criminal law sect., task force on proposed protocols for future war crimes tribunal), ATLA, Am. Polit. Sci. Assn., Pa. Bar Assn. Avocations: travel, fitness, writing. Office: Cummins & Brown 5039 Connecticut Ave NW Washington DC 20008-2056

**CUMMINS, MICHAEL WAYNE,** lawyer; b. Jacksonville, Tex., Jan. 18, 1955; s. Harry Wyndel and Wanda Jean (Childs) C.; m. Carol Ann Short, Dec. 30, 1977; children: Brian Michael, Cathryn Brooke. BBA, Ouachita Bapt. U., 1979; JD, U. Tex., 1982. Sole practitioner Law Office of Michael Cummins, Jacksonville, Tex., 1982-84; mng. ptnr. Cummins & Minton, Jacksonville, 1984-88, Cummins, Moore, Montalro & Smith, Jacksonville, 1990-93; owner Michael W. Cummins & Assocs., Jacksonville, 1994—; bd. dirs. Tex. Mcpl. Cts. Assn., 1992; faculty Tex. Mcpl. Cts. Edn. Ctr. Faculty, Austin, 1990-95. Author, Publisher: (newsletter) Insights into Estate, Tax and Financial Planning, 1991—; (curriculum) Mcpl. Ct. Process, 1992; speaker TV segments Subjects for Seniors KETK, 1993; host, producer KBJS Radio Financial Insights, 1995. Moderator Polit. Debates, Jacksonville Jaycees, 1990. Grantee: State Justice Inst., 1994. Mem. Am. Acad. Estate Planning Attys., Nat. Network Estate Planning Attys., Inst. Cert. Fin. Planners, Mensa Internat. Republican. Baptist. Avocations: flying, video production, photography, tennis. Estate planning, Taxation, general, Probate. Office: Michael W Cummins & Assocs PO Box 417 1504 E Rusk St Jacksonville TX 75766-5504

**CUMMIS, CLIVE SANFORD,** lawyer; b. Newark, Nov. 21, 1928; s. Joseph Jack and Lee (Berkie) C.; m. Ann Denburg, Mar. 24, 1956; children: Andrea, Deborah, Cynthia, Jessica. A.B., Tulane U., 1949; J.D., U. Pa., 1952; LL.M., N.Y. U., 1959. Bar: N.J. 1952. Law sec. Hon. Walter Freund, Appellate Div., Superior Ct., 1955-56; partner firm Cummis & Kroner, Newark, 1956-60; chief counsel County and Mcpl. Law Revision Commn., State of N.J., Newark, 1959-62; partner firm Schiff, Cummis & Kent, Newark, 1962-67, Cummis, Kent, Radin & Tischman, Newark, 1967-70; sr. v.p., dir. Cadence Industries, N.Y.C., 1967-70; dir. Plume & Atwood Industries, Stamford, Conn., 1969-71; chmn. Sills Cummis Radin Tischman Epstein & Gross, Newark, 1970—; dir. Essex County State Bank, Financial Resources Group; instr. Practising Law Inst. Chief counsel County and Mcpl. Revision Commn., 1959-62, N.J. Pub. Market Commn., 1961-63; counsel Bd. Edn. of South Orange and Maplewood, 1964-74, Town of Cedar Grove, 1966-70, Bd. Edn. of Dumont, 1968-72; mem. com. on rules and civil practice N.J. Supreme Ct., 1975-78. Assoc. editor NJ. Law Jour., 1961—. Trustee Newark Beth Israel Med. Ctr., 1965-75, Northfield YM-YWHA, 1968-70, U. Medicine and Dentistry N.J., 1980-84, Newark Mus., N.J. Performing Arts Ctr., Blue Cross and Blue Shield N.J.; gen. coun. N.J. Turnpike Authority, 1990-94; mem. bd. overseers U. Pa. Law Sch.; mem. bd. govs. Daus. of Israel Home for Aged, 1968-70; mem. N.J. Commn. on Statue of Liberty; mem. pres.'s coun. Tulane U., 1992—; pres. bd. dirs. Tulane Assocs., 1994-96; mem. Pres.'s commn. on White House Fellows, 1993—; dir. N.J. Regional Planning Assn. Recipient 1st Ann. Judge Learned Hand award Am. Jewish Com., 1994. 'ellow Am. Bar Found.; mem. ABA, Am. Law Inst., Am. Judicature Soc., U. Pa. Law Sch. Alumni Soc. (pres.), N.J. Bar Assn., Essex County Bar Assn., City Athletic Club (N.Y.C.), Greenbrook County Club (North Caldwell, N.J.), Stockbridge Golf Club (Mass.). Democrat. Jewish. Federal civil litigation, State civil litigation, Administrative and regulatory. Office: Sills Cummis Radin Tischman Epstein & Gross One Riverfront Pl Newark NJ 07102

**CUMPIAN, JOE G.,** lawyer; b. Crystal City, Tex., Feb. 18, 1929; s. Miguel and Maria G. Cumpian; m. Norma V. Cumpian, Feb. 4, 1961 (div. Apr. 11, 1991); children: Daniel A., Patricia M., Teresa A., Joseph S. BA, St. Mary's U., 1952, JD cum laude, 1956; diploma, Judge Adv. Gen.'s Sch., 1970. Bar: Tex. Title examiner Stewart Title Co., San Antonio, 1956-58; pvt. practice San Antonio, 1958—. Mem. St. Mary's U. Booster Club, 1948—, sec., pres. Lt. col. U.S. Army, 1956-80. Named to Hall of Fame, St. Mary's U., 1987. Mem. San Antonio Bar Assn. Democrat. Roman Catholic. Avocation: jogging. General civil litigation, Family and matrimonial, General practice. Home: 802 S Saint Marys St San Antonio TX 78205-3409

**CUNEO, DONALD LANE,** lawyer, educator; b. Alameda, Calif., Apr. 19, 1944; s. Vernon Edmund and Dorothy (Lane) c.; m. Frances Susan Huze, Aug. 8, 1981; children: Kristen Marie, Lane Michael. BA, Lehigh U., 1966; JD, Columbia U., 1970, MBA, 1970. Bar: N.Y. 1971, D.C. 1992, U.S. Claims Ct. 1972, U.S. Tax Ct. 1972, U.S. Dist. Ct. (so. dist.) N.Y. 1973, U.S. Dist. Ct. (no. dist.) 1978, U.S. Dist. Ct. D.C. 1992, U.S. Ct. Appeals (2nd cir.) 1979, U.S. Ct. Appeals (D.C. cir.) 1992, U.S. Ct. Internat. Trade 1979, U.S. Ct. Appeals (fed. cir.) 1979, U.S. Supreme Ct. 1979. Assoc. Shearman & Sterling, N.Y.C., 1971-79, ptnr., 1979-93; pres., CEO Internat. House, 1993—; sec./trustee Internat. House, N.Y.C., 1977-93. Author: (with others) Prevention and Prosecution of Computer and High Technology Crime, 1988; contbr. articles to profl. jours. Reginald Heber Smith Community Lawyer fellow U.S. Govt., N.Y.C., 1970-71. Mem. Coun. Fgn. Rels. Avocations: sports, travel. General civil litigation, Private international. Home and Office: Internat House 500 Riverside Dr New York NY 10027-3916

**CUNHA, JOHN HENRY, JR.,** lawyer; b. Cambridge, Mass., Apr. 1, 1950; s. John Henry Sr. and Dolores Antonia (de Rosas) C.; m. Catherine Rondeau, July 6, 1985; children: Christopher, Mathieu, Chloé. BA magna cum laude, Boston Coll., 1973, JD, 1977. Bar: Mass. 1977, U.S. Dist. Ct. Mass. 1978, U.S. Ct. Appeals (1st cir.) 1981, N.Y. 1986. Trial atty. Mass. Defenders Com., Boston, 1977-79; pros. atty. State Ethics Commn., Boston, 1979-81; ptnr. Salsberg & Cunha, Boston, 1981-95, Salsberg Cunha and Holcomb P.C., Boston, 1995-98; Cunha & Holcomb P.C., Boston, 1998—; instr. law Suffolk U., Boston, 1982-85, Harvard U., Cambridge, 1985-95; bd. dirs. Mass. Correctional Legal Svcs., 1996—, Ecole Bilingenal Internat. Sch. Boston, 1991-98, chmn. bd., 1994-98. Mem. Mass. Bar Assn., Boston Bar Assn. (co-chmn. indigent criminal def. com. 1985-86), Mass. Assn. Criminal Def. Lawyers, ACLU, Nat. Lawyers Guild. Democrat. Criminal, Personal injury, General civil litigation. Office: Salsberg Cunha & Holcomb PC 20 Winthrop Sq Ste 402 Boston MA 02110-1274

**CUNHA, MARK GEOFFREY,** lawyer; b. Lexington, Mass., Sept. 26, 1955; s. John Henry and Dolores (DeRosas) c.; m. Viviane Sirotto; children: Celine Yvonne, Nicholas Brian. AB magna cum laude, Cornell U., 1977; JD, Stanford U., 1980. Bar: N.Y. 1981, U.S. Dist. Ct. (so. and ea. dists.) N.Y. 1981, U.S. Ct. Appeals (2nd cir.) 1991, U.S. Tax Ct. 1992, U.S. Supreme Ct. 1996. Intern The White House, Washington, 1979-80; assoc. Simpson Thacher & Bartlett, N.Y.C., 1980-88, ptnr., 1989—; mediator comml. divsn. N.Y. State Supreme Ct., N.Y. County, 1996—; bd. dir. legal svcs. for N.Y.C., 1997—. Bd. dirs. N.Y. Lawyers for Pub. Interest, 1989—; trustee Inst. for Ednl. Achievement, 1995—, Lycee Francais N.Y., 1998—. Recipient Outstanding Vol. Lawyers award Legal Aid Soc., 1990, Pro Bono award N.Y. County Lawyers Assn., 1991. Mem. ABA, Internat. Bar Assn., N.Y. State Bar Assn. (exec. com. on comml. and fed. litigation sect.), Assn. Bar City N.Y. (chmn. com. on legal assistance, chmn. of del. to N.Y. State Bar Assn. Ho. of Dels., steering com. on legal assistance), Phi Beta Kappa. Democrat. Federal civil litigation, Insurance, General civil litigation. Home: 1150 Fifth Ave Apt 3A New York NY 10128-0724 Office: Simpson Thacher & Bartlett 425 Lexington Ave New York NY 10017-3954

**CUNNINGHAM, ANTHONY WILLARD,** lawyer; b. Lakeland, Fla., Nov. 10, 1931; s. Elmo and Anna Catherine Cunningham; m. Kathleen, 1960 (div. 1974); children: Matthew, Tracy, Melisse, Megan, Joshua, Alexandra; m. Robin Richards, Nov. 22, 1980. LLB, U. Fla., 1962. Bar: Fla. 1963, U.S. Dist. Ct. (mid. dist.) Fla. 1964, U.S. Ct. Appeals (5th cir.) 1964, U.S. Supreme Ct. 1975. Assoc. Fishback, Davis, Dominick & Troutman, Orlando, Fla., 1962-64; assoc. Nichols, Gaither, Beckham, Colson, Spence & Hicks, Miami, Fla., 1964-65, Orlando and Tampa, Fla., 1965-67; prin. Wagner, Cunningham, Vaughan & McLaughlin, P.A., Tampa, 1967-92, Cunningham Law Group, P.A., Tampa, 1992—. 1st lt. USAF, 1951-56. Mem. ATLA (bd. govs. 1979—, 90, 95), Trial Lawyers Pub. Justice (bd. dirs. 1986—, pres. elect 1990-91, pres. 1991-92), Acad. Fla. Trial Lawyers (bd. dirs., past pres. 1971—). Democrat. Avocations: boating, fishing, snow skiing. Personal injury, Product liability, General civil litigation. Office: Cunningham Law Group Ste 100 100 Ashley Dr S Tampa FL 33602-5348

**CUNNINGHAM, CRAIG CARNELL,** lawyer; b. St. Louis, Oct. 29, 1965; s. Harvey CArnell and Lillie Mae (Williams) C.; m. Sheila Robin Gibbs. BA, U. So. Calif., 1990; JD, U. Chgo., 1993. Bar: Ill. 1994, U.S. Dist. Ct. (no. dist.) Ill. 1994. Summer assoc. Sonnenschein Nath & Rosenthal, Chgo., 1991, Fried, Frank, Harris, Shriver & Jacobson, Washington, 1992; student rep. Westlaw Pub. Co., Chgo., 1992-93; legal article editor Nat. Clearing House for Legal Svcs., Chgo., 1992-93; assoc. Adler, Murphy & McQuillen, Chgo., 1993—; cert. practice Mandel Legal Aid Clinic, Chgo., 1992-93. Editor jour. U. Chgo. Law Sch. Round Table, 1993. Pres. Black Law Student Assn., Chgo., 1992; keynote spkr. African-Am. Graduation, L.A., 1990, U.S. Orgn. Student Panel, L.A., 1989. Mem. ABA, Chgo. Bar Assn., Ill. State Bar Assn., Mortar Bd. Nat. Honor Soc., Skull and Dagger Honor Soc., Mid-Day Club (jr. bd.), Pi Sigma Alpha. Aviation, General civil litigation, Securities. Home: 16 154th Pl # 2 Calumet City IL 60409-4602 Office: Adler Murphy & McQuillen 190 S La Salle St Ste 1200 Chicago IL 60603-3494

**CUNNINGHAM, DAVID FRATT,** lawyer; b. N.Y.C., May 23, 1944; s. David Fratt (dec.) and Burnley (Chenery) Wadsworth; m. Tracy Griswold, June 1966 (div. 1973); 1 child, David Fratt Jr.; m. Helen C. Sturm, Feb. 1979 (div. July 1988); children: Meghan Cunningham, Cory Cunningham; m. Janet E. Clow, Jan. 27, 1989. BA, Stanford U., 1966; JD, U. Calif., Hastings, 1969. Bar: N.Y. 1970, N.Mex. 1983. Asst. dist. atty. Manhattan Dist. Attys. Office, N.Y.C., 1969-72; chief asst. and acting spl. prosecutor Office of Spl. Narcotics Prosecutor, N.Y.C., 1972-80; chief investigative divsn. Manhattan Dist. Attys. Office, N.Y.C., 1980-83; ptnr., chief litigation sect. White, Koch, Kelly & McCarthy, PA, Santa Fe, 1983—; Commr. N.Mex. Organized Crime Commn., 1983-87; gen. counsel Zuni Tribe, 1987—. Co-author: Trial of a Criminal Case, 1980. Mem. ABA, Inn of the Ct. (Oliver Seth br. counsel 1994—). Democrat. Avocations: fly fishing, running. Federal civil litigation, State civil litigation, Criminal. Office: White Koch Kelly & McCarthy PA PO Box 787 433 Paseo De Peralta Santa Fe NM 87501-1958

**CUNNINGHAM, GARY ALLEN,** lawyer; b. Seattle, July 4, 1940; s. Chester Martin and Elsie Annette (Peterson) C.; m. Marilyn Phyllis Thunman, June 13, 1964. B in Engring., Yale U., 1962; JD, U. Wash., 1965. Bar: Wash. 1965, U.S. Dist. Ct. (we. dist.) Wash. 1965, U.S. Ct. Appeals (9th cir.) 1967, U.S. Supreme Ct. 1993. Dep. prosecutor Office King County Pros. Atty., Seattle, 1965-67; ptnr. Bishop, Cunningham & Andrews, Inc., P.S., Bremerton, Wash., 1967—. Bd. dirs. Hood Canal Environ. Coun., Seabeck, Wash., 1970—, pres., 1974, 78; bd. dirs., sec. Olympic Peninsula Kidney Ctr., Bremerton, 1980—; bd. dirs. Kitsap Land Trust, Bremerton, 1989—, pres., 1993—. Mem. ABA, Wash. State Bar Assn., Kitsap County Bar Assn. (pres. 1975-76), Kitsap Golf and Country Club, Bremerton Rotary Club. Avocations: golf, jogging, skiing, foreign travel. Probate, Real property. Home: 8411 Sunset Ln NW Seabeck WA 98380-9529 Office: PO Box 5060 Bremerton WA 98312-0469

**CUNNINGHAM, GARY H.,** lawyer; b. Grand Rapids, Mich., Jan. 11, 1953; s. Gordon H. and Marilyn J. (Lookabill) C.; m. Arlene M. Marcy, Apr. 23, 1983; children: Stephanie M., Gregory H. B.Gen. Studies, U. Mich., 1975, MA, 1977; JD, Detroit Coll. Law, 1980. Bar: Mich. 1980, U.S. Dist. Ct. Mich. 1983, U.S. Ct. Appeals (6th cir.) 1986, U.S. Ct. Appeals (Fed. cir.) 1990. Law clk. and estate adminstr. U.S. Bankruptcy Ct., Ea. Dist. Mich., Detroit, 1980-83; assoc./ptnr. Schlussel, Lifton, Simon, Rands, Galvin & Jackier, Southfield, Mich., 1983-90; ptnr./shareholder Kramer Mellen, P.C., Southfield, Mich., 1990-95; prin. shareholder Strobl Cunningham Caretti & Sharp, P.C., Bloomfield Hills, Mich., 1995—. Sr. staff mem. Detroit Coll. of Law Rev., 1978-80; contbr. articles to profl. jours. Mem. ABA (bus. law sect.), Fed. Bar Assn. (chmn. bankruptcy sect. 1989-91), Oakland County Bar Assn. (bus. law com.), State Bar of Mich. (mem. corp., fin. and bus. law sect.), Am. Bankruptcy Inst. (sponsor), Comml. Law League of Am., Detroit Econ. Club, Detroit Inst. Arts, Delta Theta Phi. Avocations: sailing, skiing, tennis. Bankruptcy, General civil litigation, Contracts commercial. Home: 2959 Cedar Ridge Dr Troy MI 48084-2613 Office: Strobl Cunningham Caretti & Sharp PC 300 E Long Lake Rd Ste 200 Bloomfield Hills MI 48304-2376

**CUNNINGHAM, JAMES PATRICK,** lawyer; b. Chgo., Mar. 15, 1937. AA, Phoenix Coll., 1956; student, Ariz. State U., 1956-58; LLB, U. Ariz., 1961. Bar: Ariz 1961, U. S. Dist. Ct. Ariz. 1963, U.S. Ct. Appeals (9th cir.) 1969, U.S. Supreme Ct. 1974, U.S. Ct. Appeals (10th cir.) 1976; cert. specialist injury and wrongful death litigation Ariz. Bd. Legal Specialization, 1991. Dep. county atty. County Atty.'s Office, Phoenix, 1961-63, spl. dep. county atty. sch. affairs, 1965-69; ptnr. Cunningham, Goodson & Tiffany, Phoenix, 1969-78, Cunningham, Tiffany & Hoffman, Phoenix, 1978-86; prin. Cunningham Law Firm, Phoenix, 1987—. Bd. dirs. Am. Ireland Fund, 1994—. Mem. ABA, ATLA, Am. Bd. Trial Advocates, Ariz. Trial Lawyers Assn. (bd. dirs.), State Bar Ariz., Maricopa County Bar Assn. Democrat. Roman Catholic. Personal injury. Office: Cunningham Law Firm 330 N 2nd Ave Phoenix AZ 85003-1517

**CUNNINGHAM, JAMES PATRICK,** lawyer; b. Providence, Nov. 1, 1950; s. John J. and Veronica C. (Williams) C.; m. Judith Kems, May 1983; children: Meredith, Jacob. AB with honors, Brown U., 1972; JD cum laude, Detroit Coll. Law, 1979. Bar. Mich. 1980, U.S. Dist. Ct. (ea. dist.) Mich. 1980. Ptnr., trial atty. Williams, Williams, Ruby & Plunkett, Birmingham, Mich., 1986—. Lt. USN, 1972-77. Fellow Am. Acad. of Matrimonial Lawyers; mem. ABA (family law sect.), State Bar Mich. (family law coun.), Oakland County Bar Assn. (past chmn. family law com., cir. ct. com., bd. dirs.), Brown U. Club (bd. dirs.), Econ. Club Detroit, Am. Inns of Ct. (master Oakland County chpt.). Avocations: gardening, travel. Family and matrimonial, State civil litigation. Office: Williams Williams Ruby & Plunkett 380 Woodward Ave Birmingham MI 48009

**CUNNINGHAM, JOEL DEAN,** lawyer; b. Seattle, Feb. 19, 1948; s. Edgar Norwood and Florence (Burgunder) C.; m. Amy Jean Radewan, Oct. 1, 1970; children: Erin Jane, Rad Norwood. BA in Econs., U. Wash., 1971, JD with high honors, 1974. Lawyer, ptnr. Williams, Kastner & Gibbs, Seattle, 1974-95; ptnr. Luvera, Barnett, Brindley, Beninger & Cunningham, Seattle, 1995—. Fellow Am. Coll. Trial Lawyers, Am. Bd. Profl. Liability Attys., Internat. Soc. Barristers; mem. Am. Bd. Trial Attys. (pres. Washington chpt. 1994), Damage Attys. Round Table, Order of Coif. Avocations: fishing, cycling, boating. Personal injury, Product liability, General civil litigation. Office: Luvera Barnett Brindley Beninger & Cunningham 6700 Columbia Ctr 701 5th Ave Seattle WA 98104-7097

**CUNNINGHAM, JORDAN DANIEL,** lawyer; b. Superior, Wis., May 9, 1951; s. Richard Michael and Dorothy H. (Mikes) C.; children: J. Benjamin, Jared Daniel, Christopher K., Morgan E.; m. Debora L. Cunningham, June 23, 1995; 1 child, Olivia A. BA, West Chester State, 1972; JD, Dickinson Sch. Law, 1976. Bar: Pa. 1976, U.S. Dist. Ct. (mid. dist.) Pa. 1979, U.S. Ct. Appeals (3d cir.) 1997, U.S. Supreme Ct. 1986. Ptnr. Cunningham & Chernicoff, P.C., Harrisburg, Pa., 1976—; lectr. Harrisburg Area C.C., mem. bd. advisors, 1980—. Bd. dirs. Harrisburg Community Theatre (pres. 1988-89). Mem. ABA, ATLA, Pa. Bar Assn., Pa. Trial Lawyers Assn., Dauphin County Bar Assn. Avocations: sailing, travel, reading, teaching. General civil litigation, Family and matrimonial, Personal injury. Office: Cunningham & Chernicoff PC 2320 N 2nd St Harrisburg PA 17110-1008

**CUNNINGHAM, JUDY MARIE,** lawyer; b. Durant, Okla., Sept. 7, 1944; d. Rowe Edwin and Margaret (Arnott) C. BA, U. Tex., 1967, JD, 1971; postgrad., Schiller Coll., Heidelberg, Fed. Republic Germany, 1976. Bar: Tex. 1972. Quizmaster U. Tex. Law Sch., Austin, 1969-71; researcher Tex. Law Rev., Washington, 1970; staff atty. Tex. Legis. Coun., Austin, 1972-75; adminstrv. law judge, dir. sales tax div., assoc. counsel Comptroller of Pub. Accounts, Austin, 1975-85; owner, editor J.C. Law Publs., Austin, 1986—; pvt. practice Austin, 1986—. Author: (with others) Texas Tax Service, 1985; pub., editor, contbr. (newsletter) Tex. State Tax Update, 1986—; contbr. articles to Revenue Adminstrn.; assoc. editor Tex. Law Rev., 1968-71. State del. Dem. Party, Ft. Worth, 1990, county del., Austin, 1972, 88, 90, 92; vol. numerous Dem. campaigns, Austin, 1972-90. Mem. Nat. Tax Assn., Industry Practitioners Liaison Group (comptr. pub. accts.), State Bar Tex. (taxation sect.), Travis County Bar (bus. corp. and taxation sect.), Tex. Taxpayers and Rsch. Assn. Avocations: traveling, cooking, reading mysteries, photography, swimming. State and local taxation, Administrative and regulatory, Legislative. Office: 4905 W Park Dr Austin TX 78731-5535

**CUNNINGHAM, KENNETH CARL,** legislative administrator; b. Lake City, Iowa, Nov. 3, 1954; s. Loren A. and Darlyne (Luhman) C.; m. Sherry Lynn Johnson, June 27, 1981; children: Kenneth Carl Jr., Jared, Marshall, Jackson. BA magna cum laude, Simpson Coll., 1977; JD, Georgetown U., 1988. Farmer Lohrville, Iowa, 1970-77; rsch. analyst Iowa Ho. of Reps., Des Moines, 1977-78; campaign asst. Tom Tauke for Congress, Dubuque, Iowa, 1978; legis. asst. Congressman Tom Tauke, Washington, 1979-80, Sen. Charles Grassley, Washington, 1981-85; legis. dir. Office of Sen. Charles Grassley, U.S. Senate, Washington, 1985-93, legis. and adminstrv. dir., 1993-95, chief of staff, legis. dir., gen. counsel, 1995—. Trustee, treas. ch., Alexandria, Va., 1991—; rsch. dirs. Jepsen for Senate, Des Moines, 1984. Named one of Outstanding Young Men of Am., Jaycees, 1987; recipient U.S. SenateLoyal Svc. award, 1993. Mem. Scholastic Honor Soc., Epsilon Sigma. Republican. Avocations: reading, woodworking. Office: US Senate 135 Hart Senate Office Bldg Washington DC 20510-0001

**CUNNINGHAM, LAWRENCE ALOYSIUS,** law educator; b. Wilmington, Del., July 10, 1962; s. John Joseph Jr. and Anne Marie (Barry) Brown. BA in Econs., U. Del., 1985; JD magna cum laude, Cardozo Law Sch., 1988. Assoc. Cravath, Swaine & Moore, N.Y.C., 1988-92; asst. prof. law Cardozo Law Sch., 1992-95, assoc. prof. law, 1995-96, prof. law, 1997—; vis. prof. law George Washington U., Washington, 1996-97, St. John's U., Queens, N.Y., 1995, 96, 97; bd. dirs. Samuel and Ronnie Heyman Ctr. on Corp. Governance, N.Y.C., 1996—; dir. nomination, shareholders' com. Shoneys Inc., 1997; dir. task force on firm structures Independence Stds. Bd., 1999—. Author: Corporate Finance and Governance, 1996, Introductory Finance and Accounting, 1997; editor symposium/book: The Essays of Warren Buffett, 1997; contbr. numerous articles to profl. jours. Mem. Omicron Delta Epsilon. Republican. Roman Catholic. Avocations: golf, windsurfing, collecting pop art. Office: Cardozo Law Sch 55 5th Ave New York NY 10003-4301

**CUNNINGHAM, PIERCE EDWARD,** lawyer, city planner; b. Cin., Aug. 18, 1934; s. Francis E. and Adelaide (Kraus) C.; m. Roberta Roche, Sept. 6, 1958; children: Pierce E., Jr. James M., Sarah Ellen, Anna C. BA, Coll. Holy Cross, 1956; LLB, Georgetown U., 1959. Bar: Ohio 1960, U.S. Supreme Ct. 1977. Atty. Hartford Accident and Indemnity Co., Cin., 1960-61; pvt. practice Hamilton, Ohio, 1961-62; asst. atty. gen. Ohio State Atty. Gen.'s Office, Columbus, 1963-70; prin. Pierce E. Cunningham and Assocs., Cin., 1964-75; ptnr. Clark & Eyrich, Cin., 1975-81, Frost & Jacobs, Cin., 1981-97; of counsel Baker Hostetler, Cleve., 1997—; chmn. Riverfront Adv. Commn., Cin., 1970-72, Zoning Bd. Appeals, Cin., 1970-72; mem. Urban Design and Rev. Bd., Cin. 1970-72, City Planning Com., Cin., 1968-73, chmn. 1970-73. Contbr. articles to profl. jours. Mem. May Festival Com., Cin., 1972-74, Cin. Bar Assn. Vol. Lawyers for Poor. Named Lawyer of Yr. Cin. Bar Assn. Vol. Lawyers for Poor, 1982-83. Mem. Am. Bd. Trial Advs., Ohio Bar Assn. (faculty continuing legal edn.), Cin. Bar Assn. (panel of neutrals CPR 1998—), Am. Arbitration Assn. (midwest region adv. coun., large complex litigation panelist), Cin. Tennis Club (pres. 1976-78), Cin. Country Club (bd. govs. 1995—), Potter Stewart Inn of Ct., Inner Cir. U.S. Senate, 1999—. Avocations: tennis, sailing. Federal civil litigation, State civil litigation, Real property. Home: 8 Hill And Hollow Ln Cincinnati OH 45208-3317 Office: Baker & Hostetler 3200 312 Walnut St Cincinnati OH 45202

**CUNNINGHAM, ROBERT D.,** lawyer. BA, Occidental Coll., Calif., 1971; JD, UCLA, 1975. Bar: Calif. 1975. Assoc. Lawler, Felix & Hall, L.A., 1975-78; atty. Buena Vista Pictures Distbn., Inc., Burbank, Calif., 1978-84, v.p., sec., gen. counsel, 1984-96; sr. v.p., sec., gen. counsel Buena Vista Pictures Distbn., Inc. (now Walt Disney Pictures & TV), Burbank, Calif., 1996—. Antitrust. Office: Walt Disney Pictures & TV 500 S Buena Vista St Burbank CA 91521-0004

**CUNNINGHAM, RYAN YERGER,** lawyer; b. Bartlesville, Okla., Jan. 5, 1970; s. Stanley Lloyd and Suzanne (Yerger) C. BA, U. Tex., 1992; JD, U. Okla., 1996. Bar: Okla. 1996. Ptnr. Cunningham & Mears, Oklahoma City, 1996—. Mem. ABA, ATLA, Okla. Bar Assn., Okla. Trial Lawyers Assn. Episcopalian. Personal injury, Insurance. Home: 5408 N Military Ave Oklahoma City OK 73118-4212 Office: 228 RS Kerr Ste 510 Oklahoma City OK 73102

**CUNNINGHAM, SAMUEL SCOT,** lawyer; b. Sidney, Nebr., Apr. 27, 1958; s. Ross C. Cunningham and Beverly K. Story; m. Guadalupe DeLeon, Aug. 8, 1987; children: Gino, Andrea, David. BA cum laude, U. Denver, 1981, JD, 1984. Bar: Colo. 1984, U.S. Dist. Ct. Colo. 1984. Contract atty. Koransky & McCullough, Denver, 1984; ho. counsel Natkin Energy Mgmt., Denver, 1985-87; gen. coun. ServiceMaster Energy Mgmt., Denver, 1987—; v.p. capital svcs. ServiceMaster Mgmt. Svcs., Englewood, Colo., 1994—. Mem. staff Tax Law Jour., 1982. Bd. dirs. C.A. Story Found., Sidney, 1992—. Finance, Education and schools. Office: ServiceMaster Mgmt Svcs 9000 E Nichols Ave Ste 150 Englewood CO 80112-3474

**CUNNINGHAM, STANLEY LLOYD,** lawyer; b. Durant, Okla., Feb. 7, 1938; s. Stanley Ryan and Hazel Dell (Dillingham) C.; m. Suzanne Yerger, Sept. 18, 1960; children: Stanley William, Ryan Yerger. BS in Geology, U. Okla., 1960, LLB, 1963. Bar: U.S. Dist. Ct. (we. dist.) Okla. 1963; U.S. Ct. Appeals (10th cir.) 1965; U.S. Supreme Ct. Okla. 1963. Atty. Phillips Petroleum Co., Oklahoma City, 1963-64, Bartlesville, Okla., 1964-71; assoc. McAfee, Taft, et al., Oklahoma City, 1971-73; mem. McAfee & Taft, Oklahoma City, 1973—; lecturer U. Okla. Coll. Law, Norman, 1977, 79, S.W. Legal Found., Dallas, 1986, 89. Contbr. articles to profl. jours. Layreader All Souls' Episcopal Ch., Oklahoma City, 1972-75. 1st lt. USAFR, 1963-72. Harry J. Brown scholar, U. Okla., 1960-63. Mem. ABA, Fed. Energy Bar Assn., Am. Soc. Internat. Law, Geological Soc. Am., Alumni Adv. Coun., U. Okla. Assoc., Oklahoma City Golf & Country Club, Order of Coif, Phi Alpha Delta, Sigma Gamma Epsilon. Republican. Episcopalian. Avocations: golf, reading. Oil, gas, and mineral, General civil litigation. Office: McAfee & Taft 2 Leadership Sq Fl 10 Oklahoma City OK 73102

**CUNNINGHAM, THOMAS JUSTIN,** lawyer; b. Hinsdale, Ill., Feb. 27, 1968; s. Thomas J. and Diane (Carlton) C.; m. Paula J. Friant, Sept. 9, 1989; children: Thomas Justin, Nicholas Joseph. BS, Ariz. State U., 1989; JD, DePaul U., 1993. Bar: Ill. 1993, U.S. Dist. Ct. (no. dist.) Ill. 1993, U.S. Ct. Appeals (7th cir.) 1993, U.S. Dist. Ct. (ctrl. dist.) Ill. 1996, U.S. Supreme Ct. 1996, Trial bar 1997. Dep. clk. U.S. Bankruptcy Ct., Chgo., 1989-90; law clk. Burke, Smith & Williams, Chgo., 1990-93; assoc. Smith, Lodge & Schneider, Chgo., 1993-98, Hopkins & Sutter, Chgo., 1998—. Contbr. articles to profl. jours. Pres. Ill. Dist. 58 Bd. Edn. Mem. Chgo. Bar Assn. (chair moot ct. com. 1995, co-editor in chief YLS jour.). Republican. Presbyterian. Avocations: hunting, fishing. Bankruptcy, Federal civil litigation, Contracts commercial. Home: 5135 Fairview Ave Downers Grove IL 60515-5211 Office: Hopkins & Sutter 3 First Nat Pla Ste 4100 Chicago IL 60602

**CUNNINGHAM, WILLIAM FRANCIS,** lawyer; b. Chgo., Feb. 24, 1945; s. Michael and Catherine B.C.; children: Kellie Marie, Kiera Megan, Micael Grant. BA, DePaul U., 1967, JD, 1971. Bar: Ill. 1971, U.S. Dist. Ct. (no. dst.) Ill. 1971. Mem. firm Gates W. Clancy, Geneva, Ill., 1971-74, O'Reilly & Quetsch, Wheaton, Ill., 1975-78; ptnr. O'Reilly & Cunningham, Norton & Mancini, 1978-95, Cunningham, Meyer & Vedrine, 1995—; lectr. to physicians on topics related to med. negligence; spl. asst. to atty. gen. State of Ill., Ill. Dept. Pub. Health; spl. asst. states atty. DuPage County Health Dept. Mem. ABA, Ill. Bar Assn., DuPage County Bar Assn., Kane County Bar Assn., Ill. Assn. Def. Trial Counsel, Soc. Trial Lawyers. Roman Catholic. State civil litigation, Insurance, Personal injury. Home: ONO64 Forbes Dr Geneva IL 60134 Office: Cunningham Meyer & Vedrine Ste B 1050 PO Box 988 Wheaton IL 60189-0988

**CUOZZI, WILLIAM F., JR.,** lawyer; b. Kearny, N.J., Jan. 4, 1920; s. William F. and Antoinette Russo Cuozzi; m. Domenica A. Baldanza, Nov. 22, 1941; children: Carol, Jo-Ellen, William III. BSc, Seton Hall U., 1942; LLB, Rutgers U., 1945. Counsel Dollin Corp., Irvington, N.J., 1946-61, Radiant Lamp, Newark, N.J., 1961-64, Syska Hennesy, N.Y.C., 1964-67; pvt. practice West Orange, N.J., 1967—. Mayor West Orange, N.J., 1974-78, councilman, 1964-74, mcpl. judge, 1992-98. Mem. Essex County Bar Assn. Democrat. Roman Catholic. Avocations: tennis, golf, theatre. Estate planning, Bankruptcy, General practice. Office: 49 Mount Pleasant Ave West Orange NJ 07052-4901

**CUPKA, BRIAN JOSEPH,** lawyer; b. Newark, Sept. 13, 1954; s. Joseph Benedict and Elizabeth Francis (O'Gorman) C.; m. Patricia Pintauro, Sept. 18, 1982; children: Matthew, Katherine. BA, St. Joseph's U., Phila., 1976; JD, Seton Hall U., 1981. Bar: N.J. 1981, U.S. Dist. Ct. N.J. 1981. Gen. counsel Theurer, Inc., Newark, 1982-84; v.p., gen. counsel and secr. Toshiba Am. Consumer Products, Inc., Wayne, N.J., 1984-98; v.p., assoc. gen. counsel Philips Consumer Comms., Murray Hill, N.J., 1998-99; spl. counsel Toshiba Am. Consumer Products, Inc., Wayne, N.J., 1999—. Avocations: basketball, soccer, skiing. Antitrust, Contracts commercial, General corporate. Office: Toshiba Am Consumer Products Inc 82 Totowa Rd Wayne NJ 07470-3191

**CURCILLO, JOSEPH A., III,** lawyer; b. Abington, Pa., Aug. 12, 1960; s. Joseph A. and Patricia A. Curcillo; m. Deborah Essis, Jan. 14, 1990; children: Olivia, Kaela. BS, Temple U., 1982, JD, 1985. Bar: Pa. 1985, U.S. Dist. Ct. (we. dist.) Pa. 1986, U.S. Dist. Ct. (ea. and mid. dists.) Pa. 1997. Asst. dist. atty. Clearfield County Dist. Atty., Clearfield, Pa., 1985-87; dep. dist. atty. Dauphin County Dist. Atty., Harrisburg, Pa., 1987-89; ptnr. MacIntyre Curcillo & MacIntyre, Harrisburg, 1989-90; dep. prosecutor York County Dist. Atty., York, Pa., 1990-91; dep. atty. gen. Atty. Gen. of Pa., Harrisburg, 1991-97; prnt. Beinhaur & Curcillo, Harrisburg, 1997—; instr. Harrisburg Area C.C. Police Acad., 1987—; mem. Crime Clinic of Greater Harrisburg, 1987—. Mem. Pa. Bar Assn., Dauphin County Bar Assn., Pa. Assn. Criminal Def. Lawyers (bd. dirs. 1998), Lower Paxton Twp. Bus. and Profl. Assn. (bd. dirs. 1998—), Internat. Brotherhood of Magicians, Psychic Entertainers Assn. Avocations: corporate entertaining, speaking. Criminal. Office: Beinhaur & Curcillo 4650 Fritchey St Harrisburg PA 17109-2813

**CURL, JEFFREY ROBERT,** lawyer; b. Lima, Ohio, Aug. 27, 1967; s. Thomas Paul and Mary Jean (Alexander) C.; m. Laurie June Lewis, Dec. 28, 1991. BA, U. Mo., Columbia, 1989, JD, 1992. Bar: Mo. 1992, U.S. Dist. Ct. (ea. dist.) Mo. 1992. Assoc. Clayton & Rhodes, Hannibal, Mo., 1992-95; ptnr. Clayton, Curl & Clayton, Hannibal, Mo., 1996-97, Clayton & Curl, Hannibal, 1997—. Bd. dirs. Marion County Health Dept., Hannibal, 1993—, Legal Svcs. of Ea. Md., St. Louis, 1995—; v.p. Marion County Dem. Orgn., 1997—; mem. Marion County Port Authority Commn., 1998—. Mem. Mo. Assn Trial Attys., Mo. Bar Assn. (rep. young lawyers sect. 1994—, exec. com. 1997—), Rotary (com. chair 1996-97, sgt. at arms 1999—). Lutheran. Avocations: golf, raquetball, tennis, politics. Family and matrimonial, Criminal, Personal injury. Office: Clayton & Curl 999 Broadway Hannibal MO 63401-4220

**CURLEY, JOHN JOSEPH,** lawyer; b. Jersey City, Mar. 11, 1948; s. William Joseph and Elizabeth Veronica (Shyne) C.; m. Natalie Ellen Feehan, June 2, 1979; children: John, Jennifer, Amanda. BA, Boston Coll., 1970; JD, Rutgers U., 1974. Bar: N.J. 1974, U.S. Dist. Ct. N.J. 1974, U.S. Ct. Appeals (3rd cir.) 1985. Assoc. Lepis & Lepis, Jersey City, 1974-78; ptnr. Lepis, Lepis & Curley, Jersey City, 1979-95, Curley & Scizruz, Hoboken, N.J., 1996—; mem. Dist. VI (Hudson County) ethics com., 1990. Trustee Boys and Girls Club of Hudson County. Mem. ABA, N.J. Bar Assn., Hudson County Bar Assn.. Roman Catholic. Real property, Condemnation, General civil litigation. Office: Curley and Scizurz Ste 210 5 Manueview Plaza Hoboken NJ 07030

**CURLEY, ROBERT AMBROSE, JR.,** lawyer; b. Boston, June 5, 1949; s. Robert Ambrose and Terese M. (O'Hara) C.; m. Kathleen M. Foley, June 10, 1972; children: Christine, Elizabeth, Margaret. AB cum laude, Harvard U., 1971; JD, Cornell U., 1974. Bar: Mass. 1974, U.S. Dist. Ct. Mass. 1975, U.S. Ct. Appeals (1st. cir.) 1976. Prin. Curley & Curley, P.C., Boston, 1974—, pres.; lectr. Mass. Continuing Legal Edn., Mass. Def. Attys., Mass. Acad. Trial Attys., Flaschner Judicial Inst., Nat. Bus. Inst. Mem. ABA, Internat. Assn. Def. Counsel, Mass. Bar Assn. (lectr., chmn. civil trial practice sect., civil litig. com. 1990-91, Mass. Def. Lawyers Assn. (co-chmn. products liability sects. 1994-96, bd. dirs. 1996—, sec. 1998—), Nat. Bus. Inst., Def. Rsch. Inst., Trial Lawyers Assn. (assoc.), Harvard Club (Hingham, treas. 1983-84, v.p. 1984-85, pres. 1985-86), Clover (Boston). Roman Catholic. Federal civil litigation, State civil litigation, Personal injury. Office: Curley & Curley PC 27 School St Ste 600 Boston MA 02108-4391

**CURNUTTE, MARK WILLIAM,** lawyer; b. Vinita, Okla., May 28, 1954; s. William Elmer and Genevieve Gertrude (Fitzgerald) C.; m. Lou Ann Coffman, Aug. 4, 1979; children: Meredith Blake, Amelia Leigh. BBA in Accountancy, U. Okla., 1976, JD, 1979. Bar: Okla. 1979, U.S. Dist. Ct. (no. dist.) Okla. 1980, U.S. Dist. Ct. (ea. and we. dists.) Okla. 1984, U.S. Tax Ct. 1979, U.S. Ct. Appeals (10th and fed. cirs.) 1980, U.S. Supreme Ct. 1984. Tax staff acct. Arthur Andersen & Co., Tulsa, 1979-81; assoc. Jones, Givens, Gotcher, Doyle & Bogan, Tulsa, 1981-84; assoc. Logan & Lowry, LLP, Vinita, Okla., 1984-87, ptnr., 1987—; bd. dirs. C&L Supply, Inc., Vinita. Trustee Craig County Law Libr., Vinita, 1984—; chmn. bd. trustees Vinita Pub. Libr., 1987-89, 91-92; treas. Vinita chpt. ARC, 1991—. Fellow Am. Coll. Trust and Estate Counsel, Okla. Bar Found.; mem. ABA (com. on estate and gift tax 1987-90, small bus. com. 1987—, com. on small law firms 1987—), Okla. Bar Assn. (title stds. com. real property sect. 1988-89, clients' security fund com. 1989-91, probate code com. 1995—, legal ethics and unauthorized practice com. 1995-97), Craig County Bar Assn. (sec.-treas. 1984-91, v.p. 1995-96, pres. 1997), U. Okla. Coll. Law Assn. (bd. dirs. 1989-91), Rotary (pres. Vinita 1988-89, Paul Harris fellow 1989), Masons, Shriners, Phi Delta Phi. Republican. Presbyterian. Avocations: hunting, fishing. Probate, Estate planning, General civil litigation. Office: PO Box 558 Vinita OK 74301-0558

**CURPHEY, WILLIAM EDWARD,** lawyer; b. Cleve., Apr. 28, 1948; s. William Edward and Gertrude (Scott) C.; m. Mary Louise Ocker, Apr. 11, 1969 (div. Mar. 1988); children: Jocelyn, Shauna, Michael; m. Jeanie Michelle Hancock, Nov. 15, 1998; children: Adam, Rachael, Mary. BA, Ohio State U., 1970; JD, Cleve. State U., 1973. Bar: Ohio 1973, Fla. 1978. Trial atty. U.S. Dept. Labor, Cleve., 1973-78; assoc. gen. counsel Harris Corp., Melbourne, Fla., 1978-86; county atty. Brevard County, Melbourne, 1986-89; assoc. Parker, Johnson, Orlando, Fla., 1989-91; of counsel Shea & Gould, Moscow, 1991-92, Stiles, Taylor & Metzler, Tampa, Fla., 1992-97; ptnr. Shumaker, Loop & Kendrick, Tampa, 1997—. Author: Effective Inter?ing, 1993. Mem. Fla. Bar Assn. (sect. chmn. 1988-89), Fla. Assn. County Attys. (pres. 1987-88). Democrat. Roman Catholic. Avocations: farming, hiking, running. Labor. Office: Shumaker Loop & Kendrick 101 E Kennedy Blvd Ste 2800 Tampa FL 33602-5153

**CURRAN, BARBARA ADELL,** retired law foundation administrator, lawyer, writer; b. Washington, Oct. 21, 1928; d. John R. and Beda (Parkins) Curran. BA, U. Mass., 1950; LLB, U. Conn., 1953; LLM, Yale U., 1961. Bar: Conn. 1953. Atty. Conn. Gen. Life Ins. Co., 1953-61; mem. rsch. staff Am. Bar Found., Chgo., 1961-93, assoc. exec. dir., 1976-86, rsch. atty., 1986-93, rsch. fellow emeritus, 1993—; vis. prof. U. Ill. Law Sch., 1965, Sch. Social Svc., U. Chgo., 1966-68, Ariz. State U., 1980; cons. in field. Author of eight books in field; contbr. articles to profl. jours. Mem. Ill. Gov.'s Consumer Credit Adv. Com., 1962-63; consumer credit adv. com. Nat. Conf. Commns. on Uniform State Laws, 1964-70; credit legis. subcom. Mayor Daley's Com. on New Residents, 1966-69; cons. Pres.'s Commn. on Consumer Interests, 1966-70, Ill. Commn. on Gender Bias in the Cts., 1987-92. Mem. ABA, Pi Beta Phi. Address: Am Bar Found 750 N Lake Shore Dr Chicago IL 60611-4403

**CURRAN, J. JOSEPH, JR.,** state attorney general; b. West Palm Beach, Fla., July 7, 1931; s. J. Joseph Sr. and Catherine (Clark) C.; m. Barbara Marie Atkins, 1959; children: Mary Carole, Alice Ann, Catherine Marie, J. Joseph III, William A. (dec.). LLB, U. Balt., 1959. Bar: Md. 1959, U.S. Dist. Ct. Md., U.S. Supreme Ct. 1987. State senator from Md., 1963-83; lt. gov. State of Md., 1983-86; atty. gen. State of Md., Balt., 1987—; mem. Md. Regional Planning Council, 1963-82. Mem. Md. Bar Assn., Balt. Bar Assn. Office: Office of Atty Gen 200 Saint Paul Pl Baltimore MD 21202-2004

**CURRAN, MARGARET E.,** prosecutor; M. Michel H. Feldhunhn; 1 child, Margee. M in Anthropology, Purdue U.; grad., U. Conn. Fed. prosecutor U.S. Atty.'s Office, 1986—; acting U.S. atty., 1998—; U.S. atty. R.I. dist. U.S. Dept. Justice, 1998—. Editor-in-chief U. Conn. Law Rev. Democrat. Office: Westminster Square Bldg 10 Dorrance St 10th Fl Providence RI 02903*

**CURRAN, MAURICE FRANCIS,** lawyer; b. Yonkers, N.Y., Feb. 20, 1931; s. James F. and Mary (O'Brien) C.; m. Deborah M., May 7, 1960; children: James, Maurice, Amy, Bridget, Ceara, Sara. Student Cathedral Coll., 1950; BA in Philosophy, St. Joseph Coll. and Sem., 1952; LLB, Fordham U., 1958. Bar: N.Y. 1958, U.S. Dist. Ct. (so. and ea. dists.) N.Y. 1960, U.S. Ct. Appeals (2d cir.) 1982, U.S. Supreme Ct. Assoc. Kelley, Drye, Newhall & Maginnes, N.Y.C., 1958-60; assoc. Wilson & Bave, Yonkers, 1960-65; div. counsel Merck & Co., Rahway, N.J., 1965-67; asst. gen. counsel E. R. Squibb & Sons, Inc., N.Y.C., 1967-70; corp. counsel, chief law dept. City of Yonkers, 1970-72; ptnr. Bleakley, Platt, Schmidt & Fritz, White Plains, N.Y., 1972-83, Banks, Curran & Keefe, Mt. Kisco, N.Y., 1983—. Past trustee, vice chmn. Westchester C.C. Capt. USMC, 1952-58. Mem. Fed. Bar Coun., N.Y. State Bar Assn., Assn. Bar City N.Y. Roman Catholic. State civil litigation, Federal civil litigation, Education and schools. Home: 388 Bronxville Rd Bronxville NY 10708-1233 Office: 61 Smith Ave Mount Kisco NY 10549-2813

**CURRAN, M(ICHAEL) SCOT,** lawyer; b. Dayton, Ohio, Feb. 7, 1952; s. John J. Curran and Patricia (Ludwig) Curran Schaffner; m. Ellen L. O'Leary, Apr. 22, 1978; children: Allison M., Scot Michael. BA, Washington & Jefferson U., 1974; JD, U. Pitts., 1977. Bar: Pa. 1977, U.S. Dist. Ct. (we. dist.) Pa. 1977, U.S. Ct. Appeals (3d cir.) 1977. Assoc. Lawrence R. Zewe Law Office, Washington, Pa., 1977-80; ptnr. Clarke & Curran, Washington, Pa., 1980-83, Saxton & Curran, Washington, Pa., 1983-86, M. Scot Curran & Assocs., Washington, Pa., 1986—. Bd. dirs. Mental Health/Mental Retardation, Washington, 1983-85; chmn. Civil Rights Com., Washington, 1988, mem., 1989-99; co-chmn. Profl. Awareness Com., Washington, 1989-99. Fellow SW Pa. Acad. Trial Lawyers (past pres. 1997); mem. Pa. Bar Assn., Pa. Trial Lawyers Assn., Washington County Bar Assn. Avocations: reading, golf. Personal injury, General civil litigation, State civil litigation. Office: M Scot Curran & Assoc 11 S College St Washington PA 15301-4821

**CURRAN, MICHAELA C.,** lawyer; b. Hollywood, Calif., Dec. 24, 1960. BA, U. Calif., Santa Barbara, 1982; JD, U. San Diego, 1987. Bar: Calif. Law clk. San Diego Superior Ct., 1986-87; law clk. to Judge John Rhoades, U.S. Dist. Ct. for So. Dist. Calif., San Diego, 1987; pvt. practice, San Diego, 1988—; seminar leader. Appellate, General civil litigation, Criminal. Office: 501 W Broadway Fl 20 San Diego CA 92101-3536

**CURRAN, PATRICK BARTON,** lawyer; b. Cleve., Sept. 30, 1953; m. Cynthia C. Majka, June 22, 1984; children: Brittany Alexandra, Alyssa Anne, Kevin Farnham. BA cum laude, SUNY, 1977; JD, N.Y. Law Sch., 1980. Bar: N.Y. 1982, U.S. Dist. Ct. (we. dist.) N.Y. 1982. Assoc. Williams, Stevens, McCarville & Frizzell P.C., Buffalo, 1982-85; assoc. Damon & Morey, Buffalo, 1985-89, ptnr., 1989—. Personal injury, General civil litigation, Health. Office: Damon & Morey 298 Main St Ste 1000 Buffalo NY 14202-4096

**CURRAN, ROBERT BRUCE,** lawyer; b. Charleston, W.Va., July 2, 1948; s. Bruce Frederick and Hazel Viola (Hoy) C.; m. Constance Marie Eggers, Jan. 24, 1970; children: Michael Robert, Laura Elizabeth, Emily Ann. BA, U. Del., 1971; JD, U. Md., 1974. Bar: Md. 1974. Ptnr. Frank, Bernstein, Conaway & Goldman, Balt., 1974-92, Whiteford Taylor & Preston, Balt., 1992—. Co-author: Tax Planning Forms for Businesses and Individuals, 1985. Mem. Md. Bar Assn. (sec. and treas. taxation sect. 1985-86, chmn. taxation sect. 1987-88). Pension, profit-sharing, and employee benefits, General corporate, Corporate taxation. Office: Whiteford Taylor & Preston 7 Saint Paul St Baltimore MD 21202-1626

**CURRAN, THOMAS J.,** federal judge; b. 1924. B of Naval Scis., Marquette U., 1945, LLB, 1948. Ptnr. Curran, Curran and Hollenback, Mauston, Wis., 1948-83; judge U.S. Dist. Ct. (ea. dist.) Wis., Milw., 1983—, now sr. judge; mem. Gov's Commn. on Crime and Law Enforcement, State of Wis. With USN, 1943-46. Mem. ABA, Am. Coll. Trial Lawyers. Office: US Dist Ct 250 US Courthouse 517 E Wisconsin Ave Milwaukee WI 53202-4500

**CURRAN, WILLIAM P.,** lawyer; b. Mpls., Feb. 27, 1946; s. William P. and Margaret L. (Killoren) C.; m. Jean L. Stabenow, Jan. 1, 1978; children: Patrick, Lisa, John. BA, U. Minn., 1969; JD, U. Calif., Berkeley, 1972. Law clk. Nev. Supreme Ct., Carson City, 1973-74, state ct. adminstr., 1973-74; assoc. Wiener, Goldwater & Galatz, Las Vegas, Nev., 1974-75; chief dept. dist. atty. Clark County Dist. Atty.'s Office, Las Vegas, 1975-79; county counsel Clark County, Las Vegas, 1979-89; pvt. practice Las Vegas, 1989-94; ptnr. Curran & Parry, Las Vegas, 1994—. Co-author: Nevada Judicial Orientation Manual, 1974. Mem. Nev. Gaming Commn., Carson City, 1989-99, chmn., 1991-99. Recipient Educator Yr. award UNLV Internat. Gaming Inst., 1998. Mem. ABA (state del. 1994—), Internat. Assn. Gaming Regulators (chmn. 1992-94), Nat. Assn. County Civil Attys. (pres. 1984-85), State Bar Nev. (pres. 1988-89), Nev. Gaming Commn. (chmn. 1989-99). Democrat. Roman Catholic. Administrative and regulatory, Land use and zoning (including planning), Real property. Office: Curran & Parry 601 S Rancho Dr Ste C-23 Las Vegas NV 89106-4825

**CURREY, REBECCA S.,** lawyer; b. Helena, Mont., Sept. 11, 1954; d. Chadwick Hainer and Dolores Johnson Smith; m. R. Scott Currey, Sept. 9, 1989. BA, Carroll Coll., 1976; JD, U. Mont., 1982. Bar: Mont. 1982, U.S. Dist. Ct. Mont. 1982, U.S. Ct. Appeals (9th cir.) 1983, Ariz. 1991, U.S. Dist. Ct. Ariz. 1992. Lawyer Smith Law Firm, P.C., Helena, 1982-87, 89-90, Asst. Atty. Gen., Phoenix, 1991-97, Mangum, Wall, Stoops & Warden PLLC, Flagstaff, Ariz., 1997—. Bd. mem., vol. RESCUE (Animal Rescue from Shelters), Phoenix; foster home Humane Soc., Phoenix, 1995—. Labor, Workers' compensation. Office: Mangum Wall Stoops & Warden PLLC PO Box 10 222 E Birch Flagstaff AZ 86002-0010

**CURRIE, CAMERON MCGOWAN,** judge; b. 1948. BA, U. S.C., 1970; JD with honors, George Washington U., 1975. Tchr. Moultrie H.S., Mt. Pleasant; law intern to magistrate judge Hon. Arthur L. Burnett U.S. Dist. Ct. D.C., 1973-74; atty. Arent, Fox, Kintner, Plotkin & Kahn, Washington, 1975-78; asst. U.S. Atty. Office U.S. Atty., Washington, 1978-80, Columbia, S.C., 1980-84; magistrate judge U.S. Dist. Ct. S.C., Columbia, 1984-86; pvt. practice Columbia, 1986-89; chief dep. atty. gen. Office Atty. Gen., State of S.C., Columbia, 1989-94; judge U.S. Dist. Ct. S.C., Florence, 1994—; adj. prof. in trial advocacy Sch. Law U. S.C., 1986-89. Assoc. editor SEC No Action Letters Index, 1972-73. Bd. dirs. Wings Inc., 1986-94, sec., 1992-94. Mem. ABA, S.C. Bar, D.C. Bar, S.C. Women Lawyers Assn. Office: US Dist Ct PO Box 2617 Florence SC 29503-2617

**CURRIER, GENE MARK,** lawyer; b. Detroit, Nov. 23, 1943; s. Harold A. and Helen K. (Carlind) C.; m. Margaret J. Currier, June 17, 1967; children: Amy, Julie, Mary, Molly. Student, U. Detroit, 1962-63, Hillsdale Coll., 1963-65, U. Mich., 1965-66; JD, Detroit Coll. Law, 1969. Bar: Mich. 1969, U.S. Dist. Ct. (ea. dist.) Mich. 1969, U.S. Ct. Appeals (6th cir.) 1973. Assoc. Mokersky, Dadeou & Currier, Inkster, Mich., 1969-71; ptnr. Alexander, Buchanan & Seavitt, Detroit, 1971-80, Highland & Currier, P.C., Southfield, Mich., 1980-92, Law of Office Gene M. Currier, P.C., Dearborn Heights, Mich., 1992—. Mem. ABA, Mich. Bar. Assn., Detroit Bar Assn., Assn. Def. Trial Counsel, Mich. Def. Trial Counsel, Def. Rsch. and Trial Lawyers Assn., Am. Arbitration Assn., Mediation Tribunal Assn., Dearborn Country Club. Avocations: reading, billiards, golf. Federal civil litigation, State civil litigation, Insurance. Home: 27104 Timber Trl Dearborn Heights MI 48127-3328 Office: PO Box 1030 Dearborn MI 48121-1030

**CURRIN, ROBERT GRAVES, JR.,** lawyer; b. Charleston, S.C., May 25, 1945; s. Robert Graves and Dorothy Anne (McNinch) C.; m. Sarah Middleton Riedell, June 21, 1969; children: Anne Cooper Burnet, Robert Graves III. AB, U. N.C., 1967; JD, U. S.C., 1970. Bar: S.C. 1970, U.S. Dist. Ct. S.C. 1971, U.S. Ct. Appeals (4th cir.) 1974; cert. mediator S.C. and U.S. Dist. Cts. Assoc. Nelson, Mullins, Riley & Scarborough, Columbia, S.C., 1970-73, ptnr., 1974-90; ptnr. Berry, Quackenbush & Stuart, Columbia, S.C., 1990-96, of counsel, 1997—; mem. uniform simplification of jury charges com. S.C. Bar, 1975-84, mem. jud. reform com. Mem. editorial bd. Barrister mag., 1977-78; contbr. articles to profl. jours. Mem. ABA (co-chmn. young lawyers sect. jud. selection com. 1973-75, exec. coun. young lawyers sect. 1974-75, state chmn. membership com. 1973-75, Cert. of Performance), S.C. Bar Assn. (chmn. com. on ann. meeting 1973), Richland County Bar Assn., Conf. Personal Fin. Law, Am. Judicature Soc. (bd. dirs. 1975-76), Order of Wig and Robe, Tarantella of Columbia, Forest Lake Club (pres. 1995-96), Alpha Tau Omega. Republican. Episcopalian. Banking, Real property, Contracts commercial. Home: 225 Spring Lake Rd Columbia SC 29206-2148

**CURRIVAN, JOHN DANIEL,** lawyer; b. Paris, Jan. 15, 1947; s. Gene and Rachel (Marash) C.; m. Patrice Salley; children: Christopher, Melissa. BS with distinction, Cornell U., 1968; MS, U. Calif.-Berkeley, 1969, U. West Fla., 1971; JD summa cum laude, Cornell Law Sch., 1978. Bar: Ohio 1978. Mng. ptnr. S.W. Devel. Co., Kingsville, Tex., 1971-76; note editor Cornell Law Rev., Ithaca, N.Y., 1977-78; prosecutor Naval Legal Office, Norfolk, Va., 1978-79, chief prosecutor, 1979-81; sr. atty. USS Nimitz, 1981-83; trial judge Naval Base, Norfolk, 1983-84; tax atty. Jones, Day, Reavis & Pogue, Cleve., 1984-88, ptnr., 1989—; adj. prof. law Case Western Res. U. Sch. Law, 1997—. Author: (with Rickert) Ohio Limited Liability Companies, 1999. Comdr. USN, 1969-84. Recipient Younger Fed. Lawyer award FBA, 1981. Mem. ABA, Nat. Assn. Bond Lawyers, Order of Coif, Tau Beta Pi, Eta Kappa Nu, Phi Kappa Phi. Taxation, general, Municipal (including bonds), General practice. Home: 12700 Lake Ave Ste 2105 Lakewood OH 44107-1506 Office: Jones Day Reavis & Pogue 901 Lakeside Ave E Cleveland OH 44114-1116

**CURRY, CLIFTON CONRAD, JR.,** lawyer; b. Tampa, Fla., July 8, 1957; s. Clifton C. and Louise (Owens) C.; m. Teresa D. Cox, Dec. 22, 1979; children: Mary Beth, Clifton C. III, Colton Cox. BS, Fla. State U., 1979; JD, Stetson U., 1981. Bar: Fla. 1982, U.S. Dist. Ct. (mid. dist.) Fla. 1982. Assoc. Mark R. Horwitz, P.A., Orlando, Fla., 1981-83; pres. Tittsworth and Curry, P.A., Brandon, Fla., 1984—, Curry and Assocs., P.A., Brandon, 1991—. Bd. dirs. Kiwanis Children's Clinic, 1988-90; vol. Missing Children's Help Ctr.; bd. dirs. Big Bros./Big Sisters, 1985-88, Rough Riders, 1987—, Brandon Outreach Clinic; chmn. Brandon Walk, March of Dimes Birth Defects Found., 1989; gen. coun. Grand Lodge of Fla. Masons, Egypt Temple Shrine, Tampa, Fla., 1996-97; active various polit. campaign coms. Recipient Alice Be. Thompkins Community Svc. award, 1991; named hon. mayor City of Brandon, 1985-86; recipient svc. award Brandon Lions Club, 1985. Mem. ABA, Assn. Trial Lawyers Am., Fla. Bar Assn., Hillsborough County Bar Assn., Brandon Bar Assn., Acad. Fla. Trial Lawyers, Brandon C. of C. (pres. 1989, bd. dirs. 1987-91, chmn. exec. bd. 1990-91, Small Bus. Leader of Yr. 1990), Kiwanis Club Brandon (past bd. dirs., pres. 1988-89), Krewe of Venus King's Guard (bd. dirs.), Fla. State Alumni Assn., Brandon Yacht Club, Ducks Unlimited, YMCA Century Club, Masons, Shriners, Scottish Rite, York Rite. State civil litigation, Condemnation, Personal injury. Office: Curry and Assocs PA 750 W Lumsden Rd Brandon FL 33511-6217

**CURRY, DANIEL ARTHUR,** judge; b. Phoenix, Mar. 28, 1937; s. John Joseph and Eva May (Wills) C.; m. Joy M. Shallenberger, Sept. 5, 1959; children: Elizabeth, Catherine, Peter, Jennifer, Julia , David. B.S., Loyola U., Los Angeles, 1957, LL.B., 1960; postgrad., U. So. Calif. Law Center, 1964-65; postgrad. exec. program, Grad. Sch. Bus., Stanford U., 1980. Bar: Calif. 1961, Hawaii 1972, N.Y. 1988, U.S. Dist. Ct. (cen. dist.) Calif. 1961, U.S. Ct. Appeals (9th cir.) 1961, U.S. Ct. Mil. Appeals 1963, U.S. Customs Ct. 1968, U.S. Dist. Ct. Hawaii 1972, U.S. Dist. Ct. (no. dist.) Calif. 1983 . Assoc. Wolford, Johnson, Pike & Covell, El Monte, Calif., 1964-65, Demetriou & Del Guercio, Los Angeles, 1965-67; counsel, corporate staff divisional asst. Technicolor, Inc., Hollywood, Calif., 1967-70; v.p., sec., gen. counsel Amfac, Inc., Honolulu, 1970-78; sr. v.p., gen. counsel Amfac, Inc., Honolulu and San Francisco, 1978-87; v.p., gen. counsel Times Mirror, L.A., 1987-92; judge Superior Ct. of State of Calif., 1992-98; assoc. justice Calif. Ct. Appeal 2d dist., L.A., 1998—; bd. regents Loyola Marymount U., Chaminade U. (hon.). Served to capt. USAF, 1961-64. Mem. ABA (hon., com. corp. law depts.), L.A. Country Club, Sigma Rho, Phi Delta Phi. Office: Calif Ct of Appeal 2d Dist 4th Fl North Tower 300 S Spring St Los Angeles CA 90013-1230

**CURRY, DONALD ROBERT,** lawyer, oil company executive; b. Pampa, Tex., Aug. 7, 1943; s. Robert Ward and Alleith Elizabeth (Elliston) C.; m. Carolyn Sue Boland, Apr. 17, 1965; 1 son, James Ward. BS, West Tex. State U., 1965; JD, U. Tex., 1968. Bar: Tex. 1968, U.S. Dist. Ct. (no. dist.) Tex. 1970, U.S. Tax Ct. 1973. Assoc., Day & Gandy, Ft. Worth, 1968-69, ptnr., 1970-72; pvt. practice, Ft. Worth, 1972—; mng. ptnr. Curry & Thornton Oil, 1981—; lectr. in field. Bd. regents West Tex. State U., Canyon, 1969-77, sec., mem. exec. com., 1972-75; mem. exec. bd. Longhorn council Boy Scouts Am., 1970—, dist. chmn., 1970-75 (recipient Silver Beaver award 1994); precinct chmn. Tarrant County (Tex.) Democratic Party, 1982-98, election judge, 1982-94; aviation adv. bd. City of Ft. Worth, 1990-95, vice chmn. bd., chmn. bd. dirs., 1994-95. Jamed E. West fellow, 1997. Fellow Tex. Bar Found.; Mem. ABA, State Bar Tex., Ft. Worth-Tarrant County Bar Assn., Ft. Worth Bus. and Estate Council, Tex. Ind. Producers and Royalty Owners Assn., Phi Alpha Delta, Phi Delta Theta. Methodist. Clubs: YMCA Century, Ft. Worth, Petroleum of Ft. Worth. General corporate, Oil, gas, and mineral. Home: 3800 Tulsa Way Fort Worth TX 76107-3346 Office: 905 Ft Worth Club Bldg Fort Worth TX 76102-4911

**CURRY, GREGORY WILLIAM,** lawyer; b. Tulsa, June 1, 1961; s. William H. and Shirley Dean (England) C.; m. Lori Lochridge, June 11, 1994; 1 child, Alanna England. Student, Loyola U., 1981; BBA, U. Okla., 1983; JD magna cum laude, Tex. Tech. U., 1989. Bar: Tex., 1989, Okla., 1996, U.S. Dist. Ct. (all dists.) Tex., Tex. Supreme Ct., U.S. Ct. Appeals (5th 7th, 8th cirs.). Landman Getty Oil Co., Midland, Tex., 1983-84, Mitchell Energy Co., Midland, 1984-86, VIP Photos, Maui, Hawaii, 1986, Thompson & Knight, Dallas, 1989—. Contbr. chpt. to book. Exec. com. mem. Nat. Marrow Donor Softball Tournament, Dallas, 1993-95, Making Strides Against Cancer, Dallas, 1995-96; com. chmn. Am. Cancer Soc. Evergreen Gala Com., Dallas, 1996-97; vol. North Tex. Legal Svcs., Dallas, 1989—; vol. judge advocacy comps. So. Meth. Law Sch., Dallas, 1989-91. Recipient Svc. award North Tex. Legal Svcs., 1989-98. Mem. Tex. Assn. of Def. Counsel (bd. dirs.), Order of Coif, Phi Kappa Phi. General civil litigation, State civil litigation, Oil, gas, and mineral. Home: 1803 Lakeshore Ct Mc Kinney TX 75070-4030 Office: Thompson & Knight 1700 Pacific Ave Ste 3300 Dallas TX 75201-4693

**CURRY, IRVING GREGG, III,** lawyer; b. Horicon, Wis., July 16, 1933; s. Irving G. and Emma Marie (Zimmerman) C.; m. Susan A. Reible, July 10, 1955; children: I. Gregg IV, Ann D. Harris. BS, Lawrence U., 1955; JD, U. Mich., 1958. Bar: Wis. 1958, U.S. Dist. Ct. (ea. dist.) Wis. 1965. Judge advocate USAF, Wichita Falls, Tex., 1958-61; assoc. McCarty & Burns, Kaukauna, Wis., 1961-65; ptnr. McCarty, Curry, Wydeven, Peeters & Haak, Kaukauna, Wis., 1965—; dir. Keller Structures, Inc., Kaukauna, Wis., 1971—; v.p. Parkside Care Ctr., Little Chute, Wis., 1991-98. Dir. Cmty. Found., Appleton, Wis., 1995—, Kaukauna Cmty. Hosp., Kaukauna, 1981-93, Kaukauna Indsl. Park, 1977-94. Recipient scholarship U. Mich., 1955. Mem. ATLA, State Bar of Wis. (dir. office mgmt.), Wis. Acad. Trial Lawyers, Outagamie County Bar Assn. (pres.). General civil litigation. Home: PO Box 62 Kaukauna WI 54130-0062 Office: McCarty Curry Wydeven Peeters & Haak PO Box 860 120 E 4th St Kaukauna WI 54130-2409

**CURRY, ROBERT LEE, III,** lawyer; b. New Orleans, Sept. 29, 1931; s. Robert Lee Jr. and Lydia (Sporl) C.; m. Courtney Davis, June 11, 1955; children: Robert Lee IV, Cynthia Curry Alexander, Thomas Davis, Kevin Courtney. BS, La. State U., 1954, JD, 1954; LLM in Taxation, NYU, 1958. Bar: La. 1954, U.S. Ct. Appeals (5th cir.) 1961, U.S. Supreme Ct. 1958. Judge advocate USAF, Wichita, Kans., 1954-56; teaching fellow NYU Sch. of Law, 1956-57; atty. advisor U.S. Tax Ct., Washington, 1957-60; atty. Theus, Grisham, Davis & Leigh, Monroe, La., 1960—; coun. mem. La. Law Inst. Coun., Baton Rouge, 1978—, pres., 1995-98. Fellow Am. Coll. Trust and Estate Counsel, Am. Coll. Tax Counsel; mem. Internat. Acad. Trust and Estate Law. Episcopalian. Estate planning, Taxation, general, General corporate. Office: Theus Grisham Davis & Leigh 1600 Lamy Ln Monroe LA 71201-3736

**CURTIN, JOHN T.,** federal judge; b. Buffalo, Aug. 24, 1921; s. John J. and Ellen (Quigley) C.; m. Jane R. Good, Aug. 9, 1952; children: Ann Elizabeth, John James, Patricia Marie, Eileen Jane, Mary Ellen, Mark Andrew, William Joseph. BS, Canisius Coll., 1945; LLB, U. Buffalo, 1949. Bar: N.Y. 1949. Pvt. practice law Buffalo, 1949-61; formerly U.S. atty. for Western Dist. N.Y., 1961-67; judge U.S. Dist. Ct. for Western N.Y., Buffalo, 1967—; previously chief judge U.S. Dist. Ct. for Western N.Y.; now sr. judge U.S. Dist. Ct. for Western N.Y., Buffalo. Served to lt. col. USMC, 1942-45, USMCR, 1952-54. Mem. ABA, N.Y. State Bar Assn., Erie County Bar Assn. Democrat. Roman Catholic. Office: US Dist Ct 624 US Courthouse 68 Court St Buffalo NY 14202-3405

**CURTIN, KEVIN GERARD,** lawyer; b. Washington, Oct. 12, 1951; s. James Andrew and Margaret Frances (Donovan) C.; m. Alice Hamilton Jackson, Apr. 8, 1978; children: Andrew, Michael, Peter. BA, Fairfield U., 1973; MA, George Washington U., 1977; JD, Georgetown U., 1982. Bar: D.C. 1982. Legis. counsel U.S. Senate Com. Commerce, Sci. and Transp., Washington, 1976-87, sr. counsel, 1987-89, chief counsel, staff dir., 1989-94, Dem. chief counsel, staff dir., 1995-96; ptnr. Bryan Cave LLP, 1996-98; pvt. practice, 1998—; adj. prof. Georgetown U., Washington, 1989-94. Mem. D.C. Bar Assn. Democrat. Roman Catholic.

**CURTIN, LAWRENCE N.,** lawyer; b. Glen Ridge, N.J., Apr. 29, 1950. BS with honors, Fla. State U., 1972, JD with honors, 1976. Bar: Fla. 1976, U.S. Dist. Ct. (no. dist.) Fla., U.S. Ct. Appeals (4th, 5th, 11th and D.C. cirs.). Law clerk to Hon. William Stafford U.S. Dist. Ct. (no. dist.) Fla., 1976-78; mem. Holland & Knight, Tallahassee. Co-author: Surface Water Pollution Control, vol. 1, 1986-96. Mem. ABA, Fla. Bar (chmn. energy law com. 1983-84), Tallahassee Bar Assn., Beta Gamma Sigma, Sigma Iota Epsilon. Environmental, Administrative and regulatory, Legislative. Office: Holland & Knight PO Drawer 810 315 S Calhoun St Ste 600 Tallahassee FL 32301-1897

**CURTIN, TIMOTHY JOHN,** lawyer; b. Detroit, Sept. 21, 1942; s. James J. and Irma Alice (Sirotti) C.; m. B. Colleen Lindsey, July 11, 1964; children: Kathleen, Mary. BA, U. Mich., 1964, JD, 1967. Bar: Ohio 1968, Mich. 1970, U.S. Dist. Ct. (no. dist.) Ohio 1968, U.S. Dist. Ct. (we. dist.) Mich. 1970, U.S. Dist. Ct. (ea. dist.) Mich. 1980, U.S. Ct. Appeals (6th cir.) 1968. Assoc. Taft, Stettinius & Hollister, Cin., 1967-70, McCobb, Heaney & Van't Hof, Grand Rapids, Mich., 1970-72; ptnr. Schmidt, Howlett, Van't Hof, Snell & Vana, Grand Rapids, 1972-83, Varnum, Riddering, Schmidt & Howlett, Grand Rapids, 1983—. Contbr. articles to legal publs. Treas. Kent County Dem. Com., 1976-78, chmn. 3rd Dist. Dem. Com., 1993—. Mem. ABA, Mich. Bar Assn., Grand Rapids Bar Assn., Fed.. Bar Assn., Am. Bankruptcy Inst., Egypt Valley C.C. Roman Catholic. Avocations: travel, fishing. Contracts commercial, Bankruptcy. Home: 448 Cambridge Blvd SE Grand Rapids MI 49506-2807 Office: Varnum Riddering Schmidt & Howlett Box 352 1700 Bridgewater Pl Grand Rapids MI 49501-0352

**CURTIS, CHARLES THACH, JR.,** lawyer; b. New Orleans, Jan. 22, 1951; s. Charles Thach and Marilyn Ellizabeth (Coons) C.; m. Marcy H. Monrose, Oct. 24, 1992; children: Sophie M., Peter T. BA, Tulane U., 1973, JD, 1976. Bar: La. 1977, U.S. Dist. Ct. (ea. dist.) La. 1979, U.S. Dist. Ct. (mid. and we. dists.) La. 1987, U.S. Ct. Appeals (5th cir.) 1981, U.S. Supreme Ct. 1983. Law clk. U.S. Dist. Ct. (ea. dist.) La., New Orleans, 1976-77; assoc. Bronfin, Heller, Feldman & Steinberg, New Orleans, 1977-79; assoc. Polack, Rosenbdfg, Rittenberg & Endom, New Orleans, 1979-82, ptnr., 1982-87; assoc. Little & Metzger, New Orleans, 1987-91; gen. counsel Pipe Liners Inc., 1991—. Bd. dirs. East Riverside Neighborhood Assn., New Orleans, 1983. Mem. ABA, Fed. Bar Assn., La. State Bar Assn., New Orleans Bar Assn. Democrat. Episcopalian. Contracts commercial, Probate, Consumer commercial. Home: 931 Henry Clay Ave New Orleans LA 70118-5934 Office: CSR Pipeline Systems 1539 Jackson Ave Fl 6 New Orleans LA 70130-5858

**CURTIS, GEORGE WARREN,** lawyer; b. Merrill, Wis., Sept. 24, 1936; s. George Gregory and Rose E. (Zimmerman) C.; m. Judith Olson, 1956 (div. 1966); m. Mary Pelman, 1967 (dec. 1973); children: George, Catherine Edwall, Eric, Greg, Paul, David; m. Mary Ruth Kersztyn, Dec. 27, 1973 (div. 1999); children: Emily, Benjamin; m. Suzette Bigler Whyte, July 10, 1999. BA, U. Minn., 1959; JD, U. Wis., 1962. Bar: Wis. 1962, Fla. 1968. Assoc. Russell & Curtis, Merrill, 1962-68; ptnr. Nolan, Engler, Yakes & Curtis, Oshkosh, Wis., 1968-74, Curtis, MacKenzie, Haase & Brown, Oshkosh, 1974-83, Curtis, Wilde & Neal, Oshkosh, 1984-96, Curtis & Neal, Oshkosh, 1997—. Mem. ATLA, Am. Coll. Trial Lawyers, Am. Bd. Trial Advocates (pres. Wis. chpt.), Wis. Acad. Trial Lawyers (bd. dirs. 1978-83, treas. 1984, sec. 1985, v.p. 1986, pres. 1987), Assn. Trial Lawyers Am. (bd. govs.), Internat. Soc. Barristers. Democrat. Avocations: conservationist, dog trainer. Personal injury, Criminal, State civil litigation. Home: 7361 Canary Rd Pickett WI 54964-9724 Office: Curtis Law Offices 2905 Universal St Oshkosh WI 54904-6341

**CURTIS, JAMES THEODORE,** lawyer; b. Lowell, Mass., July 8, 1923; s. Theodore D. and Maria (souliotis) Koutras; m. Kleanthe D. Dusopol, June 25, 1950; children: Madelon Mary, Theodore James, Stephanie Diane, Gregory Theodosius, James Theodore Jr. BA, U. Mich., 1948; JD, Harvard U., 1951; ScD (hon.), U. Mass., 1972. Bar: Mass. 1951. Assoc. Adams & Blinn, Boston, 1951-52; legal asst., asst. atty. gen. Mass., 1952-53; pvt. practice law Lowell, 1953-57; sr. ptnr. firm Goldman & Curtis, and predecessors, Lowell and Boston, 1957—. Chmn. Lowell and Greater Lowell Heart Fund, 1967-68; mem. adv. bd. Salvation Army, sec., 1956-58; mem. Bd. Higher Edn. Mass., 1967-72; elected mem. Lowell charter Commn., 1969-71; del. Dem. Party State Convs., 1956-60; trustee U. Mass., Lowell, 1963-72, chmn. bd., 1968-72; bd. dirs. U. Mass. Rsch. Found., Lowell, 1965-72, Merrimack Valley Health Planning Coun., 1969-72. Served with U.S. Army, 1943-46, spl. agt. Counter Intelligence Corps., 1945-46. Decorated Knight Order Orthodox Crusade Holy Sepulcher. Mem. ABA, ATLA, Mass. Bar Assn., Middlesex County Bar Assn., Mass. Acad. Trial Lawyers, Am. Judicature Soc., Harvard Law Sch. Alumni Assn., U. Mich. Alumni Assn., Lowell Hist. Soc., DAV, Harvard Club of Lowell (pres. 1969-71, bd. dirs.), Masons, Delta Epsilon Pi. General practice, General corporate, Real property. Home: 111 Rivercliff Rd Lowell MA 01852-1471 Office: Goldman & Curtis PC] 144 Merrimack St Ste 444 Lowell MA 01852-1789

**CURTIS, KAREN HAYNES,** lawyer; b. Laurel, Miss., Sept. 15, 1951; d. John Travis Haynes Jr. and Jeannine Burkett Tanner; m. George Ware Cornell Jr., Nov. 10, 1978; children: Laurel Elizabeth Cornell, Jaime Rodriguez Cornell. BS in Biology, Tulane U., 1973; JD summa cum laude, Nova Law Ctr., 1978. Bar: Fla. 1978; U.S. Ct Appeals (5th cir.) Fla., 1981, U.S. Ct. Appeals (11th cir.) Fla. 1981; U.S. Dist Ct. ( so. dist.) Fla. 1982, U.S. Dist Ct. (mid. dist.) Fla., 1986; U.S. Supreme Ct., 1994. Law clk. Steel, Hector & Davis, Miami, Fla., 1978; law clk. to Judge William M. Hoeveler U.S. Dist. Ct., Miami, Fla., 1978-80; assoc. Shutts & Bowen, Miami, Fla., 1980-84, ptnr., 1985-95; founding ptnr., pres. Gallway, Gillman, Curtis, Vento & Horn P.A., Miami, Fla., 1995—. Treas., dir. Church by the Sea, 1994—. Mem. ABA, Fla. Assn. Women Lawyers, Fed. Bar Assn., Dade County Bar Assn. (ins. law com. 1990-91, banking and corp. litigation com. 1992-93, appellate ct. com. 1991-92, appellate ct. rules com. 1993-96), Acad. Fla. Trial Lawyers, Assn. Trial Lawyers of Am., Supreme Ct. Historical Soc., Am. Judiciary Soc. United Church of Christ. Avocations: reading, piano, computer. Appellate, Federal civil litigation, General civil litigation. Home: 6444 Allison Rd Miami Beach FL 33141-4540 Office: Gallway Gillman Curtis Vento & Horn PA 200 SE 1st St Ste 1100 Miami FL 33131-1909

**CURTIS, LAWRENCE NEIL,** lawyer; b. Jamacia, N.Y., July 27, 1952; s. Ernest Francis and Barbara Dorothy (Malatesta) C.; m. Valeria Ann Caraldo, Nov. 1, 1975 (div. Aug. 1986); 1 child, Lauren Nicole; m. Lynn Maria Sorola, Oct. 17, 1987 (div. May 1988); m. Brenda Ann Stelly, Aug. 21, 1998. BA, St. John's U., 1974; JD, Loyola U., 1977. Bar: La. 1978, U.S. Dist. Ct. (ea. dist.) La. 1978, U.S. Dist. Ct. (we. dist.) La. 1979, U.S. Dist. Ct. (mid. dist.) La. 1991, U.S. Ct. Appeals (5th cir.) 1979. Law clk., assoc. Law Offices of Frederick J. Gisevius, Jr., New Orleans, 1977-79; assoc., ptnr. Cormier & Curtis, Lafayette, La., 1979-82, Adler, Barish, Lafayette, 1982; ptnr. J. Minos Simon Ltd., Lafayette, La., 1983-91, Curtis & Lambert, Lafayette, 1991—; master of bench Am. Inns of Ct., 1994—. Contbr. articles to profl. jours. Recipient Alumni Outstanding Achievement medal St. John's U., 1994. Mem. La. State Bar Assn. (sect. insurance, negligence and compensation), Fed. Bar Assn., ABA, Assn. Trial Lawyers of Am., La. Trial Lawyers Assn (bd. govs. 1989-91, pres. adv. coun. 1987-89), Lafayette Trial Lawyers Assn. Southeastern Admiralty Law Inst., Maritime Law Soc. U.S., Lafayette C. of C. Admiralty, Personal injury, Workers' compensation. Home: 208 Mill Valley Run Lafayette LA 70508-7052 Office: Curtis & Lambert 201 Rue Iberville Ste 300 Lafayette LA 70508-3281

**CURTIS, MARTHA YOUNG,** lawyer, partner; b. New Orleans, Aug. 20, 1965; d. Joseph McConnell Young and Lilian Helen Page; m. Mark Edward Curtis, Sept. 20, 1997. BA, Vanderbilt U., 1987; JD, Tulane U., 1990. Bar: La. 1990, U.S. Dist. Ct. (ea. and we. dists.) Ark. 1992, U.S. Dist. Ct. (ea., middle, and we. dists.) La. 1991, U.S. Dist. Ct. (no., so. and ea. dists.) Tex. 1992, U.S. Dist. Ct. (we. dist.) Tex. 1993, U.S. Dist. Ct. (no. and so. dists.) Miss. 1997, U.S. Ct. Appeals (5th cir.) 1991. Law clk., Judge Davis U.S. Ct. Appeals (5th cir.), New Orleans, 1990-91; mem. McGlinchey Stafford, New Orleans, 1991-98; assoc. Sher, Garner, Cahill, Richter, Klein, McAliston & Hilbert, 1991-97; mem. uniform rules com. of La. Bd. adv. editors Tulane Law Rev., New Orleans, sr. mng. editor, 1989-90. Mem. Nat. Inst. Trial Advocacy (grad. 1997), Assn. Women Attys., Mercy Alumnae Assn. (pres. 1995-98). Insurance, General civil litigation, Toxic tort. Office: Sher Garner Cahill Richter Klein McAliston Hilbert LLC 909 Poydras St Fl 28 New Orleans LA 70112-1017

**CURTIS, PHILIP H.,** lawyer; b. Oak Park, Ill., Jan. 22, 1946; s. Arthur R. and Shirley F. Curtis; m. Rebecca Coleman, July 24, 1971; children: Zachary Coleman, Nathaniel Lawrence. BA, Yale U., 1968; JD, Columbia U., 1971. Bar: N.Y., U.S. Dist. Ct. (so. and ea. dists.) N.Y., U.S. Dist. Ct. (ctrl. dist.) Ill., U.S. Ct. Appeal (2d, 3d and 7th cirs.), U.S. Supreme Ct. Assoc. Hughes Hubbard & Reed, N.Y.C., 1972-79, ptnr., 1980-90; ptnr. Arnold & Porter, N.Y.C., 1991—. Mem. Assn. Bar City N.Y., Yale Club of N.Y., Bridgehampton Club. Office: Arnold & Porter 399 Park Ave Fl 35 New York NY 10022-4690

**CURTIS, PHILIP JAMES,** lawyer; b. Jackson, Mich., May 28, 1945; s. Robert N. and Marjorie Louise (Balyeat) C.; m. Denise R. Curtis; children: Laura Christina, Philip Campbell, Leslie Ann. BA, U. Mich., 1967; JD, Wayne State U., 1970. Bar: Mich., U.S. Dist. Ct. (ea. dist.) Mich. 1977. Atty. Curtis, Curtis & Thomson P.C., Jackson, Mich., 1970—. Former pres., dir. Family Svc. & Children's Aid, Jackson; dir. Jackson Bus. Indsl. Devel. Co., Ltd.; former trustee Ella Sharp Mus., Jackson; dir. Jackson Y Ctr., Inc., Jackson. General corporate, Probate, Pension, profit-sharing, and employee benefits. Office: Curtis Curtis & Thomson P C PO Box 594 Jackson MI 49204-0594

**CURTZ, CHAUNCEY S.R.,** lawyer, real estate company executive; b. Ann Arbor, Mich., July 14, 1954; s. Thaddeus Bankson and Rebecca Parkhill (Reeve) C.; m. Brenda Lee Kyriss, Sept. 2, 1976; children: Lydia Lorraine, Charles Edward. Student, Georgetown U., 1972-73; BS, McGill U., 1976; JD, U. Wis., 1981. Bar: Wis. 1981, Ky. 1981, U.S. Dist. Ct. (ea. dist.) Ky. 1981, U.S. Ct. Appeals (6th cir.) 1983, U.S. Supreme Ct. 1986, U.S. Dist. Ct. (we. dist.) Ky. 1993. Assoc. Wyatt, Tarrant & Combs, Lexington, Ky., 1981-87; ptnr. Wyatt, Tarrant & Combs, Lexington, 1987-97; counsel Dinsmore & Shohl, Lexington, 1997—; sr. v.p. ops., gen. coun. Big Sandy Mgmt. Co., Inc., Lexington, 1997—; bd. dirs., sec. Curtz & Shine, Inc., Lexington, 1985—; bd. dirs., pres. CSR Curtz, Inc., Lexington, 1997—. Contbr. articles to profl. jours.; contbg. author: UK/CLE Practitioners Manual, 1989. Chmn. Lexington Arts & Cultural Coun., 1995-96; bd. dirs. Lexington Philharmonic, 1996-97, Lexington Children's Theatre, 1997-99; mem. Pritchard Com. Acad. Excellence, Lexington, 1995-98. Mem. Assn. Trial Lawyers Am., Def. Rsch. Inst., Lexington Coal Exchg. Avocations: travel, gardening, cooking, wine. Natural resources, General civil litigation, Contracts commercial. Office: Dinsmore & Shohl 250 W Main St Ste 2020 Lexington KY 40507-1714

**CURY, BRUCE PAUL,** lawyer, magistrate; b. Englewood, N.J., Mar. 19, 1942; s. Beddy Galib and Violet (Maloof) C.; m. Orahdella Elizabeth Green, Oct. 14, 1972; 1 child, Lauren Elaine. BS, U. Ky., 1965; JD, U. Louisville, 1972. Bar: Fla. 1972, U.S. Dist. Ct. (mid. dist.) Fla. 1974, U.S. Ct. Appeals (5th cir.) 1980, U.S. Ct. Appeals (11th cir.) 1982, U.S. Supreme Ct. 1976. Assoc. George McDowell P.A., Tampa, Fla., 1972-73; sole practice Tampa, 1973-76; adj. prof. bus. law U. Tampa, 1977-85; adj. prof. criminal law U. South Fla., 1984-85, lectr., 1981-87; chief asst. pub. defender Office of Pub. Defender, Tampa, 1974-85; sole practice Tampa, 1985-90; gen. counsel Fla. Dept. Transportation, Bartow, 1990—; magistrate traffic ct. Jud. 13 cir., Tampa, 1993—; chmn. Hills County Zoning Bd. Tampa, 1989-97; pres., dir. Bay Area Legal Services, Inc., Tampa, 1980-92; chmn. Hills County Land Use Appeals Bd. Tampa, 1997—. Legal counsel Big Bros./Big Sisters Greater Tampa, Inc., 1983-95; pres, bd. dirs. Rape Crisis Ctr., Tampa, 1982-84; bd. dirs. Hillsborough Edn. Found., Tampa, 1999—. Served to 1st lt. U.S. Army, 1966-69. Recipient Indigent Accused award Fla. Pub. Defender, 1985, Directors award Sexual Abuse Treatment Ctr. Tampa, 1986, President and Directors award Bay Area Legal Svcs. Tampa, 1992. Mem. Criminal Def. Lawyers Assn. Hillsborough County, Fla. Bar Assn. (mem. several sects., chmn. 13th Jud. Circuit grievance com.), Hillsborough County Bar Assn. (mem. several coms., exec. counsel trial lawyers sect.), Fla. Leadership 2000, Am. Inn of Cts. Republican. Methodist. Home: 4306 Carrollwood Village Dr Tampa FL 33624-4612 Office: Fla Dept Transportation 801 N Broadway Ave Bartow FL 33830-3809

**CURZON, THOMAS HENRY,** lawyer; b. Ft. Leonard Wood, Mo., Apr. 11, 1954; s. James E. and Vera (Roush) C.; m. Anne M. Halverhout, July 29, 1977; children: Peter Thomas, Daniel Henry. BA with highest distinction, U. Kans., 1976; JD with high honors, U. Tex., 1979. Bar: Tex. 1979, Ariz. 1980. Law clk. to Hon. James K. Logan, U.S. Ct. Appeals for 10th Circuit, Olathe, Kans., 1979-80; ptnr. Meyer, Hendricks, Osborn & Maledon, Phoenix, 1980-96, Osborn Maledon, P.A., Phoenix, 1996—; bd. dirs. Ariz. Tech.; pres. Enterprise Network, Phoenix, 1995-96. Author: Ariz. Legal Forms: Business Organizations-Corporations, 2 vols., 1990. Mem. exec. com. Ariz. Strategic Planning for Econ. Devel., Phoenix, 1990-91; bd. dirs. Downtown YMCA, Phoenix, 1997; mem. troop 644 com. Boy Scouts Am., Phoenix, 1997—. Mem. Ariz. Software Assn. (bd. dirs. 1997—). Avocations: figure skating, tae kwon do, sailing, hunting, scouting. General corporate, Securities, Mergers and acquisitions. Office: Osborn Maledon PA 2929 N Central Ave Phoenix AZ 85012-2727

**CUSACK, JAMES WESLEY,** lawyer; b. Rockville Centre, N.Y., July 30, 1966; s. James J. and Joanne W. Cusack; m. Ashley Willard Brinson, Feb. 25, 1995. BA in Econs., Fla. State U., 1988; JD, St. Thomas U., 1992. Bar: Fla. 1992, U.S. Dist. Ct. (so. dist.) Fla. 1996, U.S. Dist. Ct. (mid. dist.) Fla. 1997. Asst. state atty. 17th Jud. Cir., Ft. Lauderdale, Fla., 1992-96; atty. Ferrell, Schultz, Carter and Fertel, P.A., Miami, Fla., 1996-99, Law Office of James W. Cusack, PA, Miami, Fla., 1999—. Mem. Coral Reef Yacht Club. Roman Catholic. Avocations: fishing, hunting, skiing. General civil litigation, Criminal, Labor. Home: 6822 Mindello St Coral Gables FL 33146-3828 Office: Law Office James W Cusack PA 169 E Flagler St Miami FL 33131-1210

**CUSANO, RONALD SAMUEL,** lawyer; b. Pitts., June 28, 1951; s. Nicholas Anthony and Stella Florence C.; m. Diana Jean Stares, June 11, 1989; children: Julia Anne, Emma Maria. BA summa cum laude, U. Pitts., 1973; JD cum laude, Duquesne U., 1976. Bar: Pa. 1976, U.S. Dist. Ct. (we. dist.) Pa. 1976, U.S. Ct. Appeals (3d, 4th, D.C. cirs.). From assoc. to ptnr. Rose, Schmidt, Dixon & Hensley, Pitts., 1976-82; shareholder Corcoran, Hardesty, Whyte & Polito, Polito & Smock, Pitts., 1982-91; ptnr. Eckert, Seamans, Cherin & Mellott, Pitts., 1991-96; ptnr., co-chair environ. practice group Schnader, Harrison, Segal & Lewis, Pitts., 1996—; adj. prof. Duquesne U. Sch. of Law, Pitts., 1991-93. Recent decisions editor Duquesne Law Rev., 1976; contbr. articles on environ. issues to profl. publs. Vol. minuteman drive, St. Bernard Ch., Pitts., 1979—, fundraiser YMCA, Pitts., 1996—; mem. adv. bd. dept. geology U. Pitts., 1996—. Mem. Pa. Bar Assn. (coun., treas. sec. vice chair, chair environ. law sect. 1989-95 Cert. Recognition 1995). Achievements include trial of leading Pa. case on validity of environmental permits for municipal waste incinerators. Office: Schnader Harrison Segal & Lewis LLP 120 5th Ave Ste 2700 Pittsburgh PA 15222-3010

**CUSKADEN, EVERETT,** lawyer; b. Honolulu. BS, Ohio U., 1969; JD, U. Denver, 1973. Bar: Hawaii 1973, U.S. Dist. Ct. Hawaii 1973, U.S. Ct. Appeals (9th cir.) 1978, U.S. Supreme Ct. 1978. Dep. pub. defender State of Hawaii, Honolulu, 1974-75, dep. atty. gen., 1975-78; ptnr. Oliver Cuskaden Lee, Honolulu, 1978-88, Cuskaden & Kuyisaki, Honolulu, 1988-90; pvt. practice Honolulu, 1990—; commr. state land use commn. State of Hawaii, Honolulu, 1981-88, per diem judge, 1988—, state arbitrator, 1985—, family ct. master, 1988—. Capt. Hawaii N.G., 1980-82. Mem. Am. Arbitration Assn. (arbitrator), Waialae Country Club, Pacific Club. Family and matrimonial, General corporate, Personal injury. Office: Law Offices Everett Cuskaden ALC 1188 Bishop St Ste 1401 Honolulu HI 96813-3305

**CUSTER, ANDY M.,** lawyer; b. Bridgeport, Conn., Jan. 28, 1964; s. Keith and Caryl Sarah Custer; m. Nancy Lynn Custer, Nov. 28, 1993; 1 child, Simon Michael. BS, U. Fla., 1986; MBA, U. Miami, 1987; JD, Nova U., Ft. Lauderdale, Fla., 1992. Bar: Fla., U.S. Dist. Ct. (so. dist.) Fla. Lawyer Angel & Custer P.A., Hollywood, Fla., 1992-95, Abrams, Anton, P.A., Hollywood, 1995-96; sole practitioner Lake Worth, Fla., 1996—. Mem. Acad. Fla. Trial Lawyers (mem. leadership, membership and med. malpractice coms.), Broward County Bar Assn., Palm Beach County Bar Assn. Libel, Personal injury. Office: 515 E Las Olas Blvd Ste 1150 Fort Lauderdale FL 33301-2281

**CUSUMANO, LEANNE,** lawyer; d. Guy and Joan C.; m. Steven V. Roque, Oct. 10, 1998. BA, George Washington U., 1991; JD, Coll. William & Mary, 1994. Bar: Va. 1994, Md. 1995, D.C. 1995. Assoc. Leftwich & Douglas, Washington, 1995-97; regulatory counsel Food & Drug Adminstrn., Rockville, Md., 1997—. Mem. Prettyman-Levanthal Am. Inn of Ct. (barrister). Fax: 301-827-5562. E-mail: cusumanol@cder.fda.gov. Office: Food & Drug Adminstrn 5600 Fishers Ln Hfd 7 Rockville MD 20857-0001

**CUTCHIN, JOHN FRANKS,** lawyer; b. Roanoke Rapids, N.C., Dec. 19, 1949; s. Joseph Henry, Jr. and Janie Priscilla (Franks) C.; m. Melissa Jane Ikerd, Dec. 22, 1979; children—Jennifer Erin, Joshua Ikerd. A.B., Davidson Coll., 1972; J.D., U. N.C., 1975. Bar: N.C. 1975, U.S. Dist. Ct. (we. dist.) N.C. 1975. Assoc. Lefler, Gordon & Waddell, Newton, N.C., 1975-78; sole practice, Newton, N.C., 1978—. Campaign mgr. Judge Sam McD. Tate, Dist. Ct., 1978. Mem. N.C. Acad. Trial Lawyers, Catawba County Bar Assn. (pres. 1982-83), Lincoln County Bar Assn., Newton Mchts. Assn. (pres. 1978-80), Davidson Coll. Alumni Assn. (pres. Catawba County chpt. 1979-80), Lake Norman Jaycees (pres. 1976-77). Episcopalian. Family and matrimonial, Criminal, State civil litigation. Office: 16 S College Ave PO Box 173 Newton NC 28658-0173

**CUTCHINS, CLIFFORD ARMSTRONG, IV,** lawyer; b. Norfolk, Va., May 13, 1948; s. Clifford Armstrong III and Ann (Woods) C.; m. Jane McKenzie, Aug. 14, 1971; children: Sarah Helen, Ann Woods. BA, Princeton U., 1971; JD, MBA, U. Va., 1975. Bar: Va. 1975, U.S. Dist. Ct. (ea. dist.) Va. 1975, U.S. Ct. Appeals (4th cir.) 1975. Ptnr. McGuire, Woods, Battle & Boothe, Richmond, Va., 1975-90; sr. v.p., gen. counsel, sec. James River Corp. Va., Richmond, 1990-97, Ft. James Corp., Deerfield, Ill., 1997—; bd. dirs. Ft. James Europe N.V., Ft. James Operating Co. Bd. dirs. Arts Coun. Richmond, 1980-86, Richmond Heart Assn., 1980-83, St. Catherine's Sch., Richmond, 1983-86, Richmond Ballet, 1986-88, Richmond Children's Mus., 1986-94, Richmond on the James, 1986-88, Henrico Drs. Hosp., 1986—, Hist. Richmond Found., 1990-94, Richmond Met. Blood Svc., 1995-97, Kohl Children's Mus., Wilmette, Ill., 1998—, United Way Deerfield, 1999—; chmn. Fort James Found., 1997—. Mem. ABA, Va. Bar Assn., Country Club Va. (bd. dirs. 1990-93), Commonwealth Club (bd. dirs. 1983-86, 97—). Republican. Baptist. Avocations: golf, travel, photography. Securities, General corporate. Home: 118 Tempsford Ln Richmond VA 23226-2319 Office: Fort James Corp PO Box 89 1650 Lake Cook Rd Deerfield IL 60015-4753

**CUTLER, ARNOLD ROBERT,** lawyer; b. New Haven, Mar. 20, 1908; s. Max Nathan and Kate (Harder) C.; m. Hazel Lourie, Apr. 8, 1942; 1 son, David. B.A., Yale U., 1930, J.D., 1932; LLD (hon.), Brandeis U., 1984. Bar: Conn. 1932, Mass. 1946. Mem. staff Office Gen. Counsel Pub. Works Adminstrn., Washington, 1933-36; chief counsel Pub. Works Adminstrn. State of Wash., 1937-38; spl. asst. to chief counsel IRS, 1939-44, trial counsel New Eng. div., 1945-47; ptnr. Lourie & Cutler, Boston, 1947—; lectr. on taxation. Contbr. to books, articles to legal jours. Trustee Beth Israel Hosp.; trustee emeritus Brandeis U.; trustee, past mem. exec. com. Combined Jewish Philanthropies Greater Boston; past. bd. dirs. Nat. Jewish Welfare Bd.; past pres. Brookline, Brighton and Newton Jewish Community Ctr.; past. treas. Associated Jewish Community Ctrs. of Greater Boston; past chmn. bd. Yale Law Sch. Fund; past chmn. bequest com. Yale Law Sch. Lt. comdr. USCG, 1942-45. Fellow Am. Coll. tax Counsel, Mass. Bar Found.; mem. ABA (com. on govt. submissions 1987—, past chmn. spl. adv. exempt orgns. com. tax sect.), Mass Bar Assn., Boston Bar Assn. (past chmn. fed. tax com., former coun. mem.), Am. Law Inst., New Century Club (past pres.), Greater Boston Brandeis Club (past pres.), Yale Club, Harvard Club, Rotary (past bd. dirs.). Estate planning, Corporate taxation, Taxation, general. Office: Lourie & Cutler 60 State St Boston MA 02109-1800

**CUTLER, CHARLES EDWARD,** lawyer; b. Des Moines, Apr. 2, 1956. BS, U. Iowa, 1978, JD, 1981. Bar: Iowa 1981, U.S. Dist. Ct. (no. and so. dists.) Iowa 1981, U.S. Ct. Appeals (8th cir.) 1981. Ptnr. Patterson, Lorentzen, Duffield, Timmons, Irish, Becker & Ordway, Des Moines, 1981—. Mem. ABA, Iowa Bar Assn., Iowa Defense Lawyers Assn., Iowa Assn. Workers Compensation Lawyers, Polk County Bar Assn. Personal injury, Professional liability, Workers' compensation. Office: Patterson Lorentzen Duffield Timmons Irish Becker Des Moines 729 Insurance Exchange Bldg Des Moines IA 50309-2318

**CUTLER, LAURENCE JEFFREY,** lawyer; b. Bklyn., May 23, 1945; s. Charles and Ruth (Grossman) C.; children: Rebecca L., Mitchell A. BA, Am. U., Washington, 1967; JD, U. Ky., 1970. Bar: N.J. 1970, U.S. Dist. Ct. N.J. 1970, U.S. Supreme Ct. 1974, U.S. Ct. Appeals (3rd cir.) 1982, N.Y. 1986; cert. matrimonial arbitrator and mediator Am. Acad. Matrimonial Lawyers. Pvt. practice Morristown, N.J., 1970—; mem. coms. civil practice N.J. Supreme Ct., 1976-79, matrimonial litigation, 1980-82, family part practice, 1985-87, 98—; guest lectr. Seton Hall U. Sch. Law, 1988-90, adj. prof. law, 1992—; lectr. Am. Acad. Matrimonial Lawyers, 1985, 93, N.J. Family Part Judges' Retreat, 1989, N.J. Jud. Coll., 1990, Nat. Bus. Inst., Inc., 1992, Inst. Continuing Legal Edn. N.J., 1978—, Morris County Bar Assn., 1986, 91, N.J. State Bar Assn., 1992, Am. Trial Lawyers Assn., 1993-96, 99—. Co-author: N.J. Family Law Practice (3 vol.); contbr. articles to profl. jours. Mem. Morris Plains Juvenile Conf. Com., 1973-82; bd. trustees Morris Plains Libr. Assn., 1982-87. Recipient Tishler award, 1993, Bar Register of Pre-Eminent Lawyers, 1994—; named to Best Lawyers in Am., 1995—, Best Lawyers in N.J., 1997—. Mem. AMA (litigation sect. 1987-90), Internat. Acad. Matrimonial Lawyers (bd. govs. U.S. chpt. 1994-98), Am. Acad. Matrimonial Lawyers (bd. govs. 1989-90, 91-94, arbitration com. 1993—, chmn. mktg. com. 1991-92, membership com. 1992-93, budget and fin. com. 1990-91, editl. bd. Law Jour. 1993—, chmn. SCUBA Network 1992-93, bd. mgrs. N.J. chpt. 1981—, pres. N.J. chpt. 1985-87, chmn. nominating com. 1992-93, chmn. scholarship com. 1991-94, membership com. 1991-94), Am. Coll. Family Trial Lawyers (exec. com. 1994—), N.J. Assn. Matrimonial Arbitrators (v.p. 1993—), N.J. State Bar Assn. (exec. com. 1975-93, appellate practice com. 1993-95, curriculum com. Inst. Continuing Legal Edn. 1982-91), Morris County Bar Assn. (mem. family law com. 1973-75, 80—, chmn. 1987, chmn. matrimonial early settlement program 1976), Inn of Ct. (N.J. master family law 1993—), N.J. Bd. of Atty. (cert. matrimonial). Avocations: computers, horses. E-mail: LJC@Cutlaw.com. Family and matrimonial. Office: 60 Washington St Morristown NJ 07960-6844

**CUTLER, MIRIAM,** lawyer; b. Cambridge, N.Y., Nov. 20, 1953; d. Howard Bernard and Elaine (Niewood) C.; m. Horacio Gustavo Ferrari, Mar. 26, 1985; children: Alejandro Eric Ferrari, Corinne Bianca Ferrari. BA cum laude, Barnard Coll., 1976; JD, Yeshiva U., 1980. Bar: D.C. 1981, Va.

1986; cert. guardian ad litem Commonwealth Va. Assoc. Ginsburg, Feldman, Weil & Bress, Washington, 1980-82, Weil, Gotshal & Manges, Washington, 1982-83, Mudge Rose Guthrie Alexander & Ferdon, Washington, 1983-86; ptnr. Braverman and Cutler, Arlington, Va., 1986-88; pvt. practice Arlington, 1988—; civil magistrate, 1994—. Contbr. articles to profl. jours. Active Arlington County Cmty. Hispanic Affairs, 1992-93; bd. dirs. Friends of Argus and Aurora House, 1993-97. Mem. Am. Immigration Lawyers Assn., Va. State Bar (4th dist. com. sect. I 1998—), Arlington County Bar Assn. (mem. mediation task force and section 1994-97, treas. 1995-97, chair family law sect. 1997-99). General civil litigation, Immigration, naturalization, and customs, Family and matrimonial. Office: 2009 14th St N Ste 508 Arlington VA 22201-2514

**CUTLER, NANCY JANE,** lawyer, educator, land use planner; b. Cin., Dec. 14, 1963; d. Gilbert and Judith Cutler. BA in Psychology, U. Cin., 1986; JD, Chase Coll. Law, 1993; M of City Planning, U. Cin., 1998. Bar: Ohio. Pvt. practice law Cin., 1993—; instr. Ky. Career Inst., Florence, 1995—; adj. instr. U. Cin., 1998—; dir. planning Deerfield Twp., Loveland, Ohio, 1997—. Mem. ABA, Cin. Bar Assn., Am. Planning Assn. (planning and law divsn.), Ohio Planning Conf. Land use and zoning (including planning), General practice. Office: # 307D 4030 Mt Carmel-Tobasco Rd Cincinnati OH 45255

**CUTLER, PHILIP EDGERTON,** lawyer; b. Evanston, Ill., Mar. 18, 1948; s. John A. and Catherine (Hedman) C.; m. Barbara Anne Phippen, Oct. 27, 1948; children: David, Nathanael, Andrew. AB in History, Georgetown U., 1970; JD with honors, Northwestern U., 1973. Assoc. Perkins Coie, Seattle, 1973-79; ptnr. Sax and MacIver, Seattle, 1979-85; ptnr., shareholder Sax and MacIver merged Karr Tuttle Campbell, Seattle, 1986-89; shareholder, pres. Cutler & Nylander, Seattle, 1990—, also bd. dirs.; ct.-approved arbitrator King County Superior Ct., 1982—, U.S. Dist. Ct. (we. dist.) Wash., 1992—; mediator U.S. Dist. Ct. (we. dist.) Wash., 1982—; judge pro tem King County Superior Ct., 1993—; mem. comml. arbitration panel Am. Arbitration Assn., 1992—, mediator, 1997—; lectr., program chmn. numerous continuing legal edn. programs; mem. arbitration panel Nat. Assn. Securities Dealers, 1996—. Co-founder Country Dr. Comty. Legal Clinic, Seattle, 1974—; co-pres. parents club St. Joseph Sch., Seattle, 1984-86, mem. sch. adv. bd., 1985-88; dir. St. Joseph Endowment Fund, 1986—, St. Joseph Parish Sch. Fund, 1990—, St. George Sch. Endowment Found., Seattle, 1994—, sec., 1996—; mem. sch. adv. bd. Blanchet H.S., Seattle, 1991—, mem. devel. com., 1992—; chair Georgetown Alumni Admissions Interviewing Program, 1975—; active St. Patrick Parish, Seattle, 1974-82, St. Joseph Parish, Seattle, 1982—, Cursillo Movement, 1975-85, Cath. Archdiocese of Seattle, 1979-82, YMCA Indian Guides/Indian Princesses program, 1980-84, chief of Husky Nation, 1982-84. Mem. ABA (antitrust and litigation sects., civil practice and procedure com. antitrust sect. 1980-90), FBA (chair ct. congestion/alt. dispute resolution com. 1985—, mem. spl. alt. dispute resolution task force 1994 western dist. Wash.), Wash. State Bar Assn. (consumer protection, antitrust and unfair bus. practices sect., litigation sect., alt. dispute resolution sect.), St. Thomas More Soc. Seattle (pres. 1993-95), Georgetown Alumni Assn. (bd. dirs. 1977-80, alumni sen. 1980—), King County Bar Assn. (numerous coms.), Rainier Club, Wash. Athletic Club, Georgetown Club Wash. (pres. 1980-86, mem. exec. com. 1986—). Roman Catholic. Avocations: swimming, downhill skiing, gourmet cooking, reading, furniture-making and woodworking. Alternative dispute resolution, Appellate, Contracts commercial. Office: Cutler & Nylander 999 3rd Ave Ste 3150 Seattle WA 98104-4035

**CUTSHAW, JAMES MICHAEL,** lawyer; b. New Orleans, May 30, 1950; s. James Arthur and Leila Mays (Obier) Cutshaw Schroeder; m. Becky Lynn Simmons, Aug. 6, 1975 (div. Aug. 11, 1993); 1 child, Lewis Prentiss. BA, Tulane U., 1972; JD, La. State U., 1975. Bar: La. 1975, U.S. Dist. Ct. (we. dist.) La. 1975, U.S. Dist. Ct. (mid. dist.) La. 1977, U.S. Dist. Ct. (ea. dist.) La. 1980, U.S. Ct. Appeals (5th cir.) 1981, U.S. Supreme Ct. 1981, D.C. 1993. Law clk. La. Ct. Appeals, 3d Cir., Lake Charles, La., summer 1973, U.S. Dist. Ct. (we. dist.) La., Alexandria, 1975-77; ptnr. Howell, Schroeder & Cutshaw, Baton Rouge, 1977-81; gen. counsel La. Bankers Assn., Baton Rouge, 1981-87; counsel Phelps Dunbar, 1988—; lectr. La. Banking Sch., Baton Rouge, 1983-85; chmn. LBA Bank Counsel com., 1997-98, mem., 1994-98; chmn. LBA Security Devices Task Force, 1995-96. Editor: Louisiana Banking Laws, 1983-87; contbr. to legal bull., 1982-87, 1992—; contbr. (with Walter Stuart IV) articles to profl. jours. Chmn. bd. advs. La. State U. Sch. Social Work, 1988-92, bd. adv. 1988—; sec., vestry St. James Episcopal Ch., 1988-90; pres. Baton Rouge Symphony, 1984-85, bd. dirs., 1980-89; pres. Garden Dist. Civic Assn., 1979-81; bd. dirs. Baton Rouge English Speaking Union, 1986-92, v.p., 1988-92, treas. city club, 1989-90, sec., 1990-91, bd. dirs., 1989-92, treas. B.R. Assembly, 1991-92, exec. com. 1992-94; bd. dirs. Old State Capitol Assn., 1983-87, Sta. WRKF, 1981-88, Friends of La. Ind. Colls. and Univs., Anglo-Am. Art Mus. Mem. ABA, La. Bar Assn. (co-chmn. consumer credit com. 1982), Baton Rouge Bar Assn. (chmn. law sch. com. 1985), SAR, Baton Rouge C. of C. (chmn. state affairs council 1986-87), City Club, Mystick Krewe of Louisianians, Phi Beta Kappa, Phi Eta Sigma. Democrat. Banking, Legislative, General corporate. Home: 4045 S Ramsey Dr Baton Rouge LA 70808-1653 Office: Phelps Dunbar PO Box 4412 Baton Rouge LA 70821-4412

**CUTSUMPAS, LLOYD,** judge; b. Danbury, Conn., Oct. 14, 1933; s. John and Pauline (Dalacas) C.; m. Nicolletta Kakavas, July 31, 1960; children: John, Theodore. BBA, U. Conn., 1955; JD, Georgetown U., 1960. Bar: Conn. 1962, U.S. Dist. Ct. Conn. 1963. Pvt. practice Conn., 1962-97; ptnr. Cutsumpas, Collins, Hannafin, Garamella, Jaber and Tuozzolo, P.C., Danbury, 1962-97; judge Superior Ct., Conn., 1998—; lectr. family and bus. law Western Conn. State U., Danbury, 1980-97. Contbr. articles on family law to profl. jours. Pres. regional YMCA; pres. Parish Council Assumption Greek Orthodox Ch.; vice-chmn. Richter Park Authority. Served with U.S. Army, 1955-57. Named one of Outstanding Men of Am., Danbury Jaycees, 1967. Fellow Am. Acad. Matrimonial Lawyers (pres. Conn. chpt.); mem. ABA (family law div.), Conn. Bar Assn. (family law div., jud. com.), Danbury Bar Assn. (pres.). Democrat. Greek Orthodox. Home: 12 Maplecrest Dr Danbury CT 06811-4262

**CUTTNER, DAVID ALLAN,** lawyer; b. Bronx, N.Y., May 27, 1942; s. Louis and Beatrice Cuttner; 1 child, Wendy Lynne Arnold. BS, Mich. State U., 1964; JD, Wayne State U., 1967. Bar: Mich. 1968, U.S. Dist. Ct. 1968, U.S. Supreme Ct. 1990. Atty. David A. Cuttner, P.C., Farmington Hills, Mich., 1980—. Precinct del. Mich. Dem. Party, 1995. Capt. U.S. Army, 1968-69. Decorated Bronze Star. Mem. NRA, Mich. State Bar Assn. Jewish. Avocations: travel, fishing. Workers' compensation, Consumer commercial. Office: Ste 308 30300 Norhtwestern Hwy Farmington Hills MI 48334

**CYMROT, MARK ALAN,** lawyer; b. Queens, N.Y., Oct. 8, 1947; s. Irwin Maurice and Anne (Kipnis) C.; children: Isaac, Erin. BA, George Washington U., 1969; JD, Columbia U., 1972. Bar: D.C. 1973. Trial lawyer civil div. U.S. Dept. of Justice, Washington, 1972-77; sr. litigator Consumers Union of U.S. Inc., Washington, 1977-79; special litigation counsel civil div. U.S. Dept. of Justice, Washington, 1979-83; ptnr. Cole Corette & Abrutyn, Washington, 1983-91, Baker & Hostetler, Washington, 1991—. Contbr. articles to profl. jours. Named one of 50 Best Lawyers in Washington by Washingtonian Mag., 1992. Avocations: photography, golf. Federal civil litigation, Public international, Private international. Office: Baker & Hostetler 1050 Connecticut Ave NW Washington DC 20036-5304

**CYPSER, DARLENE ANN,** lawyer; b. Tulsa, Jan. 3, 1958; d. Donald A. and Evelyn D. (Carrigan) Chappell; 1 child, Christopher A. BA, U. Okla., 1980, JD, 1986. Bar: N.Y. 1987, Colo. 1988. Pvt. practice Boulder, Colo., 1988—. Contbr. articles to profl. jours. Vol. Boulder County Legal Svcs., 1987—, Legal Aid Soc. Westchester County, White Plains, N.Y., 1986-87; dir. Nyx Net, 1997—. Mem. Am. Geophys. Union. Avocations: macrame, hiking, photography, cooking. Computer, Environmental, Non-profit and tax-exempt organizations. Office: PO Box 2187 Boulder CO 80306-2187

**CYR, CONRAD KEEFE,** federal judge; b. Limestone, Maine, Dec. 9, 1931; s. Louis Emery and Kathleen Mary (Keefe) C.; m. Judith Ann Pirie, June 23, 1962 (dec. Mar. 1985); children: Keefe Clark, Jeffrey Louis Frederick; m. Diana Kathleen Sanborn, Sept. 25, 1987. BS cum laude, Holy Cross Coll., 1953; JD, Yale U., 1956; LLD (hon.), Husson Coll., 1991, Husson Coll., 1991. Bar: Maine 1956. Pvt. practice Limestone, 1956-59; asst. U.S. atty., Bangor, Maine, 1959-61; judge U.S. Bankruptcy Court, Bangor, 1961-81; judge U.S. Dist. Ct., Bangor, 1981-83, chief judge, 1983-89; judge U.S. Fgn. Intelligence Surveillance Ct., 1987-89; judge U.S. Ct. Appeals (1st cir.), Boston, 1989-97, sr. judge, 1997—; standing spl. master U.S. Dist. Ct., Maine, 1974-76; chief judge Bankruptcy Appellate Panel Dist., Mass., 1980-81; mem. Jud. Council for the 1st Circuit, 1987—, com. on adminstrn. of the bankruptcy system Jud. Conf. U.S., 1987—. founder, editor-in-chief Am. Bankruptcy Law Jour., 1970-81; contbg. author, editor: Collier on Bankruptcy, Vol. 10. Treas. Limestone Republican Com., 1958; chmn. Town of Limestone Budget Com., 1959; mem. steering com. U.S. AID Project for Assisting Bankruptcy and Reorgn. Procedures in Ctr. and Ea. Europe. Recipient cert. of appreciation Kans. Bar Assn., 1979, U. Maine, 1983; Nat. Judge's Recognition award Nat. Conf. Bankruptcy Judges, 1979; Key to Town Limestone, 1983; named one of Outstanding Young Men of Maine, 1963. Fellow Maine Bar Found. (charter), Am. Coll. Bankruptcy; mem. Maine Bar Assn., Penobscot Bar Assn., Nat. Conf. Bankruptcy Judges (prs. 1976-77), Nat. Bankruptcy Conf. (exec. bd. 1974-77), Am. Juticature Soc., Limestone C. of C. (pres.). Roman Catholic.

**CYR, KAREN D.,** lawyer. Gen. counsel Nuclear Regulatory Commn., Fockville, Md. Office: Nuclear Regulatory Commn 11555 Rockville Pike Rockville MD 20852-2738

**CYR, STEVEN MILES,** lawyer; b. Centralia, Wash., Mar. 8, 1948; s. Delbert Lee and Lila M. (Tatro) C.; divorced; children: Miles Lee, Lindsay Ann; m. JoAnn Cyr, Mar. 11, 1989. Student, U. S.D.; BS, Oreg. State U., 1970; JD, Lewis & Clark U., 1979. Bar: Oreg. 1979, U.S. Dist. Ct. Oreg. 1979, U.S. Tax Ct. 1979, U.S. Ct. Appeals (9th cir.) 1979. Inheritence tax examiner Oreg. Dept. Revenue, Salem, 1970-74; mgr. trust tax dept. 1st Interstate Bank of Oreg., Portland, 1974-79; ptnr. Cyr, Moe & Benner P.C., Portland, 1979-94; sr. ptnr. Cyr & Assocs. PC, Portland, 1994-98, mng. mem. legal rep., 1998—; instr. Portland State U., 1985-95. Author: Oregon Practical Probate, 1995, Oregon Estate Planning, 1997, Oregon Partnership Law, 1986-89, Mastering Estate Planning Techniques, 1998; co-author: The Oregon Trust Course, 1996-98, Fiduciary Income Tax, 1997-99, Federal Estate and Gift Tax, 1996-98. Mem. Oreg. Bar (exec. com. taxation sect. 1985-86, treas. 1986, chmn.-elect 1987, chmn. 1988, past chmn. 1989), Riverside Golf and Country Club (Portland). Avocations: skiing, golf, flying. Probate, Corporate taxation, Estate taxation. Home: 12710 SW Pacer Way Beaverton OR 97008-6908

**CZAJKOWSKI, FRANK HENRY,** lawyer; b. Bklyn., Jan. 7, 1936; m. Cecilia J. Artowicz, Sept. 3, 1955. B.A., St. John's U., Bklyn., 1957, J.D., 1959; LL.M., George Washington U., 1966. Bar: N.Y. 1960, Pa. 1970, Conn. 1974, U.S. Supreme Ct. 1964. Claims adjuster Hartford Accident & Indemnity Ins. Co., N.Y.C., 1959-60; agt. Equitable Life Assurance Soc., N.Y.C., 1960; atty. Corp. Counsel's Office, N.Y.C., 1960-62; atty. Fgn. Claims Settlement Commn., Washington, 1962-68; atty. Atlantic-Richfield Co., N.Y.C., 1968-70, Phila., 1970-72; assoc. gen. counsel Unilever U.S.A. Co., Greenwich, Conn., 1972—; instr. Fairfield U. Ctr. Lifetime Learning, 1976, Sacred Heart U., 1983; arbitrator Am. Arbitration Assn. Mem. ABA, Conn. Bar Assn., Westchester-Fairfield Corp. Counsel Assn. Republican. Roman Catholic. Labor, Pension, profit-sharing, and employee benefits, Product liability. Home: 7 Lafayette Dr Trumbull CT 06611-2751 Office: Unilever USA Co 75 Merritt Blvd Trumbull CT 06611-5435

**CZARRA, EDGAR F., JR.,** lawyer; b. Langhorne, Pa., Oct. 4, 1928; s. Edgar F. and Mary Agnes (Copeland) C.; m. Doris Catharine Lane, June 14, 1952; children: Penelope L., Edgar F. III, Jonathan C., Melanie A. BS, Yale U., 1949, LLB, 1952. Bar: U.S. Dist. Ct. D.C. 1954, U.S. Ct. Appeals (D.C. cir.) 1954, U.S. Supreme Ct. 1959. Assoc. Covington & Burling, Washington, 1952, 55-63, ptnr., 1963-97, ret., 1997; chmn. Global View Prodns., Inc. Served to lt. (j.g.) USN, 1952-55. Mem. ABA, D.C. Bar Assn., Fed. Communications Bar Assn. Administrative and regulatory, Federal civil litigation, Mergers and acquisitions. Office: Covington & Burling PO Box 7566 1201 Pennsylvania Ave NW Washington DC 20044-7566

**DABROWSKI, DORIS JANE,** lawyer; b. Paterson, N.J., May 20, 1950. BA, Rutgers U., 1972, JD, 1975. Bar: Pa. 1975, U.S. Dist. Ct. (ea. dist.) Pa. 1976, U.S. Ct. Appeals (3d cir.) 1977, N.J. 1979, U.S. Dist. Ct. N.J. 1979, U.S. Ct. Appeals (fed. cir.) 1985. Staff atty. Delaware County Legal Assistance, Chester, Pa., 1975-77; assoc. Tabas, Horwitz & Furlong (later Tabas, Furlong & Roser), Phila., 1977-83; pvt. practice Phila. and Moorestown, N.J., 1983—; arbitrator Nat. Assn. Securities Dealers, Am. Arbitration Assn., Phila. and N.J.; participant Nat. Pension Assistance Project; mem. adv. coun. 18th Police Dist., 1997—. Mem. editorial bd. Women's Rights Law Reporter, 1974-75. Dir. Well Woman, Phila., 1983-87, Pa. Pro Musica, Phila., 1983-84; mem. adv. bd. Clara Bell Duvall Edn. Fund, Phila.; mem. gov. bd. Health Systems Agy., S.E. Pa., 1980-86; mem. 18th Police Dist. Adv. Coun. Recipient Cert. of Achievement Bus. Women's Network, Phila., 1984. Mem. Nat. Employment Lawyers' Assn. (pres. Ea. Pa. chpt. 1992-98), Nat. Assn. Women Lawyers (amicus com., bd. dirs. 1994-95), Phila. Bar Assn. (mem. evidence task force 1992-93, chair support subcom. of small firm and sole practice com. 1992), Assn. for Union Democracy, Nat. Police Def. Found. (hon.), Am. Guild Organists. Labor, Pension, profit-sharing, and employee benefits, Administrative and regulatory. Office: 1308 Spruce St Philadelphia PA 19107-5812 also: 1930 Marlton Pike E Ste I48 Cherry Hill NJ 08003-4105

**DACHS, JONATHAN A.,** lawyer; b. N.Y.C., Sept. 7, 1958; s. Norman H. and Zena (Schwartz); m. Ann Turobiner, Jan. 17, 1982; children: Nina, Joshua, Julia. BA, Columbia U., 1980; JD, NYU, 1983. Bar: N.Y. 1984, U.S. Dist. Ct. (ea. and so. dists.) N.Y. 1984, U.S. Ct. Appeals (2d cir.) 1990. Assoc. Chadbourne & Parke, N.Y.C., 1983-86; assoc. Shayne, Dachs, Stanisci, Corker & Sauer, Mineola, N.Y., 1986-90, ptnr., 1990—. Author: Uninsured and Uninsured Motorist Protection, 1991, Uninsured Motorist, 1996; editor-in-chief New York Negligence Reporter, 1890-92; contbr. articles to profl. jours. Committeeman, Nassau County Dem. party, 1976-78; mem. Nassau Dem. Jud. Screening Com., 1992—. Mem. ABA, N.Y. State Bar Assn., Bar Assn. Nassau County (chair ins. law com. 1994-96), N.Y. State Trial Lawyers Assn., N.Y. County Lawyers Assn., Nassau-Suffolk Trial Lawyers Assn. Jewish. Avocations: writing, lecturing. Appellate, Insurance, Personal injury. Office: Shayne Dachs et al 250 Old Country Rd Mineola NY 11501-4299

**DADD, MARGARET BAGGOT,** lawyer; b. Portage, Wis., June 20, 1945; d. Leo James and Agatha Lucille (Mullowney) Baggot; m. Mark H. Dadd, Dec. 19, 1970; children: Molly Helen, Lucille Ann, Hayden Mark, Carolyn Maeve. BS, U. Wis., 1967, JD, 1970. Bar: Wis. 1970, N.Y. 1973. Staff atty. Milw. Legal Svcs., 1970-72, Neighborhood Legal Svcs. Buffalo (N.Y.), Inc., 1972-75, Dadd & Dadd, P.C., Attica, N.Y., 1975-91; owner, practitioner Margaret Dadd Law Office, Attica, N.Y., 1991—. Chair Wyoming County Rep. Com., Attica, 1991-97; regional dir. Cath. Charities, Buffalo, 1990—; trustee Wyoming County Bus. Devel. Corp., Warsaw, N.Y., 1991—; trustee Genessee Regional Ind. Living Ctr., Inc., sec. 1996—. Mem. Wyoming County Bar Assn. (officer 1972—). Republican. Roman Catholic. Family and matrimonial, Real property, Personal injury. Home: 166 Main St Attica NY 14011-1243 Office: 17 Exchange St Attica NY 14011-1210

**DAGGER, WILLIAM CARSON,** lawyer; b. Lancaster, Ohio, May 5, 1949; s. William Carson Sr. and Thelma (Downing) D.; m. Barbara Schaeffer, Sept. 6, 1981; children: Alison Golden; Jaclyn Hedi. AB, Kenyon Coll., 1971; postgrad., Vanderbilt U., 1971-72; JD cum laude, Suffolk U., 1978. Bar: Mass. 1979, Vt. 1981, U.S. Dist. Ct. (ea. dist.) Mass. 1979, U.S. Dist. Ct. Vt. 1981, U.S. Ct. Appeals (1st cir.) 1980, U.S. Ct. Appeals (2nd cir.) 1990. Legal asst. Bernkopf, Goodman & Baseman, Boston, 1976-78; assoc. Rodick & Flavell, Weymouth, Mass., 1978-80, Dick, Hackel & Hull, Rutland, Vt., 1980-88; ptnr. Hull, Webber, Reis & Canney, Rutland, 1989-90; pvt. practice Woodstock, Vt., 1990—; legal counsel The Howard Bank, Burlington, Vt., 1981-89, Vt. Indsl. Devel. Authority, Montpelier, 1982-84, Vt. Nat. Bank, 1990—, Woodstock Nat. Bank, 1993—, Vt. Housing Fin. Agy., 1990—, Ames Dept. Stores, 1990—, New London Trust Co., 1997—; trustee, treas. The Homestead, Inc., Woodstock, 1991-96. Com. mem. Boy Scouts Am., 1990—. Mem. ABA, Vt. Bar Assn. (jud. evaluation com. 1981), Vt. Trial Lawyers Assn. (founding mem., master Sterry R. Waterman Am. Inn of Ct. 1994—), Rotary Internat., Woodstock Rotary (pres. elect 1998-99), Sierra Club (state rep. 1973-75). General civil litigation, Contracts commercial, Real property. Home: 4702 Riverside Rd Woodstock VT 05091-9630 Office: The French Block PO Box 539 2 Central St Woodstock VT 05091-1007

**DAGHIR, GEORGE NEJM,** lawyer; b. St. Marys, Pa., Nov. 24, 1954; s. George Lewis and Wanda Marie (Richard) D. BA, Pa. State U., 1976; JD, Widener U., 1979. Bar: Pa. 1979. Ptnr. Daghir & Daghir, St. Marys, 1979—. Criminal, General practice. Office: Daghir & Daghir PO Box 404 20 N Michael St Saint Marys PA 15857-1325

**D'AGUSTO, KAREN ROSE,** lawyer; b. Phila., Jan. 4, 1952; d. Les and Anne Heilenman; m. Stephen Joseph Bernasconi, Aug. 21, 1976; children: Lesley Anne D. Bernasconi, Stephanie Kalena D. Bernasconi. BA in History cum laude, Immaculata Coll., 1974; JD, U. San Diego, 1977; postgrad., U. So. Calif., 1983—. Bar: Conn. 1977, Hawaii 1978, S.C. 1986. Tng. coord. Protection and Advocacy, Honolulu, 1978, adv. coord., 1979, staff atty., 1980-81, assoc dir., 1982, project dir., 1983—; regional coord. S.C. Protection and Adv. System, 1986-88; dep. dir. Hawaii Protection and Advocacy, 1989-91; pvt. practice law Mililani, Hawaii, 1980—; instr. Hawaii Pacific Coll., Honolulu, 1982-84; dir. Harmon-Johnson Inst., Honolulu, 1983—; adj. prof. Immaculata Coll., 1998-99; legal cons., 1999—. Author: Legal Rights of Handicapped, 1980; author, editor curriculum Vol. I Guardians Ad. Litem, 1983; editor Jour. Comparative Legis. Analysis of Protection and Advocacy System, 1991. Pres. Cen. Oahu Mental Health Ctr., Pearl City, Hawaii, 1981-82; officer Kings Grant Assn., Summerville, S.C., 1988; rep. St. Andrews Priory Parent-Tchr. Fellowship Bd., 1990-91; mem. John B. Dey PTA, mem. bd. dirs., chair legis. com.; leader Girl Scouts Am., svc. unit mgr., trainer, cons. Cape Henry Svc. unit, Colonial Coast coun.; mem. PTA legis. com.; vol. Great Neck Mid. Sch.; co-chair Tower Hill Camp Fair, 1998-99; chair family appeal Brandywine Valley Girl Scout Svc. Unit, 1996-99. Recipient Exceptional Achievement award, 1989-90, Disting. Contbn. to Civil Rights of Persons with Disabilities award, 1991, Outstanding Svc. to Hawaiis Disabled Citizens award, 1982, Outstanding Vol. of Yr. award Colonial Coast coun. Girl Scouts U.S., 1995, Vol. of Yr. award Great Neck Middle Sch., 1996; named Outstanding Adv., 1985. Mem. ABA, Hawaii State Bar Assn., S.C. Bar Assn., Conn. Bar Assn., Hawaii Lawyers Care, Am. Assn. Counsel for Children Counsel, Wimbledon on the Bay Homeowners Assn. (v.p. 1992-93, chair by-laws com. 1993-94). Personal injury, Education and schools, Civil rights.

**DAHL, EVERETT E.,** lawyer; b. Sandy, Utah, June 21, 1923; m. Ann Kosovich, June 21, 1949; children: Annette, EvAnn. BS, U. Utah, 1947, JD, 1949. Bar: Utah 1949, U.S. Dist. Ct. Utah 1959, U.S. Ct. Mil. Appeals 1959, U.S. Supreme Ct., U.S. Ct. Appeals (10th cir.). Commd. 2d lt. U.S. Army, 1943, advanced through grades to col., ret., 1975; pvt. practice Midvale, Utah, 1949—. Mayor City of Midvale, 1986-94; exec. sec. Midvale C. of C., 1950-60; bd. dirs. Rsch. Inst., 1955—; pres. Palo Verde Park, Inc., Safford, Ariz., 1970's; chmn. Salt Lake County Coun. Govts., South Valley Emergency Ctr.; bd. dirs. Trans Jordan Landfill. Mem. Res. Officers Assn. (life, dept. comdr. nat. exec. com.), Amvets (dept. pres. nat. exec. com. 1993—), VFW, Phi Kappa Phi. Avocations: fishing, golf. Environmental, Real property, Estate taxation. Office: 760 E Center St Midvale UT 84047-3208

**DAHL, LOREN SILVESTER,** retired federal judge; b. East Fairview, N.D., Mar. 1, 1921; s. William T. and Maude (Silvester) D.; m. Pamela B. Miller, Mar. 16, 1995; children by previous marriage: Candy, Walter Ray. AA, Coll. of Pacific, 1940; LLB, JD, U. Calif., San Francisco, 1949. Bar: Calif., 1950, U.S. Supreme Ct., 1957. Pvt. practice law Sacramento, 1950; sr. ptnr. Dahl, Hefner, Stark & Marois, Sacramento, 1950-80; chief judge U.S. Bankruptcy Ct. (ea. dist.) Calif., Sacramento, 1980, 86-94; chief judge emeritus, 1994—; Chmn. Conf. Chief Judges, 9th Cir., 1992. Pres. Golden Empire Coun. Boy Scouts Am., Sacramento, 1955-56, chmn. bd. trustees, 1956, exec. com. region 12, 1958, regional chmn. 1968-70, nat. exec. bd. 1968-70; Sacramento County Juvenile Justice Commn.; mem. bd. visitors McGeorge sch. law U. Pacific, 1987—; bd. dirs. Salvation Army, Sacramento, 1954-57; Sacramento Symphony Assn., 1958-59, Sacramento Safety Coun. With USAAF, 1942-46. Recipient Disting. Svc. award Jaycees, 1957, Silver Beaver award, Boy Scouts Am., 1957, Silver Antelope award, Boy Scouts Am., 1963, Disting. Eagle Scout award, Boy Scouts Am., Judge of Yr. award Sacramento County Bar Assn., 1993. Mem. U. of Pacific Alumni Assn. (pres. 1974-78, bd. regents 1980—, Disting. Alumnus award 1979), ABA, Calif. Bar Assn. (lectr. bankruptcy, continuing edn.), Am. Judicature Soc., Phi Delta Phi. Club: Del Paso Country. Lodge: Masons, Shriners, Lions (dir. Sacramento club 1952-53). Home: 842 Lake Oak Ct Sacramento CA 95864-6154

**DAHL, MICHAEL BRUCE,** lawyer; b. Princeton, N.J., Mar. 26, 1969; s. Richard Alan and Dorothy Rivers Dahl; m. Shannon McCabe, Aug. 8, 1996. BA in Polit. Sci., Colo. State U., 1991; JD, U. Pitts., 1996. Bar: N.J., Pa., U.S. Dist. Ct. N.J. Law clk. Allegheny Dist. Atty.'s Office, Pitts., summer 1993; law clk./summer assoc. Pillar, Mulroy & Ferber, Pitts., 1993-96; clk. hon. Marilyn Loftus Superior Ct. Appellate Divsn. State N.J., Morristown, 1996-97; assoc. Fox, Rothschild, O'Brien & Frankel, LLP, Lawrenceville, N.J., 1997—. Named Colo. Legis. Intern, State Colo., Denver, 1990. Mem. ABA, N.J. Bar Assn. (officer young lawyers divsn. 1998), Pa. Bar Assn., Princeton Bar Assn., Mercer County C. of C.. General corporate, Mergers and acquisitions, Securities. Office: Fox Rothschild O'Brien & Frankel LLP 997 Lenox Dr Bldg 3 Lawrenceville NJ 08648-2317

**DAHL, TYRUS VANCE, JR.,** lawyer; b. Elizabeth City, N.C., July 23, 1949; s. Tyrus Vance and Emerald (Taylor) D.; m. Susan Morrow Fitzgerald, Aug. 7, 1976 (div. Apr. 1992); children: Katherine Fitzgerald, Elizabeth Sommers. AB, Duke U., 1971; JD, U. Tulsa, 1979. Bar: Tenn. 1979, U.S. Dist. Ct. (mid. dist.) Tenn. 1979, Okla. 1981, U.S. Dist. Ct. (no. and we dists.) Okla. 1982, U.S. Ct. Appeals (10th cir.) 1982, N.C. 1985, U.S. Dist. Ct. (ea., mid., and we. dists.) N.C. 1985, U.S. Ct. Appeals (4th cir.) 1985, U.S. Supreme Ct. 1985, U.S. Ct. Appeals (6th cir.) 1987. Law clk. to chief fed. judge Nashville, 1979-81; assoc. Hall, Estill, Tulsa, 1981-84; ptnr. Womble Carlyle Sandridge & Rice, Winston-Salem, N.C., 1984—; adj. prof. clin. program, adj. prof. trail practice Sch. Law, Wake Forest U. Editor and contbr. articles to law rev. Mem. ATLA, N.C. Bar Assn., Forsyth County Bar Assn. Democrat. Methodist. Avocation: photography, music. Civil rights, Federal civil litigation, Insurance. Office: Womble Carlyle Sandridge & Rice 200 W 2nd St Winston Salem NC 27101-4019

**DAHLING, GERALD VERNON,** lawyer; b. Red Wing, Minn., Jan. 11, 1947; s. Vernon and Lucille Alfrieda (Reuter) D.; m. Edell Marie Villella, July 26, 1969; children: David (dec.), Christopher, Elizabeth, Mary. BS, Winona (Minn.) State Coll., 1968; MS, U. Minn., 1970; PhD, Harvard U., 1974; JD, William Mitchell Coll. of Law, 1980. Bar: U.S. Patent Office 1979, Minn. 1980, Ind. 1980, Pa. 1997, U.S. Dist. Ct. (so. dist.) Ind. 1980. Patent atty. Eli Lilly and Co., Indpls., 1980-84, mgr. biotech. patents, 1984-86, asst. patent counsel biotech., 1986-89, asst. patent counsel biotech. and fermentation products, 1990, asst. gen. patent counsel, 1991-95; dir. intellectual property Pasteur Mérieux Connaught, Lyon, France and Swiftwater, Pa., 1995-97; corp. v.p., dir. intellectual property Pasteur Mérieux Connaught, 1997-98; sr. v.p. intellectual property Pasteur Mérieux Connaught, Lyon, France, 1998—, Rhone Poulenc Rorer, Collegeville, Pa., 1998—. Mem. ABA, Ind. Bar Assn., Pa. Bar Assn., Am. Intellectual Property Law Assn. Democrat. Roman Catholic. Patent, Federal civil litigation, Contracts commercial. Home: 3 Jasper Ln Phoenixville PA 19460-1162 Office: 58 Ave LeClerc BP 7046, 69348 Lyon France also: 500 Arcola Rd Collegeville PA 19426-3930

**DAICHMAN, JEFFREY HOWARD,** lawyer; b. Bkln., June 2, 1948; s. Samuel and Shirley (Cooper) D.; m. Karen Gottlieb June 3, 1973; children—Joni, Michael. B.S., Rensselaer Poly. Inst., 1970; M.A., Purdue U., 1971; J.D., NYU, 1974. Bar: N.Y. 1975, U.S. Dist. Ct. (so. dist. and ea. dist.) N.Y. 1975, U.S. Ct. Appeals (2d cir.) 1975, U.S. Ct. Appeals (10th cir.) 1981, U.S. Ct. Appeals (1st cir.) 1982, U.S. Ct. Appeals (3d cir.) 1984, U.S. Supreme Ct. 1983, U.S. Ct. Appeals (4th cir.) 1985, U.S. Ct. Appeals (D.C. cir.) 1989, U.S. Ct. Appeals (9th cir.) 1993, U.S. Ct. Appeals (7th cir.) 1997. Ptnr. Kane Kessler, P.C. Mng. editor N.Y. Rev. Law and Social Change,

1973, 74. Federal civil litigation, State civil litigation, Libel. Home: 22 Fox Hill Rd Edison NJ 08820-2824 Office: Kane Kessler PC 1350 Avenue Of The Americas New York NY 10019-4702

**DAICOFF, SUSAN (SUSAN DAICOFF BASKIN),** law educator; b. Chgo., July 5, 1962; d. George Ronald and Mary Jane (Swaim) D.; m. Robert Lewis Harding, Oct. 1, 1983 (div. Mar. 1990); m. Gordon Victor Monday, Dec. 12, 1992 (div. Mar. 1994); m. Robert Neal Baskin Jr., June 22, 1996—; children: Arizona Gray, Graylin Diana. BA in Math., U. Fla., 1980, JD with honors, 1983; LLM in Taxation, NYU, 1985; MS in Clin. Psychology, U. Ctrl. Fla., 1992. Bar: Fla. 1984. Atty. Smith, Mackinnon, Mathews et al., Orlando, Fla., 1985-88; author Tax Practice Series, Tax Mgmt., Orlando, 1989; counselor III Project III of Ctrl. Fla., Orlando, 1991-92; asst. rsch. assoc. team performance lab. U. Ctrl. Fla., Orlando, 1992-93; atty. in taxation, corporate law and psychology Barnett, Bolt, Kirkwood & Long, Tampa, 1993-94; asst. prof. law Capital U. Law Sch., Columbus, Ohio, 1995—; adj. instr. Valencia Cmty. Coll., Orlando, 1988; mental health counselor intern Response, Inc., Sexual Assault Ctr., Orlando, 1992-93. Wallace scholarship NYU, 1984-85. Mem. Order of Coif, Phi Beta Kappa. Office: Captial U of Law Sch 303 E Broad St Columbus OH 43215-3200

**DAIGLE, GERALD JOSEPH, JR.,** lawyer, accountant; b. New Orleans, Sept. 13, 1957; s. Gerald J. and Anna May (Chotin) D.; m. Shannon M. Hurley, May 5, 1984; children: Gerald Joseph III, Amelie Marie Chotin, Jeanne Claire. BS in Acctg. summa cum laude, U. New Orleans, 1978; JD cum laude, Loyola U., 1983. Bar: La. 1983; CPA, La. Tax sr. Arthur Andersen & Co., New Orleans, 1978-81; mng. editor Loyola Law Rev., New Orleans, 1982-83; with Chaffe, McCall, Phillips, Toler & Sarpy, New Orleans, 1983-93. Mem. La. State Bar Assn., Beta Gamma Sigma, Beta Alpha Psi, Phi Alpha Delta. Home: 358 W Kenilworth St New Orleans LA 70124-1118 Office: 909 Poydras St Ste 2230 New Orleans LA 70112-4003

**DAIKER, PAUL B.,** lawyer; b. Oxford, Ohio, Nov. 6, 1967; s. Donald A. and Victoria A. Daiker; m. Elizabeth A. Salzarulo, June 24, 1995. BA, Vanderbilt U., 1990; JD, Cleve. State U., 1993. Bar: Ohio 1993, U.S. Dist. Ct. (no. dist.) Ohio 1996, U.S. Ct. Appeals (6th cir.) 1996. Assoc., trail lawyer Zukerman & Assocs., Cleve., 1993-96; shareholder, ptnr. Zukerman & Duiker Co., LPA, Cleve., 1996—; prosecutor Village of Moreland Hills, Ohio, 1996—. Criminal, General civil litigation, Family and matrimonial. Office: Zukerman & Daiker Co LPA 2000 E 9th St Ste 700 Cleveland OH 44115-1301

**DAIL, JOSEPH GARNER, JR.,** judge; b. Elloree, S.C., June 15, 1932; s. Joseph Garner and Esther Vernette (Harbort) D.; m. Martha E. MacReynolds; children: Edward Benjamin, Mary Holyoke. BS, U. N.C., 1953, JD with honors, 1955. Bar: N.C. 1955, D.C. 1959, Va. 1976. Pvt. practice Washington, 1959-76, McLean, Va., 1976-87; ptnr. Croft, Dail & Vance (and predecessor), 1966-76; counsel Gabeler, Ward & Griggs, 1983-87; judge U.S. adminstrv. law Fresno, Calif., 1987-94, San Francisco, 1994-97; judge U.S. adminstrv. law Tampa, 1997-99, sr. U.S. adminstrv. law judge, 1999—. Assoc. editor: N.C. Law Rev., 1954-55. Lt. USNR, 1955-59; capt. Res. (ret.). Mem. FBA, N.C. Bar Assn., D.C. Bar Assn., Transp. Lawyers Assn. (Disting. Svc. award 1976), Order of Coif, Phi Beta Kappa. Republican. Home: 103 Masters Ln Safety Harbor FL 34695-3722 Office: Times Bldg 1000 N Ashley Dr Ste 200 Tampa FL 33602-3719

**DAILEY, COLEEN HALL,** magistrate, lawyer; b. East Liverpool, Ohio, Aug. 10, 1955; d. David Lawrence and Deloris Mae (Rosensteel) Hall; m. Donald W. Dailey Jr., Aug. 16, 1980; children: Erin Elizabeth, Daniel Lester. Student, Wittenberg U., 1973-75; BA, Youngstown State U., 1977; JD, U. Cin., 1980. Bar: Ohio 1981, U.S. Dist. Ct. (no. dist.) Ohio 1981. Sr. library assoc. Marx Law Library, Cin., 1979-80; law clk. Kapp Law Office, East Liverpool, 1979, 1980-81, assoc., 1981-85; sole practice East Liverpool, 1985-95; magistrate Columbiana County, Ohio, 1995—; spl. counsel Atty. Gen. Ohio, 1985-92. Pres. Columbiana County Young Dems., 1985-87; bd. dirs. Big Bros./Big Sisters Columbiana County, Inc., Lisbon, Ohio, 1984-87, Planned Parenthood Mahoning Valley, Inc., 1993-97; trustee Ohio Women Inc., 1991-95; mem. Columbiana County Progress Coun., Inc. Mem. ABA, Ohio Bar Assn. (Ohio Supreme Ct. Joint Task Force on Gender Fairness), Ohio Assn. Magistrates (chmn. domestic rels. sect. 1998—), Columbiana County Bar Assn., East Liverpool Bus. and Profl. Women's Assn., Ohio Women's Bar Assn. (trustee 1997-99). Democrat. Lutheran. Office: Columbia County Common Pleas Court 105 S Market St Lisbon OH 44432-1255

**DAILEY, DIANNE K.,** lawyer; b. Great Falls, Mont., Oct. 10, 1950; d. Gilmore and Patricia Marie (Linnane) Halverson. BS, Portland State U., 1977; JD, Lewis & Clark Coll., 1982. Assoc. Bullivant, Houser, Bailey, et. al., Portland, Oreg., 1982-88, ptnr., 1988—. Contbr. articles to profl. jours. Mem. ABA (vice chair tort and ins. practice sect. 1995-96, chair-elect tort and ins. practice sect. 1996-97, chair tort and ins. practice sect. 1997-98, governing coun. 1992—, property ins. law com., ins. coverage litigation com., comm. com., chair task force on involvement of women 1990-93, liaison to commn. on women 1993-97, chair task force CERCLA reauthorization, litigation sect., standing com. environ. law 1996—, chair officers conf. sect. 1998—), Wash. Bar Assn., Oreg. State Bar, Oreg. Assn. Def. Counsel, Multnomah Bar Assn. (bd. dirs. 1994-95), Internat. Assn. Def. Counsel, Def. Rsch. Inst., Fedn. Ins. and Corp. Counsel. Environmental, Insurance, General civil litigation. Office: Bullivant Houser Bailey 300 Pioneer Tower 888 SW 5th Ave Ste 300 Portland OR 97204-2089

**DAILEY, GARRETT CLARK,** publisher, lawyer; b. Bethesda, Md., Mar. 22, 1947; s. Garrett Hobart Valentine and Margaret (Clark) Dailey; m. Carolynn Farrar, June 21, 1969; children: Patrick, Steven. AB, UCLA, 1969; MA, Ariz. State U., 1974; JD, U. Calif., Davis, 1977. Bar: Calif. 1977, U.S. Dist. Ct. (no. dist.) Calif. 1969. Assoc. Stark, Stewart, Simon & Sparrowe, Oakland, Calif., 1977-80; ptnr. Davies & Dailey, Oakland, 1980-85, owner, 1986-90; ptnr. Blum, Davies & Dailey, Oakland, 1985-86; pres., pub. Attys. Briefcase, Inc., Oakland, 1989—, pres., CEO, 1989—; lectr. U. Calif. Davis Sch. Law, 1988-90, Golden Gate U. Grad. Sch. Taxation, San Francisco, 1986—. Co-author: Attorney's Briefcase, Calif. Family Law, 1990-99, Calif. Evidence, 1993-99, Children and the Law, 1992-99, Calif. Lawgic Marital Termination Agreements, 1996, Calif. Divorce Guide, 1997-99, Lawgic Premarital Agreements, 1997—. Bd. dirs. Amigos de las Americas, San Ramon Valley, Calif., 1980-85, Rotary 517 Found., Oakland, 1985, Kid's Turn, 1993. Recipient Hall of Fame award Calif. Assn. Cert. Family Law Specialists, 1995. Fellow Am. Acad. Matrimonial Lawyers; mem. Assn. Cert. Family Law Specialists (Hall of Fame award 1995). Democrat. Congregationalist. Home: 1651 W Livorna Rd Alamo CA 94507-1018 Office: Attys Briefcase Inc 519 17th St Fl 7 Oakland CA 94612-1527

**DAILY, FRANK J(EROME),** lawyer; b. Chgo., Mar. 22, 1942; s. Francis Jerome and Eileen Veronica (O'Toole) D.; m. Julianna Ebert, June 23, 1996; children: Catherine, Eileen, Frank, William, Michael. BA in Journalism, Marquette U., 1964, JD, 1968. Bar: Wis. 1968, U.S. Dist. Ct. (ea. dist.) Wis. 1968, U.S. Dist. Ct. (we. dist.) Wis. 1971, U.S. Dist. Ct. (ctrl. dist.) Ill. 1990, U.S. Dist. Ct. (ea. dist.) Mich. 1994, U.S. Ct. Appeals (7th cir.) 1977, U.S. Ct. Appeals (3d and 5th cirs.) 1985, U.S. Ct. Appeals (4th, 6th, 8th, 9th, 10th, 11th cirs.) 1990, U.S. Supreme Ct. 1998, U.S. Dist. Ct. (no. dist.) Ill. 1999. Assoc. Quarles & Brady, Milw., 1968-75, ptnr., 1975—; lectr. in product liability law and trial techniques Marquette U. Law Sch., U. Wis., Harvard U. and seminars sponsored by ABA, State Bar Wis., State Bar S.D., State Bar S.C., Product Liability Adv. Coun., Chem. Mfrs. Assn., Wis. Acad. Trial Lawyers, Trial Attys. Am., Marquette U., Southeastern Corp. Law Inst., Risk Ins. Mgmt. Soc. Inc.; mem. bd. visitors Wake Forest U. Law Sch. Author: Your Product's Life Is in the Balance: Litigation Survival-Increasing the Odds for Success, 1986, Product Liability Litigation in the 80s: A Trial Lawyer's View from the Trenches, 1986, Discovery Available to the Litigator and Its Effective Use, 1986, The Future of Tort Litigation: The Continuing Validity of Jury Trials, 1991, How to Make an Impact in Opening Statements for the Defense in Automobile Product Liability Cases, 1992, How Much Reform Does Civil Jury System Need, 1992, Do Protective Orders Compromise Public's Right to Know, 1993, Developments in Chemical Exposure Cases: Challenging Expert Testimony, 1993, The Spoliation Doctrine: The Sword, The Shield and The Shadow, 1997, Trial Tested Techniques for Winning Opening Statements, 1997, Litigation in the Next Millennium -- A Trial Lawyer's Crystal Ball Report, 1998, What's Hot and What's Not in Non-Daubert Products Liability In the Seventh Circuit, 1998. Life mem. Pres.'s Coun., Marquette U., Pres.'s Cir., Boston Coll. Fellow Internat. Acad. Trial Lawyers; mem. ABA (past co-chair discovery com. litigation sect., vice chmn. products, gen. liability and consumer law com. of sect. tort and ins. practice, litigation sect. and mfrs. liability subcom.), ATLA, AAAS, Trial Atty. of Am., Wis. Bar Assn., Chgo. Bar Assn., Milw. Bar Assn., 7th Cir. Bar Assn., Am. Judicature Soc., Def. Rsch. Inst., Supreme Ct. Hist. Soc., Indsl. Truck Assn. (lawyers com.), Am. Law Inst., Product Liability Adv. Coun., Am. Agrl. Law Assn., Wis. Acad. Trial Lawyers, Assn. for Advancement of Automotive Medicine (life), Nat. I-Club U. Iowa, U. Ala. Nat. Alumni Assn., Circle of Champions. Roman Catholic. Product liability, Personal injury, General civil litigation. Office: Quarles & Brady 411 E Wisconsin Ave Ste 2550 Milwaukee WI 53202-4497

**DAILY, FREDERICK WILLIAM,** lawyer; b. Dallas, Aug. 10, 1942; s. Frederick W. and Joella (Sawyer) D.; 1 child, Frederick W. IV. BA, U. Fla., 1965, JD, 1968; LLM, Golden Gate U., 1982. Bar: Fla. 1968, Calif. 1979, U.S. Supreme Ct. 1973, U.S. Dist. Ct. (so. dist.) Fla. 1969, U.S. Dist. Ct. (no. dist.) Calif. 1982, U.S. Ct. Appeals (5th cir.) 1969, U.S. Ct. Appeals (9th cir.) 1982. Assoc. Ives & Davis, West Palm Beach, Fla., 1968-69; ptnr. Burford & Daily, West Palm Beach, Fla., 1969-73; pvt. practice West Palm Beach, Fla., 1973-79, San Francisco, 1979-82; assoc. Simpson & Gigounas, San Francisco, 1982-83; of counsel Watson & Joiner, San Francisco, 1983-86; pvt. practice San Francisco, 1986—; of counsel Tierney, Walden and Watson, 1994—; adj. prof. Golden Gate U. Sch. Taxation, San Francisco, 1997—. Author: Winning the IRS Game, 1990, Stand Up to the IRS, 1992, Tax Savvy for Small Business, 1995. Taxation, general. Office: 302 Warren Dr San Francisco CA 94131-1034

**DAILY, RICHARD W.,** lawyer; b. Boulder, Colo., Nov. 10, 1945; s. L. Donald and Lois W.; m. Patricia A. Cronin, June 30, 1986; 1 child, Samuel. BA, Antioch Coll., 1968; JD, Harvard U., 1971. Bar: Colo. 1971, U.S. Dist. Ct. Colo. 1971, U.S. Ct. Appeals (10th cir.) 1973, Fed. Cir. 1983. Assoc. Hodges, Kerwin, Otten & Weeks, Denver, 1972-73; assoc. Davis, Graham & Stubbs, Denver, 1973-79, ptnr., 1979-91; spl. counsel Burns, Wall, Smith & Mueller, P.C., Denver, 1991-93; shareholder Powers Phillips, P.C., 1994-99; ptnr. Hale Hackstaff Tymkovich ErkenBrack & Shih LLP, Denver, 1999—. Counsel Colo. Dem. Party, Denver, 1987-93; bd. dirs. Goodwill Industries Denver, 1981-87; mem. Colo. Coun. on Arts and Humanities, 1983-89. Capt. USAR, 1971-77. Mem. ABA, Colo. Bar Assn., Denver Bar Assn. Federal civil litigation, State civil litigation, Contracts commercial. Office: Hale Hackstaff Tymkovich ErkenBrack & Shih LLP 1675 Broadway Ste 2000 Denver CO 80202-4676

**DAKIN, CAROL F.,** lawyer; b. Orange, N.J., 1943. AB, Mt. Holyoke Coll., 1964; JD, U. Pa., 1969. Bar: Ohio 1969. Ptnr. Squire, Sanders & Dempsey, Cleve. Edit. bd. Cleveland-Marshall law review. Office: Squire Sanders & Dempsey 4900 Key Tower 127 Public Sq Cleveland OH 44114-1304

**DAKIN, KARL JONATHAN,** lawyer; b. Sugar Creek Twp., Kans., June 2, 1954; s. John R. and Vera (Stockabrand) D.; m. Darla Anne Click, Nov. 29, 1986; children: Tara Nicole, Emma Ariel. BBA, Washburn U., 1976; JD, WAshburn U., 1979. Bar: Colo. 1980. Legal counsel Educo Corp., Arvada, Colo., 1979-81; jr. ptnr. Corporon & Keene, Englewood, Colo., 1981-83; sr. assoc. Berkowitz, Berkowitz & Brady, Denver, 1985-86; pres. Karl J. Dakin & Assocs., P.C., Englewood, 1983-84, Karl J. Dakin, P.C., Englewood, 1986-95, Dakin LawTek LLC, Englewood, 1995—; prin. Tekquity Ventures LLC, 1998—; adj. prof. U. Denver, 1983-85, 93, 95, Met. State Coll., Denver, 1989, 90, U. Colo., 1994. Author: (seminar) Trade Secrets, 1985; co-author: Computer Law, 1990, Technology Transfer, 1991; editor: IEEE Journal on Software, 1995-97. Mem. Tech. Transfer Soc. (pres. Colo. chpt. 1992-93, nat. bd. dirs. 1994-97, v.p. fin. 1995-97, pres.-elect 1997-98), Licensing Execs. Soc., Rocky Mountain Inventors and Entrepreneurs Congress. Avocation: rowing. Intellectual property, Contracts commercial.

**DALE, ERWIN RANDOLPH,** lawyer, author; b. Herrin, Ill., July 30, 1915; s. Henry and Lena Bell (Campbell) D.; m. Charline Vincent, Aug. 27, 1955; children: Allyson Ann (Mrs. Earl A. Samson III), Kristan Charline (Mrs. Victor L. Zimmerman). BA, U. Tex., El Paso, 1937; JD, U. Tex., 1943. Bar: Tex. 1943, D.C. 1953, Mich. 1956, N.Y. 1960. Atty. IRS, 1943-56, chief reorgn. and dividend br., 1954-56; legal staff Gen. Motors Corp., 1956-57; ptnr. firm Chapman, Walsh & O'Connell, N.Y.C. and Washington, 1957-59, Hawkins, Delafield & Wood, N.Y.C., 1959-84; of counsel Hutchison, Price, Boyle & Brooks, Dallas, 1985-86, Jenkens, Hutchison & Gilchrist, Dallas, 1986, Hutchison, Price, Boyle & Brooks, Dallas, 1986-87; lectr. tax matters; dir. Md. Electronics Mfg. Corp., 1948-58; dir., treas. The Renaissance Corp., 1968-72; dir., asst. treas. Shancom Reconstrn. Corp., 1968-72, Newhaven Corp., 1968-72. Author numerous articles on fed. tax matters; bd. editors: Tex. Law Rev., 1941-42, 42-43. Mem. ABA (chmn. com. consol. returns sect. taxation 1959-60), Tex. Bar Assn., Mich. Bar Assn., N.Y. State Bar Assn. (chmn. corp. tax com. tax sect. 1967-68, mem. exec. com. 1968-70), Tax Inst. Am. (bd. dirs. 1967-69, treas. 1966), Assn. of Bar of City of N.Y., Nat. Tax Assn., Nat. Assn. Bond Lawyers, Am. Coll. Tax Counsel, Ex-Students Assn. U. Tex., Ex-Students Assn. U. Tex., El Paso, Bronxville Field Club (N.Y.), Masons. Corporate taxation, Personal income taxation. Home: 10 Holly Ln Darien CT 06820-3303

**DALE, MARGARET A.,** lawyer; b. Jersey City, N.J., June 8, 1964; d. Charles L. and Elizabeth (Brovarone) Antinori; m. James G. Dale, July 27, 1991. BA with honors, Rutgers Coll., 1986; JD, U. Chgo., 1989. Bar: N.Y. 1990, U.S. Dist. Ct. (so. and ea. dists.) N.Y. 1995. Assoc. McKenna & Cuneo, Washington, 1989-91; asst. dist. atty. Kings County, Bklyn., 1991-95; assoc. Solomon, Zauderer, Ellenhorn, Frischer & Sharp, N.Y.C., 1995—. Active Vols. of Legal Svc., N.Y.C., 1992—. Mem. N.Y. State Bar Assn. (comml. and fed. litigation sect., sec. 1996-97). Contracts commercial. Office: Solomon Zauderer Ellenhorn 45 Rockefeller Plz New York NY 10111-0100

**D'ALEMBERTE, TALBOT (SANDY D'ALEMBERTE),** academic administrator, lawyer; b. Tallahassee, June 1, 1933; m. Patsy Palmer; children: Gabrielle Lynn, Joshua Talbot. BA in Polit. Sci. with honors, U. South, 1955; postgrad., London Sch. Econs. and Polit. Sci., U. London, 1958-59; JD with honors, U. Fla., 1962. Assoc. Steel Hector & Davis, Miami, Fla., 1962-65, ptnr., 1965-84, 89-93; prof. Fla. State U., 1984—, dean, 1984-89, pres., 1994—; lectr. U. Miami Coll. Law, 1969-71, adj. prof., 1974-76; reader Fla. Bd. Bar Examiners, 1965-67; mem. jud. nominating commn. Fla. Supreme Ct., 1975-78; chief counsel Ho. Select Com. for Impeachment of Certain Justices, 1975; mem. Fla. Law Revision Coun., 1968-74; chmn. Fla. Constl. Revision Commn., 197-778. Contbr. articles to profl. jours.; articles editor U. Fla. Law Rev. Mem. Fla. Ho. Reps., 1966-72, chmn. com. on ad valorem taxation, 1969-70, chmn. judiciary com., 1971-72, mem. various coms.; chmn. Fla. Commn. on Ethics, 1974-75; trustee Miami-Dade Community Coll., 1976-84. Served with USN, 1955-58; to lt. USNR. Recipient award Fla. Acad. Trial Lawyers, 1972, 93, Fla. Patriots award Fla. Bicentennial Commn., 1976, Disting. Alumnus award U. Fla., 1977, Nelson Poynter award Fla. Civil Liberties Union, 1984, Gov.'s Emmy award Nat. Acad. TV Arts and Scis., 1985, 1st Amendment award Nat. Sigma Delta Chi/Soc. Profl. Journalists, 1986, Medal of Honor award Fla. Bar Found., 1987, Juris prudence award Anti-Defamation League of S. Fla., 1990, Fla. Acad. of Criminal Def. Lawyers Annual Justice award, 1993, Acad. of Fla. Trial Lawyers Perry Nichols award, 1993, Nat. Coun. of Jewish Women's Hannah G. Soloman award, 1996, Am. Judicature Soc. Justice award, 1996; named Outstanding First Term House Mem., 1967, Most Outstanding Mem. of House, Capital Press Corps; Rotary Found. fellowship. Mem. ABA (pres. 1991-92, chmn. spl. com. on election reform 1973-76, chmn. spl. com. on resolution of minor disputes 1976-79, chmn. spl. com. on med. malpractice 1985-86, state del. from Fla. 1980-89, commn. on governance 1983-84, rules and calender com. ho. of dels. 1982-84, commn. on women in profession 1987, chair com. rule of law project for Haiti 1993, chair nom. com. sect. dispute res. 1993, individual rights and responsibilities com., co-founder Ctrl. and East European Law Initiative, World Order Under Law award 1998, Robert J. Kutak award sect. legal edn. 1998), Fla. Bar Assn. (bd. govs. 1974-82), Dade County Bar Assn. (pres. young lawyers sect. 1965-66, bd. dirs.), Am. Judicature Soc. (pres. 1982-84), U. Fla. Law Ctr. Assn. (trustee 1967—), Order of Coif, Omicron Delta Kappa, Phi Beta Kappa. Office: Office of Pres Fla State U 211 Westcott Bldg Tallahassee FL 32306-1470

**DALEN, DUWAYNE JOHN,** lawyer; b. Campinas, Brazil, Feb. 14, 1969; s. DuWayne Russell and Joan Emily Dalen; m. Kimberly Rae Dalen, Sep. 12, 1998. BA in Polit. Sci., Wartburg Coll., 1991; JD, U. Iowa, 1994. Bar: Iowa 1994, U.S. Dist. Ct. (so. dist.) Iowa 1994. Pvt. practice Brierly Law Office, Newton, Iowa, 1994—. Legal counsel Iowa Jaycees, 1996-97; bd. dirs. Newton Cmty. Theater, 1997-98. Mem. Iowa Trial Lawyers Assn., Iowa Bar Assn., Jasper County Bar Assn. (treas. 1995-96), Newton C. of C. (bd. dirs. 1998—), Phi Delta Phi. Lutheran. Avocations: golf, hunting, fishing, singing. General civil litigation, Family and matrimonial, Personal injury. Home: 418 N 2d Ave E Newton IA 50208 Office: Brierly Law Office 211 1st Ave W Newton IA 50208-3723

**D'ALESSANDRO, DANIEL ANTHONY,** lawyer, educator; b. Jersey City, Oct. 10, 1949; s. Donato Marino D'Alessandro and Rose Teresa (Casamassimo) Drennan; m. Beth Anne Lill, Sept. 2, 1978; children: Daniel Patrick, Eric Charles. BA, St. Peter's Coll., 1971; JD, Seton Hall U., 1974; LLM in Criminal Justice, NYU, 1981. Bar: N.J. 1975, U.S. Dist. Ct. N.J. 1975, N.Y. 1982, U.S. Supreme Ct. 1985, U.S. Dist. Ct. (so. dist.) N.Y. 1989. Law clk. to presiding judge Juvenile and Domestic Relations Ct., Hudson County, N.J., 1974-75; pub. defender City of Jersey City, 1975-76; prosecutor Town of Secaucus, N.J., 1976-77; prin. D'Alessandro & Assocs., Jersey City, 1977-82; ptnr. D' Alessandro & Tutak, Jersey City, 1982-90; pres. D'Alessandro, Tutak & Aschoff, P.C., Jersey City, 1990-92; ptnr. D'Alessandro & Aschoff, P.C., Jersey City, 1993-94; pvt. practice Jersey City, 1994—; adj. prof. Middlesex County Coll., Edison, N.J., 1981-83, St. Peter's Prep., 1981-83; arbitrator automobile arbitration program N.J. Supreme Ct.; mem. ethics com. N.J. Supreme Ct. Dist. VI; counsel Employees Retirement System of Jersey City, 1985-89; vice-chair fee arbitration com. Supreme Ct. N.J. Vol. probation officer Hudson County Probation Dept., 1977; pro bono counsel Anthony R. Cucci Civic Assn., Jersey City, 1981-89; pro bono counsel Battered Women's Shelter, Jersey City, 1982; pro bono counsel Mayor's Task Force for Handicapped, Jersey City, 1985-89; v.p. Jersey City Boys Club, 1991, pres., 1993—, also trustee; baseball coach Jersey Shore Thunderbirds, N.J. AAU, 1993-99. Named Prof. of Yr., Secaucus (N.J.) Patrolmen's Benevolent Assn., 1980; recipient Disting. Svc. award Jersey City Police Dept., 1988, Cert. of Merit, N.J. Supreme Ct., Meritorious Pub. Svc. award, 1990, Outstanding Bd. Mem. award N.J. Boys Clubs Coun., 1991, Outstanding Bd. Mem. award Boys and Girls Clubs of Hudson County, 1998. Mem. ABA, N.J. State Bar Assn., Hudson County Bar Assn. (past chmn., mem. various coms., trustee, treas. 1991, sec. 1992, v.p. 1994, 95, pres-elect 1996, pres. 1997—, Outstanding Bd. Mem. award 1998). Democrat. Roman Catholic. Avocations: renovating old homes, sports, photography. General practice, Real property, State civil litigation. Office: 3279 John F Kennedy Blvd Jersey City NJ 07306-3418

**D'ALESSANDRO, DIANNE MARIE,** public defender; b. N.Y.C., Apr. 20, 1952; d. Frank and Marie A. D'A.; m. John P. Foley, July 24, 1977; children: Maria, James. BA in Psychology, Upsala Coll., East Orange, N.J., 1974; JD, N.Y. Law Sch., 1981. Bar: N.J. 1981, N.Y. 1990, U.S. Dist. Ct. N.J. 1981. Staff atty. Bergen City Legal Svc., Hackensack, N.J., 1981-83; sr. trial atty. Office Pub. Defender, Hackensack, 1983—; dist. II B ethics com., Office of Atty. Ethics of the Supreme Ct. of N.J., 1992-95; bd. dirs. Bergen County Legal Svc. Recipient citation from Susan Reisner, pub. advocate, for work done on State vs. Harris. Mem. Assn. Criminal Def. Lawyers, Women Lawyers in Bergen County. Avocations: reading, hiking, historic preservation. Office: Office of Pub Advocate/Pub Defender 60 State St Hackensack NJ 07601-5451

**DALESSANDRO, SHERRY ANN,** lawyer; b. Wilkes-Barre, Pa., Dec. 19, 1963; d. Fredrick C. and Donna R. (Evans) S.; married; children: Gabriel Justin, Nina Marie. BA, Univ. Miami, 1986; JD, Thomas M. Cooley, 1990. Bar: Pa. 1990. Law clerk Pa. Superior Ct., Wilkes-Barre, 1990-91; assoc. Laputka & Pedri, Hazleton, Pa., 1991-94; solo practioner Dalessandro Law Office, Wilkes-Barre, 1994—. Mem. ABA, Pa. Bar Assn., Pa. Trial Lawyers, Luzerne County Bar Assn. Family and matrimonial, Workers' compensation, General practice. Office: 635 Carey Ave Wilkes Barre PA 18702-1447

**DALEY, MICHAEL JOSEPH,** lawyer; b. Phila., Aug. 9, 1955; s. Robert Charles and Agnes Theresa (Brophy) D. BA with honors, U. Denver, 1977; JD, Loyola U., Chgo., 1980. Bar: Ill. 1980, U.S. Dist. Ct. (no. dist.) Ill. 1980, Trial Bar (no. dist.) Ill. 1983, U.S. Ct. Appeals (7th cir.) 1985, U.S. Supreme Ct. 1985, U.S. Dist. Ct. (no. dist.) Ind. 1994, U.S. Tax Ct. 1994. Asst. state's atty. Cook County State Atty.'s Office, Chgo., 1981-83; assoc. Nisen & Elliott, Chgo., 1983-86, ptnr., 1986—; instr. trial advocacy Loyola U. of Chgo., 1986—. Recipient Lewis Powell Medal for Advocacy, Am. Coll. Trial Lawyers, 1980, Robert Bellarmine award Loyola U. Chgo., 1995. Mem. Bar Assn. of 7th Fed. Cir., Assn. of Transp. Practitioners, Nat. Assn. R.R. Trial Counsel, Union League Club of Chgo. (pub. affairs com. 1993—). Avocations: skiing, cycling, golf. Federal civil litigation, Transportation, General civil litigation. Office: Nisen & Elliott 200 W Adams St Ste 2500 Chicago IL 60606-5283

**DALEY, SUSAN JEAN,** lawyer; b. New Britain, Conn., May 27, 1959; d. George Joseph and Norma (Woods) D. BA, U. Conn., 1978; JD, Harvard U., 1981. Bar: Ill. 1981. Assoc. Altheimer & Gray, Chgo., 1981-86, ptnr., 1986—. Mem. ABA (real property, probate and trust law sect. 1983—, chmn. welfare plans com. real property, probate and trust law sect. 1989-95, employee benefits com. taxation sect. 1984—, chmn. EEOC issues subcom. employee benefits com. taxation sect. 1990—), Nat. Assn. Stock Plan Profls. (pres. Chgo. chpt. 1995—), Ill. Bar Assn. (chmn. employee benefits divsn. fed. taxation sect. 1984-86, chmn. employee benefits sect., 1995-96, mem. employee benefits sect. 1990-97), Chgo. Bar Assn. (chmn. employee benefits divsn. fed. taxation com. 1985-86, chmn. employee benefits com. 1990-91, chmn. fed. taxatin com. 1992-93), Chgo. Coun. on Fgn. Rels. Avocation: marathons. Pension, profit-sharing, and employee benefits. Home: 1636 N Wells St Apt 415 Chicago IL 60614-6009 Office: Altheimer & Gray 10 S Wacker Dr Ste 4000 Chicago IL 60606-7407

**DALEY, TERRENCE JOSEPH,** lawyer; b. Buffalo, Aug. 27, 1954; s. Edmund Patrick and Sara Frances Daley; m. Charlotte Mary Conley, Oct. 6, 1979; children: Philip, Laura, Timothy. BA, Canisius Coll., 1976; JD, Boston Coll., 1979. Bar: Mass. 1979, N.H. 1986. Ptnr. Reardon & Reardon, Worcester, Mass., 1979-85; ptnr. Moquin & Daley, P.A., Manchester, N.H., 1985—, Boston, 1985—. Democrat. Roman Catholic. Personal injury, Workers' compensation. Office: Moquin & Daley PA 212 Coolidge Ave Manchester NH 03102-3210

**D'ALFONSO, MARIO JOSEPH,** lawyer, consultant; b. Phila., Nov. 3, 1951; s. Albert Carmine and Yolanda (Zanfrisco) D'A.; m. Rita F. Borrelli, Apr. 26, 1975; 1 child, Mario C. BA, Villanova U., 1973; JD, Widener U., 1979. Bar: Pa. 1979, N.J. 1979, U.S. Dist. Ct. (ea. dist.) Pa. 1979, U.S. Dist. Ct. N.J. 1979, U.S. Ct. Appeals (3rd dist.) 1980, U.S. Supreme Ct. 1983, U.S. Ct. Appeals (5th cir.) 1989. Assoc. Avena, Hendren & Friedman, Camden, N.J., 1979-81; ptnr. Avena, Hendren, Friedman & D'Alfonso, 1981-84, D'Alfonso & Camacho, P.A., Haddon Heights, N.J., 1984—; cons. Marbert Construction, Haddon Heights, N.J., 1982—. Mem. Am. Arbitration Assn. (Service award 1984), Assn. Criminal Def. Lawyers, Camden County Bar Assn., N.J. Trial Lawyers Assn., Phi Delta Phi (pres. 1978), Phi Kappa Phi. Roman Catholic. Criminal, Personal injury, General practice. Home: 64 Lady Diana Cir Marlton NJ 08053-3705 Office: 304 White Horse Pike Haddon Heights NJ 08035-1705

**DALLAS, WILLIAM MOFFIT, JR.,** lawyer; b. Cedar Rapids, Iowa, May 7, 1949; s. William Moffit and Winifred Mae (Lillie) D.; m. Lynne Louise Russo, July 30, 1977 (div. July 1984); m. Janet Neustaetter, Apr. 19, 1985; children: Sarah Anne, Steven Kurt. AB, Oberlin Coll., 1971; JD, Harvard U., 1974. Bar: N.Y. 1975, U.S. Dist. Ct. (so. and ea. dists.) N.Y. 1975, U.S. Ct. Appeals (2d cir.) 1976, U.S. Ct. Appeals (3d cir.) 1983, U.S. Ct. Appeals (8th cir.) 1984. Assoc. Sullivan & Cromwell, N.Y.C., 1974-82, ptnr., 1982—; fed. mediator U.S. Dist. Ct., 1995—. Contbr. articles on antitrust issues to law revs., 1978—, chpt. to book. Served to lt. USN, 1971-77. Mem. ABA, Assn. of Bar of City of N.Y. (chmn. com. on judicial admin., 1999—, sec. judiciary com. 1977-80, chmn. com. jud. adminstrn. 1999—), N.Y. County

Lawyers' Assn. (chmn. com. on trade regulation 1978-81), India House Club (N.Y.C.). Federal civil litigation, State civil litigation, Antitrust. Office: Sullivan & Cromwell 125 Broad St Fl 28 New York NY 10004-2489

**DALLER, MORTON F.,** lawyer, writer; b. Phila., Nov. 2, 1938; s. George Morton and Claire (Stritzinger) D.; m. Heide Tilda Schroeder, Dec. 23, 1966 (dec. Oct. 1982); children: Adam, Sarah; m. Margaret Ann O'Donnell, Aug. 11, 1983; children: Zachary, Nicholas. BA magna cum laude, Brown U., 1960; LLB, U. Pa., 1963. Bar: Pa., U.S. Dist. Ct. (ea., mid., and we. dists.) Pa., U.S. Ct. Appeals (3d cir.). Assoc. Rawle & Henderson, Phila., ptnr., 1964-94; ptnr. Daller Greenberg & Dietrich, Ft. Washington, Pa., 1994—; regional consel Firestone & Brush Wellman. Editor-in-chief: Product Liability Desk Reference, 1990. Mem. Phila. Assn. Def. Counse. (pres. 1990, dir. 1990-93), Phi Beta Kappa. Republican. Methodist. Avocation: sportsman. Product liability, Federal civil litigation, State civil litigation. Home: 514 Edann Rd Glenside PA 19038-1405 Office: Daller Greenberg & Dietrich Valley Green Corp Ctr 7111 Valley Green Rd Fort Washington PA 19034-2209

**DALLOSTO, RAYMOND MICHAEL,** lawyer; b. Rockford, Ill., Mar. 7, 1952; s. Raymond Anthony and Henrietta Laura (Ambrose) D.; m. Joli Denise Kolpack, June 7, 1975; children: Alisha, David, Justin. BA in History cum laude, Marquette U., 1974, JD, 1977. Bar: Wis. 1977, Ill. 1979, U.S. Dist. Ct. (ea. and we. dists.) Wis. 1977, U.S. Ct. Appeals (7th cir.) 1979, U.S. Supreme Ct. 1980. Staff atty. Milw. Legal Aid Soc., 1978; asst. pub. defender Racine County, Wis., 1977-78; legal dir. Wis. ACLU, Milw., 1978-80; felony atty. Wis. State Pub. Defender, Milw., 1980-90, tng. dir., 1984-89, 1st asst. state pub. defender in charge Milw. criminal office, 1989-90; trial atty. Gimbel, Reilly, Guerin & Brown, Milw., 1990—; adj. prof. law sch. Marquette U., Milw., 1986-90; chmn. individual rights sect. Wis. State Bar, 1983-84, criminal law sect. Wis. State Bar, 1999-00, mem. ethics com., 1990-96; frequent CLE lectr. Author: Practice Guide to Civil Rights Litigation, 1980, Attorney Fee Awards, 1981; contbr. articles to legal jours. Named Best of Bar Milw. Mag., 1985, 90. Mem. Wis. Bar Assn., Ill. Bar Assn., Milw. Bar Assn., Nat. Assn. Criminal Def. Lawyers. Avocations: travel, sailing, biking, classical music, ethnic cooking. Office: Gimbel Reilly Guerin & Brown 111 E Kilbourn Ave Milwaukee WI 53202-6611

**D'ALOISE, LAWRENCE T., JR.,** lawyer; b. Portchester, N.Y., Dec. 3, 1944; s. Lawrence Thomas and Lillian Teresa D'Aloise; children: Scott, Sean, Kimberly. BS, Holy Cross Coll., 1966; JD, Villanova U., 1969. Bar: N.Y. 1970, U.S. Dist. Ct. (all dists.) N.Y., U.S. Ct. Appeals, U.S. Supreme Ct. Ptnr. Clark, Gagliardi & Miller PC, White Plains, N.Y., 1970—. Contbr. to book. Mem. ABA, N.Y. Bar Assn., Westchester County Bar Assn. Avocation: renovating and collecting cars. Appellate, Personal injury, Product liability. Home: 130 Old Mamaroneck Rd White Plains NY 10605-2413 Office: Clark Gagliardi & Miller 99 Court St Ste 1 White Plains NY 10601-4265

**DAL SANTO, DIANE,** judge, writer; b. East Chicago, Ind., Sept. 20, 1949; d. John Quentin Dal Santo and Helen (Koval) D.; m. Fred O'Cheskey, June 29, 1985. BA, U. N.Mex., 1971; cert., Inst. Internat. and Comparative Law, Guadalajara, Mex., 1978; JD, U. San Diego, 1980. Bar: N.Mex. 1980, U.S. Dist. Ct. N.Mex. 1980. Ct. planner Met. Criminal Justice Coordinating Coun., Albuquerque, 1973-75; planning coord. Dist. Atty.'s Office, Albuquerque, 1975-76, exec. asst. to dist. atty., 1976-77, asst. dir. atty. for violent crimes, 1980-82; chief dep. city atty. City of Albuquerque, 1983; assoc. firm T.B. Keleher & Assocs., 1983-84; judge Met. Ct., 1985-89, chief judge, 1988-89; judge Dist. Ct., 1989—; mem. faculty Nat. Jud. Coll., 1990-95, 97—, bd. trustees, 1995-96. Columnist Albuquerque Jour., 1996-98. Bd. dirs. Nat. Coun. Alcoholism, 1984, S.W. Ballet Co., Albuquerque, 1982-83; mem. Mayor's Task Force on Alcoholism and Crime, 1987-88, N.Mex. Coun. Crime and Delinquency, 1987-97, bd. dirs., 1992-94, Task Force Domestic Violence, 1987-94; pres. bench, bar, media com., 1987, pres. 1992, rules of evidence com. Supreme Ct., 1993-96, chair com. access to pub. records Supreme Ct., 1988; steering com. N.Mex. Buddy Awards, 1995—; mem. Metro. Criminal Justice Coordinating Coun., 1998—. U. San Diego scholar, 1978-79; recipient Women on the Move award YWCA, 1989, Disting. Woman award U. N.Mex. Alumni Assn., 1994, Outstanding Alumnus Dept. Sociology U. N.Mex., 1995; named Woman of Yr. award Duke City Bus. and Profl. Women, 1985. Mem. ABA (Nat. Conf. State Trial Judges Jud. Excellence award 1996), LWV, AAUW, Am. Judicature Soc., N.Mex. Women's Found., N.Mex. State Bar Assn. (silver gavel award 1997), N.Mex. Women's Bar Assn. (bd. dirs. 1991-92), Albuquerque Bar Assn., Nat. Assn. Women Judges, Greater Albuquerque C. of C. (steering com. 1989), N.Mex. Magistrate Judges Assn. (v.p. 1985-89), Dist. Judges Assn. (pres. 1994-95), Pennies for Homeless. Office: Dist Ct 415 Tijeras Ave NW Albuquerque NM 87102-3252

**DALTON, ANNE,** lawyer; b. Pitts., Dec. 6, 1951; d. Thomas John and Mary Olive (Paul) D.; m. Oliver E. Martin, Dec. 26, 1987. BA in Polit. Sci., NYU, 1973; JD, Fordham U., 1977. Bar: N.Y. 1978, U.S. Dist. Ct. (so. and ea. dists.) N.Y. 1979, Pa. 1987, Fla. 1990. Assoc. Mendes & Mount, N.Y.C., 1979-80; atty. news div. ABC, N.Y.C., 1980-85; TV news producer ABC Network, N.Y.C., 1985-86; sr. atty. Radio City Music Hall Prodns., Inc., N.Y.C., 1986-87; pvt. practice Stroudsburg, Pa., 1987-91; asst. county att., asst. port authority atty. Lee County, Ft. Myers, Fla., 1991-94; pvt. practice Ft. Myers, 1994—; family law mediator Fla., 1994—, cir. civil mediator, 1995—; spl. hearing master 20th Jud. Cir., Fla., 1991—, ct. Commr., gen. master family civil and probate divsn., 1995—; adj. prof. Edison C.C., Ft. Myers, Barry U., Ft. Myers; family, cir. civil mediator, 1995. Recipient Clio award Internat. Clio Award Com., 1978. Mem. Pa. Bar Assn., Fla. Bar Assn., N.Y. Bar Assn., Lee County Bar Assn. Roman Catholic. Avocations: reading, gardening, swimming. Family and matrimonial, General practice, Real property. Office: 2044 Bayside Pkwy Fort Myers FL 33901-3102

**DALTON, JOHN JOSEPH,** lawyer; b. N.Y.C., Feb. 7, 1943; s. John Henry and Anna Veronica (Chiusano) D.; m. Martha E. Dalton, Feb. 24, 1968; children: Martha G., J. Michael, W. Brian. BBA, Fairfield U., 1964; JD, Northwestern U., 1967. Bar: Ill. 1967, Ga. 1970, U.S. Dist. Ct. (no. and mid. dists.) Ga., U.S. Dist. Ct. (no. dist.) Ill., U.S. Ct. Appeals (2d, 4th, 5th, 7th, 10th and 11th cirs.), U.S. Tax Ct., U.S. Supreme Ct. Atty. Clausen, Miller, Gorman, Caffrey & Witous, Chgo., 1967-69; ptnr. Troutman Sanders (formerly Troutman, Sanders, Lockerman & Ashmore), Atlanta, 1970—. Chmn. bd. Atlanta Vol. Lawyers Found., 1993. With U.S. Army, 1968-69. Fellow Am. Coll. Trial Lawyers, Am. Bar Found.; mem. Atlanta Bar Assn. (dir.), Piedmont Driving Club, Peachtree Golf Club. Office: Troutman Sanders 600 Peachtree St NE Ste 5200 Atlanta GA 30308-2231

**DALY, JOHN PAUL,** lawyer; b. Pitts., Aug. 6, 1939; s. John Ambrose and Cora Evelyn (Faye) D.; m. Kathleen Ellen Paul, Dec. 21, 1961. AB, U. Calif., Riverside, 1961; JD, Loyola U., Los Angeles, 1971. Bar: Calif. 1972. Dep. dist. atty. San Luis Obispo, Calif., 1971-78, dep. county counsel, 1978—; judge pro tem Calif. Superior Ct., 1985—; law prof. U. Calif. Polytech., 1979-81, lectr. Calif. Jud. Coll., 1982, post doctoral forensic psychiatry curriculum U. Calif., Atascadero State Hosp., 1987—, chmn., 1996-98; lectr. probate/med. health specialists County Counsel's Assn. Calif., 1980—; lectr. for profl. credentials cert. Calif. Assn. Pub. Adminstrs., Pub. Guardians, Pub. Conservators, 1991. Speaker Mental Health Dept. Social Svcs., San Luis Obispo, 1975—. Mem. AMA, San Luis Obispo Govt. Attys. Union (founder, pres. 1977-82, chief negotiator 1977-79), GWTA. Home: 10650 Colorado Rd Atascadero CA 93422-5706 Office: County Counsel Govt Ctr San Luis Obispo CA 93408

**DALY, JOSEPH LEO,** law educator; b. Phila., July 31, 1942; s. Leo Vincent and Genevieve Delores (McGinnis) D.; m. Kathleen Ann Dolan, July 24, 1965; children: Michael, Colleen. BA, U. Minn., 1964; JD, William Mitchell Coll. Law, 1969. Bar: Minn. 1969, U.S. Dist. Ct. Minn. 1970, U.S. Supreme Ct. 1972, U.S. Ct. Appeals (8th cir.) 1973, U.S. Ct. Appeals (D.C. cir.) 1974; cert. mediator and arbitrator alternative dispute rev. bd. Minn. Supreme Ct. Ptnr. Franke & Daly, Mpls., 1969-74; prof. law Hamline U. Sch. Law, St. Paul, 1974—; arbitrator Pub. Employment Rels. Bd., St. Paul, 1974—, Am. Arbitration Assn., N.Y.C., 1980—, U.S. Fed. Mediation and Conciliation Svc., Washington, 1988—, for the states of Minn., Hawaii, Idaho, Ind., Mass., Mich., N.D., Pa., Oreg., Wisc., V.I and City of L.A.; arbitrator Bur. Mediation Svcs., St. Paul, 1978—; vis. scholar Ctr. for Dispute Resolution, Willamette U., Salem, Oreg., 1985; facilitator Minn. Internat. Health Vols., Kenya, 1985; observer Philippine Constl. Conv., Manila, 1986; participant European Arab Arbitration Congress, Bahrain, 1987; human rights investigator in the Philippines, 1989; vis. scholar U. Oslo, 1990, 91, 92, 96, 97; lectr. on trial skills for human rights lawyers, The Philippines, 1989; lectr. to leaders at Site 2 Cambodian Refugee Camp, Thai/Cambodian border, 1989; lectr. U. Cluj-NAPACA, Romania, 1991; vis. lectr. for developing countries Internat. Bar Assn., 1991-92; lectr. U. Tirana, Albania, 1992, London, 1993, Nat. Econs. U., Hanoi, Vietnam, 1993, 94, Danang (Vietnam) Poly. U., 1993, Ho Chi Minh Econs. U., Saigon, Vietnam, 1993, U. Hanoi Law Sch., 1994, U. Modena, Italy, 1994, Hanoi, Danang and Saigon, 1995, Phnom Penh, Cambodia, 1995, Hong Kong, 1996, Shenzhen, China, 1996, Oslo, Norway, 1996, Karolinska Inst., Stockholm, 1997; vis. prof. So. Cross U., Lismore, Australia, 1998, 99, U. Bergen, Norway, 1999, Tongji U., Shanghai, China, 1999, U. Saigon, Vietnam, 1999. Co-author: The Law, the Student and the Catholic School, 1981; co-author, editor: The Student Lawyer: A High School Handbook of Minnesota Law, 1981, rev. edit., 1986, Strategies and Exercises in Law Related Education, 1981, International Law, 1993, The American Trial System, 1994; contbr. more than 50 articles to profl. jours. Mem. Minn. Legislature Task Force on Sexual Exploitation by Counselors and Therapists, St. Paul, 1984-85, Nat. Adv. Com. on Citizen Edn. in Law, 1982-85; bd. dirs. Scenic Am., Washington, 1989-92. Recipient Spurgeon award Mayor and Citizens of St. Paul and Indianhead Scouting, 1983; named a Leading Minn. Atty. in Alternative Dispute Resolution: Employment Law; fellow U. Miss. Law Sch. Mem. ABA (contbg. editor Preview of U.S. Supreme Ct. Cases mag. 1984—), Internat. Bar Assn. (London, vis. lectr. for devel. countries 1991—), Minn. State Bar Assn., Minn. Lawyers Internat. (human rights com., rep. to Philippine Constl. Conv. 1986), St. Paul Athletic Club, Phi Alpha Delta. Avocations: jogging, sailing. E-mail: jdaly@gw.hamline.edu. Office: Hamline U Sch Law 1536 Hewitt Ave Saint Paul MN 55104-1205

**DALY, JOSEPH PATRICK,** lawyer; b. Washington, Jan. 22, 1957; s. John Thomas Daly and Virginia Carol Sharp. BA, SUNY, Stony Brook, 1979; JD, George Washington U., 1982. Bar: D.C. 1982. Atty. Compt. of the Currency, Washington, 1982-85; ptnr. Muldoon, Murphy & Faucette LLP, Washington, 1985-96, mng. ptnr., 1996—. Co-author: Banking Law in the United States, 1988, 2d edit., 1992; contbg. author: Banks and Thrifts: Government Enforcement and Receivership, 1991; contbr. articles to profl. jours. Mem. ABA. Banking, General corporate, Administrative and regulatory. Office: Muldoon Murphy & Faucette 5101 Wisconsin Ave NW Ste 500 Washington DC 20016-4120

**DALY, SUSAN MARY,** lawyer; b. White Plains, N.Y., Dec. 12, 1963; d. J. Spencer and Mary E. (Kramer) D. Student, U. Madrid, 1983-85; BA, St. Lawrence U., 1985; JD, Bklyn. Law Sch., 1990. Bar: Conn. 1990, N.Y. 1991, Fla. 1991. Legal asst. Skadden, Arps, Slate, Meagher & Flom, N.Y.C., 1986-89; counsel Gilbride, Tusa, Last & Spellane, N.Y.C. and Greenwich, Conn., 1990-95, Gunster, Yoakley, Valdes-Fauli & Stewart, Ft. Lauderdale, Fla., 1995-99; trademark counsel Sundbeam Corp., 1999—. Chmn. Comm. Rev. and Project Devel., Jr. League Indian River, Vero Beach, 1997, Jr. League, Ft. Lauderdale, 1998; chmn. profl. com. United Way Indian River, 1997. Mem. ABA, Free Trade Am. (chairperson), Internat. Trademark Assn. (treaty analysis com. 1998—), Phi Beta Alpha, Kappa Kappa Gamma. Estate planning, Intellectual property, Real property. Home: 2004 Riverside Pl Apt 1 Wilton Manors FL 33305-2256

**DALY, WILLIAM JOSEPH,** lawyer; b. Bklyn., Mar. 19, 1928; s. William Bernard and Charlotte Marie (Saunders) D.; m. Barbara A. Longenecker, Nov. 19, 1955; children: Sharon, Nancy, Carol. B.A., St. John's U., 1951, J.D., 1953. Bar: N.Y. 1954, U.S. Dist. Ct. (so. and ea. dists.) N.Y. 1958, U.S. Ct. Mil. Appeals 1969, U.S. Ct. Claims 1969, U.S. Tax Ct. 1969, U.S. Supreme Ct. 1973. Assoc. Garvey & Conway, Esquires, N.Y.C., 1954-55, Wing & Wing, Esquires, N.Y.C., 1955-58; ptnr. Daly Lavery & Hall, Esquires and predecessors, Ossining, N.Y., 1958—; adj. prof. law Mercy Coll., Dobbs Ferry, N.Y. V.p. Legal Aid Soc., Westchester County, N.Y., 1983—; mem. 9th Jud. Dist. Grievance Com., 1981-89, chmn. 1988-89; spl. referee in disciplinary proceedings; trustee Supreme Ct. Libr. at White Plains, 1985—. With U.S. Army, 1946-48; ret. col. JA-AUS, 1978. Fellow Am. Bar Found., N.Y. Bar Found.; mem. ABA, N.Y. State Bar Assn. (ho. of dels. 1977-89, 90-96, exec. com. 1983-89, 90-96, v.p. 1985-89, 90-96), Westchester County Bar Assn. (pres. 1979-81, dirs. coun. 1981—), Westchester County Bar Inst. (bd. dirs. 1982-98), Ossinging Bar Assn. (pres. 1966-67), Assn. Trial Lawyers Am., N.Y. State Trial Lawyers Assn., Res. Officers Assn. U.S., Assn. U.S. Army, Skull and Circle, Phi Delta Phi. Roman Catholic. Probate, Family and matrimonial, Personal injury. Home: 232 Hunter Ave Sleepy Hollow NY 10591-1317 Office: 73 Croton Ave Ste 209 Ossining NY 10562-4971

**DALZELL, STEWART,** federal judge; b. Hackensack, N.J., Sept. 18, 1943; s. Stewart V. and Jeannette (Johnson) D.; m. Kathleen Regan, Mar. 28, 1981; children: Rebecca, Andrew. BS in Economics, U. Pa., 1965, JD, 1969. Bar: Pa. 1970, U.S. Dist. Ct. (ea. dist.) Pa. 1970, U.S. Ct. Appeals (11th cir.) 1979, U.S. Ct. Appeals (9th cir.) 1977, U.S. Ct. Appeals (Fed. cir.) 1983, U.S. Ct. Appeals (5th cir.) 1984, U.S. Ct. Appeals (2d cir.) 1986, U.S. Ct. Appeals (3d cir.) 1991, U.S. Supreme Ct. 1975. Fin. analyst NBC, N.Y.C., 1965-66; assoc. Drinker, Biddle & Reath, Phila., 1970-76, ptnr., 1976-91; judge U.S. Dist. Ct. (ea. dist.) Pa., 1991—; vis. lectr. law Wharton Sch. U. Pa., 1969-70. Contbr. articles to law revs. and profl. jours. Recipient Speiser award. Mem. Beta Gamma Sigma. Episcopalian. Avocations: movies, music. Office: US Dist Cts US Courthouse Rm 5614 601 Market St Philadelphia PA 19106-1713

**DAMASHEK, PHILIP MICHAEL,** lawyer; b. N.Y.C., May 18, 1940; s. Jacob and Esther (Sassower) D.; m. Judith Ellen Gold, Dec. 3, 1967; children: Alan S., Jonathan S., Harris R. BBA, U. Miami, 1964. Bar: N.Y. 1969, U.S. Dist. Ct. (so. and ea. dists.) N.Y. 1977. Lawyer Cosmopolitan Mut. Ins. Co., N.Y.C., 1969-70, Schneider, Kleinick, Weitz & Damashek, 1971-73; sr. ptnr. Philip M. Damashek, P.C., N.Y.C., 1974-89; ptnr. Damashek, Godosky & Gentile, 1989-94; mng. ptnr. Schneider, Kleinick, Weitz, Damashek & Shoot, 1994—; chmn. Combined Bar Assns. Jud. Screening Panel, N.Y.C., 1983-88; co-chair, trustee, co-chmn. LawPac, 1989-91; legis. appointment mem. Com. to Rev. Audio-Visual Coverage of Ct. Procs., 1993-94; exec. apptd. to govs. N.Y. Jud. Screening Com., 1997—, adv. bd. N.Y. Israel Econ. Devel. Partnership; apptd. Com. on Case Mgmt.—Office of Ct. Adminstrn., Cts. of State of N.Y., 1993, Task Force on Reducing Litigation Cost and Delay, 1st Judicial Dist., 1996—, Differentiated Case Mgmt. Project, Kings County, 1996—, Alt. Dispute Resolution Adv. Com. N.Y. State Unified Ct. Sys., 1999—, N.Y. State Jud. Salary Commn., 1997—, N.Y. State CLE Bd., 1997—; alt. dispute resolution adv. com. N.Y. State Unified Ct. Sys., 1999—; trustee N.Y. Law Sch., 1996—; mem. NYSTLA Designated Ind. Jud. Screening Panel, N.Y. County Dem. Commn., 1991—, malpractice panel Supreme Ct. of the State of N.Y., County of N.Y., 1990-91; dir. and v.p. for govt. rels. Respect for Law Alliance, Inc., 1995—. Named Lawyer of Yr., Inst. Jewish Humanities, 1990, Lawyer of the Yr., UJA Fedn., 1993. Fellow Am. Bd. Trial Advocates (life), Am. Judicature Soc., Am. Bar Found., Roscoe Pound Found., Assn. Trial Lawyers Am. (Wiedemann Wysocki citation of excellence 1990, bd. govs. 1990-92, state rels. com. 1990-92, no-fault coordinating com. 1990-92); mem. ABA, N.Y. State Bar Assn. (ct. adminstrn. com., com. jud. adminstrn. 1990-94), Assn. of Bar of City of N.Y., N.Y. State Trial Lawyers Assn. (pres. 1990-91, bd. dirs., trustee), Assn. Trial Lawyers City N.Y. (bd. dirs.), N.Y. County Lawyers Assn., Trial Lawyers for Pub. Justice (sustaining), Jewish Lawyers Guild (bd. govs.). Personal injury, State civil litigation. Office: Schneider Kleinick Weitz Damashek & Shoot 233 Broadway Fl 5 New York NY 10279-0050

**D'AMICO, ANDREW J.,** lawyer; b. Phila., Feb. 18, 1953; s. Joseph J. and Alice H. (Falotica) D'A.; m. Georgiana R. Etheridge, Feb. 25, 1978; children: Andrew J. Jr., Joseph W., Jennifer T., Theresa J. BA, St. Joseph's U., Phila., 1975; JD, Villanova U., 1978. Bar: Pa. Supreme Ct. 1978, U.S. Dist. Ct. (ea. dist.) Pa. 1979, U.S. Ct. Appeals (3d Cir.) 1981, U.S Supreme Ct. 1982. Sole practitioner Law Offices Andrew J. D'Amico, Media, Pa., 1979—. Coach Llanerch Hills Little League, Drexel Hill, Pa., 1986-96, St. Bernadette CYO Basketball, 1996—. Mem. ATLA, Pa. Trial Lawyers Assn., Del. County Bar Assn. (bd. dirs. 1991-92, 97, 98), Guy G. deFuria Am. Inn of Ct. (pres. 1995-96), Alpha Sigma Nu. Roman Catholic. Avocations: music, coaching sports, reading. General civil litigation, Personal injury, Real property. Office: PO Box 605 115 N Monroe St Media PA 19063-3037

**DAMICO, NICHOLAS PETER,** lawyer; b. Chester, Pa., June 29, 1937; s. Ralph A. and Mary C. (Ametrane) D.; m. Patricia Ann Swatek, Aug. 26, 1967; children: Christine, Gregory. BS in Acctg., St. Joseph's U. 1960, LLB, U. Pa., 1963; LLM, Georgetown U., 1967. Bar: Pa. 1963, D.C. 1967, Md. 1986. Tax law specialist IRS, Washington, 1963-66; assoc. Silverstein and Mullens, Washington, 1966-72, ptnr. 1972-76; prin. Damico & Assocs., Washington, 1976—; adj. prof. Georgetown U. Law Ctr., Washington, 1973-75. Mem. ABA. Pension, profit-sharing, and employee benefits, Estate planning, Probate. Office: 1101 17th St NW Ste 820 Washington DC 20036-4704

**DAMICO, PAUL ANTHONY,** lawyer, educator; b. Rockville Centre, N.Y., July 3, 1960; s. Anthony and Connie Ida Damico; m. Jennifer Lynn Damico, Sept. 26, 1992; children: Alec Anthony, Kyle James. BS, Fla. State U., 1983, JD, 1986. Bar: Fla. 1983, U.S. Ct. Appeals (11th cir.), U.S. Ct. Appeals (D.C. cir.), U.S. Dist. Ct. (so., mid. and no. dists.) Fla., U.S. Supreme Ct.; bd. cert. in criminal trial. Misdemeanor atty. Palm Beach County State Atty.'s Office, West Palm Beach, Fla., 1986-87, felony unit atty., 1987-89, felony unit chief, 1989-92, vice unit chief, 1992-97; felony dir. Palm Beach County Pub. Defender's Office, West Palm Beach, 1997—, chief asst., 1999—; bd. dirs. Weed/Seed Orgn., West Palm Beach, 1992—, Cmty. Ct. Task Force, West Palm Beach, 1996—, Anti-Drug Grant Com., 1996—. Mem. Republican Exec. Com., West Palm Beach, 1998—, asst. vice chair campaign endorsement committeeman dist. 6; bd. dirs. Lake Worth Criminal Justice Acad., 1998—. Mem. Kiwanis Ctrl. Palm Beach County (pres.-elect 1998), Masons. Christian. Avocations: scuba diving, golf. Office: PBC Pub Defenders Office 421 3d St West Palm Beach FL 33401

**DAMON, CLAUDIA CORDS,** lawyer; b. Heidelberg, Germany, Aug. 11, 1946; came to U.S., 1952, naturalized, 1957; d. Helmuth and Jutta Cords; married; children: Caroline, Samuel. BA, Wellesley Coll., 1967; MA, Boston U., 1968, JD, 1974. Bar: N.H. 1974, U.S. Dist. Ct. N.H. 1974. Tchr. history MacDuffie Sch. for Girls, Springfield, Mass., 1968-69; research asst. Princeton (N.J.) U., 1969-71; assoc. Sheehan, Phinney, Bass & Green P.A., Manchester, N.H., 1974-78, mem., 1979—; mem. N.H. Bd. Bar Examiners, 1980-89. Chmn. Boscawen (N.H.) Zoning Bd. Adjustment, 1976-89; bd. dirs. Manchester Girls Club, 1975-80, Manchester YMCA, 1986-95; bd. dirs. Merrimack Valley Day Care Svcs., Concord, 1983-90, pres., 1987-89; mem. steering com. N.H. Bus. Com. for the Arts, 1986—; chair Pats Peak Ednl. Found., 1994-95; bd. dirs. N.H. Legal Assistance, 1992-98, sec., 1994-98; active Concord Bd. Edn., 1997—. Mem. ABA, ATLA, N.H. Bar Assn., N.H. Trial Lawyers Assn., Am. Bd. of Trial Advocates. Democrat. Avocations: skiing, bicycling. Federal civil litigation, State civil litigation, Personal injury. Office: Sheehan Phinney Bass & Green Profl Assn PO Box 3701 Manchester NH 03105-3701

**DAMON, RICHARD EVERETT,** lawyer, educator; b. Washington, May 18, 1944; s. Sidney R. and Betty Jean Damon; m. Sheri L. Rypka, Oct. 10, 1987; children: Andrea, Jessica, Madeleine. BA with high honors, Swarthmore Coll., 1965; PhD, Columbia U., 1971; JD, Stanford U./Coll. William/Mary, 1977. Bar: Calif. 1977, U.S. Dist. Ct. Calif. 1977, U.S. Ct. Appeals (9th cir.) 1980. Asst. prof. Calif. State U., Long Beach, 1969-71, Coll. of William and Mary, Williamsburg, Va., 1971-76; Fulbright lectr. U. Clermont, Clermont-Ferrand, France, 1973-74; assoc. Lillick, McHose & Charles, San Francisco, 1977-78; law clk. to chief justice High Ct. of Am. Samoa, 1978-80; pvt. practice Santa Cruz, Calif., 1980—. Author: (book) Standing Rules of U.S. House of Representatives, 1971. Chmn. Airport Commn., Santa Cruz, 1980-82; vol. prof. San Jose State U., 1993-94. Univ. fellow Columbia U., 1965-69. Mem. Aircraft Owners and Pilots Assn. (mem. legal referral panel 1990—), Exptl. Aircraft Assn., Lawyer-Pilots Bar Assn., Santa Cruz Trial Lawyers Assn., Santa Cruz County Bar Assn., Elks. Avocations: licensed aircraft pilot, running, classical piano, traveling, reading. General civil litigation, Aviation, Intellectual property. Office: 125 Water St Ste D Santa Cruz CA 95060-2709

**DAMPIER, HAROLD DEAN, JR.,** lawyer; b. Raleigh, N.C., Feb. 28, 1962; s. Harold Dean and Janie D. Student, Am. U., 1983; BA, U. Okla., 1984; JD, South Tex. Coll. Law, 1987. Bar: Tex. 1989, U.S. Dist. Ct. (no., so., ea. and we. dists.) Tex. 1991, 92. Assoc. Law Office of Ray McQuarry, Houston, 1989; assoc. Gerald J. Goodwin & Assocs., Houston, 1989-91; ptnr. Dampier & Watson, Houston, 1991-95; pvt. practice Law Offices of Harold D. Dampier, Jr., Houston, 1995—; steering com. Multi Dist. Litigation 1038. Recipient Washington semester scholarship U. Okla., 1983; named Outstanding Freshman Sen. Okla. Intercollegiate Legislature, 1984. Mem. Assn. Trial Lawyers Am., Tex. Bar Assn., Tex. Trial Lawyers Assn. (former bd. dirs.), Houston Bar Assn. (moderator 1990—), Houston Trial Lawyers Assn. (bd. dirs., v.p.). Personal injury, State civil litigation, General civil litigation. Office: 811 Dallas St Ste 1001 Houston TX 77002-5912

**DAMSGAARD, KELL MARSH,** lawyer; b. Darby, Pa., May 16, 1949; s. Kjeld and Dorothy (Fanck) D.; m. Katherine Elizabeth Stark, June 17, 1972; children: Peter Kjeld, Christopher William, David Zentner. BA cum laude, Yale U., 1971; JD, U. Pa., 1974. Bar: Pa. 1974, U.S. Dist. Ct. (ea. dist.) Pa. 1975, U.S. Ct. Appeals (3d cir.) 1984, U.S. Ct. Appeals (D.C. cir.) 1989, U.S. Ct. Appeals (8th cir.) 1990, U.S. Ct. Appeals (10th cir.), 1991, U.S. Supreme Ct. 1991. Law clk. to judge Superior Ct. of Pa., Phila., 1974-75; assoc. Morgan, Lewis & Bockius LLP, Phila., 1975-81; ptnr. Morgan, Lewis & Bockius, Phila., 1981—, firm adminstrv. ptnr., 1996—. Mem. ABA, Phila. Bar Assn. Avocations: skiing, jogging, tennis, antiques. Federal civil litigation, State civil litigation, Product liability. Home: PO Box 141 Birchrunville PA 19421-0141 Office: Morgan Lewis & Bockius LLP 1701 Market St Philadelphia PA 19103-2903

**DAMUS, ROBERT GEORGE,** lawyer, government official; b. San Bernardino, Calif., June 24, 1945; s. Shibli and Margaret (Saliba) D.; m. Pamela Claire Aldridge, Aug. 28, 1976; children: David Alexander, Elizabeth Anne. BA magna cum laude, Harvard U., 1967, JD cum laude, 1972; BA, MA (1st class scholar), St. John's Coll., Cambridge U. (Eng.), 1969. Bar: Calif. 1972. Teaching fellow dept. econs. Harvard Coll., Cambridge, Mass., 1970-71; lectr. law U. Warwick, Coventry, Eng. 1972-73; assoc. McCutchen, Black, Verleger & Shea, L.A., 1973-80; gen. trial atty. fed. programs br., civil div., U.S. Dept. Justice, Washington, 1980-82, asst. dir., 1982-85; asst. gen. counsel Office Mgmt. and Budget, Exec. Office of Pres. of U.S., 1985-87, acting gen. counsel, 1987-88, 89-94, gen. counsel, 1994—, dep. gen. counsel, 1988-89. Recipient Spl. Achievement awards Dept. Justice, 1981, 83, Wright prize in Econs., Cambridge U. (Eng.), 1972, Sr. Exec. Svcs. Presdl. Rank Merit award of meritorious exec., 1994, disting. exec., 1995. Club: Harvard Varsity. Office: Office Mgmt & Budget Old Executive Office Bldg Washington DC 20503-0001

**DANA, FRANK J., III,** lawyer; b. Columbia, S.C., June 8, 1950; s. Frank J. Dana, Jr. and Laura Glenn McCants; m. Susan Elaine Hostetler, May 7, 1983; 1 child, Caroline. BS in Math., Davidson Col., 1972; JD, Duke U., 1975. Bar: S.C. 1975. Atty. Haynsworth, Perry, Bryant, Marion & Johnstone, Greenville, S.C., 1975-82; v.p., trust officer C & S Nat. Bank of S.C., Greenville, S.C., 1982-86; pvt. practice Greenville, S.C., 1986—. Real property, Probate, General corporate. Office: Dana Law Firm 205 N Spring St Ste 111 Greenville SC 29601-2123

**DANA, HOWARD H., JR.,** state supreme court justice. Assoc. justice Supreme Judicial Ct. of Maine, Portland, 1993—. Office: Supreme Judicial Court 142 Federal St PO Box 368 Portland ME 04112-0368*

**DANA, LAUREN ELIZABETH,** lawyer; b. Hollywood, Calif., Sept. 30, 1950; d. Franklin Eugene and Margaret Elizabeth (Nixon) D.; m. Andrew Russell Willing, May 25, 1986; 1 child, Matthew Barkan Willing. BA cum laude, Calif. State U., Northridge, 1973; JD cum laude, Southwestern U., 1982. Bar: Calif. 1982, U.S. Dist. Ct. (cen. dist.) Calif. 1983, U.S. Ct. Appeals (9th cir.) 1983, U.S. Supreme Ct. 1987. Assoc. Law Office Andrew R. Willing, Los Angeles, 1982-84; dep. atty. gen. Calif. Dept. Justice-Atty. Gen., Los Angeles, 1984—; temporary judge L.A. Mcpl. Ct. Assoc. editor legal update Police Officer Law Report, 1986-87. Recipient Am. Jurisprudence Book award Lawyers Coop. Pub. Co., 1980, Am. Jurisprudence Book award in Evidence, 1980. Mem. ABA, Fed. Bar Assn., Am. Judicature Soc., Constitutional Rights Found., Selden Soc., U.S. Supreme Ct. Hist. Soc., L.A. County Bar Assn. (conf. of delegates 1998, 99), Women Lawyers Assn. L.A., L.A. World Affairs Coun., Alliance for Children's Rights, Town Hall, Phi Alpha Delta, The Da Camera Soc. Avocations: music, collecting books on English history, reading, traveling. Office: Calif Dept Justice 300 S Spring St Los Angeles CA 90013-1230

**DANA, MARK WILLIAM,** lawyer; b. Rochester, N.Y., May 1, 1959; s. Roland Julius and Marjorie Susan (Bitten) D.; m. Dyana Ruth Koelsch, Aug. 9, 1986; children: Austin, Nathaniel, Joshua, Cassandra. BA in Comms., SUNY, Geneseo, 1981; JD, New Eng. Sch. Law, Boston, 1989. Bar: R.I. 1989, U.S. Dist. Ct. R.I. 1989. State prosecutor Dept. of Atty. Gen., Providence, 1989-92; trial lawyer Hanson, Curran, Parks & Whitman, Providence, 1992—; prof. criminal law, constl. law and agy. law C.C. R.I., Warwick, 1992-94. Del., Meeting St. Ctr., East Providence, R.I., 1994; mem. Parients Reaching Out, Warwick, 1994. Mem. ABA, R.I. Bar Assn., R.I. Criminal Def. Assn. Republican. Lutheran. General civil litigation, Criminal. Office: Hanson Curran Parks Whitman 146 Westminster St Providence RI 02903-2202

**DANAS, ANDREW MICHAEL,** lawyer; b. Redwood City, Calif., Apr. 25, 1955; s. Michael George and Marjorie Jean (Bailey) D. BA in Polit. Sci. and History, U. Conn., 1977; JD, George Washington U., 1982. Bar: D.C. 1982, U.S. Dist. Ct. (D.C. cir.), U.S. Dist. Ct. Md., U.S. Ct. Appeals (D.C., 2d, 3d, 4th, 6th, 11th and fed. cirs.), U.S. Ct. of Claims, U.S. Supreme Ct. Atty. Assn. Am. R.R.s, Washington, 1983-84; assoc. Grove Jaskiewicz & Cobert, Washington, 1984-90, Ptnr., 1991—. Contbg. author: Freewheeling; author legal column Intermodal Reporter, 1986-94; contbr. articles to profl. jours. Mem. exec. com. Friends Assisting the Nat. Symphony, Washington, 1996-97. Mem. Transp. Law Inst. (chair 1993-94), Transp. Lawyers Assn. (chair legis. com. 1995-98, co-chair 1999, Disting. Svc. award 1996), Phi Alpha Theta, Mensa. Avocations: skiing, music, travel. Private international, Federal civil litigation, Administrative and regulatory. Home: 621 Tivoli Psge Alexandria VA 22314-1932 Office: Grove Jaskiewicz and Cobert 1730 M St NW Ste 400 Washington DC 20036-4579

**DANCY, BONITA JOYCE,** lawyer; b. Balt., Jan. 21, 1946; d. Homer Benson and Joyce (Harper) D.; m. Theron Napoleon Whitaker, July 10, 1982. BA, Morgan U., 1967; MSW, U. Md., 1971, JD, 1981; Cert. in Group Therapy, U. Chgo., 1972. Bar: Md. 1981; lic. social worker, Md. Supr. family service Md. Dept. Social Services, Balt., 1967-72; adminstr. Northwest Youth Services, Balt., 1972-81; atty. adivsor, gen. counsel HHS, Balt., 1981-82; master in chancery Balt. City Cir. Ct., 1982—; assoc. prof. sociology Coppin State Coll., Balt., 1973-75; adj. prof. Morgan State Coll., Balt., 1975-81; commr. Gov.'s Landlord Tenant Law Commn., Md., 1975—; training cons. U. Md. Sch. Social Work, Balt., 1974-75. Past pres., mem. Balt. Urban League Leaguettes, 1968—; bd. dirs. Mental Health Assn. Balt., 1983, Balt. Urban League, 1981-82, v.p. Named Vol. of Yr. Balt. Urban League, 1983. Mem. ABA, Md. Bar Assn. (bd. govs. 1991-92), Md. Inst. Continuing Profl. Edn. Lawyers Inc. (bd. dirs.), Nat. Bar Assn., Nat. Assn. of Women Judges (bd. dris. Md. chpt.), Nat. Coalition of 100 Balck Women (charter), Bar Assn. Balt. City (past sec.), Monumental City Bar Assn., Phi Alpha Theta, Alpha Kappa Alpha, Rho Xi Omega (pres.).

**DANE, STEPHEN MARK,** lawyer; b. Chillicothe, Ohio, Mar. 27, 1956; s. Clyde and Rita M. (Murray) D.; m. Kim P. Piatt, July 7, 1979; children: Tara, Adam, Shannon, Alexandra, Courtney. BS with honors, U. Notre Dame, 1978; JD magna cum laude, U. Toledo, 1981. Bar: Ohio 1981, U.S. Ct. Appeals (6th and 10th cirs.) 1982, U.S. Dist. Ct. (no. dist.) Ohio 1983, U.S. Dist. Ct. (no. dist.) Tex. 1983, U.S. Ct. Appeals (5th cir.) 1984, U.S. Supreme Ct. 1985, U.S. Ct. Appeals (7th cir.) 1993. Law clk. U.S. Ct. Appeals (6th cir.), Cin., 1981-82; ptnr. Cooper, Walinski & Cramer, Toledo, 1986—; judge pro tempore Perrysburg Mcpl. Ct., 1990—. Mem. Charter Rev. Commn., Perrysburg, Ohio, 1988; pres. Perrysburg Dem. Club, 1987-88; mem. exec. com. Wood County Dem. Party, Bowling Green, Ohio, 1986-90; pres. St. Rose Peace and Justice Com., Perrysburg, 1987-92, St. John's H.S. Alumni Assn., 1988-89; chmn. Human Rights Commn. of Diocese of Toledo, 1991-93. Recipient Fair Housing award HUD, 1996, Spirit of Wood County award, 1988; named Lawyer of Yr. Lawyers Weekly, 1998; named to St. John's Jesuit H.S. Hall of Fame, 1991. Mem. ABA, Ohio State Bas Assn., Toledo Bar Assn. (chmn. fed. ct. com. 1987-89), Wood County Bar Assn.. Roman Catholic. Civil rights, Federal civil litigation, Labor. Home: 501 Hickory St Perrysburg OH 43551-2206 Office: Cooper Walinski & Cramer 900 Adams St Toledo OH 43624-1505

**DANG, MARVIN S. C.,** lawyer; b. Honolulu, Feb. 11, 1954; s. Brian K.T. and Flora (Yuen) D. BA with distinction, U. Hawaii, 1974; JD, George Washington U., 1978. Bar: Hawaii 1978, U.S. Dist. Ct. Hawaii 1978, U.S. Ct. Appeals (9th cir.) 1979. Atty. Gerson, Steiner & Anderson and predecessor firms, Honolulu, 1978-81; owner, atty. Law Offices of Marvin S.C. Dang, Honolulu, 1981—; sr. v.p., bd. dirs. Rainbow Fin. Corp., Honolulu, 1984-95; bd. dirs. Foster Equipment Co. Ltd., Honolulu, Hawaii Cmty. Reinvestment Corp.; bd. dirs. Hawaii Fin. Svcs. Assn., sec., 1991, treas., 1992, v.p., 1993, pres. 1994; vice chmn. Hawaii Consumer Fin. Polit. Action Com., 1988-95, sec./treas., 1999—; hearings officer (per diem) Adminstrv. Drivers License Revocation Office, Honolulu, 1991-95. State rep., asst. minority floor leader Hawaii State Legislature, Honolulu, 1982-84; chmn., vice chmn., mem. Manoa Neighborhood Bd., Honolulu, 1979-82, 84-87; pres., v.p., mem. Hawaii Coun. on Legal Edn. for Youth, Honolulu, 1979-86; mem. Hawaii Bicentennial Commn. of U.S. Constn., Honolulu, 1986-88. Recipient Cert. of Appreciation award Hawaii Speech-Lang.-Hearing Assn., Honolulu, 1984; named one of Ten Outstanding Young Persons of Hawaii, Hawaii State Jaycees, 1983. Mem. ABA (coun. of fund for justice and edn. 1993—, standing com. on law and electoral process 1985-89, spl. com. on youth edn. for citizenship 1979-85, 89-92, Hawaii membership chmn. 1981-93, exec. coun. young lawyers divsn. 1986-88), Hawaii State Bar Assn. (chair collection law sec. 1999—, bd. dirs. young lawyers divsn. 1990). Avocations: family, law, politics. Consumer commercial, Probate, Real property. Office: PO Box 4109 Honolulu HI 96812-4109

**D'ANGELO, CHRISTOPHER SCOTT,** lawyer; b. Phila., Aug. 30, 1953; s. George Anthony and Antonia Scott (Billett) D'A.; m. Betsy Hart Josephs, May 22, 1982; children: John Robert, Christopher Hart, Caroline Colt, Jennifer Scott. BA with honors and distinction, U. Va., 1975, JD, 1978. Bar: Pa. 1978, U.S. Dist Ct. (ea. dist.) Pa. 1978, (mid. dist.) Pa. 1992, U.S. Ct. Appeals (3d cir.) 1978, U.S. Supreme Ct. 1981. From assoc. to ptnr. Montgomery, McCracken, Walker & Rhoads, LLP, Phila., 1978-96, chmn., product liability and toxic tort sect., 1996—; sustaining mem. Products Liability Adv. Coun., 1985—, case selection com. 1988-91, experts com., 1993—, restatement project com., 1993—, exec. com. 1998—; mem. Am. Law. Inst., 1996—, mem. consultative group products liability, mem. Consultative Group-UCC, mem. trusts, 1996—; lectr., writer in law internet and tech. matters. Co-founder The Declaration (U. Va. newsweekly), 1973-75; Editor: Counsel Table, 1990-94; contbr. articles to law jours. Mem. Internat. Vis. Ctr., Phila., 1982—, bd. dirs., 1987-90, chmn. long range fin. com., 1987-89, counsel for COMPASS (young profl. and spl. events div. of ctr.), 1982-89, exec. com., 1982-89; mem. selection com. Jefferson Scholars U. Va., Phila., 1980-84, chmn., 1981-82; fundraiser U.S. Ski Team, Phila., 1979-90, chmn., 1982-83, 87; fundraiser Acad. Natural Scis., Phila, 1979-88; trustee Episcopal Acad., Merion, Pa., 1988-91, 92—; chmn. ann. giving campaigns Episcopal Acad., 1983-88; bd. mgrs. Episc. Acad. Alumni Soc., Merion, Pa., 1983-92, treas., 1984-85, v.p. 1985-88, pres. 1988-91; treas., exec. com., bd. dirs. Phila. Art Alliance, 1980-86; bd. dirs. English Speaking Union U.S., 1979-82, chmn. young mem. group, 1980-83; bd. dirs. English Speaking Union Phila., 1980-88, chmn. fin. com., 1985-88; counsel honor com. and judiciary com. U. Va., 1976-78; mem. nominating com. St. Christopher's Ch., Gladwyne, Pa., 1989-91; fundraiser Friends Sch., Haverford, Pa., 1987-89; lay reader The Ch. of the Redeemer, Bryn Mawr, Pa., 1992—, mem. capital campaign, 1993—, head usher, 1993—, vestry, 1997—; mem. trophy com. Devon (Pa.) Horse Show, 1978—; mem. com. Benjamin Franklin Inst. Nat. Meml. Awards, 1995-98. Mem. ABA (mem. sect. litigation, products liability com., sect. internat. law, corp. counsel com.), Pa. Bar Assn. (exec. com. young lawyers divsn. 1979-85, probate sect. 1979—, litigation sect. 1979—), Phila. Bar Assn. (probate sect. 1979—), Products Liability Adv. Coun. (mem. Am. Law Inst. com., mem. experts com. 1991—), Def. Rsch. Inst. (products liability com., bus. litigation com., drug and med. device com.), Fedn. of Ins. and Corp. Counsel (mem. computers and tech. com., products liability com., bus. litigation com.), Internat. Assn. Def. Counsel (mem. products liability com., mem. bus. litigation com., drug and med. device com., complex class action com., multi-nat. litigation com., computer and tech. com., author newsletters), Nat. Assn. Railroad Trial Counsel, Acad. Natural Scis., Anthenaeum, Phila. Mus. Art, Phila. Zoo, Please Touch Mus., Merion Cricket Club (Haverford), Penn Club, IV St. Club, The Assemblies, Phila. Club. Republican. Avocations: sailing, photography, travel, squash. Private international, General civil litigation, Product liability. Office: Montgomery McCracken Walker & Rhoads 123 S Broad St Fl 24 Philadelphia PA 19109-1099

**D'ANGELO-MAYER, IDA,** lawyer; b. Long Island City, N.Y., Aug. 22, 1967; d. Fileno Domenico and Nicoletta D'Angelo; m. Robert Michael Mayer, May 6, 1995; 1 child, Robert Mayer. BS, Fordham U. at Lincoln Ctr, 1988; JD, St. John's U., Jamaica, N.Y., 1992. Bar: N.Y. 1992, N.J. 1993, U.S. Dist. Ct. (ea. and so. dists.) N.Y. 1993. Assoc. atty. Law Offices of Peter T. Roach, Westbury, N.Y., 1992-94, Law Offices of Ida D'Angelo, Melville, N.Y., 1994—. Mem. ABA, N.Y. State Bar Assn., Suffolk County Bar Assn. Real property. Office: 555 Broadhollow Rd Melville NY 11747-5078

**DANIEL, J. REESE,** lawyer; b. Sanford, N.C., Dec. 24, 1924. AB, U. S.C., 1949, JD cum laude, 1956. Bar: S.C. 1955, U.S. Dist. Ct. S.C. 1956, U.S. Tax Ct. 1959, U.S. Cir. Appeals (4th cir.) 1959. Sr. ptnr. Daniel & Daniel, Litchfield, S.C.; mem. S.C. Supreme Ct. Bd. Commrs. on Grievances and Discipline, 1970-73, Columbia Zoning Bd. of Adjustment, 1970-79. Contbg. author 7 South Carolina Law Quarterly; contbr. articles to profl. jours. With USNR, 1943-46. Mem. ABA, S.C. Bar Assn. (assoc. editor S.C. Bar Assn. News Bull. 1957, editor 1958-59), Phi Delta Phi. E-mail: reesedaniel@email.msn.com. General civil litigation, Personal injury, Probate. Office: Daniel & Daniel PO Box 857 10B Pawleys Sta Hwy 17 S Pawleys Island SC 29585

**DANIEL, LANCE,** lawyer; b. St. Louis, Sept. 12, 1960; s. Robert Edward and Arlene Madeline Leber. BSBA, San Diego State U., 1985; JD, U. of the Pacific, 1988. Bar: Calif. 1989. Dep. dist. atty. Dist. Attys. Office, Sacramento, 1989; assoc. David Allen & Assocs., Sacramento, 1989-91; pvt. practice law Sacramento, 1991—; instr. paralegal studies Humphrey's Coll., Sacramento, 1996—; bd. dirs. Chai Found., Phoenix. Mem. State Bar Calif., Inns of Ct. (barrister). Avocation: collecting fountain pens, autographs, antique watches. Criminal, General civil litigation, Personal injury. Office: 1028 2nd St 3rd Fl Sacramento CA 95814-3235

**DANIEL, MELVIN RANDOLPH,** lawyer; b. Greencastle, Ind., May 15, 1942; s. Randolph Carl and Helen Marie (Hopwood) D.; m. Delynn Ann Keller, Sept. 3, 1966; children—Dia Felice, Rene Lynn. B.S., Ind. State U.-Terre Haute, 1967; J.D., Ind. U., 1972. Bar: Ind. 1972, U.S. Dist. Ct. (so. dist.) Ind. 1972, U.S. Dist. Ct. (no. dist.) Ind. 1983, U.S. Ct. Appeals (7th cir.) 1984, U.S. Ct. Appeals (5th cir.) 1988. Law editor Allen Smith Co., Indpls., 1970-72; assoc. Raber & Vandivier, Danville, Ind., 1972-73; ptnr. Raber, Vandivier & Daniel, Danville, 1973-81; assoc. Dann Pecar Newman Talesnick & Kleiman, Indpls., 1981-82; v.p., head trial dept., 1982—. Served with USN, 1959-65. Recipient Carrol prize in Advocacy, 1970, Am Jurisprudence award Lawyers Coop Pub. Co., 1970. Mem. ABA, Ind. State Bar Assn., Ind. Mcpl. Lawyers Assn., Indpls. Bar Assn., Hendricks County Bar Assn. (pres. 1977-78), Ind. State Trial Lawyers Assn., Assn. Trial Lawyers Am., Indpls. Law club, Masons. Republican. Methodist. Federal civil litigation, State civil litigation, Condemnation. Home: 499 Summit Ct Plainfield IN 46168-1076 Office: Dann Pecar Newman & Kleiman Box 82008 1 American Sq Indianapolis IN 46282-0001

**DANIEL, ROBERT MICHAEL,** lawyer; b. Rocky Mount, N.C., Aug. 21, 1947; s. Harvey Derby and Edna Lois (McCullen) D.; m. Kaye Ruth Coates, Aug. 31, 1968; children: Robert M. Jr., John Matthew. AB in Econs., U. N.C., 1968, JD, 1971. Bar: N.C. 1971, Pa. 1976; U.S. Dist. Ct. (we. dist.) Pa. 1976; U.S. Tax Ct. 1979. Judge adv. U.S. Marine Corps., 1971-74; ptnr. Smith & Daniel, Pittsboro, N.C., 1974-75; trust officer Mellon Bank, N.A., Pitts., 1975-78; assoc. Buchanan Ingersoll, Pitts., 1978-82, ptnr., 1982—. Pres. Greater Pitts. coun. Boy Scouts Am., 1996-99, bd. dirs. N.E. region. Col. USMCR, 1966-98, ret. Fellow Am. Coll. Trust and Estate Coun.; mem. Pa. Bar Assn. (real property, probate and trust law sect. 1998-99), Duquesne Club. Presbyterian. Avocations: running, reading military history. Estate planning, Probate, Estate taxation. Home: 1491 Redfern Dr Pittsburgh PA 15241-2956 Office: Buchanan Ingersoll 301 Grant St Ste 20 Pittsburgh PA 15219-1408

**DANIEL, SAMUEL PHILLIPS,** lawyer; b. Tulsa, Okla., Dec. 20, 1932; s. Samuel P. and Mary (Rumley) D.; m. Mary Lou Lowe, Feb. 24, 1982; children: Sam P. III, Theodore W., John T. BS in Philosophy and Econs., Georgetown U., 1954; JD, U. Okla., 1959. Bar: Okla. 1959, U.S. Dist. Ct. (ea., we., no. dists.) Okla. 1960, U.S. Ct. Appeals (10th cir.) 1960, U.S. Supreme Ct. 1967. With Carlson, Lupardus, Holliman & Huffman, Tulsa, 1959-65; ptnr. Doerner, Saunders, Daniel & Anderson, L.L.P., Tulsa, 1965—; adj. prof. U. Tulsa Law Sch., 1990, 92. Fellow Am. Acad. Matrimonial Lawyers, Am. Coll. Trial Lawyers; mem. Tulsa County Bar Assn. (pres. 1986-87), Am. Bar Found. (Okla. fellow), Tulsa County Bar Found. (trustee), Am. Inns of Ct. (master emeritus). Republican. Methodist. Avocations: hunting, fishing, golf. Family and matrimonial, General civil litigation. Office: Doerner Saunders Daniel & Anderson LLP 320 S Boston Ave Ste 500 Tulsa OK 74103-3725

**DANIELS, BRUCE JOEL,** lawyer; b. Denver, Apr. 16, 1935; s. Daniel Lester and Lillian Daniels; children: Julia K., Marya L., Jade A., Gregory R.S., Brenna J. AB, Ohio State U., 1957; JD, U. Mich., 1961. Bar: Fla. 1961, U.S. Dist. Ct. (middle dist.) Fla. 1962, U.S. Dist. Ct. (so. dist.) Fla. 1988. Private practice Fla., 1961-87, North Palm Beach, Fla., 1987—. Coauthor: (book) Eminent Domain, 1971. Mem. AARP (assoc. state coord. VOTE Fla. 1996—). Probate, Real property. Home: 336 Golfview Rd Apt 1018 North Palm Beach FL 33408-3513 Office: PO Box 14806 North Palm Beach FL 33408-0806

**DANIELS, DANIEL LLOYD,** lawyer; b. New Milford, Conn., Nov. 17, 1962; s. C. Ross Jr. and Fayne M. (McGrath) D.; m. Jennifer A. Matteis, Aug. 27, 1988; children: Benjamin T., Elizabeth S. AB summa cum laude, Dartmouth Coll., 1984; JD cum laude, Harvard U., 1987. Bar: N.Y. 1988, Conn. 1991. Law clk. Mass. Supreme Ct., Boston, 1987-88; assoc. Sullivan & Cromwell, N.Y.C., 1988-89; prin. Settle Agy., Inc., Danbury, Conn., 1989-91; assoc. Cummings & Lockwood, Stamford, Conn., 1991-96, ptnr., 1997—. Contbg. author: The 401 (K) Plan Handbook, 1997. Mem. Danbury Econ. Devel. Commn., 1991; bd. dirs. Cmty. Ctrs., Inc., Grenwich, Conn., 1994-96, Cmty. Answers at Greenwich Libr., 1996—. Mem. ABA, Conn. Bar Assn. (presenter 1996), N.Y. State Bar Assn., Stamford-Norwalk Regional Bar Assn., Harvard Law Sch. Assn. Conn. (trustee Stamford 1995—). Avocations: a capella singing, Gilbert and Sullivan, musical theater. Probate, Estate planning, Estate taxation. Office: Cummings & Lockwood 4 Stamford Plz Stamford CT 06902-3834

**DANIELS, JOHN DRAPER,** lawyer; b. Bklyn., Feb. 11, 1939; s. Draper L. and Louise Parker-Lux (Cort) D.; m. Sara Josephine Sears, Dec. 27, 1962; children: Stephen Draper, Elizabeth Marie, Rebecca Cort. AB, Princeton U., 1961; JD, U. Chgo., 1964. Bar: Ill. 1964, U.S. Dist. Ct. (no. dist.) Ill. 1967. Assoc. Jacobs & McKenna, Chgo., 1964-70, Law Offices Dale L. Schlafer, Chgo., 1970-73; assoc. then ptnr. Jacobs, Williams & Montgomery, Chgo., 1973-87; ptnr. Sanchez & Daniels, Chgo., 1987—; Arbitrator Cir. Ct. of Cook County. Mem. admissions screening panel Princeton Alumni Council. Capt. U.S. Army, 1964-66. Mem. ABA, Ill. Bar Assn. (chmn. ins. sect. coun.), Chgo. Bar Assn., Am. Arbitration Assn. (arbitrator 1977—), Internat. Assn. Def. Counsel, Soc. Trial Lawyers (bd. dirs. 1990, '92), Am. Bd. Trial Advs., Ill. Assn. Defense Trial Counsel, Trial Lawyers Club of Chgo., Tower of Chgo. Club (bd. trustees. 1985-87), East Bank Club. Roman Catholic. Avocations: guitar, musical composition, tennis, fishing, golf. General civil litigation, Insurance, Product liability. Home: 1611 Wilmette Ave Wilmette IL 60091-2424 Office: Sanchez & Daniels 333 W Wacker Dr Chicago IL 60606-1220

**DANIELS, JOHN HILL,** lawyer; b. Albany, N.Y., Oct. 17, 1928; s. David Samuel and Sadie (Davidson) D.; m. Helen R. Marcus, May 24, 1952; children: Marc, Scott, Seth. Grad., L.I. U., 1949; LLB, Bklyn. Law Sch., 1952; LLM, NYU, 1958. Bar: N.Y. 1954, U.S. Dist. Ct. (ea. and so. dists.) N.Y. 1954, U.S. Supreme Ct. 1958. Assoc. Friedman & Friedman, Bklyn., 1954, Finkelstein, Benton & Soll, N.Y.C., 1955-58, Levy & Kornblum, Bklyn., 1959; ptnr. Kamen & Daniels, Bklyn., 1959-61, Daniels & Daniels, Mineola, N.Y., 1983—; sole practice Roosevelt, N.Y., 1960-88, Mineola, 1975—; lectr. in field; bd. dirs. CUTCO. Candidate for judge Nassau County Dist. Ct., Mineola, 1960-63; bd. dirs. Mental Health and Alcohol, Roosevelt, 1980-92; past pres. Civic Assn. of Woodbury. Sgt. U.S. Army, 1952-54. Mem. N.Y. State Bar Assn., Nassau County Bar Assn., Nassau Lawyers Assn. L.I. (dir. 1970—, pres. 1984), Jewish Lawyers Assn. Nassau County (bd. dirs. 1964—, pres. 1985-86), Yankee Sports and Gun Club (Roosevelt) (past pres.), Lions (dir. 1960-84), Kiwanis (dir. 1978-84), epsilon Phi Alpha, Iota Theta. Criminal, Probate, Real property. Home: 29 Kodiak Dr Woodbury NY 11797-2706 Office: 114 Old Country Rd Mineola NY 11501-4400

**DANIELS, KEITH BYRON, JR.,** lawyer; b. Bloomington, Ind., Dec. 10, 1962; s. Keith Byron and Mary Avolyn (Culver) D.; m. Kathy Kay Waldsmith, Apr. 1, 1989. BA, U. Wis., Eau Claire, 1985; JD, U. Wis., Madison, 1988. Bar: Wis. 1988, U.S. Dist. Ct. (we. dist.) Wis. 1988, U.S. Ct. Mil. Appeals 1989, Ill. 1990, U.S. Dist. Ct. (ea. dist.) Wis. 1991, U.S. Ct. Appeals (7th cir.) 1991, U.S. Dict. Ct. (no. dist.) Ill. 1992. Assoc. Bolgrien, Ruth, Rentz, Mineau & Koepke, Beloit, Wis., 1988-89; staff atty. Katten, Muchin & Zavis, Chgo., 1993-94; assoc. Hanson & Peters, Chgo., 1994-98, Blatt, Hammesfahr & Eaton, Chgo., 1998—. Capt. U.S. Army, 1989-93. Recipient Army Achievement medal (3), Army Commendation medal, Meritorious Svc. medal. Mem. Chgo. Bar Assn., State Bar Wis. Presbyterian. General civil litigation, Insurance, Professional liability. Office: Blatt Hammesfahr & Eaton 333 W Wacker Dr Ste 1900 Chicago IL 60606-1293

**DANIELS, RUSSELL HOWARD,** lawyer; b. Dallas, Apr. 25, 1967; s. Charles Judd and Barbara Ann (Smith) D.; m. Pamela Beth Rhodes, June 24, 1989. BA in Criminal Justice, So. Meth. U., 1989, BA in Sociology, 1989; JD with honors, U. Tulsa, 1994. Bar: Tex. 1994, U.S. Dist. Ct. (no. and ea. dists.) Tex. 1995, U.S. Ct. Appeals (5th cir.) 1995. Law clk. Law Offices of Doug Larson, Mesquite, Tex., 1991-93, assoc., 1994—. Articles editor Tulsa Law Jour., 1993-94. Master mason Grand Lodge of Tex. A.F. & A.M., Mesquite, 1995—. Recipient Am. Jurisprudence award Lawyers Coop., 1991, 92. Mem. ABA, ATLA, Dallas Bar Assn. (cmty. involvement com. team leader 1995), State Bar of Tex., Bar Assn. Fifth Fed. Cir., Phi Delta Phi. Avocations: outdoors, travel, reading. Federal civil litigation, Civil rights. Home: PO Box 181602 Dallas TX 75218-8602 Office: Law Offices Douglas R. Larson 410 W Main St Ste 101 Mesquite TX 75149-4230

**DANIELS, TRACY ELLEN,** paralegal; b. Needham, Mass., Jan. 16, 1970; d. William Christopher and Ellen Mary D. BA, Trinity Coll., 1992; cert. in paralegal, Northeastern U., 1993. Legal asst. Olive Larsen Esq., Boston, 1993-94; legal sec. Tech. Aid Corp., Newton, Mass., 1994-96; paralegal John Hancock Mut. Life Ins. Co., Boston, 1996—. Active Campaign for Lida Harkins, Needham, 1993. Democrat. Roman Catholic. Avocations: camping, sightseeing, alumni board activities. Office: John Hancock Mut Life Ins Co 200 Clarendon St # T-55 Boston MA 02116-5021

**DANIELSON, GARY R.,** lawyer; b. Detroit, June 8, 1953; s. Ronald Gregory and Catherine (Gibson) D. BA in Psychology, Oakland U., Rochester, Mich., 1976; JD cum laude, Wayne State U., 1983. Bar: Mich. 1983, U.S. Dist. Ct. (ea. dist.) Mich., 1985, U.S. Supreme Ct. 1987. Sr. job placement counselor Ferndale (Mich.) Sch. Dist., 1976-79; employment and tng. adminstr. Oakland County Govt., Pontiac, Mich., 1979-82; sr. corp. labor rels. rep. Harper-Grace Hosps., Detroit, 1982-83; corp. labor rels. mgr. Vis. Nurse Assn., Detroit, 1983-85; atty., v.p., cons. Indsl. Rels., Inc., Detroit, 1985-90; pres. The Danielson Group, P.C., St. Clair Shores, 1990—. Pres., bd. dirs. St. Clair on Lake Condominium Assn., St. Clair Shores, Mich., 1987—. Mem. ABA, Mich. Bar Assn., Hosp. Pers. Adminstrs. Assn., Indsl. Rels. Rsch. Assn. Republican. Avocation: sailing. Civil rights, Labor. Office: Danielson Group PC 27735 Jefferson Ave Saint Clair Shores MI 48081-1309

**DANKNER, JAY WARREN,** lawyer; b. Bklyn., June 15, 1949; s. Morris and Frances Dankner; m. Iris Rose Terens, May 15, 1983; children: Danielle Renee, Nicole Beth. BA cum laude, Bklyn. Coll., 1970, JD cum laude, 1973. Bar: N.Y. 1974, Fla. 1974, U.S. Dist. Ct. (ea. and so. dists.) N.Y. 1974, U.S. Ct. Appeals (2d cir.) 1974, U.S. Supreme Ct. 1977, U.S. Dist. Ct. (no. dist.) N.Y. 1986. From assoc. to ptnr. Sullivan & Liapakis P.C., N.Y.C., 1974-94; ptnr. Dankner & Milstein, P.C., N.Y.C., 1994—; lectr. Practicing Law Inst., N.Y.C., 1983-87, N.Y. State Trial Lawyers Inst., 1985—, continuing legal edn. program Bklyn. Law Sch., 1986—, N.Y. State Bar Assn. CLE Programs, Nassau County Bar Assn., Queens Bar Assn.; mem. Bklyn. Law Rev., 1972-73; bd. dirs. Atty's Info. Exchange Group, Inc., 1981—. Author: Products Liability Practice Guide, 1988, Masters of Trial Practice, 1988, Deposing Corporate Defendants in Products Liability Actions, 1988, Trial Strategy - Plaintiffs View, 1988; contbr. articles to profl. jours. Named Best Trial Lawyers in the U.S., Town & Country, 1985. Mem. ABA, N.Y. State Bar Assn. (spl. com. on procedures for jud. discipline 1987-90), Assn. of Bar of City of N.Y. (mem. products liability com. 1993-94), Fla. Bar Assn., Assn. Trial Lawyers Am., N.Y. State Trial Lawyers Assn. (chair products liability com. 1991, 93-94), N.Y. County Lawyers Assn. General civil litigation, Personal injury, Product liability. Home: 524 E 72nd St New York NY 10021-9801 Office: Dankner & Milstein PC 41 E 57th St New York NY 10022-1908

**DANN, ERIC RAYMOND,** lawyer; b. Columbus, Ohio, Aug. 5, 1969; s. Raymond Eugene and Margaret Elizabeth (Bugden) D. AB, Dartmouth Coll., 1991; JD, Harvard U., 1996. Bar: N.Y. 1997. Assoc. Davis Polk & Wardwell, N.Y.C., 1996-99, London, 1999—. Mem. Phi Beta Kappa. Episcopalian. Home: 22 Lausdinne Rd, London W11 3LL, England Office: Davis Polk & Wardwell, 1 Fredericks Pl, London EC2R 8AB, England also: c/o Davis Polk & Wardwell 450 Lexington Ave New York NY 10017-3911

**DANNEMEYER, BRUCE WILLIAM,** lawyer; b. Santa Barbara, Calif., July 5, 1957; s. Wililam Edwin and Evelyn Mae D.; m. Deborah Ann Dannemeyer, July 30, 1983; children: Rachel, Christine, Erin. BA, Valparaiso U., 1979; JD, U. Calif., Berkeley, 1982. Atty. U.S. Dept. Interior, Washington, 1983-86; assoc. Seltzer, Caplan, Wilkins & McMahon, San Diego, 1986-87; assoc. Palmieri, Tyler, Wiener, Wilhelm & Waldson, Irvine, 1987-93, ptnr., 1993—; judge pro-tem Orange County Superior Ct., Calif., 1997. Pres. Abiding Sr. Luth. Ch., Lake Forest, Calif., 1998, chmn. planning commn., 1994-96; speaker Internat. Right of Way Assn., Orange County, 1997. Mem. Orange County Bar Assn. General civil litigation, Appellate, Condemnation. Office: Palmieri Wiener Wilhelm & Waldson 2603 Main St Ste 1300 Irvine CA 92614-4281

**DANNEN, AVRUM H.,** lawyer; b. Chgo., Dec. 16, 1935; s. Reuben L. and Lillian (Rosensen) D.; m. Bonita Dannen, Oct. 27, 1970; children: Rachel, William. BS, U. Ill., 1957; JD, DePaul U., 1961. Bar: Ill. 1961, U.S. Supreme Ct. 1971. Ptnr. Dannen, Crane, Heyman & Simon, Chgo., 1961—. Author: Alternatives for the Financially Distressed Debtor, 1985; co-author: Out of Court Compositions and Assignment for the Benefit of Creditors, 1986. With U.S. Army, 1962-63. Mem. Comml. Law League, Am. Bankruptcy Inst., Chgo. Bar Assn. (chmn. bankruptcy reorgn. 1978), Ill. State Bar Assn. (chmn. comml. banking 1987). Bankruptcy. Office: Dannen Crane Heyman Simon 135 S La Salle St Ste 1540 Chicago IL 60603-4297

**DANNENBERG, RICHARD BRUCE,** lawyer; b. N.Y.C., Jan. 10, 1931; s. Edwin V. Dannenberg and Myra Lifshutz; div.; children: Susan Dannenberg Randoing, David, Catherine Parker; m. Barbara Dannenberg, Jan. 5, 1984. BA magna cum laude, Duke U., 1952; LLB, Yale U., 1955. Bar: N.Y. 1955, U.S. Dist. Ct. (so. and ea. dists.) N.Y. 1957, U.S. Ct. Appeals (2d cir.) 1959, U.S. Supreme Ct. 1961, U.S. Ct. Appeals (5th cir.) 1978, U.S. Ct.

Appeals (11th cir.) 1984, U.S. Ct. Appeals (3d cir.) 1987, U.S. Dist. Ct. Conn. 1987. Assoc. Lipper, Shinn & Heeley, N.Y.C., 1955-58; ptnr. Lipper, Shinn, Keeley & Dannenberg, N.Y.C., 1958-68, Lipper, Keeley, Lowey & Dannenberg, N.Y.C., 1968-74, Lipper, Lowey, Dannenberg & Knapp, N.Y.C., 1974-78; prin. Lowey, Dannenberg & Knapp, P.C., N.Y.C., 1979-87; prin., CFO, Lowey, Dannenberg, Bemporad & Selinger, P.C., White Plains, N.Y., 1988—. Contbr. White Plains Beautification, 1997—, Carnegie Hall, 1994—; bd. visitors Trinity Coll., Duke U., 1990-98. Mem. ABA, Fed. Bar Coun., N.Y. State Bar Assn., Bar Assn. City of N.Y. (mem. various coms.), Yale Club N.Y.C. Avocations: tennis, music, collecting sea shells, travel, philately. Federal civil litigation, State civil litigation, Securities. Home: 34 Century Rd Purchase NY 10577 Office: The Gateway 1 N Lexington Ave White Plains NY 10601-1712

**DANNER, BRYANT CRAIG,** lawyer; b. Boston, Nov. 18, 1937; s. Nevin Earle and Marjorie (Harms) D.; m. Judith I. Baker, Aug. 23, 1958; 1 child Debra Irene. BA, Harvard U., 1960, LLB, 1963. Bar: Calif. 1963, U.S. Dist. Ct. (cen. dist.) Calif. 1963. Assoc. Latham & Watkins, L.A., 1963-70, ptnr., 1970-92; sr. v.p., gen. counsel So. Calif. Edison Co., Rosemead, Calif., 1992-95; exec. v.p., gen. counsel So. Calif. Edison Co., Rosemead, 1995—. Mem. L.A. County Bar Assn. (chmn. environ. sect. 1988-89). Avocations: fly fishing, photography. Environmental, Administrative and regulatory. Office: So Calif Edison Co 2244 Walnut Grove Ave Rosemead CA 91770-3714

**DANNHAUSER, STEPHEN J.,** lawyer; b. N.Y.C., May 23, 1950; s. Frank A. and Irene (Tinney) D.; m. Mary Elizabeth Robinson, July 1, 1973; children: Benjamin, Todd, Jess. BA with honors, SUNY, Stonybrook, 1972; JD with honors, Bklyn. Law Sch., 1975. Bar: N.Y. 1976. Atty. Weil Gotshal & Manges LLP, N.Y.C., 1975—, exec. ptnr., 1989—. Decisions editor Bklyn. Law Rev., 1974-75. Pres. N.Y. Police and Fire Windows and Children's Fund, N.Y.C., 1985—; chmn. corp. steering com. Nat. Minority Bus. Coun., N.Y.C., 1993; bd. dirs. Boys Harbor, Inc., E. Harlem, N.Y. Mem. ABA. Avocations: running, golf. Office: Weil Gotshal & Manges LLP 767 5th Ave Fl Concl New York NY 10153-0119*

**DANNOV, FRED,** lawyer; b. Chgo., Apr. 30, 1930; s. Edward Louis and Rae D.; m. Lura Juanita Craft, Dec. 25, 1952; children—David M., Dana M. BA, Westminster U., 1953; JD, U. Mo., 1959, MA, 1961. Bar: Mo. 1960, U.S. Dist. Ct. (we. dist.) Mo. 1960, U.S. Supreme Ct. 1983. Sole practice, Columbia, Mo., 1960—; asst. pros. atty. Boone County (Mo.), Columbia, 1959-61; instr. bus. law Columbia Coll., 1975-78; judge Columbia Mcpl. Ct., 1975-79. Served to lt. U.S. Army, 1953-55. Mem. Mo. Assn. of Assoc. and Mcpl. Cir. Judges (pres. 1978-79), Boone County Bar Assn., (pres. 1979-80), Mo. Bar Assn. Bankruptcy, Criminal, State civil litigation. Home: 1123 Falcon Dr Columbia MO 65201-6273 Office: 1103 E Broadway # 203 Columbia MO 65201-4909

**DANOFF, ERIC MICHAEL,** lawyer; b. Waukegan, Ill., June 30, 1949; m. Barbara Madsen, May 27, 1979; children: Nicholas Madsen Danoff, Alexander Madsen Danoff. AB, Dartmouth Coll., 1971; JD, U. Calif., Berkeley, 1974. Bar: Calif. 1974, U.S. Dist. Ct. (no., cen., ea. and so. dists.) Calif., U.S. Ct. Appeals (9th cir.), U.S. Supreme Ct. Assoc. Graham & James, San Francisco, 1974-80, ptnr., 1981-97; ptnr. Kaye, Rose & Ptnrs., San Francisco, 1998—. Contbr. articles to profl. publs. Mem. Maritime Law Assn. Admiralty, Private international, General civil litigation. Office: Kaye Rose & Ptnrs 1 California St Ste 2230 San Francisco CA 94111-5423

**D'ANTONIO, GUY JOSEPH,** lawyer; b. New Orleans, Dec. 17, 1947; s. Charles J. and Maria Morettini D'Antonio; m. Marian Bergamo; children: Amy, Alison, Adrianne. JD, Loyola U., New Orleans, 1971. Bar: La.; U.S. Supreme Ct. Asst. dist. atty. St. Tammery Parish Dist. Atty., Covington, La.; pvt. practice Slidell, La. Personal injury, General civil litigation, Land use and zoning (including planning). Office: D Antonio & Assocs 2104 1st St Slidell LA 70458-3432

**D'ANTONIO, JAMES JOSEPH,** lawyer; b. Tucson, Jan. 13, 1959; s. Lawrence Patrick and Rosemary Catherine (Kane) D'A. Student, Tufts U., 1978-79; BA, U. Ariz., 1981, JD, 1984. Bar: Ariz. 1984, U.S. Dist. Ct. Ariz. 1984, U.S. Ct. Appeals (9th cir.) 1993. Assoc. Law Office of D'Antonio and D'Antonio, Tucson, 1984-93; pvt. practice law Law Offices of James J. D'Antonio, Tucson, 1993—. Chmn. bd. govs. U. Ariz. Coll. Law, 1983-84; mem. Pima County Teen Ct. Adv. Bd; mem. Health South Rehab. Inst., Tucson Cmty. Adv. Bd.; bd. dirs. Coyote Task Force. Named Outstanding Pro Bono Lawyer Pima County Vol. Lawyers Program, 1993. Fellow Ariz. Bar Found.; mem. ABA, Assn. Trial Lawyers Am., Ariz. Bar Assn., Ariz. Trial Lawyers Assn., Pima County Bar Assn. General civil litigation, Real property, Personal injury. Office: 80 S Stone Ave Tucson AZ 85701-1713

**DANZIGER, JOEL BERNARD,** lawyer; b. N.Y.C., Oct. 17, 1932; s. Harry and Mildred (Collier) D.; m. Joan Kaufman, June 15, 1958; children: Robert, Marc, Sarah. AB, Columbia U., 1953; LLB, Yale U., 1956. Bar: N.Y. 1958, Conn. 1958, U.S. Dist. Ct. (so. and ea. dists.) N.Y. 1963, U.S. Ct. Appeals (2d cir.) 1958, U.S. Supreme Ct. 1964. Ptnr. Danziger & Markhoff, White Plains, N.Y., 1958—; adj. prof. law Bridgeport (N.Y.) Law Sch., 1982-85. Mem. ABA, N.Y. Bar Assn., Westchester County Bar Assn., Yale Club. Pension, profit-sharing, and employee benefits, Estate planning, Corporate taxation. Office: Danziger & Markhoff 123 Main St White Plains NY 10601-3104

**DANZIGER, PETER,** lawyer; b. N.Y.C., Jan. 5, 1949; s. Herbert and Eleanor (Rosner) D.; m. Joan Nelick, Aug. 15, 1970; children: Lisa, Carrie, Beth. BA, U. Vt., 1970; JD, Albany Law Sch., 1973; MS, SUNY, Albany, 1977. Bar: N.Y. 1974, U.S. Dist. Ct. (no. dist.) N.Y. 1974. Assoc. O'Connell and Aronowitz, Albany, N.Y., 1973-79, sr. ptnr., 1979—; instr. Albany Law Sch., 1972-73, SUNY at Albany, 1978-88. Author: (book) Special Education Litigation, 1989, Tapping Officials Secrets, 1989, 93; author Albany Law Rev., 1972, (newspaper column) Legal Line, 1990—; editor: Representing People with Disabilities, 1989—. Legal counsel Jewish Family Svcs. of N.E. N.Y., Albany, 1977—. Named one of Best Lawyers in Am., Woodward/White Inc., 1991—. Mem. N.Y. State Trial Lawyers Assn., Am. Trial Lawyers Assn., N.Y. State Bar Assn. (chairperson com. on mental and phys. disabilities 1989-93). Libel, Product liability, Education and schools. Office: O'Connell and Aronowitz 100 State St Ste 800 Albany NY 12207-1885

**DAO, HANH D.,** lawyer; b. Thu Duc, Vietnam, May 25, 1970; came to the U.S., 1975; s. Nhi V. Dao and Thu T. Nguyen; m. Lien B. Pham, Dec. 1, 1996; 1 child, Michael D. BS in Fin., Calif. Poly. U., Pomona, 1992; JD, Boston U., 1995. Bar: Calif., Cabazon Tribal Bar. Assoc. Law Office of Robert G. Johnson, Jr., Laguna Niguel, Calif., 1995-96; ptnr. Archer & Dao, Irvine, Calif., 1996—; gen. counsel Internat. Female Boxers Assn., Palos Verdes, Calif., 1997—, The Pet Rescue Ctr., Inc., Indio, Calif., 1998—. Mem. ABA, Young Lawyers Assn. Roman Catholic. Avocations: tennis, golf. General civil litigation, Contracts commercial, General corporate. Office: Archer & Dao 13424 Verona Tustin CA 92782-9149

**D'AQUILA, BARBARA JEAN,** lawyer; b. Virginia, Minn., Aug. 2, 1955; d. Carl Mario and Dolores (Mae) Cassagrande) D'A. BBA, U. Notre Dame (Ind.), 1977; JD, U. Minn., 1979. Bar: U.S. Dist. Ct. Minn. 1980, Minn. Supreme Ct. 1980, U.S. Ct. Appeals (8th cir.) 1981, U.S. Tax Ct. 1982, U.S. Supreme Ct. 1995; CPA, Minn. Audit acct. Arthur Andersen & Co., Mpls., summer 1977; tax acct. Peat, Marwick, Mitchell & Co., Mpls., 1979-80; law clk. Minn. Supreme Ct., St. Paul, 1980-81; assoc. Briggs & Morgan, St. Paul, 1981-83; shareholder/ptnr. Hart, Bruner & O'Brien, P.A., Mpls., 1983-91; assoc. Moss & Barnett, A Profl. Assn., Mpls., 1991-93; ptnr. Flynn & Gaskins, L.L.P., Mpls., 1993—; mem. U.S. Dist. Ct. Minn. fed. practice com., 1985-90; mem. Lawyers Trust Acct. Bd. Supreme Ct. Minn., 1993—, chair 1995—, Bar Admissions Adv. Coun. for Bd. Law Examiners, 1995—; mem. adv. com. on rules of civil procedure Minn. Supreme Ct., 1998—. Great Plains reg. rep. Am. Heart Assn., Dallas, 1989-91, chmn. bd., Mpls., 1987-88, first vice chmn., 1986-87, treas., 1984-86; sec. chmn. United Way of Mpls., 1989-91; bd. dirs. U. Minn. Law Sch., 1991—. Recipient Disting. Svc. award Am. Heart Assn., 1988. Mem. ABA (EEO com., labor and employment sect., 1992—), Minn. Bar Assn. (labor and employment law sect. 1989—), AICPA, Minn. Soc. CPAs, Beta Gamma Sigma, Beta Alpha Psi. Avocations: golf, swimming, travel, reading, theatre, arts. Labor, Federal civil litigation, State civil litigation. Office: Flynn & Gaskins LLP 2900 Met Ctr 333 S 7th St Ste 2900 Minneapolis MN 55402-2440

**DARBY, KAREN SUE,** legal education administrator; b. Columbus, Ohio, Sept. 15, 1947; d. Emerson Curtis and Kathryn Elizabeth (Bowers) Dum; m. R. Russell Darby, Dec. 21, 1974; children: David Randolph, Michael Emerson. BA magna cum laude, Capital U., Columbus, 1969; JD, Ohio State U., 1980. Bar: Ohio 1980, U.S. Dist. Ct. (so. dist.) Ohio 1981, Pa. 1998. High sch. English tchr. Columbus Pub. Schs., 1969-72; employee rels. specialist GE, Circleville, Ohio, 1972-74; mgr. EEO and manpower programs chem. met. div. GE, Worthington, Ohio, 1974-77; atty. Ohio Legal Rights Svc., Columbus, 1980-81; pvt. practice Columbus, 1981-90; assoc. dir. Ohio Continuing Legal Edn. Inst., Columbus, 1989-95; dir. Phila. Bar Edn. Ctr., 1995-97; assoc. dir. Pa. Bar Inst., Phila., 1997—; mem. rules adv. com. Supreme Ct. Ohio, Columbus, 1989-94. Author, editor: Civil Commitment in Ohio - A Manual for Respondents' Attorneys, 1980. Mem. divorce mediation panel Ohio State U. Commn. on Interprofl. Edn., Columbus, 1988-91; vol. Boy Scouts Am., Columbus, 1988-92, Columbus Pub. Schs., 1984-95. Mem. Pa. Bar Assn., Ohio State Bar Assn. (mem. family law com. 1991-95)., Assn. Continuing Legal Edn., Phila. Bar Assn. Democrat. Lutheran. Avocations: organ, piano, gardening. Office: PBI-PBEC Edn Ctr 100 Penn Sq E Philadelphia PA 19107-3322

**DARDECK, STEPHEN A.,** lawyer; b. N.Y.C., Aug. 13, 1945; s. Philip A. and Shirley R. (Hahn) D.; m. Judith K. Simpson, July 19, 1970; chi ldren: Adam, Aaron. BA, U. Pa., 1967; M in Journalism, U. Calif., Berkeley, 1968; JD, Boston U. Law Sch., 1973. Bar: Vt. 1973, U.S. Dist. Ct. Vt. 1973, U.S. Ct. Appeals (2d cir.) 1990. Dep. state's atty. Rutland County State's Atty.'s Office, Vt., 1973-78; ptnr. Tepper, Dardeck, Rutland, 1978—. Family and matrimonial, Personal injury, Real property. Office: Tepper Dardeck 73 Center St Rutland VT 05701-4046

**DARDEN, CHRISTOPHER A.,** lawyer, actor, writer. BA in Criminal Justice, Calif. State U., San Jose; JD, U. Calif., San Francisco, 1980. Bar: Calif. 1980. Former atty. Nat. Labor Rels. Bd.; former asst. head dep. in spl. investigations divsn. L.A. County Dist. Attys. Office, former dep. dist. atty. in maj. crimes divsn.; actor, writer, 1996—; assoc. prof. law Sch. Law Southwestern U., L.A., 1996—. Author: (with Jeff Walter) In Contempt, 1996. Address: Brokaw Company 9255 W Sunset Blvd Ste 804 Los Angeles CA 90069-3305 Office: Southwestern U Sch Law 675 S Westmoreland Ave Los Angeles CA 90005

**DARIO, RONALD ANTHONY,** lawyer; b. Hoboken, N.J., Aug. 12, 1968; s. Ronald Anthony and Claire D.; m. Lorraine Baumann, July 14, 1996. BA, Rutgers U., 1990; JD, Bklyn. Law Sch., 1995. Bar: N.Y., N.J., U.S. Dist. Ct., U.S. Ct. Appeals, U.S. Tax Ct. Assoc. Lenza & Agrapidis, P.C., Hackensack, N.J., 1995—. Recipient Senator Bill Bradley award, 1986, Am. Jurisprudence award, Bklyn Law Sch., 1992; Hudson County (N.J.) Bar Assn. scholar, 1993, 94. Personal injury, Municipal (including bonds), Family and matrimonial. Home: 292 E Lanza Ct Saddle Brook NJ 07663-6023 Office: Leanza & Agrapidis PC 255 Rt 17 S Hackensack NJ 07601

**DARIOTIS, TERRENCE THEODORE,** lawyer; b. Chgo., Feb. 28, 1946; s. Theodore S. and Dorothy Mizzen (Thompson) D.; m. Jeanne Elizabeth Gibbons, Oct. 24, 1970; children: Sara Mizzen, Kristin Elizabeth, Jennifer Ann. BA in Philosophy, St. Joseph's Coll., Rensselaer, Ind., 1969; JD, Loyola U., Chgo., 1973. Bar: Ill. 1973, Fla. 1975, U.S. Tax Ct. 1993, U.S. Supreme Ct., 1978. Law clk. to presiding justice Appellate Ct. of Ill. (2d dist.), Waukegan, 1973-74; assoc. Keith Kinderman, Tallahassee, 1975-76; sole practitioner Tallahassee, 1976-82; ptnr. Kahn and Dariotis, P.A., Tallahassee, 1982-96, Warfel, Goldberg, Dariotis, Waldoch & Olive, P.A., Tallahassee, 1996—; adj. prof. Fla. State U. Coll. Bus., 1987-93. Roman Catholic. Probate, Estate planning, Real property. Office: Warfel Goldberg Dariotis Waldoch & Olive PA 2120 Killarney Way Tallahassee FL 32308-3402

**DARKE, RICHARD FRANCIS,** lawyer; b. Detroit, June 17, 1943; s. Francis Joseph and Irene Anne (Potts) D.; m. Alice Mary Renger, Feb. 14, 1968; children: Kimberly, Richard, Kelly, Sean, Colin. BBA, U. Notre Dame, 1965; JD, Detroit Coll. Law, 1969. Bar: Mich. 1969. Atty. AAA, Detroit, 1969-72; assoc. Oster & Mollett P.C., Mt. Clemens, Mich., 1972-73; ptnr. Small, Darke, Oakes P.C., Southfield, Mich., 1973-77; v.p., gen. counsel, sec. Fruehauf Corp., Detroit, 1977-92; ptnr. Darke & Wilson, Grosse Pointe Woods, Mich., 1993—. Mem. ABA, Mich. Bar Assn., Detroit Bar Assn., Machinery and Allied Products Inst. (counsel), Mich. Gen. Counsel Group, Essex Country Club, Lockmoor Club. Roman Catholic. Avocation: golfing. General corporate, Private international, Real property. Home: 23173 Alger Ln Saint Clair Shores MI 48080-2624 Office: Darke & Wilson Ste 580 Pointe Plz 1925 1 Mack Ave Grosse Pointe Woods MI 48236

**DARLING, JAMES EDWARD,** lawyer; b. Rochester, N.Y., Jan. 14, 1949; s. Ralph Edward Darling and Doris Irene (Mack) Essig; m. Sandra Luz Mendoza, July 18, 1987. BA, Baylor U., 1975, JD, 1977. Bar: Tex. 1978, U.S. Dist. Ct. (so. dist.) Tex. 1979. Asst. atty. City of McAllen, Tex., 1979, atty., 1979-83; assoc. Fulbright & Jaworski, Houston, 1980-81; ptnr. Ellis, Koenek & Darling, McAllen, 1982-86; pvt. practice McAllen, 1986—; cons. Hidalgo County Elected Officials Assn., McAllen, 1987—. Trustee McAllen Firemens' Pension Bd., 1981—; campaign asst. United Way, McAllen, 1986-88; pres. McAllen Boys' Club, 1987-88. Served with USAF, 1967-71, Vietnam. Decorated D.F.C.; recipient Meritorious Service award City of McAllen, 1980. Mem. ABA, Hidalgo County Bar Assn. (bd. dirs. 1985-87, speaker 1986-87), Nat. Inst. of Mcpl. Law Officers (chmn. federalism sect. 1985), Tex. City Attys. Assn. Baptist. State and local taxation, Land use and zoning (including planning). Office: 3301 N Mccoll Rd Mcallen TX 78501-5536

**DARLING, SCOTT EDWARD,** lawyer; b. Los Angeles, Dec. 31, 1949; s. Dick R. and Marjorie Helen (Otto) D.; m. Cynthia Diane Harrah, June 1970 (div.); 1 child, Smokie; m. Deborah Lee Cochran, Aug. 22, 1981; children: Ryan, Jacob. BA, U. Redlands, 1972; JD, U.S.C., 1975. Bar: Calif. 1976, U.S. Dist. Ct. (cen. dist.) Calif. 1976. Assoc. atty. Elver, Falsetti, Boone & Crafts, Riverside, 1976-78; ptnr. Falsetti, Crafts, Pritchard & Darling, Riverside, 1978-84; pres. Scott Edward Darling, A Profl. Corp., Riverside, 1984—; grant reviewer HHS, Washington, 1982-88; judge pro tem Riverside County Mcpl. Ct., 1980, Riverside County Superior Ct., 1987-88; bd. dirs. Tel Law Nat. Legal Pub. Info. System, Riverside, 1978-80. Author, editor: Small Law Office Computer Legal System, 1984. Bd. dirs. Youth Adv. Com. to Selective Svc., 1968-70, Am. Heart Assn. Riverside County, 1978-82, Survival Ministries, 1986-89; atty. panel Calif. Assn. Realtors, L.A., 1980—; pres. Calif. Young Reps., 1978-80; mem. GI Forum, Riverside, 1970-88; presdl. del. Nat. Rep. Party, 1980-84; asst. treas. Calif. Rep. Party, 1981-83; Rep. Congl. candidate, Riverside, 1982; treas. Riverside Sickle Cell Found., 1980-82, recipient Eddie D. Smith award; pres. Calif. Rep. Youth Caucus, 1980-82; v.p. Riverside County Red Cross, 1982-84; mem. Citizen's Univ. Com., Riverside, 1978-84, World Affairs Council, 1978-82, Urban League, Riverside, 1980-82. Calif. Scholarship Fedn. (life). Named one of Outstanding Young Men in Am., U.S. Jaycees, 1979-86. Mem. ABA, Riverside County Bar Assn., Speaker's Bur. Riverside County Bar Assn., Riverside Jaycees, Riverside C. of C. Lodge: Native Sons of Golden West. Avocations: skiing, swimming, reading. Real property, Personal injury, Estate taxation. Office: 3697 Arlington Ave Riverside CA 92506-3938

**DARLING, STANTON GIRARD,** lawyer; b. Loudonville, Ohio, Apr. 13, 1920; s. Ira Jay and Pauline Esther (Miller) D.; m. Carolyn R. Miceli, Mar. 21, 1942; children: Stanton Girard II, Kaye Michele. BA, Ohio State U., 1947, JD, 1948. Bar: Ohio 1948, U.S. Dist. Bar (ea. and so. dists.) Ohio. Ptnr. Darling & Keister, Columbus, Ohio, 1948—; lectr. on real property and condominium law Ohio Bar Continuing Legal Studies, 1964-66. Author: Condominiums in Ohio, 1964. Atty. Heisey Collectors Am., Newark, Ohio, 1970—, North Market Assn., Columbus, 1985—. lst sgt. inf. AUS, 1941-45, ETO. Decorated Purple Heart with oak leaf cluster, Bronze Star with two oak leaf clusters. Mem. Ohio Bar Assn., Columbus Bar Assn. Republican. Avocations: studying antiques, art. Finance, General corporate, Probate. Home and Office: 234 Erie Rd Columbus OH 43214-3638

**DARLING, STEPHEN EDWARD,** lawyer; b. Columbia, S.C., Apr. 12, 1949; s. Norman Rushton and Elizabeth (Clarkson) D.; m. Denise Howell, June 30, 1979; children: Julia Hanley, Edward McCrady, Elizabeth Rushton. BS in Banking, Fin., Real Estate, Ins., U. S.C., 1971, JD, 1974. Bar: S.C. 1974, U.S. Dist. Ct. S.C. 1975, U.S. Ct. Appeals (4th cir.) 1975, U.S. Ct. Appeals (5th cir.) 1976, U.S. Supreme Ct. 1982. From assoc. to ptnr. Sinkler, Gibbs & Simons, Charleston, S.C., 1974-87; ptnr. Sinkler & Boyd, Charleston, 1987—. Mem. ABA, S.C. Bar Assn., S.C. Def. Trial Attys. Assn. (exec. com. 1994—), Charleston County Bar Assn. (exec. com. 1989-90, 92-93), Internat. Assn. Def. Counsel, Southeastern Admiralty Law Inst., Met. Exch. Club (Charleston) (sec. 1980). Episcopalian. Federal civil litigation, State civil litigation, Product liability. Home: 23 New St Charleston SC 29401-2405 Office: Sinkler & Boyd 160 E Bay St Charleston SC 29401-2120

**DARLOW, JULIA DONOVAN,** lawyer; b. Detroit, Sept. 18, 1941; d. Frank William Donovan and Helen Adele Turner; m. George Anthony Gratton Darlow (div.); 1 child, Gillian; m. John Corbett O'Meara. AB, Vassar Coll., 1963; postgrad., Columbia U. Law Sch., 1964-65; J.D. cum laude, Wayne State U., 1971. Bar: Mich. 1971, U.S. Dist. Ct. (ea. dist.) Mich. 1971. Assoc. Dickinson, Wright, McKean, Cudlip & Moon, Detroit, 1971-78; ptnr. Dickinson, Wright, Moon, Van Dusen & Freeman, Detroit, 1978—; adj. prof. Wayne State U. Law Sch., 1974-75, 96; commr. State Bar Mich., 1977-87, mem. exec. com., 1979-83, 84-87, sec. 1980-81, v.p., 1984-85, pres.-elect 1985-86, pres. 1986-87, coun. corp. fin. and bus. law sect. 1980-86, coun. computer law sect. 1985-88; mem. State Officers Compensation Commn., 1994-96; chair Mich. Supreme Ct. Task Force on Gender Issues in the Cts., 1987-89. Reporter: Mich. Nonprofit Corp. Act, 1977-82. Bd. dirs. Hutzel Hosp., 1984—, Mich. Opera Theater, 1985—, Mich. Women's Found., 1986-91, Detroit Med. Ctr., 1990—, Marygrove Coll., 1996—; trustee Internat. Inst. Met. Detroit, 1986-92, Mich. Met. coun. Girl Scouts U.S., 1988-91, Detroit coun. Boy Scouts Am., 1988—; mem. exec. com. Mich. Coun. for Humanities 1988-92; mem. Blue Cross-Blue Shield Prospective Reimbursement Com., Detroit, 1979-81; v.p., mem. exec. com. United Found., 1988-95; mem. Mich. Gov.'s Bilateral Trade Team for Germany, 1992-98. Fellow Am. Bar Found. (Mich. State chairperson 1990-96; mem. state officers compensation commn., 1994-96); mem. Detroit Bar Assn. Found. (treas. 1984-85, trustee 1982-85), Mich. Bar Found. (trustee 1987-94), Am. Judicature Soc. (bd. dirs. 1985-88), Internat. Women's Forum (global affairs com. 1994—), Women Lawyers Assn. (pres. 1977-78), Mich. Women's Campaign Fund (charter), Detroit Athletic Club. Democrat. General corporate, Contracts commercial, Private international. Office: Dickinson Wright Moon Van Dusen & Freeman 500 Woodward Ave Ste 4000 Detroit MI 48226-3416

**DARNALL, DARLEEN R.,** lawyer; b. Montebello, Calif., July 7, 1962; d. John Everett and Mary Irene Mock; m. Jeffrey Scott Darnall, Aug. 17, 1985 (div. Jan. 1998). BA, George Fox Coll., 1984; JD, U. Mich. Law Sch., 1989. Assoc. Honigman, Miller, Schwartz & Cohn, Detroit, 1989-90, Dykema Gossett, Detroit, 1990-92, Bullivant Houser, Portland, Oreg., 1992-95; assoc., ptnr. Davis Wright Tremaine, L.L.P., Portland, Oreg., 1995—. Pres., bd. mem. Open Adoption and Family Svcs., Portland, 1995—; mem. bd. govs. Congenital Heart Rsch. Ctr., Oreg. Health Scis. U., Portland, 1998—. Mem. Mich. Bar Assn., Washington Bar Assn., Oreg. Bar Assn., Oreg. Women Lawyers. Democrat. Mem. Soc. of Friends. Appellate, General civil litigation. Office: Davis Wright Tremain 2200 First Interstate Tower 1300 SW 5th Ave Ste 2200 Portland OR 97201-5682

**DAROSA, RONALD ANTHONY,** lawyer; b. Joliet, Ill., June 28, 1943; s. Edmund A. and Claire L. (Turner) DaR.; m. Cynthia E. Ohlenkamp; children: Ronald II, Laurel Anne, Ryan, Samantha. BS, No. Ill. U., 1965; JD, John Marshall Law Sch., 1970. Bar: Ill. 1970, U.S. Dist. Ct. (no. dist.) Ill. 1970. Asst. state's atty. DuPage County, Wheaton, Ill., 1970-71; ptnr. Mountcastle & DaRosa, P.C., Wheaton, 1971-93; sr. ptnr. DaRosa & Miller, Wheaton, 1993—; co-chmn. DuPage County Criminal Justice Council, 1979-80. Chmn. Zoning Bd. Appeals, Glen Ellyn, Ill., 1975-77; mayor Village of Glen Ellyn (cert. appreciation 1981), 1977-81; pres. Mayors and Mgrs. Conf. (cert. appreciation 1981), DuPage County, 1980-81; commr. Du Page Airport Authority, 1987-90. Recipient 10-Yr. cert. appreciation Dupage County Child Conciliation Oversight Com., 1998. Fellow Am. Acad. Matrimonial Lawyers; mem. ABA, Ill. Bar Assn., DuPage County Bar Assn. (chmn. matrimonial law com. 1981-82, bd. dirs. 1984-85). Republican. Roman Catholic. Club: Medinah Country. Family and matrimonial. Office: DaRosa & Miller 208 N West St Wheaton IL 60187-5064

**DARR, CAROL C.,** lawyer; b. Apr. 24, 1951; d. Patt M. and Justine D.; m. Albert Louis May III Dec. 19, 1992. BA, U. Memphis, 1973, JD, 1976; M.Litt, Christ's Coll., Cambridge U., 1995. Bar: Tenn. 1977, D.C. 1981. Atty. Fed. Election Commn., 1976-77; asst. counsel U.S. Senate Com. on Rules & Adminstrn., 1977-79; dep. gen counsel Carter/Mondale Presidential Com., 1979-81; in house counsel Dem. Nat. Com., 1981-82; assoc. Skadden, Arps, Slate, Meagher & Flom, 1983-85; chief counsel Dukakis/Bentsen Com., Inc., 1987-91; gen. counsel Dem. Nat. Com., 1991-92; with Clinton/Gore Transition Com., 1992-93; actg. gen. counsel, dep. gen. counsel U.S. Dept. Commerce, 1993-94; assoc. Adminstrn. Nat. Telecom. and Info. Agy., Office Internat. Affairs, 1994-96; v.p. govt. affairs Info. Tech. Industry Coun., Washington, 1996-98; sr. v.p. bus. and pub. affairs Interactive Digital Software Assn., 1998—. Author: Political Parties, Presidential Campaigns, and National Party Conventions, 1992; Contributions and Expenditures by National, State, and Local Party Conventions, 1990; Active Corporate Participation, 1993; Candidates and Parties 1982, Registration and Reporting, 1981. Recipient U. Memphis Outstanding Young Alumnus award 1982. Mem. ABA, Fed. Bar Assn. (chair. com. on political campaigns and election laws 1983-85.

**DARRELL, BARTON DAVID,** lawyer; b. Jacksonville, Tex., June 3, 1961; s. Bob and Nelda (Peeples) D. Student, Ind. U., 1979-81; BA, Ky. Wesleyan Coll., Owensboro, 1984; JD, U. Louisville, 1987. Bar: Ky. 1987, U.S. Dist. Ct. Ky. 1987. Assoc. Bell, Orr, Ayers & Moore, Bowling Green, Ky., 1987—. Chmn. bd. ARC, Bowling Green, 1989—. Mem. ABA, Ky. Bar Assn. (bd. dirs. Young Lawyers sect.), Bowling Green-Warren County Bar Assn. (community rels. com.), Bowling Green-Warren County Jaycees (atty. 1988-89, exec. bd. 1988-89), Lions. Workers' compensation, General civil litigation, Insurance. Office: Bell Orr Ayers & Moore 1010 College St # 738 Bowling Green KY 42101-2144

**DARROW, DWIGHT DANIEL,** lawyer; b. Hartford, Conn., Aug. 3, 1958; s. Daniel Porter and Lois (Kraft) D.; children: Daniel Edward, Stephen Michael. AA, U. Hartford, 1977; B, Colby Coll., 1979; JD, Marquette U., 1982. Bar: Wis. 1982, U.S. Dist. Ct. (ea. and we. dists.) 1982, U.S. Ct. Appeals (7th cir.) 1982; cert. in family law, and civil law trial advocacy, Nat. Bd. Trial Advocacy. Ptnr. Gruhle, Fessler, Van de Water and Darrow, Sheboygan, Wis., 1982-89; pres. Darrow, Dietrich & Hawley S.C., Sheboygan, 1989—; bd. dirs. Newton (Wis.) State Bank. Alderman Sheboygan Falls (Wis.) City Council, 1987-90; pres. Bowling Classic Inc., Sheboygan, 1987-91; pres. bd. dirs. Big Bros. and Big Sisters of Sheboygan County, Inc. Mem. Am. Trial Lawyers Assn. Republican. Methodist. Personal injury, General civil litigation, Family and matrimonial. Office: Darrow Dietrich & Hawley SC PO Box 1001 Sheboygan WI 53082-1001

**DARTEZ, SHANNON SEILER,** lawyer; b. New Orleans, June 25, 1968; d. Sidney Louis and Marilyn (Abbott) Seiler; m. Tim Paul Durbin, Sept. 1, 1990 (div. Aug. 1996); m. Michael Wayne Dartez, Oct. 10, 1998. BA, La. State U., 1990, JD, 1994. Bar: La., 1994, U.S. Dist. Ct. (we. dist.) La., 1994, Chitimacha Indian Tribal Ct. Assoc. Simien & Miniex, Lafayette, La., 1995-96, Hurlburt, Privat & Monrose, Lafayette, 1996—. Mem. Lafayette Young Lawyers Assn. (coord. cmty. svcs. 1996-97, treas. 1997-99, pres.-elect 1999—), Jr. League Lafayette. Republican. Roman Catholic. Workers' compensation, Insurance, Personal injury. Office: Hurlburt Privat & Monrose PO Box 4407 Lafayette LA 70502-4407

**DAS, ARUN,** lawyer; b. N.Y.C., Dec. 29, 1948; s. Kamal and Jean D.; m. Richela F. Lau, Oct. 13, 1985; 1 child, Alexander. BA with honors, Haverford Coll., 1970; JD cum laude, Boston Coll., 1981. Bar: Colo. 1981, U.S. Dist. Ct. Colo. 1981, U.S. Ct. Appeals (10th cir.) 1982. Law clk. to presiding judge U.S. Dist. Ct. Colo., Denver, 1981-82; assoc. Gorsuch,

Kirgis, Campbell, Walker & Grover, Denver, 1982-87; ptnr. Gorsuch Kirgis LLP, Denver, 1987—, exec. com., 1994-96. Mem. ABA, Colo. Bar Assn., Denver Bar Assn. (former co-chair labor law com.), Asian Am. Bar Assn. Colo. Avocations: sports, gardening. Labor, General civil litigation, Immigration, naturalization, and customs. Office: Gorsuch Kirgis LLP Ste 1000 1401 Arapahoe St Twr 1 Denver CO 80202

**DAS, KALYAN,** lawyer; b. Calcutta, India, June 23, 1956; s. Amulyaratan and Chaitaly (Mitra) D.; m. Pia Mukherjee, Feb. 18, 1986; children: Sabrina, Rahul. Barrister-at-Law, The Lincoln's Inn, London, 1979; Diploma, Assoc. of the Chartered Inst. of Arbitrators, London, 1980; LLM, NYU, 1989. Bar: Eng. 1979, Wales 1979, N.Y. 1983; advocate Supreme Ct. India, 1981; barrister and solicitor Melbourne, Australia, 1984. Barrister-at-law Fountain Ct. Temple, London, 1980-81; assoc. Malcolm A. Hoffmann, N.Y.C., 1981-82, White & Case, N.Y.C., 1983-88, Milbank, Tweed, Hadley & McCloy, N.Y.C., 1988-90; assoc. Seward & Kissel, N.Y.C., 1990-93, ptnr., 1993—. Editor: Company Law, 1980. Internat. v.p. Internat. Students' Trust, London, 1987—. Fellow Am. Coll. Investment Counsel (co-chair ann. meeting 1998); mem. ABA, N.Y. State Bar Assn., Assn. Bar City of N.Y., Am. Arbitration Assn. (panel mem.), Hon. Soc. Lincoln's Inn, Wine Soc. London, Met. Club (N.Y.C.). Avocations: sailing, tennis, travel. Banking, Contracts commercial, Finance. Home: 107 W 89th St Ph B New York NY 10024-1944 Office: Seward & Kissel 1 Battery Park Plz Fl 21 New York NY 10004-1485

**DASHOW, JULES,** lawyer; b. Bklyn., June 27, 1909; s. Raphael and Minnie D.; m. Nell Bromberg Dashow, Dec. 17, 1934; children: Russell, Deborah Beth Ruth, James. AB, U. Ill., Urbanna, 1930, JD, 1932. Bar: Ill., U.S. DIst. Ct. (so. dist.), U.S. Ct. Appeals, 1938, U.S. Supreme Ct., 1960. Sr. ptnr. Brown, Dashow, Doran, Chgo., 1932-85; mem. Am. Arbitration Assn., Chgo., 1975—; dir. Am. Res. Ins. Co., Chgo., 1970-79. Pres. North Shore Cong. Israel, Glencoe, Ill., 1965-67, Found. for Cancer Rsch., Chgo., 1975-85, New Trier Democrat Org., Winnetica Ill., 1964-72. Mem. Am. Bar Assn. Democrat. Jewish. Avocations: tennis, golf, travel. Personal income taxation, Estate taxation, Contracts commercial. Office: Altheimer & Gray 10 S Wacker Dr Fl 35 Chicago IL 60606-7482

**DASILVA, WILLARD H.,** lawyer, educator; b. Freeport, N.Y., Oct. 17, 1923; m. Frances A. DaSilva. BA, NYU, 1946; LLB, Columbia U., 1949. Bar: N.Y. 1949, U.S. Supreme Ct. 1969, U.S. Tax Ct. 1969. Sole practice, N.Y.C., 1949-70; ptnr. Goodman & DaSilva, 1970-73; sole practice, Carle Place, N.Y., 1973-76; ptnr. DaSilva & Samuelson, 1977; sole practice, Garden City, N.Y., 1978-91; ptnr. DaSilva & Keidel, Garden City, N.Y., 1992-97, DaSilva, Garson & Hilowitz LLP, 1998-99, DaSilva, Hilowitz, McEvily & Greenberg LLP, 1999—; v.p. Marcus Bros. Textile Corp., N.Y.C., 1951-63; pres. Cortley Fabrics subs. Cone Mills Corp., N.Y.C., 1964-65; lectr. Columbia U. Law Sch., Bklyn. Law Sch., St. John's Law Sch., Cardozo Law Sch., Touro Law Sch; faculty Practising Law Inst., N.Y.C., 1972—; trustee NAFA Found., 1977-85, North Shore U. Hosp., trustee, 1988-95, chair adv. bd. Family in Transition program, 1991—; mem. nat. panel of arbitrators Am. Arbitration Assn., 1965—, atty. comsn. Edn. and Assistance Corp., 1992-97. Lt. USAAF, 1942-46. Fellow ABA (mem. family law sect. 1977—, family law sect. coun. 1992—, mem. litigation sect. 1984-95, editor-in-chief Family Avocate 1981—), N.Y. State Bar Found.; mem. Am. Coll. Family Trial Lawyers (diplomate), Am. Acad. Matrimonial Lawyers (pres. 1982-84, bd. mgrs. 1977—), Assn. Trial Lawyers Am., N.Y. State Trial Lawyers Assn., N.Y. State Bar Assn. (continuing legal edn. com. 1980-90, program chmn. family law sect. 1978-82, gen. practice sect. 1988—, sec. 1994-95, mat. com. chair 1989—, council 1992—, chmn.-elect 1995-96, chmn. 1996-97), Nassau County Bar Assn., Suffolk County Bar Assn. (chmn. family law sect. 1982-84), Internat. Soc. on Family Law, Am. Soc. Writers on Legal Subjects, Phi Beta Kappa. Editor Matrimonial Law Jour., 1977-85; author N.Y. Matrimonial Practice, 1980—; editor, author Family Law Practice Systems Manual, 1982—; editor Fairshare mag., 1985—, N.Y. Matrimonial Caselaw, 1985—; editor-in-chief N.Y. Domestic Rels. Reporter, 1992—; contbr. articles to legal jours. Family and matrimonial, Real property, General civil litigation. Office: 585 Stewart Ave Garden City NY 11530-4783

**DASINGER, THOMAS EDGAR,** lawyer; b. Brewton, Ala., Mar. 9, 1968; s. Michael Anton and Sharon Rae (Hoiles) D. BS, U. South Ala., 1991; JD, U. Ala., Montgomery, 1994. Asst. dist. atty. Baldwin County Dist. Atty. Office, Bay Minette, Ala., 1994-96; assoc. James W. May & Assocs., Foley, Ala., 1997—. Episcopalian. Avocations: deep sea fishing, golf, boating. Criminal, Personal injury, Family and matrimonial. Office: James W May & Assocs PC PO Box 549 Foley AL 36536-0549

**DASTIN, ROBERT EARL,** lawyer; b. Manchester, N.H., July 19, 1934; s. Bertrand O. and Julia (Cole) D.; m. Patricia K. Linehan, Feb. 22, 1969; children: Matthew B., Robert J. BA, Boston U., 1960, JD, 1964, LLM in Taxation, 1968. Bar: N.H. 1964. Ptnr. Sheehan, Phinney, Bass & Green, P.A., Manchester, 1964—; dir. Selective Svc. for State of N.H., 1994—; chair Employer Support of Guard and Res. for N.H., 1997—; bd. dirs. Amoskeag Industries, Inc. Trustee Camp Belknap-YMCA, Concord, N.H., 1982—; bd. dirs. N.H. Cath. Charities, 1987—, N.H. YMCA, Concord, 1990—, N.H. Symphony Orch., 1995—; bd. dirs., pres. N.H. YMCA, 1994—. Brig. gen. N.H. Air N.G., 1985-94. Mem. ABA, N.H. Bar Assn., Manchester Bar Assn. Republican. Roman Catholic. Avocations: golf, gardening, skiing. General corporate, Estate planning, Non-profit and tax-exempt organizations. Office: Sheehan Phinney Bass & Green PA PO Box 3701 Manchester NH 03105-3701

**DAUBNER, SUSAN MOORE,** lawyer; b. Fairborn, Ohio, Nov. 22, 1967; d. Ralph Baldwin and Carolyn (Goodridge) Moore; m. Philip Daubner, Sept. 3, 1994. BA, U. Vt., 1990; JD, Albany Law Sch., 1994. Bar: N.Y. 1995, U.S. Dist. Ct. (we. dist.) N.Y. 1996. Assoc. Ziff, Weiermiller & Hayden, Elmira, N.Y., 1994—. Mem. N.Y. State Bar Assn. (del.). Family and matrimonial, Personal injury, Estate taxation. Office: Ziff Weiermiller & Hayden 303 William St Elmira NY 14901-2829

**DAUCHOT, LUKE LUCIEN,** lawyer; b. Ghent, Belgium, Oct. 12, 1961; came to U.S., 1972; s. Paul J. and Elise E. (Claeys) D.; m. Carol M. Manning, Jan. 2, 1987; children: Nicholas, Christopher, Elise. BA, Case Western Res. U., Cleve., 1983, JD, 1986. Bar: Ill. 1986, Ohio 1988. Assoc. Baker & McKenzie, Chgo., 1986-88, Squire Sanders & Dempsey, Cleve., 1988-92; ptnr. Thompson Hine & Flory PLL, Cleve., 1992—. Mem. Inn of Ct. (barrister), Phi Beta Kappa. Federal civil litigation, State civil litigation, Intellectual property. Office: Thompson Hine & Flory PLL 3900 Key Center 127 Public Sq Cleveland OH 44114-1216

**DAUGHERTY, FREDERICK ALVIN,** federal judge; b. Oklahoma City, Aug. 18, 1914; s. Charles Lemuel and Felicia (Mitchell) D.; m. Marjorie E. Green, Mar. 15, 1947 (dec. Feb. 1964); m. Betsy F. Amis, Dec. 15, 1965. LL.B., Cumberland U., 1933; postgrad., Oklahoma City U., 1934-35, LL.B. (hon.), 1974; postgrad., Okla. U., 1936-37; HHD (hon.), Okla. Christian Coll., 1976. Bar: Okla. 1937. Practiced Oklahoma City, 1937-40; mem. firm Ames, Ames & Daugherty, Oklahoma City, 1946-50, Ames, Daugherty, Bynum & Black, Oklahoma City, 1952-55; judge 7th Jud. Dist. Ct., Oklahoma City, 1955-61; U.S. dist. judge Western, Eastern and No. Dists. Okla., Oklahoma City, 1961—; chief judge Western Dist. Okla., Oklahoma City, 1972-82; mem. Fgn. Intelligence Surveillance Ct., 1981-88, Temporary Emergency Ct. Appeals, 1983-93, Multi dist. Litigation panel, 1980-90; mem. codes of conduct com. U.S. Jud. Conf., 1980-87. Active local ARC, 1956—, chmn., 1958-60, nat. bd. govs., 1963-69, 3d nat. vice chmn., 1968-69; active United Fund Greater Oklahoma City, 1957—, pres., 1961, trustee, 1963—; pres. Community Coun. Oklahoma City and County, 1967-69; exec. com. Okla. Med. Rsch. Found., 1966-69. With AUS, 1940-45, 50-52. Decorated Legion of Merit with 2 oak leaf clusters, Bronze Star with oak leaf cluster, Combat Infantrymans badge; recipient award to mankind Okla. City Sertoma Club, 1962, Outstanding Citizen award Okla. City Jr. C. ofC., 1965, Disting. Alumni citation Samford U., 1974, Disting. Svc. citation Okla. U., 1973, Constn. award Rogers State Coll., 1988, Pathmakers award Oklahoma County Hist. Soc., 1991; named to Okla. Hall of Fame, 1969. Mem. Fed. Bar Assn., Okla. Bar Assn., Am. Bar Found., Sigma Alpha Epsilon, Phi Delta Phi, Men's Dinner Club (Oklahoma City) (pres. 1966-69), Kiwanis (pres. 1957, lt. gov. 1959), Masons (33 degree, sovereign grand insp. gen. in Okla. 1982-86), Shriners, Jesters. Episcopalian (sr. warden 1957).

**DAUGHERTY, WALTER EMORY,** lawyer; b. Washington, May 7, 1926; s. Walter Emory and Juanita Lingle (Stanley) D.; m. Georgette Haigh, May 21, 1953 (div.); children: Mileva, Woodland, Valory; m. Yvonne Bigio. AB, Harvard U., 1949; LLB, U. Miami, 1953. Bar: Fla., U.S. Fed. Dist. Ct. 1953, U.S. Ct. Appeals (D.C. cir.) 1965, U.S. Supreme Ct. 1981. Atty. law firm Miami, 1953-55; pvt. practice Miami, Havana, Cuba, 1955-59, Miami, 1971, Boca Raton, Fla., 1983-96, Deerfield Beach, Fla., 1996—. With USN, 1944-46. Mem. Masons. Democrat. Congregationalist. Avocations: jazz drums. Immigration, naturalization, and customs, Aviation, Private international. Home and Office: Deer Creek 567 Sea Pine Ln Deerfield Beach FL 33442-1304

**DAUGHTON, DONALD,** lawyer; b. Grand River, Iowa, Mar. 11, 1932; s. F.J. and Ethel (Edwards) D.; m. Sally Daughton; children by previous marriage: Erin, Thomas, Andrew, J.P. BSc, U. Iowa, 1953, JD, 1956. Bar: Iowa, 1956, Ariz., 1958. Asst. county atty. Polk County, Des Moines, Iowa, 1956, 1958-59; atty. Snell & Wilmer, Phoenix, 1959-64, Browder and Daughton, Phoenix, 1964-65; judge Superior Ct. of Ariz., Phoenix, 1965-67, 97—; atty. Browder Gillenwater and Daughton, Phoenix, 1967-72, Daughton Feinstein and Wilson, Phoenix, 1972-86, Daughton Hawkins and Bacon, Phoenix, 1986-88; resident mng. ptnr. Brian Cave, Phoenix, 1988-92; atty. Daughton Hawkins Brockelman Guinnan and Patterson, Phoenix, 1992-97; asst. county atty. Polk County, 1958-59 chmn. Phoenix Employees Relations Bd., 1976. Pres. Maricopa County Legal Aid Soc., 1971-73. 1st lt. JAG, USAF, 1956-58. Fellow Am. Bar Found., Ariz. Bar Found. (founder); mem. ABA (bd. govs. 1989-92, exec. com. 1991-92), State Bar Ariz. (chmn. pub. rels. com. 1980-84, jud. evaluation poll com. 1984-94), Iowa State Bar, Maricopa County Bar Assn. (bd. dirs. 1962-64), 9th Cir. Jud. Conf. (lawyer rep. 1981-84, 88), Nat. Acad. Arbitrators, Chartered Inst. Arbitrators, Univ. Club. Federal civil litigation, State civil litigation. Home: 6021 N 51st Pl Paradise Valley AZ 85253-5143 Office: Superior Ct of Ariz 201 W Jefferson St Phoenix AZ 85003-2205

**DAUGHTREY, MARTHA CRAIG,** federal judge; b. Covington, Ky., July 21, 1942; d. Spence E. Kerkow and Martha E. (Craig) Piatt; m. Larry G. Daughtrey, Dec. 28, 1962; 1 child, Carran. BA, Vanderbilt U., 1964, JD, 1968. Bar: Tenn. 1968. Pvt. practice Nashville, 1968, asst. U.S. atty., 1968-69, asst. dist. atty., 1969-72; asst. prof. law Vanderbilt U., Nashville, 1972-75; judge Tenn. Ct. Appeals, Nashville, 1975-90; assoc. justice Tenn. Supreme Ct., Nashville, 1990-93; circuit judge U.S. Ct. Appeals (6th cir.), Nashville, 1993—; lectr. law Vanderbilt Law Sch., Nashville, 1975-82, adj. prof., 1988-90; mem. faculty NYU Appellate Judges Seminar, N.Y.C., 1977-90, 94—. Mem. bd. editors ABA Jour., 1995—; contbr. articles to profl. jours. Pres. Women Judges Fund for Justice, 1984-85, 1986-87; active various civic orgns. Recipient Athena award Nat. Athena Program, 1991. Mem. ABA (chmn. appellate judges conf. 1985-86, chmn. jud. div. 1989-90, ho. of dels. 1988-91, standing com. on continuing edn. of bar 1992-94, commn. on women in the profession 1994-97, bd. editors ABA Jour. 1995—), Tenn. Bar Assn., Nashville Bar Assn. (bd. dirs. 1988-90), Am. Judicature Soc. (bd. dirs. 1988-92), Nat. Assn. Women Judges (pres. 1985-86), Lawyers Assn. for Women (pres. Nashville 1986-87). Office: US Ct Appeals US Customs House 701 Broadway Rm 304 Nashville TN 37203-3944*

**DAUNT, JACQUELINE ANN,** lawyer; b. Flint, Mich., Dec. 2, 1953; d. Henry Thomas and Germaine Mary (Vanwayenbergh) D.; m. Ronald Glenn Decker, June 21, 1986. Student, Open U. Brussels, 1978-79; BA in Econs., U. Mich., 1975, JD, 1978. Bar: Calif. 1978, Mich. 1979. Assoc. Bronson, Bronson & McKinnen, San Francisco, 1979-81; assoc. Fenwick & West LLP, Palo Alto, Calif., 1981-85, ptnr., 1986—; mem. mgmt. com., co-chair mergers and acquisitions practice group Fenwick & West LLP, 1997—; bd. dirs. Assn. Software Design, Palo Alto, 1991-94. Author: (booklets) Venture Capital: A Strategy for High Tech Companies, 1989, Internat. Distribution, 1996, Mergers & Acquisitions: A Strategy for High Tech Companies, 1995; co-author: (booklets) Corporate Partnering: A Strategy for High Tech Companies, 1991, Structuring Effective Earnouts, 1991, Entering the U.S. Market: A Strategy for High Tech Companies, 1992. Mem. ABA, Calif. Bar Assn., Mich. Bar assn., No. Calif. Venture Capital Assn. (co-chmn. 1991-95). Avocations: horseback riding, skiing, reading, photography. Computer, General corporate, Mergers and acquisitions. Office: Fenwick & West Two Palo Alto Sq Ste 800 Palo Alto CA 94306

**D'AURORA, JACK,** lawyer; b. Steubenville, Ohio, Oct. 22, 1955; s. Anthony C. and Ann Marie D'Aurora; m. Kathleen C. D'Aurora, Apr. 9, 1983; children: Allison, John Joseph. BA, U. Notre Dame, 1977; JD, Georgetown U., 1987. Bar: Calif. 1987, Ohio 1991, Pa. 1991. Assoc. Baker & McKenzie, San Diego, 1987-89, Procopio Hargreaves Cory & Savitch, San Diego, 1989-91, Carlile Patchen & Murphy, Columbus, Ohio, 1991-93; of counsel Rishel & Kopech, Columbus, 1993-95, Rinehart Howarth Rishel & Kopech, Columbus, 1996—. Pres.-elect cons. bd. Downtown YMCA, Columbus, 1998. Lt. USN, 1977-85. Mem. C. of C. of Upper Arlington (pres. 1996). Democrat. General civil litigation, General corporate, Real property. Office: Rinehart Howarth et al 395 E Broad St Ste 330 Columbus OH 43215-3844

**DAUSTER, WILLIAM GARY,** lawyer, economist; b. Sacramento, Nov. 25, 1957; s. William Joe and Marianne Dauster; m. Ellen Lisa Weintraub, May 10, 1986; children: Matthew Isaac, Natanya Miriam, Emma Sophia. BA in Econs., Polit. Sci. and Internat. Rels., U. So. Calif., 1978, MA in Econs., 1981; JD, Columbia U., 1984. Bar: N.Y. 1985, U.S. Dist. Ct. (so. and ea. dists.) N.Y. 1985, D.C. 1986, U.S. Supreme Ct. 1997. Assoc. Cravath, Swaine & Moore, N.Y.C., 1984-86; chief counsel com. on budget U.S. Senate, Washington, 1986-94, acting staff dir., chief counsel, 1994, Dem. chief of staff, chief counsel, 1995-97, Dem. dep. staff dir., gen. coun. com. labor/human resources, 1997, Dem. chief of staff, chief counsel, 1997-98; counselor Wellstone Pres. Exploratory Com., Washington, 1998-99; dep. asst. to the Pres. for econ. policy, dep. dir. Nat. Econ. Coun., The White House, Washington, 1999—. Author: Congressional Budget Act Annotated, 1990, Budget Process Law Anntated, 1991, 1993; editor-in-chief Columbia Jour. Law and Social Problems, 1983-84; contbr. articles to profl. jours. Bd. visitors Columbia Law Sch., 1992—. Recipient Order of Palm, 1978; U. So. Calif. Trustee scholar, 1974, Harlan Fiske Stone scholar, 1982-84. Mem. ABA, D.C. Bar Assn., N.Y. Bar Assn., Skull and Dagger, Blue Key, Phi Beta Kappa, Phi Kappa Phi. Democrat. Jewish. Home: 9713 Connecticut Ave Kensington MD 20895-3528

**DAVENPORT, BRIAN LYNN,** lawyer; b. Spokane, Wash., June 11, 1947; s. Frank Joseph Davenport and Tolosa Ann (Wilson) Cartinella; m. Betty Jean Callahan, June 18, 1978; children: David, Bradley, Scott. BA, U. Nev., Reno, 1970; JD, Gonzaga U., 1976. Bar: Nev. 1976, U.S. Dist. Ct. Nev., 1977. Assoc. Echeverria & Osborne, Reno, Nev., 1976-78; lawyer pvt. practice, Reno, 1978-81; counsel First Interstate Bank, Reno, 1981-84; lawyer pvt. practice, Reno, 1984—; adj. prof. Old Coll. Sch. of Law, Reno, 1985-87; outside legal advisor to associated students U. Nev., Reno, 1987—. Mem. Phi Alpha Theta, Phi Kappa Phi, Pi Sigma Alpha. Avocations: camping, boating, reading, skiing, travel. Probate, Estate planning, General practice. Office: 458 Court St Reno NV 89501-1709

**DAVENPORT, GERALD BRUCE,** lawyer; b. Adrian, Mich., May 17, 1949; s. Bruce Nelson and Mildred Louise (Avis) D.; m. RoxAnn Ferguson, Dec. 27, 1975; children: Jonathan Gerald, Christopher Bruce, Timothy Charles. AB, U. Mich., 1971; JD, U. Tex., 1975. Bar: Tex. 1975, Okla. 1993. Pvt. practice Law Office of Gerald B. Davenport, Cedar Park, Tex., 1975-77; atty. Milchem Inc., Houston, 1977-81, Baker Hughes Prodn. Tools Inc., Houston, 1981-87; sr. atty. Baker Hughes Inc., Houston, 1987-88; gen. atty. environ. law Tex. Ea. Corp., Houston, 1988; atty. Browning-Ferris Industries, Houston, 1988-89, mgr. environ. law sect., 1989-92; asst. gen. counsel environ. law Mapco Inc., Tulsa, 1992-94; of counsel McKinney, Stringer & Webster, P.C., Tulsa, 1994-95; dir. Davenport & Williams, P.C., Tulsa, 1995-96; shareholder Hall, Estill, Hardwick, Gable, Golden & Nelson, P.C., Tulsa, 1996—. Contbr. articles to profl. jours. Mem. ABA, State Bar Tex. (environ. law sect.), Okla. Bar Assn. (environ. law sect.), Houston Bar Assn. (chmn. environ. law sect. 1992). Republican. Environmental, General corporate, Mergers and acquisitions. Office: Hall Estill Hardwick Gable Golden & Nelson PC 320 S Boston Ave Ste 400 Tulsa OK 74103-3704

**DAVENPORT, JAMES KENT,** lawyer; b. Dallas, Oct. 30, 1953; s. James R. and Betty Sue (Talbot) D.; m. Diana Gillingham, Aug. 16, 1980; children: Drew, Blake, Jennifer. BA, Emory U., Atlanta, 1975; MBA, Ga. State U., 1977; JD, So. Meth. U., Dallas, 1980. Bar: Tex. 1980, U.S. Dist. Ct. (no. dist.) Tex. 1980, U.S. Dist. Ct. (ea. dist.) Okla. 1988, U.S. Dist.Ct. (we. dist.) Tex. 1993, U.S. Ct. Appeals (5th cir.) 1985; bd. cert. civil trial law. Acct. Fox & Co., CPA, Dallas, 1980-81; asst. dist. atty. Dallas County Dist. Atty.'s Office, Dallas, 1981-84; assoc. Pailet & Dekan, Dallas, 1984-85, Newman, Shook & McManemin, Dallas, 1985-86; atty./shareholder Newman & Davenport, P.C., Dallas, 1986—; spkr. in field. Co-author: Bad Faith Litigation in Texas, 1996, also article in field. Mem. Tex. Bar Assn., Dallas Bar Assn. Fax: (214) 754-0936. General civil litigation, Insurance. Home: 11135 Lawnhaven Rd Dallas TX 75230-3549 Office: Newman & Davenport PC Allianz Fin Ctr LB135 2323 Bryan St Ste 2050 Dallas TX 75201-2651

**DAVEY, GERARD PAUL,** lawyer; b. Alton, Ill., May 31, 1949; s. Paul D. and Mary G. (O'Neill) D.; m. Martha Ann Florus, Aug. 13, 1977; children: Brian, Matthew, Kelly, Laura. BS, U. Ill., 1971; JD, U. Houston, 1974; MBA, Golden Gate U., 1982. Bar: Tex. 1974, Calif. 1977, U.S. Supreme Ct. 1978, U.S. Ct. Appeals (5th cir.) 1975, (9th cir.) 1978, U.S. Dist. Ct. (so. dist.) Tex. 1975, U.S. Dist. Ct. (cen. dist.) Calif. 1978, U.S. Dist. Ct. (so. dist.) Calif. 1988. Sec., counsel SW Group Fin., Houston, 1974-77; sole practice, Newport Beach, Calif., 1977-78; v.p., corp. counsel Century 21 Real Estate, Irvine, Calif., 1978-81, also sec., dir. all subsidiaries, 1980-81; prin. Davey Law Corp., Newport Beach, 1981-87; ptnr. Hatter & Davey, Attys., 1987—; lectr. Calif. Continuing Edn. of Bar. Author: Texas Law Institute of Coastal and Marine Resources, 1974; Contbr. articles to profl. jours. Bd. dirs. South Coast Symphony, Costa Mesa, Calif., 1984. Ill. Gen. Assembly scholar U. Ill., 1967-71. Mem. ABA (forum com. on franchising 1980—), Calif. Bar Assn. (franchising legis. com. 1983-86), Tex. Bar Assn., U. Houston Legal Hon. Soc., Kiwanis (Irvine). Franchising, Securities, General corporate.

**DAVEY, JOHN H.,** law librarian; b. Smyrna, Ga., Nov. 27, 1958; s. Kenneth Charles and Betty-Jo (Henderson) D. BM, Shorter Coll., Rome, Ga., 1980; MM, U. Mich., 1982. Law libr. Paul, Weiss, Rifkind Wharton & Garrison, N.Y.C., 1983-88, Dewey Ballantine, N.Y.C., 1988-90; asst. libr. Epstein Becker & Green, N.Y.C., 1990-95; head libr. Dechert Price & Rhoads, N.Y.C., 1995—. Law Lib. Assn. Greater N.Y. grant, 1995. Mem. Am. Assn. Law Librs. (social responsibilities chair 1997-98), Spl. Librs. Assn., Law Libr. Assn. Greater N.Y. (exec. bd. 1989-90, advt. chair 1991-96), Pvt. Law Libr. Assn. (advt. chair 1996-98). Democrat. Baptist. Home: 25 W 64th St Apt 7C New York NY 10023-6752 Office: Dechert Price & Rhoads 30 Rockefeller Plz Fl 22 New York NY 10112-2200

**DAVID, GEORGE A.,** lawyer; b. Miami, Sept. 27, 1961; s. Alexander E. and Patricia Anne D. BA, U. Fla., 1985, JD, 1989. Bar: Fla. 1991, U.S. Dist. Ct. (so. dist.) Fla. 1993. Lawyer Charlip Delgado & Befeler, Miami, 1990-91, Parrillo Weiss & O'Halloran, Miami, 1991-96, Thornton, Mastrucci & Sinclair, Miami, 1996-98, Ligman, Martin & Evans, Miami, 1998—. Mem. ABA, Dade County Bar Assn. Insurance, Personal injury, State civil litigation. Office: Ligman Martin & Evans 230 Catalonia Ave Coral Gables FL 33134-6705

**DAVID, MARILYN HATTIE,** lawyer, retired military officer; b. Biloxi, Miss., May 22, 1953; d. Walter Edward and Irma Lee (Shattles) D. BS in Psychology cum laude, Duke U., 1975; MA in Criminal Justice, Webster Coll., 1979; JD with honors, Tulane U., 1982; LLM Govt. Contracts and Procurement Law, George Washington U., 1996. Bar: Miss. 1982. Commd. 2d lt. USAF, 1975, advanced through grades to lt. col., 1991; base dir. telecom. USAF Security Svc., San Antonio, 1976-77, chief presentations prodn. br., 1977-79; asst. staff judge adv. civil and labor law USAF Air Tng. Command, Biloxi, Miss., 1982-83; asst. staff judge adv. criminal law USAF Air Tng. Command, Biloxi, 1983-84; chief of claims, civilian pers. and fiscal law USAF Pacific Air Force, Kunsan Air Base, Republic of Korea, 1984; area def. counsel USAF Judiciary, Kunsan Air Base, Republic of Korea, 1984-85; staff atty. telecom. law and policy Office of the Chief Regulatory Counsel, Def. Comm. Agy., Washington, 1985-87; trial atty. civilian pers. Air Force Gen. Litigation Divsn., Washington, 1987-90; team leader constant quality improvement tng. USAF Judge Adv. Gen.'s Dept., Washington, 1991-92; trial atty. fed. contract litigation USAF Contract Law Divsn., Washington, 1992-94; dep. dir. acquisition law USAF Devel. and Test Ctr., Fort Walton Beach, Fla., 1994-96; ret., 1996. Decorated Meritorious Svc. medal, Air Force Meritorious Svc. medal with four oak leaf clusters, Air Force Commendation medal, Nat. Def. Svc. medal, Air Force Overseas Ribbon, Air Force Longevity Svc. ribbon with four oak leaf clusters, Air Force Small Arms Expert Marksmanship ribbon, Air Force Tng. ribbon. Mem. NAFE, AAUW, Miss. Bar Assn., Ret. Officers Assn.

**DAVID, MONROE STEVEN,** lawyer; b. Westfield, Mass., Aug. 18, 1938; s. Casimir Steven David and Mildred Martha Mennen; m. Barbara Anne Behnke, Jan. 28, 1960; children: Stephen Mark, Todd Douglas. BA, Valparaiso U., 1960; JD, John Marshall Law Sch., 1966. Bar: Ill. 1966, Tenn. 1993, U.S. Dist. Ct. (we. dist.) Tenn. 1993. Fire marshal Republic Steel Corp., Chgo., 1960-65; dir. labor rels. Warwick Electronics, Chgo., 1966-75; dir. human resources Hunko Corp., Memphis, 1975-76; v.p. human resources Kraft Inc., Chgo., 1977-84; v.p. United Stationers Inc., Des Plaines, Ill., 1985-86; owner Franklin Printing, Memphis, 1987-90; atty. in pvt. practice Memphis, 1991—. Mem. Tenn. Bar Assn., Memphis Bar Assn. Lutheran. Avocations: woodworking, travel. General practice, General corporate, General civil litigation. Office: Law Office 7204 Skidmore Cv Memphis TN 38119-8907

**DAVID, REUBEN,** lawyer; b. Baghdad, Iraq, June 12, 1928; came to U.S., 1951; s. Isaac Solomon David and Tefaha (Nisan) Solomon D.; m. Nesta Paley David; 1 child, Aram. License in Law, Iraq Law Coll., Baghdad, 1951; BA, NYU, 1958, JD, 1962. Bar: Iraq 1951, N.Y. 1969. Asst. corp. counsel City of N.Y., 1970-76, chief legal unit dept. personnel, 1976-78; dep. dir. for legal affairs N.Y.C. Employees' Retirement System, 1978—. Mem. ABA, N.Y. State Bar Assn. General civil litigation, Pension, profit-sharing, and employee benefits. Home: 30 5th Ave New York NY 10011-8859 Office: 220 Church St Rm 1607 New York NY 10013-2904

**DAVID, ROBERT JEFFERSON,** lawyer; b. New Roads, La., Aug. 10, 1943; s. Joseph Jefferson and Doris Marie (Olinde) D.; m. Stella Marie Scott, Jan. 21, 1967; children: Robert J. Jr., Richard M. BA, Southeastern La. U., 1966; JD, Loyola U., New Orleans, 1969. Bar: U.S. Dist. Ct. (ea. dist.) La. 1969, U.S. Dist. Ct. (mid. dist.) La. 1969, U.S. Dist. Ct. (we. dist.) La. 1975. Assoc. Gainsburgh, Benjamin, Fallon, David, New Orleans, 1969-74; ptnr. Gainsburgh, Benjamin, David, New Orleans, 1974—; adj. faculty mem. Tulane U. Sch. Law, New Orleans, 1982-84, law sch. Loyola U., New Orleans, 1996; pres. Arden Cahill Acad. PTL, New Orleans, 1979-80, lectr., speaker continuing legal edn. seminars. Staff mem. Loyola U. Law Rev., 1967-69. Reader, recorder for La. Blind and Handicapped, 1986-91; charter mem. Lawyers for Alliance for Nuclear Arms Control, New Orleans, 1986—. Mem. ABA (malpractice com.), ATLA, Nat. Bd. Trial Advocacy, Am. Bd. Profl. Liability Attys., La. State Bar Assn. (asst. examiner commn. on bar admissions 1974-93, spl. ins. commn. 1974-82, med. legal interprofl. com. 1987—, co-chmn. 1991-94, contbr. Bar Assn. Jour. column on Profl. Liability 1989—), La. Bar Found., La. Trial Lawyers Assn. (bd. govs. 1981-83, 95-96, exec. com. 1996-97, coun. of dirs. 1997—, contbg. editor Civil Trial Tactics manual 1981, chmn. sect. med. malpractice 92-94, legis. com., exec. com. 1996—), Kappa Sigma, Phi Alpha Delta. Avocation: sports. Health, Personal injury, General civil litigation. Home: 21 Cypress Point Ln New Orleans LA 70131-3351 Office: Gainsburgh Benjamin David 2800 Energy Ctr New Orleans LA 70163

**DAVID, SHIRLEY HART,** law librarian; b. Camp Lejeune, N.C., Oct. 21, 1949; d. Allen Lewis Hart and Florence Marie (Novak) Rainey; m. Donald John David, June 18, 1971. BA in LS and Polit. Sci., Coll. of St. Catherine, St. Paul, 1971. Librarian Minn. State Law Library, St. Paul, 1971-83; dir. Sacramento County Law Library, Sacramento, 1983—, sec. found., 1986—;

del. White Ho. Conf. on Librs. and Info. Svcs., 1990. Recipient Liberty Bell award Sacramento County Bar Assn., 1985. Mem. Am. Assn. Law Librs. (sec.-treas. state ct. and county spl. interest sect. 1988-89, v.p., pres.elect 1998-99, exec. bd. 1990-93), Coun. Calif. County Law Librs. (v.p. 1984-86, pres. 1986-88), No. Calif. Assn. Law Librs. (v.p. 1987-88, pres. 1988-89, bd. dirs. 1989-90), Calif. Fedn. Bus. and Profl. Women, Downtown Capitol Local Orgn. (legis. chair 1985-92). Avocations: sailing, traveling, reading. Office: Sacramento County Law Libr 720 9th St Rm L6 Sacramento CA 95814-1311

**DAVID, THEODORE MARTIN,** lawyer, educator; b. Passaic, N.J., July 29, 1947. BA, Rutgers U., 1969; JD, N.Y. Law Sch., 1974; LLM in Tax Law, NYU, 1977. Trial atty. U.S. Tax Ct., Litigation Divsn., IRS, N.Y.C., 1974-78; pvt. practice law Hackensack, N.J., 1980—; prof. Fairleigh Dickinson U., Hackensack, 1980—. Contbr. articles to profl. jours. Mem. Bergen County Bar Assn. (chmn. tax com. 1980—), Bergen County Bar Found. (trustee 1991-97). Bar: N.J. 1974, U.S. Dist. Ct. N.J. 1974, U.S. Tax Ct. 1975, N.Y. 1980. Personal income taxation. Office: Two University Plaza Hackensack NJ 07446

**DAVIDSON, ANNE STOWELL,** lawyer; b. Rye, N.Y., Feb. 24, 1949; d. Robert Harold and Anne (Breeding) D. BA magna cum laude, Smith Coll., 1971; JD cum laude, George Washington U., 1974. Bar: D.C. 1975, U.S. Dist. Ct. D.C. 1975, U.S. Ct. Appeals (D.C. cir.) 1975, U.S. Supreme Ct. 1980. Asst. chief counsel drug enforcement FDA, Rockville, Md., 1974-78; counsel Abbott Labs., North Chicago, Ill., 1978-79, U.S. Pharm. Ops. Schering-Plough Corp., Kenilworth, N.J., 1979-83; sr. counsel Sandoz Pharms. Corp., Inc., East Hanover, N.J., 1983-86; v.p., assoc. gen. counsel Sandoz Pharms. Corp., Inc., East Hanover, 1987-96; assoc. gen. counsel Novartis Pharms. Corp., East Hanover, 1997—. Contbr. articles to profl. jours. Trustee N.J. Pops Orch. Recipient Dawes prize Smith Coll., 1971. Mem. ABA, Pharm. Mfrs. Assn., Food and Drug Law Inst., Non-prescription Drug Mfrs. Assn. (govt. affairs com.), Smith Coll. Club (pres. 1981-82). Republican. Presbyterian. Administrative and regulatory, General corporate, Health. Office: Novartis Pharms Corp 59 State Route 10 East Hanover NJ 07936-1005

**DAVIDSON, BARRY RODNEY,** lawyer; b. Boston, Aug. 12, 1943; s. Robert Bruce and Grace (Barry) D.; m. Paula Frances Miller, Sept. 2, 1967; children: Brent, Clay. BA, Vanderbilt U., 1964; postgrad., NYU, 1966; JD, U. Fla., 1967. Bar: Fla. 1968, U.S. Dist. Ct. (so. dist.) Fla. 1969, U.S. Ct. Appeals (5th cir.) 1971, (11th cir.) 1981, U.S. Supreme Ct. 1983, U.S. Dist. Ct. (mid. and no. dists.) Fla. 1989. Legis. aide Fla. State Senate, Tallahassee, 1968; law clk. to judge U.S. Dist. Ct. (so. dist.) Fla., Miami, 1968-70; assoc. Steel Hector & Davis, Miami, 1970-74, ptnr., 1974-87; ptnr. Coll, Davidson, Carter, Smith, Salter & Barkett, P.A., Miami, 1987—; chmn. mediation com. So. Dist. Fla., 1992-94; so. dist. rep. 11th cir. jud. conf., 1992-94; mem. Civil Justice Adv. Group So. Dist., 1992-95. Mem. Fla. Gov.'s Eminent Domain Study Com., Tallahassee, 1984-85; pres. Greater Miami Pop Warner League, Inc., 1987-89. Fellow Am. Bar Found. (life); mem. ABA, Fla. Bar Assn. (bd. govs. 1982-86, chmn. advt. com. 1977-80), Miami Vanderbilt Club (pres. 1977-80), Coral Reef Yacht Club, Ocean Reef Club, Miami Club. Democrat. Roman Catholic. Avocations: boating, skiing, golf. Antitrust, Federal civil litigation, Condemnation.

**DAVIDSON, CLIFFORD MARC,** lawyer; b. Yonkers, N.Y., Mar. 7, 1960; s. Maurice and Marilyn (Korb) D.; m. Barbara Branson, July 27, 1991. BS Pharmacy, Rutgers U., Piscataway; JD, Rutgers U., Camden. Assoc. Marmorek, Guttman & Rubenstein, N.Y.C., 1986-87, Hedman, Gibson, Costigan & Hoare, N.Y.C., 1987-88, Kenyon & Kenyon, N.Y.C., 1988-91; ptnr. Steinberg & Raskin, N.Y.C., 1991-94, Steinberg, Raskin & Davidson, P.C., N.Y.C., 1994-97; sr. ptnr. Davidson, Davidson & Kappel, LLC, N.Y.C., 1998—. Mem. Am. Pharm. Assn., Controlled Release Soc., N.J. Intellectual Property Assn., N.Y. Intellectual Property Assn. Avocations: tennis, music. Patent, Trademark and copyright. Office: Davidson Davidson & Kappel LLC 1140 Avenue Of The Americas New York NY 10036-5803

**DAVIDSON, DANIEL MORTON,** lawyer; b. Lynbrook, N.Y., July 9, 1950. BA summa cum laude, Williams Coll., 1972; JD magna cum laude, Harvard U., 1975. Bar: D.C. 1975, Calif. 1977, U.S. Tax Ct. 1979, U.S. Supreme Ct. 1992. Law clk. Mass. Supreme Ct., 1975-76; ptnr. Sidley & Austin, Washington, 1985-98, Hogan & Hartson, L.L.P., Washington, 1998—. Contbr. articles to profl. jours. Mem. ABA, D.C. Bar Assn., State Bar Calif., Phi Beta Kappa. Corporate taxation, Taxation, general, Personal income taxation. Office: Hogan & Hartson LLP 555 13th St NW Ste 900W Washington DC 20004-1109

**DAVIDSON, DAVID JOHN,** lawyer, entertainer; b. Drexel Hill, Pa., Oct. 5, 1960; s. John Thomas and Eileen G. Davidson; m. Judith Duggan, Dec. 28, 1985; children: Cody T., Jocelyn C. BA, U. Fla., 1981, JD, 1987. Bar: Fla. 1988, U.S. Dist. Ct. (mid. dist.) Fla. 1988. Probation officer Fla. Dept. Corrections, West Palm Beach, 1981-84; assoc. atty. Mateer, Harbert & Bates, P.A., Orlando, Fla., 1988-91; entertainer Sports Magic Team, Orlando, Fla., 1991—; gen. counsel Halifax Cmty. Health Sys., Daytona Beach, Fla., 1991—; chmn. Volusia County Med.-Legal Liaison, Daytona Beach, 1995; spkr. in field. Mem. Tomoka Christian Ch., Ormond Beach, Fla., 1996—; bd. counselors Bethune Cookman Coll., Daytona Beach, 1997—. Mem. Am. Health Lawyers Assn., Leadership Daytona. Avocations: playing in a band since 1993, boating, camping, sports. Health, General corporate. Office: Halifax Cmty Health Sys 303 N Clyde Morris Blvd Daytona Beach FL 32114-2709

**DAVIDSON, DAVID THEODORE,** lawyer; b. Cin., July 24, 1960; s. Elmer N. Jr. and M. Suzanne (Lamkin) D.; m. Lynn C. Bunn, June 29, 1985; children: Michael, Jonathan, Matthew. BA, Wittenberg U., Springfield, Ohio, 1983; JD, U. Toledo, 1986. Bar: Ohio 1986, U.S. Dist. Ct. (so. dist.) Ohio 1984, U.S. Ct. Appeals (6th cir.) 1995, U.S. Supreme Ct. 1995. Ptnr. Baden, Jones, Scheper & Crehan, Hamilton, Ohio, 1986-96, Davidson Law Offices, Hamilton, Ohio, 1996—. Councilman Hamilton City Coun., 1993—; treas., legal cons. Westside Little League, Hamilton, 1989—. Mem. ABA, Butler County Bar Assn. (chmn. fee arbitration 1996, bus. adv. com. 1997—), Cin. Bar Assn., Clermont County Bar Assn., Ohio Assn. Civil Trial Attys., Def. Rsch. Inst., Rotary Club. Avocations: jogging, baseball coaching. Office: 127 N 2nd St Hamilton OH 45011-2724

**DAVIDSON, FRANK PAUL,** retired macroengineer, lawyer; b. N.Y.C., May 20, 1918; s. Maurice Philip and Blanche (Reinheimer) D.; m. Izaline Marguerite Doll, May 19, 1951; children: Roger Conrad, Nicholas Henry, Charles Geoffrey. BS, Harvard U., 1939, JD, 1948; DHL (hon.), Hawthorne Coll., 1987. Bar: N.Y. 1953, U.S. Dist. Ct. (so. dist.) N.Y. 1953. Dir. mil. affairs, gen. counsel Houston C. of C., 1948-50; contract analyst Am. Embassy, Paris, 1950-53; assoc. Carb, Luria, Glassner & Cook, N.Y.C., 1953-54; pvt. practice law N.Y.C., 1955-70; founding pres., counsel, bd. dirs. The Inst. for the Future, 1967-70; rsch. assoc. MIT, Cambridge, Mass., 1970-96; also chmn. system dynamics steering com. Sloan Sch. Mgmt., coord. macro-engring. Sch. Engring., MIT; semi-ret., 1984; pres. Tch. Studies Inc., N.Y.C., 1957-96, vice chmn. Inst. for Ednl. Svcs., Bedford, Mass., 1980-84, spl. lectr. Société des Ingénieurs et Scientifiques de France, 1991, NAS del. to Renewable Resources Workshop, Katmandu, Nepal, 1981, governing bd. Channel Tunnel Study Group, 1957-85, co-founder Channel Tunnel Study Group, London, Paris, 1957, apptd. to NASA Exploration Task Force, Washington, 1989, mem. internat. sci. and tech. com. Ocean Cities Symposium, Monaco, 1995. Author: Macro: A Clear Vision of How Science and Technology Will Shape Our Future, 1983, Macro: Big is Beautiful, 1986; editor: series of AAAS books on macroengring., Tunneling and Underground Transport, 1987; co-editor: Macro-Engineering, Global Infrastructure Solutions, 1992, Solar Power Satellites, 1993, 2nd edit., 1998, Macro-Engineering and The Earth: World Projects for the Year 2000 and Beyond, 1998; mem. editorial bd. Interdisciplinary Sci. Revs., 1985—; mem. adv. bd. Tech. in Soc., 1979—, Mountain R&D, 1981—, Project Appraisal, 1986-98. Bd. dirs. Internat. Mountain Soc., Boulder, Colo., 1981—, Assn. Prospective 2100, Paris, 1997; trustee Norwich (Vt.) Ctr., 1980-83, mem. steering com. Am. Trails Network, 1986-88, bd. dirs. Am. Trails Washington, 1988-90. RCAC, 1941-46, ETO; Troop Leader 10th Cdn., Armoured Rgt. (Fort Garry Horse), Intelligence Officer and Squadron Leader, GSO III (Intelligence) Second Armoured Brigade Group, maj. Tex. State Guard; apptd. to Senate Ft. Garry Horse, 1995. Recipient Key to City Osaka, Japan, 1987; elected Mem. Honoraire, Pres. d'Honneur Assn. Louis Armand, Paris, 1996-99; Lewis Mumford Fellow Rensselaerville Inst., 1982. MEM ABA, Internat. Assn. Macro-Engring. Socs. (bd. dirs. 1987—, hon.chmn. 1997-99), Am. Soc. Macro-Engring. (bd. dirs. 1982—, vice chancellor 1983-97, pres. 1997-98, chmn. 1998), Assn. Bar of City of N.Y. (internat. law com. 1959-62), Major Projects Assn. (mem. overseas adv. com. U.K. 1995—), Knickerbocker (N.Y.C.) Club, St. Botolph (Boston) Club, MIT Quarter Century Club. Home: 26A Parker St Lexington MA 02421-4907

**DAVIDSON, GEORGE ALLAN,** lawyer; b. N.Y.C., Apr. 6, 1942; s. George Roger and Jean Allan (McKaig) D.; m. Annette L. Richter, Sept. 4, 1965; children: Emily, Charlotte. AB, Brown U., 1964; LLB, Columbia U., 1967. Bar: N.Y. 1967, U.S. Dist. Ct. (so. and ea. dists.) N.Y. 1969, U.S. Ct. Appeals (2d cir.) 1970, U.S. Supreme Ct. 1974, U.S. Tax Ct. 1974, U.S. Ct. Appeals (D.C. cir.) 1976, U.S. Dist. Ct. (no. dist.) Calif. 1980, U.S. Ct. Appeals (9th cir.) 1981, U.S. Ct. Appeals (5th cir.) 1982, U.S. Dist. Ct. (no. dist.) N.Y. 1982, U.S. Ct. Appeals (11th cir.) 1983, U.S. Ct. Appeals (1st cir.) 1986, U.S. Ct. Appeals (7th cir.) 1992. Law clk., 1967-68; assoc. Hughes Hubbard & Reed, N.Y.C., 1968-74, ptnr., 1974—; dir. P.R. Legal Def. and Edn. Fund, Inc., 1980-84, Legal Aid Soc., 1979-92, pres. 1987-89, N.Y. Lawyers for Pub. Interest, Inc., 1984-86, Columbia Law Sch. Alumni Assn., 1987-91, Practicing Attys. for Law Students, 1989—, VIP Cmty. Svcs., 1994—. Fellow Am. Coll. Trial Lawyers; mem. ABA, Internat. Bar Assn., Fed. Bar Council, Am. Law Inst., N.Y. Sci. Policy Assn., N.Y. State Bar Assn., Assn. Bar City N.Y., Nat. Assn. Coll. and Univ. Attys., Union Internationale des Avocats, Century Assn. Contbr. writings to legal publs. General civil litigation, Constitutional, Non-profit and tax-exempt organizations. Office: Hughes Hubbard & Reed LLP 1 Battery Park Plz Fl 12 New York NY 10004-1482

**DAVIDSON, GLEN HARRIS,** federal judge; b. Pontotoc, Miss., Nov. 20, 1941; s. M. Glen and Lora (Harris) D.; m. Bonnie Payne, Apr. 25, 1973; children: Glen III, Gregory P. B.A., U. Miss, 1962, J.D., 1965. Bar: Miss. 1965, U.S. Ct. Appeals (5th cir.) 1965, U.S. Supreme Ct. 1971. Asst. dist. atty. First Jud. Dist., Tupelo, Miss., 1969-74; dist. atty. First Jud. Dist., 1975; U.S. atty. U.S. Dist. Ct. (no. dist.) Miss., Oxford, 1981-85; U.S. district judge U.S. Ct. House, Aberdeen, Miss., 1985—; atty. Lee County Sch. Bd., Miss., 1974-81. Bd. dirs. Community Devel. Found., Tupelo, 1976-81; mem. exec. bd. Yocona Council Boy Scouts Am., 1972—. Served to maj. USAF, 1966-69. Mem. Fed. Bar Assn. (v.p. 1984), Miss. Bar Found., Lee County Bar Assn. (pres. 1974), Assn. Trial Lawyers Am., Miss. Prosecutors Assn. Presbyterian. Lodge: Kiwanis (pres. Tupelo 1978). Office: US Dist Ct PO Box 767 Aberdeen MS 39730-0767

**DAVIDSON, HUBERT JAMES, JR.,** lawyer, educator; b. Kosciusko, Miss., Jan. 14, 1949; s. Hubert James and Ida Mae (Hill) D.; m. Jamie Jill Alexander, May 20, 1978; children: Michael Alexander, Benjamin Hill, Elizabeth Kate. BA, U. Miss., 1971, JD, 1974. Bar: Miss. 1974. Ptnr. Carter & Davidson, Columbus, Miss., 1974—; instr. Miss. U. for Women, Columbus, 1975-86, asst. prof., 1986-90, assoc. prof., 1990-96, prof., 1996—. dir. Emergency Physicians Svcs., Columbus, 1986-95. Pres. Lowndes Cmty. Found., Columbus, 1994—; dir., v.p. Miss. Sch. for Math. and Sci. Found., Columbus, 1996—; bd. dirs. Salvation Army, Columbus, 1988—. Named Boss of the Yr., Lowndes County Legal Secs. Assn., 1978. Mem. Miss. Bar Assn. (chmn. com. on complaints 1987, co-chmn. paralegal study and cert. com. 1994), Exchange Club of Columbus (pres. 1981, dir. 1982), Columbus Lowndes C. of C. (chmn. 1992). Methodist. Avocations: tennis, reading, travel. Home: 1020 7th St N Columbus MS 39701-3408 Office: Carter & Davidson 407 7th St N Columbus MS 39701-4679

**DAVIDSON, JACK S.,** partner; b. Primrose, Ga., Feb. 11, 1922; s. Lewis M. Davidson and Getrude Louise Sullivan; children: Jack S. Jr., Linda Daniel. BBA, U. Ga., LLB; HHD, Reinhardt Coll. Judge State Ct. Jackson County, Ga., 1988, Mcpl. Ct. Jefferson, Ga., 1989-96; ptnr. Davidson, Hopkins & Booth, Jefferson, 1996—. Chmn. Jefferson City Sch. Bd.; trustee Reinhard Coll.; chmn. Jackson County Dems. Exec. Com., Jefferson. With USN, 1942-45. Mem. ABA, Jackson County Bar Assn. (pres.), Piedmont Bar Assn. (pres.). Methodist. Home: 105 Old Pendergrass Rd Jefferson GA 30549-2778 Office: Davidson Hopkins & Booth 106 Washington St Jefferson GA 30549-1003

**DAVIDSON, JAMES JOSEPH, III,** lawyer; b. Lafayette, La., July 27, 1940; s. James Joseph and Virginia Lee (Dunham) D.; m. Kay Cecile Holloway, Aug. 7, 1962; children—Kimberly Kay, James Joseph IV, Lynda Leigh, Virginia Holland. B.A., U. S.W. La., 1963; J.D., Tulane U., 1964. Bar: La. 1964, U.S. Dist. Ct. (we. dist.) La. 1965, U.S. Dist. Ct. (ea. dist.) La. 1979, U.S. Dist. Ct. (mid. dist.) 1986, U.S. Ct. Appeals (5th cir.) 1972, U.S. Supreme Ct. 1975, U.S. Ct. Appeals (11th cir.) 1981. Ptnr. Davidson, Meaux, Sonnier, McElligott & Swift, Lafayette, La., 1964—. Mem. exec. bd. Evangeline Area council Boy Scouts Am., 1969-80; trustee U. S.W. La. Found., 1981—, pres., 1988-91. Fellow Am. Bar Found. (life); mem. La. State Bar Assn. (del. 1970-96), La. Bar Found., Am. Judicature Soc., La. Assn. Def. Counsel (dir. 1975-77), Nat. Assn. R.R. Trial Counsel, Am. Bd. Trial Advocates (adv.), Am. Counsel Assn., Internat. Assn. Def. Counsel, Assn. Def. Trial Attys., Assn. Transp. Practitioners. Republican. Baptist. Federal civil litigation, State civil litigation, Condemnation. Home: 539 Girard Park Dr Lafayette LA 70503-2601 Office: PO Box 2908 Lafayette LA 70502-2908

**DAVIDSON, JEFFREY H.,** lawyer; b. Brookline, Mass., Apr. 7, 1952; s. Jacob and Bernice (Beckerman) D.; m. Cynthia J. Cohen, June 11, 1972; 1 child, Clifford. BA cum laude, Harvard U., 1973, JD cum laude, 1976. Bar: Calif. 1977, U.S. Dist. Ct. (cen. dist.) Calif. 1977, U.S. Dist. Ct. (so. dist.) Calif. 1981, U.S. Ct. Appeals (9th cir.) 1983, U.S. Dist. Ct. (no. dist.) Calif. 1986. Shareholder Stutman, Treister & Glatt, P.C., L.A., 1976—. Mem. ABA (sect. bus. law, bus. bankruptcy com., UCC com.), FBA (bankruptcy sect.), Fin. Lawyers Conf. (bd. govs. 1988-91, exec. com. 1990-91), State Bar Calif. (exec. com. bus. law sect. 1987-90, treas. bus. law sect. 1989-90, chmn. UCC com. 1986-87), L.A. County Bar Assn. (chmn. comml. law and bankruptcy sect. 1987-88, exec. com. 1985—, chmn. bankruptcy com. 1984-86, mem. nominating com. for trustees and officers 1988), Phi Beta Kappa. Bankruptcy, Contracts commercial. Office: Stutman Treister & Glatt PC 3699 Wilshire Blvd Ste 900 Los Angeles CA 90010-2766

**DAVIDSON, KENNETH LAWRENCE,** lawyer, educator; b. Tulsa, Feb. 4, 1945; s. Joe and Elsie (Hutchens) D.; m. Anne Devine; children: Rebecca Marie, Deborah Shannon. BSBA, U. Tulsa, 1968, JD, 1970; LLM, Georgetown U., 1975. Bar: Okla. 1970, U.S. Dist. Ct. (no. dist.) Okla. 1970, U.S. Ct. Mil. Appeals 1971, D.C. Ct. Appeals 1975, U.S. Supreme Ct. 1977, Ill. 1990. Assoc. CEO, assoc. legal counsel Bd. Regents Okla. State U. and A&M Colls., Stillwater, 1976-90; gen. counsel Regency Univs. System Ill. Bd. Regents, Springfield, 1990-96; parliamentarian, univ. counsel, bd. trustees No. Ill. U., DeKalb, 1995-97, counsel for governance, risk mgmt., equity svcs., 1997—; adj. assoc. prof. Coll. Edn. Okla. State U., 1986-90; adminstrv. law judge Okla. Dept. Edn., Oklahoma City, 1978-90. Bd. dirs. YMCA Aquatic Club, Stillwater, 1985-86, Judith Karman Hospice, Stillwater, 1987. Capt. JAGC, USAF, 1970-76. Decorated Meritorious Svc. medal, Commendation medal. Mem. Ill. Bar Assn., DeKalb County Bar Assn., Okla. Bar Assn., D.C. Bar Assn., Nat. Assn. Coll. and Univ. Attys., Kappa Sigma. Democrat. Insurance, Labor, Education and schools. Office: No Ill U 302 Lowden Hall Dekalb IL 60115-3080

**DAVIDSON, RICHARD DODGE,** lawyer; b. Biloxi, Miss., June 4, 1945; s. Frank William and Elaine (Dodge) D.; m. Judith C. Carey, Aug. 16, 1969; children: Christopher, Scott, Julie. BS in Engring., Princeton U., 1967; JD, Cornell U., 1970. Bar: N.Y. 1971, U.S. Supreme Ct. 1975, Fla. 1978, U.S. Dist. Ct. (middle dist.) Fla., U.S. Dist. Ct. (no. dist.) N.Y., U.S. Supreme Ct. 1975, U.S. Ct. Appeals (2nd cir.) 1971, U.S. Ct. Appeals (5th cir.) 1978, U.S. Tax Ct. 1977. Assoc. Hiscock & Barclay, Syracuse, N.Y., 1970-78, ptnr., 1978-83; resident ptnr. Hiscock & Barclay, Orlando, Fla., 1983-92; ptnr. Hiscock & Barclay, Albany, N.Y., 1992-97; of counsel Lowndes, Drosdick, Doster, Kantor & Reed, P.A., Orlando, Fla., 1997; ptnr. Lowndes, Drosdick, Doster, Kantor & Reed, P.A., Orlando, 1999—. Pres. Ecology Compliance Ltd., Syracuse, 1983; asst. town atty. Town of Manilus, N.Y., 1974-83; bd. dirs. Boys Club Cen. Fla., Orlando, 1986—, Seminole Childrens' Village, Longwood, Fla., 1987—. Mem. ABA, Fla. Bar Assn., N.Y. State Bar Assn., Orange County Bar Assn., Rotary, Princeton Club Cen. Fla. Avocations: amateur radio, youth sports, sailing. Real property. Office: Lowndes Drosdick Doster Kantor & Reed PA 215 N Eda Dr Orlando FL 32801

**DAVIDSON, ROBERT BRUCE,** lawyer; b. N.Y.C., May 6, 1945. BS in Econs. cum laude, U. Pa., 1967; JD, Columbia U., 1972. Bar: N.Y. 1973, U.S. Dist. Ct. (so. and ea. dists.) N.Y. 1973, U.S. Ct. Appeals (2d cir.) 1975, U.S. Ct. Appeals (D.C. cir.) 1981, U.S. Supreme Ct. 1979, U.S. Tax Ct. 1984, U.S. Ct. Appeals (fed. cir.) 1989, U.S. Ct. Appeals (3d cir.) 1990. Assoc. Baker & McKenzie, N.Y.C., 1972-79, ptnr., 1979—; mem. adv. bd. World Arbitration Inst., N.Y.C., 1984—. Author: (with others) Voting Laws and Procedures, 1973; also articles. Vol. U.S. Peace Corps, Philippines, 1968-70. Mem. ABA, Assn. of Bar of City of N.Y. (chair 1982-85, com. on internat. law 1986-89, com. on arbitration 1999—), Am. Fgn. Law Assn. (bd. dirs.), Maritime Law Assn. U.S., Fed. Bar Coun., Am. Arbitration Assn. (mem. internat. panel, 1997—, panel for large complex cases 1997—). Private international, Federal civil litigation, Alternative dispute resolution. Office: Baker & McKenzie 805 3rd Ave New York NY 10022-7513

**DAVIDSON, SCOTT ALLEN,** lawyer; b. Oct. 10, 1970. BS, Ind. U., 1993; JD, U. Louisville, 1996. Bar: Ky. 1996, Ind. 1998, U.S. Dist. Ct. (ea. and we. dist.) Ky. 1996. Assoc. Bennett, Bowman, Triplett & Vittitow, Louisville, Ky., 1996-98, Boehl, Stopher & Graves, Louisville, 1998—; adult advisor Ky. Teen Ct., Louisville, Ky., 1998—. Mng. editor, contbr. Jour. Family Law, 1995-96. Recipient award for scholastic excellence in property Corpus Juris Secundam, 1994-95. Mem. Ky. Bar Assn., Ky. Def. Counsel, Louisville Bar Assn., Brandeis Honor Soc. State civil litigation, Insurance, Professional liability. Office: Boehl Stopher & Graves 2300 Aegon Ctr 400 W Market St Louisville KY 40202-3346

**DAVIDSON, SHEILA KEARNEY,** lawyer; b. Paterson, N.J., Dec. 16, 1961; d. John James and Rita Barbara (Burke) Kearney; m. Anthony H. Davidson, Oct. 5, 1996; 1 child, Andrew John. BA cum laude, Fairfield U., 1983; JD, George Washington U., 1986. Bar: N.Y. 1987, U.S. Dist. Ct. (so. dist.) N.Y. 1987, D.C. 1989. Assoc. Shearson Lehman Bros., Inc., N.Y.C., 1986-87; staff atty. Nat. Assn. Securities Dealers, N.Y.C., 1987-89, regional atty., 1989-90, sr. regional atty., 1990-91; regional counsel N.Y. Life Ins. Co., N.Y.C., 1991-93, assoc. counsel, 1993-94, asst. gen. counsel, 1994-95, v.p., assoc. gen. counsel, 1995-97, sr. v.p. in charge of corp. compliance dept., 1998—. Mem. ABA, Securities Industry Assn., D.C. Bar Assn., Fairfield U. Alumni Club N.Y. (pres. 1988-90), Phi Delta Phi. Republican. Roman Catholic. Securities, Administrative and regulatory, General corporate. Office: NY Life Ins Co 51 Madison Ave New York NY 10010-1603

**DAVIDSON, STUART WEST,** lawyer; b. Natick, Mass., June 21, 1957; s. Edward William and Sonya (Westleman) D.; m. Ann Cohen, Oct. 8, 1988; 1 child, Anita Rose. BA in Polit. Sci., Johns Hopkins U., 1979; JD cum laude, Harvard U., 1982. Bar: Pa. 1982, D.C. 1983. Ptnr. Willig, Williams & Davidson, Phila., 1982—; trustee Johns Hopkins U., 1979-84; adv. coun. environ. and occupl. health Johns Hopkins U. Sch. Hygiene and Pub. Health, 1983-93; adv. coun. labor studies Pa. State U., 1985—; nat. labor adv. bd. State of Israel Bonds, 1996—; mem. lawyers coord. com. AFL-CIO; bd. dirs. Devel. Corp. of Israel. Contbr. articles to profl. jours.; speaker at various nat. conf. Mem. adv. bd. Pa. State Labor Bd.; mem. Golden Slipper Found., 1999—. Mem. ABA, Pa. Bar Assn., Phila. Bar, Am. Arbitration Assn., Indsl. Rels. Rsch. Assn., Internat. Found. Employee Benefit Funds, SHOMRIM, Omicron Delta Kappa, Phi Beta Kappa. Home: 7501 Fowler St Philadelphia PA 19128-4149 Office: Willig Williams Davidson 1845 Walnut St 24th Fl Philadelphia PA 19103-4708

**DAVIDSON, VAN MICHAEL, JR.,** lawyer; b. Baton Rouge, Nov. 26, 1945; s. Van Michael Sr. and Elizabeth Lamoine (Arnold) D.; m. Judith Ann Begue, Aug. 5, 1967; children: Van Michael III, Catherine Annette, Mary Elizabeth. BA in History, La. State U., 1968; JD, U. Miss., 1973; judge adv. gen.'s postgrad. course, 1978. Bar: Miss. 1973, U.S. Dist. Ct. (no. dist.) Miss. 1973, U.S. Ct. Mil. Appeals 1974, U.S. Supreme Ct. 1978, U.S. Ct. Claims 1979, U.S. Tax Ct. 1980, U.S. Ct. Appeals (5th cir.) 1981, La. 1982, U.S. Dist. Ct. (we. and mid. dists.) La. 1982, U.S. Dist. Ct. (no. dist.) Tex. 1982, U.S. Ct. Appeals (Fed. cir.) 1982, U.S. Dist. Ct. (so. dist.) Miss. 1985, U.S. Dist. Ct. (ea. dist.) La. 1985, D.C., 1987. Commd. 2d lt. U.S. Army, 1968, advanced through grades to maj., 1980; forward observer U.S. Army, Ft. Bragg, N.C., 1968; battery battalion officer U.S. Army, Ft. Bliss, Tex., 1968-69, battery comdr., 1969-70; command spokesman IV U.S. Army, Vietnam, 1970-71; trial counsel U.S. Army, New Ulm, Fed. Republic Germany, 1974-77; trial atty. contact appeals div. U.S. Army, Washington, 1978-81; resigned U.S. Army, 1981; ptnr. Carmouche, Gray & Hoffman, Lake Charles, La., 1981-87; sole practice Lake Charles, 1987-94; gen. counsel Stapp Towing Co. Inc., Lake Charles, 1994-97; clk. Third Circuit Ct. of Appeals, 1997—; chmn. bd. dirs. Southwest Legl Services Agy., Lake Charles. Contbr. articles to profl. jours. Lt. col. USAR, 1987. Decorated Bronze Star, Army Commendation medal, Meritorious Svc. medal with one oak leaf cluster. Mem. ABA, Fed. Bar Assn., Assn. Trial Lawyers Am., Bd. of Contract Appeals Bar Assn., Phi Delta Phi. Republican. Presbyterian. Avocations: hunting, fishing, scuba diving, playing piano, writing novels. Government contracts and claims, Federal civil litigation, Construction. Home: 1525 N Greenfield Cir Lake Charles LA 70605-5307

**DAVIES, ARTHUR B(EVERLY), III,** lawyer; b. Phila., June 29, 1924; s. Arthur B. Jr. and Margaret (Cake) D.; m. Lynda Long, July 24, 1992; children from previous marriage: Arthur Beverly IV, Jonathan E. BA, U. Va., 1948, LLB, 1949. Bar: Va., U.S. Dist. Ct. (we. dist.) Va. 1950, U.S. Dist. Ct. (ea. dist.) Va. 1964, U.S. Ct. Appeals (4th cir.) 1963, U.S. Supreme Ct. 1960. Assoc. John L. Abbot, Lynchburg, Va., 1949-50; asst. commonwealth atty. Lynchburg, 1951-55; ptnr. Hickson & Davies, Lynchburg, 1951-68, Davies, Devening & Davies, Lynchburg, 1968-91, Davies & Davies, Lynchburg, 1991—. Chmn. Kennedy Presdl. Campaign, Lynchburg, 1960. Comdr. USNR, 1942-72. Mem. ABA, Va. State Bar, Va. Bar Assn. (chmn. joint com. legal edn. 1975-77, com. hon. mems. and judges 1973-83, nominations to Supreme Ct. com. 1972-75), Lynchburg Bar Assn. (pres. 1960-61), Allegheny, Bath Highlands Bar Assn. (pres. 1996-98), Kiwanis (pres. 1962), Masons (master Hill City Lodge 1973). Avocations: hiking, hunting, reading. Probate, Estate planning, General corporate. Home: RR 1 Box 190 A Millboro VA 24460-9540 Office: Davies & Davies 802 Court St PO Box 1360 Lynchburg VA 24505-1360

**DAVIES, CALEB, IV,** lawyer; b. Hammond, Ind., Jan. 29, 1954; s. Caleb and Margaret Davies; m. Cheryl Davies, Oct. 9, 1982; children: Evan, Patrick, Ethan. BS, Ind. U., 1977; JD, Emory U., 1980. Bar: Ga. 1982, U.S. Dist. Ct. (no. dist.) Ga. 1982. Cir. mediator U.S. Ct. Appeals (11th cir.), Atlanta, 1997—; mediator, arbitrator Am. Arbitration Assn., Atlanta, 1988—, Justice Ctr. Atlanta, 1989—, U.S. Arbitration and Mediation, Atlanta, 1991, Adminstrv. Conf. of U.S., Atlanta, 1990; arbitrator Nat. Assn. Securities Dealers, Atlanta, 1992—, Ga. Dept. Community Affairs, 1992—. Organizer Soc. of Profls. in Dispute Resolution, Atlanta, 1990-92. Recognized for Pro Bono Svc. State of Ga., 1988. Mem. ABA, State Bar Ga., Atlanta Bar Assn. (chair alternative dispute resolution publs. 1992, bd. dirs. 1997-99, treas. 1999), Acad. Family Mediators. Avocations: sailing, hiking, coaching, tennis. Alternative dispute resolution, Appellate. Office: US Ct Appeals Eleventh Jud Cir 56 Forsyth St NW Atlanta GA 30303-2289

**DAVIES, CHARLES R.,** lawyer. BS, Duquesne U., 1964; JD, Georgetown U., 1967. Bar: D.C. 1968. Asst. v.p., asst. gen. counsel Geico Corp., Washington, 1978, v.p., gen. counsel, 1992—, group v.p., gen. counsel, 1999. Office: Geico Corp Gelco Plz Washington DC 20076-0001

**DAVIES, GLEN ENSIGN,** lawyer; b. Salt Lake City, Aug. 11, 1940; s. Stanley Glen and Violet Leone (Meyers) D.; m. Maurine Matheson, Dec. 17, 1965; children: Lee Ann, Jeffrey, Scott, Matthew, Alison. BS in Pol. Sci., U. Utah, 1964, JD, 1967. Bar: Utah 1967; U.S. Ct. Appeals (10th cir.) 1971, U.S. Cir. Ct. Appeals (9th cir.) 1978. Atty., shareholder Watkiss & Saperstein, Salt Lake City, 1967-92, Parsons, Davies, Kinghorn & Peters, Salt Lake City, 1992—. Del. State Dem. Conv., Salt Lake City, 1968, 70, 72, 76; voting dist. chmn. Dem. Party, Salt Lake City, 1974, 76. Mem. Evergreen Swim & Tennis Club (pres., v.p., dir., 1989-91), Order of the Coif, Nat. Bus.

Inst. Democrat. LDS Ch. Avocations: golf, photography. General civil litigation, Environmental, Natural resources. Home: 3748 S 2235 E Salt Lake City UT 84109-3332 Office: Parsons Davies Kinghorn Peters 185 S State St Salt Lake City UT 84111-1538

**DAVIES, PAUL LEWIS, JR.**, retired lawyer; b. San Jose, Calif., July 21, 1930; s. Paul Lewis and Faith (Crummey) D.; m. Barbara Bechtel, Dec. 22, 1955; children: Laura (Mrs. Segundo Mateo), Paul Lewis III. AB, Stanford U., 1952; JD, Harvard U., 1957. Bar: Calif. 1957. Assoc. Pillsbury, Madison & Sutro, San Francisco, 1957-63, ptnr., 1963-89; gen. counsel Chevron Corp., 1984-89; bd. dirs. FMC Corp. Hon. trustee Calif. Acad. Scis., trustee, 1970-83, chmn., 1973-80; pres. Herbert Hoover Found.; bd. overseers Hoover Instn., chmn., 1976-82, 91-93; hon. regent U. of Pacific, regent, 1959-90. Lt. U.S. Army, 1952-54. Mem. Bohemian Club, Pacific-Union Club, Villa Taverna, World Trade Club (San Francisco), Claremont Country Club, Lakeview (Oakland, Calif.), Cypress Point (Pebble Beach, Calif.), Sainte Claire (San Jose, Calif.), Collectors, Explorers, Links (N.Y.C.), Met. Club, Chgo. Club, Phi Beta Kappa, Pi Sigma Alpha. Republican. Office: 50 Fremont St Ste 3520 San Francisco CA 94105-2239

**D'AVIGNON, ROY JOSEPH**, lawyer; b. Dallas, July 20, 1942; s. Roy J. and Ann (Ham) D'A.; m. Tania M. Mychajlyshyn, Nov. 29, 1969; children: Larissa A., Markian W. BSS, Loyola U., New Orleans, 1964; LLB, Harvard U., 1967. Bar: Tex. 1967, Mass. 1969. Assoc. Hutchins & Wheeler, Boston, 1969-77; counsel Raytheon Co., Lexington, Mass., 1977-86, div. counsel, 1986-90, asst. gen. counsel, 1990-99; v.p., gen. counsel Simplex Time Recorder Co., Gardner, Mass., 1999—. Capt. M.I., U.S. Army, 1967-69. Mem. ABA, Mass. Bar Assn., Tex. Bar Assn., Boston Bar Assn. General corporate, Private international, Mergers and acquisitions. Office: Raytheon Co 141 Spring St Lexington MA 02421-7899

**DAVILA, EDWIN**, lawyer; b. Cleve., June 21, 1954; s. Emilio and Maltilda Davila. BA, Coll. of Wooster, Ohio, 1976; JD, Cleve. U., 1983. Bar: Ohio 1984, U.S. Dist. Ct. (so. and no. dists.) Ohio 1984, U.S. Ct. Appeals (6th cir.) 1984, U.S. Dist. Ct. (no. dist.) Tex. 1988, U.S. Ct. Appeals (5th cir.) 1988. With Prosecutor's Office City of Cleve., 1982-83; asst. atty. gen. Atty. Gen.'s Office State of Ohio, Columbus, 1983-84; law clk. Ohio Ct. Appeals, Cleve., 1984-85; assoc. Smith & Schnacke, L.P.A., Dayton, Ohio, 1985-87, Arter & Hadden, Canton, Ohio, 1987-89, Ross & Robertson, Canton, 1989-91; pvt. practice Canton, Ohio, 1991—. Mem. Am. Trial Lawyers Assn., Ohio Bar Assn., Ohio Acad. Trial Lawyers, Canton Bar Assn. Antitrust, General civil litigation, Contracts commercial. Office: 836 Savannah Ave NE Canton OH 44704-1260

**DAVILA, GREGORY DAVID**, lawyer; b. Key West, Fla., May 17, 1967; s. Helio J. and Margarita E. Davila. BA in Polit. Sci., Fla. Internat. U., 1987; JD, Stetson U., 1990. Bar: Fla. 1991. Atty. Pub. Defender's Office, Key West, 1992-94; pvt. practice Key West, 1994—. Mem. ABA, Key West Sunrise Rotary Club, Masons, Loyal Order of Moose. Criminal, Real property, State civil litigation. Office: 513 Fleming St Ste 1 Key West FL 33040-6861

**DAVIS, ALLYN WHITNEY**, lawyer; b. Lamar, Colo., July 20, 1923; s. Alan C. and Phaen D.; m. Betty J. Chambers, Oct. 6, 1963; children: Phaen, Debbie, Deanna. JD, U. Denver, 1950. Bar: Colo. 1950. Dep. D.A. Gunnison, Colo., 1952-56; atty., dep. D.A. Saguache County, Colo., 1957-61; dep. D.A. Rio Grande County, Colo., 1957-61; pvt. practice Pueblo and Florence, Colo., 1962—; city atty. Saguache Town, Colo., 1957-62. With USN, 1942-46. Mem. Masons (treas. lodge # 97 1994—). Avocations: rare coins, gardening. Real property, Family and matrimonial, General practice. Office: 204 S Pines Peak PO Box 303 Florence CO 81226-0303

**DAVIS, ALTON THOMAS**, judge; b. Petoskey, Mich., July 23, 1947; s. Alton Thomas Davis and Helen Marie (Waldron) Tull; m. Sandra Kay Shellfish; children: Brion Colleen, Colby Galen. AA, North Ctrl. Mich. Coll., 1967; BS, We. Mich. U., 1969; JD, Detroit Coll. Law, 1974. Bar: Mich., 1974. Ptnr. Kent & Davis PC, Grayling, Mich., 1975-80; pros. atty. Crawford County, Grayling, Mich., 1979-80; pvt. practice Grayling, Mich., 1980-84; judge 46th jud. cir. State of Mich., 1985—; trustee Mich. Bldg. Authority, 1984. Chmn. Crawford County Dem. Com., Grayling, 1980-84, Crawford County Fair Bd., 1990-95; area coord. for Gov. Blanchard, no. Mich., 1983-84. Mem. Rotary Club (pres. 1990-92, Paul Harris fellow), Mich. Jud. Inst. (faculty 1994—), Mich. Judges Assn. (exec. com. 1995—), Mich. State Bar Assn. (chmn. Criminal Jury Instructions com. 1995—). Episcopal. Avocations: reading, writing, fishing, travel. Office: 46th Circuit COurt 200 Michigan Ave Grayling MI 49738-1743 Home: 216 Misty Way Grayling MI 49738-8642

**DAVIS, ANDREW NEIL**, lawyer, educator; b. Boston, Nov. 7, 1959; s. Gerald Stanley and Sarah Lee D.; m. Suzanne Frances DiBenedetto, Oct. 11, 1992; children: David R. Bray, Hannah M. Davis. BS in Biology, Trinity Coll., 1981; MS in Botany, U. Mass., 1983, PhD in Botany, 1987; JD, George Washington U., 1990. Bar: Conn. 1990, U.S. Dist. Ct. Conn. 1991, Mass. 1998. Atty. Pepe & Hazard, Hartford, Conn., 1990-93, Brown, Rudnick, Freed & Gesmer, Hartford, 1993-94; ptnr. LeBoeuf, Lamb, Greene & MacRae LLP, Hartford, 1994—; adj. prof. environ. studies Conn. Coll., 1994—. Sr. author/co-author: The Home Environmental Sourcebook, 1996, ISO 14001: Meeting Business Goals Through An Effective Environmental Management System, 1998; contbr. articles to profl. jours. Mem. Leadership Greater Hartford, 1997; chmn. lake adv. commn. Town Marlborough, 1992—, mem. zoning commn., 1993-95. Recipient Hon. Sci. award Bausch & Lomb, 1977; Albert L. Deslisle Botany fellow, 1982. Mem. Am. Arbitration Assn. (environ. adv. com. 1993-95), Conn. Bar Assn. (exec. com. environ. law sect. 1996—), Conn. Bus. and Industry Assn. (environ. policies coun. 1991—), Internat. Coun. Shopping Ctrs., Conn. Groundwater Assn. Avocations: photography, sailing, scuba diving, arctic travel and reading. Environmental, Land use and zoning (including planning), Mergers and acquisitions. Office: LeBoeuf Lamb Greene MacRae LLP 225 Asylum St Hartford CT 06103-1516

**DAVIS, ANTHONY EDWARD**, lawyer; b. Portland, Aug. 29, 1971; s. Gregory A. and Constance Eileen (Paul) D. BA, Oreg. State U., 1992; JD, Stanford U., 1995. Law clk. High Ct. of Am. Samoa, Pago Pago, 1996-97; assoc. McCutchen Doyle Brown & Enersen, San Francisco, 1995-96, 97—. Avocations: kick boxing, racquet sports, snowboarding. Intellectual property, Antitrust. Office: McCutchen Doyle Brown & Enersen 3 Embarcadero Ctr San Francisco CA 94111-4003

**DAVIS, BONNIE CHRISTELL**, judge; b. Petersburg, Va., July 13, 1949; d. Robert Madison and Margaret Elizabeth (Collier) D. BA, Longwood Coll., 1971; JD, U. Richmond, 1980. Bar: Va. 1980, U.S. DDist. Ct. (ea. dist.) Va. 1980, U.S. Ct. Appeals (4th cir.) 1982. Tchr. Chesterfield County Schs., Chesterfield, Va., 1971-77; pvt. practice, Chesterfield, 1980-83; asst. commonwealth atty. Chesterfield County, 1983-93; judge Juvenile and Domestic Rels. Ct. for 12th Jud. Dist. Va., 1993—; adviser Youth Svcs. Commn., Chesterfield, 1983-93; cons. Task Force on Child Abuse, 1983-93, Met. Richmond Multi-Discipline Team on Spouse Abuse, 1983-93, Va. Dept. of Children for handbook "Step by Step Through the Juvenile Justice System in Virginia, 1988; mem. nat. adv. com. for prodn. on missing and runaway children Theatre IV; mem. adv. group to set stds. and tng. for Guardians Ad Litem, Supreme Ct. Va., 1994; chmn. jud. adminstrn. com. Jud. Conf. Va. for Dist. Cts., 1995-97; mem. state adv. com. for CASA and children's Justice Act, 1998—. Co-author: Juvenile Law and Practice in Virginia, 1994. Mem. Chesterfield County Pub. Schs. Task Force on Core Values, 1999. Mem. Va. State Bar (bd. govs. family law sect. 1997—), Va. Bar Assn., Va. Trial Lawyers Assn., Met. Richmond Women's Bar Assn., Chesterfield-Colonial Heights Bar Assn., Quota Club. Baptist. Home: 415 Lyons Ave Colonial Heights VA 23834-3154 Office: Chesterfield Juvenile and Domestic Rels Dist Ct 9600 Krause Rd Chesterfield VA 23832-6717

**DAVIS, C. VANLEER, III**, lawyer; b. Camden, N.J., 1942. AB summa cum laude, Princeton U., 1964; LLB magna cum laude, Harvard U., 1967. Bar: Pa. 1969. Law clk. to Hon. Abraham L. Freedman U.S. Ct. Appeals (3d cir.), 1967-68; ptnr. Dechert Price & Rhoads, Phila.; lectr. Pa. State U. Tax Conf., 1980, mem. planning com., 1986—, chair, 1991-92; lectr. grad. tax program Temple U., 1988-89. Author: (with Jay Zagoren) Pennsylvania Limited Liability Company Forms and Practice Manual, 1996. Mem. Phi Beta Kappa. Corporate taxation, Real property, State and local taxation. Office: Dechert Price & Rhoads 4000 Bell Atlantic Tower 1717 Arch St Ste 3 Philadelphia PA 19103-2793

**DAVIS, CHESTER R., JR.**, lawyer; b. Chgo., Aug. 30, 1930; s. Chester R. and Mead (Scoville) D.; m. Anne Meserve, Mar. 3, 1962; children: John Chester, Julia Snow, Elizabeth Meserve. Grad., Phillips Exeter Acad., 1947; A.B., Princeton, 1951; LL.B., Harvard, 1958. Bar: Ill. 1958, U.S. Dist. Ct. (no. dist.) Ill. 1958. Ptnr. Bell, Boyd & Lloyd and predecessor firms, Chgo., 1968-91; pvt. practice law Winnetka, Ill., 1991—. Assoc. Rush-Presbyn.-St. Luke's Med. Center, Chgo., 1964—, Adlai Stevenson Inst. Internat. Affairs, 1968—, Newberry Library, Chgo., 1974—; mem. Winnetka (Ill.) Zoning Commn. and Bd. Appeals, 1974-79; mem. Winnetka Plan Commn., 1976-82, 84-88; chmn. Spl. Joint. Com. of Winnetka Zoning Bd. and Plan Commn. to Revise Land Use Ordinances, 1978-83; village trustee Village of Winnetka, 1984-88; sec., bd. dirs. Vascular Disease Research Found.; mem. alumni council Phillips Exeter Acad.; chmn. Winnetka Interchurch Council, 1981-84. Served to Lt. (j.g.) USNR, 1952-56, now capt. (ret.); rear adm. Ill. Naval Militia (ret.). Decorated Navy Commendation medal, 1984; recipient New Trier Dist. award of Merit Boy Scouts Am., 1982. Mem. ABA, Ill. State Bar Assn. (mem., real property law sect. coun., 1992—), Chgo. Bar Assn. (chmn. com. civil practice 1969-70, chmn. land use and zoning com. 1980-82, chmn. real property law com. 1983-84, chmn. entertainment com. 1991-92, producer Christmas Spirits show), Am. Soc. Internat. Law, Am. Judicature Soc., Am. Arbitration Assn. (nat. panel arbitrators, mem. large complex case panel), U.S. Naval Inst., Naval Res. Assn., Am. Planning Assn., Urban Land Inst., Chgo. Mortgage Attys. Assn., Harvard Law Sch. Assn. (nat. v.p. 1970-71), Cliff Dwellers Chgo. (pres. 1993-95), Univ. Club Chgo., Econ. Club Chgo., Law Club Chgo., Legal Club Chgo., Princeton Club N.Y.C., Nassau Club, Princeton, N.J. Episcopalian. Real property, Land use and zoning (including planning), Alternative dispute resolution. Home: 670 Blackthorn Rd Winnetka IL 60093-2006 Office: PO Box 51 Winnetka IL 60093-0051

**DAVIS, CHRISTOPHER LEE**, lawyer; b. Washington, Dec. 1, 1950; s. Martin Thomas and Margaret (Babcock) D.; divorced; children: Finn Christian, Ian Dunmore. BA with honors, Middlebury Coll., 1972; JD cum laude, Union U., 1975. Bar: Vt. 1975, U.S. Dist. Ct. Vt. 1975, U.S. Ct. Appeals (2d cir.) 1975. Assoc. Gear & Kittell, Burlington, Vt., 1975-78; ptnr. Gear, Kittell & Davis, Burlington, 1979-81, Gear & Davis, Inc., Burlington, 1981-90, Gear, Davis & Kehoe, Inc., 1991-92, Langrock, Sperry & Wool, Burlington, 1992—; bd. dirs. Vt. Legal Aid, Burlington, 1983-88; mem. Vt. Profl. Conduct Bd., 1984-93, adv. com. Vt. Civil Rules, 1985-96, mem. Vt. Jud. Conduct Bd., 1998—. Chief notes editor Albany Law Rev. Bd. dirs. Children's Legal Services, Burlington, 1981-83. Mem. ABA, Vt. Bar Assn. (bd. mgrs. 1980-84), Chittenden County Bar Assn. Club: Burlington Rugby Football (pres. 1978-83, 86-88). Personal injury, General civil litigation, Criminal. Office: Langrock Sperry & Wool PO Box 721 275 College St Burlington VT 05401-8320

**DAVIS, CLAUDE-LEONARD**, lawyer, university official; b. Augusta, Ga., Feb. 16, 1944; s. James and Mary Davis; m. Margaret Earle Crowley, Dec. 30, 1965; 1 child, Margaret Michelle. BA in Journalism, U. Ga., 1966, JD, 1974. Bar: Ga. 1974. Broadcaster Sta. WKLE Radio, Washington, Ga., 1958-62; realtor Assocs. Realty, Athens, Ga., 1963-66; bus. cons. Palm Beach, Fla., 1970-71; asst. to dir. Ga. Coop. Extension Svc., Athens, 1974-81; atty. Office of Pres. U. Ga., Athens, 1981—; mem. faculty, regent Ga. Athletics Inst., 1988-98; cons. numerous agrl. chem. industry groups nationwide, 1977—, Congl. Office Tech. Assessment, Washington, 1978-79, USDA, Washington, 1979-80; del. Kellogg Nat. Leadership Conf., Pullman, Wash., 1980. Editor and contbr. Ga. Jour. of Internat. and Comparative Law, 1972-74; contbr. articles on agr. and fin. planning to profl. jours.; author and editor: DAWGFOOD: The Bulldog Cookbook, 1981, Touchdown Tailgates, 1986. Del. So. Leader Forum, Rock Eagle Ctr., Ga., 1976—; trainer Ga. 4-H Vol. Leader Assn., 1979—; vol. Athens United Way, 1980—; coordinator U. Ga. Equestrian Team, Athens, 1985-87; mem. Clarke County Sheriff's Posse, 1985—. Capt. U.S. Army, 1966-70. Chi Psi Scholar, 1965; Recipient Outstanding Alumnus award Chi Psi, 1972, Service to World Community award Chi Psi, 1975. Mem. Nat. Assn. Coll. and Univ. Attys., DAV, Poets Soc., Nat. Football Found., Am. Legion, Rotary, The President's Club (Athens), Gridiron Secret Soc., Chi Psi (advisor 1974). Baptist. Avocations: martial arts, physical fitness, creative writing, music. General corporate, Labor, Education and schools. Home: 365 Westview Dr Athens GA 30606-4635 Office: U Ga Peabody Hall Ste 3 Athens GA 30602

**DAVIS, CRESWELL DEAN**, lawyer, consultant; b. Abilene, Tex., Sept. 12, 1932; s. Emmett Dean and Marye (Creswell) D.; m. Mollie Villeret, Aug. 9, 1958; children: Addison Dean Davis, Kevin Tucker Davis. BA with honors, U. North Tex., 1953; JD, U. Tex., 1958. Bar: Tex. 1958. Asst. atty. gen. State of Tex., Austin, 1958-61; sr., mng. ptnr. Davis & Davis, P.C., Austin, 1961—; dir. Tex. Jr. Bar Conf., 1964-65. Author: Texas Legal and Consent Manual for Texas Hospitals, 1967-90; contbr. articles to profl. jours. Mem. U. North Tex. bd. regents, 1967-88, chmn., 1988; mem. U. North Tex. Health Sci. Ctr. and Tex. Coll. Osteopathic Medicine, 1967-88, chmn. 1988; adj. prof. hosp. law, Trinity U., San Antonio, 1967-90; adj. prof. pharmacy jurisprudence, U. Tex., 1969—. Recipient Disting. Svc. award Tex. Pharm. Assn., 1973, Outstanding Achievement award Tex. Assn. Life Underwriters, 1986, Outstanding Svc. award Tex. Assn. Child Care Facilities, 1984, Disting. Alumnus award U. North Tex., 1990. Mem. Rotary, Masons, Phi Alpha Delta. Episcopalian. Avocations: ranching, horses, education. General civil litigation, Administrative and regulatory, Health. Office: Davis & Davis PC 9442 N Capital Of Texas Hwy Austin TX 78759-7262

**DAVIS, CYNTHIA D'ASCENZO**, lawyer; b. Galveston, Tex., Dec. 6, 1953; d. Austin Christofer and Leah (Ellis) D'Ascenzo; 1 child, Howard Wingfield III. BA, Sam Houston State U., 1975; JD, South Tex. Coll. Law., 1983. Bar: Miss. 1987, U.S. Dist. Ct. (no. dist. so. dist.) Miss. 1987, U.S. Ct. Appeals (5th cir.). Actuarial policy analyst Am. Nat. Ins. Co., Galveston, 1975-76; tchr. ESL Texas City (Tex.) Indep. Sch. Dist., 1976-83; legal asst. Law Offices of Darrel D. Ryland, Marksville, La., 1985; pvt. practice Gloster, Miss., 1987—; atty. Town of Crosby, Miss., 1993—; mcpl. judge, Town of Gloster, 1994—; prosecutor Amite County Youth Ct., 1994—; atty. Amite County Sch. Bd., 1995—; mem. Jud. Coll. Juvenile Justice curriculum com. Treas. Amite County Hist. Soc., 1988—; mem. Miss. Animal Rescue League, Jackson, 1987—, Am. Cancer Soc., 1980—, past bd. dirs., past pub. relations chmn. Mem. ABA, Miss. Trial Lawyers Assn., S.W. Miss. Bar Assn., Miss. Bar Assn. (child advocacy com. 1990—, alternative dispute resolution com. 1991—, Pres.'s award 1990, 91, assoc. pro bono project), Miss. Women Lawyers Assn., Assn. Trial Lawyers Am., Miss. Mcpl. Judges Assn. (v.p. and pres.-elect, pres. 1999—), Miss. Capital Def. Resource Ctr. (sec., exec. com. bd. dirs.), Gloster C. of C. (sec.), Jr. League. Avocations: antiques, water skiing. Family and matrimonial, General practice, Criminal. Home: PO Box 940 Gloster MS 39638-0940 Office: 161 Main St Gloster MS 39638

**DAVIS, DALE GORDON**, lawyer; b. Akron, Ohio, Mar. 6, 1951; s. Kenneth Boone and Doris (Gordon) D.; m. Barbara Knowlton Fite, Dec. 29, 1973; children: Abigail Knowlton, Elizabeth Gordon. BA, Duke U., 1973; JD, Georgetown U., 1976. Bar: Ohio 1976, U.S. Dist. Ct. (so. dist.) Ohio 1981. Atty. McCulloch Felger Fite & Gutmann Co LPA, Piqua, Ohio, 1976-80, ptnr., 1980—. Trustee Rural Legal Aid Soc. West Ctrl. Ohio, Springfield, 1979-86, treas., 1979-84, pres., 1984-86. Mem. Ohio State Bar Assn., Miami County Bar Assn. (pres. 1990). Real property, Contracts commercial, General corporate. Office: McCulloch Felger Fite & Gutmann Co LPA PO Box 910 Piqua OH 45356-0910

**DAVIS, DARLENE ROSE**, lawyer, researcher. BA in History, U. New Orleans; postgrad., Domaine U. St. Martin D'Heres, Grenoble-Cedex, France; LLM in Taxation, U. Balt., 1994; JD, Tulane U., 1995. Bar: La. 1995, D.C. 1995. Law clk. to Hon. Louis Moore, Jr. U.S. Dist. Ct. for Ea. Dist. La., New Orleans; rsch. assoc., atty. advisor Fed. Jud. Ctr., New Orleans; sr. trial atty. U.S. EEOC, New Orleans; trial atty. environ. and natural resources divsn. U.S. Dept. Justice, Washington, 1995—; legis. counsel to Hon. William Jefferson, MC Ho. of Reps. 103d-104th Congress; tchr. ESL; spkr. Nat. Bar Assn. Nat. Conv., Chgo., 1996; organizer 1st Ann. Internat. Devel. Conf., Am. U., Washington, 1995. Bd. dirs. Visions in Action; pro bono lawyer Archdiocesan Legal Network, Washington, D.C. Arts Ctr., New Orleans Bar Assn. and New Orleans Legal Assistance Corp. Pro Bono Projects. Univ. scholar. Mem. Alpha Theta Epsilon. Home: 6101 Campus Blvd New Orleans LA 70126-2211

**DAVIS, DAVID EARL**, lawyer; b. Barberton, Ohio, Feb. 14, 1960; s. Richard D. and Darlene F. Davis; m. Deborah L. Hammond, Jan. 21, 1995. BS, Ohio State U., 1982; JD, U. Miss., 1990. Bar: Fla. 1990. Paralegal Lyle & Skipper, PA, Tampa, Fla., 1985-86; clk. U.S. Bankruptcy Ct., Tampa, 1986-87; law clk. U.S. Dept. Justice, Tampa, 1989, Pub. Defenders Office, Pascagoula, Miss., 1990; lawyer Bidwell & Assocs., Tampa, 1991-93; pvt. practice Tampa, 1993—; vol. Bay Area Legal Svcs., Tampa, 1993—. Vol. IRS Vol. Income Tax Asst. Program, Tampa, 1988—, United Way Agys., Tampa, 1992—. Mem. Fla. Bar, Hillsborough County Bar Assn., Ohio State U. Alumni, U. Miss. Alumni. Avocations: travel, boating, skiing, horseback riding. Fax: 813-250-9501. Federal civil litigation, State civil litigation, Consumer commercial. Office: 304 S Willow Ave Tampa FL 33606-2147

**DAVIS, DAVID MURREL**, lawyer; b. Shelbyville, Tenn., Sept. 11, 1947; s. Murrel Clossie and Lillie Virginia D.; m. Wanda Sue Kane Norris, May 4, 1968 (div.); children: Chris K., David A., Aimee M; m. Salee Lee, Apr. 5, 1986. BA, U. Tex., 1969, MA, 1971, JD, 1977. Bar: Tex. 1978, U.S. Dist. Ct. (we dist.) Tex. 1980, U.S. Ct. Appeals (5th cir.) 1984, U.S. Supreme Ct. 1986, cert. personal injury trial law, Tex. Bd. of Legal Specialization, 1984, civil trial advocacy, Nat. Bd. of Trial Advocacy, 1989. Assoc. Davis & Davis, P.C., Austin, Tex., 1977-85; shareholder Davis & Wilkerson, P.C., Austin, 1985—. Co-author: Texas Medical Malpractice: A Guide for the Health Sciences, 1989; editor-in-chief; Texas Health Law Reporter, 1983-94; contbr. legal articles to profl.pubis. Bd. trustees Covenant United Meth. Ch., Austin, 1982-85, 91-93; adv. bd. Am. Diabetes Assn.-Tex. Affiliate, Austin, 1984—; mem. Texas Hosp. Assn, AIDS steering com., Austin, 1988—, vice-chair, 1992-93, Defense Rsch. Inst., 1985—, Tex. Assn. of Defense Counsel, 1985—, chmn. med. malpractice com., v.p., 1995-97, Inst. for Health Policy Edn. and Rsch., Univ. of Tex. Health Sci. Ctr. at Houston, 1985—, Nat. Health Lawyers Assn., 1990—. Decorated U.S. air medal with six oak leaf clusters. Recipient Pres.' award Tex. Assn. of Defense Counsel, 1993. Mem. College of State Bar of Tex., State Bar Tex. (Litigation & Health Law sects.), Tex. State Bar Found., Travis County Bar (Litigation sect.), Fed. Bar Assn., N.W. Austin Rotary Club (Paul Harris Fellow, bd. dirs. 1985-87, pres. 1994-95, dist. gov.'s rep. 1995-96). Democrat. Methodist. Avocations: running, aerobics, photography, travel, reading. Personal injury, General civil litigation. Office: Davis & Wilkerson PC 200 One Am Ctr 600 Congress Ave Austin TX 78701-3238

**DAVIS, DAVID W.**, lawyer; b. Idaho Falls, Idaho, June 13, 1963; s. Lon F. and Mary A. Davis; m. Kim Davis, Sept. 13, 1986; children: Sarah, Joe, Rachel. BA, U. Kans., 1987; JD, U. Ariz., 1993. Assoc. Thomas Burke Law Firm, Phoenix, 1993-95, Poli & Ball, Phoenix, 1995-96, Turley Swan Childers, Phoenix, 1996—. Republican. Mem. Ch. of Jesus Christ of Latter Day Saints. Personal injury, Insurance. Home: 5301 N 85th Ave Glendale AZ 85305-3337 Office: Turley Swan Childers PC 3101 N Central Ave Ste 1300 Phoenix AZ 85012-2656

**DAVIS, DEBORAH LYNN**, lawyer; b. N.Y.C., Apr. 23, 1948; d. Melvin Jerome and Beatrice (Greenapple) D. BS, Case Western Res. U., 1970, JD, 1973. Bar: N.Y. 1974, U.S. Dist. Ct. (ea. and so. dists.) N.Y. 1974. Staff atty., dir. litigation Community Action for Legal Svcs., Inc., Bklyn., 1974-77, 78-81; atty. BLS Legal Svcs., N.Y.C., 1977-78; assoc. Gallet & Dreyer, N.Y.C., 1981-86; ptnr. Wagner, Davis & Gold, P.C., N.Y.C., 1986—. Contbg. author chpts. in book. Incorporator, officer, bd. dirs. N.Y. Svc. Program for Older People, Inc., 1978-91; mem. Family Ct. Panel Screening and Oversight com. 1st Jud. Dept., 1985-88, vice-chair screening applicants, 1985-87. Mem. N.Y. State Bar Assn., N.Y. County Lawyers Assn., N.Y. Women's Bar Assn. General civil litigation, Landlord-tenant, Real property. Office: Wagner Davis & Gold PC 99 Madison Ave New York NY 10016-7419

**DAVIS, DENNIS MILAN**, lawyer; b. Ontario, Oreg., Feb. 28, 1951; s. James Milan and Mary Louise (Meechan) D.; m. Kathryn Marie Canfield, Feb. 11, 1978. BS in Polit. Sci., U. Idaho, 1973, JD, 1977. Bar: Idaho 1977, U.S. Dist. Ct. Idaho 1977. Dep. pros. atty. Twin Falls (Idaho) County Prosecutor, 1977-78; dep. pub. defender Kootenai County Pub. Defender, Coeur d'Alene, Idaho, 1978-79; assoc. atty., ptnr. Cox & Davis Law firm, Coeur d'Alene, 1979-91; prin., atty. Witherspoon, Kelley, Davenport & Toole, P.S., Spokane, Wash., also Coeur d'Alene, 1991—. Mem. Coeur d'Alene City Planning Commn., 1985-89; mem. Idaho State Senate, Boise, 1989-94, asst. minority leader, 1993-94; mem. adv. coun. Idaho State Permanent Bldg. Fund, 1990-94, Idaho Jud. Coun., 1999—; bd. dirs. Human Rights Edn. Found., Inc., 1998—, sec., 1998—; chmn. bd. adivsors U. Idaho Rsch. Pk., 1999—. Mem. Coeur d'Alene Sunset Rotary Club. Democrat. Roman Catholic. Avocations: fly fishing, swimming, golf, bicycling. Real property, Contracts commercial, Land use and zoning (including planning). Office: Witherspoon Kelley et al The Spokesman Rev Bldg 608 Northwest Blvd Ste 401 Coeur D Alene ID 83814-2174

**DAVIS, DEREK SHANE**, lawyer; b. San Angelo, Tex., Sept. 16, 1968; s. Jim Joe and Janet (Rice) D.; m. Heather Dawn Westhoff; children: Megan Elaine, Lauren Elizabeth. BS in Pharmacy, U. Tex., 1992; JD, Tex. Tech. U., 1995. BAr: Tex. 1995, U.S. Dist. Ct. (no. dist.) Tex. 1996. Assoc. Law Offices of James C. Barber, Dallas, 1995-96, Cooper & Scully, P.C., Dallas, 1996—. Fellow Am. Soc. for Pharm. Law; mem. Tex. Pharm. Assn., Dallas Bar Assn., Dallas Assn. Young Lawyers. Personal injury, General civil litigation, Health. Office: Cooper & Scully PC 900 Jackson St Ste 100 Dallas TX 75202-4426

**DAVIS, DONALD G(LENN)**, lawyer; b. San Gabriel, Calif., Sept. 15, 1949; s. Maurice G. and Elinore C. (Leigh) D.; m. Alex Davis; children: Christian Glenn, Alexandra, Donald Glenn Jr., Regina Ann Rogers, Katherine Ann, Andrew Glenn. BS in Acctg., Calif. State U., Pomona, 1966; JD, U. So. Calif., 1969. Assoc. Adams, Duque & Hazeltine, L.A., 1968, Omlevny & Meyers, L.A., 1969-72; prof. of law Southwestern U. Law Sch., L.A., 1972-80; gen. counsel Republic Corp., L.A., 1973; ptnr. Danielson, St. Clair & Davis, L.A., 1974-77; mng. ptnr. Davis & Assocs., L.A., 1980—, DGD Enterprises P.V., L.A., 1980—, DGD Investment Banking, L.A., 1980—. Exec. editor Law Rev. jour., U. So. Calif., 1968-69. Vice-pres. student body, Calif. State U., Pomona, 1964-65; candidate 42nd Congl. Dist., Calif., 1988. Mem. ABA, L.A. Bar Assn. (chmn. securities cooperative seminar 1988, chmn. bus. lawyers sect. 1986-87), Order of Coif, Calif. Club, L.A. Yacht Club. Securities, Entertainment, Public international. Address: 1900 Ave Of Stars Ste 2600 Century City CA 90067-4507

**DAVIS, DONALD LEE**, lawyer; b. Lexington, Mo., May 24, 1953; s. Elvin Wallace and Ethel (Ikenberry) D.; m. Julie Diann Walter, Nov. 25, 1983; children: Adam Lee, Benjamin Wallace. BA, Ottawa (Kans.) U., 1976; JD, U. Nebr., 1979. Bar: Mo. 1980, U.S. Dist. Ct. (we. dist.) Mo. 1980, U.S. Ct. Appeals 1981, U.S. Supreme Ct. 1986. Pvt. practice, Kansas City, Mo., 1980—. Contbg. author: Mathew Bender's Criminal Legal Forms, 1986. Active St. Peter's Sch. Athletic Commn. Mem. Mo. Assn. Trial Attys., Kansas City Metro Bar Assn. Democrat. Episcopalian. Avocations: football, golf, barbecue. General civil litigation, Personal injury, Family and matrimonial. Home: 419 E 64th Ter Kansas City MO 64131-1127 Office: 3419 Locust St Kansas City MO 64109-2273

**DAVIS, E. MARCUS**, lawyer; b. Atlanta, Nov. 24, 1951; s. Edward Martin and Marcine (McConnell) D.; m. Sue Fouquet; children: Edward Clark, Hannah Morgan. AB in Econs., Duke U., 1973; JD, U. Ga., 1976. Bar: U.S. Supreme Ct. 1981. Ptnr. Davis, Zipperman, Kirschenbaum & Lotito, Atlanta, 1983—. Contbr. articles to profl. jours. Mem. ABA, ATLA, Ga. Trial Lawyers Assn., Ga. Criminal Def. Lawyers Assn., Nat. Bd. Trial Advocacy (cert.), Am. Bd. Profl. Liability Attys. (cert.), Lawyers Club of Atlanta. Presbyterian. Avocations: boating, painting, fishing, flying. Personal injury. Office: Davis Zipperman Kirschenbaum & Lotito 918 Ponce De Leon Ave NE Atlanta GA 30306-4212

**DAVIS, EARL PRICHARD (PAT DAVIS),** lawyer; b. Blytheville, Ark., Sept. 10, 1918; s. Thomas Wils and Nellie Pearl (Tanner) D.; widower; children: Ruth Mitchell Davis Smith, Thomas Earl. BA, S.We. Coll. (now Rhodes Coll.), Memphis, 1941; LLB, U. Va., 1947, JD, 1970. Bar: Tenn. 1947. Ptnr. Davis and Davis, Memphis, 1948-87; pvt. practice, Memphis, 1987—. Lt. col. USAF, 1941-45, ETO. General civil litigation, Probate, Personal injury. Office: 4515 Poplar Ave Ste 221 Memphis TN 38117-7506

**DAVIS, EARON SCOTT,** environmental health law consultant, lawyer; b. Chgo., Sept. 7, 1950; s. Milton and Grayce D.; m. Gilla Prizant, May 29, 1977; children: Jeremy Adam, Jonathan Michael, Daniel Benjamin. BA, U. Ill., 1972; JD, Washington U., St. Louis, 1975; MPH, UCLA, 1978. Bar: Ill. Asst. to chmn. Ill. Pollution Control Bd., Chgo., 1975-77; environ. cons. Fred C. Hart Assos., Washington, 1979-80; atty. coord. Migrant Legal Action Program, Washington, 1980-81; environ cons. Evanston, Ill., 1981—. Editor, pub. Ecol. Illness Law Report, Evanston, 1982-89; author: Toxic Chemicals: Law and Science, 1982; contbr. articles to various publs. Exec. dir. Human Ecology Action League, Evanston, 1983-84; mem. nat. adv. bd. Environ. Task Force, Washington, 1984-88, Nat. Ctr. for Environ. Health Strategies (Recognition of Excellence 1991), N.C. Ohio Coalition Against Misuse of Pesticides; mem. adv. com. D.C. Lung Assn. (spl. commendation 1981), Washington, 1980-82, Clean Air Coalition, Phila, 1983-85, U.S. EPA's Indoor Air Quality clearinghouse Planning Team, 1990-92. Recipient Presdl. award Am. Acad. Environ. Medicine, 1983, Carlton Lee award Am. Acad. Environ. Medicine, 1988, Gargoyle award Coun. for Disability Rights, 1992. Mem. Soc. Environ. Journalists. E-mail: earondavis@aol.com. Home: 643 Hibbard Rd Wilmette IL 60091-2042

**DAVIS, EDWARD BERTRAND,** federal judge; b. W. Palm Beach, Fla., Feb. 10, 1933; s. Edward Bertrand and Mattie Mae (Walker) D.; m. Patricia Lee Klein, Apr. 5, 1958; children: Diana Lee Davis, Traci Russell, Edward Bertrand, III. JD, U. Fla., 1960; LLM in Taxation, N.Y. U., 1961. Bar: Fla. 1960. Pvt. practice Miami, 1961-79; counsel High, Stack, Lazenby & Bender, 1978-79; U.S. dist. judge So. Dist. Fla., 1979—. Served with AUS, 1953-55. Mem. Fla. Bar Assn., Dade County Bar Assn. Office: US Dist Ct 301 N Miami Ave Miami FL 33128-7702

**DAVIS, EMILY S.,** lawyer; m. Matthew I. Levine; 2 children. BA cum laude, U. Mass., 1978; JD cum laude, Boston Coll., 1982. Bar: Va. 1982, N.H. 1990, U.S. Dist. Ct. Vt., U.S. Dist. Ct. N.H. Assoc. Downs, Rachlin & Martin, 1982-84; dep. state's atty. Windsor County State's Atty.'s Office, 1984-86; ptnr. Black Black & Davis, White River Junction, Vt., 1990—; adj. faculty Vt. Law Sch., 1991-94. Co-chair Citizens Justice Conf., 1998-99; mem. Commn. on the Future Vt.'s Justice Sys., 1998-99; bd. dirs. ProChoice Ct., 1982-92, co-chair, 1989-91. Mem. ABA (family law sect.), Vt. Bar Assn. (pres.-elect 1997-98, pres. 1998-99, bd. mgrs. 1993—, family law com. 1993—, long range/scope and program com. chair 1997-98, family ct. rev. com., chair rules and statutes subcom. 1997), Vt. Bar Found. (bd. dirs. 1995-98), New Eng. Bar Assn. (bd. dirs. 1995-98), Vt. Trial Lawyers Assn., Vt. Vol. Lawyers Project (Pro Bono Svc. award 1996), Windsor County Bar assn. (pres. 1991-92, v.p. 1989-91, sec.-treas. 1988-89), N.H. Bar Assn., Nat. Conf. Bar Pres. E-mail: Davis@BBDLaw.com. Family and matrimonial. Office: Black Black & Davis PO Box 796 White River Junction VT 05001-0796

**DAVIS, EVAN ANDERSON,** lawyer; b. N.Y.C., Jan. 18, 1944; s. Richard T. and Charlotte (Upham) D.; m. Mary Carroll Rothwell; 1 child, Sara Mei-Ping. BA, Harvard U., 1966; JD, Columbia U., 1969. Bar: N.Y. 1970, U.S. Dist. Ct. (so. dist.) N.Y. 1973, U.S. Ct. Appeals (2d cir.) 1973, U.S. Dist. Ct. (ea. dist.) N.Y., 1978, U.S. Supreme Ct. 1979. Law clk. to judge U.S. Ct. Appeals (D.C. cir.), 1969-70; law clk. to Justice Potter Stewart U.S. Supreme Ct., 1970-71; gen. counsel N.Y.C. Budget Bur., 1971-72; chief consumer protection div. N.Y.C. Law Dept., 1972-74; task force leader, impeachment inquiry staff U.S. Ho. of Reps., 1974; assoc. Cleary, Gottlieb, Steen & Hamilton, N.Y.C., 1975-78; ptnr. Cleary, Gottlieb, Steen & Hamilton, 1979-85, 91—; counsel to gov. of N.Y., 1985-90; vice chmn., bd. dirs. Fund for N.Y.C., 1982-85; trustee Columbia U., 1993—, mem. exec. com., 1994—, chair fin. com. Editor-in-chief Columbia Law Rev., 1968-69. Treas. Sch. for Field Studies, 1991-95; dir. Franklin and Eleanor Roosevelt Inst., 1993—, mem. exec. com., 1994—; dir. Mus. of Hudson Highlands, 1991—, Storm King Sch., 1991-98; bd. visitors Helen Hayes Hosp., 1992-98, mem. coun. fgn. rels.; chairperson N.Y. Fair Election Project, 1998—. Recipient Hopkins medal St. David's Soc., N.Y., 1988, Bruckner medal Fed. Bar Coun., 1990, Aquarium Environ. award Wildlife Conservation Soc., 1995. Mem. ABA (ho. of dels. 1983-85, 91-93, chmn. spl. com. youth edn. for citizenship 1986-88, chmn. standing com. pub. edn.), Assn. Bar City N.Y. (chmn. exec. com. 1982-83, v.p. 1983-84), Legal Aid Soc. (v.p. 1983-85, 97—, exec. com. 1992—), Am. Law Inst., N.Y. State Bar Assn. (com. to revise ethics rules 1992—, commn. on middle income access to legal svc. 1995—). Home: 6 Eagle Head Cornwall On Hudson NY 12520-1720 Office: Cleary Gottlieb Steen & Hamilton 1 Liberty Plz Fl 38 New York NY 10006-1470

**DAVIS, FLORENCE ANN,** lawyer; b. Pitts., Feb. 22, 1955; d. Richard Davis and Charlotte (Saul) McGhee; m. Kevin J. O'Brien, May 28, 1978; children: Rebecca Davis, Sarah Davis. AB, Wellesley U., 1976; JD, NYU, 1979. Bar: N.Y. 1980, U.S. Dist. Ct. (ea. and so. dists.) N.Y., N.Y. Ct. Appeals (2d cir.), U.S. Tax Ct., U.S. Supreme Ct. Assoc. atty. Sullivan & Cromwell, N.Y.C., 1979-86; litigation counsel Morgan Stanley & Co., N.Y.C., 1986-88, v.p., 1988-90, dir. compliance, 1989-90, prin., 1990-95; v.p., gen. counsel Am. Internat. Group, N.Y.C., 1995—. Root-Tilden scholar NYU Law Sch., 1976-79. Mem. Securities Industry Assn. (v.p. edn. Compliance and Legal div. 1992, exec. com. Compliance and Legal div. 1990-92). Office: American International Group Inc 70 Pine St New York NY 10270-0002*

**DAVIS, FREDERICK BENJAMIN,** law educator; b. Bklyn., Aug. 21, 1926; s. Clifford Howard and Anne Frances (Forbes) D.; m. Mary Ellen Saecker, Apr. 21, 1956; children: Judith, Robert, James, Mary. AB, Yale U., 1948; JD, Cornell U., 1953; LLM with honors, Victoria U. of Wellington (N.Z.), 1955. Bar: N.Y. 1953, Mo. 1970, Ohio 1981. Assoc. Engel Judge & Miller, N.Y.C., 1953-54; instr. U. Pa. Law Sch., 1955-56; asst. prof. NYU, 1956-57; asst. prof. U. S.D., 1957-60, assoc. prof., 1960-62; assoc. prof. Emory U., 1962-63, prof., 1963-66; prof. U. Mo.-Columbia, 1966-70, Edward W. Hinton prof. law, 1970-81, Edward W. Hinton prof. emeritus, 1981—; dean, prof. law U. Dayton Sch. Law, 1981-86; vis. prof. Wake Forest U. Sch. Law, 1980, 86-87; dean, prof. Memphis State U., 1987-92, prof. 1992-98, prof., dean emeritus, 1998—; cons. adminstrv. procedure Mo. Senate, 1974-77; vis. prof. U. Wis., 1960, George Washington U., 1965, Tulane U., 1966, U. Mo.-Kansas City, 1973, U. Ky., 1977. Contbr. numerous articles, comments, revs., notes to profl. jours. Served with USNR, 1944-46. Mem. ABA (council sect. adminstrv. law 1969-75), Am. Law Inst., Memphis South Rotary Club, Summit Club. Republican. Episcopalian. Home: 2019 Quail Creek Cv Memphis TN 38119-6410 Office: U Memphis Sch Law Memphis TN 38152-0001

**DAVIS, G. REUBEN,** lawyer; b. Muskogee, Okla., Nov. 5, 1943; s. Glenn Reuben and Margaret Elizabeth (Linebaugh) D.; m. D. Candace Jensen, June 17, 1967; children: Clay Reuben, Hayden Jensen. BA, Westminster Coll., 1966; JD, U. Okla., 1973. Bar: Okla. 1973, U.S. Dist. Ct. (no. dist.) Okla. 1973, U.S. Ct. Appeals (10th cir.) 1973, U.S. Supreme Ct. 1988. Assoc. Boone, Smith, Davis, Hurst & Dickman, Tulsa, 1973-78, ptnr., 1978—. Past pres. Tulsa Cystic Fibrosis Found., bd. dirs., 1976—; trustee Hillcrest Med. Ctr., Inc., Tulsa, 1979, Alexander Trust, Tulsa Found.; v.p., bd. dirs. Indian Nations coun. Boy Scouts Am., 1987—. Mem. ABA, Am. Inns Ct., Okla. Bar Assn., Tulsa County Bar Assn. (v.p. 1986-87, pres. 1988-89), Order of Coif. Republican. Methodist. Avocations: running, tennis, golf. Federal civil litigation, General civil litigation, State civil litigation. Office: Boone Smith Davis Hurst & Dickman 100 W 5th St Ste 500 Tulsa OK 74103-4215

**DAVIS, GENE CARLTON,** lawyer; b. Chgo., June 15, 1917; s. Carl DeWitt and Alta (Hoff) D.; m. Roberta Wilson, Mar. 14, 1942; children: Bruce Carlton, Barbara Jean. A.B., U. Chgo., 1938; LL.B., Chgo. Kent Coll. Law, 1941. Bar: Ill. 1942. Practiced in Chgo., 1942-79; with firm Isham, Lincoln & Beale, 1943-79, partner, 1953-79; individual practice law Woodstock, Ill., 1979-82; mem. firm Davis & Holmes, Lake Forest, Ill., 1982-95; dir. So. Nev. Telephone Co., 1956-60, Parker Aleshire & Co., 1962-83. Author: Estate Planning A Client's Handbook, 1967; composer: Euphonious Marcus, For Starters, At Home, Fun Time. Trustee Orchestral Assn. Chgo., v.p., 1972-76. Served with AUS, 1942-43. Fellow Am. Coll. Probate Counsel; mem. ABA, Ill. Bar Assn., Chgo. Bar Assn. (chmn. admissions com. 1955, entertainment com. 1952, probate com. 1962). Presbyterian. Clubs: Law (Chgo.), Legal (Chgo.) (pres. 1965), Onwentsia. Home: 501 Oakwood Ave Lake Forest IL 60045-1964

**DAVIS, GERALD KENNETH, JR.,** lawyer; b. Bakersfield, Calif., Apr. 7, 1966; s. Gerald Kenneth and Deloyce Rae Davis. BA in Environ. Studies, U. Kans., 1988; JD, U. Calif., Davis, 1991. Bar: Calif. 1992, Alaska 1992, U.S. Dist. Ct. Alaska 1992. Law clk. Alaska Superior Ct., Juneau, 1991-92; assoc. Law Offices of David T. Walker, Juneau, 1992—. Mem. ABA, Juneau Bar Assn. (sec. 1993-94, v.p. 1994-95). Family and matrimonial, Workers' compensation, General practice. Office: Law Office David T Walker 417 Harris St Juneau AK 99801-1048

**DAVIS, G(ILES) JACK,** lawyer; b. Dayton, Ohio, July 2, 1943; s. Giles Jack and Katherine V. Davis; m. Karen K. Snell, June 18, 1967 (div. Mar. 1978); children: Giles Jack III, Jefrey W., Christian M.; m. Arnette L. Meyers, Apr. 14, 1978; children: Annie N., Trisha M. BS, Bowling Green State U., 1965; JD, Ohio State U., 1967. Bar: Ohio 1968, U.S. Dist. Ct. (so. dist.) Ohio 1969, U.S. Supreme Ct. 1971, U.S. Tax Ct. 1972, U.S. Ct. Appeals (6th cir.) 1987. Ptnr. Baggott, Logan, Gianuglou & Davis, Dayton, 1968-74, Logan & Davis, Dayton, 1975-80, Gianuglou, Davis & Wilks, Dayton, 1980-87, Davis Law Offices, Dayton, 1987—; law dir. City of Vandalia, Ohio; asst. atty. gen. State of Ohio, Columbus, 1973-97. Pres. Vandalia Jr. Achievement, 1977. Mem. ABA, Ohio Bar Assn. (chmn. young lawyers sect. 1970), Dayton Bar Assn. (exec. com. 1978, com. profl. ethics 1984), Assn. Trial Lawyers Am., Ohio Acad. Trial Lawyers (trustee 1975-78, Disting. Svc. award 1978), Am. Arbitration Assn., Montgomery County Criminal Law Coun., Family Law Forum, Dayton Racquet Club, Masons. Personal injury, Labor, General practice. Home: 2225 Coolidge Dr Dayton OH 45419-2564 Office: 424 Patterson Rd Dayton OH 45419-4306

**DAVIS, GORDON J.,** lawyer; b. Chgo., Aug. 7, 1941. AB, Williams Coll., 1963; JD, Harvard U., 1967. Bar: Ill. 1968, N.Y. 1973, U.S. Dist. Ct. (so. and ea. dists.) N.Y. 1973. Commr. N.Y.C. Dept. Parks and Recreation, 1978-83; screening panel fed. magistrates U.S. Dist. Ct. (so. dist.) N.Y., 1983-90. Mem. N.Y. City Planning Commn., 1973-78; bd. dirs. Harlem Studio Mus., 1981, Lincoln Ctr. Performing Arts, 1983, Mcpl. Art Soc., 1983, Dance Theatre of Harlem, 1984, N.Y. Public Libr., 1993; chmn. Jazz at Lincoln Ctr., 1996. Mem. Assn. of Bar of City of N.Y. (com. to enhance profl. opportunities for minorities 1990). General corporate, Real property, Land use and zoning (including planning). Office: LeBoeuf Lamb Green & MacRae 125 W 55th St New York NY 10019-5369

**DAVIS, GREG ROBERT,** lawyer; b. N.Y.C., Dec. 30, 1967; s. Mitchell Leonard and Donna Auerbach Davis. BA, Tufts U., 1989; JD, Emory U., 1992. Bar: Ariz. 1992, U.S. Dist. Ct. Ariz. 1992, U.S. Ct. Appeals (9th cir.) 1994. Assoc. Doyle, Appel & Davis P.C., Phoenix. Office: Doyle Appel & Davis PC 4638 E Shea Blvd Phoenix AZ 85028-3072

**DAVIS, GREGG C.,** lawyer; b. Des Moines, Aug. 3, 1958; s. Charles M. and Patricia A. Davis; m. Stephanie Stuewer, Apr. 27, 1985. BA in Bus. Adminstrn., So. Meth. U., 1978; JD, Stanford U., 1982. Bar: Tex. 1982. Atty. Thompson & Knight, P.C., Dallas, 1982—. Mem. ABA, State Bar of Tex. (real property, probate and trust sect., environ. and natural resources sect.). Environmental, Real property. Office: Thompson & Knight PC 1700 Pacific Ave Ste 3300 Dallas TX 75201-4693

**DAVIS, HENRY BARNARD, JR.,** lawyer; b. East Grand Rapids, Mich., June 3, 1923; s. Henry Barnard and Ethel Margaret (Turnbull) D.; m. Margaret Lees Wilson, Aug. 27, 1946; children: Caroline Dellenbusch, Laura Davis, George B. BA, Yale U., 1945; JD, U. Mich., 1950; LLD, Olivet Coll., 1983. Bar: Mich. 1951; U.S. Dist. Ct. (we. dist.) Mich. 1956, U.S. Ct. Apls. (6th cir.) 1971, U.S. Supreme Ct. 1978. Assoc. Allaben, Wiarda, Hayes & Hewitt, 1951-52; ptnr. Hayes, Davis & Dellenbusch PLC, Grand Rapids, 1952—. Mem. Kent County Bd. Commrs., 1968-72, Community Mental Health Bd., 1970-94, past chmn.; trustee, sec. bd. Olivet Coll., 1965-91, chmn. law com., gen. counsel, 1975-91, trustee emeritus 1991—; bd. dirs. Jr. Achievement Grand Rapids, 1960-65; chair Grand Rapids Historic Preservation Com., 1977-79. Republican. Trustee, East Congregational Ch., 1979-81. Served with USAAF, 1943-46; Philippines. ABA, Mich. Bar Assn., Grand Rapids Round Table (pres. 1969). Lodge: Masons. Estate planning, Probate, Real property. Home: 30 Mayfair Dr NE Grand Rapids MI 49503-3831 Office: 535 Fountain St NE Grand Rapids MI 49503-3421

**DAVIS, HERBERT OWEN,** lawyer; b. D.C., June 11, 1935; s. Owen Steir and Claudie Lea (Pointer) D.; children: Herbert O. Jr., Ann P., Paul B. BA, U. N.C., 1957; JD, Duke U., 1960. Bar: N.C. 1960, U.S. Dist. Ct. (mid. dist.) N.C. 1960. Assoc. Smith Moore Smith Schell & Hunter, Greensboro, N.C., 1960-66, ptnr., 1966-86; ptnr. Smith Helms Mulliss & Moore, Greensboro, 1986—; bd. dirs. Custom Industries, Inc., Greensboro. Editor in chief Duke Law Jour., 1959-60. Mem. ABA, N.C. Bar Assn., Greensboro Country Club, Greensboro City Club (bd. dirs.), The Carolina Club, Phi Beta Kappa. General corporate, Mergers and acquisitions, Banking. Home: 2303 Danbury Rd Greensboro NC 27408-5123 Office: Smith Helms Mulliss & Moore 300 N Greene St Ste 1400 Greensboro NC 27401-2171

**DAVIS, J. ALAN,** lawyer, producer, writer; b. N.Y.C., Nov. 7, 1961. Student, Marlborough Coll., Eng., 1979; BA with distinction, So. Meth. U., 1983; JD with honors, U. Tex., 1987. Bar: Calif. 1988. Assoc. O'Melveny & Myers, L.A., 1987-89, Rosenfeld, Meyer & Susman, Beverly Hills, Calif., 1989-90; pvt. practice L.A., 1990-94; ptnr. Davis & Benjamin, L.A., 1995-97, Garvin, Davis & Benjamin, LLP, L.A., 1997-99; pvt. practice L.A., 1999—. Mem. Calif. Bar Assn., Beverly Hills Bar Assn. (entertainment law sect. exec. com.), Brit. Acad. Film and TV Arts, L.A. (mng. dir., bd. dirs.), British Film Office (exec. com.). Avocations: skiing, scuba diving, tennis. Entertainment, General corporate. Office: 8491 W Sunset Blvd # 1550 Los Angeles CA 90069-1911

**DAVIS, JASON MURRAY,** lawyer; b. San Antonio, June 22, 1970; s. Michael and Ann (Stenn) D. BA in Polit. Sci., Trinity U., 1992; JD, U. Tex., 1995. Bar: Tex. 1995, Fla. 1996, U.S. Dist. Ct. (no. and so. dists.) Tex. 1996, U.S. Ct. Appeals (5th cir.) 1996. Staff asst. to Senator Pete V. Domenici, U.S. Senate, Washington, 1991; rsch. asst. U. Tex., Austin, 1993; law clk. Office U.S. Atty. for Western Dist. Tex., Austin, 1995; jud. law clk. to Judge George P. Kazen, U.S. Dist. Ct. for So. Dist. Tex., Laredo, 1996; assoc. Thompson & Knight, P.C., Dallas, 1997; asst. U.S. atty. Office U.S. Atty. for So. Dist. Tex., Laredo, 1997—; lectr. continuing edn. Drug Enforcement Agy. Mem. ABA, State Bar Tex. (pro bono coll. 1997), Fla. State Bar, Young Lawyers Tex., Am. Inn Ct. (assoc.). Office: US Atty's Office 1501 Matamoros St Laredo TX 78040-4912

**DAVIS, JEFFREY ROBERT,** lawyer; b. Mineola, N.Y., Nov. 1, 1961; s. Stuart Edward and Carole Lynn Davis; m. Yasmin Suero, July 15, 1992; children: Jack Reiley, Abigail. BA, SUNY, Stony Brook, 1983; JD, U. Miami, 1986. Bar: Fla. 1986, U.S. Dist. Ct. (so. dist.) Fla. 1986. Atty. Lawrence B. Rodgers PA, Miami, Fla., 1986-88, Robert Romanga PA, Miami, 1988-89, Daryl L. Merl PA, Miami, 1989-95; ptnr. Merl & Davis PA, Miami, 1995-97, Jeffrey R. Davis PA, Miami, 1997—; dir. Dade County Trial Lawyers, 1997. Mem. ATLA, Acad. Fla. Trial Lawyers, Fla. Bar Assn. (chair grievance com. 1994-97, mem. unlicensed practice of law com. 1998—), Phi Beta Kappa. Avocations: mountain bikes, sporting clays. Personal injury, Product liability, State civil litigation. Office: Jeffrey R Davis PA 100 SE 2d St #2600 Miami FL 33131

**DAVIS, JIMMY FRANK,** assistant attorney general; b. Lubbock, Tex., June 14, 1945; s. Jack and Fern Lisemby D.; M. Joyce Zelma Hart, Nov. 6, 1976; children: Jayme Leigh, Julee Ellen. BS in Edn., Tex. Tech. U., 1968; JD, U. Tex., 1972. Bar: Tex. 1972, U.S. Supreme Ct. 1975, U.S. Dist. (no. dist.) Tex. 1976, U.S. Ct. Appeals (5th cir.) 1976, U.S. Ct. Appeals (11cir.) 1981. Asst. criminal dist. atty. Lubbock County, 1973-74, adminstrv. asst., 1976-77; county and dist. atty. Castro County, Tex., 1977-92; asst. atty. gen. Tex., 1993—. Mem. State Bar of Tex. (com. admissions dist. 16 1974-78, dist. 13 1983-92, govt. lawyers sect., coun. mem. 1991-92), Tex. Dist. and County Attys. Assn., Lubbock County Jr. Bar Assn. (pres. 1977), Tex. Tech. Ex Students Assn. (dist. rep. 1981-84, bd. dirs. 1985-90), Coll. of State Bar of Tex. (continuing legal edn. 1984-93), Kiwanis of Lubbock (pres. 1977), Kiwanis of Dimmitt (pres. 1981), Delta Theta Pi, Delta Theta Phi. Office: PO Box 5280 401 50th St Lubbock TX 79408

**DAVIS, JOHN ALBERT,** lawyer; b. Seattle, July 29, 1940; s. Carl Lee and Helen Irene (Corner) D.; m. Judith Ann colvin, June 21, 1959 (div. 1978); children: John Albert, James Colvin, Jennifer Lynn. Student, U. Calif., Berkeley, 1957-58; postgrad., Diablo Valley Coll., 1962; JD, Golden Gate U., 1970. Bar: Calif. 1971, U.S. Dist. Ct. (no. dist.) Calif. 1971, U.S. Ct. Appeals (9th cir.) 1971, U.S. Supreme Ct. 1986. Pres. Cal-State Distbrs., Oakland, Calif., 1959-78; pvt. practice Oakland, 1978-81, San Ramon, 1985—; v.p., chief operating officer Madre Mining, Ltd., Sacramento, 1981-85; pres., bd. dirs. O'Hara Resources, Ltd., Vancouver, B.C., Can., 1989—; bd. dirs. Troy Gold Industries, Ltd., Calgary, Alta., Can. Mem. Calif. Bar Asns., Commwealth Club Calif., Sequoia Woods Country Club. Republican. Presbyterian. Securities, General corporate. Office: PO Box 2096 San Ramon CA 94583-7096

**DAVIS, JOSHUA MALCOLM,** lawyer; b. Worcester, Mass., May 11, 1965; s. William Merritt and Jessica Ann (Hoffmann) D.; m. Susan Marysol Flink, Aug. 11, 1991; children: Emerson Jacob, Malcolm Christopher. BA, Swarthmore Coll., 1987; JD, U. Chgo., 1991. Bar: Mass. 1992, U.S. Ct. Appeals (10th cir.), 1992; U.S. Dist. Ct. (Mass.), 1993, U.S. Ct of Appeals (1st Cir.), 1993; U.S. Supreme Ct., 1995; U.S. Ct. of Appeals (2nd Cir.), 1997. English tchr. St. Paul's Sch., Concord, N.H., 1987-88; law clerk Hon. Stephanie K. Seymour U.S. Ct. Appeals (10th cir.), Tulsa, 1991-92; assoc. Hill & Barlow, Boston, 1992-99, mem., 1999—; tchg. asst. torts Harvard Law Sch., Cambridge, Mass., 1997, part-time lectr. law, Northeastern U. Sch. of Law, 1998. Contbr. Mass. Lawyers Weekly, 1994, 98. Mem. ABA, Mass. Bar Assn., Boston Bar Assn. Democrat. Avocations: golf, reading. Office: Hill & Barlow 1 International Pl Boston MA 02110-2602

**DAVIS, KENNETH BOONE, JR.,** dean, law educator; b. Louisville, Sept. 1, 1947; s. Kenneth Boone and Doris Edna (Gordon) D. m. Arrietta Evoline Hastings, June 2, 1984; children: Peter Hastings, Mary Elizabeth, Kenneth Boone III. AB, U. Mich., 1969; JD, Case Western Res. U., 1974. Bar: D.C. 1975, Ohio 1974. Law clk. to chief judge U.S. Ct. Appeals (9th cir.), San Francisco, 1974-75; assoc. Covington & Burling, Washington, 1975-78; prof. law U. Wis., Madison, 1978—, dean Law Sch., 1997—. Contbr. numerous articles on corp. and securities law to profl jours. Mem. ABA, Am. Fin. Assn., Am. Law Inst., Wis. Bar Assn. (reporter, corp. and bus. law com.). Office: U Wis Law Sch 975 Bascom Mall Madison WI 53706-1399

**DAVIS, KENNETH DUDLEY,** lawyer; b. Andalusia, Ala., July 6, 1958; s. Clark Kelly and Ruby Clay (Poe) D.; m. Leslie Ann McWilliams, May 17, 1986. BA, U. Ala., 1980, JD, 1983. Bar: Ala. 1983, U.S. Dist. Ct. (mid. and no. dists.) Ala. 1984, U.S. Ct. Appeals (11th cir.) 1984. Assoc. Nomberg & McCabe, Daleville, Ala., 1983-84, Cabaniss, Johnston, Gardner, Birmingham, Ala., 1984-85, Zeanah, Hust & Summerford, Tuscaloosa, Ala., 1986-89; ptnr. Zeanah, Hust, Summerford & Davis and predecessor firms, Tuscaloosa, 1989—; staff atty. Ala. Supreme Ct., Montgomery, 1984. Mem. ABA, Ala. Def. Lawyers Assn., Tuscaloosa County Bar Assn. Presbyterian. General civil litigation, Insurance, Consumer commercial. Office: Zeanah Hust Summerford & Davis PO Box 1310 Tuscaloosa AL 35403-1310

**DAVIS, KIRK STUART,** lawyer; b. Olean, N.Y., Dec. 30, 1957; s. Robert DeWitt and Joan Gracie Davis; m. Aileen Stewart, Dec. 24, 1982. BS, Stetson U., 1979, JD, 1982. Bar: Fla. 1983, U.S. Dist. Ct. (mid. dist.) Fla. 1983. Lawyer Greene, Mann, Rowe, St. Petersburg, Fla., 1983-84, Greene & Mastry, P.A., St. Petersburg, 1984-91, Elias & Davis, P.A., Clearwater, Fla., 1991-94, Annis, Mitchell, Tampa, Fla., 1995-97, Akerman, Senterfitt & Eidson, Tampa, 1997—. Mem. Fla. Bar Assn. (chair health law sect. 1992-93, chair health law cert. com. 1998-99), Bayou Club (mem. adv. bd. 1991-98, chair adv. bd. 1994-98). Avocation: golf. Health, General civil litigation. Office: Akerman Senterfitt & Eidson 100 S Ashley Dr Ste 1500 Tampa FL 33602-5314

**DAVIS, LARRY ALLEN,** lawyer; b. Chgo., June 9, 1950; s. Lee J. and Lynn (Koralchick) D.; m. Caryn Jacobs, Sept. 23, 1978; children: Shanna, Brandon, Merrill. BA, Northwestern U., 1973; JD, DePaul U., 1976. Bar: Ill. 1976, U.S. Dist. Ct. (no. dist.) Ill. 1976. Atty. Sec. of State, State of Ill., Chgo., 1976-80; pvt. practice Chgo., 1980-82; ptnr. Davis & Riebman, Des Plaines, Ill., 1982—; lectr. Ill. Inst. Continuing Legal Edn., Chgo., 1984-96. Author: (with others) Defense of DUI, 1984-96; contbr. articles to profl. jours. Cert. of Recognition NW Suburban Bar Assn., Palatine, Ill., 1985-90. Mem. Ill. State Bar Assn. (chair traffic laws and cts. sect. coun. 1992-93, Cert. of Recognition 1995), Chgo. Bar Assn. (chmn. traffic laws com. 1987-88, lectr. 1984-90, Cert. of Recognition 1995). Criminal, Administrative and regulatory, General practice. Office: Davis & Riebman Ltd 960 Rand Rd Ste 210 Des Plaines IL 60016-2355

**DAVIS, LEWIS U., JR.,** lawyer; b. Pitts., Mar. 25, 1950; s. Lewis Uber and Myrtle Elizabeth (Otte) D.; children: Shannon Lynn, Christin Lynn; m. Laraine Frazzini, May 22, 1993; 1 child, Laura Fitzgerald. BS in Engring. summa cum laude, Lehigh U., 1972; JD summa cum laude, Cornell U., 1975. Bar: Pa. 1975, U.S. Dist Ct. (we. dist.) Pa. 1975, U.S. Ct. Appeals (3d cir.) 1978. Assoc. Buchanan Ingersoll, Pitts., 1975-82, ptnr., shareholder, 1982—, v.p. tech., chief technology officer, 1994—. Contbr. articles to profl. jours. Mem. ABA, Am. Bankruptcy Inst., Pa. Bar Assn. Avocations: computers, tennis, golf. Bankruptcy, Securities, General corporate. Office: Buchanan Ingersoll One Oxford Centre 301 Grant St Fl 20 Pittsburgh PA 15219-1410

**DAVIS, LOUIS POISSON, JR.,** lawyer, consultant; b. Washington, July 17, 1919; s. Louis Poisson and Edna (Shethar) D.; m. Emily Elizabeth Carl, Feb. 7, 1943; 1 child, Cynthia. BSc, U.S. Naval Acad., 1941; postgrad., Princeton U., 1947-48; JD, Rutgers U., 1953. Bar: N.Y. 1954, Ill. 1963, U.S. Dist. Ct. (so. dist.) N.Y. 1956, U.S. Dist. Ct. (no. dist.) Ill. 1965, U.S. Supreme Ct. 1964. Mgr. engring. Esso Std. Oil, Linden, N.J., 1946-57; sr. economist, head econs. and market rsch. dept. Internat. Petroleum Co., Lima, Peru, 1957-60; asst. overseas ops. AMF Internat. Abbott Labs., North Chicago, Ill., 1962-65; gen. mgr. Far East ops. Ralston Purina Co.; pres. Ralston Purina Eastern, Hong Kong, 1966-71; dir. internat. devel. Archer Daniels Midland Internat., Decatur, Ill., 1972-74; lectr., rschr. internat. law and mgmt., N.Y.C., 1974-76; corp. rep. Europe, Mid East, Africa, Alexander & Baldwin Agribus, Inc., Abidjan, Ivory Coast, 1976, Madrid, Spain, 1977; internat. atty., cons., Sarasota, Fla., 1978-99; cons. Sarasota County Office of Sci. Advisor, 1985-86, Office of Gen. Counsel, 1989-91; vol. income tax assistance program IRS, 1983-98; cons., seminar leader Chipsoft, Inc., 1989-90; vol. atty. Gulfcoast Legal Svcs., 1987-91; instr. Sarasota Tech. Inst., 1990-98; cert. cons. Capsoft Devel. Corp. Legal Automation Software, 1991; gen. counsel Manasota Industry Coun., Inc., 1984-89; bd. dirs. Siesta Key Assn., v.p., 1993-94, 98—. Lt. comdr. USN, 1937-46. Mem. ABA, Hong Kong Country Club, Oaks Club (Sarasota). Republican. Episcopalian. General corporate, Public international, Personal income taxation. Home and Office: 620 Mangrove Point Rd Sarasota FL 34242-1230

**DAVIS, M. G.,** lawyer; b. Concho County, Tex., Nov. 11, 1930; s. Zack and Olive (Clifton) D.; m. Jeanne Focke, Feb. 7, 1959; children: Linda Jeanne, Lisbeth Dianne. BBA, Tex. Tech. U., 1952; JD, U. Tex., 1958. Bar: Tex., 1957, U.S. Supreme Ct., 1964; atty. Gen. Land Office, Austin, Tex., 1959-60, firm Smith, Porter & Caston, Longview, Tex., 1960-61; v.p. Am. Title Co. Dallas, 1961-67; owner, operator Security Land Title Co., Amarillo, Tex., 1967-69; pres. Dallas Title Co., Houston, 1969-70, Guardian Title, Houston, 1970-72, Collin County Title Co., Plano, Tex., 1972-87; pvt. practice, Plano, 1972-82; ptnr. firm Davis & Davis, Dallas, 1982-93, Davis & Sallinger, L.L.P., Dallas, 1993-98, Davis & Davis, Richardson, Tex., 1999—; guest lectr. U. Houston, Richland Jr. Coll. Chmn. Selective Service Bd. 46, 1982-92; mem. legis. task force, employer support for guard and reserve affairs TNGA. 1st lt. USAF, 1952-54; Korea. Recipient Involved Citizen award Dallas Morning News, 1980. Mem. State Bar Tex., Dallas Bar Assn., Coll. State Bar of Tex., Sons Republic Tex., Tex. Land Title Assn. (v.p. 1970-71),

Tex. Tech. Ex-Students Assn. (dir. 1961-63), Collin County Title Assn. (pres. 1977), Dallas Mortgage Bankers Assn., Collin County U. Tex. Ex-Students Assn. (pres. 1980), U. Tex. Ex-Students (exec. council 1983-86), Alpha Tau Omega. Democrat. Episcopalian. Fax: 972-690-8078. Real property. Home: 5200 Roundrock Trl Plano TX 75023-5408 Office: Davis & Davis Ste 1701 N Greenville Ave Richardson TX 75081-6271

**DAVIS, MARGUERITE HERR,** judge; b. Washington, Nov. 12, 1947; d. Norman Phillip and Margaretha Joanna (Dewaard) Herr; m. James Riley Davis, June 20, 1970; children: Amy Marguerite, Christine Riley. AA with honors, St. Petersburg J. Coll., Clearwater, Fla., 1966; BA with honors, U. of South Fla., 1968; JD with honors, Fla. State U., 1971. Bar: Fla. 1971, U.S. Dist. Ct. (no. dist.) Fla. 1971, U.S. Dist. Ct. (mid. dist.) Md. 1985, U.S. Ct. Appeals (11th cir.) 1985, U.S. Supreme Ct. 1986. Atty. workers compensation div. U.S. Dept. Labor, Tallahassee, 1971; sr. legal aide Fla. Supreme Ct., Tallahassee, 1971-85, exec. asst. to Hon. Chief Justice Alderman, 1982-84; ptnr. Swann & Haddock, Tallahassee, 1985-87, Katz, Kutler, Haigler, Alderman, Davis & Marks, Tallahassee, 1987-93; judge Dist. Ct. of Appeal (1st dist.) Fla., Tallahassee, 1993—; finalist for justice U.S. Supreme Ct., 1997. Mem. editl. bd. Trial Advocate Quar., 1991-93; contbr. chpts. to books. Mem. ABA, Fla. Bar Assn. (Tallahassee chpt., appellate ct. rules com. 1995—, appellate ct. rules com. chair, 1995-97, grievance com., disciplinary rev. com., chmn. supreme ct. local rules adv. com., jud. cir. grievance com., rules of jud. adminstrn. 1995—, chair 1997-98, jud. evaluation com. 1995—, exec. coun. appellate advocacy sect.), Fla. State Fed. Jud. Coun. (exec. dir. 1985—), Tallahassee Women Lawyers, Fla. Def. Lawyers Assn. (amicus curiae com.), Fla. Supreme Ct. Hist. Soc., Am. Arbitration Assn. (ad hoc com. stds. for appellate practice cert.), Altrusa Club of Tallahassee (treas. 1971-76), Fla. State U. Alumni Assn. (bd. dirs. 1975-76), Jud. Mgmt. Coun. (appellate ct. workload and jurisdiction com. 1996—, chair appellate rules liaison com., appellate practice and advocacy sect. 1996-98, nominated for finalist for Supreme Ct. Justice, 1997), Univ. So. Fla. (bd. dirs. Alumni Assn. 1999), Phi Theta Kappa. Methodist. Avocations: quilting, sewing, knitting, running, reading.

**DAVIS, MARK MURRAY,** lawyer; b. East Grand Rapids, Mich., Nov. 13, 1963; s. Thomas Bruce and Susan (Murray) D. BS, Mich. State U., 1986; JD, Marquette U., 1989; M in Environ. Law, Vt. Law Sch., South Royalton, 1990. Bar: Wis. 1989, Mich., U.S. Dist. Ct. (we. dist.) Mich. 1990. Atty. Vt. Office atty. Gen., Montpelier, 1989-90; asst. regional counsel Hazardous Waste br. U.S. EPA, Atlanta, 1990-92, CERCLA br. U.S. EPA, Atlanta, 1992-95; atty. Varnum, Riddering, Schmidt & Howlett,LLP, Grand Rapids, Mich., 1995—. Mem. East Grand Rapids Planning Commn., 1997—; bd. dirs. Western Mich. Environ. Action Coun., 1997—. Mem. ABA (sec. natural resources, energy and environ. law), Wis. Bar Assn., Mich. Bar Assn., Grand Rapids Bar Assn. E-mail: mmdavis@vrsn.com. Environmental. Office: Varnum Riddering et al Bridgewater Pl PO Box 352 Grand Rapids MI 49501-0352

**DAVIS, MARK RICHARD,** lawyer; b. Nov. 10, 1953. BA, U. N.Mex., 1975; JD, DePaul U., 1979. Asst. states atty., tax divsn. supr. Cook County States Atty. Office, Chgo., 1979-89; ptnr. O'Keefe Ashenden Lyons & Ward, Chgo., 1989—; adv. bd., property tax com. Civic Fedn., Chgo., 1992—; property tax adv. com. Ill. Tax Payers Fedn., Springfield, Ill., 1992—. Mem. Ill. State Bar Assn. (past chair state and local tax sect. counsel 1991—), Chgo. Bar Assn. (real estate tax com.), Phi Beta Kappa. Office: O'Keefe Ashenden Lyons & Ward 30 N Lasalle St Ste 4100 Chicago IL 60602-2507

**DAVIS, MARK WARDEN,** lawyer; b. Greenville, Miss., Sept. 17, 1958; s. Joseph Warden and Ruby Nell (Alford) D.; m. Angela Leigh Perry, Apr. 8, 1989; children: Ashleigh Elizabeth, Autumn Arissa. BS, Delta State U., 1980; JD, U. Miss., 1984. Bar: Miss. 1984, U.S. Dist. Ct. (no. and so. dist.) 1984, U.S. Ct. Appeals (5th cir.) 1984. Assoc. Hopkins, Logan, Vaughn & Anderson, Gulfport, Miss., 1984-87; ptnr. Davis & Feder, Gulfport, 1988—; speaker in field. Mem. nat. com. Miss. Young Reps., 1984-88; chmn. Gulf Coast Young Reps., 1984-88. Mem. ABA, Miss. Bar Assn., Harrison County Bar Assn., Harrison County Young Lawyers Assn. (del.), Am. Trial Lawyers Assn., Miss. Trial Lawyers Assn., Gulf Coast C. of C., Ducks Unltd., Bayou Bluff Tennis Club, Windance Country Club, Gulfport Jaycees. Methodist. Avocations: golf, tennis, fishing, hunting. Personal injury, Product liability, Admiralty.

**DAVIS, MARTHA ALGENITA SCOTT,** lawyer; b. Houston, Oct. 1, 1950; d. C.B. Scott and Althea (Lewis) Scott Renfro; m. John Whittaker Davis, III, Aug. 21, 1976 (dec. Oct. 1997); children: Marthea, John IV. BBA, Howard U., 1971, JD, 1974. Bar: Tex. 1974, U.S. Dist. Ct. (so. dist.) Tex. 1975, U.S. Ct. Appeals (5th cir.) 1976, U.S. Supreme Ct. 1980. Tax atty. Shell Oil Co., Houston, 1974-79; counsel Port of Houston Authority, 1979-89; sr. v.p., cmty. affairs officer Chase Bank Tex., 1989—; ptnr. Burney, Edwards, Hall, Hartsfield & Scott, Houston, 1975-78; bd. dirs. Unity Nat. Bank. Bd. dirs. Houston Citizens Chamber, 1980-90, Neighborhood Ednl. Ctr., Houston, 1983-87, Peoples' Workshop to Performing Arts; coord. Operation Big Vote, Washington, 1984-85; mem. planning commn. City of Houston, 1987-91; founding chair Houston Downtown Mgmt. Corp., 1991-92; pres. Greater Houston Women's Found., 1996-98; chair Third Ward Redevel. Coun., 1998. Recipient Achievement award Greek Coun., Houston, 1973; Houston's Most Influential Black Women award Black Experience Mag., Five Young Outstanding Houstonians award Houston Jr. C. of C., 1989; named one of Houston Ten Women of Distinction, Chrones and Colitis Found. and The Houston Press, 1993, one of Women on the Move, Houston Post, 1994. Mem. Nat. Bar Assn. (pres. 1990-91, sec. 1983-88, chmn. voter edn./registration com. 1985-86, Pres. award 1993, 94), Black Women Lawyers Assn. (vice chair 1983-84, Profl. Achievement award 1984), Houston Lawyers Assn. (bd. dirs. 1977-78, 85-89, pres. 1988-89), The Links (nat. and western parliamentarian 1994, Houston parliamentarian). Baptist. Admiralty, Landlord-tenant. Office: Chase Bank Tex 14 CBBE-93 PO Box 2558 Houston TX 77252-2558

**DAVIS, MARTIN CLAY,** lawyer, professor; b. Tulsa, Okla., Dec. 12, 1947; s. James William and Vera Ruby (Hatcher) D.; m. Rebecca Jo Strong, Aug. 22, 1970; children: Christopher James, Jennifer Alice. BA, U. Ark., 1970; JD, Vanderbilt U., 1973. Bar: Tex. 1973, U.S. Tax Ct. 1985, cert. specialist estate planning, probate law State Bar Tex. Assoc. atty. Gary, Thomasson, Hall & Marks, Corpus Christi, Tex., 1973-77, partner, 1977-94; partner Davis, Hutchinson & Wilkerson, LLP, Corpus Christi, Tex., 1994—; adj. prof. Corpus Christi (Tex.) State U., 1980-83, 87, Tex. A&M U.-C.C., 1993; bd. dirs. Corpus Christi Estate Planning Coun. (pres. 1985-86); pres. Am. Assn. Individual Investors, Corpus Christi subchpt., 1995-96; lectr. various profl. assns. Assoc. Editor: Vanderbilt Law Rev., 1972-73. Pres. Family Counseling Svc., Corpus Christi, 1984; trustee, chmn. United Meth. Ch., 1998. Recipient Leadership award, Corpus Christi C. of C., 1980. Fellow, Tex. Bar Found., Am. Coll. Trust & Estate Counsel; mem. ABA (subcom. chmn. taxation sect., 1975-80), State Bar Tex. (estate planning and probate law adv. commn., taxation sect.; planning com. advanced estate planning and probate course, 1982, 85, 91, planning com. wills and probate inst. 1985, 87, 88, com. to revise the Tex. Trust Act), Order of the Coif. Avocations: tennis, basketball, teaching. Estate planning, Probate. Office: Davis Hutchinson & Wilkerson LLP Frost Bank Plz Ste 1270 Corpus Christi TX 78470

**DAVIS, MICHAEL J.,** judge; b. 1947. BA, Macalester Coll., 1969; JD, U. Minn., 1972. Law clk. Legal Rights Ctr., 1971-73, atty., 1975-78; with Office Gen. Counsel Dept. Health, Edn. and Welfare, Social Security Adminstrn., Balt., 1973; criminal def. atty. Neighborhood Justice Ctr., 1974; atty., commr. Mpls. Civil Rights Commn., 1977-82; pub. defender Hennepin County, 1978-83; judge Hennepin County Mcpl. Ct., 1983-84, Hennepin County Dist. Ct. (4th jud. dist.), 1984-94, U.S. Dist. Ct. Minn., St. Paul, 1994—; constnl. law instr. Antioch Mpls. C.C., 1974; criminal def. trial practice instr. Nat. Lawyer's Guild, 1977; trial practice instr. William Mitchell Coll. Law, 1977-81, Bemidji Trial Advocacy Course, 1992, 93; adj. prof. U. Minn. Law Sch., 1982—, Hubert H. Humphrey Sch. Pub. Affairs, 1990; instr. Minn. Inst. Legal Edn., 1990—, lectr. Civil Trial Practice Inst., 1991-92; lectr. FBI Acad., 1991, 92. Recipient Outstanding Alumni award Macalester Coll., 1989, Good Neighbor award Sta. WCCO Radio, 1989. Mem. ABA, Nat. Bar Assn., Minn. Minority Lawyers Assn., Am. Inns. of Ct., Fed. Bar Assn., Fed. Judges Assn., Hennepin County Bar Assn., Minn. State Bar Assn., Minn. Lawyers Internat. Human Rights Com. (past mem. bd. dirs.), Internat. Acad. Trial Judges, Nat. Assn. for Pub. Interest Law Fellowships for Equal Justice (bd. dirs.), 8th Cir. Jury Instruction Com., U.S. Assn. Constitutional Law. Office: US Dist Ct Minn 300 S 4th St Ste 14E Minneapolis MN 55415-2251

**DAVIS, MICHAEL S.,** lawyer; b. Brookline, Mass., Aug. 1, 1947; s. Ralph and Beatrice (Levy) D.; m. Madelyn O. Davis, Aug. 16, 1970; children: Gregory, Adam, Bethany. AB, U. Rochester, 1969; JD cum laude, Boston U., 1972. Bar: N.Y. 1973, U.S. Dist. Ct. (so. and ea. dists.) N.Y. 1974, U.S. Ct. Appeals (2d cir.) 1974, U.S. Supreme Ct. 1979, U.S. Ct. Claims, 1980. Assoc. Chadbourne & Parke, N.Y.C., 1972-82; sr. counsel corp. litigation Am. Internat. Group, N.Y.C., 1982-88; ptnr. Zeichner, Ellman & Krause, LLP, N.Y.C., 1999—; asst. adj. prof. C.W. Post Ctr., L.I. U., Glen Cove, N.Y., 1975-79. Editor Boston U. Law Rev., 1970-72. Mem. Citizens Ctr. for Children of N.Y., Inc., 1978-87; pres. Pelham (N.Y.) Jewish Ctr., 1986-88. Mem. ABA, Assn. Bar City of N.Y., Am. Arbitration Assn., Huguenot Bridge Club. Democrat. Bankruptcy, General civil litigation, Insurance. Office: Zeichner Ellman & Krause 575 Lexington Ave New York NY 10022-6102

**DAVIS, MULLER,** lawyer; b. Chgo., Apr. 23, 1935; s. Benjamin B. and Janice (Muller) D.; m. Jane Lynn Strauss, Dec. 28, 1963 (div. July 1998); children: Melissa Davis Smith, Muller, Joseph Jeffrey; m. Lynn Straus, Jan. 23, 1999. Grad. with honors, Phillips Exeter (N.H.) Acad., 1953; BA magna cum laude, Yale U., 1957; JD, Harvard U., 1960. Bar: Ill. 1960, U.S. Dist. Ct. (no. dist.) Ill. 1961. Practice law Chgo., 1960—; assoc. Jenner & Block, 1960-67; ptnr. Davis, Friedman, Zavett, Kane & MacRae, 1967—; lectr. continuing legal edn., matrimonial law and litigation; legal adviser Michael Reese Med. Research Inst. Council, 1967-82. Author: (with Sherman C. Feinstein) The Parental Couple in a Successful Divorce, Illinois Practice of Family Law, 1995, 97, 98-99; mem. editl. bd. Equitable Distbn. Jour., 1984—; contbr. articles to law jours. Bd. dirs. Infant Welfare Soc., 1975-96, hon. bd. dirs., 1996—, pres., 1978-82; co-chmn. gen. gifts 40th and 45th reunions Phillips Exeter Acad., chair class capital giving, 1994-98. Capt. U.S. Army, Ill. N.G., 1960-67. Fellow Am. Acad. Matrimonial Lawyers (bd. mgrs. Ill. chpt. 1996-99), Am. Bar Found.; mem. ABA, FBA, Ill. Bar Assn., Chgo. Bar Assn. (matrimonial com. 1968-83, sec. civil practice com. 1979-80, vice chmn. 1980-81, chmn. 1981-82), Am. Soc. Writers on Legal Subjects, Chgo. Estate Planning Coun., Legal Aid Soc. (vice chmn. matrimonial bar 1991-95, vice chmn. 1995-97, chmn. 1997-99), Law Club Chgo., Tavern Club, Lake Shore Country Club, Chgo. Club. Republican. Jewish. Family and matrimonial. Home: 2110 N Fremont St Chicago IL 60614-4306 Office: Davis Friedman Zavett Kane & MacRae 140 S Dearborn St Chicago IL 60603-5202

**DAVIS, PRESTON LINDNER,** lawyer; b. Danville, Pa., Jan. 22, 1936; s. Preston B. and M. Isabelle (Lindner) D.; m. Margaret E. Whitenight, Aug. 30, 1958; children: Kerry P. Davis, Kathy J. Hrenko, Kirk P. Davis, Kelly J. Farquhar. AB, Dartmouth Coll., 1957; LLB, JD, U. Pa., Phila., 1960. Bar: Pa. 1961, U.S. Ct. Appeals (3d cir.) 1961, U.S. Dist. Ct. (mid. dist.) Pa. 1962. Law clk. to Hon. Herbert F. Goodrich U.S. Ct. Appeals (3d cir.), Phila., 1960-61; ptnr. Davis Davis & Kaar, Milton, Pa., 1961—; solicitor, Northumberland County, 1964-69, Milton Mcpl. Authority, 1980—; chmn. Milton Indsl. Authority, 1985—. Mem. exec. bd. Northumberland Rep. Party, Sunbury, Pa., 1964—. Mem. Northumberland County Bar Assn. (pres. 1984), Milton Rotary, Milton Elks Club, Milton Masons (past master), Moose, Milton Area C. of C. (past pres.). Lutheran. Avocations: sports, golf. Estate planning, General corporate, Probate. Office: Davis Davis & Kaar PO Box 319 Milton PA 17847-0319

**DAVIS, RICHARD,** lawyer; b. Miami, Fla., Sept. 12, 1943; s. James Henry and Rosa Lee Davis; m. Doreen Dolores Douglas, Mar. 20, 1970; children: Laronda Renee, Richard Quinro. BS, U. Ariz., 1969, JD, 1972. Bar: Ariz. 1972, U.S. Dist. Ct. Ariz. 1972, U.S. Ct. Appeals (9th cir.) 1974. Atty. Chandler, Tullar, Udall & Redhair, Tucson, 1972-89, Mesch, Clark & Rothschild, Tucson, 1989—. Bd. dirs. Tucson Urban League, Tucson Cmty. Found.; judge pro tem Ariz. State Bar, Pima County. Served with USAF, 1961-65. Fellow Am. Coll. Trial Lawyers, Am. Bd. Trial Advocates; mem. Ariz. State Bar assn., Pima County Bar Assn. Democrat. Avocations: travel, sports, gardening. Personal injury, Product liability, General civil litigation. Office: Mesch Clark & Rothschild 259 N Meyer Ave Tucson AZ 85701-1090

**DAVIS, RICHARD WATERS,** lawyer; b. Rocky Mount, Va., July 9, 1931; s. Beverly Andrew and Julia (Waters) D.; m. Mary Alice Woods; children: Debra, Julie, Richard Jr., Bob, Bev. B, Hampden-Sydney Coll., 1951; LLB, U. Richmond, 1959. Bar: Va. 1959. Pvt. practice Radford, Va., 1959—; dist. judge City of Radford, 1962-80; mem. Pub. Defenders Commn. Va., 1993—; mem. Va. State Bar Coun., 1989-95; assoc. prof. bus. law Radford U.; lectr. Va. Trial Lawyers Assn. Fellow Am. Coll. Trial Lawyers, Am. Bar Found., Va. Law Found.; mem. ABA. Va. Bar Assn. Personal injury, Insurance, State civil litigation. Home: 101 5th St Radford VA 24141-2401 Office: PO Box 3448 Radford VA 24143-3448

**DAVIS, ROBERT EDWARD,** state supreme court justice; b. Topeka, Aug. 28, 1939; s. Thomas Homer and Emma Claire (Hund) D.; m. Jana Jones; children: Edward, Rachel, Patrick, Carolyn, Brian. BA in Polit. Sci., Creighton U., 1961; JD, Georgetown U., 1964. Bar: Kans. 1964, U.S. Dist. Ct. Kans. 1964, U.S. Tax Ct. 1974, U.S. Ct. Mil. Appeals 1965, U.S. Ct. Mil. Review, 1970, U.S. Ct. Appeals (10th cir.) 1974, U.S. Supreme Ct. 1982. Pvt. practice Leavenworth, Kans., 1967-84; magistrate judge Leavenworth County, 1969-76, county atty., 1980-84, judge dist. ct., 1984-86; judge Kans. Ct. Appeals Jud. Br. Govt., Topeka, 1986-93; justice Kans. Supreme Ct., Topeka, 1993—; lectr. U. Kans. Law Sch., Lawrence, 1986-95. Capt. JAGC, U.S. Army, 1964-67, Korea. Mem. Am. Judges Assn., Kans. Bar Assn., Leavenworth County Bar Assn. (pres. 1977), Judge Hugh Means Am. Inn of Ct. Charter Orgn. Lawrence. Roman Catholic. Office: 301 W 10th Ave Topeka KS 66612

**DAVIS, ROBERT LARRY,** lawyer; b. Lubbock, Tex., June 6, 1942; s. R. H. and Bernice (Pray) D.; m. Peggy Saunders, Jan. 25, 1965; children: Lee Michael, Melissa Lynn. LLB with honors, Rice U., 1964; LLB (with honors), U. Tex., 1967. Bar: Tex. 1967, U.S. Dist. Ct. (we. dist.) Tex. 1969, U.S. Dist. Ct. (so. dist.) Tex. 1989. Assoc. Royston Rayzor & Cook, Houston, 1967-68; from assoc. to ptnr. Brown McCarroll & Oaks Hartline, Austin, Tex., 1968—; bus. sect. coord., mem. mgmt. com., parliamentarian, mem. exec. com. Downtown Revitalization Task Force, Austin, 1978-80. Mem., past pres. Boys Club of Austin and Travis County, 1981—; trustee Eanes Ind. Sch. Dist., Austin, 1986-93, pres., 1990-93. Mem. Assn. Atty. Mediators (pres. Cen. Tex. chpt. 1995). Methodist. Avocations: sports, music, reading. Construction, Real property, Alternative dispute resolution. Home: 36073 Pinnacle Rd Austin TX 78746 Office: Brown McCarroll 1400 Franklin Plz Austin TX 78701

**DAVIS, ROBERT LAWRENCE,** lawyer; b. Cin., Apr. 5, 1928; s. Bryan and Henrietta Elizabeth (Weber) D.; m. Mary Lee Schulte, June 14, 1952; children: Gregory, Randy, Jenny, Bradley. BA, U. Cin., 1952; JD with honors, Salmon P. Chase Coll. Law, 1958. Bar: Ohio, 1958, U.S. Supreme Ct. 1966. Assoc. Trabert & Gay, Cin., 1958-62; ptnr. Trabert, Gay & Davis, Cin., 1962-68, Gay, Davis & Kelly, Cin., 1969-71; pvt. practice, Cin., 1972—; lectr. Mt. St. Joseph Coll, 1972-82; arbitrator Am. Arbitration Assn.; assoc. adj. prof. Salmon P. Chase Coll. Sch. Law, 1969-80; lectr. Good Samaritan Hosp. Sch. Nursing, 1960-71. Pres. bd. trustees Cmty. Ltd. Care Dialysis Ctr., 1978-86; mem. Hamilton County Ohio Hosp. Commn., 1986, Kidney Found. Greater Cin., 1989, 1992. Capt. U.S. Army, 1946-48, 52-53. Decorated Bronze Star medal. Fellow Am. Coll. Trial Lawyers (state chmn. 1994-95); mem. Ohio Bar Assn., Cin. Bar Assn., Am. Bd. Trial Advs. (adv., pres. Cin. chpt. 1996), Lawyers Club (pres. 1962-63), Order of Curia, KC, Phi Delta Theta, Phi Alpha Delta, Sigma Sigma, Omicron Delta Kappa. Personal injury, State civil litigation, Probate. Home: 9969 Voyager Way Cincinnati OH 45252-1962 Office: 3600 Carew Tower Cincinnati OH 45202

**DAVIS, ROBIN JEAN,** state supreme court justice; b. Boone County, W.Va., Apr. 6, 1956; m. Scott Segal; 1 child, Oliver. BS, W.Va. Wesleyan Coll., 1978; MA in Indsl. Rels., W.Va. U., 1982, JD, 1982. With Segal & Davis L.C., 1982-96; justice W.Va. Supreme Ct. of Appeals, 1996—, chief justice, 1998—; mem. W.Va. U. Law Inst., W.Va. Bd. of Law Examiners, 1991—. Contbr. articles to W.Va. Law Rev. Mem. ABA, Assn. of Trial Lawyers of Am., Kanawha County Bar Assn., Am. Acad. Matrimonial Lawyers. Office: Supreme Ct of Appeals Bldg 1 Rm E 301 Capitol Complex Charleston WV 25305*

**DAVIS, ROLAND CHENOWETH,** lawyer; b. San Diego, Jan. 5, 1911; s. Percy Roland and Herta (Curme) D.; m. Harriet Allen, Oct. 24, 1934; children: Carolyn, Alan, Mary Anne, Roland Francis. BA, Stanford U., Palo Alto, 1932, JD, 1936. Bar: Calif. 1937, U.S. Dist. Ct. Calif. 1937, U.S. Ct. Appeals (9th cir.) 1937, U.S. Supreme Ct. 1954. Atty. Nat. Labor Bur., San Francisco, 1938-42; sect. head War Shipping Adminstrn., Washington, 1942-43; dir. Nat. Labor Bur., San Francisco, 1944-46; ptnr. Carroll, Davis & Freidenrich, San Francisco, 1947-58; sr. ptnr. Davis, Cowell & Bowe, San Francisco, 1958-87; of counsel Davis, Reno & Courtney, San Francisco, 1987—; counsel San Francisco Labor Coun. and State Coun. of Retail Clks. Unions, 1946-65; lectr. labor law Stanford U., 1950's and 60's; chmn. labor law com. San Francisco Bar Assn., 1956; chmn. labor rels. com. San Francisco Commonwealth Club, 1974-75; tchr. labor law City Coll. San Francisco, 1974-75. Parliamentarian Calif. Delegation, Nat. Dem. Conv., Phila., 1948; chmn. Dem. County Com, Santa Clara County, 1948-52; sec. state com. Dem. Party, Calif., 1952. Mem. ABA, Am. Arbitration Assn., Calif. State Bar Assn., De Anza Country Club (pres. 1976-79), Los Altos Golf and Country Club (pres. 1966), Calif. Conciliation Svc. (panel of arbitrators 1984—). Avocations: golf, gardening, reading, travelling. Labor, Pension, profit-sharing, and employee benefits, Education and schools. Home: 1620 Cowper St Palo Alto CA 94301-3619 Office: Davis Reno and Courtney 90 New Montgomery St San Francisco CA 94105-4501

**DAVIS, ROY WALTON, JR.,** lawyer; b. Marion, N.C., Jan. 15, 1930; s. Roy Walton and Mildred Gertrude (Wilson) D.; m. Madeline Burch Combs, Sept. 10, 1955; children: R. Walton III, Madeline Trent, Rebekah Wilson, Sally Fielding. BS, Davidson Coll., 1952; JD with honors, U. N.C., 1955. Bar: N.C. 1955, U.S. Dist. Ct. (we. dist.) N.C. 1960, U.S. Ct. Appeals (4th cir.) 1963. Ptnr. Davis & Davis, Marion, 1959-60; from assoc. to ptnr. Van Winkle, Buck, Wall, Starnes & Davis, Asheville, N.C., 1960—; lectr. in field. Contbr. profl. publs. Chancellor Episc. Diocese of Western N.C., Black Mountain, 1980—. With U.S. Army, 1956-59. Fellow Am. Bar Found., Am. Coll. Trial Lawyers (state chair 1994-96), Internat. Soc. Barristers; mem. ABA (tort and ins. practice and litig. sects. Ho. of Dels. 1989-92), N.C. Bar Assn. (chmn. young lawyers divsn. 1965-66), N.C. State Bar (pres. 1985-86, trustee IOLTA 1987-93), N.C. Assn. Def. Attys., Order of Coif. Democrat. State civil litigation, Federal civil litigation, Insurance. Home: 359 Country Club Rd Asheville NC 28804-2639 Office: Van Winkle Buck Wall Starnes & Davis 11 N Market St Ste 300 Asheville NC 28801-2932

**DAVIS, SAMUEL L.,** lawyer; b. Teancek, NJ, Sept. 23, 1952; s. Harold Davis and Ruth Kaufman; m. Susan Joan Agner, Dec. 29, 1985; children: Ariel, Alexa, Alana, Joshua. Grad., Tufts U., Somerville, Mass., 1973, Rutgers U., Camden, NJ, 1977. Bar: N.J. 1978, D.C. 1980. Law clerk U.S. Dist. Ct., Phila., 1975-76; law sec. Superior Ct. N.J., Hackensack, N.J., 1977-78; assoc. Liebowitz, Kraft, Liebowitz, Engelwood, N.J., 1978-79; pvt. practice Teaneck, N.J., 1979-80; founding ptnr. Davis, Saperstein & Salomon, Teaneck & N.Y.C., 1981—. Contbr. chpts. to books. Pres., founder Legal Inst. Med. Edn., Hackensack, N.J., 1988—; chmn. N.J. State Senate Auto Legis. Com., 1992-93. Mem. ABA, Am. Trial Lawyers Assn., Am. Acad. Forensic Sci. First U.S. attorney to present live testimony via video conferencing; developer of Courtcam communication system. Avocations: golf, tennis, guitar, Harleys. Office: Davis Saperstein & Salomon 375 Cedar Ln Teaneck NJ 07666-3433

**DAVIS, SCOTT JONATHAN,** lawyer; b. Chgo., Jan. 8, 1952; s. Oscar and Doris (Koller) D.; m. Anne Megan, Jan. 4, 1981; children: William, James, Peter. BA, Yale U., 1972; JD, Harvard U., 1976. Bar: Ill. 1976, U.S. Dist. Ct. (no. dist.) Ill. 1976, U.S. Ct. Appeals (7th cir.) 1977, U.S. Ct. Appeals (8th cir.) 1986. Law clk. to judge U.S. Ct. Appeals (7th cir.), Chgo., 1976-77; assoc. Mayer, Brown & Platt, Chgo., 1977-82, ptnr., 1983—. Bd. editors Harvard Law Rev., 1974-76; contbr. articles to profl. jours. V.p. Chgo. Police Bd. Mergers and acquisitions, General corporate, General civil litigation. Home: 838 W Fullerton Ave Chicago IL 60614-3236 Office: Mayer Brown & Platt 190 S La Salle St Ste 3100 Chicago IL 60603-3441

**DAVIS, STEPHEN B.,** lawyer. AB, Princeton U., 1979; MA in East Asian studies, U. Wash., 1984; JD, Columbia U., 1988. Atty. Preston, Gates & Ellis, Seattle; pres. Corbis, Seattle; bd. dirs. Lambda Legal Def. Fund, Washington, Wash. Software Alliance, Seattle. Bd. dirs. United Way of King County, Seattle, 1993—. Office: Corbis 15395 SE 30th Pl Ste 300 Bellevue WA 98007-6537

**DAVIS, SUSAN RAE,** lawyer; b. Salem, Oreg., July 15, 1948; d. William Ray and Pearl E. (Lundin) Catlin; m. Donald K. Davis, June 13, 1970. BA, U. Wash., 1969, JD, 1977. Bar: Wash. 1977, U.S. Dist. Ct. (we. dist.) Wash. 1977, U.S. Ct. Appeals (9th cir.) 1977, U.S. Dist. Ct. (ea. dist.) Wash. 1989. Writer, editor Associated Press, Seattle, 1969-70; news dir. Sta. KUUU, Seattle, 1970-71; reporter, photographer Sta. KXLY-TV, Spokane, Wash., 1971-73, Sta. KHQ-TV, Spokane, 1973-74; ptnr. Burns, Schneiderman, Davis & Finkle P.S., Seattle, 1977-86, The Davis Firm, Seattle, 1987—; instr. journalism Eastern Wash. State Coll., Spokane, 1973-74. Mem. tribunal Wash. State Human Rights Commn., Seattle, 1974-79; arbitrator King County Mandatory Arbitration Panel, Seattle, 1985—; bd. visitors U. Puget Sound, 1986-87. Mem. ATLA, Settlement Now (mediator 1988-97), Am. Bd. Trial Advs., Wash. State Bar Assn., Seattle-King County Bar Assn., Wash. State Trial Lawyers Assn. (leadership award 1984, bd. dirs. 1980-82, treas. 1982-83, v.p. west 1983-84, v.p. pub. affairs 1984-85, pres. elect 1985-86, pres. 1986-87), Wash. Women Lawyers. Democrat. Avocation: photography. Admiralty, Personal injury. Office: The Davis Firm 5301 Ballard Ave NW Seattle WA 98107-4061

**DAVIS, TERRY HUNTER, JR.,** lawyer; b. Charlottesville, Va., Mar. 19, 1931; s. Terry Hunter and Mattie May (Parsons) D.;m. Mary Jane Irwin, Sept. 3, 1960; 1 child, Terry Hunter III. BA, Va. Mil. Inst., 1953; LLB, U. Va., 1958. Bar: Va. 1958, N.Y. 1959. Assoc. Thacher, Proffitt, Prizer, N.Y.C., 1958-60; law clk. Chief U.S. Dist. Judge, Norfolk, Va., 1960-61; assoc., ptnr. Taylor, Gustin, Harris, Norfolk, 1961-88; ptnr. Harris, Fears, Davis, Lynch & McDaniel, Norfolk, 1988—. Contbg. author Virginia Lawyer's Basic Practice Handbook, 1964. Chmn. Norfolk Electral Bd., 1971-72. 1st lt. U.S. Army, 1953-55. Mem. ABA, Va. Bar Assn., Va. State Bar (com. mem. 1972-73), Norfolk/Portsmouth Bar (com. chmn. 1962-63), SAR (treas. 1962-64), Kiwanis. Republican. Episcopalian. Avocations: jogging, tennis. General civil litigation, Insurance, Personal injury. Home: 7451 N Shore Rd Norfolk VA 23505-1770 Office: Harris Fears Davis Lynch & McDaniel 5735 Poplar Hall Dr Norfolk VA 23502-3813

**DAVIS, THOMAS E.,** lawyer; b. Gadsden, Ala., June 29, 1945; s. Truman Hoyt and Willia Mae Davis; m. Diane K. Davis, Oct. 22, 1966; children: Ashley, Stacy. BS, Auburn (Ala.) U., 1966; JD, Samford U., Birmingham, Ala., 1969. Bar: Ala. 1973, U.S. Dist. Ct. (no. dist.) Ala. 1970, U.S. Ct. Appeals (5th cir.) 1975, U.S. Ct. Appeals (11th cir.) 1981, U.S. Ct. Appeals (fed. cir.) 1983, U.S. Supreme Ct. 1973. Pvt. practice Gadsden, 1969—. General civil litigation, Personal injury, General practice. Office: 740 Forrest Ave Gadsden AL 35901-3639

**DAVIS, THOMAS HILL, JR.,** lawyer; b. Raleigh, N.C., June 11, 1951; s. Thomas Hill and Margie Wayne (Perry) D.; m. Julia Dee Wilson, May 31, 1980; children: Thomas Hill III, Alexander Erwin, Julia Hadley, Hunter McDowell. BA, N.C. State U., 1973; JD, Wake Forest U., 1976. Bar: N.C. 1976, U.S. Dist. Ct. (ea. and middle dist.) N.C. 1976, U.S. Ct. Appeals (11th cir.) 1982, U.S. Ct. Appeals (4th cir.) 1986, U.S. Supreme Ct. 1979. Reporter Winston-Salem (N.C.) Jour., 1974-76; asst. atty. N.C. Dept. Justice, Raleigh, 1976-88; gen. ptnr. Poyner & Spruill, Raleigh, 1988—; arbitrator Am. Arbitration Assn., Charlotte, N.C., 1990—; lectr. Campbell U. Sch. Law, Buies Creek, N.C., 1992. Supplement editor: Construction Litigation, 1992; contbg. author: Public & Private Contracting in North Carolina, 1985, North Carolina Adminstrative Law, 1996; contbr. articles to profl. jours. Mem. N.C. R.R. Legis. Study Commn., Raleigh, 1985-87; legal counsel N.C. Aeronautics Coun., Raleigh, 1981-88. Capt. N.C. State Def. Militia, 1993—.

Mem. N.C. Bar Assn. (Appreciation award 1989), Wake County Bar Assn. (VLP award 1995), North Hills Club, Lions. Democrat. Presbyterian. Avocations: fly fishing, wing shooting, photography, tennis. Construction, Labor, Condemnation. Home: 608 Blenheim Pl Raleigh NC 27612-4943 Office: Poyner & Spruill 3600 Glenwood Ave Raleigh NC 27612-4945

**DAVIS, TIMOTHY DONALD,** lawyer; b. Anniston, Ala., July 1, 1965; s. William Donald and Anne (Cartwright) D.; m. Lisa Beth Singer, Oct. 9, 1993; 1 child, Emma Pauline. BA in Econs., Rhodes Coll., 1987; JD, U. Va., 1990. Bar: Ala. 1990, D.C. 1992. Atty., shareholder Gordon, Silberman, Wiggins & Childs, P.C., Birmingham, 1990—; adv. bd. T.A. Lewis & Assocs., Inc., Birmingham. Mem. ABA (real property sect. 1993—). Republican. Methodist. Avocation: golf. Fax: 205-254-1500. E-mail: tdavis@gswc.com. Real property, General corporate, Banking. Office: Gordon Silberman Wiggins & Childs PC 1400 South Trust Tower Birmingham AL 35203

**DAVIS, VICKI,** prosecutor; b. Oceanside, Calif., July 8, 1958; d. Booker T. and Ruby H.; m. Jordan T. AA, Bishop State Jr. Coll., Mobile, Ala., 1978; BA, U. Ala., 1978-80; JD, Cumberland Sch. Law, Birmingham, Ala., 1983-87. Bar: Ala., U.S. Dist. Ct. (so. dist.) Ala. Staff atty. Legal Aide Soc., Birmingham, 1988-91; staff atty. Mobile County Dist. Atty.'s Office, 1991-92, murder team leader, 1995—; staff atty. Childe Advocacy Ctr., Mobile, 1992-95. Bd. dirs. Penolope House, Mobile, 1997—, Acad. Pub. Safety, Mobile, 1997—; mem. Alice Meadows Coun., Mobile. Mem. Paul Brock Inns of Ct. Baptist. Home: 1361 Goodman Ave Mobile AL 36605-2560 Office: Mobile County Dist Atty Office 205 Government St Mobile AL 36644-0001

**DAVIS, VIRGINIA ESTELLE,** lawyer; b. Orange, N.J., Mar. 23, 1947; d. A. Arthur and Mildred (Harr) D.; m. James C. Pitney Jr. Sept. 20, 1975; Children: Thaddeus, Alexandra, Kristian. BA, Skidmore Coll., 1969; MA, U. Denver, 1971; JD cum laude, Seton Hall U., 1974. Bar: N.J. 1974, U.S. Dist. Ct. N.J. 1974, Maine 1977, U.S. Dist. Ct. Maine 1978, U.S. Ct. Appeals (1st cir.), U.S. Ct. Appeals D.C. 1985. Law sec. Frederick Hall Assoc., N.J., 1974-75; assoc. Pitney, Hardin, Kipp, N.J., 1975-77; atty. AT&T, N.J., 1977-78; assoc. Verrill & Dana, Augusta, Maine, 1978-79; atty. Natural Resources Coun. Maine, Augusta, 1979-84; gen. counsel Maine State Housing Authority, Augusta, 1984-86; ptnr. Preti, Flaherty et al, Augusta, 1986—. Bd. dirs. Maine Chamber and Bus. Alliance; bd. dirs. Literacy Vols. of Am., Augusta affiliate. Avocations: sailing, riding, skiing, gardening, rowing. Environmental. Office: Preti Flaherty 45 Meml Cir PO Box 1058 Augusta ME 04332-1058

**DAVIS, WALTER LEE,** lawyer; b. Chgo., Aug. 14, 1954; s. Walter Lee Williams and Emily (Phillips) Davis; m. Karen Knight, Aug. 17, 1984; children: Terry, Devin, Alissha. BA, Pitzer Coll., 1976; JD, U. San Francisco, 1979. Bar: Calif. 1980. Dep. city atty. City Atty.'s Office, San Francisco, 1980-86; trial assoc. Kincaid, Gianunzio et al, Oakland, Calif., 1986-90; prin. Davis & Hoh, Alamo, Calif., 1990—; judge pro tem Alameda County Mcpl. Ct., Pleasanton, Calif., 1990—; arbitrator Alameda County Superior Ct., Oakland, 1990—, settlement commr., Alameda County Superior Ct., 1991—. Mem. ABA, Am. Trial Lawyers Assn., State Bar Calif., Ea. Alameda Bar Assn., Charles Houston Bar Assn., Alameda County Bar Assn., Centra Costa County Bar Assn., Alameda-Contra Costa Trial Lawyers Assn. Avocations: music, radio-controlled vehicles. Personal injury, General civil litigation, Civil rights. Office: Davis & Hoh 3189 Danville Blvd Ste 150 Alamo CA 94507-1982

**DAVIS, WENDY BETH,** law educator; b. Lynn, Mass., July 19, 1956; d. Charles Fred and Thelma Elaine (Berry) D. BA, U. Mass., 1980; JD, Boston Coll. Law Sch., 1985. Bar: N.H. 1985, Mass. 1986. Assoc. Bingham Dana & Gould, Boston, 1986-88, Peabody & Brown, Boston, 1988-90; v.p. Shawmut Bank, Boston, 1990-96; instr. Suffolk U. Law Sch., Boston, 1997—; adj. faculty Northeastern U., Boston, 1996—, New Eng. Banking Inst., Boston, 1994-97; cons. Fleet Bank, Boston, 1996-97. Bd. dirs. Respond Shelter for Battered Women, Somerville, Mass., 1994-95. Avocations: biking, hiking, flying. Office: Suffolk U Law Sch Temple St Archer Bldg Boston MA 02114

**DAVIS, WILLIAM EUGENE,** federal judge; b. Winfield, Ala., Aug. 18, 1936; s. A.L. and Addie Lee (Lenahan) D.; m. Celia Chalaron, Oct. 3, 1963. J.D., Tulane U., 1960. Bar: La. 1960. Assoc. Phelps Dunbar Marks Claverie & Sims, New Orleans, 1960-64; ptnr. Caffery Duhe & Davis, New Iberia, La., 1964-76; judge U.S. Dist. Ct., Lafayette, La., 1976-83, U.S. Ct. Appeals (5th Cir.), Lafayette, 1983—. Mem. ABA, La. Bar Assn., Maritime Assn. U.S. Republican. Office: US Ct Appeals 800 Lafayette St Ste 500 Lafayette LA 70501-6800

**DAVIS, WILLIAM HOWARD,** lawyer; b. Monmouth, Ill., May 24, 1951; s. Orville Francis and Alice Gertrude (Hennenfent) D.; m. Susan Claire Parris, April 11, 1981; children: Benjamin Patrick, Jackson Mitchell, Claire Marie. BA with honors, U. South Fla., 1974; JD with high honors, Fla. State U., 1977. Bar: Fla. 1977, U.S. Dist. Ct. (no. dist.) Fla. 1977, U.S. Dist. Ct. (mid. dist.) Fla. 1986, U.S. Ct. Appeals (11th cir.) 1986, U.S. Supreme Ct. 1993. Assoc. Thompson, Wadsworth, Messer & Rhodes, Tallahassee, 1977-80; ptnr. Wadsworth & Davis, P.A., Tallahassee, 1980—; instr. law Fla. State U., 1976-77. Editor notes and comments Fla. State U. Law Rev., 1976-77. Bd. dirs. Legal Aid Found., Inc., 1980-81, Fla. Legal Svcs., Inc., 1988-96, pres., 1993; pres. student govt., chmn., state coun. student body pres. State U. Sys. Fla., 1973-74. Mem. Acad. Fla. Trial Lawyers, Fla. Bar Assn. (2d cir. judge nominations commn. 1986-90, chmn. 2d cir. jud. grievance com. 1988-90), Fla. Bar Found. (bd. dirs. 1993-94, 97—, legal assistance to poor grant com. 1993—, exec. com. 1998—), Tallahassee Bar Assn. (bd. dirs. 1982-88, pres. 1986-87), Fla. Assn. Criminal Def. Lawyers, Am. Inns of Ct. (master of bench emeritus, exec. com. Tallahassee 1994—), Cath. Charities (bd. dirs. Tallahassee region 1995—, pres. 1999), Gulf Winds Track Club, Capital Tiger Bay Club, Omicron Delta Kappa, Phi Sigma Alpha. Democrat. Immigration, naturalization, and customs, State civil litigation, Federal civil litigation. Home: 914 Mimosa Dr Tallahassee FL 32312-3012 Office: Wadsworth & Davis PA 203 N Gadsden St Ste 1 Tallahassee FL 32301-7633

**DAVIS, WILLIAM J.,** lawyer; b. East Liverpool, Ohio, May 14, 1948; s. Earl L. and Dorothy Ann Davis; m. Darlene K. Davis, Feb. 26, 1977. BA, Ohio State U., 1970, JD, 1973. Bar: Ohio 1973, W.Va. 1986, Pa. 1987. Assoc. Aronson, Fineman Law Offices, East Liverpool, 1973-84; ptnr. Aronson, Fineman & Davis Co. LPA, East Liverpool, 1984—. Mem. Assn. Trial Lawyers Am., Am. Bd. Profl. Liab. Attys. (diplomat), Ohio Acad. Trial Lawyers (trustee 1985-87), Ohio State Bar Assn. (coun. dels. 1992—), Pa. Bar Assn., W.Va. Bar Assn., Nat. Bd. Trial Advocacy (civil diplomat), Laywer Pilots Bar Assn., Rotary Club. Personal injury, Product liability, Insurance. Office: Aronson Fineman & Davis Co LPA 124 E 5th St East Liverpool OH 43920-3031

**DAVIS, WILLIAM MAXIE, JR.,** lawyer; b. Elizabethtown, N.C., June 7, 1932; s. Willie Maxie and Lucy Victoria (Dowless) D.; m. Shirley Jane Smith, Mar. 24, 1987. B. Gen. Edn., U. Nebr., 1965; MA, U. So. Calif., 1970; JD, N.C. Cen. U., 1986. Bar: N.C. 1986, U.S. Dist. Ct. (we., ea. and mid. dists.) N.C., U.S. Ct. Appeals (4th cir.), U.S. Supreme Ct. 1989. Commd. 2d lt. U.S. Air Force, 1958, advanced through grades to lt. col, 1974, ret., 1975; asst. county mgr., personnel officer, dir. of planning, dir. of emergency mgmt. Bladen County, Elizabethtown, 1976-83; asst. pub. defender N.C. 26th Jud. Dist., Charlotte, 1986—; dir. plans, programs U.K. Comm. Region, Eng., 1967-71; chief systems implementations br. USAF, Hdqrs. SAC, 1971-73; chief career devel., assignments for communications-electronics officers USAF, 1973-75. Pres. Help Every Loving Parent, 1988—; county dir. Boy Scouts Am., Bladen County, N.C., 1976; pres. bd. dirs. Vistana SPA Condo Homeowners Assn., 1992—. Profiled in Champion mag., 1992. Mem. N.C. Bar, N.C. Acad. Trial Lawyers, Elizabethtown-White Lake C. of C. (bd. dirs. 1975-77), Nat. Bd. Trial Advocacy (cert. criminal trial advocacy 1993), Am. Legion, VFW, DAV. Home: PO Box 35006 Charlotte NC 28235-5006 Office: Office Pub Defender 720 E 4th St Charlotte NC 28202-2802

**DAVIS-MORRIS, ANGELA ELIZABETH,** lawyer; b. Natchez, Miss., Feb. 21, 1967; d. Fred H. and Marie (Herring) Davis; m. Raymond Joe Morris, Sept. 14, 1996. BS, U. So. Miss., 1989; JD, U. Miss., 1992. Bar: Miss. 1992, U.S. Dist. Ct. (so. dist.) Miss. 1992, U.S. Ct. Appeals (5th cir.) 1992. Paralegal Al Shiyou, Atty. at Law, Hattiesburg, Miss., 1988-89; law clk. Hickman, Goza & Gore, Attys., Oxford, Miss., 1990-92; pvt. practice Hattiesburg, 1992—; spkr. in field. Mem. Area Devel. Partnership, Hattiesburg, 1995—. Mem. ABA, Nat. Orgn. Social Security Claimants Reps. (sec. 5th cir.), Fifth Cir. Orgn. of Social Security Claimants Reps. (sec. 1998—), Miss. Bar Assn., South Cen. Miss. Bar Assn., Kiwanis (co-editor newsletter 1995-96). Avocations: target shooting, music performance, volleyball, travel, reading. Criminal, Bankruptcy, Administrative and regulatory. Office: 301 W Pine St Hattiesburg MS 39401-3829

**DAVISON, ROBERT P., JR.,** lawyer; b. Burlington, Vt., July 30, 1937; s. Robert P. and Janet Elizabeth (Miller) D.; m. Marlene P. Paradee, June 19, 1959; children Stephanie, Heidi, Robert P. III. BA, U. Vt., 1959; LLB, U. Va., 1962. Bar Vt. 1962, U.S. Dist. Ct. Vt. 1962. Dir. C & I Girdler Internat. S.A., Brussels, 1965-67; exec. v.p. Devel. Fin. Corp. S.A., Brussels, 1967-69; pres. TSI Lesiure Corp., Hempstead, N.Y., 1970-71; prin. Robert P. Davison Jr., P.C., Stowe, Vt., 1971—; chmn., founder Mt. Trust Corp., Stowe, Vt., 1976-80. Capt. U.S. Army, 1963-65. Mem. Vt. Bar Assn. (chmn. property law sec. 1975-80, chmn. banking law sec. 1977-80), Vt. Trial Lawyers Assn., Assn. Trial Lawyers Am., Ethan Allen Club, Lake Mansfield Trout Club, N.Y. Yacht Club. Republican. Congregationalist. Avocations: sailing, skiing, polo, golf, mountaineering. General civil litigation, Criminal, Federal civil litigation. Office: PO Box 299 Stowe VT 05672-0299

**DAVIS-YANCEY, GWENDOLYN,** lawyer; b. Jackson, Mich., Apr. 6, 1955; d. Wendell Norman Sr. and Jean Davis; children: Natosha, Michael, Nicole, Jennifer, Cyril; m. Kenneth Donald Yancey, Dec. 9, 1995. BS, Wayne State U., 1990; JD, U. Detroit-Mercy, 1994. Bar: Mich., U.S. Dist. Ct. (ea. dist.) Mich.; cert. tchr., Mich. Legal sec. Dykema, Gossett, Detroit; chemistry tchr. Detroit Bd. Edn., 1990-92; atty. Misdemeanor Def.'s Office, Detroit, 1994-95, Legal Aid and Def.'s Office, Detroit, 1995-96, Davis-Yancey Law Office P.L.L.C., Southfield, Mich., 1996—; ptnr., owner Men's Legal Svc., 1999—. Mem. ABA, State Bar of Mich. (family law sect., real estate sect., bus. law sect., litig. sect.), Wayne County Family Law Bar. Family and matrimonial, Real property. Office: Davis-Yancey Law Office PLLC # 703A W 15565 Northland Dr Southfield MI 48075

**DAWE, JAMES ROBERT,** lawyer; b. Bristol, Conn., Aug. 12, 1945; s. John Grosvenor and Madeline Rose (Pilbin) D.; m. Mary Gardner, July 5, 1970; children: Emily, Jeremy, Sarah. BA, Lehigh U., 1967; M City Planning, San Diego State U., 1974; JD, U. San Diego, 1976. Bar: Calif. 1976, U.S. Dist. Ct. (so. dist.) Calif. 1976. Atty. Seltzer Caplan Wilkins & McMahon, San Diego, 1976—. Chair Urban Librs. Coun., Evanston, Ill., 1993-94, San Diego Pub. Libr. Commn., 1986-94; chair Libr. Calif. Bd., Sacramento; past chair Downtown San Diego Partnership, San Diego City Mgr. Ballot com. Mem. ABA (real property sect.), Urban Land Inst., Calif. Bldg. Industry Assn. (legal action com.). Land use and zoning (including planning), Administrative and regulatory, Environmental. Office: Seltzer Caplan Wilkins & McMahon 750 B St Ste 2100 San Diego CA 92101-8177

**DAWSON, DENNIS RAY,** lawyer, manufacturing company executive; b. Alma, Mich., June 19, 1948; s. Maurice L. and Virginia (Baker) D.; m. Marilynn S. Gordon, Nov. 26, 1971; children: Emily Lynn, Brett Thomas. AA, Gulf Coast Coll., 1968; AB, Duke U., 1970; JD, Wayne State U., 1973. Bar: Mich. 1973, U.S. Dist. Ct. (ea. dist.) Mich. 1973, U.S. Dist. Ct. (we. dist.) Mich. 1975. Assoc. Watson, Wunsch & Keidan, Detroit, 1973-75; mem. Coupe, Ophoff & Dawson, Holland, Mich., 1975-77; staff atty. Amway Corp., Ada, Mich., 1977-79; corp. counsel Meijer, Inc., Grand Rapids, Mich., 1979-82; sec., corp. counsel Tecumseh Products Co., 1982-92; corp. counsel, asst. sec. Holnam Inc., Dundee, Mich., 1992-93; v.p., gen. counsel, sec. Denso Internat. Am. Inc., 1993—; exec. com. Bank of Lenawee, Adrian, Mich., 1984-93, also bd. dirs.; adj. prof. Aquinas Coll., Grand Rapids, 1978-82; govt. regulation and litigation com. Outdoor Power Equipment Inst. Inc., Washington, 1982-92. Trustee Herrick Meml. Hosp., 1988-91, Tecumseh Civic Auditorium, 1986-89; mem. adv. coun. Montessori Children's House and Acad., Adrian, 1987-93. Mem. ABA, Mich. State Bar Assn., Am. Soc. Corp. Secs., Am. Corp. Counsel Assn., Mich. Mfrs. Assn. (lawyers com. 1987-92), Lenawee C. of C. (bd. dirs. 1988-92). General corporate. Office: Denso Internat America Inc PO Box 5133 24777 Denso Dr Southfield MI 48034-5244

**DAWSON, JOHN E.,** lawyer; b. Ogden, Utah, Dec. 5, 1957; s. Joseph and Verla (Simpson) D. BS in Acctg., Weber State U., 1983; JD, Brigham Young U., 1988; LLM in Taxation, U. San Diego, 1993. Bar: Nev. 1988, Utah 1989. Assoc. Kent J. Dawson chartered, Las Vegas, 1988-90, Jeffrey L. Burr & Assocs., Las Vegas, 1990-95, Marquis & Aurbach, Las Vegas, 1995—. Estate planning, Probate, Estate taxation. Home: 3052 Sabine Hill Ave Henderson NV 89052-3029 Office: 228 S 4th St Las Vegas NV 89101-5705

**DAWSON, NORMA ANN,** lawyer; b. L.A., Sept. 11, 1950; d. Emmett Chamberlain and B. Louise Dawson. BA, Pa. State U., 1971; JD, U. Mich., 1974. Bar: Calif. 1979, U.S. Dist. Ct. (cen. dist.) Calif. 1979, U.S. Ct. Appeals (9th cir.), 1979, U.S. Supreme Ct. 1984, U.S. Dist. Ct. (so. dist.) Calif. 1991, U.S. Dist. Ct. (ea. and no. dists.) Calif. 1993. Compliance atty. Penncorp Fin., Inc., Santa Monica, Calif., 1980-87; assoc. Mathon & Rosensweig, Beverly Hills, Calif., 1987-89, Stone & Hiles, Beverly Hills, 1989-94; pvt. practice L.A., 1994—; judge pro tem L.A. Cts., 1989—. Bd. dirs. Open Fist Theatre Co., Hollywood, Calif., 1991-94. Mem. Calif. State Bar (probation monitor 1984-96), Los Angeles County Bar Assn., Beverly Hills Bar Assn. (mandatory fee arbitrator 1984—), Women Lawyers Assn. L.A. General civil litigation, Personal injury. Office: 1940 Westwood Blvd PMB 245 Los Angeles CA 90025-4614

**DAWSON, STEPHEN EVERETTE,** lawyer; b. Detroit, May 14, 1946; s. Everette Ivan and Irene (Dresser) D.; m. Consiglia J. Bellisario, Sept. 20, 1974; children: Stephen Everette Jr., Gina C., Joseph J. BA, Mich. State U., 1968; MA, U. Mich., 1969, JD, 1972. Bar: Mich. 1972, U.S. Dist. Ct. (ea. dist.) Mich. 1972, U.S. Supreme Ct. 1978, U.S. Ct. Appeals (6th cir.) 1980. Assoc. Dickinson, Wright, Moon, Van Dusen & Freeman, Detroit, 1972-79; ptnr. Dickinson, Wright, PLLC, Bloomfield Hills, Mich., 1979—; adj. prof. law U. Detroit, 1986-88. Mem. ABA, Am. Coll. Real Estate Lawyers, Mich. State Bar Assn. (mem. coun. real property law sect. 1986—, chairperson 1992-93), Phi Beta Kappa. Republican. Avocations: jogging, reading. Real property, Contracts commercial, Landlord-tenant. Office: Dickinson Wright PLLC 525 N Woodward Ave Ste 2000 Bloomfield Hills MI 48304-2970

**DAWSON, THOMAS WINTER,** prosecutor; b. Corpus Christi, Tex., Sept. 4, 1943; s. Winter Wood and Helen Virginia (Moore) D.; m. Susan Carole Simpson, Apr. 24, 1971; children: Susan Caroline, Virginia Katherine. BS in Chemistry, U. So. Miss., 1966; JD, U. Miss., 1969. Bar: Miss. 1969, U.S. Supreme Ct. 1975, U.S. Ct. Appeals (5th cir.) 1975. Assoc. Bourdeaux & Jones, Meridian, Miss., 1969-72; trial atty. U.S. Dist. Justice, Washington, 1973-75; asst. U.S. atty. U.S. Atty.'s Office, Oxford, Miss., 1975-97, 98—; assoc. ind. counsel Whitewater Investigation, Little Rock/Washington, 1997-98; sr. litigation counsel U.S. Dept. of Justice, 1989—; instr. FBI Acad., Quantico, Va., 1987, 90, Atty. Gen.'s Advocacy Inst., Washington, 1990; lectr. Miss. Trial Lawyers Assn., Biloxi, 1990. Recipient Ednl. Svc. award FBI, 1989. Mem. Miss. Bar Assn. Baptist. Avocations: hunting, fishing, college football. Home: 206 Woodland Hills Dr Oxford MS 38655-9770 Office: US Atty's Office 911 Jackson Ave E Oxford MS 38655-3632

**DAY, CHRISTOPHER MARK,** lawyer; b. Atlantic City, N.J, May 24, 1968; s. Frederick Nicholes and Judith Lee Day. BA in Polit. Sci., Stockton State U., 1990; JD, Widener U., 1994. Bar: N.J. 1994, Pa. 1994, U.S. Dist. Ct. N.J. 1994. Law clk. Hon. Richard J. Williams, Assignment Judge Superior Ct., Atlantic City, 1994-95; assoc. Cooper Perskie Law Firm, Atlantic City, 1995-98, Petro Cohen Law Firm, Atlantic City, 1998—. Bd. mem. Chief Arthur Brown Meml. Scholarship Found., 1992—, Chelsea Neighborhood Assn., 1995—; co-chmn. Attys. Reaching Others, 1995—. Mem. Atlantic County Bar Assn. (trustee 1998—), N.J. Workers Compensation Am. Inns Ct., Jr. C. of C. Workers' compensation, Personal injury, Criminal. Home: 46 S Laclede Pl Atlantic City NJ 08401-5806 Office: Petro Cohen Law Firm 2111 New Rd Northfield NJ 08225-1512

**DAY, EDWARD FRANCIS, JR.,** lawyer; b. Portland, Maine, Nov. 4, 1946; s. Edward Francis and Anne (Rague) D.; m. Claire Ann Nicholson, June 27, 1970; children: Kelley Ann, John Edward. BA, St. Anselm Coll., 1968; JD cum laude, U. Maine, 1973; LLM in Taxation, NYU, 1976. Bar: N.J. 1973, U.S. Dist. Ct. N.J. 1973, U.S. Tax Ct. 1974, N.Y. 1981. Assoc. Hannoch, Weisman, Stern & Besser, Newark, 1973-74; assoc. Carpenter, Bennett & Morrissey, Newark, 1974-78, ptnr., 1979-93, sr. ptnr., 1994-98, of counsel, 1999—; instr. employee benefits and comml. law The Am. Coll., Valley Forge, Pa., 1981-82; bd. dirs. Weiss-Aug. Co., Inc., East Hanover, N.J., Main Tape Co., Tinton Falls, N.J., exec. v.p., gen. counsel, 1999—. Editor Maine Law Rev., 1972-73. Mem., vice-chmn. Allenhurst (N.J) Bd. Adjustment, 1983-85; mem., vice-chmn. Allenhurst Planning Bd., 1985-87; mem. Nat. Ski Patrol, Denver, 1985—; scoutmaster Monmouth coun. Boy Scouts Am., Ocean Twp., 1987-90; mem. 10th Mountain Divsn. Assn., Aspen, Colo., 1996—. Served in U.S. Army, 1968-70. Named One of Outstanding Young Men of Am., 1979; Ford Found. scholar, 1966-68. Mem. ABA, N.J. Bar Assn., Essex County Bar Assn., Estate Planning Coun. No. N.J., Am. Legion, Deal (N.J.) Golf and Country Club (bd. dirs. 1985-92, sec. 1991-92), Jersey Coast Club of Red Bank (v.p. 1976-77). Roman Catholic. Avocations: golf, skiing, piano. Contracts commercial, Probate, Real property. Home: 225 Spier Ave Allenhurst NJ 07711-1120 Office: Carpenter Bennett & Morrissey 3 Gateway Ctr Newark NJ 07102-4079 also: Main Tape Co 2 Hance Ave Eatontown NJ 07724-2726

**DAY, GREGORY THOMAS,** lawyer; b. L.A., Apr. 17, 1964; s. Arthur John and Margaret Genevieve Day. BA in History, Humboldt State U., 1986; JD, U. Oreg., 1995. Bar: Oreg. 1995. Atty. Hydes & Day, Canyon City, Oreg., 1995-98, Myrick, Seagraves et al, Grants Pass, Oreg., 1998—. Capt. U.S. Army, 1989-92, Oreg. Army NG, 1992—. Mem. U.S. Armor Assn., Am. Legion, Elks, Delta Sigma Phi. Republican. Roman Catholic. E-mail: gtd@raguefirm.com. General civil litigation, Family and matrimonial, Criminal. Office: Myrick Seagraves Adams & Davis 600 NW 5th St Grants Pass OR 97526-2024

**DAY, JAMES MCADAM, JR.,** lawyer; b. Detroit, Aug. 18, 1948; s. James McAdam and Mary Elizabeth (McGibbon) D.; m. Sally Marie Sterud; children: Cara McAdam, Brenna Marie, Michael James. AB, UCLA, 1970; JD magna cum laude, U. Pacific, 1973. Bar: Calif. 1973, U.S. Dist. Ct. (no. dist.) Calif. 1973, U.S. Ct. Appeals (9th cir.) 1975. Assoc. Downey, Brand, Seymour & Rohwer, Sacramento, 1973-78, ptnr., 1978—, chmn. natural resources dept., 1985-90; mng. ptnr. Downey, Brand, Seymour & Rohmer, Sacramento, 1990-94, 97—. Contbr. articles to profl. jours. Pres., bd. dirs. Sacramento Soc. for Prevention of Cruelty to Animals, 1976-79, Children's Home Soc. of Calif., Sacramento, 1979-85; bd. dirs. Sta. KXPR/KXJZ, Inc. Pub. Radio, Sacramento, 1984-94, chmn., 1990-93; bd. dirs. Calif. State Libr. Found., 1995—, chmn., 1995—. Mem. ABA (natural resources sect. 1998), Calif. Bar Assn. (exec. com. 1985-89, chmn. real property law sect. 1988), Rocky Mountain Mineral Law Found., No. Calif. Assn. Petroleum Landmen, Calif. Mining Assn., U. Pacific McGeorge Law Sch. Alumni Assn. (bd. dirs. 1980-83). Avocations: yacht racing and cruising, fishing. Office: Downey Brand Seymour & Rohwer 555 Capitol Mall Fl 10 Sacramento CA 95814-4504

**DAY, JOHN ARTHUR,** lawyer; b. Madison, Wis., Sept. 21, 1956; s. John Donald and Elinor Roletta (Heath) D. BS, U. Wis., Platteville, 1978; JD, U. N.C., 1981. Bar: Tenn. 1981, U.S. Dist. Ct. (mid. dist.) Tenn. 1981, U.S. Ct. Appeals (6th cir.) 1982; civil cert. Nat. Bd. Trial Advocacy 1991. Assoc. Boult Cummings Conners & Berry, Nashville, 1981-86, ptnr., 1987-92; shareholder Branham & Day, P.C., 1993—; mem. Civil Justice Reform Act adv. group U.S. Dist. Ct. (mid. dist.) Tenn., 1991-95; bd. dirs. Nat. Bd. Trial Advocacy. Co-author: Tennessee Law of Comparative Fault, 1997; founder, editor Tenn. Tort Law Letter, 1995—; contbr. articles to profl. jours. Com. mem. Cohn Roundtable, Nashville, 1988; assoc. Harry Phillips Inn of Ct., 1990-92. Mem. Tenn. Trial Lawyers Assn. (bd. govs. 1984-85, treas. 1985-89, v.p. 1989-93, pres. 1993-94, immediate past pres. 1994-95, legal edn. com. chairperson 1985-86, legis. com. chairperson 1987-90, CLE com. 1984-97, pub. rels. com. 1986-88, long range planning com. 1991-93), Assn. Trial Lawyers Am. (Tenn. pub. rels. rep. 1986-87, people's law sch. com. co-chairperson 1986-88, pub. rels. com. 1986-91, chairperson 1988-89, edn. com. 1987-88, pub. affairs com. 1987-89, publs. com. 1990-93, vice chmn. 1991-93, co-chairperson 1992-93, key person com. 1987-89, nursing home litigation group 1985-89, chmn. 1987-89, mem. exec. com. 1994-95, chair pres.'s coun. 1994-95), Nashville Bar Assn. (bd. dirs. 1998—, circuit and chancery ct. com. vice-chairperson 1988, chairperson 1989, fee disputes com. 1984-85, 87, vice chmn. 1988, chmn. 1989, bd. dirs. 1998—), Lawyers Involved for Tenn. (trustee 1988—), Tenn. Bar Assn. (local rules com. 1986-87, mem. litigation sect. coun. 1989-90, nat. bd. trial advocacy, bd. dirs. 1998—, stds. com. 1998—). Democrat. Personal injury. Home: 18107 Crowne Brook Cir Franklin TN 37067-1676 Office: Branham & Day PC 150 4th Ave N Ste 1950 Nashville TN 37219-2427

**DAY, RICHARD EARL,** lawyer, educator; b. St. Joseph, Mo., Nov. 2, 1929; s. William E. and Geneva C. (Miller) D.; m. Melissa W. Blair, Feb. 2, 1951; children: William E., Thomas E. BS, U. Pa., 1951; JD with distinction, U. Mich., 1957. Bar: Ill. 1957, D.C. 1959, S.C. 1980. Assoc. Kirkland & Ellis, Chgo., 1957-58, Howrey Simon Baker & Murchison, Washington, 1958-61; asst. prof. law U. N.C., Chapel Hill, 1961-64; assoc. prof. Ohio State U., Columbus, 1964-66, prof., 1966-75; prof. U. S.C., Columbia, 1975-76, 80-86, dean, 1977-80, John William Thurmond chair disting. prof. law, 1986-99, disting. prof. law emeritus, 1999—; cons. U.S. Office Edn., 1964-66; course dir. Ohio Legal Ctr. Inst. Columbus, 1970-75; vis. prof. law U. Southampton (Eng.), fall 1988. Author: The Intensified Course in Antitrust Law, 1972, rev. edit., 1974; book rev. editor Antitrust Bull., 1968-71, adv. bd., 1971—; adv. bd. Antitrust and Trade Regulation Report, 1973-76, Jour. Reprints for Antitrust Law and Econs., 1974—. Ohio commr. Nat. Conf. on Uniform State Laws, 1967-75, S.C. commr., 1977-80; mem. Ohio Gov.'s Adv. Coun. Internat. Trade, 1972-74, S.C. Jud. Coun., 1977-80; chmn. S.C. Appellate Def. Coun., 1977-80, S.C. Com. Intellectual Property and Unfair Trade Practices Law, 1981-87. Lt. USNR, 1952-55. Named John William Thurmond Disting. Prof. Law. Mem. ABA, S.C. Bar Assn. (bd. govs. 1977-80), Am. Law Inst. Methodist. Antitrust, Trademark and copyright. Home: 204 Saint James St Columbia SC 29205-3074 Office: U SC Law Ctr Main And Green Sts Columbia SC 29208-0001

**DAY, ROLAND BERNARD,** retired chief justice state supreme court; b. Oshkosh, Wis., June 11, 1919; s. Peter Oliver and Joanna King (Wescott) D.; m. Mary Jane Purcell, Dec. 18, 1948; 1 dau., Sarah Jane. B.A., U. Wis., 1942, J.D., 1947. Bar: Wis. 1947. Trainee Office Wis. Atty. Gen., 1947; assoc. mem. firm Maloney & Wheeler, Madison, Wis., 1947-49; 1st asst. dist. atty. Dane County, Wis., 1949-52; partner firm Day, Goodman, Madison, 1953-57; firm Wheeler, Van Sickle, Day & Anderson, Madison, 1959-74; legal counsel mem. staff Sen. William Proxmire, Washington, 1957-58; justice Wis. Supreme Ct., Madison, 1974-95, chief justice, 1995-96; Mem. Madison Housing Authority, 1960-64, chmn., 1961-63; regent U. Wis. System, 1972-74. Served with AUS, 1943-46. Mem. ABA, State Bar Wis., Am. Trial Lawyers Assn., Ygdrasil Lit. Soc. (pres. 1968), Madison Torske Klubben, Masons (33rd degree). Mem. United Ch. of Christ. Clubs: Madison, Madison Lit.

**DAY, STUART REID,** lawyer; b. Laramie, Wyo., July 2, 1959; s. Richard Erwin and Evelyn (Reid) D.; m. TimAnn Day, Jan. 18, 1980; children: Shelby Rochelle, Erica Rachel. BS, Ariz. State U., 1981; JD, U. Wyo., 1984. Assoc. Williams, Porter, Day & Neville, Casper, Wyo., 1984-87, ptnr., 1987—; mem. unauthorized practice of law com. Wyo. State Bar. Mem. ABA, ATLA, Wyo. Bar Assn. (bd. dirs., vice chmn., bd. CLE 1992-93, chmn. bd. CLE 1994-95), Colo. Bar Assn., Def. Rsch. Inst., Natrona County Bar Assn. (treas. 1989, v.p. 1990, pres. 1991), Casper C. of C. (bd. dirs. 1989-91, 97—). General civil litigation, Personal injury, Education and schools. Office: PO Box 10700 Casper WY 82602-3902

**DAYE, CHARLES EDWARD,** law educator; b. Durham, N.C., May 14, 1944; s. Eccleasiastes and Addie Lula (Roberts) D.; m. Norma Lowery, Dec. 19, 1976; stepchildren: Clarence L. Hill, III, Tammy H. Roundtree. Student, N.C. Central U., 1966; JD, Columbia U., 1969. Bar: N.Y. 1970, D.C. 1971, N.C. 1975, U.S. Supreme Ct. 1979. Assoc. Dewey, Ballantine, Bushby, Palmer & Wood, N.Y.C., 1969; law clk. U.S. Ct. Appeals (6th cir.), 1969-70; assoc. Covington & Burling, Washington, 1970-72; prof. law Sch. Law U. N.C., Chapel Hill, 1972-81, 85—, Henry Brandis prof. law, 1991—; dean, prof. law Sch. Law, N.C. Central U., Durham, 1981-85; cons. N.C. Dept. Adminstrn., 1975; mem. Triangle Housing Devel. Corp., 1973—, chmn. 1977-93; chair N.C. Poverty Project, 1990—. Author: (with Mandelker et al) Housing and Community Development, 1981, 2d edit., 1989, 3rd edit., 1999, (with Morris) N.C. Law of Torts, 2d edit., 1999; contbr. articles to profl. jours. Mem. ABA (mem. commn. on minorities in the profn. 1990-95, pres. law sch. admission coun. 1991-93), N.C. Assn. Black Lawyers (Lawyer of Yr. 1980, pres. 1976-78, exec. sec. 1979—), N.C. Bar Assn. Democrat. Baptist. E-mail: edaye@email.unc.edu. Home: 3400 Cambridge Rd Durham NC 27707-4508 Office: Univ NC Law Sch Chapel Hill NC 27599-0001

**DAYNARD, RICHARD ALAN,** law educator; b. N.Y.C., July 19, 1943; s. David M. and Sarah (Weidenbaum) D.; m. Carol S. Iskols, Aug. 9, 1975; children: David J., Gabriela C. BA, Columbia U., 1964, MA in Sociology, 1970; JD, Harvard U., 1967; PhD in Urban Studies and Planning, MIT, 1980. Bar: N.Y. 1967, U.S. Ct. Appeals (6th cir.) 1986, U.S. Supreme Ct. 1986, U.S. Ct. Appeals (11th cir.) 1987, U.S. Ct. Appeals (5th cir.) 1996. Law clk. 2d cir. U.S. Ct. Appeals, N.Y.C., 1967-68; teaching fellow Columbia U., N.Y.C., 1968-69; asst. prof. law Northeastern U., Boston, 1969-71, assoc. prof. law, 1971-73, prof. law, 1973—; lectr. Tufts Med. Sch., Boston, 1975-89; internat. lectr. and cons. Editor-in-chief Tobacco Products Litigation Reporter, 1985—; assoc. editor: Tobacco Control: An Internat. Jour., 1998—; contbr. articles in field to profl. jours. Chmn. Tobacco Products Liability Project, Boston, 1984—; pres. Group Against Smoking Pollution of Mass., Boston, 1983—, Clean Indoor Air Ednl. Found., Boston, 1983-92, Tobacco Control Resource Ctr., Inc., Boston, 1993—; pres. Stop Teenage Addiction to Tobacco, 1996-98. Mem. ABA, Am. Pub. Health Assn., Law and Soc. Assn., Phi Beta Kappa. Home: 90 Commonwealth Ave Boston MA 02116-3040 Office: Northeastern U Sch Law 400 Huntington Ave Boston MA 02115-5005

**DAYTON, CHARLES KELLY,** lawyer; b. Belvidere, Ill., May 16, 1939; s. Charles F. and Marie Dayton; m. Kathleen Hanegan; children: Michael, James. BA, Dartmouth Coll., 1961; JD, U. Mich., 1964. Bar: Minn. 1964, Wis. 1988. Ptnr. Gray Plant Mooty & Bennet, Mpls., 1964-71; legal dir. Minn. Pub. Interest Rsch. Group, Mpls., 1971-72; founding ptnr. Pepin Dayton Herman & Graham, Mpls., 1973-88; ptnr. Leonard, Street & Deinard, Mpls., 1988—; adj. prof. U. Minn. Law Sch., Mpls., 1983-84. Dir. Environ. Law and Policy Ctr., Chgo., 1996—; bd. dirs. Elmer L. and Eleanor Andersen Found., St. Paul, 1997, Nat. Inst. for the Environment, Washington, 1992—. Named Environmentalist of Decade, Northstar chpt. Sierra Club, 1982, Pro Bono Vol. award Minn. Ctr. for Environ. Advocacy, Disting. Svc. award Minn. Justice Found., 1997. Mem. Hennepin County Bar Assn. (chair environ. law com. 1994-99). Avocations: sailing, cross country skiing, canoeing. E-mail: ckd1665@leonard.com. Home: 12001 Golden Acre Dr Minnetonka MN 55305-2831 Office: Leonard Street and Deinard 150 S 5th St Ste 2300 Minneapolis MN 55402-4238

**DEACHMAN, ROSS VARICK,** lawyer; b. Plymouth, N.H., Mar. 13, 1942; s. W. John Deachman and H. Annie Griffin; m. Nancy L. Stone, Aug. 30, 1967; children: Amy E., William John IV. BA, U. N.H., 1964; JD, Boston U., 1967. Assoc. Burns, Bryant, Hinchey & Nadeau, Dover, N.H., 1967-70; ptnr. Murphy and Deachman, Plymouth, 1971-74; owner Deachman Law Office, Plymouth, 1974-89; ptnr. Deachman & Cowie, P.A., Plymouth, 1989—; dir., sec. N.H. Bar Assn., 1975-80; pres. Grafton County Bar Assn., 1980. Author: Bi-Centennial of the Grafton County Bar Association, 1993; editor: 25th Reunion Class of 1964, 1989. Moderator Town of Holderness, N.H., 1988—; sch. bd. mem. Pemi-Baker Co-op Sch. Dist., Plymouth, 1989—. Real property, Probate, Estate planning. Office: Deachman & Cowie PA PO Box 96 66 Main St Plymouth NH 03264-1451

**DEACON, JOHN C.,** lawyer; b. Newport, Ark., Sept. 26, 1920. BA, U. Ark., 1941, JD, 1948. Bar: Ark. 1948. Ptnr. Barrett & Deacon, Jonesboro, Ark.; commr. from Ark. to Nat. Conf. Commrs. on Uniform State Laws, 1966—, chmn. exec. com., 1977-79, pres. 1979-81. Recipient Ark. Outstanding Lawyer-Citizen award, 1973. Fellow Am. Coll. Trial Lawyers, Internat. Acad. Trial Lawyers (bd. d irs. 1978-84), Southwestern Legal Found. (trustee 1975-95, chmn. Research Fellows 1983-85); mem. Craighead County Bar Assn. (pres. 1968-69), N.E. Ark. Bar Assn. (pres. 1966-68), Ark. Bar Assn. (pres. 1970-71), ABA (chmn. sect. bar activities 1967-68, Ark. del. 1967-79, bd. govs. 1980-83, 92-93, chair sr. lawyers divsn. 1994-95), Am. Counsel Assn. (pres. 1974-75), Am. Bar Found. (pres. 1994-96), Internat. Assn. Def. Counsel, Nat. Assn. R.R. Trial Lawyers, Delta Theta Phi. General practice, General civil litigation. Office: PO Box 1700 Jonesboro AR 72403-1700 Office: Barrett & Deacon PA Union Planters Bank Building 300 S Church St Jonesboro AR 72401-2911

**DEACY, THOMAS EDWARD, JR.,** lawyer; b. Kansas City, Mo., Oct. 14, 1918; s. Thomas Edward and Grace (Scales) D.; m. Jean Freeman, July 10, 1943 (div. 1988); children: Bennette Kay Deacy Kramer, Carolyn G., Margaret Deacy Vickrey, Thomas, Ann Deacy Krause; m. Jean Holmes McDonald, 1988. J.D., U. Mo., 1940; M.B.A., U. Chgo., 1949. Bar: Mo. 1940, Ill. 1946. Practice law Kansas City, 1940-42; ptnr. Taylor, Miller, Busch & Magner, Chgo., 1946-55, Deacy & Deacy, Kansas City, 1955—; lectr. Northwestern U., 1949-55, U. Chgo., 1950-55; dir., mem. exec. com. St. L.-S.F. Ry., 1962-80; dir. Burlington No. Inc., 1980-86; mem. U.S. team Anglo-Am. Legal Exchange, 1973, 77. Mem. Juv. Protective Assn. Chgo., 1947-55, pres., bd. dirs., 1950-53; mem. exec. bd. Chgo. coun. Boy Scouts Am., 1952-55; pres. Kansas City Philharmonic Orch., 1961-63, chmn. bd. trustees, 1963-65; trustee Sunset Hill Sch., 1963-73; trustee, mem. exec. com. u. Kansas City, 1963—; trustee Mo. Law Sch. Found., pres., 1973-77, Kans. chpt. The Nature Conservancy, 1994—. Capt. AUS, 1942-45. Fellow Am. Coll. Trial Lawyers (regent 1968—, treas. 1973-74, pres. 1975-76), Am. Bar Found; mem. Am. Law Inst., Jud. Conf. U.S. (implementation com. on admission of attys. to fed. practice 1979-86), ABA (commn. standards jud. adminstrn. 1972-74, standing com. fed. judiciary 1974-80), Ill. Bar Assn., Chgo. Bar Assn., Mo. Bar, Kansas City Bar Assn., Lawyers Assn. Kansas City, Chgo. Club, La Jolla (Calif.) Country Club, La Jolla Beach and Tennis Club, Kansas City Club, Kansas City Country Club, River Club, Quod Erat Bonus Homo Honor Soc., Beta Gamma Sigma, Sigma Chi. Appellate, Banking, General civil litigation. Home: 2724 Verona Cir Shawnee Mission KS 66208-1265 Office: 920 Main St Ste 1900 Kansas City MO 64105-2010

**DEAGAZIO, CHRISTOPHER RICHARD,** lawyer; b. Boston, Apr. 30, 1970; s. Richard J. and Ann Y. DeAgazio. BA, U. Richmond, 1992; JD, Suffolk U., 1995. Assoc. Crowe & Casey, P.C., Boston, 1995-96, Perkins, Smith & Cohen, LLP, Boston, 1997—. Roman Catholic. General corporate, Real property, Bankruptcy. Office: Perkins Smith & Cohen LLP One Beacon St Boston MA 02108

**DEAGOSTINO, THOMAS M.,** lawyer; b. Flint, Mich., July 15, 1957; s. Thomas V. and Barbra (Bean) DeA.; m. Mary P. Kasper, Dec. 26, 1987; children: Mia Rose, T. Anthony. BSBA, Ctrl. Mich. U., 1979; JD, U. Detroit, 1982. Bar: Mich., 1982, Fla., 1983, U.S. Dist. Ct. (ea. dist. so. divsn.) Mich., 1982. Assoc. Powers, Chapman, DeAgostino & Meyers, Troy, Mich., 1982-93; ptnr. Potter, Carniak, Anderson & DeAgostino, Auburn Hills, Mich., 1993—. Mem. ATLA, Oakland County Bar Assn. (vice chair negligence sect. 1998—, chmn. elect), Fla. Bar Assn., Mich. Trial Lawyers Assn. Avocations: fly fishing, skiing, travel. Personal injury, Professional liability, Product liability. Office: Potter Carniak Anderson & DeAgostino 2701 University Dr Ste 223 Auburn Hills MI 48326-2565

**DEAL, JAMES EDWARD,** lawyer; b. Brazil, Ind., Oct. 25, 1957; s. Charles Edward and Margaret Ann (Evans) D.; m. Kathy Louise Wells, Sept. 18, 1982; children: Suzanne Emily, Jana Louise, Evan W. BA, Ind. State U., 1979; JD, Ind. U., 1982. Bar: Ind. 1982, U.S. Dist. Ct. (so. dist.) Ind. 1982. Assoc. Sacopulos, Crawford & Johnson, Terre Haute, Ind., 1982-83; pvt. practice Brazil, Ind., 1983—; prosecuting atty. 13th jud. cir., 1991-94. Mem. Brazil Concert Band, 1974—. Named One of Outstanding Young Men Am., 1985. Mem. Christian Legal Soc., Ind. Bar Assn. (county contact person young lawyers sect. 1986—), Clay County Bar Assn., Rotary. Republican. Avocations: handbell choir, reading, exercise, family activities. General practice, Criminal, Government contracts and claims. Home: 5066 W State Road 340 Brazil IN 47834-7869 Office: 11 W National Ave Brazil IN 47834-2536

**DEAL, JASON J.,** lawyer; b. Ft. Gordon, Ga., Jan. 30, 1968; s. J. Nathan and Sandra (Dunagan) D.; m. Denise Dianne Fallin, May 18, 1996. BS in Biology, Furman U., 1990; JD, U. Ga., 1996. Bar: Ga. 1996. Constituent svcs. asst. U.S. Senator Sam Nunn, Washington, 1993; assoc. Thompson, Fox, Chandler, Homans & Hicks, Dawsonville, Ga., 1996-98; asst. dist. atty. Northeastern Jud. Cir., Gainesville, Ga., 1998—; county atty., Dawson County, Dawsonville, 1997-98. 1st lt. U.S. Army, 1990-92. Republican. Baptist. Avocations: farming, horse training, hunting. Office: Dist Atty's Office Hall County Court House PO Box 1690 Gainesville GA 30503-1690

**DEAL, JOHN CHARLES,** lawyer; b. Kenton, Ohio, Jan. 5, 1947. BS, Ohio State U., 1969, JD cum laude, 1974. Bar: Ohio 1974, U.S. Dist. Ct. (no. and so. dists.) Ohio 1977, U.S. Ct. Appeals (D.C. cir.) 1979, U.S. Dist. Ct. (ea. dist.) Ky. 1980, U.S. Ct. Appeals (6th cir.) 1983, U.S. Ct. Appeals (8th cir.) 1988, U.S. Supreme Ct. 1988, U.S. Ct. Appeals (4th and 5th cirs.) 1990, U.S. Ct. Fed. Claims 1993. Reg. counsel FDIC, Columbus, 1976-85; of counsel Kegler Brown Hill & Ritter, Columbus, 1985—. Contbr. articles to profl. jours. Mem. ABA (bus. law sect., chair regulatory enforcement, dir. liability subcom. of Banking Law Com. 1985-90), Ohio State Bar Assn. (chair banking, comml. and bankruptcy law com. 1992-94), Columbus Bar Assn. Administrative and regulatory, Banking, Contracts commercial. Office: Kegler Brown Hill & Ritter 65 E State St Ste 1800 Columbus OH 43215-4295

**DEAMER, MICHAEL LYNN,** lawyer, accountant; b. Aurora, Ill., Apr. 8, 1946; s. Jack C. and Jean A. (Purdie) D.; m. Evelyn W. Warren, Sept. 12, 1969; children—Michelle, Tracy, Debbie, Robin, Michael. B.A. in Acctg., U. Utah, 1970, J.D., 1973. Bar: Utah 1973, U.S. Ct. Appeals (5th, 9th and 10th cirs.), U.S. Tax Ct. 1973, U.S. Supreme Ct. 1976; C.P.A., Utah. Assoc., McKay Burton et al, Salt Lake City, 1973-74; asst. atty. gen. State of Utah, Salt Lake City, 1974-76, chief dep. atty. gen., 1976-80; corp. counsel Skyline Exploration, 1980-82; adj. prof. mgmt. and bus. law U. Utah, 1984—. Recipient Silver Beaver award Boy Scouts Am., 1996. Republican. Lodge: Kiwanis. Insurance, General civil litigation, Taxation, general. Office: Randle Deamer Zarr McConkie & Lee PC 139 E South Temple Ste 330 Salt Lake City UT 84111-1169

**DEAN, BEALE,** lawyer; b. Ft. Worth, Feb. 26, 1922; s. Ben J. and Helen (Beale) D.; m. Margaret Ann Webster, Sept. 3, 1948; children: Webster Beale, Giselle Liseanne. BA, U. Tex., Austin, 1943, LLB, 1947. Bar: Tex. 1946. Asst. dist. atty. Dallas, 1947-48; assoc. Martin, Moore & Brewster, Ft. Worth, 1948-50; mem. Martin, Moore, Brewster & Dean, 1950-51, Pannell, Dean, Pannell & Kerry (and predecessor firms), 1951-65; ptnr. Brown, Herman, Scott, Young & Dean, Ft. Worth, 1965-71, Brown, Herman, Scott, Dean & Miles, Ft. Worth, 1971-98, Brown, Herman, Dean, Wiseman, Liser & Hart, LLP, Ft. Worth, 1998—; spl. asst. atty. Gen. Tex., 1959-61. Regent Nat. Coll. Dist. Attys., 1985—. With AUS, 1942-45, ETO. Mem. ABA, Bar Assn. Fifth Fed. Cir., Ft. Worth-Tarrant County Bar Assn. (past pres. 1971-72, Blackstone award 1991), Am. Coll. Trial Lawyers, State Bar Tex. (dir. 1973-75), Am. Bar Found., Tex. Bar Found. (charter mem.), Ft. Worth Boat Club, Ridglea Country Club, Ft. Worth Club. Presbyterian. Federal civil litigation, General civil litigation, State civil litigation. Office: 200 Ft Worth Club Bldg Fort Worth TX 76102-4905

**DEAN, BILL VERLIN, JR.,** lawyer; b. Oklahoma City, Jan. 11, 1957; s. Bill V. and Mary Lou (Dorman) D.; m. Christine Potter; children: Bill V. III, Mary Megan. BS, Cen. State U., 1978; JD, Oklahoma City U., 1981. Bar: Okla. 1982, U.S. Dist. Ct. (we. dist.) Okla. 1983, (no. dist.) Okla. 1986, (ea. dist.) Okla. 1987, Tex. 1990, N.Y. 1992, U.S. Ct. Appeals (10th cir.) 1986; lic. real estate broker and ins. agt. Second dep. assessor Okla. County Assessor, Oklahoma City, 1978-80; atty. Struthers Oil and Gas Corp., Oklahoma City, 1980-82; cons. Bill Dean & Co., Jones, Okla., 1978—; ptnr. Dean & Assocs. P.C., Jones, Okla., 1982—; pres. Dean Ins. Agy. Ltd., 1986—, Casualty Corp. Am., Inc., 1999—; bd. dirs. Union Mut. Ins. Co.; CEO Casualty Corp. of Am., Inc., 1990—. Mem. Okla. County Bar Assn., Okla. Bar Assn., Tex. Bar Assn., N.Y. Bar Assn., Shriners. Methodist. Banking, Insurance, Real property. Home: 200 Cherokee St Jones OK 73049-7709 Office: Dean & Assocs P C PO Box 1060 110 E Main St Jones OK 73049-7706

**DEAN, CHRISTINE WITCOVER,** lawyer; b. Washington, May 23, 1947; d. Henry Wallace and Kate (Briggs) Witcover; m. Joseph Wayne Dean, May 22, 1977; children: Joseph Jefferson, Katherine Briggs. AB, Sweet Briar Coll., 1968; JD, Duke U., 1971. Bar: N.C. 1971, U.S. Dist. Ct. (ea. dist.) N.C., 1972, U.S. Ct. Appeals (4th cir.) 1973, U.S. Supreme Ct. 1983, Fed. Cir. Ct. Appeals 1986. Assoc. attorney N.C. Dept. Justice, Raleigh, 1971-72; asst. U.S. attorney U.S. Attorney Office, Raleigh, 1973-78, 87—; partner Dean & Dean, Raleigh, 1978-85; pvt. practice Raleigh, 1985-87; judge Siegal Moot Court Competition, Durham, N.C., 1993-95. Vice chmn. Govs. Council Drug Abuse, Raleigh, 1986-92. Mem. Braxton Craven Inn of Court (master attorney 1993-97, master attorney emeritus 1998). Republican. Episcopalian. Avocations: horseback riding, tap dancing. Office: US Attorneys Office EDNC 310 New Bern Ave Rm 800 Raleigh NC 27601-1461

**DEAN, JAMES BENWELL,** lawyer; b. Dodge City, Kans., May 23, 1941; s. James Harvey and Bess (Benwell) D.; m. Sharon Ann Carver, Sept. 1, 1962 (div. 1991); m. Patricia A. Bostick, Aug. 23, 1993 (div. 1999); children: Cynthia G. Dean Vosburgh, James M. Student, Southwestern Coll., 1959-60, U. Colo., 1961; BA, Kans. State U., 1962; JD, Harvard U., 1965. Bar: Colo. 1965, U.S. Dist. Ct. Colo. 1965, U.S. Tax Ct. 1966, Nebr. 1971, U.S. Ct. Appeals (10th cir.) 1971. From assoc. to ptnr. Tweedy & Mosley, Denver, 1965-71, Kutak Rock Cohen Campbell Garfinkle & Woodward, Omaha, 1971-73; ptnr. Mosley, Wells & Dean, Denver, 1973-77, Kutak Rock & Huie, Denver, 1977-81, James B. Dean, P.C., Denver, 1981-91, Dean, McClure, Eggleston & Husney, Denver, 1991-95; James B. Dean, PC, Denver, 1995—; spl. asst. atty. gen. State of Colo., Denver, 1989—; lectr. U. Ark. Law Sch., Fayetteville, 1982-86, C.C. Aurora, Colo., 1996-97. Coeditor Agricultural Law Jour., 1979-84; contbr. articles to profl. jours. Mem. ABA (advisor bd. forum com. on rural lawyers and agrl. bus. 1983-89), Nebr. Bar Assn., Colo. Bar Assn. (sec. agrl. law sect. 1991-94, bd. dirs. 1989—), Denver Bar Assn., Am. Agrl. Law Assn. (pres. elect 1985-86, pres. 1986-87, bd. dirs. 1981-83, Disting. Svc. award 1989). Republican. Avocations: photography, woodworking, hiking, piano. General corporate, Contracts commercial, Mergers and acquisitions. Office: 4155 E Jewell Ave Ste 703 Denver CO 80222-4511

**DEAN, JAY DOUGLAS,** lawyer; b. Monterey Park, Calif., Feb. 19, 1950; s. J. Donovan and Doris (Mattson) D.; m. Jeanette Wasserstein, Feb. 14, 1986; children: Ezekiel, Jessica. BA, Occidental Coll., L.A., 1972; Cert. d'Etudes Pol., Inst. d'et. Pol. de Paris, 1976; MIA, Columbia U., 1988; JD, Yale U., 1988. Bar: N.Y. 1989, U.S. Dist. Ct. (so. and ea. dists.) N.Y. 1989, U.S. Ct. Appeals (2d cir.) 1998. Vol. U.S. Peace Corps, Chad, Africa, 1973-75; asst. editor The Paris Metro, 1976-77; reporter Ridgecrest Daily Independence, Ridge Crest, Calif., 1978, Glendale (Calif.) News-Press, 1979-80; newsperson UPI, N.Y.C., Washington, 1981-84; assoc. Curtis, Mallet, Prevost, Colt & Mosle, N.Y.C., 1988-90, Shea & Gould, N.Y.C., 1990-91, Berlack, Israels & Liberman, N.Y.C., 1991-93; asst. corp. counsel N.Y.C. Dept. Law, 1994—. Contbr. German translations, articles to profl. jours. Dir. 370 Tenants Corp., N.Y.C., 1993—. Recipient Award for Best Photo Story, Cath. Press Assn., 1981, Argonaut award for playwriting Occidental Coll., 1972; Peace Corps fellow Columbia U., 1984-85. Mem. ABA, Assn. of the Bar of City of N.Y. Jewish. Avocation: bonsai. General civil litigation. Home: 370 Riverside Dr Apt 9E New York NY 10025-2107 Office: NYC Law Dept 100 Church St New York NY 10007-2601

**DEAN, JON,** lawyer; b. Ventura, Calif., July 19, 1969; s. Larry Victor and Josephine (Mejia) D. BA in Polit. Sci., UCLA, 1992; JD, U. Calif., Berkeley, 1996. Bar: Calif. 1996, U.S. Dist. Ct. (ctrl. dist.) Calif. 1996. Law clk. to Hon. H. Andrew Hauk U.S. Dist. Ct. (ctrl. dist.) Calif., L.A., 1996-97; assoc. Kirkland & Ellis, L.A., 1997-98, Berman, Blanchard, Mousner & Resser, L.A., 1998—. Winner James Patterson McBaine Honors Moot Ct. Competition, 1996. Mem. ABA, L.A. County Bar Assn. Democrat. Avocations: basketball, golf. General civil litigation, Intellectual property, Entertainment. Home: 750 S Bundy Dr Apt 102 Los Angeles CA 90049-4954 Office: 4727 Wilshire Blvd Ste 500 Los Angeles CA 90010-3848

**DEAN, LAWRENCE KENYON,** lawyer; b. Columbus, Ohio, June 17, 1949; m. Josephine Dean; 1 child, Evelyn Maria; m. Linda Curell. AB in History with honors, U. Calif., Berkeley, 1971; JD, Am. U., 1975. Bar: Colo. 1976, U.S. Dist. Ct. Colo. 1976. Coach, YMCA Youth Sports, Colorado Springs, 1989, 90, 92; bd. dirs. Colorado Youth Symphony Assn., 1993—; commr. Old Lawyers Basketball Assn., Colorado Springs, 1990-91, 94-99. Regents scholar, 1967-71. Mem. Colo. Bar Assn. (fin. com.), El Paso County Bar Assn. (fin. com.), Colo. Trial Lawyers Assn., Nat. Assn. Counsel for Children. Democrat. Avocations: church activities, basketball, hiking, Nordic and Alpine skiing. Family and matrimonial, Juvenile, Criminal. Office: 419 N Cascade Ave Colorado Springs CO 80903-3324

**DEAN, ROBERT STUART,** lawyer; b. N.Y.C., Mar. 22, 1952; s. Leo J. and Sonia (Margolin) D.; m. Lynn W.L. Fahey, July 31, 1983; children: Alexander, Benjamin. BA, Northwestern U., 1973; diploma in advanced internat. studies, Johns Hopkins U., Bologna, Italy, 1974; JD, NYU, 1977. Bar: N.Y. 1978, U.S. Dist. Ct. (ea. and so. dists.) N.Y. 1979, U.S. Ct. Appeals (2d cir.) 1979, U.S. Supreme Ct. 1986. Assoc. appellate counsel Criminal Appeals Bur., Legal Aid Soc., N.Y.C., 1977-79, sr. supervising atty., 1979-97; atty.-in-charge Ctr. for Appellate Litigation, N.Y.C., 1997—; adj. asst. prof. law NYU Sch. Law, N.Y.C., 1995-97; adj. prof. law Bklyn. Law Sch., N.Y.C., 1998-99. Co-author: New York Pretrial Criminal Procedure, 1996. Mem. New York County Lawyers Assn., Assn. Bar City N.Y. Appellate, Criminal. Office: Ctr for Appellate Litigation 74 Trinity Pl New York NY 10006-2003

**DEAN, RONALD GLENN,** lawyer; b. Milw., Feb. 18, 1944; m. Mary Blumberg, Jan. 25, 1969; children: Elizabeth Lucile, Joshua Henry. BA, Antioch Coll., 1967; JD, U. Wis. 1970. Bar: Wis. 1970, Calif. 1971; assoc. Mink & Neiman, L.A., 1971; pvt. practice, L.A., 1971-74; ptnr. Margolis, McTernan, Scope & Sacks, L.A., 1974-77; pvt. practice, Pacific Palisades, 1977—; mem. judge pro-tem program L.A. County Bar, 1978-91; judge pro tem Beverly Hills Mcpl. Ct., 1980-90; arbitrator L.A. Superior Ct., 1980—, L.A. County Fee Dispute Panel, 1979-86, 94—, Santa Monica Mcpl. Ct., 1980—; referee for disciplinary matters State Bar Ct., 1980-88, supervising referee, 1984-88, rev. dept. 1988-90, judge pro tem 1990-94. Bd. dirs. Pacific Palisades Residents Assn., 1983—, pres., 1985-88; counsel to Pacific Palisades Cmty. Coun., 1983-92; C. of C. rep. to Cmty. Coun., 1995—; mem. Councilman's Citizen Adv. Com. to Develop Palisades Specific Plan, 1983-85; bd. govs. Pacific Palisades Civic League, 1987-89; exec. bd. Pacific Palisades Dem. Club, 1990—, pres., 1991, 96; mem. Palisades P.R.I.D.E., 1996—, pres., 1997-98, bd. dirs. Fellow Coll. Labor & Employment Lawyers; mem. Am. Arbitration Assn. (panel 1974-95), ABA (co-chmn. employee benefits com, labor sect., bd. sr. editors Employee Benefits Law 1995-98, plaintiff co-chair, nat. insts. subcom.), BNA Pension and Benefits Reporter (adv. bd. 1995—), Wis. Bar Assn., Calif. Bar Assn., Calif. State Bar (chmn. pension and trust benefits com. of labor sect. 1984), L.A. County Bar Assn. Antioch Alumni Assn. (dir. 1982-88), Pacific Palisades (Calif.) C. of C. (bd. dirs. 1995—). Pension, profit-sharing, and employee benefits, Personal injury. Office: 15135 W Sunset Blvd Ste 280 Pacific Palisades CA 90272-3735

**DEANE, RICHARD H., JR.,** federal judge; b. 1952. BA, U. Ga., 1974, JD, 1977; LLM, U. Mich., 1979. Asst. U.S. atty. No. Dist. Ga.; magistrate judge U.S. Dist. Ct. (no. dist.) Ga., Atlanta, 1994-98; U.S. atty. No. Dist. Ga., Atlanta, 1998—. Office: 1800 US Courthouse 75 Spring St SW Atlanta GA 30335-1700

**DEANE, RUTH M.,** lawyer; b. Providence, R.I., Dec. 21, 1950; m. Barry S. Glick, June 17, 1989. BS, Kean Coll., BA. Pvt. practice Lincoln Park, N.J., 1995—. Real property, Personal injury, Probate.

**DEANGELO, CHARLES SALVATORE,** lawyer; b. Jamestown, N.Y., Oct. 10, 1955; s. John P. and Santina M. DeAngelo; m. Deborah M. Mason, Aug. 20, 1977; children: Kara, Jonathan, Matthew. BS, Cornell U., 1977, MS, 1978; JD, Georgetown U., 1981. Bar: D.C. 1982, N.Y. 1984, U.S. Dist. Ct. (we. dist.) N.Y. 1992, U.S. Ct. Appeals (3d cir.) 1982, U.S. Ct. Appeals (fed. cir.) 1985. Law clk. Cafferky, Powers, Jordan & Lewis, P.C., Washington, 1979-80; law clk. Internat. Brotherhood of Teamsters, Washington, 1980-81, staff atty., 1981-84; campaign mgr. Stan Lundine for Congress, Jamestown, N.Y., 1984; assoc. Fessenden & Laumer, Jamestown, 1985-87; ptnr. Fessenden, Laumer & DeAngelo, Jamestown, 1987—. Mem. Pub. Schs. Effective Schs. Com., Jamestown, 1992; lector St. James Roman Cath. Ch., Jamestown, 1994—; coach Youth Soccer, Hockey, T-Ball, Jamestown, 1993—. Alpern Edn. scholar, Cornell U., 1977. Mem. N.Y. State Bar Assn., Jamestown Bar Assn. (chmn. continuing edn. com. 1993, chmn. criminal def. com. 1990-94), N.Y. State Trial Lawyers Assn., Marco Polo Club, Elks. Democrat. Avocations: running, reading, card collecting, spectator sports, children. General civil litigation, General practice, Labor. Office: Fessenden Laumer & DeAngelo PO Box 590 81 Forest Ave Jamestown NY 14701-6605

**DEARIE, RAYMOND JOSEPH,** federal judge; b. 1944. AB, Fairfield U., 1966; JD, St. John's U., 1969. Pvt. practice law Shearman & Sterling, N.Y.C., 1969-71, Surrey & Morse, N.Y.C., 1977-80; chief Appeals div. U.S. Dept. Justice, 1971-74, chief gen. crimes sect., 1974-76, chief Criminal div., 1976-77; exec. asst. U.S. Atty.'s Office, 1977; asst. U.S. atty. U.S. Dist. Ct. (ea. dist.) N.Y., 1971-77, chief asst. U.S. atty., 1980-82, U.S. atty., 1982-86; judge U.S. Dist. Ct. (ea. dist.) N.Y., Bklyn., 1986—. Contbr. articles to profl. jours. Bd. dirs. Daytop Village, L.I. Coll. Hosp. Mem. ABA, N.Y. State Bar Assn., Assn. of Bar of City of N.Y., Fed. Bar Coun. Office: US Dist Ct 225 Cadman Plz E Brooklyn NY 11201-1818

**DEASON, EDWARD JOSEPH,** lawyer; b. Pasadena, Calif., July 5, 1955; s. Edward Patrick Deason and Marye Annette (Erramouspe) Kennedy; m. Charlotte Thunberg, Aug. 1, 1987; children: Keelin Marie, Erin Michelle. BA, Loyola Marymount U., 1977, JD, 1982. Bar: Calif. 1983, U.S. Dist. Ct. (ctrl. dist.) Calif. 1983, U.S. Dist. Ct. (ea. dist.) Calif. 1987, U.S. Ct. Appeals (9th cir.) 1993, U.S. Supreme Ct. 1994. Assoc. Law Offices Edwin C. Martin, L.A., 1983-86; ptnr. Martin & Deason, L.A., 1986-94; pvt. practice L.A., 1994—. Mem. ATLA, Consumer Attys. of Calif., Trial Lawyers for Pub. Justice, L.A. Lawyers Club, Loyola Scott Moot Ct. Democrat. Roman Catholic. Personal injury. Office: 21515 Hawthorne Blvd Ste 1000 Torrance CA 90503-6505

**DEASON, HEROLD MCCLURE,** lawyer; b. Alton, Ill., July 24, 1942; s. Ernest Wilburn and Mildred Mary (McClure) D.; m. Wilma Lee Kaemmerle, June 18, 1966; children: Sean, Ian, Whitney. BA, Albion Coll., 1964; JD, Northwestern U., 1967. Bar: Mich. 1968. Assoc. Bodman, Longley & Dahling, LLP, Detroit, 1967-74, ptnr., 1975—; city atty. Grosse Pointe Pk., Mich., 1978—. Vice chmn. Detroit, Windsor Freedom Festival, 1978-92; bd. dirs. Spirit of Detroit Assn., 1980—. Recipient Spirit of Detroit award, Detroit City Coun., 1986. Mem. ABA, Mich. Assn. Mcpl. Attys. (pres. 1995-97), Detroit Bar Assn., Can.-U.S. Bus. Assn. (v.p. 1997—), Grosse Pointe Yacht Club (commodore 1992-93), Detroit Racquet Club, Windsor Club, Clinton River Boat Club. General corporate, Mergers and acquisitions, Municipal (including bonds). Home: 1044 Kensington Ave Grosse Pointe Park MI 48230-1437 Office: Bodman Longley Dahling LLP 100 Renaissance Ctr Fl 34 Detroit MI 48243-1001

**DEATHERAGE, WILLIAM VERNON,** lawyer; b. Drumright, Okla., Apr. 17, 1927; s. William Johnson and Pearl Mae (Watson) D.; m. Priscilla Ann Campbell, Sept. 16, 1932; children: Thomas William, Andrea Susan. BS, U. Oreg., 1952, LLB with honors, 1954. Bar: Oreg. 1954, U.S. Dist. Ct. Oreg. 1956. Ptnr. Frohnmayer, Deatherage, Pratt, Jamieson & Clarke & Moore, Medford, Oreg., 1954—; bd. dirs. Oreg. Law Inst., U. Oreg. Found. Served with USN, 1945-48. Mem. Am. Coll. Trial Lawyers, Internat. Acad. Trial Lawyers, Delta Theta Phi, Rogue Valley Country Club (pres. 1988), Rogue River Valley Univ. Club. Democrat. Episcopalian. Federal civil litigation,

State civil litigation, Insurance. Address: 2592 E Barnett Rd Medford OR 97504-8345

**DEATLEY, JAMES HARRY,** prosecutor. BBA cum laude, Baylor U., 1972, JD, 1974. Bar: Fla., Tex., U.S. Dist. Ct. (no. dist.) Fla, U.S. Dist. Ct. (ea., we. and so. dists.) Tex., U.S. Ct. Appeals (5th and 11th cirs.). Asst. staff judge advocate Brooks AFB, 1975-76; area def. counsel Torrejon AFB, Madrid, Spain, 1976-78; cir. def. counsel Maxwell AFB, Montgomery, Ala., 1978-82; asst. fed. pub. defender No. Dist. Fla., 1979-80; pvt. practice, 1980-82; exec. asst. U.S. atty. Ea. Dist. Tex., 1982-85; asst. U.S. atty., chief Austin-Waco divsns. West Dist. Tex., 1985-89, 1st asst.-criminal, 1990-93, U.S. atty., 1993-96, sr. litigation counsel, 1996-97; U.S. atty. So. Dist. Tex., 1997—; speaker in field. Contbr. articles to profl. jours. Recipient Atty. Gen.'s award for disting. svc., 1996. Office: US Attys Office PO Box 61129 Houston TX 77208-1129

**DEAVER, PHILLIP LESTER,** lawyer; b. Long Beach, Calif., July 21, 1952; s. Albert Lester and Eva Lucille (Welton) D. Student, USCG Acad., 1970-72; BA, UCLA, 1974; JD, U. So. Calif., 1977. Bar: Hawaii 1977, U.S. Dist. Ct. Hawaii 1977, U.S. Ct. Appeals (9th cir.) 1978, U.S. Supreme Ct. 1981. Assoc. Carlsmith, Wichman, Case, Mukai & Ichiki, Honolulu, 1977-83, ptnr., 1983-86; ptnr. Bays, Deaver, Hiatt, Lung & Rose, Honolulu, 1986, mng. ptnr., 1986-95. Contbr. articles to profl. jours. Dir. Parents and Children Together. Mem. ABA (forum com. on the Constrn. Industry), AIA (affiliate Hawaii chpt.), Am. Arbitration Assn. (arbitrator). Construction, General civil litigation. Home: 2471 Pacific Heights Rd Honolulu HI 96813-1029 Office: Bays Deaver Hiatt Lung & Rose PO Box 1760 Honolulu HI 96806-1760

**DEAVERS, MARIBETH,** lawyer; b. Niles, Ohio, Apr. 30, 1959; d. Ralph Edward and Kathleen Ann Melvch; m. J. Todd Deavers, May 19, 1989. BA in Microbiology/Zoology, Miami U., 1982; JD cum laude, Capital U. Law Sch., 1991. Bar: Ohio 1991, U.S. Dist. Ct. (so. dist.) Ohio 1991, U.S. Dist. Ct. (no. dist.) Ohio 1997; U.S. Ct. Appeals (6th cir.) 1992; U.S. Patent and Trademark Office, 1994. Legal Downes & Hurst, Columbus, Ohio, 1990-94; law clk. Supreme Ct. of Ohio, Columbus, 1990; atty. Cen. Ohio Transit Authority, Columbus, 1994-96, Manos, Martin, Pergram & Browning, Columbus and Delaware, Ohio, 1996—; magistrate Ct. of Common Pleas - Juv. Div., Delaware, 1996—; rschr. Battelle Meml. Inst., Columbus, 1983-85; microbiologist L.J. Minor Corp., Cleve., 1986-87, Borden, Inc., Columbus, 1987-89. Author: (book) Civil Service Law in Ohio, 1993. Bd. dirs. Del. Area C. of C., 1998—, Sunbury Big Walnut C. of C., Ohio, 1998—, St. John Learning Ctr., Columbus, 1992—, Big Bros./Big Sisters, Delware, 1996—, adv. coun., 1996—; mem. com. United Way, Delaware, 1998—, devel. coun. Grady Meml. Hosp., Delaware, 1997—. Recipient Dir.'s award Big Bros./Big Sisters, Delaware, 1997. Mem. Ohio State Bar Found. (Cmty. Svc. award for Lawyers Under 40 1997), Ohio State Bar Assn. (bd. govs. 1999—), Delaware Bar Assn., Columbus Bar Assn., Rotary (bd. dirs./sgt.-at-arms Sunbury Galena club 1998—). Avocations: gardening, landscaping, cooking, bicycling, running. Labor, Contracts commercial, Intellectual property. Office: Manos Martin Pergram & Browning 40 N Sandusky St Ste 200 Delaware OH 43015-1995

**DEBEAUBIEN, HUGO H.,** lawyer; b. Detroit, Sept. 20, 1948; s. Phillip Frances and June (Hesse) deB.; m. Mary Lazenby, Apr. 30, 1977; 1 child, Hugo Samuel. BS in Bus., Fla. State U., 1970; JD, Stetson U., 1973. Bar: Fla. 1973, U.S. Dist. Ct. (mid. dist.) Fla. 1974, U.S. Supreme Ct. 1978, U.S. Ct. Appeals (11th cir.) 1981. Asst. state atty. Fla. 9th Jud. Cir. Ct., Orlando, 1973-76; ptnr. Drage, deBeaubien, Orlando, 1976-79; ptnr., pres. Drage, deBeaubien, Knight & Simmons, Orlando, 1980-87, Drage, deBeaubien, Knight, Simmons, Romano and Neal, Orlando, 1987-98; ptnr. Drage, deBeaubien, Knight, Simmons, Mantzaris and Neal, Orlando, 1999—; lectr. Fla. Bar Assn., 1981-83. Mem. ATLA, Nat. Assn. Criminal Def. Lawyers, Fla. State U. Alumni Assn. (bd. dirs. 1986-93, sec. 1993-94, treas. 1995-96, v.p. 1996-97, chmn.-elect 1997-98, chmn. 1998—), Univ. Club Orlando, Country Club Orlando. Republican. Methodist. Avocations: golf, tennis. State civil litigation, Criminal, Family and matrimonial. Home: 1125 Belleaire Cir Orlando FL 32804-6703 Office: Drage deBeaubien Knight Simmons Mantzaris & Neal 322 N Magnolia Ave Orlando FL 32801-1609

**DEBERARDINE, ROBERT,** lawyer; b. Bklyn., June 29, 1958; s. Roger B. and Rose Ann DeBerardine; m. Cara Mia Williams, Nov. 24, 1991; children: Maximilla Williams, Emanuella Williams. BSChemE cum laude, Lafayette Coll., 1980; JD magna cum laude, Cornell U., 1983. Bar: U.S. Patent Office. Assoc. Jones, Day, Reavis & Pogue, L.A., N.Y.C., Dallas, 1983-91; ptnr. Brobeck, Phleger & Harrison, Palo Alto, Calif., 1992—; head litigation Brobeck, Phleger & Harrison, Austin. Mem. State Bar N.Y., State Bar Calif., State Bar Tex., Order of the Coif. Avocations: writing, outdoor sports, family. E-mail: rdeberardine@brobeck.com. Fax: 512-477-5426. Patent, Trademark and copyright. Office: Brobeck Phleger & Harrison 111 Congress Ave Austin TX 78701-4050

**DEBEVOISE, DICKINSON RICHARDS,** federal judge; b. Orange, N.J., Apr. 23, 1924; s. Elliott and Josephine (Richards) D.; m. Katrina Stephenson Leeb, Feb. 24, 1951; children: Kate, Josephine Debevoise Davies, Mary Debevoise Rennie, Abigail D. Byrne. BA, Williams Coll., 1948; LLB, Columbia U., 1951. Bar: N.J. 1953, U.S. Supreme Ct. 1956. Law clk. to Hon. Phillip Forman, chief judge U.S. Dist. Ct. for Dist. N.J., 1952-53; assoc. firm Riker, Emery & Danzig, Newark, 1953-56; partner firm Riker, Danzig, Scherer, Debevoise & Hyland, Newark, 1957-79; judge U.S. Dist. Ct. for N.J., 1979—; adj. prof. constitutional law Seton Hall U., 1992-94; pres. Newark Legal Services Project, 1965-70; chmn. N.J. Gov.'s Workmen's Compensation Study Commn., 1972-73; mem. N.J. Supreme Ct. Adv. Com. on Jud. Conduct, 1974-78; chmn. N.J. Disciplinary Rev. Bd., 1978-79; mem. Lawyers Adv. Com. for 3d Circuit, 1975-79, chmn., 1979; chmn. N.J. Legal Services Adv. Council, 1976-78. Asso. editor: N.J. Law Jour, 1959-79. Trustee Ramapo Coll., N.J., 1969-73, chmn. bd., 1971-73; trustee Williams Coll., 1969-74, Fund for N.J., 1985—; trustee Hosp. Ctr. at Orange, N.J., v.p., 1975-79; pres. Democrats for Good Govt., 1956-60, active various presdl., senatorial, gubernatorial campaigns; active St. Stephens Episcopal Ch. Sgt. U.S. Army, WWII, 1st lt. Korean War. Decorated Bronze Star. Fellow Am. Bar Found.; mem. ABA, N.J. Bar Assn., Fed. Bar Assn. (v.p. 1976), Assn. Fed. Bar State N.J. (v.p. 1977-79), Essex County Bar Assn. (treas. 1960-64, trustee 1968-71), Am. Law Inst., Judicature Soc., Columbia Law Sch. Assn. (bd. dirs., pres. 1992-94). Office: US Dist Ct PO Box 999 Newark NJ 07101-0999

**DEBEVOISE, ELI WHITNEY, II,** lawyer; b. Morristown, N.J., Feb. 8, 1953. BA, Yale Coll., 1974; JD, Harvard U., 1977. Bar: D.C. Law clk. to William J. Holloway Jr. U.S. Ct. Appeals (10th cir.) Okla., Oklahoma City, 1978-79; ptnr. Arnold & Porter, Washington, 1979—. Mem. ABA (coun. mem. sect. on internat. law and practice), Am. Soc. Internat. Law (exec. coun.). Private international, General corporate, Banking. Office: Arnold & Porter 555 12th St NW Washington DC 20004-1206

**DE BRIER, DONALD PAUL,** lawyer; b. Atlantic City, Mar. 20, 1940; s. Daniel and Ethel de B.; m. Nancy Lee McElroy, Aug. 1, 1964; children: Lesley Anne, Rachel Wynne, Danielle Verne. B.A. in History, Princeton U., 1962; LL.B. with honors, U. Pa., 1967. Bar: N.Y. 1967, Tex. 1977, Utah 1983, Ohio 1987. Assoc. firm Sullivan & Cromwell, N.Y.C., 1967-70, Patterson, Belknap, Webb & Tyler, N.Y.C., 1970-76; v.p., gen. counsel, dir. Gulf Resources & Chem. Corp., Houston, 1976-82; v.p. law Kennecott Corp. (former subs. BP America Inc.), Salt Lake City, 1983-89; assoc. gen. counsel BP America Inc., Cleve., 1987-89; gen. counsel BP Exploration Co. Ltd., London, 1989-93; exec. v.p., gen. counsel Occidental Petroleum Corp., L.A., 1993—. Bd. dirs. L.A. Philharm., 1995—. Served to lt. USNR, 1962-64. Mem. Calif. Club, Riviera Tennis Club. General corporate, General practice, Private international. Home: 699 Amalfi Dr Pacific Palisades CA 90272-4507 Office: Occidental Petroleum Corp 10889 Wilshire Blvd Los Angeles CA 90024-4201

**DEBUNDA, SALVATORE MICHAEL,** lawyer; b. Phila., June 17, 1943; s. Salvatore and Marie Ann (Carilli) DeB.; children: Lauren, David. BS in Econs., U. Pa., 1965, JD, 1968. Bar: Pa. 1968, U.S. Supreme Ct. 1977. Law clk. to justice Phila. Ct. of Common Pleas, 1968-69; asst. gen. counsel ARA Services, Inc., Phila., 1969-74; sr. assoc. Cohen, Verlin, Sherzer & Porter, Phila., 1974-75; v.p., sec., gen. counsel AEL Industries, Inc., Montgomeryville, Pa., 1975-80; v.p., gen. counsel Cooper Assocs., Inc., Marlton, N.J., 1980-81; v.p. cable TV devel. Greater Media, Inc., East Brunswick, N.J., 1981-85; ptnr., chmn. media/entertainment law group Fox, Rothschild, O'Brien & Frankel, Phila., 1985-91; shareholder, dir. Pelino & Lentz, PC, Phila., 1991—. Mem. ABA, Pa. Bar Assn., Phila. Bar Assn., Fed. Comm. Bar Assn. Avocations: sports, owning thoroughbred horses. Communications, General corporate, Entertainment. Office: Pelino & Lentz PC One Liberty Pl 32d Fl Philadelphia PA 19103-7393

**DEC, FRANCIS P.,** lawyer; b. Auburn, N.Y., Mar. 24, 1969; s. Walter F. and Maryann Dec; m. Jacklyn M. Venditti, Oct. 20, 1994; children: David Anthony, Courtney Elizabeth, Michael Patrick. BA, Coll. St. Rose, 1993; JD, U. Buffalo, 1996. Bar: N.Y. 1996, U.S. Dist. Ct. (we. dist.) N.Y. 1996, U.S. Tax Ct. 1996, U.S. Bankruptcy Ct. 1996. Assoc. Horwitz & Fine PC, Buffalo, N.Y., 1996-97; prin. Dec & Assocs. PC, Clarence, N.Y., 1997—. Contbr. articles to mag. Lectr. Ea. States Divsn. Kirby, N.Y., N.J., 1997-98; fin. means com. chair Our Lady Pompeii Ch., Lancaster, N.Y., 1998—. Mem. ABA, N.Y. State Bar Assn. Democrat. Roman Catholic. Estate planning, General corporate, General practice. Office: Dec & Assocs PC 8940 Main St Clarence NY 14031-1959

**DECARLO, DONALD THOMAS,** lawyer, insurance company executive. BA in Econs., Iona Coll., 1960; JD, St. John's U., 1969. Bar: N.Y. 1970, U.S. Dist. Ct. (so. and ea. dists.) 1972, U.S. Supreme Ct. 1973; cert. reins. arbitrator. Asst. regional sales dir. Govt. Employees Ins. Co., 1962-71; lawyer, counsel Lee, McCarthy & Derosa, 1971-72; v.p., gen. counsel Nat. Coun. on Compensation Ins., 1972-86; sr. v.p. Am. Ins. Assn., N.Y.C., 1986-87; sr. v.p., gen. counsel Comml. Ins. Resources, Inc., N.Y.C., 1987-96; dep. gen. counsel Travelers Corp., 1991-96; gen. counsel Travelers Ins. Cos., 1994-96; exec. v.p., gen. counsel Gulf Ins. Co., N.Y.C., 1987-97; ptnr. Lord, Bissell & Brook, 1997—; apptd. master arbitrator N.Y. Inst. Supt.; adj. prof. NYU, Coll. Ins.; mem. Def. Rsch. Inst.; mem. N.Y. State commrs. N.Y. State Fund, 1997—. Author: (with D.J. Gruenfeld) Stress in the American Workplace--Alternatives for the Working Wounded, 1989, (with M. Minkowitz) Workers Compensation Insurance and Law Practice--The Next Generation, 1989; contbr. articles to profl. jours. Mem. ABA (past chmn. workers' compensation com., chair corp. counsel com. 1992-93), Assn. of Bar of City of N.Y. (ins. com.), Queens County Bar Assn. (past chmn. ins. com.), N.Y. State Bar Assn. (worker's compensation), N.Y. County Lawyers Assn. (chair workers' compensation com. 1993). Alternative dispute resolution, Insurance, Workers' compensation. Home: 200 Manor Rd Douglaston NY 11363-1130 Office: Lord Bissell & Brook 1 Penn Plz New York NY 10119-0002

**DECHAINE, DEAN DENNIS,** lawyer; b. Lake Oswego, Oreg., Dec. 12, 1936; s. Bennet Dennis and Hazel Pearl (Vose) DeC.; m. Joan Carolyn Mann, Sept. 29, 1963; children: Michael, Beth, Eve. BS, Portland State U., 1959; LLB, U. Va., 1964. Bar: Va. 1964, Oreg. 1964, Wash. 1986, U.S. Dist. Ct. Oreg. 1964, U.S. Dist. Ct. (we. dist.) Wash. 1986, U.S. Ct. Appeals (9th cir.) 1966, U.S. Ct. Internat. Trade 1996. Rsch. asst. to U.S. senator from Oreg. Richard L. Neuberger, Washington, 1959-60; legis. asst. to U.S. senator from Oreg. Hall S. Lusk, Washington, 1960; ptnr. Miller, Nash, Wiener, Hager & Carlsen, Portland, 1964—; sec., legal counsel World Forestry Ctr., Portland, 1965—. Contbr. article to profl. jour. Chair Portland State U. Alumni Assn., 1967-68, Portland State U. Alumni Bd., 1986-89; scoutmaster Boy Scouts Am., Lake Oswego, 1983-86; program chair continuing legal edn. Oreg. State Bar, 1971, chair aviation sect. 1989-90, chair admiralty sect., 1983-84, 1997—. With U.S. Army, 1960-61. Mem. Maritime Law Assn. U.S. (proctor). Admiralty, Aviation, Environmental. Home: 443 Country Club Rd Lake Oswego OR 97034-2107 Office: Miller Nash Wiener Hager & Carlsen 111 SW 5th Ave Ste 3400 Portland OR 97204-3604

**DECKELMAN, ARTHUR D.,** lawyer, motion picture line producer; b. Balt., Apr. 21, 1929; s. Ruben and Ida (Havelock) D.; m. Wilma Schoenbuch, June 1961 (dec. Aug. 1974); 1 child, Daniel J.; m. Jennifer Hull, Nov. 5, 1977; children: Jennette, Erica. BBA in Acctg., U. Miami, 1953, LLB/JD, 1957; LLM, NYU, 1961; MBA in Taxes, Golden Gate U., 1982. Bar: Fla. 1953, N.Y. 1961, Calif. 1977, U.S. Dist. Ct. (so. dist.) Fla. 1964, U.S. Dist. Ct. (mid. dist.) Fla. 1982, U.S. Dist. Ct. (ctrl. dist.) Calif. 1977, U.S. Ct. Appeals (5th and 9th cirs.), U.S. Supreme Ct. 1964. Auditor Coopers Lybrandt, N.Y.C., 1957-61; assoc. atty. Hammer Rothblatt, N.Y.C., 1961, Walters, Moore & Costanzo, Miami, 1961-68; sole practitioner Miami, 1968-76; ptnr. Hillsinger & Costanzo, L.A., 1977-82, Hillsinger, Costanzo, Deckelman & Mason, Clearwater, Fla., 1982-84; sole practitioner Palm Harbor, Fla., 1984—; bd. dirs. New Focus Films, Inc., Orlando, Fla. Contbg. author: Criminal Law of New York, 1960, Successful Techniques for Criminal Trials, 1961, Art of Cross Examination, 1971, Fundamentals of Criminal Advocacy, 1974, others. Bd. dirs. Suncoast YMCA, Clearwater, 1983; mem. adv. bd. Salvation Army, Clearwater. With JAGC, U.S. Army, 1953-55, Japan. Mem. ABA, ATLA, Clearwater Bar Assn., Rotary Internat. (pres. Clearwater 1997, Paul Harris fellow 1985). Democrat. General practice, Entertainment. Address: 36402 US Hwy 19 N Palm Harbor FL 34684-1330

**DECKER, DAVID ALFRED,** lawyer; b. Waukegan, Ill., Nov. 30, 1937; s. Alfred D. and Marian (Bellows) D.; m. Mary Louise Kirby, Apr. 1, 1967; children: Kathleen, David Jr., Michael. Grad. in Liberal Arts, Lake Forest Coll., 1960; JD, Northwestern U., 1963. Bar: Ill. 1964. Atty. Pretzel & Stouffer, Chgo., 1964-65, Phillip E. Howard, Chgo., 1965-67, Howard & Decker, Chgo., 1967-79, David Decker & Assoc., Waukegan, Ill., 1969-87, Decker and Linn, Ltd., Waukegan, Ill., 1987—. Cpl. U.S. Army, 1956-58. Fellow Internat. Acad. Trial Lawyers, Am. Coll. Trial Lawyers; mem. Am. Trial Lawyers Assn. (bd. govs. 1980—), Ill. State Bar Assn. (pres. 1994-95), Ill. Trial Lawyers Assn. (pres. 1985-86). Democrat. Roman Catholic. Avocations: golf, literature, jazz. Personal injury, State civil litigation. Office: Decker and Linn Ltd 215 N Utica St Waukegan IL 60085-4235

**DECKER, JOHN ROBERT,** lawyer; b. Milw., Apr. 29, 1952; s. John Anthony and Margaret Eleanor (Cook) D.; m. Sandra Jean Kuelz, May 25, 1974; 1 child: Jennifer. BA, U. Wis., 1974; JD, Marquette U., 1977. Bar: Wis. 1977, U.S. Ct. Appeals (7th cir.) 1978, U.S. Supreme Ct. 1990. Assoc. Michael, Best & Friedrich, Madison, Wis., 1977-80; assoc. Michael, Best & Friedrich, Milw., 1980-84, ptnr., 1984-91; pvt. practice law Milw., 1991-92; pres. Decker & Gunta, S.C., Milw., 1992-98, Decker Corp., Milw., 1998—; instr. Milw. Sch. Engring., 1987—; mem. Wis. Jud. Coun., 1989-90, Wis. Bd. of Attys. Profl. Responsibility, 1989-90; hearing examiner, 1991—; mem. Wis. Equal Justice Task Force, 1989-91. Author: Construction Claims Under Wisconsin Law, 1988; co-author: Special Verdict Formulation in Wis., 1977; exec. editor Marquette U. Law Rev., 1976-77. Trustee Mt. Zion Luth. Ch., 1986-89, pres., 1988-89. Mem. ABA (ho. of dels. 1984-88, 93, 95-96, governing com. of forum on constrn. industry 1987-89, 91-95, achievement award 1985), Wis. Bar Assn. (bd. govs. 1984-92, exec. com. 1984-85, 87-92, chmn. bd. 1987-88, pres. 1990-91, chmn. constrn. and pub. contract law sect. 1992-94, chmn. constrn. lien law revision com. 1994-99). General civil litigation, Real property, Construction. Home and Office: 2611 N 89th St Milwaukee WI 53226-1807

**DECKER, KURT HANS,** lawyer, educator, author; b. Sept. 23, 1946; s. Hans Emil and Gertrude Elsa (Nestler) D.; m. Hilary McAllister, Aug. 13, 1973; children: Kurt Christian, Allison McAllister. BA in History, Thiel Coll., 1968; MPA, Pa. State U., 1973; JD, Vanderbilt U., 1976; LLM in Labor, Temple U., 1980. Bar: Pa. 1976, U.S. Tax Ct. 1977, U.S. Ct. Internat. Trade 1977, U.S. Ct. Claims 1979, U.S. Dist. Ct. (mid. dist.) Pa. 1976, U.S. Dist. Ct. (ea. dist.) Pa. 1980, U.S. Ct. Appeals (3d cir.) 1980, U.S. Supreme Ct. 1980. Asst. atty. gen. Gov.'s Office Pa. Bur. Labor Rels., Harrisburg, 1976-79; ptnr. Stevens & Lee, Reading, Pa., 1979—; adj. prof. indsl. rels. St. Francis Coll., Pa., 1985—, Widener Sch. Law, Harrisburg, Pa., 1993—; seminar spkr.; rschr. in field. Author: Employee Privacy: Law and Practice, 1987, Employee Privacy Forms and Procedures, 1988, A Manager's Guide to Employment Privacy: Law, Procedures and Policies, 1989, The Individual Employment Rights Primer, 1991, Covenants Not to Compete, 1993, Drafting and Revising Employment Policies and Handbooks, 1994, Privacy in the Workplace: Rights, Procedures and Policies, 1994, Hiring Legally: A Guide for Employees and Employers, 1999; co-author: Drafting and Revising Employment Contracts, 1991, Drafting and Revising Employment Handbooks, 1991, Individual Employee Rights in a Nutshell, 1995; editor: Jour. Individual Employment Rights, 1992—; adminstrv. editor Vanderbilt Jour. Transnat. Law; bd. editors Jour. Collective Negotiations in Pub. Sector, 1982—; contbr. chpts. to books, articles to profl. jours. With U.S. Army, 1968-72. Decorated Army Commendation medal. Mem. ABA (sect. labor and employment law), Pa. Bar Assn. (sect. labor and employment law), Phila. Bar Assn. (News Media award 1985), Berks County Bar Assn., Soc. for Human Resource Mgmt., Sigma Phi Epsilon, Phi Alpha Delta. Lutheran. Labor. Office: Stevens & Lee 111 N 6th St Reading PA 19601-3501

**DECKER, MICHAEL LYNN,** lawyer, judge; b. Oklahoma City, May 5, 1953; s. Leroy Melvin and Yvonne (Baird) D.; m. Robin Strom, July 25, 1987. BA, Oklahoma City U., 1975, JD, 1978; grad., Nat. Jud. Coll., U. Nev., Reno, 1990. Bar: Okla. 1978, U.S. Ct. Appeals (10th cir.) 1979, U.S. Dist. Ct. (we. dist.) Okla. 1985, U.S. Supreme Ct. 1994. Assoc. Bay, Hamilton, Lees, Spears, and Verity, Oklahoma City, 1978-80; assoc. dir. devel. Oklahoma City U., 1980-81, asst. dean, Sch. of Law, 1981-82; sr. oil and gas adminstrv. law judge Okla. Corp. Commn., Oklahoma City, 1982-92, sr. asst. gen. counsel oil and gas conservation, 1992-95, deputy gen. counsel oil and gas conservation, 1995—; campaign staff intern U.S. Senator Henry Bellmon's Re-election Campaign, 1974; mem. Civil Arbitration Panel, U.S. Dist. Ct. (we. dist.) Okla., 1985—; seminar spkr. Am. Inst. Profl. Geologists (Okla. sect.), 1985; mem. dean's adv. com. Oklahoma City U. Law Sch., 1986; mem. sys. rev. bd. Okla. Corp. Commn., 1990-93, mem. process mgmt. rev. team, 1995-96; lectr. adminstrv. law Vanderbilt U. Sch. Law, 1993. Trustee Oklahoma City U., 1989-91, mem. alumni bd. dirs., 1988-95, also mem. devel. com., long range planning com. and adminstrv. liaison com.; mem. com. of twenty Oklahoma City Art Mus., 1987-95, co-chair omelette party, 1990; vol. Contact Teleminster, Oklahoma City, 1986-91, bd. dirs., 1987-90; mem. rev. bd. Okla. Corp. Commn., 1990; mem. adminstrv. bd. St. Luke's United Meth. Ch., 1988-92, chair missions com., 1993-94; bd. dirs. March of Dimes, Western Okla., 1990-93; mem. Class XI Leadership Oklahoma City, 1993; area rep. Okla. Mozart Fest., Bartlesville, 1988—. Mem. Okla. Bar Assn. (mineral law sect., environ. law sect.), Okla. County Bar Assn. (exec. com. young lawyers sect. 1978-82, mem. law day com. 1979-88, chmn. law day luncheon spkr. com. 1985-88), Oklahoma City Mineral Lawyers Soc., Lions, Phi Alpha Delta, Lambda Chi Alpha (treas. bldg. corp. 1984-89, pres. 1989-91, Outstanding Alumnus award 1983), Oklahoma City Dinner Club, Lester Raymer Soc. (Lindsborg, Kans.). Republican. Administrative and regulatory, Oil, gas, and mineral. Home: 2008 NW 44th St Oklahoma City OK 73118-1902 Office: Okla Corp Commn State Capitol Complex Jim Thorpe Bldg PO Box 52000-2000 Oklahoma City OK 73152-2000

**DECUZZI, JAMES,** public official, lawyer; b. N.Y.C., Mar. 7, 1958; s. Frank J. and Florence (Meyers) DeC. BA magna cum laude, SUNY, Albany, 1980; JD, Rutgers U., 1983. Bar: N.Y. 1984, U.S. Dist. Ct. (so. and ea. dists.) N.Y. 1985, U.S. Ct. Appeals (2d cir.) 1989, U.S. Supreme Ct. 1990, U.S. Tax Ct. 1992. Legal coord. N.Y.C. Dept. Correction, 1983-84; confidential law asst. appellate divsn. N.Y. State Supreme Ct., 2d Dept., 1984-85; assoc. atty. Koeppel Sommer & Del Casino, Mineola, N.Y., 1985-91; ptnr. DeCuzzi & Getzler, N.Y.C., 1993-96; adminstrv. law judge N.Y.C. Housing Authority, 1995-96; commr. Tax Commn. of City of N.Y., N.Y.C., 1996, pres., 1997—; mem. Mayor's Cabinet, N.Y.C., 1997—; mem. Mayor's Com. on City Marshals, N.Y.C., 1994—; mentor N.Y. Vol. for Youth Campaign, N.Y.C.; sustaining life mem. Queens Farm Mus., mem. nat. bd. dirs., Cooley's Anemia Found., Inc. Recipient Man of Yr. award Italian-Ams. for Better Govt. of N.Y., Inc., 1997, NYC Coun. Outstanding Citizen citation, Nassau Cty's Commty Svc. award., Italian-Amer. Federation of Brooklyn and Queens Commty. Svc. award, named Principal for a Day Pub. Sch. #159 Queens. Mem. N.Y. State Bar Assn., Columbian Lawyers' Assn. Nassau County Inc. (bd. dirs. 1989—, pres. 1994-95), Coalition of Italo-Am. Assns. Inc. (bd. dirs. 1987-96, bd. advisors 1997—), Confederation Columbian Lawyers Assns. (co-founder 1994, gov. coun. 1994-95), Lt. Joseph Petrosino Lodge of Order Sons of Italy in America, NY, NY (charter mem., 1999, trustee, 1999—), Amer. Australian Assn., Italy-Am. C. of C. Office: NYC Tax Commn Mcpl Bldg 1 Centre St New York NY 10007

**DEEGEAR, JAMES OTIS, III,** lawyer; b. Dallas, Oct. 11, 1948; s. James O. Jr. and Madeleine (Couch) D.; m. Pamela Word; children: James O. IV, Frances S., Cynthia S. AA, San Antonio Coll., 1968; BA, U. Tex., 1971, JD, 1974. Bar: Tex. 1974, U.S. Dist. Ct. (we. dist.) Tex. 1980. Assoc. Law Offices of Rudy Rice, San Antonio, 1974-75; ptnr. Collins, DeWall & Deegear, San Antonio, 1975-79, Davis, Smith & Davis, San Antonio, 1979-82; counsel Southers & Lyons, Inc., San Antonio, 1983; pvt. practice law San Antonio, 1983—. Chmn. Leadership San Antonio, 1986-87; pres. Elf Louise, San Antonio, 1987-91. Fellow Tex. Bar Found., San Antonio Bar Found.; mem. State Bar of Tex., San Antonio Bar Assn. (bd. dirs. 1981-83), Assn. Trial Lawyers Am., Tex. Trial Lawyers Assn. (bd. dirs. 1984-89), San Antonio Trial Lawyers Assn. (pres. 1980-81). Avocations: community interests, reading, sports. General civil litigation, Personal injury, Criminal. Office: PO Box 1124 Boerne TX 78006-1124

**DEENER, JEROME ALAN,** lawyer; b. Newark, Jan. 23, 1943; s. Harry Simon and Ann Deener; m. Brenda Diane Appelbaum, June 28, 1965; children: Elisa Teri Deener-Agus, Shira Ann, Avi Michael. BS in Acctg., Pa. State U., 1965; JD, Bklyn. Law Sch., 1968; LLM in Taxation, NYU, 1971. Bar: N.Y. 1968, N.J. 1972, U.S. Dist. Ct. N.Y. 1971, U.S. Ct. Appeals 1981. Sr. tax acct. Arthur Andersen, N.Y.C., 1968-71; tax assoc. Herbert M. Gannet, Esq., Newark, 1971-72, Gruen, Sorkow & Sorkow, Hackensack, N.J., 1972-74; ptnr. Deener & Fond, Hackensack, 1974-79; sr. ptnr. Jerome A. Deener, P.C., Hackensack, 1980—, Deener Feingold & Stern, Hackensack, 1980—. contbr. articles to profl. jours. Past pres. Solomon Schechter Day Sch., Cranford, N.J., 1983-84. Fellow Am. Coll. Trust and Estate Counsel; mem. Estate Planning Coun. Bergen County (pres. 1973). Jewish. Avocations: travel, tennis, photography, bike riding, hiking. Taxation, general, Estate taxation, Estate planning. Office: Deener Feingold & Stern PC Two University Plaza Hackensack NJ 07601

**DEERSON, ADELE SHAPIRO,** lawyer, educator; b. N.Y.C., July 14, 1924; d. Samuel and Marion (Pestreich) Shapiro; m. Nathan Deerson, Sept. 8, 1946; children—Bruce Alan, Jayne Ellen. B.A., Hunter Coll., 1944; J.D. magna cum laude, Bklyn. Law Sch., 1946, J.S.D. magna cum laude, 1949. Bar: N.Y. 1946. Atty., Henry H. Salzberg, N.Y.C., 1946-49; trial counsel Cosmopolitan Mut., N.Y.C., 1959-78; sole practice, Nassau County, N.Y., 1949—; asst. prof. N.Y. Inst. Tech., 1968, assoc. prof., 1969-78, prof. law, 1978—; prof. no-fault arbitrator, N.Y., 1990—. Author: Learning Manual Business Law, 1978. Staff editor Jour. Legal Services Edn. Arbitrator, Am. Arbitration Assn., Small Claims Ct., Civil Ct., Dist. Ct. Nassau, N.Y. Recipient Cert. of Appreciation, Judges Civil Ct., Queens, 1977, N.Y.C. Family Ct. 1977. Mem. Queens County Bar Assn., Nassau County Bar Assn., Nat. Assn. Bus. Law Tchrs., Assn. Arbitrators, Nassau-Suffolk Women's Bar Assn., Delta Mu Delta. Lodge: B'nai B'rith (v.p. 1956-58). Contracts commercial, General practice. Home: 7612 176th St Flushing NY 11366-1514

**DEFEIS, ELIZABETH FRANCES,** law educator, lawyer; b. N.Y.C.; d. Francis Paul and Lena (Amendola) D. BA, St. John's U., 1956, JD, 1958, JSD (hon.), 1984; LLM, NYU, 1971; postgrad., U. Milan, Italy, 1963-64, Inst. Internat. Human Rights, 1991. Bar: N.Y. 1959, U.S. Dist. Ct. (fed. dist.) 1960, U.S. Dist. Ct. (so. dist.) N.Y. 1961, U.S. Supreme Ct. 1965, U.S. Dist. Ct. (ea. dist.) N.Y. 1978, N.J. 1983. Asst. U.S. atty. So. Dist. N.Y., Dept. Justice, 1961-62; atty. RCA Corp., 1962-63; assoc. Carter, Ledyard & Milburn, N.Y.C., 1963-69; atty. Bedford Stuyvesant Legal Svcs. Corp., 1969-70; prof. law Seton Hall U., Newark, 1971—, dean Sch. Law, 1983-88; vis. prof. St. Louis U. Sch. Law, 1988, St. John's U. Sch. Law, 1990, U. Milan, Italy, 1996; Fulbright-Hays lectr., Iran, India, 1977-79; lectr. Orgn. Security and Cooperation in Europe, Russia, Turkmenistan, Tajikistan, Azerbaijan; vis. scholar Ctr. Study of Human Rights, Columbia U., 1989; project dir. TV series Women and Law, 1974-80; narrator TV series Alternatives to Violence, 1981—; mem. com. women and cts. N.J. Supreme Ct., 1982-95; trustee Legal Svcs. N.J., 1983-88; mem. 3rd Cir. Task Force on Equality in the Cts., 1995—; tech. cons. on Constitution of Armenia, 1992-95; project dir. T.V. series Pub. Internat. Law.; legal expert Armenia election OSCE, 1998. Chair

Albert Einstein Inst., Boston, 1995—. Fulbright-Hays scholar Milan, Italy, 1963-64, Fulbright-Hays, Orgn. for Security and Cooperation in Europe scholar, Armenia, Russia, Italy, 1996; Ford Found. fellow, 1970-71. Mem. ABA, Nat. Italian Am. Bar Assn. (dir.), Columbian Lawyers Assn., Assn. of Bar of City of N.Y. (chair internat. law com., coun. internat. affairs), N.J. Bar Assn., Nat. Italian Am. Found. Office: Seton Hall U Law Sch One Newark Ctr Newark NJ 07102

**DEFFNER, ROGER L.,** lawyer, investment counselor; b. Merrill, Wis., Aug. 17, 1945; s. Oscar A. and Elsie E. (Liebers) D. B.S. in Chem. Engring., U. Wis.-Madison, 1968, J.D., 1973. Bar: Wis. 1973, U.S. Dist. Ct. (we. dist.) Wis. 1973. Chem. engr. prodn. and research, spl. products div. NCR, Portage, Wis., 1968-69; chem. engr. plant modernization Olin Chem., Baraboo, Wis., 1969-70; pres., owner Deffner Law Firm, S. C., Wausau, 1973—; gen. ptnr. D&D Investments, Wausau, 1974—; advisor N. Central Tech. Inst., Wausau, 1977-98; lectr. Mt. Senario Coll., Upper Iowa U., N. Ctrl. Tech. Coll.; dir. Wausau Kayak/Canoe Corp., 1992—, Crossroads Mental Health Svcs., Inc., Wausau Area Builders Assn. Co-author: Legal Systems Inc., 1977-78. Mem. Wausau C. of C., Jaycees (life, bd. dirs. Portage 1969, pres. 1970, state v.p. Madison 1971, dir. Wausau 1974. Republican. Lutheran and Polish Catholic. Club: Wausau Noon Optimists (life, internal v.p. 1985-86, pres. 1986-87). Lodge: Elks, Fraternal Triangle. Consumer commercial, Real property, General practice. Address: Deffner Law Firm 1803 Stewart Ave Wausau WI 54401-5374

**DEFOOR, J. ALLISON, II,** lawyer, state agency officer; b. Coral Gables, Fla., Dec. 6, 1953; s. James Allison Sr. and Marjorie (Keen) DeF.; m. Terry Ann White, June 24, 1977; children: Melissa Anne, Mary Katherine, James Allison III. BA, U. So. Fla., 1976; JD, Stetson U., 1979; MA, U. So. Fla., 1979; postgrad., Harvard U., 1989; STD, So. Fla. Ctr. Theol. Studies, 1999. Bar: Fla. 1979, U.S. Dist. Ct. (so. dist.) Fla. 1980, U.S. Ct. Appeals (5th cir.) 1981, U.S. Ct. Appeals (11th cir.) 1982. Asst. pub. defender, 1979-80; asst. state's atty. 16th Cir., Key West, Fla., 1980-83, dir. narcotics task force, 1981-83; judge Monroe County, Plantation Key, Fla., 1983-87; assoc. Cunningham, Albritton, Lenzi, Warner, Bragg & Miller, Plantation Key, 1987-89; sheriff Monroe County, Fla., 1989-90; sr. v.p. CEO Wackenut Monitoring Systems Inc., Coral Gables, Fla., 1991-92; gen. counsel, sec. HEM Pharm. Corp., Phila. and Key Largo, 1992-93; ptnr. Hershoff, Lupino DeFoor & Gregg, Tavernier, Fla., 1993-99; Everglades policy coord. State of Fla., Office of Gov., Tallahassee, 1999—; adj. faculty St. Leo Coll., Key West, 1980-81, U. So. Fla., Ft. Myers, 1981-82, Fla. Internat. U., Miami, 1985, U. Miami Law Sch., 1985-99 ; faculty Nat. Jud. Coll., Reno, Nev., 1985-86. Editor U. Miami Law Rev., 1985; author: (books) DeFoor & Schultz, Fla. Civil Procedure Forms with Practice Commentary, 1989, Odet Philippe, Peninsular Pioneer, 1997 (Safety Harbor Mus., Fla.). Chmn. Monroe County Rep. Exec. Com., 1987-88, 94, state committeeman, 1994-99; mem . Fla. Rep. Exec. Com., 1995-96, 97-99; del. Rep. Nat. Conv., 1992; Rep. nominee for Lt. Gov. of Fla., 1990; trustee Gov.'s Commn. Sustainable Fla., Fla. Dispute Resolution Consortium. Named one of Five Outstanding Young Men in Fla., Jaycees, 1984, Ten Outstanding Young Men in Am., Jaycees, 1985; recipient Merit award Fla. Crime Prevention Commn., 1982, Leadership Fla. Class V. Mem. ABA, Fla. Bar (bd. govs. 1995-97), Monroe County Bar Assn., Mensa, Fla. Keys Bar Assn., Ocean Reef Club (Key Largo, Fla.), Islamorada Fishing Club, Key West Yacht Club, Explorer's Club (New York), Upper Keys Rotary (pres. 1987-88). Republican. Episcopalian. Avocations: scuba diving, sailing, golf. Environmental, Technology. Home: 359 River Plantation Rd Crawfordville FL 32327 Office: State of Fla Office of Gov 1501 The Capitol Tallahassee FL 32099-6001

**DEFOREST, STEPHEN ELLIOTT,** lawyer; b. Seattle, Sept. 16, 1933; s. Elliott and Helen Tyson Hart; m. Sylvia Lynn Agathon, June 14, 1958; children: Christopher Elliott, John Andrew, Katherine Elizabeth. BA, Yale U., 1955; JD, Harvard U., 1960. Bar: Wash. 1960, U.S. Dist. Ct. (we. dist.) Wash. 1961, U.S. Ct. Appeals (9th cir.) 1961, U.S. Supreme Ct. 1972. Assoc. Riddell, Riddell & Williams, Seattle, 1960-64; ptnr. Riddell, Williams, Bullitt & Walkinshaw, Seattle, 1964-95; prin., shareholder Graham & James, LLP/Riddell Williams P.S., Seattle, 1995—. Bd. dirs. United Way King County, Seattle, 1975-79, chmn. planning and allocation, 1978-80; trustee Nature Conservancy Wash., Seattle, 1993—. Lt. (j.g.) USN, 1955-57. Mem. ABA, King County Bar Assn. (pres. 1981-82), Wash. State Bar Assn. (pres. 92-93), King County Pub. Defenders (trustee 1975-77). Avocations: hiking, cross-country skiing, squash. Pension, profit-sharing, and employee benefits, Labor, General corporate. Office: Graham & James LLP Et Al 1001 4th Ave Ste 4500 Seattle WA 98154-1192

**DEFOREST, WALTER PATTISON, III,** lawyer; b. Ft. Sill, Okla., Dec. 4, 1944; s. Walter P. Jr. and Mary E. (Miller) DeF.; m. Anna Thun. BA, U. Pitts., 1966; JD, Harvard U., 1969. Bar: Pa. 1970, U.S. Ct. Appeals (2d and 3d cirs.) 1973, U.S. Ct. Appeals (4th, 5th and D.C. cirs.) 1978, U.S. Ct. Appeals (10th cir.) 1981, U.S. Ct. Appeals (11th cir.), U.S. Ct. Appeals (7th cir.) 1986, U.S. Ct. Appeals (fed. cir.) 1995, U.S. Supreme Ct. 1974, W.Va. 1997. Assoc. Reed, Smith, Shaw & McClay, Pitts., 1969-77, ptnr., 1978-93; ptnr. DeForest & Koscelnik, Pitts., 1994—; instr. Grad. Sch. Indsl. Adminstrn. Carnegie Mellon U., Pitts., 1974-75. Mem. adv. com. Big Bros. and Big Sisters Western Pa., Pitts., 1984—; bd. dirs. Pa. Small Bus. Advocacy Coun., Harrisburg, 1984-89, 92. Mem. ABA (litigation, labor sects.), Pa. Bar Assn. (litigation, labor sects.), Allegheny County Bar Assn. (litigation sect., fed. ct. sect.). Labor, General civil litigation, Administrative and regulatory. Office: DeForest & Koscelnik 3000 Koppers Bldg 436 7th Ave Pittsburgh PA 15219-1826

**DEFRANCESCHI, GARY M.,** lawyer; b. Bklyn., June 18, 1967; s. Joseph and Evelyn M. DeFranceschi; m. Kathleen A. Brady, Oct. 26, 1991. AB, Muhlenberg Coll., Allentown, Pa., 1989; JD cum laude, Widener U., 1993. Bar: N.J. 1993, Pa. 1993, U.S. Dist. Ct. N.J. 1993. Rsch. asst. Widener Sch. Law, Wilmington, Del., 1989-90; law clk. U.S. Bankruptcy Ct., Dist. of Del., 1994; atty. Hoechst Celanese Corp., Bridgewater, N.J., 1995-97; sr. atty. Hoechst Marion Roussel, Bridgewater, 1998—. Mem. law rev. Vol. State Rep. com. of Del., Wilmington, 1991. Mem. ABA, Am. Corp. Counsel Assn., Phi Delta Phi. Roman Catholic. General corporate, Contracts commercial. Office: Hoechst Marion Roussel Rte 202-206 Bridgewater NJ 08807

**DEGARIS, ANNESLEY HODGES,** lawyer, educator; b. Birmingham, Ala., June 23, 1963; s. John A. Jr. and Lena Kate (Hodges) DeG.; m. Ashley H. DeGaris, July 1, 1995. BS in Pub. Adminstrn. magna cum laude, Samford U., 1985; JD magna cum laude, Cumberland Sch. Law, 1988; LLM, U. Melbourne, Australia, 1992. Bar: Ala. 1989, U.S. Dist. Ct. (no. dist.) Ala. 1989, U.S. Ct. Appeals (11th cir.) 1992, U.S. Dist. Ct. (mid. dist.) Ala. 1995, U.S. Dist. Ct. (so. dist.) Ala. 1996, U.S. Supreme Ct. 1995. Jud. law clk. U.S. Dist. Ct., Huntsville, Ala., 1988-89; staff atty. U.S. Ct. Appeals 11th Cir., Atlanta, 1991-93; assoc. Johnson & Cory, Birmingham, 1993-95; ptnr. Cory, Watson, Crowder & DeGaris, Birmingham, 1995—; adj. prof. Emory U. Sch. Law, Atlanta, 1992-93; prof. constnl. law Birmingham Sch. Law, 1993—. Casenote editor Cumberland Law Rev.; contbr. articles to profl. jours. Rotary Found. scholar Rotary Internat., Australia, 1990. Mem. ATLA, ABA, Ala. Trial Lawyers Assn., Vestavia Hills Rotary. Avocations: backpacking, travel. Personal injury, Aviation, Product liability. Office: Cory Watson Crowder & DeGaris PC 2131 Magnolia Ave S Birmingham AL 35205-2808

**DEGENER, CAROL MARIE-LAURE,** lawyer; b. N.Y.C., Sept. 4, 1961; d. John Michael and Marie-Laure Murat (Frank) D. BA, Columbia U., 1983, MA, 1984; JD, Harvard U., 1987. Bar: Mass. 1988, N.Y. 1990. Assoc. corp. fin. Goldman Sachs & Co., N.Y.C., 1987-89; assoc. corp. dept. Donovan Leisure Newton & Irvine, N.Y.C., 1989-95, Seward & Kissel, N.Y.C., 1996—. Mem. N.Y. State Bar Assn. (com. on securities regulation 1993—), Bar Assn. City N.Y. (com. on corp. law 1991—), New York County Lawyers' Assn. (com. on securities and exchs. 1991—), Harvard Law Sch. Assn. N.Y. Office: Seward & Kissel 1 Battery Park Plz Fl 20 New York NY 10004-1405

**DEGNAN, JOHN MICHAEL,** lawyer; b. Mpls., Apr. 2, 1948; s. John F. and Lorraine A. D.; m. Barbara B. Degnan; children: John Patrick, Amy Marie, David Charles. BA, U. Minn., 1970; JD, William Mitchell Coll. Law, 1976. Bar: Minn. 1976, U.S. Dist. Ct. Minn. 1976, U.S. Ct. Appeals (8th cir.) Minn. 1976, U.S. Supreme Ct. 1976. Ins. underwriter Marsh & McLennan, Mpls., 1973-76; lawyer, pres. Bassford, Heckt, Lockhart, Tresdell, Briggs & Mullin, P.A., Mpls., 1976—; lectr. in field. Bd. dirs. Hennepin County Pub. Libraries, 1980-84, Storefront Youth Action, 1981-83, Mediation Ctr., 1991—. 1st lt. U.S. Army, 1971-72, Vietnam. Mem. ABA, Minn. State Bar Assn. (ins. com., lectr. convs. 1984-85, civil trial cert. governing coun., cert. trial specialist), Hennepin County Bar Assn. (mem. professionalism com.), Nat. Bd. Trial Advocacy (cert. civil trial specialist), Am. Bd. Trial Advocates, Minn. Def. Lawyers Assn (bd. dirs. 1986—, pres. 1990-91), Minn. Soc. Hosp. Attys., Def. Rsch. Inst., Am. Soc. Law and Medicine, Richfield Jaycees (past pres.). Avocations: running, tennis, golf, boating, sports. Personal injury, Insurance, State civil litigation. Office: Bassford Lockhart Tresdell & Briggs 3550 Multifoods Tower Minneapolis MN 55402

**DE GOFF, VICTORIA JOAN,** lawyer; b. San Francisco, Mar. 2, 1945; d. Sidney Francis and Jean Frances (Alexander) De G.; m. Peter D. Coppelman, May 2, 1971 (div. Dec. 1978); m. Richard Sherman, June 16, 1980. BA in Math. with great distinction, U. Calif., Berkeley, 1967, JD, 1972. Bar: Calif. 1972, U.S. Dist. Ct. (no. dist.) Calif. 1972, U.S. Ct. Appeals 1972, U.S. Supreme Ct. 1979; cert. appellate law specialist, 1996. Rsch. atty. Calif. Ct. Appeal, San Francisco, 1972-73; Reginald Heber Smith Found. fellow San Francisco Neighborhood Legal Assistance Found., 1973-74; assoc. Field, De Goff, Huppert & McGowan, San Francisco, 1974-77; pvt. practice Berkeley, Calif., 1977-80; ptnr. De Goff and Sherman, Berkeley, 1980—; lectr. continuing edn. of bar, Calif., 1987, 90-92, U. Calif. Boalt Hall Sch. Law, Berkeley, 1981-85, dir. appellate advocacy, 1992; cons. Calif. Civil Practice Procedure, Bancroft Whitney, 1992; mem. Appellate Law Adv. Commn., 1995; apptd. applicant evaluation and nomination com. for State Bar Ct. by Calif. Supreme Ct., 1995; pvt. atty., clk. ct. com. Calif. Ct. Appeals, 1997-99; mem. com. on appellate practice ABA, 1997. Author: (with others) Matthew Bender's Treatise on California Torts, 1985. Apptd. to adv. com. Calif. Jud. Coun. on Implementing Proposition 32, 1984-85; mem. adv. bd. Hastings Coll. Trial and Appellate Adv., 1984-91; expert 20/20 vision project, commn. on future cts. Jud. Coun. Calif., 1993, apptd. to appellate standing adv. com., 1993-95; apptd. to Appellate Indigent Def. Oversight Adv. Com., State of Calif., 1995—; com. on appellate stds. of ABA Appellate Judges Conf., 1995-96; com. on appellate practice ABA, 1997; adv. bd. Witkin Legal Inst., Bancroft Whitney, 1996—; bd. dirs. Calif. Supreme Ct. Hist. Soc. (sec. 1999—), State Bar Calif., Appellate Law Cons. Group, 1994-95; appointee 9th Jud. Cir. Hist. Soc. Hon. Cecil Poole Biography Project, 1998. Fellow Woodrow Wilson Found., 1967-68. Mem. Calif. Trial Lawyers Assn. (bd. govs. 1980-88, amicus-curiae com. 1981-87, editor-in-chief assn. mag. 1980-81, Presdl. award of merit 1980, 81), Calif. Acad. Appellate Lawyers (sec.-treas. 1989-90, 2d v.p. 1990-91, 1st v.p. 1991-92, pres. 1992-93), Am. Acad. Appellate Lawyers, Edward J. McFetridge Am. Inn of Cts. (counsellor 1990-91, edn. chmn. 1991-92, social chmn. 1992-93, v.p. 1993-94, pres. 1994-95), Boalt Hall Sch. Law U. Calif. Alumni Assn. (bd. dirs. 1989-91), Order of Coif. Jewish. General civil litigation, Personal injury. Office: 1916 Los Angeles Ave Berkeley CA 94707-2419

**DEGRANDI, JOSEPH ANTHONY,** lawyer; b. Hartford, Conn., 1927; m. Yolanda Salica; children: Terese, Lisa, Donna. BS, Trinity Coll., Hartford, 1949; MS, George Washington U., 1950, LLB, 1952. Bar: D.C. 1952, U.S. Supreme Ct. 1956. Ptnr. Beveridge, DeGrandi, Weilacher & Young, Washington, 1962—; mem. adv. bd. Marymount Sch., Arlington, Va., pres., 1969-72; mem. Pres.'s Adv. Com. on Indsl. Innovation, 1978-79; legal advisor U.S. delegation Diplomatic Conf. for Revision of Paris Conv., Nairobi, Kenya, 1981, Treaty on Harmonization of Patent Laws, The Hague, 1991. Recipient Disting. Alumnus award George Washington U., 1982. Fellow Am. Bar Found.; mem. FBA, IBA, ABA (chmn. sect. patent, trademark and copyright law 1981-82, dep. del. 1986-89, del. to ho. of dels. 1989—, nominating com. 1989-92, 98—), Inter-Am. Bar Assn., Nat. Coun. Patent Law Assns. (sec. 1971-75, adv. panel 1975-79), The Fed. Cir. Bar Assn., Bar Assn. D.C. (bd. dirs. 1968-69, chmn. patent, trademark and copyright law sect. 1967-68), D.C. Bar Assn. (chmn. divsn. patent, trademark and copyright law 1978-79), N.Y. Intellectual Property Law Assn., Patent Lawyers Club Washington (pres. 1959), Nat. Lawyers Club (bd. govs. 1984-92, v.p. 1989-92, acting pres. 1991-92), Am. Judicature Soc., Am. Intellectual Property Law Assn. (bd. mgrs. 1976-79, 2d v.p. 1984-85, 1st v.p. 1985-86, pres.-elect 1986-87, pres. 1987-88), Giles S. Rich Am. Inn of Ct. (master emeritus), Patent and Trademark Inst. Can., Internat. Assn. for Protection Indsl. Property (treas.-gen. 1989—), Chartered Inst. Patent Agts. (Gt. Britain), Internat. Patent and Trademark Assn. (exec. com. 1978-83, 89—, v.p. 1983-89), Licensing Execs. Soc., Inter-Am. Assn. Indsl. Property, Internat. Intellectual Property Assn. (exec. com. 1989—), Federation Internationale des Conseils en Propriete Industrielle, Thomas Moore Soc. Am., Internat. Club Washington (bd. govs. 1991-95), Rotary, Nu Beta Epsilon. Lodge: Rotary. Trademark and copyright, Patent. Office: Smith Gambrell & Russell LLP Intellectual Property Gr 1850 M St NW Ste 800 Washington DC 20036-5819 *Died July 17, 1999.*

**DEGRANDPRE, CHARLES ALLYSON,** lawyer; b. Manchester, N.H., July 7, 1936; s. Arthur Vital and Andrea Amanda (L'Etoile) DeG.; m. Patricia Rahn DeGrandpre, Oct. 9, 1982. AB, Clark U., 1958; JD, U. Mich., 1961. Bar: N.H. 1961, U.S. Dist. Ct. N.H. 1964, U.S. Supreme Ct. 1969. Dir. McLane, Graf, Raulerson & Middleton, P.A., Portsmouth, N.H., 1968—; trustee, chair Smith Found., Manchester, 1986—; bd. dirs. Piscataqua Cmty. Found., 1990-97. Author: Probate Law and Procedure, 1990, 2d edit., 1996, Wills, Trusts and Gifts, 1992, 3d edit., 1997. Chair bd. trustees Canterbury Shaker Village, 1992-97; trustee Strawbery Banke Mus., 1996—; chmn. bd. dirs. N.H. Bar Found., 1997—. Recipient N.H. Vol. of Yr. award Office of Gov., Concord, N.H., 1982. Fellow Am. Coll. Trust and Estate Counsel; mem. N.H. Bar Assn. (Pres.'s award 1983). Avocations: hiking, reading, wine. Estate planning, Probate, General corporate. Home: 60 Pleasant Point Dr Portsmouth NH 03801-5265 Office: McLane Graf Raulerson & Middleton PO Box 4316 30 Penhallow St Portsmouth NH 03801-3816

**DEGUILIO, JON E.,** lawyer; b. Hammond, Ind., June 15, 1955; s. Ernest Michael and Jeanne (Hochis) D.; m. Barbara Jo Wieser, Oct. 3, 1981; 1 child, Suzanne Jeanne. BA, U. Notre Dame, 1977; JD, Valparaiso U., 1981. Bar: Ind. 1981, U.S. Dist. Ct. (so. dist.) Ind. 1981, U.S. Dist. Ct. (no. dist.) Ind. 1981. Pub. defender Lake County Ct., Crown Point, Ind., 1984-87; dep. prosecutor Lake County Prosecutor's Office, Crown Point, 1981-84; 87-94; assoc. James Wieser Law Offices, Highland, Ind., 1981-93; U.S. atty. no. dist. Ind. Dept. Justice, Dyer, 1993-99; atty. Highland Police Commn., Highland, Ind., 1987— and Highland Water Bd., 1987—; legal advisor, Lake County Sheriff, Crown Point, Ind., 1986-87; atty. Hammond and East Chgo. Fedn. of Tchrs., 1986—. Councilman Hammond City Council, 1984-87; mem. Lake County Med. Ctr. Devel. Agy., 1988—, Greater Hammond Community Services, 1987—; treas. Little Calumet River Basin Com., 1986. Mem. Lake County Bar Assn. (bd. dirs. 1988-90), Justinian Soc. Democrat. Avocations: basketball, bolf, reading. General practice, Education and schools. Home: 8944 Liable Rd Hammond IN 46322-2248 Office: 1001 Main St Ste A Dyer IN 46311-1234*

**DEHAVEN, MICHAEL ALLEN,** lawyer; b. Richmond, Ind., May 24, 1950; s. Thomas A. and Sara Alice (Kerlin) DeH.; m. Wanda C. McDaniel; children: A. Kyle, Scott K., Abigail S. BA cum laude, Purdue U., 1972; JD, Washington U., 1975. Bar: Mo. 1975. Assoc. Thompson & Mitchell, St. Louis, 1975-80, ptnr., 1981-92, co-chair corp. dept., 1987-92; sr. v.p., gen. counsel, sec. Direct Response Group Capital Holding Corp., Valley Forge, Pa., 1994; ptnr. Bryan Cave, 1994-95; sr. v.p., gen. counsel BJC Health System, St. Louis, 1995—; adv. dir. Bank of South County. Mem. exec. com. Arts and Edn. Roundtable of Greater St. Louis; v.p. devel. bd. St. Louis Children's Hosp.; past vice chmn. R&D commn. United Way of Greater St. Louis; bd. dirs Allendale Mut. Ins. Co., Barnes Jewish West County Hosp. Mem. ABA, Mo. Bar Assn., Bar Assn. of Met. St. Louis, Mo. Athletic Club, Old Warson Country Club. Presbyterian. Banking, Contracts commercial, General corporate. Office: BJC Health System 4444 Forest Park Ave Ste 500 Saint Louis MO 63108-2297

**DEHERRERA, JUAN LEO,** lawyer; b. Costilla, N.Mex., Sept. 25, 1939; s. Gilbert and Maria (Arellano) DeH.; m. Dora O. Garcia, Dec. 31, 1964; children: Kelly, Michelle, Amy, Karen. BA, U. Wyo., 1968, JD, 1971. Bar: Wyo. 1971, U.S. Dist. Ct. Wyo. 1971, U.S. Ct. Appeals (10th cir.) 1973, U.S. Supreme Ct. 1975. Atty. gen. State of Wyo., Cheyenne, 1971-74; atty. pvt. practice, Cheyenne, 1974-78, Legal Aid Southeast Wyo, Cheyenne, 1978-79, pvt. practice, Rawlins, Wyo., 1979—; bd. dirs. Equality State Bank, Cheyenne, 1977—, Equality Bankshares, Multi-Bank Holding Co., 1983—. With U.S. Army, 1960-66. Mem. Wyo. State Bar Assn., Wyo. Trial Lawyers Assn., Carbon County Bar Assn., VFW, Disabled Am. Vets., Am. Legion, U. Wyo. Alumni. General civil litigation, Criminal, Bankruptcy. Home: 1715 Inverness Blvd Rawlins WY 82301-4205 Office: PO Box 71 Rawlins WY 82301-0071

**DEHN, FRANCIS XAVIER,** lawyer, journalist; b. Bronx, N.Y., Aug. 12, 1957; s. Francis X. and Irene (Canning) D. BSFS in Internat. Politics, Georgetown U., 1979; JD, Harvard U., 1983; MS in Journalism, Columbia U., 1991. Bar: N.Y. 1985. Atty. Webster & Sheffield, N.Y.C., 1985-90; reporter Sta. WPDE-TV, Florence/Myrtle Beach, S.C., 1991-93; atty. Gersten, Savage, Kaplowitz & Curtin, 1993-95; reporter Court TV, 1995-97; ptnr. Jacobs, deBrauwere & Dehn LLP, 1998—. Orgn. dir. O'Rourke for Gov. campaign, 1986. Mem. Phi Beta Kappa. Roman Catholic. General civil litigation, Libel, Entertainment. Office: Jacobs deBrauwere & Dehn LLP Fl 17 445 Park Ave New York NY 10022-2606

**DE HOYOS, DEBORA M.,** lawyer; b. Monticello, N.Y., Aug. 10, 1953; d. Luis and Marion (Kinney) de H.; m. Walter C. Carlson, June 20, 1981; children: Amanda, Greta, Linnea. BA, Wellesley Coll., 1975; JD, Harvard U., 1978. Bar: Ill. 1978, U.S. Dist. Ct. (no. dist.) Ill. 1980. Assoc. Mayer, Brown & Platt, Chgo., 1978-84, ptnr., 1985—, mng. ptnr., 1991—; bd. dirs. Northwestern Healthcare; bd. trustees Providence St. Mel. Sch. Contbr. chpt. to Securitization of Financial Assets, 1991. Chmn. strategic issues com. Econ. Devel. Commn., Chgo., 1992; trustee Chgo. Symphony Orch. Bd. dirs. Chicagoland C. of C. Office: Mayer Brown & Platt 190 S La Salle St Ste 3100 Chicago IL 60603-3441

**DEIANA, ROBERT VINCENT,** lawyer; b. Milford, Mass., July 19, 1937; s. Frank John and Mary Frances (Oates) D.; m. Mary Theresa Murray, July 20, 1963; children: Robert V. Jr., Thomas F. BS, Holy Cross, 1959; LLB, Georgetown U., 1962. Bar: Mass. 1962, U.S. Dist. Ct. Mass. 1966. Trial atty. Liberty Mut. Ins. Co., Worcester, Mass., 1966-70; ptnr. Mirick, O'Connell, DeMallie & Lougee, Worcester, Mass., 1970—. Moderator Town of Grafton, 1969-87. Lt. USN, 1962-65. Fellow Am. Bar Found. (life), Mass. Bar Found. (life); mem. Mass. Bar Assn. (v.p. 1984-86, treas. 1986-87). Avocations: tennis, skiing, phys. fitness, reading. Alternative dispute resolution, General civil litigation, Professional liability. Home: 8 Merriam Rd Grafton MA 01519-1216 Office: Mirick O'Connell DeMallie & Lougee 100 Front St Worcester MA 01608-1402

**DEIKMAN, EUGENE LAWRENCE,** lawyer; b. Denver, Nov. 27, 1927; s. Herman and Eva (Lader) D.; m. Dolores Korosec, 1952 (div. 1964); children: Diana Wong, Jill, Alan; m. Doris A. Walker, Sept. 2, 1967 (div. May 1984); 1 child, Jane; m. Roberta Brozovich, May 21, 1998. LLB, U. Colo., 1951. Bar: Colo. 1953, U.S. Dist. Ct. Colo, 1955, U.S. Ct. Appeals (10th cir.) 1956. Ptnr. Menin & Deikman, Denver, 1954-59, Montfort, Wilson & Deikman, Denver, 1959-62; sole practice Denver, 1962-79; pres. Eugene Deikman, P.C., Denver, 1979—; cons. Crusade for Justice, Denver, 1972-79. Treas., trustee Mus. Contemporary Art/Denver. Mem. Colo. Bar Assn., Colo. Trial Lawyers Assn., Nat. Lawyers Guild (founder Denver chpt., Founder cert. 1987). Democrat. Avocations: painting, art criticism. photography, skiing, tennis. General civil litigation, Criminal, Personal injury. Office: 1700 Broadway Ste 1200 Denver CO 80290-1201

**DEISLEY, DAVID LEE,** lawyer; b. Lancaster, Pa., July 9, 1956; s. William J. and Ruth R. (Reamer) D.; m. Susan Gorey, July 19, 1980; children: Lara, Daniel, Anne. AB, Brown U., 1978; JD, U. Utah, 1983. Bar: Utah 1983, U.S. Ct. Appeals (10th cir.) 1986. Legis. asst. to senator John Heinz, Washington, 1978-80; jud. clk. to hon. judge David Winder U.S. Dist. Ct., Salt Lake City, 1983-84; assoc. Van Cott, Bagley, Salt Lake City, 1984-88; assoc. Parsons, Behle & Latimer, Salt Lake City, 1988-90, mem., 1990—, chair natural resources dept., 1993—. Trustee Rocky Mountain Mineral Law Found., 1997—. Mem. Utah Bar Assn. (chair mining natural resources sect. 1990-91, Dist. Pro Bono Atty. 1988). Avocations: skiing, hiking, tennis. Natural resources, Environmental. Office: Parsons Behle & Latimer 201 S Main St Salt Lake City UT 84111-2215

**DEITZLER, HARRY G.,** lawyer; b. South Charleston, W.Va., Mar. 24, 1951; s. James Edward and Betty Jean (Luchtemeyer) D.; m. Kathe Frances Elswick, June 24, 1989; children: Erin Lindsay, Bradford James. BS, W.Va. U., 1973, JD, 1976; postgrad., Nat. Coll. of Dist. Attys., U. Houston, 1977-81. Bar: W.Va. 1976, U.S. Dist. Ct. (so. and no. dists.) W.Va. 1976, U.S. Ct. Appeals (4th cir.) 1989. Asst. prosecuting atty. Wood County, Parkersburg, W.Va., 1976-79; prosecuting atty. Wood County, Parkersburg, 1979-88; staff atty. Preiser Law Offices, Charleston, W.Va., 1988-89; chief criminal div. Preiser Law Offices, Charleston, 1989-90; ptnr. Hill, Peterson, Carper, Bee & Deitzler, Charleston, 1990—; coord. state prosecuters W.Va., 1985-88. Author: (manual) Indictment Manual for West Virginia Prosecuters, 1985. Elected Prosecuting Atty. Wood County, Parkersburg, 1980, 84; elected officer Wood County Dem. Exec. Com., 1980-88; candidate for Atty. Gen. of W.Va., 1988. Mem. ATLA (instr. Nat. Coll. Advocacy 1995, 96), Trial Lawyers for Pub. Justice (bd. dirs. 1992—, state coord. 1992-95), W.Va. Trial Lawyers Assn. (bd. govs., exec. com.), W.Va. State Bar (exec. com. Young Lawyer sect. 1977-79, criminal law com. 1979—), Nat. Dist. Attys. Assn. (state dir. 1984-85), Masons, Shriners. Presbyterian. Avocations: running, skiing, family activities. Personal injury, Product liability, Criminal. Home: 4910 Kanawha Ave SE Charleston WV 25304-2004 Office: Hill Peterson Carper Bee & Deitzler 500 Tracy Way Charleston WV 25311-1555

**DEJARNETTE, ELLIOTT HAWES,** lawyer; b. Charlottesville, Va., Nov. 14, 1951; s. Joseph Spencer and Ruby Marise (Larrabee) DeJ.; m. Mary Kathleen Dodd, July 11, 1981; children: Elliott Hawes V, James Coleman, Elizabeth Trueheart. BA, U. Va., 1974; JD, U. Richmond, 1978. Bar: Va. 1978. Pvt. practice, 1978—; spl. justice Culpeper County Gen. Dist. Ct., Culpeper, Va., 1980—. Democrat. Episcopalian. Avocations: tennis, basketball, soccer. Real property, Estate planning, Criminal. Home: 215 W Park Ave Culpeper VA 22701-3443 Office: 114 N Main St Culpeper VA 22701-3026

**DE JONG, DAVID SAMUEL,** lawyer, educator; b. Washington, Jan. 8, 1951; s. Samuel and Dorothy (Thomas) De J.; m. Tracy Ann Barger, Sept. 23, 1995; 1 child, Jacob Samuel. BA, U. Md., 1972; JD, Washington and Lee U., 1975; LLM in Taxation, Georgetown U., 1979. Bar: Md. 1975, U.S. Dist. Ct. Md. 1977, U.S. Tax Ct. 1977, U.S. Ct. Appeals (4th cir.) 1978, U.S. Supreme Ct. 1979, D.C. 1980, U.S. Dist. Ct. D.C. 1983, U.S. Ct. Claims, U.S. Ct. Appeals (fed. cir.) 1983; CPA, Md.; cert. valuation analyst. Atty. Gen. Bus. Svcs., Inc., Rockville, Md., 1975-80; ptnr. Stein, Sperling, Bennett, De Jong, Driscoll, Greenfeig & Metro P.A., Rockville, 1980—; adj. prof. Southea. U., Washington, 1979-85, Am. U., Washington, 1983—; instr. U. Md., College Park, 1986-87, Montgomery Coll., Rockville, 1983. Co-author: (ann. book) J.K. Lasser's Year-Round Tax Strategies, 1989—; editor Notes and Comments, Washington and Lee U. Law Rev., 1974-75. V.p. Seneca Whetstone Homeowners Assn., Gaithersburg, Md., 1981-82, pres. 1982-83. Mem. ABA, AICPA, Am. Assn. Atty.-CPAs (bd. dirs. 1997—, sec. 1998-99, treas. 1999—), Md. Bar Assn., Montgomery County Bar Assn. (chmn. tax sect. 1991-92, treas. 1996-97), D.C. Bar Assn., Md. Assn. CPAs, D.C. Inst. CPAs, Nat. Assn. Cert. Valuation Analysts, Inst. Bus. Appraisers, Phi Alpha Delta. Corporate taxation, Personal income taxation, Estate taxation. Office: 25 W Middle Ln Rockville MD 20850-2214

**DE JULIO, LOIS A.,** lawyer; b. Newark, Oct. 23, 1947; s. Maurice Ennio and Minnette (Palermo) De J. BA with honors, Douglass Coll., New Brunswick, N.J., 1969; JD with honors, Rutgers U., Newark, 1973. Bar: N.J. 1973, N.Y. 1983, U.S. Dist. Ct. N.J. 1973, U.S. Supreme Ct., 1979. Dep. atty. gen. Appellate sect. N.J. Atty. Gen.'s Office, East Orange, 1973-76; assoc. Cummin, Dunn, Horowitz & Pashman, Hackensack, N.J., 1976-77; asst. dep. pub. defender Appellate sect. N.J. Pub. Defender's Office, East Orange, 1977-79, 1st asst. dep. pub. defender, 1979-89; asst. dep. pub. defender Hudson trial region N.J. Pub. Defender's Office, Jersey City, 1989—; mem. N.J. Supreme Ct. Com. on Model Jury Charges, Trenton,

1995-96. Author: (tng. manual) Outline of New Jersey Search and Seizure Law, annually. Trustee Bloomfield (N.J.) Fedn. Music, 1988—. Mem. Hudson County Bar Asn., Assn. Criminal Def. Lawyers N.J. (trustee 1986-96), Nat. Assn. Criminal Def. Lawyers, Phi Beta Kappa. Avocation: playing clarinet in Bloomfield Civic Band. Office: NJ Pub Defenders Office Hudson Trial Region 438 Summit Ave Jersey City NJ 07306-3158

**DE KOSTER, JOHN G.,** lawyer; b. Berea, Ohio, May 23, 1950; s. Lucas J. and Dorothea L. De Koster; m. Glenda F. Alons, Aug. 19, 1972; children: Lucas, Philip. BS in Polit. Sci., Iowa State U., 1972; JD, U. Colo., 1975. Bar: Iowa 1975, U.S. Supreme Ct. 1978. Atty., advisor U.S. Dept. of Interior, Washington, 1975-79; ptnr. De Koster & De Koster, Hull, Iowa, 1979—; bd. dirs. Iowa State Bank, Hull, Mut. Fire and Auto Ins. Co., Cedar Rapids. Named Citizen of Yr. Hull Bus. and Profl. Club, 1997; recipient Cmty. Svc. award Modern Woodmen, Hull, 1987. Fellow Iowa State Bar Found.; mem. Iowa State Bar Assn. (bd. govs. 1994-99), Sioux County Bar Assn. (pres. 1996-98), Kiwanis. Office: De Koster & De Koster 1106 Main St Hull IA 51239-0801

**DEKOSTER, LUCAS J(AMES),** lawyer; b. Hull, Iowa, June 18, 1918; s. John and Sarah Katherine (Poppen) DeK.; m. Dorothea LaVonne Hymans, Dec. 30, 1942; children—Sarah K, Jacqueline A., John G., Claire E., Mary D. B.S. in Mech. Engring. Iowa State U., 1939; J.D. cum laude, Cleve.-Marshall Law Sch., 1949. Bar: Iowa, 1952. Aerospace research scientist NACA, Hampton, Va., 1940-44, Cleve., 1944-49; patent atty., agt. J.D. Douglass Co., Cleve., 1949-51; sole practice, Hull, 1952-79; ptnr. DeKoster & DeKoster, Hull, 1979—; mem. Iowa Senate, 1964-82; pres. Mut. Fire and Auto Ins. Co., Cedar Rapids, Iowa, 1979-90; mem. Iowa Bd. Edn. (formerly Iowa Bd. Pub. Instrn.), Des Moines, 1982-88, chmn., 1984. Mem. ABA, Iowa Bar Assn. (chmn. com. 1983-87), Iowa Intellectual Property Law Assn. Republican. Mem. Reformed Ch. in Am. Lodge: Kiwanis (lt. gov. 1984). Avocations: reading, travelling. Patent, Trademark and copyright. Office: 1106 Main St Hull IA 51239

**DE LA CARRERA, MIGUEL ANTONIO,** lawyer, judge; b. Havana, Cuba, Feb. 5, 1955; came to U.S., 1960; s. Antonio Miguel and Gloria Maria (Coll) de La C.; m. Aurora Rosario Rangel, Nov. 24, 1984; children: Miguel Arturo, Andréз Antonio, Daniel Alejandro. BA, Yale U., 1977; JD, Columbia U., 1982. Bar: N.J. 1982, U.S. Dist. Ct. N.J. Staff atty., mem. adj. faculty Essex-Newark Legal Svcs.-Seton Hall Law Sch., 1982-85; ptnr. Carrera & Carrera, Paterson, N.J., 1985—; judge mcpl. ct. City of Paterson, 1993—. Trustee Essex-Newark Legal Svcs., 1987-89, Passaic County C.C., Paterson, 1989—. Mem. Passaic County Bar Assn. (fee arbitration com. 1993-95, trustee 1997—), Lions (past pres. local club). Democrat. Family and matrimonial, Personal injury, Bankruptcy. Office: Carrera & Carrera 998 Madison Ave Paterson NJ 07501-3636

**DELA CRUZ, JOSE SANTOS,** retired state supreme court chief justice; b. Saipan, Commonwealth No. Mariana Islands, July 18, 1948; s. Thomas Castro and Remedio Sablan (Santos) Dela C.; m. Rita Tenorio Sablan, Nov. 12, 1977; children: Roxanne, Renee, Rica Ann. BA, U. Guam, 1971; JD, U. Calif., Berkeley, 1974; cert., Nat. Jud. Coll., Reno, 1985. Bar: No. Mariana Islands, 1974, U.S. Dist. Ct. No. Mariana Islands 1978. Staff atty. Micro. Legal Svcs. Corp., Saipan, 1974-79; gen. counsel Marianas Pub. Land Corp., Saipan, 1979-81; liaison atty. CNMI Fed. Laws Commn., Saipan, 1981-83; ptnr. Borja & Dela Cruz, Saipan, 1983-85; assoc. judge Commonwealth Trial Ct., Saipan, 1985-89; chief justice Supreme Ct. No. Mariana Islands, 1989-95; retired, 1995; mem. Conf. of Chief Justices, 1989-95, Adv. Commn. on Judiciary, Saipan, 1980-82; chmn. Criminal Justice Planning Agy., Saipan, 1985-95. Mem. Coun. for Arts, Saipan, 1982-83; chmn. Bd. of Elections, Saipan, 1977-82; pres. Cath. Social Svcs., Saipan, 1982-85. Mem. No. Marianas Bar Assn. (pres. 1984-85). Roman Catholic. Avocations: golf, reading, walking. Office: Commonwealth Supreme Ct Civic Ctr Saipan MP 96950 *There is an inherent goodness in every person, no matter how bad that person may appear. Recognizing that goodness in each gives us hope that the future of mankind will not be destructive.*

**DE LA FE, ERNESTO JUAN,** lawyer; b. Cardenas, Matanzas, Cuba, Sept. 22, 1953; came to U.S., 1960; s. Ernesto Genaro and Juana Luisa (Vadillo) de la F.; m. Silvia Maria Matos, June 18, 1977; children: Ernest, Brian, Steven, Pedro. AA in Bus., Miami Dade C.C., 1974; BS in Mktg., Fla. Atlantic U., 1976; JD, U. Miami, 1985. Bar: Fla. 1985. Assoc. Floyd Pearson Richman Greer Weil Zach & Brumbaugh, Miami, Fla., 1985-88; ptnr. Perez-Abreu, Zamora, de la Fe & Hillman Waller, Coral Gables, Fla., 1988-92; pvt. practice, Coral Gables, 1992—. Trustee Cuban Am. Nat. Found., Miami, 1989-92; v.p. Free Cuba Polit. Action Com., Miami, 1994—. Mem. Cuban Am. Bar Assn. Republican. Roman Catholic. Avocations: vegetable gardening, photography, computers. Personal injury, General civil litigation, Real property. Address: 6701 Sunset Dr Ste 100 Miami FL 33143-4529

**DELAFUENTE, CHARLES,** lawyer, educator, journalist; b. N.Y.C., Oct. 6, 1945; s. Maurice and Rose (Schulder) De La F.; m. Jill Rosenfeld, Apr. 8, 1979; children: Marc, Carla. Student, Queens Coll., Flushing, N.Y., 1962-66; BA, SUNY, Albany, 1979; JD cum laude, Yeshiva U., N.Y.C., 1981. Bar: N.Y. 1982, D.C. 1985. Night city editor N.Y. Post, N.Y.C., 1969-78; assoc. Herzfield & Rusin, N.Y.C., 1981-83; atty. Fed. Jud. Ctr., Washington, 1984-85; fgn. desk editor UPI, Washington, 1985-87; asst. city editor Daily News, N.Y.C., 1987-90; asst. mng. editor Times Union, Albany, N.Y., 1990-94; dep. met. editor Daily News, N.Y.C., 1949-95; editor Record, Troy, N.Y., 1995-96; ptnr. Forman & De La Fuente, Latham, N.Y., 1997-98; staff editor N.Y. Times, 1998—; del. N.Y. State Fair Trial/Free Press Com., Albany, 1994-96; adj. prof. George Washington Coll. Law, Washington, 1985-87, Cardozo Law Sch. Yeshiva U., 1989-90. Mem. ABA, N.Y. State Bar Assn., Order of Barristers. Constitutional, Libel, Appellate.

**DE LA GARZA, CHARLES H.,** lawyer; b. Hamilton AFB, Calif., Sept. 21, 1948; s. Porfirio N. and Maria (Larralde) De La G.; m. Margaret Waldner, Feb. 6, 1971; children: Christian L., Todd O. BSChemE, Lamar U., 1970; JD cum laude, South Tex. Coll. Law, 1976. Bar: Tex. 1976, U.S. Ct. Appeals (5th cir.) Tex. 1981, U.S. Ct. Appeals (11th cir.) Tex. 1983, U.S. Dist. Ct. (so. dist.) Tex. 1985, U.S. Dist. Ct. (we. dist.) Tex. 1992, U.S. Patent and Trademark Office. Process engr. ARCO, Houston, 1970-72, supr./foreman, 1972-76; assoc. Arnold, White & Durkee, Houston, 1976-82, shareholder, 1982—. Editor Tex. State Bar Newsletter, 1989-93; contbr. chpt.: Unfair Competition, 1987. Fellow Houston Bar Found.; mem. Houston Bar Assn. (sustaining), Order of the Lytae, Blue Key, Tau Beta Pi, Phi Eta Sigma, Delta Theta Phi, Omega Chi Epsilon. Avocations: tennis, snow skiing, cooking. Federal civil litigation, Patent, Trademark and copyright. Office: Arnold White & Durkee 750 Bering Dr Ste 200 Houston TX 77057-2132

**DELAHUNTY, JANE GOODMAN,** judge, mediator, psychologist; b. Johannesburg, South Africa, Feb. 17, 1952; came to U.S., 1975; d. Roy and Myrtle Ianthe Fraser; m. Oscar Goodman, Oct. 11, 1976 (div. July 1993); m. Roderick C. Smoleniec-Delahunty; 1 child, Sorcha Delahunty. BA, U. Witwatersrand, South Africa, 1972; MA, U. Witwatersrand, 1973; JD, U. Seattle, 1983; PhD, U. Wash., 1986. Bar: Wash. 1983, U.S. Dist. Ct. (we. dist.) Wash. 1983. Assoc. Bricklin & Gendler, Seattle, 1983-84; trial atty. U.S. EEOC, Seattle, 1984-98; litigation atty. Frank & Rosen, Seattle, 1988-92; adminstrv. judge U.S. EEOC, L.A., 1992—; mediator, arbitrator JAMS/ Endispute, so. Calif., 1994—; adj. prof. law U. Seattle, 1990-91, Whittier Law Sch., Costa Mesa, Calif., 1998—. Editor: Washington Lawyers Practice Manual, 1989-90; editor Psycology, Public Policy and Law, 2000—; mem. editl. bd. Law and Human Behavior, 1990—, Behavioural Scis. and the Law, 1999—, Perspectives in Psychology and Law, 1995—; contbr. more than 50 articles to profl. jours. Fellow APA; mem. ABA, Am. Psychology-Law Soc. (pres. 1994-95). Home: 2407 Calle Maderia San Clemente CA 92672-4404 Office: 255 E Temple St Fl 4 Los Angeles CA 90012-3334

**DELANEY, HERBERT WADE, JR.,** lawyer; b. Leadville, Colo., Mar. 30, 1925; s. Herbert Wade and Marie Ann (Garbarino) DeL.; m. Ramona Rae Ortiz, Aug. 6, 1953; children: Herbert Wade III, Paula Rae, Bonnie Marie. BSBA, U. Denver, 1949, LLB, 1951. Bar: Colo. 1951, U.S. Supreme Ct. 1959. Pvt. practice, Denver, 1953-64, 1965-91, 94—; mem. firm DeLaney and Sandven, P.C., 1992-94; faculty U. Denver, Colo., 1960-61, 89; ptnr. DeLaney & West, Denver, 1964-65. Capt. JAG's Dept., USAF, 1951-53. Mem. Colo. Bar Assn., Denver Bar Assn., Am. Legion, Masons, Elks, Phi Alpha Delta. State civil litigation, Bankruptcy, Personal injury. Office: 50 S Steele St Ste 660 Denver CO 80209-2811

**DELANEY, RAIGHNE C.,** lawyer; b. Phila., Apr. 25, 1967; s. Arthur J. and Maria B. D.; m. Sherry A Kuczynski Delaney, Jan. 12, 1991; 1 child, Eleana Alice. BA in Econ., Temple U., Phila., 1989; JD, George Washington U., 1995. Bar: Va. 1995, D.C. 1996, U.S. Supreme Ct. 1999. Assoc. Murray & Jacobs, Alexandria, Va., 1995-97; mem. Pompan, Murray, Ruffner & Werfel PLC, Alexandria, Va., 1997—; mem. Northern Va. Dental Soc. Peer Review Com., Fairfax, Va., 1996—. Mem. Alexandria C. of C. Legis. Com., 1996—. 1st lt. U.S. Army, 1989-92. Mem. Alexandria Bar Assn., Am. Legion, VFW, Disabled Am. Vets. Roman Catholic. General civil litigation. Office: Pompan Murray Ruffner & Werfel PLC 601 King St Ste 400 Alexandria VA 22314-3105

**DE LASA, JOSÉ M.,** lawyer; b. Havana, Cuba, Nov. 28, 1941; came to U.S., 1961; s. Miguel and Conchita de Lasa; m. Maria Teresa Figueroa, Nov. 23, 1963; children: Maria Teresa, José, Andrés, Carlos. BA, Yale U., 1968, JD, 1971. Bar: N.Y. 1973. Assoc. Cleary, Gottlieb, Steen & Hamilton, N.Y.C., 1971-76; legal dept. Bristol-Myers Squibb Co., N.Y.C., 1976-94; sr. v.p., sec. and gen. counsel Abbott Labs., 1994—; lectr. internat. law, various locations. Bd. dirs. Chgo. Children's Mus., 1995—, The Resource Found., 1989—, Internat. Inst. Rural Reconstrn., 1989—. Mem. ABA, N.Y. County Bar Assn., Assn. of Bar of City of N.Y. Roman Catholic. Private international, General corporate, Health. Office: Abbott Laboratories D-364 AP6D-2 100 Abbott Park Rd North Chicago IL 60064-3500

**DELAUGHTER, JERRY L.,** lawyer; b. Brookhaven, Miss., Oct. 24, 1944; s. Hardy L. and Eloise (Hayes) Del.; m. Linda Marie Bacchiocchi; children: Hardy Isaac, Sarah Emilia. BA, U. Miss., 1969, JD, 1978; postgrad., U. Calif., Santa Barbara, 1973-74. Bar: Miss. 1978, U.S. Dist. Ct. (no. and so. dists.) Miss. 1978, U.S. Ct. Appeals (5th and 11th cirs.) 1979, Calif. 1982. Law clk. U.S. Dist. Ct. (so. dist.) Miss., 1978-79; assoc. Eaton & Cottrel, Gulfport, Miss., 1979-81, Cappello & Foley, Santa Barbara, 1981, Hatch & Parent, Santa Barbara, 1983; pvt. practice law Santa Barbara, 1984-91, Brookhaven, 1991—; vol. tchr. legal asst. program U. Calif., Santa Barbara, 1984-85; contracts negotiator Santa Barbara Rsch. Ctr., 1986-89. Editor in chief Jour. of Space Law, 1977-78. Deacon, Sun. sch. supt., instr. New Converts. Capt. USAF, 1969-73. Mem. Calif. Bar Assn., Miss. Bar Assn., Lincoln County Bar Assn., Phi Gamma Delta, Phi Alpha Delta. Avocation: bicycling. General civil litigation, General practice, Personal injury. Home and Office: PO Box 21433 Santa Barbara CA 93121-1433

**DELAYO, LEONARD J., JR.,** lawyer; b. New Rochelle, N.Y., Aug. 17, 1949; s. Leonard J. Sr. and Helen (Griffith) DeL.; m. Jean Ann Jourdan; children: Francesca Marie, David Joseph. BA, U. N.Mex., 1971, JD, 1974. Bar: N.Mex. 1974, U.S. Dist. Ct. 1974, U.S. Ct. Appeals (10th cir.) 1974, U.S. Supreme Ct. 1978. Atty. Toulouse, Krehbeil & DeLayo, Albuquerque, 1974-79, DeLayo, Olson & Blueher, Albuquerque, 1979-86, Leonard J. DeLayo, Jr., PC, Albuquerque, 1986—; bd. dirs. First State Bancorp., Albuquerque. Mem. bd. edn. Albuquerque Pub. Schs., 1987—, pres., 1992-93, 96—. Mem. ABA, U.S. Supreme Ct. Bar Assn., State Bar Assn. N.Mex. Office: 817 Gold Ave SW Albuquerque NM 87102-3014

**DEL BUONO, JOHN ANGELO,** lawyer; b. Waterbury, Conn., Jan. 30, 1928; s. Nicola and Raffaela (Cusano) Del B.; m. Barbara Rae Ellingsworth, Jan. 27, 1950; children: Mary Ann, John Nicholas, Barbara Joan, Joseph Frederick, Susan Mae, Sally Ann, Deborah Jean, Catherine Jane. Student, U. Conn., 1945-46, 47-48; LLB, U. Okla., 1951. Bar: Okla. 1950, Conn. 1955; U.S. Dist. Ct. Conn., 1956. Assoc. Cheek, Cheek & Cheek, Oklahoma City, 1950-51; claims adjuster USF & G Ins. Co., Waterbury, 1952-55; pvt. practice Waterbury, 1955-90, Watertown, Conn., 1990—. Co-author: When Two Become One, 1976 (Nat. Cath. Press award 1977). Pres. Civitan Club, Waterbury, 1956-57, Waterbury Jr. Bar Assn., 1956-57; mem. Rep. Town Com., Waterbury, 1963-65; bd. dirs. Conn. TBI Assn., Rocky Hill, 1982-85. With U.S. Army, 1946-47. Mem. Waterbury Bar Assn., Conn. Bar Assn., Am. Trial Lawyers Assn., Conn. Trial Lawyers Assn. Roman Catholic. Avocation: ball room dancing. Personal injury, Workers' compensation, Probate. Home: 615 Northfield Rd Watertown CT 06795-1502 Office: 680 Main St Watertown CT 06795-2655

**DE LEON, ALBERT VERNON,** lawyer; b. Oakland, Calif., Sept. 14, 1947; s. Alfred Vernon and Mona Janice (Young) De L.; m. Lauren Adams, Aug. 28, 1982. BA, CCNY, 1972; JD, U. San Diego, 1976. Bar: N.Y. 1979, U.S. Supreme Ct. 1995. Atty. IRS, Washington, 1977-78; v.p., counsel Nat. Westminster Bancorp Inc., Jersey City, N.J., 1978-94; prin. The Secura Group, N.Y.C., 1995-97; v.p., gen. counsel, sec. Skandinaviska Enskilda Banken, N.Y.C., 1997—. Banking, General corporate, Computer. Address: 140 8th Ave Apt 2P Brooklyn NY 11215-1744 Office: 245 Park Ave Fl 42 New York NY 10167-4299

**DE LEON, JOHN LOUIS,** public defender; b. North Miami, Fla., Feb. 14, 1962; s. Leon Juan and Lydia (Diaz Cruz) de L. AB cum laude, U. Miami, 1983; JD, Georgetown U., 1986; M in Internat. Affairs, Columbia U., 1992. Bar: Fla. 1987, U.S. Supreme Ct. 1993. V.p. Bristol Investment Group, Coral Gables, Fla., 1982-85; jud. intern to Judge Francis Bason Fed. Bankruptcy Ct., Washington, 1986; asst. pub. defender Office Pub. Defender for 11th Jud. Cir., Miami, 1987—; law clk. Geiger, Riggs & Freud, P.A., Miami, Fla., 1986-87; mem. bd. arbitrators Nat. Assn. Security Dealers, N.Y.C., 1989; press officer, intern. Delegation of the Commn. of the European Communities, UN, N.Y.C., 1990; mem. steering com. Georgetown Criminal Justice Clinic, Georgetown U. Law Ctr. Bd. dirs. Citykids, Inc., Miami, 1986; mem. adv. bd. Douglas MacArthur Sr. H.S., Miami; mem. audience devel. commn. Mus. Contemporary Arts, North Miami, Fla.; bd. dirs. Urban Environment League, Miami. Mem. ABA, Cuban Am. Bar Assn., Nat. Assn. Criminal Def. Lawyers, Am. Civil Liberties Union, Fla. Assn. Pub. Defenders, ACLU (bd. mem. Dade County chpt., pres.), Amnesty Internat., Golden Key, Phi Delta Phi, Phi Kappa Phi, Pi Sigma Alpha. Roman Catholic. Avocations: reading, politics, arts. Home: 1805 Ixora Rd Miami FL 33181-2309 Office: Pub Defender Svc 1320 NW 14th St Miami FL 33125-1609

**DE LEON, RUBEN L.,** lawyer; b. Habana, Cuba, Jan. 26, 1955; came to U.S., 1960; s. Ruben and Maria C. (Grau) deL.; m. Juana Maria de Leon. BA in Politics & Pub. Affairs, U. Miami, 1977; JD, Nova U., 1980. Bar: Fla. 1980, U.S. Dist. Ct. (so. dist.) Fla. 1980. Assoc. Law Offices of Gaston R. Alvarez, Miami, 1980-82; pvt. practice Miami, 1982—; cons. Ram-Mart Investments, Inc., Miami, 1982-85, Edclamer Corp., Miami, 1985-87; mem. nominating com. Fla. Bar, 1995. Campaign worker Rep. Party Nat. Conv., Miami, 1972. Recipient Cert. of Appreciation, Pres. of the U.S., Washington, 1972. Mem. ABA, Assn. Trial Lawyers Am., Cuban-Am. Bar Assn., Nova Univ. Internat. Law Soc., Nova Univ. Alumni Assn. Roman Catholic. Family and matrimonial, Criminal, Personal injury. Office: 1900 Coral Way Ste 301 Miami FL 33145-2661

**DELIN, SYLVIA KAUFMAN,** lawyer; b. Detroit, Nov. 10, 1945; d. Ira G. and Lillian (Farbman) Kaufman; m. Robert B. Smith, June 13, 1971 (div.); children: David, Mark, Barbara. Student, U. Sheffield, Eng., 1965-66; BA, U. Mich., 1967; JD, Loyola U., Chgo., 1973. Bar: Ill. 1973, U.S. Dist. Ct. (no. dist.) Ill. 1980, U.S. Ct. Appeals (7th cir.) 1981, U.S. Supreme Ct. 1982, Mich. 1986, U.S. Ct. Appeals (6th cir.) 1989. Pvt. practice, Flossmoor, Ill., 1975-86, Southfield, Mich., 1986-96, Birmingham, Mich., 1996—. Author: Two Against One, 1964, Out of the Slums, 1968. Mem. ABA, Mich. Bar Assn., Oakland County Bar Assn. (family law and juvenile law coms.), Women Lawyers Assn. of Mich. Republican. Jewish. Family and matrimonial, General practice, General civil litigation. Home: 1285 Ruffner Ave Birmingham MI 48009-7173 Office: 400 W Maple Rd Ste 200 Birmingham MI 48009-3351

**DE LIO, ANTHONY PETER,** lawyer; b. Bklyn., June 29, 1928; s. David V. and Margaret M. De L.; m. Marie DiTrani, July 19, 1952; children: Anthony P., Donna Marie Maistros, Lois Anne Cromwell; m. Margit Kaye, May 2, 1992. BS in Physics, Poly Inst. Bklyn., 1953; JD with honors, George Washington U., 1957. Bar: D.C. 1957, Conn. 1958, U.S. Dist. Ct. Conn. 1958. With patent dept. Bendix Corp., Washington, 1954-56; patent advisor U.S. Navy Dept., Washington, 1957; assoc. Blair & Spencer, Stamford, Conn., 1957-60; ptnr. Spencer, Rockwell & Bartholow, Stamford, 1960-62, Rockwell & De Lio, New Haven, 1962-64, De Lio and Libert, New Haven, 1981-84, De Lio & Assocs., New Haven, 1984-91, De Lio & Peterson, New Haven, 1991—; lectr. in field. Contbr. articles to legal jours. Chmn. Hamden Planning and Zoning Commn., 1969-81; alt. commr. Hamden Zoning Bd. Appeals, 1981-85. Served with USMC, 1946-48. Mem. ABA, Am. Intellectual Property Law Assn., Conn. Intellectual Property Law Assn., Internat. Intellectual Property Law Assn., Quinnipiack Club (New Haven), New Haven Country Club, Amity Club (New Haven), Alpha Phi Delta. Democrat. Roman Catholic. Patent, Trademark and copyright, Intellectual property. Office: 121 Whitney Ave New Haven CT 06510-1242

**DELL, ERNEST ROBERT,** lawyer; b. Vandergrift, Pa., Feb. 6, 1928; m. Karen D. Reed, May 8, 1965; children: Robert W., John D., Jane C. B.S., U. Pitts., 1949, M.Litt., 1953; J.D., Harvard U., 1956. Bar: Pa. 1957, U.S. Supreme Ct. 1961; C.P.A., Pa. Ptnr. firm Reed Smith Shaw & McClay, Pitts., 1956—; adj. prof. law Duquesne U. Law Sch., Pitts., 1960-86; bd. dirs. Atty's. Liability Assurance Soc. Inc., Chgo., Atty's. Liability Assurance Soc. (Bermuda) Ltd. Mem. ABA, Fed. Bar Assn., Pa. Bar Assn., Allegheny County Bar Assn., AICPAs, Pa. Inst. CPAs. Banking, General corporate, Corporate taxation. Home: 119 Riding Trail Ln Pittsburgh PA 15215-1521 Office: Reed Smith Shaw & McClay Mellon Sq 435 6th Ave Ste 2 Pittsburgh PA 15219-1886

**DELLA ROCCO, KENNETH ANTHONY,** lawyer; b. Bridgeport, Conn., Sept. 5, 1952. BA, Sacred Heart U., Fairfield, Conn., 1974; JD, U. Bridgeport, 1982. Bar: Conn. 1983, U.S. Dist. Ct. Conn. 1985, N.Y. 1988, U.S. Supreme Ct. 1991. Assoc. Cummings & Lockwood, Stamford, Conn., 1982-88; asst. gen. counsel Melville Corp., Rye, N.Y., 1988-90, dir. legal affairs, counsel, 1990-94, asst. corp. sec., 1990-95, v.p. legal affairs, gen. counsel, 1994-95; counsel Cacace, Tusch & Santagata, Stamford, 1996—. Mem. ABA, Conn. Regional Bar Assn., N.Y. State Bar Assn. General corporate, Real property, Mergers and acquisitions. Office: Cacace Tusch and Santagata 777 Summer St Stamford CT 06901-1022

**DELLINGER, WALTER ESTES, III,** law educator, lawyer; b. Charlotte, N.C., May 15, 1941; s. Walter Estes and Grace Phelan (Lawing) D.; m. Anne Elizabeth Maxwell, June 12, 1965; children—Hampton, Andrew. AB with honors, U. N.C., 1963; LLB, Yale U., 1966. Bar: N.C. 1970. Assoc. prof. law U. Miss., 1966-68; law clk. to Justice Hugo L. Black, U.S. Supreme Ct., 1968-69; assoc. prof. law Duke U., 1969-72, prof. law, 1972-93, 98—; assoc. dean Duke U. Law Sch., 1974-76, acting dean, 1976-78; vis. prof. U. So. Calif. Law Ctr., 1973-74, U. Mich. Law Sch., 1977, Cath. U. Leuven, Belgium, 1985; prof. in residence U.S. Dept. Justice, Washington, 1980-81; asst. atty. gen. for legal counsel U.S. Justice Dept., Washington, 1993-96; acting Solicitor Gen. of the U.S., 1996-97; cons., draftsman N.C. Criminal Code Commn., 1970-78. Mem. bd. editors Yale Law Jour., 1965-66. Rockefeller Found. Humanities fellow, 1981-82. Mem. Am. Bar Assn., N.C. State Bar. Democrat. Home: 604 E Franklin St Chapel Hill NC 27514-3822 Office: Duke U Sch Law Box 90389 Science Dr & Towerview Rd Durham NC 27708

**DELLOFF, STEFAN T.,** lawyer; b. N.Y.C., Apr. 15, 1942. AB, Rutgers U., 1963; JD, NYU, 1972. Bar: N.J. 1972. Revenue officer IRS, N.Y.C., 1966-72; exec. asst. Motivation and Tng. Programs, Fair Lawn, N.J., 1972—; pvt. practice, Fair Lawn, 1972—. Construction. Office: 518 Essex Pl Fair Lawn NJ 07410-1012

**DELLO IACONO, PAUL MICHAEL,** lawyer; b. Brookline, Mass., July 26, 1957; s. John B. Jr. and Marie J.C. (Beaulieu) D.-I.; m. Donna M. Lynch, Jan. 10, 1981; children: Brad Michael, Andrea Marie. BA, St. Anselm Coll., 1979; JD, Suffolk U., 1982. Bar: Mass. 1982. V.p. Housing Dynamics, Boston, 1978-82; counsel DMC Energy Inc., Boston, 1982-85; exec. dir. Brockton (Mass.) Cen., Inc., 1985-89; Ea. regional counsel Proven Alternatives, Inc., Waltham, Mass., 1990-94; contracts mgr. Duke Solutions, Inc., Boston, 1995-98; asst. gen. counsel Duke Energy Corp., Boston/Charlotte, Mass./N.C., 1998—. Mem. devel. staff Vt. State Prison, 1978; apptd. mem. Citizens Adv. Commn., Boston, 1986-98; alt. atty. mem. Weymouth Zoning Bd. Appeals. Mem. Mass. Bar Assn., Delta Sigma Rho, Tau Kappa Alpha, Pi Gamma Mu. Democrat. Roman Catholic. Avocations: gardening, electronics, computers. Contracts commercial, General corporate. Home: 42 Weyfair Path Weymouth MA 02190-2638 Office: Duke Solutions Inc 1 Winthrop Sq Boston MA 02110-1209

**DEL NEGRO, JOHN THOMAS,** lawyer; b. Springfield, Mass., Oct. 2, 1948; s. Angelo Antonio and Marguerite (Garofalo) Del N.; m. Linda Anne Mayberry, July 6, 1973. BA, George Washington U., 1970; JD, Cornell U., 1975. Bar: Conn. 1975, U.S. Dist. Ct. Conn. 1978, U.S. Tax Ct. 1981. Assoc. Murtha, Cullina, Richter & Pinney, Hartford, Conn., 1975-81; ptnr. Murtha, Cullina, Richter & Pinney, Hartford, 1982-95, Del Negro, Feldman & Volpe, LLC, Hartford, 1995—. Author: (with Levenson) Depreciation and Investment Tax Credits, 1983. Dir. Conn. Opera Assn., 1990—, Watkinson Sch., 1992—. Mem. ABA, Conn. Bar Assn. (tax exec. com. 1992—). General corporate, Health, Taxation, general. Office: Del Negro Feldman & Volpe LLC Goodwin Sq 225 Asylum St Hartford CT 06103-1516

**DELO, ELLEN SANDERSON,** lawyer; b. Nassawadox, Va., Nov. 29, 1944; d. Robert G. and Daisy B. (Hitchens) Sanderson; m. Arthur C. Delo Jr., Mar. 20, 1971; 1 child, Marjorie Cotton Delo. BA, U. Richmond, 1966; JD, Rutgers U., 1977; LLM, NYU, 1985. Bar: N.J., 1977, U.S. Dist. Ct. N.J., 1977, U.S. Tax Ct., 1987, U.S. Ct. Appeals (2nd cir.) 1997, D.C. 1999. Law clk. to Hon. John J. Geronimo N.J. Superior Ct., 1977-78; assoc. Lamb Hutchinson Chappell Ryan & Hartung, Jersey City, 1978-80, Chasan Leyner Holland & Tarrant, Jersey City, 1980-84; assoc. Stryker Tams & Dill, Newark, 1985-92, ptnr., 1993-98; exec. compensation assoc. Bachelder Law Offices, N.Y.C., 1998—; lectr. on tax issues. Contbr. articles to profl. jours. Lay reader Summit Ridge Nursing and Rehab. Ctr., West Orange, N.J., Inglemoor Care Ctr., Livingston, N.J. Mem. ABA (tax sect., employee benefits com.). Democrat. Episcopalian. Avocation: animal welfare organizations and activities. Corporate taxation, Pension, profit-sharing, and employee benefits, State and local taxation. Home: 340 Montrose Ave South Orange NJ 07079-2439

**DELOACH, HARRIS E(UGENE), JR.,** lawyer, manufacturing company executive; b. Columbia, S.C., Aug. 7, 1944; s. Harris Eugene and Julia (Murdock) DeL.; m. Louise Hawes, June 12, 1969; children: Harris Eugene III, John Wilson Malloy, Jeanette Hawes. BBA, U.S.C., 1966; JD, 1969. Bar: S.C. 1969, U. S.Dist. Ct. S.C. 1969, U.S. Ct. Appeals (4th cir.) 1974. Ptnr., Wilmeth & DeLoach, Hartsville, S.C., 1972-85; v.p., gen. counsel Sonoco Products Co., Hartsville, 1986-90, exec. v.p. 1996—; v.p. HDFP, 1990-92; bd. dirs. Bank of Hartsville, Coker's Pedigreed Seed Co., Hartsville, Sonoco Products Co. Trustee Coker Coll., Hartsville, 1974-79, vice chmn., 1979; chmn. bd. trustees Byerly Hosp., Hartsville, 1976-79, chmn. 1997; chmn. bd. dirs. Thomas Hart Acad., Hartsville, 1984. Served to capt. USAF, 1969-72. Recipient Algernon Sydney Sullivan award Coker Coll., 1985, Disting. Alumnus award U. So. Calif., 1998. Mem. ABA, S.C. Bar Assn., 4th Jud. Cir. Assn. S.C. (v.p. 1974-78), Darlington County Bar Assn. (pres. 1984), Hartsville C. of C. (pres. 1977). Presbyterian. Lodge: Rotary (pres. Hartsville club 1977, Citizen of Yr. of Hartsville club 1980). General corporate, Banking, General practice. Home: 620 W Home Ave Hartsville SC 29550-4430 Office: Sonoco Products Co 2D N St Hartsville SC 29550

**DELONG, RAY,** editor. Copy editor Dayton (Ohio) Jour. Herald, 1972-73; editor, reporter Chgo. Daily News, 1973-78; city editor Columbia Missourian, summer 1980; freelance writer, 1978—; with ABA, 1986—, now editor Bus. Law Today, Litigation Docket; asst. prof. journalism U. Ill., 1978-84; asst. prof. Medill Sch. Journalism, Northwestern U., 1984-86; lectr. Univ. Coll., Northwestern U., 1985—. Office: ABA Publishing 750 N Lake Shore Dr Chicago IL 60611-4403

**DELORENZO, PAUL E.,** lawyer; b. Schenectady, N.Y., Dec. 13, 1964; s. Thomas E. and Patricia A. DeL. BS in Fin., Siena Coll., 1988; JD, Pace U., 1991. Ptnr. DeLorenzo, Pasquariello, Wieskopf & Gorman, Schenectady, N.Y., 1992—. Town atty. Town of Rotterdam, N.Y., 1997—. Mem. ABA, N.Y. State Trial Lawyers Assn., Schenectady County Bar Assn., Internat. Italian Am. Bar Assn. (co-founder), KC. Republican. Avocations: cooking, golf, scuba diving, exercising, boating. Federal civil litigation, Criminal, Personal injury. Home: 22 N Church St Schenectady NY 12305-1607 Office: DeLorenzo Pasquariello Wieskopf & Gorman 201 Nott Ter Schenectady NY 12307-1025

**DEL PAPA, FRANKIE SUE,** state attorney general; b. 1949. BA, U. Nev.; JD, George Washington U., 1974. Bar: Nev. 1974. Staff asst. U.S. Senator Alan Bible, Washington, 1971-74; assoc. Law Office of Leslie B. Grey, Reno, Nev., 1975-78; legis. asst. to U.S. Senator Howard Cannon, Washington, 1978-79; ptnr. Thornton & Del Papa, 1979-84; pvt. practice Reno, 1984-87; sec. of state State of Nev., Carson City, 1987-91; atty. gen. State of Nev., 1991—. Mem. Sierra Arts Found. (bd. dirs.), Trust for Pub. Land (adv. com.), Nev. Women's Fund. Democrat. Office: Office of Atty Gen Capitol Complex 100 N Carson St Carson City NV 89701-4717*

**DEL RASO, JOSEPH VINCENT,** lawyer; b. Phila., Dec. 21, 1952; s. Vincent and Dolores Ann (D'Adamo) Del R.; m. Anne Marie McGloin, Apr. 17, 1982; children: Joseph Vincent Jr., Katherine Anne, Marianna. BS in Acctg., Villanova U., 1974, JD, 1983. Bar: Pa., 1983, Fla. 1988. Exec. v.p. Belgrade Constrn., Inc., Wayne, Pa., 1974-80; atty. SEC, Washington, 1983-85; assoc. Dechert, Price & Rhoads, Washington, 1986-88; ptnr. Holland & Knight, Ft. Lauderdale, Fla., 1988-92, Stradley, Ronon, Stevens & Young, Phila., 1992-98, Pepper Hamilton LLP, Phila., 1998—; bd. dirs. Nat. Italian-Am. Found., Belgrade Constrn., Inc., Telespectrum Worldwide, Inc. Co-editor-in-chief Villanova Jour. Law and Investment Mgmt. Bd. consultors Villanova U. Sch. Law. Mem. Broward County Bar Assn., ABA, Villanova U. Alumni Assn. (class agt. 1974—), Union League Phila., Aronimink Golf Club. Republican. Roman Catholic. Securities, General corporate. Office: Pepper Hamilton LLP 18th & Arch Sts 3000 Two Logan Sq Philadelphia PA 19103

**DEL RUSSO, ALESSANDRA LUINI,** law educator; b. Milan, Italy, Jan. 2, 1916; d. Avvocato Umberto and Candita (Recio) Luini; m. Carl R. del Russo, Apr. 12, 1947; children: Carl Luini, Alexander David. PhD in History with honors, Royal U., Milan, 1939; SJD summa cum laude, Royal U., Pavia, Italy, 1943; LLM in Comparative Law, George Washington U., Washington, 1949. Bar: Md. 1956, Md. Ct. Appeals, Ct. of Appeals (Milano) 1947, U.S. Ct. Appeals (D.C. cir.) 1950, U.S. Supreme Ct. 1955. Legal adviser Allied Mil. Govt. and Ct., Milan, 1945-46, U.S. Consulate Gen., Milan, 1946-47; pvt. practice Washington, Bethesda, Md., 1950-58; atty. adviser Legis. Ref. Libr. of Congress, Washington, 1958-59; atty. U.S. Commn. on Civil Rights, Washington, 1959-61; prof. Howard U. Sch. Law, Washington, 1961-81, dir. grad. program, 1972-74; prof. emerita Howard U. Sch. Law, 1981—; adj. prof. Stetson U. Coll. Law, St. Petersburg, Fla., 1980-95, adj. prof. emerita, 1995—; professorial lectr. George Washington U. Law Ctr., 1970-80; mem. legal cons. com. U.S. Commn. on Status of P.R., Washington, 1965-66; lectr. in field. Author: International Protection of Human Rights, 1971; editor and chmn. of symposium on International Law of Human Rights, Howard U. Sch. of Law, Washington, 1965; contbr. numerous articles to internat. and Am. profl. jours. Rsch. grant Howard U., 1963. Mem. ABA, Brit. Inst. Internat. and Comparative Law, Am. Soc. Internat. Law. Republican. Roman Catholic. Achievements include 1st woman to receive LLM in Comparative Law from George Washington U. Avocations: travels, foreign languages, collecting antique books, genealogy. Home: 400 Ocean Trail Way Apt 908 Jupiter FL 33477-5527

**DELSTON, ROSS SCHEONBERG,** lawyer; b. N.Y.C., Aug. 7, 1951; s. Vernon and Ethel Scheonberg D.; m. Nancy Baker, July 21, 1974; childre; Rachel, Jill. BA, George Washington U., 1973, JD, 1976. Bar: D.C. Counsel Export-Import Bank of U.S., Washington, 1976-86; counsel Fed. Deposit Ins. Corp., Washington, 1986-88, asst. gen. counsel assisted acquisitions, 1988-91; of counsel Jones, Day, Reavis & Pogue, Washington, 1991-94; atty. pvt. practice, Washington, 1994—; cons. in field. Mem. ABA (banking law com.), D.C. Bar Assn. (membership benefits com.). Jewish. Office: 3013 Beech St NW Washington DC 20015-2203

**DEL TUFO, ROBERT J.,** lawyer, former US attorney, former state attorney general; b. Newark, Nov. 18, 1933; s. Raymond and Mary (Pellecchia) Del T.; m. Katherine Nouri Hughes; children: Barbara, Ann, Robert, David. B.A. cum laude in English, Princeton U., 1955; J.D., Yale U., 1958. Bar: N.J. 1959. Law sec. to chief justice N.J. Supreme Ct., 1958-60; assoc. firm Dillon, Bitar & Luther, Morristown, N.J., 1960-62, ptnr., 1962-74; asst. prosecutor Morris County, N.J., 1963-65; 1st asst. prosecutor, 1965-67; 1st asst. atty. gen. State of N.J., 1974-77; dir. criminal justice, 1976-77; U.S. atty. Dist. of N.J., Newark, 1977-80; prof. Rutgers U. Sch. Criminal Justice, 1979-81; ptnr. firm Stryker, Tams & Dill, 1980-86, Hannoch Weisman, 1986-90; atty. gen. State of N.J., 1990-93; ptnr. Skadden, Arps, Slate, Meagher & Flom, N.Y.C. and Newark, 1993—; commr. N.J. State Commn. of Investigation, 1981-84; instr. bus. law Fairleigh-Dickinson U., 1964; mem. N.J. State Bd. Bar Examiners, 1967-74; mem. criminal law drafting com. Nat. Conf. Bar Examiners, 1972—; bd. dirs. Nat. Victim Ctr., 1995—; Nat. Italian Am. Found., 1995—, Integrity Inc., 1995—, John Cabot U. in Rome, 1997—, N.J. Pub. Interest Law Ctr., 1996—, Daytop Village Found., 1998—, Planned Parenthood, 1999—; mem. com. on character N.J. Supreme Ct., 1982-84; spl. master, fed. jail overcrowding litigation, Essex County, 1989-90. Bd. editors Yale U Law Jour; contbr. articles to profl. jours. Mem. law enforcement adv. com. County Coll. of Morris, 1970-85; mem. Morris County Ethics Com., 1968-71, Morris County Jud. Selection Com., 1970-72, Essex County Jud. Selection Com., 1982-84; v.p., mem. exec. com. United Fund of Morris County, 1966-70; chmn. Morris Twp. Juvenile Conf. Com., 1963-74; bd. dirs. Nat. Found. March of Dimes, 1966-68, Vis. Nurse Assn. Morris County, 1963-70, Morristown YMCA, 1970-74; trustee Newark Acad., 1976-95, 97—, pres. bd. dirs. 1983-87; bd. regents St. Peter's Coll., 1979-85. Fellow Am. Bar Found.; mem. Am., N.J., Morris County bar assns., Nat. Dist. Attys. Assn., Yale Law Sch. Assn. (exec. com. 1978-84), Order of Coif. Home: 13 Ober Rd Princeton NJ 08540-4917 Office: Skadden Arts Slate Meagher & Flom One Newark Ctr Newark NJ 07102 also: 919 3rd Ave New York NY 10022-3902

**DELUCA, ANTHONY R.,** lawyer, arbitrator; b. Phila., May 6, 1948; s. Antonio. BA with honors, Ctrl. High Sch., Phila., 1965; BA, Temple U., 1969; JD, U. Balt., 1976. Asst. gen. coun. Dept. Pub. Welfare, Phila., 1978-79; assoc. Michael J. Pepe, PC, Phila., 1979-85; trial assoc. Margolis, Edelstein, Phila., 1985-86; trial splst. Hartford Ins. Co., Phila., 1986-97; sr. trial atty. Nationwide Enterprises, Phila., 1997—. Mem. Justinian Soc. (bd. dirs. 1991-94). Insurance. Home: 51 Longview Dr Springfield PA 19064-1642 Office: Nationwide Enterprises 1515 Market St Lbby 4 Philadelphia PA 19102-1901

**DE LUCA, THOMAS GEORGE,** lawyer; b. Jersey City, Dec. 28, 1950; s. Michael Anthony and Estelle Theresa (Wickiewicz) De L.; m. Annette Catherine Pandolfo, Aug. 16, 1975; children: Michele, Thomas, Rachel. BS in Econs., St. Peters Coll., Jersey City, 1972; JD, Seton Hall U., 1978. Bar: N.J. 1978, U.S. Dist. Ct. 1978, N.Y. 1981, U.S. Dist. Ct. (so. and ea. dists.) N.Y. 1981, U.S. Ct. Appeals (2d cir.) 1986, U.S. Ct. Appeals (3d cir.) 1987, U.S. Claims Ct. 1989, U.S. Dist. Ct. (we. dist.) N.Y. 1990, U.S. Dist. Ct. (no. dist.) N.Y. 1991, U.S. Supreme Ct. 1987. Supervising underwriter Fireman's Fund Ins. Cos., Newark, 1972-77; assoc. Sellar, Richardson & Stuart, Newark, 1978-80; assoc. Postner & Rubin, N.Y.C., 1980-84, ptnr., 1985-93; ptnr. De Luca & Forster, Cranford, N.J., 1994—. Mem. ABA, N.J. Bar Assn., N.Y. County Lawyers Assn. Roman Catholic. Construction, State civil litigation, Federal civil litigation. Home: 14 Kilmer Dr Colonia NJ 07067-1213 Office: De Luca and Forster 11 Commerce Dr Cranford NJ 07016-3501 also: 1 N Broadway White Plains NY 10601-2310

**DELUCE-TAYLOR, PENNY JANE,** lawyer; b. Kapuskasing, Ont., July 15, 1965; came to U.S., 1990; BA with honors, York U., Ont., 1988; JD, Hamline U., 1991. Bar: Minn. 1991, U.S. Dist. Ct. Minn. 1992. Private practice St. Paul, 1992—. Family and matrimonial. Office: 2353 Rice St Ste 203 Roseville MN 55113-3721

**DEL VALLE, TERESA JONES,** lawyer; b. Dayton, Ohio, July 20, 1965; d. Roy and Carmen D. Jones; m. Rene R. Del Valle, July 18, 1998. BS, Ariz. State U., 1988; JD, U. Houston, 1993. Bar: Tex. 1993, U.S. Dist. Ct. (so. and ea. dists.) Tex. 1994. Underwriter Prudential Property and Casualty Ins. Co., Scottsdale, Ariz., 1988-90; assoc. Doyle, Rider, Restrepo, Harvin & Robbins, LLP, Houston, 1993-97, Cash, Jones & Springhetti, LLP, Houston, 1997—. Fellow Tex. Bar Found.; mem. Tex. Young Lawyers Assn. (v.p. 1998-99, sec. 1997-98, bd. dirs. 1995-98, Pres.' award of merit 1994-97), Houston Young Lawyers Assn. (bd. dirs. 1994-95), Aspiring Youth Found. (bd. dirs. 1997-98), Houston Lawyers Found. (trustee 1998-99). Roman Catholic. General civil litigation. Office: Cash Jones Springhetti LLP 600 Travis St Ste 6710 Houston TX 77002-3000

**DEL VECCHIO, DEBRA ANNE,** lawyer; b. Milford, Conn., June 19, 1958; d. Daniel Thomas and Carmela Theresa DelV.; m. Scott Douglas Houseman, Sept. 7, 1985; children: Haley Elizabeth, Luke. BA English/Polit. Sci. magna cum laude, Boston U., 1980; JD cum laude, Suffolk Law Sch., 1983. Bar: Mass. 1983, U.S. Dist. Ct. Mass. 1984, U.S. Ct. Appeals (1st cir.) 1984. Law clk. to justices Superior Ct., Boston, 1983-84; trial atty. tax divsn. criminal sect. we. region U.S. Dept. Justice, Washington, 1984-87; asst. dist. atty. Middlesex County Dist. Atty.'s Office, Cambridge, Mass., 1987-91; assoc. Smith, Duggan & Johnson, Boston, 1991-95; pvt. practice, 1995-96; ptnr. Del Vecchio & Houseman, 1997—. Mem. Mass. Bar Assn., Essex County Bar Assn. Workers' compensation, Criminal, General civil litigation. Office: 15 Front St Salem MA 01970-3707

**DEMARCO, ANTHONY J., JR.,** lawyer; b. Bklyn., June 27, 1928; s. Anthony J. and Clementine (Corazza) D.; (div.) children—Angela J., Jennifer C. B.S., Manhattan Coll., 1952; J.D., St. John's U., 1958; postgrad. NYU, Grad. Sch. Law 1960 Bar: N.Y. 1958. Atty. Hartford Accident and Indemnity Co., 1956-58; sole practice, 1958-76, trial counsel Anthony J. DeMarco Jr., P.C., 1976—. Bd. dirs. and counsel S.I. Hosp. Heart Assn., S.I. Artificial Kidney Fund. Served with USMC, 1946-48. Fellow Am. Bd. Trial Advocates; mem. ABA (com. on litigation, com. on trial evidence 1977—), N.Y. State Bar Assn. (permanent chmn. trial adv. and scholarship com., exec. com. trial lawyers sect., chmn. 1984—, faculty, lectr. com. on continuing legal edn.), Bklyn. Bar Assn., Kings County Defenders Assn., Columbia Lawyers Assn., Fed. Bar Council, Nat. Trial Advocacy Assn. (assoc. dir.), N.Y. State Trial Lawyers Assn., N.Y. County Lawyers Assn. Federal civil litigation, State civil litigation, Criminal. Office: 26 Court St Suite 2803 Brooklyn NY 11242

**DEMARCO, G. LAWRENCE,** lawyer; b. Stratford, N.J., Dec. 3, 1968; s. James J. and Linda (Acchione) DeM. BA, Dickinson U., 1990; JD, Villanova U., 1993. Ptnr. DeMarco & DeMarco, Phila. Majority insp. Dem. party, Phila., 1993-98. Roman Catholic. Avocations: soccer, Internet surfing. Fax: 2155465246. E-mail: Gennarro@aol.com. Office: DeMarco & DeMarco 1420 Walnut St Philadelphia PA 19102-4017

**DEMARIA, ANTHONY NICHOLAS,** lawyer; b. N.Y.C., Aug. 3, 1969; s. Anthony Nicholas and DeLores Ruth DeMaria; m. Kimberly Diane Paul, July 20, 1991; 1 child, Alec William. BA, U. Calif., Davis, 1991; postgrad., Regent U., 1992-93; JD, U. San Diego, 1995. Bar: Calif. 1995, Colo. 1997. Atty. McCormick, Barstow Sheppard Wayte & Carruth, Fresno, Calif., 1995—. Mem. Christian Legal Soc. (pres. 1997-98), U. San Diego, St. Thomas More Soc. (pres. 1994-95), Order of Coif. Republican. Roman Catholic. Avocations: basketball, swimming, southern and civil war history, reading. General civil litigation, Personal injury, Product liability. Office: McCormick Barstow Sheppard Wayte and Curruth 5 River Park Pl E Fresno CA 93720-1501

**DEMARIA, JOSEPH CARMINUS,** lawyer; b. Phila., June 21, 1947; s. Joseph and Mary A. DeMaria. AB in Politics, St. Joseph's Coll., Phila., 1969; JD, Villanova U., 1972. Bar: Pa. 1972, U.S. Dist. Ct. (ea. dist.) Pa. 1972, U.S. Ct. Appeals (3rd cir.) 1982, U.S. Supreme Ct. 1982, Conn. 1988. Staff atty. Southeastern Pa. Transportation Authority, Phila., 1972-78; mng. atty. Aetna Life and Casualty, Phila., 1978-87; asst. v.p., staff counsel ops. Aetna Life and Casualty, Hartford, Conn., 1987-91; claim counsel Aetna Life & Casualty, Phila., 1991-96; pvt. practice Phila., 1972—. Mem. Am. Corp. Counsel Assn., Pa. Bar Assn., Def. Rsch. Inst., Assn. Calif. Tort Reform, Fedn. of Ins. and Corp. Counsel, Pa. Bar Assn., Phila. Bar Assn., Pa. Def. Inst., Phila. Assn. Def. Counsel, John Peter Zenger Law Soc., German Am. Police Assn., German Soc. Pa., FOP. Republican. Roman Catholic. Avocations: tennis, music, science fiction, scale modeling. Insurance, General civil litigation, Probate. Home and Office: 237 Weadley Rd King Of Prussia PA 19406-3746

**DE MARINO, THOMAS JOHN,** lawyer; b. Greensburg, Pa., Nov. 24, 1937; s. Thomas Camille and Sue Eleanor (Nicholson) de M.; m. Elizabeth Hamilton Bardsley, Aug. 22, 1959 (div. Aug. 1978); children: Jeffrey, Lynn; m. Joyce Hobson Le, May 18, 1979 (dec. Sept. 1995). BA, Dickinson Coll., 1959, JD, 1962. Bar: Pa. 1963, Colo. 1965; U.S. Dist. Ct. Colo. 1965, U.S. Ct. Appeals (10th cir.) 1965, U.S. Supreme Ct. Assoc. Hamilton, Darmo, Malloy, Phila., 1963; ptnr. firm Ellison, de Marion & Knapp, Denver, 1965-76, de Marino & Knapp, Denver, 1976-77, Sheldon, Bayer, McLean & Glasman, Denver, 1978; Colo. mng. atty. law dept. litigation divsn. Travelers Ins. Co., Denver, 1979-93; dir. Weinberger & Kanan, P.C., Denver, 1994-98; adminstrv. law judge Colo. Divsn. Workers Comp., 1999—. Author: Colorado Workers Compensation Law and Practice, 1984; contbr. articles to legal jours. Pres. Denver Lyric Opera Co., 1973; treas. Colo. Mountain Club Found., Denver, 1984. Fellow Am. Bar Found., Colo. Bar Found.; mem. Colo. Bar Assn. (bd. govs. 1985-90, chmn. interprofl. com. 1983, chmn. worker's compensation sect. 1983, vice chmn., litigation sect. coun. 1988), Denver Bar Assn. (pres. 1997, 1st v.p. 1988, bd. trustees 1991-94, chmn. barristers benefit ball com. 1989, Merit award 1995), Colo. Def. Lawyers Assn. (v.p. 1975, pres. 1976), Def. Rsch. Inst. (exceptional performance citation 1977), Colo. Mountain Club (bd. dirs. Denver 1974). Republican. Congregationalist. Insurance, Personal injury, Workers' compensation. Office: 1700 Broadway Ste 1910 Denver CO 80290-1901

**DEMARTIN, CHARLES PETER,** lawyer; b. N.Y.C., Aug. 21, 1952; s. Samuel Peter and Rose Marie (Parisi) DeM.; m. Frances Gloria Vitrano, Apr. 4, 1981; children: Stephen, Charles, Joseph. BS, SUNY, Binghamton, 1974; JD, St. John's U., Jamaica, N.Y., 1977. Bar: N.Y. 1978, D.C. 1978, U.S. Dist. Ct. (ea. and so. dists.) N.Y. 1978, U.S. Ct. Appeals (2d cir.) 1983; U.S. Dist. Ct. Ariz., 1993. Assoc. Hartman & Lerner, Mineola, N.Y., 1978-80; pvt. practice law Garden City, N.Y., 1980, 85-87; counsel Curtis, Zaklukiewicz, Vasile & Devine, Merrick, N.Y., 1980-82, 85-87; ptnr. DeMartin, Kranz, Davis & Hersh, Hauppauge, N.Y., 1981-85, Damadeo & DeMartin, Hicksville, N.Y., 1987-88; pvt. practice law Huntington, N.Y., 1989-92; ptnr. McCarthy, McCarthy & DeMartin, Huntington, 1992-94; pvt. practice law Huntington, N.Y., 1994—. Mem. N.Y. State Bar Assn., Nassau County Bar Assn., D.C. Bar Assn., Brookville Country Club. Republican. Roman Catholic. Avocations: golf, sports, photography. General civil litigation, General corporate, Personal injury. Home: 2 Bluebird Ln Huntington NY 11743-6502 Office: 870 W Jericho Tpke Huntington NY 11743-6037

**DEMBLING, PAUL GERALD,** lawyer, former government official; b. Rahway, N.J., Jan. 11, 1920; s. Simon and Fannie (Ellenbogen) D.; m. Florence Brotman, Nov. 22, 1947; children: Ross Wayne, Douglas Evan, Donna Stacy. B.A., Rutgers U., 1940, M.A., 1942; J.D., George Washington U., 1951. Bar: D.C. 1952. Grad. asst., teaching fellow Rutgers U., 1940-42; economist Office Chief Transp., Dept. Army, 1942-45; since practiced in Washington; indsl. relations NACA, 1945-51, spl. counsel, legal adviser, gen. counsel, 1951-58; asst. gen. counsel NASA, 1958-61, dir. legis. affairs, 1961-63, dep. gen. counsel, 1963-67, gen. counsel, 1967-69, chmn. bd. contract appeals, 1958-61, vice chmn. inventions and contbns. bd., 1959-67; mem. and alt. rep. U.S. del. UN Legal Subcom. Com. on Outer Space, 1964-69; gen. counsel GAO, 1969-78; partner Schnader, Harrison, Segal & Lewis, Washington, 1978-93, sr. counsel, 1994—; prin. author NASA Act, 1958; professorial lectr. George Washington U. Law Sch., 1965-86. Co-author: Federal Contract Management, 1988, Essentials of Grant Law Practice, 1991; editor in chief Fed. Bar Jour., 1962-69; contbr. articles to profl. jours. Recipient Meritorious Civilian Service award War Dept., 1945; Disting. Service medal NASA, 1968; Nat. Civil Service League award, 1973. Fellow AIAA (chmn. com. law and sociology 1969-71), Nat. Contract Mgmt. Assn. (bd. advisers 1973—), Nat. Acad. Pub. Adminstrn., Am. Bar Found. (life); mem. ABA (coun., public contract law sec. 1983-84, vice chmn. 1984-85, chmn. elect 1985-86, chmn. 1986-87), FBA (nat. coun. 1963—, pres. Capitol Hill chpt. 1977-78, nat. sec. 1978-79, pres.-elect 1981-82, nat. pres. 1983-84, bd. dirs. bldg. corp. 1989—), D.C. Bar (mem. steering com. govt. contracts and litigation sect. 1989-95), Procurement Roundtable (bd. dirs. 1984—, vice chmn. 1988—), Internat. Inst. Space Law (pres. Am. assn. 1970-72, Internat. Astronaut. Fedn. award 1992), Cosmos Club, Nat. Lawyers Club, Phi Delta Phi. Government contracts and claims, Public international. Home: 11625 Pamplona Blvd Boynton Beach FL 33437-4077 Office: Schnader Harrison Segal & Lewis 1300 I St NW Washington DC 20005-3314

**DE MENT, IRA,** judge; b. Birmingham, Ala., Dec. 21, 1931; s. Ira Jr. and Helen (Sparks) DeM.; m. Ruth Lester Posey; 1 child, Charles Posey. AS, Marion Mil. Inst., 1951; AB, U. Ala., 1953, LLB, 1958, JD, 1969. Bar: Ala. 1958, U.S. Dist. Ct. (mid. dist.) Ala. 1958, U.S. Ct. Appeals (5th cir.) 1958, U.S. Supreme Ct. 1966, U.S. Dist. Ct. (so. dist.) Ala. 1967, U.S. Dist. Ct. D.C. 1972, U.S. Ct. Appeals (D.C.) 1972, U.S. Tax Ct. 1972, U.S. Customs and Patents Appeals 1976, U.S. Dist. Ct. (no. dist.) Ala. 1977. U.S. Ct. Appeals (11th cir.), 1981, U.S. Ct. Mil. Appeal 1972. Law clk. Sup. Ct. Ala., 1958-59; asst. atty. gen. State of Ala., 1959, spl. asst. atty. gen., 1966-69, 81-92; asst. U.S. atty., Montgomery, Ala., 1959-61; pvt. practice Montgomery, 1961-69, 77-92; U.S. dist. judge (mid. dist.) Ala., 1992—;acting U.S. atty. Mid. Dist. Ala. 1969, U.S. atty., 1969-77; asst. atty., legal advisor to police and fire depts. City of Montgomery, 1965-69; instr. Jones Law Sch., 1962-64; instr. Montgomery Police Acad. 1964-77; lectr. constl. law Ala. Police Acad., 1971-75; instr. law enforcement U. Ala., 1967, mem. adj. faculty New Coll., 1974-75, adj. prof. psychology, 1975-92; spl. counsel to Gov. State Ala., 1980-88, gen. counsel Commn. on Aging, 1980-82. Lt. col. USAR, 1953-74; maj. gen. USAFR ret. Recipient Disting. Service award Internat. Assn. Firefighters, 1975; Rockefeller Pub. Service award, Woodrow Wilson Sch. Pub. and Internat. Affairs Princeton U., 1976; named Alumnus of Yr. Marion Mil. Inst., 1988, Significant Sig award Sigma Chi Fraternity, 1998, Judicial Award of Merit Ala. State Bar., 1998. Mem. ABA, Fed. Bar Assn., D.C. Bar Assn., Ala. Bar Assn. (mem. editorial adv. bd. The Alabama Lawyer 1966-72), Am. Judicature Soc.,Nat. Assn. Former U.S. Attys., Phi Alpha Delta. Republican. United Methodist. Clubs: Masons, Shriners. Address: PO Box 2149 Montgomery AL 36102-2149

**DEMENT, JAMES ALDERSON, JR.,** lawyer; b. Clinton, Okla., Sept. 11, 1947; s. James Alderson and Ruby (Weaver) DeM.; m. Sally Anne Wylder, June 6, 1970; children: Stephen, Suzanne, Jonathan. BA summa cum laude, Tex. Christian U., 1969; JD in Internat. Affairs, Cornell U., 1972. Bar: N.Y. 1973, Tex. 1974. Assoc. Alexander & Green, N.Y.C., 1972-73; assoc. Baker & Botts, Houston, 1977-85, ptnr., 1985-98—; ptnr., chmn. corp. tax and internat. sect. Butler & Binion, LLP, Houston, 1985-97; adj. prof. U. Houston, 1987-88. Mem. edtl. rev. bd. The Internat. Lawyer, 1987-94. Trustee Houston Ballet Found., 1989-96, Brazos Presbyn. Homes, Inc., 1990-96. Capt. USAF, 1973-77. Fellow Tex. Bar Found.; mem. State Bar Tex. (internat. law sect., chmn. 1989-90), Internat. and Comparative Law Ctr. Southwestern Legal Found. (adv. coun. 1986—), Houston Bar Assn. (internat. law sect., pres. 1989-90). Presbyterian. Private international. Office: Baker & Botts LLP 1 Shell Plz 910 Louisiana St Houston TX 77002-4991

**DE MEO, ANTONIA M.,** lawyer; b. Stanford, Calif., Feb. 12, 1967; d. Anthony S. and Geraldine B. De M. BA, Wellesley Coll., 1989; JD, Lewis & Clark U., 1994. Bar: Oreg. 1994, Wash. 1996, U.S. Dist. Ct. Oreg. 1995, U.S. Dist. Ct. (ea. and we. dists.) Wash. 1997, U.S. Ct. Appeals (9th cir.) 1995. Assoc. Harrang Long Gary Rudnick, Eugene, Oreg., 1994-96, Markowitz, Herbold, Glade & Mehlhaf, Portland, Oreg., 1996—; mem. panel Lewis & Clark Coll., 1996, 97, ABA, San Francisco, 1997; guest spkr. Wash. Women Lawyres, Vancouver, 1998, So. Nev. Assn. Women Attys., Las Vegas, 1998. Author: (with others) Posttrial Matters, 1996, How to Develop the Marketing and Rainmaking Skills Necessary to be Successful in Today's Legal Market, 1997; contbr. articles to profl. jours. Bd. dirs. Portland Habilitation Ctr., 1997—. Recipient 3d pl. writing award Am. Indian Law Rev., 1993-94. Mem. Oreg. Women Lawyers (bd. dirs. 1995—), Oreg. State Bar Assn. (exec. com. bus. litig. sect. 1997—, ho. dels. 1997—), Oreg. Wellesley Club (bd. dirs. 1996—), Wellesley Coll. Alumni Assn. (regional career svcs. rep. 1997—), Lane County Women Lawyers (steering com. 1995), Multnomah Bar Assn. (young lawyers divsn. pub. svc. com. 1997-98), Portland City Club. Avocations: ballet, yoga, art history, rollerblading, reading. General civil litigation, Contracts commercial. Office: Markowitz Herbold Glade & Mehlhaf 1211 SW 5th Ave Ste 3000 Portland OR 97204-3730

**DEMER, MARGARET E.,** lawyer; b. Cleve.. BS in Edn., Kent State U., 1941; LLB, JD, Ind. U., 1958. Bar: Ind. 1958, Ohio 1959. Pvt. practice law Cleve., 1958—; pers. specialist U.S. Govt., Washington, 1979-82. Sgt. WAC, 1942-46. Mem. Garfield Heights Womens Club. Republican. Mem. United Ch. of Christ. Probate, Real property, Family and matrimonial. Home and Office: 11429 Bradwell Rd Garfield Hts OH 44125-3505

**DEMING, BRUCE ROBERT,** lawyer; b. Balt., July 27, 1964; s. Robert Hershel and Beverly Ann Deming; m. Jeffrey Scott Byrne, June 1, 1996; 1 child, Anna Robin Byrne-Deming. BS, U. Colo., 1986; JD, Harvard U., 1992. Bar: Calif. 1996, U.S. Dist. Ct. (no. and so. dists.) 1996. Sr. acct. Price Waterhouse, Denver, 1986-89; law clk. to Judge Skinner U.S. Dist. Ct., Boston, 1992-93; assoc. Farella, Braun & Martel LLP, San Francisco, 1993-98; v.p., gen. counsel Tier Tech., Inc., Walnut Creek, Calif., 1998—; co-founder, bd. dirs. Computer Repeats, Inc., Boulder, Colo., 1986-89; founder, co-chair Harvard Law Sch. Gay, Lesbian and Bisexual Alumni Com., Cambridge, Mass., 1992-96; cooperating atty. ACLU, 1993-96. Avocation: skiing. Mergers and acquisitions, Securities, General corporate. Office: Tier Tech Inc 1350 Treat Blvd Walnut Creek CA 94596-2133

**DEMING, FRANK STOUT,** lawyer; b. Oswego, Kans., Aug. 12, 1927; s. Robert Orin Jr. and Helen Josephine (Stout) D.; m. Carolyn Ruth Kauffman, June 24, 1950; children: Frank S. Jr., Christiana Deming Jacobsen, David M., Robert W. BS in Econs., U. Pa., 1949, LLB, 1952. Bar: Pa. 1953, U.S. Dist. Ct. (ea. dist.) Pa. 1953, U.S. Ct. Appeals (3d cir.) 1953, U.S. Ct. Appeals (9th cir.) 1965. Assoc., then ptnr., now of counsel Montgomery, McCracken, Walker & Rhoads, Phila., 1952—; bd. dirs. New Covenant Trust co. Contbr. articles to profl. jours. Trustee Bricker Found., Phila., 1980—, Presbyn. Ch. (U.S.A.) Found., Jeffersonville, Ind., 1989-94, chmn., 1993, mem. gen. assembly coun., Louisville, 1990-91; dir. Presbyn. Children's Village, 1992-94. Sgt. U.S. Army, 1946-47. Fellow Am. Coll. Trust and Estate Counsel; mem. ABA, Pa. Bar Assn., Phila. Bar Assn., Mil. Figure Collectors Am., Phi Delta Theta, Beta Alpha Psi, Beta Gamma Sigma. Republican. Avocations: travel. Estate planning, Probate, Estate taxation. Home: Riddle Village 410 Hampton Media PA 19063-6009 Office: Montgomery McCracken Walker & Rhoads 123 S Broad St Fl 25 Philadelphia PA 19109-1029

**DEMING, STUART HAYDEN,** lawyer; b. Kalamazoo, Mich., Dec. 17, 1951; s. Ned Wesley and Anne Kingsbury (Gower) D. Student, Williams Coll., 1970-71; BA, U. Mich., 1973, JD, 1977, MBA, 1978. Bar: Mich. 1977, U.S. Ct. Appeals (D.C. cir.) 1984, U.S. Ct. Internat. Trade 1991; CPA, Mich. Law clk. to Hon. Wendell A. Miles U.S. Dist. Ct., Grand Rapids, Mich., 1978-79; asst. U.S. atty. U.S. Dept. Justice, Grand Rapids, 1980-83; atty. SEC, Washington, 1983-85; trial atty. U.S. Dept. Justice, Washington, 1985-87, spl. prosecutor, 1992; assoc. Steptoe & Johnson, Washington, 1987-90; exec. asst. 1990 Econ. Summit, Houston; spl. asst. U.S. Dept. Def., Washington, 1991-92; resident advisor Lithuanian Govt., Vilnius, 1994; advisor Ethiopian Spl. Prosecutor, Addis Ababa, 1994; pvt. practice Kalamazoo, 1994—. Contbr. articles to profl. publs. Vol. Garry E. Brown Campaign, Kalamazoo, 1978, Bush-Quayle Campaign, 1987-88; del. George Allen Campaign, Va., 1993. Mem. ABA (chmn. com. 1992-95), AICPA, State Bar Mich. (chmn. com. 1994-95), Atlantic Coun. of U.S. Republican. Avocations: travel, sports, politics, reading. Private international, Public international, General corporate. Home: 1246 W Kilgore Rd Kalamazoo MI 49008-3502 Office: 229 E Michigan Ave Ste 340B Kalamazoo MI 49007-6400

**DEMITCHELL, TERRI ANN,** law educator; b. San Diego, Apr. 10, 1953; d. William Edward and Rose Annette (Carreras) Wheeler; m. Todd Allan

DeMitchell, Aug. 14, 1982. AB in English with honors, San Diego State U., 1975; JD, U. San Diego, 1984; MA in Edn., U. Calif., Davis, 1990; EdM, Harvard U., 1997. Bar: Calif. 1985, U.S. Dist. Ct. (so. dist.) Calif. 1985; cert. elem. tchr., Calif. Tchr. Fallbrook (Calif.) Union Elem. Sch. Dist., 1976-86; adminstrv. asst. gen. counsel San Diego Unified Sch. Dist., 1984; assoc. Biddle and Hamilton, Sacramento, 1986-88; instr. U. N.H., 1990-93; teaching asst. U. Calif., Davis, 1987. Author: The California Teacher and the Law, 1985, The Law in Relation to Teacher, Out of School Behavior, 1990, Censorship and the Public School Library: A Bicoastal View, 1991; contbr. chpt. to book: The Limits of Law-Based School Reform, 1997. Ava. Calif. Bar Assn., Internat. Reading Assn.

**DEMLOW, JAMES CARL,** judge; b. Ft. Collins, Colo., Aug. 7, 1945; s. Ernest Carl and Evelyn Louise Demlow; m. Delsa Beth Demlow; children: Debbie, Trissie. BSME, Colo. State U., 1967; JD, Denver U., 1973. Bar: Colo. 1973, U.S. Dist. Ct. Colo. 1973, U.S. Ct. Appeals (10th cir.) 1973, U.S. Supreme Ct. 1977. Engr. Martin Marietta, Colo., 1967-73; pvt. practice Colo., 1973-74; county atty. Jefferson, Colo., 1974-78; magistrate 1st Jud. Dist., Golden, Colo., 1978-82, judge, 1982—. Mem. Gov.'s Task Force on Domestic Violence, Colo., 1994—. Mem. Colo. Trial Judges Assn. (pres. 1994-95), Colo. County Judges Assn. (pres. 1993-94), Mensa, Optimist Club (dir. 1978—), Lakewood Swim Club (dir. 1976-82), Phi Delta Theta. Avocations: cycling, jogging. Office: 1st Jud Dist 100 Jefferson County Pkwy Golden CO 80401-6000

**DEMOFF, MARVIN ALAN,** lawyer; b. L.A., Oct. 28, 1942; s. Max and Mildred (Tweer) D.; m. Patricia Caryn Abelov, June 16, 1968; children: Allison Leigh, Kevin Andrew. BA, UCLA, 1964; JD, Loyola U., L.A., 1967. Bar: Calif. 1969. Asst. pub. defender Los Angeles County, 1968-72; ptnr. Steinberg & Demoff, L.A., 1973-83, Craighill, Fentress & Demoff, L.A. and Washington, 1983-86; of counsel Mitchell, Silberberg & Knupp, L.A., 1987—. Mem. citizens adv. bd. Olympic Organizing Com., L.A., 1982-84; bd. trustees Curtis Sch., L.A., 1985-94, chmn. bd. trustees, 1988-93; sports adv. bd. Constitution Rights Found., L.A., 1986—. Mem. ABA (mem. forum com. on entertainment and sports), Calif. Bar Assn., UCLA Alumni Assn., Phi Delta Phi. Avocations: sports, music, art. Entertainment, Sports. Office: Mitchell Silberberg Knupp Los Angeles CA 90064

**DEMOND, WALTER EUGENE,** lawyer; b. Sacramento, Oct. 15, 1947; s. Walter G. and Laura (Bartlett) D.; m. Kari Demond; 1 child, William. BA, U. Tex., 1969, JD with honors, 1976. Bar: Tex. 1976. With Clark, Thomas & Winters, Austin, 1976—; mem. mgmt. com. Clark, Thomas & Winters, 1984-94, 97—, CFO, 1984—. Capt. USAF, 1970-74. Fellow Am. Bar Found., Tex. Bar Found.; mem. ABA (vice chmn. gas com. pub. utility, comm. and transp. law sect. 1986-91, 97—, chmn. gas com. 1991-93, pub. utility comm. and transp. law sect.), State Bar of Tex. (adminstrv. law com. 1984-87). Avocations: sailing, jogging. Administrative and regulatory, Public utilities. Office: Clark Thomas & Winters 700 Lavaca St Austin TX 78701-3102

**DEMOPULOS, HAROLD WILLIAM,** lawyer; b. Providence, R.I., Jan. 14, 1924; s. George K. and Grace (Loures) D.; m. Frances Scorzoni, June 10, 1967; children—Amelia Hannah, Abigail Mary. BA, Brown U., 1948; JD, U. Miami, 1952. Bar: Fla. 1952, R.I. 1953, U.S. Dist. Ct. (so. dist.) Fla. 1952, U.S. Dist. Ct. R.I. 1953. Sole practice, Providence and Bristol, R.I., 1953—; Patentee in field. Clk. R.I. State Senate Jud. Com., 1953-54; atty. labor rels. bd. R.I. Dept. Labor, 1968-70; mem. dist. adv. coun. SBA, 1970-78, mem. adv. bd. State of R.I. Briston County Cable Area; probate judge Town of Bristol (R.I.), 1973-74; bd. dirs. Bristol Land Trust Corp. Pres., Bristol C. of C., 1970s; mem. corp. Roger Williams Coll., Bristol; v.p. Bristol Art Mus., 1970s; treas., bd. dirs. Coggeshall Farm Mus. Inc.; incorporator, bd. dirs. Prepaid Legal Service Corp. R.I. With U.S. Army, 1942-46. Mem. R.I. Bar Assn. (pres. 1984—), ABA, Fla. Bar Assn., R.I. Law Inst. (bd. dirs.), R.I. Law Found., Order of Ahepa (pres. Sophocles chpt. 1958, dist. gov. 1966-67), Rotary, Brown Club (pres. R.I. 1975). Republican. Greek Orthodox. Probate, Personal injury, General practice. Office: Westminster Square Bldg 10 Dorrance St Ste 634 Providence RI 02903-2018

**DEMOREST, MARK STUART,** lawyer; b. Chambley, France, Mar. 14, 1957; came to U.S., 1960; s. Raymond Phillip and Maud Jane (Dahle) D.; m. Patricia Louise Button, July 28, 1979; children: Melissa, Matthew, Kristin, Kevin, Ryan. AB magna cum laude, Harvard U., 1979; JD magna cum laude, U. Mich., 1983. Bar: Mich. 1983, US Dist. Ct. (ea. dist.) Mich. 1983, U.S. Ct. Appeals (6th cir.) 1984, U.S. Ct. Appeals (7th cir.) 1986, U.S. Supreme Ct. 1993, U.S. Dist. Ct. (cen. dist.) Ill. 1995, U.S. Ct. Appeals (4th cir.) 1995, U.S. Dist. Ct. (we. dist.) Mich. 1996. Assoc. Dykema Gossett, Detroit, 1983-85, Simpson & Moran, Birmingham, Mich., 1985-87; ptnr. The Robert P. Ufer Partnership, Bloomfield Hills, Mich., 1987-92, Hainer, Demorest & Berman, P.C., Troy, Mich., 1993-98; pvt. practice, 1998—. Mem. ABA, State Bar Mich., Def. Rsch. Inst., Oakland County Bar Assn., Harvard Club of Ea. Mich. (schs. com.), Order of Coif. Methodist. Avocation: sports. General corporate, General civil litigation, Labor. Office: 19853 Outer Dr Ste 300 Dearborn MI 48124-2066

**DEMOSS, HAROLD RAYMOND, JR.,** federal judge; b. Houston, Tex., Dec. 30, 1930; s. Harold R. and Jessy May (Cox) DeM.; m. Judith Phelps; children: Harold R. III, Louise Holland. BA, Rice U., 1952; LLB, U. Tex., 1955. Assoc. Bracewell & Patterson, Houston, 1957-61, ptnr., 1961-91; judge U.S. Ct. of Appeals (5th cir.), HOUSTON, 1991—. Area chmn. Bush Congl. Campaign, Houston, 1968; Harris County vice chmn. Tower Senate Campaign, Houston, 1972, Ford/Dale Campaign, 1976; Harris County chmn. Loeffler for Gov. Primary, 1986; Harris County co-chmn. Reagan/Bush Campaign, 1980, 84; Tex. State chmn. Bush for Pres. Primary, 1979-80, Tex. vice chmn., 1988; mem. platform group Bush for Pres., Washington, 1988; rsch. analyst Bush/Quayle Campaign, 1988; del. Rep. State Conv., Houston, 1968; dist. del. at large Rep. Nat. Conv., Houston, 1980, alternate del. at large, 1984, 88; vestryman St. Martin's Episcopal Ch., Houston, 1968-72; mem. exec. bd. Episcopal Diocese Tex., 1983-86, chmn. planning com., 1985-88, del. Diocesan Conv., 1976-88; chmn. bd. Tex. Bill Rights Found., Houston, 1969-70; bd. dirs. Amigos de las Americas, 1974-76; pres. Tanglewood Homeowners Assn., 1987. Sgt. U.S. Army, 1955-57. Fellow Tex. Bar Assn. (life); mem. ABA, Internat. Bar Assn., Am. Judicature Soc., Maritime Law Assn. U.S., Houston Bar Assn. (bd. dirs. 1969-71, 1st v.p. 1972-73), Tex. Assn. Def. Counsel (bd. dirs. 1972-74), The Houston Club, The Houstonian Club. Avocations: fishing, waterskiing. Office: US Courthouse 515 Rusk St Ste 12015 Houston TX 77002-2605*

**DEMOSS, JON W.,** insurance company executive, lawyer; b. Kewanee, Ill., Aug. 9, 1947; s. Wendell and Virginia Beth DeMoss; m. Eleanor T. Thornley, Aug. 9, 1969; 1 child, Marc Alain. BS, U. Ill., 1969, JD, 1972. Bar: Ill. 1972, U.S. Dist. Ct. (cen. dist.) Ill. 1977, U.S. Supreme Ct. 1978, U.S. dist. Ct. (no. dist., trial bar) Ill. 1983. In house counsel Assn. Ill. Electric Coop., Springfield, 1972-74; registered lobbyist Ill. Gen. Assembly, Springfield, 1972-74; asst. dir. Ill. Inst. for CLE, Springfield, 1974-85; exec. dir. Ill. State Bar Assn., 1986-94; pres., CEO ISBA Mut. Ins. Co., Chgo., 1994—. Bd. dirs. Springfield Symphony Orch., 1982-87, Ill. Inst. for CLE, 1986-89, Nat. Assn. of Bar Related Ins. Cos., 1989, pres., elect., 1998-99; bd. dirs. Lawyers Reins. Co., 1997—; bd. visitors John Marshall Law Sch., 1990—. Capt. U.S. Army, 1972. Fellow Am. Bar Found. (life, co-chmn. projects to prepare Appellate Handbook 1978, 90), Ill. Bar Found. (bd. dirs. 1983-85); mem. ABA (mem. ho. of dels. 1979-85, 89, 91, 93-94), Nat. Conf. Bar Pres., Ill. State Bar Assn. (pres. 1984-85, bd. govs. 1975-85, chmn. com. on scope and correlation of work 1982-83, chmn. budget com. 1983-85, chmn. legis. com. 1983-84, 85, chmn. com. on merit selection of judges 1977, del. long-range planning conf. 1972, 78, liaison to numerous coms. and sects.), Chgo. Bar Assn., Lake County Bar Assn., U. Ill. Coll. Dean's Club, La Chaine des Rotisseurs (Chgo.), Ordre Mondial des Gourmet Degustateurs (Chgo.), Les Gourmets (Chgo.). Home: 180 Norwich Ct Lake Bluff IL 60044-1914 Office: ISBA Mutual Ins Co First National Plaza 20 S Clark St Ste 910 Chicago IL 60603-1898

**DEMPSEY, BERNARD HAYDEN, JR.,** lawyer; b. Evanston, Ill., Mar. 29, 1942; s. Bernard H. and Margaret C. (Gallagher) D.; m. Cynthia T. Dempsey; children: Bernard H. III, Matthew B., Kathleen N., Rose Maureen G., Alexandra C., Anastasia M. BS, Coll. Holy Cross, 1964; JD, Georgetown U., 1967. Bar: Fla. 1968, D.C. 1979. Law clk. to chief judge U.S. Dist. Ct. (mid. dist.) Fla., 1967-69; asst. U.S. Atty. Mid. Dist. Fla., 1969-73; pvt. practice, 1973—; lectr. trial tactics seminars. Contbr. articles to legal jours. Recipient John Marshall award U.S. Dept. Justice, 1972, U.S. Atty's Outstanding Performance award 1970, 71, 72, 73. Mem. ABA, ATLA, NACDL, Fla. Bar Assn., Am. Judicature Soc., Fla. Bar Found., Univ. Club (Orlando), Winter Park (Fla.) Racquet Club, Delta Theta Pi. Republican. Roman Catholic. Federal civil litigation, State civil litigation, Criminal. Office: Dempsey & Sasso NationsBank Ctr 390 N Orange Ave Ste 2700 Orlando FL 32801-1643

**DEMPSEY, EDWARD JOSEPH,** lawyer; b. Lynn, Mass., Mar. 13, 1943; s. Timothy Finbar and Christine Margaret (Callahan) D.; m. Eileen Margaret McManus, Apr. 15, 1967; children: Kristen A. Stofi, Katherine B. Aydin, Shelagh E., James P. *Grandparents James and Catherine (Naegle) Dempsey having emigrated from Rosscarerry, Ireland and grandparents Matthew and Catherine Callahan having emigrated from Cork, Ireland, Edward Dempsey honored their memory by registering his Irish citizenship* AB, Boston Coll., 1964; JD, Cath. U. Am., 1970. Bar: D.C. 1970, Conn. 1982. Assoc., Arent, Fox, Kintner, Plotkin & Kahn, Washington, 1970-72, Akin, Gump, Strauss, Hauer & Feld, Washington, 1972-75; supervisory trial atty. EEOC, Washington, 1975-79; assoc. Whitman & Ransom, Washington, 1979-81, Farmer, Wells, McGuinn & Sibal, Washington, 1981-82; ptnr. Farmer, Wells, Sibal & Dempsey, Washington and Hartford, Conn., 1983-84; dir. indsl. relations and labor counsel United Technologies Corp., Hartford, 1985—. Capt. USNR (ret.). Mem. ABA. *Edward Dempsey was editor-in-chief of the Catholic University Law Review from 1969-1970. He represented Sikorsky Aircraft Corporation before the Connecticut Supreme Court in the cases Parsons v. Sikorsky Aircraft and Cotto v. Sikorsky Aircraft. Before retiring from the U.S. Naval Reserve in 1991, he had served as Commanding Officer-Reserve Crew (SELRPS Coordinator) U.S.S. Steinaker (DD-863) and at the Naval War College, Newport, R.I.* Labor, Civil rights, Federal civil litigation. Office: United Techs Bldg Hartford CT 06101

**DEMURO, PAUL ROBERT,** lawyer; b. Aberdeen, Md., Mar. 21, 1954; s. Paul Robert and Amelia C. DeMuro; m. Susan Taylor, May 26, 1990; children: Melissa Taylor, Natalie Lauren, Alanna Leigh. BA summa cum laude, U. Md., 1976; JD, Washington U., 1979; MBA, U. Calif., Berkeley, 1986. Bar: Md. 1979, U.S. Dist. Ct. Md. 1979, D.C. 1980, U.S. Dist. Ct. D.C. 1980, U.S. Dist. Ct. (ea. dist.) Calif. 1986, U.S. Ct. Appeals (4th cir.) 1981, U.S. Tax Ct. 1981, Calif. 1982, U.S. Dist. Ct. (no. dist.) Calif. 1982; CPA, Md. Assoc. Ober, Grimes & Shriver, Balt., 1979-82; ptnr. Carpenter et al, San Francisco, 1982-89, McCutchen, Doyle, Brown & Enerson, San Francisco, 1989-93, Latham & Watkins, San Francisco, 1993—; bd. dirs. FMA Learning Solutions Inc. Author: The Financial Managers Guide to Managed Care and Integrated Delivery Systems, 1995, The Fundamentals of Managed Care and Network Development, 1999; co-author: Health Care Mergers and Acquisitions: The Transactional Perspective, 1996, Health Care Executives' Guide to Fraud and Abuse, 1998; editor, contbg. author Integrated Delivery Systems, 1994; article and book rev. editor Washington U. Law Qrtly., St. Louis, 1975-76. Mem. San Francisco Mus. Modern Art, 1985—; bd. dirs sch. health Calif. State U., 1992—. Fellow Healthcare Fin. Mgmt. Assn. (bd. dirs. No. Calif. chpt. 1990-93, 99—, sec. 1999—, nat. principles and practices bd. 1992-95, vice chair 1993-95, nat. bd. dirs. 1995-97, exec. com. 1996-97, chair compliance officers forum adv. coun. 1998—); mem. ABA (health law sect., chair transactional and bus. health care interest group 1998—), L.A. County Bar Assn. (health law sect.), Calif. Bar Assn., San Francisco Bar Assn., AICPA, Am. Health Lawyers Assn. (fraud and abuse and self-referral substantive law com. 1998—, task force on best practices in advising clients), The IPA Assn. Am. (mem. legal adv. coun. 1996—), Med. Group Mgmt. Assn. Republican. Health, Mergers and acquisitions, Administrative and regulatory. Office: Latham & Watkins 505 Montgomery St Ste 1900 San Francisco CA 94111-2552

**DEMUTH, ALAN CORNELIUS,** lawyer; b. Boulder, Colo., Apr. 29, 1935; s. Laurence Wheeler and Eugenia Augusta (Roach) DeM.; m. Susan McDermott; children: Scott Lewis, Evan Dale, Joel Millard. BA in Econs. & Gen. Studies magna cum laude, U. Colo., 1958, LLB, 1961. Bar: Colo. 1961, U.S. Dist. Ct. Colo. 1961, U.S. Ct. Appeals (10th cir.) 1962. Assoc. Akolt, Turnquist, Shepherd & Dick, Denver, 1961-68; ptnr. DeMuth & DeMuth, Denver, 1968—. Conf. atty. Rocky Mountain Conf. United Ch. of Christ, 1970-95; bd. dirs. Friends of U. Colo. Libr., 1978-86; bd. dirs., sponsor Denver Boys Inc., 1987-93, sec., 1988-89, v.p., 1989-90, pres., 1992-93; bd. dirs. Denver Kids, Inc., 1993—, Children's Ctr. for Arts and Learning, 1995—; mem. bd. advisors Lambuth Family Ctr. of Salvation Army, 1994—, chmn., 1994—; bd. advisors Metro Denver Salvation Army, 1988—, vice chmn. 1994-96. Mem. ABA, Colo. Bar Assn., Denver Bar Assn., Denver Rotary (bd. dirs. 1996-98), Phi Beta Kappa, Sigma Alpha Epsilon, Phi Delta Phi. Republican. Mem. United Ch. of Christ. Real property, Consumer commercial, Bankruptcy. Office: DeMuth & DeMuth 990 S High St Denver CO 80209-4551

**DEMUTH, C. JEANNE,** lawyer. JD, Kans. U., 1983. Bar: Kans. 1983, Calif. 1985, Tex. 1989; CPA, Kans. Taxation, general, Bankruptcy, Personal income taxation. Home: 3503B Cedar Knolls Dr Kingwood TX 77339-2468

**DEMUTH, LAURENCE WHEELER, JR.,** lawyer, utility company executive; b. Boulder, Colo., Nov. 22; s. Laurence Wheeler and Eugenia Augusta (Roach) DeM.; m. Paula Phipps, Mar. 7, 1987; children: Debra Lynn, Laurence Wheeler III, Brant Hill. AB, U. Colo., 1951, LLB, 1953. Gen. atty. Mountain State Telephone and Telegraph Co., Denver, 1968, v.p., gen. counsel, 1968-84, sec., 1974-84; exec. v.p., gen. counsel, sec. U.S. West, Inc., Englewood, Colo., 1984-92; ret. U.S. West, Inc., Englewood, 1992. Dist. capt. Rep. Precinct Com., 1957-70' trustee Lakewood (Colo.) Presbyn. Ch., 1965-68; bd. dirs. Colo. Epilepsy Assn., 1973-79; bd. litigation Mountain States Legal Found., 1980-89; Colo. Commr. on Uniform State of Laws, 1997—. Mem. ABA, Colo. Bar Assn. (chmn. ethics com. 1973-74, bd. govs., fellow found.), Denver Bar Assn., Am. Judicature Soc., Colo. Assn. Corp. Counsel (pres.), Order of Coif, Phi Beta Kappa, Pi Gamma Mu. Clubs: University, Metropolitan. Communications, General corporate. Office: US West Inc 9785 S Maroon Cir Ste 210 Englewood CO 80112-5918

**DENARO, CHARLES THOMAS,** lawyer; b. Phila., Aug. 16, 1953; s. Anthony Carmen and Alfia Dorothy (Nucifora) D.; m. Carol Anne Lewis, Apr. 24, 1983; children: Kristin Anne, Samantha, Kandace. BA, Villanova U., 1975, JD, 1978. Bar: Pa. 1978. Gen. counsel Pilgrim Life Ins. Co., Folcroft, Pa., 1979-87; exec. v.p. Pilgrim Ins. Group, Folcroft, 1987-93; corp. counsel Corp. Life Ins. Co., West Chester, Pa., 1993-94; sec., assoc. gen. counsel Reliance Standard Life Ins. Co., Phila., 1995—; bd. dirs. Pilgrim Life Ins. Co., Folcroft, Delphi Project Found. Mem. ABA, Pa. Bar Assn., Assn. Trial Lawyers Am. Republican. Roman Catholic. General corporate, Insurance, Pension, profit-sharing, and employee benefits.

**DENARO, GREGORY,** lawyer; b. Rochester, N.Y., Dec. 10, 1954; m. Nancy Cardiff; children: Adrienne, Gregory, Madeline. BA, U. Rochester, 1976; JD, U. Miami, 1979. Bar: Fla. 1979, U.S. Dist. Ct. (so. dist.) Fla. 1979, U.S. Ct. Appeals (5th and 11th cirs.) 1981, U.S. Supreme Ct. 1984, N.Y. 1985, U.S. Dist. Ct. (mid. dist.) Fla. 1986, U.S. Ct. Appeals (D.C. cir.) 1989, U.S. Dist. Ct. (we. dist.) Tex. 1990, U.S. Ct. Appeals (4th cir.) 1992. Pub. defender Dade County, Miami, Fla., 1979-82; sr. ptnr. Gregory C. Denaro P.A., Miami, 1982—; advisor nat. mock trial U. Miami Law Sch., 1984—. Mem. ABA (criminal law sect.), Dade County Bar Assn., Assn. Trial Attys., Nat. Assn. Criminal Def. Lawyers, Fla. Assn. Criminal Def. Lawyers (bd. dirs. 1997, 98). Criminal. Office: Coconut Grove Bank Bldg 2701 S Bayshore Dr Ste 605 Coconut Grove FL 33133-5360

**DENCKER, LESTER J.,** lawyer; b. Milw., Apr. 27, 1914; s. Charles W. and Barbara M. (Haubert) D.; m. Cecilia F. Wellington, June 17, 1944. PhB, Marquette U., 1938, JD, 1940. Bar: Wis. 1940, U.S. Dist. Ct. (ea. and we. dists.) Wis. 1940, U.S. Supreme Ct. 1954, U.S. Ct. Appeals (7th cir.) 1973. Pvt. practice, Milw.; treas. Milw. Bar Found. Pres. adv. coun. to mayor City of Milw., 1954, sec. mcpl. mass transp. com., 1954-55, mem. July 4 com., 1957-62; chmn. bd. trustees Milwaukee County War Meml. Corp., 1989; pres. Upper Fond du Lac Capitol Drive Advancement Assn., 1958-60. Recipient Disting. Pub. Svc. award Milwaukee County Bd. Suprs., 1994, Standing Ovation award Greater Milw. Conv. and Visitors Bur., 1997. Mem. ABA, Am. Judicature Soc., State Bar Assn. Wis. (emeritus), Milw. Bar Assn. (chmn. spkrs. bur. 1957-59, memls. com. 1964-94, Spl. Svc. award 1998), St. Thomas More Lawyers Soc. (pres. 1974), CBI Vets. Assn. (co-founder, 1st nat. comdr. 1948-49), Marquette U. Law Alumni Assn. (pres. 1953-54), VFW (life), Elks. (exalted ruler Milw. 1965), Lions (pres. Milw. 1954). Probate, Real property, Estate taxation. Office: 9205 W Center St Ste 202 Milwaukee WI 53222-4548

**DENECKE, DAVID ROCKEY,** corporate and real estate lawyer; b. Portland, Oreg., May 31, 1949; s Arno Harry and Selma Jane (Rockey) D.; m. Gail Neuburg, June 14, 1974; children: Christl Marcelle, Samantha Jane. Student, Oreg. State U., 1967-69, U. Pavia, Italy, 1969-70; BA in History, U. Oreg., 1971; LLB, Lewis and Clark U., 1978. Bar: Oreg. 1978, U.S. Dist. Ct. Oreg. 1980, U.S. Ct. Appeals (9th cir.) 1981, U.S. Dist. Ct. Calif. 1994. Law clk. to Hon. Charles CCrookham U.S. Dist. Ct., Portland, 1975-76; law clk. to presiding justice Multnomah County Cir. Ct., Portland, 1977-78; assoc. Thompson, Adams, Beaverton, Oreg., 1978-82; asst. gen. counsel, asst. v.p., asst. sec. Amfac Inc., Beaverton, 1982-87, v.p., dep. gen. counsel, 1988—. bd. dirs. N.W. Portland Neighborhood Assn., pres. Hillside Neighborhood Assn.; mem. City of Portland Towing Bd., 1978-80; adv. com. Dept. of Transp., City of Portland; ecotrust adv. com. Martindale Hubbel AV rating. Mem. ABA, Oreg. Bar Assn. (continuing legal edn. com. 1980-81, fee arbitration panel 198-86), Multnomah and Washington County Bar Assn., Am. Frozen Food Inst. (chmn. atty's com.), Am. Judicature Soc. Mergers and acquisitions, Real property, Trademark and copyright. Office: 1150 Pioneer Twr Portland OR 97204

**DENES, RICHARD FORD,** lawyer; b. Newark, Feb. 3, 1955; s. Meyer Jacob and Rosalind (Buchsbaum) D.; m. Laura Ann Von Thron, Nov. 20, 1977; children: Matthew, Amanda. BS, Rider Coll., 1976; JD, Seton Hall U., 1980. Bar: N.J. 1980, U.S. Dist. Ct. N.J. 1980, U.S. Supreme Ct. 1984. Supervising auditor Prudential Ins. Co., Newark, 1976-78; auditor Gen. Services Adminstrn., N.Y.C., 1978-80; asst. prosecutor Hudson County, Jersey City, 1980-85; assoc. Citrino, DiBiasi and Katchen, Nutley, N.J., 1985-86; ptnr. DiBiasi, Ruddy and Denes, Nutley, 1986-87; sole practice Fairfield, N.J., 1988—; mcpl. prosecutor Township of Caldwell, N.J., 1991-94; hearing officer Rent Leveling Office, Orange, N.J., 1987-89; adj. instr. Jersey City State Coll., 1985-87, Upsala Coll., East Orange, N.J., 1987-89, Caldwell (N.J.) Coll., 1990; police instr. Jersey City Police Acad., 1983-86. Author: (with others) Criminal Procedure in New Jersey, 1984; contbr. mag. articles on security mgmt. Mem. Essex County Bar Assn., Cedar Grove Jaycees (Jaycee of the Yr. 1990), Omicron Delta Kappa. Criminal, Personal injury, General civil litigation. Home: 7 Robin Ln Cedar Grove NJ 07009-1806 Office: Fairfield Commons 271 Rte 46 W Ste F207 Fairfield NJ 07004-2418

**DENGER, MICHAEL L.,** lawyer; b. Davenport, Iowa, Sept. 8, 1945; s. Ralph Henry and Bernice Marie (Cederberg) D.; m. Mary Elizabeth Colbert, Aug. 30, 1969; children: Lorna Marie, Mary Catherine, Rachel Anne. BS with highest distinction, Northwestern U., 1967; JD cum laude, Harvard U., 1970. Bar: D.C. 1970, U.S. Ct. Appeals (D.C. cir.) 1971, U.S. Supreme Ct. 1978. Assoc. atty. Sutherland, Asbill & Brennan, Washington, 1970-76, ptnr., 1976-92; ptnr. Gibson, Dunn & Crutcher LLP, Washington, 1992—; speaker on antitrust, trade regulation numerous groups. Bd. editors Antitrust Report, 1992—; contbr. articles to profl. jours. Mem. nat. adv. coun. Northwestern U. Sch. Speech, Evanston, Ill., 1990—. 2d lt. USAR, 1970. Mem. ABA (vice chair antitrust law sect. 1985-86, sec. antitrust law sect. 1988-91, chair-elect antitrust law sect. 1991-92, chair antitrust law sect. 1992-93, chair edit. bd. antitrust sect. Federal and State Price Discrimination Law 1991, co-editor in chief antitrust sect. State Antitrust Practice and Statutes 3 vols. 1990, vice chair edit. bd. antitrust sect. Antitrust Law Devels. 2d edit. 1984), Columbia Country Club (Chevy Chase, Md.). Republican. Roman Catholic. Avocations: tennis, collecting military miniatures, military history, bridge. Antitrust, Federal civil litigation. Home: 5802 Kirkside Dr Chevy Chase MD 20815-7118 Office: Gibson Dunn & Crutcher LLP 1050 Connecticut Ave NW Ste 900 Washington DC 20036-5306

**DENHAM, VERNON ROBERT, JR.,** lawyer; b. Atlanta, Apr. 18, 1948; s. Vernon Robert and Sara Elizabeth (Robertson) D.; m. Susan Elizabeth Willis, Mar. 19, 1974; children: Whitney Willis, Tyler Willis. Student, Rensselaer Poly. Inst., 1966-68; BSE, U. Mich., 1970, MSE, 1972; JD with honors, U. Fla., 1979. Bar: Fla. 1979, Ga. 1979, U.S. Dist. Ct. (no. dist.) Ga. 1979, U.S. Ct. Appeals (11th cir.) 1981. Engr. Ford Motor Co., Dearborn, Mich., 1972-73; assoc. Powell, Goldstein, Frazer & Murphy, Atlanta, 1979-86, ptnr., 1986—; mem. case notes com. U.S. Dist. Ct. (no. dist.) Ga., Atlanta, 1980-86, mem. magistrate merit selection panel, 1983. Lt. USNR, 1973-76. Mem. ABA (natural resources law sect., litigation sec., corp. and bus. sect.), Am. Chem. Soc., Internat. Soc. Regulatory Toxicology and Pharmacology, Fla. Bar (gen. practice trial sect., environ. and land use law sect.), State Bar Ga. (litigation and environ. sects.), Atlanta Bar Assn. (litigation, environ. sects., vice chair environ. sect. 1992-93, chair 1993-94), Order of Coif, Tau Beta Pi. General civil litigation, Environmental, Toxic tort. Home: 1433 Sheridan Walk NE Atlanta GA 30324-3253 Office: Powell Goldstein Frazer & Murphy 191 Peachtree St NE Fl 16 Atlanta GA 30303-1740

**DENIRO, MARY LYN S.,** lawyer; b. Salt Lake City, Feb. 15, 1959; d. Ted Gordon and Marilyn Valoe (Butcher) Symes; m. Dan DeNiro. BS magna cum laude, U. Utah, 1980; JD magna cum laude, Fordham U., 1992. Bar: N.Y. 1993. Exec. asst. to chmn. ASARCO Inc., N.Y.C., 1983-91, legal asst., 1991-92; jud. clk. U.S. Dist. Ct. (ea. dist.) N.Y., Bklyn., 1992-93; assoc. Davis, Polk & Wardwell, N.Y.C., 1993—. Mem. Assn. of Bar of City of N.Y., Order of Coif, Phi Kappa Phi, Phi Eta Sigma. Office: Davis Polk & Wardwell 450 Lexington Ave New York NY 10017-3911

**DENISON, MARY BONEY,** lawyer; b. Wilmington, N.C., June 8, 1956; d. Leslie Norwood Jr. and Lillian (Bellamy) Boney; children: Mary Catesby Bellamy, James Wholley IV. AB, Duke U., 1978; JD, U. N.C., 1981. Bar: N.Y. 1982, U.S. Dist. Ct. (so. and ea. dists.) N.Y. 1983, U.S. Ct. Appeals (2d cir.) 1984, D.C. 1988, U.S. Dist. Ct. D.C. 1988, U.S. Ct. Appeals (D.C. cir.) 1988. Assoc. Law Office William G. Kaelin, N.Y.C., 1981-82, Smith, Steibel, Alexander & Saskor, N.Y.C., 1982-86; assoc. Graham & James, Washington, 1986-91, ptnr., 1992-96; ptnr. Farkas & Manelli PLLC, Washington, 1996—. Vol. Legal Aid Soc., N.Y.C., 1983-86. Mem. ABA, Internat. Trademark Assn. (subcom. chair 1998-00), The French Am. C. of C. of Washington (treas. 1991-97). Democrat. Episcopalian. General civil litigation, Private international, Trademark and copyright. Office: Farkas & Manelli PLLC 2000 M St NW Ste 700 Washington DC 20036-3364

**DENIUS, FRANKLIN WOFFORD,** lawyer; b. Athens, Tex., Jan. 4, 1925; s. S.F. and Frances (Cain) D.; m. Charmaine Hooper, Nov. 19, 1949; children: Frank Wofford, Charmaine. B.B.A., LL.B., U. Tex. Bar: Tex. 1949. Pvt. practice Austin, 1949—; past pres., chief exec. officer, chmn. bd., dir. So. Union Co.; past legal counsel Austin Better Bus. Bur.; dir., chmn. bd. emeritus So. Union Co., 1991—; advt. dir. Chase Bank Tex., Austin. Chmn. spl. schs. div. United Fund, 1960, Pacesetters div., 1961, Schs. div., 1964; 1st v.p. United Fund; chmn. steering com. sch. bond campaign, past trustee Austin Ind. Sch. Dist., 1964; past pres. Young Men's Bus. League Austin; past pres., exec. council Austin Ex-Students Assn. U. Tex.; past co-chmn. LBJ U Tex. Library Found.; mem. chancellor's council, pres.'s assos. U. Tex.; bd. dirs. Tex. Research League; advisory trustee Schreiner Coll.; chmn. capital planning com. Longhorn Adv. Coun., U. Tex., mem. Longhorn Legacy Com; chmn. Austin Leadership Coun., U. Tex. Devel. Office; mem. U. Tex. Devel. bd. Decorated Silver Star medal with 3 oak leaf clusters, Purple Heart; recipient Outstanding Young Man of Austin award Jr. C. of C., 1959; named Disting. Alumnus U. Tex. Ex-Students Assn., 1991. Mem. ABA, Tex. Bar Assn., Travis County Bar Assn., Tex. Philos. Soc., Longhorn Club (past pres.), West Austin Optimists (past dir.), Headliners (pres., sec. bd. trustees, exec. com.), Masons. Presbyterian (deacon, elder). Home: 3703 Meadowbank Dr Austin TX 78703-1025 Office: Chase Bank Bldg 700 Lavaca St Ste 700 Austin TX 78701-3102

**DENMARK, WILLIAM ADAM,** lawyer; b. N.Y.C., July 30, 1957; s. Jerome and Frieda (Pollack) D.; m. Carol J. Sack, Apr. 20, 1986; children: Andrea K., Julie E. AB, Cornell U., 1979; JD, U. Pa., 1982. Bar: Pa. 1982, U.S. Dist. Ct. (ea. dist.) Pa. 1982. Assoc. Ballard, Spahr, Andrews & Ingersoll, Phila., 1982-86; assoc. Jacoby Donner & Jacoby, P.C., Phila., 1986-89, shareholder, 1989—. Contbr. articles to profl. jours. Mem. ABA,

Phila. Bar Assn. (vice chair mergers and acquisitions com. bus. law sect. 1994-95, constrn. law and comml. leases com. real property sect.), Del. Valley Soc. Assn. Execs., Phi Beta Kappa. Avocations: jogging, tennis, reading. Real property, Contracts commercial, Estate planning. Office: Jacoby Donner PC 1515 Market St Ste 2000 Philadelphia PA 19102-1920

**DENNEEN, JOHN PAUL,** lawyer; b. N.Y.C., Aug. 18, 1940; s. John Thomas Denneen and Pauline Jane Ludlow; m. Mary Veronica Murphy, July 3, 1965; children: John Edward, Thomas Michael, James Patrick, Robert Andrew, Daniel Joseph, Mary Elizabeth. BS, Fordham U., 1963; JD, Columbia U., 1966. Bar: N.Y. 1966, U.S. Ct. Appeals (2d cir.) 1974, U.S. Dist. Ct. (so. and ea. dists.) N.Y. 1975, Mo. 1987. Assoc. Seward & Kissel, N.Y.C., 1966-75; sr. v.p., gen counsel, sec. GK Techs., Inc., Greenwich, Conn., 1975-83; exec. v.p., gen. counsel, sec. Chromalloy Am. Corp., St. Louis, 1983-87; ptnr. Bryan Cave LLP, St. Louis, 1987-99, of counsel, 1999—; exec. v.p. corp. devel. and legal affairs Gabriel Comms., Inc., St. Louis, 1999—. Mem. ABA, Internat. Bar Assn., N.Y. State Bar Assn., N.Y.C. Bar Assn., Bar Assn. Met. St. Louis. Mergers and acquisitions, Securities, Communications. Office: Gabriel Comms Inc 16090 Swingley Ridge Rd Ste 500 Chesterfield MO 63017-6029

**DENNIN, TIMOTHY J.,** lawyer; b. Dearborn, Mich., May 18, 1956; s. William Edward and Clare S. (Syron) D. BA, Coll. Holy Cross, 1978; JD, St. John's U., 1983. Bar: Mass. 1983, N.Y. 1984. Asst. dist. atty. Dist. Atty.'s Office, Mineola, N.Y., 1983-87; staff atty. divsn. enforcement U.S. Securities Exch., Washington, 1987-89; ptnr. Timothy J. Dennin, P.C., N.Y.C., 1990—; faculty mem. practicing law Inst. on Securities Arbitration. Contbr. articles to profl. jours. Sponsor Rotary Club, L.I., 1994—. Mem. Assn. Bar City N.Y. (securities and commodities law panel), Pub. Investors Arbitration Bar Assn. Republican. Roman Catholic. Avocations: reading, running, fishing. Securities.

**DENNIS, ANDRE L.,** lawyer; b. Burton-on-Trent, Eng., May 15, 1943; came to U.S., 1946; m. Julie B. Carpenter; 1 child, Matthew A. BA, Cheyney U., 1966; JD, Howard U., 1969, LLD, 1993. Bar: Pa. 1970, D.C. 1969, U.S. Dist. Ct. (ea. dist.) Pa. 1970, U.S. Ct. Appeals (3d cir.) 1977, U.S. Supreme Ct. 1990. Ptnr. Stradley, Ronon, Stevens & Young LLP, Phila., 1969—. Bd. dirs. Phila. Facilities Mgmt. Corp., 1996-97, Vols. for the Indigent Program, Phila., 1988-95. Recipient Judge William H. Hastie award NAACP Legal Def. and Ednl. Fund, Inc., 1995, Martin Luther King Jr. Humanities award Salem Bapt. Ch., 1993; Hon. fellow U. Pa. Law Sch., 1999. Mem. ABA (sect. on litig. coun. 1996—, Pro Bono Publico award 1994), Pa. Bar Assn. (ho. of dels. 1988—), Am. Coll. Trial Lawyers, Am. Law Inst., Nat. Bar Assn., Phila. Bar Assn. (chancellor 1993), Am. Inns of Ct. Constitutional, Contracts commercial. Office: 2600 One Commerce St 2005 Market St Philadelphia PA 19103-7042

**DENNIS, ANTHONY JAMES,** lawyer; b. Manchester, Conn., Feb. 11, 1963; s. Anthony James and Barbara Frances D. BA cum laude, Tufts U., 1985; JD, Northwestern U., Chgo., 1988. Bar: Conn. 1988, U.S. Dist. Ct. Conn. 1988, D.C. 1989. Assoc. Robinson & Cole, Hartford, Conn., 1988-89; atty. Aetna, Inc., Hartford, 1989-92, counsel, 1992—; TV and radio talk show guest. Author: The Rise of the Islamic Empire and the Threat to the West, 1996; co-author: Healthcare Antitrust: Strategies for Changing Provider Organizations, 1994; contbr. articles to profl. jours. Mem. Conn. Bar Assn. (subcom. chmn. 1990-93, exec. com. 1990—, com. chmn. 1990—, treas. 1993-94, vice-chmn. 1994-95, chmn. 1995—), D.C. Bar Assn., Nat. Health Lawyers Assn., Wadsworth Atheneum, KC (past grand knight). Antitrust, General corporate, Health. Home: PO Box 837 South Windsor CT 06074-0837 Office: Aetna Inc Hartford CT 06156-0001

**DENNIS, BENJAMIN FRANKLIN, III,** lawyer, aerospace engineer; b. N.Y.C., June 1, 1942; s. Benjamin Franklin and Margaret Mary (Duggan) Dennis; m. Marilyn Ruth Scully, Aug. 14, 1971; children—Laura Meghan, Benjamin Franklin IV. BA magna cum laude, Fairleigh Dickinson U., 1979; JD Georgetown U., 1991. Bar: Md., U.S. Dist. Ct. Md. Missile systems engr. Sperry Gyro, Lake Success, N.Y., 1966-69; computer programmer Litton Sweda ARS, Morristown, N.J., 1970-72; systems designer Digital Computer Controls, Fairfield, N.J., 1972-75; pres., cons. Dennis-Weingarten Assocs., Mt. Freedom, N.J., 1975-84; mgr. software engrng. Conrac/Lear Siegler Avionics, Caldwell, N.J., 1980-82; mgr. engrng. computer services Litton Amecom, College Park, Md., 1984-86; project mgr. FAA/DIA/DOJ programs Data Transformation Corp., Silver Spring, Md., 1986—; pvt. practice law, 1991—. Leader Boy Scouts Am., 1989—, staff dist. tng., 1992—. With U.S. Army, 1963-66. Mem. ABA, Md. Bar Assn., Montgomery County Bar Assn, Am. Inn of Ct. (sec./treas. 1990), Sons of St. Patrick (life), Masons (jr. warden 1991). Roman Catholic. Bankruptcy, Family and matrimonial, Computer. Office: Data Transformation Corp 200 N Adams St Rockville MD 20850-1829

**DENNIS, EDWARD S(PENCER) G(ALE), JR.,** lawyer; b. Salisbury, Md., Jan. 24, 1945; s. Edward Spencer and Virginia (Monroe) D.; m. Lois Juliette Young, Dec. 27, 1969; 1 son, Edward Brookfield. BS, U.S. Mcht. Marine Acad., 1967; LLD, U. Pa., 1973. Bar: Pa. 1973. Law clk. Hon. A. Leon Higginbotham, Jr., U.S. Dist. Ct., Phila., 1973-75; asst. U.S. atty. U.S. Atty. Office, Phila., 1975-80, dep. chief. criminal div., 1978-80; chief narcotic and dangerous drug sect. U.S. Dept. Justice, Washington, 1980-83, asst. atty. gen. criminal div., 1988-90, acting dep. atty. gen., 1989; U.S. atty. Ea. Dist. Pa., Phila., 1983-88; ptnr., co-chair corp. investigations, criminal def. practice Morgan, Lewis & Bockius, Phila., 1990—; adj. prof. Law Sch. U. Pa. Fellow Am. Coll. Trial Lawyers; mem. ABA, Nat. Bar Assn., Phila. Bar Assn., Internat. Soc. Barristers. Federal civil litigation, Criminal. Office: Morgan Lewis & Bockius 1701 Market St Philadelphia PA 19103-2903 also: 1800 M St NW Washington DC 20036-5802

**DENNIS, JAMES LEON,** federal judge; b. Monroe, La., Jan. 9, 1936; s. Jenner Leon and Hope (Taylo) D.; m. Gwen Nicolich; children: Stephen James, Gregory Leon, Mark Taylo, John Timothy. B.S. in Bus. Adminstrn, La. Tech. U., Ruston, 1959; J.D., La. State U., 1962; LL.M., U. Va., 1984. Bar: La. 1962. Assoc. firm Hudson, Potts & Bernstein, Monroe, 1962-65; ptnr. Hudson, Potts & Bernstein, 1965-72; judge 4th Dist. Ct. La. for Morehouse and Ouachita Parishes, 1972-74, La. 2d Circuit Ct. Appeals, 1974-75; assoc. justice La. Supreme Ct., 1975-95; coord. La. Constnl. Revision Commn., 1970-72; del., chmn. judiciary com. La. Constnl. Conv., 1973; judge U.S. Ct. Appeals Fifth Cir., New Orleans, 1995—; Mem. La. Ho. of Reps., 1968-72; chmn. La. Commn. on Bicentennial U.S. Constn. With U.S. Army, 1955-57. Served with AUS, 1955-57. Mem. ABA (com. on appellate practice), La. Bar Assn., 4th Jud. Bar Assn. Methodist. Club: Rotary. Office: US Courthouse 600 Camp St New Orleans LA 70130-3425

**DENNIS, RALPH EMERSON, JR.,** lawyer; b. Marion, Ind., Dec. 19, 1925; s. Ralph Emerson Sr. and Martha Elnora (Bahr) D.; m. Virginia Lea Harter, June 19, 1949 (dec. Oct. 1981); children: Nancy J. Barefoot, Kathleen Ann Polk, Amel Joseph, Mary Elizabeth Saler, Ralph E. III; m. Barbara Grose, May 31, 1985. BS, Dartmouth Coll., 1946; JD, Ind. U., 1950. Bar: Ind. 1950, U.S. Supreme Ct. 1971. Sr. ptnr. Dennis, Cross, Raisor, Jordan & Marshall, P.C., Muncie, Ind., 1956-80, Dennis, Raisor, Wenger & Haynes, P.C., Muncie, 1980-85, Dennis & Wenger, P.C., Muncie, 1985-86, Dennis, Wenger & Orlosky, P.C., Muncie, 1986—; chmn. bd. dirs. Lift-A-Loft Corp., Muncie. City judge, Muncie, 1951-59, city atty., 1964-67; trustee Muncie Community Schs., 1960-63. With USN, 1944-46. Recipient Disting. Service award, Muncie Jaycees, 1959, Good Govt. award, Muncie Jaycees, 1959. Mem. ABA, Ind. Bar Assn. Republican. Lutheran. Club: Del. Country (Muncie). Lodges: Elks, Masons. General corporate, Estate planning, Probate. Home: 411 N Greenbriar Rd Muncie IN 47304-3717 Office: Dennis Wenger & Abrell PC 324 W Jackson St Muncie IN 47305-1625

**DENNIS, THOMAS G.,** lawyer; b. Hartford, Conn., Jan. 16, 1942; s. Vincent William and Theresa Elizabeth D.; m. Carol Ann Higgins, Aug. 24, 1964; children: Thomas G. Jr., Kristen Marie. BA, U. Conn., 1964, JD, 1967. Bar: Conn. 1967, U.S. Dist. Ct. Conn. 1968, U.S. Ct. Appeals (2d cir.) 1969. Law clk. Hon. T. Emmet Clarie U.S. Dist. Ct., Hartford, Conn., 1967-68; ptnr. Updike, Kelly & Spellacy P.C., Hartford, 1968-72; atty. Town of S. Windsor, Conn., 1971-77; lawyer pvt. practice, South Windsor, 1972-80; chief fed. defender Fed. Defender Office Conn. Dist., Hartford, 1980—; incorporator Hartford Hosp., 1980-85; mem. adv. bd. Santoro, Inc., Newington, Conn., 1994—. Mng. editor Conn. Law Rev., 1967, contbr. articles 1966-67. Mem. Conn. Bar Assn. Office: Fed Defender Office 241 Main St Fl 1-2 Hartford CT 06106-5325

**DENNIS, TRICIA L.,** lawyer; b. Shelbyville, Tenn., Nov. 19, 1955; d. Halbert Floyd and Elizabeth (Tittsworth) Dennis; m. Michael F. Mustafa, May 27, 1989; 1 child, Katherine Emel Mustafa. BS, Vanderbilt U., 1978, MS, 1982; JD, U. Tenn., Knoxville, 1987. Bar: Tenn. 1982. Adminstr. cmty. programs Tenn. Dept. Mental Health/Mental Retardation, Nashville, 1982-84; jud. clk. to Hon. Vann Owens and Howell Peoples 11th Jud. Dist. Tenn., Chattanooga, 1987-88; sole practitioner Chattanooga, 1988—; spkr. in field. Precinct chair Hamilton County Dem. Party, Chattanooga, 1986—, mem. exec. com., 1986—; active Tenn. Assn. Retarded Citizens, Tenn. Brain Injury Found. Mem. Chattanooga Trial Lawyers Assn. (bd. dirs. 1988-91, 93-95, sec. 1991-92, prs. 1992-93). Methodist. Personal injury, Workers' compensation, Federal civil litigation. Office: 6400 Lee Hwy Ste 102 Chattanooga TN 37421-2452

**DENNIS, WARREN LEWIS,** lawyer, partner; b. Toms River, N.J., Sept. 24, 1948; s. Joseph Lewis Dennis and Sylvia Cooper Dennis-Kaye; m. Diane Lipton, Dec. 1968; children: Joanne Ivy, Seth Joseph. BS, U. Pa., 1970, JD, 1972. Bar: Pa., 1972, U.S. Dist. Ct. (ea. dist.) Pa., 1972, U.S. Dist. Ct. D.C., 1972, U.S. Ct. Appeals (3d, 4th, 5th, D.C. and Fed. cir.), 1972, U.S. Claims Ct., 1972, U.S. Supreme Ct., 1975; admitted pro hoc vice in various U.S. Dist Cts. Trial atty., Atty. Gen. Honors Program U.S. Dept. Justice, Washington, 1972-77, head fin. discrimination task force, 1974-77; ptnr. Troy, Malin & Pottinger, Washington/L.A., 1977-82; ptnr., D.C. litigation practice head Ballard, Spahr, Andrews and Urgersoll, Wash./Phila., 1982-89; ptnr., head D.C. office Proskauer, Rose LLP, Wash./N.Y.C., 1989—; mem. adv. bd. Practicing Law Inst., chmn. and participant numerous programs and seminars; lectr. Nat. Inst. Consumer Fin. Law, Nat. Law Jour. Press, Am. Coll. Mortgage Attys., Fed. Res. Bank N.Y., Fed. Res. Bd., Mass. Banking Commn., many others; presenter testimony before various Congl. coms. on consumer credit protection and civil rights. Chmn. editl adv. bd. Bank Bailout Litigation News; mem. adv. bd. Comml. Lending Litigation News; mem. editl. dv. bd. Consumer Fin. Svcs. Law Report; mem. litigation adv. bd. Documentary Credit World Inst. Internat. Banking Law and Practice; exec. com. Consumer Fin. Quarterly; co-author monographs for program faculties; contbr. chpts. to books.; co-author (with J. Stanley Pottinger) Federal Regulation of Banking: Redlining and Community Reinvestment, 1980; author (manuals) The Community Reinvestment Act: Strategies for Compliance; A Comprehensive Manual for Managing Officers of Financial Institutions, 1978, Developing Policies and Procedures Under the Federal Home Loan Bank Board's Nondiscrimination Regulations and Guidelines, 1978, The Integrated Compliance Program: A Comprehensive Guide to ECOA, Regulation B and Fair Housing, 1978; contbr. numerous articles to profl. jours.; invited panelist on legal affairs TV programs, including Burden of Proof, CNN Town Meetings, Larry King Live, Frontline with Ted Koppel, CNN's Inside Politics, Fox Morning News. Co-founder Shelter Project, Washington; vice chair Washington region bd. Anti-Defamation League, chair devel. com., mem. task force on black-jewish relationships, nat. Anti-Defamation League; bd. dirs. Jewish Cmty. Ctr. Greater Washington, 1995-97; no. Va. Zamler, Nat. Yiddish Book Ctr.; pro bono litigant, NAACP Legal Def. Fund, Ms. Found., Anti-Defamation League; chair bus. adv. bd. of 501(c)(3) entitles pub. Bibl. Archeology Rev., Bible Rev., Moment Mag., Archeol. Odyssey. Mem. ABA (sects. on litigation, corps., banking and bus. law; mem. com. on consumer fin. svcs., former co-chair litigation subcom.), Am. Trial Lawyers Assn., Fed. Bar Assn. Bar Assn. D.C., Pa. Bar Assn., Comml. Bar Assn. London (N.Am. hon. com.), B'nai B'rith (nat. commr.). Fax: 703-356-5344, 202-416-6856. E-mail: wdennis@proskauer.com. Federal civil litigation, Banking, Administrative and regulatory. Office: 1233 20th St NW Ste 800 Washington DC 20036-2377

**DENNISON, DONALD LEE,** lawyer; b. Dec. 5, 1932; s. Robert Irving and Hannah W. Dennison; m. Tina L. Dennison, Feb. 12, 1955; children: Scott A., Carol R., David R. BSME, Carnegie Inst. Tech., Pitts., 1955; JD, George Washington U., 1961. Bar: Va. 1969, U.S. Supreme Ct. 1965, U.S. Ct. Appeals (fed. cir.) 1969, Md. 1968, D.C. 1962, U.S. Ct. Appeals (4th cir.) 1970. Examiner U.S. Patent Office, Washington, 1957-60; ptnr. Dennison & Dennison, Washington, 1960-66, Dennison, Meserole, Pollack & Scheiner, Arlington, Va., 1966-98, Dennison, Meserole, Scheiner & Schultz, 1999—. Pres. Met. Washington Soccer Referees Assn., 1980-83. 1st lt. U.S. Army, 1954-57. Mem. Internat. Trademark Assn., European Cmty. Trademark Assn. Republican. Patent, Trademark and copyright, Computer. Home: 11209 Farmland Dr North Bethesda MD 20852-4521 Office: Dennison Meserole Scheiner & Schultz 1745 Jefferson Davis Hwy Arlington VA 22202-3402

**DENNISTON, BRACKETT BADGER, III,** lawyer; b. Oak Park, Ill., July 23, 1947; s. Brackett Badger Jr. and Frances Ann (Jones) D.; m. Kathleen Foley, Aug. 2, 1975; children: Alexandra, Brackett Badger IV, Elizabeth. AB, Kenyon Coll., 1969; JD, Harvard U., 1973. Bar: Mass. 1974, U.S. Dist. Ct. Mass. 1975, U.S. Dist. Ct. (we. dist.) Tex. 1987, U.S. Ct. Appeals (1st cir.) 1975, U.S. Ct. Appeals (D.C. cir.) 1976, U.S. Ct. Appeals (7th cir.) 1978, U.S. Ct. Appeals (10th cir.) 1981, U.S. Supreme Ct. 1981. Law clk. to judge U.S. Ct. Appeals for 9th Cir., Honolulu, 1973-74; assoc. Goodwin, Procter & Hoar, Boston, 1974-81, ptnr., 1981-82, 86-93, mem. exec. com., 1990-93; chief major frauds unit U.S. Atty.'s Office, Boston, 1982-86; chief legal counsel Gov. of Mass., Boston, 1993-96; v.p., sr. counsel litigation GE, Fairfield, Conn., 1996—. Class chmn. Kenyon Coll., Gambier, Ohio, 1979-90; mem. Duxbury (Mass.) Zoning Bd. Appeals, 1980-92, chmn., 1984-90. Recipient Dir.'s award for superior achievement U.S. Dept. Justice, 1986. Mem. Mass. Bar Assn. (chmn. coun. jud. adminstrn. sect. 1989-90, jud. adminstrv. coun. 1987-90, 95-96, criminal justice sect. 1986—, litig. sect. 1988—). General civil litigation, Securities, Criminal. Office: GE Co 3137 Easton Tpke Fairfield CT 06432-1008

**DENNISTON, JOHN ALEXANDER,** lawyer; b. Evanston, Ill., Feb. 27, 1958; s. John Lauren and Rose Mary Denniston; m. Dena Louise Lyon, May 27, 1989; children: Lauren Christine, Kathleen Taylor. BA, U. Mich., 1980, JD, 1983. Bar: Calif. 1983. Assoc. Brobeck, Phleger & Harrison, San Francisco, Palo Alto, Calif., 1983-90; ptnr. Brobeck, Phleger & Harrison, Palo Alto and San Diego, 1990—; bd. dirs. San Diego Venture Group, 1996—. General corporate, Intellectual property, Securities. Office: Brobeck Phleger & Harrison 550 W C St San Diego CA 92101-3540

**DENNY, COLLINS, III,** lawyer; b. Richmond, Va., Dec. 5, 1933; s. Collins Jr. and Rebecca (Miller) D.; m. Anne Carples, June 28, 1957; children: Collins IV, William R., Katharine M. AB, Princeton U., 1956; LLB, U. Va., 1961. Bar: Va. 1961, U.S. Dist. Ct. (ea. dist.) Va. 1962, U.S. Ct. Appeals (4th cir.) 1962. U.S. Tax Ct. 1971, U.S. Ct. Claims 1976. Assoc. Denny, Valentine & Davenport, Richmond, 1961-67; ptnr. Mays & Valentine LLP, Richmond, 1967—, mng. ptnr., 1992-93; gen. counsel, corp. sec. Coastal Lumber Co., Weldon, N.C., 1980—; gen. counsel Bear Island Timberlands Co., L.L.C., Ashland, Va., 1985—, Bear Island Paper Co., L.L.C., 1985—. Contbr. chpt. to book, articles to profl. jours. Lt. USNR, 1956-66. Mem. ABA (chmn. exempt orgns. subcom., tax sect. 1971-86), Va. Bar Assn. (chmn. jr. bar 1965-66), Va. State Bar (com. chmn. 1981-83), Va. Tax Rev. (adv. bd. 1978—), Va. Forestry Assn., Richmond Feeder Cattle Assn. (pres. 1972-77), Princeton Alumni Assn. Va. (pres. 1974-78), Richmond-First Club (pres. 1969-70), Deep Run Hunt Club (pres. 1986-88), Va. Country Club. Episcopalian. Avocations: horse sports, tree farming, agriculture. General corporate, Taxation, general, Natural resources. Home: 1230 Millers Ln Manakin Sabot VA 23103-2720 Office: Mays & Valentine LLP 1111 E Main St PO Box 1122 Richmond VA 23218-1122

**DENNY, GREGORY TODD,** lawyer; b. Birmingham, Ala.. BA, U. Ala., 1988; JD, Cumberland U., 1991. Atty. Powell & Denny P.C., Birmingham, Ala. Avocations: surfing, yachting, scuba diving, ballroom dancing, hang gliding. Office: Powell & Denny PC 1320 Alford Ave Ste 201 Birmingham AL 35226-3159

**DENSLEY, JAMES ALBERT,** lawyer; b. Murray, Utah, Sept. 15, 1950; s. Hilton and Margaret Densley; m. Kathleen Goetz, Aug. 10, 1974. BA in Econs., U. Wash., 1972; JD, Seattle U., 1976. Bar: Wash. 1976, U.S. Dist. Ct. (we. dist.) Wash. 1977. Pvt. practice Tacoma, 1976-77; dep. prosecutor Pierce County, Tacoma, 1977—. Contbr. articles to profl. jours. Lt. col. U.S. Army, 1972—, res. Mem. Wash. State Bar Assn., Gigharbor Sportsman's Club. Environmental, Land use and zoning (including planning), Public utilities. Office: Pierce County Prosecutors 930 Tacoma Ave S Tacoma WA 98402-2105

**DENSMORE, DOUGLAS WARREN,** lawyer; b. Jan. 30, 1948; s. Warren Orson and Lois Martha (Ery) D.; m. Janet Roberta Broadley, Oct. 26, 1973; children: Bradley Wythe, Andrew Fitz Douglas. AB, Coll. of William and Mary, Williamsburg, Va., 1970; JD cum laude, U. Toledo, 1975. Bar: Ohio 1976, U.S. Dist. Ct. (no. dist.) Ohio, Va. 1980, U.S. Dist. Ct. (ea. and we. dists.) Va. 1980, U.S. Ct. Appeals (4th cir.) 1980, U.S. Supreme Ct., 1997. Assoc. Gertner, Barkan & Robon, Toledo, 1975-77, Shumaker, Loop & Kendrick, Toledo, 1977-79; corp. counsel Dominion Bankshares Corp., Roanoke, Va., 1979-80; assoc. Woods, Rogers, Muse, Walker & Thornton, Roanoke, Va., 1980-84; ptnr. Woods, Rogers & Hazlegrove, Roanoke, Va., 1984-96, Flippin, Densmore, Morse, Rutherford and Jessee, Roanoke, Va., 1996—. Co-author: Examining the Increase in Federal Regulatory Requirements and Penalties: Is Banking Facing Another Troubled Decade?, 1995; contbr. articles to profl. jours. Bd. dirs. Orgn. Aiding Rehab., Roanoke, 1983-88; chmn. lawyer's sect. Cancer Crusade, Roanoke, 1984; v.p. Blue Ridge Highlands Scottish Festival, Roanoke, 1988-91, pres., 1992, bd. dirs. New Century Tech. Coun.; Vet. Corps of Artillery N.Y., Army-Navy Union. Decorated Venerable Order St. John (Eng.), Companion of the O'Conor Don (Ireland), Royal Order of Don Carlos I (Portugal), knight grand cross Order of St. Catherine, knight comdr. of justice Order of St. Lazarus, first class Order of Polonia Restituta (Poland), knight grand cross Order of the Temple, knight comdr. Order of Crown of Thorns, knight grand cross Order of St. Michael and St. George, knight grand cross Orthodox Order St. John, knight Order of St. John, Knights of Malta, knight grand cross Order of Holy Cross of Jerusalem, knight grand cross with collar Order of St. Gregory, knight grand cross Order of St. Stephen, Royal Ukranian Order of St. Vladimir the Great, knight grand cross Greek Order of St. Denis of Zante, Order of the White Eagle. Fellow Baskerville Soc. (U.K.); mem. ABA (banking law com. 1988—, uniform comml. code com. 1988—), Va. Bar Assn. (corp. code com. 1984—), Bar Assn. City of Roanoke (bd. dirs. 1998—), Scottish Soc. Va. Highlands (v.p. 1994-95, pres. 1995-96, bd. dirs. 1992—), Brit. Manorial Soc. (Lord of Stratford St. Andrew), Augustan Soc., English Speaking Union (v.p. 1998, 99), Soc. of St. George, Kiwanis Internat., Masons (32 degree, master, jr. deacon 1992), Shriners, Royal Order of Scotland, Shenandoah Club (Roanoke, Va.), Roanoke Country Club, Farmington Country Club (Charlottesville, Va.), Hunting Hills Country Club (Roanoke). Episcopalian. Avocations: golf, gardening, reading. General corporate, Banking, General civil litigation. Office: 2625 S Jefferson St Roanoke VA 24014-3315

**DENSON, ALEXANDER BUNN,** federal magistrate judge; b. Rocky Mount, N.C., Nov. 11, 1936; s. Samuel Leland and Elizabeth Pearl (Bunn) D.; children: Rebecca Anne Denson, Matthew Robert. BS, N.C. State U., 1959; LLB, Duke U., 1966. Bar: N.C. 1966. Assoc. Yarborough, Blanchard & Tucker, Raleigh, 1966-68; ptnr. Blanchard, Tucker, Twiggs & Denson, Raleigh, 1968-81; U.S. magistrate judge U.S. Dist. Ct. (ea. dist.), Raleigh, 1981—; OSHA adminstrv. law judge cons. N.C. Dept. Labor, Raleigh, 1978-81. Pres. Sir Walter Lions Club, 1982-83, Symphony Soc., Wake County chpt., 1975-76; founder Raleigh-Wake County Coalition for Homeless, 1987—; deacon Pullen Meml. Bapt. Ch., 1989-91; founding mem. Am. Shroud of Turin Assn., 1990-92; dir. Community Alternative Support Abodes for Mentally Ill Homeless, 1992—, chair 1996-98; elder Westminster Presbyn. Ch., 1998—. Lt. USNR, 1959-63. Recipient Outstanding Contbns. to Human Rels. and Human Svc. recognition, Gov., Raleigh Mayor, City Council, 1989. Mem. Wake County Duke Bar Assn. (past pres.). Republican. Avocations: gardening, chess. Office: US Dist Ct Po Box 25610 310 New Bern Ave Raleigh NC 27611-5610

**DENT, EDWARD DWAIN,** lawyer; b. Ft. Worth, Dec. 23, 1950. BA, Tex. Christian U., 1973; JD, St. Mary's U., Tex., 1976. Bar: Tex., U.S. Dist. Ct. (no. and so. dists.) Tex., U.S. Supreme Ct. Atty., ptnr. Kugle, Stewart, Dent, Frederick, Ft. Worth, 1979-89; founder Dent Law Firm, Ft. Worth, Dallas, 1990—. Bd. dirs. Greater Boys/Girls Clubs, Ft. Worth, 1989—, Westside Little League. Recipient Hist. Preservation award Tarrant County Hist. Coun., 1992. Mem. ATLA, U.S. Supreme Ct. Hist. Soc., Tex. Trial Lawyers (bd. dirs. 1989—), Tarrant County Trial Lawyers (bd. dirs. 1988-89, officer 1989), Trial Lawyers for Pub. Justice, Ft. Worth Club, Colonial Country Club, Million Dollar Advocacy Soc. (life). Democrat. Personal injury, Insurance. Office: Dent Law Firm 1120 Penn St Fort Worth TX 76102-3417

**DENTEN, CHRISTOPHER PETER,** lawyer; b. Oakland, Calif., Apr. 23, 1964; s. Richard and Waltraud Denten; m. Mary McLaughlin, May 18, 1996. BA, U. Calif., Berkeley, 1986; JD, U. San Francisco, 1990. Bar: Calif. 1991, U.S. Dist. Ct. (no. dist.) Calif. 1991, U.S. Ct. Appeals (9th cir.) 1991; CPA, Colo. Tax profl. KPMG Peat Marwick, Oakland, 1988-92; sr. tax analyst Cisco Sys., Inc., San Jose, Calif., 1992-97; mgr. legal affairs and taxation Network Assocs., Inc. (formerly McAfee, Inc.), Santa Clara, Calif., 1997—. Named to Outstanding Young Men of Am., 1982; Brother Gary Stone Meml. scholar, 1982. Mem. AICPA, Santa Clara Bar As, U. Calif. Berkeley Alumni Assn., U. San Francisco Law Sch. Alumni Assn. Republican. Roman Catholic. Avocations: marathons, golf, art, travel. General corporate, Mergers and acquisitions, Corporate taxation. Home: PO Box 117932 Burlingame CA 94011-7932 Office: Network Assocs Inc 3965 Freedom Cir Santa Clara CA 95054-1203

**DENTICE, M. ANGELA,** lawyer; b. Milw., Sept. 29, 1948; d. Joseph E. and Frances M. (Alioto) D.; m. Benn Di Pasquale, Jan. 4, 1997; 1 child, Adam Samuel Bottoni. BBA, Marquette U., 1970, JD cum laude, 1985; MS, U. Wis., Milw., 1974. Tchr. of handicapped children Mequon (Wis.) Pub. Schs., 1971-75; adminstr. vocat. program, supr. programs for handicapped Milw. Pub. Schs., 1975-82; lectr. grad. and undergrad. courses U. Wis., Milw., 1978-79; shareholder Cannon & Dunphy S.C., Brookfield, Wis., 1999—; advisor trial practice course Marquette U., Milw., 1986—; lectr. in field. Bd. dirs. St. Francis Children's Ctr., Glendale, Wis., 1980's. Mem. ATLA (state del. 1996-98), Assn. Women Lawyers, Wis. Bar Assn., Wis. Acad. Lawyers (v.p. 1999—). Avocations: running, music, piano. Personal injury. Office: Hausmann McNally SC 633 W Wisconsin Ave Ste 2000 Milwaukee WI 53203-1957

**DENTON, MICHAEL DAVID, JR.,** lawyer; b. Oklahoma City, Okla., Sept. 21, 1963; s. Michael David and Nancy Marie (Boone) D.; m. Kristin Marie Drea; 1 child, Michael David III. BSBA, Southwestern Okla. State U., 1987; JD, U. Okla., 1990. Bar: Okla. 1991, U.S. Dist. Ct. (no., ea. and we. dists.) Okla. 1991, U.S. Dist. Ct. (cen. dist.) 1997. Law clk., intern, assoc. Edmonds Cole Hargrave Givens & Witzke, Oklahoma City, 1989-92; assoc. A. Scott Johnson & Assoc., Oklahoma City, 1992-95, Huddleston, Pike & Assoc., 1995-96, Hiltgen & Brewer, P.C., 1996-98; pvt. practice Mustang, Okla., 1998—. Mem. First Bapt. Ch., Mustang, Okla., 1980—. With U.S. Army, 1985-87. Mem. ABA, Defense Rsch. Inst., Okla. Trial Lawyers Assn., Okla. Bar Assn., Canadian County Bar Assn., Okla. County Bar Assn. (chmn. athletic com., 1994-98, exec. dir. young lawyer divsn. 1992-98), Sigma Tau Gamma (chpt. advisor 1991-92, chpt. counselor 1991-97, Outstanding Athlete award, 1987, Super Sig Tau 1987). Republican. Avocations: fishing, hunting, basketball, tinkering, children. Personal injury, Labor, Product liability. Office: Ste 114 464 Financial Ctr Ter Mustang OK 73064

**DENYS, SYLVIA,** lawyer; d. Joseph and Louise D. BA in Philosophy and English with honors, Duquesne U., 1970, MA in English, 1977, JD, 1979. Bar: Pa. 1979, U.S. Dist. Ct. (we. dist.) Pa. 1979, U.S. Ct. Appeals (3d cir.), 1994. Atty. Neighborhood Legal Svcs. Assn., Pitts., 1979-81; jud. law clk. Superior Ct. Pa., Pitts., 1981-82; asst. prof. Duquesne U. Grad. Sch. Bus. and Sch. Bus., 1982-89; pvt. practice, Pitts., 1982-91, 93—; tchr. Acad. for Advancement Sci., Pecs, Hungary, 1992-93; adj. prof. Duquesne U. Sch. Bus., 1990-91; vis. prof. Sch. Medicine, Pecs, 1991-92; adj. prof. Janus Pannonius Sch. Law, Pecs, Hungary, 1991-92lectr. and presenter in field. Mem. editl. bd. Duquesne Law Rev., 1978-79; contbr. articles to profl. jours. Legal coun., bd. dirs. Pitts. Deaf Theatre, Pitts., 1984-85; bd. dirs. YWCA,

Pitts., 1984, Blind Outdoor Leisure Devel., Pitts., 1994-95; rev. com. United Way, Pitts., 1982-86; citizens assembly mem. Health and Welfare Planning Allegheny County, Pitts., 1982-85; v.p. UN Assn. Pitts., 1984-85, bd. dirs., 1982-85; vol. atty. Legal Resources for Women, Pitts., 1997, Neighborhood Legal Svcs. Assn., Pitts., 1994—; adv. bd. Radio Info. Svc., Pitts., 1994-95, vol. atty., 1996-97; govtl. activities com. United Cerebral Palsy, Pitts., 1994-96; dir. legal project for deaf and hard of hearing Pitts. Hearing, Speech and Deaf Svcs., 1995-96; tutor goodwill literacy program Allegheny County Jail, Pitts., 1995-96; membership com. World Affairs Coun., Pitts., 1983-85. Hunkele Found. grantee, Brussels, 1988, U.S. Info. Agy. grantee U. Pitts., 1992-93; Fulbright-Hayes fellow Coun. for Internat. Exch. of Scholars, 1990; selected mem. Team '92 Delegation of Commn. of European Communities, 1989-91. Mem. ABA (editor-in-chief Internat. Aspects of Antitrust Law newsletter 1984-86, del. to European Union 1989), ACLU (lawyers com. 1994-98), Fed. Bar Assn. (steering com., publicity chmn. Western Pa. chpt. 1995—), Am. Inns of Ct., Pa. Bar Assn. (legal svcs. to persons with disabilities com. 1994—, civil and equal rights com. 1994-98, LINK project for disabled children 1997-98), Allegheny County Bar Assn. (antitrust and class action com., court rules com., editl. bd. Pitts. Legal Jour. 1982-88, pub. svc. com., civil rights com., internat. twinning com. 1994-98), Womens Bar Assn. Allegheny County, World Federalists, Amnesty Internat., Lawyers Com. for Human Rights. Avocations: languages, cultures, arts, nature, gourmet cooking. Civil rights, Labor. Home: 4609 Bayard St Pittsburgh PA 15213-2755 Office: 429 Forbes Ave Pittsburgh PA 15219-1622

**DEORCHIS, VINCENT MOORE,** lawyer; b. N.Y.C., Aug. 25, 1949; s. Mario E. and Frankie (Moore) DeO.; m. Donna B., July 24, 1971; children: Vincent Scott, Dana Lauren. BA, Fordham Coll., 1971, JD, 1974. Bar: N.Y. 1975, U.S. Dist. Ct. (so. and ea. dists.) N.Y. 1975, U.S. Ct. Appeals (2d cir.) 1975, U.S. Supreme Ct. 1985, U.S. Ct. Appeals (3d cir.) 1989, U.S. Dist. Ct. (so. dist.) Tex. 1992, U.S. Ct. Appeals (4th cir.) 1996. Assoc. Haight, Gardner, Poor & Havens, N.Y.C., 1974-84; ptnr. DeOrchis & Ptnrs., N.Y.C., 1984-97, DeOrchis, Walker & Corsa, LLP, N.Y.C., 1997—. Co-author: Attorney's Practice Guide to Negotiations, 1985. Pres. North Stratmore Civic Assn., Manhasset, N.Y., 1978-82. Mem. ABA (com. on maritime litig.), Maritime Law Assn. (bd. dirs., chmn. com. on carriage of goods by sea), Assn. Transp. Practitioners, N.Y. County Lawyer's Assn. (com. on maritime and admiralty law), Propeller Club U.S. Avocation: sailing. Admiralty, Insurance, Federal civil litigation. Office: DeOrchis Walker & Corsa 2d Flr One Battery Park Plaza New York NY 10004-1480

**DEPAOLO, JOHN P.,** lawyer; b. Buffalo, Jan. 5, 1961. BA, SUNY, Buffalo, 1987; JD, U. Dayton, 1990. Bar: N.Y. 1990, Mass. 1990, U.S. Dist. Ct. 1990. Trial atty. MacCarthy, Pojani & Hurley, Mass., 1990-92, Prosecutor's Office, Worcester, Mass., 1992—. Bankruptcy, General civil litigation, Estate taxation. Office: Dist Atty 2 Main St Rm 42 Worcester MA 01608-1116

**DEPASCALE, DIANE KAPPELER,** lawyer; b. Dayton, Ohio, July 1, 1957; d. Robert L. and L. Ann Kappeler; m. Vincent N. DePascale, July 11, 1992. BA in Pol. Sci., U. Dayton, 1978, JD, 1981. Bar: Ohio 1981, U.S. Dist. Ct. (so. dist.) Ohio 1981, U.S. Ct. Appeals (6th cir.) 1986, U.S. Supreme Ct. 1986, U.S. Dist. Ct. (no. dist.) Ohio 1996. Law clk. to Judge Michael Merz, Mcpl. Ct., Dayton, 1980; assoc. Biegel, Kirkland & Berger, Dayton, 1981-84; pvt. practice, Dayton, 1984-92; ptnr. DePascale Law Offices, Columbus, Dayton, Ohio, 1992—; facilitator 1991 Bench-Bar Conf.; mem. Ohio Supreme Ct. Task Force on Ct. Costs & Indigent Defense, 1991-92, Dayton Bar Assn. Vol. Lawyer's Project, 1990-92, Ohio Supreme Ct. Com. Study Impact of Substance Abuse on the Cts., 1989-90; adj. prof. U. Dayton, 1986—; visiting referee Montgomery County Domestic Ct., 1986. Named Outstanding Lawyer Greater Dayton Vol. Lawyer's Project, 1992. Mem. Dayton Bar Assn., Columbus Bar Assn. (family law com.), Ohio Bar Assn. (chmn. criminal justice com., 1991-93, family law com.), Ohio Assn. Criminal Def. Lawyers. Republican. Roman Catholic. Avocations: model railroads, toy poodle. Criminal, Family and matrimonial, Appellate. Office: DePascale Law Offices 786 Northwest Blvd Columbus OH 43212-3832 also: 120 W 2d St Dayton OH 45402-1604

**DEPAUL, ANTHONY KENNETH,** lawyer; b. Chester, Pa., Feb. 9, 1939; s. Samuel DePaul and Lucille DiNicola; m. Joanne J. Machristie, June 30, 1984. BA, Widener U., 1959; JD, Georgetown U., 1962. Bar: D.C. 1964, U.S. Ct. Mil. Appeals 1968, Pa., U.S. Supreme Ct. 1975. Pub. defender Media, Pa., 1970-75; pro bono def. counsel for indigent accused Phila., 1984-90; instr. U.S. Mil. Acad., West Point, N.Y., 1965-70; prof. law Widener U., Chester, Pa., 1970-90, St. Joseph's U., Phila., 1975-92; solicitor mcpl. fire cos., 1970-90. Co-author: USMA-Analysis of Academy Laws, 1970. Maj. U.S. Army, 1966-70. Recipient Alumni Svc. award Widener U. Mem. AAUP, Pa. Bar Assn., Phila. Bar Assn. General practice, Juvenile, Real property. Home: 23 Medbury Rd Wallingford PA 19086-6602

**DEPEW, CHAUNCEY MITCHELL, III,** lawyer; b. Summit, N.J., May 15, 1968; s. Chauncey Mitchell Depew and Judith Lynne Purcell; m. Lisa Anne Stinnett Depew, Aug. 15, 1992; 1 child, Chauncey Mitchell IV. BA, DePauw U., 1990; JD, U. Mo., 1993. Bar: Kans. 1993. Asst. city atty. City of Overland Park, Kans., 1993-95; ptnr. Lance Hanson, L.L.C., Overland Park, 1995—; city prosecutor City of Merriam, Kans., 1996—. Mem. Johnson County Bar Assn. Republican. Presbyterian. Home: 9544 Roe Ave Shawnee Mission KS 66207-3557 Office: Lance E Hanson LLC 3145 Broadway St Kansas City MO 64111-2405

**DEPEW, SPENCER LONG,** lawyer; b. Wichita, Kans., June 6, 1933; s. Claude I. and Frances Ann (Bell) D.; m. Donna Wolever, Dec. 28, 1957; children: Clifford S., Sally F. AB, U. Wichita, 1955; LLB, U. Mich., 1960. Bar: Kans.; U.S. Dist. Ct. Kans.; U.S. Supreme Ct. Mem. Depew and Gillen, LLC, Wichita; mem. Interstate Oil and Gas Compact Commn., Oklahoma City. With U.S. Army, 1955-57, Germany. Mem. IPAA, Kans. Ind. Oil and Gas Assn. Oil, gas, and mineral, Estate planning, General corporate. Home: 6322 E English St Wichita KS 67218-1802 Office: Depew and Gillen LLC 151 N Main St Ste 800 Wichita KS 67202-1409

**DEPPER, ESTELLE M.,** lawyer; b. Oakland, Calif., May 13, 1942; d. Martin S. and Estelle D. Depper. BA, U. Calif., Berkeley, 1964, JD, 1967. Bar: Calif. 1967. V.p., mng. sr. counsel Wells Fargo Bank, San Francisco, 1982-98; sole practitioner San Francisco, 1998—. Author: California Trust Administration, 1998. Bd. dirs. Holy Names H.S., Oakland, 1996—. Mem. ABA (chair com. on adminstrn. and distbn. of trusts 1989-93), Calif. State Bar (exec. com. for estate planning sect. 1979-81), San Francisco Bar Assn. (chair probate and trust law sect. 1979-80), Alameda County Bar Assn. Probate. Office: 8041 Phaeton Dr Oakland CA 94605-4214

**DEPPMAN, JOHN C.,** lawyer; b. Evanston, Ill., Sept. 25, 1943; s. George and Elsie Jane (Erickson) D.; divorced; children: Ann, Jed, Benj. BS, Middlebury Coll., 1965; JD, Georgetown U., 1969. Bar: Vt. 1969. State's atty. Addison County, Middlebury, Vt., 1972-74; pvt. practice Middlebury, Vt., 1974-90; ptnr. Deppman & Foley, Middlebury, 1990—; pres. Am. Land Title, Inc., Middlebury, 1984—. Selectman Town of Middlebury, 1970-72. Mem. ABA, Vt. Bar Assn., Addison County Bar Assn. (past pres.). Republican. Avocation: cross-country ski marathons, birding. General practice. Home: 8 Northshore Dr Burlington VT 05401-1255 Office: PO Box 688 Middlebury VT 05753-0688

**DEPREZ, DEBORAH ANN,** lawyer; b. Cleve., July 8, 1952; d. Frank Robert and Patricia Ann (Tees) D. BA, Boston Coll., 1974; JD, Northwestern U., 1977. Bar: Mich. 1977. Ptnr. Foster, Swift, Collins & Coey, P.C., Lansing, Mich., 1977-84; northern zone dir. Mich. Edn. Assn., East Lansing, Mich., 1984-89; ptnr. Sinas, Dramis, Brake Boughton, McIntyre & Reisig, P.C., Lansing, 1989—. Mem. State Bar of Mich., Assn. Trial Lawyers Am., Ingham County Bar Assn. Roman Catholic. Avocations: gardening, skiing, traveling, bicycling. Personal injury, Pension, profit-sharing, and employee benefits, Workers' compensation. Office: Sinas Dramis Law Firm 520 Seymour Ave Lansing MI 48933-1118 Home: 13270 Grand River Ave Eagle MI 48822-9701

**DEPUY, WALTER ALBERT, JR.,** prosecutor; b. Salem, Oreg., Nov. 12, 1958; s. Walter Albert Sr. and Mabel Lois (Hoof) DeP.; m. Naomi Ruth Basto, Oct. 1, 1994. BS, Oreg. State U., 1980; JD, U. Puget Sound, 1983. Bar: Wash. 1983. Dep. prosecutor Pierce County Prosecutor's Office, Tacoma, 1984-88, Clark County Prosecutor's Office, Wash., 1990—, Cowlitz County Prosecutor's Office, Longview, Wash., 1991-92; pvt. practice Tacoma, 1988-90; cons. USN, 1988-89; keynote speaker Juvenile Justice Jud. Tng. Conf., S.C., 1988; speaker Nat. Child Advocacy Ctr., Austin, Tex., 1987. Speaker Pierce County Health Dept., Tacoma, 1988. Mem. ABA, Wash. State Bar Assn. Republican. Avocations: reading, flying, photography, golf. Home: 3054 Yolanda Ave Springfield OR 97477-1757

**DERBY, ERNEST STEPHEN,** federal judge; b. Boston, July 10, 1938; s. Elmer Goodrich and Lucy (Davis) D.; m. Gretel Hanauer, June 10, 1961; children: Anne Gray, Michael Stephen. AB with distinction, Wesleyan U., 1960; LLB cum laude, Harvard U., 1965. Bar: Md. Ct. Appeals 1965, U.S. Dist. Ct. Md. 1966, U.S. Ct. Appeals (4th cir.) 1968, U.S. Supreme Ct. 1973. Law clk. to presiding justice U.S. Dist. Ct. Md. and U.S. Ct. of Appeals 4th cir., 1965-66; assoc. Piper & Marbury, Balt., 1966-71, ptnr., 1973-87; asst. atty. gen. Atty. Gen. Md., 1971-73; judge U.S. Bankruptcy Ct., Balt., 1987—; adj. faculty U. Md. Sch. Law, 1987, 90—. Pres. Dismas Ho., Balt. Inc., 1969—; trustee Enoch Pratt Free Libr., Balt., 1977-93. Fellow Am. Coll. Bankruptcy, Md. Bar Found.; mem. Md. State Bar Assn., Anne Arundel County Bar Assn., Paca/Brent Am. Inn of Ct. (pres. 1993-94). Office: US District Court US Courthouse 101 W Lombard St Rm 9442 Baltimore MD 21201-2626

**DERDENGER, PATRICK,** lawyer; b. L.A., June 29, 1946; s. Charles Patrick and Drucilla Marguerite (Lange) D.; m. Jo Lynn Dickins, Aug. 24, 1968; children: Kristin Lynn, Bryan Patrick, Timothy Patrick. BA, Loyola U., L.A., 1968; MBA, U. So. Calif., 1971, JD, 1974; LLM in Taxation, George Washington U., 1977. Bar: Calif. 1974, U.S. Ct. Claims 1975, Ariz. 1979, U.S. Ct. Appeals (9th cir.) 1979, U.S. Dist. Ct. Ariz. 1979, U.S. Tax Ct. 1979, U.S. Supreme Ct. 1979; cert. specialist in tax law. Trial atty. honors program U.S. Dept. Justice, Washington, 1974-78; ptnr. Lewis and Roca, Phoenix, 1978—; adj. prof. taxation Golden Gate U., Phoenix, 1983-87; mem. Ariz. State Tax Ct. Legis. Study Commn., Tax Law Specialist Commn., Ariz. Property Tax Oversight Commn.; appt. Ariz. Property Tax Oversight Commn., 1997—. Author: Arizona State and Local Taxation, Cases and Materials, 1983, Arizona Sales and Use Tax Guide, 1990, Advanced Arizona Sales and Use Tax, 1987-96, Arizona State and Local Taxation, 1989, 93, 96, Arizona Sales and Use Tax, 1988-96. Arizona Property Taxation, 1993-96, ABA Sales and Use Tax Deskbook, Property Tax Deskbook. Past pres., bd. dirs. North Scottsdale Little League; apptd. Ariz. Property Tax Oversight Commn. Served to capt. USAF, 1968-71. Recipient U.S. Law Week award Bur. Nat. Affairs, 1974. Mem. ABA (taxation sect., various coms.), Ariz. Bar Assn. (taxation sect., former chair sect. taxation, former treas., chmn. state and local tax com., chmn. continuing legal edn. com., tax adv. com., others, mem. tax law specialist commn.), Maricopa County Bar Assn., Inst. Sales Taxation, Nat. Tax Assn., Inst. Property Taxation Met. C. of C., Ariz. C. of C. (chair tax com.), U. So. Calif. Alumni Club (past pres., bd. dirs.), Phi Delta Phi. State and local taxation, Corporate taxation, Taxation, general. Home: 10040 E Happy Valley Rd Scottsdale AZ 85255-2395 Office: Lewis and Roca 2 Renaissance Plz 40 N Central Ave Ste 1900 Phoenix AZ 85004-4429

**DERENSIS, PAUL,** lawyer; b. Boston, July 3, 1944; s. Pardo and Tatiana (Bramorska) D.; m. Sheila B., Aug. 25, 1968 (div. 1983); children: Allyson, Jennifer, Heather, Karen, Will; m. Linda A. Fraze, Oct. 6, 1990; children: Parker L., Lindsey A. BA, Harvard U., 1966, JD, 1969. Bar: N.Y. 1970, Mass. 1975, U.S. Supreme Ct. 1982, U.S. Ct. Appeals (2nd cir.) 1975, U.S. Ct. Appeals (1st cir.) 1976), U.S. Dist. Ct. (so. and ea. dists.) N.Y. 1971, U.S. Dist. Ct. Mass. 1975. Assoc. Poletti Freidin Prashker Feldman & Gartner, N.Y.C., 1969-75; dir./shareholder Powers & Hall Profl. Corp., Boston, 1975-84; dir., shareholder Deutsch Williams Brooks DeRensis Holland & Drachman, P.C., Boston, 1984—; Essex County atty., Mass., 1987-92; town counsel Town of Nantucket, 1986—, Town of Randolph, 1990—, Town of Cohasset, 1996—, Town of Carlisle, 1999—. Contbr. articles to profl. jours. Mem. Planning Bd. Town of Sherborn (Mass.), 1990-93, mem. bd. of selectmen, 1996—, chmn., 1997—; mem. Sherborn Housing Partnership, Woodhaven Study Com., 19993; chmn. Sherborn Groundwater Protection Com., 1992—, mem. adv. com., 1994-95, chmn. s.w. water area protection adv. com., 1995—. Mem. ABA (chmn. subcommn. on tort liability for use of computer systems, sect. on sci. and tech. 1988-91), Assn. Bar City N.Y., Mass. Bar Assn., Boston Bar Assn., Mass. Assn. City Solicitors and Town Counsel. Municipal (including bonds), General corporate, Insurance. Office: Deutsch Williams Brooks DeRensis Holland & Drachman 99 Summer St Fl 13 Boston MA 02110-1235

**DERIC, ARTHUR JOSEPH,** lawyer, management consultant, health coop trustee; b. Phila., July 20, 1926; m. Claire Brandt, June 26, 1954; children: John Mark, Beverly Joyce, Alexa Dru. BA in Polit. Sci., Temple U., 1950, JD, 1953; MBA, U. Pa., 1959. Bar: Pa. 1953, U.S. Dist. Ct. (ea. dist.) Pa. 1953. Law clk. Ct. of Common Pleas, Phila., 1953-55; claims atty. USF & G Ins. Co., Phila., 1955-59; adj. lectr. ins., risk mgmt. Wharton Sch. U. Pa., Phila., 1959; mgr. ins., risk mgmt. and employee benefit divsn. Am. Mgmt. Assn. Inc., N.Y.C., 1959-69; assoc. prof. Bucks County C.C., Newtown, Pa., 1965-70; v.p. Fred S. James & Co. Inc., N.Y.C., 1970-82; pres., gen. counsel Deric Assocs., Inc., Ft. Washington, Pa., 1982-96; founding trustee Am. Coop. Health Trust, Lansdale, Pa., 1996. Editor: The Total Approach to Employee Benefits, 1967; author, editor, cons. speeches, books, articles and monographs on bus., estate, and health risk mgmt. Capt. U.S. Army, 1944-56. Mem. ABA, Internat. Ins. Hall of Fame (emeritus elector), Scabbard and Blade, Conwell Inn of Phi Delta Phi (past pres.), Pi Gamma Mu. Avocations: golf, bridge, reading, swimming, grandparenting. Alternative dispute resolution, Constitutional, Health.

**DE RODON, MIRIAM NAVEIRA,** supreme court justice; b. Santurce, P.R., July 28, 1934; married; 2 children. BA, Mount St. Vincent Coll., N.Y., 1956; JD, U. P.R. Law Sch., 1960; LLM, Columbia U., 1969; postgrad., Leiden U., Holland, 1971-72; LLD, U. Georgetown Sch. Law, 1990. Law clerk P.R. Supreme Ct., 1963-71, asst. atty. gen. Dept. Justice, 1966-73, asst. solicitor gen. Dept. Justice, 1973-76, assoc. justice, 1985—, pres. judicial commn. on gender bias, 1992—; tchr. Law Sch. U. P.R., 1971-72; atty. pvt. practice, 1976-85; prof. Sch. Law Inter-Am. U. Office: Supreme Ct PO Box 2392 San Juan PR 00902-2392

**DERON, EDWARD MICHAEL,** lawyer; b. Detroit, Dec. 18, 1945; m. Jana Lene Berlenbach, Aug. 12, 1977. BS, Wayne State U., 1968, JD cum laude, 1972; LLM in Taxation, NYU, 1973. Bar: Mich. 1972, U.S. Ct. Appeals (6th cir.) 1973, U.S. Tax Ct. 1974. Assoc. Evans & Luptak, Detroit, 1973-79, ptnr., 1980—. With U.S. Army, 1969-71, ETO, Germany. Mem. ABA, Mich. Bar Assn. (chmn. taxation sect., estates and trusts com. 1994-96, taxation sect. coun. 1996—, editor Mich. Tax Lawyer 1998-99) Detroit Bar Assn. (co-chmn. taxation com. 1984-86), Fin. and Estate Planning Coun. Detroit, Detroit Athletic Club, Rotary, KC. Taxation, general, Estate planning, General corporate. Office: Evans & Luptak 2500 Buhl Building Detroit MI 48226-3674

**DE ROSE, JOHN PATRICK,** lawyer; b. Chgo., July 31, 1943; s. John Patrick Sr. and Dorothy Delores (De Munnick) DeR.; m. Donna Mary Fogarty, Nov. 26, 1972; children: Justin Patrick, Caitlyn Fogarty. B. in Classical Arts, Loyola U., Chgo., 1965, JD, 1968. Bar: Ill. 1968, U.S. Dist. (no. dist.) Ill. 1977. Asst. state's atty. Cook County State's Atty. Office, Chgo., 1970-77; pvt. practice Chgo., 1977-86; pvt. practice law John P. De Rose & Assocs., Chgo., 1986—; panel atty. Fed. Def. Office, Chgo., 1977--. With U.S. Army, 1968-70. Decorated Army Commendation medal. Mem. ABA, Ill. Bar Assn., Criminal Def. Assn., W. Suburban Bar Assn. (bd. govs. 1978—). Roman Catholic. Criminal, Civil rights, General civil litigation. Home: 615 N York Rd Hinsdale IL 60521-3532 Office: John P De Rose & Assocs 200 S Frontage Rd Hinsdale IL 60521-6915

**DERR, ALLEN R.,** lawyer; b. Boise, Idaho, Apr. 5, 1928. BA in Journalism, U. Idaho, 1951, JD, 1969; postgrad., U. Ill., 1955-56. Bar: Idaho 1959, U.S. Dist. Ct. Idaho 1959, U.S. Cir. Ct. (9th cir.) 1964, U.S. Supreme Ct. 1971. Asst. atty. gen. State of Idaho, 1959-60; pvt. practice Boise, 1960—; speaker, lectr., master ceremonies, radio and T.V. panalist. Editor and asst. exec. dir. Tau Kappa Epsilon Nat. Mag.; contbr. articles to profl. jours. Past state pres. Young Dem. Club for Idaho.. Recipient Disting. Svc. award, Tau Kappa Epsilon, 1955. Mem. Am. Legion (past comdr.), Idaho Press Club (bd. dirs.). Personal injury, Criminal, Probate. Home: 199 N Capitol Blvd Apt 1005 Boise ID 83702-5982 Office: PO Box 1006 Boise ID 83701-1006

**DERRICK, GARY WAYNE,** lawyer; b. Enid, Okla., Nov. 3, 1953; s. John Henry and Leota Elaine (Glenn) D.; m. Susan Adele Goodwin, Dec. 22, 1979 (div. June 1981); m. Francys Hollis Johnson, May 3, 1986; children: Meghan, Drew, Jane. BA in History, English, Okla. State U., 1976; JD, U. Okla., 1979. Bar: Okla. 1979. Assoc. Andrews, Davis, Legg, Bixler, Milsten & Price, Oklahoma City, 1979-84, ptnr., 1985-90; of counsel McKinney, Stringer & Webster, P.C., Oklahoma City, 1990-93; ptnr. Derrick & Briggs, Oklahoma City, 1994—; active Securities Law and Acctg. Group, Oklahoma City, 1979—; chmn. Gen. Corp. Act Commn., Okla., 1984—, chmn. Securities Liaison Com., Okla., 1985-86; lectr. sem. Okla. Corp. Act, 1986—. Conbg. author: Oklahoma Business Organizations. Mem. Okla. State U. Found., Stillwater, 1983-89, U. Okla. Found., Norman, 1982—; mem. condr.'s circle Okla. Symphony Orch., 1981-88; bd. dirs. Hist. Preservation, Inc., 1990—. Mem. ABA (taxation and corp. sect., banking and bus. law sect.), Okla. Bar Assn. (chmn. bus. assn. sect. 1985-87, outstanding contbn. to continuing legal edn., Earl Sneed award 1997), Oklahoma County Bar Assn. (bd. govs. young lawyers div. 1981-82), Am. Soc. Corp. Secs. (pres. Okla.-Ark. chpt. 1994-95), Oklahoma City Boat Club. Republican. Episcopalian. Avocations: sailing, violin. Securities. Home: 500 NW 15th St Oklahoma City OK 73103-2102 Office: Derrick & Briggs Bank One Ctr 20th Fl 100 N Broadway Ave Oklahoma City OK 73102-8606

**DERRICK, JAMES V., JR.,** lawyer; b. Graham, Tex., Jan. 8, 1945. BA with honors, U. Tex., 1967, JD with honors, 1970. Bar: Tex. 1970. Jud. clk. U.S. Ct. Appeals (5th cir.), 1970-71; ptnr. Vinson & Elkins, Houston, from 1977; sr. v.p., gen. counsel Enron Corp., Houston, 1991—; adj. prof. U. Tex. Law Sch., 1984-90. Assoc. editor Tex. Law Rev., 1969-70. Mem. ABA, State Bar Tex., Houston Bar Found., Houston Bar Assn., Chancellors, Order of Coif, Houston Grand Opera (bd. dirs.), Soc. for Performing Arts, Found. for Jones Hall, U. Tex. Law Sch. Alumni Bd. (exec. com.). Address: Enron Global Power to Pipelines LLC PO Box 1188 Houston TX 77251-1188 also: Enron Corp 1400 Smith St Houston TX 77002-7311*

**DERRICK, RAYMOND TODD,** lawyer; b. Delhi, La., Mar. 1, 1967; m. Bobbie Moore, June 26, 1993; children: Jesse Adam, Robert Cole. AA, Enterprise State Jr. Coll., Enterprise, Ala., 1988; BA magna cum laude, U. Ala., 1990, JD, 1994. Bar: Ala. 1994, U.S. Dist. Ct. (mid. dist.) Ala. 1994, U.S. Ct. Appeals (11th cir.) 1995, U.S. Dist. Ct. (no. dist.) Ala. 1998. Lawyer Cobb & Shealy PA, Dothan, Ala., 1994—. Served with U.S. Army, 1985-92, with USNGR, 1985-92. Mem. Ala. Def. Lawyers, Ala. Trial Lawyers, Houston County Bar (sec. 1998—), Phi Beta Kappa. General civil litigation. Office: Cobb & Shealy PO Box 6346 Dothan AL 36302-6346

**DERSHEM, LARRY DOUGLAS,** lawyer, legal administration; b. Dayton, Ohio, May 11, 1948; s. William Aaron and Helen Marie (Ullery) D.; m. Hoa Thuy Le, July 5, 1980; children: Michelle Le, Kristin Lynn. AB, UCLA, 1973; MLS, U. Calif., Berkeley, 1974; JD, U. San Diego, 1978. Bar: Calif. 1979, U.S. Dist. Ct. (so. dist.) Calif. 1979. Catalog libr. U. San Diego Sch. Law, 1974-77; assoc. law libr. San Diego County Law Libr., 1977-87; dir. law libr. Nat. Univ. Sch. Law, San Diego, 1987-93; br. svcs. libr. Los Angeles County Law Libr., L.A., 1993-94; reference libr., computer rsch. specialist U. San Diego Sch. Law, 1994-97; pvt. practice San Diego, 1979-97; dir. classificaton standards Lexis Nexis, Miamisburg, Ohio, 1997—. Author: California Legal Research Handbook, 1995; compiler loose-leaf books Libr. of Congress. With USNR, 1968-69. Mem. Am. Assn. Law Librs., San Diego County Bar Assn., So. Calif. Assn. Law Librs. Republican. Avocations: computer programming, piano, drums. E-mail: larry.dershem@lexis-nexis.com. Office: Lexis Nexis 9595 Springboro Pike Miamisburg OH 45342

**DERSHOWITZ, ALAN MORTON,** lawyer, educator; b. Bklyn., Sept. 1, 1938; s. Harry and Claire (Ringel) D.; m. Carolyn Cohen; children: Elon Marc, Jamin Seth, Ella Kaille Cohen Dershowitz. BA magna cum laude, Bklyn. Coll., 1959; LLB magna cum laude, Yale U., 1962; MA (hon.), Harvard Coll., 1967; LLD (hon.), Yeshiva U., 1989; PhD (hon.), Haifa U., 1993; JD (hon.), Syracuse U., 1997. Bar: D.C. 1963, Mass. 1968, U.S. Supreme Ct. 1968. Law clk. to chief judge David L. Bazelon, U.S. Ct. Appeals, 1962-63; to justice Arthur J. Goldberg, U.S. Supreme Ct., 1963-64; mem. faculty Harvard Law Sch., 1964—, prof. law, 1967—, Felix Frankfurter Prof. of Law, 1993—; fellow Ctr. for Advanced Study of Behavioral Scis., 1971-72; Cons. to dir. NIMH, 1967-69, (Pres.'s Commn. Civil Disorders), 1967, (Pres.'s Com. Causes Violence), 1968, (NAACP Legal Def. Fund), 1967-68, NIMH Pres.'s Commn. Marijuana and Drug Abuse, 1972-73, Coun. on Drug Abuse, 1972—, Ford Found. Study on Law and Justice, 1973-76; rapporteur Twentieth Century Fund Study on Sentencing, 1975-76. *Professor Alan Dershowitz of Harvard Law School has been described by Newsweek as "the nation's most peripatetic civil-liberties lawyer and one of its most distinguished defenders of individual rights." Time called him "the top lawyer of last resort in the country--a sort of judicial St. Jude." Business Week characterized him as "a feisty civil libertarian and one of the nation's most prominent legal educators." He has been profiled by every major magazine ranging from Life ("iconoclast and self-appointed scourge of the criminal justice system"); to Esquire ("the country's most articulate and uncompromising protector of criminal defendants").* Author: (with others) Psychoanalysis, Psychiatry and the Law, 1967, Criminal Law: Theory and Process, 1974, The Best Defense, 1982, Reversal of Fortune: Inside the von Bulow Case, 1986, Taking Liberties: A Decade of Hard Cases, Bad Laws and Bum Raps, 1988, Chutzpah, 1991, Contrary to Popular Opinion, 1992, The Abuse Excuse, 1994, The Advocate's Devil, 1994, Reasonable Doubts, 1996, The Vanishing American Jew, 1997, Sexual McCarthyism: Clinton, Starr and the Emerging Constitutional Crisis, 1998, Just Revenge, 1999; contbr. articles to profl. jours.; editor-in-chief Yale Law Jour., 1961-62. Chmn. civil rights com. New England region Anti-Defamation League, B'nai B'rith, 1980-85; bd. dirs. ACLU, 1968-71, 72-75, Assembly Behavioral and Social Scis. at Nat. Acad. Scis., 1973-76. Guggenheim fellow, 1978-79; recipient hon. doctorates from Hebrew Union, Monmouth. Mem. Order of Coif, Phi Beta Kappa. Jewish. Office: Harvard Law Sch 1575 Massachusetts Ave Cambridge MA 02138-2801

**DERWART, A. REES,** lawyer; b. Indiana, Pa., Aug. 14, 1944; s. August Michael and Margaret Jane (Rees) D. BA, Dickinson Coll., Carlisle, Pa., 1966; MSLS, Case Western Res. U., 1967; JD, NYU, 1980. Bar: N.Y. 1981, Pa. 1993. Catalog libr. Berkeley Div. Sch., New Haven, Conn., 1969-71; adminstr. Yale Psychiat. Inst., New Haven, 1971-77; assoc. Hughes Hubbard & Reed, N.Y.C., 1980-91; pvt. practice Indiana, Pa., 1991—. Editor-in-chief NYU Jour. of Internat. Law and Politics, 1979-80; contbg. author: (CD-ROM) Business Transactions PowerLink, 1997. Office: 555 Chestnut St Indiana PA 15701-1967

**DERWIN, JORDAN,** lawyer, consultant, actor; b. N.Y.C., Sept. 15, 1931; s. Harry and Sadie (Baruch) D.; m. Barbara Joan Concool, July 4, 1956 (div. 1969); children: Susan Lee, Ellen; m. Joan Linda Wolfberg, May 6, 1973. BS, NYU, 1953, JD, 1959. Bar: N.Y. 1959, U.S. Dist. Ct. (so. and ea. dists.) N.Y. 1960, U.S. Ct. Appeals (2d. cir.) 1960, U.S. Supreme Ct. 1962. Arthur Garfield Hays rsch. fellow NYU, 1958-59, rsch. assoc. Duke U. Sch. of Law, Durham, N.C., 1959-60; assoc. Brennan, London, Buttenwieser, N.Y.C., 1960-64; sole practice Jordan Derwin, N.Y.C., 1964-70; gen. counsel N.Y.C. Off Track Betting Corp., 1970-74; assoc. gen. counsel Gen. Instrument Corp., N.Y.C., 1974-79; cons., 1980—; instr. basic life support, CPR and advanced 1st aid: ARC, 1988—, Am. Heart Assn., 1989—, Nat. Safety Coun., 1991—; instr. trainer basic cardiac lifesupport Am. Heart Assn., 1990—, mem. affiliate faculty, 1997—; emergency med. technician N.Y. State, 1990—; v.p., gen. counsel Cen. Park Med. Unit, Inc., N.Y.C., 1991—; del. N.Y.C. Ctrl. Labor Coun., 1996—. Author (with F. Hodge O'Neal), Expulsion or Oppression of Business Associates: Squeeze Outs in Small Business, 1960; actor in various films including Stardust Memories, 1980, Rollover, 1981, I'm Dancing as Fast as I Can, 1982, Hard Feelings, 1984, Cotton Club, 1984, One Down Two to Go, 1986, Cadillac Man, 1990, McBain 1991, Ambulance, 1992, Extreme Measures, 1996, Private Parts, 1997, TV programs including Nurse, Today's FBI, Another World, As The World Turns, Guiding Light, All My Children, One Life To Live, Loving, Saturday Night Live, Late Night and Late Show With David Letterman,

Conan O'Brien Show, TV commls. 1980—; contbr. articles to prof. jours. Lt. j.g., USNR, 1953-56, Korea, Vietnam. Mem. SAG (dir. nat. bd. 1982—, nat. exec. com., 1983—, sec. N.Y. br. 1983-87, 12th nat. v.p. 1984-87, 4th nat. v.p. 1987-89, 1st v.p. N.Y. br. 1987-89, 2d v.p. N.Y. br. 1989-91, 95—, 3d v.p. N.Y. br. 1993-95), AFTRA (dir. N.Y. local bd. 1980-83, 87-90, dir. nat. bd. 1981-92, Ken Harvey award for outstanding svc. to the mem. 1998), Am. Soc. Mag. Photographers, Nat. Press Photographers Assn., Motion Picture Players Welfare Fund (trustee 1987—), Actors Equity Assn., Associated Actors and Artistes Am. AFL-CIO (del. internat. bd. 1984-94, 97—, ctrl. labor coun. N.Y.C. 1996—), Phi Delta Phi. Labor, Legislative, General corporate. Home and Office: 305 E 86th St New York NY 10028-4702

**DERZAW, RICHARD LAWRENCE,** lawyer; b. N.Y.C., Mar. 6, 1954; s. Ronald Murray and Diana (Diamond) D.; m. Susan Katz, 1993. BA magna cum laude, Fairleigh Dickinson U., 1976; JD, Ohio No. U., 1979. Bar: Fla. 1979, U.S. Dist. Ct. (so. dist.) Fla. 1981, U.S. Ct. Appeals (5th cir.) 1981, U.S. Ct. Appeals (11th cir.) 1981, (2d cir.), 1988, N.Y. 1982, N.C. 1995, U.S. Dist. Ct. (so. dist.) N.Y. 1985, (ea. dist.) N.Y. 1986, U.S. Tax Ct. 1986, U.S. Supreme Ct., 1988. Sole practice, Boca Raton, Fla., 1979-82, N.Y.C., 1982—. Mem. ABA, N.Y. State Bar Assn., N.C. Bar Assn., Fla. Bar Assn., Am. Arbitration Assn., Assn. of Bar of City of N.Y., Fed. Bar Coun., Phi Alpha Delta, Phi Zeta Kappa, Phi Omega Epsilon. Lodge: Lions of Boca Raton (treas. 1981-82). General corporate, Contracts commercial, General civil litigation. Office: 635 Madison Ave Rm 400 New York NY 10022-1009

**DESAI, AASHISH Y.,** lawyer; b. Chgo., Oct. 7, 1968; s. Yadvendra and Shradhha Desei. BA in Econs., U. Tex., 1991; JD, U. Houston, 1996. Bar: Calif. 1996, U.S. Dist. Ct. (ctrl. dist.) Calif. 1996, U.S. Dist. Ct. Colo. 1998. Tchg. asst. U. Houston Law Ctr., 1994-95; summer assoc. Thompson & Knight, Dallas, 1994-95; jud. clk. Hon. Judge Maloney U.S. Ct. Appeals (5th cir.), Dallas, 1994-95; assoc. Law Offices of Alan Rubinstein, L.A., 1996-97, Mower, Koeller, Nebeker, Carlson & Haluck, Irvine, Calif., 1997—. Mem. ABA, Orange County Bar Assn. Avocations: golf, jazz, blues guitar, tennis, family. General civil litigation, Labor, Personal injury. Home: 9 Darlington Irvine CA 92620-0221 Office: Mower Koeller Nebeker Carlson & Haluck 108 Pacifica PO Box 19799 Irvine CA 92623-9799

**DESAI, JIGNASA,** lawyer; b. India, Dec. 12, 1969; came to U.S., 1971; d. Dinker and Bharti Desai. BA, Rutgers Coll., 1991; JD, Rutgers U., Camden, N.J., 1994; student, U. Exeter, Eng., 1989. Bar: N.J. 1994, U.S. Dist. Ct. N.J. 1995. Jud. clk. to two judges New Brunswick, N.J., 1994-95; assoc. Lomurro, Davison, Eastman & Munoz, P.A., Freehold, N.J., 1995-98, sr. assoc., 1998-99; gen. counsel Dept. Def./Comms.-Electronics Command, Ft. Monmouth, N.J., 1999—; mcpl. prosecutor Twp. of Millstone, N.J., 1997-99; asst. twp. atty. Twp. of Manalapan, N.J., 1996-99. Trustee Legal Aid Soc., Monmouth County, 1996—. Mem. N.J. State Bar Assn. (minorities sect.), Women Lawyers in Monmouth, Rutgers Law Alumni Assn. (bd. dirs. 1994—). Government contracts and claims, Labor. Office: Office of the Chief Counsel Dept of Def US Army Hdqrs CECOM AMSEL-LG-A Fort Monmouth NJ 07703-5000

**DE SALVA, CHRISTOPHER JOSEPH,** lawyer; b. Milw., June 16, 1950; s. Salvadore Joseph and Elaine Mae De S.; m. Erika Marie De Salva, May 24, 1975; 1 child, Jessica Anne. BA in Polit. Sci., St. Vincent Coll., 1972; JD summa cum laude, Am. Coll. Law, 1987; MBA, Calif. Coast U., 1993, postgrad., 1994. Bar: Calif. 1994, U.S. Dist. Ct. (ctrl. dist.) Calif. 1995, U.S. Ct. Fed. Claims 1995, U.S. Tax Ct. 1995. Founder, owner C.J. De Salva & Assocs. Investment and Mktg. Svcs. of La Quinta (now C.J. De Salva & Assocs., La Quinta, 1979—; pvt. practice La Quinta, Calif., 1994-98, Indio, Calif., 1994—, San Diego, 1996-98; ceo, pres. The Kings Vault Gallery, Inc., 1985; adj. faculty property law Am. Coll. Law, Brea, Calif., 1989-90, 92-95; life and disability ins. agent C.J. De Salva Ins. Agency 1978—; real estate broker De Salva Realty Calif., 1980—, realtor, 1985-94; tax cons., preparer Christopher De Salva Tax Cons.; cons. Christopher De Salva Bus. and Mgmt. Cons.; lectr. property law. Am. Coll. Law. Author: NAFTA, The Hidden Agenda, 1995. 1st lt. USMC, 1974-77. Vietnam. Am. Jurisprudence award Am. Coll. Law. Mem. ABA, Assn. Trial Lawyers, Vietnam Era Vet., Vet. of Latin Am., Nat. Soc. Pub. Accts (cert. 1984), Calif. Bar Assn. Avocations: music, sports, writing songs, flying. Criminal, General civil litigation, Estate taxation. Office: 45-902 Oasis St Ste D Indio CA 92201

**DESANTIS, RICHARD A.,** lawyer; b. Long Branch, N.J., May 10, 1931; s. Peter and Maria DeSantis; m. Charlan K. (div. Aug. 1975); children: Sheri, Laurie. BA (hons.) summa cum laude, Rutgers Univ., 1953; JD, Yale Law Sch., 1958. Bar: Calif. 1960, U.S. Dist. Ct. (cen. dist.) Calif. 1960, U.S. Cir. Cts. (9th cir.) 1960, U.S. Cir. Cts. (5th cir.) 1990, U.S. Supreme Ct. 1971, U.S. Tax Ct. 1971, U.S. Ct. Internat. Trade 1981. Assoc. legal staff Securities Exchange Commn., L.A., 1959-60; spl. deputy atty., gen. deputy, spl. dist. atty. State of Calif., L.A., 1960-62; assoc. Zagon, Aaron & Schiff, Beverly Hills, Calif., 1962-64; ptnr. DeSantis & Baumeister, Beverly Hills, Calif., 1964-66, DeSantis, Gordon, Lipstone & Rich, Beverly Hills, Calif., 1965-71; proprietor Law Office Richard A DeSantis, Century City, Calif., 1971—; CEO Acoustica Assocs., L.A., 1964-70; chmn. bd. Montessori Schs. Inc., Pasadena, Calif., 1968-72. Author: The Class Actions Primer, 1975, Corridors of Securities Litigation, 1981; editor: USC Class Actions Manual, 1974. Bd. dirs., v.p. program Valley Cultural Ctr., Woodland Hills, Calif., 1993-95. 1st lt. U.S. Army, 1953-56, PTO. Decorated Silver Star Purple Heart Def. Svc. medal U.S. Army, 1955. Mem. ABA (securities reg. commn. 1970-90). Avocations: producer classical/semi classical musical productions. Securities, Real property, General civil litigation. Office: Law Offices Richard A DeSantis 4872 Topanga Canyon Blvd # 155 Woodland Hills CA 91364-4229

**DESANTO, JAMES JOHN,** lawyer; b. Chgo., Oct. 12, 1943; s. John Joseph and Erminia Asunda (Cassano) DeS.; m. Denise Clare Caneva, Feb. 3, 1968; children: Carrie Ann, James Thomas, John Joseph. BA, U. Ill., 1965; JD, DePaul U., 1969. Bar: Ill. 1969, U.S. Dist. Ct. (no. dist.) Ill. 1969, U.S. Ct. Appeals (7th cir.) 1972, U.S. Supreme Ct. 1974; cert. mediator 19th Jud. Circuit, Ill., 1996. Asst. state's atty. Waukegan, Ill., 1969-72; assoc. Finn, Geiger & Rafferty, Waukegan, 1972-74; ptnr. Rawles, Katz & DeSanto, Waukegan, 1975-80; pvt. practice law Waukegan, 1980-88; sr. ptnr. DeSanto & Bonamarte, Waukegan, 1988-91; pvt. practice law Libertyville, Ill., 1991—, James J. DeSanto and Assocs., 1992—; lectr. in trial technique and practice Ill. Inst. for CLE and Ill. State Bar Assn.; lectr. in bus. law Coll. of Lake County, 1974-84; bd. dirs. Ill. State Bar Assn. Mut. Ins. Co., 1989—, chairperson com. on finance and investment 1995-97, sec./treas., 1999—; mem. ad hoc com. on profl. quality in the practice of law State Bar Assn., 1995—. Co-editor Tort Trends newsletter, 1988-91. Trustee Village of Libertyville, 1991-93. Fellow Ill. Bar Inst.; mem. ATLA, Ill. Bar Assn. (chmn. fin. and budget com. of assembly 1988-89, chmn. tort law sect. coun. 1991-92, co-editor Tort Trends newsletter 1988-91, mem. standing com. on legislation 1995—), Lake County Bar Assn. (sec. 1979-80, 2d v.p. 1991-92, pres. 1993-94), Lake County Trial Lawyers Assn. (sec. 1985—), Jefferson Inns of Ct., Libertyville Rotary (pres. 1990-91). Avocations: golf, fishing. State civil litigation, Personal injury, Federal civil litigation. Home: 1209 St William Dr Libertyville IL 60048-1275 Office: 339 N Milwaukee Ave Libertyville IL 60048-2279

**DESARIO, DANIEL J.,** lawyer; b. Coral Gables, Fla., Mar. 2, 1953; s. Edith R. D.; divorced; 1 child, Steven J. BBA cum laude, U. Miami, 1975; JD, UCLA, 1982. Bar: Calif. Pvt. practice L.A.; pres. Nat. Bar Rev., L.A. and San Francisco, 1994—. Contbr. articles to profl. jours. Mem. Calif. Trial Lawyers Assn., L.A. County Bar Assn. General civil litigation, Contracts commercial, Criminal. Office: Daniel J Desario & Assocs 1875 Century Park E Ste 600 Los Angeles CA 90067-2507

**DE SHIELDS-MINNIS, TARRA R.,** lawyer; b. Balt.; d. Lawrence Franklin DeShields and Ramona Fleurette Brown. BA, U. Md., 1984; JD, U. Balt., 1987. Bar: Md., U.S. Dist. Ct. Md. 1990, U.S. Ct. Appeals (4th cir.), U.S. Supreme Ct. 1993. Jud. clk. Md. Ct. of Spl. Appeals, 1987-88; asst. state's atty. Office of the State's Atty., Montgomery County, 1988-90; asst. atty. gen. Office of the Atty. Gen., Balt., 1990-96; asst. U.S. atty. U.S. Atty.'s Office, Balt., 1996—. Recipient Am. Jurisprudence award Lawyer's Cooperative Pub. Co., 1988; Supreme Ct. fellow Nat. Assn. of Attys. Gens., 1993. Mem. Md. State Bar Assn., Nat. Bar Assn. Roman Catholic. Avocations: reading, antique shopping, racquetball. Office: US Attys Office 101 W Lombard St Baltimore MD 21201-2626

**DE SIMONE, DOMINIC J.,** lawyer; b. Phila., Dec. 3, 1964; s. Joseph and Joanne De Simone; m. Maria Chiara Lombardi, Sept. 29, 1990. BS, Drexel U., 1988; JD, Temple U., 1995. Bar: Pa., N.J. Assoc. Sonnenblick-Goldman Corp., Moorestown, N.J., 1987-89; sr. banking officer Liberty Bank, Phila., 1989-91; asst. v.p. PNC Bank Nat. Assn., Phila., 1991-95; assoc. Ballard Spahr Andrews & Ingersoll LLP, Phila., 1995—. Mem. ABA, Pa. Bar Assn., Phila. Bar Assn., N.J. Bar Assn. Avocations: travel, golf. Banking, Finance, Real property. Office: Ballard Spahr Andrews & Ingersoll LLP 1735 Market St Fl 51 Philadelphia PA 19103-7501

**DESISTO, JOHN ANTHONY,** lawyer; b. Denver, Apr. 10, 1959; s. John Anthony and Patricia Ann DeSisto; m. Storm Diane Griffin, Mar. 27, 1982; children: Tyler, Danielle. BS magna cum laude, U. Utah, 1981, MS, 1985; JD, U. Denver, 1989. Bar: Colo. 1989, U.S. Dist. Ct. Colo. 1989, Calif. 1995. Assoc. Kirkland & Ellis, Denver, 1989-95; ptnr. Kirkland & Ellis, L.A., 1995-96, Featherstone & Shea, Denver, 1996-99, Featherstone DeSisto LLP, Denver, 1999—. Scoutleader Boy Scouts Am., Denver, 1984-86. Mem. Colo. Bar Assn., Denver Bar Assn., Order of St. Ives. General civil litigation, Contracts commercial, Environmental. Office: Featherstone DeSisto LLP 600 17th St Ste 2500 Denver CO 80202-5402

**DESLER, PETER,** lawyer; b. Troy, N.Y., Oct. 2, 1947; s. Joseph Francis and Helen (Meagher) D.; m. Cynthia Lee Hymes, Sept. 20, 1980; children: Frances Lauren, Audrey Rose, Emily Helen. BA, Providence Coll., 1969; JD, Coll. William and Mary, 1972. Bar: Va. 1972, Calif. 1975, Idaho 1992, U.S. Dist. Ct. (ea. dist.) Va. 1972, U.S. Dist. Ct. (no. dist.) Calif. 1975, U.S. Dist. Ct. (ea. dist.) Calif. 1982, U.S. Dist. Ct. Idaho 1992, U.S. Mil. Appeals 1972, U.S. Ct. Appeals (4th cir.) 1974. Atty. litigation dept. The Pentagon, U.S. Army, Washington, 1972-74; atty. Presidio of San Francisco, 1974-77; assoc. Law Offices of Yanello & Flippen, San Francisco, 1979-81, Law Offices of Berger & Taggart, San Francisco, 1981-86; pvt. practice San Rafael, Calif., 1986-92, Boise Arbitration/Mediation Svcs., Boise, Idaho, 1992—; faculty Dominican Coll., San Rafael, Calif., 1980-88, U. San Francisco, 1989-92, Boise State U., 1992—; judge pro tempore Marin County Superior Ct., 1985-92, Marin County Mcpl. Ct. 1983-92. Capt. U.S. Army, 1972-76. Mem. Bar Assn. San Francisco (arbitrator 1986-92), Marin County Bar Assn. (arbitrator1986-92), Am. Arbitration Assn. (arbitrator 1986—), Idaho Bar Assn. (arbitrator 1992—, alt. dispute resolution sect. gov. council mem.), Idaho Mediation Assn., U.S. Arbitration & Mediation Inc. Avocations: motorcycling, golf, skiing, music, mountain biking, fishing. General civil litigation, Alternative dispute resolution, General practice. Office: Boise Arbitration Mediation Svcs 104 Rush Creek Rd Boise ID 83716-3172

**DESMARAIS, MICHAEL GEORGE,** lawyer; b. Oakland, Calif., Jan. 11, 1948; s. Alfred W. and Evelyn G. Desmarais; m. Karen Hales, Mar. 26, 1989; 1 child, Brian. AB, U. Calif., Davis, 1970; JD, U. Calif., San Francisco, 1973. Bar: Calif. 1973. Ptnr. Hoge, Fenton, Jones & Appel, San Jose, Calif., 1981-91, Lakin Speais, Palo Alto, Calif., 1991—; bd. dirs. Ct. Designated Child Advocates, San Jose. Contbr. articles to profl. publs. Mem. State Bar Calif. (mem. exec. com., estate planning, probate and trust sect.), Santa Clara County Bar Assn. (exec. com., estate planning, probate and trust sect.), Order of Coif. Roman Catholic. Estate planning, Probate. Office: Temmerman & Desmarais LLP 1550 S Bascom Ave Ste 240 Campbell CA 95008-0638

**DESMOND, SUSAN FAHEY,** lawyer; b. Greenville, Miss., Feb. 24, 1961; d. Richard Paul and Bonnie Jean (Williams) Fahey; m. John Michael Desmond; May 28, 1994; children: Meghan, Kelsey. BA in English and History, U. Miss., 1982; JD, U. Tenn., 1985. Bar: Miss. 1985, Colo. 1996, La. 1998. Assoc. Robertshaw, Terney & Noble, Greenville, Miss., 1985-86, Miller, Milam & Moeller, Jackson, Miss., 1986-89; assoc. Phelps Dunbar, Jackson, Miss., 1989-92, ptnr., 1992-97; ptnr. Phelps Dunbar, New Orleans, 1998—. Author: Employment Issues for Hospital Supervisors, 1996; editor: Mississippi Pro Bono Material, 1989. bd. dirs. Am. Cancer Soc. Hinds County Unit, Jackson, Miss., 1990-96. Mem. Jackson Young Lawyers (dir. 1991-93, merit award 1988), Am. Bar Assn./Young Lawyers (labor com. chmn., Chgo., 1990-92), Miss. Bar Assn. (dir. 1990-92, Outstanding Young Lawyer 1997). Republican. Roman Catholic. Avocations: tennis, reading. Labor, Civil rights, Immigration, naturalization, and customs. Office: Phelps Dunbar 400 Poydras St New Orleans LA 70130-3245

**DESO, ROBERT EDWARD, JR.,** lawyer; b. Albany, N.Y., Mar. 20, 1943; s. Robert Edward and Mary Audrey (Donahue) D.; m. Alice Rae Jones, Oct. 28, 1967; children: Robert, Susan, Karen, Kathleen. BSFS, Georgetown U., 1965; JD, U. Va., 1968. Bar: Va. 1968, D.C. 1973, U.S. Ct. Mil. Appeals 1968, U.S. Dist. Ct. D.C. 1977, U.S. Dist. Ct. (ea. dist.) Va. 1975, U.S. Ct. Claims 1975, U.S. Ct. Appeals (D.C. cir.) 1988. Spl. asst. to Judge Advocate Gen. U.S. Army-Pentagon, Washington, 1972-73; asst. gen. counsel Met. Police Dept., Washington, 1973-75, dep. gen. counsel, 1975-78; ptnr./prin. Deso & Greenberg, P.C., Washington, 1978-90; ptnr., prin. Deso, Thomas, Spevack & Weitzman, Washington, 1990—. Researcher/author: Law at War, 1975. Scoutmaster Boy Scouts Am., Falls Church, Va., 1981-84; legis. chmn. PTA, McLean, Va., 1985-88. Capt. U.S. Army. 1968-73. Decorated Bronze Star medal. Mem. ABA, Va. Bar Assn., Bar Assn. of D.C. Roman Catholic. Lodge: Fraternal Order of Police. Labor, General practice, General civil litigation. Office: Deso Thomas Spevack & Weitzman 1828 L St NW Ste 660 Washington DC 20036-5112

**DESSEM, R. LAWRENCE,** dean, law educator; b. Berea, Ohio, May 16, 1951; s. Ralph Eugene and Jane Elizabeth (Brightbill) D.; m. Beth Ann Taylor, May 20, 1973; children: Matthew, Lindsay, Emily. BA, Macalester Coll., 1973; JD, Harvard U., 1976. Bar: Ohio 1976, D.C. 1979, Tenn. 1985. Law clk. to presiding judge U.S. Dist. Ct. (no. dist.) Ohio, Cleve., 1976-78; asst. gen. counsel NEA, Washington, 1978-80; trial atty. civil div. U.S. Dept. Justice, Washington, 1980-84, sr. trial counsel, 1984-85; assoc. prof. law coll. of law U. Tenn., Knoxville, 1985-92, prof. law coll. of law, 1992-95, assoc. dean, 1993-95; dean Mercer U., Macon, Ga., 1995—; mem. faculty Legal Edn. Inst., U.S. Dept. Justice, San Francisco, 1985, Nat. Inst. for Trial Adv., Chgo., 1987-90; reporter Adv. Group on Litigation Cost and Delay, Tenn., 1991-95; mem. Tenn. Supreme Ct. Commn. on Dispute Resolution, 1992-94. Author: Pretrial Litigation, 1991, 2d edit., 1996; contbr. articles to profl. jours. Nat. Merit scholar 1969. Fellow Am. Bar Found., Lawyer's Found. of Ga.; mem. ABA (co-chair dean's workshop 1998-99), Tenn. Bar Found., Am. Law Inst., Phi Beta Kappa. Office: Mercer U Law Sch 1400 Coleman Ave Macon GA 31207-0003

**DETERMAN, DON PAUL,** lawyer; b. Sacramento, Nov. 9, 1938; s. Charles Kenneth and Winnifred Ann D. BS, U. Calif., 1961, Sacramento State, 1963; JD, Calif. Western, 1967. Bar: Calif. 1969, U.S. Cir. Ct. (9th cir.) 1970, U.S. Tax. Ct. 1973. Acct. Touche, Ross & Co., San Diego, 1966-67; counsel Irvin Kahn Orgn., San Diego, 1967-72; treas. U.S. Elevator, San Diego, 1972; v.p., counsel Sheltert Island Properties, San Diego, 1973-74; v.p. Vidcom, San Diego, 1975-90; pvt. practice San Diego, 1990—; dir. Sail Bay Shores, San Diego, 1975-80. Author: Grand Larceny by Power, 1970, What is Gambling?, 1973. Dir. Rep. Advocates, San Diego, 1970-80. With USAFR, 1961-67. Recipient Bank of Am. award, 1958. Mem. Tau Kappa Epsilon (pres. 1964-65). Roman Catholic. Avocations: stamp collecting, tennis, golfing, sports cards. Home: 3920 Riviera Dr San Diego CA 92109-5835

**DETHOMASIS, CRAIG CONSTANTINE,** lawyer, educator; b. Glen Cove, N.Y., Oct. 2, 1958. AA, U. Fla., 1978, BS, 1980, JD, 1983. Bar: Fla. 1983. Asst. pub. defender Pub. Defender's Office, Gainesville, Fla., 1983-87; atty. Silverman, Wilkov, DeThomasis & Buchanan, Gainesville, 1987-90, DeThomasis & Buchanan P.A., Gainesville, 1990—; adj. prof. law U. Fla. Coll. Law, Gainesville, 1990—; chmn. grievance com. Fla. Bar 8th Jud. Cir., Gainesville, 1994-97. Bd. dirs. Children's Home Soc.-Mid. Fla. Divsn., Gainesville, 1994—; mem. Leadership Gainesville, Gainesville Co. of C., 1996. Mem. Fla. Assn. Criminal Def. Lawyers (treas., v.p., pres. 1994-96), Eighth Jud. Cir. Assn. Criminal Def. Lawyers, Eighth Jud. Cir. Bar Assn., J.C. Adkins Inn of Ct. (master 1995—). Criminal. Office: DeThomasis & Buchanan PA 1800 N Main St Gainesville FL 32609-8606

**DETISCH, DONALD W.,** lawyer; b. Erie, Pa., May 5, 1941; s. John Jacob and Myra Detisch; m. Sue Bardwell, May 3, 1969; children: Blakeslee, Jennifer, Sara. BA, Pa. State U., 1963; JD, U. Calif., San Francisco, 1970. Bar: Calif. 1971, U.S. Dist. Ct. (so. dist.) Calif. 1973, U.S. Dist. Ct. (ctrl. dist.) Calif. 1995, U.S. Ct. Appeals (9th cir.) 1973. Claims adjuster Liberty Mut., L.A., 1963-64; dep. city atty. San Diego Atty.'s Office, 1971-83; ptnr. Detisch & Christensen, San Diego, 1983—. Contbr. articles to profl. jours. Lt. USN, 1964-67, Vietnam. Mem. San Diego County Bar Assn. (chmn. eminent domain sect.). Republican. Lutheran. Avocations: sports, jogging, fishing, backpacking, music. General civil litigation, Condemnation, Real property. Office: Detisch & Christensen 444 W C St Ste 200 San Diego CA 92101-3582

**DETJEN, DAVID WHEELER,** lawyer; b. St. Louis, Jan. 25, 1948; s. Don Wheeler and Shirley (Pence) D.; m. Barbara Louise Morgan, Jan. 6, 1973; children: Andrea Marlene, Erika Alexandra. *David Detjen is 3rd generation of lawyers in the Detjen family to represent European and American clients since his great-grandfather, Gustav Detjen, emigrated to the U.S. from Germany in 1890 and became a lawyer. Gustav (who, at the end of his career, received the Bundesverdienstkreuz from the German government) and his son, C. Wheeler Detjen, carried on general law practice as Detjen and Detjen in St. Louis for nearly 50 years, handling matters for U.S. and European clients and also for German and Swiss consulates there, while David Detjen practices law in NYC, representing primarily clients from Germany and other European countries doing business in the U.S.* AB magna cum laude, Washington U., 1970, JD, 1973; postgrad., Eberhard-Karls-Universitaet, Tuebingen, Fed. Republic of Germany, 1969-70. Bar: Mo. 1973, U.S. Supreme Ct. 1976, U.S. Ct. Appeals (8th cir.) 1976, N.Y. 1981. Law clk. to chief judge U.S. Ct. Appeals (8th cir.), St. Louis, 1973-75; assoc. Lewis, Rice, Tucker, Allen & Chubb, St. Louis, 1975-80; assoc. Walter, Conston, Alexander & Green, P.C., N.Y.C., 1980-83, ptnr., 1983—; affiliate office resident Walter, Conston, Alexander & Green, P.C., Bangkok, 1991-92; lectr. in law Washington U., St. Louis, 1975-80. Author: Distributorship Agreements in the U.S., 1983, 2d edit., 1989, The Germans in Missouri, 1900-1918: Prohibition, Neutrality and Assimilation, 1985, Licensing Technology and Trademarks in the United States, 1988, 2d edit., 1997, Establishing a United States Joint Venture with a Foreign Partner, 1988, 3d edit., 1993, United States Joint Ventures with International Partners, 1999; bd. dirs. Felix Schoeller Tech. Papers Inc., 1998—. Mem. Wash. U. Law Sch. Nat. Coun., 1989—; sec. German Forum, N.Y.C., 1988—, bd. dirs. 1995—; mem. St. Louis County Rep Cen. Com., 1976-83, Am. Coun. on Germany; co-pres. King-Merritt Comty. Assn., Greenwich, Conn., 1997—; trustee Am. Inst. Contemporary German Studies at Johns Hopkins U., 1999—. Recipient Disting. Alumnus award Law Sch. Wash. U., 1998. Mem. ABA, N.Y. State Bar Assn. (exec. editor Internat. Law Practicum 1988—, mem. exec. com. internat. law and practice sect. 1999—), Assn. Bar City N.Y., German Am. Law Assn., German am. Round Table, William G. Eliot Soc. of Washington U. (N.Y. chmn. 1993—), Deutscher Verein Club N.Y.C. (bd. dirs. 1994-97, 99—), Order of Coif, Delta Phi Alpha. Presbyterian. General corporate, Private international, Mergers and acquisitions. Home: 35 Stonehedge Dr S Greenwich CT 06831-3220 Office: Walter Conston Alexander & Green 90 Park Ave Fl 14 New York NY 10016-1387

**DETTINGER, WARREN WALTER,** lawyer; b. Toledo, Feb. 13, 1954; s. Walter Henry and Elizabeth Mae (Zoll) D.; m. Patricia Marie Kasper, June 21, 1975; children: John Robert, Laura Marie. BS cum laude, U. Toledo, 1977, JD magna cum laude, 1980. Bar: Ohio 1980, U.S. Dist. Ct. (no. dist.) Ohio 1980, U.S. Ct. Appeals (6th cir.) 1980, U.S. Tax Ct. 1981. Law clk. to presiding judge U.S. Ct. Appeals (6th cir.), Grand Rapids, Mich., 1980-81; assoc. Fuller & Henry, Toledo, 1981-84; atty. Sheller-Globe Corp., Toledo, 1984-87; v.p., gen. counsel Diebold, Inc., Canton, Ohio, 1987—. Mem. ABA, Ohio Bar Assn., Stark County Bar Assn., Am. Corp. Counsel Assn., Mfr.'s Alliance (law coun. II), Brookside Country Club, Phi Kappa Phi. Roman Catholic. Avocations: golf, travel, photography, tennis. General corporate, Computer, Private international. Home: 5237 Birkdale St NW Canton OH 44708-1825 Office: Diebold Inc 5995 Mayfair Rd PO Box 3077 North Canton OH 44720-8077

**DETTMER, MICHAEL HAYES,** lawyer; b. Detroit, June 6, 1946; s. Frank Arthur and Mary Frances (Conway) D.; m. Teckla Ann Getts, Aug. 15, 1969; children: Bryn Patrick, Janna Hayes. BS, Mich. State U., 1968; JD, Wayne State U., 1971. Bar: Mich. 1971, U.S. Dist. Ct. (we. dist.) Mich. 1992. Atty. Dettmer Thompon Parsons, Traverse City, Mich., 1972-90; pres., CEO Mich. Lawyer Mutual Ins. Co., Southfield, Grand Rapids, Mich., 1990-93; U.S. atty. we. dist. Mich. U.S. Dept. Justice, Grand Rapids, 1994—; lectr. in field. Contbr. articles to profl. jours. Pres. Traverse City Montessori Ctr., 1978-83; commr. Traverse City Human Rights Commn.; chmn. Grand Traverse County Dem. Party, 1986. Fellow Am. Bar Found., Mich. State Bar Found.; mem. ABA, State Bar of Mich. (pres. 1993-94, commr. No. Mich. and Upper Peninsula 1986-94, exec. com. bd. commrs. 1988-94, com. on legislation 1990-91, task force on professionalism 1988-90, co-chair standing com. on professionalism 1992—, chair Upper Mich. lawyers com. 1986-94, rep. assembly 1977-80, 88-94, atty. discipline bd. hearing panelist 1980-88), Am. Bd. Trial Advocates, Nat. Bd. Trial Advocacy (cert. 1981—). Democrat. Presbyterian. Office: 330 Ionia PO Box 208 Grand Rapids MI 49501-0208

**DEUTSCH, ANDREW L.,** lawyer; b. Chgo., Feb. 23, 1952; m. Cynthia Babcock; children: Jonathan, Laura. AB, Vassar Coll., 1973; cert. d'etudes politiques, Inst. Polit. Studies, Paris, 1974; JD, Yale U., 1977. Bar: N.Y. 1978, Ill. Assoc. Cahill Gordon & Reindel, N.Y.C., 1977-81; assoc. Milgrim, Thomajan & Lee PC, N.Y.C., 1981-88, mem., 1988-92; mem. Varet, Marcus & Fink, N.Y.C., 1992-93, Varet & Fink, N.Y.C., 1993-95; ptnr. Piper & Marbury LLP, N.Y.C., 1995—. Mem. ABA, Copyright Soc. U.S.A. (libel def. resource com.), Assn. Bar City N.Y. Jewish. Intellectual property, Libel, Trademark and copyright. Office: Piper & Marbury LLP 29th Fl 1251 Ave of Americas New York NY 10020

**DEUTSCH, GERALD S.,** lawyer; b. Bronx, Apr. 9, 1937; s. David and Margaret (Stern) D.; m. Linda E. Finkestein, Dec. 24, 1961; children: Daniel, Jonathan. BBA, CCNY, 1958; JD, Bklyn. Coll., 1962. CPA. Atty., acct. pvt. practice, 1962—. Home: 10 Hummingbird Dr Roslyn NY 11576-2507 Office: 3101 Hempstead Tpke Ste 121 Levittown NY 11756-1317

**DEUTSCH, STEPHEN B.,** lawyer; b. N.Y.C., Jan. 3, 1944; s. A. William and Rose (Berkowitz) D.; m. Jane M. Burnat, Nov. 23, 1986; children: Nancy, Jeffrey, Elizabeth. SB, MIT, 1965, PhD, 1969; JD, Harvard U., 1974. Bar: Mass. 1975, U.S. Dist. Mass., U.S. Ct. Appeals (1st cir.), U.S. Supreme Ct. Law clk. Supreme Judicial Ct. Mass., Boston, 1974-75; assoc. Foley, Hoag & Eliot, Boston, 1975-80, ptnr., 1981—. Mem. ABA, Mass. Bar Assn., Boston Bar Assn. Intellectual property, General civil litigation, Labor. Office: Foley Hoag & Eliot 1 Post Office Sq Ste 1700 Boston MA 02109-2170

**DEUTSCH, STUART LEWIS,** law educator; b. Bronx, N.Y., Dec. 11, 1945; s. Abraham and Ruth (Zarkower) D.; m. Elizabeth A. Burki, Mar. 12, 1969 (div. 1985); 1 son, Michael J.; m. Holly W. Gauthier, May 17, 1986. BA, U. Mich., 1966; JD, Yale U., 1969; LLM, Harvard U., 1974. Bar: Calif. 1971, Ill. 1978, U.S. Dist. Ct. (no. dist.) Ill. 1978. Assoc. Olwine, Connolly, Chase, O'Donnell & Weyher, N.Y.C., 1969-70; assoc. prof. law U. Santa Clara, Calif., 1970-75; prof. law Chgo. Kent Coll. Law Ill. Inst. Tech., 1976-99, assoc. dean, 1987-90, 95-96, 1997-99, interim dean, 1996-97; dean, prof. of law Rutgers U., Newark, N.J., 1999—; fellow in law and humanities Harvard Law Sch., Cambridge,Mass., 1973-74; vis. assoc. prof. U&. Ill. Coll. Law, Champaign, 1975-76; cons. various law firms and communities, Chgo., 1976--. Author: Deutsch's Illinois Environmental Statutes Annotated, West, 1999; editor Land Use and Environment Law Rev., 1982—; contbr. articles on land use and environment to profl. jours. Hearing officer Chgo. Commn. on Human Rels., 1992-98; chmn. bd. North Suburban Housing Ctr., Wilmette, Ill., 1983-87; chmn. adv. com., Eviction Ct., Chgo., 1986-89; chmn. interfaith Housing Devel. Corp., Wilmette, 1984-87; mem. atty. gen.'s Adv. Com. to Handicapped, Chgo., 1986-92; mem. attys.' revolving fund leadership coun. Met. Open Community Chgo., 1978-91. Named Outstanding Faculty Mem., Student Bar Assn., Ill. Inst. Tech., 1987, recipient Harold Washington Svc. award Black Students Assn., 1988, Distinguished Svc. award Chgo.-Kent Law Sch. Assn., 1998. Mem. ABA, State Bar Ill.,

Internat. Council Environ. Law. Democrat. Jewish. Environmental, Land use and zoning (including planning). Home: 224 Warwick Ave South Orange NJ 07079-2443 Office: Rutgers Univ Newark Sch of Law Kent Coll Law 15 Washington St Newark NJ 07102-3105

**DEVALL, JAMES LEE,** lawyer; b. Kansas City, Kans., Aug. 22, 1941; s. William Edward and Marie Etta (Culp) D.; m. Donna Jean Gould, Aug. 14, 1964; children: Carrie, David, John. BA, U. Kans., 1963; MA, Tufts U., 1964; JD, U. Calif., Berkeley, 1967. Bar: U.S. Dist. Ct. D.C. 1968, U.S. Ct. Appeals (D.C. and 9th cirs.) 1973, U.S. Supreme Ct. 1973. Legis. officer U.S. Bur. of the Budget, Washington, 1967-69; dir. legislation D.C. Govt., Washington, 1969-72; ptnr. Zuckert, Scoutt & Rasenberger, LLP, Washington; mem. CCH Aviation Law Coun., 1999—; adj. prof. law Am. U., 1998—. Mem. ABA, Fed. Bar Assn., Internat. Bar Assn., D.C. Bar Assn. Administrative and regulatory, Aviation, Private international. Home: 6125 33d St NW Washington DC 20015-2403 Office: Zuckert Scoutt & Rasenberger 888 17th St NW Ste 600 Washington DC 20006-3959

**DEVAN, MARK ROY,** lawyer; b. Cleve., May 30, 1948; s. Marco Dominic and Melba Juanita (Mauer) DeV. BA, Ashland (Ohio) Coll., 1971; JD, Cleve. U., 1974. Bar: Ohio 1974, U.S. Dist. Ct. (no. dist.) Ohio 1974, U.S. Ct. Appeals (6th cir.) 1975, U.S. Supreme Ct. 1982. Staff atty. Legal Aid Soc., Cleve., 1975-77; staff atty. pub. defender's office County of Cuyahoga, Cleve., 1977-79; pvt. practice Cleve., 1979-92; ptnr. Berkman, Gordon, Murray & DeVan, Cleve., 1992—. Contbr. articles to profl. jours. Fellow Am. Bd. Criminal Lawyers, Am. Coll. Trial Lawyers; mem. Ohio Bar Assn., Ohio Assn. Criminal Def. Lawyers (bd. dirs. 1988—, v.p. publs. 1989—, pres. 1993-94), Cuyahoga County Criminal Def. Lawyers Assn. (bd. dirs. 1985—, chmn. Amicus com. 1985, 86, chmn. grand jury com. 1986-88, lawyers assistance com. 1986, chmn. resource panel 1986, ann. meeting com. 1986—, pres. 1988-89), Nat. Assn. Criminal Def. Lawyers (death penalty com. 1983-84, vice chmn. hot line panel experts 1986, legis. com. 1987-90), Am. Inns of Ct. (master bencher). Democrat. Roman Catholic. Criminal, Personal injury. Office: 2121 Illuminating Bldg Cleveland OH 44113

**DEVANEY, DONNA BROOKES,** lawyer; b. Orlando, Fla., Sept. 7, 1972; d. Edward Nolan and Carolyn (Jessen) B.; m. David Brooks DeVaney, May 24, 1997. BS, Auburn U., 1993; JD, Stetson U., 1997. Bar: Fla. 1997, U.S. Dist. Ct. (mid. dist.) Fla. 1997, U.S. Dist. Ct. (so. and no. dists.) Fla. 1999, U.S. Ct. Appeals (11th cir.) 1999. Atty. Carlton, Fields, Ward, Emmanuel, Smith and Cutler, Tampa, Fla., 1997—. Vol., Soc. for Prevention of Cruelty to Animals, Largo, Fla., 1996—, Hillsborough Reads, Tampa, 1998—. Mem. ABA, Fed. Bar Assn., Fla. Bar Assn., Hillsborough County Bar Assn., Ferguson White Inn of Ct. Avocations: boating, swimming, running. General civil litigation, Federal civil litigation, State civil litigation. Office: Calrton Fields et al One Harbour Pl Tampa FL 33601

**DEVASTO, DIANE V.,** judge; b. Ft. Worth, Apr. 19, 1951; d. Aaron J. Vinson and Sarah C. (Price) Olson. BA, Baylor U., 1972, JD, 1974. Bar: Tex. 1974. Asst. city atty. City of Tyler, Tex., 1974-75, cmty. devel. coord., 1975-80; pvt. practice with emphasis in real estate and oil and gas, 1980-83; interim dir. Juvenile Attention Ctr., Smith County, Tex., 1981; alt. mcpl. ct. judge City of Tyler, 1981-83; presiding judge City of Tyler Mcpl. Ct., 1983-94; judge Smith County Ct. at Law, 1995, 241st Dist. Ct., 1995—; mem. Smith County Juvenile Bd.; bd. dirs. Tex. Mcpl. Cts. Edn. Ctr./Tex. Mcpl. Cts. Assn., 1987-94. Bd. dirs. Children's Village, 1995—, PATH, 1992—; mem. Tex. Commn. on Jud. Efficience, 1995; mem. pub.policy com. Tex. Coun. Family Violence, 1992-94; mem. Smith County Bail Bond Bd., 1988-94, chair, 1990, vice chair, 1989, 92; mem. Tex. Supreme Ct. Jud. Edn. Exec. Com., 1992-93. Mem. Smith County Bar Assn., Baylor Law Alumni Assn., Delta Theta Phi. Office: 241st Dist Ct 100 N Broadway Ave Tyler TX 75702-7236

**D'EVEGNEE, CHARLES PAUL,** lawyer; b. Liege, Belgium, Aug. 4, 1939; came to U.S., 1959; s. Charles Clement and Fernande Francoise (Godet) Devignez; m. Marie-Therese L. Barnich, Apr. 17, 1962; children: Chantal E., Charles D. BA, Brigham Young U., 1966; MA, U. Conn., Storrs, 1969; JD, U. Conn., West Hartford, 1974. Bar: Va. 1991, U.S. Banktuptcy Ct. (ea. dist.-Richmond divsn.), U.S. Dist. Ct. 9ea. dist.) Va., U.S. Ct. Appeals (4th cir.), U.S. Supreme Ct. Group pension underwriter Conn. Gen. Life Ins. Co., Bloomfield, 1969-72; legal cons. Frank B. Hall & Co., N.Y.C., 1974-76; regional counsel Meidinger & Assocs., Richmond, Va., 1976-78; dir. Office Benefits Devel., Commonwealth of Va., Richmond, 1978-91; pvt. practice, Ashland, Va., 1991—. Co-author: European Antitrust Law, 1976. Mem. Va. Gov.'s U.S. Savs. Bond Com., Richmond, 1986; rep. exec. bd. State's United Appeals of Greater Richmond Community Chest, 1989. With U.S. Army, 1960-63. Mem. ABA, Va. State Bar Assn., Hanover Bar Assn., Richmond Bar Assn. Avocations: travel, landscaping, sports. General practice, Private international, Workers' compensation. Home: 6034 Northfall Creek Pkwy Mechanicsville VA 23111-7522 Office: 130 Thompson St Ste D Ashland VA 23005-1512

**DEVENS, CHARLES J.,** lawyer; b. Chgo., Apr. 16, 1952; s. Joseph F. and Phyllis E. (Guenther) D.; m. Darci L. Walker, Jan. 15, 1987; children: Andrew Wagner, Amy Wagner, Adam Wagner, Mallory L. Devens, Patrick C. Devens. BS, U. Ill., 1974, JD, 1977. Bar: Ill., 1977; U.S. Dist. Ct. (cen. dist.) Ill., 1977. Asst. county prosecutor Marion County Prosecutor's Office, Indpls., 1976-77; asst. state's atty. Vermillion County State's Atty., Danville, Ill., 1977-78; assoc. Manion, Janov & Edgar, Ltd., Danville, 1978-80; ptnr. Manion, Janov, Edgar & Devens, Ltd., Danville, 1980-82; mng. ptnr. Manion, Devens & McFetridge, Ltd., Danville, 1982—; city atty. City of Georgetown, Ill., 1992—. Author: (book) Worker's Comp for the Worker, 1994. Vice-chmn. Vermilion County Airport Authority, Danville, 1992—, Vermilion County Dem. Party, Danville, 1982-83; v.p. Women's Shelter, Danville, 1979-81. Mem. K.C., Elks. Workers' compensation, Insurance, Personal injury. Office: Manion Devens & McFetridge 24 E North St Danville IL 61832-5804

**DEVER, VERONICA MCNAMARA,** prosecutor; b. Cleve., May 27, 1940; d. Hugh and Margaret O'Grady (McNamara) D. AB, Ursuline Coll., 1962; MSW, St. Louis U., 1966; JD, Cleve. State U., 1970. Social worker Cuyahoga County Child Welfare Dept., Cleve., 1963-67; psychiat. social worker Criminal Psychiat. Clinic, Cleve., 1966-71; prosecutor City of Cleve., 1971-73; atty. inspector State of Ohio, Columbus, 1973-75; dir. legal aid Erie County, Sandusky, Ohio, 1975-80, prosecutor child support, 1980-86; prosecutor Vermilian, Ohio, 1983-93; prosecutor child support Cuyahoga County, 1986—. Mem. Ohio Pub. Def. Assn. (pres. 1976-77, bd. dirs. 1976-81), Erie County Bar Assn. (treas. 1975-82), Ohio Family Support Assn. (pres. 1985-96, bd. dirs. 1981—), Kapa Beta Pi. Roman Catholic. Avocations: classical music, ice skating, hiking, travel, white water rafting. Office: Cuyahoga County Prosecutor Rm 74 One Lakeside Cleveland OH 44113

**DEVEREAUX, WILLIAM P.,** lawyer, military officer; b. Boston, Nov. 12, 1952; s. William Joseph and Geraldine Louise O'Connor D.; m. Amy Ruth Hryt, July 8, 1988; 1 child, William Gerald. BA in History with honors, Wesleyan U., 1975; JD, Suffolk U., 1979. Bar: R.I. 1979, Mass. 1979, U.S. Dist. Ct. R.I. 1983, U.S. Dist. Ct. Mass. 1990, U.S. Ct. Appeals Armed Forces 1992. Commd. ensign USN, 1979, advanced through grades to capt., 1999; with USN and USNR, 1979—; asst. atty. gen. State R.I., Providence, 1983-87; ptnr. Fontaine Croll & Devereaux, Woonsocket, R.I., 1987-91, McGovern Noel & Benik, Providence, 1991—. Author: Guide to Grand Jury Service, 1987. Bd. dirs. Providence Ctr., 1995—. Mem. R.I. Bar Assn., R.I. Superior Ct. (mem. superior ct. bench and bar com.), R.I. Jud. Nominating Commn. (vice-chair 1994-98), No. R.I. C. of C. (mem. exec. success com. 1997—). Democrat. Roman Catholic. Avocations: kayaking, ice hockey. Fax: 401-824-5175. E-mail: MNB@Law.com. General civil litigation, Criminal, Insurance. Home: 30 Lincoln Dr North Smithfield RI 02896-6956 Office: McGovern Noel & Benik 1 Bankboston Plz Ste 1800 Providence RI 02903-2419

**DEVERS, PETER DIX,** lawyer; b. N.Y.C., Mar. 13, 1938. BS, Holy Cross Coll., 1961; JD, NYU, 1964. Bar: N.Y. 1965, U.S. Dist Ct. (so. and ea. dists.) N.Y. 1965, U.S. Ct. Appeals (2d cir.) 1965. Assoc. Shearman & Sterling, N.Y.C., 1965-73; v.p., counsel Equitable Life Assurance Soc. U.S., N.Y.C., 1973—. Mem. Assn. Life Ins. Counsel, Am. Arbitration Assn., N.Y. State Bar Assn., Phi Delta Phi. Insurance, Finance, Real property. Office: Equitable Life Assurance Soc US 787 7th Ave Fl 38 New York NY 10019-6018

**DEVGUN, DHARMINDER SINGH,** lawyer; b. Dudley, U.K., Nov. 27, 1967; came to U.S., 1990; s. Mohan Singh and Kirpal Kaur Devgun; m. Amrit Bhooi, May 4, 1994. LLB with honors, U. Birmingham, 1990; JD with high distinction, U. Iowa, 1993. Bar: Minn. 1993, U.S. Ct. Internat. Trade 1997. Assoc. Faegre & Benson, Mpls., 1993-96, Doherty, Rumble & Butler, St. Paul, 1996-98; sr. corp. counsel The St. Paul Cos., Inc., 1998—; lectr., adj. prof. William Mitchell Coll. of Law, St. Paul, 1994—. Author: Doing Business in the United Kingdom, 1998; editor-in-chief Transnational Law and Contemporary Problems, 1992-93; contbr. articles to profl. jours. Active Leadership St. Paul, 1998—. Mem. ABA, Minn. State Bar Assn., Order of Coif. Avocations: writing, computers. Private international, General corporate, Mergers and acquisitions. Office: St Paul Cos Inc Mail Code 515A 385 Washington St Saint Paul MN 55102-1309

**DEVINE, ANTOINE MAURICE,** lawyer; b. Milw., Apr. 19, 1957; s. John and Marietta Elizabeth D.; m. Jeanne Nicole Covington, Aug. 2, 1991 (div. 1994). BS in Fin., Jackson State U., 1979; JD, U. Tex., 1991. Bar: Calif. 1993. Asst. auditor Trustmark Bank, Jackson, Miss., 1979-81; sr. compliance examiner NASD Regulation, Inc., Dallas, 1981-84; adminstr., pres. Hall Securities Corp./Funding Capital, Inc., Dallas, 1985-86; pres. Devine Fin. Svcs., Bedford, Tex., 1987-88; assoc. Dennis & Coscia, San Diego, 1993-95; staff atty. San Diego Gas & Elec., 1995; corp. counsel Global Resource Investments, Ltd., Carlsbad, Calif., 1997-98; sr. assoc. Evers & Hendrickson, San Francisco, 1998—. Basketball coach Jackie Robinson YMCA, San Diego, 1994-97. Democrat. Avocations: golf, tennis, softball, jazz. General corporate, Private international, Securities. Home: 3 Shoreline Ct Richmond CA 94804-4586 Office: Evers & Hendrickson LLP 155 Montgomery St Fl 12 San Francisco CA 94104-4105

**DEVINE, DONN,** lawyer, genealogist, former city official; b. South Amboy, N.J., Mar. 30, 1929; s. Frank Edward and Emily Theresa (DeRevere) D. m. Elizabeth Cecilia Baldwin, Nov. 23, 1951; children: Edward (dec.), Mary Elizabeth, Martin Joseph. BS, U. Del., 1949; JD with honors, Widener U., 1975. Bar: Del. 1975, U.S. Dist. Ct. Del. 1976, U.S. Supreme Ct. 1997; cert. genealogist and cert. genealogy instr. Bd. for Cert. Genealogists; cert. Am. Inst. Cert. Planners. Devel. chemist Allied Chem. Corp., Claymont, Del., 1950-52; newspaper writer, editor corp. publs. Atlas Powder Co., Wilmington, Del., 1952-60; mgmt. cons., 1960-68; dir. renewal planning City of Wilmington, 1968-79, dep. dir. planning, 1979-80, dir. planning, 1981-85; cons. Wilmington City Coun., 1985—; pvt. practice, 1985—; archival cons. Cath. Diocese Wilmington, 1989—; spl. counsel Del. Div. Alcoholism, Drug Abuse and Mental Health, 1990-93; trustee Bd. for Cert. Genealogists, 1992—; mediator Del. Superior Ct., 1998—. Author: Delaware National Guard, A Historical Sketch, 1968, DeRevere Family of Peekskill, New York, 1982; editor Del. Geneal. Soc. Jour., 1980-81, Cultural Resources Survey of Wilmington, Del., 1982-84; assoc. editor Del. Jour. Corp. Law, 1974-75. Past bd. dirs. Wilmington Small Bus. Devel. Corp., Wilmington Econ. Devel. Corp.; past officer Delmarva Ecumenical Agy.; emeritus bd. dirs., past officer Geriatric Svcs. Del.; past officer Christina Cultural Arts Ctr., Cath. Interracial Coun., Del. chpt. ACLU, Maplewood Housing for Elderly, St. Mary's-St. Patrick's Parish Coun. With USAR, 1950-54; brig. gen. Del. Army N.G., 1954-84, ret. Decorated Meritorious Svc. medal. Mem. Am. Planning Assn., Am. Chem. Soc., Del. Bar Assn., Del. Soc. SAR (past pres.), Nat. Geneal. Soc. (bd. dirs. 1994—), Assn. Cath. Diocesan Archivists (bd. dirs. 1993-95), Del. Geneal. Soc. (past pres.), Ft. Delaware Soc. (recognition award), Old Bohemia Hist. Soc. (bd. dirs. 1992—), Univ. and Whist Club, Chemists Club N.Y.C., Ancient Order Hibernians, Phi Kappa Phi, Delta Theta Phi. Democrat. Land use and zoning (including planning), Intellectual property. Home: 2004 Kentmere Pkwy Wilmington DE 19806-2014

**DEVINE, EDMOND FRANCIS,** lawyer; b. Ann Arbor, Mich., Aug. 9, 1916; s. Frank B. and Elizabeth Catherine (Doherty) DeV.; m. Elizabeth Palmer Ward, Sept. 17, 1955; children: Elizabeth Palmer, Stephen Ward, Michael Edmond, Suzanne Lee. AB, U. Mich., 1937, JD, 1940; LLM, Cath. U. Am., 1941. Bar: Mich. 1940, U.S. Dist. Ct. (ea. dist.) Mich. 1940, U.S. Ct. Appeals (6th cir) 1974, U.S. Supreme Ct. 1975. Spl. agt. FBI, 1941-43; chief asst. prosecutor Washtenaw County (Mich.), Ann Arbor, 1947-53, prosecuting atty., 1953-58; ptnr. DeVine & DeVine, Ann Arbor, 1958-74, DeVine, DeVine, Kantor & Serr, Ann Arbor, 1974-84; sr. ptnr. Miller, Canfield, Paddock & Stone, Ann Arbor, 1984-92, of counsel, 1992—; lectr., asst. prof., adj. prof. U. Mich. Law Sch., 1949-79. Co-author: Criminal Procedure, 1960. Bd. dirs. Youth for Understanding, Inc., Ann Arbor, 1966-70. Lt. USNR, 1943-46, PTO. Decorated Bronze Star with combat v. Fellow Am. Bar Found. (cons. 1956-61), Am. Coll. Trial Lawyers, Mich. Bar Found.; mem. ABA, State Bar Mich. (bd. commrs., chmn. judiciary com. 1976-85, mem. rep. assembly, chmn. rules and calendar com.1971-76, co-chair U.S. Cts. com. 1986-87), Internat. Assn. Def. Counsel, U.S. Supreme Ct. Hist. Soc., Ann Arbor C. of C. (chmn. bd. 1971), Detroit Athletic Club, Barton Hills Country Club, Pres.'s Club. U. Mich., Varsity M Club, Order of Coif, Barristers, Phi Delta Phi, Phi Kappa Psi. Republican. Roman Catholic. Avocations: golf, jogging, reading. General civil litigation, Federal civil litigation, State civil litigation. Home: 101 Underdown Rd Ann Arbor MI 48105-1078 Office: Miller Canfield Paddock & Stone 101 N Main St Fl 7 Ann Arbor MI 48104-5507

**DEVINE, EUGENE PETER,** lawyer; b. Albany, N.Y., Oct. 14, 1948; s. Eugene Peter and Phyllis Jean (Albanese) D.; m. Debra Ann Ziamandanis, Apr. 11, 1992; children: Kimberly, Tracy, Adrianne, Madeline. JD, Union U., 1975. Bar: N.Y. 1975, U.S. Dist. Ct. (no. dist.) N.Y. 1975, U.S. Supreme Ct. 1980. Asst. N.Y. Pub. Defender, Albany County, 1976-85; ptnr. Cooper, Erving & Savage, Albany, 1975-85, Devine, Piedment & Rutnik, 1985-91; chief pub. defender Albany County, 1994—; of counsel Carter Conboy, 1995—; chief atty. Albany County Dept. Social Svcs., 1985-88. Bd. dirs. Ronald McDonald House, Albany, 1980—, founding mem.; committeeman Albany County Dem. Com., 1979—; treas. com. to elect Jim Tully N.Y. State Compt. N.Y. State Compt., N.Y.C., 1980, vice chmn. Albany Med. Ctr. Found., 1994—. Mem. Woolferts Roost Country Club, Steuben Athletic Club, Albany Sons of St. Patrick (pres. 1984). Criminal, Labor, General practice. Office: Carter Conboy Case Blackmore Napierski & Maloney 20 Corporate Woods Blvd Ste 8 Albany NY 12211-2362

**DEVINE, JOHN MICHAEL,** lawyer; b. Albany, N.Y., Oct. 21, 1947; s. John Joseph and Veronica Theresa D.; children: John Michael II, Gregory Joseph. BA in English, Manhattan Coll., 1969; JD, Albany Law Sch., 1973. Bar: N.Y. and U.S. Dist. Cts., 1974. Asst. corp. counsel City of Albany, 1974-78, exec. dep. corp. counsel, 1979-84; asst. county atty. County of Albany, 1984-93; airport counsel, Albany County Airport, 1984-91. Bd. dirs. YMCA, Albany, 1981-89, Rensselaer (N.Y.) Boys and Girls Club, 1986—. With USAR, 1969-75. Recipient Outstanding Svc. award Rensselaer Boys and Girls Club, 1990; named Rotarian of Yr. Albany Airport Rotary Club, 1990. Mem. N.Y. State Bar Assn., Albany County Bar, Knights of Columbus, Troy (N.Y.) Country Club. Democrat. Roman Catholic. Avocations: golf, yoga, reading. Office: 600 Broadway Albany NY 12207-2205

**DEVINE, SHANE,** federal judge; b. Feb. 1, 1926. B.A., U. N.H., 1949; J.D., Boston Coll., 1952. Bar: N.H. 1952. Formerly ptnr. Devine, Millimet, Stahl & Branch, Manchester, N.H.; judge U.S. Dist. Ct. N.H., 1978—, chief judge, now sr. judge, 1992—. Mem. ABA, N.H. Bar Assn. (pres. 1973-74), Manchester Bar Assn. Office: US Dist Ct NH 55 Pleasant St Rm 511 Concord NH 03301-3954

**DEVINE, WILLIAM FRANKLIN,** lawyer; b. Norfolk, Va., Apr. 19, 1961; s. Patrick C. and Linda (Dofflemoyer) D.; m. Alicia Taylor Scott, May 26, 1990; children: William Franklin, Wyatt T. BA in Politics, Washington and Lee U., 1983; JD, Coll. of William and Mary, 1986. Bar: Va. 1986. Prin. atty. Hofheimer, Nusbaum, McPhaul & Samuels, P.C., Norfolk, 1986—. Sec., counsel The AIDS Fund, Inc., Norfolk, 1991—. Mem. ABA, Va. Bar Assn., Va. Trial Laywers Assn., Norfolk-Portsmouth Bar Assn. (exec. com. Young Lawyers sect. 1987-95). Democrat. Roman Catholic. Avocations: golf, gardening, walking. General civil litigation, Contracts commercial. Office: Hofheimer Nusbaum PC PO Box 3460 1700 Dominion Tower Norfolk VA 23514

**DEVINS, ROBERT SYLVESTER,** lawyer; b. N.Y.C., Mar. 19, 1949; s. Arthur Sylvester and Judith Delores (Whelan) D. BA, Tulane U., 1971; JD, Emory U., 1978. Bar: Ga. 1978, Fla. 1981, U.S. Dist. Ct. (no. dist.) Ga. 1978, U.S. Tax Ct. 1978, U.S. Ct. Appeals (5th cir.) 1978, U.S. Supreme Ct. 1982, U.S. Dist. Ct. (mid. dist.) Ga. 1994. Pvt. practice Atlanta, 1978—. Lt. USN, 1971-75. Mem. ABA, Internat. Bar Assn. (vice chmn. criminal law sect. 1985-87, chmn. 1987-89. rep. UN Conf. 1987, 89), Inter Am. Bar Assn., Nat. Assn. Criminal Def. Lawyers, Ga. Assn. Criminal Def. Lawyers, Assn. Trial Lawyers Am., Ga. Trial Lawyers Assn., Union International des Avocats. Avocation: reading. Criminal, General civil litigation, Family and matrimonial. Home: 1489 Leafmore Pl Decatur GA 30033-2050 Office: 1776 Peachtree St NW Atlanta GA 30309-2307

**DEVITA, DANIELLE,** lawyer; b. Passaic, N.J., Apr. 27, 1970. BA, Skidmore Coll., 1992; JD, Seton Hall U., Newark, 1996. Bar: N.J. 1996, U.S. Dist. Ct. (N.J.) 1996. Law clk. to Hon. Joseph F. Scancarella presiding civil judge Passaic County Superior Ct., Passaic, N.J., 1996-97, law clk. to Hon. Joseph A. Falcone assignment judge, 1996-97; assoc. Price, Meese, Shulman & D'Arminio, P.C., Woodcliff Lake, N.J., 1997—. Mem. steering com. March of Dimes, Pine Brook, N.J., 1997—. Mem. N.J. Bar Assn., Passaic County Bar Assn., Bergen County Bar Assn. Land use and zoning (including planning), Bankruptcy, General civil litigation. Office: Price Meese Shulman & D'Arminio PC 50 Tice Blvd Woodcliff Lake NJ 07675-7654

**DEVLIEGER, TRACY BLAKE,** lawyer; b. Darby, Pa., Aug. 6, 1959; d. Edward J. and Marian J. Blake; m. Pierre J. DeVlieger, Feb. 7, 1987; children: Dana, Blake, Madeline. BA magna cum laude, U. Notre Dame, 1981; JD cum laude, Villanova U., 1984. Bar: Pa. 1984, U.S. Dist. Ct. (ea. dist.) Pa. 1984, U.S. Ct. Appeals (3d cir.) 1984. Jud. clk. U.S. Dist. Ct. (ea. dist.) Pa., Phila., 1984-86; assoc. Schnader, Harrison Segal & Lewis, Phila., 1986-91; ptnr. Lamb, Windle & McErlane P.C., West Chester, Pa., 1991—; mem. Chester County Estate Planning Coun., West Chester, 1993-98. Mem. Chester County Bar Assn., Order of Coif, Phi Beta Kappa. Avocations: sports, traveling. Estate planning, Probate, Estate taxation. Office: Lamb Windle & McErlane PC 24 E Market St West Chester PA 19382-3151

**DEVLIN, FRANCIS JAMES,** lawyer; b. N.Y.C., Apr. 12, 1943; s. Francis James and Marie A. (Portley) D.; m. Patricia Ann Scheid, Feb. 23, 1969; children: Christopher James, Kimberley Ann. BA magna cum laude, Providence Coll., 1964; JD, Fordham U., 1967. Bar: N.Y. 1968, Tex. 1979, U.S. Ct. Appeals (5th and 11th cirs.) 1981, U.S. Supreme Ct. 1993. Assoc. Rogers and Wells, N.Y.C., 1967-72; counsel Standard Oil Co. N.J., N.Y.C., 1972, Exxon Corp., N.Y.C., 1973-78; counsel Exxon Co., U.S.A., Houston, 1978-90, sr. counsel, 1990—, coord. gen. comml. practice group, 1996—. Articles editor: Fordham Law Review, 1966-67. Bd. dirs. Our Lady of Guadalupe Sch., Houston, 1994-99 (chmn. 1998—). Mem. ABA (vice-chmn. petroleum and mktg. com., natural resources, energy and environ. law sect.), Tex. State Bar (Bar Jour. com. 1995-98, unauthorized practice of law com. 1989-92), Coll. of State Bar Tex., Am. Petroleum Inst. (chmn. subcom. on mktg. law, gen. com. law, chmn. 1990-92, 97-98, vice-chmn. 1992-94, 98—), Tex. Mid-Continent Oil and Gas Assn. (chmn. mktg. subcom. legal com. 1982—), Soc. Friendly Sons of St. Patrick in City N.Y. Republican. Roman Catholic. Franchising, Antitrust, Legislative. Home: 12625 Memorial Townhouse #112 Houston TX 77024 Office: Exxon Co USA 800 Bell St Rm 1859 Houston TX 77002-7497

**DEVLIN, JAMES RICHARD,** lawyer; b. Camden, N.J., July 7, 1950; s. Gerald William and Mary (Hand) D.; children: Grace, Jennifer, Kristen. BS in Indsl. Engring., N.J. Inst. Tech., 1972; JD, Fordham U., 1976. Bar: N.J. 1976, N.Y. 1977, U.S. Ct. Appeals (D.C. cir.) 1982. Various mgmt. positions in Long Lines Sect. AT&T, N.Y.C., 1972-76; counsel Long Lines Sect. AT&T, Bedminster, N.J., 1976-82; counsel AT&T, N.Y.C., 1982-83; gen. atty. comm. sect. AT&T, Basking Ridge, N.J., 1983-86; v.p., gen. counsel telephone United Telecomm., Inc., Westwood, Kans., 1987-88; exec. v.p. gen. counsel and external affairs Sprint Corp., Westwood, 1989—; bd. dirs. Transfinancial Holdings, Inc., Lenexa, Kans.; pres. bd. dirs. Ctr. Mgmt. Assitance, 1993-97; mem. bd. overseers N.J. Inst. Tech., 1997—. Past pres., bd. dirs. Ctr. for Mgmt. Assistance, Kansas City, Mo., 1993-96; bd. dirs. Heart of Am. United Way, Minority Supplier Coun., Kansas City; mem. bd. overseers N.J. Inst. Tech. Mem. ABA (past chmn. comm. com. pub. utility law sect.), Am. Arbitration Assn., Fed. Comm. Bar Assn. Administrative and regulatory, General corporate, Communications. Home: 4104 W 123rd St Leawood KS 66209-2220 Office: Sprint Corp 2330 Shawnee Mission Pkwy Westwood KS 66205-2090

**DEVLIN, JOHN GERARD,** lawyer, author; b. Phila., Apr. 26, 1955; s. John and Catherine (Flannery) D.; m. Maureen Borneman, June 17, 1978; children: Caitlin, Colin, Courtenay, Conor. BA, Temple U., 1977, JD, 1980, LLM, 1996. Bar: Pa. 1980, N.J. 1992. Assoc. Spencer, Sherr & Moses, Norristown, Pa., 1980-82, Deasey, Scanlan & Bender, Phila., 1982-84; mng. atty. Devlin Assocs., P.A., Phila., 1984—. Author: Tort Liability for Bad Faith Claims, 1995. Mem. Union League Club, Phi Beta Kappa. Insurance, General civil litigation. Office: 1515 Market St Ste 2010 Philadelphia PA 19102-1920

**DEVOTO, LOUIS JOSEPH,** lawyer; b. Jersey City, July 27, 1965; s. Richard Louis and Concetta Ann DeVoto; m. Anne M. Hayes, June 1, 1991; children: Thomas, Emily, Caroline. BS in Mgmt., St. Joseph's U., Phila., 1987; JD, Ohio No. U., 1993. Bar: N.J. 1993, U.S. Dist. Ct. N.J. 1993, Pa. 1994, U.S. Ct. Appeals (3d cir.), 1995, U.S. Dist. Ct. (ea. dist.) Pa. 1998, U.S. Supreme Ct. 1999. Jud. clk. to Hon. Marvin E. Schlosser, N.J. Superior Ct., Mt. Holly, 1993-94; assoc. Ferrara & Rossetti, P.A., Cherry Hill, N.J., 1994-97; ptnr. Ferrara, Rossetti & DeVoto, P.A., Cherry Hill, 1998—; guest spkr. Gloucester County Coll., 1996. Exec. editor Ohio No. U. Law Rev., 1992-93. Mem. bldg. com. Our Lady Queen of Peach Ch., West Milford, N.J., 1987-88; sponsor annual fundraising banquet March of Dimes Found., Cherry Hill, N.J., 1994—, Bancroft Found., Phila., 1998; coach Marlton (N.J.) Rec. Coun., 1995; trustee Bancroft Brain Injury Svcs. Corp., 1999—. Fellow Camden County Bar Found.; mem. ATLA (guest spkr. N.J. affiliate 1997), Am. Arbitration Assn. (adv. com.), N.J. Bar Assn., Trial Attys. N.J. (trustee 1999—), Trial Lawyers for Pub. Justice, Camden County Bar Assn. (personal injury law com.), Burlington County Bar Assn. (civil practice com.). Roman Catholic. Avocations: golf, ice hockey, rollerblading. Fax: 856-661-0369. E-mail: ldevoto@njinjurylaw.com. Personal injury, Product liability, General civil litigation. Office: Ferrara Rossetti & DeVoto 601 Longwood Ave Cherry Hill NJ 08002-2856

**DEVRIES, DONALD LAWSON, JR.,** lawyer; b. Phila., May 1, 1947; s. Donald Lawson and Jeanne (Coleman) DeV.; m. Nancy Shafer, Aug. 10, 1977; children: Donald Lawson III, Emily Shafer; stepdaughter: Alison Brady Beale. BA with honors, Dartmouth Coll., 1969; JD with honors, U. Md., 1973. Bar: Md. 1973, U.S. Dist. Ct. Md. 1973, U.S. Ct. Appeals (4th cir.) 1976, U.S. Ct. Appeals (D.C. cir.) 1989, U.S. Dist. Ct. D.C. 1991. Assoc. Semmes, Bowen & Semmes, Balt., 1973-80, ptnr., chmn. med. malpractice dept., 1980-88; founding ptnr. Goodell, DeVries, Leech & Gray, Balt., 1988—; chmn. dept. med. malpractice Semmes, Bowen & Semmes, 1980-88; mem. faculty Md. Inst. Continuing Profl. Edn. for Lawyers, 1984-95; gov.'s task force on Med. Malpractice Ins., 1985; master Am. Inns of Court, 1986-90. Contbr. Md. Law Rev., 1973. Trustee Roland Pk. Country Sch., 1987-94, Woodbourne Ctr., 1981-88; trustee, exec. com. South Balt. Gen. Hosp., 1983-88; mem. Canons and Other Bus. Coms. of Episcopal Diocese Md., 1984-95; vestryman St. David's Ch., 1982-85; bd. dirs. Md. affiliate Am. Heart Assn., 1986-90, co-chmn. Heart Ball, 1986, 87, 88, chmn. solicitation com. Shock Trauma Gala, 1988, 89, co-chmn., 1990, 91, bd. visitors Shock Trauma, 1989-93, chmn. 1990-93; chmn. Emergency Med. Svcs. Bd., Md., 1992—; mem. joint exec./legis. task force on med. malpractice ins., Md., 1985; mem. com. on uninsured persons Gov.'s Commn. on Health Care Policy and Financing, 1988-90. Mem. ABA (spkr. ann. meeting 1984, moderator, program planner ann. meeting medicine and law com. 1986, 88, vice chmn. medicine and law com. torts and ins. practice sect. 1982-89, med. adv. panel medicine and law com. 1986-87, forum com. health law 1984—, faculty nat. inst. on med. malpractice 1987, 88, 89, 90, chmn. medicine and law com., torts and ins. practice sect. 1988-89), Internat. Assn. Ins. Counsel, Internat. Assn. Def. Counsel (faculty trial acad. 1991, moderator, program planner 1992, vice chmn. med. malpractice com. for newsletters 1989-90, program chmn. 1990-92, chmn. med. malpractice com. 1992-94, chmn. def. counsel com. 1997-99, exec. com. 1999—, George W. Yantey Meml. award 1998), Internat. Soc. Barristers, Assn. Def. Trial Attys., Am. Bd. Trial Advocates (pres. Md. chpt. 1993-95, nat. bd. dirs. 1993—), Md. State Bar Assn. (spl. com. on health claims arbitration 1983), Md. Trial Lawyers Assn. (faculty 1983, 85), Md. Assn. Def. Trial Counsel, Def. Rsch. Inst., Wednesday Law Club, Maryland Club, Chesapeake Bay Yacht Club. Republican. Personal injury, Product liability, Professional liability. Office: Goodell DeVries Leech & Gray LLP 1 South St Ste 200 Baltimore MD 21202-3298

**DEVRIES, JAMES HOWARD,** lawyer; b. Chgo., Mar. 17, 1932; s. James and Ruth Frances (Heuman) DeV.; m. Eleanor Newport Smith, Mar. 3, 1956; children: Sara, James, Peter, Adam, Mary. BS in Bus. Mgmt., U. Colo., 1954; JD with distinction, U. Mich., 1961. Bar: Ill. 1961. Assoc. Hopkins & Sutter, Chgo., 1961-62; ptnr. McBride & Baker, Chgo., 1963-82; chmn., chief exec. officer LaserVideo, Inc., Chgo., 1982-88; vice chmn. Disc Mfg. Inc., Chgo., 1991-97; exec. v.p., sec. Quixote Corp., Chgo., 1969-97, ret., 1997, also bd. dirs., 1969—; pres. Legal Techs. Inc., Chgo., 1993-96, also bd. dirs. Pres. Library Internat. Relations, Chgo., 1980-83; dir. Internat. Trade Club, Chgo., 1974-76. Served to lt. USN, 1954-58. Mem. Univ. Club (Chgo.), Am. Corp. Counsel Assn., Michigan Shores Club (Wilmette, Ill.). Avocation: photography. Administrative and regulatory, Intellectual property, Private international. Home: 467 Willow Rd Winnetka IL 60093-4140 Office: Quixote Corp 1 E Wacker Dr Chicago IL 60601-1802

**DEW, THOMAS EDWARD,** lawyer; b. Detroit, Feb. 13, 1947; s. Albert Nelson and Irene Theresa (Morris) D.; m. Gail Ruth Tuesink, June 27, 1970. BA, U. Mich., 1969; JD, Detroit Coll. Law, 1974. Bar: Mich. 1974, U.S. Dist. Ct. (ea. dist.) Mich. 1974, U.S. Tax Ct. 1980. Agt. IRS, Detroit, 1969-74; trust officer Ann Arbor (Mich.) Trust Co., 1974-75, asst. v.p., 1975-78; ptnr. Conner, Harbour, Dew, Ann Arbor, 1978-83, Harris, Lax, Guenzel & Dew, Ann Arbor, 1983-87; private practice Thomas E. Dew Profl. Corp., Ann Arbor, 1987-88; prin. Dever and Dew Profl. Corp., Ann Arbor, 1988-99, Wise & Marsac, Detroit, 1999—; lectr. Am. Coll., Bryn Mawr, Pa., 1979-82, Am. Inst. Paralegal Studies, Detroit, 1982. Mem. Ann Harbor Housing Commn., 1979-81, pres. 1981. Named Law scholar, Sigma Nu Phi, 1974. Fellow Mich. State Bar Found.; mem. State Bar Mich., Washtenaw County Bar Assn., Washtenaw Estate Planning Coun. (pres. 1979-80), New Enterprise Forum. Republican. Presbyterian. Estate taxation, Probate, General corporate. Office: Dever and Dew Profl Corp 339 E Liberty St Ste 310 Ann Arbor MI 48104-2258

**DEWEIL, DAWN SUSAN,** lawyer; b. Passaic, N.J., July 1, 1957; d. Ralph Earl and Thelma Susan (Schwartz) DeW.; m. Jonathan Stuart Blausten, Oct. 12, 1989. BA, Rutgers U., 1979; JD, N.Y. Law Sch., 1987. Bar: N.J. 1987, N.Y. 1988, U.S. Dist. Ct. (so. and ea. dists.) N.Y. 1994, U.S. Dist. Ct. N.J. 1994. Asst. regional counsel U.S. Dept. Health and Human Svcs., N.Y.C., 1987-88; assoc. atty. N.Y.C. Police Dept., N.Y.C., 1988-89, Heidell Pittoni Murphy & Bach, N.Y.C., 1989-93; mng. atty. breast implant litigation unit Schneider Kleinick Weitz Damashek & Shoot, N.Y.C., 1993—; lectr. Prentice Hall Law and Bus., 1994; guest commentator Court TV, 1995, 97. Mem. editl. bd. Medical and Legal Aspects of Breast Implant Litigation. Mem. Am. Trial Lawyers Assn., N.Y. Bar Assn., Metro. Women's Bar Assn., N.Y. State Trial Lawyers Assn. General civil litigation, Personal injury, Product liability. Office: Schneider Kleinick Weitz Damashek & Shoot 233 Broadway Fl 5 New York NY 10279-0050

**DEWELL, JULIAN C.,** lawyer; b. San Antonio, Feb. 13, 1930; s. Julian and Hope (Correll) D.; m. Alice Jane Palmer, Aug. 28, 1954; children: Gwen A. Dewell Brown, Jane H., Laura M. BS, Trinity U., 1952; LLD, U. Wash., Seattle, 1957. Bar: Wash. 1957, Calif. 1958, U.S. Ct. of Appeals (9th cir.) 1958. Trial lawyer (anti trust) U.S. Dept. Justice, San Francisco, 1957-59; assoc. Howe, Davis, Riese & Jones, Seattle, 1959-63; ptnr. Anderson Hunter Law Firm, Everett, Wash., 1963—. Freeholder City of Everett, Wash., 1966-67, mem. Growth Mgmt. Com., 1982, mem. shoreline mgmt. rev. com., 1998-99; mem. bd. Everett Sch. Dist., 1966-71; bd. dirs. Snohomish County Land Trust, 1989-93, Law Fund, 1992-98. Named to Law Sch. Honor Grad. Program, U.S. Dept. Justice, San Francisco, 1957. Fellow Am. Coll. Trial Lawyers; mem. ABA, Wash. Bar Assn. (disciplinary bd. 1974-77, bd. govs. 1980-83, advt. task force, 1985-86, Professionalism award 1991, Merit award 1998), Calif. Bar Assn. Democrat. Unitarian. Avocations: sailing, hiking, tennis. General civil litigation, Civil rights, Environmental. Home: 609 Maulsby Ln Everett WA 98201-1031 Office: Anderson Hunter Firm PO Box 5397 Everett WA 98206-5397

**DEWEY, ANNE ELIZABETH MARIE,** lawyer; b. Balt., Mar. 16, 1951; d. George Daniel and Elizabeth Patricia (Mohan) D.; children: Brendan M., Andrew P., Meghan E. BA, Mich. State U., 1972; JD, U. Chgo., 1975; grad., Stonier Grad. Sch. Banking, East Brunswick, N.J., 1983. Bar: D.C. 1976. Legal clk. and atty. FTC, Washington, 1975-78; atty. and sr. atty. Comptr. of Currency, Dallas and Washington, 1978-86; assoc. gen. counsel, gen. counsel, spl. counsel Farm Credit Adminstrn., McLean, Va., 1986-92; counsel, closed bank litig. and policy sect. FDIC, Washington, 1993-94; gen. counsel Office of Fed. Housing Enterprise Oversight, HUD, Washington, 1994—. Mem. ABA (bus. law sect., mem. banking law com., co-chair banking & fin. sevcs. com., adminstrv. law & regulatory practice sect. 1997—), FBA (bd. dirs. D.C. chpt. 1988-91, banking law com. exec. coun. 1995—), Women in Housing and Fin. (bd. dirs. 1982-83, gen counsel 1991-93), D.C. Bar Assn., Exchequer Club. Roman Catholic. Office: Office Fed Housing Enterprise Oversight 1700 G St NW Fl 4 Washington DC 20552-0003

**DEWITT, ANTHONY LOUIS,** lawyer; b. Kansas City, Mo., Sept. 3, 1955; s. Alvin Lewis Lowe and Mary Anna Gower Hall; m. Elizabeth Johanna Wood, July 12, 1982; children: Geoffrey, Meghan, Zachary. AS in Respiratory Therapy, Creighton U., 1981; B in Health Adminstrn., Ottawa (Kans.) U., 1986; JD, St. Louis U., 1993. Cert. respiratory therapy technician; registered respiratory therapist Nat. Bd. Respiratory Care. Staff therapist Kirksville (Mo.) Osteo. Hosp., 1980-81; dir. spl. procedures St. Mary's Hosp, West Palm Beach, Fla., 1982-83; dir. cardiopulmonary svcs. Blessing Hosp., Quincy, Ill., 1983-88; adminstr. pulmonary and neurology Mt. Sinai Med. Ctr., Hartford, Conn., 1988; adminstrv. dir. cardiopulmonary svcs. St. Charles Hosp., Toledo, 1988-90; adminstrv. editor ABA Fidelity and Surety News, St. Louis, 1992-93; law clk. to Judge Edward D. Robertson Jr. Mo. Supreme Ct., Jefferson City, 1993-94; assoc. atty. Shamberg, Johnson & Bergman, Overland Park, Kans., 1993—. Legal corr. Merion Publs., 1988-94; mng. editor St. Louis U. Pub. Law Rev., 1993; mem. editl. bd. Am. Assn. Respiratory Care, Dallas, 1986-90; contbr. articles to profl. jours. Bd. dirs. Adams County Heart Assn., Quincy, 1988. Sgt. U.S. Army, 1976-80, Korea. St. Louis U. scholar, 1991-93. Mem. ABA, Kansas City Met. Bar Assn., Kans. Trial Lawyers Assn., Mo. Trial Lawyers Assn., Order of the Woolsack, Alpha Sigma Nu. Avocations: computers, writing, reading good literature. Personal injury, Civil rights, Toxic tort. Home: 1225 W Poplar St Olathe KS 66061-5088

**DEWITT, BRIAN LEIGH,** lawyer; b. Pitts., June 3, 1959. BA with honors, U. Calif. Santa Cruz, 1982; MPhil, U. Oxford, Eng., 1985; JD, Stanford U., 1989. Bar: Calif. 1990. Assoc. Morrison & Foerster, L.A., 1989-91; pvt. practice L.A., 1992—. Recipient Overseas Rsch. Student award Chancellor of Colls. & Univs. of U.K., 1984. Mem. L.A. Bar Assn. Real property, Contracts commercial, Estate planning. Office: 2500 Via Cabrillo Marina San Pedro CA 90731-7222

**DEWITT, CHARLES BENJAMIN, III,** lawyer, educator; b. Glendale, Calif., Nov. 29, 1952; s. Charles Benjamin Jr. and Lucille Ann (Johnston) deW.; m. Karen Denise Blackwood, Dec. 29, 1979. BA magna cum laude, Pacific Union Coll., 1973; JD, U. So. Calif., 1976; MA, U. Memphis, 1995. Bar: Tenn. 1984, U.S. Dist. Ct. (we. dist.) Tenn. 1984, D.C. 1989. Atty., agy. mgr., v.p. SAFECO/Chgo. Title Ins., Memphis, 1980-91; regional underwriting counsel Commonwealth Land Title Ins. Co., 1991-93; asst. prof., instr. U. Memphis, 1986—, asst. dean paralegal, 1993-96., asst. dean law sch., 1996—. Contbr. articles to profl. jours. Registrar gen. Washington Family Descendants;. Mem. Memphis Bar Assn., Tenn. Land Title Assn. (sec.-treas. 1983-87), U. S.C. Alumni Assn. (life), Order Crown of Charlemagne, Kiwanis, Mensa, Phi Alpha Theta, Phi Kappa Phi, Phi Alpha Delta. Real property, Education and schools. Home: 2488 Cedarwood Dr Germantown TN 38138-5802 Office: U Memphis Sch Law PO Box 526513 Memphis TN 38152-0001

**DEWOLFE, RUTHANNE K. S.,** lawyer, psychologist; b. Milw., Aug. 14, 1933; d. Erich Max and Mary Elizabeth (Stork) Sobota; m. Alan S. Dewolfe Aug. 24, 1952 (div. July 1986); children: Kyle A., Hillary S., Elena M. BA, Heidelberg Coll., Tiffin, Ohio, 1954; PhD, Northwestern U., 1960; JD, DePaul U., Chgo., 1976; LLM, DePaul U., 1985. Bar: Ill. 1976, U.S. Dist. Ct. (no. dist.) Ill. 1976, U.S. Ct. Appeals (7th cir.) Ill. 1980, U.S. Supreme Ct. 1982; registered psychologist, Pa., Ill. Staff psychologist Hines VA Hosp., 1960-62; pvt. parctice psychology Chgo., 1962—; staff atty. Legal Asst. Found., Chgo., 1975-77, supr. atty., 1980-97; regional atty. U.S. Civil Rights Commn., Chgo., 1977-80; pvt. practice, 1997—; adj. faculty criminal justice dept. U. Ill., Chgo., 1980-86; lectr. in field. Contbr. numerous articles and papers to various publs. Mem. Ill. State Bar Assn. (chairperson com. on corrections 1985-87, 95-96, chairperson com. on mentally disabled 1982-83), Chgo. Bar Assn. (chairperson com. on civil rights 1981-82), Women's Bar Assn., Internat. Fedn. Women Lawyers, John Howard Assn. (v.p. 1985-91), Sigma Xi. Civil rights, Appellate, Constitutional. Home: 811 Colfax St Evanston IL 60201-2420

**DEWOSKIN, ALAN ELLIS,** lawyer; b. St. Louis, Sept. 10, 1940; s. Samuel S. and Lillian (Sachs) DeW.; m. Iris Lynn Shapiro, Aug. 15, 1942; children: Joseph, Henry, Franklin. BA, Washington U., St. Louis, 1962, JD, 1965; postgrad. U.S. Army Command and Gen. Staff Coll., 1978, U.S. Army War Coll., 1985. Bar: Mo. 1968, U.S. Dist. Ct. (ea. dist.) Mo. 1968, Ill. 1999, U.S. Ct. Claims 1997, U.S. Ct. Appeals (8th cir.) 1969, U.S. Ct. Appeals (Armed Forces) 1976, U.S. Supreme Ct. 1990. Pvt. practice law, St. Louis, 1968-82, prin. Alan E. DeWoskin, P.C., St. Louis, 1982—. Active Boy Scouts Am. Col. JAGC, USAR Ret., 1962-92. Recipient U.S. Legion of Merit, 1992. Fellow Am. Bar Found., Mo. Bar Found.; mem. ABA (chmn. gen. practice sect. 1985-86, mem. Ho. of Dels., 1986-87, assembly del. 1988-91, standing com. mil. law, 1988-91, standing com. assembly resolutions 1988-91, vice chmn. task force solo and small firm practitioners), ATLA, Mo. Bar Assn. (chmn. gen. practice com. 1987-90, chmn. computer interest groups 1988-90), Bar Assn. Met. St. Louis (mem. exec. com. 1993-94, bd. govs. 1994-95, chmn. solo and small firm sect., 1993-95, exec. com. 1993-94, bd. govs. 1994-95, chair sect. solo and small firms practitioners 1993-95), Mo. Assn. Trial Attys., St. Louis Bar Found (disting. fellow), Masons (past master, dir. 1972—). General practice, State civil litigation, Federal civil litigation. Home: 14030 Deltona Dr Chesterfield MO 63017-3311 Office: 225 S Meramec Ave Ste 426 Saint Louis MO 63105-3511

**DEWSNUP, RALPH L.,** lawyer; b. Salt Lake City, Mar. 13, 1948; s. Edwin Grant and Mary Jeannette (Fairbanks) D.; m. Mary C. Dewsnup, Mar. 26, 1971; children: Emily, Rebecca, Hillary, Nathan, Heidi. BA, U. Utah, 1972; JD, Brigham Young U., 1977. Bar: Utah, 1977; U.S. Dist. Ct. Utah, 1977, U.S. Ct. Appeals (10th cir.) 1978, U.S. Supreme Ct., 1985. Asst. trust officer Tracy Collins Bank and Trust, Salt Lake City, 1971-74; col. Utah Air Nat. Guard, Salt Lake City, 1967—; law clk. Hansen & Orton, Salt Lake City, 1975-77; assoc. Hansen & Thompson, Salt Lake City, 1977-80; ptnr. Hansen, Thompson & Dewsnup, Salt Lake City, 1980-83, Hansen & Dewsnup, Salt Lake City, 1983-90; shareholder, officer Wilcox, Dewsnup & King, Salt Lake City, 1990-97; pres. Dewsnup, King & Olsen, 1998—. Stake pres. LDS Ch., Salt Lake City, 1988-97, bishop, 1985-88; chmn. prelitigation task force Divsn. of Occpl. and Profl. Lics., Salt Lake City, 1995-96. Mem. ATLA, Utah State Bar, Temple Bar Found. (trustee 1996-98), Aldon J. Anderson Am. Inn of Ct. (pres. 1991-92), Utah Trial Lawyers Assn. (pres. 1990-92, gov. 1987—), Am. Inns of Ct. Found. (trustee, mem. exec. com. 1988-98). Republican. Avocations: music (piano, banjo and guitar), woodworking, basketball. Personal injury. Home: 1407 E Stratford Ave Salt Lake City UT 84106-3527 Office: Dewsnup King & Olsen 36 S State St Salt Lake City UT 84111-1401

**DEZZANI, DAVID JOHN,** lawyer; b. Oakland, Calif., July 31, 1936; s. Maurice Joseph and Henryetta Esther (Greene) D.; m. Rochelle Lee Renner, Nov. 17, 1967; children—Scott, John, Michael, Douglas. Student, U. Vienna, 1960; B.A., U. Calif.-Berkeley, 1961, J.D., 1965; postgrad. U. Tuebingen, Fed. Republic Germany, 1962-63. Bar: Calif. 1965, Hawaii 1966, U.S. Supreme Ct. 1975. Assoc. Goodsill Anderson Quinn & Stifel, Honolulu, 1965-70, ptnr., 1970—. Rotary Found. fellow, 1962; Ford Found. grantee, 1964. Fellow Am. Coll. Trial Lawyers; mem. ABA, Hawaii State Bar Assn. (bd. dirs. 1992-93, 96-98), Calif. State Bar Assn., Am. Bd. Trial Advs. (adv.). Federal civil litigation, State civil litigation, Libel. Office: PO Box 3196 Honolulu HI 96801-3196

**DIAKOS, MARIA LOUISE,** lawyer; b. Buffalo, Jan. 31, 1959; d. Louis K. and Deanna (Doerr) D.; m. Michael Manolitsas. BA in Polit. Sci., SUNY, Buffalo, 1979, JD, 1982. Bar: N.Y. 1983. Assoc. counsel divsn. corps. N.Y. Dept. of State, Albany, 1982-84; assoc. Sargent & Repka, P.C., Cheektowaga, N.Y., 1984-85; pvt. practice Amherst, N.Y., 1985—; hearing officer small claims assessment rev. 8th Jud. Dist. N.Y. Supreme Ct., Buffalo, 1986-97; sr. closing atty. Pub. Abstract Corp., Ticor Title Ins. Co., Niagara Sq. Abstract Co., Buffalo, 1995—. Founding mem. joint pub. policy com. Hellenic Am. Women, Washington; mem. parish coun. Hellenic Orthodox Ch. of Annunciation, Buffalo, 1985-88, 93-98, parish legal advisor, 1995-98, treas., 1995, interim treas., sec., 1996. Mem. Women's Philoptochos Com. (recording sec. 1984-85, corr. sec. 1995-97), Buffalo and Western N.Y. Women in Travel, Variety Club Women. Democrat. Eastern Orthodox. Avocations: travel, cruising, spectator sports, sewing, cooking. General practice, Estate planning, Real property. Home: 9 Omega Dr Rochester NY 14624-5415 Office: 1449 Eggert Rd Amherst NY 14226-3356

**DIAMANT, WILLIAM,** lawyer; b. Johnstown, Pa., May 30, 1928; s. James and Anna (Papanicholau) D.; m. Bertha Polydoros, Nov. 27, 1951; children—Anna Woods, Elaine Sikorski, Christine Kipp, James. B.S., U. Pitts., 1952, J.D., 1955; grad. in trust adminstrn. Naval Justice Sch., 1956; postgrad. Northwestern U., 1967. Bar: Pa. 1955, Ill. 1958, U.S. Dist. Ct. (no. dist.) Ill. 1984. Title legal officer Chgo. Title & Trust Co., 1957-62; v.p., gen. counsel Unibanctrust Co., Chgo., 1962-78; v.p., trust dept. head, counsel 1st Nat. Bank of Elgin, Ill., 1978-81; sr. v.p., gen. counsel, sec. bd. dirs. Elmhurst Nat. Bank, Ill., 1981-83; sole practice, Hinsdale, Ill., 1983—; tchr. Am. Inst. Banking, Chgo., 1972—. Sec. Sch. Bd. Unit Dist. 401, Elmwood Park, Ill., 1972-78. Served with USMC, 1949; capt. Res. (ret.). Recipient Meritorious Service award Sch. Bd. Unit Dist. 401, 1978, Disting. Service award Am. Inst. Banking, 1982. Mem. Ill. Bar Assn., Pa. Bar Assn., Chgo. Bar Assn., DuPage County Bar Assn. Club: Ahepa (Chgo.) (pres. 1960-62). Lodge: Elks. Probate, Real property, General corporate. Office: 119 E Ogden Ave Hinsdale IL 60521-3541

**DIAMOND, BERNARD ROBIN,** lawyer; b. Bronx, N.Y., July 3, 1944; m. Elizabeth Heimbuch, Oct. 20, 1976; children: Jessica, Carey, Erin. BA, Rutgers U., 1966; JD, Bklyn. Law Sch., 1972. Bar: N.Y. 1973, U.S. Dist. Ct. (so. and ea. dists.) N.Y. 1973, U.S. Ct. Appeals (2d cir.) 1974. Gen. counsel The Trump Orgn., N.Y.C., 1995—. Mem. Assn. of the Bar of the City of N.Y. Real property. Office: Trump Orgn 725 5th Ave Fl 26 New York NY 10022-2520

**DIAMOND, DAVID HOWARD,** lawyer; b. N.Y.C., June 24, 1945; s. Philip and Betty (Resnikoff) D.; m. Barbara R. Jacobs, Sep. 6, 1969; children: John, Andrew, Jill. BA, SUNY, Binghamton, 1967; JD, Georgetown U., Washington, D.C., 1970. Bar: Va. 1970, D.C. 1971, N.J. 1972, N.Y. 1973, U.S. Supreme Ct. 1982, U.S. Dist. Ct. Asst. gen. counsel Nat. Treas. Employees Union, Washington, D.C., 1970-71; trial atty. Nat. Labor Relations Bd., Newark, N.J., 1971-73; assoc. Putney, Twombly, Hall & Hirson, N.Y.C., 1973-76; ptnr. Guggenheimer & Untermeyer, N.Y.C., 1976-86, Summit, Rovins & Felderman, N.Y.C., 1986-89, Patterson, Belknap, Webb & Tyler, N.Y.C., 1989-91, Proskauer, Rose LLP, N.Y.C., 1991—. Contbg. editor: Developing Labor Law, 1975-82. Pres., dir. Birchwood Civic Assn., Jericho, N.Y., 1985—; trustee Jericho Libr. Bd., 1994—. Mem. ABA (sect. labor and employment law, com. fed. labor standards), N.Y. State Bar Assn. (com. on individual and employee rights). Avocations: biking, tennis, whitewater rafting. Labor, Civil rights, Health. Home: 18 Briar Ln Jericho NY 11753-2212 Office: Proskauer Rose LLP 1585 Broadway New York NY 10036-8200

**DIAMOND, EUGENE CHRISTOPHER,** lawyer, hospital administrator; b. Oceanside, Calif., Oct. 19, 1952; s. Eugene Francis and Rosemary (Wright) D.; m. Mary Theresa O'Donnell, Jan. 20, 1984; children: Eugene John, Kevin Seamus, Hannah Rosemary, Seamus Michael, Maeve Therese. BA, U. Notre Dame, 1974; MHA, St. Louis U., 1978, JD, 1979. Bar: Ill. 1979. Staff atty. AUL Legal Def. Fund, Chgo., 1979-80; adminstrv. asst. Holy Cross Hosp., Chgo., 1980-81, asst. adminstr., 1981-82, v.p., 1982-83, counsel to adminstr., 1980—, exec. v.p., 1983-91; exec. v.p., COO St. Margaret Mercy Healthcare Ctrs., Hammond, Ind., 1991-93, pres. CEO, 1993; cons. Birthright of Chgo., 1979—, mem. benefit com., 1981—; bd. dirs. Hammond C. of C., 1993, North West Ind. Forum. Mem. Ill. State Bar Assn., Chgo. Bar Assn. Mgmt. Roman Catholic. Health. Office: St Margaret Mercy Healthcare Ctrs 5454 Hohman Ave Hammond IN 46320-1999

**DIAMOND, GUSTAVE,** federal judge; b. Burgettstown, Pa., Jan. 29, 1928; s. George and Margaret (Solinsky) D.; m. Emma L. Scarton, Dec. 28, 1974; 1 dau., Margaret Ann; 1 stepdau., Joanne Yoney. A.B., Duke U., 1951; J.D., Duquesne U., 1956. Bar: Pa. bar 1958, U.S. Ct. Appeals bar 1962. Law clk. to judge U.S. Dist. Ct., Pitts., 1955-61; 1st asst. U.S. atty. Western Dist. Pa., 1961-62, U.S. atty., 1963-69; partner firm Cooper, Schwartz, Diamond & Reich, Pitts., 1969-75; formerly individual practice law Washington, Pa.; former solicitor Washington County, Pa.; judge U.S. Dist. Ct. Western Dist. Pa.; chief judge U.S. Dist. Ct. (we. dist.) Pa., 1992-94, sr. judge, 1994—; chmn. Jud. Conf. Com. on Defender Svcs. Mem. ABA, Fed. Bar Assn., Pa. Bar Assn., Allegheny County Bar Assn., Washington County Bar Assn. Office: US Dist Ct 821 US Courthouse 7th St Rm 2 Pittsburgh PA 15219

**DIAMOND, JEFFREY BRIAN,** lawyer; b. N.Y.C., Sept. 17, 1950; s. Norman and Sylvia (Kurinsky) D.; m. Evalynn Joyce Stern, Apr. 15, 1977. BA, Dickinson Coll., 1972; JD, Pepperdine U., 1976. Bar: N.Mex. 1976, U.S. Dist. Ct. N.Mex. 1980, U.S. Ct. Appeals (10th cir.) 1985. Ptnr. Shuler & Diamond, Carlsbad, N.Mex., 1976-77, Paine, Blenden & Diamond, Carlsbad, N.Mex., 1977-92; prin. Jeffrey B. Diamond P.A., Carlsbad, N.Mex., 1992—; atty. Eddy County, Carlsbad, 1983-84. Chmn. Eddy County Dems., Carlsbad, 1981-85; pres. Carlsbad Jewish Congregation, 1979-81, Carlsbad Mental Health Assn., 1985-89, also founder Carlsbad Area Counselling and Resource Ctr., 1977-83, also bd. dirs.; sec. Eddy County Sheriff's Posse, 1987-90; pres. Carlsbad Mcpl. Schs. Bd. Edn., 1989-91; bd. dirs. Anti-Defamation League (B'nai Brith), 1990—, Boys and Girls Club of Carlsbad. Mem. ABA, ATLA, N.Mex. Bar Assn., Eddy County Bar Assn., N.Mex. Trial Lawyers Assn., Elks. Personal injury, Pension, profit-sharing, and employee benefits, Family and matrimonial. Home: 1427 Verdel Ave Carlsbad NM 88220-9233 Address: PO Box 1866 Carlsbad NM 88221-1866

**DIAMOND, JOSEF,** lawyer; b. L.A., Mar. 6, 1907; s. Michael and Ruby (Shifrin) D.; m. Violett Diamond, Apr. 2, 1933 (dec. 1979); children: Joel, Diane Foreman; m. Ann Dulien, Jan. 12, 1981 (dec. 1984); m. Muriel Bach, 1986. BBA, U. Wash., 1929, JD, 1931. Bar: Wash. 1931, U.S. Dist. Ct. (we. dist.) Wash. 1932, U.S. Ct. Appeals (9th cir.) 1934, U.S. Supreme Ct. 1944. Assoc. Caldwell & Lycette, Seattle, 1931-35; ptnr. Caldwell, Lycette & Diamond, Seattle, 1935-45, Lycette, Diamond & Sylvester, Seattle, 1945-80; ptnr. Diamond & Sylvester, Seattle, 1980-82, of counsel, 1982-88; of counsel Short, Cressman & Burgess, Seattle, 1988—; chmn. bd. Diamond Parking Inc., Seattle, 1945-70; cons. various businesses. Bd. dirs. Am. Heart Assn., 1960; chmn. Wash. Heart Assn., 1962. Col. JAGC, U.S. Army, WWII. Decorated Legion of Merit. Mem. Wash. Bar Assn., Assn. Trial Lawyers Wash., Seattle Bar Assn., Mil. Engrs. Soc., Wash. Athletic Club, Bellevue Athletic Club, Harbor Club, Rainier Club. Contracts commercial, Construction, General corporate. Office: 3000 First Interstate Ctr 999 3d Ave Seattle WA 98104-4019

**DIAMOND, JOSEPH,** lawyer; b. Washington, Dec. 22, 1935; s. Leo Aaron and Dora S. D.; m. Susan Kaplan, Dec. 25, 1965; children: Sara, David. A.B., Columbia U., 1957; LL.B., Cornell U., 1960. Bar: N.Y. 1961, D.C. 1964, U.S. Supreme Ct. 1964. Assoc. LeBoeuf, Lamb & Leiby, N.Y.C., 1961-63; mem. Melrod, Redman & Gartlan, Washington, 1963-65; compt. of currency Office of Chief Counsel U.S. Dept. Treasury, Washington, 1966-67; assoc. Rogers & Wells, N.Y.C., 1967-69; ptnr. Rogers & Wells, 1969-83; ptnr. Skadden, Arps, Slate, Meagher & Flom, N.Y.C., 1983-92, of counsel, 1992-95; sr. counsel Shaw, Pittman, Potts & Trowbridge, N.Y.C., 1995—; Legal adv. com. to nat. ctr. on fin. svcs. U.S. Army. Mem. ABA (vice chair com. on ins. regulation 1987-92). Banking, Insurance. Office: Shaw Pittman Potts Trowbridge 1675 Broadway New York NY 10019-5820

**DIAMOND, MARIA SOPHIA,** lawyer; b. Portland, Oreg., Aug. 29, 1958; d. Harry and Nitsa (Fotiou) D. BA in Eng. cum laude, U. Wash., 1980; JD, U. Puget Sound, 1983. Bar: Wash. 1983, U.S. Dist. Ct. (we. dist.) Wash. 1983, U.S. Ct. Appeals (9th cir.) 1985. Contract atty. Levinson, Friedman, Vhugen, Duggan & Bland, Seattle, 1983-84, assoc., 1985-90, ptnr., 1990—. Mem. ABA, ATLA, FBA, Wash. State Trial Lawyers Assn. (bd. govs. 1992—), King County Bar Assn., Hellenic Bar Assn., U. Wash. Alumni Assn., Nat. Order Barristers, Alpha Gamma Delta. Admiralty, Insurance, Personal injury. Office: Levinson Friedman Vhugen Duggan & Bland 600 University St Ste 2900 Seattle WA 98101-4156

**DIAMOND, PAUL STEVEN,** lawyer; b. Bklyn., Jan. 2, 1953; s. George and Anna (Jaeger) D.; m. Robin Nilon. BA magna cum laude, Columbia U., 1974; JD, U. Pa., 1977. Bar: Pa. 1977, U.S. Dist. Ct. (ea. dist.) Pa, 1979, U.S. Ct. Appeals (3d cir.) 1979, U.S. Supreme Ct. 1983. Asst. dist. atty. Phila. Dist. Atty. Office, 1977-83; law clk. Supreme Ct. Pa., Phila., 1980; assoc. Dilworth, Paxson, Kalish & Kauffman, Phila., 1983-85, ptnr., 1986-91; ptnr. Obermayer, Rebmann, Maxwell & Hippel, Phila., 1992—; lectr. Temple U. Sch. Law, Phila., 1990-92; mem. civil prodecural rules com. Supreme Ct. Pa., 1995—, fed. judicial nominating commn., 1995—; treas. Pa. lawyers fund for client security bd. Supreme Ct. Pa., 1999. Author: Federal Grand Jury Practice and Procedure, 1990, rev. 2nd edit., 1993; vice-chmn. Amicus Curiae Briefs Comm., 1995—. Mem. ABA (criminal justice sect., Amicus Curiae briefs subcom. 1983—, grand jury subcom. 1991—), Am. Law Inst., Pa. Bar Assn., Phila. Bar Assn. Republican. Jewish. General civil litigation, Constitutional, Criminal. Office: Obermayer Rebmann Maxwell & Hippel One Penn Ctr 19th Fl 1617 John F Kennedy Blvd Philadelphia PA 19103

**DIAMOND, PHILIP ERNEST,** lawyer; b. L.A., Feb. 11, 1925; s. William and Elizabeth (Weizenhaus) D.; m. Dorae Seymour (dec.); children: William, Wendy, Nancy; m. 2d, Jenny White Carson. B.A., UCLA, 1949, M.A., 1950; J.D., U. Calif., Berkeley, 1953. Bar: Calif. 1953, U.S. Dist. Ct. (no., ea. and cen. dists.) Calif. 1953, U.S. Ct. Appeals (9th cir.) 1953. Law clk. to presiding justice Calif. Dist. Ct. Appeals, 1953-54; assoc. Landels & Weigel, San Francisco, 1954-60; ptnr. Landels Weigel & Ripley, San Francisco, 1960-62; sr. ptnr. Landels, Ripley & Diamond, San Francisco, 1962-93—; pres. Diamond Wine Mchts., San Francisco, 1976—; bd. dirs. Yasutomo & Co. Pres. Contra Costa Sch. Bd. Assn., 1966-68. With USN, 1943-46. Mem. ABA, Am. Arbitration Assn., Calif. State Bar Assn., San Francisco Bar Assn., Phi Beta Kappa. Democrat. Clubs: Commonwealth, Mchts. & Exch. Contracts commercial, General corporate, Real property. Office: 350 The Embarcadero San Francisco CA 94105-1204

**DIAMOND, PRISCILLA SEIDERMAN,** lawyer; b. Miami, Fla., Sept. 28, 1940; d. Emanuel and Miriam Seiderman; m. Ivan Marshall Diamond, Dec. 23, 1962; children: Elizabeth, Daniel. BA, U. Fla., 1962; JD cum laude, U. Louisville, 1979. Bar: Ky. 1979, U.S. Dist. Ct. (ea. dist., we. dist.) Ky. 1979, U.S. Ct. Appeals (6th dist.), 1979. Assoc. Pallo & White, Louisville, 1979-81; ptnr. White & Diamond, Louisville, 1981-82; pvt. practice Louisville, 1983—. Mem. ABA, Jefferson County Women Lawyers Assn. (pres. 1982), Am. Trial Lawyers Assn., Nat. Employment Lawyers Assn., Ky. Bar Assn., Louisville Bar Assn. Avocations: dressage. Office: 200 S 5th St Louisville KY 40202-3215

**DIAMOND, RICHARD SCOTT,** lawyer; b. Newark, June 26, 1960; s. Robert and Arlene (Cohen) D.; m. Denise E. Block, Nov. 12, 1988. BA in Econs./Bus., Rutgers U., 1981; JD, Seton Hall U., 1984. Bar: N.J. 1984, Fla. 1991, U.S. Dist. Ct. N.J. 1984; cert. matrimonial lawyer, cert. divorce mediator. Jud. clk. to judge State of N.J., Union County, N.J.; assoc. Law

Firm of Robert Diamond, Springfield, N.J.; ptnr. Diamond Hodes & Diamond, Springfield, Gourvitz, Diamond, Hodes, Braun & Diamond, Springfield, Diamond & Diamond P.A., Millburn, N.J.; lectr. TV and radio broadcasts. Contbr. articles to profl. jours. Mem. Union County Bar Assn. (matrimonial practice, exec. com.), Essex County Bar (matrimonial practice), N.J. State Bar (matrimonial practice, lectr., speaker). Avocations: racquetball, tennis, running. Family and matrimonial, General civil litigation. Office: Diamond & Diamond PA 225 Millburn Ave Ste 208 Millburn NJ 07041-1712

**DIAMOND, STANLEY,** lawyer; b. New York, Dec. 14, 1929; s. Herman and Lee (Semsker) D.; m. Harriet Diamond, (div. Jan. 1975); children: Jessica, Nancy; m. Ethel Spector Person, July 16, 1978; children: Louis Sherman, Lloyd Sherman. BBA, City Coll. N.Y., 1951; JD, NYU, 1954. Bar: NY, Canal Zone, U.S. Ct. Appeals (3rd cir.). Ptnr. Maxwell & Diamond, N.Y., 1956-71; sr. v.p., exec. v.p. Prel Corp., Saddle Brook, NJ, 1971-72; pres. DKB Enterprises, Inc., Paramus, NJ, 1973-75, Landall Corp., Hackensack, NJ, 1975-77; ptnr. Herrick, Feinstein, N.Y., 1977-85; pres. Am. Midland Corp., N.Y., 1984-86; chmn. Castle Sr. Living, Teaneck, NJ, 1986—; counsel Rosenman & Colin, N.Y., 1986—; adj. prof. NYU Sch. of Law, 1973-92. Rsch. editor NYU Law Review. Mem. zoning bd. of appeals, Village of Ardsley, N.Y., 1973-77. Recipient Edward H. Dixon prize scholarship. Mem. ABA, N.Y. State Bar Assn., N.Y. County Lawyers Assn., Vanderbilt Assn., Weinfield Assoc., Friar's Club; life mem. Gallatin Assn. of N.Y. General corporate, Real property, Health. Home: 135 Central Park W New York NY 10023-2413 Office: Castle Sr Living, LLC 405 Cedar Ln Teaneck NJ 07666-1739

**DIAMOND, STANLEY JAY,** lawyer; b. Los Angeles, Nov. 27, 1927; s. Philip Alfred and Florence (Fadem) D.; m. Lois Jane Broida, June 22, 1969; children: Caryn Elaine, Dana Beth. B.A., UCLA, 1949; J.D., U. So. Calif., 1952. Bar: Calif. 1953. Practiced law Los Angeles, 1953—; dep. Office of Calif. Atty. Gen., Los Angeles, 1953; ptnr. Diamond & Tilem, Los Angeles, 1957-60, Diamond, Tilem & Colden, Los Angeles, 1960-79, Diamond & Wilson, Los Angeles, 1979—; lectr. music and entertainment law UCLA; Mem. nat. panel arbitrators Am. Arbitration Assn. Bd. dirs. Los Angeles Suicide Prevention Center, 1971-76. Served with 349th Engr. Constrn. Bn. AUS, 1945-47. Mem. ABA, Calif. Bar Assn., Los Angeles County Bar Assn., Beverly Hills Bar Assn., Am. Judicature Soc., Calif. Copyright Conf., Nat. Acad. Rec. Arts and Scis., Zeta Beta Tau, Nu Beta Epsilon. Entertainment. Office: 12304 Santa Monica Blvd Fl 3D Los Angeles CA 90025-2551

**DIAZ, JOHN ANDREW,** patent lawyer; b. Freeland, Pa., Oct. 21, 1930; s. Andrew and Angelina Diaz; children: John Andrew II, Patrick, Kathryn Elizabeth. BSChemE, Lehigh U., 1952; JD, George Washington U., 1959. Bar: N.Y. 1961, U.S. Dist. Ct. (so. and ea. dists.) N.Y. 1962, U.S. Ct. Appeals (9th cir.) 1967, U.S. Ct. Appeals (2d cir.) 1969, U.S. Supreme Ct. 1969, U.S. Ct. Appeals (fed. cir.) 1982. Patent atty. Morgan & Finnegan, N.Y.C., 1960—. With U.S. Army, 1952-56. Mem. ATLA, AIPLA, ABA, Am. Coll. Trial Lawyers, N.Y. Patent Law, N.Y.C. Bar Assn. Intellectual property. Office: Morgan & Finnegan 345 Park Ave Fl 22 New York NY 10154-0053

**DIAZ, RAMON VALERO,** retired judge; b. Manila, Oct. 13, 1918; came to Guam, 1951; s. Vicente and Bibiana (Valero) D.; m. Josefina Dela Concepcion, July 3, 1945; children: Marilu, Mariles, Maribel, Marilen, Maryann, Anthony, Vincent, Ramon, Maricar. PhB, U. St. Tomas, Manila, 1940, LLB, 1941; grad. U.S. Army J.A.G. Sch., 1945; Diploma Jud. Skills, Am. Acad. Jud. Edn., 1984. Bar: Philippines 1941, Guam 1956, U.S. Ct. Appeals (9th cir.) 1966, High Ct. of Trust Territories 1977, No. Marianas 1985. Assoc. Diokno Law Office, Manila, 1943-44; pvt. practice, Guam, 1960-80; judge Superior Ct. of Guam, Agana, 1980-94; ret. 1994; mem. U.S. Selective Service Bd. Appeals, Guam, 1950-62. Permanent deacon Roman Catholic Ch. Judge Adv. Gen.'s Svc., Philippine Army, 1941-51. Mem. Am. Judges Assn., Nat. Council Juvenile and Family Ct. Judges, VFW II and POW. Survivor Bataan Death March, 1942. Home: PO Box 22978 Barrigada GU 96921-2978

**DIAZ-ARRASTIA, GEORGE RAVELO,** lawyer; b. Havana, Cuba, Aug. 20, 1959; came to U.S., 1968; s. Ramon Fuentes and Elihut (Ravelo) D.-A.; m. Maria del Carmen Gomez, Aug. 6, 1983. BA in History, Rice U., 1980; JD, U. Chgo., 1983. Bar: Tex. 1983, U.S. Dist. Ct. (so. dist.) Tex. 1985, U.S. Ct. Appeals (5th and D.C. cirs.) 1985, U.S. Supreme Ct. 1992, U.S. Dist. Ct. (no., we. and ea. dists.) Tex. 1994. Assoc. Baker & Botts, Houston, 1983-88, Deaton & Briggs (formerly Deaton, Briggs & McCain), Houston, 1988-90; ptnr. Gilpin, Paxson & Bersch, LLP, Houston, 1991-98, Schirrmeister Ajamie LLP, Houston, 1998—. Fellow Tex. Bar Found., Houston Bar Found.; mem. ABA, Am. Judicature Soc., Am. Soc. Internat. Law, State Bar of Tex., Houston Bar Assn., Coll. of State Bar Tex. Republican. Roman Catholic. E-mail: gdarrastia@shirr-aj.com. Construction, Consumer commercial, Education and schools. Home: 3794 Drake St Houston TX 77005-1118 Office: Schirrmeister Ajamie LLP 711 Louisiana St Ste 2150 Houston TX 77002-2720

**DIAZ-GRANADOS, RAFAEL ANDRES,** lawyer; b. Bogota, Colombia, Feb. 2, 1973; s. Pedro Rafael and Sonia Diaz-Granados; m. Sonja Natasha Noah, Aug. 13, 1995; children: Sriyani Ninotchka, Katja Sofia. BA, Harvard U., 1993; JD, Georgetown U., 1996. Bar: N.Y. 1997. Legal intern SEC, Washington, 1994-95; law clk. Covington & Burling, Washington, 1995-96; assoc. Baker & McKenzie, N.Y.C., summer 1995, O'Melveny & Myers LLP, N.Y.C., 1996—. Contbr. articles to profl. jours. Mem. ABA, N.Y. State Bar Assn., N.Y. County Bar Assn. Private international, General corporate, Finance. Office: O'Melveny & Myers LLP 153 E 53rd St Fl 54 New York NY 10022-4611

**DIB, ALBERT JAMES,** lawyer; b. Detroit, Oct. 14, 1955; s. James Benjamin and Salma (Nacoud) D.; m. Dana Santerini, 1994. BA, U. Mich., 1977; JD, Wayne State U., 1980; cert., U. Exeter, England, 1980. Bar: Mich. 1981, U.S. Dist. Ct. (ea. dist.) Mich. 1981, U.S. Ct. Appeals (6th cir.). Law clerk Lopatin, Miller, Freedman, Bluestone, Erich, Rosen & Bartnik, Detroit, 1978-80, assoc., 1981-81; ptnr. Dib and Fagan P.C., Detroit, 1987—; mediator Macomb County; moot ct. judge Detroit Coll. Law, 1984; instr. Cen. Mich. U., 1988. Vestryman Christ Episcopal Ch., Detroit, 1974-77. Recipient Cert. Achievement Mich. High Sch. Mock Trial Tournament, 1984. Mem. ABA, ATLA (cert. trial advocacy 1984, instr. trial advocacy 1987 birth trauma litig. gp.), Mich. Trial Lawyers Assn. (sustaining, past exec. bd.), Detroit Bar Assn. (speakers bur. com. 1986, Negligence law com. 1986), Oakland Bar Assn., Macomb Bar Assn. (spkr. 1984), Wayne County Mediator (med. malpractice panel), Anthony Wayne Soc. Office: Dib and Fagan PC The Globe Bldg 407 E Fort St Ste 401 Detroit MI 48226-2956

**DIBBLE, FRANCIS DANIEL, JR.,** lawyer; b. Holyoke, Mass., Mar. 1, 1947; s. Francis Daniel and Rita (Egan) D.;; m. Mary Harris Dibble, June 26, 1971. AB, Amherst Coll., 1971; JD magna cum laude, Suffolk U., 1974. Bar: Mass. 1974, U.S. Dist. Ct. Mass. 1975, U.S. Dist. Ct. Conn. 1978, U.S. Dist. Ct. (ea. dist.) Mich. 1984, U.S. Ct. Appeals (1st cir.) 1987, U.S. Ct. Appeals (D.C. cir.) 1981, U.S. Supreme Ct. 1984. Law clk. to justice Supreme Jud. Ct. of Mass., Boston, 1974-75; from assoc. to mng. ptnr. Bulkley, Richardson and Gelinas, Springfield, Mass., 1975-94; chmn., exec. com. Bulkley, Richardson and Gelinas, Springfield, 1997—; instr. Western New Eng. Law Sch., Springfield, 1979. Contbr. articles to profl. jours. Bd. dirs. Amherst Coll. Alumni Coun. Mem. ABA (antitrust law sect., criminal antitrust com.), Mass. Bar Assn., Hampden County Bar, Boston Bar Assn., East Chop Assn., East Chop Yacht Club. Antitrust, General civil litigation, Family and matrimonial. Home: 180 Eton Rd Longmeadow MA 01106-1516 Office: Bulkley Richardson & Gelinas LLP BayBank Tower Ste 2700 1500 Main St Springfield MA 01115-0001

**DICARA, PHYLLIS M.,** lawyer; b. Winsted, Conn., Mar. 22, 1957; d. Philip and Lois (Place) DiC.; m. Frank DeMaio, Mar. 23, 1997. BS, St. Joseph's Coll., 1979; JD, Syracuse U., 1982. Bar: Conn. 1982. Assoc. Tulisano & Lifshitz, Rocky Hill, Conn., 1982-86; atty. Stillman & DiCara, Rocky Hill, 1986-93; sole practice law Rocky Hill, 1993—. Bd. dirs., pres. Providence Crandall Ctr. for Women, New Britian, Conn., 1995—. Family and matrimonial, Probate, General practice. Office: 750 Old Main St Rocky Hill CT 06067-1567

**DICARLO, DOMINICK L.,** federal judge; b. Bklyn., Mar. 11, 1928; m. Esther Hansen (dec.); children: Vincent, Carl, Robert, Barbara DiCarlo Basgaard; m. Susan L. Hauck. BA, St. John's Coll., 1950, LLB, 1953; LLM, NYU, 1957. Asst. U.S. atty. Eastern Dist. N.Y., 1959-62, chief organized crime and racketeering sect.; spl. asst. to U.S. atty., 1962; counsel to minority leader N.Y. Council, 1962-65; mem. N.Y. State assembly, 1965-81, dep. minority leader, 1975-78; vice chmn. N.Y. State Legis. Commn. Crime, 1969-70, Select Commn. Correctional Insts. and Programs, 1972-73; asst. sec. state for internat. narcotics matters Dept. State, Washington, 1981-84; rep. U.S. Commn. on narcotic drugs of econ. and social coun. UN, 1982-84; judge U.S. Ct. Internat. Trade, N.Y.C., 1984-91, chief judge, 1991-96, sr. status, 1996—. Office: US Ct Internat Trade 1 Federal Plz New York NY 10278-0001

**DI CARLO, PATRICK CONNORS,** lawyer; b. Atlanta, Dec. 28, 1968; s. Nancy Anne Connors. BA, U. Ga., 1991, JD cum laude, 1993. Bar: Ga. 1994, U.S. Dist. Ct. (so. and mid. dists.) Ga. 1994, U.S. Ct. Appeals (11th cir.) 1994. Rsch./tchg. asst. U. Ga. Law Sch., Athens, 1992-93; intern Hall County Dist. Atty.'s Office, Gainesville, Ga., 1993; law clk. Fortson, Bentley & Griffen, Athens, Ga., 1993-94; assoc. Oliver, Maner & Gray, Savannah, Ga., 1994-96, Carter & Ansley, Atlanta, 1996—. Democrat. Avocation: carpentry. General civil litigation, Pension, profit-sharing, and employee benefits.

**DICEMBRE, MICHAEL DOMINICK,** lawyer; b. St. Petersburg, Fla., July 17, 1968; s. John and Nancy D.; 1 child, John L. BA in Econs., Rollins Coll., 1990; JD, U. Fla., 1993. Bar: Fla. 1994, U.S. Dist. Ct. (no. dist.) Fla. 1994. Assoc. Huntley, Johnson & Assocs., Gainesville, Fla., 1993-96; atty. pvt. practice, Orlando, Fla., 1996—. Mem. ABA, Nat. Assn. Criminal Defense Lawyers, Assn. Trial Lawyers Am. Criminal. Office: 37 N Orange Ave # 404 Orlando FL 32801-2449

**DI CHIARA, GERALD J.,** lawyer; b. N.Y.C., May 12, 1951; s. Salvatore and Lee (Amato) Di C.; m. Lisa Mirabile, June 4, 1977; children: Lauren, Gerald. BA, CUNY, 1972; JD, Widener U., Wilmington, Del., 1975. Bar: N.Y. 1976, U.S. Dist. Ct. (ea. and so. dists.) N.Y. 1976, U.S. Ct. Appeals (2d cir.) 1982, U.S. Supreme Ct. 1984, U.S. Ct. Appeals (3d cir.) 1991. Assoc. atty. Legal Aid Soc., N.Y.C., 1975-78; ptnr. Di Chiara & Moringello, Bklyn., 1978-80, Bogucki, Scotto & Di Chiara, N.Y.C., 1980-85; pvt. practice, N.Y.C., 1985—. Mem. ABA, Nat. Assn. Criminal Def. Attys., Bklyn. Bar Assn. (speaker's panel 1983), Columbia Lawyers Assn. (pres. 1982-83, jud. screening panel 1982, 83, trustee 1983—). Avocations: music, guitar. Criminal. Home: 404 Park Ave S New York NY 10016-8404

**DICHNER, ELLEN,** lawyer; b. Mar. 1, 1951. BA, Oberlin Coll., 1973; JD, Northeastern U., 1981. Atty. NLRB Region 2, N.Y.C., 1982-85, N.Y. State Atty. Gen., N.Y.C., 1985-86; atty., assoc. ptnr. Gladstein, Reif & Meginniss, N.Y.C., 1986-90, ptnr., 1990—. Mem. Bar City N.Y. (labor com. 1992-95). Labor. Office: Gladstein Reif & Meginniss 361 Broadway Ste 610 New York NY 10013-3903

**DICHTER, BARRY JOEL,** lawyer; b. Brookline, Mass., Feb. 19, 1950; s. Irving Melvin and Arlene Dichter; m. Judith Rand, Oct. 22, 1972; children: Rebecca Lynn, Jason Benjamin. AB magna cum laude, Harvard U., 1972, JD cum laude, 1975. Bar: Mass. 1975, N.Y. 1976, U.S. Dist. Ct. (so. and ea. dists.) N.Y. 1976, D.C. 1980, U.S. Dist. Ct. D.C. 1980, U.S. Ct. Appeals (D.C. cir.) 1985. Assoc. Webster & Sheffield, N.Y.C., 1975-82; assoc. Cadwalader, Wickersham & Taft, N.Y.C., 1983-84, ptnr., 1984—; lectr. in field. Contbg. editor: Collier on Bankruptcy, 15th edit., rev. Vice chmn. Harvard Law Sch. Fund, Cambridge, Mass., 1984-88, class agt., 1988—; bd. dirs. Children's Corner, Inc., 1990-95, treas., 1992-95; mem. exec. com., bankruptcy and reorgn. group of lawyers divsn. N.Y. United Jewish Appeal. Mem. ABA (mem. task force on Sect. 110 1991-92, mem. task force on emerging issues in the transp. industry 1992-96, mem. task force on Article 9 securitization issues), Assn. of Bar of City of N.Y. (mem. bankruptcy com. 1986-89, 91-94). Bankruptcy. Office: Cadwalader Wickersham & Taft 100 Maiden Ln New York NY 10038-4818

**DICHTER, MARK S.,** lawyer; b. Phila., Jan. 22, 1943; s. Harry B. and Mollie (Silverstein) D.; m. Tobey Gordon, Aug. 17, 1969; children: Aliza, Melissa. BSEE, Drexel U., 1966; JD magna cum laude, Villanova U., 1969. Bar: Pa. 1969, U.S. Ct. Appeals (3d cir.) 1969, U.S. Supreme Ct. 1979. Assoc. Morgan, Lewis & Bockius, LLP, Phila., 1969-76, ptnr., 1976—, chmn. labor and employment law sect. Co-author: Employee Dismissal Law: Forms and Procedures, 1986-91; editor-in-chief Ann. Supplement Employment Discrimination Law, 1984-89; co-editor: Employment-at-will, 1985, 86, State-by-State Survey, 1984-89; adv. bd. Disability Law Reporter. Bd. dirs., sec. Urban League Phila.; bd. dirs., v.p. Wilma Theater; bd. consultors Villanova U. Sch. Law; bd. dirs. Pub. Interest Law Ctr. Phila. Mem. ABA (labor and employment law sect. mgmt., mem. gov. coun. 1991—, co-chmn. equal opportunity com. 1986-89, litigation sect., employment law com.), Fed. Bar Assn. (equal employment com. vice-chmn. 1983-86), Nat. Employment Law Inst. (adv. bd. 1984—), Am. Employment Law Counsel (bd. dirs.), Am. Coll. Employment Lawyers, Def. Rsch. Inst. (chmn. employment law com. 1989-93). Fax: 215-963-5299. E-mail: dich5291@mlb.com. Labor. Home: 1017 Clinton St Philadelphia PA 19107-6016 Office: Morgan Lewis & Bockius 1701 Market St Philadelphia PA 19103-2903

**DICK, SHERYL LYNN,** lawyer; b. Kansas City, Mo., Apr. 9, 1954; d. Robert Dean and Margaret Louise (Adamson) Dick; BS, U. Kans.-Lawrence, 1976; JD, Washburn U., 1983. Bar: Kans. 1983, Mo. 1990. Tchr., Shawnee Mission (Kans.) Pub. Schs., 1977-80; atty. Mut. Benefit Life Ins. Co., Kansas City, Mo., 1984-93, Ahrens Fin. Sys., Inc., Overland Park, Kans., 1997—. Contbr. Washburn Law Jour., 1982, tech. editor, 1982-83. Mem. ABA, Kans. Bar Assn., Mo. Bar Assn., Kansas City Met. Bar Assn., Phi Delta Phi (vice magister 1981-82). Insurance, Pension, profit-sharing, and employee benefits.

**DICK, TERÉSE MARGARET,** defender; b. Milw., Aug. 30, 1960; d. Norman Franklin and Patricia Louise (Swift) D. BA in Sociology and Law Enforcement, Marquette U., 1982, MA, 1985, JD, 1990. Bar: Wis. 1990, U.S. Dist. Ct. (ea. and we. dist.) Wis. 1990. Pub. defender State of Wis., Milw., 1990—. Office: State Pub Defender of Wis 819 N 6th St Milwaukee WI 53203-1606

**DICKERMAN, DOROTHEA WILHELMINA,** lawyer; b. Washington, Apr. 2, 1958; d. John Melville and Serafina Amelia (Peoria) D.; m. Richard Kevin Anthony Becker, May 24, 1986. BA summa cum laude, Amherst (Mass.) Coll., 1980; JD, U. Chgo., 1983. Bar: U.S. Ct. Appeals (D.C. cir.) 1983, Va. Supreme Ct. 1990. Salesperson Dickerman Realty, Washington, 1976-83; assoc. Shaw, Pittman, Potts & Trowbridge, Washington, 1983-86; from assoc. to ptnr. Stohlman, Beuchert, Egan & Smith, Washington, 1986-97; with Andrews & Kurth, LLP, Washington, 1997—. Member endowment com. Western Presbyn. Ch., Washington, 1991—; mem. alumni bd. Amherst Coll., N.Y.C., 1983-87; sec. Amherst Club of Washington, 1987-88. Mem. DAR, Comml. Real Estate Women, Congl. Country Club. Avocations: ballet, theology, golf, fine arts. Contracts commercial, Finance, Real property. Office: Andrews & Kurth LLP 1701 Pennsylvania Ave NW Washington DC 20006-5805

**DICKERSON, CLAIRE MOORE,** lawyer, educator; b. Boston, Apr. 1, 1950; d. Roger Cleveland and Ines Idelette (Roullet) Moore; m. Thomas Pasquali Dickerson, May 22, 1976; children: Caroline Anne, Susannah Moore. AB, Wellesley Coll., 1971; JD, Columbia U., 1974; LLM in Taxation, NYU, 1981. Bar: N.Y. 1975, U.S. Dist. Ct. (ea. and so. dists.) N.Y. 1975, U.S. Ct. Appeals (2d cir.) 1975, U.S. Supreme Ct. 1980. Assoc. Coudert Brothers, N.Y., 1974-82, ptnr., 1983-86; ptnr. Schnader, Harrison, Segal & Lewis, N.Y., 1987-88, of counsel, 1988—; assoc. prof. law St. John's U., Jamaica, N.Y., 1986-88, prof., 1989—. Author: Partnership Law Adviser; contbr. articles to profl. jours. Trustee Rye (N.Y.) Presbyn. Nursery Sch., 1988-90. Mem. ABA, Assn. of Bar of City of N.Y., Union Internat. des Avocats, Shenorock Club. Democrat. General corporate, Private international. Office: St John's U Sch Law Grand Central And Utopia Pky Jamaica NY 11439-0002

**DICKEY, DAVID HERSCHEL,** lawyer, accountant; b. Savannah, Ga., Dec. 31, 1951; s. Grady Lee and Sara (Leon) D.; m. Carolyn Amanda Brooks, June 11, 1983; children: David Bradford, Carolyn Amanda. BBA in Acctg. and Fin., Armstrong State Coll., 1974; M in Accountancy, U. Ga., 1977, JD, 1977. Bar: Ga. 1978, U.S. Dist. Ct. (so. dist.) Ga. 1978, U.S. Dist. Ct. (no. dist.) Ga. 1980, U.S. Ct. Claims 1978, U.S. Tax Ct. 1978, U.S. Ct. Appeals (5th and 11th cirs.) 1978, U.S. Supreme Ct. 1981; CPA, Ga.; accredited estate planner. Assoc., acct. Thompson and Benken, Attys., Savannah, 1977-79; pub. acct. Arthur Andersen & Co., Atlanta, 1979-81; assoc. Oliver Maner & Gray, Attys., Savannah, 1981-82, ptnr., 1982—; pres. Savannah Estate Planning Coun., 1986-87, chmn. bd., 1987-88; bd. dirs. Chatham-Savannah Citizen's Advocacy; mem. legal adv. bd. Small Bus. Coun. Am., Inc., 1989—; pres. Seminar Group, Inc., 1989—, Hist. Investment Properties, Inc., 1991—. Mem. staff Ga. Law Rev., 1975. Bd. dirs. Savannah Theatre Co., 1984, Savannah chpt. Am. Cancer Soc., 1986-91, Hist. Savannah Found., Inc., 1988-94; chmn., trustee Armstrong State Coll. Alumni Endowment Fund, Inc., 1991; chmn. lawyers div. Chatham County United Way, 1992; commdr. Francis S. Barton Camp No. 93 Sons Confederate Vets., 1997-98. Recipient Outstanding Svc. award Am. Cancer Soc., 1987, Outstanding Alumni Svc. award Armstrong State Coll., 1992; named to Leadership Savannah, Savannah C. of C., 1984-86. Fellow Am. Coll. Trust and Estate Counsel; mem. AICPA, ABA (estate and gift tax com. taxation sect. 1990—), Ga. Bar Assn., Savannah Bar Assn., Ga. Soc. CPAs, Am. Assn. Atty.-CPAs, First City Club (bd. dirs. Savannah 1987-90), Chatham Club, Rotary Club Skidaway Island (bd. dirs. 1997). Avocations: history, genealogy, music, computers, historic rehab. Estate planning, Probate, Taxation, general. Home: 4 Springfield Pl Savannah GA 31411-2132 Office: Oliver Maner & Gray 218 W State St Savannah GA 31401-3232

**DICKEY, HARRISON GASLIN, III,** lawyer; b. Mpls., June 26, 1937; s. Charles Lonsdale and Elizabeth Eakin (Haumerson) D.; m. Linda Strickland (div. Oct. 1981); children—Susan Elizabeth, Jennifer Lynn; m. Foye Jean Turner, Sept. 7, 1982. B.A., U. So. Calif., 1959; J.D., U. Ariz., 1962. Bar: Ariz. 1963, U.S. Dist. Ct. Ariz. 1963, U.S. Ct. Claims 1974, U.S. Tax Ct. 1974. Asst. atty. City of Tucson, Ariz., 1963-65; assoc., then ptnr. Holesapple-Conner-Jones-McFall & Johnson, 1965-72; sole practice Harrison G. Dickey, P.C., Tucson, 1972-87, 95—; ptnr. Dickey & Brady, 1987-95. Mem. Bd. Adjustments dist. #1, Pima County, Ariz., 1991-98. Served to 1st lt. USNG, 1962-68. Fellow Ariz. Bar Found. (founder); Ariz. Bar Assn., Pima County Bar Assn., Alpha Tau Omega, Phi Delta Phi. Republican. Federal civil litigation, General civil litigation, Construction. Home: 6593 N Shadow Run Dr Tucson AZ 85704-6936 Office: 2200 E River Rd Ste 101 Tucson AZ 85718-6515

**DICKEY, JOHN HARWELL,** lawyer; b. Huntsville, Ala., Feb. 22, 1944; s. Gilbert McClain and Marjorie Loucille (Harwell) D.; m. Nancy Margaret Eagar, Nov. 24, 1984; children: Marjorie Ruth, Gilbert Charles. BA, Samford U., 1966; JD, Cumberland Sch. of Law, 1969. Bar: Tenn. 1971, U.S. Dist. Ct. (ea. dist.) Tenn. 1972. Adminstrv. asst. Dist. Atty.'s Office, Huntsville, 1969-70; law clerk domestic and juvenile divsn. Cir. Ct., Huntsville, 1970-72; trial lawyer Legal Aid Soc., Chattanooga, 1972-75; pvt. practice Chattanooga, 1975-77, Fayetteville, Tenn., 1977-89; dist. pub. defender 17th jud. cir. State of Tenn., Fayetteville, 1989-98; pvt. practice, Fayetteville, Tenn., 1998—; mem. continuing edn. com. Pub. Defenders Conf., Tenn., 1990-92, mem. long range planning com., 1991-93, mem. legis. com., 1990-93, mem. exec. com., Mid. Tenn. rep., 1993-94. Lectr. Fayetteville-Lincoln County Leadership Tng. Program, 1989—; mem. adv. bd. Community Correction South Ctrl. Tenn., Fayetteville, 1989—; mem. Bedford County Dem. Club, 1989—. Mem. Nat. Assn. Criminal Def. Lawyers, Tenn. Bar Assn., Tenn. Assn. Criminal Def. Lawyers (membership com. 1989—, juvenile law com. 1988—, Disting. Svc. award 1990, 91, 92), Marshall County Bar Assn., Fayetteville-Lincoln County Bar Assn. (treas. 1977, sec. 1978, v.p. 1979, pres. 1980), Fayetteville-Lincoln County C. of C., Elks, Masons (jr. steward 1991, sr. steward 1992, jr. deacon 1993, jr. warden 1994, sr. warden 1995, worshipful master 1996), York Rite Mason, Scottish Rite Mason (32 degree), Shriners (sgt.-at-arms 1993, v.p. 1994, dir. pub. rels. 1994, 96—, pres. 1995), Internat. Platform Assn., Order of Ea. Star (chaplain 1993-94), Tenn. 4-H Found. Democrat. Methodist. Avocations: hunting, fishing, canoeing, kayaking. Constitutional, Criminal, Juvenile. Home: 122 Brookmeade Dr Fayetteville TN 37334-2046 Office: 105 Main Ave S Fayetteville TN 37334-3057

**DICKEY, JOHN M.,** lawyer; b. Indpls., Aug. 23, 1964; s. Robert F. and Patricia A. D.; m. Debra A. Kishton, July 28, 1990; children: Zachary John, Kyle Andrew. BS, Youngstown State U., 1987; JD, Ohio No. U., 1992. Lawyer Stading & Assocs., El Paso, Tex., 1992-96; sole practice law El Paso, 1996—. Mem. ABA, Tex. Bar Assn., N.Mex. Bar Assn., El Paso Bar Assn. Avocation: running. General civil litigation, Insurance, Personal injury. Office: 1520 N Campbell St El Paso TX 79902-4219

**DICKEY, JOHN W.,** lawyer; b. Springfield, Mo., 1927. AB, U. Mo., 1950; BA, Oxford (Eng.) U., 1952, MA, 1956; LLB, Harvard U., 1954. Bar: Mo. 1954, N.Y. 1955, Eng. and Wales 1999. Sr. counsel Sullivan & Cromwell, London. Mem. Am. Coll. Trial Lawyers. Office: Sullivan & Cromwell, 9A Ironmonger Ln, London EC2V 8EY, England

**DICKEY, SAMUEL STEPHENS,** lawyer; b. Wichita Falls, Tex., Feb. 14, 1921; s. Charles Wallis and Edoline (Stephens) D.; m. Betty Alice Long, June 18, 1949; children: Andrew Charles, Stuart Gilbert. Student, SW Mo. State U., 1942; AB, Drury Coll., 1943; JD, U. Mo., 1949. Bar: Mo. 1948, U.S. Dist. Ct. (we.) Mo. 1949. Ptnr. Haymes Dickey & Dickey, Springfield, Mo., 1949-59, Chinn White & Dickey, Springfield, Mo., 1959-60, White & Dickey, Springfield, Mo., Dickey, Allemann, Chaney & McCurry, Springfield, Mo., 1960-94, Dickey & Allemann, Springfield, 1995-99; pvt. practice Springfield, 1999—; bd. dirs. Citizens Bank Rogerville. With USN 1941-63. Avocations: reading, golf. Estate planning, Probate. Office: 2636 E Glenwood St Springfield MO 65804-3422

**DICKGRAFE, SHARON LOUISE,** lawyer; b. Herington, Kans., Aug. 5, 1964; d. Harold D. and Betty J. Chalker; m. Daniel W. Dickgrafe. BS in Family Econs., Kansas State U., 1986; JD, U. Kans., 1989. Bar: Kans. 1989. Assoc. Foulston & Siefkin, Wichita, Kans., 1989-92; asst. city atty. City of Wichita, 1992—. Office: City of Wichita City Hall 13th Fl 455 N Main St Wichita KS 67202-1600

**DICKINSON, TEMPLE,** lawyer; b. Glasgow, Ky., Mar. 13, 1956; s. Lewis and Selma (Goodman) D.; m. Jan Marie Wussow, Oct. 7, 1995. AB, Transylvania U., 1978; JD, Harvard U., 1984. Bar: Mass. 1985, N.Y. 1990, Ky. 1995, U.S. Dist. Ct. Mass. 1985, U.S. Ct. Appeals (1st cir.) 1988. Assoc. Casner, Edwards & Roseman, Boston, 1984-88; asst. dist. atty. Kings County Dist. Atty.'s Office, Bklyn., 1988-95; ptner. Gillenwater, Hampton and Dickinson, Glasgow, Ky., 1995—. Democrat. Mem. Disciples of Christ. Avocation: theater. Criminal, Personal injury. Office: Gillenwater Hampton et al 103 E Main St Glasgow KY 42141-2835

**DICKS, SARAH HOUSTON,** lawyer; b. Ft. Polk, La., Jan. 26, 1954; d. Donald Eugene and Esther (Cowan) H.; m. Michael E. Fox, May 26, 1973 (dec. apr. 1983); children: Nathaniel, Eliza, Isaac; m. James K. Dick, Dec. 21, 1993. BA, Purdue U., 1976; MAT, De Pauw U., 1983; JD, Ind. U., 1989. Dep. prosecutor Tippecanoe County, Lafayette, Ind., 1989-94; assoc. Heide Sandy Deets Kennedy, Lafayette, 1994-96; pvt. practice Waynetown, Ind., 1996—; pub. defender, Montgomery County, Crawfordsville, Tippecanoe County, Lafayette, Fountain County, Covington, Ind. Criminal, Family and matrimonial, Juvenile. Office: 102 E Washington St Waynetown IN 47990

**DICKSON, BRENT E(LLIS),** state supreme court justice; b. July 18, 1941; m. Jan Aikman, June 8, 1963; children: Andrew, Kyle, Reed. BA, Purdue U., 1964; JD, Ind. U., Indpls., 1968; LittD, Purdue U., 1996. Bar: Ind. 1968, U.S. Ct. Appeals (7th cir.) 1972, U.S. Supreme Ct. 1975; cert. civil trial adv., NBTA. Pvt. practice Lafayette, Ind., 1968-85; sr. ptnr. Dickson, Reiling, Teder & Withered, 1977-85; justice Ind. Supreme Ct., Indpls.,

1986—; adj. prof. Sch. of Law Ind. U., 1992—. Past pres. Tippecanoe County Hist. Assn.; mem. dean's adv. coun. Sch. Liberal Arts Purdue U., 1990-94; mem. adv. bd. Heartland Film Festival, 1995—. Office: Ind Supreme Ct 304 Statehouse Indianapolis IN 46204-2213*

**DICKSON, ROBERT JAY,** lawyer; b. Waukegan, Ill., Sept. 20, 1947; s. Robert Jay and Suzanne Elizabeth (Smith) D.; m. J. Alyson Younghusband, June 21, 1969; children: Peter M., Joshua H., Theodore F., Ian A. BA, Northwestern U., 1969; JD, U. Ill., Champaign, 1972. Bar: Alaska 1972, U.S. Dist. Ct. Alaska 1972, U.S. Ct. Appeals (9th cir.) 1972, U.S. Supreme Ct. 1973. Assoc. Atkinson, Conway & Gagnon, Anchorage, 1972—, ptnr., 1974—; mem. Forum Com. Constrn. Industry, 1978—. Co-author: Alaska Construction Law, 6th rev. edit., 1986, Alaska Construction Law, 1998, Advanced Construction Law in Alaska, 1999, Sourcebook on Construction Contracting, 1999. Mem. community adv. bd. Providence Health System Alaska, Anchorage; bd. dirs. Alaskan Scottish Club, 1973-88, Meier Lake Conf. Ctr., Wasilla, Alaska, 1979-88, Homer (Alaska) Soc. Natural History, 1985-89, Alaska Ctr. for the Performing Arts, 1990-91, Anchorage Sch. Bus. Ptnrships., 1995—, Alaska Support Industry Alliance, 1997—, Govs. Prayer Breakfast, 1997—; bd. dirs. Anchorage Symphony Orch., 1987—, pres., 1989-91, 99—; bd. dirs., chmn. Russian-Alaska Acad. Fine Arts, 1996—; chmn. bd. trustees Robert E. and Margaret E. Lyle Trust, 1996—. Mem. ABA, Alaska Bar Assn., Anchorage Bar Assn., Am. Acad. Healthcare Attys., Assoc. Gen. Contractors (legal affairs com. Alaska chpt.), Anchorage C. of C., Commonwealth North Club, Capt. Cook Athletic Club (Anchorage). Episcopalian. Avocations: piano, boating. General civil litigation, Health, Construction. Office: Atkinson Conway & Gagnon 420 L St Anchorage AK 99501-1937

**DICKSON, VICTOR PAUL,** lawyer; b. Pensacola, Fla., Aug. 20, 1950; s. Victor Lewis and Mary (Sasnette) D.; m. Paige Stenstrom, May 14, 1988. BA, U. West Fla., 1973; JD, Stetson U., 1976. Bar: Fla. 1976, Tex. 1979; bd. cert. criminal law splist. Tex. Bd. Legal Splization, 1988, bd. cert. Criminal Trial Adv. Nat. Bd. Trial Advocacy, 1992. Asst. pub. defender 20th Cir. Pub. Defenders Off., Naples, Fla., 1977-78; asst. city atty. City Atty.'s Office, Ft. Worth, 1979-84; asst. dist. atty. Tarrant County Criminal Dist. Atty.'s Off., Ft. Worth, 1984-94; pvt. practice Ft. Worth, 1994—. Criminal. Home: 2318 W Magnolia Ave Fort Worth TX 76110-1125 Office: PO Box 11611 Fort Worth TX 76110-0611

**DICKSTEIN, JOAN BORTECK,** arbitrator, conflict management consultant; b. Phila., June 20, 1919; d. Joseph and Mary (Leibovitz) Borteck; m. Benjamin Dickstein, Dec. 24, 1939; children: Howard, Kenneth, Mary. BA, Antioch Coll., 1974; MA in Sociology, U. Pa., 1978. Phila. coord. Gt. Books Found., Chgo., 1960-64; moderator, panelist Panel of Am. Women, Phila., 1964-73; trainer sensitivity courses Phila. Fellowship commn., 1966-69; rsch. assoc., cons. U. Pa. Human Resources Ctr., Phila., 1969-73; arbitrator comty. disputes Am. Arbitration Assn., Phila., 1969-82, Mcpl. Ct. of Phila., 1974-80, Commn. on Human Rels., Phila., 1979-82; facilitator interfaith dialogue Elkins Park (Pa.) Interfaith Dialogue, 1987—; guest lectr. conflict mgmt. La Salle Coll., Phila., 1971-74; mem. adv. com. Episcopal Comty. Svcs., Phila., 1972-73; cons. staff devel. Covenant House Health Svc., Phila., 1979-80. V.p. Phila. chpt. Am. Jewish Com., Phila., 1970-73; study tour mem. Scandinavia, World Future Soc., Washington, 1974; study tour mem. Mid. East, United Presbyn. Ch., Roman Cath. Conf., Am. Jewish Com., N.Y.C., 1976; bd. dirs. Or Hadash Congregation, Ft. Washington, Pa., 1990-93; peer counselor Women's Ctr., Jenkintown, Pa., 1987—. Recipient Human Rights award City of Phila. Commn. on Human Rels., 1982. Democrat. Jewish. Avocations: Great Books discussion programs, interfaith dialogue, aeorbics, crossword puzzles, volunteering at women's ctr. Home: 8325 Fairview Rd Elkins Park PA 19027-2120

**DICKSTEIN, MICHAEL ETHAN,** lawyer; b. Montreal, Sept. 8, 1959; s. Joseph and Barbara Dickstein. AB, Harvard U., 1981, JD, 1985. Bar: Calif. 1985. Assoc. Heller, Ehrman, White & McAuliffe, San Francisco, 1985-91, ptnr., 1992; atty./mediator/cons. in pvt. practice, 1993—; judge pro tem/mediator San Francisco and Alameda Superior and Mcpl. Cts., 1992—; mediation and negotiation instr. Stitt, Feld, Handy, Houston, 1996—; lectr. in appellate advocacy Boalt Law Sch., U. Calif., Berkeley, 1990. Labor, Alternative dispute resolution, General civil litigation.

**DICKSTEIN, SIDNEY,** lawyer; b. Bklyn., May 13, 1925; s. Charles and Pearl (Stahl) D.; m. Barbara H. Duke, Sept. 20, 1953; children: Ellen Simeon, Matthew Howard, Nancy Joy. A.B., Franklin and Marshall Coll., Lancaster, Pa., 1947; J.D., Columbia U., 1949. Bar: N.Y. 1949, D.C. 1959. Law clk. to Joseph Richter, N.Y.C., 1949-50; assoc. law office Herman E. Cooper, 1950-53; founder Dickstein & Shapiro, N.Y.C., 1953; sr. ptnr. successor firm Dickstein, Shapiro, Morin & Oshinsky, Washington, 1953-97, sr. counsel, 1998—. Trustee Franklin and Marshall Coll., 1978—. Served with AUS, 1943-44, USNR, 1944-46. Mem. ABA, Bar Assn. D.C., Am. Jewish Com. (pres. Washington chpt. 1999—, mem. nat. bd. govs.). Antitrust, General corporate, Securities. Home: 9050 Bradgrove Dr Bethesda MD 20817-3003 Office: Dickstein Shapiro Morin & Oshinsky 2101 L St NW Washington DC 20037-1524

**DICLERICO, JOSEPH ANTHONY, JR.,** federal judge; b. Lynn, Mass., Jan. 30, 1941; s. Joseph Anthony and Ruth Adel (Cummings) DiC.; m. Laurie Breed Thomson, July 27, 1975; 1 child, Devon Thomson. BA, Williams Coll., Williamstown, Mass., 1963; LLB, Yale U., 1966. Bar: N.H. 1967, U.S. Dist. Ct. N.H. 1967, U.S. Ct. Appeals (1st cir.) 1973, U.S. Supreme Ct. 1975. Law clk. to presiding justice U.S. Dist. Ct. N.H., Concord, 1966-67, N.H. Supreme Ct., Concord, 1967-68; assoc. Cleveland Waters & Bass, Concord, 1968-70; asst. atty. gen. State of N.H., Concord, 1970-77; assoc. justice N.H. Superior Ct., Concord, 1977-91, chief justice, 1991-92; chief judge U.S. Dist. Ct. N.H., Concord, 1992-97; chmn. Superior Ct. sentence rev. disvn., 1987-92. Fellow Am. Bar Found. (life), N.H. Bar Found. (jud.); mem. N.H. Bar Assn (nat. conf. state trial judges 1986-92, nat. conf. fed. trial judges, 1992-96, mem. com. on codes of conduct jud. conf. of U.S. 1994—, dist. judge rep. from 1st cir. to Jud. Conf. of U.S. 1997—), Phi Beta Kappa. Republican. Roman Catholic. Avocation: gardening. Office: 55 Pleasant St Concord NH 03301-3954

**DICUS, BRIAN GEORGE,** lawyer; b. Kansas City, Mo., Oct. 29, 1961; s. Clarence Howard and Edith Helen (George) D.; m. Vali Ann Venner, Dec. 14, 1985; children: Brian George, Cady Alyssa. BA, So. Meth. U., 1984, JD, 1987. Bar: Tex. 1987, U.S. Dist. Ct. (no. dist.) Tex. 1988; bd. cert. estate planning and probate law Tex. Bd. Legal Specialization. Assoc. Thorp & Sorenson, Dallas, 1987-89, Joseph E. Ashmore Jr., P.C., Dallas, 1989-92; pvt. practice Dallas, 1992—. Chmn. local alumni student recruiting program So. Meth. U., Dallas, 1989-90. Fellow Tex. Bar Found.; mem. Tex. Bar Assn., Dallas Bar Assn., Phi Alpha Delta, Pi Sigma Alpha. Probate, General civil litigation, Estate planning. Home: 2336 Serenity Ln Heath TX 75032-1922 Office: 5910 N Central Expy Ste 920 Dallas TX 75206-5159

**DICUS, STEPHEN HOWARD,** lawyer; b. Kansas City, Mo., Mar. 3, 1948; s. Clarence Howard and Edith Helen (George) D.; children: Brett S., Adam J. AB, U. Mo., 1970; JD, U. Mo., Kansas City, 1973. Bar: Mo. 1973, U.S. Dist. Ct. (we. dist.) Mo. 1973. Assoc. Dietrich, Davis, Dicus, Rowlands, Schmitt & Gorman, Kansas City, 1973-78; ptnr. Armstrong Teasdale, Schlafly, Davis & Dicus (formerly Dietrich, Davis, Dicus, Rowlands, Schmitt & Gorman), Kansas City, 1979-91, Dicus Davis Sands & Collins, P.C., Kansas City, 1991—. Mem. ABA, Kansas City Met. Bar Assn., Estate Planning Soc. Kansas City, Rotary Club. Presbyterian. Avocations: tennis, golf, skiing. Estate planning, Probate, Real property. Home: 12019 Ensley Ln Shawnee Mission KS 66209-1069 Office: Dicus Davis Sands & Collins PC 1100 Main St Ste 1930 Kansas City MO 64105-5175

**DI DOMENICO, PHILIP,** lawyer; b. Manhasset, N.Y., Mar. 11, 1962; s. Philip and Marie di D. BA, Fairfield U., 1984; JD, Boston U., 1988. Bar: Hawaii 1991, Mass. 1994, N.Y. 1997; U.S. Dist. Ct. Hawaii 1991, U.S. Dist. Ct. Mass. 1994, U.S. Dist. Ct. (so. dist. N.Y.) 1997; U.S. Ct. Appeals (9th cir.) 1991, U.S. Ct. Appeals (1st cir.) 1994, U.S. Ct. Appeals (2d cir.) 1997. Counsel CIC Aviation S.A., Nice, France, 1988-91; assoc. Greeley, Walker & Kowen, Honolulu, 1991-92; ptnr. Cabinet di Domenico, Paris, 1992-94; assoc. City, Hayes, Meagher & Dissette, Boston, 1994-97; ptnr. Law Offices of Philip di Domenico, N.Y.C., 1997—. Avocat Accredite, Consulate of France, Boston, 1995-97. Private international, General civil litigation, Contracts commercial. Office: 520 W 112th St Apt 5A New York NY 10025-1603

**DIEFENBACH, DALE ALAN,** law librarian, retired; b. Cleve., Aug. 14, 1933; s. Walter Ewald and Alice Naomi (Austin) D.; m. Olga Maspaitella, Jan. 20, 1973; 1 stepson, Andrew Ivan Ward. BA, Baldwin-Wallace Coll., 1955; MLS, U. Hawaii, 1970. Fgn. svc. officer U.S. Dept. State, 1961-68; reference libr. Cornell U. Law Libr., Ithaca, N.Y., 1970-87; sr. reference libr. Harvard U. Law Libr., Cambridge, Mass., 1987-97, ret., 1997; reference libr., adj. assoc. prof. law libr. Barry U. Orlando (Fla.) Sch. Law Euliano Law Libr., 1998—. Lt. (j.g.) USNR, 1956-60, Philippines. Recipient Ficken Meml. award Baldwin-Wallace Coll., Berea, Ohio, 1988. Mem. ALA, Am. Assn. Law Librs. Democrat. Fax: 407-275-3654. Home: 500 Windmeadows St Altamonte Springs FL 32701-3572 Office: Barry U Orlando Sch Law Euliano Law Libr 6441 E Colonial Dr Orlando FL 32807-3650

**DIEGUEZ, RICHARD PETER,** lawyer; b. Bklyn., Apr. 25, 1960. BA cum laude, Manhattanville Coll., 1982; JD, NYU, 1985. Bar: Conn. 1986, N.Y. 1987, U.S. Dist. Ct. (so. and ea. dists.) N.Y. 1987, U.S. Supreme Ct. 1990. Assoc. Morgan Lewis & Bockius, N.Y.C., 1985-86, Battle Fowler, N.Y.C., 1987; pvt. practice in internat. entertainment law Roslyn Heights, N.Y., 1987—; speaker various nat. trade cons., confs. and ednl. instns.; mgr. Lisa Lisa. Editor-in-chief Jour. Internat. Law and Politics, 1985; contbr. articles to law jours. and numerous nat. mags. and trade publs.; appeared on various TV talk shows. Founder, chmn. The Federalist Soc., N.Y.C., 1984. Mem. Nassau County Bar Assn. Avocations: writing, painting, music, recording, composing. Entertainment, General practice, Estate planning. Office: 192 Garden St Ste 2 Roslyn Heights NY 11577-1012

**DIEHL, RICHARD PAUL,** lawyer; b. Toledo, Dec. 25, 1940; s. Clair Bertrand and Josephine Frances (Kwiatkowski) D.; m. Laura Gean Carpenter, Mar. 26, 1966; children: Michelle, Michael. BS in Mech. Engring., U. Mich., 1963; MBA, Tulane U., 1972; JD, U. Detroit, 1983. Bar: Mich. 1983, U.S. Dist. Ct. (ea. dist.) Mich. 1983, U.S. Supreme Ct. 1988, U.S. Ct. Fed. Claims 1990, U.S. Ct. Appeals (6th cir.) 1991, U.S. Ct. Appeals (fed., D.C. cirs.) 1992), U.S. Dist. Ct. (we. dist.) Mich. 1996. Commd. 2d lt. U.S. Army, 1963, advanced through grades to col., ret., 1986; pres. Diehl & Sobczak, P.C., Troy, Mich., 1986—; adj. prof. bus. Am. Tech. U., Killeen, Tex., 1977-78; adj. prof. law U. Detroit, 1987-89. Contbr. articles to profl. jours. Decorated 2 Silver stars, five Bronze stars, 2 Purple Hearts, 2 Legions of Merit Meritorious Svc. medal, Army Commendation medal, 3 Air medals, Cross of Gallantry. Mem. Am. Def. Preparedness Assn., Assn. U.S. Army, Oakland County Bar Assn., Fed. Bar Assn., U. Mich. Alumni Assn., Elks. Avocations: hunting, fishing, sports. Government contracts and claims, General practice. Office: 1105 Kingsview Ave Rochester Hls MI 48309-2510

**DIEHL, THOMAS JAMES,** lawyer; b. Cin., June 5, 1963; s. James Harrison and Sally (Patton) D.; m. Donna T. Lutz, May 9, 1992. BS, Miami U., 1985; JD, U. Cin., 1988. Bar: Ohio 1988. Assoc. Shulman & Hall, Dayton, Ohio, 1988-89; ptnr. Sheets, Ernst & Diehl, Lebanon, Ohio, 1989—. Mem. Ohio Acad. Trial Lawyers, Ohio State Bar Assn., Warren County Bar Assn. Personal injury, Criminal. Home: 445 Stolle Dr Springboro OH 45066-8621 Office: Sheets Ernst & Diehl 304 E Warren St Lebanon OH 45036-1854

**DIEHM, JAMES WARREN,** lawyer, educator; b. Lancaster, Pa., Nov. 6, 1944; s. Warren G. and Verna M. (Hertzler) D.; m. Cathleen M. Hohmeier; children: Elizabeth Ann, Rebecca Jane. B.A., Pa. State U., 1966; J.D., Georgetown U., 1969. Bar: D.C. 1969, V.I. 1975, Pa. 1988. Asst. U.S. atty. Washington, 1970-74; asst. atty. gen. Atty. Gen.'s Office U.S. V.I., St. Croix, 1974-76; from assoc. to ptnr. Isherwood, Hunter & Diehm, St. Croix, 1976-83; U.S. atty. U.S. V.I., 1983-87; prof. law Widener U., 1987—; bar examiner U.S. V.I. Bar, 1979-87. Mem. ABA. Republican. Lutheran. Office: Widener U Sch Law 3800 Vartan Way PO Box 69382 Harrisburg PA 17106-9382

**DIENES, LOUIS ROBERT,** lawyer; b. New Brunswick, N.J., Apr. 17, 1966; s. Louis S. and Rosemary T. D. AB, U. Calif., Berkeley, 1990; JD, Stanford U., 1994. Bar: Calif. 1994. Assoc. Baker & McKenzie LLP, Palo Alto, Calif., 1994-96, Pennie & Edmonds LLP, Palo Alto, 1996-99, Gibson Dunn & Crutcher LLP, N.Y.C., 1999—. Mem. Santa Clara Bar Assn. (co-chmn. high tech law sect. 1998-99), Federalist Soc. (chmn. biotech. com. 1998-99), Phi Beta Kappa. Intellectual property, Contracts commercial, General corporate. Office: Gibson Dunn & Crutcher LLP 200 Park Ave New York NY 10021

**DIENSTAG, CYNTHIA JILL,** lawyer, childcare business owner; b. N.Y.C., Apr. 17, 1962; d. Jack Jacob Helman and Roni Helene (Turk) Setti; div.; children: Marissa, Allison. AA, Fla. State U., 1981; BS, Fla. Internat. U., 1983; JD, U. Miami, 1988. Bar: Fla. 1989; cert. family law mediator, Fla. Judicial asst. Cir. Judge Frederick N. Barad, Miami, Fla., 1982-85; assoc. Brenner & Dienstag, P.A., Miami, Fla., 1988-90, Weissman & Greenblatt, Ft. Lauderdale, Fla., 1990-91, Elser, Greene & Hodor, Miami, 1991-93; pvt. practice Coconut Grove, Fla., 1993—. Active lectr., participant Schs.; mem. professionalism and ethics com., family law com., Dade County Bar, 1992-97; mem. support issues and gen. masters com. Fla. Bar. Mem. ABA (family law sect.), Fla. Assn. Women Lawyers. Republican. Jewish. Family and matrimonial. Office: 2601 S Bayshore Dr Ste 1400 Miami FL 33133-5413

**DIERKING, JOHN RANDALL,** lawyer; b. Valparaiso, Ind., Oct. 28, 1957; s. Edwin John and Rachel Ann Dierking; m. Lavinia Georgia Jean Keefer, June 29, 1979; 1 child, Sarah Elizabeth. BSBA, U. Ctrl. Fla., Orlando, 1978; JD with honors, U. Fla., 1991. Bar: Fla. 1992, U.S. Dist. Ct. (mid. dist.) Fla. 1992. Account mgr. NCR Corp., Orlando, 1979-82; asst. v.p., human resources adminstr. Am. Pioneer Savs. Bank, Orlando, 1982-89; atty. Holland & Knight LLP, Orlando, 1992—. Chair ptnrs. in bus. com. Lake Eola Charter Sch., Orlando, 1998. Mem. South Lake Kiwanis Club (bd. dirs. 1995—), Tiger Bay Club, Order of Coif. Avocations: swimming, travel, theater. General corporate, Contracts commercial. Office: Holland & Knight LLP 200 S Orange Ave Ste 2600 Orlando FL 32801-3449

**DIETEL, JAMES EDWIN,** lawyer, consultant; b. Dallas, Sept. 14, 1941; s. Bernhard Herman and Gladys Ellen D.; m. Elizabeth Nathan, May 9, 1964; 1 child, Elizabeth Lindsay. BSME, So. Meth. U., 1964; JD, George Washington U., 1969; LLM in Internat. Trade, Georgetown U., 1977; MBA, U. Pa., 1992. Bar: D.C. 1971, U.S. Dist. Ct. D.C. 1971, U.S. Ct. Appeals (D.C. cir.) 1975, U.S. Supreme Ct. 1975, Va. 1990. Engr. CIA, Washington, 1964-70; program evaluation officer CIA, 1970-73, assoc. gen. counsel, 1979-80, from assoc. dep. gen. counsel to insp., 1980-93, with office exec. dir., 1993-94; counsel for info. policy, 1994-95; participant ann. jud. conf. U.S. Ct. Appeals (D.C. cir.), 1986; speaker, ltr. and presenter in field. Author: Leading a Law Practice to Excellence, 1992, Sustaining Law Practice Excellence, 1995, Designing Effective Records Retention Compliance Program, 1993, Leaders' Digest: A Review of the Best Books on Leadership, 1995; contbr. articles to profl. jours. Mem. ABA (coun. mem. law practice mgmt. sect., chmn. govt. and pub. sector lawyers divsn.), Coll. Law Practice Mgmt., Cosmos Club, Pi Tau Sigma, Kappa Mu Epsilon, Kappa Alpha.

**DIETZ, CHARLTON HENRY,** lawyer; b. LeMars, Iowa, Jan. 8, 1931; s. Clifford Henry and Mildred Verna (Eggensperger) D.; m. Viola Ann Lange, Aug. 17, 1952; children: Susan (Mrs. Jay Kakuk), Robin (Mrs. Jack Mayfield), Craig. BA, Macalester Coll., 1953; JD, William Mitchell Coll. Law, 1957, LLD, 1993. Bar: Minn. 1957. Mem. pub. rels. staff 3M, St. Paul, 1952-58, atty., 1958-70, assoc. counsel, asst. sec., 1970-72, asst. gen. counsel, 1972-75, sec., 1972-76, gen. counsel, 1975-92, v.p. legal affairs, 1976-88, sr. v.p., 1988-93; bd. dirs. Ea. Heights Bank, 1972-99, chmn. bd., 1981-93; bd. dirs. Mairs & Power Mutual Funds, 1994—; mem. adv. bd. UFE; instr. William Mitchell Coll. Law, 1960-74, trustee, 1974-86, 87-96, pres., 1980-83. Bd. dirs. St. Paul Area YMCA, 1973-80, chmn. 1978-80, Minn. Citizens Coun. on Crime and Justice, 1976-88, pres., 1982-84, St. Paul United Way, 1980-95, Ramsey County Hist. Soc., 1979-86, St. Paul Lowertown Redevel. Corp., 1988-94, Minn. Hist. Soc., 1993—, Supreme Ct. Hist. Soc., 1991—, Children's Health Care, 1994—; trustee United Theol. Sem., 1976-82, Macalester Coll., 1983-89, Wilder Found., 1989—, chmn., 1996—; mem. Conferees of Minn. Citizens Conf. on Cts.; bd. dirs. Masonic Cancer Ctr. Fund, 1984—, pres. 1994-97. Fellow Am. Bar Found.; mem. ABA, Fedn. Bar Assn., Minn. Bar Assn., Ramsey County Bar Assn., Assn. Gen. Counsel, Am. Judicature Soc. (bd. dirs. 1989-95), Am. Law Inst., Masons, Shriners, Jesters. Republican. Mem. United Ch. of Christ. General corporate. Home: 1 Birch Ln Saint Paul MN 55127-6402

**DIETZ, ROBERT BARRON,** lawyer; b. San Diego, May 14, 1942; s. J. Thomas and Mary Agnes (Barron) D.; m. Grace Louise Purcell, Aug. 19, 1967; children: Thomas E., Michael B., Denis P., M. Alison. AB, Coll. Holy Cross, 1964; JD, Cornell U., 1968. Bar: N.Y. 1968, U.S. Dist. Ct. (no. dist.) N.Y. 1968, U.S. Dist. Ct. (so. and ea. dists.) N.Y. 1973, U.S. Supreme Ct. 1974. Asst. dist. atty. County of Dutchess, Poughkeepsie, N.Y., 1969-70, confidential law clk. to surrogate of Dutchess County, 1970-73; corp. counsel City of Poughkeepsie, 1973-75; assoc. Garrity & Dietz, Poughkeepsie, 1969-73, ptnr., 1973-75; assoc. Gellert & Cutler, P.C. and predecessor firms, Poughkeepsie, 1975-78, ptnr., 1978-86; pvt. practice law Poughkeepsie, 1986-94; ptnr. Dietz & Dietz, Poughkeepsie, 1995—; lectr. Dutchess C.C., Poughkeepsie, 1985—; mem. grievance com. 9th Jud. Dist., N.Y., 1987-95; bd. dirs. Youth Resource Devel. Corp., chmn., 1992-95. Bd. dirs. Mid Hudson Workshop for Disabled, Sports Mus. Dutchess County; chmn. Mid Hudson adv. bd. Salvation Army; bd. trustees Vassar-Warner Home; bd. counsellors The Children's Home of Poughkeepsie, Inc.; bd. dirs. Dutchess County coun. Boy Scouts Am.; former mem. City of Poughkeepsie Recreation Commn.; bd. dirs. Greystone Programs, Inc. Fellow Dist. 721 Rotary, Poughkeepsie, 1964-65. Mem. ABA, N.Y. State Bar Assn., Dutchess County Bar Assn., Poughkeepsie C. of C., Kiwanis (pres. Poughkeepsie club 1974-75). Republican. Roman Catholic. Avocations: golf, tennis, reading, baseball card collecting. General practice, Probate, Real property. Office: 2 Cannon St Poughkeepsie NY 12601-3229

**DIETZ, ROBERT LEE,** lawyer; b. Miami, Fla., Apr. 28, 1958; s. Edward William and Anna C. D.; m. Laura Sanders, May 8, 1982; children: John Edward, Stephanie Elizabeth. BA with honors, Eckerd Coll., St. Petersburg, Fla., 1979; JD, Vanderbilt U., 1982. Bar: Fla. 1984; cert. workers' compensation, 1992—; Supreme Ct. cert. cir. civil mediator, 1995—. Atty. Zimmerman, Shuffield, Kiser & Sutcliffe, P.A., Orlando, Fla., 1984—. Contbr. articles to profl. jours. Vice chair S.E. region bd. dirs. Canine Companions for Independence, Orlando, 1991-93; alumni bd. dirs., 1992-97, chair alumni capital campaign Eckerd Coll., 1994-97. Recipient McArthur Alumni award Eckerd Coll., 1993. Mem. ABA (nat. chair ABA TIPS, workers compensation and employer liability com. 1995-96), The Fla. Bar (workers compensation rules com. 1988-91), Orange County Bar Assn. (chmn. workers compensation com. 1996-97, Guardian ad Litem of the Yr. 1996), Fla. Def. Lawyers Assn. (chair workers compensation com. 1989-96, bd. dirs. 1991-95, sec.-treas. 1996-97, pres. 1998-99, Pro Bono award 1996), Civitan Internat. (Disting. gov. 1993-94, internat. mem. mktg. com. 1994-96, Club Honor key East Orlando club 1994, Winter Park Club 1996, College Park Club 1996, Dist. Honor key Sunshine dist. 1994, Region II Honor key 1995). Avocations: indoor soccer, speed chess, golf, tennis. Fax: 407-425-1537. E-mail: rdietz@zsks.com. Workers' compensation. Home: 2534 Shrewsbury Rd Orlando FL 32803-1336 Office: Zimmerman Shuffield Kiser & Sutcliffe PA 315 E Robinson St Ste 600 Orlando FL 32801-4308

**DIETZ, ROBERT SHELDON,** lawyer; b. N.Y.C., Aug. 21, 1950; s. Sheldon and Annabel (Hagyard) D. Student, Harvard U., 1968-70; BA, Oxford U., 1974, MA, 1977; JD cum laude, U. Miami, 1982. Bar: Fla. 1983, La. 1983, D.C. 1987. Law clk. U.S. Dist. Ct. (ea. dist.) La., New Orleans, 1985-87; assoc. Milling, Bensen, Woodward, Pierson & Miller, New Orleans, 1983-85, Stroock & Stroock & Lavan, Washington, 1987-89; counsel merchant marine and fisheries com. Ho. Reps., Washington, 1989-90; assoc. LeBoeuf, Lamb, Leiby & MacRae, Washington, 1990—. Admiralty, Legislative. Home: 2310 Ashmead Pl NW Washington DC 20009-1439 Office: LeBoeuf Lamb Leiby & MacRae 1875 Connecticut Ave NW Washington DC 20009-5728

**DIETZEN, CHRISTOPHER J.,** lawyer; b. Yakima, Wash., Mar. 8, 1947; s. John Frederick and Elizabeth P. (Schneider) D.; m. Peggy Marie Regan, Dec. 27, 1969; children: Stacey, Mark, Lisa, John. BS, Gonzaga U., 1969, JD, 1973. Bar: Wash. 1973, Minn. 1978; cert. civil trial advocate, civil trial specialist. Assoc. Richter, Wimberley & Ericson, Spokane, Wash., 1973-78, Larkin, Hoffman, Daly & Lindgren, Mpls., 1978-83; ptnr., 1983—. Mem. Durenberger vol. com., 1990—, Grams vol. com. 1992—; mem. Mpls. Reapportionment Commn., 1991-92; deanery rep. ann. Cath. appeal, 1991-94; chair Outreach Panel-fin. coun. Archdiocese St. Paul & Mpls., 1994—. Mem. Eminent Domain Soc., Minn. State Bar Assn. (summer reporter), Hennepin County Bar Assn. (gov. coun. environ., natural resource sect. 1990—). Republican. Roman Catholic. Avocations: fishing, running, hiking. General civil litigation, Environmental, Condemnation. Home: 21 E 107th Street Cir # E Bloomington MN 55420-5311 Office: Larkin Hoffman Daly 7900 Xerxes Ave S Ste 1500 Minneapolis MN 55431-1128

**DIFILIPPO, FERNANDO, JR.,** lawyer; b. West Palm Beach, Fla., Feb. 24, 1948; s. Fernando Sr. and Quintina (Alo) D.; m. Kay DiFilippo (dec. 1986); children: Francesca, Jay B.; m. Wanda Rayle, Nov. 12, 1989. BA in History magna cum laude, Georgetown U., 1970, JD cum laude, 1973. Bar: N.Y. 1973. Assoc. Sullivan & Cromwell, N.Y.C., 1973-76; ptnr. Baker & McKenzie, Washington, 1977-85; sr. v.p., gen. counsel, sec. Balt. Fed. Fin. F.S.A., 1985-87; exec. v.p., gen. counsel, sec. Home Shopping Network, Inc., St. Petersburg, Fla., 1987—. Author: (with others) Merger Jurisdiction for FMC. Chmn. Life With Cancer, Fairfax, Va., 1987. Mem. ABA, N.Y. Bar Assn., D.C. Bar Assn., Phi Alpha Beta, Phi Beta Kappa. General corporate, Securities. Office: Home Shopping Network Inc 2505 118th Ave N Saint Petersburg FL 33716-1920

**DIFRONZO, MICHAEL A.,** lawyer, accountant; b. Billings, Mont., Sept. 23, 1968; s. Michael J. and Ashlea C. DiFronzo. BS in Acctg., Mont. State U., 1991; JD, U. Mont., 1994; LLM in Tax, NYU, 1997. Mont. 1994, Nev. 1995, DC 1998, U.S. Ct. Appeals. 1998. Sr. tax cons. Deloitte & Touche, Reno, 1994-96; internat. tax mgr. Deloitte & Touche, Washington, 1997—. Contbr. articles to profl. jours. Mem. ABA, Mont. Bar Assn., Nev. Bar Assn., D.C. Bar Assn., Mont. Bd. CPAs. Corporate taxation, Taxation, general, Public international. Office: Deloitte & Touche Nat Tax Office 555 12th St NW Ste 500 Washington DC 20004-1200

**DIFRUSCIA, ANTHONY R.,** lawyer, real estate executive; b. Lawrence, Mass., June 5, 1940; s. Carmine and Sebastina (Tine) DiF.; m. Kathleen Sullivan; children: Marc Anthony, Kara Ann, Tamra Lee, Daniel Anthony. B, Emerson Coll.; JD, New Eng. Sch. Law, 1966. Bar: Mass. 1967. Sr. ptnr. Lawrence, 1967—; pres. A.D. Devel., Inc., Lawrence; pres., treas. A.D. Mgmt., Lawrence. Mem. Mass. Ho. of Reps., 1965-72. Roman Catholic. Office: 260 Haverhill St Lawrence MA 01840-1208

**DIGGES, EDWARD S(IMMS), JR.,** business management consultant; b. Pitts., June 30, 1946. AB, Princeton U., 1968; JD, U. Md., 1971. Bar: Md. 1972, U.S. Supreme Ct. 1975. With staff of gov. State of Md., Annapolis, 1973; ptnr. Piper & Marbury, Washington and Balt., 1977-84; founding ptnr. Digges, Wharton & Levin, Annapolis, 1984-89; corp. cons. various corps., Towson, Md., 1989—; bd. dirs. Televest Comms., LLC, Corp. Comms. Mgmt. Group, LLC; instr. advanced bus. law Johns Hopkins U., 1975-78; lectr. civil procedure U. Balt. Law Sch., 1976-78; mem. govs. commn. to revise Md. code, 1978-90. Contbr. articles to profl. jours. Mem. Alumni Council Mercersburg Acad., 1982-88, pres. 1987-88; bd. advisors Indian Creek Sch., 1982-88, chmn. 1986-88; pres. Beacon Hill Community Assn., 1978-86. ROTC, U.S. Army, 1970-71. Mem. Md. State Bar Assn. (bd. govs. 1972-84), Am. Law Inst., Am. Bd. Trial Adv. (pres. Md. chpt. 1984-89), Inn XIII, Am. Inns of Ct. (Master of the Bench 1986-89), Scribes. Democrat. Roman Catholic. Clubs: So. Md. Soc. (bd. govs., pres. 1988), Mid Ocean (Bermuda), Princeton Club of N.Y. Product liability. Home: PO Box 42737 Baltimore MD 21284-2737

**DIGGS, BRADLEY C.,** lawyer; b. Missoula, Mont., Sept. 18, 1948. BA magna cum laude, Amherst Coll., 1970; JD cum laude, Harvard U., 1973. Bar: Wash. 1973. Mng. ptnr. Davis Wright Tremaine, Seattle. Mem. ABA, Phi Beta Kappa. Consumer commercial, General corporate. Office: Davis

Wright Tremaine 2600 Century Sq 1501 4th Ave Ste 2600 Seattle WA 98101-1688

**DIGIACOMO, PAULA COSENZA,** assistant prosecutor; b. Kingston, N.Y., Apr. 20, 1968; d. Richard Francis and Joan Wanda Cosenza; m. Richar Joseph DiGiacomo, June 28, 1997. BA, Fordham U., 1990; JD, Duquesne U., 1993. Bar: Pa. 1993, N.Y. 1994, U.S. Dist. Ct. (we. dist.) Pa. 1st asst. atty. Crawford County Dist. Atty.'s Office, Meadville, Pa., 1994—. Vol. Am. Cancer Soc., Crawford County, 1994-98. Mem. Am. Inn Ct., Pa. Bar Assn., Crawford County Bar Assn. Office: Crawford County Dist Atty Diamond Park PA 16335

**DI GIULIAN, BRUNO L.,** lawyer; b. West Palm Beach, Fla., Dec. 24, 1933; s. Angelo and Teresita Irma Di Giulian; m. Patsy R. Sammons, July 30, 1960; children: Teri, Bee Gee, Angelo. BA, Stetson U., 1954; JD, Yale U., 1957. Bar: Fla. 1957, U.S. Dist. Ct. (no. dist.) Fla. 1959, U.S. Dist. Ct. (so dist.) Fla. 1965, U.S. Ct. Appeals (11th cir.) 1981; cert. mediator. Assoc. Coe, Richardson & Broberg, Palm Beach, 1957-58; rsch. assoc. to chief justice Glenn Terrell Fla. Supreme Ct., Tallahassee, 1958-60; city atty. City of Pompano Beach, Fla., 1960-63; pvt. practice law Ft. Lauderdale, Fla., 1964-94; of counsel Ruden, McClosky, Smith, Schuster & Russell, P.A., Ft. Lauderdale, 1994—; bd. dirs. BankAtlantic; chmn. 17th Cir. Trial Ct. Nominating Coun., 1971-76. Trustee St. Thomas Aquinas Found., 1979-81. Recipient Young Man of the Yr. award Pompano Beach Jaycees, 1963. Mem. Fla. Bar (vice-chmn. com. on econs. 1966-71, chmn. group legal svc. com. 1975, real property and probate law sect. 1976-90, family law sect. 1978-94), Broward County Bar Assn. (chmn. 17th cir. grievance com. A 1969, treas. 1969-70, pres. 1971-72), Phi Delta Phi. Roman Catholic. Avocations: travel, languages, computers. Alternative dispute resolution, State civil litigation, Family and matrimonial. Home: 12045 NW 62d Ct Coral Springs FL 33076-1906 Office: Ruden McClosky Smith Schuster & Russell PA 200 E Broward Blvd Fort Lauderdale FL 33301-1963

**DIGNAM, ROBERT JAMES,** lawyer; b. Evergreen Park, Ill., June 26, 1960; s. Donald Robert and Geraldine Renetta Dignam; m. Wendy Sue Bouché, July 27, 1996; 1 child, Henry Robert; 1 step-son Kenneth Anthony. BA, St. Xavier U., 1983; JD, Valparaiso U., 1986. Bar: Ind. 1986, U.S. Dist. Ct. (no. and so. dist.) Ind. 1986, U.S. Ct. of Appeals (7th cir.) 1993, U.S. Supreme Ct. 1993. Assoc. Spangler, Jennings and Dougherty, P.C., Merrillville, Ind., 1986-96, ptnr., shareholder, 1997—. Author: (with others) Indiana Evidence Workshop, 1996, 97. Mem. ABA, Lake County Ind. Bar Assn., Def. Rsch. Inst., Calumet Am. Inn of Ct. (barrister). Avocations: running, marathons. Professional liability, Federal civil litigation, Civil rights. Office: Spangler Jennings & Dougherty PC 8396 Mississippi St Merrillville IN 46410-6316

**DIGNAN, THOMAS GREGORY, JR.,** lawyer; b. Worcester, Mass., May 23, 1940; s. Thomas Gregory and Hester Clare (Sharkey) D.; m. Mary Anne Connor, Sept. 16, 1978; children: Kellyanne E., Maryclare E. BA, Yale U., 1961; JD, U. Mich., 1964. Bar: Mass. 1964, U.S. Supreme Ct. 1968. Assoc. firm Ropes & Gray, Boston, 1964-74; ptnr. firm Ropes & Gray, 1974—; spl. asst. atty. gen. State of Mass., 1974-76; dir. Boston Edison Co.; trustee BEC Energy, NSTAR. Asst. editor: Mich. Law Rev., 1963-64; contbr. articles to profl. jours. Bd. dirs. Family Counseling and Guidance Ctrs., Inc., 1967-76, 78-94, v.p., 1983-87, pres., 1987-89; trustee Cath. Charitable Bur. of Boston, Inc., 1994-97, Dana Hall Sch., 1994—; bd. dirs. Gov.'s Mgmt. Task Force, 1979-81, Mass. Moderator's assn., 1994—; mem. fin. com. Town of Sudbury, 1982-85, moderator, 1985—; bd. advisors Environ. Law Ctr., Vt. Law Sch., 1981—; mem. vis. com. U. Mich. Law Sch.; corporator Emerson Hosp., 1989—. Mem. ABA, Mass. Bar Assn., Boston Bar Assn., Assn. Internationale du Droit Nucleaire, Am. Nuclear Soc., Am. Law Inst., Downtown Club, Nashawtuc Country Club, Order of the Coif, Phi Delta Phi. Republican. Roman Catholic. Federal civil litigation, Nuclear power, Environmental. Home: 8 Saddle Ridge Rd Sudbury MA 01776-2772 Office: Ropes & Gray One International Pl Boston MA 02110

**DIJKMAN, CHRISTIANA,** lawyer; b. Den Haag, The Netherlands, Sept. 5, 1964; came to U.S., 1974; d. Eduard Albertus and Hendricka Johanna Dijkman. BA in History, Tex. A&M U., 1987; postgrad., U. Tulsa, 1989-90; JD, U. Houston, 1992. Bar: Tex. 1992, U.S. Dist. Ct. (so., no. and ea. dists.) Tex. 1993, U.S. Ct. Appeals (5th cir.) 1996. Assoc. atty. So. Pacific, Houston, 1992-93; assoc. Hirsch Sheiness Glover, Houston and Brownsville, Tex., 1994-95, Phillips & Akers, Brownsville, 1995-97; dir. atty. Phillips & Akers, Houston, 1998—. Mem. Order of the Barons, Order of Coif. Avocations: scuba diving, running, aerobics, bicycling. General civil litigation, Personal injury, Labor. Office: Phillips & Akers 3400 Phoenix Tower 3200 Southwest Fwy Houston TX 77027-7528

**DIKEOU, GEORGE DEMETRIOS,** lawyer; b. Denver, Sept. 2, 1938; s. James George and Minnie A. (Girk) D.; m. Debby E. Wing, June 12, 1960 (div. June 1975); children: Erica, Carissa; m. Yonnie Kay Bell, June 18, 1977; 1 child, Damara. BA in Econs., Colo. Coll., 1960; cert. completion, U. Edinburgh, 1961; JD, Stanford U., 1964. Bar: Colo. 1965, Calif. 1965, U.S. Dist. Ct. Colo. 1965, U.S. Ct. Appeals (10th cir.) 1965, U.S. Ct. Claims 1980, U.S. Supreme Ct. 1980. Assoc. Holland & Hart, Denver, 1964-66; ptnr. Davies, St. Veltrie & Dikeou, Denver, 1966-72; asst. atty. gen. State of Colo., Denver, 1972-81, spl. asst. atty. gen., 1981-85; mng. ptnr. Roan & Grossman, Denver, 1981-82; ptnr. Gorsuch, Kirgis, Denver, 1982-85, Faegre & Benson, Denver, 1985-89; pvt. practice Englewood, Colo., 1989—; asst. atty. gen. Colo. Dept. Hwys., Denver, 1966-72; gen. counsel Health Scis. Ctr. U. Colo, 1972-77, instr. Dept. Preventative Medicine, 1972-80, clin instr., 1980-82, asst. prof. sch. nursing, 1978-80, adj. asst. prof. health adminstrn. Grad. Sch. Bus. Adminstrn., 1982—, vice chancellor for legal affairs and risk mgmt., 1980-81, mem. trust adv. bd., 1976-84, asst. Univ. counsel, 1972-77; instr. Webster U. Grad. Sch., Denver, 1983-88; bd. dirs. COPIC Trust, Denver; exec. v.p. COPIC Ins. Co., Denver. Pres. Wellshire Homeowner's Assn., 1969-71; chmn. adv. com. Regional Cancer Ctr., Denver, 1977-79; bd. dirs. for Neurologic Diseases, Rocky Mountain Multiple Sclerosis Found., Denver, 1979-92; bd. dirs. Family Support Svcs., Inc., Denver., 1982-84, Timber Ridge Homeowners Assn., Dillon, Colo., 1986-97, Wilderness Homeowners Assn., Dillon, 1986-92; bd. vis. Stanford U. Sch. Law, 1985-91. Recipient Mack Easton Distinguished Svc. award U. Colo., 1987, Outstanding Faculty MHA program award U. Colo., 1997. Mem. ABA, Colo. Bar Assn. (interprofl. com. 1987-89) Calif. Bar Assn., Denver Bar Assn. (interprofl. com. 1987-89), Soc. Law and Medicine. Health, Legislative, Insurance.

**DIKTAS, CHRISTOS JAMES,** lawyer; b. Hackensack, N.J., June 17, 1955; s. Christos James and Elpiniki (Angelou) D. Student U. Salonika (Greece), 1976, U. Copenhagen (Denmark), 1976. BA, Montclair State U., 1977; JD, Calif. Western Sch. Law, 1981; diploma. Rutgers U., 1992. Bar: N.J. 1982, U.S. Dist. Ct. N.J. 1982, N.Y. 1989, U.S. Supreme Ct. 1989. Law sec. Honorable James F. Madden, Superior Ct. Judge, Hackensack, N.J., 1981-82; sr. assoc. Klinger, Nicolette, Mavroudis & Honig, Hackensack, 1982-85; ptnr. Montecallo & Diktas, Hackensack, 1985-86; ptnr., Biagiotti, Marino, Montecallo & Diktas, Hackensack, 1986-89; ptnr., Diktas & Habeeb, North Bergen, N.J., 1989-94; ptnr. Diktas Gillen, 1995—. asst. counsel Bergen County, 1986-87; atty. zoning bd. adjustment Borough of Cliffside Park, N.J., 1986-94; atty. planning bd. Borough of Ridgefield, N.J., 1987—, Borough atty. Bogota, N.J., 1989-91; bd. edn. atty., Bogota, 1992-95; labor counsel Bergen County, N.J., 1990—; borough atty. Fairview, N.J., 1994-95; borough atty., Cliffside Park, 1994—; atty. planning bd. City of Garfield, N.J., 1994—; adj. prof. law Montclair (N.J.) State U., 1988—. Editor lead articles Calif. Western Internat. Law Jour., 1980-81. Campaign dir. Kingman for Senate Com., Bergen County, N.J., 1983; mcpl. coord. Kean for Gov. campaign, 1985; asst. treas. Arthur F. Jones for Congress, 9th Congl. Dist., 1986. Mem. ABA, N.J. Bar Assn., Bergen County Bar Assn., Order of Am. Hellenic Edn. Progressive Assn., Phi Alpa Delta (parliamentarian Campbell E. Beaumont chpt. 1978-81). Greek Orthodox. Lodge: Sons of Pericles (5th dist. gov. 1976-77, supreme gov. 1977-78). Real property, Contracts commercial, General practice. Home: 445 Oncrest Ter Cliffside Park NJ 07010-2814 Office: Diktas Gillen 596 Anderson Ave Cliffside Park NJ 07010-1831

**DILL, WILLIAM ALLEN,** lawyer; b. Sharon, Pa., May 18, 1918; s. Harry Armitage and Mary Rose (McCann) D.; m. Marjorie Croft, Sept. 3, 1946; children—Mary Alyson, Laurie Ann, Thomas Allen. B.S., U. Pitts., 1940, J.D., 1948. Bar: Pa. 1949. Pilot, Pan Am. Airways, North and South Atlantic, N.Y.C., 1941-42, Central and South Am., Miami, 1942-43; spl. lectr. U. Pitts. Sch. Transp., 1946-48; assoc. Fruit & Francis, Sharon, 1949-68; ptnr. Fruit Dill, Goodwin & Scholl, Sharon, 1968—; asst. dist. atty., 1952-54; solicitor City of Sharon, 1958-68; spl. dep. atty. gen., 1966-71; lectr. Pa. Bar Inst., Def. Research Inst., Pa. Def. Inst., Am. Arbitration Assn. Rep. state committeeman, 1954-78. Served to capt. USNR, 1944-70, ret. Mem. Am. Jurisprudence Soc., Pa. Bar Assn., Mercer County Bar Assn. (pres. 1969). State civil litigation, Probate, Workers' compensation. Home: 219 Case Ave Sharon PA 16146-3427 Office: 32 Shenango Ave Sharon PA 16146-1502

**DILLAHUNTY, WILBUR HARRIS,** lawyer; b. Memphis, June 30, 1928; s. Joseph S. and Octavia M. (Jones) D.; 1 child, Sharon K. JD, U. Ark., 1954. Bar: Ark. 1954. City atty. West Memphis, Ark., 1958-68; U.S. atty. (ea. dist.) Little Rock, 1968-79; exec. asst. adminstr. SBA, Washington, 1979-80; prin. Dillahunty Law Firm, Little Rock, 1980—; chancery and probate judge 6th Jud. Dist., 6th Divsn., Little Rock, 1997—. Served to lt. U.S. Army, 1945-48, ETO. Mem. ABA, Pulaski Bar Assn., Nat. Assn. Former U.S. Attys. (pres. 1991—), Am. Inns of Ct. (pres. William R. Overton chpt. 1989-90). Federal civil litigation, State civil litigation. Home: 9710 Catskill Rd Little Rock AR 72227-5562

**DILLARD, CYNTHIA LYNN,** lawyer; b. Columbia, Mo., July 3, 1964; d. Robert Howard and Martha Ann Dillard. Student, Vanderbilt U., 1982-83; BS, S.E. Mo. State U., 1986; JD, U. Mo., Columbia, 1990. Bar: Mo. 1990, Kans. 1991. Atty. Blackwell Sanders et al, Kansas City, Mo., 1990-92, Bryan Cave LLP, Kansas City, Mo., 1992—. Adminstrv. asst. Mayor's Fast Forward Com., Kansas City, 1996—; vol. Jr. League Kansas City, Mo., 1991—. Mem. Am. Bankruptcy Inst., Kansas City Met. Bar Assn. (bankruptcy com. 1990—), Cen. Exch. (chair membership com. 1992—), Workout Profls. Assn. (pres. of bd.), Kansas City Club. Roman Catholic. Bankruptcy. Office: Bryan Cave LLP 3500 1 KC Pl 1200 Main St Kansas City MO 64105-2122

**DILLARD, JOHN MARTIN,** lawyer, pilot; b. Long Beach, Calif., Dec. 25, 1945; s. John Warren and Clara Leora (Livermore) D.; student U. Calif., Berkeley, 1963-67; BA, UCLA, 1968; JD, Pepperdine U., 1976; m. Patricia Anne Yeager, Aug. 10, 1968; children: Jason Robert, Jennifer Lee. Instr. pilot Norton AFB, Calif., 1973-77. Bar: Calif., 1976. Assoc. Magana, Cathcart & McCarthy, L.A., 1977-80, Lord, Bissell & Brook, L.A., 1980-85; of counsel Finley, Kumble, Wagner, 1985-86, Schell & Delamer, 1986-94, Law Offices of John M. Dillard, 1986—, v.p., gen. counsel, dir. Resort Aviation Svcs, Inc., Calif., 1988-93; mng. ptnr. Natkin & Weisbach, So. Calif., 1988-89; arbitrator Orange County Superior Ct.; atty. settlement officer U.S. Dist. Ct. Ctrl. Dist. Calif. Active Am. Cancer Soc.; bd. dirs. Placentia-Yorba Linda Ednl. Found., Inc. Capt. USAF, 1968-73, Vietnam. Mem. ATLA (aviation litigation com.), Am. Bar Assn. (aviation com.), Orange County Bar Assn., Fed. Bar Assn., L.A. County Bar Assn. (aviation com.), Century City Bar Assn., Internat. Platform Assn., Res. Officers Assn., Orange County Com. of 100, Sigma Nu. Construction, Personal injury, General civil litigation. Home: 19621 Verona Ln Yorba Linda CA 92886-2858 Office: 313 N Birch St Santa Ana CA 92701-5263

**DILL CHADICK, TERRI,** lawyer; b. Little Rock, Feb. 4, 1970; d. Charles Wayne and Doris Lynn Dill; m. Vincent O. Chadick. BA, U. Ark., Fayetteville, 1992, JD with honors, 1995. Atty. Armstrong Allen Prewitt Gentry Johnson & Holmes, Memphis, 1995-96, Kiesewetter Wise Kaplan Schwimmer & Prather, Memphis, 1996-97, Conner & Winters, Tulsa and Fayetteville, Ark., 1997—. Mem. Ark. Bar Assn., Okla. Bar Assn., Tulsa County Bar Assn. Labor. Office: Conner & Winters 100 W Center St Fayetteville AR 72701-6078

**DILLIN, S. HUGH,** federal judge; b. Petersburg, Ind., June 9, 1914; s. Samuel E. and Maude (Harrell) D.; m. Mary Eloise Humphreys, Nov. 24, 1940; 1 child, Patricia Wright. A.B. in Govt, Ind. U., 1936, LLB, 1938, LLD, 1992; D of Civil Law (hon.), Ind. State U., 1990. Bar: Ind. 1938. Ptnr. Dillin & Dillin, Petersburg, 1938-61; U.S. dist. judge So. Dist. Ind., 1961—, chief judge, 1982-84; mem. Jud. Conf. U.S., 1979-82, mem. exec. com., 1980-82, mem. Jud. Conf. Com. on Ct. Adminstrn., 1983-89, chmn. subcom. on fed.-state rels., 1983-89; mem. Jud. Panel on Multidist. Litigation, 1983-92; sec. Pub. Svc. Commn. Ind., 1942; mem. Interstate Oil Compact Commn., 1949-52, 61. Mem. Ind. Ho. of Reps. from Pike and Knox Counties, 1937, 39, 41, 51, floor leader, 1951; mem. Ind. Senate from Pike and Gibson Counties, 1959-61, pres. pro tem, 1961. Capt. AUS, 1943-46. Recipient Disting. Alumnus award Ind. U. Coll. Arts and Scis., 1985, Ind. U. Sch. Law, 1987. Mem. Am. Bar Assn., Ind. State Bar Assn., Fed. Bar Assn., 7th Cir. Judges Assn. (pres. 1977-79), Am. Judicature Soc., Delta Tau Delta, Phi Delta Phi. Democrat. Presbyn. Club: Indianapolis Athletic. Office: US Dist Ct 255 US Courthouse 46 E Ohio St Indianapolis IN 46204-1903

**DILLING, KIRKPATRICK WALLWICK,** lawyer; b. Evanston, Ill., Apr. 11, 1920; s. Albert W. and Elizabeth (Kirkpatrick) D.; m. Betty Ellen Bronson, June, 1942 (div. July 1944); m. Elizabeth Ely Tilden, Dec. 11, 1948; children: Diana Jean, Eloise Tilden, Victoria Walgreen, Albert Kirkpatrick. Student, Cornell U., 1939-40; BS in Law, Northwestern U., 1942; postgrad., DePaul U., 1946-47, L'Ecole Vaubier, Montreux, Switzerland; Degré Normal, Sorbonne U., Paris. Bar: Ill. 1947, U.S. Dist. Ct. (no. dist.) Ill., Ind., Mich., Md., La., Tex., Okla., Wis., Idaho, U.S. Ct. Appeals (2nd, 3rd, 5th, 7th, 8th, 9th, 10th, 11th, fed. and D.C. cirs.), U.S. Supreme Ct. Ptnr. Dilling and Dilling, Chgo., 1948—; counsel Cancer Control Soc., Nat. Coun. for Improved Health; bd. dirs. Klaire Labs., Nutradelle Labs., Ltd., V.E. Irons, Inc.; v.p. Midwest Medic-Aide, Inc.; spl. counsel Herbalife (U.K.) Ltd., Herbalife Australasia Pty., Ltd.; lectr. on pub. health law. Contbr. articles to pub. health pubs. Bd. dirs. Adelle Davis Found., Liberty Lobby. 1st lt. AUS, 1943-46. Recipient Humanitarian award Nat. Health Fedn. Mem. ABA, Ill. Bar Assn., Chgo. Bar Assn., Assn. Trial Lawyers Am., Cornell Soc. Engrs., Am. Legion, Air Force Assn., Pharm. Advt. Club, Rolls Royce Owners' Club, Tower Club, Cornell U., Chicago Club, Delta Upsilon. Republican. Episcopalian. Health, Administrative and regulatory, Federal civil litigation. Home: 1120 Lee Rd Northbrook IL 60062-3816

**DILLION, GREGORY LEE,** lawyer; b. Lima, Ohio, June 21, 1954; s. James A. and Wanda L. Dillion; m. Cynthia S. Shimon, Oct. 1, 1983; children: Blake A., Ross A., Colton A., Jason A., Jordan N. BA with distinction, Cornell U., 1977; JD with honors, U. Tex., 1980. Bar: Calif. 1980, U.S. Dist. Ct. (no. & cen. dists.) Calif. 1980, U.S. Ct. Appeals (9th cir.) 1981, U.S. Dist. Ct. (so. & ea. dists.) Calif. 1986, U.S. Supreme Ct. Assoc. Lillick, McHose & Charles, L.A., 1980-83; ptnr. Newmeyer & Dillion, Newport Beach, Calif., 1984—. Mem. 552 Club of Hoag Meml. Hosp., Newport Beach, 1983—; bd. dirs. Newport Beach Little League, 1995—. Mem. ABA, ATLA, State Bar Calif., Orange County Bar Assn. (bus. litigation sect. 1985—, real estate sect. 1990—, constrn. law and ins. law sects. 1990—), Big Canyon Country Club, Phi Kappa Phi. Avocations: surfing, snowboarding, golf. Construction, Insurance. Home: 7 Bodega Bay Dr Corona Del Mar CA 92625-1002 Office: Newmeyer & Dillion North Tower 6th Fl 3501 Jamboree Rd Newport Beach CA 92660-2939

**DILLON, CLIFFORD BRIEN,** retired lawyer; b. Amarillo, Tex., Oct. 25, 1921; s. Clifford Newton and Leone (Brien) D.; m. Audrey Catherine Johnson, Jan. 16, 1945; children: Audrey Catherine Dillon Peters (dec. Nov. 1997), Robert Brien, Douglas Johnson. B.B.A., U. Tex., 1943, LL.B. with honors, 1947. Bar: Tex. 1947. Practiced in Houston, 1947-87; ptnr. Baker & Botts, 1957-87, ret. ptnr., 1987—; mem. faculty Southwestern Legal Found., 1968-87. Author articles in field. Life mem., bd. dirs. U. Tex. Health Sci. Ctr., Houston; past mem. antitrust adv. bd. Bur. Nat. Affairs; past bd. dirs. Houston Vis. Nurses Assn.; bd. visitors, life mem. Mc Donald Obs. and Astronomy, 1986—. Fellow ABA (chmn. sect. antitrust law 1975-76, Ho. of Dels. 1974-75, 85-87, bd. govs. 1985-87), State Bar Tex., Am. Judicature Soc., Tex. Bar Found., Houston Bar Found.; mem. Houston Bar Assn., Houston C. of C., U.S. C. of C. (past mem. adv. coun. antitrust policy), Phi Kappa Psi, Phi Delta Phi. Presbyterian. Clubs: Houston Country (Houston), Petroleum (Houston); Riverhill Country (Kerrville, Tex.), Old Baldy (Saratoga, Wyo.).. Antitrust. Office: Baker & Botts 3000 One Shell Plaza Houston TX 77002

**DILLON, JAMES JOSEPH,** lawyer; b. Rockville Ctr., N.Y., June 18, 1948; s. James Martin and Rosemary (Peter) D.; m. Martha Stone Wiske, Mar. 19, 1977; 1 child, Eleanor. BA, Fordham U., 1970, Oxford U., 1972; JD, Harvard U., 1975; MA, Oxford U., 1982. Bar: Mass. 1975, U.S. Dist. Ct. Mass. 1976, U.S. Ct. Appeals (1st cir.) 1978, U.S. Ct. Appeals (5th cir.) 1986, U.S. Ct. Appeals (6th cir.) 1996, U.S. Ct. Appeals (11th cir.) 1995, U.S. Supreme Ct. 1990. Assoc. Goodwin, Procter & Hoar LLP, Boston, 1975-83, ptnr., 1983—; dir. Beth Israel Deaconess Med. Ctr. Obstetrics and Gynecology Found., Inc., overseer Huntington Theatre Co. Mem. ABA, Mass. State Bar Assn., Boston Bar Assn. Democrat. Club: St. Botolph (Boston). Federal civil litigation, State civil litigation, Product liability. Office: Goodwin Procter & Hoar LLP Exchange Pl Boston MA 02109-2803

**DILLON, JOSEPH FRANCIS,** lawyer; b. Bklyn., Oct. 15, 1938; s. Joseph and Elizabeth (Sullivan) D.; m. Pamela Margaret Higbee, May 15, 1966 (div. Feb. 1972); children: Elizabeth Margaret, J. Alexander; m. Diane L. Long, Mar. 17, 1978. BBA, St. John's U., 1960; LLB, U. Va., 1963. Bar: Va. 1963, N.Y. 1964, U.S. Tax Ct. 1965, Mich. 1968, Ohio 1975, Fla. 1983. Tax trial atty. IRS, Washington and Detroit, 1963-68; mem. Raymond & Dillon, P.C., Detroit, 1969-93, Dykema Gossett PLC, Detroit, 1993-97, Cox, Hodgman & Giarmarco, P.C., Detroit, 1997—; adj. prof. taxation U. Detroit Law Sch., 1977-87; spkr., planning chmn. Inst. CLE Programs; mem. magistrates merit selection panel and profl. assistance com. U.S. Dist. Ct. for Ea. Dist. Mich.; mem. U.S. Ct. Internat. Trade. Bd. dirs., mem. exec. com. Met. Ctr. for High Tech., Detroit, 1993-96. Cpl. USAR, 1958-64. Fellow Mich. State Bar Found.; mem. ABA (taxation and internat. sects. 1963—), FBA (officer, pres. Detroit chpt. 1978-82), Mich. Bar Assn. 1988—, (taxation counsel 1979-82, internat. sec. 1990—), Detroit Bar Assn. (taxation com. 1973—), Va. Bar Assn., N.Y. State Bar Assn., Ohio Bar Assn., Fla. Bar Assn., Am. Judicature Soc., Am. C. of C. in Japan, London Ct. of Internat. Arbitration, Inter-Pacific Bar Assn., Internat. Bar Assn., Greater Detroit-Windsor Japan Am. Soc. (bd. dirs. 1992—), Japanese Bus. Soc. Detroit Found. (v.p. 1992—), Greater Detroit C. of C. (nominating com. for dirs.), French-Am. C. of C. of Detroit (bd. dirs. 1997—), Detroit Athletic Club, Lochmoor Club, Vineyards Country Club, World Trade Club, Econ. Club (Detroit). Republican. Roman Catholic. Avocations: golf, squash, skiing. Fax: (248) 528-2773. E-mail: CHG@CHGLAW.COM. Taxation, general, General corporate, Private international. Office: Cox Hodgman & Giarmarco PC 5th Fl Columbia Ctr 201 W Big Beaver Rd Troy MI 48084-4152

**DILLON, KAREN,** editor. Editor in chief The American Lawyer, N.Y.C. Office: American Lawyer Media 105 Madison Ave Fl 7 New York NY 10016-7418

**DILORENZO, LOUIS PATRICK,** lawyer; b. Waterloo, N.Y., Nov. 3, 1952; s.Luigi and Theresa Marie (Grieco) D.; m. Deborah Joan Boudreau, Aug. 18, 1973; children: Louis Patrick, Lisa Marie, Laura Gabriel. Student, U.S. Mil. Acad., West Point, 1970-72; BA, Syracuse U., 1973; JD, SUNY, Buffalo, 1976. Bar: N.Y. 1977, U.S. Dist. Ct. (no. dist.) N.Y. 1977, U.S. Supreme Ct. 1988. Assoc. Bond, Schoeneck & King, Syracuse, 1976-84; ptnr. Bond, Schoeneck & King, 1985—, chair recruiting com., chair labor and employment law dept.; co-chair employment law litigation group, adj. prof. Syracuse U. Sch. Mgmt., 1988—; participant NYU Annual Conf. on Labor, 1989. Author: Syracuse Law Jour., 1978, Jour. of Coll. and U. Law Jour., 1980, N.Y. State Bar Jour., 1982; author: (with others) Corporate Counseling, 1988, Public Sector Labor Law, 1988; bd. editors N.Y. State Bar Jour., 1998—. Bd. dirs. Syracuse Opera Co., 1986. Fellow ABA Coll. Employment and Labor Law; mem. ABA, Nat. Assn. Coll. and Univ. Attys., N.Y. State Bar Assn. (mem. ho. of dels. 1984-90, 99—, chmn. young lawyers sect. 1987, chmn. labor rels. com. 1988, chair CLE com. 1990-93, chair labor and employment law sect. 1994). Republican. Roman Catholic. Avocations: golf, tennis, reading. Labor, Federal civil litigation. Office: Bond Schoeneck & King 1 Lincoln Ctr Fl 18 Syracuse NY 13202-1324

**DILTS, JON PAUL,** law educator; b. Monterey, Ind., Sept. 7, 1945; s. Charles Albert and Janet Cecilia (Keitzer) D.; m. Anne Williams Avirett, Aug. 21, 1971; children: Christopher, Andrew. BA, Saint Meinrad Coll., 1967; MA, Ind. U., 1974; JD, Valparaiso U., 1981. Bar: Ind. 1981, U.S. Dist. Ct. (so. dist.) Ind. 1981. Reporter Peru (Ind.) Daily Tribune, 1972-73, wire editor, 1973-76, city editor, 1976-78; law clk. Ind. Ct. Appeals, Indpls., 1981-82; asst. prof. Ind. U., Bloomington, 1982-88, assoc. prof., 1988—, assoc. dean, 1985—. Author: The Magnificent 92 Indiana Courthouses, 1992; co-author: Media Law, 1994, 97; mem. editl. bd. Comms. Law & Policy, 1998—. Trustee Saint Meinrad Coll., Sch. Theology, 1996-98; mem. exec. bd. dirs. Hoosier Trails Coun., Boy Scouts Am., Bloomington, 1992-93. With U.S. Army, 1968-71. Mem. Assn. for Edn. in Journalism and Mass Comm. (head law divsn. 1987-88), Soc. Profl. Journalists, AP Mng. Editors Assn., Rotary. Democrat. Roman Catholic. Avocations: skiing, hiking, backpacking, canoeing, sailing. Office: Ind U Sch Journalism 940 E 7th St Bloomington IN 47405-7108

**DILWORTH, GEORGE THAYER,** prosecutor; b. Camp LeJeune, N.C., Mar. 26, 1956; s. Warden and Elizabeth Dilworth; m. Sarah H. Clark, June 28, 1986; children: Molly, Joseph, Katherine. BA, Yale U., 1980; JD, Boston Coll., 1987. Bar: Maine 1987, Mass. 1987. Spl. asst. U.S. Sen. Paul Tsongas, Boston, 1981-84; law clk. to presiding judge Gene Carter U.S. Dist. Ct. Maine, Portland, 1987-88; assoc. Drummond, Woodson & MacMahon, Portland, 1988-91; asst. U.S. atty. U.S. Atty.'s Office, Portland, 1991—; adj. faculty mem. U. Maine Law Sch., Portland, 1997, 99. Bd. dirs. Merrill Meml. Libr., Yarmouth, Maine, 1997—. Mem. Maine State Bar Assn. (gov. 1989-91). Office: US Atty's Office 100 Middle St Ste 10 Portland ME 04101-4159

**DIMARCO, FRANK PAUL,** lawyer; b. N.Y.C., Oct. 7, 1945; s. Dominick and Serafina (Musca) D.; m. Carmelina Ventura DiMarco, July 24, 1971; children: Frank, Paul, Elena. BA, CUNY, 1967; JD, N.Y. Law Sch., 1970. Bar: N.Y. Assoc. Lifschutz & Polland, N.Y.C., 1971-86; atty. pvt. practice, New Rochelle, N.Y., 1986—; dir., treas. New Rochelle Bar Assn., 1986—; arbitrator City of New Rochelle, 1984—; adv. bd. New Rochelle YMCA, 1987—; commr. Bd. of Assessment Review, New Rochelle, 1977—. Dir., treas. New Rochelle Neighborhood and Civic Assn., 1976—; lectr. Calabria Mutual Aid Soc., New Rochelle, N.Y., 1975—; lector Blessed Sacrament Ch., New Rochelle, N.Y., 1990—. Recipient Mayor's Commendation, New Rochelle, 1986, 1991, New Rochelle City Coun. Cert. Appreciation, 1986, N.Y. State Senate Outstanding Achievement Medal, 1991, 97, 98, Congrnl. Proclamation, 1997, N.Y. State Assembly Citation, 1997, Sons of Italy Profl. Achievement award 1997, Westchester County Bd. Legislator's Proclamation, 1991, 97, New Rochelle YMCA Joseph Charla award, 1998. Mem. New Rochelle Bar Assn., Westchester County Bar Assn., Columbian Lawyers Assn., N.Y. County Lawyers Assn., Bronx-New Rochelle Elks, Calabria Mutual Aid Soc. Democrat. Roman Catholic. Avocations: reading, gardening, softball, cooking. General practice, Probate, Real property. Home: 21 Pintard Ave New Rochelle NY 10801-7119 Office: 20 Cedar St New Rochelle NY 10801-5247

**DI MASCIO, JOHN PHILIP,** lawyer; b. Bklyn., Feb. 4, 1944; s. Eugenio and Stella (Scheuermann) Di M.; m. Angela Piccininni, Apr. 2, 1967 (div. 1980); children: John Philip, Jr., Christine, Thomas; m. Linda Nick, Oct. 19, 1997. BA, C.W. Post Coll., 1975; MA, L.I. U., 1976; postgrad., NYU, 1976-79; JD, St. John's U., 1983. Bar: N.Y. 1984, U.S. Dist. Ct. (ea. and so. dists.) N.Y. 1984, U.S. Ct. Appeals (2d cir.) 1984, U.S. Supreme Ct. 1997, U.S. Ct. Appeals for Armed Forces 1997, U.S. Ct. of Fed. Claims, 1997, U.S. Ct. Appeals (fed. cir.) 1997. Sr. ct. officer N.Y. State Supreme Ct., Mineola, 1970-82; assoc. Joel R. Brandes, P.C., Garden City, N.Y., 1984; pvt. practice N.Y., 1984-87; ptnr. Di Mascio, Meisner & Koopersmith, Carle Place, 1987-93; sole practice Garden City, 1993—. Contbg. author Ann. Survey. With USN, 1962-69. Recipient various acad. awards. Mem. ABA (bus. law, health law and family law sects.), N.Y. State Bar Assn. (family law com. 1982), Nassau County Bar Assn. (vice-chmn. matrimonial com. sup. ct. com., fam. ct. com. 1984, co-editor monthly publ. Recent Decisions), Am. Inns of Ct. (N.Y. family law chpt.). Avocations: photography, boating. General civil litigation, Family and matrimonial. Office: 300 Garden City Plz Garden City NY 11530-3302

**DIMES, EDWIN KINSLEY,** lawyer; b. Hartford, Conn., Apr. 13, 1923; s. Alfred Eustace and Charlotte (Miller) D.; m. Edwina May Adams, Feb. 3, 1945 (div. 1981); chldren: Martha, Deborah, Kimberley; m. S. Antoinette Morton, Dec. 29, 1990. BA, Conn. Wesleyan U., Middletown, 1947; JD, Yale U., 1950. Bar: Conn. 1950, U.S. Tax Ct. 1960, U.S. Supreme Ct. 1960. From assoc. to ptnr. Wake, See, Dimes and Bryniczka, Westport, Conn., 1950—; state trial referee State of Conn., 1985—. Chmn. bd. fin. City of Westport, 1979-97. 2d lt. USAF, 1943-45. Mem. ABA, Westport Bar Assn., Conn. Bar Assn. (bd. govs.). Republican. Congregationalist. Avocations: boating, tennis. Real property, Family and matrimonial, General practice. Home: 70 Morningside Dr S Westport CT 06880-5415 Office: Wake See Dimes and Brynicza 27 Imperial Ave Westport CT 06880-4303

**DIMMICK, CAROLYN REABER,** federal judge; b. Seattle, Oct. 24, 1929; d. Maurice C. and Margaret T. (Taylor) Reaber; m. Cyrus Allen Dimmick, Sept. 10, 1955; children: Taylor, Dana. BA, U. Wash., 1951, JD, 1963; LLD, Gonzaga U., 1982, CUNY, 1987. Bar: Wash. 1953. Asst. atty. gen. State of Wash., Seattle, 1953-55; pros. atty. King County, Wash., 1955-59, 60-62; sole practice Seattle, 1959-60, 62-65; judge N.E. Dist. Ct. Wash., 1965-75, King County Superior Ct., 1976-80; justice Wash. Supreme Ct., 1981-85; judge U.S. Dist. Ct. (we. dist.) Wash., Seattle, 1985-94, chief judge, 1994-97, sr. judge, 1997—; chmn. Jud. Resources Com., 1991-94, active, 1987-94. Recipient Matrix Table award, 1981, World Plan Execs. Council award, 1981, Vanguard Honor award King County of Washington Women Lawyers, 1996, Honorable mention U. Wash. Law Rev., 1997, Disting. Alumni award U. Wash. Law Sch., 1997. Mem. ABA, Am. Judges Assn. (gov.), Nat. Assn. Women Judges, World Assn. Judges, Wash. Bar Assn., Am. Judicature Soc., Order of Coif (Wash. chpt.). Office: US Dist Ct 713 US Courthouse 1010 5th Ave Ste 713 Seattle WA 98104-1191

**DIMMITT, LAWRENCE ANDREW,** lawyer; b. Kansas City, Kans., July 20, 1941; s. Herbert Andrew and Mary (Duncan) D.; m. Lois Kinney, Dec. 23, 1962; children: Cynthia Susan, Lawrence Michael. BA, Kans. State U., 1963, MA, 1967; JD, Washburn U., 1968. Bar: Kans. 1968, U.S. Dist. Ct. Kans. 1968, U.S. Ct. Appeals (10th cir.) 1969, Mo. 1973, N.Y. 1975, U.S. Supreme Ct. 1986. Atty. Southwestern Bell Telephone Co., Topeka, 1968-73; atty. Southwestern Bell Telephone Co., St. Louis, 1973-74, gen. atty. regulation, 1979; atty. AT&T, N.Y.C., 1974-79; gen. atty. Kans. Southwestern Bell Telephone Co., Topeka, 1979-94; ret., 1994; adj. prof. telecomms. law Washburn U. Sch. Law, 1996-99. Bd. dirs. First United Meth. Ch., Topeka, 1979-84, mem. nominating com., 1985-87; bd. dirs. Sunflower Music Festival, 1993-94; mem. master planning com. Historic Ward-Meade Park, 1998-99. Recipient commendation Legal Aid Soc. Topeka, 1986, 90, 93. Mem. Kans. Bar Assn. (pres. adminstrv. law sect. 1985-86, bd. editors newsletter), Topeka Bar Assn., Phi Alpha Delta (alumni bd. 1986-88, 1993-97), Rotary (bd. dirs., 2d vice-pres. 1999—). Administrative and regulatory, Public utilities, Federal civil litigation. Home: 3123 SW 15th St Topeka KS 66604-2515

**DINAN, CHRISTOPHER CHARLES,** lawyer, mediator; b. Winchester, Mass., May 27, 1955; s. Edward Joseph and Catherine Marie Dinan; m. Judy Ann Parlin, Sept. 10, 1989; children: Sean Christopher, Elyse Catherine. BA, Harvard Coll., 1977; JD, U. Maine, 1982. Bar: Maine 1982, U.S. Dist. Ct. Maine 1982. Ptnr. Monaghan, Leahy, Hochadel & Libby, Portland, Maine, 1982—. Mem. Zoning Bd. Appeals, Portland, Maine, 1986-89. Mem. ATLA, Maine State Bar Assn., Maine Trial Lawyers Assn., Def. Rsch. Inst. Avocations: golf, skiing, running. Personal injury, Insurance, General civil litigation. Office: Monaghan Leahy Hochadel & Libby 95 Exchange St Ste 300 Portland ME 04101-5044

**DINAN, DONALD ROBERT,** lawyer; b. Nashua, N.H., Aug. 28, 1949; s. Robert J. and Jeanette F. (Farland) D.; m. Amy Littlepage, June 24, 1978; 1 child: Emma. BS in Econs., U. Pa., 1971; JD, Georgetown U., 1974; LLM, London Sch. Econs., 1975. Bar: Mass. 1976, D.C. 1977, N.Y. 1986, U.S. Supreme Ct. 1979, U.S. Ct. Internat. Trade 1982. Atty. advisor U.S. Internat. Trade Commn., Washington, 1976-81, chief patent br., 1981-82, chief unfair imports investigation div., 1981-82; ptnr. Adduci Dinan & Mastriani, Washington, 1982-88, Fitzpatrick, Cella, Harper & Scinto, Washington, 1988-90, O'Connor & Hannan, Washington, 1990-98, Hall Estill, 1998—; prof. internat. trade Georgetown U., Wharton Econs. Soc.; prin. Coun. for Excellence in Govt. Mem. Mayor's Internat. Adv. Coun., Washington, D.C. Regulatory Reform Com.D.C., Washington Dem. State Com., gen. counsel, 1988-92, 94—. Mem. ABA, Fed. Bar Assn., ITC Trial Laywers Assn., Am. Intellectual Property Law Assn. (chmn. internat. trade com., export lic. com.). Democrat. Roman Catholic. Private international, Federal civil litigation, Intellectual property. Home: 221 9th St SE Washington DC 20003-2112 Office: Hall Estill Hardwick Gable Goldin & Nelson 1120 20th St NW Ste 750 Washington DC 20036-3406

**DINARDO, JOSEPH,** lawyer; b. Rochester, N.Y., Jan. 6, 1947; s. Carmen and Bertha Mascirelli DiN. B.A., SUNY, Buffalo, 1968, J.D., 1972. Bar: N.Y. 1973, U.S. Ct. Appeals (2d cir.) 1974, Pa., Ohio, Mich. Assoc. The DiNardo Law Firm. Recipient Outstanding Citizen award Erie County Coll., 1994. Statler trustee, 1992. Mem. Trial Lawyers Am., N.Y. State Bar Assn., Erie County Bar Assn., Brotherhood Locomotive Engrs. (counsel), United Transp. Union (counsel). Recipient Book award Bancroft-Whitney, 1969. Federal civil litigation, State civil litigation, Probate. Office: Dinardo Law Firm 2430 N Forest Rd Ste 195 Getzville NY 14068-1535

**DINEEN, JOHN K.,** lawyer; b. Gardiner, Maine, Jan. 21, 1928; s. James J. and Eleanor (Kelley) D.; m. Carolyn Foley Reardon (dec. 1982); children: Jane, Martha, Louisa, Jessica, John; m. Susan Lowell Wales, Aug. 15, 1986; children: Theodore, Ralph, Andrew. BA, U. Maine, 1951; JD, Boston U., 1954. Bar: Maine 1954, Mass. 1954. Ptnr. Weston, Patrick & Stevens, Boston, 1954-67, Peabody & Arnold, Boston, 1967-70, 91—, Gaston & Snow, Boston, 1970-91; spl. asst. atty. gen. Commonwealth of Mass., Boston, 1965-67; bd. dirs. exec. com. Fiduciary Trust Co., Boston, P&O Properties Boston, Inc., London; dir. Dingle Am. Properties Ltd., Dingle, County Kerry, Ireland, 1973—; pres., trustee Boston Local Devel. Corp., 1982—. Trustee emeritus Waring Sch., Beverley, Mass., 1981—, Cambridge (Mass.) Coll.; trustee U.S.S. Constn. Mus., 1993—; trustee, chmn. Nahant (Mass.) Pub. Libr., 1996—; former trustee Boston U. Med. Ctr., Winsor Sch. Emmanuel Coll., Boston, Hebron Acad., Maine; trustee Boston Aid to the Blind, 1994—. With U.S. Army, 1946-48. Mem. Boston Bar Assn., Mass. Bar Assn., Boston Law Sch. Alumni Assn. (exec. com. 1989-91), Marshall Street Hist. Soc., Tavern Club, Union Club, Cary Street Club, Apollo Club, Norway Weary Club. Republican. Roman Catholic. Real property. Home: 40 Pleasant St Nahant MA 01908-1632 Office: Peabody & Arnold 50 Rowes Wharf Fl 7 Boston MA 02110-3342

**DINGFELDER, JUSTIN,** lawyer; b. Fureth, Germany, Mar. 30, 1936; came to U.S., 1939; s. Sigbert and Elizabeth (Neu) D.; m. Adele Garten, June 30, 1963; 1 child, Sara. ALA, U. Minn., 1956, BBA, 1958, JD, 1961. Bar: Minn. 1961, U.S. Dist. Ct. Minn. 1964, U.S. Supreme Ct. 1967, U.S. Dist. Ct. D.C. 1969. Atty. VA, St. Paul, 1961-65, Washington, 1970-72; atty. Dept. HEW, Washington, 1965-70; atty. FTC, Washington, 1972-75, asst. dir., 1975—. Contbr. articles to profl. jours. Vice chmn. Combined Fed. Campaign, FTC, Washington, 1983. With U.S. Army, 1954-62. Mem. Fed. Bar Assn. (nat. treas. 1986-93, chair rules com. 1994-95, pres. D.C. chpt. 1975-76, editor jour. 1973-74, Disting. Svc. award 1977, Commendation awards 1989, 93). Avocation: tennis. Home: 1830 Nigel Ct Vienna VA 22182-3430 Office: Federal Trade Commn 6th & Pennsylvania Ave NW Washington DC 20580-0001

**DINGUS, JONATHAN WESLEY,** prosecutor, lawyer; b. Cin., June 21, 1963; s. Doyle Ross and Helen Hartman Dingus; m. Nancy Kazmierski, Aug. 17, 1991; 1 child, Abigail. BS, Fla. State U., 1984; JD, U. Fla., 1988. Asst. pub. defender Pub. Defenders Office, Lake City, Fla., 1989-90; asst. state atty. State Attys. Office, Panama City, Fla., 1990—. Office: State Attys Office 910 Harrison Ave Panama City FL 32401-2528

**DINKINS, CAROL EGGERT,** lawyer; b. Corpus Christi, Tex., Nov. 9, 1945; d. Edgar H. Jr. and Evelyn S. (Scheel) Eggert; m. Bob Brown; children: Anne, Amy. BS, U. Tex., 1968; JD, U. Houston, 1971. Bar: Tex. 1971. Prin. assoc. Tex. Law Inst. Coastal and Marine Resources, Coll. Law U. Houston, Tex., 1971-73; assoc., ptnr. Vinson & Elkins, Houston, 1973-81, 83-84, 85—, mem. mgmt. com., 1991-96; asst. atty. gen. environ. and natural resources Dept. Justice, 1981-83, U.S. dep. atty. gen., 1984-85; chmn. Pres.'s Task Force on Legal Equity for Women, 1981-83; mem. Hawaiian Native Study Commn., 1981-83; dir. Nat. Consumer Coop. Banks Bd., 1981, mem. Texas Parks Wildlife Com. Author articles in field. Chmn. Tex. Gov.'s Flood Control Action Group 1980-81; commr. Tex. Parks and Wildlife Dept., 1997—; bd. dirs. The Nature Conservancy, 1996—, Oryx Energy Co., 1990-95, U. Houston Law Ctr. Found., 1985-89, 96-98, Environ. and Energy Study Inst., 1986-98, Houston Mus. Natural Sci. 1, 1986-98, Tex. Nature Conservancy, 1985—, chair, 1996—. Mem. ABA (ho. of dels., past chmn. state and local govt. sect., immediate past chair sect. nat. resources, energy, and environ. law, standing com. on Fed. Judges 1997-98; bd. editors ABA Jour.), Fed. Bar Assn. (bd. dirs. Houston chpt. 1986), State Bar Tex., Houston Bar Assn., Tex. Water Conservation Assn., Houston Law Rev. Assn. (bd. dirs. 1978). Republican. Lutheran. Environmental. Office: Vinson & Elkins 2300 First City Tower 1001 Fannin St Ste 3300 Houston TX 77002-6706*

**DINNING, WOODFORD WYNDHAM, JR.,** lawyer; b. Demopolis, Ala., Aug. 15, 1954; s. Woodford W. and Gladys (Brown) D.; m. Tammy E. Cannon, May 27, 1994. AS, U. Ala., 1976, JD, 1979. Bar: Ala. 1979, U.S. Dist. Ct. (so. dist.) Ala. 1980. Mcpl. judge City of Demopolis, 1980-93, 98—; ptnr. Lloyd, Dinning, Boggs & Dinning, Demopolis, 1979—; mcpl. judge City of Linden, Ala., 1997—; pres. and bd. dirs. Tenn. Tom Motel, Inc.; atty. Marengo County Commn. and City of Linden, Ala. Mem. U. Ala. Alumni Assn. (chmn. 1985-86). Avocations: water skiing, snow skiing. State civil litigation, Contracts commercial, Family and matrimonial. Office: Lloyd Dinning Boggs & Dinning PO Drawer Z Demopolis AL 36732

**DINSMOOR, ROBERT DAVIDSON,** judge; b. El Paso, Tex., May 19, 1955; s. William Bell Jr. and Mary (Higgins) D. BA in Polit. Sci., Brigham Young U., 1979, JD, 1982. Bar: Tex. 1983, U.S. Dist. Ct. (we. dist.) Tex. 1985, U.S. Ct. Appeals (5th cir.) 1986, U.S. Supreme Ct. 1987. Rsch. assoc. J. Reuben Clark Law Sch., Brigham Young U., Provo, Utah, 1981-82; asst. dist. atty. El Paso (Tex.) Dist. Atty., 1983-90; dist. ct. judge State of Tex., El Paso, 1991—; spkr. Tex. County Judges Assn., 1992, 1992 Ann. Mex. Am. Bar Assn. of Tex. Conf., 1992, 97, St. Mary's U. Law Sch. Ethics Seminar, 1999, El Paso Bar Assn. Ethics Seminar, 1997-99, also various h.s. and mid. schs., El Paso, 1988—; co-founder El Paso Criminal Law Study Group. Contbr. articles to profl. jours. Bd. dirs. S.W. Repertory Orgn., El Paso, 1994-95; Sunday Sch. pres. Latter Day Saints Ch., 5th ward, El Paso, 1993-95; exec. sec. to bishop, 1995—. Recipient Outstanding Achievement award El Paso Young Lawyers Assn., 1990, Outstanding Jurist award, 1999. Mem. State Bar Tex. (mem. indigent representation com. 1994-98, 99—, victim/witness com. 1992-95, 97-98, 99—), El Paso Bar Assn. (mem. legal bar com., libr. com., criminal law com., others 1986—, bd. dirs. 1993-96, sec. 1996-97, treas. 1997-98, v.p. 1998-99, pres.-elect 1999—). Democrat. Avocations: playing piano, writing music, bicycle riding, basketball, accordion playing. Office: 120th Dist Ct County Bldg Rm 605 500 E San Antonio Ave El Paso TX 79901-2419

**DIODOSIO, CHARLES JOSEPH,** lawyer; b. Pueblo, Colo., Apr. 27, 1951; s. Warren Joseph and Lucille Julia Diodosio. BSChemE, U. Colo., 1973; JD, Northwestern U., 1976. Assoc. McDermott, Will & Emery, Chgo., 1976-80; internat. counsel Beatrice Co., Chgo., 1980-84, v.p. Asia devel., 1984-88; chmn. TMGC Ltd., Chgo., 1988—. Mem. ABA, Ill. Bar. Home: 822 W Oakdale Ave Chicago IL 60657-5122

**DION, ALAN,** lawyer; b. Providence, R.I., Dec. 29, 1950; s. Ernest Lionel and Jean L. (Lehman) D.; m. Joan Zeccola, Apr. 24, 1993. BS, Worcester (Mass.) Tech., 1972; MS, U. R.I., 1975; JD, Suffolk U., 1985. Bar: Mass. 1985, R.I. 1989. Air program engr. U.S. EPA, Atlanta, 1979-81; air compliance engr. U.S. EPA, Boston, 1981-86; asst. regional counsel U.S. EPA, Atlanta, 1986-97, sr. atty., 1998—. Office: EPA 61 Forsyth St SW Ste 9t25 Atlanta GA 30303-8960

**DIORIO, ROBERT MICHAEL,** lawyer, public official; b. Phila., Aug. 5, 1947; s. Carl and Yolanda D. (DiJohn) DiO.; m. Bianka M. Chojnacki; children: Danielle, Stephanie Lauren. BA in Polit. Sci., Pa. State U., 1969; JD, Temple U., 1973. Cert. elem. tchr., Pa. Pvt. practice Media, Pa., 1973—; asst. pub. defender Delaware County, Media, 1974-76, asst. dist. atty., 1976-79, support master, 1980, custody conciliator, 1980-97; solicitor, controller Delaware County, 1985-90; ptnr. DiOrio & Sereni LLP, Media, Pa., 1989—; spl. solicitor City of Springfield, Pa., Upper Darby Sch. Dist.; solicitor County Svcs. for Aging, Delaware County Bd. Prison Insps., S.E. Delco Sch. Dist. Commr. Springfield Twp. Bd. of Commrs., 1977-87, pres. 1981-87; bd. dirs. Deaf Hearing Comm. Ctr., Springfield, Immaculata (Pa.) Coll. Pres. Council, Met. Hosp., Phila., Delaware County Regional Water Quality Control Authority, 1987-89; mem. Delaware County Leadership Adv. Bd., Delaware County Bur. Elections. Mem. ATLA, Pa. Bar Assn., Pa. Assn. Trial Lawyers, Delaware County Bar Assn. (sect. dir. 1976, 93-95), Delaware County C. of C. (chmn. family bus. com.), Pa. State U. Alumni Assn. (pres.), Lions. Republican. Roman Catholic. Avocations: golf, skiing. Fax: (610) 891-0652. General civil litigation, Family and matrimonial, Personal injury. Home: 3 Springton Pointe Dr Newtown Square PA 19073-3931 Office: DiOrio & Sereni LLP Front and Plum Sts Media PA 19063

**DIPACE, STEVEN B.,** lawyer; b. Leominster, Mass., July 17, 1948; s. B. Vincent and Lucille C. (Boucher) DiP.; m. Gail S. Moskowitz, May 29, 1971; children: Angela Val, Michael Steven. BA, Brandeis U., 1970; JD, Suffolk U., 1974. Bar: Mass. 1974, U.S. Dist. Ct. Mass. 1974. Pvt. practice Fitchburg, Mass., 1974—; counsel No. Worcester County Bd. of Realtors, Fitchburg, 1987—. Mem. Montachusett Regional Planning Commn., Fitchburg, 1980, Leominster Planning Bd., 1980-81; chmn. Leominster Zoning and Appeals Bd., 1981-87. Mem. Mass. Bar Assn., No. Worcester County Bar Assn. (exec. bd. 1989-92). Avocation: coach youth sports. Real property, Probate, General practice. Home: 40 Wilder Ln Leominster MA 01453-6640 Office: 348 Lunenburg St Ste 201 Fitchburg MA 01420-4566

**DIPIETRO, MARK JOSEPH,** lawyer; b. Memphis, Aug. 25, 1947; s. Joseph Mark and Anne E. (Dorsey) DiP.; m. Kathleen Ann (Rafferty), June 22, 1968; children: Mark, Lora, Matthew. BA in Chemistry, So. Ill. U., 1969; JD, John Marshall Law Sch., 1976. Bar: Ill. 1976, Minn. 1983. Chemist Univ. Conn. Med. Sch., Hartford, 1969-70, VA Hosp., Indpls., 1970-71, U.S. Steel Corp., Gary, Ind., 1971-76; atty. Standard Oil of Ind. (now BP-Amoco), Chgo., 1976-81; from assoc. to ptnr. Merchant and Gould PA, Mpls., 1981-91; sr. v.p., sec. Merchant & Gould PA, St. Paul, 1992—. Mem. Met. Airport Sound Abatement Com., Mpls., 1984. Mem. ABA, AAAS, Internat. Bar Assn., Am. Intellectual Property Assn., Minn. Intellectual Property Assn., Ramsey County Bar Assn. Roman Catholic. Avocations: reading, bicycling, aerobics, piano. Fax: 612 371-5323. Patent, Intellectual property. Home: 815 Fairview Ave S Saint Paul MN 55116-2161 Office: Merchant & Gould 3100 Norwest Ctr 90 S 7th St Minneapolis MN 55402-4131

**DISALVO, THEODORE L.,** lawyer; b. Bethpage, N.Y., June 17, 1960; s. Charles Joseph and Marion Veronica DiSalvo; m. Rita M. McConaghy, July 14, 1984; children: Theodore Francis, Matthew Daniel. AS, Johnson and Wales U., 1981, BS in Hotel/Restaurant Mgmt. cum laude, 1984; JD, Suffolk U., 1988. Bar: Mass. 1988, U.S. Dist. Ct. Mass. 1989, U.S. Ct. Appeals (1st cir.) 1989, Fla. 1991, U.S. Dist. Ct. (so. dist.) Fla. 1992. Assoc. Schrieber & Assocs., Salem, Mass., 1988-89, Connolly & Fiengold, Wakefield, Mass., 1989, Gibson & Behman, Burlington, Mass., 1989-90, Heinrich, Gordon, Batchelder et al, Ft. Lauderdale, Fla., 1991, Paxton, Crow, Bragg, Smith et al, West Palm Beach, Fla., 1991-94; ptnr. Kogan & DiSalvo, Boca Raton, Fla., 1994—. Mem. ABA, ATLA, Acad. Fla. Trial Lawyers, South Palm Beach County Bar Assn. (chmn. civil practice com. 1995-96), Palm Beach County Bar Assn. (cir. ct. civil practice com. 1995—), Fla. Bar Assn. (grievance com. 1997—, unlicensed practice of law com. 1995-97), Med.-Legal Soc., Golden Quill Soc., Phi Delta Phi. Avocations: photography, camping, music. E-mail: TLDiSalvo@aol.com. Personal injury, Product liability, Insurance.

**DISHER, DAVID ALAN,** lawyer, geophysical research consultant; b. Chgo., Apr. 15, 1944; s. Hugh George and Beatrice Rose (Selmanovitz) D.; children: Karl Theodore, Carol Ann; m. Clara Hoffman, Sept. 17, 1991. BS in Elec. Engring., MIT, 1965, MS in Elec. Engring., 1966; JD, U. Houston, 1983. Bar: Tex. 1984, U.S. Ct. Appeals (5th cir.) 1984, U.S. Tax Ct. 1984, U.S. Dist. Ct. (so. dist.) 1986, U.S. Supreme Ct. 1987. Mathematician Shell Devel., Houston, 1966-68; sr. engr. Tex. Instruments, Stafford, 1968; dir. rsch. GEOCOM, New Orleans, 1969-70; cons., inventor Disher Consulting Svc., Houston, 1970-73; pres., chmn. bd. Seismic Programming Internat., 1973-84, 1974-84; pvt. practice law LaMarque, Tex., 1984-99; pvt. prac. Houston, TX, 1999—; v.p. St. Vincent's House, Galveston, Tex.; ind. geophys. rsch. cons. Contbr. articles to Geophysics. Mem. Concerned Citizens Galveston County, 1986—; precinct chmn., Galveston, 1980-84. Mem. ABA, NAACP, ACLU, Mainland Bar (treas.), Galveston Family Law Bar (treas.). E-mail: disherdave@aol.com; fax: 713-961-9402. Family and matrimonial, Criminal, Personal income taxation. Office: 3318 Mercer St Houston TX 77027-6020

**DISHEROON, FRED RUSSELL,** lawyer; b. Hot Springs, Ark., Nov. 21, 1931; s. Andrew Russell and Ruth Fayrene (Bearden) D.; m. Laurel Joan Picou, Apr. 1, 1961 (div. Dec. 1977); children: Terri Suzanne, John Frederick; m. Diane L. Donley, Apr. 8, 1989; 1 child, Travis William. AB, Hendrix Coll., 1953; JD, So. Meth. U., 1956; LLM in Environ. Law, George Washington U., 1976. Bar: Tex. 1956, U.S. Ct. Appeals (1st, 5th, 6th, 8th, 9th, 10th, 11th D.C. and fed. cirs.), U.S. Supreme Ct. 1964, Va. 1974. Atty. Superior Ins. Co., Dallas, 1960-64; claims atty. Sentry Ins. Co., Dallas, 1964-67; litigation counsel Stigall, Maxfield & Collier, Dallas, 1967-69; sole practice Dallas, 1969-70; asst. gen. counsel for litigation C.E. U.S. Army, Washington, 1970-75; spl. litigation counsel Dept. Justice, Washington, 1975—; instr. environ. law U. Ala.-Huntsville, 1979-82; lectr. law George Washington U., 1981-86; vis. rsch. specialist U. Calif., Davis, 1990. Co-author: Sustainable Environmental Law, 1993, Water Law, Trends, Policies and Practice, 1995; editor Southwestern Law Jour., 1955-56. Col. JAGC, USAR. Recipient numerous outstanding performance awrds U.S. Army, Dept. Justice, Sr. Exec. Svc. meritorious award Dept. Justice, 1984, Outstanding Civilian Svc. medal Dept. Army. Mem. Sr. Execs. Assn. Home: 3508 Riverwood Rd Alexandria VA 22309-2720 Office: Dept Justice Environ & Natural Resources Divsn 601 Pennsylvania Ave NW Ste 110 Washington DC 20004-2601

**DISIBIO, CAROL LYNN KRIDLER,** lawyer; b. Tarentum, Pa., July 13, 1949; d. William Wesley and Janet Louise (Lobaugh) Kridler; m. Ralph Robert DiSibio, June 6, 1987; children: Dean, Doreen. BA in Polit. Sci., U. Pitts., 1971, JD, 1974. Bar: Pa. 1974, U.S. Dist. Ct. (we. dist.) Pa. 1974. Atty. Neighborhood Legal Svcs., Pitts., 1974-80; dep. atty. gen. Pa. Bur. Consumer Protection, Pitts., 1980-81; contract mgmt. staff Westinghouse Elec. Corp., Pitts., 1981-85, mgr. licensing and adminstrn., 1985-86, mgr. nuclear svcs. contracts, 1986-87; sr. counsel Westinghouse Hanford Co., Richland, Wash., 1987-90; dep. gen. counsel Westinghouse Hanford Co., Richland, 1990-93; litigation cons. Westinghouse Elec. Corp. Pitts., 1993-96; asst. gen. counsel United States Enrichment Corp., 1996-98; instr. U. Pitts., Pa., 1980-85. Co-author: (booklet) Lawsuits Without Lawyers, 1994. Bd. mem. Camp Fire, Richland, 1988-90. Mem. Humane Soc. of the U.S., World Wildlife Found., Nature Conservancy. Avocations: golf, piano, reading, word games, cooking. Government contracts and claims, General corporate, Contracts commercial. Home: 22 Scotland Dr Reading PA 19606-9544

**DISSEN, JAMES HARDIMAN,** lawyer; b. Pitts., Jan. 26, 1942; s. William Paul and Kathryn Grace (Reilly) D.; m. Shirley Ann Stark, Dec. 17, 1976; children: Elizabeth Ann, William Stark, Anna Kathryn. BS, Wheeling (W.Va.) Jesuit U., 1963; MBA, Xavier U., Cin., 1966; JD, Duquesne U., Pitts., 1972. Bar: Pa. 1972, U.S. Dist. Ct. (we. dist.) Pa. 1972, W.Va. 1973, U.S. Dist. Ct. (so. dist.) W.Va. 1973, U.S. Supreme Ct. 1976. Spl. agent Counter Intelligence U.S. Army Intelligence Corps, 1963-66; personnel mgr. Columbia Gas of Pa., Inc., Uniontown, 1969-73; dir. labor rels. Columbia Gas Transmission Corp., Charleston, W.Va., 1973-84, dir. personnel and labor rels., 1984-87, dir. employee rels., 1987-96; v.p. Columbia Nat. Resources, Charleston, W.Va., 1996—; bd. dirs. Fourth Venture Investment Group, Inc.; adj. prof. W.Va. Grad. Coll., 1996-97, Wheeling Jesuit U., 1997, U. Charleston, 1998; vice-chmn., exec. com., bd. dirs. Star U.S.A. Fed. Credit Union. v.p., bd. trustees Highland Hosp., 1991—; vice chmn., exec. com. Star USA Fed. Credit Union. Mem. ABA, W.Va. State Bar, Soc. Human Resource Mgmt., W.Va. C. of C. (chmn. human resource com.), St. Thomas Moore Soc., Charleston Tennis Club. Republican. Roman Catholic. Avocation: golf. Labor. Home: 1501 Brentwood Rd Charleston WV 25314-2307 Office: Columbia Natural Resources 900 Pennsylvania Ave Charleston WV 25302-3548

**DITKOWSKY, KENNETH K.,** lawyer; b. Chgo., July 12, 1936; s. Samuel J. and Lillian (Plavnik) D.; m. Judith Goodman, Aug. 9, 1959; children—Naomi, Deborah, R. Benjamin. B.S., U. Chgo.; J.D., Loyola U., Chgo. Bar: Ill. 1961, U.S. Dist. Ct. (no. dist.) Ill. 1962, U.S. Ct. Apls. (7th cir.) 1973, U.S. Tax Ct. 1973, U.S. Sup. Ct. 1975. Ptnr., Ditkowsky & Contorer, Chgo., 1961—. Mem. Ill. Bar Assn. General practice, Federal civil litigation, State civil litigation. Office: Ditkowsky & Contorer 2626 W Touhy Ave Chicago IL 60645-3110

**DITO, JOHN ALLEN,** lawyer; b. Oakland, Calif., June 8, 1935; s. Peter Louis and Anne Marie (Sullivan) D.;. BA, Stanford U., 1957; LLB, Harvard U., 1961. Bar: Calif. 1962. Pvt. practice law L.A., 1961-72; ptnr. Buchalter, Nemer, Fields & Younger, L.A., 1972—; cons. Calif. Continuing Edn. of Bar, 1983-85. Contbr. articles on litigation practice to profl. publs. 1st lt. U.S. Army, 1957-58. Univ. Honors scholar Stanford U. Mem. ABA, Calif. Bar Assn., L.A. County Bar Assn., Irish-Am. Bar Assn. (pres 1992), Assn. Bus. Trial Lawyers, Am. Mensa Club (N.Y.C.), Sierra Club. Democrat. Roman Catholic. Avocations: reading, skiing. Federal civil litigation, General civil litigation, State civil litigation. Home: 5019 Jarvis Ave La Canada Flintridge CA 91011-1640 Office: Buchalter Nemer Fields & Younger 660 Newport Center Dr Newport Beach CA 92660-6401

**DITTER, J. WILLIAM, JR.,** federal judge; b. Phila., Oct. 19, 1921. *Father, a congressman from 1933 until his death in 1943, lead the efforts before World War II to obtain legislation for a two ocean navy. The USS J. William Ditter (DM31), a destroyer mine-layer, was named in his honor as is the chapel at the Naval Air Station, Willow Grove, Pennsylvania. Cousin, Dorothy Gondos Beers, was full professor and dean of women at American University, Washington, DC. Cousin, Edward G. Biester, was a state judge, 1949-70, and his son, Edward G. Biester, Jr., a member of congress, Attorney General of Pennsylvania, and is now a state judge in Bucks County, Pennsylvania.* B.A., Ursinus Coll., 1943, LL.D., 1970; LL.B., U. Pa., 1948. Bar: Pa. 1949. Clk. Ct. Common Pleas, Montgomery County, Pa., 1948-51; asst. dist. atty. Montgomery County, 1951, 53-55, 1st asst. dist. atty., 1956-60; mem. firm Ditter and Jenkins and predecessor firm, Ambler, Pa., 1953-63; judge Ct. Common Pleas, Montgomery County, 1964-70; judge U.S. Dist. Ct. Ea. Dist. Pa., Phila., 1970-86, sr. judge, 1986—; lectr. Villanova U. Past pres. bd. trustees Calvary Methodist Ch.; charter pres. Ambler Jaycees, 1954-55; bd. dirs. Riverview Osteo. Hosp., Norristown, Pa., 1964-71; bd. consulters Villanova U. Sch. Law, 1977—. Served to capt. USNR, 1943-68. Recipient Disting. Alumnus award Ambler High Sch., 1986; named Alumnus of Yr., Ursinus Coll., 1980. Mem. Am., Fed., Pa., Montgomery County bar assns., Hist. Soc. U.S. Dist. Ct. Eastern Dist. Pa. (incorporator, bd. dirs.). Office: US Dist Ct 3118 601 Market St Philadelphia PA 19106-1713

**DITTMAR, DAWN MARIE,** lawyer; b. Aberdeen, Md., Dec. 13, 1955; d. Robert William Grady and Diane Elizabeth (Canepi) Katz; m. Walter. BA in Polit. Sci., SUNY, 1982; JD, U. Bridgeport, 1985. Rsch. asst. Tuv Rheinland, Mt. Kisco, N.Y., 1982; clk. Danbury (Conn.) Superior Ct, 1985-86; pvt. practice Ridgefield, Conn., 1986-98, Brookfield, Conn., 1998—. Mem. Conn. Bar Assn. Republican. Roman Catholic. Avocations: ballet, yoga, reading, theater. Personal injury, Criminal, Family and matrimonial.

Home: 261 Wilton Rd Ridgefield CT 06877 Office: 60 Old New Milford Rd Brookfield CT 06804-2430

**DIVER, COLIN S.,** dean, law educator; b. 1943. BA, Amherst Coll., 1965; LLB, Harvard U., 1968; MA, U. Pa., 1989; LLD, Amherst Coll., 1990. Bar: Mass. 1968. Spl. counsel Office of the Mayor, Boston, 1968-71; asst. sec. consumer affairs Exec. Office Consumer Affairs, Boston, 1971-72; undersec. adminstrn. Exec. Office Adminstrn. and Fin., Boston, 1972-74; assoc. prof. Boston U., 1975-81, prof., 1981-89, from assoc. dean to dean, 1985-89; dean, Bernard G. Segal prof. U. Pa., Phila., 1989—; cons. Adminstrv. Conf. of U.S., 1980-88. Chmn. Mass. State Ethics Com., 1983-89; mem. adv. com. on enforcement policy NRC, 1984-85. Office: U Pa Law Sch 3400 Chestnut St Philadelphia PA 19104-6204

**DIVITO, JOSEPH ANTHONY,** lawyer; b. Shirley, Mass., Jan. 6, 1953; s. John and Gloria DiVito; m. M. Theresa DiVito, Sept. 5, 1997; children: Brian, Lisa, Thomas. BS, Springhill Coll., 1974; JD, Stetson U., 1977. Bar: Fla. 1977, Ohio 1978, U.S. Dist. Ct. (mid. dist.) Fla. 1980, U.S. Supreme Ct. 1988. Atty. Whitney & Monlar, Columbus, Ohio, 1977-80, DiVito & Higham, P.A., St. Petersburg, Fla., 1980—; spkr. in field. Pres. Sunshine City, St. Petersburg, 1984; baseball and soccer coach Osceola Little League and Youth Soccer, Seminole, Fla., 1990-96. Mem. Nat. Diocesan Attys. Assn. (U.S. Cath. Conf. 1991—), Fla. Bar (chmn. benefits com. 1992), St. Petersburg Bar Assn. (exec. com. 1986-88, 97—). Non-profit and tax-exempt organizations, Real property, Probate. Office: DiVito and Higham PA 4514 Central Ave Saint Petersburg FL 33711-1097

**DIXON, CARL FRANKLIN,** lawyer; b. Mansfield, Ohio, Feb. 17, 1948; s. Carl Hughes and Elizabeth (Kauffman) D.; m. Barbara Wagner, Dec. 27, 1969 (div. 1990); children: Clare Elizabeth, Jane Allison. B.A., Ill. Wesleyan U., 1970, B.S., 1970; M.A. Fletcher Sch. Law and Diplomacy div. Tufts U., 1971; JD, U. Chgo., 1974. Bar: Ill. 1975, U.S. Dist. Ct. (no. dist.) Ill. 1975, Ohio 1983. Assoc., Keck, Mahin & Cate, Chgo., 1974-78; ptnr. Dixon & Kois, Chgo., 1978-82; assoc. Porter, Wright, Morris & Arthur, Cleve., 1982-85, ptnr., 1986-87; v.p., sec., gen. counsel Weston, Inc., Cleve., 1987-90; counsel Beeler, Schad & Diamond, P.C., Chgo., 1990-93; nat. exec. dir. Nat. Kidney Cancer Assn., Evanston, Ill., 1994—. Recipient Adlai E. Stevenson award UN Assn., 1970; Edward R. Murrow fellow, 1971. bd. dirs. Chgo. Opera Theatre, 1992—. Mem. ABA, Am. Lung Assn. (trustee 1986—), Chgo. Regional Alumni Assn. Ill. Wesleyan U. (pres. 1997—), Kenilworth (Ill.) Club, North Shore Country Club (Glenview, Ill.), Phi Kappa Phi. Republican. Episcopalian. Real property, Federal civil litigation, General corporate. Home: 628 Brier St Kenilworth IL 60043-1061

**DIXON, E. A., JR.,** lawyer; b. Bryn Mawr, Pa., Dec. 12, 1939; m. Margaret Kennedy Cortright; children: Thomas W.W., Abigail C., Marion W., Meghan. AB, Princeton U., 1962; JD with honors, George Washington U., 1967. Bar: Pa. 1968, U.S. Dist. Ct. (ea. dist.) 1968. Assoc. Montgomery, McCracken, Walker & Rhoads, Phila., 1967-69; assoc. resident counsel Industrial Valley Bank, Phila., 1970-73; ptnr. Hepburn, Ross, Wilcox & Putnam, Phila., 1974-78; owner wholesale nursery business, 1979-85; atty. Monumental Title Corp., Severna Park, Md., 1985-86; mgr. comml. divsn. The Sentinel Title Corp., Balt., 1987-89; regional underwriting counsel Nations Title Ins. (formerly Nat. Attys and TRW Title), Trevose, Pa., 1989-96; sr. title counsel Lawyers Title Ins. Corp., Phila., 1996; N.J. area counsel Lawyers Title Ins. Corp., Iselin, 1997; counsel Stewart Title Guaranty Co., Wayne, Pa., 1998—; seminar spkr. Nat. Bus. Inst., N.J., 1995-96, Title Acad. N.J., 1995—. Contbr. articles to co. publs., 1990—. Mem. Quaker City Farmers. 2d lt. USAF, 1963-64. Mem. Pa. Land Title Assn. (exec. com. 1993-96), Pa. Bar Assn., The Phila. Club, Ardossan Beagles, Princeton Club (Phila.), St. Andrew's Soc. (Phila.), Montrose Club. Libertarian. Episcopalian. Avocations: horticulture, sailing, fly fishing, tennis. Office: 900 W Valley Rd Wayne PA 19087-1830

**DIXON, EDWARD KENNETH,** lawyer; b. Pitts., Sept. 21, 1952; s. Francis Kenneth and Mary Agnes (Barry) D.; children: Erika, Connor, Jamey. BA, So. Ill. U., 1974; MSW, U. Pitts., 1976; JD, Duquesne U., 1984. Bar: Pa. 1986, U.S. Dist. Ct. (we. dist.) Pa. 1986. Law clk. to judge Francis A. Barry Commonwealth Ct. of Pa., Pitts., 1985-87; staff atty. Faderewski & Herrington, Pitts., 1987-88; assoc. Zimmer Kunz, Pitts., 1988-93, shareholder, 1988—. Mem. Allegheny County Bar Assn. Workers' compensation.

**DIXON, HARRY D., JR. (DONNIE DIXON),** prosecutor; b. Waycross, Ga., Nov. 6, 1953; s. Harry D. Sr. and Ruth (Starling) D.; m. Elizabeth Tonning, Apr. 19, 1980; 2 children. AB in History, Valdosta State Coll., 1974; JD, U. Ga., 1977. Bar: Ga. 1977, U.S. Dist. Ct. Ga. 1978, U.S. Ct. Appeals 1979. Law clk. to Hon. Marvin Hartley, Jr. Superior Ct. for Mid. Jud. Cir., 1977-78; asst. dist. atty. Waycross Jud. Cir, 1977-79, dist. atty., 1983-94; atty. Bennett, Pedrick and Bennett, 1979-83; U.S. atty. for so. dist. Ga. U.S. Dept. Justice, Savannah, 1994—. Office: US Atty So Dist GA 100 Bull St Ste 201 Savannah GA 31401-3305

**DIXON, JEROME WAYNE,** lawyer; b. Shreveport, La., July 7, 1955; s. Huey P. Dixon and Myrtle Martin. BA, U. Calif., Santa Cruz, 1981; JD, So. U., Baton Rouge, La., 1986. Bar: La. 1988, U.S. Dist. Ct. (mid. dist.) La. 1988, U.S. Dist. Ct. (ea. dist.) La. 1989, U.S. Dist. Ct. (we. dist.) La. 1989, U.S. Dist. Ct. (no. dist.) Calif., 1989, U.S. Ct. Appeals (5th cir.) 1989. Pvt. practice Baton Rouge, 1988—; staff atty. Legis. Bur. La. Senate, Baton Rouge, 1988-96; La. State senate atty. for rsch. svcs., 1991-96. Coach Baker Brownfield Athletic Assn., Baton Rouge, 1990, Glen Oaks Athletics, Baton Rouge, 1989. Mem. ABA, ATLA, La. Trial Lawyers Assn., Baton Rouge Bar Assn. (v.p. 1997, pres. 1998), Kiwanis (v.p. 1989). Insurance, Juvenile, Criminal. Office: PO Box 44360 Baton Rouge LA 70804-4360

**DIXON, NANCY,** lawyer; b. Kansas City, Mo., Mar. 17, 1950; d. David Joel and Mary Frances (Riggs) D. AB, Carleton Coll., 1972; JD, U. Colo., 1977. Bar: Colo. 1977, Ariz. 1978, Mo. 1983. Assoc. Bader & Cox, Denver, 1980-82, Wassberg, Gallagher & Jones, Kansas City, Mo., 1983-86; pvt. practice, Kansas City, 1986-87, 88-89; of counsel Wilder & Hipsh, Kansas City, 1987-88; atty. Sprint, Kansas City, 1989—; bd. dirs. Kansas City Met. Bar Found. Pres. Com. for County Progress, Kansas City, 1998—, exec. com. 1994—; class agt. Alumni Annual Fund, Carleton Coll., Northfield, Minn., 1992—; commr. Jackson County Merit Commn., Kansas City, 1993—; v.p. Greater Kansas City Women's Polit. Caucus, Kansas City, 1994-97; v.p. Save, Inc., Kansas City, 1997—; house com. Ctrl. Exch., Kansas City, 1994-96. Mem. Mo. Bar Assn., Kansas City Met. Bar Assn., Ctrl. Exch. Democrat. Presbyterian. Labor. Home: 141 W 61st Ter Kansas City MO 64113-1455 Office: Sprint 8140 Ward Pky Kansas City MO 64114-2050

**DIXON, NICOLE FRANCIS,** financial executive, lawyer; b. Bklyn., Mar. 31, 1969; d. Reginald Clark and Bobsie (Binns) Dixon. BA, Fisk U., 1991; JD, U. Miami, 1996. Bar: Fla. 1997. Asst. mgr. Champs Sports, Nashville, Tenn., 1991-93; pro player stadium Cmty. Rels. Coord., Miami, 1996-97; law clk. Zemel & Kaufman PA, Aventura, Fla., 1996; legal intern Magistrate Judge L. Johnson, Miami, 1996-97; fin. planner, registered rep. Prudential Individual Fin. Svcs., Ft. Lauderdale, Fla., 1997—. Mem. ABA, Fla. Bar, Sports Lawyers Assn., Dade County Bar Assn., Delta Sigma Theta.

**DIXON, PAUL EDWARD,** lawyer, metal products and manufacturing company executive, lawyer; b. Bklyn., Aug. 27, 1944; s. Paul Stewart and Bernice (Mathisen) D.; BA, Villanova U., 1966; JD, St. Johns U., 1972; m. Kathleen Constance Kayser, Sept. 23, 1967; children: Jennifer Pyne, Paul Kayser, Meredith Stewart. Admitted to N.Y. State bar, 1972, U.S. Supreme Ct., 1976; assoc. mem. firm Rogers & Wells, N.Y.C., 1972-77; sec., asst. gen. counsel Volvo of Am. Corp., Rockleigh, N.J., 1977-79, v.p., gen. counsel, 1979-81; v.p., gen. counsel, sec. Reichhold Chems. Inc., 1981-88; sr. v.p., gen. counsel, sec. The Warnaco Group Inc., 1988-91; v.p., gen. counsel, sec. Handy & Harman, N.Y.C., 1992—; chmn. Teeches Ltd., Bermuda. Mem. ABA, Assn. Bar City N.Y., N.Y. State Bar Assn., U.S. Supreme Ct. Hist. Soc., Am. Corp. Counsel Assn. Club: Bedford Golf and Tennis Club. General corporate. Office: Handy & Harman 555 Theodore Fremd Ave Rye NY 10580-1451

**DIXON, WILLIAM CORNELIUS,** lawyer; b. Dexter, N.Y., July 1, 1904; s. Frank and Celia (Potter) D.; m. Arvilla Pratt, Nov. 20, 1934; children—Anne Arvilla, Nancy Cornelia. A.B., U. Mich., 1926, J.D., 1928. Bar: Ohio 1928, Calif. 1948, Supreme Ct. U.S 1948. Assoc. Holliday-Grossman-McAfee, Cleve., 1928-32; asst. dir. law Cleve., 1932-33, practiced law, 1933-38; justice Supreme Ct. Ohio, 1938; spl. asst. in anti-trust div. to atty. gen. U.S. Dept. Justice, 1944-54, chief asst. trial sect. anti-trust div., 1945, apptd. chief West Coast offices Anti-trust div., 1946, chief trial counsel for Govt. U.S. versus Standard Oil Co. Calif. et al, 1948, chief Los Angeles Office, 1948-54; pvt. law practice Los Angeles, 1954-59; asst. atty. gen. in charge state anti-trust enforcement Calif., 1959-63; legal adviser and mem. Joint War and State Depts., Zaibatsu Mission to Japan, 1946. Dir. relief for Ohio under Emergency Relief Act, 1938-39; moderator Los Angeles Assn. Congl. Chs., 1957; moderator Congl. Conf. So. Calif. and S.W., 1960; mem. constn. commn. United Ch. of Christ; mem. United Ch. Bd. for Homeland Ministries, 1962-65. Papers included in Truman Library, Library of Contemporary History, U. Wyo., Ohio State U. and UCLA libraries. Mem. Calif., Los Angeles bar assns., Delta Sigma Rho, Pi Kappa Alpha. Democrat. Antitrust. Home: 1590 W San Marcos Blvd Apt 168 San Marcos CA 92069-4076 *The past and unachieved goals in life soon pass into history. The goals of today become the achievements and successes of tomorrow.*

**DIXON, WRIGHT TRACY, JR.,** lawyer; b. Raleigh, N.C., Oct. 7, 1921; s. Wright T. and Marion Jefferson (Homes) D.; m. Elizabeth Prince Nufer, June 3, 1950; children: Wright III, William N., Elizabeth Prince. AB, Duke U., 1947; LLB, U. N.C., 1951. Bar: N.C. 1951, U.S. Dsit. Ct. (ea., mid. and we. dists.), N.C. 1951, U.S. Ct. Appeals (4th cir.) 1956; cert. mediator, N.C. Ptnr. Bailey & Dixon, Raleigh, N.C., 1956—; mem. Bd. of Adjustments, Raleigh, 1960-74, chmn., 1969-74. Jr. warden, sr. warden, mem. vestry St. Michael's Episcopal Ch., Raleigh; trustee So. Sem. Va., 1961-81, N.C. Clinent Security Fund, 1986-91. With USMC, 1943-59. Fellow Am. Bar Found.; mem. ABA (del. 1984-88), N.C. State Bar (counselor 1979-86, pres. 1985-86, Gen. Practice Hall of Fame 1997), Wake County Bar Assn. (pres. 1976, mem. N.C. commn. on code recodification 1979-81, hon. bd. mem. 1995, Joseph Branch professionalism award 1996), Raleigh Kiwanis Club (pres.), Sphinx Club (pres.), Carolina Country Club, Capital City Club. Avocations: golf, woodworking, genealogy, tennis, reading. Administrative and regulatory, Insurance, General civil litigation. Home: 414 Marlowe Rd Raleigh NC 27609-7018 Office: Bailey & Dixon PO Box 1351 2 Hannover Sq Raleigh NC 27602

**DJINIS, STEPHANIE ANN,** lawyer; b. Huntington, N.Y., June 1, 1964; d. James John and Norma Miriam Xupolos; m. Peter George Djinis, Sept. 19, 1992; 1 child, Elizabeth. AB, Duke U., 1984; JD, Columbia U., 1987. Bar: D.C. 1989, N.Y. 1988. Assoc. Kirkpatrick and Lockhart LLP, Washington, 1987-94, ptnr., 1995-99; ptnr. Law Offices Stephanie A. Djinis, 1999—. Product liability, General corporate. Office: Law Offices Stephanie A Djinis 7918 Jones Beach Dr Ste 600 McLean VA 22102

**DJOKIC, WALTER HENRY,** lawyer; b. Schwaforden, Germany, Sept. 12, 1947; came to U.S., 1951, naturalized, 1959; s. Radovan and Martha (Schulenburg) D.; divorced; 1 child, Joshua David. B.A., U. Ill., 1969; J.D., DePaul U., 1972. Bar: Ill. 1972, Ariz. 1980. Assoc., Wachowski & Wachowski, Chgo., 1972-73; atty. Pretzel & Stouffer, Chartered, Chgo., 1973-79; ptnr., 1979-85, Wood, Lucksinger & Epstein, Chgo., 1985-86, Finley Kumble Wagner, Heine, Underberg, Manley, Myerson & Casey, Chgo., 1986-88; of counsel McCullough, Campbell & Lane, 1988-93, Conrad, Scherer & James, 1994-96, Miller, Kagan, Rodriguez & Silver, 1996—. Mem. Chgo. Bar Assn., Ill. State Bar Assn., State Bar of Ariz., State Bar of Fla. Personal injury, Federal civil litigation, State civil litigation. Office: Finley Kumble Wagner et al 250 S Australian Ave West Palm Beach FL 33401-5018

**DJORDJEVIC, MICHAEL M.,** lawyer; b. Rochester, Pa., Sept. 20, 1952; s. Vlastimir and Vera D.; m. Mary C. Djordjevic, Aug. 24, 1974; children: Charles, Thomas, Gregory. BA, Allegheny Coll., 1974; JD, Case We. Res. U., 1977. Assoc. Smith & Smith, Avon Lake, Ohio, 1977-86; assoc. Jacobson, Maynard, Tuschman & Kalur, Cleve., 1986-87, prin., 1987-94; prin. Michael M. Djordjevic Attys. at Law, Akron, Ohio, 1994—. Alden scholar Allegheny Coll., 1972-73. Mem. Am. Trial Lawyers Assn., Ohio Acad. Trial Lawyers, Pi Gamma Mu. Avocation: motorcycle sports riding. General civil litigation, Personal injury, Professional liability. Office: 17 S Main St # 201 Akron OH 44308-1803

**DLUGOFF, MARC ALAN,** lawyer; b. N.Y.C., Oct. 6, 1955; s. Arnold M. and Ruth B. (Schnall) D. AB, Colgate U., 1976; JD, Hofstra U., 1980; LLM in Taxation, NYU, 1981. Bar: N.Y. 1981, D.C. 1985, Calif. 1988. Law clk. to presiding justice U.S. Tax Ct., Washington, 1981-83; assoc. Mudge, Rose, Guthrie, Alexander & Ferdon, N.Y.C., 1983-85; assoc. Milbank, Tweed, Hadley & McCloy, N.Y.C., 1985-89, ptnr., 1989-93; counsel Roberts & Holland, N.Y.C., 1993-94; pres., CEO Atlantic Advisory Corp., N.Y.C., 1995—. Fund raiser lawyers div. United Jewish Appeal, N.Y.C. chpt., 1986-90. Charles Dana scholar Colgate U., 1976. Mem. ABA, N.Y. State Bar Assn., Assn. of Bar of City of N.Y., State Bar of Calif., Phi Beta Kappa. Jewish. Private international, General corporate, Taxation, general. Home: 130 Water St New York NY 10005-1615 Office: Atlantic Advisory Corp 237 Park Ave Fl 21 New York NY 10017-3140

**DOAN, XUYEN VAN,** lawyer; b. Hadong, Vietnam, Apr. 1, 1949; came to U.S., 1975; s. Quyet V. Doan and Binh T. Kieu; m. Binh Thanh Tran, 1980; children: Quy-Bao, Ky-Nam. Licence en droit, U. Saigon Law Sch., Vietnam, 1971; MBA, U. Ark., 1977; JD, U. Calif., Hastings, 1982. Bar: Saigon 1972, Calif. 1982. Sole practice Costa Mesa and San Jose, Calif., 1982-84; ptnr. Doan & Vu, San Jose, 1984-90; prin. Law Offices of Xuyen V. Doan, 1990-95; ptnr. Doan & Tran, San Jose, 1995—; founder, coord. VietLawyers Com., Calif. and Vietnam. Author: Of the Seas and Men, 1985, also other publs. in English and Vietnamese. Named Ark. Traveler Ambassador of Good Will, State of Ark., 1975. Email: JD@VietLawyers.com. General corporate, Immigration, naturalization, and customs, Private international. Office: 2114 Senter Rd Ste 20 San Jose CA 95112-2608

**DOBBERSTEIN, ERIC,** lawyer; b. Las Vegas, Sept. 19, 1961; s. Herbert Emil and Ruth Ferris (Young) D.; children: Eric Rashon, Ian Cordell, Nyles Elijah. Student, U. Nev., 1981; BA, U. Nev., Las Vegas, 1985; JD, Thurgood Marshall Sch. of Law, 1988. Bar: Nev. 1989, U.S. Dist. Ct. Nev. 1989, U.S. Ct. Appeals (9th cir.) 1990. Asst. law libr. Libr. Mgmt. Svc., Houston, 1987-88; lawyer, law clk. Zervas & Evans, Las Vegas, 1986-89; lawyer Keith Gregory, Ltd., Las Vegas, 1989, Morton & McCullough, Las Vegas, 1990-91; pvt. practice Henderson, Nev., 1991—; arbitrator Eighth Jud. Dist. Ct., Las Vegas, 1992—; Justice of Peace Pro Tempore, 1999—; referee small claims ct., traffic court, 1998-99. Editor (notes) Thurgood Marshall Law Rev., 1988. Planning commr. City of Henderson, Nev., 1994-97. Mem. ABA, State Bar of Nev., Nev. Trial Lawyers Assn., Clark County Bar Assn., State Bar of Nev. (mem. fee dispute com., atty. disciplinary bd. 1998—). Democrat. Avocation: sports. Personal injury, Bankruptcy, Family and matrimonial. Office: 1399 Galleria Dr Ste 201 Henderson NV 89014-6664

**DOBBINS, CARYL DEAN,** lawyer; b. Indpls., July 3, 1947; s. Caryl L. and Janet (Matlock) D.; m. Amanda M. Cline, Nov. 22, 1972 (div. Jan. 1977); 1 child, Heather Lynn; m. Barbara J. Perry, Nov. 10, 1977; 1 child, Jason Dean. BS, Purdue U., 1969; postgrad., Valparaiso (Ind.) U., 1969-70; spl. med. student, Ind. U. Med. Sch., 1970-72; JD, Ind. U., Indpls., 1972; postgrad., Oxford (Eng.) U. and Brunel U., 1971. Bar: Ind. 1972, U.S. Dist. Ct. (so. dist.) Ind. 1972, U.S. Ct. Appeals (7th cir.) 1973, U.S. Supreme Ct. 1987. Chief law clk. to chief judge U.S. Dist. Ct. for So. Dist. Ind., Indpls., 1972-74; pros. atty. 18th jud. cir. State of Ind., 1975-78; dir. child support State of Ind., Indpls., 1979; pvt. practice, Greenfield, Ind., 1979—; dir. Ind. Law Enforcement Asst. Adminstrn., 1976-78; bd. dirs. Ind. Pros. Atty. Coun., 1976-78. Recipient Am. Farmer degree Future Farmers Am., 1967, Preservation award Greenfield Hist. Landmarks, 1984. Mem. ABA (gen. practice link bar leader award 1997), Ind. Bar Assn. (del. 1988-98, chair gen. practice, solo and small firm sect. 1996-97, chair, law practice mgmt. 1998-99), Ind. Bar Found. (master fellow), Hancock County Bar Assn., C. of C. Greater Hancock County and Greenfield (bd. dirs. 2d v.p. 1990, 1st v.p. 1991, pres. 1992, chmn. bd. dirs. 1993), Rotary (bd. dirs. 1991-94, Paul Harris fellow), Sertoma (treas. Greenfield 1982-84, sec. 1984-85, pres. 1985-86, chmn. bd. dirs. 1986-87, internat. del. 1983-86, Community Achievement award 1986), Farm House, Phi Alpha Delta. Avocations: gardening, travel. Personal injury, Probate, Criminal. Home: 4392 E 100 S Greenfield IN 46140-9758 Office: 19 W Main St Greenfield IN 46140-2340

**DOBBS, C. EDWARD,** lawyer, educator; b. Richmond, Va., July 15, 1949; s. Glenn Wellington and Sara Catherine (Judy) D.; m. J. Elisabeth Kuypers, Aug. 29, 1981; children: Elisabeth Peyten, Edward Palmer, Virginia Whitney. BA, Davidson Coll., 1971; JD, Vanderbilt U., 1974. Bar: Ga. 1974, U.S. Dist. Ct. (no., mid. dists.) Ga. 1974, U.S. Ct. Appeals (11th and 5th crcts.) 1974. Ptnr. Kutak Rock, Atlanta, 1974-83, Parker, Hudson, Rainer & Dobbs, LLP, Atlanta, 1983—; adj. prof. Emory Law Sch., Atlanta, 1987-92; mem. adv. bd. Atlanta Legal Aid Soc., 1980-82. Author: Reorganization Under Chapter 11 of the Bankruptcy Code, 1979, Enforcement of Security Interests in Personal Property, 1978. Bd. dirs., trustee Trinity Sch., Inc., Atlanta, 1992-96; chmn. Ga. Fin. Lawyers Conf., 1995—; bd. dirs. Comm. Fin. Assn. Edn. Found., 1996—. Fellow Am. Coll. Bankruptcy, Ga. Bar Found., Am. Coll. Comml. Fin. Laws (bd. regents 1990—, pres. 1996-98); mem. ABA (chmn. young lawyers divsn. 1981-82), Am. Arbitration Assn., Southeastern Bankruptcy Law Inst. (bd. dirs., chmn. 1992-93), Order of Coif, Omicron Delta Kappa. Presbyterian. Avocations: golf, tennis, fishing, trees. Bankruptcy, Banking. Office: Parker Hudson Rainer & Dobbs LLP 1500 Marquis Two Tower 285 Peachtree Center Ave NE Atlanta GA 30303-1229

**DOBIN, EDWARD I.,** lawyer; b. Binghamton, N.Y., Jan. 30, 1936; s. David I. and Frances (Lieber) D.; m. Gloria Schreiber, Aug. 16, 1959; children: Marc S., Nanette, Andrea. Student, Cornell U., 1953-54; BS, Franklin & Marshall Coll., 1957; LLB, U. Pa., 1960. Bar: Pa. 1961, U.S. Dist. Ct. (ea. dist.) Pa. 1961, U.S. Ct. Appeals (3d cir.) 1973, U.S. Supreme Ct. 1974. Assoc. Curtin and Heefner, Morrisville, Pa., 1961-66, ptnr., 1967-87, 95—, mng. ptnr., 1988-94. Trustee Adath Israel Congregation, Trenton, N.J., 1972-81; chmn. Mid Atlantic Ter. ARC, Phila., 1988-92, bd. dirs. Lower Bucks chpt., Langhorne, Pa., 1978—, pres., 1983-84; bd. dirs. Abrams Hebrew Acad., Yardley, Pa., 1975—, pres., 1980-84; chmn. Jewish Fedn. of Phila.-Buck Co. div., 1991-93, bd. dirs., 1994—. Fellow Am. Bar Found. (life), Pa. Bar Found.; mem. ABA, Pa. Bar Assn., Bucks County Bar Assn. (bd. dirs. 1971-72, treas. 1973-74, pres. 1981-82); mem. Nat. Assn. Bond Lawyers, Pa. Assn. Bond Lawyers (founder, bd. dirs. 1988-93, pres. 1990-91). Jewish. Municipal (including bonds), General corporate. Home: 250 Woodhill Rd Newtown PA 18940-2514 Office: Curtin and Heefner 250 N Pennsylvania Ave Morrisville PA 19067-1104

**DOBRA, CHARLES WILLIAM,** lawyer; b. Chgo., Oct. 7, 1944; s. Charles William and Mary Jean Dobra; m. Elaine J. Dobra, Aug. 21, 1998; 1 child, Christine J. AA, Chgo. City Jr. Coll., 1964; BA, DePaul U., 1967; MS, Iowa State U., 1969; JD, John Marshall Law Sch., Chgo., 1975. Bar: Ill. 1975, U.S. Dist. Ct. (no. dist.) Ill. 1975, U.S. Dist. Ct. (ea. dist.) 1977, U.S. Ct. Appeals (7th cir.) 1981, U.S. Ct. Mil. Appeals 1984. Tchg. and rsch. asst. Iowa State U., Ames, 1968, 69; asst. atty. gen. Office Ill. Atty. Gen., Springfield, 1975-78; ptnr. Geinko, Pulke & Dobra, Schaumburg, Ill., 1978-82, Geinko & Dobra, Bloomingdale, Ill., 1982-87; pvt. practice, Roselle, Ill., 1987—; bd. dirs. Bloomingdale Bank & Trust. Contbr. articles to law jours. Comdr. USNR. Mem. Chgo. Soc. of Clubs, Meadow Club, Rotary (pres. Bloomingdale-Roselle 1996-98). Libertarian. Roman Catholic. Avocation: sporting clays and upland game hunting. Personal injury, Bankruptcy, Real property. Office: 675 E Irving Park Rd Roselle IL 60172-2311

**DOBSON, ROBERT ALBERTUS, III,** lawyer, executive, volunteer; b. Greenville, S.C., Nov. 27, 1938; s. Robert A. Jr. and Dorothy (Leonard) D.; m. Linda Josephine Bryant, Nov. 18, 1956; children: Robert, William, Michael, Daniel, Jonathan, Laura (dec.); m. Catherine Elizabeth Cornmesser, Sept. 17, 1983; children: Andrew, Thomas. BS in Acctg. summa cum laude, U. S.C., 1960, JD magna cum laude, 1962. Asst. dean of students U. S.C., 1960-62; pvt. practice pub. acctg. Greenville, 1962-64; ptnr. Dobson & Dobson, Greenville, 1964-93; chmn., bd. trustees Limestone Coll., 1987-89. *Practiced tax and corporate law for thirty years pioneering the professional corporation concept for physicians, dentists and other professionals in South Carolina. Left his law practice in 1993 to devote full time to Christian ministry. Dobson Ministries supplies spiritual materials, support and encouragement to the elderly in nursing homes and to children in orphanages and shelters throughout the United States. Partners with and supports other ministries, including Homeless Children International and Campus Crusade for Christ. Extensively involved in numerous philanthropies.* Contbr. articles on tax and acctg. to profl. jours. Lay minister St. Francis Episcopal Ch., Greenville; chmn. bd. Dobson Tape Ministry, Homeless Children Internat., Inc.; bd. dirs. A Child's Haven, Inc., Found. for the Multihandicapped, Deaf and Blind, Spartanburg, S.C.; mem. adv. bd. Salvation Army, Greenville; chmn. fund raising com. Sch. Ministries, Inc., 1997-98; mem. history's handful Campus Crusade for Christ. Mem. ABA, S.C. Bar Assn., AICPAs, Am. Assn. Attys. and CPAs, S.C. Assn. Pub. Accts., Block C Assn. The Group, U. S.C. Alumni Assn. (cir. v.p.), Kappa Sigma (chmn. legal com. 1989-93, dist. grand master 1971—, Nat. Dist. Grand Master of the Yr. 1986, John G. Tower Disting. Alumni award 1997, Stephen Alonzo Jackson award 1998), Phi Beta Kappa. Episcopalian. Lodges: Sertoma Internat. (dist. treas.), Sertoma Sunrisers (pres. Greenville club). General corporate, Estate planning, Taxation, general. Home: 1207 Pelham Rd Greenville SC 29615-3643 Office: 1306 S Church St Greenville SC 29605-3814

**DOCKRY, KATHLEEN A.,** lawyer; b. Denville, N.J., Nov. 6, 1953; d. Joseph M. and Margaret (McAndrew) D.; m. Peter N. Perretti, III, June 20, 1979. BA cum laude, Duke U., 1976; JD with honors, Rutgers U., 1982. Bar: N.J. 1983. Law clerk U.S. Ct. Appeals (3d cir.), Newark, N.J., 1982-83; assoc. Lowenstein, Sandler, Roseland, N.J., 1983-87; asst. gen. counsel Asarco, Inc., N.Y.C., 1987-93; gen. counsel Castrol North Am., Wayne, 1993-95, v.p., gen. counsel, 1995-96, sr. v.p. human resources, adminstrn. & law, 1996-98; pres. Burmah Castrol Holdings Inc., Wayne, 1998—. Editor-in-Chief: Rutgers Law Review, 1981-82. Pres. Essex Youth Theater, Montclair, N.J., 1995—; trustee Bloomfield Coll. Mem. Am. Corp. Counsel Assn. General corporate. Home: 115B Undercliff Rd Montclair NJ 07042-1617 Office: Burmah Castrol Holdings Inc 1500 Valley Rd Wayne NJ 07470-8427

**DOCKSEY, JOHN ROSS,** lawyer; b. Milw., Sept. 4, 1951; s. John Warren and Marilyn Ruth (Skinner) D.; m. D. Christine Bjorum, May 21, 1988; children; John Thomas, Adam Christopher. BS, U.S. Mil. Acad., 1973; JD, U. Minn., 1981. Bar: Ill. 1981, U.S. Dist. Ct. (no. dist.) Ill. 1981. Assoc. Sonnenschein Nath & Rosenthal, Chgo., 1981-88; ptnr. Sonnenschein Moth & Rosenthal, Chgo., 1988—, chmn. corp. practice group, 1998—; bd. dirs. Daubert Industries, Oak Brook, Ill., Gullikson Found., Chgo. Contbr. articles to profl. jours. Capt. U.S. Army, 1973-78. Decorated Army Commendation medal. Mem. Met. Club, West Point Soc. Chgo. (v.p. 1984-86), Royal Melbourne Country Club. Avocations: skiing, family, golf. Mergers and acquisitions, General corporate, Private international. Office: Sonnenschein Nath & Rosenthal 8000 Sears Tower Chicago IL 60606

**DODD, HIRAM, JR.,** lawyer; b. Birmingham, Ala., Aug. 13, 1946; s. Hiram and Mary (Martin) D.; m. Annie Mayhall, Dec. 17, 1970; children: Hiram III, Brian Alan, Amie Michelle. BA, Samford U., 1968, JD, 1971. Pvt. practice law Birmingham. Mem. Ala. Bar Assn., Ala. Criminal Def. Lawyers Assn., Greater Birmingham Criminal Def. Lawyers Assn. Republican. Episcopalian. Criminal, Transportation. Office: 2107 5th Ave N Ste 100 Birmingham AL 35203-3325

**DODD, JERRY LEE,** lawyer; b. Bakersfield, Calif., Nov. 16, 1953; s. James Luther and Juanita Louise (Holmes) D.; m. Phena Fite, Jan. 9, 1972; children: Jody, Kimberly, Kristy, Julie, Timothy, Andrew, Matthew, Lindsey, Allison, Daniel. BS magna cum laude, U. Ark., 1975; MBA, Monmouth Coll., 1978; JD, Rutgers U., 1979. Bar: N.J. 1979, Pa. 1983, Minn. 1988; CPA. Commd. 2d. lt. USAF, 1975, advanced through grades to capt.; auditor A.F. Audit Agy. USAF, Wrightstown, N.J., 1975-78; base counsel USAF, Alexandria, La., 1979-81, def. counsel, 1981-82; contract trial atty. A.F. Contract Law Ctr. USAF, Dayton, Ohio, 1982-86; ret. USAF, 1986; govt. contracts counsel U.S. Army 7th Signal Command, Ft. Richie, Md., 1986-87; group counsel Honeywell, Mpls., 1987-90; divsn. counsel Harsco-

BMY Wheeled Vehicles Divsn., Marysville, Ohio, 1990—. Mem. ABA (com. mem.), Assn. Corp. Counsels Am. (bd. dirs.), Ohio Bar Assn. (com. mem.), Union County Bar Assn., Ark. Soc. CPAs. Government contracts and claims, Corporate taxation, General corporate. Home: 2217 Marshrun Ct Grove City OH 43123-1877 Office: Harsco BMY Wheeled Vehicles 3735 Grantz Rd Grove City OH 43123

**DODDS, FRANCES ALISON,** lawyer; b. Cleve., July 2, 1950; d. Warwick Moorin and Stella Bette (Kowalski) D.; m. Jorge Luis Cubas, June 6, 1975 (div.); 1 child, Alexa Victoria; m. Ronald W. Fleming, Aug. 20, 1993. BA, U. Denver, 1972; JD, Harvard U., 1975. Bar: Ill 1975, U.S. Dist. Ct. (no. dist.) Ill. 1976, U.S. Ct. Appeals (7th cir.) 1972, U.S. Ct. Appeals (fed. cir.) 1982. Assoc. Holleb. Gerstein & Glass, Chgo., 1975-81, ptnr., 1981-82; ptnr. Holleb & Coff, Chgo., 1982-91; of counsel Shaheen, Lundberg, Callahan and Orr, Chgo., 1991-94, Altheimer & Gray, Chgo., 1994-96, Shaheen, Orr, Pearce, Griffin & Staat P.C., Chgo., 1996—; mem. faculty Ill. CPA Found., Chgo., 1986-91, Am. Conf. Inst., 1991-92, N.W. Ctr. for Profl. Edn., Seattle, 1986-87; counsel Chgo. Office Leasing Brokers Assn., 1983—. Contbr. over 60 articles and interviews on rehabs. leasing, brokerage, ins. and environ. topics for Fed. Rsch. Press, Brownstone Pub., others; also seminars, panel and radio presentations. Trustee, chmn. Lincoln Park Co-op Nursery Sch., Chgo., 1987-88; bd. dirs. Cactus Theater, Chgo., 1988-89. Mem. ABA (chmn. housing ct. com. 1980-81), Assn. Women in Real Estate (bd. dirs. 1989-91), Chgo. Real Estate Exec. Women (sec. 1987-89, v.p. 1989-91, pres. 1991-92), Chgo. Bar Assn. (chmn. HUD 1979-80, bd. dirs. Young Lawyers 1980-82). Real property, Non-profit and tax-exempt organizations, Landlord-tenant. Office: Shaheen Orr Pearce Griffin & Staat PC 20 N Wacker Dr Ste 2900 Chicago IL 60606-3101

**DODDS, MICHAEL BRUCE,** lawyer; b. Spokane, Wash., June 27, 1952; s. Bruce Alison and Janet Lorraine (Swanbeck) D.; m. Karen Lynn Sifford, Jan. 5, 1972; children: Jennifer Ann, Stephanie Marie, Alexander Michael, Matthew Tyler. BA, Gonzaga U., 1974, JD, 1979. Bar: Wash. 1980, U.S. Dist. (ea. dist.) Wash. 1983, U.S. Dist. Ct. (we. dist.) Wash. 1987, U.S. Ct. Appeals (9th cir.) 1994, U.S. Supreme Ct. 1987. Dep. prosecutor Okanogan (Wash.) County, 1980-87, Clark (Wash.) County, 1987—. Served to 2d lt. U.S. Army, 1974-76. Recipient Excellence in Performance award Clark County, 1995. Mem. Clark County Bar Assn., Wash. State Bar Assn., Nat. Dist. Attys. Assn., Phi Alpha Delta. Republican. Lodge: Eagles, Moose. Home: 2104 NE Cranbrook Dr Vancouver WA 98664-2960 Office: Clark County Prosecuter's Office PO Box 5000 Vancouver WA 98666-5000

**DODELL, SUE ELLEN,** lawyer; b. N.Y.C., June 16, 1955; d. Martin Samuel and Carrye Lorch (Weisberg) Dodell; m. Joel Gary Chaiken, Aug. 19, 1984; children: Benjamin, Aviva, Joshua (dec.). AB, Mt. Holyoke Coll., 1976; JD, Columbia U., 1978. Bar: N.Y. 1979, U.S. Dist. Ct. (so. dist.) N.Y. 1979. Assoc. Parker Chapin, N.Y.C., 1978-79; asst. corp. counsel N.Y.C. Law Dept., 1979-83; dep. gen. counsel N.Y.C. Comptroller, 1983—. Mem. Phi Beta Kappa. Office: NYC Comptroller 1 Centre St Rm 518 New York NY 10007-1602

**DODGE, JAMES WILLIAM,** lawyer, educator; b. Springfield, Ill., Sept. 14, 1967; s. James U. and Nancy C. (Donaldson) D.; m. Cynthia Joy Selby, July 19, 1991; children: James A., Adrienne R.M. BS, U. Ill., 1989; JD, So. Ill. U., 1992. Bar: Ill. 1992, U.S. Dist. Ct. (ctrl. dist.) 1992, U.S. Ct. Appeals (7th cir.) 1993, U.S. Tax Ct. 1993. Pvt. practice Springfield, 1992-93; asst. atty. gen. Ill. Atty. Gen.'s Office, Springfield, 1993-97; first asst. state's atty. Christian County State's Atty.'s Office, Taylorville, Ill., 1997-99; legal counsel judiciary com. Ill. Senate Dem. Leader's Office, Springfield, Ill., 1999—; instr. MacMurry Coll., Jacksonville, 1998—; instr. Robert Morris Coll., Springfield, 1993-99. Author: A Brief Survey of Limited Liability Partnership Law in Illinois, 1996; contbr. articles to profl. jours. Ky. Col., Commonwealth of Ky., 1994. Fellow Ill. Bar Found.; mem. ABA, Ill. State Bar Assn. (mem.law-related edn. to pub. com. 1994-97, Christian County Bar Assn. (v.p. 1998—), Ask a Lawyer Day vol. 1994—, h.s. mock trial evaluator 1994—), Sangamon County Bar Assn. (dir. Young Lawyer's divsn. 1993-98), Acad. Legal Studies in Bus., Sangamo Club, Masons, Phi Alpha Delta. Episcopalian. Office: Ill Senate Dem Leader's Office State Capitol Rm 309 Springfield IL 62706-0001

**DODGE, JONATHAN KAREL,** lawyer; b. Kansas City, Mo., Sept. 8, 1949; s. Milton and Selma (Krulevitz) D.; m. Vita Mary Marino, May 15, 1983; children: Monica, Claudia. BA magna cum laude, Harvard U., 1972; JD, Georgetown U., 1977. Bar: N.Y. 1978. Assoc. Skadden, Arps, Slate, Meagher & Flom, N.Y.C., 1977-83; v.p., sec., gen. counsel Graphic Scanning Corp., Teaneck, N.J., 1983-86, DeGeorge Fin. Corp., Cheshire, Conn., 1993—; ptnr. Ashinoff, Ross & Korff, N.Y.C., 1986-90, Andrews & Kurth, Houston, 1990-92. General corporate, Contracts commercial, Securities. Office: DeGeorge Home Alliance Inc 591 Park Ave New York NY 10021-7361

**DODGE, MANNETTE ANTILL,** lawyer; b. Galveston, Tex., June 15, 1951; d. Don Arthur Sr. and Anna Maud (Morse) D.; m. Neil Howard Cogan, Apr. 26, 1981; children: Hillel Avidan Dodge-Cogan, Chava Lilit Dodge-Cogan, Saraleah Ariel Dodge-Cogan, Aviel Rahel Dodge-Cogan, Eliya Yacova Dodge-Covan. BA, Southwestern U., 1973; JD, So. Meth. U., 1977. Bar: Tex. 1977, U.S. Dist. Ct. (no. dist.) Tex. 1978. Asst. atty. gen. State of Tex., Dallas, 1977-79; corp. counsel Dr. Pepper Co., Dallas, 1979-81, Pepsi Co. Inc., Dallas, 1981-83; ptnr. Dodge & Loeffler, Dallas, 1983-86; exec. dir. Dallas Civil Liberties Union, 1985-86. Producer: film Battered Wives: The Next Step, 1984. V.p. adminstrn. Dallas Area Women's Polit. Caucus, 1982—, bd. dirs., chair commn. on ch. state; mem. Am. Jewish Congress, Dallas, 1981-86; bd. dirs. Domestic Violence Intervention Alliance Dallas Inc., 1980-85, chair legal com.; bd. dirs. Elizabeth Ives Acad., 1995—, Congregation Beth El Keser Israel, 1996—, Ezra Acad., 1997—; adv. bd. Talmed Torah Mejnuhad, 1995—. Fellow Tex. Bar Found.; mem. Tex. Bar Assn. (trustee ins. trust, pres. women and the law sect. 1982, chair com. on com. devel.), Dallas Bar Assn. (sec./treas., bd. dirs. 1984-85). Democrat. Civil rights, General corporate, Legislative. Home: 25 Woodside Ter New Haven CT 06515-2020

**DODGE, NANCY O'CONNELL,** lawyer; b. Bridgeport, Conn., Feb. 13, 1947; d. James J. and Katherine (Lyons) O'Connell; m. George Evan Dodge, May 17, 1975; children: Joshua, Amy, Jed, Casey. Degree, Manhattanville Coll., 1968, Boston Coll., 1971. Bar: Conn. 1971, N.H. 1976, R.I. 1980. Assoc. Coles, O'Connell, Dolan & McDonald P.C., Bridgeport, Conn., 1971-75, Nardone, Turo, Naccarato, Westerly, R.I., 1979-88; ptnr. Chernick & Dodge, Westerly, R.I., 1988-92; sole practitioner Westerly, R.I., 1992—; town solicitor Town of New Shoreham, R.I., 1985-89, probate judge, 1989-97; spl. probate judge Town of Hopkinton, R.I., 1992-96; zoning commn. task force Westerly, 1992-97. Mem. Westerly sch. com., 1990—, chmn., 1994-96, vice chair, 1996—; bd. dirs. Bishop Hendricken H.S., Warwick, R.I., 1996—. Democrat. Roman Catholic. Home and Office: 49 Sherwood Dr Westerly RI 02891-3701

**DODGEN, ANDREW CLAY,** lawyer; b. LaGrange, Ga., Apr. 8, 1961; s. Walter Eugene Dodgen and Mary Lucy (Thomason) Fuller; m. Lisa Jean Morris, July 7, 1979; children: Andrew Lee, Alexander Morris, Benjamin Michael. BA in History and Religion, LaGrange (Ga.) Coll., 1983; JD, Mercer U., 1986. Bar: Ga. 1986, U.S. Dist. Ct. (mid. dist.) Ga. 1986. Ptnr. Moore & Dodgen, Columbus, Ga., 1986—. * Mem. ABA, Assn. Trial Lawyers Am., State Bar Ga., Ga. Trial Lawyers Assn., Columbus Lawyers Club. Baptist. Criminal, Personal injury, Family and matrimonial. Office: Moore & Dodgen 846 Second Ave PO Box 1297 Columbus GA 31902-1297

**DODSON, F. BRIAN,** lawyer; b. Pitts., Oct. 2, 1948; s. James W. and Bernice F. (Fitzgerald) D.; m. Lisa Aloe, Dec. 23, 1971; children: Meredith, Chelsea, William, Timothy. BS, Pa. State U., 1970; JD, U. Pitts., 1974; LLM in Taxation, NYU, 1975. Tax atty. Cauley, Birsic & Conflenti, Pitts., 1975-78; pres., CEO Luzerne Coal Co., Pitts., 1978-85; cons. Pitts., 1985-89; pres., CEO Multisearch, Inc., Pitts., 1989-92; pvt. practice Pitts., 1992—; bd. dirs. Imperial Land Corp., Pitts. Commr. Fox Chapel Area Youth Svcs., Pitts., 1993—; pres. Coalition for Quality Edn., Pitts., 1993—. With U.S. Army, 1973-79. Mem. ABA, Allegheny County Bar Assn. Estate planning, Estate taxation, Corporate taxation. Home: 203 Staffordshire Dr Pittsburgh PA 15238-1631 Office: 9800 Mcknight Rd # 332A Pittsburgh PA 15237-6003

**DODSON, GERALD PAUL,** lawyer; b. Pitts., Sept. 15, 1947; s. Paul C. and Eileen (Lebo) D.; m. Patricia Lawrence, May 31, 1981. BSME, Lafayette Coll., 1969; JD, U. Md., 1972; LLM, George Washington U., 1977. Bar: Calif., Pa., DC; registered to practice U.S. Patent and Trademark Office. Asst. county solicitor Allegheny County Law Dept., Pitts., 1972-75; staff atty. U.S. Dept. of Interior, Washington, 1976-78; chief counsel U.S. House of Reps., subcom. on Health & Environ., Washington, 1978-88; ptnr. Townsend & Townsend, San Francisco, 1988-92, Howard, Rice & Nemerovski, San Francisco, 1992-95, Arnold, White & Durkee, Menlo Park, Calif., 1995—. Mem. San Francisco Patent & Trademark Law Assn. Democrat. Intellectual property. Office: Arnold White & Durkee 155 Linfield Dr Menlo Park CA 94025-3741

**DODSON, TAMMY ROSE,** lawyer; b. Topeka, Kans., Aug. 16, 1963; d. Paul Thomas and Rosemary (Garretson) D. BS in Journalism, U. Kans., 1985, MPA, 1990; JD, Washburn U., 1994. Staff attorney Legal Svcs. of Southeast Kansas, 1994-96, Shook, Hardy & Bacon LLP, Kansas City, 1996—. Mem. Am. Bar Assn., Mo. Bar Assn., Kans. Bar Assn., Kans. City Metropolitan Bar Assn. Democrat. Office: Shook Hardy & Bacon LLP One Kansas City Pl 1200 Main St Kansas City MO 64105-2118

**DOERR, JEFFREY MARK,** lawyer; b. Ames, Iowa, Jan. 23, 1956; s. LaVern Hollis and Hedy Neuman D.; m. Karen June Kruse, Aug. 2, 1980; children: Tyler Ryan, Melissa Ann. BSc, U. Nebr., 1974, JD, 1982. Bar: Nebr., U.S. Dist. Ct. Nebr. Lawyer Person, Dier, Person & Osborn, Holdrege, Nebr., 1982-83; partner Kryger & Doerr, Neligh, Nebr., 1984-89; pvt. practice Neligh, 1989-95; partner Smith & Doerr, PC, Neligh, 1995-97; pvt. practice Neligh, 1997—; adv. bd. Antelope County Recycling Neligh, 1990—; commr. Neligh Housing Authority, 1993—. Attorney coach Neligh/Oakdale High Sch. mock trial team, 1985—. Mem. Nebr. Criminal Defense Attorney's Assn., Neligh Rural Vol. Fire Dept., Delta Sigma Pi (outstanding pledge 1976-77, outstanding active 1978, outstanding alumni 1980). Republican. Methodist. Avocations: umpire, coaching, weight lifting, running. Criminal. Home: RR 2 Box 37A Neligh NE 68756-9612 Office: PO Box 166 Neligh NE 68756-0166

**DOERR, STEPHEN,** lawyer; b. Misawa AFB, Japan, Jan. 30, 1953. BS, Eastern N.Mex. U., 1977; JD, U. N.Mex., 1980. Bar: N.Mex. 1980, U.S. Dist. Ct. N.Mex. 1984, U.S. Dist. Ct. (ea. dist.) Okla. Ptnr. Doerr & Knudson, Clovis, N.Mex.; bus. law and real property instr. Eastern N.Mex. U., 1982-84; bar commr. Fifth Bar Dist. Curry, Roosevelt, and Quay Counties. With USMC, 1972. Mem. ABA, ATLA, State Bar N.Mex. (pres.), N.Mex. Trial Lawyers Assn., Roosevelt County Bar Assn. (pres. 1984-85), Curry County Bar Assn. (pres. 1983, v.p. 1982), Curry-Roosevelt County Bar Assn. (pres. 1986), Phi Kappa Phi, Delta Theta Pi. Personal injury, Product liability, Family and matrimonial. Office: Doerr & Knudson PA 600 Mitchell St Clovis NM 88101-7358*

**DOETSCH, DOUGLAS ALLEN,** lawyer; b. Lake Charles, La., Nov. 6, 1957; s. Gerald Allen and Marjorie Ruth (Hess) D.; m. Susan Allene Manning, Aug. 24, 1985. BA magna cum laude, Kalamazoo Coll., 1979; JD, Columbia Law Sch., 1986. Assoc. Cleary, Gottlieb, Steen & Hamilton, N.Y.C., 1986-88, Mayer, Brown & Platt, Chgo., 1988—; dir. Columbia Jour. of Transnational Law, N.Y.C., 1985—. Private international, Finance, General corporate. Office: Mayer Brown & Platt 190 S La Salle St Ste 3100 Chicago IL 60603-3441

**DOHERTY, BRIAN JOHN,** lawyer; b. Milw., July 27, 1969; s. John Michael and Carol Ann Doherty; m. Michelle Elizabeth Rondeau, May 9, 1998. BA, St. Norbert Coll., 1991; JD, U. Mo., 1994. Bar: Mo. 1994, U.S. Dist. Ct. (we. dist.) Mo. 1994, Kans. 1995, U.S. Dist. Ct. Kans. 1995. Atty. Field, Gentry & Benjamin P.C., Kansas City, Mo., 1994—; barrister Ross T. Roberts Inn of Ct., 1996—. Recipient Guy A. Thompson award Mo. Law Rev., 1993, 94. Mem. ABA, Lawyers Assn. of Kansas City, Kansas City Met. Bar Assn. Avocations: sailing, golfing. General civil litigation, Insurance, Product liability. Office: Field Gentry & Benjamin 4600 Madison Ave Ste 210 Kansas City MO 64112-3019

**DOHERTY, DANIEL JOSEPH, III,** lawyer; b. Washington, May 14, 1964; s. Daniel Joseph Jr. and Gail Howard D. BA, Wake Forest U., 1986; JD, W.Va. U., 1989. Bar: W.Va. 1990, D.C. 1991, U.S. Supreme Ct. 1994, Md. 1997. Assoc. atty. John P. Ball Law Offices, Morgantown, W.Va., 1991-95; assoc. investigator D.J. Doherty & Assocs., Davidsonville, Md., 1995-96; rsch. assoc. Callahan & Callahan, Crofton, Md., 1996-98, assoc., 1998—. Legal counsel Annapolis Jaycees, Md., 1998—; ice hockey coach U.S. Naval Acad. Mem. Md. Bar Assn., D.C. Bar Assn., W.Va. Bar Assn., Anne Arundel County Bar Assn., Prince George's County Bar Assn. Independent. Roman Catholic. Avocation: coaching collegiate ice hockey. General practice, Probate, General corporate. Office: Callahan & Callahan 2133 Defense Hwy Crofton MD 21114-2436

**DOHERTY, REBECCA FEENEY,** federal judge; b. Ft. Worth, June 3, 1952; d. Charles Edwin Feeney and Annabelle (Knight) Smith; divorced; 1 child, George Jason. BA, Northwestern State U., 1973, MA, 1975; JD, La. State U., 1981. Bar: La. 1981, U.S. Dist. Ct. (mid., ea. and we. dists.) La. 1981, U.S. Ct. Appeals (5th cir.) 1981, U.S. Dist. Ct. (so. dist.) Tex. 1986, U.S. Dist. Ct. (ea. dist.) Tex. 1989. Assoc. Onebane, Donohoe, Bernard, Torian, Diaz, McNamara & Abell, Lafayette, La., 1981-84, ptnr., 1985-91; U.S. dist. ct. judge We. Dist. La., Lafayette, 1991—; adj. instr. Northwestern State U., Natchitoches, La., 1975; co-dir. secondary level gifted and talented program Webster Parish, La., 1978. Contbr. articles to profl. jours.; mem. La. Law Rev., 1980, 81. Recipient Am. Jurisprudence award Lawyers Coop. Pub. Co., 1980, Career Achievement award 1991; inducted into La. State U. Law Ctr. Hall of Fame, 1987. Mem. ABA, La. Bar Assn., La. Assn. Def. Counsel, La. Assn. Trial Lawyers, Acadian Assn. Women Attys., Order of Coif. Office: US Dist Ct 800 Lafayette St Ste 4900 Lafayette LA 70501-6800

**DOHERTY, ROBERT CHRISTOPHER,** lawyer; b. Elizabeth, N.J., Sept. 3, 1943; s. Christopher Joseph and Marie Veronica (McLaughlin) D.; m. Sarajane Frances Doherty, June 12, 1965; children: Dennis Michael, Amy Elizabeth, Tracey Carolan. AB, St. Peter's Coll., 1965; JD, Seton Hall U., 1970. Bar: N.J. 1970, U.S. Ct. Appeals (3rd cir.) 1982, U.S. Supreme Ct. 1977. Asst. prosecutor Union County, Elizabeth, N.J., 1971-72; mem. Schumann, Hession, Kennelly & Dorment, Jersey City, 1972-73, Robert D. Younghans, Westfield, N.J., 1973-76; ptnr. Doherty & Kopnicki, Westfield, 1976-87; county counsel Union County, Elizabeth, 1981-88; assoc. Nelinson, Roche & Carter, East Orange, N.J., 1988-92, Stanley Marcus, Newark, 1992-98, Weiner Lesniak, Parsippany, N.J., 1998—. Mem. ABA, N.J. Bar Assn., Union County Bar Assn., Essex County Bar Assn., N.J. Assn. County Counsels. Republican. Roman Catholic. State civil litigation, Personal injury, General practice. Home: 771 Fairacres Ave Westfield NJ 07090-2027 Office: Weiner Lesniak 299 Cherry Hill Rd Parsippany NJ 07054-1111

**DOHRMANN, JEFFREY CHARLES,** lawyer; b. Lock Haven, Pa., Dec. 27, 1959; s. Bernhard Dohrmann and Mary Elaine (Teichman) Genevish; m. Madeline Erica Jacobs (div. 1984); m. Melanie Kay Bagley, Dec. 2, 1986; children: Peter Geanacopoulos, Philip Geanacopoulos, Caitlin Dohrmann, Colin Dohrmann. BA, Pa. State U., 1982; JD magna cum laude, Widener U., 1993. Bar: Pa. 1993, U.S. Dist. Ct. (mid. dist.) Pa. 1993, U.S. Ct. Appeals (3d cir.) 1994. Paralegal Bernhard Dohrmann, Lock Haven, 1982-83; litigation paralegal Rieders, Travis, Mussina, Humphrey & Harris, Williamsport, Pa., 1983-93, lawyer, 1993—. Actor, dir. numerous plays, 1977—. Bd. dirs., mem. Cmty. Theater League, Williamsport, 1987-89, 93—, v.p. prodn., 1987-89. Mem. ATLA, Fed. Bar Assn., Pa. Trial Lawyers Assn. (publs. com. 1993-94). Avocations: acting, directing, writing, soccer coaching, hunting. Civil rights, Personal injury, Criminal. Office: Rieders Travis et al 161 W 3rd St Williamsport PA 17701-6407

**DOHSE, ROBERTA SHELLUM,** lawyer; b. Cin., Dec. 29, 1949; d. Harold and Ruth (Torgleson) Shellum; m. Craig Dohse, May 25, 1984 (div. Nov. 1993); children: Gretchen, Kari, Christian. BA, U. Calif., Berkeley, 1971; JD with hons., U. Houston, 1991. Bar: Tex. 1992, U.S. Dist. Ct. (so. dist.) Tex. 1992, U.S. Dist. Ct. (no. dist.) Tex. 1997. Instr., program coord., legal support svcs. North Harris Coll., Houston, 1984-92; assoc. Bishop, Peterson & Sharp, Houston, 1992; lawyer pvt. practice Houston, 1993-95; assoc. Wetzel & Herron, The Woodlands, Tex., 1995-96, Chaves Gonzales & Hobl, L.L.P., Corpus Christi, Tex., 1997—. Mem. cutting horse com. Houston Livestock Show and Rodeo, 1988-93, legal adv. com. North Harris Coll., Houston. Mem. ABA, Tex. Bar Assn., Corpus Christi Bar Assn., Order of Coif, Phi Beta Kappa, Order of Barons, Phi Delta Phi. Presbyterian. Contracts commercial, Probate. Home: 4621 Hogan Dr Corpus Christi TX 78413-2136 Office: Chaves Gonzales & Hoblit 2000 Frost Bank Tower 802 N Carancahua St Corpus Christi TX 78470-0002

**DOKE, MARSHALL J., JR.,** lawyer; b. Wichita Falls, Tex., June 9, 1934; s. Marshall J. and Mary Jane (Johnson) D.; m. Betty Marie Orsini, June 2, 1956; children: Gregory J., Michael J., Laetitia Marie. BA magna cum laude, Hardin-Simmons U., 1956; LLB magna cum laude, So. Meth. U., 1959. Bar: Tex. 1959. Assoc. Thompson, Knight, Wright & Simmons, Dallas, 1959, 62-65; founding ptnr. Rain Harrell Emery Young & Doke, Dallas, 1965-87, Doke & Riley, Dallas, 1987-92; ptnr. McKenna & Cuneo, 1993-96, Gardere & Wynne, L.L.P., Dallas, 1996—; gen. counsel Tex. Rep. Party, 1976-77; mem. adv. coun. U.S. Ct. Fed. Claims, 1982—. Author: Ann. Procurement Rev., Govt. Contractor Briefing Papers, Contract Changes, Fed. Contract Mgmt., 1982—, also articles; editor-in-chief: Southwestern Law Jour., 1958-59; editor: ABA Ann. Devels. in Govt. Contract Law, 1975-78 . Pres. Hope Cottage-Children's Bur., Inc., 1969-70, Hope Cottage Found., 1997—; mem. bd. visitors Law Sch., So. Meth. U., 1966-69, McDonald Obs., U. Tex., 1990—; dir. Tex. Hist. Found., 1993—, v.p., 1996-98; mem. law com., bd. trustees So. Meth. U., 1977-78; bd. dirs., pres. World Trade Assn., Dallas-Ft. Worth, 1979-80; chmn. bd. dirs. Internat. Trade Assn. Dallas/Ft. Worth, 1993-94; bd. dirs., sec. Theater Trustees Am., 1983-93; chmn. Mayor's Internat. Com., City of Dallas, 1984-87, mem. Judicial Nominating Commn., 1997—. 1st lt. JAGC, U.S. Army, 1959-62. Fellow Am. Bar Found., Tex. Bar Found.; mem. ABA (chmn. sect. pub. contract law 1969-70, ho. of dels. 1970-72, 74—, bd. govs. 1980-82, nominating com. 1988-91, chmn. conf. sect. dels. 1991—), Tex. Bar Assn., U.S. Ct. of Fed. Claims Bar Assn. (bd. govs. 1987—, pres. 1996), Bd. of Contract Appeals Bar Assn. (pres. 1988-90, bd. govs. 1988—), Am. Bar Retirement Assn. (bd. dirs., trustee 1980-84, pres 1982-90), Nat. Conf. Lawyers and CPAs (co-chmn. 1983-85), Nat. Contract Mgmt. Assn. (nat. bd. advisors 1983—), Dallas C. of C. (chmn. internat. com. 1979-83). E-mail: dokm@gardere.com. Construction, Government contracts and claims, Private international. Home: 6910 Dartbrook Dr Dallas TX 75240-7926 Office: Gardere & Wynne Thanksgiving Tower Ste 3000 Dallas TX 75201-7254

**DOKURNO, ANTHONY DAVID,** lawyer; b. Gardner, Mass., Mar. 14, 1957; s. Anthony Chester and Damey Anteena (Aleson) D.; m. Andee J. Rappazzo. BA, Holy Cross Coll., 1979; JD, Vt. Law Sch., 1982; postgrad., Johns Hopkins U., 1993-94. Bar: Mass. 1982, U.S. Ct. Appeals for the Armed Forces 1986, U.S. Supreme Ct. 1987. Pvt. practice law Fitchburg, Mass., 1982-86; appellate counsel Navy-Marine Corps Appellate Rev. Activity, Washington, 1986-88; atty. admiralty div. JAG, Washington, 1988-90, atty. ops. and mgmt., 1991-93. Assoc. counsel, bd. vets. appeals Dept. Vets. Affairs, 1994-96; analyst Dept. of Def., 1996—. Comdr. USNR, 1998—. Mem. Maritime Law Assn., Nat. Cryptologic History Found., Am. Legion, Naval Res. Assn., Mensa, Phi Beta Kappa. Administrative and regulatory, Admiralty, Public international. Home: 200 N Pickett St Apt 1504 Alexandria VA 22304-2127

**DOLAN, ANDREW KEVIN,** lawyer; b. Chgo., Dec. 7, 1945; s. Andrew O. and Elsie (Grafner) D.; children: Andrew, Francesca, Melinda. BA, U. Ill., Chgo., 1967; JD, Columbia U., 1970, MPH, 1976, DPH, 1980. Bar: Wash. 1980. Asst. prof. law Rutgers-Camden Law Sch., N.J., 1970-72; assoc. prof. law U. So. Calif., L.A., 1972-75; assoc. prof. pub. health U. Wash., Seattle, 1977-81; ptnr. Bogle & Gates, Seattle, 1988-93; pvt. practice law, 1993—. Commr. Civil Svc. Commn., Lake Forest Park, Wash., 1981; mcpl. judge City of Lake Forest Park, 1982-98. Russell Sage fellow, 1975. Mem. Order of Coif, Washington Athletic Club. Avocation: book collecting. Health, Administrative and regulatory, Pension, profit-sharing, and employee benefits. Office: 5800 Columbia Ctr 701 5th Ave Seattle WA 98104-7097

**DOLAN, BRIAN THOMAS,** lawyer; b. Springfield, Ill., Dec. 27, 1940; s. William Stanley and Dorotha Caroline (Battles) D.; m. Kathleen Lois Smith, Sept. 14, 1963; children: Elizabeth Beaumont, Leslie Caroline. AB, Stanford U., 1963, JD, 1965. Bar: Calif. 1966, Colo. 1966, D.C. 1980. Capt. USAF, 1966-70; ptnr. Davis, Graham & Stubbs LLP, Denver, Boulder, 1970—. Finance, Natural resources. Office: Davis Graham & Stubbs LLP 370 17th St Ste 4700 Denver CO 80202-5682

**DOLAN, EDWARD CHARLES,** lawyer; b. N.Y.C., Sept. 25, 1953; s. Eamonn Ignatius and Mary Theresa (Golden) D.; m. Margaret Mary Vaughan, Nov. 29, 1980; children: Caroline, William. BA, Columbia U., 1975; JD, Georgetown U., 1978. Bar: Md. 1978, D.C. 1979, U.S. Dist. Ct. Md. 1980, U.S. Dist. Ct. D.C. 1980, U.S. Supreme Ct. 1983, U.S. Ct. of Appeals (4th cir.), U.S. Dist. Ct. Colo. 1997. Intern Office of U.S. Atty., ea. dist., N.Y., 1977; law clk. Dept. Justice Drug Enforcement Adminstrn., Washington, 1978; assoc. Beckett Cromwell & Myers, Bethesda, Md., 1978-84; assoc. Hogan and Hartson L.L.P., Washington, D.C., 1984-87, counsel, 1987-89, ptnr., 1989—; Chandler Bankruptcy Inn of Ct., Washington, 1990—; mem. standing com. local rules Bankruptcy Ct., Md., 1984—, chair, 1996-97. Author: (with others) The Law of Distressed Real Estate, 1988, Practice Manual for the Maryland Lawyer, 1989, 2d edit., 1992; contbg. author: Environmental Aspects of Real Estate Transactions, 1995. Pres. De Chantal Parish Home and Sch. Assn., Bethesda, 1990-92; active De Chantal Parish Sch. Bd., Bethesda, 1992-96, pres., 1994-96; mem. parents' coun. St. Anselm's Abbey Sch., Washington, 1995—; active Columbia Coll. Secondary Schs. Com., N.Y.C., 1978-92; class co-chmn. Columbia Coll. Club, Washington, 1990-92. Mem. ABA, Md. State Bar Assn., Montgomery County Bar Assn. (chmn. bankruptcy com. 1990-91), Prince George's County Bar Assn. (spl. com. on professionalism 1988-90), Bankruptcy Bar Assn. (Md. pres. 1989-90, dir. 1988—), D.C. Bar Assn. (chmn. bus. bankruptcy com. 1995—). Banking, Bankruptcy, General civil litigation. Office: Hogan and Hartson LLP 555 13th St NW Ste 800E Washington DC 20004-1161

**DOLAN, JAMES BOYLE, JR.,** lawyer; b. Memphis, Tenn., Aug. 1, 1944; s. James B. and Agnes (Kett) D. AB, Boston Coll., 1966; JD, Cornell U., 1969; diploma, U.S. Army War Coll., 1989. Bar: Mass. 1969, U.S. Dist. Ct. Mass. 1972, U.S. Ct. Appeals (1st cir.) 1980, U.S. Supreme Ct. 1986. Assoc. Badger, Parrish, Sullivan and Frederick, Boston, 1969-70; assoc. Badger, Sullivan, Kelley and Cole, Boston, 1972-79, ptnr., 1979-90; ptnr. Badger, Dolan, Parker and Cohen, Boston, 1990—; arbitrator Am. Arbitration Assn., Boston; chmn. hearing com. Bd. Bar Overseers; mem. bd. editors Defense Counsel Jour. Capt. U.S. Army, 1970-72. Mem. ABA, Mass. Bar Assn. (artibration fee disputes tribunal, ethics com., def. rsch. inst., products liability com., agrl., constrn., mining and indsl. equipment specialized litigation group), Internat. Assn. Def. Counsel, Boston Athenaeum, Supreme Judicial Ct. Hist. Soc., Mil. Hist. Soc. Mass., Res. Officers Assn., Army and Navy Club, Downtown Club. Independent. Roman Catholic. Avocations: reading, travel. E-mail address: jamesd@badgerlaw.com. Personal injury, Insurance, Product liability. Office: Badger Dolan Parker Cohen 2 Oliver St Boston MA 02109-4901

**DOLAN, JAMES VINCENT,** lawyer; b. Washington, Nov. 11, 1938; s. John Vincent and Philomena Theresa (Vance) D.; m. Anne McSherry Reilly, June 18, 1960; children: Caroline McSherry, James Reilly. AB, Georgetown U., 1960, LLB, 1963. Bar: U.S. Dist. Ct. 1963, U.S. Ct. Appeals (D.C.) cir. 1964, U.S. Ct. Appeals (4th cir.) 1976. Law clk. U.S. Ct. Appeals D.C., 1963-64; assoc. Steptoe & Johnson, Washington, 1964-71, ptnr., 1971-82; mem. Steptoe & Johnson Chartered, Washington, 1982-83; v.p. law Union Pacific R.R., Omaha, 1983—. Co-author: Construction Contract Law, 1981; contbr. articles to legal jours.; editor-in-chief: Georgetown Law Jour., 1962-63. Mem. ABA, Nebr. Bar Assn., D.C. Bar Assn., Barristers, Congl. Country Club (v.p. 1982, pres. 1983), Omaha Country Club. Republican. Roman Catholic. General corporate, Public utilities, Federal civil litigation. Home: 1909 County Road 8 Yutan NE 68073-5013 Office: Union Pacific RR 1416 Dodge St Omaha NE 68179-0002

**DOLAN, JOHN F.,** lawyer; b. Cleve., Oct. 19, 1925; s. John Francis and Lillian Marie (Courtad) D.; m. Rose M. Fitzsimmons, June 13, 1953 (dec.); children: Patricia Ann, John Patrick, Mary Bridget, Margaret Mary, Ann Marie, Kathleen Marie, Michael Anthony, Daniel Joseph. AB, Harvard U., 1947; JD, LLB, Western Res. U., 1949. Asst. dir. law City of Cleve., 1951-56, chief of litigation, 1955-56; dir. law City of Shaker Heights, Ohio, 1956-57; asst. gen. atty. N.Y.C., Penn Cen. Conrail, Cleve., 1957-78; sole practice Cleve., 1978—. Served to lt. (j.g.) USN, 1943-46. Mem. Ohio State Bar Assn., Cleve. Bar Assn. Democrat. Roman Catholic. General civil litigation, Federal civil litigation, State civil litigation. Home: 6038 Magnolia Stedman Rd Mayville NY 14757-9620

**DOLAN, LOUIS EDWARD, SR.,** lawyer, insurance company executive; b. Youngstown, Ohio, Feb. 29, 1920; s. William Patrick Dolan and Anna Walberga Holl; m. Jacqueline Le Mortland; children: Patrick Louis, Amy Jane Tychsen, Louis Edward Jr., Paul William. BA, Youngstown Coll., 1943; DL, Case We. Res., 1947. Bar: Ohio, Minn. Ptnr. Horace Andrews & Dolan, Cleve., 1948-57; gen. counsel The Ohio Co., Columbus, 1957-62; exec. v.p. Nationwide Corp., Columbus, 1962-65; pres. John Alden Life Ins. Co. subs. Gamble-Skogmo, Mpls., 1968-77; vice chair bd., gen. counsel Gamble-Skogmo, Mpls., 1977-79; exec. v.p., pres. and chair acceleration U.S. Life Corp. N.Y.C., Dublin, Ohio, 1979-88; ret., 1988; dir. subs. Nationwide, Gamble-Skogam, Capital Sq. Cols., Pk. Loan Co., others, 1957-87. Contbr. articles to profl. jours. Capt. U.S. Army, 1943-45. Republican. Avocations: flying, jogging, fishing, motor boats, travelling. Home: 3374 Gunston Rd Alexandria VA 22302-2133

**DOLAN, PATRICK DANIEL,** lawyer; b. N.Y.C., Apr. 28, 1961; s. Patrick A. and Sarah A. Dolan; m. Marie Whelan, June 9, 1990; children: Elizabeth, Rebecca. BA, Swarthmore Coll., 1983; JD, U. Chgo., 1987. Bar: N.Y. 1988. Assoc. Simpson Thacher & Bartlett, N.Y.C., 1987-90, Weil Gotshal & Manges, N.Y.C., 1990-96; ptnr. Dechert Price & Rhoads, N.Y.C., 1998—, of counsel, 1996-98. Contbr. articles to profl. jours. Finance, Contracts commercial. Office: Dechert Price & Rhoads 30 Rockefeller Plz Fl 23 New York NY 10112-0002

**DOLAN, THOMAS JOSEPH,** judge; b. Bronx, N.Y., Oct. 24, 1943; s. Joseph William and Helen Winnifred (Hannigan) D.; m. Barbara Louise Nuesell, Apr. 6, 1968; children—Claire Jean, Claudia Barbara. B.S., Fordham U., 1965; J.D., St. John's U., 1968. Bar: N.Y. 1968, U.S. Ct. Mil. Appeals 1969, U.S. Dist. Ct. (so. and ea. dists.) N.Y. 1975, U.S. Supreme Ct. 1980. Asst. dist. atty. Office of Dist. Atty. Dutchess County, Poughkeepsie, N.Y., 1973-92, county court judge, Dutchess County, 1993—. Served to capt. JAGC, U.S. Army, 1968-73, Vietnam. Decorated Bronze Star (2), Army Commendation medal (2). Mem. N.Y. State Bar Assn., Dutchess County Bar Assn. Republican. Roman Catholic. Clubs: So. Dutchess Exchange (Fishkill, N.Y.). Home: Neville Rd Wappingers Falls NY 12590 Office: County Court 10 Market St Ste 7 Poughkeepsie NY 12601-3233

**DOLCE, JULIA WAGNER,** lawyer; b. West Palm Beach, Fla., Aug. 13, 1959; d. Arthur Ward and Ruth Alice (Shingler) W. BSBA, So. Meth. U., 1980; JD, Marquette U., 1985. Bar: Wis. 1985, U.S. Dist. Ct. (ea. and we. dists.) Wis. 1985, Fla. 1989, U.S. Dist. Ct. (so. and mid. dists.) Fla. 1990, U.S. Supreme Ct. 1993. Atty. Marcus Corp., Milw., 1986-88; judicial asst. Fla. State Ct. Appeals (4th dist.), West Palm Beach, Fla., 1989; ptnr. Wagner, Nugent, Johnson & McAfee, West Palm Beach, 1990-95; atty. pvt. practice, West Palm Beach, 1995—. Bd. dirs. Hope House of the Palm Beaches, West Palm Beach, 1993-97. Avocation: reading. General civil litigation, Personal injury, Probate.

**DOLEAC, CHARLES BARTHOLOMEW,** lawyer; b. New Orleans, Sept. 20, 1947; s. Cyril Bartholomew and Emma Elizabeth (St. Clair) D.; m. Denise Kilfoyle, Feb. 2, 1972; children: Keith Gabriel, Jessa Lee. BS cum laude, U. N.H., 1968; JD, NYU, 1971. Bar: Mass. 1972, N.H. 1972, Maine 1973. Law clk. to Justice Grimes N.H. Supreme Ct., Concord, 1972-73; assoc. Boynton, Waldron, Dill & Aeschliman, Portsmouth, N.H., 1973-76; ptnr. Boynton, Waldron, Doleac, Woodman & Scott, Portsmouth, 1977—; appointed mediator N.H. Superior Ct., 1992—; del. to tour Chinese legal system Chinese Ministry Justice, 1982; del. to People's Republic of China/U.S. joint session on trade investments and econ. law Chinese Ministry Justice/U.S. Dept. Justice, Beijing, 1987; propr. Portsmouth Athenaeum; moderator seminars on ethics for Leaders & Comparative Cultures and Values/East & West Aspen Inst., 1990-95, 97-98; mem. faculty Southwestern Legal Found. Ctr. for Law Enforcement Ethics, 1993—; adv. bd. mem. Southwestern Law Enforcement Inst., 1995—; mem. faculty Southwestern Legal Found. Internat. & Comparative Law Ctr., 1997—; official guest Fgn. Ministry Japan, Tokyo, 1998. Contbr. articles to profl. jours. Mem. citizens adv. coun. Portsmouth Cmty. Devel. Program, 1976-77; incorporator N.H. Charitable Found.; pres., bd. dirs. Seacoast United Way; chmn. Portsmouth Bd. Bldg. Appeals, 1976-77; chmn. stewardship com. Soc. Preservation New Eng. Antiquities, 1980-84, also trustee; pres. bd. trustees Strawbery Banke Mus., 1985-88; founder Daniel Webster Inn of Ct., 1993, Charles C. Doe Inn of Ct., 1994, Portsmouth Peace Treaty Forum, 1994; founder, pres. Japan-Am. Soc. N.H., 1988. NEH fellow, Aspen Inst.; named Citizen of Yr. Portsmouth, N.H., 1991. Fellow N.H. Bar Found; mem. ATLA, Mass. Bar Assn., Maine Bar Assn., N.H. Bar Assn., N.H. Trial Lawyers Assn., Maine Trial Lawyers Assn. Avocations: masters swimming. Contracts commercial, General civil litigation. Home: Little Harbor Rd Portsmouth NH 03801 Office: Boynton Waldron Doleac Woodman & Scott PA 82 Court St Portsmouth NH 03801-4414

**DOLIN, LONNY H.,** lawyer; b. Youngstown, Ohio, Jan. 24, 1954; d. Lawrence Joseph and Sonya (Sacks) Heselov ; m. Gordon S. Black, Aug. 20, 1988; children: Nathaniel, Brooke, Aaron, Benjamin, Lindsay. AB, Georgetown U., 1976; JD, Cath. U., 1979. Bar: Vt. 1980, N.Y. State Bar 1984, U.S. Dist. Ct. (we. dist.) N.Y. 1984. Assoc. Downs, Rachlin & Martin, Burlington, Vt., 1979-81; pvt. practice Burlington, 1981-84; assoc., then ptnr. Harris, Beach, Wilcox, Rubin & Levey, Rochester, N.Y., 1984-90; ptnr. Harris, Beach & Wilcox, Rochester, N.Y., 1990—; of counsel to U.S. Congressman Fred J. Eckert, N.Y.; bd. dirs. Monroe County Legal Services Corp. Mem. Pittsford Town and County Com., N.Y., 1983—, Town of Pittsford Bd. of Zoning Appeals, N.Y., 1984—, vice chair 1990; chmn. Monroe County Comparable Worth Task Force, Rochester, 1985—, Fred J. Eckert Women's Adv. Council, Rochester, 1985—; del. The Jud. Dist. N.Y., Rochester, 1985—, chair 1990; bd. dirs. Nat. Council Jewish Women. Recipient Corpus Juris Secundum award West Pub. co., 1979. Mem. ABA, Vt. Bar Assn., N.Y. Bar Assn., Monroe County Bar Assn. (mem. practice and perf. com.), Greater Rochester Women's Bar Assn. (treas. 1986), Assn. Trial Lawyers Am., N.Y. State Trial Lawyers Assn., Genesee Valley Trial Lawyers Assn. (treas. 1990). Republican. Avocations: golf, skiing, tennis. State civil litigation, Federal civil litigation, Personal injury. Home: 9 Hidden Springs Dr Pittsford NY 14534-2897 Office: Harris Beach & Wilcox 130 Main St E Rochester NY 14604-1687

**DOLINER, NATHANIEL LEE,** lawyer; b. Daytona Beach, Fla., June 28, 1949; s. Joseph and Asia (Shaffer) D.; m. Debra Lynn Simon, June 5, 1983. BA, George Washington U., 1970; JD, Vanderbilt U., 1973; LLM in Taxation, U. Fla., 1977. Bar: Fla. 1973, U.S. Tax Ct. 1973, U.S. Dist. Ct. (mid. dist.) Fla. 1974. Assoc. Smalbein, Eubank, Johnson, Rosier & Bussey, P.A., Daytona Beach, Fla., 1973-76; vis. asst. prof. law U. Fla., Gainesville, 1977-78; assoc. Carlton, Fields, Ward, Emmanuel, Smith & Cutler, P.A., Tampa, Fla., 1978-82; shareholder Carlton, Fields, Ward, Emmanuel, Smith & Cutler, P.A., Tampa, 1982—, chmn. corp. and securities dept., 1984-96, treas., 1985-86, co-chair bus. transactions dept., 1996-98, chair bus. transactions dept., 1998—; spkr. NYU Real Estate Tax Inst., 1989, 94, Advanced Tax Inst., Balt., 1994, ABA Presdl. Showcase Programs ABA Ann. Conv., 1993-96; co-chmn., spkr. ABA mergers and Acquisitions Inst., N.Y.C., 1996 2d Ann. Inst. Negotiating Bus. Acquisitions, Chgo., 1997, 3d Ann. Inst., New Orleans, 1998. Adv. bd. Mergers and Acquisitions Law Report. Bd. dirs. Big Bros./Big Sisters Greater Tampa, Inc., 1980-82, Child Abuse Coun., Inc., 1986-95, asst. treas., 1987-88, treas., 1988-89, pres.-elect 1989-90, pres., 1990-91; dist. commr. Gulf Ridgecoun. Boy Scouts Am., 1983; bd. dirs. Tampa Jewish Fedn. Bd., 1988-91, Mus. Sci. and Industry, Tampa, 1994—, exec. com., 1994—, sec. 1995-97, first vice chair, 1997—; mem. alumni bd. Vanderbilt Law Sch., 1998—, bd. dirs., exec. com. Hillel Sch. Tampa, 1998—, first vice chair, 1999—. Fellow Am. Bar Found., Am. Coll. Tax Counsel; mem. ABA tax sect. (vice chmn. continuing legal education com. 1986-88, chmn. 1988-90, mem. bus. law sect. com. negotiated acquisitions, vice chair 1997-98, chair 1998—, chmn. task force preliminary and ancillary agreements, 1992-95, mem. acquisition rev. subcom. 1992-95, chair program letters of intent in bus. transactions 1993, chair programs subcom. 1995-98, exec. com. 1995—, co-chair program mergers of for-profit and not-for-profit hosps. 1996, spkr. not for profit corps. 1997), Am. Law Inst., Fla. Bar Assn. (mem. exec. coun. tax sect. 1980-83, tax cert. com. 1987-88, vice chair 1988-89, chair 1989-90), Greater Tampa C. of C. (chmn. Ambassadors Target Task Force of Com. of 100 1984-85, 87-88, chair geographic task force 1989-90, vice chmn. govt. fin. and taxation coun. 1987-88, chmn. 1988-89, bd. govs. 1990-93, exec. com. 1992, chmn. govtl. affairs dept., 1992), Anti-Defamation League (regional bd. mem. 1986-90, exec. com. 1987-90), Tampa Club (bd. dirs. 1987-92, sec. 1987-89, pres. 1990-91). Mergers and acquisitions, Taxation, general, General corporate. Home: 13341 Golf Crest Cir Tampa FL 33624-4648 Office: Carlton Fields Ward Emmanuel Smith & Cutler PA Ste 500 777 S Harbour Island Blvd Tampa FL 33602-5729

**DOLLARS, ROBERT ALAN,** lawyer; b. Indpls., May 12, 1961; s. B.D. and Anna S. (Schofield) D.; m. Margaret A. Johnson, Feb. 29, 1992. BA (hons.), Univ. Tex., 1983, JD, 1986. Bar: Tex. 1986. Assoc. Small, Craig & Werkentuin, Austin, Tex., 1986-88, Flahive, Ogden & Latson, Austin, Tex., 1988—. Office: Flahive Ogden & Latson PO Box 13367 Austin TX 78711-3367

**DOLLIVER, JAMES MORGAN,** retired state supreme court justice; b. Ft. Dodge, Iowa, Oct. 13, 1924; s. James Isaac and Margaret Elizabeth (Morgan) D.; m. Barbara Babcock, Dec. 18, 1948; children: Elizabeth, James, Peter, Keith, Jennifer, Nancy. BA in Polit. Sci. with high honors, Swarthmore Coll., 1949; LLB, U. Wash., 1952; D in Liberal Arts (hon.), U. Puget Sound, 1981. Bar: Wash. 1952. Clk. to presiding justice Wash. Supreme Ct., 1952-53; pvt. practice Port Angeles, Wash., 1953-54, Everett, Wash., 1961-64; adminstrv. asst. to Congressman Jack Westland, 1955-61, Gov. Daniel J. Evans, 1965-76; justice Supreme Ct. State of Wash., 1976-99, chief justice, 1985-87; adj. prof. U. Puget Sound Sch. Law, 1988-92. Chmn. United Way Campaign Thurston County, 1975; chmn. Wash. chpt. Nature Conservancy, 1981-83; pres. exec. bd. Tumwater Area coun. Boy Scouts Am., 1972-73, Wash. State Capital Hist. Assn., 1976-80, 85—, also trustee, 1983-84; trustee Deaconess Children's Home, Everett, 1963-65, U. Puget Sound, 1969—, chair exec. com., 1990-93, Wash. 4-H Found., 1977-93, Claremont (Calif.) Theol. Sem., assoc. mem., Community Mental Health Ctr., 1977-84; bd. mgrs. Swarthmore Coll., 1980-84; bd. dirs. Thurston Mason Community Health Ctr., 1977-84, Thurston Youth Svcs. Soc., 1969-84, also pres., 1983, mem. exec com. 1970-84, Wash. Women's Employment and Edn., 1982-84; mem. jud. coun. United Meth. Ch., 1984-92, gen. cong., 1970-72, 80—, gen. bd. ch. and soc., 1976-84; adv. coun. Ret. Sr. Vol. program, 1979-83; pres. Wash. Ctr. Law-related Edn., 1987-89, bd. dirs. 1987-95; bd. dirs. World Assn. for Children and Parents, 1987-93; trustee U. Wash. Law Sch. Found., 1982-90, Olympic Park Inst., 1988-94; mem. bd. visitors U. Wash. Sch. Social Work, 1987-93; chair bd. visitors U. Puget Sound Sch. Law, 1988-90, bd. visitors, 1988-93; chmn. bd. dirs. Pub. Lands Employee Recognition Fund, 1994—; mem. bd. dirs. St. Peter Hosp. Med. Rehab. Community Adv. Bd., 1993—. With USN, 1943-45; ensign USCG, 1945-46. Recipient award Nat. Council Japanese Am. Citizens League, 1976; Silver Beaver award, 1971; Silver Antelope award, 1976. Mem. ABA, Wash. Bar Assn., Am. Judges Assn., Am. Judicature Soc., Pub. Broadcast Found. (bd. dirs. 1982-95), Masons, Rotary, Phi Delta Theta, Delta Theta Phi.

**DOLSON, EDWARD M.,** lawyer; b. Kansas City, Mo., Sept. 21, 1939; s. Ralph H. and Elinor M. Dolson; m. Kay M. Clancy, Aug. 10, 1963; children: Michael, Patricia, Jennifer. BSBA, U. Kans., 1960; JD, U. Mich., 1963. Bar: N.Y. 1963, N.Y. Dist. Ct. (so. dist.) N.Y., Mo. 1966, U.S. Dist. Ct. (we. dist.) Mo., U.S. Dist. Ct. (ctrl. dist.) Wis., U.S. Ct. Claims, U.S. Ct. Appeals (7th, 8th and 10th cirs.). Assoc. Reid & Priest, N.Y.C., 1963-66; ptnr. Dietrich, Davis et al, Kansas City, Mo., 1966-90, Armstrong, Teasdale et al, Kansas City, 1990-92, Smith, Gill et al, Kansas City, 1992-95, Swanson, Midgley, Gangwere, Kitchin & McLarney LLC, Kansas City, 1995—. Co-author: Missouri Corporate Forms Practice, 1981; contbg. author: Missouri Bar Supplement, 1981, Speaker ABA Forum on Franchising, 1988. Chmn. Alliance for Safer Met. Kansas City, 1971-73; fin. chmn. Visitation Ch., Kansas City, 1993; mem. fin. com., bd. dirs. St. Joseph Health Ctr., Kansas City, 1989-92; tutor Laubach Lit. Soc., Kansas City, 1998. Mem. Lawyers Assn. Kansas City (pres. 1991), mem. Found. (pres. 1992), Kansas City Met. Bar Assn. (chmn. franchise law com. 1983-87), Heartland Franchise Assn. (founder, bd. dirs. 1989—), U. Mich. Club Kansas City (pres. 1974-77). Banking, Franchising, Mergers and acquisitions. Office: Swanson Midgley Gangwere Kitchin & McLarney LLC 1500 Commerce Trust Bldg 2420 Pershing Rd Ste 400 Kansas City MO 64108-2505

**DOLT, FREDERICK CORRANCE,** lawyer; b. Louisville, Oct. 10, 1929; s. O. Frederick and Margaret A. (Corrance) D.; m. Lucy M. Voelker, Dec. 8, 1960; 1 child, Frederick C. Jr. JD, U. Louisville, 1952. Bar: Ky. 1952, U.S. Ct. Appeals (6th cir.) 1965, U.S. Supreme Ct. 1972, La. 1982. Assoc. Morris & Garlove, Louisville, 1955-59; sole practice Louisville, 1959-70, 79—; ptnr. Leibson, Dolt & McCarthy, Louisville, 1970-73. Mem. Inner Circle Advocates, 1981. Served with U.S. Army, 1953-55. Mem. ABA, Ky. Bar Assn. (chmn. ins. negligence sect. 1968-70, mem. Ho. of Dels. 1970-80), Assn. Trial Lawyers Am. (state del. 1965-70), Ky. Trial Lawyers Assn. (pres. 1970). Republican. Presbyterian. Avocation: golf. Federal civil litigation, State civil litigation. Home: 19634 Lost Creek Dr Fort Myers FL 33912-5539 Office: 310 Starks Bldg Louisville KY 40202

**DOMALAKES, PAUL GEORGE,** lawyer; b. Frackville, Pa., Mar. 21, 1951; s. John George and Sara Jane (Wetzel) D.; m. Patricia Marie Kiefer, Oct. 5, 1985; children: Meredith Ann, Ann Patricia, Paul Luke, Madeline Claire. BA, Allentown Coll., 1973; JD, Dickinson Coll., 1976. Bar: Supreme Ct. Pa. 1976, U.S. Dist. Ct. (ea. dist.) Pa. 1977, U.S. Supreme Ct. 1992. Ptnr. Rubright, Domalakes, Troy & Miller, Frackville, 1980—. Pres. bd. dirs. Intermediate Unit No. 29 Bldg. Authority, Marlin, Pa., 1983—; dir. Annunciation B.V.M. Ch. Choir, Frackville, 1984—; bd. dirs., founding mem. Pa. Shakespeare Festival. Mem. Pa. Bar Assn. Republican. Roman Catholic. Workers' compensation, General practice, Criminal. Office: Rubright Domalakes Troy & Miller PO Box 9 Frackville PA 17931-0009

**DOMBROWSKI, GERALD MICHAEL,** lawyer; b. Chgo., Aug. 1, 1964; s. Leo Joseph and Mary Cecelia D.; m. Pamela A. Dombrowski. BA in Sociology and Polit. Sci., U. Ill., 1986; JD, Ill. Inst. Tech., 1992. Bar: Ill., U.S. Dist. Ct. (no. dist.) Ill. Asst. state's atty. Lake County, Waukegan, Ill., 1992-96; assoc. Sanchez & Daniels, Chgo., 1996—; arbitrator Cook County Dist., Chgo., 1997—. State civil litigation, Insurance, General civil litigation. Office: Sanchez & Daniels 333 W Wacker Dr Ste 500 Chicago IL 60606-1225

**DOMBROWSKI, RAYMOND EDWARD, JR.,** lawyer; b. Phila., Aug. 27, 1954; s. Raymond Edward Sr. and Josephine Louise (DiBartolo) D.; m. Sylvia Ann Klinedinst, Oct. 27, 1984. BS, U.S. Merchant Marine Acad., Kings Point, N.Y., 1976; JD, Temple U., 1979, LLM in Taxation, 1982. Bar: Pa. 1979, N.J. 1979, U.S. Tax Ct. 1980. Tax atty. Schnader, Harrison, Segal & Lewis, Phila., 1979-85, Bell Atlantic Corp., Phila., 1985-86; exec. v.p., counsel Bell Atlantic Capital Corp., Phila., 1987—; counsel, treasury and fin. matters Bell Atlantic NSI, 1994-97; gen. atty., fin. Bell Atlantic Group, N.Y.C., 1997—. Lt. USNR, 1976-82. Mem. ABA, Pa. Bar Assn., Phila. Bar Assn., Riverton Country Club. Republican. Roman Catholic. Avocations: golf, sailing. Corporate taxation, Finance, Mergers and acquisitions. Home: 120 Glenwood Rd Haddonfield NJ 08033-3427 Office: Bell Atlantic Capital Corp 1717 Arch St Fl 32 Philadelphia PA 19103-2713

**DOMENICO, CALVIN J., JR.,** lawyer; b. Rome, N.Y., Aug. 8, 1951; s. Calvin J. Sr. and Mary (DeSimone) D.; m. Nancy MacDougall, Aug. 17, 1974; children: Carrie M., Aimee E., Calvin J. III. AAS, Jefferson C.C., Watertown, N.Y., 1971; BS, Rochester Inst. Tech., 1973; JD, Ohio No. U., 1976. Bar: N.Y. 1977, U.S. Dist. Ct. (no. dist.) N.Y. 1978, Fla. 1988. Assoc. Russo Law Offices, Rome, N.Y., 1977-80; ptnr. Russo & Domenico, Rome, 1980-85; pvt. practice Rome, 1985—. Mem. Am. Trial Lawyers Assn., Fla. Bar Assn. Criminal, Family and matrimonial, Personal injury. Office: 1919 Black River Blvd N Rome NY 13440-2446

**DOMINGUE, C. DEAN,** patent attorney; b. Lafayette, La., July 26, 1957; s. Fred Allen and Marie Louise (Angelle) D.; m. M. Denise Broussard, May 1, 1981; children: Angelle Marie, Simone Justine. BS in Petroleum Engring., U. Southwestern La., 1980; JD, La. State U., 1987. Bar: La. 1987, U.S. Dist. Ct. (we. and ea. dists.) La., U.S. Patent and Trademark 1989. Reservoir and prodn. engr. Marathon Oil Co., Lafayette, La., 1980-84; rsch. asst. Mineral Law Inst. La. State U., Baton Rouge, 1985-86; litigation assoc. Voorhies & Labbe, Lafayette, 1986-90; sr. patent atty. Halliburton Corp., Duncan, Okla., 1990-92; patent litigating atty. Roy, Kiesel, Aaron & Tucker, Baton Rouge, 1992-93; patent counsel Baker Hughes INTEQ, Houston, 1993-94; sr. ptnr. Domingue & Delaune, Lafayette, 1994—. Mem. ABA, La. Bar Assn. (editor The Promulgator 1994-95), bd. dirs.), Lafayette Bar Assn., Lafayette C. of C., Houston Intellectual Property Law Assn., Soc. Petroleum Engrs. (instr. oil and gas law), Am. Intellectual Property Law Assn., U. Southwestern La. Alumni Assn., La. State U. Alumni Assn. Democrat. Roman Catholic. Avocations: sailing, tennis. Patent, Trademark and copyright, Intellectual property. Office: Domingue & Delaune 1003 Hugh Wallis Rd Ste I Lafayette LA 70508-2528

**DOMINGUEZ, A(L) M(ANUEL), JR.,** prosecutor; b. San Juan, P.R., Mar. 12, 1943; s. A.M. Dominguez and Olga (Berrios) Winston; children: Steven Kline, Angelica M., Adrian N., Paul A. BA, Fresno State Coll., 1968; JD, U. Colo., 1971. Bar: Colo. 1971, U.S. Dist. Ct. Colo. 1971. Computer programmer Continental Tel. Co., Bakersfield, Calif., 1966-68; pvt. practice Greeley, Colo., 1971-88; dist. atty. 19th Jud. Dist. Colo., Greeley, 1988—; mem. nominating com. 19th Jud. Dist. Colo., 1978-82; grader Colo. Bar Exam, 1978-83; mem. sentencing subcom. Colo. Criminal Justice Commn., 1991—. Actor, Independence Stampede Troupe, 1983—, Greeley Civic Theatre, 1983—. Mem. Civil Svc. Commn., City of Greeley, 1978-82; pres. Child Abuse Prevention, Inc., 1978-82, Parent Child Learning Ctr., 1982-84, Rehab. and Vis. Nurses Assn. Weld County, 1981-84; chmn. Dist. 6 Hispanic Employment Task Force, 1986-88; bd. dirs. No. Colo. Med. Ctr. Found., 1986-92; mem. sexual assault task force U. No. Colo., 1989—, mem. drug and alcohol awareness task force, 1990; active United Way, other civic orgns.; Colo. co-chairperson Lawyers for Pres. Bush, 1992. With USAF, 1961-65. Mem. ABA, APHA, Colo. Bar Assn. (bd. govs. 1993—), Colo. Dist. Attys. Assn. (treas. 1993—, pres. 1995), Weld County Bar Assn. (pres. young lawyers divsn. 1975), Nat. Dist. Attys. Assn., Rotary, Weld/Greeley C. of C. (bd. dirs. 1990—). Republican. Roman Catholic. Avocations: community theater, river rafting, photography, physical fitness. Office: 19th Jud Dist Colo PO Box 1167 Greeley CO 80632-1167

**DOMINGUEZ, DANIEL R.,** judge; b. 1945. BA, Boston U., 1967; LLB cum laude, U. P.R., 1970. Bar: P.R. Atty. Hector M. Laffitte Law Offices, 1970-72; ptnr. Laffitte, Dominguez & Totti, 1973-84, Dominguez & Totti, 1983-94; judge U.S. Dist. Ct. P.R., San Juan, 1994—; gov. Adv. Com. on Labor Policy, 1984; mem. bd. Fed. Bar Examiners U.S. Dist. Ct. P.R., 1989-94, mem. Civil Justice Reform Act Adv. Group, 1991-94; mem. merit selection com. for Appointment of U.S. Magistrate Judges, 1993; mem. com. for jud. reform Gov. P.R., 1993-94. Mem. Berwind Country Club, Hyatt Dorado Beach Country Club. Office: US Dist Ct PR US Courthouse CH-129 150 Ave Carlos Chardon San Juan PR 00918-1703

**DOMINICK, PAUL ALLEN,** lawyer; b. Orangeburg, S.C., Feb. 13, 1954; s. Allen Etheredge and Ruby Estelle (Pardue) D.; m. Sharon Norment, May 15, 1982. BA, U. S.C., 1976; JD, Washington & Lee U., 1979. Bar: S.C. 1979, U.S. Dist. Ct. S.C. 1980, U.S. Ct. Appeals (4th cir.) 1982. Assoc. Nexsen, Pruet, Jacobs & Pollard, Columbia, S.C., 1979-85, ptnr., 1985-87; ptnr. Nexsen, Pruet, Jacobs, Pollard & Robinson, Charleston, S.C., 1987—. Bd. dirs., Columbia Forum; bd. dirs., participant Leadership Columbia-Columbia C. of C., 1986. Mem. ABA (chair bus. torts com. and ins. practice sect 1995-96), S.C. Bar Assn., S.C. Def. Trial Attys. Assn., Richland County Bar Assn., Columbia Forum, Com. of 100, Columbia 100 (pres. 1983-84), Sertoma (pres. 1987-88), Phi Beta Kappa. Presbyterian. Federal civil litigation, State civil litigation, Securities. Home: 1548 Strathmore Ln Mount Pleasant SC 29464-8164 Office: Nexsen Pruet Jacobs Pollard & Robinson PO Box 486 Charleston SC 29402-0486

**DOMINIK, JACK EDWARD,** lawyer; b. Chgo., July 9, 1924; s. Ewald Arthur and Gertrude Alene (Crotzer) D.; children: Paul, David, Georgia Lee, Elizabeth, Sarah, Clare. BSME with distinction, Purdue U., 1947; JD, Northwestern U., 1950. Bar: Ill. 1950, U.S. Patent Office 1953, Wis. 1959, Fla. 1964, U.S. Dist. Ct. (ea. dist.) Wis. 1959, U.S. Supreme Ct. 1965, U.S. Dist. Ct. (no. dist.) Ohio 1962, U.S. Dist. Ct. (so. dist.) Ill. 1965, U.S. Ct. Appeals (7th and 9th cirs.) 1965, U.S. Ct. Appeals (4th cir.) 1973, U.S. Dist. Ct. (so. dist.) Fla. 1974, U.S. Ct. Appeals (5th cir.) 1977, U.S. Dist. Ct. (mid. dist.) Fla. 1979, U.S. Ct. Appeals (fed. cir.) 1983, U.S. Ct. Appeals (11th cir.) 1984, U.S. Ct. Appeals (2d cir.) 1987. Assoc. Carlson, Pitzner, Hubbard & Wolfe, Chgo., 1950-54; ptnr. Ooms and Dominik, Chgo., 1954-59, White & Hirshboeck, Milw., 1959-62; ptnr. Dominik, Knechtel, DeMeur & Samlan, Chgo., 1962-78, Miami, Fla., 1978—. Served to 1st lt., C.E. AUS, 1943-46, ETO. Mil. govt. judge, 1945-46. Mem. ABA, Wis. Bar Assn., Fla. Bar Assn., Chgo. Bar Assn., Am. Patent Law Assn., Chgo. Patent Law Assn. (chmn. taxation com. 1966, 69-70), Milw. Patent Law Assn., Patent Law Assn. So. Fla. (founder, dir. 1982—, past pres.), Chgo. Yacht Club, Union League Club, Tau Beta Pi, Pi Tau Sigma, Tau Kappa Alpha. Avocation: flying. Federal civil litigation, Intellectual property, Private international. Home: 14751 Lewis Rd Miami Lakes FL 33014-2731 Office: 6175 NW 153rd St Hialeah FL 33014-2435

**DONA, NOREEN,** lawyer; b. Webster, Mass., June 17, 1961; d. George William and Mary Phil (Viley) D. BS, Quinnipiac Coll., Hamden, Conn., 1983; JD, Southwestern Sch. Law, L.A., 1990. Sr. tax acct. Far West Savs. & Loan Assn., Newport Beach, Calif., 1985-87; tax specialist KPMG Peat Marwick, Long Beach, Calif., 1990-92; pvt. practice Huntington Beach, Calif., 1992—; vol. atty. L.A. County Bar AIDS Project, L.A. and Orange County, 1993, Pub. Law Ctr., Santa Ana, Calif., 1993; mediator Cmty. Svc. Programs, Inc., Irvine, Calif., 1992-94. Lit. vol. Lit. Vols. Am., Huntington Beach, Calif., 1992-93; U.S. probation officer, Santa Ana, Calif., 1997—. Mem. Orange County Bar Assn. Avocations: snow skiing, reading, bicycling. Office: 18685 Main St Ste A276 Huntington Beach CA 92648-1723

**DONAHEY, RICHARD STERLING, JR.,** lawyer, real estate broker; b. Cin., July 12, 1941; s. Richard Sterling Sr. and Martha (Magann) D.; m. Isabelle Harner, Dec. 7, 1963 (div. Dec. 1970); m. Patricia Geiger, Dec. 4, 1971; children: Richard III, John, Timothy. B in Engring., Ohio State U., 1965, JD, 1967. Bar: Ohio 1970. Engr. in tng. James Guthrie Assoc., Columbus, Ohio, 1965-68; ptnr. Twyford & Donahey, Columbus, 1968—; real estate broker Richard S. Donahey, Realtor, Columbus, 1975—; pres. Courthouse Sq. Properties, Inc., Columbus, 1970-88, Black Acre Farms, Inc., Columbus, 1977--, Brewer's Alley Restaurant, Columbus, 1980-89. Chmn. Ohio Young Dems., Columbus, 1965. With U.S. Army, 1959-60. Mem. Ohio Bar Assn. (com. chmn. 1970), Am. Trial Lawyers Assn., Am. Bd. Realtors, Ohio Acad. Trial Lawyers (com. chmn. 1969-72), Mensa, Farm Bur., Franklin County Trial Lawyers Assn. (officer 1972-73). Democrat. Presbyterian. Avocations: skiing, hiking, farming. Personal injury, Criminal, Family and matrimonial. Home: 393 Westland Ave Columbus OH 43209-1663 Office: Twyford & Donahey 495 S High St Columbus OH 43215-5058

**DONAHOE, DANIEL BRENNEN,** lawyer; b. Pitts., Apr. 3, 1960; s. Thomas Kernan and Anna Mae (Lawrence) D.; m. Virginia O'Friel; children: Erin, Lauren. BA, Carnegie Mellon U., 1982; JD, Duquesne U., 1990. Bar: Pa. 1990, U.S. Dist. Ct. (we. dist.) Pa. 1990. Organized crime info. specialist FBI, Pitts., 1983-90; atty. Burns, White & Hickton, Pitts., 1990—. Democat. Roman Catholic. Federal civil litigation, General civil litigation, State civil litigation. Home: 220 Bernice St Pittsburgh PA 15237-2235

**DONAHOE, PETER ALOYSIUS,** lawyer. BA in Polit. Sci., U. Wash., Seattle, 1957; JD, Harvard U., 1960. Bar: Hawaii 1961. Assoc. Carlsmith, Carlsmith, Wichman & Case, Hilo, Hawaii, 1960-63; staff Senate Majority Hawaii State Senate, Honolulu, 1963; dep. Atty. Gen. anti-trust divsn. State of Hawaii, Honolulu, 1963-65; asst. U.S. Atty. U.S. Dept. Justice, Honolulu, 1965-67; ptnr. Robertson, Castle & Anthony, Honolulu, 1967-71; pvt. practice Honolulu, 1973-91; dir. Atty.'s and Judge's Assistance Program Supreme Ct. for State of Hawaii, Honolulu, 1993—; vis. prof. polit. sci. Am. Coll. Switzerland, Leysan, 1971-73; chmn. liquor commn., City and County of Honolulu, 1969; lectr. Hawaii Inst. CLE. Contbr. articles to profl. jours. Mem. Hawaii State Bar Assn. Home: 47-516 Hui Iwa St Kaneohe HI 96744-4615

**DONAHOO, THOMAS MITCHELL,** lawyer; b. Jacksonville, Fla., Dec. 22, 1939; s. John William and Margaret Jeanne Donahoo; m. Hazel Elizabeth Harby, Aug. 4, 1962; children: Thomas Mitchell Jr., Elizabeth Earle. BSBA, U. Fla., 1962; JD, Samford U., 1965; LLM, NYU, 1966. Bar: Fla. 1965, Ala. 1965. Assoc. Donahoo & Rogers, Jacksonville, 1966-69, ptnr., 1969-81; shareholder, pres., atty. Donahoo Donahoo & Ball, Jacksonville, 1981-98, Donahoo Ball McMenamy & Johnson, Jacksonville, 1998—. Contbr. chpts. (book) Florida Corporate Practice, 1983. Trustee Jacksonville U., 1976—, Episcopal H.S. Found., 1992—. Fellow Am. Coll. Trust and estate Counsel; mem. Fla. Bar Assn. (chair tax sect. 1986-87, chair tax cert. 1990), Jacksonville Bar Assn. (tax sect. 1980). Episcopalian. Avocations: golf, hunting, fishing, travel, music. Estate taxation, Personal income taxation, Taxation, general. Home: 4364 Mcgirts Blvd Jacksonville FL 32210-5941 Office: Donahoo Ball McMenamy & Johnson PA 50 N Laura St Ste 2925 Jacksonville FL 32202-3677

**DONAHUE, CHARLES BERTRAND, II,** lawyer; b. Hampton, Iowa; s. Charles B. and Alta M. (Sykes) D.; m. Brenda K. Kumpf (div. Dec. 1980); children: Kaylie Elizabeth, Megan E. (dec.). AB, Harvard U., 1959; JD cum laude, Cleve. State U., 1967. Bar: Ohio, 1967, Fla., 1970. Commd. 2d lt. USAF, 1959, advanced through grades to capt., 1962, res., 1969; contracting officer USAF, McGuire AFB, N.J., 1959-62; subcontract adminstr. Westinghouse, Pitts., 1962-63; contract adminstr. TRW, Inc., Cleve., 1963-67; atty., ptnr. Calfee Halter & Griswold, Cleve., 1967-79; founder, ptnr. Donahue & Scanlon, Cleve., 1979—. Trustee Cleve. Artists Fuond., 1998; civil svc. commn. City Westlake, Ohio, 1995-96. Avocations: cooking, reading, travel. General corporate, Mergers and acquisitions, Estate planning. Home: 827 Brick Mill Run Westlake OH 44145-1602 Office: Donahue & Scanlon 3300 Terminal Tower Cleveland OH 44113

**DONAHUE, CHARLOTTE MARY,** lawyer; b. Columbus, Ohio, Sept. 29, 1954; d. Patrick Henry and Helen Dillon (Meany) D. AB, Holy Cross Coll., 1976; JD, U. Toledo, 1983. Bar: Pa. 1984, D.C. 1985, U.S. Dist. Ct. (ea. dist.) Pa. 1985, U.S. Ct. Appeals 3d cir.) 1985, U.S. Supreme Ct. 1990, Mass. 1992. Jud. clk. to presiding justice Commonwealth Ct. Pa., Phila., 1983-84; spl. asst. U.S. atty. U.S. Dist. Ct. (ea. dist.) Pa., Phila., 1987-90; atty. HUD, Phila., 1984-93, Boston, 1993—. Mem. Fed. Bar Assn., Pa. Bar Assn., Mass. Bar Assn., D.C. Bar Assn., Order of Barristers, Internat. Platform Assn., Supreme Ct. Hist. Soc. Home: 40 Meredith Cir Milton MA 02186-3916 Office: HUD Thomas P O'Neill Jr Fed Bldg 10 Causeway St Boston MA 02222-1092

**DONAHUE, JOHN EDWARD,** lawyer; b. Milw., Aug. 22, 1950; s. Joseph Robert and Helen Ann (Kelly) D.; m. Maureen Dolores Hart, Sept. 20, 1974; children: Timothy Robert Hart, Michael John Hart. BA with honors, Marquette U., 1972; JD, U. Wis., Madison, 1975. Bar: Wis. 1975, U.S. Dist. Ct. (we. and ea. dists.) Wis. 1975. Assoc. Weiss, Steuer, Berzowski and Kriger, Milw., 1975-80; ptnr. Weiss, Berzowski, Brady & Donahue LLP, Milw., 1981—; guest lectr. Marquette U. Law Sch., Milw., 1976-90; presenter programs Wis. Inst. CPAs, 1984—, Minn. Soc. CPAs, 1992—; expert witness The Best Lawyers in Am., 1995-96, 97-98, 99—. Past chmn. bd. trustees, past chmn. bd. dirs., past chmn. bd. govs., trustee, exec. com., com. chmn. Mt. Mary Coll., Milw., 1984—, past pres., bd. dirs. com. chmn. Met. Milw. Civic Alliance, 1980—, Children's Hosp. Found., Milw., 1984—; mem. steering com. Greater Milw. Initiative, 1989-92; v.p., bd. dirs. Future Milw., 1984-88; council bd., com. chmn., scoutmaster, Boy Scouts Am., 1990—. Recipient citation Milwaukee County Bd. Suprs., 1990, spl. svc. award Met. Milw. Civil Alliance, 1990, silver beaver award Boy Scouts Am., 1995; named outstanding instr. AICPA, 1991. Mem. ABA, Wis. Bar Assn., Milw. Bar Assn., Wis. Retirement Plan Profls., Greater Milw. Employee Benefits Coun., Kiwanis Club (pres. Milw. unit 1989-90, Outstanding Kiwanian 1989-97, Kiwanian of Yr. 1993). Pension, profit-sharing, and employee benefits, General corporate, General practice. Office: Weiss Berzowski Brady & Donahue LLP 700 N Water St Milwaukee WI 53202-4206

**DONAHUE, JOSEPH GERALD,** lawyer; b. Waterville, Maine, Oct. 16, 1951; s. Gerald L. and Gertrude (Poulin) D.; m. Rita P. Bouchard, Aug. 31, 1974; children: Kathryn, Joseph, James. AB, Bowdoin Coll., Brunswick, Maine, 1974; JD, Boston U., 1977. Bar: Mass.. 1977, Maine 1978, U.S. Dist. Ct. Maine 1978, U.S. Ct. Appeals (1st cir.) 1984, U.S. Supreme Ct. 1985, U.S. Ct. Appeals (D.C. cir.) 1986. Law clk. Maine Supreme Jud. Ct., Portland, 1978-79; atty. examiner Maine Pub. Utilities Commn., Augusta, 1979-82, gen. counsel, 1982-89; assoc. Preti, Flaherty, Beliveau, Pachios & Haley, Augusta, Maine, 1989-93, ptnr., 1994—. Mem. Fed. Comm. Bar Assn. Public utilities, Communications, FERC practice. Home: 74 Lincoln Ave Gardiner ME 04345-2518 Office: Preti Flaherty Beliveau Pachios & Haley 45 Memorial Cir Ste 2 Augusta ME 04330-6494

**DONAHUE, MICHAEL JOSEPH,** lawyer; b. Manchester, N.H., Dec. 28, 1947; s. Francis Lawler and Laura (Veroneau) D.; m. Diane Landry, May 26, 1973; children: Sarah, Kerry. AB, Holy Cross Coll., Worcester, Mass., 1970; JD, U. Pa., Phila., 1973. Bar: N.H. 1973, U.S. Dist. Ct. N.H. 1977, U.S. Ct. Appeals (1st cir.) 1982, U.S. Ct. Mil. Appeals 1991. Ptnr. Kearns, Colliander, Donahue & Tucker, P.A., Exeter, N.H., 1977-85, Donahue, Tucker & Ciandella, Exeter, 1985-91. Bd. dirs. Greater Seacoast United Way, 1985-92; v.p., sec., bd. trustees Strawberry Banke Mus., 1992-98. Capt. JAGC, USNR, 1970-98. Mem. ABA, N.H. Bar Assn. (bd. dirs. mcpl. law sect. 1984-86). Roman Catholic. E-mail: dtclawyers@aol.com. Land use and zoning (including planning), Environmental, Real property. Home: 8 Old Locke Rd North Hampton NH 03862-2236 Office: Donahue Tucker & Ciandella 225 Water St/PO Box 630 Exeter NH 03833-0630

**DONALD, NORMAN HENDERSON, III,** lawyer; b. Denver, Nov. 1, 1937; s. Norman Henderson Jr. and Angelene (Pell) D.; m. Alice Allen, Oct. 31, 1970 (div. Aug. 1980); children: Norman H. IV (dec.), Helen P.; m. Kathryn Akers, Sept. 26, 1981 (div. Jan. 1998). AB, Princeton U., 1959; LLB, Harvard U., 1962. Bar: N.Y. 1962. Assoc. Davis, Polk & Wardwell, N.Y.C., 1962-67; assoc. Skadden, Arps, Slate, Meagher & Flom, N.Y.C., 1967-68, ptnr., 1968-94; chmn. bd. dirs. Norwil Holdings, Inc., N.Y.C., Atlanta and Sarasota, Solarmax Corp., Sarasota. Mem. Assn. of Bar of City of N.Y., Practising Law Inst. (editor Reit Restructuring 1977—), St. Paul's Sch. Alumni Assn. (v.p., bd. dirs. 1984-86), Union Club (N.Y.C.), Racquet Club (N.Y.C.), Gold Creek Club (Dawsonville, Ga.). Republican. Episcopalian. General corporate. Home: Mistral Farms 1544 Bailey Waters Rd Dawsonville GA 30534-1807 Office: care Brock Fensterstock et al 153 E 53rd St New York NY 10022-4611

**DONALDSON, ARTHUR JOSEPH,** lawyer; b. N.Y.C., Mar. 29, 1938; s. Francis Leo and Mabel J. (Erckert) D.; children: Sheelagh, Shannon, Sean, Seamus; m. Nancy Donaldson. BA, Cath. U. Am., Washington, 1960, JD, 1963. Bar: D.C. 1965, N.C. 1966, U.S. Dist. Ct. (mid. dist.) N.C. 1967, U.S. Ct. Appeals (4th cir.) 1968, U.S. Supreme Ct. 1974. Spl. agt. FBI, 1963-67; pvt. practice law Salisbury, N.C., 1967-88; ptnr. Donaldson & Horsley, Greensboro, N.C., 1988—. Contbr. articles to profl. jours. Candidate N.C. Supreme Ct., 1986, 88. Mem. Nat. Lawyers Assn., Rep. Nat. Lawyers Assn., N.C. Rep. Lawyers Assn. (pres., founder 1981). Roman Catholic. Avocations: travel, woodworking, gardening, model trains. Personal injury, Product liability. Home: 1806 Northbay Dr Browns Summit NC 27214-9681 Office: Donaldson & Horsley PA 208 W Wendover Ave Greensboro NC 27401-1307

**DONALDSON, CRAIG JOHN,** lawyer; b. Princeton, N.J., Mar. 3, 1949; s. John Welsh and Gloria Tempest (Bonner) D.; m. Phyllis Ann Golden, July 28, 1978; children: Stephanie Ann, Craig John. BA in Polit. Sci., Farleigh Dickinson U., 1971; JD, U. Mo., Kansas City, 1975. Bar: Tenn. 1975, N.J. 1991, U.S. Dist. Ct. N.J. 1991, U.S. Dist. Ct. (we. and middle dist.) Tenn. 1975, U.S. Dist. Ct. (no. dist.) Miss. 1981, U.S. Ct. Appeals (8th cir.) 1980, U.S. Ct. Appeals (11th cir.) 1984, U.S. Ct. Appeals (6th cir.) 1985, U.S. Ct. Appeals (3d cir.) 1991, U.S. Supreme Ct. 1985. Assoc. Armstrong, Allen, Braden, Goodman et al., Memphis, 1975-78; ptnr. Heiskell, Donelson, Bearman et al, Memphis, 1978-86, Dearborn & Ewing, Nashville, Tenn., 1986-91; counsel Riker, Danzig, Scherer, Hyland & Perretti, Morristown, N.J., 1991—. Mem. ABA, Am. Bankruptcy Inst. Avocations: golf, antiques, reading. Bankruptcy, Contracts commercial, Federal civil litigation. Office: Riker Danzig Scherer Hyland & Perretti Hdqrs Pla One Speedwell Ave Morristown NJ 07962-1981

**DONALDSON, JOHN WEBER,** lawyer; b. Lebanon, Ind., Oct. 13, 1926; s. Fred R. and Esther Ann (Coombs) D.; m. Sara Jane Rudolph, Nov. 22, 1953; children: Carmen Donaldson Yanney, Catherine Donaldson Buckallew, J. Bradford. AB, DePauw U., 1951; JD, Ind. U., 1954. Bar: Ind. 1954, U.S. Dist. Ind. 1954, U.S. Supreme Ct. 1973. Sole practice law Lebanon, Ind., 1958-76; ptnr. Hutchinson & Donaldson, Lebanon, 1954-58, Donaldson & Andreoli, Lebanon, 1976-81, Donaldson, Andreoli & Truitt, Lebanon, 1982—; city atty. City of Lebanon, 1965-66; mem. Ind. Gen. Assembly, 1956-58, 60-92, criminal law study commn., 1969-89, commn. on trial cts., 1987-90; chmn. Gov.'s Task Force on Drunk Driving, 1982-88. Served with USN, 1944-49; ATO. Recipient Disting. Svc. award Jaycees, 1958, Boone County Citizen of Yr. award, 1992. Mem. ABA, Ind. Bar Assn., Boone County Bar Assn., Ind. Criminal Law Study Commn., Ind. Trial Lawyers Assn., Lebanon Jaycees, Ind. Def. Lawyers Assn., DAV, Am. Legion, Elks, Kiwanis (pres. 1964). Republican. Presbyterian. Avocation: tennis. State civil litigation, Family and matrimonial, Criminal. Address: 129 N Meridian St Lebanon IN 46052-2263

**DONALDSON, MICHAEL CLEAVES,** lawyer; b. Montclair, N.J., Oct. 13, 1939; s. Wyman C. and Ernestine (Greenwood) D.; m. Diana D., Sept. 12, 1969 (div. 1979); children: Michelle, Amy, Wendy; m. Mimi Schwied, Sept. 14, 1991. BS, U. Fla., 1961; JD, U. Calif., Berkeley, 1967. Bar: Calif. 1967, U.S. Dist. Ct. (cen. dist.) Calif. 1967, U.S. Ct. Appeals (9th cir.) 1967. Assoc. Harris & Hollingsworth, L.A., 1969-72; ptnr. McCabe & Donaldson, L.A., 1972-79; pvt. practice Law Office of M.C. Donaldson, L.A., 1979-90; ptnr. Dern & Donaldson, L.A., 1990-94, Berton & Donaldson, Beverly Hills, Calif., 1994—; lectr. in field; judge, preliminary and finalist judge Internat. Emmys; preliminary judge Night Time Emmys; gen. counsel Ind. Feature Project West, Internat. Documentary Assn. Author: EZ Legal Guide to Copyright and Trademark, 1995, (booklet) Something Funny Happened on the Way to Dinner, 1976; contg. author: Conversations with Michael Landon, 1992, Negotiating for Dummies, 1996, Clearance & Copyright What the Independent Filmmaker Needs to Know, 1997. Bd. dirs. Calif. Theatre Coun., L.A. 1st lt. USMC, 1961-64. Mem. ABA (entertainment and sports sect.), NATAS, Nat. Acad. Cable Broadcasting, Beverly Hills Bar Assn. (chmn. entertainment sect.), L.A. Copyright Soc. Republican. Avocations: photography, writing, gardening, hiking, skiing. Entertainment, Intellectual property. Home: 2074 Benedict Canyon Dr Beverly Hills CA 90210-1404 Office: Berton & Donaldson 9595 Wilshire Blvd Ste 711 Beverly Hills CA 90212-2507

**DONALDSON, STEVEN BRYAN,** lawyer; b. Vincennes, Ind., Sept. 23, 1963; s. Steve Donaldson and Lynne Raye (Wilson) Murray. BA, Ind. U., 1985, JD, 1988. Bar: Ind. 1988, U.S. Dist. Ct. (no. and so. dists.) Ind. 1988. Assoc. Berry Capper & Tulley, Crawfordsville, Ind., 1988-94; ptnr. Berry Capper Donaldson & Tulley, Crawfordsville, Ind., 1995-96; prin. S. Bryan Donaldson, Crawfordsville, Ind., 1997—. Judge teen ct. Youth Svc. Bur., Crawfordsville, 1993; chmn. bd. trustees 1st United Meth. Ch., Crawfordsville, 1994-97; mem. Montgomery County Cultural Found., Crawfordsville, 1994—. Mem. Ind. Bar Assn., Montgomery County Bar Assn., Kiwanis (bd. dirs. Crawfordsville 1992-94). Republican. Avocations: bowling, golf, spectator sports, reading. General practice, Consumer commercial, Family and matrimonial. Home: 1270 Lake Vista Dr Crawfordsville IN 47933-8940 Office: 134 W Main St Crawfordsville IN 47933-1718

**DONDANVILLE, PATRICIA,** lawyer; b. Anchorage, Alaska, Mar. 21, 1956; d. Leo John and Ann Louise (Mosey) D.; m. Emily Grace, Edward James. BA in Am. Studies, U. Notre Dame, 1978; JD, U. Va., 1981. Bar: Ill. 1981. Assoc. Schiff Hardin & Waite, Chgo., 1981-87, ptnr., 1988—. Bd. dirs. Nat. Ctr. for Laity, Chgo., 1986—. Mem. ABA, Chgo. Bar Assn., Notre Dame Club Chgo. (bd. govs., scholarship found. 1988—), The Economic Club Chgo. Contracts commercial, Finance, General corporate. Office: Schiff Hardin & Waite 7200 Sears Tower Chicago IL 60606

**DONEGAN, CHARLES EDWARD,** lawyer, educator; b. Chgo., Apr. 10, 1933; s. Arthur C. and Odessa (Arnold) D.; m. Patty Lou Harris, June 15, 1963; 1 son, Carter Edward. B.S.C., Roosevelt U., 1954; M.S., Loyola U., 1959; J.D., Howard U., 1967; LL.M., Columbia, 1970. Bar: N.Y. 1968, D.C. 1968, Ill. 1979. Pub. sch. tchr. Chgo., 1956-59; with Office Internal Revenue, Chgo., 1959-62; labor economist U.S. Dept. Labor, Washington, 1962-65; legal intern U.S. Commn. Civil Rights, Washington, summer 1966; asst. counsel NAACP Legal Def. Fund, N.Y.C., 1967-69; lectr. law Baruch Coll., N.Y.C., 1969-70; asst. prof. law State U. N.Y. at Buffalo, 1970-73; assoc. prof. law Howard U., 1973-77; vis. assoc. prof. Ohio State U., Columbus, 1977-78; asst. regional counsel U.S. EPA, 1978-80; prof. law So. U., Baton Rouge, 1980—; sole practice law Chgo. and Washington, 1984—; arbitrator steel industry, 1972, U.S. Postal Svc., New Orleans, D.C. Superior Ct., 1987—, Fed. Mediation and Conciliation Svc., 1985—, N.Y. Stock Exch.; vis. prof. law La. State U., summer 1981, N.C. Cen. U., Durham, 1988—, So. U., Baton Rouge, spring 1992; real estate broker; mem. bd. consumer claims Dist. D.C., 1988—; mem. Mayor's Transition Task Force, Washington, 1995; moot ct. judge Georgetown U. Law Sch., Washington, 1987—, Howard U. Law Sch., Washington, 1987—, Balsa, 1987—; spkr., participant nat. confs. on law, edn. and labor rels. Author: Discrimination in Public Employment, 1975; Contbr. articles to profl. jours., to Dictionary Am. Negro Biography. Active Ams. for Dem. Action; me. adv. com. D.C. Bd. of Edn. Named one of Top 42 Lawyers in Washington Area, Washington Afro-Am. Newspaper, 1993, 94, 95, 96' Ford Found. scholar, 1965-67. Columbia U., 1972-73, NEH Postdoctoral fellow in Afro-Am. studies Yale U., 1972-73. Mem. ABA (vice chmn. edn. and curriculum com. local govt. law sect. 1972-80, pub. edn. com. sect. local govt. 1974-84, chmn. liaison com. AALS, 1984, chair arbitration sect.), Nat. Bar Assn. (labor and employment law sect., steering com.), D.C. Bar Assn., Washington Bar Assn. (chmn. legal edn. com.), Chgo. Bar Assn., Fed. Bar Assn., Cook County Bar Assn., Am. Arbitration Assn. (arbitrator), D.C. Fee Arbitration Bd. (bd. govs. 1990—), Nat. Conf. Black Lawyers (bd. organizers), Nat. Futures Assn. (arbitrator), Nat. Assn. Securities Dealers (arbitrator), Assn. Henri Capitant, Roosevelt U. Alumni Assn. (rep. at George Washington U. 175th anniversary charter day convocation 1996), Loyola U. Alumni Assn. (v.p. Washington), Howard U. Alumni Assn. (rep. at Hunter Coll. Centennial 1970), Columbia U. Alumni Assn. (v.p. law Washington), Alpha Phi Alpha, Phi Alpha Kappa, Phi Alpha Delta. Alternative dispute resolution, General practice, Labor. Home: 4315 Argyle Ter NW Washington DC 20011-4243 Office: Ste 900 South Bldg 601 Pennsylvania Ave NW Washington DC 20004-2601 also: 311 S Wacker Dr Ste 4550 Chicago IL 60606-6622 *I have always tried to do my best and never give in to obstacles. I have also been blessed with wonderful parents, relatives, friends, teachers and mentors who had confidence in me.*

**DONEGAN, JOSEPH MICHAEL,** lawyer; b. Englewood, N.J., Sept. 17, 1961; s. James J. and Mary C. Donegan; m. Darlene A. Donegan, Nov. 17, 1993; 1 child, Lindsay A. BA in Acctg., Pace U., 1983; JD, Widener Sch. of Law, 1987. Bar: N.J. 1987, Pa. 1987, N.Y. 1993, U.S. Tax Ct., 1993. Atty. Courter, Kobert, Laufer, Purcell & Cohen, Morristown, N.J., 1987-93; pvt. practice Morristown, 1993-96; ptnr. Purcell, Ries, Shannon, Mulcahy & O'Neill, Bedminster, N.J., 1996—. Editor Del. Jour. of Corp. Law, 1986-87. Commn. N.J. Commn. on Aging, Trenton, 1995-97, N.J. Uniform Legislation, Trenton, 1998—. Mem. N.J. Bar Assn. (chair corp. and individual tax sect. 1995-97). Republican. Avocations: golfing, marathon running. Estate planning, Probate, Estate taxation. Home: 1511 Long Hill Rd Millington NJ 07946-1813 Office: Purcell Ries Shannon Mulcahy & O'Neill One Pluckemin Way Bedminster NJ 07921

**DONES-CARSON, KATHIE DENISE,** lawyer; b. Flint, Mich., May 28, 1951; d. Kenneth Dobson Dones and Edwyna Lucille (Goodwin) Anderson; m. Russell Arthur Carson Sr., May 16, 1972; children: Kori Eileen Carson, Russell Arthur Jr. BS in Polit. Sci. and English, U. Mich., Ann Arbor and Flint, 1979; JD, Wayne State U., 1982, postgrad.. PhD program, 1994—. Bar: Mich. 1982. Investigator, consumer protection divsn. County Prosecutor, Flint, 1975-78; law clk., corp. counsel City of Flint, 1982, asst. city atty., 1982-84, dep. ombudsman, 1984-87; sole practitioner Flint, 1987-90; legal coun., dir. rsch. and analysis divsn. Detroit City Coun., 1990—; adj. instr. U. Mich., Flint, 1990; entrepreneurship instr. Met. Chamber, Flint, 1987-90. Mem. NAACP (cons., bd. mdm. legal/edn. 1984-92), ABA, Nat. Black Women's Polit. Caucus, Women's Informal Network (150 Most Influential Black Women Met. Detroit 1997), Nat. League of Cities (bd. mem. Women in Mcpl. Govt. 1995—), Detroit Urban League. Episcopalian. Avocations: writing poetry and prose, gourmet cooking, African-American literature and art, computers and internet research. Office: Detroit City Council Rsch & Analysis Divsn 2 Woodward Ave Rm 1320 Detroit MI 48226-3448

**DONILON, THOMAS E.,** federal official; b. Providence, May 14, 1955; m. Catherine Russell, Dec. 14, 1991. BA summa cum laude, Cath. U., 1977; JD, U. Va., 1985. Bar: D.C. With office congrl. liaison White House, 1977-79; nat. del. selection coord., nat. conv. dir. Carter-Mondale Presdl. Campaign, 1979-80; lectr. politics Cath. U. Am., 1981; nat. campaign coord. Mondale for Pres. Campaign, 1983-84; assoc. O'Melveny & Myers, Washington, 1985-92, ptnr., 1992-93; asst. sec. pub. affairs bur. pub. affairs Dept. of State, Washington, 1993—; chief of staff to sec. of state Washington, 1994-99; gen. counsel Fannie Mae, Washington, 1999—; cons. CBS News, 1988; presdl. debate coord. Clinton-Gore Presdl. Campaign, 1992; mem. Clinton-Gore Presdl. Transition Team, 1992-93. Mem. editorial bd. U. Va. Law Rev., 1982-83. Mem. ABA, Coun. on Fgn. Rels., Phi Beta Kappa. Office: Fannie Mae 3900 Wisconsin Ave NW Washington DC 20016-2892*

**DONKER, NORMAN WAYNE,** prosecutor; b. Shelby, Mich., Apr. 16, 1955; s. Marvin C. and N. Lorrene (Miller) D.; m. H. Maureen, July 10, 1987; children: Erin Elizabeth, Jonathan Russell. BS in Polit. Sci., magna cum laude, Grand Valley State, 1977, BS in History, magna cum laude, 1977; JD cum laude, Wayne State U., 1980. Bar: Mich.; U.S. Dist. Ct. (ea. dist.) Mich.; U.S. Ct. Appeals (6th cir.); U.S. Supreme Ct. Asst. prosecuting atty. Clare County, Harrison, Mich., 1980; asst. prosecuting atty. Midland (Mich.) County, 1981, sr. asst. prosecuting atty., 1981-85, chief asst. prosecuting atty., 1985-88, prosecuting atty., 1989—. Bd. dirs. Voluntary Action Ctr., Midland, 1985-91, Ernie Wallace Meml. Blood Bank, 1994—, ARC, Midland, 1995—; mem. Mich. Cmty. Corrections Bd. Mem. Pros. Atty. Assn. Mich. (pres. 1997, bd. dirs. 1990—). Office: Midland Co Prosecutor Offc 301 W Main St Midland MI 48640-5162

**DONLEY, DENNIS W.,** lawyer; b. Denver, Mar. 20, 1974; s. Dennis W. and Linda Jo D. BS summa cum laude, U. Mary Hardin-Baylor, 1995; JD, U. Tex., 1997. Bar: Tex. Clk. to Judge Paul Davis 200 Dist. Ct., Austin, Tex., 1996; intern/clk. to Justice James A. Baker Tex. Supreme Ct., Austin, 1997; clk. Scott, Douglas & McConnico, Austin, 1997; assoc. Naman, Howell, Smith & Lee, Austin, 1997—. Campaign vol. Gov. Bush, Austin; vol. Habitat for Humanity, Austin, Meals on Wheels, Austin. Mem. Tex. Young Lawyer Assn. (com. on voter edn., com. dropout prevention), Austin Young Lawyer Assn. (com. teen ct., cmty. svcs. com.). Republican. Avocations: boxing, reading, running, power lifting. General civil litigation, Administrative and regulatory, General corporate. Office: Naman Howell Smith & Lee PC 1900 Bank One Tower Austin TX 78701

**DONNALLY, ROBERT ANDREW,** lawyer, real estate broker; b. Washington, July 10, 1953; s. Reaumur Stearnes and Katherine Ann (Sutliff) D.; m. Patricia Kane Broderick, Dec. 30, 1977; 1 child, Danielle Christine. BA in Psychology, U. Md., 1976; JD, U. Balt., 1980; cert. in bus., Stanford U., 1996. Bar: Md. 1980, Calif. 1986. Pvt. practice Oxen Hill, Md., 1980-81; rsch. contract staff officer Dept. Def., Ft. Meade, Md., 1981-85; with legal and contractual ops. ARGOSystems, Inc., Sunnyvale, Calif., 1985-90; asst. dir. Inst. Def. Analyses, San Diego, 1990-91; dep. chief counsel ARGOSystems, Inc., 1991-93, chief counsel, corp. sec., 1993-98; chief counsel comms. and infomanagement divsn. Boeing Co., 1997-98; gen. counsel, mng. ptnr. BT Comml. Real Estate, Palo Alto, Calif., 1998—. Editor-in-chief The Forum, 1979-80. Active The Pillars Soc./United Way, 1991—. Waxter Legal scholar U. Baltimore, 1978. Mem. Am. Corp. Counsel, Nat. Contract Mgmt. Assn., Md. Bar Assn., Calif. Bar Assn., Assn. of Silicon Valley Brokers, Tae Kwon Do Assn. (Black Belt), Black Belt, Kukkiwon World Tae Kwon Do Assn. Avocations: martial arts, marathons, hiking, travel, reading. General corporate, Real property, General practice. Office: BT Comml Real Estate 2445 Faber Pl Ste 250 Palo Alto CA 94303-3316

**DONNAN, SUSAN L.,** lawyer; b. Natchez, Miss., Dec. 14, 1946; d. Leon A. and Annette (West) D.; m. Elliot Di Beaudoin, (dec. Dec. 1996); 1 child, Marian Morris. BS, Tougaloo Coll., Jackson, Miss., 1967; JD, Southern U., 1984. Bar: La. 1984, U.S. Dist. Ct. (mid. dist.) La. 1984. Assoc. Schaeffer & Schaeffer, New Orleans, 1985-86; ptnr. Dersona & Donnan, Baton Rouge, 1986—. Mem. Phi Alpha Delta, Delta Sigma. State civil litigation, Federal civil litigation, Immigration, naturalization, and customs. Office: Dersona & Donnan 4420 North Blvd Ste 102 Baton Rouge LA 70806-3919

**DONNELL, BRIAN JAMES,** lawyer; b. Glen Cove, N.Y., Oct. 27, 1955; s. John Francis and Margaret (Grosek) D.; m. Karen Wachtell, June 20, 1981. BA in Polit. Sci. & Econs, Trinity Coll., 1977; JD cum laude, Boston Coll., 1980. Bar: Conn. 1980, U.S. Dist. Ct. Conn. 1981, U.S. Supreme Ct. 1991, U.S. Ct. Appeals (2nd cir.) 1994. From assoc. to ptnr. Halloran & Sage LLP, Hartford, Conn., 1980—. Editor-in-chief Boston Coll. Law Sch., 1979, Uniform Comml. Code Reporter-Digest, 1980. Mem. U. Hartford Constrn. Inst., 1987—. Mem. ABA, Conn. Bar Assn. (sects. on antitrust, constrn. law exec. com., comml. and bankruptcy law), Hartford County Bar Assn., Am. Arbitration Assn. (panel arbitrators constrn. industry), Pi Gamma Mu. Republican. General civil litigation, Construction, Contracts commercial. Office: Halloran & Sage LLP 1 Goodwin Sq Hartford CT 06103-4300

**DONNELLA, MICHAEL ANDRE,** lawyer; b. Great Lakes, Ill., Oct. 16, 1954; s. Joseph Anthony and Jacqueline (Reddick) D. BA in Mathematics, Wesleyan U., Middletown, Conn., 1976; JD, U.Chgo., 1979. Bar: Ga. 1979, U.S. Ct. Appeals (D.C. and 11th cirs.) 1980, N.J. 1987. Assoc. Troutman, Sanders et al, Atlanta, 1979-83; atty. AT&T So. Region, Atlanta, 1983-86; sr. atty. AT&T Internat., Basking Ridge, N.J., 1986-95; divsn. counsel Am. Home Products Corp., St. Davids, PA, 1995—; vis. prof. Nat. Urban League Black Exec. Exchange Program, 1986, Huston-Tillotson Coll., Austin, Tex. Interviewer Wesleyan Schs. Com., Middletown, 1976—; counsel Ga. Legis. Black Caucus, Atlanta, 1982-86; mem. visitors com. U. Chgo. Law Sch., 1989-92. Named to 100 Black Men of N.J., Inc. Black Elected Ofcls. Found. Roman Catholic. Avocations: jazz, sports. Private international, Public utilities, General corporate. Office: Am Home Products Corp 170 N Radnor Chester Rd Wayne PA 19087-5221

**DONNELLY, DANIEL PATRICK,** lawyer; b. Nyack, N.Y., May 29, 1933; s. Daniel Patrick and Elizabeth (Quinn) D.; m. Sheila Catherine Flanagan, Feb. 16, 1963; children: Maureen, John. AB, Fordham Coll., 1955, LLB, 1960. Bar: N.Y. 1960, Ind. 1972, U.S. Dist. Ct. (so. and ea. dists.) N.Y. 1966, U.S. Dist. Ct. (no. dist.) N.Y. 1972, U.S. Ct. Appeals (2d cir.) 1966, U.S. Ct. Appeals (8th cir.) 1978, U.S. Ct. Appeals (11th cir.) 1984, U.S. Ct. Appeals (1st cir.) 1981. Assoc. Deforest, Elder & Mulreaney, N.Y.C., 1960-62; asst. atty. Dept. Justice, N.Y.C., 1962-66; assoc. Kreindler & Kreindler, N.Y.C., 1966-69; mem. Healey & Donnelly, N.Y.C., 1969-72; prin. Law Office Daniel Donnelly, Garrison, N.Y., 1972—; accident prevention counselor FAA, 1986—; mem. annual symposium bd. advisors Jour. Air Law & Commerce, So. Meth. U., 1987—. Contbr. articles to profl. jours. Intelligence analyst Counter Intelligence Corps, U.S. Army, 1955-57. Mem. ABA (aviation and space law com. 1974-86), ATLA, Assn. of Bar of City of N.Y. (chmn. aero. law com. 1980-83, Fed. Bar Coun. (chmn. aero. com. 1970-72), N.Y. County Lawyers Assn. (com. aero. law 1971-74), Nat. Transp. Bar Assn. Democrat. Avocations: flying, foreign travel. General civil litigation, Product liability, Aviation. Home: Crossfields Garrison NY 10524 Office: Law Office Daniel Donnelly Garrisons Landing Garrison NY 10524

**DONNELLY, JAMES CORCORAN, JR.,** lawyer; b. Newton, Mass., June 10, 1946; s. James C. Sr. and Margery J. (MacNeil) D.; m. Carol R. Burns, June 28, 1968; children: James C. IV, Sarah Y. BA, Dartmouth Coll., 1968;

JD, Boston Coll., 1973. Bar: Mass. 1973, U.S. Dist. Ct. Mass. 1974, U.S. Ct. Appeals (7th cir.) 1979, U.S. Ct. Appeals (1st cir.) 1983, U.S. Tax Ct. 1988, U.S. Dist. Ct. (no. dist.) Ohio 1991, U.S. Ct. Appeals (2d cir) 1994. From assoc. to ptnr. Hale & Dorr, Boston, 1973-84; sr. ptnr. Mirick, O'Connell, DeMallie & Lougee, Worcester, Mass., 1985—, chmn. litigation dept., 1993-97; bd. dirs. C.P. Bourg, Inc., New Bedford, Mass. Editor-in-chief 1972 Annual Survey of Mass. Law. Corporator Greater Worcester Cmty. Found., 1986—, mem. monitoring and evaluation com., 1997—; trustee Higgins Armory Mus., Worcester, 1985—, pres. 1994-97, Worcester Art Mus., 1987-88; councilor Am. Antiquarian Soc., 1996—, treas., 1997—. Fellow Mass. Bar Found., 1994; mem. ABA, Mass. Bar Assn., Worcester County Bar Assn. (co-chmn. fed. ct. com. 1995—), Dartmouth Lawyers Assn., Worcester Club (bd. dirs. 1995-98), Dartmouth Club Ctrl. Mass. (exec. com. 1996—, pres. 1997—), Dartmouth Coll. Club (Officers exec. com. 1997—, v.p. 1998—).que. Avocations: sailing, skiing, bicycling, hiking, history. General civil litigation, General corporate, Health. Home: 285 Salisbury St Worcester MA 01609-1661 Office: Mirick O'Connell 100 Front St Worcester MA 01608-1402

**DONNELLY, KEVIN WILLIAM,** lawyer; b. Rockville Centre, N.Y., Sept. 25, 1954; s. William Lorne and Marie Grace (Busch) D.; m. Judith Marcia Brier, July 19, 1986; children: Lisa, Jennifer. BS, Boston Coll., 1976, JD, 1979; MBA, Dartmouth Coll., 1982. Bar: N.Y. 1980, Mass. 1980, U.S. Supreme Ct. 1999. Tax atty. Exxon Corp., N.Y.C., 1979-80; assoc. Hemenway & Barnes, Boston, 1982-83; v.p., gen. counsel The Yankee Cos. Inc., Boston, 1983-88, Nortek, Inc., Providence, 1988—. Mem. ABA, Mass. Bar Assn. General corporate, Mergers and acquisitions, General civil litigation. Home: 11 Foxhunt Trl Walpole MA 02081-2270 Office: Nortek Inc 50 Kennedy Plz Ste 1700 Providence RI 02903-2360

**DONNELLY, PAUL E.,** lawyer; b. Kansas City, Mo., Jan. 12, 1948. AB, St. Louis U., 1970, JD, 1973. Bar: Mo. 1973. Law clerk to Hon. William H. Becker U.S. Dist. Ct. (we. dist.) Mo., 1973-75; counsel U.S. Senator Stuart Symington, 1975-77; mem. Stinson, Mag & Fizzell, Kansas City, Mo. Editorial bd. St. Louis U. Law Jour., 1972-73. Mem. ABA, Mo. Bar, Kansas City Met. Bar Assn. Labor. Office: Stinson Mag & Fizzell PO Box 419251 Kansas City MO 64141-6251

**DONNEM, ROLAND WILLIAM,** lawyer, hotel owner, developer; b. Seattle, Nov. 8, 1929; s. William Roland and Mary Louise (Hughes) D.; m. Sarah Brandon Lund, Feb. 18, 1961; children: Elizabeth Prince, Sarah Madison. BA, Yale U., 1952; JD magna cum laude, Harvard U., 1957. Bar: N.Y. 1958, U.S. Dist. Ct. (ea. and so. dists.) N.Y. 1959, U.S. Ct. Appeals (2d cir.) 1959, U.S. Ct. Claims 1960, U.S. Tax Ct. 1960, U.S. Supreme Ct. 1963, U.S. Ct. Appeals (3d cir.) 1969, D.C. 1970, U.S. Ct. Appeals (D.C. cir.) 1970, Ohio 1976, U.S. Dist. Ct. (no. dist.) Ohio 1980, U.S. Ct. Appeals (7th cir.) 1980, U.S. Ct. Appeals (6th cir.) 1984. With Davis Polk & Wardwell, N.Y.C., 1957-63, 64-69; law sec. appellate divsn. N.Y. Supreme Ct., N.Y.C., 1963-64; dir. policy planning antitrust divsn. Justice Dept., Washington, 1969-71; v.p., sec., gen. counsel Standard Brands Inc., N.Y.C., 1971-76; from v.p. law to sr. v.p. law and casualty prevention Chessie System, Cleve., 1976-86; ptnr. Meta Ptnrs., real estate devel., 1984-89, mng. ptnr., 1989—, registered security rep., 1985-90; bd. dirs., gen. counsel Acorn Properties, Inc., Cleve., 1985—, pres., 1989—; bd. dirs., gen. counsel Meta Devel. Corp., Cleve., 1985—, pres., 1989—; bd. dirs., gen. counsel Meta Properties, Inc., Cleve., 1988—, pres., 1989—; founding mem., bd. dirs. Assn. Sheraton Franchisees N.Am., 1997—. Mem. editl. bd. Harvard Law Rev., 1955-57. Bd. dirs., fin. v.p. Presbyn. Home for Aged Women, N.Y.C., 1972-76; bd. dirs., treas. James Lenox Ho., Inc., 1972-76; trustee Food and Drug Law Inst., 1974-76; trustee, sec. Brick Presbyn. Ch., N.Y.C., 1974-76; sec. class of 1952, Yale U., 1992-97; bd. dirs. Yale Alumni Fund, 1990-95; chmn. Cleve. Area Yale Campaign, 1991-97. Lt. (j.g.) USNR, 1952-54. Fellow Timothy Dwight Coll., Yale U., 1987—. Mem. D.C. Bar Assn., Ohio Bar Assn., Greater Cleve. Bar Assn., Am. Law Inst. (life), Am. Arbitration Assn. (nat. panel arbitrators), Def. Orientation Conf. Assn. (bd. dirs. 1996—), Yale U. Alumni Assn. Cleve. (treas. 1982-84, del. 1984-87, trustee 1984-93, adv. coun. 1993—), Yale U. Alumni Assn. (bd. govs. 1987-90), Union Club (N.Y.C. and Cleve.), Capitol Hill Club (Washington), Washington Chevy Chase Club, Cleve. Racquet Club, Kirtland Club (Cleve.), Met. Club (Washington), Phi Beta Kappa. Republican. Presbyterian. Home: 2945 Fontenay Rd Shaker Heights OH 44120-1726 Office: 3619 Park East Dr Ste 214 Beachwood OH 44122-4312

**DONNER, HENRY JAY,** lawyer; b. Atlantic City, N.J., Sept. 1, 1944; s. Harry and Sylvia (Payes) D.; m. Katherine Weiner, Dec. 20, 1969; children: Benjamin James, Melissa Faith. BA, Am. U., 1966; JD, Villanova U., 1969. Bar: Pa. 1969, U.S. Dist. Ct. (ea. dist.) Pa. 1969, U.S. Ct. Appeals (3d cir.) 1983. Staff mem. U.S. Senator Joseph A. Clark, Washington, 1965-68; assoc. Dilworth, Paxson, Kalish and Levy, Phila., 1969-74; ptnr. Jacoby, Donner & Jacoby, Phila., 1974-82; sr. mem. Jacoby Donner, P.C., Phila., 1982—; lectr. Nat. Home Builders Assn., Pa. State U., State Coll., 1989-90. Author: West Legal Forms: Specialized Forms, Vol. 27, Chpt. 8, Building Agreements. Mem. sch. com. Germantown Friends Sch., 1993—; bd. dirs. Germantown Jewish Ctr., 1989-91. Mem. ABA, Phila. Bar Assn. (exec. com. real property sect. 1987-96, chmn. constrn. law com., real property sect. 1986-89, chmn. real property sect. 1993, bd. govs. 1993), Constrn. Fin. Mgmt. Assn. (bd. dirs. Phila. chpt. 1990-95), Union League Phila., Germantown Cricket Club. Construction, General civil litigation, Professional liability. Office: Jacoby Donner PC 1515 Market St Ste 2000 Philadelphia PA 19102-1920

**DONNER, TED A.,** lawyer; b. N.Y.C., Nov. 22, 1960; s. Robert A. and Barbara (Wood) D.; m. Leslie Lynn Wasserman, Sept. 16, 1990; children: Alexandra Sofia, Samuel Joseph. BA, Roosevelt U., 1987; JD, Loyola U., 1990. Bar: U.S. Dist. Ct. Ill. 1990. Assoc. Rock, Fusco, Reynolds & Garvey, Chgo., 1990-94, Altheimer & Gray, Chgo., 1994—; instr. Loyola U. Chgo. Sch. Law, 1990-96. Author: Attorney's Practice Guide to Negotiations, 2d edit., 1995-99, Jury Selection Strategy & Science, 2d edit., 1990-99, Jury Selection Handbook, 1999. Mem. ATLA, ABA, Am. Soc. Trial Consultants, Am. Soc. Legal Writers, Internat. Platform Assn., DuPage County Bar Assn., Chgo. Bar Assn., Alpha Sigma Nu. General civil litigation, Antitrust, Insurance. Office: Altheimer & Gray 10 S Wacker Dr Fl 35 Chicago IL 60606-7482

**DONNICI, PETER JOSEPH,** lawyer, law educator, consultant; b. Kansas City, Mo., Sept. 5, 1939; s. Albert H. and Jennie (Danubio) D.; m. Diane DuPlantier, July 27, 1985; children: JuliaAnn Donnici Clifford, Joseph A., Joann Donnici Powers. BA, U. Mo., Kansas City, 1959, JD, 1962; LLM, Yale U., 1963. Bar: Mo. 1963, U.S. Supreme Ct. 1966, Calif. 1969. Asst. prof. law U. San Francisco, 1963-65, assoc. prof., 1965-68, prof., 1968-91, prof. emeritus, 1992—; assoc. Law Offices Joseph L. Alioto, San Francisco, 1967-72; sole practice San Francisco, 1974—; ptnr. Donnici & LuPo, San Francisco, 1982-92, Donnici, Kerwin, Phillips & Donnici, San Francisco, 1993—; chmn. L.L. Hillblom Found. & Charitable Trust, 1995—; asst. prosecutor Jackson County Prosecutor's Office, Mo., 1963; cons. to Office of Mayor of San Francisco, 1968-72; No. Calif. bd. dirs. Coun. on Legal Ednl. Opportunity, San Francisco, 1969-70; conciliator for housing discrimination cases HUD, San Francisco, 1976; cons. Calif. Consumer Affairs' Task Force on Electronic Funds Transfer, Sacramento, 1978-79; bd. dirs. Air Micronesia, Inc., DHL Internat., Ltd., Bermuda, Continental Micronesia; spl. counsel and del. to internat. confs. Commonwealth of No. Mariana Islands, 1983-84; faculty adviser U. San Francisco Law Rev., 1966-91; bd. counselors U. San Francisco, 1993—. Editor-in-Chief: U. Mo., Kansas City Law Rev., 1961-62; contbr. articles to profl. jours., 1964—. Lawyers' com. for Urban Affairs, San Francisco, 1965-68. Wilson scholar U. Mo.-Kansas City, 1956-62; Sterling fellow Law Sch., Yale U., 1962-63. Mem. Bench and Robe, Phi Delta Phi. Democrat. Roman Catholic. Home: 190 Cresta Vista Dr San Francisco CA 94127-1635 Office: One Post St Ste 2450 San Francisco CA 94104

**DONOFRIO, COLLEEN GRACE,** lawyer, consultant; b. Washington, Dec. 3, 1958; d. Thomas Francis and Yvonne (Garsick) Grace; m. John Richard Donofrio; children: Rae-Ellen Lynn, Mary Elizabeth. BSChemE, Rutgers Coll. Engring., Piscataway, N.J., 1982; BA in Econs., Rutgers U., New Brunswick, N.J., 1982; JD, Rutgers Sch. Law, Camden, N.J., 1986. Bar: N.J. 1986. Power engr. Stone and Webster, Cherry Hill, N.J., 1982-84; environ. engr. U.S. EPA Region III, Phila., 1984-86; environ. practitioner Babst Calland Clements & Zom, P.C., Pitts., 1986-89, Phila., 1989—. Sunday Sch. tchr. Trinity United Meth. Ch., Mullica Hill, N.J., 1998. Mem. AIChE, AIChE-Delaware Valley Environ. Breakfast Club. Democrat. Meth. Avocations: needlework, hiking. Environmental. Office: Babst Collard Clements & Zom PC 1 S Penn Sq Philadelphia PA 19107-3519

**DONOHOE, CHARLES RICHARD,** general patent counsel; b. Iowa City, Apr. 29, 1941; s. Charles Joseph and Sarah Henrietta D.; m. Kathryn Ann Lyons, Apr. 20, 1968; children: Kelly, Patrick, Mark, Charles Jr. BSEE, Ohio State U., 1964, MSEE, 1965; JD, George Washington U., 1970. Bar: Md. 1970, D.C. 1973. Engr. GM, Milford, Mich., 1965-68; patent engr. Burroughs Corp., Washington, 1968-70; assoc. atty. Pennie & Edmonds, N.Y.C., 1970-73; ptnr. Cushman, Darby & Cushman, Washington, 1973-89; gen. patent consul, v.p. Samsung Electronics Co. Ltd., Washington and Seoul, 1989—; lectr. Patent Resources Group, Washington, 1977-88, Kyoto U. Comparative Law Conv., Tokyo, 1984. Co-author: Advanced Patent Prosecution, 1977; patentee in field. Mem. Am. C. of C., Seoul, Korea, 1988—. Recipient Caldwell scholarship Ohio State U., 1964. Mem. ABA, Am. Intellectual Property Assn., Md. Bar Assn., Customs and Internat. Trade Bar Assn., Seoul Club, Am. C. of C., Manor Country Club. Democrat. Roman Catholic. Avocations: golf, tennis. Patent, Trademark and copyright, Private international. Home: 15309 Basswood Ct Rockville MD 20853-1801 Office: Samsung Electronics 2445 M St NW Washington DC 20037-1435 also: Samsung Main Bldg 10th Fl, 250 Taepyung-Ro, Chung-Ku, Seoul Republic of Korea

**DONOHOE, JEROME FRANCIS,** lawyer; b. Yankton, S.D., Mar. 17, 1939; s. Francis A. and Ruth D.; m. Elaine Joyce Bush, Jan. 27, 1968; 1 child, Nicole Elaine. BA, St. John's U., 1961; JD cum laude, U. Minn., 1964. Bar: Ill. 1964, S.D. 1964. Atty. Atchison, Topeka & Santa Fe Ry. Co., Chgo., 1967-73, gen. atty., 1973-78; gen. counsel corp. affairs Santa Fe Industries Inc., Chgo., 1978-84; v.p. law Santa Fe Industries, Inc., Chgo., 1984-90, Santa Fe Pacific Corp., Chgo., 1984-94; ptnr. Mayer, Brown & Platt, Chgo., 1990-99; sr. ptnr. Mayer, Brown & Platt, 1999—. Mem. corp. coun. Interlochen (Mich.) Ctr. for Arts, 1987—; bd. dirs. Better Govt. Assn., 1989—. Capt. JAGC, U.S. Army, 1964-67. Fellow Ill. Bar Found.; mem. ABA (sect. vice chair, chair membership and railroad coms., pub. utility, comm. and transp. law sect.), Northwestern U. Assocs., Northwestern U. Corp. Counsel Ctr., Chgo. Club, Chgo. Athletic Assn., Michigan Shores Club (Wilmette, Ill.). General corporate, Administrative and regulatory, Securities. Office: Mayer Brown & Platt 190 S La Salle St Ste 3100 Chicago IL 60603-3441

**DONOHOE, JOHN JOSEPH,** lawyer; b. Iowa City, Jan. 19, 1962; s. John Lawrence and Janet Donohoe; m. Lori Young, Aug. 9, 1986; children: Kelsey Young, Zachary, Emilie. BA, U. Iowa, 1984; JD, Creighton U., 1987. Bar: Colo. 1987, U.S. Dist. Ct. Colo. 1987. Ptnr. Shakeshaft, Chernushin & Donohoe, Colorado Springs, Colo., 1987—. Mem. Colo. Bar Assn., Colo. Criminal Def. Bar Assn. Avocations: softball, basketball, skiing. Criminal, General civil litigation, Family and matrimonial. Office: Shakeshaft Chernushin & Donohoe 1530 S Tejon St Colorado Springs CO 80906-2214

**DONOHUE, BRIAN E.,** lawyer; b. Troy, N.Y., Feb. 18, 1951; s. Edward Joseph and Sibyl (Douglas) D.; m. Mary Kathryn O'Connor, Apr. 20, 1985; 1 child, Justin O'Connor. BA cum laude, SUNY, Albany, 1974; JD, Albany Law Sch., 1983. Bar: N.Y. 1984, U.S. Dist. Ct. (no. dist.) N.Y. 1988, U.S. Dist. Ct. Vt. 1991. Adminstrv. asst. N.Y. State Senate, Albany, 1971-76, rsch. fellow, 1976-80; instr. legal writing Albany Law Sch., 1982-83; atty. Frost & Donohue, P.C., Troy, 1984—. Contbr. articles to profl. jours. Poll watcher, vol. Albany County Dem. Com., Albany, 1984; vol. supr. ARC, Troy and Albany, 1975-79, 83-87. Mem. ABA, N.Y. State Bar Assn., Assn. Trial Lawyers Am., Rensselaer County Bar Assn., N.Y. State Trial Lawyers Assn. Republican. Roman Catholic. Avocations: golf, tennis, flying, skydiving, mountain climbing. Personal injury, Criminal. Home: 3 Windfield Ln Troy NY 12180-9652 Office: Frost & Donohue PC 112 State St Ste 1320 Albany NY 12207-2024

**DONOHUE, JOHN JOSEPH,** law educator; b. Alexandria, Va., Jan. 30, 1953; s. Mildred (Sileo) Donohue; m. Marijke Rijsberman, Dec. 27, 1986 (div.); 1 child, Lauren Elizabeth; m. Maureen O'Kicki, Oct. 25, 1995; 1 child, Aidan John. BA, Hamilton Coll., 1974; JD, Harvard U., 1977; PhD, Yale U., 1986. Bar: Conn. 1977, D.C. 1978. Assoc. Covington & Burling, Washington, D.C., 1978-81; fellow Civil Liability Program, Law Sch. Yale U., New Haven, 1985-86; rsch. fellow Am. Bar Found., Chgo., 1986-95; Class of 1967 James B. Haddad prof. law Northwestern U., Chgo., 1994-95; prof. Stanford (Calif.) Law Sch., 1995—. Contbr. articles to profl. jours. Mem. ABA, Am. Econ. Assn., Phi Beta Kappa. Office: Stanford Law Sch Crown Quad Stanford CA 94305

**DONOHUE, JOHN PATRICK,** lawyer; b. N.Y.C., Sept. 16, 1944; s. Joseph Francis and Catherine Elizabeth (Feeney) D.; m. Patricia Ann Holly, June 11, 1977; children: Eileen Mary, Anne Catherine. B.A., Providence Coll., 1966; J.D., Catholic U. Am., 1969. Bar: N.Y. 1973, U.S. Ct. Appeals (2d cir.) 1973, U.S. Ct. Appeals (fed. cir.) 1974, N.J. 1975, U.S. Dist. Ct. N.J. 1975, U.S. Dist. Ct. (so., ea. dists.) N.Y. 1975, U.S. Supreme Ct. 1978, D.C. 1981, Pa. 1986. Spl. agt. FBI, Washington, 1969-71; assoc. Donohue & Donohue, N.Y.C., 1971-74, ptnr., 1974—; adj. prof. law internat. bus. transactions Seton Hall U. Sch. Law, Newark, 1986-94. Author book sect. Customs Fraud Section on Business Crimes, 1982; co-author: The Prevention and Prosecution of Computer and High Technology Crime. Bd. dirs. Maritime Exch. Delaware River and Bay; mem. bd. regents Cath. U. Am., 1990—, chmn. 1997—; trustee Rosemont (Pa.) Sch., chmn. 1996—; mem. bd. visitors Cath. U. Sch. Law, 1998—. Named Man of Yr., Phila. Customs, Brokers and Forwarders Assn., 1984. Mem. Customs and Internat. Trade Bar Assn., Pa. State Bar Assn. Republican. Roman Catholic. Private international, Immigration, naturalization, and customs, Federal civil litigation. Office: Donohue & Donohue 232 S 4th St Philadelphia PA 19106-3704

**DONOHUE, MICHAEL JOSEPH,** judge; b. Holyoke, Mass.; s. David I. and Mary (Fitzgerald) D.; m. Adeline L. O'Neil (dec. Mar. 1986); children: Michael J., Adeline L., Owen B., Anne C., Quentin, Maria. Student N. Tex. U., 1943, Stanford U., 1944, U. Pa., 1944; BA, U. Mass., 1947; LLB, Boston U., 1950. Bar: Mass. 1950. Pvt. practice law, Holyoke, Mass., 1950-63; presiding justice Holyoke Dist. Ct., 1963-89, retired; asst. city solicitor Holyoke, 1959-60; pub. adminstr. Hampden County (Mass.), 1959-64; pub. (newspaper) Hello Holyoke, 1990—. Chmn. Internat. Conf. on Judges on Violence and Terrorism; past pres. Am. Judges Found.; mem. exec. bd. Am. Coalition Against Crime, pres., 1983; mem. bldg. authority U. Mass. With AUS, 1943-46. Recipient award of merit Am. Judges Assn.; Centennial award Boston U. Mem. Judges of Am. (pres. 1982), Am. Judges Assn. (past pres.), Mass. Judges Conf., U. Mass. Alumni Assn. (past pres.), World Jurist Assn. (dir. pub. info.). Lodge: KC (past grand knight). Co-author: R, 1983; editor Judicial Hilites; editor Court Rev., Mass. Judges' Conf. Newsletter, 1988-89. Office: PO Box 390 Holyoke MA 01041-0390 also: 188 Chestnut St Holyoke MA 01040-4341

**DONOHUE, ROBERT JOHN,** lawyer; b. Orange, N.J., Oct. 12, 1934; s. Walter Joseph and Helen Gray (Quinby) D.; m. Patricia McKenzie, Sept. 28, 1958; children: Christine, Colleen, Robert, Daniel, David, Michael, Mary. AB, Villanova U., 1957; JD, Georgetown U., 1960. Bar: Pa. 1961, U.S. Supreme Ct. 1969. Assoc. Reilly & Pierce, Upper Darby, Pa., 1961-64, Kardas & Donohue, Upper Darby, 1965-73, Cantwell & Donohue, Upper Darby, 1974-77; sr. ptnr. Donohue McKee, Mattson & Green, Havertown, Pa., 1978—; bd. dirs. various mfg. cos. Bd. dirs. Community YM-YWCA, 1976-84, chmn. bd., 1980-84; bd. dirs. St. Vincent's Home for Children, 1975-81, Jay Lau Meml. Scholarship Fund, 1979—; govt. appeal agt. U.S. Selective Service System, 1968-72; bd. dirs. Southeastern Del. County chpt. ARC, 1980-82; vice chmn. Upper Darby Mayor's Blue Ribbon Panel for 69th St., 1976-77. Served with U.S. Army, 1960-61. Mem. ABA, Pa. Bar Assn., Delaware County Bar Assn., Am. Judicature Soc., Am. Arbitration Assn. (nat. panel arbitrators 1965—), Am. Legion, Phi Alpha Delta (life), Undine Barge Club, Lions (pres. 1966—). Writer children's short stories. General practice, Probate, General corporate. Home: 1217 Mason Ave Drexel Hill PA 19026-2511 Office: Donohue McKee Mattson & Green Drexel Ave Havertown PA 19083-5796

**DONOVAN, CHARLES STEPHEN,** lawyer; b. Boston, Feb. 28, 1951; s. Alfred Michael and Maureen (Murphy) D.; m. Lisa Marie Dicharry, Apr. 21, 1979; children: Yvette, Martine, Neal. BA, Haverford Coll., 1974; JD, Cornell U., 1977. Bar: Mass. 1977, La. 1977, Calif. 1982, U.S. Supreme Ct. 1988. Atty. Phelps, Dunbar, Marks, Claverie & Sims, New Orleans, 1977-81, Dorr, Cooper & Hays, San Francisco, 1981-84, Walsh, Donovan, Lindh & Keech LLP, San Francisco, 1984—; instr. maritime law Calif. Maritime Acad., Vallejo, 1982—; spl. advisor U.S. State Dept., 1993-96. Contbr. numerous articles to profl. jours. Recipient Gustavus H. Robinson prize Cornell Law Sch., 1977. Mem. ABA (chmn. admiralty and maritime law com. Chgo. 1989-90), Internat. Bar Assn., Maritime Law Assn. U.S. (chmn. com. on maritime criminal law 1998—, chmn. subcom. on maritime liens and mortgages 1994—), Tulane Admiralty Inst. (permanent adv. bd.), Marine Exch. (bd. dirs. San Francisco Bay region 1993-96). Avocations: skiing, hiking, mandolin, guitar, sailing. Admiralty, General civil litigation, Private international. Office: Walsh Donovan Lindh & Keech LLP 595 Market St Ste 2000 San Francisco CA 94105-2831

**DONOVAN, MAUREEN DRISCOLL,** lawyer; b. N.Y.C., Dec. 2, 1940; d. Bartholomew Driscoll and Josephine (Keohane) Driscoll. AB, Coll. of New Rochelle, 1962; LLB with honors, Fordham U., 1966. Bar: N.Y. 1966, U.S. Supreme Ct. 1971, U.S. Ct. Appeals (2d cir.) 1975, U.S. Dist. Ct. (so. dist.) N.Y. 1976. Assoc. White & Case LLP, N.Y.C., 1966-75, ptnr., 1975—. Trustee St. Barnabas Hosp., Bronx, N.Y., 1992—, chair fin. com. 1997—, vice chair bd., 1998—; trustee N.Y. Urban Coalition, N.Y.C., 1990-94. Mem. ABA, Princeton Club (N.Y.), Coral Beach Club (Paget, Bermuda), Englewood (N.J.) Field Club. Estate planning, Pension, profit-sharing, and employee benefits, Probate. Office: White & Case LLP 1155 Avenue of the Americas New York NY 10036-2711

**DONOVAN, MICHAEL SHAUN,** lawyer; b. Helena, Mont., Aug. 29, 1951; s. Michael E. and Marjorie C. (Emery) D.; m. Patricia A. Steinbacher, June 16, 1979; children: Michael, Colin, Maura. BS in Biol. Scis., Stanford U., 1973; JD, U. Mont., 1979. Bar: Mont. 1979, U.S. Dist. Ct. Mont. 1979, U.S. Ct. Appeals (9th cir.) 1990. County atty. Mineral County, Superior, Mont., 1979—. Past pres., treas. Superior Lions Club, 1980—; bd. dirs. Mineral County Boy Scout Coun., 1983-89; chmn. Mineral County Dems., 1989; incorporator/trainer Mineral County Helpline, 1989—. Mem. State Bar Mont., Mont. County Attys. Assn. (bd. dirs. 1989—, pres. 1997—), Ancient Order Hibernans. Roman Catholic. Avocations: woodworking, photography, golf. Office: Mineral County Atty 300 River Superior MT 59872

**DONOVAN, RICHARD EDWARD,** lawyer; b. Cleve., Dec. 3, 1952; s. Richard A. and Eileen (Karthaus) D.; m. Ellen Brode, June 16, 1979; children: Colin, Ryan Michael, Patrick. BS, U. Notre Dame, 1974; JD, Rutgers U., 1977. Bar: N.Y. 1978, U.S. Dist. Ct. (ea. dist.) N.Y. 1978, N.J. 1985, U.S. Dist. Ct. N.J. 1985, U.S. Ct. Appeals (2d cir.) 1987, U.S. Supreme Ct. 1990. Assoc. Breed, Abbott & Morgan, N.Y.C., 1977-80; assoc. Kelley, Drye & Warren LLP, N.Y.C., 1980-86, ptnr., 1987—. Mem. ABA, Assn. Bar City N.Y. (com. prof. and jud. ethics 1997—), N.J. Bar Assn., Rutgers Alumni Coun., N.Y. State Bar Assn. (sec. comml. and fed. litigation sect. 1988-90), Fed. Bar Coun., Assn. Fed. Bar N.J. General civil litigation, Antitrust, Health. Home: 61 Oak Ridge Ave Summit NJ 07901-4306 Office: Kelley Drye & Warren 5 Sylvan Way Parsippany NJ 07054-3813

**DONOYAN, GARY LEON,** lawyer; b. L.A., Oct. 1, 1962; s. Leon Souren and Karin Donoyan; m. Harumi Aoto Donoyan, Mar. 8, 1988; children: Leon Arthur, Martin Alexander. BA, UCLA, 1986; JD, Hofstra U., 1994. Bar: N.Y. 1995, U.S. Dsit. Ct. (so. and ea. dists.) N.Y. 1995. Paralegal Baker & McKenzie, N.Y.C., 1990-91; atty. Law Offices of Norman Kaplan, Great Neck, N.Y., 1995-97, Law Firm of Hugh H. Mo, N.Y.C., 1997—. Pres. James Monroe Owners Co-op, Forest Hills, N.Y., 1995-97; mem. coun. Grace Luth. Ch., Forest Hills, 1994-97. Mem. ABA, N.Y. State Bar Assn., Assn. Bar City N.Y., New York County Lawyers Assn. Democrat. General civil litigation, Bankruptcy, Real property. Office: Law Firm of Hugh H Mo 225 Broadway Rm 2702 New York NY 10007-3001

**DOOLEY, JOHN AUGUSTINE, III,** state supreme court justice; b. Nashua, N.H., Apr. 10, 1944; s. John A. and Edna Elizabeth (Elwell) D.; m. Sandra C. Sapp, Dec. 19, 1970. BS, Union Coll., 1965; LLB, Boston Coll., 1968. Bar: Vt. 1968. Law clk. to presiding judge U.S. Dist. Ct. Vt., 1968-69; asst. dir. Vt. Legal Aid, 1969-72, dir., 1972-78; legal counsel to gov. of Vt., 1985; sec. of adminstrn. State of Vt., 1985-87; assoc. justice Vt. Supreme Ct., 1987—; part-time U.S. magistrate for Vt., from 1971. Co-author: Cases and Materials on Urban Poverty Law, 1974. Mem. Vt. Bar Assn. Office: Vt Supreme Ct 109 State St Montpelier VT 05609-0001*

**DOPF, GLENN WILLIAM,** lawyer; b. N.Y.C., June 6, 1953; s. William Bernard and Doris Virginia (Roxby) D. BS cum laude, Fordham Coll., 1975; JD, Fordham U., 1979; LLM, NYU, 1983. Bar: N.J. 1979, U.S. Dist. Ct. N.J. 1979, N.Y. 1980, U.S. Dist. Ct. (so. and ea. dists.) N.Y. 1980, U.S. Ct. Appeals (2d cir.) 1980, U.S. Ct. Internat. Trade 1981, U.S. Supreme Ct. 1983. Assoc. Martin, Clearwater & Bell, N.Y.C., 1980-81; ptnr. Kopff, Nardelli & Dopf, N.Y.C., 1982—. Mem. ABA, Assn. Bar City N.Y. State civil litigation, Federal civil litigation, Insurance. Office: Kopff Nardelli & Dopf 440 9th Ave Fl 15 New York NY 10001-1688

**DOPKIN, MARK DREGANT,** lawyer; b. Balt., Jan. 14, 1943; s. Wilford and Beverly (Dregant) D.; m. Ilene Kleinman, Mar. 21, 1967 (div.); children: Rebecca, Peter; m. Deborah Cohn, May 28, 1984. BA, Union Coll., Schenectady, 1964; JD, U. Md., 1967. Bar: Md. 1967, U.S. Dist. Ct. Md. 1968, U.S. Supreme Ct. 1974. Assoc. Blades & Rosenfeld, Balt., 1968-71; assoc. Kaplan, Heyman, Greenberg, Engelman & Belgrd, P.A., Balt., 1971-76, ptnr., 1977-98; ptnr. Tydings & Rosenberg LLP, Balt., 1998—; mem. Real Property Records Improvement Fund Oversight Com., 1995—. Mem. Gov.'s Salary Rev. Com., Md., 1980-85, Balt. County Charter Rev. Com., 1977-79; treas. Congressman Benjamin L. Cardin, Balt., 1985—; 1st v.p. Har Sinai Cong., Balt., 1987-89, pres., 1989-91, trustee, 1973-75, 77-80, 86—; active various charitable orgns. With U.S. Army, 1967-73. Fellow Md. Bar Found.; mem. ABA, Bar Assn. Balt. City, Md. Bar Assn. Democrat. Jewish. Real property, General corporate, Land use and zoning (including planning). Office: Tydings & Rosenberg LLP 100 E Pratt St Fl 26 Baltimore MD 21202-1009

**DORADO, MARIANNE GAERTNER,** lawyer; b. Neptune, N.J., May 18, 1956; d. Wolfgang Wilhelm and Marianne L. (Weber) Gaertner; m. Richard Manuel Dorado, Oct. 1, 1982; children: Marianne Christine, Kathleen Gina. BA, Yale U., 1978; JD, U. Mich., 1981. Bar: N.Y. 1982, U.S. Supreme Ct. 1993. Ptnr. Chimel Dorado, N.Y.C., 1998—; bd. dirs. Blue Heron Theater, N.Y.C. Contbr. articles to profl. jours. Extern office legal advisor U.S. Dept. State, Washington, 1980. Republican. Roman Catholic. Mergers and acquisitions, General corporate, Securities. Office: Chimel Dorado 14th Fl 1180 Ave of Americas New York NY 10036

**DORAN, JOHN ALAN,** lawyer; b. Bronx, N.Y., May 25, 1962; s. Robert James Finbar and Patricia Roche D.; m. Carolann Cervetti, Feb. 27, 1966. BA in Comm., Polit. Sci., Loyola Marymount U., 1985; JD, Vanderbilt U., 1988. Bar: Ariz. 1988 (exec. com. labor sect. 1996—), U.S. Ct. Appeals (9th cir.) 1988, U.S. Dist. Ct. Ariz. 1988, U.S. Ct. Appeals (5th cir.) 1999. Summer assoc. O'Fluherty, Prestholt & Bennington, L.A., 1986, Lillick, McHose & Charles, L.A., 1987; summer assoc. Streich, Lang, Weeks & Carden, Phoenix, 1987, assoc., 1988-94; assoc. Bryan Cave LLP, Phoenix, 1994-97, ptnr., 1997—. Contbg. author: Ariz. Employment Law Handbook, 1995—, The Employer's Handbooks, 1996, 97, 98, Internat. Legal Strategies, 1998; co-author Mass. Law Rev., 1992; exec. editor Ariz. Labor Letter, 1993—. Bd. dirs. N.E. Training Inst., Phoenix, 1994-96; mem. planning com. Labor Letters, Inc. Bass, Berry & Sims scholar Vanderbilt U., 1988, Vanderbilt Bar Assn. scholar, 1988. Mem. Ariz. Assn. Def. Counsel Vanderbilt Alumni Assn., Delta Sigma Phi. Avocations: Irish history, golfing. Labor, Appellate. Office: Bryan Cave LLP 2 N Central Ave Ste 2200 Phoenix AZ 85004-4406

**DORAN, WILLIAM MICHAEL,** lawyer; b. Albany, N.Y., May 26, 1940; s. James R. and Lorene Tinsley (Nees) D.; m. Susan Coryell Lloyd; children:

Melissa, Heather, Leigh. BS in Journalism, Northwestern U., 1962; LLB, U. Pa., 1966. Assoc. Morgan, Lewis & Bockius, Phila., 1967-76, ptnr., 1976—; dir. SEI Corp.; trustee SEI Liquid Asset Trust, SEI Daily Income Trust, SEI Tax Exempt Trust, SEI Instl. Managed Trust, SEI Index Funds, SEI Internat. Trust, The Advisors Inner Cir. Fund, The Arbor Fund, Inventor Funds, Incs. Vice chmn. World Affairs Coun. Phila. Mem. ABA, Pa. Bar Assn., Phila. Bar Assn., Nat. Assn. Bond Lawyers. Finance, Banking, General corporate. Home: 27 Druim Moir Ln Philadelphia PA 19118-4134 Office: Morgan Lewis & Bockius LLP 1701 Market St Philadelphia PA 19103-2903

**DORCHAK, THOMAS J.,** lawyer; b. Cleve., Aug. 31, 1940; s. Joseph J. and Julia H. D.; m. Eileen C. Coakley, June 27, 1964; children: Joshua, Andrew, Claire Marie, Sarah T. BA with honors, Xavier U., 1962; JD, Boston Coll., 1965. Bar: Ohio 1966, U.S. Dist. Ct. (no. dist.) Ohio 1970, U.S. Ct. Appeals (6th cir.) 1981. In house def. atty. Allstate Ins. Co., Cleve., 1969-73; assoc. Bertsch Edelman & Fludine, Cleve., 1973-76; pvt. practice Cleve., 1976-92; assoc. The Crombie Law Firm, North Olmsted, Ohio, 1993—. Actor cmty. theater. General practice, Family and matrimonial, General civil litigation. Office: The Crombie Law Firm 4615 Great Northern Blvd North Olmsted OH 44070-3426

**DORDELL, TIMOTHY PAUL,** lawyer; b. Mpls., June 26, 1962. BA summa cum laude, St. Olaf Coll., Northfield, Minn., 1984; student, Cambridge (Eng.) U., 1983; JD cum laude, U. Minn., 1987. Bar: Ariz. 1987, Minn. 1989, U.S. Dist. Ct. Ariz. 1987, U.S. Dist. Ct. Minn. 1991. Atty. Streich Lang, Phoenix, 1987-89; v.p., gen. counsel Twin Star Prodns., Inc., Scottsdale, Ariz., 1989-91; atty. Fredrikson & Byron, Mpls., 1992-96; sr. atty. Ecolab Inc., St. Paul, 1996—. Bd. dirs. Minn. AIDS Project, Mpls., 1996—. Mem. Phi Beta Kappa, Phi Alpha Theta. Mergers and acquisitions, Private international. Office: Ecolab Inc 370 Wabasha St N Saint Paul MN 55102-1349

**DOREMUS, OGDEN,** lawyer; b. Atlanta, Apr. 23, 1921; s. C. Estes and Mary (McAdory) D.; m. Carolyn Wooten Greene, Aug. 30, 1947 (dec. Aug. 1989); children: Celia Jane, Frank O., Dale Marie Doremus; m. Linda Parker, Dec. 4, 1992. BA, Emory U., 1946, JD, 1949. Bar: Ga. 1947. Asst. solicitor gen. Atlanta, 1947-49; ptnr. firm Smith Field Doremus & Ringel, Atlanta, 1949-60, Falligant, Doremus and Karsman, Savannah, Ga., 1960-72, Doremus, Jones & Smith, P.C., Metter, Ga., 1972-94; of counsel Karsman, Brooks & Callaway, 1994—; prof. Woodrow Wilson Sch. Law, Atlanta, 1948-50; judge State Ct. Candler County, Ga., 1985—; pres. Ga. Coun. State Ct. Judges, 1990-91; mem. Jud. Coun. State of Ga., 1989-91, Unified Trial Ct. Commn., 1997; mem. ct. futures com. State Bar Ga., 1996—; bd. dirs. Ctr. for Law in the Pub. Interest, 1996—; judge Mcpl. Ct., Metter, Ga., 1997—; mem. commn. on judiciary Supreme Ct. Ga., 1999—. Mem. editorial adv. bd. Environ. Law, Reporter, 1969-80. Scoutmaster Boy Scouts Am., Atlanta, 1951-60, commn., 1961-70; chmn. Ga. Day and Savannah Arts Festival, 1968-72; mem. Atlanta City Coun., 1950-53; mem. Savannah Govtl. Reorgn. Commn., 1960-61, Ga. Ct. Futures Commn., 1991-93, 97—; adv. com. Nat. Coastal Zone Mgmt. Coun., 1978-86; trustee Ga. Conservancy; bd. dirs. Legal Environ. Assistance Found., 1983-86, Ga. Hazardous Waste Authority, 1989—, Chatham Environ. Forum, 1990-93; mem. strategic planning com. Coun. State Ct. Judges Ga., 1996—; bd. dirs. Coastal Environ. Orgn. Ga., 1998—. Served with USAAC, 1942-46, ETO. Named Young Man of Yr. Atlanta, 1951; recipient Thomas H. gignilliat award Cultural Progress of Savannah, 1969, Tradition of Excellence award Ga. State Bar, 1988, 1st Ann. Coun. of State Cts. award named Ogden Doremus in his honor, 1993. Mem. ABA (chmn. environ. law com., gen. practice 1976-77), State Bar Ga. (chmn. ins. law sect. 1963-67, 77-83, cert. mediator Ga. commn. on dispute resolution), Savannah Bar Assn., Ga. Inst. Trial Advocacy (chmn. 1984-89), Izaak Walton league (founder Ga. chpt. 1950), Sierra Club (exec. com. Chattahoochee chpt. 1965-75, chair Legal Com. Sierra Club-Ga. chpt., Lifetime Achievement Ga. environ. coun. Citizenship award), Common Cause, Chatham Club, Chatham Tennis Club, Willow Lake Country Club, Atlanta Soc. General civil litigation, Environmental, Alternative dispute resolution. Home: RR 2 Box 188A Metter GA 30439-9570 Office: Doremus and Assocs Courthouse Sq PO Box 702 Metter GA 30439-0702 *It has been my experience that a love for this earth and all that it has is the most precious of our possessions. My hope is that love and kindness become universal.*

**DORFMAN, FREDERICK NILES,** lawyer; b. Phila., Sept. 28, 1952; children: Audrey, Robert. BS, Drexel U., 1975; JD, Pepperdine U., 1978. Bar: Pa. 1978, N.J. 1978, U.S. Ct. Appeals (3d cir.) 1985, Fla. 1992. Atty. Aetna Ins. Co., Phila., 1989-91, Phila. Fraternal Order Police Law Firm, Phila., 1991-92, Fireman's Fund Ins. Co., Phila., 1992-94; pvt. practice, Phila., 1978-89, King of Prussia, Pa., 1995—. Cubmaster Cub Scouts Am., Radnor, Pa., 1992-96. Mem. Pa. Bar Assn., Montgomery County Bar Assn. Workers' compensation, Personal injury, State civil litigation. Office: 677 W Dekalb Pike Ste 2D King Of Prussia PA 19406-3065

**DORGAN, JAMES RICHARD,** lawyer, educator; b. Jacksonville, Fla., Aug. 6, 1968; s. John Alston Jr. and Virginia (Zirkel) D. BA in English, Spring Hill Coll., Mobile, Ala., 1991; JD, Miss. Coll., 1995. Bar: Ala. 1996, U.S. Dist. Ct. (so. and mid. dists.) 1996. Pvt. practice Fairhope, Ala., 1996—; adj. prof. U. Mobile, 1997—, Spring Hill Coll., 1997—. Mem. Mobile Bar Assn., Baldwin County Bar Assn. General practice. Office: 314 Magnolia Ave Ste B Fairhope AL 36532-2434

**DORIA, ANTHONY NOTARNICOLA,** college dean, educator; b. Savona, Italy, June 2, 1927; s. Vito Sante and Jolanda (Giampaolo) Notarnicola. M.B.A., Wharton Sch., U. Pa., 1953; LL.M. (equivalent), U. Paris, 1960; D.Jr., U. Rome, 1962. Prof. history, bus. and internat. law Community Coll. at Suffolk County, Selden, N.Y., 1960-65, L.I. U., Southampton, N.Y., 1964-65; founder, pres. Royalton Coll. Sch. Internat. Affairs, S. Royalton, Vt., 1965-72; founder, dean Vt. Law Sch., 1972-74; dean Royalton Coll. Sch. Internat. Affairs (Royalton Coll. Law Study Center), 1974-92; prof. internat. law U. China, Beijing, 1992—; dir. grad. sch. program Internat. Bus. and Law - Hong Kong Ctr.; dir. grad. sch. program internat. bus. and law Hong Kong Ctr.; cons. internat. law and orgns.; panelist Am. Arbitration Assn.; mem. Vt. Gov.'s Commn. on Student Affairs, 1972-75. Author: Italy and the Free World, 1945, The Conquest of the Congo, 1947, Influences in the Making of Foreign Policy in the United States of America, Great Britain and France, 1953, Introduction to the Study of International Law, 1990. Candidate for U.S. Senate, 1986. Served with underground resistance movement World War II. Recipient Merit cert. UN; citation Boy Scouts Am., 1965. Mem. Am. Judicature Soc., Internat. Bar Assn., Internat. Law Assn., Am. Soc. Internat. Law, AAUP, Acad. Polit. Sci., Noble Assn. Chevaliers Pontificaux (life), Elysee (Paris), Penn and Pencil, Rotary (pres. 1990-91). Home: The Royalton Inn South Royalton VT 05068 Office: Royalton Coll Law Study Ctr South Royalton VT 05068

**DORIS, ALAN S(ANFORD),** lawyer; b. Cleve., June 18, 1947; s. Sam E. and Rebecca (Sunshine) D.; m. Nancy Rose Spitzer, Jan. 10, 1976; children: Matthew, Lisa. AB and BS in Bus. cum laude, Miami U., Oxford U., 1969; JD cum laude, Harvard U., 1972. Bar: Ohio 1972, U.S. Dist. Ct. (no. dist.) Ohio 1972, U.S. Tax Ct. 1972, U.S. Ct. Appeals (6th cir.) 1972. Assoc. Stotter, Familo, Cavitch, Elden & Durkin, Cleve., 1972-77; ptnr. Elden & Ford, Cleve., 1978-79, Benesch, Friedlander, Coplan & Aronoff, Cleve., 1980—. Editor: Ohio Transaction Guide. Treas. Hawthorne Valley Country Club, Cleve., 1984-85; chmn. Cleve. Tax Inst., 1994. Mem. ABA (chmn. capital recovery com. taxation sect. 1994-96). Avocation: golf. Corporate taxation, Taxation, general, Personal income taxation. Office: Benesch Friedlander Coplan & Aronoff 2300 American Rd Cleveland OH 44144-2301

**DORNAN, KEVIN WILLIAM,** lawyer; b. Rockville Centre, N.Y., Apr. 13, 1952; s. William G. and Grace M. (Maher) D. BA, Johns Hopkins U., 1973; student, U. Heidelberg, Germany, 1973-74; MA, U. N.C., 1975, Catholic U., 1979; JD, U. Md., Balt., 1987. Bar: Md. 1988, U.S. Dist. Ct. Md. 1988, U.S. Ct. Appeals (2nd, 4th, and D.C. cir.) 1988, U.S. Dist. Ct. (ea. and we. dist.) Ark. 1992, D.C. 1993, U.S. Dist. Ct. D.C. 1994, Fla. 1996, U.S. Ct. Appeals (11th cir.) 1996, U.S. Dist. Ct. (mid. dist.) Fla. 1997, U.S. Dist. Ct. (we. dist.) Tex. 1999, U.S. Supreme Ct. 1999. Assoc. Finley, Kumble, Wagner, Washington, 1987-88, Pillsbury, Madison & Sutro, Washington, 1989-91; sr. assoc. Winthrop, Stimson, Putnam & Roberts, Washington, 1991-94; prin. Law Offices of Kevin W. Dornan, North Bethesda, Md., 1994-96; sr. assoc. Salem, Saxon & Nielsen, PA, Tampa, Fla., 1997; gen. counsel Internat. Carrier Exch., Inc., Jacksonville, Fla., 1997—; adj. prof. Eckerd Coll. Bus. and Environ. Law, St. Petersburg, Fla., 1996—, St. Leo Coll. Bus. Ethics, St. Leo, Fla., 1996-97. Editor Md. Law Rev., 1986-87; contbr. article to profl. jour. Mem. adv. bd. Clinton-Gore Com., Washington, 1995-96; chair nat. alumni sch. com. Johns Hopkins U., Washington, 1976-82. Asper fellow U.S. Dist. Ct. Md., 1986, fellow U. N.C., 1974-75, Boston U., 1975-76; Rothenberg scholar U. Md., 1986-87. Mem. ABA, FBA, Md. State Bar Assn., D.C. Bar Assn., Fla. Bar. Democrat. Roman Catholic. Communications, Environmental, General corporate. Home: 700 Boardwalk Dr Apt 721 Ponte Vedra Beach FL 32082-6261 Office: 8421 Baymeadows Way Ste 1 Jacksonville FL 32256-1218

**DORNBUSCH, ARTHUR A., II,** lawyer; b. Peru, Ill., Nov. 8, 1943; s. Arthur A. Sr. and Genevieve C. (Knudtson) D.; children: Kimberly, Brendan, Courtney, Eric; m. Jacqueline Bahrs Montanus, Feb. 10, 1996. BA, Yale U., 1966; LLB, U. Pa., 1969. Bar: N.Y. 1970, U.S. Ct. Appeals. (2d cir.) 1971, U.S. Dist. Ct. (so. and ea. dists.) N.Y. 1971. Assoc. Dewey, Ballantine, Bushby, Palmer & Wood, N.Y.C., 1969-72; asst. gen. counsel Boise Cascade Corp., N.Y.C., 1972-75; asst. gen counsel Teleprompter Corp., N.Y.C., 1975-76; asst. gen. counsel Engelhard Industries div. Engelhard Minerals and Chem. Corp., Edison, N.J., 1976-80; v.p., gen. counsel Minerals and Chems. divsn. Engelhard Corp., Edison, 1980-84; v.p., gen. counsel, sec. Engelhard Corp., Iselin, N.J., 1984—. Mem. Pelham (N.Y.) Union Free Sch. Bd., 1979-82. Mem. ABA, N.Y. State Bar Assn., Assn. Bar City N.Y., Am. Corp. Counsel Assn., Am. Intellectual Property Law Assn., Am. Soc. Corp. Secs., Mfrs. Alliance for Productivity and Innovation. Antitrust, Patent, General corporate. Office: Engelhard Corp PO Box 770 101 Wood Ave S Iselin NJ 08830-2703

**DORNE, DAVID J.,** lawyer; b. Chgo., Dec. 9, 1946. BS magna cum laude, U. Ill., 1969; MSc, London Sch. Econs., 1970; JD cum laude, Boston U., 1973. Bar: N.Y. 1973, U.S. Ct. Appeals (2d cir.) 1973, U.S. Tax Ct. 1973, U.S. Dist. Ct. (so. dist.) N.Y. 1975, Calif. 1978. Mem. Seltzer Caplan Wilkins & McMahon P.C., San Diego. Mem. City of San Diego Charter Rev. Commn., 1989—. Mem. ABA (taxation sect., corp., banking and bus. law sect.), State Bar Calif. (taxation sect., real property law sect., chmn. personal income tax subcom. 1982-84), San Diego County Bar Assn., Assn. of Bar of City of N.Y. (taxation sect.), Beta Gamma Sigma. Taxation, general, Real property, General corporate. Office: Seltzer Caplan Wilkins & McMahon PC 2100 Symphony Tower 750 B St San Diego CA 92101-8114

**DORNETTE, W(ILLIAM) STUART,** lawyer, educator; b. Washington, Mar. 2, 1951; s. William Henry Lueders and Frances Roberta (Hester) D.; m. Martha Louise Mehl, Nov. 19, 1983; children: Marjorie Frances, Anna Christine, David Paul. AB, Williams Coll., 1972; JD, U. Va., 1975. Bar: Va. 1975, Ohio 1975, U.S. Dist. Ct. (so. dist.) Ohio, 1975, D.C. 1976, U.S. Ct. Appeals (6th cir.) 1977, U.S. Supreme Ct. 1980. Assoc. Taft, Stettinius & Hollister, Cin., 1975-83, ptnr., 1983—; instr. law U. Cin., 1980-87, adj. prof., 1988-91. Co-author: Federal Judiciary Almanac, 1984-87. Mem. Ohio Bd. Bar Examiners, 1992-93, Hamilton County Republican Exec. Com., 1982—; bd. dirs. Zool. Soc. Cin., 1983-94, Cin. Parks Found., 1995—. Mem. Cin. Bar Assn., Fed. Bar Assn., Ohio State Bar Assn., Am. Phys. Soc. Republican. Methodist. Federal civil litigation, State civil litigation, Sports. Home: 329 Bishopsbridge Dr Cincinnati OH 45255-3948 Office: 1800 Star Bank Ctr 425 Walnut St Cincinnati OH 45202-3923

**DORNFELD, SHARON WICKS,** lawyer; b. Detroit, Jan. 22, 1952; d. John Hoddard and Mary Catherine (Hogan) Wicks; m. William Harlan Dornfeld, Dec. 30, 1977; 2 children. BA, U. Mich., 1974, JD, 1981. Bar: Conn. 1982; U.S. Dist. Ct. Conn. 1983, U.S. Supreme Ct. 1996. Pvt. practice Danbury, Conn., 1988—. Bd. dirs. A Better Chance in Ridgefield, Conn., 1985-91; parking violations hearing officer Town of Ridgefield, 1988—; mem. Office of Child Advocate Adv. Com., 1996—. Mem. ABA, Nat. Assn. Counsel Children, Conn. Bar Assn., Danbury Bar Assn. (pres. 1995). Democrat. Christian Scientist. Family and matrimonial, Juvenile, General civil litigation. Office: 42 Main St Ste 1 Danbury CT 06810-3015

**DOROCKE, LAWRENCE FRANCIS,** lawyer; b. Chgo., Oct. 4, 1946; s. Walter P. and Effie M. (Gillis) D.; m. Diane L. Roberts, June 22, 1968; children: Todd D., Rob L., Jill A. BS in Econs., Purdue U., 1968, MS in Indsl. Relations, 1970; JD magna cum laude, Ind. U., 1973. Bar: Ind. 1973, U.S. Dist. Ct. (so. dist.) Ind. 1973, Iowa 1974, U.S. Ct. Appeals (7th cir.). Asst. mgr. personnel Comml. Solvents Corp., Terre Haute, Ind., 1970-71; law clk. to chief justice U.S. Dist. Ct. (so. dist.) Iowa, Des Moines, 1973-75; ptnr. Dann, Pecar, Newman & Kleiman P.C., Indpls., 1975—. Mem. ABA, Ind. Bar Assn., Indpls. Bar Assn. Roman Catholic. Real property, General corporate, Landlord-tenant. Home: 308 W Haydn Dr Ste 1316 Carmel IN 46032-7047 Office: Dann Pecar Newman & Kleiman PO Box 82008 1 American Sq Ste 2300 Indianapolis IN 46282-0001

**DORR, ROBERT CHARLES,** lawyer; b. Denver, Jan. 7, 1946; s. Owen and Rose Esther (Tudek) D.; m. Sandra Leah Gehlsen, Feb. 26, 1972; children: Bryan, Aric. BSEE, Milw. Sch. Engring., 1968; MSEE, Northwestern U., 1970; JD, U. Denver, 1975. Bar: Colo. 1975, U.S. Dist. Ct. Colo. 1975, U.S. Patent Office 1975. Mem. tech. staff Bell Labs., Naperville, Ill., 1968-72, patent staff, Denver, 1975-76; ptnr. Dorr, Carson, Sloan & Birney, P.C., Denver, 1976-86, sr. ptnr., 1986—; ptnr. Internat. Practicum Inst., Denver, 1979—; seminar speaker various profl. orgns. Co-author: Protecting Trade Secrets, Patents and Copyrights, 1995, 3rd edit., 1999, Protecting Trade Dress, 1992, 2d edit., 1999; contbr. articles to profl. jours. Active Citizens Com. for Retention of Judges, Denver, 1984. Milw. Sch. Engring. scholar, 1964-68; named Outstanding Young Man Am., 1976. Mem. ABA, Colo. Bar Assn. (pres. patent, trademark, copyright sect.), Douglas-Elbert County Bar Assn. (pres. 1983), IEEE, AAAS, Sigma Xi. Roman Catholic. Patent, Trademark and copyright, Computer. Home: 1755 S Hwy 83 PO Box 116 Franktown CO 80116-0116 Office: Dorr Carson Sloan & Birney PC 3010 E 6th Ave Denver CO 80206-4328

**DORR, RODERICK A.,** lawyer; b. Oklahoma City, Aug. 10, 1937; s. Clyde H. and Mary A. D. BS in Aero. Engring., U. Okla., 1961, JD, 1975. Bar: Okla., N.Mex., Calif., U.S. Dist. Ct. N.Mex. 1975, U.S. Dist. Ct. (no., ctrl., ea., so. dists.) Calif. 1983, U.S. Ct. Appeals (9th cir.) 1988, U.S. Ct. Appeals (10th cir.) 1977, U.S. Supreme Ct. 1982. Fighter pilot USAF, 1961-67, USAR, Dallas, 1967-72; comml. airline pilot Braniff Airways, Dallas, 1967-72; assoc. Civerolo, Hansen & Wolf, Albuquerque, 1975-77; asst. atty. gen. State of N.Mex., Santa Fe, 1977-78; ptnr. Terrazaz & Dorr, P.A., Santa Fe, 1978-81; asst. dist. atty. 1st Jud. Dist., Santa Fe, 1981-83; assoc. Thomas H. Lambert, P.C., San Diego, 1983, Pothier, Moore & Hinricks, Santa Ana, Calif., 1983, Magana, Cathcart et. al., L.A., 1984-93; pvt. practice Albuquerque, 1995, 96—; assoc. John A. Budagher & Assocs., Albuquerque, 1993-95; ptnr. Moore, Brewer & Burbott, La Jolla, Calif., 1995-96. Capt. USAF; LCDR USNR. Mem. N.Mex. Trial Lawyers Assn., Lawyer Pilots Bar Assn., Albuquerque Bar Assn. Aviation, Personal injury, General civil litigation. Office: 4159 Montgomery Blvd NE Albuquerque NM 87109-6742

**DORRIER, LINDSAY GORDON, JR.,** lawyer; b. Scottsville, Va., Aug. 27, 1943; s. Lindsay Gordon and Anne Shirley (Bruce) D.; m. Jane Ikenberry, Feb. 14, 1982; children: Margaret Anne, Lindsay Gordon III. BA, Trinity Coll., 1966; JD, U. Va., 1972; MBA, James Madison U., 1987; LLM, U. Va., 1989. Bar: Va. 1972, U.S. Dist. Ct. (we. dist.) Va. 1972. Law clk. to presiding judge U.S. Dist. Ct. (we. dist.) Va., Roanoke, 1972-73; assoc. Paxson, Smith, Boyd, Gilliam & Gouldman, Charlottesville, Va., 1973-76; sole practice Charlottesville, 1976-80; commonwealth atty. Albemarle County, Charlottesville, 1980-90; dir. Va. Dept. Criminal Justice Svcs., Richmond, 1990-94; pvt. practice Scottsville, Va., 1994—. Pres. Charlottesville-Albemarle Mental Health Assn., 1974-75, bd. dirs., 1973-76; pres. Jefferson Area Community Corrections Resources Bd., 1981-83, bd. dirs., 1981-90; mem. Albemarle County Bd. Suprs., 1976-80; Dem. candidate for Congress from 7th dist. Va., 1982; bd. dirs. Charlottesville-Albemarle United Way, 1983-90, Tandem Sch., 1987-91, James River Alcohol Safety Action Program, 1988-90; mem. Va. Dem. Leadership Com., 1989-93; co-chair Richmond One-to-One Partnership, 1992-94. Lt. col. JAGC, USAR, 1966-95. Mem. Nat. Criminal Justice Assn. (bd. dirs. 1990-94), Va. Bar Assn., Va. Assn. Local Exec. Constl. Officers (bd. dirs. 1982-86, pres. 1986-87), Va. Assn. Comml. Attys. (bd. dirs. 1984-90), Albemarle Hist. Soc. (pres. 1976-78), Fraternal Order Police, Am. Legion. Criminal, Probate.

**DORRIS, DAVID VERNON,** lawyer; b. Herrin, Ill., May 10, 1947; s. Cecil Vernon and Nora Madelene D.; children: David N., Amelia S., Daniel V.; m. Leigh Anne Lynch, Oct. 15, 1994; 1 child, Stephanie. BA in History, Blackburn Coll., 1969; JD, U. Ill., 1973. Bar: Ill. 1973. Asst. state's atty. McLean County State's Atty., Bloomington, Ill., 1973-74; atty. Jerome Mirza & Assocs., Ltd., Bloomington, Chgo., 1974—; bd. dirs. Ill. Inst. Continuing Legal Edn., Springfield, 1991-93. Mem. Ill. Trial Lawyers Assn. (pres. 1995-96), Ill. State Bar Assn. (chair tort & civil practice sect. coun. 1990-91). Democrat. Mem. Disciples of Christ Ch. Avocations: fast pitch softball, basketball, woodworking. Office: 705 E Washington St Bloomington IL 61701-4105

**DORSEN, DAVID M(ILTON),** lawyer; b. N.Y.C., Oct. 10, 1935; s. Arthur and Tanya (Stone) D.; m. Margaret L. Stern, Mar. 5, 1969 (div. Feb. 1976); m. Kenna D. Peusner, Jan. 24, 1997. AB, Harvard U., 1956, JD, 1959. Bar: N.Y. 1960, D.C. 1960, U.S. Supreme Ct. 1977. Assoc. Kaye, Scholer, Fierman, Hays & Handler, N.Y.C., 1960-64; asst. U.S. atty. U.S. Dist. Ct. (so. dist.) N.Y., 1964-69; dep. commr. and 1st dep. commr. N.Y.C. Dept. Investigation, 1969-73; asst. chief counsel Senate Watergate Com., Washington, 1973-74; ptnr. Sachs, Greenebaum & Tayler, Washington, 1974-91; of counsel Hughes Hubbard & Reed, Washington, 1991-94; pvt. practice Washington, 1994-98; of counsel Wallace King Marraro & Branson PLLC, Washington, 1998—; vis. lectr. pub. policy studies Terry Sanford Inst. Pub. Policy, Duke U., Durham, N.C., 1995—. Contbg. editor, wine and food editor The Washingtonian Mag., 1982—; assoc. prodr. Tolstoy, 1996; columnist The Hill, Washington, 1998—. Mem. D.C. Bar Assn. (chmn. arbitration bd. 1982-84), Internat. Club of Washington (chief counsel 1981-89). General civil litigation, Libel, Alternative dispute resolution. Home: 3501 Davis St NW Washington DC 20007-1426 Office: 1735 New York Ave NW Ste 400 Washington DC 20006-5209

**DORSEN, NORMAN,** lawyer, educator; b. N.Y.C., Sept. 4, 1930; s. Arthur and Tanya (Stone) D.; m. Harriette Koffler, Nov. 25, 1965; children: Jennifer, Caroline Gail, Anne. BA, Columbia U., 1950; LLB magna cum laude, Harvard U., 1953; postgrad., London Sch. Econs., 1955-56; LLD (hon.), Ripon Coll., 1981, John Jay Coll. Criminal Justice, 1992. Bar: D.C. 1953, N.Y. 1954. Law clk. to chief judge Calvert Magruder U.S. Ct. Appeals, Boston, 1956-57; law clk. to Justice John Marshall Harlan U.S. Supreme Ct., Washington, 1957-58; assoc. Dewey, Ballantine, Bushby, Palmer & Wood, N.Y.C., 1958-60; prof. law NYU Sch. Law, N.Y.C., 1961-81, Stokes prof., 1981—, dir. Hays civil liberties program, 1961—, dir. global law sch. program, 1994-96, chmn., 1996—; vis. prof. law London Sch. Econs., 1968, U. Calif., Berkeley, 1974-75, Harvard U., 1980, 83, 84; cons. U.S. Commn. on Violence, 1968-69, Random House, 1969-73, B.B.C., 1969-73, U.S. Commn. on Social Security, 1979-80, Native Am. Rights Fund, 1978-89; exec. dir. spl. com. on courtroom conduct Assn. Bar N.Y.C., 1970-73; chmn. Com. for Pub. Justice, 1972-74; vice chmn. HEW sec.'s rev. panel on new drug regulation, 1975-76, chmn., 1976-77; mem. N.Y.C. Commn. on Status of Women, 1978-80; chmn. Sec. of Treasury's Citizen Rev. Panel on Good O' Boy Round-up, 1995-96. Author: (with others) Political and Civil Rights in U.S., 3d edit., 1967, 4th edit., Vol. I, 1976, Vol. II, 1979, Frontiers of Civil Liberties, 1968, Discrimination and Civil Rights, 1969, (with L. Friedman) Disorder in the Court, 1973, (with S. Gillers) Regulation of Lawyers, 1985, 2d edit., 1989; editor: The Rights of Americans, 1971, (with S. Gillers) None of Your Business, 1974, Our Endangered Rights, 1984, The Evolving Constitution, 1987, (with others) Human Rights in Northern Ireland, 1991. 1st lt. JAGC, U.S. Army, 1953-55. Recipient medal French Minister of Justice, 1983; Fulbright Disting. Prof., Argentina, 1987, 88. Fellow Am. Acad. Arts and Scis.; mem. ABA (chmn. com. free speech and press 1968-70), ACLU (gen. counsel 1969-76, pres. 1976-91), Am. Law Inst., Coun. on Fgn. Rels., Lawyers Com. Human Rights (chmn. bd. dirs. 1995—), Lawyer Com. Civil Rights, Internat. Assn. Constnl. Law (exec. com.), U.S. Assn. Constnl. Law (pres. 1996—), Soc. Am. Law Tchrs. (pres. 1973-75), Thomas Jefferson Ctr. for Free Expression (trustee). Home: 146 Central Park W New York NY 10023-2005 Office: NYU Sch Law 40 Washington Sq S New York NY 10012-1005

**DORSEY, JAMES BAKER,** surgeon, lawyer; b. Saratoga Springs, N.Y., Aug. 29, 1927; s. Francis Edward and Katherine (Baker) D.; m. Patricia Ann Walsh, June 10, 1950; children: Katherine, Mary Lee, Pamela, Suzanne, James B., Jr., Alison. BA, Brown U., 1949; LLB, Union U. Sch., 1952, JD, 1991; MD, N.Y. Med. Coll., 1957. Bar: N.Y. 1953, Mass. 1988, U.S. Supreme Ct. 1982; lic. physician, N.Y., Mass., Calif. Intern Greenwich Hosp., Conn., 1957-58; resident White Plains Hosp., N.Y., 1958-59, Lenox Hill Hosp., N.Y.C., 1961-64; chmn. dept. surgery Saratoga Hosp., Saratoga Springs, 1976-79, 85-87; cons. surgeon Wesley Nursing Homes, Saratoga Springs, 1964—. Bd. dirs. Saratoga YMCA, Saratoga Springs, 1971-72; pres. Saratoga Springs Hist. Soc., 1972-74. Diplomate Am. Bd. Surgery. Fellow ACS, Am. Coll. Legal Medicine; mem. Saratoga County Bar Assn., Saratoga County Med. Soc. (pres. 1982-85), Med. Soc. N.Y., Mass. Med. Soc., N.Y. State Bar Assn., Mass. Bar Assn., AMA. Republican. Roman Catholic. Lodge: Elks, K.C. Personal injury, Product liability. Office: 112 S Broadway Adirondack Trust Bldg St 1 Saratoga Springs NY 12866

**DORSEY, PETER COLLINS,** federal judge; b. New London, Conn., Mar. 24, 1931; s. Thomas F., Jr. and Helen Mary (Collins) D.; m. Cornelia McEwen, June 26, 1954; children: Karen G., Peter C., Jennifer S., Christopher M. B.A., Yale U., 1953; J.D., Harvard U., 1959. Ptnr. Flanagan, Dorsey & Flanagan, New Haven, 1963-74; U.S. atty. Dept. Justice, New Haven, 1974-77; ptnr. Flanagan, Dorsey & Mulvey, New Haven, 1977-83; judge U.S. Dist. Ct. Conn., New Haven, 1983-99, chief judge, 1994-98, now sr. judge; mem. Jud. Conf. of U.S. Cts., 1995-98. Councilman Town of Hamden, Conn., 1961-69; town atty., 1973-74; commr. Bd. of Police, Hamden, 1977-81. Served to lt. comdr., USNR, 1953-56. Fellow Am. Coll. Trial Lawyers; mem. ABA (mem. house of dels. 1974-78), Conn. Bar Assn. (bd. govs. 1968-70, 74-78, pres. 1978), Am. Coll. Trial Lawyers, Conn. Def. Lawyers Assn. (pres. 1974), Am. Inns of Ct. Hartford (pres. 1991-93). Roman Catholic. Office: US Dist Ct 141 Church St New Haven CT 06510-2030

**DORSEY, RICHARD P., III,** lawyer, former state legislator; b. St. Louis, Sept. 7, 1959; s. Richard P. and Dolores (McNamara) D.; m. Elaine F. Dochnal; 1 child, Catherine Lian. BSBA, St. Louis U., 1981, MBA, 1984, JD, 1984. Bar: Mo. 1985, U.S. Dist. Ct. (ea. and we. dists.) Mo. 1985, U.S. Supreme Ct. 1991, U.S. Ct. Appeals (8th cir.) 1996. Assoc. Niedner, Niedner, Ahlheim & Bodeux, St. Charles, Mo., 1985-90; ptnr. Niedner, Ahlheim, Bodeux and Dorsey, St. Charles, 1990-95; mem. Ahlheim & Dorsey LLC, St. Charles, Mo., 1995—, Mo. Ho. of Reps., 1991-93; spl. counsel Ohio Atty. Gen., 1999—. Bd. dirs. St. Charles County ARC, 1985-91, Eagle Scout Assn., St. Louis, 1987-93, 94—, Florissant Twp. Dem. Party, 1987—, Ferguson Twp. Dem. Club, 1994—, Florissant Valley Shelter Workshop, 1990—, Florissant Valley Jaycees, 1990—, mem. bd. dirs., 1990-95, 96-99, pres., 1995-96; mem. bd. dirs. St. Louis High Alumni, 1994—, Florissant Rotary Club, 1997-98; mem. bd. St. Louis U. Sch. Bus. Adminstrn., 1995—; commr. Boy Scouts Am., St. Louis, 1984-92; mem. Cath. Commn. on Scouting, St. Louis, 1984—. Recipient Polaris award St. Louis Area coun. Boy Scouts Am., 1986, St. George award Boy Scouts Am., 1987; named One of Ten Outstanding Young Missourians, Mo. Jaycees, 1992. Mem. Bar Assn. Met. St. Louis, Mo. Bar Assn., St. Charles County Bar Assn., Assn. Trial Lawyers Am., Mo. Assn. Trial Attys., U.S. Jr. C. of C. (amb. 1998). Democrat. Roman Catholic. General practice, Taxation, general, Bankruptcy. Home: 16 Harneywold Dr Saint Louis MO 63136-2402 Office: Ahlheim & Dorsey LLC 2209 1st Capitol Dr Saint Charles MO 63301-5809

**DORSI, STEPHEN NATHAN,** lawyer, real estate development consultant; b. Bklyn., June 2, 1947; s. Stephen Nathan and Fannie (Christopher) D.; m. Phyllis Elizabeth Blastervold, Aug. 12, 1976; 1 child, Michael. AA, Pasadena City Coll., 1968; BA, Calif. State U., L.A., 1970; JD, Golden Gate U., 1973. Bar: Calif. 1973, U.S. Dist. Ct. (no. dist.) Calif. 1973, U.S. Dist. Ct. (cen. dist.) Calif. 1974, U.S. Ct. Appeals (9th cir.) 1973. Sole practitioner San Luis Obispo, Calif., 1974—; bd. dirs. Sta. KCBX Pub. Radio, San Luis Obispo, 1975—. Author: Horse Trader's Guide, 1987. Bd. bldg. trustee San

Luis Obispo Art Ctr., 1976—. Avocations: flying, youth sports coach and referee, Scouting. Estate planning, Trademark and copyright, Real property. Home: PO Box 1253 San Luis Obispo CA 93406-1253 Office: 1026 Chorro St San Luis Obispo CA 93401-3230

**DORTCH, CLARENCE, III,** lawyer; b. Talladega, Ala., May 16, 1962; s. Clarence Jr. and Peggy (White) D.; m. Floretta James, Dec. 21, 1985; children: Clarence IV, Thayer Johnetta. BA, Talladega Coll., 1983; JD, Temple U., 1986. BarL Ala. 1987, U.S. Dist Ct. (no. dist.) Ala. 1987. Law clk. Love, Love & Love, Talladega, 1985-86, Reid & Thomas, Attys., Anniston, Ala., 1986, Schoel, Ogle, & Benton, Birmingham, Ala., 1968-87, Ala. Supreme Ct., Birmingham, 1988-89; assoc. Oscar W. Adams III law offices, Birmingham, 1987-88; pvt. practice Birmingham, 1989—. Mem. Ala. Lawyers Assn., Nat. Bar Assn., Magic City Bar Assn., Assn. Trial Lawyers Am., Internat. Platform Assn., Alpha Phi Alpha, Phi Alpha Theta. Democrat. Methodist. Personal injury, Bankruptcy, Criminal. Home: 106 Harrison Dr Talladega AL 35160-2317 Office: 2000 1st Ave N Ste 450 Birmingham AL 35203-4125

**DORWART, DONALD BRUCE,** lawyer; b. Zanesville, Ohio, Dec. 12, 1949; s. Walter G. and Katherine (Kachmar) D.; m. Judith K. Coleman, Aug. 21, 1971; children: Claire Lauren, Hillary Beth. BA, Vanderbilt U., 1971; JD, Washington U., St. Louis, 1974. Bar: Mo. 1974, U.S. Dist. Ct. (ea. dist.) Mo. 1974. Assoc. Thompson Coburn LLP, St. Louis, 1974-79, ptnr., 1980—; dir. New Energy Corp. Ind., 1992-95. Contbr. articles to profl. jours. Mem. ABA, Maritime Law Assn. U.S. (proctor, mem. maritime fin. com. 1980—), Bar Assn. Met. St. Louis (chair securities regulation com. 1979), Focus St. Louis (mem. selection com. 1990-91, mem. fin. com. 1990—, mem. implementation steering com. 1988-90), Noonday Club. Mergers and acquisitions, Admiralty, General corporate. Office: Thompson Coburn 1 Mercantile Ctr Ste 3300 Saint Louis MO 63101-1643

**DOST, MARK W.,** lawyer; b. Attleboro, Mass., May 22, 1955; s. Raymond and A. Louise (Fraser) D.; m. Karen M. Sullivan, Aug. 1976; children: Christopher, Stephen, Gregory, Isaac. AB summa cum laude, U. Mass., 1978; JD cum laude, Boston Coll., 1981. Bar: Conn. 1981, U.S. Dist. Ct. Conn. 1986, U.S. Tax Ct. 1985. Atty. Gager & Henry, Waterbury, Conn., 1981-95; ptnr. Tinley, Nastri, Renehan & Dost, Waterbury, 1995—. Author: (with John V. Galiette) Planning for Retirement Benefit Distributions, 1995, 2d revised edit., 1999. Fellow Am. Coll. Trust and Estate Counsel; mem. ABA, Conn. Bar Assn. (exec. com., elder law sect. 1991—, exec. com., estates and probate sect. 1991—, chair elder law sect. 1994-96, chair publs. com. 1997—), Nat. Acad. Elder Law Attys. Estate planning, Probate, Estate taxation. Office: Tinley Nastri Renehan Dost 60 N Main St Waterbury CT 06702-1403

**DOSTART, PAUL JOSEPH,** lawyer, investor and director; b. Riceville, Iowa, Nov. 12, 1951; s. Leonard Atchison and Lois Marie Dostart; m. Joyce Alene Sicking, Aug. 14, 1976; children: Zachariah Paul, Samuel Paul. BS, Iowa State U., 1973; JD, U. Houston, 1977; LLM in Taxation, NYU, 1978. Bar: Tex, 1977, Calif. 1978; CPA, Ill. Mng. dir., prin. Torrey Venture Group, LaJolla, Calif., 1993—; mng. ptr. Dostart, Clapp & Coveney LLP; adj. prof. U. San Diego, 1986-90; bd. dirs. various cos., 1990—. Editor Houston Law Rev.; contbr. articles to profl. jours. founder U. Houston Tax Law Soc.; bd. dirs. Christian Exec. Officers, 1988-91, pres., 1989-90. Lasker scholar, NYU, Nat. Merit scholar. Fellow Am. Bar Found. (life); mem. ABA (chmn. various subcoms. sect. taxation 1982—, exempt orgns. com. 1977—), Calif. Bar Assn. (tax and bus. sects.), San Diego County Bar Assn. (chmn. tax sect. 1989), San Diego Tax Practitioners Group, Am. Electronics Assn. (San Diego coun. exec. com. 1993-95), World Trade Assn. (bd. dirs.), Order of Barons (chancellor), Phi Delta Phi (magister Hutcheson Inn.). Presbyterian. General corporate, Non-profit and tax-exempt organizations, Taxation, general. Office: Dostart Clapp & Coveney LLP 4370 La Jolla Village Dr San Diego CA 92122-1249

**DOTTEN, MICHAEL CHESTER,** lawyer; b. Marathon, Ont., Can., Feb. 23, 1952; came to U.S., 1957; s. William James and Ona Adelaide (Sheppard) D.; m. Kathleen Curtis, Aug. 17, 1974 (div. July 1991); children: Matthew Curtis, Tyler Ryan; m. Cheryl Calvin, Apr. 16, 1994. BS in Polit. Sci., U. Oreg., 1974, JD, 1977. Bar: Idaho 1977, Oreg. 1978, U.S. Dist. Ct. Idaho 1977, U.S. Dist. Ct. Oreg. 1978, U.S. Ct. Appeals (9th cir.), U.S. Ct. Appeals (D.C. cir.) 1987, U.S. Ct. Claims 1986, U.S. Supreme Ct. 1996. Staff asst. U.S. Senator Bob Packwood, Washington, 1973-74; asst. atty. gen. State of Idaho, Boise, 1977-78; chief rate counsel Bonneville Power Adminstrn., Portland, 1978-83; spl. counsel Heller, Ehrman, White & McAuliffe, Portland, 1983-84, ptnr., 1985-98, 99; gen. counsel PG&E Gas Transmission, N.W. Corp., Portland, 1998-99; utility com. mem. Ctr. for Pub. Resources, N.Y.C., 1992—. Coun. Emanual Hosp. Assocs., Portland, 1988-92; bd. dirs. William Temple House, 1995—, chmn. devel. com., 1996-98, v.p., 1997-98, pres., 1998—; active Portland Interneighborhood Trans. Rev. Commn., 1986-88. Hunter Leadership scholar U. Oreg., 1973, Oreg. scholar, 1970. Mem. ABA (chmn. electric power com. sect. natural resources 1985-88, coun. liaison energy com. 1990-93, coordinating group on energy law 1992-96), Fed. Bar Assn. (pres. Oreg. chpt. 1989-90, Chpt. Activity award 1990, Pres. award 1988-89), Oreg. State Bar (chmn. dispute resolution com. 1986-87), U. Oreg. Law Sch. Alumni Assn. (pres. 1989-92), Multnomah Athletic Club. Democrat. Episcopalian. Avocations: snow skiing, golf, hiking, travel, racquetball. Administrative and regulatory, Public utilities, FERC practice. Office: PG&E Gas Transmission NW Corp 2100 SW River Pky Portland OR 97201-8009

**DOTY, DAVID SINGLETON,** federal judge; b. Anoka, Minn., June 30, 1929. BA, U. Minn., 1961, LLB, 1961; LLD (hon.), William Mitchell Coll. Law. Bar: Minn. 1961, U.S. Ct. Appeals (8th and 9th cirs.) 1976, U.S. Supreme Ct. 1982. V.p., dir. Popham, Haik, Schnobrich, Kaufman & Doty, Mpls., 1962-87, pres., 1977-79; instr. William Mitchell Coll. Law, Mpls., 1963-64; judge U.S. Dist. Ct. for Minn., Mpls., 1987—. Mem. Adv. Com. on Civil Rules, 1992-98, Adv. Com. on Evidence Rules, 1994-98; trustee Mpls. Libr. Bd., 1969-79, Mpls. Found., 1976-83. Fellow ABA Found.; mem. ABA, Minn. Bar Assn. (gov. 1976-87, sec. 1980-83, pres. 1984-85), Hennepin County Bar Assn. (pres. 1975-76), Am. Judicature Soc., Am. Law Inst. Home: 23 Greenway Gables Minneapolis MN 55403-2145 Office: US Dist Ct 14 W US Courthouse 300 S 4th St Minneapolis MN 55415-1320

**DOTY, SALLY BURCHFIELD,** lawyer; b. Kosciusko, Miss., Dec. 22, 1966; d. Charles Edward and Betty Prewitt Burchfield; m. W. Don Doty, June 4, 1988; children: Mary Eleanor, Sarah Caroline. BA, Miss. U. for Women, 1988; JD, Miss. Coll., 1991. Bar: Miss. 1991, U.S. Dist. Ct. (no. and so. dists.) Miss. 1991, U.S. Ct. Appeals (5th cir.) 1991. Assoc. Wells, Moore, Simmons & Neal, Jackson, Miss., 1991-93, Allen, Allen, Boerner & Breeland, Brookhaven, Miss., 1997—; dir. legal writing Miss. Coll. Sch. of Law, Jackson, 1994-96. Author chpt.: Mississippi Civil Procedure, 1995. Mem. ABA, Miss. Bar Assn., Lincoln County Bar Assn. Methodist. General civil litigation, Civil rights, General corporate. Home: 312 Becker St Brookhaven MS 39601-3214 Office: Allen Allen Boerner & Breeland 214 Justice St Brookhaven MS 39601-3325

**DOUAIHY, TONI PATRICIA,** lawyer; b. St. Louis, Jan. 27, 1967; d. Lynn Louis and Mary Gail Surrett; m. Thomas Zakhia Douaihy, Dec. 3, 1987; children: Salim Zakhia, Noah Zakhia. BA in History, BA in Spanish, U. Mo., 1991; JD, Washington U., St. Louis, 1994. Bar: Mo. 1994, Ill. 1995. Of counsel The May Dept. Stores Co., St. Louis, 1993—. Vol. lawyer Legal Svcs. Eastern Mo., St. Louis, 1994—; mem. Compton Heights Assn., St. Louis, 1996—. Mem. Bar Assn. Metro. St. Louis. Republican. Avocations: reading, gourmet cooking, gardening. Labor, Federal civil litigation, State civil litigation. Office: The May Dept Stores Co 611 Olive St Ste 1750 Saint Louis MO 63101-1721

**DOUB, WILLIAM OFFUTT,** lawyer; b. Cumberland, Md., Sept. 3, 1931; s. Albert A. and Fannabelle (Offutt) D.; m. Mary Graham Boggs, Sept. 12, 1959; children: Joseph Peyton, Albert A., II. A.B., Washington and Jefferson Coll., 1953; LL.B., U. Md., 1956. Bar: Md. 1956, D.C. 1974. With law dept. B. & O. R.R., 1955-57; assoc. Bartlett Poe & Claggett, Balt., 1957-61; ptnr. Niles Barton & Wilmer, Balt., 1961-71; commr. AEC, 1971-74; ptnr. LeBoeuf, Lamb, Leiby & MacRae, Washington, 1974-77, Doub, Muntzing and Glasgow, Washington, 1977-91, Newman & Holtzinger, P.C., Washington, 1991-94, Morgan Lewis & Bockius, Washington, 1995—; chmn. Minimum Wage Commn., Balt., 1964-66; peoples' counsel Md. Pub. Service Commn., 1967-68, chmn., 1968-71; vice chmn. Washington Met. Area Transit Commn., 1968-71; mem. President's Air Quality Adv. Bd., 1970-71; mem. exec. adv. com. FPC, 1969-71, Nat. Gas Survey, 1975-78; pres. Great Lakes Conf. Pub. Utility Commrs., 1971; mem. nat. adv. bd. Am. Nat. Standards Inst., 1975-80; mem. Md. Adv. Com. Retardation, 1969-71. Mem. Adminstrv. Conf., U.S., 1973-75; chmn. U.S. Energy Assn., Inc., World Energy Conf., 1978-80, U.S. del., 1974, 77, 80, 83, 86, 89, 92, 95, 98; vice chmn. World Energy Conf., 1986-88, hon. vice chmn., 1988—; mem. adv. groups Nat. Acad. Pub. Adminstrn., NSF; presdl. appointee as rep. to So. States Energy Bd., 1983-90; bd. govs. Mid. East Inst. of U.S., 1982-86, 88-94, 95—; mem. exec. com. Thomas Alva Edison Found., 1983-90, 85-90; presdl. appointee 33d Ann. Conf. of Internat. Atomic Energy Agy., 1989. Recipient Nat. Energy award U.S. Energy Assn., 1998. Mem. Met. Club. Nuclear power, Public utilities, Legislative.

**DOUCHKESS, GEORGE,** lawyer; b. N.Y.C., Apr. 19, 1911; s. Frank A. and Dorothy (Grunberg) D.; m. Sonia Sloshay; children—Donald, Barbara. B.B.A. in Acctg., CCNY, 1936; J.D., Bklyn. Law Sch., 1939. Bar: N.Y. 1940, U.S. dist. Ct. (ea. dist.) N.Y., U.S. Dist. Ct. (so. dist.) N.Y. 1951, U.S. Supreme Ct. 1992. Claim supr. Aetna Casualty & Surety Co., N.Y.C., 1940-44; compensation hearing attorney Liberty Mut. Ins. Co., N.Y.C., 1944-47; compensation atty. Preferred Accident & Ins. Co., N.Y.C., 1947-51; U.S. supt. compensation claims div., compensation atty. Gen. Fire & Casualty Co., N.Y.C., 1951-65; compensation atty. Zurich Am. Ins. Co., N.Y.C., 1965-96. Mem. Torch and Scroll. Republican. Administrative and regulatory, Workers' compensation. Home: 715 Park Ave New York NY 10021-5047

**DOUDNA, HEATHER LYNN,** lawyer; b. Fairfax, Va., Sept. 4, 1968; d. Donald Alexander Britton and Beth Ann Dalessandra; 1 child, Sydney Elizabeth. BS in Fin., Fla. State U., 1990; JD, Stetson U., 1993. Bar: Fla. 1993; U.S. Dist. Ct. (mid. dist. Fla.) 1994. Law clk. Clearwater, Fla., 1994; corporate counsel Adminstrn. Inc, Clearwater, 1994—. Mem. Clearwater Bar Assn. Avocations: kayaking, bicycling. General corporate, Consumer commercial, Labor. Office: Adminstrn Inc 2536 Countryside Blvd Fl 6 Clearwater FL 33763-1639

**DOUGAN, STACEY PASTEL,** lawyer; b. Pitts., Feb. 20, 1963; d. Donald Joseph and Patricia Janeda Dougan; m. Marvin Paul Pastel II, Apr. 28, 1991; 1 child, Justin, Matthew Pastel. BA in Polit. Sci., U. Miami, 1985; JD, Fla. State U., 1991; LLM with high honors, Columbia U. Pro se law clk. to Hon. Patricia Fansett & G. Kendall Sharp U.S. Dist. Ct. (mid. dist.) Fla., Orlando, 1991-92; asst. pub. defender Office of Pub. Defender of Broward County, Ft. Lauderdale, Fla., 1992-96; assoc. Greenberg Traurig, Miami, Fla., 1996—; bd. dirs. Legal Svcs. of Greater Miami. Vol. atty. Guardian Ad Litem Program, 11th Cir., Miami, 1997-98; mem. Fla. Coalition Against Domestic Violence, Tallahassee, 1997—. Harlan Fiske Stone scholar Columbia U.; Pub. Svc. fellow Fla. Bar Found., 1988-91. Mem. Fla. Assn. Women Lawyers, Dade County Bar Assn. (guardian ad litem Put Something Back program 1996-98). General civil litigation, General corporate. Home: 1301 NE 101st St Miami Shores FL 33138-2610 Office: Greenberg Traurig 1221 Brickell Ave Miami FL 33131-3224

**DOUGHERTY, CHARLES RAYMOND,** lawyer; b. Buffalo, Jan. 21, 1954; s. Charles H. Dougherty and Anne E. Carey; m. Lisa Lee, Oct. 10, 1993; children: Pamela, Charles L., Memphis. BA, Hampshire Coll., 1975; JD, Boston U., 1980. Bar: Mass. 1980. Law clk. U.S. Ct. Appeals (1st cir.), Boston, 1980-81; from assoc. to mem. Hill & Barlow, Boston, 1981—. Gen. counsel ACLU, Boston; bd. dirs. BBB, Boston, 1996-97. Office: Hill & Barlow One International Pl Boston MA 02114

**DOUGHERTY, GERARD MICHAEL,** lawyer; b. Glen Cove, N.Y., May 11, 1959; s. Joseph John and Gina (DeGeorge) D.; m. Sherry Dougherty, Oct. 15, 1988; children: Briana Kristin, Danielle Caitlyn. BS in Mktg. and Econs., St. Johns U., 1981; JD, Southwestern U., 1984. Bar: Calif. 1985. Assoc. Matthew Biren & Assocs., L.A., 1984-87, Alfonso, Klonsky & Sternberg, Woodland Hills, Calif., 1987-89, Anderson Krehbiel McCreary, Westlake Village, Calif., 1989-95; ptnr. Dougherty and Waters, Simi Valley, Calif., 1995-97; prin. Dougherty & Landon, P.L.C., Westlake Village, Calif., 1997-98; sr. ptnr. Dougherty & Landon, P.L.C., Thousand Oaks, 1999—. Co-host Law Talk, KVEN Radio, Ventura, Calif. Coach Simi Valley Boys and Girls Club, 1995—; v.p. Simi Valley Rep. Club, 1996-97; bd. mem. Calif. Congress Reps., 1997—. Mem. Ventura County Bar Assn., Bus. Networking Internat., Westlake Village, Entrepreneurs United (Conejo Valley), Kiwanis. Roman Catholic. Avocations: ice and roller hockey, boating, camping. General civil litigation, Family and matrimonial, Construction. Office: Dougherty & Landon 2660 Townsgate Rd Ste 400 Thousand Oaks CA 91361-5715

**DOUGHERTY, JOHN CHRYSOSTOM, III,** lawyer; b. Beeville, Tex., May 3, 1915; s. John Chrysostom and Mary V. (Henderson) D.; m. Mary Ireland Graves, Apr. 18, 1942 (dec. July 1977); children: Mary Ireland, John Chrysostom IV; m. Bea Ann Smith, June 1978 (div. 1981); m. Sarah B. Randle, 1981 (dec. June 1997). BA, U. Tex., 1937; LLB, Harvard U., 1940; diploma, Inter-Am. Acad. Internat. and Comparative Law, Havana, Cuba, 1948. Bar: Tex. 1940. Atty. Hewit & Dougherty, Beeville, 1940-41; ptnr. Graves & Dougherty, Austin, Tex., 1946-50, Graves, Dougherty & Greenhill, Austin, 1950-57, Graves, Dougherty & Gee, Austin, 1957-60, Graves, Dougherty, Gee & Hearon, Austin, 1961-66, Graves, Dougherty, Gee, Hearon, Moody & Garwood, Austin, 1966-73, Graves, Dougherty, Hearon, Moody & Garwood, Austin, 1973-79; ptnr. Graves, Dougherty, Hearon & Moody, Austin, 1979-93, sr. counsel, 1993—; ret., 1997; spl. asst. atty. gen., 1949-50; Hon. French Consul, Austin, 1971-86; lectr. on tax, estate planning, probate code, community property problems; mem. Tex. Submerged Lands Adv. Com., 1963-72, Tex. Bus. and Commerce Code Adv. Com., 1964-66, Gov.'s Com. on Marine Resources, 1970-71, Gov.'s Planning Com. on Colorado River Basin Water Quality Mgmt. Study, 1972-73, Tex. Legis. Property Tax Com., 1973-75. Co-editor: Texas Appellate Practice, 1964, 2d edit., 1977; contbr. Bowe, Estate Planning and Taxation, 1957, 65; Texas Lawyers Practice Guide, 1967, 71, How to Live and Die with Texas Probate, 1968, 7th edit., 1995, Texas Estate Administration, 1975, 78; mem. bd. editors: Appellate Procedure in Tex., 1964, 2d edit., 1982; contbr. articles to legal jours. Bd. dirs. Tex. Beta Students Aid Fund, 1949-84, Grenville Clark Fund at Dartmouth Coll., 1976-90, Umlauf Sculpture Garden, Inc., 1990-91, New Life Inst., 1993—; past bd. dirs. Advanced Religious Study Found., Holy Cross Hosp., Sea Arama, Inc., Nat. Pollution Control Found., Austin Nat. Bank; trustee St. Stephen's Episcopal Sch., Austin, 1969-83, Tex. Equal Access to Justice Found., 1986-90, U. Tex. Law Sch. Found., 1974—; mem. adv. com. Legal Assts. Tng. Inst., U. Tex., 1990—; mem. vis. com. Harvard Law Sch., 1983-87. Capt. C.I.C., AUS, 1941-44, JAGC, 1944-46, maj. USAR. Decorated Medaille Française, France, Medaille d'honneur en Argent des Affairs Etrangeres, France, chevalier l'Ordre Nat. du Merite. Fellow Am. Bar Found., Tex. Bar Found., Am. Coll. Trust and Estate Counsel, Am. Coll. Tax Counsel; mem. ABA (ho. of dels. 1982-88, standing com. on lawyers pub. responsibility 1983-85, mem. spl. com. on delivery legal svcs. 1987-91, com. legal problems of the elderly 1997—), Am. Arbitration Assn. (nat. panel arbitrators 1958-90), Travis County Bar Assn. (pres. 1979-80), Internat. Acad. Estate and Trust Law (exec. coun. 1988-90), State Bar Tex. (chmn. sect. taxation 1965-66, pres. 1979-80, com. legal svcs. to the poor 1986-94), Am. Judicature Soc. (bd. dirs. 1985-87), Am. Law Inst. (adv. com. project law governing lawyers 1990-97), Tex. Supreme Ct. Hist. Soc. (trustee, chmn. 1999—), Philos. Soc. Tex. (pres. 1989, bd. dirs. 1989—), Harvard Law Sch. Assn. (mem. com. on pub. svc. law 1990-95, chmn. 1990-95, coun. 1991-95, exec. com. 1992-95), Tex. Appleseed, Inc. (bd. dirs. 1996—), Rotary. Presbyterian. E-mail: cdougherty@gdhm.com. Estate planning, Probate, Estate taxation. Home: 6 Green Ln Austin TX 78703-2515 Office: 515 Congress Ave Ste 2300 Austin TX 78701-3503 also: PO Box 98 Austin TX 78767-0098

**DOUGHERTY, RONALD WILLIAM,** lawyer; b. Canton, Ohio, Dec. 6, 1932; s. Russell Dewey and Agnes Elizabeth (Arnold) D.; m. Carole Dee Stover, Aug. 28, 1954; children: Kerry Jane, Russell Delbert. BA, Dartmouth Coll., 1954; JD, U. Va., 1960. Ptnr. Krugliak, Wilkins, Griffiths and Dougherty, Canton, Ohio, 1960—; bd. dirs. Ohio Printing Co., Ohio Law Abstract Publ. Co.; asst. solicitor City of Canton, 1966-68; lectr. legal seminars. Sec. bd. trustees Christ Prsbyn. Ch., Canton, 1972-74; mem. exec. com. Rep. Party, Stark County, Ohio; mem. allocations coun. United Way Star County, chmn., 1989, chmn. legal divsn., Rainbow Club, Stark County Bluecoats. Lt. capt. USAF, 1954-57. Recipient awards Ohio Jaycees, Canton Jaycees, Svc. award Buckey Coun. Boy Scouts Am., 1974. Fellow Ohio State Bar Found. (life); mem. ABA, Stark County Bar Assn. (pres. 1983-84, chmn. pub. defender commn. 1976—), Ohio State Bar Assn. (coun. dels. 1978-84, exec. com. 1985-88, bd. govs. 1991-94, chmn. budget and hdqs. com. 1987-88, 93-94, media law com., family law com.), Pro Football Hall of Fame Enshrinees (civic dinner com. 1989, 90, 91, gen. vice-chmn. festival 1991, chmn. 1992-96, chmn. steering com. 1993, alumni assn. 1993-96, gen. counsel), Ohio Acad. Trial Lawyers, Assn. Trials Lawyers Am., Canton Regional C. of C. (chmn. city-county govt. affairs com. 1986-92, chmn. regionalization com. 1990-92, chmn. annexation com. 1990-92, bd. trustees 1991-97, vice-chmn. bd. 1993, sr. vice-chmn. bd. 1994, chmn. bd. 1995), Ohio Jaycess (former legal counsel 1965-66, award), Shady Hollow Country (chmn. long range planning com. 1990, pres. 1978), Canton (bd. trustees 1988-93), Dartmouth (pres. N.E. Ohio 1978—). Home: 340 Lakecrest St NW Canton OH 44709-1510 Office: Krugliak Wilkins Griffiths & Dougherty 4775 Munson St NW Canton OH 44718-3612

**DOUGHTY, MARK ANTHONY,** lawyer; b. Pasadena, Calif., Aug. 18, 1951; s. Lawrence Richard and Bertha Lou D.; children: Matthew James, Luke Anthony. BA in Bus. Law, Calif. State U., Chico, 1976; JD, U. Pacific, Sacramento, Calif., 1979. Bar: Calif. 1979, U.S. Dist. Ct. (ea. dist.) Calif. 1979. Law clk. Calif. Ct. Appeals (5th cir.), Fresno, Calif., 1979-80; assoc. Ashby and Guth, Yuba City, Calif., 1980-82; ptnr. Ashby, Guth and Doughty, Yuba City, 1982-86, Ashby & Doughty, Yuba City, 1986-92; prin. Law Offices of Mark A. Doughty, Yuba City, 1992—. Pres. Russian Radio Bible Inst. em. Network Profls. Yuba City, Consumer Attys. of Calif. (bd. govs. 19th dist.), Fellowship of Christian Businessmen. Republican. Avocations: fathering, golf, private pilot, hunting, boating. Fax: 530-674-1180. E-mail: mark@golaw.com. General civil litigation, Estate planning, Personal injury. Home: 1691 Corsica Dr Yuba City CA 95993-1124 Office: Law Offices of Mark A Doughty 1528 Poole Blvd Ste A PO Box 3420 Yuba City CA 95992

**DOUGLAS, AARON KIRK,** legal firm marketing executive; b. Springfield, Oreg., Aug. 9, 1961; s. Robert Daniel and Emily B. Buss. BA, U. Oreg., 1983; Paralegal Cert., Edmonds (Wash.) C.C., 1993. Broadcast news writer, reporter KPNW AM/FM, Eugene, Oreg., 1980-83; weekend assignment news editor KEZI-TV 9, Eugene, 1982-83; office mgr., mktg. coord. Eugene Mcpl. Ct., 1983-88, Hult Ctr. for the Performing Arts, Eugene, 1983-88; TV news writer KIRO-TV 7, Seattle, 1988-89; legal sec., paralegal Law Offices of Steven J. Fields, Seattle, 1989-96; paralegal, newsletter editor, mktg. adminstr. Lane Powell Spears Lubersky LLP, Seattle, 1995-98; client svcs. dir. Barran Liebman LLP, Portland, Oreg., 1998—. Vocalist local group High Society Jazz Ensemble. Bd. dirs., v.p. Epilepsy Found. Oreg., Portland, 1999—. Mem. Soc. for Profl. Acct. and Atty. Marketers (unofcl. chair). Democrat. Mem. Sci. of the Soul Ch. Home: 17567 NW Sauvie ISL Rd Portland OR 97231 Office: Barran Liebman LLp 601 SW 2nd Ave Fl D Portland OR 97204-3154

**DOUGLAS, ANDREW,** state supreme court justice; b. Toledo, July 5, 1932; 4 children. J.D., U. Toledo, 1959. Bar: Ohio 1960, U.S. Dist. Ct. (no. dist.) Ohio 1960. Former ptnr. Winchester & Douglas; judge Ohio 6th Dist. Ct. Appeals, 1981-84; justice Ohio Supreme Ct., 1985—; mem. nat. adv. bd. Ctr. for Informatics Law John Marshall Law Sch., Chgo.; former spl. counsel Atty. Gen. of Ohio; former instr. law Ohio Dominican Coll. Served with U.S. Army, 1952-54. Recipient award Maumee Valley council Girl Scouts U.S., 1976, Outstanding Service award Toledo Police Command Officers Assn., 1980, Toledo Soc. for Autistic Children and Adults, 1983, Extra-Spl. Person award Central Catholic High Sch., 1981, Disting. Service award Toledo Police Patrolman's Assn., 1982, award Ohio Hispanic Inst. Opportunity, 1985, Disting. Merit award Alpha Sigma Phi, 1988, Gold "T" award U. Toledo, First Amendment award Cen. Ohio Chpt. Soc. Profl. Journalists Sigma Delta Chi, 1989; named to Woodward High Sch. Hall of Fame. Mem. Toledo Bar Assn., Lucas County Bar Assn., Ohio Bar Assn., Toledo U. Alumni Assn., U. Toledo Coll. Law Alumni Assn. (Disting. Alumnus award 1991), Internat. Inst., North Toledo Old Timers Assn., Old Newsboys Goodfellow Assn., Pi Sigma Alpha, Delta Theta Phi. Office: Ohio Supreme Ct 30 E Broad St Fl 3 Columbus OH 43266-0001*

**DOUGLAS, JAMES MATTHEW,** law educator; b. Onalaska, Tex., Feb. 11, 1944; s. Desso D. and Mary L. (Durden) D.; div.; children: DeLicia, Renee. BA in Math., Tex. So. U., 1966; JD, 1970; MS Law, Stanford U., 1971. Bar: Tex. 1970. Programmer analyst Singer Gen. Precision Co., Houston, 1966-70, 71-72; asst. prof. law Tex. So. U., Houston, 1971-72; asst. prof. Cleve. State U., Cleve.-Marshall Coll. Law, 1972-75; asst. prof., asst. dean student affairs, 1974-75; assoc. prof. law, assoc. dean Coll. of Law Syracuse (N.Y.) U., 1975-80; prof. law Northea. U., Boston, 1980-81; dean, prof. law Tex. So. U., Houston, 1981-95, provost, v.p. acad. affairs, 1995, pres., prof. 1995—; mem. Law Sch. Admissions Coun.; cons. computer law and computer contracts; bd. dirs. Civil Ct. Legal Svcs., Gulf Coast Legal Found.; bd. dirs. Boy Scouts Am., mem. exec. com., 1998—. Mem. editl. bd. The Tex. Lawyer. Mem. ABA (mem. affirmative action com.), Tex. Bar Assn., Houston Bar Assn., Hiscock Legal Soc. (dir.), Houston C. of C. (mem. chmns. club), Greater Houston Partnership (bd. of dir.). Home: 5318 Calhoun Rd Houston TX 77021-1714 Office: Tex U Thurgood Marshall Law Sch Bldg 3100 Cleburne St Houston TX 77004-4501

**DOUGLAS, JAMES MCCRYSTAL,** lawyer; b. Wantagh, N.Y., 1956. Student, Bucknell U.; BA, SUNY, Binghamton, 1978; JD cum laude, Fordham U., 1981. Bar: N.Y. 1982. Ptnr. Skadden, Arps, Slate, Meagher & Flom LLP, N.Y.C. Mem. Fordham Law Rev., 1980-81. Office: Skadden Arps Slate Meagher & Flom LLP 919 3rd Ave New York NY 10022-3902

**DOUGLAS, OLLIS, JR.,** public defender; b. Brunswick, Ga., Jan. 18, 1940; s. Ollis Sr. and Amanda (Evan) D.; 1 child, Michael Tyrone. BS in Polit. Sci., Tenn. State U., Nashville, 1968; JD, Rutgers U., Newark, 1972. Bar: N.J. 1972. Nat. dir. Pan African Skills, N.Y.C., 1970-73; asst. dep. Office Pub. Defender, Newark, 1973—. Civil rights worker SNCC, 1964-70. Mem. ABA, Garden State Bar Assn. Baptist. Avocations: reading, politics. Home: 25 Clifton Ave # D-711 Newark NJ 07104-1872 Office: Office Pub Defender 31 Clinton St Newark NJ 07102-3719

**DOUGLAS, ROBERT EDWARD,** lawyer; b. Filbert, Pa., Apr. 8, 1928; s. Guy Carlton and Ruth (See) D.; married Sept. 12, 1957 (widowed 1963); children: Ann Douglas Keesler, Robert E. Jr.; m. Nancy Sue McNary, Feb. 13, 1965. BS, W.Va. U., 1952, LLB, 1956. Bar: W.Va. 1956. Pvt. practice Charleston, W.Va., 1956—; sec. Appalachian Tire Products, Charleston, 1976—; regional counsel Georgia-Pacific, W.Va., 1978—. 1st lt. USAF, 1946-48. Mem. ABA, Def. Research Inst., Shriners (potentate Beni Kedem Temple 1984), Charleston Boat Club, Phi Delta Phi. Republican. Presbyterian. Avocation: boating. General civil litigation, Condemnation, General practice. Home: 608 Bendview Dr Charleston WV 25314-1515 Office: Douglas Law Offices 1701 Bank One Ctr 707 Virginia St E Charleston WV 25301-2702

**DOUGLASS, FRANK RUSSELL,** lawyer; b. Dallas, May 29, 1933; s. Claire Allen and Caroline (Score) D.; m. Carita Calkins, Feb. 5, 1955 (div. 1983); children: Russell, Tom, Andrew, Cathy; m. Betty Elwanda Richards, Dec. 31, 1983. BBA, Southwestern U., 1953; LLB, U. Tex., 1958. Bar: Tex. 1957, U.S. Dist. Ct. (we. dist.) Tex. 1960, U.S. Dist. Ct. (so. dist.) Tex. 1981, U.S. Dist. Ct. (no. dist.) Tex. 1985, U.S. Dist. Ct. (ea. dist.) Tex. 1987, U.S. Supreme Ct. 1964, U.S. Ct. Appeals (5th cir.) 1985; cert. in civil trial law, and oil, gas and mineral law. Various positions to ptnr. McGinnis, Lochridge & Kilgore, Austin, Tex., 1957-76; sr. ptnr. Scott, Douglass & McConnico, Austin, 1976—; bd. dirs. Mallon Resources, Denver, Rio Petroleum Co., Amarillo, Tex; trustee Southwestern U., Georgetown, Tex. (distinguished alumnus 1999). Contbr. articles to profl. jours. City atty., Westlake Hills, Tex., 1968. Served as airman USAF, 1953-55. Named Dist. Alumus Southwestern U., 1999. Fellow Am. Coll. Trial Lawyers; mem. ABA (natural resources law sect., coun. 1987-90, litig. sect.), Am. Inns of Ct., State Bar of Tex., Tex. Bar Found., The Tex. Ctr. for Legal Ethics and Professionalism (founding), Dallas Bar Assn., The Littlefield Soc. U. Tex.

(charter). Oil, gas, and mineral, General civil litigation, Administrative and regulatory. Home and Office: 10424 Woodford Dr Dallas TX 75229-6317

**DOUGLASS, JOHN JAY,** lawyer, educator; b. Lincoln, Nebr., Mar. 9, 1922; s. Edward Lyman and Edna Marie (Ball) D.; m. Margaret Casteel Pickering, Aug. 31, 1946; children: Carrie Bess, Timothy Pickering, Margaret Marie. AB with distinction, U. Nebr., 1943; JD with distinction, U. Mich., 1952; MA, George Washington U., 1963; LLM, U. Va., 1973; postgrad., Army War Coll., 1963. Bar: Nebr. 1952, Mich. 1952, Tex. 1975. Infantry officer U.S. Army, 1943-52, advanced through grades to col., 1966, judge adv., 1952-74; judge adv. U.S. Army, Vietnam, 1968-69; mil. judge U.S. Army, Ft. Riley, Kans., 1969-70; comdt. U.S. Army JAG Sch., Charlottesville, Va., 1970-74; ret. U.S. Army, 1974; dean emeritus Nat. Coll. Dist. Attys., Houston, 1974-94; prof. U. Houston, 1974—; advisor on criminal law to Albania, 1991; advisor on elections to Ukraine, 1993; advisor Russian procuracy, 1994, Ukraine procuracy, 1995. Author: Ethical Concerns in Prosecution, 1988, 93; contbr. articles to profl. jours. Judge Harris County Absentee Voting, Houston, 1980-92. Decorated D.S.C., Legion of Merit, Bronze Star. Fellow Am. Bar Found.; mem. ABA (ho. of dels. 1980-96, chmn. standing com. on law and electoral process 1987-90), Tex. Bar Assn. (penal code and criminal process com. 1988-90), Order of Coif, Houston City Club, Army and Navy Club, Alpha Tau Omega. Avocation: tennis. Home: 25 T 14 E Greenway Plz Houston TX 77046-1400 Office: U Houston Law Ctr Houston TX 77204-0001

**DOUGLASS, ORION LORENZO,** lawyer, judge; b. Savannah, Ga., Feb. 22, 1947; s. Otha Lafayette Sr. and C. Veronica (Redd) D.; m. Shirley Ann Hill, June 29, 1952; children: Orion Jr., Omar Lorne, Odet Lenore. BA, Holy Cross Coll., 1968; JD, Washington U., St. Louis, 1971. Staff atty. Legal Aid Soc., St. Louis, 1972-74; asst. cir. atty. City of St. Louis, 1973-74; staff atty. Hill, Jones & Farrington, Atlanta, 1974-75; pvt. practice Brunswick, 1975-92; judge Recorder's Ct., City of Brunswick, 1981-92, State Ct., Glynn County, Brunswick, 1993—. Panel mem. Spl. Adv. Bd. for Handicapped, State of Ga., 1985—. Mem. Ga. Bar Assn., Mo. Bar Assn. Presbyterian. Avocations: golf, music. Home: 642 Johnson Rd Saint Simons GA 31522 Office: 1516 Goodyear Ave Brunswick GA 31520-6661

**DOUMAR, GEORGE R. A.,** lawyer; b. Norfolk, Va., Apr. 8, 1961; s. Albert George and Betty Grace (Turner) D.; m. Victoria Berberi, Mar. 21, 1990; Lia Alexandra, Celine Maris. BS in Fgn. Svc., Georgetown U., 1983; JD, U. Va., 1986. Bar: Va. 1986, D.C. 1988, U.S. Dist. Ct. (ea. dist.) Va. 1990, U. S. Ct. Appeals (4th cir.) 1990. Assoc. Cleary, Gottlieb, Steen & Hamilton, Washington, 1986-88, 90—, London, 1988-90. Mem. ABA, Assn. Trial Lawyers Am., Order of Coif. Republican. Roman Catholic. Federal civil litigation, Product liability. Home: 2042 Reynolds St Falls Church VA 22043-1633 Office: 1752 N St NW Washington DC 20036-2907

**DOUMAR, ROBERT GEORGE,** judge; b. Feb. 17, 1930; m. Dorothy Ann Mundy; children: Robert G., Charles C. BA, U. Va., 1951, LLB, 1953, LLM, 1988. Assoc. Venable, Parsons, Kyle & Hylton, 1955-58; sr. ptnr. Doumar, Pincus, Knight & Harlan, 1958-81; judge U.S. Dist. Ct. (ea. dist.) Va., Norfolk, 1981—; now sr. judge U.S. Dist. Ct. (ea. dist.) Va. Lt. USAF. Mem. ATLA, Am. Judicature Soc., Def. Rsch. Inst., Internat. Soc. Barristers, Va. Conf. of Local Bar Assns., Va. Assn. Trial Lawyers. Roman Catholic. Office: US Dist Ct US Courthouse 600 Granby St Ste 344 Norfolk VA 23510-1923

**DOUSE, STEVEN CARL,** lawyer; b. Hastings, Mich., Sept. 9, 1948; s. Adolph, Jr. and Rose Marie (Laeder) D.; m. Karen Elizabeth Murray, Aug. 14, 1971; children: Katherine Emily, Christopher Murray. BA, Mich. State U., 1970; JD, U. Mich., 1973. Bar: Mich. 1973, Tenn. 1988, U.S. Dist. Ct. (ea. dist.) Mich. 1974, U.S. Dist. Ct. (mid. dist.) Tenn. 1988, U.S. Ct. Appeals (6th and 7th cirs.) 1995, U.S. Supreme Ct. 1980. Law clk. to hon. judge John Feikens U.S. Dist. Ct. (ea. dist.) Mich., Detroit, 1973-74; trial atty., asst. sect. chief Antitrust Div. U.S. Dept. Justice, Washington, 1974-87; ptnr. King & Ballow, Nashville, 1987;, 1988—; staff atty. Nat. Commn. for the Rev. of Antitrust Laws and Procedures, Washington, 1978-79; adj. prof. Vanderbilt Law Sch., 1996—. Note editor Mich. Jour. of Law Reform, 1972-73. Recipient Lewis Honigman Meml. award U. Mich. Law Sch., 1973. Mem. ABA, Tenn. Bar Assn., Soc. Barristers, Nashville Bar Assn., Fed. Bar Assn. (pres. Nashville chpt.). Presbyterian. Avocation: running. Antitrust, General civil litigation, Labor. Home: 5116 Woodland Hills Dr Brentwood TN 37027-5826 Office: King & Ballow 1100 Union St Plz 315 Union St Nashville TN 37201-1401

**DOUTHAT, JAMES FIELDING,** lawyer; b. Cin., June 16, 1942; s. Anderson Wade II and Lutie Tom (Walcott) D.; m. Ann Scott Thompson, Aug. 6, 1966; children: J. Fielding, Ann Scott. BA, Hampden-Sydney Coll., 1964; LLB cum laude, Washington & Lee U., 1967. Bar: U.S. Ct. Appeals (4th cir.), Va. 1967, U.S. Dist. Ct. (we. dist.) Va., 1971. Ptnr. Hazlegrove, Dickenson & Rea, Roanoke, Va., 1971-85, Woods, Rogers & Hazlegrove, Roanoke, 1985—. Editor Washington & Lee Law Rev., 1967. Pres. The Achievement Ctr., Roanoke, 1987. Capt. U.S. Army, 1967-71. Avocations: cars, hunting, shooting. Bankruptcy, Contracts commercial, Land use and zoning (including planning). Home: 3625 Ridgewood Ln SW Roanoke VA 24014-3029 Office: Woods Rogers & Hazlegrove 10 S Jefferson St Ste 1201 Roanoke VA 24011-1319

**DOUVILLE, LOUISE M.,** lawyer; b. Ottawa, Ont., Can., May 6, 1960; came to U.S., 1972; d. Elmer Louis and Joy Claire (Sours) D.; m. Raymond M. Sanchez, Jr., Nov. 23, 1991; children: Raymond III, Jasmine, Cody, Lauren. BA, U. Calif., Riverside, 1980; JD, Western State U., Fullerton, 1987. Bar: Calif. 1987, U.S. Ct. Appeals (9th cir.) 1989, U.S. Dist. Ct. (cen. dist.) Calif. 1989, U.S. Supreme Ct. 1995. Assoc. Garrett, Fisher, Jensen & Sanders, Tustin, Calif., 1988-89, Madory, Booth, Zell & Pleiss, Tustin, Calif., 1989-95, Beam, Brobeck & West, Santa Ana, Calif., 1995—. Avocations: computers, painting, travel, piano. Personal injury, General civil litigation. Office: Beam Brobeck & West 600 W Santa Ana Blvd Ste 1000 Santa Ana CA 92701-4586

**DOVE, JEFFREY AUSTIN,** lawyer; b. Syracuse, N.Y., Sept. 21, 1959; s. Austin and Jane (Mooney) D.; m. Cathy Stein, Oct. 12, 1985. BA cum laude, Middlebury Coll., 1981; JD, Syracuse U., 1984. Bar: N.Y. 1985, U.S. Dist. Ct. (no. and we. dists.) N.Y. 1985, U.S. Dist. Ct. (we. dist.) Wis. 1994. Ptnr. Menter, Rudin & Trivelpiece, P.C., Syracuse, 1984—; lectr., author N.Y. State Bar Assn., Nat. Bus. Inst. Mem. ABA, N.Y. Bar Assn., Onondaga County Bar Assn., Ctrl. N.Y. Bankruptcy Bar Assn. (pres. 1997, founding mem., dir.), Capitol Region Bankruptcy Bar Assn. Bankruptcy, Contracts commercial, General civil litigation. Office: Menter Rudin & Trivelpiece 500 S Salina St Ste 500 Syracuse NY 13202-3300

**DOW, JOSEPH SHEFFIELD,** lawyer; b. Boston, Mar. 18, 1925; s. John Abraham Dow and Yamna Maloof; children: Rachel Mary Dow-Tehrani, Sarah Yameen. AB cum laude, Bates Coll., Lewiston, ME, 1948; LLB, JD, Harvard, Cambridge, Mass., 1951. Bar: Mass. 1951, U.S. Dist. Ct. 1954. Pvt. practice Boston & Brookline, Mass., 1951—. Contbr. articles to profl. jours. Overseer of pub. welfare, Boston, 1960-70; 1st Lt. U.S. Army. Mem. Brookline Town Meeting, Brookline Arts Coun. Harvard Club, Boston Host Lions Club. General practice, Personal injury, Immigration, naturalization, and customs. Home and Office: 92 Newton St Brookline MA 02445-7407

**DOW, WILLIAM F.,** lawyer; b. New Haven, Dec. 7, 1941; s. William French and Mary Carolyn (Grandel) D.; m. Diane Ruth McClure, July 15, 1967; children: Brian, Nancy, Tony, Andy, Tina, Mary, Becky. BA, Yale U., 1963; LLB, U. Pa., 1968. Bar: Conn., Fla., U.S. Dist. Ct. Conn., U.S. Dist. Ct. D.C., U.S. Dist. Ct. (mid. dist.) Fla., U.S. Ct. Appeals (2d and 3d cir.), D.C., U.S. Supreme Ct. Staff atty. Fla. Migrant Legal Svcs., 1968-69, Neighborhood Legal Svcs. Program, Washington, 1969-70, Pub. Defender Svc., Washington, 1970-74; asst. U.S. atty. U.S. Atty. for Dist. of Conn., New Haven, 1974-76; ptnr. Jacobs, Grudberg, Belt & Dow, New Haven, 1976—. Campaign mgr. Einhorn for Mayor, New Haven, 1992; trustee Hopkins Sch., New Haven, 1988-98; bd. edn. St. Aedans, New Haven, 1981-82. Recpient Commendation Dept. Justice, 1976. Mem. Conn. Criminal Def. Lawyers Assn. (pres. 1991-92, Pres.'s Commendation 1991), Conn. Bar Assn. (chmn. exec. for criminal justice 1991-94), New Haven County Bar Assn., Assn. Trial Lawyers Am., Conn. Trial Lawyers Assn. Democrat. Roman Catholic. Avocations: tennis, little league. Criminal, State civil litigation, General civil litigation.

**DOWD, CLARK WAYNE,** lawyer, state legislator; b. Texarkana, Ark., Nov. 1, 1941; s. Tillman Harold and Blanche Ethel (Pope) D.; m. Carolyn Margaret Walker, Apr. 17, 1965; children: Chad Everett, Joseph Walker. BBA, So. State Coll., 1966; LLB, U. Ark., 1967. Bar: Ark. 1966, Tex. 1968, U.S. Supreme Ct. 1974. Dep. pros. atty. 8th Jud. Cir. Ct., Texarkana, 1967-68; city atty. City of Texarkana, 1971; ptnr. Dowd, Harrelson, Moore & Giles, Texarkana, 1980—; mem. Ark. State Senate, Little Rock, 1979—. Mem. Texarkana Bar Assn. (pres.). Democrat. Methodist. Avocations: hunting, fishing, canoeing, camping. Home: 12 Northern Hills Pl Texarkana AR 71854-8213

**DOWD, DAVID D., JR.,** federal judge; b. Cleve., Jan. 31, 1929; m. Joyce; children—Cindy, David, Doug, Mark. B.A., Coll. Wooster, 1951; J.D., U. Mich., 1954. Ptnr. Dowd & Dowd, Massillon, Ohio, 1954-55, ptnr., 1957-75; asst. pros. atty. Stark County, 1961-67, pros. atty., 1967-75; judge Ohio 5th Dist. Ct. Appeals, 1975-80, Ohio Supreme Ct., 1980-81; ptnr. Black, McCuskey, Souers & Arbaugh, Canton, Ohio, 1981-82; judge U.S. Dist. Ct. (no. dist.) Ohio, 1982—, now sr. judge, 1996—. Office: US Dist Ct 2 S Main St Akron OH 44308-1813

**DOWD, EDWARD L., JR.,** prosecutor; s. Edward L. Dowd; m. Jill Goessling; 3 children. JD with distinction, St. Mary's Univ. With Dowd, Oates & Dowd; from asst. atty. to chief narcotics sect. U.S. Atty.'s Office, 1979-84; pvt. practice, 1984-93; atty. ea. judicial dist. U.S. Dept. Justice, St. Louis, 1993—; regional dir. south central region Pres.'s Organized Crime Drug Enforcement Task Force. Office: US Attys Office 401 US Court & Custom House 1114 Market St Saint Louis MO 63101-2043

**DOWD, STEVEN MILTON,** lawyer; b. Tyler, Tex., Feb. 1, 1951; s. Loyd Robertus and Roy Frances (Dickard) D.; m. Pamela Gayle Blacklock, Apr. 6, 1974; children—Anna Lisa, Lydia Caroline. B.A., Austin Coll., 1973; J.D., Baylor U., 1975; LL.M., So. Meth. U., 1977. Bar: Tex. 1975, U.S. Dist. Ct. (so. dist.) Tex. 1983, U.S. Dist. Ct. (ea. dist.) Tex. 1985. Tax Atty. Exxon Corp., Houston, 1977-79, Tyler, Tex., 1979-84; pvt. practice 1984-86; assoc. Covington & Reese, Houston, 1982-84; asst. gen. counsel Temple-Eastex Inc., Diboll, Tex., 1986-92; co-owner Panola County Abstract and Title Co., 1992—; pvt. practice, 1992—; dist. judge 123rd Jud. Dist. Ct., Panola and Shelby Counties, 1995-97. Bd. dirs. Noonday Holiness Camp, Hallsville, Tex. Mem. Panola County Bar Assn. Baptist. State civil litigation, Banking, Real property. Home and Office: 300 Martin Ln Carthage TX 75633-2233

**DOWDEY, LANDON GERALD,** lawyer; b. Washington, Aug. 2, 1923; s. Landon Ashton Dowdey and Dorothy M. Fogarty; m. Mary M. Shinners, June 7, 1947 (dec. June 1989); children: Patrick F., Kathleen M., Martin Joseph. BS in Edn., U. Pa., 1946; JD, Georgetown U., 1948. Bar: U.S. Ct. Appeals (D.C., fed., 2nd, 3rd, 4th, 6th, 7th and 9th cirs.), U.S. Supreme Ct. 1952. Assoc. Levi H. David & E.L. Sheehan, Washington, 1948-57; ptnr. Dowdey & Bartow, Washington, 1958-66, Dowdey, Levy & Cohen, Washington, 1966-72, Dowdey & Urbina, Washington, 1972-76; pvt. practice Washington, 1977—. Editor: Journey to Freedom, 1969 (Nat. Book award 1969), The Four Zoas, 1983. Lawyer Dem. State Com. D.C., Washington, 1968-90. Pvt. U.S. Army, 1943-44. Roman Catholic. Appellate, Federal civil litigation, Constitutional. Office: 2000 L St NW Ste 200 Washington DC 20036-4924

**DOWDLE, PATRICK DENNIS,** lawyer; b. Denver, Dec. 8, 1948; s. William Robert and Helen (Schraeder) D.; m. Eleanor Pryor, Mar. 8, 1975; children: Jeffery William, Andrew Peter. BA, Cornell Coll., Mt. Vernon, Iowa, 1971; JD, Boston U., 1975. Bar: Colo. 1975, U.S. Dist. Ct. Colo. 1975, U.S. Ct. Appeals (10th cir.) 1976, U.S. Supreme Ct. 1978. Acad. dir. in Japan Sch. Internat. Tng., Putney, Vt., 1974; assoc. Decker & Miller, Denver, 1975-77; ptnr. Miller, Makkai & Dowdle, Denver, 1977—; designated counsel criminal appeals Colo. Atty. Gens. Office, Denver, 1980-81; guardian ad litem Adams County Dist. Ct., Brighton, Colo., 1980-83; affiliated counsel ACLU, Denver, 1980—. Mem. Colo. Bar Assn., Denver Bar Assn. (various coms.), Porsche Club of Am. Avocations: scuba diving, photography, wine making, travel, skiing. General civil litigation, Real property, Bankruptcy. Home: 3254 Tabor Ct Wheat Ridge CO 80033-5367 Office: Miller Makkai & Dowdle 2325 W 72nd Ave Denver CO 80221-3101

**DOWDY, JOHN VERNARD, JR.,** lawyer, educator, arbitrator, mediator; b. Malakoff, Tex., July 3, 1942; s. John Vernard Sr. and Johnnie Dena (Riley) D.; m. Sarah Ellen Chambers, June 13, 1964; children: Rebekah Anne, Susannah Lynn. BSc in Phys. Edn., Baylor U., 1966, JD, 1968. Bar: Tex. 1968, U.S. Dist. Ct. (no. dist.) Tex. 1972, U.S. Dist. Ct. (ea. dist.) Tex. 1980. Assoc. Warwick, Jenkins Law Firm, Waxahachie, Tex., 1968-69, Atkins, Carpenter & Dowdy, Arlington, Tex., 1969-72, Duke, Rosenberry & Dowdy, Arlington, 1972-74; pvt. practice law Arlington, 1974—; lectr. bus. law U. Tex., Arlington, 1974—. Mem. ptnrs. in search of ednl. excellence Arlington Ind. Sch. Dist., 1989-90; pres., bd. dirs. AWARE Found., Inc., Arlington, 1989—. Mem. ABA, Assn. Attorney-Mediators, Christian Legal Soc., State Bar Tex., Arlington Bar Assn. Baptist. Avocations: amateur baseball, backpacking, running, phys. fitness, handball. Probate, General corporate, Alternative dispute resolution. Home: 3706 Shadycreek Dr N Arlington TX 76013-1017 Office: 2403 Cales Dr Arlington TX 76013-1304

**DOWELL, JAMES DALE,** lawyer; b. Goose Creek, Tex., July 17, 1932; s. James Dale and Margaret (King) D.; m. Patricia Jo Skaggs, Feb. 2, 1957; children: Terry Dowell Owens, James Dale III. BA, Tex. A&M U, 1954; LLB, U. Tex., 1957. Bar: Tex. 1956, U.S. Dist. Ct. (ea. dist.) Tex. 1958, U.S Ct. Appeals (5th cir.) 1964, U.S. Supreme Ct. 1969. Assoc. King, Sharfstein & Rienstra, Beaumont, Tex., 1957-63, ptnr., 1963-68; ptnr. Rienstra, Rienstra & Dowell, Beaumont, 1968-85, Rienstra, Dowell & Flatten, Beaumont, 1985—. Mem. Tex. Dem. Exec. Com., 1966-68, del. Nat. Conv., 1976—. Mem. ABA, State Bar Tex., Tex. Bar Found., Jefferson County Bar Assn. (pres. 1978-79), Def. Rsch. Inst., Tex. Assn. Def. Counsel, Beaumont Country Club, Beaumont Club (bd. dirs. 1975-77), Rotary, Phi Gamma Delta. Methodist. Avocations: reading. General civil litigation, Insurance, Personal injury. Home: 6275 Wilchester Ln Beaumont TX 77706-4328 Office: 595 Orleans St Beaumont TX 77701-3214

**DOWER, HARRY ALLEN,** lawyer; b. Bethlehem, Pa., Nov. 29, 1918. AB, Lafayette Coll., 1940; JD, Yale U., 1948. Bar: Pa. 1949, U.S. Supreme Ct. 1974. Sole practice Allentown, Pa., 1949—; gen. counsel Alpo Pet Foods div. Allen Products Co., 1964-69; adj. prof. law Lehigh U., Bethlehem, 1969-84. Author: (with Charles Vihon) Cases on Legal Problems of Business in Free Society, 1973. Legal counsel ACLU of Lehigh Valley, Pa., 1950-86; trustee Allentown br. NAACP Scholarship Fund, 1965-75; bd. dirs. Wiley House, Bethlehem, 1973-82. Mem. Pa. Bar Assn. Pension, profit-sharing, and employee benefits, General civil litigation. Home: 1665 Lehigh Pky N Allentown PA 18103-2913 Office: PO Box 950 Allentown PA 18105-0950

**DOWIS, LENORE,** lawyer; b. N.Y., Nov. 7, 1934; d. Thomas and Julianna (Csitkovits) Esteves; children: Daniel, Lenore, Denise, Jonathan. AAS, Suffolk County Community Coll., 1981; BA, SUNY, Stony Brook, 1983; JD, Touro Coll., 1987. Bar: N.Y. 1988, N.J. 1988, U.S. Dist. Ct. N.J. 1988, U.S. Dist. Ct. (so. and ea. dists.) N.Y. 1992, U.S. Ct. Mil. Appeals 1993, U.S. Ct. Claims 1993, U.S. Ct. Appeals (fed. cir.) 1993, U.S. Supreme Ct. 1993. Tel. operator N.Y. Tel. Co., L.I., 1951-58; real estate sales agt. Gen. Devel. Corp., Hauppauge, N.Y, 1974-75; ptnr., owner Davis Trucking Co., Huntington, N.Y., 1957-67; student law clk. to assoc. judge appellate div. U.S. Supreme Ct. N.Y., Bklyn., 1986; staff atty. Nassau/Suffolk Law Svcs., Bay Shore, N.Y., 1988; pvt. practice, Smithtown, N.Y., 1988—. Mem. ABA, Suffolk County Bar Assn., N.Y. State Bar Assn., Phi Theta Kappa, Alpha Beta Gamma. Republican. Family and matrimonial, General practice, Administrative and regulatory. Home and Office: 33 Beverly Rd Smithtown NY 11787-5324

**DOWLING, JOAN E.,** lawyer; b. N.Y.C., July 11, 1953; d. James J. and Natalie E. Dowling. BA, Marywood Coll., 1975; cert. attendance, Temple U., 1978, Athens (Greece) U., 1978; JD, Seton Hall U., 1979. Bar: N.J. 1980, U.S. Dist. Ct. N.J. 1980, U.S. Supreme Ct. 1985. Pvt. practice law Plainfield, N.J., 1981—; atty. Zoning Bd. Adjustment, Middlesex Borough, N.J., 1989—. Trustee Union County Legal Svcs., Elizabeth, N.J., 1986-91; bd. dirs. Rolling Hills Girl Scout Coun., North Branch, N.J., 1988-94, v.p., 1995—; pres. Middlesex (N.J.) Borough Sr. Citizen Housing Corp., 1994—. Recipient Outstanding Citizen award Middlesex Borough Coun., 1985, Outstanding Cmty. Svc. Resolution, Union County Bd. Freeholders, Elizabeth, 1986, Honor award Rolling Hills Girl Scout Coun., North Branch, 1995, Thanks award, 1997. Mem. Women Lawyers in Union County (treas. 1992-93, v.p. 1994-96, pres. 1996-98). Democrat. Roman Catholic. Avocation: canoeing. Real property, Land use and zoning (including planning), Family and matrimonial. Office: 404 E Front St Plainfield NJ 07060-1342

**DOWLING, VINCENT JOHN,** lawyer; b. N.Y.C., Dec. 20, 1927; s. Victor Hurlin and Joan Agnes (Reardon) D.; m. Jane Cooney, Apr. 16, 1958; children: Vincent John, Jr., Douglas J., S. Colin, Joseph G. B.S., Lehigh U., 1949; J.D., U. Conn., 1957. Bar: Conn. 1957, Mass. 1985, Fla. 1986, U.S. Dist. Ct. Conn. 1958, U.S. Ct. Appeals (2d cir.) 1960, U.S. Ct. Claims 1986. Chief mfg. engr. Veeder-Root, Inc., Hartford, Conn., 1949-58; ptnr. Dowling & Dowling, Hartford, 1958-65; ptnr. Cooney, Scully & Dowling, Hartford, 1965—; lectr. constrn. law. Served to capt. U.S. Army, 1951-53. Mem. ASME, ABA, Conn. Bar Assn. (mem. liaison com. with cts., constrn. law com., aleternat dispute resolution com., chmn. specialization com.), Am. Arbitration Assn., Nat. Panel Constrn. Arbitrators and Mediators, Fed. Bar Assn., Mass. Bar Assn., Fla. Bar Assn., Internat. Bar Assn., Diocesan Attys. Assn., Hartford Golf Club, Hartford Club, John's Island Club (Vero Beach, Fla.), Kappa Alpha Soc. Roman Catholic. Construction, Federal civil litigation, Alternative dispute resolution. Address: 10 Columbus Blvd Hartford CT 06106-1976

**DOWNER, ROBERT NELSON,** lawyer; b. Newton, Iowa, July 15, 1939; s. Lowell William and Mabel Mary (Hannon) D.; m. Jane Alice Glafka, May 29, 1971; children: Elise Michele, Andrew Nelson. BA, U. Iowa, 1961, JD, 1963. Bar: Iowa 1963, U.S. Dist. Ct. (so. dist.) Iowa 1963, U.S. Dist. Ct. (no. dist.) Iowa 1964, U.S. Supreme Ct. 1995. Assoc. Meardon Law Office, Iowa City, 1963-68; mem. Meardon, Sueppel & Downer PLC and predecessor firms, Iowa City, 1969—; dir., sec. KZIA, Inc., Iowa City, 1975—, Iowa City Tennis & Fitness Ctr., 1987-93; trustee The Oaknoll Found., Iowa City, 1990-98; dir. Christian Retirement Svcs., Inc., Iowa City, 1967-82, Iowa State Bar Found., 1996—. Pres. Greater Iowa City Area C. of C., 1979; bd. trustees Iowa City Pub. Libr., 1971-75, chair, 1973-74; chair adminstrv. bd. First United Meth. Ch., Iowa City, 1985-87; del. Rep. Nat. Conv., New Orleans, 1988; mem. Iowa Supreme Ct. Commn. on Continuing Legal Edn., 1975-83, Task Force on Domestic Abuse, 1993-94; bd. dirs. Iowa City Area Devel. Group, 1993—, chmn., 1996-97. Recipient Excellence in Svc. award Legal Svcs. Corp. Iowa, 1996. Fellow Am. Coll. Trust & Estate Counsel, Am. Bar Found., Iowa State Bar Found.; mem. ABA, Iowa State Bar Assn. (chair probate, property and trust law com. 1988-90, chair probate sect. 1990-93, v.p. 1993-94, pres.-elect 1994-95, pres. 1995-96), Johnson County Bar Assn. (pres. 1976), Rotary Club Iowa City (pres. 1988-89). Republican. Methodist. Probate, General corporate, Banking. Home: 2029 Rochester Ct Iowa City IA 52245-3246 Office: Meardon Sueppel Downer & Hayes PLC 122 S Linn St Iowa City IA 52240-1830

**DOWNES, JAMES J.,** lawyer; b. La Crosse, Wis., Oct. 14, 1944; s. James Richard and Dorothy Elizabeth Downes; m. Susan Downes, Jan. 25, 1969; children: Ian, Kevin. AB, Mt. St. Mary's Coll., 1966; JD, N.Y. Law Sch., 1969. Bar: N.Y. 1969, U.S. Dist. Ct. (so. dist.) N.Y. 1973, U.S. Dist. Ct. (no. dist.) N.Y. 1998, U.S. Ct. Appeals (2d cir.) 1974, U.S. Supreme Ct. 1974. Asst. dist. atty. Westchester County Dist. Atty.'s Office, White Plains, N.Y., 1969-71; assoc. Clark, Gagliardi & Miller, White Plains, N.Y., 1971-82; founding ptnr. Rende, Ryan & Downes, White Plains, N.Y., 1982—; spkr. Westchester County Bar Trial Lawyers, 1980—. Commr. Pound Ridge (N.Y.) Recreation Commn., 1987-94; pres. Bedford (N.Y.) Pound Ridge Little League, 1986-97. Mem. ATLA, N.Y. State Trial Lawyers, Westchester County Bar Assn., Lambda Iota Tau. Avocations: running, reading. Personal injury, General civil litigation. Office: Rende Ryan & Downes 202 Mamaroneck Ave Ste 601 White Plains NY 10601-5308

**DOWNES, WILLIAM F.,** judge; b. 1946. BA, U. North Tex., 1968; JD, U. Houston, 1974. Ptnr. Clark and Downes, Green River, Wyo., 1976-78; mem. Brown & Drew, Casper, Wyo., 1978-94; dist. judge U.S. Dist. Ct. Wyo., Casper, Wyo., 1994—. Capt. USMC, 1968-71. Mem. Wyo. State Bar, Natrona County Bar Assn., Casper Petroleum Club, Wyo. Athletic Club. Office: US Dist Ct 111 S Wolcott St Rm 210 Casper WY 82601-2534

**DOWNEY, BRIAN PATRICK,** lawyer; b. Pitts., Sept. 1, 1964; s. Edmond John and Mary Elizabeth (Wallace) D.; m. Linda Alice McKay, Oct. 9, 1993. BA, Dartmouth Coll., 1987; JD, Dickinson Sch. of Law, 1990. Bar: Pa. 1990, U.S. Dist. Ct. (we. dist.) Pa. 1991, U.S. Dist. Ct. (ea. and mid. dists.) Pa. 1994, U.S. Ct. Appeals (3rd cir.) 1994. Assoc. counsel Eckert Seamans Cherin & Mellott, Pitts., 1990-92; asst. counsel Pa. Dept. of Labor, Harrisburg, 1992-94; assoc. atty. Pepper Hamilton, LLP, Harrisburg, 1994—. Mem. Friends of Tom Foley Com., Harrisburg, 1994. Mem. ABA, Pa. Bar Assn., Dauphin County Bar Assn. Democrat. Roman Catholic. Avocations: creative writing, golf, reading fiction. Product liability, General civil litigation, Environmental. Office: Pepper Hamilton LLP 200 One Keystone Plz Harrisburg PA 17108

**DOWNEY, RICHARD LAWRENCE,** lawyer; b. Washington, Apr. 3, 1948; s. William G. and Laufey A. D.; m. Pamela L. Drewry, July 10, 1971; children: Anna Christine, Laura Michele, Richard Lawrence, Patricia Kathleen. BA, Randolph-Macon Coll., 1970; JD, Hamline U., 1977. Bar: Va. 1978, U.S. Dist. Ct. (ea. dist.) Va. 1978, U.S. Ct. Appeals (4th cir.) 1978, U.S. Supreme Ct. 1983, U.S. Tax Ct. 1990, U.S. Claims Ct. 1990; diplomate Nat. Bd. Trial Advocacy, cert. civil trial adv. Assoc. Downey & Lennhoff, Springfield, Va., 1978-80; pvt. practice, Fairfax, Va., 1980-82; sr. ptnr. Duvall, Blackburn, Hale & Downey, Fairfax, 1982-92; pvt. practice, Fairfax, Va., 1993—. Served to lt. col., USAR. Named Outstanding Young Man of Am., U.S. Jaycees, 1982. Mem. ABA, ATLA, Va. State Bar Assn., Va. Trial Lawyers Assn., Fairfax Bar Assn. (gen. dist. cts. com. 1984-86, cir. ct. com. 1988-89), Nat. Lawyers Assn., Christian Legal Soc., Fairfax County C. of C. (internat. trade com., planning and land use com., legis. com. 1984), Phi Alpha Delta. Republican. Lodge: Rotary. General civil litigation, General corporate, Contracts commercial. Address: 4118 Leonard Dr Fairfax VA 22030-5118

**DOWNEY, WILLIAM J., III,** lawyer; b. Newton, Mass., July 27, 1947; s. William J. and Marie Louise (Dupuis) D.; m. Leslie Ann Shields, Oct. 7, 1975 (div. 1979); 1 dau., Jessica Ann; m. 2d, Sherrill R. Gould, Aug. 15, 1982 (div. 1987); 1 dau., Julie Samantha; m. Lisa G. Russell, Feb. 14, 1992. Student, Grinnell (Iowa) Coll., 1965; BS magna cum laude, Northeastern U., Boston, 1983; JD cum laude, Suffolk U. Law Sch., 1988. Bar: Calif. 1988, U.S. Dist. Ct. (ctrl. and so. dists.) Calif. 1992, U.S. Dist. Ct. (ea. and no. dists.) Calif. 1995, 96. Assoc. Kananack, Murgatroyd, Baum & Hedlund (and predecessor firms), 1988-92; shareholder Baum, Hedlund, Aristei, Guilford & Downey, L.A., 1993—; mem. steering com. Prozac products liability Eli Lilly & Co., mem. plaintiff's steering com. Perris Valley air crash, Northridge earthquake litigation, Fialuridine Product liability cases, Washington. Recipient Am. Jurisprudence award, 1987. Mem. State Bar Calif., Consumer Attys. Calif., Phi Delta Kappa, Phi Delta Phi. Aviation, Personal injury, Product liability. Office: Baum Hedlund Aristei Guilford & Downey 12100 Wilshire Blvd Ste 950 Los Angeles CA 90025-7107

**DOWNIE, ROBERT COLLINS, II,** lawyer; b. Panama Canal Zone, Feb. 18, 1965; s. Robert Wahl Downie and Margaret Brandon Ausley; m. Robyn Elizabeth McGuire, Sept. 1, 1994. BA in English, Davidson Coll., 1987; JD, Fla. State U., 1989. Bar: Fla. 1990, U.S. Dist. Ct. (mid. and no. dists.) Fla. 1996, U.S. Ct. Appeals (11th cir.) 1996. Assoc. Oertel, Hoffman, Fernandez & Cole, Tallahassee, Fla., 1990-94; shareholder Mathews & Downie, Tallahassee, 1994-97; assoc. Brown, Ward et al, Orlando, 1997—. Administrative and regulatory, Environmental, State civil litigation. Office: Brown Ward et al 111 N Orange Ave Ste 875 Orlando FL 32801-2346

**DOWNING, CARL SELDON,** lawyer; b. Memphis, Jan. 22, 1935; s. Carl E. and Edna (Southall) D.; m. Mar. 6, 1960; children: Douglas Southall, Carl Andrew, Catherine Barrett. BSCE, U. Miss., 1956, LLB with distinction, 1963. Bar: Miss. 1963, La. 1964. Engr. DuPont Corp., Birmingham, Ala., 1960; ptnr. The Kullman Firm, New Orleans, 1963—; exec. com. New Orleans Bar Assn., 1983-87. Exec. com. New Orleans Bar Assn., 1983-87; bd. dirs. U. Miss. Found., 1984-88, U. Miss. Alumni Assn., 1987-89; bd. govs. Newman Sch., 1983-93. Mem. Phi Delta Theta (Outstanding Miss. Alpha chpt. alumnus 1985). Labor, Mergers and acquisitions, General corporate. Office: The Kullman Firm PO Box 60118 1100 Poydras St Ste 1600 New Orleans LA 70163-1600

**DOWNING, JAMES CHRISTIE,** lawyer; b. Los Angeles, Dec. 17, 1924; s. Dorman Perkins and Merle Grace (Christie) D.; m. Betty Griggs, Dec. 23, 1949; children: Colleen, James, Kimberly, Kelly, Kathleen. BS, U. Calif., 1949; LLB, U. Calif.-San Francisco, 1952. Bar: Calif. 1953, U.S. Dist. Ct. (no. dist.) Calif. 1953, U.S. Dist. Ct. (ea. dist.) Calif. 1975, U.S. Ct. Appeals (9th dir.) 1953. Assoc. Walkup, Downing, Shelby, Bastian, Melodia, Kelly & O'Reilly, and predecessors, San Francisco, 1954-59, ptnr., 1959-70, exec. v.p., 1970-84; ptnr. Downing & Downing, 1985—; lectr. Calif. Continuing Edn. of Bar Program. Served in AC, U.S. Army, 1943-45. Decorated Air medal with 5 oak leaf clusters. Fellow Am. Coll. Trial Lawyers; mem. ABA, State Bar Calif., Bar Assn. San Francisco (vice chmn. trial practice com. 1970), San Francisco Trial Lawyers Assn. (pres. 1972), Am. Bd. Trial Advs. (nat. exec. com. 1970-73, nat. sec. 1971, nat. chmn. membership 1972-73, 76-77, nat. pres. 1974, pres. San Francisco chpt. 1974, Calif. Trial Lawyer of Yr. 1978), Internat. Soc. Barristers, Internat. Acad. Trial Lawyers, Trader Brown Soc. Republican. Federal civil litigation, State civil litigation. Office: Downing & Downing PO Box 398 Middletown CA 95461-0398

**DOWNING, LAWRENCE DEWITT,** lawyer; b. McPherson, Kans., Aug. 2, 1936; s. Wayne Curtis and Waneta Corinne (DeWitt) D.; m. Kristi Karen Anderson, June 19, 1960 (div. 1983); children: Kyia, Christopher; m. Ann Marie Lucke, June 2, 1985. BS, Iowa State U., 1958; JD, U. Minn. 1962. Bar: Minn. 1962, U.S. Dist. Ct. Minn. 1962, U.S. Supreme Ct. 1978. Chemist Procter & Gamble, Cin., 1958-59; ptnr. O'Brien, Ehrick, Wolf, Deaner & Downing, Rochester, Minn., 1962-90; pvt. practice Rochester, 1990—; owner Lawrence Downing & Assocs., Rochester, 1990—. Trustee John Muir Trust, U.K., 1988—; past mem. Minn. Gov.'s Task Force on Environ. Compact of the States; mem. hon. com. Earth Day, 1990; past mem., chmn. subcom. Minn. Gov.'s Task Force on Energy Policy; past mem. Minn. Gov.'s Power Plan Sitting Adv. Com., Olmsted County Environ. Environ. Quality Commn. Fellow Am. Acad. Matrimonial Lawyers; mem. ABA (family law sect.), Minn. Bar Assn. (bd. dirs. family law sect. 1978-79), 3d Dist. Bar Assn., Olmsted County Bar Assn. (pres. 1985-86), Sierra Club (mem. exec. com. 1984-88, 5th officer 1984-85, sec. 1985-86, v.p. for adminstv. law 1988-92, bd. dirs. 1983-89, pres. 1986-88, pres. Sierra Club Found. 1989-92, mem. numerous nat. coms. and task forces). Family and matrimonial. Office: Lawrence Downing & Assocs 330 Norwest Ctr 21 1st Ave SW Rochester MN 55902-3033

**DOWNS, CLARK EVANS,** lawyer; b. Boston, July 30, 1946; s. Willis A. and Josephine Joyce (Evans) D.; m. Emilie Louise Hartnett, Aug. 17, 1968; children: Elizabeth Morgan, Julia Clark. AB in English Lit., Boston U., 1968, JD cum laude, 1973. Bar: Ill. 1973, D.C. 1981. Assoc. Isham Lincoln & Beale, Washington, 1973-80, ptnr., 1981-87; ptnr. Jones Day Reavis & Pogue, Washington, 1988—. Mem. editl. adv. bd. CCH Power and Telecom. Law. Trustee, sec. Found. Energy Law Jour., Washington, 1989-93; trustee Mt. Ida Coll., Newton Centre, Mass., 1994-98, chair, 1989-98; trustee Nat. Presbyn. Sch., Washington, 1986-90, Nat. Presbyn. Ch., Washington, 1991-93, Chevy Chase Presbyn. Ch., Washington, 1981-84. Fellow Am. Bar Found.; mem. ABA (ho. of dels. 1995-97), Fed. Energy Bar Assn. (chmn. program com. 1985-86, bd. dirs. 1986-89), FERC (Practice Procedure Manual editl. adv. bd. 1996—), D.C. Bar (chmn. lawyers counseling com. 1989). Avocations: cello, folk music, choral music. FERC practice, Public utilities, Finance. Office: Jones Day Reavis & Pogue 51 Louisiana Ave NW Washington DC 20001-2113

**DOWNS, J. ANTHONY,** lawyer; b. Evanston, Ill., May 16, 1960; s. Anthony and Katherine W. Downs; m. Jin-Kyung Kim, July 21, 1990; children: Matthew, Jonathan. AB in Econs., Princeton U., 1982; JD, U. Chgo., 1986. Bar: Mass., U.D. Dist. Ct. Mass., U.S. Ct. Appeals (1st and 2d cirs.), U.S. Supreme Ct. Law clk. to Judge James L. Oakes U.S. Ct. Appeals (2d cir.), Brattleboro, Vt., 1986-87; law clk. to Chief Justice William H. Rehnquist U.S. Supreme Ct., Washington, 1987-88; ptnr. Goodwin, Procter & Hoar LLP, Boston, 1988—. Mem. ABA, Boston Bar Assn. General civil litigation, Antitrust, Intellectual property. Office: Goodwin Procter & Hoar LLp Exchange Pl Boston MA 02109-2803

**DOWNS, THOMAS EDWARD, IV,** lawyer; b. South Amboy, N.J., Sept. 27, 1950; s. Thomas Edward III and Theresa Mary (Jaje) D.; m. Marie Popik, Oct. 6, 1979; children: Thomas Edward V, Lauren Ann. BA, St. Peter's Coll., 1972; JD, Seton Hall U., 1975. Bar: N.J. 1975, U.S. Dist. Ct. N.J. 1975, U.S. Dist. Cts. (so. and ea. dists.) N.Y. 1981. Law clk. to presiding judges Middlesex County, N.J., 1975; assoc. Irving Tabman, Old Bridge, N.J., 1975-76; ptnr. Tabman, Downs & McDonnell, Old Bridge, 1976-77, Tabman & Downs, Old Bridge, 1978-82; pvt. practice Old Bridge, 1982—; South Amboy Mcpl. pros., 1977—, Sayreville Mcpl. pros., 1987-90, 94—. Sec. South Amboy Shade Tree com., 1974; co-chmn. South Amboy Blood Bank; pres. South Amboy Young Dem. Orgn.; dep. chmn. Sayreville Dem. Orgn., 1992—. Mem. Assn. Trial Lawyers Am., N.J. State Trial Lawyers Assn., Middlesex County Bar Assn., N.J. State Bar Assn., Lions (pres. South Amboy chpt. 1984). Roman Catholic. Real property, Family and matrimonial, Criminal. Home: 26 Carter Pl Sayreville PO Box Parlin NJ 08859 Office: PO Box 498 Old Bridge NJ 08857-0498

**DOYLE, ANTHONY PETER,** lawyer; b. Washington, July 13, 1953; s. Francis X. and Anna (Klekotka) D.; m. Maria H. Duda, Aug. 13, 1977; children: Jeffrey Anthony, Joseph Edward, Natalie Maria, Andrew Michael. AA, Berkshire Community Coll., Pittsfield, Mass., 1972-75; BS magna cum laude, Worcester State Coll., 1977; JD, Western New Eng. Coll., 1980. Bar: Mass. 1980; U.S. Dist. Ct. Mass. 1981; U.S. Ct. Appeals (1st cir.) 1981, U.S. Supreme Ct. 1999. Pvt. practice Pittsfield, 1980-84; ptnr. Doyle & Cormier, Pittsfield, 1985-88, Barry, Doyle & Cormier, Pittsfield, 1989, Barry & Doyle, Pittsfield, 1989—. Pres. Hospice of Cen. Berkshire, Pittsfield, 1988-90; v.p. HospiceCare of the Berkshires, Pittsfield, 1990-92, pres. 1992—; bd. dirs. Dalton (Mass.) Youth Ctr., 1986-89, Community Recreation Assn., Dalton, 1989-95; exec. com. Appalachian Trails Dist. Boy Scouts Am., Dalton, 1989-96; mem. Zoning Bd. Appeals, Dalton, 1995—, chmn., 1997—, Dalton Coun. Aging, 1997—. Recipient commendation Western Mass. Pro Bono Referral Svc., 1983-87. Mem. Mass. Bar Assn., Berkshire Bar Assn. (exec. com. 1989-91, v.p. 1997—). Roman Catholic. Avocations: skiing, tennis. General practice, Personal injury, Probate. Home: 108 Barton Hill Rd Dalton MA 01226-2005 Office: Barry & Doyle 8 Bank Row Ste 2 Pittsfield MA 01201-6224

**DOYLE, AUSTIN JOSEPH,** lawyer; b. Atlanta, Aug. 2, 1941; s. Austin Joseph Sr. and Marguerite Clare (Sheridan) D.; m. Marian Frances Murphy, June 24, 1980; children: Kelly, Deborah. BBA, U. Notre Dame, 1963; JD, Am. U., 1973. Bar: D.C. 1974, U.S. Dist. Ct. D.C. 1974, U.S. Tax Ct. 1974, U.S. Ct. Appeals (D.C. cir.) 1986, U.S. Ct. Appeals (9th cir.) 1990, U.S. Ct. Appeals (5th cir.), 1994; CPA, D.C. CPA Williams & Connolly, Washington, 1967-73; sole practice Washington, 1973—. Served to 1st lt. U.S. Army, 1963-65. Mem. ABA, Internat. Assn. Fin. Planners, Nat. Network of Estate Planning Attys., D.C. Bar Assn., Am. Assn. Atty. CPA's, Greater Washington Soc. CPA's. Roman Catholic. Taxation, general, Estate planning, Criminal. Office: 3201 New Mexico Ave NW Washington DC 20016-2756

**DOYLE, DAVID PERRIE,** lawyer; b. Orange, N.J., May 11, 1960; s. Ralph Thomas and Dorothy (Trevorrow) D.; m. Ana Linda Day, Mar. 7, 1987. BA, Emory U., 1982; JD, Rutgers U., 1985; LLM in Taxation, N.Y.U., 1990. Bar: N.J. 1986, U.S. Dist. Ct. N.J. 1986, U.S. Tax Ct. 1988, U.S. Dist. Ct. (so. dist.) N.Y. 1998. Law clk. to presiding judge Tax Ct. N.J., Trenton, 1985-86; assoc. Pitney, Hardin, Kipp & Szuch, Morristown, N.J., 1986-92, counsel, 1993-94, ptnr., 1995—. Mem. ABA (tax sect., mem. employee benefits com.), N.J. State Bar Assn. (tax sect., past chair employee benefits com.). Taxation, general, Pension, profit-sharing, and employee benefits. Office: Pitney Hardin Kipp & Szuch PO Box 1945 Morristown NJ 07962-1945

**DOYLE, DENNIS THOMAS,** lawyer; b. White Plains, N.Y., Apr. 9, 1943. BA, Boston Coll., 1965; JD, Fordham U., 1968. Bar: U.S. Dist. Ct. (so. and ea. dists.) N.Y., U.S. Supreme Ct. With O'Connor, McGuiness, Conte, Doyle & Oleson, White Plains, 1969—. Mem. ABA, ATLA, Fedn. Ins. and Corp. Counsel, Trial Lawyers Assn., N.Y. State Bar Assn. Conservative. Roman Catholic. Avocation: Religious education instructor. Federal civil litigation, General civil litigation, State civil litigation. Office: O'Connor McGuiness Conte Doyle & Oleson One Barker Ave Ste 675 White Plains NY 10601-1517

**DOYLE, GERARD FRANCIS,** lawyer; b. Needham, Mass., Oct. 25, 1942; s. John Patrick and Catherine Mary (Lawler) D.; BS in Indsl. Adminstrn., Yale U., 1966; JD, Georgetown U., 1972; m. Paula Marie Dervay, May 14, 1983; children: Laura Dervay, Meredith Lawler, Philip John. Bar: D.C. 1973, U.S. Dist. Ct. D.C. 1973, U.S. Ct. Fed. Claims 1976, U.S. Ct. Appeals (fed. cir.), 1982, U.S. Supreme Ct. 1982. Group head for operating submarine reactors and reactor tech. Div. Naval Reactors, AEC, Washington, 1970-72; atty. firm Morgan, Lewis & Bockius, Washington, 1972-76; legal counsel Am. Nuclear Energy Council, Washington, 1975-76; ptnr. Cotten, Day & Doyle, Washington, 1976-87; ptnr. Doyle & Savit, Doyle, Simmons & Bachman, and Doyle & Bachman, Washington, 1987—; legal counsel Assn. Fed. Data Peripheral Suppliers, Washington, 1979; dir. M Internat., Inc.; author and lectr. in field. Columnist Federal Computer Week, 1989. With USN, 1966-71. Recipient Outstanding Young Man of Year award, 1976. Mem. ABA (mem. coun. publ. contract law sect. 1989-92), D.C. Bar Assn., Fed. Bar Assn., Am. Arbitration Assn. (panel arbitrators), Nat. Contract Mgmt. Assn. Republican. Roman Catholic. Clubs: Met. (Washington), Yale, Washington Golf and Country. Government contracts and claims, Computer. Home: 901 Whann Ave Mc Lean VA 22101-1570 Office: Doyle & Bachman 4245 Fairfax Dr Arlington VA 22203-1606

**DOYLE, JAMES E(DWARD),** state attorney general; b. Washington, Nov. 23, 1945; s. James E. and Ruth (Bachhuber) D.; m. Jessica Laird, Dec. 21, 1966; children: Augustus, Gabriel. Student, Stanford U., 1963-66; AB in History, U. Wis., 1967; JD cum laude, Harvard U., 1972. Bar: Ariz. 1973, Wis. 1975, U.S. Dist. Ct. N.Mex. 1973, U.S. Dist. Ct. Ariz. 1973, U.S. Dist. Ct. Utah 1973, U.S. Dist. Ct. (we. dist.) Wis. 1975, U.S. Dist. Ct. (ea. dist.) Wis. 1976, U.S. Ct. Appeals (10th cir.) 1974, U.S. Ct. Appeals (7th cir.) 1985, U.S. Supreme Ct. 1989. Vol. Peace Corps, Tunisia, 1967-69; atty. DNA Legal Svcs., Chinle, Ariz., 1972-75; ptnr. Jacobs & Doyle, Madison, Wis., 1975-77; dist. atty. Dane County, Madison, 1977-83; ptnr. Doyle & Ritz, Madison, 1983-90; of counsel Lawton & Cates, Madison, 1990-91; atty. gen. State of Wis., Madison, 1991—. Mem. ABA, Wis. Bar Assn. (bd. dirs. criminal law sect. 1988), 7th Cir. Bar Assn. (chair criminal law sect. 1988-89). Democrat. Roman Catholic. Office: Office Atty Gen Dept Justice 123 W Washington Ave Rm 117 Madison WI 53702-0009

**DOYLE, JOHN C.,** lawyer; b. L.A., Sept. 5, 1953; s. John Joseph and Patricia Ann (McGrath) Cheap; m. Mary Lynne Schlotterbeck, Oct. 28, 1984; children: Eamon Keenan, Lindsey Karen. BA, U. Santa Clara, 1975, JD, 1978. Bar: Calif. 1978, U.S. Dist. Ct. (cen. dist.) Calif. 1979, U.S. Ct. Appeals (9th cir.) 1994, U.S. Supreme Ct. 1994. Law clk. to Hon. Francis C. Whelan U.S. Dist. Ct., L.A., 1978-79; assoc. Haight, Dickson, Brown & Bonesteel, L.A., Washington, 1979-82, Iorillo & Karp, L.A., 1982-87; dir. Hosp, Granieri & Cairns, Pasadena, Calif., 1987-93; ptnr. Cairns, Doyle, Lans, Nicholas & Soni, Pasadena, Calif., 1993-99; founding ptnr. Ongkeko, Doyle & Nicholas, Pasadena, 1999—; arbitrator L.A. County Superior Ct., 1984-93; judge pro tempore L.A. County Superior Ct., 1993—. Bd. dirs. Ctr. for Children, Pasadena, 1990-93; mem. instl. rev. bd. Childrens Hosp. L.A., 1983-90, bd. dirs. Mem. Def. Rsch. Inst., Assn. So. Calif. Def. Counsel, L.A. County Bar Assn., Pasadena Bar Assn. Roman Catholic. Avocations: hiking, backpacking, voice, skiing. Insurance, General civil litigation, Product liability. Office: Ongkeko Doyle & Nicholas 225 S Lake Ave Fl 9 Pasadena CA 91101-3005

**DOYLE, JUSTIN EMMETT,** lawyer, government official; b. Rochester, N.Y., Aug. 12, 1935; s. Emmett L. and Marion E. (Holihan) D.; m. Deborah Shea, Aug. 26, 1961; children: Christine, Clare, Thomas. BA with honors, U. Rochester, 1957; LLB, Cornell U., 1962. Bar: Calif. 1963, N.Y. 1964. Assoc. Gibson, Dunn & Crutcher, Los Angeles, 1962-64, Harris, Beach, et al, Rochester, N.Y., 1964-68; assoc. Nixon, Hargrave, Devans & Doyle, Rochester, 1968-73, ptnr., 1974-92; atty. U.S. Fgn. Svc., Agy. Internat. Devel., Washington, 1992-93; legal adv. USAID, Cairo, 1993-97; sr. regional legal adv. USAID Regional Ctr. for So. Africa, 1998—. Contbr. tax articles to profl jours.; speaker in field. Served to lt. (j.g.) USN, 1957-59. Recipient Citation for Service Nat. Gov.'s Assn., 1986. Mem. ABA, N.Y. Bar Assn., Calif. Bar Assn., Order of Coif. Republican. Roman Catholic. Club: Tennis of Rochester (Pittsford, N.Y.). Avocations: tennis, skiing, investments, reading. Office: USAID Regional Ctr for So Africa USAID/Botswana Dept State Washington DC 20521-0001

**DOYLE, JUSTIN P,** lawyer; b. Rochester, N.Y., Oct. 26, 1948; s. Justin Joseph and Jane Martha (Kreag) D.; m. Mary Elizabeth Mayer; children: Mary, Joe. BA, Dartmouth Coll., 1970; JD, Cornell U., 1974. Bar: N.Y. 1974. From assoc. to ptnr. Nixon, Hargrave, Devans & Doyle, Rochester, 1974-99; ptnr. Nixon Peabody LLP (formerly Nixon, Hargrave, Devans & Doyle), Rochester, 1999—. Mem. N.Y. Bar Assn., Monroe County Bar Assn. General corporate, Mergers and acquisitions, Securities. Home: 252 Overbrook Rd Rochester NY 14618-3648 Office: Nixon Peabody LLP Clinton Sq PO Box 1051 Rochester NY 14603-1051

**DOYLE, MARK ANTHONY,** lawyer; b. Louisville, Feb. 26, 1971; s. Joe Doyle and Betsy Brodnax. BBA, S.W. Tex. State U., 1992; JD, Tex. Wesleyan Sch. Law, 1995. Bar: Tex. 1995, U.S. Dist. Ct. (no. and ea. dists.) Tex. 1995. Atty. Bush, Hauder & Adkerson, Dallas, 1995-99, Smith & Knott, Dallas, 1999—. Mem. State Bar Tex. (litigation sect.), Dallas Bar Assn. (tort and ins. sect.), Dallas Assn. Young Lawyers. Personal injury, Insurance, Workers' compensation. Office: Smith & Knott 380 Founders Sq 900 Jackson St Dallas TX 75202-4436

**DOYLE, MICHAEL ANTHONY,** lawyer; b. Atlanta, Nov. 4, 1937; s. James Alexander and Wilma (Summersgill) D.; children: John, David, Peter; m. Bernice H. Winter, Nov. 12, 1977. BA, Yale U., 1959, LLB, 1962. Bar: Ga. 1961, D.C. 1967, U.S. Dist. Ct. D.C. 1967, U.S. Dist. Ct. (no. dist.) Ga. 1962, U.S. Ct. Appeals (5th cir.) 1962, U.S. Ct. Appeals (11th cir.) 1982, U.S. Ct. Appeals (D.C. cir.) 1968, U.S. Supreme Ct. 1972, U.S. Ct. Appeals (4th cir.) 1985. Assoc. Alston, Miller & Gaines, Atlanta, 1962-67; ptnr. Alston & Bird, and predecessor, Atlanta, 1967—. Bd. dirs. Atlanta Legal Aid Soc., 1969-84, pres., 1975-76; bd. dirs. Ga. Legal Services Program; mem. Leadership Atlanta, 1974. Served to lt. USNR, 1964-69. Mem. ABA, State Bar Ga., Atlanta Lawyers Club, Master, Bleckley Inn of Court, Assn. Yale Alumni, Yale Law Sch. Assn. (nat. v.p. 1982-85, mem. exec. com. 1978-85, chmn. planning com. 1988-90, pres. 1991-92, chmn. exec. com. 1992-94). Roman Catholic. Clubs: Piedmont Driving, Commerce, Yale of Ga. (pres. 1982-84), Yale of N.Y. State civil litigation, Federal civil litigation, Antitrust. Office: Alston & Bird 4200 One Atlantic Ctr 1201 W Peachtree St NW Atlanta GA 30309-3424

**DOYLE, RICHARD HENRY, IV,** lawyer; b. Elgin, Ill., Aug. 8, 1949; s. Richard Henry and Shirley Marian (Ohms) D.; m. Debbie Kay Cahalan, Aug. 2, 1975; children: John Richard, Kerry Jane. BA, Drake U., 1971, JD, 1976. Bar: Iowa 1976, U.S. Dist. Ct. (no. and so. dists.) Iowa 1977, U.S. Ct. Appeals (8th cir.) 1977, U.S. Supreme Ct. 1986. Asst. atty. gen. Iowa Dept. Justice, Des Moines, 1976-77; assoc. Lawyer, Lawyer & Jackson, Des Moines, 1977-79; assoc. Law Offices of Verne Lawyer & Assocs., Des Moines, 1979-93, Reavely, Shinkle, Bauer, Scism, Reavely & Doyle, Des Moines, 1993, Michael J. Galligan Law Firm, P.C., Des Moines, 1994-96. Contbr. articles to profl. jours. With U.S. Army, 1971-73. Fellow Iowa Acad. Trial Lawyers; mem. ABA, ATLA, Iowa Trial Lawyers Assn., Iowa Bar Assn., Iowa State Bar Assn., Polk County Bar Assn., SAR (registrar Iowa 1983-94, v.p. 1994-97, chancellor 1997-99), Order of the Founders and Patriots of Am., Phi Alpha Delta (chpt. pres. 1975). Personal injury, State civil litigation. Home: 532 Waterbury Cir Des Moines IA 50312-1316 Office: Galligan Tully Doyle & Reid PC The Plaza 300 Walnut St Ste 5 Des Moines IA 50309-2258

**DOYLE, ROBERT EUGENE, JR.,** lawyer; b. St. Simons Island, Ga., Sept. 5, 1948; s. Robert Eugene and Elizabeth Anne (Webb) D.; m. Kristina Maria Kost, Nov. 27, 1971; children: K. Maria, R. Eugene III, Emily Anne. BA, George Washington U., 1970; JD, Stetson U., 1975. Bar: Fla. 1975, U.S. Dist. Ct. (mid. and so. dists.) Fla. 1976, U.S. Ct. Appeals (5th cir.) 1981, U.S. Ct. Appeals (11th cir.) 1985, U.S. Supreme Ct. 1994; cert. Nat. Bd. Trial Advocacy. Ptnr. Asbell, Hains & Doyle, Naples, Fla., 1975-93, Quarles & Brady, Naples, 1993—; mem. code and rules of evidence com. Fla. Bar, 1988—, chair, 1993-94. Pres. Fillabelly Found., Naples, 1993-95. 1st lt. USMC, 1971-75. Mem. ABA, ATLA, Am. Inns of Ct. (barrister Thomas S. Biggs chpt. 1995). Democrat. Presbyterian. Avocations: fishing, flying. General civil litigation, Construction. Office: Quarles & Brady 4501 Tamiami Trl N Ste 300 Naples FL 34103-3023

**DOYLE, THOMAS EDWARD,** lawyer, educator; b. Washington, Mar. 11, 1963; s. Joseph Thomas Doyle and Elizabeth Brown Preston; m. Ferhan K. Doyle, Oct. 4, 1992; children: Alexis Shannon, Dominic Thomas. BS, U. Md., 1985; JD, George Mason U., 1989. Bar: U.S. Ct. Appeals Md. 1991, U.S. Dist. Ct. Md. 1992, D.C. 1993, U.S. Supreme Ct. 1997, U.S. Dist. Ct. D.C. 1997. Atty., law clk. Van Grack, Axelson & Williamowsky, Rockville, Md., 1989-91; pvt. practice Rockville, 1991-92; ptnr. Siegel & Doyle L.L.C., Rockville, 1992—; adj. prof. Montgomery Coll., Takoma Park, Md., 1991—; mem. adv. bd. D.C. Consumer Protection Law Ctr., Washington, 1997—; founder, exec. dir. Consumer Law Ctr. Md., Rockville, 1997—. Dir. Joseph T. Doyle Meml. Scholarship, Montgomery Coll., 1992. Recipient Am. Jurisprudence awards for excellence in consumer fin. law and pub. fin. law, 1989. Mem. ATLA, ABA, Md. State Bar Assn., D.C. Bar Assn. Personal injury, General civil litigation, Sports. Office: Galt Siegel & Doyle LLC 101 N Adams St Rockville MD 20850-2217

**DOZIER, LESTER ZACK,** lawyer; b. Spring City, Tenn., Nov. 28, 1940; s. Lester Zack and Maude (Valentine) D.; m. Brenda Jean Bankston, Feb. 24, 1963; children: Lester Zack III, Bankston Jerome, John William David. Grad., Gordon Mil. Coll., 1960; BA, U. Ga., 1962, JD, 1964. Bar: Ga. 1963, U.S. Dist. Ct. (mid. dist.) Ga., U.S. Ct. Appeals (5th and 11th cirs.). Ptnr. Dozier, Sikes, Grist & Brock, Macon, Ga.; judge Mcpl. Ct., Macon, 1967-68. Bd. dirs. Big Bros. Assn., Macon, 1974, Mid. Ga. Area Planning Commn., Macon, 1974. 1st lt. U.S. Army, 1964-66, ETO. Mem. ATLA, Ga. Trial Lawyers Assn. (v.p. 1984-86), Mid. Ga. Trial Lawyers Assn. (pres. 1986), Ga. Bar Assn., Macon bar Assn. (pres. 1972-73), Elks (exalted ruler 1977-78, 82-83). Baptist. Personal injury, Insurance, State civil litigation. Home: 2281 Vineville Ave Macon GA 31204-3129 Office: Dozier Sikes Grist and Brock 327 3rd St Macon GA 31201-3312

**DRABKIN, MURRAY,** lawyer; b. N.Y.C., Aug. 3, 1928; s. Max Drabkin and Minnie (Masin) Weiner; m. Mary Elizabeth Hooper, Nov. 27, 1971. AB, Hamilton Coll., 1950; LLB, Harvard U., 1953. Bar: D.C. 1953, U.S. Ct. Appeals (D.C. cir.) 1954, N.Y. 1966, U.S. Supreme Ct. 1972. Counsel com. on judiciary U.S. Ho. of Reps., Washington, 1957-66; spl. asst. to mayor City of N.Y., 1966-68; pvt. practice N.Y.C. and Washington, 1968-82; ptnr. Cadwalader, Wickersham & Taft, Washington, 1983-92; ret., 1992; ptnr. Hopkins & Sutter, Washington, 1992—; dir. Conn. State Revenue Task Force, 1969-71; mem. adv. com. FRS, Washington, 1970-71, D.C. Tax Revision Com., 1976-77; lectr. law George Washington U., Washington, 1978-80. Contbr. articles to profl. jours. Served with USN, 1953-57, to lt. commdr. USNR. Mem. D.C. Bar Assn., Assn. Bar City N.Y. (com. on mcpl. affairs 1989-92), N.Y. County Lawyers Assn. (chmn. com. on bankruptcy 1987-88), Nat. Bankruptcy Conf. (chmn. com. on R.R. reorgn. 1984—, chmn. com. on bankruptcy crimes 1994-98), Cosmos Club, Harvard Club of N.Y.C., Harvard Club of Washington (bd. dirs. 1996-98), Chesapeake Bay Bermuda 40 Assn., Phi Beta Kappa, Delta Sigma Rho. Bankruptcy, State and local taxation. Office: Hopkins & Sutter 888 16th St NW Ste 600 Washington DC 20006-4135

**DRACHMAN, ALLAN WARREN,** lawyer, director; b. Bklyn., Apr. 5, 1937; s. Norman and Marion (Soifer) D.; m. Judy, June 10, 1962; children: Neil, Amy. AB (cum laude), Brandeis U., 1958; LLB, Harvard Law Sch., 1961. Bar: Mass. 1961, U.S. Ct. Appeals (1st cir.) Mass. 1961. Atty. Schneider, Bronstein & Shapiro, Boston, 1961-66; corp. counsel City Boston Law Dept., 1966-70; ptnr. Deutsch, Holtz and Drachman, Boston, 1970-71; atty. sole practice Boston, 1971-73; ptnr., dir. Holtz & Drachman, P.C., 1973-77; dir. Allan W. Drachman, P.C., Boston, 1978-82, Holland, Crowe & Drachman, P.C., Boston, 1982-86, Deutsch Williams et al, Boston, 1986—. Labor. Home: 304 Dahlia Dr Wayland MA 01778-2825

**DRAGOO, DENISE ANN,** lawyer; b. Colorado Springs, Colo., Mar. 28, 1952; d. Harold E. and Irma A. Dragoo; m. Craig W. Anderson, Nov. 25, 1977. BA with distinction in History, U. Colo., 1973; cert. planning U. Utah, 1976, JD, 1976; LLM in Environ./Land Use Law, Washington U., St. Louis, 1977. Bar: Utah 1978. Mem. staff Environ. Law Inst., Washington, 1977; spl. asst. atty. gen. for energy and natural resources, State of Utah, Salt Lake City, 1978-81; shareholder VanCott Bagley Cornwall & McCarthy, 1995-98; ptnr. Shell & Wilmer, LLD, 1998—. Mem. coal com. Western States Policy Office, 1980-81. Named Woman Lawyer of Yr., Women Lawyers of Utah, 1997. Fellow Am. Bar Found.; mem. Utah State Bar (bd. bar commrs. 1991—, jud. conduct com. 1993-98, Natural Resources Lawyer of Yr. 1985, Edward Clyde Disting. Svc. award 1996), ABA (chair SONREEL pub. lands com., mining com. 1999—), Rocky Mountain Mineral Law Assn. (trustee 1987—), Utah Petroleum Assn., Utah Mining Assn. (pub. lands com.), Utah Bar and Gavel Soc. Contbr. articles on environ. law to profl. jours.; editorial bd. Jour. Contemporary Law, 1975-76. Environmental, Natural resources, Real property. Home: 1826 Hubbard Ave Salt Lake City UT 84108-1362 Office: Shell & Wilmer 111 E Broadway Ste 900 Salt Lake City UT 84111-5235

**DRAKE, CHRISTOPHER TODD,** lawyer; b. Peoria, Ill., Dec. 12, 1967; s. Bernard Lee and Roseann Peyronet Drake; m. Janet Stansberry, May 24, 1997. BA, U. Ill., 1991; JD, U. Colo., 1996. Bar: Colo. 1996, U.S. Dist. Ct. Colo. 1997, U.S. Ct. Appeals (10th cir.) 1997. Paralegal Heyl, Royster, Voelker & Allen, Peoria, 1992-93; student atty. Boulder (Colo.) Dist. Attys. Office, 1995; assoc. Richman & Hensen, P.C., Denver, 1996—. Mem. Jour. Internat. Environ. Law and Policy. Mem. Colo. Bar Assn. (interprofl. com. 1998—), Denver Bar Assn. (legal edn. com. 1997-98). Avocations: skiing, golfing, softball, travel. Personal injury, General civil litigation, Appellate. Office: Richman & Hensen PC 1775 Sherman St Ste 1717 Denver CO 80203-4318

**DRAKE, EDWIN P.,** lawyer; b. Battle Creek, Mich., Mar. 18, 1960; s. Ross Burton and Mary (Smith) D.; m. Janet Anne Van Dongen, May 9, 1981; children: Caleb, Rachel, Bethany, Hannah. BS, Olivet Nazarene U., Kankakee, Ill., 1981£; JD, U. Tenn., Knoxville, 1984, MBA, 1984. BAr: Pa. 1984. Atty. Alumnium Co. Am., Pitts., 1985-90, counsel, 1991—. Student materials editor U. Tenn. Law Rev., Knoxville, 1982-84. Mem. Order of Coif. Avocations: dramatic musical theatre acting, slot car collecting. Antitrust, General corporate, Mergers and acquisitions. Office: Aluminum Co Am 201 Isabella St Ste 6014 Pittsburgh PA 15212-5858

**DRAKE, WILLIAM FRANK, JR.,** lawyer; b. St. Louis, Mar. 29, 1932; s. William Frank and Beatrice Drake; m. Martha Minohr Mockbee. BA, Principia Coll., 1954; LLB, Yale U., 1957. Bar: Pa. 1958. Practice Phila., 1958-68, 84—; mem. firm Montgomery, McCracken, Walker & Rhoads, 1958-68, 87-96, of counsel, 1984-87, 96—; sr. v.p., gen. counsel Alco Std. Corp., 1968-79, 96-98, sr. v.p. adminstrn., 1979-83; chmn., CEO Alco Health Svcs. Corp., 1983-84, vice chmn., 1984-98, also bd. dirs.; vice chmn., gen. counsel Alco Standard Corp. (now Ikon Office Solutions Inc.), 1996-98. Trustee Peoples Light & Theatre Co., Malvern, Pa. With U.S. Army, 1957-58. Mem. ABA, Pa. Bar Assn., Phila. Bar Assn., Union League (Phila.), Roaring Fork Club (Basalt, Colo.), Wilmington (Del.) Country Club, First Troop, Phila. City Calvary. General corporate, Pension, profit-sharing, and employee benefits, Securities. Office: Montgomery McCracken Walker & Rhoads 123 S Broad St Fl 24 Philadelphia PA 19109-1099

**DRAPER, CARL R.,** lawyer; b. Springfield, Mo., Apr. 18, 1955. BA, Bradley U., 1976; JD, U. Ill., 1981. Bar: Ill. 1981, U.S. Dist. Ct. (ctrl. dist.) Ill. 1982. Assoc. McConnell Kennedy Quinn & Johnston, Peoria, Ill., 1981-82; asst. atty. gen. Office of Ill. Atty. Gen., Springfield, 1982-84; legal counsel to gov. Office of Ill. Gov., Springfield, 1984-87; ptnr. Feldman, Wasser, Draper & Benson, Springfield, 1987—. Mem. ABA, Ill. State Bar Assn. (law office mgmt. com. 1993—). Civil rights, Administrative and regulatory, Family and matrimonial. Office: Feldman Wasser Draper & Benson 1307 S 7th St Springfield IL 62703-2460

**DRAPER, GERALD LINDEN,** lawyer; b. Oberlin, Ohio, July 14, 1941; s. Earl Linden and Mary Antoinette (Colotto) D.; m. Barbara Jean Winter, Aug. 26, 1960; children: Melissa Leigh Price, Stephen Edward Draper. BA, Muskingum Coll., 1963; JD, Northwestern U., 1966. Bar: Ohio, 1966, U.S. Dist. Ct. (so. dist.) Ohio, 1966, U.S. Ct. Appeals (6th cir.), 1975, U.S. Supreme Ct., 1980. Ptnr. Bricker & Eckler, Columbus, Ohio, 1966-88, Thompson, Hine & Flory, Columbus, 1989-95, Draper, Hollenbaugh, Briscoe, Yashko & Carmany, Columbus, 1996—. Trustee, past pres. Wesley Glen Retirement Ctr., Columbus, 1979-95; trustee Muskingum Coll., New Concord, Ohio, 1988-92, 93—, vice chair, 1994—; trustee, pres. Wesley Ridge Retirement Ctr., 1995—. Fellow Am. Coll. Trial Lawyers, Am. Bd. Trial Advocates; mem. ABA (Ho. of Dels.), Ohio State Bar Assn. (pres. 1990-91), Ohio State Bar Found. (trustee 1992-97), Columbus Bar Assn. (pres. 1982-83, Bar Svc. medal 1998), Columbus Bar Found. (pres. 1984-86), Nat. Conf. of Bar Found. (trustee 1987-90, 91-94), Ohio Continuing Legal Edn. Inst. (trustee 1992-98, chair 1997-98), Ohio Assn. Hosp. Attys., Def. Rsch. Inst. Avocations: travel, golf, photography. General civil litigation, Professional liability, Insurance. Office: Draper Hollenbaugh Briscoe Yashko and Carmany LPA 175 S 3rd St Ste 1250 Columbus OH 43215-5199

**DRAPER, STEPHEN ELLIOT,** lawyer, engineer; b. Columbus, Ga., Mar. 17, 1942; s. Philip Henry and Ethel Illges (Woodruff) D.; m. Lucy Leila Hargrett, June 20, 1970; 1 child, Jessie Roxanne. BS, U.S. Mil. Acad., 1964; MBA, C.W. Post/L.I. U., 1976; JD, Ga. State U., 1992; MSCE, PhD, Ga. Inst. Tech., 1971, 81. Registered profl. engr., Ga., Fla. Commd. 2d. lt. U.S. Army, 1964, advanced through grades to col., retired, 1984; forensic engr. Atlanta, 1984-86; pres. and tech. dir. Draper Engring. Rsch., Atlanta, 1986-93, The Draper Group, Atlanta, 1993—. Contbr. articles to profl. jours. Bd. dirs. J.W. & E.I. Woodruff Found., Columbus, Ga., 1991—, Met. Boys Club, Columbus, 1981-84; mem. long-range planning com. Atlanta Area Coun., Boys Scouts Am., 1972; trustee the Foxcroft Sch., Middleburg, Va., 1994; bd. visitors U. Ga. Libr., 1997—; mem. svc. acad. selection bd. U.S. Senate, 1998—. Decorated Gallantry Cross with Silver Star, Legion of Merit, Bronze Star (2), Soldier's medal, Purple Heart (3), Air medal (2), Army Commendation medal (4), others; recipient Am. Jurisprudence award Ga. State U., 1992, Spl. Actions award Women's Equity Action League, 1976. Mem. ABA, ASCE, NSPE, Am. Water Resources Assn., Nat. Acad. Forensic Engrs., Capital City Club, Commerce Club, Sea Island Beach Club. Avocations: travel, history, sports, phys. fitness. Environmental, Real property, Natural resources. Office: The Draper Group 1401 Peachtree St NE Ste 500 Atlanta GA 30309-3000

**DRAUGHON, SCOTT WILSON,** lawyer, social worker; b. Muskogee, Okla., June 17, 1952; s. Arthur Eugene and Helen Carrie (Vanhooser) D. AA, Tulsa Jr. Coll., 1972; BA, Okla. State U., 1974; JD, U. Tulsa, 1977; postgrad., Oxford U., Eng., 1978; MSW, U. Okla, 1992. Bar: Okla. 1979, U.S. Dist. Ct. (no. dist.) Okla. 1980, U.S. Claims Ct., U.S. Tax Ct. 1979, U.S. Ct. Appeals (10th cir.) 1984, U.S. Supreme Ct. 1984. Lic. social worker with clin. specialty cert. Sole law practice Tulsa, 1979—; stockbroker, 1983-93; pvt. practice fin. planning Tulsa, 1984—; aftercare dept. coord. Tulsa Boys' Home, 1992-94; pvt. practice social worker, 1994—; legal counsel Tulsa City-County Health Dept., 1996-97; clin. social worker Cushing (Okla.) Regional Hosp., 1996—; founder, exec. dir. The Fin. Hotline, Tulsa, 1984—; adj. faculty Tulsa Jr. Coll., 1986-87; student intern, social work dept. Laureate Psychiat. Clinic and Hosp., summer 1991; v.p. govtl. and pub. affairs Okla. Credit Union League, Inc., 1988-90, dir. rsch./info. Okla. Credit Union League Affiliates, 1991. Active Indian Affairs Commn. City of Tulsa, 1989-91, 20th Anniversary Com. Leadership Tulsa, Inc., 1992—, class IX grad.; mem. exec. bd. Tulsa Assn. Vol. Adminstrs., 1994—; bd. dirs. Arts and Humanities Coun., Tulsa, 1982-83, Ea. Okla. chpt. March of Dimes, 1989-90, Internat. Coun. Tulsa, 1987-91, Tulsa County Regional Planning Coord. Bd. Svcs. to Children and Youth, 1992—; mem. exec. com. Corp. Vol. Coun. Greater Tulsa, 1990; chmn. pub. rels. com., exec. com. Tulsa Human Rights Commn., 1987-88; mem., vol. Tulsa Global Alliance, 1999—; registered lobbyist Okla. Credit Union League Affilliate, 1988-90; student intern Social Svcs. Dept. St. Frances Hosp., 1992; mem. Okla. Human Rights Commn., 1997—; mem. state assn. com. Leadership Okla., Inc., 1998—, chmn. Program Comm. Okla. Human Rights Commn.; mem. World Fedn. on Mental Health, 1999—, Internat. Fedn. of Social Workers, 1999—. Mem. NASW (treas. Okla. chpt. 1992-94), Assoc. mem., Okla. Assn. of Mcpl. Atty. (assoc.), Okla. Bar Assn., Masons, Shriners, Phi Delta Phi (life), Cushing Rotary Club, 1997—. Republican. Methodist. Avocations: travel, photography, reading, gardening, cooking. Labor, Health, Estate planning. Office: Cushing Regional Hosp 1027 E Cherry Cushing PO Box 1409 Cushing OK 74023-1409

**DREIER, WILLIAM ALAN,** lawyer; b. N.Y.C., Sept. 18, 1937; s. Henry M. and Mildred R. Dreier; m. Sandra F. Hollander, June 12, 1960; children: Susan Dreier Wishnow, David H. BS, MIT, 1958; JD, Columbia U., 1961. Bar: N.J. 1961, U.S. Dist. Ct. N.J. 1961, U.S. Supreme Ct. 1969, U.S. Ct. Claims 1972, U.S. Ct. Appeals (3d cir.) 1972, N.Y. 1988. Law clk. to Hon. Sidney Goldmann Superior Ct. N.J., Trenton, 1961-62, judge law divsn., 1976-80, judge chancery divsn., 1980-83; judge appellate divsn. Superior Ct. N.J., Springfield, 1983-84, presiding judge, 1984-98; assoc. Gordon, Mackenzie & Welt, Elizabeth, 1962-65; ptnr. Mackenzie, West & Dreier, Elizabeth, 1965-73; judge Union County Dist. Ct. and Union County Ct., Elizabeth, 1973-76; ptnr. Norris, McLaughlin & Marcus, Somerville, N.J., 1998—; lectr. N.J. Inst. for CLE, 1978, 80, 82-96, 98, Nat. Jud. Coll., U. Nev., Reno, 1982-90, N.J. Jud. Coll., 1977—, N.J. Inst. Mcpl. Attys., 1969-72, Seton Hall Law Sch., 1992—, Rutgers U. Law Sch., 1995, U. Mich. Law Sch., 1996, U. Tex. Law Sch., 1998, also numerous others; corp. counsel City of Plainfield, N.J., 1969-73; mem. bd. visitors Columbia U. Law Sch., N.Y.C., 1993—; mem. com. on continuing profl. edn., product liability adv. group Am. Law Inst.-ABA, 1985-97; mem. standing com. on evidence N.J. Supreme Ct., 1981—, on jud. salaries and pensions, 1992%, civil practice, 1979-90; arbitrator, mediator Graduate Ctr. Dispute Settlement, Washington; panel Distinguished Neutrals CPR Inst. Dispute Resolution. Author: Secured Financing under the Uniform Commercial Code, 1963, 5th edit., 1979, Products Liability and Toxic Torts Law in New Jersey—A Practitioner's Guide, 1978, 6th edit., 1988, Secured Transactions under the Revised Uniform Commercial Code, 1981, 3d edit., 1989, Chancery Practice in New Jersey, 1983, 4th edit., 1997, New Jersey Products Liability and Toxic Torts Law, 1995, 96, 98, 99; mem. editl. bd. N.J. Law Jour., 1998—; contbr. articles to law jours. Mem. Plainfield City Coun., 196-69; treas., dist. committeeman Plainfield Rep. City Com., 1963. eamed Plainfield's Outstanding Citizen, Plainfield Jaycees, 1972; recipient Jud. Achievement award Nat. Inst. for Child Custody and Divorce Awareness, 1979, Alfred C. Clapp award for excellence N.J. Inst. CLE, 1993. Fellow Am. Bar Found. (life); mem. ABA, Am. Law Inst., N.J. Bar Assn., Plainfield P.B.A. (hon. life), Twin Brooks Country Club (pres. bd. govs. 1997), Richard J. Hughes Am. Inn Ct. (master 1988—). Avocations: golf, classical music. Fax: 908-722-0755. E-mail: wadreier@nm&mlaw.com. Product liability, General civil litigation, Alternative dispute resolution. Home: 48 Skyline Dr Warren NJ 07059-6718 Office: Norris McLaughlin & Marcus 721 Rts 202-206 Somerville NJ 08876-1018

**DREIZE, LIVIA REBBEKA,** lawyer; b. Jan. 14, 1964. BS in Hotel and Restaurant Mgmt., Fla. Internat. U., 1988; postgrad., U. Complutense de Madrid, 1990; JD summa cum laude, Pontifical Cath. U. P.R., Ponce, 1992. Bar: P.R. 1993, Fla. 1994, D.C. 1996, U.S. Dist. Ct. (so. dist.) Fla. 1995. Assoc. Law Offices of Nathan D. Clark, Miami, Fla., 1993-96; mng. ptnr. Damera & Dreize, P.A., Miami, 1996—; lectr. Fla. Internat. U., Miami, 1998. mem. Law Rev., Pontifical Cath. U. P.R., 1990-92. Recipient Acad. Excellence award P.R. Bar Assn., 1992. Mem. ATLA, Dade County Bar Assn. General corporate, Family and matrimonial, Immigration, naturalization, and customs. Office: Damera & Dreize PA 201 W Flagler St Miami FL 33130-1510

**DRENDEL, KEVIN GILBERT,** lawyer; b. Boston, Dec. 29, 1959; s. Gilbert Xavier and Carol Katherine D.; m. Elizabeth Rosemary Caron, Feb. 24, 1961; childen: Nathan Xavier, Tyler Kevin, Jonathan David, Nicholas Raymond, Ryan Joseph. B Spl. Studies, Cornell Coll., 1982; JD, No. Ill. U., 1991. Bar: Ill. 1991, U.S. Dist. Ct. (no. dist. Ill.) 1992. With Drendel, Schanlaber, Horwitz, Tatnall & McCracken, Aurora, Ill., 1991-94; ptnr. Drendel, Tatnall, Hoffman & McCracken, Batavia, Ill., 1994-96, Drendel, Tatnall & Hoffman, Batavia, 1996-97, Drendel, Tatnall, Batavia, 1998—. Trustee Am. Cancer Soc., Batavia, 1995-96. Recipient award for Outstanding Scholastic Achievement, West Pub., 1991. Mem. Ill. State Bar Assn., Kane County Bar Assn. (chmn. mem. com. 1995-98, dir. 1999—), Christian Legal Soc. Avocations: musky fishing, cigars. Municipal (including bonds), Probate, General practice. Office: Drendel Tatnall 201 Houston St Ste 300 Batavia IL 60510-1960

**DRENGLER, WILLIAM ALLAN JOHN,** lawyer; b. Shawano, Wis., Nov. 18, 1949; s. William J. and Vera J. (Simmonds) D.; m. Kathleen A. Hintz, June 18, 1983; children: Ryan, Jeffrey, Brittany. BA, Am. U., 1972; JD, Marquette U., 1976. Bar: Wis. 1976, U.S. Dist. Ct. (ea. and we. dists.) Wis. 1976. Assoc. Herrling, Swain & Drengler, Appleton, Wis., 1976-78; dist. atty. Outagamie County, Appleton, 1979-81; corp. counsel Marathon County, Wausau, Wis., 1981-96, Drengler Law Firm, Wausau, 1997—; vice chmn. Wis. Equal Rights Coun., 1978-83, Wis. Coun. on Criminal Justice, Madison, 1983-87. Nat. pres. Future Bus. Leaders Am., 1967-68; mem. nat. Dem. delegation, 1974-76; mem. adminstrv. com. Wis. Dems., Madison, 1977-81, 86-88; chmn. local Selective Svc. Bd., Wausau, 1982-89; mem. adv. bd. Wausau Salvation Army, 1986—; judge adv. officer Wis. Army N.G., 1989-96; bd. dirs. Wausau Youth/Little League Baseball, 1988—, team mgr., 1994—. Mem. ABA (chair com. on govt. lawyers, sect. state and local govt. 1991-93, bylaws com. govt. and pub. sect. lawyers divsn. 1993-98), KC, Nat. Assn. County Civil Attys. (dir. 1986-88, v.p. 1988-91, pres. 1991-92), Nat. Assn. Counties (bd. dirs. 1991-92, taxation and fin. steering com. 1991-93, deferred compensation adv. com. 1993-95, justice and pub. safety steering com. 1993-94), State Bar Wis. (govt. lawyers divsn., bd. dirs. 1982-86, sec. 1986-87, pres. 1989-91, professionalism com. 1987-91, 92—), Nat. Eagle Scout Assn., Kiwanis (lt. gov. 1985-86, club pres. 1989-90, chair past lt. govs. coun. 1990-91), Elks. Roman Catholic. Avocations: baseball, camping, fishing, gardening, tennis. General practice, Legislative. Office: PO Box 5152 609 Scott St Wausau WI 54402-5152

**DRENNAN, JOSEPH PETER,** lawyer; b. Albany, N.Y., Apr. 15, 1956; s. Richard Peter and Ann Marie (Conlon) D.; m. Adriana Sonia Miramontes, Sept. 26, 1987; children: Patricia Solange, Monica Adriana, Michael Robert II. BA in Polit. Sci., U. Richmond, 1978; JD, Cath. U. of Am., Washington, 1981. Bar: D.C. 1981, U.S. Dist. Ct. D.C. 1983, U.S. Ct. Appeals (fed. cir.) 1983, Va. 1984, U.S. Ct. Appeals (D.C. cir.) 1984, U.S. Dist. Ct. (no. dist.) Va. 1987, U.S. Ct. Appeals (4th cir.) 1987, U.S. Dist. Ct. (no. dist.) Miss. 1988, U.S. Dist. Ct. Md. 1990, U.S. Dist. Ct. (ea. dist.) Mich. 1991. Pvt. practice law Washington, 1981—. Mem. ATLA, Bar Assn. D.C., Am. Bankruptcy Inst., Alexandria Bar Assn., Va. Trial Lawyers Assn., Trial Lawyers Met. Washington. Republican. Roman Catholic. Club: U. Washington. Personal injury, Federal civil litigation. Home: 9616 Dominion Forest Cir Fredericksbrg VA 22408-9505 Office: 2121 Eisenhower Ave Alexandria VA 22314-4688

**DRESCHER, JOHN WEBB,** lawyer; b. Norfolk, Va., May 13, 1948; s. Otto Charles and Anne Best (Webb) D.; m. Dale McKeithan Moore, June 13, 1970; 1 child, Ryan. BA, Hampden-Sydney Coll., 1970; JD, U. Richmond, 1973. Bar: Va. 1973, U.S. Supreme Ct. 1980, U.S. Ct. Appeals (4th cir.) 1985, U.S. Dist. Ct. (ea. dist.) Va. 1976. Assoc. Brydges, Hammers & Hudgins, Virginia Beach, 1973-74; asst. atty. Office of Commonwealth Atty., Virginia Beach, 1974-75; assoc. Pickett, Spain & Lyle, P.C., Virginia Beach, 1976-78; ptnr. Pickett, Lyle , Siegel, Drescher & Croshaw P.C., Virginia Beach, 1979-87, Breit, Drescher & Breit, P.C., Norfolk, 1988—. Pres. Hampden-Sydney Alumni Assn., Tidewater, Va., 1970—. Named among best lawyers in Am. Naifch & Smith, 1995—. Fellow Am. Bd. Trial Advocates; mem. ATLA, Va. Trial Lawyers Assn. (bd. govs. 1990—), Nat. Assn. Criminal Def. Lawyers, Am. Inns Ct., Norfolk-Portsmouth Bar Assn., U. Richmond Law Sch. Alumni Assn., Va. Beach Bar Assn. (pres. 1990). Democrat. Episcopal. Avocations: physical fitness, golf. Personal injury, Product liability, Civil rights. Home: 925 Holladay Pt Virginia Beach VA 23451 Office: Breit Drescher & Breit 1000 Dominion Twr 999 Waterside Dr Ste 1000 Norfolk VA 23510-3304

**DRESCHER, KATHLEEN EBBEN,** lawyer; b. Kaukauna, Wis., May 17, 1963; d. Willard Peter and Helen Mary (Joyce) Ebben; m. Park Morris Drescher, Aug. 12, 1989; children: John Park, William Morris. BA, Lawrence U., 1985; JD, Washington U. St. Louis, 1989. Bar: Mo. 1989, Wis. 1992. Assoc. Popkin & Stern, St. Louis, 1989-90; ptnr. Drescher & Drescher, St. Louis, 1990-92; shareholder Drescher & Drescher, S.C., Appleton, Wis., 1992—. Pres. bd. dirs. Emergency Shelters, Appleton, 1992—; bd. dirs. Child Care Resource and Referral, Appleton. Mem. ABA, Wis. Bar Assn., Mo. Bar Assn., Outagamie County Bar Assn. Avocation: tennis. General practice, Real property, Estate planning. Home: 14 Lamplighter Ct Appleton WI 54914-6519 Office: Drescher & Drescher SC 100 W Lawrence St Fl 3D Appleton WI 54911-5773

**DRESCHER, PARK MORRIS,** lawyer; b. St. Louis, Apr. 20, 1963; s. John Morris and Katherine (White) D.; m. Kathleen Ebben, Aug. 12, 1989; children: John Park, William Morris. BA, Lawrence U., 1985; JD, St. Louis U., 1988. Bar: Mo., 1989, Wis., 1992, U.S. Ct. of Appeals (8th cir.), 1989. Assoc. Biggs & Hensley, P.C., St. Louis, 1988-90; ptnr. Drescher & Drescher, S.C., Appleton, Wis., 1990—. Trustee The Mari Taniguchi Found., Appleton, 1997—; mem. small bus. sect. Appleton Area C. of C., 1997. Mem. ABA, Wis. Bar Assn., Mo. Bar Assn., Outagamie County Bar Assn. Avocation: tennis. Office: Drescher & Drescher SC 100 W Lawrence St Appleton WI 54911-5773

**DRESSER, RAYMOND H., JR.,** lawyer; b. Sturgis, Mich., Feb. 23, 1931; s. Raymond H. and Lola (Juckette) D.; m. Gretchen G. Meier, Aug. 7, 1954; children—John, Amy, Marcia. B.A. cum laude, Amherst Coll., 1953; J.D., U. Mich., 1956. Bar: Mich. 1956, U.S. Dist. Ct. (we. dist.) Mich. 1958, U.S. Ct. Appeals (6th cir.) 1958. Ptnr. Dresser & Dresser et al, Sturgis, 1956-85; sr. ptnr. Dresser, Dresser, Gilbertt & Haas P.C., Sturgis, 1986—; city atty. City of Sturgis, 1962-84. Bd. dirs. Mich. Assn. Professions, 1981-85; bd. dirs. Glen Oaks Community Coll. Found., Jane A. Sturges Meml. Home Assn., Sturgis, Econ. Devel. Corp. Sturgis; elder Sturgis Presbyn. Fellow Am. Coll. Probate Counsel; mem. Am. Judicature Soc., ABA, State Bar Mich. (bd. dirs. 1980-92, treas. 1985-88, chair probate and trust law sect. 1995-96, Roberts P. Hudson award), Klinger Lake Country Club (pres. 1978), Rotary (pres. 1960-61), Shriners. Republican. Probate, General corporate, Corporate taxation. Office: 112 S Monroe St Sturgis MI 49091-1729

**DRESSER, WILLIAM CHARLES,** lawyer; b. Phila., June 24, 1955; s. Richard M. and Peggy Dresser; m. Anne Ingels Dresser, Feb. 8, 1997; 1 child, Michael. BA, Denison U., 1977; JD, Hastings Coll. of Law, 1982. Bar: Calif. 1982, U.S. Dist. Ct. (no. dist.) Calif. 1982, U.S. Dist. Ct. (ea. dist.) Calif. 1984. Atty. Breakstone & Cotsirillos, San Francisco, 1982-83, Cal Farm Ins., Berkeley, 1983-88; ptnr. Tarkington, O'Connor and O'Neill, San Jose, Calif., 1988-94; pvt. practice San Jose, 1994—. Editor Exile, 1977. Mem. Santa Clara County Bar Assn. (chair conf. dels. 1997-98, chair labor law exec. com. 1996). Avocations: soccer, baseball, chess. General civil litigation, Insurance, Personal injury. Office: 4 N 2nd St Ste 275 San Jose CA 95113-1323

**DRETZIN, DAVID,** lawyer; b. N.Y.C., July 24, 1928; s. Isadore and Clara Yohalem D.; m. Joanna Merlin, Mar. 1, 1964; children: Rachel Dretzin Goodman, Julie Y. BA, Reed Coll., 1951; MA, U. Chgo., 1952; JD, Yale U., 1959. Bar: N.Y.; U.S. Dist. Ct. (so. dist.) N.Y. Asst. gen. counsel ILGWU, N.Y.C., 1959-62; assoc. Finkelstein, Benton & Soll, N.Y.C., 1962-66; ptnr. Heller & Dretzin, N.Y.C., 1966-68; pvt. practice N.Y.C., 1968-70; ptnr., counsel Dretzin, Kauff, McClain & McGuire, N.Y.C., 1970-90; ptnr. Stroock & Stroock & Lavan, N.Y.C., 1990-93; pvt. practice N.Y.C., 1994—; dir. Floating Hosp., N.Y.C., Theatreworks U.S.A., N.Y.C. Author: PLI Publs. on Employment Law. Pvt. U.S. Army, 1954-56. Mem. Bar Assn. of City of N.Y. (mem. com. on labor and employment law 1995-97). Democrat. Jewish. Avocations: tennis, music, books. Labor, Entertainment. Office: 1251 Avenue Of The Americas New York NY 10020-1104

**DREW, GAYDEN, IV,** lawyer; b. Memphis, Jan. 21, 1953; s. Gayden III and Betty Lee (Hancock) D.; m. Leigh Ann McCord, Nov. 3, 1984; children: Gayden V, James Logan. BS in Psychology, U. Tenn., 1975; JD, Memphis State U., 1979. Bar: Tenn., 1980, U.S. Dist. Ct. (we. dist.) Tenn., 1980, U.S. Ct. Appeals (6th cir.) 1988. Atty. Wilson, McRae, Ivy, Sevier, McTyier and Strain, Memphis, 1980-82, Hill, Boren, Drew and Martindale, Jackson, Tenn., 1982-95, Drew and Martindale, P.C., Jackson, Tenn., 1996—; spkr. Med. Ednl. Svcs., Nashville, 1992, Tenn. Trial Lawyers Assn., 1988, 89, 95, 96, 97. Contbr. articles to The Trial Mag., profl. jours. V.p. YMCA, Jackson, 1992, bd. dirs., 1991—; commr. World Tennis Ball League, Memphis, 1982-90. Mem. Am. Trial Lawyers Assn., Tenn. Trial Lawyers Assn., Tenn. Bar Assn., Jackson-Madison County Bar Assn., Sigma Alpha Epsilon Alumni Assn. (alumni pres. 1980), Jackson Country Club, Men's Golf Assn. (pres. 1993, bd. dirs. 1994-97). Episcopalian. Avocations: golf, jogging. Workers' compensation, Personal injury. Home: 18 Deepwood Dr Jackson TN 38305-9679 Office: Drew and Martindale PC 470 N Parkway Ste C Jackson TN 38305-2843

**DREXEL, BARON JEROME,** lawyer; b. Miami Beach, Fla., Sept. 3, 1954; s. Gustave L. and Dorris J. (Haas) D. AA, U. Fla., 1973; BA, U. Calif. Berkeley, 1979; MA in Econs., U. Miami, 1983, JD cum laude, 1985. Bar: Fla. 1985, Calif. 1987, U.S. Ct. Appeals (9th cir.) 1987, U.S. Ct. Appeals (11th cir.) 1989, U.S. dist. Ct. (no. dist.) Calif. 1986, U.S. Dist. Ct. (ctrl. dist.) Calif. 1987, U.S. Dist. Ct. (so. dist.) Calif. 1988. Survey crew mem. U.S. Forest Svc., Hayfork, Calif., 1979; sales rep. real estate Allen Morris Co., Miami, Fla., 1981-82; assoc. Shutts & Bowen, Miami, 1985-88, Lasky, Haas, Cohler & Munter, San Francisco, 1988-89, Aiken, Kramer & Cummings, Oakland, Calif., 1989-92, Bostwick & Tehin, San Francisco, 1992-95; pvt. practice Oakland, 1995—. Recipient J.B. Spence award U. Miami Law Rev. Mem. Order of Coif. Co-trial couns. for $15.4 million verdict. Avocations: computers, travel, photography, chess, writing poetry. Personal injury, Civil rights, General civil litigation. Office: 312 Lee St Apt 1 Oakland CA 94610-4356

**DREXEL, RAY PHILLIPS,** lawyer; b. Cleve., Aug. 28, 1949; s. Gordon Arthur and Jean Elizabeth (Phillips) D.; m. Beverly Lynn Beall, June 26, 1971; children—Kate Phillips, Alexander Ray. B.S., Ohio State U., 1971; J.D., Capital U., 1974. Bar: Ohio 1974, U.S. Dist. Ct. (so. dist.) Ohio 1975, U.S. Supreme Ct. 1978. Staff atty. Buckeye Fed. Savs. & Loan Assn., Columbus, Ohio, 1974-82; ptnr. Hilliard, Ramsey & Drexel, Columbus, 1982-85, Hilliard, Ramsey, Drexel & DePew, 1985-86, Hilliard, Drexel & DePew, 1986-89, Hilliard & Drexel, 1989-93, Buckley King & Bluso, 1994—. Second v.p. Annehurst Village Residents Assn., Westerville, Ohio, 1983-86 . Arnold Cohn Meml. scholar, 1970-71. Mem. Columbus Bar Assn., Mid Ohio Savs. and Loan Attys. Assn. (pres. 1978-80), Franklin County Trial Lawyers, Nat Mgmt Assn. (pres. Buckeye Fed. chpt. 1980-81). Republican. Methodist. Lodge: Masons. State civil litigation, Consumer commercial, General practice. Office: Buckley King & Bluso 10 W Broad St Ste 1300 Columbus OH 43215-3482

**DREXLER, KENNETH,** lawyer; b. San Francisco, Aug. 2, 1941; s. Fred and Martha Jane (Cunningham) D.; BA, Stanford U., 1963; JD, UCLA, 1969. Bar: Calif. 1970. Assoc., David S. Smith, Beverly Hills, Calif., 1970, McCutchen, Doyle, Brown and Enersen, San Francisco, 1970-77; assoc. Chickering & Gregory, San Francisco, 1977-80, ptnr., 1980-82; ptnr. Drexler & Leach, San Rafael, Calif., 1982—. Served with AUS, 1964-66. Mem. Calif. State Bar (resolutions com. conf. of dels. 1979-83, chmn. 1982-83, adminstrn. justice com. 1983-89, chmn. 1987-88, adv. mem. 1990—), Marin County Bar Assn. (bd. dirs. 1985-87), Bar Assn. San Francisco (dir. 1980-81), San Francisco Barristers Club (pres. 1976, dir. 1975-76), Marin Conservation League (bd. dirs. 1985-97, 98—). General practice, Estate planning. Office: 1330 Lincoln Ave Ste 300 San Rafael CA 94901-2143

**DREYER, JOHN EDWARD,** lawyer; b. Chgo., Feb. 22, 1929; s. Felix Edward and Marie Ann (Bungert) D.; m. Shirley Ann Fenhaus, May 29, 1954 (div.); children: Thomas, Laura, Gregory, Michael; m. Nancy A. Mickelson. BS, Loyola U., Chgo., 1951; JD, DePaul U., 1953. Bar: Ill. 1953, U.S. Dist. Ct. (no. dist.) Ill. 1953, U.S. Ct. Appeals (7th cir.) 1953, U.S. Ct. Mil. Appeals 1954. Jr. ptnr. Sears Streit, Tyler & Dreyer, Chgo. and Aurora, Ill., 1961-63; sr. ptnr. Dreyer, Foote & Streit, Assocs., Aurora, 1963-84; sr. ptnr. Dreyer, Foote, Streit, Furgason & Slocum, P.A., 1984-94, of counsel, 1994—; dir. Valley Nat. Bank Aurora. Bd. dirs. Family Support Ctr., Aurora, 1975-86 . Served to 1st. lt. JAGC, U.S. Army, 1953-56. Mem. Ill. State Bar Assn. (assembly 1972-78), Kane County Bar Assn., ABA, Am. Judicature Soc., Ill. Soc. Trial Lawyers, Nat. Assn. R.R. Trial Counsel, Phi Alpha Delta, Pi Gamma Mu. Club: Moose. Bd. editors DePaul Law Rev., 1952-53. State civil litigation, Labor. Home: 3 S 611 Finley Rd Sugar Grove IL 60554 Office: Dreyer Foote Streit Furgason & Slocum PA 900 N Lake St Ste 1 Aurora IL 60506-2578

**DREYFUSS, STEPHEN LAWRENCE,** lawyer; b. N.Y.C., May 28, 1949; s. Joseph David and Janet Roslyn (Schuman) D.; m. Lillian Francine Pliner, June 24, 1984; children: Katherine Marielle, Caroline Pliner. Student U. Paris, 1969-70; AB magna cum laude, Princeton U., 1971; JD (Harlan Fiske Stone scholar), Columbia U., 1974. Bar: N.J. 1974, N.Y. 1975, D.C. 1976. Law clk. to U.S. Dist. Judge, U.S. Dist. Ct., Newark, 1974-76; asst. dist. atty., N.Y. County, N.Y., 1976-79; assoc. Hellring, Lindeman, Goldstein, & Siegal, Newark, 1979-82, ptnr., 1983—. Mem. adv. com. dept. Romance langs. and Lits. Princeton U., 1989—, chmn., 1997—. Bd. dirs. French-Am. C. of C. in the U.S., Inc., N.Y.C., 1985—, nat. sec., 1987-90, v.p., 1991—. Co-author: (handbook) Special Considerations in Cases Involving Foreign Parties, 1992. Mem. N.J. State Bar Assn. (vice chair internat. law and orgns. sect. 1992—, chair com. on transnational litigation and arbitration 1992-93, vice chair antitrust law com. 1993-97, chair Com. on Internat. Trade and Investment, 1995), Assn. Fed. Bar State N.J., Union Internat. des Avocats (mem. bd. gov. U.S. nat. com., 1994—, del. gen. assembly, 1994—, conseiller du pres. 1997—), Europe/USA 2000, Ivy Club. Private international, Federal civil litigation, Antitrust. Home: 5 Holly Dr Short Hills NJ 07078-1317 Office: Hellring Lindeman Goldstein & Siegal One Gateway Ctr Newark NJ 07102-5386

**DRIBIN, MICHAEL A.,** lawyer; b. 1951. BA, Northwestern U., 1972; JD, Loyola U., Chgo., 1975; LLM in Taxation, U. Miami, 1979. Bar: Ill. 1975, Fla. 1975. Mem. Broad and Cassel, Miami, Fla. Fellow Am. Coll. Trust and Estate Counsel; mem. Fla. Bar (bd. cert. estate planning and probate lawyer bd. legal specialization and edn.). Probate, Estate planning, Estate taxation. Office: Broad and Cassel 201 S Biscayne Blvd Ste 3000 Miami FL 33131-4399

**DRINKO, JOHN DEAVER,** lawyer; b. St. Marys, W.Va., June 17, 1921; s. Emery J. and Hazel (White) D.; m. Elizabeth Gibson, May 14, 1946; children: Elizabeth Lee Sullivan, Diana Lynn Martin, John Randall, Jay Deaver. AB, Marshall U., 1942; JD, Ohio State U., 1944; postgrad., U. Tex. Sch. Law, 1944; LLD (hon.), Marshall U., 1980, Ohio State U., 1986, John Carroll U., 1987, Capital U., 1988, Cleve. State U., 1990; DHL (hon.), David N. Myers Coll., 1990, U. N.H., 1992, Baldwin-Wallace Coll., 1993, Ursuline Coll., 1994, Notre Dame Coll., 1997, U. Rio Grande, 1999. Bar: Ohio 1945, D.C 1946, U.S. Dist. Ct. (no. dist.) Ohio 1958. Assoc. Baker & Hostetler, Cleve., 1945-55, ptnr., 1955-69, mng. ptnr., from 1969, sr. adviser to mng. com.; chmn. bd. Cleve. Inst. Electronics Inc., Double D Ranch Inc., Ohio; bd. dirs. Cloyes Gear and Products Inc., McGean-Rohco Worldwide Inc., Orvis Co. Inc., Preformed Line Products Inc., The Standard Products Co. Trustee Elizabeth G. and John D. Drinko Charitable Found., Orvis-Perkins Found., Thomas F. Peterson Found., Mellen Found., The Cloyes-Myers Found., Marshall U. Found.; founder Consortium of Multiple Sclerosis Ctrs., Mellen Conf. on Acute and Critical Care Nursing, Case Western Res. U. Disting. fellow Cleve. Clinc Found., 1991; Ohio State Law Sch. Bldg. named in his honor, 1995, libr. at Marshall U. named in his honor, 1997; inducted into Bus. Hall of Fame, Marshall Univ., 1996. Mem. ABA, Am. Jud. Assn., Bar Assn. Greater Cleve., Greater Cleve. Growth Assn., Ohio State Bar Assn., Jud. Conf. 8th Jud. Dist. (life), Soc. Benchers, Case Western Res. U. Law Sch. Assn., Cleve. Play House, Cleve. Civil War Round-table, Mayfield Country Club, Union Club, The Club at Soc. Ctr., O'Donnell Golf Club,

Order of Coif, 33o Scottish Rite Mason, Knight Templar, York Rite, Euclid Blue Lodge No. 599 (Jesters, Shrine, Grotto). Republican. Presbyterian. Home: 4891 Middledale Rd Cleveland OH 44124-2522 also: 1245 Otono Dr Palm Springs CA 92264-8445 Office: Baker & Hostetler 1900 E 9th St Ste 3200 Cleveland OH 44114-3475

**DRISKILL, ROGER MERRILL,** lawyer; b. Ft. Collins, Colo., Oct. 31, 1949; s. S.D. and Ardis Loree Driskill; m. Kay M. Kaplan, Aug. 2, 1974; children: Jennifer Lynn, Susan Loree. BA, S.W. Bapt. Coll., Bolivar, Mo., 1971; JD, U. Mo., 1974. Bar: Mo. 1974, U.S. Dist. Ct. (we. dist. Mo.) 1974. Pvt. practice Richmond, Mo., 1974-91, Liberty, Mo., 1991—. City counselor City of Richmond, Mo., 1975-85. 1st lt. U.S. Army Nat. Guard, 1974-80. Republican. Baptist. Office: 19 N Water St Liberty MO 64068-1747

**DROGIN, SUSAN F.,** lawyer; b. Bayonne, N.J., Apr. 17, 1956; d. Morris and Shirley Drogin. BA, Tufts U., 1976; JD, Boston U., 1979. Bar: Mass. 1979, U.S. Dist. Ct. Mass., U.S. Ct. Appeals (1st cir.). Assoc. Corwin & Corwin, Boston, 1979-84; enforcement atty. U.S. SEC, Boston, 1984-86; sr. assoc. Looney & Grossman, Boston, 1986-94; pvt. practice, of counsel Spencer & Stone, Boston, 1995—; arbitrator NYSE, NASD, Boston, 1984—. Author: Arbitrating Securities INdustry Disputes, 1995, 96. Mem. Boston Bar Assn. Avocations: gardenign, swimming, reading. Securities, Appellate, General civil litigation. Office: Spencer & Stone 50 Beacon St Fl 2D Boston MA 02108-3524

**DROLLA, JOHN CASPER DODT, JR.,** lawyer; b. New Orleans, Sept. 29, 1944; s. John Casper Drolla Sr. and Edna Florence (Bauerfeind) Dempsey. AS, Tarleton State Univ., 1960; BA, Univ. Tex., 1963, JD, 1972. Bar: U.S. Ct. Appeals (fifth cir.) 1976, 82, U.S. Dist. Ct. (we. dist.) Tex. 1974, U.S. Ct. Military Appeals 1988. Commander 25th Trans Co. Honor Guard Fort Sam, Houston, 1965-67; briefing clerk Judge Leon Douglas Tex. Ct. Criminal Appeals, Austin, 1972-73, rsch. asst. Judge Leon Douglas, 1973-74; assoc. Philip & Norris, Inc., Austin, 1974-76; rsch. asst. Judge Leon Douglas Tex. Ct. Criminal Appeals, Austin, 1976-77; sr. atty. Law Office of John C.D. Drolla,Jr., Austin, 1977—; lectr. in field. Contbr. numerous articles to profl. jours. Bd. dirs. Tex. Embassy Mus., 100 Club Austin, 1990—, Track 7 Field official, Olympic Games, L.A., 1984, U.S. Olympic Com. Adminstrv. staff U.S. Olympic Festival, 1993, Track & Field Official USATF Nat. Jr. Olympics, San Jose, Calif., 1995, Houston, 1996, Track & Field Official X Paralympic Games, Atlanta, 1996, coun. mem. Habitat for Humanity, 1993-95; bd. dirs. Tex. Military Forces Mus., Tex., 1996—. Col. USAR 1985. Decorated Silver Star, 1968, Bronze Star, 1968, Def. Meritorious Svc. medal, 1993, Meritorious Svc. medal with two Oak Leaf clusters, 1970, 84, 93, Army Commendation medal with one oak leaf cluster, 1967, 76, Army Achievement medal, 1986, Nat. Def. Svc. medal with one bronze svc. star, 1970, 92, Vietnam Svc. medal with 4 bronze svc. stars, 1970, Armed Forces Res. medal with hour Glass, 1980, 83, Army Res. Components Achievement medal with 3 oak leaf clusters, 1976, 80, 84, Army Svc. ribbon, 1981, Overseas Svc. ribbon, 1981, and others. Mem. State Bar Tex., State Bar Tex. Real Estate (probate and trust sect., family law sect., banking and bus. law sect.), Travis County Bar Assn., Fed. Bar Assn. (treas. 1994-95, prog. com. chair 1994-95, del. nat. conv. 1995, 97, sec. 1995-96, vice pres. 1996-97, pres. elect 1997-98, pres. 1998-99). Avocations: track and field official, stamp collecting, sport cars, outdoor and water related sports. General civil litigation, Real property, General practice. Office: The Town Lake Bldg 512 E Riverside Dr Ste 105 Austin TX 78704-1356

**DRONEY, CHRISTOPHER F.,** judge; b. June 22, 1954; m. Elizabeth Kelly, Oct. 13, 1979; children: Sarah Elizabeth, Emily Christine, Katherine Fitzgerald. BA, Coll. Holy Cross, 1976; JD, U. Conn., 1979. Ptnr. Reid & Riege, P.C., Hartford, Conn., 1983-93; U.S. atty. for dist. of Conn. U.S. Dept. Justice, New Haven, 1993-97; judge U.S. Dist. Ct., Conn., 1997—. Notes and comments editor Conn. Law Rev., 1978-79. mem. U.S. atty. gen. adv. com., 1996-97. Office: 450 Main St Hartford CT 06103-3022

**DROPKIN, CHARLES EDWARD,** lawyer; b. N.Y.C., Dec. 17, 1951; s. Harry and Jeanette Dropkin; m. Jeanine Deborah Love, Nov. 5, 1983; children: Melissa Emily, Rebecca Allyson. BA, Williams Coll., 1974; JD, Harvard U., 1977. Bar: N.Y. 1978, U.S. Dist. Ct. (so. and ea. dist.) N.Y. 1978, U.S. Ct. Appeals (2d cir.) 1981, U.S. Supreme Ct. 1981. With Milbank Tweed Hadley & McCloy, N.Y.C., 1977-94; chair banking and fin. instns. dept. Proskauer Rose LLP, N.Y.C., 1994—. Editl. adv. bd. Banking Policy Report, 1994—; contbg. author: Securities Lending and Repurchase Agreements, 1997; contbr. articles to profl. jours. Mem. Assn. of the Bar of the City of N.Y., N.Y. State Bar Assn. (exec. com. comml. and fed. litigation sect. 1989-91, creditors rights and banking litigation com. 1995—), B'Nai B'rith. Avocation: golf. Contracts commercial, General corporate, General civil litigation. Home: 177 Laurel Dr Oradell NJ 07649-2422 Office: Proskauer Rose LLP 1585 Broadway New York NY 10036-8200

**DROSSEL, NORLEN ELTOFT,** lawyer; b. San Mateo, Calif., Jan. 8, 1944; d. Norman J. and Helen (Eltoft) D.; m. Robert P. Anderson, Nov. 22, 1977; children: Signe Anderssel, Jared Anderssel. AB, U. Calif., Berkeley, 1965; JD, San Francisco Law Sch., 1979; LLM, Golden Gate U., 1985. Bar: Calif. 1979. Law clk. to superior ct. judge San Francisco, 1978-79; ptnr. Law Offices Anderson & Drossel, Berkeley, 1980—; judge/referee pro tem Alameda County Superior Ct., Oakland, Calif., 1988-93; panel mem. Ct. Appointed Atty. Juvenile Ct., Berkeley, 1980-88; bd. dirs. Donald McCullum Youth Ct., Child Assault Prevention. Bd. dirs., cons. editor Calif. Conservatorships and Guardians, 1990, Calif. Will Drafting Practice, 1992. Bd. dirs. ARC, Oakland, 1985-91; mem. com. Alta Bates Hosp., Berkeley, 1988-91. Mem. Berkeley-Albany Bar Assn. (past bd. dirs.), Alameda County Bar Assn., Women Lawyers Alameda County (past bd. dirs., editor newsletter 1981-83). Democrat. Fax: (510) 845-6419. E-mail: androssl@ix.netcom.com. Home: 1149 Euclid Ave Berkeley CA 94708-1602 Office: 2041 Bancroft Way Ste 207 Berkeley CA 94704-1406

**DROUGHT, JAMES L.,** lawyer; b. San Antonio, May 8, 1943; s. James L. and Juanita Herff Drought; m. Joane Bennett, Nov. 25, 1966; children: James L. III, Henry Patrick IV, Elizabeth H. BBA, U. Tex., 1966; JD, S. Mary's Sch. Law, San Antonio, 1969. Bar: Tex. 1969, U.S. Dist. Ct. (so. and we. dists.) Tex. 1975, U.S. Ct. Appeals (5th cir.) 1975, U.S. Supreme Ct. 1975; bd. cert. civil trial law Tex. Bd. Legal Specialization. Assoc. Law Office of Thomas Drought, San Antonio, 1969-73; ptnr. Brite Drought Bubbitt & Halter, San Antonio, 1973-88, Brite & Drought, San Antonio, 1988-93, Drought & Pipkin LLP, San Antonio, 1993-98, Drought, Drought, & Bobbitt, San Antonio, 1998—. Past pres. Sarah Roberts Fench Home, San Antonio, 1985-86, Boysville, Inc., San Antonio, 1994. Fellow Tex. Bar Found., San Antonio Bar Found.; mem. ABA, State Bar Tex. (mem. grievance com. 1996—). General civil litigation. Office: Drought Drought & Bobbit LLP 112 E Pecan St San Antonio TX 78205-1512

**DROWOTA, FRANK F., III,** state supreme court justice; b. Williamsburg, Ky., July 7, 1938; married; 2 children. B.A., Vanderbilt U., 1960, J.D., 1965. Bar: Tenn. 1965, U.S. Dist. Ct. Tenn. 1965. Sole practice, 1965-70; chancellor Tenn. Chancery Ct. Div. 7, 1970-74; judge Tenn. Ct. Appeals, Middle Tenn. Div., 1974-80; assoc. justice Tenn. Supreme Ct., Nashville, 1980-89, chief justice, 1989-93, assoc. justice, 1993—. Served with USN, 1960-62. Office: Tenn Supreme Ct 318 Supreme Ct Bldg 401 7th Ave N Nashville TN 37219-1406*

**DROZIN, GARTH MATTHEW,** lawyer; b. Albany, N.Y., Dec. 10, 1953; s. Harold and Harriet D.; m. Renee Marie McMurray, May 24, 1987. BA, SUNY, Plattsburgh, 1975; MM, N. Tex. State U., 1977; D in Mus. Arts, Cornell U., 1981; JD, Southwestern U. Sch. Law, 1987. Bar: Calif. 1987, U.S. Dist. Ct. Calif. 1987, Mass. 1993, D.C. 1993. Instr. N. Tex. State U., Denton, Tex., 1975-77; dir. Auralisms Ensemble, Ithaca, N.Y., 1978-84; editor, musicologist Calouste Gulbenkian Found., Lisbon, Portugal, 1981-82; faculty composer, lectr. SUNY, Binghamton, N.Y., 1982-83; Fulbright prof. U.F.R.J. Nat. Sch. Music, Rio de Janeiro, Brazil, 1983; dep. dist. atty. Los Angeles County, 1988-90; atty. Kirtland & Packard, L.A., 1990-95, The Infinity Group, L.A., 1997—; judge pro tem L.A. County, Calif., 1988—; arbitrator Ventura County, Calif., 1993—, also mandatory settlement conf. officer and judge pro tem, 1993—. Composer Parabolics, 1980, Systemics, 1978, Sacred Service, 1979; editor Law Rev., 1985-86. Recipient Fulbright Sr. Scholar award Fulbright Commn., 1983, Darmstadt City Ring Fellowship award Internationales Music Institut, 1982, Cornell U. Western Soc. Dissertation Grant Cornell U., 1981. Mem. ABA, ASCAP, Percussive Arts Soc. (chpt. pres. 1981-82), State Bar Calif., Phi Mu Alpha Sinfonia. Democrat. Jewish. Avocations: exotic birds, chess, skiing, karate, languages. Construction, Personal injury, Professional liability. Home: 8545 Sale Ave West Hills CA 91304-2255 Office: The Infinity Group 3660 Wilshire Blvd Ste 614 Los Angeles CA 90010-2712

**DRUCKER, JACQUELIN F.,** lawyer, arbitrator, mediator, educator, author; b. Celina, Ohio, Oct. 15, 1954; d. Jack Burton and Dorothea (Eckenstein) Davis; m. John H. Drucker, Sept. 8, 1990. BA with distinction and honors, Ohio State U., 1977, JD with honors, 1981. Bar: Ohio 1981, N.Y. 1992, U.S. Supreme Ct. 1989. Legis. asst. Speaker of Ohio Ho. of Reps., Columbus, 1974-78; rsch. asst., lobbyist United Auto Workers, Columbus, 1978-81; labor atty. Porter, Wright, Morris & Arthur, Columbus, 1981-84; gen. counsel Ohio Employment Rels. Bd., Columbus, 1984-86, exec. dir., 1986-88, vice chmn., 1988-90; pvt. practice arbitration and mediation N.Y.C. and Ohio, 1990—; dir. labor mgmt. programs sch. indsl. and labor rels. Cornell U., 1994-97; dir. programs for neutrals Cornell U. Sch. of Indsl. and Labor Rels., 1996—; dir. for ednl. svcs. Cornell/PERC Inst. on Conflict Resolution, 1998—; cons. to W.J. Usery Ctr. for Workplace, Ga. State U.; counsel to Gov.'s Task Force on Collective Bargaining, Columbus, 1983-84; adj. prof. labor law Franklin U., Columbus, 1988-89; mem. panel of arbitrators Fed. Mediation and Conciliation Svc., Am. Arbitration Assn., Employment ADR Roster of Neutrals of Am. Arbitration Assn., N.Y. State Employment Rels. Bd.; mem. roster of neutrals N.Y.C. Office of Collective Bargaining; mem. panel V.I. Pub. Employment Rels. Bd., N.J. Pub. Employment Rels. Commn., N.Y. Pub. Employment Rels. Bd.; mem. permanent arbitration panel United Mine Workers and Bituminous Coal Operators Assn., Am. Postal Workers Union, U.S. Postal Svc., Off-Track Betting Corp. and Local 32E, State of N.Y. and Pub. Employees Fedn., State of N.Y. and Civil Svc. Employees Assn., Consolidated Edison and Utility Workers Local 1-2, U. Cin. and Dist. 925, Beth Isreal Med. Ctr. and 1199 Nat. Health and Human Svcs. Employees Union; cons. labor mgmt. cooperation, 1996—; lectr., spkr. in field. Author: Collective Bargaining Law in Ohio, 1993; editor L.I. Indsl. Rels. Quar.; contbg. editor Pub. Sector Labor and Employment Law supplement, 1995, Pub. Sector Labor and Employment Law, 2d edit.; assoc. editor Discipline and Discharge in Arbitration, 1998; contbg. editor: Public Sector Labor and Employment Law, 2nd edit., 1998; contbr. numerous articles to profl. jours. Mem. ABA (labor and employment law sect., co-chair tng. devel. sub-com. of ADR com., dispute resolution sect.), Nat. Acad. Arbitrators, Ohio State Bar Assn., Assn. of Bar of City of N.Y., N.Y. State Bar Assn. (labor and employment law sect. sec.-elect, sec. 1997-98, co-chair ADR in employment com. 1998—), N.Y. County Lawyers Assn. (labor rels. com., co-chair), Nassau County Bar Assn., Suffolk County Bar Assn., Indsl. Rels. Rsch. Assn. (N.Y. chpt., Cleve. chpt., L.I. chpt.), Soc. Fed. Labor Rels. Profls. Jewish. Labor, Alternative dispute resolution, Administrative and regulatory. Office: 432 E 58th St # 2 New York NY 10022-2331

**DRUCKER, MICHAEL STUART,** lawyer; b. Brookline, Mass., May 14, 1968; s. C. Gerard and Marjorie (Epstein) D.; m. Laura Ann Sugar, June 14, 1997. BA, U. Mich., 1990; JD, Suffolk U., 1993. Bar: Ga. 1993, Mass. 1993. Assoc. counsel The Collegiate Licensing Co., Atlanta, 1993—. Avocations: travel, sports, Am. lit., dining. Trademark and copyright, Sports, General corporate. Office: The Collegiate Lic Co Ste 102 320 Interstate North Pkwy SE Atlanta GA 30339-2205

**DRUCKER, RICHARD ALLEN,** lawyer; b. N.Y.C., Mar. 30, 1952; s. Charles and Bette Drucker; m. Jeanmarie Hamilton, Sept. 30, 1989; children: Richard Allen Jr., Hamilton Charles. BA, U. Vt., 1974; JD, U. Va., 1977. Bar: N.Y. 1978. Law clk. to Hon. William H. Webster, U.S. Ct. Appeals for 8th Cir., St. Louis, 1977-78; ptnr. Davis Polk & Wardwell, N.Y.C., 1978—. Contbr. articles to profl. jours. Mem. ABA, N.Y. State Bar Assn., Assn. Bar City N.Y. (Asian affairs com. 1998-99), Coun. Fgn. Rels. Avocations: golf, running, classical music. Securities, Finance. Office: Davis Polk & Wardwell 450 Lexington Ave New York NY 10017-3911

**DRUKER, JAMES OWEN,** lawyer; b. Cambridge, Mass., Apr. 9, 1942; s. Melvin and Charlotte (Zelermyer) D.; m. Joan Eleanora Smith, June 9, 1968; children—Scott Michael, Brian Daniel. A.B. in Polit. Sci., U. N.C., 1963; J.D., Boston Coll. Law, 1969. Bar: Mass. 1969, U.S. Ct. Appeals (1st cir.) 1969, U.S. Supreme Ct. 1973, U.S. tax Ct. (2d cir.) 1974, N.Y. 1974, Fla. 1979. Dep. asst. atty. gen. Dept. Atty. Gen. Mass., 1969-70; spl. atty. U.S. Dept. Justice, Washington, 1970-73; asst. U.S. atty., chief spl. prosecutions Eastern Dist. N.Y., Bklyn., 1974-75; asst. dist. atty. chief rackets, Nassau County, N.Y., Mineola, 1976-78; mng. ptnr. Kase & Druker, Garden City, N.Y., 1978—; lectr. in field. Recipient Meritorious Service award Justice Dept., 1974. Mem. ABA, Fla. Bar Assn., Mass. Bar Assn., N.Y. State Bar Assn., Nassau County Bar Assn., Am. Inns of Ct. (Master of Bench 1988), Theodore Roosevelt Inn of Ct. Personal income taxation, Criminal. Home: 140 W End Ave Apt 11C New York NY 10023-6152 Office: Kase & Druker 1325 Franklin Ave Suite 225 Garden City NY 11530

**DRUMKE, MICHAEL WILLIAM,** lawyer; b. Chgo., Mar. 29, 1966; s. Ronald Alfred and Sandra Drumke; m. Jody L. Pabst, Jan. 2, 1993. BA cum laude, Tufts U., 1988; JD, U. Wis., 1991. Bar: Wis. 1991, Ill. 1992, Ind. 1995; U.S. Dist. Ct. (we. dist. Wis.) 1991, U.S. Dist. Ct. (no. dist. Ill.) 1992, U.S. Dist. Ct. (ea. dist. Wis.) 1995, U.S. Dist. Ct. (no. and so. dists. Ind.) 1995. Intern to chief justice Supreme Ct. of Wis., Madison, 1991; law clk. to presiding justices Dane County Cir. Ct., Madison, Wis., 1991-92; assoc. Taylor, Miller, Sprowl, Hoffnagle & Merletti, Chgo., 92-94, Segal McCambridge Singer & Mahoney, Ltd., Chgo., 1994—; spkr. in field. Contbr. articles to profl. jours. Mem. ABA, Ill. Bar Assn., State Bar Wis., Chgo. Bar Assn. Toxic tort, Insurance, Environmental. Office: Segal McCambridge Singer & Mahoney Ltd One IBM Plaza Ste 200 Chicago IL 60611

**DRUMMOND, CECIL G.,** lawyer; b. Stillwater, Okla., Apr. 1, 1940; s. Gent Drummond and Leva Lorraine Fairweather; m. Mary Carol Chamlee, July 24, 1965 (div. Feb. 1979); children: Susan L. Brewer, Carolyn B. Leary, Cecil G. Drummond II. BS in Agriculture, Okla. State U., 1963; JD, Okla. U., 1967. Bar: Okla. 1967, U.S. Dist. Ct. (no. dist.) Okla. 1967, U.S. Dist. Ct. (we. dist.) Okla. 1967, U.S. Claims Ct. Partner Boettcher & Drummond, Tulsa, Okla.; adv. bd. Selective Svc. Sys., Osage County, Okla., 1968-70. Pres., dir. Pawhuska (Okla.) C. of C., 1969-71; county chmn. U.S. Savings Bonds, Osage County, 1968-72; dir. Osage County Cattlemen's Assn., 1969; chmn. Pawhuska (Okla.) United Fund, 1970; dir. Osage County Legal Aid Assn., 1970; delegate Democratic Nat. Convention, Miami, Fla., 1972, Democratic Platform com., Washington, 1972. With USNGR, 1963-71. Mem. Okla. Trial Lawyers (dir. 1970-72). Avocations: raising horses, teaching children to ride and work with horses. Home: 12601 S Mingo Rd Bixby OK 74008-2143 Office: Boettcher & Drummond 5200 S Yale Ave Ste 402 Tulsa OK 74135-7489

**DRUMMOND, ERIC HUBERT,** lawyer; b. Alamogordo, N.Mex., Nov. 16, 1959; s. Howard and Rosaline Drummond; m. Elizabeth Ann Bruch, May 19, 1990; 1 child, Jordan Eric. BA, U. Tex., 1989, JD, 1992. Bar: Tex. 1993. Assoc. Bickerstaff, Heath & Smiley, LLP, Austin, Tex., 1992-98, Casey, Gentz & Sifuentes, LLP, Austin, 1998—; judge mock trial and moot ct. Bd. Advs., Austin, 1992—. Bd. dirs. Legal Aid Ctrl. Tex., Austin, 1996—, Big Bros.-Big Sisters, Austin, 1998—. Mem. Fed. Comm. Bar Assn., Travis County Bar Assn. Avocations: running, backpacking, mountain climbing. Administrative and regulatory, Communications, Public utilities. Office: Casey Gentz & Sifuentes LLP Ste 1060 919 Congress Ave Austin TX 78701-2444

**DRUNGOLE, PAULA ELAINE,** lawyer; b. Starkville, Miss., Mar. 29, 1963; m. George W. Ellis; three children. BS, Rust Coll., 1983; JD, U. Kans., 1986. Bar: Miss. 1986, U.S. Dist. Ct. (no. and so. dists.) Miss. 1986, U.S. Ct. Appeals (5th cir.) 1986, U.S. Supreme Ct. 1986. Legal intern, supr. Kans. Defender Project, Lawrence, 1984-86; assoc. Jackson M. Brown Law Firm, Starkville, 1987-93; sole practice Starkville, 1993—; prof. Miss. State U., Starkville, 1987—. Bd. dirs. Judicare, Inc., Columbus, Miss. Methodist Leadership grantee, 1982. Mem. Assn. Trial Lawyers Am., Miss. Trial Lawyers Assn., Miss. Women Lawyers Assn., Bus & Profl. Women, Rust Alumni Club (sec. Starkville chpt. 1986—), Zeta Phi Beta. Methodist. Criminal, Family and matrimonial, Personal injury. Office: PO Box 186 Starkville MS 39760-0186

**DRYDEN, ROBERT EUGENE,** lawyer; b. Chanute, Kans., Aug. 20, 1927; s. Calvin William and Mary Alfreda (Foley) D.; m. Jetta Rae Burger, Dec. 19, 1953; children: Lynn Marie, Thomas Calvin. AA, City Coll., San Francisco, 1947; BS, U. San Francisco, 1951, JD, 1954. Bar: Calif. 1955; diplomate Am. Bd. Trial Advocates (pres. San Francisco chpt. 1997). Assoc. Barfield, Dryden & Ruane (and predecessor firm), San Francisco, 1954-60, jr. ptnr., 1960-65, gen. ptnr., 1965-89; sr. ptnr. Dryden, Margoles, Schimaneck, Kelly & Wait, San Francisco, 1989—; lectr. continuing edn. of the bar, 1971-77; evaluator U.S. Dist. Ct. (no. dist.) Calif. Early Neutral Evaluation Program; master atty. San Francisco Am. Inn of Ct. Mem. bd. counsellors U. San Francisco, 1993—. With USMCR, 1945-46. Fellow Am. Coll. Trial Lawyers, Am. Bar Found., Internat. Acad. Trial Lawyers; mem. ABA, San Francisco Bar Assn., Assn. Def. Counsel (bd. dirs. 1968-71), Def. Rsch. Inst., Internat. Assn. Ins. Counsel, Fedn. Ins. Counsel, Am. Arbitration Assn., U. San Francisco Law Soc. (mem. exec. com. 1970-72), U. San Francisco Alumni Assn. (mem. bd. govs. 1977), Phi Alpha Delta. Product liability, Insurance, Personal injury. Home: 1320 Lasuen Dr Millbrae CA 94030-2846 Office: Dryden Margoles Schimaneck Kelly & Wait 1 California St Ste 2600 San Francisco CA 94111-5427

**DRYDEN, WOODSON E.,** lawyer; b. Anadarko, Okla., Dec. 21, 1924; s. Harry Ernest and Ruth Sally (Woodson) D.; divorced; children: Judith, Carol, Kim, Christine, Erich. BBA, Kans. U., 1948; LLB, Tex. U., 1951. Sole practice Beaumont, Tex., 1951—. With USNR, 1942-46. Mem. Tex. Trial Lawyers Assn. (pres. 1972-73). Democrat. Episcopalian. Personal injury. Home: 6625 Windwood Ln Beaumont TX 77706-4239 Office: 915 Goodhue Bldg Beaumont TX 77706-6229

**DRYVYNSYDE, GEOFFREY BERESFORD,** lawyer, law educator, utilities commission counsel; b. Vancouver, B.C., Can., Oct. 27, 1964; came to U.S. 1981; s. Beresford O'Neil and Ann Christine D. AB, Stanford U., 1985; JD, Yale U., 1988. Assoc. Cooley, Godward LLP, San Francisco, 1991-92; staff counsel Calif. Pub. Utilities Commn., San Francisco, 1993—; prof. law New Coll. Law Sch., San Francisco, 1994—. Achievements include key membership on legal team advising on California's electricity deregulation. Administrative and regulatory, Appellate. Office: State Pub Utility Commn 505 Van Ness Ave Fl 5 San Francisco CA 94102-3214

**DUARTE, LEROY WILSON,** lawyer; b. Carlsbad, N.Mex., Dec. 7, 1947; s. Abel Felix and Lorenza (Wilson) D.; m. Romaine Elizabeth Serna, Dec. 19, 1982 (div. May 1991); children: Marsella, Camilla, Joile, LeAnn. BS, U. N.Mex., 1977, JD, 1983. Bar: N.Mex. 1983, U.S. Dist. Ct. N.Mex. 1984, U.S. Ct. Appeals (10th cir.) 1983. Ednl. counselor LULAC Ednl. Svcs. Ctr., Albuquerque, 1977-78; dir. Job Corp Recruiting Program League of United Latin Am. Citizens, Albuquerque, 1978; atty., pvt. practice Albuquerque, 1983—. Chmn., bd. dirs. Operation Svc. Employment Rehab., Albuquerque, 1978-80; mem. LULAC Coun. 8020, Albuquerque, 1977-80. With USN, 1967-69. Mem. N.Mex. Trial Lawyers Assn., Albuquerque Bar Assn. Roman Catholic. Avocations: golf, handball, fishing, outdoor recreation. Criminal, Personal injury, General practice. Office: 1500 Mountain Rd NW Albuquerque NM 87104-1359

**DUBÉ, LAWRENCE EDWARD, JR.,** lawyer; b. Chgo., Sept. 25, 1948; s. Lawrence Edward and Rosemary Nora (Cooney) D.; m. Paula Ann Goodgal, Jan. 10, 1982; 1 child, Charles Bernard. BA in Polit. Sci. cum laude, Knox Coll., 1970; JD with distinction, U. Iowa, 1973. Bar: Ill. 1973, Md. 1982, Pa. 1982, D.C. 1983, U.S. Supreme Ct., 1987. Field atty. NLRB, Chgo., 1973-80, supr. atty., 1980-81; sole practice Balt., 1981-85; assoc. Grove, Jaskiewicz, Gilliam & Cobert, Washington, 1985-87; ptnr. Dubé & Goodgal, P.C., Balt., 1987—. Author: Management on Trial-The Law of Wrongful Discharge, 1987, New Employment Issues: How to Shield your Business from Costly Lawsuits, 1988, Employment References and the Law, 1989; co-author: The Maryland Employer's Guide to Labor and Employment Law, 1984. Mem. Am. Arbitration Assn. (arbitrator), Nat. Assn. Securities Dealers (arbitrator). Labor, Pension, profit-sharing, and employee benefits, Federal civil litigation. Home: 622 W University Pky Baltimore MD 21210-2908 Office: Dubé & Goodgal PC 2400 Boston St Ste 407 Baltimore MD 21224-4787

**DUBER, MICHAEL JOSEPH,** lawyer; b. Columbus, Ohio, Mar. 3, 1947; s. Herbert Charles and Pauline Selma (Yaross) D.; m. Cindy A. Roller, Feb. 29, 1976; children: Herbert, Brandon, Craig. BS in Bus. Adminstrn., Ohio State U., 1970; JD, U. Cin., 1973. Bar: Ohio 1973, U.S. Dist. Ct. (no. dist.) Ohio 1973. Assoc. F.J. Bentoff Co., L.P.A., Cleve., 1973-79; ptnr. Bentoff & Duber Co., L.P.A., Cleve., 1979—; instr. Ohio Paralegal Inst., Cleve., 1984. Mem. Holden Arboretum, Cleve., 1978—. Mem. Ohio Bar Assn., Cleve. Bar Assn. (vice-chmn. workers' compensation sect.), Cuyhoga County Bar Assn., Cleve. Law Library Assn., Ohio Acad. Trial Lawyers, Tau Epsilon Phi. Democrat. Jewish. Workers' compensation. Home: 3952 White Oak Trl Cleveland OH 44122-4722 Office: Bentoff and Duber Co LPA 230 Leader Bldg Cleveland OH 44114

**DUBIN, JAMES MICHAEL,** lawyer; b. N.Y.C., Aug. 20, 1946; s. Benjamin and Irene (Wasserman) D.; m. Susan Hope Schraub, Mar. 15, 1981; children: Alexander Philip, Elizabeth Joy. BA, U. Pa., 1968; JD, Columbia U., 1974. BAr: N.Y. 1975, D.C. 1984, U.S. Dist. Ct. (so. and ea. dists.) N.Y. 1975, U.S. Ct. Appeals (2d cir.) 1975. Assoc. Paul, Weiss, Rifkind, Wharton & Garrison, N.Y.C., 1974-82, ptnr., 1982—, chmn. corp. dept., 1995-99; bd. dirs. FOJP Svc. Corp., 1988—, Conair Corp., 1995—, Carnival Corp., 1995—. Mem. bd. editors Columbia Law Rev., 1973-74. Bd. dirs. YM-YWHA of Mid-Westchester, Scarsdale, N.Y., 1983-86, chmn. budget and fin. com., 1984-85; bd. dirs., mem. exec. com. Nat. Found. Advancement in Arts, 1991&, vice chmn., 1994-99; trustee Solomon Schechter Sch. Westchester, 1991—, vice chmn., 1997—, chmn. ann. fund, 1993-96, chmn. devel. com., 1994-97, v.p., sec., 1996-97; bd. dirs. Jewish Guild for the Blind, 1989—, mem. exec. com., 1991—, sec., 1992-94, chmn., 1995-99; trustee Jewish Cmty. Ctr. of Harrison, 1994-97, mem. bd. edn., 1987-90; chmn. Cable Oversight Com., Harrison, N Y., 1983-85. With U.S. Army, 1969-71. Mem. ABA, Assn. Bar City N.Y., Am. Arbitration Assn. (comml. panel arbitrators 1989—), Sunningdale Country Club (bd. govs. 1989—, v.p. 1992—), The Dukes Golf Club, Colony Club, Phi Delta Phi. Securities, Mergers and acquisitions, General corporate. Office: Paul Weiss Rifkind Wharton & Garrison Ste 3700 1285 Avenue Of The Americas New York NY 10019-6028

**DUBINA, JOEL FREDRICK,** federal judge; b. 1947. BS, U. Ala., 1970; JD, Cumberland Sch. Law, 1973. Pvt. practice law Jones, Murray, Stewart & Yarbrough, 1974-83; law clk. to presiding judge U.S. Dist. Ct. (mid. dist.) Ala., Montgomery, 1973-74, U.S. magistrate, 1983-86, U.S. Dist. judge, 1986-90; judge U.S. Ct. Appeals (11th cir.), 1990—. Mem. FBA (pres. Montgomery chpt. 1982-83), Nat. Coun. U.S. Magistrate Judges, Fed. Judges Assn. (bd. dirs.), Supreme Ct. Hist. Soc., Ala. State Bar Assn., 11th Cir. Hist. Soc., Montgomery County Bar Assn. (chmn. Law Day com. 1975, constrn. and bylaws com. 1977-80, grievance com. 1981-83), Cumberland Sch. Law Alumni Assn., Lions, Am. Inn of Cts. (pres. Montgomery chpt. 1993-94), Phi Delta Phi. Office: US Cir Ct Appeals 11th Cir PO Box 867 Montgomery AL 36101-0867

**DUBINER, MICHAEL,** lawyer; b. N.Y.C., Jan. 9, 1954; s. Morris and Ann D.; m. Nancy Susan Tilles, May 31, 1975; children: David, Jeannie. BA, CUNY, 1975; JD, U. Miami, 1978. Bar: Fla. 1978, U.S. Dist. Ct. (so. dist.), U.S. Supreme Ct. 1983. Atty. PB County Pub. Defenders Office, West Palm Beach, Fla., 1978-81, Dubiner & Blumberg, PA, Boynton Beach, Fla., 1981-95; pvt. practice West Palm Beach, 1995-97; atty. Dubiner & Wilensky, P.A., West Palm Beach, 1997—; founding chmn. Domestic Violence Counsel Palm Beach County, 1995-97. Recipient Fla. Bar Pres. Pro Bono award Fla. Bar Assn., 1985. Criminal, Family and matrimonial. Office: Dubiner & Wilensky PA 515 N Flagler Dr Ste 325 West Palm Beach FL 33401-4349

**DUBINSKY, DONNA,** mediator; b. Little Neck, N.Y., June 8, 1965; d. Michael and Priscilla Dikman; m. Eric Dubinsky; children: Julie, Jason. BS, St. John's Coll., Jamaica, N.Y., 1987; JD, Hofstra U., 1990. Bar: N.Y. 1990.

Assoc. Dikman & Dikman, Lake Success, N.Y., 1990-95; prin. Dubinsky Assocs., Carle Place, N.Y., 1995—. Office: Dubinsky Assocs 1 Old Country Rd Ste 370 Carle Place NY 11514-1894

**DUBOFF, SCOTT M.**, lawyer; b. Chgo., June 19, 1947. BA, U. Wis., 1969, JD cum laude, 1973. Bar: Wis. 1973, D.C. 1975. Atty. office of gen. counsel Fed. Power Commn., 1973-75, atty. office of solicitor, 1975-77; ptnr. Wright & Talisman. Mem. ABA (mem. natural resources sect.), D.C. Bar (mem. environ., energy and natural resources divsn. 1983—). Office: Wright & Talisman 1200 G St NW Ste 600 Washington DC 20005-3838

**DUBOIS, JAN ELY**, federal judge; b. Phila., Jan. 17, 1931; s. M. Norman and Syd (Stern) DuB.; m. Ruth Harberg, Aug. 19, 1956; children: Marc Norman, Jon Stuart, Peter Andrew, Pamela Sue. BS, U. Pa., 1952; LLB, Yale U., 1957. Law clk. civil div. U.S. Dept. of Justice, Washington, 1956; law clk. to Hon. Harry E. Kalodner Phila., 1957-58; atty. White and Williams, Phila., 1958-64, ptnr., 1964-88; judge U.S. Dist. Ct. (ea. dist.) Pa., Phila., 1988—. Trustee Phila. Bar Found., 1981-89, pres. 1987; trustee Reform Congregation Keneseth Israel, Elkins Park, Pa., pres., 1985-87. 1st lt. U.S. Army, 1952-54, cpt. U.S.A.R., ret. Recipient John Currier Gallagher prize Yale U., 1957. Mem. ABA, Pa. Bar Assn., Phila. Bar Assn. (chmn. medico-legal com. 1981), Yale Law Sch. Assn. of Phila. (past pres.), Yale Club. Office: US Dist Ct 12613 US Courthouse 601 Market St Philadelphia PA 19106-1713

**DUBOIS, JONATHAN DELAFIELD**, lawyer; b. N.Y.C., Feb. 15, 1941; s. John Delafield and Elizabeth (Gibson) D.; m. Elizabeth Bartholet, June 9, 1962; 1 child, Derek Delafield; m. Ann Hewitt Doe, Nov. 18, 1971; children: Nicholas Brooks, Alice Haven. BA, Harvard U., 1962, LLB, 1965. Bar: N.Y. With evaluation sect. Dept. Justice, Washington, 1965-68; atty. Cravath, Swaine & Moore, N.Y.C., 1968-73; ptnr. Coudert Brothers, N.Y.C., 1973-96, Morgan, Lewis & Bockius, N.Y.C., 1996—; bd. dirs. U.S. Guaranteed Fin. Corp., Wilmington, Del., Christiania Capital Corp., Wilmington, Del. Mem. ABA, N.Y. Bar Assn., N.Y.C. Bar Assn., Harvard Club (N.Y.C.), Indian Harbor Yacht Club (dir., counsel 1990—), Greenwich Field Club. Democrat. Home: 707 Steamboat Rd Greenwich CT 06830-7114 Office: Morgan Lewis & Bockius 101 Park Ave Fl 46 New York NY 10178-0060

**DUBOVE, FERNANDO ANIBAL**, lawyer; b. Bellville, Argentina, Feb. 29, 1960; came to U.S., 1966; s. John C. and Clodis Dubove. BA, U. Tex., 1983, JD, 1986. Bar: Tex. 1986, U.S. Dist. Ct. (no. dist.) Tex. 1986. Asst. dir. Tex. project Nat. Immigration Forum, Austin, 1987-88; legis. liaison State Bar Tex., Austin, 1989-90; staff atty. Diocesan Migrant and Refugee Svcs., El Paso, 1991-92; atty. Ronquillo & DeWolf, Austin and Dallas, 1993-96; sole practitioner Dallas, 1997—; counsel to House Jud. Com., Tex. Legislature. Mem. Am. Immogration Lawyers Assn., State Bar Tex. (immigration law com.). Avocation: photography. Office: 3102 Maple Ave Ste 400 Dallas TX 75201-1261

**DUBROFF, DIANA D.**, lawyer, TV producer; b. N.Y.C., Mar. 4, 1909; d. Meyer and Gussie (Ginsburg) Leibow; BS, Hunter Coll., 1928; JD, Bklyn. Law Sch., 1931; m. Alexander DuBroff (dec.); children: Elinor, William. Tchr. young children, 1928-65; mem. staff Family Law Practice, 1970-85; tchr. pub. schs., N.Y.C., 1971—; founder, dean Practising Justice Inst., 1971-80; producer cable TV series Practical Justice by a Creative Lawyer. Columnist Let's Look at the Law. Designer concept of divorce and homemaker ins.; organizer groups to insure child support; developer personalized affordable settlement strategies. Home and Office: 12 W 72nd St New York NY 10023-4163

**DUBUC, CARROLL EDWARD**, lawyer; b. Burlington, Vt., May 6, 1933; s. Jerome Joachim and Rose (Bessette) D.; m. Mary Jane Lowe, Aug. 3, 1963; children; Andrew, Steven, Matthew. *Carroll Dubuc's son, Steven, is an environmental lawyer with a major Washington,D.C. law firm. Andrew is in the drywall construction business in Washington, Virginia, Maryland and London. Matthew sells computer technology equipment to the Department of Defense.* BS in Acctg., Cornell U., 1955; LLB, Boston Coll., 1962; postgrad., NYU, 1963-64. Bar: N.Y. 1963, Va. 1999; U.S. Dist. Ct. (so. and ea. dists.) N.Y. 1964, U.S. Ct. Appeals (2d cir.) 1965, U.S. Supreme Ct. 1970, D.C. 1972, U.S. Ct. Appeals (D.C. cir.) 1972, U.S. Dist. Ct. D.C. 1973, U.S. Ct. Claims 1975, U.S. Ct. Appeals (4th cir.) 1977, U.S. Ct. Appeals (7th cir.) 1984, U.S. Ct. Appeals (9th cir.) 1985, U.S. Ct. Appeals (5th cir.) 1986, U.S. Ct. Appeals (fed. cir.) 1988, U.S. Ct. Internat. Trade 1988, U.S. Ct. Appeals (6th cir.) 1989, Va. 1999; cert. ct. mediator 1998. Assoc. Haight, Gardner, Poor & Havens, N.Y.C., 1962-70, ptnr., 1970-75; resident ptnr. Finley Kumble Wagner Heine Underberg Manley Myerson & Casey, Washington, 1983-87, Laxalt, Washington, Perito & Dubuc, Washington, 1988-90; Washington, Perito & Dubuc Laxalt, Washington, Perito & Dubuc, 1990-91; ptnr. Graham & James, 1991-95, of counsel, 1996-98; of counsel Cohen Gettings & Dunham, 1998—. *Carroll Dubuc has over 35 years of responsible experience as a trial lawyer and counselor to major U.S. and international airlines and their insurers. She is now acting as a mediator/arbitrator in similar technical multi-party protracted disputes. Also, mediator for mediating employment, product liability, aviation, insurance international claims, partnership bankruptcy and unfair competition matters.* Capt. AC USN, 1954-59. Mem. AIAA, ABA (chmn. aviation and space law com. 1985-86, subcom. aviation ins., subcom. internat. practice 1985-87, vice chmn. alternative resolution com., mktg. legal svcs. com. 1991-92, vice chmn. ins. com. 1982-84), N.Y. State Bar Assn. (past chmn. aviation law com.), D.C. Bar Assn., Va. Bar Assn., Assn. of Bar of City of N.Y. (aeroav. com.), Fed. Cir. Bar Assn., 5th Fed. Cir. Bar Assn., Fed. Bar Coun., Nat. Transp. Safety Bd. Bar Assn., Maritime Law Assn. U.S., Naval Aviation Command (vice comdr.), Internat. Assn. Def. Counsel (chmn. alternqte dispute resolution sec., aviation transp. 1996—), Helicopter Assn. Internat., Transp. Lawyers Assn., Assn. Trial Lawyers Am., Def. Assn. N.Y., Boston Coll. Law Sch. Alumni (pres. Washington chpt. 1992-96), Assn. Transp. Practitioners, Internat. Soc. Air Safety Investigators, Soc. Sr. Aerospace Execs., Internat. Aviation Club, Washington chpt. Aero Club, Nat. Aerunautic Assn., French-Am. C. of C., N.Y. Athletic Club, Cornell Club, Wings Club, Congrl. Country Club, Sigma Chi. Aviation, Alternative dispute resolution, Federal civil litigation.

**DUCHENE, TODD MICHAEL**, lawyer; b. Akron, Ohio, June 19, 1963; s. Glenn Robert DuChene and Judith Ann (Dipnall) Kehoe; m. Jennifer Lee Belt, May 25, 1990; children: Elizabeth, Margaret, Emily. BA in Polit. Sci. with honors, Coll. of Wooster, 1985; JD, U. Mich., 1988. Bar: Ohio 1988. Assoc. Baker & Hostetler, Cleve., 1985-93; sr. v.p., gen. counsel, sec. Office Max, Inc., Shaker Heights, Ohio, 1993-96; v.p., gen. counsel, sec. Fisher Scientific Internat. Inc., Hampton, N.H., 1996—. Securities, General corporate, Mergers and acquisitions. Office: Fisher Scientific Internat 1 Liberty Ln Hampton NH 03842-1808

**DUCHEZ, NEIL ANDRE**, lawyer; b. Cleve., June 2, 1946; s. Louis John and Margaret Mary DuChez; m. Gayle Elizabeth Hatton, Apr. 28, 1973; children: Elizabeth, Cheryl, Neil. BSChemE, Cleve. State U., 1969, JD, 1972. Bar: Ohio 1972, U.S. Dist. Ct. (no. dist.) Ohio 1972, U.S. Ct. Appeals (6th cir.) 1973, U.S. Patent and Trademark Office 1973, U.S. Supreme Ct. 1976, U.S. Ct. Appeals (fed. cir.) 1978. Assoc. Bosworth, Sessions & McCoy, Cleve., 1972-74; staff atty. Sherwin Williams Co., Cleve., 1974-78; assoc. patent and trademark counsel Alcan Aluminum Corp., Cleve., 1978-80; ptnr. Renner, Otto, Boisselle & Sklar, PLL, Cleve., 1980—. Mem. Cleve. Intellectual Property Law Assn. (treas. 1981-83, v.p. 1996-97, pres. 1999—). Intellectual property. Office: Renner Otto Boisselle & Sklar PLL 1621 Euclid Ave Fl 19 Cleveland OH 44115-2107

**DUCKETT, JOAN**, law librarian; b. Bklyn., Oct. 21, 1934; d. Stephen and Mary (Wehrum) Kearney; m. Richard Duckett, Aug. 25, 1956; children: Richard, David, Daniel, Deirdre. BA, Kean Coll., 1974; MLS, Rutgers U., 1977; JD, Suffolk U., 1983; postgrad., Oxford (Eng.) U., 1986. Bar: Mass. 1983, U.S. Ct. Appeals (fed. cir.) 1984. Media specialist Oak Knoll Sch., Summit, N.J., 1976-80; law clk. Dist. Atty. Suffolk County, Boston, 1982; vol. atty. Cambridgeport Problem Ctr., Cambridge, Mass., 1984-85; reference libr. Harvard Law Sch. Libr., Cambridge, 1982-84, coord. The New Eng. Law Libr. Consortium, 1984-87, head reference svcs., 1987—, profl. devel. com., chmn. Bryant fellowship award panel, 1987—. Contbr. articles to profl. jours. Protocol hostess L.A. Olympic Com., 1984. Fellow Mass. Bar Found.; mem. Mass. Bar Assn., Boston Bar Assn., Am. Assn. Law Librs., Law Librs. New Eng., Assn. Boston Law Librs., Alpha Sigma Lambda, Beta Phi Mu. Office: Harvard Law Sch Libr Langdell Hall Cambridge MA 02138

**DUCKSTAD, JON R.**, lawyer, educator; b. Beaver Creek, Minn., June 4, 1934; s. Norman Brown and Mary Josephine (Holbert) D.; m. Joan Victoria McCrory, Feb. 5, 1967; children: Julie, Patricia, Marjorie Duckstad Coluccio. BA, Luther Coll., 1956; LLB, JD, William Mitchell Coll. Law, 1962. Asst. atty. St. Paul City Atty., 1963-70; asst. pub. defender Ramsey County, St. Paul, 1973-98; pvt. practice St. Paul, 1998—; adj. prof. William Mitchell Coll. Law, St. Paul, 1973-98; mem., atty. civil commitment def. panel Probate Ct., Ramsey County, Minn., 1971—; mental illness, dangerous def. atty. jud. appeal panel Minn. Supreme Ct., 1973—. Sgt. med. corps U.S. Army, 1956-58. Mem. Ramsey County Bar assn. (pres. 1995-96). Avocations: hunting, fishing. Criminal, Mental health, Personal injury. Office: 46 4th St E Saint Paul MN 55101-1121

**DUCKWORTH, MARVIN E.**, lawyer, educator; b. Aug. 16, 1942; s. Marvin E. and Maryann Duckworth; children: Matthew, Brian, Jennifer, Jeffrey. BS in Indsl. Engring., Iowa State U., 1964; JD, Drake U., 1968. Bar: Iowa 1968, U.S. Dist. Ct. (no. and so. dists.) Iowa 1969. Assoc. Davis, Huebner, Johnson & Burt, Des Moines, 1968-70; asst. prof. Drake U., 1970-71, lectr. law, 1971-85, assoc. dean clin. programs, 1986—; shareholder Hopkins & Huebner, P.C., Des Moines, 1971—; spkr. in field. Pres. Drake Law Bd. Counselors, 1991-92, Drake Law Endowment Trust, 1995-96. Named Alumnus of Yr. Drake Law Sch., 1997. Fellow Iowa Bar Found.; mem. ABA (chmn. workers compensation and employers liability law 1986-87, vice hmn. toxic and hazardous substances and environ. law com. 1989-93), Iowa Bar Assn. (pres. young lawyers sect. 1977-78, Merit award 1982, chair workers compensation sect. 1992-93), Def. Rsch. Inst., Fedn. Ins. and Corp. Counsel (workers compensation com.), Iowa Assn. Workers Compensation Lawyers (pres. 1988-89), Iowa Acad. Trial Lawyers, Order of Coif. State civil litigation, Insurance, Workers' compensation. Office: 2700 Grand Ave Ste 111 Des Moines IA 50312-5215

**DUDEN, PAUL RUSSELL**, lawyer, managing partner; b. Portland, Oreg., Sept. 1, 1940; s. Harold Pennoyer Duden and Helen Pearson Campbell; m. Martha Anderson, Nov. 9, 1985; children: Emily, Andrew, Lessie, Gurney. BS, U. Oreg., 1963, LLB, 1966. Bar: Oreg. 1966, U.S. Dist. Ct. Oreg. 1966, U.S. Ct. Appals (5th cir.) 1966, U.S. Supreme Ct. 1977. Assoc. Tooze, Kerr, Tooze & Peterson, Portland, 1966-70, ptnr., 1970-72; mng. ptnr. Tooze, Duden, Creamer, Frank & Hutchinson, Portland, 1972—. Bd./dirs. Riverdale Sch. Dist., Portland, 1972-80; commr. Palatine Hill Water Act, Portland, 1982—; bd. dirs. Easter Seal Soc. Oreg., 1967—. Fellow Am. Coll. Trial Lawyers; m. Am. Bd. Trial Advocates, Internat. Assn. Def. Counsel, Def. Rsch. Inst. General civil litigation, Product liability, Toxic tort. Home: 250 SW Carey Ln Portland OR 97219-7973 Office: Tooze Duden Creamer Frank & Hutchinson 333 SW Taylor St Portland OR 97204-2413

**DUDLEY, EVERETT HASKELL, JR.**, lawyer; b. Fitchburg, Mass., June 2, 1930; s. Everett H. Sr. and Marguerite I. (Connors) D.; m. Joyce Pettapiece, Aug. 23, 1952; children: Everett H. III, Lisa R. McKim. AA, Boston U., 1950, BS, 1954; JD, U. Miami, 1960. Bar: Mass. 1961, Fla. 1960, U.S. Dist. Ct. (so. dist.) Fla. 1961, U.S. Supreme Ct. 1964. Assoc. Sams, Anderson, Alper, Meadows & Spencer, Miami, Fla., 1960-61; ptnr. Stamey, Kravitz & Dudley, Hialeah, Fla., 1961-63, Kravitz, Dudley & Dean, Hialeah, Fla., 1963-69, Kravitz, Dudley & Duckworth, Hialeah, Fla., 1972-79, Weintraub, Weintraub, Seiden, Dudley & Press, Miami, Fla., 1979-85; judge Criminal Ct. of Record, Miami, Fla., 1969-71, City of Miami Springs, Fla., 1971-73; pres., prin. Everett H. Dudley Jr., P.A., Ft. Lauderdale, Fla., 1985-89; ptnr. Keeley, Hayes, Dudley, Johnson, Roberts, Keeley, Hayes & Dudley, Boca Raton, Fla., 1989-95, Keeley, Hayes, Dudley, Cappeller & Meeker, Boca Raton, 1995—. Founder, pres. Coun. on Drug Edn., Miami, 1970-72; chmn. Nat. Cancer Cytology Ctr., 1961-79, Miami Springs Charter Bd., 1974, Miami Springs Code Rev. Bd., 1975; cons. Dade County Drug Abuse Adv. Bd., 1971-75; mem. Dade County Secretariat on Crime and Law Enforcement, 1971-72; bd. dirs. Dade County Crime Commn., 1971-81. With USMC, 1953-56. Recipient Citizen of Yr. award Op. Self-Help, 1970, Disting. Svc. award City of Miami Springs, 1974; commd. Ky. Col., Commonwealth of Ky., 1990. Mem. ABA, Assn. Trial Lawyers Am., Am. Judicature Soc., Mass. Bar Assn., Fla. Bar Assn., Am. Arbitration Assn., Navy League of U.S. (judge adv. Delray Beach coun. 1990—), Masons, Shriners, Delta Theta Phi, Sigma Alpha Epsilon. General practice, General civil litigation, Probate. Office: Keeley Hayes Dudley Cappeller & Meeker 2424 N Federal Hwy Boca Raton FL 33431-7735

**DUDLEY, GEORGE ELLSWORTH**, lawyer; b. Earlington, Ky., July 14, 1922; s. Ralph Emerson and Camille (Lackey) D.; m. Barbara J. Muir, June 28, 1950 (dec. Feb. 1995); children: Bruce K., Camille Dudley McNutt, Nancy S., Elizabeth Dudley Stephens. BS in Commerce, U. Ky., 1947; JD, U. Mich., 1950. Bar: Ky. 1950, D.C. 1951, U.S. Dist. Ct. (we. dist.) Ky. 1962, U.S. Ct. Appeals (6th cir.) 1987. Assoc. Gordon, Gordon & Moore, Madisonville, Ky., 1950-51; pvt. practice law Louisville, 1952-59; ptnr. Brown, Ardery, Todd & Dudley, Louisville, 1959-72; ptnr. Brown, Todd & Heyburn, Louisville, 1972-92, of counsel, 1992—, mem. mgmt. com., 1972-90, chmn., 1989-90. Pres. Ky. Easter Seal Soc., Louisville, 1971-72; treas. Ky. Dem. Party, Frankfort, 1971-74; bd. dirs. Alliant Adult Health Svcs., Louisville, 1976—; 1st v.p. Nat. Easter Seal Soc., Chgo., 1981. Capt. inf. U.S. Army, 1943-46, ETO; capt. JAGC, U.S. Army, 1951-52. Mem. ABA, Ky. Bar Assn., Louisville Bar Assn., U.S. 6th Cir. Jud. Conf. (life), Harmony Landing Country Club (pres. 1978-79), Tavern Club, Barristers Soc., Omicron Delta Kappa. Presbyterian. Avocations: golf, tennis, travel, sports spectator. Home: 1905 Crossgate Ln Louisville KY 40222-6405 Office: Brown Todd & Heyburn 3200 Providian Louisville KY 40202

**DUDLEY, TODD STEVEN**, lawyer; b. Dallas, Apr. 17, 1970; s. Charles Dudley and Rebecca Chenoweth; m. Stephanie Renè Crossley. BA in Polit. Sci., So. Meth. U., 1992, BA in Sociology, 1992; JD, St. Mary's U., San Antonio, 1995. Bar: Tex. 1995. Pvt. practice Ft. Worth, 1995-98, Austin, Tex., 1998—. Mem. Tex. Criminal Def. Lawyers Assn. Criminal, Juvenile. Office: 400 W 15th St Ste 1410 Austin TX 78701-1648

**DUE, DANFORD ROYCE**, lawyer; b. Louisville, Sept. 28, 1948; s. Victor T. and Betty (Duffy) D.; m. Susan L. Landrum, Aug. 14, 1971; children: Stephen L., Michael R. BA, Vanderbilt U., 1970; JD cum laude, Ind. U., 1973. Bar: Ind. 1973, U.S. Dist. Ct. (so. dist.) Ind. 1973, U.S. Dist. Ct. (no. dist.) Ind. 1980, U.S. Ct. Appeals (7th cir.) 1986. Assoc. Stewart, Irwin, Gilliom, Fuller & Meyer, Indpls., 1973-79, ptnr., 1979-84; ptnr. Stewart, Due, Doyle & Pugh, Indpls., 1984—. Contbg. author (Continuing Legal Edn. series) Uninsured/Underinsured Motorist Coverage in Indiana, 1988, The Wrongful Death Case in Indiana, 1989, Sucessful Handling of Wrongful Death Cases: The Experts Share Their Secrets, 1998. Bd. mgrs. Baxter YMCA, Indpls., 1983—. Mem. ABA, Def. Rsch. Inst., Ind. State Bar Assn., Ind. Def. Lawyers Assn., Johnson County Bar Assn. Avocations: golf, reading, mountain hiking, fishing. General civil litigation, Insurance, Personal injury. Home: 524 Ho Hum Ct Greenwood IN 46142 Office: Stewart Due Miller & Pugh 55 Monument Circle 900 Circle Tower Indianapolis IN 46204

**DUELL-CAZES, TRACY LEIGH**, lawyer; b. Mpls., July 25, 1962; d. Delmar Alvin and Donna Mae Duell; m. Lary Alan Cazes, Mar. 30, 1996. AS in Acctg., De Anza Coll., 1983; BS in Acctg., Calif. State U., Chico, 1985; JD, Santa Clara U., 1989. Bar: Calif. 1989. Dep. pub. defender Stanislaus County Pub. Defender's Office, Modesto, Calif., 1990-91; ptnr. Bohn, Duell & Steinmetz, San Jose, Calif., 1993-95; pvt. practice San Jose, Calif., 1989-90, 91-93, 95—; sponsor Divorcenet, 1997—; lectr. Santa Clara County Bar Assn., 1997—. Contbr. articles to profl. jours. Judge pro tem Santa Clara County Superior Ct., San Jose, 1997—. Recipient Pro Bono Vol. award Santa Clara County Pro Bono Project, 1998. Mem. Santa Clara County Bar Assn. (exec. com. family law sect. 1997—, co-chair exec. com. criminal law sect. 1996), Calif. Pub. Defender's Assn., Calif. Attys. for Criminal Justice. Avocations: golf, reading, travel. E-mail: tcazes@pacbell.net. Family and matrimonial, Criminal. Office: 181 Devine St San Jose CA 95110-2403

**DUES, THEODORE ROOSEVELT, JR.**, lawyer; b. Montgomery, W.Va., June 23, 1953; s. Theodore Roosevelt and Mary Lucille (White) D.; m. Mona Lisa Day, Aug. 25, 1979; children: Theodore Roosevelt III, Ryah Leigh. BBA, W.Va. U., 1975, JD, 1978. Bar: W.Va. 1978, U.S. Dist. Ct. (no. and so. dist.) W.Va. 1978, U.S. Ct. Appeals (4th cir.) 1978. Pvt. practice, Fayetteville, W.Va., 1978-79, Charleston, W.Va., 1979-81; sr. ptnr. Dues, Tyree & Hicks, Charleston, 1981-83, Dues & Tyre, Charleston, 1983-85; sole practice, Charleston, 1985—, hearing examiner W.Va. Human Rights Commn., Charleston, 1981-90; mem. bd. govs. W.Va. State Bar, 1985—. Bd. dirs. Family Svcs. United Way Agy., Charleston, 1983—, Appalachian Rsch. and Def. Fund, Charleston, 1979-83, Legal Aid Soc., 1981-84; commr. Kanawha County Dep. sheriffs, 1984—, City of Charleston Fire Dept., 1987—; pres. Kanawha County Civil Svc. Commn., 1987-90; trustee, supt. Sunday sch. First Bapt. Ch. London, 1991—; mem. Gov.'s Task Force on Pers., 1992—; bd. dirs. Adult Basic Edn., 1991—; appointed chair Martin Luther King, Jr. Holiday Commn., 1995. Named Most Outstanding Black Atty., Black Am. Law Students, 1982. Mem. NAACP (W.Va. legal redress com. 1978—, chmn. Charleston legal redress com. 1983—), Mountain State Bar Assn. (pres. 1988-90, chmn. bd. dirs. 1990—), W.Va. State Bar Assn. (jud. improvement com. 1983—). Office: Daniel Boone Bldg 405 Capitol St Charleston WV 25301-1716

**DUESENBERG, RICHARD WILLIAM**, lawyer; b. St. Louis, Dec. 10, 1930; s. (John August) Hugo and Edna Marie (Warmann) D.; m. Phyllis Evelyn Buehner, Aug. 7, 1955; children: Karen, Daryl, Mark, David. BA, Valparaiso U., 1951, JD, 1953; LLM, Yale U., 1956. Bar: Mo. 1953. Prof. law NYU, N.Y.C., 1956-62, dir. law ctr. publs., 1960-62; sr. atty. Monsanto Co., St. Louis, 1963-70, asst. gen. counsel, asst. sec., 1975-77, sr. v.p., sec., gen. counsel, 1977-96; dir. law Monsanto Textiles Co., St. Louis, 1971-75; corp. sec. Fisher Controls Co., Marshalltown, Iowa, 1969-71, Olympia Industries, Spartanburg, S.C., 1974-75; vis. prof. law U. Mo., 1970-71; faculty Banking Sch. South, La. State U., 1967-83; vis. scholar Cambridge U., England, 1996; vis. prof. law St. Louis U., 1997-98. Author: (with Lawrence P. King) Sales and Bulk Transfers Under the Uniform Commercial Code, 2 vols, 1966, rev., 1984, New York Law of Contracts, 3 vols, 1964, Missouri Forms and Practice Under the Uniform Commercial Code, 2 vols, 1966; editor: Ann. Survey of Am. Law, NYU, 1961-62; mem. bd. contbg. editors and advisors: Corp. Law Rev, 1977-86; contbr. articles to law revs., jours. Mem. lawyers adv. coun. NAM, Washington, 1980, Adminstrv. Conf. U.S., 1980-86, legal adv. com. N.Y. Stock Exch., 1983-87, corp. law dept. adv. coun. Practising Law Inst., 1982; bd. dirs. Bach Soc., St. Louis, 1985-86, pres., 1973-77; bd. dirs. Valparaiso U., 1977—, chmn. bd. visitors law sch., 1966—, Luth. Charities Assn., 1984-87, vice chmn., 1986-87; bd. dirs. Luth. Med. Ctr., St. Louis, 1973-82, vice chmn., 1975-80; bd. dirs. Nat. Jud. Coll., 1984-90, St. Louis Symphony, 1988—, Opera Theatre St. Louis, 1988—, Luth. Brotherhood, Mpls., 1992—, Liberty Fund, Inc., Indpls., 1997—. Served with U.S. Army, 1953-55. Named Disting. Alumnus Valparaiso U., 1976. Fellow Am. Bar Found.; mem. ABA (chmn. com. uniform comml. code 1976-79, coun. sect. corp., banking and bus. law 1979-83, sec. 1983-84, chmn. 1986-87), Mo. Bar Assn., Am. Law Inst., Mont Pelerin Soc., Nat. Jud. Coll. (bd. dirs. 1984-90), Order of Coif, Bach Soc., Am. Soc. Corp. Sec. (bd. chmn. 1987-88), Assn. Gen. Coun., Am. Arbitration Assn., St. Louis Club. Contracts commercial, General corporate, General practice. Home: 1 Indian Creek Ln Saint Louis MO 63131-3333

**DUESENBERG, ROBERT H.**, lawyer; b. St. Louis, Dec. 10, 1930; s. Hugo John August and Edna Marie (Warmann) D.; m. Lorraine Freda Hall, July 23, 1938; children: Lynda Renee, Kirsten Lynn, John Robert. BA, Valparaiso (Ind.) U., 1951, LLB, 1953; LLM, Harvard U., 1956. Bar: Mo. 1953, U.S. Supreme Ct. 1981, Va. 1993. Pvt. practice St. Louis, 1956-58; atty. Wabash R.R. Co., St. Louis, 1958-65, Norfolk & Western Ry. Co., St. Louis, 1962-65; atty., assoc. gen. counsel Pet Inc., St. Louis, 1965-77, v.p., assoc. gen. counsel, 1977-80, v.p., gen. counsel, 1980-83; v.p., gen. counsel Gen. Dynamics Corp., Falls Church, Va., 1984-91, sr. v.p. and gen. counsel, 1991-93; ret., 1993; bd. dirs. VisionAire Corp., St. Louis, Valparaiso (Ind.) U. Contbr. numerous articles to profl. jours. Sec., treas., legal advisor Am. Kantorei, St. Louis, 1970-75; mem. Coun. on World Affairs, St. Louis, 1975—, Mo. Coordinating Bd. for Higher Edn., Jefferson City, 1976-83, chmn., 1978-81; mem. pres.'s coun. Valparaiso (Ind.) U., 1979—, bd. dirs., 1995—; bd. dirs. Higher Edn. Loan Authority, 1982-84; mem. adv. bd. Northwestern U. Corp. Counsel Ctr., 1988—, chmn. adv. bd., 1992; bd. dirs. Opera Theatre of St. Louis, 1988—. Cpl. U.S. Army, 1953-55. Recipient Disting. Alumnus award Valparaiso U., 1982. Mem. ABA, Va. Bar Assn., Mo. Bar Assn., St. Louis Bar Assn. (chmn. antitrust com. 1971-73, v.p. bus. law sect. 1972-73, chmn. 1973-74), Am. Law Inst., Gen. Counsels Assn., Machine and Allied Products Inst. (legal counsel 1986—), Am. Corp. Counsel Assn., S.W. Legal Found. (adv. bd.), Aerospace Industry Assn. (legal com. 1981-88), Bach Soc. of St. Louis (bd. dirs.). Republican. Lutheran. General corporate, Government contracts and claims. Home: 10171 Castlewood Ln Oakton VA 22124-3027 Office: Gen Dynamics Corp 3190 Fairview Park Dr Ste 1 Falls Church VA 22042-4523

**DUFF, BRIAN BARNETT**, federal judge; b. Dallas, Sept. 15, 1930; s. Paul Harrington and Frances Ellen (FitzGerald) D.; m. Florence Ann Buckley, Nov. 27, 1953; children: F. Ellen, Brian Barnett Jr., Roderick FitzGerald, Kevin Buckley, Daniel Harrington. AB in English, U. Notre Dame, 1953, postgrad., 1997—; JD, DePaul U., Chgo., 1962. Bar: Ill. 1962, Mass. 1962, U.S. Dist. Ct. (no. dist.) Ill. 1962, U.S. Supreme Ct. 1968. Mgmt. trainee, multiple line underwriter Continental Casualty Co., Chgo., 1956-60; mgmt. cons. Booz, Allen and Hamilton, Chgo., 1960-62; asst. to chief exec. officer Bankers Life and Casualty Co., Chgo., 1962-67; atty. Sloan & Bragiel, Chgo., 1965-68; exec. v.p., gen. counsel R.H. Gore Co., Chgo., 1968-69; atty. Brian B. Duff & Assocs., Chgo., 1969-76; judge Cir. Ct. Cook County Ill., Chgo., 1976-85; judge U.S. Dist. Ct. (no. dist.) Ill., Chgo., 1985—, now sr. judge; rep. Ill. Gen. Assembly, Springfield, 1971-76; chmn. House Judiciary Com., 1973-74, minority whip, 1975-76; vis. com. Coll. Law U Chgo., 1977-79; lectr. Law Sch. Loyola U., 1978-79; adj. prof. John Marshall Law Sch., 1985-90, DePaul U. Sch. Law, 1990. Served to lt (j.g.) USN, 1953-56. Mem. ABA, Chgo. Bar Assn., Fed. Judges Assn., Am. Judicature Soc., Nat. Lawyers Club, Inc., (hon.), Legal Club Chgo. (hon.), Law Club, Ill. State Bar Assn. Roman Catholic. Avocations: fishing, reading, travel, writing. Office: US Dist Ct 219 S Dearborn St Chicago IL 60604-1702

**DUFF, WILLIAM BRANDON**, lawyer; b. Flushing, N.Y., June 1, 1949; s. Daniel Vincent and Priscilla (Booth) D.; m. Terri Ann Sherman, June 16, 1985; children: Elizabeth, Madeleine. AB, Coll. of Holy Cross, 1971; JD, Georgetown U., 1975. Bar: D.C. 1975, U.S. Dist. Ct. (D.C.) 1975, U.S. Ct. Appeals (D.C. cir.) 1975, N.Y. 1983. Assoc. McChesney & Pyne, Washington, 1975-78, Carter, Ledyard & Milburn, N.Y.C., 1980-84; lawyer pvt. practice, N.Y.C., 1984-86; ptnr., dept. head DeForest & Duer, N.Y.C., 1986-96, Baer, Marks & Upham, N.Y.C., 1996—; instr. in Fed. Employee Benefit Plans Law, Georgetown U. Sch. Continuing Edn., Washington, 1977, 78. Mem. legislature, City of Greenwich, Conn., 1994—. Pension, profit-sharing, and employee benefits, Labor. Office: Baer Marks & Upham LLP 805 3d Ave New York NY 10022

**DUFFETT, BENTON SAMUEL, JR.**, lawyer; b. Kansas City, Mo., Dec. 22, 1936; s. Benton S. Sr. and Carabel (Marvin) D.; m. Virginia M. Keys, June 23, 1962 (dec. Mar. 1998); children: Benton S., III, Robert J., David J. BS in Chem., U. Kans., 1959; JD in Law, U. Mich., 1962. Bar: D.C. 1963, Va. 1978. From assoc. to partner Burns, Doane, Swecker & Mathis LLP, Alexandria, Va., 1963—. Mem. ABA, Am. Intellectual Property Law Assn., Nat. Assn. Plant Patent Owners, Am. Chem. Soc., Am. Soc. Hort. Sci., Am. Hort. Soc., Royal Hort. Soc., Can. Ornamental Plant Found., Internat. Community of Breeders of Asexually Reporduced Ornamental and Fruit-Tree Varieties. Intellectual property. Office: Burns Doane Swecker Mathis LLP 1737 King St Ste 500 Alexandria VA 22314-2727

**DUFFEY, WILLIAM SIMON, JR.**, lawyer; b. Phila., May 9, 1952; s. William Simon and Elinor (Daniluk) D.; m. Betsy Byars, Dec. 17, 1977; children: Charles, Scott. BA in English, honors, Drake U., 1973; JD cum laude, U. S.C., 1977. Bar: S.C. 1977, Ga. 1982, U.S. Dist. Ct. (no., mid. and so. dists.) Ga. 1982, U.S. Ct. Appeals (llth cir.) 1983, U.S. Supreme Ct., 1992. Atty. Nexson, Pruet, Jacobs & Pollard, Columbia, S.C., 1977-78, King & Spalding, Atlanta, 1982-94; dep. ind. counsel Office of the Ind. Counsel, Little Rock, 1994-95; ptnr. King & Spalding, Atlanta, 1995—. Articles editor S.C. Lawyer, 1990-94. Pres. Pine Hills Civic Assn., Atlanta, 1984-88; trustee Drake U.; mem. Atlanta Task Force Neighborhood Buyouts, 1986, Ga. Rep. Found., Leadership Atlanta; chmn. bd. dirs. Ga. Wilderness Inst., 1992—; mem. Peachtree Rd. Race Com., 1993—, chmn. Ga. Good Govt. Com.; chmn. bd. advisors Coverdell Leadership Inst., 1995—. Mem. Altanta Bar Assn. (chmn. alt. dispute resolution com. 1984-88), Lawyers Club, Atlanta Track Club (gen. counsel 1993—), Nat. Practitioners Advisory Coun. The Fed. Soc. Republican. Avocation: running. Federal civil litigation, State civil litigation. Home: 4825 Franklin Pond NE Atlanta GA 30342-2765 Office: King & Spalding 191 Peachtree St NE Ste 40 Atlanta GA 30303-1763

**DUFFY, EDMUND CHARLES,** lawyer; b. N.Y.C., Jan. 16, 1942; s. Thomas and Helen (Fisher) D.; m. Terry L. Davis, Oct. 21, 1973; children: Elisabeth, Margot. AB in Eng., Boston Coll., 1963; LLB, Columbia U., 1966. Bar: N.Y. 1967. Assoc. Cravath, Swaine & Moore, N.Y.C., 1968-77; from assoc. to ptnr. Skadden, Arps, Slate, Meagher & Flom, N.Y.C., 1977—. Served to capt. U.S. Army, 1966-68, Vietnam. Mem. ABA, N.Y. State Bar Assn. General corporate, Private international, Securities. Home: 15 W 81st St New York NY 10024-6022 Office: Skadden Arps Slate Meagher & Flom 919 3rd Ave New York NY 10022-3902

**DUFFY, JAMES F.,** lawyer; b. N.Y.C., Jan. 13, 1949; s. Hugh B. and Winifred V. (Hogarty) D.; m. Carol Wallis, June 11, 1983; children: Katherine, Elizabeth. BA, Fordham U., 1970; JD, NYU, 1976. Bar: N.Y. 1977. Assoc. Lord, Day & Lord, N.Y.C., 1976-87; asst. gen. counsel corp. law and fin. GTE Corp., Stamford, Conn., 1987-89; sr. v.p., gen. counsel Am. Stock Exch., Inc., N.Y.C., 1989-94, exec. v.p., gen. counsel, 1994-99. Mem. ABA, Assn. of the Bar of the City N.Y. Securities, Administrative and regulatory, General corporate.

**DUFFY, JAMES FRANCIS, III,** lawyer; b. Providence, Jan. 28, 1956; s. James Francis Jr. and Eileen (Barry) D. BA, U. R.I., 1978; JD, Harvard U., 1981. Bar: Mass. 1981, U.S. Dist. Ct. Mass. 1982. Assoc. Peabody & Brown, Boston, 1981-89, ptnr., 1989—. Mem. ABA, Boston Bar Assn. (real estate steering com. 1991-93, chmn. equity fin. com. of real estate sect. 1991-93), Mass. Bar Assn. E-mail: jduffy@peabodybrown.com. Securities, Real property, Finance. Home: 17 Jackson Rd Somerville MA 02145-2908 Office: Peabody & Brown 101 Federal St Fl 11 Boston MA 02110-1800

**DUFFY, JOHN FITZGERALD,** law educator; b. Pittsfield, Mass., Nov. 22, 1963; s. Thomas Francis and Noreen (Brett) D.; m. Anne Sprightley Ryan, July 3, 1998; 1 child, Clara Trinity. AB in Physics cum laude, Harvard Coll., 1985; JD cum laude, U. Chgo., 1989. Bar: Pa. 1991, D.C. 1994, U.S. Patent and Trademark Office 1996. Law clk. to Hon. Stephen Williams U.S. Ct. of Appeals for the D.C. Cir., Washington, 1989-90; atty. advisor Office of Legal Counsel, U.S. Dept. Justice, Washington, 1990-92; law clk. to Hon. Antonin Scalia U.S. Supreme Ct., Washington, 1992-93; assoc. Covington & Burling, Washington, 1993-96; asst. prof. law Cardozo Law Sch., Yeshiva U., N.Y.C., 1996—. Avocation: distance running. Office: Cardozo Sch Law 55 5th Ave Fl 10 New York NY 10003-4391

**DUFFY, KEVIN THOMAS,** federal judge; b. N.Y.C., Jan. 10, 1933; s. Patrick John and Mary (McGarrell) D.; m. Irene Krumeich, Nov. 9, 1957; children: Kevin Thomas, Irene Moira, Gavin Edward, Patrick Giles. AB, Fordham Coll., 1954, LLB, 1958. Bar: N.Y. 1958. Clk. to chief circuit judge N.Y.C., 1955-58; asst. chief criminal div. U.S. Atty.'s Office, N.Y.C., 1958-61; assoc. Whitman, Ransom & Coulson, N.Y.C., 1961-66; ptnr. Gordon & Gordon, N.Y.C., 1966-69; regional adminstr. SEC, N.Y.C., 1969-72; judge U.S. Dist. Ct. (so. dist.), N.Y., 1972—; adj. prof. securities law Bklyn. Law Sch., 1975-80; prof. trial advocacy NYU, 1982-84, Pace Law Sch., 1984-85, Fordham Law Sch., 1993—. Author: Cross-Examination of Witnesses: The Litigator's Puzzle, 1990, Impeachment of Witnesses, 1990. Recipient Achievement in Law award Fordham Coll. Alumni Assn., 1976, Alumni Gold medal Fordham Law Sch., 1984, Kupferman's award Laymen's Nat. Bible Assn., 1992, Disting. Pub. Svc. award N.Y. County Lawyers' Assn., Lifetime Achievement award SEC, 1995. Mem. ABA, Am. Bar Assn., N.Y. State County Bar Assn., Westchester County Bar Assn., Assn. of Bar of City of N.Y., Fed. Bar Council (trustee 1970-72), Fordham Law Sch. Alumni Assn. (trustee 1969—, v.p.). Clubs: Merchants (N.Y.C.). Office: US Dist Ct US Courthouse 40 Foley Sq New York NY 10007-1502

**DUFFY, MARTIN PATRICK,** lawyer; b. Louisville, Feb. 2, 1942; s. Martin Joseph and Elsie (Shrader) D.; m. Virginia Schoo, Mar. 20, 1970; children: Timothy Brian, Kathleen Kelly. AB in English, U. Notre Dame, 1964; JD, U. Louisville, 1975. Bar: Ky. 1975, U.S. Tax Ct. 1980. Ptnr. Olson, Baker, Henriksen & Duffy, Louisville, 1978-79, Wyatt, Tarrant & Combs, Louisville, 1979--. Bd. dirs. Bellarmine Coll. Overseers, Louisville, 1974-80; trustee St. Mary & Elizabeth Hosp., Louisville, 1980-86, chmn. bd. 1982-85. With U.S. Army, 1964-65, 68-69. Mem. ABA, Ky. Bar Assn., Louisville Bar Assn. Democrat. Roman Catholic. Avocations: running, golf. Estate taxation, Probate, Estate planning. Office: Wyatt Tarrant & Combs 2700 Citizens Plz Louisville KY 40202

**DUFFY, STEPHEN WILLIAM,** lawyer; b. Ft. Walton Beach, Fla., July 11, 1953; s. Peter Joseph and Adelaide Dorothy D.; m. Linda Grieve, July 4, 1981; children: Hilary Anne, Stephen William, Jr. BA, U. Calif., Berkeley, 1973; postgrad., Duke U., 1975; JD, Southern Meth. U., 1978. Staff atty. Legal Svcs. Corp. Western Carolina, Inc., Greenville, S.C., 1980-81; assoc. counsel Petroleum Corp., Breckenridge, Tex., 1981-83; asst. gen. counsel P&O Falco, Inc., Shreveport, La., 1983-85; gen. counsel Breck Operating Corp., Breckenridge, 1985-88; asst. gen. cousel EnRon Oil Trading & Transp., Houston, 1988-93; v.p., gen. counsel Eott Energy Corp., Houston, 1993—. Mem. S.C. Bar, Tex. Bar Assn. Republican. Roman Catholic. Oil, gas, and mineral, General corporate, Mergers and acquisitions. Office: Eott Energy Corp 1330 Post Oak Blvd Ste 2700 Houston TX 77056-3060

**DUFFY, WILLIAM J.,** lawyer; b. Allentown, Pa., Nov. 25, 1954; s. James Edward and Shirley Ritter Duffy; m. Teri S. Anderson, Aug. 30, 1986; children: Lucas James, Katherine Jeanne. BS, U. Del., 1976; MS, Pa. State U., 1983; JD, U. Denver, 1986. Bar: Colo. 1986, U.S. Dist. Ct. (D.C. dist.), U.S. Ct. Appeals (10th cir.). Assoc. Kelly Standsfield/O'Donnel, Denver, 1986-89; dir. Parcel Mauro Hultin & Spaanstra, Denver, 1989-98, Parcel Mauro, PC, Denver, 1998—; ptnr. Davis Graham & Stubbs, LLC, Denver, 1999—. Environmental, Federal civil litigation, Natural resources. Office: Davis Graham & Stubbs 370 17th St Ste 4700 Denver CO 80202-5682

**DUFOUR, RICHARD JOSEPH,** district attorney; b. Milw., Aug. 3, 1956; s Robert Alfred and Claire Lorraine (Gamache) D.; m. Shelley Sue Freitag, Oct. 1, 1983; 1 child, Genevieve Claire. BA cum laude, Marquette U., 1978, JD, 1981. Bar: Wis., U.S. Dist. Ct. Wis. Assoc. Rudolph, Kubasta, Rathjen & Murach, Wautoma, Wis., 1981-85; ptnr. Kubasta, Rathjen, Murach, Dufour & Bickford, Wautoma, 1985-90; dist. atty. Marquette County, Wis., Montello, 1990—; cons. Dept. of Justice, Madison, 1992—; com. mem. Statewide Prosecutor Edn. and Tng. Bd. Wis. Dist. Atty.'s Assn., Info. Tech. Com., Madison, 1995—. Bd. dirs. Waushara Industries, Wautoma, 1985-91, United Cerebral Palsy, Winnebagoland, Oshkosh, Wis., 1991—, Madison, 1995—, Marquette County Hist. Soc., Westfield, Wis., 1996. Recipient Am. Jurisprudence award Lawyer's Coop. Pub., 1979, Lawyer's Coop. Pub., 1981. Mem. Rotary Club of Montello (pres. 1994-95), Phi Alpha Theta. Republican. Roman Catholic. Avocations: golf, computers, skiing, working with youth. Home: PO Box 54 494 S Lake St Montello WI 53949 Office: Marquette County Dist Attys Office PO Box 396 77 W Park St Montello WI 53949-9366

**DUGAN, JOHN F.,** lawyer; b. Phila., May 25, 1935; s. Albert C. and Helen Josephine (Pritchard) D.; m. Colette Gregory, Jan. 18, 1987. AB, U. Pa., 1956, LLD, 1960. Bar: Pa. 1961, U.S. Ct. Appeals (3d cir.) 1961, Va. 1966, U.S. Supreme Ct. 1967. Assoc. Obermayer Rebmann Maxwell & Hippel, Phila., 1960-66; of counsel Reynolds Metals Co., Richmond, Va., 1966-69, Pennwalt Corp., Phila., 1969-71; ptnr. Berkman Ruslander, Pitts., 1971-85, Kirkpatrick & Lockhart, Pitts., 1985—; labor rels. law rep. mgmt., Kirkpatrick & Lockhart. Mem. Pitts. Field Club, Duquesne Club, Order of the Coif, Phi Beta Kappa. Republican. Labor. Office: Kirkpatrick & Lockhart 1500 Oliver Building Pittsburgh PA 15222-2312

**DUGAN, JOHN R.,** lawyer; b. Washington, Apr. 5, 1943; s. Thomas J. and Mary A. (McDevitt) D.; divorced; children: John Jr., Joseph, Katherine, Christina, David, Matthew. AB, Coll. Holy Cross, 1965; JD, George Washington U., 1968. Bar: Md. 1968, Va. 1972, U.S. Dist. Ct. (D.C.) 1968. Law clk. to Hon. Judge Matthew McGuire U.S. Dist. Ct., Washington, 1968-69; asst. U.S. atty. D.C., 1969-78; assoc. atty. Levitan, Ezrin, Cramer, West & Weinstein, Chevy Chase, Md., 1978-80; pvt. practice Rockville, Md., 1980—. Mem. D.C. Bar Assn., Va. State Bar Assn. Roman Catholic. Federal civil litigation, State civil litigation, Insurance. Office: 27 Wood Ln Rockville MD 20850-2228

**DUGAN, KEVIN F.,** lawyer; b. Kingston, N.Y., Oct. 30, 1959; s. Owen F. and Helen A. (Frost) D.; m. Diane Tremaine, Dec. 30, 1988; children: Molly, Brighid, Owen. BS, Fla. State U., 1981; JD, Stetson Coll. Law, 1985. Bar: Fla. 1985, U.S. Dist. Ct. (mid. dist.), Fla., 1986, U.S. Ct. Appeals (11th cir.) 1987, N.H. 1991, U.S. Supreme Ct. 1991. Lawyer Woodworth & Dugan, St. Petersburg, Fla., 1985-90, Abramson, Reis, Brown & Dugan, Manchester, N.H., 1990—, Masterson, Rogers, Woodworth, Masterson & Lopez, St. Petersburg, 1998—. Mem. ATLA, N.H. Trial Lawyers Assn. (Bd. Govs. award 1997, bd. govs. 1995—, pres. 1999—), N.H. Bar Found., Inns of Ct. Democrat. Roman Catholic. Personal injury. Office: Abramson Reis Brown & Dugan 1819 Elm St Manchester NH 03104-2910

**DUGAN, ROBERT JOHN,** lawyer; b. Pontiac, Mich., Dec. 25, 1945; s. John A. and Margaret E. Dugan; m. Jean L. Scott, May 23, 1970; children: Karen J., Stephen R. BA, U. Mich., 1968, JD, 1971. Bar: Mich. 1971, U.S. Dist. Ct. (we. dist.) Mich. 1971. Assoc., shareholder Mohney Goodrich & Titta PC, Grand Rapids, Mich., 1971-86; atty., shareholder Rhoades McKee Boer Goodrich & Titta, Grand Rapids, 1986—. Elder Presbyn. Ch., Grand Rapids. Mem., trustee Grand Rapids Bar Assn. Republican. Real property, General corporate, Estate planning. Home: 7329 Oliver Woods Dr SE Grand Rapids MI 49546-9707 Office: Rhoades McKee Boer Goodrich & Titta 161 Ottawa Ave NW Ste 600 Grand Rapids MI 49503-2766

**DUGAN, TERRENCE LEE,** lawyer; b. Bryson City, N.C., June 21, 1959; s. Harold R. and Elizabeth Mary D.; m. Peggy Kolber, Feb. 15, 1987; children: Erin, Jonathan, Brendan. BA, Vanderbilt U., 1981, JD, 1984. Bar: N.Y. 1984. Assoc. Sage, Gray, Todd & Sims, N.Y.C., 1984-87; assoc. Chadbourne & Parke, N.Y.C., 1987; assoc. Simpson, Thacher & Bartlett, N.Y.C., 1987-96, counsel, 1997—; gen. counsel Parallel Capital Corp., N.Y.C., 1996-97. Mem. ABA, Assn. of the Bar of the City of N.Y. (energy com. 1997-99). Finance, Contracts commercial, Real property. Office: Simpson Thacher & Bartlett 425 Lexington Ave Fl 15 New York NY 10017-3954

**DUGAS, LOUIS, JR.,** lawyer; b. Beaumont, Tex., Dec. 12, 1928; s. Louis and Loney (Duron) D.; m. Frances Elizabeth Tuley, Feb. 3, 1956; children: Mary Hester Dugas Koch, Kerry Beth Dugas Davidson, Louis Claiborne, Evin Garner, Reagan Taylor. AA, Lamar Jr. Coll., 1950; BBA in Banking and Fin., U. Tex., 1956, LLB, 1960. Bar: Tex. 1960, U.S. Ct. Appeals (5th cir.) 1972, U.S. Ct. Appeals (11th cir.) 1984, U.S. Supreme Ct. 1967. Pvt. practice, 1960—; mem. Tex. Ho. of Reps., 1954-60; justice of the peace, Orange County, Tex., 1963; spl. counsel D.C. com. U.S. Ho. of Reps., 1967; dist. and county atty., Orange County, 1968-72; former tchr. Tex. history and govt., Lamar U. Former columnist The Opportunity Valley News; columnist Orange County Record, 1993—. Regent Nat. Criminal Def. Coll., Mercer Law Sch., Macon, Ga.; explorer leader Boy Scouts Am., 1963; comdr. Am. Legion Post, 1967; mem. bd. Adjustments, City of Orange, 1967; founder "Les Acadiens du Texas"; pres. Orange County Hist. Soc., 1974-76; active Orange Art League; bd. dirs. Orange Community Players, 1977-82; tchr. Cajun French Orange City Parks and Recreation Dept., 1980-81; nominee Rep. Party for 2d Congl. Dist., Tex., 1984; pres. Lamar U. Friends of the Arts, 1985-86; adminstrv. bd. First United Meth. Ch., Orange, 1983, 84, 85. Sgt. USMC, 1950-52, Korea. Mem. Tex. Bar Assn. (sec. criminal law sect. 1969, 72), Orange County Bar Assn. (pres. 1979), Nat. Assn. Criminal Def. Lawyers (bd. dirs. 1982-88), Tex. Criminal Def. Lawyers Assn. (bd. dirs. 1976-88, pres. 1985-86, contbr. to pub. The Voice), Tex. Criminal Def. Lawyers Inst. (pres. 1986), Tex. Assn. Bd. Cert. Specialists in Criminal Law (pres. 1983), Tex. Criminal Def. Lawyers (sec.-treas. 1981), VFW, Gulf Coast Leathernecks (founder 1995), Optimists Club, Phi Alpha Delta. Avocations: historical research, bird watching, photography, conchology, writing. General civil litigation, Criminal, Civil rights. Home: 1802 16th St Orange TX 77630-3309 Office: 1804 16th St Orange TX 77630-3309

**DUGGAN, JENNIFER E.,** lawyer; b. Berkeley, Calif., July 1, 1969; d. Peter Logan Duggan and Judith Diana Wilbur. BA, U. Calif., Davis, 1992; JD, U. Oreg., 1996. Bar: Calif. 1996, U.S. Dist. Ct. (ea. dist.) Calif. Lawyer Porter, Scott, Weiberg & Delehant, Sacramento, 1996—; adv. bd. mem. Law and Entrepreneurship Ctr., U. Oreg. Sch. Law, Eugene, 1997—. Editor-in-chief Jour. Environ. Law and Litigation, 1995-96. Mem. Calif. State Bar. Federal civil litigation, State civil litigation, Civil rights. Office: Porter Scott Weiberg & Delehant 350 University Ave Ste 200 Sacramento CA 95825-6581

**DUGGAN, JOHN PETER,** lawyer; b. Newark, June 28, 1946; s. Patrick Joseph and Mary Ellen (Gallagher) D.; m. Bernadine Ann Lehman, Oct. 24, 1976; children: Erin, Sean, Mary Kate. BA, Montclair State U., 1968; JD with honors, Rutgers U., 1973. Bar: N.J. 1973, U.S. Dist. Ct. N.J. 1973, U.S. Supreme Ct. 1982, U.S. Ct. Appeals (3d cir.) 1988. Asst. prosecutor Middlesex County Prosecutor's Office, New Brunswick, N.J., 1973-78; assoc. Francis H. Wolff, P.A., Red Bank, N.J., 1978-80; ptnr. Wolff, Helies & Duggan, P.A., Red Bank, 1980—. Mem. ABA, N.J. Def. Assn., N.J. Bar Assn., Monmouth County Bar Assn. (chmn. civil practice com. 1990-91, 92-93, 96-97, 97—, sec. 1997—). Federal civil litigation, General civil litigation, State civil litigation. Office: Wolff Helies & Duggan PA 188 E Bergen Pl Red Bank NJ 07701-2161

**DUGGAN, PATRICK JAMES,** federal judge; b. 1933. BS in Econs., Xavier U., 1955; LLB, U. Detroit, 1958. Pvt. practice law Brashear, Duggan & Tangora, 1959-76; judge Wayne County Cir. Ct., 1977-86, U.S. Dist. Ct. (ea. dist.) Mich., Detroit, 1987—; adj. prof. Madonna U., Livonia, Mich., 1975-93. Chmn. Livonia Family YMCA, 1970-71; mem. bd. trustees Madonna U., 1970-79. Mem. Mich. Jaycees (pres. 1967-68). Office: US Dist Ct 251 Theodore Levin US Courthouse 231 W Lafayette Blvd Detroit MI 48226-2700

**DUGGAN, PATRICK O'NEILL,** lawyer; b. West Branch, Mich., May 28, 1953; s. William and Marjorie Rose (Moates) D.; m. Debra Gene DeCourcy, Nov. 27, 1971; children: Margaret May, Gene Patrice. BA, Mich. State U., 1975; JD, Wayne State U., 1978. Bar: Mich. 1978. Retail clk. Golden's Men's Shop, West Branch, 1968-71; tour guide of capitol State of Mich., Lansing, 1972-75; paralegal, law clk. Edgar Dietrich, Atty., Detroit, 1976-77; adminstrv. asst. to cir. judge County of Wayne, Detroit, 1977-79; asst. prosecutor County of Bay, Bay City, Mich., 1979-83, chief asst. prosecutor, 1983-88, appointed dep. county exec., civil counsel to county, 1989—. Speaker, trainer Bay County Women's Crisis Ctr., 1985—; bd. dirs. BASIS Corp. Alcohol and Substance Abuse Svcs., Bay City, 1982-83; elder First Presbyn. Ch., 1988-90. Mem. Bay County Bar Assn. (sec.-treas. 1986-88). Democrat. Avocations: photography, hiking, softball. Home: 407 Birney St Essexville MI 48732-1670 Office: Bay County Exec Office 515 Center Ave Bay City MI 48708-5941

**DUGGINS, DAVID DRYDEN,** lawyer; b. Wichita, Kans., June 9, 1937; s. Frank Hall and Camille (Wilson) D.; m. Elizabeth Laudeman, Nov. 4, 1967; children: David Dryden II, William Scott. BA, Tulane U., 1960, LLB, 1962. Bar: La. 1962. Landman Chevron Oil Co., 1962; ptnr. Newman, Duggins, Drolla & Gamble, 1967-74; pvt. practice New Orleans, 1974—. V.p. adv. bd. Salvation Army of New Orleans, pres., 1994-95; mem. La. Civil Svc. League, Jefferson Parish Charter Adv. Bd., Velocity Found., La. Coun. for Music and Performing Arts; founder, past pres. Jeuness D'Orleans; mem. adv. bd. St. Martin's Episcopal Sch.; past chmn. bd. St. George's Episcopal Sch.; mem. alumni bd. Metairie Park Country Day Sch.; mem. La. State Civil Svc. Commn., Preservation Resource Ctr.; mem. arson com. New Orleans Fire Dept. Recipient Monte M. Leman award La. Civil Svc. League; named Vol. of Yr., Salvation Army, 1992. Mem. Rotary Club of New Orleans (pres. 1995-96). Republican. Methodist. Avocations: hunting, fishing, gourmet cooking, renovations, antiques. Consumer commercial. Home: 32 Orpheum Ave Metairie LA 70005-4524 Office: 916 Lafayette St New Orleans LA 70113-1014

**DUHE, JOHN MALCOLM, JR.,** judge; b. Iberia Parish, La., Apr. 7, 1933; s. J. Malcolm and Rita (Arnandez) D.; children: Kim Duhe Holleman, Jeanne Duhe Sinitier, Edward M., M. Bofill. Student Washington and Lee U., 1951-53, BBA, Tulane U., 1955, LLB, 1957. Atty. Helm, Simon, Caffery & Duhe, New Iberia, La., 1957-78; dist. judge State of La., New Iberia, 1979-84; judge U.S. Dist. Ct. (we. dist.) La., Lafayette, 1984-88; cir. judge, U.S. Ct. Appeals (5th cir.), Lafayette, 1988-99, sr. judge, 1999—. Assoc. editor Tulane Law Rev., 1956, editor-in-chief, 1967. Mem. Order Coif, Omicron delta Kappa, Kappa Delta Phi. Office: US Ct Appeals 556 Jefferson St Ste 200 Lafayette LA 70501-6945*

**DUHIG, DIANE,** lawyer; b. Washington, June 22, 1959; m. Steven David Duhig, Oct. 11, 1998. AB, St. Louis U., 1984; JD, Cath. U. Am., 1987. Bar: Md. 1987, D.C. 1995. Assoc. McNamee Hosea Jernigan & Scott, Greenbelt, Md., 1986-90; staff atty. EEOC, Washington, 1990-94; assoc. Swick & Shapiro, Washington, 1994—. Vice chmn. Vote Know Coalition, Md., 1992; treas. Lake Village Manor HOA, Md., 1998—. Mem. D.C. Bar Assn. Labor, Civil rights, General civil litigation. Office: Swick & Shapiro PC 1225 Eye St NW Ste 1290 Washington DC 20005-3975

**DUKE, GEORGE F.,** lawyer; b. N.Y.C., Aug. 21, 1935; s. David S. and Marlene D.; m. Eugenie Arnold (div. 1985); children: Jonas, Nina; m. Shirley Kison, Sept. 4, 1988. BA magna cum laude, Tufts U., 1956; JD, Harvard U., 1959. Law clk. Calif. Ct. of Appeal, 1960-61; assoc. Leonard, Dole & Formichelli, San Francisco, 1961-66; directing atty. Calif. Rural Legal Assistance, Santa Rosa, 1966-67; dir. Calif. Indian Legal Svcs., Berkeley, 1968-71; cons. Carnegie Endowment for Internat. Peace, Geneva, Switzerland, 1972; pvt. practice law San Francisco, 1973—; lectr. Boalt Hall Law Sch., Berkeley, 1975-78, U. Calif., Davis, 1980. Ford Found. grantee, 1971-72. Mem. Calif. Bar Assn., Bar Assn. of San Francisco, Phi Beta Kappa. Avocations: music, hiking. Fax: 415-389-9828. Health. Office: 50 Monte Cimas Ave Mill Valley CA 94941-1742

**DUKE, MIRIAM D. WANSLEY,** prosecutor; m. W. Maxwell Duke; 1 child, Amanda. BA, Ga. State U., 1972; JD, Emory U., 1975. Bar: Ga. 1975. Asst. dist. atty. Dist. Atty.'s Office, Perry, Ga., 1975-79; asst. U.S. atty. U.S. Atty.'s Office, Macon, Ga., 1979-98, sr. litigation counsel, 1989-90, chief criminal divsn., 1990-94, sr. litigation counsel, 1995-98; retired, 1998; instr., lectr. Atty. Gen.'s Advocacy Inst., 1987-98; evaluator Dept. Justice Office of Legal Rev., 1990-98. Contbr. articles to profl. jours. Mem. Gov.'s Coun. on Criminal Justice, 1992-94; del. Peach County 3d Dist., Rep. Party, 1994-96, del. state conv., 1994-96, 3d dist. state conv. com. 1995-96; mem. state-wide law enforcement com. Senator Paul Coverdell, 1995-96, local adv. com. Peach County, 1995—; dir. Boys and Girls Club of Mid. Ga., 1996-98; mem. Career Women's Network, 1995-98, Women's Polit. Orgn., 1994-96, Am. Humane Soc., 1985—, Peach County Hist. Soc., 1990-98, Leadership Macon, 1988—; troop leader Girl Scouts U.S., 1985-87; vol. Bib County Emergency Mgmt. Agy., Salvation Army, Leukemia Soc. Am., others. Recipient Award for Outstanding Performance, FBI, Washington, 1985, 87, Dir.'s Award for Outstainding Performance, 1992, 93, 96, Cert. of Merit, U.S. Ho. of Reps., 1977, Outstanding Asst. Dist. Atty., Dist. Atty.'s Assn. of Ga., 1977, Outstanding Career Woman, Houston County, 1977, Outstanding Pub. Ofcl., Houston County C. of C., 1978, Award for Outstanding Performance, IRS, 1987, Commr.'s award, 1990, Award of Excellence, Dept. of Def. Inspector Gen.'s Office, Washington, 1989, Cert. of Excellence, Air Force Office of Spl. Investigation, Dist. 7, Melbourne, Fla., 1990, Outstanding Prosecution award, Washington, 1991, Dir.'s award Exec. Office of U.S. Attys., Dept. Justice, Washington, 1991. Mem. Fed. Bar Assn. (sec. 1993, pres.-elect 1994, pres. 1995, Outstanding Young Lawyer award 1985), Ga. Bar Assn., Macon Bar Assn., Ga. Pub. Safety Tng. Assn. (instr. 1990-98), Ga. Assn. Women Lawyers, Houston County Bar Assn. (treas. 1975-79), Nat. Assn. of asst. U.S. Attys. (del. 1991-98). Home: Duke Rd 638 Duke Rd Fort Valley GA 31030-7306 Office: US Attorneys Office 433 Cherry St Macon GA 31201-7919

**DUKE, THOMAS HARRISON,** lawyer; b. Pensacola, Fla., June 23, 1957; s. Alexander Gilliam and Margie Ellen (Harrison) D.; m. Janice Conway, June 11, 1983; children: Alexander, Haley. BS, Fla. State U., 1979; JD, Samford U., 1984. Assoc. Bell, Hahn & Schuster, P.A., Pensacola, 1986-88; shareholder Baker & Duke, P.A., Pensacola, 1988-91; shareholder, pres. Baker, Duke & Tipton, P.A., Pensacola, 1991-93; pres. Baker & Duke, P.A., Pensacola, 1993-96, Baker, Duke & Holman, P.A., Pensacola, 1997—. Mem. Assn. Trial Lawyers Am., Acad. Fla. Trial Lawyers, Escambia Santa-Rosa Bar Assn. (unauthorized practice of law standing com., children and the law com., med. liaison com., bar/realtor com.). Avocations: boating, diving, golf. State civil litigation, Insurance, Personal injury. Home: 4195 Madura Rd Gulf Breeze FL 32561-3544 Office: Baker Duke & Holman PA 15 W La Rua St Pensacola FL 32501-3933

**DUKES, JAMES OTIS,** lawyer; b. Quitman, Miss., Aug. 4, 1946; s. James O. and Helen (Carlson) D.; m. Leslie Ann McIntyre, Jan. 24, 1970; children: Leslie Macon, William James. BS in Math., U. Miss., 1968, MS in Math., 1970, JD, 1975. Bar: Miss. 1975, U.S. Dist. Ct. (no. and so. dists. Miss.) 1975, U.S. Ct. Appeals (5th cir.) 1981, U.S. Supreme Ct. 1993. Law clk. to chief judge U.S. Dist. Ct. (so. dist.) Miss., Biloxi, 1975-77; assoc. Bryant, Stennis & Colingo, Gulfport, Miss., 1977-79; ptnr. Bryant, Clark, Dukes, Blakeslee, Ramsay & Hammond, PLLC, Gulfport, Miss., 1979—. Vestry, jr. warden, sr. warden St. Peters Episc. Ch., Gulfport, 1976-83, 94-95; pres. standing com. Episcopal Diocese Miss., Jackson, 1989, exec. com., 1990—, v.p., 1992—. 1st lt. U.S. Army, 1969-71. Fellow Miss. Bar Found. (trustee 1995—); mem. ABA, Fed. Bar Assn., Def. Rsch. Inst., Assn. Def. Trial Attys., Southeastern Admirality Inst., Am. Coll. Trial Lawyers, Am. Bd. Trial Advocates, Miss. Bar Assn. (pres. 1999—), Miss. Def. Lawyers Assn. (bd. dirs. 1991-94, v.p. 1995), Harrison County Bar Assn. (sec. 1979-80, v.p. 1989-91, pres. 1992-93), Harrison County Jr. Bar Assn. (pres. 1981-82), Am. Inns. of Ct., Rotary. Insurance, Personal injury, Professional liability. Home: 149 Bayou Cir Gulfport MS 39507-4623 Office: Bryant Clark Dukes Blakeslee Ramsay & Hammond 2223 14th St Gulfport MS 39501-2064

**DUKES, KATHARINE LEE,** lawyer; b. Washington, July 31, 1968; d. Mack Gerald and Elizabeth (McClellan) Fleming; m. Glenn Edward Dukes, Sept. 4, 1993. BA in History, Rice U., 1990; JD, U. Tex., 1993. Bar: Tex. 1993, U.S. Dist. Ct. (ea. dist.) Tex. 1994, U.S. Ct. Appeals (5th cir.) 1994, U.S. Dist. Ct. (we. dist.) Tex. 1995, U.S. Supreme Ct. 1998. Jud. law clk. U.S. Dist. Ct. (ea. dist.) Tex., Marshall, Tex., 1993-94, U.S. Ct. Appeals (5th cir.), Tyler, Tex., 1994-95; jud. law clk. to Hon. Capelle U.S. Ct. Appeals (5th cir.), Austin, 1995-96; assoc. Cantilo Maisel & Hubbard LLP, Austin, 1996-98; staff atty. 3d Ct. Appeals, Austin, 1998-99; jud. law clk. U.S. Dist. Ct. (we. dist.) Tex., Austin, 1999—. Mem. ABA, Travis County Bar Assn., Austin Young Lawyers Assn. Democrat. Presbyterian. Avocations: musical theater, vocal ensemble. Office: Chambers of US Magistrate Judge Capelle 200 W 8th St Austin TX 78701-2325

**DULANEY, RICHARD ALVIN,** lawyer; b. Charlottesville, Va., Oct. 18, 1948; s. Alvin Tandy and Susie Lucille (Sims) D. B.A., Yale U., 1971; J.D., Coll. William and Mary, 1977. Bar: Va. 1977, U.S. Dist. Ct. (ea. dist.) Va. 1978. V.p. Christian Ctr., Charlottesville, Va., 1972-73; rsch. asst. Marshall-Wythe Sch. Law, Williamsburg, Va., 1975; assoc. Niles & Chapman, Remington, Va., 1977-79; gen. ptnr. Niles, Dulaney & Parker, Culpeper, Va., 1980-92; of counsel Chandler, Franklin, and O'Bryan, Culpeper, Va., 1988—; ptnr. Niles Duleney Parker and Lauer LLP, Culpeper, 1992—; bd. dirs. Rappahanock Legal Svcs., Fredericksburg, Va., 1981-83. Bd. dirs. Christian Ctr., Syria, Va., 1974-89, U. Sci. and Philosophy Swannanoa, Waynesboro, Va., 1985—, The Quest Inst., Charlottesville, Va., 1986-87; mem. bd. Zoning Appeals, Culpeper County, Culpeper, Va., 1983-90. Mem. Culpeper Bar Assn. (pres. 1985-86), New Haven chpt. Pierson Fellowship Club, Omicron Delta Kappa. Personal injury, Insurance, Entertainment. Home: PO Box 511 Culpeper VA 22701-0511 Office: Niles Dulaney Parker & Lauer LLP PO Box 190 Culpeper VA 22701-0190

**DULAURENCE, HENRY J., III,** lawyer; b. Cleve., Aug. 5, 1939; s. Henry J. Jr. and Sarah Hawley DuLaurence; m. Nancy A. Novince, Dec. 15, 1965 (div. Aug. 15, 1997); children: Henry IV, Hawley, Tara. BA, Williams Coll.,

1962; JD, Western Res. U., 1967. Bar: Mass. 1968. Legal aid City of Cleve., 1965-67; corp. counsel Liberty Mut. Ins. Co., Boston, 1967-70, litigation counsel, 1970-95; pvt. practice Boston, 1995—; time stds. cons., Boston and Cambridge, 1988. Bd. dirs. Copley Soc., Boston, 1968-74, Fuller Mus. Art, Brockton, Mass., 1969-74, Archives of Am. Art-Smithsonian, Boston, 1981—; chmn. WGBH Auction, Cambridge, 1983-93; mem. adv. bd. Pub. Action for Arts, 1989—. Recipient Muse award for outstanding charitable work Mayor's Office of Cultural Affairs, Boston, 1995. Avocations: fine art and antiques, tennis, guitar playing and performing, acting in movies, sailboat racing. Personal injury, General civil litigation, Labor. Office: Union Estates 4302 Eighth St Charlestown MA 02129

**DULAUX, RUSSELL FREDERICK,** lawyer; b. West New York, N.J., Dec. 30, 1918; s. Frederick and Theresa A. (Noble) L.; m. Ann deFriedberg, Aug. 22, 1962 (dec.); m. Eva DeLuca, Dec. 24, 1985. Student, Drake's Bus. Sch., 1937; Student, Pace Inst., 1938-40, Fordham U., 1946-48; LLB summa cum laude, N.Y. Law Sch., 1950; postgrad., Pace Coll., 1951, Columbia U., 1955. Bar: N.Y. 1951, U.S. Dist. (so. dist.) N.Y. 1951, U.S. Ct. Appeals (2d cir.) 1951, U.S. Ct. Claims 1952, U.S. Tax Ct. 1952, U.S. Dist. Ct. (ea. dist.) N.Y. 1953, U.S. Ct. Customs and Patent Appeals 1963, U.S. Ct. Mil. Appeals 1963, U.S. Supreme Ct. 1963. Mem. staff N.Y. State Dept. Law, Richmond County Investigations, 1951-54, N.Y. State Exec. Dept. Office of Commr. of Investigations, 1954-57; comptroller-counsel Odyssey Productions, Inc., 1957-59; ptnr. Ryan, Murray & Laux, N.Y.C., 1951-61, Ryan & Laux, N.Y.C., 1961; pvt. practice N.Y.C., 1961—. Served with AUS, 1940-46; capt. JAG, vet. corps. of arty. State of N.Y., 1975-92, maj., 1992—; spl. agt. counter intelligence corps and security intelligence corps; col. U.S. Army. Recipient Eloy Alfaro Grand Cross Republic of Panama, Cert. of World Leadership for Leadership and Achievement, 1987, Cert. of Merit for Disting Achievement, 1984, Cert. for Internt. Contemporary Achievement for Outstanding Contbr. to Soc., 1984, Disting. Leadership award for Contbns. to the Legal Profession, Award of Merit for Outstanding Profl. and Pub. Svc., Guglielono Marconi Bronze award, 1987; inducted Hall of Fame for Contbn. to Legal Profession. Mem. NATAS, Bronx County Bar Assn. (Townsend Wandell Gold medal), Met. Opera Guild, Internat. Platform Assn., VFW (adjutant Floyd Gibbons Post 500, Cert. of Recognition and Appreciation Polit. Action Com. 1990, Cert. of Svc. on Pres. Rehab. Com. Vets. sect.), Order of Lafayette, Am. Def. Preparedness Assn., Sons Union Vets. Civil War, Soc. Am. Wars, Nat. Sojourners, Heroes of '76, Navy League, St. Andrews Soc. N.Y., St. George Soc. N.Y., Soc. Friendly Sons St. Patrick, English Speaking Union, Asia Soc., China Inst. Am., Army and Navy Union USA, Am. Legion (past post comdr. admen's post 209), Mid Manhattan C. of C., Res. Officers Assn. U.S. (col.), Humanity Against Hatred, Delta Theta Phi, Lambs Club, Knights Hospitaller of St. John of Jerusalem, Grand St. Boys' Club, Soldiers' Club, Sailors' and Airmen's Club, Order Ea. Star, Masons (past comdr. N.Y. Masonic War Vets), Shriners, Knights of Malta, Knights of St. George, Sovereign Mil. Order of Temple of Jerusalem. Probate, Real property, Estate taxation. Office: FDR Station PO Box 477 New York NY 10150-0477

**DULCHINOS, PETER,** lawyer; b. Chicopee Falls, Mass., Feb. 2, 1935; s. George and Angeline D.; children: Matthew George, Paul Constantine, Gregory Peter. BSEE, MIT, 1956, MSEE, 1957; MS in Engring. Mgmt., Northeastern U., 1965; JD, Suffolk U., 1984. Bar: Mass. 1984, U.S. Dist. Ct. (Mass.) 1984, U.S. Ct. Appeals (1st cir.) 1985, U.S. Supreme Ct. 1988, U.S. Patent and Trademark Office 1989, U.S. Claims Ct. 1989. With Sylvania Co., Waltham, Mass., 1957-61, Needham, Mass., 1963-66; with Tech Ops, Burlington, Mass., 1961, RCA, Burlington, 1962-63, Raytheon Co., Bedford, Mass., 1966—; computer ops. mgr. tactical software devel. facility Patriot Ground Computer System, 1977-86, intellectual property mgr., 1986—; lectr. Fitchburg State Coll., 1985—; corporator Ctrl. Savs. Bank, Lowell, Mass., 1980-92; sec.-treas. U. Lowell Bldg. Authority, 1974-85; mem. statewide adv. coun. Dept. Mental Health, 1996—. Mem. statewide adv. coun. Dept. Mental Retardation, 1993-96; mem. human studies subcom. Bedford VA Hosp., 1987-90; pres. Chelmsford Rep. Club, 1964-70; chmn. Chelmsford Rep. Town Com., 1972-76, 80—; assoc. town counsel Tyngsborough, Mass., 1985-87; mem., former chmn. Chelmsford Bd. Health, 1972-87, 93—; mem. Nashoba Tech. High Sch. Com., 1970-71; trustee, chmn. Medfield State Hosp., 1993—; v.p. Greater Lowell Comprehensive Cmty. Support Systems Bd. Dept. Mental Health, 1994—; mem. State Mental Health Planning Coun., 1999—. 2d lt. U.S. Army, 1957-58. Mem. Mass. Bar Assn., Boston Patent Law Assn., Raytheon Employees Profl. Assn. (treas. 1998, pres. 1999). Republican. Greek Orthodox. Intellectual property, Trademark and copyright, Probate. Home: 17 Spaulding Rd Chelmsford MA 01824-1021 Office: Raytheon Co 50 Apple Hill Dr Tewksbury MA 01876-1198

**DULIN, THOMAS N.,** lawyer; b. Albany, N.Y., May 26, 1949; s. Joseph Paul and Mary Carol (Keane) D.; m. Pamela Lee Kendall, May 14, 1983; 1 children: Chelsea K., Danielle Y. Boshea, Amanda L. Boshea, Thomas M. Boshea. BA, Siena Coll., 1972; JD, Western New England U., 1976. Bar: N.Y. 1977, U.S. Dist. Ct. (no. dist.) N.Y. 1977, U.S. Supreme Ct. 1984. Asst. dist. atty. Albany County, 1977-81; assoc. McCarthy & Evanick, Albany, 1981-83; sole practice Albany, 1983-88; sr. ptnr. Dulin, Harris & Bixby, Albany, 1988-92; ptnr. Gerstenzang, Weiner & Gerstenzang, Albany, 1992-93, The Dulin Law Firm, Albany, 1993—; staff atty. Albany County Pub. Defender's Office, 1983—. Bd. dirs. Big Bros. and Sisters of Albany County, Inc., 1983-92, pres., bd. dirs. , 1988-90. Mem. ABA, N.Y. State Bar Assn. (lectr. criminal justice sect.), Nat. Assn. Criminal Def. Lawyers, N.Y. State Assn. Criminal Def. Lawyers, Capital Dist. Trial Lawyers Assn., Albany County Bar Assn., Assn. Trial Lawyers Am., N.Y. State Trial Lawyers Assn. Democrat. Avocations: skiing, golfing, swimming. Criminal, Personal injury. Home: 2 Country Rdg Schenectady NY 12304-2531 Office: 4 Tower Pl Exec Park Tower Albany NY 12203

**D'ULL, WALTER,** lawyer; b. Vienna, Austria, May 23, 1931; s. Leon D'U.; m. Roberta Gail Rubin, Nov. 1, 1964; children: Leon, Victoria. BA, N.Y. U., 1950; JD, Yale U., 1953. Bar: N.Y. 1954, U.S. Supreme Ct. 1967. Law clk. to Hon. Ben Harrison Fed. Dist. Ct., L.A.; private practice N.Y.C., 1954—. Pub. (jour.) N.J. Computer News, 1995; inventor airplane baby seat. Mem. Bar Assn. N.Y.C., Pub. Investors Arbitration Bar Assn. Alternative dispute resolution, Securities, Real property. Office: 223 E 62nd St New York NY 10021-7685

**DUMVILLE, S(AMUEL) LAWRENCE,** lawyer; b. Richmond, Va., Mar. 14, 1953; m. Frances Adair Davis, Oct. 24, 1981; 2 children. BA, Washington and Lee U., 1975; JD, Coll. William and Mary, 1978. Bar: Va. 1978, U.S. Dist. Ct. (ea. dist.) Va. 1978, U.S. Ct. Appeals (4th cir.) 1979, U.S. Dist. Ct. (we. dist.) Va. 1981. Assoc. Breeden, Howard & MacMillan, Norfolk, Va., 1978-85; ptnr. Breeden, MacMillan & Green, PLC, Norfolk, 1985-95; bd. dirs. Breeden Adams Found., 1992-95. Mem. adv. bd. Back Bay Restoration Found., Virginia Beach, 1982-87; fin. chair, mem. adminstrn. bd. St. Andrew's United Meth. Ch., Virginia Beach, 1992—, del. to ann. conf., 1989-92, pres., 1995-97; treas., bd. dirs. Larkspur Civic League, 1989-92, 94—; pres. Norfolk Law Libr. Found., 1989; bd. dirs. Norfolk Law Libr., 1986-91. Mem. Va. Bar Assn., Norfolk-Portsmouth Bar Assn. (bd. dirs. 1988-89), Virginia Beach Bar Assn., Va. Assn. Def. Counsel. Republican. Avocations: deep sea sport fishing, sporting clays. Federal civil litigation, General civil litigation, Insurance. Office: Independence Law Ctr 4356 Bonney Rd Ste 2-102 Virginia Beach VA 23452-1200

**DUNAGAN, WALTER BENTON,** lawyer, educator; b. Midland, Tex., Dec. 11, 1937; s. Clinton McCormick and Allie Mae (Stout) D.; m. Tera Childress, Feb. 1, 1969; children: Elysha, Sandi. BA, U. Tex., 1963, JD, 1965, postgrad., 1965-68. Bar: Tex. 1965, Fla. 1970, U.S. Dist. Ct. (mid. dist.) Fla. 1971, U.S. Ct. Appeals (11th cir.) 1982. Corp. atty. Gulf Oil, New Orleans, 1968-69, Getty Oil Co., L.A., 1969—, Westinghouse/Econocar, Internat., Daytona Beach, Fla., 1969-72; assoc. Becks & Becks, Daytona Beach, 1973-75; prin. Walter B. Dunagan, Daytona Beach, 1975—; cons. Bermuda Villas Motel, Daytona Beach, Buccanneer Motel, Daytona Beach, Pelican Cove West Homeowners Assn., Edgewater, Fla. Organizer Interfaith Coffee House, New Orleans; tchr., song leader various chs.; chief Indian guide/princess program YMCA, Daytona Beach; bd. dirs. Legal Aid, Daytona Beach. Lance cpl. USMC. Mem. Volusia County Bar Assn., Lawyers Title Guaranty Fund, Phi Delta Phi. Avocations: reading, languages. Family and matrimonial, Real property, Consumer commercial. Home: 714 Egret Ct Edgewater FL 32141-4120 Address: 1141 S Ridgewood Ave Daytona Beach FL 32114-6149

**DUNCAN, ED EUGENE,** lawyer; b. Gary, Ind., Dec. 10, 1948; s. Attwood and Freddie Leon (Ballard) D.; m. Patricia Louise Revado, Sept. 8, 1973 (div.); children: Kristin, Anika, Gregory. BA, Oberlin Coll., 1970; JD, Northwestern U., 1974. Bar: Ohio 1974, U.S. Dist. Ct. (no. dist.) Ohio 1977, U.S. Supreme Ct. 1977. Assoc. Arter & Hadden, Cleve., 1974-82, ptnr., 1982—. Bd. mem. Glenville br. YMCA, Cleve., 1979—, Ohio Bd. of Bldg. Standards, Columbus, 1986-89; trustee Legal Aid Soc., Cleve., 1990-91. Mem. Ohio Bar Assn., Cleve. Bar Assn., Minority Ptnrs. in Majority Corp. Law Firms, Internat. Assn. Def. Counsel. Avocations: writing, reading. General civil litigation, Insurance, Personal injury. Home: 935 Roland Rd Cleveland OH 44124-1033 Office: Arter & Hadden 925 Euclid Ave Ste 1100 Cleveland OH 44115-1475

**DUNCAN, JOHN DEAN, JR.,** lawyer; b. Detroit, Nov. 25, 1950; s. John Dean Duncan and Ann Marie (Bruton) Bridges; m. Vickie Renee Olafson, May 10, 1986; children: Katherine Lund, John Dean III. Student, USAF Acad., 1969-71; BA, Cath. U., 1973, JD, 1976; MPA, Harvard U., 1991. Bar: U.S. Ct. Appeals Md. 1976, U.S. Ct. Appeals D.C. 1978, U.S. Supreme Ct. 1980. Law clk. to presiding justice 6th Jud. Ct., Rockville, Md., 1976-77; sr. asst. state's atty. Montgomery County, Rockville, 1977-81; sr. trial atty. pub. integrity sect., criminal div. Dept. Justice, Washington, 1981-87; chief counsel to Inspector Gen. Dept. State, Washington, 1987-98, sr. seminar, 1998—; career mem. Sr. Exec. Svc. U.S., 1987—. Mem. admissions com. J.F. Kennedy Sch. of Govt., Harvard U., Cambridge, Mass., 1991; bar liaison Law Related Edn. Project of Md., 1979-80; alumni rep. nat. phonethon Cath. U., Washington, 1980. Named one of Outstanding Young Men Am., 1980. Mem. D.C. Bar Assn., Mountgomery County Bar Assn. (editor manual on local practice and procedure 1980), Nat. Dist. Attys. Assn., Aircraft Owners and Pilots Assn. Avocations: flying, alpine skiing, squash, sports car driving, jogging. Office: Dept State Nat Sec Council The White House Washington DC 20520-0001

**DUNCAN, NORA KATHRYN,** lawyer; b. Chgo., Feb. 23, 1946; d. Robert Ferrie and Elise Grace (Walker) D. BA in Sociology, MacMurray Coll., 1968; JD, La. State U., 1973; LLM in Internat. and Comparative Law, George Washington U., 1979. Bar: La. 1973, U.S. Dist. Ct. (mid. dist.) La. 1974, U.S. Supreme Ct. 1978, D.C. 1979, U.S. Dist. Ct. (we. dist.) La. 1981, U.S. Ct. Appeals (5th and 11th cirs.) 1981. Staff atty. La. Dept. of Justice, Baton Rouge, 1973-76; contract counsel lands and natural resource La. Dept. of Justice, Washington, 1976-78; staff atty. La. Dept. of Justice, Shreveport, 1980; assoc. Cady & Thompson, Shreveport, 1981-82; ptnr. Cady, Thompson & Duncan, Shreveport, 1983; pvt. practice Shreveport, 1984-86, 87-88; ptnr. Walker, Tooke, Perlman & Lyons, Shreveport, 1986; atty. U.S. Immigration and Naturalization Service Dept. Justice, Oakdale, La., 1988-92, ret., 1992; instr., dir. paralegal studies program Draughon Bus. Coll., 1987. Atty., speech writer Gahagan for U.S. Senate, Augusta, 1978; bd. dirs. Better Bus. Bur., Shreveport, 1985-86; lit. tutor and trainer Allen Parish Libraries Adult Literacy Program; pres. Oakdale-Elizabeth Branch Friends of the Library, 1994-96; founder, 1st pres. Reading Edn. for Adult Devel.-READ, 1997—. Paul Harris fellow Rotary Found., 1981. Mem. Toastmasters Internat. (area 11 gov. 1986-87, area 18 gov. 1994-95, pres. local chpt. 1986, 88, 94, named dist. 68 Gov. of Yr. 1987, dist. 25 Govt. of the Yr. 1995), Rotary (dist. 6290 group study exch. team leader 1997), Rotarian of the Yr. 1994-95, sec. 1995-96). Republican. Oil, gas, and mineral, Immigration, naturalization, and customs, Probate.

**DUNCAN, PRISCILLA BLACK,** lawyer; b. Centerville, Ind., Oct. 18, 1948; d. Paul Herbert and Bonnie (Clevenger) Hedges; m. Charles Le Roy Black Jr., Nov. 7, 1975 (dec. Oct. 1982); m. Donald Arthur Duncan. BA, DePauw U., 1970; JD, U. Ala., 1997. Bar: Ala. 1997, U.S. Dist. Ct. (mid. dist.) Ala. 1997. Asst. libr. Centerville (Ind.) Twp. Libr., 1968-70; newswriter Palladium Item, Richmond, Ind., 1970-74, AP, Atlanta, 1974; editor, columnist Columbus (Ga.) Ledger-Enquirer, 1974-92; dir. consumer affairs Ala. Office of Atty. Gen., Montgomery, 1993-97; assoc. Taber, Rountree, Singleton & Lyons, Montgomery, 1997-98; ptnr. P.B. Duncan & Assocs., Montgomery, 1998—. Mem. Montgomery County Dem. exec. com., 1998—; mem. Good Govt., Montgomery, 1997-98. Mem. ATLA, Ala. Trial lawyers Assn., Montgomery County Trial Lawyers Assn., Ala. Bar Assn. Democrat. Episcopalian. Avocations: politics, reading. General civil litigation, Contracts commercial, Labor. Office: PB Duncan & Assocs 472 S Lawrence St Ste 204 Montgomery AL 36104-4261

**DUNCAN, RICHARD ALAN,** lawyer; b. Mpls., July 8, 1963. BA in Econs. summa cum laude, Yale U., 1985, JD, 1988. Bar: Minn. 1988, U.S. Ct. Appeals (8th cir.) 1988, U.S. Ct. Appeals (9th cir.) 1990, U.S. Ct. Appeals (10th cir.) 1998, U.S. Supreme Ct. 1991. Assoc. Faegre & Benson, LLP, Mpls., 1988-95, ptnr., 1996—. Mem. exec. com. North Star chpt. Sierra Club, 1988-91, 95-98. Mem. Phi Beta Kappa. Antitrust, Environmental, Native American. Office: Faegre & Benson LLP 90 S 7th St Ste 2200 Minneapolis MN 55402-3901

**DUNCAN, SARAH BAKER,** judge; b. Waco, Tex., May 23, 1955; d. Malcolm Perry and Mary Ruth (Norris) D. BA with honors, U. Tex., 1977, JD with honors, 1984. Bar: Tex. 1984; cert. in civil appellate law Tex. Bd. Legal Specialization. Assoc. Fulbright & Jaworski, Austin and Houston, 1984-88, Minton, Burton, Foster & Collins, Austin, 1988-89; assoc., participating assoc. Soules & Wallace, P.C., San Antonio, 1989-90; pvt. practice San Antonio, 1990-91; of counsel Fulbright & Jaworski, LLP, San Antonio, 1991-93, Denton McKannie & Navarro, San Antonio, 1994; justice Fourth Ct. Appeals, San Antonio, 1995—; mem. Supreme Ct. Adv. Com. on the Rules of Civil Procedure, Austin, 1993-97; tri-chair Gender Bias Task Force, San Antonio, 1995—; mem. Task Force on Funding Jud. Efficiency Commn., Austin, 1995-96; coun. mem. Appellate Practice Sect., State Bar Tex., 1996-98. Contbg. author: Texas Appellate Practice Manual, 1993; mem. Tex. Law Rev./U. Tex. Sch. Law, Austin, 1982-84. Fellow Am. Bar Found., Tex. Bar Found., San Antonio Bar Found.; mem. State Bar Tex. (appellate sect., jud. sect.), San Antonio Bar Assn. (appellate sect.), Bar Assn. Fifth Fed. Cir., Bar U.S. Supreme Ct. Avocations: gardening, reading, computers, cross-country skiing. Office: Fourth Ct Appeals 300 Dolorosa Ste 3200 San Antonio TX 78205-3037

**DUNCOMBE, RAYNOR BAILEY,** lawyer; b. Washington, July 17, 1942; s. Raynor Lockwood and Avis Ethel (Bailey) D.; m. Janice Assunta Rini, Apr. 12, 1969; children: Christina Luccioni, Raynor Luccioni. AB, Franklin and Marshall Coll., 1965; JD, Syracuse U., 1968. Bar: N.Y. 1972, U.S. Dist. Ct. (no. dist.) N.Y. 1972. Staff atty. State of N.Y., Albany, 1968-70; mgmt. trainee State Bank Albany, 1970-72; staff atty. Vibbard, Donaghy & Wright, Schoharie, N.Y., 1972-73, F. Walter Bliss, Esq., Schoharie, 1973-74; pvt. practice Schoharie, 1974—; chmn. bd. dirs. Fulmont Mut. Ins. co., Mohawk Minden Ins. Co.; town atty. seven towns, one village and one water dist. in Schoharie County, 1975—; adminstr. Assigned Counsel Program, 1975—; sch. atty. Middleburgh (N.Y.) Schs., 1981-85, 97—; atty. Schoharie County, 1982-87, 90-91, Schoharie County Hist. Soc., 1975—; mem. Tax Cons. Tech. Adv. Group, Catskill Watershed Corp., 1998—. Rep. committeeman Schoharie county, 1984-92; dist. commr. Boy Scouts Am., 1987-92, asst. scoutmaster, 1988-91, Explorer advisor, 1991—, dist. chmn., 1992-95, asst. coun. commr., 1995-96, coun. commr. 1996-99, coun. pres. 1999—; elder Presbyn. Ch., 1992-98, mem. pers. com. Albany Presbytery of Presbyn. Ch., 1998—; chmn. Middleburgh Rep. Town Com., 1995—, personnel com. Albany Presbyn. Mem. ABA, N.Y. State Bar Assn., Schoharie County Bar Assn. (sec.-treas. 1975—), Rotary (past pres.), Masons (past master), Lions. Avocations: camping, cross country skiing, collecting stamps. General practice. Home: RR 2 Box 360 Middleburgh NY 12122-9415 Office: PO Box 490 319 Main St Schoharie NY 12157

**DUNDAS, PHILIP BLAIR, JR.,** lawyer; b. Middletown, Conn., Apr. 29, 1948; s. Philip Blair and Madolyn Margaret Dundas; m. Elizabeth Anne Adorno, Aug. 9, 1969; children: Philip Blair III, Chapman P. BA, Wesleyan U., Conn., 1970; JD, Washington and Lee U., 1973. Bar: N.Y. 1974. Assoc. Shearman & Sterling, N.Y.C., 1973-81, ptnr., 1981—, ptnr. in charge of Abu Dhabi, United Arab Emirates Office, 1981—. Mem. ABA, Internat. Bar Assn., N.Y. State Bar Assn., Assn. Bar City N.Y., Union Internationale des Avocats, Clinton Country Club. Private international, General corporate, Finance. Home: 288 Old Kelsey Point Rd Westbrook CT 06498-2132

**DUNDON, THOMAS H.,** lawyer; b. Anniston, Ala., Nov. 28, 1951; s. Harry Benedict Dundon and Kathleen Bright; children: Catherine Jane, Jeffrey Thomas. BS, Coll. of William and Mary, 1973, JD, 1976. Bar: Tenn. 1976, U.S. Dist. Ct. (mid. dist.) Tenn. 1978, U.S. Dist. Ct. (we. dist.) Tenn. 1984, U.S. Dist. Ct. (ea. dist.) Tenn. 1987, U.S. Supreme Ct. Atty. Neal & Harwell, Nashville, Tenn., 1976—. Fellowship Nashville Bar Found., 1998. Mem. ABA, Tenn. Bar Assn., Nashville Bar Assn. Avocation: aviation. Aviation, General civil litigation, Criminal. Office: Neal & Harwell 150 4th Ave N 2000 First Union Tower Nashville TN 37219

**DUNE, STEVE CHARLES,** lawyer; b. Vithkuqi, Korca, Albania, June 15, 1931; s. Costa Pappas and Evanthia (Vangel) D.; m. Irene Duff Boudreau, Sept. 4, 1955; children: Michelle Dune Hopper, Christopher Michael. AB, Clark U., 1953; JD, NYU, 1956. Bar: N.Y. 1957. Law clk. U.S. Ct. Appeals 1st Cir., 1956-57; from assoc. to ptnr. Cadwalader, Wickersham & Taft, N.Y.C., 1957-95; counsel Albanian-Am. Enterprise Fund, 1995-96. Trustee Clark U., Worcester, Mass., 1974-86, 93-97, hon. trustee, 1997—, vice-chmn. bd. dirs., 1980-84, chmn. bd. dirs., 1984-86, chmn. presdl. search com., 1983-84, mem. pres.'s coun., 1987-90; dir. Albanian Children Fund, 1998—, chmn. Albanian-Am. C. of C., 1995-96. Root-Tilden scholar, 1953-56. Mem. ABA (internat. law and practice sect.), N.Y. State Bar Assn., Assn. Bar City N.Y. (com. on Ea. European affairs 1992-95, admiralty com. 1976-79, 87-90), Maritime Law Assn. U.S. (marine fin. com. 1980-95), Internat. Bar Assn. (bus. and law sect. Ea. European Forum), India House, Phi Beta Kappa. Admiralty, Contracts commercial, General corporate. Home and Office: PO Box 456 98 Barrett Hill Rd Brooklyn CT 06234-1500 *Commitment, determination and perseverance are a person's best allies in solving any problem, meeting any challenge or realizing upon any opportunity of life.*

**DUNFEE, THOMAS WYLIE,** law educator; b. Huntington, W.Va., Nov. 15, 1941; s. Wylie Ray and Chloe Edith (Wylie) D.; m. Dorothy Jane Taylor, Aug. 26, 1967; children: John Wylie, Jennifer Sue, Shannon Elizabeth. AB, Marshall U., 1963; JD, NYU, 1966, LLM, 1969. Instr. N.Y. Inst. Tech., 1965-68; asst. prof. Ill. State U., Normal, 1968-70; asst. prof. Ohio State U., Columbus, 1970-72, assoc. prof., 1972-74; assoc. prof. legal studies Wharton Sch., U. Pa., Phila., 1974-79, prof., 1979—, Kolodny prof. social responsibility, 1982—, chmn. dept. legal studies, 1980-84, 87-91, dir. Wharton ethics program, 1995-96, dir. Zicklin Ctr. for Bus. Ethics Rsch., 1997—; vis. prof. U. Fla., 1989, U. Newcastle, Australia, 1981, 85, Georgetown U., 1994; cons. United Way of Am., McGraw-Hill, Nynex, Citibank, GM, Honda, SmithKline & Beecham, AT&T. Author: Business and Its Legal Environment, 1992, Modern Business Law, 1996; editor: Business Ethics: Japan and the Global Economy, 1993, (with Thomas Donaldson) Ethics in Business and Economics, 2 vols., 1997, Ties That Bind: A Social Contracts Approach to Business Ethics, 1999; editor-in-chief Am. Bus. Law Jour., 1976-79; contbr. articles to profl. jours. Grantee Exxon Found., 1985-86, Kemper Found., 1993. Mem. Acad. Legal Studies in Bus. (pres. 1989-90, Disting. Sr. Faculty award for Excellence 1991), Soc. Bus. Ethics (pres. 1995-96). Home: 517 Arthur Dr Cherry Hill NJ 08003-3005

**DUNHAM, DOUGLAS SPENCE,** lawyer; b. Anchorage, Apr. 11, 1943; s. Alexander Spence and Thelma Gladys (Akridge) D.; m. Ellen Marie Bailey, Mar. 22, 1980; children: Dana Addison, Michael Jens. BA in Econs., Willamette U., 1965, JD cum laude, 1969; LLM, Harvard U., 1975. Bar: Wash. 1969, U.S. Dist. Ct. Wash. 1970, U.S. Ct. Appeals (9th cir.) 1970, U.S. Supreme Ct. 1979. Dep. pros. atty. King County, Seattle, 1969-72, sr. dep. pros. atty., 1973; assoc. Skeel, McKelvy, Henke, Evenson & Betts, Seattle, 1973-78; mem. staff Crane, Dunham & Drury PLLC, Seattle, 1978—. Contbg. editor Willamette U. Law Rev., 1969, Wash. Lawyer Practise Manual, 1972-83. Mem. Wash. State Bar Assn. (bd. examiners 1980-81, sec.-treas. trial sect. 1983-85, chairperson 1986-88, dist. counsel disciplinary bd. 1985—, hearing officer disciplinary bd. 1998—), Seattle-King County Bar Assn. (trustee young lawyers sect. 1977-80, treas. 1978-79). State civil litigation, Federal civil litigation, General practice. Home: 10770 Valmay Ave NW Seattle WA 98177-5337 Office: Crane Dunham & Drury PLLC 701 5th Ave Ste 5700 Seattle WA 98104-7028

**DUNHAM, FRANK WILLARD,** lawyer; b. Phila., Sept. 16, 1942; m. Elinor Rockwell, Dec. 25, 1965; children: Frank W. III, John Durgin. BS, Va. Tech. U., 1965; JD, Catholic U., Washington, 1970. Bar: Va. 1970, U.S. Dist. Ct. (ea. dist.) Va. 1970, D.C. 1970, U.S. Dist. Ct. D.C. 1970, U.S. Ct. Appeals (4th cir.) 1971, U.S. Ct. Appeals (3d cir.) 1975, U.S. Tax Ct. 1983, U.S. Supreme Ct. 1980. Naval architect Naval Sea Systems Command, Arlington, Va., 1965-71; law clk. U.S. Dist. Ct., Alexandria, Va., 1970-71; asst. U.S. atty. Justice Dept., Alexandria, 1971-76; 1st asst. U.S. atty. U.S. Dept. Justice, Alexandria, 1976-78; assoc. Leonard, Cohen, Gettings and Sher, Arlington, 1978-83; ptnr. Cohen, Gettings, Alper and Dunham, Arlington, 1983-90, Cohen, Gettings & Dunham, Arlington, 1991—. Contbr. article to profl. jour. Dir. Ft. Hunt Youth Athete Assn., Fairfax County, Va., 1980—; mem. 10th jud. dist. grievence com. Recipient Disting. Svc. award Waynewood Civic Assn., 1985. Mem. Fed. Bar Assn. (pres. No. Va. chpt. 1998-99), Alexandria Bar Assn., Va. Trial Lawyers Assn. (chmn. criminal law sect. 1991-92), Va. Assn. Def. Attys., Arlington County Bar Assn. Avocations: tennis, coaching baseball. Federal civil litigation, Criminal, Personal injury. Office: Cohen Gettings & Dunham 2200 Wilson Blvd Ste 800 Arlington VA 22201-3375

**DUNHAM, WOLCOTT BALESTIER, JR.,** lawyer; b. N.Y.C., Sept. 14, 1943; s. Wolcott Balestier and Isabel Caroline (Bosworth) D.; m. Joan Scott Findlay, Jan. 26, 1974; children: Mary Findlay, James Wolcott. AB magna cum laude, Harvard U., 1965, LLB cum laude, 1968. Bar: N.Y. 1969. Vol. VISTA, 1968-69; assoc. Debevoise & Plimpton and predecessor Debevoise, Plimpton, Lyons & Gates, N.Y.C., 1969-76, ptnr., 1977—; exec. dir. N.Y. State Exec. Adv. Commn. on Ins. Industry Regulatory Reform, 1982. Co-author: Insurance M&A, 1997—; contbr. articles to profl. jours.; gen. editor and chpt. author, New York Insurance Law, 1991, and ann. supplements. Treas., trustee Fund for Astrophys. Rsch., N.Y.C., 1970—, sec., 1970-84, pres., 1984—; bd. dirs. UN Assn., N.Y.C., 1973-79, vice chmn., 1975-79, adv. coun., 1992—; vestry mem. St. James Ch., N.Y.C., 1987-93, clk., 1988-93, jr. warden, 1993-94, sr. warden, 1994-95, chancellor, 1994—; bd. dirs. Neighborhood Coalition for Shelter, Inc., 1983—; pres., bd. dirs. East Side Cmty. Ctr., Inc., 1988—; bd. dirs. Dutchess Land Conservancy, 1996—; bd. mgrs. Shekomeko Valley Farm Assn., LLC, 1996—. Fellow Am. Coll. Investment Counsel; mem. ABA (chmn. com. on ins. sect. adminstrv. law 1979-83), Assn. Bar City N.Y. (com. on ins. 1981-87, chmn. com. 1984-87), Union Internationale des Avocats, Am. Soc. Internat. Law, Harvard Law Sch. Assn. N.Y.C. (dir. 1978-81). Episcopalian. General corporate, Securities, Insurance. Office: Debevoise & Plimpton 875 3rd Ave Fl 23 New York NY 10022-6256

**DUNIPACE, IAN DOUGLAS,** lawyer; b. Tucson, Dec. 18, 1939; s. William Smith and Esther Morvyth (McGeorge) D.; m. Janet Mae Dailey, June 9, 1963; children: Kenneth Mark, Leslie Amanda. BA magna cum laude, U. Ariz., 1961, JD cum laude, 1966. Bar: Ariz. 1966, U.S. Supreme Ct. 1972, Nev. 1994, Colo. 1996. Reporter, critic Long Branch (N.J.) Daily Record, 1963; assoc. firm Jennings, Strouss, Salmon & Trask, Phoenix, 1966-69; assoc. Jennings, Strouss & Salmon, PLC, Phoenix, 1969-70, ptnr., 1971-93, mem., 1993—, chmn. comml. practice dept., 1998—. Comments editor Ariz. Law Rev., 1965-66. Reporter Phoenix Forward Edn. Com., 1969-70; mem. Phoenix Arts Commn., 1990-93, chmn., 1992-93; bd. mgmt. Downtown Phoenix YMCA, 1973-80, chmn. 1977-78; bd. dirs. Phoenix Met. YMCA, 1976-87, 88—, chmn. 1984-85; bd. mgmt. Paradise Valley YMCA, 1979-82, chmn. 1980-81; bd. mgmt. Scottsdale/Paradise Valley YMCA, 1983, mem. legal affairs com. Pacific Region YMCA, 1978-81; chmn. YMCA Ariz. State Youth and Govt. Com., 1989-95; bd. dirs. The Schoolhouse Found. 1990-96, pres. 1990-94, Kids Voting, 1990-94, Beaver Valley Improvement Assn. 1977-79, Pi Kappa Alpha Holding Corp., 1968-72, The Heard Mus. 1993-94, Ariz. Bar Found., 1996—, treas. 1998-99, v.p. 1999—; trustee Paradise Valley Unified Dist. Employee Benefit Trust, 1980-93, chmn. 1987-93, Sch. Theology, Claremont, Calif. 1994—; trustee First Meth. Found. of Phoenix, 1984-93, 99—; mem. Greater Paradise Valley Cmty. Coun., 1985-87; bd. dir. Heart Mus. Coun., 1990-95, pres. 1993-94; mem. Ariz. Venture Capital Conf. Planning Com., 1994—, mem. exec. com. 1997—, vice chmn. 1999—; mem.

Assn. for Corp. Growth, 1995-96, Ariz. Bus. Leadership Assn., 1996—; bd. visitors U. Ariz. Law Coll., 1996—. Capt. AUS, 1961-63. Mem. State Bar Ariz. (securities regulation sect. 1970—, chmn. 1991-92, mem. com. unauthorized practice of law 1972-84, chmn. 1975-83, mem. bus. law sect. 1981—, chmn. 1984-85), State Bar Nev., State Bar Colo., Am., Fed. (pres. Ariz. chpt. 1980-81), Maricopa County Bar Assns. (bd. dirs. Corp. Coun. divsn. 1996-99), Ariz. Zool. Soc., U. Ariz. Law Coll. Assn. (bd. dirs. 1983-90, pres. 1985-86, bd. visitors 1996—), Smithsonian Assn., U. Ariz. Alumni Assn. (bd. dirs. 1985-86), Ariz. Club, Renaissance Club, Orange Tree Club, Masons, Kiwanis (pres. Phoenix 1984-85, disting. lt. gov. 1986-87, S.W. dist. cmty. svc. chmn. 1987-88, dist. activity com. coord. 1988-89, dist. laws and regulation chmn. 1989-90, 92-93, 95-96, asst. to dist. gov. for club svcs. 1990-91, field dir. 1991-92, dist. conv. chmn. 1993-94, pub. rels. chmn. 1996-98, mem. internat. com. on Project 39, 1988-89, internat. com. On to Anaheim 1990-91, internat. com. on leadership tng. and devel. 1991-92, 93-94, trustee SW dist. found. 1987-92, 1st v.p. 1990-92), Phi Beta Kappa, Phi Kappa Phi, Phi Delta Phi, Phi Alpha Theta, Sigma Delta Pi, Phi Eta Sigma, Pi Kappa Alpha (nat. counsel 1968-72). Democrat. Methodist (mem. met. Phoenix commn. 1968-71, lay leader 1975-78, trustee 1979-81, pres. 1981; mem. Pacific S.W. ann. conf. 1969-79, lawyer commn. 1980-85, chancellor Desert S.W. ann. conf. 1985—). Securities, General corporate, Banking. Home: 4147 E Desert Cove Ave Phoenix AZ 85028-3514 Office: Jennings Strouss & Salmon PLC 2 N Central Ave Fl 14 Phoenix AZ 85004-4471

**DUNKIN, ELLEN R.,** lawyer; b. Flushing, N.Y., Sept. 23, 1958; d. Sol R. and Leonore C. Dunkin; m. Joseph Michaeli, Aug. 16, 1981; 3 children. BA, SUNY, Albany, 1979; JD, St. John's Sch. Law, Jamaica, N.Y., 1982. Bar: N.Y. 1983. Assoc. Willkie Farr & Gallagher, N.Y.C., 1982-86; atty. Marsh & McLennan Cos., N.Y.C., 1986-90, sr. atty., 1990-95; sole practitioner Larchmont, N.Y., 1995-98; gen. counsel Risk and Ins. Mgmt. Soc. Inc., N.Y.C., 1998—. Bd. dirs. Mamaroneck (N.Y.) Schs. Found., 1997—; trustee Westchester Jewish Ctr., Mamaroneck, 1989—. Mem. N.Y. State Bar Assn., Assn. Bar City N.Y., Am. Corp. Counsel Assn., Am. Soc. Assn. Execs. Avocations: tennis, skiing. General corporate, Non-profit and tax-exempt organizations, Pension, profit-sharing, and employee benefits. Office: Risk and Ins Mgmt Soc 655 3d Ave New York NY 10017

**DUNKLE, KURT HUGHES,** lawyer; b. St. Petersburg, Fla., Aug. 23, 1961; s. Harry Newton and Caroline (Hughes) D.; m. Cathleen Brooke, May 16, 1987. AB, Duke U., 1983; JD, U. Fla., 1987. Bar: Fla. 1987. Shareholder Rogers, Towers, Bailey, Jones & Gay, 1995—; past mem. bd. govs., treas. young lawyers divsn. Fla. Bar, 1992—; past chmn. cmty. adv. bd. WJCT (local PBS-TV and radio), 1994-95. Construction, General civil litigation, Contracts commercial. Office: Rogers Towers Bailey Jones & Gay 1301 Riverplace Blvd Ste 1500 Jacksonville FL 32207-1811

**DUNKUM, BETTY LEE,** lawyer; b. Farmville, Va., Jan. 23, 1968; d. Wesley Earl Jr. and Elizabeth Burnette D. BA magna cum laude, Williams Coll., 1990; JD cum laude, Harvard U., 1995. Bar: Calif. 1995, D.C. 1998, U.S. Supreme Ct. 1999. Intern Office of U.S. Congressman L.F. Payne, Washington, 1989, budget com. assoc., 1990-92; legal asst. U.S. Nat. Labor Rels. Bd., Washington, 1993; assoc. McDermott, Will & Emery, Washington, 1994; atty. Howarth & Smith, L.A., 1995-96; law clk. Sr. U.S. Dist. Judge Jackson Kiser, Danville, Va., 1996-97; atty. Preston, Gates, Ellis & Rouvelas Meeds, Washington, 1997-99, Christian Legal Soc., Annandale, Va., 1999—. Cons. Mass. Mus. Contemporary Art, North Adams, 1988-90. Mem. ABA, Christian Legal Soc., Harvard Law Sch. Christian Fellowship Alumni Assn. (alumni coord. 1995-99), Phi Beta Kappa. Avocations: swimming, photography, travel. Fax: 703-642-1075. E-mail:bldunkum@aol.com. General civil litigation, Civil rights, Constitutional. Office: Christian Legal Soc 4208 Evergreen Ln Ste 222 Annandale VA 22003-3251

**DUNLAP, F. THOMAS, JR.,** lawyer, electronics company executive; b. Pitts., Feb. 7, 1951; s. Francis Thomas and Margaret (Hubert) D.; m. Kathy Dunlap; children: Bridgette, Katie. B.S.E.E., U. Cin., 1974; J.D., U. Santa Clara, Calif., 1979. Bar: Calif., 1979, U.S. Dist. Ct. (no. dist.) Calif. 1979. Mgr. engring. Intel Corp, Santa Clara, Calif., 1974-78, adminstr. tech. exchange, 1978-80, European counsel, 1980-81, sr. atty., 1981-83, gen. counsel, sec., 1983-87, v.p., gen. counsel, sec., 1987—. drafter, lobbyist Semiconductor Chip Protection Act, 1984. Republican. Roman Catholic. Avocation: jogging. Office: Intel Corp Ste 4 2200 Mission College Blvd Santa Clara CA 95054-1549*

**DUNLAP, TAVNER BRANHAM,** lawyer; b. Lexington, Ky., Oct. 19, 1953; s. Tavner and Anna (Miller) D.; m. Celia Muller, Aug. 18, 1979; children: Sarah Jordan, Tavner Alexander. BS in Psychology, Denison U., 1976; JD, U. Dayton, 1980. Bar: Ohio 1980, Ky. 1981. Ptnr. Dunlap & Dunlap, Lexington, 1981-86, Bunch & Brock, Lexington, 1986-90; v.p. Sugar Hill Farm, Inc., Versailles, Ky., 1986-95, pres., 1995—; v.p. Pisqah Community Assn., 1990; counsel Pisqah Community Hist. Assn., 1991; gen. ptnr. Dunlap Farm Mgmt. Ptnrs. Scoutmaster Lexington Boy Scouts Am., 1982-85, advancement chmn. Blue Grass Counsel, 1998—; dir. Woodford County Red Cross, 1994-97; treas. New Union Christian Ch., 1998, 99. Mem. ABA, Fed. Bar Assn., Ky. Bar Assn., Fayette Bar Assn., Fed. Tax Ct. Bar Assn. Democrat. Avocation: scuba diving. Family and matrimonial, Personal income taxation, Consumer commercial. Office: 2600 Paynes Mill Rd Versailles KY 40383-9204

**DUNLAY, CATHERINE TELLES,** lawyer; b. Cin., Apr. 5, 1958; d. Paul Albert and Donna Mae Telles; m. Thomas Vincent Dunlay, July 10, 1981; children: Christine Jennifer, Thomas Paul, Brian Patrick. Student, Ind. U., 1976-78; BA in English Lit. summa cum laude, U. Cin., 1981; JD summa cum laude, Ohio State U., 1984. Bar: Ohio 1984. Teaching asst., legal rsch. and writing Ohio State U. Coll. of Law, Columbus, 1982; law clk. Brownfield, Bowen & Bally, Columbus, 1983; assoc. Schottenstein, Zox & Dunn, LPA, Columbus, 1984-91, atty., principal, 1991—. Mng. editor Ohio State Law Jour., 1983-84; co-author Health Span, 1993, Akron Law Rev., Fall 1993; co-editor Health Law Jour. of Ohio, 1994-95. Grad. Columbus Leadership Program, 1991; mem. admissions/inclusiveness com. United Way of Franklin County, Columbus, 1991-94, 96. Recipient C. Simeral Bunch award for Acad. Excellence, Ohio State U., 1984, Law Jour. Past Editors award, 1984. Mem. ABA, Ohio State Bar Assn. (vice chair healthcare law com. 1998—), Columbus Bar Assn., Ohio Women's Bar Assn., Women Lawyers of Franklin County (trustee, treas. 1990-93, 91-92), Am. Health Lawyers Assn., Soc. of Ohio Hosp. Attys., Order of the Coif. Roman Catholic. Avocations: cooking, hiking, camping, reading. Health, General corporate, Securities. Office: Schottenstein Zox & Dunn 41 S High St Ste 2600 Columbus OH 43215-6109

**DUNLAY, F. CHARLES,** lawyer; b. Pitts., Feb. 22, 1966; s. Frank C. and Paricia A. (Whalen) D.; m. Haley Astrid Reed, June 20, 1998. BS, Tex. Christian U., 1988; JD, U. Kans., 1991; student, London U., 1986-87. Bar: Kans. 1991, U.S. Dist. Ct. Kans. 1991, U.S. Dist. Ct. (we. dist.) Mo., 1992, Mo. 1992, U.S. Ct. Appeals (10th cir.). Pvt. practice Overland Park, Kans., 1991-96; asst. county counselor Wyandotte County (Kans.) Counselor's Office, Kansas City, 1996-97; ast. counsel Unified Govt. of Wyandotte County and City of Kansas City, 1997—; legal advisor Police Dept. City of Kansas City, 1998; coord. student mediation program, Lincoln Preparatory Sch., Kansas City, Mo., 1993-95. Bd. dirs. Sudden Infant Death Suyndrome Devel. Bd., Kansas City, 1994-96; legal advisor Unified Govt. Human Svcs. standing com., Kansas Ciaty, 1997-98, Wyandotte County Park Bd., 1996-97. Mem. Kans. Bar Assn., Wyandotte County Bar Assn. E-mail: fcdunlay@toto.net. Home: 106 Cambridge St Kansas City KS 66103-2219 Office: Unified Govt Wyandotte County and Kansas City 710 N 7th St Fl 2D Kansas City KS 66101-3077

**DUNLEVY, WILLIAM SARGENT,** lawyer; b. Burbank, Calif., June 5, 1952; s. Roy William and Zella LaVerne (Singleton) D.; m. Margaret Joy Lehman Dunlevy, June 22, 1974; children: Thomas William, Gregory Michael. BA, U. Calif., Davis, 1974; JD, UCLA, 1977. Bar: Calif. 1977. Lawyer Law office of Robert Silver, Ventura, Calif., 1977-80, Taylor, Churchman & Lingl, Camarillo, Calif., 1980-84, Liebmann & Dunlevy, Camarillo, Calif., 1984-88, James P. Lingl & Assoc., Camarillo, Calif., 1988-97, Knopfler & Robertson, Camarillo, Calif., 1998—; editor Inst. Channel Islands chpt. Cmty. Assn., Ventura, Calif., 1984—, pres., 1986-87. Pres. Ventura (Calif.) Downtown Lions Club, 1985-86; bd. mem. Am. Youth Soccer Orgn., Ventura, Calif., 1986-88, 90-96. Mem. Community Assn. Inst., Poinsetta Lodge. Republican. Baptist. Avocations: photography, hiking. Real property, Estate planning. Office: Knopfler & Robertson 1200 Paseo Camarillo Ste 170 Camarillo CA 93010-6085

**DUNN, DAVID NORMAN,** lawyer; b. Blossburg, Pa., Dec. 13, 1954; s. Lawrence E. and Barbara (Perrin) D.; m. Kirsten E. Beske, Aug. 16, 1997. BS, Cornell U., 1977; JD, MS in Environ. Law, Vt. Law Sch., 1981. Bar: D.C. 1981, U.S. Dist. Ct. D.C., U.S. Ct. Appeals (D.C. cir.), Mass. 1988, U S. Dist. Ct. Mass., Vt. 1996, U.S. Dist. Ct. Vt., U.S. Ct. Appeals (1st cir.). Assoc. Warren & Assocs., Washington, 1981-84, Glassie, Pewett, Dudley, Beebe, Shanks, Washington, 1984-88, Peabody & Arnold, Boston, 1988=94; sr. counsel Recoll Mgmt. Corp., Boston, 1994-96; ptnr. Potter Stewart, Jr. Law Offices, P.C., Brattleboro, Vt., 1996—. Banking, Contracts commercial, Bankruptcy. Home: 774 Stickney Brook Rd Dummerston VT 05301-8670 Office: 205 Main St Ste 3D Brattleboro VT 05301-2868

**DUNN, EDWARD THOMAS, JR.,** lawyer, educator; b. L.A., Dec. 7, 1954; s. Edward Thomas and Beverly Jean (Dixon) D.; m. Marcy Jean McNeely, Nov. 5, 1977; children: Charles Jason Thomas, Laura Brianna, Kaeli Carissa Michele, Edward Thomas IV. BA, Biola U., 1977; postgrad., U. Calif., Irvine, 1980-81; JD, Southwestern U., 1984. Bar: Calif. 1985, U.S. Dist. Ct. (cen. dist.) Calif. 1985, U.S. Dist. Ct. (ea., no. and so. dists.) Calif. 1986, U.S. Ct. Appeals (9th cir.) 1985, U.S. Supreme Ct. 1989. Mem. minority staff com. on rules Ho. of Reps., Washington, 1976-77; asst. v.p., br. mgr. Downey Savs. & Loan Assn., Rolling Hills Estates, Calif., 1977-80; sr. atty. Calif. Ct. Appeal, Santa Ana, 1989, 97—; assoc. prof. law Orange County U., Newport Beach, 1990-94; pros. Orange County Dist. Atty. Office, Santa Ana, 1985-97; adj. prof. law Western State U., Fullerton, Calif., 1991—, Whittier Law Sch., 1997—. Bd. dirs. Whittier Christian H.S., La Habra, Calif., 1995—; assoc. mem. ctrl. com. Orange County Calif. Rep. Orgn., 1997-99; candidate Orange County Superior Ct. Judge, 1996; mem. First Evang. Free Ch. of Fullerton, 1964—, elder, 1995-99. Named Atty. of Yr. Constnl. Rights Found., 1988, Vol. of Yr. Calif. Rep. Orgn., 1997. Mem. Orange County Bar Assn. (ethics com. 1992-96, Cert. of Recognition 1995, appellate com. 1992-95), Orange County Attys. Assn. (bd. dirs. 1993-94), Calif. Family Support coun. (appellate com. 1975-95). Calif. Dist. Attys. Assn. (appellate com. 1987-96), Calif. State Bar (cert. specialist in criminal law). Avocations: keyboards, writer, musical arranger, sailing. Office: Calif Ct Appeal 4th Dist Divsn 3 925 N Spurgeon St Santa Ana CA 92701-3700

**DUNN, EDWIN RYDELL,** lawyer; b. Boston, July 24, 1942; s. Richard Joseph and Clara Hudson (Rydell) D.; m. Kathleen Lynch, July 23, 1966; children—Jeanne, Kathleen, Anne, Daniel. B.A., U. Notre Dame, 1964; J.D. cum laude, Northwestern U., Chgo., 1967. Bar: Ill. 1967. Assoc., Baker & McKenzie, Chgo., 1967-73, ptnr., 1973—. Mem. ABA, Ill. Bar Assn., Chgo. Bar Assn. General corporate, Mergers and acquisitions, Securities. Office: Baker & McKenzie 1 Prudential Pla 130 E Randolph St Ste 3700 Chicago IL 60601-6342

**DUNN, HERBERT IRVIN,** lawyer; b. Balt., July 19, 1946; s. Albert M. and Hilda F. (Winakur) D.; m. Marsha Edith Greenfield, Apr. 1, 1979; children: Marla Phyllis, Jonathan Howard. BS with high honors, U. Md., 1969, JD, 1971. Bar: Md. 1971, D.C. 1971, U.S. Ct. Claims 1972, U.S. Tax Ct. 1972, U.S. Dist. Ct. D.C. 1971, U.S. Ct. Appeals (D.C. cir.) 1971, U.S. Supreme Ct. 1975. Atty.-adviser Office of Gen. Counsel U.S. Gen. Acctg. Office, Washington, 1971-83, sr. atty., 1983—. Served with USAR, 1968-74. Mem. FBA (treas. younger lawyers divsn. 1977-79, nat. coun. 1978-79, 91—, Capitol Hill chpt. exec. coun. 1975-83, v.p. 1990-91, pres.-elect 1991-92, pres. 1992-93, v.p. D.C. cir. 1994—), Md. Bar Assn., Northwest Br. Citizens Assn. (sec. 1988-95, 1st v.p. 1995-99), Omicron Delta Epsilon. Office: 441 G St NW Washington DC 20548-0001

**DUNN, JAMES FRANCIS,** lawyer; b. Joliet, Ill., Nov. 28, 1945; s. John J. and Rita Ann (Flanagan) D.; m. (div.); children: Amy Ann, Jennifer Elizabeth; m. Mary Jean Wolke, Oct. 19, 1985; children: Michael James, Molly Kathleen. BA, U. St. Thomas, 1968; JD magna cum laude, William Mitchell Coll. Law, 1974. Bar: Minn. 1974, U.S. Ct. Appeals (8th cir.) 1974, U.S. Dist. Ct. Minn. 1975, U.S. Supreme Ct. 1981, Wis. 1987, U.S. Dist. Ct. (we. dist.) Wis. 1989, U.S. Dist. Ct. N.D. 1990. From claim rep. to sr. claim rep. Aetna Casualty and Surety Co., Mpls., 1968-74; assoc. Robins, Kaplan, Miller & Ciresi, St. Paul, 1974-76; ptnr. Liefschultz & Dunn, St. Paul, 1976-81, Dunn & Johnson, St. Paul, 1981-83; pres. James F. Dunn & Assoc., P.A., St. Paul, 1983-93; pres., ptnr. Dunn & Elliott, P.A., St. Paul, 1993—; legal writing instr. Hamline U. Sch. Law, St. Paul, 1974-75. Named one of Minn. Outstanding Attys., Am. Rsch. Corp., Mpls., 1994. Mem. ABA, ATLA, Am. Arbitration Assn., Minn. State Bar Assn. (cert. specialist in civil trial advocacy), Ramsey County Bar Assn., Hennepin County Bar Assn., Wis. State Bar Assn., Def. Rsch. Inst., Minn. Def. Lawyers Assn., Minn. Trial Lawyers Assn. Avocations: cycling, reading. Insurance, Personal injury, Product liability. Home: 13877 17th St N Stillwater MN 55082-1746 Office: Dunn & Elliott PA 2177 Youngman Ave Ste 100 Saint Paul MN 55116-3042

**DUNN, JOHN BENJAMIN,** lawyer; b. Washington, July 12, 1948; s. Read P. and Barbara (Butts) D.; m. Virginia Ann Hughes, July 3, 1983; children: Lily Conti, Noah Benjamin. BA, Ohio Wesleyan U., Delaware, 1970; JD, George Washington U., 1973. Bar: D.C. 1973, Md. 1974, U.S. Ct. Appeals (D.C. cir.) 1974. Assoc. Schultz & Overby, Washington, 1973-76, Law Offices of Daniel E. Schultz, Washington, 1976-80; prin. Schultz & Dunn Chartered to Schultz Dunn & Murray Chartered, Washington, 1980-85; sole practice Takoma Park, Md., 1985—. Estate planning, Family and matrimonial, Probate. Office: 7030 Carroll Ave Ste 2 Silver Spring MD 20912-4448

**DUNN, KENNETH CARL,** lawyer; b. Eldora, Iowa, July 3, 1956. AB summa cum laude, Duke U., 1978; JD, Stanford U., 1982. Bar: Ill. Assoc. Gardner, Carton & Douglas, Chgo., 1982-89, equity ptnr., 1990-95; v.p., assoc. gen. counsel John Nuveen & Co., Chgo., 1995; asst. gen. counsel Ameritech Corp., Chgo., 1995—. Author: (periodicals) 6th Annual NYU Institute on Corporate Tax Planning, 1984, Topics in Health Care Financing, 1991. Bd. dirs. Marcy-Newberry Assn., Chgo., 1988-94, co-chmn., 1994—. Mem. Environ. Defense Club, Wilderness Soc., Sierra Club. Avocations: mountain climbing, backpacking, travel, reading, movies. General corporate, Mergers and acquisitions, Securities. Office: Ameritech Corp 30 S Wacker Dr Fl 34 Chicago IL 60606-7402

**DUNN, LARRY K.,** lawyer; b. Oaha, Hawaii, Apr. 3, 1948; s. Norman Dunn and Anne Martin; m. Kathleen Lillo, March 23, 1968; children: Jennifer, Karena, Jeffrey, Lindsay. AA, Western Nev. Cmty. Coll., 1977; BA, U. Nev., 1980; JD, McGeorge Sch. Law, 1984. Bar: Nev. 1984. Law clerk County Pub. Defenders Office, Sacramento, Calif., 1982-84; deputy dist. attorney Washoe County Dist. Attorney, Reno, Nev., 1984-86; criminal defense attorney Larry K. Dunn Chartered, Reno, Nev., 1986—; lectr. High Sierra Police Acad., Reno, 1994—. With U.S. Army, 1967-72. Mem. Am. Legion. Republican. Episcopalian. Avocations: golf, ocean fishing, guitar. Criminal. Office: Larry K Dunn Chartered 1440 Haskell St Reno NV 89509-2843

**DUNN, MARK L.,** lawyer; b. N.Y., Aug. 2, 1960; s. James N. and Mary K. D. BA in Econs., St. John Fisher Coll., 1982; JD, Union U., 1986. Bar: N.Y., U.S. Dist. Ct. (no. dist.) N.Y., U.S. Ct. Appeals (2d cir.), U.S. Supreme Ct. Atty. Martin, Ganotis, Brown, Mould & Currie, PC, Syracuse, N.Y., 1986—; Vol. Onondaga Small Claims Arbitration. Coach IHM CYO, Syracuse, 1993-98; mem. fin. com. St. Margarets Ch., Syracuse, 1996-98. Mem. ABA (mem. litig. sect.), N.Y. State Bar Assn. (mem. torts, ins. and compensation law sect.). General civil litigation, Personal injury. Office: Martin Ganotis Brown Mould & Currie PC 5790 Widewaters Pkwy Ste 6 De Witt NY 13214-1850

**DUNN, MELVIN EDWARD,** retired judge; b. Chgo., Oct. 31, 1933; s. Raymond E. and Josephine (Fitzgerald) D.; m. Judith Wilkinson, Oct. 28, 1972; children: Lori, Richard A. Vester Jr., Jonathan T. Vester, Geoffrey A. Vester, andrea Lynn. JD, Ill. Inst. Tech., 1971. Bar: Ill. 1971. Owner Melvin E. Dunn, Ltd., Elburn, Ill., 1972-82; assoc. judge 16th Jud. Cir., Kane County, Ill., 1982-86; cir. judge, 1986—, presiding judge family divsn., 1986-89, presiding judge chancery divsn., 1989—. Served with USCG, 1952-56. Mem. Am. Acad. Matrimonial Lawyers (bd. mgrs. Ill. chpt.), Ill. Bar Assn. (chmn. family law sect. coun.), Kane County Bar Assn. Lutheran.

**DUNN, M(ORRIS) DOUGLAS,** lawyer; b. Ionia, Mich., Nov. 1, 1944; s. Morris Frederick and Lola Adella (Gee) D.; m. Jill Lynn Fasbender, July 22, 1967; children: Brooks, Gillian, Joshua. BS in Mech. Engring., U. Mich., 1967; JD, Vanderbilt U., 1970. Bar: 1971, U.S. Dist. Ct. (so. dist.) N.Y. 1972, U.S. Ct. Appeals (2d cir.) 1973, U.S. Supreme Ct. 1978. Assoc. Winthrop Stimson, Putnam & Roberts, N.Y.C., 1970-78, ptnr. 1978-84; sr. v.p., mng. dir. Shearson Lehman Bros. Inc., N.Y.C., 1984-85; ptnr. Milbank, Tweed. Hadley & McCloy, N.Y.C., 1985—. Contbr. articles to profl. jours. Fellow Am. Bar Found., ABA (fed. regulation of securities com. bus. law sect. mem. 1981—, chair pub. utility, comms. and transp. law sect. 1997-98, bd. govs. 1998—); mem. Assn. Bar City N.Y. (chmn. nuclear tech. and law com. 1976-77), Internat. Bar Assn. (com. chmn. 1990-94), Alumni Bd. Vanderbilt U. Law Sch. (1987-90), Down Town (N.Y.C.), Canoe Brook Country Club (Summit, N.J.), Park Ave. Club (Florham Park, N.J.). Securities, Public utilities, Mergers and acquisitions. Office: Milbank Tweed Hadley & McCloy 1 Chase Manhattan Plz Fl 47 New York NY 10005-1413

**DUNN, RANDY EDWIN,** lawyer; b. Hutchinson, Kans., Oct. 8, 1954; s. Roy Edwin and Joan Irene (Farney) D.; m. Michelle Renee Sandwith, Dec. 18, 1976 (div. Aug. 1979); 1 child, Brandi Dawn Sandwith; m. Rosalind O'Nita Heiman, Dec. 22, 1990. BA magna cum laude, Wichita State U., 1977; JD, U. Colo., 1983. Bar: Colo. 1983, U.S. Dist. Ct. Colo. 1986. Store and sales mgr. Pop Shoppe, Inc., Wichita, Kans., 1976-77; sales rep. Lifesavers, Inc., Wichita, 1977-80; asst. mgr. Quik Trip, Inc., Wichita, 1980; assoc. McIntyre & Varallo, P.C., Greeley, Colo., 1983-85; pvt. practice law Denver, 1985-87; ptnr. Dean & Dunn, P.C., Denver, 1987-89; assoc. Lau & Choi, P.C., Denver, 1989-90, Baker & Hostetler, Denver, 1991, Hopper & Kanouff, P.C., Denver, 1991-95; pvt. practice law Denver, 1995—. Mem. ABA, Colo. Bar Assn., Denver Bar Assn., Masons. Democrat. General corporate, Communications, General civil litigation. Office: Clanahan Tanner Downing and Knowlton PC 730 17th St Ste 500 Denver CO 80202-3580

**DUNN, ROBERT LAWRENCE,** lawyer; b. Westerly, R.I., Jan. 2, 1938. BA, Cornell U., 1958; JD magna cum laude, Harvard U., 1962. Bar: N.Y. 1962, Calif. 1966, U.S. Dist. Ct. (no. dist.) Calif. 1966, U.S. Ct. Appeals (9th cir.) 1966, U.S. Dist. Ct. (ea. dist.) Calif. 1970, U.S. Supreme Ct. 1984, U.S. Dist. Ct. (cen. dist.) Calif. 1987. Law clk. to cir. judge U.S. Cir. Ct., Hartford, Conn., 1962-63; assoc. Paul, Weiss, Rifkind, Wharton & Garrison, N.Y.C., 1963-65, Bancroft, Avery & McAlister, San Francisco, 1965-71; ptnr. Bancroft & McAlister, San Francisco, 1971-93, Cooper, White & Cooper, San Francisco, 1993—. Author: Recovery of Damages for Lost Profits, 1978, rev. edit., 1998, Recovery of Damages for Fraud, rev. edit., 1995, Expert Witnesses: Law and Practice, 1996; contbr. articles to profl. jours. Mem. planning commn. Town of Corte Madera, Calif. 1974-78, mem. town coun., 1978-84, mayor, 1979, 82; bd. dirs. Merola Opera Program, 1995—, Philharmonia Baroque Orch., San Francisco, 1991-94. 1st lt. U.S. Army, 1958-59. Avocations: travel, scuba diving, opera, lit. General civil litigation, State and local taxation. Office: Cooper White & Cooper 201 California St San Francisco CA 94111-5002

**DUNN, WILLIAM BRADLEY,** lawyer; b. Newark, Dec. 2, 1939; s. Ernest William and Ruth Harriet (Bradley) D.; m. Judy Ann Shepherd, Aug. 2, 1988; children: John, Peter, Brian, Kelly. AB, Muskingum Coll., 1961; JD, U. Mich., 1964. Bar: Mich. 1964. Mem. Clark Hill PLC (formerly Clark, Klein & Beaumont), Detroit, 1964—; lectr. in field. Contbr. articles to legal jours. Mem. ABA (chair sect. real property, probate and trust law 1989-90, mem. ho. of dels. 1990-98, mem. standing com. on professionalism 1993-96, mem. standing com. on ethics and profl. responsibility 1998—), Am. Coll. Real Estate Lawyers (pres. 1983-84), Urban Land Inst., Internat. Assn. Attys. and Exec. Corporate Real Estate. Episcopalian. Real property, Contracts commercial. Home: 6398 Catalpa Ct Troy MI 48098-2231 Office: Clark Hill PLC 500 Woodward Ave Ste 3500 Detroit MI 48226-3435

**DUNNE, GERARD FRANCIS,** lawyer; b. Huntington, N.Y., Aug. 23, 1947; s. Frank and Adele A. (Malerba) D.; m. Judith Ellen Gordon, Dec. 5, 1976; 1 child, Heather Chelsey. B in Engring., Manhattan Coll., 1969; JD, U. Balt., 1974. Bar: D.C. 1974, N.Y. 1974, U.S. Patent Office, U.S. Dist. Ct. (ea. and so. dists.) N.Y. 1976, U.S. Ct. Appeals (fed. cir.) 1982, U.S. Ct. Appeals (2d and 8th cirs.) 1985, U.S. Supreme Ct. 1987. Examiner patents U.S. Patent Office, Washington, 1969-74; assoc. Law Offices of Albert C. Johnston P.C., N.Y.C., 1974-76; assoc. Wyatt, Gerber, Burke & Badie, N.Y.C., 1976-82, ptnr., 1982-94. Mem. ABA, Assn. of Bar of City of N.Y., Fed. Bar Council, Am. Intellectual Property Law Assn. Federal civil litigation, Patent, Trademark and copyright. Home: 89-04 63rd Ave Flushing NY 11374-2815 Office: 156 5th Ave Ste 1223 New York NY 10010-7002

**DUNNILL, WILLIAM CONNOR,** lawyer; b. Murfreesboro, Tenn., May 16, 1968; s. William Arthur and Alice Connor Dunnill; m. Susan Shawner, July 20, 1991; 1 child, John Connor. BA, U. Tex., 1990; MBA, U. Tex., Dallas, 1995; JD, Tex. Wesleyan U., 1995. Bar: Tex., U.S. Dist. Ct. (no. and ea. dists.) Tex. Assoc. Law Office Joel Steed, Dallas, 1996—. State civil litigation, Insurance, Personal injury. Office: Law Office of Joel Steel PC 5910 N Central Expy Ste 650 Dallas TX 75206-5138

**DUPLANTIER, ADRIAN GUY,** federal judge; b. New Orleans, Mar. 5, 1929; s. F. Robert and Amelie (Rivet) D.; m. Sally Thomas, July 15, 1951; children: Adrian G., David L., Thomas, Jeanne M., Louise M., John C. J.D. cum laude, Loyola U., New Orleans, 1949; LLM, U. Va., 1988. Bar: La. 1950, U.S. Supreme Ct. 1954. Pvt. practice law New Orleans, 1950-74; judge Civil Dist. Ct. Parish of Orleans, 1974-78; judge U.S. Dist. Ct., New Orleans, 1978-94, sr. judge, 1994—; part-time prof. code of civil procedure Loyola U., 1951—, lectr. dental jurisprudence, 1960-67, lectr. English dept., 1948-50, chmn. law sch. vis. com., 1995-97; mem. La. State Senate, 1960-74; 1st asst. dist. atty. New Orleans, 1954-56; mem. Jud. Conf. of U.S. Bankruptcy Rules Adv. Com., 1994-96, chmn. 1997—. Editorial bd.: Loyola Law Rev, 1947-48; editor-in-chief, 1948-49. Del. Democratic Nat. Conv., 1964; pres. Associated Cath. Charities New Orleans, Social Welfare Planning Council Greater New Orleans; mem. adv. bd. St. Mary's Dominican Coll., 1970-71, Ursuline Acad., 1968-73, Mt. Carmel Acad., 1965-69; chmn. pres.'s adv. council Jesuit High Sch., 1979—, Boys Hope, 1980—; active Assn. Retarded Children. Recipient Meritorious award New Orleans Assn. Retarded Children, 1965; Gov.'s Cert. of Merit, 1970. Mem. ABA (award 1960), La. Bar Assn., New Orleans Bar Assn., Jud. Conf. of U.S., Order of Coif, Alpha Sigma Nu. Office: US Dist Ct C-205 US Courthouse 500 Camp St New Orleans LA 70130-3313

**DUPLECHIN, D. JAMES,** lawyer; b. Rayne, La., Aug. 1, 1967; s. Kermit Joseph and Neva (Boudreaux) D.; m. Deborah Lynn McEachern, Oct. 13, 1990; children: Ryan James, Andrew David. BS, Troy State U., 1990, MPA, 1991; JD, Birmingham U. Sch. Law, 1996. Bar: Ala. 1997, U.S. Dist. Ct. (mid. dist.) Ala. 1997. Case mgr. Norris & Assocs., Birmingham, 1991-95; intern McCallum & Assocs., Birmingham, 1996; from law clk. to assoc. Powell, Powell & Powell, Crestview, Fla., 1996—; adv. coun. USAF Tactical Air Warfare Ctr., Eglin AFB, Fla., 1988-91, 8th Tactical Fighter Wing, Kunsan Air Base, South Korea, 1987-88. Mem. ABA, Ala. State Bar Assn., ATLA, Acad. Fla. Trial Lawyers. Roman Catholic. Personal injury, Workers' compensation, State civil litigation. Office: Powell Powell & Powell 422 N Main St Crestview FL 32536-3540

**DUPONT, ANTOINETTE L.,** judge; b. N.Y.C., Jan. 10, 1929; d. Albert J. Loiacono and Helen Utano; m. Albert W. Cretella Jr., Aug. 24, 1990; children: Ellen, Antonia, William. AB, Brown U., 1950; JD, Harvard U., 1954; LLD (hon.), Conn. Coll., 1998. Judge Hartford (Conn.) Superior Trial Ct., 1977-83; chief judge Appellate Ct. of Conn., Hartford, 1984-98, sr. judge, 1998—. Office: Appellate Ct of Conn 95 Washington St Hartford CT 06106-4406

**DUPONT, MICHAEL RICHARD,** lawyer; b. Ft. Dix, N.J., Sept. 28, 1961; s. Arnold Richard and Doris Ann (Murphy) DuP. Student, LeMoyne Coll.,

1979-80, Loyola U., Chgo., 1981-83, Loyola U., Rome, 1982; JD, John Marshall Law Sch., 1986. Bar: N.J. 1986, U.S. Dist. Ct. N.J. 1986, U.S. Tax Ct. 1987, U.S. Ct. Appeals (3d cir.) 1987, D.C. 1992. Ptnr. McKenna, Leone & DuPont, Red Bank, N.J., 1986—; pub. defender Belmar, Bradly Beach, South Belmar, Sea Bright, N.J. Sec. Food Bank of Momouth and Ocean Counties. Mem. ABA, N.J. Bar Assn., Monmouth County Bar Assn. (mem. real estate workers compensation and banking com.), Monmouth County Ethics Com. Roman Catholic. Avocations: fishing, backetball, golf, reading. Banking, Personal injury, Bankruptcy. Office: McKenna Leone & DuPont PO Box 610 Red Bank NJ 07701-0610

**DUPONT, RALPH PAUL,** lawyer, educator; b. Fall River, Mass., May 21, 1929; s. Michael William and Gertrude (Murphy) D.; children: Ellen O'Neill, Antonia Chafee, William Albert. AB cum laude with highest honors in Am. Civilization, Brown U., 1951; JD cum laude, Harvard U., 1956. Bar: Conn. 1956, U.S. Supreme Ct. 1967; diplomate Nat. Bd. Trial Advocacy; cert. civil trial specialist, Conn. Assoc. Davies, Hardy & Schenck, N.Y.C., 1956-57; ptnr. Copp & Dupont, New London, Conn., 1957-60; mem. Suisman, Shapiro & Wool, New London, 1961-63; ptnr. Dupont & Dupont (and successor firms), New London, 1963-91; of counsel Durant, Nichols, Houston, Mitchell & Sheahan, Bridgeport, Conn., 1992-97; ptnr. Dupont and Radlauer LLP, New London, Conn., 1997—; instr. Am. history and bus. law Mitchell Coll., New London, 1955, 57-58, trustee, 1991-94; instr. bus. law U. New Haven, 1998; vis. prof. Northeastern U. Sch. Law, 1977-78; vis. prof. law Bridgeport Law Sch. Quinnipiac Coll., 1991-92, We. New Eng. Coll. Law, 1992-94; lectr.-on-law U. Conn. Sch. Law, 1980-86; mem. exec. bd., adj. prof. Quinnipiac Coll. Sch. Law, Hamden, Conn., 1994-96; trustee Anne S.K. Brown Mil. Collection, Brown U., 1988-94, presiding trustee, 1990-92; mem. Conn. Legal Svcs. Adv. Coun., 1980-82; pres. Conn. Acad. Cert. Trial Lawyers, 1998—. Author: Litigation in 1 Attorney's Desk Library, 1994, Dupont On Connecticut Civil Practice, 1998. Mem. bd. edn. New London, Conn., 1959-61; Dem. candidate for Conn. Senate, 1960; trustee U.S. Atlantic Tuna Tournament, 1984-85, pres. 1988-90. Lt. (j.g.) USNR, 1951-53. Named Outstanding Young Man of Yr. Conn. Jr. C. of C., 1960; recipient Disting. Svc. award Greater New London Jr. C. of C., 1960. Fellow Am. Coll. Trust and Estate Counsel; mem. ATLA, ABA, FBA, Conn. Bar Assn., Conn. Bar Found. (bd. dirs. 1975-79), Internat. Acad. Trust and Estate Law, Harvard U. Law Sch. Assn., Harvard Club, Delta Sigma Rho, Kappa Sigma. Roman Catholic. Home: PO Box 710 New London CT 06320-0710 Office: Dupont and Radlauer LLP PO Box 710 165 State St New London CT 06320-6397

**DUPONT, WESLEY DAVID,** lawyer; b. Putnam, Conn., Nov. 1, 1968; s. Thomas Edward Sr. and Patricia Fay Dupont. BA magna cum laude, Brown U., 1992; JD with honors, U. Conn., 1995. Bar: Conn. 1995, N.Y. 1995, U.S. Dist. Ct. Conn. 1995. Assoc. Kelley Drye & Warren LLP, Stamford, Conn., 1995—; sec. Fano Securities LLC, Greenwich, Conn., 1997—, Fano Holdings Corp., 1998—. Contbr. articles to profl. jours. Atty., Stamford Symphony, 1998—. Mem. ABA, Conn. Bar Assn., N.Y. State Bar Assn., The Corp. Bar, Phi Delta Phi. Avocations: fly-fishing, running, golf. Mergers and acquisitions, Securities, General corporate. Office: Kelley Drye & Warren LLP 281 Tresser Blvd Stamford CT 06901-3229

**DUPRIEST, DOUGLAS MILLHOLLEN,** lawyer; b. Ft. Riley, Kans., Dec. 28, 1951; s. Robert White and Barbara Nadine (Millhollen) DuP. AB in Philosophy with high honors, Oberlin Coll., 1974; JD, U. Oreg., 1977. Bar: Oreg. 1977, U.S. Dist. Ct. Oreg. 1977, U.S. Ct. Appeals (9th cir.) 1977. Assoc. Coons & Anderson and predecessors, Eugene, Oreg., 1977-81, Hutchinson, Harrell et al, 1981; ptnr. Hutchinson, Anderson, Cox, Coons & DuPriest and predecessors, 1982—; adj. prof. sch. law U. Oreg., 1986; mem. task forces Wetlands Mgmt., 1988-89, 92-93. Author: (with others) Land Use, 1982, Administrative Law, 1985; contbg. editor Real Estate & Land Use Digest, 1983-86; articles editor, mng. bd. mem. U. Oreg. Law Rev., 1976-77. Bd. dirs. Home Health Agy., Eugene, 1977-79, pres., 1978-79; bd. dirs. Oreg. Environ. Coun., Portland, 1979-84, pres., 1980-81; mem. Lane Econ. Com., 1989-91; chair voters pamphlet com. Eugene City Club, 1993. Recipient Disting. Svc. award Oreg. Environ. Coun., 1988. Mem. Oreg. Bar Assn. (exec. com. real estate and land use sect. 1978-81). General practice, Land use and zoning (including planning), Real property. Home: 225 Dartmoor Dr Eugene OR 97401-6620 Office: Hutchinson Anderson Cox Coons & DuPriest 777 High St Ste 200 Eugene OR 97401-2750

**DUQUETTE, DAVID JOSEPH, JR.,** lawyer; b. Boston, May 12, 1964; s. David Joseph and Joan (Culverhouse) D.; m. Patricia Mae Doykos; 1 child, John Culver. AB, Princeton U., 1986; JD, U. Va., 1991. Bar: N.Y. 1992, Mass. 1992. Assoc. Rogers & Wells, N.Y.C., 1991-96; ptnr. Duquette & Assoc. PC, N.Y.C., 1996—. Mem. Racquet & Tennis Club. Office: Duquette & Assoc PC 34 Chambers St Ste 200 Princeton NJ 08542-3700

**DUQUETTE, DONALD NORMAN,** law educator; b. Manistique, Mich., Apr. 3, 1947; s. Donald Francis and Martha Adeline (Rice) D.; m. Kathy Jo Loudenbeck, June 17, 1967; 1 child, Gail Jean. BA, Mich. State U., 1969; JD, U. Mich., 1974. Bar: Mich. 1975. Children's caseworker Mich. Dept. Social Svcs., Muskegon, 1969-72; asst. prof. pediatrics and human devel. Mich. State U. Coll. Human Medicine, East Lansing, 1975-76; clin. prof., dir. child advocacy law clinic U. Mich., Ann Arbor, 1976—, co-dir. interdisciplinary project on child abuse and neglect, 1979-89, dir. permanency planning legal svcs., 1984—, dir. interdisciplinary grad. edn. in child abuse-neglect, 1986-92, dir. Kellogg child welfare law program, 1995-98; bd. visitors U. Ariz. Sch. of Law, 1995-99; legal cons. U.S. Children's Bur., Pres. Clinton's Initiative on Adoption and Foster Care, 1997-98; bd. dirs. Nat. Assn. Counsel for Children, 1999—. Author: Advocating for the Child, 1990, Michigan Child Welfare Law, 1990, rev. edit., 1994; mem. editl. bd. Child Abuse and Neglect Internat. Jour., 1985-90; conbr. articles to profl. jours. Commr. Washtenaw County Bd. Commrs., 1981-88; bd. dirs. Children's Trust Fund for Prevention of Child Abuse, 1983-85; mem. Permanency Planning Com. Mich. Supreme Ct., 1982-85, Probate Ct. Task Force, 1986-87, Govs. Task Force on Children's Justice, 1992—. Named Citizen of Yr. Huron Valley NASW, Ann Arbor, 1985; recipient Rsch. in Advocacy award Nat. Ct. Apptd. Spl. Advocate Assn., Seattle, 1985, Outstanding Legal Advocacy award Nat. Assn. of Counsel for Children, 1996, Hicks Child Welfare Leadership award Mich. Fedn. Children's Agys., 1998. Mem. Am. Profl. Soc. on Abuse of Children, Mich. State Bar (co-chair Children's Task Force 1993-95). Democrat. Unitarian. Avocations: piano, sailing. Home: 1510 Linwood Ave Ann Arbor MI 48103-3659 Office: U Mich Sch Law Child Advocacy Law Clinic 625 S State St Ann Arbor MI 48109-1215

**DURAN, STANLEY JOHN,** lawyer; b. Balt., Aug. 11, 1953. BS, U. Md., 1975; MBA, Loyola Coll., 1982; JD, William Mitchell Coll., 1987. Bar: Minn. 1987, D.C. 1989, Md. 1989; CPA, Md. Fin. acctg. mgr. Joseph E. Seagram & Sons, Inc., Balt., 1976-79; hotel acctg. mgr. Marriott Corp., Washington, 1979-82; contract adminstrn. mgr. PHH Inc., Hunt Valley, Md., 1982-84; assoc. atty. Hogan & Hartson, Balt., 1988-90; v.p. BEI/Ritz, Bloomington, Minn., 1991-92; shareholder Felhaber, Larson, Fenlon & Vogt, Mpls., 1992—; adj. prof. fin. U. St. Thomas, Mpls. Mem. ABA, AICPA, Nat. Assn. Indsl. and Office Properties, Minn. State Bar Assn., Minn. Soc. CPAs, Hennepin County Bar Assn. Avocation: keeping up with my two sons. Mergers and acquisitions, General corporate, Finance. Office: Felhaber Larson Fenlon and Vogt PA 601 2nd Ave S Ste 4200 Minneapolis MN 55402-4305

**DURAND, JEAN-PAUL,** lawyer, business consultant; b. Olean, N.Y., June 24, 1970. BA, U. Fla., 1992; JD, Stetson U., 1996; postgrad. in MBA program, U. Fla., 1999. Bar: Fla. 1996, U.S. Dist. Ct. (ctrl. dist.) Fla. 1996. Sole practitioner Clearwater, Fla. Mem. Assn. Trial Lawyers of Am., Def. Rsch. Inst., Fla. Def. Lawyers Assn., Hillsborough County Bar Assn., Tampa C. of C. Private international, General corporate, State civil litigation. Home and Office: 309 Venetian Dr Clearwater FL 33755

**DURAND, WHITNEY,** lawyer; b. Chattanooga, Aug. 9, 1942; s. Harry W. and Patricia (Hardy) D.; m. Sarah C. Chrystal, Sept. 16, 1967; children: James T., Stephen C., Sarah W. BA, U. N.C., Chapel Hill, 1964; JD, Harvard U., Cambridge, Mass., 1967. Bar: Tenn. 1967. Assoc. Miller & Martin, Chattanooga, 1967-71, ptnr., 1971-98; mng. dir. Advance Decisions, LLC, 1998—; of counsel Miller & Martin, 1999—. Pres. Chattanooga Symphony and Opera, 1985; candidate U.S. Congress Tenn. 3d Dist., 1987-88, 93-94; dir. United Way, 1986-92, Tonya Meml. Found., 1986—, The Enterprise Fund, 1989-92, Allied Arts Greater Chattanooga, 1990-94, McCallie Sch., 1990-95, Tenn. Indsl. and Agrl. Devel. Commn., 1992-95; mem. fin. coun. Dem. Nat. Com., 1992-94. Democrat. Episcopalian. Avocations: tennis, running, comtemporary fiction. General corporate, Estate planning. Home: 1914 E Brow Rd Signal Mountain TN 37377-3321 Office: Miller & Martin 1000 Volunteer Bldg Chattanooga TN 37402-2289

**DURANT, MARC,** lawyer; b. N.Y.C., Jan. 17, 1947; s. Sidney Irwin and Estelle (Haas) D.; m. Karen Rose Baker, June 9, 1968 (div. 1975); children: Lauren, Elyssa; m. Rita Mary Tatar, Dec. 31, 1979; children: David, Alexander. BS, Cornell U., 1968; JD, Harvard U., 1968-71. Bar: Pa. 1972, U.S. Dist. Ct. (ea. dist.) Pa. 1972, U.S. Supreme Ct. 1980, U.S. Ct. Appeals (3d cir.) 1981, N.Y. 1991. Law clk. U.S. Dist. Ct., Wilmington, Del., 1971-72; assoc. Schnader, Harrison, Segal & Lewis, Phila., 1972-75; asst. U.S. Atty. U.S. Dept. Justice, Phila., 1975-77; dep. chief criminal divsn.v. U.S. Atty.'s Office, Phila., 1977-81; ptnr. Durant and Durant, Phila., 1981—. Mem. ABA, FBA, Nat. Assn. Criminal Def. Lawyers, Pa. Bar Assn., Phila. Bar Assn. Federal civil litigation, Criminal. Office: Durant & Durant 325 Chestnut St Philadelphia PA 19106-2614

**DURANTE, CHARLES JOSEPH,** lawyer, sportswriter; b. Phila., Oct. 26, 1951; m. Janice Floyd, Aug. 24, 1985. BA with honors, Haverford Coll., 1973; JD, Villanova U., 1977, LLM, 1983. Bar: Del. 1977, Pa. 1980, U.S. Dist. Ct. Del. 1979, U.S. Ct. Appeals (3rd cir.) 1979, U.S. Dist. Ct. Pa. 1996. Sportswriter Phila. Inquirer, 1974-80; dept. atty. gen. State of Del., 1978-81; asst. solicitor City of Wilmington, Del., 1981-85; assoc. Richards, Layton & Finger, Wilmington, 1985-88; ptnr. Connolly, Bove, Lodge & Hutz, 1988—. Parliamentarian Del. Dem. Com., 1990—. Mem. Broadcasters Assn. (pres. 1986-87, sec., treas. 1987—), Pen and Pencil Club (Phila.). Democrat. Taxation, general, Probate, Contracts commercial. Office: Connolly Bove Lodge & Hutz 1220 N Market St Fl 10 Wilmington DE 19801-2552

**DURANTE, JAMES PETER,** lawyer; b. N.Y.C., July 17, 1914; s. Salvatore and Grace (Rocco) D.; m. Joan Marilyn Durante (dec.). LLB, St. John's U., Queens, N.Y., 1938. Bar: N.Y. 1939, U.S. Dist. Ct. (so. dist.) N.Y. 1947, U.S. Supreme Ct. 1956. Ptnr. Reavis & McGrath, 1962-80, Fulbright & Jaworski, N.Y.C., 1990—; mediator Citizen Dispute Settlement Program, Sarasota, Fla., 1983—; arbitrator Better Business Coun., Sarasota, Fla.; testified as a labor arbitrator, mediation expert U.S. Congress Judiciary Com. Author: Law of Sports, 1950. With USMC, 1942-43. Mem. ABA (labor arbitration com.). Alternative dispute resolution, Labor. Home: 565 Longboat Club Rd Longboat Key FL 34228-3822

**DURBIN, RICHARD LOUIS, JR.,** lawyer; b. Gary, Ind., Dec. 23, 1955; s. Richard Louis and Carolyn Martha (Bohrer) D.; m. Diana Cabaza Durbin, June 2, 1979; children: Louis Eloy, Laura Elena. Student, Rutgers U., 1973-75; BA, U. Chgo., 1977; JD, U. Tex., 1980. Bar: Tex. 1980. Law clk. to presiding judge U.S. Dist. Ct. (we. dist.) Tex., San Antonio, 1980-82; assoc. Susman, Godfrey & McGowan, Houston, 1982-83; asst. U.S. atty. Organized Crime Drug Enforcement Task Force U.S. Atty.'s Office (we. dist.), San Antonio, 1983-88, chief criminal sect., 1988-90, 98—, chief narcotics sect., 1990-92, chief appellate sect., 1992-98; chief Organized Crime Drug Enforcement Task Force U.S. Atty.'s Office (we. dist.), 1997-98; adj. prof. law St. Mary's U. Sch. of Law, 1995—; instr. U.S. Atty. Gen. Adv. Inst., Washington, 1987-99. Editor Tex. U. Law Rev., 1979-80. Interviewer U. Chgo. Alumni Schs. Com., San Antonio, 1984-97. Recipient Dir.'s award Tex. Dept. Pub. Safety, Austin, 1985. Mem. Tex. State Bar, Coll. State Bar Tex., Order of Coif, Phi Beta Kappa. Office: US Attys Office 601 NW Loop 410 Ste 600 San Antonio TX 78216-5512

**DURGOM-POWERS, JANE ELLYN,** lawyer; b. Denver, Sept. 1, 1948; d. John Albert and Rosemarie (Scordino) Durgom. BSIM in Econs., Purdue U., 1971; JD, Georgetown U., 1974. Bar: N.Y. 1975, U.S. Dist. Ct. (so. dist.) N.Y. 1975, U.S. Ct. Appeals (2d cir.) 1975, U.S. Supreme Ct. 1978, Ill. 1981, D.C. 1987, U.S. Dist. Ct. (no. dist.) Ill. 1989, Wyo. 1994. Asst. dist. atty. N.Y.C., 1974-76; spl. asst. narcotics prosecutor Office of Spl. Prosecution, N.Y.C., 1976-78; atty. GM Corp., N.Y.C., 1978-81; gen. counsel Genway Corp., Chgo., 1981-83, Nissan Motor Acceptance Corp., Carson, Calif., 1983-87; cons. Nissan Motor Corp., Ltd., Carson, 1987-88; ptnr. Williams and McCarthy law firm, Rockford, Ill., 1988-97; pres., gen. counsel Antel Internat., Inc., 1997-98; pres., CEO Warrne Industries, 1998—; bd. dirs. Internat. Sch. Rock Valley Coll., Rockford. Co-author: (books) Federal Regulation of Consumer Credit, 1981, Jury Instructions for Civil-Criminal RICO Cases. Chosen by Rockford mag. as one of city's most interesting people, 1989; recipient cert. Spl. U.S. Congressional Recognition for Outstanding & Invaluable Cmty. Svc., 1995, Nat. Humanitarian Svc. award to Am. MIA's and POW's of the SE Asia War Nat. League of Families, 1995. Mem. ABA (v.p. RICO subcom. 1974-75), N.Y. Bar Assn., Washington D.C. Bar Assn., Ill. Bar Assn., Rockford C. of C. (bd. dirs.). Avocations: collecting art, antiques. Private international, General corporate, Contracts commercial.

**DURHAM, BARBARA,** state supreme court justice; b. 1942. BSBA, Georgetown U.; JD, Stanford U. Bar: Wash. 1968. Former judge Wash. Superior Ct., King County; judge Wash. Ct. Appeals; assoc. justice Wash. Supreme Ct., 1985—, chief justice, 1995-99, justice, 1999—. Office: Wash Supreme Ct Temple of Justice PO Box 40929 Olympia WA 98504-0929

**DURHAM, CHRISTINE MEADERS,** state supreme court justice; b. L.A., Aug. 3, 1945; d. William Anderson and Louise (Christensen) Meaders; m. George Homer Durham II, Dec. 29, 1966; children: Jennifer, Meghan, Troy, Melinda, Isaac. A.B., Wellesley Coll., 1967; J.D., Duke U., 1971. Bar: N.C. 1971, Utah 1974. Sole practice law Durham, N.C., 1971-73; instr. legal medicine Duke U., Durham, 1971-73; adj. prof. law Brigham Young U., Provo, Utah, 1973-78; ptnr. Johnson, Durham & Moxley, Salt Lake City, 1974-78; judge Utah Dist. Ct., 1978-82; assoc. justice Utah Supreme Ct., 1982—. Pres. Women Judges Fund for Justice, 1987-88. Fellow Am. Bar Found.; mem. ABA (edn. com. appellate judges' conf.), Nat. Assn. Women Judges (pres. 1986-87), Utah Bar Assn., Am. Law Inst. (coun. mem.), Nat. Ctr. State Courts (bd. dirs.), Am. Inns of Ct. Found. (trustee). Office: Utah Supreme Ct PO Box 140210 Salt Lake City UT 84114-0210

**DURHAM, JOHN,** prosecutor. Dep. U.S. atty. State of Conn., New Haven. Office: Conn Fin Ctr 157 Church St Ste 23D New Haven CT 06510-2100*

**DURHAM, J(OSEPH) PORTER, JR.,** lawyer, educator; b. Nashville, May 11, 1961. AB in Polit. Sci. and History cum laude, Duke U., 1982, JD, 1985. Bar: Tenn. 1985, Md. 1988. Ptnr. Miller & Martin, Chattanooga, 1990-96; ptnr. Baker, Donelson, Bearman & Caldwell, Chattanooga, 1997—, chmn. corp. dept., 1998—; adj. prof. dept. acctg. and fin. U. Tenn., Chattanooga, 1992-98; participant Russian tax code adv. group. Editor Duke Law Mag., 1984-85; contbr. articles to legal pubs. Mem. Balt. Citizens Planning and Housing Assn., 1988-90; career edn. spkr. Explorer Scout program Boy Scouts Am., 1985, 88, 90-92; mem., v.p. bd. dirs., chmn. fin. com. Waxter Ctr. Found., 1989-91; mem., sec. bd. dirs. Assn. for Visual Artists, 1993-96; trustee Good Shepherd Sch., 1992-93; chmn. spl. mgmt. com. Nashville Rehab. Hosp., 1995; trail maintenance vol. U.S. Pk. Svc., 1993-95; mem. adv. com. Chattanooga State Tech. C.C. Recipient Outstanding Svc. award Waxter Ctr. Found., 1991. Mem. ABA, Tenn. Bar Assn., Md. Bar Assn., Duke U. Law Sch. Alumni Assn. (bd. dirs. 1994-97), Duke U. Gen. Alumni Assn. (bd. dirs. 1986-92, exec. com. 1989-92). General corporate, Mergers and acquisitions, Securities. Home: 600 W Brow Rd Lookout Mountain TN 37350-1118 Office: Baker Donelson Bearman & Caldwell 1800 Republic Ctr 633 Chestnut St Chattanooga TN 37450-4000

**DURHAM, RICHARD MONROE,** lawyer; b. Winston-Salem, N.C., July 7, 1954; s. George Washington and Martha Rebecca (Teague) D.; m. Tina Marie Tunks, Dec. 1, 1984; children: Eric Patrick, Sarah Kathryn. BA with honors, U. N.C., 1976, JD, 1979. Bar: N.C. 1982, U.S. Dist. Ct. (ea. and mid. dists.) N.C., 1982, U.S. Ct. Appeals (4th cir.) 1983, U.S. Supreme Ct. 1986, U.S. Dist. Ct. (we. dist.) N.C., 1992. Legal asst. Robert A. Ades & Assocs., PC, Springfield, Va., 1980-82; assoc. H. Weldon Lloyd, Esq., Henderson, N.C., 1982-83, Jenkins, Lucas, Babb and Rabil, Winston-Salem, 1983-85, James J. Booker, PA, Winston-Salem, 1985-87; sole practice Winston-Salem, 1987—; instr. Nat. Bus. Inst., Inc. Bd. trustees Home Moravian Ch. Mem. N.C. Bar Assn., N.C. Acad. of Trial Lawyers, N.C. Coll. of Advocacy, ATLA, Ardmore Comty. Club, U. N.C.-Charlotte Alumni Assn. (bd. govs.), Phi Delta Phi (exchequer 1977-79). Democrat. Avocations: basketball, tennis, music. State civil litigation, Personal injury, Workers' compensation. Home: 2313 Walker Ave Winston Salem NC 27103-4331 Office: 8 W 3rd St Ste 360 Winston Salem NC 27101-3923

**DURHAM, ROBERT DONALD, JR.,** state supreme court justice; b. Lynwood, Calif., May 10, 1947; s. Robert Donald Durham and Rosemary Constance (Brennan) McKelvey; m. Linda Jo Rollins, Aug. 29, 1970; children: Melissa Brennan, Amy Elizabeth. BA, Whittier Coll., 1969; JD, U. Santa Clara, 1972; LLM in the Judicial Process, U. Va., 1998. Bar: Oreg. 1972, Calif. 1973, U.S. Dist. Ct. Oreg. 1974, U.S. Ct. Appeals (9th cir.) 1980, U.S. Supreme Ct. 1987. Law clk. Oreg. Supreme Ct., Salem, 1972-74; ptnr. Bennett & Durham, Portland, Oreg., 1974-91; assoc. judge Oreg. Ct. Appeals, Salem, 1991-94; assoc. justice Oreg. Supreme Ct., Salem, 1994—; mem. adv. com. to Joint Interim Judiciary Com., 1984-86; chair Oreg. Commn. on Adminstrv. Hearings, 1988-89; faculty Nat. Jud. Coll., Reno, Nev., 1992; mem. Case Disposition Benchmarks Com., 1992-93, Coun. on Ct. Procedures, 1992-93, 95—; mem. Oreg. Rules of Appellate Procedure Com., 1998—. Mem. ACLU Lawyer's Com., Eugene and Portland, Oreg., 1978-91. Recipient award for civil rights litigation ACLU of Oreg., 1988, Ed Elliott Human Rights award Oreg. Edn. Assn., Portland, 1990. Mem. Am. Acad. Appellate Lawyers (ninth cir. screening com. 1991—, rules com. 1994, co-chair appellate cts. liaison com. 1994), Oreg. Appellate Judges Assn. (pres. 1996-97), Oreg. State Bar (chair labor law sect. 1983-84, adminstrv. law com. govt. law sect. 1986), Willamette Valley Inns of Ct. (master of bench, team leader 1994—). Office: Oreg Supreme Ct 1163 State St Salem OR 97310-1331

**DURHAM, SIDNEY DOWN,** lawyer; b. Detroit, Dec. 27, 1943; s. Robert Harris and Mary Louise (Edwards) D.; m. Julia Crane; 1 child, Emily Bartlett Crane Durham. BA, U. Mich., 1966; JD, Wayne State U., 1969. Bar: Mich. 1969, U.S. Dist. Ct. (we. dist.) Mich. 1969. Ptnr. Butler, Durham & Willoughby, Kalamazoo, Mich., 1989—. Fellow Am. Acad. Matrimonial Lawyers, Mich. State Bar Found.; mem. ABA (family law sect.), State Bar Mich. (family law, real property and probate law sects.), Fedn. of Fly Fishermen, Ducks Unltd. (chmn. S.W. Mich. chpt., sponsor), Safari Club Internat. Episcopalian. Avocations: horseback riding, duck hunting, trout fishing, big game hunting. General corporate, Family and matrimonial, Estate planning. Home: 6820 N 37th St Richland MI 49083-9687 Office: Butler Durham & Willoughby 202 N Riverview Dr Kalamazoo MI 49004-1310

**DURHAM, WILLIAM ANDREW,** lawyer; b. Paris, Tex., Mar. 21, 1956; s. James David and Ruby (Bartlett) D.; m. Susan Margaret Gallagher, Sept. 30, 1982; children: Andrew Gallagher, Margaret Rudyard. BA cum laude, Tex. A&M U., 1978; JD cum laude, U. Houston, 1981. Bar: Tex. 1981, U.S. Dist. Ct. (so. and ea. dists.) Tex. 1981, U.S. Ct. Appeals (5th cir.) 1982, U.S. Dist. Ct. (no. dist.) Tex. 1983, U.S. Supreme Ct. 1990. Assoc. Eastham, Watson, Dale & Forney, Houston, 1981-84, ptnr., 1984-98, mng. ptnr., 1998—. Bd. dirs. Casa Juan Diego, Houston, 1986—. Mem. State Bar Tex., Houston Bar Assn., Maritime Law Assn. Republican. Episcopalian. Admiralty, Federal civil litigation, Insurance. Office: Eastham Watson Dale & Forney Niels Esperson Bldg 20th 808 Travis St Houston TX 77002-5706

**DURIC, NICHOLAS M.,** lawyer; b. Chgo., Mar. 16, 1960; s. Marko and Joka Duric; m. Milena Duric, June 14, 1986; children: Mark, Marissa, Nina. BBA, Loyola U., 1982, JD, 1985. Bar: U.S. Dist. Ct. (no. dist.) Ill. 1985, U.S. Ct. Appeals (7th cir.) 1994. Assoc. Clausen Miller, Chgo., 1985-88, Fagel and Haber, Chgo., 1988-89; gen. counsel United Savs. of Am., Chgo., 1984-92; prin. Law Offices of Nicholas M. Duric, Chgo., 1992—; chmn. U.S. Dept. of Edn. First Bd., Washington, 1991-93; bd. dirs. Ill. Real Esate Appraisal Bd., Springfield. Real property, Banking, General civil litigation. Office: 4849 N Milwaukee Ave Chicago IL 60630-2171

**DURIE, JACK FREDERICK, JR.,** lawyer; b. Lexington, Ky., Jan. 25, 1944. BS, U. Ky., 1966, JD, 1969. Bar: Ky. 1969, Fla. 1969, U.S. Ct. Mil. Appeals 1970, U.S. Dist. Ct. (so. dist.) Fla. 1974, U.S. Ct. Appeals (5th cir.) 1974, U.S. Dist. Ct. (mid. dist.) Fla. 1978, U.S. Ct. Appeals (11th cir.) 1982, U.S. Supreme Ct. 1975; bd. cert. civil trial lawyer, Fla.; cert. mil. judge 1971. Pvt. practice Orlando, Fla., 1979—. Capt. JAGC, USAF, 1970-74. Mem. ABA, Ky. Bar Assn., Fla. Bar Assn. (chmn. aviation and space law com. 1978-79, vice chmn. 1980-81), Orange County Bar Assn., Dade County Bar Assn. (bd. dirs. 1976-78, pres. young lawyers sect. 1978-79), Assn. Trial Lawyers Am., Acad. Fla. Trial Lawyers, Lawyer-Pilots Bar Assn., Lances, Men's Jr. Hon. Fraternity, Nat. Acctg. Hon., Beta Alpha Psi, Sigma Chi, Phi Delta Phi. Office: 1000 E Robinson St Orlando FL 32801-2024

**DURIO, WILLIAM HENRY,** lawyer; b. Crowley, La., May 15, 1947; s. Lennard Edwin and Helen Hazel (Miller) D.; m. Rita Jane Putch, June 6, 1971; children: Matthew, Caroline. BS, U. Southwestern La., 1970; JD, La. State U., 1975. Sole practice Lafayette, La., 1976-78, 83-89; ptnr. Hughes Durio & Grant, Lafayette, 1978-83; gen. counsel Global Industries Ltd., Maurice, La., 1990-91; sole practice Lafayette, 1991—; adj. prof. mineral law U. Southwestern La., Lafayette, 1983-84. With U.S. Army, 1970-72. Mem. La. State Bar Assn., Lafayette Town House Club, Order of Troubadours. Avocations: running, fishing, scuba diving, hunting, traveling. Oil, gas, and mineral, Natural resources, Probate. Home: 608 Claymore Dr Lafayette LA 70503-4020

**DURKIN, ALBERT EUGENE,** lawyer; b. Evergreen Park, Ill., June 5, 1952; s. Albert and Geraldine M. (Ryan) D.; m. Anita M. Nosmar, Apr. 2, 1977 (div. May 1982); m. Kathleen L. Sieber, Oct. 7, 1983; children: Jessica, Alison. BA, Lewis U., Romeoville, Ill., 1974; JD, DePaul U., 1977. Bar: Ill. 1977, U.S. Dist. Ct. (no. dist.) Ill. 1977. Atty. Carr & O'Rourke Assocs., Chgo., 1977-80, A. Denison Weaver Ltd., Chgo., 1980-82; pvt. practice, Chgo., 1982-84; ptnr. Alfieri, Abbene, Durkin & Dailey, Chgo., 1984-90, Grotefeld, Johnson, Pekola & Durkin, Chgo., 1990-91; assoc. Nolan Law Group, Chgo., 1991—. Mem. adv. bd. Mercy Hosp. Chgo., 1994—. Mem. ATLA, Ill. Bar Assn., Ill. Trial Lawyers Assn., Chgo. Bar Assn., Lewis U. Alumni Assn. (pres. 1983-85). Roman Catholic. Avocations: his home and family. Aviation, Personal injury, Product liability. Office: Nolan Law Group 20 N Clark St Chicago IL 60602-4109

**DU ROCHER, JAMES HOWARD,** lawyer; b. Racine, Wis., Aug. 4, 1945; s. Howard James and Frances Ann (Rasmussen) Du R.; m. Rosalyn Ann, Sept. 2, 1972; children: Jessica Lynn, James Howard, Emily Rosalyn. Student, U.S. Mil. Acad., 1963-65, Ripon Coll., 1965-66; JD, U. Wis., 1969. Bar: Wis. Assoc. Stewart, Peyton, Crawford & Josten, Racine, 1969-78; pres. Du Rocher, Murphy, Murphy & Schroeder, S.C., Racine, 1978-96, Du Rocher Law Offices, S.C., 1996—; bd. dirs., Careers Industries, Inc., pres., 1988-89. Bd. dirs. Racine Area United Way, 1973-79, v.p., 1977-79; chmn. Park Trails Dist. Boy Scouts Am., 1979-82; bd. dirs. Careers for Retarded Adults, Inc., 1982, pres., 1983, 90; bd. dirs. A-Center of Racine, Inc., 1978-85, pres., 1985; bd. dirs. Careers Industries Support Found., Inc., 1993—; deacon Atonement Luth. Ch., Racine, 1978-81; mem. adv. bd. Children's Svc. Soc. Wis. Capt. JAGC, U.S. Army, 1969-73. Decorated Bronze Star. Mem. State Bar Wis., Mason, Rotary (pres. Racine-West club 1998-99). General corporate, Probate, Real property. Home: 5531 Whirlaway Ln Racine WI 53402-1865 Office: 827 Main St PO Box 1406 Racine WI 53401-1406

**DURONI, CHARLES EUGENE,** retired lawyer, food products executive; b. McCune, Kans., Apr. 9, 1933; s. Charley S. and Dorothy M. D.; m. Charlene D. White, Feb. 18, 1978; children: Renee, Ashley, Michele, Lance. B.S., U. Kans., 1955; LL.B., U. Wis., 1962. Bar: Wis. 1962, Pa. 1979, U.S. Supreme Ct. 1979, U.S. Dist. Ct. (mid. dist.) Pa. 1980, U.S. Ct. Appeals (3d cir.) 1982. Staff atty. FTC, 1962-64; staff counsel Rockwell Internat. Co., Pitts., 1964-68; sr. atty. H.J. Heinz Co., Pitts., 1968-77; sr. assoc. counsel, asst. gen. counsel Hershey (Pa.) Foods Corp., 1977-79, v.p., gen. counsel, 1979-93; ret., 1993; bd. dirs. U.S. Trademark Assn., 1972-76; trustee Food & Drug Law Inst. Served with USAF, 1955-59. Mem. ABA (com. corp. law depts., com. corp. counsel), Wis. Bar Assn., Pa. Bar Assn., Lancaster County Bar Assn., Am. Law Inst., Atlantic Legal Found., The Bus. Roundtable (lawyers steering com.), Cen. Pa. Corp. Lawyers Group, Grocery Mfrs. Am. (legal com.), Sigma Chi, Phi Delta Phi, Met. Club (N.Y.C.). General corporate, General practice. Home: 928 Forest Rd Lancaster PA 17601-2203 *Of the highest importance in the legal and business world is the exercise of imaginative good judgment consistently exercised with a sensitivity to others.*

**DUROSE, RICHARD ARTHUR,** lawyer; b. Cleve., Nov. 6, 1937; s. Arthur H. and Helen G. (Doran) DuR.; m. Nancy Ann Hunter, Aug. 9, 1959; children: Steven A., Carolyn M., Douglas H. AA, Graceland Coll., 1957; BA, Ohio State U., 1959, JD, 1962. Bar: Ohio 1962, Fla. 1988. Atty., ptnr. Foley & Lardner, Orlando, 1990—. Contbr. articles to profl. jours. Mem. ABA, Fla. Bar Assn., Ohio Bar Assn., Def. Rsch. Inst., Quest, Inc. (pres. 1993-94),Isleworth Country Club. Democrat. Avocations: tennis, golf. Labor. Office: Foley & Lardner 111 N Orange Ave Ste 1800 Orlando FL 32801-2386

**DUROSS, CHARLES EDWARD, IV,** lawyer; b. N.Y.C., Nov. 23, 1970; s. Charles E. Duross (dec.) and Mary M. Walsh. BA, U. Mich., 1993, JD, 1996. Bar: Mich. 1996, U.S. Dist. Ct. (we. dist.) Mich. 1997, U.S. Ct. Internat. Trade 1997, U.S. Dist. Ct. D.C. 1999. Law clk. Law Offices of Edward C. Bou, P.C., Washington, 1993-94; summer law clk. hon. Nicholas S. Nunzio Superior Ct. D.C., Washington, 1994; assoc. Kirkland & Ellis, Washington, 1996—. Vol. atty. Lawyers Com. for Human Rights, Washington, 1996—; mem. Dem. Leadership Coun., Washington, 1998—; bd. mem. Choice in Dying, Washington, 1998—. Mem. ABA, State Bar Mich., D.C. Bar, Inc. Soc. Irish-Am. Lawyers, Ancient Order Hibernians. Roman Catholic. Avocations: jogging, bowling, football, hockey. Product liability, General civil litigation, Immigration, naturalization, and customs. Office: Kirkland & Ellis 655 15th St NW Ste 1200 Washington DC 20005-5793

**DURR, MALCOLM DANIEL,** lawyer; b. Bond County, Ill., Apr. 22, 1917; s. Eckard Karol and Bertha (Mitchell) D.; children: Franklin Mitchell, Bradford Karol, Christopher Hubbard. BA, U. Ill., 1938, LLB, JSD, 1940. Bar: Ill. 1940, U.S. Dist. Ct. (so. dist.) Ill. 1940). Pvt. practice Alton, Ill., 1940—; counsel Smith, Wesson & Fiocchi, Alton, 1970-73; atty. City of Alton, 1940-41, corp. counselor, 1949-53; asst. state's atty. Madison County, Ill., 1952-56. Maj. USAAF, 1941-51. Decorated DFC (4), Air medals (5), Croix DeGuerre and Etoile D'Argent, France, 1947; recipient Commemorative medal 50th Ann. of WW II, Russia, 1998. Mem. Madison County Bar Assn., Masons. Contracts commercial, General corporate, Estate planning. Office: 307 Henry St Ste 415 Alton IL 62002-6326

**DURRETT, JAMES FRAZER, JR.,** lawyer; b. Atlanta, Mar. 23, 1931; s. James Frazer and Cora Frazer (Morton) D.; m. Lucretia McPherson, June 9, 1956; children: James Frazer III, William McPherson, Lucretia Heston Miller, Thomas Ratcliffe. AB, Emory U., 1952; postgrad., Princeton U., 1952-53; LLB cum laude, Harvard U., 1956. Bar: Ga. 1955. Ptnr. Alston & Bird (and predecessor firm), Atlanta, 1956-97, retired, 1997; adj. prof. Emory U. Law Sch., 1961-77. Trustee Student Aid Found., The Howard Sch. Mem. Am. Law Inst. (adv. estate and gift tax project, restatement, second. property, Fed. Income Tax project), Capital City Club, Harvard Club (Atlanta). Presbyterian. Estate planning, General corporate, Taxation, general. Home: 3483 Ridgewood Rd NW Atlanta GA 30327-2417 Office: Alston & Bird 1 Atlantic Ctr 1201 W Peachtree St NW Ste 4200 Atlanta GA 30309-3424

**DURST, ROBERT JOSEPH, II,** lawyer; b. Pitts., Jan. 23, 1943; s. Robert J. and Catherine (Thomas) D.; m. Sandra A. Cattani; children—Thomas Sandberg, Eric Francis. B.A., Gettysburg Coll., 1964; J.D., Villanova U., 1967. Bar: Pa. 1967, N.J. 1968, U.S. Dist. Ct. (we. dist.) Pa. 1967, U.S. Dist. Ct. (N.J.) 1968, U.S. Supreme Ct. 1973. Corp. staff atty. Alcoa, Pitts., 1967; assoc. Herr & Fisher, Flemington, N.J., 1967-76; ptnr. Bernhard, Durst & Dilts, Flemington, 1976-89, Stark & Stark, Princeton, N.J., 1989—; board cert. matrimonial atty. N.J. Supreme Ct., 1982—; lectr., author on divorce and family law. With USMC, 1960-64. Fellow Am. Acad. Matrimonial Lawyers (pres. N.J. chpt. 1998-99); mem. ABA, Am. Trial Lawyers Assn., N.J. Bar Assn. (former mem. exec. com. family law sect.), Hunterdon County Bar Assn., Mercer County Bar Assns., Am. Coll. Family Trial Lawyers (diplomate). Family and matrimonial. Home: 28 Marvin Ct Lawrenceville NJ 08648-2112 Office: Stark & Stark PO Box 5315 Princeton NJ 08543-5315

**DUSHMAN, LOWELL EDWARD,** lawyer; b. Chgo., Nov. 22, 1932; s. Gabriel and Augustine (Maille) D.; m. Margaret Rudy, June 25, 1955; children: Laurie, Susan, Richard. BA, So. Meth. U., 1954, JD, 1956. Bar: Tex. 1956, U.S. Dist. Ct. (no., ea., dists.) Tex., U.S. Ct. Appeals (5th cir.), U.S. Supreme Ct. Assoc. Elmo Irby & Baylor Brown, Ft. Worth, 1956-59; ptnr. Ramfield & Dushman, Ft. Worth, 1960-65; sole practice Ft. Worth, 1965-70; assoc. Dushman & Denbow, Ft. Worth, 1970-71; ptnr. Dushman & Friedman P.C., Ft. Worth, 1984-98; sole practitioner Ft. Worth, 1972-83, 99—. Trustee Melvin Belli Found., Ft. Worth. Mem. ABA, Assn. Trial Lawyers Am., State Bar of Tex., Tarrant County Bar Assn., Tex. Trial Lawyers Assn., Am. Bd Trial Advocacy (v.p. 1988, pres. 1989), Ft. Worth Tarrant County Trial Lawyers (v.p. 1968, dir. 1968-74, 97-99), Elks (exalted ruler Ft. Worth chpt. 1965-66). Avocations: boating, swimming, reading, ranching. Personal injury, Alternative dispute resolution, Insurance. Office: Lowell E Dushman 1300 Summit Ave Ste 700 Fort Worth TX 76102-4424

**DUSSAULT, WILLIAM LEONARD ERNEST,** lawyer; b. New Westminster, B.C., Can., May 9, 1947; came to U.S., 1960; s. Eugene Leo and Louise (Hobbs) D.; m. Kate Stitt, Jan. 19, 1999; 1 child, Amy Louise. BA, U. Wash., 1969, JD, 1972. Bar: Wash. 1972, U.S. Dist. Ct. (we. dist.) Wash. 1973, U.S. Supreme Ct. 1982. Ptnr., prin. Law Offices of William L.E. Dussault P.S., Seattle, 1972-84; sole practice Seattle, 1984—; adj. prof. U. Wash. Sch. Law, dept. spl. edn. Cen. Wash. U.; mem. faculty U. Wash. Sch. Nursing; guest lectr. U. Oreg., Seattle U.; judge pro-tempore Seattle Mcpl. Ct.; cons. Guardian, Advocacy and Protective Services Program, Oreg., supt. of pub. instruction, devel. disabilities planning council, protection and advocacy agy., Assn. for Retarded Citizens, Devel. Diabilities Residential Service Assn., Coalition for Spl. Edn. State of Wash., Assn. Retarded Citizens, div. mental health State of Oreg., Devel. Disabilities Council State of Mont., Dept. Edn. States of N.D. and Kans., Protection Advocacy Agy. State of Tenn., Northwest Assn. Rehab. Industries. Mem. Editorial bd. The Assn. for the Severely Handicapped; author: drafted legislation concerning edn. rights of the handicapped; conbr. articles to profl. jours. Counsel The Assn. for the Severely Handicapped; bd. dirs. trustee Found. for the Handicapped; former mem. Wash. Spl. Edn. Commn., Wash. State Legis. Rev. Com. Spl. Edn., Gov.'s Com. on Employment of the Handicapped, Wash. State Human Rights Commn. Adv. Council for the Physically, Mentally and Sensory Handicapped; vol. atty. Wash. Assn. for Persons with Disabilities; vol. Wash. State Spl. Olympics; bd. dirs. Wash. State Disabilities Polit. Action Com. Served to capt. USAR, 1967-75. Mem. ABA (family law com. on mental disability, cons. to guardianship/limited guardianship report 1981) , Wash. Bar Assn. (civil rights com.), Seattle-King County Bar Assn. Administrative and regulatory, Probate, Mental health. Office: 219 E Galer St Seattle WA 98102-3730

**DUTILE, FERNAND NEVILLE,** law educator; b. Lewiston, Maine, Feb. 15, 1940; s. Wilfred Joseph and Lauretta Blanche (Cote) D.; m. Brigid Dooley, Apr. 4, 1964; children: Daniel, Patricia. AB, Assumption Coll., 1962; JD, U. Notre Dame, 1965. Bar: Maine 1965. Atty. U.S. Dept. Justice, Washington, 1965-66; prof. law Cath. U. Am., Washington, 1966-71, U. Notre Dame Law Sch., Ind., 1971—; bd. dirs. Ind. Lawyers Commn., Indpls., 1975-85, Legal Services of No. Ind., South Bend, 1975-83; dir. South Bend Work Release Ctr., 1973-75, Ind. Criminal Law Study Commn., 1991—. Editor: Legal Education and Lawyer Competency, 1981; author: Sex, Schools and the Law, 1986; co-editor: Early Childhood Intervention and Juvenile Delinquency, 1982; The Prediction of Criminal Violence, 1987; co-author: State and Campus, 1984. Democrat. Roman Catholic.

**DUTKO, MICHAEL EDWARD,** lawyer; b. Memphis, Jan. 18, 1954; s. Edward James and Norma Dean (Sparks) D.; m. Bettie Ballowe, Mar. 14, 1981; children: Michael, Christina, Ashley. BA, Biscayne Coll., 1978; JD, Nova U., 1984. Police officer, detective Ft. Lauderdale (Fla.) Police Dept., 1976-81; pros., asst. state atty. Broward State Atty.'s Office, Ft. Lauderdale, 1984-86; assoc. Kay & Bogenschutz, P.A., Ft. Lauderdale, 1986-90; ptnr. Kay, Bogenschutz & Dutko, Ft. Lauderdale, 1990-92, Bogenschutz & Dutko, P.A., Ft. Lauderdale, 1992—. Mem. Broward Assn. Criminal Def. Lawyers. Democrat. Roman Catholic. Avocations: golf, boxing, motorcycles. Criminal. Office: Bogenschutz & Dutko PA 600 S Andrews Ave Ste 500 Fort Lauderdale FL 33301-2851

**DUTTON, CLARENCE BENJAMIN,** lawyer; b. Pitts., May 31, 1917; s. Clarence Benjamin and Lillian (King) D.; m. Marian Jane Stevens, June 21, 1941; children: Victoria Lynn Dutton Sheehan, Barbara King Dutton Morgan. BS with distinction, Ind. U., 1938, JD with high distinction, 1940, LLD, 1970. Bar: Ind. 1940. Instr. bus. law Ind. U. Sch. Bus., 1940-41; atty. E.I. duPont de Nemours & Co., Inc., Wilmington, Del., 1941-43; asst. prof. law Ind. U. Sch. Law, 1946-47; pvt. practice, Indpls., 1947—; bd. dirs. Sarkes Tarzian, Inc.; mem. Ind. Jud. Study Commn., 1965-74; regional adv. group Ind. U. Sch. Medicine, 1966-75; mem., sec. Ind. Civil Code Study Commn., 1967-73; mem. Ind. Commn. on Uniform State Laws, 1970—, chmn., 1980-91, life mem., 1991. Author: (bus. law sect.) Chemical Business Handbook, 1954; contbr. articles to profl. jours. Bd. dirs. Found. Ind. U. Sch. Bus., Found. Econ. and Bus. Studies; mem. bd. visitors Ind. U. Sch. Law, 1971—, chmn., 1974-75; bd. dirs. Soc. for Advanced Study, Ind. U., 1984-95, pres., 1985-87; mem. Acad. Alumni Fellows, Ind. U. Sch. Law, 1988. Comdr. USNR, 1943-45. Recipient Ind. Bar Found. 50-Yr. award, 1992, Ind. U. Disting. Alumni Svc. award, 1995. Mem. ABA (ho. of dels. 1960-62, state del. 1967-72, bd. govs. 1971-74, chmn. gen. practice sect. 1971-72), Ind. State Bar Assn. (bd. mgrs. 1957-63, pres. 1961-62), Indpls. Bar Assn. (v.p. 1957), Ind. Soc. Chgo., Lawyers Club (pres. 1959-60), Indpls. Country Club (pres. 1955), Columbia Club, Woodstock Club, Wilderness Country Club (Naples, Fla., dir. 1991-94). Republican. Presbyterian. Construction, General corporate, Probate. Home: 1402 W 52d St Indianapolis IN 46228-2317

**DUTTON, MARK ANTHONY,** lawyer; b. Moulton, Ala., Jan. 24, 1964; s. William B. and Judith C. (Barrett) D. BA, Huntingdon Coll., Montgomery, Ala., 1987; JD, Samford U., 1990. Bar: Ala. 1991, U.S. Dist. Ct. (no. dist.) Ala. 1991, U.S. Ct. Appeals (11th cir.) 1991. Pvt. practice Moulton, Ala., 1991—. Exec. committeeman Dem. Party, Lawrence County, Ala., 1993—. Mem. Ala. Bar Assn., Ala. Trial Lawyers Assn., Masons. Democrat. Baptist. Avocations: racquetball, politics, reading. General civil litigation, State civil litigation, Criminal. Home: 14220 Market St Moulton AL 35650-1442 Office: 714 East St Moulton AL 35650-1668

**DUTTON, STEPHEN JAMES,** lawyer; b. Chgo., Sept. 20, 1942; S. James H. and Marjorie C. (Smith) D.; m. Ellen W. Lee; children: Patrick, Mark. BS, Ill. Inst. Tech., 1965; JD, Ind. U., 1969. Bar: Ind. 1969, U.S. Dist. Ct. (so. dist.) Ind. 1969, U.S. Ct. Appeals (7th cir.) 1972, U.S. Ct. Appeals (D.C. cir.) 1980, U.S. Supreme Ct. 1978. With McHale, Cook & Welch, P.C., Indpls., 1969-86, Dutton & Overman, P.C., 1986-91, Dutton & Bailey, P.C., 1991-94, Locke, Reynolds, Boyd & Weisell, 1994-99, Leagre, Chandler & Millard, LLP, Indpls., 1999—; mem. Com. on Law of Cyberspace Bus. Law Sect. Mem. ABA. Securities, General corporate, Computer. Home: 3705 Spring Hollow Rd Indianapolis IN 46208-4169 Address: 201 N Illinois St Ste 1000 Indianapolis IN 46204-4227

**DUUS, GORDON COCHRAN,** lawyer; b. Ridley Park, Pa., Oct. 17, 1954; s. Frank Martin and Shirley (Cochran) D.; m. Mary Ellen Moses, Nov. 9, 1985; children: Alexander, Hannah, Julianne. BA magna cum laude, U. Pa., 1977; JD with honors, George Washington U., 1981. Bar: D.C. 1981, N.J. 1982, Calif. 1987, U.S. Dist. Ct. N.J. 1982, U.S. Supreme Ct. 1989. Assoc. Previti, Todd, Gemmel, Fitzgerald & Nugent, Linwood, N.J., 1982-87; ptnr., chmn. environ. law dept. Margolis, Chase, Kosicki, Aboyoun & Hartman, Verona, N.J., 1987-90, Cole, Schotz, Meisel, Forman & Leonard, Hackensack, N.J., 1990—; mem. faculty Cook Coll. of Rutgers U., New Brunswick, N.J., 1991-99, Nat. Bus. Insts., Saddlebrook, N.J., 1992, Govt. Inst., Atlantic City, 1995; spkr. in field. Contbr. articles to profl. jours. Mem. ABA, N.J. Bar Assn., Bergen County Bar Assn. Environmental, Real property, Land use and zoning (including planning). Office: Cole Schotz Meisel Forman & Leonard 25 Main St Hackensack NJ 07601-7015

**DUVAL, STANWOOD RICHARDSON, JR.,** judge; b. New Orleans, Feb. 8, 1942; m. Deborah Barnes, Jan. 20, 1979. BA, La. State U., 1964, LLB, 1966. Ptnr. Duval, Funderburk, Sundbery & Lovell, 1966-94; dist. judge U.S. Dist. Ct. (ea. dist.), La., 1994—. Mem. City of Houma Charter Commn., 1975, vice chmn. Charter Commn., 1980-81, Terrebonne Port Commn., 1987-88. Mem. ABA, Am. Trial Lawyers Assn., La. State Bar Assn., Terrebonne Parish Bar Assn., La. Trial Lawyers Assn. (bd.. gov. 1976-77), Whiskey Pass Silver King Assn., Houma-Terrebonne Jaycees. Avocations: traveling, scuba diving, hunting, fishing, performing arts. Office: U S Dist Ct Ea Dist 500 Camp St Rm C-368 New Orleans LA 70130-3313

**DUVIN, ROBERT PHILLIP,** lawyer; b. Evansville, Ind., May 18, 1937; s. Louis and Henrietta (Hamburg) D.; m. Darlene Chmiel, Aug. 23, 1961; children: Scott A., Marc A., Louis A. BA with honors, Ind. U., 1958, JD with highest honors, 1961; LLM with highest honors, Columbia U., 1963. Bar: Ohio 1964. Since practiced in Cleve.; pres. Duvin, Cahn & Hutton, 1972—; lectr. law schs.; labor adviser corps., cities and hosps. Contbr. to books and legal jours.; bd. editors: Ind. Law Jour., 1961, Columbia Law Rev., 1963. Served with AUS, 1961-62. Mem. Am., Fed., Ohio, Cleve. bar assns. Jewish. Clubs: Cleve. Racquet, Beechmont Country, Soc., Canterbury Golf Club. Labor. Home: 2775 S Park Blvd Cleveland OH 44120-1669 Office: Duvin Cahn & Hutton Erieview Tower 1301 E 9th St Ste 2000 Cleveland OH 44114-1886

**DUVIVIER, KATHARINE KEYES,** lawyer, educator; b. Alton, Ill., Jan. 1, 1953; d. Edward Keyes and Marjorie (Attebery) DuV.; m. James Wesley Perl, Mar. 30, 1985 (div. Aug. 1997); 2 children: Alice Katharine Perl, Emmett Edward Perl. BA in Geology and English cum laude, Williams Coll., 1975; JD, U. Denver, 1982. Bar: Colo. 1982, U.S. Dist. Ct. Colo. 1982, U.S. Ct. Appeals (10th cir.) 1982. Intern-curator Hudson River Mus., Yonkers, N.Y., 1975; geologist French Am. Metals Corp., Lakewood, Colo., 1976-79; assoc. Sherman & Howard, Denver, 1982-84, Arnold & Porter, Denver, 1984-87; atty. Office of City Atty., Denver, 1987-90; sr. instr. sch. law Univ. Colo., 1990—; chair Appellate Practice Subcommittee. Contbr. articles to profl. jours. Mem. Denver Botanic Garden, 1981-88; vol. Outdoor Colo., Denver, 1985-87, 1998—. Mem. ABA (vice chmn. subcom. 1985-91), Colo. Bar Assn., Boulder Bar Assn., Boulder Women's Bar Assn. (pres. 1991-93), Alliance Profl. Women (bd. dirs. 1985-90, pres. 1988-89), Work and Family Consortium (bd. dirs. 1988-90), St. Ives, William Coll. Alumni Assn. (co-pres. Colo. chpt. 1984-86), Phi Beta Kappa. Avocations: geology, hiking, skiing, dancing, swimming. Home: 4761 Mckinley Dr Boulder CO 80303-1142 Office: U Colo Sch Law PO Box 401 Boulder CO 80303

**DUZEY, ROBERT LINDSEY,** lawyer; b. Long Beach, Calif., Nov. 15, 1960; s. Donald Bohdan and Noreen (Rosen) D.; m. Susan Misook Yoon, Mar. 14, 1987; children: Dylan Grey, Zenon Drake. BA, U. Calif., Irvine, 1984; JD, Western State U., Fullerton, Calif., 1994. Bar: Calif. 1994., U.S. Dist. Ct. (so., ctrl., ea. and no. dists.) Calif., U.S. Ct. Appeals (9th cir.). Claims rep., mgr. Farmers Ins. Group, Santa Ana, Calif., 1985-89; risk mgr. Dollar Rent A Car, Irvine, 1989-93; law clk. Callahan, McCune & Willis, Tustin, Calif., 1994-96; atty. Madigan, Evans & Boyer, Costa Mesa, Calif., 1996-98, Law Offices of Robert Lindsey Duzey, Costa Mesa, 1998—. Recipient Am. Jurisprudence award, 1993. Mem. ATLA, ABA, Orange County Bar Assn., Fed. Bar Assn., Risk and Ins. Mgmt. Soc. (bd. dirs. 1991-93), Orange County Barristers, Orange County Trial Lawyers Assn., Def. Rsch. Inst., Assn. So. Calif. Def. Counsel, Am. Inns of Ct., Peter M. Elliot Inn, L.A. County Bar Assn., Long Beach Bar Assn., Delta Theta Phi. Avocations: golf, gardening, skiing, cigars. Fax: (562) 862-7721. E-mail: RDuzey@aol.com. General civil litigation, Product liability, Insurance. Office: Law Offices Robert Lindsey Duzey 9900 Lakewood Blvd Ste 250 Downey CA 90240-4038

**DVORAK, RICHARD DEE,** lawyer; b. Mpls., May 31, 1958; s. Delano Dvorak and Barbara Mataya; m. Sherry A. Page, Sept. 13, 1985; children: Eric, Bryon, Daine, Paige. BGS, Roosevelt U., 1986; JD, IIT-Chgo. Kent, 1992. Bar: Ill. 1991, Kans. 1992, Mo. 1993, U.S. Dist. Ct. (no. dist.) Ill., U.S. Dist. (we. dist.) Mo., U.S. Dist. Ct. Kans., U.S. Ct. Appeals for Armed Forces. Pension asset analyst The No. Trust Co., Chgo., 1988-92; lease analyst Claire's Stores, Inc., Elk Grove Village, Ill., 1990-92; pvt. practice Overland Park, Kans., 1992-95; ptnr. Tomes & Dvorak, Leawood, Kans., 1995—. Sgt. USMC, 1976-84. General civil litigation, Criminal, Personal injury. Office: Tomes & Dvorak 5001 College Blvd Ste 214 Leawood KS 66211-1618

**DWORKIN, MICHAEL LEONARD,** lawyer; b. Bridgeport Ct., Oct. 10, 1947; s. Samuel and Frances (Stein) Dworkin; m. Christina Lyn Hildreth, Sept. 25, 1977; children: Jennifer Hildreth, Amanda Hildreth. BA in Gov. with honors, Clark U., 1969; JD with honors, George Washington U., 1973. Bar: D.C. 1973, Calif. 1975, U.S. Ct. Appeals (9th cir.) 1982, U.S. Supreme Ct. 1978, U.S. Claims Ct. 1983. Atty. FAA, Washington, Los Angeles, 1973-77, United Airlines, San Francisco, 1977-81; pvt. practice, San Francisco, 1981-95, San Mateo, Calif., 1995—; instr. Embry Riddle Aeronautical U., San Francisco, 1980-81; dir. Poplar Ctr., San Mateo, Calif., 1979-86. Benefactor Hiller No. Calif. Aviation Mus. Jonas Clark scholar Clark U., 1966-69. Mem. ABA, Lawyer Pilot's Bar Assn., Nat. Transp. Safety Bd. Bar Assn. (regional v.p. 1986-87, 90—, chmn. rules com. 1985—), Aircraft Owners and Pilots Assn., Conn. Aviation Hist. Assn., Benefactor-Hiller Aviation Mus., San Mateo County Bar Assn., Bar Assn. San Francisco, Internat. Soc. Air Safety Investigators (bd. dirs. San Francisco regional chpt. 1988-89), State Bar Calif., D.C. Bar Assn., Regional Airline Assn., Commonwealth Club of Calif., New England Air Mus. Jewish. E-mail: law@avialex.com. Aviation, Contracts commercial, Insurance. Office: 155 Bovet Rd Ste 455 San Mateo CA 94402-3112

**DWORNIK, FRANCES PIERSON,** lawyer; b. Newport News, Va., Nov. 5, 1956; d. John Clayton and Frances Ann Pierson; m. David Dwornik, Mar. 9, 1991. BA with distinction, U. Va., 1979; JD, Coll. William and Mary, 1985. Bar: Va. 1985, U.S. Dist. Ct. (ea. dist.) Va. 1986. Assoc. Odin, Feldman and Pittleman, P.C., Fairfax, Va., 1985-89, ptnr., 1989—. Symposium editor, exec. bd.: William and Mary Law Review, 1985. Mem. ABA (regional III trial competition organizing com. 1988, 90), Va. Bar Assn. (labor and employment sect.), No. Va. Young Lawyers Assn. (v.p. 1986-87, pres. 1987-88). Labor, General civil litigation, General corporate. Office: Odin Feldman and Pittleman 9302 Lee Hwy Ste 1100 Fairfax VA 22031-1215

**DWORSKY, CLARA WEINER,** lawyer, former merchandise brokerage executive; b. N.Y.C., Apr. 28, 1918; d. Charles and Rebecca (Becker) Weiner; m. Bernard Ezra Dworsky, Jan. 2, 1944; 1 child, Barbara G. Goodman. BS, St. John's U., N.Y.C., 1937, LLB, 1939, JD, 1968. Bar: N.Y. 1939, U.S. Dist. Ct. (ea. dist.) N.Y. 1942, U.S. Dist. Ct. (so. dist.) Tex. 1993, U.S. Ct. Appeals (9th cir.) 1994, U.S. Ct. Appeals (5th cir.) 1995. Pvt. practice N.Y.C., 1939-51; assoc. Bessie Farberman, N.Y.C., 1942; clk., sec. U.S. Armed Forces, Camp Carson, Colo., Camp Claiborne, La., 1944-45; abstractor, dir. Realty Title, Rockville, Md., 1954-55; v.p. Kelley & Dworsky Inc., Houston, 1960—; appeals agt. Gasoline Rationing Apls. Bd., N.Y.C., 1942; bd. dirs. Southlan Sales Assocs., Houston. Vol. ARC, N.Y.C.; vice chmn. War Bond pledge drive, Bklyn.; vol. Houston Legal Found., 1972-73; pres. Women's Aux. Washington Hebrew Acad., 1958-60, v.p. bd. trustees, 1959-60; co-founder, v.p. S. Tex. Hebrew Acad. (now Hebrew Acad.), Houston, 1970-75, hon. pres. women's divsn., 1973. Recipient Cert. award Treas. of U.S., 1943; Commendation Office of Chief Magistrate of City N.Y., 1948; Pietas medal St. Johns U., 1985. Mem. ABA (chmn. social security com., sr. lawyers divsn. 1989-93, 95—, chairsubcom. 1993-95, mem. sr. lawyers divsn. coun. 1989-95, mem. editl. bd. sr. lawyers divsn. pub. Experience), N.Y. State Bar Assn., Fed. Bar Assn. (vice chair for programs, sr. lawyers divsn. 1994-96, dep. chair 1996-97, chmn. 1997-98, chmn. soc. sec. com. south Tex. chpt. 1998—), Houston Bar Assn. (sec. social security sect. 1995-96), Nat. Assn. Women Lawyers (chmn. organizer Juvenile Delinquency Clinic N.Y. 1948-51), St. Johns U. Alumni Assn. (coord. Houston chpt. 1983—, pres. 1986), Delphians Past Pres.'s Club, Amit Women Club, Hadassah. Jewish. Pension, profit-sharing, and employee benefits. Home: 9726 Cliffwood Dr Houston TX 77096-4406

**DWYER, DIANE MARIE,** lawyer, judge; b. Amityville, N.Y., Nov. 5, 1958; d. Joseph R. and Geraldine (Burchell) D. BA, Molloy Coll., 1980; JD, St. John's U., 1983. Bar: N.Y. 1983, U.S. Supreme Ct. 1991. Assoc. Deutsch & Schneider, Bklyn., 1983-84; pvt. law practice Wantagh, N.Y., 1984—; dist. ct. judge, 1999—; dep. county atty. Nassau County, N.Y., 1984-91; hearing examiner Nassau County Family Ct., 1991-88; advisor community legal instrn. program St. John's U., Jamaica, N.Y., 1984. Mem. ABA, Nassau County Bar Assn. (com. mem. 1987—), Nassau County Women's Bar Assn. (bd. dirs. 1993—), Molloy Coll. Alumni Assn. (v.p. 1986-89, pres. 1989-92, admissions recruiter 1988—). General civil litigation, Criminal, Family and matrimonial. Home: 2300 Willow St Wantagh NY 11793-4227

**DWYER, JAMES FRANCIS,** lawyer; b. Syracuse, N.Y., Aug. 19, 1930; s. Andrew F. and Berthe E. (Traub) D.; m. Ellen A. O'Shea, Oct. 22, 1960; children: Thomas A., Anthony F., Sarah E. BBA, St. Bonaventure U., 1953; LLB, Syracuse U., 1960. Bar: N.Y. 1960. Atty., ptnr. Grossman, Kinney, Dwyer & Harrigan PC and predecessor firms, Syracuse, 1961—; mem. Onondaga County Criminal Justice Adv. Bd., Syracuse, 1994—;. Bd. dirs. Hiscock Legal Aid Soc., 1983— (pres. 1983-84); town justice Marcellus, N.Y., 1983—; mem. Onondaga County Magistrate's Assn., 1983— (v.p. 1989, pres. 1990), N.Y. State Magistrate's Assn., 1983—, St. Francis Xavier Ch. parish coun., Marcellus, 1969-93 (pres. 1988-91, lay lector 1969—); village atty., Marcellus, 1967—. Capt. USNR (active duty 1953-57), 1952-78. Mem. ABA (standing com. on lawyer referral and info. svc. 1998—), N.Y. State Bar Assn. (at-large mem. exec. com., mem. Ho. Dels. 1998—, chmn. gen. practice sect. 1986, mem. gen. practice, real estate, trust and estates, mcpl. environ. law sects., spl. com. on atty. competency 1987-88, spl. com. to consider proposed plan for mandatory pro bono svcs. 1989, pres.'s com. on access to justice 1990—, spl. com. on atty. professionalism 1989-94, com. on advt. and referral svc. 1997—, chmn. lawyer referral info. svc. 1991-97), Onondaga County Bar Assn. (pres. 1982, chmn. grievance com. 1977, mem. 5th dist. appellate divsn. 4th dept. grievance com. 1978-86, 94—, rep. N.Y. State Bar Assn. Ho. Dels. 1985-90). Republican. Roman Catholic. Avocations: golf, travel. General practice, Municipal (including bonds), Real property. Office: Grossman Kinney Dwyer & Harrigan PC 2 Clinton Sq Atrium #215 Syracuse NY 13202-1042

**DWYER, JOHN RYAN, JR.,** lawyer; b. Erie, Pa., Nov. 13, 1940; s. John Ryan and Virginia (Rentz) D.; m. Barbara Maley, Dec. 28, 1963; children: Malia, Ryan, Nedra, Matthew, Bridget. Student, U. Notre Dame, 1958-59; BS, U.S. Mil. Acad., 1963; JD magna cum laude, U. Miami, Fla., 1973. Bar: Hawaii 1974, U.S. Dist. Ct. Hawaii 1974, U.S. Ct. Appeals (9th cir.) 1985. Commd. 2d lt. U.S. Army, 1963, advanced through grades to capt., resigned, 1968; asst. v.p. Sunbeam and Holsum Bakeries, Erie, 1969-71; assoc. Conroy Hamilton Gibson Nickelsen Rush and Moore, Honolulu, 1974-77; ptnr., pres. Dwyer, Imanaka, Schrafff and Kudo, Honolulu, 1977—; prof. U. Hawaii, 1979-89. Bd. dirs. Friends of Children's Advocacy Ctr., Honolulu, 1987—, Friends of Foster Kids, Honolulu, 1989—; Bd. dir., 1st v.p. Girl Scout Coun. Hawaii, 1998. Mem. Am. Coll Real Estate Lawyers, Rotary Club Honolulu (pres. 1992—). Avocations: jogging, golf, surfing. Real property, Contracts commercial, General civil litigation. Home: 1639 Ulueo St Kailua HI 96734-4460 Office: Dwyer Imanaka Schraff and Kudo 900 Fort Street Mall Honolulu HI 96813-3721

**DWYER, RALPH DANIEL, JR.,** lawyer; b. New Orleans, Apr. 23, 1924; s. Ralph Daniel Sr. and Carolyn (Nolting) D.; m. Gwendolyn Betpouey, Feb. 12, 1955; children: Ralph, Bridget Mary, Frederick Henry, Patrick Rees, John Betpouey, Timothy Paul, Kathleen Mary, Mary Megan, Pegeen Mary. BS in Econs., Loyola U., New Orleans, 1943; Japanese area and lang. program, U. Chgo., U. Mich., 1943-45; JD, Loyola U., New Orleans, 1950; grad., Army War Coll., 1976. Bar: La. 1950. Law clk. to judges Civil Dist. Ct., Parish Orleans, 1950-51; pvt. practice, New Orleans, 1950—. Mem. La. Civil Service League, 1968—, bd. govs., 1984—; past pres. Japanese Soc. New Orleans. Served to col. AUS, La. N.G., 1978, ret. Decorated Order of Sacred Treasure (Japan), Order of Medallion of St. Louis, Archdiocese of New Orleans, 1982; recipient Monte M. Lemann award La. Civil Svc. League, 1982, 84, La. Disting. Svc. medal 1978. Mem. La. State Bar Assn. (com. on law reform 1971-82, ho. of dels. 1975-77), New Orleans Bar Assn.

(3d v.p. 1968-69), St. Thomas More Cath. Lawyers Assn. (pres. 1968-70). Democrat. Roman Catholic. Avocations: reading, family, fly-fishing. General civil litigation, Civil rights, Alternative dispute resolution. Home and Office: 1622 Cadiz St New Orleans LA 70115-4816

**DWYER, WILLIAM L.**, federal judge; b. Olympia, Wash., Mar. 26, 1929; s. William E. and Ila (Williams) D.; m. Vasiliki Asimakopulos, Oct. 5, 1952; chldren: Joanna, Anthony, Charles. BS in Law, U. Wash., 1951; JD, NYU, 1953; LLD (hon.), Gonzaga U., 1994. Bar: Wash. 1953, U.S. Ct. Appeals (9th cir.) 1959, U.S. Supreme Ct. 1968. Law clk. Supreme Ct. Wash., Olympia, 1957; ptnr. Culp, Dwyer, Guterson & Grader, Seattle, 1957-87; judge U.S. Dist. Ct. (we. dist.) Wash., Seattle, 1987—; now sr. judge U.S. Dist. Ct. (we. dist.) Wash. Author: The Goldmark Case, 1984 (Gavel award ABA 1985, Gov.'s award Wash. 1985). 1st lt. U.S. Army, 1953-56. Recipient Outstanding Svc. award U. Wash. Law Rev., 1985, Helen Geisness disting. Svc. award Seattle-King County Bar Assn., 1985, Disting. Alumnus award U. Wash. Sch. of Law, 1994, W.G. Magnuson award King County Mcpl. League, 1994, Judge of Yr. Wash. State Trial Lawyers, 1994, Outstanding Jurist award Am. Bd. Trial Advocates, Washington, 1998, William L. Dwyer Outstanding Jurist Award, King County Bar Assn., 1998. Fellow Am. Coll. Trial Lawyers, Am. Bar Found., Hon. Order of Coif; mem. ABA, Inter-Am. Bar Assn., Am. Judicature Soc., Supreme Ct. Hist. Soc., 9th Cir. Hist. Assn. Office: US Dist Ct 502 US Courthouse Seattle WA 98104-1189

**DYAL, LUCIUS MAHLON, JR.**, lawyer; b. Gadsden, Ala., Mar. 30, 1937; s. Lucius M. and Juliet (McCall) D.; m. Kay Rankin, Jan. 27, 1968; children: Juliet, Caroline, Lucius M. III. BS in Civil Engring., Auburn U., 1959; JD, U. Fla., 1966. Bar: Fla. 1966, U.S. Dist. Ct. (mid. dist.) Fla. 1966, U.S. Ct. Claims 1995, Internat. Ct. Trade 1995; cert. internat. and civil law notary, Fla.; bd. cert. in internat. law. Commd. 2d. lt. U.S. Army, 1959, advanced through grades to capt., 1965, resigned, 1967; attorney Shackleford, Farrior, Stallings & Evans, Pa., Tampa, Fla., 1966—, pres., 1989-93. Mem. USF Engring. adv. bd. (chmn. 1999—). Mem. ABA, Am. Bar Found., Bar of Lima Peru, Bar of Rep. Honduras, Soc. Internat. Bus. Fellows (pres., chmn. 1995-97), Mus. Sci. Industry Found. (pres., chmn. 1994-96), Tampa C. of C. Private international, Labor, Construction. Office: Shackleford Farrior Stallings & Evans 501 E Kennedy Blvd Ste 1400 Tampa FL 33602-4991

**DYE, ALAN PAGE**, lawyer; b. Eustis, Fla., Apr. 4, 1946; s. Harlan Page and Maryse Jean (Tyre) D.; m. Rebecca Deen Comer, June 12, 1972; children: Katherine Ann, Andrew. AB in Econs., Duke U., 1968; JD, U. Fla., 1971; LLM, NYU, 1973. Bar: Fla. 1971, U.S. Ct. Claims 1974, U.S. Tax Ct. 1974, D.C. 1975, U.S. Ct. Appeals (10th cir.) 1975, U.S. Dist. Ct. D.C. 1976, U.S. Supreme Ct. 1976. Dir. Ea. Water Law Ctr., Gainesville, Fla., 1971-72; assoc. Webster, Chamberlain & Bean, Washington, 1975-79, ptnr., 1979—. Author: Association Legal Check List, 1983; contbr. articles to profl. jours. Bd. dirs. United Children's Fund, Washington, 1987—, Cancer Rsch. Found. Am., Washington, 1986—, chmn., 1994-96, Capitol Hill Restoration Soc., Washington, 1975-79, Am. Franklin Friends Com., 1991-95, Lee-Fendall House, 1992—, Freedom House, 1996—. Capt USAR, 1972-80. Mem. ABA, Am. Coll. Tax Counsel. Republican. Presbyterian. Avocations: golf, skiing, tennis. Non-profit and tax-exempt organizations, Taxation, general, General corporate. Office: Webster Chamberlain & Bean Ste 1000 1747 Pennsylvania Ave NW Washington DC 20006-4693

**DYE, DAVID ALAN**, lawyer, educator; b. Lexington, Mo., Sept. 11, 1950; s. Donald Alfred and Dorothy Sue D.; m. Julia Yolanda Zapata, June 21, 1979; 1 child, Soyal Chaski; m. Dora J. Lew, Aug. 8, 1997; 1 child, David A. BA, U. Mo., 1972, JD, 1976. Sole pra ctice, Kansas City, Mo., 1976-91; sole practice, 1991-97, co-founder, dir. Edn. for the Consortium for Advanced Legal Edn., 1997—; prof., coordinator legal asst. program Mo. Western State Coll., St. Joseph, 1977—; cons. in field; mem. bd. advisors for paralegal edn. Little, Brown and Co., 1991—; organizer, condr. nat. and regional seminars, confs. and workshops on legal assts. programs. Contbr. articles to profl. jours. Co-founder, pres. Mid-Coast Radio Project, Inc., 1978-79, bd. dirs., 1978-80, chmn. adv. coun., 1980—; legal cons. Greater Kansas City Epilepsy League, pres., 1982-84, mem. exec. com., 1984-87, bd. dirs. 1978-87; mem. ho. of dels. Epilepsy Found. Am., 1982-83; trustee Legal Aid Western Mo., 1987—. State of Mo. grantee, 1980, 82. Mem. ABA (law practice mgmt. sect.), Mo. Bar Assn. (past chmn. legal asst. com., law practice mgmt. com., tech. com., gen. practice com.), Kansas City Met. Bar Assn., Am. Assn. for Paralegal Edn. (organizer, pres. 1986-88, bd. dirs. 1983-88, past pres.' coun. 1988—, editor The Paralegal Educator), Nat. Assn. of Legal Assts. (assoc.). General practice. Home: 578 Farallon Ave Pacifica CA 94044-1439 Office: Consortium Advanced Legal Edn 735 Hickey Blvd Pacifica CA 94044-1214

**DYE, RALPH DEAN, JR.**, lawyer; b. Zanesville, Ohio, Sept. 10, 1931; s. Ralph Dean Sr. and Mary Elizabeth (Coulson) D. BSBA, Ohio State U., 1953; LLB, Youngstown (Ohio) U., 1958. Bar: Ohio 1958. Mgmt. trainee, cost acct. U.S. Steel Corp., Youngstown, 1953-58; pvt. practice McConnelsville, Ohio. Republican. Methodist. Avocations: collecting banks, hunting, fishing. General practice, Probate. Office: PO Box 178 Mc Connelsville OH 43756-0178

**DYE, WILLIAM ELLSWORTH**, lawyer; b. Detroit, Oct. 15, 1926; s. Edward Ellsworth and Elizabeth (Esther Bloom) D.; m. Joy Ann Kuehneman, Apr. 28, 1956 (div.); children: Constance, Elizabeth, William. BA, U. Wis., 1948, LLB, 1951. Bar: Wis., 1951. Assoc. John F. Thompson, Racine, Wis., 1951-75; ptnr. Heft, Dye, Paulson & Nichols, Racine, 1975-87; ptnr. Foley, Dye, Foley and Tollaksen, S.C., Racine, 1987-92, Coates, Dye, Foley & Shannon, S.C., Racine, 1993-98, Dye, Foley, Krohn & Shannon, S.C., Racine, 1998—; instr. U. Wis. Law Sch., 1970-71. Bd. Visitors U. Wis., 1982-85. With U.S. Army, 1946-47. Mem. ABA, State Bar Wis. (bd. govs. 1972-78), Racine County Bar Assn. (pres. 1985-86). Republican. Episcopalian. Clubs: Racine Country, U. Milw., Somerset of Racine. Banking, Consumer commercial, General corporate. Home: 111 11th St Racine WI 53403-1966 Office: Dye Foley Krohn & Shannon 1300 S Green Bay Rd Racine WI 53406-4469

**DYEKMAN, GREGORY CHRIS**, lawyer; b. Ft. Collins, Colo., Aug. 2, 1955; s. Elmer Clifford and Patsy Joyce (Hill) D. BS with honors, U. Wyo., 1977, JD, 1980. Bar: Wyo. 1980, U.S. Dist. Ct. Wyo. 1980, U.S. Ct. Appeals (10th cir.) 1980, U.S. Tax Ct. 1981, U.S. Supreme Ct. 1988, U.S. Claims Ct. 1990. Assoc. Dray, Madison & Thomson, P.C., Cheyenne, Wyo., 1980-82, shareholder, 1983-96; Dray, Thomson & Dyekman, P.C., 1996—; adj. prof. law U. Wyo., 1993, 98, chmn. law shc. liaison com., 1998—. Editor-in-chief Land and Water Law Rev., 1978-79. Mem. dist. com. Boy Scouts Am., Cheyenne, 1980-83, 87-88, dist. chmn., 1987-88, fin. chmn., 1995-96; bd. counsel Symphony and Choral Soc. of Cheyenne, 1983-88; pres. Cheyenne Family YMCA, 1984-85, bd. dirs., 1982-88, YMCA Endowment Bd., 1993—; pres., elder 1st Presbyn. Ch., Cheyenne, 1983-85, treas., 1986—; bd. dirs. Meals on Wheels Found., 1993—, v.p., 1995, pres.-elect, 1996, pres., 1997-98; cabinet mem. United Way, 1997; bd. trustees Long's Peak coun. Boy Scouts Am., 1998—, v.p. endowment. Mem. ABA, Laramie County Bar Assn. (sec., treas. 1985-86), Wyo. Trial Lawyers Assn. (editor newsletter 1983—), Kiwanis Found. (bd. dirs. 1993-95, pres. 1995), Cheyenne Kiwanis Club (bd. dirs. 1998—). Republican. Avocations: music composition, sports, internet. Federal civil litigation, State civil litigation, Banking. Home: 5010 Mccue Dr Cheyenne WY 82009-4815

**DYER, CHARLES ARNOLD**, lawyer; b. Blairstown, Mo., Aug. 29, 1940; s. Arnold and Mary Charlotte (West) D.; children: Kristine, Erin, Kathleen, Kerry. BJ, U. Mo., 1962; JD, U. Calif., 1970. Bar: Calif. 1971, U.S. Sup. Ct. 1976. Ptnr., Dyer & White, Menlo Park, Calif.; judge Pro Tem Mcpl. and Superior Ct., San Mateo County, Pro Tem Superior Ct. Santa Clara County, arbitrator and mediator; lectr. in field. Bd. dirs. Boys Club of San Mateo, 1971-83, pres., 1975; mem. exec. council Boys Clubs of the Bay Area, 1977-83; mem. Democratic Nat. Fin. Com., 1978. Capt. USNR, 1963-93, ret. Mem. Calif. Bar Assn., San Mateo County Bar Assn., Santa Clara County Bar Assn., Palo Alto Bar Assn., Assn. Trial Lawyers Am., Consumer Attys. Calif., Consumer Attys. San Mateo County, Assn. Atty. Mediators, Trial Lawyers Pub. Justice, Am. Bd. Trial Advs., Nat. Bd. Trial Advocacy, Am. Arbitration Assn. Roman Catholic. State civil litigation, Federal civil litigation. Office: Dyer & White 800 Oak Grove Ave Menlo Park CA 94025-4477

**DYER, CROMWELL ADAIR, JR.**, lawyer, international organization official; b. St. Louis, Sept. 9, 1932; came to The Netherlands, 1973; s. Adair and Tompie Leora (Giles) D.; m. Margaret Copeland Peickert, June 12, 1958 (div. Aug. 1976); children: Gretchen, Jack, Julie, Stephen; m. Susan Aynesworth, Aug. 20, 1977; stepchildren: Carol Godso, Amanda McDonough, Donne Brown. BA, U. Tex., 1954; JD, 1961; LLM, Harvard U., 1971. Bar: Tex. 1961, U.S. Dist. Ct. (no dist.) Tex. 1965, U.S. Dist. Ct. (ea. dist.) Tex. 1966, U.S. Ct. Appeals (5th cir.) 1965, U.S. Ct. Appeals (11th cir.) 1982. Law clk. FTC, Washington, 1960; assoc. Branscomb, Gary, Thomasson & Hall, Corpus Christi, Tex., 1961-62; staff atty. So. Union Gas Co., Dallas, 1962-64; assoc. Dedman & May, Dallas, 1964-65, White, McElroy & White, Dallas, 1965-67; sole practice, 1967-73; sec. Hague Conf. on Pvt. Internat. Law, The Hague, The Netherlands, 1973-78; 1st sec., 1978-93, dep. sec. gen., 1993-97, observer, cons. to intergovtl. orgns., 1976-97; lectr. Asser Coll. Europe, 1992-96, Davis Sch. Law U. Calif. Davis, 1996, Brigitte M. Bodenheimer Meml. Lecture on the Family, 1996; condr. seminars. Author: Globalization of Child Law The Role of the Hague Conventions, 1999; co-author: Report on Trusts and Analogous Institutions, 1982; contbr. articles to profl. jours. Mem. jury for award of Diploma in Internat. Law Hague Acad., 1980, 84, 85, 86, 87, 91, 94, 95, 96, dir. studies, 1985, course on Unfair Competition in Pvt. Internat. Law, 1998. Lt. (j.g.) USN, 1954-57. Mem. ABA, ATLA, Am. Soc. Internat. Law, Am. Fgn. Law Assn., Inter-Pacific Bar Assn., Inter-Am. Bar Assn., Travis County Bar Assn., Dallas Bar Assn., Internat. Soc. Family Law, Assn. Louis Chatin pour la Def. des Droits de l'Enfant (Paris), Club du jeudi (pres. 1983-85, The Hague). Fax: (512) 231-9498. E-mail: adyer@jump.net. Private international, Public international. Office: 9130 Jollyville Rd Ste 250 Austin TX 78759-7473

**DYER, GREGORY CLARK**, lawyer, mediator; b. Stanford, Calif., May 29, 1947; s. Allen Clayton (dec.) and Mary Louise (Sutter) D.; m. Karyne Lee Clough, June 28, 1980; children: Ash, Chelsea. Grad., Webb Sch., 1965; BA, Stanford U., 1970, JD, 1971. Bar: Calif. 1972, U.S. Ct. Appeals (9th cir.) 1972, U.S. Dist. Ct. (no. dist.) Calif. 1972; cert. specialist estate planning, trust and probate law, Bd. Legal Specialization of State Bar of Calif. Pvt. practice Marin County, Calif., 1972—; referee, arbitrator, mediator, judge pro tem Marin County Superior Ct. Bd. dirs. Legal Aid Soc., Marin, 1979-81; coach Mill Valley Soccer Club; basketball coach YMCA, Cath. Youth Orgn.; mgr. Mill Valley Little League. Mem. Marin County Bar Assn. (bd. dirs. 1980-82, treas. 1985, pres. 1987), Rotary (pres. local club 1984-85, area rep. 1986-87, leader fgn. exch. team 1981, 87, dist. treas. 1991-92), Scott Valley Swim and Tennis Club (bd. dirs. 1976-80). Avocations: travel, tennis, scuba diving, photography. Estate planning, Probate, Alternative dispute resolution. Office: 103 E Blithedale Ave Ste 3 Mill Valley CA 94941-2062

**DYER, J.W.**, lawyer; b. San Juan, Tex., June 9, 1953; s. Malcolm G. and Mary A. D.; m. Cecily S., Aug. 14, 1976; children: Sarah, Noah, Briannah, Micah. BSCE, Tex. A&M U., 1976; JD, U. Tex., 1986. Bar: Tex. 1987. Engr. Sigler Winston & Greenwood, Weslaco, Tex., 1980-84; atty. Jarvis & Kittleman, McAllen, Tex., 1986-92, pvt. practice, McAllen, Tex., 1992-93, Dyer, Cavazos & Kimbal, McAllen, Tex., 1993-94, Dyer, Caclaux & Cavazos, McAllen, Tex., 1994, Dyer & Assocs., McAllen, Tex., 1994-98, Dyer & Denham, McAllen, Tex., 1998—; trial cons. Insights, McAllen, 1992—; farming Capote Farms, Inc., Pharr, Tex., 1976—, land devel., 1996—. Scoutmaster Boy Scouts Am., Rio Grande Coun., 1992—. 1st lt. U.S. Army, 1976-86. Mem. Tex. Soc. Profl. Engrs., Tex. Soc. Profl. Surveyors, Tex. State Bar Assn., Coll. of State Bar of Tex. Avocations: camping. General civil litigation, Contracts commercial, Environmental. Office: Dyer & Denham 3700 N 10th St Ste 105 Mcallen TX 78501-1774

**DYER, SUE MCCLURE**, lawyer, nurse; b. Louisville, May 6, 1962; d. John Rutledge and Frances June McClure; m. Kendall Aaron Dyer, June 27, 1998. BSN, U. Ky., 1987, JD, 1996. Bar: Tenn. 1996, U.S. Dist. Ct. (mid. dist.) Tenn. 1996, U.S. Dist. Ct. (we. dist.) Tenn. 1997, U.S. Dist. Ct. (ea. dist.) Tenn. 1998, U.S. Ct. Appeals (D.C. cir.); RN, Ky. Nurse U. Ky. Med. Ctr., Lexington, 1987-93; assoc. Bass, Berry & Sims, Nashville, 1996—. Mem. ABA, Nashville Bar Assn., Am. Health Lawyers Assn. Republican. Christian. Health, General civil litigation. Office: Bass Berry & Sims PLC 2700 First American Ctr Nashville TN 37238

**DYKES, LILLIAN ELISE LEVY**, lawyer; b. New Orleans, Sept. 30, 1946; d. Lewis Harris and Phyllis Marie-Louise (Williams) Levy; m. Osborne Jefferson Dykes III, Dec. 31, 1965 (div. 1970). BA, Memphis State U., 1973, JD, 1975. Bar: Tenn. 1975, U.S. Dist. Ct. (we. dist.) Tenn. 1979. Atty. Tenn. Dept. Mental Health, Memphis, 1975-78; assoc. James F. Schaeffer, Memphis, 1978-79, Wilson, McRae, Ivy, McTyre, Sevier, Strain, Memphis, 1979-84; sole practice, Memphis, 1985—; assoc. prof. U. Tenn. Ctr. for Health Scis., Memphis, 1976-77; actress Berlin Internat. Theatre, 1966-67, Memphis Little Theatre, 1969—, Am. Community Theatre Conf., 1973. Mem. adv. bd. Lowenstein House, Memphis, 1979-81; jud. candidate Circuit Ct. Shelby County, Tenn., 1982; pres. Cooper-Young Community Assn., Memphis, 1984-85; bd. dirs. Theatre Memphis, 1985-87. Named One of Outstanding Young Women Am., Girl Scouts U.S., 1986. Mem. ABA, Assn. Trial Lawyers Am., Memphis Trial Lawyers Assn., Memphis-Shelby County Bar Assn. (ethics com. 1986-87, impaired attys. com. 1987). Democrat. Roman Catholic. Clubs: Am. Businesswomen's, Tennessee (Memphis). Lodge: Zonta. Personal injury, Labor, Family and matrimonial. Home: 2076 Evelyn Ave Memphis TN 38104-5416 Office: 22 N 2nd St Ste 400 Memphis TN 38103-2639

**DYMER, MARILYN**, lawyer; b. Canonsburg, Pa.., Aug. 15, 1947; d. Paul Francis and Mary Jane (Black) Stabile; m. Larry Gene Smith, Apr. 19, 1990. BSN, Duquesne U., 1969; M in Nursing Edn., U. Pitts., 1978; JD, U. Mo., Kansas City, 1987. Bar: Mo. 1987, Kans. 1988, U.S. Ct. Fed. Claims 1993; RN, Mo. Staff nurse various specialties various orgns., 1969-76; clin. dir. John J. Kane Hosp., Pitts., 1978-79; dir. patient care Vis. Nurse Assn., Kansas City, Mo., 1979-81; DON Northside Home Health Care, Inc., Chgo., 1981-82; dir. edn. Lee's Summit (Mo.) Cmty. Hosp., 1982-84; of counsel Lantz Welch P.C. & James Bartimus, P.C., Kansas City, 1987-90; assoc. Bartimus, Kavanaugh et al., Kansas City, 1990-92, ptnr., 1992-94; owner Dymer Med.-Legal Cons., Kansas City, 1994—; mem. adv. bd. for nursing U. Mo., Kansas City, 1979-81; testified U.S. Senate Hearings on the Elderly, Kansas City, Kans., 1981; pres. Health Educator's Alliance, Kansas City, 1983-84; bd. govs. Mo. Assn. Trial Attys., Jefferson City, Mo., 1991-94; chairperson med.-legal com. Kansas City (Mo.) Met. Bar Assn., 1994; bd. dirs., chairperson gender issue com. Assn. for Women Lawyers of Greater Kansas City. Chief rschr. Litigation, 1987; cons. editor Kansas City Nursing Mag., 1981. Mem. Am. Coll. Legal Medicine, Law Found., Nursing Entrepreneurs, Phi Delta Phi (officer, treas.), Sigma Theta Tau. Avocations: camping, traveling, physical fitness. Personal injury. Home and Office: 6432 Mcgee St Kansas City MO 64113-2334

**DYWAN, JEFFERY JOSEPH**, judge; b. Hammond, Ind., Apr. 26, 1949; s. Joseph Michael and Florence Marie (Buda) D.; m. Jacque Ann Shulmistras, June 20, 1971; children: Dina, Abigail, Kathryn. BS in Indsl. Engring., Purdue U., 1971; JD, Valparaiso U., 1974. Bar: Ind. 1974, U.S. Dist. Ct. (no. and so. dists.) Ind. 1974, U.S. Ct. Appeals (7th cir.) 1975, Ill. 1984, U.S. Dist. Ct. (no. dist.) Ill. 1986. Assoc. Breclaw & Dywan, Griffith, Ind., 1974-77; sole practice Griffith, 1977-81; dep. prosecuting atty. Lake County, Crown Point, Ind., 1978-80, pub. defender, 1981-83; assoc. Chudom & Meyer, Schererville, Ind., 1981-89; ptnr. O'Drobinak, Dywan & Austgen, Crown Point, 1989-91; judge Lake Superior Ct., Hammond, Ind., 1991-98; chief judge Lake Superior Ct., Hammond, 1998—; instr. Calumet Coll., Hammond, Ind., 1974-76, Ind. Vocat. and Tech. Coll., Gary, Ind., 1978-79. Mem. Ind. State Bar Assn., Lake County Bar Assn., Am. Judicature Soc., KC. Roman Catholic. Office: Lake Superior Ct 232 Russell St Hammond IN 46320-1814

**EABY, CHRISTIAN EARL**, lawyer, small business owner; b. Reading, Pa., June 16, 1945; s. David Russell and Pearl Haller (Root) E.; m. Dace Rekis, Jan. 4, 1986. BA in Univ. Studies, U. N.Mex., 1976, JD, 1980. Bar: N.Mex. 1980, Pa. 1990, U.S. Dist. Ct. (ea. dist.) Pa. 1992. Tchr. Albuquerque Pub. Schs., 1976; ednl. dir. N.Mex. Pub. Employees Coun., 1977; tutor Am. Indian Law Ctr. U. N.Mex., 1978-79; pvt. practice Albuquerque, 1980-90; owner Eby Clock Co., New Holland, Pa., 1990-95; pvt. practice New Holland, 1990—; past legal coun. N.Mex. Vietnam Vets. of Am. Contbr. articles to profl. jours. Bd. dirs. U. N.Mex. Cancer Ctr., 1984-92, Albuquerque United Artists Downtown Ctr. for Arts, Ea. Lancaster County Sch., 1990-93; pres. Coalition Albuquerque Neighborhoods, 1983-85, Nob Hill Neighborhood Assn., 1980-86; mem. task force Albuquerque Goals Com.; founding dir., sec. Nob Hill Main St., 1987; founding dir. Casa Esperanza Cancer Patients Homes, 1987. Mem. ABA, ATLA (product liability sect.), Am. Arbitration Assn., Am. Numismatic Assn., N.Mex. Bar Assn., N.Mex. Trial Lawyers Assn., Albuquerque Bar Assn., Pa. Bar Assn. (workers' compensation sect.), Lancaster Bar Assn., Pa. Trial Lawyers Assn., Nat. Assn. Watch and Clock Collectors, Nat. Trust Hist. Preservation, Hist. Preservation Trust of Lancaster County, Lancaster Mennonite Hist. Soc., Lancaster Hist. Soc., Hist. Soc. of Cocalico Valley, Eby Family Assn. (pres. 1992—). Avocations: geneology, numismatics, horology, restoring 1727 family home. Fax: 717-656-3434. E-mail: cee@eabylaw.com. Personal injury, Workers' compensation, Product liability. Home: 405 Peters Rd New Holland PA 17557-9389 Office: 352 E Main St Ste 230 Leola PA 17540-1961

**EAGAN, CLAIRE VERONICA**, magistrate judge; b. Bronx, N.Y., Oct. 9, 1950; d. Joseph Thomas and Margaret (Lynch) E.; m. M. Stephen Barrett, Aug. 25, 1978 (div. 1984); m. Anthony J. Loretti, Jr., Feb. 13, 1988. Student, U. Fribourg, Switzerland, 1970-71; BA, Trinity Coll., Washington, 1972; postgrad., U. Paris, 1972-73; JD, Fordham U., 1976. Bar: N.Y. 1977, Okla. 1977, U.S. Dist. Ct. (no. dist.) Okla. 1977, U.S. Ct. Appeals (10th cir.) 1978, U.S. Supreme Ct. 1980, U.S. Dist. Ct. (we. dist.) Okla. 1981, U.S. Ct. Appeals (5th cir.) 1982, U.S. Dist. Ct. (ea. dist.) Okla. 1988, U.S. Ct. Appeals (Fed. cir.) 1990. Mem. Hall, Estill, Hardwick, Gable, Golden & Nelson, Tulsa, 1978-98, shareholder, 1981-98, also bd. dirs., exec. com.; magistrate judge U.S. Dist. Ct. (no. dist.) Okla., Tulsa, 1998—. Editor Fordham Law Rev., 1975-76. Bd. dirs. Cath. Charities, Tulsa, 1983-98, Cystic Fibrosis Found., Tulsa, 1982-84; mem. Jr. League Tulsa, Inc., 1983—; trustee Gannon U., Erie, Pa., 1995-98; bd. dirs. Okla. Sinfonia, Tulsa, 1982-86; adj. settlement judge, Tulsa County, 1990-97. Fellow Am. Bar Found.; mem. Tulsa County Bar Assn., 10th Cir. Jud. Conf., Am. Inns of Ct. (chpt. pres. 1999—). Republican. Roman Catholic. Federal civil litigation, General civil litigation, State civil litigation. Office: US Dist Ct No Dist Okla 333 W 4th St Ste 411 Tulsa OK 74103-3819

**EAGAN, WILLIAM LEON**, lawyer; b. Tampa, Fla., Feb. 10, 1928; s. John Robert and Margaret (Williams) E.; m. Marjorie Young, Mar. 6, 1949; children—Barbara Anne, Rebecca Elizabeth, Laurel Lea. Student U. Tampa, 1959, LL.B., U. Fla., 1961. Bar: Fla. 1961, U.S. Dist. Ct. (mid. dist.) Fla. 1959, U.S. Dist. Ct. (so. dist.) Fla. 1962, U.S. Ct. Appeals (5th cir.) 1972; bd. cert. civil trial lawyer, Fla. Assoc. Dexter, Conlee & Bissell, Sarasota, Fla., 1961-62; ptnr., v.p. Arnold, Matheny & Eagan, P.A., Orlando, 1962—; mem. Fla. Bar Ninth Circuit Grievance Com., 1982-84; mediator Family Law Mediation Program. Articles editor U. Fla. Law Rev., 1961. Chmn. bd. trustees First Baptist Ch. Winter Park, Fla., 1970-72, chmn. bd. deacons, 1967-69; active Indsl. Devel. Commn. Mid-Fla., Orlando, 1979-84. Served to seaman 2d class USN, 1945-46. Mem. Acad. Fla. Trial Lawyers, Am. Trial Lawyers Assn., Lawyers Title Guaranty Assn., Orange County Bar Assn. (exec. council), Order of Coif, Phi Alpha Delta, Phi Kappa Phi. Republican. Baptist and Methodist. Clubs: University, Citrus (Orlando). Federal civil litigation, State civil litigation, Real property. Office: Arnold Matheny & Eagan PA 801 N Magnolia Ave Ste 201 Orlando FL 32803-3842

**EAGEN, WILLIAM JAMES**, lawyer; b. Port Huron, Mich., July 10, 1950; s. Richard Bernard and Dorothy Sondae (Di Duca) E.; m. Sheri Lynn Tomlin, Jan. 5, 1974; children: Rochelle Sondae, Vincent James, Anthony Richard Thomas. BS in Physics, Santa Clara U., 1972, JD, 1977. Bar: Calif. 1977. Pres. W.J. Eagen, Atty. at Law, San Jose, Calif., 1977—. Mem. Calif. State Bar, Santa Clara County Bar. Avocations: backpacking, hunting, baseball. E-mail: wjeagenesq@aol.com. Criminal, Family and matrimonial, Estate planning.

**EAGLE, LESLIE ANNE**, lawyer, hospital administrator; b. Pomona, Calif., Feb. 3, 1967; d. John Worley Jr. and Gwendolyn (Rogers) E.; m. Paul Russell Dennis, Sept. 21, 1996. BA, UCLA, 1989; JD, Loyola U., 1993. Bar: Calif. 1993, U.S. Dist. Ct. (ctrl. dist.) Calif. 1993. Assoc. Law Offices of Robert L. Hunter, Santa Monica, Calif., 1993-95, Sullivan, Walsh & Wood, L.A., 1995-96; adminstrv. coord. Cedars-Sinai Medical Ctr., L.A., 1996—. Mem. Am. Bar Assn., L.A. County Bar Assn., Am. Soc. Parenteral Enteral Nutrition. Avocations: wakeboarding.

**EAGLES, SIDNEY SMITH, JR.**, judge; b. Asheville, N.C., Aug. 5, 1939; s. Sidney Smith Sr. and Mildred Truman (Brite) E.; m. Rachel Phillips, May 22, 1965; children: Virginia Brite, Margaret Phillips. BA, Wake Forest U., 1961, JD, 1964. Bar: N.C. 1964. Revisor Gen. Statutes Commn., Raleigh, N.C., 1967-70; asst. atty. gen. legis. drafting service Office Atty. Gen. N.C., Raleigh, 1970-74, dep. atty. gen. spl. prosecution divsn., 1974-76; counsel to speaker N.C. State Legislature, Raleigh, 1976-80; ptnr. Eagles Hafer & Hall, Raleigh, 1977-82; judge N.C. Ct. Appeals, Raleigh, 1983—, chief judge, 1998—; adj. prof. Campbell U. Sch. Law, 1977—; chmn. N.C. Jud. Stds. Commn., 1994-96; mem. faculty Appellate Judges Sch. Law Sch. NYU, N.Y.C., 1993—. Co-author: North Carolina Criminal Procedure Forms, 1975, 3d edit., 1989; contbr. articles to profl. jours. V.p. Raleigh Jaycees, 1972-73; mem. Senatorial Dist. Dem. Com., 1979-81; bd. dirs. Wake County (N.C.) Symphony Soc., 1980-81, Women's Aid of Wake County, 1978—; bd. elders, bd. deacons, trustee, tchr. Sunday sch. Hillyer Meml. Christian Ch., 1980—, chmn bd., 1989; bd. visitors Wake Forest U. Sch. Law; trustee and vice chair Barton Coll. Served to capt. USAF, 1964-67; col., ret. 1991. Named Disting. Law Alumnus, Wake Forest U., 1981; N.C. Justice Found. fellow, 1972. Mem. ABA (chmn. appellate judges conf. 1993-94, mem. appellate jud. edn. com. 1994—, ho. of dels. 1992—), Am. Law Inst. (uniform laws conf. 1968-83, 92—), N.C. Bar Assn. (v.p. 1989-90), Wake county Bar Assn. (chmn. exec. com. 1975), N.C. State Bar, Execs. Club (pres. 1985), Kiwanis (disting. pres. Raleigh 1986-87, disting. lt. gov. 1995, Kiwanian of Yr. award 1989), Phi Delta Phi, Phi Alpha Delta (James Iredell award 1990). Avocations: politics, reading. Office: NC Ct of Appeals PO Box 888 Raleigh NC 27602-0888

**EAKIN, MARGARETTA MORGAN**, lawyer; b. Ft. Smith, Ark., Aug. 27, 1941; d. Ariel Thomas and Oma (Thomas) Morgan; m. Harry D. Eakin, June 7, 1959; 1 dau., Margaretta E. B.A. with honors, U. Oreg., 1969, J.D., 1971. Bar: Oreg. 1971, U.S. Dist. Ct. Oreg. 1973, U.S. Ct. Appeals (9th cir.) 1977. Law clk. to chief justice Oreg. Supreme Ct., 1971-72; Reginald Heber Smith Law Reform fellow, 1972-73; house counsel Hyster Co., 1973-75; assoc. N. Robert Stoll, 1975-77; mem. firm Margaretta Eakin, P.C., Portland, Oreg., 1977—; tchr. bus. law Portland State U., 1979-80; speaker; mem. state bd. profl. responsibility Oreg. State Bar, 1979-82; vol. lawyer FEMA, 1995—. Mem. bd. visitors U. Oreg. Sch. of Law, 1986-93, vice chair, 1989-91, chair, 1992-93; mem. ann. fund com. Oreg. Episc. Sch., 1981, chmn. subcom. country fair, 1981; sec. Parent Club Bd., St. Mary's Acad., 1987; mem. Oreg. State. Bar Com. on Uniform State Laws, 1989-93, vol. lawyer Fed. Emergency Mgmt. Assn., 1995—. Paul Patterson fellow. Mem. ABA, Assn. Trial Lawyers Am., Oreg. Trial Lawyers Assn., Oreg. Bar Assn., Multnomah County Bar Assn. (jud. selection com. 1992-94), 1000 Friends of Oreg., City Club. Federal civil litigation, State civil litigation, Contracts commercial. Office: 30th Fl Pacwest Ctr 1211 SW 5th Ave Portland OR 97204-3713

**EAKINS, WILLIAM SHANNON**, lawyer; b. Glen Cove, N.Y., July 22, 1951; s. William Shannon and Jean (Pickup) E.; 1 child, Amelia Moore. BA, Yale U., 1974; JD, Cornell U., 1977. Lawyer, trust adminstr. Morgan Bank, N.Y.C., 1977-81; tax counsel com. on taxation and investigations N.Y. State Senate, Albany, 1981-84; assoc. Gelberg & Abrams, N.Y.C., 1981-84; assoc. Phillips, Nizer, Benjamin, Krim & Ballon, N.Y.C., 1984-88, ptnr., 1989-92; ptnr., chair trusts and estates dept. Olshan, Grundman, Frome & Rosenzweig, N.Y.C., 1993-98; of counsel Rosen & Reade, LLP, N.Y.C., 1998, Forsythe, Patton, Ellis, Lipsett & Savage, N.Y.C.; bd. dirs. Asehalt Green Inc. Contbr. articles to profl. jours. Vice chmn. N.Y. Rep. County Com., N.Y.C., 1985-89, exec. com., 1979-87, dist. leader, 1979-87; vice chmn. Manhattan Community Bd. No. 8, N.Y.C., 1980-84, 93-97; Rep., Ind. Neighbors and Conservative candidate for N.Y. State Assembly, 1992. Mem. N.Y. State Bar Assn., Assn. Bar City N.Y. (mem. com. on estate and gift taxation, mem. com. on N.Y. state legislation), Yale Club. Republican. Presbyterian. E-mail: wmeakins@aol.com. Probate, Estate taxation,

General civil litigation. Office: Forsythe Patton Ellis Lipsett & Savage 420 Lexington Ave New York NY 10170-0002

**EALY, JONATHAN BRUCE,** lawyer; b. L.A., Apr. 20, 1960; s. Donald Rae and Cynthia Howland (Pike) E. AB cum laude, Harvard U., 1982; JD, Duke U., 1985. Bar: Alaska 1986, U.S. Ct. Appeals (9th cir.) 1986. Clk. judge Karen Hunt Alaska Superior Ct., Anchorage, 1985-86; assoc. Taylor & Hintz, Anchorage, 1986-89, Heller, Ehrman, White & McAuliffe, Anchorage, 1989-93; gen. counsel Borisovich Internat., Inc., Anchorage, 1993—; of counsel Partnow, Sharrock & Tindall, Anchorage, 1995—; bd. dirs. Borealis Brewing Co.; prin. Na'au, Inc., 1998—. Author: Third Story, 1998. Pres. Anchorage Youth Ct., 1993-94, legal advisor, 1989-92; bd. dirs. Kids Voting Alaska, Anchorage, 1993. Mem. Anchorage Bar Assn. (pres. 1994, v.p. 1993, pres. young lawyers sect. 1988-90). Private international, State civil litigation, General civil litigation. Office: 510 L St Ste 500 Anchorage AK 99501-1956

**EAMES, ROBERT NEWTON,** lawyer; b. Tyler, Tex., Oct. 18, 1945; s. Newton Lincoln and Helen Keith Eames; m. Phyllis Ann Prenevost, June 26, 1970; children: Erin, Brant. BA, Tex. Tech. U., 1967, JD, 1970. Bar: Tex. Felony prosecutor Dist. Atty.'s Office, Denton, Tex., 1971-72; ptnr. Griffin, Shelton & Eames, Denton, 1972-80; pres., shareholder Philips & Hopkins, PC, Denton, 1980-94, Philips, Hopkins, Eames, Cobb, Denton, 1994—. Contbr. scholarly articles to law jours. Bd. dirs. Little League Baseball, Denton, 1987-92. Mem. State Bar of Tex. (mem. dist. 14-B grievance com. 1993-95, chair dist. 14-B grievance com. 1995-96, pattern jury charge com. 1994-98), Tex. Acad. Family Law Specialists, North Tex. Family Law Specialists Assn. (dir. 1988-92), Denton Bar Assn. (pre.), Alliance Bar Assn. Avocations: golf, flying. Family and matrimonial. Office: Philips Hopkins Eames & Cobb 525 N Locust St Denton TX 76201-4127

**EARLE, ROBERT RAY,** lawyer; b. Rayville, La., Dec. 24, 1937; s. Ranklin W. Earle and Mary Mildred (Girod) Muirhead; m. Bobbye Jane Fletcher, Dec. 20, 1958; children: Robert C., Leigh Angela Earle Lyles. BS, N.E. La. U., 1960, postgrad. in edn., 1969-71; MEd, Miss. Coll., 1968; JD, So. U., 1984. Bar: La. 1984, U.S. Dist. Ct. (we. and ea. dists.) La. 1984, U.S. Ct. Appeals (5th cir.) 1984. Elem. tchr. Ouachita Parish System, Lake Providence, La., 1960-61, tchr., coach, 1965-66, 69-72; tchr., coach East Carroll Parish System, Lake Providence, La., 1966-69, asst. prin., 1972-74; tchr., coach Union Parish System, Farmerville, La., 1974-81; pvt. practice Farmerville, 1984—; bd. dirs. D'Arbonne Bank, Farmerville, La. Trustee Farmerville United Meth. Ch., 1985—. Mem. ABA, La. Bar Assn. (del. 1984—), Assn. Trial Lawyers Am., La. Trial Lawyers Assn. (president's adv. coun.), La. Criminal Def. Lawyers Assn., Lake D'Arbonne Country Club (bd. dirs. 1985—), Lions (v.p. Farmerville 1986). Democrat. Avocations: golf, flying. Criminal, Banking, Personal injury. Home and Office: PO Box 518 Farmerville LA 71241-0518

**EARLEY, MARK LAWRENCE,** state attorney general; b. Norfolk, Va., July 26, 1954; s. Whitmel Franklin and Ann Harris Earley; m. Cynthia Ellen Breithaupt, June 5, 1982; children: Rachel, Justin, Mark, Jr., Mary Catherine, Franklin Edward, Anne Harris. BA in Religion, Coll. William and Mary, 1976, JD, 1982. Bar: Va. Ptnr. Tavss, Fletcher, Earley and King, P.C., Norfolk, 1982-97; senator Senate of Va., 1987-97; atty. gen. Commonwealth of Va., 1998—; Senate Rep. Whip, 1993; mem. privileges and elections com. Va. State Senate, 1993—, cts. justice com., 1988—, local govt. com., 1988—, rehab. and social svcs. com., 1988—; chmn. local govt. charter subcom. Va. State Senate, 1992—; mem. Gov.'s Commn. Parole Abolition and Sentencing Reform, 1994, Gov.'s Commn. Champion Schs., 1994, State Water Commn., 1994, Commn. Preservation of Capitol, 1994, Adv. Commn. Welfare Reform, 1994, Commn. Youth's Juvenile Detention Task Force, 1994, Commn. Sentencing and Parole Policies and the Need to Establish Truth in Sentencing, 1993—, Quadrennial Review Panel for Child Support Guidelines, 1994, Poverty Commn., 1992-93, Chowan River Commn., 1988—, Commn. Youth's Task Force, 1992-94; mem. environ. quality and natural resources com. So. Legis. Conf., 1994; mem. family ct. pilot project com. Supreme Ct. Va., 1989-93. Del. Rep. Nat. Conv., 1988, 92, mem. platform com., 1992; founding mem. Rep. Leadership Network; hon. chmn. Va. chpt. United Negro Coll. Fund, 1990; mem. Atlantic Shores Bapt. Ch.; mem. Chesapeake Cmty. Svcs. Bd., 1985-87; mem. Chesapeake Cmty. Corrections Resources Bd., 1985-87, vice-chmn., 1986-87; mem. Leadership Hampton Roads, 1990; bd. dirs. Comprehensive Health Investment Project, 1994, Va. CARES, Inc., 1993—, Tidewater Legal Aid, 1993—; Chesapeake bd. dirs. Commerce Bank, 1993—. Recipient Environ. award Port Folio Mag., 1990, Appreciation award Va. Crime Prevention Assn., Outstanding Alumnus and Disting. Pub. Svc. award Presdl. Classroom for Young Ams., 1994; Henry Toll fellow Coun. State Govts., 1994. Mem. Am. Trial Lawyers Assn., Nat. Rep. Legislators Assn. (bd. dirs. 1990-97; Legislator of Yr. award 1997), Va. State Bar, Va. Bar Assn., Va. Trial Lawyers Assn., Chesapeake Bar Assn., Norfolk-Portsmouth Bar Assn., Tidewater Pro Bono Program, Rotary Club, Great Bridge Sertoma Club. Office: Office of Atty Gen 900 E Main St Richmond VA 23219-3513 also: PO Box 36347 Richmond VA 23235-8007

**EARLS, DONALD EDWARD,** lawyer; b. Bluefield, W.Va., Oct. 15, 1941; s. Willie Hoge and Zella (Hunnicutt) E.; m. Sandra Elizabeth Stallard, Apr. 10, 1968; children: Shawn, Julia, Matthew (dec.), Mark. AB, Clinch Valley Coll., Wise, Va., 1961; BS, U. Va., 1963; JD, Wash. and Lee U., 1971. Bar: Va. 1971. Law clk. Hon. Emory Widner U.S. Dist. Ct. (we. dist.) Va., Abingdon, 1971-72; assoc. Cline & McAfee, Norton, Va., 1972-77; ptnr. Earls, Wolfe & Farmer, Norton, Va., 1977-81; pvt. practice Norton, Va., 1981—. Chmn. Rep. Party, City of Norton. Capt. USAF, 1963-67, Vietnam. Mem. Delta Theta Phi. Episcopalian. Avocations: tropical fish, gardening, painting. Criminal, General civil litigation, Personal injury. Home: PO Box 1005 Norton VA 24273-0892 Office: 936 Park Ave Norton VA 24273

**EARLY, ALEXANDER RIEMAN, III,** judge; b. Phila., Sept. 22, 1917; s. A.R. Jr. and Elizabeth Frances (Dence) E.; m. Mary Celeste Worland, Aug. 15, 1959; children: A.R. IV, Lucia C. STroh, Elizabeth V., John Drennan V. BA, Cornell U., 1983; LLB, Harvard U., 1941. Bar: Calif. 1946. Pvt. law practice L.A., 1946-50; sr. atty. Divsn. of Hwys., State of Calif., 1950-55; asst. U.S. atty. Lands divsn. U.S. Dept. Justice, L.A., 1955-57; asst. county counsel Los Angeles County, Calif., 1957-72; judge Superior Ct., L.A., 1972-87, by assignment, 1987—; adj. prof. Southwestern Law Sch., L.A., 1970-79. Contbr. articles to profl. jours. Mgr. internat. fedn. rels. boxing venue 1984 Olympics. Comdr. USNR, 1941-46. Decorated comdr. Order Polonia Restituta (Poland); knight grand cross Order of Holy Sepulchre (Vatican). Mem. Nat. Conf. State Tax Judges, Calif. Soc. Sons of Revolution (pres., Disting. Svc. award), Soc. War of 1812 (vice pres. gen., Disting. Svc. award), Soc. Cincinnati, Md. Hist. Soc., U.S. Naval Inst. Roman Catholic. Avocations: American history, genealogy, camellia seedlings. Home: 3017 Kirkham Dr Glendale CA 91206-1127

**EARLY, BERT HYLTON,** lawyer; b. Kimball, W.Va., July 17, 1922; s. Robert Terry and Sue Keister (Hylton) E.; m. Elizabeth Henry, June 24, 1950; children—Bert Hylton, Robert Christian, Mark Randolph, Philip Henry, Peter St. Clair. Student, Marshall U., 1940-42; A.B., Duke U., 1946; J.D., Harvard U., 1949. Bar: W.Va. 1949, Ill. 1963, Fla. 1981. Assoc. Fitzpatrick, Marshall, Huddleston & Bolen, Huntington, W.Va., 1949-57; asst. counsel Island Creek Coal Co., Huntington, W.Va., 1957-60, assoc. gen. counsel, 1960-62; dep. exec. dir. ABA, Chgo., 1962-64, exec. dir., 1964-81; sr. v.p. Wells Internat., Chgo., 1981-83, pres., 1983-85; pres. Bert H. Early Assocs. Inc., Chgo., 1985-94, Early Cochran & Olson, Chgo., 1994-98; of counsel Early Cochran & Olson, 1998—; dir. Am. Bar Found., Chgo., 1993-95; instr. Marshall U., Huntington, W.Va., 1950-53; legal search cons. and lectr. in field. Bd. dirs. Morris Meml. Hosp. for Crippled Children, 1954-60, Huntington Pub. Libr., 1951-60, W.Va. Tax Inst., 1961-62, Huntington Mus. Art, 1961-62; mem. W.Va. Jud. Coun., 1960-62, Huntington City Coun., 1961-62; bd. dirs. Cmty. Renewal Soc., Chgo., 1965-76, United Charities Chgo., 1972-80, Hinsdale (Ill.) Hosp. Found., 1987-93, Internat. Bar Assn. Found., 1987-89; bd. dirs. Am. Bar Endowment, 1983-95, sec., 1987-89, treas., 1989-91, v.p., 1991-93, pres., 1993-95, dir. emeritus, 1995—; mem. vis. com. U. Chgo. Law Sch., 1975-78; trustee Davis and Elkins Coll., 1960-63; mem. Hinsdale Plan Commn., 1982-85. 1st lt. AC, U.S. Army, 1943-45. Fellow Am. Bar Found., Ill. Bar Found. (charter); mem. ABA (ho. of dels. 1958-59, 84-93, chmn. young lawyers divsn. 1957-58, Disting. Svc. award young lawyers divsn. 1983), Am. Law Inst. (life), Internat. Bar Assn. (asst. sec. gen. 1967-82), Nat. Legal Aid and Defender Assn., Legal Aid Soc. Chgo., Am. Judicature Soc. (bd. dirs. 1981-84), Fla. Bar, W.Va. Bar Assn., Chgo. Bar Assn. Presbyterian. Office: Early Cochran & Olson Inc 401 N Michigan Ave Ste 515 Chicago IL 60611-4280

**EARLY, ERIC PETER,** lawyer; b. Ann Arbor, Mich., Aug. 20, 1958; s. George Early and Suzanne Rosa Schneider; m. Deborah Lynn Glasser, Aug. 10, 1986 (div. Mar. 1998); children: Alexander, Lauren. Degree, NYU, 1981; JD, Southwestern. U., L.A., 1992. Bar: Calif., 1993. Atty. Haight, Brown & Bonestell, Santa Monica, Calif., 1993-95, Christensen, Miller, Fink, Jacobs, Glaser, Weil & Shapiro, L.A., 1993—. Author children's animated films. Avocations: writing, skiing, reading. Fax: 310-282-6227. E-mail: eearly@chrismill.com. General civil litigation, Entertainment. Office: Christensen Miller Fink Jacobs Glaser Weil & Shapiro LLP 2121 Ave Of Stars Fl 18 Los Angeles CA 90067-5010

**EARLY, JAMES H., JR.,** lawyer; b. Henderson, N.C., May 6, 1939; s. James Howard and Nettie Anna (Hicks) E.; m. Ida Patricia Robinson; children: James H. III, Anna Elizabeth, Mary Elizabeth. AA, Mars Hill Coll., 1960; BA, Wake Forest U., 1962, LLB, 1964, JD, 1970. Bar: N.C. 1964, U.S. Dist. Ct. (mid. dist.) N.C. 1970, U.S. Ct. Appeals (4th cir.) 1995; cert. mediator Superior Cts. of N.C., 1992. Pvt. practice Winston-Salem, 1964—; mediator Adminstrv. Office of the Cts. of N.C., 1992—; mediator Am. Arbitration Assn., 1992—. Contbr. articles to profl. jours. With U.S. Army, 1957. Chmn. fundraising Cub Scouts/Boy Scouts Am., Little League, Pop Warner, Indian Guides, March of Dimes, others. With U.S. Army. Mem. ABA, ATLA, N.C. Bar Assn. (chmn. continuing legal edn. subcom., mem. effectiveness and quality of life com., moderator skills course com.), , Forsyth County Bar Assn. (sec. 1970-71), N.C. Acad. Trial Lawyers, Phi Alpha Delta (alumni advisor 1969-84, Outstanding Alumnus award 1967), Kiwanis (pres. 1989-90, 91-92), Masons. Baptist. Avocations: hunting, fishing, walking horses, bird dogs, racing. Personal injury, Labor, General corporate. Home: 519A S Salisbury St Mocksville NC 27028-2529 Office: 1320 Westgate Center Dr Winston Salem NC 27103-2933

**EARNEST, G. LANE,** lawyer; b. Pueblo, Colo., May 12, 1938; s. George Sites and Lucia Hopkins Earnest; m. Barbara Kelly, June 4, 1960; children: Hillary E., Keith L. BA in Polit. Sci. and Econs., U. Colo., 1960, JD, 1963. Bar: Colo. 1963, U.S. Dist. Ct. Colo. 1963. Ptnr. Caplan and Earnest, LLC, Boulder, Colo., 1969—; mem. hearing panel grievance com. Colo. Supreme Ct., 1977-88. Contbr. articles to profl. jours. Mem. Boulder Devel. Commn., 1996; chmn. March of Dimes Campaign, 1968; elder 1st Presbytn. Ch., Boulder, 1972-75, 83-86, instr. Bethel Bible series, 1978—, sr. pastor nominating com. 1990-92; chmn. citizens adv. coun. Boulder H.S., 1982-83; bd. dirs. Hist. Boulder, Inc., 1979-85, exec. com., 1983; profl. divsn. chmn. Boulder County United Way, 1990, chmn. campaign, 1993; vol. Meals on Wheels, Boulder, 1986—. Capt. U.S. Army, 1963-66. Recipient Disting. Citizen of Yr. Boulder County award Longs Peak coun. Boy Scouts Am., 1994. Fellow Am. Bar Assn. Found.; mem. ABA, Am. Acad. Hosp. Attys., Colo. Bar Assn. (bd. govs. 1972, 90-93, exec. coun. real estate sect. 1983-87, health law sect. 1990—, chmn. lawyer's fidelity fund com. 1981-87, chmn. young lawyers sect. 1971-72), Boulder County Bar Assn. (pres. 1972-73), U. Colo. Alumni Assn. (pres. 1974-75, Cmty. Svc. award 1982, Recognition medal 1975). Avocations: skiing, scuba diving, golf, travel. Contracts commercial, General corporate, Health. Office: Caplan and Earnset LLC 2595 Canyon Blvd Ste 400 Boulder CO 80302-6737

**EASLEY, GLENN EDWARD,** lawyer; b. Vandalia, Mo., Mar. 6, 1952; s. Frank Edward and Betty Evalena (McCollum) E.; m. Mary Catherine Albrecht, May 26, 1978; children: Matthew Edward, Sarah Elaine. BA, U. Mo., 1974, JD, 1977. Bar: Mo. 1977, U.S. Dist. Ct. (we. dist.) Mo. 1977, U.S. Dist. Ct. (ea. dist.) Mo. 1978. Assoc. atty. Hyde, Purcell, Wilhoit, Edmundson & Merrell, Poplar Bluff, Mo., 1977-80, John Schwabe & Assocs., Columbia, Mo., 1980-97; mediator State Mo., Divsn. Workers Compensation, Jefferson City, 1997—. Mem. Boone County Bar Assn., Cole County Bar Assn. Baptist. Alternative dispute resolution, Workers' compensation. Home: 12501 State Rd N Columbia MO 65203-9804 Office: State Mo Divsn Workers Comp 3315 W Truman Blvd Jefferson City MO 65109-6805

**EASLEY, MARJORIE MAE,** retired legal administrator; b. Fulton County, Ill., Mar. 6, 1935; d. Calvin Leo and Rita Jean (Henderson) Bainter; m. David L. Easley, Apr. 10, 1954 (dec. May 1992); children: James David, Joseph Leon, Julie Ann Easley Smick. Grad. high sch. Legal sec. Arthur D. Young, Atty., Lewistown, Ill., 1954-56, Martin M. Love, Atty., Lewistown, Ill., 1964-78; clk., recorder Fulton County, Lewistown, Ill., 1978-82; data processing cons. Fidlar Chambers Co., Moline, Ill., 1982-87; legal adminstr. Davis & Morgan Law Firm, Peoria, Ill., 1987-89, Husch & Eppenberger Law Firm, Peoria, Ill., 1989-97. Mem. Ctrl. Ill. Legal Adminstrs. (treas. 1991-92, sec. 1995-96, sec-treas. 1996-97), Nat. Assn. Cert. Profl. Secs. (cert. profl. sec.). Republican. Presbyterian. Avocations: reading, travel. Home: 14425 E Depler Springs Hwy Lewistown IL 61542-8435

**EASLEY, MICHAEL F.,** state attorney general; b. Rocky Mount, N.C., 1950; m. Mary Pipines; 1 child, Michael F., Jr. BA in Polit. Sci. cum laude, U. N.C., 1972; JD cum laude, N.C. Ctrl. U. Dist. atty. 13th Dist., N.C., 1982-91; pvt. practice Southport, N.C., 1991-93; atty. gen. N.C., 1993—. Contbr. numerous articles in field. Recipient Pub. Svc. award U.S. Dept. Justice, 1984. Pres. N.C. Conf. Dist. Attys.; mem. N.C. Dist. Attys. Assn. (past pres., legis. chmn.). Avocations: hunting, sailing, woodworking. Office: Justice Department/Attorney General PO Box 629 114 West Edenton St Raleigh NC 27602-0629*

**EASON, MARCIA JEAN,** lawyer; b. Dallas, Aug. 31, 1953; d. John Keller and Sara Marguerite (Prindle) McCarron; m. S. Lee Meredith, Sept. 12, 1981 (div. Oct. 1989); m. David O. Eason, Aug. 21, 1993; stepchildren: Chelsea, Shannon, Valerie. BA magna cum laude, Trinity U., 1975; JD, U. Houston, 1979. Bar: Tex. 1978, U.S. Dist. Ct. (so. dist.) Tex. 1978, U.S. Ct. Appeals (5th cir.) 1979, Tenn. 1985, U.S. Dist. Ct. (ea. dist.) Tenn. 1985, U.S. Supreme Ct. 1985, U.S. Ct. Appeals (6th cir.) 1986, U.S. Ct. Appeals (4th cir.) 1994. Ptnr. Byrnes & Martin, Houston, 1984-85, Miller & Martin, Chattanooga, 1987—. Pres., bd. dirs. Chattanooga's Kids on the Block, 1987-94; bd. dirs. AIM Ctr, Chattanooga, 1993—; campaign chair, atys. divsn. United Way, Chattanooga, 1994, leadership campaign chair, 1998. Mem. ABA, Tenn. Bar Assn., Chattanooga Bar Assn. (com. chair 1985-86), Tenn. Lawyers Assn. for Women (co-chair com. 1994, treas. 1995-97, pres. 1998). General civil litigation, Professional liability, Insurance. Home: 33 Rock Crest Dr Signal Mountain TN 37377-2326 Office: Miller & Martin 832 Georgia Ave Ste 1000 Chattanooga TN 37402-2289

**EASTAUGH, ROBERT L.,** state supreme court justice; b. Seattle, Nov. 12, 1943. BA, Yale U., 1965; JD, U. Mich., 1968. Bar: Alaska 1968. Asst. atty. gen. State of Alaska, 1968-69, asst. dist. atty., 1969-72; lawyer Delaney, Wiles, Hayes, Reitman & Brubaker, Inc., 1972-94; assoc. justice Alaska Supreme Ct., 1994—. Office: Alaska Supreme Court 303 K St Anchorage AK 99501-2013*

**EASTER, SCOTT BEYER,** lawyer; b. Seattle, Apr. 13, 1949; s. Frank Kenneth and Marjorie (Beyer) E.; m. Gay Lynn Garbe, Dec. 28, 1974; children: Renee Marie, Shane Barrett. BA in Econs. magna cum laude, U. Wash., 1971; JD, Stanford U., 1974. Bar: Wash. 1974, U.S. Dist. Ct. (we. dist.) Wash. 1978, U.S. Dist. Ct. (ea. dist.) Wash. 1994, U.S. Ct. Appeals (9th cir.) 1988. Dep. prosecutor King County Prosecutor, Seattle, 1974-76; assoc. King, Davidson & Dzeisler, Kirkland, Wash., 1976-79; assoc. Montgomery, Purdue, Blankinship & Austin P.L.L.C., Seattle, 1979-82, mem., 1983—; lectr. U. Wash., Seattle. Mem. ABA (litigation sect. 1985—, health law sect. 1992—), Wash. State Bar Assn. (litigation sect. 1986—, health law sect. 1992—), Seattle-King County Bar Assn. (chair legal auth. com. 1985-87), Phi Beta Kappa. Avocation: skiing. General civil litigation, Health, Insurance. Office: Montgomery Purdue Blankinship & Austin PLLC 701 5th Ave Ste 5800 Seattle WA 98104-7096

**EASTER, TIMOTHY LEE,** lawyer, judge; b. Radford, Va., Mar. 2, 1960; s. Clyde E. and Ethel (Stoneman) E.; m. Colette Rives, Oct. 22, 1983; children: Amy Marie, Emily Virginia. BA, David Lipscomb U., Nashville, 1982; JD, Nashville Sch. Law, 1989. Bar: Tenn. 1989, U.S. Supreme Ct. 1993, U.S. Dist. Ct. (mid. dist.) Tenn. 1994. Asst. dist. atty. State of Tenn., Franklin, 1989-94; pvt. practice Brentwood, Tenn., 1994—; judge Cir. Ct. 21st Dist. State of Tenn., 1998—. Mem. Tenn. Bar Assn., Williamson County Bar Assn., Brentwood Rotary, John Marshall Inn of Ct. (master of bench). General civil litigation, Bankruptcy, Criminal. Office: 8210 Halford Pl Brentwood TN 37027-6704

**EASTERBROOK, FRANK HOOVER,** federal judge; b. Buffalo, Sept. 3, 1948; s. George Edmund and Vimy (Hoover) E. B.A., Swarthmore Coll., 1970; J.D., U. Chgo., 1973. Bar: D.C. Law clk. to judge U.S. Ct. Appeals, Boston, 1973-74; asst. to solicitor gen. U.S. Dept. Justice, Washington, 1974-77, dep. solicitor gen. of U.S., 1978-79; asst. prof. law U. Chgo., 1978-81, prof. law, 1981-84, Lee & Brena Freeman prof., 1984-85; prin. employee Lexecon Inc., Chgo., 1980-85; sr. lectr. U. Chgo., 1985—; judge U.S. Ct. Appeals (7th cir.), Chgo., 1985—; mem. adv. com. on tender offers SEC, Washington, 1983. Author: (with Richard A. Posner) Antitrust, 1981, (with Daniel R. Fischel) The Economic Structure of Corporate Law, 1991; editor Jour. Law and Econs., Chgo., 1982-91; contbr. articles to profl. jours. Trustee James Madison Meml. Fellowship Found., 1988—. Recipient Prize for Disting. scholarship Emory U., Atlanta, 1981. Mem. AAAS, Am. Law Inst., Mont Pelerin Soc., Order of Coif, Phi Beta Kappa. Office: US Ct Appeals Everett McKinley Dirksen Fed Bldg 219 S Dearborn St Ste 2746 Chicago IL 60604-1803*

**EASTERLING, CHARLES ARMO,** lawyer; b. Hamilton, Tex., July 22, 1920; s. William Hamby and Jennie (Arilla) E.; m. Irene A. Easterling, Apr. 25, 1943; children: Charles David, Danny Karl, Jan Easterling Petty. BBA, Baylor U., 1951; LLB, 1951, JD, 1969. Bar: Tex. 1950, U.S. Supreme Ct. 1954. Sr. asst. city atty. City of Houston, 1952-64; sole practice Houston, 1964-70; city atty. Pasadena, Tex., 1970-82; of counsel Easterling and Easterling, Houston, 1982—; instr. So. Tex. Coll. Law, 1954-69. Lt. col. (ret.) USAFR. Mem. Houston-Harris County Bar Assn., Masons (33d degree, inspector gen. hon.), Shriners, Jesters, Arabia Temple Shrine (past potentate), Red Cross Constantine (past sovereign) Phi Alpha Delta. Democrat. Medthodist. Fax: (713) 228-4072. E-mail: eal@insync.net. General practice, Probate, Workers' compensation.

**EASTIN, KEITH E.,** lawyer; b. Lorain, Ohio, Jan. 16, 1940; s. Keith Ernest and Jane E. (Heimer) E. A.B., U. Cin., 1963, M.B.A., 1964; J.D., U. Chgo., 1967. Bar: Ill. 1967, Tex. 1974, Calif. 1975, U.S. Supreme Ct. 1975, D.C. 1983. Atty. Vedder, Price, Kaufman & Kammholz, Chgo., 1967-73; v.p., sec., gen. counsel Nat. Convenience Stores, Inc., Houston, 1973-79; ptnr. Payne, Eastin & Widmer, Houston, 1977-83; dep. under sec. U.S. Dept. Interior, 1983-86; prin. dep. asst. sec. USN, 1986-88; ptnr. Hopkins & Sutter, Washington, 1989-91; sr. v.p. Guy F. Atkinson Co., San Francisco, 1991-92; dir. environ. svcs. Deloitte & Touche, Washington, 1992—; sr. v.p., gen. counsel Guy F. Atkinson Co., 1991-92; dir. Nat. Money Orders Inc., Feast & Co., Inc., Kempco Petroleum Co., Bertman Drilling Co., Pacific Options, Inc., Del Rey Food Svcs., Inc., Stratford Feedyards, Inc., Deloitte & Touche, 1993-98, Pricewaterhouse Coopers, 1998—; prin. Westec Environ., Inc., Reno, 1993—. Bd. dirs. Theatre Under the Stars, Houston, Statue of Liberty-Ellis Island Found.; mem. exec. com. Harris County Republican Party, 1976-83. Mem. ABA, Ill. Bar Assn., Tex. Bar Assn., D.C. Bar Assn., State Bar Calif., Knights Templar, Beta Gamma Sigma, Phi Delta Phi, Beta Theta Pi. Clubs: University (Houston); Capitol Hill (Washington). Construction, General corporate, Environmental. Home and Office: 101 Westheimer Rd Apt F Houston TX 77006-3360

**EASTLAND, S. STACY,** lawyer; b. Houston, Oct. 27, 1948; s. Seaborn and Anne (Stacy) E.; m. Tara Gardner, Mar. 24, 1972; children: Tara Doran, Seaborn Gardner. BS, Washington & Lee U, 1971; JD, U. Tex., 1974. Assoc. Baker & Botts, Houston, 1974-81, ptnr., 1982—; bd. dirs. Houston Estate and Fin. Forum, Camp Mystic, Inc.; mem. Tex. Bd. Legal Specialization in Estate Planning and Probate Law. Bd. dirs. Oscar Neuhaus Found., St. John Meml. Endowment Fund, Houston chpt. Ortin Soc., DePelchin Children's Ctr., Inst. Child and Family Svcs.; trustee Kelsey-Seabold Found. Fellow Am. Coll. Probate Counsel; mem. ABA (coun. 1990—, publs. coord. probate and trust divsn. 1992-93, bylaws and handbook com. 1992—, sec. adv. Revision Uniform Partnership Act 1987—, publs. com. 1992-93, budget and fin. com. 1991-92, chair divsn. coord. ann. meeting programs 1987-89), Am. Coll. Trust and Estate Counsel (bd. regents, chmn. transfer tax study com. 1988-93), Tex. State Bar Assn., Houston Bar Assn., Houston Country Club, Tex. Allegro Club. Episcopalian. Avocations: tennis, golf. Estate planning, Probate, Estate taxation. Home: 3730 Piping Rock Ln Houston TX 77027-4032

**EASTMAN, JENNIFER,** lawyer; b. Greenwich, Conn., Oct. 30, 1942; d. Lucius and Sarah (Frost) E. BA magna cum laude, Brandeis U., 1968; C.A.S., Harvard U., 1980; JD cum laude, Suffolk U., 1982. Bar: Mass. 1983. Instr. Framingham (Mass.) State Coll., 1984—; pvt. law practice Westwood, Mass., 1985—; instr. Clark U., Worcester, Mass., 1991—; mediator State Claims Ct., Plymouth, Mass., 1997—. Contbr. articles to profl. jours. Democrat. Avocations: literature, art, music, swimming. General corporate. Office: PO Box 470 Westwood MA 02090-0470

**EASTWOOD, MARY,** retired lawyer, womens rights advocate; b. Wiota, Wis., June 1, 1930; d. Ralph Edwin and Selma Viola (Berget) E. BS in Edn., U. Wis., 1951, JD, 1955. Social studies and history tchr. Potosi (Wis.) High Sch., 1951-53; staff atty. Hwy. Laws Project NAS, Washington, 1955-60; atty. advisor Office Legal Counsel U.S. Dept. Justice, Washington, 1960-79; assoc. spl. council U.S. Merit Syss. Protection Bd., Washington, 1979-82, acting spl. counsel, 1980-81; pres. Equal Opportunity Conss., Inc., Lanham, Md., 1984-88; technical sec. Pres.'s Commn. Status of Women, 1962-63. Contbr. articles to profl. jours., chpts. to books. Founding mem. NOW, Washington, 1966, Federally Employed Women, Washington, 1968, Human Rights for Women, Washington, 1968; pres. Nat. Woman's Party, Washington, 1989-91, South Wayne (Wis.) Women's Club, 1994-98; v.p. Veteran Feminists of Am., 1997-98; exec. bd. dirs. Lafayette County Home and Cmty. Edn., 1997-98. Recipient Jessie Bernard award Ctr. Women Policy Studies, 1989, Veteran Feminists of Am. award, 1996, Disting. Alumnus award U. Wis., Platteville, 1998. Mem. Lafayette County Hist. Soc., Monroe (Wis.) Swiss Attic Questers (treas. 1998—), Sons of Norway. Avocations: music, photography, flowers, cats.

**EASUM, NANCY G.,** lawyer; b. Monmouth, Ill., Sept. 1, 1956; d. Forrest G. and Mary L. (Galbreath) E. BA, Ill. Wesleyan U., 1978; JD, Valparaiso U., 1981. Bar: Ill. 1981. Asst. state's atty. Christian County State's Attys. Office, Taylorville, Ill., 1982-83; dep. gen. counsel Ill. Sec. of State, Springfield, 1983-99; spl. counsel to dir. Ill. State Police, Springfield, 1999—. Mem. adv. bd. Ill. Traffic Ct. Mem. Ill. State Bar Assn. (former chmn. traffic laws and cts.), Altrusa Internat. (pres. 1990-92), Altrusa Club of Springfield Found. (Internat. Found. legal advisor). Avocations: walking, bowling, music. Office: Ill State Police 201 E Adams St Ste 100 Springfield IL 62701-1100

**EATON, JAY,** lawyer; b. Waterloo, Iowa, Feb. 24, 1946. BBA, U. Iowa, 1968, JD with honors, 1971. Bar: Iowa 1971, Ohio 1972, Wis. 1977. Assoc. Nyemaster, Goode, Voigts, West, Hansell & O'Brien, Des Moines. Mem. ABA, Iowa State Bar Assn. (v.p. 1997-98, pres. 1998—), Polk County Bar Assn. (bd. dirs. 1989-97, pres. 1992-93). E-mail: je@nyemaster.com. General civil litigation, Contracts commercial, Environmental. Office: Nyemaster Goode Voigts West Hansell & O'Brien PC 700 Walnut St Ste 1600 Des Moines IA 50309-3800*

**EATON, JOE OSCAR,** federal judge; b. Monticello, Fla., Apr. 2, 1920; s. Robert Lewis and Mamie (Gireadeau) E. AB, Presbyn. Coll., 1941, LLD (hon.), 1979; LLB, U. Fla., 1948. Pvt. practice law Miami, Fla., 1948-51, 55-59; asst. state atty. Dade County, Fla., 1953; circuit judge Miami, 1954-55, 59-67; mem. Fla. Senate, 1956-59; mem. law firm Eaton & Achor, Miami, 1955-58, Sams, Anderson, Eaton & Alper, Miami, 1958-59; judge U.S. Dist. Ct. (so. dist.) Fla., 1967-83, chief judge, from 1983, now sr. judge; Instr. law

U. Miami Coll. Law, 1954-56. Served with USAAF, 1941-45; Served with USAF, 1951-52. Decorated D.F.C., Air medal. Methodist. Club: Kiwanian.

**EATON, JOEL DOUGLAS,** lawyer; b. Miami, Fla., Oct. 31, 1943; s. Joe Oscar and Patricia (MacVicar) E.; m. Mary Benson, June 24, 1967; children: Douglas, Darryl, David. BA, Yale U., 1965; JD, Harvard U., 1975. Bar: Fla. 1975, U.S. Dist. Ct. (so. dist.) Fla. 1976, U.S. Ct. Appeals (5th cir.) 1976, U.S. Supreme Ct. 1978, U.S. Ct. Appeals (11th cir.) 1981, U.S. Ct. Appeals (Fed. cir.) 1996. Ptnr. Podhurst, Orseck, Josefbert, Eaton, Meadow, Olin & Perwin, P.A. and predecessors, Miami, 1975—. With USN, 1965-71. Decorated Air medal with Bronze Star and numeral 14, Navy Commendation medal with 2 gold stars, Cross of Gallantry (Viet Nam). Mem. ABA, ATLA, Am. Law Inst., Acad. Fla. Trial Lawyers, Fla. Bar Assn. (appellate rules com. 1981—, chmn. 1989-90, jud. evaluation com. 1995-98, Fla. std. jury instn. com. 1998—). Democrat. State civil litigation, Federal civil litigation, Appellate. Office: Podhurst Orseck Josefsberg Eaton Meadow Olin & Perwin PA 25 W Flagler St Ste 800 Miami FL 33130-1720

**EATON, LARRY RALPH,** lawyer; b. Quincy, Ill., Aug. 18, 1944; s. Roscoe Ralph and Velma Marie (Beckett) E.; m. Janet Claire Rosen, Oct. 28, 1978. B.A., Western Ill. U., 1965; J.D., U. Mich., 1968. Bar: Ill. 1968, U.S. Dist. Ct. (no. dist.) Ill. 1976, U.S. Supreme Ct. 1978, U.S. Ct. Appeals (D.C. cir.) 1984, U.S. Ct. Appeals (7th cir.) 1989. U.S. Peace Corps vol. Instr. law U. Liberia Sch. Law, Monrovia, 1968-70; lawyer Forest Park Found., Peoria Heights, Ill., 1970-71; asst. atty. gen. State of Ill., Springfield, 1971-75; ptnr. Peterson & Ross and predecessor firms, Chgo., 1975-94; founder Blatt, Hammesfahr & Eaton, Chgo., 1994—; instr. environ. law Quincy Coll., Ill., 1973-75; mem. Ill. Indsl. Pollution Control Financing Authority, 1979; bd. dirs. Near North Montessori Sch., 1989-95, vice chair 1992-95. Contbg. writer Chgo. Daily Law Bull., 1975-77; field editor Pollution Engring., 1976. Fellow Ill. Bar Found. (charter); mem. ABA (environ. ins. litigation task force 1990—), Atticus Finch Inn of Ct., Ill. Bar Assn. (chmn. environ. control law sect. 1976-77, mem. coun. 1973-77, 1990-94, editor sect. newsletter 1972-77, mem. assembly 1980-86, 89-92), Chgo. Bar Assn. (environ law sect. 1990—), Bar Assn. for 7th Jud. Cir., Law Club Chgo. Environmental, Insurance, Federal civil litigation.

**EATON, MICHAEL WILLIAM,** lawyer, educator; b. Dallas, July 28, 1958; s. Charles H. and Helen Gilbough (Miller) E. BS in Polit. Sci., So. Meth. U., 1980, JD, 1984; postgrad., U. Tex., Dallas, 1997—. Bar: Tex. 1984, U.S. Dist. Ct. (no. dist.) Tex. 1985, U.S. Ct. Appeals (5th cir.) 1986, U.S. Supreme Ct. 1988. Asst. gen. counsel Kirby Oil Co., Inc., Dallas, 1984-85; ptnr. Leonard & Eaton, Dallas, 1985-86; assoc. Page & Addison, P.C., Dallas, 1986-87; pvt. practice Dallas, 1987—; pres. San Jacinto Investments Group, 1992—; lectr. in econs. El Centro (Tex.) Coll., 1995—; lectr. in constl. law U. Tex., Dallas, 1996—; founder, dir. Tex. Jury Rsch. Inst., 1996—; founding ptnr. Affordable Housing Solutions, 1998—. Co-author: Expert Witnesses in The Courtroom, 1996; reviewer Am. Jour. of Polit. Sci., 1994—. Vol. Texans for Bush/Quayle, Dallas, 1988; del. John Connolly for Pres. Campaign, Dallas, New Orleans, 1980; north Tex. youth coord. William P. Clements for Gov. Campaign, Dallas, Ft. Worth, Denton, 1978; So. Meth. U. re-election chmn. John Tower for U.S. Senate Campaign, Dallas, 1978. Mem. Nat. Audubon Soc., Nature Conservancy, State Bar Tex., Tex. Young Lawyers Assn., Dallas Assn. Young Lawyers, Assn. Trial Lawyers Am., Lawyers Concerned for Lawyers (officer Dallas Lawyers Concerned Lawyers 1996-97, 1997—), Smithsonian Instn. Nat. Arbor Day Found., Phi Alpha Delta, Ancient Order of Hibernians (pres. 1998—). Republican. Roman Catholic. Avocations: golf, gourmet cooking, travel. General civil litigation, Family and matrimonial, State civil litigation. Office: 4151 Belt Line Rd Ste 124 Dallas TX 75244-2323 also: 704 Oakwood Tower 3626 N Hall St Dallas TX 75219-5107

**EATON, PHILLIP DALE,** lawyer; b. Tulsa, July 4, 1940; s. Elmer Dale and Mozelle (Villings) E.; m. Shirley Ann Rosa, Aug. 20, 1961; children: Christopher Dale, Jeffrey Phillip. AA, Santa Ana Coll., 1967; JD, Pepperdine U. Sch. Law, 1972. Bar: Calif. 1972, U.S. Dist. Ct. Ctrl. Dist. Calif. 1973, U.S. Dist. Ct. (so. dist. ) Calif. 1988, U.S. Ct. Appeals (9th cir.) 1975. Police officer Santa Ana (Calif.) Police Dept., 1962-68; investigator Dist. Atty., Santa Ana, 1968-72; sole practice law Santa Ana, 1972—; instr. Santa Ana Coll., 1971-84. Mem. Redevel. Commn. Orange, Calif., 1980-82; mem. Citizen's Adv. Bd., Santa Ana, 1988-89. Served in U.S. Army, 1957-60. Mem. U.S. Sailing Assn. (bd. dirs.), Yacht Racing Union So. Calif. (commodore), So. Calif. Yachting Assn. (bd. dirs. 1993-96, judge advocate 1999), Assn. Orange Coast Yacht Clubs (commodore 1992), Am. Legion, Dana West Yacht Club. Office: 888 W Santa Ana Blvd Ste 150 Santa Ana CA 92701-4576

**EAYRS, SONJA TROM,** lawyer; b. Austin, Minn., Oct. 4, 1958; d. Lowell I. and Evelyn G. (Gross) Trom; m. Douglas A. Eayrs; children: Rebekah K., Kathleen R. BA, Carleton Coll., 1985; JD, Marquette U., 1989. Bar: Minn. 1989, Wisc. 1989, Fla. 1999. Assoc. Moss & Barnett, PA, Mpls., 1989-91, Goff, Kaplan & Wolf, PA, St. Paul, 1991-95; ptnr. Zalk & Eayrs, PA, Mpls., 1995-99; chair Ramsey County Family Law sect., St. Paul, 1995-96. Contbr. articles to profl. jours. Family and matrimonial.

**EBEL, DAVID M.,** federal judge; b. 1940. BA, Northwestern U., 1962; JD, U. Mich., 1965. Law clk. assoc. justice Byron White U.S. Supreme Ct., 1965-66; pvt. practice Davis, Graham & Stubbs, Denver, 1966-88; judge U.S. Ct. Appeals (10th cir.), Denver, 1988—; adj. prof. law U. Denver Law Sch., 1987-89; sr. lectr. fellow Duke U. Sch. Law, 1992-94. Mem. Am. Coll. Trial Lawyers, Colo. Bar Assn. (v.p. 1982), Jud. Conf. U.S. (com. on codes of conduct 1991-98, co-chair 10th cir. gender bias task force 1994—). Office: US Ct Appeals 1823 Stout St Rm 109L Denver CO 80257-1823

**EBELL, C(ECIL) WALTER,** lawyer; b. Baker, Oreg., June 26, 1947; s. Cecil John and Sylvia Jean (Malone) E.; m. Dianna Rae Gentry, June 2, 1980; children: Anne, Erik, Michael. BS, Oreg. State U., 1970; MS, U. No. Colo., 1973; JD, Lewis and Clark Coll., 1977. Bar: Oreg. 1977, Alaska 1978, U.S. Ct. Appeals (9th cir.) 1981, U.S. Supreme Ct. 1985, Wash. 1990. Pvt. practice Portland, Oreg., 1977-78; ptnr. Hartig, Rhodes, Norman & Mahoney, Anchorage, 1978-84, Jamin, Ebell, Bolger & Gentry, Kodiak, Alaska, 1984-97, Jamin, Ebell, Schmitt & Mason, Seattle, 1997—. Press sec., Clay Myers for Gov. campaign, Oreg., 1974. Capt. USMC, 1970-73. Mem. ABA, Assn. Trial Lawyers Am., Rotary. Democrat. Avocations: photography, fishing, skiing. Admiralty, General corporate, Native American. Office: Jamin Ebell Schmitt Mason 300 Mutual Life Bldg 605 1st Ave Seattle WA 98104-2207

**EBERHARD, ERIC DRAKE,** lawyer; b. Alliance, Ohio, Sept. 21, 1945; s. Edward G. and Margaret R. (Drake) E. BA, Western Reserve U., 1967; JD, U. Cin., 1970; LLM, George Washington U., 1972. Bar: Ohio 1970, D.C. 1971, N.Mex. 1973, Navajo Nation 1978, U.S. Ct. Appeals (D.C. cir.) 1979, U.S. Ct. Appeals (9th and 10th cirs) 1980, U.S. Ct. Appeals (fed. cir.) 1981, U.S. Supreme Ct. 1983, Wash. 1994. Assoc. Price & Scherr, Washington, 1971-72; staff atty. Legal Aid Soc. Cin., 1972-73, DNA-People's Legal Services, Window Rock, Ariz., 1973-78; ptnr. Luebben & Eberhard, Albuquerque, 1978; pvt. practice Albuquerque, 1978-82; dep. atty. gen. Navajo Nation Dept. Justice, Window Rock, 1982-84; exec. dir. Navajo Nation Washington Office, Washington, 1984-87; of counsel Gover, Stetson & Williams, Washington, 1987-88; counsel, minority staff dir. U.S. Senate Select Com. Indian Affairs, Washington, 1988-91; legis. counsel U.S. Senator John McCain, Washington, 1991-93; counsel U.S. Senate Com. Indian Affairs, 1993-95; mng. ptnr. Dorsey & Whitney, Seattle, 1995-99, mem. exec. com., 1999—. Recipient Outstanding Contbns. award Navajo Nation Ct. Appeals, Window Rock, 1984. Mem. D.C. Bar Assn., Navajo Nation Bar Assn. Administrative and regulatory, Environmental, Legislative. Office: Dorsey & Whitney Second & Seneca Bldg 1420 5th Ave Ste 4200 Seattle WA 98101-2375

**EBERHARDT, DANIEL HUGO,** lawyer; b. Milw., Feb. 19, 1938; s. Erwin M. and Hazel M. (Daley) E.; m. Josephine E. Jeka, Sept. 10, 1960; children: Daniel Hugo Jr., Mark John. BS, Colo. State U., 1962; JD, Marquette U., 1968. Bar: Wis. 1968, U.S. Dist. Ct. (ea. dist.) Wis. 1968. Assoc. Morrissy, Morrissy, Sweet & Race, Elkhorn, Wis., 1968-70; ptnr. Sweet & Eberhardt, Elkhorn, 1970-76; sole practice Elkhorn, 1976—; commr. Walworth County Cir. Cts., 1975—. Served to 1st lt. U.S. Army, 1962-65, AUS. Mem. ABA, Wis. Bar Assn., Walworth County Bar Assn. (sec., treas. 1983-85, v.p. 1985-86, pres. 1986-87), VFW (comdr. 1980-81). Republican. Roman Catholic. Lodge: Rotary (pres. 1980-81). Family and matrimonial, Probate, Real property. Home: N6601 Peck Station Rd Elkhorn WI 53121-3247 Office: 18 S Broad St PO Box 258 Elkhorn WI 53121-0258

**EBERHARDT, GRETCHEN ANN,** lawyer, hearing officer; b. Denver, Feb. 9, 1964; d. Robert Schuler and Lusetta Mary (Bush) E. BA in Sociology, U. Colo., 1986; JD, Whittier Coll., 1991. Bar: Colo. 1992, U.S. Ct. Appeals (10th cir.) 1992. Flight attendant Continental Airlines, Denver, 1987-88; due process hearing officer Colo. Dept. Edn., Denver, 1991—; ptnr. Eberhardt & Eberhardt, Littleton, Colo., 1991—; spkr. estate planning seminars AARP, Denver, 1996; phone-in cons. Law Line 9—Legal Questions, Channel 9, Sta. KUSA, Denver, 1994—. Vol., supr. Rocky Mountain PBS, Denver, 1993—; chmn. Arapahoe County Young Reps., Aurora, Colo., 1992-97; chmn. 26th Rep. Senatorial Dist., Arapahoe County and Jefferson County, 1997-99. Mem. Colo. Bar Assn., Arapahoe County Bar Assn. Republican. Roman Catholic. Avocations: traveling, skiing, swimming, reading, hiking. Estate planning, Personal injury, Family and matrimonial. Office: Eberhardt & Eberhardt 8441 W Bowles Ave Ste 210 Littleton CO 80123-9501

**EBERHARDT, ROBERT SCHULER, JR.,** lawyer; b. Denver, Aug. 13, 1928; s. Robert Schuler and Kathryn Marie (Babington) E.; m. Lusetta Mary Bush, Aug. 6, 1955; children: Robert S. III, Gretchen Ann, Derek Bush, Krista Kathryn. BJ, U. Colo., 1952, JD, 1955; postgrad., Georgetown U. Law Sch., 1953-54. Bar: Colo. 1955, Denver 1955. Sole practice Littleton, Colo., 1955—. Rep. Colo. State Legis., Denver, 1960-65. Served with U.S. Army, 1947-48. Mem. Phi Delta Phi, Sigma Delta Chi. Personal injury, Probate, Estate taxation. Home: 3811 Edward Rd Princeville Kavai HI 96722 Office: 8441 W Bowles Ave Suite 210 Littleton CO 80123

**EBERSOLE, JODI KAY,** lawyer; b. Pitts., Mar. 15, 1966; d. Denver J. Weigel and JoAnn Ramsey; m. Gary R. Ebersole, Nov. 3, 1990. BA in Social Work, Elizabethtown Coll., 1987; JD, Widener U., 1990. Bar: Md. 1990, D.C. 1991, U. S. Dist. Ct. Md. 1991, U.S. Ct. Appeals (4th cir.) 1991, U.S. Ct. Appeals (3d cir.) 1994. Assoc. Thieblot, Ryan, Martin & Ferguson, Balt., 1990-96; assoc. Ferguson, Schetelich & Heffernan, Balt., 1996-97, ptnr., 1997—. Mem. Md. State Bar Assn., Def. Rsch. Inst., Bar Assn. Balt. City (sec. young lawyers divsn. 1998—). Insurance, Professional liability, Personal injury. Office: Ferguson Schetelich & Heffernan 1401 Nations Bank Ctr 100 S Charles St Baltimore MD 21201-2725

**EBERT, GARY ANDREW,** lawyer; b. Sandusky, Ohio, May 15, 1950; s. Harry J. and Virginia M. Ebert; m. Pamela M. Wentz, Aug. 5, 1972; children: Caroline, Amanda, Brian. BS in Bus. Adminstrn., Ashland U., 1972; JD, Cleveland Marshall U., 1975. Bar: Ohio 1978, U.S. Dist. Ct. (no. dist.) Ohio 1978. Ptnr. Coltman, Ebert & Valore, Fairview Park, Ohio, 1978-91, Seeley, Savidge & Ebert, Cleve., 1991—; law dir. City of Bay Village, 1986—. Councilman City of Bay Village, Ohio, 1981-86; pres. St. Rapael's Athletic Commn., Bay Village, 1997—. Mem. Ohio State Bar Assn., Cuyahoga County Law Dir. Assn., Internat. Mpcl. Lawyers Assn. Avocations: coaching youth basketball and baseball, golf. General corporate, Estate planning, Municipal (including bonds). Home: 153 Kensington Cir Bay Village OH 44140-1060 Office: Seeley Savidge & Ebert 800 Bank One Ctr Cleveland OH 44114

**EBERT, LAWRENCE BURTON,** lawyer; b. Bronxville, N.Y., Jan. 14, 1949; s. Burton Eidell and Mildred Elizabeth (Hearting) E.; m. Rebeccca Ann Vares, Aug. 3, 1997. BS, U. Chgo., 1971, JD, 1993; PhD, Stanford U., 1975. Bar: N.Y. 1994, U.S. Dist. Ct. (ea. and so. dists.) N.Y. 1995, Fed. Cir. Ct. 1995. Staff scientist Exxon Corp. Rsch., Annandale, N.J., 1975-90; assoc. Pennie & Edmonds LLP, N.Y.C., 1993-98, Kenyon & Kenyon, N.Y.C., 1998—. Contbr. numerous sci. and legal articles to profl. jours. Fannie and John Hertz Found. fellow, 1971-75. Mem. ABA, Am. Phys. Soc., Am. Chem. Soc. Intellectual property, Patent, Trademark and copyright. Home: 390 Garretson Rd Bridgewater NJ 08807-1967 Office: Kenyon and Kenyon 1 Broadway New York NY 10004-1007

**EBERT, MICHAEL,** lawyer; b. N.Y.C., Jan. 9, 1917; s. Abraham and Bessie (Alster) E.; m. Rosalind Lein, June, 1941; 1 child, Carl. BS, CCNY, 1940; LLB, N.Y. Law Sch., 1952. Bar: N.Y. 1953, U.S. Dist. Ct. (so. and ea. dists.) N.Y. 1960, U.S. Ct. Appeals (Fed. cir.) 1982. Patent advisor U.S. Army Radar Labs., Belmar, N.J., 1942-44, Radiation Labs. MIT, Boston, 1944-46, NV Phillips of Holland, Irvington, N.Y., 1946-53; assoc. Kenyon & Kenyon, N.Y.C., 1953-60; ptnr. Lewy, Rosoff & Stern, N.Y.C., 1960-66, Hopgood, Calimafde et al, N.Y.C., 1966—; adj. prof. Cooper Union Sch. Engring., N.Y.C., 1983—; bd. dirs. Fluoramics, Inc., N.J., 1975—. Pres. East Side Democrats, N.Y.C., 1955-57. Sgt. U.S. Army Signal Corps, 1943-44. Mem. ABA, N.Y. Patent Law Assn. Patent, Education and schools. Office: Hopgood Calimafde et al 60 E 42nd St New York NY 10165-0006

**EBINER, ROBERT MAURICE,** lawyer; b. Los Angeles, Sept. 2, 1927; s. Maurice and Virginia (Grand) E.; m. Paula H. Van Sluyters, June 16, 1951; children: John, Lawrence, Marie, Michael, Christopher, Joseph, Francis, Matthew, Therese, Kathleen, Eileen, Brian, Patricia, Elizabeth, Ann. J.D., Loyola U., Los Angeles, 1953. Bar: Calif. 1954, U.S. dist. Ct. (cen. dist.) Calif. 1954. Solo practice, West Covina, Calif., 1954—; judge pro tem Los Angeles Superior Ct., 1964-66, arbitrator, 1979—; judge pro tem Citrus Mcpl. Ct., 1966-70; mem. disciplinary hearing panel Calif. State Bar, 1968-75. Bd. dirs. West Covina United Fund, 1958-61, chmn. budget com. 1960-61; organizer Joint United Funds East San Gabriel Valley, 1962, bd. dirs. 1961-68; bd. dirs. San Gabriel Valley Cath. Social Services, 1969—, pres., 1969-72; bd. dirs. Region II Cath. Social Service, 1970—, pres. 1970-74; trustee Los Angeles Cath. Welfare Bur. (now Cath. Charities), 1978—; charter bd. dirs. East San Gabriel Valley Hot Line, 1969-74, sec., 1969-72; charter bd. dirs. N.E. Los Angeles County unit Am. Cancer Soc., 1973-78, chmn. by-laws com. 1973-78; bd. dirs. Queen of the Valley Hosp. Found., 1983-89; organizer West Covina Hist. Soc., 1982—; active Calif. State Dem. Cen. Com., 1963-68; mng. meet dir. Greater La Puente Valley Spl. Olympics, 1985-88, Bishop Amat Relays, 1981-94; mem. MSAC Relays com., 1978-94; campaign mgr. Congressman Ronald B. Cameron, 1964. With U.S. Army, 1945-47. Recipient Los Angeles County Human Relations Commn. Disting. Service award, 1978, Thomas A. Kiefer Humanitarian award, 1993. Named West Covina Citizen of Yr., 1986, San Gabriel Valley Daily Tribune's Father of Yr., 1986. Mem. ABA, Calif. Bar Assn., Los Angeles County Bar Assn. (arbitrator 1975—), Fed. Ct. So. Dist. Calif. Assn., Los Angeles Trial Lawyers Assn., Eastern Bar Assn. Los Angeles County (pres. Pomona Valley 1965-66), West Covina C. of C. (pres. 1960), Am. Arbitration Assn. (arbitrator 1965—). Clubs: K.C., Bishop Amat High Sch. Booster (bd. dirs. 1973—, pres. 1978-80), Kiwanis (charter West Covina, pres. 1976-77, lt. gov. div. 35 1980-81, Kiwanian of Yr. 1978, 82, Disting. Lt. Gov. 1980-81, bd. dirs. Cal-Nev-Ha Found. 1986—). Avocations: collector of historical olympic and political memorabilia. State civil litigation, Personal injury, Probate. Office: 1000 E Garvey Ave S Ste 365 West Covina CA 91790-2900

**EBITZ, ELIZABETH KELLY,** lawyer; b. LaPorte, Ind., June 9, 1950; d. Joseph Monahan and Ann Mary (Barrett) Kelly; m. David MacKinnon Ebitz, Jan. 23, 1971 (div. 1981). AB with honors, Smith Coll., 1972; JD cum laude, Boston U., 1975. BAr: Maine 1979, Mass. 1975, U.S. Dist. Ct. Mass. 1976, U.S. Dist. Ct. Maine 1979, U.S. Ct. Appeals (1st cir.) 1976, U.S. Supreme Ct. 1982. Law clk. Boston Legal Assistance Project, 1973-75; law clk., assoc. Law Offices of John J. Thornton, Boston, 1974-76; ptnr. Ebitz & Zurn, Northampton, Mass., 1976-79; assoc. Gross, Minsky, Mogul & Singal, Bangor, Maine, 1979-80; pres. Elizabeth Kelly Ebitz P.A., Bangor, 1980-92, Ebitz & Thornton, P.A., 1993—. Pres. Greater Bangor Rape Crisis Bd., 1983-85; bd. dirs. Greater Bangor Area Shelter, 1985-92, 93-99, Maine Women's Lobby, 1986-89, No. Maine Bread for the World, 1987-90; bd. dirs. Am. Heart Assn., Maine, 1989—, chair, 1993-95; mem. various peace, feminist and hunger orgns., Bangor, 1982—. Named Young Career Woman of Hampshire County, Nat. Bus. and Profl. Women, Northampton, 1979. Mem. ABA, ATLA, Sigma Xi. Democrat. Roman Catholic. Family and matrimonial, Personal injury, Pension, profit-sharing, and employee benefits. Home: 111 Maple St Bangor ME 04401-4031 Office: 15 Columbia St PO Box 641 Bangor ME 04402-0641

**EBLIN, ROBERT L.,** lawyer; b. Columbus, Ohio, Apr. 21, 1963. AB cum laude, Harvard U., 1985; JD summa cum laude, Ohio State U., 1991. Bar: Ohio 1991, U.S. Dist. Ct. (so. dist.) Ohio 1991, U.S. Ct. Appeals (6th cir.) 1992, U.S. Supreme Ct. 1997. Assoc. Schwartz Warren & Ramirez, Columbus, 1991-96, Arter & Hadden LLP, Columbus, 1997—; adj. prof. law Ohio State U., Columbus, 1997. Contbg. author: Looking at Law School, 3d edit., 1990, 4th edit., 1997, Liability of Corporate Officers and Directors, 6th edit., 1999. Mem. Ohio Human Rights Bar Assn. (trustee 1989-93, 99—), Profl. Liability Underwriting Soc., Order of Coif. General civil litigation, Labor. Office: Arter & Hadden LLP 10 W Broad St Ste 2100 Columbus OH 43215-3422

**EBNER, RUTH,** lawyer; b. Wolfratzhausen, Germany, Aug. 10, 1947; came to U.S., 1949; d. Alexander and Helen (Walrauch) E.; m. Mark Green, Nov. 25, 1979 (div. Aug. 1981); 1 child, Noah Abram. BA cum laude, U. Ill., Chgo., 1967; MA, U. Ill., Urbana, 1971; JD magna cum laude, Southwestern U., 1980. Bar: Calif., 1981; U.S. Dist. Ct. (cen. dist.) Calif. 1981, U.S. Ct. Appeals (9th cir.) 1982. Tchr. Chgo. Pub. Schs., 1969-71; asst. head overseas pub. rels. Hebrew U., Jerusalem, 1973-75; tchr. Goldwater H.S., Eilat, Israel, 1975-76; dep. city atty. City of L.A., 1983—; legal advisor Planned Parenthood, Manhattan Beach, Calif., 1992-93, L.A. Women's Shakespeare Co., L.A., 1992-93; legal council Jewish Fedn., L.A., 1993-97. Mem. Santa Monica (Calif.) City Coun., 1994—. Recipient Dynamic Woman award Santa Monica C. of C., 1996, Congl. Commendation award U.S. Congress, 1997. Avocations: scuba diving, painting. Office: Office of City Atty 1645 Corinth Ave # 211 Los Angeles CA 90025-3150

**ECABERT, PETER LEO,** lawyer, accountant; b. Greenville, Ohio, Sept. 10, 1948; s. C.M. and Mary M. (Richard) E.; children: Christina Lynn, Angela Marie. BSBA in Acctg., Georgetown U., 1970; postgrad., Exeter (Eng.) U., 1973; JD with distinction, Ohio No. U., 1974; LLM in Taxation, Boston U., 1977. Bar: Ohio 1974, U.S. Dist. Ct. (ea. dist.) Ky. 1977, Ky. 1978, U.S. Tax Ct. 1979, U.S. Ct. Claims 1981; CPA, Ky. Tax sr. Deloitte Haskins & Sells, Boston, 1974-77, Lexington, Ky., 1977-79; assoc. Stites & Harbision, Lexington, Ky., 1979-81, ptnr., 1981-88; assoc. gen. counsel Deloitte Haskins & Sells, N.Y.C., 1988-90; mem. firm McBrayer, McGinnis, Leslie & Kirkland, Lexington, Ky., 1990-92; ptnr. Scoville, Cessna, Crawford & Ecabert, Lexington, Ky., 1992-95; pvt. practice Lexington, Ky., 1995—; speaker in field. Mng. editor: Ohio No. U. Law Review, 1972-74. Mem. ABA, Ky. Bar Assn. (past chmn. taxation sect.), Ohio Bar Assn., Fayette County Bar Assn., Am. Inst. CPAs, Ky. Soc. CPAs, Am. Arbitration Assn., Willis Legal Hon. Soc., Phi Kappa Phi. Republican. Roman Catholic. E-mail: pecabert@aol.com. General civil litigation, Estate planning. Office: Chevy Chase Plz 836 E Euclid Ave Ste 207 Lexington KY 40502-1777

**ECHOLS, DOUGLAS ALLEN,** lawyer; b. Farmington, N.Mex., Jan. 7, 1955; s. Jack A. and Della Mae (Allred) E.; m. Evangeline R. Cochran, Aug. 6, 1994. AA, San Juan Coll., Farmington, 1975; BA, N.Mex. State U., 1977; JD, U. Okla., 1979. Bar: N.Mex. 1980, U.S. Dist. Ct. N.Mex. 1980, U.S. Ct. Appeals (10th cir.) 1980. Shareholder Tansey Law Firm, Farmington, 1980-97; shareholder Rosebrough, Thrower & Echols, Farmington, 1997-98; asst. city atty. Farmington, 1998—. Del. San Juan County Dem. Com., 1980, 84, 86, 88, 90, 92, 94. Recipient Trial Advocacy Pro Bono award Legal Svcs. of San Juan County, 1995. Mem. N.Mex. Bar Assn., San Juan County Bar Assn., Order of Coif, Masons, Elks. s. Democrat. Methodist. Municipal (including bonds), Administrative and regulatory, Banking. Office: City of Farmington 800 Municipal Dr Farmington NM 87401-2663

**ECHOLS, ROBERT L.,** federal judge; b. 1941. BA, Rhodes Coll., 1962; JD, U. Tenn., 1964. Law clk. to Hon. Marion S. Boyd U.S. Dist. Ct. (we. dist.) Tenn., Nashville, 1965-66; legis. asst. Congressman Dan Kuykendall, 1967-69; ptnr. Baily, Ewing, Dale & Conner, Nashville, 1969-72, Dearborn & Ewing, Nashville, 1972-92; fed. judge U.S. Dist. Ct. (mid. dist.) Tenn., Nashville, 1992—, chief judge, 1998—. With U.S. Army, 1966; col. Tenn. Army N.G., 1969—. Mem. ABA, Am. Bar Found., Am. Coll. Mortgage Attys., Fed. Judges Assn., Tenn. State-Fed. Jud. Coun., Am. Judicature Soc., Tenn. Bar Found., Tenn. Bar Assn., Nashville Bar Assn., Nashville Bar Found., Harry Phillips Am. Inn of Ct., Jud. Br. Com. U.S. Jud. Conf. Office: US Dist Ct 801 Broadway Ste 824 Nashville TN 37203-3868

**ECHSNER, STEPHEN HERRE,** lawyer; b. Columbus, Ind., Dec. 25, 1954; s. Herman Joseph and Virginia Blair (Lechleiter) E. BA, Marquette U., 1977; JD, St. Louis U., 1980. Bar: Fla. 1980, U.S. Dist. Ct. (no. dist.) Fla. 1980, U.S. Ct. Appeals (5th and 11th cirs.) 1980, U.S. Dist. Ct. (mid. dist.) Fla. 1988, U.S. Supreme Ct. 1988. Assoc. Levin, Middlebrooks, Thomas, Mitchell, Green, Echsner, et al, Pensacola, Fla., 1980-85, ptnr., 1985—. Mem. ABA, Assn. Trial Lawyers Am., Acad. Fla. Trial Lawyers. Roman Catholic. Personal injury, Insurance. Home: 23 N Sunset Blvd Gulf Breeze FL 32561-4051 Office: Levin Middlebrooks Thomas Mitchell Green Echsner et al PO Box 12308 Pensacola FL 32581-2308

**ECK, JOHN TERRENCE,** lawyer; b. Mpls., Jan. 4, 1969; s. Terrence J. and Nancy Eck; m. Tammy L. Eck. BA in Polit. Sci., So. Meth. U., 1991, BS in Econs., 1991; JD, U. Okla., 1994. Assoc. Law Offices Robert T. Stites, Ft. Worth, 1994—. Office: Law Offices of Robert T Stites 933 W Weatherford St Fort Worth TX 76102-1800

**ECK, ROBERT JOSEPH,** lawyer; b. St. Louis, Mo., Mar. 10, 1939; s. Joseph A. and Virginia M. (Bruhin) E.; m. Carol J. Sawicki, May 21, 1966; children: Stephanie, Renee, Justin. BSCE, Washington U., St. Louis, 1961, JD, 1964. Bar: Mo. 1964, U.S. Supreme Ct. 1970, N.Y. 1981. Pvt. practice St. Louis, 1964-71; assoc. gen. counsel Seven-Up Co., St. Louis, 1971-80; v.p., assoc. gen. counsel Philip Morris Mgmt. Corp., Rye Brook, 1980—. Mem. ABA, Internat. Bar Assn., U.S. Trademark Assn. (dir., pres. 1987-88), Met. St. Louis Assn. Protection of Indsl. Property, Inter-Am. Assn. Indsl. Property. Republican. Roman Catholic. Trademark and copyright. Home: 245 Daybreak Rd Southport CT 06490-1011 Office: Philip Morris Mgmt Corp 800 Westchester Ave Rye Brook NY 10573-1322

**ECKER, HOWARD,** lawyer; b. N.Y.C., June 10, 1946; s. David and Sylvia (Goldstein) E.; children: David, Ashley. BA, U. Mich., 1967; JD, NYU, 1971. Bar: Nev. 1973, U.S. Dist. Ct. Nev. 1974, U.S. Ct. Appeals (9th cir.) 1976, U.S. Supreme Ct. 1976. Pub. defender Clark County Pub. Defender's Office, Nev., 1973-77; ptnr. Ecker & Standish, Chtd., Clark County, Nev., 1977—; apptd. settlement judge in appeals Nev. Supreme Ct., 1997—; guest lectr. in field. Mem. Nev. Employee Mgmt. Rels. Bd., Las Vegas, 1990-94. Mem. ATLA, State Bar Nev. (bd. govs. 1984-90), Clark County Bar Assn., Nev. Trial Lawyers Assn. (bd. govs. 1977-89, pres. 1985-86), Nev. Am. Inns of Ct. (barrister 1990-93, master 1993—). Avocations: travel, golf, reading. Family and matrimonial. Office: Ecker & Standish Chtd 300 S 4th St Ste 611 Las Vegas NV 89101-6017

**ECKERT, MICHAEL LOUIS,** lawyer; b. Oshkosh, Wis., Jan. 14, 1950; s. Vincent Edward and Eileen Margaret (Lienum) E.; m. Mary Patricia Kroll, May 27, 1972; children—Brian W., Jeffrey V., Matthew J. BA, U. Wis., 1972, JD, 1975. Bar: Wis. 1975, U.S. Dist. Ct. (ea. and we. dists.) Wis. 1975, U.S. Ct. Appeals (7th cir.) 1976. ptnr. Eckert Law Office, Rhinelander, Wis., 1975-85; owner, Eckert Law Office, Rhineland, Wis., 1985-93; ptnr., Eckert Law Office, Rhinelander, 1993—. teaching atty. U. Wis. Law Sch., 1983, 86. Bd. dirs. Rhinelander Indsl. Devel. Corp., 1982—, Sacred Heart-St. Mary's Hosp., 1982—, Community Mental Health Services, 1986—, Sta. WXPR-FM Pub. Radio, 1986—, Older Am. Service Bur., 1986—, White Pines Community Broadcasting, 1987—. Recipient Wall Street Jour. Student Achievement award Dow-Jones, Inc., 1972. Mem. ABA, Oneida-Vilas-Forest County Bar Assn. (pres. 1982-83), Fedn. Ins. and Corp. Counsel, Def. Rsch. Inst., Civil Trial Counsel Wis. (pres. 1997-98), Internat. Assn. Def. Counsel, Kiwanis. Republican. Roman Catholic. Insurance, State civil litigation, Personal injury. Home: 1526 Riverglen Ave Rhinelander WI 54501-2400 Office: Eckert Kost & Vocke PO Box 1247 Rhinelander WI 54501-1247

**ECKL, WILLIAM WRAY,** lawyer; b. Florence, Ala., Dec. 2, 1936; s. Louis Arnold and Patricia Barclift (Dowd) E.; m. Mary Lynn McGough, June 29, 1963; children—Eric Dowd, Lynn Lacey. B.A., U. Notre Dame, 1959, LL.B., U. Va., 1962. Bar: Va. 1962, Ala. 1962, Ga. 1964. Law clk. Supreme

Ct. of Ala., 1962; ptnr. Gambrell, Harlan, Russell & Moye, Atlanta, 1965-68, Swift, Currie, McGhee & Hiers, Atlanta, 1968-82, Drew, Eckl & Farnham, Atlanta, 1983—. Served to capt. JAGC, USAR, 1962-65. Mem. Def. Research Inst., State Bar of Ga. Roman Catholic. Clubs: Lawyers of Atlanta, Brookwood Hills. Product liability, Insurance, Personal injury. Home: 348 Camden Rd NE Atlanta GA 30309-1513 Office: Drew Eckl & Farnham 880 W Peachtree St PO Box 7600 Atlanta GA 30357-0600

**ECKMAN, DAVID WALTER,** lawyer; b. Ogden, Utah, Oct. 23, 1942; s. Walter and Ann-Marie Pauline Eckman; m. Laurie Alden Waters, Aug. 28, 19. Student, Rice U., 1960-61; B.A. with honors, U. Tex., Austin, 1964, J.D. (Sam D. Hanna scholar), 1967. Bar: Tex. 1967, Calif. 1976, U.S Ct. Appeals (5th cir.) 1983. With Exxon Co., U.S.A. div. Exxon Corp., 1967-78; mem. Prudhoe Bay Law Task Force Exxon Co., U.S.A. div. Exxon Corp., Houston and Los Angeles, 1974-75; counsel Pacific Region Exxon Co., U.S.A. div. Exxon Corp., Los Angeles, 1975-77; counsel hdqrs. Exxon Co., U.S.A. div. Exxon Corp., Houston, 1977-78; gen. counsel Natomas N.Am. Inc., Houston, 1978; v.p.-legal, corp. chief legal counsel Natomas N.Am. Inc., 1978-82; sole practice Houston, 1982—. Vestryman, dir. Christian edn. All Sts. Episcopal Ch., Corpus Christi, 1968-70; leader adult study St. Mark's Episcopal Ch., Houston, 1971-74; v.p. St. Mark's Sch. PTO, 1981-82; vol. Bible Study tchr., one-on-one counseling Tex. Dept. Criminal Justice, Houston, 1983-94; lay reader St. John the Divine Episc. Ch., Houston, 1982—, leader adult study, 1983-86, 94—; bd. mem. Houston Legal Clin., 1999—; mem. St. Patrick's Sch. Bd., Thousand Oaks, Calif., 1976-77; pres. Houston Youth Soccer Assn., 1979-81, bd. dirs., 1979-83; pres. Neartown Soccer Club, 1980-83; v.p. Old Braeswood Civic Assn., 1982-85; bd. dirs. Friends of Pyramid House, Inc., 1985-95. Recipient Am. Jurisprudence award in antitrust law U. Tex., 1967. Mem. Tex. State Bar, Calif. State Bar, Houston Bar Assn., Full Gospel Bus. Men's Fellowship Internat. (v.p. downtown Houston chpt. 1985-89), Lambda Chi Alpha, Phi Delta Phi. General practice, Family and matrimonial, General corporate. Office: 3730 Kirby Dr Ste 1200 Houston TX 77098-3979

**ECKWEILER, KARL TERRANCE,** lawyer; b. Bridgeport, Conn., Apr. 18, 1961; s. Henry Williams and Elaine Ann Eckweiler; m. Beth Ann Bailey, Feb. 4, 1984; children: Talbot, Karsen, Tucker, Dane. BSBA, Bryant Coll., 1983; JD, U. Bridgeport, 1987. Bar: Conn. 1987, U.S. Dist. Ct. Conn. 1988. Materials mgr. Consolidate Mobile Diesel Equipment Co., Waterbury, Conn., 1983-84; supr. United Parcel Svc., Stratford, Conn., 1984-85; counsel dept. environ., health and safety Xerox Corp., Stamford, Conn., 1987—. Corporator Lower Naugatuck Valley Boys Club, Shelton, 1997-98. Mem. Am. Corp. Counsel Assn., Huntington/Shelton Exch. Club (bd. dirs. 1998). Avocations: hunting, fishing, camping. Environmental, Product liability. Office: Xerox Corp 800 Long Ridge Rd Stamford CT 06902-1288

**EDEE, JAMES PHILIP,** lawyer; b. Pawnee City, Nebr., Oct. 12, 1929; s. Allen Barnett and Helen (Reavy) E.; m. Sheila Grainger, Nov. 15, 1951; children: Alix Nardone, Eric Edee, Brooke Stark. BS in Law, U. Nebr., 1952, JD, 1954; MBA, Ga. State U., 1971; LLM in Taxation, Emory U., 1975. Bar: Nebr. 1954, U.S. Dist. Ct. Nebr. 1954, Ga. 1958, U.S. Dist. Ct. (no. dist.)Ga. 1973, U.S. Tax Ct. 1973, U.S. Supreme Ct. 1973. Trust rep. 1st Atlanta Bank, 1956-61; atty. estate tax IRS, Atlanta, 1961-73; sole practice Atlanta, 1973—. Served to capt. USAF, 1954-56. Mem. Lawyers Club Atlanta, Atlanta Estate Planning Council. Republican (precinct chmn.). Presbyterian. Club: Cherokee. Probate, Estate taxation, Estate planning. Home: 2639 Battle Overlook NW Atlanta GA 30327-1202 Office: 2639 Battle Overlook NW Atlanta GA 30327-1202

**EDELBAUM, PHILIP R.,** lawyer; b. Bklyn., June 2, 1936; s. Maurice and Selma (Samuels) E.; m. Corinne Edelbaum, May 29, 1960 (div. Mar. 1974); children: Stacey K. Boretz, Evan Mark. BA, Adelphi U., 1957; LLB, NYU, 1960. Bar: N.Y. 1961, U.S. Dist. Cts. (so. and ea. dists.) N.Y. 1962, U.S. Ct. of Appeals (2d cir.) 1964, (3d cir.) 1977, U.S. Supreme Ct. 1965. Atty. criminal div. Legal Aid Soc., N.Y.C., 1961-63; pvt. practice N.Y.C., 1963—; faculty Nat. Inst. Trial Advocacy-N.E. Region, Nat. Inst. Trial Advocacy-N.E. Master Advocates, Hempstead, N.Y., 1985—, Cardozo Law Sch. intensive trial advocacy program, 1993—, ABA/USTA Trademark Trial Advocacy Inst., 1993—, Widener U. Sch. Law intensive trial advocacy program, 1995—; faculty trial techniques program Hofstra U. Sch. of Law, Hempstead, 1985—. Chmn. pool feasibility com. Town of Eastchester, N.Y., 1971-72. Mem. Nat. Def. Lawyers Criminal Cases, N.Y. Criminal Bar Assn., N.Y. State Bar Assn., Assn. of Bar of City of N.Y. (com. on criminal cts. op. and budget 1988-92, chmn. com. on criminal advocacy 1995—, mem. coun. criminal justice 1992—, com. to study alts. to incarceration and probation 1993-94, numerous sub-coms. on criminal justice 1988—). Avocations: classical music, bird watching, N.Y. Mets, cooking. Criminal. Home: 345 E 93rd St New York NY 10128-5515 Office: 100 Church St New York NY 10007-2601

**EDELL, MARC ZANE,** lawyer; b. Newark, Nov. 13, 1950; s. E. Joseph and Beverlee Edell; children: Eric, Steven, Alison. BS, Boston U., 1972; JD cum laude, N.Y. Law Sch., 1975. Bar: N.J. 1975, U.S. Dist. Ct. N.J. 1975, U.S. Supreme Ct. 1981, N.Y. 1982, U.S. Dist. Ct. (ea. and so. dists.) N.Y. 1982, U.S. Ct. Appeals (3rd cir.) 1982, U.S. Ct. Appeals (4th cir.) 1986, U.S. Ct. Fed. Claims, 1992; cert. civil trial lawyer Supreme Ct. N.J. Law sect. to hon. John C. Demos Superior Ct. N.J., 1975-76; assoc. Porzio, Bromberg & Newman, P.C., Morristown, N.J., 1976-81; prin. Porzio, Bromberg & Newman, P.C., Morristown, N.J., 1981-86, Budd Larner Gross Rosenbaum Greenberg & Sade, P.C., Short Hills, N.J., 1986-94, Edell & Assocs., P.C., Morristown, N.J., 1995—; adj. prof. Rutgers Law Sch., 1992-96, N.Y. Law Sch., 1993-97; spkr. in field. Contbr. articles to profl. jours. Named Trial Lawyer of Yr., Trial Lawyers for Pub. Justice, 1988. Fellow Am. Coll. Trial Lawyers, Internat. Soc. Barristers; mem. ABA, FBA, Am. Bd. Trial Advs., N.J. State Bar Assn. (bd. dirs. product liability and toxic tort sect., co-chair com. on mass tort litigation 1993-94), N.Y. State Bar Assn., Trial Attys. N.J., Morris County Bar Assn., U.S. V.I. Bar Assn., Vanderbilt Inns Ct. (Essex County chpt.). Office: Edell & Assocs PC PO Box 2355 1776 On The Green Morristown NJ 07960

**EDELMAN, ALAN IRWIN,** lawyer; b. Poughkeepsie, N.Y., June 14, 1958; s. Edwyn Herman and Shirley Frances (Kandel) E.; m. Erica Joy Schwartz, Aug. 16, 1981; children: Leah Hanit, Avram Natan, Samuel Aaron. BA, Cornell U., 1980; JD, Boston U., 1983. Bar: D.C. 1983, U.S. Dist. Ct. D.C. 1985, U.S. Supreme Ct. 1991. Atty. enforcement div. SEC, Washington, 1983-86, atty. Office of Gen. Counsel, 1986-87; counsel U.S. Senate Permanent Subcom. on Investigations, Washington, 1987-97, U.S. Senate Com. on Govtl. Affairs, 1997—. Edward F. Hennessy scholar Boston U., 1983. Mem. ABA, Fed. Bar Assn. Office: US Senate 326 Dirksen Senate Bldg Washington DC 20510-0001

**EDELMAN, BERNARD PAUL,** lawyer, counselor. BA with high distinction, U. Mich., 1981; JD, Northwestern U., 1985. Bar: Ill. 1985, U.S Dist. Ct. (no. dist.) Ill. 1985. Assoc. Friedman & Koven, Chgo., 1985-86; ptnr. Rosenthal & Schanfield, Chgo., 1987-94, Arnstein & Lehr, Chgo., 1994—; spl. asst. atty. gen. Ill. Atty. Gen.'s Office, Springfield, 1997—; spl. hearing officer Ill. Dept. Profl. Regulation, Chgo., 1996, Office Banks & Real Estate State Ill., Chgo., 1997—; chairperson Cook County Mandatory Ct. Annex Arbitration Program, Chgo., 1994—. Co-founder, pres., bd. dirs. The LaSalle St. Coun., Chgo., 1991—; bd. dirs. LaSalle St. Found., Chgo., 1994—; rep. City of Chgo., Dept. Cultural Affairs, North LaSalle St. Project, Project Adv. Panel, 1998—. Angell Scholar U. Mich., 1981; Crain's Chgo. Bus. honoree 40 Under 40, 1993. Mem. Econ. Club Chgo., Execs. Club Chgo., Mid Day Club (Chgo.), Pi Sigma Alpha. Avocations: golf, tennis, political history, photography. Fax: (312) 876-0288. E-mail: bpe@arnstein.com. General civil litigation, General corporate, Real property. Office: Arnstein & Lehr 120 S Riverside Plz Fl 12 Chicago IL 60606-3913

**EDELMAN, PAUL STERLING,** lawyer; b. Bklyn., Jan. 2, 1926; s. Joseph S. and Rose (Kaminsky) E.; m. Rosemary Jacobs, June 15, 1951; children: Peter, Jeffrey. AB, Harvard U., 1946, JD, 1950. Bar: N.Y. 1951, U.S. Dist. Ct. (so. and ea. dists.) N.Y. 1954, U.S. Ct. Appeals (2d cir.) 1965, U.S. Supreme Ct. 1967. Ptnr. Kreindler & Kreindler, N.Y.C., 1953-95, counsel, 1996—; legal advisor Andrea Doria TV show, 1984, QE2 TV show, 1995. Author: Maritime Injury and Death, 1960; editor: Maritime Law Reporter, 1987—, Marine Laws, 1993, 94; columnist N.Y. Law Jour. Served with U.S. Army, 1944-46. Fellow N.Y. Bar Found.; mem. ABA (past chmn. admiralty com., toxic and hazardous substances litigation com., mem. long range planning com. 1982-84, 88—, mem. TIPS council 1984-88, Soviet-Am lawyers conf. Moscow 1987, 94, TIPS lawyers conf. Russia 1993), Maritime Law Assn. (rep. to law of the sea seminar Moscow, 1994), N.Y. State Bar Assn. (INCL award 1980, 90, 93, chmn. INCL sect. 1982-83, editor Ins. Jour. 1973—), Assn. Trial Lawyers Am. (past chmn. admiralty coms.), Maritime Law Assn., World Peace Through Law Ctr., Hudson Valley Tennis Club, Hastings on Hudson (past chmn., planning bd.). Democrat. Jewish. Admiralty, Personal injury, Private international. Home: 57 Buena Vista Dr Hastings On Hudson NY 10706 Office: 100 Park Ave New York NY 10017-5516

**EDELSTEIN, DAVID NORTHON,** federal judge; b. N.Y.C., Feb. 16, 1910; s. Benjamin and Dora (Mancher) E.; m. Florence Koch, Feb. 18, 1940; children: Jonathan H., Jeffrey M. BS, Fordham U., MA, LLB. Bar: N.Y., Ct. Appeals Paris. Practiced in N.Y.C.; atty. claims divsn. U.S. Dept. Justice, 1944; asst. U.S. atty. So. Dist. N.Y., 1945-47, spl. asst. to atty. gen. in charge of lands divsn., 1947-48, asst. atty. gen. in charge customs divsn., 1948-51; judge U.S. Dist. Ct. So. Dist. N.Y., N.Y.C., 1951-94, chief judge, 1971-80, sr. judge, 1994—; former elected mem. Jud. Conf. U.S.; rep. Nat. Conf. Fed. Trial Judges, also mem. exec. and program coms., 1975-86; assisted Pres.'s Temporary Commn. on Employee Loyalty, preparation of report, 1946; mem. legis. com. Attys. Gen. Conf. on Crime, 1950; former mem. steering com. N.Y. Fed. Exec. Bd.; former mem. planning commn. Met. Conf. Chief Judges; founder student litigation tng. program So. Dist. N.Y.; mem. com. courtroom facilities Jud. Adminstrv. Div.; mem. White Plains Courthouse Com., 1983—, mem., former chmn. rules com.; former mem. nat. adv. bd. Ctr. for the Study of the Presidency; former mem. planning and program com. Jud. Conf. (2d cir.), mem. Jud. Adminstrn. Div. Com. to coordinate revision of Code of Jud. Conduct, mem. com. on jury charge simplification; mem. Com. So. Dist. N.Y. Ct. History. Author: The Ethics of Dilatory Motion Practice: Time for Change, 1976; co-author: Jouralist Privilege and the Criminal Defendant, 1979, The Continued Role of the Judiciary in Securities After McMahon, 1988; contbr. articles to Fordham Law Rev., Securities Arbitration, N.Y. Law Jour. Bd. advisors Health Edn. Found.; moderator Jud. Conf. on Legalization of Drugs in U.S.; former hon. mem. Beth Israel Med. Ctr., Interfaith Movement, Internat. Trade Divsn. of Wall St. Synagogue; former participant 23d annual Air War Coll. nat. security forum Chopin Found. Recipient medal of recognition Interfaith Movement, 1964, Humanitarian award N.Y. Philanthropic League, Juristic Excellence award Fed. Bar Coun., The Forum Club, Svc. Beyond Self award Rotary Internat. N.Y. Coun. Explorer Divsn. award, Jud. Recognition award Assn. Bar City N.Y., Greater N.Y. Coun., Explorer's Divsn. award for serving youth, 1979, Dean's medal of recognition Fordham U., 1990, Gold Medal Honor for Achievement award; named to James Monroe H.S. Hall of Fame, Hon. Mem. Crew of USS Franklin D. Roosevelt, Hon. Order of Ky. Cols.; included in Am. Jury Trial Found. A Tribute to Trial by Jury; former fellow Am. Bar Found. Mem. ABA (spl. com. to survey legal needs 1971-77, past chmn. speedy trial planning group, subcom. on planning for Dist. Cts., jud. adminstrn. div. lawyers conf. state and fed. practice com. 1989-90, lawyers conf. civil justice reform initiatives com. 1993—), Nat. Conf. Fed. Trial Judges (liaison to ABA), Fed. Bar Assn. (past pres. Empire chpt., past nat. del., past jud. selection com., past alt. del. ho. of dels), Maritime Lawyers Assn. (jud.), ATLA (hon.), Nat. Lawyers Club (hon.), Fordham Alumni Assn. (bd. dirs.), Lawyers Assn. Textile Industry (1st hon.), Pan Am. Med. Soc. (hon.), Phi Delta Phi (hon.). Office: US Dist Ct US Courthouse Foley Sq New York NY 10007-1501

**EDELSTEIN, PETER MICHAEL,** lawyer; b. N.Y.C., Jan. 11, 1943. BA, Boston U., 1964, JD, 1966; LLM, NYU, 1967. Bar: N.Y. 1966, Fla. 1978, Conn. 1982, U.S. Supreme Ct. 1977. Ptnr. Rockwood, Edelstein & Duffy, PC, Briarcliff Manor, N.Y., 1972-84; assoc. Peschio, Rockwood, Edelstein & Duffy, PA, Pompano Beach, Fla., 1978-84; ptnr. Edelstein & Lochner, Mt. Kisco, N.Y., 1984—; prof. law Pace U., Pleasantville, N.Y., 1973—, mem. adv. com. Law Sch., 1974—. Author: The Lender Liablity Deskbook, 1992; contbr. articles to profl. jours. Bd. dirs. Putnam Community Hosp., 1978. Recipient Kenan award Pace U., 1995-96, named Tchr. of Yr., 1992. Mem. ABA, N.Y. State Bar Assn. (spkr.), Conn. Bar Assn., Fla. Bar Assn., Ossining Bar Assn. (pres. 1974), Westchester Bar Assn. (editor-in-chief 1978-83, bd. dirs. 1981-87). Banking, Contracts commercial, General corporate. Office: Edelstein & Lochner 491 Lexington Ave Mount Kisco NY 10549-2717

**EDEN, NATHAN E.,** lawyer; b. Key West, Fla., Mar. 24, 1944; s. Delmar M. and Lois (Archer) E.; m. Cindy Pike, Jan. 4, 1964 (div. Mar. 1984); 1 child, Jennifer S. BA, U. Fla., 1966; JD magna cum laude, Stetson U., 1969. Bar: Fla. 1969, U.S. Dist. Ct. (so. and mid. dists.) Fla. 1969, U.S. Ct. Appeals (5th cir.) 1969, U.S. Ct. Appeals (11th cir.) 1982. Assoc. Nelson, Stinnett, Surfus, et al, Sarasota, Fla., 1969; ptnr. Feldman & Eden & predecessors, Key West, 1970-84; sole practice Key West, 1984—; of counsel Lazzara and Paul, P.A., Tampa, 1982—; bd. atty. Utility Bd. of Key West, 1974—; asst. pub. defender State of Fla., Key West, 1970, county solicitor State of Fla., Key West, 1970-72; chief asst. state atty State of Fla., Key West, 1972-74; U.S. magistrate, U.S. Dist. Ct. (so. dist.) Fla., 1974-78. Mem. jud. nominating com. 16th Jud. Cir. State of Fla., 1995, bd. dirs. Hospice Monroe County. Mem. Acad. Trial Lawyers, Fla. Acad. Trial Lawyers, Nat. Assn. Criminal Def. Lawyers, Fla. Bar Assn. (bd. govs. 1976-80), North Am. Hunt Club, NRA. Democrat. Avocations: hunting, softball, jogging, basketball. Criminal, Personal injury. Office: 402 Appleroouth Ln Key West FL 33040-6557 also: Lazzara and Paul PA Ste 2001 606 Madison St Tampa FL 33602-4017

**EDENFIELD, BERRY AVANT,** federal judge; b. Bulloch County, Ga., Aug. 2, 1934; s. Perry and Vera E.; m. Vida Melvis Bryant, Aug. 3, 1963. B.B.A. U. Ga, 1956, LL.B., 1958. Bar: Ga. 1958. Partner firm Allen, Edenfield, Brown & Wright (and predecessors), Statesboro, Ga., 1958-78; judge U.S. Dist. Ct. (so. dist.) Ga., Savannah, 1978-90, chief judge, 1990-97, judge, 1997—. Mem. Ga. Senate, 1965-66. Office: US Dist Ct PO Box 9865 Savannah GA 31412-0065

**EDENFIELD, JAMES FRANKLIN,** lawyer; b. Swainsboro, Ga., Dec. 17, 1949; s. James Otis and Bernice Lorine (Tucker) Drake; m. Joyce Marilyn Sloan Ramsey, Apr. 7, 1972 (div. May 1985); children: Sloan, Taylor; m. Dabney Harris Adams, May 25, 1985; children: Rocky, Curry, Cameron Brazzell. AB in History, U. Ga., 1971, JD cum laude, 1975. Ptnr. Spivey, Carlton & Edenfield, 1975—; county atty., atty. Emanuel Med. Ctr.; spl. trial counsel Emanuel County Devel. Authority; spl. bond counsel to the joint devel. authority Emanuel County and City of Swainsboro; interim state ct. solicitor State Ct. of Emanuel County, 1995-97, state ct. solicitor, 1997—. Former mem. Swainsboro Jaycees; former chmn. Emanuel County United Way; former mem. Savannah Coun. for Girl Scouts of Am.. Mem. Ga. Bar Assn. (middle cir. rep. to bd. govs., chmn. unauthorized practice of law com.), Middle Jud. Cir. Bar Assn., Emanuel County Bar Assn. (pres.). Avocations: woodworking, scuba diving, skiing, reading, cooking. General civil litigation, General practice, Insurance. Office: Spivey Carlton & Edenfield PC 210 N Main St Swainsboro GA 30401-3536

**EDENHOFER, CARL R.,** lawyer; b. Oak Park, Ill., Aug. 12, 1958. BS in History, No. Ariz. U., 1980; JD, Hamline U., 1983. Bar: Wis. 1983—, U.S. Dist. Ct. (ea. dist.) 1983—, U.S. Dist. Ct. (we. dist.) 1983—, 7th Cir. Ct. Appeals 1983—. Atty. Joling Rizzo & Willems S.C., Kenosha, Wis., 1983-86; atty., mng. ptnr. Joling Edenhofer & Van Cura, Kenosha, 1986-88, Joling Edenhofer & Assoc. S.C., Kenosha, 1988-95; atty., CEO Edenhofer Law Offices, S.C., Salem, Wis., 1995—; prof. Carthage Coll., Kenosha, 1988—, mem. adv. bd. paralegal program, 1988-95. Editor: Ob-Gyn Malpractice, 1986; contbr. articles to profl. jours. Bd. dirs. Plan Commn., Brighton, 1995—. Mem. Assn. Trial Lawyers Am. 1985—, Inadequate Security Litigation Group (treas. 1996—), State of Wis. Bar Assn. (sole small firm com. 1995—). Avocations: fishing, hiking, softball. Personal injury, Product liability, Estate planning. Office: Edenhofer Law Offices SC 23042 75th St Salem WI 53168-9465

**EDER, ELAINE ANNMARIE,** lawyer; b. Chgo., Apr. 25, 1953; d. Kurt Eduard and Violet Alvy (O'Malley) E.; m. Alfred Ernest Moreau, Oct. 9, 1982; children: Elizabeth, Andrew, Eileen. BA, Northwestern U., Evanston, Ill., 1973; JD, Emory U., 1975. Bar: Ga. 1976, Mass. 1977. Law clk. Mass. Land Ct., Boston, 1976-77; atty., advisor Army Armament Material Readiness Command, Rock Island, Ill., 1977-80; atty. Gen. Svcs. Adminstrn., Chgo., 1980-83; trial atty. procurement law, chief counsel USCG, Washington, 1983-95, chief trial atty., chief office of procurement law, 1995—, ADR coord., 1998—; mem. alumni admissions coun. Northwestern U., No. Va., 1988—; founding bd. dirs., vice-chair Our Kids Inc. USCG, Washington, 1991-93. Apptd. mem. Early Childhood Edn. Adv. Com., Arlington, Va., 1993-95, Arts Edn. Adv. Com., Arlington, 1995—; vol. Kennedy Ctr., Washington, 1995—; active Arlington PTA. Mem. Fed. Bar Assn. (pub. contract law sect.), Bds. of Contract Appeals Bar Assn., State Bar Ga. Office: USCG 2100 2d St SW Washington DC 20093

**EDER, TODD BRANDON,** lawyer; b. Englewood, N.J., Sept. 12, 1954; s. Harold Norman Eder and Jan (Schaffer) LeWinter; m. Lois Ann Friedman, July 31, 1983. B.A. in History magna cum laude, Boston U., 1977; J.D., U. Tulsa, 1980. Bar: N.J. 1980, U.S. Dist. Ct. N.J. 1980, N.Y. 1981, U.S. Dist. Ct. (so. dist.) N.Y. 1981, (ea. dist.) N.Y. 1981, U.S. Tax Ct. 1981, U.S. Ct. Claims 1981, U.S. Ct. Mil. Appeals 1981, U.S. Ct. Internat. Trade 1981, Fla. 1982, U.S. Ct. Appeals (3d cir.) 1982, (2d cir.) 1984, U.S. Supreme Ct. 1985; cert. civil trial atty., N.J. Congl. intern Robert F. Drinan, Washington, 1977; law librarian asst U. Tulsa Coll. Law Library, 1978-79; legal intern John B. Jarboe, Tulsa, 1979-80; law clk. Harold N. Eder, N.Y.C., 1980; asst. prosecutor Hudson County Prosecutor's Office, Jersey City, 1980-83; assoc. Morgan, Melhuish, Monaghan, Arvidson, Abrutyn & Lisowski, Livingston, N.J., 1984-87; ptnr. Garruto Cantor Trial Lawyers, P.C., East Brunswick, N.J., 1987-97; sole practitioner, East Brunswick, 1997—. Trustee United Way of Ctrl. N.J., 1997—, mem. exec. bd., 1998—. Mem. ATLA, Trial Lawyers Assn. N.J., N.Y. Bar Assn., N.J. Bar Assn., Middlesex County Bar Asn., Middlesex County Trial Lawyers Assn., East Brunswick Regional C. of C. Phi Delta Phi. State civil litigation, Federal civil litigation, Personal injury. Office: 646 Highway 18 Bldg B East Brunswick NJ 08816-3711

**EDERLE, DOUGLAS RICHARD,** investment manager; b. St. Louis, Aug. 10, 1962; s. Richard Joseph and Mary Ellen (Gorman) E.; m. Virginia Foss Mara, June 5, 1988; children: Ryan Douglas, William Gorman, Samuel Mara, Katherine Rose. BS in Acct. magna cum laude, U. Ill., 1984; JD, Harvard U., 1987. Bar: Tex. 1987, Mass. 1989. Assoc. Hughes & Luce, Dallas, 1987-88; ptnr. Testa, Hurwitz & Thibeault, Boston, 1989-98; sr. v.p., mng. dir. Pell, Rudman Trust Co., N.A., Boston, 1998—. Bd. advisors Project Bug Light, Little Angels Fund; treas. Duxbury Edn. Found. Mem. ABA, Tex. Bar Assn., Mass. Bar Assn., Boston Bar Assn. Roman Catholic. Avocations: golf, basketball, tennis. Home: PO Box 1942 32 Hounds Ditch Ln Duxbury MA 02332-4421 Office: Pell Rudman Trust Co NA 100 Federal St Ste 3700 Boston MA 02110-1802

**EDGAR, CHARLES WESLEY, III,** lawyer; b. Springfield, Ohio, Mar. 4, 1953; s. Charles Wesley and Rosemary (Neal) E.; children: Michael Damon, Mathew Christopher, Marc Benjamin. BA, Wittenberg U., 1975; JD, U. Miami, 1979. Bar: Fla. Assoc. gen. counsel Continental Mortgage Investors, Coral Gables, Fla., 1979-80; assoc. Greenberg, Traurig, et al, Miami, Fla., 1980-86; shareholder Greenberg, Traurig, et al, West Palm Beach, Fla., 1986-93, Levine, Frank, Edgar and Telepman, P.A., Palm Beach Gardens, Fla., 1993—; adj. prof. U. Miami Sch. Law, Coral Gables, 1982-85; adv. bd. U. Miami Inst. Condominium and Cluster Devel., Coral Gables. Columnist The Observer, 1994. Chair adv. coun. on cmty. assn. mgrs. State of Fla., Tallahassee; chair Tradewinds dist. Boy Scouts Am., West Palm Beach, 1989, v.p. fin. Gulf Stream Coun.; v.p. Gulf Stream Coun. Boy Scouts Am., 1996—; elder Palms West Presbyn. Ch., Royal Palm Beach, Fla., 1992. Recipient Dist. award of Merit, Boy Scouts Am., 1989. Mem. Palm Beach Polo and Country Club. Republican. Presbyterian. Avocations: golf, camping, canoeing. Real property, Land use and zoning (including planning). Office: Levine Frank Edgar & Telepman PA Ste 114 11380 Prosperity Farms Rd Palm Beach Gardens FL 33410-3464

**EDGAR, GEORGE LUKENS,** lawyer; b. Elkins Park, Pa., Nov. 2, 1941; s. George Barnes and Anne Lukens Edgar; m. Anne Harlan, Sept. 6, 1969; children: Gillian Lukens Curran, Jonathan Harlan. AB, Dartmouth Coll., 1963, BME, 1964; JD, George Washington U., 1970. Bar: D.C. 1970, U.S. Dist. Ct. D.C. 1970. Assoc. Morgan Lewis & Bockius, Washington, 1970-73, ptnr., 1973-83; ptnr. Newman & Holtzinger, Washington, 1983-94, Morgan Lewis & Bockius, Washington, 1994—; mem. steering group, lawyers com. Nuclear Energy Inst., Washington, 1994-98. Lt. USN, 1964-69. Mem. Washington Golf and Country Club, Long Cove Club. Avocations: golf, fishing. Nuclear power. Office: Morgan Lewis and Bockius LLP 1800 M St NW Washington DC 20036-5802

**EDGAR, R(OBERT) ALLAN,** federal judge; b. Munising, Mich., Oct. 6, 1940; s. Robert Richard and Jean Lillian (Hansen) E.; m. Frances Gail Martin, Mar. 30, 1968; children: Amy Elizabeth, Laura Anne. BA, Davidson Coll., 1962; LLB, Duke U., 1965. Bar: Tenn. 1965. From assoc. to ptnr. Miller & Martin, Chattanooga, 1967-85; judge U.S. Dist. Ct. (ea. dist.) Tenn., Chattanooga, 1985—; mem. com. ct. adminstrn. and case mgmt. Jud. Conf. of the U.S. Mem. Tenn. Ho. of Reps., Nashville, 1970-72, Tenn. Wildlife Resources Commn., Nashville, 1979-85. Served to capt. U.S. Army, 1966-67, Vietnam. Decorated Bronze Star, 1967. Mem. Fed. Bar Assn., Chattanooga Bar Assn. Episcopalian. Office: US Dist Ct PO Box 1748 960 Georgia Ave Chattanooga TN 37402-2220

**EDGE, KATHRYN REED,** lawyer; b. Birmingham, Ala., Feb. 15, 1946; d. William Alvin and Charlotte Rowena (Rickles) Reed; m. Michael Wayne Edge, Aug. 18, 1967 (div. 1979); 1 child: Michael Lawrence. BA, Vanderbilt U., 1967; JD, Nashville Sch. Law, 1983. Bar: Tenn. 1983. Staff atty. Tenn. Dept. Fin. Instns., Nashville, 1983-, gen. counsel/asst. commr., dep. commr.; ptnr. Miller & Martin, Nashville, 1994—; instr. law Nashville Sch. Law, 1995—; co-chair Tenn. Supreme Ct. Commn. on Gender Fairness, 1994—; past mem. adv. bd. So. Banking Law Conf. Contbr. articles to profl. jours. Mem. Tenn. Dem. Party Compliance Counsel, 1998—; mem. Nashville Sch. Law fundraising com.; mem. Tenn. Bankers Assn. lawyers com., 1997—, govt. rels. com., 1997—. Recipient cert. of appreciation Tenn. Supreme Ct., 1996. Mem. ABA (mem. bus. law sect., banking law com., former chair subcom. on state banking law devels.; mem. commn. on pub. understanding about the law, Achievement award young lawyers divsn. 1992-93), Am. Bar Found., Tenn. Bar Assn. (bd. govs. 1993—, mem. exec. com., v.p. 1993—, mem. editl. bd. TBALink 1996—, mem. publs. com. 1996—, fin. com. 1993—, treas. 1993-97, mid. Tenn. gov. 1997-98, chair bar ctr. and capital campaign com. 1998-99, chair drafting com. on policy on response to unjust criticism of the judiciary 1997-98, chair commn. on women and minorities in the profn. 1992-93, mem. 1993-97, mem. pub. edn. about judiciary com., participant Tenn. Conclave on Legal Edn. 1997, Pres.'s award for svc. 1996), Tenn. Lawyers Assn. for Women (charter mem., pres. 1990-91, editor IN RE TLAW 1997—), Nashville Bar Assn. (past chair Nashville lawyers concerned for lawyers com., mem. bar mentoring com. 1995—, chair 1997-98), Lawyers Assn. for Women, (Marion Griffin chpt., Nashville; pres. 1987-88), Tenn. Bar Found., Nashville Bar Found. (mem. grant rev. com. 1995-98, mem. history project com. 1998—), Harry Phillips Am. Inn of Ct. Democrat. United Methodist. Avocations: reading poetry, photography, dogs. Administrative and regulatory, Banking, Mergers and acquisitions. Office: Miller & Martin LLP 832 Georgia Ave Chattanooga TN 37402-2207

**EDGEMON, PAULINE DIANE,** lawyer; b. Palo Alto, Calif., Dec. 30, 1960; d. Hugh Boswell and Margot Allen Hudson; m. Dennis Michael Edgemon, May 30, 1992; 1 child, Grayson Michael. BA in History, UCLA, 1983; JD, Southwestern U., 1987. Bar: Calif. 1987, U.S. Dist. Ct. (ctrl. dist.) Calif. 1987. Assoc. Freid & Goldsman, L.A., 1987-91, Diamond, Bennington & Simborg, Corte Madera, Calif., 1991-98; ptnr. The Edgemon Law Firm, Corte Madera, 1998—. E-mail: pauline@dbslaw.com. Family and matrimonial. Office: The Edgemon Law Firm 770 Tamalpais Dr Ste 306 Corte Madera CA 94925-1737

**EDIN, CHARLES THOMAS,** lawyer; b. Williston, N.D., Mar. 23, 1955; s. Charles Crane and A. Borgni (Skorpen) E.; children: Charles, Taylor Marie. BA summa cum laude, Concordia Coll., 1978; JD with honors, U.N.D., 1983. Bar: N.D. 1984, U.S. Dist. Ct. N.D. 1984, U.S. Ct. Appeals (8th cir.) 1984. With Landman Westex Petroleum Corp., Bismarck, N.D., 1980-82; ptnr. Zuger Kirmis & Smith, Bismarck, 1984-94; pvt. practice Bismarck, 1995—; spl. asst. atty. gen. State of N.D., Bismarck, 1998—.

Precinct committeeman Rep. Party, Bismarck, 1990. Burtness scholar U. N.D., 1983. Mem. ABA (litigation and natural resources sects.), N.D. Bar Assn. (mineral title stds. com. real property sect.), Burleigh County Bar Assn., Rocky Mountain Mineral Law Found. (N.D. case law reporter Mineral Law Newsletter 1988-96). Lutheran. General civil litigation, Insurance, Real property. Office: PO Box 2391 Bismarck ND 58502-2391

**EDLES, GARY JOEL,** lawyer; b. N.Y.C., Feb. 27, 1941; s. Allen Irving and Helen (Hurowitz) E.; m. Nadine Cohen, Feb. 15, 1973. BA, Queens Coll., 1962; JD, NYU, 1965; LLM, George Washington U., 1966, DJuridical Sci., 1975. Bar: N.Y. 1966, U.S. Ct. Appeals (D.C. cir.) 1970. Staff atty. Civil Aeronautics Bd., Washington, 1967-75, assoc. gen. coun., 1975-77, dep. gen. coun., 1977-80; dir. office of procs. Interstate Commerce Commn., Washington, 1980-81; adminstrv. appeals judge Nuclear Regulatory Commn., Washington, 1981-87; gen. coun. Adminstrv. Conf. U.S., Washington, 1987-95; fellow Am. U., 1995; faculty Dept. Justice Legal Edn. Inst., 1982-97; vis. prof. U. Sheffield, Eng., 1994, U. Hull, Eng., 1997—. Co-author: Federal Regulatory Process, 2d edit., 1989; contbr. articles to profl. jours. Mem. ABA, Fed. Bar Assn. (chmn. adminstrv. law sect. (1989-91). Home: 10 Keldgate, Beverley HU17 8HY, England

**EDLITZ, SANDRA B.,** judge; children: Mark, Tracy. Grad., Barnard Coll.; Masters degree, Hunter Coll.; JD, Pace U., 1981. Tchr. h.s. English N.Y.C. Pub. Sch. Sys.; family ct. hearing examiner, 1991-96; family ct. judge Family Ct., Yonkers, N.Y., 1996—; law guardian Family Ct.; assigned counsel Family and local Criminal Ct.; ct. atty. to supervising judge Family Ct., Manhattan. Bd. dirs. Am. Red Cross, Westchester Chpt., Pace U. Sch. Law Alumni Assn., Westchester Benjamin N. Cardozo Soc. Mem. Nat. Assn. Women Judges, Am. Assn. Women Judges, Assn. Women Judges of State of N.Y., Women's Bar Assn. of State of N.Y. (state dir., bd. dirs.), Westchester Women's Bar Assn. (chairperson family, matrimonial and jud. coms.), Westchester County Bar Assn., White Plains Bar Assn. Fax: 914-966-6861. Office: Family Ct of State of NY County of Westchester 53 S Broadway Yonkers NY 10701-4011

**EDMONDS, THOMAS ANDREW,** legal association administrator; b. Jackson, Miss., July 5, 1938. B.A., Miss. Coll., 1962; LL.B., Duke U., 1965. Bar: Fla. 1965, Va. 1981. Pvt. practice law Orlando, Fla., 1965-66; assoc. prof. law U. Miss., Oxford, 1966-70; assoc. prof.law Fla. State U., Tallahassee, 1970-74, prof., 1974-77; dean Sch. Law, U. Richmond (Va.), 1977-87, U. Miss. Sch. Law, University, 1987-89; exec. dir. Va. State Bar, Richmond, 1989—; vis. assoc. prof. Duke U., 1968-69; vis. prof. McGeorge Sch. Law of the Univ. of the Pacific, 1975-76. Served with USMC, 1957-60. Office: VA State Bar 707 E Main St Ste 1500 Richmond VA 23219-2800

**EDMONDS, THOMAS H.,** lawyer; b. Boston, Oct. 30, 1961; s. George H. and Patricia (Hope) E.; m. Ann Slocum, June 4, 1989; children: Alexander G.S., Timothy D.S. BA, Ohio Wesleyan U., 1983; JD, Lewis and Clark Coll., 1990. Bar: Oreg. 1990, U.S. Dist. Ct. Oreg. 1990. Dep. dist. atty. Multnomah County Dist. Attys. Office, Portland, Oreg., 1990—; vis. lawyer Crown Prosecution Svc., London, 1993-94. Capt. USMC, 1983-86, 91. Avocations: running, squash, golf, skiing, wine. Office: Multnomah County Dist Atty 1021 SW 4th Ave Ste 600 Portland OR 97204-1110

**EDMONDS, THOMAS LEON,** lawyer, management consultant; b. Borger, Tex., May 10, 1932; s. Cline Azel and Flora (Love) E.; m. Virginia Marguerite Leon, June 20, 1960; 1 child, Stephanie Lynn. BS in Chem. Engring., Tex. Tech. U., 1953, JD, 1973. Bar: Tex. 1974, U.S. Tax Ct. 1975, U.S. Ct. Appeals (5th cir.) 1975, U.S. Dist. Ct. (no. dist.) Tex. 1976, U.S. Supreme Ct. 1996. Registered profl. engr., Tex. Engr. computers-exec. dept. Phillips Petroleum, Bartlesville, Okla., 1953-67; mktg. specialist Control Data, Dallas, 1967-68; exec. v.p. CUI, Austin, Tex., 1968-70; mgmt. cons. Mcauto, St. Louis, 1970-71; sr. ptnr. Edmonds & Assocs., Borger, 1973—; city atty. City of Borger, 1991—; treas., dir. Ram Biochems., Inc. Bd. dirs., pres. chancellor's coun. Tex. Tech U.; bd. dirs. Can. River Mcpl. Water Authority, Hutchinson County Tex. Hist. Commn., chmn. Mem. Borger Bar Assn. (pres. 1998—), Borger Country Club. Environmental, Estate planning, Intellectual property. Home: 210 Broadmoor St Borger TX 79007-8210 Office: PO Box 985 Borger TX 79008-0985

**EDMONDSON, FRANK KELLEY, JR.,** lawyer, legal administrator; b. Newport, R.I., Aug. 27, 1936; s. Frank Kelley Sr. and Margaret (Russell) E.; m. Christiane Semirot, Mar. 5, 1959 (div. Sept. 1969); children: Mylene Anne, Yvonne Marie, Catherine May; m. Elaine Sueko Kaneshiro, Aug. 17, 1970 (div. June 1992); m. Karen Louise Bishop, Feb. 27, 1993 (div. Feb. 1996). BBA, Ind. U., 1958; MBA, So. Ill. U., 1978; JD, U. Puget Sound, 1982. Bar: Wash. 1982, U.S. Dist. Ct. (we. dist.) Wash. 1983. Commd. 2d lt. USAF, 1959, advanced through grades to maj., 1969, ret., 1979; contracts specialist Wash. State Lottery, Olympia, 1982-85, asst. contracts adminstr., 1985-87; contracts officer 1989 Washington Centennial Commn., 1987-90; fin. svc. officer Office of the Adminstr. for the Cts., 1990-92; contracts officer, office of adminstr. for the cts. State of Wash. Supreme Ct., Olympia, 1992—; mem. Seattle U. Sch. Law, Law Alumni Soc. Nat. Coun., 1997—, scholarship com. Wash. State Employees Credit Union, 1995—. Bd. dirs. Friends of Chambers Creek, Tacoma, 1981-90; mem. pro bono panel Puget Sound Legal Assistance Found., Olympia, 1985-90; mock trial program com. Youth and Govt. YMCA, 1994-96. Mem. ABA, Wash. State Bar Assn. (spl. dist. counsel 1993-95), Thurston County Bar Assn., Govt. Lawyers Bar Assn. (sec. 1985-86, 1st v.p. 1986-87, pres. 1987-89, liaison to Wash. State Bar Assn. 1989-93), Beta Gamma Sigma, Coll. Club. Home: 6600 Miner Dr SW Tumwater WA 98512-7282 Office: State of Wash Supreme Ct Office of Adminstr for Cts PO Box 41170 Olympia WA 98504-1170

**EDMONDSON, JAMES LARRY,** federal judge; b. Jasper, Ga., July 14, 1947; s. James George and Betty Ruth (Holcomb) E.; m. Eugenia Dettelbach (div. 1992); children: Kelley Eugenia, Alexandra Lisa. BA, Emory U., 1968; JD, U. Ga., 1971; LLM in Jud. Process, U. Va., 1989. Bar: Ga. 1971. Law clk. to dist. judge U.S. Dist. Ct. (no. dist.) Ga., Gainesville, 1971-73; instr. in trial practice U. Ga. Sch. Law, Athens, 1975-84; assoc. Webb, Fowler, Tanner & Edmondson, Lawrenceville, Ga., 1973-76, ptnr., 1976-81; mem. firm Tennant, Davidson & Edmondson, P.C., Lawrenceville, 1982-86; judge U.S. Ct. Appeals (11th cir.), Atlanta, 1986—; instr. U. Ga. Sch. Law, 1975-84. Contbr. articles to legal jours. Trustee Inst. Continuing Legal Edn., 1980-84. Mem. State Bar Ga. (bd. govs. 1982-86), Gwinnett County Bar Assn. (pres. 1980-81), Fellows Ga. Bar Found. (charter), Old War Horse Lawyers Club, Order of Barristers, Pi Sigma Alpha. Episcopalian. Office: US Ct Appeals 11th Circuit 56 Forsyth St NW Atlanta GA 30303-2205*

**EDMONDSON, PAUL WILLIAM,** lawyer; b. Dar Es Salaam, Tanzania, Apr. 13, 1955; s. William Brockway and Donna (Kiechel) E.; m. Susan Haude, May 6, 1978; children: Michael Ruslan, Mary Elizabeth. AB, Cornell U., 1976; JD, Am. U., 1981. BAr: D.C. 1981, U.S. Dist. Ct. D.C 1981, U.S. Ct. Appeals (D.C. cir.) 1981. Staff archaeologist Atlantic Testing Labs., Syracuse, N.Y., 1976-78; sr. atty., atty. advisor U.S. GAO, Washington, 1981-87; counsel Nat. Trust for Historic Preservation, Washington, 1987-93, dep. gen. counsel, 1993-96, gen. counsel, corp. sec., 1996-98, v.p., gen. counsel, 1998—. Co-author: Procedural Due Process in Plain English, 1994; contbg. editor Heritage Resources Law, 1998; contbr. articles to profl. jours. Non-profit and tax-exempt organizations, Land use and zoning (including planning), Environmental. Office: Nat Trust for Hist Preservation 1785 Massachusetts Ave NW Washington DC 20036-2117

**EDMONDSON, WILLIAM ANDREW,** state attorney general; b. Washington, Oct. 12, 1946; m. Linda Larason; children: Mary Elizabeth, Robert Andrew. BA in Speech Edn., Northeastern State U., Tahlequah, Okla., 1968; JD, U. Tulsa, 1978. Mem. Okla. Legislature, 1974-76; intern Office Dist. Atty., Muskogee, Okla., 1978—, asst. dist. atty., 1979, chief prosecutor, 1982—, dist. attorney, 1982-92; pvt. practice atty. Muskogee, 1979-82, Green & Edmondson, 1992-94; atty. gen. State of Okla., 1994—. With U.S. Navy, 1968-72. Named Outstanding Dist. Atty., State of Okla., 1985. Mem. Okla. Bar Assn., Okla. Dist. Attys. Assn. (pres. 1983—). Office: Office Atty Gen 2300 N Lincoln Blvd Rm 112 Oklahoma City OK 73105-4894

**EDMONSON, ALDERT ROOT,** legal association administrator, lawyer; b. Raleigh, N.C., July 29, 1947; s. Richard Tyler and Olivia Smith (Root) E.; m. Susan Alice McDermott, Aug. 25, 1973; children: Ashley Lange, Justin Chambers. AB, U.N.C., 1971; JD, N.C. Ctrl. U., 1976. Bar: N.C. 1976, U.S. Ct. Appeals (4th cir.) 1981, U.S. Supreme Ct. 1981. Partner Jernigan & Edmonson, Raleigh, N.C., 1976-79; dep. counsel N.C. State Bar, Raleigh, 1979-81, counsel, 1981-91, dep. counsel, 1991—; adj. prof. N.C. Ctrl. U. Sch. Law, Durham, 1993—. Dir. Carolina Legal Assistance, Raleigh, 1979-95, Capital Area YMCA, Raleigh, 1990-92; jr. warden St. Michaels Epsicopal Ch., Raleigh, 1992. With U.S. Army, 1968-70. Mem. N.C. Bar Assn., Nat. Orgn. Bar Counsel (dir., 1988-91), Wake County Bar Assn. (bd. dirs. 1990-91, 1999-2000, Pres.'s Award of Excellence 1998), Tenth Judicial Dist. Bar (bd. dirs., 1990-91, 1999-2000). Democrat. Episcopalian. Avocation: basketball. Home: 2508 Stafford Ave Raleigh NC 27607-7243 Office: NC State Bar 208 Fayetteville Street Mall Raleigh NC 27601-1310

**EDMUNDS, JOHN SANFORD,** lawyer; b. L.A., Jan. 3, 1943; s. Arthur Edmunds and Sarah Bernadine (Miles) E.; m. Virginia Maejan Ching, Nov. 30, 1975; children: Laura, Shauna. AB, Stanford U., 1964; JD, U. So. Calif., 1967. Bar: Hawaii 1972, U.S. Dist. Ct. Hawaii, U.S. Ct. Appeals (9th cir.), U.S. Supreme Ct. Chief dep. pub. defender State of Hawaii, 1970-72, spl. dep. atty. gen., 1974-75; acting chief justice Supreme Ct., Republic of Marshall Islands, 1980-81; ptnr. Edmunds & Verga, Honolulu, 1981-97, Edmunds, Maki, Versa and Thorn, Honolulu, 1997—; adj. prof. law U. Hawaii, 1976-77, 85-89; counsel Hemmeter Investment Co., Obayashi Corp., Shell Oil Co., Nestle, U.S.A., Inc., Bank of Am. Bd. dirs. Legal Aid Soc. Hawaii, 1974-75. Fellow Internat. Acad. Trial Lawyers, Am. Coll. Trial Lawyers (state chmn. 1991-92, nat. com. legal ethics and profl. responsibility 1994—), Internat. Soc. Barristers, Am. Bar Found.; mem. ABA, ACLU (bd. dirs. 1969-73, pres. 1971-73, adv. counsel 1974-75), Hawaii Bar Assn., Assn. Trial Lawyers Am., Hawaii Acad. Plaintiffs Attys (bd. govs. 1995—), Master of Bench, Am. Inns. of Ct. E-Mail: 71330.2466@compuserve.com. Personal injury, General civil litigation, Criminal. Office: Edmunds Maki Verga & Thorn 841 Bishop St Ste 2104 Honolulu HI 96813-3921

**EDMUNDS, MICHAEL WINTERTON,** lawyer; b. Chgo., Oct. 4, 1967; s. Clifford Galloway Jr. and Marilyn Winterton Edmunds; m. Alice Aline Parke, Aug. 7, 1993. BA in Polit. Sci., Brigham Young U., 1992; JD, U. Mich., 1996. Bar: Mich. 1996, U.S. Dist. Ct. (ea. dist.) Mich. 1996, U.S. Dist. Ct. (we. dist.) Mich. 1997, U.S. Ct. Appeals (6th cir.) 1998. Assoc. Gault Davison P.C., Flint, Mich., 1993—. Democrat. Mem. LDS Ch. Avocations: hunting, fishing, woodworking, saxophone, scouting. General civil litigation, Contracts commercial, Civil rights. Home: 224 E Court St Apt 502 Flint MI 48502-1633 Office: Gault Davison PC 432 N Saginaw St Fl 10 Flint MI 48502-2013

**EDMUNDS, NANCY GARLOCK,** federal judge; b. Detroit, July 10, 1947; m. William C. Edmunds, 1977. BA cum laude, Cornell U., 1969; MA in Teaching, U. Chgo., 1971; JD summa cum laude, Wayne U., 1976. Bar: Mich. 1976. With Plymouth Canton Public Schools, 1971-73; law clk. Barris, Sott, Denn & Driker, 1973-75; law clk. to Hon. Ralph Freeman U.S. Dist. Ct. (ea. dist.) Mich., 1976-78; ptnr. litigation sect. Dykema Gossett, 1984-92, resident Oakland County, 1986-92; judge U.S. Dist. Ct. (ea. dist.) Mich., 1992—; trustee Hist. Soc. U.S. Dist Ct. (ea. dist.) Mich. Bd. trustees Temple Beth El; mem. bus. and profl. women's divsn., lawyers' divsn. Jewish Welfare Fedn./Allied Jewish Campaign; mem. Saginaw Valley State U. Bd. Control, 1991-92. Mem. ABA, Fed. Judges Assn., Nat. Assn. Women Judges, Federalist Soc., State Bar Mich. (chair U.S. cts. com. 1990-91). Avocations: skiing, reading. Office: US Dist Ct US Courthouse #211 231 W Lafayette Blvd Detroit MI 48226-2700

**EDOZIEN, MARGARET EKWUTOZIA,** lawyer; b. Ibadan, Nigeria, Aug. 31, 1959; came to U.S., 1970; d. Joseph Chike and Modupe Clara (Smith) E. BA, Duke U., 1981; JD, U. N.C., 1984; BL, Nigerian Law Sch., Lagos, 1985; LLM, Georgetown U., 1990. Bar: N.Y. 1986, Nigeria, 1985, Ct. of Internat. Trade, 1990. Assoc. Stewart and Stewart, Washington, 1990-93; v.p., counsel Meridien Corp., N.Y.C., 1993—. Mem. ABA. Private international, Contracts commercial, Administrative and regulatory. Office: Meridien Corp 126 E 56th St New York NY 10022-3613

**EDSON, CHARLES LOUIS,** lawyer, educator; b. St. Louis, Dec. 14, 1934; s. Harry G. and Mildred (Solomon) E.; m. Susan Kramer, Mar. 29, 1959; children: Richard, Nancy, Margaret. AB, Harvard U., 1956, LLB, 1959. Bar: Mo. 1959, U.S. Supreme Ct. 1966, D.C. 1967. Assoc. Lewis, Rice, Tucker, Allen & Chubb, St. Louis, 1959-65; chief ops. officer Legal Svcs. Program, OEO, Washington, 1966-67; gen. counsel Pres.'s Commn. on Postal Orgn., Washington, 1967-68; chief pub. housing sect. Officer of Gen. Counsel, HUD, Washington, 1968-70; ptnr. Lane and Edson, P.C., Washington, 1970-89, Kelley, Drye & Warren, Washington, 1989-93, Peabody & Brown, Washington, 1993-99, Nixon Peabody, Washington, 1999—; adj. prof. law Georgetown U. Law Sch., Washington, 1970-76; HUD coord. Pres. Carter's Transition Staff, 1976-77. Co-author: A Practical Guide to Low and Moderate Income Housing, 1972, A Leased Housing Primer, 1975, A Section 8 Deskbook, 1976, Guide to Federal Housing Programs, 1982, Secondary Mortgage Market Guide, 1985, HDR Affordable Seniors Housing Handbook, 1986. Councilman Town of Somerset, Md., 1976-78; trustee Md. Hist. Trust, 1995—. With USNR, 1953-61. Alt. White House fellow, 1965. Mem. ABA (chmn. forum com. on affordable housing and comm. devel. 1991-93, chmn. spl. housing and urban devel. 1987-90), Harvard U. Law Sch. Assn. D.C. (pres. 1972-73), Cosmos Club (Washington). Real property. Home: 5802 Surrey St Chevy Chase MD 20815-5419 Office: 1255 23rd St NW Ste 800 Washington DC 20037-1125

**EDWARDS, ARTHUR ADEN,** lawyer; b. St. George's, Grenada, June 28, 1964; came to U.S., 1982; s. Walter and Muriel Edwards; m. Ursula Albert, Aug. 16, 1997; children: Johnathan Arthur, Daniel Jeremy. BBA, CUNY (Baruch Coll.), N.Y.C., 1988; MA, CUNY, Bklyn. Coll., 1991; JD, U. Buffalo, 1994. Bar: N.Y. 1997, U.S. Dist. Ct. (so. and ea. dists.) N.Y. 1997. Asst. supr. Mfrs. Hanover Trust, N.Y.C., 1982-87; ct. clk. Office of Ct. Adminstrn., S.I., N.Y., 1987; labor rels. asst. N.Y.C. Health and Hosps. Corp., 1990-91; asst. dist. atty. Office of N.Y. County Dist. Atty., N.Y.C., 1994-96; assoc. Law Office of Earle C. Roberts, Bklyn., 1996-97; owner, prin. Law Office of Arthur A. Edwards, Bklyn., 1997—. Criminal, Real property, General corporate. Office: 1988 Bedford Ave Brooklyn NY 11225-5711

**EDWARDS, BLAINE DOUGLASS,** lawyer; b. Borger, Tex., Sept. 30, 1961; s. Charles Afton and Harriett (Hauser) E.; m. Jill Summers Hendrickson, Sept. 1, 1984; children: Audrey Summers, Cole Douglass. BBA in Acctg. and Fin., Tex. A&M U., 1984; JD magna cum laude, St. Mary's U., 1990. Bar: Tex. 1990, U.S. Dist. Ct. (so., no., and ea. dists.) Tex. 1991, 96, U.S. Ct. Appeals (5th cir.) 1992. Oil and gas/real estate lending officer InterFirst Bank, San Antonio, 1984-87; participating assoc. Fulbright & Jaworski, LLP, Houston, 1990-95, Shook, Hardy & Bacon, LLP, Houston, 1995—; adj. prof. law South Tex. Coll. of Law Tex. A&M U., Houston. Co-author: Texas Environmental Law Handbook, 1990, 92; editor St. Mary's Law Jour., 1989-90; contbr. articles to profl. jours. Mem. Phi Delta Phi. Avocations: reading, snow skiing, golfing. General civil litigation, Environmental, Toxic tort. Office: Shook Hardy & Bacon Ste 1600 600 Travis St Houston TX 77002

**EDWARDS, BOYKIN, JR.,** lawyer; b. Atlanta, Mar. 10, 1950; m. Jean Elizabeth Henderson, June 28, 1975; children: Rachelle, Tonya. BBA, Morris Brown Coll., 1972; JD, John Marshall Law Sch., Atlanta, 1985. Bar: Ga. 1987, U.S. Dist. Ct. (no. dist.) Ga. 1987. Claims rep. Liberty Mut. Ins. Co., Atlanta, 1972-75; spl. claims rep. Nationwide Ins. Co., Atlanta, 1975-87; sole practice Decatur, Ga., 1987—; appointed spl. master Supreme Ct. of Ga., 1999. Pres. Morris Brown 50-50, Atlanta, 1987-88; bd. stewards St. Philip A.M.E. Ch., Atlanta, 1987-88. Mem. ABA, State Bar of Ga. Avocations: spectator sports, bowling, jazz. Personal injury, Insurance, General practice. Office: 3951 Snapfinger Pkwy Decatur GA 30035-3203

**EDWARDS, CHARLENE VERNELL,** lawyer; b. Henderson, N.C., July 29, 1968; d. Robert Johnson and Edith Vernell (Allred) E. BA cum laude, Campbell U., 1990, JD, 1993. Bar: N.C. 1993, U.S. Dsit. Ct. (ea. dist.) N.C. 1995, U.S. Dist. Ct. (mid. dist.) N.C. 1998. Ptnr. Hartley & Edwards, Lillington, N.C., 1993—; gen. counsel Harnett County Humane Soc., Lillington, 1994—; child support enforcement atty. County of Harnett, 1994—; adj. prof. Campbell U., 1995—, dir. mock trials program. Editor: Campbell Law Observer, 1992-93; editor N.C. Supreme Ct. Active Harnett County Rep. Ctrl. Com., 1986—. Recipient Outstanding Alumni award Campbell U., 1996. Mem. N.C. Assn. Women Attys., N.C. Acad. Trial Lawyers, N.C. Bar Assn., Harnett County Bar Assn., Federalist Soc. (pres., sec. 1990—, John Madison award 1993), Pi Gamma Mu. Roman Catholic. Avocations: writing novels, red wolf preservation. State civil litigation, Criminal, Family and matrimonial. Home: PO Box 1462 Buies Creek NC 27506-1462 Office: Hartley & Edwards PO Box 966 Lillington NC 27546-0966

**EDWARDS, CHRISTINE ANNETTE,** lawyer, securities firm executive; b. Ft. Monmouth, N.J., Aug. 30, 1952; d. Harry W. Jr. and Elizabeth Power; m. John H. Edwards, Aug. 24, 1974; children: Lindsey, John. BA, U. Md., College Park, 1974; JD with honors, U. Md., Balt., 1983. Bar: Md. 1983, D.C. 1984, Ill 1990. With Sears, Roebuck and Co., Md., 1971-81; sr. paralegal, staff asst. Sears, Roebuck and Co., Washington, 1981-83, atty. govt. affairs, 1983-87; asst. v.p., dir. govt. affairs Dean Witter Fin. Svcs. Group, Washington, 1987-88; v.p., gen. counsel Dean Witter Fin. Svcs. Group, Lincolnshire, Ill., 1988-89, sr. v.p., 1989-91; exec. v.p., sec., chief legal officer Dean Witter Fin. Svcs. Group, N.Y.C., 1991-97; exec. v.p., chief legal officer, corp. sec. Morgan Stanley Dean Witter & Co. (merger Dean Witter Discover & Co. with Morgan Stanley & Co. Inc.), N.Y.C., 1997—; mem. bd. Fin. Svcs. Coun., Washington, 1990—; bd. trustees Nat. Found. for Consumer Credit Counseling Svcs., Silver Spring, Md., 1990-92; mem. Women in Housing and Fin., Washington, 1982—, SAI Letigation Com., 1995—, N.Y. Stock Exchange Legal Adv. Com., 1992-95; bd. dirs. Chgo. Bd. of Options Exchange, SPS Transaction Svcs. Inc.; exec. v.p., chief legal officer, corp. sec. CLO Roundtable, 1995—. Recipient Disting. Mem. award Women in Housing and Fin., Washington, 1988; named 1 of 50 Top Women Lawyers Nat. Law Journal, 1998. Mem. ABA, Securities Industry Assn. (mem. fed. regulation com. 1990—). Securities. Office: Morgan Stanley Dean Witter & Co Law Dept 1585 Broadway Fl 38 New York NY 10036-8200*

**EDWARDS, CHRISTOPHER ALAN,** lawyer; b. Lafayette, La., Apr. 4, 1958; s. Nolan J. and Eleanor V. (Byrne) E.; m. Laura Ann Dailey, May 19, 1984; children: Evan Trigg, Laura Hodges. BS, Tulane U., 1980; JD, La. State U., 1983. Bar: La., U.S. Supreme Ct. Assoc. Edwards, Stefanski & Barousse, Crowley, La., 1983-88; ptnr. Edwards Law Firm, Lafayette, La., 1988—. With USN, 1976-78. Mem. ABA, KC, La. Trial Lawyers Assn., Lafayette Bar Assn. Democrat. Avocations: hunting, shooting, computers. Personal injury, Pension, profit-sharing, and employee benefits. Office: PO Box 2970 Lafayette LA 70502-2970

**EDWARDS, DANIEL PAUL,** lawyer; educator; b. Enid, Okla., Apr. 15, 1940; s. Daniel Paul and Joye Virginia (van Horn) E.; m. Virginia Lee Kidd, Mar. 27, 1976; children: Austin Daniel, David Paul, Anne Marie. BA, U. Okla., 1962; JD, Harvard Law Sch., 1965. Bar: Colo. 1965, Hawaii, 1987, Ariz. 1988. Ptnr., v.p. Cole, Helox, Tolley, Edwards & Keene, P.C., Colorado Springs, 1965-82; sole practice, Colorado Springs, 1983-94; ptnr. Edwards & Sabo, Colorado Springs, 1994—; lectr. law Colo. Coll., 1976-87. Pres. Springs Area Beautiful Assn., 1978. Mem. ABA, Colo., Ariz. and Hawaii Bar Assn., Harvard Law Sch. Assn. Colo. (pres. 1986-87), El Paso Club, Broadmoor Golf Club, Cheyenne Mt. Club, Garden of the Gods Club, Kapalua Tennis Club, Phi Beta Kappa, Phi Delta Theta. Republican. Presbyterian. Estate planning, Real property, Securities.

**EDWARDS, DANIEL WALDEN,** lawyer; b. Vancouver, Wash., Aug. 7, 1950; s. Chester W. Edwards and Marilyn E. Russell; m. Joan S. Heller, Oct. 18, 1987; children: Nathaniel, Matthew, Stephen, Alexander. BA in Psychology magna cum laude, Met. State Coll., Denver, 1973, BA in Philosophy, 1974; JD, U. Colo., 1976. Bar: Colo. 1977, U.S. Dist. Ct. Colo. 1977. Dep. pub. defender State of Colo., Denver, 1977-79, Littleton, 1979-81, Pueblo, 1981-86; head office pub. defender State of Colo., Brighton, 1987-89; mem. jud. faculty State of Colo., 1988-91; sole practitioner Denver, 1991-93; magistrate Denver Juvenile Ct., 1993—; instr. sch. of law U. Denver, 1988-91, adj. prof., 1991—, coach appellate advocacy team, 1991—; adv. coun. Colo. Legal Svcs., 1989—; adj. mem. Colo. Supreme Ct. Grievance Com., 1991—. Author: Basic Trial Practice: An Introduction to Persuasive Trial Techniques, 1995. Mem. visual arts com. City Arts III, 1989-90, com. chmn., mem. adv. coun., 1991; bd. dirs. Metropolitan State Coll. Alumni Assn., 1991-92; vol. lectr. CSE Thursday Night Bar Pro Se Divorce Clinic, 1991—. Named Pub. Defender of Yr. Colo. State Pub. Defender's Office, 1985, Outstanding Colo. Criminal Def. Atty., 1989. Mem. ABA, Assn. Trial Lawyers Am., Colo. Bar Assn., Adams County Bar Asss., Denver Bar Assn., Met. State Coll. Alumni Assn. (bd. dirs. 1991—). Home: 2335 Clermont St Denver CO 80207-3134 Office: Denver Juvenile Ct Divsn 6 City and County Bldg Denver CO 80202

**EDWARDS, EDITH MARTHA,** lawyer; b. Great Neck, N.Y., Mar. 7, 1945; d. Paul Walter and Alice Matilda (Hansen) Steen; m. Thomas Murray Edwards Sr., Dec. 27, 1966; children: Janice Audrey, Thomas Murray Jr. BS, Coker Coll., 1967; JD, Olgethorpe U., 1981. Bar: Ga. 1982, U.S. Dist. Ct. (no. dist.) Ga. 1983, U.S. Supreme Ct. 1986. Atty. Ga. Legal Svcs., Nashville, 1983-84; asst. dist. atty. Alapaha Cir., Ga., 1984-86; asst. dist. Cherokee Jud. Cir., Ga., 1987; atty. pvt. practice, Valdosta, Ga., 1988—. Republican. Episcopalian. Avocation: art. Criminal, Family and matrimonial. Home and Office: 508 Gornto Rd Valdosta GA 31602-1602

**EDWARDS, HARRY LAFOY,** lawyer; b. Greenville, S.C., July 29, 1936; s. George Belton and Mary Olive (Jones) E.; m. Suzanne Copeland, June 16, 1956; 1 child, Margaret Peden. LLB, U. S.C., 1963, JD, 1970. Bar: S.C. 1963, U.S. dist. Ct. S.C. 1975, U.S. Ct. Apls. (4th cir.) 1974. Assoc. Edwards and Edmunds, Greenville, 1963; v.p., sec., dir. Edwards Co., Inc., Greenville, 1963-65; atty. investment legal dept. Liberty Life Ins. Co., Greenville, 1965-67, asst. sec., asst. v.p., head investment legal dept., 1967-70; asst. sec. Liberty Corp., 1970-75; asst. v.p. Liberty Life Ins. Co., 1970-75; sec. Bent Tree Corp., CEL, Inc., 1970-75; sec., dir. Westchester Mall, Inc., 1970-75; asst. sect. Libco, Inc., Liberty Properties, Inc., 1970-75; pvt. practice, Greenville, 1975—. Editor U. S.C. Law Rev., 1963. Com. mem. Hipp Fund Spl. Edn., Greenville County Sch. System; mem. Boyd C. Hipp II Scholarship Com., Wofford Coll. Spartanburg, S.C.; mem. scholarship com. Liberty Scholars, U. S.C., 1984, 86-99. With USAFR, 1957-64. Mem. ABA, S.C. Bar Assn., Greenville County Bar Assn., Phi Delta Phi, Greenville Lawyers, Poinsett Club (Greenville). Baptist. General corporate, Estate planning, Real property. Home: 106 Ridgeland Dr Greenville SC 29601-3017 Office: PO Box 10350 Greenville SC 29603-0350

**EDWARDS, HARRY T.,** federal judge; b. N.Y.C., Nov. 3, 1940; s. George H. E. and Arline (Ross) Lyle; children: Brent, Michelle. BS, Cornell U., 1962; JD, U. Mich., 1965. Assoc. firm Seyfarth, Shaw, Fairweather & Geraldson, Chgo., 1965-70; prof. law U. Mich., 1970-76, 77-80; vis. prof. law Harvard U., 1975-76, prof., 1976-77; now judge U.S. Ct. Appeals, Washington, 1980—; vis. prof. Free U. Brussels, 1974; dir. AMTRAK, 1977-80, chmn. bd., 1979-80; disting. lectr. law Duke U., 1983-85; lectr. law Georgetown Law Ctr., 1986-87; chief judge U.S. Ct. Appeals (D.C. cir.), Washington, 1994—; adj. prof. law NYU Law Sch., 1990—; lectr. Harvard Law Sch., 1982-88, Mich. Law Sch., 1989—. Mem. Adminstrv. Conf. of U.S., 1976-80. Co-author: Labor Relations Law in the Public Sector, 1975, 79, 85, Lawyer as a Negotiator, 1977, Collective Bargaining and Labor Arbitration, 1979, Higher Education and the Law, 1979. Mem. Nat. Acad. Arbitrators (dir. 1975-80, v.p. 1978-80), Am. Acad. Arts and Scis., Am. Arbitration Assn. (dir. 1979-80), Am. Bar Assn. (sec. sect. labor law 1976-77), Am. Law Inst., Order of Coif. Office: US Ct Appeals 333 Constitution Ave NW Washington DC 20001-2866

**EDWARDS, JAMES ALFRED,** lawyer; b. Orlando, Fla., Feb. 18, 1954. BA in Psychology with high honors, Auburn U., 1976; JD with high honors, U. Fla., 1979. Bar: Fla. 1979, U.S. Dist. Ct. (no. dist.) Fla. 1979, U.S. Dist. Ct. (mid. and so. dists.) Fla. 1981, U.S. Ct. Appeals (5th cir.) 1979, U.S. Ct. Appeals (11th cir.) 1982, U.S. Supreme Ct. 1984; bd. cert. civil trial lawyer Fla. Bar Assn. Ptnr. Rumberger, Kirk & Caldwell, Orlando, Fla., 1979-89, Roth, Edwards & Smith, P.A., Orlando, Fla., 1989—; sustaining mem. Product Liability Adv. Coun., Detroit, 1989—. Mem. Fla. Bar Assn. (cert. civil trial lawyer, mem. trial lawyers, appellate practice sects.), Orange County Bar Assn. Avocations: fishing, water skiing, snow skiing, coaching youth basketball. Fax: 407-599-7797. E-mail: jedwards@rothedwardssmith.com. Product liability, Federal civil litigation, State civil litigation. Office: Roth Edwards & Smith PA 800 S Orlando Ave Maitland FL 32751-5685

**EDWARDS, JAMES EDWIN,** lawyer; b. Clarkesville, Ga., July 29, 1914; s. Gus Calloway and Mary Clara (McKinney) E.; m. Frances Lillian Stanley, Nov. 22, 1948; children: Robin Anne Edwards Kaylor, James Christopher, Clare Edwards Weber. Student U. Tex. 1931-33; B.A., George Washington U., 1935, J.D. cum laude, 1946. Bar: Fla. 1938, Va 1987. Practice law, Cocoa, Fla., 1938-42; hearing and exam. officer USCG, 1943-45; div. asst. State Dept., Washington, 1945-50; practice law Ft. Lauderdale, Fla., 1951-55, 59-77; mem. firm Bell, Edwards, Coker, Carlon & Amsden, Ft. Lauderdale, 1956-59; sole practice, Coral Springs, Fla., 1977-81, 84-85; asst. city atty. Fort Lauderdale, 1961, 63-65; mem. firm. Edwards & Leary, Coral Springs, 1981-84; mem. panel Am. Arbitration Assn., 1984—; sole practice, Albemarle County, Va., 1987-88, Charlottesville, Va., 1988—. Author: Myths About Guns, 1978. Commr., Coral Springs, 1970-76, mayor, 1972-74; mem. bd. suprs. Sunshine Water Mgmt. Dist., 1976-80; chmn. Ft. Lauderdale for Eisenhower, 1952; pres. Fla. Conservative Union, Broward County, 1976. Served to lt. USCGR, 1943-45, to lt. col. JAG, USAFR, 1950-68. Recipient 50-Yr. award Fla. Bar, 1988. Mem. SAR, English Speaking Union Club (Charlottesville), The Ret. Officers Assn., Air Force Assn., Rotary. Estate planning, Probate, Estate taxation. Office: Commonwealth Ctr 300 Preston Ave Ste 312 Charlottesville VA 22902-5044

**EDWARDS, JOHN DUNCAN,** law educator, librarian; b. Louisiana, Mo., Sept. 15, 1953; s. Harold Wenkle and Mary Elizabeth (Duncan) E.; m. Beth Ann Rahm, May 21, 1977; children: Craig, Martha, Brooks. BA, Southeast Mo. State U., 1975; JD, U. Mo., Kansas City, 1977; MALS, U. Mo., Columbia, 1979. Bar: Mo. 1978, U.S. Dist. Ct. (we. dist.) Mo. 1978. Instr. legal research and writing U. Mo., Columbia, 1978; dir. legal research and writing, librarian U. Mo., 1979-80; pub. svcs. librarian Law Sch., U. Okla., Norman, 1980-81; assoc. librarian Law Sch., U. Okla., 1981-84, adj. instr. sch. library sci., 1983-84; prof. law, dir. law library law sch. Drake U., Des Moines, 1984—; adj. instr. Columbia Coll., 1979-80; cons. Cleveland County Bar Assn., 1984. Contbr. articles to profl. jours. Cons. Friends Drake U. Libr., 1985—; coach, mgr. Westminster Softball Team. Des Moines, 1987-94; pres. Crestview Parent-Tchr. Coun., Des Moines, 1988-90; trustee Westminster Presbyn. Ch., Des Moines, 1988-89, treas., 1990, pres., 1991; mem. Clive City Coun., 1995—, mayor pro tem, 1998—; trustee Des Moines Metro Transit Authority, 1996—, chmn. bd. dirs., 1997-98, sec., treas., 1996. Recipient Presdl. award Drake U. Student Bar Assn., 1987; named Outstanding Vol., Crestview Elem. Sch., 1989-90. Mem. Am. Assn. Law Librs. (chmn. awards com. 1987-88, chmn. grants com. 1996-97, chmn. scholarship com. 1998-99), Mid-Am. Assn. Law Librs. (chmn. resource sharing 1986-93, v.p. 1994-95, pres. 1995-96), Mid-Am. Law Sch. Librs., Consortium (pres. 1986-88), Delta Theta Phi, Beta Phi Mu. Avocations: softball, tennis. Office: Drake U Libr Law Sch 27th & Carpenter Sts Des Moines IA 50311

**EDWARDS, JOHN MAX, JR.,** lawyer; b. Greenville, Miss., Sept. 2, 1961; s. John Max and Barbara Ann (Bivens) E.; m. Elizabeth L. Thurman, June 25, 1989; 1 child, John Max III. BA in Accountancy, U. Miss., 1984, M of Accountancy, 1987, JD, 1988. Bar: Miss. 1988, U.S. Dist. Ct. (no. and so. dists.) Miss. 1988, U.S. Ct. Appeals (5th cir.) 1988. Assoc. Holcomb, Dunbar, Oxford, Miss., 1988-91; ptnr. Webb, McLaurin & O'Neal, Tupelo, Miss., 1991-94, Tutor, Henry & Edwards, Tupelo, 1994—. Com. mem. Ducks Unltd., Tupelo, 1993—. 2d lt. Miss. Army N.G., 198th AC, 1987-89. Mem. ABA, Miss. Bar Assn., Miss. Def. Lawyers Assn., Miss. Claims Assn., Lee County Bar Assn., Phi Delta Phi. Methodist. Avocations: duck hunting, fishing, tennis. General civil litigation, Insurance, Education and schools. Office: Tutor Henry & Edwards 306 Troy St Tupelo MS 38804-4830

**EDWARDS, MARK BROWNLOW,** lawyer; b. Asheville, N.C., Nov. 14, 1939; s. Mark and Sarah Juanita (Whitaker) E.; m. Doris Julian Reynolds, June 26, 1966; children: Mark Brownlow Jr., Elizabeth Reynolds. AB, Duke U., 1961, JD, 1963. Bar: N.C. 1963. Ptnr. Poyner & Spruill, L.L.P., Charlotte, N.C., 1988-98, of counsel, 1998—. Author: North Carolina Probate Handbook, 1994, What You Need to Know About Wills, Trusts, Estates in North Carolina, 1994. Vice chmn. The Meth. Home, Inc., Charlotte, 1980-94, chmn., 1994-99. Fellow Am. Coll. Trust and Estates Counsel, Order of Coif., Phi Beta Kappa. Methodist. Avocations: music, pub. speaking, writing. Estate planning, Probate, Estate taxation. Office: Poyner & Spruill 100 N Tryon St Ste 4000 Charlotte NC 28202-4010

**EDWARDS, MARK E.,** healthcare company lawyer; b. Iowa City, Iowa, July 25, 1950. BBA, U. Iowa, 1972; JD, Vanderbilt U., 1975. Assoc. Fisher & Phillips, 1979-86; ptnr. Ford & Harrison, 1986-90; labor counsel Hosp. Corp. Am., 1990-94; chief labor counsel Columbia/HCA Healthcare Corp., Nashville, 1994—. Capt. USAF, 1975-79. Mem. ABA, Ga. Bar Assn., Iowa Bar Assn., Tenn. Bar Assn. Office: Columbia/HCA Healthcare Corp 2501 Park Plz Nashville TN 37203-1512*

**EDWARDS, NINIAN MURRY,** judge; b. St. Louis, Jan. 11, 1922; s. N. Murry and Mabel E. (Dailey) E.; m. Mary Catherine McKeown, May 12, 1944; children: Katherine S. Edwards Burckhalter, Barbara Edwards Perkins. JD, U. Mo., 1947. Trial lawyer St. Louis area, 1947-65; cir. judge St. Louis County, Clayton, Mo., 1965-66, 70-88, sr. judge, arbitrator, mediator, 1988—. Coun. mem. City of Kirkwood, Mo., atty., 1968-70. Maj. USAFR, 1950-90, ret. Mem. Mo. Bar Assn. (past bd. govs.), Bar Assn. Met. St. Louis, St. Louis County Bar Assn. (Disting. Svc. award 1970), Nat. Coun. Juvenile and Family Ct. Judges (bd. trustees, past sec., treas., v.p., pres. elect 1990, pres. 1991-92), Phi Delta Phi. Democrat.

**EDWARDS, PRISCILLA ANN,** paralegal, business owner; b. Orlando, Fla., Sept. 28, 1947; d. William Granville and Bernice Royster. Paralegal cert., U. Calif., Berkeley, 1994. Paralegal Charles R. Garry Esquire, San Francisco, Calif., 1989-90, Marvin Cahn Esquire, San Francisco, 1990-91; owner, mgr. Fed. Legal Resources, San Francisco, 1991—; speaker Sonoma State U., Santa Rosa, Calif., 1993. Publisher: (book) Zero Weather, 1981. Recipient Wiley W. Manuel award for pro bono legal svcs. Bd. Govs. State Bar of Calif., 1994, 95, 96, 97, 98. Episcopalian. Avocations: horseback riding, mountain biking. Office: Fed Legal Resources 345 Franklin St San Francisco CA 94102-4427

**EDWARDS, RICHARD LANSING,** lawyer; b. Wilmington, Del., Apr. 16, 1944; s. Robert Wilson Jr. and Eleanor (Inscho) E.; m. Betsey Ann Barney, Aug. 24, 1980; children: Beth, Melissa, Jeffrey, Jason, Karen. BS in Indsl. Engring., Lehigh U., 1966; JD, Northeastern U., 1980. Bar: Mass. 1980, U.S. Dist. Ct. Mass. 1981, U.S. Ct. Appeals (1st cir.) 1983, U.S. Supreme Ct. 1985, U.S. Dist. Ct. Conn. 1998. Lawyer Craig & Macauley, Boston, 1980-83; lawyer, shareholder Campbell, Campbell & Edwards, P.C. (and predecessor firm), Boston, 1983—. Contbr. articles to profl. jours. Capt. USAF, 1966-70. Decorated Bronze star. Mem. ABA (tort and ins. practice and litigation sect. 1984—), Mass. Bar Assn. (civil litigation sect. 1983—), Def. Rsch. Inst. (products liability com., chmn. 1997-99, chmn. duty to warn and labeling subcom. 1985-88, steering com. 1988—), Internat. Assn. of Def. Counsel (chmn. advocacy practice and procedure com. 1993-95), Mass. Def. Lawyers Assn., Soc. of Automotive Engrs., Product Liability Adv. Coun., Boston Bar Assn. Product liability, Personal injury, Construction. Office: Campbell Campbell & Edwards PC One Constitution Plaza Boston MA 02129

**EDWARDS, ROBERT LEON,** lawyer; b. Greenville, N.C., Oct. 14, 1940; s. Lennie Wardell Edwards and Dorothy Tyson Stewart; m. Kathryn Elizabeth Oakes, Aug. 17, 1963; children: Robert Jr., Stewart. BA, East Carolina U., 1962; LLB, U. N.C., 1965. Bar: N.C., U.S. Tax Ct.; CPA. Tax acct. Ernst & Young, Winston-Salem, N.C., 1965-69; from assoc. to ptnr. Kilpatrick Stockton, Winston-Salem, 1969—; bd. dirs. Wilson-Covington Co., Winston-Salem, Covington-Ring Co., Winston-Salem; v.p. Covington-Wilson, Inc., Winston-Salem, 1996—, Ardmore Terrace, Inc., Winston-Salem, 1996—, Cloverdale Apts., Inc., Winston-Salem, 1996—, Wilson-Covington Co., Covington-Ring Co. Com. mem. Triad United Meth. Home Estate Planning Coun., Winston-Salem, 1990—; former pres. Y-Men's Club, Winston-Salem; past budget com. United Way, Winston-Salem; past bd. dirs. Winston-Salem Little League. Mem. N.C. Assn. CPAs, N.C. Bar Assn., Forsyth County Bar Assn., Kiwanis Club, Forsyth County Club. Avocations: golf, snow skiing, platform tennis, walking, exercise. Estate planning, Probate, Taxation, general. Office: Kilpatrick Stockton LLP 1001 W 4th St Winston Salem NC 27101-2410

**EDWARDS, ROBERT NELSON,** lawyer; b. Sugar Creek, Pa., May 25, 1946; s. Robert Francis and Kathryn Lucille (Nelson) E.; m. Joyce Mary Olejar, July 14, 1973; 1 child: Suzanne Kathryn. BS cum laude, St. Louis U., 1967; postgrad. St. Mary's U. Sch. Law, San Antonio, 1970-72; J.D., Seton Hall U., 1977. Bar: N.J. 1977, U.S. Dist. Ct. N.J. 1977, U.S. Tax Ct. 1979, N.Y. 1990. Assoc., Frank J. Planer, Hackensack, N.J., 1977-78; assoc. Michael J. Mella, Fair Lawn, N.J., 1978-79; sole practice, Elmwood Park, N.J., 1979-83; corp. atty., asst. nat. mgr. of contracts The Perkin-Elmer Corp., Oceanport, N.J., 1983-85; v.p., gen. counsel, sec. Info. Sci. Inc., Montvale, N.J., 1985-92; v.p., gen. counsel, asst. sec. Fedders Corp., Liberty Corner, N.J., 1992—. Councilman, Borough of Elmwood Park, N.J., 1983-85; commr. Vol. Fire Dept., Elmwood Park, 1983-85. Served to sgt USAF, 1968-72. Recipient Am. Jurisprudence award Bancroft-Whitney Co., St. Mary's U. Sch. Law, 1970, 71; Mgmt. Achievement award The Perkin-Elmer Corp., 1983. Mem. ABA, Computer Law Assn., N.J. Corp. Counsel Assn., Phi Delta Phi, Alpha Eta Rho. Republican. Roman Catholic. Clubs: Rotary (Elmwood Park, v.p. 1982-83), Homeowners Assn. (sec. 1979). Lodge: Elks. General corporate, Securities, Computer. Home: 497 Calvin St Washington Township NJ 07675-4401 Office: 505 Martinsville Rd Liberty Corner NJ 07938

**EDWARDS, STEVEN ALAN,** lawyer; b. Louisville, Apr. 3, 1956; s. Herbert Martin and Mary Catherine (Hill) E.; children: Matthew Wilson, Mark Alan. AB, Western Ky. U., 1978; JD, U. Louisville, 1985. Bar: Ky. 1985, U.S. Dist. Ct. (we. dist.) Ky. 1986, U.S. Ct. Appeals (6th cir.) 1993, U.S. Ct. Mil. Appeals. Assoc. Westfall, Talbott & Woods, Louisville, 1985-92, Woodward, Hobson & Fulton, Louisville, 1992-94, Hirn Doheny & Harper, Louisville, 1994-96, Bowles, Rice, McDavid, Graff & Love, Louisville, 1996—. Vol. Arbitrator Better Bus. Bur., Louisville, 1985-90. Capt. USAR, 1988—. Mem. ABA (outreach program nat. pub. svc. conf. 1987, 90), Ky. Bar Assn., Louisville Bar Assn. (sec. young lawyers sect. 1987, exec. com. 1986—, chmn. cmty. svc. com. 1986—, chmn. driving-under-influence edn. com. 1991, treas. 1991, chmn.-elect 1990, bd. dirs. 1993—, chmn. young lawyers sect. 1993—), Delta Theta Phi. Democrat. Lutheran. Avocations: Tae Kwon Do, sports, music, travel. General civil litigation, Health, Personal injury. Office: Bowles Rice McDavid Graff & Love 633 Starks Bldg 455 S 4th Ave Louisville KY 40202-2593 Address: 607 Sausburn Oaks Dr Louisville KY 40214-5685

**EDWARDS, THOMAS ASHTON,** lawyer; b. McKeesport, Pa., June 29, 1960; s. Thomas and Gladys (Ashton) E.; m. Jeannette Maria Valls, June 5, 1987. BSBA, Duquesne U., 1982; MBA in Fin., U. Miami, 1987; JD, Duquesne U., 1991. Bar: Fla. 1992, Pa. 1992, D.C. 1993, Minn. 1994. Asst. contr. 1st Home Savs. Assn., Pitts., 1983-87; contr. Concord-Liberty Savs. Bank, Monroeville, Pa., 1987-89; exec. asst. Investment Timing Svcs., Inc., Pitts., 1989-90; law clk. Welch and Gold, Evashavik and Della Vecchia, Pitts., 1990-91; assoc. Valls Enterprises, Miami, Fla., 1991—; ptnr. Quintana, Arboleya, Delgado de Aranas & Edwards, Coral Gables, Fla.; exec. v.p. ProSolve Techs., Inc., Miami; cons., bus. mgr. Behavior Cons., Monroeville, 1986-91; legal rsch. teaching asst. Duquesne U. Sch. Law; jud. clk. U.S. Dist. Ct. (we. dist.) Pa. Mng. editor Juris mag., 1988-89. Mem. Coral Gables Bar Assn., Dade County Bar Assn., Dade City Bar Assn., Cuban Am. Bar Assn., Phi Alpha Delta. Democrat. Presbyterian. Avocations: running, golf, reading. General civil litigation, General corporate, Real property. Office: Valls Mgmt Group Corp Counsel 700 SW 36th Ave Miami FL 33135-4124 also: Arboleya & Edwards # 1000 2100 Ponce De Leon Blvd Coral Gables FL 33134-5226 also: ProSolve Techs Inc 2100 Ponce De Leon Blvd Coral Gables FL 33134-5215

**EDWARDS, VAN EVERETTE, III,** lawyer; b. Johnston, S.C., July 6, 1946; s. Van Everette Jr. and Mary (Gavin) E.; m. Bettie Ford, July 25, 1970; children: Virginia Gavin, Meredith Pepper. BA, U. S.C., 1968, JD, 1975; postgrad., U. Va., 1969-70. Bar: S.C. 1975, Eng. and Wales, 1998. Assoc. atty. Henderson, Salley, Lynn & Farmer, Aiken, S.C., 1975-77; atty. Harry S. Dent & Assocs., Columbia, S.C., 1977-81; dep. gen. counsel, sr. v.p. Policy Mgmt. Sys. Corp., Columbia, 1981—. Bd. dirs. S.C. Philharm. Orch., Columbia, 1996—, S.C. Humanities Coun., Columbia, 1997—, Lawyers for civil Justice, Columbia, 1996-98, Midlands Internat. Trade Assn., Columbia, 1995-97; v.p. Opera Guild of Greater Columbia, 1998—. Methodist. Avocations: history, jogging, weightlifting. Intellectual property, Private international, Contracts commercial. Office: Policy Mgmt Sys Corp One PMSC Ctr Blythewood SC 29016

**EDWARDS, WILLIAM JOSEPH,** lawyer, educator; b. Balt., May 18, 1962; s. Ronald and Kathleen (Marshall) E. BA, Loyola Coll., Balt., 1985; JD, Western State U., San Diego, 1991. Bar: U.S. Dist. Ct. (no. dist.) Calif. 1994. Intern Office of The Pub. Defender, Annapolis, Md., 1984-85; law clerk Goldberg, Frant & Hall, San Diego, 1987-88, Pfeffer and Turner, San Diego, 1988-89, Office of Pub. Defender, San Diego, 1989-90, Sheela and Sheela, San Diego, 1990-91; law clk. Office of Pub. Defender, San Bernardino, Calif., 1990-91; atty., law clk. Riverside County, Calif., 1991-95; dep. pub. defender Office of Pub. Defender, Riverside, Calif., 1995—; instr. Phillips Coll., Riverside, Calif., 1993-94, U. Calif., Irvine, 1994—; cons. in field. Law rev. staff writer, 1989, notes editor, 1990, asst. exec. editor, 1991; contbr. publs. to profl. jours. Bd. dirs. Assn. Retarded Citizens, Calif. Loyola Coll. Senatorial scholar, 1981; Joyce Yoshioka scholar Calif. Attys. for Criminal Justice, 1994-95; named Profl. of Yr., Assn. Retarded Citizens of Calif., 1995. Mem. ABA (criminal law sect., planning bd. human and civil rights and criminal and juvenile justice com.) Nat. Assn. Criminal Def. Lawyers (drunk driving advocacy com., death penalty commn., NLADA, death penalty litigation sect., criminal justice task force for persons with devel. disabilities, chair criminal justice process com.), Calif. Attys. for Criminal Justice, Calif. Pub. Defenders Assn., Calif. State Bar Assn. (criminal law sect.). Home: 4068 52nd St San Diego CA 92105-2224 Office: Office of Public Defender 46209 Oasis St Ste 314 Indio CA 92201-5903

**EDWARDS, WILLIAM THOMAS, JR.,** lawyer, internet referral consultant; b. Eglin AFB, Fla., Feb. 8, 1956; s. William Thomas and Josephine (Fabian) E.; m. Karen Sue Foulk, July 1, 1978; children: Jennifer, Ali. BA, Fla. State U., 1977, JD, 1980. Bar: Fla. 1980, U.S. Dist. Ct. (mid. dist.) Fla. 1981, U.S. Ct. Claims 1981, U.S. Tax Ct. 1981, U.S. Ct. Appeals (11th cir.) 1983. Assoc. William T. Lassiter Jr., P.A., Jacksonville, Fla., 1980-82; sole practice Middleburg, Fla., 1982-93, 95-98, The Edwards Law Firm, P.A., Orange Park, Fla., 1999—; owner Edwards Internat., 1994—. Pres. Middleburg Bus. Council, 1985, 87, v.p., 1984. Mem. Am. Acad. Estate Planning Attys., Fla. Bar Assn., Clay County Bar Assn., Clay County C. of C. (bd. dirs. 1985, 87-90, chmn. film liaison com. 1990-91, chmn. mil. affairs com. 1990, v.p. membership svcs. 1990), KC. Republican. Roman Catholic. Avocation: travel, reading, walking. Estate planning, Probate, Contracts commercial.

**EFFEL, LAURA,** lawyer; b. Dallas, May 9, 1945; d. Louis E. and Fay (Lee) Ray; m. Marc J. Patterson, Sept. 19, 1992; 1 child, Stephen. BA, U. Calif., Berkeley, 1971; JD, U. Md., 1975. Bar: N.Y. 1976, U.S. Dist. Ct. (so. and ea. dists.) N.Y. 1976, U.S. Ct. Appeals (2d cir.) 1980, U.S. Supreme Ct. 1980, D.C. 1993, N.C. 1998. Assoc. Burns Jackson Miller Summit & Jacoby, N.Y.C., 1975-78, Pincus Munzer Bizar & D'Alessandro, N.Y.C., 1978-80; v.p., sr. assoc. counsel Chase Manhattan Bank, N.A., N.Y.C., 1980-96; counsel Baker & McKenzie, N.Y.C., 1996-99; gen. counsel Garban Cos., 1999—; bd. dirs. Bklyn. Legal Svcs. Corp. A. Mem. ABA (litigation sect. co-chair com. on midyear and regional meetings 1997-98) , Am. Corp. Counsel Assn. (dir. emeritus, pro bono svc. award 1989), Assn. of Bar of City of N.Y. (com. on lectures and continuing edn. 1991-96, com. on banking law 1997-99, com. on state cts. 1999—). General civil litigation, Finance, Labor. Office: Garban 55th Fl 2 World Trade Ctr Fl 55 New York NY 10048-5597

**EFFROS, ROBERT CARLTON,** lawyer; b. N.Y.C., Dec. 5, 1933. AB, Harvard Coll., 1954, LLB, 1957; LLM, Georgetown U., 1965. Bar: N.Y. 1959, D.C. 1964. Atty. Fed. Res. Bank N.Y., N.Y.C., 1959-63; asst. gen. counsel Internat. Monetary Fund, Washington, 1963—; adj. prof. Washington Coll. Law Am. U., 1983—. Editor: Emerging Financial Centers, 1982, Current Legal Issues Affecting Central Banks, vol I, 1992, vol. 2, 1994, vol. 3, 1995, Payment Systems of the World, 1994; contbr. articles to profl. publs. Mem. ABA. Office: Internat Monetary Fund 700 19th St NW Washington DC 20431-0001

**EFRON, MORTON LEON,** lawyer; b. N.Y.C., Jan. 10, 1938; s. Frank S. and Mary (Freedman)E.; m. Anita Schwartz, June 7, 1964; children: Jessica M., Matthew L. BA in Econs., U. Mich., 1959, JD, 1962; postgrad., U. Chgo., 1963. Bar: Ind. 1962, U.S. Dist. Ct. (no. dist.) Ind. 1962. Ptnr. Efron and Efron, P.C., Hammond, Ind., 1962—; chmn. bd. dirs., Western State Bank, Howard City, Mich. Bd. dirs., Hammond Legal Aid Soc., 1962-88. Mem. Ind. State Bar Assn., Hammond Bar Assn., Lake City Bar Assn. Office: Efron and Efron PC 5246 Hohman Ave Fl 5 Hammond IN 46320-1733

**EFSTRATION, GARY GERASIMOS,** lawyer; b. Drexel Hill, Pa., Nov. 18, 1963; s. Michael and Mary Efstration; m. Angela Tsoflias, May 25, 1991; children: Michael, Kalliopi. BA in Econs., Villanova U., 1989; JD, Widener U., Harrisburg, Pa. and Del., 1992. Bar: Pa. 1992. Rsch. asst. Widener U., Harrisburg, 1990; law clk. to Hon. Wayne G. Hummer, Lancaster, Pa., 1992-93; assoc. Pyfer & Reese, Lancaster, 1993-96; pvt. practice, Lancaster, 1996—. Mem. Am. Hellenic Ednl. and Progressive Assn. (pres. 1998). Office: 129 E Orange St Fl 3D Lancaster PA 17602-2851

**EFTIMOFF, KATERINA,** lawyer, chemical engineer, consultant; b. Columbus, Ohio, May 18, 1967; d. Boris and Millie Eftimoff. BSChemE, Ohio State U., 1989; JD, Capital U., 1994. Bar: Ohio 1994, U.S. Dist. Ct. (so. dist.) Ohio 1994. Assoc. Porter, Wright, Morris & Arthur, Columbus, 1994—; cons. Andersen Cons., Columbus, 1989-91. Editor The Affiliate, 1997—. Pres. Greater Franklin County (Ohio) chpt. Am. Diabetes Assn., 1998; pres. German Village Sertoma, Columbus, 1997; bd. dirs. Bravo (Opera Columbus), 1996-98; mem. alumni adv. bd., bd. dirs. Capital U. Law Sch., Columbus, 1998—. Recipient Outstanding Young Citizen award Columbus C. of C., 1997, Forty Under 40 award Bus. First, 1997, Cmty. Svc. award Columbus Dispatch, 1997. Mem. ABA (affiliate outreach program team young lawyer's divsn.), Columbus Bar Assn. (chmn. young lawyers divsn. 1996-98). Environmental, General civil litigation, Administrative and regulatory. Office: Porter Wright Morris & Arthur 41 S High St Ste 2800 Columbus OH 43215-6194

**EGAN, ALECE BLANCHE,** lawyer, mediator; b. Dallas, July 21, 1934; d. Edwin Lawrence Blanche and Alece Catherine (Poirier) Prather; m. William F. Egan, Dec. 26, 1952 (div. 1976); children: Eileen Marie, Catherine C. Egan Goetzke, Peggy Egan Holmes, Mary E.; m. John R. MacKinnon, Apr. 12, 1980 (div. 1987). BS summa cum laude, U. Houston, 1962, JD cum laude, 1964. Bar: Tex. 1964, U.S. Dist. Ct. (so. dist.) Tex. 1964, U.S. Ct. Appeals (5th cir.) 1964, N.Mex. 1987. Assoc. Fulbright & Jaworski, Houston, 1964-67; pvt. practice law Pearland, Tex., 1967-75, Houston, 1975-81, 81-86; assoc. Irving Stern, Houston, 1981; pvt. practice law Albuquerque, 1987-97; assoc. Wheeler, McElwee & Sprague, P.C., Albuquerque, 1987; coord. mediation project Harris County Family Dist. Ct., Houston, 1985-86; co-founder and trainer Mediation Tng. of the S.W., 1985—. Editor-in-chief U. Houston Law Rev., 1963. Mem. Tex. Assn. Famly Mediators (founding mem.), N.M. Mediation Assn. (founding mem.), Albuquerque Philatelic Soc., Ind. Order Foresters. Democrat. Roman Catholic. Avocations: camping, gardening, writing, travel, Indian studies. Family and matrimonial, Estate planning.

**EGAN, CHARLES JOSEPH, JR.,** lawyer, greeting card company executive; b. Cambridge, Mass., Aug. 11, 1932; s. Charles Joseph and Alice Claire (Ball) E.; m. Mary Bowersox, Aug. 6, 1955; children: Timothy, Sean, Peter, James. AB, Harvard U., 1954; LLB, Columbia U., 1959. Bar: N.Y. 1960, Mo. 1973. Assoc. Donovan, Leisure, Newton & Irvine, N.Y.C., 1959-62; ptnr. Hall, McNicol, Marett & Hamilton, N.Y.C., 1962-68; v.p., gen. counsel Thomson & McKinnon Securities, N.Y.C., 1969-70, Hallmark Cards, Inc., Kansas City, Mo., 1972—; bd. dirs. Am. Multi Cinema, Inc., Kansas City, Mo. Trustee Notre Dame de Sion Sch., Kansas City, 1973-77, Pembroke Country Day Sch., Kansas City, 1976-82, Kansas City Art Inst., 1995—; bd. dirs. Kansas City YMCA, 1976-80; mem. dean's coun. Columbia Law Sch., 1991—; vice chmn. Harvard Coll. Fund, 1994—. Served to 1st lt. USMC, 1954-56. Mem. Mo. Bar Assn., Kansas City Lawyers Assn., Harvard Alumni Assn. (pres. 1989-90, exec. com. 1987—), Century Assn., Somerset Club, Harvard Club of N.Y., Harvard Club of Kansas City (pres. 1985-87). Roman Catholic. General corporate, Antitrust, Taxation, general. Office: Hallmark Cards Inc 2501 Mcgee St Kansas City MO 64108-2600

**EGAN, JAMES E.,** lawyer; b. Chgo., Aug. 29, 1945; s. James B. and Ruth E.; m. Catherine L. Connors Egan, July 7, 1967; children: Carrie J. Baffes, Martin W., Jarac, Stephen J. BS in Mktg., U. Ill., Champaign, 1968; JD, IIT Chgo.-Kent Coll. Law, 1973. Assoc. atty. Gavowich, Falowich, McSteen & Shelan, Joliet, Ill., 1973-78; ptnr. McSteen, Phelan & Egan, Joliet, Ill., 1978-86, Phelan, Egan & Nolan, Joliet, Ill., 1986-96, pvt. practice, Joliet, Ill., 1996—; asst. pub. defender Will County, Joliet, Ill., 1974—; U.S. Bankruptcy trustee, Joliet, Ill., 1978-84. Mem. Will County Bar Assn. (sec-treas, 1992), Ill. State Bar Assn. Bankruptcy, Criminal, Family and matrimonial. Home: 525 Cornelia St Joliet IL 60435-6039 Office: 57 N Ottawa St Joliet IL 60432-4389

**EGAN, JOSEPH RICHARD,** lawyer, nuclear engineer; b. Melrose, Minn., Nov. 18, 1954; s. Richard B. and Lucienne M. (Gosselin) E.; m. Patricia Pierson, Nov. 8, 1997. BS in Physics, MIT, 1977, MS in Nuclear Engring., 1979, MS in Tech. and Policy, 1979; JD, Columbia U., 1986. Bar: N.Y. 1986, D.C. 1992. Nuclear reactor engr. Commonwealth Edison Co., Chgo., 1979-80; energy supply planning analyst Argonne (Il.) Nat. Lab., 1980-81; nuclear licensing engr. N.Y. Power Authority, White Plains, 1982-83; assoc. LeBoeuf, Lamb, Leiby & MacRae, N.Y.C., 1985-91; ptnr. Shaw, Pittman, Potts & Trowbridge, Washington, 1991-94; chmn. Egan & Assocs., P.C., Washington, 1994—; cons. Lawrence Berkeley Lab., 1980, World Info. Systems, Cambridge, 1982, East-West Ctr., Honolulu, 1983, UN World Commn on Environ. and Devel., Geneva, 1985. Contbg. author: Nuclear Energy Law after Chernobyl, 1988; contbr. articles to profl. jours. Recipient Wertheimer prize, 1986; Harlan Fiske Stone scholar, 1986. Mem. Fed. Energy Bar Assn., N.Y. State Bar Assn., Internat. Nuclear Law Assn., Am. Nuclear Soc., Nat. Assn. Rocketry, Sigma Xi. Avocations: piano, writing, travel. Nuclear power, FERC practice, Public utilities. Home: 1007 Kimberly Ct Great Falls VA 22066-1546 Office: Egan & Assocs PC 2121 K St NW Ste 800 Washington DC 20037-1829

**EGBERT, RICHARD MICHAEL,** lawyer; b. Newton, Mass., Feb. 13, 1947; s. Marcus Manuel and Annette Honey (Segal) E.; m. D. Patricia Egbert, Oct. 27, 1990; children: Shea N., Danielle F., Manuel R. BBA, U. Mass., 1969; JD, Northeastern U., 1972. Bar: Mass. 1972, U.S. Dist. Ct. Mass. 1973, U.S. Ct. Appeals (1st cir.) 1974, U.S. Supreme Ct. 1980. Founder Law Offices of Richard M. Egbert, Boston, 1972—. Dir. Nat. Coun. Northeastern U., Boston, 1996—; mem. Chancellors Coun., U. Mass., Amherst, 1993—. Mem. ABA, Nat. Assn. Criminal Def. Lawyers, Mass. Assn. Criminal Def. Lawyers (pres. 1999). Criminal. Office: 99 Summer St Boston MA 02110-1213

**EGENOLF, ROBERT F.,** lawyer; b. San Francisco, Jan. 23, 1946; s. John D. and Virginia (Kirkland) Butler; m. Judy Wish, Jan. 23, 1970; children: Cristi Michelle, Jonah Wish. BA, U.S. Internat. U., San Diego, 1970; JD, Calif. Western U., San Diego, 1973; LLM, U. Miami, Fla., 1974. Bar: Calif. 1973, U.S. Tax Ct. 1974. Assoc. Blum & Blum, Oakland, Calif., 1974-75; ptnr. Westwick & Collison, Santa Barbara, Calif., 1976-80, Egenolf & Moore, Santa Barbara, 1980-94; pres., founder Calif. Exchange Corp., Santa Barbara, 1984-90, Santa Barbara Exch. Corp., 1984-90, 97—, First Exch. Corp., Santa Barbara, 1988-90, Amherst Exch. Corp., Santa Barbara, 1989—; instr., lectr. Santa Barbara City Coll., 1987—; lectr. in real estate exch. seminars Lawyers Throughout the U.S., 1987—. Bd. dirs. Tri Counties Devel. Disabilities Bd., Santa Barbara, 1977-78, Child Abuse Listening Mediation, Santa Barbara, 1979-80, Ensemble Theatre Project, Santa Barbara, 1981-83, Santa Barbara City Coll. Theatre Group, 1983-84; trustee Laguna Blanca Sch., 1997—; dir. Am. Inst. Food and Wine, 1991-93, Santa Barbara Wine Auction, 1993-94, Semana Nautica Masters Volleyball Tournament, 1993-97; mem. polit. action com. Planned Parenthood, 1995; mem. fin. devel. steering com. Santa Barbara Contemporary Arts Forum, 1995-96. With USN, 1967-69, PTO. Mem. Calif. Bar Assn. (co-chair joint tax subsect. 1990-95), Santa Barbara Bar Assn. (bd. dirs. 1978, 95—, pres. elect 2000), Barristers Santa Barbara (pres. 1976-77). Avocations: pilot, volleyball. E-mail: egenolf@agenolf.com. Real property, Taxation, general, Estate planning. Office: Egenolf Assocs LLP 130 E Carrillo St Santa Barbara CA 93101-2111

**EGER, JOHN MITCHELL,** lawyer, educator; b. Chgo., Jan. 16, 1940; s. Elvin William and Elizabeth (Kleinman) E.; m. Judith Prescott, June 16, 1962 (div. Sept. 1982); children: Mark, Laura; m. Mary Ann Jackson, Dec. 23, 1982; children: John, Matthew. BA in English, Va. Mil. Inst., 1962; JD, John Marshall Law Sch., 1970. Bar: Ill. 1970, U.S. Ct. Appeals (7th cir.) 1970, D.C. 1972. Exec. mgr. AT&T, Chgo., 1965-70; assoc. Menk, Johnson & Bishop, Chgo., 1970; legal advisor gen. counsel FCC, Washington, 1971, legal advisor chmn., 1971-73; dep. dir. White House Office of Telecommunications Policy, Washington, 1973-74, dir., 1974-76; sole practice Washington, 1976-81; sr. v.p. CBS, Inc., N.Y.C., 1981-86; sole practice N.Y.C., 1986—; Van Deerlin endowed prof. communications and pub. policy San Diego State U., 1990—, dir. Internat. Ctr. for Communications, 1990—; trustee Internat. Inst. Communications, London, 1986—; adviser Fletcher Sch. Law and Diplomacy, 1984—. Mem. editorial bd. The Info. Soc., 1988—; contbr. articles to profl. jours. Served to 1st lt. U.S. Army, 1962-65. trustee Internat. Inst. Communications, London, 1986—; adviser Fletcher Sch. Law and Diplomacy, 1984—; pres. San Diego Communications Coun., 1991—. Republican. Episcopalian. Club: Cosmos (Washington). Lodge: Masons. Communications, Private international, Public international. Home: 2717 Caminito Prado La Jolla CA 92037-4010 Office: San Diego State U San Diego CA 92182-0412

**EGGERT, RUSSELL RAYMOND,** lawyer; b. Chgo., July 28, 1948; s. Ralph A. and Alice M. (Nischwitz) E.; m. Patricia Anne Alegre, 1998. AB, U. Ill., 1970, JD, 1973; postgrad., Hague Acad. Internat. Law, The Netherlands, 1972. Bar: Ill. 1973, U.S. Supreme Ct. 1979. Assoc. U. Ill., Champaign, 1973-74; asst. atty. gen. State of Ill., Chgo., 1974-79; assoc. O'Conor, Karaganis & Gail, Chgo., 1979-83; legal counsel to Ill. atty. gen., Chgo., 1983-87; ptnr. Mayer, Brown & Platt, Chgo., 1987—. Contbr. various articles to profl. jours. Mem. ABA. Democrat. Environmental, Administrative and regulatory, General civil litigation. Office: Mayer Brown & Platt 190 S La Salle St Ste 3100 Chicago IL 60603-3441

**EGGLESTON, JON R.,** lawyer. JD, Cornell U., 1971; LLM, Georgetown U., 1975. Bar: Vt. 1971. Ptnr. Miller, Eggleston & Cramer, Burlington, Vt. Mem. Vt. Bar Assn. (bd. mgrs. 1994—, pres.-elect 1998-99). Office: Miller Eggleston & Cramer Ltd PO Box 1489 Burlington VT 05402-1489*

**EGINTON, WARREN WILLIAM,** federal judge; b. Bklyn., Feb. 16, 1924. AB, Princeton U., 1948; LLB, Yale U., 1951. Bar: N.Y. 1952, Conn. 1954. Assoc. Davis Polk & Wardwell, N.Y.C., 1951-53; ptnr. Cummings & Lockwood, Stamford, Conn., 1954-79; judge U.S. Dist. Ct., Bridgeport, Conn., 1979—. Mem. ABA, Am. Judicature Soc., Am. Bar Found., Conn. Bar Assn., Fed. Bar Coun., Fed. Bar Assn., Ins. Jud. Adminstrn., Jud. Leadership Devel. Coun., Fgn. Policy Assn. Office: US Dist Ct 915 Lafayette Blvd Ste 335 Bridgeport CT 06604-4706

**EHLINGER, RALPH JEROME,** lawyer; b. Oconto, Wis., Mar. 22, 1941; s. Jerome Nicholas and Margaret Ann (Otradovec) E.; m. Nancy L. McKinley, Dec. 26, 1966 (div. Oct. 1986); children: Nicholas Joseph, Martha Johanna; m. Mary Verstegen, Sept. 25, 1987; children: Autumn V., Andrea V., Jessa V. BA in Philosophy, St. Paul Sem., 1963; JD, Georgetown U., 1968. Bar: Wis. 1968, U.S. Dist. Ct. (ea. dist.) Wis. 1969, U.S. Dist. Ct. (we. dist.) Wis. 1977, U.S. Ct. Appeals (7th cir.) 1983, U.S. Supreme Ct. 1986, D.C. 1988, U.S. Ct. Appeals (4th cir.) 1988. Ptnr. Meissner, Tierney, Ehlinger & Whipp, Milw., 1968-86; pvt. practice Milw., 1986-87; counsel Casson, Harkins & LaPallo, Washington, 1987-88; pres. Ehlinger & Krill, SC, Milw., 1988—; adj. prof. law Marquette U. Law Sch., 1999—; dir. Milw. Bar Assn., 1990-93. Articles editor: The Georgetown Law Jour., 1967-68 (Outstanding Editor 1968); editor-in-chief: The Milwaukee Lawyer, 1982-84. Trustee Wis. Sch. Profl. Psychology, Milw., 1990-93; bd. pres. Grand Ave Club, Milw., 1990-92, Mental Health Assn., Milw., 1992-93; dir. Centro Legal Por Derechos Humanos, 1996—. Mem. ATLA, Am. Judicature Soc., Wis. Acad. Trial Lawyers, Milw. Bar Assn. Found. (pres. 1994-97), Nordic Ski Club (life), Milw. Bar Assn. (Lawyer of Yr. award 1997). Democrat. Roman Catholic. Avocations: instrumental and vocal music, cross-country skiing, backpacking, canoeing, poetry. General civil litigation, Health, General corporate. Office: Ehlinger & Krill SC 316 N Milwaukee St Ste 410 Milwaukee WI 53202-5832

**EHMANN, ANTHONY VALENTINE,** lawyer; b. Chgo., Sept. 5, 1935; s. Anthony E. and Frances (Verweil) E.; m. Alice A. Avina, Nov. 27, 1959; children: Ann, Thomas, Jerome, Gregory, Rose, Robert. BS, Ariz. State U., 1957; JD, U. Ariz., 1960. Bar: Ariz. 1960, U.S. Tax Ct. 1960, U.S. Sup. Ct. 1968; CPA, Ariz.; cert. tax specialist, trusts and estates specialist. Spl. asst. atty. gen., 1961-68; mem. Ehmann and Hiller, Phoenix, 1969—. Republican dist. chmn. Ariz., 1964; pres. Grand Canyon council Boy Scouts Am., 1987-89, mem. exec. com., 1981—; v.p. western region Boy Scouts Am., 1991—; mem. bd. dirs. Nat. Catholic Com. on Scouting, 1995—. Recipient Silver Beaver award Boy Scouts Am., 1982, Bronze Pelican award Cath. Com. on Scouting, 1981, Silver Antelope award Boy Scouts Am., 1994. Fellow Am. Coll. Trusts & Estate Counsel; mem. State Bar Ariz. (chmn. tax sect. 1968, 69), Central Ariz. Estate Planning Council (pres. 1968, 69). Republican. Roman Catholic. Clubs: KC (grand knight 1964, 65) (Glendale, Ariz.), Serra Internat. (pres. Phoenix club 1992-93, dist. gov. Ariz. 1993-95), Knight of Holy Sepulchre, Knight of Malta. Pension, profit-sharing, and employee benefits, Estate planning, Corporate taxation. Office: Ehmann & Hiller 2525 E Camelback Rd Ste 720 Phoenix AZ 85016-4229

**EHRENWERTH, DAVID HARRY,** lawyer; b. Pitts., Apr. 22, 1947; s. Ben and Beatrice Lee (Schwartz) E.; m. Judith B. Ehrenwerth; children: Justin Reid, Lindsey Royce. BA, U. Pitts., 1969; JD, Harvard U., 1972. Bar: Pa. 1972, U.S. Dist. Ct. (we. dist.) Pa. 1972, U.S. Ct. Appeals (3d cir.) 1976. Asst. atty. gen. Commonwealth of Pa., Pitts., 1972-74; assoc. Kirkpatrick & Lockhart, Pitts., 1974-79, ptnr., 1979—. Pres. Pitts. chpt. Am. Jewish Com., 1988-90, nat. bd. govs., 1991-95, chmn. Pitts. chpt., 1996-98; mem. nat. adv. coun. Fed. Nat. Mortgage Assn., 1984-85; bd. dirs. Pa. Bd. Vocat. Rehab., Harrisburg, 1983-88, United Jewish Fedn., Pitts., 1991-93, Presbyn. U. Hosp., Pitts., 1993-94, Riverview Ctr. for Jewish Srs., 1991-93, U. Pitts. Cancer Inst., 1995—; bd. dirs. Montefiore Hosp., Pitts., 1985-93, treas., 1989, vice chmn., 1990-92, chmn., 1992-93; bd. govs. Pa. Econ. League, Western Region, 1999—. Named Pittsburgher to Watch Pitts. Mag., 1980. Mem. Pa. Bar Assn. (chmn. real estate fin. com. 1985-87), Allegheny County Bar Assn. (chmn. real property sect. 1989), Harvard U. Law Alumni Assn. Western Pa. (pres. 1986-87), Concordia Club, Westmoreland Country Club, Heinz Fifty-Seven Club (chmn. 1974-91), Duquesne Club, Phi Beta Kappa. Republican. Jewish. Avocations: tennis, golf. Real property, Finance, Securities. Home: 413 Windmere Dr Pittsburgh PA 15238-2440 Office: Kirkpatrick & Lockhart 1500 Oliver Building Bldg Pittsburgh PA 15222-2312

**EHRLICH, JEROME HARRY,** lawyer; b. Bklyn., Jan. 22, 1937; s. Harvey I. and Jeanne S. (Bayer) E.; m. Deena Rosenfeld, Feb. 15, 1987. BBA, CCNY, 1958; LLB, NYU, 1962. Bar: N.Y. 1962, U.S. Dist. Ct. (ea. and so. dists.) N.Y. 1964, U.S. Ct. Appeals (2nd cir.) 1965, U.S. Ct. Mil. Appeals 1966, U.S. Supreme Ct. 1966. Ptnr. Jaspan, Ginsberg, Ehrlich, Schlesinger & Hoffman, Garden City, N.Y., 1964-91, Ehrlich, Frazer & Feldman, Garden City, N.Y., 1992—. Mem. panel mediators and fact-finders Nassau County Pub. Employment Rels. Bd., Mineola, N.Y., 1969—; mem. adv. bd. Little Village Sch. for Handicapped Children, Garden City, N.Y., 1979—, N.Y. State Sch. Music Assn., 1987—. Staff sgt. USAR, 1962-68. Mem. ABA, N.Y. State Assn. Sch. Attys. (pres. 1983), N.Y. State Bar Assn., Nassau County Bar Assn. (chair edn. law com. 1994-96), Theodore Roosevelt Am. Inns. of Ct. Education and schools, Labor, General practice. Office: Ehrlich Frazer & Feldman 1415 Kellum Pl Garden City NY 11530-1695

**EHRLICH, RAYMOND,** lawyer; b. Swainsboro, Ga., Feb. 2, 1918; s. Ben and Esther Ehrlich; m. Miriam Bettman, Nov. 27, 1975; stepchildren: Jack Bettman, Gerald Bettman, Zelda Bettman, Carol Ann B. Berkowitz. BS, U. Fla., 1939, JD, 1942. Bar: Fla. 1942, U.S. Dist. Ct., U.S. Ct. Appeals (11th cir.), U.S. Supreme Ct. Ptnr. Mathews Osborne Ehrlich et al., Jacksonville, Fla., 1946-81; justice Supreme Ct. Fla., Tallahassee, 1981-91, chief justice, 1988-90; ptnr. Holland & Knight, Jacksonville, Fla., 1992—; jurist-in-residence Fla. State U. Coll. Law, 1991. Spl. counsel to U.S. Senator Bob Graham, 1991. Served to comdr. USN, 1942-46. Mem. ABA, Fla. Bar Assn., Jacksonville Bar Assn., Am. Coll. Trial Lawyers, Internat. Acad. Trial Lawyers, Am. Law Inst. Personal injury, Professional liability. Office: Holland & Knight 50 N Laura St Ste 3900 Jacksonville FL 32202-3622

**EHRLICH, STEPHEN RICHARD,** lawyer; b. Rockville Centre, N.Y., Dec. 28, 1949; s. Harry Simon and Ida G. (Lable) E. BA, U. Pa., 1971; JD, U. Denver, 1977. Bar: Colo. 1977, U.S. Dist. Ct. Colo. 1977. Pvt. practice Denver, 1977—. Mem. Assn. Trial Lawyers Am., Colo. Bar Assn., Colo. Trial Lawyers Assn., Denver Bar Assn. Avocations: skiing, tennis, bicycling. Personal injury, Criminal, State civil litigation. Home: 534 E 7th Ave Denver CO 80203-3883 Office: 847 Sherman St Denver CO 80203-2913

**EHRLICH, SUSAN ANNE,** judge; b. Dec. 26, 1948; d. Lee and Mildred Josephine (Cohen) E.; m. James C. Hair, Jr., July 16, 1978; children: Lee M.E., Caitlin A.E. AB, Wellesley Coll., 1978; JD, Ariz. State U., 1974. Bar: Ariz., D.C.; U.S. Ct. Appeals (1st, 2nd, 4th, 5th, 6th, 7th, 8th, 9th, 10th and D.C. cirs.), U.S. Dist. Ct. of Ariz., U.S. Supreme Ct. Rsch. analyst Civil Rights Divsn. U.S. Dept. Justice, Washington, 1970-71; law clk. to chief justice Ariz. Supreme Ct., 1974-76; pvt. practice Ariz., 1976-77; atty. Civil Divsn. U.S. Dept. Justice, Washington, 1978-80; asst. U.S. atty. Dist. of Ariz., 1981-89; judge Ariz. Ct. of Appeals, Phoenix, 1989—. Author: Handbook: Appeals in the Ninth Circuit, 1987, 89; co-author: The Ability of the Mentally Retarded to Plead Guilty, 1975, Tribute to Justice Jack D.H. Hays, 1995. Mem. Mayor's Task Force on Domestic Violence; mem. steering com. Phoenix Violence Prevention Initiative; bd. dirs. U. Ariz. Law Coll. Assn., others. Mem. ABA (mem. task force on the federalization of criminal law, appellate judges' conf. edn. com.), Am. Law Inst., Ariz. State, Tribal and Federal Ct. Forum, Phoenix Mcpl. Ct. Jud. Selection Adv. Bd. (chair), Ariz. Judges' Assn., Lorna E. Lockwood Inn of Ct. (past pres.), Ariz. Women Lawyers' Assn. (past pres.). Office: Ariz Ct of Appeals 1501 W Washington St Phoenix AZ 85007-3231

**EICHER, DONALD E., III,** lawyer; b. Vicksburg, Miss., July 26, 1969; s. Donald E. Jr. and Rosemary E. Eicher; m. Amy Christine Carlson, May 30, 1998. BBA cum laude, U. Miss., 1991, JD, 1994. Bar: Miss. 1994, U.S. Dist. Ct. (no. and so. dists.) Miss. 1994, U.S. Ct. Appeals (5th cir.) 1994, Ala. 1996, U.S. Dist. Ct. (ctrl. dist.) Ala. 1999, U.S. Ct. Appeals (11th cir.) 1999. Assoc. McTeer Assocs., Greenville, Miss., 1994-96, William L. Brambach, Columbus, Miss., 1996; atty. Malone Law Firm PLLC, Ridgeland, Miss., 1996-97; assoc. McDavid Noblin & West PLLC, Jackson, Miss., 1997—. Mem. ABA, Miss. Oil and Gas Lawyers Assn., Hinds County Bar Assn. Consumer commercial, Real property, Oil, gas, and mineral. Home: 1431 Sheffield Dr Jackson MS 39211-5631 Office: McDavid Noblin West PLLC 248 E Capitol St Ste 840 Jackson MS 39201-2505

**EICKMEYER, EVAN,** lawyer; b. South Laguna Beach, Calif., Apr. 6, 1968; s. Thomas L. and Joyce B. Eickmeyer; m. Stephanie R. Wood, July 13, 1991. BA, U. So. Calif., 1990; JD, U. of the Pacific, 1993. Bar: Calif. 1993, U.S. Dist. Ct. (ea. dist.) Calif. 1993, U.S. Ct. Appeals (9th cir.) 1996, U.S. Dist. Ct. (ctrl. dist.) Calif. 1998, U.S. Supreme Ct. 1999. Dep. dist. atty. Sacramento (Calif.) County Dist. Atty.'s Office, 1994-95; assoc. McKinley & Smith, Sacramento, 1995—. Mem. Nat. Eagle Scouts Assn. (life). Republican. Mem. LDS Ch. General civil litigation, Appellate, Personal injury. Office: McKinley & Smith 3435 American River Dr Ste B Sacramento CA 95864-5743

**EIDSON, FRANK M.,** lawyer; b. Orlando, Fla., Aug. 19, 1961; s. George T. Jr. and Elsie (McCoy) E. BA cum laude, Vanderbilt U., 1984; JD, U. Fla., 1987. Atty. Maguire, Voorhis & Wells, Orlando, 1987-88, Griffin & Linder, Orlando, 1988-90, Frank M. Eidson, Esquire, Orlando, 1990—. Mem. Fla. Acad. Trial Lawyers (com. continuing edn. 1989—), Lawyers of Am., Orange County Bar Assn., Orlando C. of C., Citrus Club, YMCA, Touchdown Club (bd. dirs. 1991—). Avocations: hunting, fishing, water skiing, basketball. Personal injury, Workers' compensation. Office: PO Box 4908 Orlando FL 32802-4908

**EIDSON, JAMES ANTHONY,** lawyer; b. Atlanta, June 3, 1952; s. Howard Curtis and Emma Delores (Wilson) E.; m. Dianne Claudia Chesslock, Jan. 9, 1982. BS in Psychology cum laude, Ga. State U., 1977; JD cum laude, Mercer U., Macon, Ga., 1980. Bar: Ga. 1980; U.S. Ct. Appeals (11th cir.) 1984, U.S. Dist. Ct. (no. dist.) 1981, U.S. Dist. Ct. (mid. dist.) 1982, U.S. Dist. Ct. (so. dist.) 1982, U.S. Ct. Appeals (5th cir.) 1981. Assoc. atty. Powell, Goldstein, Frazier and Murphy, Atlanta, 1980-83; ptnr. Eidson & Assocs., P.C., Atlanta, 1983—; city atty. City of East Point, Ga., 1983-90, City of Fairburn, Ga., 1986-96; dir. First Bank of Ga., East Point, 1988—, First Bankshares, Inc., Hapeville, Ga., 1994—. Author: (Jour.) Mercer Law Review, 1978. Lt. USMC, 1969-80. Mem. Atlanta Lawyers Club, 191 Club. Republican. Methodist. Avocations: sailing, hunting. General civil litigation, Product liability. Home: 2515 Habersham Rd NW Atlanta GA 30305-3557 Office: Eidson & Assocs PC 600 S Central Ave Atlanta GA 30354-1928

**EIDSON, PATRICK SAMUEL,** lawyer; b. Athens, Ga., May 17, 1967; s. Caswell S. and Elizabeth J. Eidson; m. Marsa Wilkinson, Sept. 7, 1997. BS in Agr., U. Ga., 1991; JD, Samford U., 1996. Bar: Ga. 1996. Law clk. judge Mike McCormick Birmingham, Ala., 1995; rsch. asst. Gov. Albert P. Brewer, Birmingham, 1995; pub. defender Birmingham, 1996; litigation atty. Beauchamp & Assocs., Albany, Ga., 1996—; mem.-at-large Cumberland Trial Adv. Bd., Birmingham, 1995-96. Mem. election com. Mark Taylor State Senate, Albany, 1996, Michael Meyer Von Boemer State Senate, Albany, 1998. Mem. ATLA, ABA, Trial Lawyers for Pub. Justice, Ga. Trial Lawyers Assn., Ga. State Bar (mem. exec. com. young lawyers divsn. 1998—), Phi Delta Phi. Baptist. Avocation: American motorcycle riding. General civil litigation, Personal injury. Office: Beauchamp & Assocs 323 Pine Ave Albany GA 31701-2575

**EIERMANN-WEGENER, DARLENE MAE,** paralegal; b. New Orleans, June 10, 1959; d. Wilbur Joseph and Dorothy M. (Walton-Palmer) Eiermann; m. Edmund T. Wegener, Jr., Apr. 26, 1991. Student, U. New Orleans, 1991—. Cert. paralegal. Adminstrv. asst. Jefferson Parish Coun., Gretna, La., 1980; sec. Robin Towing Corp., Harvey, La., 1980-83; legal sec. Oster & Wegener, APLC, New Orleans, 1983-86, paralegal, 1986—. Candidate for justice of the peace, Ward 8, St. Tammany parish, 1996. Mem. Assn. Trial Lawyers of Am., New Orleans Paralegal Assn., La. State Paralegal Assn., Nat. Paralegal Assn., Mensa, Beta Sigma Phi, others. Republican. Lutheran. Avocations: reading, researching, attaining political office, continuing education. Office: Oster & Wegener PO Box 5747 Slidell LA 70469-5747

**EIKNER, TOD BAYARD,** lawyer; b. Ft. Lauderdale, Fla., Sept. 8, 1967; s. Charles Buford and Jacqueline (Tod) E.; m. Paola Parra, Oct. 24, 1998. JD, Mercer U., 1994. Bar: Fla. 1994, Ga. 1994, U.S. Dist. Ct. (mid. dist.) Fla. 1994, U.S. Dist. Ct. (so. dist.) Ga. 1994. Atty. Cole, Stone, Stoudemire, Morgan & Dore, P.A., Jacksonville, Fla., 1994—. Mem. Jacksonville Claims Assn. (membership chmn., bd. dirs. 1994-98). Insurance, Personal injury, Product liability. Office: Cole Stone et al 76 S Laura St Ste 1700 Jacksonville FL 32202-5444

**EILAND, GARY WAYNE,** lawyer; b. Houston, Apr. 25, 1951; s. William N. and Louise A. (Foltin) E.; m. Sandra K. Streetman, Aug. 4, 1973; children: Trina L., Peter T. BBA, U. Tex., 1973, JD, 1976. Bar: Tex. 1976, U.S. Ct. Claims 1977, U.S. Ct. Appeals (5th cir.) 1978, U.S. Ct. Appeals (11th cir.) 1981, U.S. Supreme Ct. 1989. Assoc. Wood, Lucksinger & Epstein, Houston, 1976-81, ptnr., 1981-91; ptnr. Vinson & Elkins L.L.P., Houston, 1991—; co-chair health industry group, 1996—; lectr. Aspen Health Care Industry seminars, Aspen Pubs., Inc., Rockville, Md., 1978-89, HLO Health Care seminars, 1990-91. Mem. Tex. Bar Assn. (chmn. health law sect. 1991-92), Am. Acad. Healthcare Attys. (bd. dirs. 1991-97, pres. 1996-97), Am. Health Lawyers Assn. (past pres., exec. com. 1997-98), Healthcare Fin. Mgmt. Assn. Region 9 chpt. liaison rep. 1994-95), Assn. Am. Med. Colls., Houston Ctr. Club, Bentwater Country Club. Health, Administrative and regulatory, Government contracts and claims. Home: 23319 Holly Hollow Tomball TX 77375-3684 Office: Vinson & Elkins LLP 1001 Fannin St Ste 2300 Houston TX 77002-6760

**EILEN, HOWARD SCOTT,** lawyer, mediator; b. N.Y.C., Mar. 28, 1954; m. Sharon R. Kornbluth, Oct. 21, 1979; children: Michael, Jeffrey. BA summa cum laude, CUNY, 1975, MA, 1975; JD, St. John's U., 1979. Bar: N.Y. 1980, U.S. Tax Ct. 1980, U.S. Dist. Ct. (so., ea. dists.) N.Y. 1980, U.S. Dist. Ct. (ea. dist.) Mich. 1982. Assoc. Bloom & Tese, N.Y.C., 1980-83; ptnr. Bloom & Eilen, N.Y.C., 1983-86, 87-94; of counsel Spengler, Carlson, Gubar, Brodsky & Frischling, N.Y.C., 1986-87; ptnr. Lehman & Eilen, Uniondale, N.Y., 1994—; Arbitrator Nat. Assn. Securities Dealers, Inc., Nat. Futures Assn., Am. Arbitration Assn., U.S. Arbitration and Mediation, Inc., Mediator Nat. Assn. Sec. Dealers, Inc., Spl. Master N.Y. Supreme Ct., Faculty Practising Law Inst., Sec. Arbitration Program. Contbg. editor Futures Tribune Mag., Japan. Mem. N.Y. County Lawyers Assn. (com. on securities and exchanges 1983—, chmn. subcom. on commodities regulation, com. on arbitration and conciliation 1990—), Nassau County Bar Assn. (securities law com.). Securities, General civil litigation, Alternative dispute resolution. Office: Lehman & Eilen LLP Ste 505 50 Charles Lindbergh Blvd Uniondale NY 11553-3612

**EILERAAS, KARINA ASTRID,** legal assistant; b. Duluth, Minn., July 26, 1971; d. Kåre Meling and Ruth Janette (Nilsen) E. BA with high honors, Wesleyan U., 1993; postgrad., Northwestern U., 1995—. Cons. Andersen Consulting, Hartford, Conn., 1993-94; tchr. French Northwestern U., Evanston, Ill., 1996-97; legal asst. Sidley & Austin, Chgo., 1997—. Contbr. essays, poems, photographs numerous jours. Vol. ACLU, Chgo., 1990, Planned Parenthood, Middletown, Conn., 1990-91; crisis adv. Rape Victim Advs., Chgo., 1995—. Avocations: biking, photography, hiking, travel, guitar. Home: 401 W Webster Ave Apt 503 Chicago IL 60614-3864 Office: Sidley & Austin 3 S Dearborn St Chicago IL 60603-2301

**EIMER, NATHAN PHILIP,** lawyer; b. Chgo., June 26, 1949; s. Irving A. and Charlotte Eimer; m. Kathleen L. Roach; children: Micah Jacob, Noah Joseph, Daniel Jordan, Anna Beatrice. AB in Econs. magna cum laude, U. Ill., 1970; JD cum laude, Northwestern U., 1973. Bar: Ill. 1973, U.S. Supreme Ct. 1978, N.Y. 1985, Tex. 1998. Assoc. Sidley & Austin, Chgo., 1973-80, ptnr., 1980—; adj. prof. Law Sch., Northwestern U., Chgo., 1989-96. Note and comment editor Northwestern U. Law Rev., 1972-73. Bd. dirs. Chgo. Lawyers Com. for Civil Rights, 1991—, pres., 1993-94; bd. dirs. UNICEF, 1992-93, Infant Welfare Soc., Chgo., exec. v.p., 1992-96, pres., 1996-98; mem. adv. bd. Children & Family Justice Ctr., Northwestern U. Legal Clinic, 1996-98. Mem. ABA, Midday Club Chgo. General civil litigation, Antitrust. Office: Sidley & Austin 1 First Natl Plz Ste 5300 Chicago IL 60603-2003

**EINHORN, DAVID ALLEN,** lawyer; b. Bklyn., Dec. 11, 1961; s. Harold and Jane Ellen (Wiener) E. BA in Computer Sci. magna cum laude, Columbia U., 1983, JD, 1986. Bar: N.Y. 1987, D.C. 1988, U.S. Dist. Ct. (so. and ea. dists.) N.Y. 1989, U.S. Ct. Appeals (fed. cir.) 1992, U.S. Dist. Ct. (no. dist.) Calif. 1994. Assoc. Kaye, Scholer, Fierman, Hays & Handler, N.Y.C., 1986-89; ptnr. Anderson Kill & Olick, PC, N.Y.C., 1989—; columnist Grapevine; lectr. Am. Conf. Inst. Editor-in-chief Law and Technology for the New Millenium, 1997—; contbr. articles to profl. jours. Lt. col. N.Y. Guard, 1987—. Harlan Fiske Stone scholar Columbia U., 1985; recipient Nat. prize Nathan Burkan Copyright Essay Competition, 1985; named to Order of Merit, Les Amis du Vin, 1982. Mem. ABA (chmn. software patent subcom. 1988-91, software licensing subcom. 1991-97, software copyright subcom. 1995-96), Am. Israel Pub. Affairs Com., Am. Intellectual Property Law Assn. (chmn. software copyright subcom. 1999—), N.Y. Intellectual Property Law Assn., Internat. Trademark Assn. (chmn. com. on electronic info. 1994-95), D.C. Bar Assn. (computer law sect.), Columbia Soc. Law and Tech. (pres. 1985-86), Licensing Execs. Soc. (lectr.), N.Y. Soc. Mil. and Naval Officers (v.p. 1995—), Wine Lovers Internat. (v.p., bd. dirs. 1994—, Order of Merit 1997), Tasters Guild (v.p., bd. dirs. 1997—), Untitled Theater Co. #61, Ltd. (chmn. bd. dirs., producing dir., treas. 1994—). Jewish. Democrat. Avocations: tennis, racquetball, wine tasting, marksmanship. Computer, Patent, Trademark and copyright. Home: 2373 Broadway Apt 802 New York NY 10024-2835 Office: Anderson Kill & Olick PC 1251 Ave of the Americas New York NY 10020-1182

**EINHORN, HAROLD,** lawyer, writer; b. N.Y.C., Dec. 17, 1929; s. Abe and Pauline (Miller) E.; m. Jane Ellen, June 16, 1957; children: David, Edward. AB, NYU, 1951, MA, 1957; JD, Columbia U., 1960. Bar: N.Y. 1961, U.S. Ct. Appeals (fed. cir.) 1966. Pat. atty. Exxon Rsch. and Engring. Co., Linden, N.J., 1960-65; sr. pat. atty. Exxon Rsch. and Engring. Co., Linden, 1965-72, pat. csl., 1972-81; gen. tech. atty. Exxon Chem. Co., Linden, 1982-94; v.p. Exxon Chem. Patents Inc., 1989-94; of counsel Skadden, Arps, Slate, Meagher & Flom, N.Y.C., 1994-96, Ostrolenk, Faber, Gerb & Soffen, N.Y.C., 1996-97; ptnr. Ostrolenk, Faber, Gerb, N.Y.C., 1997—; lectr. Practicing Law Inst., Am. Mgmt. Assn., World Trade Inst., Franklin Pierce Law Sch., Can. Inst., Bridgeport U., Seton Hall U., N.J. Inventor's Congress, N.Y. State Bar Assn., Internat. Patent Club, ABA, Corp. Patent Seminar, joint seminar N.Y., Conn., Phila. law assns., Assn. Bar City N.Y., Insight Info. Inc.; mem. adj. faculty John Marshall Law Sch., 1993—, Practicing Law Inst. patent bar rev. program, 1995—, Fordham Law Sch., 1998—; bd. advisors BNA's World Licensing Law Report. Author: Patent Licensing Transactions, 2 vols., rev. ann., 1970—; contbg. author: Domestic and International Licensing of Technology, 1980, Domestic and Foreign Technology Licensing, 1984, Trends in Biotechnology and Chemical Patent Practice, 1989, Antitrust Law Developments, 3rd edit., 1991; bd. adv. BNA's World Lic. Law Report; contbr. articles to profl. jours. Bd. trustees Temple B'nai Israel, Elizabeth, N.J., 1980—, pres., 1985-89. Served with CIC, U.S. Army, 1953-55. Mem. ABA (subcom. chmn. 1981, 85, 86, 89, 91, chmn. com. internat. tech. transfer 1992, 93, chmn. com. rights of contractors with U.S. govt. 1994, 95, 96, 97, 98, chmn. com. expert witnesses 1998, 99), N.Y. Patent Law Assn. (assoc. editor bull. 1968-76, lectr.), Licensing Execs. Soc. (lectr.), Am. Intellectual Property Law Assn. (lectr.), Rochester Patent Law Assn. (lectr.), Assn. Corp. Patent Counsel (lectr.), Intellectual Property Owners Assn. (chmn. subcom. U.S. licensing devels.), Assn. of Bar of City of N.Y. (chmn. subcom. antitrust and licensing). Patent, Antitrust. Home: 382 Orenda Cir Westfield NJ 07090-2927 Office: 1180 Avenue Of The Americas New York NY 10036-8401

**EISCHEN, JAMES JOHN, JR.,** lawyer; b. Great Lakes, Ill., July 30, 1962; s. James J. and Nada M. (Tangway) E.; m. Cyndi J. Dillon, Dec. 27, 1986; children: James J. III, Faith Elizabeth. BA in English, Creighton U., 1984; JD, U. Calif., Davis, 1987. Bar: Calif. 1987, U.S. Dist. Ct. (so. dist.) Calif. 1987, U.S. Ct. Appeals (9th cir.) 1987. Assoc. Higgs, Fletcher & Mack, San Diego, 1987-89, Lillick & McHose, San Diego, 1989-90; sole practitioner San Diego, 1990-91; prin. Shannahan, Smith & Dailey, La Jolla, Calif., 1991-92; mng. prin. Smith, Dailey & Eischen, La Jolla, 1992—. Contbr. articles to profl. jours. Bd. dirs. San Diego YMCA Camping Svcs., St. Augustine H.S., 1997—. Mem. ABA (real property, probate and trust law com.), San Diego Bar Assn. (ethics, bus./corp. and real property sects.), San Diego Yacht Club (flag mem. 1990—). Republican. Roman Catholic. General civil litigation, Contracts commercial, Condemnation. Office: Eischen & Assocs 836 Prospect St Ste 1 La Jolla CA 92037-4213

**EISELE, GARNETT THOMAS,** federal judge; b. Hot Springs, Ark., Nov. 3, 1923; s. Garnett Martin and Mary (Martin) E.; m. Kathryn Freygang, June 24, 1950; children: Wendell A., Garnett Martin II, Kathryn M., Jean E. Student, U. Fla., 1940-42, Ind. U., 1942-43; AB, Washington U., 1947; LLB, Harvard U., 1950, LLM, 1951. Bar: Ark. 1951. Practiced in Hot Springs, 1951-52, Little Rock, 1953-69; assoc. Wootten, Land and Matthews, 1951-52, Owens, McHaney, Lofton & McHaney, 1956-60; asst. U.S. atty. Little Rock, 1953-55; pvt. practice law, 1961-69; judge U.S. Dist. Ct. (ea. dist.) Ark., 1970—, chief judge, 1975-91, sr. judge, 1991—; legal adviser to gov. Ark., 1966-69. Del. Ark. 7th Constl. Conv., 1969-70; trustee U. Ark., 1969-70. Served with AUS, 1943-46, ETO. Mem. ABA, Ark. Bar Assn., Pulaski County Bar Assn., Am. Judicature Soc., Am. Law Inst. Office: US Dist Ct PO Box 3684 Little Rock AR 72203-3684

**EISELE, JOHN EUGENE,** lawyer; b. Mpls., Apr. 22, 1938; s. James William and Fayloa Geneva E.; m. Patricia Anne Thornburg, Mar. 2, 1962 (div. Feb. 1981); children: John Michael, William Todd. BA, Ind. U., 1961, JD, 1968. Bar: Ind. 1968, U.S. Dist. Ct. Ind. 1968, U.S. Supreme Ct. 1990. Personnel, foreman GM, Anderson, Ind., 1964-68; hearing officer Ind. Pub. Svc. Commn., Indpls., 1968-70; deputy prosecutor Madison County, Anderson, 1970, pub. defender, 1971-76, atty., 1968—. Mem. Anderson Police Merit Commn., 1997—. 1st lt. U.S. Army, 1962-64. Mem. Ind. Bar Assn., Ind. Trial Lawyers Assn., Madison County Bar Assn. (pres. 1989), Am. Legion, Anderson Country Club (sec./bd. dirs. 1991-94), Exch. Club. Avocations: fishing, jogging, weightlifting. Home: 514 Ironwood Ln Anderson IN 46011-1650 Office: Eisele Lockwood & Eisele 200 E 11th St Ste 100 Anderson IN 46016-1779

**EISEMAN, NEAL MARTIN,** lawyer; b. Perth Amboy, N.J., Dec. 13, 1955; s. Lawrence and Ethel (Goldenberg) E.; m. Lynda Bolnick, Sept. 4, 1988. BA in Journalism, Polit. Sci., George Washington U., 1978; JD, St. John's U., 1981. Bar: N.Y. 1982, N.J. 1981, U.S. Dist. Ct. N.J. 1981, U.S. Dist. Ct. (ea. dist., so. dist.) N.Y. 1982, U.S. Ct. Appeals (2d cir.) 1984, U.S. Supreme Ct. 1985. Assoc. Goetz, Fitzpatrick & Flynn, N.Y.C., 1981-86, ptnr., 1987—, mng. ptnr., 1999—; panel of arbitrators, Am. Arbitration Assn., N.Y.C., 1987; arbitrator small claims dept. N.Y. Civil Ct., 1990—; prof. diploma program in bldg. constrn. mgmt. Real Estate Inst. N.Y.U., 1990—. Construction, State civil litigation, General corporate. Office: Goetz Fitzpatrick Most & Bruckman LLP 1 Penn Plz Ste 4401 New York NY 10119-0196

**EISEN, ERIC ANSHEL,** lawyer; b. N.Y.C., Apr. 9, 1950; s. Morton and Victoria (Goldstein) E.; m. Claire L. Shapiro, Jan. 6, 1979; children: Rebecca, Jennifer, Melissa. AB, U. Mich., 1971, JD magna cum laude, 1975. Bar: Alaska 1976, D.C. 1977, Md. 1988. Law clk. to presiding justice Alaska Supreme Ct., Fairbanks, 1975-76; assoc. Covington & Burling, Washington, 1976-81; assoc. Birch, Horton, Bittner, Washington, 1981-85, ptnr., 1985-93; ptnr. Eisen Law Offices, Bethesda, Md., 1993—; speaker various seminars and colloquia on energy and bus. matters. Contbr. articles legal publs. Pres. Wildwood Hills Citizens Assn., Bethesda, Md., 1987—; sec. N. Bethesda Cong. Citizens Assns., 1989-90. Mem. Fed. Energy Bar Assn. (antitrust com.), D.C. Bar Assn., Montgomery County Bar Assn. (intellectual property and litigation sects.), Toastmasters, Order of Coif. Avocation: woodworking. Administrative and regulatory, FERC practice, General civil litigation. Office: Eisen Law Office 10028 Woodhill Rd Bethesda MD 20817-1218

**EISEN, SAUL,** lawyer; b. Cleve., July 26, 1935; s. Ben and Manya (Parsons) E.; m. Hermine Beth Greene, Dec. 16, 1961; children: Barbara, Brian, Abigail. BA, Case Western Res. U., 1957, LLb, 1959. Bar: Ohio 1960, U.S. Dist. Ct. (no. dist.) Ohio 1960, U.S. Supreme Ct. 1960. Ptnr. Blane, Eisen & Wasserman, Cleve., 1960-63, Starkoff, Yelsky & Eisen, Cleve., 1963-73, Yelsky, Eisen & Singer, Cleve., 1973-80, Javitch & Eisen Co., L.P.A., Cleve., 1981-92, Javitch, Block, Eisen & Rathbone, Cleve., 1992—. Bd. dirs., pres. Beachwood (Ohio) Sch. Bd., 1972—; pres. Friends of Beachwood Library, 1982-87; acting judge Shaker Heights Ohio Mcpl. Ct., 1994—. Mem. Nat. Assn. Bankruptcy Trustees (chmn. membership com. 1988—, past pres.), Cleve. Bar Assn. (sec. bankruptcy sect. 1988—), Cuyahoga County Bar Assn. (chmn. bankruptcy sect. 1988—, trustee, 1st v.p.), Masons (pres. 1969). Bankruptcy, Consumer commercial. Home: 25010 Duffield Rd Cleveland OH 44122-3263 Office: Jacitch Block Eisen & Rathbone 1300 E 9th St Cleveland OH 44114-1503

**EISEN, STEVEN JEFFREY,** lawyer; b. Nashville, May 14, 1958; s. Harvey and Ann Eisen; m. Gay Lisa Levine, June 26, 1988. BA in Econs., Northwestern U., 1979; MBA, Vanderbilt U., Nashville, 1983; JD, Vanderbilt U., 1983. Bar: Tenn 1983, U.S. Dist. Ct. (mid. dist.) Tenn., U.S. Ct. Appeals (6th cir.). Assoc. Bone, Langford & Armistead, Nashville, 1983-87; ptnr. Baker, Donelson, Bearman & Caldwell, Nashville, 1988—. European Inst. scholar, 1980, Owen scholar, 1979. Mem. ABA, Tenn. Bar Assn., Nashville Bar Assn. Avocations: tennis, boating. Banking, Securities, General corporate. Office: Baker Donelson Bearman & Caldwell 511 Union St Ste 1700 Nashville TN 37219-1737

**EISENBERG, BRUCE ALAN,** lawyer; b. Balt., Dec. 3, 1952; s. Leonard E. and Elaine Bondy Eisenberg; m. Doreen E. Caplan, Aug. 30, 1977; children: Brett H., Lindsay A. BA, Yale U., 1974; JD, U. Pa., 1977. Bar: Pa. 1977, D.C. 1979, Md. 1979. Assoc. Pepper Hamilton & Scheetz, Phila., 1977-78; law clk. to Hon. Raymond Broderick, U.S. Dist. Ct. for Ea. Dist. Pa., Phila., 1978-79; ptnr. Cohen Snyder Eisenberg & Katzenberg, Balt., 1979—. Avocations: softball, soccer, racquetball. Personal injury, Criminal. Home: 2103 Burdock Rd Baltimore MD 21209-1001 Office: Cohen Snyder Et Al 347 N Charles St Baltimore MD 21201-4307

**EISENBERG, HOWARD BRUCE,** law educator; b. Chgo., Dec. 9, 1946; s. Herman Levy and Margie M. (Meyers) E.; m. Phyllis Terry Borenstein, Aug. 25, 1968; children: Nathan, Adam, Leah. BA, Northwestern U., 1968; JD, U. Wis., 1971. Bar: Wis. 1971, D.C. 1980, Ill. 1983, U.S. Dist. Ct. (ea. and we. dists.) Wis. 1971, U.S. Dist. Ct. (so. and ctrl. dists.) Ill. 1983, U.S. Ct. Appeals (7th cir.) 1971, U.S. Ct. Appeals (8th cir.) 1983, U.S. Supreme Ct. 1974, U.S. Ct. Appeals (D.C. cir.) 1978, U.S. Dist. Ct. (ea. and we. dists.) Ark. 1991. Mem. staff Wis. Judicare Legal Svcs. Agy. OEO, Madison, 1968-71; law clk. to justice Wis. Supreme Ct., 1971-72; asst. state pub. defender State of Wis., 1972, state pub. defender, 1972-78; dir. defender div. Nat. Legal Aid and Defender Assn., Washington, 1978-79, exec. dir., 1979-83; assoc. prof. law, dir. clin. edn. So. Ill. U., Carbondale, 1983-91, assoc. prof., 1983-87, prof., 1987-91; dean Sch. Law, prof. law U. Ark. at Little Rock, 1991-95; dean, prof. law Sch. Marquette U., 1995—; mem. Wis. Bd. Bar Examiners, 1996—; dir. Coalition for Legal Assn., 1981-82, Ill. Guardianship and Protective Svcs. Assn., 1990-91; Ark. Continuing Legal Edn. Bd., 1991-95, Pulaski County Bar Assn., 1991-95, Ark. Inst. Continuing Legal Edn., Assn. Religiously Affiliated Law Schs.; chair Fed. Judicial Nominating Commn., Ea. Dist., Wis., 1995—. Ill. State scholar, 1964-68; NDEA grantee, 1967. Bd. dirs. Hospice So. Ill., 1988-91, Milw. Legal Aid Soc., 1997—. Mem. ABA, Am. Acad. Appellate Lawyers, Nat. Acad. Elder Law Attys., State Bar Wis., Wis. Assn. Criminal Attys., Ark. State Bar Assn., 7th Circuit Bar Assn., Ill. State Bar Assn., Milw. Bar Assn. (bd. mem. 1997—), Equal Justice Coalition (bd. mem. 1998—), Nat. Assn. Criminal Def. Lawyers, Northwestern U. Alumni Assn., Wis. U. Alumni Assn., Phi Beta Kappa. Democrat. Jewish. Contbr. articles to profl. jours. Office: Marquette U Sch of Law PO Box 1881 Milwaukee WI 53201-1881

**EISENBERG, STEVEN KEITH,** lawyer; b. Phila., July 24, 1970; s. Stuart A. and Marsha Z. Eisenberg; m. Sasha R. Eisenberg, June 25, 1995. BA, Cornell U., 1991; JD, MBA, Temple U., 1995. Bar: Pa. 1995, N.J. 1995, U.S. Dist. Ct. N.J., U.S. Dist. Ct. (ea. dist.) Pa., U.S. Ct. Appeals (3d cir.). Pvt. practice, Doylestown, Pa., 1995—, N.J., 1995—. Pres. bd. dirs. Fireside Cmty. Assn., Doylestown, 1996—. Mem. Pa. Bar Assn., N.J. Bar Assn. Democrat. Jewish. General corporate, Contracts commercial, Estate planning. Home: 5974 Raintree Ct Doylestown PA 18901 Office: 603 Horsham Rd Apt B Horsham PA 19044-4201 also: 1 Greentree Ctr Ste 201 Marlton NJ 08053-3105

**EISENBERG, SUSAN MARY,** retired employment representative; b. Duquesne, Pa., July 24, 1929; d. John and Maria (Sokolvsky) Boronkay; m. Jack Cleon Seidling, Sept. 18, 1949 (wid. Feb. 1979); children: Cheryl Susan Seidling Lindsey, Janet Marie Seidling Kelly, David John Seidling; m. Ronald John Eisenberg, Sept. 26, 1992. Student, LaSalle Inst., 1947-48; fin., N.Y. Inst. of Fin., 1964. Lic. ins. agt. Pa., stockbroker. Paralegal A.J. Rosenbleet, McKeesport, Pa., 1949-51, Stokes & Lurie, Clairton, Pa., 1952-56; asst. mgr. Bernstein & Co., McKeesport, 1963-64; stockbroker Chaplin McGuiness Co., Pitts., 1965-66; account exec. Bache & Co., Pitts., 1966-75; employee rep. Dept. of Labor and Industry, McKeesport, 1975-91. Author/editor: (newsletter) Sr. Ams. Newsletter, 1981—. Girl Scout leader Girl Scouts U.S., West Mifflin, Pa., 1956-61, troop cons., 1957-58; telephone reassurance vol. Contact Pitts., Inc., N. Versailles, Pa., 1995; vol. Eye & Ear Hosp., Pitts., 1995-96; eucharistic minister, N. Versailles, 1993-96; founder, travel chair ALPS, Inc., v.p. 1982-83; founder, pres. Sr. Ams. Club, Inc., 1981-91. Recipient Senatorial citation Pa. Senate, 1988, Lt. Gov.'s proclamation Sate of Pa., 1988, People Who Care award Pa. Sec. of Labor, 1990. Mem. VFW Aux. (parliamentarian, trustee 1997—), Am. Legion Aux. (pres., v.p., mem. chair 1980-84), St. Stephens Ladies Guild (pres. 1983-84). Avocations: playing organ, reading, dancing, gardening, charitable volunteering. Home: 3035 Fairway Dr Fort Pierce FL 34982-4319

**EISENBERG, THEODORE,** law educator; b. Bklyn., Oct. 26, 1947; s. Abraham Louis and Esther (Waldman) E.; m. Lisa Wright, Nov. 27, 1971; children: Katherine Wright, Ann Marie, Thomas Peter. BA, Swarthmore, Pa. Coll., 1969; JD, U. Pa., 1972. Bar: Pa. 1972, N.Y. 1974, U.S. Ct. Appeals (2d cir.) 1974, Calif. 1977. Law clk. U.S. Ct. Appeals, D.C. Cir., 1972-73; law clk. to U.S. Supreme Ct. Justice Earl Warren, 1973; assoc. Debevoise & Plimpton, N.Y.C., 1974-77; prof. law UCLA Law Sch., 1977-81; prof. law Cornell U. Law Sch., Ithaca, N.Y., 1981-96, Henry Allen Mark prof. law, 1996—; vis. prof. law Harvard U. Law Sch., 1984-85; vis. prof. Law, Stanford U. Law Sch., 1987. Author: Civil Rights Legislation, 1981, 4th edit. 1996; Bankruptcy and Debtor-Creditor Law, 1984, 2d edit. 1988; mem. adv. bd. Law and Society Rev., Am. Law and Econ. Rev., Justice System Jour.; contbr. articles to profl. jours. Am. Bar Found. grantee, NSF grantee. Fellow Royal Statis. Soc.; mem. ABA, Assn. Bar City N.Y., Law and Soc. Assn., Am. Law and Econ. Assn., Am. Bankruptcy Inst. Office: Cornell U Law Sch Myron Taylor Hall Ithaca NY 14853

**EISENBERG, VIVIANE,** lawyer; b. Brussels, Belgium, July 18, 1952; came to the U.S., 1975; d. Samuel Eisenberg and Laura Preiss; m. Richard Mellen, Dec. 5, 1980; children: Joshua, Alex, Ruby. Attended, U. Brussels, 1970-75; LLM, Columbia U., 1976. Bar: N.Y., 1977. Assoc. Proskauer Rose Goetz & Menelsohn, N.Y., 1976-80; v.p., chief counsel Home Box Office, N.Y., 1980—. Democrat. General corporate, Entertainment, Intellectual property. Office: Home Box Office 1100 Avenue Of The Americas New York NY 10036-6712

**EISENHAUER, WAYNE HAROLD,** lawyer; b. Salem, Mass., Apr. 15, 1949. BA, Tufts U., 1971; JD, Boston Coll., 1974. Bar: Mass. 1974, U.S. Dist. Ct. Mass. 1976, U.S. Ct. Appeals (1st cir.) 1977, U.S. Supreme Ct. 1977. Pvt. practice law Danvers, Mass., 1974—; v.p., bd. dirs. Eisenhauers & Co., Inc., Danvers, 1971—; ret.; pres., bd. dir. Small Bus. Econs., Danvers, 1988—; corporator Danvers Savs. Bank, 1977, Beverly (Mass.) Hosp., 1988. Mem. Danvers Town Meeting, 1979; chmn. Danvers Preservation Commn., 1988, mem.; bd. dirs. Danvers Hist. Soc., Danvers Town Meeting. Mem. ABA, Mass. Bar Assn., Boston Bar Assn., Mass. Conveyancers, Mass. Assn. Bank Counsel, Greater Salem Bd. Realtors, Corinthian Yacht Club. General corporate, Probate, Real property. Office: 66 Elm St PO Box 119 Danvers MA 01923-0119

**EISGRUBER, CHRISTOPHER L.,** law educator; b. West Lafayette, Ind., Sept. 24, 1961; s. Ludwig Maria and Eva R. Eisgruber; m. Lori A. Martin, June 14, 1987. AB in Physics, Princeton U., 1983; MLitt in Politics, Oxford U., 1987; JD, U. Chgo., 1988. Law clk. Judge Patrick Higginbotham, Dallas, 1988-89, Justice John Paul Stevens, Washington, 1989-90; asst. prof. NYU Sch. Law, N.Y.C., 1990-93, assoc. prof., 1993-95, prof. law, 1995—. Editor in chief U. Chgo. Law Rev., 1987-88; co-convenor Colloquium in Constl. Theory, 1993-97. Rhodes Scholar, 1983. Office: NYU Sch Law 40 Washington Sq S New York NY 10012-1005

**EISMAN, CLYDE JAY,** lawyer; b. N.Y.C., Oct. 23, 1967; s. Stanley and Beatrice Eisman. BA, Oberlin Coll., 1989; JD with honors, Tulane U., 1994. Bar: N.Y. 1995, U.S. Dist. Ct. (so. and ea. dist.) N.Y. 1995. Trade advisor South Korean Govt., 1990-91; law clk. Gen. Counsel's Office U.S. Dept. Def., Pentagon, 1992; pvt. practice N.Y.C., 1995—; adj. instr. Baruch Coll., Manhattan; arbitrator; instr. legal rsch. and writing Legal Aid Soc., 1997; mediator various orgns. Contbr. articles to profl. jours. Mem. N.Y. County Lawyers Assn. (bd. dirs., chair solo and small firm com.), Am. Inn of Ct., Assn. of the Bar of the City of N.Y. Federal civil litigation, State civil litigation. Office: 220 E 23rd St Ste 307 New York NY 10010-4606

**EISNER, ELLIOTT ROY,** lawyer; b. Cleve., Jan. 8, 1945; s. Sydney S. and Dorothy Regina (Haber) E.; m. Adele Levine, Oct. 28, 1967 (div. 1984); children: Jonathon, Samantha; m. Mary Lynn Winter, May 10, 1986. BA, Ohio State U., 1966; JD, Cleve. State U., 1970. Bar: Ohio 1970, Nev. 1986. Assoc. gen. counsel Cardinal Fed. Savs. Bank, Cleve., 1972-84, Valley Bank of Nev., Las Vegas, 1984-89; assoc. Vargas & Bartlett, Las Vegas, 1989-94; ptnr. Kummer, Kaempfer, Bonnza & Renshaw, 1994—. Mem. Nev. Bar Assn. Real property, Banking, Contracts commercial. Office: Kummer Kaempfer Bonner & Renshaw 3800 Hqward Hughes Pkwy Fl 7 Las Vegas NV 89109-0925

**EISZNER, JAMES RICHARD, JR.,** lawyer; b. Chicago Heights, Ill., June 6, 1953; s. James R. Sr. and Joyce Carolyn (Holland) E.; m. Barbara Lynn Bonavita, Aug. 15, 1976; children: Nicole, James, Richard. AB, Princeton U., 1975; JD, NYU, 1978. Bar: N.Y. 1979, U.S. Dist. Ct. (so. and ea. dists.) N.Y. 1979, U.S. Supreme Ct. 1982, U.S. Ct. Appeals 1982, Mo. 1997. Assoc. Lord, Day & Lord, N.Y.C., 1978-86; ptnr. Coudert Brothers, N.Y.C., 1986-97, Shook, Hardy & Bacon, LLP, Kansas City, 1997—. Mem. ABA, Hallbrook Country Club. Republican. Presbyterian. Antitrust, Federal civil litigation, Criminal. Home: 11704 Norwood Dr Leawood KS 66211-3002 Office: Shook Hardy & Bacon LLP 1200 Main St One Kansas City Pl Kansas City MO 64105-2118

**EKKER, HENRY MAYER,** lawyer; b. Sharon, Pa., Feb. 28, 1939; s. David Leonard and Sedalia (Mayer) E.; m. Kathryn Glick, May 30, 1965; children: Steven, Sedalia, Gregory, Laura. BA, U.Mich., 1961, JD, 1964. Bar: Pa. 1965, U.S. Tax Ct. 1969, U.S. Ct. Internat. Trade 1971. From assoc. to mng. ptnr. Ekker, Kuster & McConnell (formerly Cusick, Madden, Joyce & McKay), Sharon, 1965—; bd. dirs. FNB Corp., FNB of Pa., First Nat. Trust Co., First Nat. Bank of Pa., Shenango Valley Indsl. Devel. Corp. Pres., dir. Temple Beth Israel, Sharon; bd. dirs. United Way Mercer County, Pa, Shenango Valley Redevel. Authority. Mem. Mercer County Bar Assn. (pres., chmn. family law divsn.), Sharon C. of C. (bd. dirs.), Fraternal Order of Police (recipient Man of Yr. award). Republican. Jewish. Avocations: sports memorabilia, travel. Estate planning, General corporate, Family and matrimonial. Office: Ekker Kuster & McConnell PO Box 91 First Western Bank Bldg Sharon PA 16146 also: 3545 E State St Hermitage PA 16148-3413 also: 210 S Market St New Wilmington PA 16142-1239

**EKLUND, PAUL G.,** lawyer, author, psychotherapist; b. Seattle, Sept. 4, 1951; s. Bruce G. and Alice J. Eklund; divorced; children: Bruce, Ben, Brie Anna. BS in Psychology, U. Wash., 1972; MA in Clin. Psychology, Western Sem., Portland, Oreg., 1980; JD, U. Puget Sound/Seattle U., 1987. Bar: Wash. 1988, Hawaii 1994, U.S. Dist. Ct. Wash., U.S. Dist. Ct. Hawaii. Mgr. United Airlines, Seattle, 1972-78; psychotherapist Seattle, 1978-88; atty. Moren, Lageschulte, Cornell, Seattle, 1987-88; sole practitioner Seattle, 1989—; judge pro tem City of Seattle-Tacoma, 1995; mediator/arbitrator King County Superior Ct., Seattle, 1995—. Co-author counseling text; author: (nonfiction) Pathways Through Pain, 1998. Mem. Human Rels. Commn., City of Tacoma, 1982; bd. dirs. Seattle Christian Sch., 1996-98, Alpine Boys Ranch, Wash., 1976-77, 94-96, Ctr. for Conflict Mgmt., Seattle, 1995-97; bd. dirs., chmn. MVP Relief Agy., Seattle, 1994-96; bd. dirs., v.p. Vision-Heir, Inc.. Recipient Human Rels. award Western Sem., 1980. Mem. Wash. Bar Assn., Hawaii Bar Assn. Avocations: foreign languages (Swedish, French, Spanish, German), hiking, travel. Private international, Labor, General civil litigation. Home: PO Box 547 Winthrop WA 98862-0547

**EKWEM, ROBERTSON M.,** lawyer; b. Lagos, Nigeria, Oct. 16, 1962; s. Chief B.N. and Lolo Briget (Oforha) E. BBA in Banking and Fin., Tex. So. U., Houston, 1987; JD, Thurgood Marshall Sch. Law, Houston, 1994. Bar: Tex. 1994, U.S. Dist. Ct. (so. and ea. dists.) Tex. 1995, U.S. Ct. Appeals (5th cir.) 1995. Pvt. practice Houston, 1994—. Mem. ABA, Houston Bar Assn., Assn. Trial Lawyers Am., Houston Young Lawyers Assn., NAACP, Harris County Criminal Lawyers Assn., Tex. Trial Lawyers Assn., Phi Alpha Delta. Roman Catholic. Avocations: reading, travel, jazz music, dancing, biking. General civil litigation, Criminal, Personal injury. Home: 6601 Sands Point Dr Apt 55 Houston TX 77074-3738 Office: 8323 Southwest Fwy Ste 555 Houston TX 77074-1609

**ELA, WILLIAM MACHARG,** judge, mediator, arbitrator; b. Grand Junction, Colo., May 11, 1923; s. Wendell Dennett and Lucy Ferril Ela; m. Shirley P. Phillips, Oct. 3, 1946; children: Beth Ela Wilkens, Wendell Phillips, Thomas Nelson, Daniel Dennett, Steven Dean. LLB, Harvard U., 1949; D for Pub. Svc., Mesa State Coll., 1993. Bar: Colo. 1949, U.S. Dist. Ct. Colo. 1949. Pvt. practice Adams, Heckman, Traylor & Ela, Grand Junction, 1949-65; dist. ct. judge, chief judge State of Colo., Grand Junction, 1965-87, sr. dist. judge, 1987-99; faculty, faculty advisor Nat. Jud. Coll., Reno, 1966-75. Contbr. articles to profl. jours. Mem. Grand Junction Lion's Club, 1955-98; trustee, pres. Goodwin Found., Grand Junction, 1975-98; founding co-chmn. Grand Junction Mesa County Riverfront Commn., 1988-96. Lt. (j.g.) USN, 1944-46, ATO, PTO. Fellow Am. Coll. Trust and Estates Coun.; mem. ABA, Colo. Bar Assn. (sect. chmn., v.p. 1958), Mesa County Bar Assn. (pres. and numerous coms. 1949-88). Avocations: cross country skiing, bicycling, fishing, gardening, astronomy. Home and Office: 3051 L Rd Hotchkiss CO 81419-9407

**ELBERGER, RONALD EDWARD,** lawyer; b. Newark, Mar. 13, 1945; s. Morris and Clara (Denes) E.; m. Rena Ann Brodey, Feb. 15, 1975; children: Seth, Rebecca. AA, George Washington U., 1964, BA, 1966; JD, Am. U., 1969. Bar: Md. 1969, D.C. 1970, Ind. 1971, U.S. Ct. Appeals (7th cir.) 1971, U.S. Supreme Ct. 1973. Atty. Balt. Legal Aid Bur., 1969-70; chief counsel Legal Services Orgn., Indpls., 1970-72; ptnr. Elberger & Stanton, Indpls., 1974-76, Bose, McKinney & Evans, Indpls., 1976—; asst. sec., v.p., litigation counsel Emmis Comm. Corp., 1986—; v.p. Cardboard Shoe Prodns., Inc., 1989—, Worldwide Slacks, Inc., 1994—. Mem., v.p. Med. Licensing Bd. Ind., 1982-98; pres., chmn. bd. dirs. Ind. Civil Liberties Union, Indpls., 1972-77, bd. dirs., 1972, 80-82; bd. dirs. ACLU, N.Y.C., 1972-77, Jewish Cmty. Rels. Coun., 1997—; trustee Children's Mus. of Indpls., 1994—. Reginald Heber Smith fellow U. Pa., 1969-71. Mem. ABA, Ind. Bar Assn., Md. Bar Assn., D.C. Bar Assn., Indpls. Bar Assn. Democrat. Jewish. Avocations: fishing, music, gardening. Federal civil litigation, State civil litigation, Entertainment. Office: Bose McKinney & Evans 2700 First Indiana Pla 135 N Pennsylvania St Indianapolis IN 46204-2400

**ELBERT, CHARLES STEINER,** lawyer; b. St. Louis, May 18, 1950; s. Harold I. and Carol B. (Steiner) E.; m. Karen Berry, Dec. 9, 1979; children: Matthew Berry, Lisa Beth. AB, Washington U., St. Louis, 1972; JD cum laude, St. Louis U., 1976. Bar: Mo. 1976, Ill. 1977, U.S. Dist. Ct. (ea. and we. dists.) Mo. 1977, U.S. Ct. Appeals (8th cir.) 1977, U.S. Supreme Ct. 1985. Assoc. Kohn, Shands, Elbert, Gianoulakis & Giljum, St. Louis, 1976-81, ptnr., 1982—; spl. rep. 22d Jud. Bar Com., St. Louis, 1978-88; spk. labor and employment law CLEs. Contbr. articles to profl. jours. Trustee Clayton Gardens Neighborhood Assn., Mo., 1983-84, 85-86, pres., 1984-85; bd. dirs. St. Louis chpt. Am. Diabetes Assn., 1998—, St. Louis chpt. Am. Jewish Com., 1994-97, sec. 1994-97; v.p. Nursery Found., St. Louis, 1988-89, bd. dirs., Mo. Coalition Against Censorship, 1986-92, sec., 1988-92; mentor Dunbar Sch., 1995—. Mem. Mo. Bar Assn. (labor law com. 1977—), Ill. State Bar Assn., ABA (labor law sect. 1984—, corp., banking and bus. law sect., 1987—), Bar Assn. Met. St. Louis (labor law com. 1977—, grievance com. 1978-87 ). Jewish. Labor, General corporate, Real property. Home: 8137 University Dr Saint Louis MO 63105-3726 Office: Kohn Shands Elbert et al One Mercantile Ctr 24th Fl Saint Louis MO 63101

**ELCANO, MARY S.,** lawyer, federal agency administrator. BA cum laude, Lynchburg Coll., 1971; JD, Cath. U., Washington, 1976. Litigation atty. Balt. Legal Aide Bur., 1976; staff atty. Office Solicitor Dept. Labor, 1979; gen. trial and appellate atty. Office Labor Law U.S. Postal Svc., 1982, exec. dir. Office EEO, 1984, regional dir. human resources N.E. region, 1987, sr. v.p., gen. counsel, 1992—. Office: US Postal Svc 475 L'enfant Plz SW Washington DC 20260-1100

**ELDEN, GARY MICHAEL,** lawyer; b. Chgo., Dec. 11, 1944; s. E. Harold and Sylvia Arlene (Diamond) E.; m. Phyllis Deborah Mandler, Apr. 20, 1975; children: Roxanna Mandler, Erica Mandler. BA, U. Ill., 1966; JD, Harvard U., 1969. Bar: Ill. 1969, U.S. Dist. Ct. (no. dist.) Ill. 1969, U.S. Ct. Appeals (7th cir.) 1973, U.S. Supreme Ct. 1973, U.S. Dist. Ct. (ea. dist.) Mich. 1985, U.S. Ct. Appeals (8th cir.) 1988, U.S. Ct. Appeals (6th and 10th cirs.) 1990, U.S. Dist. Ct. (ea. dist.) Wis. 1992. Ptnr. Kirkland & Ellis, Chgo., 1969-78, Reuben & Proctor, Chgo., 1978-86, Isham, Lincoln & Beale, Chgo., 1986-88, Grippo & Elden, Chgo., 1988—. Contbr. articles to profl. jours. Fellow Am. Coll. Trial Lawyers; mem. ABA, Chgo. Bar Assn. (sec. com. appellate procedures 1975-77), Chgo. Coun. Lawyers, Appellate Lawyers Assn. (bd. dirs. 1975-77), Met. Club. Federal civil litigation, General civil litigation, Insurance. Home: 3750 N Lake Shore Dr Chicago IL 60613-4238 Office: Grippo & Elden 227 W Monroe St Ste 3600 Chicago IL 60606-5098

**ELDER, JAMES CARL,** lawyer; b. Detroit, Mar. 11, 1947; s. Carl W. and Alta M. (Bradley) E.; m. Margaret Ford, Apr. 6, 1974; children: James B., William J., Michael L., Samuel F. BA, U. Okla, 1969, JD, 1972. Bar: Okla. 1972, U.S. Dist. Ct. (we. dist.) Okla. 1972. Ptnr., dir. Crowe & Dunlevy, Oklahoma City, 1972-82; dir., mem. Mock, Schwabe, Waldo, et. al., Oklahoma City, 1982-96, 98—; ptnr. Gable Gotwals Mock Schwabe Kihle Gaberino, 1996-98. Nat. coun. rep. Last Frontier Coun. Boy Scouts Am., 1989—, pres., 1997-99; trustee Norman (Okla.) Pub. Sch. Found., 1989—, pres., 1995-97; elder Meml. Presbyn. Ch., Norman, clk. of session, 1992-95; dir. Cmty. Coun. Ctrl. Okla., 1999—. Recipient Silver Beaver award Boy Scouts Am., Oklahoma City, 1988, Silver Antelope award, 1999. Fellow Okla. Bar Found. (life), Baden Powell World Fellowship; mem. ABA (mem. title ins. com. real property, probate and trust law sect. 1993—, chmn. closing issues subcom. 1995—), Rotary, Beta Theta Pi Corp. of Okla. (trustee, v.p., chpt. counselor 1975-85, pres. 1995—). Avocations: scouting, skiing, reading. Real property, Contracts commercial, Banking. Office: Mock Schwabe Waldo et al 211 N Robinson 2 Leadership Sq 14th Fl Oklahoma City OK 73102

**ELDER, LAMAR ALEXANDER, JR.,** lawyer; b. Athens, Ga., June 16, 1945; s. Lamar Alexander Sr. and Johnnie Lucile (Aycock) E.; m. Jane Ellen Lindauer, July 25, 1970; children: Jennifer, Jonathan. AB, U. Ga., 1967, JD, 1970. Bar: Ga. 1970, U.S. Supreme Ct. 1974, U.S. Dist. Ct. (so. dist.) Ga. 1985. Assoc. Cook, Pleger & Noell, Athens, 1970-71; asst. gen. counsel USDA, Atlanta, 1975-77; assoc. J. Harold Mimbs, Hazlehurst, Ga., 1977-79; sole practice Hazlehurst, 1979—; atty. Jeff Davis County, Hazlehurst, 1980—; judge Mcpl. Ct. of Hazlehurst, 1985-86. Mem. Dem. Exec. Com., Jeff Davis County, Ga., 1980—; chmn. adminstrv. bd. 1st United Meth. Ch., Hazlehurst, 1985. Capt. JAGC USAF, 1971-75. Mem. Ga. Bar Assn., Hazlehurst-Jeff Davis County C. of C. (bd. dirs. 1980—, past pres.). Lodge: Rotary (bd. dirs. Hazlehurst chpt. 1982-84, v.p. 1984-85, pres. 1985-86). Avocations: fishing, gardening, refinishing antiques. General practice, State civil litigation, Real property. Home: 11 Woodhaven Dr Hazlehurst GA 31539-6615 Office: # 7 Jeff Davis St PO Box 632 Hazlehurst GA 31539-0632

**ELDERGILL, KATHLEEN,** lawyer; b. Mt. Kisco, N.Y., Jan. 16, 1953; d. William E. and Isabel (Rodgers) E.; m. Bruce S. Beck, Apr. 10, 1990; children: Jacob, Louis. BA in Anthropology, U. Conn., 1976, JD, 1981. Cert. civil trial advocacy. Assoc. Beck & Pagano, Manchester, Conn., 1981-83; ptnr., then prin. Beck & Eldergill P.C., Manchester, 1983—; mem. Fed. Grievance Com., New Haven, 1993-96, chair, 1996—. Mem. legal adv. bd. Conn. Fund for Environment, 1994—. Fellow Am. Coll. of Trial Lawyers; mem. Am. Trial Lawyers Assn., Conn. Employment Lawyers Assn., Nat. Employment Lawyers Assn., Conn. Trial Lawyers Assn. Labor, Civil rights, General civil litigation. Office: Beck & Eldergill PC 447 Center St Manchester CT 06040-3998

**ELDREDGE, GEORGE BADGE,** lawyer; b. Jasper, Tex., Mar. 2, 1950; s. Inman Fowler Jr. and Marjorie Lee (Badge) E.; m. Debra Lynn Campbell, Oct. 4, 1975; children: George Badge Jr., Christopher Campbell. BA, La. State U., 1972, JD, 1974. Bar: La. 1975, Tex. 1975, U.S. Dist. Ct. (mid. dist.) La. 1985, U.S. Ct. Appeals (5th cir.) 1985, U.S. Dist. Ct. (ea. and we. dists.) La. 1987, U.S. Ct. Mil. Appeals 1975. Instr. Far East div. U. Md., Misawa, Japan, 1977-80, L.A. Community Coll., Misawa, Japan, 1977-80; dep. gen. counsel La. Dept. Natural Resources, Baton Rouge, 1981-84; gen. counsel La. Dept. Environ. Quality, Baton Rouge, 1984-85; v.p., gen. counsel, bd. dirs. Marine Shale Processors, Inc., Morgan City, La., 1986-99;

ptnr. Eldredge and Eldredge Attys. at Law, Baton Rouge, 1985—. Author: (with others) Louisiana Environmental Handbook, 1992. Webelos leader Boy Scouts Am., Baton Rouge, 1989-91, asst. scoutmaster, 1990-96, scoutmaster, 1997—. Capt. USAF, 1975-81. Mem. ABA (nat. resources sect.), Tex. Bar Assn. (environ. sect.), La. Bar Assn. (environ. sect.), Baton Rouge Bar Assn. Roman Catholic. Environmental, General corporate, Administrative and regulatory. Office: Eldredge and Eldredge Attys at Law 10641 Lindsey Ln Saint Francisville LA 70775-5249

**ELDRIDGE, DOUGLAS ALAN,** lawyer; b. Boulder, Colo., Mar. 15, 1944; s. Douglas Hilton and Clara Effie (Young) E.; m. Benna June Germann, June 24, 1967; children: Heather Dana, Ethan Douglas, Hilary Beca. BA, Yale U., 1966; LLB, U. Pa., 1969; cert., Nat. Inst. Trial Advocacy, Boulder, 1973. Bar: N.Y. 1972, U.S. Dist. Ct. (no. dist.) N.Y. 1973, U.S. Supreme Ct. 1975. Staff atty. Onondaga Neighborhood Legal Svcs., Syracuse, N.Y., 1971-74, exec. dir., 1974-76; counsel N.Y. State Divsn. of Substance Abuse Svcs., Albany, 1976-79; dep. counsel N.Y. State Health Dept., Albany, 1979-80; dep. counsel N.Y. State Energy Office, Albany, 1980-82, asst. counsel, 1982-87; gen. counsel Commn. for Siting Low-Level Radioactive Waste Disposal Facilities, Troy, N.Y., 1987-95; sole practice, 1995—; govt. affairs counsel N.Y. Rehab. Assn., Inc. Contbr. articles to legal jours. Bd. dirs. Coun. Cmty. Svcs. United Way of Northeastern N.Y., Albany, 1980-90, pres., 1986-88; bd. dirs. United Way Ea. N.Y., 1986-88, Mohawk-Hudson Found., 1986-89. Recipient Reginald Heber Smity Cmty. Lawyer fellowship OEO, 1969-71. Mem. N.Y. State Bar Assn., Albany County Bar Assn. (chair legis. com. 1998—), Onondaga County Bar Assn., Assn. of Bar of City of N.Y., Yale Alumni Schs. Com., Yale Alumni Assn. Northeastern N.Y., Assn. of Yale Alumni (rep. 1985-88, 94-97), University Club (bd. dirs. 1998—). Home: 9 Pinedale Ave Delmar NY 12054-3012

**ELDRIDGE, JOHN COLE,** judge; b. Balt., Nov. 13, 1933; s. Arthur Clement and Bertha Jean (Klitch) E.; m. Dayne S. Worsham, July 15, 1961; children: Kathryn Chandler, John Cole. B.A., Harvard U., 1955; LL.B., U. Md., 1959. Bar: Md. 1960, D.C. 1961. Law clk. to chief judge U.S. Ct. Appeals 4th Circuit, 1959-61; trial atty. appellate sect., civil div. Dept. Justice, 1961-67, asst. chief appellate sect., 1967-69; chief legis. officer, counsel Staff of Gov. of Md., 1969-74; judge Ct. Appeals Md, Annapolis, Md., 1974—; Chmn. Md. Adv. Bd. Correction, 1969-70; dir. Annapolis Fine Arts Found., 1974-77. Mem. Anne Arundel County Bar Assn., Annapolis Yacht Club. Democrat. Methodist. Office: Ct Appeals Md Court of Appeals Bldg 361 Rowe Blvd Annapolis MD 21401-1672*

**ELDRIDGE, RICHARD MARK,** lawyer; b. Okmulgee, Okla., June 20, 1951; s. H.G. and Marcheta (Barnes) E.; m. Nellene Jane Mark, Aug. 20, 1971; children: Richard Mark Jr. (dec.), Christopher Bryan, Ryan Matthew, Michael Jonathan. BA, Okla. State U., 1973; JD, U. Tulsa, 1975. Bar: Okla. 1976; U.S. Dist. Ct. (no. dist.) Okla. 1976, U.S. Dist. Ct. (ea. dist.) Okla. 1989; U.S. Ct. Appeals (10th cir.) 1977, U.S. Dist. Ct. (we. dist.) Okla. 1991. Ptnr. Jacobus, Green & Eldridge, Tulsa, 1976-78; spl. judge Dist. Ct., Tulsa, 1979-82; ptnr. Rhodes, Hieronymus, Jones, Tucker & Gable, Tulsa, 1982—; adj. prof. Oral Roberts U., Tulsa, 1985. Tchr. Couples for Christ, Asbury United Meth. Ch., Tulsa, 1979—; pres., sec. Christian Businessmen's Com., Tulsa, 1981-93; chmn. Asbury Presch. Bd., Tulsa, 1985-95; trustee Metro Christian Acad., 1998—. Recipient Cert. of Achievement, Am. Acad. Jud. Edn., 1979. Mem. Okla. Bar Assn., Tulsa County Bar Assn. Democrat. Avocation: basketball. State civil litigation, Federal civil litigation, Personal injury. Home: 2916 E 88th St Tulsa OK 74137-2507 Office: Rhodes Hieronymus et al 100 W 5th St Ste 400 Tulsa OK 74103-4287

**ELDRIDGE, TRUMAN KERMIT, JR.,** lawyer; b. Kansas City, Mo., July 27, 1944; s. Truman Kermit and Nell Marie (Dennis) E.; m. Joan Ellen Jurgeson, Feb. 9, 1965; children: Christina Joanne, Gregory Truman. AB, Rockhurst Coll., 1966; JD, U. Mo., Kansas City, 1969. Bar: Mo. 1969, U.S. Dist. Ct. (we. dist.) Mo. 1969, U.S. Ct. Appeals (8th cir.) 1977, (10th cir.) 1995, U.S. S. Ct., 1992, U.S. Dist. Ct. Kans. 1998. Assoc. Morris, Foust, Moudy & Beckett, Kansas City, 1969-70; assoc. Dietrich, Davis, Dicus, Rowlands & Schmitt, Kansas City, 1971-74, ptnr., 1975; ptnr. Armstrong, Teasdale, LLP, Kansas City, 1989—. Author: (with others) Missouri Environmental Law Handbook, 1990, 2d edit., 1993, 3d edit., 1997; contbr. articles to profl. jours. Chmn. bd. dirs. Loretto Sch., Kansas City, 1981-83; mem. Friends of Art, Nelson Atkins Gallery, Kansas City, 1980—; mem. Energy and Environ. Commn. City of Kansas City, 1990-91, 1994, bd. dirs. Sheffield Pl., 1997—, vice chair, 1998—. Mem. ABA, Def. Rsch. Inst., Mo. Bar Assn., Kansas City Met. Bar Assn. (fed. ct. com., vice chair 1989-90, chair 1990-91), Mo. Orgn. Def. Lawyers, Greater Kansas City C. of C. (mem. environ. com. 1989—), Kansas City Club (athletic com. 1990—, chair 1995—, house com. 1993-96, 98—, long range planning com. 1993-97, bd. dirs. 1997—). Roman Catholic. Avocations: sailing, reading, photography, raquetball. General civil litigation, Environmental, Product liability. Home: 448 W 68th Ter Kansas City MO 64113-1933 Office: Armstrong Teasdale LLP 2345 Grand Blvd Ste 2000 Kansas City MO 64108-2617

**ELDRIDGE, WILLIAM PHILLIP,** lawyer; b. Midland City, Ala., May 20, 1948; s. Lennie Jonathan and Gaynell Eldridge; m. Brenda Joyce Marshall, Oct. 5, 1968; 1 child, Heather Michelle. BS, U. Ala., 1973, JD, 1976. Bar: Ala. 1977, U.S. Dist. Ct. Ala. 1978, U.S. Ct. Appeals (5th cir.) 1979, U.S. Supreme Ct. 1994. Asst. atty. gen. Ala. Atty. Gen.'s Office, Montgomery, 1977-79; pvt. practice Hartford, Ala., 1979—; mcpl. judge City of Hartford, Ala., 1979—; county atty. Geneva County Commn., 1981-94; city atty. City of Slocomb, Ala., 1986-94; chmn. bd. Wiregrass Hosp., Geneva, 1995—; mem. Statewide Planning Com. Adminstrv. Office of Ct., 1996. Mem. Geneva County Athletic Club (past pres. 1993), Hartford Lions Club. With U.S. Army, 1969-71. Democrat. Baptist. Avocations: golf, tennis, swimming, antique collecting. State civil litigation, Family and matrimonial, Criminal. Home: 509 S 2nd Ave Hartford AL 36344-1744 Office: W Phil Eldridge 206 W Commerce St Hartford AL 36344-1605

**ELFMAN, ERIC MICHAEL,** lawyer; b. Phila., Oct. 24, 1954; s. Isaac Selig and Mae (Kline) E.; m. Barbara Cecile Feldstein, Oct. 9, 1982; children: Elizabeth, Bradley, Todd. BS in Econs., U. Pa., 1975, MS in Acctg., 1976; JD, George Washington U., 1980. Bar: Calif. 1980, U.S. Tax Ct. 1981, Mass. 1986; CPA, Pa. Acct. Peat, Marwick, Mitchell and Co., Phila., 1976-77; assoc. Pettit & Martin, San Francisco, 1980-83; assoc. office of tax legis. counsel U.S. Dept. of Treas., Washington, 1983-85; ptnr. Ropes & Gray, Boston, 1985—. Mem. ABA (chair corporate tax com. 1996-97, taxation sect.), AICPA, Mass. Soc. CPAs, Boston Bar Assn. Corporate taxation, Personal income taxation, General corporate. Home: 19 Gypsy Trl Weston MA 02493-1607 Office: Ropes & Gray One Internat Pl Boston MA 02110-2624

**ELFVIN, JOHN THOMAS,** federal judge; b. Montour Falls, N.Y., June 30, 1917; s. John Arthur and Lillian Ruth (Dorning) E.; m. Peggy Pierce, Oct. 1, 1949. B.E.E., Cornell U., 1942; J.D., Georgetown U., 1947. Bar: D.C. 1948, N.Y. 1949. Confidential clk. to U.S. Circuit Ct. Judge E. Barrett Prettyman, 1947-48; asst. U.S. atty., Buffalo, 1955-58; U.S. atty. Western Dist. N.Y., 1972-75; with firm Cravath, Swaine & Moore, N.Y.C., 1948-51, Dudley, Stowe & Sawyer, Buffalo, 1951-55, Lansdowne, Horning & Elfvin, Buffalo, 1958-69, 70-72; justice N.Y. Supreme Ct., 1969; judge U.S. Dist. Ct., Buffalo, 1975—, now sr. judge; Mem. bd. suprs. Erie County, N.Y., 1962-65, mem. bd. ethics, 1971-74, chmn., 1971-72; mem., minority leader Buffalo Common Council Delaware Dist., 1966-69. Mem. Am. Judicature Soc., Erie County Bar Assn., Engring. Soc. Buffalo (pres. 1958-59), Tech. Socs. Niagara Frontier (pres. 1960-61), Phi Kappa Tau, Delta Sigma Chi. Republican. Clubs: Cornell (pres. 1957-58); City (Buffalo), Buffalo Country, Saturn. Office: US Dist Ct 716 US Courthouse 68 Court St Buffalo NY 14202-3405

**ELIASON, RUSSELL ALLEN,** judge; b. Mpls., Jan. 28, 1944; s. Walter Joseph and Hazel Agnes Pearl (Jensen) E.; m. Karen L. Stevens; children: Nathaniel, Heidi, Justine, Danielle. Student U. Minn., 1964-65, JD, 1970; BA, Yale U., 1967; student Wake Forest U. Sch. Law, 1967-68. Bar: Minn. 1970, Iowa 1971, N.C. 1973, Nebr. 1975, U.S. Dist. Ct. (no. dist.) Iowa 1971, U.S. Dist. Ct. (mid. dist.) N.C. 1974, U.S. Dist. Ct. Nebr. 1975, U.S. Ct. Appeals (8th cir.) 1971, U.S. Ct. Appeals (4th cir.) 1976. Law clk. to judge U.S. Ct. Appeals 8th Cir., 1970-71; asst. U.S. atty. Dept. Justice, Sioux City, Iowa, 1971-72; law clk. to judge U.S. Dist. Ct. Mid. Dist. N.C., 1972-74; assoc. Ryan, Scoville & Uhlir, South Sioux City, Nebr., 1974-75; asst. U.S. atty. Dept. Justice, Greensboro, N.C., 1975-76; U.S. magistrate judge U.S. Dist. Ct. Mid. Dist. N.C., Winston-Salem, 1976—; lectr. in field; active law-sch. skills programs. Trumpeter Salem Band, Old Salem Band. Mem. ABA, N.C. Bar Assn., Forsyth County Bar, Minn. Bar Assn., Nebr. Bar Assn., Sons of Norway, Phi Alpha Alpha Delta. Mem. Moravian Ch. Office: 224 Fed Bldg 251 N Main St Winston Salem NC 27101-3914

**ELIOT, THEODORE QUENTIN,** lawyer; b. Tulsa, Mar. 18, 1954; s. Theodore Quentin and Norma Jo (Jones) E.; m. Judith Rae Seymour, May 16, 1954. BA, Drake U., 1976; JD, U. Okla., 1979. Bar: Okla. 1979, U.S. Dist. Ct. (no., we. and ea. dists.), U.S. Ct. Appeals (10th cir.). Assoc. Gable & Gotwals, Inc., Tulsa, 1979-85, ptnr., 1985—. Mem. ABA, Okla. Bar Assn., Tulsa Bar Assn., Summit Club. Avocations: hunting, sports, reading. Federal civil litigation, General civil litigation, Bankruptcy. Office: Gable & Gotwals 15 W 6th St Ste 2000 Tulsa OK 74119-5447

**ELIZONDO, LUIS A.,** lawyer, rancher; b. Alice, Tex., Aug. 2, 1958; s. Luis and Olga (Cantu) E.; m. Rosa Elena Garza, June 21, 1986 (div. Oct. 1995); 1 child, Luis Gabriel; m. Rosario Angelica Gonzalez, July 10, 1998; stepchildren: Christina Lopez, Monica Garza. BA, U. Tex., 1980; JD, Tex. So. U., 1985. Bar: Tex. 1986. Assoc. Law Offices of Albert Huerta, Corpus Christi, 1986-88, Allison and Huerta, Corpus Christi, 1988-97, Huerta, Hastings, Allison, 1997—. Mem. Corpus Christi Bar Assn., Tex. Trial Lawyers Assn. Federal civil litigation, State civil litigation, Insurance. Office: Huerta Hastings & Allison 924 Leopard St Corpus Christi TX 78401-2423

**ELKIND, LAURA PETERSON,** lawyer; b. Beaumont, Tex., Sept. 5, 1959; d. Harold Leo and Marjorie Anne (Hunter) Peterson; m. Peter Jay Elkind, Oct. 22, 1994; children: Stephen, George, Landon, Adele. BA, Wellesley Coll., 1981; JD with honors, U. Tex., 1985. Bar: Tex. 1985, U.S. Dist. Ct. (no. dist.) Tex. 1987, U.S. Ct. Appeals (5th cir.) 1987. Assoc. Small, Craig & Werkenthin, Austin, Tex., 1985-87; assoc. Locke Purnell Rain Harrell, Dallas, 1987-93, shareholder, 1994-95; shareholder Thompson & Knight, P.C., Dallas, 1996—. Bd. dirs. Freedom of Info. Found. of Tex., Dallas, 1993—, treas., 1994-95, v.p., 1996-97. Wellesley scholar, 1981. Mem. ABA (forum on comms. law), Dallas Bar Assn. (vice chair media rels. com. 1993, chair 1994). General civil litigation, Communications, Libel. Office: Thompson & Knight PC 1700 Pacific Ave Ste 3300 Dallas TX 75201-4693

**ELKINS, BRIAN EDWARD,** lawyer; b. Spokane, Wash., Dec. 6, 1955; s. Albert Lee and Phyllis L. Elkins; m. Melissa L. Scott, Apr. 11, 1998. B of Bus., U. Idaho, 1979, JD, 1983. Bar: Idaho 1983, U.S. Dist. Ct. Idaho 1983, U.S. Supreme Ct. 1994; cert. criminal trial specialist, Idaho Trial Lawyers Assn. Law clk. Blaine County Dist. Ct., Hailey, Idaho, 1983-85; dep. prosecutor Blaine County Prosecuting Atty., Hailey, Idaho, 1985, pub. defender, 1986-91; ptnr. Roark & Elkins, Hailey, Idaho, 1986, Roark, Donovan, Praggastis & Elkins, Hailey, Idaho, 1986-88; pvt. practice Ketchum, Idaho, 1988—. Mem. Nat. Assn. Criminal Def. Lawyers, Idaho Assn. Criminal Def. Lawyers (bd. dirs. 1998), Idaho Bar Assn., Am. Inns of Ct. Avocations: private pilot, running, kayaking, adventure travel, mountain biking. Criminal. Office: Brian E Elkins PC PO Box 766 Ketchum ID 83340-0766

**ELKINS, DAVID MARK,** lawyer; b. N.Y.C., Nov. 18, 1966; s. Robert William and Ellyn Faith (Appleman) E. BA in English, U. Va., 1988; JD cum laude, Boston Coll., 1991. Bar: N.Y. 1992, U.S. Dist. Ct. (ea. and so. dists.) N.Y. 1993. Assoc. Cahill Gordon & Reindel, N.Y.C., 1991-94, Greenberg Traurig Hoffman Lipoff Rosen & Quentel, N.Y.C., 1994—. General civil litigation, Intellectual property, Securities. Office: Greenberg Traurig et al 200 Park Ave Fl 14 New York NY 10166-1400

**ELKINS, ROBERT NEAL,** lawyer; b. Tampa, Fla., Dec. 11, 1944. BA, Vanderbilt U., 1967; MBA, U. So. Miss., 1972; JD, U. Ga., 1976. Bar: Ga. 1976, Fla. 1976, U.S. Dist. Ct. (mid. and no. dists.) Ga. With Las Vegas City Attys. Office, 1976-77; asst. dist. atty. Office of Dist. Atty., Athens, Ga., 1978-83; ptnr. Fortson Bentley & Griffin, Athens, 1983—; mem. adv. com. Athens Tech. Paralegal Studies, 1983—. Bd. dirs. Athens Clark Libr., 1980-96, Clark County unit Am. Cancer Soc., 1980—; mem. Leadership Athens, 1983. Capt. USAF, 1968-73. Mem. Western Cir. Bar Assn. (sec.-treas. 1985-86, pres. 1999—). Avocations: flying, sailing, biking. General civil litigation, Personal injury. Office: Fortson Bentley & Griffin PO Box 1744 Athens GA 30603-1744

**ELKINS, S. GORDON,** lawyer; b. Phila., Dec. 21, 1930; m. Ethel Bronstein, June 16, 1957; children: Tod, Adam, Peter, Douglas. BS, Temple U., 1952; LLB, Yale U., 1955. Bar: Pa. 1956, U.S. Dist. Ct. (ea. dist.) Pa. 1956, U.S. Ct. Appeals (3d cir.) 1956, U.S. Ct. Appeals (6th cir.) 1979, U.S. Supreme Ct. Assoc. Stradley, Ronon, Stevens & Young, Phila., 1955-62, ptnr., 1962—; speaker on surety and fidelity matters to ABA, Practicing Law Inst., Internat. Assn. Def. Counsel, also others, on antitrust matters to Wood Machinery Mfrs. Assn., Fluid Power Distbr. Assn., Am. Brush Mfrs. Assn., Nat. Welding Supply Assn.; former trial cons. Cmty. Legal Svcs. Phila.; bd. dirs. Entertainment Comm., Inc. Contbr. articles to legal publs. Past pres. Melrose Park Improvement Assn.; former panel mem. Philadelphians for Equal Justice; bd. dirs. Phila. and Pa. chpts. ACLU, pres. Greater Phila. chpt., 1976-81; frequent speaker at meetings, participant various TV and radio panels on civil liberties matters; mem. Cheltenham Twp. Govt. Study Commn., 1974-76. Mem. ABA (fidelity and surety law com. tort ins. practice sect., past vice chair), Phila. Bar Assn., Internat. Assn. Def. Counsel (fidelity and surety law com.), Fedn. Ins. and Corp. Counsel (fidelity com.), Forum Com. for Constrn. Industry, Def. Rsch. Inst., Defenders Assn. Phila. (past bd. dirs.). Antitrust, Insurance, Product liability. Office: Stradley Ronon et al 2600 One Commerce Sq Philadelphia PA 19103

**ELKINS-ELLIOTT, KAY,** law educator; b. Dallas, Nov. 21, 1938; d. William Hardin and Maxidine (Sadler) E.; m. Michael Gail Hodgson, July 7, 1960 (div. Dec. 1974); children: Michael Brett, Ashley Kim, Samantha; m. Frank Wallace Elliott, Aug. 15, 1983. AA with honors, Stephens Coll., 1958; JD, U. Okla., 1964; LLM, So. Meth. U., 1984; MA, U. Tex., Dallas, 1990. Bar: Okla. 1964, Tex. 1982, U.S. Dist. Ct. (no. dist.) Tex. 1982, U.S. Supreme Ct. 1984, U.S. Dist. Ct. (we. dist.) Okla. 1989. Assoc. Ben Hatcher and Assocs., Oklahoma City, Okla., 1964-65; dir., gen. counsel Take-A-Tour Swaziland, Mbabane, Swaziland, 1966-74; atty. Dept. Health and Human Svcs., Dallas, 1975-80; hearing officer EEOC, Dallas, 1980-84; atty. pvt. practice, Dallas, 1984-92; vis. assoc. prof. Tex. Wesleyan U. Sch. Law, Dallas, 1992-95; arbitrator State Farm Ins., Dallas, 1991-96; adj. prof. Wesleyan U. Sch. Law, 1995—, coach nat. ABA champion negotiation team, 1998; mediator pvt. practice, Dallas, 1991—; coord. cert. in conflict resolution program Tex. Woman's U., 1996—; cons. in field. Author: (with others) West Texas Practice, 1995. Mem. ABA (peer mediation and cmty. com. 1997—, alternative dispute resolution sect.), Tex. Bar Assn. (ADR sect. coun. mem. 1998—, chair Cont. Legal Edn. com.), Tex. Bar Found., Tex. Initiatives for Mediation in Edn. (founder, planning com. 1993-95), Soc. for Profls. in Dispute Resolution (pres. Dallas region 1995-97), Tex. Assn. Mediators, Assn. Atty. Mediators, Dallas Bar Assn. (coun. mem. 1993-94), Acad. Family Mediators, Toastmasters (v.p. 1993-94, pres. 1996-97), AIM for Peacepath. Avocations: singing, public speaking, peer mediation training. Home: 2120 N Rough Creek Ct Granbury TX 76048-2903 Office: 2401 Turtle Creek Blvd Dallas TX 75219-4712

**ELLARD, GEROGE WILLIAM,** lawyer; b. Rochester, N.Y., Mar. 22, 1960; m. Jan E. Ellard. BS in Polit. Sci., U.S. Naval Acad., 1983; JD, U. San Francisco, 1991. Bar: Calif. 1992, U.S. Ct. Appeals (9th cir.). Atty. Hassard Bonnington, San Francisco, 1991-96, Saucedo & Corsiglia, San Jose, Calif., 1996—. Lt. U.S. Navy, 1883-88. Personal injury, Professional liability. Office: Saucedo & Corsiglia 50 W San Fernando St Ste 425 San Jose CA 95113-2433

**ELLBOGEN, ANDREW D.,** lawyer; b. Chgo., Apr. 16, 1963; s. David F. and Elaine S. Ellbogen; m. Dana Korman, July 16, 1995; 1 child, Lauren Elizabeth. BS, U. Iowa, 1985, JD, 1988. Bar: Ill. 1988. Atty. Conklin & Roadhouse, Chgo., 1989; ptnr. Kopka, Landau and Pinkus, Chgo., 1989—. Surrogate spke. Clinton Campaign, Chog., 1992, 96. Mem. Chgo. Bar Assn., Chgo. Hist. Soc., Lincoln Park Zool. Soc. Avocations: politics, tennis, racquetball, reading of history and study of demographics. General civil litigation, Product liability, Appellate. Home: 2626 N Lakeview Ave Apt 1802 Chicago IL 60614-1812

**ELLEFSON, VANCE E.,** lawyer; b. St. Charles, Ill., Jan. 28, 1943; m. Maria Elzbieta Samotyj; children: Sara, Edward, Matthew. JD, Loyola U., New Orleans, 1972. Bar: La. 1972, Tex. 1991, U.S. Dist. Ct. (ea., we. and mid. dists.) La. 1972, U.S. Dist. Ct. (so. dist.) Tex. 1991, U.S. Ct. Appeals (5th cir.) 1972, U.S. Ct. Appeals (11th cir.) 1982, U.S. Supreme Ct. 1980. Sole practitioner Metairie, La., 1972—. Contbr. articles to profl. jours. Served with USMC, 1960-66. Mem. Internat. Assn. Ins. Counsel, Def. Rsch. Inst. Avocations: travel, trekking, hiking. Aviation, Admiralty, Insurance. Office: 3445 N Causeway Blvd Ste 501 Metairie LA 70002-3723

**ELLERBY, JAMES EDWARD, JR.,** judge; b. Valhalla, N.Y., May 27, 1959; s. James Edward Sr. and Harriet Ellerby. BA cum laude, Columbia Coll., 1981, MS, 1984, JD, 1986. Bar: N.Y. 1987, U.S. Dist. Ct. (so. and ea. dists.) N.Y. 1992, U.S. Ct. Appeals (2d cir.) 1993. Adj. instr. Hudson County C.C., Jersey City, 1986-88; asst. counsel Mayor's Office of Midtown Enforcement City of N.Y., 1986-88; litigation assoc. Fennel & Minkoff, N.Y.C., 1988-89; of counsel Law Firm of Gail Butler, N.Y.C., 1989-92; adminstrv. law judge Environ. Control Bd., N.Y.C., 1992-93; adj. instr. John Jay Coll. Criminal Justice CCNY, 1992-93; of counsel McCarthy & Sullivan, N.Y.C., 1984-95; pvt. practice James Edward Ellerby, Jr., Esq., N.Y.C., 1995; adminstrv. law judge N.Y. State Dept. Social Svc., N.Y.C., 1995—. Mem. Assn. Bar of City of N.Y. Home: James Ellerby Esq 80 Longdale Ave White Plains NY 10607

**ELLETT, JOHN SPEARS, II,** retired taxation educator, accountant, lawyer; b. Richmond, Va., Sept. 17, 1923; s. Henry Guerrant and Elizabeth Firmstone (Maxwell) E.; m. Mary Ball Ruffin, Apr. 15, 1950; children: John, Mary Ball, Elizabeth, Martha, Henry. BA, U. Va., 1948, JD, 1957, MA, 1961; PhD, U. N.C., 1969; CPA, Va., La.; bar: Va. 1957. Lab. instr. U. Va., Charlottesville, 1953-58; instr. Washington and Lee U., 1958-60; asst. prof. U. Fla., 1967-71; assoc. prof. U. New Orleans, 1971-76, prof. taxation, 1976-94, prof. emeritus, 1994—; trainee Va. Carolina Hardware Co., Richmond, 1948-51; acct. Equitable Life Assurance Soc., Richmond, 1951-52; staff acct. Musselman & Drysdale, Charlottesville, 1952-54; staff acct. R.M. Musselman, Charlottesville, 1957-58; mem. U. New Orleans Oil and Gas Acctg. Conf., 1973-92; bd. dirs., publicity chmn. U. New Orleans Energy Acctg. and Tax Conf., 1993-94, bd. dirs. publicity com.; pres. Maxwelton Farm and Timber Corp., 1994—; treas. U. New Orleans Estate Planning Seminar, 1975-78, lectr. continuing edn.; CPCU instr. New Orleans Ins. Inst., 1975-78. Served with AUS, 1943-46. Mem. AICPA, Am. Acctg. Assn., Am. Assn. Atty.-CPAs (chmn. ptnrship. taxation continuing edn. com. 1989, ptnrship. taxation com. 1990, organized La. chpt., v.p. 1991-93), Va. Soc. CPAs, Soc. La. CPAs, Va. Bar Assn. Democrat. Episcopalian. Author books; contbr. articles to prof. jours. Home: 177 Maxwelton Rd Charlottesville VA 22903-7859

**ELLICKSON, ROBERT CHESTER,** law educator; b. Washington, Aug. 4, 1941; s. John Chester and Katherine Heilprin (Pollak) E.; m. Ellen Zachariasen, Dec. 19, 1971; children—Jenny, Owen. A.B., Oberlin Coll., 1963; LL.B., Yale U., 1966. Bar: D.C. 1967, Calif. 1971. Atty. adviser Pres.'s Com. on Urban Housing, Washington, 1967-68; mgr. urban affairs Levitt & Sons Inc., Lake Success, N.Y., 1968-70; prof. law U. So. Calif., Los Angeles, 1970-81, Stanford U., Calif., 1981-85; Robert E. Paradise prof. of natural resources law, Stanford U., Calif., 1985-88; Walter E. Meyer prof. of property and urban law, Yale U., New Haven, Conn., 1988—, dep. dean, 1991-92. Author: (with Tarlock) Land-Use Controls, 1981, Order Without Law, 1991 (Triennial award Order of the Coif), (with Rose & Ackerman) Perspectives on Property Law, 2d edit., 1995. Mem. Am. Acad. Arts & Scis., Am. Law Inst. Office: Yale U Law Sch PO Box 208215 New Haven CT 06520-8215

**ELLICOTT, JOHN LEMOYNE,** lawyer; b. Balt., May 26, 1929; s. Valcoulon LeMoyne and Mary Purnell (Gould) E.; m. Mary Lou Ulery, June 19, 1954 (dec. Jan. 1995); children: Valcoulon, Ann; m. Beatrice Berle Meyerson, Sept. 14, 1996. AB summa cum laude, Princeton U., 1951; LLB cum laude, Harvard U., 1954. Bar: D.C. 1957, U.S. Supreme Ct. 1959. Assoc. Covington & Burling, Washington, 1958-65, ptnr., 1965-98, chmn. mgmt. com., 1986-90, sr. counsel, 1998—. Pres. Fairfax County Fedn. Citizens Assn., Va., 1964; mem. governing bd. Nat. Cathedral Sch., Washington, 1973-80, 85-88, 89-90, chmn., 1978-79; trustee Landon Sch., Bethesda, Md., 1972-76; bd. dirs. Protestant Episc. Cathedral Found., Washington, 1980-88. Mem. ABA (sect. internat. law and practice), Washington Inst. Fgn. Affairs, Phi Beta Kappa. Democrat. Private international, Administrative and regulatory, General corporate. Home: 5117 Macomb St NW Washington DC 20016-2611 Office: Covington & Burling 1201 Pennsylvania Ave NW PO Box 7566 Washington DC 20044-7566

**ELLICOTT, VERNON L.,** lawyer; b. Calif., July 2, 1954; s. Vernon L. and Edna Ellicott; children by previous marriage: Christine, Meaghan, Jillian, Danielle; m. Lareita Tharp, Feb. 14, 1997. BA, George Fox U., Newberg, Oreg., 1976; MDiv, Fuller Theol. Sem., 1979; D Ministry, Tex. Christian U., 1988; JD, Southwestern U., 1994. Bar: Calif. 1994, U.S. Dist. Ct. (ctrl. dist.) Calif. 1994. Assoc. R. Reinjohn, L.A., 1993-96; pvt. practice, Westlake Village, Calif., 1996—. Mem. Conejo Substance Abuse Adv. Com., Thousand Oaks, Calif., 1998, chmn., 1999. Bankruptcy, Family and matrimonial. Office: 920 Hampshire Rd Ste 25 Westlake Vlg CA 91361-2816

**ELLIGETT, RAYMOND THOMAS, JR.,** lawyer; b. N.Y.C., June 5, 1953; s. Raymond Thomas Elligett and Jane (Klein) Elligett-Leitner; m. Cheryl Eileen Roberts, Jan. 4, 1986. BA in Math., U. Fla., 1975; JD, Harvard U., 1978. Bar: Fla. 1978, U.S. Dist. Ct. (mid. dist.) Fla. 1979, U.S. Dist. Ct. (so. dist.) Fla. 1981, U.S. Ct. Appeals (11th cir.) 1981. Ptnr. Shackleford, Farrior, Stallings & Evans, P.A., Tampa, Fla., 1978-90, Schropp, Buell & Elligett, P.A., Tampa, 1990—. Contbr. articles to law jours. Mem. ABA, Fla. Bar Assn. (appellate rules com. 1982-87, jud. adminstrn. com. 1988—, appellate practice sect. 1994—, chair 1996-97), Hillsborough County Bar Assn. (pres. 1997-98), Temple Ter. C. of C. Democrat. Methodist. General civil litigation, Environmental, Insurance. Office: Schropp Buell & Elligett PA 401 E Jackson St Tampa FL 33602-5233

**ELLIN, MARVIN,** lawyer; b. Balt., Mar. 6, 1923; s. Morris and Goldie (Rosen) E.; m. Stella J. Granto, Aug. 2, 1948; children: Morris, Raymond, Elisa. JD, U. Balt., 1953. Bar: Md. 1953, U.S. Supreme Ct. 1978; diplomate Am. Bd. Forensic Examiners. Practice law Balt., 1953—; mem. firm Ellin & Baker, 1957—; specialist in med. malpractice law; cons. on med. and legal trial matters; lectr. ACS, U. Md. Law Sch., U. Balt. City, Yale U. Sch. Medicine, Johns Hopkins Hosp., U. Calif., San Francisco, U. N.J.; former mem. chmn.'s adv. coun. com. on judiciary U.S. Senate. mem. editl. adv. bd.: Ob/Gyn Malpractice Prevention; contbr. chpts. on med. malpractice to various profl. publs. including Radiation Therapy of Benign Diseases. Fellow Internat. Acad. Trial Lawyers; mem. ABA, Am. Soc. Law and Medicine. General civil litigation, Personal injury. Home: 13414 Longnecker Rd Glyndon MD 21071-4805 Office: 1101 Saint Paul St Baltimore MD 21202-2662

**ELLIOT, CAMERON ROBERT,** lawyer; b. Portland, Oreg., Jan. 6, 1966; s. James Addison and Dianne Louise (Youngblood) E. BS, Yale U., 1987; JD, Harvard U., 1996. Bar: Calif. 1996, D.C. 1999. Jud. clk. U.S. Dist. Ct., Reno, 1996-98; atty. civil divsn. U.S. Dept. Justice, Washington, 1998—. Editor-in-chief: (jour.) Harvard Environ. Law Rev., 1995-96. Mem. Reno Environ. Bd., 1996-97. Lt. USN, 1987-92. Home: 1725 17th St NW Apt 112 Washington DC 20009-2414 Office: US Dept Justice Civil Divsn Washington DC 20530-0001

**ELLIOT, N. FRANK,** lawyer; b. New Orleans, July 29, 1966; s. Norvall Francis and Alberta Cuccia E.; m. Michelle Marie Monistere, Aug. 6, 1994; 1 child, Michael Etienne. BA, Southwestern U., 1988; JD & MBA, Loyola U., 1994. Bar: La. 1994, U.S. Ct. Appeals (5th cir.) 1994, U.S. Ct. Appeals (5th cir.) 1994, U.S. Dist. Ct. )we. dist.) La. 1994. Jud. law clk. U.S. Dist. Ct., Lake Charles, La., 1994-95; assoc. Badon & Ranier, Lake Charles, La., 1995—. Democrat. Roman Catholic. Avocations: hunting, fishing. Appellate, Environmental, Toxic tort. Office: Badon & Ranier 1818 Ryan St Lake Charles LA 70601-6052

**ELLIOT, RALPH GREGORY,** lawyer; b. Hartford, Conn., Oct. 20, 1936; s. K. Gregory and Zarou (Manoukian) E. BA, Yale U., 1958, LLB, 1961. Bar: Conn. 1961, U.S. Dist. Ct. Conn. 1963, U.S. Ct. Appeals (2d cir.) 1966, U.S. Ct. Appeals (Fed. cir.) 1993, U.S. Ct. Appeals (1st cir.) 1997, U.S. Supreme Ct. 1967. Law clk. to assoc. justice Conn. Supreme Ct., Hartford, 1961-62; assoc. Alcorn, Bakewell & Smith, Hartford, 1962-67, ptnr., 1967-83; ptnr. Tyler, Cooper & Alcorn, Hartford, 1983—; adj. prof. law U. Conn., Hartford, 1973—; sec. Superior Ct. Legal Internship Com., Conn., 1971—; chmn. Superior Ct. Legal Specialization Screening Com., Conn., 1981—, U.S. Dist. Ct. Panel Spl. Masters, Hartford, 1983-88. Chmn. bd. editors Conn. Law Tribune, 1986-87. Chmn. Constn. Bicentennial Commn., Conn., 1986-91; mem. Criminal Justice Commn. Conn., 1991-95. Recipient Fenton P. Futtner award Conn. Reps., 1993. Fellow Am. Bar Found.; mem. ABA (standing com. on ethics and profl. responsibility 1989-95, standing com. on profl. discipline 1998—, ho. of dels. 1983-87), Conn. Bar Assn. (officer, bd. govs. 1971-79, 83-87, pres. 1985-86, John Eldred Shields Disting. Profl. Svc. award 1993), Am. Law Inst., Yale Law Sch. Assn. (pres. 1988-90, chmn. exec. com. 1990-92), Yale Club (pres. 1977-79, Nathan Hale award 1984, Betty McCallip Meml. award 1991), Hartford, Grad. Club (New Haven), Phi Beta Kappa. Republican. Episcopalian. Federal civil litigation, State civil litigation, Libel. Office: Tyler Cooper & Alcorn City Pl Fl 35 Hartford CT 06103

**ELLIOTT, BRADY GIFFORD,** judge; b. Harlingen, Tex., Nov. 26, 1943; s. Clyde Andres Elliott and Mildred (Parker) Bounds; m. Rhea Elizabeth Ricks, May 15, 1967; children: Adrian Winthrope, Jason Lawrence. BBA, McMurray Coll., 1970; JD, South Tex. Coll. Law, 1973. Bar: Tex. 1973, U.S. Dist. Ct. (so. dist.) Tex. 1974, U.S. Tax Ct. 1974, U.S. Ct. Appeals (5th cir.) 1974, U.S. Supreme Ct. 1979, U.S. Ct. Appeals (11th cir.) 1981. Asst. sec., asst. treas., asst. gen. counsel Gordon Jewelry Corp., Houston, 1970-79; sec., gen. counsel Oshman's Sporting Goods, Inc., Houston, 1979-82; sole practice, Sugar Land, Tex., 1982-88; legal counsel Ft. Bend C. of C., Sugar Land, Tex., 1982-88; mcpl. judge Missouri City, Tex., 1983-88; judge 268th Dist. Ct., Fort Bend County, Tex., 1988—. Bd. dirs. Ft. Bend chpt. Texans' War on Drugs, Sugar Land, 1981-94; bd. dirs. Ft. Bend Boys Choir, 1984-94. Mem. ABA, Houston Bar Assn., Fort Bend County Bar Assn., Masons, Rotary (treas. 1983-85). Republican. Methodist. Office: County Ct House Richmond TX 77469

**ELLIOTT, CLIFTON LANGSDALE,** lawyer; b. Kansas City, Mo., Oct. 26, 1938; s. John Miller and Kate (Langsdale) E.; m. Bronwyn Ann Reese, Mar. 31, 1963 (div. Mar. 1983); children—Evan R., Kate L.; m. Marjorie A. Critten, Apr. 4, 1987. B.A., Dartmouth Coll., 1960; J.D., Northwestern U., 1963. Bar: Mo. 1963, Wash. 1991, Calif. 1992, U.S. Dist. Ct. (we. and ea. dists.) U.S. Ct. Appeals (8th cir.) 1965, U.S. Ct. Appeals (4th cir.) 1968, U.S. Ct. Appeals (D.C. cir.) 1973, U.S. Ct. Appeals (10 cir.) 1975, U.S. Ct. Appeals (2d, 5th and 9th cirs.) 1980, U.S. Supreme Ct. 1979. Assoc., ptnr. Spencer, Fane, Britt & Browne, Kansas City, Mo., 1963-79; ptnr. Elliott & Kaiser, Kansas City, 1979-87, Smith, Gill, Fisher & Butts, Kansas City, 1987-88, Watson, Ess, Marshall & Enggas, Kansas City, 1988-91; of counsel, ptnr. Davis Wright Tremaine, Seattle, 1991—; instr. labor law U. Mo., 1966; spl. counsel Am. Hosp. Assn., 1973-75; mem. U.S. C. of C. Nat. Labor Relations Act Task Force, 1980—. Mem. ABA, Mo. Bar, Wash. State Bar, Calif. Bar, Am. Soc. Hosp. Attys. (ad hoc com. labor relations 1975—). Contbr. articles to profl. jours. Avocations: boating, fishing. Labor. Office: Davis Wright Tremaine 1501 4th Ave Ste 2600 Seattle WA 98101-1688

**ELLIOTT, EDWIN DONALD, JR.,** law educator, federal administrator, environmental lawyer; b. Chgo., Apr. 4, 1948; s. Edwin Donald and Mary Jane (Bope) E.; m. Geraldine Gennet (div. 1980); m. Mary Ellen Savage, Nov. 22, 1980; children: Eve Christina, Ian Donald. BA, Yale U., 1970, JD, 1974. Bar: D.C. 1975, U.S. Dist. Ct. D.C. 1975, U.S. Ct. Appeals (2d cir.) 1982. Law clk. to judge U.S. Dist. Ct. D.C., Washington, 1974-75, U.S. Ct. Appeals, Washington, 1975-76; assoc. Leva, Hawes et al, Washington, 1976-80; assoc. prof. law Yale U., New Haven, 1981-84, prof. law, 1984-89, 91-92; asst. adminstr., gen. counsel U.S. EPA, Washington, 1989-91; Julien & Virginia Cornell chair environ. law and litigation Yale U., New Haven, 1992-94, adj. prof. law, 1994—; cons. Fried, Frank, Harris, Shriver & Jacobson, N.Y.C., Washington, 1991-93; ptnr., head of DC Environ. Practice Fried, Frank, Harris, Shriver & Jacobson, Washington, 1993-96; ptnr. Paul, Hastings, Janofsky & Walker, Washington, 1996—; adj. prof. law Georgetown U., Washington, 1997—; advisor Fed. Cts. Study Com., UN Environment Programme, 1993; cons. Asian Devel. Bank, 1994, Carnegie Com. Sci., Tech. and Govt., 1989-93, chair Role of Sci. and Risk Assessment; with Nat. Environ. Policy Inst., 1994—, Overseas Pvt. Investment Corp., Washington, 1983-85, Adminstrv. Conf. U.S., 1987-89, Aetna Ins. Co., 1987-89, G.D. Searle Co., 1988-89; spl. litigation counsel GE Co., Fairfield, Conn., 1985-89; gen. series editor Prentice Hall Environ. Series. Co-author: Sustainable Environmental Law, 1993; contbr. articles on evolutionary theories of law, adminstrv. law, constl. law, environ. and toxic tort law to profl. jours. Resources for the Future fellow, 1989. Mem. ABA (vice chmn. com. on separation of powers 1985-89, jud. rev. 1992—, environ. values 1993—, chair govt. policy liaison), Environ. Law Inst., Gruter Inst. for Law and Behavioral Rsch. (adv. bd. 1986—), Nat. Environ. Policy Inst. (chair sci. and risk assessment), Yale Club N.Y.C., New Haven Lawn Club. Republican. Presbyterian. Home: 826 A St SE Washington DC 20003-1340 also: 56 Beach Ave Milford CT 06460-8156 Office: Paul Hastings Janofsky & Walker 1299 Pennsylvania Ave NW Washington DC 20004-2400 also: Yale Law Sch PO Box 208215 New Haven CT 06520-8215

**ELLIOTT, FRANK WALLACE,** lawyer, educator; b. Cotulla, Tex., June 25, 1930; s. Frank Wallace and Eunice Marie (Akin) E.; m. Winona Trent, July 3, 1954 (dec. 1981); 1 child, Harriet Lindsey; m. Kay Elkins, Aug. 15, 1983. Student, N.Mex. Mil. Inst., 1947-49; BA, U. Tex., 1951, LLB, 1957. Bar: Tex. 1957, U.S. Supreme Ct. 1962, U.S. Ct. Mil. Appeals 1974, U.S. Dist. Ct. (no. dist.) Tex. 1987, U.S. Ct. Appeals (5th cir.) 1988. Asst. atty. gen. State of Tex., 1957; briefing atty. Supreme Ct. Tex., 1957-58; prof. U. Tex. Law Sch., 1958-77; dean, prof. law Tex. Tech U. Sch. Law, 1977-80; pres. Southwestern Legal Found., 1980-86; ptnr. Baker, Mills & Glast, Dallas, 1987-88; of counsel Ramirez & Assocs., 1988—; dean Dallas/Ft. Worth Sch. Law, 1989-92; dean Sch. Law Tex. Wesleyan U., 1992-94, prof., 1992—; parliamentarian Tex. Senate, 1969-73; dir. rsch. Tex. Constl. Revision Commn., 1973. Author: Texas Judicial Process, 2d edit., 1977, Texas Trial and Appellate Practice, 2d edit., 1974, Cases on Evidence, 1980, West's Texas Forms, 20 vols., 1977—, West's Texas Practice, vol. 11, 1990, vol. 14, 1996. Served with U.S. Army, 1951-53, 73-74. Decorated Purple Heart. Mem. ABA, Judge Advs. Assn., Am. Judicature Soc., Am. Bar Found., Tex. Bar Found., Dallas Bar Found., Am. Law Inst., N.Mex. Mil. Inst. Alumni Hall of Fame. Federal civil litigation, State civil litigation, Private international. Home: 2120 N Rough Creek Ct Granbury TX 76048-2903 Office: 1515 Commerce Fort Worth TX 76102-6509

**ELLIOTT, JAMES ROBERT,** federal judge; b. Gainesville, Ga., Jan. 1, 1910; s. Thomas M. and Mamie Lucille (Glenn) E.; m. Brownie C. Buck, Aug. 3, 1949; children: Susan G., James Robert. Ph.B., Emory U., 1930, LL.B., 1934. Bar: Ga. 1934. Pvt. practice law Columbus, Ga., 1934-62; judge U.S. Dist. Ct. (mid. dist.) Ga., Columbus, 1962—; Mem. Ga. Ho. of Reps., 1937-43, 47-49; Democratic nat. committeeman, 1948-56. Served as lt. USNR, 1943-46, PTO. Mem. Ga. Bar Assn., Kiwanis, Lambda Chi Alpha, Phi Delta Phi, Omicron Delta Kappa. Home: 2612 Carson Dr Columbus GA 31906-1563 Office: US Dist Ct 120-12th St Rm 224 PO Box 2017 Columbus GA 31902-2017

**ELLIOTT, JAMES SEWELL,** lawyer; b. Augusta, Ga., Dec. 30, 1922; s. Lester Franklin and Frances (Sewell) E.; m. Mary Jones Grace, June 25, 1947; children: James Sewell Jr., Lester Franklin III, Walter Grace, Randolph Squire, Robert Bruce. BS, The Citadel, 1943, U.S. Mil. Acad., 1946; JD, Mercer U., 1952. Bar: Ga. 1952, U.S. Dist. Ct. (mid. dist.) Ga. 1953, U.S. Ct. Appeals (11th cir.) 1953, U.S. Supreme Ct. 1959. Asst. U.S. atty. U.S. Dist. Ct. (mid. dist.) Ga., Macon, 1953-57; prin. Law Offices of J. Sewell Elliott, Macon, Ga., 1957—. Mem. Ga. Ho. of Reps. 107th dist., Atlanta, 1966; chmn. exec. com. Bibb County Reps., Macon, 1985. Maj. USAR, 1946-58. Mem. ABA, Ga. Bar Assn., Macon Bar Assn. Episcopalian. Lodge: Kiwanis (pres. Macon). General practice, General corporate, State civil litigation. Office: 544 Mulberry St Macon GA 31201-2770

**ELLIOTT, JAMES WARD,** lawyer; b. Norwich, N.Y., Mar. 4, 1954; m. Susan Talbot, Dec. 22, 1979; children: Shawn, Chris. BA, SUNY, Oneonta, 1976; JD, Union U., Albany, N.Y., 1979. Bar: N.Y. 1980, U.S. Dist. Ct. (no. dist.) N.Y. 1980, U.S. Ct. Mil. Appeals 1980, Va. 1991. Procurement and govt. contracts counsel Grumman Aerospace Corp., Bethpage, N.Y., 1986-89; corp. counsel McDermott, Inc. subs. BWX Techs., Inc., Lynchburg, Va., 1989—. With JAGC, U.S. Army, 1980-86; lt. col. USAR. Mem. Hazardous Waste Action Coalition, Nat. Security Indsl. Assn. (subcom. law), Am. Arbitration Assn. (panel of arbitrators). Republican. Government contracts and claims, Environmental, Nuclear power. Office: BWX Tech Inc Law Dept Mt Athos Rd State Rt 726 Lynchburg VA 24506-1165

**ELLIOTT, RICHARD HOWARD,** lawyer; b. Astoria, N.Y., Apr. 30, 1933; m. Judith A. Kessler, Dec. 26, 1956; children—Marc Evan, Jonathan Hugh, Eve; m. 2d, Diane S. Schaefer, Nov. 18, 1978; children—Alexis, Sara Jane, Benjamin, David. B.S., Lehigh U., 1954; J.D. cum laude, U. Pa., 1962. Bar: U.S. Dist. Ct. (ea. dist.) Pa. 1962, Pa. Supreme Ct. 1962, U.S. Ct. Appeals (3d cir.) 1963, U.S. Dist. Ct. (mid. dist.) Pa. 1976. Assoc. Clark, Ladner, Fortenbaugh & Young, Phila., 1962-69; ptnr., 1970-75; ptnr. Elliott & Magee, Doylestown, Pa., 1976—; moderator Permanent Jud. Commn., Presbytery of Phila.; v.p., dir. Bucks County Soc. Prevention Cruelty to Animals; pres., dir. Pa. Soc. for Prevention of Cruelty to Animals. Gen. Counsel, dir. Pa. Fedn. Humane Socs., adj. faculty Bucks County Cmty. Coll.; mem. Pa. Navigation Commn., 1977-80. Lt. USN, 1954-59. Mem. ABA, Pa. Bar Assn., Phila. Bar Assn., Bucks County Bar Assn. Democrat. General civil litigation, General practice, Probate. Home: 1205 Victoria Rd Warminster PA 18974-3923 Office: Elliott & Magee 1795 S Easton Rd Doylestown PA 18901-2837

**ELLIOTT, SCOTT,** lawyer, theater artistic director; b. San Jose, July 26, 1957; s. Roland Meredith and Sandra Gale (Deem) E.; m. Nancy Marie Oller, Apr. 6, 1979; children: Tristan Robin, Jordan Brook, Robin Sage, Forest Dream. BA in Drama magna cum laude, Calif. State U. Stanislaus, Turlock, 1979; JD, U. Oreg., 1987. Bar: Oreg. 1987, U.S. Dist. Ct. Oreg. 1988, U.S. Ct. Appeals (9th cir.) 1992. Assoc. Larry O. Gildea, Eugene, Oreg., 1987-88, Thorp, Dennet, Purdy & Golden, Springfield, Oreg., 1988; law clk. U.S. Dist. Ct. Nev., Las Vegas, 1988-89; ptnr. Green & Elliott, Lincoln City, Oreg., 1989-95; assoc. Thorp, Purdy, Jewett, Urness & Wilkinson, Springfield, Oreg., 1995-96, Wine, Weller, Ehrlich and Green, Lincoln City, 1996-98; pvt. practice Lincoln City, 1998—. Mem. choir Congl. Ch., 1997—, youth athletic coach, 1990-94, 97; pres. PTA, 1995, 97-98; founder, artistic dir. Cmty. Family Players, 1997—. U. Oreg. Theatre grad. tchg. fellow, 1979-80. Avocations: family, gardening, theatre, singing. Personal injury, Civil rights, General civil litigation. Office: 2137 NW Highway 101 Ste B Lincoln City OR 97367-4214 also: Lincoln City Congl Ch 1760 NW 25th Lincoln City OR 97367

**ELLIOTT, THOMAS CLARK, JR.,** lawyer; b. Portland, Maine, July 10, 1955; s. Thomas Clark and Lucille Eda (Davis) E.; m. Kathleen J. Swan, Dec. 31, 1985; 1 child, Devin Lundeen. BA, DePauw U., 1977; JD, Ill. Inst. Tech., 1981. Bar: Ill. 1981, U.S. Dist. Ct. (no. dist.) Ill. 1981, U.S. Dist. Ct. (ea. dist.) Mich. 1984, U.S. Dist. Ct. 9ea. dist.) Wis. 1988, U.S. Dist. Ct. (ctrl. dist.) Ill. 1995), U.S. Ct. Appeals (7th cir.) 1981, U.S. Ct. Appeals (fed. cir.) 1983. Assoc. McDougall, Hersh & Scott, Chgo., 1981-87, Jones, Day, Reavis & Pogue, Chgo., 1987-88, Niro, Scavone, Haller, Niro & Rockey, Chgo., 1988-89; ptnr. Rockey, Rifkin, Ryther, Chgo., 1989-96; shareholder Dressler, Rockey, Milnamow & Katz, Chgo., 1997—. Mem. ABA, Chgo. Bar Assn., Intellectual Property Law Assn. Chgo. Intellectual property. Office: Dressler Rockey Milnamow & Katz 4700 Two Prudential Plz Chicago IL 60601

**ELLIS, ALFRED WRIGHT (AL ELLIS),** lawyer; b. Cleve., Aug. 26, 1943; s. Donald Porter and Louise (Wright) E.; m. Kay Genseke, June 1965 (div. 1976); 1 child, Joshua Kyle; m. Sandra Lee Fahey, Feb. 11, 1989. BA with honors, U. Tex., Arlington, 1965; JD, So. Meth. U., 1971. Bar: Tex., U.S. Dist. Ct. (no., so., ea. and we. dists.) Tex., U.S. Ct. Appeals (5th cir.), U.S. Supreme Ct.; cert. personal injury and civil trial lawyer. Atty. Woodruff, Kendall & Smith, Dallas, 1972; ptnr. Woodruff & Ellis, Dallas; pvt. practice Dallas, 1983-96; of counsel Howie & Sweeney, 1996—; instr. So. Meth. U. Law Sch. Trial Advocacy; past pres. Law Focused Edn., Inc. Past mem. City of Dallas Urban Rehab. Standards Bd., Dallas Assembly, Salesmanship Club, Dallas; bd. dirs. Dallas Habitat for Humanity, 1998—, treas., 1999; trustee Hist. Preservation League, 1992-94; tournament dir. Dallas Regional Golden Gloves Tournament, 1976-96; pres., bd. dirs. Dallas Coun. on Alcoholism, 1980. Capt. U.S. Army, 1965-69. Fellow Roscoe Pound Found.; named one of Outstanding Young Mem of Am., 1977, named Boss of Yr. Dallas Assn. Legal Secs., 1978; recipient Certs. of Recognition (8) D.I.S.D., 1971-83, Wall St. Jour. award So. Meth. U. Law Sch., 1972, Hayward McMurray award Dallas Jaycees, 1975-76, Spl. Recognition award All Sports Assn., 1977, Cert. of Appreciation for Exceptional and Disting. Vol. Svc. Gov. Mark White, 1983, Community Spirit award Dallas Bus. Jour., 1993, Disting. Svc. award Dallas All Sports Assn., 1993,award Nancy Garms Meml. for outstanding Contr. to Law Focus Edn., 1996-Leon Jaworski award. Fellow Tex. Bar Found. (sustaining life), Dallas Bar Found. (trustee); mem. ATLA, Am. Bd. Trial Advocates (diplomate, sec.-treas. Dallas chpt. 1998, pres. 1999), Am. Coll. Legal Medicine (assoc.), Legal Svcs. of North Tex. (bd. dirs., Outstanding Svc. award 1990), State Bar Tex. (lectr. seminars, bd. dirs. 1991-94, 95, Excellence in Diversity award 1994, Outstanding 3d Yr. Dir. award, Judge Sam Williams Local Bar Leadership award), Dallas Bar Assn. (bd. dirs. 1978, chmn. bd. dirs. 1986, v.p. 1987-88, pres. 1990), Dallas Trial Lawyers Assn. (pres. 1977, Disting. Cmty. Svc. award 1990), Tex. Trial Lawyers Assn., Tex. Equal Access to Justice Found. (bd. dirs. 1994-96), Coll. State Bar of Tex. (bd. dirs. 1997—), Dallas All Sports Assn. (pres.-1980), Tex. Commn. for Lawyer Discipline, Tex. Ctr. for Legal Ethics and Professionalism (bd. dirs. 1999—), Tex. Legal Svcs. Ctr. (bd. dirs. 1999—). Avocations: tennis, skiing. Personal injury, General civil litigation, Insurance. Office: 2911 Turtle Creek Blvd Ste 1400 Dallas TX 75219-6258

**ELLIS, ANDREW JACKSON, JR.,** lawyer; b. Ashland, Va., June 23, 1930; m. Dorothy L. Lichliter, Apr. 24, 1954; children: Elizabeth E. Attkisson, Andrew C., William D. AB, Washington and Lee U., 1951, LLB, 1953. Bar: Va. 1952. Ptnr. Campbell, Ellis & Campbell, Ashland, 1955-70, Mays, Valentine, Davenport & Moore, Richmond, Va., 1970-88; ptnr. Mays & Valentine, Richmond, 1988-96, sr. counsel, 1998—; substitute judge County of Hanover (Va.) Ct., 1958-63, commonwealth atty., 1963-70, county atty., 1970-78; substitute judge 15th jud. dist., 1990-96; judge 15th dist Juvenile and Domestic Rels. Ct., 1996-98; mem. capital adv. bd. NationsBank of Va., 1960-93. Mem. Ashland Town Coun., 1956-63, mayor, 1958-63; trustee J. Sargent Reynolds C.C., 1972-80. 1st lt. U.S. Army, 1953-55. Fellow Am. Coll. Trial Lawyers, Va. Law Found.; mem. Am. Judicature Soc., Va. Bar Assn., Va. State Bar (coun. 1968-74), Va. Trial Lawyers Assn., S.R., Kiwanis. Episcopalian. General civil litigation, Condemnation, Insurance. Home: 15293 Old Ridge Rd Beaverdam VA 23015-1610 Office: PO Box 1122 Richmond VA 23218-1122

**ELLIS, DONALD LEE,** lawyer; b. Dallas, Oct. 2, 1950; s. Truett T. and Rosemary (Tarrant) E.; children: Angela Nicole, Laura Elizabeth, Natalie Dawn, Donald Lee II. BS, U. Tulsa, 1973; JD, Oklahoma City U., 1976. Bar: Tex. 1979, Okla. 1977, U.S. Dist. Ct. (ea. dist.) Tex. 1978, U.S. Dist. Ct. (we. dist.) Okla. 1978, U.S. Ct. Appeals (5th cir.) 1984, U.S. Supreme Ct., 1984, U.S. Ct. Appeals (11th cir.). Spl. agt. FBI, Washington, 1976-78; asst. dist. atty. Smith County, Tyler, Tex., 1979-80; mem. firm Barron & Ellis, Tyler, 1980-84, Ellis & Woods law firm, 1984-85; sole practice, Tyler, 1985—. Bd. dirs. Mental Health Assn., Tyler, 1983-87. Mem. Assn. Trial Lawyers Am., Tex. Bar Assn., Okla. Bar Assn., Smith County Bar Assn., Soc. Former Spl. Agts. FBI, Tex. Trial Lawyers Assn., FBI Agents Assn., Lawyers-Pilot Bar Assn. Personal injury. Home: PO Box 131221 Tyler TX 75713-1221 Office: 217 W Houston St Tyler TX 75702-8137

**ELLIS, DORSEY DANIEL, JR.,** lawyer, educator; b. Cape Girardeau, Mo., May 18, 1938; s. Dorsey D. and Anne (Stanaland) E.; m. Sondra Wagner, Dec. 27, 1962; children: Laura Elizabeth, Geoffrey Earl. BA, Maryville Coll., 1960; JD, U. Chgo., 1963; LLD, Maryville Coll., 1998. Bar: N.Y. 1967, U.S. Ct. Appeals (2d cir.) 1967, Iowa 1976, U.S. Ct. Appeals (8th cir.) 1976. Assoc. Cravath, Swaine & Moore, N.Y.C., 1963-68; assoc. prof. U. Iowa, Iowa City, 1968-71, prof., 1971-87, v.p. fin. and univ. svcs., 1984-87, spl. asst. to pres., 1974-75; dean Washington U. Sch. Law, St. Louis, Mo., 1987-98, prof. law, 1998-99; disitng. prof. law, 1999—; vis. mem. sr. common room Mansfield Coll., Oxford U., Eng., 1972-73, 75; vis. prof. law Emory U., Atlanta, 1981-82, Victoria U., New Zealand, 1999; vis. sr. rsch. fellow Jesus Coll. Oxford U., Eng., 1998; bd. dirs. Maryville Coll., 1989-98, 99—. Contbr. articles to profl. jours. Trustee Mo. Hist. Soc., St. Louis, 1995—. Nat. Honor scholar U. Chgo., 1960-63; recipient Joseph Henry Beale prize, 1961, Alumni award Maryville Coll., 1988. Mem. ABA, Am. Law Inst., Bar Assn. Metro St. Louis, Mound City Bar Assn., Iowa Bar Assn., AALS Acad. Resource Corps., Order of Coif. Antitrust, Personal injury. Home: 6901 Kingsbury Blvd Saint Louis MO 63130

**ELLIS, FREDRIC LEE,** lawyer; b. Springfield, Mass., Nov. 21, 1957; s. Irving Donald and Evelyn Gladys (Melnick) E.; m. Wendy J. Murphy, Oct. 21, 1988; children: Grant, Taylor, Reed, Cameron. BA, Hampshire Coll., Amherst, Mass., 1979; JD cum laude, Harvard U., 1983. Bar: Mass. 1983, U.S. Dist. Ct. Mass. 1983, U.S. Ct. Appeals (1st cir.) 1983, U.S. Ct. Appeals (11th cir.) 1994. Law clk. to Justice Raya Dreben Mass. Appellate Cr., Boston, 1983-84; asst. dist. atty. Dist. Atty.'s Office, Cambridge, Mass., 1984-86, dep. chief Appeals and Tng. Bur., 1986-87; ptnr. Gilman, McLaughlin & Hanrahan, Boston, 1987-96; owner Ellis & Rapacki, Boston, 1996—. Mem. bd. editors med./Legal Aspects of Breast Implants, 1996—. Named Lawyer of Yr., Mass. Lawyers Weekly, 1996, Outstanding Civil Trial Atty., Middlesex Bar Assn., 1998. Mem. ATLA, Mass. Bar Assn. Personal injury, Product liability, General civil litigation. Office: Ellis & Rapacki 85 Merrimac St Ste 300 Boston MA 02114-4715

**ELLIS, GEORGE DAWLIN,** lawyer; b. Little Rock, June 26, 1946; s. Dawlin C. and Joan Marie (Savage) E.; m. Selena T. Duncan, Jan. 25, 1969; children: John Andrew, Mary Elizabeth. BA, Little Rock U., 1969; JD, U. Ark., 1972. Bar: Ark. 1972, U.S. Dist. Ct. (ea. dist.) Ark. 1972, U.S. Ct. Appeals (8th cir.) 1974, U.S. Supreme Ct. 1975. Atty. Ark. Ins. Dept., Little Rock, 1972; sole practice Little Rock, 1972-73; assoc. Spitzberg, Mitchell & Hays, Little Rock, 1973-74, Boswell Law Firm, Bryant, Ark., 1974-80; ptnr. Gibson & Ellis, Benton, Ark., 1980-91; prin. Ellis Law Firm, Benton, 1991—. Mem. Ark. Govs. Mansion Commn., Little Rock, 1984-92; chmn. Benton Planning Commn.; bd. dirs. Saline County Boys Club, Benton, 1980-83. Mem. ABA, Ark. Bar Assn. (chmn. young lawyers sect. 1974-75), Saline County Bar Assn. (pres. 1975-76), Assn. Trial Lawyers Am., Ark. Trial Lawyers Assn. Democrat. Episcopalian. Insurance, Federal civil litigation, State civil litigation. Office: Ellis Law Firm 126 N Main St Benton AR 72015-3765

**ELLIS, JAMES D.,** communications executive, corporate lawyer; b. 1943. BBA, U. Iowa, 1965; JD, U. Mo., 1968. Bar: Mo. 1968, U.S. Ct. Appeals (D.C. cir.) 1977, Tex. 1980. Atty. AT&T, 1972-74, AT&T Long Lines, 1974-77; atty. gen. depts. AT&T, 1977-79; gen. atty. Southwestern Bell Telephone Co., San Antonio, 1979-83; v.p., gen. counsel Bellcore, 1983-84, Southwestern Bell Telephone Co., Tex., 1984-86; v.p., gen. counsel, sec. Southwestern Bell Telephone Co., 1986-88; sr. v.p., gen. counsel Southwestern Bell Corp., 1988-89; sr. exec. v.p., gen. counsel SBC Comm., San Antonio, 1989—. With U.S. Army, 1968-72. Office: SBC Communications Inc 175 E Houston St San Antonio TX 78205-2233*

**ELLIS, JAMES REED,** lawyer; b. Oakland, Calif., Aug. 5, 1921; s. Floyd E. and Hazel (Reed) E.; m. Mary Lou Earling, Nov. 18, 1944 (dec.); children: Robert Lee, Judith Ann (dec.), Lynn Earling, Steven Reed. B.S., Yale, 1942; J.D., U. Wash., 1948; LL.D., Lewis and Clark U., 1968, Seattle U., 1981, Whitman Coll., 1992. Bar: Wash. 1949, D.C. 1971. Ptnr. Preston, Thorgrimson, Horowitz, Starin & Ellis, Seattle, 1952-69, Preston, Thorgrimson, Starin, Ellis & Holman, Seattle, 1969-72, Preston, Thorgrimson, Ellis, Holman & Fletcher, Seattle, 1972-79; sr. ptnr. Preston, Thorgrimson, Ellis & Holman, Seattle, 1979-90, Preston, Thorgrimson, Shidler, Gates & Ellis, Seattle, 1990-92; ret., of counsel Preston, Gates & Ellis, Seattle, 1992—; chmn., CEO Wash. State Convention and Trade Ctr., Seattle, 1986—; dep. pros. atty. King County, 1952; gen. counsel Municipality of Met. Seattle, 1958-79; dir., mem. exec. com. Key Bank of Wash., 1969-94, KIRO, Inc., 1965-95; dir. Blue Cross of Wash. and Alaska, 1989-98. Mem. Nat. Water Commn., 1970-73; mem. urban transp. adv. council U.S. Dept. Transp., 1970-71; mem. Wash. Planning Adv. Council, 1965-72; mem. Washington State Growth Strategies Commn., 1989-90; pres. Forward Thrust Inc., 1966-73; chmn. Mayors Com. on Rapid Transit, 1964-65; trustee Ford Found., 1970-82, mem. exec. com., 1978-82; bd. regents U. Wash., 1965-77, pres., 1972-73; trustee Resources for the Future, 1983-92; mem. council Nat. Mcpl. League, 1968-76, v.p., 1972-76; chmn. Save our Local Farmlands Com., 1978-79, King County Farmlands Adv. Commn., 1980-82; pres. Friends of Freeway Park, 1976—; bd. dirs. Nat. Park and Recreation Assn., 1979-82; trustee Lewis and Clark U., 1988-94; pres. Mountains to Sound Greenway Trust, Inc., 1991—; trustee Henry M. Jackson Found., 1992—. 1st lt. USAAF, 1943-46. Recipient Bellevue First Citizen award, 1968, Seattle First Citizen award, 1968, Nat. Conservation award Am. Motors, 1968, Distinguished Service award Wash. State Dept. Parks and Recreation, 1968, Distinguished Citizen award Nat. Municipal League, 1969, King County Distinguished Citizen award, 1970, La Guardia award Center N.Y.C. Affairs, 1975, Environ. Quality award EPA, 1977, Am. Inst. for Public Service Nat. Jefferson award, 1974, U. Wash. Recognition award, 1981, State Merit medal State of Wash., 1990, Nat. Founders award Local Initiatives Support Corp., 1992, Henry M. Jackson Disting. Pub. Svc. medal, 1998. Fellow Am. Bar Found.; mem. ABA (ho. dels. 1978-82, past chmn. urban, state and local govt. law sect.), Nat. Assn. Bond Lawyers (com. standards of practice), Wash. Bar Assn., Seattle Bar Assn. (Pres.'s award 1993), D.C. Bar Assn., Am. Judicature Soc., Acad. Pub. Adminstrn., Coun. on Fgn. Rels., Mcpl. League Seattle and King County (past pres.), Order of Hosp. of St. John of Jerusalem, AIA (hon.), Order of Coif (hon.), Phi Delta Phi, Phi Gamma Delta, Rainier Club (Seattle). General practice, Municipal (including bonds). Home: 903 Shoreland Dr SE Bellevue WA 98004-6738 Office: 3000 Columbia Seafirst Ctr 701 5th Ave Seattle WA 98104-7097

**ELLIS, JEFFREY ORVILLE,** lawyer; b. Parsons, Kans., Mar. 9, 1944; s. Orman Carl Ellis and Esther Jane (Landreth) Ellis-Hett; m. Carol Lynne Byington, Aug. 6, 1966; children: Robert James, Jeffrey Todd. BS, U. Kans., 1966; JD, Washburn U., 1977. Bar: Kans. 1977, U.S. Dist. Ct. Kans. 1977, Mo. 1993. Tchr. Shawnee Mission (Kans.) Dist. Schs., 1966-68; atty., ptnr. Holbrook, Ellis & Heaven, Shawnee Mission, 1977-91, Lathrop & Gage, L.C., Kansas City, Mo., 1991—; bd. dirs. United Community Svcs., Johnson County, Johnson County Health Partnership; speaker in field. Author, editor: Handbook for Peer Review, 1992. Chmn. task force Gov.'s Commn. on Health Care, Topeka, 1989-90; mem. Legis.'s Commn. on Health Care Svcs., Topeka, 1987-90; chmn. Kans. Rep. Party, 3d Congl. Dist., 1990-92. Capt. U.S. Army, 1966-74, Vietnam. Mem. Am. Health Lawyers Assn., Kans. Assn. Hosp. Attys. (bd. dirs. 1987-90, pres. 1992-93), Kansas Head Injury Assn. (bd. dirs. 1987-91), Greater Kansas City C. of C. (chmn. task force 1991-93), Rotary (pres. Overland Park 1992). Republican. Presbyterian. Avocations: golf, bicycling. Health, General corporate, Insurance. Home: 183 Hillcrest Rd W Shawnee Mission KS 66217-8731 Office: Lathrop & Gage LC 1050 Corporate Woods Overland Park KS 66210-2019

**ELLIS, LESTER NEAL, JR.,** lawyer; b. Washington, Aug. 1, 1948; s. Lester Neal and Marie (Brooks) E. BS, U.s. Mil. Acad., 1970; JD, U. Va., 1975. Bar: Va. 1975, U.S. Ct. Appeals (5th cir.) 1977, D.C. 1978, U.S. Ct. Appeals (4th and D.C. cirs.) 1979, U.S. Ct. Appeals (11th cir.) 1982, N.C. 1985, U.S. Dist. Ct. (ea., mid., we. dists.) N.C., U.S. Dist. Ct. (ea., we. dists.) Va., U.S. Ct. Claims. Trial atty. litigation divsn. Office of JAG, U.S. Dept. Army, Washington, 1975-78; assoc. Hunton & Williams, Richmond, Va., 1978-84; ptnr. Hunton & Williams, Raleigh, 1984—. Maj. U.S. Army, 1970-78, col. USAR, 1993-99. Recipient Judge Paul Brosman award U.S. Ct. Mil. Appeals, 1975. Mem. ABA (chair comml. torts commn., tort and ins. practice sect., editor-in-chief tort and Ins. Law Jour., chair-elect trial techniques com.), Va. Bar Assn. (spl. issues com. 1982—), D.C. Bar Assn.

(ct. rules com., Wake County bd. elections 1986-93, chmn. 1987-93), Phi Kappa Phi. Republican. Episcopalian. General civil litigation, Environmental. Home: 2608 Dover Rd Raleigh NC 27608-2032 Office: Hunton & Williams One Hanover Sq PO Box 109 Raleigh NC 27602-0109

**ELLIS, ROBERT BRYAN, JR.,** lawyer; b. Rome, Ga., June 9, 1957; s. Robert Bryan and Ferris Opal (Everett) E. BA cum laude, Mercer U., 1978, JD, 1981. Bar: Ga. 1981, U.S. Dist. Ct. (no. dist.) Ga. 1981, U.S. Ct. Appeals Ga. 1981, U.S. Dist. Ct. (mid. dist.) Ga. 1986. Law clk. to presiding judge Rome Jud. Cir. Ct., Ga., 1981-82; asst. dist. atty. Alapaha Jud. Cir. Ct., 1982-86; pvt. practice Nashville, Ga., 1986-88; dist. atty. Alapaha Jud. Cir. Ct., Ga., 1989—; judge City of Nashville, 1986-88, City of Alapaha, 1986-88. Mem. ABA, Jaycees (v.p. Berrrien County chpt. 1984-85). Democrat. Baptist. Avocations: hunting, fishing, running. Criminal, Family and matrimonial, General civil litigation. Office: PO Box 125 115 N Davis St Nashville GA 31639-2161

**ELLIS, SHARON HENDERSON,** arbitrator, mediator; b. Wenatchee, Wash., May 31, 1944; d. Marvin T. and Nola Henderson; m. Alfred D. Ellis, Aug. 1972. BA, U. Wash., 1967; JD, Suffolk U., 1975. Adminstrv. law judge Mass. Labor Rels. Com., Boston, 1978-81; arbitrator, mediator Brookline, Mass., 1982—. Contbg. author: (book) Labor and Employment Arbitration. Tchr., vol. U.S. Peace Corps, Tunisia, 1967-69. Mem. Am. Arbitration Assn., Nat. Acad. Arbitrators (regional chair 1997-99), Mass. Bar Assn., Soc. Profls. in Dispute Resolution. E-mail: sharonhendersonellis@juno.com. Office: 36 Salisbury Rd Brookline MA 02445-2105

**ELLIS, STUART L.,** lawyer; b. Milw., Dec. 16, 1952; s. Lester S. and Luverne A. Ellis. BA, U. Wis., 1975; JD, John Marshall Sch. Law, 1981. Bar: Ill. 1981, U.S. Dist. Ct. (no. dist.) Ill. 1981, Wis. 1985. Ptnr. Karp and Ellis, Chgo., 1981—. Mem. Ill. State Bar, State Bar Wis., Chgo. Bar Assn. Personal injury, Workers' compensation. Office: 77 W Washington St Ste 1020 Chicago IL 60602-2805

**ELLIS, THOMAS SELBY, III,** judge; b. Bogota, Columbia, May 15, 1940; came to U.S., 1951; s. Thomas Selby and Anne Leete (Sachs) E.; m. Rebecca Lynn Garron, Sept. 23, 1995; children: Alexander Reed, Parrish Selby. B.S.E., Princeton U., 1961; J.D. magna cum laude (Knox fellow), Harvard U., 1969; diploma in law Magdalen Coll. Oxford (Eng.) U., 1970. Assoc., Hunton & Williams, Richmond, Va., 1970-76, ptnr., 1976-87; judge U.S. Dist. Ct. (ea. dist.) Va., Alexandria, 1987—; temporary mem. sr. common rm. U. Coll., Oxford, 1984. lectr. law Coll. William & Mary, Williamsburg, Va., 1981-83; mem. adv. coun. dept. astrophysics Princeton U., 1984—; speaker in field. Office: US Dist Court 401 Courthouse Sq Alexandria VA 22314-5704

**ELLIS, TIMOTHY DAVID,** lawyer; b. L.A., Aug. 28, 1968; s. Raymond Dewitt and Gretchen (Morris) E. BA, U. Chgo., 1990; JD, U. Mich., 1994. Bar: Calif. 1994. Assoc. Sheppard Mullin Richter & Hampton, L.A., 1994-97, Hancock Rothert & Bunshoft, L.A., 1998—. Office: Hancock Rothert & Bunshoft 515 S Figueroa St Los Angeles CA 90071-3301

**ELLIS, WILLIAM R.,** lawyer; b. Pitts., Aug. 14, 1949; s. Edwin Francis and Mary Jane Ellis; m. Deborah L. Ellis, Mar. 14, 1981; children: Catherine, Deborah, Jennifer, Jillian. BA, U. Dayton, 1970; JD, Duquesne U., 1975. Assoc. Leventon & Leventon, Pitts., 1975-79, Waite, Schneider, Bayless & Chesley, Cin., 1979-84; ptnr. Wood & Lamping LLP, Cin., 1984—. Office: Wood & Lamping LLP 600 Vine St Cincinnati OH 45202-2400

**ELLISON, JAMES OLIVER,** federal judge; b. St. Louis, Mo., Jan. 11, 1929; s. Jack and Mary (Patton) E.; m. Joan Roberts Ellison, June 7, 1950; 1 son, Scott. Student, U. Mo., Columbia, 1946-48; B.A., U. Okla., 1951, LL.B., 1951. Bar: Okla. Pvt. practice law Red Fork, Okla., 1953-55; ptnr. Boone, Ellison & Smith, Davis & Minter, 1955-79; judge U.S. Dist. Ct. (no. dist.) Okla., Tulsa, 1979—, chief justice, now sr. judge. Trustee Hillcrest Med. Center, Institution Programs, Inc.; elder Southminster Presbyterian Ch. Served to capt., inf. AUS, 1951-53. Mem. ABA, Okla. Bar Assn., Tulsa County Bar Assn., Alpha Tau Omega. Office: US Dist Ct The Fed Bldg 224 S Boulder Ave Tulsa OK 74103-3006

**ELLISON, PATRICIA LEE,** lawyer; b. Elizabeth, N.J., Oct. 17, 1943; d. Harry C. and Leila D. Ellison. BA, Denison U., 1965; student, U. Paris, France, 1963-64; MA, U. Calif., Riverside, 1967; JD cum laude, U. San Diego, 1973. Bar: Calif. 1973, N.Y. 1983. Fin. analyst NASA, Greenbelt, Md., 1967-68; rsch. atty. Dist. Atty.'s Office, San Diego, 1973-74; assoc. atty. Butler Ruff & Harrigan, San Diego, 1974-75; ptnr. Ellison Eichten & Bell, San Diego, 1975-82; sole practice Kingston, N.Y., 1983—. Bd. dirs. Ulster County YWCA, Kingston, 1988-91, pres. bd. dirs., 1992; chairperson Dem. Com. Town of Shandaken, N.Y., 1993—. Recipient Internat. Acad. Trial Lawyers Advocacy award, 1973. Mem. Alpha Chi Omega. Avocations: music, piano, gardening. Pension, profit-sharing, and employee benefits, Probate, Family and matrimonial. Office: 175 Clinton Ave PO Box 1717 Kingston NY 12402-1717

**ELLMANN, DOUGLAS STANLEY,** lawyer; b. Detroit, July 15, 1956; s. William Marshall and Sheila Estelle (Frenkel) E.; m. Claudia Joan Roberts, Feb. 16, 1985; children: Ben Bosworth, Liam Roberts. AB, Occidental Coll., 1978; JD, U. Mich., 1982. Bar: Mich. 1982, U.S. Dist. Ct. (ea. dist.) Mich. 1982, U.S. Ct. Appeals (6th cir.) 1982. Assoc. Butzel, Keidan, Simon, Myers & Graham, Detroit, 1982-84; ptnr. Ellmann & Ellmann, Detroit, 1984-86; atty. Wise & Marsac, Detroit, 1987-89; U.S. panel trustee, 1989—; prin. Ellmann & Ellmann, P.C., Ann Arbor, Mich., 1989—; spl. asst. atty. gen., 1986; sec. bankruptcy trustees U.S. Bankruptcy Ct. (ea. dist.) Mich., 1993—, mem. bench bar com., 1994—. Author: Selected Issues in Asset Protection, 1994, My Advice: Next Time Go Solo, 1994, LWUSA; co-author: Winning Labor Arbitrations, 1987. Founder Amnesty Internat., Detroit, Lawyer's Support Network; mem. nat. com. U. Mich. Law Sch. Fund, 1986—. Mem. ABA (vice chair bankruptcy com. 1995—), Mich. Bar Assn. (rep. assembly 1983-89, 90-92, exec. counsel young lawyers sect. 1985-87, mem. client security fund com. 1987-95), State Bar Mich. (mem. manditory CLE com. 1989-96, chmn. 1995-96), Washtenaw County Bar Assn. (chmn. banking, bus., bankruptcy com. 1995—). Contracts commercial, General civil litigation, Bankruptcy. Home: 4575 W Loch Alpine Dr Ann Arbor MI 48103-9081 Office: 308 W Huron St Ann Arbor MI 48103-4204

**ELLMANN, WILLIAM MARSHALL,** lawyer, mediator, arbitrator, researcher; b. Highland Park, Mich., Mar. 23, 1921; s. James I. and Jeannette (Barsook) E.; m. Sheila Estelle Frenkel, Nov. 1, 1953; children: Douglas S., Carol E., Robert L. Student, Occidental Coll., 1939-40; AB, U. Mich., 1946; LLB, Wayne State U., 1951. Bar: Mich. 1951. Pvt. practice law Detroit, 1951—; ptnr. Ellmann & Ellmann, 1970—; spl. com. atty. gen. Mich. to study use state troops in emergencies, 1964-65; mem. exec. Inst. Continuing Legal Edn., 1964-68; mem. Mich. Employment Rels. Commn., 1973—, chmn., 1983-86; commr. Mackinac Island State Park Commn., 1979-85, chmn., 1983-86; panel mem. numerous orgns. Author: Of Hemingway, Toscanni and Arbitration: Practical Considerations for Preparing Winning Cases, 1985, A Reply to the Ambassador on Russia, 1991, (with Douglas S. Ellmann) Winning Labor Arbitrations, 1987; contbr. articles to profl. jours. With USAAF, 1942-46. Fellow Am. Bar Found.; mem. ABA (ho. of dels. 1969-72), Am. Arbitration Assn. (mem. adv. council), Nat. Acad. Arbitrators, Detroit Bar Assn. (vice chmn. pub. relations com. 1959), State Bar Mich. (commr. 1959-69, pres. 1966-67, co-chmn. com. on qualification jud. candidates 1970-78, mem. Detroit News secret witness panel 1983), Practicing Law Inst. (adv. council 1969-70, spl. asst. atty. gen. 1970-78), Sigma Nu Phi. General practice, Probate, Labor. Home: 28000 Weymouth Ct Farmington Hills MI 48334-3267 Office: Ellmann & Ellmann 308 W Huron St Ann Arbor MI 48103-4204

**ELLSWORTH, JOHN DAVID,** lawyer; b. Clarion, Iowa, Nov. 13, 1944; s. John Alfred and Marjorie Eileen (Smith) E.; m. Jane Porteous, July 9, 1975; children: John P., Charles G. AB, Carleton Coll., 1966; JD, Harvard U., 1969; LLM, Georgetown U., 1974. Bar: Nebr. 1969, D.C. 1972, U.S. Ct. Appeals (8th cir.) 1972. Law clk. to judge U.S. Ct. Appeals (8th cir.), St. Louis, 1971-72; atty., advisor SEC, Washington, 1972-74; from assoc. to ptnr. Ober, Kaler, Grimes & Shriver, Washington, 1974-80; ptnr. Kutak, Rock & Campbell, Omaha, 1980-81; pvt. practice Omaha, 1981-90; prin. Lieben, Whitted, Houghton, Slowiaczek & Cavanagh, Omaha, 1990—; pres. Broker-Dealer Communications Ltd., Omaha, 1983—. Author: How to Register the DPP Broker-Dealer, 1982, How to Operate the DPP Broker-Dealer, 1984, Real Estate Syndication Handbook, 1984. Served to capt. USAR, 1970-78. Mem. Real Estate Securities and Syndication Inst. (chmn. various coms.), Nat. Assn. Securities Dealers (real estate com.), Nebr. Environ. Trust, Audubon Soc. Nebr. Republican. Presbyterian. Club: Omaha. Avocations: hunting, fishing. Securities, Corporate taxation, Personal income taxation. Office: 2027 Dodge St Ste 100 Omaha NE 68102-1229

**ELLSWORTH-UNGERMAN, BETTY MARIE,** lawyer; b. Humansville, Mo., July 20, 1959; d. David McDonald and Betty Frances Ellsworth; m. Steve A. Ungerman, Nov. 27, 1994; children: Meyer David, Megan Harper. BS, U. Mo., Rolla, 1980; MBA, Oklahoma City U., 1986; JD, So. Meth. U., 1990. Bar: Tex. 1990. Assoc. Baker & Botts, Dallas, 1990-92; staff atty. FINA, Inc., Dallas, 1992-95, sr. atty., 1995-97; dir. investor rels. PetroFina, Dallas, 1997—; spker for CLE course, 1994. Trustee So. Meth. U., Dallas; bd. dirs. Women's Ctr. Dallas; room mother Solomon Schechter Acad. Mem. Jr. League Dallas. Intellectual property, General practice. Office: PetroFina PO Box 2159 Dallas TX 75221-2159

**ELLWANGER, THOMAS JOHN,** lawyer; b. Summit, N.J., Feb. 26, 1949; s. James Warren and Lorean (Nicholson) E.; children: James Hunter, Margaret Lorean. BA, Northwestern U., 1970; JD, U. Fla., 1974. Bar: Fla. 1975, U.S. Dist. Ct. (mid. dist.) Fla. 1976, U.S. Ct. Appeals (11th cir.) 1976, U.S. Dist. Ct. (so. dist.) Fla. 1977, U.S. Tax Ct. Mem. Fowler, White, Gillen, Boggs, Villareal & Banker P.A., Tampa, Fla., 1975—; instr. law U. Fla., Gainesville, 1975; adj. prof. Stetson U. Coll. Law, 1997—. Editor: Gadsden County Times, 1970-72. Pres. Neighborhood Housing Services Hyde Park, Tampa, 1978. Fellow Am. Coll. Trust and Estate Counsel, Fla. Bar (cert. tax lawyer), Hillsborough County Bar Assn. (chmn. com. probate liaison 1985-86, real property probate and trust law sect. 1987-89), Tampa Bay Estate Planning Counsel (pres. 1994-95). Democrat. Avocations: music. lit., sports. Estate planning, Probate, Estate taxation. Office: Fowler White Gillen Boggs Villareal & Banker PA 501 E Kennedy Blvd Ste 1700 Tampa FL 33602-5239

**ELMORE, EDWARD WHITEHEAD,** lawyer; b. Lawrenceville, Va., July 15, 1938; s. Thomas Milton and Mary Norfleet (Whitehead) E.; m. Gail Harmon, Aug. 10, 1968; children: Mary Jennifer, Edward Whitehead Jr. B.A., U. Va.-Charlottesville, 1959, J.D., 1962. Bar: Va. 1962. Assoc. firm Hunton & Williams, Richmond, Va., 1965-69; staff atty. Ethyl Corp., Richmond, 1969-78, asst. gen. counsel, 1978-79, gen. counsel, 1979-80, gen. counsel., sec., 1980-83, v.p., gen. counsel, sec., 1983-94, spl. counsel to exec. com., corp. sec., 1994-97; sr. v.p., gen. counsel, sec. Albemarle Corp., Richmond, 1994—. Served to capt. AUS, 1962-65. Decorated Army Commendation medal. Mem. ABA, Va. Bar Assn., Internat. Bar Assn., Va. State Bar, Am. Corp. Counsel Assn., Bar Assn. Richmond, Am. Soc. Corp. Secs., Raven Soc., Phi Beta Kappa. General corporate. Home: 2901 W Brigstock Rd Midlothian VA 23113-6335 Office: Albemarle Corp 330 S 4th St Richmond VA 23219-4350

**ELROD, EUGENE RICHARD,** lawyer; b. Roanoke, Ala., May 14, 1949; s. James Woodrow and Selma Fromer (Steinbach) E. AB, Dartmouth Coll., 1971; JD, Emory U., 1974. Bar: Ga. 1974, D.C. 1976, U.S. Ct. Appeals (D.C. cir.) 1985, U.S. Ct. Appeals (5th cir.) 1987, U.S. Dist. Ct. D.C. 1987, U.S. Ct. Appeals (11th cir.) 1987, U.S. Supreme Ct. 1987, U.S. Ct. Appeals (10th cir.) 1997. Trial atty. Fed. Power Com., Washington, 1974-76; atty.-advisor Fed. Energy Adminstrn., Washington, 1977; assoc. Sidley & Austin, Washington, 1977-80, ptnr., 1981—; mem. adv. bd. The Keplinger Cos., Houston. Mem. selection com. for Woodruff scholars Emory U. Law Sch., Dartmouth '71 Exec. Com. Mem. ABA, D.C. Bar Assn., Ga. Bar Assn., Fed. Energy Bar Assn. (chmn. oil pipeline com. 1982-83, tax com. 1980-81, 92-95, liaison with adminstrv. law judges 1986-87, ethics com. 1997—), Dartmouth Club (exec. com. class of 1971), Book Club of Calif. Avocations: running, book collecting, gardening. FERC practice, Administrative and regulatory. Home: 4300 Hawthorne St NW Washington DC 20016-3571 Office: Sidley & Austin 1722 I St NW Fl 7 Washington DC 20006-3795

**ELROD, LINDA DIANE HENRY,** lawyer, educator; b. Topeka, Kans., Mar. 6, 1947; d. Lyndus Arthur Henry and Marjorie Jane (Hammel) Allen; divorced; children: Carson Douglas, Bree Elizabeth. BA in English with honors, Washburn U., 1969, JD cum laude, 1971. Bar: Kans. 1972. Instr. U. S.D., Topeka, 1970-71; research atty. Kans. Jud. Council, Topeka, 1972-74; asst. prof. Washburn U., Topeka, 1974-78, assoc. prof., 1978-82, prof. law, 1982-93; disting. prof., 1993—; vis. prof. law U. San Diego, Paris Summer Inst., 1988, 90, Washington U. Sch. Law, St. Louis, 1990, 98, summer 1991, 93. Author: Kansas Family Law Handbook, 1983, rev. edit., 1990, supplement, 1993, Child Custody Practice and Procedure, 1993, supplements, 1994-97, 99; co-author: Principle of Family Law, 1999, Kansas Family Law Guide, 1999; editor Family Law Quar., 1992—; contbr. articles to profl. jours. Pres. YWCA, Topeka, 1982-83; vice-chair Kans. Commn. on Child Support, 1984-87, Supreme Ct. Com. on Child Support, 1989—; chair Kans. Cmty. Svc. Orgn., 1986-87; adv. bd. CASA, 1997—. Recipient Disting. Service award Washburn Law Sch. Assn., 1986; named woman of distinction YWCA, 1997. Mem. ABA (coun. family law sect. 1988-92, sec. 1998, vice-chair, 1999, chair Schwab Meml. Grant Implementation 1984-87, co-chair Amicus Curiae com. 1987-92), Topeka Bar Assn. (sec. 1981-85, v.p. 1985-86, pres. 1986-87), Kans. Child Support Enforcement Assn. (bd. dirs. 1988—, Child Support Hall of Fame 1990), Kans. Bar Assn. (sec.-treas. 1988-89, com. ops. and fin. 1988, pres. family law sect. 1984-86, Disting. Svc. award 1985), NONOSO, Phi Kappa Phi, Phi Alpha Delta Alumni Assn. (justice 1976-77), Phi Beta Delta, Kappa Alpha Theta (pres. alumnae chpt. 1995-97). Presbyterian. Avocations: bridge, reading, quilting. Office: Washburn U Law Sch 17th and College Topeka KS 66621

**ELSASS, TOBIAS HAROLD,** lawyer; b. Lima, Ohio, Mar. 20, 1954; s. Donald Harold and Donna (Bruner) E.; m. Vickie S. Marsh, Dec. 31, 1977 (div. Mar. 18, 1980); m. Linda Kay Parker, Mar. 26, 1983; children: Ashley, Donald. BA, Ohio State U., 1976; JD, Capitol U., 1980. Bar: Ohio 1980, U.S. Dist. Ct. (so. dist.) Ohio 1983. Law clk. Franklin County Probate Ct., Columbus, 1976-79; assoc. Wilcox, Schlosser & Bendig Co., LPA, Columbus, 1979-80; pvt. practice Columbus, 1980—. Originator, organizer Werewolf Open Golf Classic, Columbus, 1986—. Numerous Merit awards Creative Living Assn., Columbus, 1986—. Mem. Ohio Bar Assn., Columbus Bar Assn., Trial Lawyers Am. Republican. Methodist. Avocations: golf, running, fishing, skiing, scuba diving. Family and matrimonial, Probate, Real property. Office: 4937 W Broad St Columbus OH 43228-1646

**ELSBERG, DAVID DONALD,** lawyer; b. Washington, Jan. 19, 1951; s. Paul and Elizabeth Margaret (Swartz) E.; m. Susan Finley, June 5, 1987; children: Elizabeth Hazen, Emily Reka. BA with distinction, U. Va., 1973, MA, 1975; JD, U. Richmond, 1978. Bar: Va. 1978, D.C. 1979. Atty. Law Office of John Smith, Falls Church, Va., 1978-79; assoc. Taylor & Clemente, Alexandria, Va., 1979-81; atty. Flow General, Tysons Corner, Va., 1981-82; ptnr. McGinley & Elsberg, Alexandria, 1982—; part-time faculty No. Va. C.C., Alexandria, 1981-84; faculty Nat. Bus. Inst., Inc., Eau Claire, Wis., 1996; agy. rep. Va. Retirement Sys., Richmond, 1986—. Mem. Va. Bar Assn., D.C. Bar Assn., Alexandria Bar Assn., Kiwanis. Banking, Real property. Home: 11345 River Rd Mason Neck VA 22079-4221 Office: McGinley & Elsberg 627 S Washington St Alexandria VA 22314-4109

**ELSEN, SHELDON HOWARD,** lawyer; b. Pitts., May 12, 1928; m. Gerri Sharfman, 1952; children: Susan Rachel, Jonathan Charles. AB, Princeton U., 1950; AM, Harvard U., 1952, JD, 1958. Bar: N.Y. 1959, U.S. Supreme Ct. 1971. Ptnr. Orans, Elsen & Lupert, N.Y.C., 1965—; adj. prof. law Columbia U. Law Sch., 1969—; chief counsel N.Y. Moreland Act Commn. on UDC, 1975-76; asst. U.S. atty. So. Dist. N.Y., 1960-64; cons. Pres.'s Commn. Law Enforcement Adminstrn. Justice, 1967; mem. faculty Nat. Inst. Trial Advocacy, 1973; mem., panel chmn. 1st dept. disciplinary com. N.Y., 1990-96. Contbr. articles to legal jours. Fellow Am. Coll. Trial Lawyers; mem. Assn. of Bar of City of N.Y. (v.p. 1988-89, chmn. com. on fed. legislation 1969-72, chmn. com. on fed. cts. 1983-86, chmn. nominating com. 1986-87, chmn. com. amenities in land use process for N.Y.C. 1987-88), Am. Law Inst., Phi Beta Kappa. Federal civil litigation, State civil litigation, Criminal. Home: 50 Fenimore Rd Scarsdale NY 10583-2251 Office: 1 Rockefeller Plz New York NY 10020-2102

**ELSMAN, JAMES LEONARD, JR.,** lawyer; b. Kalamazoo, Sept. 10, 1936; s. James Leonard and Dorothy Isabell (Pierce) E.; m. Janice Marie Wilczewski, Aug. 6, 1960; children—Stephanie, James Leonard III. *Grandaftaher Leonard Elsman, immigrated into the US in early 1900s, from The Netherlands (Freesland), but mother's lineage was Native Indian, German, English and Irish. All Common people who believed the Bible re lineage: "And He made from one (common origin, one source, one blood) all nations of men to settle on the face of the earth." - The Amplified Bible - Zondervan Acts 17:26.* B.A., U. Mich., 1958, J.D., 1962; postgrad., Harvard Div. Sch., 1958-59. Bar: Mich. 1963. Clk. Mich. Atty. Gen.'s Office, Lansing, 1961; atty. legal dept. Chrysler Corp., Detroit, 1962-64; founding ptnr. Elsman, Young, O'Rourke, Bruno & Bunn, Birmingham, Mich., 1964-72; pvt. practice Elsman Law Firm, Birmingham, 1972—; owner Radio Sta. WOLY, Battle Creek, Mich. Author: The Seekers, 1962; screenplay, 1976, 200 Candles to Whom?, 1973; contbr. articles to profl. jours.; Composer, 1974, 76; talk show host Citizen's Court, TV-48, Detroit. Mem. Regional Export Expansion Coun., 1966-73, Mich. Ptnrs. for Alliance for Progress, 1969-80; cand. U.S. Senate, 1966, 76, 94, 96, U.S. Ho. of Reps., 1970. Rockefeller Bros. Found. fellow Harvard Div. Sch., 1959. Mem. ABA, Am. Soc. Internat. Law, Econ. Club Detroit, World Peace Through Law Center, Full Gospel Businessmen, Bloomfield Open Hunt Club, Pres. Club (U. Mich.), Circumnavigators Club, Naples Bath and Tennis, Rotary. Republican. Mem. Christian Ch. Private international, Personal injury, Product liability. Home: 4811 Burnley Dr Bloomfield Hills MI 48304-3781 Office: 635 Elm St Birmingham MI 48009-6768 *Christianity is not a religion. It is knowing Jesus, i.e. God, personally. It does not hinge on man's works or effort. Christianity is the only way to God, as Christ is the only Mediator between God and man. Choose! You can be sincerely wrong and still go to Hell eternally. Just A country lawyer in a big city, representing the common man in mass tort and class actions and other litigation, whose priority client is Jesus.*

**ELSON, CHARLES MYER,** law educator; b. Atlanta, Nov. 12, 1959; s. Edward Elliott and Suzanne (Goodman) E.; m. Aimee F. Kemker, Dec. 18, 1993. AB magna cum laude, Harvard U., 1981, postgrad., 1981-82; JD, U. Va., 1985. Bar: N.Y. 1987, D.C. 1988, U.S. Dist. Ct. (so. and ea. dists.) N.Y. 1987, U.S. Ct. Appeals (11th cir.) 1987. Law clk. to judge U.S. Ct. Appeals (11th cir.), Atlanta, 1985-86; assoc. Sullivan & Cromwell, N.Y.C., 1986-90; asst. prof. Stetson U. Coll. Law, St. Petersburg, Fla., 1990-93, assoc. prof., 1993-96, prof., 1996—; vis. prof. law U. Ill., Champaign-Urbana, 1995, Cornell U. Law Sch., Ithaca, N.Y., 1996, U. Md. Law Sch., Balt., 1998; cons. Holland & Knight, 1995—, Towers, Perrin, 1998; bd. dirs. Nuevo Energy Co., Sunbeam Corp., Gulfcoast Legal Svcs. Corp. Bd. dirs. Big Apple Circus, Ltd., N.Y.C., 1987-93, Circon Corp., 1997-99, Investor Responsibility Rsch. Ctr., 1999—; trustee Talladega Coll., 1994—, Tampa Mus. Art, 1993—. Salvatori fellow Heritage Found., 1993-94. Mem. ABA, Am. Law Inst., Assn. Bar City N.Y., Chevaliers du Tastevin, Down Town Assn., Nat. Assn. Corp. Dirs. (adv. coun. 1997—, commn. dir. compensation 1995, commn. dir. professionalism 1996, com. on securities litig. reform and fraud detection 1997, com. on succession planning 1998, com. on audit coms. 1999), Harvard Club N.Y.C., Univ. Club N.Y.C. Home: 3315 W Mullen Ave Tampa FL 33609-4657 Office: Law Coll 1401 61st St S Saint Petersburg FL 33707-3246

**ELSTEAD, JOHN CLIFTON,** lawyer; b. San Bernardino, CA, Nov. 11, 1942; s. Lawrence Martin and Eleanor Elizabeth (Clifton) E.; 1 child, Logan Elizabeth. BA, U. Calif., Riverside, 1964; MA, U. West Fla., 1971; JD, U. Calif., Berkeley, 1974. Bar: Calif. 1974, U.S. Dist. Ct. (no. dist.) Calif. 1974, U.S. Dist. Ct. (cent. dist. Calif. 1975, U.S. Dist. Ct. (so. dist.) Calif. 1979, U.S. Supreme Ct. 1982. Lawyer Wells & Chesney, Oakland, Calif., 1974-77, Sterns, Smith, Elstead & Walker, San Francisco, 1977-86; pvt. practice Pleasanton, Calif., 1986—; tchg. fellow internat. law U. Pisa, Italy, 1973-74. Naval aviator, USN, 1966-71. Democrat. Roman Catholic. Avocations: reading, handball. Personal injury, Appellate, Aviation. Office: 5820 Stoneridge Mall Rd Ste 203 Pleasanton CA 94588-3200

**ELSTER, J. ROBERT,** lawyer; b. Mar. 10, 1938; m. Suzan Douglas, July 9, 1960; children: John Robert Jr., Mary Douglas Peters. BA in History, Rice U., 1959; JD, Duke U., 1964. Bar: N.C. 1964, U.S. Dist. Ct. N.C. 1964, U.S. Ct. Appeals (4th cir.) 1964, U.S. Supreme Ct. 1972. Assoc. Petree & Stockton, Winston-Salem, N.C., 1964-70; ptnr. Kilpatrick Stockton LLP (formerly Petree & Stockton), 1970—; adj. prof. law Wake Forest U., 1995-96. Contbr. articles to profl. publs. Bd. dirs. YMCA, 1978-80, Summit Sch., Winston-Salem, 1978-81, Forsyth County Day Sch., Winston-Salem, 1981-83; bd. trustees Centenary United Meth. Ch., 1988-91. Capt. USMC, 1959-61. Master Inns of Ct.; mem. Am. Coll. Trial Lawyers (trial comp. com. 1987-92, trial advocacy com. 1992—), N.C. Assn. Def. Attys. (pres. 1978-79), Forsyth County Bar Assn. (sec. 1966-67), N.C. Bar Assn. (bd. govs. 1987-90, mem. ethics and grievance com. 1986-89, endowment com. 1990—, chair professionalism com. 1996-99), Rotary (bd. dirs. 1984-89, pres. 1987-88). Republican. Federal civil litigation, State civil litigation.

**ELVE, DANIEL LEIGH,** lawyer; b. Holland, Mich., July 10, 1953; s. Albertus Henry and Ruth Elaine (Workman) E. AA, Grand Rapids (Mich.) Jr. Coll., 1973; BA, La. State U., 1975, JD, 1978. Bar: Mich. 1978, U.S. Dist. Ct. (we. dist.) Mich. 1978, U.S. Ct. Appeals (6th cir.) 1992. Adminstrv. asst. Detroit Tigers Baseball Club, 1979-81; lawyer Rhoades, McKee, Boer, Goodrich & Titta, Grand Rapids, 1982—; adj. instr. bus. law Grand Rapids C.C., 1985—. Active Pro Sports Kent County, Grand Rapids, 1990—, YMCA, 1992—. Mem. State Bar Mich., Detroit Bar Assn., Grand Rapids Bar Assn., Detroit Tiger Alumni Assn. (com. mem.). Avocation: baseball scouting. Criminal, General civil litigation, Education and schools. Office: Rhoades McKee Boer Goodrich & Titta 161 Ottawa Ave NW Grand Rapids MI 49503-2701

**ELWELL, CELIA CANDACE,** legal assistant; b. Ardmore, Okla., Oct. 12, 1954; d. James B. and Audra Eve (Wolleson) Baxter; m. Phillip B. Elwell, Aug. 11, 1973; 1 child, Christopher Brent. Cert. legal asst., U. Okla., 1986. Clk. Okla. Gas and Electric Co., Oklahoma City, 1973-82; legal sec. various law firms, Oklahoma City, 1982-84; legal asst. Robert Shoemaker, Esq., Oklahoma City, 1984-85; legal asst. to justice Supreme Ct. Okla., Oklahoma City, 1985-87; legal asst. Fellers, Snider, Blankenship, Bailey & Tippens, Oklahoma City, 1987-90, Linn & Helms, Oklahoma City, 1990; legal asst. office of mcpl. counselor City of Oklahoma City, 1990—; adj. instr. U. Okla., Norman, 1986—, adv. com. legal asst. dept. edn. coll. law; mem. approval commn. on-site evaluation team ABA, 1994; lectr. in field. Author: Study Guide for West's Paralegal Today, 2d edit., 1999; co-author: Practical Legal Writing for Legal Assistants, 1996, NFPA PACE Study Manual, 1996; contbr. articles to profl. jours. Mem. Am. Assn. Paralegal Edn., Cen. Okla. Assn. Legal Assts. (2d v.p. 1989-90, sec. 1988), Nat. Fed. Paralegal Assns., Kans. Legal Assts. Soc. Methodist. Home: 1714 Barb Dr Norman OK 73071-3026 Office: Office Mcpl Counselor Ste 400 200 N Walker Ave Oklahoma City OK 73102-2232

**ELWIN, JAMES WILLIAM, JR.,** dean, lawyer; b. Everett, Wash., June 28, 1950; s. James William Elwin and Jeannette Georgette (Zichy-Litscheff) Sherman; m. Regina K. McCabe, Oct. 25, 1986. BA, U. Denver, 1971, MA, 1972; JD, Northwestern U., 1975. Bar: Ill. 1975, U.S. Dist. Ct. (no. dist.) Ill. 1975, U.S. Ct. Appeals (7th cir.) 1977, U.S. Supreme Ct. 1980, U.S. Ct. Fed. Claims 1989. Trial atty. antitrust divsn. U.S. Dept. Justice, Chgo., 1975-77; asst. dean Sch. Law Northwestern U., Chgo., 1977-82, assoc. dean, 1982—; exec. dir. Corp. Counsel Ctr., 1984—; planning dir. Corp. Counsel Inst., Garrett Corp. and Securities Law Inst., Chgo., 1983—; dir. Short Course for Pros. Attys., 1981—, Short Course for Def. Lawyers in Criminal Cases, Chgo., 1979—. Bd. dirs. Legal Assistance Found. of Chgo., 1985-97; vice chmn. Gov.'s Adv. Coun. on Criminal Justice Legis., 1986-91. Fellow German Acad. Exch. Svc., 1986; Fulbright scholar, Germany, 1990. Mem. Chgo. Coun. Fgn. Rels. (mem. Chgo. com.), Chgo. Bar Assn. (bd. mgrs. 1983-85), Chgo. Bar Found. (bd. dirs. 1985-93, pres. 1989-91), Ill. Inst. Continuing Legal Edn. (bd. dirs. 1978-90, chmn. 1987-88), Am. Law Inst., Legal Club (pres. 1991-92), Univ. Club, Law Club City of Chgo., Phi Beta

Kappa, Pi Gamma Mu. Office: Northwestern U Sch Law 357 E Chicago Ave Chicago IL 60611-3059

**ELY, JOHN P.,** lawyer; b. Lubbock, Tex., Apr. 21, 1945; s. John O. and Laverne (Barton) E.; m. Julie McCall Sherman, Dec. 27, 1967. B.A., U. N.H., 1967; J.D., Boston U., 1976. Bar: Mass. 1977, U.S. Dist. Ct. Mass. 1977, U.S. Dist. Ct. Conn. 1980, U.S. Supreme Ct. 1980. Sole practice, Agawam, Mass., 1977-78; assoc. Laming, Smith, et al, Springfield, Mass., 1978-80; jr. ptnr. Auchter, Bozenhard & Socha, Springfield, 1980-83, ptnr., 1984-85; ptnr. Bozenhard, Socha, Ely & Kolber, Springfield, 1985—. Served to 1st lt. USMCR, 1968-71. Mem. Marine Corps Assn., 3d Marine Div. Assn., ABA, Mass. Bar Assn., Hamdpen County Bar Assn., Mass. Conveyancers Assn. Real property, Probate, General practice. Office: Bozenhard Socha Ely & Kolber 1275 Elm St Ste 3 West Springfield MA 01089-1890

**ELY, WAYNE ARLEN,** lawyer; b. Phila., Sept. 7, 1966; s. Jack and Joan (Mullen) E.; m. Margaret Astrid Kenyon, Oct. 17, 1998. BA in Journalism summa cum laude, Temple U., Phila., 1990, JD cum laude, 1993. Bar: Pa. 1993, U.S. Dist. Ct. (eastern dist.) Pa., 1994, U.S. Ct. Appeals (3rd cir.), 1998. Freelance journalist, 1986-90; assoc. Britt, Hankins, Schaible & Moughan, Phila., 1993, Kolman & Lea, Langhorne/Allentown, Pa., 1993-94, McLafferty, Cohen & Stein, Phila., 1994-96, Villari & Golomb, Phila., 1996-97; firm counsel Timothy M. Kolman & Assoc., Langhorne, Pa., 1997—. Contbr. articles to profl. jours. Recipient Keystone Press award, 1990, American Jurisprudence award, 1991, Barrister's award for excellence in trial advocacy, Temple U., 1993, mem. Temple U. Moot Ct. Hon. Soc.; named Temple U. President's scholar, 1990. Mem. Diver's Alert Network. Avocations: scuba diving, archeology, epigraphy (Egyptian and Maya Hieroglyphs). Labor, Professional liability, Federal civil litigation. Office: Timothy M Kolman & Assocs 225 N Flowers Mill Rd Langhorne PA 19047-1679

**EMANUEL, TODD POWELL,** lawyer; b. Skokie, Ill., Oct. 25, 1968; s. Barry Howard and Rosalie Karen Emanuel. BA, U. Calif., Berkeley, 1990; JD, U. San Francisco, 1993. Bar: Calif. 1994. Intern Atty. Gen.'s Office, San Francisco, 1992-93; dep. dist. atty. San Mateo County Dist., Redwood City, Calif., 1994-96; pvt. practice, Redwood City, 1996—; coach mock trial team Menlo-Atherton H.S., Calif., 1996—. Mem. exec. com. Svc. League, Redwood City, 1998; mem. San Mateo County Pvt. Defender Program, 1996—. Mem. San Mateo County Barristers (officer). Personal injury, Criminal, General civil litigation. Office: 702 Marshall St Ste 310 Redwood City CA 94063-1824

**EMBRY, STEPHEN CRESTON,** lawyer; b. Key West, Fla., Feb. 13, 1949; s. Jewell Creston and Julia Martine (Taylor) E.; m. Priscilla Mary Brown, Aug. 21, 1971; children: Nathaniel, Julia, Jessamyn. BA, Am. U., 1971; JD, U. Conn., 1976. Bar: Conn. 1976, U.S. Dist. Ct. Conn. 1976, U.S. Ct. Appeals (2d, 5th and 9th cirs.). Staff aide to Pres. The White House, Washington, 1969-72; assoc. Turner & Hensley, Great Bend, Kans., 1976, O'Brien, Shafner, Bartinik, & Stuart, Groton, Conn., 1976-85, Embry and Neusner, Groton, Conn., 1985—. Editor: Longshore and Harborworkers Textbook; mem. editl. bd. Matthew Bender, BRB Reporter; contbr. articles to profl. publs. Mem. Groton Rep. com., 1976-83, North Stonington Rep. com., 1984-88; chmn. Groton Housing Authority, 1979-80. Mem. ATLA (chair workers compensation sect. 1984-85, bd. dirs. workplace injury litigation group), Maritime Claimants Attys. Assn. (bd. dirs. 1980—), Conn. Trial Lawyers, Conn. Bar Assn. (exec. bd.), Thames Club, Grange. Democrat. Workers' compensation, Personal injury, Product liability.

**EMENS, J. RICHARD,** lawyer; b. Jackson, Mich., May 3, 1934; s. John R. and Aline (Brainerd) E.; m. Mary Francis, July 31, 1957 (div. Aug. 1980); children: Anne, John D., Alaine, Elizabeth; m. Beatrice Wolper, Aug. 31, 1983; children: Renee, Jennifer. BA, DePauw U., 1956; JD, U. Mich., 1959. Bar: Mich. 1959, Ohio 1964. Ptnr. McInally, Rosenfeld & Emens, Jackson, 1959-64, Emens and Ashworth, Marion, Ohio, 1964-68; dir. Emens, Kegler, Brown, Hill & Ritter, Columbus, Ohio, 1968-97, mng. dir., 1984-95; ptnr. Chester, Willcox & Saxbe LLP, Columbus; trustee Ea. Mineral Law Found., pres., 1982-83. Contbg. author: Coal Law and Regulations Treatise, 1983; contbr. articles to law jours. Co-founder Emens scholars program Ball State U. Muncie, Ind., 1977—; trustee, chmn. bd. trustees Franklin U., Columbus, 1995-96; past chmn. fin. com. Franklin County Rep. Com.; former trustee and pres. Friends of Librs. Ohio State U. Mem. Internat. Bar Assn. (subcom.), Columbus Area C. of C. (edn. com. 1989—), Rotary, Phi Beta Kappa. Avocations: travel, reading, fishing. Private international, General corporate, Estate planning. Office: Chester Willcox & Saxbe 17 S High St Ste 900 Columbus OH 43215-3442

**EMERSON, DOUGLAS THEODORE,** lawyer; b. Sept. 25, 1952; s. Douglas Theodore and Dora Mae (Angle) E. BA, U. Nev., Las Vegas, 1985; JD, Calif. Western Sch. Law, 1987. Bar: Tex. 1988, U.S. Dist. Ct. (no. dist.) Tex. 1988, U.S. Ct. Appeals (5th cir.) 1994. Assoc. Parkhill, Parkhill, Cowden & Runge, Grand Prairie, Tex., 1987-89; pvt. practice, Ft. Worth, 1989-92; ptnr. Law Offices Nekhom, Behr, Barnett & Emerson, Ft. Worth, 1992-95; pvt. practice Ft. Worth, 1995—. With USMC, 1971-73. Mem. State Bar of Tex., Tarrant County Bar Assn., Tex. Criminal Def. Lawyers Assn., Tarrant County Criminal Def. Lawyers Assn., Phi Alpha Delta. Criminal, General civil litigation, General practice. Office: 131 E Exchange Ave Ste 230 Fort Worth TX 76106-8253

**EMERSON, JOHN WILLIAMS, II,** lawyer; b. Greeneville, Tenn., Nov. 9, 1929; s. John Williams and Dorothy Mae (Moore) E.; m. Carolyn Rose Buchanan, Dec. 21, 1956; children: John Williams III, Amy Elizabeth, Emily Alicia. JD, Vanderbilt U., 1960. Bar: Fla. 1960, Tenn. 1960, U.S. Dist. Ct. (so. dist.) Fla. 1961, U.S. Ct. Appeals (5th cir.) 1961, U.S. Supreme Ct. 1968, U.S. Dist. Ct. (ea. dist.) Tenn. 1982, U.S. Ct. Appeals (6th cir.) 1983, U.S. Dist. Ct. (mid. dist.) Tenn. 1988, U.S. Dist. Ct. (mid. dist.) Fla. 1990. Ins. agt. Emerson Ins. Agy., Greeneville, 1949-56; instr. Peabody Coll., Nashville, 1958-59; assoc. Henderson, Franklin, Starnes & Holt, Ft. Myers, Fla., 1960-63; ptnr. Parks & Emerson, Naples, Fla., 1963-72, Treadwell, Emerson & Elkins, Naples, 1972-79, Emerson & Emerson P.C., Johnson City, Tenn., 1979-83, Emerson & Emerson P.A., Naples, 1983—; judge Small Claims Ct., Collier County, Naples, Fla., 1963-64. Col. aide de camp gov.'s staff State of Tenn., 1963-66; lt. gov. dist. 11 Fla. Dist. of Kiwanis, 1970-71. Capt. U.S. Army, 1950-54, Korea. Fellow Fla. Kiwanis Found. (life); mem. ABA, The Fla. Bar (bd. govs. young lawyers sect. 1963-66), Fla. Acad. Trial Lawyers, Assn. Trial Lawyers Am., Araba Temple (Ft. Myers, Fla.), Masons (32 Degree). Democrat. Presbyterian. Avocations: boating, travel. Private international, Contracts commercial, Real property. Home: 1935 Seville Blvd Apt 112 Naples FL 34109-3367 Office: Emerson & Emerson PA PO Box 1675 Naples FL 34106-1675

**EMERSON, WILLIAM HARRY,** lawyer, retired, oil company executive; b. Rochester, N.Y., Jan. 13, 1928; s. William Canfield and Alice Sarah (Adams) E.; m. Jane Anne Epple, Dec. 27, 1956; children: Elizabeth Anne, Carolyn Jane. BA, Cornell U., 1951, LLB, 1956. Bar: Ill. 1974. Atty. Amoco Corp., 1956-91; sec., dir. Amoco Gas Co., 1979-91. Pres., dir. Undercroft Montessori Sch., Tulsa, 1965-67, Tulsa Figure Skating Club, 1969; bd. dirs. Lake Forest (Ill.) Found. for Hist. Preservation, 1983—; mem. vestry Ch. Holy Spirit, Lake Forest. Federal civil litigation, State civil litigation, FERC practice. Home: 593 Greenvale Rd Lake Forest IL 60045-1526

**EMGE, DEREK JOHN,** lawyer; b. Glendale, Calif., Aug. 27, 1967; s. Carl Richard and Heather Anne Emge; m. Suzanne Katleman, Aug. 5, 1989; children: Zachary Brayton, Allison Leigh. BA, Claremont McKenna Coll., Claremont, Calif., 1989; JD, U. San Diego, 1992. Bar: Calif. 1992, U.S. Dist. Ct. (so. dist.) Calif. 1992. Atty. Edwards, White & Sooy, San Diego, 1992-96, Booth, Mitchel & Strange, San Diego, 1996-99; prin. Gilliland & Emge, LLP, San Diego, 1999—. Author: Hidden Trails of San Diego, 1994. Mem. Consumer Lawyers of San Diego. Avocations: cycling, running, backpacking. General civil litigation, Professional liability, Contracts commercial. Office: Gilliland & Emge LLP 29th Fl 402 W Broadway Fl 29 San Diego CA 92101-3542

**EMMERT, STEVEN MICHAEL,** lawyer; b. Zanesville, Ohio, July 6, 1957; s. Edward Francis and Doris Jean (Sigrist) E.; m. Margaret Teresa Brosnan, Aug. 8, 1981; 1 child, Denys Patrick. BA with distinction, Ohio State U., 1979, JD, 1982. Bar: Ohio 1982, U.S. Dist. Ct. (so. dist.) Ohio 1984. Staff atty. Ohio Dept. Energy, Columbus, 1981-83, Ohio Bur. Workers' Compensation, Columbus, 1983; adminstrv. law judge energy Ohio Dept. Devel., Columbus, 1983-85; sr. atty. Online Computer Library Ctr., Dublin, Ohio, 1985—. Participant, supr. Vol/ Income Tax Assistance IRS, 1981-82. Named one of Outstanding Young Men Am. U.S. Jaycees, 1983-88. Mem. Ohio Bar Assn., U.S. Tennis Assn. Democrat. Roman Catholic. Club: Ohio State U. Karate. Avocations: tennis, golf, karate. Computer, Labor, General corporate. Home: 13890 Lewis Mill Way Chantilly VA 20151-2324 Office: Online Computer Library Ctr Inc 6565 Frantz Rd Dublin OH 43017-3395

**EMRICH, EDMUND MICHAEL,** lawyer; b. N.Y.C., Apr. 12, 1956; s. Edmund and Mary Ann (Picarella) E. BA, SUNY, Albany, 1978; JD, Hofstra U., 1981. Bar: N.Y. 1982, U.S. Dist. Ct. (so. and ea. dists.) N.Y. 1982, U.S. Ct. Appeals (2d cir.) 1987. Law clk. to presiding justice U.S. Bankruptcy Ct. (ea. dist.) N.Y., Westbury, 1982-83; assoc. Levin & Weintraub & Crames, N.Y.C., 1983-90; assoc. Kaye, Scholer, Fierman, Hays & Handler, N.Y.C., 1990-92, ptnr., 1993—; local rules com. U.S. Bankruptcy Ct. (ea. dist.) N.Y., 1985-86; mem. local rules drafting subcom. U.S. Bankruptcy Ct. (so. dist.) N.Y., 1985-86, 95-98. Mem. Hofstra U. Law Rev., 1981-82. Mem. ABA, N.Y. State Bar Assn., Am. Bankruptcy Inst. Avocations: golf, tennis, wine collecting. Bankruptcy. Home: 300 E 85th St New York NY 10028-4500 Office: Kaye Scholer Fierman Hays & Handler 425 Park Ave New York NY 10022-3506

**EMRY, FREDERIC GRANT,** lawyer; b. Spokane, Wash., Jan. 30, 1939; s. Merle F. and Grace (Humphreys) E.; m. Connie M. McGreevy, June 4, 1966; children: Deric, Kris, Karin, Geoff. BS in Econs., U. Pa., 1961; LLB, Gonzaga U., Spokane, Wash., 1965; LLM in Taxation, NYU, 1966. Bar: Wash. 1965, U.S. Tax Ct. 1965, U.S. Dist. Ct. (ea. dist.) Wash. 1965. Ptnr. Paine, Hamblen, Coffin, Brooke & Miller, Spokane, Wash., 1967—; past chmn. Wash. State Legal Ethics Com.; adj. prof. Gonzaga Law Sch. Mem. ABA (sec. real property trust and probate, taxation sect.), Am. Coll. Probate Counsel (fellow). Estate planning, Probate.

**ENDEMAN, RONALD LEE,** lawyer; b. Riverside, Calif., May 13, 1936; s. Walter Metsger and May Florence (Higdon) E.; m. Judith Lynn Sherman, May 27, 1959; children—Michael Scott, Melissa May. B.A., U. Calif.-Riverside, 1959; J.D., U. So. Calif., 1966. Bar: Calif. 1967, U.S. Dist. Ct. (so. dist.) Calif. 1967, U.S. Ct. Claims 1972, U.S. Ct. Appeals (9th cir.) 1973, U.S. Supreme Ct. 1972. Trial atty. Calif. Legal Div., San Diego, 1967-71; ptnr. Jackson, Turner, Endeman & Mulcare, Burlingame, Calif., 1971-73; ptnr. Jennings, Engstrand & Henrikson, San Diego, 1973-87; ptnr. Endeman, Lincoln, Turek & Heater, 1987—. Mem. State Bar Com. on Condemnation, 1987-89. Mem. ABA, Calif. Bar Assn., San Diego County Bar Assn., Assn. Trial Lawyers Am., Calif. Trial Lawyers Assn., San Diego County Trial Lawyers Assn., Am. Arbitration Assn., Internat. Right of Way Assn., Guild of Real Estate Appraisers (Man of Yr. 1971). Republican. Condemnation. Home: 10602 Noakes Rd La Mesa CA 91941-5776 Office: 600 B St Ste 2400 San Diego CA 92101-4582

**ENDIEVERI, ANTHONY FRANK,** lawyer; b. Syracuse, N.Y., May 21, 1939; s. Santo and Anne Rose (Zeolla) E.; m. Arlene Rita McDonald, May 20, 1967; children: Anne C., Steven A. BA, Syracuse U., 1961, LLB, 1965, JD, 1968. Bar: N.Y. 1967, U.S. Dist. Ct. (no. dist.) N.Y. 1967, U.S. Ct. Appeals (2d cir.) 1969, U.S. Supreme Ct. 1970; cert. civil trial lawyer Nat. Bd. Trial Advocacy. Assoc. Ronald Crowley, Atty., North Syracuse, N.Y., 1965-67, Love, Balducci & Scacciz, Syracuse, 1967; pvt. practice law Camillus, N.Y., 1968—; appellate counsel Hiscock Legal Aid, Syracuse, 1968-70; asst. corp. counsel, housing code prosecutor City of Syracuse, 1970-74; participant Nat. Coll. Advocacy, 1981-83, 86; lectr. Melvin Belli seminar, San Francisco, 1987, 93, Kansas City, Mo., 1988, Boston, 1989, San Diego, 1990; spkr. in field. Mem. ministry program Syracuse Diocese Pre-Deacon Study, 1980-82. Maj. USMCR, 1972-88, ret. Mem. ATLA (spkr. nat. conv. 1990, seminar 1990, ultimate trial advocacy course 1 991), Assn. Trial Lawyers Am. Coll. Advocacy, N.Y. Bar Assn., N.Y. State Bar Assn., Onondaga County Bar Assn., N.Y. Trial Lawyers Assn., Nat. Brain Injury Assn., N.Y. Brain Injury Assn. Democrat. Roman Catholic. Professional liability, Personal injury, Product liability. Home: 205 Emann Dr Camillus NY 13031-2009

**ENDRISS, MARILYN JEAN,** lawyer; b. New Haven, June 27, 1953. BA, Duke U., 1975; JD, Golden Gate U., 1981. Bar: Wash. 1981, U.S. Dist. Ct. (we. dist.) Wash., U.S. Ct. Appeals (9th cir.) 1990. Staff atty. N.W. Women's Law Ctr., Seattle, 1981-82; pvt. practice Seattle, 1982-83; legal advisor Seattle Human Rights Dept., 1984, mgr. enforcement divsn., 1984-87; assoc. Law Office Judith Lonnquist, Seattle, 1987-90; prin. Endriss & Shear, PS, Seattle, 1990-95; pvt. practice Seattle, 1995-99; adminstrv. judge U.S. Equal Employment Opportunity Commn., 1999—. Mem. King County Affirmative Action Adv. Com., Seattle, 1986-88; mem. Edmonds Sch. Dist. Citizens Planning Com., 1993—, chair 1994-96. Mem. ABA (labor and employment law and ind. rights and responsibilities sects., plaintiff contact Seattle EEOC/ABA joint tng. initiative program 1999—), Nat. Women and the Law Assn. (bd. dirs. 1985-86, mem. steering com. various confs.), Seattle-King County Bar Assn. (labor law sect.), Nat. Employment Lawyers Assn., Wash. Employment Lawyers Assn. (chair 1993-99), Wash. Pattern Jury Instrn. Com., Wash. Women Lawyers, Wash. State Bar Assn. (mem. civil rights com. 1987-90, chairperson 1989-90), N.W. Women's Law Ctr. (mem. legal com. 1981-89, bd. dirs. 1983-87, pres. 1985-87). Civil rights, Labor, Administrative and regulatory. Office: US Equal Employment Opportunity Commn Seattle Dist Office 909 1st Ave Ste 400 Seattle WA 98104-1055

**ENERSEN, BURNHAM,** lawyer; b. Lamberton, Minn., Nov. 17, 1905; s. Albert H. and Ethel (Rice) E.; m. Nina H. Wallace, July 21, 1935; children: Richard W., Elizabeth. A.B., Carleton Coll., 1927, L.H.D., 1974; LL.B., Harvard U., 1930. Bar: Calif. 1931. Assoc. McCutchen, Doyle, Brown & Enersen, San Francisco, 1930-43, ptnr., 1943-78, counsel, 1978—; dir. Pomfret Estates, Inc., Calif. Student Loan Fin. Corp., 1981-90; chmn. Gov.'s Com. Water Lawyers, 1957; mem. Calif. Jud. Coun., 1960-64; vice chmn. Calif. Constn. Revision Commn., 1964-75; mem. com. to rev. Calif. Master Plan for Higher Edn., 1971-72. Mem. Calif. Citizens Commn. for Tort Reform, 1976-77; bd. dirs. Assn. Calif. Tort Reform, 1979-93, chmn., 1979-80; mem. Calif. Postsecondary Edn. Com., 1974-78; bd. dirs. Criminal Justice Legal Found., 1982-94, chmn. bd. trustees, 1985-86; bd. dirs. Fine Arts Mus. Found., 1983-94, pres. bd. trustees, 1987-92; pres. United Bay Area Crusade, 1962, United Crusades of Calif., 1969-71; trustee Mills Coll., 1972-82, chmn., 1976-80. Fellow Am. Bar Found.; mem. ABA (ho. of dels. 1970-76), State Bar Calif. (pres. 1960), Bar Assn. San Francisco (pres. 1955), Assn. of Bar of City of N.Y., Am. Judicature Soc., Am. Law Inst., Calif. C. of C. (dir. 1962-78, pres. 1971), Calif. Hist. Soc. (bd. trustees 1976-78, 83-89), Bohemian Club, Pacific-Union Club, Commercial Club (pres. 1966), Commonwealth Club Calif., San Francisco Golf Club, Cypress Point Club. General practice, Real property. Home: 1661 Pine St Apt 1111 San Francisco CA 94109-0413 Office: 3 Embarcadero Ctr San Francisco CA 94111-4003

**ENGBERS, JAMES AREND,** lawyer; b. Grand Rapids, Mich., Dec. 11, 1938; s. Martin Hoffius and Harriet Jean (Riddering) E.; m. Harriet M. Wissink, Sept. 13, 1960; children: Charles M., James A., Nancy L. Falk, David W. LLB, Hope Coll., Holland, Mich., 1960; JD, Wayne U., 1963. Bar: Mich. 1963, U.S. Dist. Ct. (we. dist.) Mich. 1963. Mem. firm Miller, Johnson, Snell & Cummiskey, P.L.C., Grand Rapids, Mich., 1963—. Mem. State Bar Mich. (standing com. on character and fitness 1993-97), Grand Rapids Bar Assn. (trustee 1972-73), Rotary Club. Republican. Presbyterian. Avocations: golf, tennis, reading, photography. Bankruptcy, General corporate, Contracts commercial. Office: Miller Johnson Snell & Cummiskey PLC 800 Calder Plaza Bldg Grand Rapids MI 49503-2250

**ENGEBRETSON, ANDREW PETER,** lawyer; b. Starbuck, Minn., Aug. 21, 1932; s. Herman Ferdinand and Agnes Serina (Knutson) E.; m. Fay Louise Amundson, Nov. 28, 1959 (div. Apr. 1970); children: Peter, Sarah; m. Rachel Wayne Warrick, June 16, 1970; 1 child, Margaret. BA cum laude, St. Olaf Coll., 1954; JD, U. Minn., 1959. Assoc. Rudolph L. Swore, Alexandria, Minn., 1959-61, Ernest H. Steneroden, St. Paul, 1968-69; ptnr. Engebretson Law Offices, St. Paul, 1969-94, pvt. practice, 1995—. Conv. del. Ramsey County Republicans, St. Paul, 1974-90, congrl. candidate, St. Paul, 1976. With U.S. Army, 1955-56. Mem. ABA, Minn. Bar Assn., Minn. Trial Lawyers Assn., Am. Trial Lawyers Assn., Mason. Republican. Lutheran. Avocations: fishing, chess, fgn. lang. studies, non-fiction books. Personal injury, Workers' compensation. Office: Engebretson Law Offices 200 Plato Blvd E Saint Paul MN 55107-1618

**ENGEL, ALBERT JOSEPH,** federal judge; b. Lake City, Mich., Mar. 21, 1924; s. Albert Joseph and Bertha (Bielby) E.; m. Eloise Ruth Bull, Oct. 18, 1952; children: Albert Joseph III, Katherine Ann, James Robert, Mary Elizabeth. Student, U. Md., 1941-42; A.B., U. Mich., 1948, LL.B., 1950. Bar: Mich. 1951. Ptnr. firm Engle & Engel, Muskegon, Mich., 1952-67; judge Mich. Circuit Ct., 1967-71; judge U.S. Dist. Ct. Western Dist. Mich., 1971-74; circuit judge U.S. Ct. Appeals, 6th Circuit, Grand Rapids, Mich., 1974-88, chief judge, 1988-89, sr. judge, 1989—. Served with AUS, 1943-46, ETO. Fellow Am. Bar Found.; mem. ABA, Fed. Bar Assn., Mich. Bar Assn., Cin. Bar Assn., Grand Rapids Bar Assn., Am. Judicature Soc., Am. Legion, Phi Sigma Kappa, Phi Delta Phi. Episcopalian. Club: Grand Rapids Torch. Home: 5497 Forest Bend Dr SE Ada MI 49301-9079 Office: US Ct Appeals 100 E 5th St Ste 418 Cincinnati OH 45202-3911 also: 640 Federal Bldg 110 Michigan St NW Grand Rapids MI 49503-2313

**ENGEL, DAVID LEWIS,** lawyer; b. N.Y.C., Mar. 31, 1947; s. Benjamin and Selma (Fruchtman) E.; m. Edith Greetham Smith, June 9, 1973; children: Richard William, Jonathan Martin. AB in Gen. Studies in Econ. cum laude, Harvard U., 1967, JD magna cum laude, 1973; Disting. Naval grad., U.S. Naval Officer Candidate Sch., 1969. Bar: Mass. 1975. Law clk. to Judge Henry J. Friendly U.S. Ct. Appeals (2nd cir.), N.Y.C., 1973-74; assoc. Goodwin, Procter & Hoar, Boston, 1974-76, 79-80; asst. prof. law Stanford U., Calif., 1976-79; ptnr. Berman, Dittmar & Engel, P.C., Boston, 1980-84, Bingham Dana LLP, Boston, 1984—. Contbr. article to Stanford Law Rev., 1979; pres. Harvard Law Rev., 1972-73. Mem. bd. visitors Stanford U. Law Sch., 1982-84; bd. dirs. Project Joy, 1995—. Lt. (j.g.) USNR, 1969-71. Named John Harvard scholar, Harvard Coll. scholar, Nat. Merit scholar, 1964-67; recipient Sears prize, 1968, John Bingham Hurlbut award, 1979. Mem. ABA, Boston Bar Assn. (working group of task force on revision of Mass. corp. statute 1987—), Phi Beta Kappa. General corporate, Securities. Office: Bingham Dana LLP 150 Federal St Boston MA 02110-1713

**ENGEL, JOHN CHARLES,** lawyer, lobbyist; b. Milw., Aug. 24, 1955; s. Russell Bernard Glen and Helen Marie (Poh) E.; m. Debra Ann McCall, Apr. 17, 1982; children: Stephanie, Jacqueline, Elizabeth, Thomas. BA, U. Wis., Milw., 1982, MLS, 1983; JD, Marquette U., 1986. Bar: Wis. 1986, U.S. Dist. Ct. (ea. dist.) Wis. 1986, U.S. Dist. Ct. (we. dist.) Wis. 1987, U.S. Supreme Ct. 1989. Staff atty. Wis. Credit Union League, Pewaukee, Wis., 1986-93, mgr. tech. dept., 1993-94, sr. mgr. tech. dept., 1994-96, staff atty. compliance, rsch. and publs., 1996-99, league compliance counsel, 1999—; bd. dirs. Outpost Natural Foods Coop., pres., 1991, sec., 1992-93. Active Mil. Dems. Mem. ACLU, Wis. Bar Assn., Phi Alpha Theta. Roman Catholic. Avocation: genealogy. Banking, Consumer commercial, General corporate. Home: 2359 S 78th St West Allis WI 53219-1857 Office: Wis Credit Union League N25w23131 Paul Rd Pewaukee WI 53072-5734

**ENGEL, RALPH MANUEL,** lawyer; b. N.Y.C., May 13, 1944; s. Werner Herman and Ruth Fredericke (Friedlander) E.; m. Diane Linda Weinberg, Aug. 10, 1968; children—Eric M., Daniel C., Julie R. BA in Econs. with highest honors, NYU, 1965, JD, 1968. Bar: N.Y. 1968, U.S. Supreme Ct. 1972. Assoc. Gilbert, Segall and Young, N.Y.C., 1968-71, Trubin Sillcocks Edelman & Knapp, N.Y.C., 1971-76; assoc., then ptnr. Summit Rovins & Feldesman and predecessor firms, N.Y.C., 1976-91; ptnr. Rosen & Reade, LLP, N.Y.C., 1991—; lectr. Sch. Law, Fordham U., 1990-91. Contbr. articles to legal and other publs.; editor-in-chief The Commentator, NYU, 1968. Mem. Planning Com., Larchmont, N.Y., 1992—. Fellow Am. Coll. Trust and Estate Counsel; mem. N.Y. State Bar Assn. (trust and estate law sect. com. on practice and ethics 1991—, elder law sect., com. on guardianships and fiduciaries 1991-97, com. on estates and tax planning 1997—), Assn. Bar City of N.Y. (com. on estate and gift taxation 1992-95, chmn. subcom. on splitting and combining trusts 1994-95, chmn., subcom. on spousal rights 1994-95, com. on trusts, estates and surrogate's cts. 1997—), N.Y. County Lawyers' Assn. (sect. on estates, trusts and surrogate's court practice 1999—), Estate Planning Coun. Westchester County (bd. dirs. 1985-91). Probate, Estate planning, Estate taxation. Home and Office: 6 Rockwood Dr Larchmont NY 10538-2537 Office: 757 3rd Ave New York NY 10017-2013

**ENGEL, RICHARD LEE,** lawyer, educator; b. Syracuse, N.Y., Sept. 19, 1936; s. S. Sanford and Eleanor M. (Gallop) E.; m. Karen K. Engel, Dec. 26, 1965; children: Todd Sanford, Gregg Matthew. BA, Yale U., 1958, JD, 1981. Bar: N.Y. 1961. Law asst. justices Appellate Divsn. N.Y. 4th Jud. Dist., 1961-63; law clk. judge N.Y. Supreme Ct., 1963-65; sr. ptnr. Nottingham, Engel, Gordon & Kerr LLP, Syracuse, 1970—; adj. prof. law Syracuse U. Coll. of Law; arbitrator, mediator law and medicine, equine law Coll. Law trial practice Am. Arbitration Assn., Resolute Sys., Inc.; lectr. in field. Contbr. articles to profl. jours. Pres. Temple Soc. Concord, 1985-87; bd. dirs. Am. Field Svcs. Intercultural Programs, Inc., 1974-81. Mem. ABA, Am. Coll. Legal Medicine, N.Y. State Bar Assn., Onondaga Bar Asn. (mem. trial lawyers com. 1978-80, chmn. med. legal liaison com. 1976-77, chmn. spl. ins. com. 1988, Bench and Bar com. 1991, found. bd. 1992-98, grievance com. 1998), N.Y. State Trial Attys. Assn., Upstate Trial Attys. Assn. (pres. 1973-74, chmn. bd. 1974-77), Thoroughbred Owners and Breeders Assn. (owners coun.), Def. Rsch. Inst., Inc., Cavalry Country, Saratoga Reading Rooms, Inc., Yale (pres. Ctrl. N.Y.). General practice, General corporate, General civil litigation. Home: Brockway Ln Fayetteville NY 13066 Office: Nottingham Engel Gordon & Kerr LLP One Lincoln Ctr 8th Flr Syracuse NY 13202

**ENGEL, RICHARD W., JR.,** lawyer; b. St. Louis, Aug. 9, 1941; s. Richard W. and Marian P. Engel; m. Tamara A. Kenny, May 15, 1967; 1 child, Elias. BSBA, St. Louis U., 1983; JD, U. Mo., 1987. Bar: Mo. 1987, Ill. 1988, U.S. Dist. Ct. (ea. dist.) Mo. 1987, U.S. Dist. Ct. (we. dist.) Mo. 1987, U.S. Dist. Ct. (so. dist.) Ill. 1988, U.S. Dist. Ct. (no. dist.) Ill. 1988, U.S. Ct. Appeals (8th cir.) 1989, U.S. Supreme Ct. 1997. Assoc. Armstrong Teasdale, St. Louis, 1987-94, ptnr., 1994—; mng. mem. First Fin. Group, St. Louis, 1994—; bd. dirs. ACM Acquisitions Inc., St. Louis. Mem. Mo. Bar Assn. (rep. 1988-94). Avocations: golf, tennis, reading. Contracts commercial, Bankruptcy, General corporate. Office: Armstrong Teasdale 211 N Broadway Ste 2600 Saint Louis MO 63102-2733

**ENGEL, TALA,** lawyer; b. N.Y.C.; d. Volodia Vladimir Boris and Risia (Modelevska) E.; m. James Colias, Nov. 22, 1981 (dec. Nov. 1989). *Ms. Engel's mother Risia, escaped Tzarist Russia by crawling through a minefield at the border with her parents and sister, Musia Kadany. Her mother attended the Conservatory of Kiev. Aunt Musia won two scholarships to Julliard School of Music and spent the rest of her life teaching there. Father Vladimir, escaped Tzarist Russia by leaving through the yet unmarked border through Georgia into Turkey. Brother Alex Engel, BS MIT, 1952, works for Jet Propulsion Laboratories on their mission to Mars. Husband James, was a criminal investigator for the US and States Attorney and the Secretary of State in Chicago. He was in the business of cost efficient development of real estate into rental property in Washington.* AA, U. Fla., 1952; BA in Russian and Spanish, U. Miami, 1954; JD, U. Miami, Coral Gables, 1957; postgrad., Middlebury Coll., 1953. Bar: Fla. 1957, U.S. Dist. Ct. (so. dist.) Fla. 1957, U.S. Dist. Ct. (no. dist.) Ill. 1962, U.S. Supreme Ct., 1965, D.C. 1982. Sole practice Miami, Fla. and Chgo., 1957-61, 66-86; pvt. practice immigration atty. Washington, 1987—; atty. Immigration and Naturalization Service, Chgo., 1961-62; parole agt. Ill. Youth Commn., Chgo., 1963-66. Editor The Editor, 1956. Bd. dirs. Cordi-Marian Settlement, Chgo., 1977-93. Mem. ABA, Ill. Bar Assn. (gen. assembly 1984-86), Chgo. Bar Assn. (devel. of law com. 1985-87), Chgo. Bar Found., Fed. Bar Assn., Nat. Lawyers Club, Fla. Bar Assn., Am. Immigration Lawyers Assn., Alpha Lambda Delta. Avocations: traveling, theater, singing, writing, Russian and Spanish langs. Fax: 202-244-6893. E-mail: TalaEngel@aol.com. Immigration, naturalization, and customs. Home and Office: 2800 Quebec St NW Apt 1027 Washington DC 20008-1237

**ENGELHARDT, JOHN HUGO,** lawyer, banker; b. Houston, Feb. 3, 1946; s. Hugo Tristram and Beulah Lillie (Karbach) E.; m. Jasmin Inge Nestler, Nov. 12, 1976; children: Angelique D, Sabrina N. BA, U. Tex., 1968; JD, St. Mary's U., San Antonio, 1973. Bar: Tex. 1973. Tchr. history Pearsall H.S., Tex., 1968-69; pvt. practice, New Braunfels, Tex., 1973-75; examining atty. Comml. Title Co., San Antonio, 1975-78, San Antonio Title Co., 1978-82; pvt. practice, New Braunfels, 1982—; adv. dir. M Bank Brenham, Tex., 1983-89. Fellow Coll. State Bar Tex.; mem. ABA, Pi Gamma Mu. Republican. Roman Catholic. Real property, Probate.

**ENGELMAN LADO, MARIANNE L.,** civil rights lawyer, educator; b. N.Y.C., Sept. 28, 1962; d. Irwin and Rosalyn (Ackerman) Engelman; m. Fred Alexander Lado, July 22, 1989; children: Nathan Alejandro, Elana Rosa. BA, Cornell U., 1984; JD, U. Calif., Berkeley, 1987; MA, Princeton U., 1989. Bar: N.Y. 1988, U.S. Dist. Ct. (so. and ea. dists.) N.Y. 1990. Staff atty. NAACP Legal Def. and Ednl. Fund, Inc., N.Y.C., 1989-97; asst. prof. Sch. Pub. Affairs, Baruch Coll., N.Y.C., 1997-99; gen. counsel N.Y. Lawyers for Pub. Interest, N.Y.C., 1999—; pro bono atty. NAACP Legal Def. and Ednl. Fund, Ind., 1997-99. Office: NY Lawyers for Pub Interest 151 W 30th 11th Fl New York NY 10001

**ENGELS, PATRICIA LOUISE,** lawyer; b. Joliet, Ill., July 2, 1926; d. Fred Bridges and Loretta Mae (Fisk) B.; m. Henry William Engels, Feb. 1, 1947; children: Patrick Henry, Michael Bruce, Timothy William. BS in Edn., Olivet Nazarene Coll., 1970, MEd, 1971; JD, John Marshall Law Sch., 1979. Bar: Ill. 1979, Ind. 1979; cert. elem. and high sch. tchr., edn. adminstrn., Ill. Tchr. Bourbonnais (Ill.) and Momence (Ill.) Unit Schs., 1970-76; instr. Kankakee (Ill.) Community Coll., 1975; sole practice Ind. and Ill., 1979—; qualified divorce mediator, 1991—. Active Lake Village (Ind.) Civic Assn., 1980—; edn. coord. St. Augusta Ch., Lake Village, 1985-89. Avocations: exercise, swimming, sewing, country dancing, reading. Mem. ABA, Ind. Bar Assn., Ill. Bar Assn., Pub. Defender Bar Assn., Theta Chi Sigma, Kappa Delta Pi. Roman Catholic. Avocations: exercise, swimming, sewing, dancing, reading. Family and matrimonial, Estate planning, Real property. Home: 16905A E 3250N Rd Momence IL 60954-3852 Office: Engels Law Office 16905A E 3250N Rd Momence IL 60954-3852

**ENGERRAND, KENNETH G.,** lawyer, educator; b. Atlanta, June 30, 1952; s. Gabriel H. and Doris A. (Dieskow) E.; m. Anne Walts, Mar. 16, 1985; children: Caroline Elizabeth Turner, Catherine Anne Denton. BA, Fla. State U., 1973; JD, U. Tex., 1976. Bar: Tex. 1976, U.S. Dist. Ct. (so. dist.) Tex. 1977. U.S. Ct. Appeals (5th cir.) 1978, U.S. Supreme Ct. 1980, U.S. Ct. Appeals (11th cir.) 1981, U.S. Dist. Ct. (ea. dist.) Tex. 1987. Assoc. Royston, Rayzor, Vickery & Williams, Houston, 1976-80, Brown, Sims & Ayre, Houston, 1980; v.p., gen. counsel Huthnance Offshore Corp., Houston, 1980-86; ptnr. Brown, Sims, Wise & White, Houston, 1986—; adj. prof. law S. Tex. Coll. Law, Houston, 1979-93. Columnist The Reporter, 1984-87; contbr. articles to profl. jours.; faculty advisor to spl. maritime edits. S. Tex. Law Jour., 1981-86. Fund drive vol. Houston Grand Opera, 1985-93, trustee, 1986-93. Named Best Prof., S. Tex. Coll. Law, Houston, 1981-82, 83-84; recipient Outstanding Contbn. to Community award, Houston Jaycees, 1983. Mem. ABA (vice chmn. admiralty and maritime law com., tort and ins. practice sect. 1986-89), Def. Rsch. Inst., Maritime Law Assn., Order of Coif, Phi Beta Kappa, Phi Delta Phi. Republican. Methodist. Avocations: legal writing, cultivating roses. Admiralty, General corporate, Federal civil litigation. Home: 10603 Twelve Oaks Dr Houston TX 77024-3135 Office: Brown Sims Wise & White 2000 Post Oak Blvd Ste 2300 Post Oak Central Houston TX 77056

**ENGLAND, AUSTIN HINDS,** lawyer; b. Abilene, Tex., Mar. 21, 1964; s. Joe Pope and Mary Jeanett (Hinds) E.; m. Dayna Carroll Warren, July 23, 1988; 1 child, Griffith Dry. BBA in Fin., Econs., Baylor U., 1987; JD, U. Ark., 1990. Bar: Tex. 1990, U.S. Dist. Ct. (no. dist.) Tex. 1990. Assoc. Fanning, Harper & Martinson, Dallas, 1990-94; counsel Fujitsu Network Transmission Systems, Inc., Richardson, Tex., 1994-95; assoc. Friedman & Assocs., Dallas, 1995—; speaker on Tex. Ins. Laws, 1992-93. Vol., speakers bur., Clinton & Gore Campaign, Dallas, 1992. Mem. Tex. State Bar Coll. Episcopalian. Avocations: old house remodeling, reading, basketball. General corporate, Labor, Contracts commercial. Office: Friedman & Assocs 570 Preston Commons W 8117 Preston Rd Dallas TX 75225-6332

**ENGLAND, JOHN MELVIN,** lawyer, clergyman; b. June 29, 1932; s. John Marcus and Frances Dorothy (Brown) E.; m. Jane Cantrell, Aug. 2, 1953; children: Kathryn Elizabeth, Janette Evelyn, John William, Kenneth Paul, James Andrew, Samuel Robert. Student, Ga. State U., 1951-53; JD, U. Ga., 1956; BD magna cum laude with honors Theology, Columbia Theol. Sem., Decatur, Ga., 1964. Bar: Ga. 1959, U.S. Dist. Ct. (no. dist.) Ga. 1967, U.S. Ct. Mil. Appeals 1976, U.S. Ct. Appeals (5th cir.) 1967, U.S. Ct. Appeals (11th cir.) 1981, U.S. Supreme Ct. 1977, U.S. Dist. Ct. (mid. dist.) Ga. 1986, U.S. Dist. Ct. (so. dist.) Ga. 1991, U.S. Dist. Ct. (no. dist.) Tex. 1991; ordained to ministry Presbyn. Ch., 1964. Spl. agt. FBI, Washington, 1956-57, Indpls., 1957-59, Charlotte, N.C., 1959, Greenville, S.C., 1959-60; student supply pastor Bethel and Buford Presbyn. Chs., Atlanta, 1960-63; pastor Mullins (S.C.) Presbyn. Ch., 1964-67; asst. dist. atty. Fulton County, Ga., 1967-75; sr. ptnr. England and Weller, Atlanta, 1975-88, England, Wearer & Kytle, 1988-94, England & McKnight, 1994—; legal seminar lectr. and spkr. throughout the country under auspices of Christian orgns.; gal. pros. for gov. Ga., 1976-79; spl. cons. on appellate reform Supreme Ct. Ga., 1979-80; state bar rep. to Superior Ct. Uniform Rules Com. Coun. Superior Ct. Judges, 1984, 93. Elder, tchr., evangelism coord. Presbyn. Ch. USA; chmn. Christian Bus. Men's Coms. of U.S.A., Atlanta, 1971-73, chmn. internat. conv., Atlanta, 1979, bd. dirs., 1971-81. Mem. ABA, ATLA, State Bar Ga., Atlanta Bar Assn., Lawyers Club Atlanta, Ga. Trial Lawyers Assn., Nat. Assn. Criminal Def. Lawyers, Ga. Assn. Criminal Def. Lawyers, North Fulton Bar Assn. General civil litigation, Criminal, Personal injury. Office: England & McKnight 9040 Roswell Rd Ste 410 Atlanta GA 30350-1863

**ENGLAND, KATHLEEN JANE,** lawyer; b. Boston, July 29, 1953; d. Frank W. and Kathleen E. (Van DenHouten) E. BA cum laude, Mich. State U., 1975; postgrad., U. Exeter, summer 1977; JD, Suffolk U., Boston, 1978. Bar: Mass. 1979, Nev. 1979, U.S. Dist. Ct. Nev. 1980, U.S. Ct. Appeals (9th cir.) 1980. Intern Middlesex Dist. Atty. Bur., Cambridge, Mass., 1978; law clk. Withington, Cross, Park & Groden, Boston, 1976-78; law clk. City of Las Vegas, Nev., 1978-79, dep. city atty., 1979-82; assoc. Vargas & Bartlett, Las Vegas, 1982-89; ptnr. Combs & England, Las Vegas, 1989-93; pres. England & Assocs., Las Vegas, 1994—; bd. dirs., legal counsel Planned Parenthood So. Nev., Las Vegas; mem. Nev. Supreme Ct. Task Force on Gender Bias, 1987—; bd. dirs. Nat. Conf. Women's Bar Assn., 1992—; vice chair, chair character and fitness com. State Bar of Nev., 1993—. Contbr. articles to profl. jours. Bd. dirs. Nat. Kidney Found. of So. Nev., Las Vegas, 1983, U. Nev., Las Vegas Womens Ctr.; active Amnesty Internat., Campaign for Choice, 1990, Nev. Women's Lobby, chair Ethics Review Bd. City Las Vegas, 1994-97. Recipient Woman of Yr. award Desert Sands Bus. & Profl. Women's Club, 1993; named Disting. Woman of So. Nev., 1992, Woman of Achievement, Legal Women's Coun., C. of C., 1994, Women Helping Women award Soroptimist Internat. of Greater Las Vegas, 1995. Mem. ABA, AAUW, So. Nev. Assn. Women Attys., Nev. Inn of Ct. (chmn. programs 1992-95), State Bar Nev. (founder chair young lawyers sect.). Avocations: travel, reading, horseback riding. Federal civil litigation, State civil litigation, Labor. Office: England & Assocs 700 S 3d St Las Vegas NV 89101

**ENGLAND, LYNNE LIPTON,** lawyer, speech pathologist, audiologist; b. Youngstown, Ohio, Apr. 11, 1949; d. Sanford Y. and Sally (Kentor) Lipton; m. Richard E. England, Mar. 5, 1977. BA, U. Mich., 1970; MA, Temple U., 1972; JD, Tulane U., 1981. Bar: Fla. 1982, U.S. Dist. Ct. (mid. dist.) Fla. 1982, U.S. Ct. Appeals (11th cir.) 1982; cert. clin. competence in speech pathology and audiology. Speech pathologist Rockland Children's Hosp., N.Y., 1972-74, Jefferson Parish Sch., Gretna, La., 1977-81; audiologist Rehab. Inst. Chgo., 1974-76; assoc. Trenam, Simmons, Kemker, Scharf, Barkin, Frye & O'Neill, Tampa, Fla., 1981-84; asst. U.S. atty. for Middle Dist. Fla. Tampa, 1984-87; asst. U.S. trustee, 1987-91; ptnr. Stearns, Weaver, Miller, Weissler, Alhadeff & Sitterson, P.A., 1991-94, Prevatt, England & Taylor, Tampa, Fla., 1994—. Editor Fla. Bankruptcy Casenotes, 1983. Recipient clin. assistantship Temple U., 1972-74. Mem. ATLA, Comml. Law League, Am. Speech and Hearing Assn., Tampa Bay Bankruptcy Bar Assn. (dir. 1990-95), Am. Bankruptcy Inst., Fla. Bar Assn., Hillsborough County Bar Assn., Order of Coif. Jewish. Avocations: tennis, golf, playing French horn and piano. Bankruptcy. Office: PO Box 2920 1 Tampa City Ctr Ste 1700 Tampa FL 33602-5843

**ENGLAND, RUDY ALAN,** lawyer; b. Snyder, Tex., Sept. 29, 1959; s. Bud and Imo D. (Witcher) E.; m. Zenda Cherie Ball, Mar. 24, 1978 (div. June 1988); children: Aaron, Kyle; m. Susan Ann Steadman, Mar. 10, 1990 (div. Dec. 1998). AA summa cum laude, Western Tex. Coll., 1979; BS summa cum laude, U. Houston, 1986, JD, 1989. Bar: Tex. 1990, U.S. Dist. Ct. (so. dist.) Tex. 1990, U.S. Dist. Ct. (no., ea. and we. dists.) Tex. 1994, U.S. Ct. Appeals (5th cir.) 1990. Adminstrv. asst. Tartan Oil & Gas, Houston, 1981-82; div. order analyst Moran Exploration, Inc., Houston, 1982-83; sr. lease analyst Integrated Energy Inc., Houston, 1983-84; landman Cambridge Royalty Co., Houston, 1984-85; supr. div. orders MCO Resources Inc., Houston, 1985-87; assoc. Hutcheson & Grundy, L.L.P., Houston, 1989-96, ptnr., 1997-98; of counsel Haynes and Boone LLP, Houston, 1998—. Mem. Houston Law Rev., 1988-89, bd. dirs. Houston Law Rev. Alumni Assn., 1996-97, v.p. 1997-98, pres., 1998-99. Mem. taxi squad U. Houston, 1991; mgr. Little League Baseball, 1993-96; bd. dirs. Braeburn Little League, 1995-96. Mem. Am. Assn. Profl. Landmen, Coll. of State Bar, State Bar Tex. (professionalism com. 1996—), Houston Bar Assn. (lawyers for literacy com. 1991-92, lawyers in pub. schs. com. 1995-98), Tex. Young Lawyers Assn. (bd. dirs. 1993-95, liaison to Tex. lawyer's creed com. of State Bar 1994-95, co-chmn. profl. and grievance awareness com. 1994-95, chmn. profl. com. 1993-94, mem. legis. com. 1990-93, vice chmn. legis. com. 1993-94, mem. local affiliates com. 1991-92, dropout prevention com. 1991-92, Tex. Young Lawyer Assn. sect. Tex. Bar Jour. com., 1991-93, profl. and ethics com. 1995-96, outstanding young lawyer com. 1995-96), Houston Young Lawyers Assn. (bd. dirs. 1991-93, sec. 1993-94, chmn. professionalism com. 1991-92, chmn. Law Day com. 1992-93, award achievement com. 1993-94, chmn. ops. com. 1993-94, outstanding young lawyers com. 1991-92, Liberty Bell award com. 1992-93), Houston Prodrs.' Forum, U. Houston Law Ctr. Alumni Assn. (bd. dirs. 1997-98), Cougar Cager Club. Mem. Unity Ch. of Christianity. Avocations: golf, snow skiing. General civil litigation, Oil, gas, and mineral, Securities. Office: Haynes & Boone LLP 1000 Louisiana St Ste 4300 Houston TX 77002-5020

**ENGLE, DAVID SCOTT,** lawyer; b. Normundy, Mo., Oct. 6, 1963; m. Diana E. Peterson Engle, Aug. 12, 1989; children: Kayla Breanne, Kaitlyn Jo, David Austin. BA, Cen. Wash. U., 1989; JD, Thomas Cooley Law Sch., 1992. Bar: Wash. 1992, U.S. Dist. Ct. (we. dist.) Wash. 1992, U.S. Dist. Ct. (ea. dist.) Wash. 1993, U.S. Dist. Ct. (no. dist.) Calif. 1994, U.S. Ct. Appeals (9th cir.) 1994. Assoc. Am. Bankruptcy Clinic, Tacoma, 1992-93, Law Offices of Leon Najman, Seattle, 1993-94; assoc., mng. atty. Hessinger & Assocs. of Wash. PC, Kent, 1994-95; assoc. Law Offices of John Graham, Bellevue, Wash., 1995-97, Goldberg, Fancher & Jones PLLC, Seattle, 1997-98, Dohrety & Fleury LLC, Tacoma, 1998-99. Family and matrimonial, Bankruptcy, Personal injury. Office: PO Box 1294 Maple Valley WA 98038-1294

**ENGLERT, ROY THEODORE, JR.,** lawyer; b. Alexandria, Va., Dec. 5, 1958; s. Roy Theodore and Helen Frances (Wiggs) E. AB, Princeton U., 1978; JD, Harvard U., 1981. Ct. law clk. U.S. Ct. Appeals-D.C. Cir., Washington, 1981-82; assoc. Wilmer, Cutler & Pickering, Washington, 1982-86; asst. to the solicitor gen. U.S. Dept. Justice, Washington, 1986-89; assoc. Mayer, Brown & Platt, Washington, 1989-90, ptnr., 1991—. Tech. official judo Centennial Olympic Games, Atlanta, 1996. Presbyterian. Avocation: judo. Appellate, Administrative and regulatory, Antitrust. Home: 411 S Pitt St Alexandria VA 22314-3713 Office: Mayer Brown & Platt 1909 K St NW Washington DC 20006-1101

**ENGLISH, CAROLINE TURNER,** lawyer, educator; b. Rochester, N.Y., Aug. 18, 1970; d. Charles Shoemaker and Marian Taglang Turner; m. Mark English, Aug. 6, 1994. BA, Denison U., 1992; JD, George Washington U., 1996. Bar: Va. 1996, U.S. Ct. Fed. Claims 1997, D.C. 1999. Assoc. Arent Fox Kintner Plotkin & Kahn, Washington, 1996—. Mem. Va. Trial Lawyers Assn. Democrat. General civil litigation, Criminal, Bankruptcy. Office: Arent Fox Kintner Plotkin & Kahn 1050 Connecticut Ave NW Ste 500 Washington DC 20036-5339

**ENGLISH, CHARLES ROYAL,** lawyer; b. Santa Monica, Calif., Apr. 9, 1938; s. Charles James and Antoinette Frieda (Schindler) E.; m. Marylyn Gray, Sept. 6, 1969; children: Mitchell Lloyd, Charles James, Julia Catherine. Santa Monica City Coll., 1958; BS, UCLA, 1961, UCLA, 1965. Bar: Calif. 1966. Sole practice Santa Monica, 1967; with L.A. County Pub. Defender's Office, 1967-78, sr. trial dep., 1978; ptnr. Chaleff, English and Catalano and predecessor Lafaille, Chaleff & English, Santa Monica, 1978-97; propr. Law Office of Charles R. English, 1997-98, English & Gold, Santa Monica, 1998—; lectr. in field. With USAR, 1961-67. Mem. ABA (criminal justice sect coun. 1992, chmn. standards com. 1997-98), Santa Monica Bar, State Bar Calif., Criminal Cts. Bar Assn., Bur. Automotive Repair, L.A. County Bar Assn. (trustee 1980-83, pres. found 1990-91), UCLA Law Alumni Assn. (pres. 1980), Chancery Club (treas. 1997, sec. 1998), Olde Bailey. Criminal, Juvenile. Home and Office: 1337 Ocean Ave Santa Monica CA 90401-1029

**ENGLISH, JOHN DWIGHT,** lawyer; b. Evanston, Ill., Mar. 28, 1949; s. John Francis English and Mary Faye (Taylor) Butler; m. Claranne Kay Lundeen, Apr. 22, 1972; children: Jennifer A., Katharine V., Margaret E. BA, Drake U., 1971; JD, Loyola U., 1976. Bar: Ill. 1976, U.S. Dist. Ct. (no. dist.) Ill. 1976, U.S. Tax Ct. 1977. Assoc. Bentley DuCanto Silvestri & Forkins, Chgo., 1976-79; ptnr. Silvestri Mahoney English & Zdeb, Chgo., 1979-81; assoc. Coffield Ungaretti & Harris, Chgo., 1981-83, ptnr., 1983—; instr. estate planning Loyola U., Chgo., 1982-87. Bd. dirs. Prince of Peace Luth. Sch., Chgo., 1977-83, Bethesda Home for the Aged, Chgo., 1988-89, Luth. Family Mission, Chgo., 1985-91; alderman Park Ridge (Ill.) City Coun., 1991-95. Mem. Ill. State Bar Assn., Chgo. Bar Assn. (chmn. div. II probate practice com.), Phi Beta Kappa. Lutheran. Estate planning, Probate, Estate taxation. Home: 631 Wisner St Park Ridge IL 60068-3428 Office: Ungaretti & Harris 3500 Three 1st Nat Bank Plz Chicago IL 60602

**ENGLISH, R(OBERT) BRADFORD,** marshal; b. Jefferson City, Mo., Apr. 12, 1952; s. Robert Deaton and Peggy Louise (Dickson) E.; m. Marsha Lynn Mills, Mar. 17, 1979; children: Lindsay Renee, Amy Leigh. BS in Criminal Justice, Lincoln U., 1982; MPA, U. Mo., 1984. Residential juvenile counselor Cole County Juvenile Ctr., Jefferson City, Mo., 1972-74; patrolman Jefferson City Police Dept., 1975-76, detective, 1976-78; comdr. Mo. Capitol Police, Jefferson City, 1978-79, police chief, 1979-94; marshal U.S. Marshal Svc., Kansas City, Mo., 1994—; chmn. ct. security com. U.S. Dist. Ct. (we. dist.) Mo., Kansas City, 1995—. Chmn. bd. dirs. Capitol Area Cmty. Svc. Agy., Jefferson City, 1994. Named Statesman of Month, News Tribune Co., 1994. Mem. Am. Soc. Indsl. Security (cert. protection profl.), Internat. Assn. Chiefs of Police, Internat. Assn. Bomb Technicians and Investigators, Masons. Democrat. Avocations: golf, scuba diving, walking, weight lifting. Office: US Marshal Svc 811 Grand Blvd Ste 509 Kansas City MO 64106-1904

**ENGLISH, WILLIAM DESHAY,** lawyer; b. Piedmont, Calif., Dec. 25, 1924; s. Munro and Mabel (Michener) English; m. Nancy Ames, Apr. 7, 1956; children: Catherine, Barbara, Susan, Stephen. AB in Econs., U. Calif., Berkeley, 1948; JD, U. Calif., 1951. Bar: Calif. 1952, D.C. 1972. Trial atty, spl. asst. to atty. gen. U.S. Dept. Justice, Washington, 1953-55; sr. atty. AEC, Washington, 1955-62; legal advisor U.S. Mission to European Communities, Brussels, 1962-64; asst. gen. counsel internat. matters COMSAT, Washington, 1965-73; counsel Internat. Telecommunication Satellite Orgn., 1965-73; v.p., gen. counsel, dir. COMSAT Gen. Corp., 1973-76; sr. v.p. legal and govtl. affairs Satellite Bus. Systems, McLean, Va., 1976-86; v.p., gen. counsel Satellite Transponder Leasing Corp. (IBM), McLean, 1986-87; pvt. practice, McLean, 1987—; counsel Am. Space Transp. Assn., 1987-93, Washington Space Bus. Roundtable; gen. counsel Iridium, LLC, 1992-96, spl. counsel, 1996—. With USAAF, 1943-45. Decorated air medal. Fellow Coun. on Econ. Regulation, 1985-91; mem. ABA, AIAA (chmn. com. legal aspects aeronautics and astronautics, chmn. allocation space launch risks subcom. 1987, chmn. orbital debris legal subcom.), Am. Competitive Telecommunications Assn. (bd. dirs. 1976-84, pres. 1983), D.C. Bar Assn., Fed. Communications Bar Assn., State Bar Calif., Fgn. Policy Discussion Group, Metropolitan. Administrative and regulatory, Private international, Legislative. Home: 7420 Exeter Rd Bethesda MD 20814-2352

**ENGLISH, WOODROW DOUGLAS,** lawyer; b. San Antonio, Dec. 1, 1941; s. Woodie Douglas Jr. and June Louise (Wasik) E.; m. Marcia Anne Mathwig, Dec. 19, 1969 (div. Aug. 1981); children: Kristina Renee, David Douglas; m. Carol Jordan, July 11, 1987; children: Leanne Alexander Cassidy, Lisa Alexander Cook. BS in Physics, Trinity U., 1967; JD, Western State U., 1981. Bar: Calif. 1989, U.S. Patent Office 1982, U.S. Supreme Ct. 1992. Sales engr. Mfrs. Rep., Seattle, 1972-75; real estate salesperson, broker Sherwood & Roberts Realtors & Coldwell Banker, Seattle, 1975-78; safety engr. Boeing Aerospace, Seattle, 1978-79; ins. agt., broker Farmers Ins. Group, San Diego, 1979-81; U.S. patent agt. Dept. Def., China Lake, Calif., 1981-87; corp. counsel Del Mar Avionics, Irvine, Calif., 1987-97; pvt. practice Ventura, Calif., 1991—; real estate broker, Ventura, ins. broker, Ventura. Capt. USAF, 1961-65. Mem. Masons, Shriners, Elks, Kiwanis, Am. Legion, Sigma Pi Sigma, Phi Alpha Delta, Nu Beta Epsilon. Republican. Avocation: flying. Intellectual property, Trademark and copyright, Patent. Home: 1215 Lost Point Ln Oxnard CA 93030-6770 Office: County Sq Profl Offices 674 County Square Dr Ventura CA 93003-5454

**ENGORON, ARTHUR FREDERICKS,** law clerk; b. N.Y.C., May 22, 1949; s. Malcolm Wilson and Edna June (Fredericks) E.; 1 child, Ian Abbie Intrator. BA, Columbia Coll., 1972; JD, NYU, 1979. Bar: N.Y., U.S. Dist. Ct. (so. and ea. dists.) N.Y. 1980, U.S. Supreme Ct. 1996. Assoc. Olwine, Connelly, Chase, O'Donnell & Weyher, N.Y.C., 1979-81, Pryor, Coshman, Sherman & Flynn, N.Y.C., 1981-83; prin. law clk. Martin Schoenfeld N.Y. State Supreme Ct., N.Y.C., 1991—. Author: Manual for Small Claims Arbitrators, 1998. Newsletter editor Park River Ind. Dems., N.Y.C., 1994-96. Mem. Assn. of the Bar of the City of N.Y. (chairperson civil ct. com.), Assn. Small Claims Arbitrators (2d v.p.). Democrat. Avocations: politics, computers, chess, art, physical fitness. Home: 255 W 84th St Apt 11E New York NY 10024-4325 Office: NY State Supreme Ct 60 Centre St Rm 517 New York NY 10007-1402

**ENGWALL, GREGORY BOND,** lawyer; b. Sioux City, Iowa, May 23, 1950; s. Glen Leslie and Maxine Lillian (Bond) E.; m. Jeanne Ann Van Drasek, July 22, 1977; children: Thomas Gregory, Daniel Henry, Laura Ann. BA, Gustavus Adolphus Coll., 1972; JD, U. Minn., 1975. Bar: Minn. 1975. Assoc. Larson Law Office, Winthrop, Minn., 1975-94; sole practitioner Engwall Law Office, Winthrop, 1995—. Mem. Minn. State Bar Assn., Guild of St. Ansgar, K.C., Mensa, Iota Delta Gamma. Republican. Roman Catholic. Probate, Real property, General practice. Home: 1690 S Grade Rd SW Hutchinson MN 55350-6728 Office: Engwall Law Office 110 E 2d St PO Box D Winthrop MN 55396

**ENIS, THOMAS JOSEPH,** lawyer; b. Maryville, Mo., July 2, 1937; s. Herbert William and Loretta M. (Fitzmaurice) E.; m. Harolyn Gray Westhoff, July 24, 1971; children: Margaret Elizabeth, David Richard, John Anthony, Brian Edward. B.S., Rockhurst Coll., 1958; J.D., U. Mo.-Columbia, 1966. Bar: Mo. 1966, Okla. 1973. Law clk. U.S. Dist. Ct. (we. dist.) Mo., 1966-67; prof. coll. law U. Okla., Norman, 1967-74, assoc. dean, 1970-74; atty. Southwestern Bell Tel. Co., Oklahoma City, 1974-79; ptnr. Bulla and Enis, Oklahoma City, 1979-81; pvt. practice Law Offices of Thomas J. Enis, Oklahoma City, 1981-87; of counsel Fellers, Snider, Blankenship, Bailey & Tippens, Oklahoma City, 1988-89, ptnr., 1990—; lectr. Okla. Bar Rev., 1968-96, 98—. Bd. dirs. Okla. Symphony Orch., 1978-88, legal counsel, 1981-88; spl. counsel Okla. Ethics Commn., 1986-88; trustee Okla. County Law Libr., 1989-91; Judge Temp. Ct. of Appeals Okla., 1991-92. Mem. ABA, Okla. Bar Assn., Mo. Bar Assn., Oklahoma County Bar Assn., Order of Coif, Phi Delta Phi. Republican. Roman Catholic. Editor-in-chief Mo. Law Rev., 1965-66. Oil, gas, and mineral, Environmental, General civil litigation. Home: 3016 Stoneybrook Rd Oklahoma City OK 73120-5716 Office: 100 N Broadway Ave Ste 1700 Oklahoma City OK 73102-8805

**ENNIS, EDGAR WILLIAM, JR.,** lawyer; b. Macon, Ga., May 20, 1945; s. Edgar W. and Nelle (Branan) E.; m. Judith Anne Godfrey, June 29, 1974; children: William, Branan. BS in Engring. Sci., USAF Acad., Colorado Springs, Colo., 1967; JD, U. Ga., 1971. Bar: Ga. 1971. Commd. 2d lt. USAF, 1967, advanced through ranks to capt., 1970, resigned, 1975; asst. U.S. atty. U.S. Atty.'s Office-Mid. Dist. of Ga., Macon, 1975-88; U.S. atty. U.S. Dept. Justice, Macon, 1988-93; of counsel Haynsworth, Baldwin, Johnson & Harper, Macon, 1993-97; ptnr. Haynsworth, Baldwin, Johnson & Greaves LLC, Macon, 1998-99, Constangy, Brooks & Smith LLC, Macon, 1999—. Labor, Federal civil litigation, Environmental. Office: Constangy Brooks & Smith LLC 577 Mulberry St Ste 710 Macon GA 31201-8588

**ENOCH, CRAIG TRIVELY,** state supreme court justice; b. Wichita, Kans., Apr. 3, 1950; s. Donald Kirk and Margery (Trively) E.; m. Kathryn Stafford Barker, Aug. 2, 1975. BA, So. Meth. U., 1972, JD, 1975; LLM, U. Va., 1992. Bar: Tex. 1975, U.S. Dist. Ct. (no. dist.) Tex. 1976, U.S. Ct. Appeals (5th cir.) 1979. Assoc. Burford, Ryburn & Ford, Dallas, 1975-77; ptnr. Moseley, Jones, Enoch & Martin, Dallas, 1977-81; judge 101st Dist. Ct., Dallas, 1981-87; chief justice Tex. Ct. Appeals (5th dist.), 1987-92; justice Tex. Supreme Ct., Austin, 1993—. Mem. exec. bd. Sch. Law So. Meth. U., 1990—; chmn. Canterbury House Collegiate Chapel, Dallas, 1982-84; chmn. subcom. Scouting for the Handicapped, Circle 10 Coun., Dallas, 1982-84; exec. vice chmn. track and field events area 10 Spl. Olympics, Dallas, 1984-85. Capt. USAFR, 1973-81. Recipient Disting. Alumni award for judicial svc. So. Meth. U. Sch. of Law, 1999. Fellow Am. Bar Found., Tex. State Bar Found., Dallas Bar Found.; mem. ABA (mem. exec. bd. appellate judges conf. jud. divsn.), Am. Law Inst., Dallas Bar Assn. Republican. Episcopalian. Home: 2614 Maria Anna Rd Austin TX 78703-1656

**ENRIGHT, THOMAS MICHAEL,** lawyer; b. Chgo., Feb. 28, 1954; s. George F. and Loraine Marie (Dunn) E.; m. Susan Marie Cartee; children: Matthew, Meghan. BS, Ill. State U., 1976; JD, John Marshall Law Sch., 1980. Bar: Ill. 1980, Fla. 1989, U.S. Dist. Ct. (no. dist.) Ill. 1980, U.S. Ct. Appeals D.C. 1990. Instr. St. Xavier Coll., Chgo., 1984—; atty., ptnr. Parrillo Weiss & O'Halloran, Chgo., 1980—; instr. St. Xavier Coll. Graham Sch. Mgmt., Chgo., 1989—. Mem. Ill. State Bar Assn., Chgo. Bar Assn., Fla. Bar Assn., Ill. Assn. Def. Trial Counsel. Avocations: scuba diving, boating. General civil litigation, Personal injury, Insurance. Office: Parrillo Weiss & O'Halloran 77 W Wacker Dr 50th Fl Chicago IL 60601-1604

**ENRIGHT, WILLIAM BENNER,** judge; b. N.Y.C., July 12, 1925; s. Arthur Joseph and Anna Beatrice (Plante) E.; m. Bette Lou Card, Apr. 13, 1951; children—Kevin A., Kimberly A., Kerry K. BA, Dartmouth, 1947; LLB, Loyola U. at L.A., 1950. Bar: Calif. 1951; diplomate: Am. Bd. Trial Advs. Dep. dist. atty. San Diego County, 1951-54; ptnr. Enright, Levitt, Knutson & Tobin, San Diego, 1954-72; judge U.S. Dist. Ct. (so. dist.) Calif., San Diego, 1972-90, sr. judge, 1990—; Mem. adv. bd. Joint Legis. Com. for Revision Penal Code, 1970-72, Calif. Bd. Legal Specialization, 1970-72; mem. Jud. Council, 1972; Bd. dirs. Defenders, 1965-72, pres., 1972. Served as ensign USNR, 1943-46. Recipient Honor award San Diego County Bar, 1970; Extraordinary Service to Legal Professions award Mcpl. Ct. San Diego Jud. Dist., 1971. Fellow Am. Coll. Trial Lawyers, Am. Bar Found.; mem. ABA, San Diego County Bar Assn. (dir. 1963-65, pres. 1965), State Bar Calif. (gov. 1967-70, v.p. 1970, exec. com. law in a free soc. 1970—), Dartmouth Club San Diego, Am. Judicature Soc., Alpha Sigma Nu, Phi Delta Phi. Club: Rotarian. Office: US Dist Ct 4145 US Courthouse 940 Front St San Diego CA 92101-8994

**ENSLEN, RICHARD ALAN,** federal judge; b. Kalamazoo, May 28, 1931; s. Ehrman Thrasher and Pauline Mabel (Dragoo) E.; m. Pamela Gayle Chapman, Nov. 2, 1985; children—David, Susan, Sandra, Thomas, Janet, Joseph, Gennady. Student, Kalamazoo Coll., 1949-51, Western Mich. U., 1955; LL.B., Wayne State U., 1958; LL.M., U. Va., 1986. Bar: Mich. 1958, U.S. Dist. Ct. (we. dist.) Mich. 1960, U.S. Ct. Appeals (6th cir.) 1971, U.S. Ct. Appeals (4th cir.) 1975, U.S. Supreme Ct 1975. Mem. firm Stratton, Wise, Early & Starbuck, Kalamazoo, 1958-60, Bauckham & Enslen, Kalamazoo, 1960-64, Howard & Howard, Kalamazoo, 1970-76, Enslen & Schma, Kalamazoo, 1977-79; dir. Peace Corps. Costa Rica, 1965-67; judge

Mich. Dist. Ct., 1968-70; U.S. dist. judge Kalamazoo, 1979—, chief judge, 1995—; mem. faculty Western Mich. U., 1961-62, Nazareth Coll., 1974-75; adj. prof. polit. sci. Western Mich. U., 1982—. Co-author: The Constitution Law Dictionary: Volume One, Individual Rights, 1985; Volume Two, Governmental Powers, 1987, Constitutional Deskbook: Individual Rights, 1987, (with Mary Bedikian and Pamela Enslen) Michigan Practice, Alternative Dispute Resolution, 1998. Served with USAF, 1951-54. Recipient Disting. Alumni award Wayne State Law Sch., 1980, Disting. Alumni award Western Mich. U., 1982; Outstanding Practical Achievement award Ctr. Pub. Resources, 1984; award for Excellence and Innovation in Alternative Dispute Resolution and Dispute Mgmt., Legal Program; Jewel Corp. scholar, 1956-57; Lampson McElhorne scholar, 1957. Mem. ABA (standing com. on dispute resolution 1983-90), Mich. Bar Assn., Am. Judicature Soc. (bd. dirs. 1983-85), Sixth Cir. Jud. Coun. Office: US Dist Ct 410 W Michigan Ave Kalamazoo MI 49007-3757

**ENWALL, MICHAEL R.,** lawyer; b. Greeley, Colo., May 16, 1942; s. Ivan Edward and Dorothy Belle (Iveland) E.; m. July 20, 1964 (div. Sept. 1969); 1 child, Timothy Sean. BA, U. Colo., 1965, JD, 1969. Bar: Colo., U.S. Dist. Ct. (ea. dist.) Tex. Law clk. U.S. Dist. Ct., Denver, 1969-70; atty. Metro Denver Legal Aid, Denver, 1970-74, Colo. Pub. Defender, Greeley, 1979-77; pvt. practice Boulder, 1977-82, 87—; judge Boulder Dist. Ct., 1982-87; instr. Sch. of Law U. Colo., Boulder, 1986-97; pres. Colo. Criminal Def. Bar, Denver, 1991-92. Recipiednt Jonathan Olom award Colo. Criminal Def. Bar, 1998. Democrat. Avocations: bicycling. Criminal, General civil litigation, Family and matrimonial. Office: Enwall & Grant LLC 720 Pearl St Boulder CO 80302-5006

**ENZEL, DAVID H.,** lawyer; b. Pitts., Jan. 21, 1955; s. Abram and Dora Enzel. BA, U. Pitts., 1976, JD, 1979. Bar: Pa. 1979, D.C. 1981. Chief atty. for fair housing enforcement HUD, Washington, 1979-91; spl. counsel Office of Thrift Supervision, Washington, 1991—. Mem. Phi Beta Kappa. Avocation: running. Office: Office Thrift Supervision 1700 G St NW Washington DC 20552-0004

**ENZLER, SHERRY A.,** lawyer; b. St. Louis, June 19, 1954; d. Hugh Joseph and Doreen Joan E. BA, U. Minn., 1976; MPA, U. So. Calif., 1978; JD, William Mitchell Coll. Law, 1985. Spl. asst. to asst. sec. U.S. Dept. Interior, Washington, 1976-79; program evaluation specialist Minn. Legis. Auditor, St. Paul, 1979-83; asst. atty. gen. Minn. Atty. Gen.'s Office, St. Paul, 1985-97; atty. Doherty, Rumble & Butler, St. Paul, 1997—; adj. prof. William Mitchell Coll. Law, St. Paul, 1990-93, 95—. Mem. Minn. Women Lawyers, Minn. State Bar Assn. (coun. 1994-98, diverity com. 1996—). Office: Doherty Rumble & Butler 30 E 7th St 2800 Minn World Trade Ctr Saint Paul MN 55101

**EORY, JOHN STEPHEN,** lawyer; b. New Brunswick, N.J., Nov. 26, 1947; s. Stephen and Margaret (Park) E.; m. Jennifer Eory, July 11, 1993; children: Katherine, Stephen. BA, Temple U., 1970, JD, 1975. Bar: N.J. 1975, U.S. Supreme Ct. 1980. Jud. law clk. Camden, N.J., 1975-76; assoc. Forkin Segal & Dugan, Cherry Hill, N.J., 1976-85, Parker McCay & Criscuolo, Marlton, N.J., 1985-89; ptnr. Klein Cettci Italden & Eory, Haddonfield, N.J., 1989-92, Ulrichsen Amarel & Eory, Skillman, N.J., 1992—; instr. N.J. Inst. Cont. Legal Edn., New Brunswick, N.J., 1993—. TV panelist Rutgers Forum, 1993. With U.S. Army, 1970-72. Fellow Am. Acad. Matrimonial Lawyers; mem. ABA. Avocations: music, literature. Family and matrimonial. Office: 47 Tamarack Cir Skillman NJ 08558-2019

**EPPERSON, JOEL RODMAN,** lawyer; b. Miami, Fla., Aug. 29, 1945; s. John Rodman and Ann Louise (Barrs) E.; m. Gretchen Jean Meyer, Apr. 16, 1968; children: Joel Rodman, David Michael, Sandra Elizabeth. BS, U. South Fla., 1967; JD, South Tex. Coll., 1976. Bar: Fla. 1976, U.S. Dist. Ct. (mid. dist.) Fla. 1976, U.S. Ct. Appeals (5th cir.) 1976, U.S. Supreme Ct. 1979, U.S. Ct. Appeals (11th cir.) 1991. Asst. states atty. State of Fla., Tampa, 1976-79; ptnr. Bryant & Epperson, 1979-86, Assocs. & Bruce L. Scheiner, Ft. Myers, Fla., 1987-88; ptnr. Epperson & Stahl, Ft. Myers, 1988-90, Epperson & DeMinico, Tampa/Ft. Myers, 1991-92, Epperson & Assocs., P.A., Tampa/Ft. Myers, 1993—. Served to capt. USMC, 1968-72. Mem. ABA, ATLA, Acad. Fla. Trial Lawyers Assn., Lee County Bar Assn., Hillsborough County Bar Assn. Democrat. Personal injury. Home: 1306 Anglers Ln Lutz FL 33549-5040 also: Epperson & Assocs 1719 W Kennedy Blvd Tampa FL 33606-1643

**EPPERSON, KRAETTLI QUYNTON,** lawyer, educator; b. Ft. Eustis, Va., May 2, 1949; s. Dimpster Eugene Sr. and Helen Walter (Davidson) E.; m. Kay Lawrence, Aug. 22, 1970; children: Kraettli L., Kristin J., Kevin Q., Keith W. BA in Polit. Sci., U. Okla., 1971; MS in Urban and Policy Scis., SUNY, Stony Brook, 1974; JD, Oklahoma City U., 1978. Bar: Okla. 1979, U.S. Dist. Ct. (we. dist.) Okla. 1984, Fed. Claims Ct. 1997. Urban planner Gov.'s Office of Community Affairs and Planning, Oklahoma City, 1974-75; adminstr. of pub. transp. planning Okla. Dept. of Transp., Oklahoma City, 1975-79; title examiner Lawyers Title of Oklahoma City, Inc., 1979-80; gen. counsel, v.p. Am. First Land Title Ins. Co., Oklahoma City, 1980-82; assoc. Ferguson & Litchfield, Oklahoma City, 1982-85; assoc. Ames & Ashabranner, Oklahoma City, 1986-88, ptnr., 1989-93; ptnr. Cook & Epperson, Oklahoma City, 1994-97; sole practitioner Oklahoma City, 1997—; adj. prof. law Okla. land titles Oklahoma City U., 1982—; instr. real property Okla. Bar Rev., 1998—; instr. real property titles Grad. Realtors Inst., 1998—. Contbr. articles to profl. jours. Asst. scoutmaster Boy Scouts Am., Oklahoma City, 1984-88, 93—, asst. cubmaster, 1989-90, cubmaster, 1990-91, webelos leader, 1991-93, 94-95. 2d lt. USAR, 1971. Mem. ABA (vice chmn. conveyancing com. 1987-88, 93-94, chmn. 1991-93, chmn. state customs and practice subcom. 1987-88, project chmn. title exam. standards 1988—), Am. Land Title Assn. (legis. com. 1981-82, jud. com. 1981-82), Okla. Bar Assn. (real property sect. 1979—, dir. 1982-88, 94-95, chmn. 1985-86, project chmn. Okla. Title Exam. Standards Handbook project 1982-85, mem. title exam. standards com. 1980—, chmn. 1992—, legis. liaison com. 1986-92, co-chmn. abstracting standards com. 1982-84), Oklahoma City Real Property Lawyers Assn. (dir. 1985-91, pres. 1990-91), Oklahoma City Comml. Law Attys. Assn. Republican. Episcopalian. Avocations: skeet, storytelling, camping. Real property, General civil litigation, Land use and zoning (including planning). Home: 3029 Rock Ridge Ct Oklahoma City OK 73120-5731 Office: 5901 N Western Ave Ste 200 Oklahoma City OK 73118-1235

**EPPES, SHARON MARIE,** lawyer; b. Wilmington, Del., Dec. 31, 1964; d. James Edward and Doris Marie Lister; m. David Charles Eppes, Sept. 22, 1990 (div. Aug. 1996); children: Marissa Lee, Cara Marie. BA, U. Del., 1987; JD, Widener U., 1990. Bar: Del. 1992, U.S. Dist. Ct. Del. 1992. Instr. Del. Tech. and C.C., Newark, 1989-92; assoc. Becker & Becker, P.A., Wilmington, Del., 1990—; speaker Nat. Bus. Inst., Wilmington, 1998, 99. V.p. Dewey Beach Civic League, Del., 1994-96. Mem. Del. State Bar Assn., Elks. Republican. Roman Catholic. Avocation: skating, karate. Family and matrimonial, Personal injury, General civil litigation. Home: 222 Plymouth Rd Wilmington DE 19803-3117 Office: Becker & Becker PA 913 Market St Ste 702 Wilmington DE 19801-4924

**EPPES, WALTER W., JR.,** lawyer; b. Meridian, Miss., Oct. 9, 1929; s. Walter W. Sr. and Mary (Seymour) E.; m. Katherine Bailey, Oct. 17, 1952; children: Kathy Eppes Yarborough, Susan Eppes Whitehead. Student, U. Ala., Tuscaloosa, 1947-50; LLB, U. Miss., 1952. Bar: Miss. 1952, U.S. Dist. Ct. (so. dist.) Miss. 1952, U.S. Ct. Appeals (5th cir.) 1952. Adjuster U.S. Fidelity & Guaranty, Co., Meridian, 1952-54; ptnr. Shumate & Eppes, Meridian, 1954-63, Huff, Williams, Gunn, Eppes & Crenshaw, Meridian, 1963-73, Eppes, Watts & Shannon, Meridian, 1973-95, Eppes & Carter, Meridian, 1995—. Author: (with others) Mississippi Law Institute, 1975. Pres. Roundtable Investors, Meridian, 1992. Mem. Am. Bd. Trial Advs. (diplomate), Miss. Bar (pres. 1985-86), Internat. Soc. Barristers (gov. 1968—), Internat. Assn. Def. Counsel (comm. chmn. 1960—), Downtown Club Meridian (pres. 1972), Northwood Country Club (bd. dirs. 1972). Republican. Presbyterian. Avocation: hunting. Insurance, Public utilities, Professional liability. Home: 4833 15th Pl Meridian MS 39305-1736 Office: Eppes & Carter Attys PO Box 3037 Broadmoor Mart Meridian MS 39303

**EPSTEIN, ALAN BRUCE,** lawyer; b. Passaic, N.J., Sept. 20, 1944; s. Jerome P. and Stella M. (Goldfinger) E.; m. Eve Teichholz, June 21, 1966; children: Jason, Dylan. BA, Temple U., 1967, JD, 1969. Bar: Pa. 1970, U.S. Dist. Ct. (ea. dist.) Pa. 1970, U.S. Ct. Appeals (3d cir.) 1972, U.S. Ct. Appeals (5th cir.) 1977, U.S. Dist. Ct. (cen. and we. dists.) Pa. 1987, U.S. Supreme Ct. 1988. Assoc. firm Freedman, Borowsky & Lorry, Phila., 1969-77; ptnr. firm Jablon, Epstein, Wolf, & Drucker, Phila., 1977—; pres. Judicate Nat. Pvt. Ct. System, Phila., 1983-88. Fellow Pa. Bar Found.; mem. Phila. Trial Lawyers Assn. (bd. dirs. 1980-84), Pa. Trial Lawyers Assn. (bd. govs. 1984-86), Assn. Trial Lawyers Am., ABA, Phila. Bar Assn., Pa. Bar Assn., Temple Am. Inn of Ct. (bd. dirs. 1994—). Jewish. Federal civil litigation, Civil rights, Labor. Home: 404 S Camac St Philadelphia PA 19147-1112 Office: Jablon Epstein Wolf & Drucker The Bellevue 9th Fl Broad St At Walnut Philadelphia PA 19102

**EPSTEIN, BRUCE HOWARD,** lawyer, real estate broker; b. Dallas, Jan. 30, 1952; s. Raymond Howard and Thelma (Romotsky) E.; m. Toni Rosas, Aug. 28, 1988; children: Marianne Corinne, Peter Louis. Student, U. Calif., San Diego, 1970-71; AB in Polit. Sci. with honors, U. Calif., Riverside, 1974; JD, U. Calif., San Francisco, 1977. Bar: Calif. 1977, U.S. Dist. Ct. (no. dist.) Calif. 1977, U.S. Dist. Ct. (cen., ea. and so. dists.) Calif, 1990, U.S. Ct. Appeals (9th cir.) 1990, U.S. Supreme Ct. 1990; lic. real estate broker, Calif. Dep. dist. atty. San Bernardino County Dist. Atty.'s Office, San Bernardino, Calif., 1977-83; sr. assoc. Atwood, Hurst, Knox & Anderson, San Jose, Calif., 1983-85; dep. city atty. San Jose City Atty.'s Office, 1985-86; sole practitioner Campbell, Calif., 1985-87; asst. v.p. Lawyers Title Ins. Corp., Pasadena, Calif., 1987—, Lawyers Title Co., Pasadena, 1987—; counsel, sec. Land Title Ins. Co., Pasadena, 1987—, Land Am. Fin. Group, Pasadena, 1998—, Transnation Title Ins. Co., Pasadena, 1998—, Commonwealth Land Title Ins. Co., Pasadena, 1998—; asst. v.p. Land Am. Fin. Group, Pasadena, 1998—; real estate broker, Burbank, Calif., 1983—; lectr. Evergreen Coll., San Jose, 1986-87; instr. Minimum Continuing Legal Edn., 1997—, Escrow Agent Profl. Devel., 1997—; mem. claims awareness com. Calif. Land Title Assn., 1997—; pres. Robert Louis Stevenson Sch. Site Coun., 1997—. Mem. Am. Diabetes Assn., 1977—, Nat. Space Soc., 1992—, Smithsonian Instn., 1990—, Jewish Found. for the Righteous, 1990—, Am. Air Mus. in Britain; v.p. Temple Beth Emet, Burbank, Calif. Mem. Calif. State Bar Assn., Los Angeles County Bar Assn., Nat. Air and Space Soc., Am. Mus. Natural History, Anti Defamation League, Greater Los Angeles Zool. Assn., Descanso Gardens Guild, Natural History Mus. Los Angeles County, Calif. Sci. Ctr., Zool. Soc. of San Diego. Democrat. Jewish. Avocations: writing, sports, painting. Real property, General civil litigation. Office: Land Am 55 S Lake Ave Ste 600 Pasadena CA 91101-2688

**EPSTEIN, ELAINE MAY,** lawyer; b. Phila., May 29, 1947; d. Sidney and Helen (Brill) Epstein; m. James A. Krachey, July 25, 1987; stepchildren: Ross Krachey, Anna Krachey. BA, U. Pa., 1968; MA, Yale U., 1971; JD, Northeastern U., 1976. Assoc. Law Offices of P.J. Piscitelli, Brockton, Mass., 1975-78; ptnr. LoDolce & Epstein, Brockton, 1978-94, Todd & Weld, Boston, 1994—; mem. Bd. Bar Overseers, Boston, 1984-88; trustee Mass. Continuing Legal Edn., Boston, 1991-93. Mem. editl. bd. Mass. Lawyers Weekly, 1993-98. Fellow Mass. Bar Found. (trustee 1993-98); mem. ABA, Mass. Bar Assn. (pres. 1992-93), Women's Bar Assn. (pres. 1979-80). Democrat. Jewish. Family and matrimonial, Appellate, General civil litigation. Home: 4 Manns Hill Cres Sharon MA 02067-2267 Office: Todd & Weld 28 State St Fl 31 Boston MA 02109-1775

**EPSTEIN, JUDITH ANN,** lawyer; b. L.A., Dec. 23, 1942; d. Gerald Elliot and Harriet (Hirsh) Rubens; m. Joseph I. Epstein, Oct. 4, 1964; children: Mark Douglas, Laura Ann. AB, U. Calif., Berkeley, 1964; MA, U. San Francisco, 1974, JD, 1977. Bar: Calif. 1978, U.S. Dist. Ct. (no. dist.) Calif 1978, U.S. Supreme Ct. 1983, U.S. Ct. Appeals (9th cir.) 1984. With social svcs. dept. Sutter County, Yuba City, Calif., 1964-66; bus. devel. assoc. Yuba County C. of C., Marysville, Calif., 1968-70; rsch. clk. Calif. Supreme Ct., San Fransisco, 1977; ptnr. Crosby, Heafey, Roach & May, Oakland, Calif., 1978-91; gen. counsel and sec. Valent USA Corp., 1991-98; exec. dir. East Bay/The Commonwealth Club of Calif., 1998—; lectr. U. Calif. Grad. Sch. Journalism in Media Law, Berkeley, 1987-91; bd. dirs. Sierra Pacific Steel, Hayward, Calif.; adj. prof. U. San Francisco, 1999—. Bd. dirs., v.p. Oakland Ballet, 1980-92; mem. bd. counselors U. San Francisco Sch. Law, 1994; trustee U. San Francisco, 1996—; bd. dirs. San Francisco Bay area Girl Scouts U.S., 1998—. Recipient Pres.'s award Oakland Ballet, James Madison Freedom of Info. award Soc. Profl. Journalists, 1992; award for Disting. Achievement, Girl Scouts U.S., 1995. Fellow Am. Bar Found.; mem. Calif. Women Lawyers Assn., Alameda Bar Assn., Berkeley Tennis Club. Libel, General corporate, Antitrust. Office: Valent USA Corp 1333 N California Blvd Ste 600 Walnut Creek CA 94596-4558

**EPSTEIN, MICHAEL ALAN,** lawyer; b. N.Y.C., June 26, 1954; s. Herman and Lillian (King) E. BA, Lehigh U., 1975; JD, NYU, 1979. Bar: N.Y., 1980, US. Dist. Ct. (so., ea. dists.) N.Y., 1980. Ptnr. Weil, Gotshal & Manges, N.Y.C., 1979—; lectr. in field. Author: Modern Intellectual Property, 1984, 3d edit., 1994, International Intellectual Property, 1992; editor: Corporate Counsellors Deskbook, 1982, 3d edit., 1990, Biotechnology Law, 1988, The Trademark Law Revision Act, 1989, Trade Secrets, Restrictive Covenants and Other Safeguards, 1986, Online-Internet Law, 1997, Epstein on Intellectual Property, 1998; co-editor, mem. editl. bd. Jour. Proprietary Rights, The Computer Lawyer, The Intellectual Property Strategist, The Cyberspace Lawyer; contbr. articles to profl. jours. Trustee Jonas Salk Found., Am. Health Found. Donald L. Brown fellow in trade regulation NYU Sch. Law, 1978-79. Mem. ABA, N.Y. State Bar Assn. Antitrust, Computer, Trademark and copyright. Home: 1020 Park Ave New York NY 10028-0913 Office: Weil Gotshal & Manges 767 5th Ave Fl Concl New York NY 10153-0119

**EPSTEIN, SHERRY STEIN,** lawyer; b. Idaho Falls, Idaho, Jan. 15, 1960; d. Seymour S. and Lucille R. (Richman) S. AB, Vassar Coll., 1981; JD, U. Pitts., 1985; MBA, Cleveland State U., 1994. Bar: Pa. 1985, U.S. Dist. Ct. (we. dist.) Pa. 1985, D.C. 1986, Ohio 1986, Fla. 1986, U.S. Dist. Ct. (no. dist.) Ohio 1986, U.S. Ct. Appeals (3d cir.) 1986, U.S. Ct. Appeals (6th cir.) 1987, U.S. Dist. Ct. D.C. 1988, U.S. Ct. Appeals (D.C. cir.) 1989, U.S. Supreme Ct. 1990. Account rep. West Svcs., Inc., Pitts., 1985-86; law clk. to judge Superior Ct. Pitts., 1986; assoc. Wickens, Hazen & Panza, Lorain, Ohio, 1986-88; legal counsel Advanced Med. Systems, Inc., Geneva, Ohio, 1988-95; sr. atty. Reminger & Reminger Co., L.P.A., Cleve., 1995; legal counsel ATC Lighting & Plastics, Inc., 1996—; bd. dirs. Lorain County Legal Aid Soc., Elyria, Ohio, 1988-89, Ash/Craft Industries; interviewer Cleve. and Cuyahoga Counties Joint Com. on Applications for Cuyahoga County for admission to Supreme Ct. of Ohio, Cleve., 1987-94; instr. Am. Inst. Paralegal Studies, Cleve., 1988-90; v.p., bd. dirs. Tree of Knowledge Learning Ctr. Inc., 1999—. Bd. dirs. Case Western Res. U. Friends of Eldred Theater, 1995—, Starting Point, 1996—, Mt. Sinai Cmty. Ptnrs., 1995—. Mem. ABA, Fla. Bar Assn., D.C. Bar Assn., Ohio Bar Assn., Cleve. Bar Assn., Ashtabula County Bar Assn. Avocation: teaching. Administrative and regulatory, General corporate, Environmental. Office: ATC Lighting & Plastics Inc 107 N Eagle St Geneva OH 44041-1161

**EPSTEIN, WILLIAM HARVEY,** patent lawyer; b. Bklyn., Sept. 27, 1933; s. Morris and Sylvia Epstein; m. Elaine Rosenstock, Apr. 3, 1960; children: Eric, Ellen Epstein Brunsberg. BS, Columbia U., 1955, BS in Chem. Engring., 1956; JD, George Washington U., 1960. Bar: N.J. 1960. Asst. patent counsel Nopco Chem. Co., Newark, 1962-64; atty. Blum, Moscovitz, Friedman & Kaplan, N.Y.C., 1964-66; assoc. patent counsel, asst. sec. Hoffmann-La Roche Inc., Nutley, N.J., 1966—. Home: 71 Pomona Rd Suffern NY 10901-1919 Office: Hoffmann-La Roche Inc 340 Kingsland St Nutley NJ 07110-1199

**ERGAZOS, JOHN WILLIAM,** lawyer; b. Canton, Ohio, Nov. 26, 1924; s. Manso Aristidis and Ella (Wongler) E.; m. Margaret Berbeles, Oct. 22, 1950; children: John William Jr., Veronica. BA, Kent State U., 1948; LLB, McKinley Law Sch., 1952. Bar: Ohio 1952, U.S. Dist. Ct. 1954. Pvt. practice Canton, Ohio, 1952—; bd. dirs. Factory Indsl. Maintenance Co., Kimdot Travel, Inc. Com. mem. Greater Canton C. of C., 1981-91. 2d lt. U.S. Army, 1943-46, ETO. Named Man of the Yr., St. Haralambos Men's Club, Canton, 1979. Mem. Am. Trial Lawyers Assn., Ohio State Bar Assn., Stark County Bar Assn., Order of Ahepa (pres. 1985-89), Eagles, Elks. Office: 300 National City Bank Bldg Canton OH 44702

**ERHART, JAMES NELSON,** lawyer; b. Flushing, N.Y., Mar. 18, 1953; s. Nelson S. and Gloria (Wagner) E.; m. Suzanne Marie Stahl, Oct. 25, 1980. BA, Coll. of Holy Cross, 1975; JD, Detroit Coll. Law, 1979. Bar: Mich. 1979, U.S. Dist. Ct. (ea. and we. dists.) Mich. 1979. Assoc. John H. McKaig, II, Mancelona, Mich., 1979-81; ptnr. Murphy and Erhart, Petoskey, Mich., 1981-88, Marco, Litzenburger, Smith, Brown & Erhart, P.C., Petoskey, 1988-91, Smith & Erhart P.C., 1991-95; atty. pvt. practice, 1995-98; ptnr. Stroup, Erhart & Wurster, Petoskey, Mich., 1998—. Bd. dirs. Big Bros.-Big Sisters, Kalkaska, Antrim County, 1980-81. Mem. Mich. Bar Assn., Charlevoix-Emmet County Bar Assn., State Bar of Mich. (rep. assembly 1992—, liaison to No. Mich. 1997—). Roman Catholic. Avocations: skiing, boating. General civil litigation, Personal injury, Family and matrimonial. Office: Stroup Erhart & Wurster 7 Pennsylvania Plz Petoskey MI 49770-2460

**ERHART, JOHN JOSEPH,** lawyer; b. Rush City, Minn., May 20, 1952; m. Debra Elaine Borris, Oct. 22, 1988; children: Laura Frances, Jenna Rae. BA, St. John's U., 1974; JD, Georgetown U., 1977. Bar: Minn. 1977, U.S. Dist. Ct. Minn. 1977, U.S. Ct. Appeals (8th cir.) 1978. Law clk. Judge Gerald W. Heaney U.S. Ct. Appeals (8th cir.), Duluth, Minn., 1977-79; shareholder Fredrikson & Byron, Mpls., 1979—. Taxation, general, Mergers and acquisitions, General corporate. Office: Fredrikson & Byron 1100 International Ctr 900 2nd Ave S Minneapolis MN 55402-3314

**ERICKSON, DAVID BELNAP,** lawyer; b. Ogden, Utah, Oct. 13, 1951; s. Eldred H. and Lois (Belnap) E.; m. Julie Ann Hill, Apr. 19, 1974; children: Rachel, John, Michael, Jared, Emily, Steven, Katherine, Daniel, Elizabeth. BA, Brigham Young U., 1975; MEd, Utah State U., 1979; JD, Gonzaga Sch. Law, 1982. Bar: Utah 1982, U.S. Claims Ct. 1990, U.S. Dist. Ct. Utah 1982, U.S. Ct. Appeals (10th cir.) 1984, U.S. Ct. Appeals (9th cir.) 1987, U.S. Supreme Ct. 1987. English tchr., debate coach Bonneville High Sch., Ogden, 1976-79; law clk. U.S. Atty.'s Office, Spokane, Washington, 1980-81; law clk. to judge U.S. Dist. Ct., Salt Lake City, 1982-83; with Kirton, McConkie & Poelman, Salt Lake City, 1983-92; sr. counsel Intermountain Health Care, Salt Lake City, 1992—. Co-author: Utah Appellate Practice Manual, 1986, Utah Sr. Citizen's Handbook, 1987; editor-in-chief Gonzaga Law Rev., 1981-82; assoc. editor: Utah Barrister, 1986-87, Utah Bar Jour., 1988—. Mem. LDS Hosp. Bioethics Com.; mem. planning and zoning commn. Pleasant View City, 1991-95, chmn., 1994-95, mem. city coun., mayor protempor, 1998—; chmn. Weber View Dist. Boy Scouts Am., 1993-95; trustee Utah Alliance for Health Care, 1994-99. Mem. ABA (litigation sect.), Utah Bar Assn. (law jour. com., bridging the gap com., needs of the elderly com., legal and med. com., examiner constl. law bar, assoc. editor Utah Bar jour.), Salt Lake County Bar Assn., Weber County Bar Assn.,Am. Health Lawyers Assn., Phi Delta Phi. Mem. LDS Ch. Federal civil litigation, State civil litigation, Health. Office: Intermountain Health Care 36 S State St Fl 22 Salt Lake City UT 84111-1401

**ERICKSON, DIANE QUINN,** lawyer, artist, small business owner; b. La Grange, Ill., Oct. 8, 1959; d. Stanley Brittian Sr. and Marilyn Agnes (Miller) Quinn; m. Russell Lee Erickson, Mar. 9, 1985. BS in Psychology, U. Ill., 1981; JD, Valparaiso U., 1984. Bar: Ill. 1985. Assoc. Dreyer, Foote, et al, Aurora, Ill., 1984-87; trust officer, atty. 1st Nat. Bank Des Plaines, Ill., 1987-89; owner Erickson Art & Frame, Naperville, Ill., 1988—. Mem. Brain Rsch. Found. Mem. NAFE, Ill. Bar Assn., DuPage County Bar Assn., N.W. Suburban Bar Assn., Chgo. Bar Assn. Lutheran. Avocations: tennis, travel, dance, skiing. Estate planning, Probate, Real property. Home: 6413 Greene Rd Woodridge IL 60517-1485 Office: 1807 S Washington St Ste 115 Naperville IL 60565-2051

**ERICKSON, JOHN RICHARD,** lawyer; b. Port Washington, N.Y., Sept. 19, 1942; s. John Sebastian and Rita Helen Erickson; m. Suzanne George, Oct. 26, 1968; children: John Todd, Jill Elizabeth. AB, Brown U., 1964; JD, Harvard U., 1967; LLM, Georgetown U., 1975. Bar: Mass. 1967, D.C. 1972, U.S. Dist. Ct. D.C. 1972, U.S. Ct. Appeals (D.C. cir.) 1972, U.S. Ct. Appeals (7th cir.) 1973, U.S. Supreme Ct. 1973, Va. 1975, U.S. Dist. Ct. (ea. and we. dists.) Va. 1975, U.S. Ct. Appeals (2d and 4th cirs.) 1975, Md. 1984, U.S. Dist. Ct. Md. 1984, U.S. Ct. Appeals (11th cir.) 1997. Assoc., then ptnr. Loomis, Owen, Fellman & Coleman, Washington, 1972-78, Pierson, Ball & Dowd, Washington, 1978-89; ptnr. Reed Smith Shaw & McClay, LLP, McLean, Va., 1989—. Capt. USMC, 1968-72. Mem. Va. Bar Assn., Fairfax Bar Assn., Tower Club. Labor, General civil litigation. Home: 12082 Chancery Station Cir Reston VA 20190-3286 Office: Reed Smith Shaw & McClay LLP 8251 Greensboro Dr Ste 1100 Mc Lean VA 22102-3844

**ERICKSON, ROBERT STANLEY,** lawyer; b. Kemmerer, Wyo., Apr. 17, 1944; s. Stanley W. and Dorothy Marie (Johnson) E.; m. Alice Norman, Dec. 27, 1972; children: Robert Badger, Erin Elizabeth, Andrew Carl, Scott Stanley, Courtney Ellen, Brennan Marie. BS in Bus., U. Idaho, 1966; JD, U. Utah, 1969; LLM in Taxation, George Washington U., 1973. Bar: U.S. Supreme Ct. 1973, U.S. Ct. Appeals (9th cir.) 1980, U.S. Dist. Ct. Idaho 1973, U.S. Tax Ct. 1969, Idaho 1973, Utah 1969. Assoc. atty. Office of Chief Counsel, Dept. Treasury, Washington, 1969-73; assoc. Elam, Burke, Jeppesen, Evans & Boyd, Boise, Idaho, 1973-77; ptnr. Elam, Burke, Evans, Boyd & Koontz, Boise, 1977-81; spl. counsel Holme Roberts & Owen, Salt Lake City, 1981-83; ptnr. Hansen & Erickson, Boise, 1983-85, Hawley Troxell Ennis & Hawley, Boise, 1985—. Contbr. articles to profl. jours. Named Citizen of Yr., Boise Exch. Club, 1980. Fellow Am. Coll. of Trust and Estate Counsel (past Idaho chmn. 1993—); mem. ABA (sect. on taxation, com. state and local taxes), IRS/Western Region Bar Assn. (mem., past chmn. liaison com. Idaho co-chair local task force IRS non-filer program 1993), Idaho State Bar (founding chmn. taxation, probate and trust law sect.), Utah State Bar (tax and estate planning sect.), Boise Estate Planning Council, Idaho State Tax Inst. (exec. com., numerous other local and nat. coms.). Mem. LDS Ch. Estate planning, Probate, Corporate taxation. Office: Hawley Troxell Ennis & Hawley First Interstate Ctr 877 Main St Ste 1000 Boise ID 83702-5884

**ERICKSON, WILLIAM HURT,** retired state supreme court justice; b. Denver, May 11, 1924; s. Arthur Xavier and Virginia (Hurt) E.; m. Doris Rogers, Dec. 24, 1953; children: Barbara Ann, Virginia Lee, Stephen Arthur, William Taylor. Degree in petroleum engring., Colo. Sch. Mines, 1947; student, U. Mich., 1949; LLB, U. Va., 1950. Bar: Colo. 1951. Pvt. practice Denver; justice Colo. Supreme Ct., 1971-96, chief justice, 1983-86; faculty NYU Appellate Judges Sch., 1972-85; mem. exec. Commn. on Accreditation of Law Enforcement Agys., 1980-83; chmn. Pres.'s Nat. Commn. for Rev. of Fed. and State Laws Relating to Wiretapping and Electronic Surveillance, 1976. Chmn. Erickson Commn., 1997. With USAAF, 1943. Recipient Disting. Achievement medal Colo. Sch. Mines, 1990. Fellow Internat. Acad. Trial Lawyers (former sec.), Am. Coll. Trial Lawyers, Am. Bar Found. (chmn. 1985), Internat. Soc. Barristers (pres. 1971); mem. ABA, (bd. govs. 1975-79, former chmn. com. on standards criminal justice, former chmn. coun. criminal law sect., former chmn. com. to implement standards criminal justice, mem. long-range planning com., action com. to reduce ct. cost and delay), Colo. Bar Assn. (award of merit 1989), Denver Bar Assn. (past pres., trustee), Am. Law Inst. (coun.), Practising Law Inst. (nat. adv. coun., bd. govs. Colo.), Freedoms Found. at Valley Forge (nat. coun. trustees, 1986—), Order of Coif, Scribes (pres. 1978). Home: 10 Martin Ln Englewood CO 80110-4821

**ERICKSTAD, RALPH JOHN,** judge, retired state supreme court chief justice; b. Starkweather, N.D., Aug. 15, 1922; s. John T. and Anna Louisa (Myklebust) E.; m. Lois Katherine Jacobson, July 30, 1949; children:. Student, U. N.D., 1940-43; B.Sc. in Law, U. Minn., 1947, JD, 1949. Bar: N.D. 1949. Practiced in Devils Lake, 1949-62; State's atty. Ramsey County, 1953-57; mem. N.D. Senate from, Ramsey County, 1957-62; asst. majority floor leader N.D. Senate from, 1959, 61; assoc. justice Supreme Ct. N.D., Bismarck, 1963-73, chief justice, 1973-93, surrogate judge; treas. N.D. States Attys. Assn., 1955, v.p., 1956; mem. N.D. Legislative Research Com., 1957-59, N.D. Budget Bd., 1961-63, Gov. N.D. Spl. Com. Labor, 1960. Past mem. exec. com. Mo. Valley council Boy Scouts Am.; chmn. bd. trustees Mo. Valley Family YMCA, 1966-77. Served with USAAF, 1943-45, ETO. Recipient Silver Beaver award Boy Scouts Am., 1967, Sioux award U. N.D., 1973, 1st Disting. Service award Missouri Valley Family YMCA, 1978, Disting. Service award Nat. Ctr. for State Cts., 1989, N.D. Nat. Leadership award of excellence, 1987, "Chief Justice Ralph J. Erickstad Eagle Class" named in his honor, Frontier trails dist., No. Lights council, Boy Scouts Am., 1983. Mem. ABA, N.D. Bar Assn. (disting. svc. award 1988), Burleigh County Bar Assn., State Justice Inst. (bd. dirs. 1987-90), Nat. Conf. Chief Justices (exec. council 1977-78, 1980-82, pres. 1983-84), Am. Judicature Soc. (Herbert Harley award 1992), Am. Law Inst., Nat. Ctr. for State Cts. (pres. 1983-84), Task Force on Pub. Image of Cts., Williamsburg Conf.-State Courts: A Blueprint for the Future, 1978, Am. Legion (life). Lutheran (del. 1st biennial conv., mem. nominating com.). Clubs: Am. Legion, VFW, Kiwanian. Office: ND Supreme Ct Judicial Wing 1st Fl 600 E Boulevard Ave Bismarck ND 58505-0660

**ERICSON, JAMES DONALD,** lawyer, insurance executive; b. Hawarden, Iowa, Oct. 12, 1935; s. Elmer H. and Martha (Sydness) E.; children: Linda Jean, James Robert. B.A. in History, State U. Iowa, 1958, J.D., 1962. Bar: Wis. 1965. Assoc. Fitzgerald, Brown, Leahy, McGill & Strom, Omaha, 1962-65; with Northwestern Mut. Life Ins. Co., Milw., 1965—, asst. to pres., 1972-75, dir. policy benefits, 1975-76, v.p., gen. counsel, sec., 1976-80, sr. v.p., 1980, exec. v.p., 1987, pres., 1990; chief operating officer Northwestern Mut. Life Ins. Co., 1991-93, pres., CEO, 1993—; dir. MGIC Investment Corp., Green Bay Packaging Inc., Am. Coun. Life Ins., Kohl's Corp., Consol. Papers, Inc., Northwestern Mut. Investment Svcs.; chair Am. Coun. Life Ins. Bd. dirs. Wis. Taxpayers Alliance, Competitive Wis., Inc., Greater Milw. Com., Milw. Redevel. Com., Marcus Ctr. for the Performing Arts, United Way, Met. Milw. Assn. Commerce, Med. Coll. Wis., Milw. Sch. Engring.; trustee Lawrence U., Com. for Econ. Devel., Boys and Girls Club Greater Milw. Mem. ABA, Assn. Life Ins. Counsel (hon.), Wis. Bar Assn., Milw. Club (bd. dirs.), Phi Beta Kappa. Republican. Presbyterian. General corporate. Office: Northwestern Mut Life Ins Co 720 E Wisconsin Ave Milwaukee WI 53202-4703

**ERICSON, ROGER DELWIN,** lawyer, forest resource company executive; b. Moline, Ill, Dec. 21, 1934; s. Carl D. and Linnea E. (Challman) E.; m. Norma F. Brown, Aug. 1, 1957; children: Catherine Lynn, David. AB, Stetson U., DeLand, Fla., 1958, JD, 1958; MBA, U. Chgo., 1971. Bar: Fla. 1958, Ill. 1959, Ind. 1974. Atty. Brunswick Corp., Skokie, Ill., 1959-62; asst. sec., asst. gen. counsel Chemetron Corp., Chgo., 1962-73; asst. v.p. Inland Container Corp., Indpls., 1973-75, v.p., gen. counsel, sec., 1975-83; v.p., gen. counsel, sec. Temple-Inland, Inc., 1983-94, of counsel, 1994—; v.p., sec. bd. dirs. Inland Container Corp.; dir., pres., co-CEO Kraft Land Svcs., Inc., Atlanta, 1978-88; bd. dirs., v.p. Guaranty Holdings Inc., Dallas; v.p. Temple-Inland Fin. Svcs., Inc., Austin, 1990-94; bd. dirs. Temple-Inland Forest Products, Temple-Inland Real Estate Investment, Inc., Temple-Inland Realty Inc. Trustee Chgo. Homes for Children, 1971-74; mem. alumni coun. U. Chgo., 1972-76; mem. Palatine Twp. Youth Commn., 1969-72; sect. chmn. Chgo. Heart Assn., 1972, 73; alumni bd. dirs. Stetson U.; bd. dirs. Temple-Inland Found; mem. Safe and Drug-Free Comm. Collier County Sch. Bd., 1996—. Mem. ABA, Am. Arbitration Assn. (nat. panel of comml. arbitrators), Am. Soc. corp. Secs., Am. Forest Products Assn. (past mem. govt. affairs com. and legal com.), Am. Corp. Counsel Assn., Ill Bar Assn., Ind. Bar Assn., Fla. Bar Assn., Chgo. Bar Assn., Indpls. Bar Assn. (chmn. corp. counsel sect., mem. profl. responsibility com. 1982), Collier County Bar Assn., Indpls. C. of C. (mem. govt. affairs com.), Plum Grove Club (pres. 1967), Collier's Reserve Country Club, Omicron Delta Kappa, Phi Delta Phi. General corporate, Antitrust, Administrative and regulatory. Home: 12502 Colliers Reserve Dr Naples FL 34110-0915 Office: Temple-Inland Inc Drawer N Diboll TX 75941 *Concentrate on the desired final result of any activity. Never forget your family, co-workers, friends.*

**ERICSSON, RICHARD L.,** lawyer; b. 1948. BA, U. S.D., JD. Bar: S.D. 1974. Ptnr. Ericsson Ericsson & Leibel, Madison, S.D. Mem. State Bar S.D. (pres.-elect). Office: Ericsson Ericsson & Leibel 100 N Egan Ave Madison SD 57042-2909*

**ERIKSEN, RICHARD EUGENE,** lawyer; b. Orange, N.J., Mar. 7, 1945; s. Richard Raymond and Mary Helen (Moreschi) E.; m. Valerie Jean Herbert, Jan. 15, 1972; children: Christian Richard, Laura Jeanne. BA, Rutgers U., 1967, JD, 1973; postgrad., London U., 1973-74; LLM, Georgetown U., 1981. Bar: N.J. 1975, D.C. 1978, U.S. Ct. Appeals (5th cir.) 1975, U.S. Supreme Ct 1980. Law clk. to judge U.S. Dist. Ct. (ea. dist.) La., 1974-76; exec. atty. Spl. Ct. Regional Rail Reorgn. Act 1973, Washington, 1976-97, U.S. Dist. Ct. D.C., 1997—. Lt. (j.g.) USCG, 1968-71. Mem. ABA (internat. law, law practice and mgmt. and adminstrv. law sects.). Home: 3521 Slade Run Dr Falls Church VA 22042-3923 Office: US Dist Ct 333 Constitution Ave NW # 20001 Washington DC 20001-2802

**ERISMAN, JAMES A.,** lawyer; b. Wilmington, Del., Jan. 29, 1940; s. Hudson H. and Madeleine (Poinsett) E.; m. Jane Sarius, June 12, 1965; children: James B., Samantha S. BS, U. Del., 1963; JD, Dickinson Sch. Law, Carlisle, pa., 1966. Bar: Del. 1966, U.S. Dist. Ct. Del. 1967, U.S. Supreme Ct. 1972; diplomate Nat. Bd. Trial Advocacy. Military judge USMC, 1969-70; dep. atty. gen. State of Del., Wilmington, 1970-72; spl. rate counsel Del. Pub. Svc. Commn., Dover, 1972-73; ptnr. Daley, Erisman, vanOgtrop, Wilmington and Newark, 1972—, Daley, Erisman & Van Ogtrop. Contbr. articles to profl. jurs. With USMC, 1967-70. Mem. Am. Bd. Trial Advocates (pres. 1996), Assn. Trial Lawyers Am. (bd. govs. 1985-94, trustee 1988-91, 93-95, 97—), Million Dollar Advocates Forum, Del. Trial Lawyers Assn. (pres. 1982-83, 85-86). Personal injury, Professional liability, Insurance. Home: 1224 King St Wilmington DE 19801-3232 Office: Daley Erisman vanOgtrop & Hudson 715 N King St Wilmington DE 19801-3503

**ERLEBACHER, ARLENE CERNIK,** retired lawyer; b. Chgo., Oct. 3, 1946; d. Laddie J. and Gertrude V. (Kurdys) Cernik; m. Albert Erlebacher, June 14, 1968; children: Annette Doherty, Jacqueline Erlebacher. BA, Northwestern U., 1967, JD, 1973. Bar: Ill. 1974, U.S. Dist. Ct. (no. dist.) Ill. 1974, U.S. Ct. Appeals (7th cir.) 1974, Fed. Trial Bar, 1983, U.S. Supreme Ct. 1985. Assoc. Sidley & Austin, Chgo., 1974-80, ptnr., 1980-95, ret., 1996. Fellow Am. Bar Found.; mem. Order Coif. Federal civil litigation, State civil litigation, Product liability.

**ERLITZ, STEPHEN W.,** lawyer; b. Bklyn., Oct. 21, 1937; s. Lawrence I. and Gussie Erlitz; m. Gail M. Saltz, July 11, 1965; 1 child, Dana Erlitz Gutt. BA, Bklyn. Coll., 1959, JD, 1962. Bar: N.Y., Fla. Assoc. Shapiro & Brown, N.Y.C., 1963-64, Daniel Segal, N.Y.C., 1964-65, Murray Segal, N.Y.C., 1965-66; pvt. practice Bklyn., 1967-69, 82—; ptnr. Bacine & Erlitz, Bklyn., 1969-77, Segal, Lilling & Erlitz, N.Y.C., 1977-82. Trustee Village of East Rockaway, N.Y., 1995—. With USAR, 1962-68. Mem. Sheepshead Bay C. of C. (Gratitude award 1986). Avocations: reading, politics. General practice, Probate, Family and matrimonial. Home: 16A Murdock Rd East Rockaway NY 11518-1601 Office: 2623 E 16th St Brooklyn NY 11235-3805

**ERNST, DANIEL PEARSON,** lawyer; b. Des Moines, Sept. 30, 1931; s. Daniel Ward and Thea Elaine (Pearson) E.; m. Ann Robinson, April 14, 1956; children: Ellen, Daniel R., Ruth Ann. BA, Dartmouth Coll., 1953; JD, U. Mich., 1956. Bar: Iowa 1956, Ill. 1964, Mich. 1980. Assoc. Clewell Cooney & Fuerste, 1960-64; ptnr. Nelson Stapleton & Ernst, Stapleton & Ernst, Stapleton Ernst & Sprengelmeyer, East Dubuque, Ill., Nelson Stapleton & Ernst & Sprengelmeyer, Dubuque, Iowa, 1964-79; pvt. practice Dubuque, 1979-80; ptnr. Ernst & Cody, Dubuque, 1981-84, Daniel P. Ernst, P.C., Dubuque, 1984-90, Vincent Roth & Ernst, P.C., Galena, Ill., 1991; pub. defender State of Iowa, Dubuque, 1991-96; pvt. practice Dubuque, 1997—; U.S. trustee 1979-91. Capt. USAF, 1957-60. Mem. ABA, Iowa State Bar Assn. (bd. govs. 1985-89), Dubuque County Bar Assn. (2d v.p. 1979-80, 1st v.p. 1980-81, pres. 1981-82), Ill. State Bar Assn., Jo Daviess County Bar Assn., State Bar Assn. Mich., Grand Traverse-Leelanau-Antrim Bar Assn., Nat. Assn. Criminal Def. Lawyers, Nat. Legal Aid and Defenders Assn. Democrat. Avocations: swimming, sailing. Office: Attorney-at-Law 899 Mount Carmel Rd Dubuque IA 52003-7946

**ERRICO, MELISSA,** lawyer; b. Waterbury, Conn., Mar. 14, 1969; d. John and Carol Ann (Summa) E. BA, U. Ariz., 1991; JD, Washburn U., 1994. Bar: Ariz., U.S. Dist. Ct. Ariz. Assoc. Virgelli & Bryson, Tucson, 1994—. Republican. Roman Catholic. Personal injury, Family and matrimonial, Appellate. Office: Vingelli and Bryson 33 N Stone Ave Ste 750 Tucson AZ 85701-1429

**ERSEK, GREGORY JOSEPH MARK,** lawyer, business administrator; b. Cleve., Aug. 30, 1956; s. Joseph Francis and Mary H. (Hurchanik) E. AB, Columbia U., 1977; MBA, U. Pa., 1979; JD, U. Fla., 1984; cert. cir. civil mediator, Fla. Internat. U., 1998. Bar: Fla. 1986, U.S. Dist. Ct. (so. dist.) Fla. 1987. Cons. fin. valuation Am. Appraisal Co., Princeton, N.J., 1979-80; mgr. import-export Marie L. Veslie Co., Coral Gables, Fla., 1980-85; assoc. Lunny, Tucker, Karns & Brescher, Ft. Lauderdale, Fla., 1986; dir. legal dept. Horizons Rsch. Labs. Inc., Ft. Lauderdale, 1986-89, sr. corp. planner, 1988-89; gen. counsel Unisco Corp., Ft. Lauderdale, 1989-93, TRICORD Corp., Ft. Lauderdale, 1990-93, Irish Times, Inc., Ft. Lauderdale, 1993-97; dir. corp. fin. dept. & sr. corp. counsel Canton Fin. Svcs. Corp., subs. Cyber Am. Corp., Salt Lake City, 1995-96; gen. counsel Greenstreet Capital Corp., Investment Bankers, Las Vegas, 1996—, Gaelic Pub. Devel., Inc., Ft. Lauderdale, 1998—; sec.-treas., dir. Sorkar Group, Inc., Ft. Lauderdale, 1987-89; CEO Am. CompuShopper, Inc., 1989-98; with legal dept. Pfizer Inc., N.Y.C., 1983; co-founder, mgr. Poland/U.S. Trade and Mktg. Consortium, 1989—; mem. Philip C. Jessup Internat. Moot Ct. team, 1983; gen. counsel Biltmore Vacation Resorts, Inc., f/k/a Cyber Information, Inc., Las Vegas, 1997—, Avalon Group, Inc., Cedar Rapids, Iowa, 1997—. Editor Medscanner, med. industry newsletter, 1987-89. Mem. venture coun. forum. Mem. Fla. Bar Assn., Utah Bar (securities sect.), Nat. Assn. Securities Dealers (nat. arbitration com.), Coun. on Fgn. Rels. (local com.), Wharton Club South Fla. Republican. Episcopalian. Avocations: travel, books, entrepreneurship, internat. bus. ventures, mergers and acquisitions. Private international, Mergers and acquisitions, Securities. Home and Office: 17820 NW 18th Ave Miami FL 33056-4949

**ERSKINE, MATTHEW FORBES,** lawyer; b. Worcester, Mass., May 13, 1959; s. Linwood Mandeville Jr. and Margaret (Ayers) E.; m. Carolyn Woodbury Davis, June 8, 1985; children: Nathaniel Avery Kidder, Adele Woodbury, Amelia Forbes. BA, Carleton Coll., 1982; JD, Suffolk U., Boston, 1987. Bar: Mass. 1987. Law clk. Fletcher, Tilton & Whipple, Worcester, 1983-84; mem. Peters & Erskine, Worcester, 1987-94; ptnr. Erskine & Erskine, Worcester, 1994—; clk. Goddard/Homestead Inc., Worcester, 1988-95. Mem. Weld Com., Worcester, 1990, 94, 96; mem. clk. Paxton (Mass.) Conservation Commn., 1988—; pres. Worcester Forum Theatre, 1990-92; trustee Quinsigamond C.C., 1993—; dir. Family Svcs. of Cen. Mass., 1995—; dir. Cmty. Healthlink, 1992-95. Mem. Estate and Bus. Planning Coun., Worcester Com. on Fgn. Rels., Worcester Econ. Club, Rotary (Worcester Club). Republican. Congregationalist. Avocations: farming, military history, theater. Estate planning, Estate taxation, Probate. Office: Erskine & Erskine 30 Highland St Worcester MA 01609-2704

**ERSTAD, LEON ROBERT,** lawyer; b. Tyler, Minn., Aug. 3, 1947; s. Clifford and Josie (Dellberg) E.; m. Nancy Youel, July 19, 1969; children: Eric, Andrew, Jonathan. BSBA, U. Minn., 1969; JD cum laude, Temple U., 1976. Bar: Minn. 1976, U.S. Dist. Ct. Minn. 1976, U.S. Ct. Appeals (8th cir.) 1992, U.S. Supreme Ct. 1994; cert. ct. mediator. Ptnr. Chadwick, Johnson & Condon, P.A., Mpls., 1976-90, Erstad & Riemer P.A., 1990—; adj. instr. law William Mitchell Coll., St. Paul, 1985-94; spkr. at profl. seminars. Contbr. articles to profl. jours. Bd. dirs. Loring Nicollet Cmty. Ctr., Mpls., 1981-91, Minn. Returned Peace Corps Vols., Mpls., 1980-86, pres., 1980-81; trustee Lynnhurst Congrl. Ch., 1997—, deacon, 1994-97. Named alumni of notable achievement U. Minn. Mem. ABA, Minn. State Bar Assn., Minn. Def. Lawyers Assn., Def. Rsch. Inst., Def. Lawyers Assn. (bd. dirs. 1999—). General civil litigation, Insurance, Environmental. Home: 4700 Dupont Ave S Minneapolis MN 55409-2324 Office: Erstad & Riemer PA 1000 Northland Plz Minneapolis MN 55431

**ERTEL, ALLEN EDWARD,** lawyer, former congressman; b. Williamsport, Pa., Nov. 7, 1936; s. Clarence and Helen (Froehner) E.; m. Catharine Bieber Klepper, June 20, 1959; children: Taylor John (dec.), Edward Barnhardt, Amy Sara. BA, Dartmouth Coll., 1958, MSBA, MS, 1959; LL.B., Yale U., 1965. Bar: Pa., Del., U.S. Supreme Ct. Law clk. U.S. Dist. Ct. of Del., 1965-66; ptnr. Candor, Youngman, Gibson & Gault, Williamsport, 1967-72, Ertel & Kieser, Williamsport, 1972-76; dist. atty. Lycoming County, Pa., 1967-76; mem. 95th-97th Congresses from 17th Pa. Dist.; ptnr. Reed Smith Shaw & McClay, Williamsport, 1985-88; pvt. practice Williamsport, 1988—. del. Democratic. Nat. Conv., 1972; Dem. nominee for gov. of Pa., 1982, for atty. gen. of Pa., 1984. Served with USN, 1959-62. Mem. Pa. Bar Assn., Del. Bar Assn., Dartmouth Soc. Engrs., Lions. Lutheran. Environmental, General corporate, Personal injury. Home: 2245 Heim Hill Rd Montoursville PA 17754-9699 Office: 605 W 4th St Williamsport PA 17701-5901

**ERVIN, EDIE RENEE,** lawyer; b. Magnolia, Ark.; d. James E. Jr. and Ginger Ervin. BA, Hendrix Coll., 1988; JD with high honors, U. Ark., Little Rock, 1993. Bar: Ark. 1993, U.S. Dist. Ct. Ark. 1993, U.S. Ct. Appeals (8th cir.) 1993. Jud. law clk. ea. dist. U.S. Dist. Ct. Ark., Little Rock, 1994; lawyer Williams & Anderson LLP, Little Rock, 1995—. Federal civil litigation, State civil litigation, Product liability. Office: Williams & Anderson 111 Center St Fl 22 Little Rock AR 72201-4402

**ERVIN, MARK ALAN,** lawyer; b. Muncie, Ind., Apr. 23, 1959; s. Ben and Martha Elizabeth (Shelley) E.; m. Molly M. Garrett, July 1, 1995; children: Zachary Christopher, Priscilla Noelle. BS, Ball State U., Muncie, Ind., 1981, MA, 1985; JD, Ind. U., Indpls., 1992. Legis. intern Ind. State Senate, Indpls., 1980; adminstrv. asst. alumni program Ball State U., 1981-83, asst. dir. alumni and devel. program, 1983-88, dir. alumni constituent program, 1988-90. Bd. dirs. Delaware County Mental Health Assn., 1993—, pres., 1997-98. John R. Emens scholar Ball State U., 1977. Mem. Ball State U. Alumni Assn., Jaycees (bd. dirs. Muncie chpt. 1986-89, v.p. 1988), Muncie Exchange Club (bd. dirs. 1996—, pres.-elect 1999-2000). Avocations: golf, tennis, sports, music, photography. Home: 8614 E Windsor Rd Selma IN 47383-9667 Office: Beasley Gilkison Retherford Buckles & Clark 110 E Charles St Muncie IN 47305-2400

**ERVIN, SAMUEL JAMES, III,** federal judge; b. Morganton, N.C., Mar. 2, 1926; s. Sam Ervin. B.S., Davidson Coll., 1948; LL.B., Harvard U., 1951. Bar: N.C. Pvt. practice law Morganton, 1952-57; solicitor Burke County (N.C.) Criminal Ct., 1954-56; mem. firm Patton, Ervin & Starnes and predecessors, Morganton, 1957-67; judge Superior Ct. 25th Jud. Dist. N.C., 1967-80; judge U.S. Ct. Appeals (4th cir.), Morganton, N.C., 1980-89, 96—, chief judge, 1989-96. Pres. Davidson Coll. Nat. Alumni Assn., 1973-74; trustee Davidson Coll., 1982-94, Grace Hosp., Inc., 1992—. Named Young Man of Yr. Morganton Jaycees, 1954. Office: US Ct Appeals One North Square PO Box 1488 Morganton NC 28680-1488*

**ERVIN, SPENCER,** lawyer; b. Bala, Pa., Nov. 25, 1932; s. Spencer and Miriam Williams (Roberts) E.; m. Florence Wetherill Schroeder, Sept. 12, 1964; children: Margaret, Mary, Miriam, Helen. AB, Harvard U., 1954, JD, 1959. Bar: Pa. 1960, Maine 1995, U.S. Supreme Ct. 1963. Staff counsel Philco Corp., Phila., 1959-62; assoc. Ringe & Dewey, Phila., 1962-64; ptnr. Ringe, Tate & Ervin, Phila., 1964-72, Gratz, Tate, Spiegel, Ervin & Ruthrauff, Phila., 1972-92, Hepburn, Willcox, Hamilton & Putnam, Phila., 1992-96, Largay Law Offices, Bangor, Maine, 1996-97; pvt. practice Bass Harbor, Maine, 1998—. Bd. dirs., officer Neighborhood Club, Bala Cynwyd, Pa., 1969-89. Lt. USNR, 1954-56. Republican. Episcopal. General civil litigation, General practice, Bankruptcy. Home and Office: PO Box 383 Bass Harbor ME 04653-0383

**ERWIN, H. ROBERT,** lawyer; b. L.A., May 19, 1945; s. Howard R. and Nina B. Erwin; m. Nancy Smick, Sept. 9, 1967; children: Meghan, Kate, Benson, Carter. BA, Purdue U., 1967; JD, Georgetown U., 1972. Bar: Md. 1973, D.C. 1972, U.S. Dist. Ct. Md. 1973, U.S. Ct. Appeals (4th cir.) 1985. Dir. Consumer Law Ctr. Legal Aid Bur., Balt., 1972-78; cons., Office of Consumer Affairs U.S. Dept. Energy, Washington, 1978; chief Consumer Protections Divsn. Office of Atty. Gen., Balt., 1979-82; ptnr. Pretl & Erwin, P.A., Balt., 1983-95, The Erwin Law Firm, P.A., Balt., 1996—; guest lectr., moot ct. judge U. Md. Sch. Law, Balt., 1988, 91-94; adv. bd. St. Ambrose Legal Svcs., Balt., 1994—. Contbr. chpt. to book. Pres., bd. mem. League for the Disabled, Balt., 1989-98; chpt. mem. Cathedral of the Incarnation, Balt., 1987-89. With U.S. Army, 1969-71. Mem. Am. Trial Lawyers Assn., Md. Trial Lawyers Assn., Md. State Bar Assn., Nat. Assn. Consumer Advocates, Engring. Soc. Consumer commercial, Product liability. Office: The Erwin Law Firm PA 111 W Monument St Baltimore MD 21201-4707

**ERWIN, JUDITH ANN (JUDITH ANN PEACOCK),** writer, photographer, lawyer; b. Decatur, Ga., Jan. 4, 1939; d. Milo Eugene and Lucy Isabelle (Simpson) Peacock; m. William Wofford Erwin, Sept. 5, 1959 (div. Mar. 1982); children: William Wofford Jr., Allison Sheridan (Norton). AA, Fla. C.C., 1987; BA summa cum laude, Jacksonville U., 1989; JD, U. Fla., 1993. Photography instr., freelance writer Jacksonville, Fla., 1986-91, freelance dance photographer, 1984-91; theater and dance critic Folio Weekly, Jacksonville, Fla., 1987-89; writer dance VUE mag.; founder On Our Own, 1991; pvt. practice lawyer; pres. Ballet Guild, Jacksonville, 1973-75, Ballet Repertory Jacksonville, 1979-80; freelance costume designer, Jacksonville, 1981-86; mem. grand rev. dance panel Fla. Dept. Cultural Affairs, 1996, 97; seminar spkr. in field. Mem. editorial staff Kalliope, Jour. Women's Art, 1989-91; editor-in-chief U. Fla. Jour. of Law and Pub. Policy, fall 1993; editor Jacksonville Trial Lawyers Newsletter. Mem. del.'s council Art's Assembly Jacksonville, 1979-80. Mem. AAUW, ATLA, Nat. Soc. Arts and Letters, Nat. League Am. Pen Women, Fla. Bar Assn., Jacksonville Bar Assn., Jacksonville Women Lawyers Assn., Phi Kappa Phi, Phi Theta Kappa. Democrat. Episcopalian.

**ERWIN, LAWRENCE WARDE,** lawyer; b. Portland, Oreg., Dec. 10, 1948; s. Warde Hagaman and Mary Lou Erwin; m. Lillian Erwin, 1982 (div. 1988); 1 child, Stephen. BS, U. Oreg., 1970; JD, N.W. Sch. Law, Portland, 1973. Bar: Oreg. 1973, Alaska 1976, Nev. 1985, U.S. Dist. Ct. Oreg. 1973, U.S. Dist. Ct. Alaska 1976, U.S. Tax Ct. 1988. Ptnr. Erwin, Lamb & Erwin, P.C., Portland, 1973-75, Boyko & Assocs., Anchorage, 1975-81; pvt. practice Law Offices of Lawrence Erwin, Bend, Oreg., 1981-86; ptnr. Babb, Auedoveca & Erwin, Bend, Oreg., 1986-94; pvt. practice Law Offices of Lawrence Erwin, Bend, Oreg., 1994—. Mem. Oreg. State Bar (profl. responsibility com. 1989), Ctrl. Oreg. Bar Assn. (sec. treas. 1990). Republican. Presbyterian. Real property, Bankruptcy, Personal injury. Office: Law Office Lawrence Erwin 221 NW Lafayette Ave Bend OR 97701-1927

**ERWIN, RICHARD CANNON, SR.,** federal judge; b. McDowell County, N.C., Aug. 23, 1923; s. John Adam and Flora (Cannon) E.; m. Demerice Whitley, Aug. 25, 1946; children: Richard Cannon, Jr., Aurelia Whitley. BA, Johnson C. Smith U., 1947; LLB, Howard U., 1951; LLD, Pfeiffer Coll., 1980, Johnson C. Smith U., 1981. Bar: N.C. 1951, U.S. Supreme Ct. 1974. Practice law Winston-Salem, N.C., 1951-77; judge N.C. Ct. Appeals, 1978; judge U.S. Dist. Ct. (mid. dist.) N.C., 1980-88, chief judge, 1988-92, sr. judge, 1992—; rep. N.C. Gen. Assembly, chmn. hwy. safety com.; mem. law bd. vis. Wake Forest U., 1984—. Trustee Forsyth County Legal Aid Soc., Amos Cottage, Inc.; chmn. bd. trustees Bennett Coll.; bd. dirs. N.C. 4-H Devel. Fund, Inc.; bd. visitors Div. Sch., Duke U.; trustee Children's Home, Winston-Salem; mem. steering com. Winston-Salem Found.; bd. dirs. United Fund; bd. dirs., pres. Citizens Coalition Forsyth County and Anderson High Sch., PTA; mem. N.C. Bd. Edn., 1971-77, N.C. State Library Bd. Trustees, 1968-69; mem., chmn. personnel com. Winston-Salem/Forsyth County Sch. Bd.; chmn. bd. trustees St. Paul United Methodist Ch. Mem. N.C. Bar Assn. (v.p. 1983-84), N.C. Assn. Black Lawyers, Forsyth County Bar Assn. (pres.), N.C. State Bar. Office: US Dist Ct Federal Bldg #246 251 N Main St Winston Salem NC 27101-3914

**ERZEN, MARK D.,** lawyer; b. Alton, Ill., July 5, 1954; s. Richard G. and Edith R. E.; m. Marian S. Erzen, Apr. 9, 1983; children: Christa, Robert. BS, Mich. State U., 1975; JD, U. Mich., 1980. Assoc. Kirkland & Ellis, Chgo., 1980-83, Schuyler, Roche & Zwirner, Chgo., 1983-87; owner Visc, Inc., Chgo., 1987-89; atty. Karaganis & White Ltd., Chgo., 1989—. Fax: 312-836-9083. E-mail: MarkúErzen@K-W.com. Office: Karaganis & White Ltd 414 N Orleans St Ste 810 Chicago IL 60610-4482

**ESCARRAZ, ENRIQUE, III,** lawyer; b. Evergreen Park, Ill., Aug. 30, 1944; s. Enrique Jr. and Mary Ellen (Bandy) E.; children from previous marriage; Erin Christine, Martina Mary; m. Patricia Jane Escarraz; children: Sarah Ellen, James Lee, Jason F. BA, U. Fla., 1966, JD, 1968. Bar: Fla. 1969, U.S. Dist. Ct. (so. and mid. dists.) Fla. 1969, U.S. Ct. Appeals (5th cir.) 1971, U.S. Ct. Appeals (11th cir.) 1981. VISTA atty. Community Legal Counsel, Chgo., 1968-69; mng. atty. Fla. Rural Legal Services, Ft. Myers, 1969-71; pvt. practice law St. Petersburg, Fla., 1971-82, 85-87, 88—; ptnr. Anderson & Escarraz, St. Petersburg, 1982-85; asst. gen. counsel U. South Fla., 1987-88; assoc. James L. Eskald Law Office, Largo, Fla., 1988; part-time atty. Pub. Defender's Office Fla. 6th Cir., St. Petersburg, 1973-74; bd. dirs. Gulf Coast Legal Svcs., Inc., 1989—, pres., 1994-96. Vol. Cmty. Law Prog., Inc.; coord. James B. Sanderlin for Judge, Pinellas County, Fla., 1972-76; mem. ACLU Legal Panel, St. Petersburg, 1972—; cooperating atty. NAACP Legal Panel, St. Petersburg, 1972—; cooperating atty. NAACP Legal Def. Edn. Funds, Inc., N.Y.C., 1973—; pres. Creative Care, Inc., Clearwater, Fla., 1974-80; mem. allocations com. United Way, Pinellas County, 1976, 1978-81; pres., treas. Cmty. Youth Svcs., Inc., St. Petersburg, 1977-82; co-chmn. Blue Ribbon Com. Pinellas County Dem. Exec. Com., 1977-82; mem. Fla. HRS Dist. V Adv. Coun., Pinellas County, 1982, St. Petersburg Human Rels. Rev. Bd., 1984, 90—, St. Petersburg Adult Cmty. Band, 1989—, Greater St. Petersburg Second Time Around Marching Band, 1990-92; mem. adv. bd. Jacquelyn Elvera Hodges Johnson Fund, 1990—. Mem. ABA, ATLA, FBA, Nat. Assn. Social Security Claimant Reps., Pinellas County Trial Lawyers Assn., St. Petersburg Bar Assn. (pro bono com. 1988, 95—), Bayshore Runners Club, Greater Pinellas County Dem. Club (sec.-treas. 1989-97, bd. dirs. 1997—), Road Runners Club Am. Workers' compensation, Civil rights, Pension, profit-sharing, and employee benefits. Office: 2121 5th Ave N Saint Petersburg FL 33713-8013 also: PO Box 847 Saint Petersburg FL 33731-0847

**ESCHBACH, JESSE ERNEST,** federal judge; b. Warsaw, Ind., Oct. 26, 1920; S. Jesse Ernest and Mary W. (Stout) E.; m. Sara Ann Walker, Mar. 15, 1947; children: Jesse Ernest III, Virginia. BS, Ind. U., 1943, JD with distinction, 1949, LLD (hon.), 1986. Bar: Ind. 1949. Ptnr. Graham, Rasor, Eschbach & Harris, Warsaw, 1949-62; city atty. Warsaw, 1952-53; dep. pros. atty. 54th Jud. Circuit Ct. Ind., 1952-1954; judge U.S. Dist. Ct. Ind., 1962-81; chief judge U.S. Dist. Ct. Ind., 1974-81; judge U.S. Ct. Appeals (7th cir.), W. Palm Beach, Fla., 1981-85, sr. judge, 1985—; Pres. Endicott Church Furniture, Inc., 1960-62; sec., gen. counsel Dalton Foundries, Inc., 1957-62. Editorial staff: Ind. Law Jour, 1947-49. Trustee Ind. U., 1965-70. Served with USNR, 1943-46. Hastings scholar, 1949; Recipient U.S. Law Week award, 1949. Mem. U.S. C. of C. (labor relations com. 1960-62), Warsaw C. of C. (pres. 1955-56), Nat. Assn. Furniture Mfrs. (dir. 1962), Ind. Mfrs. Assn. (dir. 1962), ABA, Ind. Bar Assn. (bd. mgrs. 1953-54, ho. dels. 1950-60), Fed. Bar Assn., Am. Judicature Soc., Order of Coif. Presbyn. Club: Rotarian (pres. Warsaw 1956-57). Home: 11709 N Lake Dr Boynton Beach FL 33436-5518 Office: US Ct Appeals 7th Cir 253 US Courthouse 701 Clematis St West Palm Beach FL 33401-5101

**ESDALE, R. GRAHAM, JR.,** lawyer; b. Birmingham, Ala., June 3, 1957; s. Robert Graham and Angelyn (Brown) E.; m. Leigh-Ann Hibbett, June 2, 1990; 1 child, Whitney Angelyn. BS, Auburn U., 1980; JD, U. Ala., 1989. Bar: Ala. 1989, U.S. Dist. Ct. (no. dist.) Ala. 1989, U.S. Dist. Ct. (mid. and so. dists.) Ala. 1994, U.S. Ct. Appeals (11th cir.) 1994. Dist. sales rep. Fram Corp., Birmingham, Ala., 1980-83; dist. mgr. Gates Rubber Co., Birmingham, Ala., 1983-86; assoc. White, Dunn & Booker, Birmingham, Ala., 1989-90; dep. dist. atty. Jefferson County Dist. Atty.'s Office, Birmingham, Ala., 1990-94; assoc. Emond & Vines, Birmingham, Ala., 1994-96; assoc., shareholder Beasley, Allen, Crow, Methvin, Portis & Miles, Montgomery, Ala., 1996—. Contbr. articles to profl. jours. Mem. ATLA (bd. govs., exec. com. 1996-98), ABA, Ala. Trial Lawyers Assn., Birmingham Bar Assn., Mobile Bar Assn., Montgomery County Bar Assn., Tobacco Trial Lawyers Assn. (exec. com.). Product liability, Personal injury, General civil litigation. Office: Beasley Allen Crow Et Al 218 Commerce St Montgomery AL 36104-2540

**ESHER, JACOB AARON,** lawyer, mediator; b. Boston, Oct. 25, 1950; s. Eli Abraham and Irma (Hoffman) Etscovitz; m. Susan Riedle Foucault, June 1975 (div. Sept. 1979); m. Linda Ann Robinson, May 9, 1984; children: Joel Harry Robinson, Samantha Blihn Robinson. BA, Brandeis U., 1972; JD magna cum laude, U. San Francisco, 1977. Bar: Calif. 1977, Mass. 1985, U.S. Dist. Ct. (no. dist.) Calif. 1977, U.S. Dist. Ct. (ea. dist.) Calif. 1979, U.S. Dist. Ct. Mass. 1985. Assoc. Murphy, Weir & Butler, San Francisco, 1977-79; assoc. counsel, legal dept. Bank of Am., San Francisco, 1979-82; pvt. practice Law Offices of Jacob Aaron Esher, Petaluma, Calif., 1982-84;

ptnr. Riemer & Braunstein, Boston, 1984-90, Rubin and Rudman, Boston, 1990-99; sr. mediator JAMS/Endispute, Boston, 1996—; ptnr. Riley & Esher, Cambridge, 1999—. Author: (manual) Mediation Manual, ABI, 1996, (songs) Blindspot, 1998; contbr. chpt. to Theory and Practice. Mem. Am. Bankruptcy Inst. (chair ADR subcom. 1994—), Boston Bar Assn. (chair ADR subcom. 1995-98). Bankruptcy, Contracts commercial, Alternative dispute resolution. Office: Riley & Esher LLP 69 Thordike St Cambridge MA 02141

**ESKELSON, SCOTT P.,** lawyer; b. Logan, Utah, June 20, 1953; s. Ross W. and Bernice P. Eskelson; m. Lesley Prince, Sept. 16, 1976 (div. Apr. 1991); m. Ronda J. Storer, June 1, 1996; children: Brandon, Heather, Matthew, Mandy. BS in Prelaw, Utah State U., 1976; JD, U. Utah, 1979. Asst. gen. counsel Del E Webb Corp., Phoenix, 1979-83; atty. Petersen, Moss, Olsen Carr Eskelson & Hall, Idaho Falls, Idaho, 1983—. Recipient Outstanding Svc. award Idaho State Bar, Boise, 1993. Avocation: member National Ski Patrol, fly fishing. Probate, State and local taxation, Real property. Office: Petersen Moss Olsen Carr Eskelson & Hall 485 E St Idaho Falls ID 83402-3522

**ESKEW, BENTON,** judge; b. Bastrop, Tex., Sept. 2, 1961; s. Charles Allen and Vina M. (Sims) E. BBA, Baylor U., 1984, JD, 1986. Bar: Tex., U.S. Dist. Ct. (no. and we. dists.) Tex.; ordained Bapt. minister. Assoc. McCamish, Ingram, Martin & Brown, Austin, Tex., 1986-88, Naman, Howell, Smith & Lee, Austin, 1989-91; ptnr. Eskew & Goertz, Bastrop, Tex., 1992-94; judge Bastrop County, Tex., 1994—. Bd. dirs. Child Protective Svcs. Bd., Bastrop, 1994—, Bastrop Boys and Girls Club, 1998—. Mem. Bastrop C. of C., Masons, York Rite, Scottish Rite, Shriners, Lions Club, Kiwanis Club. Home: PO Box 1120 Bastrop TX 78602-1120 Office: Bastrop County Ct Law 804 Pecan St Bastrop TX 78602-3846

**ESKEY, LEO JOSEPH,** lawyer; b. Lincoln, Nebr., July 4, 1946; s. Joseph George and Hanora Cecilia (Malone) E.; m. Garland Louise Kiner, June 27, 1969; 1 child, Joseph Charles. BA, U. Nebr., 1969, JD, 1971. Bar: Nebr. 1971, U.S. Supreme Ct. 1978. Assoc. atty. Harry Stephens Law Office, Fremont, Nebr., 1971-75; ptnr. Eskey & Gless Law Office, Fremont, Nebr., 1975-81; pvt. practice Fremont, Nebr., 1981—; police judge, Fremont, Nebr., 1972; spl. prosecutor Washington County, Fremont, 1985, Dodge County, 1975-99. Mem. St. Patrick's Ch. (finance com. mem 1993-95, ch. coun. mem. 1992-95), Fremont, Nebr.; chmn. alternate Dodge County Bd. Mental Health, 1985—. Mem. Nebr. State Bar Assn., Dodge County Bar Assn., Nebr. Trial Attys. Assn., Nebr. Criminal Def. Attys. Assn., Fremont Area Svc. Club, Fremont Golf Club. Roman Catholic. Family and matrimonial, Juvenile, Criminal. Office: Leo J Eskey Law Office 16 Bell Ctr Fremont NE 68025-3100

**ESKIN, BARRY SANFORD,** court investigator; b. Pitts., Mar. 6, 1943; s. Saul and Dorothy (Zaron) E.; m. M. Joyce Rosalind, Sept. 12, 1965; 1 child, David. AA, L.A. City Coll., 1963; BA, Calif. State U., L.A., 1965; JD, Citrus Belt Law Sch., 1976. Bar: Calif. 1976. Social service worker San Bernardino (Calif.) Dept. Pub. Social Services, 1965-77; assoc. Law Office of Lawrence Novack, San Bernardino, 1978; ct. investigator San Bernardino Superior Ct., 1978, supervising investigator, 1978—; pro bono atty. Mex. Am. Commn., 1977-78. Mem. ARC Svc. Ctr. Advising Bd., San Bernardino, 1980-82; bd. dirs. Golden Valley Civ. Assn., San Bernardino, 1978-81, Congregation Emanuel, San Bernardino, 1984-87, bd. dirs. 1994-96. Mem. ABA, Calif. Assn. of Superior Ct. Investigators (pres. 1980-81, treas. 1984-85, bd. dirs.), San Bernardino County Bar Assn., Alpha Phi Omega. Democrat. Jewish. Avocations: reading, photography, baseball. Office: San Bernardino Superior Ct 351 N Arrowhead Ave Rm 200 San Bernardino CA 92401-1605

**ESPERON, ROSARIA RODRIGUEZ,** lawyer; b. N.Y.C., Nov. 17, 1950; d. Victor Tomas and Raimunda (Fuentes) R.; m. Carlos Esperon, July 3, 1965; children: Carlos Louie, Raimunda. BA, Fordham, U., 1976; JD, Hofstra U., 1980. Bar: N.Y. 1981. Pub. info. specialist N.Y. Divsn. Human Rights, N.Y.C., 1976-77; vis. atty., staff counsel P.R. Legal Def. Fund, N.Y.C., 1980-85; adminstrv. law judge N.Y. Workers' Compensation, N.Y.C., 1985-87; asst. gen. counsel AFSCME, Inc., Dist. Council 37, N.Y.C., 1987-90; asst. dep. comptroller N.Y. Comptroller's Office, N.Y.C., 1990-94, dep. comptroller, claims and contracts, 1994—. Co-editor: (brochurs) How to Become a Lawyer, 1990. Treas., vice-chmn. MFY Legal Svcs., Inc., N.Y.C., 1972-90; vice-chmn. Grand St. Guild Housing Co., N.Y.C., 1973-90; chmn. Joint Planning Coun. on Housing, N.Y.C., 1976-80; mem. Ctr. Social Welfare, Policy and Law, Washington, 1980-85, N.Y. Civil Liberties Union, N.Y.C., 1987-90. Recipient Cmty. Activist award Kings County Dist. Atty., 1995; named to Celebrating Women, N.Y. Women's Found., 1992, 50 Successful Women, El Diario-La Presena, 1996. Mem. P.R. Bar Assn., Hispanic Nat. Bar Assn. Jehovah's Witness. Avocations: reading, sewing, teaching and preaching about Jehovah's kingdom. Office: NY City Office of the Comptroller 1 Centre St Rm 1200 New York NY 10007-1602

**ESPOSITO, CHERYL LYNNE,** lawyer; b. Cleve., Dec. 13, 1964; d. John N. Nard and Patricia A. (Manilla) E.; m. John J. Nebel III, Oct. 20, 1990: children: Deanna Teresa, Dominic Franklyn. BA in Polit. Sci., U. Pitts., 1986, cert. in East Asian studies, 1986, JD, 1989. Bar: Pa. 1989, U.S. Dist. Ct. Pa. 1989. Assoc. Riley & DeFalice, P.C., Pitts., 1989-93, Cauley & Conflenti, Pitts., 1993-94; Marshall, Dennehey, Warner, Coleman & Goggin, Pitts., 1994-97; atty. Warner, Coleman & Goggin, Pitts., 1994-97, Gigler & Joyal, Pitts., 1997—. Soprano U. Pitts. Choral Soc., 1986-91; cantor St. James Ch., Wilkinsburg, Pa., 1991-92, St. Maurice Ch., Forest Hills, Pa., 1992—; mem. steering com. Tribute for First 100 Women Lawyers in Allegheny County, 1992, Tribute to the Female Judiciary of Pa., 1993-94. Mem. ABA (tort and ins. div.), Pa. Bar Assn., Allegheny County Bar Assn., Am. Inn of Ct. (charter), Japan-Am. Soc. Pitts., St. Thomas More Soc. Roman Catholic. General civil litigation, Personal injury. Office: Gigler & Joyal 500 Grant St Ste 2720 Pittsburgh PA 15219-2510

**ESPOSITO, DENNIS HARRY,** lawyer; b. Providence, June 30, 1947; s. Harry Victor and Irene Rose (Radoccia) E.; m. Susan Audrey Cohen, Sept. 28, 1985; children: Matthew Perry, Lauren Elizabeth, Adam Aarons. BS, Boston Coll., 1969; JD, Boston U., 1974. Bar: R.I. 1974, U.S. Dist. Ct. R.I. 1974, Mass. 1984. Assoc. Goldman & Biafore, Providence, 1974-81; ptnr. Vrana, Cunha & Esposito, Providence, 1981-84; pvt. practice, Providence, 1984-91; of counsel McGregor, Shea & Doliner, Boston, 1987-91; ptnr., chmn. environ. practice group Adler Pollock and Sheehan, 1991—; legal counsel Coastal Resources Mgmt., Providence, 1974-81, Narragansett Bay Water Quality Mgmt. Dist. Commn., Providence, 1980-85; adj. prof. environ. law Sch. Law Roger Williams U. Alt. designee R.I. State Planning Council, 1980; legal advisor R.I. Constl. Conv. Commr., 1986-87, R.I. Environ. Quality Study Commn., 1988-90; adminstrv. hearing officer R.I. Dept. of Environ. Mgmt., 1987-89; gov.'s task force for Statutory Reorgn. R.I. Dept. Environ. Mgmt. and Coastal Resources Mgmt. Coun., 1989-90; mem. Gov.'s Commn. on Individual Sewage Disposal Systems and Freshwater Wetlands, 1995. Maj. USAFR, ret. Mem. ABA, R.I. Bar Assn. (chmn. environ. law com. 1985-95), R.I. Trial Assn. Environmental, General practice, General civil litigation. Office: Adler Pollock & Sheehan 2300 Hospital Trust Tower Providence RI 02903-2443

**ESPOSITO, JOSEPH ANTHONY,** lawyer; b. Spokane, Wash., Oct. 4, 1941; s. Charles Esposito and Angela (Migliuri) E.; m. Joyce A. Chastek, Aug. 7, 1966; children: Kate, Molly, Jill, Sara, Amy. BBA, Gonzaga U., 1963, JD, 1969. Bar: Wash., U.S. Dist. Ct. Wash., U.S. Ct. Appeals (9th cir.). Law clk. to presiding justice Wash. State Ct. Appeals, Spokane, 1969-70; lawyer in prin. Dellwo, Rudolph and Grant, Spokane, 1970-73; ptnr. Trezona Lorenz and Esposito, Spokane, 1973-85; prin. Esposito, Tombari and George, Spokane, 1985—. Trustee St. Joseph's Children's Home, Spokane, 1970-85, Gonzaga Preparatory Sch., 1982-88; legal counsel, bd. dirs. Spokane Jr. C. of C., 1969-75; bd. dirs. Spokane Legal Svcs. Bd., 1970-75. Recipient service award Spokane Jr. C. of C., 1973. Mem. Wash. Bar Assn., Manito Golf and Country Club, Rotary. Roman Catholic. Avocations: golf, skiing, fly fishing, hunting. Bankruptcy, Contracts commercial, Real property. Office: Esposito Tombari and George 960 Paulsen Bldg Spokane WA 99201

**ESPOSITO, JOSEPH LOUIS,** lawyer; b. New Haven, Conn., Nov. 2, 1941; s. Joseph Henry and Camille (Carrano) E.; m. Nancy Giller, June 17, 1967 (div. 1973); m. Maddalena Fiorillo, Dec. 17, 1977 (div. 1986); 1 child, Giulio; m. Katherine Valenzuela, Oct. 26, 1996. BS, Fairfield U., 1964; MA, NYU, 1968, PhD, 1970; JD, U. Ariz., 1986. Bar: Ariz. 1987, U.S. Dist. Ct. (9th cir.) Ariz. 1987, U.S. Supreme Ct. 1991, U.S. Ct. Appeals (fed. cir.) 1998. Assoc. prof. philosophy Bradley U., Peoria, Ill., 1968-70; prof. philosophy Bradley U., Peoria, 1970-76; editor, 1974-80; with various bus. ventures, 1981-88; assoc. Smitherman and Sacks, Tucson, 1987-88; ptnr. Smitherman, Sacks and Esposito, Tucson, 1988-89, Smitherman & Esposito, Tucson, 1989-91; pvt. practice Tucson, 1992—; rsch. prof. Inst. for Studies in Pragmatism, Tex. Tech. U., Lubbock, 1975-84. Author five philosophy books; contbr. articles to profl. jours. Mem. Am. Philos. Assn. Avocation: travel. General civil litigation, Civil rights, Labor. Office: 630 N Craycroft Rd Ste 250 Tucson AZ 85711-1456

**ESPOSITO, JOSEPH PAUL,** lawyer; b. Niagara Falls, N.Y., Sept. 4, 1953. BA, SUNY, Buffalo, 1975; JD, NYU, 1978. Bar: N.Y. 1979, D.C. 1980, U.S. Ct. Appeals (2d cir.), U.S. Ct. Appeals (4th cir.), U.S. Ct. Appeals (6th cir.), U.S. Ct. Appeals (11th cir.). Law clk. U.S. Dist. Ct. No. Ind., Hammond, 1978-79, U.S. Ct. Appeals (6th cir.), Akron, Ohio, 1979-80; assoc. Cahill, Gordon & Reindel, N.Y.C., 1980-82, Steptoe & Johnson, Washington, 1982-87; assoc., then ptnr. Heron Burchette Ruckert & Rothell, Washington, 1987-90; of counsel, then ptnr. Akin Gump Strauss Hauer & Feld, Washington, 1990—. Mem. ABA (sect. litigation), Phi Beta Kappa. Federal civil litigation, State civil litigation. Office: Akin Gump et al 1333 New Hampshire Ave NW Washington DC 20036-1511

**ESRICK, JERALD PAUL,** lawyer; b. Moline, Ill., Oct. 1, 1941; s. Reuben and Nancy (Parson) E.; m. Ellen Feinstein, June 18, 1966; children: Sara Elizabeth, Daniel Michael. BA, Northwestern U., 1963; JD, Harvard U., 1966. Bar: Ill. 1966, U.S. Dist. Ct. (no. dist.) Ill. 1967, U.S. Supreme Ct. 1974, U.S. Ct. Appeals (9th cir.) 1985, U.S. Ct. Appeals (7th cir.) 1967. Law clk. U.S. Dist. Ct. (no. dist.) Ill., 1966-68; assoc. Wildman, Harrold, Allen & Dixon, Chgo., 1968-73, ptnr., 1973—, also chmn. firm mgmt. com., 1987-90; lectr. Northwestern U., 1984-93, Coll. Arts and Scis. bd. advs., 1993—, Nat. Panel Comml. Arbitrators, Am. Arbitration Assn. Pres. bd. trustees Nat. Lekotek Ctr., Evanston, Ill., 1989-93, U.S. Toy Libr. Assn., 1987-88; bd. dirs. Evanston Mental Health Assn., 1984-86, Fund for Justice, 1969-95, Lawyers' Com. for Civil Rights, 1974-84. Fellow Am. Coll. Trial Lawyers; mem. ABA, Ill. State Bar Assn., Chgo. Coun. Lawyers (bd. dirs., sec., founding mem.), Chgo. Bar Assn., Legal Club Chgo. Avocations: running, skiing, sailing, windsurfing, classical music. E-mail esrick@whad.com. Antitrust, General civil litigation, General corporate. Home: 1326 Judson Ave Evanston IL 60201-4720 Office: Wildman Harrold Allen & Dixon 225 W Wacker Dr Ste 3000 Chicago IL 60606-1224

**ESSAYE, ANNE ELIZABETH,** lawyer; b. Arlington, Mass., Apr. 2, 1960; d. Anthony Foley and Eileen (Flaherty) Essaye; m. Scott Nord Lurie, Oct. 28, 1988; children: Christopher, Andrew. AB, Duke U., 1982; JD, Georgetown U., 1988. Bar: N.C. 1988, U.S. Dist. Ct. (ea. dist.) N.C. 1988, U.S. Dist. Ct. (we. dist.) N.C. 1989, U.S. Dist. Ct. (mid. dist.) N.C. 1991, U.S. Ct. Appeals (4th cir.) 1989. Ptnr. Kilpatrick Stockton (formerly Petree Stockton), Raleigh, N.C., 1988-91, Charlotte, N.C., 1991—; mem. Civil Justice Reform Act Com., We. Dist. N.C., 1996-98. Bd. dirs. Seigle Ave. Presch., Charlotte, 1995-99; vol. United Way, Charlotte, 1996-97, Dem. Nat. Com. Vol. Lawyers Program, N.C., 1992, 96. Mem. N.C. Bar Assn. (dir. young lawyers divsn. 1994-96, Outstanding Young Lawyer of Yr. 1995, co-chair diversity in the profession com. 1994-96). Health, Administrative and regulatory. Office: Kilpatrick Stockton LLP 3500 One First Union Ctr Charlotte NC 28202

**ESSER, CARL ERIC,** lawyer; b. Montclair, N.J., Feb. 12, 1942; s. Josef and Elly (Graber) E.; m. Barbara A. B. Stelzer, Oct. 12, 1968; children: Jennifer, Eric, Brian. AB, Princeton U., 1964; JD, U. Mich., 1967. Bar: Pa. 1967. Assoc. firm Reed Smith Shaw & McClay LLP, Phila., 1967-72, ptnr., 1973—. With USMCR, 1960-66. Mem. ABA, Pa. Bar Assn., Phila. Bar Assn., Pa. Soc. Healthcare Attys. (bd. dirs.), Pa. Lawyers Fund for Client Security (bd. dirs., chmn.), Octavia Hill Assn. (bd. dirs., asst. sec.), Racquet Club, Penllyn Club (bd. govs.), Mfrs. Golf and Country Club. Republican. Securities, Health, Banking. Office: Reed Smith Shaw & McClay LLP 2500 One Liberty Pl Philadelphia PA 19103

**ESSER, CHRISTINE D.,** lawyer; b. Linton, Ind., Dec. 29, 1967; d. William D. Bakeis and Roberta A. Gilmore Wiley. BS, Millsaps Coll., 1990; JD, Drake U., 1994. Bar: Wis. 1995, U.S. Dist. Ct. (ea. and we. dists.) Wis., U.S. Ct. Appeals (7th cir.). Jud. law clk. to Hon. Marsha K. Ternus Iowa Supreme Ct., Des Moines, 1994-95; assoc. Kasdorf, Lewis & Swietlik, Milw., 1995—. Editor-in-chief Drake Law Rev., 1993-94. Coach, Stillwell Jr. H.S. Mock Trial Team, Des Moines, 1994; tutor Gateway's Paths to Adult Literacy Program, Milw.; chair young lawyer's pub. com. Def. Rsch. Inst., 1997-99. Nat. Tutor of Yr. Gateway, 1998. Mem. Order of Coif, Order of Barristers. Insurance. Office: Kasdorf Lewis & Swietlik 1551 S 108th St Milwaukee WI 53214-4020

**ESSEX, MAUREEN FRANCES,** defender; b. Worcester, Mass., Nov. 16, 1960; d. Michael Joseph Essex and Karen Claire Boden. AB in History and Sociology, Mount Holyoke Coll., 1982; JD, Georgetown U., 1985. Bar: Md. 1986, D.C. 1989. Asst. pub. defender Md. Office of the Pub. Defender, Rockville, 1986—; adj. prof. U. Md. Law Sch., Balt., 1997. Guest lectr. U.S. Info. Agy., Uzbekistan, 1998. Mem. ABA, Nat. Assn. Criminal Def. Lawyers, Md. Criminal Def. Attys. Assn., Bar Assn. Montgomery County. Office: Office of the Pub Defender 27 Courthouse Sq Rockville MD 20850-2325

**ESSIEN, VICTOR KWESI,** lawyer, law librarian; b. Obuasi, Ashanti, Ghana, Apr. 22, 1952; came to U.S., 1981; s. Joseph William and Cecilia Bernice (Renner) E.; m. Ophelia Opoku-Pare, Aug. 12, 1978; children: Bernice, Victor Kwesi Jr. LLB, U. Ghana, 1973, LLM, 1976; LLM in Internat. Law, NYU, 1982, JSD, 1985. Bar: Ghana 1977, N.Y. 1985, U.S. Dist. Ct. (ea. and so. dists.) N.Y. 1985. Lectr. law U. Ghana, Legon, 1976-77, U. Jos (Nigeria), 1977-81; of counsel Deguzman, Essien & Ragland, N.Y.C., 1985-89, Law Offices of Victor Essien, N.Y.C., 1990—; adj. prof. law, internat. law libr. Fordham Law Sch., N.Y.C.; cons. Frost & Sullivan, N.Y.C., 1985-87; legal asst. U.S.-Iran Claims Tribunal, The Hague, Netherlands, 1986; cons. United Nation Centre for Transnat. Corps., 1989—. Contbr. articles to legal jours. Herzfeld scholar NYU, 1982, Robert Marshall fellow, 1982-83. Mem. N.Y. State Bar Assn., Am. Assn. Law Librs. (West Pub. Co. scholar 1986), Am. Fgn. Law Assn., Internat. Third World Legal Studies Assn. Roman Catholic. Avocations: music, drama. Immigration, naturalization, and customs, Private international, Family and matrimonial. Home: 110 W Highland Pky Roselle NJ 07203-2540 Office: Fordham U Law Sch 140 W 62nd St New York NY 10023-7407

**ESSLING, WILLIAM WARREN,** lawyer; b. Eveleth, Minn., July 18, 1915; s. Victor Emanuel and Marjorie Marie (McGrath) E.; m. Margaret Rose Geblin, Sept. 12, 1935; children: William M., James M., David E., Margaret M., Joel. BS, U. Minn., 1937; LLB, St. Paul Coll. Law, 1939; JD, William Mitchell Coll. Law, 1969. Bar: Minn. 1939, U.S. Dist. Ct. Minn. 1946, U.S. Bd. Appeals 1949, U.S. Claims Ct. 1951, U.S. Ct. Appeals (8th cir.) 1959, U.S. Supreme Ct. 1959, Minn. Bd. Tax Appeals 1963, U.S. Ct. Appeals (7th cir.) 1981, U.S. Ct. Appeals (fed. cir.) 1986. Spl. asst. atty. gen. State of Minn., St. Paul, 1950-56, mem. bd. tax appeals, tax ct., 1963-67; 1st asst. U.S. atty. for dist. of Minn. U.S. Dept. Justice, St. Paul, 1956-60; spl. asst. to atty. gen. Robert F. Kennedy, U.S. Dept. Justice, St. Paul and Washington, 1961-63; prin. Essling Ltd., St. Paul; law clk. to Hon. George F. Sullivan U.S. Dist. Ct., St. Paul, 1936-39; pvt. practice Eveleth and Deluth, Minn.; pvt. practice, State Farm Mutual Ins. Co., Eveleth and Duluth; 1st asst. U.S. atty. HLS attys., St. Paul; spl. asst. to dep. atty. gen. Minn. A.G. Lord and Mondale; now pvt. practice St. Paul; adj. prof. law St. Paul Coll. Law, William Mitchell Coll. of Law, both St. Paul, 1969. Bd. dirs. Boundary Water Landowners Assn., 1975—. With USN, 1945. Mem. ABA, Ramsey County Bar Assn., Minn. State Bar, St. Paul Athletic Club. Democrat. Roman Catholic. Avocations: hunting, fishing, travel, baseball. Home: 1404 Lincoln Ave Saint Paul MN 55105-2216 Office: Essling Ltd 1217 7th St W Saint Paul MN 55102-4197

**ESSLINGER, JOHN THOMAS,** lawyer; b. Ephrata, Pa., Aug. 11, 1943; s. Doster Alvin and Lucy Mildred (Ream) E.; m. Patricia Lynn Smith, Aug. 15, 1970; 1 child, John David. BA, Yale U., 1965; JD, Georgetown U., 1973. Bar: D.C. 1973, U.S. Dist. Ct. D.C. 1974, U.S. Supreme Ct. 1974, U.S. Ct. Appeals (D.C. cir.) 1974. Assoc. Morgan, Lewis & Bockius, Washington, 1973-76; ptnr. Schmeltzer, Aptaker & Shepard, P.C., Washington, 1976—. Capt. USMC, 1966-70, Vietnam. Decorated Purple Heart, Bronze Star, Gold Star. Mem. ABA, Bar Assn. D.C., D.C. Bar Assn., Maritime Adminstrv. Bar Assn. Episcopalian. Avocations: golf, wine, baseball. Federal civil litigation, Labor, Transportation. Home: 9102 Brierly Rd Chevy Chase MD 20815-5655 Office: Schmeltzer Aptaker & Shepard PC 2600 Virginia Ave NW Ste 1000 Washington DC 20037-1905

**ESSMYER, MICHAEL MARTIN,** lawyer; b. Abilene, Tex., Dec. 6, 1949; s. Lytle Martin Essmyer and Roberta N. Essmyer Nicholson; m. Cynthia Rose Piccolo, Dec. 27, 1970; children: Deanna, Mike, Brent Austin. BS in Geology, Tex. A&M U., 1972; postgrad., Tex. Christian U., 1976; JD summa cum laude, South Tex. Coll. Law, 1980. Bar: Tex. 1980, U.S. Dist. Ct. (no., so., ea. we. dists) Tex. 1982, U.S. Ct. Appeals (5th cir.) 1981, U.S. Ct. Appeals (9th cir.) 1990, U.S. Ct. Appeals (1st cir.) 1993, U.S. Ct. Appeals (7th cir.) 1995, U.S. Ct. Appeals (fed. cir.) 1985, U.S. Ct. Claims, 1981, U.S. Supreme Ct. 1991. Briefing atty. Supreme Ct. Tex., Austin, 1980-81, Haynes & Fullenweider, Houston, 1981-89, Essmyer & Hanby, Houston, 1989-92; atty. Essmyer & Assocs., Houston, 1992-94; pres. Essmyer & Tritco, LLP, Houston, 1994-95, Essmyer, Tritco & Clary, LLP, Houston, 1995-99, Essmyer & Tritco, LLP, Houston, 1999—. Lead article editor South Tex. Law Jour., 1979. Dem. candidate for state rep., Bryan, Tex., 1972; del. Dem. Party, Houston, 1982, 84; precinct chmn. Harris County Dem. Exec. Com., Houston, 1983-86. Capt. USAF, 1972-78. Nat. Merit Scholar, 1968-72. Mem. ABA, Houston Bar Assn., Tex. Trial Lawyers Assn. (assoc. dir. 1996—), Harris County Trial Lawyers Assn. (dir. 1997—), Assn. Trial Lawyers Am., Tex. Criminal Def. Lawyers Assn., Tex. Bar Found., Harris County Criminal Lawyers Assn. (dir. 1986-87), Fed. Bar Assn., Houstonian Club, The Doctor's Club of Houston. Roman Catholic. E-mail: essmyer@flash.net. Criminal, Personal injury, Federal civil litigation. Home: 1122 Glourie Dr Houston TX 77055-7506 Office: Essmyer & Tritico LLP 4300 Scotland St Houston TX 77007-7328

**ESTEP, ARTHUR LEE,** lawyer; b. Forsyth, Mo., Dec. 4, 1932; s. Raymond B. and Nancy Mabel (Melton) E.; m. Joan Marie Hayes, June 16, 1956; 1 child, Sallie Ann Estep Warren. BS, U. Mo., 1954; JD, U. Ariz., 1959, honors grad., 1989. Bar: Ariz. 1959, Calif. 1959. Trust officer 1st Nat. Bank, San Diego, 1959-60; dep. city atty. City of San Diego, 1960-71; pvt. practice San Diego, 1961—. Bd. visitors U. Ariz., Tucson, 1986-96. 1st lt. USMC, 1950-56, Korea. Recipient Outstanding Svc. to Legal Profession award San Diego Bar Assn., 1986. Diplomate Am. Bd. Trial Advs. (pres. San Diego chpt. 1991, mem. nat. bd. dirs. 1990-96). General civil litigation. Office: Estep & Warren 2257 Front St San Diego CA 92101-1999

**ESTES, ANDREW HARPER,** lawyer; b. Pecos, Tex., Dec. 16, 1956; s. Bobby Frank and Gayle (Harper) E.; m. Deidre Dement, Mar. 19, 1976; children: Andrew Kimble, Jada Catherine. BA, Tex. Tech U., 1977; JD, Baylor Sch. Law, 1979. Bar: Tex. 1980, U.S. Dist. Ct. (no. dist.) Tex. 1980, U.S. Dist. Ct. (we. dist.) Tex. 1981, U.S. Ct. Appeals (5th cir.) 1982, U.S. Supreme Ct. 1983, U.S. Tax Ct., U.S. Ct. Appeals (10th cir.) 1987. Ptnr. Lynch, Chappell & Alsup P.C., Midland, Tex., 1980—; mem. admissions com. Dist. 16, State Bar Tex., 1982-85, bd. dirs., 1999—. Mem. Tex. Tech. U. Coll. Edn. Devel. Coun., Lubbock, 1986-87; vol. Big Bros., Midland, 1983—, bd. dirs., 1985-89; bd. dirs. Hearthstone Temporary Children's Shelter, 1988-92. Named Big Brother of Yr., Big Bros./Big Sisters of Midland, 1985; recipient Trimble Vol. Svc. award, Leadership Midland Alumni, 1986, Pro Bono Atty. award West Tex. Legal Svcs., 1991. Mem. ABA, Midland County Young Lawyers Assn. (sec., treas. 1987-88, Outstanding Young Lawyer of Midland County 1992), Midland County Bar Assn. (sec., treas. 1987-88, v.p. 1992-93, pres. elect. 1993-94, pres. 1995-96), State Bar Tex. (Dist. 16B grievance com. 1990-93, chmn. 1992-93), Tex. Young Lawyers Assn. (bd. dirs. 1987-89), Tex. Bd. Legal Specialization (cert.), Phi Delta Phi. Presbyterian. Federal civil litigation, State civil litigation. Home: 1404 Princeton Ave Midland TX 79701-5760 Office: Lynch Chappell & Alsup PC The Summit Bldg 300 N Marienfeld St Fl 7 Midland TX 79701-4345

**ESTES, CARL LEWIS, II,** lawyer; b. Ft. Worth, Feb. 9, 1936; s. Joe E. and Carroll E.; m. Gay Gooch, Aug. 29, 1959; children: Adrienne Virginia, Margaret Ellen. B.S., U. Tex., 1957, LL.B., 1960. Bar: Tex. 1960. Law clk. U.S. Supreme Ct., 1960-61; assoc. firm Vinson & Elkins, Houston, 1961-69; ptnr. Vinson & Elkins, 1970—. Bd. dirs. Houston Grand Opera Assn., Houston Arboretum. Fellow Am. Bar Found., Tex. Bar Found.; mem. ABA, Internat. Bar Assn., Am. Law Inst., Am. Coll. Probate Counsel, Tex. Bar Assn., Internat. Fiscal Assn., Internat. Acad. Estate and Trust Law. Fellow Am. Bar Found., Tex. Bar Found.; mem. ABA, Internat. Bar Assn., Am. Law Inst., Am. Coll. Probate Counsel, Tex. Bar Assn., Internat. Fiscal Assn., Internat. Acad. Estate and Trust Law, Asia Soc. (bd. dirs.). Corporate taxation, Personal income taxation, Private international. Office: Vinson & Elkins 3300 First City Towers Houston TX 77002

**ESTES, RICHARD MARTIN,** lawyer; b. N.Y.C., June 27, 1933; s. Jack Estes and Irene Eva (Dessauer) Schwarz; m. Pamela Jane Graine, Mar. 18, 1965; children: Kenneth Murray, William Jonathan, Jessica Jane. BA, Yale Coll., 1955; LLB, Columbia U., 1959; LLM in Taxation, NYU, 1962. Bar: N.Y. 1959, Fla. 1976; U.S. Supreme Ct. 1962. Assoc. White & Case, N.Y.C., 1959-62, Root, Barrett, Cohen Knapp & Smith, N.Y.C., 1962-65; asst. tax counsel Rockefeller Family & Assocs., N.Y.C., 1965-68; tax counsel Bear, Stearns & Co., N.Y.C., 1968-70; assoc. to ptnr. Spear & Hill, N.Y.C., 1970-75; founding ptnr. Christy & Viener, N.Y.C., 1976-98, Salans, Hertzfeld, Heilbronn, Christy & Viener, N.Y.C., 1999—; lectr. in field. Contbr. articles to profl. jours. Trustee, sec., nomination com. N.Y.C. Police Found., 1971—; bd. mem., v.p., sec. Yale Project 55, Inc., N.Y.C., 1993—; trustee, treas. 1010 Tenants Corp., N.Y.C., 1988—. Maj. USAR, 1955-65. Honored as co-founder N.Y.C. Police Found., 1991. Mem. ABA, Assn. of the Bar of the City of N.Y. (libr. com.), N.Y. State Bar Assn. (tax sect.), Fla. Bar Assn., Univ. Club (coun., libr. and art com. 1976—), Grolier Club, Harmonie Club, Beach Point Club. Avocations: antiquarian book collector, fitness, reading, travel. Taxation, general, Pension, profit-sharing, and employee benefits, General corporate. Office: Salans Hertzfeld Heilbronn Christy & Viener 620 5th Ave New York NY 10020-2402

**ESTES, ROYCE JOE,** lawyer; b. Topeka, Kans., Mar. 30, 1944; s. Joseph Sumner and Mildred Eve (Lunday) E.; m. Marla Ann Hampton, June 13, 1964; children—Gina Christine, Darin Wesley, Erika Alynn. B.A., Kans. State U., 1968; J.D., U. Mo., 1972, LL.M., 1975. Bar: Mo. 1972, Ill. 1976. Ptnr. firm Linde, Thomson, Fairchild, Langworthy & Kohn, Kansas City, Mo., 1972-75; asst. gen. counsel A.E. Staley Mfg. Co., Decatur, Ill., 1975-79; assoc. gen. counsel Anheuser-Busch Cos., Inc., St. Louis, 1979-82, sr. assoc. gen. counsel, 1983, dep. gen. counsel, 1983-90, v.p., dep. gen. counsel, 1992-95, v.p. corp. law antitrust, mktg. & distbn., 1995—; dir. Metal Container Corp., Sunset Hills. Staff mem. U. Mo. Law Rev., 1970-71. Served with USN, 1969-70. Law Found. scholar U. Mo., 1967-68. Mem. ABA, Mo. Bar Assn., Ill. State Bar Assn. Antitrust, General corporate. Home: 628 Wood Fern Dr Ballwin MO 63021-5865 Office: Anheuser Busch Cos Inc One Busch Pl Saint Louis MO 63118*

**ESTES, STEWART ANDREW,** lawyer; b. Tucson, Feb. 22, 1960; s. L. Donald and Y.L. Charlene (Stewart) E. BA in Polit. Sci., U. Ariz., 1982; JD, U. N.Mex., 1985. Bar: Wash. 1985, U.S. Dist. Ct. (ea. and we. dist.) 1985), U.S. Ct. Appeals (9th cir.) 1985, U.S. Supreme Ct. 1994. Jud. intern Supreme Ct. of N.Mex., Albuquerque, 1985; assoc. Winston & Cashatt, Spokane, Wash., 1985-86, Keating, Bucklin & McCormack, Seattle, 1992—; staff atty. Spokane Legal Svc. Ctr., Spokane, 1986-87; asst. atty. gen. State of Wash. Office of Atty. Gen., Olympia, 1987-92. Contbr. articles to profl. jours. Mem. Wash. State Bar Assn. (legal aid com. 1989-92, civil rights com. 1995-97, ct. rules and procedures 1997—), Wash. Def. Trial Lawyers (amicus and seminar coms. 1992—). Federal civil litigation, Civil rights, Municipal (including bonds). Office: Keating Bucklin McCormack 800 5th Ave Ste 4141 Seattle WA 98104-3175

**ESTEVE, EDWARD V.,** lawyer; b. N.Y.C., May 29, 1937; s. Edward J. and Maria Ignacia (Alcaraz) E.; m. Mildred Briand, June 10, 1961; children: Greg, Christopher, Kimberly. Grad., NYU, 1959; LLB, JD, N.Y. Law Sch., 1962. Ptnr. Taitz, Bernard & Esteve, Patchogue, N.Y., to 1997, Pelletreau & Pelletreau, Patchogue, 1997—; adj. prof. Touro Coll. Law, Huntington, N.Y., 1995—; mem. com. on character and fitness, 2d dept. N.Y. Appellate Divsn., 1991—. Bd. dirs. Brookhaven Meml. Hosp., Patchogue, 1995—; v.p., officer Suffolk Acad. Law, 1977-89. Mem. N.Y. State Bar Assn. (gen. practice sect. 10th and 11th jud. dist. v.p. 1981-82, pres. com. access justice 1990-96), Suffolk County Bar Assn. (pres. 1989-90, bd. dirs. and exzc. com. 1977-93). Avocation: aviation. General civil litigation, Real property, Criminal. Office: Pelletreau & Pelletreau PO Box 110 20 Church St Patchogue NY 11772-3564

**ESTILL, JOHN STAPLES, JR.,** lawyer; b. Grapevine, Tex., Jan. 20, 1919; s. John Staples and Ada Beauchamp (Chambers) E.; m. Dorothy Finlayson, Nov. 27, 1940; children: John S. III, James Calloway, Sally Finlayson Muhlbach. BS in Commerce, Tex. Christian U., 1940; JD, So. Meth. U., 1948. Bar: Tex. 1948, U.S. Dist. Ct. (no. dist.) Tex. 1948, Kans. 1958, Okla. 1966, U.S. Ct. Appeals (5th cir.) 1973, D.C. 1978, U.S. Supreme Ct. 1978. Pvt. practice law Ft. Worth, 1948-50; asst. atty. U.S. Dept. Justice, Ft. Worth, 1950-53; atty. Sinclair Oil & Gas Co., Ft. Worth, 1953-57, Tulsa, 1965-66; atty., gen. atty. Sinclair Pipe Line Co., Independence, Kans., 1957-65; atty. Hall, Estill, Hardwick, Gable, Golden & Nelson, P.C., Tulsa, 1966-76, pres., 1976-90, of counsel, 1990—; sec. Sinclair Pipe Line Co., Independence, 1964-65, Williams Pipe Line Co., Tulsa, 1969-87. Served to lt. USNR, 1942-46. Mem. ABA, Okla. Bar Found. (trustee 1984-87), D.C. Bar Assn., Kans. Bar Assn., Tex. Bar. Assn., Tulsa County Bar Assn., Colonial Country Club. Republican. Methodist. Avocation: golf. Transportation, General corporate, Administrative and regulatory. Address: 320 S Boston Ave Ste 400 Tulsa OK 74103-3704

**ESTREICHER, SAMUEL,** lawyer, educator; b. Bergen, Democratic Republic Germany, Sept. 29, 1948; came to U.S., 1951; s. David and Rose (Abramowicz) E.; m. Aleta Glaseroff, Aug. 10, 1969; children: Michael, Hannah. BA, Columbia U., 1970, JD, 1975; MS in Labor Rels., Cornell U., 1974. Bar: N.Y. 1976, D.C. 1978, U.S. Dist. Ct. (so. and ea. dists.) N.Y., U.S. Ct. Appeals (2d and 11th cirs.), U.S. Supreme Ct. Law clk. to assoc. judge U.S. Ct. Appeals (D.C. cir.), 1975-76; assoc. Cohn, Glickstein, Lurie, Ostrin & Lubell, N.Y.C., 1976-77; law clk. to assoc. justice Lewis F. Powell Jr. U.S. Supreme Ct., Washington, 1977-78; prof. law NYU, 1978—; of counsel Cahill, Gordon & Reindel, N.Y.C., 1984-98; labor and employment counsel O'Melveny & Myers LLP, N.Y.C., 1998—; vis. prof. law Columbia U., 1984-85; dir. NYU-Inst. Jud. Adminstrn., 1991—, Ctr. for Labor and Employment Law at NYU Sch. Law, 1996—. Author: Redefining the Supreme Court, 1986, Labor Law and Business Change, 1988, The Law Governing the Employment Relationship,1990, 2d edit., 1992, Labor Law: Text and Materials, 4th edit., 1996, Procs. of 49th NYU Annual Conference on Labor, 1997, Employee Representation in the Emerging Workplace: Alternatives/Supplements to Collective Bargaining, 1999, Sexual Harassment in the Workplace, 1999; contbr. articles to profl. jours.; editor-in-chief Columbia U. Law Rev., 1974-75. Pulitzer Fund scholar, 1966-70; Herbert H. Lehman fellow, 1970-72. Mem. ABA (labor and employment law sect. 1978—), N.Y. State Bar Assn. (labor and employment law sect. 1980—), Assn. Bar City N.Y. (chmn. labor and employment law com. 1984-87), Am. Law Inst. Office: O'Melveny & Myers LLP 153 E 53d St New York NY 10022-4611

**ETHRIDGE, LARRY CLAYTON,** lawyer; b. Houston, Feb. 27, 1946; s. Robert Pike and Gladys Jeannette (Grant) E.; m. Edith Kirkbride Gilbert, May 21, 1977; children: Elizabeth Kirkbride, Grant Harbin. BA, Duke U., 1968; JD cum laude, U. Louisville, 1975. Bar: Ky. 1975, U.S. Dist. Ct. (we. dist.) Ky. 1980, U.S. Ct. Appeals (6th cir.) 1981. Intern Adv. Commn. on Intergovtl. Rels., Washington, 1975-76; asst. dir. model procurement code project ABA, Washington, 1976-80; ptnr. Mosley, Clare & Townes, Louisville, 1980-97, Ackerson Mosley & Yann, 1997—; cons. ABA model procurement code project, Washington, 1980-82; panel mem. N.Y. State Procurement Rev., 1984—. Co-author: Supplement to Annotations on the Model Procurement Code, 1991, Annotations, 3d edit., 1996. Elder Highland Presbyn. Ch., Louisville, clk. of session, 1989-90, 96—; vol. Am. Cancer Soc.; gen. counsel Mobile Riverine Force Assn., 1995—. Lt. USNR, 1969, Vietnam, Cambodia, and Japan. Recipient Disting. Svc. award Nat. Inst. Govtl. Purchasing, 1987. Fellow Am. Bar Found. (life); mem. ABA (chmn. coord. com. on a model procurement code 1985-96, co-chmn. model procurement code revision project steering com. 1997—, coun. mem., state and local govt. law sect. 1988—, sect. publs. dir. 1990-93, comms. dir. 1993-95, sec. 1995-96, vice-chmn. 1996-97, chmn. elect 1997-98, chmn. 1998-99, Donald M. Davidson award), AAA Ky. (bd. dirs. 1990-96, sec., gen. counsel 1996—) , Ky. Bar Assn., Louisville Bar Assn. (co-chmn. golf com.), Jefferson Fordham Soc., U. Louisville Law Alumni Assn. (pres. 1990-92), U. Louisville Alumni Assn. (exec. com., bicentennial history com. 1994—, Alumni Svc. award), Duke Club Ky. (pres. 1992-94), Waggener H.S. Alumni Assn. (pres. 1996-97), Univ. of La. Club (bd. dirs. 1997—). Republican. Presbyterian. Avocations: gardening, travel, golf, bicycling, reading. General civil litigation, Government contracts and claims, Construction. Home: 2402 Longest Ave Louisville KY 40204-2125

**ETHRIDGE, ROBERT MICHAEL,** lawyer; b. Macon, Ga., Sept. 21, 1960; s. Robert Ernest and Sandra (Grimsley) E.; m. Jane West, Aug. 1982 (div. Apr. 1985); m. Harriet Woods, Dec. 10, 1989; 1 child, Anna Margaret. BA, Miss. Coll., Clinton, 1982; MDiv, So. Bapt. Theol. Sem., Louisville, 1986; JD, U. Ga. Atty. Webb, Carlock, Copeland, Semler & Stair, Atlanta, 1988—. Mem. Ga. Bar Assn., Atlanta Bar Assn., Gwinnett Bar Assn., Lawyers Club. Avocation: music. General civil litigation, Family and matrimonial, Construction. Office: Webb Carlock 2600 Marquis Two Tower 285 Peachtree Center Ave NE Atlanta GA 30303-1229

**ETKIND, STEVEN MARK,** lawyer; b. N.Y.C., Nov. 25, 1961; s. Irving M. and Judith Ann (Conrad) E.; m. Lanie Debra Padzensky, Nov. 30, 1986. BA in Econs., Brandeis U., 1983; JD, Tulane U., 1986. Bar: N.Y. 1987. Tax assoc. Stephen I. Soble & Co., N.Y.C., 1986-87, Spicer & Oppenheim, N.Y.C., 1987—. Contbr. articles on estate planning and taxation to profl. publs. Office: Kleinberg Kaplan Wolff Cohen PC 551 5th Ave Fl 18 New York NY 10176-1800

**ETTERS, RONALD MILTON,** lawyer, government official; b. San Antonio, Nov. 6, 1948; s. Milton William and Ilse Charlotte (Ostler) E.; m. Anna Colleen Wesson, Feb. 12, 1977; children: William Lawrence, Elizabeth Charlotte, Margaret Lawreen. BA magna cum laude, Am. U., 1971, JD, 1976. Bar: Va. 1976, U.S. Ct. Appeals (D.C. cir.) 1977, U.S. Dist. Ct. (ea. dist.) Va. 1978, U.S. Ct. Appeals (4th and 9th cirs.) 1978, U.S. Supreme Ct. 1979, D.C. 1980, U.S. Dist. Ct. D.C. 1980, U.S. Ct. Appeals (1st and 2d cirs.) 1980, U.S. Ct. Appeals (7th cir.) 1981, U.S. Ct. Appeals (3rd, 11th and Fed. cirs.) 1982, U.S. Ct. Appeals (5th cir.) 1983. Intern to gen. counsel Adminstrv. Office of U.S. Cts., Washington, 1970-71; fed. mgmt. intern IRS, Washington, 1971-72, labor rels. officer, 1972-75; ptnr. Nusbaum & Etters, Burke, Va., 1976-80; hearing officer, chief hearing officer Nat. Mediation Bd., Washington, 1975-80, gen. counsel, 1980—; with Sigma Alpha, 1971; justice Phi Alpha Delta, 1975; professorial lectr. Am. U., Washington, 1978-83; adj. prof. law Georgetown U., Washington, 1985-88. Sr. bd. editors The Railway Labor Act, 1991—. Mem. ABA (co-chmn. com. on railway and airline labor law 1987-93), Christian Legal Soc., Nat. Lawyers Assn. Home: PO Box 2374 Centreville VA 20122-2374 Office: Nat Mediation Bd 1301 K St NW East Tower Washington DC 20005

**ETTINGER, JOSEPH ALAN,** lawyer; b. N.Y.C., July 21, 1931; s. Max and Frances E.; children: Amy Beth, Ellen Jane. BA, Tulane U., 1954, JD with honors, 1956. Bar: La. 1956, Ill. 1959. Asst. corp. counsel City of Chgo., 1959-62; pvt. practice, Chgo., 1962-73, 76-80; sr. ptnr. Ettinger & Schoenfield, Chgo., 1980-92; pvt. practice, Chgo., 1993—; assoc. prof. law Chgo.-Kent Coll., 1973-76; chmn. Village of Olympia Fields (Ill.) Zoning Bd. Appeals, 1969-76; chmn. panel on corrections Welfare Coun. Met. Chgo., 1969-76; spl. state appellate defender State of Ill., 1997-98. Contbr. articles to profl. publs. Capt. JAGC, U.S.Army, 1956-59. Recipient svc. award Village of Olympia Fields, 1976. Mem. Chgo. Bar Assn., Assn. Criminal Def. Lawyers (gov. 1970-72). Criminal, Personal injury, Federal civil litigation.

**EUBANK, CHRISTINA,** oil company executive; b. Temple, Tex., Jan. 17, 1944; d. G. R. and Catherine (Andrews) E. B.A., Baylor U., 1966, J.D., 1973. Bar: Tex. 1973. Atty., Champlin Petroleum Co., Ft. Worth, Tex., 1973-76, asst. gen. atty., 1976-78, staff atty., 1978-79, sr. staff atty., 1979-81, gen. atty., 1981-83, sr. gen. atty., 1983-84, asst. gen. counsel, 1984—. Contbg. author, mem. task force Presdl. Commn. War on Waste, 1984; contbr. Baylor Law Rev. Recipient Am. Jurisprudence award, 1973; Presdl. Letter of Commendation, 1982, Disting. Alumnae award Hill Coll., 1987. Mem. ABA, Tex. Bar Assn., Am. Corp. Counsel Assn., Am. Labor Lawyers Assn. (pres.). Greek Orthodox. Clubs: Shady Oaks Country, Woman's, Petroleum. Administrative and regulatory, Labor. Home: 1239 Roaring Springs Rd Fort Worth TX 76114-4489 Office: Union Pacific Resources Co 801 Cherry St Fort Worth TX 76102-6803

**EUBANKS, GARY LEROY, SR.,** lawyer; b. North Little Rock, Ark., Nov. 22, 1933; s. Herman and Gertrude (Carmack) E.; m. Mary Joyce Gathright, 1955 (div. 1966); children: Gary Leroy Jr., Bobby Ray; m. Beverly Gayle Mauldin, Apr. 21, 1971 (div. 1983); 1 child, Shane Mauldin; m. Elizabeth Duncan, Dec. 18, 1987. JD, U. Ark., 1960. Bar: Ark. 1960, U.S. Dist. Ct. Ark. 1960, U.S. Supreme Ct. 1970. Ptnr. Bailey, Jones, and Eubanks, Little Rock, 1960-63, Eubanks and Deane, Little Rock, 1963-65, Eubanks, Hood, and Files, Little Rock, 1965-69, Eubanks, Files and Hurley, Little Rock, 1969-76, Haskins Eubanks and Wilson, Little Rock, 1976-79, Gary Eubanks and Assocs., Little Rock, 1979—. Mem. Ark. Ho. of Reps., 1963-66, Pulaski County (Ark.) Sch. Bd., 1967. Served with USN, 1952-54. Mem. ABA, Ark. State Bar Assn., Pulaski County Bar Assn., Ark. Trial Lawyers Assn., Assn. Trial Lawyers Am., Am. Bd. Trial Advocacy (civil trial advocate). Democrat. Methodist. Personal injury. Home: 211 Scenic Dr Hot Springs National Park AR 71913-7729 Office: PO Box 3887 Little Rock AR 72203-3887

**EUBANKS, RONALD W.,** lawyer, broadcaster; b. Montgomery, Ala., Sept. 17, 1946; s. William Shell and Violet Lavern (Walker) E.; 1 child, Edward Todd; m. Anna Shaw; stepdaughter, Jennifer Shaw. Student, Auburn U., 1964-65; BA, U. Ala., 1968; JD, U. Utah, 1974. Bar: Utah 1974, Nebr. 1979, Minn. 1983, Wash. 1985, U.S. Ct. Appeals (10th cir.) 1977, U.S. Ct. Appeals (8th cir.) 1979, U.S. Supreme Ct. 1977, U.S. Ct. Appeals (9th cir.) 1985. Gen. mgr. Sta. WVMI and Sta. WQID, Biloxi Gulfport, Miss., 1968-71; with FCC, Washington, 1974-75; assoc. Hansen & Hansen, Salt Lake City, 1975-77; with law dept. Union Pacific R.R., Omaha, 1977-83; asst. gen. counsel Burlington No. R.R. Co., St. Paul, 1983-84, gen. counsel western region, 1984-87; v.p. law and corp. affairs Glacier Park Co., 1987-88; exec. v.p. Ecos Corp., 1988; CEO Capital Comms., Montgomery, 1991-97; pres. ET Comms., Montgomery, 1988-97; sr. regional v.p. So. Star Comm., 1997—; dir. Camas Prairie R. R., Longview Switching Co. Co-author: Practical Law in Utah, 1978, Defense of Mary Carter, 1984; contbr. articles to profl. publs. Bd. dirs., mem. exec. com., legal counsel Utah Boys Ranch, Salt Lake City, 1977-79; bd. dirs. Children and Youth Svcs., Salt Lake City, 1977-84, Nebr. affiliate Am. Diabetes Assn., 1982-83, Greater Montgomery Sickle Cell Found., 1990—, Ala. Broadcasters Assn., 1998—; co-chmn. Montgomery Father and Son Banquet Com., 1993—; bd. dirs., mem. exec. com. Montgomery Mental Health Assn., 1995—, treas., 1996—; bd. dirs., mem. exec. com. Montgomery Area Coun. on Aging; bd. advisors, dept. comm. Ala. State U., 1995—. Recipient Friend of Youth award YMCA, 1993; named Role Model of Yr. Southlawn Sch., 1996-97. Mem. ABA (sect. on litigation, coms. on publs. and trial techniques, sect. on tort and ins. practice, com. on r.r. law), Washington State Bar Assn., Seattle-King County Bar Assn., Wash. R.R. Assn. (chmn. 1984-87), Def. Rsch. Inst. (chmn. com on r.r. law 1984-86, mem. com. on practice and procedure), Jason's Soc., Phi Alpha Delta, Alpha Tau Omega. Presbyterian. Home: 9750 Vaughn Rd Pike Road AL 36064-2751 Office: Capital Comm 648 Perry St Montgomery AL 36104

**EUGENE, JOHN,** lawyer; b. Glen Cove, N.Y., Aug. 18, 1940; s. Edward and Asimina (Stergionis) E. BS, St. Peter's Coll., Jersey City, 1961; JD, Rutgers U., Newark, 1964. Bar: N.J. 1966, D.C. 1968, U.S. Dist. Ct. N.J. 1966, U.S. Supreme Ct. 1970, N.Y. 1972, Fla. 1977, U.S. Dist. Ct. (so. and ea. dists.) N.Y. 1984. Spl. agt. U.S. Treasury Dept., Washington, 1965-67; pvt. practice, Metuchen, N.J., 1967—. Mem. Nat. Coll. Criminal Def. Lawyers (grad. charter class 1972). Criminal, General practice, Probate. Office: 475 Main St PO Box 449 Metuchen NJ 08840-0449

**EUSTICE, FRANCIS JOSEPH,** lawyer; b. LaCrosse, Wis., Feb. 2, 1951; s. Frank R. and Cecelia T. (Babler) E.; m. Mary J. McCormick, July 28, 1971; children: Cristen L., Tara L. BS in Chemistry, Kansas Newman Coll., 1976; JD, U. Wis., 1980. Bar: Wis. 1980, U.S. Dist. Ct. (ea. and we. dists.) Wis. 1980, U.S. Tax Ct. 1981, U.S. Ct. Appeals (7th cir.) 1990, U.S. Dist. Ct. (no. dist.) Ill. 1993. With Eustice, Albert & Laffey, S.C. and predecessor firms, Sun Prairie, Wis., 1980—; bd. dirs., pres. Sun Prairie Devel. Corp., 1989—. Bd. dirs. Exch. Ctr. for Prevention of Child Abuse, Inc., Dane County, Wis., 1984-95. Sgt. USAF, 1973-77. Mem. Wis. Bar Assn., Dane County Bar Assn., Sun Prairie C. of C. (bd. dirs., pres., amb. 1987—), Sun Prairie Exch. Club (sec., pres., bd. dirs. 1980—). Roman Catholic. Contracts commercial, Banking, General corporate. Office: PO Box 590 100 Wilburn Rd Ste 202 Sun Prairie WI 53590-1478

**EUSTICE, JAMES SAMUEL,** legal educator, lawyer; b. Chgo., June 9, 1932; s. Burt C. and Julia (Bohon) E.; m. LaVaun Schild, Jan. 29, 1956 (dec. 1994); m. Carol Fonda, Nov. 1995; children: Cynthia, James M. BS, U. Ill., 1954, LLB, 1956; LLM in Taxation, NYU, 1958. Bar: Ill., 1956, N.Y., 1958. Assoc. White & Case, N.Y.C., 1958-60; prof. law NYU, N.Y.C., 1960—; counsel Kronish Lieb, N.Y.C., 1970—. Mem. ABA, N.Y. State Bar Assn., Am. Coll. Tax Counsel, Order of Coif. Republican, Presbyterian. Club: University (N.Y.C.). Author: (with Bittker) Federal Income Taxation of Corporations and Shareholders, 1994, (with Kuntz) Federal Income Taxation of Subchapter S Corporations, 1993. Office: NYU Sch Law 40 Washington Sq S New York NY 10012-1005

**EUSTIS, JEFFREY MURDOCK,** lawyer; b. Glen Cove, N.Y., Sept. 30, 1947; s. Richard Spellman and Lenore (Murdock) E.; m. Teresa Ann Wolber, Apr. 23, 1983; children: Ian Campbell, Ross Camden. AB, Harvard U., 1970; JD, U. Puget Sound, 1979. Bar: Wash. 1979, U.S. Dist. Ct. (we. dist.) Wash. 1981, Alaska 1982, U.S. Dist. Ct. Alaska 1982. Atty. Leed Law Offices, Seattle, 1979-81, Trustees for Alaska, Anchorage, 1981-84; pvt. practice J. Richard Aramburu, Seattle, 1985—; founder and dir. 1000 Friends of Wash., Seattle, 1991—, Wash. Wildlife Fedn., Pullman, 1989-91, Northwest Rivers Coun., Seattle, 1986-89, 97. Contbr. chpt. to book Treatist, 1984, 89, 96; editor: Environmental Law Newsletter, 1986-89. Drafter Citizens for Balanced Growth, Seattle, 1990. Mem. Wash. State Bar Assn. (bd. dirs. land use sect. 1990-93), Seattle/King County Bar Assn. (com. chair 1987-89). Democrat. Avocations: environmental activist, Nordic skiing (nat. and world cup competitor). Land use and zoning (including planning), Environmental, Real property. Office: 505 Madison St Ste 209 Seattle WA 98104-1138

**EUSTIS, RICHMOND MINOR,** lawyer; b. New Orleans, Nov. 24, 1945; s. David and Molly Cox (Minor) E.; m. Catherine Luise Baños, Apr. 15, 1971; children: Richmond Minor Jr., Julie Bransford, Joshua Leeds, Molly Minor. BA in Econs., U. Va., 1967; JD, Tulane U., 1970. Bar: La. 1970. Assoc. Phelps Dunbar, New Orleans, 1970-75; ptnr. Monroe and Lemann, New Orleans, 1975-96; founder, ptnr. Eustis & O'Keefe, LLC, New Orleans, 1996—. Bd. dirs. Children's Bur., 1976-88, treas., 1984. Mem. ABA, La. Bar Assn., New Orleans Bar Assn. (chmn. torts and ins. com. 1992-95), Maritime Law Assn., S.E. Admiralty Law Inst., Boston Club, La. Club. Republican. Episcopalian. Avocation: fishing. Admiralty, General civil litigation, Insurance. Home: 289 Audubon St New Orleans LA 70118-4841 Office: Eustis & O'Keefe 228 Saint Charles Ave Ste 1010 New Orleans LA 70130-2686

**EVANS, ALLENE DELORIES,** lawyer; b. Cin., Oct. 4, 1951; d. Allen Douglas and Margaret (Spradley) E. Student, U. Ams., Cholula, Mex., 1971; BA, Adams State Coll., 1972; JD cum laude, U. Minn., 1977. Bar: Minn. 1977, Tex. 1983, U.S. Dist. Ct. (no., so., ea., we. dists.) Tex. 1983, U.S. Dist. Ct. Minn. 1977, U.S. Ct. Appeals (5th and 9th cirs.), U.S. Supreme Ct. Assoc. Broeker, Hardfelt, Mpls., 1977-80; assoc. counsel Northwestern Nat. Life Ins. Co., Mpls., 1980-82; asst. city atty. City of Corpus Christi, Tex., 1983-84; asst. dist. atty. Nueces County, Corpus Christi, Tex., 1984-85; asst. atty. gen. Atty Gen.'s Office, Austin, Tex., 1985-91; mem. bd. dirs. Tex. State Bd. Ins., Austin, 1991-94; capital ptnr. Edwards, Perry & Haas, LLP, Austin, Corpus Christi, 1994—; expert witness on NAFTA Tex. Legislature and U.S. Congress; speaker to bar, industry and govt. groups on ins. regulations, anti-trust issues. Recipient Tex. Outstanding Pub. Svc. award Consumers' Union, Tex. Consumer Assn., Tex. Gray Ptnrs. Mem. Tex. Bar Assn. (chair anti-trust and bus. litigation sect. 1993-94), Tex.-Mex. Bar Assn (bd. dirs. Corpus Christi 1998-2000). Democrat. Presbyterian. Product liability, Insurance, Antitrust. Office: Edwards Perry & Haas LLP 2100 Frost Bank Plz Corpus Christi TX 78403

**EVANS, CHARLES GRAHAM,** lawyer; b. Charlottesville, Va., Sept. 13, 1949; s. Kerr Stewart and Josephine (Smith) E.; m. Nancy M. Lee, Dec. 29, 1984; children: Charles G. IV, Elizabeth Q. BA with distinction, U. Va., 1972, JD, 1976. Bar: Va. 1976, U.S. Dist. Ct. (we. dist.) Va. 1976, Alaska 1977, U.S. Ct. Appeals (4th cir.) 1977, U.S. Dist. Ct. Alaska 1978, U.S. Ct. Appeals (9th cir.) 1978, U.S. Supreme Ct. 1993. Assoc. Law Offices J. Anthony Smith, Anchorage, 1977-78; partner Smith & Gruening, Anchorage, 1978-84, Smith Robinson & Greuning, Anchorage, 1984-85, Smith Robinson Gruening & Brecht, Anchorage, 1985-86, Smith Gruening Brecht Evans & Spitzfaden, Anchorage, 1986-87, Wohlforth Flint & Gruening, Anchorage, 1987-88; pvt. practice Law Offices Charles Evans, Anchorage, 1988—; dir. Post-Conviction Assistance Project, Charlottesville, Va., 1974-76; mem. Anchorage Hazardous Materials Commn., 1990-92. Dir. Anchorage Audubon Soc., 1979-92, Nat. Audubon Soc., N.Y.C., 1987-92. Mem. ABA (fidelity & surety law section legis reporter), Va. State Bar, Alaska Bar Assn. (arbitrator 1989-92). Avocations: birding, fishing, wilderness recreation. General civil litigation, Consumer commercial, Construction. Office: 4201 Tudor Centre Dr Ste 108 Anchorage AK 99508-5914

**EVANS, DOUGLAS HAYWARD,** lawyer; b. Providence, R.I., July 21, 1950; s. Jerrold Merton and Gladys Jean (Snelgrove) E.; m. Sarah Edwards Cogan, May 28, 1983; children: Anne Morrill, Thomas Taylor Seelye, Elizabeth Hayward. AB, Franklin & Marshall Coll., 1972; JD, Cornell U., 1975. Bar: N.J. 1975, U.S. Dist. Ct. N.J. 1975, N.Y. 1976, U.S. Dist Ct. (so. dist.) N.Y. 1991. Assoc. Windels, Marx, Davies & Ives, N.Y.C., 1975-85; assoc. Sullivan & Cromwell, N.Y.C., 1985-90, spl. counsel, 1990—; faculty NYU Inst. Fed. Taxation, N.Y.C., 1984; counsel, treas., pres. St. David's Soc. State of N.Y., N.Y.C., 1985—; bd. dirs. Friends of Washington Sq. Park, 1989—, Washington Sq. Assn., 1992—. Co-Author: Estate Accounting, 1980, Probate and Estate Administration, 1982, Administration of Estates, 1985, Settling An Estate, 1989; Editor-in-Chief and Co-Author: Probate and Administration of New York Estates, 1995; also articles. Trustee Franklin & Marshall Coll., 1994—, Grace Ch. Sch., N.Y.C., 1997—; mem. Ch. Club of N.Y. Fellow Am. Coll. of Trust and Estate Coun.; mem. ABA, N.J. Bar Assn., N.Y. State Bar Assn. (estate litig. and adminstrn. of trusts and estates com., com. on Cont. Legal Edn.; chmn. 1991-94), N.Y. County Lawyers Assn. (com. for not-for-profit orgns.), Phi Beta Kappa, Phi Delta Phi, Phi Alpha Theta, Pi Gamma Mu. Episcopalian. Estate planning, Probate, Estate taxation. Home: 43 Fifth Ave New York NY 10003-4368 Office: Sullivan & Cromwell 125 Broad St Fl 28 New York NY 10004-2489

**EVANS, G. ANNE,** lawyer; b. Eastland, Tex., Feb. 24, 1954; d. Travis Clay and Maude Velma (DeMoss) E.; children: Courtney Faith, Alexandria Brooke. BA in Psychology, U. Nebr., Omaha, 1988; JD, U. Nebr., Lincoln, 1991. Bar: Nebr. 1991, U.S. Dist. Ct. Nebr. 1991, U.S. Ct. Appeals (8th cir.) 1992. Pvt. practice, Omaha, 1991—. Mm. ABA (vice chair solo practioners/small firm com.), Nat. Assn. Criminal Def. Lawyers, Nebr. State Bar Assn., Nebr. Criminal Def. Attys. Assn., Am. Inns of Ct. (co-founder Omaha chpt.), Golden Key, Phi Alpha Delta, Psi Chi. Democrat. Roman Catholic. Avocations: theatre, hiking, climbing, calligraphy. Criminal, Family and matrimonial, Personal injury.

**EVANS, JAMES E.,** lawyer; b. 1946. BA, Mich. State U., 1968; JD, Ohio State U., 1970. Bar: Ohio 1971. Assoc. Keating, Muething & Klekamp, 1971-76; v.p., gen. counsel Am. Fin. Corp., Cin., 1976—, now sr. v.p. General corporate, Securities. Office: Am Fin Corp 1 E 4th St Cincinnati OH 45202-3717

**EVANS, JAN ROGER,** lawyer; b. Camden, N.J., Nov. 25, 1942; s. Gordon Russell and Gloria Beulah (Smith) E.; m. Michaelyn P. Evans, Aug. 10, 1963; children: Janell Patrice, Jessica Ann. BA, Rutgers U., Camden, N.J., 1964; JD, U. Wis., 1967; LLM, Temple U., Phila., 1988. Bar: N.J. 1968, U.S. Dist. Ct. N.J. 1968, U.S. Ct. Appeals (3d cir.) 1986, U.S. Supreme Ct. 1987. Assoc. Taylor, Bischoff, Neutze & Williams, Camden, N.J., 1967-70; assoc. counsel N.J. Mfrs. Ins. Co., West Trenton, 1970-72, Yeager, Evans & O'Brien, Camden, N.J., 1973-75; ptnr. Evans & O'Brien, Audubon, N.J., 1975-79; pvt. practice Medford, N.J., 1979-98; with Evans Faccenda Karpf, Medford, 1998—; gen. counsel Victims of Compensation Abuses Under the Law, Westville, N.J. Mem. Am. Trial Lawyers Assn., N.J. Trial Lawyers Assn. Personal injury, Workers' compensation, Labor. Home: 156 Atsion Rd Medford NJ 08055-1311 Office: 152 Himmelein Rd Ste 8 Medford NJ 08055-9316

**EVANS, JEFFREY ALLEN,** lawyer; b. Washington; s. Thomas Jay and Ann Evans. BA in Polit. Sci. with honors, U. Calif., Berkeley, 1992; JD, U. Va., 1997. Intern Select Com. on Narcotics Abuse and Control, Washington, 1987; programmer Montgomery Securities, San Francisco, 1991-92; snowboard instr. Aspen Ski Co., Snowmass, Colo., 1993-94; summer assoc. Freshfields, London, 1995, Davis Polk & Wardwell, N.Y.C., 1996, Covington & Burling, Washington, 1996, O'Melveny & Myers, Newport Beach, Calif., 1997; summer assoc. Wilson Sonsini Goodrich & Rosati, Palo Alto, Calif., 1997, assoc., 1998—; jud. clk. Hon. Raymond A. Jackson U.S. Dist. Ct. for the Ea. Dist. Va., Norfolk, 1997-98; assoc. Wilson Sonsini Goodrich & Rosati, Palo Alto, Calif., 1998—. Mng. editor Va. Jour. Internat. Law, 1995-97; mem. editl. bd. Va. Law Rev., 1996-97. Mem. Phi Delta Phi, Pi Kappa Alpha (Alpha Sigma chpt. sec. 1989-90), Order of the Coif, Order of Omega. Avocations: travel, golf, snowboarding.

**EVANS, LANCE T.,** lawyer; b. Lubbock, Tex., Nov. 2, 1963; s. Tim Evans and Mary Ann Fergus-Evans. BA in English, Tex. Tech. U., 1988, JD, 1991. Asst. dist. atty. Tarrant County Offic of Dist. Attys., Ft. Worth, 1991-95; pvt. practice Law Office of Evans, Gandy, Daniel and Moore, Ft. Worth, 1996—; mem. faculty Criminal Trial Advocacy Inst., Huntsville, Tex., 1997-98. Mem. Tarrant County Bar Assn., Tex. State Bar Assn., Coll. of State Bar of Tex., Tarrant County Criminal Def. Lawyers Assn. (v.p. 1998), Tex. Criminal Def. Lawyers Assn., Inn of Ct. Criminal, Juvenile. Office: Evans Gandy Daniel & Moore 115 W 2d Ste #202 Fort Worth TX 76102

**EVANS, LARRY G.,** lawyer; b. Gary, Ind., Nov. 18, 1939; s. Gene Henley and Josephine Belle Evans; m. Gene Hilda Rosenthal, Dec. 16, 1961; children: Dec. 10, 1979; m. Laura T. Saims, Oct. 4, 1981; children: Carolyn, Kim, Eric, August. AB, Valparaiso U., 1960, JD, 1962. Bar: Ind. 1962, U.S. Dist. Ct. Ind., U.S. Supreme Ct. Dep. prosecuting atty. Porter County, Valparaiso, Ind., 1963; atty. Hoeppner, Wagner Evans, Valparaiso, 1963—; prof. Valparaiso Sch. of Law, 1972-80; chmn. N.W. Ind. Pub. Broadcasting, Merrillville, Ind. Contbr. articles to profl. jours. Mem. ABA, Fed. Bar Assn. (pres. 1985), Ind. Bar Assn., Porter County Bar Assn. Labor, Federal civil litigation, Product liability. Office: Hoeppner Wagner & Evans 103 Lincolnway Valparaiso IN 46383-5637

**EVANS, LAWRENCE E.,** lawyer, educator; b. Houston, Mar. 30, 1950; s. Lawrence Edgar and Edith (Kinzy) E.; m. Nancy Campbell, Aug. 20, 1977; children: Christopher, Laura. BA, Washington & Lee U., 1973; JD, South Tex. Coll., 1977. Bar: Tex. 1977, Mo. 1989. Lawyer Gunn, Lee & Miller, Houston, 1977-88, Herzog, Crebs & McGhee, St. Louis, 1988—; adj. prof. Washington Univ., St. Louis, 1996. Mem. Metro. Bar Assn. St. Louis (chmn. Patent, Trademark and Copyright sect. 1994), Internat. Trademark Assn., Am. Intellectual Property Law Assn. Intellectual property, Patent, Trademark and copyright. Office: Herzog Crebs & McGhee One City Ctr 24th Fl Saint Louis MO 63101

**EVANS, LAWRENCE JACK, JR.,** lawyer, judge; b. Oakland, Calif., Apr. 4, 1921; s. Lawrence Jack and Eva May (Dickinson) E.; m. Marjorie Hisken, Dec. 23, 1944; children: Daryl S. Kleweno, Richard L., Shirley J. Coursey, Donald B. Diplomate Near East Sch. Theology, Beirut, 1951; MA, Am. U. Beirut, 1951; grad. Command and Gen. Staff Coll., 1960; PhD, Brantridge Forest Sch., Sussex, Eng., 1968; JD, Ariz. State U., 1971; grad. Nat. Jud. Coll., 1974. Bar: Ariz. 1971, U.S. Dist. Ct. Ariz. 1971, U.S. Ct. Claims 1972, U.S. Customs Ct., 1972, U.S. Tax Ct. 1972, U.S. Ct. Customs and Patent Appeals 1972, U.S. Ct. Appeals (9th cir.) 1972, U.S. Supreme Ct. 1975. Enlisted U.S. Navy, 1938-41, U.S. Army, 1942-44, commd. 2d lt. U.S. Army, 1944, advanced through ranks to lt. col., 1962; war plans officer, G-3 Seventh Army, 1960-62, chief, field ops. and tactics divsn., U.S. Army Spl. Forces, 1963, chief spl. techniques divsn., U.S. Army Spl. Forces, 1964, unconventional warfare monitor, U.S. Army Spl. Forces, 1964-65; ops. staff officer J-3 USEUCOM, 1965-68; mem. Airborne Command Post Study Group, Joint Chiefs of Staff, 1967; ret., 1968; mem. faculty Ariz. State U., 1968; sole practice law, cons. on Near and Middle Eastern affairs, Tempe, Ariz., 1971-72, 76—; v.p., dir. Trojan Investment & Devel. Co., Inc., 1972-75; active Ariz. Tax Conf., 1971-75; mem. adminstrv. law com., labor mgmt. rels. com., unauthorized practice of law com. Ariz. State Bar. Author: Legal Aspects of Land Tenure in the Republic of Lebanon, 1951, International Constitutional Law, (with Helen Miller Davis) Electoral Laws and Treaties of the Near and Middle East, 1951; contbr. articles to mags., chpts. to books. Chmn. legal and legis. com. Phoenix Mayor's Com. To Employ Handicapped, 1971-75; active Tempe Leadership Conf., 1971-75; chmn. Citizens Against Corruption in Govt., 1976-95; mem. Princeton Coun. on Fgn. and Internat. Studies, 1968; comdr. Ranger Area-Ariz., Ranger Region-West, 1993—. Decorated Silver Star, Legion of Merit, Bronze Star, Purple Heart, Combat Infantryman badge, Master Parachutist badge, Aircrewman badge; named Outstanding Adminstrv. Law Judge for State Service for U.S., 1974; named to U.S. Army Ranger Hall of Fame, 1981. Fellow Coll. of Rites of U.S.A.; mem. Ranger Bns. Assn. World War II (life), Tempe Rep. Mens Club (v.p., bd. dirs. 1971-72), U.S. Army Airborne Ranger Assn. (life), Mil. Order Purple Heart (life), NRA (official referee, life), Masonic Order of the Bath, The Philatethes Soc., Ye Antient and Old Order of Corks, Order of the Secret Monitor, BL (twice past master Thunderbird Lodge # 48 Phoenix, past master Ariz. Rsch. Lodge # 1), Order Ky. Colonels, Sovereign Mil. Order of Temple of Jerusalem (grand avocat pro tem 1993, grand officier 1993), Knight Commdr. Grace Sovereign Mil. Order St. John Jerusalem (Knights Hospitallers), Grand Chpt. Royal Arch Masons Ariz. (grand lectr.), Fraternal Order of Medieval Knighthood, Internat. (sovereign venerable master Ariz. Coll. 1988-93, supreme sovereign grand master 1991), YR (past high priest, past thrice illustrious master, twice eminent past comdr., Knight Templar Cross of Honor, 1988, Orator Order of High Priesthood, Grand Chpt. YRM 1989, pres. Grand Coun. Holy Order of High Priesthood of Ariz. 1996-97, York Rite Mason of Decade, Scottsdale YRB 1989), SR (32, ritual dir.), Chief Adept Ariz. Coll. Socs. Rosicruceana In Civitatibus Foederatis IX Degree, Grand Commandery of Knights Templar of Ariz. (grand insp. gen. 1990-91), Grand Royal Arch Masons Ariz. (grand lectr. 1995-96), Masons (knight U.S.A., Chevalier and Ami du Patriarchate, KCM Ordo Sancti Constantini Magni), Order of Secret Monitor, So. Calif. Rsch. Lodge, Royal Order of Scotland, Comdr. Ranger Area-Ariz. (Ranger Region- West Red 1993), Mil. Order of World Wars (historian, archivist), The Nat. Sojourners Inc., United Assn. (life, local #469 Phoenix), Phi Delta Phi, Delta Theta Phi, Alpha Rho of Theta Chi. Episcopalian. General corporate, General practice. Home: 539 E Erie Dr Tempe AZ 85282-3712

**EVANS, MICHELLE LEE,** lawyer, educator; b. Ft. Sam Houston, Tex., June 22, 1970; d. William H. and Linda Lee (Johnson) E.; m. Richard L. Marryott, Aug. 2, 1996. BS, U. Tex., San Antonio, 1991; JD, St. Mary's U., San Antonio, 1995. Bar: Tex. 1995. Rsch. asst. St. Mary's U. Sch. Law, San Antonio, 1994-95; jud. intern U.S. Dist. Ct., San Antonio, 1995; real estate instr. Am. Coll. Real Estate, San Antonio, 1996-97; instr. Alamo Real Estate Inst., San Antonio, 1997—, Tex. Luth. U., San Antonio, 1997—; paralegal instr. U. Tex., San Antonio, 1997—; prof. San Antonio Coll., 1997—; pvt. practice San Antonio, 1995—; cmty. edn. instr. Northside Ind. Sch. Dist., San Antonio, 1990—. Co-author: Texas Real Estate Contracts, 1999; contbr. articles to profl. jours. Fundraiser March of Dimes, San Antonio, 1991-96. Mem. ABA, Am. Chem. Soc., Real Estate Educators Assn., San Antonio Bar Assn., Greater San Antonio C. of C., San Antonio Women's C. of C., Tex. Real Estate Tchrs. Assn., Phi Delta Phi, Alpha Chi. Address: 700 N St Marys San Antonio TX 78205-3507

**EVANS, ORINDA D.,** federal judge; b. Savannah, Ga., Apr. 23, 1943; d. Thomas and Virginia Elizabeth (Grieco) E.; m. Roberts O. Bennett, Apr. 12, 1975; children: Wells Cooper, Elizabeth Thomas. B.A., Duke U., 1965; J.D. with distinction, Emory U., 1968. Bar: Ga. 1968. Assoc. Fisher & Phillips, Altanta, 1968-69; assoc. Alston, Miller & Gaines, Atlanta, 1969-74, ptnr., 1974-79; judge U.S. Dist Ct. (no. dist.) Ga., Atlanta, 1979—; adj. prof. Emory U. Law Sch., 1974-77; counsel Atlanta Crime Commn., 1970-71. Recipient Disting. award BBB, 1972. Mem. Atlanta Bar Assn. (dir. 1979). Democrat. Episcopalian. Office: US Dist Ct 1988 US Courthouse 75 Spring St SW Atlanta GA 30303-3309

**EVANS, PAUL VERNON,** lawyer; b. Colorado Springs, Colo., June 19, 1926; s. Fred Harrison and Emma Hooper (Austin) E.; m. Patricia Gwyn Davis, July 27, 1964; children: Bruce, Mike, Mark, Paul. B.A. cum laude, Colo. Coll., 1953; J.D., Duke U., 1956. Bar: Colo. 1956, U.S. Dist. Ct. Colo. 1956, U.S. Supreme Ct. 1971, U.S. Ct. Appeals (10th cir.) 1974. Field mgr. Keystone Readers Service, Dallas, 1946-50; sole practice Colorado Springs, 1956-60; ptnr. Goodbar, Evans & Goodbar, 1960-63; sr. ptnr. Evans & Briggs Attys., Colorado Springs, 1963-95; city atty. City of Fountain, Colo., 1958-62, City of Woodland Park, Colo., 1962-78; atty. Rock Creek Mesa Water Dist., Colorado Springs, 1963—. Author instruction materials. Precinct com. man Republican Com., Colorado Springs, 1956-72. Served with USNR, 1944-46, PTO. Recipient Jr. C. of C. Outstanding Achievement award, 1957. Mem. Colo. Mining Assn., Am. Jud. Soc., ABA, Colo. Bar Assn. (com. chmn. 1966-67, 84), El Paso County Bar Assn. (com. chmn. 1956—0, Assn. Trial Lawyers Am., Colo. and Local Trial Lawyers, Tau Kappa Alpha (pres.), Phi Beta Kappa. Republican. Club: Optimist (pres. 1966-67). General practice, Family and matrimonial, Personal injury. Home: 244 Cobblestone Dr Colorado Springs CO 80906-7624 Office: 227 E Costilla St Colorado Springs CO 80903-2103

**EVANS, ROBERT DAVID,** legal association executive; b. Vergennes, Vt., Mar. 1, 1945. BA, Yale U., 1966; JD, U. Mich., 1969. Bar: Ill. 1969. Assoc. Sachnoff Schrager Jones & Weaver, Chgo., 1969-72; asst. dir. divsn. pub. svc. activities ABA, Chgo., 1972-73; asst. dir. govtl. rels. office ABA, Washington, 1973-78, assoc. dir. govtl. rels. office, 1978-82, dir. govtl. affairs office, 1982—, assoc. dir., dir. Washington Office, 1988—. Mem. Washington Grove (Md.) Town Coun., 1977-81, Washington Grove Town Planning Commn., 1977-81; mayor Washington Grove, 1981-83; vice chmn. assns. divsn. Nat. Capital Area United Way, 1986, chmn., 1987. Recipient Spl. Achievement award Nat. Legal Aid and Defender Assn., 1990. Fellow ABA, Am. Bar Found. Home: PO Box 332 Washington Grove MD 20880-0332 Office: ABA 740 15th St NW Fl 8 Washington DC 20005-1022

**EVANS, ROBERT WHITESIDE, III,** lawyer; b. Pottstown, Pa., Dec. 24, 1951; s. Robert Whiteside Jr. and Julia (Gutshall) Evans. BA, Haverford Coll., 1973; JD, Villanova U., 1976. Bar: Pa. 1976, Md. 1982. Assoc. Mauger & Spare, Pottstown, 1976-79; ptnr. Mauger, Spare & Evans, Pottstown, 1979-81; sr. trust officer First Nat. Bank Md., Balt., 1981-85; pvt. practice Pottstown, 1987-89; gen. counsel Am. Inst. Metaphysics Studies, Washington, 1986-89, resident staff Kriplau Ctr., 1989—; cons. adult mentor, 1990—. Pres. Pottstown Pub. Libr., 1979-81. Mem. ABA, Pa. Bar Assn., Montgomery Bar Assn. Republican. Avocation: macrobiotic cooking. Probate, Real property. Home: 351 Highland Rd Pottstown PA 19464-4407 Office: 29 N Hanover St Pottstown PA 19464-5485

**EVANS, ROGER,** lawyer; b. Syracuse, N.Y., Apr. 18, 1951; s. David Longfellow and Louise Maude (Crawford) E.; children: Jonathan Longfellow, Gillian Crawford, Catherine Leigh, Skylar Elizabeth; m. Catherine Stayman, Aug. 4, 1989. AB, Cornell U., 1974; postgrad., Columbia U., 1976-77; JD, Harvard U., 1977. Bar: Ohio 1977, U.S. Dist. Ct. (no. dist.) Ohio 1978, Tex. 1981, U.S. Dist. Ct. (no. dist.) Tex. 1981, U.S. Dist. Ct. (so. dist.) Tex. 1997, U.S. Ct. Appeals (5th, 6th and 11th cirs.) 1981, U.S. Ct. Appeals (10th cir.) 1982, U.S. Tax Ct. 1989, U.S. Dist. Ct. (we. dist.) Tex. 1998. Assoc. Jones, Day, Reavis & Pogue, Cleve., 1977-81, Dallas, 1981-84; ptnr. Shank, Irwin & Conant, Dallas, 1985, Gardner, Carton & Douglas, Dallas, 1986-88, Vinson & Elkins, Dallas, 1988-91; pvt. practice Dallas, 1991—; gen. counsel Equest, Inc., Dallas, 1986-88; instr. trial advocacy So. Meth. U. Sch. Law, instr. law and econs.; instr. labor law Baylor U.; mem. faculty Nat. Inst. Trial Advocacy. Gen. counsel, bd. dirs. Freedom Ride Found., Dallas, 1985-86; mem. cmty. svcs. bd. mgmt. YMCA, 1990-92; bd. dirs. Legal Svcs. Corp. North Tex., 1991-92; mem. adv. bd. dirs. Providence Christian Schs. of Tex., Inc., 1995—. Recipient Advocacy award Dallas Epilepsy Assn., 1995. Mem. Tex. Bar Assn., Cornell U. Alumni Assn. (class pres. 1984-89), Harvard U. Law Sch. Alumni Assn. No. Ohio (sec. 1978-81), Harvard Club. Republican. Presbyterian. Federal civil litigation, State civil litigation, Labor. Office: 2708 Fairmount St Ste 210 Dallas TX 75201-1961

**EVANS, TERENCE THOMAS,** federal judge; b. Milwaukee, Wisc., Mar. 25, 1940; s. Robert Hansen and Jeanette (Walters) E.; m. Joan Marie Witte, July 24, 1965; children: Kelly Elizabeth, Christine Marie, David Rourke. BA, Marquette U., 1962, JD, 1967. Bar: Wis. 1967. Law clk. to justice Wis. Supreme Ct., 1967-68; dist. atty. Milw. County, 1968-70; pvt. practice law Milw., 1970-74; cir. judge State of Wis., 1974-80; judge U.S. Dist. Ct. (ea. dist) Wis., Milw., 1980-95, U.S. Ct. Appeals (7th cir.), 1995—. Mem. ABA, State Bar Wis., Milw. Bar Assn. Roman Catholic. Office: US Courthouse & Federal Bldg 517 E Wisconsin Ave Rm 721 Milwaukee WI 53202-4504*

**EVANS, THOMAS S.,** lawyer; b. Coral Gables, Fla., July 27, 1943; s. Robert C. and Wilma A. Evans; m. Cynthia P. Faigle, Aug. 1, 1970; children: Elizabeth S., David T. BA, Duke U., 1965, JD, 1969; postgrad., U. Ceylon, 1965-66. Bar: Mich. 1969, N.Y. 1971, Fla. 1977, U.S. Dist. Ct. (no. dist.) N.Y. 1971, U.S. Ct. Appeals (2d cir.) 1977, U.S. Supreme Ct. 1980. Assoc. Warner, Norcross & Judd, Grand Rapids, Mich., 1969-70; from assoc. to sr. ptnr. Bond, Schoeneck & King, LLP, Syracuse, N.Y., 1971—; mem. adv. bd. law tech. and mgr. program, Syracuse U. Coll. of Law, 1985-90. Bd. dirs., pres. Friends of Burnet Park Zoo, Syracuse, 1984-90; trustee Manlius Pebble Hill Sch., syracuse, 1992-98, Syracuse U. Theatre, Syracuse, 1986-92, 98—. Mem. ABA, N.Y. State Bar Assn., Onondaga County Bar Assn., Nat. Assn. of Col./Univ. Attys., Greater Syracuse C. of C. (bd. dirs. 1992—). Republican. Avocations: golf, racquetball, cross-country skiing, hunting, fishing. General corporate, Intellectual property, Non-profit and tax-exempt organizations. Office: Bond Schoeneck & King LLP One Lincoln Ctr Syracuse NY 13202

**EVANS, THOMAS WILLIAM,** lawyer; b. N.Y.C., Dec. 9, 1930; s. William J. and R. Helen (Stenvall) E.; m. Lois deBaun Logan, Dec. 22, 1956; children: Heather, Logan, Paige. BA, Williams Coll., 1952; JD, Columbia U., 1958; EdD, Piedmont Coll., 1993. Bar: N.Y. 1958, U.S. Supreme Ct. 1961. Assoc. Simpson, Thacher & Bartlett, N.Y.C., 1958-64; asst. coun. to spl. state commn. of investigation, spl. dep. asst. N.Y. Atty. Gen., N.Y.C., 1964-65; assoc. Mudge Rose Guthrie Alexander & Ferdon, N.Y.C., 1965-66, ptnr., 1967-93, of counsel, 1993-94; of counsel Andrews & Kurth, Washington, 1995—; founder MENTOR, nat. law-related edn. program for pub. sch. students, 1983. Author: The School in the Home, 1973, Admissions Practices (Center for Public Resources), 1986, Mentors, 1992. Chmn. Nat. Symposium on Partnerships in Edn., 1983-90; chmn. bd. trustees Columbia U. Tchrs. Coll., 1991-98, trustee, 1985—, adj. prof. of ednl. adminstrn., 1992-95; co-chmn. N.Y. Korean Vets. Meml. Commn.; chmn. The Mentor Ctr., L.C., 1998—. With USMC, 1952-54. Mem. ABA, Fed. Bar Coun. (pres. 1989-90, trustee 1981—), Century Assn. Republican. Episcopalian. Federal civil litigation, State civil litigation. Home: 10245 Collins Ave Bal Harbour FL 33154-1407 Office: Andrews & Kurth LLP 1701 Pennsylvania Ave NW Washington DC 20006-5805

**EVANS, WAYNE LEWIS,** lawyer; b. Bluefield, W.Va., Mar. 30, 1954; s. Douglas Evan and Wanda (Shrewsberry) E.; m. Cheryl Jane Richardson, June 28, 1980; children: Lisa Marie, Jason Lloyd. BA summa cum laude, U. N.C., Greensboro, 1976; MS, Radford U., 1978; diploma, Roanoke Police Acad., 1980; JD, Wake Forest U., 1984. Bar: W.Va. 1984, U.S. Dist. Ct. (so. dist.) W.Va. 1984, U.S. Ct. Appeals (4th cir. 1989); cert. Va. Cert. Bds. Zoning Appeals Programs. Probation/parole officer Va. Dept. Corrections, Tazewell, Va., 1976-77; dep. sheriff Roanoke County Sheriff Dept., Salem, Va., 1979-81; summer assoc. Katz Kantor & Perkins, Bluefield, W.Va., 1982; sr. assoc. Katz, Kantor & Perkins, Bluefield, 1985—; summer assoc. Gardner, Moss, Brown & Rocovich, Roanoke, 1983; assoc. Law Office of John H. Shott, Bluefield, 1984-85; v.p., sec. WELD Enterprises, 1989-95; mem. Campaigning With Lee-Civil War Roundtable, Va. Tech., 1994, 95, 96, 97; speaker at seminars. Mem. Bd. Zoning Appeals, Bluefield, 1991—; participant Career Awareness, Mercer County (W.Va.) Schs., 1989, 92; coach Odyssey of the Mind, Tazewell County (Va.) Schs., 1994, 95, 96, 97, judge, 1999; vol. United Way, Mercer and Tazewell Counties, 1989; chmn. com. PTA, Dudley Primary Sch; leader Boy Scouts Am., Bluefield, Va., 1996—; pres. Graham Middle Sch. PTA, Bluefield, 1997—; pres. Graham H.S. Band Boosters, 1999-00. Mem. ATLA, W.Va. Trial Lawyers Assn., Fincastle Country Club, Phi Beta Kappa, Psi Chi, Phi Kappa Phi. Avocations: golf, tennis, Civil War history. General civil litigation, Personal injury, Health. Home: 45 College Dr Bluefield VA 24605-1736 Office: Katz Kantor and Perkins 307 Federal St Bluefield WV 24701-3005

**EVANS, WILLIAM DAVIDSON, JR.,** lawyer; b. Memphis, Jan. 20, 1943; s. William D. and Maxey (Carter) E.; m. Eileen McKenna, June 19, 1971; children: William D., Carter M., Alexander B. BA, Vanderbilt U., 1965; JD, U. Tenn., 1968; LLM, Georgetown U., 1985. Bar: Tenn. 1968, D.C. 1988, Md. 1996. Spl. agt. FBI, N.Y.C., 1968-72; ptnr. Glankler, Brown, Gilliland, Chase, Robinson & Raines, Memphis, 1972-82; trial atty. environ. enforcement sect. U.S. Dept. of Justice, Washington, 1982-86; of counsel Washington, Perito & Dubuc, Washington, 1986-91, Graham & James, Washington, 1991-93; ptnr. Rich and Henderson, P.C., Annapolis, Md., 1993-98; sr. asst. county atty. Anne Arundel County Office of Law, Annapolis, 1998—. Editor Digest Environ. Law of Real Property, 1986-90, Environ. Hazards, 1989-90; contbr. articles to profl. jours. Mem. environ. issues grop George Bush for Pres. Campaign, Washington, 1987-88, Robert Dole for Pres. Campaign, Washington, 1995-96. Mem. ABA, D.C. Bar Assn., Md. Bar Assn., Environ. Law Inst. Republican. Roman Catholic. Environmental, Labor, General civil litigation. Home: 4949 Hillbrook Ln NW Washington DC 20016-3208 Office: Anne Arundel County Office Law 2660 Riva Rd Annapolis MD 21401-7305

**EVANS, WILLIAM WALLACE,** lawyer; b. St. Louis, Jan. 20, 1923; s. John Franklin and Elizabeth (Dearing) E.; m. Theodora Louise Cofer, June 6, 1944 (wid. Oct. 1993); children: John Dearing, Nancy Elizabeth. LLB, Washington U., St. Louis, 1948; student, Maryville (Tenn.) Coll., 1940-43. Bar: Mo. 1948, U.S. Dist. Ct. (ea. dist.) Mo. 1948, U.S. Ct. Appeals (8th cir.) 1948. Ptnr. Evans & Dixon, St. Louis, 1948-93, of counsel, 1993—. Recipient ann. award of honor, Lawyers Assn. of St. Louis, 1997. Fellow Am. Coll. Trial Lawyers, Internat. Acad. Trial Lawyers; mem. Internat. Assn. Ins. Counsel, St. Louis Bar Assn., ABA, Mo. Bar Assn. (Lon O. Hocker Meml. Trial Lawyers award 1958), Order of the Coif, Phi Kappa Delta. Republican. Avocations: bird dogs and hunting, fishing, golf. General civil litigation, Insurance, Personal injury. Office: Evans & Dixon 1200 St Louis Pl 1200 N Broadway Saint Louis MO 63102-2206

**EVANS, WINTHROP SHATTUCK,** airline captain, lawyer; b. Santa Monica, Calif., June 21, 1939; s. Clifford E. and Luella (Wyble) E.; m. Carlene D. Buschena, June 26, 1965; children—Theresa, Shalene, Shanna, Michelle. A.A., Fullerton Coll., 1969; B.A., Calif. State U.-Fullerton, 1973; J.D., Western State U., Fullerton, 1980. Bar: Calif. 1980. Enlisted in U.S. Navy, 1957, commd. ensign, 1961, advanced through grades to lt. comdr., 1969; served with U.S. Naval Reserve, 1965-76, ret. lt. comdr., 1976; airline capt. Am. Airlines, L.A., 1965-97; pvt. practice law, Placentia, Calif., 1980—; substitute tchr. Western State U.; litigation atty. Fair Housing coun. Orange County. Mem. Calif. Bar Assn., Orange County Bar Assn., Aircraft Owners and Pilots Bar Assn. Republican. Roman Catholic. Probate, Personal injury, Landlord-tenant. Office: PO Box 532 Placentia CA 92871-0532

**EVE, ROBERT MICHAEL, JR.,** lawyer; b. Charlotte, N.C., Apr. 26, 1953; s. Robert Michael and Carolyn Elizabeth (Roesel); m. Kimberly Denise Davenport, June 9, 1984. B.A. with honors, U. N.C.; J.D. cum laude Samford U. Bar: Ala. 1978, N.C. 1979, U.S. Dist. Ct. (mid. dist.) Ala. 1978, U.S. Dist. Ct. (we. dist.) N.C. 1979, U.S. Ct. Appeals (4th cir.) 1980. Dep. clk. Superior Ct., Mecklenburg County, N.C., 1972-73; dep. sheriff, 1974-75; law clk. to justice Supreme Ct. of Ala., Montgomery, 1978-79; assoc. Bailey, Brackett and Brackett, P.A., Charlotte, N.C., 1979-84; ptnr. Justice Eve and Edwards, P.A., Charlotte, 1984—; law clk. U.S. Dist. Ct. (no. dist.) Ala., 1978. Mem. Mecklenburg County Eagle Scout Rev. Bd., Boy Scouts Am.; Recipient Order of the Old Well, U. N.C., 1975. Mem. N.C. Bar Assn., N.C. Acad. Trial Lawyers, Mecklenburg County Bar Assn. (exec. com.). Lutheran. Club: Order of the Arrow. Editor-in-chief Cumberland Law Rev., 1977-78; contbr. articles on law to profl. jours. State civil litigation, Personal injury, Contracts commercial. Home: 2000 Brandon Cir Charlotte NC 28211-1615 Office: BB&T Ctr 200 S Tryon St 1801 East Blvd Charlotte NC 28203-5825

**EVELAND, THOMAS SHAW,** judge; b. Detroit, Nov. 24, 1941; s. De Forest H. and Florence May E. BA, U. Mich., 1963, JD, 1965. Bill drafter Legis. Svc. Bur., Lansing, Mich., 1966-69; pvt. practice Lansing, 1969-88; judge cir. ct. Eaton County, Charlotte, Mich., 1989—. Pres. Eaton (Mich.) Shelter/Siren, Charlotte, Mich., 1994—, Eaton Area Habitat for Humanity, Charlotte, 1995—, Eaton County Cmty. Found., 1996—, Eaton County Comty. Corrections, 1998—; elder First Presbyn. Ch., 1991. Mem. Mich. Judges Assn. (head com. 1995), Eaton County Bar Assn. (pres. 1995). Avocations: gardening, reading, guilding. Office: Courthouse Charlotte MI 48813

**EVELETH, JANET STIDMAN,** law association administrator; b. Balt., Sept. 6, 1950; d. John Charles and Edith Janet (Scales) Stidman; m. Donald P. Eveleth, May 11, 1974. BA, Washington Coll., 1972; MS, Johns Hopkins U., 1973. Counselor Office of Mayor, Balt., 1973-75; asst. dir. Gov. Commn. on Children, Balt., 1975-78; lobbyist Balt., 1978-80; comm. specialist Med. Soc., Balt., 1980-81; dir. pub. affairs Mid-Atlantic Food Dealers, Balt., 1981-84; dir. comm. Home Builders Assn., Balt., 1984-87, Md. Bar Assn., Balt., 1987—. Contbr. articles to profl. jours. Recipient Gov. citation State of Md., 1993, Citizen citation City of Balt., 1993. Mem. NAFE, Am. Soc. Profl. Women, Md. Soc. Assn. Execs. (pres. 1992-93), Nat. Assn. Bar Execs. (chmn. pub. rels. sect. 1994-95, achievement award 1995, ABA's E.A. Wally Richter award 1997), Alpha Chi Omega, Pi Lambda Theta. Office: Md Bar Assn 520 W Fayette St Baltimore MD 21201-1781

**EVERBACH, OTTO GEORGE,** lawyer; b. New Albany, Ind., Aug. 27, 1938; s. Otto G. and Zelda Marie (Hilt) E.; m. Nancy Lee Stern, June 3, 1961; children: Tracy Ellen, Stephen George. BS, U.S. Mil. Acad., 1960; LLB, U. Va., 1966. Bar: Va. 1967, Ind. 1967, Calif. 1975, Mass. 1978. Counsel CIA, Langley, Va., 1966-67; corp. counsel Bristol-Meyers Co., Evansville, Ind., 1967-74, Alza Corp., Palo Alto, Calif., 1974-75; sec., gen. counsel Am. Optical Corp., Southbridge, Mass., 1976-81; assoc. gen. counsel Warner-Lambert Co., Morris Plains, N.J., 1981-83; v.p. Kimberly-Clark Corp., Neenah, Wis., 1984-86, sr. v.p., gen. counsel, 1986—, sr. v.p. law & govt. affairs, 1988—. Served with U.S. Army, 1960-63. Mem. Am. Bar Assn., Mass. Bar Assn., Ind. Bar Assn., Calif. Bar Assn. Office: Kimberly-Clark Corp DFW Airport Sta PO Box 619100 Dallas TX 75261-9100

**EVERETT, CARL BELL,** lawyer; b. Plainfield, N.J., Mar. 23, 1947; s. Edward F. and Catherine (Bell) E.; m. Julie Elizabeth Lund, June 25, 1971; children: Andrew, Martha. BS Chem. Engring., MIT, 1969; JD, U. Houston, 1973. Bar: Tex. 1974, Del. 1974, Pa. 1987, U.S. Dist. Ct. Del. 1977, U.S. Dist. Ct. (ea. dist.) Pa. 1987, U.S. Ct. Appeals (6th cir.) 1977, U.S. Ct. Appeals (5th cir.) 1978, U.S. Ct. Appeals (1st cir.) 1979, U.S. Ct. Appeals (D.C. cir.) 1979. Sr. counsel E.I. du Pont de Nemours & Co. Inc., Wilmington, Del., 1974-86, Liebert, Short, FitzPatrick & Hirshland, Phila., 1986-87; with Saul, Ewing, Remick & Saul, Phila., 1987—. Environmental. Home: 214 Elm Ave Swarthmore PA 19081-1427 Office: Saul Ewing Remick & Saul 3800 Centre Sq W Philadelphia PA 19102

**EVERETT, C(HARLES) CURTIS,** retired lawyer; b. Omaha, Aug. 9, 1930; s. Charles Edgar and Rosalie (Cook) E.; m. Joan Rose Bader, Sept. 7, 1951; children: Jeffrey, Ellen, Amy, Jennifer. BA cum laude, Beloit Coll., 1952; JD, U. Chgo., 1957. Bar: Ill. 1957. Pvt. practice Chgo., 1957-91; ptnr. Bell, Boyd, Lloyd, Haddad & Burns, 1965-81, successor firm Bell, Boyd & Lloyd, 1981-91; v.p. law, sec., gen. counsel AMRE, Inc., Dallas, 1991-96; v.p. law, sec., gen. counsel, bd. dirs. Am. Remodeling, Inc., Dallas, 1992-96; v.p. Canre Remodeling, Inc., Dallas, 1992-94; v.p., sec. Hans Bader, Cons., Inc., Clearwater, Fla., 1954-99, also bd. dirs.; vis. com. U. Chgo. Law Sch., 1986-89; lectr. Ill. Inst. CLE. Mem. editl. bd. U. Chgo. Law Rev., 1956-57; contbr. articles to profl. jours. Chmn. So. Suburban area Beloit Coll. Ford Found. challange program, 1964-65; pres. The Players, Flossmoor, 1970-71; bd. govs. Lake Shore Dr. Condominium Assn., 1986-91. With AUS, 1952-54. Mem. ABA, Ill. Bar Assn., Chgo. Bar Assn. (mem. securities law com. 1960-91), U. Chgo. Law Sch. Alumni Assn. (dir. 1973-76, pres. Chgo. chpt. 1979-80), Legal Club, Law Club, Monroe Club (bd. govs. 1976-97), Univ. Club Chgo., Order of DeMolay (past master counselor Rock River chpt.), Order of Coif, Sigma Chi, Phi Alpha Delta. Mem. Cmty. Ch. (deacon). General corporate, Securities, Mergers and acquisitions. Home: 532 Long Reach Dr Salem SC 29676-4214

**EVERETT, JAMES JOSEPH,** lawyer; b. San Antonio, May 7, 1955. BA, St. Mary's U., San Antonio, 1976; JD, Tex. So. U., 1980. Bar: U.S. Dist. Ct. Ariz. 1987, U.S. Tax Ct. 1980, U.S. Ct. Appeals (9th cir.) 1988. Sr. trial atty. IRS, Phoenix, 1980-87; ptnr. Brnilovich & Everett, Phoenix, 1987-89; pvt. practice Law Offices of James J. Everett, Phoenix, 1989—; of counsel Broadbent, Walker & Wales, 1991-95. Mem. ATLA, ABA (bus. and tax sects.), Fed. Bar Assn., Tex. Bar Assn., Ariz. Bar Assn., State Bar Ariz. (cert. tax specialist), Maricopa County Bar Assn., Ariz. Tax Controversy Group, Valley Estate Planners (Phoenix), Ctrl. Ariz. Estate Planners, Ariz. Soc. Boutiques, St. Thomas Moore Soc. (fee arbitration com.). Corporate taxation, Estate taxation, Personal income taxation. Office: 608 E Missouri Ave Phoenix AZ 85012-1377

**EVERETT, JOHN PRENTIS, JR.,** lawyer; b. Shreveport, La., Dec. 17, 1941; s. John Prentis and Doris (Waguespack) E.; m. Mary Jane Spaht, Nov. 5, 1966 (div. 1979); 1 child, John Prentis III; m. Katherine Coghlan, June 25, 1981. BS, La. State U., 1966, JD, 1966. Bar: La. 1966, U.S. Ct. Mil. Appeals 1968, U.S. Supreme Ct. 1970. Ptnr. Kantrow Spaht Weaver & Walter, Baton Rouge, 1970-78; dir. Camp Carmouche Palmer Barsh & Hunter, Lake Charles, La., 1978-90, Carmouche Law Firm, Lake Charles, 1990-95; ptnr. Wright and Everett, L.L.C., Lake Charles, 1995—; pres. Imperial Calcasieu Title Corp. Maj. JAGC, USMC, 1967-70. Fellow Am. Coll. Mortgage Attys., La. Bar Found. (bd. dirs. 1998—; mem. La. Bar Assn. (ho. of dels. 1996—). Real property, Contracts commercial, Consumer commercial. Home: 4563 Pete Seay Rd Sulphur LA 70665-8264 Office: Wright and Everett LLC 203 W Clarence St Lake Charles LA 70601-5229

**EVERETT, PAMELA IRENE,** legal management company executive, educator; b. L.A., Dec. 31, 1947; d. Richard Weldon and Alta Irene (Tuttle) Bunnell; m. James E. Everett, Sept. 2, 1967 (div. 1973); 1 child, Richard Earl. Cert. Paralegal, Rancho Santago Coll., Santa Ana, Calif., 1977; BA, Calif. State U.-Long Beach, 1985; MA, U. Redlands, 1988. Owner, mgr. Orange County Paralegal Svc., Santa Ana, 1979-85; pres. Gem Legal Mgmt. Inc., Fullerton, Calif., 1986—; co-owner Bunnell Publs., Fullerton, Calif., 1992-96, The Millennium Network, 1997; instr. Rancho Santiago Coll., 1979—, chmn. adv. bd., 1980-85; instr. Fullerton Coll., 1989—, Rio Hondo Coll., Whittier, Calif., 1992-94; advisor Nat. Paralegal Assn., 1982—, Saddleback Coll., 1985—, North Orange County Regional Occupational Program, Fullerton, 1986—, Fullerton Coll. So. Calif. Coll. Bus. and Law; bd. dirs. Nat. Profl. Legal Assts. Inc., editor PLA News. Author: Legal Secretary Federal Litigation, 1986, Bankruptcy Courts and Procedure, 1987, Going Independent--Business Planning Guide, Fundamentals of Law Office Management, 1994. Republican. Avocation: reading. Office: 406 N Adams Ave Fullerton CA 92832-1605

**EVERETT, STEPHEN EDWARD,** lawyer; b. Shreveport, La., Jan. 16, 1944; s. Rufus Webb and Myrtie (Morgan) E.; m. Patricia Hostetter, Jan. 19, 1965; children—Michael Stephen, Morgan Terez. B.A., La. Tech. U., 1965;

J.D., Tulane U., 1967. Bar: La. 1967, U.S. Dist. Ct. (ea. dist.) La. 1968, U.S. Dist. Ct. (we. dist.) La. 1969, U.S. Ct. Appeals (5th cir.) 1976, U.S. Dist. Ct. (mid. dist.) La. 1982, U.S. Supreme Ct. 1983. Assoc. Montgomery, Barnett, Brown & Read, New Orleans, 1967-69, Gravel & Burnes, Alexandria, La., 1969-73; sole practice, Alexandria, 1973—. Mem. La. Trial Lawyers Assn., Assn. Trial Lawyers Am., La. Nature Conservancy, LEICA Hist. Soc. Am., Friends of Pub. Broadcasting. Republican. Unitarian. Criminal, Civil rights, Federal civil litigation. Home: 8512 Fairway Dr Pineville LA 71360-2618 Office: 823 Johnston St Alexandria LA 71301-7636

**EVERS, WILLIAM C., III,** lawyer; b. Alton, Ill., June 13, 1945; s. William C. Evers Jr. and Doroty M. Gehrecke; m. Lynda Sue Vandewater, Dec. 22, 1973; children: Caren E. and W. Clark. BA, Blackburn Coll., 1967; JD, U. Kans., 1972. Bar: Kans. 1972, Ill. 1972, U.S. Dist. Ct. (so. and cen. dists.) Ill. 1972, U.S. Ct. Appeals (7th cir.) 1973, U.S. Tax Ct. 1993. Asst. atty. U.S. Dept. Justice, East St. Louis, 1972-76; pvt. practice Collinsville, Ill., 1976—; asst. atty. gen. State of Ill., Springfield, 1979-82; atty. for sec. of state State of Ill., Springfield, Ill., 1988-90; asst. state's atty. Madison County, Edwardsville, Ill., 1980-85. Precinct committeeman Republican Com., Collinsville, Ill., 1976—. Presbyterian. Avocations: History, Politics, Economics. Probate, General practice, Real property. Office: 212 E Main St Collinsville IL 62234-3005

**EVERS, WILLIAM DOHRMANN,** lawyer; b. San Francisco, May 6, 1927; s. Albert John and Sepha (Pischel) E.; m. Edwina Bigelow Benington, Aug. 26, 1950 (div. May 1978); children: Elliot B., Anne B., Albert John II, William Dohrmann; m. Britte-Marie Emblad, May 27, 1978. BA, Yale U., 1949; LLB, JD, U. Calif., Berkeley, 1952. Bar: Calif. 1952. Assoc. Chickering & Gregory, San Francisco, 1953-56; legal asst. to commr. SEC, 1956-57; assoc. atty. Allen, Miller, Groezinger, Keesling & Martin, San Francisco, 1957-60; ptnr. Pettit, Evers & Martin, San Francisco, 1960-78; chmn. On-Line Bus. Sys., Inc., 1980-82; chmn., CEO Precision Techs., 1982-87; ptnr. Chickering & Gregory, San Francisco, 1986-89, Sullivan, Roche & Johnson, San Francisco, 1989-95, Miller, Mailliad & Culve LLP, San Francisco, 1995-96, Evers & Andelin LLP, San Francisco, 1996-97, Evers & Hendrickson LLP, 1997—; bd. dir. Comml. Bank San Francisco, Boreal Ridge Corp. Pres. Econ. Devel. Council City and County of San Francisco, 1978-80; chmn. San Francisco Bay Conservation and Devel. Commn., 1972-75; pres. Calif. Roadside Council, 1959-60; chmn. SPUR, San Francisco, 1975-78; chmn. assistance and adv. council Calif. Gov.'s Office Planning and Research, 1977-78; founder, pres. Planning and Conservation League, 1965-68; mem. air quality adv. bd. EPA, 1970-73; vice chmn. San Francisco Republican County Central Com., 1959-63; trustee Marin County Day Sch., 1967-70, 79-82, Katherine Branson Sch., 1976-78; bd. dirs. Yosemite Nat. Inst., 1981—, chmn. 1988-90; mem. governing council Wilderness Soc., Washington, 1984-96; chmn. Calif. Capital Access Forum, 1996—. With USNR, 1944-45. Mem. ABA, San Francisco Bar Assn., State Bar Calif., Bohemian Club. Clubs: Bohemian (San Francisco). General corporate, Securities, Mergers and acquisitions. Home: 2019 Lyon St San Francisco CA 94115-1609 *Intelligence, industry, integrity and humor are the essential elements for business or professional success and, of these, integrity is the most important.*

**EVERSON, MARTIN JOSEPH,** lawyer; b. San Francisco, Feb. 8, 1948; s. Joseph Martin and Virginia (Smith) E.; m. Lucille Jacobsen, Apr. 10, 1981; children: Diana, Andrew, Cynthia. BA, Georgetown U., 1970; JD, U. Calif., San Francisco, 1977. Bar: Calif. 1977, U.S. Dist. Ct. (no. dist.) Calif. 1977. Dep. dist. atty. San Mateo County Dist. Atty.'s Office, Redwood City, Calif., 1977-78; assoc. Anderson, Galloway & Lucchese, Walnut Creek, Calif., 1978-85, ptnr., 1985—. Capt. USMC, 1971-74. Mem. ABA, Assn. Def. Counsel, Dep. Dist. Atty. Assn., Am. Bd. Trial Advocates, Alameda County Bar Assn., Contra Costa County Bar Assn. Roman Catholic. Avocations: golf, fishing. Insurance, Personal injury, Product liability. Office: Anderson Galloway & Lucchese 1676 N California Blvd Ste 500 Walnut Creek CA 94596-4183

**EVERSON, STEVEN LEE,** lawyer, real estate executive; b. Philippi, W.Va., June 16, 1950; s. Billie Lee and Mildred Ann (Hill) E.; m. Donna Janine Chmielarz, May 29, 1976; 1 child, Michael. BA in Math. magna cum laude, W. Va. U., 1972; JD, Northwestern U., 1979. Bar: Colo. 1979. Tax sr. acct. Deloitte, Haskins & Sells, Colorado Springs, Colo., 1979-82; v.p., sec., treas. The Schuck Corp., Colorado Springs, 1982—; instr. real estate U. Colo. Bd. dirs., sec., past chmn. Pikes Peak Found. for Mental Health, Colorado Springs, 1986—, Boys and Girls Club of Pikes Peak Region, Colorado Springs, 1987-90; mem. UCCS Exec. Club, Colorado Springs, 1988-90; treas. Steve Schuck for Gov. Com., 1988—; project bus. instr. Jr. Achievement, 1985-87. Capt. USAF, 1972-76. Mem. Phi Beta Kappa. Republican. Mem. Ch. of Christ. Avocations: racquetball, skiing, softball, golf, tennis, vol. coaching youth sports teams. Real property, Taxation, general, Personal income taxation. Home: 1690 Colgate Dr Colorado Springs CO 80918 Office: Schuck Communities Inc 2 N Cascade Ave Ste 1280 Colorado Springs CO 80903-1631

**EWALD, REX ALAN,** lawyer; b. Elmhurst, Ill., Aug. 14, 1951; s. Wallace J. and Maybelle (Rhea) E.; m. Sharon M. Frame, Nov. 6, 1971; children: Jennifer, Jeffrey. BS, U. Wis., Platteville, 1973; JD, U. Wis., Madison, 1978. Bar: Wis. 1979, U.S. Dist. Ct. (we. dist.) Wis. 1979. Assoc. Regez Callahan & Knoke, Monroe, Wis., 1979-80; pvt. practice Monroe, 1981-83, 88—; ptnr. Ewald & Duxstad, Monroe, 1983-84, Ewald Duxstad & Vale, Monroe, 1984-88; lectr. on atty. desktop computers, 1988. Mem. ABA, Wis. Bar Assn. (chmn. resource tech. com. 1987-91), Green County Bar Assn. (pres. 1984-85), Jaycees (v.p. Monroe 1981-82), Optimists. Avocations: basketball, youth sports promotion. Banking, General practice. Home: 719 15th Ave Monroe WI 53566-1460 Office: 1750 10th St Monroe WI 53566-1827

**EWAN, DAVID E.,** lawyer; b. Camden, N.J., June 23, 1959; s. Eugene H. and Catherine T. (Stannard) E. BA, Dickinson Coll., 1981; JD, Rutgers U., 1991. Bar: N.J. 1991, Pa. 1991, Fla. 1992, Colo. 1994, U.S. Dist. Ct. N.J. 1991, U.S. Ct. Appeals (3d cir.) 1992. Legal intern Camden County Prosecutor, 1989; law clk. U.S. Ct. Appeals (3d cir.), Phila., 1990-91; assoc. Begley, McCloskey & Gaskill, Moorestown, N.J., 1991—; sr. adj. prof. paralegal program Burlington County Coll., Pemberton, N.J., 1996—. Real property. Home: 400 N Haddon Ave Unit 50 Haddonfield NJ 08033-1731 Office: Begley McCloskey & Gaskill 40 E Main St Moorestown NJ 08057-3310

**EWAN, WILLIAM KENNETH,** lawyer; b. Riverdale, Md., May 15, 1943; s. Richard Kenneth and Dorothy Alice (Spencer) E.; m. Naomi Ruth Browne, July 31, 1971; 1 child, Andrea Sue. BS, Ind. U., 1964, JD, 1967. Bar: Ind. 1967, U.S. Dist. Ct. (so. dist.) Ind. 1967, U.S. Ct. Mil. Appeals 1976. Pvt. practice law Lawrenceburg, Ind., 1974—. Unit sec. Salvation Army, chmn. kettle drive; bd. dirs. United Fund of Dearborn County Inc., Lawrenceburg, 1985. Capt. USNR, 1967-99. Decorated Navy Achievement medal. Mem. Ind. State Bar Assn., Dearborn-Ohio County Bar Assn. (pres. 1976-78), Ind. U. Alumni Assn., Ind. U. Alumni Club Dearborn County (pres. 1976), Am. Legion. Methodist. Avocations: photography, hiking Appalachian trail, sailing, golf. Military, Probate, Real property. Home: 9636 Old State Road 350 Aurora IN 47001-9343 Office: 210 W High St Lawrenceburg IN 47025-1910

**EWBANK, THOMAS PETERS,** lawyer, retired banker; b. Indpls., Dec. 29, 1943; s. William Curtis and Maxine Stuart (Peters) E.; m. Alice Ann Shelton, June 8, 1968; children: William Curtis, Ann Shelton. Student, Stanford U., 1961-62; AB, Ind. U., 1965, JD, 1969. Bar: Ind. 1969, U.S. Tax Ct. 1969, U.S. Dist. Ct. (so. dist.) Ind. 1969, U.S. Supreme Ct. 1974; cert. trust & fin. advisor. Legis. asst. Ind. Legis. Coun., 1966-67; estate and inheritance tax adminstr. mchts. Nat. Bank, Indpls., 1967-69; assoc. Hilgedag, Johnson, Secrest and Murphy, Indpls., 1969-71; asst. gen. counsel Everett I. Brown Co., Indpls., 1971-72; with Mchts. Nat. Bank & Trust Co. (now Nat. City Bank), Indpls., 1972-95; from probate adminstr. to pres. Mechants Capital Mgmt., Inc., Ind., 1990-93; ptnr. Krieg DeVault Alexander & Capehart Law Firm, Indpls., 1995—. Contbr. articles to profl. jours. Asst. treas. Ruckelshaus for U.S. Senator Com., 1968; candidate for Ind. Legislature, 1970, 74; bd. dirs. Noble Found. Ind., 1997—, Indpls. Art Ctr., Ruth Lilly Found., 1997—, Ctr. Philanthropy, Inc. U., Indpls., 1998—, Benjamin Harrison Home Found., 1994—, v.p., 1996-98, pres., 1998—; chmn. adv. com. ARC, 1987—. Fellow Ind. Bar Found. (life patron); mem. Estate Planning Coun. Indpls. (pres. 1982-83), Indpls. Bar Assn., Ind. Bar Assn., Indpls. Bar Found. (treas 1976-81), Blue Key, Meridian Hills Country Club, Masons, Kiwanis (Circle K Internat. trustee 1963-64, pres. 1964-65, chmn. internat. com. 1988-90, George Hixson Diamond fellow, treas. Indpls. club 1980-81, 84-85 designated maj. builder 1983). Republican. Baptist. Home: 1280 Laurelwood Carmel IN 46032-8752 Office: One Indiana Sq Ste 2800 Indianapolis IN 46204-2017

**EWELL, A. BEN, JR.,** lawyer, businessman; b. Elyria, Ohio, Sept. 10, 1941; s. Austin Bert and Mary Rebecca (Thompson) E.; m. Suzanne E.; children: Austin Bert III, Brice Ballantyne, Harrison Dale. BA, Miami U., Oxford, Ohio, 1963; JD, Hasting Coll. Law, U. Calif., San Francisco, 1966. Bar: Calif. 1966, U.S. Dist. Ct. (ea. dist.) Calif. 1967, U.S. Supreme Ct. 1982, U.S. Ct. Appeals (9th cir.) 1967. Pres. A.B. Ewell, Jr., A. Profl. Corp., Fresno, 1984-98, The Clarksfield Co., Inc., Fresno, 1989—; formerly gen. counsel to various water dists. and assn.; gen. counsel, chmn. San Joaquin River Flood Control Assn., 1984-88; CEO Millerton New Town Devel. Co., 1988-94, chmn., 1994-96; pres. Millerton Open Space and Natural Resource Plan, 1999—; mem. task force on prosecution, cts. and law reform Calif. Coun. Criminal Justice, 1971-74; mem. Fresno Bulldog Found., Calif. State U.; mem. San Joaquin Valley Agrl. Water commn., 1979-88; co-chmn. nat. adv. coun. SBA, 1981, 82, mem. 1981-87; bd. dirs. Fresno East Cmty. Ctr., 1971-73; mem. Fresno County Water Adv. Com., 1989, Fresno Cmty. Coun., 1972-73; chmn. various area polit. campaigns and orgns., including Reagan/Bush, 1984, Deukmejian for Gov., 1986; mem. adv. com. St. Agnes Med. Ctr. Found., 1983-89; trustee U. Calif. Med. Edn. Found., 1989-90, Fresno Met. Mus. Art, History and Sci., active, 1989—, mem. adv. coun., 1993-94; bd. dirs. Citizens for Cmty. Enrichment, Fresno, 1990-93; mem. Police Activities League, 1995—, Fresno Conv. and Visitors Bur., 1997—; bd. dirs. Fresno Volleyball Club, 1998—. Mem. Millerton Lake C. of C., Brighton Crest Country Club (pres. 1989-96), Cooper River Country Club, Phi Alpha Delta, Brighton Crest Golf and Country Club, Sigma Nu. Congregationalist. Real property, General corporate, Public utilities. Office: 410 W Fallbrook Ave Ste 102 Fresno CA 93711-6191

**EWEN, PAMELA BINNINGS,** lawyer; b. Phila., Mar. 22, 1944; d. Walter James and Barbara (Perkins) Binnings; m. Jerome Francis Ayers, Aug. 22, 1965 (div. July 1974); 1 child, Scott Dylan; m. John Alexander Ewen, Dec. 13, 1974. BA, Tulane U., 1977; JD cum laude, U. Houston, 1979. Bar: Tex. 1979, U.S. Dist. Ct. (so. dist.) Tex. 1981, U.S. Ct. Appeals (5th cir.) 1981. Law clk. Harris, Cook, Browning & Barker, Corpus Christi, Tex., 1977-79; assoc. Kleberg, Dyer, Redford & Weil, Corpus Christi, 1979-80; atty. law dept. Gulf Oil Corp., Houston, 1980-84; assoc. Baker & Botts, L.L.P., Houston, 1984-88, ptnr., 1988—. Author: Faith On Trial, 1999. La. Legis. scholar, New Orleans, 1976-77. Mem. ABA (forum com. on franchising 1983-85, corp., banking, bus. law sect., 1984—, law practice mgmt. sect., subcom. Women Rainmakers Assn.), Am. Petroleum Inst. (spl. subcom. to gen. com. on law, com. on product liability 1982-85), Tex. State Bar (com. on uniform communal code 1988—), Tex. Assn. Bank Coun. (bd. dirs. 1994-97), Jr. Achievement S.E. Tex. (bd. dirs. 1997—), Order of Barons. Finance, Contracts commercial, General corporate. Office: Baker & Botts 3000 1 Shell Plz Houston TX 77002

**EWERT, QUENTIN ALBERT,** lawyer, consultant; b. Griggsville, Ill., Aug. 19, 1915; s. Albert Merritt and Anna Mabel (Beard) E.; m. Frances Norfleet, Dec. 25, 1941; children: David Norfleet, Gregory Albert, Catherine Ann, Mary Frances, Jane Cranston; m. Arlayne Joy Brown, May 1973 (div. June 1981). BA, Mich. State U., 1938; JD, U. Mich., 1946. Bar: Mich. 1946. Atty. Auto Owners Ins. Co., Lansing, Mich., 1946-47; ptnr. Ewert and Fagan, Lansing, Mich., 1947-48; sole practice Lansing, Mich., 1948-53; pres., bd. chmn. Guardsman Ins. Co., Pasadena, Calif., 1953-55; ptnr. Loomis, Ewert, Ederer, Parsley, Davis & Gotting, P.C., Lansing, 1955-87, of counsel, 1988—; owner, bd. chmn. Communications, Inc., Grand Rapids, Mich., 1972-87; cons. TIE/communications, Inc., Shelton, Conn., 1988-91. Met. area chmn. Rep. party, Lansing, 1952. Served to lt. cmdr. USNR, 1941-45. Mem. Kiwanis (Lansing), The Springs Country Club. General corporate, Public utilities. Home (winter): 11 Mount Holyoke Dr Rancho Mirage CA 92270-3667 Office: Loomis Ewert Parsley Davis & Gotting 232 S Capitol Ave Ste 1000 Lansing MI 48933-1526

**EWING, KY PEPPER, JR.,** lawyer; b. Victoria, Tex., Jan. 7, 1935; s. Ky Pepper and Sallie (Dixon) E.; m. Almuth Rott, Apr. 6, 1963; children: Kenneth Patrick, Kevin Andrew, Kathryn Diana. B.A. cum laude, Baylor U., 1956; LL.B. cum laude, Harvard U., 1959. Bar: D.C. 1959, U.S. Supreme Ct 1963. Assoc. firm Covington & Burling, Washington, 1959-64; partner firm Prather, Seeger, Doolittle, Farmer & Ewing, Washington, 1964-77; dep. asst. atty. gen. antitrust div. Dept. Justice, Washington, 1978-80; ptnr. Vinson & Elkins, Washington, 1980—; dir., sec. Washington Inst. Fgn. Affairs. Co-editor-in-chief: State Antitrust Practice and Statutes, 3 Vols., 1990; mem. antitrust adv. bd. Antitrust and Trade Regulation Report Bur. Nat. Affairs, 1990—; mem. edit. bd. Antitrust Report Matthew Bender & Co., 1993—. Pres. Potomac Valley League, 1977, Carderock Springs Citizens Assn., 1975-78. Fellow Am. Bar Found.; mem. ABA (chmn. legis. com. antitrust sect. 1987-91, coun. antitrust sect. 1991-94, fin. officer antitrust sect. 1994-96, chmn. FTC/Dept. Justice working group 1994-97, mem. ho. of dels. 1996-98, vice chair antitrust sect. 1998-99, chair elect 1999—), D.C. Bar Assn., Am. Soc. Internat. Law, Internat. Bar Assn., Met. Club. Democrat. Episcopalian. Antitrust, Federal civil litigation, Environmental. Home: 8317 Comanche Ct Bethesda MD 20817-4561 Office: Vinson & Elkins 1455 Pennsylvania Ave NW Fl 7 Washington DC 20004-1013

**EWING, MARY ARNOLD,** lawyer; b. Shreveport, La., Feb. 21, 1948; d. George and Christine (Cocek) Hengy; m. Robert Craig Ewing, Aug. 30, 1981; 1 child, Kyle Ross. BA, U. Colo., 1972; JD, U. Denver, 1975. Bar: Colo. 1975, U.S. Supreme Ct. 1979. Assoc. Johnson & Mahoney, Denver, 1975-80; ptnr. Branney, Hillyard, Ewing & Barnes, Englewood, Colo., 1980-85, Bucholtz, Bull & Ewing, Denver, 1985-96, Ewing & Ewing PC, Englewood, Colo., 1996—; asst. prof. law U. Denver, 1977-78, part time prof. 1978—; mem. faculty Nat. Inst. Trial Advocacy, 1984-89; instr. nat. session 1984, 85, 87, Nat. Bd. Trial Advocacy, regional session, 1984-89. Chmn. Denver County Task Force, 1976-77, mem., 1990; treas. Cen. Com. 1st Congl. Dist., 1976-77; v.p. Young Rep. League Denver, 1975, pres., 1976; mem. govt. relations com. Jr. Symphony Guild, 1978—; mem. legal com. County Horse Assn., 1990—. Mem. ABA, Colo. Bar Assn. (ethics com.), Denver Bar Assn. (vice chmn. new lawyers assistance com. 1977), Colo. Women's Bar Assn., Internat. Platform Assn., Mountain States Combined Tng. Assn., Rocky Mountain Dressage Soc. (sec. High Plains chpt. 1979-80, chmn. constn. and by-laws com. 1988—), Assn. Trial Lawyers Am., Colo. Trial Lawyers Assn. (bd. govs., chmn. interprofl. com. 1980—, bd. dirs. polit. action com. 1989—), Douglas County Bar Assn., Am. Arbitration Assn., Nat. Bd. Trial Advocacy (cert. 1983), Am. Trakehner Assn., Rocky Mountain Trakehner Assn. (v.p. 1987), Arapahoe Hunt Club, Greenwood Athletic Club, Kappa Beta Pi (pres. 1977-78). Personal injury, Workers' compensation, Labor. Home: Nonesuch Farms 4256 S Perry Park Rd Sedalia CO 80135 Address: 8400 E Prentice Ave Ste 1115 Englewood CO 80111-2923

**EWING, ROBERT CLARK,** lawyer; b. Lower Merion, Pa., Nov. 26, 1957; m. Cheralynn Kennedy, Mar. 22, 1986; children: Edward, Jaesun; stepchildren: Kristin, Shannon. BS in Fin., Pa. State U., 1980; JD, Villanova U., 1983. Bar: Pa. 1983, U.S. Dist. Ct. (ea. dist.) Pa. 1985, U.S. Ct. Appeals (3rd cir.) 1987, U.S. Supreme Ct. 1987. Ranger Pa. State Park Svc., 1976-78, Valley Forge Nat. Park, 1979; police officer Ocean City (Md.) Police Dept., 1980-81, Springfield Twp. Delaware County, 1992-99; assoc. Lagoy & Lyons, West Chester, Pa., 1983-86, Ronald H. Silverman, P.C., King of Prussia, Pa., 1986-88, Anthony J. McNulty & Assocs., Media, Pa., 1988-91; pvt. practice Media, Pa., 1991—. Contbr. articles to profl. jours. Mem. Lima (Pa.) Fire Co., 1973—, bd. dirs., 1981-88; mem. Media (Pa.) Fire Co., 1988—; bd. dirs. Hank Nacrelli Scholarship Fund, 1988-97, Delaware County Emergency Health Svcs. Coun., 1986-93; active Delaware County Critical Incident Stress Mgmt. Program, Media, 1987—. Mem. Delaware County Bar Assn., Delaware County Firemen's Assn., Assn. Trial Lawyers Am., Pa. Trial Lawyers Assn. General civil litigation, Family and matrimonial, Real property. Office: 115 N Monroe St PO Box 1468 Media PA 19063-8468

**EXNICIOS, VAL PATRICK,** lawyer; b. New Orleans, Aug. 29, 1959; s. Samuel Richard and Glendora Marie (de Bouchel) E.; m. Carol Ann Carlton (div.); m. Victoria Cotton, Jan. 1997; 1 child, Valerie Marie. BA in Polit. Sci., U. New Orleans, 1986; JD, Loyola U., New Orleans, 1989. Bar: La. 1989, U.S. Dist. Ct. (ea. and mid. dists.) La. 1990. Assoc. Liska, Exnicios & Nungesser, New Orleans, 1989-93, ptnr., 1993-95, mng. dir., 1995—. Author case note Loyola Law Rev., 1989. Pres. Lawyers Against Crime Inc., New Orleans, 1996—; bd. dirs. St. Thomas More Soc., New Orleans, 1996—. Mem. ATLA, La. State Bar Assn. (environ. law sect., sect. on ins., negligence, compensation and admiralty law), New Orleans Bar Assn., La. Trial Lawyers Assn., Cosmopolitan Club of New Orleans (pres. 1994-96). Republican. Roman Catholic. Avocations: skiing, water skiing. Toxic tort, Personal injury, General civil litigation. Office: Liska Exnicios & Nungesser 9701 Lake Forest Blvd New Orleans LA 70127-5402

**EXTEIN, MARK CHARLES,** lawyer; b. St. Louis, 1951; s. Alvin M. and Leadora S. Extein; m. Lynn Peak, Dec. 26, 1976; children: Brian, Jonathan. AB, Princeton U., 1972; JD, Harvard U., 1976. Bar: Pa. 1976, N.Y. 1979, Fla. 1985, U.S. Dist. Ct. (mid. dist.) Fla., U.S. Ct. Appeals (11th cir.) Assoc. Ballard Spahr Andrews & Ingersoll, Phila., 1976-78, Rosenman & Colin, N.Y.C., 1979-84; assoc. Foley & Lardner, Orlando, Fla., 1985-86, ptnr., 1987—; Bd. dirs. BOMA-Orlando, 1995-96. General corporate, Real property. Office: Foley & Lardner 111 N Orange Ave Ste 1800 Orlando FL 32801-2386

**EYDELSHTEYN, SIMON MARK,** lawyer; b. Chernovtsy, Ukraine, Russia, Oct. 18, 1950; came to U.S., 1992; s. Mark A. and Eva S. (Isayeva) E.; m. Svetlana V. Gordan, Feb. 21, 1980; 1 child, Paul. MSME, Tashkent State Poly. U., Russia, 1972; JD, Tashkent State U., Russia, 1977; LLM, Wayne State U., 1996. Bar: Russia 1977, Mich. 1995. Rschr. Rsch. Inst., Tashkent, 1972-77; atty. Specialized Law Firm, Tashkent, 1977-92; assoc. Berry Moorman, P.C., Birmingham, Mich., 1993—. Author: Taxation of Foreign Corporations in Russia, 1995, Foreign Invesment in Russia, 1996, An Introduction to Russia Labor Legislation, 1996. Mem. Union of Lawyers of Uzbekistan, Uzbek State Sci. and Tech. Soc., Russian-Am. Inst. Indsl. Mgmt. (bd. dirs.), Mich. State Bar Assn., Oakland County Bar Assn. Public international, Immigration, naturalization, and customs, Private international. Office: Berry Moorman PC 255 E Brown St Ste 320 Birmingham MI 48009-6209

**EYLER, BONNIE,** lawyer; b. Cumberland, Md.; d. George Raphael and Elizabeth (Binnix) E. BS in Nursing, Widener U., 1969; MS, Boston U., 1974; JD, Nova U., 1983. Bar: Fla. 1984, U.S. Dist. Ct. (so. dist.) Fla. 1984. Registered nurse at several hosps. in the Boston and Phila. areas, 1974-84; assoc. Conrad, Scherer & James, Ft. Lauderdale, Fla., 1984—. Mem. Am. Acad. Hosp. Attys., Fla. Assn. Hosp. Attys., Am. Assn. Nurse-Attys., Fla. Assn. Def. Lawyers, Assn. Trial Lawyers Am. Health, Personal injury, State civil litigation. Home: 20694 NW 29th Ave Boca Raton FL 33434-4348 Office: Sonneborn Rutter Cooney Klingensmith & Eyler PA 1545 Centrepark Dr N West Palm Beach FL 33401-7414

**EYLER, JAMES R.,** judge; b. Westminster, Md., July 13, 1942. AB, U. Md., 1964, LLB magna cum laude, 1967. Bar: Md. 1967, D.C. 1976. Law clk. Ct. Appeals Md., 1967-68; mem. Miles & Stockbridge, Balt., 1968-95; judge Ct. Spl. Appeals Md., Towson, 1995—. Rsch. editor Md. Law Rev., 1966-67. Mem. ABA, Md. State Bar Assn., Bar Assn. Balt. City, Order of Coif. Office: HD Ct of Special Appeals County Cts Bldg Rm M-13 401 Bosley Ave Towson MD 21204-4420

**EYMANN, RICHARD C.,** lawyer; b. Hanover, N.H., June 6, 1945. BS, U. Oreg., 1968; JD, Gonzaga U., 1976. Bar: Wash. 1976, U.S. Dist. Ct. (ea. dist.) Wash. 1978, U.S. Ct. Appeals (9th cir.) 1987, U.S. Dist. Ct. (we. dist.) Wash. 1989, U.S. Supreme Ct. 1995. Ptnr. Feltman, Gebhardt, Eymann & Jones, Spokane, Wash. Mem. ABA (founder, chmn. nat. appellate advocacy competition 1975-84, bd. advs. 1985-93), ATLA, Wash. State Bar Assn. (bd. govs. 1997-98, pres. elect 1998-99), , Wash. State Trial Lawyers Assn. (bd. govs. 1984-86, 88-95, legis. steering com. 1990-96, membership chair 1984-85, v.p. East 1991-92, fin. com. 1994-95, Trial Lawyer of Yr. 1995, pres. 1996-97), Wash. Trial Lawyers for Pub. Justice (bd. dirs. 1994-98), Spokane County Bar Assn., Am. Inns of Ct. (barrister 1986, master of the bench 1990, Charles L. Powell & Inn pres. 1991-93). E-mail: rceymann@fgej.com. Office: Feltman Gebhardt Eymann & Jones PS 14th Fl Paulsen Ctr Spokane WA 99201*

**EYSTER, CHARLES RICHARD,** lawyer, oil and gas exploration executive; b. Ballinger, Tex., Dec. 2, 1930; s. Charles Francis and Mildred Maurine (Butler) E.; m. Agnes Christian Welsh, Feb. 11, 1961; children: Richard, Maury, John. BBA, Tex. A&M U., 1953; LLB, U. Tex., 1958. Bar: Tex. 1957, U.S. Supreme Ct. 1967. Lawyer Coastal States, Corpus Christi, Tex., 1959-61; head land and legal svcs. Alamo Gas, San Antonio, Tex., 1961-64; lawyer Forest Oil, San Antonio, 1964-68; pvt. practice law San Antonio, 1968—; mgr. Corcel, LC, Waco, Tex., 1992—, Agarita Trading Co., LLC, San Antonio, 1996—. Capt. USMC, 1953-61, Korea. Episcopalian. Avocations: family, oil and gas exploration. Oil, gas, and mineral, Natural resources. Home: 240 E Huisache Ave San Antonio TX 78212-3029 Office: 405 North Saint Marys Ste 930 San Antonio TX 78205-1713

**EZERSKY, WILLIAM MARTIN,** lawyer; b. N.Y.C., Sept. 14, 1951; s. Abraham David and Ada Ezersky; m. Karen Gail Hecht, June 30, 1985. BA in Communications, Philosophy, Queens Coll., 1974; JD, Hofstra U., 1977. Bar: N.Y. 1979, U.S. Dist. Ct. (so. and ea. dists.) N.Y. 1979. Sole practice N.Y.C., 1979—. Mem. ABA. Bar Assn. City N.Y., N.Y. State Trial Lawyers Assn., N.Y. County Trial Lawyers Assn., Queens Bar Assn., Jewish Lawyers Guild. Democrat. Jewish. Lodge: Masons. Avocations: rowing, walking, sailing, tennis, swimming. Personal injury, Criminal, State civil litigation. Office: 3333 New Hyde Park Rd New Hyde Park NY 11042-1205

**EZOLD, NANCY O'MARA,** lawyer; b. Laconia, N.H., July 21, 1942; d. Francis L. and Edna Mae (Jackson) O'Mara; m. William L. Keenan; children: Christopher E. Ezold, Matthew F. Ezold. BA, U. Maine, 1964; JD, Villanova U., 1980. Bar: Pa. 1980, U.S. Dist. Ct. (ea. dist.) Pa. 1980, U.S. Ct. Appeals (3rd and fed. cirs.) 1982, U.S. Claims Ct. 1989, U.S. Dist. Ct. (mid. dist.) Pa. 1989, U.S. Supreme Ct. 1989, U.S. Dist. Ct. Ariz. 1991. Adminstrv. positions fed., state and local govt. agys., 1964-77; assoc. Kirschner, Walters & Willig, Phila., 1980-81, Phillips & Phelan, Phila., 1981-83, Wolf Block Schorr & Solis-Cohen, Phila., 1983-89, Rosenthal & Ganister, West Chester, Pa., 1990-94; pres., chief counsel BES Environ. Specialists, Larksville, Pa., 1989-90; pvt. practice Bala Cynwyd, Pa., 1994—. Chmn. Women's Law Project, Phila., 1995. Named Feminist of Yr., Feminist Majority Found., 1993. Mem. ATLA, NAFE, Phila. Bar Assn., Nat. Assn. Women Lawyers (pres.' award 1991). Fax #: (610) 660-5595. E-mail: ezoldlaw@msn.com. Office: 401 E City Ave Ste 904 Bala Cynwyd PA 19004-1131

**EZRA, DAVID ALAN,** federal judge; b. 1947. BBA magna cum laude, St. Mary's U., 1969, JD, 1972. Law clk. Office of Corp. Counsel City and County Honolulu, 1972; mem. firm Greenstein, Cowen & Frey, 1972-73, Anthony, Hoddick, Reinwald & O'Connor, 1973-80, Ezra, O'Connor, Moon & Tam, 1980-88; dist. judge U.S. Dist. Ct., Hawaii, 1988-98, chief judge, 1998—; adj. prof. law Wm. S. Richardson Sch. Law, 1978—; exec. com. 9th cir. Jud. Conf. Co-editor, author: Hwaii Construction Law - What to Do and When, 1987; editor: Hawaii Collection Practices Manual. 1st lt. USAR 1971-77. Daugherty Fund scholar, 1971, San Antonio Bar Assn. Aux. scholar, 1972. Mem. ABA, U.S. Fed. Judges Assn. (bd. dirs., exec. com.), Dist. Judges Assn. (v.p. 9th cir.), Hawaii State Bar, Am. Arbitration Assn., Delta Epsilon Sigma, Phi Delta Phi. Office: US Dist Ct 300 Alamoana Blvd C-400 Honolulu HI 96803

**FAAL, EDI M. O.,** lawyer; b. Gambia, Africa, 1954; came to U.S., 1974; BS, Fla. Internat. U.; Barrister at Law, Mid. Temple Inns Ct., London; JD, Western State U., Fullerton, Calif., 1982. Bar: U.K., Wales, Calif., Ind., U.S. Supreme Ct. Adj. prof. U. So. Calif. Law Ctr., L.A. Named Lawyer of Yr., Langston Bar Assn. L.A., 1994; recipient Pres.'s award L.A. Criminal Cts. Bar Assn., Legal Champion award Ohio Criminal Def. Bar Assn. Office: 221 N Figueroa St Ste 1200 Los Angeles CA 90012-2646

**FABBRINI, RICHARD ROBERT,** lawyer; b. Chgo., Nov. 21, 1949; s. Robert Raymond and Frances Elizabeth (Mushong) F.; m. Connie Sue Sommer, June 26, 1971 (div. Mar 1997); children: Carrie, Jennifer, Maria. BB, We. Ill. U., 1971; JD, U. Louisville, 1974. Bar: Ill.; CPA Ill. Tax supr. Touche Ross & Co., Chgo., 1975-79; v.p., tax Lane Industries, Inc., Northbrook, Ill., 1979—. Bd. dirs. Chgo. Lighthouse, 1987-92. Mem. ABA, AICPA, Ill. Bar Assn., Ill. CPA Soc. Office: Lane Industries Inc 1200 Shermer Rd Northbrook IL 60062-4500

**FABE, DANA ANDERSON,** judge; b. Cin., Mar. 29, 1951; d. George and Mary Lawrence (Van Antwerp) F.; m. Randall Gene Simpson, Jan. 1, 1983; 1 child, Amelia Fabe Simpson. B.A., Cornell U., 1973; J.D., Northeastern U., 1976. Bar: Alaska 1977, U.S. Supreme Ct. 1981. Law clk. to justice Alaska Supreme Ct., 1976-77; staff atty. pub. defenders State of Alaska, 1977-81; dir. Alaska Pub. Defender Agy., Anchorage, from 1981; judge Superior Ct., Anchorage; justice Alaska Supreme Ct., Anchorage, 1996—. Named Alumna of Yr., Northeastern Sch. Law, 1983. Mem. Nat. Assn. Women Judges, Alaska Bar Assn., Anchorage Assn. Women Attys. Office: Alaska Supreme Ct 303 K St Fl 5 Anchorage AK 99501-2013

**FABEL, THOMAS LINCOLN,** lawyer; b. St. Paul, Feb. 12, 1946; s. George Forest and Beatrice Evelyn (Ostrom) F.; m. Jean Marquerite Hoisser, Nov. 21, 1946; children: Jessica, Anne, Leah, Theodore. BA, Carleton Coll., 1968; JD, U. Chgo., 1971; LLD (Hon.), William Mitchell Coll. Law, 1988. Bar: Minn. 1971; U.S. Dist. Ct. Minn. 1972; U.S. Ct. Appeals (8th cir.) 1974; U.S. Supreme Ct. 1976. Special asst. atty. gen. Minn. Atty. Gen., St. Paul, 1971-73, deputy atty. gen., 1973-87; ptnr. Lindquist & Vennum, Mpls., 1987-97, 99—; dep. mayor City of St. Paul, 1998; adj. faculty William Mitchell Coll. Law, St. Paul, 1982—. Mem. Minn. Bar Assn., Ramsey County Bar Assn., Rotary. General civil litigation. Home: 1550 Edgewater Ave Saint Paul MN 55112-3630 Office: Lindquist & Vennum 444 Cedar St Saint Paul MN 55101-2179

**FABER, DAVID ALAN,** federal judge; b. Charleston, W.Va., Oct. 21, 1942; s. John Smith and Wilda Elaine (Melton) F.; m. Deborah Ellayne Anderson, Aug. 24, 1968; 1 dau., Katherine Peyton. B.A., W.Va. U., 1964; J.D., Yale U., 1967; LLM, U. Va., 1998. Bar: W.Va. 1967, U.S. Ct. Mil. Appeals 1970, U.S. Supreme Ct. 1974. Assoc. Dayton, Campbell & Love, Charleston, W.Va., 1967-68, Campbell, Love, Woodroe, 1972-74; ptnr. Campbell, Love, Woodroe & Kizer, Charleston, 1974-77, Love, Wise, Robinson & Woodroe, Charleston, 1977-81; U.S. atty. U.S. Dept. Justice, Charleston, 1982-86; ptnr. Spilman, Thomas, Battle & Klostermeyer, Charleston, 1987-91; judge U.S. Dist. Ct. (so. dist.) W.Va., Bluefield, 1991—; counsel to ethics commn. W.Va. State Bar, Charleston, 1974-76. Served to capt. USAF, 1968-72, to col. W.Va. Air N.G., 1978-92. Nat. law scholar Yale Law Sch. New Haven, 1964-65. Mem. W.Va. State Bar, W.Va. Bar Assn., Phi beta Kappa. Republican. Episcopalian. Office: US Dist Ct PO Box 4068 601 Federal St Ste 2303 Bluefield WV 24701-3033

**FABER, KEITH L.,** lawyer; b. Troy, Mo., Jan. 19, 1966; s. Joeseph and Patsy Faber. BS in Pub. Adminstrn., Oakland U., 1988; JD, Ohio State U., 1991. Bar: Ohio 1991, Ind. 1991, U.S. Dist. Ct. (no. and so. dists.) Ind. 1991, U.S. Dist. Ct. (no. dist.) Ohio 1994. Assoc. Barnes & Thornburg, Ft. Wayne, Ind., 1991-93; atty. Buck Berry Landau & Breunig, Indpls., 1993; house counsel Celina (Ohio) Group, 1993—; legal advisor Ohio Mock Trial Program. Advisor Explorer troop Boy Scouts Am., Celina, 1994; instr. CPCU program, Celina, 1994; Bd. dirs. Mercer County YMCA. Mem. ABA, Ohio State Bar Assn. (pub. understanding of law com. 1993—, chairperson newspaper editl. bd. Laws You Can Use), Ind. State Bar Assn., Am. Corp. Coun. Assn. Insurance, State civil litigation, Personal injury. Office: Celina Group 1 Insurance Sq Celina OH 45822-1690

**FABER, PETER LEWIS,** lawyer; b. N.Y.C., Apr. 29, 1938; s. Alexander W. and Anne L. Faber; m. Joan Schuster, June 14, 1959; children: Michael, Julia, Thomas. AB, Swarthmore Coll., 1960; LLB, Harvard U., 1963. Bar: N.Y. 1964. Assoc. Wiser, Shaw, Freeman, Ickes & Williams, Rochester, N.Y., 1963-65; assoc. Parker, Chapin & Flattau, N.Y.C., 1965-66; ptnr. Harter, Secrest & Emery, Rochester, N.Y., 1966-82; ptnr. Winthrop, Stimson, Putnam & Roberts, N.Y.C., 1982-84, Kaye, Scholer, Fierman, Hays & Handler, N.Y.C., 1984-95, McDermott, Will & Emery, 1995—; mem. adv. com. NYU Ann. Inst. on State & Local Taxation; mem. N.Y. State Coun. on Fiscal and Econ. Priorities, 1991-95. Chmn. Rochester Econ. Devel. Com., 1979-82; pres. Rochester Philharmonic Orch., Inc., 1980-82; bd. dirs. Met. Rochester Devel. Council, Harley Sch., 1978-81; mem. fin. com. Monroe County Dem. Party, 1979-82; active N.Y.C. Partnership. Fellow Am. Bar Found., Am. Coll. Tax Counsel; mem. ABA (chmn. tax sect. 1991-92, vice chmn. 1986-88, chmn.-elect 1990-91, chmn. com. corp. stockholder relationships tax sect. 1980-82, liaison to IRS for North Atlantic region, vice chmn. spl. com. on integration 1979-81, sec. tax sect. 1984-86), N.Y. State Bar Assn. (chmn. sect. taxation 1976-77, exec. com. sect. taxation 1969—), N.Y. C. of C. (chmn. tax. com. 1988—, trustee 1989—, exec. com. 1990—), Monroe County Bar Assn., Am. Law Inst. (tax project adv. group), Rochester Area C. of C. (trustee 1980-82). Contbr. articles to profl. jours. Corporate taxation, State and local taxation. Home: 300 Central Park W New York NY 10024-1513 Office: McDermott Will & Emery 50 Rockefeller Plz New York NY 10020-1605

**FABER, ROBERT CHARLES,** lawyer; b. N.Y.C., June 26, 1941; s. Sidney G. and Beatrice (Siebert) F.; m. Carol Z. Zimmerman, Aug. 15, 1965; 1 child, Susan Faber. BA, Cornell U., 1962; JD, Harvard Law Sch., 1965. Bar: N.Y. 1966; U.S. Dist. Ct. (so. dist.) N.Y. 1967; U.S. Ct. Appeals (2nd cir.); U.S. Ct. Appeals (fed. cir.) 1982; U.S. Supreme Ct. 1971; U.S. Patent and trademark Office 1967. Atty., ptnr. Ostrolenk, Faber, Gerb & Soffen, LLP, N.Y.C., 1965—; lecturer Practicing Law Inst., N.Y.C., 1974—. Author: Landis on Mechanics of Patent Claim Drafting, 3d edit. 1990, 4th edit. 1996. Mem. Am. Intellectual Property Law Assn., N.Y. Intellectual Property Law Assn., Harvard Club of N.Y. Intellectual property, Patent, Trademark and copyright. Office: Ostrolenk Faber Gerb & Soffen LLP 1180 Ave of Americas New York NY 10036-8401

**FABIAN, EMIL MICHELLE,** lawyer; b. Wiltshire, Eng., Mar. 1, 1954. BA, U. Nebr., 1977, JD, 1980. Bar: Nebr., 1980, U.S. Ct. Appeals (8th cir.), 1989, U.S. Supreme Ct., 1986. Ptnr. Fabian & Thielen, Omaha, 1983—. Contbr. articles to profl. jours. Mem. Nebr. Criminal Def. Attys. Assn. (bd. dirs. 1980—). Democrat. Roman Catholic. Avocations: family. Criminal. Office: Fabian & Thielen PO Box 7567 4939 S 24th St Omaha NE 68107-2706

**FABIO, THEA MARIE,** lawyer; b. Boston, Mar. 8, 1955; d. Faust F. and Mary R. (Bonafede) F.; m. Richard L. Merrill, Aug. 4, 1979; children: Alessandra, Maria, Livia. BA, Smith Coll., 1976; JD, U. Tex., 1979. Bar: Tex. 1979, Mass. 1987, U.S. Dist. Ct. (so. dist.) Tex. 1980, U.S. Ct. Appeals (5th cir.) 1980. Atty. Groom, Miglicco & Gibson, Houston, 1979-85; shareholder/ptnr. Botschen & Fabio, Houston, 1986-87; pvt. practice Thea M. Fabio, Houston, 1987-90; ptnr. Fabio & Merrill, Houston, 1990—; vol. Houston Vol. Lawyers Program, 1988—; trainer Alternative Dispute Resolution, Houston, 1987-90; pres. Univ. Pl. Assn., 1999—. Pres. Southgate Civic Club, Houston, 1992-97; troop leader San Jacinto Girl Scouts, Houston, 1996—; chair various coms. Roberts Elem. Sch., Houston, 1989—. Mem. Houston Bar Assn., Smith Coll. Club Houston, Univ. Place Assn. (pres. 1996—). Family and matrimonial, Probate, General practice. Office: Fabio and Merrill 4543 Post Oak Place Dr Ste 120 Houston TX 77027-3103

**FACEY, JOHN ABBOTT, III,** lawyer; b. Springfield, Mass., June 14, 1950; s. John Abbott Jr. and Mary Agnes (Murphy) F.; m. Patricia Marie Otto, Sept. 27, 1975; children: Justin Abbott, Christopher John, Michael Edward. BA, Coll. of the Holy Cross, 1972; JD, Suffolk U., 1975. Bar: Mass. 1975, Vt. 1976, U.S. Dist. Ct. Vt. 1977. Assoc. Bishop & Crowley, Rutland, Vt., 1975-81; ptnr. Keyser, Crowley, Banse & Facey, Rutland, 1981-90, Reiber Kenlan Schwiebert Hall & Facey, P.C., Rutland, 1990—. Corporator Rutland Regional Med. Ctr.; trustee Rutland Free Libr., 1988-94, pres., 1989-90; bd. dirs. Downtown Devel. Corp., 1990-94; mem. Rutland City Planning Commn., 1994—, chair, 1996—. Mem. ABA, Mass. Bar Assn., Vt. Bar Assn., Rutland County Bar Assn., New Eng. Land Title Assn., Rotary (bd. dirs. 1989—, pres. 1991-92). Republican. Roman Catholic. Avocation: skiing. Real property, Land use and zoning (including planning), Municipal (including bonds). Home: 82 Davis St Rutland VT 05701-3308 Office: Reiber Kenland Schwiebert Hall & Facey 71 Allen St Rutland VT 05701-4570

**FADAOL, ROBERT FREDERICK,** lawyer; b. Opelousas, La., Oct. 3, 1939; s. Joseph Charles and Marie (Nassar) F.; m. Carolyn Ann Chapman, Jan. 1, 1970; children: Charles, Tracy, Robert. BS in Pharmacy, Auburn U., 1962; JD, Loyola U., New Orleans, 1970. Bar: La. 1971, U.S. Dist. Ct. (ea. and mid. dists.) La. 1971, U.S. Ct. Appeals (5th cir.) 1971, U.S. Dist. Ct. (we. dist.) La. 1975, U.S. Ct. Appeals (11th cir.) 1980, U.S. Tax Ct. 1984, U.S. Ct. Appeals (fed. cir.) 1994, U.S. Supreme Ct. 1976. Sole practice New Orleans, 1971—; judge ad hoc Parish Ct., 1986. Served to 2nd lt. U.S. Army, 1962-67. Mem. ABA, La. Bar Assn., Assn. Trial Lawyers Am., La. Trial Lawyers Assn. Republican. Roman Catholic. General corporate, Insurance, Probate. Home: 348 Terry Pky Gretna LA 70056-2637 Office: 1108 Stumpf Blvd Gretna LA 70053-3612

**FADELEY, EDWARD NORMAN,** retired state supreme court justice; b. Williamsville, Mo., Dec. 13, 1929; m. Nancie Peacocke, June 11, 1953; children: Charles, Shira; m. Darian Cyr, Sept. 12, 1992. A.B., U. Mo., 1951; J.D. cum laude, U. Oreg., 1957. Bar: Oreg. 1957, U.S. Supreme Ct. 1968. Practice law Eugene, Oreg., 1957-88; mem. Oreg. Ho. of Reps., 1961-63; mem. Oreg. Senate, 1963-87, pres., 1983-85; justice Oregon Supreme Ct., 1989-98; ret., 1998; mem. jud. working group Internat. Water Tribunal, Amsterdam, The Netherlands 1991-95; invitee Rio Environ. Conf., 1992, Indigenous Peoples of World Conf., New Zealand, 1993; adj. prof. law U. Oreg.; formerly gen. couns., bd. officer for rsch. corp., fin. instn. Advisor, counsellor to Pres. Clinton, others; chmn. Oreg. Dem. party, 1966-68; chmn. law and justice com. Nat. Conf. Legislators, 1977-78; adv. com. to State and Local Law Ctr., Washington; participants com. Washington Pub. Power Supply System, 1982-88; candidate for nomination for gov., 1986; bd. dirs. Wayne Morse Hist. Park. Lt. USNR, 1951-54. Recipient First Pioneer award U. Oreg., 1980, Assn. Oreg. Counties award for leadership in the reform of state ct. system, 1982. Mem. ABA (internat. law, pub. utility law), Oreg. State Bar Assn. (chmn. uniform laws com. 1962-64), Order of Coif, Alpha Pi Zeta, Phi Alpha Delta. Democrat. Methodist. Avocations: canoeing, backpacking, hunting, riding, poetry.

**FAERBER, CHARLES N.,** editor; b. Wakefield, R.I., July 11, 1944. BA, Dartmouth Coll., 1966; MS, San Diego State U., 1977. Newspaper reporter/editor, 1972-78; v.p. legis. affairs Nat. Notary Assn. Editor Nat. Notary mag., Notary Bull. Served with USN, 1967-72. Office: Nat Notary Assn Box 2402 9350 DeSoto Ave Chatsworth CA 91313-2402

**FAGAN, CHRISTOPHER BRENDAN,** lawyer; b. South Bend, Ind., Sept. 1, 1937; s. Christopher J. and Clara A. (Poirier) F. ;m. Mary K. O'Neill, Feb. 11, 1961 (div. July 1977); children: Kathleen, Patricia, Colleen, Matthew, Timothy, Daniel; m. Janyce R. Brock, Sept. 1, 1978 (div. May 1997); m. Barbara A. Vargo, Apr. 10, 1999. BSME, U. Notre Dame, 1959; JD, Georgetown U., 1965. Bar: Ohio 1965, U.S. Dist. Ct. (no. dist.) Ohio 1967. Patent examiner U.S. Patent Office, Washington, 1963-65; patent atty. Eaton Corp., Cleve., 1965-67; assoc. Fay, Sharpe, Beall, Fagan, Minnich & McKee, Cleve., 1967-70, ptnr., 1970—. Lt. USN, 1959-63. Mem. Ohio State Bar Assn., Cleve. Bar Assn., Am. Patent Law Assn., Cleve. Patent Law Assn. Republican. Roman Catholic. Patent, Trademark and copyright. Home: 3040 N Windsor Ct Westlake OH 44145-6717 Office: Fay Sharpe Beall Fagan Minnich & McKee 1100 Superior Ave E Ste 700 Cleveland OH 44114-2518

**FAGERBERG, ROGER RICHARD,** lawyer; b. Chgo., Dec. 11, 1935; s. Richard Emil and Evelyn (Thor) F.; m. Virginia Fuller Vaughan, June 20, 1959; children: Steven Roger, Susan Vaughan, James Thor, Laura Craft. B.S. in Bus. Adminstrn., Washington U., St. Louis, 1958, J.D., 1961, postgrad., 1961-62. Bar: Mo. 1961. Grad. teaching asst. Washington U., St. Louis, 1961-62; assoc. firm Rassieur, Long & Yawitz, St. Louis, 1962-64; ptnr. Rassieur, Long, Yawitz & Schneider and predecessor firms, St. Louis, 1965-91; pvt. practice St. Louis, 1991—. Mem. exec. com. Citizens' Adv. Council Pkwy. Sch. Dist., 1974—, pres.-elect, 1976-77, pres., 1977-78; bd. dirs. Parkway Residents Orgn., 1969—, v.p., 1970-73, pres., 1973—; scoutmaster Boy Scouts Am., 1979-83; Presbyn. elder, 1976—, pres. three local congs. 1968-70, 77-78, 83-84. Mem. ABA, Mo. Bar Assn., St. Louis Bar Assn., Christian Bus. Men's Com. (bd. dirs. 1975-78, 87-91), Full Gospel Bus. Men's Fellowship, Order of Coif, Omicron Delta Kappa, Beta Gamma Sigma, Pi Sigma Alpha, Phi Eta Sigma, Phi Delta Phi, Kappa Sigma. Republican. Lodges: Kiwanis (bd. dirs. 1988-91), Masons, Shriners. General corporate, Probate, Taxation, general. Home and Office: 13812 Clayton Rd Chesterfield MO 63017-8407

**FAGG, GEORGE GARDNER,** federal judge; b. Eldora, Iowa, Apr. 30, 1934; s. Ned and Arleene (Gardner) F.; m. Jane E. Wood, Aug. 19, 1956; children: Martha, Thomas, Ned, Susan, George, Sarah. BS in Bus. Adminstrn., Drake U., 1956, JD, 1958. Bar: Iowa 1958. Ptnr. Cartwright, Druker, Ryden & Fagg, Marshalltown, Iowa, 1958-72; judge Iowa Dist. Ct., 1972-82; judge U.S. Ct. Appeals (8th cir.), 1982-99, sr. judge, 1999-; mem. faculty Nat. Jud. Coll., 1979. Mem. ABA, Iowa Bar Assn., Order of Coif. Office: US Ct Appeals US Courthouse Annex 110 E Court Ave Ste 455 Des Moines IA 50309-2044

**FAGUNDES, JOSEPH MARVIN, III,** lawyer; b. Modesto, Calif., Feb. 26, 1953; s. Joseph M. Jr. and Laura Florence (Bavaro) F.; m. Kathryn J., July 9, 1995; children: Brie M., Mia N., Tiffany W. BA, U. Calif., Berkeley, 1976; JD, U. Hawaii, 1980. Bar: Hawaii 1980, U.S. Dist. Ct. Hawaii 1980, U.S. Ct. Appeals (9th cir.) 1983. Assoc. Gallup, Mah, Van Pernis & Ihara, Kailua-Kona, Hawaii, 1980-82; ptnr. Gallup, Van Pernis & Fagundes, Kailua-Kona, 1982-84, Fagundes & Seiter, Kailua-Kona, 1984-87; pvt. practice Kailua-Kona, 1987—; founder West Hawaii Law Clinic, Kailua-Kona, 1988-91. Mem. ABA, Hawaii Bar Assn. (bd. dirs. 1987-91), West Hawaii Bar Assn. (bd. dirs. 1987-89, 90-91, pres. 1988-89), Legal Aid Soc. Hawaii (bd. dirs. 1987-89), Hawaii Fishing and Boating Assn. (bd. dirs. 1986—), Hawaii Island Portuguese C. of C., Waikiki Yacht Club, Heeia Bay Fishing Club (pres. 1989—), Hawaii Big Game Fishing Club, Phi Delta Phi. Avocations: sportfishing, motorcycling, music. Admiralty, General civil litigation, Real property. Address: Hualalai Ctr 75-170 Hualalai Rd Ste D214 Kailua Kona HI 96740-1737

**FAHEY, HALLIE JOAN MILLER,** lawyer; b. McHenry, Ill., July 2, 1965; d. Charles Peter and Joan Kathryn (Bauer) Miller; m. Brian Joseph Fahey, Nov. 18, 1995; 1 child, Cameron Miller Fahey. BS, Butler U., 1987; postgrad., Boston Coll., 1987-88; JD, U. Ill., 1990. Bar: Ill. 1990. Assoc. Schiff Hardin & White, Chgo., 1990-95, Blatt Hammesfahr & Eaton, Chgo., 1995-97, Bates Meckler Bulger & Tilson, Chgo., 1997—. Republican. Roman Catholic. Avocations: photography, architecture. Office: Bates Meckler Bulger & Tilson 8300 Sears Tower Chicago IL 60606

**FAHEY, HELEN F.,** prosecutor. Atty. U.S. Dept. Justice, Alexandria, Va., 1993—. Office: US Attys Office 2100 Jamieson Ave Alexandria VA 22314-5702*

**FAHNER, TYRONE C.,** lawyer, former state attorney general; b. Detroit, Nov. 18, 1942; s. Warren George and Alma Fahner; BA, U. Mich., 1965; JD, Wayne State U., 1968; LLM, Northwestern U., 1971; m. Anne Beauchamp, July 2, 1966; children—Margaret, Daniel, Molly. Bar: Mich. 1968, Ill. 1969, Tex. 1984, U.S. Dist. Ct. (ea. dist.) Mich. 1968, U.S. Dist. Ct. (no. dist.) Ill. 1969, U.S. Ct. Appeals (7th cir.) 1969, U.S. Ct. Appeals (5th cir.) 1981. asst. U.S. atty. for No. Dist. Ill., Chgo., 1971-75, dep. chief consumer fraud and civil rights, 1973-74, chief ofcl. corruption, 1974-75; ptnr. Freeman, Rothe, Freeman & Salzman, Chgo., 1975-77; dir. Ill. Dept. Law Enforcement, Springfield, 1977-79; ptnr. Mayer, Brown & Platt, Chgo., 1979-80, 83—; Co-chmn of managmnt comm., Mayer, Brown & Platt, 1998—; atty. gen. State of Ill., Springfield, 1980-83; instr. John Marshall Law Sch., 1973-76, 78-84; pvt. sector rep. UNCTAD; former chmn. Coun. Great Lakes Govs.; chmn. Govs. Adv. Bd. Law Enforcement, 1980-83, Ill. Jud. Inquiry Bd. 1988-92, Chgo., Com. Honest Elections, 1984-92, Com. Internat. Trade and Tourism, Chgo. com. Chgo. Coun. Fgn. Rels. Mem. Toronto sister city com. Chgo. Sister Cities Internat. Program; bd. dirs. Mex.-Am. Legal Defense and Ednl. Fund; mem. corp. adv. com. U. Mich. Coll. Lit., Sci. & The Arts, mem. major gifts com.; Mex.-Am. Legal Def. and Ednl. Fund; mem. William J. Fulbright bd. fgn. scholarships USIA, 1988-93; active Law Sch.'s Com. Visitors Wayne State U., U.S. Info. Agy., Ill. Racing Bd., 1979-80, United Cerbral Palsy, Chgo., 1981-84, Epilepsy Found. Greater Chgo., Evanston Hist. Soc., Bureau Ednl. and Cultural Affairs, 1988-93. Mem. ABA, Am. Coll. Trial Lawyers, Internat. Assn. Gaming Attys., Mich. Bar Assn., Tex. Bar Assn., Chgo. Bar Assn., Law Club Chgo., Am. Inns of Ct. (Chgo. chpt.), Ill. Ambs. (bd. dirs., past pres.), Northwestern U. Sch. Law Alumni Assn. (bd. dirs. 1990-95, chmn. Class 1967 James B. Haddad professorship fundraising com.), Econ. Club of Chgo., Chgo. Club, Chgo. Commonwealth Club, Legal Club Chgo., Am. Effective Law Enforcement (com. cts. and justice), Commercial Club Chgo., U. Mich. Major Gifts com., Just The Beginning Found. Republican. Lutheran. Antitrust, Federal civil litigation, Securities. Office: Mayer Brown & Platt 190 S La Salle St Ste 3100 Chicago IL 60603-3441

**FAHRNBRUCH, DALE E.,** retired state supreme court justice; b. Lincoln, Nebr., Sept. 13, 1924; s. Henry and Bessie M. (Osborne) F.; m. Margaret L. Hunt, July 4, 1952; children: Rebecca Kay Fahrnbruch Braymen, Daniel D. (dec.). AD in Journalism, U. Nebr., 1948, BS in Law, 1950; JD, Creighton U., 1951; LLM, U. Va., 1986. Bar: Nebr. 1951, U.S. Ct. Appeals (8th cir.) 1969. City editor Jour. Newspaper, Lincoln, 1951-52; asst., then dep. county atty. Lancaster County, Lincoln, Nebr., 1952-55; chief dep. county atty. Lancaster County, Lincoln, 1955-59; ptnr. Beynon, Hecht & Fahrnbruch, Lincoln, 1959-73; dist. judge Nebr. Lincoln, 1973-87; justice Nebr. Supreme Ct., Lincoln, 1987-97.

**FAHY, JOSEPH THOMAS,** lawyer; b. Uxbridge, Mass., July 9, 1919; s. John Francis and Josephine Mary (Rooney) F.; m. Marie C. McOsker, May 7, 1955; children: Margaret Ellen, Joseph Thomas Jr., John Fergus, Mary Celine. AB, Coll. of Holy Cross, 1941; LLB, Harvard U., 1948. Bar: Mass. 1948, U.S. Dist. Ct. Mass. 1954, U.S. Ct. Appeals (1st cir.) 1971, U.S. Supreme Ct. 1971. Assoc. Peabody, Brown, Rowley & Storey, Boston, 1948-56, ptnr., 1957-80; prin. Joseph T. Fahy, P.C., Boston, 1981-92; ptnr. Peabody & Brown, P.C., Boston, 1981-92, counsel, 1992-99; counsel Nixon Peabody LLP, Boston, 1999—. Mem. ABA, Boston Bar Assn., Harvard U. Law Sch. Assn., Alpha Sigma Nu, Delta Epsilon Sigma, Holy Cross Club (past bd. dirs.), Harvard Club, K.C. Avocation: American history. General civil litigation, Condemnation, General practice. Office: Nixon Peabody LLP 101 Federal St Fl 11 Boston MA 02110-1832

**FAIGNANT, JOHN PAUL,** lawyer, educator; b. Proctor, Vt., Mar. 24, 1953; s. Joseph Paul and Ann (DeBlasio) F.; children: Janelle, Melissa. BA, U. New Haven, 1974; JD, George Mason U., 1978. Bar: Va. 1978, Vt. 1979, U.S. Dist. Ct. Vt. 1979, U.S. Ct. Appeals (4th cir.) 1979, U.S. Supreme Ct. 1992. Assoc. Griffin & Griffin, Rutland, Vt., 1978-79; assoc. Miller, Norton & Cleary, Rutland, 1979-84, ptnr., 1984-87; ptnr. Miller, Cleary and Faignant PC, Rutland, 1988-91, Miller & Faignant, Ltd., Rutland, 1991-97, Miller Faignant & Whelton PC (now Miller Faignant & Behrens), Rutland, 1997—; adj. prof. Coll. St. Joseph, Rutland, 1982-90. Mem. Rutland Town Fire Dept., 1989—; mem., pres. No. New England Def. Counsel, 1995-96. Mem. Va. Bar Assn., Vt. Bar Assn., Assn. Trial Lawyers Am., Def. Rsch. Inst., Am. Bd. Trial Advocates. Roman Catholic. Avocation: antique trucks. Insurance, Personal injury, General civil litigation. Home: RR 1 Box 3762 Rutland VT 05701-9214 Office: Miller Faignant & Behrens PC 36 Merchants Row PO Box 6688 Rutland VT 05702-6688

**FAILINGER, MARIE ANITA,** law educator, editor; b. Battle Creek, Mich., June 29, 1952; d. Conard Frederick and Joan Anita (Lang) F.; children: Joanna, Kristina. BA, Valparaiso U., 1973, JD, 1976; LLM, Yale U., 1983; postgrad., U. Chgo., 1990. Bar: Ind. 1976, U.S. Dist. Ct. (no. dist.) Ind. 1976, U.S. Dist. Ct. (so. dist. ) Ind. 1977, U.S. Ct. Appeals (7th cir.) 1979, Minn. 1984, U.S. Supreme Ct. 1980. Prof. of law Hamline U., St. Paul, 1983—, assoc. dean, 1990-93. Editor: Jour. of Law and Religion, 1988—; contbr. articles, book revs. to profl. publs. Mem. Am. Indian Rsch. and Policy Inst., 1993—; sec. Church Innovations Inst.; treas. Luth. Innovations. Mem. Minn. Women Lawyers (bd. dirs. 1989-90), Am. Assn. Law Schs. (chair poverty sect. 1984-88, exec. com. law and religion sect.), Ctrl. Minn. Legal Svcs. Bd., Nat. Equal Justice Libr. (bd. dirs. 1989—). Democrat. Mem. Evang. Luth. Ch. Am. Office: Hamline U Sch Law 1536 Hewitt Ave Saint Paul MN 55104-1284

**FAILLACE, CHARLES KENNETH,** lawyer; b. Mineola, N.Y., Nov. 4, 1956; s. Frank A. and Natalie (Gavin) F. BS cum laude, Boston Coll., 1978; JD, Hofstra U., 1981. Bar: N.Y. 1983, U.S. Dist. Ct. (so. and ea. dists.) N.Y. 1983, U.S. Ct. Appeals ((2d cir.) 1985, Mass. 1995, U.S. Dist. Ct. Mass. 1995. With Evans, Orr, Pacelli, Norton & Laffan, PC, N.Y.C., 1982; assoc. Kopff, Nardelli & Dopf, N.Y.C., 1982-98; ptnr. DuBois, Billig, Loughlan, Conaty & Weisman, Mineola, N.Y., 1998—. Mem. ABA, N.Y. State Med. Malpractice Bar Assn., N.Y. Trial Lawyers Assn., Def. Rsch. Inst., Nassau County Bar Assn. Personal injury, Professional liability, State civil litigation. Home: 23 Waverly Pl Apt 5K New York NY 10003-6717

**FAIN, JOEL MAURICE,** lawyer; b. Miami Beach, Fla., Dec. 11, 1953; s. William Maurice and Carolyn Genievive (Baggett) F.; m. Moira Joan Slocum, June 15, 1974; children: Hannah Ruth, Dylan Michael, Rachel Joan. BA, Yale U., 1975; JD, U. Conn., 1978. Bar: Conn. 1978, U.S. Dist. Ct. Conn. 1978, U.S. Ct. Appeals (2d cir.) 1989, U.S. Supreme Ct. 1999. Assoc. Kahan, Kerensky, Capossela, Levine & Breslau, Vernon, Conn., 1978-83, ptnr., 1984-90; mng. ptnr. Kahan, Kerensky, Capossela, Levine & Breslau, 1990-91; ptnr. Morrison, Mahoney & Miller, Hartford, Conn., 1992—. Chmn. Youth Adv. Bd., Tolland, Conn., 1983-92; chmn. Tolland Town Coun., 1995—. Mem. ABA, Conn. Bar Assn., Tolland County Bar Assn. (pres. 1991-92), Assn. Trial Lawyers Am., Conn. Trial Lawyers Assn., Lions (pres. 1987-88). Democrat. Congregationalist. Personal injury, State civil litigation, Federal civil litigation. Home: 76 Tolland Grn Tolland CT 06084-3044 Office: Morrison Mahoney & Miller 100 Pearl St Hartford CT 06103-4506

**FAIRBAIRN, SYDNEY ELISE,** lawyer; b. Fullerton, Calif., Feb. 20, 1963; d. Robin H. and Yvonne A. Fairbairn. BA in Rhetoric, U. Calif., Berkeley, 1982, BA in Anthropology, 1982; JD, Golden Gate U., 1985. Pvt. practice law San Rafael, Calif. Atty. YWCA, San Anselmo, Calif., 1995—. Mem. Marin County Bar Assn. (chair ins. sect. 1999—), Marin County Women's Bar, Mission San Rafael Rotary Club. Democrat. General civil litigation, Real property, Personal injury. Office: Ste A-110 Seven Mt Lassen Dr San Rafael CA 94903

**FAIRBANKS, ROBERT ALVIN,** lawyer; b. Oklahoma City, July 9, 1944; s. Albert Edward and Lucille Imogene (Scherer) F.; m. Linda Gayle Geer, Aug. 26, 1967; children: Chele Lyn, Kimberly Jo, Robert Alvin II, Michael Albert, Richard Alan, Joseph Alexander. BS in Math., U. Okla., 1967, JD, 1973; MBA, Oklahoma City U., 1970, MCJA, 1975; LLM, Columbia U., 1976; MA, Stanford U., 1984; MEd, Harvard U., 1993. Bar: Okla. 1974, U.S. Dist. Ct. (we. dist.) Okla. 1974, U.S. Ct. Customs and Patent Appeals 1974, U.S. Ct. Mil. Appeals, 1974, U.S. Tax Ct. 1974, U.S. Claims Ct. 1975, U.S. Customs Ct. 1975, U.S. Ct. Appeals (10th cir.) 1975, U.S. Supreme Ct. 1977, U.S. Dist. Ct. (ea. dist.) Okla. 1984, Minn. 1993. Commd. 2d lt. USAF, 1967, advanced through grades to capt., 1970; col. USAFR, 1986; asst. staff judge adv., chief of claims div. Office of Staff Judge Adv., Tinker AFB, Okla., 1974-75; legal asst. to Justice William A. Berry, Okla. Supreme Ct., 1977; pvt. practice Norman, Okla., 1974—; v.p. St. Gregory's U., Shawnee, Okla., 1997—; instr. bus. adminstrn. U. Md. Far East div., Nha Trang, Viet Nam, 1970-71, Rose State Coll., Midwest City, Okla., 1974; rsch. assoc. in law U. Okla., Norman, 1974, spl. lectr., 1974-75, vis. asst. prof., 1976-77, adj. prof. law, 1984—; vis. asst. prof. law Oklahoma City U., 1977; asst. prof. law U. Ark., Fayetteville, Arks., 1977-81; assoc. prof. law La. State U., Baton Rouge, 1981; rsch. asst. dept. family, community and preventative medicine Stanford (Calif.) Med. Sch., 1981-82; adj. asst. prof. govt. contract law Air Force Inst. Tech., Wright-Patterson AFB, Ohio, 1985—; v.p. St. Gregory's U., Shawnee, Okla.; cons. Cheyenne Tribe, Clinton, Okla., 1977-81, 90, Citizens Band of Pottawatomie Tribe, Shawnee, Okla., 1977-79, Inst. for Devel. of Indian Law, Washington, 1976-81; dir. Native Am. Coll. Prep. Ctr. Bemidji State U., Minn., 1993—. Editor-in-chief Am. Indian Law Rev., 1973; editor Okla. Law Rev., 1971-73; producer, dir.:

(with Barbara P. Ettinger) "Aa-Niin" film, 1994; author book revs.; contbr. articles to profl. jours. Mem. bd. control Fayetteville (Ark.) City Hosp., 1977-81; cubmaster Boy Scouts Am., Norman, 1982-83, asst. scoutmaster, Stanford, 1981, scoutmaster, Norman, 1990-91, com. mem., den leader, 1988; softball coach Jr. High Girls League, Fayetteville, 1977-81; mem. adv. bd. Native Am. Prep. Sch., Santa Fe; pres., chmn. bd. Native Am. Coll. Prep. Ctr., Bemidji, Minn.; mem. exec. adv. bd. Aerospace Sci. and Tech. Edn. Ctr. of Okla., Okla. City Univ. U.S. Dept. Edn. fellow Stanford U. Med. Sch.; Charles Evans Hughes fellow Columbia U. Law Sch., 1976; Sequoyah fellow Assn. Am. Indian Affairs, 1975-76; Mellon fellow Harvard U. Sch. Edn., 1993; nominee Pulitzer prize for Disting. Commentary, 1997. Mem. ABA, Okla. Bar Assn., Fed. Bar Assn., Am. Trial Lawyers Assn., Okla. Trial Lawyers Assn., Okla. Indian Bar Assn., Oklahoma County Bar Assn., Assn. Am. Law Schs., N.G. Assn. U.S., Air Force Assn. (life), Res. Officers Assn. (life), Nat. Contract Mgmt. Assn., Soc. Logistics Engrs., Phi Alpha Delta, Phi Delta Epsilon, Phi Delta Kappa. Republican. Roman Catholic. Personal injury, Pension, profit-sharing, and employee benefits, Entertainment. Office: 2212 Westpark Dr Norman OK 73069-4012

**FAIRCHILD, RAYMOND FRANCIS,** lawyer; b. Springfield, Ill., June 29, 1946; s. Francis M. and Estelle G. Fairchild; m. Ann Louise Templeton, Dec. 28, 1968. BA, U. Ill., 1968; JD, Ind. U., 1971. Bar: Ind. 1971, U.S. Dist. Ct. (so. dist.) Ind. 1971, U.S. Ct. Appeals (7th cir.) 1989. Sole practice Indpls., 1971—. Mem. Assn. Trial Lawyers Am., N.Y. State Trial Lawyers Assn., Ind. Trial Lawyers Assn. Club: Manor House, Skyline (Indpls.). Personal injury, State civil litigation, Federal civil litigation. Office: 2501 E South St Columbus IN 47201-8637

**FAIRCHILD, THOMAS E.,** federal judge; b. Milw., Dec. 25, 1912; s. Edward Thomas and Helen (Edwards) F.; m. Eleanor E. Dahl, July 24, 1937; children: Edward, Susan, Jennifer, Andrew. Student, Princeton, 1931-33; A.B., Cornell U., 1934; LL.B., U. Wis., 1938. Bar: Wis. 1938. Practiced Portage, Wis., 1938-41, Milw., 1945-48, 53-56; atty. OPA, Chgo., Milw., 1941-45; hearing commr. Chgo. Region, 1945; atty. gen. Wis., 1948-51; U.S. atty. for Western Dist. Wis., 1951-52; justice Supreme Ct. Wis., 1957-66, U.S. Ct. Appeals for 7th Circuit, 1966—. Dem. candidate Senator from Wis., 1950, 52. Mem. ABA, Wis. Bar Assn., Fed. Bar Assn., Milw. Bar Assn., 7th Cir. Bar Assn., Dane County Bar Assn., Am. Judicature Soc., Am. Law Inst., Phi Delta Phi, KP. Democrat. Mem. United Ch. of Christ. Office: US Courthouse Rm 2764 219 S Dearborn St Chicago IL 60604-1702

**FAIRLEIGH, MARGARET HILLS,** lawyer; b. Atlanta, Apr. 11, 1912; d. Albert Lymanand Georgia Belle (Burns) Hills; m. George DuRelle Fairleigh, June 29, 1951 (dec. June 1978); children: Kathryn Fairleigh Allen, Henrietta Fairleigh Sparacino. LLB, Woodrow Wilson Coll. Law, Atlanta, 1939. Bar: Ga. 1940, U.S. Dist. Ct. (no. dist.) Ga. 1942, U.S. Ct. Appeals (5th cir.) 1949, U.S. Supreme Ct. 1954, U.S. Ct. Appeals (11th cir.) 1981. Assoc. Poole, Pearce & Graham, Atlanta, 1942-51; ptnr. Poole, Pearce & Hall (Poole, Pearce & Cooper), Atlanta, 1951-71; pvt. practice Decatur, Ga., 1971—. Pres. Atlanta Legal Aid Soc., 1966; vice-chmn. DeKalb County Salary Study Commn. for Statutory Pub. Employees, 1969; mem. Gov.'s Commn. on Status of Women, 1968-70; mem. Atlanta Estate Planning Coun.; treas. DeKalb Estate Planning Coun. Mem. Ga. Assn. Women Lawyers (pres. 1947-48), Ga. State Bar Assn., DeKalb County Bar Assn., DeKalb C.of C. (bd. dirs. 1976-78). Democrat. Presbyterian. Avocations: gardening, reading, travel, animals. Office: PO Box 15097 Atlanta GA 30333-0097

**FAIRMAN, MARC P.,** lawyer; b. May 25, 1945. BA, U. Calif., Berkeley, 1967; JD cum laude, Harvard U., 1970. Bar: Calif. 1971. Ptnr. McDermott, Will & Emery, Menlo Park. Northern Calif. adv. bd. Entrepreneurship Inst.; bd. trustees Mills Coll. Mem. Am. Inns of Ct., Assn. of Bus. Trial Lawyers. General civil litigation, Antitrust, Securities. Office: McDermott Will & Emery 2700 Sand Hill Rd Menlo Park CA 94025-7020

**FAISS, ROBERT DEAN,** lawyer; b. Centralia, Ill., Sept. 19, 1934; s. Wilbur and Theresa Ella (Watts) F.; m. Linda Louise Chambers, Mar. 30, 1991; children: Michael Dean Faiss, Marcy Faiss Ayres, Robert Mitchell Faiss, Philip Grant Faiss, Justin Cooper. *Robert Faiss's grandchildren are Stephanie Jane Faiss, Branden Faiss, Khristopher Robert Faiss, Adelaide Chambers Ayres and Eliza Pennington Ayres. Son Michael Faiss is a regional restaurant manager in California. Daughter Marceline Ayres is an educator in Massachusetts. Son Robert Mitchell Faiss owns an electrical contracting company in Nevada. Sons Philip Faiss and Justin Cooper are involved in the entertainment industry in California.* BA in Journalism, Am. U., 1969, JD, 1972. Bar: Nev. 1972, D.C. 1972, U.S. Dist. Ct. Nev. 1973, U.S. Supreme Ct. 1977, U.S. Ct. Appeals (9th cir.) 1978. City editor Las Vegas (Nev.) Sun, 1957-59; pub. info. officer Nev. Dept. Employment Security, 1959-61; asst. exec. sec. Nev. Gaming Commn., Carson City, 1961-63; exec. asst. to gov. State of Nev., Carson City, 1963-67; staff asst. U.S. Pres. Lyndon B. Johnson, White House, Washington, 1968-69; asst. to exec. dir. U.S. Travel Adminstrn., Washington, 1969-72; ptnr., chmn. adminstrv. law dept. Lionel, Sawyer & Collins, Las Vegas, 1973—; mem. bank secrecy Act Adv. Group U.S. Treasury. Co-author: Legalized Gaming in Nevada, 1961, Nevada Gaming License Guide, 1988, Nevada Gaming Law, 1991, 95, 98. Recipient Bronze medal Dept. Commerce, 1972, Chris Schaller award We Can, Las Vegas, 1995, Lifetime Achievement award Nev. Gaming Attys. Assn., 1997; named One of 100 Most Influential Lawyers in Am. and premier U.S. gaming atty., Nat. Law Jour., 1997. Mem. ABA (chmn. gaming law com. 1985-86), Internat. Assn. Gaming Attys. (founding, pres. 1980), Nev. Gaming Attys. Administrative and regulatory, Legislative, Libel. Office: Lionel Sawyer & Collins 300 S 4th St Ste 1700 Las Vegas NV 89101-6053

**FAITH, STANLEY O.,** lawyer; b. New Albany, Ind., Nov. 28, 1944; s. Albert L. and Mary Alice (Beanblossom) F.; m. Judy A. Lone, July 9, 1989; 1 child, Kimberly Ann Ransom. BS in Edn., Ind. U., 1966; MS in Edn., Ind. U., New Albany, 1979; JD, Ind. U., 1982. Bar: Ind. 1982, U.S. Dist. Ct. (no. and so. dists.) Ind. 1982. Tchr. Brownsburg (Ind.) Sch. Corp., 1966-67, N.W. Hendricks Sch. Corp., Lizton, Ind., 1967-70; sales rep. Amsco Publs., N.Y.C., 1970-77; legal intern/investigator Greene County Prosecutor's Office, Bloomfield, Ind., 1980-82; chief dep. prosecutor Floyd County Prosecutor's Office, New Albany, 1982-86, prosecutor, 1986—. Bd. dirs. So. Ind. Christian Leadership Conf., Jeffersonville, 1993, Dem. Men's Club, New Albany, 1994-95. Recipient Drum Maj. award So. Ind. So. Christian Leadership Conf., 1994. Mem. NAACP, Nat. Dist. Atty.'s Assn., Ind. Prosecuting Atty.'s Coun. Avocations: astronomy, horseback riding. Home: 9145 Nina Dr Georgetown IN 47122-8929 Office: Floyd County Prosecutors Office 249 City County Bldg New Albany IN 47150

**FAIZAKOFF, DANIEL BENJAMIN,** lawyer; b. N.Y.C., June 22, 1971; s. Yoseff and Gloria Faizakoff. BA, Yeshiva U., 1993; JD, Benjamin N. Cardozo Sch. Law, 1996. Bar: N.Y., U.S. Dist. Ct. (so. and ea. dists.) N.Y., N.J., U.S. Dist. Ct. N.J. Assoc. Lester Schwab Katz & Dwyer, N.Y.C., 1996—. Mem. ABA, N.Y. County Lawyers Assn., N.Y. State Bar Assn. General civil litigation, Product liability, Toxic tort. Office: Lester Schwab Katz & Dwyer 120 Broadway Fl 38 New York NY 10271-0071

**FALCAO, LINDA PHYLLIS,** lawyer, former screenwriter; b. Lisbon, Portugal, June 1, 1960; came to U.S., 1961; d. John Moniz and Phyllis Margaret (Fleming) F.; 1 child, Lauren N. BS in Econs., BA, U. Pa., 1982, JD, 1985. Assoc. Schnader, Harrison, Segal & Lewis, Phila., 1985-86; law clk. Hon. Phyllis W. Beck Superior Ct. Pa., 1986-88, 92; assoc. Dechert, Price & Rhoads, Phila., 1989-92; freelance writer Wynnewood, Pa., 1993-96; shareholder Salmanson and Falcão, LLC, Phila., 1997—. Author: (screenplay) Pattern and Practice, 1993, Millennium, 1996. Presdl. scholar Commn. Presdl. Scholars, Washington, 1978. Mem. Phi Beta Kappa, Beta Gamma Sigma. General civil litigation, Civil rights, Health. Office: Salmanson & Falcão LLC Ste 703 1608 Walnut St Philadelphia PA 19103

**FALCON, RAYMOND JESUS, JR.,** lawyer; b. N.Y.C., Nov. 17, 1953; s. Raymond J. and Lolin (Lopez) F.; m. Debra Mary Bomeisl, June 4, 1977; children: Victoria Marie, Mark Daniel. BA, Columbia U., 1975; JD, Yale U., 1978. Bar: N.Y. 1979, U.S. Dist. Ct. (so. and ea. dist.) N.Y. 1979, U.S. Ct. Appeals (D.C. and 2d cirs.) 1983, Fla. 1987, N.J. 1988, U.S. Dist. Ct. N.J. 1988. Assoc. Webster and Sheffield, N.Y.C., 1978-82; ptnr. Falcon and Hom, N.Y.C., 1982-85; sr. atty. Degussa Corp., Ridgefield Park, N.J., 1985-88, v.p., sec., gen. counsel, 1989-94; pvt. practice Woodcliff Lake, N.J., 1994-95; ptnr. Falcon & Singer PC, Woodcliff Lake, 1995—. Contbr. articles to profl. jours. Dem. candidate Town Justice, Town of Rye, N.Y., 1983; Dem. jud. del., Westchester, N.Y., 1984-89. Mem. ABA, N.J. State Bar Assn., Fla. Bar Assn., Bergen County Bar Assn., Nat. Acad. Elder Law Attys., Park Ridge Rotary (bd. dirs. 1997—), Columbia Alumni of Westchester County (v.p., bd. dirs. 1983-90, 97—). General corporate, Contracts commercial, Estate planning. Home: 582 Colonial Rd River Vale NJ 07675-6107 Office: 172 Broadway River Vale NJ 07675-8077 also: 14 Harwood Ct Scarsdale NY 10583-4121

**FALCONER, THOMAS ROBERT,** paralegal; b. Jersey City, N.J., Sept. 23, 1964; s. Charles Edward Falconer and BarbaraAnn Rose (Wohlleben) Weber; m. Karen Ann Swauger, May 14, 1989; children: Jessica Lynn, Rebecca Jo. Paralegal cert., Katharine Gibbs Sch., 1993. Pro-bono paralegal Joseph Fortunato, Esq., Montclair, N.J., 1993; pro-bono/intern paralegal Gary D. Grant, Esq., Morristown, N.J., 1993, paralegal, 1993-94; freelance paralegal Falconer Paralegal Svcs., Lake Hiawatha, N.J., 1994-97, Hopatcong, N.J., 1998—; notary public State of N.J., 1993—. CPR instr. Am. Red Cross, Morris County, N.J., 1990, standard first-aid instr., 1990; mem. Better Bus. Bur. No. N.J., 1996. With N.J. Army Nat. Guard, 1983—. Mem. NRA (life), Nat. Fedn. of Ind. Businesses, Nat. Notary Assn., Morris County Bar Assn. (assoc.). Methodist. Home: 30 Williams Trail Hopatcong NJ 07843-1123 Office: Falconer Paralegal Svcs 30 Williams Trl Hopatcong NJ 07843-1123

**FALENDER, DEBRA ANN,** lawyer, educator; b. 1948. AB, Mt. Holyoke Coll., 1970; JD, Ind. U., 1975. Bar: Ind. 1975, U.S. Dist. Ct. (so. dist.) Ind. 1975. Clk. to Judge Robert H. Staton Ind. Ct. Appeals, Indpls., 1975-76; asst. prof. law Ind. U. Sch. Law, Indpls., 1976-79, assoc. prof. law, 1979-85, prof. law, 1985—, assoc. dean, 1989-90; speaker in field. Contbr. articles to books and profl. jours. Recipient Outstanding New Prof. award Student Bar Assn. of Ind. U. Sch. Law, 1977-78. Mem. ABA (com. on creditors' rights in estates and trusts, sect. of real property, probate and trust law 1985-91), Ind. State Bar Assn. (probate reform com. sect. of probate, trust and real property 1995—, rights of surviving spouses subcom., will subcom. legislation com. of probate, trust and real property sect. 1986-87, chair notice to creditors subcom. of legislation com. of probate, trust and real property sect. 1986-89), Indpls. Bar Assn. (estate planning sect. coun. 1993-95), estate planning sect. coun. nominating com. 1991, estate planning sect. coun. 1988-90). Office: Ind Univ Sch Law 735 W New York St Indianapolis IN 46202-5222

**FALEY, R(ICHARD) SCOTT,** lawyer; b. Trenton, N.J., Aug. 18, 1947; s. Henry and Winifred (Goeke) F.; m. Josepha Ann Bartlett, Aug. 29, 1970; children: Scott Joseph, Zachary Lorin, Katherine Winifred. BA, Georgetown U., 1969, JD, 1972; LLM, George Washington U., 1975. Bar: D.C. 1973, U.S. Tax Ct. 1973, U.S. Dist. Ct. D.C. 1973, Mont. 1996. Assoc., ptnr. Danzansky, Dickey, Tydings, Quint & Gordon, Washington, 1972-78; prin. R. Scott Faley, P.C., Washington, 1978—; bd. dir. Fed. Employees News Digest, Inc., Fairfax, Va., 1980—; bd. dir., pres. NCC Trout Unltd., 1985—; del. Mid Atlantic Coun. Trout Unltd., 1985—, v.p., 1992—; bd. dirs. Falling Springs Greenway, Inc., Chambersburg, Pa. Inst. for Safety Analysis, Inc., Rockville, Md., 1980-89. Contbr. articles to profl. jours. Mem. instnl. rev. com. Sibley Meml. Hosp., Washington, 1980—. Capt. USAF, 1974. Mem. ABA, FBA, Univ. Club, Boca Bay Pass Club, Alpha Phi Omega, Phi Alpha Delta. Roman Catholic. Pension, profit-sharing, and employee benefits, Estate planning, Taxation, general. Home: 25 Primrose St Chevy Chase MD 20815-4228 Office: Ste 401 5100 Wisconsin Ave NW Washington DC 20016-4119

**FALK, JAMES HARVEY, SR.,** lawyer; b. Tucson, Aug. 17, 1938; s. George W. and Elsie L. (Higgins) F.; m. Bobbie Jo Vest, July 8, 1960; children: James H. Jr., John Mansfield, Kathryn Colleen. BS, BA, U. Ariz., 1960, LLB, 1965, JD, 1965. Bar: Ariz. 1965, U.S. Dist. Ct. Ariz. 1968, U.S. Dist. Ct. D.C. 1971, U.S. Dist. Ct. Md., 1990, U.S. Ct. Appeals (fed., 4th, 6th and 9th cirs.) 1981, U.S. Ct. Claims 1985, U.S. Supreme Ct. 1972. Counsel El Paso (Tex.) Natural Gas Co., 1965-66, The Anaconda Co., Tucson, 1967-68; ptnr. Waterfall Economidis, Falk & Caldwell, Tucson, 1968-71; staff asst. to pres. Office of the Pres., Washington, 1971-73; assoc. dir. Domestic Coun., The White House, Washington, 1973-76; assoc. Touche Ross & Co., Washington, 1976-78; ptnr. Coffey, McGovern, Noel & Novogroski, Washington, 1978-81, Larkin, Noel & Falk, Washington, 1981-86, Thompson & Mitchell, Washington, 1986-87, McGovern, Noel & Falk, Ltd., Washington, 1987-90, Falk & Causey, Washington, 1991-92; prin. Falk Law Firm, Washington, 1993—; rep. of U.S. Pres. to state and local govts., D.C., U.S. ters., 1974-75, U.S. Govs. Conf., 1974-75, U.S. Conf. Mayors, 1974-75, U.S. Del. Peoples Republic of China, 1974; asst. city prosecutor, city atty., Tucson, 1966-67; chmn. Tucson Transit Authority, 1971-72; apptd. D.C. Bar Jud. Evaluation Com., 1992-95, 95-98. Mem. ABA. Republican. Congregationalist. Government contracts and claims, General corporate, Federal civil litigation. Home: 9430 Cornwell Farm Rd Great Falls VA 22066-2702 Office: Falk Law Firm 2445 M St NW Washington DC 20037-1435

**FALK, JOHN MANSFIELD,** shareholder; b. Tucson, May 6, 1964; s. James Harvey Sr. and Bobbie Jo (Vest) F.; m. Jacqueline Stacey Gray, July 22, 1968; 1 child, John Mansfield Jr. BA with honors, Washington and Lee U., 1986, JD, 1990. Bar: Va. 1991, D.C. 1993, U.S. Ct. Appeals (4th cir.) 1991, U.S. Ct. Appeals (D.C. cir.) 1993, U.S. Dist. Ct. (ea. dist.) Va. 1991, U.S. Dist. Ct. D.C. 1993, U.S. Fed. Ct. Claims 1993, U.S. Tax Ct. 1996, U.S. Supreme Ct. 1997. Asst. to pres. Support Sys. Assoc., Inc., Northport, N.Y., 1986-87; assoc. McGovern, Noel & Falk, Washington, 1990-93, Falk & Causey, Washington, 1993-94; v.p., shareholder The Falk Law Firm, plc, Washington, 1994—; Chmn. contact com., white book revisions com. Washington & Lee U., 1986, student affairs com., 1989-90, sec. Washington alumni chpt., 1992-94, v.p., 1994-95, pres., 1995-98. Bd. dirs. Congl. Award Found., Washington, 1990—, vice-chmn., 1990—. Recipient Congl. award Gold medal U.S. Congress, 1986, Significant Achievement award Sigma Delta Chi, 1990, Frank G. Gillman award Washington and Lee U., 1990, Univ. Svc. award, 1990. Mem. ABA, Fed. Cir. Bar Assn., Va. Bar Assn., D.C. Bar Assn. Episcopalian. Avocations: horse racing, hunting, fishing, tennis. Government contracts and claims, Private international, Legislative. Office: The Falk Law Firm plc 2445 M St NW Ste 260 Washington DC 20037-1435

**FALK, KENNETH B.,** lawyer; b. Bklyn., June 17, 1938; s. Abraham N. and Rose Falk; m. Genette Lebron, Jan. 2, 1988; children: Jonathan, Joan. BS in Acctg., Queen's Coll., 1959; JD, NYU, 1962. Law clk. Hon. J. Spencer Ball U.S. Ct. Appeals (4th cir.), Charlotte, N.C., 1962-63; capt., judge advocate USAF, 1963-66; assoc. Maxwell & Diamond, N.Y.C., 1966-74; shareholder Maxwell & Diamond, Woodbridge, N.J., 1974-91, Deutch & Falk, Woodbridge, N.J., 1991—. Mem. N.Y. Bar Assn., N.J. Bar Assn., Order of Coif. Contracts commercial, General corporate, Mergers and acquisitions. Home: 212 Water St Perth Amboy NJ 08861-4427 Office: Deutch & Falk 843 Rahway Ave Woodbridge NJ 07095-3699

**FALK, LAUREN WEISSMAN,** lawyer; b. Newark, Apr. 8, 1959; d. Joseph and Florence Weissman; m. William J. Falk, July 26, 1981; children: David, Evan, Alex. Student, Hebrew U., Jerusalem, Israel, 1978; BA, Lehigh U., 1980; JD, U. Bridgeport Sch. of Law, 1983. Bar: N.Y. 1984, U.S. Ct. Appeals (2d cir.) 1984, N.J. 1984, U.S. Ct. Appeals (3d cir.) 1984, U.S. Dist. Ct. N.J. 1984. Assoc. John Walsh, N.Y.C., 1984; corp. counsel Clark (N.J.) Distbrs., 1985; assoc. Craner, Nelson, Satkin & Glazner, South Plains, N.J., 1986; sole practitioner Lauren W. Falk, Clark, 1987-90; assoc. Robert S. Ellenport, P.A., Clark, 1990-93; sole practice Clark, 1991—; atty. zoning of adjustment Twp. Clark, 1993—. Pres. Sisterhood Temple Beth O-r, Clark, 1992-94, trustee, rep., 1988—. Mem. ABA, N.J. Bar Assn., N.Y. State Bar Assn., Union County Bar Assn., Clark Rotary (pres. 1995—). Jewish. Avocations: musician, tennis, Hebrew lang., Jewish culture. Real property, Consumer commercial, General civil litigation. Home: 61 Summit Ct Westfield NJ 07090-2834 Office: 840 N Wood Ave Linden NJ 07036-4038

**FALK, ROBERT HARDY,** lawyer; b. Houston, Dec. 27, 1948; s. Arnold Charles and Sara Holmes (Pierce) F.; m. Donna Kay Watts, Aug. 18, 1973 (div. Apr. 1990); children: Dorian Danielle, Dillon Holmes; m. Patricia K. Stampley, Nov. 5, 1994. BS summa cum laude, U. Tex., 1971; BA cum laude, Austin Coll., 1972; JD, U. Tex., 1975. Bar: Tex. 1975, D.C. 1977, U.S. Dist. Ct. (so. dist. Tex.) 1975, U.S. Patent Office, U.S. Ct. Appeals (5th cir.) 1976, Ct. Customs and Patent Appeals 1976, N.C. 1979, U.S. Dist. Ct. (we. dist. N.C.) 1982, U.S. Dist Ct. (no. dist. Tex.) 1984, U.S. Ct. Appeals (fed. cir.) 1982, U.S. Ct. Appeals (5th cir.) 1983, U.S. Ct. Internat. Trade 1985, U.S. Dist. Ct. (no. dist.) Tex. 1987. Process engr. Exxon Co., USA, Baytown, Tex., 1971-72; atty. Pravel, Wilson & Gambrell, Houston, 1975-77; patent and trademark counsel Organon Inc. div. Akzona, Inc., Asheville, N.C., 1977-84; ptnr. Hubbard, Thurman, Tucker & Harris, Dallas, 1984-91; dir. Geary, Glast & Middleton, P.C., Dallas, 1992; mng. ptnr. Falk, Vestal & Fish, LLP, Dallas, 1992—. Pres. Haw Creek Vol. Fire Dept., Asheville, 1980-84; deacon Cen. Christian Ch., Dallas, 1985-89. Fellow U. Tex., 1972. Mem. ABA, ATLA, Am. Patent Law Assn., Tex. Bar Assn., N.C. Bar Assn., D.C. Bar Assn., Dallas Bar Assn., Dallas Patent Law Assn., Licensing Execs., Univ. Club (Dallas), Gleneagles Country Club (Plano), Plaza of the Ams. Club (Dallas). Republican. Avocations: golf, fishing. Patent, Trademark and copyright, Federal civil litigation. Home: 6016 Parksedge Ln Dallas TX 75252-2695 Office: 700 N Pearl St Ste 970 Dallas TX 75201-2838

**FALKNER, WILLIAM CARROLL,** lawyer; b. Baird, Tex., Mar. 26, 1954; s. Vernon Lee and Eunice Vera (Fore) F.; m. Linda May (Tilley), May 23, 1987; children: Heather Lynn, Holly Ann. BA in Govt., Tarleton State U., Stephenville, Tex., 1976; JD, Stetson U., Gulfport, Fla., 1984. Bar: Fla. 1984, U.S. Dist. Ct. (mid. dist.) Fla. 1985, U.S. Ct. Appeals (11th cir.) 1985. Asst. co. atty., sr. asst. co. atty. Pinellas County Atty.'s Office, Clearwater, Fla., 1985—. Editor Res Ipsa, Clearwater, Fla., 1992-93; contbr. articles to profl. jours. Lt. col. U.S. Army Res., 1976—. Mem. ABA, Fla. Bar Assoc., Clearwater Bar Assoc. Baptist. Avocations: reading, writing, sports, biblical studies. Office: Pinellas County Atty's Office 315 Court St Clearwater FL 33756-5165

**FALL, ROBERT J.,** lawyer; b. Homestead, Pa., July 22, 1955; s. Philip J. and Alice A. Fall; m. Patricia A. Hammerton, Oct. 16, 1982; children: Meghan, Kelsey. BS in Sociology, St. Joseph's Coll., Rensselaer, Ind., 1977; JD, Ohio No. U., 1980. Bar: Pa. 1980, U.S. Dist. Ct. (we. dist.) Pa. 1980. Atty. Neighborhood Legal Svcs. Assn., Pitts., 1980-82, Wymard, Dunn, Gurdon, Fall, Pitts., 1982-90, Babb, Fall & Assocs. P.C., Pitts. and Wexford, Pa., 1990-96; sole practitioner Pitts. and Wexford, 1996—. Bd. dirs. St. Nicholas Ch., Homestead, Pa., 1980-85, Cmty. Alcoholism Svcs. of Beaver County, Beaver, Pa., 1981-90; mem. McCandless (Pa.) Rep. Com., 1990—; vol. firefighter Ingomar Vol. Fire Co., McCandless, 1998; mgr., coach McCandless Athletic Assn., 1992—. Family and matrimonial, Probate, General practice. Office: 11676 Perry Hwy Wexford PA 15090-7201

**FALLEK, ANDREW MICHAEL,** lawyer; b. Bklyn., Aug. 15, 1956; m. Elaine Friedman, June 4, 1984. BA, U. Pa., 1978; JD, Vanderbilt U., 1981. Bar: N.Y. 1982, U.S. Dist. Ct. (so. and ea. dists.) N.Y. 1985, U.S. Ct. Appeals (2d cir.) 1991, U.S. Ct. Appeals (D.C. cir.) 1993. Assoc. Belson, Connolly & Belson, N.Y.C., 1981-84; pvt. practice Bklyn., 1984—. Mem. editl. bd., articles editor Bklyn. Barrister. Mem. N.Y. State Bar Assn., Bklyn. Bar Assn. (judiciary com., continuing legal educator com.), Def. Rsch. Inst. Labor, General civil litigation, Product liability. Office: 32 Court St Ste 1401 Brooklyn NY 11201-4441

**FALLER, RHODA DIANNE GROSSBERG,** lawyer; b. N.Y.C., Dec. 21, 1946; d. Benjamin and Marion (Mediasky) Sragg; m. Stanley Grossberg, Apr. 12, 1973 (div. Oct. 1983); children: Joseph Seth, Daniel Benjamin; m. Bernard Martin Faller, May 31, 1987. BS, SUNY, Stony Brook, 1967; MS, Pace U., 1973; JD, N.Y. Law Sch., 1978. Bar: N.Y. 1979, N.J. 1979, U.S. Dist. Ct. N.J. 1979, Fla. 1980, U.S. Dist. Ct. (ea. and so. dists.) N.Y. 1982, Ky. 1996, U.S. Dist. Ct. (ea. dist.) Ky. 1997. Assoc. Fuchsberg & Fuchsberg, N.Y.C., 1982-91, DeBlasio & Alton, P.C., N.Y.C., 1991-95, Rhoda Grossberg Faller, Esq., Teaneck, 1995-96, Becker Law Office, Louisville, Ky., 1997—. Mem. Assn. Trial Lawyers Am., Nat. Assn. Women Bus. Owners, Ky. Acad. Trial Attys., Ky. Bar Assn., N.Y. State Trial Lawyers Assn., N.Y. State Bar Assn., Fla. Bar Assn., Louisville Bar Assn., Women Lawyers Assn. Democrat. Jewish. Personal injury. Home: 213 Mockingbird Gardens Dr Louisville KY 40207-5718 Office: Becker Law Office 800 Browns Ln Louisville KY 40207-4009

**FALLER, SUSAN GROGAN,** lawyer; b. Cin., Mar. 1, 1950; d. William M. and Jane (Eagen) Grogan; m. Kenneth R. Faller, June 8, 1973; children: Susan Elisabeth, Maura Christine, Julie Kathleen. BA, U. Cin., 1972; JD, U. Mich., 1975. Bar: Ohio 1975, Ky. 1989, U.S. Dist. Ct. (so. dist.) Ohio 1975, U.S. Ct. Claims 1982, U.S. Ct. Appeals (6th cir.) 1982, U.S. Supreme Ct. 1982, U.S. Tax Ct. 1984, U.S. Dist. Ct. (ea. dist.) Ky. 1991, U.S. Dist. Ct. (ea. dist.) Ky., 1991. Assoc. Frost & Jacobs, Cin., 1975-82, ptnr. 1982—. Assoc. editor Mich. Law Rev., 1974-75; contbg. author: LDRC 50-State Survey of Media Libel and Privacy Law, 1982—. Bd. dirs. Summit Alumni Coun., Cin., 1983-85; trustee Newman Found., Cin., 1980-86, Catholic Social Svc., Cin., 1984-93, nominating com., 1985-88, sec., 1990; mem. Class XVII Leadership Cin., 1993-94; mem. exec. com., sec. def. counsel sect. Libel Def. Resource Ctr., 1998—; parish coun. St. Monica-St. George Ch., 1997—. Recipient Career Women of Achievement award YWCA, 1990. Mem. ABA (co-editor newsletter media litigation 1993-97), FBA, Ky. Bar Assn., No. Ky. Bar Assn., No. Ky. Women's Bar Assn., Ohio Bar Assn. (bd. govs. litigation sect.), Cin. Bar Assn. (com. mem.), Potter Stewart Inn of Ct., Greater Cin. Women Lawyer's Assn., U. Cin. Alumni Assn., Arts and Scis. Alumni Assn. (bd. gov.'s U. Cin. Coll. 1988—), U. Mich. Alumni Assn., Mortar Bd., Women Entrepreneurs (pres. 1988-89), Leland Yacht Club, Lawyers Club, Coll. Club, Clifton Meadows Club, Phi Beta Kappa, Theta Phi Alpha. Roman Catholic. General civil litigation, Libel, Taxation, general. Home: 5 Belsaw Pl Cincinnati OH 45220-1104 Office: Frost & Jacobs LLP 2500 PNC Ct 201 E 5th St Ste 2500 Cincinnati OH 45202-4182 *Notable cases include: Cin. Bell vs. Gates, libel; Lusby vs. Cin. Mag., libel.*

**FALLIS, NORMA ELEANOR,** lawyer, radiologist; b. Virelin, Man., Can., June 15, 1924; d. Francis Norman and Frances Irene Graham; m. F. Evan Lynn, Oct. 1, 1943 (div. Sept. 1945); m. Roy H.D. Harris, Jan. 1, 1954; 1 child, Sarah Tracy. BSc, U. Sask., Can., 1952; MD, U. Alta., Can., 1956; JD, South Tex. Law Sch., 1991. Bar: Tex.; diplomate Am. Bd. Internal Medicine, Am. Bd. Radiology, Tex. Bd. Med. Examiners. Resident Baylor U. and Johns Hopkins U., 1957-59; fellow in clin. pharmacology Johns Hopkins U., Balt., 1959-61; asst. prof. U. Miss., Jackson, 1961-63; staff dept. radiology VA Hosp., Houston, 1969-73; asst. prof. radiology Baylor U., Houston, 1973-82; pvt. practice Houston. Contbr. articles to profl. jours. Mem. AMA, Tex. Med. Assn., Harris County Med. Assn. Democrat. Episcopalian. Probate, Animal welfare. Home: 2922 W Holcombe Blvd Houston TX 77025-1501 Office: PO Box 540248 Houston TX 77254-0248

**FALLON, ELDON E.,** judge; b. New Orleans, Feb. 16, 1939; s. Edward and Delia (Koster) F.; m. Cecile Fallon, Sept. 28, 1967. BA, Tulane U., 1960, JD, 1962; LLM, Yale U., 1963. Bar: La. 1962. Assoc. Kierr & Gainsburgh, 1962-66; ptnr. Gainsburgh, Benjamin & Fallon, New Orleans, 1966-95; judge U.S. Dist. Ct., New Orleans, 1995—; adj. prof. Tulane U. Author: Trial Handbook For Louisiana Lawyers, 1981; contbr. articles to profl. jours. Fellow Am. Bar Found., Am. Coll. Trial Lawyers, La. Bar Found. (bd. dirs., pres. 1995-96); mem. La. Bar Assn. (sec. treas. 1984, pres. 1985-86). Office: US Courthouse 500 Camp St New Orleans LA 70130-3313

**FALLON, KIERAN PATRICK,** lawyer; b. Providence, Oct. 31, 1955; s. Patrick Joseph and Mary (Ryan) F. BA, Boston Coll., 1977, JD, 1980. Bar: Mass. 1980, R.I. 1981, Fla. 1982. Law clk. to Hon. David Nelson U.S. Dist. Ct., Mass., 1980; law clk. to Hon. Thomas Kelleher R.I. Supreme Ct., 1980-81; asst. state atty. Dade County, 1982-85; assoc. William Cagney, P.A., 1985-87; pvt. practice Miami, 1988—.

**FALSGRAF, WILLIAM WENDELL,** lawyer; b. Cleve., Nov. 10, 1933; s. Wendell A. and Catherine J. F.; children: Carl Douglas, Jeffrey Price, Catherine Louise. AB cum laude, Amherst Coll., 1955, LLD (hon.), 1986; JD, Case Western Res. U., 1958. Bar: Ohio 1958, U.S. Supreme Ct. 1972. Ptnr. Baker & Hostetler, Cleve., 1971—. Chmn. vis. com. Case Western Res. U. Law Sch., 1973-76; trustee Case Western Reserve U., 1978-90, chmn. bd. overseers, 1977-78; trustee Cleve. Health Mus., 1975-90, Hirom Coll., 1989—; chmn. bd. trustees Hiram Coll., 1990-99. Recipient Disting. Service award; named Outstanding Young Man of Year Cleve. Jr. C. of C., 1962. Fellow Am. Bar Found., Ohio Bar Found.; mem. ABA (chmn. young lawyers sect. 1966-67, mem. ho. of dels. 1967-68, 70—, bd. govs. 1971-75, pres. 1985-86, bd. dirs. Am. Bar Endowment 1974-84, 87-97), Am. Bar Ins. Plans Cons. (pres. 1991—), Ohio Bar Assn. (mem. coun. of dels. 1968-70), Cleve. Bar Assn. (trustee 1979-82), Amherst Alumni Assn. (pres. N.E. Ohio 1964), Union Club, The Country Club. Environmental, General corporate, Probate. Home: 616 North St Chagrin Falls OH 44022-2514 Office: Baker & Hostetler LLP 3200 National City Ctr Cleveland OH 44114-3485

**FALSTROM, KENNETH EDWARD,** lawyer; b. San Luis Obispo, Calif., June 25, 1946; s. William and Irene (Carroll) F.; children: Kenneth Todd, Tricia Karen. BA, UCLA, 1967; JD, U. Calif., Berkeley, 1970. Bar: Calif. 1971, U.S. Dist. Ct. (cen. dist.) Calif. 1977. Rsch. asst. Ctr. Study Dem. Insts., Santa Barbara, Calif., 1971; atty. Law Office Christopher Zayic, Santa Barbara, Calif., 1972; pvt. practice Santa Barbara, Calif., 1973—. Bd. dirs. Hope Sch. Dist. Santa Barbara, 1972-80. General practice. Office: 1530 Chapala St Santa Barbara CA 93101-3017

**FALVEY, PATRICK JOSEPH,** lawyer; b. Yonkers, N.Y., June 29, 1927; s. Patrick J. Falvey and Nora Rowley Falvey; m. Eileen Ryan, June 29, 1963; 1 child, Patrick James. Student, Iona Coll., 1944-47; JD cum laude, St. John's U., Jamaica, N.Y., 1950. Bar: N.Y. 1951, U.S. Supreme Ct. 1972. Law asst. Port Authority of N.Y. and N.J., 1951, atty., 1951-65, chief condemnation and litigation, 1965-67, asst. gen. counsel, 1967-72, gen. counsel, 1972-91, gen. counsel, asst. exec. dir., 1979-87, dep. exec. dir., 1987-91, spl. counsel, 1991—; advisor U.S. del. to UN Com. on Internat. Trade Law, U.S. State Dept. Pvt. Trade Law; advisor to U.S. del. UN diplomatic confs. on treaty on liability of ops. of transport terminals; N.Y. County Lawyers Assn., 1992—. With USN, 1945-46. Recipient Howard S. Cullman Disting. Svc. medal Port Authority of N.Y. and N.J., 1982, 91; Loftus award and Trustee's Honoree Iona Coll., 1982. Fellow Am. Bar Found.; mem. ABA (chmn. urban state and local govt. law sect. 1983-84, vice-chmn. model procurement code project 1979—, sect. del. 1987-90), FBA, Airport Operators Coun. Internat. (legal com.), Assn. Bar City N.Y., N.Y. County Lawyers Assn., Nat. Inst. Mcpl. Law Officers, Internat. Assn. Ports and Harbors (hon., legal counsellors com., arbitrator, mediator trade and comml. matters, cons. transp. and trade studies), Woodlawn Comm. Assn. (counsel 1996—). Address: PM 81 Pondfield Rd #338 Bronxville NY 10708-3818

**FALVEY, W(ILLIAM) PATRICK,** judge; b. Penn Yan, N.Y., Aug. 31, 1946; s. William Jennings and Thelma Rosetta (Hall) F.; m. Suzanne G. Christensen, Sept. 14, 1968; children: Scott P., Jennifer G. BA, Hobart Coll., 1968; JD, John Marshall Law Sch., 1975; postgrad., U. Nev., 1994. Bar: N.Y. 1976, U.S. Dist. Ct. (we. dist.) N.Y. 1979, U.S. Supreme Ct. 1984. Confidential law clerk N.Y. State Supreme Justice, Penn Yan, 1976-77; atty. Dept. Social Svcs. Yates County, Penn Yan, 1976-77, pvt. practice, 1976-88, asst. pub. defender, 1977-80, acting dist. atty., 1980-81, dist. atty., 1981-88, judge surrogate and family ct., acting Supreme Ct. Justice, 1988—; mem. alternatives to incarceration com. Yates County; mem. Yates County Custody and Visitation Mediation Bd., 1995—; adv. com. Finger Lakes Vol. Lawyer's Svc., Geneva, N.Y., 1989-91; chair bd. trustees Yates County Law Libr.; jud. adv. coun. Seventh Jud. Dist. Mem., sec. Yates County Republican Com., Penn Yan, 1977-81; mem. Yates County Coop. Farm & Craft Market, Penn Yan, 1976-79; bd. dirs. Lit. Vols., Penn Yan, 1979-83; mem., pres. Yates County Profl. & Health Adv. Com., Penn Yan, 1980-88. 1st lt. U.S. Army, 1969-71, Vietnam. Recipient N.Y. State Conspicuous Svc. Cross, Hon. Hugh R. Carey Gov. N.Y., 1979. Ctr. for Dispute Settlement's Disting. Jurist award, 1996. Mem. Am. Judges Assn., Am. Judicature Soc., Ontario/Yates Magistrates Assn., N.Y. Bar Assn., N.Y. State, County, Family and Surrogate Judges Assn., Yates County Bar Assn. (past pres.), VFW, Am. Legion (post comdr. 1981). Fax: (315) 536-5190. Office: Yates County Cts 108 Court St Penn Yan NY 14527-1102

**FALVO, MARK ANTHONY,** lawyer; b. Boston, June 11, 1960; s. Carl Albert and Thelma Ann (Evans) F. BA in Polit. Sci., Pa. State U., 1982; JD, Ohio No. U., 1988. Bar: Pa. 1990, U.S. Supreme Ct. 1997; cert. solicitor County Treas.'s Office 1993. Account exec., pub. rels. staff, broadcaster Clearfield (Pa.) Broadcasters, Inc., 1975-82, 91; account exec., pub. rels. staff Ctr. Comm., Inc., State College, Pa., 1982-83, Gilcom Comm., Inc., Altoona, Pa., 1983-84, State College Broadcasters, Inc., 1984-85; pub. rels. mgr. dept. arts and comm. Ohio No. U., Ada, 1985-88; law clk., atty. Ct. Common Pleas of Clearfield County-Pa. 46th Jud. Dist., 1988-93; pvt. practice Clearfield, 1993—; intern Hill, Morgan & Africa, Warren, Pa., summer 1986, Dist. Atty.'s Office Clearfield County, summer 1987; county coord. Clearfield County Statewide Mock Trial Competition, 1989-96; dist. coord. Pa. Statewide Mock Trial Competition, 1991-95, regional coord., 1993-94; dir. Boy Scouts of Am., Law and Law Enforcement Explorers Post, 1992-94; coord. Teen Ct. Program, Clearfield County, 1992—; law clk., atty. Ct. Common Pleas of Clearfield County, Pa., 46th Jud. Dist., 1998—; others. Campaign staff congressman William F. Clinger, Jr., State College, 1984; bd. dirs., vice-chmn. ARC/Clearfield Chpt., 1989-95; bd. dirs., mem. Am. Cancer Soc./Clearfield County, 1989-93; bd. dirs., treas. Pa. State Alumni Assn., DuBois, 1989-95; vol. Clearfield Sr. Little League Baseball, 1975-82, Clearfield Little League Baseball, 1999—; mem. Clearfield County Crimestoppers, 1998. Recipient Spl. Recognition award Pa. Ho. of Reps., Harrisburg, 1988, Spl. Recognition award Pa. Senate, Harrisburg, 1988, Spl. Recognition award U.S. Congress, 1988, Law Mentoring Program award Conf. of County Bar Leaders, Harrisburg, 1991, Street Law Program award Conf. of County Bar Leaders, Harrisburg, 1991, Outstanding Young Alumni award Pa. State U., DuBois, 1992, Spl. Recognition award Teen Ct. Program Clearfield County, 1996. Mem. ABA (Pub. Svc. award 1990, 91, 98), Pa. Bar Assn., Clearfield County Bar Assn. (v.p. 1998—, rep. under 35 1989-98, chmn. young lawyers divsn. 1989-98, exec. com. 1989—, chmn. Law Day 1989, 90, 91, 92, 97, 98, mem. Law Day com. 1993, 94, 95, 96, 98), Sports, Art and Entertainment Law Com., The Forum on Entertainment and Sports Industries, Clearfield County Pa. Bar Inst. (chmn. CLE 1998—). Democrat. Methodist/Roman Catholic. Avocations: painting, tennis, golf, music, skiing. General practice, Communications, Entertainment. Home and Office: 7 Bigler Rd Clearfield PA 16830-1762

**FAMULARO, JOSEPH L.,** prosecutor; b. Mt. Olivet, Ky., Nov. 6, 1942. BA, Loyola U., New Orleans, 1964; JD, U. Ky., 1967. Clk. to Hon. Mac Swinford U.S. Dist. Ct. Ky.; atty. Ky. Atty. Gen. Office; legal officer Ky. State Police; 1st asst. and U.S. atty. for ea. dist. Ky. Office U.S. Atty., 1977-81; chief dep. atty. gen. Office Atty. Gen. Ky., 1982-86; 1st asst. county atty. Fayette County Attys. Office, 1988-89; commr. pub. safety Lexington Fayette Urban County, Ky., 1990-93; now U.S. atty. for ea. dist. Ky. U.S. Dept. Justice, Lexington. Office: US Atty Ea Dist Ky PO Box 3077 Lexington KY 40588-3077*

**FANCHER, RICK,** lawyer; b. Tucson, July 27, 1953; s. James Richard and Margaret Mae (Gum) F.; m. Cecelia Francis Baney, July 12, 1975; children: Jeffery Reed, Ashley Kristin. BA, Trinity U., 1975; JD, U. Tex., 1978. Bar: Tex. 1979, U.S. Dist. Ct. (we. and so. dists.) Tex. 1981, U.S. Ct. Appeals (5th cir.) 1981. Law clk. U.S. Dist. Ct., Corpus Christi, Tex., 1978-80; asst. atty. City of Corpus Christi, 1980; assoc. Gibbins, Burrow & Bratton, Austin, Tex., 1981, John L. Johnson, Corpus Christi, 1982-85; ptnr. Thornton, Summers, Biachlin, Dunham & Brown, Corpus Christi, 1985—. Mem. Tex. Bar Assn., Tex. Bd. Legal Specialization (cert. personal injury trial law). Democrat. Avocations: jogging, bicycling, hunting, golf. Insurance, Personal injury, Product liability. Home: 4502 Lake Bistineau Dr Corpus Christi TX 78413-5261 Office: Thornton Summers Biechlin Dunham & Brown Ste 600 Am Bank Pla Corpus Christi TX 78475

**FANCIULLO, WILLIAM PATRICK,** lawyer; b. S.I., N.Y., Nov. 20, 1953; s. Gilbert Louis and Betty Elaine (Beyer) F.; m. Gunilla G. Fanciullo, July 25, 1981 (dec.); children: Chirstina Marie, Matthew William, James Eric. BA magna cum laude, SUNY, Albany, 1975; JD, SUNY, Buffalo, 1979. Bar: N.Y. 1980, U.S. Dist. Ct. (no. dist.) N.Y. 1980, U.S. Ct. Appeals (9th cir.) 1980, U.S. Ct. Appeals (2d cir.) 1981, U.S. Dist. Ct. (we. dist.) N.Y. 1990, U.S. Supreme Ct. 1992. Trial atty. honor grads. program U.S. Dept. Justice, Washington, 1979-80; asst. U.S. atty. U.S. Dept. Justice, Albany, 1980-89; pvt. practice, Albany, 1989—; speaker in field. Recipient commendation FBI, 1985, 87, Dir.'s award for superior performance U.S. Dept. Justice, 1988. Mem. ABA (sects. on litigation and criminal justice), N.Y. State Bar Assn. (trial lawyers and criminal law sect.), Nat. Assn. Criminal Def. Lawyers, Albany County Bar Assn. (former chmn. fed. practice com.), Capital Dist. Trial Lawyers Assn. General civil litigation, Criminal, Personal injury. Home: 214 Woodscape Dr Albany NY 12203-5604 Office: 61 Columbia St Albany NY 12210-2736

**FANKHAUSER, ALLEN,** lawyer, consultant; b. Humboldt, Nebr., Aug. 25, 1950; s. Elsworth and Luella (Kerl) F.; m. Trudy Dee Carsh, Aug. 1, 1970; children: Shannon, Matthew, Bryce. BS in Bus. Adminstrn., U. Nebr., 1972, JD, 1975. Bar: Nebr. 1975, U.S. Dist. Ct. Nebr. 1975. Ptnr. Kotouc Fankhauser & Maschman, Humboldt, 1975-93; pvt. practice Fankhauser Law Offices, Humboldt, 1993—; ptnr. ATT-EMT, Med. Legal, Falls City, Nebr., 1988—. Contbr. articles to profl. jours. Bd. dirs. Colonial Acres Nursing Home, Inc., Humboldt, 1987—; legal counsel Nebr. Jaycees, Lincoln, 1976-78; tng. officer/emergency med. technician Humboldt Rescue, 1977—. Recipient Kimball award, 1989; named EMT-A of Yr., Nebr. EMT Assn. 1992. Fellow Nebr. State Found. (bd. dir. 1991—); mem. Nebr. State Bar Assn. (com. on inquiry 1st Dist. 1990—). Republican. Methodist. Avocations: pre-hospital medical care, teaching. General practice, Estate planning, Family and matrimonial. Office: Fankhauser Law Offices 713 4th St Humboldt NE 68376

**FANNING, ELEANOR,** lawyer; b. Warren, Ohio, May 19, 1949; d. Arthur and Irene Lillian (Elefant) F. BA, Syracuse U., 1968; JD, Temple U., 1974. Bar: Pa. 1974. Law clk. Isaac S. Garb, Pres. Judge Bucks County, Doylestown, Pa., 1974-75; mental health rev. officer County of Bucks, Doylestown, 1975—; sole practice law, Trevose, Pa., 1980—. V.p. Fedn. Mercer and Bucks Counties; bd. dirs. Abrams Hebrew Acad., Big Sister, Phila., 1982-84. Recipient Sara A. Shulman award Temple U. Law Sch., 1974. Mem. ABA, Pa. Bar Assn., Bucks County Bar Assn. Democrat. Family and matrimonial, General practice, Personal injury. Office: Ste 204 Two Neshaminy Interplex Trevose PA 19053

**FANNING, NITA KISSEL,** lawyer; b. Waco, Tex., 1953. BA, Baylor U., 1976, JD, 1978. Bar: Tex. 1979, U.S. Dist. Ct. (we. dist.) Tex. 1994. Pvt. practice Waco, 1978-80, 81-83; atty. Law Office of Burt Berry, Dallas, 1980, Heart of Tex. Legal Svcs., Waco, 1989-92; pvt. practice Law Offices of Nita Fanning, Waco, 1992—; mem. estate planning coun. Baylor U., 1997—. Bd. dirs. Family Abuse Ctr., Waco, 1997—. Mem. ABA, Am. Trial Lawyers Assn., Tex. Trial Laywers, State Bar Tex. (history and traditions com. 1991-93). Family and matrimonial, Personal injury, Estate planning.

**FANONE, JOHN R.,** lawyer; b. Chgo., June 24, 1950; s. Antonio and Elda Anna (Alfieri) F.; m. Kathleen Sharon Peters, Aug. 27, 1977; children: Christopher, John, Kimberly. BSEE, Purdue U., 1972; JD, John Marshall Law Sch., 1975. Bar: Ill. 1975, Tex. 1993, U.S. Ct. Appeals (7th cir.) 1985, U.S. Ct. Appeals (11th cir.) 1996, U.S. Dist. Ct. (no. dist.) Ill. 1976, U.S. Dist. Ct. (ctrl. dist.) Ill. 1991, U.S. Dist. Ct. Ariz. 1991, U.S. Dist. Ct. (we. dist.) Mich. 1995. Pvt. practice Chgo., 1975-78; asst. atty. gen. State of Ill., Chgo., 1978-81; assoc. Robert D. Kolar & Assocs., Chgo., 1981—. Contbr. articles to profl. publs. Insurance, Product liability, Criminal. Office: Robert D. Kolar & Assocs Ltd 233 S Wacker Dr Ste 22 Chicago IL 60606-6427

**FANONE, JOSEPH ANTHONY,** lawyer; b. Sharon, Pa., Apr. 14, 1949; s. Anthony and Nancy Fanone; children: Michael, Kathleen, Peter. AB, Georgetown U., 1971, JD, 1974. Bar: Pa. 1974, D.C. 1980. Asst. atty. gen. Pa. Dept. of Justice, 1974-77; assoc. Squire, Sanders & Dempsey, Washington, 1977-81; assoc. Ballard, Spahr, Andrews & Ingersoll, Washington, 1981-83, ptnr., 1983-94; ptnr. Piper & Marbury, Washington, 1994-95, Ballard, Spahr, Andrews & Ingersoll, Washington, 1996—. Mem. ABA. Finance. Office: Ballard Spahr Andrews & Ingersoll 601 13th St NW Ste 1000 Washington DC 20005-3807

**FANOUS, NIKKI HOBERT,** lawyer; b. Lubbock, Tex., July 2, 1967; d. Tony R. Hobert and Ann A. (Moorhouse) Gibbs; m. David Elias Fanous, Apr. 27, 1996. BA, So. Meth. U., 1987; JD, La. State U., 1993. Bar: Tex. 1993. Assoc. Page & Addison, P.C., Dallas, 1994-96, Jackson Walker, L.L.P., Ft. Worth, 1996—. Mem. ABA, State Bar Tex., Dallas Bar Assn., Dallas Assn. Young Lawyers, Tarrant County Bar Assn. Republican. Presbyterian. Avocations: travel, reading, scuba diving. Real property, General corporate, Landlord-tenant. Office: Jackson Walker LLP 301 Commerce St Ste 2400 Fort Worth TX 76102-4124

**FANT, PHILIP ARLINGTON,** lawyer; b. N.Y.C., Mar. 14, 1952; m. Carol A. Glaser, Sept. 21, 1991; children: Jennifer, Thomas. BA, Tulane U., 1974, JD, 1977. Bar: La. 1977, Calif. 1991. Atty. Leach, Paysse & Baldwin, New Orleans, 1977-87, Montgomery, Barnett, New Orleans, 1987-91; pvt. practice San Francisco, 1991—. Mem. Maritime Law Assn. Roman Catholic. Admiralty, Transportation, Insurance. Office: 88 Kearny St Ste 1000 San Francisco CA 94108-5530

**FARAGO, JOHN MICHAEL,** law educator, hearing officer, consultant; b. N.Y.C., Mar. 8, 1951; s. Ladislas and Liesel (Mroz) F.; m. Sharon Cramer, Nov. 11, 1972 (div.); m. Jeanne Elaine Martin, Dec. 5, 1985; 1 child, Max Farago; stepchildren: Belle Iskowitz, Sarah Iskowitz. BA, Harvard U., 1972, MAT, 1972; JD, NYU, 1978, postgrad., 1975-78. Assoc. dean, prof. Valparaiso (Ind.) U. Sch. Law, 1978-82; assoc. dean, prof. CUNY Law Sch., N.Y.C., 1982-86, dir. systems, assoc. prof., 1986-90, assoc. prof., 1992—; assoc. dean for acad. affairs N.Y. Law Sch., N.Y.C., 1990-92; spl. edn. hearing officer Ind. Edn. Dept., 1979-82, N.Y.C. Bd. Edn., 1982—; hearing officer N.Y. State vocat. Edn., N.Y.C., 1993—; adj. prof. Tchrs. Coll., 1998—; cons. in field. Co-author: Junk Food, 1978; editor: The Family, 1975; editl. bd. Ctr. for Computer-Assisted Legal Instrn., 1997—; contbr. articles to profl. jours. Search coord., chancellor search N.Y.C. Bd. Edn., 1995. Home: 1225 Park Ave New York NY 10128-1758 Office: CUNY Law Sch 65-21 Main St Flushing NY 11367

**FARAH, BENJAMIN FREDERICK,** lawyer; b. Cleve., Mar. 29, 1956; s. Benjamin Hallack and Janice Elizabeth (Gassan) F.; m. Ann Ruth Livingston, Sept. 8, 1984; children: Benjamin Livingston, Mary Elizabeth. BBA, George Washington U., 1978; JD, Case Western Res. U., 1981. Bar: Ohio 1981, U.S. Dist. Ct. (no. dist.) Ohio 1981, U.S. Tax Ct. 1981, U.S. Ct. Appeals (6th cir) 1983, U.S. Supreme Ct. 1984. Assoc. Steuer, Escovar & Berk, Cleve., 1981-85; pvt. practice Rocky River, Ohio, 1985—; of counsel Homer S. Taft & Assocs., Rocky River, 1989; prin. Taft Farah and Assocs., P.A., 1990; sole practitioner, 1992; sec. Ohio Assn. R.R. Passengers, 1990-94, gen. counsel, 1990—. Mem. ABA, Ohio Bar Assn., Cleve. Bar Assn., Masons, Phi Alpha Delta. Republican. General corporate, Probate, Estate planning. Home: 2323 Winfield Ave Rocky River OH 44116-2868 Office: 1154 Linda St Ste 175 Cleveland OH 44116-1877

**FARBER, BERNARD JOHN,** lawyer; b. London, Feb. 27, 1948; came to U.S., 1949; s. Solomon and Regina (Wachter) F.; m. Mary Lee Mueller, Feb. 14, 1987; children: Zachary, Anne. BS, U. of State of N.Y., Albany, 1978; JD, Ill. Inst. Tech., 1983. Bar: Ill. 1983, U.S. Dist. Ct. (no. dist.) Ill. 1983, U.S. Ct. Appeals (7th cir.) 1985, U.S. Tax Ct. 1986, U.S. Ct. Mil. Appeals 1986, U.S. Supreme Ct. 1987, U.S. Ct. Appeals (6th cir.) 1988, U.S. Ct. Appeals (4th cir.) 1989, U.S. Ct. Appeals (11th cir.) 1990. Instr. legal writing Chgo.-Kent Law Sch. Ill. Inst. Tech., 1983-85, computer rsch. atty., 1985-86, adj. prof. law, 1987—; legal editor Longman Fin. Svcs., Chgo., 1986-87; rsch. counsel publs. Ams. for Effective Law Enforcement, Chgo., 1987—; instr. Law Scholastic Aptitude Test; preparation course BAR/BRI, Chgo., 1984-88; v.p. Brickton Montessori Sch., Chgo., 1992-93; sec. bd. dirs., 1993-95. Mng. editor: Chgo.-Kent Law Rev., 1981-82, editor-in-chief, 1982-83; co-author: Protective Security Law, 1996; editor: (with others) Dow Jones-Irwin Handbook of Micro Computer Applications in Law, 1987, Illinois Law of Criminal Investigation, 1986; contbr. articles to profl. jours. Elected mem. Local Sch. Coun., Agassiz Elem. Sch., Chgo., 1996—, chmn., 1999—. Mem. ABA, Ill. State Bar Assn., Chgo. Bar Assn., Sci. Fiction Rsch. Assn., Mensa. Avocations: history, computers, science fiction. E-mail: bernfarber@aol.com. Civil rights, Criminal. Home and Office: 1126 W Wolfram St Rear Chicago IL 60657-4330

**FARBER, DONALD CLIFFORD,** lawyer, educator; b. Columbus, Nebr., Oct. 19, 1923; s. Charles and Sarah (Epstein) F.; m. Ann Eis, Dec. 28, 1947; children: Seth, Patricia. BS in Law, U. Nebr., 1948, JD, 1950. Bar: N.Y. 1950. Assoc. Newman, Hauser & Teitler, N.Y.C., 1950-58; sole practice N.Y.C., 1958-80; of counsel Conboy, Hewitt, O'Brien & Boardman, N.Y.C., 1980-84; ptnr. Tanner Propp Fersko & Sterner, N.Y.C., 1984-95, Farber & Rich LLP, N.Y.C., 1995-98; of counsel Hartman & Craven LLP, N.Y.C., 1998—; prof. law York U., Toronto, Ont., Can., 1970, 72-73; prof. theatre law Hofstra Law Sch., Hempstead, N.Y., 1974-75; prof. New Sch. for Social Rsch., N.Y.C., 1972—, Hunter Coll., 1978. Author: From Option to Opening, 1968, 4th edit., 1st Limelight edit., 1988, Producing on Broadway, 1969, Actor's Guide: What You Should Know About the Contracts You Sign, 1971, Producing, Financing and Distributing Film, 1973, 2d edit., 1991, The Amazing Story of the Fantasticks: America's Longest Running Play, 1991, Producing Theatre: A Comprehensive Legal and Business Guide, 1981, 3d Limelight edit., 1997, Common Sense Negotiation-The Art of Winning Gracefully, 1996; gen. editor (10 vol. series, author theatre vol.) Entertainment Industry Contracts-Negotiating and Drafting Guide. With AUS, 1941-44, ETO. Mem. Order of Coif, Hon. Law Soc. Fax: (212) 223-0467. Entertainment. Home: 14 E 75th St New York NY 10021-2657 Office: Hartman & Craven LLP 11th Fl 460 Park Ave New York NY 10022-1987

**FARBER, HOWARD,** lawyer; b. N.Y.C., Dec. 7, 1931; s. Joseph and Mamie (Aronson) F.; m. June R. Polinger, Dec. 20, 1953; children: Shelly G., Carol R. BBA, CCNY, 1953; MS, Columbia U., 1957; JD, Temple U., 1972. Bar: Pa. 1972, Del. 1972, U.S. Dist. Ct. (ea. dist.) Pa. 1972, U.S. Ct. Appeals (3d cir.) 1975, U.S. Supreme Ct. 1975, N.Y. 1980. Ptnr. Farber & Halligan, P.C., Media, Pa., 1972-80; pvt. practice law Media, 1980-89; ptnr. Farber & Farber, Media, 1989—; solicitor Twp. of Marple, Pa., 1975-78. Bd. dirs. Marple-Newton Sch. Dist., Newton Square, Pa., 1972-75. Served with U.S. Army, 1954-56. Recipient Disting. Service to Community award Marple Township Bd. Coms., 1978, Outstanding Service to Edn., Pa. Sch. Bds. Assn., 1976. Mem. ABA, Pa. Bar Assn., Pa. Trial Lawyers Assn., Delaware County Bar Assn. Personal injury, Probate, Workers' compensation. Office: 1 Veterans Sq Media PA 19063-3216

**FARBER, SIDNEY THEODORE,** lawyer; b. Buffalo, Sept. 16, 1948; s. Jacob Jason and Dorothy Farber; m. Deborah Gerber, Oct. 12, 1981; children: Matthew, Jonathon, Rebecca. BA, SUNY, Buffalo, 1970, JD, 1973. Bar: N.Y. 1974, U.S. Dist. Ct. (we. dist.) N.Y. 1975, U.S. Supreme Ct. 1980. Spl. asst. pub. defender Monroe County Pub. Defender's Office, Rochester, N.Y., 1974-87; town justice Town of Penfield, N.Y., 1987—; ptnr. Farber & Farber, Penfield, 1987—; faculty mem., instr. N.Y. State Office of Ct. Adminstrn., N.Y.C., 1993—. founding mem. Monroe County Cmty. Svc. Sentencing Program, 1987—; mgr., coach, sponsor Penfield Little League, 1990—, bd. dirs. 1990—; cmty. career advisor Penfield H.S. Internship Program, 1993—; founder Student Ct. Program, Penfield. Adelbert Moot scholarship SUNY Buffalo, 1973. Mem. N.Y. State Magistrates Assn. (1st v.p. 1998, Magistrate of Yr. 1998). Republican. Avocations: reading, travel, golf, tennis, coaching. Family and matrimonial, Probate, Real property. Office: Farber & Farber 2140 Penfield Rd Penfield NY 14526-1736

**FARBER, STEVEN GLENN,** lawyer; b. Phila., July 20, 1946; s. Isadore Irving and Sylvia (Galperin) F.; children: Jamie, Daniel, Zoey, Avi. BBA, Temple U., 1968, JD, 1972. Bar: Pa. 1972, U.S. Dist. Ct. (ea. dist.) Pa. 1972, U.S. Dist. Ct. Appeals (3d cir.) 1972, N.Mex. 1975, U.S. Dist. Ct. N.Mex. 1975, U.S. Ct. Appeals (10th cir.) 1979, U.S. Supreme Ct. 1980. Asst. defender Pub. Defender Assn. Phila., 1972-74; acting dist. pub. defender State of N.Mex., Santa Fe, 1975-76, asst. atty. gen., 1976-78; pvt. practice Santa Fe, 1978—; mem. N.Mex. Bd. Legal Specialization, 1986-90, chmn., 1991-93. Elected city councilor City of Santa Fe, 1992-96, mem. Santa Fe Mcpl. Home Rule Charter Commn., 1997; bd. dirs. Ptnrs. in Edn., 1997—, Temple Beth Shalom, 1997—, Santa Fe County United Way, 1998—. Mem. Nat. Assn. Criminal Def. Lawyers (vice-chmn. continuing legal edn. com. 1990-91), N.Mex. Lawyers Guild (pres. 1980-81), N.Mex. State Bar Assn. (bd. dirs. criminal law sect. 1980-83, chmn. 1981-82), N.Mex. Criminal Def. Lawyers Assn. (bd. dirs. 1991, treas. 1996), First Jud. Dist. Criminal Def. Lawyers Assn. (sec. 1999). Democrat. Jewish. Criminal, Civil rights, Personal injury. Office: PO Box 2473 306 Catron St Santa Fe NM 87504-2473

**FARICY, JOHN HARTNETT, JR.,** lawyer; b. Augsburg, Germany, Nov. 5, 1955; came to U.S., 1956; s. John Hartnett and Mary Helen Sarah (Bowe) F. BA, Tulane U., 1977; JD, William Mitchell Coll. Law, St. Paul, 1982. Bar: Minn. 1982, U.S. Dist. Ct. Minn. 1983, U.S. Ct. Appeals (2d cir.) 1987, U.S. Supreme Ct. 1988. Ptnr. Faricy & Roen, P.A., Mpls., 1996—. Mem. Univ. Club of St. Paul. General civil litigation, Toxic tort, Insurance. Office: Faricy & Roen PA 150 S 5th St Minneapolis MN 55402-4200

**FARINA, JAMES L.,** lawyer; b. Chgo., June 7, 1954; s. Louis P. and Rose (Torina) F.; m. Rita Marie Sassetti, July 25, 1981; children: Lauren, Nicholas, Lisa, Michael. BS, Ill. State U., Normal, 1976; JD, IIT, 1979. Bar: Ill. 1979, U.S. Dist. Ct. (no. dist.) Ill. 1980, U.S. Ct. Appeals (7th cir.) 1991, U.S. Dist. Ct. (ctrl. dist.) Ill. 1992. Asst. pub. defender Cook County, Chgo., 1979-80; assoc. Perz and McGuire, Chgo., 1981-86, J. Dillon Hoey, P.C., Chgo., 1987-90; ptnr. Hoey and Farina, Chgo., 1990-97, Hoey, Farina and Downes, Chgo., 1997—. Mem. United Transp. Union (local 1299), Acad. Rail Labor Attys., ATLA, Ill. Trial Lawyers Assn. Roman Catholic. Criminal, Transportation, Personal injury. Home: 7833 Courtland Pkwy Elmwood Pk IL 60707 Office: Hoey Farina and Downes 542 S Dearborn St Chicago IL 60605-1508

**FARINA, JOHN,** lawyer; b. Rockville Center, N.Y., Oct. 20, 1959; s. Joseph P. Farina and Marilyn A. Echkoff; m. Julia Pressly, May 30, 1987; children: Matthew, Timothy, Nicholas. BA, Villanova U., 1981; JD, Suffolk U., 1985. Bar: Mass. 1985, Fla. 1986. Law clk. U.S. Ct. Appeals (4th dist.), West Palm Beach, Fla., 1985-86; assoc. Winthrop Stimson Putnam & Roberts, Palm Beach, Fla., 1986-90, Edwards & Angell, Palm Beach, 1990-94; ptnr. Boyes & Farina, West Palm Beach, 1994—; mem. Fla. Probate Rules Com., Fla. Bar Greivance Com., 1998—. Mem. Palm Beach County Bar Assn. Avocations: trap and skeet shooting, running, tennis. State civil litigation, Probate. Home: 131 Thornton Dr Palm Beach Gardens FL 33418-8089 Office: Boyes & Farina PA 1601 Forum Pl Ste 900 West Palm Beach FL 33401-8105

**FARINA, MARIO G.,** lawyer; b. Newark, Nov. 1, 1927; s. Gerardo and Marianna F.; m. Lois R. Wachman, Apr. 11, 1955; children: Jay E., Wendy D., F. William. BS in Edn., Montclair State U., 1949; MA in Adminstrn., Seton Hall U., 1955, JD, 1960. Bar: N.J. 1963, N.Y. 1982, U.S. Dist. Ct. N.J. 1963, U.S. Supreme Ct. 1977. Atty. N.J. Pub. Defenders Office, Elizabeth, 1968-86; pvt. practice Clark, N.J., 1963—. Sgt. U.S. Army, 1950-52. Mem. Union County Bar Assn. Democrat. Roman Catholic. Avocation: writing. Criminal, Juvenile, State civil litigation. Office: 990 Raritan Rd Clark NJ 07066-1740

**FARLESS, FLOYD HUGH,** lawyer; b. Rome, Ga., Apr. 28, 1950; s. Floyd and Ruby Lee (Hilburn) F.; m. Lila Dolora Lloyd, Feb. 12, 1977; children: Evan, Anna, Emma. BA, Auburn U., 1972; LLB, Cumberland Sch. of Law, Birmingham, Ala., 1976. Bar: Ga. Assoc. Clary, Kent, Rome, 1976-80; ptnr. Farless, Newton, Wyatt, Rome, 1980-82, Farless & Newton, Rome, 1982—. Precinct pres. Rep. Party of Ga.'s Floyd County, Rome, 1997—; pres. treas. bd. dirs. Floyd County Wildlife Assn., Rome, 1966-94. Capt. USAR. Mem. F&AM, Am. Legion. LDS. Avocations: fishing, camping, history. Home: 5878 Alabama Hwy NW Rome GA 30165-8812 Office: Farless & Newton 15A E 5th Ave Rome GA 30161-3125

**FARLEY, BARBARA SUZANNE,** lawyer; b. Salt Lake City, Dec. 13, 1949; d. Ross Edward Farley and Barbara Ann (Edwards) Farley Swanson; m. Arthur Hoffman Ferris, Apr. 9, 1982 (div. 1995); children: Barbara Whitney, Taylor Edwards; m. Michael L. Levine, Aug. 9, 1999. BA with honors, Mills Coll., 1972; JD, U. Calif.-Hastings, San Francisco, 1976. Bar: Calif. 1976. Extern law clk. to justice Calif. Supreme Ct., San Francisco, 1975; assoc. Pillsbury, Madison & Sutro, San Francisco, 1976-78, Bronson, Bronson & McKinnon, San Francisco, 1978-80, Goldstein & Phillips, San Francisco, 1980-84; ptnr., head litigation Rosen, Wachtell & Gilbert, San

Francisco, 1984-89; of counsel Lempres & Wulfsberg, Oakkland, Calif., 1989—; arbitrator U.S. Dist. Ct. (no. dist.) Calif., San Francisco, 1981—, Calif. Superior Ct., San Francisco, 1984-89; judge pro tem San Francisco Mcpl. Ct., 1983—; probation monitor Calif. State Bar, 1990—; speaker Nat. Bus. Inst. Estate Adminstrn. Contbg. author Calif. Continuing Edn. of the Bar, N at. Bus. Inst.; mng. editor Hastings Coll. of Law-U. Calif.-San Francisco Constl. Law Quar., 1975-76; civil litigation reporter. Mills Coll. scholar, 1970-72, U. Calif.-Hastings, San Francisco scholar, 1973-76. Mem. ATLA, San Francisco Bar Assn., Calif. Trial Lawyers Assn., San Francisco Trial Lawyers Assn., Alameda Bar Assn. General civil litigation, Probate.

**FARLEY, DANIEL W.,** utility company executive, lawyer; b. Syracuse, N.Y., Dec. 6, 1955. BS, Clarkson U., 1978; JD, Syracuse U., 1981. Bar: N.Y. 1984. Adminstr. N.Y. State Electric & Gas Co., Binghamton, 1981-86; asst. to sec. N.Y. State Electric and Gas Co., Ithaca, 1986-87, asst. sec., 1987, corp. sec., 1987—, v.p., sec., 1991; sec. Energy East Corp.; v.p., sec., dir. XEnergy Enterprises, Inc.; sec. Energy East Enterprises Inc., Energy East Solutions, Inc., NYSEG Solutions, Inc., N.H. Gas Corp., Cayuga Energy, Inc., Senaca Lake Storage, Inc., Energy East Telecomms., Inc., So. Vt. Natural Gas Corp.; clk. Xenergy, Inc. Bd. dirs., treas., sec. The NYSEG Found., Inc. Office: NY State Electric & Gas Co PO Box 5224 Binghamton NY 13902-5224

**FARLEY, JOHN JOSEPH, III,** federal judge; b. Hackensack, N.J., July 30, 1942; s. John Joseph and Patricia (Earle) F.; m. Kathleen Mary Wells, June 27, 1970; children: Maura, Brendan, Thomas, Caitlin. AB in Econs., Holy Cross Coll., 1964; MBA, Columbia, 1966; JD cum laude, Hofstra U., 1973. Bar: N.Y. 1974, D.C. 1975, U.S. Supreme Ct. 1977. Trial atty. torts sect. civil div. U.S. Dept. Justice, Washington, 1973-78, asst. dir. torts br. civil div., 1978-80, dir. torts br. civil div., 1980-89; judge U.S. Ct. of Appeals for Vets. Claims, Washington, 1989—; mem. faculty OPM Exec. Seminar Ctrs., Denver, 1980—; lectr. Atty. Gen's. Advocacy Inst., Washington, 1976-89, FBI Acad., Quantico, Va., 1978-88. Editor-in-chief Hofstra Law Rev., 1971-73; contbr. articles to profl. jours. Bd. dirs. Amputee Coalition of Am., 1997-98. Served to capt. U.S. Army, 1966-70, Vietnam. Decorated Bronze Star with V device and 3 oak leaf clusters, Purple Heart with oak leaf cluster; recipient Sr. Exec. Service Spl. Achievement award U.S. Dept. Justice, 1984, Civil Div. Spl award U.S. Dept. Justice, 1980; Samuel Bronfman fellow, 1964-65, Dean's award for Disting. Hofstra Law Sch. Alumni, 1995, Disting. Alumni medal Hofstra U. Sch. of Law, 1986. Mem. Fed. Bar Assn. (1st chmn. vets. law sec. 1990-91). Roman Catholic. Avocations: skiing, tennis, bicycling, reading. Office: US Court Of Appeals for Vets Claims 625 Indiana Ave NW Ste 900 Washington DC 20004-2917

**FARLEY, MARGARET M.,** lawyer; b. San Francisco, Jan. 8, 1958; d. James V. and Margaret M. (Bertolli) Farley; m. Raymond W. Laing; 1 child, Brendan. BA, Loyola Marymount U., L.A., 1980; JD, U. San Francisco, 1983. Bar: Calif. 1984, U.S. Dist. Ct. Calif. 1984, U.S. Ct. Appeals (9th cir.). Assoc. Freitas, McCarthy, Bettini et al, San Rafael, Calif., 1983-84, Goshkin Pollatsek Meredith & Lee, San Francisco, 1984-87, John Parente, San Francisco, 1987-88, Laughlin Falbo Levy & Moressi, San Francisco, 1988-92; ptnr. Ropers & Farley, San Rafael, 1992-96; pvt. practice San Rafael, 1996—. Mem. Rotary Club of Ctr. Marin (dir. 1995-97). General civil litigation, Insurance, Education and schools. Office: 100 Smith Ranch Rd Ste 306 San Rafael CA 94903-1994

**FARLEY, TERRENCE P.,** prosecutor, lecturer; b. Jersey City, Jan. 16, 1943; s. Terrence Joseph and Jacqueline (Taub) F.; m. Marilyn M. Willadsen, Apr. 14, 1967 (div. Oct. 1997); children: Terrence R., Karin A. Farley Killian. BA in History and Polit. Sci., Parsons Coll., Fairfield, Iowa, 1963; JD, Rutgers U., Newark, 1966. Bar: N.J. 1967, U.S. Dist. Ct. N.J. 1967, U.S. Supreme Ct.; cert. instr. N.J. Police Tng. Commn. Jud. clk. Superior Ct. N.J., Toms River, 1966-67; atty. Novins Farley, Grossman & York, Toms River, 1967-87; dir. Nat. Drug Prosecution Ctr., Alexandria, Va., 1992-94, N.J. Divsn. Criminal Justice, Trenton, 1994-97; 1st asst. prosecutor Ocean County Prosecutors Office, Toms River, 1987-92, 1997—; instr. Nat. Inst. Trial Advocacy, Widener U. Sch. Law; cons. peer rev. programs Office of Justice Programs, Dept. Justice; mem. N.J. Atty. Gen.'s Narcotics Intervention Plan Task Force. Editor: Beyond Convictions: Prosecutors as Community Leaders in the War on Drugs, 1993; contbr. articles to profl. jours. Mem. Ocean County Emergency Mgmt. Coun. Recipient Exceptional Svc. award Ocean County Crime Prevention Officers, others. Mem. ABA, N.J. Bar Assn., Ocean County (past pres.) Bar Assn., Internat. Assn. Chiefs of Police (cmty. oriented policing com.). Office: Ocean County Pros Office 119 Hooper Ave Toms River NJ 08753-7605

**FARLEY, THOMAS T.,** lawyer; b. Pueblo, Colo., Nov. 10, 1934; s. John Baron and Mary (Tancred) F.; m. Kathleen Maybelle Murphy, May 14, 1960; children: John, Michael, Kelly, Anne. BS, U. Santa Clara, 1956; LLB, U. Colo., 1959. Bar: Colo. 1959, U.S. Dist. Ct. Colo. 1959, U.S. Ct. Appeals (10th cir.) 1988. Dep. dist. atty. County of Pueblo, 1960-62; pvt. practice Pueblo, 1963-69; ptnr. Phelps, Fonda & Hays, Pueblo, 1970-75, Petersen & Fonda, P.C., Pueblo, 1975—; bd. dirs. Pub. Svc. Co. Colo., Denver, Norwest Pueblo, Norwest Sunset, Found. Health Systems, Inc., Colo. Public Radio. Minority leader Colo. Ho. of Reps., 1967-75; chmn. Colo. Wildlife Commn., 1975-79, Colo. Bd. Agr., 1979-87; bd. regents Santa Clara U., 1987—; commr. Colo. State Fair; trustee Cath. Found. Diocese of Pueblo, Great Outdoors Colo. Trust Fund. Recipient Disting. Svc. award U. So. Colo., 1987, 93, Bd. of Regents, U. Colo., 1993. Mem. ABA, Colo. Bar Assn., Pueblo C. of C. (bd. dirs. 1991-93), Rotary. Democrat. Roman Catholic. Education and schools, Health, Administrative and regulatory. Office: Petersen & Fonda PC 650 Thatcher Bldg Pueblo CO 81003

**FARMER, GARY MICHAEL,** judge; b. Toledo, Ohio, Aug. 28, 1940; s. James Alphonso Farmer and Jeannette Elizabeth Bowser; m. JoAnn Patricia Hines, Oct. 5, 1963; children: Gary M. Jr., Linda Kathleen. AA, Broward C.C., 1968; BA, Fla. Atlantic U., 1970; JD, U. Toledo, 1973. Bar: Ohio 1973, Fla. 1974, U.S. Supreme Ct. 1976. Law clk. to judge N. Walinski U.D. Dist. Ct., Toledo, 1973-75; ptnr. Abrams Anton P.A., Hollywood, Fla., 1975-82, Goldberg Young, P.A., Ft. Lauderdale, Fla., 1982-84; owner, ptnr. Gary M. Farmer, P.A., Ft. Lauderdale, 1984-91; dist. ct. judge State of Fla., West Palm Beach, Fla., 1991—. Mng. editor U. Toledo Law Rev., 1972-73. With USMC, 1958-61. Named to Alumni Hall of Fame Fla. Atlantic U., 1992, Disting. Alumnus Broward C.C., 1978. Office: Dist Ct Appeal 4th Dist 1525 Palm Beach Lakes Blvd West Palm Beach FL 33401-2301

**FARMER, WILLIAM DAVID,** lawyer; b. Wilmington, N.C., Mar. 3, 1962; s. William Henry Jr. and Marilyn (Meyers) F. BA in Psychology, U. N.C., Wilmington, 1985; JD, St. Mary's U., San Antonio, 1990. Bar: Tex. 1990. Law clk. Tinsman & Houser, Inc., San Antonio, 1990-91; assoc. Johnson, Curney & Fields, P.C., San Antonio, 1991—, recruiting coord., 1991-93; legal cons. Purely Phys. Exercise Studio, San Antonio, 1990—. Mem. ABA, State Bar Tex., San Antonio Bar Assn., Phi Delta Phi. Presbyterian. Avocations: aerobic exercise, tennis, collecting antiques, reading, TV trivia. Insurance, General practice, Personal injury. Office: Johnson Curney & Fields PC 613 NW Loop 410 Ste 800 San Antonio TX 78216-5509

**FARNAM, THOMAS CAMPBELL,** lawyer, educator; b. Indpls., Feb. 13, 1945; s. Frederick Dean Farnam and Isabelle (Campbell) Fearheiley; children: Rachel Anne Stujenske, Thomas Matthews. BS, Butler U., 1966; JD, Ind. U., Indpls., 1970; LLM in Taxation, Georgetown U., 1973. Bar: Ind. 1970, U.S. Dist. Ct. (so. dist.) Ind. 1970, U.S. Ct. Appeals (7th cir.) 1970, U.S. Tax Ct. 1970, Mo. 1983, U.S. Supreme Ct 1991. Asst. dir. advanced underwriting Indpls. Life Ins. Co., 1970-72; tax atty., employee benefits specialist Emerson Electric Co., St. Louis, 1973-78; benefits cons. Alexander & Alexander, St. Louis, 1978-79; asst. v.p. pension profit sharing Centerre Trust, St. Louis, 1979-82; dir. of pensions St. Louis Home Builders Assn., St. Louis, 1982-83; v.p., gen. counsel, benefits cons. Pension Assocs., Inc., St. Louis, 1983-84; pvt. practice T.C. Farnam & Assocs., St. Louis, 1984-92; adj. prof. Webster U., St. Louis, 1984-93; pvt. practice The Farnam Law Firm, 1993—; bd. dirs. Small Bus. Coun. Am., Washington, Newman Ctr. of Washington U., St. Louis; mem. exec. com. Employee Benefits Assn. of St. Louis, 1985-99, Art St. Louis, Inc.; mem. steering com. WEB, St. Louis, 1987-90. Contbr. chpt. to book and articles to profl. jours. Trustee Eugene Field Found., St. Louis, 1986—; pres. of trustee Wydown Terr., Clayton, Mo., 1982-93; com. chmn. troop 21 Boy Scouts Am., Clayton, 1989-92, asst. scoutmaster, 1992-98, post advisor Explorer Post 9021, Clayton, 1996-97; mem. parish coun. St. Joseph's Ch., Clayton, 1982-85. Fellow Am. Coll. Tax Counsel; mem. ABA (taxation, bus. & labor sect., employee benefit coms.), Mo. State Bar Assn., Ind. State Bar Assn., Bar Assn. Met. St. Louis (chair employee benefits com. 1986-93), Noonday Club. Republican. E-mail: tcf@farnamlaw.com. Avocation: restoring 356 Porsches, photography, computers, cooking. Pension, profit-sharing, and employee benefits, Corporate taxation, Personal income taxation. Office: The Farnam Law Firm One Metropolitan Sq 211 N Broadway Ste 2940 Saint Louis MO 63102-2733

**FARNAN, JOSEPH JAMES, JR.,** federal judge; b. Phila., June 15, 1945; s. Joseph James and Philomena (DeLaurentis) F.; m. Patricia Candice Winner, June 28, 1969. BA, King's Coll., (Pa.), 1967; JD, U. Toledo Coll. Law, 1970. Bar: N.J. 1970, Del. 1972. Dir. crime justice program Wilmington Coll., New Castle, Del., 1970-73; pvt. practice law Wilmington, 1973-76; asst. pub. defender State Del., Wilmington, 1973-75; county atty. New Castle County, Wilmington, 1976-79; chief dep. atty. gen. Del. Dept. Justice, Wilmington, 1979-81; U.S. atty. U.S. Dept. Justice, Wilmington, 1981-85; judge U.S. Dist. Ct. Del., Wilmington, 1985—, now chief judge. Mem. ABA, Del. State Bar Assn., N.J. State Bar Assn., Am. Trail Lawyers Assn., Fed. Bar Assn. Republican. Roman Catholic. Office: US Dist Ct Federal Bldg 6325 844 N King St Ste 27 Wilmington DE 19801-3519

**FARNELL, ALAN STUART,** lawyer; b. Hartford, Conn., Mar. 14, 1948; s. Denis Frank and Katherine Dorothy (Dettenborn) F.; m. Roberta Ann Arquilla, May 21, 1983; children: Thomas Alan, Jeffrey Stuart. B.A. with honors, Trinity Coll., 1970; J.D., Georgetown U., 1973. Bar: D.C. 1973, N.Y. 1975, Ill. 1980, U.S. Dist. Ct. (no. dist.) Ill. 1980, U.S. Ct. Appeals (7th cir.) 1980. Assoc. Kaye, Scholer, Fierman, Hayes & Handler, N.Y.C., 1973-79; assoc. Isham, Lincoln & Beale, Chgo., 1979-83, ptnr., 1983—; gen. counsel 1550 N. State Pkwy. Condominium Assn., Chgo., 1984—; gen. counsel, bd. govs. Ginger Creek Community Assn., Oak Brook, Ill., 1984—. Editor Georgetown Law Jour., 1972-73. Mem. ABA. Club: Butterfield Country (Oak Brook). Federal civil litigation, General corporate, Securities. Home: 1 Pembroke Ln Oak Brook IL 60523-1726

**FARNHAM, CLAYTON HENSON,** lawyer; b. New Brunswick, N.J., Aug. 18, 1938; s. Richard Bayles and Naomi Shropshire (Henson) F.; m. Katharine Gross, Sept. 16, 1967; children: Julia Kernan, Richard Bayles II. BA, U. of the South, 1961; LLB, U. Ga., 1967. Bar: Ga. 1968, U.S. Dist. Ct. (no., so. and mid. dists.) Ga. 1968, U.S. Supreme Ct. 1978, U.S. Dist. Ct. (no. dist.) Miss. 1978, U.S. Ct. Appeals (5th. cir., 11th cir.) 1968, (4th cir.) 1980, U.S. Ct. Appeals (8th cir.) 1992. Law clk. to judge U.S. Dist. Ct., Atlanta, 1967-69; from assoc., to ptnr. Swift, Currie, McGhee & Hiers, Atlanta, 1969-82; ptnr. Drew, Eckl & Farnham, Atlanta, 1982—. Contbr. articles to profl. jours. Lt. (j.g.) USNR, 1961-64. Mem. ABA (coun. TIPS sect. 1989-92), Internat. Assn. Def. Counsel (com. chmn. 1987-89), Ansley Golf Club, Lawyer's Club Atlanta, Old War Horse Lawyer's Club. Insurance, Federal civil litigation, State civil litigation. Home: 30 Inman Cir NE Atlanta GA 30309-3332 Office: Drew Eckl & Farnham 800 W Peachtree St NW PO Box 7600 Atlanta GA 30357-0600

**FARNSWORTH, E(DWARD) ALLAN,** lawyer, educator; b. Providence, June 30, 1928; s. Harrison Edward and Gertrude (Romig) F.; m. Patricia Ann Nordstrom, May 30, 1952; children: Jeanne Scott, Karen Ladd, Edward Allan (dec.), Pamela Ann. BS, U. Mich., 1948; MA, Yale U., 1949; JD (Ordronaux prize 1952), Columbia U., 1952; LLD (hon.), Dickenson Law Sch., 1988; Docteur en Droit (hon.), U. Paris, 1988, U. Louvain, 1989. Bar: D.C 1952, N.Y. 1956. Mem. faculty Columbia U., N.Y.C., 1954—, prof. law, 1959—, Alfred McCormack prof. law, 1970—; vis. prof. U. Istanbul, U. Dakar, 1964, U. Paris, 1974-75, 90, 93, Harvard Law S ch., 1970-71, Stetson Coll. Law, 1991, 94, U. Mich., 1994; mem. faculty Salzburg Seminar Am. Law, 1963, Columbia-Leyden-Amsterdam program on Am. law, 1964, 69, 73, 85, San Diego Inst. Internat. and Comparative Law, Paris, 1982, 94, Tulane Summer Inst. Practice, Paris, 1995, 98, 99, Rhodes, 1996, China Ctr. for Am. Law Study, Beijing, 1986; dir. orientation program on Am. law Assn. Am. Law Schs., 1965-68; U.S. rep. UN Commn. on Internat. Trade Law, 1970-81; reporter Restatement of Contracts 2d, 1971-80; cons. N.Y. State Law Revision Commn., 1956, 58, 59, 61, P.R. comml. code revision, 1988-91; mem. coms. validity and agy. internat. sales contracts Internat. Inst. Unification Pvt. Law, Rome, 1966-72, mem. governing coun., 1978—; mem. adv. com. on pvt. internat. law Sec. of State, 1985-89; spl. counsel city reorgn. N.Y.C. Coun., 1966-68; U.S. del. Vienna Conf. on Internat. Sales Law, 1980, Bucharest and Geneva Conf. on Internat. Agy., 1979, 83. Author: Changing Your Mind: The Law of Regretted Decisions, 1998, An Introduction to the Legal System of the United States, 3d edit., 1993; (with J. Honnold, S. Harris, C. Mooney, and C. Reitz) Cases and Materials on Commercial Law, 5th edit., 1993; (with W.F. Young) Cases and Materials on Contracts, 5th edit., 1995, Cases and Materials on Negotiable Instruments, 4th edit., 1993, Treatise on Contracts, 1982, 3d edit., 1999; (with V. Mozolin) Contract Law in the USSR and the United States, 1987, Farnsworth on Contracts, 3 vols., 1990, 2nd edit., 1998, United States Contract Law, 1992, 2d revised edit, 1999. Capt. USAAF, 1952-54. Fellow British Acad.; mem. ABA (Theberge award for pvt. internat. law 1996), Am. Philos. Soc., Am. Law Inst., Assn. of Bar of City of N.Y. (chmn. com. on fgn. and comparative law 1967-70, chmn. spl. com. on products liability 1979-82), Phi Beta Kappa, Phi Delta Phi. Unitarian. Home: 201 Lincoln St Englewood NJ 07631-3158 Office: Columbia U 435 W 116th St New York NY 10027-7201

**FARNSWORTH, T. BROOKE,** lawyer; b. Grand Rapids, Mich., Mar. 16, 1945; s. George Llelwyn and Gladys Fern (Kennedy) F.; children: Leslie Erin, T. Brooke. BS in Bus., Ind. U., 1967; JD, Ind. U., Indpls., 1971. Bar: Tex. 1971, U.S. Dist. Ct. (so. dist.) Tex. 1972, U.S. Tax Ct. 1972, U.S. Ct. Appeals (5th cir.) 1977, U.S. Ct. Appeals D.C. Cir. 1977, U.S. Supreme Ct. 1978, U.S. Ct. Appeals (11th cir.) 1982, U.S. Dist. Ct. (we. dist.) Tex. 1988, U.S. Dist. Ct. (no. dist.) Tex. 1994. Adminstrv. asst. to treas. of State of Ind. Indpls., 1968-71; assoc. Butler, Binion, Rice, Cook & Knapp, Houston, 1971-74; counsel Damson Oil Corp., Houston, 1974-78; prin. Farnsworth & Assocs., Houston, 1978-90, Farnsworth & von Berg, Houston, 1990—; bd. dirs., corp. sec. Lomax Exploration, Inc. Contbr. articles on law to profl. jours. Mem. ABA, Fed. Bar Assn., State Bar Tex., Houston Bar Assn., Fed. Energy Bar Assn., Assn. Trial Lawyers Am., Tex. Trial Lawyers Assn., Comml. Law League Am., Petroleum Club (Houston), Champions Golf Club. Republican. Mem. Christian Ch. General civil litigation, Contracts commercial, Oil, gas, and mineral. Home: 17302 Atherington Pl Spring TX 77379-6231 Office: Farnsworth and von Berg 333 N Sam Houston Pkwy E Ste 30 Houston TX 77060-2414

**FARON, ROBERT STEVEN,** lawyer; b. N.Y.C., Jan. 10, 1947; s. Jack and Ceil Faron; m. Linda A. Baumann, May 18, 1975; children: Gregory Andrew, Douglas James, Daniel Scott. BS in Engring., Princeton U., 1968; JD, Columbia U., 1975. Bar: D.C. 1975, U.S. Ct. Appeals (D.C. cir.) 1978, U.S. Ct. Appeals (4th cir.) 1986, U.S. Ct. Claims 1986. Systems engr. IBM Corp., Holmdel, N.J., 1968-69; atty. U.S. Dept. of Commerce, Washington, 1975-76; fgn. svc. officer U.S. Dept. of State, Washington, 1976-77; assoc. LeBoef, Lamb, Leiby & MacRae, Washington, 1977-82; of counsel Lane & Mittendorf, Washington, 1982-84, Brown, Roady, Bonvillian & Gold, Washington, 1984-85; ptnr. Alagia, Day, Marshall, Mintmire & Chauvin, Washington, 1986-90; dep. asst. gen. counsel for environ. Dept. of Energy, Washington, 1990-93; asst. gen. counsel Amerada Hess Corp., 1993-97; sr. advisor PHB Hagler Bailly, Inc., Washington, 1997—. Contbr. articles to profl. jours. Capt. USAF, 1969-72. Mem. ABA (chmn. TIPS energy resources law com. 1988-89, 91-97, mem. TIPS profl. issues com. 1989-92, coordinating group energy law 1989-94), Assoc. Internat. de Droit des Assurances (chmn. U.S. pollution law working party 1986-89). Environmental, Insurance, Private international. Office: PHB Hagler Bailly Inc 1776 Eye St NW Ste 600 Washington DC 20006-3700

**FARQUHAR, ROBERT MICHAEL,** lawyer; b. Chelsea, Mass., Apr. 28, 1954; s. Robert Vociel and Helen Margaret (Stevens) F.; m. Carol Elizabeth Auch, Dec. 16, 1978; children: Stephanie Elizabeth, Andrew Michael. BS, So. Meth. U., 1977, JD, 1980. Bar: Tex. 1980, U.S. Dist. Ct. (no. and ea. dists.) Tex. 1980, U.S. Ct. Appeals (5th and 11th cirs.) 1980, U.S. Supreme Ct. 1990; cert. bus. bankruptcy law Tex. Bd. Legal Specialization. Assoc. Carter Jones MaGee Rudberg Moss & Mayes, Dallas, 1980-82; ptnr. Johnson & Cravens, Dallas, 1982-88; shareholder Winstead Sechrest & Minick, P.C., Dallas, 1988—. Mem. ABA, Dallas Bar Assn. Republican. Episcopalian. Avocations: bicycling, computers. Bankruptcy, Computer. Office: Winstead Sechrest Minick PC 1201 Elm St Ste 5400 Dallas TX 75270-2199

**FARR, G(ARDNER) NEIL,** lawyer; b. L.A., Jan. 9, 1932; s. Gardner and Elsie M. (Schuster) F.; m. Lorna Jean, Oct. 26, 1957; children: Marshall Clay, Jennifer T., Thomas M. BA, U. Calif., Berkeley, 1957, JD, U. Calif., San Francisco, 1960. Bar: Calif. 1961, U.S. Supreme Ct. 1977. Cert specialist family law Calif. Bd. Specialization, 1980. Dep. dist. atty. Solano County, 1961-66; recreation commr. City of Fairfield, 1964-66; dep. dist. atty. Kern County, 1966-69; ptnr. Young, Wooldridge, Paulden, Self, Farr & Hugie (now Law Offices of Young Wooldridge), Bakersfield, Calif., 1969—; dir. Cen. Calif. Appellate Program, Inc.; judge protem Kern County Superior Ct. Chmn. Kern County Juvenile Justice Commn. With USNR, 1949-53. Mem. ABA, Calif. Bar Assn., Kern County Bar Assn. (pres. 1984, past pres. family law sect.). Fax: (805) 327-1087. Family and matrimonial. Office: Young Wooldridge 1800 30th St Fl 4 Bakersfield CA 93301-1919

**FARRAR, STANLEY F.,** lawyer; b. Santa Ana, Calif., 1943. BS, U. Calif., Berkeley, 1964, JD, 1967. Bar: Calif. 1968, N.Y. 1969. Mem. Sullivan & Cromwell, L.A. Mem. ABA (chmn. subcom. on bank holding cos. and nonbank activities banking law com. 1980-85, chmn. letters credit subcom. uniform comml. code com. 1982-88, sect. bus. law), State Bar Calif. (chmn. fin. instns. com. 1981-82). Banking, Mergers and acquisitions, Securities. Office: Sullivan & Cromwell 1888 Century Park E Los Angeles CA 90067-1702

**FARRELL, MICHAEL W.,** state supreme court justice. Grad., U. Notre Dame; MA, Columbia U.; JD, Am. U. Law clerk to Assoc. Judge John P. Moore Md. Ct. Spl. Appeals, 1973; atty. criminal divsn. U.S. Dept. Justice; chief appellate divsn. Office U.S. Atty. D.C., 1982-89; assoc. judge Ct. Appeals, 1989—; chmn. Eng. dept. Georgetown Prep. Sch. Office: Ct Appeals 500 Indiana Ave NW Rm 6000 Washington DC 20001-2131

**FARRELL, SCOT JERARD,** executive, accountant; b. Houston, June 16, 1959; s. James W. and Betty Moorin F.; m. Sherri Komorn, Dec. 22, 1985; children: Ariana, Lauren, Matthew. BS, Lehigh U., 1981. Supr. Coopers & Lybrand, N.Y.C., 1981-82, Houston, 1982-85; acctg. mgr. A-Z Internat. Tool, Houston, 1985; chief fin. officer Fulbright & Jaworski, Houston, 1986—. Co-author: Poems of Lehigh, 1981. Mem. AICPA, Tex. Soc. CPAs, Assn. Legal Adminstrs. (Houston chpt. adv. bd. 1988-90). Avocations: cooking, bicycling, family. Home: 4913 Laurel St Bellaire TX 77401-4426 Office: Fulbright & Jaworski 1301 Mckinney St Ste 5100 Houston TX 77010-3031

**FARRELL, TERESA JOANNING,** lawyer; b. L.A., Sept. 17, 1958; d. Harold T. and Helen Dolores Joanning; m. Michael P. Farrell, Oct. 18, 1986. BA, U. Calif., San Diego, 1980; JD, U. Calif., San Francisco, 1986. Bar: Calif. 1986, U.S. Dist. Ct. (ctrl. dist.) Calif. 1987. Assoc., spl. counsel Gibson, Dunn & Crutcher LLP, Irvine, Calif., 1986-98, ptnr., 1999—. Bd. dirs. Second Harvest Food Bank, Orange, Calif., 1993—, The Harvesters, Newport Beach, Calif., 1993—. Mem. Calif. State Bar Assn. (real property sect.), Internat. Coun. Shopping Ctrs. Real property, Finance, Landlord-tenant. Office: Gibson Dunn & Crutcher LLP 4 Park Plz Ste 1400 Irvine CA 92614-8557

**FARRELL, THOMAS DINAN,** lawyer; b. Chgo., Feb. 14, 1948; s. Francis George and Marian F.; m. Elizabeth Ann McElyea, Apr. 26, 1975; children: Brian, Timothy. AB in Politics, Princeton U., 1970; JD, U. Calif., Berkeley, 1973. Bar: N.J. 1974, Calif. 1977, N.Y. 1987. Asst. counsel Nat. Gambling Commn., Washington, 1974-76; asst. U.S. atty. U.S. Dept. Justice, L.A., 1976-78; assoc. Pitney, Hardin & Kipp, Morristown, N.J., 1978-80; v.p. Hilton Hotels Corp., Beverly Hills, Calif., 1980-82, Harrah's, Atlantic City, 1982-85; sr. v.p., gen. counsel Trusthouse Forte, Inc., N.Y.C., 1985-90; sr. v.p. devel. Hilton Hotels, 1990-94; exec. v.p. devel. Airport Group Internat., Glendale, Calif., 1994-96; v.p. Hyatt Internat. Corp., Chgo., 1996—. Commr. Alcoholic Beverage Study Commn., Trenton, N.J., 1983-85. Served to capt. USAR, 1972-80. Nat. Merit Scholar 1966. Mem. N.J. Bar Assn. (chmn. casino law com. 1984-85). Episcopalian. General corporate, Private international, Real property. Home: 612 Marlin Ln Carlsbad CA 92009-4685 Office: Hyatt Internat Corp 200 W Madison St Chicago IL 60606-3414

**FARRELL, TRENT D.,** lawyer, consultant; b. Waco, Tex., July 31, 1969; s. Robert Carl and Linda Carol Farrell; m. Tricia Anne Wills, Aug. 15, 1998. BA, Baylor U., 1993; JD, Wesleyan U., Ft. Worth, 1997. Bar: Tex. 1997; cert. mediator. Congl. intern U.S. Congressman Chet Edwards, Waco, Tex., 1992; assoc. Corbin & Assocs., Betton, Killeen, Copperas Cove, Tex., 1997—; legal cons. T.B.K. Enterprises, Inc., Round Rock, Tex., 1997—; mediator, Copperas Cove, 1997—. Editor Mgr.'s Legal Guide, 1992. Named to Outstanding Young Men of Am., 1992, 98. Mem. Delta Theta Phi, Alpha Chi, Omicron Delta Kappa. Office: Corbin & Assocs 90 Cove Terrace Ste 202 Copperas Cove TX 76522

**FARRIOR, J. REX, JR.,** lawyer; b. Tampa, Fla., June 5, 1927; s. J. Rex and Lera Spotswood (Finley) F.; children: J. Rex III, Preston Lee, Hugh Nunnally, Robert Pendleton. Student Auburn U., 1945-46; B.S. in Bus. Adminstrn., U. Fla., 1949, J.D., 1951. Bar: Fla. 1951. Assoc. Shackleford, Farrior, Stallings & Evans, P.A. and predecessors, Tampa, Fla., 1951-55, ptnr., 1955—, sr. ptnr., past pres., also bd. dirs.; owner Rocking F Ranch, Ocala, Fla.; permanent guest lectr. U. Fla., Coll. Engring.; lectr. U. Fla., Stetson U.; mem. Fed. Jud. Nominating Comm., 1980-88; bd. dirs. Flagship Bank Tampa East. Pres. Round Table of Tampa, 1965; trustee U. Fla. Law Ctr. Assocs., 1989—, Cmty. Found. Greater Tampa, 1993—. With USNR, World War II. Named to Hall of Fame, U. Fla., 1951. Fellow Am. Coll. Trust and Estate Counsel, Am. Bar Found. (life); mem. ABA (ho. of dels. 1976-81, award of Merit), Fla. Bar (pres. Fla. young lawyers sect. 1958, pres. 1975-76, Most Outstanding Local Bar Pres. 1977, award of Merit), Hillsborough County Bar Assn. (pres. 1966), Acad. Fla. Trial Lawyers, Am. Judicature Soc., Inter-Am. Bar Assn., Am. Counsel Assn. (bd. dirs. 1973—, pres. 1983-84), Assn. Trial Lawyers Am., Greater Tampa C. of C. (bd. govs.), Phi Delta Phi, Kappa Alpha Alumni Assn. (pres. 1957). Presbyterian. Clubs: Rotary, Sertoma (founder Tampa club 1952, pres. 1964), Masons, Shriners, Mystic Krewe of Gasparilla (capt. 1970-72, King LX 1973, Court of Honor medal Kappa Alpha Order 1991). General corporate, Probate, Estate planning. Office: Shackleford Farrior Stallings & Evans PO Box 3324 Tampa FL 33601-3324

**FARRIS, FRANK MITCHELL, JR.,** retired lawyer; b. Nashville, Sept. 29, 1915; s. Frank M. and Mary (Lellyett) F.; m. Genevieve Baird, June 7, 1941; 1 dau., Genevieve B. B.A., Vanderbilt U., 1937; postgrad. N.Y. Law Sch., 1938-39. Bar: Tenn., 1939, U.S. Tax Ct., 1948, U.S. Supreme Ct., 1968. Conciliation commr. in bankruptcy U.S. Dist. Ct. Middle Dist. Tenn., 1940-42; ptnr. Farris, Warfield & Kanaday, and predecessors, Nashville, 1946-98; gen. counsel, trustee George Peabody Coll. for Tchrs., 1968-79; counsel 3d Nat. Corp., Nashville, Cherokee Equity Corp., Nashville. Commr. Watkins Inst., Nashville, 1953-95; trustee Vanderbilt U., 1979—; chmn. bd. Oak Hill Sch., Nashville, 1968-74, 80-81. Mem. ABA, Tenn. Bar Assn., Nashville Bar Assn. Banking, General corporate, Estate planning. Home: 940 Overton Lea Rd Nashville TN 37220-1503

**FARRIS, JEROME,** federal judge; b. Birmingham, Ala., Mar. 4, 1930; s. William J. and Elizabeth (White) F.; widower; children: Juli Elizabeth, Janelle Marie. BS, Morehouse Coll., 1951, LLD, 1978; MSW, Atlanta U., 1955; JD, U. Wash., 1958. Bar: Wash. 1958. Mem. Weyer, Roderick, Schroeter and Sterne, Seattle, 1958-59; ptnr. Weyer, Schroeter, Sterne & Farris and successor firms, Seattle, 1959-61, Schroeter & Farris, Seattle, 1961-63, Schroeter, Farris, Bangs & Horowitz, Seattle, 1963-65, Farris, Bangs & Horowitz, Seattle, 1965-69; judge Wash. State Ct. of Appeals, Seattle, 1969-79, U.S. Ct. of Appeals (9th cir.), Seattle, 1979—; lectr. U. Wash. Law Sch. and Sch. of Social Work, 1976—; mem. faculty Nat. Coll. State Judiciary, U. Nev., 1973; adv. bd. Nat. Ctr. for State Cts. Appellate Justice Project, 1978-81; founder First Union Nat. Bank, Seattle, 1965, dir.,

1965-69; mem. U.S. Supreme Ct. Jud. Fellows Commn., 1997—; mem. Jud. Conf. Com. on Internat. Jud. Rels., 1997—. Del. The White House Conf. on Children and Youth, 1970; mem. King County (Wash.) Youth Commn., 1969-70; vis. com. U. Wash. Sch. Social Work, 1977-90; mem. King County Mental Health-Mental Retardation Bd., 1967-69; past bd. dirs. Seattle United Way; mem. Tyee Bd. Advisers, U. Wash., 1984—, bd. regents, 1985—, pres., 1990-91; trustee U. Law Sch. Found., 1978-84; mem. vis. com. Harvard Law Sch., 1996—. With Signal Corps, U.S. Army, 1952-53. Recipient Disting. Service award Seattle Jaycees, 1965, Clayton Frost award, 1966. Fellow Am. Bar Found. (sec. of fellows 1998); mem. ABA (exec. com. appellate judges conf. 1978-84, 87—, chmn. conf. 1982-83, del. jud. adminstrn. coun. 1987-88), Wash. Council on Crime and Delinquency (chmn. 1970-72), Am. Bar Found. (bd. dirs. 1987, exec. com. 1989—), State-Fed. Jud. Council of State of Wash. (vice-chmn. 1977-78, chmn. 1983-87), Order of Coif (mem. law rev.), U. Wash. Law Sch. Office: US Ct Appeals 9th Cir 1030 US Courthouse 1010 5th Ave Seattle WA 98104-1195

**FARROW, SALLIE,** lawyer; b. Plainfield, N.J., Dec. 31, 1942; d. James R. and Sallie A. (Mitchell) Rivera; 1 child, Richard H. Staton Jr. BA with honors, U. Denver, 1974; JD, U. Nebr, 1976. Bar: Nebr. 1977, U.S. Ct. Appeals (8th cir.) 1978. Laborer Standard Plastics, Plainfield, N.J., 1960-64; sr. line clk. N.J. Bell Telephone, Elizabeth, 1964-68; underwriter Allstate Ins., Murray Hill, N.J., 1969-72; asst. gen. counsel, sec. Mut. Omaha Ins. Co., Omaha, Nebr., 1977-87; assoc. cousel, sec. N.Y. Life Ins. Co., N.Y.C., 1987—; mem. Creighton U. Speakers Series, Omaha, 1981; ACE counselor SBA, Omaha, 1980—. Panelist U.S. Office Edn., Washington, 1978; organizer, advisor Metro Sci. and Engring. Fair Inc., Omaha, 1982—; chairperson Boy Scouts Am., Omaha, 1982, cons.,1983; cons. Adopt A Sch. Program, Omaha, 1986; mentor Legal Outreach, Inc., 1991. Mem. ABA, Nat. Bar Assn. (com. mem., mng. editor law jour. 1986), Nebr. Bar Assn. (mng. editor Law Jour. 1986), Kappa Delta Phi, Phi Alpha Delta. Democrat. Avocations: jogging, tapestry, collecting books, aerobics. Securities, General corporate, Insurance. Office: New York Life Ins Co 51 Madison Ave Rm 105B New York NY 10010-1603

**FARRUG, EUGENE JOSEPH, SR.,** lawyer; b. Detroit, May 22, 1928; s. Michael and Bridget Mary (Foley) F.; m. Dolores Marie Augustine, Apr. 14, 1951; children: Elizabeth Marie Streit, Eugene Joseph Jr., Matthew Augustine, Pamela Ann, Bridget Louise, Donna Michele. BBA, U. Mich., 1950, JD, 1958. Bar: Ill. 1958, U.S. Dist. Ct. (no. dist.) Ill. 1958; U.S. Supreme Ct. 1980. With Lincoln-Mercury div. Ford Motor Co., Dearborn, Mich., 1950, Aircraft Engine div., Chgo., 1951; assoc. McKenna, Storer, Rowe, White & Farrug, Chgo., 1958-62, ptnr., 1962-92; of counsel, 1992—. Mem. Citizens of Greater Chgo., 1970-80, pres., 1976-79. Served with USN, 1951-55. McGreggor Fund scholar, 1946; Mich. Bd. Realtors scholar, 1949. Mem. Ill. Bar Assn., Chgo. Bar Assn., DuPage County Bar Assn., Am. Judicature Soc., Cath. Lawyers Guild, Phi Alpha Delta. Lodge: Kiwanis (pres. 1964). State civil litigation, Personal injury, Federal civil litigation. Home: 122 5th St Hinsdale IL 60521

**FARRY, MICHAEL ALLEN,** lawyer; b. Knoxville, Tenn., Aug. 25, 1957; s. Joseph Mitchell and Betty (Bolten) F.; m. Julia Worthington, Feb. 5, 1983; children: Robert Mitchell, Thomas Worthington. BS, U. Tenn., 1979; JD, U. S.C., 1982. Bar: S.C. 1982, U.S. Dist. Ct. S.C. 1982, U.S. Ct. Appeals (4th cir.) 1982, U.S. Supreme Ct. 1986. Assoc. Horton, Drawdy, Ward & Johnson, P.A., Greenville, S.C., 1982-84; ptnr. Horton, Drawdy, Ward & Johnson, P.A., Greenville, 1985—. General civil litigation, Workers' compensation, Insurance. Home: 10 Running Springs Ct Greer SC 29650-3037 Office: Horton Drawdy Ward & Black 307 Pettigru St Greenville SC 29601-3112

**FARSJO, FRED A.,** lawyer; b. Tucson, June 20, 1953; s. Tallak Thomason and Lillian Viola (Erickson) F.; m. Dorothy Ann Farsjo, Aug. 20, 1974 (div. Nov. 1986); children: Christopher Michael, Kirsten Rene; m. Patricia Lynn Payne, May 18, 1991; 1 child, Matthew Tyler. BSBA, U. Ariz., 1975, JD, 1979, M in Acctg., 1980. Bar: Ariz. 1979, U.S. Dist. Ct. Ariz. 1990, U.S. Ct. Appeals 1981, U.S. Tax Ct. 1981. Assoc. Bilby, Shoenhair, Warnock & Dolph, Tucson, 1979-81, O'Connell & Assocs., Tucson, 1981-83; inhouse counsel, v.p. fin. Empire West, Tucson, 1983-85; inhouse counsel, v.p. devel. Clifton & Assocs., Tucson, 1985-86; assoc. Harrison, Rollman & Gabroy, Tucson, 1986-90, Gabroy, Rollman & Bossé, Tucson, 1990—. Bd. dirs. YMCA, Tucson, 1988-95; lawyer Habitat for Humanity, Tucson, 1980-83. Mem. State Bar of Ariz. (real estate coun. 1983—, subcom. chmn. CLE 1986-87, sec. exec. coun. 1989-90), Order of Coif, Alpha Kappa Psi. Lutheran. Avocations: racquetball, weight lifting, camping. Estate planning, Real property, Probate. Home: 5760 E Territory Ave Tucson AZ 85750-1801 Office: Gabroy Rollman & Bossé 3507 N Campbell Ave Ste 111 Tucson AZ 85719-2000

**FARTHING, EDWIN GLENN,** lawyer; b. Greensboro, N.C., July 2, 1947; s. Edwin Harold Glenn and Martha Rachel (Harris) F.; life ptnr. Thomas Edwin Fancher; 1 child, Lyle Britton. BA, U. N.C., 1969, JD, 1972. Bar: N.C 1972, U.S. Dist. Ct. (we. dist.) N.C. 1976, U.S. Ct. Appeals (4th cir.) 1982. Assoc. Smathers & Ferrell, Hickory, N.C., 1972; ptnr. Smathers, Ferrell & Farthing, Hickory, 1973, Smather & Farthing, Hickory, 1973-78, Farthing & Cheshire, Hickory, 1978-81, Tate, Young, Morphis, Bach & Farthing, Hickory, 1982-94; pvt. practice Law Office Edwin G. Farthing, Hickory, 1995—; bd. dirs. N.C. Legal Edn. Assistance Fund, Raleigh, 1990-98. Elder Northminster Presbyn. Ch., Hickory, 1982-85, 89-92; precinct chmn. Catawba County Rep. Com., Hickory, 1993—; bd. dirs. N.C. Pride Polit. Action Com., Raleigh, 1993-97; mem. Hickory Cmty. Rels. Coun., 1995—. Mem. Mem. N.C. State Bar, N.C. Assn. Def. Attys. (sec.-tras. 1989-92), N.C. Bar Assn., Catawba County Bar Assn., N.C. Gay and Lesbian Attys. (pres. 1996-97). Avocations: politics, reading, boating, snow skiing. General practice, Civil rights, Alternative dispute resolution. Office: PO Box 9294 Hickory NC 28603-9294

**FARUKI, CHARLES JOSEPH,** lawyer; b. Bay Shore, N.Y., July 3, 1949; s. Mahmud Taji and Rita (Trownsell) F.; m. Nancy Louise Glock, June 5, 1971 (div. Oct. 1995); children: Brian Andrew, Jason Allen, Charles Joseph Jr.; m. Michelle F. Zalar, June 15, 1996. BA summa cum laude, U. Cin., 1971; JD cum laude, Ohio State U., 1973. Bar: Ohio 1974, U.S. Dist. Ct. (no. and so. dists.) Ohio 1975, U.S. Ct. Appeals (9th cir.) 1977, U.S. Tax Ct. 1977, U.S. Supreme Ct. 1977, U.S. Ct. Appeals (6th cir.) 1978, U.S. Dist. Ct. (no. dist.) Tex. 1979, U.S. Dist. Ct. (ea. dist.) Ky. 1982, U.S. Ct. Appeals (D.C. cir.) 1982, U.S. Ct. Customs and Patent Appeals 1982, U.S. Ct. Appeals (4th cir.) 1986, U.S. Ct. Appeals (2d cir.) 1989, U.S. Ct. Appeals (fed. cir.), 1991, U.S. Ct. Appeals (8th cir.) 1997. Assoc. Smith & Schnacke, Dayton, Ohio, 1974-78; ptnr. Smith & Schnacke, Dayton, 1979-89; founder, mng. ptnr. Faruki Gilliam & Ireland, PLL, Dayton, 1989—; Mem. bd. dirs. Smith & Schnacke, Dayton, 1980-88; lectr. various continuing legal edn. programs. Contbr. articles in field. Served to capt. U.S. Army Res., 1971-79. Fellow Am. Bar Found., Am. Coll. Trial Lawyers (complex litigation com.); mem. ABA, Fed. Bar Assn. (officer and exec. com. Dayton chpt. 1988-93, pres. 1991-92), Ohio State Bar Assn. (bd. govs. Antitrust sect. 1992—), Dayton Bar Assn. (officer 1992-94, pres. 1994-95), Def. Rsch. Inst., Human Factors and Ergonomics Soc. (affiliate mem.), Fed. Cir. Bar Assn. Avocation: numismatics. Antitrust, General civil litigation, Federal civil litigation. Home: 300 Fairforest Cir Dayton OH 45419-1308 Office: Faruki Gilliam & Ireland PLL 600 Courthouse Plz SW Dayton OH 45402

**FASCETTA, CHRISTOPHER M.,** lawyer; b. N.Y.C., Apr. 27, 1966; s. Salvatore Charles and Mary Barbara Fascetta; m. Patricia Ann Salloom, July 25, 1998. BA, Washington Coll., 1988; JD, Widener U., 1991. Bar: Md. 1991, U.S. Dist. Ct. Md., 1992. Assoc. Rodgers and Dickerson, P.C., Timonium, Md., 1991-95, Law Offices Robert Grossbart, Balt., 1995-97; sr. assoc. Rodgers and Dickerson, P.C., Lutherville, Md., 1997—. Mem. Harford County Rep. Com., Bel Air, Md., 1998—, Balt. County Rep. Com., Towson, Md., 1995-98. Mem. Bankruptcy Bar Assn. (adv. bd. 1992—), Kappa Alpha (alumni advisor 1990—). Roman Catholic. Avocations: golf, camping. Bankruptcy, General corporate, Consumer commercial. Home: 481 Copeland Rd Fallston MD 21047-2924 Office: Rodgers and Dickerson PC 1301 York Rd Ste 500 Heaver Plaza Lutherville MD 21093

**FASON, RITA MILLER,** lawyer; b. Fargo, N.D., July 12, 1935; d. John Maurice Miller and Mary Dullea; divorced; children: Catherine, John, William, Richard. BA in History, Rice Inst., 1957; JD, U. Houston, 1979. Bar: Tex. 1979. With John Graml & Assocs., Houston, 1979-80; ptnr. Brady & Fason, Houston, 1981-82; pvt. practice Houston, 1982—. Eucharistic min. St. Anne's Cath. Ch., Houston, 1988—; pres. bd. dirs. Wellsprings, Houston, 1989-95. Mem. Assn. Women Attys. (com. 1979—). Avocations: gardening, traveling. Family and matrimonial, Probate. Home: 2121 Peckham St Houston TX 77019-6431 Office: 3212 Smith St Ste 202 Houston TX 77006-6622

**FASS, PETER MICHAEL,** lawyer, educator; b. Bklyn., Apr. 11, 1937; s. Irving and Bess (Fordin) F.; m. Deborah K. Orshan, May 6, 1989; 1 child, Olivia Jae; children from previous marriage: Brian Samuel, Lyle Williams. BS in Econs. with honors, U. Pa., 1958; JD cum laude, Harvard U., 1961; LLM, NYU, 1964. Bar: N.Y. 1965; CPA. From assoc. to ptnr. Carro, Spanbock, Fass, Geller, Kaster & Cuiffo, N.Y.C., 1968-86; ptnr. Kaye, Scholer, Fierman, Hayes & Handler, N.Y.C., 1988-95, Battle Fowler LLP, N.Y.C., 1995—; adj. asst. prof. real estate NYU; lectr. Practising Law Inst., N.Y. Law Jour., Instl. mag., Ill. Inst. Continuing Legal Edn.; spl. cons. Calif. Commr. of Corps Real Estate Adv. Com.; mem. ad hoc com. Real Estate Securities and Syndication Inst., chmn. regulatory legis and taxation com., 1975-76; mem., dir. participant/real estate com. NASD, 1991-94. Co-author: Tax Advantaged Securities, 1977—, Real Estate Syndication Handbook, 1985-87, Tax Aspects of Real Estate Investments, 1988, Blue Sky Practice Handbook, 1987—, Real Estate Investment Trusts Handbook, 1987—, S Corporation Handbook, 1985—, Tax Advantaged Securities Handbook, 1979—; contbr. articles to profl. jours. Recipient Haskins award for outstanding achievement in N.Y. State C.P.A.s exam., 1964. Mem. ABA (chmn. real estate investment com., real property, probate and trust sect.), N.Y. State Bar Assn., Am. Inst. CPA's, N.Y. State Soc. CPA's, Pi Lambda Phi, Beta Gamma Sigma, Beta Alpha Psi. Securities, Taxation, general, Trademark and copyright. Home: 115 Central Park W New York NY 10023-4153 Office: Battle Fowler LLP 75 E 55th St New York NY 10022-3205

**FASSETTO, EUGENE A.,** lawyer; b. Salinas, Calif., Feb. 25, 1950; s. Eugene Edward and Dorothy Marguerite Fassetto; m. Deborah D. Bruzda, July 2, 1976; children: Gina Marie, Angela Denise, Anthony Edward. Student, U. Calif., Berkeley, 1968-71; BA in Microbiology, Oreg. State U., 1976; JD, Willamette U., 1984. Bar: Oreg. 1984. Ops. mgr. Beaver State Movers, Corvallis, Oreg., 1977-81; jud. clk. Oreg. Supreme Ct., Salem, 1984-86; atty. Stoel Rives LLP, Portland, Oreg., 1986—. Mem. adv. bd. Austitic Children's Activity Program, Portland, Oreg., 1987—. Mem. Oreg. State Bar (chair real estate and land use sect. 1996-97, mem. exec. com. use sect. 1990-98). Real property. Office: Stoel Rives LLP 900 SW 5th Ave Ste 2600 Portland OR 97204-1268

**FAST, KENNETH H.,** lawyer; b. Newark, Apr. 4, 1929; s. Moe M. and Eva H. (Hurwitz) F.; m. Judith Nicholson, Nov. 23, 1969; children—Jonathan Nicholson, Madelaine M. BA, Lafayette Coll., 1951; LLB, Yale U., 1954. Bar: N.J. 1954, D.C. 1954, U.S. Ct. Appeals (D.C. cir.) 1954, U.S. Ct. Appeals (3d cir.) 1958, U.S. Supreme Ct. 1960. Ptnr., Fast & Fast, East Orange, N.J., 1957-86; ptnr. Fox & Fox, Newark, 1987—. Trustee, Weisberger Found. for Aged, Poor and Needy, East Orange, 1969—. 1st lt. USAF, 1955-57. Mem. N.J. State Bar Assn., Essex County Bar Assn., Title Abstracter's Assn. Real property, Contracts commercial, Landlord-tenant. Home: 91 Fairfield Dr Short Hills NJ 07078-1718

**FASTIFF, WESLEY J.,** lawyer; b. Fall River, Mass., July 19, 1932; s. Jacob Fastiff and Ida Bertman; m. Bonnie Barmon, Dec. 29, 1963; children: Pamela Fastiff Ellman, Eric Barmon Fastiff. LLB, Harvard U., 1959. Bar: Calif., D.C., U.S. Dist. Ct. (no., ea., ctrl. dist.) Calif., U.S. Ct. Appeals (2nd, 9th cir.), U.S. Supreme Ct. Lawyer, chmn. bd. Littler Mendelson, San Francisco, 1963—. With USN, 1954-56. Labor. Office: Littler Mendelson 650 California St Fl 20 San Francisco CA 94108-2702

**FAULKNER, ANDREW MONTGOMERY,** lawyer; b. New Rochelle, N.Y., 1959. BA magna cum laude, Cornell U., 1981; JD, Columbia U., 1986. Bar: N.Y. 1987. Ptnr. Skadden, Arps, Slate, Meagher & Flom LLP, N.Y.C., 1985—. Stone scholar. Finance. Office: Skadden Arps Slate Meagher & Flom LLP 919 3rd Ave New York NY 10022-3902

**FAUPEL, MARIAN L.,** lawyer; b. Detroit, July 30, 1943; d. William Barrett and Jay Elizabeth Locke; m. Kirk Arthur Faupel, Mar. 27, 1965; 1 child, Corey Barrett. AB in English, U. Mich., 1965; JD, Wayne State U., 1983. Bar: Mich., U.S. Dist. Ct. (ea. dist.) Mich., U.S. Supreme Ct. Assoc. Smith, Hirsch, Brody & Weingarden, Detroit, 1983-84, Hill, Lewis, Adams, Goodrich & Tait, Ann Arbor, 1984-86, Burnham, Connolly, Oesterle & Henry, Ann Arbor, 1986-88; of counsel Schlussel, Lifton, Simon, Rands, Galvin & Jackier, P.C., Ann Arbor, 1988-90; sole shareholder Faupel & Assocs., Ann Arbor, 1990—; presenter in field. Survey editor Wayne Law Rev., 1982-83; contbr. articles to profl. jours. Trustee Saline Bd. Edn., 1978-90; past dir. Washtenaw Sch. Officers Assn.; chmn. Indsl. Devel. Commn., 1970-80; v.p. United Fund, 1970-80; pub. rels. cons. Saline Cmty. Hosp., ARC, Saline Area Schs. William D. Traitel scholar Wayne State U. Law Sch., 1982-83; recipient Cert. Achievement, Washtenaw County Bar Assn., 1986; named Michiganians of Yr. award Detroit News, 1994. Mem. Mich. Bar Assn. (mem. rep. assembly 1987-93), Washtenaw County Bar Assn. (editor 1985-95), Kappa Tau Alpha. Episcopalian. Avocations: couture sewing and writing. Office: Faupel & Assocs 303 Detroit St Ste 200 Ann Arbor MI 48104-1126

**FAURI, ERIC JOSEPH,** lawyer; b. Lansing, Mich., Feb. 16, 1942; s. Fedele Fauri and Iris M. Petersen; m. Sherrill Lynn Nurenberg, July 15, 1969; children—Lauren, Nadia, Kirk. B.A., U. Del., 1963; J.D. with distinction, U. Mich., 1966. Bar: Mich. 1967, U.S. Dist. Ct. (ea. dist.) Mich. 1967, U.S. Dist. Ct. (we. dist.) Mich. 1972, U.S. Ct. Appeals (6th cir.) 1974. Assoc. Dykema, Gossett, Spencer, Goodnow & Trigg, Detroit, 1966-71; Parmenter Forsythe, Rude et al, Muskegon, Mich., 1971-73; ptnr. Parmenter, Forsythe, Rude et al, Muskegon, 1973—; Parmenter O'Toole, 1992—. Served to capt. U.S. Army, 1967-68. Mem. ABA, State Bar Mich. Banking, Contracts commercial. Office: Parmenter O'Toole 175 W Apple Ave PO Box 786 Muskegon MI 49443-0786

**FAUST, JONATHAN JAY,** lawyer; b. Scarsdale, N.Y., Sept. 5, 1968; s. David I. and Marilyn S. Faust; m. Nancy Anne Knox, June 28, 1997. BA in Polit. Sci. with honors, U. Mich., 1990; JD, Columbia U., 1993. Assoc. Rosenman & Colin LLP, N.Y.C., 1993-98, 98—; sr. atty. Claims Resolution Tribunal for Dormant Accts., Zürich, Switzerland, 1998; spl. asst. dist. atty. Manhattan Dist. Attys. Office, N.Y.C., 1994-97. Avocations: rock climbing, exercise, football, dog. General civil litigation, Environmental. Home: 139 W 74th St Apt 1B New York NY 10023-2270 Office: Rosenman & Colin LLP 575 Madison Ave Fl 26 New York NY 10022-2585

**FAWCETT, ROBROY RONALD,** lawyer; b. San Bernardino, Calif., June 25, 1960; s. Kenneth Cannon Fawcett and Patricia Marlene Quinn; m. Jane Moraes, June 28, 1986; children: Robroy, Andrew, Michelle. BS in Electronic Engring., Calif. State Poly. U., 1984, BS in Physics, 1984; JD, Brigham Young U., 1992. Bar: Calif. 1992, U.S. Dist. Ct. (ctrl. dist.) Calif. 1993. Electronic engr. Hughes Aircraft Co., El Segundo, Calif., 1985-86; optoelectronic design engr. space comm. divsn. TRW, Redondo Beach, Calif., 1987-88; sr. product mktg. engr. Advanced Optoelectronics, ASEC, Industry, Calif., 1988-89; assoc. Pretty, Schroeder, Breuggeman, L.A., 1992-96, Fitch, Even, Tabin & Flannery, La Jolla, Calif., 1996-97, Gray Cary Ware Friendrich, San Diego, 1997—. Mem. San Diego Intellectual Property Law Assn. Avocations: tennis, swimming. Intellectual property, Patent. Office: Gray Cary Ware & Freidenrich 401 B St Ste 1700 San Diego CA 92101-4240

**FAWELL, BLANCHE HILL,** lawyer; b. Champaign, Ill., Sept. 23, 1955; d. David Bennett and Blanche Elaine Hill; m. Jeffrey Bruce Fawell, Aug. 21, 1983; children: Daniel, Timothy, Joseph. BA, Am. U., 1977; JD, Loyola U., Chgo., 1980. Bar Ill. 1980, U.S. Dist. Ct. (no. dist.) Ill. 1980, U.S. Ct. of Appeals (cir.) 1981. Asst. sales atty. DuPage County States Atty. Office, Wheaton, Ill., 1980-85; ptnr. Fawell, Fawell & Kavvadias, Wheaton, 1986—; bd. dirs. Suburban Bank & Trust Co., Elmhurst, Ill. Gen. counsel Ill. Rep. Party, Chgo., 1997—; sec., founding mem. Ill. Lincoln Excellence in Pub. Svc. Series, Naperville, 1994. Republican. Criminal, Immigration, naturalization, and customs, Election. Office: Fawell Fawell & Kavvadias 2100 Manchester Rd Ste 101 Wheaton IL 60187-4582

**FAWER, MARK S.,** lawyer; b. N.Y.C., Sept. 6, 1961; s. Martin S. and Ellen S. F.; m. Melissa Greenberg, Jan. 14, 1989; children: Zoe Sydney, Hallie Devorah. BA, U. Pa., 1983, JD, 1986. Bar: N.Y. 1987. Assoc. Rogers & Wells, N.Y.C., 1986-89, Richards & O'Neil, N.Y.C., 1989-92, Kramer, Levin & Naftalis, N.Y.C., 1992-97; ptnr. Moses & Singer LLP, N.Y.C., 1997—. Contbr. articles to profl. jours. Mem. ABA (mem. hotels and hospitality issues subcom. real propert commn. 1998—), N.Y. State Bar Assn. (mem. comml. leasing com. 1996—), Assn. Bar City N.Y. (mem. state legis. com. 1998—). Real property, Banking, Finance. Office: Moses & Singer LLP 1301 Ave of Americas New York NY 10019

**FAWSETT, PATRICIA COMBS,** federal judge; b. 1943. BA, U. Fla., 1965, MAT, 1966, JD, 1973. Pvt. practice law Akerman, Senterfitt & Edison, Orlando, Fla., 1973-86; commr. 9th Cir. Jud. Nominating Commn, 1973-75, Greater Orlando Crime Prevention Assn., 1983-86; judge U.S. Dist. Ct. (mid. dist.) Fla., Orlando, 1986—. Trustee Loch Haven Art Ctr., Inc., Orlando, 1980-84; commr. Orlando Housing Authority, 1976-80, Winter Park (Fla.) Sidewalk Festival, 1973-75; bd. dirs. Greater Orlando Area C. of C., 1982-85. Mem. ABA (trial lawyers sect., real estate probate sect.), Am. Judicatures Soc., Assn. Trial Lawyers Am., Fla. Bar Found. (bd. dirs. grants com.), Commn. on Access to Cts., Fla. Coun. Bar Assn. Pres.'s (pres., bd. dirs. 9th cir. grievance com.) Osceola County Bar Assn., Fla. Bar (bd. govs. 1983-86, budget com., disciplinary rev. com., integration rule and bylaws com., com. on access to legal system, bd. of cert., designation and advt., jud. adminstrn., selection and tenure com., jud. nominating procedures com., pub. rels. com., ann. meeting com., appellate rules com., spl. com. on judiciary-trial lawyer rels., chairperson midyr. conv. com., bd. dirs. trial lawyers sect.), Orange County Bar Assn. (exec. coun. 1977-83, pres. 1981-82, trustee Legal Aid Soc. 1977-81), Order of Coif, Phi Beta Kappa. Office: US Dist Ct Federal Bldg 80 N Hughey Ave Ste 611 Orlando FL 32801-2231

**FAX, CHARLES SAMUEL,** lawyer; b. Balt., Sept. 12, 1948; s. David Hirsch and Eleanor Shirley (Lobe) F.; m. Nancy Lee Gruenberg, 1980 (div. 1995); children: Joanna May, Benjamin Zachary; m. Michele Weil, 1996. BA, Johns Hopkins U., 1970; JD with honors, George Washington U., 1973. Bar: D.C. 1974, N.Y. 1974, Md. 1990. Office of dist. atty. N.Y.C. (Bronx county), 1973-74; assoc. Truitt & Fabrikant, Washington, 1974-75; assoc. Chapman, Duff & Paul, Washington, 1975-79, ptnr., 1979-84; ptnr. Porter, Wright, Morris & Arthur, Washington, 1985-89; sr. ptnr., chmn. lit. dept. Shapiro and Olander, Balt., 1989—, mem. exec. com., 1999—; gen. counsel Parents and Children Together, Inc., 1992-98; apptd. mediator Cir. Ct. for Balt. City, 1994-98; spl. outside litigation counsel Commonwealth P.R. Dept. Justice, 1998—; mem. faculty Exec. Enterprises, Inc., N.Y.C., Chgo., 1985-86; lectr. fed. personnel litigation Adminstrv. Law Inst., Washington, Chgo., San Francisco, 1982-83; lectr. Md. Mcpl. League, 1990-98; book rev. Cleve. Plain Dealer. Contbr. articles to newspapers and mags. Mem. Washington com. for Sch. Arts and Scis., Johns Hopkins U., 1987-89. Mem. D.C. Bar, Johns Hopkins U. Soc. for 2d Decade, Tudor and Stuart Club, Johns Hopkins Club, Alpha Delta Phi. Democrat. Jewish. Home: 10720 Gloxinia Dr N Bethesda MD 20852-3404 Office: Shapiro and Olander 36 S Charles St Ste 2000 Baltimore MD 21201-3147

**FAY, JOHN FARRELL,** lawyer; b. Medford, Mass., Jan. 12, 1946; s. Edward Thomas Fay and Bridgett Kathleen Clancy; m. Paula Ann Monroe, Aug. 20, 1994. BS in Fin., Merrimack Coll., 1968; JD, Wstn. State U. Sch. Law, 1977. Sole practice law San Diego, 1979-86; atty. Law Offices of Leon Schneider, Beverly Hills, Calif., 1986-89; trial counsel Seigfried & Jensen, Salt Lake City, 1990-96, Tesch, Thompson & Fay, Park City, Utah, 1996-97; sole practice law Park City, 1998—. Author: Arbitrating Personal Injury Claims, 1992; contbr. articles to profl. jours. Mem. ATLA, Utah Trial Lawyers Assn. (bd. govs., state del. to ATLA), Utah State Bar Assn., Calif. State Bar Assn. Avocations: biking, skiing, reading, writing. Insurance, State civil litigation, Product liability. Office: 1662 Bonanza Dr Park City UT 84060-7225

**FAY, PETER THORP,** federal judge; b. Rochester, N.Y., Jan. 18, 1929; s. Lester Thorp and Jane (Baumler) F.; m. Claudia Pat Zimmerman, Oct. 1, 1958; children: Michael Thorp, William, Darcy. B.A., Rollins Coll., 1951, LL.D., 1971; J.D., U. Fla., 1956; LL.D., Biscayne Coll., 1975. Bar: Fla. 1956, U.S. Supreme Ct. 1961. Ptnr. firm Nichols, Gaither Green, Frates & Beckham, Miami, Fla., 1956-61, Frates, Fay, Floyd & Pearson (and predecessors), Miami, 1961-70; prof. Fla. Jr. Bar Practical Legal Inst., 1959-65; judge U.S. Dist. Ct. for So. Fla., Miami, 1970-76, U.S. Ct. Appeals (5th cir.), 1976-81; judge U.S. Ct. Appeals (11th cir.), 1981-94, sr. judge, 1994—; lectr. Fla. Bar Legal Inst., 1959—; faculty Fed. Jud. Center, Washington, 1974-94; mem. Jud. Conf. Com. for Implementation Criminal Justice Act, 1974-82, Adv. Com. on Codes of Conduct, 1980-87, Adv. Com. on Appellate Rules, 1987-90; co-chmn. Nat. Jud. Coun. for State and Fed. Cts., 1990—. Mem. Orange Bowl Com., 1974—; dist. collector United Fund, 1957-70; mem. adminstrv. bd. St. Thomas U., 1970—; trustee U. Miami, Fla., 1989—; mem., supr. Ind. Counsel, 1994—. With USAF, 1951-53. Mem. Law Sci. Acad., Fla. Acad. Trial Attys., Am., Fla., Dade County, John Marshall (past pres.) bar assns., Fla. Council of 100, U. Fla. Alumni Assn. (dir.), Miami C. of C., Medico Legal Inst., Order of Coif, Phi Delta Phi (past pres.), Omicron Delta Kappa (past pres.), Pi Gamma Mu (past pres.), Phi Kappa Phi, Phi Delta Theta (past sec.). Republican. Roman Catholic. Clubs: Wildcat Cliffs (N.C.); Snapper Creek Lakes (Miami), Coral Oaks (Miami), Miami. Office: US Ct Appeals 11th Cir 99 NE 4th St Rm 1255 Miami FL 33132-2140

**FAYE, RICHARD BRENT,** lawyer; b. San Francisco, Jan. 25, 1945; s. Robert Ray and Rose (Weinberg) F.; m. Anne Marie Maughan, Aug. 1, 1970; children—Patrick Terence, Timothy Richard. BA, San Francisco State U., 1966, MA, 1968; JD, U. San Francisco, 1975. Bar: Calif. 1975, U.S. Dist. Ct. (no. dist.) Calif. 1975. Assoc. Graves & Allen, Oakland, Calif., 1976-77; staff counsel Calif. State Banking Dept., San Francisco, 1977-80; assoc. Rosenblum, Rabkin, Parish, Jack Bashli & Bacigalupi, San Francisco, 1980-82; assoc. Lillick & Charles, San Francisco, 1982-84, ptnr., 1984—; mem. supt. com. fin. code revisions, 1977-78, Calif. Bar fin. instns. com., 1982-85, Calif. Supt. Banks Regulation Task Force, 1985-86. Asst. editor law rev. 1975. Mem. ABA, San Francisco Bar Assn., St. Thomas More Soc. U. San Francisco Law Assembly. Democrat. Roman Catholic. Avocations: reading, running, hiking, music. Banking, Securities, General corporate. Office: Lillick & Charles 2 Embarcadero Ctr San Francisco CA 94111-3823

**FAYETTE, KATHLEEN OWENS,** lawyer; b. N.Y.C., Feb. 28, 1939; d. Edward Francis and Margaret Grace (Quigley) Owens; m. Alan Gerard Fayette, June 15, 1963; children: Stephen, Suzanne, Christopher. AB, Marymount Coll., N.Y.C., 1960; JD, Pace U., White Plains, N.Y., 1979. Asst. MHLS atty. Appellate divsn. N.Y. State Supreme Ct., N.Y.C., 1979-82; instr. law Interboro Inst., 1983-84; ct. liaison Project Greenhope, N.Y.C., 1985-87; dir. alternative to incarceration N.W. Bronx Cmty. and Clergy Coalition, N.Y.C., 1987-89; ct. liaison Children's Village, Dobbs Ferry, N.Y., 1989-91; lectr., cons. on the legal rights of the mentally disabled; cons. alternative incarceration. Author: The Bar is Closed, 1986; columnist You and the Law, 1982-83. Cons., dir. Bishop-Browne Project, Fla., 1994—; pro bono child welfare advocate Guardian ad Litem Program, Fla., 1992—. Mem. Pace U. Sch. Law Alumni Assn., Marymount Coll. Alumni Assn. Roman Catholic. Avocations: curling, skeet shooting, scuba diving. Fax: 561-451-3035. General practice, Family and matrimonial, Juvenile.

**FAZIO, D. FREDRICO,** lawyer; b. Bradford, Pa., July 25, 1940; s. Joseph Richard and Florence Fazio; m. Nancy Kretzschmar, May 4, 1963; children: Joseph R. III, Quinn. BS, Fla. State U., 1962; JD, U. Miami, Fla., 1967. Bar: Fla. 1967, U.S. Dist. Ct. (so. dist.) Fla. 1967. Assoc. Hawkesworth & Kay, Miami; ptnr. Fazio, Dawson, DiSalvo, Cannon, Abers & Podrecca, Ft. Lauderdale, Fla., 1969—; bd. dirs. Lucor, Inc. Mem. Downtown Devel. Authority, Ft. Lauderdale, 1992—, chmn., 1995, also sec. of bd.; bd. dirs. Boys Town of Fla., 1969-89. Mem. Am. Bd. Trial Advocates (pres., bd. dirs. 1992—), Ocean Reef Club. Avocations: golf, sailing. Home: 2887 Riverland Rd Fort Lauderdale FL 33312-4456 Office: Fazio Dawson DiSalvo Cannon

Abers & Podrecca 633 S Andrews Ave Ste 500 Fort Lauderdale FL 33301-2862

**FAZIO, JAMES VINCENT, III,** lawyer; b. Rome, N.Y., Mar. 8, 1969; s. James Vincent Jr. and Elaine Marie F. BA, Colgate U., 1991; JD, Syracuse U., 1995. Bar: Calif. 1996; U.S. Dist. Ct. (so., no., ea. and cen. dists.) Calif. 1996. Assoc. McKenna & Cuneo LLP, San Diego, 1995-97, Cooley Godward LLP, San Diego, 1997—. Mem. ABA, San Diego County Bar Assn. (mem. legis. com. 1997—), La Jolla Kiwanis Club. Avocations: skiing, rock climbing. General civil litigation. Office: Cooley Godward LLP 4365 Executive Dr Ste 1100 San Diego CA 92121-2133

**FAZIO, PETER VICTOR, JR.,** lawyer; b. Chgo., Jan. 22, 1940; s. Peter Victor and Marie Rose (LaMantia) F.; m. Patti Ann Campbell, Jan. 3, 1966; children: Patti-Marie, Catherine, Peter. AB, Holy Cross Coll., Worcester, Mass., 1961; JD, U. Mich., 1964. Bar: Ill. 1964, D.C. 1981, Ind. 1993, U.S. Dist. Ct. (no. dist.) Ill. 1965, U.S. Ct. Appeals (7th cir.) 1972, U.S. Supreme Ct. 1977, U.S. Ct. Appeals (D.C. cir.) 1988. Assoc. Schiff, Hardin & Waite, Chgo., 1964-70, ptnr., 1970-82, 84—; exec. v.p. Internat. Capital Equipment, Chgo., 1982-83, also dir., 1982-85, sec., 1982-87; bd. dirs. Planmetrics Inc., Chgo., 1984-92, Chgo. Lawyers Commn. for Civil Rights Under Law, 1976-82, co-chmn., 1978-80; bd. dirs. Seton Health Corp. No. Ill., Chgo 1987-90, vice chmn., 1989-90. Trustee Barat Coll., Lake Forest, Ill., 1977-82; bd. dirs. St. Joseph Hosp., Chgo., 1990-95, mem. exec. adv. bd. 1984-89, chmn., 1986-89; vice chmn. bd. dirs. Cath. Health Ptnrs., 1995—; dir. exec. com. Ill. Coalition, 1994—, Northwest Ind. Forum, 1994-98. Mem. ABA (mem. coun. 1991-94, vice-chmn. sect. pub. utlity, transp. and comm. law), Ill. State Bar Assn., Chgo. Bar Assn., Fed. Bar Assn., Fed. Energy Bar Assn., Edison Electric Inst. (vice chmn. legal com., chmn. legal exec. adv. com.), Am. Gas Assn. (mem. legal com.), Am. Soc. Corp. Secs., Met. Club (Chgo.), Econ. Club of Chgo., Commercial Club of Chgo. Public utilities, Contracts commercial, FERC practice. Office: Schiff Hardin & Waite 6600 Sears Tower 233 S Wacker Dr Chicago IL 60606-6473

**FEAR, RALPH J.,** prosecutor; b. Lone Pine, Calif., Oct. 4, 1941; s. Ralph A. and Elisa V. (Carrasco) F.; m. Suzanne C. Dunne, Nov. 17, 1973; children: Patrick, Andrew. BA magna cum laude, U. San Diego, 1963; LLB, Loyola U., L.A., 1966. Dep. dist. atty. County of San Diego, San Diego, 1969—. Adult leader Boy Scouts Am., San Diego, 1986—; bd. govs. Standly Jr. H.S., San Diego, 1987-88, University City H.S., San Diego, 1992-93. Lt., U.S. Army Inf., 1967-69. Recipient Bronze Pelican, Cath. Boy Scouts, San Diego, 1989. Mem. Nat. Dist. Attys. Assn., Calif. Dist. Attys. Assn., San Diego Dist. Attys. Assn. Avocations: family history, music, reading, travel, theatre, cooking. Office: Dist Attys Office County of San Diego PO Box 1011 San Diego CA 92112-1011

**FEATHERLY, HENRY FREDERICK,** lawyer; b. Stillwater, Okla., Aug. 10, 1930; s. Henry Ira and Lucy Anne (Borsch) F.; m. Dorcas Diane Rowley, July 19, 1952; children—Henry Frederick, Charles Alan. B.S., Okla. State U., Stillwater, 1952; LL.B., Okla. U., Norman, 1957. Bar: Okla. 1957, U.S. Dist. Ct. (we. and ea. dists.) Okla. 1957, U.S. Ct. Appeals (10th cir.) 1958. Assoc. Pierce, Mock & Duncan, Oklahoma City, 1957-63; ptnr. Chiles & Featherly, Oklahoma City, 1963-64; sole practice, Oklahoma City, 1964-66; ptnr. Lamun, Mock, Featherly, Baer & Timberlake, Oklahoma City, 1966-85; ptnr. Lamun, Mock, Featherly, Kuehling & Cunningham, Oklahoma City, 1986—. Mem. commrs. staff Dan Beard Dist. council Boy Scouts Am., 1966-89, Last Frontier council; trustee Heritage Hall Sch., Oklahoma City, 1974-77. Mem. ABA, Okla. Bar Assn., Oklahoma County Bar Assn., Am. Trial Lawyers Assn., Okla. Trial Lawyers Assn., Okla. Assn. Def. Counsel, Am. Judicature Soc. Republican. Methodist. Lodge: Lions (pres. 1970-71, 83-84). Workers' compensation, State civil litigation, Federal civil litigation. Home: 2433 NW 46th St Oklahoma City OK 73112-8307

**FEATHERSTONE, BRUCE ALAN,** lawyer; b. Detroit, Mar. 2, 1953; s. Ronald A. and Lois R. (Bosshart) F.; children: Leigh Allison, Edward Alan. BA cum laude with distinction in Econs., Yale U., 1974; JD magna cum laude, U. Mich., 1977. Bar: Ill. 1977, Colo. 1983, U.S. Dist. Ct. (no. dist.) Ill. 1978, U.S. Dist. Ct. Colo. 1983, U.S. Ct. Appeals (5th cir.) 1980, U.S. Ct. Appeals (7th cir.) 1981, U.S. Ct. Appeals (10th cir.) 1983, U.S. Ct. Appeals (9th cir.) 1991, U.S. Supreme Ct. 1984. Assoc. Kirkland & Ellis, Denver, 1977-83, ptnr., 1983-96; ptnr. Featherstone & Shea, LLP, Denver, 1996—. Articles editor U. Mich. Law Rev., 1976-77. Mem. ABA (litigation sect.), Colo. Bar Assn., Denver Bar Assn., Order of Coif. Avocations: swimming, biking, running. Federal civil litigation, State civil litigation, Environmental. Home: 725 Saint Paul St Denver CO 80206-3912 also: PO Box 1467 Denver CO 80201-1467 Office: Featherstone & Shea LLP 600-17th St Ste 2500 Denver CO 80202-5402

**FEAVEL, PATRICK MCGEE,** lawyer, mediator; b. Appleton, Wis., Dec. 15, 1949; s. Norman William and Lillian Estelle (Bucklew) F.; m. Kathleen Sonoe Thompson, Feb. 11, 1989; 1 child, Justin Michael. AA, Long Beach City Coll., 1973; BA, Northeast La. U., 1978; JD with honors, Loyola U., 1982. Bar: Calif., U.S. Dist. Ct. (ctrl. dist.) Calif. 1983, U.S. Dist. Ct. (ea. dist.) Calif. 1988. Assoc. Law Offices of Ron Minkin, L.A., 1981-83, Long & Levitt, L.A., 1983-84, Parkinson, Wolf & Leo, Century City, Calif., 1984-85; ptnr. Dunnion Law Firm, Monterey, Calif., 1985—. Assoc. editor Internat. and Comparative Law Jour., 1981. Mem. bd. dirs. Transp. Agy. of Monterey County, 1994. Mem. Monterey County Bar Assn., Phi Beta Kappa. Republican. Roman Catholic. Avocations: competitive bicyclist (U.S. Cycling Fedn.), debate. Insurance, Personal injury, State civil litigation. Home: 3074 Crescent Ave Marina CA 93933-3530 Office: Dunnion Law Firm 2711 Garden Rd Monterey CA 93940-5304

**FEAZELL, VIC,** lawyer; b. Monroe, La., June 8, 1951; 1 child, Gregory Victor. BA, Mary Hardin Baylor Coll., 1972; JD, Baylor U., 1979. Bar: Tex. 1979, U.S. Dist. Ct. (5th cir.) 1988, U.S. Dist. Ct. (no. dist) 1988, U.S. Dist. Ct. (so. dist), 1989. Dir. drug abuse treatment program Mental Health-Mental Retardation, Waco, Tex., 1975-79; pvt. practice Waco, 1979-82; dist. atty. McLennan County, Tex., 1983-88; pvt. practice Austin, Tex., 1989-94; of counsel Rosenthal and Watson, Austin, 1995—; pres. McLennan County Peace Officers Assn., Waco, 1984-87; pro bono def. counsel Henry Lee Lucas, 1989-94; expert legal corr. O.J. Simpson Trial, KTBC T.V. Primary character: Careless Whispers, 1986 (Edgar award 1986); exec. prodr. Rhinos; pres. One Horn Prodns.; contbr. articles to profl. jours. Del. State Dem. Conv., Houston, 1988. Named Outstanding Young Alumni, U. Mary Hardin Baylor, Belton, Tex., 1985, Peace Officer of Yr., Waco JC's, 1986. Mem. Nat. Assn. Criminal Def. Lawyers (life), Tex. Trial Laywers Assn., Tex. Criminal Def. Lawyers Assn., State Bar Tex., Bar of U.S. Fifth Cir. Avocation: flim making. E-mail: vic@rhinosthemovie.com. Criminal, Entertainment, General civil litigation.

**FECHTEL, VINCENT JOHN,** legal administrator; b. Leesburg, Fla., Aug. 10, 1936; s. Vincent John and Annie Jo (Hayman) F.; m. Dixie Davenport, Feb. 1992; children: John, Katherine, Elizabeth D., MaryKatherine. BSBA, U. Fla., 1959. Mem. Fla. Ho. of Reps., 1972-78, Fla. Senate, 1978-80; parole commr. U.S. Dept. Justice, Chevy Chase, Md., 1983-96. Served with USNR and Fla. Nat. Guard. Mem. Alpha Tau Omega. Republican. Roman Catholic. Home: 1101 S 9th St Leesburg FL 34748-6843

**FECIK, SHELLEY ANN,** lawyer, prosecutor; b. Pitts., Aug. 5, 1971; d. George Eugene and Theresa Ann Fecik. BA, U. Pitts., 1993; JD, Cleveland-Marshall Law Sch., 1996. Bar: Ohio 1996, Pa. 1997. Asst. pub. advocate Dept. Pub. Advocacy, Hazard, Ky., 1996-98; asst. dist. atty. Blair County Dist. Atty.'s Office, Hollidaysburg, Pa., 1998—. Recipient Oral Advocacy award Order of Barristers, 1996. Mem. Blair County Bar Assn. Republican. Roman Catholic. Avocations: photography, skiing, art, music, yoga. Office: Dist Atty's Office Blair County Courthouse Hollidaysburg PA 16648

**FEDDE, G(ABRIEL) BERNHARD,** retired lawyer; b. Bklyn., Mar. 7, 1909; s. Bernhard Andreas and Anna Mathea (Heggelund) F.; m. Johanna Borrevik, Aug. 14, 1957; m. Elizabeth Amy Ralston, Oct. 9, 1938 (div. 1955). AB, Williams Coll., 1930; postgrad., U. Munich, 1930-31, Columbia U., 1933-35; JD, U. Oreg., 1936; AM, Oreg. State U., 1964. Bar: Oreg. 1936. Pvt. practice law Eugene, Oreg., 1938-43, Portland, Oreg., 1955-90; with forest svc. Civil Pub. Svc., Cascade Locks, Oreg., 1943-46; head relief mission Am. Friends Svc. Com., Oberhausen, Germany, 1946-48; lawyer Luth. World Fedn., Palestine, 1949-50; adj. prof. Portland State U., 1955-90. Author: Norwegian-Swedish Crisis of 1905, 1964, also monographs. Mem. Scandinavian Heritage Found. (pres. 1985-90, bd. dirs. 1990—), Oreg. UN Assn. (bd. dirs. 1954—), Norsemen's Fedn. Oreg. (pres. 1982-91), Scandinavian Club of Portland (pres. 1977-82). Lutheran. Home: 1919 NW Ramsey Crest Portland OR 97229-4209

**FEDE, ANDREW THOMAS,** lawyer, educator; b. Jersey City, N.J., Jan. 20, 1956; s. Andrew Paul and Dorothy Marie Fede. BA, Montclair State U., 1978; JD, Rutgers U., 1982. Bar: N.J. 1982, U.S. Dist. Ct. N.J., 1982, U.S. Ct. Appeals (3d cir.) 1986, U.S. Supreme Ct. 1987. Assoc. Contant, Scherby & Atkins, Hackensack, N.J., 1982-90, ptnr., 1991—; atty. Borough of Bogota, 1992, 96—, Bogota Planning Bd., 1985-86, Borough of Maywood, 1993-94, 98—, Hasbrouck Heights Planning Bd., 1991-94, Borough of Norwood, 1998; adj. prof. Montclair State U., 1985—. Author: People Without Rights: An Interpretation of the Fundamentals of the Law of Slavery in the U.S. South, 1992; contbr. articles to profl. jours. Rep. County Committeeman, 1979-95; pres. Bd. Health, Bogota, 1983-89. Mem. ABA, N.J. Bar Assn., Bergen County Bar Assn., Am. Soc. for Legal History. Avocation: legal history. General civil litigation, Municipal (including bonds), General practice. Office: Contant Scherby & Atkins 33 Hudson St Hackensack NJ 07601-6902

**FEDER, ARTHUR A.,** lawyer; b. N.Y.C., Mar. 23, 1927; s. Leo and Bertha (Franklin) F.; m. Ruth Musicant, Sept. 4, 1949; children: Gwen Lisabeth, Leslie Margaret, Andrew Michael. BA, Columbia Coll., 1949; LLB, Columbia U., 1951. Bar: N.Y. 1951. Assoc. Fulton Walter & Halley, 1951-53; rsch. asst. Am. Law Inst. Fed. Income, Estate and Gift Tax Project, 1953-54; assoc., ptnr. Roberts & Holland, N.Y.C., 1954-66; ptnr. Willkie, Farr & Gallagher, N.Y.C., 1966-69; ptnr. Fried, Frank, Harris, Shriver & Jacobson, N.Y.C., 1970-94, of counsel, 1994—; sr. adv. to exec. com. Herzog, Heine, Geduld Inc., 1996—; lectr. in law Columbia U., 1961-63; lectr. Am. Law Inst., NYU Inst. on Fed. Taxation, Practicing Law Inst., various profl. groups. Editor Columbia Law Rev., 1949-51; contbr. articles to profl. jours. With USN, 1945-46. Fellow Am. Coll. Tax Counsel; mem. ABA (taxation sect., chmn. com. on real property tax problems 1964-66, com. on legis. drafting 1968-84), Assn. of Bar of City of N.Y. (various coms.), N.Y. State Bar Assn. (taxation sect., co-chmn. various coms. 1982-86, sec. 1987-88, 2d vice chmn. 1988-89, vice chmn. 1989-90, chmn. 1990-91), Internat. Fiscal Assn. (coun. U.S.A. br. 1984-91), Am. Law Inst. (tax adv. group fed. income tax project), Univ. Club, Phi Beta Kappa. Democrat. E-mail: afeder@herzog.com. Fax: 201-418-5293. Corporate taxation, Estate taxation, Taxation, general. Home: 25 W 81st St New York NY 10024-6023 Office: Herzog Heine Geduld Inc 525 Washington Blvd Jersey City NJ 07310-1690

**FEDER, HELENE TERRY,** lawyer. BA in English, UCLA, 1980; JD, Southwestern U., 1991; LLM, George Washington U., 1993. Bar: Calif. 1991, D.C. 1994. Legal intern U.S. Internat. Trade Commn.; legis. asst. intern Congresswoman Ileana Ros-Lehtinen. Home: 10490 Wilshire Blvd Apt 505 Los Angeles CA 90024-4657

**FEDER, ROBERT,** lawyer; b. N.Y.C., Nov. 29, 1930; s. Benjamin and Bertha (Bloodstein) F.; m. Marjorie Feder, Dec. 3, 1950; children: Susan E., Judith D., Benjamin D., Jessica R., Abigail M. BA cum laude, CCNY, 1953; LLB, Columbia U., 1953. Bar: N.Y. 1953, U.S. Tax Ct. 1956, U.S. Dist. Ct. (so. dist.) N.Y. 1973. V.p., gen. counsel Presdl. Realty Corp., White Plains, N.Y., 1953-71; ptnr. Cuddy & Feder & Worby, White Plains, 1971—; bd. dirs. Westchester County (N.Y.) Legal Aid Soc., 1972—, pres., 1974-78; adj. prof. sch. bus. Columbia U., 1988-89; bd. dirs. Presdl. Realty Corp. (Amex), Interplex Industries, Inc., Healthstar Network, Inc. Pres., White Plains Community Action Program, 1967-69; bd. dirs. White Plains Hosp. Ctr., 1978—, also sec., treas., chmn. 1992-97; commr. White Plains Housing Authority, 1984—; trustee SUNY-Purchase Coll. Found., 1988—, vice-chmn., 1995—; adj. prof. Pace U. Law Sch., 1985-87. Mem. ABA, N.Y. State Bar Assn., White Plains Bar Assn., Westchester County Bar Assn., Am. Coll. Real Estate Lawyers. Real property, Environmental, General corporate. Home: 9 Oxford Rd White Plains NY 10605-3602 Office: Cuddy & Feder & Worby 90 Maple Ave White Plains NY 10601-5105

**FEDER, SAUL E.,** lawyer; b. Bklyn., Oct. 8, 1943; s. Joseph Robert and Toby Feder; m. Marcia Carrie Weinblatt, Feb. 25, 1968; children: Howard Avram, Fayge Miriam, Tamar Miriam, Michael Elon, David Ben-Zion Aaron, Alexandra Rachel, Evan Daniel. BS, NYU, 1965; JD, Bklyn. Law Sch., 1968. Bar: N.Y. 1969, U.S. Ct. Appeals (2d cir.) 1969, U.S. Ct. Claims 1970, U.S. Customs Ct. 1972, U.S. Supreme Ct. 1972, U.S. Ct. Customs and Patent Appeals 1974. Mng. lawyer Queens Legal Services, Jamaica, N.Y., 1970-71; ptnr. Previte-Glasser-Feder & Farber, Jackson Heights, N.Y., 1972-73, Hein-Waters-Klein & Feder, Far Rockaway, N.Y., 1973-78, Regosin-Edwards-Stone & Feder, N.Y.C., 1979—; spl. investigator Bur. Election Frauds, Atty. Gen.'s Office, N.Y.C., 1976-77, spl. dep. atty. gen., 1969-70; arbitrator, consumer counsel small claims div. Civil Ct. City of N.Y., 1974—. Pres. Young Israel Briarwood, Queens, N.Y., 1978; chmn. polit. affairs com. Young Israel Staten Island, 1985—; rep. candidate State of N.Y. Assembly, Queens, 1976; chmn. Stat Pac Polit. Action Com., Young Israel Staten Island Pub. Affairs Com. Mem. N.Y. Bar Assn., Queens County Bar Assn. Nassau County Bar Assn., Am. Judges Assn., N.Y. Trial Lawyers Assn., Richmond County Bar Assn., Com. on Law and Pub. Affairs, Internat. Acad. Law & Sci., Am. Jud. Soc., Soc. Med. Jurisprudence, Am. Arbitration Assn. Republican. Contracts commercial, General practice, State civil litigation. Home: 259 Ardmore Ave Staten Island NY 10314-4349 Office: Regosin Edwards Stone & Feder 225 Broadway Rm 515 New York NY 10007-3059

**FEDER, STEVEN J.,** lawyer; b. Phila., Nov. 1, 1963; s. Stanley J. and Marcella S. Feder; m. Marla Stein, June 22, 1986; children: Sarah, Jack. BS in Edn., Temple U., 1985, JD, 1988. Bar: Pa. 1988. Corp. counsel Mediq Inc., Pennsauken, N.J., 1990-95; sr. assoc. Ballard, Spahr, Andrews & Ingersoll, Phila., 1995-98; ptnr. White & Williams, LLP, Phila., 1998—. Mem. ABA, Pa. Bar Assn., Phila. Bar Assn. Securities, Mergers and acquisitions, General corporate. Office: White & Williams LLP One Liberty Pl 1650 Market St Ste 1800 Philadelphia PA 19103-7304

**FEELEY, KELLY A.,** lawyer; b. Malden, Mass., Apr. 13, 1969; d. Thomas M. and Joan M. F. BA, U. Mass., 1991; JD, Suffolk U., 1994. Bar: Mass. 1994, U.S. Dist. Ct. Mass. 1995. Vol. atty. Office of Atty. Gen. Mass., Boston, 1995-96; atty. Law Office of Kevin F. Carney, Burlington, Mass., 1995—. Mem. Mass. Bar Assn. Democrat. Family and matrimonial, General practice, State civil litigation. Office: Law Office Kevin F Carney 44 Mall Rd Ste 206 Burlington MA 01803-4530

**FEERICK, JOHN DAVID,** dean, lawyer; b. N.Y.C., July 12, 1936; s. John D. and Mary J. F.; m. Emalie Platt, Aug. 25, 1962; children: Maureen, Margaret, Jean, Rosemary, John, William. B.S., Fordham U., 1958, LL.B., 1961; hon. degree, Coll. New Rochelle, 1991. Bar: N.Y. 1961. Assoc. Skadden, Arps, Slate, Meagher & Flom, N.Y.C., 1961-68; partner Skadden, Arps, Slate, Meagher & Flom, 1968-82; dean Fordham U. Sch. Law, 1982—. Author: From Failing Hands: The Story of Presidential Succession, 1965, The 25th Amendment, 1976; co-author: The Vice Presidents of the United States, 1967, NLRB Representation Elections-Law, Practice and Procedure, 1980; also articles; editor-in-chief Fordham Law Rev., 1960-61. Chmn. N.Y. State Commn. Govt. Integrity, 1987-90. Recipient Eugene J. Keefe award Fordham U. Law Sch., 1975, 85, spl. award Fordham U. Law Rev. Assn., 1977. Fellow Am. Bar Found.; mem. ABA (chmn. spl. com. election law and voter participation 1976-79, spl. award 1966), N.Y. State Bar Assn. (chmn. com. fed. constrn. 1979-83, exec. com. 1985-87), Assn. Bar City N.Y. (v.p. 1986-87, pres. 1992-94), Am. Arbitration Assn. (chair exec. com. 1995, chair Fund for Modern Cts. 1995—), Fordham U. Law Sch. Alumni Assn. (dir. 1972—, medal of achievement 1980); Phi Beta Kappa. *

**FEFFER, GERALD ALAN,** lawyer; b. Washington, Apr. 24, 1942; s. Louis Charles and Elsie (Glick) F.; children: Andrew, John, Keith. BA with honors, Lehigh U., 1964; JD, U. Va., 1967. Bar: N.Y. 1968, D.C. 1980. Assoc. Mudge, Rose, Guthrie & Alexander, N.Y.C., 1967-71; asst. U.S. atty. So. Dist. N.Y., 1971-76, asst. chief criminal div., 1975-76; ptnr. Kostelanetz & Ritholz, N.Y.C., 1976-79; dep. asst. atty. gen. tax div. Dept. Justice, Washington, 1979-81; ptnr. Steptoe & Johnson, Washington, 1981-86, Williams & Connolly, Washington, 1986—. Mem. editl. bd. Busniess Crimes Bulletin: Compliance and Litigation, Health Care Fraud and Abuse Newsletter; contbr. articles to profl. jours. Fellow Am. Coll. Tax Counsel, Am. Coll. Trial Lawyers; mem. ABA (criminal justice litigation and taxation sects.), Nat. Inst. on Criminal Tax Fraud (chmn.), Nat. Assn. Criminal Def. Lawyers. Criminal. Home: 3000 Garrison St NW Washington DC 20008-1032 Office: Williams & Connolly 725 12th St NW Washington DC 20005-5901

**FEFFER, JOANNA WAHL,** lawyer; b. New Hyde Park, N.Y., May 30, 1969; d. Michael and Judith Wahl; m. Nicholas W.O. Feffer. BA, Rollins Coll., 1991; JD, Hofstra U., 1994; LLM, Fordham U., 1995. Bar: N.Y. 1998, U.S. Dist. Ct. (so. dist.) N.Y. 1998. Legal asst. Parker, Duryee, Rosoff, Haft PC, N.Y.C., 1995-97; ptnr. Feffer & Feffer, LLC, N.Y.C., 1997—; sponsorship cons. HMG Worldwide, N.Y.C., 1994—. Mem. N.Y. Bar Assn., Bar Assn. City of N.Y., U.S. Equestrian Team, Am. Horse Show Assn. Avocation: horseback riding competition. Sports, Real property, State civil litigation. Office: Feffer & Feffer LLC 529 5th Ave Fl 8 New York NY 10017-4608

**FEIERSTEIN, MARK ERROL,** lawyer; b. N.Y.C., May 22, 1948; s. Lester and Rose (Feingersh) F. BA, Miami U., Oxford, Ohio, 1970; MS in Bus., L.I. U., 1975; JD, N.Y. Law Sch., 1979. Bar: N.Y. 1979, U.S. Tax Ct., 1988. Assoc. Olvaney, Eisner and Donnelly, N.Y.C., 1977-79, Oppenheim, Appel and Co., N.Y.C., 1981-82; law guardian Family Ct. of N.Y., Westchester; atty. Article 18-B Panel, Westchester; of counsel Thomas and Sykes, Yonkers, N.Y., 1985-86; adminstrv. law judge N.Y.C. Taxi and Limousine Commn., N.Y.C. Parking Violations Bur., 1984-93, N.Y.C. Environ. Control Bd., 1987-99; arbitrator Civil Ct. of N.Y.C., N.Y. Stock Exch., 1988, Nat. Assn. Securities Dealers, 1989; hearing officer N.Y.C. Transit Adjudication Bur., Bklyn., 1987-88; expert in credit card fraud Tech. Adv. Svc. for Attys., Blue Bell, Pa. Author: Emergency Guidelines to Assist Individuals and Businesses Counter Credit Card Fraud, 1992. Mem. Bronx Citizens Com., N.Y., 1986. Mem. ABA, N.Y. State Bar Assn., N.Y. Law Sch. Alumni Assn., Am. Arbitration Assn. Jewish. Avocations: movies, theater, reading.

**FEIG, EDWARD STEVEN,** lawyer; b. Bklyn., July 19, 1963; s. Seymour Ira Feig and Gloria Louise Gold; m. Ellen Beth Rosner, Oct. 1, 1988; children: Benjamin Peter, Samantha Alex. BA in Polit. Sci., SUNY, Binghamton, 1985; JD magna cum laude, N.Y. Law Sch., 1988. Bar: N.Y., U.S. Dist. Ct. (so. dist.) N.Y., U.S. Ct. Appeals (fed. cir.). Assoc. Weil Gotshal & Manges, N.Y.C., 1988-94; assoc. Baer Marks & Upham LLP, N.Y.C., 1994-97, ptnr., 1998—; Articles editor N.Y. Law Sch. Law Rev., 1986-87. Mem. ABA (sect. litigation, sect. bus. law). Avocation: musician. General civil litigation, Securities, General corporate. Office: Baer Marks & Upham 805 3rd Ave Fl 19 New York NY 10022-7598

**FEIGEN, BRENDA S.,** literary manager, lawyer, motion picture producer; b. Chgo., July 7, 1944; d. Arthur Paul Feigen and Shirley (Bierman) Feigen Kadison; children: Alexis Feigen Fasteau. BA in Math. cum laude, Vassar Coll., 1966; JD, Harvard U., 1969. Bar: Mass. 1970, N.Y. 1971. Chief analyst Boston Redevel. Authority, 1969; assoc. firm Rosenman, Colin, Kaye, Petschek, Freund & Emil, N.Y.C., 1970; pvt. practice N.Y.C., 1970—; founder, coordinating dir. Women's Action Alliance, N.Y.C., 1970-72; co-founder Ms. Mag., 1971; dir. Nat. Women's Rights project ACLU, N.Y.C., 1972-74; ptnr. firm Fasteau and Feigen, N.Y.C., 1974-80; assoc. firm Hess, Segall, Guterman, Pelz & Steiner, N.Y.C., 1980-81; atty., motion picture agt. William Morris Agy., N.Y.C., 1982-87; pres. Brenda Feigen Prodns., N.Y.C., L.A., 1987-97; ptnr. Baxter/Feigen Prodns., 1919-92, Berton & Feigen, Beverly Hills, 1992-94; of counsel Berton & Donaldson, Beverly Hills, 1994-96; pres. Feigen/Parrent Lit. Mgmt., Bel Air, Calif., 1995—; co-pres. Reel Life Women Prodn. Co., Bel Air, 1996—; adj. instr. law Coll. New Rochelle, 1976; prof. UCLA Ext., 1990; guest spkr., panelist numerous confs., seminars; panelist Harvard Law Sch. seminar, 1999, Yale Law Sch. seminar, 1999, Calif. Lawyers for Arts, 1999; co-chair Practicing Law Inst. Seminars on Entertainment Law, 1987, 88, Harvard Law and Harvard Bus. Schs. Entertainement Law Conf., 1999, Vassar Coll. Symposium on Entertainment Industry, 1998; practicing Law Inst., 1987, 88; bd. dirs. Calif. Lawyers for the Arts, 1996—; panelist AFI/Cinetex Conf., 1990, SAG Women's Conf., 1990, Show Coalition, L.A., 1990-92; emerita mem. bd. dirs. Women's Action Alliance. Film prodr. Orion Pictures (film) NAVY SEALS, 1990; contbr. chpt. to book and articles to mags. Mem. adv. bd. Working Women United, nat. adv. bd. Take Our Daus. to Work, 1993—; bd. dirs. Film Forum, 1986-90, Calif. Lawyers for the Arts, 1996—; mem. Pen Ctr. USA West, 1996—, Authors' Guild, 1996—, Harvard Com. Entertainment, Sports and Cyberspace Law, 1997—; candidate for N.Y. State Senate, 1978. Hon. Pres.'s fellow Columbia U., 1977, 78; participant Exec. Seminar, Aspen Inst., 1979. Mem. NOW (nat. legis. v.p., bd. dirs. 1970-71), Show Coalition (bd. govs. 1990-92), N.Y. Women in Film (bd. dirs. 1985-86), Women's Action Alliance (co-founder, dir.), Nat. Women's Polit. Caucus (co-founder, nat. adv. com.). Democrat. Entertainment, Intellectual property, Civil rights. Office: 10158 Hollow Glen Cir Los Angeles CA 90077-2112

**FEIGENBAUM, BARRY S.,** lawyer; b. Hartford, Conn., Oct. 1, 1957; s. Harold H. and Lucille Blum F.; m. Lisa Kalb, May 19, 1985; children: Melanie, David. BBA in Acctg., George Washington U., 1978; JD, U. Conn., 1981. Bar: Conn. 1981, U.S. Dist. Ct. Conn. 1981, U.S. Supreme Ct. 1984, U.S. Ct. Appeals (1st and 2d cirs.), U.S. Tax Ct., U.S. Claims Ct. Assoc. Byrne, Shechtman & Slater, Hartford, Conn., 1981-84, Silverstone & Koontz, Hartford, Conn., 1985; assoc. gen. counsel Coleco Industries, Inc., West Hartford, Conn., 1986-89; ptnr. Rogin, Nassau, Caplan, Lassman & Hirtle, Hartford, 1989—. Mem. Am. Bankruptcy Inst., Conn. Bar Assn. Contracts commercial, Bankruptcy, General corporate. Office: Rogin Nassau Caplan Lassman & Hirtle 185 Asylum St Hartford CT 06103-3408

**FEIGENBAUM, EDWARD D.,** legal editor, publisher, consultant; b. Rochester, N.Y., Mar. 16, 1958; s. Samuel and Norma Feigenbaum; m. Ann Elizabeth Andrews, Aug. 6, 1983; children: Edward Andrews, Breanna Layne. BA with honors, Ind. U., 1978, MBA, JD, 1982. Bar: Ind. 1983, U.S. Dist. Ct. (no. and so. dists.) Ind. 1983. Sr. staff assoc. Inst. for Rsch. in Pub. Safety, Bloomington, Ind., 1977-83; dir. legal affairs Coun. State Govts., Lexington, Ky., 1983-87; legal counsel, dir. mktg. Hudson Inst., Indpls., 1987-89; editor, pub. Ind. Legislative Insight, Indpls., 1989—, Ind. Gaming Insight, Indpls., 1993—, Ind. Edn. Insight, Indpls., 1997—; researcher D.T. Skelton Svc. Assocs. Inc., Bloomington, 1983-88. Contbr. numerous articles to profl. jours. Chmn. City of Bloomington Environ. Quality & Conservation Commn., 1982, mem. Redistricting Com., 1982-83, City of Noblesville (Ind.) Planning Commn., 1989-96; co-chair election subcom. of urban, state and local govt. law govt. ops. com. 1994-96. Mem. ABA (vice chmn. com. election law adminstrv. law sect. 1984-90), Coun. on Govtl. Ethics Laws (steering com. 1987-90), Am. Polit. Sci. Assn., Midwest Polit. Sci. Assn., Ind. State Bar Assn. (chair govtl. practice sect. 1991-92), Columbia Club. Avocation: collecting polit. memorabilia. Home: 5537 Salem Dr N Carmel IN 46033-8582 Office: INGroup PO Box 383 Noblesville IN 46061-0383

**FEIGENBAUM, LARRY SETH,** lawyer; b. Long Branch, N.J., Oct. 2, 1956; s. Harvey and Gloria F.; m. Lori Pam Fischer; children: Amanda Beth, Corey Michael. BS in Environ. Planning & Design, Rutgers U., 1980; JD, NYU, 1987. Bar: N.J. 1987, U.S. Dist. Ct. N.J. 1987, N.Y. 1988, D.C. 1989. Assoc. Bathgate, Wegener, Wouters & Neumann, Newark, 1987-89; gen. atty. Hoffmann-LaRoche Inc., Nutley, N.J., 1989-92; sr. atty. Hoffmann-LaRoche Inc., Nutley, 1992-95, sr. counsel, 1996—. Trustee Downtown West Orange (N.J.) Alliance, 1998-99. Mem. N.J. State Bar Assn., N.Y. State Bar Assn. Avocations: softball, cycling, hiking, swimming. Construction, Environmental, Land use and zoning (including planning). Home: 14 Shelley Ter West Orange NJ 07052-1833 Office: Hoffmann-LaRoche Inc 340 Kingsland St Nutley NJ 07110-1199

**FEIGHNY, MICHAEL LOUIS,** lawyer; b. Mpls., Mar. 20, 1943; s. Louis S. and Bride (Gaetz) F.; m. Hie Jean Kim, Mar. 25, 1983; children: Eileen Kimberly, Seita Kathleen, Edward Jackson. BA in History, Tex. A&M U., 1965; JD, U. Tex., 1968; LLM, George Washington U., 1982. Bar: Calif. 1973, Ct. Mil. Appeals 1974, U.S. Supreme Ct. 1988. Commd. 2d lt. U.S.

Army, 1968, advanced through grades to lt. col., 1985; chief counsel U.S. Army Korea Contracting Agy., Seoul, 1987-89; ret. U.S. Army Korea Contracting Agy., 1989; contract law atty. U.S. Army Korea Contracting Agy., Seoul, 1989-91; dist. counsel Far East Dist. U.S. Army C.E., Seoul, 1991-95; divsn. counsel Pacific Ocean divsn. U.S. Army C.E., Honolulu, 1995—. Decorated Legion of Merit, Bronze Star medal. Mem. VFW, Assn. U.S. Army, Ex-Students Assn. U. Tex., Assn. Former Students Tex. A&M. Avocations: philately, numismatics. Government contracts and claims, Military, Public international. Home: 46-323 Kumoo Loop Kaneohe HI 96744-3532 Office: US Army CE Pacific Ocean Divsn Bldg 230 Fort Shafter HI 96858-0001

**FEIJOO, JOHN,** lawyer; b. Bklyn., Nov. 30, 1966; s. Juan and Eladia (Garcia) F.; m. Stephanie Roters, June 4, 1994. BA, NYU, 1988; JD, Bklyn. Law Sch., 1991. Bar: Conn. 1992, N.Y. 1993, U.S. Dist. Ct. (ea. and so. dists.) N.Y. 1994. Intern Dist. Atty. King's City, Bklyn., 1990; atty. Previte Farber & Rosen PC, Rego Pk., N.Y., 1990—. Avocations: golf, travel. Family and matrimonial, Contracts commercial, Personal injury. Office: Previte Farber & Rosen PC 97-77 Queens Blvd Rego Park NY 11374

**FEIKENS, JOHN,** federal judge; b. Clifton, N.J., Dec. 3, 1917; s. Sipke and Corine (Wisse) F.; m. Henriette Dorothy Schulthouse, Nov. 4, 1939; children: Jon, Susan Corine, Barbara Edith, Julie Anne, Robert H. A.B., Calvin Coll., Grand Rapids, Mich., 1938; J.D., U. Mich., 1941; LL.D., U. Detroit, 1979, Detroit Coll. Law, 1981. Bar: Mich. 1942. Gen. practice law Detroit; dist. judge Ea. Dist. Mich., Detroit, 1960-61, 70-79, chief judge, 1979-86, sr. judge, 1986—; past co-chmn. Mich. Civil Rights Commn.; past chmn. Rep. State Central Com.; past mem. Rep. Nat. Com.; mem. com. visitors U. Mich. Law Sch. Past bd. trustees Calvin Coll. Fellow Am. Coll. Trial Lawyers; mem. ABA, Detroit Bar Assn. (dir. 1962, past pres.), State Bar Mich. (commr. 1965-71), U. Mich. Club (com. visitors). Office: US Dist Ct 851 Theodore Levin US Ct 231 W Lafayette Blvd Detroit MI 48226-2700

**FEIL, FRANK J., JR.,** lawyer; b. Racine, Wis., Sept. 17, 1926; s. Frank J. and Catherine (Kropp) F.; m. Ada Hanley, Aug. 2, 1958 (dec. 1963); children: Elizabeth, Marilyn; m. Joan Marie Brenner, July 22, 1989; 1 child, Rachel. BA, U. Wis., Madison, 1950; JD, U. Wis., 1952. Asst. dist. atty. Racine (Wis.) County, 1954-58; pvt. practice Racine. With USN, 1944-46, PTO. General practice, Probate, Personal injury. Office: 610 S Main St Racine WI 53403-1258

**FEILER, MICHAEL BENJAMIN,** lawyer; b. Miami, Fla., Nov. 23, 1964; s. Barton C. and Linda Q. (Goldman) F.; m. Anna Marie Prozzillo, Mar. 30, 1990. BS in Polit. Sci., Fla. State U., 1987; JD with honors, U. Fla., 1992. Bar: Fla. 1996, U.S. Dist. Ct. Fla. 1997, U.S. Ct. Appeals (11th cir.) 1997. Atty. High, Stack, Lazenby, Palahach, Platt & Feiler, Coral Gables, Fla., 1993—; dir. Eric Stack Meml. Found., Melbourne, Fla., 1996—. Best Buddies citizen Best Buddies Internat., Miami, 1993—, celebration of friendship com., 1997. Mem. ABA, Assn. Trial Lawyers Am., Acad. Fla. Trial Lawyers, Dade County Trial Lawyers Assn., Dade County Bar Assn., Coral Gables Bar Assn. Jewish. Avocation: golf. General civil litigation, Professional liability, Civil rights. Office: High Stack Lazenby Platt & Feiler 3929 Ponce De Leon Blvd Coral Gables FL 33134-7323

**FEIN, ROGER GARY,** lawyer; b. St. Louis, Mar. 12, 1940; s. Albert and Fanny (Levinson) F.; m. Susanne M. Cohen, Dec. 18, 1965; children: David I., Lisa J. Student, Washington U., St. Louis, 1959, NYU, 1960; BS, UCLA, 1962; JD, Northwestern U., 1965; MBA, Am. U., 1967. Bar: Ill. 1965, U.S. Dist. Ct. (no. dist.) Ill. 1968, U.S. Ct. Appeals (7th cir.) 1968, U.S. Supreme Ct. 1970. Atty. divsn. corp. fin. SEC, Washington, 1965-67; ptnr. Arvey, Hodes, Costello & Burman, Chgo., 1967-91, Wildman, Harrold, Allen and Dixon, Chgo., 1992—; co-chair Corp., Securities and Tax Practice Group; mem. Securities Adv. Com. to Sec. State Ill., 1973—, chmn., 1973-79, 87-93, vice-chmn., 1983-87, chmn. emeritus, 1994—; spl. asst. atty. gen. State of Ill., 1974-83, 85—; spl. asst. state's atty. Cook County, Ill., 1989-90; mem. Appeal Bd., Ill. Law Enforcement Commn., 1980-83; mem. lawyer's adv. bc. So. Ill. Law Jour., 1980-83; mem. adv. bd. securities regulation and law report Bur. Nat. Affairs Inc., 1985—; lectr., author on land trust financing, consumer credit and securities law. Mem. Bd. Edn., Sch. Dist. No. 29, Northfield, Ill., 1977-83, pres., 1981-83; mem. Pub. Vehicle Ops. Citizens Adv. coun. City Chgo., 1985-86; mem. Chgo. regional bd. Anti-Defamation League of B'nai B'rith, 1975-91, vice chmn., 1980-88, mem. exec. com. Greater Chgo./Upper Midwest Region, 1996—; chmn. lawyers' com. for ann. telethon Muscular Dystrophy Assn., 1983; past bd. dirs. Jewish Nat. Fund, Am. Friends Hebrew U., Northfield Comty. Fund. Recipient Sec. State Ill. Pub. Svc. award, 1976, Citation of Merit, WAIT Radio, 1976, Sunset Ridge Sch. Comty. Svc. award, 1984, City of Chgo. Citizen's award, 1986; named one of Leading Ill. Attys., 1997. Fellow Am. Bar Found., Ill. Bar Found. (bd. dirs. 1978-88, v.p. 1982-84, pres. 1984-86, chmn. Fellows 1983-84, chmn., past pres. adv. com. 1988-90, Cert. of Appreciation 1985, 86, Stalwart fellow 1997), Chgo. Bar Found; mem. ABA (state regulation of securities com. 1982—, Ill. liaison of com., ho. of dels. 1981-85, chmn. subcom. liaison with securities adminstrs. and NASD 1998—), Ill. State Bar Assn. (bd. govs. 1976-80, del. assembly 1976-88, sec. 1977-78, cert. of appreciation 1980, 88, chmn. Bench and Bar com. 1982-83, chmn. Bench and Bar sect. coun., 1983-84, chmn. bar elections supervision com. 1986-87, chmn. assembly com. on hearings 1987-88, mem. com. on jud. appointments 1987-90), Chgo. Bar Assn. (mem. task force delivery legal svcs. 1978-80, cert. of appreciation 1976, chmn. land trusts com. 1978-79, chmn. consumer credit com. 1977-78, chmn. state securities law subcom. 1977-79), Decalogue Soc. Lawyers, Northwestern U. Sch. of Law Alumni Assn. (dir.), Standard Club, Legal Club Chgo., Tau Epsilon Phi, Alpha Kappa Psi, Phi Delta Phi. General corporate, Mergers and acquisitions, Securities. Office: Wildman Harrold Allen & Dixon 225 W Wacker Dr Ste 3000 Chicago IL 60606-1224

**FEINBERG, CHERYL LACKMAN,** lawyer, mediator; b. Long Beach, Calif., May 29, 1957; d. Lawrence H. and Etta D. Lackman; children: Craig, Adriana. BA, UCLA, 1980; JD, Western State U., Fullerton, Calif., 1985. Bar: Calif. 1986, U.S. Dist. Ct. (ctrl. dist.) Calif. 1987, U.S. Ct. Appeals (9th cir.) 1987; cert. tchr., Calif. Atty. Law Offices of Lawrence H. Lackman, Long Beach, 1986—; mediator L.A. Superior Ct., Norwalk, Calif., 1996—, The Mediation Ctr., Costa Mesa, Calif., 1994—; instr. legal aspects of real estate Long Beach City Coll., 1989—; arbitrator Long Beach Bar Assn., 1990—. Cmty. atty. advisor The Jr. League of Long Beach, 1991-95; mem. exec. task force, fund raising com. Legal Aid Found. Long Beach, 1990-97; legal vol. Stand Down 1997, 98, Long Beach. Mem. Long Beach Bar Assn. (bd. govs. 1991-92, 96-97, sec./treas. 1998, v.p. 1999, Women Lawyers of Long Beach (pres. 1989-90), Calif. Women Lawyers (bd. govs. 1990-91), So. Calif. Mediation Assn. (chair Mediation Week 1997). Office: Law Offices Lawrence H Lackman 3740 Long Beach Blvd Long Beach CA 90807-3310

**FEINBERG, DYANNE ELYCE,** lawyer; b. Bklyn., Dec. 4, 1959; d. Arthur Irving and Bernice Bauer Feinberg; m. Timothy D. Henkel, May 2, 1992. BA with high honors, U. Fla., 1980, JD with honors, 1983. Bar: Fla. 1983, U.S. Dist. Ct. (so. dist.) Fla. 1985, U.S. Ct. Appeals (11th cir.) 1987. Law clk. to Hon. Wilkie D. Ferguson Jr. Third Dist. Ct. Appeals Fla., Miami, 1983-85; ptnr. Gilbride Heller & Brown, P.A., Miami, 1985—. Mem. ABA, Dade County Bar Assn., Fla. Assn. Women Lawyers (treas. 1997-98), Dade Bus. and Profl. Women's Club (pres. 1994-95), Kiwanis of Miami (pres. 1997-98). General civil litigation, Contracts commercial, Securities. Office: Gilbride Heller & Brown 1 Biscayne Tower Ste 1570 Miami FL 33131-1816

**FEINBERG, GREGG MICHAEL,** lawyer; b. Allentown, Pa., June 7, 1958; s. Alan Morton Feinberg and Elaine Joyce (Saslow) Snyder; m. Cynthia Ann McDonnell, Sept. 24, 1983; children: Brendan Nathaniel, Casey Lynn. BA, U. Pitts., 1980, JD, 1983. Bar: Pa. 1983, U.S. Dist. Ct. (ea. dist.) Pa. 1983, U.S. Tax Ct. 1986. V.p., gen. counsel Rothrock Motor Sales, Inc., Allentown, 1983-87; pvt. practice Allentown, 1987-88; ptnr. Black, McCarthy, Eidelman & Feinberg, Allentown, 1988-92; sole practice Allentown, 1992—; lectr. in field. Mem. Northeast Tier Venture Capital Group, 1987—. Mem. ABA, Am. Trial Lawyers Assn., Pa. Bar Assn., Pa. Creditor's Bar Assn. (founder), Lehigh County Bar Assn. (Legal Eagle award 1988), Ea. Dist. Bankruptcy Conf., Comml. Law League Am. (vice chmn. Fair Debt Collection Practice Act Com.), Nat. Assn. Retail Collection Attys. Avocations: golf, flying, paddle tennis, skiing. Consumer commercial, General corporate, General practice. Office: Ste 301 1390 Ridgeview Dr Allentown PA 18104-9065

**FEINBERG, JACK,** lawyer; b. Atlantic City, Mar. 24, 1949; s. Jules and Sara Rae (Schleimer) F.; m. Judy I. Levine, July 27, 1972; children—Jason B., Jamie L. B.A., Syracuse U., 1971; J.D., U. Akron, 1974. Bar: N.J. 1974, U.S. Dist. Ct. N.J. 1974, U.S. Supreme Ct. 1986. Ptnr. firm Goldenberg, Mackler & Feinberg, Atlantic City, 1974-81, Mairone, Biel, Zlotnick, & Feinberg, Atlantic City, 1982—; sole practice, Ventnor, N.J., 1981-82. Contbr. articles to profl. jours. County com. mem. Atlantic County Democrats, 1979; bd. dirs. Atlantic Cape March of Dimes; mem., legal counsel to bd. dirs. Maine Mammal Study Ctr. Named Boss of Yr., Atlantic County Legal Secs., 1980. Mem. ABA, Atlantic County Bar Assn., Assn. Trial Lawyers Am., N.J. Trial Lawyers Assn., Nat. Health Lawyers Assn., Greater Atlantic City Jaycees (legal counsel 1975-76, pres. 1976-77). Democrat. Jewish. Personal injury, Professional liability, Banking. Office: Mairone Biel Zlotnick Feinberg & Griffith 3201 Atlantic Ave Atlantic City NJ 08401-6216

**FEINBERG, JACK E.,** lawyer; b. Phila., Dec. 9, 1929; s. Joseph and Mary C. F.; m. Phyllis B., Oct. 28, 1958; children: Arthur C., Donald J. AB, Temple U., 1952, LLB, JD, 1957. Bar: Pa., U.S. Dist. Ct. (ea. and mid. dists.) Pa., U.S. Ct. Appeals (3rd cir.), U.S. Supreme Ct. Atty. Feinberg & Silva, Phila., 1957—. Contbr. articles to profl. jours. Capt. U.S. Army, 1952-54. Mem. Lawyer's Club. Personal injury, Professional liability, Product liability. Office: Feinberg & Silva 2000 Market St Ste 1805 Philadelphia PA 19103-3293

**FEINBERG, ROBERT I(RA),** lawyer; b. Boston, Jan. 6, 1956; s. Philip I. and Evelyn Helene (Hurvitz) F.; m. Lisa Michelle Palmer, Aug. 18, 1991; children: Perry, Justin. BA magna cum laude, Brown U., 1978; JD, U. Pa., 1981. Bar: Mass. 1982, Fla. 1985. Assoc. Parker, Coulter, Daley & White, Boston, 1981-83; ptnr. Feinberg and Alban, P.C., Brookline and Boston, Mass., 1984—; v.p. MVP Assocs., Brookline, 1980-87. Author: Jewish Voting Patterns in America, 1978. Active Anti-Defamation League, Boston, 1987—. Mem. Mass. Acad. Trial Attys. (lectr., mem. bd. govs. 1991—), Mass. Bar Assn., Boston Bar Assn., Nat. Polit. Action Com. (Washington). Jewish. Avocations: baseball, politics. Personal injury, General civil litigation, Insurance. Home: 1650 Commonwealth Ave West Newton MA 02465-2821 Office: Feinberg & Alban PC 141 Tremont St Boston MA 02111-1209

**FEINBERG, ROBERT JULIAN,** judge; b. Plattsburgh, N.Y., Feb. 13, 1924; s. Benjamin Franklin and Leah (Mendelsohn) F.; m. Laurie Covert, Mar. 22, 1974. BA, Yale U., 1945, JD, 1947. Bar: N.Y. 1948; cert. circuit ct. civil mediator 1994, Fla. Assoc. Costello, Cooney & Fearon, Syracuse, N.Y., 1947-50; mem. Feinberg, Jerry & Lewis, Plattsburgh, 1950-60; sole practice Plattsburgh, 1961-67; mem. Jerry, Lewis, Feinberg & Lyon, Plattsburgh, 1967-70; judge Clinton County (N.Y.) Ct. and Family Ct., Plattsburgh, 1970-88; civil mediator Circuit Ct. Fla., Delray Beach, 1994—; asst. atty. gen. N.Y. State, 1948; mem. N.Y. State Assembly, 1957-64. Mng. editor Yale Law Jour., 1946-47. Mem. N.Y. State Bar Assn., Clinton County Bar Assn. (past pres.), Am. Judges Assn., Rotary (past pres.) Elks (past dist. dep., grand exalted ruler), Masons (32 deg.), Shriners, Moose, B'nai B'rith (past pres.), Yale Club N.Y.C., Grad. Club (New Haven, Conn.), Delray Beach. (Fla.) Club. Republican. Jewish. Address: PO Box 827 Plattsburgh NY 12901-0827 Also: PO Box 1220 Delray Beach FL 33447-1220

**FEINBERG, WILFRED,** federal judge; b. N.Y.C., June 22, 1920; s. Jac and Eva (Wolin) F.; m. Shirley Marcus, June 23, 1946; children: Susan Stelk, Jack Feinberg, Jessica Twedt. BA, Columbia U., 1940, LLB, 1946, LLD (hon.), 1985; LLD (hon.), Syracuse U., 1985, Bklyn. Law Sch., 1998. Bar: N.Y. 1947. Law clk. Hon. James P. McGranery U.S. Dist. Ct. (ea. dist.) Pa., 1947-49; assoc. Kaye, Scholer, Fierman & Hays, N.Y.C., 1949-53; ptnr. McGoldrick, Dannett, Horowitz & Golub, N.Y.C., 1953-61; dep. supt. N.Y. State Banking Dept., N.Y.C., 1958; judge U.S. Dist Ct. (so. dist.), N.Y.C., N.Y., 1961-66; judge U.S. Ct. Appeals (2nd cir.), N.Y.C., N.Y., 1966—, chief judge, 1980-88, sr. judge, 1991—; mem. U.S. Jud. Conf. U.S., 1980-88, chmn. exec. com., 1987-88, mem. Devitt award com., 1989, 90, mem. long-range planning com., 1991-96; Madison lectr. NYU Law Sch., 1983; Sonnett lectr. Fordham U. Law Sch., 1984; Inaugural Howard Kaplan Meml. lectr. Hofstra U. Law Sch., 1986; The Future of Justice lectr. Inst. of Comparative Law, Chuo U., Japan, 1991. Editor-in-chief Columbia Law Rev, 1946; contbr. to profl. jours. and mags. With AUS, 1942-45. Recipient Learned Hand medal for excellence in fed. jurisprudence, 1982, Gold medal, award for disting. svc. in the law N.Y. State Bar Assn., 1990, medal for excellence Columbia Law Alumni Assn., 1990, Pursuit of Justice award Internat. Assn. Jewish Lawyers and Jurists, 1993, Disting. Pub. Svc. award N.Y. County Lawyers Assn., 1994, Edward Weinfeld award N.Y. County Lawyers Assn., 1995; Ann. Wilfred Feinberg Prize named in his honor for best student work at Columbia Law Sch. related to fed. cts., 1998. Mem. ABA, Assn. of Bar of City of N.Y., N.Y. County Lawyers Assn., Am. Judicature Soc., Am. Law Inst., Phi Beta Kappa. Office: US Ct Appeals 2nd Cir Room 2004 US Court House Foley Sq New York NY 10007-1501

**FEINMARK, PHYLLIS S. KAPLAN,** lawyer; b. Washington, Jan. 31, 1954. BA, Johns Hopkins U., 1975; JD, George Washington U., 1978. Bar: Md. 1978, D.C. 1991, U.S. Dist. Ct. Md. 1979, U.S. Ct. Appeals (4th cir.) 1979. Atty. advisor USDA, Washington, 1978-80; environ. cons. Royal Swedish Acad. Sci., Swedish Dept. Agr., Stockholm, 1980-83; asst. dist. counsel U.S. Army C.E., N.Y.C., 1985-90; sr. asst. regional counsel EPA, N.Y.C., 1990—; lectr. on environ. law. Office: US EPA 290 Broadway New York NY 10007-1823

**FEINSMITH, PAUL LOWELL,** lawyer; b. N.Y.C., July 30, 1941; s. Sydney William and Esther (Gell) F.; m. Sherry Raphael, May 28, 1967 (div. 1972); children—Jeremiah R., Deborah Gardner; m. Alicia Goldstein, Nov. 18, 1979; 1 child, Sylvie G. B.A., U. Pa., 1962; J.D., NYU Sch. Law, 1965. Bar: N.J., 1965, Ill., 1969, Fla., 1981. Assoc. Platoff, Heftler, Harker & Nashel, Esqs, Union City, N.J., 1965-69; v.p., gen. counsel Elgin & Waltham Watch Cos., Chgo., 1969-79, N.Y.C., 1972-76, Miami, Fla., 1979-82; ptnr. Hoffman, Larin & Feinsmith, North Miami Beach, Fla., 1982-88; sole practice, Ft. Lauderdale, Hollywood and Miami Beach, Fla., 1990—. Pres. Nat. Kidney Found. Fla., 1981-85; mem. exec. com. Renal Network, 1982—; pres. NAPHT, 1984-86; co-founder, former chmn. Nat. Renal Coalition, Fla. Renal Coalition; mem. Broward County Dem. Exec. Com., Fla., 1994—. Mem. ABA, Chgo. Bar Assn., Fla. Bar Assn. Democrat. Jewish. Club: New York University (N.Y.C.). Lodge: B'nai B'rith. Real property, Landlord-tenant, General corporate. Home: 1730 N 55th Ave Hollywood FL 33021-3934 Office: 1111 Lincoln Rd Miami FL 33139-2452

**FEINSTEIN, FRED IRA,** lawyer; b. Chgo., Apr. 6, 1945; s. Bernard and Beatrice (Mines) F.; m. Judy Cutler, Aug. 25, 1968; children: Karen, Donald. BSC, DePaul U., 1967, JD, 1970. Bar: Ill. 1970, U.S. Supreme Ct. 1977. Ptnr. McDermott, Will & Emery, Chgo., 1976—; lectr. in field. Pres., Skokie/Evanston (Ill.) Action Council, 1981-84; bd. dirs. Temple Judea Mizpah, Skokie, 1982-84, Deborah Goldfine Meml. Cancer Research, 1968—, YMCA of Chgo., 1985—. Mem. Ill. Bar Assn., Am. Coll. Real Estate Lawyers, Union League, Blue Key, Beta Gamma Sigma, Beta Alpha Psi, Pi Gamma Mu, Lambda Alpha. Contbr. articles to profl. jours. Real property, Bankruptcy, Environmental. Office: McDermott Will & Emery 227 W Monroe St Ste 3100 Chicago IL 60606-5096

**FEINSTEIN, MILES ROGER,** lawyer; b. Camden, N.J., June 25, 1941; s. Louis Emory and Sylvia K. (Jacobs) F.; m. Lydia Ann Sopoliga, Sept. 12, 1976; children: Bari, Matthew, Elizabeth. BA, Rutgers U., 1963; JD, Duke U., 1966. Bar: N.J. 1966, U.S. Dist. Ct. N.J. 1966, U.S. Ct. Appeals (3d cir.) 1967, U.S. Ct. Appeals (2d cir.) 1971. Pvt. practice Clifton, N.J., 1967—; mem. Passaic Criminal Justice commn.; mem. com. on drugs and cts.; mem. speedy trial com. N.J. Supreme Ct.; expert commentator Nat. Courtroom TV; lectr. in field. Author: Historical Development of Pineys of Southern New Jersey. Trustee Passaic County Heart Fund, 1970-93, Passaic County Cancer Soc.; chmn. Passaic County March of Dimes, 1989. Named Man of Yr., Passaic County Heart Fund, 1976, Passaic County Cancer Soc., 1978, Passaic County coun. Boy Scouts Am., 1978, Passaic County Bad Guys Charitable Orgn., 1974; recipient award Passaic Civic Orgn., Humanitarian award Unico, 1976, Nationwide Bail Bonds award Policeman's Benevolent Assn., Disting. Svc. award, 1980, 84, 85, History prize Soc. Colonial Wars; subject of numerous legal articles. Mem. ABA, Assn. Trial Lawyers Am., Nat. Assn. Criminal Def. Lawyers, Fed. Bar Assn., N.J. Bar Assn., N.J. Assn. Criminal Def. Lawyers (former trustee, treas., v.p., pres. 1990-91), N.J. Assn. of Trial Lawyers (bd. govs. 1992-93), Passaic County Bar Assn. (chmn. criminal law com. 1990-93), Phi Beta Kappa, Phi Delta Phi, Phi Alpha Theta (Henry Rutgers scholar). Avocations: sports, theatre, collecting stamps. Criminal. Office: 1135 Clifton Ave Clifton NJ 07013-3642

**FEINSTEIN, NATHAN B.,** lawyer; b. Phila., Nov. 13, 1929; s. Oscar and Donia (Weiner) F.; m. Joanne S. Polk, Jan. 5, 1959; children: Elliot Abraham, Michael Joel. BA in Polit. Sci., Pa. State U., 1951; LLB, Yale U., 1954. Bar: Pa. 1955, Md. 1988, D.C. 1988, U.S. Ct. Appeals (3d and 4th cirs.), U.S. Supreme Ct. 1981. Law clk. to Hon. T. McKean Chidsey Pa. Supreme Ct., Phila., 1956-57; assoc., ptnr. Cohen, Shapiro, Polisher, Sheikman and Cohen, Phila., 1957-83; ptnr. Dilworth, Paxson, Kalish and Kauffman, Phila., 1984-87, Piper & Marbury LLP, Washington, 1987—. With U.S. Army, 1956-57. Fellow Am. Coll. of Bankruptcy; mem. ABA (chair bus. bankruptcy com. 1989-93, chair joint com. on bankruptcy ct. structure 1993-97), Pa. Bar Assn. (chair com. on legal ethics and profl. responsibility 1983-84), Md. Bar Assn., D.C. Bar Assn., Phila. Bar Assn. (chair profl. guidance com. 1980-81). Democrat. Jewish. Bankruptcy, Contracts commercial. Office: Piper & Marbury LLP 1200 19th St NW Fl 7 Washington DC 20036-2430

**FEINSTEIN, STEPHEN MICHAEL,** lawyer; b. Stamford, Conn., Jan. 19, 1959; s. Norton Perry and Phyllis Marilyn (Fabel) F.; m. Bonnie Helene Litsky, Aug. 27, 1989; children: Shayna Justine, Maxwell Benjamin, Sydney Ilana. BA, U. Conn., 1981; JD, Quninnipiac Coll., 1984. Bar: Conn. 1984, U.S. Dist. Ct. Conn. 1985. Assoc. Feinstein & Hermann, Norwalk, Conn., 1984-91; ptnr. Feinstein & Hermann, P.C., Norwalk, Conn., 1991—; instr. Conn. Inst. Paralegal Studies, Stamford, 1994—; bd. dirs. Conn. State Law Libr. Adv. Com., Hartford, Conn., 1993—. Chmn. adult adv. bd. B'nai B'rith Youth Orgn., New Haven, 1994-96. Mem. Assn. Trial Lawyers Am., Conn. Bar Assn., Conn. Trial Lawyers Assn., Friends of Stamford Law Libr. (pres. 1992-94, v.p. 1994). Republican. Jewish. General practice, General civil litigation, Criminal. Home: 21 Ludlow Mnr Norwalk CT 06855-2010 Office: Feinstein and Hermann PC 5 Myrtle St Norwalk CT 06855-1315

**FEIT, DAVID JONATHAN,** lawyer; b. Bklyn., May 22, 1963; s. Dov and Anna F. BA magna cum laude, U. Pa., 1985; JD, UCLA, 1988. Bar: N.J. 1988, U.S. Dist. Ct. N.J. 1988, N.Y. 1989. Assoc. Warshaw Burstein Cohen et al, N.Y.C., 1988-92, David S. Kriss Law Office, N.Y.C., 1992-94; ptnr. Kriss & Feit, N.Y.C., 1994—. Mem. Young Mortgage Brokers Assn. Democrat. Jewish. Real property, Finance, Contracts commercial. Home: 19 E 80th St Apt 2C New York NY 10021-0109 Office: Kriss & Feit 360 Lexington Ave New York NY 10017-6502

**FEIT, GLENN M.,** lawyer; b. Elizabeth, N.J., Oct. 16, 1929; s. Charles Theodore and Beatrice (Esther) F.; m. Rona F. Gottlieb, June 14, 1953 (div. 1974); children: Glenn M., John Paul, Adam Gibbs (dec.); m. Barberi Platt Paull. BS in Econ., U. Pa., 1951; JD magna cum laude, Harvard U., 1957. Bar: N.Y. 1958, U.S. Dist. Ct. (2d dist.) 1959). Assoc. Cravath, Swaine & Moore, N.Y.C., 1957-64; ptnr. London, Buttenwieser & Chalif, N.Y.C., 1965-70, Feit & Ahrens, N.Y.C., 1970-88, Feit & Shor, N.Y.C., 1988-89, Proskauer Rose LLP, N.Y.C., 1989—; bd. dirs. C&D Techs., Inc., Blue Bell, Pa., Blair Industries, Inc., Scott City, Mo.; sec. Charterhouse Group Internat., Inc., N.Y.C. Mem. editl. bd. Harvard Law Rev., 1955-57. Bd. dirs. Friends of the IDF, N.Y.C. Lt. USN, 1951-54. Mem. ABA, Assn. Bar City N.Y., Aircraft Owners and Pilots Assn., Exptl. Aircraft Assn., Tailhook Assn., Harvard Club, Seaplane Pilots Assn. General corporate, Mergers and acquisitions, Securities. Office: Proskauer Rose LLP 1585 Broadway New York NY 10036-8200

**FEKETE, GEORGE OTTO,** judge, lawyer, pharmacist; b. Budapest, Hungary; s. Bela and Ilona (Meer) F.; m. Amy Zheng; children: Jacqueline Kim, Jeanette Lee. BS in Psychology, Wayne State U.; PhD, U. So. Calif.; postgrad. in psychology, Calif. State U., Long Beach; JD, Pepperdine U., 1973. Bar: Calif. 1973, U.S. Dist. Ct. (so. dist.) Calif. 1973, U.S. Supreme Ct. 1980, U.S. Dist Ct. (no. dist.) Calif. 1986. Chief pharmacist Hylo Drug Co., Huntington Beach, Calif., 1970; pres. G.O. Fekete Law Corp., Anaheim, Calif., 1973-86; lead trial lawyer Melvin Belli Law Offices, San Francisco, 1986-88; ind. trial specialist, superior ct. apptd. arbitrator San Francisco and Bay Area, 1988—; judge pro tem. Served to maj. USAF, 1954-59. Mem. ABA, Assn. Trial Lawyers Am., Calif. Trial Lawyers Assn. (legis. com. 1976-78), Orange County Trial Lawyers Assn (bd. dirs. 1977). Personal injury, Insurance, State civil litigation.

**FELD, ALAN DAVID,** lawyer; b. Dallas, Nov. 13, 1936; s. Henry R. and Rose (Scissors) F.; m. Anne Sanger, June 1, 1957; children: Alan David, Elizabeth S., John L. B.A., So. Methodist U., 1957, LL.B., 1960. Bar: Tex. 1960. Since practiced in Dallas; from ptnr. to chmn. bd. Akin, Gump, Hauer, Strauss & Feld, Dallas, 1960-96, sr. exec. ptnr., 1996—; lectr. Southwestern U. Med. Sch.; chmn. Tex. State Securities Bd.; bd. dirs. Clear Channel Comms., Inc., Ctr. Point Properties, Inc. Contbr. articles to legal jours. Bd. trustees Brandeis U., AMR Advantage Funds; bd. dirs. Dallas Day Nursery Assn., Timberlawn Found., Dallas Symphony Orch. Mem. Am., Tex., D.C., Dallas bar assns., Salesmanship Club, Dallas Club, Royal Oaks Country Club, Phi Delta Phi. General corporate, Mergers and acquisitions, Securities. Home: 4235 Bordeaux Ave Dallas TX 75205-3717 Office: Akin Gump Strauss Hauer & Feld 1700 Pacific Ave Ste 4100 Dallas TX 75201-4675

**FELD, FRANKLIN FRED,** lawyer, accountant; b. Bklyn., July 17, 1923. BBA, CCNY, 1947; LLD, Seton Hall U., 1961. Bar: N.J. 1963, U. S. Dist. Ct. N.J. 1963, U.S. Tax Ct. 1963; CPA, N.J. Pvt. practice acctg. New Brunswick, N.J., 1950-55; ptnr. Feld & Beck, CPAs, New Brunswick, 1955-78; pvt. practice law New Brunswick, 1963-78; pvt. practice law and acctg. Highland Park, 1978-94; ptnr. Feld & Rathser, 1994—; asst. law dir. City of New Brunswick, 1968-74; dist. supr. inheritance tax bur. N.J. Dept. Taxation, New Brunswick, 1974-89. Mem. ABA, N.J. Bar Assn., Middlesex County Bar Assn. (pres. 1987-88), Am. Assn. CPAs. Avocations: tennis, swimming, reading. Probate, Real property, Taxation, general. Office: 321 Raritan Ave Highland Park NJ 08904-2701

**FELDBERG, MICHAEL SVETKEY,** lawyer; b. Boston, May 21, 1951; s. Sumner Lee Feldberg and Eunice (Svetkey) Cohen; m. Ruth Lazarus, Sept. 23, 1978; children: Rachel, Jesse, Ben. BA, Harvard U., 1973, JD, 1977. Bar: N.Y. 1978, U.S. Dist. Ct. (ea. and so. dists.) N.Y. 1978, U.S. Ct. Appeals (2d cir.) 1983, U.S. Supreme Ct. 1994. Assoc. Orans, Elsen, Polstein & Naftalis, N.Y.C., 1977-80; asst. U.S. atty. So. Dist. of N.Y., N.Y.C., 1981-84; ptnr. Shea & Gould, N.Y.C., 1985-91, Schulte Roth & Zabel, N.Y.C., 1991—. Bd. dirs. 92d St. YMCA, N.Y.C., Child Devel. Rsch., N.Y.C., 1988—. Mem. Assn. Bar City N.Y. (criminal law com., com. on the judiciary, com. on profl. responsibility). Federal civil litigation, Criminal, State civil litigation. Office: Schulte Roth & Zabel 900 3rd Ave Fl 19 New York NY 10022-4774

**FELDER, MYRNA,** lawyer; b. N.Y.C., Apr. 19, 1941. BA magna cum laude, Brown U., 1961; JD cum laude, NYU, 1971. Bar: N.Y. 1971, U.S. Dist. Ct. (so. and ea. dists.) N.Y. 1974, U.S. Ct. Appeals (2nd cir.) 1977, U.S. Supreme Ct. 1978. Ptnr. Raoul Lionel Felder P.C., N.Y.C., 1972—; lawyer; b. N.Y.C., Apr. 19, 1941. B.A. magna cum laude, Brown U., 1961; J.D. cum laude, N.Y.U., 1971. Bar: N.Y. 1971, U.S. dist. ct. (so. and ea. dists.) N.Y. 1974, U.S. Ct. Apls. (2d cir.), 1977, U.S. Sup. Ct. 1978. ptnr. Raoul Lionel Felder, P.C., N.Y.C., 1972—; lectr., cons. in field. Mem. N.Y. State Civil Practice Adv. Com., chair subcom. Matrimonial Procedures, 1983—. Editor-in-chief The Matrimonial Strategist, 1985-89; bimonthly columnist New York Law Journal; contbr. chpts. to books. Mem. ABA, N.Y. State Bar Assn. (chair cts. of appellate jurisdiction com., 1988-92), Assn. Bar City N.Y., Women's Bar Assn. State N.Y. (dir. 1980-85, chmn. com. on matrimonial law 1984-85, pres. 1986-87), N.Y. Women's Bar Assn. (pres. 1976-77), Order of Coif, Phi Beta Kappa. Editor-in-chief: The Matrimonial Strategist, 1985-89; bimonthly columnist New York Law Jour.; contbr. chpts. to books. Mem. ABA, N.Y. State Bar Assn. (chair cts. of appellate jurisdiction com. 1988-92), Assn. Bar City of N.Y., Women's Bar Assn., State N.Y. (dir. 1980-85, chmn. com. on matrimonial law 1984-85, pres. 1986-87), N.Y. Women's Bar Assn. (pres. 1976-77), Order of the Coif, Phi Beta Kappa. Family and matrimonial. Home: 60 Sutton Pl S # 19AS New York NY 10022-4168 Office: Raoul Lionel Felder PC 437 Madison Ave New York NY 10022-7001

**FELDER, RAOUL LIONEL,** lawyer; b. N.Y.C., May 13, 1934; s. Morris and Millie (Goldstein) F.; m. Myrna Felder, May 26, 1963; children: Rachel, James. BA, NYU, 1955; JD, NYU, Switzerland, 1959; postgrad., U. Bern, Switzerland, 1955-56; hon. degree of fellow in jurisprudence, Oxford U., 1995. Bar: N.Y. 1959, U.S. Dist. Ct. (so. and ea. dists.) N.Y. 1962, U.S. Ct. Appeals (2d cir.) 1962, U.S. Supreme Ct. 1970. Pvt. practice N.Y.C., 1959-61, 64—, asst. U.S. atty., 1961-64; mem. faculty Practicing Law Inst., 1979, Marymount Coll., 1982—, Ethical Culture Sch., 1981, 82; moderator Nat. Conf. on Child Abuse, 1989; apptd. to N.Y.C. Cultural Affairs Adv. Commn., 1995—, State Commn. on Child Abuse, 1996. Author: Divorce: The Way Things Are, Not the Way Things Should Be, 1971, Lawyers Practical Handbook to the New Divorce Law, 1981, Raoul Felder's Encyclopedia of Matrimonial Clauses, 1990, updated, 1991—, Getting Away with Murder, 1996, Restaurant Guide to Los Angeles and New York, 1996, Survival Guide to New York, 1997; columnist Fame mag., 1988-92, Am. Women Mag., 1994, N.Y. Daily News Sundays, 1995; contbr. articles on law to profl. jours. and N.Y. Times; editorials to Newsweek mag., Harper's Bazaar mag., Newsday newspaper, N.Y. Post, The Guardian (London), Penthouse mag., Cosmopolitan mag., N.Y. Times; commentator Cable News Network, 1989, BBC World Wide, 1994, 95, 97, Crossing the Line, 1997-99, The Felder Report, 1998-99; guest commentator Court TV, 1992, bd. advisors, 1992-95, editl. contr.; (documentary) Survival Guide to New York, 1998; host (TV series) Metrolaw, 1995—; host (radio talk show) The Felder Report. Chmn. Nat. Kidney Found. Auction, also N.Y. Fund; chmn. Dinner Jerusalem Reclamation Project; grand marshall U.S.A. Day Washington, Israel Day Parade, N.Y.C.; bd. dirs. Big Apple Greeters, Cop Care, Hosp. Audiences Inc., Nat. Kidney Found. Named Man of Yr. Bklyn. Sch. for Spl. Children, Met. Geriatric Ctr., Shield Inst., 1997; recipient Defender of Jerusalem medal, 1990, Crimebusters award Take Back N.Y., 1996. Mem. ABA (judge nat. finals client counseling competition), Assn. of Bar of City of N.Y. (spl. com. matrimonial law 1975-77), N.Y. State Trial Lawyers Assn. (past chmn. matrimonial law 1974-75), Am. Arbitration Assn., N.Y. Women's Bar Assn., Minion of the Stars (chmn. bd. 1993). Family and matrimonial, Appellate, General practice. Home: 60 Sutton Pl S New York NY 10022-4168 Office: 437 Madison Ave New York NY 10022-7001

**FELDERSTEIN, STEVEN HOWARD,** lawyer; b. Rochester, N.Y., Oct. 28, 1946; s. Lester and Ruth (Tatelbaum) F.; m. Sandra Lynn Goldman, Aug. 26, 1969; 1 child, Janis. BA, SUNY, 1968; JD, U. Calif., San Francisco, 1973. Bar: Calif. Law clk. U.S. Dist. Ct., Sacramento, 1973-75; ptnr. Felderstein Rosenberg & McManes, Sacramento, 1978-86, Diepenbrock, Wulff, Plant & Hanmegan, Sacramento, 1986-98, Felderstein Willoughby & Pascuzzi LLP, Sacramento, 1999—. Contbr. articles to profl. jours. Bd. trustees Jewish Fedn. Sacramento Region, 1990-95. Mem. Calif. Bar Assn. (uniform comml. code com. bus. sect. 1983-85), Calif. Continuing Edn. of Bar (lectr. 1987—), Practicing Law Inst. (lectr. 1995—), Am. Coll. Bankruptcy, Calif. Bankruptcy Forum (v.p. 1998, pres. 1998-99). Bankruptcy, Contracts commercial. Office: Felderstein Willoughby & Pascuzzi LLP 400 Capitol Mall Ste 1450 Sacramento CA 95814-4434

**FELDKAMP, JOHN CALVIN,** lawyer, educational administrator; b. Milw., Sept. 5, 1939; s. Leroy Lyle and Dorothea Arpke (Reineking) F.; m. Barbara Joan Condon, June 30, 1962; children: John Calvin, Stephen Patrick, Amy Genevieve. BA, U. Mich., 1961, JD, 1965. Bar: Mich. 1970, N.J. 1980, D.C. 1983. Asst. to v.p. U. Mich., Ann Arbor, 1964-66, dir. housing, 1966-77; gen. mgr. svcs. Princeton U., N.J., 1977-82; pvt. practice law, Ann Arbor, 1970-77, Princeton, 1977-82; assoc. Caplin & Drysdale, Washington, 1982-85; assoc., exec. dir. Brown & Wood, N.Y.C., 1985—; exec. dir. Brown & Wood, N.Y.C. Councilman, City of Ann Arbor, 1967-69; hearing referee Mich. Civil Rights Commn., Lansing, 1975-77. Mem. Rotary (bd. dirs. Ann Arbor 1970-77, Princeton 1978-82). General practice. Home: 229 E 79th St New York NY 10021-0866 Office: Brown & Wood 1 World Trade Ctr Fl 58 New York NY 10048-0557*

**FELDMAN, ARNOLD H.,** lawyer; b. Yonkers, N.Y., Aug. 22, 1931; s. Joseph and Minnie Sarah Feldman; m. Carole Linzer, Jan. 29, 1956; children: Tamar Feldman Miller, Deena Feldman Altman, David, Nathan. BA, Yeshiva U., 1952; JD, Rutgers U., 1981. Bar: Pa. 1981, N.J. 1981, U.S. Dist. Ct. (ea. dist.) Pa. 1981, U.S. Dist. Ct. N.J. 1981, U.S. Ct. Appeals (3d cir.) 1981, U.S. Tax Ct. 1981; ordained as rabbi, 956. Atty. Ballen Gertel and Feldman, Camden, N.J., 1982-89, Feldman and Hildebrand, Cherry Hill, N.J., 1989—. Labor, Personal injury, Federal civil litigation. Office: Feldman and Hildebrand PC 802 Kings Hwy N Cherry Hill NJ 08034-1512

**FELDMAN, DAVID SCOTT,** lawyer; b. New Haven, Conn., Apr. 15, 1963; s. Gerald and Elaine Hope (Levin) F.; m. Karen Elizabeth Hilliard, Aug. 18, 1991; children: Brandan Taft, Tyler Benjamin. BS, So. Conn. U., 1985; JD, U. Bridgeport, 1988. Bar: Conn. 1988, U.S. Dist. Ct. Conn. 1989. Law clk. Zeisler & Zeisler, Bridgeport, Conn., 1987-88, atty., 1988—; v.p. Student Bar Assn. U. Bridgeport Sch. Law, 1987-88. Mem. ABA, Am. Trial Lawyers Assn., Conn. Trial Lawyers Assn., Conn. Bar Assn., Greater Bridgeport Bar Assn. Personal injury, Product liability, Workers' compensation. Office: Zeisler & Zeisler 558 Clinton Ave Bridgeport CT 06605-1701

**FELDMAN, DONALD,** lawyer; b. Bronx, N.Y., July 10, 1935; s. Irving Feldman; m. Patsy Jane Bee, Apr. 18, 1963. BS, Cornell U., 1956; student, Stanford U., 1956-57, NYU, 1958; LLB, U. Miami, 1960. Bar: Fla. 1960, U.S. Dist. Ct. (so. dist.) Fla. 1963, U.S. Ct. Appeals (11th cir.) 1981, U.S. Tax Ct., U.S. Supreme Ct. 1970. Atty. Kaplan and Ser, Miami, Fla., 1960-63; mng. ptnr. Feldman, Abramson, et al., Miami, 1965-83, Feldman & Levy, P.A., Miami, 1983-89; sr. litigator Kaplan & Bloom, P.A., Miami, 1989-90, Sherr, Tiballi, et al., Ft. Lauderdale, Fla., 1990-91, Weiss & Handler, P.A., Boca Raton, Fla., 1991—; lectr. cuban atty. program U. Miami Law Sch., 1963-64; instr. continuing legal edn. The Fla. Bar, 1970-75. Featured in Fortune Mag., 1985. With USCGR, 1961-64. Mem. ATLA, The Fla. Bar. Personal injury, General civil litigation. Office: Weiss & Handler PA 2255 Glades Rd Ste 218A Boca Raton FL 33431-7392

**FELDMAN, ELDA BEYLERIAN,** lawyer; b. Beirut, Nov. 14, 1966; d. Hagop Garbis and Jacqueline Beylerian. BA, Yale U., 1988; JD, Rutgers U., Newark, 1991. Bar: N.J. 1991, U.S. Dist. Ct. N.J. 1991, N.Y. 1992, U.S. Dist. Ct. (so. and ea. dists.) N.Y. 1996. Clk. Hon. Geoffrey Gaulkin presiding judge of N.J. Superior Ct.-Appellate Divsn., Jersey City, 1991-92; assoc. Varet Marcus & Fink, N.Y.C., 1992-93, Budd Larner Gross Rosenbaum Greenberg & Sade, Short Hills, N.J., 1993-96; first liaison to Republic of Armenia ABA Ctrl. and East European Law Initiative, Washington, 1996-97; assoc. LeBoeuf Lamb Greene & MacRae, Newark, 1997—. Editor-in-chief Women's Rights Law Reporter, 1990-91. Mem. N.J. State Bar Assn., Bar Assn. of the City of N.Y. Armenian Apostolic. Fax: 973-643-6111. Federal civil litigation, Insurance, Public international. Office: LeBoeuf Lamb Greene & MacRae One Riverfront Plaza Newark NJ 07102

**FELDMAN, HOWARD WILLIAM,** lawyer; b. Chgo., July 18, 1946; s. Nathan and Sylvia (Greenberg) F.; m. Beryl Dale Fruchter, July 12, 1970; children: Neal J. (dec.), Stephen D., Shira B. BS, Purdue U., 1968; JD, Ind. U., 1973. Bar: Ill. 1973, U.S. Dist. Ct. (cen. dist.) Ill. 1975, U.S. Ct. Appeals (7th cir.) 1975, U.S. Supreme Ct. 1977. Asst. atty. gen. Office Ill. Atty. Gen., Springfield, 1973-79; gen. counsel Capital Deve. Bd., Springfield, 1979-82; pvt. practice Springfield, 1982-86; ptnr. Feldman & Wasser, Springfield, 1987-95, Feldman, Wasser, Draper & Benson, Springfield, 1996—. Chmn. Springfield Fair Housing Bd., 1986-93; mem. Springfield Human Rights Commn., 1986-93. Mem. ABA, Ill. Bar Assn. Jewish. Avocations: amateur radio, woodworking. Construction, General civil litigation, Civil rights. Office: Feldman Wasser Draper & Benson 1307 S 7th St Springfield IL 62703-2460

**FELDMAN, JOEL HARVEY,** lawyer; b. Bklyn., July 12, 1954; s. William Carl and Arline (Karu) F. BA, Georgetown U., 1976; JD, Duke U., 1979. Bar: Fla. 1979, U.S. Dist. Ct. (so. dist.) Fla. 1980, U.S. Ct. Appeals (11th cir.) 1980, U.S. Supreme Ct. 1986. Assoc. Lavalle, Wochna, Rutherford & Brown, Boca Raton, Fla., 1979-81; ptnr. Weiss & Feldman, P.A., Boca Raton, 1981-83, Feldman & Mallinger, P.A., Boca Raton, 1983-84, Friedman, Leeds, Shorenstein, Feldman, Mallinger & Kaplan, P.A., Boca Raton, 1984-88, Feldman, Mallinger & Brown PA, 1988-91; prin. Joel H. Feldman, P.A., 1991-95. Pres. Florence Fuller Child Devel. Ctr.; chmn. legal com. Anti-Defamation League, 1990—; mem. Am.-Jewish Com. Mem. ABA, Fla. Bar Assn. (chmn. grievance com. 15-F 1988-89, real property, probate, trust law, family law sect.), Palm Beach County Bar Assn. (cmty. svc. award 1994), South Palm Beach County Bar Assn. Democrat. Jewish. Lodge: Kiwanis (bd. dirs. West Boca Raton club 1981—, youth services award, 1984, pres. 1991). Avocations: tennis, golf. State civil litigation, Family and matrimonial, Real property. Office: 4800 N Federal Hwy Ste 2070 Boca Raton FL 33431-5188

**FELDMAN, MARTIN L. C.,** federal judge; b. St. Louis, Jan. 28, 1934; s. Joseph and Zelma (Bosse) F.; m. Melanie Pulitzer, Nov. 26, 1958; children: Jennifer Pulitzer, Martin L.C. Jr. B.A., Tulane U., 1955, J.D., 1957. Bar: La., Mo. 1957. Law clk. to Hon. J.M. Wisdom, U.S. Ct. Appeals, 1958-59; assoc. Bronfin, Heller, Feldman & Steinberg, New Orleans, 1959-60; ptnr. Bronfin, Heller, Feldman & Steinberg, 1960-83; judge U.S. Dist. Ct., New Orleans, 1983—; trustee, former chmn. Sta. WYES-TV; spl. counsel to Gov. of La., 1979-83. Contbr. articles to profl. jours. Former nat. sec. Anti-Defamation League; former pres. bd. mgrs. Touro Infirmary; bd. dirs. Public Broadcasting Service. Mem. ABA (chair nat. conf. of fed. trial judges 1996-97), La. Bar Assn. (chmn. law reform com. 1981-82), Mo. Bar Assn., Am. Law Inst., Order of Coif. Republican. Jewish. Home: 12 Rosa Park New Orleans LA 70115-5044 Office: US Dist Ct Chambers of Judge Feldman 500 Camp St New Orleans LA 70130-3313

**FELDMAN, MONROE JOSEPH,** lawyer; b. Bronx, N.Y., May 27, 1949; s. Samuel C. and Sylvia (Libin) F. BA, L.I. U., 1972; JD, John Marshall Law Sch., Atlanta, 1975. Bar: Ga. 1975, U.S. Dist. Ct. (no. dist.) Ga. 1975, U.S. Ct. Appeals (5th cir.) 1975, U.S. Ct. Appeals (4th cir.) 1976, U.S. Tax Ct. 1978, U.S. Supreme Ct. 1979, U.S. Ct. Appeals (11th cir.) 1982. Mem. lawyer panel AOPA Legal Svcs. Plan, Fredricksburg, Md., 1984—; speaker in field. Pub. affairs officer, legal officer, lt. col. Civil Air Patrol Ga. Wing, Dobbins AFB, Marietta, Ga., 1984—; mem. citizens adv. council Cobb County, Ga., 1984-86; instr. Peace Officer Stds. and Tng. Coun. Ga. Mem. ABA, ATLA, Atlanta Bar Assn., Nat. Assn. Criminal Def. Lawyers, Pilots Internat. Assn., Lawyers-Pilots Bar Assn., Ga. Trial Lawyers Assn., Ga. Assn. Criminal Def. Lawyers. Democrat. Avocations: flying, motocycles. Criminal, Insurance, Personal injury. Office: 1518 Monroe Dr NE Atlanta GA 30324-5320

**FELDMAN, PHILLIP,** lawyer; b. N.Y.C., Apr. 26, 1932. BS, Calif. State, 1956; MBA, U.S.C., 1963, JD, 1966. Pvt. practice Law Offices of Phillip Feldman, Sherman Oaks, Calif., 1967—. Fellow Am. Bd. of Profl. Liability Attorneys (chair cert. commn.). Professional liability. Office: 15250 Ventura Blvd Ste 604 Sherman Oaks CA 91403-3218

**FELDMAN, RICHARD DAVID,** lawyer; b. N.Y.C., May 12, 1949; m. Leslie Lerman, May 23, 1974; children: Rachel Ann, Elizabeth Sara. BA, Bklyn. Coll., 1971; JD, N.Y. Law Sch., 1974. Bar: N.Y. 1975, U.S. Dist. Ct. (ea. and so. dists.) N.Y. 1975. Assoc. Curtis Hart & Zaklukiewicz, Merrick, N.Y., 1975-78, Friedlander Gaines Cohen Rosenthal & Rosenberg, N.Y., 1978-81, Zimmerman & Zimmerman, N.Y.C., 1981-85, Sanders Block & Byrne, Mineola, N.Y., 1985-87, Raoul Lionel Felder, N.Y.C., 1987-89; pvt. practice Lake Success, N.Y., 1989—; gen. counsel BLDG Mgmt. Co., Inc; cons. ADA Compliance Group, N.Y.C. Mem. N.Y. State Bar Assn., Assn. of Bar of City of N.Y. Real property, Contracts commercial, Family and matrimonial.

**FELDMAN, ROGER DAVID,** lawyer; b. N.Y.C., Apr. 7, 1943; s. Louis and Dora (Goldsmith) F.; m. Gail Steg, May 31, 1969; children: Rebecca, Seth. AB, Brown U., 1962; LLB, Yale U.; MBA, Harvard U. Bar: N.Y. 1966, D.C. 1977. Ops. rsch. analyst Office Asst. Sec. Def., Washington, 1967-68; staff asst. Office of Pres. U. S., Washington, 1968-69; assoc. LeBoeuf Lamb Leiby & MacRae, 1969-75; ptnr. Le Boeuf Lamb Leiby & MacRae, 1977-83; dep. asst. adminstr. FEA, Washington, 1975-77; mng. ptnr. project fin. group Nixon Hargrave Devans & Doyle, Washington, 1983-89; head ptnr. project fin. group McDermott Will & Emery, Washington, 1989-97; chair project fin. group Bingham Dana LLP, 1997—; mem. fin. adv. bd. EPA, 1989-92; bd. dirs. R.J. Rudden & Assocs. Inc., Bingham Consulting Group, LLC, Cogeneration Inst., pub.-pvt. venture divsn. Am. Road and Transp. Builders, 1991-93, N.E. Energy and Commerce Assn.; pres. Nat. Coun. for Pub. & Pvt. Partnerships, 1983-98, chair, 1998—; mem. bd. advisors Inst. Gas Tech., Infrastructure Fin. *Roger Feldman is a leading advisor on techniques for projects and structured financing of energy and infrastructure projects and services. The Project Finance Group which he chairs is active throughout the U.S. and internationally in structuring, negotiating, and providing the legal framework for the finance of infrastructure, electric power, water, transportation, and facilities.* Author: (with others) Infrastructure Finance: Tools for the Future, 1988, Public-Private Ventures in Transportation, 1990, Comprehensive Guide to Water and Wastewater Finance, 1991, Privatization of Public Utilities, 1995, Privatization, 1995; mem. bd. editors Yale Law Jour., 1964-65, Jour. Project Fin., 1995—, Constrn. Bus. Rev., 1992—; Washington editor Cogeneration and Power Marketing Monthly Letter, 1987—, Mcht. Power Monthly, 1998—, Strategic Planning for Energy and the Environment, 1992— (Author of the Yr. 1998); contbr. articles to profl. jours. Mem. ABA (chmn. energy law com. 1980-83, alt. energy sources com. 1981-84, 86-90, chmn. environ. values com. 1983-89, com. on privatization 1985-90, chmn. energy fin. 1990-91), Fed. Energy Bar Assn. (chmn. cogeneration com. 1981-82), Nat. Coun. for Pub.-Pvt. Partnerships (Outstanding Contbn. to Privatization award), N.Y. Bar Assn., D.C. Bar Assn. (chair internat. fin. and investment com. 1998—), Assn. Energy Engrs. (Cogeneration Profl. of Yr. 1990), Phi Beta Kappa. Finance, FERC practice, Transportation. Office: Bingham Dana LLP 1200 19th St NW Ste 400 Washington DC 20036-2427

**FELDMAN, STANLEY GEORGE,** state supreme court justice; b. N.Y.C., N.Y., Mar. 9, 1933; s. Meyer and Esther Betty (Golden) F.; m. Norma Arambula; 1 dau., Elizabeth L. Student, U. Calif., Los Angeles, 1950-51; LL.B., U. Ariz., 1956. Bar: Ariz. 1956. Practiced in Tucson, 1956-81; ptnr. Miller, Pitt & Feldman, 1968-81; justice Ariz. Supreme Ct., Phoenix, 1982—, chief justice, 1992-97; lectr. Coll. Law, U. Ariz., 1965-76, adj. prof., 1976-81. Bd. dirs. Tucson Jewish Community Council, U. Ariz. Found., 1999—. Mem. ABA, Am. Bd. Trial Advocates (past pres. So. Ariz. chpt.), Ariz. Bar Assn. (pres. 1974-75, bd. govs. 1967-76), Pima County Bar Assn. (past pres.), Am. Trial Lawyers Assn. (dir. chpt. 1967-76). Democrat. Jewish. Office: Ariz Supreme Ct 1501 W Washington St Phoenix AZ 85007-3231

**FELKER, ROBERT STRATTON,** lawyer; b. Portland, Oreg., Mar. 14, 1942; s. Samuel Alfred and Helen (Stratton) F.; m. Betty Brocato, March 4, 1947; children: Nadine, Robert Jr., Troy. BA, U. Puget Sound, Tacoma, Wash., 1964; JD, U. Oreg., Eugene, 1967. Bar: Wash. 1967, U.S. Dist. Ct. Wash. 1969. Asst. atty. gen. Wash. State Atty. Gen.'s Office, Olympia, Wash., 1967-69; partner Tanner, McGavick, Felker, Fleming, Burguss & Lazares and predecessor firm, Tacoma, 1970-79; pvt. practice Tacoma, 1979—. Inventor water treatment processes; developer computer software co. Mem. Am. Trial Lawyers Assn., Wash. Bar Assn., Wash.State Trial Lawyers Assn., Pierce County Bar Assn., Tacoma Christian Lawyers, Arabian Horse Assn. (bd. dirs. 1989), Tacoma City Club. Avocations: raising Arabian horses, racing & collecting sports cars, boating. General civil litigation, Personal injury, General practice. Home: 9309 Crescent Valley Dr NW Gig Harbor WA 98332-7520 Office: 202 E 34th St Tacoma WA 98404-1503

**FELL, JAMES F.,** lawyer; b. Toledo, Ohio, Nov. 18, 1944; s. George H. Fell and Bibianne C. (Hebert) Franklin; children from a previous marriage: Jennifer A., Brian F.; m. Betty L. Wenzel, May 23, 1981. BA, U. Notre Dame, 1966; JD, Ohio State U., 1969. Bar: N.Y. 1970, Calif. 1972, Idaho 1978, Wash. 1981, Oreg. 1984, U.S. Ct. Appeals (9th cir.) 1983, U.S. Dist. Ct. Idaho 1978. Assoc. Breed, Abbott & Morgan, N.Y.C., 1969-72; ptnr. McKenna & Fitting, L.A., 1972-78; atty. Office Atty. Gen., State of Idaho, Boise, 1978-79; dir. policy and administrn. Idaho Pub. Utilities Commn., Boise, 1979-81; gen. counsel, dep. dir. Northwest Power Planning Coun., Portland, Oreg., 1981-84; ptnr. Stoel Rives LLP, Portland, 1984—. Mem. ABA (pub. utility law sect.), Oreg. State Bar (exec. com. pub. utility law sect.). Public utilities. Office: Stoel Rives LLP 900 SW 5th Ave Ste 2600 Portland OR 97204-1268

**FELL, RILEY BROWN,** lawyer; b. New Orleans, Apr. 28, 1921; s. William Riley Brown and Lucy Agnes (Alcantara) F.; m. Mildred Elizabeth Gause, Aug. 21, 1947 (dec. July 1995); children: Damon, Martha, Mark, Michael, Brigid, James (dec.), Monica, Mary, Grace, Gerard. BSME, La. Poly. Inst., Ruston, 1943; LLB, Tulane U., 1947. Bar: La. 1947, Okla. 1961, U.S. Ct. Appeals (5th and 10th cirs.), U.S. Supreme Ct. 1957, U.S. Dist. Ct. (we. and ea. dists.) La., U.S. Dist. Ct. (no. and ea. dists.) Okla., U.S. Dist. Ct. (so. dist.) Ill., U.S. Dist. Ct. (so. dist.) Miss., others. Lawyer Hunt Oil Co., Shreveport, 1947-55, The Ohio Oil Co., Shreveport, Tulsa, 1955-63; divsn. atty. Marathon Oil Co., Tulsa, 1963-72; gen. counsel Loop Inc., New Orleans, 1972-79; ptnr. Barham & Churchill, New Orleans, 1979-82; sole practice law New Orleans, Tulsa, 1982—; legal com. Interstate Oil Compact Commn., Tulsa, 1966-70, New Orleans, 1973-81. Served in U.S. Navy, 1944-45. Mem. ABA, Am. Petroleum Inst. (chmn. subcom. 1969-81), Serra Club. Republican. Roman Catholic. Avocations: church choir, cooking, aerobics, mentoring, tutoring. Alternative dispute resolution, Environmental, Oil, gas, and mineral. Home: 4231 S Sandusky Ave Tulsa OK 74135-2860

**FELLER, ROBERT H.,** lawyer; b. N.Y.C., July 12, 1952; s. M. Toby and Dorothy Feller; m. Aida V. Mendoza, Oct. 27, 1984; 1 child, Marcos. BS, Union Coll., 1974; JD, Albany Law Sch., 1977; MBA, Rensselaer Poly. Inst., 1995. Bar: N.Y. 1977, U.S. Dist. Ct. (no. dist.) N.Y. Asst. corp. counsel N.Y. State Environ. Facilities Corp., Albany, N.Y., 1978-80; asst. counsel N.Y. State Dept. Environ. Conservation, Albany, 1980-86, asst. commr., 1986-95; clin. prof. Rensselaer Poly. Inst., Troy, N.Y., 1993-97; ptnr. Feller & Ferrentino, Albany, 1995—; dir. regulatory affairs Air Resources Group, Albany, 1997—; bd. dirs. Ctr. for Environ. Innovation, 1997—. Contbr. articles to profl. jours. Mem. adv. bd. Guilderland (N.Y.) Sch. Dist., 1998; pres. Turning Point II Condominiums, Albany, 1983-90. Mem. N.Y. State Bar Assn. (exec. com. environ. law sect. 1995—, Albany Law Sch. Alumni Assn. (steering com. 1995—). Avocations: tournament bridge, hiking. Environmental, Land use and zoning (including planning), Administrative and regulatory. Office: Feller & Ferrentino 488 Broadway Ste 512 Albany NY 12207-2935

**FELLERS, RHONDA GAY,** lawyer; b. Gainesville, Tex., July 20, 1955; d. James Norman and Gaytha Ann (Sanders) F.; m. Bruce C. Hinton, Oct. 15, 1981 (div. Oct. 1985). BA, U. Tex., 1977, JD, 1980; LLM in Taxation, U. Denver, 1987. Bar: Tex. 1981, Colo. 1981, U.S. Dist. Ct. (no. dist.) Tex. 1982, U.S. Dist. Ct. Colo. 1985, U.S. Tax Ct. 1985, U.S. Ct. Appeals (5th cir.) 1986, U.S. Ct. Appeals (10th cir.) 1989, U.S. Supreme Ct. 1993, U.S. Ct. Claims 1993. Assoc. Walters & Assocs., Lubbock, Tex., 1981-83; gen. counsel Security Nat. Bank, Lubbock, 1983; sole practice Lubbock, 1983-87; assoc. Melvin Coffee & Assocs., P.C., Denver, 1984-85, 87-90; atty. adviser U.S. Tax Ct., Washington, 1990-94; pvt. practice Pinehurst, Tex., 1994-98; with Arthur Andersen LLP, Houston, 1998—. Mem. ABA, State Bar Tex., Colo. Bar Assn., Houston Bar Assn. Avocations: golf, tennis, photography. Office: 711 Louisiana St Ste 1300 Houston TX 77002-2716

**FELLMAN, GERRY LOUIS,** lawyer, arbitrator; b. Omaha, May 22, 1932; s. Charles and Rose Mae (Shyken) F.; m. Jane Hallock, July 25, 1964. BS in Law, U. Nebr., 1954, JD, 1956; MA, U. Minn., 1959. Bar: Nebr. 1956, Calif. 1964, U.S. Supreme Ct. 1982; cert. Mediator. Field atty. NLRB, L.A., 1959-63; atty. div. labor law enforcement State of Calif., L.A., 1964-66; sole practice L.A., 1967-83; assoc. Ibanez & Fellman, L.A., 1968-75; sole practice Pasadena, Calif., 1984—; arbitrator labor-mgmt. disputes Am. Arbitration Assn., 1967—, Fed. Mediation and Conciliation Svc., 1968—, Calif. State Mediation and Conciliation Svc., 1967—, UCLA, 1977-89, L.A. City Employee Rels. Bd., 1973—, E.E.O.C. Mediation Panel, 1996—; bd. dirs. Claremont Dispute Resolution Ctr. Contbr. numerous articles to legal jours. Bd. dirs. Legal Aid Found. L.A., 1974-83, pres., 1981-82. With U.S. Army, 1956-58. Mem. Nat. Acad. Arbitrators (chmn. So. Calif. region 1980-82, bd. dirs. 1997—), Indsl. Rels. Rsch. Assn. (past pres. So. Calif. chpt. 1976-77), ABA, Calif. Bar Assn., L.A. County Bar Assn. (exec. com. labor and employment sect.), Pasadena Bar Assn., Nebr. Bar Assn., Soc. for Profl. in Dispute Resolution, Southern Calif. Mediation Assn. Jewish. General practice, Probate, Alternative dispute resolution. Office: 745 S Marengo Ave Ste 10 Pasadena CA 91106-3687

**FELLMAN, RICHARD MAYER,** lawyer; b. Omaha, May 30, 1935; s. Leon E. and Frances (Green) F.; m. Beverly Bloom, Jan. 12, 1964; children: Susan, Deborah, Jonathan, Daniel. BA in Polit. Sci., U. Nebr., 1957, JD, 1959. Bar: Nebr. 1959, U.S. Dist. Ct. Nebr. 1959. Farm editor, reporter Lincoln (Nebr.) Star, 1956-58; state capitol reporter AP, Lincoln, 1958; assoc. Marks, Clare, Hopkins & Rauth, 1960-64; ptnr. Fellman & Stern, 1965-73, Fellman Law Offices, 1973-86, Fellman, Moylan, Natvig & Kelly, Omaha, 1987—. Chair jud. subcom. Nebr. State Legis. on No Fault Divorce, 1973-74; bd. dirs. Vol. Bur., 1965-67; bd. dirs. NCCJ, 1968-72, Omaha-Douglas County Health Dept., 1977-80; mem. Omaha-Douglas Bldg. Commn., 1977-80; bd. dirs. Metro Area Planning Agy., Omaha, 1979; founding bd. dirs. Omaha Coun. on Domestic Violence, current chair of legis. com.; hon. bd. dirs. Alzheimer's Assn., Omaha, 1997-98; bd. dirs. Omaha Symphony Assn.; bd. dirs., officer Beth El Synagogue, Omaha; chmn. Omaha com. Anti-Defamation League, 1967-70; mem. Nat. Civil Rights Com. and Law Com., 1965—; bd. dirs. Jewish Fedn. Omaha, 1969-72; founding pres. Omaha Jewish Day Sch. (now Friedel Acad.), 1970; gen. men's chair United Jewish Appeal, 1968; bd. dirs. Omaha Jewish Press, J.C.C. Libr. Br., Nebr. Jewish Hist. Soc., Jewish Coll. Learning; organizer, chair Nebr. Dem. State Reform Commn., 1971; mem. Douglas County Bd. Commrs., 1977-80, chair of bd., 1980; senator State of Nebr., 1973-74, mem. jud. com. and govt., mil. and vets. affairs com.; mem. Mid-Am. coun. adv. bd. Boy Scouts Am., 1983—, cub and scout troop committeeman, 1980-87, chair coun. Jewish cmty. relationships com., 1985-96. Capt. USAR, 1959-66. Recipient Humanitarian of the Yr. award Sons of Italy, 1977. Mem. Nebr. Trial Lawyers Assn. (bd. dirs. 1971-72, legis. com. 1992-95), Nebr. Bar Assn. (chmn. family law com. 1971-72, 75-76), Omaha Bar Assn. (chair com. on domestic violence 1996, Pro Bono Publico award 1972), Rotary, Delta Sigma Rho, Zeta Beta Tau. Democrat. Jewish. Fax: 402-341-8159. Family and matrimonial, Personal injury, Workers' compensation. Home: 12206 Leavenworth Rd Omaha NE 68154 Office: Fellman Moylan Natvig & Kelly 100 Continental Bldg 209 S 19th St Omaha NE 68102-1755

**FELLMETH, ROBERT CHARLES,** law educator; b. Lake City, Fla., Sept. 21, 1945; s. Robert Butler and Jane Zenith F.; m. Jill D. Heiman, Dec. 17, 1967; children: Michael Q., Aaron X.; m. Julie Barbara D'Angelo, Aug. 4, 1996. BA, Stanford U., 1967; JD, Harvard U., 1970. Bar: Calif. 1971, U.S. Dist. Ct. (so. dist.) Calif. 1979, U.S. Ct. Appeals (9th cir.) 1984, U.S. Supreme Ct. 1985. Assoc. Ctr. for Study of Responsive Law, Washington, 1969-73; dep. DA, asst. U.S. Atty. Offices of D.A. and U.S Atty., San Diego, 1973-82; Price prof. pub. interest law U. San Diego, 1977—, dir. Ctr. Pub. Interest Law, Children's Adv. Inst., 1980—; state bar discipline monitor separate office, Calif., 1987-92. Author: The Politics of Land, 1972, (report) California Children's Budget 1998-99, 1998, California Children's Budget, 1999-00, 1999; co-author: Interstate Commerce Omission, 1970, California White Collar Crime, 1996. Chair, bd. dirs. Pub. Citizen Found., Washington, 1992—; bd. dirs. Consumer's Union, 1981-85, Calif. Common Cause, 1986-91; cmty. champion Civil Justice Found., Ill., 1998; chmn. athletic commn. State of Calif., 1977-81. Mem. Nat. Assn. Child Advocates (bd. dirs., counsel to bd. 1992—), Nat. Assn. Counsel for Children (bd. dirs. 1991—). Avocations: Native American artifacts and art, whaling and nautical artifacts, parrots. Office: Children's Advocacy Inst 5998 Alcala Park San Diego CA 92110-2429

**FELLOWS, HENRY DAVID, JR.,** lawyer; b. N.Y.C., Dec. 17, 1954; s. Henry D. Sr. and Mary (Stecko) F.; m. Pam Neal Fellows, May 15, 1982; children: Christopher, Suzanne, Thomas. BSBA, Bucknell U., 1975; JD, Georgetown U., 1978. Bar: Ga. 1978, U.S. Dist. Ct. (no. dist.) Ga. 1978, U.S. Ct. Appeals (11th cir.) 1978, U.S. Supreme Ct. 1997. Law clk. to hon. judge Charles A. Moye Jr. U.S. Dist. Ct. (no. dist.) Ga., Atlanta, 1978-80; assoc. Hurt, Richardson, Garner, Todd & Cadenhead, Atlanta, 1981-87, ptnr., 1987-92; ptnr. Fellows, Johnson & LaBriola, LLP (and predecessor firm), Atlanta, 1993—. Mem. ABA, Ga. Bar Assn., Atlanta Bar Assn. (chmn. ct. com. 1992-98, bd. dirs. litigation sect. 1999—), Lawyers Club of Atlanta. Avocations: tennis, piano. Federal civil litigation, General civil litigation. Office: Fellows Johnson & LaBriola LLP Peachtree Ctr # 2300 South 225 Peachtree St NE Atlanta GA 30303-1701

**FELLRATH, RICHARD FREDERIC,** lawyer; b. Dearborn, Mich., Nov. 30, 1940; s. Jerome John and Jane Elizabeth (Ayers) F.; m. Barbara Ann Osani, Oct. 14, 1966; children: Richard F., Jr., Christina Joyce. BA, U. Notre Dame, 1963; JD, U. Detroit, 1966. Bar: Mich. 1967, D.C. 1969, U.S. Ct. Mil. Appeals 1967, U.S. Supreme Ct. 1970, U.S. Ct. Appeals (6th cir.) 1984, U.S. Ct. Claims 1987. Judge adv. U.S. Army, Balt., 1967-71; ptnr. Milmet & Vecchio P.C., Detroit, 1971-85; sr. atty. Miller, Canfield, Paddock & Stone, Detroit, 1985-91, Fitzgerald & Dakmak, P.C., Detroit, 1991-96. Contbr. articles to profl. jours. Capt. U.S. Army, 1967-71. Mem. ABA, Fed. Bar Assn. (Detroit bankruptcy chm. 1985-87), Am. Bankruptcy Inst., State Bar Mich., SAR, Sons Union Vets Civil War. Republican. Roman Catholic. Avocations: stamps, windsurfing, ancient coins, mil. miniatures, genealogy. Fax: 313-961-3132. Bankruptcy, Government contracts and claims. Home: 4056 Middlebury Dr Troy MI 48098-3620 Office: 600 Ford Bldg Detroit MI 48226

**FELNER, RICHARD M.,** real estate consultant, lawyer; b. N.Y.C., Mar. 27, 1936; s. Theodore I. and Sylvia L. Felner; m. Linda Marks Vogel, Dec. 15, 1963 (div. May 1994); children: Andrew, David, Julie. AB, Cornell U., 1958; LLB, Columbia U., 1961. Bar: N.Y. Supreme Ct. 1962. Intern Senator Jacob Javits U.S. Senate, Washington, 1958; spl. asst. to Senator Jacob Javits U.S. Senate, N.Y.C., 1958-61; assoc. Hays, Sklar & Hertzberg, N.Y.C., 1961-62, Cole and Dietz, N.Y.C., 1962-65; assoc. counsel N.Y. State Joint Legis. Com. to Revise the Banking Law, N.Y.C. and Albany, 1962-65; co-chief exec. The Fabric Tree Ind., N.Y.C., 1966-77; gen. counsel, sec. Brooks Fashion Stores, Inc., N.Y.C., 1978-85; exec. v.p., dir. Worths Stores, Inc., N.Y.C. and St. Louis, 1985-91; chmn. Richard M. Felner Assocs., N.Y.C., 1991—; bd. dirs. Ames Dept. Stores, Inc., Rocky Hill, Conn. Active Westchester (N.Y.) County Rep. Com., 1968-85; mem. various adv. coms. Town of Mamaroneck, N.Y., 1970-85. Mem. Internat. Coun. Shopping Ctrs., Assn. Bar City N.Y. Office: 200 E 57th St New York NY 10022-2860

**FELOS, GEORGE JAMES,** lawyer; b. N.Y.C., Mar. 23, 1952; s. James George and Jean (Rodis) F.; m. Constance M. Felos; 1 child, Alexander James. BA cum laude, Queens Coll. N.Y., 1973; JD, Boston U., 1976. Bar: Mass. 1977, Fla. 1977, U.S. Dist. Ct. (mid. dist.) Fla. 1978, U.S. Ct. Appeals (11th cir.) Fla. 1992, U.S. Supreme Ct. 1984. Assoc. Law Office of John N. Samaha, St. Petersburg, Fla., 1978-79; prin. Law Office of George Felos, St. Petersburg, 1979-80; ptnr. Felos & Felos, Dunedin, Fla., 1980—; legal advisor Soc. for Right to Die, 1992—. Chmn. bd. dirs. Hospice of Fla. Suncoast, 1996-98. Mem. Fla. Bar Assn., Clearwater County Bar Assn., Am.-Hellenic Ednl. Progressive Assn. (gov. 1986—), Nat. Assn. Security Dealers (arbitrator), Am. Arbitration Assn. (cert.). Greek Orthodox. Avocations: astronomy, tennis, gardening, baseball, piano. General civil litigation, Contracts commercial, Personal injury. Office: Felos & Felos 640 Douglas Ave Dunedin FL 34698-7001

**FELPER, DAVID MICHAEL,** lawyer; b. Springfield, Mass., Dec. 17, 1954; s. Lawrence Allen and Edith Charlotte (Flesher) F.; m. Kimberlee White, May 19, 1979; children: Andrew Martin, Evan Matthew, Scott Tyler. BA in Polit. Sci., George Washington U., 1976; JD cum laude, Western New Eng. Coll., 1980. Bar: Mass. 1980, U.S. Dist. Ct. Mass. 1981, U.S. Ct. Appeals (1st cir.) 1987. Assoc. Michelman & Feinstein, Springfield, 1980-82; asst. regional counsel Dept. Social Services, Commonweatlh of Mass., Springfield, 1982-83; labor relations counsel Sprague Electric Co., Lexington, Mass., 1983-87; assoc. Bowditch & Dewey, Framingham, Mass., 1987-92; ptnr. Bowditch & Dewey, Framingham, 1992—; lectr. various human resource orgns. throughout U.S., 1984—; pres. Valley Tech. Ednl. Found. Inc., 1998—; corporator Milford-Whitinsville Regional Hosp. Bd. dirs. United Way of Tri-County, Hopedale Youth Baseball Assn. Inc.; fin. com. Town of Hopedale. Mem. Mass. Bar Assn. (labor law com., labor and employment sect. coun.), Worcester County Bar Assn. (labor and employment law com.), Blackstone Valley C. of C. (dir.). Avocations: golf, running, reading. Labor, Pension, profit-sharing, and employee benefits, Workers' compensation. Office: Bowditch & Dewey PO Box 9320 Framingham MA 01701-9320

**FELS, CHARLES WENTWORTH BAKER,** lawyer; b. Cin., Feb. 26, 1943; s. Rendigs Thomas and Beatrice Carmichael (Baker) f.; m. Joy Mary Bothwell, April 26, 1975; children: Sarah Victoria Bothwell, Andrew Christian Graham Carmichael. BA in English Lit., Stanford U., 1965; MA in Am. Colonial History, Vanderbilt U., 1972, JD, 1974. Bar: Tenn. 1974, U.S. Ct. Appeals (6th cir.) 1975, U.S. Ct. Appeals (11th cir.) 1987, U.S. Supreme Ct. 1988. Vol. U.S. Peace Corps, Dodoma and Moshi, Tanzania, 1965-67; teaching asst. history Vanderbilt U., Nashville, 1968-69; vis. reader Brit. Mus., London, 1970; asst. U.S. atty. U.S. Dept. Justice, Nashville, 1974-77, Knoxville, 1982-84; articled clk. Morris, Fletcher & Cross, Brisbane, Queensland, Australia, 1977-79; asst. dist. atty. Knox County Dist. Atty's Office, Knoxville, Tenn., 1979-82; ptnr. Ritchie, Fels & Dillard P.C., Knoxville, 1984—; instr. Nat. Criminal Def. Coll., Macon, Ga., 1987—; vis. lectr. FBI, Quantico, Va.; mem. faculty U. Tenn. Coll. Trial Advocacy; continuing legal edn. speaker, Tenn., Ga., Kans., S.C., Tex., Calif., Colo., Ill., N.Y., R.I., Wash., Fla., Mass., Ixtapa, Mex. Editor spl. projects Vanderbilt Law Rev., 1974. Weldon B. White scholar Vanderbilt U. Sch. Law, 1973-74. Mem. ABA, Nat. Assn. Criminal Def. Lawyers (com. continuing legal edn. 1987-88, bd. dirs. 1989-95), Tenn. Bar Assn., Tenn. Assn. Criminal Def. Lawyers (chmn. continuing legal edn. com. 1987-88, bd. dirs. 1986-95), Les Cheneaux Club (Marquette Island, Mich.). Democrat. Criminal, Constitutional. Office: Ritchie Fels & Dillard PC 606 W Main Ave PO Box 1126 Knoxville TN 37901-1126

**FELSENTHAL, STEVEN ALTUS,** lawyer; b. Chgo., May 21, 1949; s. Jerome and Eve (Altus) F.; m. Carol Judith Greenberg, June 14, 1970; children: Rebecca Elizabeth, Julia Alison, Daniel Louis Altus. AB, U. Ill., 1971; JD, Harvard U., 1974. Bar: Ill. 1974, U.S. Dist. Ct. (no. dist.) Ill. 1974, U.S. Ct. Claims 1975, U.S. Tax Ct. 1975, U.S. Ct. Appeals (7th cir.) 1981. Assoc. Levenfeld, Kanter, Baskes & Lippitz Chgo., 1974-78, ptnr. Levenfeld & Kanter, Chgo., 1978-80; ptnr. Levenfeld, Eisenberg, Janger, Glassberg & Lippitz, Chgo., 1980-84; sr. ptnr. Sugar, Friedberg & Felsenthal, Chgo., 1984—; lectr. Kent Coll. Law, Ill. Inst. Tech., Chgo., 1978-80. Mem. ABA, Ill. State Bar Assn., Chgo. Bar Assn., Chgo. Coun. Lawyers, Harvard Law Soc. Ill., Phi Beta Kappa. Clubs: Standard, Harvard (Chgo.). Taxation, general, Estate planning, General corporate. Office: Sugar Friedberg & Felsenthal 30 N La Salle St Ste 2600 Chicago IL 60602-2506

**FELTER, EDWIN LESTER, JR.,** judge; b. Washington, Aug. 11, 1941; s. Edwin L. Felter and Bertha (Peters) Brekke; m. Yoko Yamauchi-Koito, Dec. 26, 1969. BA, U. Tex., 1964; JD, Cath. U. of Am., 1967. Bar: Colo. 1970, U.S. Dist. Ct. Colo. 1970, U.S. Ct. Appeals (10th cir.) 1971, U.S. Supreme Ct. 1973, U.S. Tax Ct. 1979, U.S. Ct. Claims 1979, U.S. Ct. Internat. Trade 1979. Dep. pub. defender State of Colo., Ft. Collins, 1971-75; asst. atty. gen. Office of the Atty. Gen., Denver, 1975-80; state adminstrv. law judge Colo. Divsn. of Adminstrv. Hearings, Denver, 1980-83, chief adminstrv. law judge, 1983—; disciplinary prosecutor Supreme Ct. Grievance Com., 1975-78. Contbg. editor Internat. Franchising, 1970. Mem. Colo. State Mgmt. Cert. Steering Com., 1983-86; No. Colo. Criminal Justice Planning Coun., Ft. Collins, 1973-75; bd. dirs., vice chmn. The Point Cmty. Crisis Ctr., Ft. Collins, 1971-73; mem. Denver County Dem. Party Steering Com., 1978-79, chmn. 12th legis. dist., 1978-79; bd. dirs., pres. Denver Internat. Program, 1989-90. Mem. ABA, Nat. Conf. Adminstrv. Law Judges (chair), Colo. Bar Assn. (chmn. grievance policy com. 1991-94, interprofl. com. 1995—), Arapahoe County Bar Assn., Denver Bar Assn., Nat. Assn. Adminstrv. Law Judges (pres. Colo. chpt. 1982-84, Nat. Fellowship winner 1994), Am. Inns of Ct. (master level 1996—). Office: Colo Divsn Adminstrv Hearings 1120 Lincoln St Ste 1400 Denver CO 80203-2140

**FELTER, JOHN KENNETH,** lawyer; b. Monmouth, N.J., May 9, 1950; s. Joseph Harold and Rosanne (Bautz) F. BA magna cum laude, MA in Econs., Boston Coll., 1972; JD cum laude, Harvard U., 1975. Bar: Mass. 1975, U.S. Dist. Ct. Mass. 1976, U.S. Ct. Appeals (1st cir.) 1977, U.S. Supreme Ct. 1982, U.S. Tax Ct. 1993. Assoc. Goodwin, Procter & Hoar, Boston, 1975-83, ptnr., 1983—; spl. asst. gen. Commonwealth of Mass., 1982-84, 94-95; spl. counsel Town of Plymouth, Mass., Town of Salisbury, Mass., Town of Edgartown, Mass.; spl. outside counsel City of Boston, 1990-92; mem. devel. com. Greater Boston Legal Svcs., 1982—, bd. dirs., 1980—, mem. exec. com., 1989-93; mem. faculty Mass. Continuing Legal Edn., Inc., Boston. Mem. adv. com. The Boston Plan for Excellence in Pub. Schs.; mem. elem. edn. com. Blue Ribbon Commn. on Cmty. Learning Ctrs.; VIP panelist Easter Seals Telethon, Boston, 1978-79. Fellow Mass. Bar Found.; mem. ABA (litigation sect., gen. practice sect., mem. personal rights litigation com. environ. law sect., mem. ABA-Am. Law Inst. com. on continuing edn.), Am. Arbitration Assn. (comml. arbitrator), Mass. Bar Assn. (co-chmn. edn. com. pub. law sect.), Boston Bar Assn. (bd. dirs. law firm resources project 1985—, mem. coll. and univ. law com. 1986—, chmn. fed. rules com. litigation sect. 1994), Greater Boston C. of C. (mem. edn. com., mem. health care com.). Federal civil litigation, State civil litigation, Education and schools. Office: Goodwin Procter & Hoar Exchange Pl 53 State St Ste 20 Boston MA 02109-2881

**FELTES, CHARLES VICTOR,** lawyer; b. St. Charles, Ill., Apr. 9, 1947; s. Victor P. and Ramona R. (Nagle) F.; m. Susan Joyce Seidelman, Nov. 21, 1975; children: Jennifer, Katherine, Victor, Laura. BS, U. Wis., 1969; JD, U. Ill., 1973. Bar: Ill. 1973, Wis. 1975, U.S. Dist. Ct. (no. dist.) Ill. 1973, U.S. Dist. Ct. (we. dist.) Wis. 1976. Assoc. Tyler, Peskind & Solomon, Aurora, Ill., 1973-75; assoc. Kostner, Ward & Koslo, Osseo, Wis., 1975-84, ptnr., 1984-94; atty. pvt. practice, Osseo, Wis., 1995—. Mem. Wis. Bar Assn., Ill. Bar Assn., Tri-County Bar Assn. (pres. 1996), Osseo Comml. Club (pres. 1983). Republican. Roman Catholic. General practice, General civil litigation, Personal injury. Home: 1049 N East St PO Box 54 Osseo WI 54758-0054 Office: 13819 W 7th St Osseo WI 54758-0785

**FELTY, KRISS DELBERT,** lawyer; b. Cleve., May 5, 1954; s. John Gilbert and Stephanie (Kriss) F. BA in Psychology, Case Western Res. U., 1976; postgrad., Cleve. State U., 1977-79; JD, U. Akron, Ohio, 1983. Bar: Ohio 1983, Tex.1988, Wis. 1989, U.S. Dist. Ct. Ohio 1983, U.S. Ct. Appeals (6th cir.) 1984, Fla. 1985, U.S. Supreme Ct. 1986. Assoc. Dennis Reimer Co., LPA, Twinsburg, Ohio, 1983-87; mng. ptnr. Shapiro & Felty, Independence, Ohio, 1987--. Mem. ABA, Fla. Bar Assn., Ohio Bar Assn., Greater Cleve. Bar Assn., Cuyahoga County Bar Assn., Mortgage Bankers Assn. Am., Ohio Mortgage Bankers Assn., Mortgage Bankers Assn. Met. Cleve., Phi Kappa Theta (trustee 1973-74). Avocations: golf, swimming, reading, music, leaded glass lamps. Real property, Bankruptcy, Consumer commercial. Office: Shapiro & Felty 800 W Saint Clair Ave Fl 2 Cleveland OH 44113-1205

**FENDLER, OSCAR,** lawyer; b. Blytheville, Ark., Mar. 22, 1909; s. Alfred and Rae (Sattler) F.; m. Patricia Shane, Oct. 26, 1946; children: Tilden P. Wright III (stepson), Frances Shane. B.A., U. Ark., 1930; LL.B., Harvard, 1933. Bar: Ark. bar 1933. Practice in Blytheville, 1933-41, 46—; spl. justice Ark. Supreme Ct., 1965; Mem. Ark. Jud. Council, 1959- 60; pres. Conf. Local Bar Assn., 1958-60; pres. bd. dirs. Ark. Law Rev., 1961-67; mem. Ark. Bd. Pardons and Paroles, 1970-71. Mem. Miss. County Democratic Central Com., 1948—. Served with USNR, 1941-45. Fellow Am. Coll. Trust and Estate Counsel, Am. Bar Found.; mem. ABA (chmn. gen. practice sect. 1966-67, mem. council sect. gen. practice 1964—, ho. dels. 1968-80, mem. com. edn. about Communism 1966-70, com. legal aid and indigent defendants 1970-73, chmn. com. law lists 1973-76, Founders award 1992), Ark. Bar Assn. (chmn. exec. com. 1956-57, pres. 1962-63), Am. Judicature Soc. (dir. 1964-68), Scribes, Nat. Conf. Bar Presidents (exec. council 1963-65), Blytheville C. of C. (past v.p., dir.), Navy League, Am. Legion. Club: Blytheville Rotary (past pres.). General practice, General civil litigation, Probate. Home: 1062 Hearn St Blytheville AR 72315-2659 Office: 104 N 6th St Blytheville AR 72315-3315

**FENECH, JOSEPH CHARLES,** lawyer; b. London, May 28, 1950; came to U.S., 1953; s. Carmel John and Elizabeth Frances (Borg) F.; m. Cynthia A. Rennie, June 14, 1980 (div. 1998); children: Paul C., Peter J., Elizabeth F. BA with honors, Mich. State U., 1972; JD, U. Mich., 1975. Bar: Mich. 1975, U.S. Dist. Ct. (ea. dist.) Mich. 1975, U.S. Ct. Appeals (6th cir.) 1977, Ill. 1980, U.S. Dist. Ct. (no. dist.) Ill. 1980, U.S. Dist. Ct. (ctrl. dist.) Ill. 1993, U.S. Dist. Ct. (ea. dist.) Wis. 1993, U.S. Ct. Appeals (7th cir.) 1980, U.S. Supreme Ct. 1993, U.S. Tax Ct. 1993. Law clk. Washtenaw Cir. Ct., Ann Arbor, Mich., 1975-76; asst. atty. gen. State of Mich., Detroit, 1976-80; labor rels. counsel McDonald's Corp., Oak Brook, Ill., 1980-82, sr. internat. atty., 1982-84; sr. mem. Fenech & Assoc., Oak Brook, Ill., 1985—. Contbr. articles to profl. jours. Bd. dirs. Cath. Charities Diocese of Joliet, Ill.; active Family Focus, Mich., 1979-80, Internat. Found. Employee Benefit Plans, Brookfield, Wis., 1980-83, Chmns. Club Ctrl.; mem. bd. govs. DuPage Hosp., Ctrl. DuPage Hosp. Tree Life, Ctrl., Glen Oaks Med. Ctr., Tree of Life, Rep. Campaign Coun., 1995; supt. adv. com. Naperville Cmty. Sch. Dist. 203; improvement com. Mill St. Sch., Naperville; charter mem. Marklund Children's Home Endowment; bd. govs. Ctrl. DuPage Hosp. Named Regents scholar U. Mich., 1973, 74, 75, Trustees scholar Mich. State U., 1969-72. Mem. ABA, Ill. State Bar Assn., Mich. Bar assn., DuPage Estate Planning Coun., U. Mich. Lawyers Club, Ill. Bankers Assn., Ill. Mortgage Bankers Assn., Internat. Platform Assn. Am. Hosp. Assn. (sr. mem.), Am. Acad. Healthcare Attys. (sr. mem.). General corporate, Private international, Contracts commercial. Office: Fenech & Pachulski PC 1 Lincoln Ctr Ste 840 Oakbrook Ter IL 60181-4265

**FENET, ROBERT WICKLIFFE,** lawyer; b. Lake Charles, La., Dec. 16, 1947; m. Sally Elizabeth Gamblin, Aug. 26, 1972; children: Charles, Lydia, Andrew, Hilary. BSc in Indsl. Engring., Ga. Inst. Tech., 1969; JD, La. State U., 1972; Cert. de Langue Francaise, U. Paris Sorbonne, 1972; Cert. Pratique de Langue Francaise, U. Grenoble, France, 1973. Law clk. 3d Circuit Ct. Appeals, Lake Charles, La., 1973-74, 14th Jud. Dist. Ct., Lake Charles, La., 1973-74; ptnr. Woodley, Williams, Fenet, Boudreau, Norman & Brown, Lake Charles, La., 1974-97; spl. counsel internat. affairs Breazeale, Sachse & Wilson, Baton Rouge, 1997—; spl. counsel City of Lake Charles, 1977-83; impartial hearing officer State of La., 1978-83; spl. dep. atty. gen. State of La., 1988—. Mem. vestry Episc. Ch. Good Shepherd; bd. dirs. Am. Cancer Soc.. With USNR, 1965-70. Named Hon. Ins. Commr. State of La. Mem. ABA, S.W. La. Bar Assn., La. Bar Assn., Am. Assn. Average Adjusters, British Assn. Average Adjusters of U.S., Maritime Law Assn. U.S., Southeastern Admiralty Law Inst., Union des Avocates Internat., Nat. Assn. Profl. Surplus Lines Offices, Ltd., La. Surplus Lines Assn., France Amerique (pres.), Rotary, S.W. La. C. of C. (mem. legis. affairs com.). Camelot Club, City Club Baton Rouge, Country Club Lake Charles. Avocation: photography. Home: 7522 Rienzi Blvd Baton Rouge LA 70809-1122 Office: Breazeale Sachse & Wilson 1 American Pl 23rd Flr PO Box 3197 Baton Rouge LA 70821-3197

**FENNELL, DANIEL JOSEPH, II,** lawyer; b. Berlin, Germany, June 2, 1966; came to U.S., 1968; s. Daniel Joseph Fennell and Peg Hess-Fennell. AB with honors, Brown U., 1989; JD, Rutgers U., 1994. Bar: Pa. 1995, N.J. 1995, U.S. Dist. Ct. N.J. 1995, U.S. Dist. Ct. (ea. dist.) Pa. 1998. Staff atty. Ct. Common Pleas, Norristown, Pa., 1994-95, Supreme Ct. Pa., Phila., 1995-96; atty. Yost & Tretta, Phila., 1996-98, White & Williams, Phila., 1998—. Mem. Phila. World Affairs Counsel, 1996—. Mem. ABA, Pa. Bar Assn., Montgomery County Bar Assn., St. Thomas More Soc. Roman Catholic. General civil litigation, Appellate. Home: 4201 Wilson Blvd # 110 Arlington VA 22203-1859 Office: White & Williams 1800 One Liberty Pl Philadelphia PA 19103

**FENNELL, MONICA ANN,** lawyer; b. Evanston, Ill., Apr. 2, 1965; d. Frank L. and Kay L. F.; m. David N. Gellman, Aug. 19, 1995; 1 child, Hannah Gellman. BA cum laude, Williams Coll., 1987; JD, Georgetown U. Law Ctr., 1993. Bar: Wis. 1993, Ill. 1994, U.S. Dist. Ct. (no. dist.) Ill. 1994. Assoc. Michael, Best & Friedrich, Milw., 1993-94, Gardner, Carton & Douglas, Chgo., 1994-97, Sonnenschein, Nath & Rosenthal, Chgo., 1998—. Social action com. Temple Sholom, Chgo., 1996—. Mem. ABA, Chgo. Bar Assn. Democrat. Federal civil litigation, General civil litigation, State civil litigation. Office: Sonnenschein Nath & Rosenthal 8000 Sears Tower Chicago IL 60606

**FENNING, LISA HILL,** federal judge; b. Chgo., Feb. 22, 1952; d. Ivan Byron and Jean (Hennigar) Hill; m. Alan Mark Fenning, Apr. 3, 1977; 4 children. BA with honors, Wellesley Coll., 1971; JD, Yale U., 1974. Bar: Ill. 1975, Calif. 1979, U.S. Dist. Ct. (no. dist.) Ill., U.S. Dist. Ct. (no., ea., so. & cen. dists.) Calif., U.S. Ct. Appeals (6th, 7th & 9th cirs.), U.S. Supreme Ct. 1989. Law clk. U.S. Ct. Appeals 7th cir., Chgo., 1974-75; assoc. Jenner and Block, Chgo., 1975-77, O'Melveny and Myers, L.A., 1977-85; judge U.S. Bankruptcy Ct. Cen. Dist. Calif., L.A., 1985—; bd. govs. Nat. Conf. Bankruptcy Judges, 1989-92; pres. Nat. Conf. of Women's Bar Assns., N.C., 1987-88, pres.-elect, 1986-87, v.p., 1985-86, bd. dirs.; lectr., program coord. in field; bd. govs. Nat. Conf. Bankruptcy Judges Endowment for Edn., 1992—, Am. Bankruptcy Inst., 1994-97; mem., bd. advisors Nat. Jud. Edn. Program to Promote Equality for Women and Men in the Cts., 1994—. Mem., bd. advisors: Lawyer Hiring & Training Report, 1985-87; contbr. articles to profl. jours. Durant scholar Wellesley Coll., 1971; named one of Am's. 100 Most Important Women Ladies Home Jour., 1988, one of L.A.'s 50 Most Powerful Women Lawyers, L.A. Bus. Jour., 1998. Fellow Am. Bar Found., Am. Coll. Bankruptcy (bd. regents 1995-98); mem. ABA (standing com. on fed. jud. improvements 1995-98, mem. commn. on women in the profession 1987-91, Women's Caucus 1987—, Individual Rights and Responsibilities sect. 1984—, bus. law sect. 1986—, bus. bankruptcy com.), Nat. Assn. Women Judges (nat. task force gender bias in the cts. 1986-87, 93-94), Nat. Conf. Bankruptcy Judges (chair endowment edn. bd.), Am. Bankruptcy Inst. (nominating com. 1994-95, bd. steering com. statis. project 1994-96), Calif. State Bar Assn. (chair com. on women in law 1986-87), Women Lawyers' Assn. L.A. (ex officio mem., bd. dirs., chmn., founder com. on status of women lawyers 1984-85, officer nominating com. 1986, founder, mem. Do-It-Yourself Mentor Network 1986-96), Phi Beta Kappa. Democrat. Office: US Bankruptcy Ct 255 E Temple St Rm 1682 Los Angeles CA 90012-3334

**FENSKE, KARL ARTHUR,** lawyer; b. Orange, N.J., July 5, 1950; s. Arthur Gottfried and Helen Fenske. BA, Drew U., 1974; LLB, Seton Hall U., 1977. Trial atty. Morristown, N.J., 1977—; mem. Morristown Bd. Adjustment, 1988-92; atty. Morristown Planning Bd., 1996-97; bd. dirs. Alfre, Inc., Morristown. Author: N.J. Environmental Commission Handbook, 1973. Active Morristown Dem. Com., 1988-97. Mem. N.J. Bar Assn., Morris County Bar Assn. Federal civil litigation, State civil litigation, Environmental. Office: 26 Park Pl Morristown NJ 07960-3944

**FENSOM, JAMES B.,** lawyer; b. Port St. Joe, Fla., Feb. 25, 1950; s. Paul Sherwood and Elizabeth (Ball) F.; m. Jan Lehman, July 14, 1973; children: Meredith, Stuart. BS, Auburn (Ala.) U., 1972; JD, Fla. State U., 1975. Bar: Fla. 1975, U.S. Dist. Ct. (no. dist.) Fla. 1978, U.S. Ct. Appeals (11th cir.) 1979. Legis. asst. U.S. Congress, Washington, 1975-76; with felony divsn. State Atty.'s Office, Panama City, Fla., 1976-78; ptnr. Barron, Redding, Hughes, Fite, Bassett, Fensom & Sanborn, PA, Panama City, 1979—; bd. dirs. SouthTrust Bank, Panama City; bd. govs. 14th Jud. Cir. Grievance Com., Panama City, 1990-91. Mem. Bay County Bar Assn. (prs. 1980), Fla. Bar (bd. govs. 1992-96, exec. com. 1995), St. Andrews Yacht Club (bd. dirs. 1996—). Avocations: navigation and cruising, flats fishing, hunting. General civil litigation, Personal injury, Insurance. Office: Barron Redding et al 220 Mckenzie Ave Panama City FL 32401-3129

**FENSTER, HERBERT LAWRENCE,** lawyer; b. N.Y.C., Mar. 29, 1935; s. Oscar Samuel and Bessie Estelle (Schafran) F.; m. Gail Frances Meier, Apr. 18, 1964; children—Christopher Lawrence, Jennifer Gail, Jonathan Adam; m. Jane Porter Elam Allen, Dec. 31, 1993. A.B., U. Pa., 1957, M.A., 1958; J.D., U. Va., 1961. Bar: Va. 1961, D.C. 1962, U.S. Supreme Ct. 1967, Colo., 1993. Assoc., Sellers, Conner & Cuneo, Washington, 1961-66, ptnr., 1967-78, sr. ptnr., 1978-80; sr. ptnr. McKenna, Conner & Cuneo, 1980-90, McKenna & Cuneo, 1990—. Author treatise Anti Deficiency Act, ABA, 1979. Litigation counsel Reagan-Bush Campaign Com., Washington, 1980-83, pres.'s pvt. sector survey Grace Commn., 1982—; bd. dirs. Nat. Chamber Litigation Ctr., Washington, 1983—; bd. dirs. Keewaydin Found., Middlebury Vermont, 1982—, also trustee, corp. dir. Fellow Assn. Trial Lawyers Am.; mem. ABA, Fed. Bar Assn., D.C. Bar Assn., Am. Law Inst. Republican. Episcopalian. Clubs: Metropolitan, University. Government contracts and claims, Product liability, Environmental. Home: 845 6th St Boulder CO 80302-7418 Address: 370 17th St Denver CO 80202-1370

**FENSTER, ROBERT DAVID,** lawyer; b. N.Y.C., Sept. 25, 1946; s. Alfred Howard and Esther (Eisenberg) F.; m. Janet Lynne Shanes, July 27, 1969; children: Lori Beth, Eric Steven. BA, Queens Coll., 1968; JD, Bklyn. Law Sch., 1973. Bar: N.Y. 1974, U.S. Dist. Ct. (so. and ea. dists.) N.Y. 1974, U.S. Supreme Ct. 1977. Investigator, prosecutor N.Y. Stock Exchange, N.Y.C., 1972-73; assoc. various law firms, Rockland County, N.Y., 1973-80; ptnr. Fenster & Weiss, New City, 1980—; bd. dirs. Brit. Pub. Corp., various other corps. Advisor Clarkstown Youth Ct., New City, N.Y., 1982; bd. dirs. Legal Aid Soc., Rockland County, 1974-78, Nyack Hosp. Found., Good Samaritan Hosp. Found. Mem. ABA, N.Y. State Bar Assn., Rockland County Bar Assn., Am. Arbitration Assn. (arbitrator). General corporate, Real property, General civil litigation. Office: Fenster & Weiss 337 N Main St Ste 11 New City NY 10956-4310

**FENSTER, SIDNEY J.,** judge; b. N.Y.C.; s. Morris and Regina Fenster; m. Annette Drucker, June 18, 1949; children: Regina, Albert, Mark, Joan. BS in Commerce, U. Md., 1939; LLB, JD, Fordham U., 1945. Bar: N.Y. 1945, U.S. Supreme Ct. 1985. Formal referee dept. of fin. City of N.Y., 1954-65; adminstrv. judge U.S. Govt./Social Security adminstrn., Detroit, Queens, N.Y.C., 1965-90; pvt. practice Whitestone, N.Y., 1990—. Mem. Fordham Law Alumni Assn.

**FENTON, THOMAS CONNER,** lawyer; b. Cin., Feb. 9, 1954; S. William Conner and Virginia (Rawnsley) F.; m. Karen Lois Haswell, Oct. 20, 1979; children: Margaret Lois, Rebecca Conner, Robert Ellis. BA, Centre Coll., 1976; JD, Ohio State U., 1979. Bar: Ky. 1979, U.S. Dist. Ct. (we. dist.) Ky. 1979, U.S. Ct. Appeals (D.C. cir.) 1981, U.S. Dist. Ct. (ea. dist.) Ky. 1985, U.S. Ct. Appeals (6th cir.) 1986. Assoc. Greenebaum, Treitz, Brown & Marshall, Louisville, 1979-85, ptnr., 1985-88; v.p., counsel Nat. City Bank Ky., Louisville, 1989-93; counsel Nat. City Corp., Cleve., 1989-93; v.p. human resources Nat. City Processing Co., Louisville, 1993-95; of counsel Morgan & Pottinger PSC, Louisville, 1996—; lectr. Ohio Bankers Assn. Sch. of Human Resources Adminstrn., 1989-91. Author: Affirmative Action Relevant to Bankers, 1996. Bd. dirs. Elder Serve Inc., Louisville, 1983-91, 95—, sec. 1984-86, v.p., 1986-87, pres., 1987-90; bd. dirs. Louisville Youth Choir, Inc., 1996—, chmn., 1997—. Mem. Ky. Bar Assn. (chmn. labor rels. law sect. 1981-83), Louisville Bar Assn. Methodist. Labor, Contracts commercial, Banking. Home: 11003 Fox Moore Ct Louisville KY 40223-5531 Office: Morgan & Pottinger PSC 601 W Main St Louisville KY 40202-2976

**FERENCZ, BRADLEY,** judge; b. Queens, N.Y.; s. Murray Eugene and Regina Lorrain (Ingelberg). F.; m. Dulce Rodrequez, July 8, 1984; children: Margot Melissa Ferencz, Alexander Mikel Ferencz. BA, Ohio State U., 1969; JD, Rutgers U., 1971, postgrad., 1976-78. Bar: N.J. 1972, U.S. Dist. Ct. N.J. 1972, U.S. Supreme Ct. 1977, U.S. Ct. Appeals (3d cir.) 1980. Staff legal svcs. Middlesex County, N.J., 1972-76; pvt. practice Woodbridge, Highland Pk., N.J., 1976-80; supr. litigation Office Pub. Defender, Middlesex, 1979-84, 1st asst. dep., 1984-86, dir., 1986—; apptd. superior ct. judge Middlesex County, 1997—; adj. prof. Rutgers U., 1985-89. Trustee Middlesex County Bar Found., 1993—, Middlesex County Legal Svcs., 1981—, N.J. State Bar Found., scholarship com., fellowship com., mock trial com.; adv. com. mem. Puerto Rican Assn. Human Devel., 1993—, Middlesex County Coll. Divsn. Social Scis. and Humanities, 1991—. Mem. Nat. Assn. Criminal Def. Lawyers, N.J. State Bar Assn. (trustee criminal sect.), N.J. Assn. Criminal Def. Lawyers, Middlesex County Bar Assn. (pres. 1990-91, pres. elect 1989-90, 1st v.p. 1988-89, 2d v.p. 1987-88, sec. 1986-87, treas. 1985-87, trustee 1985-87, publicity and pub. rels. com., criminal practice com.), Assn. County Bar Pres., New Brunswick Bar Assn. Office: Middlesex County Court House 1 Kennedy Sq New Brunswick NJ 08901-1952

**FERGUS, GARY SCOTT,** lawyer; b. Racine, Wis., Apr. 20, 1954; s. Russell Malcolm and Phyl Rose (Muratore) F.; m. Isabelle Sabina Beekman, Sept. 28, 1985; children: Mary Marckwald Beekman Fergus, Kirkpatrick Russell Beekman Fergus. SB, Stanford U., 1976; JD, U. Wis., 1979; LLM, NYU,

1981. Bar: Wis. 1979, Calif. 1980. Assoc. Brobeck, Phleger & Harrison, San Francisco, 1980-86, ptnr., 1986—, mng. ptnr. products liability, ins. coverage, environ. and antitrust/appellat practices, 1996—, mgr. product liability/ins. coverage, environ. and antitrust, 1996—. Arch. computerized case mgmt. sys. Vol. San Francisco Leadership. Mem. ABA. Product liability, Transportation, Toxic tort. Home: 3024 Washington St San Francisco CA 94115-1618 Office: Brobeck Phleger & Harrison 1 Market Plz Ste 341 San Francisco CA 94105-1420

**FERGUSON, C. ROBERT,** lawyer, educator; b. Long Beach, Calif., Dec. 31, 1938; s. Frank H. and Ruth S. Ferguson; m. Kathryn Jane Weaver, Apr. 10, 1965 (div. June 25, 1995); children: Sharon Anne, Robert Timothy; m. Peggy Burke Daniell, Nov. 19, 1995. AB in Econs., U. So. Calif., 1961, JD, 1965. Bar: Calif. 1966, U.S. Dist. Ct. (ctrl. dist.) Calif. 1966, U.S. Ct. Appeals (9th cir.) 1987, U.S. Supreme Ct. 1975. Assoc. Musick, Peeler & Garrett, L.A., 1965-69, Hayes & Hume, Beverly Hills, Calif., 1969-74; pvt. practice Pasadena/Claremont, Calif., 1974—; adj. prof. physics U. La Verne (Calif.) Coll. Law, Calif., 1993—, adj. prof. evidence, 1994—; mem. Alcohol and Drug Abuse Com. Calif. State Bar, 1990-91; instr. astronomy and bus. law Chapman U., 1992-93; mem. adv. bd. La Verne Coll. Law, 1998—; arbitrator Am. Arbitration Assn., Nat. Arbitration Forum. Editor: Tall Tales and Memories, 1987. Mem. Stony Ridge Obs., 1985—, pres., 1994-97; co-founder, bd. govs. Mt. Wilson (Calif.) Inst., 1987—, COO, 1987-91; lectr., cons. Californians for Redevel. Edn., South Gate, 1996—; bd. dirs. Clan Fergusson Soc. N.Am., 1997—, regional v.p., pres. elect.; mem. L.A. Opera League. With U.S. Army, 1961-62. Decorated Knight, Knights Templar of Jerusalem, 1998. Mem. Univ. Club Pasadena, Univ. Club Claremont, Beta Theta Pi (past pres.). Avocations: astronomy, mountaineering, dry fly fishing, skiing. Land use and zoning (including planning), General civil litigation, General corporate. Office: C Robert Ferguson Atty at Law 237 W 4th St Claremont CA 91711-4710

**FERGUSON, DONALD LITTLEFIELD,** lawyer; b. Greenville, S.C., June 10, 1930; s. H. L. and Anne (Littlefield) F.; m. Barbara Wilson, May 20, 1961; children: Donald L. Jr., David Wilson, Robert Neil. BA, Furman U., 1951; LLB, Tulane U., 1954. Bar: S.C. 1954, U.S. Ct. Mil. Appeals 1955, U.S. Dist. Ct. S.C. 1957, U.S. Ct. Appeals (4th cir.) 1974. Assoc. Haynsworth, Marion, McKay & Guerard, Greenville, 1954-61, ptnr., 1961—, sr. ptnr., ret. Capt. USAF, 1954-57. Mem. ABA, Am. Judicature Soc., S.c. Bar Assn., Poinsett Club, Phi Kappa Phi, Phi Delta Phi. Baptist. Federal civil litigation, General civil litigation, State civil litigation. Home: 612 Roper Mountain Rd Greenville SC 29615-4227 Office: Haynsworth Marion McKay & Guerard 75 Beattie Pl Greenville SC 29601-2130

**FERGUSON, FRED ERNEST, JR.,** lawyer; b. Phoenix, June 8, 1935; s. Helen (Wilson) Ferguson; m. June, 1957 (div. Sept. 1970); 1 child, SueAnn; m. Patricia Sue Wooden, Sept. 25, 1970; 1 child, Fred E. III. BS, Ariz. State U., 1958; LLB, U. Ariz., 1963. Bar: Ariz. 1963, U.S. Dist. Ct. Ariz. 1963, U.S. Ct. Appeals (9th cir.) 1976, U.S. Supreme Ct. 1977. Ptnr. Evans, Kitchel & Jenckes, P.C., Phoenix, 1963-89, Lewis and Roca, Phoenix, 1989-91, Gust Rosenfeld, Phoenix, 1991—. Advisor YWCA of Maricopa County, Phoenix; trustee Rocky Mountain Mineral Law Found., 1979-88, 91-94, 98—; Christown YMCA, Phoenix, 1987-90; chmn. legis. dist. Phoenix Reps.; pres. bd. dirs. Lit. Vols. Maricopa County, 1992-94. Fellow Ariz. Bar Found.; mem. Kiwanis (pres. Camelback chpt. 1988-89). Republican. Episcopalian. Natural resources, Real property, Private international. Office: Gust Rosenfeld 201 N Central Ave Ste 3300 Phoenix AZ 85073-3300

**FERGUSON, GERALD PAUL,** lawyer; b. Teaneck, N.J., Oct. 17, 1951; s. James Richard and Ilene Veronica (Meyer) F.; m. Nancy Ivers, Aug. 20, 1977; 1 child, James Ralph. BA, Fairleigh Dickinson U., 1974; JD, Capital U., 1979. Bar: Ohio 1979, U.S. Dist. Ct. (so. dist.) Ohio 1980, U.S. Ct. Appeals (6th cir.) 1986, U.S. Supreme Ct. 1990. Ptnr. Vorys, Sater, Seymour and Pease, Columbus, 1979—; mem. rules adv. com. Ohio Supreme Ct., Columbus, 1993. Mem. ABA (litigation sect., mem. trial evidence subcom. 1985-86), Ohio State Bar Assn. (mem. jud. adv. and legal reform com., unauthorized practice law com. 1985-90), Columbus Bar Assn. (chmn. juror subcom. 1979-86). Republican. Roman Catholic. Avocations: tennis, golf, fishing. Federal civil litigation, State civil litigation, Intellectual property. Office: Vorys Sater Seymour & Pease 52 E Gay St Columbus OH 43215-3161

**FERGUSON, JAMES CURTIS,** lawyer; b. Spartanburg, S.C., Aug. 13, 1948; s. Napoleon and Elmira (Bennett) F.; m. Gloria Boatner, Aug. 3, 1976 (div. Feb. 1986); children: Troy, Aqua. Student, Friendship Jr. Coll., 1967-69; BA cum laude, Hiram Scott Coll., 1970; JD, So. U., 1975. Bar: La. 1976, U.S. Dist. Ct. (mid. dist.) La. 1976, U.S. Ct. Appeals (fifth cir.) 1976, U.S. Supreme Ct. 1982. Mng. atty. Capital Area Legal Svcs., Baton Rouge, 1976-80; pvt. practice Ferguson & Assocs., Baton Rouge, 1980—. Recipient Leadership award and medal Am. Legion, I Dare You award Readers Digest; Earl Warren scholar; Reginald Huber Smith fellow. Avocations: sports, reading, writing, cooking, counseling. General civil litigation, Civil rights, Franchising. Home: 5929 Hartford Ave Baton Rouge LA 70812-2236 Office: Ferguson & Assocs 343 3rd St Ste 410 Baton Rouge LA 70801-1309

**FERGUSON, JOHN MARSHALL,** retired federal judge; b. Marion, Ill., Oct. 14, 1921; s. John Marshall and Vessie (Widdows) F.; m. Jeanne Harmon, Sept. 23, 1950; children: Marcia Ferguson Velde, Mark Harmon, John Scott, Mary Sue. Student, So. Ill. U., 1939-41, S.E. Mo. Tchrs. Coll., 1941; LLB, JD, Washington U., St. Louis, 1948. Bar: Ill. 1949, U.S. Ct. Appeals (7th cir.) 1956, U.S. Supreme Ct. 1960. Asst. mgr. I.W. Rogers Theaters, Inc., Anna, Ill., 1934-42; atty. U.S. Fidelity & Guaranty Co., St. Louis, 1948-51; assoc. Baker, Kagy & Wagner, East St. Louis, Ill., 1951-56; ptnr. Baker, Kagy & Wagner, 1956-59, Wagner, Ferguson, Bertrand & Baker, East St. Louis and Belleville, Ill., 1959-72; magistrate judge U.S. Dist. Ct. (so. dist.) Ill., 1990-94; pres. bd. Arch Aircraft, Inc., 1966-68; disciplinary commr. Ill. Supreme Ct., 1957-90, mem. joint com. on revision disciplinary rules, 1972-74; mem. hearing bd. Ill. Registration and Disciplinary Commn., 1974-90; pres. 1st Dist. Fedn. Bar Assns. Precinct committeeman Stookey Twp., St. Clair County (Ill.) Republican Com., 1958-62; Bd. dirs., v.p. East St. Louis chpt. ARC. Capt. AUS, 1942-45. Mem. ABA, Ill. Bar Assn. (prof. responsibility com. 1975-86, chmn. 1983-84), St. Clair County Bar Assn., 7th Fed. Cir. Bar Assn. (bd. govs.), East St. Louis City Club (pres. 1960-61), Ill. Club (govs., pres. 1966-67), East St. Louis City Club (pres. 1960-61), Ill. Club (gov., pres. 1966-67), St. Clair Country Club (Belleville, pres. 1972-73), Masons, Elks, Delta Theta Phi. Home: 12 Oak Knoll Belleville IL 62223-1817

**FERGUSON, JOHN R.,** lawyer; b. Youngstown, Ohio, May 23, 1934; s. Hugh and Grace (Pearson) F.; m. Janine D. Harris, Febr. 1, 1980; children: Lorna Elizabeth, Scott Richard, Robert Ian, Brigit Grace, Rachel Anna. B, Ohio State U., Columbus, 1957; JD, Case Western Reserve U., Cleve., 1963. Bar: D.C. Ptnr. Baker & Hostetler, Cleve. & Washington, 1963-81, Pettit & Martin, Washington, 1979-81; mng. ptnr. Peabody Lambert Meyers, Washington, 1981-84; head of litigation Swindler & Berlin, Washington, 1984—; dir. Silver Hilton Lodge, 1995-98. V.p. Turkey Neck Loop Assn., Swanton, Mass., 1996-98. Capt. U.S. Marines, 1959-63. Mem. Deep Creek Lake Yacht Club. Avocations: fly fishing, skiing, boating. Federal civil litigation, Administrative and regulatory, Antitrust. Office: Swidler & Berlin 3000 K St NW Fl 3 Washington DC 20007-5109

**FERGUSON, MILTON CARR, JR.,** lawyer; b. Washington, Feb. 10, 1931; s. Milton Carr and Gladys (Emery) F.; m. Marian Evelyn Nelson, Aug. 21, 1954; children: Laura, Sharon, Marcia, Sandra. B.A., Cornell U., 1952; LL.B., 1954; LL.M., N.Y. U., 1960. Bar: N.Y. State 1954. Trial atty. tax div. Dept. Justice, Washington, 1954-60; asst. atty. gen. Dept. Justice, 1977-81; asst. prof. law U. Iowa, 1960-62; assoc. prof. N.Y.U., 1962-65; prof. N.Y. U., 1965-77; vis. prof. law Stanford (Calif.) U., 1972-73; of counsel Wachtell, Lipton, Rosen & Katz, N.Y.C., 1969-76; ptnr. Davis Polk & Wardwell, N.Y.C., 1981—; spl. cons. to Treasury Dept., Commonwealth P.R., 1974. Author: (with others) Federal Income Taxation Legislation in Perspective, 1965, Federal Income Taxation of Estates and Beneficiaries, 1970, 2d edit., 1994. Trustee NYU Law Ctr. Found., Lewis and Clark Coll. Mem. ABA (chmn. tax sect. 1993-94), N.Y. State Bar Assn., Soc. Illustrators. Corporate taxation, Taxation, general. Home: 32 Washington Sq W New York NY 10011-9156 Office: Davis Polk & Wardwell 450 Lexington Ave New York NY 10017-3911

**FERGUSON, PAUL F., JR.,** lawyer; b. Bethesda, Md., Aug. 1, 1957; s. Paul F. and Mary T. Ferguson; m. Kara Knapo, Jan. 27, 1984; children: Cassie, Katlyn, Trey, Timothy. BA, Rice U., 1979; JD, U. Houston, 1982. Bar: Tex., Colo., U.S. Dist. Ct. (ea. dist.) Tex., U.S. Ct. Appeals (5th cir.), U.S. Supreme Ct. Ptnr. Perdue, Turner & Berry, Houston, 1982-89, Provost & Umphrey, Beaumont, Tex., 1989—. Mem. Tex. State Bar Assn., Colo. State Bar Assn., Jefferson County Bar Assn., Port Arthur Bar Assn., Internat. Soc. Barristers, Am. Bd. Trial Advocates, Million Dollar Advocates Forum. Democrat. Baptist. Personal injury, Product liability. Office: Provost & Umphrey PO Box 4905 Beaumont TX 77704-4905

**FERGUSON, RALPH ALTON, JR. (SONNY FERGUSON),** circuit court judge; b. St. Louis, Mar. 23, 1948; s. Ralph Anderson and Mary P. Ferguson; m. Pennye Michelle Boackle, Oct. 8, 1972; children: Trey, Lorie, Jamie. BS in Bus., Auburn (Ala.) U., 1970; JD, Cumberland Sch. Law, Birmingham, Ala., 1973. Bar: Ala. 1974, U.S. Dist. Ct. (all dists.) Ala. 1974, U.S. Ct. Appeals (11th cir.) 1978. Sales clk., security Yeildings, Birmingham, 1970; lumber sales Southeastern Treated, Birmingham, 1971; head coach all sports Briarwood Christian, Birmingham, 1971-73; lawyer Lindberg, Lindberg & Leach, Birmingham, 1974-76, Leach, Dillard & Ferguson, Birmingham, 1976-80, Hampe, dillard & Ferguson, Birmingham, 1980-88, Dillard & Ferguson, Birmingham, 1988-95; circuit judge State of Ala., Birmingham, 1995—. Student/adult leader Fellowship of Christian Athletes, Birmingham, 1966—; mem. Monday Morning Quarterback, Birmingham, 1988—. Sgt. Air N.G., 1966-72. Named Nat. Lineman/Southeastern, Sports Illus./SEC, 1969. Mem. Ala. Bar Assn., Birmingham Bar Assn. (exec. com. 1994-97), Birmingham Bar Found., Am. Acad. Adoption Lawyers. Republican. Roman Catholic. Avocations: handball, football, basketball, boating. Office: Jefferson County Courthouse 716 21st St N Birmingham AL 35263-0110

**FERGUSON, ROBERT L., JR.,** lawyer; b. Cambridge, Mass., Mar. 31, 1945; s. Robert L. and Mary Jane (Campbell) F.; m. Pamela Gail Fuller, Apr. 20, 1968; children: Colleen B. Ferguson Driscoll, R. Christopher, P. Scott, Elizabeth E. BS in Elec. Engring., U. Md., College Park, 1968; JD, U. Md., Balt., 1972. Bar: Md. Assoc. engr. Bethlehem Steel Corp., Balt., 1968-69; assoc. engr. Balt. Gas & Electric, 1969-71, engr., 1971-73; assoc. Allen, Thieblot & Alexander, Balt., 1973-77, ptnr., 1977-88; ptnr. Thieblot, Ryan, Martin & Ferguson, Balt., 1988-96, Ferguson, Schetelich & Heffernan, P.A. and predecessor, Balt., 1996—. Pres. Balt. Coalition Against Substance Abuse, 1991-96; v.p. Balt. Prevention Coalition, 1995-96. Recipient Spl. award for legal excellence Md. Bar Found., 1995. Mem. Md. State Bar Assn. (past chmn. litigation sect.), Bar Assn. Balt. City (pres. 1998-99). Roman Catholic. Avocations: reading, sports, music. General civil litigation, Insurance, Aviation. Office: Ferguson Schetelich & Heffernan PA 1401 NationsBank Ctr 100 S Charles St Baltimore MD 21201-2725

**FERGUSON, ROYCE ALLAN, JR.,** lawyer; b. Spokane, Wash., Oct. 11, 1948; s. Royce Allan and Norma Jean (Hoskinson) F.; m. Mary Louise McKean, Dec. 27, 1974 (div. Mar. 1981); m. Peggy Hellen Tingley, Dec. 12, 1981 (div. June 1996); children: Sheila Rae, Royce Allan III, Scott Taylor. AA, Everett C.C., 1969; BA, Western Wash. U., 1971; JD, Gonzaga U., 1974. Bar: Wash. 1974, Ariz. 1983, U.S. Dist. Ct. (we. dist.) Wash. 1974, U.S. Ct. Appeals (9th cir.) 1981, U.S. Supreme Ct. 1981. Assoc., Michelson & Gallagher, Lynnwood, Wash., 1974-76; sole practice, Everett, Wash., 1976-79; sr. ptnr. Ferguson, Maynard, Miller & Wolff, Everett, 1979-89; pvt. practice, 1989—; referral atty. 2nd Amendment Found. Wash. State, Bellevue, 1982—, NRA, 1982—; Author: Washington Criminal Practice and Procedure, vols. 12 and 13, 1984, 2nd edit.; co-author: Washington Criminal Law, vol. 13A, 1990. Del. Wash. State Rep. Conv., 1976, 80; bd. dirs. Mental Health Svcs. Snohomish County, Inc., 1979. Mem. Wash. Trial Lawyers Assn., Wash. State Bar Assn. (mem. editl. adv. bd. 1984-90), Wash. Assn. Criminal Def. Lawyers, Wash. Arms. Coll. Club. Criminal, State civil litigation, Federal civil litigation. Office: 2931 Rockefeller Ave Everett WA 98201-4019

**FERGUSON, STEVEN E.,** lawyer; b. Oklahoma City, Apr. 26, 1955; m. Shelly J. Smith, Aug. 5, 1977; children: Steven E. Jr., Cicely J. BA, U. Okla., 1977; JD, Oklahoma City U., 1980. Bar: Okla. 1980. Ptnr. Crabb, Ferguson & Riesen, Oklahoma City. Family and matrimonial, Criminal, Personal injury. Office: Crabb Ferguson & Riesen 5101 N Classen Blvd Ste 301 Oklahoma City OK 73118-4433

**FERGUSON, THOMAS CROOKS,** lawyer; b. Nov. 27, 1933; s. Thomas C. and Grace (Crooks) F.; children: Leslie Mead, Ian Thomas. AB, Vanderbilt U., 1955, JD, 1959; cert., Hague Acad. Internat. Law, 1958; postgrad., Kenney Sch. Govt., Harvard U., 1985. Bar: Ill. 1960, Ky. 1961, D.C. 1993. Bd. mem. Mead Johnson Found., 1960-70; mktg. mgr. Pharmaseal Labs., 1962-75; pres. Atlantic Salvage Corp., 1975-78, Brevard Marina, 1977-82; dir. Eastern Caribbean Peace Corps, 1982-84; dep. commr. Immigration and Naturalization Service Dept. Justice, 1984-87; U.S. amb. to Brunei Darussalam, 1987-89; pres. Airscan Internat., Indialantic, Fla., 1989-91; pvt. practice Washington, 1991—. With U.S. Army, 1955-56. Recipient Comdr.'s medal for civilian svc. Grenada, 1983. Mem. ABA, Fed. Bar Assn. Clubs: Offshore Cruising of Calif., Eau Gallie Yacht. Avocations: sailing, tennis, diving. Home: 6781 Linford Ln Jacksonville FL 32217-2660 Office: 336 S Carolina Ave SE Washington DC 20003-4223

**FERGUSON, V. KEITH,** lawyer; b. Wilkin, Minn., May 1, 1932; s. Vernon Henry and Clarice Adeline F.; m. Mary Louise Scott, July 1, 1956; Bryan, Brent, Perry, Holly, Wade. JD, Drake U., 1958. Bar: Iowa. Ptnr. McCarville, Bennet, Berser, Ferguson, & Wilke, Ft. Dodge, Iowa, 1965-78; pvt. practice Ft. Dodge, Dayton, Iowa, 1978—; city atty. Dayton, Iowa, 1968-95; trustee Dayton Light & Power, 1971-96. Pres. Cmty. Club, Dayton, 1967-74, Lions Club, Dayton, 1998—. With U.S. Army, 1953-55. General practice. Home: PO Box 67 Dayton IA 50530-0067 Office: 35 S Main St Dayton IA 50530

**FERGUSON, WARREN JOHN,** federal judge; b. Eureka, Nev., Oct. 31, 1920; s. Ralph and Marian (Damele) F.; m. E. Laura Keyes, June 5, 1948; children: Faye F., Warren John, Teresa M., Peter J. B.A., U. Nev., 1942; LL.B., U. So. Calif., 1949; LL.D. (hon.), Western State U., San Fernando Valley Coll. Law. Bar: Calif. 1950. Mem. firm Ferguson & Judge, Fullerton, Calif., 1950-59; city atty. for cities of Buena Park, Placentia, La Puente, Baldwin Park, Santa Fe Springs, Walnut and Rosemead, Calif., 1953-59; mcpl. ct. judge Anaheim, Calif., 1959-60; judge Superior Ct., Santa Ana, Calif., 1961-66, Juvenile Ct., 1963-64, Appellate Dept., 1965-66; U.S. dist. judge Los Angeles, 1966-79; judge U.S. Circuit Ct. (9th cir.), Los Angeles, 1979-86; sr. judge U.S. Ct. Appeals (9th cir.), Santa Ana, 1986—; faculty Fed. Jud. Ctr., Practising Law Inst., U. Iowa Coll. Law, N.Y. Law Jour.; assoc. prof. psychiatry (law) Sch. Medicine, U. So. Calif.; assoc. prof. Loyola Law Sch. Served with AUS, 1942-46. Decorated Bronze Star. Mem. Phi Kappa Phi, Theta Chi. Democrat. Roman Catholic. Office: US Courthouse 411 W 4th St Ste 10-080 Santa Ana CA 92701-8001 *Having been born and raised in Nevada, I have adopted an old prospector's philosophy: "Live today; look every man in the eye; and tell the rest of the world to go to hell."*

**FERGUSON, WHITWORTH, III,** consulting company executive; b. Buffalo, Aug. 16, 1954; s. Whitworth Jr. and Elizabeth (Rice) F.; m. Mary Barstow, May 30, 1981 (div. 1993). BA in Econs., St. Lawrence U., Canton, N.Y., 1976; MBA in Fin., U. Pa., 1978; JD, Cornell U., 1981; MDiv, Princeton Theol. Sem., 1999. Bar: Ill. 1981, N.Y. 1983. Assoc. McDermott, Will & Emery, Chgo., 1981-82, Damon & Morey, Buffalo, 1982-84; officer fin. planning Key Trust Co., Buffalo, 1984-86; pres. Alpine Sports, Ltd., Williamsville, N.Y., 1986-90, Buffalo Consulting Co., Buffalo, 1990-94; editor The Economist Intelligence Unit, N.Y.C., 1994-96; cons. The Wharton Sch., 1996—; mng. dir. The NORAM Group, Ltd., Buffalo, 1990-94. Bd. dirs. Senecare Corp., 1983-88; bd. dirs. YMCA Greater Buffalo, 1985-94, vice chmn., 1988-90; ho. of dels. United Way Buffalo and Erie County, 1984-94; chmn. campaign for creativity Creative Edn. Found.; advisor ctr. entrepreneurial leadership Sch. Mgmt., SUNY, Buffalo, 1991-94; dir. Western N.Y. Venture Assn., 1991-94; mem. Westminster Presbyn. Trustees, 1989-91, chmn. stewardship, 1989, v.p., 1990, pres., 1991; ruling elder, 1992; advisor Ctr. for Entrepreneurship, Canisius Coll., 1992-94; active Brick Presbyn. Ch. Mem. ABA, Brick Presbyn. Ch.

**FERGUSON, WILLIAM I.,** judge; b. Feb. 22, 1949; s. William A. and Evalyn F.; m. Susan L. Ferguson, 1983. BS, Mo. Valley Coll., 1971; JD, IIT, 1975. Assoc. judge DuPage Jud. Ctr., Wheaton, Ill. Mem. Ill. State Bar Assn. (assembly mem. 1996—, Hon. Mention 1996-97), DuPage County Bar Assn. (bd. dirs. 1991-94, past pres. 1994, 96, pres. 1997—). Presbyterian. Office: DuPage Jud Ctr 501 N County Farm Rd Wheaton IL 60187-3942

**FERN, CAROLE LYNN,** lawyer; b. Freeport, N.Y., Sept. 2, 1958; m. Tariq Rafique. BA, Johns Hopkins U., 1980; JD, Harvard U., 1983. Bar: N.Y. 1983, Calif. 1987. Assoc. Donovan, Leisure, Newton & Irvine, N.Y.C., 1983-87, Shearman & Sterling, N.Y.C., 1987-91, Berlack, Israels & Liberman, LLP, N.Y.C., 1991-92; ptnr. Berlack, Israels & Liberman, N.Y.C., 1993—. Dep. counsel Dukakis for Pres. Mem. N.Y.C. Bar Assn., Am. Arbitration Assn. (panel of arbitrators), N.Y. County Lawyers Assn. (Supreme Ct. com.), Phi Beta Kappa. Democrat. Unitarian. Avocation: tennis, jogging. Bankruptcy, General civil litigation. Office: Berlack Israels & Liberman 120 W 45th St New York NY 10036-4041

**FERNANDEZ, DENNIS SUNGA,** lawyer, electrical engineer, entrepreneur; b. Manila, June 3, 1961; came to U.S., 1972; s. Gil Conui and Imelda Sunga (Miller) F.; m. Irene Y. Hu, Aug. 26, 1989; children: Megan H., Jared R. BSEE, Northwestern U., 1983; JD, Suffolk U., 1989. Bar: Mass. 1989, U.S. Dist. Ct. Mass. 1989, D.C. 1990, U.S. Ct. Appeals (Fed. cir.) 1990, Calif, 1991. Engr. NCR, Ft. Collins, Colo., 1983-84; product mgr. Digital Equipment Corp., Hudson, Mass., 1984-86; program mgr. Raytheon, Andover, Mass., 1986-88; engr. Racal, Westford, Mass., 1988-89; assoc. Nutter, McClennen & Fish, Boston, 1989-91, Fenwick & West, Palo Alto, Calif., 1991-94; v.p. Walden Internat. Investment Group, San Francisco, 1995-96, Singapore Techs./Vertex Mgmt., 1996-97, Neo Paradigm Labs., Inc., 1997-98; ptnr. Dennis & Irene Fernandez LLP, 1998—. Contbr. articles to profl. jours. Mem. IEEE, Sci. and Tech. Adv. Coun. (dir.). Patent, Computer.

**FERNANDEZ, FERDINAND FRANCIS,** federal judge; b. 1937. BS, U. So. Calif., 1958, JD, 1963; LLM, Harvard U., 1963. Bar: Calif. 1963, U.S. Dist. Ct. (cen. dist.) Calif. 1963, U.S. Ct. Appeals (9th cir.) 1963, U.S. Supreme Ct. 1967. Elec. engr. Hughes Aircraft Co., Culver City, Calif., 1958-62; law clk. to dist. judge U.S. Dist. Ct. (cen. dist.) Calif., 1963-64; pvt. practice law Allard, Shelton & O'Connor, Pomona, Calif., 1964-80; judge Calif. Superior Ct. San Bernardino County, Calif., 1980-85, U.S. Dist. Ct. (cen. dist.) Calif., L.A., 1985-89, U.S. Ct. Appeals (9th cir.), L.A., 1989—; Lester Roth lectr. U. So. Calif. Law Sch., 1992. Contbr. articles to profl. jours. Vice chmn. City of La Verne Commn. on Environ. Quality, 1971-73; chmn. City of Claremont Environ. Quality Bd., 1972-73; bd. trustees Pomona Coll., 1990—. Fellow Am. Coll. Trust and Estate Counsel; mem. ABA, State Bar of Calif. (fed. cts. com. 1966-69, ad hoc com. on attachments 1971-85, chmn. com. on adminstrn. of justice 1976-77, exec. com. taxation sect. 1977-80, spl. com. on mandatory fee arbitration 1978-79), Calif. Judges Assn. (chmn. juvenile cts. com. 1983-84, faculty mem. Calif. Jud. Coll. 1982-83, faculty mem. jurisprudence and humanities course 1983-85), Hispanic Nat. Bar Assn., L.A. County Bar Assn. (bull. com. 1974-75), San Bernardino County Bar Assn., Pomona Valley Bar Assn. (co-editor Newsletter 1970-72, trustee 1971-78, sec.-treas. 1973-74, 2d v.p. 1974-75, 1st v.p. 1975-76, pres. 1976-77), Estate Planning Coun. Pomona Valley (sec. 1966-76), Order of Coif, Phi Kappa Phi, Tau Beta Pi. Office: US Ct Appeals 9th Cir 125 S Grand Ave Ste 602 Pasadena CA 91105-1621

**FERNANDEZ, FRANCES GARCIA,** lawyer; b. New Rochelle, N.Y., May 14, 1960; d. Marcelino Francis and Elizabeth Lee (Edge) Garcia; m. Ricardo A. Fernandez, Apr. 1, 1989. BSN, Vanderbilt U., 1983; JD, Stetson U., 1987. Bar: Fla. 1987, U.S. Ct. Appeals (11th cir.) 1988, U.S. Dist. Ct. (mid. dist.) Fla., 1988. Staff nurse Tampa (Fla.) Gen. Hosp., 1983-86, dir. risk mgmt., 1992—; assoc. Shackleford, Farrior, Stallings, Tampa, 1987-88, Shear, Newman, Hahn & Rosenkranz, Tampa, 1988-91, Stephens, Lynn, Klein & McNicholas, Tampa, 1991, 92—. Bd. dirs. Fla. West Coast chpt. Chrons & Colitus Found. Am., Tampa, 1992; atty., guardian Guardian Ad Litem, Tampa, 1988—. Mem. ABA, Fla. Bar, Hillsborough County Bar Assn., Jr. League Tampa. Personal injury, Health, Administrative and regulatory. Office: 101 E Kennedy Blvd Ste 2500 Tampa FL 33602-5150

**FERNANDEZ, HERMES A., III,** lawyer; b. Queens, N.Y., Aug. 22, 1955; s. Hermes Alexander and Helen Gloria (Hall) F.; m. Theresa Anne Dehm, Sept. 10, 1977; children: Holly Kathryn, Amy Elizabeth, Daniel Dehm. BA with honors, LeMoyne Coll., 1977; JD magna cum laude, Syracuse U., 1981. Bar: N.Y. 1982, U.S. Dist. Ct. (no. dist.) N.Y. 1991, U.S. Ct. Appeals (2d cir.) 1991, U.S. Ct. Appeals (5th cir.) 1984. Jud. clk. Hon. John MacKenzie U.S. Dist. Ct. (ea. dist.) Va., Norfolk, 1981-82; trial atty. civil divsn. U.S. Dept. Justice, Washington, 1982-86; asst. counsel to gov. State of N.Y., Albany, 1986-90; assoc., ptnr. Bond, Schoeneck & King, LLP, Albany, 1990—. Author articles. Mem. Citizens Budget Adv. Com., Albany, 1996—; v.p. Homeless and Travelers Aid Soc., Albany, 1991—, also past pres.; chair legis. com. MS Soc. N.E. N.Y., Albany, 1997—. Mem. N.Y. State Bar Assn. (health law sect., legis. policy com.), Am. Health Lawyers Assn., Univ. Club. Avocations: golf, history. Administrative and regulatory, Health, Government contracts and claims. Office: Bond Schoeneck & King LLp 111 Washington Ave Albany NY 12210-2202

**FERNANDEZ, JOSE WALFREDO,** lawyer; b. Cienfuegos, Cuba, Sept. 19, 1955; came to U.S., 1967; s. Jose Rigoberto and Flora (Gomez) F.; m. Andrea Gabor, June 22, 1985. BA, Dartmouth Coll., 1977; JD, Columbia U., 1980. Bar: N.Y. 1981, N.J. 1981, U.S. Dist. Ct. (so. dist.) N.Y. 1981, U.S. Dist. Ct. N.J. 1981. Assoc. Curtis, Mallet, Prevost, Colt & Mosle, N.Y.C., 1981-84; assoc. Baker & McKenzie, N.Y.C., 1984-89, ptnr., 1989-96; ptnr. O'Melveny & Myers, L.L.P., N.Y.C., 1996—; adj. prof. N.Y. Law Sch., 1984-87. Contbr. articles to profl. jours. Bd. dirs. Ballet Hispanico, Ceiba Prodns., WBGO-FM Newark Pub. Radio. Mem. ABA (com. Inter-Am. law 1985—, Ctrl. Am. task force 1985-92, presdl. commn. L.Am. 1986-91), N.Y.C. Bar Assn. (com. fgn. and comparative law, chmn. Inter-A m. affairs com. 1996-98, city bar fund 1999—), U.S.-Spain C. of C. (bd. dirs. 1999), Brazilian-U.S. C. of C. (bd. dirs. 1994-99). Avocations: sports, non-fiction writing, travel. Private international, Contracts commercial, Banking. Home: 508 E 87th St New York NY 10128-7602 Office: O'Melveny & Myers LLP Citicorp Ctr 153 E 53rd St Fl 53D New York NY 10022-4611

**FERNANDEZ, RICARDO ANTONIO,** lawyer; b. Tampa, Fla., Feb. 28, 1955; s. Ramon Vega and Josephine (Giglio) F.; m. Fran Gracia, Apr. 1, 1989 (div. Aug. 1995); 1 child, Michael Anthony. BA, U. Fla., 1975; JD, Stetson U., 1978. Bar: Fla. 1978, Calif. 1982. Atty. USN JAG Corps, San Diego, 1979-84; shareholder Shackleford, Farrior et al, Tampa, Fla., 1984-96, Bavol Bush & Sisco, Tampa, Fla., 1996—; mem. steering com. Def. Rsch. Inst., Chgo., 1990—. Contbr. articles to profl. jours.; editor (newsletter) Rx for the Def., 1998. Pres. Guardian Ad Litem Guild, Tampa, 1994-95. Lt. USN, 1979-84. Fellow Am. Bar Found.; mem. Fla. Bar Assn. (gov. 1995-97, Pro Bono Svc. award 1990), Calif. Bar Assn., Hillsborough County Bar Assn. (pres. 1994-95, Jimmy Kynes Pro Bono Svc. award 1990). Avocations: reading, scuba diving, fishing. Personal injury, Product liability, General civil litigation. Office: Bavol Bush & Sisco 100 S Ashley Dr Ste 2100 Tampa FL 33602-5311

**FERNANDEZ, WILLIAM WARREN, SR.,** lawyer; b. Washington, Aug. 31, 1943; s. Gumersindo Alonso and Kathryn Naomi (Nycum) F.; m. Linda J.; children: William Warren, James Robert, Rosemarie Patricia. A.A., U. Fla., 1964, B.A., 1967, J.D., 1969. Bar: Fla. 1969, U.S. Dist. Ct. (mid. dist.) Fla. 1970, U.S. Ct. Claims 1973, U.S. Tax Ct. 1973, U.S. Ct. Appeals (5th cir.) 1972, U.S. Ct. Appeals (11th cir.) 1981, U.S. Supreme Ct. 1972. Staff atty. Law, Inc. of Hillsborough County (Fla.), 1969-70; assoc. Pope & Burton, P.A., Tampa, Fla., 1970-71; ptnr. Fernandez & Scarito, Orlando, Fla., 1971-79; sole practice, Orlando, 1979—; mem. Fla. Bar Study and Standardization of Disciplinary Enforcement Com., 1972-73, client security fund, 1993—; chmn. Winter Springs beautification bd., 1994-95, mem. planning and zoning bd., local planning agy., 1995—, chmn., 1996-98; treas. Citrus coun. Girl Scouts U.S., 1997-98; chmn. Altamonte Springs Code Enforcement Bd., 1982-88. Mem. Altamonte Springs (Fla.) Charter Revision Commn., 1974, 79, 85; mem. citizens adv. com., sec. Seminole County Expressway Authority, 1984—; bd. dirs. Fla. Symphony Youth Orch., 1988-89;

bd. dirs. Muscular Dystrophy Assn. Am., 1972-77, pres., 1975-76; bd. dirs. Seminole County Mental Health Ctr., Inc., 1979-84, pres., 1982-83; bd. dirs. Council of 100 of Seminole County (Fla.), 1975—, pres., 1978-80, 83—, sec., 1980-83 ; bd. dirs. T.H.E. Wayfarer Inc. (Transp. for Handicapped and Elderly), Orlando, 1976-79, treas., 1977-79; bd. dirs. Easter Seals Soc. Orange, Seminole and Osceola, 1978-79, coun. rep. to Seminole Sunshine State House. Served with U.S. Army, 1968-69. Recipient various civic awards, including certs. of appreciation from Muscular Dystrophy Assn., Easter Seals, YMCA, T.H.E. Wayfarer, Inc., Seminole County Mental Health Ctr. Service award City Altamonte Springs, 1974, 83. Mem. ABA, Orange County Bar Assn., Assn. Trial Lawyers Am., Orange County Legal Aid Soc., Aircraft Owners and Pilots Assn., Acad. Fla. Trial Lawyers, Ranchlands Homeowner's Assn. (v.p. 1994-95, pres. 1995—). . Roman Catholic.pres. 1995—), Fla. Trailblazers, Triple Horse Club. Democrat. Roman Catholic. Fax: 407-699-6877. E-mail: wm.w.fernandez@abanet.org. General practice, Real property, Alternative dispute resolution. Office: 250 Panama Rd E Winter Springs FL 32708-3516

**FERNÁNDEZ-GONZÁLEZ, JUSTO,** lawyer, legal assistance director; b. San Gaspar, Jalisco, Mexico, Oct. 18, 1952; came to U.S., 1966; s. Feliciano and Paula (González) Fernández; m. Bernice Armijo-Fernández, Feb. 1984 (div.); children: Justo, Natalia, Maclovio, Rene. AA, Reedley Coll., 1973; BA, UCLA, 1976, student, 1978; JD, U. Calif. Hastings, San Francisco, 1981. Bar: Tex. 1983, U.S. Ct. Appeals (5th cir.) 1984, U.S. Dist. Ct. (no. and we. dists.) Tex. 1986, U.S. Supreme Ct. 1990. Staff atty. North Cen. Tex. Legal Aid, Dallas, 1984-86; staff atty. El Paso (Tex.) Legal Assistance, 1986, supr., 1986-87, dep. dir., 1987-89, exec. dir., 1989—. Bd. dirs. Tex. Legal Svcs. Ctr., Austin, 1986—, Cen. de Medico Del Valle, El Paso, 1990—, Alternative Dispute Resolution, El Paso, 1989—, Project Adv. Group region 7, Washington, 1985—; adv. com. United Way, El Paso, 1990. Reginald Heber Smith fellow Legal Svcs. Corp., Washington, 1981-84; named Most Outstanding Atty. North Cen. Legal Svcs., Dallas, 1985, Atty. of Yr., Tex. Clients Coun., 1992. Mem. Tex. Bar Assn., Fed. Bar Assn., Mexican-Am. Bar, Coll. of the State Bar. Avocations: jogging, swiming, reading, raising pigeons. Home: 2325 San Diego Ave El Paso TX 79930-1322 Office: El Paso Legal Assistance 1301 N Oregon St El Paso TX 79902-4025

**FERNICOLA, GREGORY ANTHONY,** lawyer; b. Orange, N.J., Jan. 3, 1957; s. Anthony R. and Vera A. (Merlo) F. BS, St. Francis Coll., 1978; MBA, Rutgers U., 1980; JD cum laude, Georgetown U., 1985. Bar: N.Y. 1986, N.J. 1986, U.S. Dist. Ct. N.J. 1986; CPA, N.Y. Acct. Price Waterhouse & Co., N.Y.C., 1980-82; assoc. Spengler, Carlson et al, N.Y.C., 1985-87, Skadden, Arps, Slate, Meagher & Flom, N.Y.C., 1987-92; ptnr., 1993—. Sr. editor Law and Policy in Internat. Bus., 1984-85. Mem. Georgetown U. Nat. Law Alumni Bd., 1993-95. Mem. ABA, AICPA, Assn. Bar City N.Y. Roman Catholic. Avocations: underwater archaeology, sailing, fishing, distance swimming. Finance, Securities, General corporate. Home: 300 W 23rd St New York NY 10011-2210 Office: Skadden Arps Slate Meagher & Flom 919 3rd Ave New York NY 10022-3902

**FERNSTRUM, DAVID ROSS,** lawyer; b. Detroit, Mar. 24, 1950; s. Richard Franklin and Margaret Elizabeth (Mehlhope) F.; m. Marilyn Jeanne Waite, June 3, 1972; children: Megan, Tait. BA, Ohio Wesleyan U., Delaware, 1972; JD, Wayne State U., Detroit, 1975. Bar: Mich. 1975, U.S. Dist. Ct. (we. dist.) Mich. 1975, U.S. Dist. Ct. (ea. dist.) Mich. 1977, U.S. Dist. Ct. (no. dist.) Ky. 1981. Clk. Mich. State Appellate Defender's Office, Detroit, 1974-75; assoc. Clary, Nantz, Wood, Hoffius, Rankin & Cooper, Grand Rapids, Mich., 1975-81; shareholder Clary, Nantz, Wood, Hoffius, Rankin & Cooper, Grand Rapids, 1981-83; ptnr. Mika, Meyers, Beckett & Jones, Grand Rapids, 1984; v.p. Atmosphere Processing, Inc., Holland, Mich., 1985; ptnr. Mika, Meyers, Beckett & Jones, Grand Rapids, 1986—; lectr. Grand Valley State U., Allendale, Mich., 1989-92. Mem. Planning Commn., East Grand Rapids, Mich., 1987-88. Mem. ABA (chair subcom. rights of union mems. and non mems., com. on state and local govt., bargaining and employment law, sect. labor and employment law 1984—), Grand Rapids Bar Assn. (sec. labor and employment law, chair 1999). Avocations: boating, golf, photography. Labor. Office: Mika Meyers Beckett & Jones 200 Ottawa Ave NW Ste 700 Grand Rapids MI 49503-2421

**FERO, DEAN JOHN,** lawyer; b. Rochester, N.Y., July 1, 1930; s. Victor Warren and Nina D. F.; m. Karolina Seidenbusch, Mar. 18, 1972; children: Shela Karolina, Matthew J. History & Econs., Hobart Coll., 1953; LLB, Syracuse U., 1956, JD, 1968. Bar: N.Y., U.S. Dist. Ct. (no, ea. and we. dists.) N.Y. Atty. Castle Fitch Swan & DeVidio, Rochester, N.Y., 1956-58, Hon. J. Eugene Goddard, Rochester, N.Y., 1958-64, Damico & Fero, Rochester, N.Y., 1964-84, Fero, Pilato & Ingersoll, Rochester, N.Y., 1984—. Mem. N.Y. State Bar Assn. Episcopalian. Avocations: hunting, fishing, reading. Estate planning, Family and matrimonial, General practice. Office: Fero Pilato & Ingersoll 183 E Main St Ste 1350 Rochester NY 14604-1674

**FERRANTE, R. WILLIAM,** lawyer; b. Dearborn, Mich., Feb. 1, 1942; s. Carmen Oral and Angel Agnes (Gallo) F.; m. Karen Sue Swanson, Aug. 22, 1964; children: Christopher A., Paul A. BA, Claremont McKenna Coll., 1964; MBA, U. Calif., Berkeley, 1969; JD, U. San Diego, 1976. Bar: Calif. 1976, U.S. Dist. Ct. (so. dist.) Calif. 1976, U.S. Dist. Ct. (ctrl. dist.) Calif. 1990. Dep. city atty. City Prosecutor's Office, San Diego, 1977-78; sr. atty. Pacific Bell, San Diego, 1978-90; sole practitioner Oceanside, Calif., 1990—. Chmn. Bonsall (Calif.) Planning Commn., 1988-94, Santa Margarita Family YMCA, Vista, Caif., 1985-86; trustee MiraCosta Coll., Oceanside, 1981-82. Named Boss Cum Laude, San Diego Legal Secs., 1984. Mem. Calif. Bar Assn., Bar Assn. No. San Diego County, Bonsall C. of C. (bd. dirs. 1993-96). General corporate, Estate planning, State civil litigation. Home: PO Box 714 Bonsall CA 92003-0714 Office: 4128 Avenida De La Plata Ste A Oceanside CA 92056-6001

**FERRANTI, THOMAS, JR.,** lawyer; b. Bklyn., Mar. 14, 1969; s. Thomas and Janet Rose (Giordano) F.; m. Renée Esposito, July 11, 1998. BA, St. John's U., N.Y.C., 1991, JD, 1994. Bar: N.Y. 1995, N.J. 1995, D.C. 1995. Dietary aide S.I. (N.Y.) U. Hosp., 1987-1993; intern Dept. of Investigation, N.Y.C., 1990, Justice Finnegan, N.Y. State Supreme Ct., Queens, 1990; legal intern Macy's Northeast, N.Y.C., 1991, N.Y.C. Coun., S.I., 1992; intern Supreme Ct. trial divsn. Richmond County Dist. Atty., S.I., 1993-94; tchr. law Monsignor Farrell H.S., S.I., 1994-95; pvt. practice, S.I., 1995—; lawyer, witness Criminal Trial Inst., St. John's U., 1991-94, Civil Trial Inst., 1991-94; tutor, counselor Student Network Accessing Counselor Program, 1991-94; fire fighter N.Y.C. Fire Dept., 1993—. Gen. mgr., pres. Sta. WMOC, S.I., 1989-91. St. John's U. scholar, 1988-91. Mem. ABA, N.Y. State Bar Assn., Nat. Italian-Am. Bar Assn., Golden Key, Lambda Kappa Phi, Kappa Gamma Pi, Iota Alpha Sigma (pres. 1990-91). Roman Catholic. Avocations: aquarium hobbyist, weight training, science fiction, coin collecting, travel. Fax: 718-948-5000. Probate, Real property, General practice. Home: 99 Pitney Ave Staten Island NY 10309-1918 Office: 11 Sunfield Ave Staten Island NY 10312-1414

**FERRARI, GARY JOHN,** lawyer; b. Ill., Oct. 14, 1958; s. John Joseph and Geraldine May F. AA, Ill. Valley C.C., 1978; BA, U. Ill., 1980, JD, 1983. Bar: Ill. 1983, U.S. Ct. Mil. Appeals 1986, U.S. Dist. Ct. (cen. dist.) Ill. 1987, U.S. Dist. Ct. (no dist.) Ill. 1990. Atty. Goldsworthy, Fifield & Hasselberg, Peoria, Ill., 1987-90, John E. Mitchell Law Offices, Peoria, Ill., 1990—. Pres. Peoria Italian-Am. Soc., 1998—; sec. Peoria Area Ethnic Assn., 1997—. Lt.USNR, 1983-86. Mem. KC, Am. Legion. Roman Catholic. Workers' compensation. Home: 6710 N Fawndale Dr Peoria IL 61615-2315 Office: Law Offices John Mitchell 415 NE Jefferson Ave Peoria IL 61603-3725

**FERRELL, MILTON MORGAN, JR.,** lawyer; b. Coral Gables, Fla., Nov. 6, 1951; s. Milton M. and Annie (Blanche) Bradley; m. Lori R. Sanders, May 22, 1982; children: Milton Morgan III, Whitney Connolly. BA, Mercer U., 1973, JD, 1975. Bar: Fla. 1975. Asst. state's atty. State's Atty.'s Office, Miami, 1975-77; ptnr. Ferrell & Ferrell, Miami, 1977-84; sole practice Miami, 1985-87; ptnr. Ferrell & Williams, P.A., Miami, 1987-90, Ferrell & Fertel, P.A., Miami, 1990-98, Ferrell Schultz Carter & Fertel P.A., 1999—. Trustee Mus. Sci. and Space Transit Planetarium, 1977-82; mem. Ambs. of Mercy, Mercy Hosp. Found., Inc., 1985-94; trustee, mem. legal com., chair com. U. Miami Project to Cure Paralysis, 1985-94; bd. trustees Eaglebrook Sch., 1995-98, Robinson Charitable Found., 1993—. Fellow Nat. Assn. Criminal Def. Lawyers, Am. Bd. Criminal Lawyers (bd. govs. 1981-82, sec. 1983-84, v.p. 1984-86, pres. 1987-88); mem. ABA (grantee 1975), Fla. Bar Assn. (jury instrns. com. 1987-88, chmn. grievance com. 11-L 1989-91), Dade County Bar Assn. (bd. dirs. 1977-80), mem. Performing Arts Ctr. Found. Greater Miami, Bath Club (bd. govs. 1992-95), Miami Club, Banker's Club, Cat Cay Yacht Club, Inc. (bd. dirs. 1997—, treas. 1998-99, pres. 1999—), Indian Creek Country Club, LaGorce Country Club, Fisher Island Club. Federal civil litigation, State civil litigation, Criminal. Home: Bay Point 4511 Lake Rd Miami FL 33137-3372 Office: Ferrell Schultz Carter & Fertel PA 201 S Biscayne Blvd Ste 1920 Miami FL 33131-4329

**FERRELL, SUSAN R.,** lawyer; b. Muncy, Pa., Jan. 13, 1959; d. Robert Walton and Lorma Rae (Egli) F.; m. David Edward Troller, Aug. 31, 1985; children: Katharine, Andrew, Robert. BA, Pa. State U., 1980; JD, Coll. William and Mary, 1983. Bar: Pa. 1983, Ohio 1986. Assoc. Mitchell, Mitchell & Gray, Williamsport, Pa., 1983-85; asst. dist. atty. Lycoming County, Williamsport, 1984; assoc. Hollingworth & Sunderland, Cin., 1986-89; law clk. to judge U.S. Dist. Ct. (so. dist.) Ohio, Cin., 1990—; adj. prof. sch. of law U. Dayton, 1997. pres. elect Jr. League Cin., 1999-00; bd. sec. Family Nurturing Ctr. Ky., Edgewood, 1993-96; mem. chancel choir Armstrong Chapel United Meth. Ch., Cin., 1995—; bd. mem. Village Views, Terrace Park, Ohio, 1994-98. Mem. ABA. Avocations: volunteer work, music, writing. Office: Potter Stewart US Courthouse 100 E 5th St Ste 801 Cincinnati OH 45202-3927

**FERRELL, WAYNE EDWARD, JR.,** lawyer; b. Pascagoula, Miss., Jan. 26, 1946; s. Wayne E. and Bessie (Ryals) F.; m. Susan Jane Nicholson, Mar. 28, 1970; children: Taylor N., Matthew G. B.A. in Bus. Adminstrn. & Econs., Millsaps Coll., 1969; J.D., Miss. Coll. Sch. Law, 1975; LL.M. in Aviation and Space Law, McGill U., 1981. Bar: Miss. 1976, U.S. Dist. Cts. (so. and no. dists.) Miss. 1976, U.S. Ct. Appeals (5th and 11th cirs.) 1978, U.S. Supreme Ct. 1985; lic. instrument-rated comml. pilot. Assoc. Satterfield, Allred & Colbert, Jackson, Miss., 1976-78; assoc., ptnr. Cothren, Pittman & Ferrell, Jackson, 1978-81; sole practice, Jackson, 1981-83, 95—; ptnr. Ferrell & Hubbard, Jackson, 1983-94. Mem. class of 1992-93 Leadership Jackson, Miss. Served to Lt. Col., Dep. Comdr. Maintenance, Miss. Air N.G., 1970-92. Named Alumnus of Yr., Miss. Coll. Sch. Law, 1983. Fellow ABA (mem. young lawyers divsn. 1984—); mem. Nat. Transp. Safety Bd. Bar Assn. (v.p.), Nat. Football Players Assn. (agent), Nat. Basketball Players Assn. (agent), Am. Soc. Internat. Law, Assn. Trial Lawyers of Am. (aviation sect.), Miss. Young Lawyers Assn. (sec. 1980-81), Brain Injury Assn. of Miss., Inc. (bd. dirs. 1995—, treas. 1995-96, v.p. 1996-99), Miss. Trial Lawyers Assn., bd. govs. 1982-83, chmn. products liability com. 1982-83, aviation com. 1982-83), Miss. Bar Assn. (ethics com., 1984-87, character and fitness com., 1982-87, Young Lawyers sect. 1976-82, sec. 1980-81), Miss. Coll. Sch. of Law Alumni Assn. (pres. 1979-80, bd. dirs. 1978-79, 80-81), Hinds County Trial Lawyers Assn., Hinds County and Am. (mem. aviation and space law com., torts and ins. practices 1976—, internat. ins. com. internat. law 1976-86, aviation com. litigation 1980—, forum com. air space law 1984—, young lawyers liason standing com. aeronautical law 1982-85), Inst. Air and Space Law Assn., Lawyer-Pilots Bar Assn., Metro Jackson Sports Mktg. Coun., Phi Alpha Delta (charter mem. Virgil A. Griffin chpt.). Methodist. Aviation, Personal injury, Admiralty. Home: 5326 Red Fox Rd Jackson MS 39211-4626 Office: 405 Tombigbee St PO Box 24448 Jackson MS 39225-4448

**FERREN, JOHN MAXWELL,** lawyer; b. Kansas City, Mo., July 21, 1937; s. Jack Maxwell and Elizabeth Anne (Hansen) F.; m. Ann Elizabeth Speidel, Sept. 4, 1961 (div.); children: Andrew John, Peter Maxwell; m. Linda Jane Finkelstein, June 17, 1994. AB magna cum laude, Harvard U., 1959, LLB, 1962. Bar: Ill. 1962, Mass. 1967, D.C. 1970. Assoc. Kirkland, Ellis, Hodson, Chaffetz & Masters, Chgo., 1962-66; dir. Neighborhood Law Office Program, Harvard U. Law Sch., Cambridge, Mass., 1966-68; teaching fellow, dir. Neighborhood Law Office Program, Harvard Law Sch. (Legal Svcs. Program), Cambridge, 1968-69, lectr. law, dir., 1969-70; ptnr. Hogan & Hartson, Washington, 1970-77; assoc. judge D.C. Ct. Appeals, 1977-97, Corp. Counsel, Washington, 1997—; mem. disciplinary bd. D.C. Ct. Appeals, 1972-76; mem. exec. com., bd. dirs. Council on Legal Edn. for Profl. Responsibility, 1970-80; exec. com. Washington Lawyers Com. for Civil Rights Under Law, 1970-77. Contbr. articles to profl. jours. Treas., bd. dirs. Firman Neighborhood House, Chgo., 1964-66; legis. subcom. on consumer credit Chgo. Commn. on Human Rels. Com. on New Residents, 1964-66; bd. dirs. Frederick B. Abramson Meml. Found., 1991-97, People's Devel. Corp., Washington, 1970-74, George A. Wiley Meml. Fund, 1974-84, Nat. Resource Ctr. for Consumers of Legal Svcs., 1973-77, Ctr. for Law and Edn., Cambridge, Mass., 1989-94; originator, chmn. Neighborhood Legal Advice Clinics, Ch. Fedn. Greater Chgo., 1964-66; exec. com. of legal adv. com. Nat. Com. Against Discrimination in Housing, 1974-77; steering com. Nat. Prison Project of ACLU Found., 1975-77. Fellow Am. Bar Found.; mem. ABA (Commn. on Nat. Inst. Justice 1972-80, mem. consortium on legal svcs. and pub. 1972-73, 76-79, chmn. 1979-82, chmn. spl. com. on pub. interest practice 1976-78), Am. Law Inst., Phi Beta Kappa. Presbyterian. Office: Office of the Corp Counsel 441 4th St NW # 1060N Washington DC 20001-2714

**FERRER, RAFAEL DOUGLAS PAUL,** lawyer; b. Seattle, Apr. 12, 1957; s. Rafael George and Barbara (Gould) F. BA in Acctg., U. Wash., 1979; JD, U. Puget Sound, 1982. Bar: Wash. 1985, U.S. Ct. Appeals (9th cir.) 1986. Acct. Lallman & Feldman, Ketchum, Idaho, 1980; tax profl. Touche Ross & Co., Seattle, 1981-82; securities syndicator Brouner Securities, Seattle, 1983; legal intern Davies Pearson, Tacoma, Wash., 1984; Ferrer Law Offices P.C. Seattle, 1985—; bd. dirs. Paisans on First, Seattle, Ferrer Law Offices. Mem. Poncho Arts Found., Seattle, 1982, Madrona Community Group, Seattle, 1985; bd. dirs. Westboro Assn., Federal Way, Wash., 1981. Served with U.S. Marine Corps, 1975-80. Recipient Mr. Seattle 1st Place award IFBB Affiliate, 1978, Mr. Wash. 2d Place award IFBB Affiliate, 1978. Mem. ACLU, Wash. State Bar Assn., Assn. Trial Lawyers Am., Seattle King County Bar Assn., Wash. State Trial Lawyers Assn., Constrn. Fin. Mgmt. Assn., Phi Delta Phi. Republican. Congregationalist. Avocations: skiing, skydiving, scuba diving, mountain climbing, sailing. General corporate, General civil litigation, Contracts commercial. Home: 710 Lakeside Ave S Apt 118 Seattle WA 98144-3335 Office: First Interstate Ctr 999 3rd Ave Ste 3105 Seattle WA 98104-4001

**FERRERI, VITO RICHARD,** lawyer; b. Phila., Feb. 17, 1949; s. Vito and Lucrecia (Poleo) F.; 1 child, Michelle Lee. BA, U. Pitts., 1970; JD, Rutgers U., 1973; postgrad. Nat. Coll. Advocacy, 1976. Bar: N.J. 1973, U.S. Dist. Ct. N.J. 1973, U.S. Supreme Ct. 1977, U.S. Ct. Appeals (3d cir.) 1978. Ptnr., Moss, Thatcher, Moss, McNeill & Ferreri, Runnemede, N.J., 1972-86, V. Richard Ferreri, P.C., 1986—; arbitrator Am. Arbitration Assn., Somerset, N.J., 1980—, adv. bd., 1985—; prosecutor Voorhees Twp., 1973-75, Washington Twp., 1973-75, Mantua Twp., 1975-79, Berlin Borough, 1979-82; spl. investigating prosecutor Washington Twp., 1986; pub. defender Voorhees Twp., 1989; judge Voorhess Twp. Mcpl. Ct., 1989-91, Barrington Borough Mcpl. Ct., 1990-96. Trustee St. Andrew the Apostle Roman Cath. Ch., 1987-89; mem. Camden County Rep. Exec. Com., 1986-89. Named One of Outstanding Young Men of Am. 1981-84. Mem. Camden N.J. State Bar Assn., County Bar Assn., Assn. Trial Lawyers Am. General practice, State civil litigation, Family and matrimonial. Office: V Richard Ferreri PC 200 Haddonfield Rd Ste 202 Gibbsboro NJ 08026-1239

**FERRINI, JAMES THOMAS,** lawyer; b. Chgo., Jan. 14, 1938; s. John B. and Julia (Marre) F.; m. Jeanne Marie Fontana, June 8, 1963; children: Anthony, Mary Caren, Emily, Joseph, Danielle. JD, Loyola U., 1963. Bar: U.S. Supreme Ct. 1963, U.S. Ct. Appeals (7th cir.) 1967, U.S. Ct. Appeals (8th cir.) 1969, U.S. Ct. Appeals (3d cir.) 1975, U.S. Ct. Appeals (6th cir.) 1982, U.S. Ct. Appeals (10th cir.) 1984, U.S. Ct. Appeals (4th cir.) 1987, U.S. Ct. Appeals (9th cir.) 1989. Sr. ptnr. Clausen Miller Gorman Caffrey & Witous, P.C., Chgo., 1963—; mem. pattern jury instructions Ill. Supreme Ct. Commn., Chgo., 1978-94. Contbr. articles to profl. jours. Mem. Mary Seat of Wisdom Parish, Park Ridge. Fellow Am. Acad. Appellate Lawyers; mem. ABA, Ill. Bar Assn., Chgo. Bar Assn. (chmn. civil practice com.), Ill. Assn. Def. Trial Counsel, Appellate Lawyers Assn. (pres. Chgo. chpt. 1978, 79), Justinian Soc. Roman Catholic. Avocations: handball, sailing, skiing, cooking. General civil litigation, Insurance, Personal injury. Office: Clausen Miller PC 10 S La Salle St Ste 1600 Chicago IL 60603-1098

**FERRIS, DONALD WILLIAM, JR.,** lawyer; b. Terre Haute, Ind., Jan. 18, 1951; s. Donald W. and Margaret L. (Rademaker) F.; m. Heidi L. Salter, May 28, 1995. BA, U. Notre Dame, 1973; JD, U. Mich., 1976. Bar: Mich. 1976, U.S. Dist. Ct. (ea. dist.) Mich. 1980, U.S. Dist. Ct. (we. dist.) Mich. 1988, U.S. Ct. Appeals (6th cir.) 1982, U.S. Supreme Ct., 1987. Sr. asst. pub. defender Washtenaw County Pub. Defender, Ann Arbor, 1976-80; pvt. practice Ann Arbor, 1980-95; ptnr. Ferris & Salter, P.C., Ann Arbor, 1995—; instr. Washtenaw C.C., Ann Arbor, 1980-84. Mem. ATLA, Nat. Assn. Criminal Def. Lawyers, Washtenaw Trial Lawyers Assn. (pres. 1996-97), Criminal Def. Lawyers of Washtenaw County (pres. 1994-96), Washtenaw County Bar Assn. (chmn. criminal sect. 1986-90), Mich. Trial Lawyers Assn. (adv. bd. 1996-97). Democrat. Avocations: golf, travel. Personal injury, Criminal, General civil litigation. Office: Ferris & Salter PC 4158 Washtenaw Ave Ann Arbor MI 48108-1004

**FERRIS, WILLIAM MICHAEL,** lawyer; b. Jackson, Mich., May 1, 1948; s. Franklyn C. and Betty J. (Dickerson) F.; m. Cynthia L. Muffitt, June 26, 1970 (div.); 1 child, Christina M.; m. Kathleen S. Santacroce, Mar. 21, 1987; stepchildren: Michael W. Santacroce, Megan D. Santacroce. BS with distinction, U.S. Naval Acad., 1970; JD summa cum laude, U. Balt., 1978, LLM in Taxation, 1994. Commd. ensign USN, 1970, advanced through grades to lt., 1974, resigned active duty, 1977; staff atty. Md. Legis., Annapolis, 1977-78, 80-81; assoc. Semmes, Bowen & Semmes, Balt., 1978-80; ptnr. Ferris & Robin, Annapolis, 1981-83, Krause & Ferris, Annapolis, 1983-87, Michaelson, Krause & Ferris, PA, Annapolis, 1987-91, Krause & Ferris, Annapolis, 1991—; adj. faculty Anne Arundel C.C., 1988—, U. Balt. Sch. Law, 1997—. Author: Maryland Style Manual for Statutory Law, 1985; article supr. Md. Annotated Code, 1981-84. Elder Woods Meml. Presbyn. Ch., Severna Park, Md., 1980—; chmn. Com. to rev. Anne Arundel County Code, Annapolis, 1985-86; temporary zoning hearing officer, Anne Arundel County, Annapolis, 1984-87; hearing officer Anne Arundel County Bd. Edn., Annapolis, 1990—; pres. Md. Bd. Dental Examiners, Balt., 1987-88; mem. inquiry com. Md. Atty. Grievance Commn., 1987—; ; mem. Md. Commn. on Jud. Disabilities, 1995—; treas. Bay Hills Cmty. Assn., 1990-96. Comdr. USNR, 1984-91, ret. Mem. ABA, Md. State Bar Assn., Maritime Law Assn., Anne Arundel County Bar Assn. Republican. Avocations: golfing, running, tennis. General civil litigation, Family and matrimonial, Military. Home: 606 Bay Green Dr Arnold MD 21012-2009 Office: Krause & Ferris 196 Duke Of Gloucester St Annapolis MD 21401-2515

**FERRITER, MAURICE JOSEPH,** lawyer; b. Holyoke, Mass., Aug. 14, 1930; s. John J. and Aldea F.; m. Margaret; children: Maurice J., John J., Mary M., Joseph P. AA, Holyoke Jr. Coll., 1952; BA, U. Mass., 1979; JD, Western New Eng. Law Sch., Springfield, Mass., 1957. Bar: Mass. 1957, U.S. Dist. Ct. Mass. 1960, U.S. Supreme Ct. 1967, U.S. Ct. Appeals (1st cir.) 1980. Sr. ptnr. Lyon, Ferriter & Fitzpatrick, LLP, Holyoke, 1957—; chmn. bd. dirs. emeritus Ferriter, Scobbo, Sikora, Singal, Caruso & Rodophele, P.C., Boston; gen. counsel emeritus Mass. Mcpl. Wholesale Electric Co.; arbitrator AAA. Dir. Holyoke Heritage Park R.R.; trustee Providence Health Sys., Greater Holyoke, Inc.; trustee, former chmn. bd. Holyoke C.C., Providence Ministries Needy; former city solicitor, Holyoke. With U.S. Army, 1948-51. Recipient Outstanding Servant of Pub. award Springfield TV Sta. WWLP Channel 22, 1976, Spl. Svc. award Mcpl. Electric Assn. Mass., 1981, award of merit Bur. Exceptional Children, 1979, Cmty. Svc. award YMCA, 1989, Disting. Alumni award Holyoke C.C., 1983, Outstanding Significant Achievement award Rotary, 1996; named Person of Yr., N.E. Pub. Power Assn., 1992, Peace and Justice award Providence Ministries, 1999. Fellow Mass. Bar Found.; mem. ATLA, Am. Pub. Power Assn. (Individual Achievement award 1998), Mass. Bar Assn., Hampden County Bar Assn., Holyoke Bar Assn., Mass. Acad. Trial Lawyers, Am. Judicature Soc. (MBA fee arbitration com.), Holyoke C. of C. (past pres., Bus. Man of Yr. award 1990, Appreciation award 1975). General corporate, Administrative and regulatory, Municipal (including bonds). Home: 31 Longfellow Dr Holyoke MA 01040-1290 Office: Whitney Place 14 Bobala Rd Holyoke MA 01040-9632

**FERRO, ELIZABETH KRAMS,** lawyer; b. Cheverly, Md., Oct. 14, 1948; d. Harry Francis and Jeanne Elizabeth (Edwards) Krams; children: Stephen Christopher, Elizabeth Juliet, Alexander Eli; m. Jose M. Ferro, Oct. 7, 1994. BS magna cum laude, U. Md., 1977; JD, George Washington U., 1982. Bar: D.C. 1983. Adminstr. Raleigh Stores Corp., Washington, 1973-83; atty. Lansfam Mgmt. Corp., Balt., 1983—, corp. sec., 1986—. V.p., dir. Sidney Lansburgh III Found., 1989—; bd. dirs. Debel Foods Corp., Elizabeth, N.J., 1986. Mem. ABA, D.C. Bar Assn., Alpha Sigma Lambda, Phi Kappa Phi. Roman Catholic. Estate planning, General practice. Home: 10210 Riggs Rd Hyattsville MD 20783-1213 Office: Lansfam Mgmt Corp 300 E Lombard St Ste 1900 Baltimore MD 21202-6739

**FERRUCCI, JOSEPH PETER,** lawyer; b. Providence, Sept. 8, 1964; s. John B. and Filomina (Rosati) F.; m. Angela M. Bucci, Aug. 12, 1990 (div. Apr. 1992); m. Leslie L. Manning, Nov. 4, 1993; children: Gabriella Mina, Samantha Christina. BS, U. R.I., 1986; JD, Suffolk U., Boston, 1989. Bar: R.I. 1989. Law clk. to Hon. Francis J. Boyle, Chief Judge U.S. Dist. Ct. R.I., Providence, 1989-90; assoc. Hinckley, Allen & Snyder, Providence, 1990-95; ptnr. D'Amico, Burchfield & Ferrucci, Providence, 1996—. Exec. editor Suffolk U. Law Rev., 1988, also contbr. articles. Mem. R.I. Bar Assn., Mass. Bar Assn. Avocations: auto racing, golf. Office: D'Amico Burchfield & Ferrucci 728 Valley St Providence RI 02908-4855

**FERSHEE, SUSAN JOYCE,** lawyer; b. Battle Creek, Mich., Apr. 20, 1947; d. James Fershee and Marian (Paden) Metcalf; m. Daniel Bernard Keating, Aug. 29, 1970 (div. Apr. 1974); m. George Frederick Wolfgang Hauck, Sept. 7, 1974. BA in Fgn. Langs., Maryville Coll., 1969; postgrad., U. Tuebingen, Germany, 1969-70; MA in German Lit., Ohio State U., 1972; JD, U. Mo.-Kansas City, 1988. Bar: Mo. 1988. Instr. German & French Tri-State U., Angola, Ind., 1972-74; self employed translator Angola, 1974-75; adminstrv. asst. Faultless Starch/Bon Ami Co., Kansas City, Mo., 1976-85; assoc. Law Office of Dennis W. Jennings, Kansas City, Mo., 1990-92; ptnr. Budesheim, Schlegel & Durbin, Kansas City, Mo., 1993-95; of counsel Boyd, Kenter & Stewart, LLC and predecessor, Kansas City, Mo., 1995—; judge moot ct. competition U. Mo.-Kansas City Sch. Law, 1990. Active Country Club United Meth. Ch., Kansas City, Mo., 1976—; rep. Cuban detainees Project Due Process, Leavenworth, Kans., 1988. Fulbright Found. fellow, 1969-70. Mem. ATLA, Assn. Women Lawyers (treas. 1993-95), Kansas City Metro. Bar Assn., Mo. Assn. Trial Attys., Nat. Orgn. Social Security Claimants Reps. Democrat. Avocations: choral singing, piano, reading, theater, symphony. Pension, profit-sharing, and employee benefits. Home: 5724 McGee St Kansas City MO 64113-2130 Office: 1150 Grand Blvd Ste 250 Kansas City MO 64106-2309

**FERSHTMAN, JULIE ILENE,** lawyer; b. Detroit, Apr. 3, 1961; d. Sidney and Judith Joyce (Stoll) F.; m. Robert S. Bick, Mar. 4, 1990. Student, Mich. State U., 1979-81, James Madison Coll., 1979-81; BA in Philosophy and Polit. Sci., Emory U., 1983, JD, 1986. Bar: Mich. 1986, U.S. Dist. Ct. (ea. dist.) Mich. 1986, U.S. Ct. Appeals (6th cir.) 1987, U.S. Dist. Ct. (we. dist.) Mich. 1993. Assoc. Miller, Canfield, Paddock and Stone, Detroit, 1986-89; assoc. Miro, Miro & Weiner P.C., Bloomfield Hills, Mich., 1989-92; pvt. practice, Bingham Farms, Mich., 1992—; adj. prof. Schoolcraft Coll., Livonia, Mich., 1994—; lectr. in field. Author: Equine Law & Horse Sense, 1996; contbr. article to Barrister Mag. Bd. dirs. Franklin Cmty. Assn., 1989-92, sec., 1991-92; mem. Franklin Planning Commn., 1993-94. Recipient Nat. Ptnr. in Safety award Assn. for Horsemanship Safety and Edn., 1997, Outstanding Achievement award Am. Riding Instrs. Assn., 1998; named one of Crain's Detroit Bus. "40 Bus. Leaders Under 40", 1996. Mem. ABA (planning bd. litigation sect. young lawyers divsn., honoree Barrister mag., 1995, FBA (courthouse tours com. Detroit chpt., featured in Barrister mag. in 21 Young Lawyers Leading US and the 21st Century 1995), State Bar Mich. (exec. coun. young lawyers sect. 1989-96, bd. commrs. 1994-96, 99—, sec.-treas. bd. commrs. 1991-93, vice chmn. 1993-94, chmn. elect 1994-95, chmn. 1995-96, professionalism com. 1997—, grievance com. 1997-99, structure and governance com. 1997—, rep. assn. 1997—, clk. 1999—), Oakland County Bar Assn. (prof. com. 1995—, Inns of Ct. com. 1995—, chair 1998—), Markel Equestrian Safety Bd., Women Lawyers Assn., Mich. Soc. Coll. Journalists, Phi Alpha Delta, Omicron Delta Kappa, Phi Sigma Tau, Pi Sigma Alpha. Avocations: horse showing, writing, music, art. Insurance, Labor, General civil litigation. Home: 31700 Briarcliff Rd Franklin MI

48025-1273 Office: 30700 Telegraph Rd Ste 3475 Bingham Farms MI 48025-4571

**FETTER, JEFFREY MICHAEL,** lawyer; b. Elmira, N.Y., Feb. 8, 1955; s. William and Mary Fetter; m. Anne Fetter; children: Jennifer, Joseph, Daniel. BS, SUNY, Geneseo, 1977; JD, Ohio No. U., 1983. Bar: N.Y. 1983. Assoc. Moot Sprague Law Firm, Buffalo, 1982-85; ptnr. Scolaro, Shulman, Cohen, Lawler & Burstein, P.C., Syracuse, N.Y., 1985—. Bd. dirs. Onandaga County Cultural Resources Coun., 1999—; mem. bus. adv. coun. Sch. Bus., SUNY-Geneseo, 1997—; sec. parish coun. St. Charles Borromeo Ch., 1992-93, pres. parish coun., 1993-94. Mem. ABA, N.Y. State Bar Assn. (ho. of dels. 1993-94, chair young lawyers sect. 1991-92, exec. com. gen. practice sect. 1995—, chair 1997-98, membership com. 1996—), Pa. Bar Assn., Onondaga County Bar Assn., N.Y. State Bar Found. Office: Scolaro Shulman et al 90 Presidential Plz Syracuse NY 13202-2240

**FETTERMAN, JAMES CHARLES,** lawyer; b. Charleston, W.Va., Apr. 13, 1947; s. Kenneth Lee and Sara Jane (Shaffer) F.; children: Janet, Paula, Kenneth, David. BA, Miss. State U., 1969, MA, 1970; JD, U. Miss., Oxford, 1972; MBA, St. Louis U., 1985. Bar: Miss. 1972, Sarasota County, U.S. Dist. Ct. (no. dist.) Miss. 1972, U.S. Ct. Mil. Appeals 1972, U.S. Dist. Ct. (mid. dist.) Fla. 1986, U.S. Tax Ct. 1986, U.S. Ct. Appeals (11th cir.) 1986. Staff atty. First Miss. Corp., Jackson, 1976-77; cert. of need adminstr. Office of Gov. State of Miss., Jackson, 1977-78; adminstrator, prin. investigator Miss. Bd. Nursing, Jackson, 1978-79; asst. prof., head dept. fin. Jackson State U., 1979-82; asst. prof. dept. mgmt sci. St. Louis U., Mo., 1982-86; ptnr. Borza Fetterman, Sardelis, Chartered, Sarasota, 1986-89, James C. Fetterman, P.A., Sarasota, Fla., 1989—; sr. res. adviser to gen. counsel and assoc. gen. counsel Def. Lobistics Agy., 199--94; assoc. prof. U. Sarasota, 1987—; judge advocate I.M.A. USAF, 1987; spl. master for zoning and code enforcement Sarasota County, 1991—; vol. counsel Am. Radio Relay League, 1995—; legal advisor Family Forum, CompuServe, 1996—. Editor Midwest Law Review U. Kans., 1984-86, also textbooks. Bd. dirs., v.p., chaperone Sarasota Boy's Choir, 1992-93; asst. scoutmaster Boy Scouts Am., 1991-95, 99—, scoutmaster, 1995-98, scoutmaster nat. jamboree troop, 1998, dist. com., 1998-99; bd. dirs. Fla. Inst. Traditional Chinese Medicine, 1998—, chmn. bd. dirs., 1998—. Capt. USAF, 1972-76, ETO; col. res. 1972—. Named one of Outstanding Young Men of Am., Jaycees, 1982; recipient award of merit Boy Scouts Am., 1998. Mem. Am. Bus. Law Assn., Res. Officer Assn. (Sarasota chpt. pres. 1989-91, v.p. 1991-92), Fla. Bar (vice chmn. mil. law com. 1991-94, chmn. 1994-95), Ret. Officer's Assn. (bd. dirs. Sarasota chpt. 1991-93), Am. Legion, Nat. Eagle Scout Assn. Republican. Roman Catholic. Avocations: running, swimming, ham radio. General corporate, Bankruptcy, Education and schools. Office: 4521A Bee Ridge Rd Sarasota FL 34233-2517

**FETZER, MARK STEPHEN,** lawyer; b. Louisville, Oct. 10, 1950; s. Sherrill Lee and Betty Ann (Meyer) F.; m. Pamela Ferrell, May 8, 1982; children: Martha Meyer, John Mark. Student, Purdue U., 1968-70; BA, U. Ky., 1973; JD, U. Denver, 1976. Bar: Colo. 1979, U.S. Dist. Ct. Colo. 1979. Sr. landman Minerals Svc. Co., Grand Junction, Colo., 1976-79; mgr. land & pub. affairs Marline Oil Corp., Danville, Va., 1980-85; mgr. R.R., utility & govtl. acquisition Dallas Area Rapid Transit, 1986-88; environ. counsel Cura, Inc., Dallas, 1989-91; dir., environ. counsel Terra-Mar, Inc., Dallas, 1991-92; environ. counsel Infodata Systems, Inc., Falls Church, Va., 1992-94; project mgr. Walcoff & Assocs., Inc., Fairfax, Va., 1994; sr. regulatory analyst Ecology and Environment, Inc., Idaho Falls, Idaho, 1995—. Mem. ABA, Colo. Bar Assn., Rocky Mountain Mineral Law Found., Air and Waste Mgmt. Assn. Evangelist. Avocation: bicycling. Environmental, Nuclear power, Real property.

**FEUER, PAUL ROBERT,** lawyer; b. Bayshore, N.Y., Oct. 7, 1956; s. Lloyd A. and Joyce S. Feuer; m. Shari S. Feuer, Oct. 27, 1990. BA, Drew U., 1978; JD, Widener Law Sch., 1981. Bar: N.Y., 1986, U.S. Dist. Ct. (ea. dist.) N.Y., 1986, U.S. Dist. Ct. (so. dist.) N.Y., 1986. Intern U.S. Atty Dist. Del., Wilmington, 1980, Delaware County Dist. Atty., Chester, Pa., 1981; asst. dist. atty. Suffolk County Dist. Atty., Riverhead, N.Y., 1981-87; ptnr. Zwissler, Diedolf, Feuer & Volkmann, LLP, Patchogue, N.Y., 1987—. Legis. officer Patchogue Bay Power Squadron, 1988—; apt. rental rev. com. Village Patchogue. Mem. ABA, N.Y. State Bar Assn., Suffolk County Bar Assn., Suffolk County Criminal Bar Assn., Lions Club (pres. 1997). Personal injury, General practice, Criminal. Office: Zwissler Diedolf Feuer & Volkmann PO Box 936 Patchogue NY 11772-0936

**FEUERSTEIN, ALAN RICKY,** lawyer; b. Buffalo, Oct. 24, 1950; s. Aaron Irving and Doris Jean (Davis) F.; m. June, 1973 (div. Jan. 1984); children: Marni Lauren, Jami Lynn; m. Susan T. Skop, Dec. 31, 1986; children: Christopher Borkowski, Philip Borkowski. BS cum laude, SUNY, Buffalo, 1974; LLB, U. Toledo, 1977. Bar: N.Y. 1978, Territorial and Dist. Ct. V.I. 1989, U.S. Supreme Ct. 1991, Fed. Ct. Puerto Rico 1993. Assoc. Law Offices of Salvatore Martoche, Buffalo, 1977-79; ptnr. Martoche & Feuerstein, Buffalo, 1979-81; lectr. Erie County Cen. Police Svcs. Acad., Buffalo, 1981-82; pvt. practice Buffalo, 1981-93; ptnr. Feuerstein & Santapia, Buffalo, 1993-94; prin. Law Offices of Alan R. Feuerstein, Buffalo, 1994-97; ptnr. Feuerstein & Smith, LLP, Buffalo, 1998—; lectr. Daemen Coll. Consortium, Buffalo, 1980-81; cons. in field. Mem. Erie County Reps., Buffalo, 1979—. Mem. Niagara Club, St.Thomas Yacht Club, The Buffalo Launch Club, Confrérie de la Chåne des Rôtisseurs (chevalier). Republican. Jewish. Civil rights, General civil litigation, Personal injury. Office: 17 St Louis Pl Buffalo NY 14202-1502 also: Woods & Woods 1 Comptroller Plz San Juan PR 00917 also: PO Box 502008 Saint Thomas VI 00805-2008

**FEUERSTEIN, BERNARD A.,** lawyer; b. Bklyn., Aug. 17, 1928; s. Emil and Rae (Diamond) F.; m. Irene A. Marcus, Apr. 3, 1955; children: Susan, Barbara, Steven. AB, NYU, 1946, LLM, 1956; JD cum laude, Harvard U., 1949. Bar: NY 1950. Tchg. fellow U. Chgo. Law Sch., 1949-50; asst. dist. atty. New York County, N.Y.C., 1951; from assoc. to ptnr. Scribner & Miller, N.Y.C., 1953-62; ptnr. various law firms, N.Y.C., 1962-80, Baer, Marks & Upham LLC, N.Y.C., 1980—; dir., sec. Dale Carnegie & Assocs., Inc., Garden City, N.Y., 1978—. Trustee, counsel Ctr. Preventive Psychiatry, White Plains, N.Y., 1978-97, World Edn. Svcs., N.Y.C., 1992-95. 1st lt. U.S. Army, 1951-53. Mem. ABA, Assn. Bar N.Y.C. General corporate, Securities, Intellectual property. Office: Baer Marks & Upham LLP 805 3rd Ave New York NY 10022-7513

**FEUERSTEIN, DONALD MARTIN,** lawyer; b. Chgo., May 30, 1937; s. Morris Martin and Pauline Jean (Zagel) F.; m. Dorothy Rosalind Sokolsky, June 3, 1962 (dec. Mar. 1978); children: Eliza Carol, Anthony David; m. Summer Donna Berben, May 25, 1987; 1 child, Ashley Paul. BA magna cum laude, Yale U., 1959; JD magna cum laude, Harvard U., 1962. Bar: N.Y. 1962. Assoc. firm Cleary, Gottlieb, Steen & Hamilton, N.Y.C., 1962-63; law clk. to U.S. dist. judge N.Y.C., 1963-65; assoc. firm Saxe, Bacon & Bolan, N.Y.C., 1965; asst. gen. counsel, chief counsel instl. investor study SEC, Washington, 1966-71; ptnr., counsel Salomon Bros., N.Y.C., 1971-81, mng. dir., sec., 1981-91; exec. v.p., chief legal officer Salomon, Inc., 1991; spl. asst. U.S. Dept. Edn., Washington, 1993-94, sr. advisor, 1994—; spl. cons. Intersch. Group, N.Y.C., 1991-93. Editor Harvard Law Rev., 1960-62; mem. editl. adv. bd. Securities Regulation Law Jour., 1973-90; bd. editors Nat. Law Jour., 1978-90. Mem. vis. com. Northwestern U. Law Sch., 1975-78; bd. dirs. 1st All Children;s Theatre, 1976-85, chmn., 1976-82; mem. long-range planning and capital campaign coms. Brearley Sch., N.Y.C., 1981-83; mem. adv. bd. Solomon R. Guggenheim Mus., N.Y.C., 1984-91, chmn. bus. com., 1988-91, mem. internat. coun., 1991—; bd. dirs. Arts and Bus. Coun., 1980-85, v.p., 1985-88; trustee, v.p., mem. exec. com. Dalton Sch., 1983-89, 90-93; mem. dean's adv. coun. Harvard U. Law Sch., 1988-95, mem. steering com. and capital campaign, 1991-95; mem. com. on univ. resources Harvard U., 1988—; mem. vis. com. Harvard Grad. Sch. Edn., 1993-99; mem. tech. adv. coun., 1996—; chmn. tech. com. Georgetown Day Sch., 1997—, trustee, 1997—. Mem. ABA, Phi Beta Kappa, Pi Sigma Alpha. General corporate, Securities, General practice. Home: 6430 Bradley Blvd Bethesda MD 20817-3246 Office: US Dept Edn Office Dep Sec 400 Maryland Ave SW Washington DC 20202-0001

**FEUVREL, SIDNEY LEO, JR.,** lawyer, educator; b. Birmingham, Ala., June 7, 1948; s. Sidney Leo and Tommie Eula (Nolan) F.; m. Glenda Kay Erwin, May 8, 1970 (div. 1979); 1 child, William Michael; m. Lillian Torrence, Apr. 22, 1989. BA, Mercer U., 1978, JD, 1981; student comparative criminal law, Moscow U., Russia, 1979; student East-West trade law, Warsaw U., Poland, 1979; student U.S. govt. law studies, U. Utah, 1980. Bar: Fla. 1981, Ga. 1981, U.S. Dist. Ct. (no. dist.) Ga. 1981, U.S. Dist. Ct. (mid. dist.) Fla. 1983, U.S. Ct. Appeals (11th cir.) 1983, U.S. Supreme Ct. 1989; cert. mediator and arbitrator, Federal Dist. Ct., U.S. Bankruptcy Ct. (mid. dist.), Fla. Air traffic controller FAA, Memphis, 1970-74, Atlanta, 1974-76; pvt. practice law Atlanta, 1981, Orlando, Fla., 1981—; adj. prof. Fla. Inst. Tech., Melbourne, 1983-91, Velenica C.C., Orlando, 1990—, Webster U., Orlando, 1990—; cert. family mediator, ins. mediator, county ct. mediator Fla. Supreme Ct. Bd. dirs. Griffin Prep. Sch., Ga., 1977. With USN, 1966-69, Vietnam 1967-68. Mem. ATLA, Rotary (treas. 1985), 3d Degree Mason, 32 Degree Scottish Rite Mason, Noble of Shrine (Atlanta), Orange County Bar Assn. (pro bono panel), Am. Arbitration Assn. (apptd. panel of arbitrators), Am. Trial Lawyers Assn., Acad. of Fla. Trial Lawyers. Avocations: travel, snow skiing, scuba diving, private piloting. Personal injury, General corporate, Criminal.

**FEVURLY, KEITH ROBERT,** educational administrator; b. Leavenworth, Kans., Oct. 30, 1951; s. James R. Fevurly and Anne (McDade) Barrett; m. Peggy L. Vosburg, Aug. 4, 1978; children: Rebecca Dawn, Grant Robert. BA in Polit. Sci., U. Kans., 1973; JD, Washburn U. of Topeka Sch. Law, 1976; postgrad., U. Mo. Sch. Law, 1984; MBA, Regis U., 1988; LLM, U. Denver, 1992. Bar: Kans. 1977, Colo. 1986; cert. fin. planner. Sole practice Leavenworth, 1977; atty. estate and gift tax IRS, Wichita and Salina, Kans., Austin, Tex., 1977-83; atty., acad. assoc. Coll. for Fin. Planning, Denver, 1984-91, program dir., 1991-95, v.p. edn., 1995-98; COO U. St. Augustine (Fla.) for Health Scis., 1998—; adj. prof. taxation Met. State Coll., Denver; adj. faculty in retirement planning and estate planning Coll. Fin. Planning. Contbg. author tng. modules, articles on tax mgmt., estate planning. Mem. Colo. Bar Assn., Toastmasters Internat., Rotary Internat., Delta Theta Phi, Pi Sigma Alpha. Republican. Presbyterian. Avocations: softball, racquetball. Home: 505 Hoot Owl Ct Saint Augustine FL 32084-7972 Office: U St Augustine for Health Scis 1 University Blvd Saint Augustine FL 32086-5799

**FEWELL, CHARLES KENNETH, JR.,** lawyer; b. Washington, Jan. 26, 1943; s. Charles Kenneth and Mary Amanda (Hunt) F.; m. Christine Baker Huff, Jan. 23, 1971; children: Anna Catherine, John Maenner. BA magna cum laude, Dartmouth Coll., 1964; JD, Harvard U., 1967. Bar: N.Y. 1968, U.S. Dist. Ct. (so. dist.) N.Y. 1970, U.S. Ct. Appeals (2d cir.) 1975. Law clk. U.S. Dist. Ct. (so. dist.) N.Y,, N.Y.C., 1967-68; assoc. White & Case, N.Y.C., 1968-75; v.p., counsel Nat. Westminster Bank, N.Y.C., 1975-80; sr. counsel, sr. v.p. Deutsche Bank AG, N.Y.C., 1980-92; chief counsel, mng. dir. Deutsche Bank N.Am., 1992-97; ptnr. Eaton & Van Winkle, N.Y.C., 1998—; bd. dirs. Deutsche Bank Trust Co., Deutsche Fin. Svcs. Can. Corp.; v.p., sec. Deutsche Bank Fin., Inc., N.Y.C., 1980-97. Mem. ABA (banking com. 1980—, co-chair internat. banking and fin. com. 1995-98), Inst. Internat. Bankers (legis. and regulatory com. 1988-97), German Am. Law Assn. (dir. 1982—), N.Y. State Bar Assn. (internat. banking and securities markets 1987—, internat. employment law 1992—), Assn. Bar City N.Y. (banking law sect. 1992-95), Phi Beta Kappa. E-mail: cfewell@evw.com. Banking, Private international, General corporate. Office: Eaton & Van Winkle Three Park Ave New York NY 10016-2078

**FIALA, DAVID MARCUS,** lawyer; b. Cleve., Aug. 1, 1946; s. Frank J. and Anna Mae (Phillips) F. BBA, U. Cin., 1969; JD, Chase Coll. No. Ky. State U., 1974. Bar: Ohil, 1974, U.S. Tax Court, 1974. Assoc. Benesch, Friedlander, Coplan and Aronoff, Cin., 1971-78; ptnr. Benesch, Friedlander, Coplan and Aronoff, 1979-92, Rice & Fiala, 1992-94; sole practice Cin., 1995—; lectr. Southwestern Ohio Tax Inst., 1978-79, 88, Cin. Bar Assn. Estate Planning Inst., 1989. Bd. dirs. Elkhorn Collieries; trustee, sec. Sta. WCET-TV, Cin., 1983-87, auction chmn., 1979, chmn. 1987-90, trustee emeritus, 1990—; trustee Jr. Achievement Greater Cin., 1979-93, 1999—, Mental health Svcs. West, 1974-83, Contemporary Dance theatre, 1974-80. Personal income taxation, Probate, Estate planning.

**FIALKY, GARY LEWIS,** lawyer; b. Lawrence, Mass., July 24, 1942; s. Paul James and Estelle F. (Gottlieb) F.; m. Elaine N. Scotch, Aug. 19, 1967; children: Jeffrey, Joshua. BA, Am. Internat. Coll., Springfield, Mass., 1964; JD, Suffolk U., Boston, 1967; LLM in Taxation, Boston U., 1968. Bar: Mass. 1967, U.S. Dist. Ct. Mass. 1969, U.S. Dist. Ct. Conn. 1975. Ptnr. Alpert & Fialky, Springfield, Mass., 1968-75, Bacon & Wilson, P.C., Springfield, 1975—. Bd. trustees Am. Internat. Coll., Springfield, 1984-88, Wilbraham & Monson Acad., 1986—; adv. bd. Western New Eng. Coll. Tax Adv. Bd. Mem. Estate Planning Coun. of Hampden County (pres. 1973, 74, 75), Springfield Tax Club (pres. 1985), Springfield C. of C. (pres. 1998—). Avocations: skiing, tennis, reading, running. General corporate, Probate, Mergers and acquisitions. Office: Bacon & Wilson PC 33 State St Springfield MA 01103-2003

**FIANDACH, EDWARD LOUIS,** lawyer; b. Rochester, N.Y., Jan. 10, 1953; s. Samuel and Mayme Eleanor (Schifino) F.; m. Mary Louise Ferrari, Sept. 2, 1979. BA, St. John Fisher Coll., 1975; JD, Union U., 1978. Bar: N.Y. 1979, U.S. Dist. Ct. (we. dist.) N.Y. 1981, U.S. Ct. Appeals (2nd cir.) 1988, U.S. Supreme Ct. 1988. Ptnr. Fiandach & Fiandach, Rochester, 1979—; pres. MTC Publs. Inc.; instr. E. Irondequoit Ctrl. Sch. Dist. Adult Edn., Rochester. Author: NY DWI, 1992; author (with others) Erwin's Defense of Drunk Driving, 1992, Zett's New York Criminal Practice, 1990; columnist N.Y. DWI; editor: Fiandach's NY DWI Bulletin; contbr. numerous articles to mags. and profl. jours. Mem. N.Y. Lawyers Against the Death Penalty. Mem. N.Y. State Bar Assn., Assn. Trial Lawyers Am., N.Y. State Trial Lawyers Assn., Nat. Inst. for Trial Advocacy, Criminal Defense League, Genesee Valley Trial Lawyers Assn., Greater Rochester Assn. Women Attys., Monroe County Bar Assn. (criminal justice sect., coms.: mandatory pro bono svc., judiciary, long range planning, personal injury, bench-bar), Univ. Club Rochester. Democrat. Roman Catholic. Avocations: skiing, sports cars, dogs, reading. Criminal, Personal injury, Computer. Home: 335 Warren Ave Rochester NY 14618-4317 Office: Fiandach & Fiandach 100 Allens Creek Rd Rochester NY 14618-3303

**FICEK, VINCE H.,** lawyer; b. Dickinson, N.D., Feb. 24, 1949; s. Vince F. and Emily L. (Kralicek) F.; m. Roxanne Herberholz, Apr. 23, 1994; children: Mariah Kelsey, Delanie Chelsey. BA in Social Sci., U. N.D., 1971, JD, 1976. Bar: N.D. 1976, U.S. Dist. Ct. N.D. 1979. Trust officer 1st Nat. Bank & Trust, Dickinson, 1976-77; pvt. practice, Dickinson, 1978-92; ptnr. Reichert Buresh Herauf & Ficek, P.C., Dickinson, 1993-96, Ficek & Buresh, P.C., Dickinson, 1997—; city atty. City of Dickinson, 1980-91; petroleum landman, Dickinson, 1979-81. Candidate for N.D. Ho. of Reps., 1989, 91. Mem. N.D. Trial Lawyers Assn. (bd. govs., sec., treas., v.p., 1990-94, pres. elect 1994-95, pres. 1995-96), Stark-Dunn County Bar Assn. (pres. 1980-81), S.W. Jud. Dist. Bar Assn. (sec.-treas. 1994-96, pres. 1996-98), State Bar Assn. (bd. govs. 1996-98). Democrat. Roman Catholic. Avocations: snow skiing, trout fishing, reading, golfing, fishing. Personal injury, Criminal, General civil litigation. Office: Ficek & Buresh PC PO Box 1224 Dickinson ND 58602-1224

**FICHERA, LEWIS CARMEN,** lawyer; b. Woodbury, N.J., July 16, 1949; s. Paul Benjamin and Mary (Cristaudo) F. BSBA, Villanova U., 1971; JD, Widener U., 1982. Bar: N.J. 1984, Pa. 1984. Cost analyst Catalytic, Inc., Phila., 1974-76; field cost analyst Catalytic, Inc., Balt., 1976-77; cost analyst Catalytic, Inc., London, 1977-78; chief cost analyst Catalytic, Inc., Phila., 1978-82; ptnr. Cristaudo & Fichera, West Deptford, N.J., 1984-86; pvt. practice West Deptford, 1987—; pres. Diversified Funding Svcs., Inc. Active Cristaudo for N.J. Ho. of Reps. campaign, 1988. With USANG, 1971-77. Mem. Am. Cash Flow Assn., Cash Flow Profls. Network (sec.), N.J. State Bar ASsn., Pa. Bar Assn., Gloucester County Bar Assn., Fitness Unltd., Nat. Orgn. of Social Security Claimant's Reps., Nat. Orgn. of Vet.'s Advocates, Cherry Hill Regional C. of C. Republican. Roman Catholic. General practice, Probate, Pension, profit-sharing, and employee benefits. Home: 773 Atlantic Ave Sewell NJ 08080-1502 Office: Sherwood Sq 943 Kings Hwy Paulsboro NJ 08066

**FICKLER, ARLENE,** lawyer; b. Phila., Apr. 21, 1951. BA cum laude, U. Pa., 1971, JD cum laude, 1974. Bar: Pa. 1974, D.C. 1980, U.S. Supreme Ct. 1989. Ptnr. Hoyle Morris & Kerr LLP, Phila.; staff atty. Commn. on Revision of Fed. Ct. Appellate System, 1974-75; exec. asst. Bicentennial Com. Jud. Conf. of U.S., 1975-76. Comment editor U. Pa. Law Rev., 1973-74; contbr. articles to law jours. Pres. U. Pa. Law Sch. Alumni Bd. Mgrs., 1997-99; trustee Jewish Fedn. of Greater Phila., 1981-88, 89-93, 94-98, 99—, Phila. Bar Found., 1993-98, Jewish Cmty. Ctrs. of Phila., 1997—, asst. treas., 1999—; treas. HIAS Immigration Svcs. Phila., 1999—; active Jewish Cmty. Rels. Coun. Greater Phila., 1983-94, 98—; mem. United Jewish Appeal Nat. Young Women's Leadership Cabinet, 1982-87; v.p. Phila. chpt. Am. Jewish Congress, 1995—. Recipient Mrs. Isidor Kohn Young Leadership award Jewish Fedn. Greater Phila. Mem. ABA, Am. Law Inst., Am. Bar Found., Pa. Bar Assn., D.C. Bar, Phila. Bar Assn. (chmn. fed. cts. com. 1992), Fed. Bar Coun. of Second Cir. General civil litigation, Product liability, Toxic tort. Office: Hoyle Morris & Kerr LLP 1650 Market St Ste 1 Philadelphia PA 19103-7397

**FIEBACH, H. ROBERT,** lawyer; b. Paterson, N.J., June 7, 1939; s. Michael M. and Silvia Irene (Nadler) F.; m. Elizabeth D. Carlton, Mar. 17, 1984; children: Michael, Emma; children by previous marriage: Jonathan, Rachel. B.S., U. Pa., 1961, LL.B. cum laude, 1964. Bar: Pa. 1965, U.S. Supreme Ct. 1971. Law clk. to Chief Judge Biggs U.S. Ct. Appeals for 3d Cir., 1964-65; assoc. Wolf, Block, Schorr and Solis-Cohen, Phila., 1965-71, ptnr., 1971-79, sr. ptnr., 1979-95; sr. mem. Cozen & O'Connor, Phila., 1995—; permanent mem. U.S. Jud. Conf. for 3d cir., 1967—; mem. Pa. Supreme Ct. Adv. Com. on Appellate Rules, 1987-93, Commn. on Jud. Elections, 1997—; arbitrator, mediator U.S. Dist. Ct. (ea. dist.) Pa., Am. Arbitration Assn., 1966—; bd. dirs. Pa. Capital Case Resource Ctr. Contbg. author: Business and Commercial Litigation in the Federal Courts, 1998; rsch. editor U. Pa. Law Rev., 1964-65; contbr. articles to legal jours. Past mem. Phila. adv. bd. Anti-Defamation League of B'nai Brith, Greater Phila. Regional Commn. on Law and Social Action, Am. Jewish Congress; bd. dirs. Greater Phila. chpt. ACLU, past chmn. criminal justice and police practices com.; past bd. dirs. Pa. chpt. ACLU. Fellow Am. Coll. Trial Lawyers; mem. ABA (bd. govs. 1997—, Ho. of Dels., pres. nat. caucus state bar assns. 1994-95, chmn. standing com. on lawyers profl. liability 1994-95, past chmn. jud. performance and conduct com., jud. adminstrn. divsn., 1989-91, litig. sect., 1988 midyear meeting host com.), Pa. Bar Assn. (pres.-elect 1992-93, pres. 1993-94, bd. govs. 1987-95, ho. of dels. 1983—, Pa. Bar Trust 1996—, past vice chmn. jud. selection com., past chmn. jud. retention election com. 1980-83, chmn. com. on profl. liability 1984-87, past chmn. polit. action com. for merit retention of judges 1980-83, Spl. Achievement award 1986), Phila. Bar Assn. (bd. govs. 1983-87, past chmn. fed. cts. com., past vice chmn. arbitration com., past mem. spl. com. to study appellate cts., past chmn. spl. com. on ins. 1983-84, civil jud. procedures com., spkr. various panels), Pa. Bar Inst. (bd. dirs. 1984-90), Defender Assn. Phila. (bd. dirs.), Am. Judicature Soc. (state membership chmn. 1988), Phila. Trial Lawyers Assn. (past chmn. bus. litig. com., bd. dirs. 1989-90), Soc. of Fellows, Am. Bar Found., Order of Coif (past dir. U. Pa. chpt.). Federal civil litigation, State civil litigation. Home: 301 Delancey St Philadelphia PA 19106-4208 Office: Cozen & O'Conner 1900 Market St Fl 3 Philadelphia PA 19103-3572

**FIEGER, GEOFFREY NELS,** lawyer; b. Detroit, Dec. 23, 1950; s. Bernard Julian and June Beth (Oberer) F.; m. Kathleen Janice Podwoiski, June 25, 1983. BA, U. Mich., 1974, MA, 1976; JD, Detroit Coll. Law, 1979. Bar: Mich. 1979, U.S. Dist. Ct. (ea. dist.) Mich. 1979, Fla. 1980, U.S. Dist. Ct. (mid. dist.) Fla. 1980, Ariz. 1980. Ptnr. Fieger Fieger & Schwartz, P.C., Southfield, Mich., 1979—. V.p. Orgns. United to Save Twp., West Bloomfield, Mich., 1987. Mem. ABA, Detroit Bar Assn., Assn. Trial Lawyers Am. Unitarian. Avocations: running, swimming. Federal civil litigation, Personal injury, State civil litigation. Office: Fieger Fieger & Schwartz PC 19390 W 10 Mile Rd Southfield MI 48075-2463

**FIELD, DAVID ANTHONY,** lawyer; b. N.Y.C., Mar. 25, 1934; s. Arthur N. and Rose F.; m. Ellen J. Hirshon, Apr. 1, 1958; children: Mitchell, Lawrence. BA, Tufts U., 1955; JD, Columbia U., 1958; LLM, NYU, 1965. Bar: N.Y. 1958, U.S. Dist. Ct. (so. and ea. dists.) N.Y., U.S. Tax Ct., U.S. Supreme Ct. Ptnr. Field, Florea & Field, N.Y.C., 1959-62, DiFalco, Field, Lomenzo & Turret, N.Y.C., 1962-78, Field, Lomenzo & Turret, N.Y.C., 1978—. Exec. com. Five Young Dem. Club, Woodmere, N.Y., 1964-66; pres. Hewlett Park Civic Assn., Woodmere, 1963-64. Mem. N.Y. State Trial Lawyers Assn., N.Y.C. Bar Assn. Avocations: golf, boating. Family and matrimonial, General civil litigation, Probate. Office: Field Lomenzo Turret 205 Lexington Ave Fl 17 New York NY 10016-6070

**FIELD, DAVID ELLIS,** lawyer; b. Washington, Feb. 3, 1953; s. Ellis Arrington and Phyllis Martina (Anderson) F. BA, U. Va., 1975, MEd, 1976; JD, George Mason U., 1983. Bar: Va. 1983, D.C. 1990, Md. 1991, U.S. Dist. Ct. (ea. dist.) Va. 1984, U.S. Ct. Appeals (4th cir.) 1985. Assoc. Law Offices Alphonse Audet, Fairfax, Va., 1984; asst. commonwealth's atty. Office of Fairfax County, Va., 1984-87; assoc. Miller & Bucholtz, P.C., Reston, Va., 1987-89, Falcone & Rosenfeld, Ltd., Fairfax, 1989, Lewis, Dack, Paradiso, O'Connor & Good, Wasington, 1989-91, Deckelbaum, Ogens & Fischer, Wasington, 1991-92; atty. Alan S. Toppelberg & Assocs., Washington, 1992-94; ptnr. Field & Cram, Fairfax, Va., 1994-98; pvt. practice Fairfax, Va., 1998—; asst. city atty. City of Fairfax, 1988-89. Mem. Am. Arbitration Assn., Va. Coll. Criminal Def. Attys., Fairfax Bar Assn., Delta Theta Pi. Democrat. Presbyterian. Criminal, Personal injury, General civil litigation. Office: 10605 Judicial Dr Ste B6 Fairfax VA 22030-5167

**FIELD, HAROLD BASIL,** lawyer; b. Phila., Nov. 6, 1955; s. Andrew Holmes Field and Helen May Ellsworth; m. Kathleen cottrell, June 20, 1981; children: Lydia Elizabeth, Russell Ellsworth. BA magna cum laude, U. Calif., San Diego, 1977; JD, U. Wash., 1980. Bar: Wash. 1980, U.S. Dist. Ct. (we. dist.) 1981, U.S. Dist. Ct. (ea. dist.) 1993. Ptnr. Murray, Dunham & Murray, Seattle, 1980—. Insurance, Personal injury. Office: Murray Dunham & Murray 900 4th Ave Ste 3200 Seattle WA 98164-1058

**FIELD, JOSEPH HOOPER,** judge; b. Weston, Mass., Dec. 28, 1946; s. Edward Olsen and Harriet Margaret (Jacobs) F.; m. Georgina Munson Ducey, Aug. 1, 1970; children: Charles H., Elizabeth M., William O. AB, Harvard U., 1969; JD, U. Maine, 1976. Bar: Maine, 1976, U.S. Dist. Ct. Maine 1976, U.S. Ct. Appeals (1st cir.) 1984, Mass. 1977, U.S. Dist. Ct. Mass. 1977, U.S. Supreme Ct. 1982. Asst. dist. atty. Maine Prosecutorial Dist. VI, Bath, Maine, 1976-80; ptnr. Loyd, Bumgardner & Field, Brunswick, Maine, 1980-90; judge Maine Dist. Ct., Bath, 1990—. Chmn. Coastal Waters Commn., Freeport, Maine, 1980-88. Comdr. USCG Res., 1973-93. Mem. Wolf Neck Club (pres. 1987-89, 91-93), Harraseeket Yacht Club. Avocations: sailing, music. Office: Maine Dist Ct RR 1 Box 310 Bath ME 04530-9704

**FIELD, KATHLEEN COTTRELL,** lawyer; b. Honolulu, Dec. 30, 1955; d. Harold Everett Cottrell and Ann (Pappenhagen) Reimann; m. Harold B. Field, June 20, 1981; children: Lydia Elizabeth, Russell Ellsworth. BA, Coll. of Idaho, 1978; JD, U. Wash., 1981, MA, 1982. Bar: Wash. 1982, U.S. Dist. Ct. (we. dist.) Wash. 1984. Dep. prosecutor Snohomish County, Everett, Wash., 1982-88; pvt. practice Lynnwood, Wash., 1988—; judge pro tem. City of Edmonds, 1989—, City of Lynnwood, 1990—; mem. Nat. Task Force on Juvenile Sexual Offending, Denver, 1987-94; mem. Gov.'s Juvenile Justice Adv. Com., 1987-93; bd. dirs. Columbia Legal Svcs. Bd. dirs. Open Door Theatre, 1984-94, pres., 1988-89; bd. dirs. Wash. Assn. Child Abuse Couns., 1985-91, co-chair advocacy com., 1985-87; bd. dirs. Snohomish County Child Abuse Coun., 1984-87, chair legis. com.; active Snohomish County Children's Commn., 1986-87; founder A Better Way Mediation & Arbitration Svcs., Inc., 1996—. Recipient Award for Extraordinary Pro Bono Svc. Hours Snohomish County Legal Svcs., Everett, 1992, Pro Bono Lawyer of Yr. award, 1994, Lawyer of Yr. award Snohomish County Bar Assn., 1999. Mem. Wash. State Bar Assn. (hearings examiner 1998), Wash. Women Lawyers Assn. (Passing the Torch award 1995), Wash. State Trial Lawyers Assn., Soc. Profls. Dispute Resolution, Acad. Family Mediators. Fax: 425-774-2034. Personal injury, Family and matrimonial, Alternative dispute resolution. Office: 5800 236 St SW Mountlake Terrace WA 98043

**FIELD, RICHARD CLARK,** lawyer; b. Stanford, Calif., July 13, 1940; s. John and Sally Field; m. Barbara Faith Butler, May 22, 1967 (dec. Apr. 1984); 1 child, Amanda Katherine; m. Eva Sara Halbreich, Dec. 1, 1985. BA, U. Calif., Riverside, 1962; JD, Harvard U., 1965. Bar: Calif. 1966, U.S. Supreme Ct., 1971, U.S. Ct. Appeals (9th cir.) 1979. Assoc.

Thompson & Colegate, Riverside, 1965-69; ptnr. Adams, Duque & Hazeltine, Los Angeles, 1970-89, mem. mgmt. com., 1981-84, chmn. litigation dept., 1985-89; ptnr. Cadwalader, Wickersham & Taft, Los Angeles, 1989-97, McCutchen, Doyle, Brown & Enersen, LLP, Los Angeles, 1997—. Bd. dirs. ARC, L.A., 1984-93, 97—. Mem. ABA (litigation, torts and ins. practice sects., bus. torts com., products, gen. liability and consumer law com.), Los Angeles County Bar Assn. (trial lawyers sect.), Assn. Bus. Trial Lawyers (bd. govs. 1978-82), Am. Arbitration Assn. (comml. arbitration panel). Episcopalian. General civil litigation, Product liability, Insurance. Office: McCutchen Doyle Brown & Enersen LLP 355 S Grand Ave Ste 4400 Los Angeles CA 90071-3106

**FIELD, ROBERT EDWARD,** lawyer; b. Chgo., Aug. 21, 1945; s. Robert Edward and Florence Elizabeth (Aiken) F.; m. Jenny Lee Hill, Aug. 5, 1967; children: Jennifer Kay, Kimberly Anne, Amanda Brooke. BA, Ill. Wesleyan U., 1967; MA, Northwestern U., 1969, JD, 1973. Bar: Ill. 1973, U.S. Dist. Ct. (no. dist.) Ill. 1974, U.S. Supreme Ct. 1979. Exec. dir. Winnetka Youth Orgn., Ill., 1969-73; assoc. Seyfarth, Shaw, Fairweather & Geraldson, Chgo., 1973-79, ptnr., 1979-93; ptnr. Field, Golan & Swiger, Chgo., 1993—; bd. dirs. Gt. Lakes Fin. Resources, Matteson, Ill., 1983—, vice chmn., 1988-91, chmn. 1991—; bd. dirs. Chgo. chpt. Ill. Wesleyan U. Assocs.; chmn. bd. dirs. 1st Nat. Bank of Blue Island, 1989—, Bank of Homewood, 1988—; bd. dirs. Winchester Mfg. Co., Wood Dale, Ill., Ludell Mfg. Co., Milw.; dir. Comml. Resources Corp., Naperville, Ill., 1984-93; dir., sec. Ellis Corp., Itasca, Ill., 1980—; chmn. bd. dirs. Cmty. Bank of Homewood-Flossmoor, Ill., 1983-92, Bank of Matteson, Ill., 1992—; mem. State Banking Bd. Ill., 1993-97. Bd. dirs. Ctr. for New Beginnings, 1997—, Family Svc. Ctrs. Cook County, Matteson, 1979—, treas., 1981-82, pres. 1986-88, chmn., 1988-93; pres. Lakes of Olympia Condominium Assn., 1987-89; trustee Village of Olympia Fields, Ill., 1981-89, pres., 1991-97; trustee Ill. Wesleyan U., 1990—, treas. 1994—; bd. dirs. Northwestern U. Sch Law Alumni Assn., 1990-94. Mem. ABA, Ill. Bar Assn., Am. Bankers Assn., Ill. Bankers Assn., United Meth. Bar Assn. (v.p. Chgo. chpt. 1989), Chgo. Bar Assn., Bankers Club of Chgo., Union League Club Chgo., Calumet Country Club. Banking, Contracts commercial, Real property. Home: 3424 Parthenon Way Olympia Fields IL 60461-1321 Office: Field Golan & Swiger 3 1st Nat Plz Ste 1500 Chicago IL 60602

**FIELDS, BERTRAM HARRIS,** lawyer; b. Los Angeles, Mar. 31, 1929; s. H. Maxwell and Mildred Arlyn (Ruben) F.; m. Lydia Ellen Minevitch, Oct. 22, 1960 (dec. Sept. 1986); 1 child, James Eldar, m. Barbara Guggenheim, Feb. 21, 1991. B.A., UCLA, 1949; J.D. magna cum laude, Harvard U., 1952. Bar: Calif. 1953. Practiced in Los Angeles, 1955—; assoc. firm Shearer, Fields, Rohner & Shearer, and predecessor firms, 1955-57, mem. firm, 1957-82; ptnr. Greenberg, Glusker, Fields, Claman & Machtinger, 1982—. Author: (as D. Kincaid) The Sunset Bomber, 1986, The Lawyer's Tale, 1992, (as B. Fields) Royal Blood Richard III and the Mystery of the Princes, 1998; mem. bd. editors: Harvard Law Rev., 1953-55. Bd. dirs. U. So. Calif. Annenberg Sch. Comm. 1st. lt. USAF, 1953-55, Korea. Mem. ABA, L.A. County Bar Assn., Coun. Fgn. Rels. Subject of profiles Calif. Mag., Nov. 1987, Avenue Mag., Mar. 1989, Am. Film Mag., Dec. 1989, Vanity Fair Mag., Dec. 1993, Harvard Law Sch. Bull., spring 1998, London Sunday Telegraph, June 1999, Sunday New York Post, July 1999. Office: Greenberg Glusker Fields Claman & Machtinger Ste 2000 1900 Avenue Of The Stars Los Angeles CA 90067-4590

**FIELDS, BRIAN JAY,** lawyer; b. L.A., Oct. 17, 1962; s. Edwin L. and Judith L. (Feder) F.; m. Diana Denman, Apr. 10, 1994; 1 child, Daniella Corinne. BA in History, U. So. Calif., 1985; JD, Loyola U., L.A., 1998. Bar: Calif. 1985, U.S. Dist. Ct. (ctrl. dist.) Calif. 1993. Extern U.S. Dist. Ct., L.A., 1985; assoc. Lynberg & Watkins, L.A., 1988-91; legal counsel Thrifty Payless Corp., L.A., 1991-95, Alpha Therapeutic Corp., L.A., 1995-97; sr. counsel WellPoint Health Networks, Inc., L.A., 1997—; mediator, arbitrator L.A. Superior/Mcpl. Cts., 1992. Mem. L.A. County Barristers (vice chmn. 1993, corp. counsel com., moot ct. juror 1992). Avocations: golf, tennis, history. Administrative and regulatory, Health, Insurance. Office: WellPoint Health Networks Inc 21555 Oxnard St Fl 1 Woodland Hills CA 91367-4943

**FIELDS, JOHN NORRIS,** judge, educator; b. Niles, Mich., July 21, 1950; s. Donald H. and June N. Fields; m. Karin S. Fields, Sept. 11, 1976; 2 children. BA, Mich. State U., 1972, JD, 1976. Bar: Mich. 1976, U.S. Dist. Ct. (we. dist.) Mich. 1976, U.S. Supreme Ct. 1993. Asst. pros. atty. Berrien County Mich., St. Joseph, 1976-80, 5th dist. judge, 1980-94, 2d cir. judge, 1994—, chief judge, 1996—; adj. asst. prof. U. Notre Dame, Ind., 1991—. Dir. 4-H Found., Berrien County, 1984—; mem. exec. bd. dirs. Boy Scouts Am., Kalamazoo, Mich., 1984-88. Mem. ABA, State Bar Mich., Berrien County Bar Assn. Avocation: travel. Office: Berrien County Trial Ct 811 Port St Saint Joseph MI 49085-1183

**FIELDS, RICHARD CHARLES,** lawyer; b. Waterloo, Iowa, Jan. 10, 1931; s. George H. and Emily H. Fields; m. Shirley Izawa, Nov. 25, 1957; children: Stephanie, Diana, Deborah (dec.), Steven. AB magna cum laude, Harvard U., 1952; JD, U. Denver, 1964. Bar: Colo. 1964, Idaho 1966, U.S. Dist. Ct. Colo. 1964, U.S. Dist. Ct. Idaho 1966, U.S. Ct. Appeals (10th cir.) 1965, U.S. Ct. Appeals (9th cir.) 1968. Reporter, editor AP, Boise, Idaho and Helena, Mont., 1952-60; editor, supr. The Martin Co., Littleton, Colo., 1960-64; staff atty. NLRB, Denver, 1964-66; ptnr. Moffatt, Thomas, Barrett, Rock & Fields, Boise, 1966—; sec. Boise Indsl. Found., 1970—; sec./past pres. Greater Boise Rotary Found., 1980—; mem. adv. bd. Literacy Lab, Boise, 1995—; lawyer rep. 9th Cir. Jud. Conf., 1983-86. Dir., chmn. Ada County Paramedics, Boise; commr. Boise City Personnel Commn., 1995—; pres. Boise Philharmonic Assn., 1993-95; mem. Salvation Army Adv. Bd., Boise, 1973—. 1st lt. USAF, 1952-57. Mem. Idaho State Bar (commr. 1980-83, pres. 1982, Outstanding Svc. award 1990, Profl. award 1992), Am. Health Lawyers Assn., Am. Bd. Trial Advs. (state chmn.), Am. Coll. Trial Lawyers (state chmn.), Am. Employment Law Coun., Western States Bar Conf. (past pres.), Jackrabbit States Bar (past chancellor), Rotary (Boise chpt. pres., dist. gov.), Order of St. Ives. Methodist. Avocations: fishing, photography, travel, music, golf. Health, Labor, Insurance. Home: 3800 Mountain View Dr Boise ID 83704-3548 Office: Moffatt Thomas Barrett Rock and Fields PO Box 829 Boise ID 83701-0829

**FIELDS, TIMMY LEE,** lawyer; b. Richmond, Va., Mar. 10, 1966; s. A. Wilson and Patricia Ruth Fields. Student, Emory and Henry Coll., 1984-86; BA, Tulane U., 1991; JD, Loyola U., New Orleans, 1996. Bar: La. 1997. Assoc. Law Offices John Sullivan, New Orleans, 1997-98; ptnr. Bombardier & Fields, LLP, New Orleans, 1998-99; pvt. practice New Orleans, 1999—. Active Forum for Equality, New Orleans, 1990—; bd. dirs. Belle Reve Hospice, New Orleans, 1997—. Mem. ABA, La. Bar Assn. Republican. Baptist. Avocations: antiques, travel. Personal injury, Estate planning, General practice. Home: 1901 Prytania St Apt 1 New Orleans LA 70130-5366 Office: Bombardier & Fields LLP 8428 Oak St New Orleans LA 70118-2046

**FIELKOW, ARNOLD DAVID,** lawyer; b. Appleton, Wis., Feb. 12, 1956; s. Jack and Dorothy (Rosenburg) F.; m. Susan Karen Schriber, Dec. 3, 1983. BA in Polit. Sci., Northwestern U., 1978; postgrad., U. Wis., 1978-80; JD, U. Fla., 1981. Bar: Ill. 1981, Wis. 1981, U.S. Dist. Ct. (no. dist.) Ill. 1981. Assoc. Leahy & Eisenburg Ltd., Chgo., 1981-86; ptnr. Grossman, Soloman & Fielkow, Lincolnwood, Ill., 1986—. Mem. Ill. Bar Assn., Chgo. Bar Assn. Democrat. Jewish. Avocations: athletics, travel. Insurance, Personal injury, Sports. Home: 2081 Kinsmon Dr Marietta GA 30062-8137 Office: So League of Prof Baseball 1 Depot St Ste 300 Marietta GA 30060-1909

**FIERKE, THOMAS GARNER,** lawyer; b. Boone, Iowa, Nov. 12, 1948; s. Norman Garner and Mary Margaret (Mullen) F.; m. Susan Marie Butler, July 17, 1976 (div. Mar. 1983); m. Debra Lynn Clayton, Sept. 17, 1988; children: Veronica Helen, Caroline Margaret. BSMetE, Iowa State U., 1971; JD, U. Minn., 1974; LLM, Boston U., 1978. Bar: Ill. 1974, U.S. Dist. Ct. Mass. 1976, U.S. Dist. Ct. (no. dist.) Ill. 1976, U.S. Ct. Appeals (1st cir.) 1976, U.S. Tax Ct. 1978, U.S. Supreme Ct. 1978, Mass. 1980, N.Y. 1981, U.S. Ct. Appeals (fed. cir.) 1989. Commd. 2nd lt. U.S. Army, 1971, advanced through grades to capt., resigned, 1980; trial ct. prosecutor Ft. Devens, Mass., 1974-77; group judge adv. 10th Spl. Forces Group, 1975-78; chief adminstrv. law sect. Ft. Devens, 1977-78; chief legal counsel, contracting officer U.S. Def. Rep., Am. Embassy, Tehran, Iran, 1979; chief adminstrv. law Ft. Devens, 1979-80; judge adv. gen. corps, 1974-80; atty., advisor Army Materiel Command, 1980-82; mgr. contracts policy and review Martin Marietta Michoud Aerospace, Martin Marietta Corp., New Orleans, 1982; gen. counsel Lockheed Martin Manned Space Sys., Lockheed Martin Corp., New Orleans, 1984—; apptd. to La. Gov.'s Mil. Adv. Commn., 1991—; bd. dirs. La. Orgn. for Jud. Excellence, 1988—; mem. La. state com. Employer Support of Guard and Res., 1988—, regional ombudsman, 1989-92, dep. state ombudsman, 1992-94, state ombudsman, 1994—, chmn. New Orleans sect., 1992-94. Col. USAR, 1995. Recipient Most Valuable Employer Support for the Guard and Res. award, NASA Pub. Svc. medal, 1992, La. Cross Merit award State of La., 1994, 4 Outstanding Vol. Svc. medals Dept. Def., 1994, 96, 97, Legion of Merit, 1998. Mem. Am. Corp. Counsel Assn. (bd. dirs. New Orleans chpt. 1987—, v.p. 1989-90), Internat. Assn. Def. Counsel. Republican. Episcopalian. Avocations: snow skiing, reading, running. General civil litigation, General corporate, Government contracts and claims. Office: Lockheed Martin Michoud Space Sys PO Box 29304 New Orleans LA 70189-0304

**FIERST, FREDERICK UDELL,** lawyer; b. Washington, July 12, 1948; s. Herbert Abner and Edith Udell Fierst; m. Eva Christiana Lauber, Apr. 17, 1981; children: Benjamin Thomas, Daniel Lauber, Sonya Elene. BA magna cum laude, Tufts Coll., 1970; JD, Columbia U., 1976. Bar: N.Y. 1977, Mass., 1981. Assoc. Peter Eikenberry, N.Y.C., 1976-78; jr. ptnr. Parcher and Herbert, N.Y.C., 1978-79; ptnr. Fierst & Neiman, Northampton, Mass., 1981-94, Fierst & Pucci LLP, Northampton, 1995—. Watson fellow, 1971. E-mail: fred@ent-atty.com. Entertainment. Home: 10 Park St Florence MA 01062-1206 Office: Fierst and Pucci LLP 64 Gothic St Northampton MA 01060-3042

**FIESCHKO, JOSEPH EDWARD, JR.,** lawyer; b. Chgo., July 11, 1953; s. Joseph E. and Antoinette Jane Fieschko; m. Regina Calkins, Oct. 2, 1982; 1 child, Zander Lewis. BA, Brown U., 1975; JD, U. Pitts., 1978. Bar: Pa. 1978, U.S. Ct. Appeals (3d cir.) 1978, U.S. Dist. Ct. (we. dist.) Pa. 1978. Assoc. Shire & Bergstein, Monessen, Pa., 1978-81; pvt. practice Fieschko & Assocs., Pitts., 1981—. Mem. ATLA, Pa. Trial Lawyers Assn., Brown Alumni Club of Pitts. (trustee 1992—). Democrat. Roman Catholic. Personal injury, Pension, profit-sharing, and employee benefits, Bankruptcy. Home: 697 Valleyview Rd Pittsburgh PA 15243-1015 Office: 2200 Koppers Bldg 438 Grant St Pittsburgh PA 15219-2402

**FIFIELD, WILLIAM O.,** lawyer; b. Crown Point, Ind., May 25, 1946. BS with honors, Purdue U., 1968; JD cum laude, Harvard U., 1971. Bar: Ill. 1971, Tex. 1998. Assoc. Sidley & Austin, Dallas, 1971-77, ptnr., 1977—, mng. ptnr., 1996—; bd. dirs. Kimberly-Clark Corp. Office: Sidley & Austin 717 N Harwood St Ste 3400 Dallas TX 75201-6538

**FIFLIS, TED JAMES,** lawyer, educator; b. Chgo., Feb. 20, 1933; s. James P. and Christine (Karakitsos) F.; m. Vasilike Pantelakos, July 3, 1955; children: Christina Eason, Antonia Fowler, Andreanna Lawson. BS, Northwestern U., 1954; LLB, Harvard U., 1957. Bar: Ill. 1957, Colo. 1975, U.S. Supreme Ct. 1984. Pvt. practice law Chgo., 1957-65; mem. faculty U. Colo. Law Sch., Boulder, 1965—; prof. U. Colo. Law Sch., 1968—; vis. prof. NYU, 1968, U. Calif., Davis, 1973, U. Chgo., 1976, U. Va., 1979, Duke U., 1980, Georgetown U., 1982, U. Pa., 1983, Am. U., 1983, Harvard U., 1988; Lehmann Disting. vis. prof. Washington U., 1991; cons. Rice U. Author: (with Homer Kripke, Paul Foster) Accounting for Business Lawyers, 1970, 3rd edit., 1984, Accounting Issues for Lawyers, 1991; editor-in-chief Corp. Law Rev., 1977-88; contbr. articles to profl. jours. Mem. ABA, Am. Assn. Law Schs. (past chmn. bus. law sect.), Colo. Bar Assn. (mem. coun. sect. of corp., banking and bus. law 1974-75), Am. Law Inst., Colo. Assn. Corp. Counsel (pres. 1998—). Greek Orthodox. Home: 1340 Bluebell Ave Boulder CO 80302-7832 Office: Univ Of Colo Law Sch Boulder CO 80309-0001

**FIGARI, ERNEST EMIL, JR.,** lawyer, educator; b. Navasota, Tex., Feb. 18, 1939; s. Ernest Emil and Louise (Campbell) F.; children: Alexandra Caroline, Audrey Elizabeth. BS, Tex. A&M U., 1961; LLB, U. Tex.-Austin, 1964; LLM, So. Meth. U., 1970. Bar: Tex. 1964, U.S. Ct. Appeals (5th cir.) 1965, U.S. Dist. Ct. (no. dist.) Tex. 1964, U.S. Supreme Ct. 1967. Law clerk to judge U.S. Dist. Ct. (no. dist.) Tex., Dallas, 1964-65; assoc. Coke & Coke, Dallas, 1965-70, ptnr., 1970-75; ptnr. Johnson & Swanson, Dallas, 1975-86, Figari & Davenport, Dallas, 1986—; adj. prof. law So. Meth. U., Dallas, 1974-79, 81-82, U. Tex., 1980 . Contbr. articles to legal jours. Fellow ABA, Tex. Bar Found., Dallas Bar Found.; mem. State Bar Tex., ABA. Roman Catholic. Federal civil litigation, State civil litigation. Office: Figari & Davenport 4800 Nations Bank Pla 901 Main St Ste 4800 Dallas TX 75202-3796

**FIGNAR, EUGENE MICHAEL,** financial company executive, lawyer; b. Hazleton, Pa.; s. Basil W. and Helen (Hannock) F.; m. Rosemary Casey. BBA, King's Coll., Wilkes-Barre, Pa., 1967; JD, Duquesne U., 1972. Bar: Pa. 1972, U.S. Dist. Ct. (we. dist.) Pa. 1972, Conn. 1988, N.Y. 1998; lic. real estate broker, N.Y., Conn. Counsel Westinghouse Electric Corp., Pitts., 1972-80; asst. gen. counsel Champion Internat. Corp., Stamford, Conn., 1980-81; v.p., gen. counsel, sec. Merrill Lynch Realty, Stamford, Conn., 1981-82; v.p., gen. counsel, sec. Merrill Lynch Mortgage, Stamford, Conn., 1982-84, v.p. quality, product devel., 1985-88, also bd. dirs.; sr. v.p., sr. lending officer The Bank Mart, Bridgeport, Conn., 1988-90; pres., CEO TDS Fin., Inc., Stamford, 1990—. Mem. bus. adv. coun. King's Coll., Wilkes-Barre, 1985—; mem. bus. adv. coun. Norwalk C.C., 1996—; bd. dirs. Ea. Fairfield County United Way, 1988-94; bd. dirs., vice chmn. Bridgeport Regional Counsel for Homeless, 1989-94. Sgt. U.S. Army, 1969-71. Mem. Am. Arbitration Assn., Real Estate Fin. Assn., N.Y. State Bar Assn., West End Yacht Club, Old Greenwich Yacht Club. Democrat. Catholic. Avocations: sailing, bicycling, model railroading, gardening. Home: 21 West End Ave Old Greenwich CT 06870-1611 Office: TDS Fin Inc 2001 W Main St Stamford CT 06902-4501

**FIHN, JEFFREY GLASER,** lawyer; b. St. Louis, Sept. 1, 1949; s. Jay Lofton and Carol (Glaser) F.; m. Gloria Jean Bratnick, Oct. 10, 1975. BSBA, Washington U., St. Louis, 1972; JD, U. La Verne, 1976. Bar: Ind. 1977, U.S. Dist. Ct. (so. dist.) Ind. 1977, U.S. Ct. Appeals (7th cir.) 1980, U.S. Supreme Ct. 1980, Nev. 1983, U.S. Dist. Ct. Nev. 1984, U.S. Ct. Appeals (9th cir.) 1986. Subrogation atty. Underwriters Adjusting Co., Chgo., 1978-79; assoc. Watson, Gleason & Hay, Indpls., 1977-78; dep. atty. gen. State of Ind., Indpls., 1979-84; staff-in-house atty. Travel Am., Las Vegas, 1984-86; insolvency counsel Ind. Dept. Ins., Indpls., 1986-88; claims counsel Vasa North Atlantic Ins. Co., Indpls., 1988-91; def. counsel Ind. Law Enforcement Acad., Indpls., 1987—; arbitrator Better Bus. Bur., Indpls., 1988—; sr. claim rep. Farmers Ins. Co., 1996; mem. arbitration panel Inter Ins. Co., 1996. Host and guest of Legally Speaking, Sta. WICR-FM, Indpls., 1987—. Chmn. adv. com. Town of Fishers, Ind. Recipient plaque Ind. Dept. Hwys., 1983. Mem. ABA, Indpls. Bar Assn. (mem. realtor/lawyer subcom.), Ind. State Bar Assn., Nev. Bar Assn. Republican. Jewish. Avocations: golf, photography, music, bridge.

**FILAN, PATRICK J.,** lawyer; b. Toledo, Ohio, Sept. 1, 1956; s. James K. and Nancy L. (Lillis) F.; m. Jessica B. Filan, July 2, 1988; children: Anja, Sofia, Eva, Sogmul. AB, Duke U., 1978; JD, Ohio State U., 1982. Ptnr. Rosenblum & Filan, Stamford, Conn. Editor ABA Medicine-Law Com. Newsletter, 1990—. Mem. ABA (vice chair medicine and law com. 1990—), Conn. Bar Assn. (vice chair med.-legal com. 1991—), Def. Rsch. Inst. Personal injury, Product liability, Labor. Office: Rosenblum & Filan 1 Landmark Sq Ste 500 Stamford CT 06901-2617 also: 400 Madison Ave New York NY 10017-1909

**FILES, JASON DANIEL,** lawyer; b. Little Rock, Ark., Nov. 28, 1967; s. Jack Dale and Jo Anne Files. BA, Rhodes Coll., 1990; JD, U. Ark., 1995. Atty. Gary Eubanks & Assoc., Little Rock, 1995-97, Howell, Trice and Hope, Little Rock, 1997—. Mem. Am. Inns of Ct., Ark. Trial Lawyers Assn., Ark. Bar Assn. Personal injury, Criminal, Family and matrimonial. Office: Howell Trice and Hope 211 S Spring St Little Rock AR 72201-2405

**FILI, DENISE M.,** lawyer; b. Balt., Apr. 16, 1960; d. Robert Charles and Shirley Lillian Franke; m. Salvatore Fili, Sept. 24, 1988; children: Liana, Joseph and Michalina (triplets). BA, Loyola U., Balt., 1982; JD, U. Md., Balt., 1985. Bar: Md. 1986, U.S. Dist. Ct. Md. 1986. Asst. state's atty. Balt. City State's Attys. Office, 1986—, sr. trial atty., 1990-96, supr. misdemeanor unit, 1996—; instr. Balt. City Police Dept., 1995—. Mem. Md. Bar Assn., Md. State's Attys. Assn. (instr. trial advocacy 1997—). Avocations: real estate, investments, baking. Office: State's Atty's Office Rm 454 Clarence Mitchell Jr Ct Hse Baltimore MD 21202

**FILINGO, MICHAEL ANTHONY,** lawyer; b. Easton, Pa., July 5, 1957; s. Michael A. Sr. and Rose M. (Gigliotti) F.; m. Wanda M. Stauffer, July 23, 1988. BA cum laude, Moravian Coll., 1979; JD, Capital U., 1982. Bar: Pa. 1982, U.S. Dist. Ct. (ea. dist.) Pa. 1982, U.S. Ct. Appeals (3d cir.) 1984. Atty. Zito, Martino & Karasek, Bangor, Pa., 1982-84, Cassebaum, McFall & Molnar, Bangor, 1984-86; pvt. practice Wind Gap, Pa., 1986—; asst. pub. defender Northampton County, Easton, Pa., 1986—; mcpl. solicitor Portland (Pa.) Borough, 1994—. Swimming and boating instr. for mentally retarded Robert F. Moll Camp, 1978, 79. Named Eagle Scout Boy Scouts Am., 1971; recipient Black belt in Shorin Ryu Karate Nazareth Karate Acad., 1990. Mem. Pa. Assn. of Criminal Def. Attys., Pa. Borough Solicitors Assn., Northampton County Bar Assn. (county fee dispute com. 1993—, county criminal rules com. 1993—), Pa. Bar Assn., Phi Alpha Theta, Delta Theta Phi. Avocations: Shorin Ryu karate, swimming, reading. Office: 116 S Broadway Wind Gap PA 18091-1424

**FILIPPINE, EDWARD LOUIS,** federal judge; b. 1930. A.B., St. Louis U., 1951, J.D., 1957. Bar: Mo. 1957. Pvt. practice law St. Louis, 1957-77; spl. asst. atty. gen. State of Mo., 1963-64; chief judge U.S. Dist. Ct. (ea. dist.) Mo., St. Louis, 1977-95, sr. judge, 1995—, 1995—. Served with USAF, 1951-53. Mem. ABA, Mo. Bar Assn., Bar Assn. Met. St. Louis, St. Louis County Bar Assn., Lawyers Assn. of St. Louis. Office: US Dist Ct 1114 Market St Rm 329 Saint Louis MO 63101-2038

**FILLER, GARRET I.,** lawyer. BS in Applied Econs. with distinction, Cornell U., 1990; LLD, Cornell U. Law Sch., 1993. Bar: N.J. 1993, N.Y. 1993. Mktg. program mgr. Atalanta Corp., Elizabeth, N.J., 1987-89; intern Borough Pres's. Office, Staten Island, N.Y., 1990-91; law clerk U.S. Dist. Ct. (no. dist.) N.Y., Binghamton, 1992; assoc. Cadwalader, Wickersham & Taft, N.Y.C., 1993-97; v.p., assoc. counsel D.E. Shaw & Co., L.P., N.Y.C., 1997—. Mem. ABA (mem. regulation futures derivative instruments com., subcom. investment cos. investment advisers), N.Y. State Bar Assn. (mem. securities regulation com., futures and derivative law com., futures regulation com.), Securities Industry Assn. (investment co. com.). Avocations: wine collecting, scuba diving, hiking, canoeing, horseback riding.

**FILLER, RONALD HOWARD,** lawyer; b. St. Louis, Apr. 11, 1948; s. Leon Isaac and Jeanette Frances (Sanofsky) F.; m. Paula; children: Stephen Paul, Lindsay Ann. BS, U. Ill., 1970; JD, George Washington U., 1973; LLM in Taxation, Georgetown U., 1976. BAr: D.C. 1973, Ill. 1976, N.Y. 1993. Atty. SEC, Washington, 1973-76; assoc. Abramson & Fox, Chgo., 1976-77; assoc. counsel Conti Cmty. Svc., Chgo., 1977-78, dir. mgmt. accounts, 1978-80; mng. ptnr. Filler Zaner & Assocs., Chgo., 1980-85; ptnr. Vedder, Price, Kaufman & Kammholz, Chgo., 1985-93, corp. practice leader, 1989-91, mem. exec. com., 1991-93; dir. futures adminstrn. Lehman Bros., Inc., 1993—; dir. Commodities Law Inst., Ill. Inst. Tech./Chgo-Kent Law Sch., 1978-97, adj. prof. law, 1977-93, bd. overseers, 1982-97; lectr. Commodities Ednl. Inst., 1977-89; adj. prof. law Bklyn. Law Sch., 1994-96. Contbr. articles to jours. and futures mags. Named one of top 315 lawyers State of Ill., 1991. Mem. ABA (chmn. sub futures commn. mchts. 1986—), Nat. Futures Assn. (bd. dirs. 1984-87), Am. Arbitration Assn. (arbitrator), Mid Am. Commodity Exch. (bd. dirs. 1984-86), Chgo. Bar Assn. (chmn. commodities law com. 1981-82, vice chmn. fin. and legal svcs. com. 1988-89, co-vice chmn. large law firm com. 1991-92), Nat. Assn. Futures Traders Assn., Futures Industry Assn. (bd. dirs. 1990-92, exec. com. Chgo. divsn. 1986-88, exec. com. Law and Comp. divsn. 1985-90, 92—, sec. 1995-98, pres. 1998—), N.Y. State Bar Assn., Ill. State Bar Assn. Democrat. Jewish. Fax: 212 526-6193. E-mail: RFiller@LEHMAN.com. Contracts commercial, Commodities, Securities. Home: 54 Collinwood Rd Maplewood NJ 07040-1038 Office: Lehman Bros Inc Am Exp Tower 3 World Fin Ctr Fl 8 New York NY 10285-0001

**FILPI, ROBERT ALAN,** lawyer; b. Chgo., Oct. 8, 1945; s. John Andrew and Eunice Lorraine (Taylor) F.; m. Janice Elizabeth Crusoe, June 24, 1967; children—Jennifer Anne, Christopher Alan, Emily Elizabeth. B.A. in History, magna cum laude, Harvard U., 1967; J.D., Northwestern U., 1970. Bar: Ill. 1970, U.S. Dist. Ct. (no. dist.) Ill. 1971, U.S. Ct. Appeals, 7th cir. 1971, U.S. Supreme Ct. 1975. Asst. U.S. atty. No. Dist. Ill., Chgo., 1971-75; dep. chief U.S. atty. No. Dist. Ill., Civil Div., Chgo., 1975-76; ptnr. Stack & Filpi, Chgo., 1976—. Assoc. editor Jour. Criminal Law, Criminology and Police Sci., 1969-70. Coach, Spring Lake Sports League, Lincolnshire, Ill., 1984-91 ; mem. Village of Lincolnshire Plan Commn., 1984-94 . Recipient Hyde prize Northwestern U. Sch. Law, 1967. Mem. Chgo. Bar Assn. Clubs: Union League, Harvard. General civil litigation, General corporate, General practice. Office: 140 S Dearborn St Ste 411 Chicago IL 60603-5201

**FILSON, J. ADAM,** lawyer; b. N.Y.C., Nov. 5, 1964; s. Brent F. and E. Magalis (Riera) F.; m. Amy Cott, July 25, 1993; 1 child, Calvin Cott. BA, Princeton U., 1988; JD, St. John's U., Jamaica, N.Y., 1995. Bar: Mass. 1995. Paralegal Simpson Thacher & Bartlett, N.Y.C., 1988-90, Marks & Murase, N.Y.C., 1991-92; credit analyst Barclays Bank PLC, N.Y.C., 1990-91; assoc. Grinnell, Dubendorf & Smith LLP, Williamstown, Mass., 1995—. Bd. govs. The See Fund, Williamstown, 1997—. 1st lt. USAR, 1994—. Mem. ABA, Mass. Bar Assn., Berkshire Bar Assn., Williamstown C. of C. (bd. dirs. v.p. 1998—). General corporate, Land use and zoning (including planning), Real property. Office: Grinnell Dubendorf & Smith One Bank St Williamstown MA 01267

**FINA, PAUL JOSEPH,** lawyer; b. Chgo., Mar. 1, 1959; s. Paul Emil and Vera Christiane (Mutzbauer) F.; m. Robyn Leann Hughes, May 24, 1986; 1 child, Paul George. BA in Econs., U. Ill., 1982, MA, 1983; JD, DePaul U., Chgo., 1987. Bar: Ill. 1988, U.S. Dist. Ct. (no. dist.) Ill. 1990, U.S. Ct. Appeals (7th cir.) 1990, U.S. Supreme Ct. 1991. Assoc. Haskin, Taylor & McDonough, Wheaton, Ill., 1988-90, Komessar & Wintroub, Chgo., 1990-94; pvt. practice Law Office of Paul J. Fina, Chgo., 1994—; mem. bus. faculty Coll. of DuPage, Glen Ellyn, Ill., 1986—, Aurora (Ill.) U., 1997—. Gen. counsel Housing Helpers, Inc., Riverside, Ill., 1991—. DePaul law grantee, 1985. Mem. ABA, Ill. BAr Assn., Assn. Trial Lawyers Am., DuPage County Bar Assn. (civil practice com.), Phi Alpha Delta. Roman Catholic. Avocations: music performance, athletics. Personal injury, State civil litigation. Home: 101 Red Fox Run Montgomery IL 60538-2914 Office: 30 N La Salle St Ste 1530 Chicago IL 60602-2503

**FINAN, CHRISTINE DENISE,** lawyer; b. Barberton, Ohio, Dec. 3, 1958; d. Frank Bissett and Virginia Joyce Duncan; m. Michael John Wartko, Oct. 31, 1981 (div. Apr. 1986); 1 child, Michael Jonathan Wartko. BA in Social Work, Akron U., 1983, JD, 1990. Pvt. practice Stow, Ohio, 1992-97; atty. Slater & Zurz, Akron, 1997—. Mem. Ohio Bar Assn., Akron Bar Assn. (mem. family law sect. 1993—, vol. legal svcs. project 1995—). Family and matrimonial, Juvenile. Office: Slater and Zurz 1 Cascade Plz Ste 2210 Akron OH 44308-1135

**FINBERG, JAMES MICHAEL,** lawyer; b. Balt., Sept. 6, 1958; s. Laurence and Harriet (Levinson) F.; m. Marian D. Keeler, June 28, 1986. BA, Brown U., 1980; JD, U. Chgo., 1983. Bar: Calif. 1984, U.S. Dist. Ct. (no. dist.) Calif. 1984, U.S. Dist. Ct. (ea. dist.) Calif. 1987, U.S. Ct. Appeals (9th and fed. cirs.) 1987, U.S. Dist. Ct. Hawaii, 1988, U.S. Supreme Ct. 1994. Law clk. to assoc. justice Mich. Supreme Ct., 1983-84; assoc. Feldman, Waldman and Kline, San Francisco, 1984-87, Morrison and Foerster, 1987-90; ptnr. Lieff, Cabraser, Heimann & Bernstein, L.L.P., San Francisco, 1991—; adv. com. local rules for securities cases U.S. Dist. Ct., Calif., 1996. Exec. editor U. Chgo. Law Rev., 1982-83. Mem. ABA (chmn. securities subcom. class and derivative action com. 1998—), ACLU (bd. dirs. No. Calif. chpt. 1995), Bar Assn. San Francisco (bd. dirs. 1999—, jud. evaluation com. 1994, bd. dirs. 1998—), Calif. Bar Assn. (mem. standing com. on legal svcs. to poor 1990-94, vice-chmn. 1993-94), Lawyers Com. for Civil Rights of San

Francisco Bay Area (bd. dirs. 1992-98, fin. chmn. 1992-95, sec. 1996, co-chmn. 1997-98). Federal civil litigation, Securities. Office: Lieff Cabraser Heimann & Bernstein LL 275 Battery St Fl 30 San Francisco CA 94111-3305

**FINBERG, JEANNE,** lawyer; b. Balt., Nov. 20, 1952; d. Laurence and Harriet (Levinson) F.; m. Kem Holland Cook, Apr. 20, 1980; 1 child, Keegan Cook Finberg. AB, Stanford U., 1974; JD, U. San Francisco, 1979. Bar: Calif., Ariz., U.S. Supreme Ct., U.S. Ct. Appeals D.C. Cir., U.S. Ct. Appeals (9th, 8th, 4th, 6th cirs.), U.S. Dist. Ct. (no. and cen. dists.) Calif., U.S. Dist. Ct. Ariz. VISTA atty. Sr. Adults Legal Assistance, San Jose, Calif., 1979-80; staff atty. Legal Aid Soc. of San Mateo, Redwood City, Calif., 1980-82; assoc. DeConcini, McDonald, Brammer, Yetwin, Lacey, Tucson, Ariz., 1982; atty./law clk. U.S. Dist. Ct., Tucson, 1983-85; staff atty. So. Ariz. Legal Aid, Tucson, 1985-86; directing atty. San Fernando Valley Neighborhood Legal Svc., Pacoima, Calif., 1986-88; staff atty. Nat. Sr. Citizens Ctr., L.A., 1988-93; sr. atty./policy analyst Consumers Union, San Francisco, 1993-97, Nat. Ctr. for Youth Law, San Francisco, 1997—; exec. bd. dirs. Health Access, San Francisco; bd. dirs. Internat. Inst. of the East Bay, Oakland, Calif. Contbr. articles to profl. jours., publs. Avocations: lit., opera, theatre. Office: Nat Ctr for Youth Law 114 Sansome St Ste 900 San Francisco CA 94104-3820

**FINCH, EDWARD RIDLEY, JR.,** lawyer, diplomat, author, lecturer; b. Westhampton Beach, N.Y., Aug. 31, 1919. AB with Atwater honors, Princeton U., 1941; JD, NYU, 1947; LLD (hon.), Mo. Valley Coll., 1963; DSc (hon.), Cumberland Coll., 1985. Bar: N.Y. 1948, U.S. Supreme Ct. 1953, D.C. 1978, Fla. 1980, Pa. 1992. Ptnr. Finch & Schaefler, N.Y.C., 1950-85; of counsel Le Boeuf, Lamb, Leiby & MacRae, N.Y.C., 1986-88; commr. City of N.Y., 1955-58; v.p. gen. counsel, dir. St. Giles Found., 1994—, Am. Internat. Petroleum Corp., 1988-92; U.S. del. 4th UN Congress, Geneva, 1970, 5th UN Congress, Japan, 1975; U.S. spl. ambassador to Panama, 1972; legal advisor, mem. U.S. Del. UNISPACE II , 1982, UNISPACE III, Vienna, Austria, 1999; lectr. in field. Author: Holes in Your Pockets, 3rd edit., Astro Business-A Guide to Commerce and Law of Outer Space, Judicial Politics; contbr. articles to legal and sci. jours. Pres., bd. dirs. St. Nicholas Soc. N.Y., 1948—; past pres. N.Y. Inst. Spl. Edn., 1950—; bd. govs. Nat. Space Soc., 1984—; mem. faculty adv. com. dept. politics Princeton U.; treas. Jessie Ridley Found., N.Y.C., Finch Trusts; pres. Adams Meml. Fund Inc.; trustee St. Andrew's Dune Ch., Southampton, Cathedral of St. John the Divine, 1989-92; bd. dirs. Am. Found. Cancer Rsch.; life trustee Met. Mus. of Art, N.Y.C.; trustee Whittell Trust. Col. JAG, USAFR, 1941-72. Decorated U.S. Legion of Merit with oak leaf cluster; order Brit. Empire; Knight Order St. John; officer French Legion of Honor, Disting. Eagle Scout, Coun. of Am. Ambassadors. Fellow Am. Bar Found. (chmn. aerospace coun. sect. sci. and tech 1986-92); mem. ABA (ho. of dels. 1971-72, chmn. corp. lawyers sr. lawyer divsn., chmn. aerospace law divsn. internat. law sect.1973-79), AIAA (sr.), Fed. Bar Assn., Inter-Am. Bar Assn. (Hallgartern telecommunications award 1991), N.Y. State Bar Assn. (internat. law and practice sec., chmn. arms control and nat. security com.), Pa. Bar Assn., Fla. Bar Assn., Assn., Bar City of N.Y., Internat. Bar Assn., Judge Advs. Assn. U.S. (past pres.), Am. Law Inst., Am. Judicature Soc. (sr.), Internat. Astronautical Acad. (full elected mem.), Internat. Inst. Space Law (Lifetim Disting. Svc. award 1997), Am. Arbitration Assn. (panelist), Univ. Clubs of Wash. and N.Y., Union League Club, Union Club, Princeton Club (bd. govs. 1982—), L.I. Club, Bathing Corp. of Southampton, Westhampton Country Club. Fax: 212-327-0593. E-mail: erfinchjr@aol.com. Non-profit and tax-exempt organizations, Estate taxation, Securities. Office: 862 Park Ave New York NY 10021-1806

**FINCH, FRANK HERSCHEL, JR.,** lawyer; b. Mpls., Mar. 13, 1933; s. Frank H. and Louise A. (Henry) F.; m. Margaret Lee Samuel, June 13, 1953; children: Frank H. III, Lani D.L. BA, Harvard U., 1953; LLB, Harvard U. Law Sch., 1959. Bar: Conn. 1959, U.S. Supreme Ct. 1967. Assoc. Howd & Lavieri, Winsted, Conn., 1959-61; ptnr. Howd, Lavieri & Finch, Winsted, 1961—; pros. atty. Conn. Cir. Ct., 1961-78; adv. bd. Conn. Bank and Trust Co., 1976—; bd. dirs. Northwest Conn. Health Corp. Chmn., bd. dirs. Winsted Meml. Hosp., 1975-77; chmn. personnel com. Town of Barkhamsted, Conn., 1984—; mem. regional adv. coun. N.W. Conn. C.C.; vice-chmn. bd. trustees N.W. Conn. YMCA. Lt. USNR, 1953-59. Mem. ABA, Conn. Bar Assn. (chmn. standing com. on admissions 1978—, bd. govs. 1985—), Litchfield County Bar Assn. (pres. 1974-76, grievance com. 1982-86, state trial referee 1984—), Am. Arbitration Assn. (arbitrator 1975—), Nat. Assn. Dist. Attys., N.W. Conn. C. of C. (bd. dirs. 1978—, chmn. 1980-81, sec. 1985-89, v.p. 1989—). Club: University (exec. com. 1985—), Rotary (pres. Winsted club 1967-68). General corporate, Real property, General practice. Office: Howd Lavieri & Finch PO Box 1080 682 Main St Winsted CT 06098-1515

**FINCH, MICHAEL PAUL,** lawyer; b. Galveston, Tex., Jan. 4, 1946; s. Albert Lynn and Ila Belle (Robertson) F.; m. Rebecca Jean Minnear, Dec. 27, 1969; children: Michael Paul, Rachelle Jean. BEE cum laude, Rice U., 1969, MEE, 1969; JD magna cum laude, U. Houston, 1972. Bar: Tex. 1973. Petroleum engr. Exxon Corp., Houston, 1969-72; assoc. Vinson & Elkins, Houston, 1972-79, ptnr., 1980—. Dir. Houston Pops Orch., 1988-89; bd. dirs. Rice Engring. Alumni, 1994-98. Mem. ABA, Tex. Bar Assn., Houston Bar Assn., Am. Contact Bridge League (life master 1964—). Republican. Methodist. Clubs: Houston Ctr., Rice U. (founder). Avocations: electronics, woodworking, snow skiing, piano. Securities, General corporate, Mergers and acquisitions. Home: 12531 Overcup Dr Houston TX 77024-4915 Office: Vinson & Elkins 2300 First City Tower 1001 Fannin St Ste 3300 Houston TX 77002-6706

**FINCH, RAYMOND LAWRENCE,** judge; b. Christiansted, St. Croix, V.I., Oct. 4, 1940; s. Wilfred Christopher and Beryl Elaine (Bough) F.; m. Anne Marie Mohammed, May 8, 1996; children—Allison, Mark, Jennifer. A.B., Howard U., 1962, J.D., 1965. Bar: V.I. 1971, Third Circuit Ct. of Appeals 1976. Law clk. Judge's Municipal Ct. of V.I., 1965-66; partner firm Hodge, Sheen, Finch & Ross, Christiansted, 1970-75; judge Territorial Ct. of V.I., Charlotte Amalie, 1975-86, Ct. of Appeals, V.I., Charlotte Amalie, 1986-94; judge U.S. Dist. Ct. of V.I., 1994—, chief judge, 1999—; instr. Grad. div., Coll. of V.I., Am. Inst. Banking, 1976—. Bd. dirs. Boy Scouts Am., Boys Club Am. Served to capt. U.S. Army, 1966-69. Decorated Army Commendation medal, Bronze Star medal. Mem. Am. Judges Assn., Am., Nat. bar assns., Internat. Assn. Chiefs of Police. Democrat. Lutheran. Office: PO Box 24051 Christiansted VI 00824-0051

**FINCH, SUSAN CHLOË,** mediator, therapist; b. Norfolk, Va., Apr. 24, 1962; d. Charles Warren Wagner and Patsy Ann (Barker) Carlin; m. Patrick Kenneth Finch, Aug. 10, 1985; children: Ryan Patrick, Hannah Chloë. BA in Psychology, San Diego State U., 1985; MA in Marriage and Family Therapy, U. So. Calif., 1992, MA in Sociology, 1992, postgrad., 1992—. Cert. family life educator Nat. Coun. on Family Rels.; registered marriage, family, child counselor intern, Calif. Tchg. asst., asst. lectr. dept. sociology U. So. Calif., L.A., 1985-88, therapist trainee, 1987-89, academic advisor, 1988-91; mediator intern Family Ct. Svcs./Conciliation Ct., L.A., 1989-90, family counselor, 1990-96, sr. family mediator, 1996—. Contbr. article to profl. jour., chpt. to book. Mem. Lancaster (Calif.) Child Abuse Task Force, 1996-97. Mem. Am. Assn. Marriage and Family Therapy, Am. Sociol. Assn., Nat. Coun. Family Rels. Episcopalian. Office: Mediation and Conciliation Svc 1040 W Avenue J Rm 218 Lancaster CA 93534-3329

**FINCK, BARRY RUSSELL,** lawyer; b. Warwick, R.I., Oct. 2, 1969; s. Keith Barry and Mary Anne Ryan F. BA, Boston Coll., 1991; JD, U. Denver, 1995. Bar: Colo. 1995. Atty. pvt. practice, Denver, 1995—. Mem. Colo. Bar Assn., Colo. Criminal Def. Assn. Criminal, Family and matrimonial, Bankruptcy. Office: 1490 Lafayette St Ste 407 Denver CO 80218-2394

**FINCK, KEVIN WILLIAM,** lawyer; b. Whittier, Calif., Dec. 14, 1954; s. William Albert and Ester (Gutbub) F.; m. Kathleen A. Miller, Oct. 7, 1989. BA in History, U. Calif., Santa Barbara, 1977; JD, U. Calif., San Francisco, 1980. Bar: Calif. 1980. lectr. Internat. Bar Assn., Learning Annex. Author: California Corporation Start Up Package and Minute Book, 1982, 9th edit., 1998; contbr. articles to various profl. jours. Avocations: hiking, golf, skiing. General corporate, Private international, Contracts commercial. Office: Ste 1670 Two Embarcadero Ctr San Francisco CA 94111

**FINCKE, WARING ROBERTS,** lawyer; b. Pasadena, Calif., Nov. 4, 1945; s. John Meigs and Harriet Coleman (Roberts) F.; m. Gretchen Mary Loyster, Mar. 28, 1972; children: Brian Bronaugh, Kari Bronaugh, Laura Roberts Fincke. BJ, U. Wis., 1973, JD, 1975. Bar: Wis. 1975, U.S. Dist. Ct. Appeals (3rd cir.) 1976, U.S. Ct. Appeals (7th cir.) 1979. Law clk. to presiding justice U.S. Dist. Ct. (mid. dist.) Pa., Williamsport, 1975-76; pvt. practice law Montoursville, Pa., 1976-79; ptnr. Ellis & Fincke, State College, Pa., 1977-79; assoc. Shellow, Shellow & Glynn, S.C., Milw., 1979-82; staff atty. pub. defender's office State of Wis., 1982-87; pvt. practice law West Bend, Wis., 1987; ptnr. Dvorak & Fincke, Milw., 1987-96; pvt. practice West Bend, Wis., 1998—. Mem. ABA, Wis. Bar Assn. (chair criminal law sect. 1994-97), Wis. Assn. Criminal Def. Lawyers (bd. dirs. 1988—), Nat. Assn. Criminal Def. Lawyers. Avocations: gardening, computer research, camping. E-mail: wrfincke@mail.execpc.com. Criminal, Constitutional, Environmental. Home: 6945 Colt Cir West Bend WI 53090-9326 Office: 1784 Barton Ave Ste 17 West Bend WI 53090-5418

**FINE, A(RTHUR) KENNETH,** lawyer; b. N.Y.C., June 29, 1937; s. Aaron Harry and Rose (Levin) F.; m. Ellen Marie Jensen, July 11, 1964; children: Craig Jensen, Ricki-Barie, Desiree-Ellen. AB, Hunter Coll., 1959; JD, Columbia U., 1963; CLU, Coll. Ins., 1973; diploma, Command and Gen. Staff Coll., 1978. Bar: N.Y. 1974; registered rep. and limited prin. Nat. Assn. Securities Dealers, Inc. Joined U.S. Army N.G., 1955, advanced through grades to maj., 1973, ret., 1980; cons. U.S. Life Ins. Co., N.Y.C., 1970-74, atty., 1975-78, asst. gen. counsel, 1978; asst. counsel USLIFE Corp., N.Y.C., 1978-79, assoc. counsel, 1979-93; v.p., counsel Western Res. Life Assurance Co. Ohio, Clearwater, Fla. Mem. ABA, Soc. Fin. Svc. Profls., N.Y. State Bar Assn., N.G. Assn. U.S., Militia Assn. N.Y. (chmn. vet. officers com. 1981-90), Am. Legion (7th regt. post), Ret. Officers Club St. Petersburg, Fla. Republican. Lutheran. Administrative and regulatory, General corporate, Insurance. Home: 5953 36th Ave N Saint Petersburg FL 33710-1835 Office: Western Res Life Assurance Co of Ohio PO Box 5068 Clearwater FL 33758-5068

**FINE, J. DAVID,** lawyer; b. N.Y.C., Jan. 30, 1951; s. Phillip and Irma (Miller) F.; m. Judith Lynn McMillan, June 6, 1984. BSFS, Georgetown U., 1970; LLB, McGill U., Montreal, Que., 1973, BCL, 1974; LLM, Columbia U., 1978. Bar: We. Australia, 1987, High Ct. Australia, 1987, Oreg., 1992, U.S. Dist. Ct. Oreg., 1994. Asst. prof. U. Melbourne, Australia, 1974-76; clin. instr. Osgoode Hall Law Sch., Toronto, Ont., Can., 1976-77; Jervey fellow comp. law Columbia U., N.Y.C., 1977-79; assoc. prof. Loyola U., New Orleans, 1979-84, Macquarie U., Sydney, Australia, 1984-86; prof. U. Western Australia, Perth, 1986-91; pvt. practice Ashland, Oreg., 1992—; traffic safety commr., City of Ashland, 1997-99. contbr. articles to profl. jours. City councilman City of Ashland, 1999—. Mem. Internat. Trademark Assn., So. Oreg. Internat. Trade Coun. (charter mem.), Oreg. State Bar Assn. (continuing legal edn. com. 1995-98), Jackson County Bar Assn. (sec. 1999), Ashland Gun Club. Jewish. Avocations: reading, shooting, cooking, fly fishing. Intellectual property, Private international, General corporate. Home: 735 Frances Ln Ashland OR 97520-3411 Office: 50 3rd St PO Box 66 Ashland OR 97520-0166

**FINE, RICHARD ISAAC,** lawyer; b. Milw., Jan. 22, 1940; s. Jack and Frieda F.; m. Maryellen Olman, Nov. 25, 1982; 1 child, Victoria Elizabeth. BS, U. Wis., 1961; JD, U. Chgo., 1964; PhD in Internat. Law, U. London, 1967, cert., 1965, 66; cert. comparative law, Internat. U. Comparative Sci., Luxembourg, 1966; diplôme supérieur, Faculté Internat. pour l'Enseignement du Droit Comparé, Strasbourg, France, 1967. Bar: Ill. 1964, D.C. 1972, Calif. 1973. Trial atty. fgn. commerce sect. antitrust div. U.S. Dept. Justice, 1968-72; chief antitrust div. Los Angeles City Atty.'s Office, also spl. counsel gov. efficiency com., 1973-74; prof. internat., comparative and EEC antitrust law U. Syracuse (N.Y.) Law Sch. (overseas program), summers 1970-72; individual practice Richard I. Fine and Assocs., Los Angeles, 1974—; mem. antitrust adv. bd. Bur. Nat. Affairs, 1981—; bd. dirs. Citizens Island Bridge Co., Ltd., 1992—; vis. com. U. Chgo. Law Sch., 1992-95; hon. consul gen. Kingdom of Norway, 1995—. Contbr. articles to legal publs. Bd. dirs. Retinitis Pigmentosa Internat., 1985-90. Mem. ABA (chmn. subcom. internat. antitrust and trade regulation, internat. law sect. 1972-77, co-chmn. com. internat. econ. orgn. 1977-79), ATLA, Am. Soc. Internat. Law (co-chmn. com. corp. membership 1978-83, exec. coun. 1984-87, budget com. 1992-97, regional coord. for L.A. 1994—, 1995 ann. program com. 1994-95, corr. editor Internat. Legal Materials 1983—), Am. Fgn. Law Assn., Internat. Law Assn., Brit. Inst. Internat. and Comparative Law, State Bar Calif. (chmn. antitrust and trade regulation law sect. 1981-84, exec. com. 1981-87), L.A. County Bar Assn. (chmn. antitrust sect. 1977-78, exec. com. sect. internat. law 1993—, treas. 1997), Ill. Bar Assn., Am. Friends London Sch. Econs. and Polit. Sci. (bd. dirs. 1984—, chmn. So. Calif. chpt. 1984—, chmn. L.A. adv. com.), L.A. World Affairs Coun. (internat. cir. 1990—), Phi Delta Phi. Antitrust, Federal civil litigation, State civil litigation. Office: 10100 Santa Monica Blvd Los Angeles CA 90067-4003

**FINE, ROGER SETH,** pharmaceutical executive, lawyer; b. Bklyn., Sept. 22, 1942; s. Jack F. and Mildred (Perlmutter) F.; m. Rebecca Gold, June 14, 1964; children: David, Adam. BA, Columbia Coll., 1963; LLB, NYU, 1966. Bar: N.Y. 1966, U.S. Dist. Ct. (so. dist.) N.Y. 1967, U.S. Ct. Appeals (2d cir.) 1967. Assoc. Cahill, Gordon & Reindel, N.Y.C., 1966-74; gen. atty. Johnson & Johnson, New Brunswick, N.J., 1974-78; asst. gen. counsel Johnson & Johnson, New Brunswick, 1978-84, assoc. gen. counsel, 1984-91, v.p. adminstrn., mem. exec. com., 1991-95, v.p., gen. counsel, mem. exec. com., 1996—. Mem. ABA. Home: 26 Brook Dr Milltown NJ 08850-1932 Office: Johnson & Johnson 1 Johnson And Johnson Plz New Brunswick NJ 08933-0002

**FINE, STEPHANIE BETH,** lawyer; b. Phila., July 3, 1970. BA, Temple U., 1992; JD, Widener U., 1995. Bar: N.J. 1995, Pa. 1996. Law clk. to Hon. I. Raymond Kramer Phila. Ct. Common Pleas, Phila., 1993; lawyer Law Office of Joseph LaRosa, Phila., also Clementon, N.J., 1993-96, Feder, DellaGuardia & Feldman, Phila., 1996—. Mem. ABA, Pa. Bar Assn., Tau Epsilon Rho. General civil litigation, General practice, Workers' compensation. Office: Feder DellaGuardia et al 1515 Locust St Fl 6 Philadelphia PA 19102-3726

**FINE, TONI MICHELE,** law educator; b. N.Y.C., Feb. 7, 1961; d. Seymour and Wilma Gangel Fine. BA, SUNY, Binghamton, 1983; JD, Duke U., 1986. Bar: Pa. 1986, D.C. 1988, U.S. Ct. Appeals (D.C. cir.) 1988. Assoc. Crowell & Moring, Washington, 1986-93; lawyering instr. NYU Law Sch., N.Y.C., 1993-95, coord. Master Comparative Jurisprudence program, 1995-98, assoc. dir. global law sch. program, 1998—, acting dir. LLM (CJ) program, 1999—; assoc. professorial lectr. in law George Washington U. Law Ctr., Washington, 1992-93. Author: Americal Legal Systems: A Resource and Reference Guide, 1997; contbr. articles to profl. jours. Mem. Am. Assn. Law Schs. (exec. bd. sect. on grad. programs for fgn. students 1997—), Phi Beta Kappa, Pi Sigma Alpha. Office: NYU Sch of Law 40 Washington Sq S New York NY 10012-1005

**FINE, WILLIAM IRWIN,** lawyer; b. Hammond, Ind., Feb. 2, 1951; s. Leonard and Sylvia (Appleman) F.; m. Adele Barbara Hult; children: Rachel, Sarah, Rebecca. AB, Ind. U., 1973, JD, 1976; MA, Purdue U., 1996. Bar: Ind. 1976, U.S. Dist. Ct. (no. dist.) Ind. 1987. Assoc. Efron, Efron & Komyatte, Hammond, 1977-79, Efron and Efron, Hammond, 1979-88; pvt. practice, Highland, Ind., 1988—. Mem. Ind. State Bar Assn., Lake County Bar Assn., Phi Beta Kappa. Real property, Probate, Contracts commercial. Home: 1341 Fitzgerald Dr Munster IN 46321-4203 Office: 2833 Lincoln St Ste F Highland IN 46322-1924

**FINEGAN, COLE,** lawyer; b. Tulsa, Oct. 1, 1956; s. Philip Cole and Margaret (Hudson) F.; m. Robin Fudge, Dec. 29, 1984; children: Jordan Nicole, Ryan Andrew. BA in English, U. Notre Dame, Ind., 1978; JD, Georgetown U., 1987. Legis. asst., adminstrv. asst. Ctrl. Dist.-1st Dist. Okla., Tulsa and Washington, 1978-87; assoc. Brownstein Hyatt Farber & Strickland, Denver, 1987-91, shareholder, 1993—; dir. Office Policy and Initiatives Gov. State of Colo., Denver, 1991-93. Staff mem. The Tax Lawyer, 1984-86. Bd. mem. Greater Denver Corp., 1993-96, State Bd. of Agr., 1997—, I Have A Dream Found.; bd. trustees State Colls. Colo., 1993-97; bd. mem. Auvaria Higher Edn. Commn., 1993-95. Democrat. Roman Catholic. Home: 1934 Forest Pkwy Denver CO 80220-1337 Office: Brownstein Hyatt Farber & Strickland 410 17th St Fl 22 Denver CO 80202-4402

**FINEMAN, GARY LEE,** lawyer; b. Chgo., Oct. 3, 1960; s. Morris Fineman and Sharon Audrey Singer. BA, Mich. State U., 1983; JD cum laude, Thomas M. Cooley Law Sch., 1988. Bar: Mich. 1988, Ill. 1989. V.p., sr. atty. Gt. Lakes Nat. Bank, Ann Arbor, Mich., 1993—. Banking, Consumer commercial, General corporate. Home: 29584 Sierra Point Cir Farmingtn Hls MI 48331-1477 Office: Gt Lakes Nat Bank 401 E Liberty St Ann Arbor MI 48104-2207

**FINEMAN, S. DAVID,** lawyer; b. Phila., Oct. 23, 1945. B.A., Am. U., 1967; J.D. with honors, George Washington U., 1970. Bar: Pa. 1971, U.S. Dist. Ct. (ea. dist.) Pa., U.S. Ct. Appeals (3d cir.) Pa. 1980. Trial atty. Defender Assn., Phila., 1971-72; law clk. Superior Ct. Commonwealth Pa., 1972-73; mng. ptnr. Fineman & Bach, P.C., Phila., 1981—, Fineman & Bach, 1987—; instr. bus. law Temple U., 1974-83; mem. Phila. Planning Commn., 1989-91; mem. Industry Policy Adv. Com. to Advise Sec. of Commerce on Internat. Trade Issues, 1994—. Bd. govs. U.S. Postal Svc., 1995—, chmn. compensation com., 1997—. Mem. Phila. Bar Assn., Pa. Bar Assn., Pa. State Trial Lawyers Assn., Am. Bar Assn., Def. Rsch. Inst. General civil litigation, Administrative and regulatory, Insurance. Home: 335 Woodley Rd Merion Station PA 19066-1430 Office: 1608 Walnut St Ste 19 Philadelphia PA 19103-5443

**FINER, WILLIAM A.,** lawyer; b. Bklyn., Nov. 10, 1942; s. Samuel and Rachel Finer; 1 child, Jessica Rose. AB in Econs., Calif. State U., Long Beach, 1969; JD, Loyola U., L.A., 1972. Bar: Calif. 1972, U.S. Dist. Ct. (cen. dist.) Calif. 1972. Sole practitioner Palos Verdes Estates, Calif., 1973-76, Torrance, Calif., 1977-85; mng. dir. Bell, Fainsbert & Finer, El Segundo, Calif., 1985-87, Finer, Kim & Stearns, Torrance, 1988—; counsel Palos Verdes Art Ctr., Rolling Hills Estates, Calif., 1988-92, pres.-elect, 1992-94, pres. 1994-95; counsel, bd. dirs. Palos Verdes Beach and Athletic Club, Palos Verdes Estates, 1990-94, South Bay Svc. Ctr., Torrance, 1978-92. Mem. City Coun. of Palos Verdes Estates, 1994—, mayor pro tem, 1995-96, mayor, 1996-97. With USN, 1960-63. Mem. ABA, Los Angeles County Bar Assn., South Bay Bar Assn., Kiwanis (pres. 1988-90). Republican. Avocation: bicycling. Real property, Taxation, general, Estate planning. Office: 3424 W Carson St Ste 500 Torrance CA 90503-5723

**FINERTY, JOHN DANIEL, JR.,** lawyer; b. Milw., Sept. 27, 1965; s. John Daniel and Karen Ann Siewart Finerty; m. Kathryn Ann Lonsdorf, Apr. 5, 1966; 1 child, Justine Marie. BBA, U. Wis., Madison, 1988; JD, Marquette U., 1992; MA in Econs., U. Wis., Milw., 1999. Bar: Wis. 1992, U.S. Ct. Appeals (7th cir.) Ill. 1993, U.S. Ct. Appeals (11th cir.) Ga., U.S. Ct. Appeals (10th cir.) Colo. 1995. Assoc. Krukowski & Costello, S.C., Milw., 1992-95, Kravit, Gass, Hovel & Leitner, Milw., 1995—. Contbr. articles to profl. jours. Pres. planning commn. St. John's Cathedral, Milw., 1995. Named 40 under 40 Award Bus. Jour., 1995. Mem. State Bar of Wis., Seventh Cir. Bar Assn., Milw. Bar Assn. Democrat. Labor, Federal civil litigation, State civil litigation. Office: Kravit Gass Hovel & Leitner SC 825 N Jefferson St Milwaukee WI 53202-3721

**FINESILVER, JAY MARK,** lawyer; b. Denver, June 10, 1955; s. Sherman G. and Annette (Warren) F.; m. Debra K. Wilcox, Apr. 6, 1979 (div.); children: Justin, Lauren. BA, Washington U., St. Louis, 1977; JD, U. Denver, 1980. Bar: Colo. 1981, U.S. Dist. Ct. Colo. 1980, U.S. Ct. Appeals (7th and 10th cirs.) 1981. Law clk. to judge U.S. Ct. Appeals (7th cir.), Chgo., 1980-81; assoc. Rothgerber, Appel & Powers, Denver, 1981-85, Elrod, Katz, Preeo & Look, Denver, 1985-86; pvt. practice Denver, 1986-90; v.p. corp. affairs Daniels Communications Inc., Denver, 1990—; instr. Denver Paralegal Inst., 1987-88. Author: Colorado Foreclosure and Bankruptcy, 1988; contbr. articles to profl. jours. Pres. Denver Citizenship Day Com., 1983-86, Mayfair Neighbors, Inc., Denver, 1984-87. Named Outstanding Neighbor Mayfair Neighbors Inc., 1988. Mem. ABA, Washington U. Alumni Assn. (Colo. chmn. 1982-87). Avocations: fishing, skiing, photography, creative writing, Southwestern art. Real property, Consumer commercial, Communications. Office: Ste 460 3200 Chevy Creek South Dr Denver CO 80209

**FINGERMAN, ALBERT R.,** lawyer; b. Cin., Sept. 29, 1920; s. Louis and Freda (Skyletsky) F.; m. Shirley Eskind, June 2, 1946; children—Naomi Osher, David, Joel, Jeremy. LL.B., U. Cin., 1948. Bar: Ohio 1948, U.S. Supreme Ct. 1955. Assoc. Schmidt, Effron, Josselson & Weber, Cin., 1970-83; ptnr. Fingerman, Guckenberger & Assocs., Cin., 1983-88, Fingerman, Guckenberger & Gehrig, Cin., 1988-93; ptnr., Fingerman, Gehrig & Gelwicks, Cin., 1993—; guest instr. U. Cin. Law Sch., Chase Coll. Law, No. Ky. State Coll. Past chmn. Woodward High Sch. Alumnal Endowment Fund. Served with USAAF, 1941-45. Decorated Air medal with oak leaf cluster. Mem. ABA (past mem. bar pres. sect.), Ohio Bar Assn. (past com. chmn.), Cin. Bar Assn. (past pres.), Lawyers Club Cin. Mem. B'nai B'rith (past pres. Cin.). General practice, Criminal, Probate. Office: 36 E 4th St Ste 1140 Cincinnati OH 45202-3809

**FINIZIO-BASCOMBE, JAMIE JULIA,** lawyer; b. Phila., Jan. 29, 1967; d. Rick Finizio; m. Timothy Paul Bascombe, Nov. 5, 1994. BSBA in Fin., U. Fla., 1989; JD, Nova Law Sch., 1993. Clk. English Solicitors, London, 1992; ptnr. Montero, Finizio, Velasquez & Weissing, Ft. Lauderdale, Fla., 1993—. Pres. Coalition Hispanic Am. Women, Broward County; bd. dirs. Ft. Lauderdale Sister Cities Internat., PACE Girls Ctr. Mem. Fla. Bar Young Lawyers (bd. govs.), Broward County Bar Assn. (bd. dirs. young lawyers divsn.). Republican. Roman Catholic. Avocations: water skiing, travel, languages.

**FINK, DAVID HOWARD,** lawyer; b. Detroit, Sept. 25, 1952; s. Samuel R. and Bertha B. (Slutsky) F.; m. Trudy Ellen Gealer, July 5, 1981; children: Nathan, Lauren. BA magna cum laude, Harvard Coll., 1974, JD cum laude, 1977. Bar: Mich. 1977, U.S. Ct. Appeals (6th and 7th cirs.), U.S. Supreme Ct. Asst. corp. counsel City of Detroit, 1977-78; ptnr. Cooper, Fink & Zausmer, P.C., Detroit, 1978—. Mem. Dem. Party 18th Congl. Dist. Exec. Com., Oakland County, Mich., 1969-71, Southeast Mich. Coun. Gov. Task Force on Environ. Regulation, Citizens Advisory Group to Ad Hoc Com. on Revitalizing our Mich. Cities, Mich. Ho. of Reps. Hon. scholar Harvard Coll., 1970. Mem. ABA, Oakland County Bar Assn., Washtenaw County Bar Assn., Ingham County Bar Assn., Detroit Bar Assn., Greater Detroit C. of C. (energy and environ. policy com.).

**FINK, EDWARD MURRAY,** lawyer, educator; b. N.Y.C., Mar. 11, 1934; s. Nathaniel and Elsa Charlotte (Lenrow) F.; divorced; children: Jeffrey Neil, Andrea Sue; m. Rita Toby Cohen, Aug. 11, 1985. BS in Chemistry, CCNY, 1955; JD, Georgetown U., 1959. Bar: D.C. 1960, U.S. Dist. Ct. D.C. 1960, U.S. Ct. Appeals (D.C. cir.) 1960, N.Y. 1962, N.J. 1970, U.S. Dist. Ct. N.J. 1970, U.S. Patent and Trademark Office 1960. Patent examiner U.S. Patent Office, Washington, 1955-60; atty. Bell Labs., Murray Hill, N.J., 1960-83, Bell Comm. Rsch. Inc., Livingston, N.J., 1984-91, Edward M. Fink, P.A., Edison, N.J., 1991—; adj. prof. torts, bus. law and civil litigation Middlesex County Coll., Edison, N.J., 1980—; adj. prof. partnerships and corps, contract law Montclair State U., Upper Montclair, N.J., 1984—. Mem. ABA, Am. Intellectual Property Assn., N.J. Patent Law Assn., N.J. State Bar Assn., Middlesex County Bar Assn., D.C. Bar Assn., N.Y. State Bar Assn. Democrat. Jewish. Patent, General practice, Real property. Home and Office: 51 Jamaica St Edison NJ 08820-3726

**FINK, GORDON IAN,** lawyer, educator; b. Detroit, July 13, 1953; s. Joseph Louis and Charlotte (Shulman) F. AB, U. Calif., Santa Barbara, 1975; JD, Calif. Western U., San Diego, 1978. Bar: Nev., Pa., D.C. Sportscaster Sports Chatter Sta. KUVU-TV, Las Vegas, Nev., 1976-83; intern, law clk. Nev. Supreme Ct., Carson City, 1978; staff atty. U.S. Senate Commerce Com., Washington, 1978-83; pvt. practice Washington, 1983-84; sportscaster Sports Open Line Sta. KOWN, Washington, 1985—; instr. in polit. sci. U. Nev., Las Vegas, 1984—; pvt. practice Las Vegas, 1984—; dep. atty. gen. State of Nev., 1993—; sportscaster Runnin Rebel Basketball, Las Vegas, 1987—; scouting cons. Seattle Supersonics, 1993. Mem. Clark County Dem.

Cen. Com., Las Vegas, 1989—. Mem. ABA, D.C. Bar Assn., Pa. Bar Assn., Nev. Bar Assn., Forum Com. on Communications Law, Pi Sigma Alpha. Communications, Administrative and regulatory, Labor. Home and Office: 1761 Seneca Ln Las Vegas NV 89109-3178

**FINK, JOSEPH ALLEN,** lawyer; b. Lexington, Ky., Oct. 4, 1942; s. Allen Medford and Margaret Ruth (Draper) F.; children: Alexander Mentzer, Justin McGranahan. Student, Wayne State U., 1960-61; BA, Oberlin Coll., 1964; JD, Duke U., 1967. Bar: Mich. 1968, U.S. Dist Ct. (ea. dist.) Mich. 1968, U.S. Dist. Ct. (we. dist.) Mich. 1974, U.S. Ct. Appeals (6th cir.) 1987, U.S. Supreme Ct. 1998. Assoc. Dickinson, Wright, McKean & Cudlip, Detroit, 1972-75, Lansing, Mich., 1968-75; ptnr. Dickinson Wright PLLC, Lansing, 1976—; instr. U.S. Internat. U. Grad. Sch. Bus., San Diego, 1971; adj. prof. trial advocacy Thomas M. Cooley Law Sch., Lansing, 1984-85; mem. com. on local rules U.S. Dist. Cts., 1985; chmn. trial experience sub-com. U.S. Dist. Ct. (we. dist.) Mich., 1981. Contbg. author: Construction Litigation, 1979, Legal Considerations in Managing Problem Employees, 1988, Michigan Civil Procedure During Trial, 2d edit., 1989; contbr. articles to profl. jours. Bd. dirs. Lansing 2000 Inc., 1985-92; bd. trustees Olivet (Mich.) Coll., 1985-94; mem. bd. advisors Mich. State U. Press, 1993-96. Lt. JAGC, USNR, 1968-72. Fellow Mich. State Bar Found.; mem. Fed. Bar Assn., State Bar of Mich. (chmn. local disciplinary com. 1983—, mem. com. for U.S. Cts. 1984), Mich. Def. Trial Counsel Assn. Episcopalian. Avocations: writing, reading, golf. Federal civil litigation, General civil litigation, Insurance. Home: 1356 Hickory Island Dr Haslett MI 48840-8944 Office: Dickinson Wright PLLC 215 S Washington Sq Ste 200 Lansing MI 48933-1816

**FINK, NORMAN STILES,** lawyer, educational administrator, fundraising consultant; b. Easton, Pa., Aug. 13, 1926; s. Herman and Yetta (Hyman) F.; m. Helen Mullen, Sept. 1, 1956; children: Hayden Michael, Patricia Carol. AB, Dartmouth Coll., 1947; JD, Harvard U., 1950. Bar: N.Y. 1951, U.S. Dist. Ct. (ea. and so. dists.) N.Y. 1954, U.S. Supreme Ct. 1964. Mem. legal staff Remington Rand, Inc., N.Y.C., Washington, 1949-54; ptnr. Lans & Fink, N.Y.C., 1954-68; counsel devel. program U. Pa., Phila., 1969-80; v.p. devel. and univ. rels. Brandeis U., Waltham, Mass., 1980-81; dep. v.p. devel., alumni rels., assoc. gen. counsel devel. Columbia U., N.Y.C., 1981-89; sr. counsel John Grenzebach & Assocs., Inc., Chgo., 1989-91; cons. v.p. Engle Consulting Group, Inc., Chgo. Editor: Deferred Giving Handbook, 1977; author: (with Howard C. Metzler) The Costs and Benefits of Deferred Giving, 1982. V.p. Am. Australian Studies Found.; mem. bd. vis. Brevard (N.C.) Coll., 1995—, life trustee, 1999, Warren Wilson Coll., 1997—. With U.S. Army, 1945-46. Recipient Alice Beeman award for excellence in devel. writing Coun. Advancement and Support of Edn., 1984, Silver medal for fundraising comms., Conn. Adv. and Support of Edn., 1988; Lilly Endowment grantee, 1979-80. Mem. ABA (mem. com. on exempt orgns. sect. taxation and com. estate planning and drafting, charitable givint), Coun. Advancement and support of Edn. (various coms.), Am. Arbitration Assn. (panelist), Assn. of Bar of City of N.Y.C. (com. on tax-exempt orgns. 1987-90), Dartmouth Lawyers Assn., Harvard Law Sch. Assn., Nat. Soc. Fund Raising Execs (Contbn. to Knowledge award 1985), Harvard Club Western N.C. Democrat. Jewish. Education and schools, Non-profit and tax-exempt organizations, Estate planning.

**FINK, ROBERT STEVEN,** lawyer, writer, educator; b. Bklyn., Dec. 7, 1943; s. Samuel Miles and Helen Leah (bogen) F.; m. Abby Deutsch, Mar. 20, 1980; children: Juliet Leah, Robin Rachel. Diploma, U. Vienna, 1962; BA, Bklyn. Coll., 1965; JD, NYU, 1968, LLM, 1973. Bar: N.Y. 1969, U.S. Dist. Ct. (so. and ea. dists.) N.Y. 1970, U.S. Tax Ct. 1970, U.S. Ct. Appeals (2d cir.) 1970, U.S. Supreme Ct. 1972, U.S. Dist. Ct. (we. dist.) N.Y. 1975, U.S. Ct. Claims 1984, U.S. Dist. Ct. (no. dist.) N.Y. 1985, U.S. Ct. Appeals (fed. cir.) 1990, U.S. Ct. Internat. Trade 1998. Assoc. Kostelanetz & Ritholz, N.Y.C., 1968-75, ptnr., 1975-87; ptnr. Kostelantez, Ritholz, Tigue and Fink, N.Y.C., 1987-94, Kostelanetz & Fink, N.Y.C., 1994—; lectr. in field; expert witness IRS; mem. adv. com. tax divsn. Dept. Justice; chmn. IRS/Bar Liaison Com. N.E. Region, 1996-99; adj. prof. law NYU. Author: Tax Fraud: Audits, Investigations, Prosecutions, 2 vols., 1980, 18th rev. edit., 1999; co-author: How to Defend Yourself Against the IRS, 1985, You Can Protect Yourself from the IRS, 1987, 2d rev. edit., 1988; dept. editor Jour. of Taxation; contbr. numerous articles in field to profl. jours. Fellow Am. Coll. Tax Counsel; mem. ABA (chmn. com. civil and criminal tax penalties 1983-85, chmn. task force for revision of tax penalties 1982), N.Y. State Bar Assn. (chmn. com. criminal and civil tax penalties 1982-85, 88-90, chmn. compliance and unreported income 1985-87, chmn. commodities and fin. futures 1987-88, chmn. com. compliance and penalties 1991-93, chmn. com. compliance practice and proceduce 1993—, mem. house of dels. 1995-97), Fed. Bar Assn., N.Y. County Lawyers Assn. (chmn. com. taxation 1988-92, 969-7, bd. dirs. 1989-95), Assn. of Bar of City of N.Y., Am. Arbitration Assn. (arbitrator). Federal civil litigation, Taxation, general, Criminal. Office: Kostelanetz & Fink 530 Fifth Ave New York NY 10036

**FINK, STEVEN D.,** lawyer; b. Akron, Ohio, Mar. 3, 1952; s. Raymond and Dona (Dryden) F. BA, U. Colo., 1975; JD, U. Denver, 1979. Bar: Colo. 1979, U.S. Dist. Ct. Colo. 1979. Atty. Denver, 1979—. Mem. Colo. Bar Assn., Interprofessional Com. Democrat. Episcopalian. Avocations: bicycling, skiing, camping. General practice, General civil litigation, Family and matrimonial. Home: 1632 Bellaire St Denver CO 80220-1047 Office: 316 E 7th Ave Denver CO 80203-3623

**FINK, THOMAS MICHAEL,** lawyer; b. Huntington, Ind., Oct. 6, 1947; s. Francis Anthony and Helen Elizabeth (Hartman) F.; m. Sheila Ann Jeffers, Aug. 11, 1973; children: Mark, Matthew, Megan. BBA, U. Notre Dame, 1970; JD, Northwestern U., 1973. Bar: Ind. 1973, U.S. Dist. Ct. (no. dist.) Ind. 1973. Assoc. Barrett & McNagny, Ft. Wayne, Ind., 1973-78, ptnr., 1979—; speaker Estate Planning Coun., Ft. Wayne, 1987—. Pres. Bishop Luers H.S. Bd. Edn., Ft. Wayne, 1992-93; bd. dirs. Ft. Wayne Cmty. Found. Bus. Edn. Fund, 1990—; bd. dirs., treas. Planned Giving Coun. N.E. Ind., 1995—. Mem. Ft. Wayne Country Club, Notre Dame Club of Ft. Wayne, Beta Gamma Sigma. Roman Catholic. Avocations: coaching basketball, golf, tennis, travel. Estate planning, Probate, Estate taxation. Home: 1302 Sunset Dr Fort Wayne IN 46807-2952 Office: Barrett & McNagny 215 E Berry St Fort Wayne IN 46802-2705

**FINKEL, BARRY I.,** lawyer; b. N.Y.C., Aug. 5, 1958; s. Albert and Roslyn F.; m. Susan Kelly Young, Sept. 11, 1961; children: Chase, Spencer, Brent. BS in Mgmt., Tulane U., 1980; JD, Nova U., 1983. Bar: Fla.; U.S. Dist. Ct. (so. dist.) Fla.; U.S. Ct. Appeals (11th cir.). Ptnr. Finkel & Finkel, PA, Pompano Bell, Fla., 1983-95; pres. Barry I. Finkel, PA, Ft. Lauderdale, 1995—. Mem. N. Broward Bar (pres. 1990-91), Broward County Bar (pres. family law sect. 1995-96, dir. 1997—). Avocations: skiing, diving, running. Family and matrimonial. Office: 2400 E Commercial Blvd Ste 800 Fort Lauderdale FL 33308-4033

**FINKEL, MIRIAM JO,** lawyer; b. Elizabeth, N.J., July 14, 1964; d. Paul and Estelle Finkel. BA, Emory U., 1986; JD, U. Dayton, 1993. Bar: N.J. 1993, N.Y. 1994. V.p., compliance mgr. Salomon Smith Barney, N.Y.C., 1994—. Mem. Assn. of the Bar of City of N.Y. (vol. atty.). Jewish. Avocations: jogging, aerobics, music, travel, cooking. Securities. Home: 200 W 60th St Apt 4D New York NY 10023-8503 Office: Salomon Smith Barney 250 West St Fl 10 New York NY 10013-2300

**FINKEL, SANFORD NORMAN,** lawyer; b. Troy, N.Y., Oct. 19, 1946; s. Max and Mildred (Fares) F.; m. Amy Lynn Gordon, Oct. 13, 1974 (div. July 1984); children: Marcy Jennifer, Melanie Gordon. BA, SUNY, Buffalo, 1968; JD, Union U., 1974. Bar: N.Y 1975, U.S. Dist. Ct. (no. dist.) N.Y. 1975. Tchr. sci. Enlarged City Sch. Dist. of Troy, N.Y., 1968-71; pvt. practice Troy, 1975—; counsel to dem. study group N.Y. State Assembly, Albany, 1977-78; instr. paralegal studies Jr. Coll. Albany divsn. Russell Sage Coll., 1977-81; dep. corp. counsel City of Troy, 1990-94. Mem. Rensselaer County Bar Assn. Avocations: reading, numismatics, philately, travel. General civil litigation, Family and matrimonial, Personal injury. Home: 19 Capitol Pl Rensselaer NY 12144-9658 Office: 68 2nd St Troy NY 12180-3932

**FINKELSTEIN, ALLEN LEWIS,** lawyer; b. N.Y.C., Mar. 19, 1943; s. David and Ella (Miller) F.; m. Judith Elaine Stutman, June 20, 1964 (div. Mar. 1980); children: Jill, Jennifer; m. Shelley Gail Barone, June 15, 1980; 1 child, Amanda. BS, NYU, 1964; JD, Bklyn. Law Sch., 1967; MBA, L.I. U., 1969. Bar: N.Y. 1968, U.S. Dist. Ct. (ea. and so. dists.) N.Y. 1973, U.S. Ct. Appeals (2d cir.) 1973, U.S. Supreme Ct. 1976, U.S. Tax Ct. 1979. Ptnr. Finkelstein, Bruckman, Wohl, Most & Rothman, N.Y.C., 1974-97; sr. ptnr. Pressman Finkelstein, N.Y.C., 1997-99; ptnr. Schwarzfeld Ganfer & Shore, N.Y.C., 1999—; asst. prof. L.I. U., N.Y.C., 1969-73, adj. assoc. prof., 1973-74; bd. dirs. Amotrophic Laterial Sclerosis Assn. Mem. ABA (bus. law and family law sect.), N.Y. State Bar Assn., Assn. of Bar of City of N.Y., Queens County Bar Assn. Jewish. Lodge: Masons. Real property, General corporate, Family and matrimonial. Home: 425 E 63rd St New York NY 10021-7804 Office: Schwarzfeld Ganfer & Shore 360 Lexington Ave New York NY 10017-6502

**FINKELSTEIN, DANIEL,** lawyer, educator; b. Phila., Oct. 24, 1927; s. Morris and Bertha (Lindenbaum) F.; m. Janet Finkelstein, Sept. 7, 1959; children: Beth Pellino, Robert. BS, NYU, 1949; JD, Bklyn. Law Sch., 1955. Bar: N.Y. 1956, U.S. Dist. Ct. N.Y. 1959, U.S. Ct. Appeals (2d cir.) 1966, U.S. Supreme Ct. 1963; lic. real estate broker, N.Y.; lic. real estate instr. N.Y.C. Bd. Edn. Real estate broker, 1949-52; with Pub. Housing and Site Mgmt., N.Y.C. Housing Authority, 1952-54; supr. relocation and site mgmt. for schs., roads Bd. of Estimate, Bur. of Real Estate, 1954-56; formulator, tchr. Real Estate for the Layman program Evander Childs Evening Adult Edn. Ctr., 1956-59; supr. relocation/site mgmt. Title 1 Urban Renewal Projects N.Y.C. Bd. of Estimate, Bur. of Real Estate, 1956-59; ptnr. Finkelstein Newman LLP, N.Y.C., 1959—; asst. counsel, asst. chief enforcement atty. N.Y. State Temporary Housing Rent Commn., 1956-59; adj. prof. real estate NYU Sch. of Continuing and Profl. Studies, 1991—; formulator, presenter Safe Housing for Children course Grad. Sch. Social Studies, Fordham U.; arbitrator small claims sect. Civil Ct., 1992—; lectr. and presenter in field. Author: Landlord and Tenant Practice in New York, 1997; contbr. articles to law jours. Past counsel, chmn. bd. govs. Civil Assn. of the Mahopacs; mem. Dem. County Com., N.Y. County, 1998—, Putnam County, 1971-73. Recipient Presdl. Cert. of Appreciation, Pres. Kennedy, 1961, Pres. Johnson, 1965, Pres. Nixon, 1970, Pres. Ford, 1975, 76, Svc. award Am. Arbitration Assn., 1964. Mem. ABA, Am. Judges Assn., Am. Judicature Assn., Assn. Small Claims Arbitrators of Civil Ct. of City of N.Y. (bd. dirs.), N.Y. State Bar Assn. (cert. Appreciation for Outstanding Contbn. to Continued Legal Edn. 1989), N.Y. State Trial Lawyers Assn., N.Y. County Lawyers' Assn. (bd. dirs., Cert. Appreciation for Outstanding Pro Bono Activities 1991, 92, 93, 96, 97, 98, Cert. Appreciation for Outstanding Contbn. to Continued Legal Edn. 1982, 83, 91, 93, 97-98), Bronx County Bar Assn., Masons, Mahopec-Carmel Dem. Club (past pres.). Landlord-tenant. Office: Finkelstein Newman LLP 185 Madison Ave New York NY 10016-4325

**FINKELSTEIN, JAY GARY,** lawyer; b. Riverdale, Md., July 22, 1953; s. Harry and Gertrude Finkelstein; m. Susan Carole Slatkin, Oct. 4, 1980; children: Jeffrey, Rachel, Andrew. AB, Princeton U., 1975; JD, Harvard U., 1978. Bar: D.C. 1978, U.S. Dist. Ct. Md. 1978. Law clk. to hon. Frank A. Kaufman U.S. Dist. Ct. Md., Balt., 1978-79; assoc. Bergson Borkland, Margolis & Adler, Washington, 1979-82; assoc. Piper & Marbury LLP, Washington, 1982-85, ptnr., 1986—. Contbg. editor: How to Keep Your Company Out of Court, 1984. Dir. Charles E. Smith Jewish Day Sch., Rockville, Md., 1995—. Avocation: travel. General corporate, Finance, Securities. Office: Piper & Marbury LLP 1200 19th St NW Fl 7 Washington DC 20036-2430

**FINKELSTEIN, JOSEPH SIMON,** lawyer; b. Vineland, N.J., Feb. 28, 1952; s. Absalom and Goldie (Cukier) F.; m. Sara M. Green, May 30, 1976; children: Adam, Julia, Seth. BA, Rutgers U., 1973; JD, U. Pa., 1976. Bar: Pa. 1976, N.J. 1976, U.S. Supreme Ct. 1982. Assoc. Wolf, Block, Schorr and Solis-Cohen, Phila., 1976-85, ptnr., 1985—. Mem. exec. bd. young leadership coun. bd. Fedn. Jewish Agys., Phila., 1986-88; mem. Nat. Young Leadership cabinet United Jewish Appeal, 1987-91; pres. Perelman Jewish Day Sch., 1996-99; bd. dirs. Temple Beth Hillel, Beth El, State of Israel Bonds, Phila.; mem. Wexner Heritage Found., 1991-95; exec. com., bd. dirs., chair funds. distbn. United Way of Southeastern Pa., 1997-99; trustee Jewish Fedn. of Greater Phila., 1996-99. Recipient New Life/New Leadership award State of Israel, 1989. Mem. ABA, Internat. Coun. Shopping Ctrs., Pa. Bar Assn., N.J. Bar Assn., Phila. Bar Assn. Real property, Contracts commercial. Home: 716 Oxford Rd Bala Cynwyd PA 19004-2112 Office: Wolf Block Schorr & Solis-Cohen 1650 Arch St Fl 22D Philadelphia PA 19103-2029

**FINKELSTEIN, MARCIA LYN,** lawyer; b. N.Y.C., Dec. 27, 1961; d. Bernard and Adele (Levine) F. BA magna cum laude, U. Pa., 1983; JD, Vanderbilt Law Sch., 1986. Admitted to N.Y. State Bar. Ptnr. Lamb & Barnosky LLP, Melville, N.Y. Mem. ABA, N.Y. Bar Assn., Suffolk County Bar Assn., Women's Bar Assn. Real property, Contracts commercial, General corporate.

**FINKELSTEIN, STUART M.,** lawyer; b. N.Y., 1960. BBA with distinction, U. Mich., 1982, JD cum laude, 1985. Bar: N.Y. 1986. Assoc. Skadden, Arps, Slate, Meagher & Flom LLP, N.Y.C., 1985-93, ptnr., 1993—. Corporate taxation, Taxation, general. Office: Skadden Arps Slate Meagher & Flom LLP 919 3rd Ave New York NY 10022-3902

**FINLEY, CHAMDLER R.,** lawyer; b. Miami Beach, Fla., Oct. 2, 1963. BA, Emory U., 1985, B of Music Performance/Polit. Sci., 1985, JD, 1988. Bar: Fla. 1988, U.S. Dist. Ct. (so. dist.) Fla. 1989. Ptnr. Stuber & Finley, West Palm Beach, Fla., 1988-92; talent agt. Image Models Talent Agy., Miami Beach, Fla., 1992—; ptnr. Finley & Assocs., West Palm Beach, 1992—; sports agt. Internat. Polo & Equestrian Sports Agy., West Palm Beach, 1994—; legal counsel, state bd. Fla. Motion Picture T.V. Assn., Palm Beach County, 1995—, Finley Music and Entertainment, 1998—. legal counsel Palm Beach County Work Force Devel. Bd., 1988—; bd.dirs. Fla. Philharmonic, West Palm Beach, 1997—. Entertainment, Immigration, naturalization, and customs, Public international. Office: The Immigration Office A Law Firm Ste 520 1645 Palm Beach Lakes Blvd West Palm Beach FL 33401-2217 also: 710 Washington Ave # 5 Miami Beach FL 33139-6248 also: 1515 N Federal Hwy Ste 300 Boca Raton FL 33432-1994

**FINLEY, KERRY A.,** lawyer; b. Iowa CIty, Iowa, June 15, 1965; d. Thomas A. and Diane Deckard F.; m. Roger A. Dahl, Dec. 14, 1996; children: Beckett, Deckard. BA, Dartmouth Coll., 1987; JD, U. Iowa, 1990. Bar: N.Y. 1991, Iowa 1993. Assoc. Willkie, Farr & Gallagher, N.Y.C., 1990-93; ptnr., shareholder Finley, Alt, Smith, Scharnberg, Craig, Hilmes & Gaffey, Des Moines, 1993—. Mem. ABA, Iowa Bar Assn., Polk County Bar Assn., C. Edwin Moore Am. Inn of Ct. (barrister). Democrat. General civil litigation, Appellate, Professional liability. Home: 712 50th St Des Moines IA 50312-1810 Office: Finley Alt Smith Scharnberg Craig Hilmes & Gaffey 604 Locust St Des Moines IA 50309-3705

**FINMAN, SHELDON ELIOT,** lawyer, mediator; b. Tampa, Fla., Aug. 25, 1943; s. Oscar E. and Shirley E. Finman; m. Bonnie I. Finman, Jan. 16, 1966 (div. Sept. 1976); 1 child, Seth; m. Lynn E. Finman, June 18, 1978; children: Jennilynn, Julia Lynn. BA, U. Fla., 1965, JD, 1971. Bar: Fla. 1971; cert. family law mediator and arbitrator. Assoc. Robinson, Ginsburg et al, Sarasota, Fla., 1971-73; assoc. Allen Knudsen et al, Ft. Myers, Fla., 1973-75, ptnr., 1975-77; pvt. practice Ft. Myers, 1977—; family law mediator Sheldon E. Finman Mediation Svcs., Ft. Myers, 1983—. Pro bono atty. Guardian Ad Litem Program, Ft. Myers, 1996—; exec. bd. Lee County YMCA, Ft. Myers, 1976-80, S.W. Fla. Sports Assn., Inc., Ft. Myers, 1976—. Capt. U.S. Army, 1966-68. Mem. Fla. Bar Assn. (bd. cert. marital and family law), Acad. of Family Mediators, Assn. of Family Law Profls. (exec. bd., pres. 1995-97), Calusa Inn of Ct. (master). Avocations: health and fitness, racquetball, hiking, reading. Family and matrimonial. Office: 2215 1st St Fort Myers FL 33901-2901

**FINMAN-PINCE, TERRY J.,** lawyer; b. San Francisco; d. Ted and Susan Finman. BS, U. Wis., 1977, JD, 1982. Bar: Wis. 1982, Ill. 1982. Fin. planner Waddell & Reed, Chgo., 1985-89; atty. Schiller, DuCanto & Fleck, Chgo., 1982-85, Axley Brynelson, Madison, 1990-94, Brennan, Steil, Basting & MacDougall, Janesville, Wis., 1994—. Mem. ABA, Wis. Bar Assn., Ill. Bar Assn., Dane County Bar Assn., Rock County Bar Assn. Family and matrimonial, General corporate, Health. Office: Brennan Steil Basting & MacDougall SC 1 E Milwaukee St Janesville WI 53545-3011

**FINN, ANNE-MARIE,** lawyer; b. Providence, R.I.; d. James and Elizabeth (McDole) Hultquist; m. S. Michael Finn, May 29, 1982. BA, Providence (R.I.) Coll., 1979; JD, Boston U., 1983. Bar: Mass. 1983, R.I. 1989, U.S. Dist. Ct. Mass. 1984, U.S. Dist. Ct. R.I. 1990. Attorney Lynch & Lynch, Easton, Mass., 1984—. Mem. Am. Bar Assn. Personal injury, Insurance, General civil litigation. Office: Lynch & Lynch 45 Bristol Dr South Easton MA 02375-1916

**FINN, JERRY MARTIN,** lawyer; b. Newark, Dec. 10, 1932; s. Harry and Miriam (Dichne) F.; m. Terri Lowen, June 13, 1954; children: David, Lawrence, Brian. BA, Emerson Coll., 1954; JD, Boston U., 1956. Bar: Mass. 1956, U.S. Dist. Ct. Mass. 1956, N.J. 1959, U.S. Dist. Ct. N.J. 1959, U.S. Supreme Ct. 1965. Assoc. Greenstone & Greenstone, Newark, 1959-62; ptnr. Goldberger & Finn, West Orange, N.J., 1962-92, Schneider, Goldberger, Cohen, Finn, Solomon, Leder et al, 1992—. Mem. ABA, Assn. Trial Lawyers Am. (pres. N.J. br., chmn. nat. legis. 1964). Democrat. Jewish. Avocations: profl. and coll. soccer referee, breeder and exhibitor of doberman pinschers. Workers' compensation, Personal injury, Labor. Home: 42 Bailey Hollow Rd Morristown NJ 07960-6203 Office: Schneider Goldberger Cohen Finn Solomon Leder & Montalb 1700 Galloping Hill Rd Kenilworth NJ 07033-1303

**FINN, JOHN STEPHEN,** lawyer; b. Chgo., Dec. 18, 1951; s. Matthew Thomas and Mary (Martin) F.; m. Sarah Sanderford, Nov. 27, 1982; children: Caitlin, Erin. BA with high honors, Lehigh U., 1973; JD, U. Denver, 1975. Bar: Colo. 1976, U.S. Dist. Ct. Colo. 1976, U.S. Ct. Appeals (10th cir.) 1986, U.S. Ct. Appeals (8th cir.) 1988. Assoc. Nelson and Harding, Denver, 1976-78, ptnr., 1979-88; ptnr. Stettner, Miller & Cohn, P.C., Denver, 1989—; instr. program for advanced profl. devel. U. Denver, 1984; lectr. various continuing legal edn. programs and profl. assn. lectures, Denver, 1985—. Mem. ABA, Colo. Bar Assn. (constrn. law forum), Colo. Contractors Assn., Denver Bar Assn., Constrn. Fin. Mgmt. Assn., Rocky Mountain Lehigh Alumni Assn. (sec.), Met. Irish Counsellors Soc. (founding mem.). Avocations: tennis, golf, piano, jazz. General civil litigation, Contracts commercial, Construction. Office: Stettner Miller & Cohn PC 1380 Lawrence St Ste 1000 Denver CO 80204

**FINNARN, THEODORE ORA,** lawyer; b. Greenville, Ohio, Aug. 20, 1949; s. Theodore Lincoln and Jeannie (Kelman) F.; B.Ed., Miami U., 1972; J.D. cum laude, U. Toledo, 1976; m. Holly C. Bankson, Sept. 15, 1973; children—Shawn April, Theodore O., Thomas A., Alexander H., Alison C. Bar: Ohio 1976, U.S. Dist. Ct. (so. dist.) Ohio 1978. Acting dir. Preble County Community Action Com., 1973, program developer, 1972-73; chief agrl. engr. Finnarn Farms, Greenville, Ohio, 1976—; individual practice law, Greenville, 1976—; sec.-treas. Finnarn Devel. Corp., 1977—. Bd. dirs. Darke County Center for Arts; active Greenville Friends of the Library, 1977—; sec.-treas. Greenville Boys Clubs, Inc., 1977—. Mem. Assn. Trial Lawyers Am., Ohio Acad. Trial Lawyers, Am., Ohio, Darke County bar assns., Ohio Farmers Union, Darke County Farmers Union (sec.-treas.), Scribes, Phi Alpha Delta. Democrat. Presbyterian. Editor articles in legal jours. Estate planning, Probate, Bankruptcy. Home: 3153 Us Route 127 Greenville OH 45331-9717 Office: 201 E 5th St Greenville OH 45331-1937

**FINNEGAN, HUGH PATRICK,** lawyer; b. N.Y.C., May 7, 1958; s. Philip Joseph and Nora Mary (Kilkenny) F.; m. Peggy Donlon, Dec. 27, 1981; children: Philip James, Mary Kate, Conor John, Daniel Joseph. AB, Fordham U., 1980, JD, 1983. Bar: N.Y. 1984. Assoc. Sage, Gray, Todd & Sims, N.Y.C., 1983-86, DeForest & Duer, N.Y.C., 1986-87, Siller, Wilk, Mencher & Simkin, N.Y.C., 1987-90; spl. counsel Siller, Wilk & Mencher, N.Y.C., 1991, ptnr., 1992—; bd. dirs. New Ground Inc. Bd. dirs. Rockville Ctr. Basketball League. Mem. N.Y. State Bar Assn., Com. on Comml. Leasing and Litig. (real property law sect., environ. law sect.), Com. on Comml. Fin., Rural Resettlement (USA) Ltd. (pres.), New Ground Inc. (sec.), Ireland-U.S. Coun. Avocations: sports, charity. Real property, Contracts commercial, Finance. Office: Siller Wilk LLP 747 3rd Ave New York NY 10017-2803

**FINNERTY, JOSEPH GREGORY, JR.,** lawyer; b. Balt., Jan. 25, 1937; s. Joseph Gregory and Sara Virginia (Porter) F.; m. Alice Ann Fannon, Sept. 14, 1958 (div. May 1989); children: Sara F. Kelly, Joseph G. III, Alice Ann Martin, Thomas P., Kathleen F. Curtis, Eileen F. McCoy; m. Deborah Barrett, Oct. 20, 1989; 1 child, Bridget P. BS in Physics, Loyola Coll., 1958; JD, U. Md., 1963. Bar: Md. 1963, D.C. 1981, N.Y. 1993. Law clk. Supreme Bench, Balt., 1960-63; assoc. Piper & Marbury, Balt., 1963-66; ptnr. Gallagher, Evelins & Finnerty, Balt., 1966-71; gen. counsel The Ryland Group, Columbia, Md., 1971-72; ptnr. Piper & Marbury, N.Y.C., 1972—. 2nd lt. U.S. Army, 1958-59. Fellow Am. Coll. Trial Lawyers, Am. Bar Found.; mem. ABA, N.Y. State Bar Assn., Md. State Bar Assn. Avocation: farming. General civil litigation, Professional liability, Product liability. Home: 300 E 56th St New York NY 10022-4136 Office: Piper & Marbury 1251 Avenue Of The Americas New York NY 10020-1104

**FINNERTY, JOSEPH GREGORY, III,** lawyer; b. Balt., Apr. 25, 1960; s. Joseph Gregory Jr. and Alice Ann (Fannon) F.; m. Amy Caroline Shull, Nov. 12, 1988 (div. 1999); children: Katherine Pagett, Alice Olivia. AB in English Lit., Hamilton Coll., 1982; JD, U. Md., Balt., 1987. Bar: N.Y. 1988. Assoc. Rogers & Wells, N.Y.C., 1988-94; prin. ptnr. McCarrick, Finnerty & Mayer, N.Y.C., 1994-96; ptnr. Piper & Marbury, L.L.P., N.Y.C., 1996—. Mem. ABA, Assn. Bar City N.Y. Federal civil litigation, Securities, Insurance. Office: Piper & Marbury LLP 1251 Avenue Of The Americas New York NY 10020-1104

**FINNEY, ERNEST ADOLPHUS, JR.,** state supreme court chief justice; b. Smithfield, Va., Mar. 23, 1931; s. Ernest A. Sr. and Collen (Godwin) F.; m. Frances Davenport, Aug. 20, 1955; children: Ernest A. III, Lynn Carol (Nikky) Finney, Jerry Leo. BA, Claflin Coll., 1952; JD, S.C. State U., 1954, LHD (hon.), 1996; HHD (hon.), Claflin Coll., 1977; LLD, U. S.C., 1991, The Citadel, 1995, Johnson C. Smith U., 1995, Morris Coll., 1996; LHD (hon.), Coll. of Charleston, 1995; LLD, Morris Coll., 1996. Bar: S.C. 1954, U.S. Dist. Ct. S.C. 1957, U.S. Ct. Appeals (4th cir.) 1964. Pvt. practice law Conway, S.C., 1954-60, Sumter, S.C., 1960-66; with Finney and Gray, Attys. at Law, Sumter, 1966-76; mem. S.C. Ho. of Reps., Columbia, 1973-76; judge S.C. Cir. Ct., Columbia, 1976-85; assoc. justice S.C. Supreme Ct., Columbia, 1985-94, chief justice, 1994—. Chmn. S.C. Legis. Black Caucus, Columbia, 1973-75; chmn. bd. dirs. Buena Vista Devel. Corp., Sumter, 1967—; mem. S.C. State Elections Commn., Columbia, 1968-72; trustee Claflin Coll., Orangeburg, S.C., 1986—, chmn. bd. trustees, 1987-95; sch. law minority adv. com. U. S.C., 1988—. Recipient Disting. Alumni of Yr. award Nat. Assn. Equal Opportunity Edn., 1986, Achievement award C. of C., Sumter, 1986, Presdl. Citation Morris Coll., Sumter, 1986, Wiley A. Branton award NBA, 1998, Afro Am. Achievement award Turner Broadcasting Sys., 1998; named 1987 Citizen of Yr. Charleston (S.C.) Med. Soc., 1987; inductee Nat. Black Coll. Alumni Hall of Fame, 1988. Mem. ABA, Am. Judges Assn., Am. Law Inst. (bd. dirs.), Conf. Chief Justices (bd. dirs.), Sumter County Bar, S.C. Bar, Assn. Trial Lawyers Am., Nat. Bar Assn. (appellate com.), S.C. Trial Lawyers Assn. (hon.), Masons, Shriners. Methodist. Avocations: reading, fishing, golf. Home: 24 Runnymede Blvd Sumter SC 29153-8742 Office: SC Supreme Ct PO Box 11330 Columbia SC 29211-1330 Office: PO Box 1309 Sumter SC 29151-1309

**FINNIGAN, JOHN JULIUS, JR.,** lawyer; b. Cin., May 22, 1955; s. John J. Sr. and Virginia (Habermehl) F.; m. Cynthia S. Mason, Dec. 20, 1981; children: Patrick K., Jennifer R., Timothy J. BA in Psychology, U. Cin., 1976; postgrad., Miami U., Oxford, Ohio, 1973-75; JD, U. Cin., 1979. Bar: Ohio 1979, U.S. Dist. Ct. (so. dist.) Ohio 1979, U.S. Ct. Appeals (6th cir.) 1985, U.S. Dist. Ct. (ea. dist.) Ky. 1986, Ky. 1997. Law clk. to judge U.S. Dist. Ct. (so. dist.) Ohio, Cin., 1979-81; assoc. Frost & Jacobs, Cin., 1981-83, McCaslin, Imbus & McCaslin, Cin., 1984-96; sr. counsel Cinergy Corp., 1996—; lectr. Chase Coll. Law No. Ky. U., Highland Heights, 1983-84; barrister Potter Stewart Am. Inn Ct., Cin., 1986-88. Contbr. articles to profl. publs. Mem. Ohio Bar Assn., Cin. Bar Assn., Ohio Assn. Civil Trial Attys., Def. Rsch. Inst. Republican. Roman Catholic. Avocations: sports, reading, travel. E-mail: jfinnigan@cinergy.com. Personal injury, Public utilities, Labor. Home: 128 Winding Brook Ln Terrace Park OH 45174-1035 Office: Cinergy Corp Legal Dept 2500 Atrium II PO Box 960 Cincinnati OH 45201-0960

**FINSTAD, SUZANNE ELAINE,** writer, producer, lawyer; b. Mpls., Sept. 14, 1955; d. Harold Martin and Elaine Lois (Strom) F. Student, U. Tex., 1973-74; BA in French, U. Houston, 1976, JD, 1980; postgrad., London Sch. Econs., 1980, U. Grenoble, France, 1979. Bar: Tex. 1981. Legal asst. Butler & Binion, Houston, 1976-78, law clk., 1978-81, assoc., 1982; spl. counsel Ad Litem in the Estate of Howard Hughes Jr., Houston, 1981; mng. ptnr. Finstad & Assoc., Houston, 1990—. Author: Heir Not Apparent, 1984 (Frank Wardlaw award 1984), Ulterior Motives, 1987, Child Bride, 1997, Sleeping With the Devil, 1991, co-prodr. (TV), 1997; collaborator Queen Noor biography; screenwriter, exec. prodr.: (feature film) Elvis' Child Bride, 1999. Named to Order of Barons, Bates Coll. Law, 1979-80. Mem. Order of Barons. General practice, Entertainment, Criminal. Office: Joel Gotler Renaissance Agy 9220 W Sunset Blvd West Hollywood CA 90069-3501

**FINUCANE, LEO GERARD,** lawyer; b. Dublin, Ireland, Mar. 28, 1957; came to U.S., 1960; s. Thomas and Mary T. (Morrissey) F.; m. Carol Andersen, Mar. 19, 1983; children: Sara, Adair, Connor. BA, Boston Coll., 1979; JD, Buffalo Law Sch., 1982. Assoc. Hirsch and Burke, P.C., Rochester, N.Y., 1983-85, Robert J. Burke, Rochester, N.Y., 1986-87; litigation assoc. Osborn, Reed, Vandevate & Burke, Rochester, N.Y., 1987-91; ptnr. Finucane & Hartzell, Pittsford, N.Y., 1991—; legal adivsor Cure Childhood Cancer Assn., Rochester, 1992—. Author (video) Why Do You Need a Lawyer If You Are Buying or Selling a House, 1993. Bd. dirs. Bishop Sheen Ecumenical Housing Found., Inc., Rochester, 1992-94. Mem. Am. Trial Lawyers Assn., N.Y. State Bar Assn., Monroe County Bar Assn. (personal injury com. 1983—). Democrat. Roman Catholic. Avocations: running, music. Personal injury, General civil litigation, Real property. Office: Finucane and Hartzell 6 N Main St Pittsford NY 14534-1310

**FIORE, KEVIN JOHN,** lawyer; b. Pitts., Oct. 11, 1956; s. Marshall Michael Fiore and Ruth Helen Bindas; m. Ann M. Fiore, Aug. 22, 1977 (div. Aug. 1993); children: Thomas M., Daniel K., Julie L. Bar: Pa., Fla., U.S. Dist. Ct. (we. dist.) Pa. Atty. Picadio, McCall, Miller & Norton, Pitts. Mem. Pa. Bar Assn., Fla. Bar Assn., Allegheny Bar Assn. Construction, Real property, Contracts commercial. Office: Picadio McCall Miller & Norton 600 Grant St Pittsburgh PA 15222

**FIORE, ROBERT J.,** lawyer; b. Miami, Fla., Apr. 22, 1961; s. Robert Victor and Angela (Vaccaro) F. BA, Biscayne Coll., 1983; JD, U. Fla., 1986. Bar: Fla. 1986, U.S. Dist. Ct. 1987. Assoc. Floyd Pearson et al, Miami, Fla., 1986-94, ptnr., 1994-96; ptnr. Russomanno Fiore & Borrello, Miami, Fla., 1996-98; sole practitioner Miami, 1998—; spkr. Acad. Fla. Trial Lawyers, Dade County Trial Lawyers Assn.; program chair The Stephen R. Covey Professionalism Program for Lawyers, Judges & Staff. Mem. steering com., com. of 100 Big Bros./Big Sisters of Greater Miami, 1994; co-organizer Halloween for Hurricane Kids, 1992. Mem. ATLA (chair new lawyers divsn. 1995-96, vice chair 1994-95, bd. govs. 1996—, Most Dedicated Pub. Servant award 1994, Nat. Pub. Svc. award 1994, Most Outstanding Young Lawyers Sect. Nat. award 1995), Acad. Fla. Trial Lawyers (chair young lawyers sect. 1994-95, chair elect 1993-94, sec. 1993, program chair ultimate trial notebook seminar 1994, bd. dirs. 1993—), Dade County Trial Lawyers Assn. (bd. dirs. 1992—, sec. 1993-94, treas. 1994-95, pres. elect 1995-96, pres. 1996-97, Exceptional Svc. and Leadership award 1996), Dade County Bar Assn. (bd. dirs. 1997—, chair meetings and luncheons com. 1993-94). Democrat. Roman Catholic. Avocations: fitness, nutrition, health. General civil litigation, Personal injury, Insurance. Office: 22 W Flagler St Miami FL 33130-1802

**FIORENTINO, CARMINE,** lawyer; b. Bklyn., Sept. 11, 1932; s. Pasquale and Lucy (Coppola) F. LL.B., Blackstone Sch. Law, Chgo., 1954, John Marshall Law Sch., Atlanta, 1957. Bar: Ga, D.C., U.S. Supreme Ct., U.S. Dist. Ct. D.C., U.S. Ct. Appeals (2d cir.), U.S. Dist. Ct. (no. dist.) Ga., U.S. Ct. Appeals (5th cir.), U.S. Ct. Claims. Mem. N.Y. State Workmen's Compensation Bd., N.Y. State Dept. Labor, 1950-53; ct. reporter, hearing stenographer N.Y. State Com. State Counsel and Attys., 1953; public relations sec. Indsl. Home for Blind, Bklyn., 1953-55; legal stenographer, researcher, law clk., Atlanta, 1955, 57-59; sec. import-export firm, Atlanta, 1956; sole practice, Atlanta, 1959-63, 73—; atty., advisor, trial atty. HUD, Atlanta and Washington, also legal counsel Peachtree Fed. Credit Union, 1963-74; acting dir. Elmira (N.Y.) Disaster Field Office, HUD, 1973; former candidate U.S. Adminstrv. Law Judge. Recipient State of Victory World Culture prize. Mem. Smithsonian Instn., pres., dir., gen. counsel The Hexagon Corp., Republican Nat. Com., Rep. Presdl. Task Force, Nat. Hist. Soc.; Inducted into Rep. Presdl. Legion Merit, 1993; Life Dynamics fellow; mem. Atlanta Hist. Soc., Atlanta Bot. Gardens, Am. Mus. Natural History, Mus. Heritage Soc. Mem. ABA, Fed. Bar Assn., Atlanta Bar Assn., Decatur-DeKalb Bar Assn., Am. Judicature Soc., Old War Horse Lawyers Club, Assn. Trial Lawyers Am., AAAS, Internat. Platform Soc., Nat. Audubon Soc. Presbyterian. Clubs: Toastmasters, Gaslight, Sierra. Writer non-fiction and poetry; composer songs and hymns. General corporate, General practice, Personal injury. Home and Office: 4717 Roswell Rd NE Apt R4 Atlanta GA 30342-2915

**FIORENTINO, THOMAS MARTIN,** transportation executive, lawyer; b. Washington, Aug. 4, 1959; s. Thomas Martin Sr. and Julia (Bray) F.; m. Mary Ann Hammer, June 12, 1983; children: Sara Elizabeth, Caroline McKay, Thomas Martin III. BA, U. Fla., 1980; JD, Mercer U., 1983. Bar: Fla. 1984. Claims rep. Seaboard System R.R., Evansville, Ind., 1983-84; claims atty. Seaboard System R.R., Jacksonville, Fla., 1984-86; dir. risk mgmt. CSX Corp., Jacksonville, 1986-87; asst. to pres. CSX Tech., Jacksonville, 1987-89; chief of staff Fed. R.R. Adminstrn., 1989-90; counselor to dep. sec. of transp. Office of the Sec., Dept. Transp., Washington, 1990-91; asst. v.p. pub. affairs CSX Transp., Jacksonville, 1991-94, v.p. govt. affairs, 1994-95, v.p. corp. comms. and pub. affairs, 1995—. Mem. bd. visitors The Bolles Sch., 1990-96; bd. dirs. St. Mark's Episcopal Day Sch., 1992-94, Theatreworks, 1992-95, Boys and Girls Clubs of N.E. Fla., 1992-95, Mus. Sci. and History, 1993-96, Jacksonville Urban League, 1993-95, I.M. Sultzbacher Ctr. for the Homeless, 1994-95, Gov. Coun. Sustainable Devel., 1996-97, Children's Home Soc. of Jacksonville, 1996-98, James Madison Inst., 1997—, Fla. Theatre, 1997-99, Ronald McDonald House, 1998—; bd. mem. Jacksonville Port Authority, 1999; chmn. Bapt. Health Sys. Found., 1992—; mem. Fourth Cir. Jud. Nominating Commn., 1988. Mem. Fla. Bar Assn., Fla. C. of C., Jacksonville C. of C., First Coast Mfrs. Assn., The Capital Hill Club, River Club, Marsh Landing Country Club, The Lodge and Bath Club (Ponte Vedra Beach), Fla. Coun. Econ. Edn., Phi Delta Phi, Fla. C. of C. (bd. trustees 1996—), Jacksonville C. of C. (bd. trustees 1995-96). Republican. Presbyterian. Avocation: golf, tennis. Home: 140 Indian Hammock Ln Ponte Vedra Beach FL 32082-2155

**FIORETTI, MICHAEL D.,** lawyer; b. Phila., Mar. 25, 1946; s. Michael R. and Mafalda (Fala) F. BS, St. Joseph's U., Phila., 1967; JD, Villanova U., 1972. Bar: Pa. 1972, N.J. 1981. Sr. ptnr. Law Offices of Michael D. Fioretti, Phila., 1972—; sole propietor Law Offices of Michael D. Fioretti, Cherry Hill, N.J., 1981—. Author: Divorce Rules and Practice Manual. With U.S. Army, 1968-70, Vietnam. Roman Catholic. Family and matrimonial. Office: Bourse Bldg Ste 790 111 S Independence Mall E Philadelphia PA 19106-2515 also: 1765 Springdale Rd Cherry Hill NJ 08003-2177

**FIORETTI, ROBERT WILLIAM,** lawyer; b. Chgo., Mar. 8, 1953; s. Edward E. and Helene (Krypcio) F. BA, U. Ill., 1975; JD, No. Ill. U., 1978. Bar: Ill. 1978, U.s. Dist. Ill. 1978, N.Y. 1981, U.S. Supreme Ct. 1981. Asst. corp. counsel City of Chgo., 1978-82, sr. supervising atty., 1982-86; litigation chief Shain, Firsel & Burney, Chgo., 1986-88; ptnr. Fioretti & Des Jardins Ltd., Chgo., 1989—. Contbr. articles to law rev. Bd. dirs. Historic Pullman Found., Chgo., 1992—, Chgo. Vol. Legal Svcs. Found., 1997—; mem. pres.' coun. U. Ill. Found., Champaign, 1993—; mem. bd. visitors No. Ill. U., DeKalb, 1992, mem. alumni coun. coll. law, 1991—, pres. alumni coun., 1994—; pres. Historic Pullman Found., 1995—; mem. Friends of S Hosp. Named Outstanding Young Alumni No. Ill. U., 1994. Mem. FBA (bd. dirs.), Chgo. Athletic Assn. (bd. dirs. 1993-97, v.p. 1995-97), No. Ill. U. Alumni Assn. (bd. dirs. 1997—). Office: Fioretti & Des Jardins Ltd 8 S Michigan Ave Chicago IL 60603-3357

**FIORITO, EDWARD GERALD,** lawyer; b. Irvington, N.J., Oct. 20, 1936; s. Edward and Emma (DePascale) F.; m. Charlotte H. Longo; children—Jeanne C., Kathryn M., Thomas E., Lynn M., Patricia A. BSEE, Rutgers U., 1958; JD, Georgetown U., 1963. Bar: U.S. Patent and Trademark Office 1960, Va. 1963, N.Y. 1964, Mich. 1970, Ohio 1975, Tex. 1984. Patent staff atty. IBM, Armonk, N.Y., 1958-69; v.p. patent and comml. relations Energy Conversion Devices, Troy, Mich., 1969-71; mng. patent prosecution Burroughs Corp., Detroit, 1971-75; gen. patent counsel B.F. Goodrich Corp., Akron, Ohio, 1975-83; dir. patents and licensing Dresser Industries, Inc., Dallas, 1983-93; alt. mem. Dept. Commerce Adv. Commn. on Patent Law Reform, 1991-92; spl. master, arbitrator, neutral evaluator, expert providing opinion testimony in intellectual property litigation, 1986—; U.S. del. to World Intellectual Property Orgn. Diplomatic Conf., 1991. Bd. dirs. Akron's House Extending Aid on Drugs, 1976. Mem. ABA (chmn. sci. and tech. sect. 1984-85, vice chair intellectual property law sect.), IEEE, Tex. Bar Assn. (chmn. intellectual property law sect. 1990-91), Internat. Assn. for Protection Indsl. Property (exec. bd. 1989—), Assn. Corp. Patent Counsel (exec. com. 1982-84), Tau Beta Pi. Roman Catholic. Avocations: music, running. Patent, Trademark and copyright, Intellectual property. *Those of you who have received gifts in great abundance at the beginning of your journey here, should remember to use them before your journey ends in the service of your creator who gave them to you.*

**FIRESTONE, CHARLES MORTON,** lawyer, educator; b. St. Louis, Oct. 16, 1944; s. Victor and Betty (Solomon) F.; m. Pattie Winston Porter, Apr. 19, 1975; children: Laurel, Asa. BA, Amherst Coll., 1966; JD, Duke U., 1969. Bar: D.C. 1969, U.S. Ct. Appeals (D.C. cir.) 1970, U.S. Ct. Appeals (5th cir.) 1972, U.S. Ct. Appeals (9th cir.) 1973, U.S. Ct. Appeals (2d cir.) 1975, U.S. Ct. Appeals (3d cir.) 1976, U.S. Ct. Appeals (8th cir.) 1977, U.S. Supreme Ct. 1977, Calif. 1983. Litigation atty. FCC, Washington, 1969-73; dir. litigation Citizens Comm. Ctr., Washington, 1973-77; adj. prof. law, dir. comm. law program UCLA, 1977-86; counsel Mitchell, Silberberg & Knupp, L.A., 1983-90; vis. lectr. UCLA Sch. Law, 1986-90; exec. dir. comm. and society program Aspen Inst., 1989—, exec. v.p. policy programs and internat. activities, 1998—; faculty adviser Fed. Comm. Law Jour., L.A., 1977-86; counsel statewide TV debates LVW Calif., 1978-90, counsel Calif. media Dukakis-Bentsen Com.; co-cmmn. adv. com. LWC Calif. Speak Out 1998 Election Project; pres. Bd. Telecom. Commrs., City of La., 1984-86; mem. nat. adv. bd. Privacy and Am.Bus., 1993—; mem. Commn. on Radio and Tv Policy, 1996. Author: (with Ellen Mickiewiz) Television and Elections, 1992, (with Donald R. Browne and Mickiewicz) Television/Radio News and Minorities, 1994, (with Robert Entman, Dee Reid and Mickiewicz) Television, Radio & Privatization, 1998, (with Craig L. Lamay and Mickiewicz) Television Autonomy & the State, 1999; editor: Television for the 21st Century: The Next Wave, 1993, (with Jorge Reina Schement) Toward An Information Bill of Rights and Responsibilities, 1995, (with Amy Korzick Garmer) Creating a Learning Society: Initiatives for Education and Technology, 1996, (with Anthony Corrado) Elections in Cyberspace: Toward A New Era in American Politics, 1996, (with Garmer) Digital Broadcasting and the Public Interest, 1998; contbr. articles to profl. jours., chpts. to books. Bd. dirs. Corp. for Disabilities and Telecom., L.A., 1980-82; bd. dirs. KCRW Found., Santa Monica, Calif., 1982-90, vice chmn., 1987-90; trustee Ctr. for Law in Pub. Interest, 1988-89; mem. adv. com. campaign Mondale for Pres., L.A., 1984. Recipient cert. of commendation Mayor of L.A., 1986, resolution commendation award City Coun. L.A., 1986; Luther Ely Smith scholar and Andrew Laurie scholar Amherst Coll., 1965-66. Mem. ABA (chmn. broadcast and spectrum use com., sect. sci. and tech. 1981-83, chmn. electronic campaigning com. 1984-86), Fed. Comm. Bar Assn., Soc. Satellite Profls. (sec. bd. dirs. So Calif. chpt. 1984-87), Coun. Fgn. Rels., Cosmos Club. Jewish. Office: 1 Dupont Cir NW Ste 700 Washington DC 20036-1133

**FIRESTONE, ERIC A.,** lawyer; b. Columbus, Ohio, May 29, 1953. BS, Ohio State U., 1975; JD, U. Akron, 1978. Bar: Ohio 1978. Pvt. practice Canton, Ohio. Den leader Boy Scouts Am., Canton, 1998. Mem. Ohio Bar Assn., Stark County Bar Assn., Stark County Acad. Trial Lawyers. Personal injury. Home: 327 Hillview Cir NW Canton OH 44709-1438 Office: 2800 Market Ave N Canton OH 44714-1781

**FIRESTONE, GARY,** lawyer; b. Montreal, Quebec, Can., May 27, 1952; s. E. Harvey Firestone and Dorothy F. McCauley; m. M. Jane Burns, June 8, 1976; 1 child, Elliot T. BA, McGill U., 1974, MA, 1979; JD, U. Ariz., 1987. Bar: Oreg. 1987, Wash. 1994, U.S. Dist. Ct. Oreg. 1991, U.S. Dist. Ct. (we. dist.) Wash. 1995, U.S. Ct. Appeals (9th and D.C. cirs.) 1990. Atty. Heller Ehrman White & McAuliffe, Portland, Oreg., 1989-93, O'Donnell, Ramis, Crew, Corrigan & Bachrach, Portland, 1993—. Editor Ariz. U. Law Rev., 1986-87. Avocations: coaching soccer and basketball, chess. Municipal (including bonds), Land use and zoning (including planning). Office: O'Donnell Ramis Crew Corrigan & Bachrach 1727 NW Hoyt St Portland OR 97209-2242

**FIRETOG, THEODORE WARREN,** lawyer; b. Bklyn., Sept. 18, 1950; s. Max E. and Ilene (Volk) F.; m. Kathleen Ann Neudecker, Feb. 21, 1980; children: Heather, Philip, Trevor. BS in Natural Resources, U. Mich., 1974, MS in Natural Resources, 1976; JD, SUNY, Buffalo, 1979. Bar: N.Y. 1980, U.S. Dist. Ct. (ea. dist.) N.Y. 1986, U.S. Dist. Ct. (so. dist.) N.Y. 1986. Dir. nature and conservation Nassau County coun. Boy Scouts Am., N.Y., 1967-73; teaching fellow dept. natural resources U. Mich., Ann Arbor, 1975-76; staff atty. Environ. Law Inst., Washington, 1979-80; atty., advisor EPA, Washington, 1980-85; sr. assoc. Rivkin, Radler, Dunne & Bayh, Uniondale, N.Y., 1985-87; environ. counsel Shea & Gould, N.Y.C., 1987-94; with Jaspen, Ginsberg, Schlesinger, Silverman & Hoffman, Garden City, N.Y., 1994-95; pvt. practice Farmingdale, N.Y., 1995—; lectr. various environ. seminars. Contbr. articles to profl. jours. Mem. com. Nassau County Dem. Com., 1987—. Sea Grant Law fellow U. Buffalo, 1977; recipient Cert. of award EPA, 1985. Mem. ABA (natural resources divsn.), Environ. Law Inst. (assoc.), N.Y. Bar Assn., Suffolk County Bar Assn. Jewish. Environmental. Office: 111 Thomas Powell Blvd Farmingdale NY 11735-2251

**FIRKSER, ROBERT M.,** lawyer; b. Phila., Mar. 16, 1953; s. Benjamin and Agnes F.; m. Judith J. Farrell, June 24, 1978; children: Stephen, Ryan, David, Carolyn. BA, St. Joseph's Coll., 1975; JD, U. Miami, 1978. Bar: Pa., U.S. Dist. Ct. (ea. dist.) Pa., U.S. Ct. Appeals (3rd cir.), U.S. Supreme Ct., Ct. Common Pleas. Assoc. Thomas R. Kimmel, Folcroft, Pa., 1978-80; ptnr. Kimmel & Firkser, Springfield, Pa., 1980-92, DelSordo, Firkser & Donze, Media, Pa., 1992—. Editor: Del. County Legal Jour., 1985. dir. Wallingford-Swarthmore (Pa.) Sch. Bd., 1991—, pres., 1996-97; founder, co-commr. daniel e. Murtaugh, Jr. Young Lawyers' Sect. Softball League; past bd. dirs. Child Guidance and Mental Health Clinic of Del. County, Inc., Del. County Immediate Unit. Mem. Pa. Bar Assn. (ho. of dels. 1983-86, real property and probate sect., civil litigation sect.), Pa. Trial Lawyers' Assn., Del. County Bar Assn. (chmn. citizens' conf. com. 1985, jud. retention com. 1990, arbitration com. 1993—, mem. civil trial practices com., civil rules com., civil justice adv. com., real estate practices com., civil legal edn. com.), Guy G. deFuria Am. in of Ct. (pres. 1993-94). Fax: 610-565-9853. General civil litigation, Personal injury, Probate. Office: DelSordo Firkser & Donze 333 W Baltimore Pike Media PA 19063-5625

**FIRST, HARRY,** law educator; b. 1945. BA, U. Pa., 1966, JD, 1969. Bar: Pa. 1969, N.Y. 1979. Law clk. to justice Supreme Ct. Pa., 1969-70; atty. U.S. Dept. Justice, Washington, 1970-72; asst. prof. U. Toledo Coll. Law, 1972-76; vis. assoc. prof. NYU Law Sch., N.Y.C., 1976-77, assoc. prof., 1977-79, prof., 1979—; counsel Loeb & Loeb, N.Y.C. and Los Angeles. Mem. editorial bd.: Pa. Law Rev. Mem. Pa. Law Rev., Order of Coif, Phi Beta Kappa. Office: NYU Law Sch 40 Washington Sq S New York NY 10012-1099

**FISCH, EDITH L.,** lawyer; b. N.Y.C., Mar. 3, 1923; d. Hyman and Clara L. Fisch; m. Steven Ludwig Werner, Dec. 14, 1963 (dec.). BA, Bklyn. Coll., 1945; LLB, Columbia U., 1948, LLM, 1949, J.Sc.D, 1950. Bar: N.Y. 1948, U.S. Supreme Ct. 1957. Grad. asst. Columbia U. Law Sch., N.Y.C., 1948, fellow in law, 1949-50; assoc. firm Conrad & Smith, N.Y.C., 1951-57; pvt. practice N.Y.C., 1957-62, 65—; asst. prof. law N.Y. Law Sch., 1963-65; counsel firm Brodsky, Lenett & Altman, N.Y.C., 1973-75; pres. Lond Publs., 1958—; ednl. dir. Found. for CLE, 1964—; editor N.Y.C. Charter and Adminstrv. Code, 1965-81; presenter lectures, seminars and courses for profl. groups. Author: The Cy Pres Doctrine in the U.S., 1950, (with others) State Laws on the Employment of Women, 1953, Lawyers in Industry, 1956, Fisch on New York Evidence, 1959, 2d edit., 1977, (with others) Charities and Charitable Foundations, 1974; contbr. numerous articles to legal publs. County committeewoman 7th Dist. N.Y. Dem. Party, 1949-52; bd. dirs., treas. nat. women's com. Brandeis U., 1964-68. Mem. AAUW, N.Y. Women's Bar Assn. (pres. 1970-71, bd. dirs. 1971-73, adv. coun. 1974—), Nat. Assn. Women Lawyers, Assn. Bar City N.Y. (chmn. libr. com. 1991-94), Bklyn. Coll. Lawyers Group (rec. sec. 1961-63, bd. govs. 1963-65), Am. Arbitration Assn. (nat. panelist), Acad. Polit. Sci., Alumni Assn. Columbia U., Bklyn. Coll. Alumni Assn. Probate, Appellate. Home: 250 W 94th St New York NY 10025-6954 Office: 33 Call Hollow Rd Pomona NY 10970-2702

**FISCH, JOSEPH,** lawyer; b. N.Y.C., Apr. 7, 1939; s. Israel Ben Zion and Esther Leah (Spielvogel) F.; m. Norma Potter, Aug. 7, 1960; children: Adam Jeffrey, Jennifer Anne, Rachel Lynne. BA, Tufts U., 1960; JD, NYU, 1963, LLM in Taxation, 1969. Bar: N.J. 1964, U.S. Dist. Ct. N.J. 1964, U.S. Tax Ct. 1966, U.S. Supreme Ct. 1969, U.S. Ct. Appeals (3d cir.) 1971. Law clk. to judge N.J. Superior Ct., Jersey City, 1963-64; assoc. Hannock, Wiseman, Stern and Besser, Newark, 1964-65, Blume and Kalb, Newark, 1965-66; sole practice Somerset, N.J., 1966-87, Kendall, N.J., 1987—; asst. prof. Rutgers U., New Brunswick, N.J., 1971-81; arbitrator Am. Arbitration Assn., 1969-97, N.J. Superior Ct., Somerville, 1985-89; atty. Franklin Twp. Rent Leveling Bd., Somerset, 1980-91; mem. malpractice panel N.J. Supreme Ct., 1980-84; atty. Franklin Twp. Bd. Adjustment, Somerset, 1991—. Contbr. articles to law jours. Pres. Franklin Twp. Jaycees, 1967-68, Franklin Housing and Neighborhood Devel. Corp., Somerset, 1975-78, Temple Beth El Men's Club, Somerset, 1971-72, trustee, 1970, 97—. Mem. ABA, N.J. Bar Assn., Somerset County Bar Assn., Rotary (Franklin Twp. bd. dirs. 1987-88). Republican. Jewish. Avocations: tennis, golf, skiing, sailing. State civil litigation, Real property, General practice. Office: 3084 State Route 27 Ste 7 Kendall Park NJ 08824-1657

**FISCHBACH, DONALD RICHARD,** lawyer; b. Ventura, Calif., Sept. 26, 1947; s. Richard A. and Ruth (Blevins) F.; m. Linda Say, Nov. 22, 1986; children: Amy, Sara, Andrea, Sean. BS in Bus. adminstrn. with honors, Calif. State Poly. Coll., 1969; JD, U. Calif., San Francisco, 1972. Bar: Calif. 1972. Assoc. Baker, Manock & Jensen, Fresno, Calif., 1972-75, ptnr., 1976—; adj. asst. prof. San Joaquin Coll. Law., Fresno, 1980-82; commr. jud. State Bar Calif., 1983; lectr. in field. Vol. atty. Fresno County Legal Services, 1973-79; chmn. fund raising United Way, 1979, Am. Cancer Soc., 1980-81, bd, dirs, 1980-82, Fresno Met. Mus., 1982, Rally for Ratcliffe, 1983, Valley Childrens Hosp., 1986; bd. dirs. Fresno County Legal Services, 1976-79. Mem. ABA (del. young lawyers div. 1977-79), Calif. Bar Assn. (treas. young lawyers assn. 1978, 1st v.p. 1979, bd. dirs. 1976-79, Pres.'s Pro Bono Svc. award 1988), Fresno County Bar Assn. (pres. 1985, v.p. 1984, bd. dirs. 1975, 78-81, 1983—), State Bar Calif. (bd. govs., pres. 1994-95), Assn. Trial Lawyers Am., Calif. Trial Lawyers Assn., Fresno County Young Lawyers Assn. (pres. 1975, bd. dirs. 1975-79), No. Calif. Def. Counsel Assn., So. Calif. Def. Coun. Assn., Fresno Trial Lawyers Assn. (bd. dirs., officer 1978-82), Def. Rsch. Inst. State civil litigation, Personal injury, Insurance. Home: 520 E Summerdale Ct Fresno CA 93720-0893 Office: Baker Manock & Jensen 5260 N Palm Ave Ste 421 Fresno CA 93704-2222

**FISCHBACH, ROBERT,** lawyer, musician; b. Havre de Grace, Md., Dec. 22, 1953; s. Joseph W. and Beatrice (Eckstein) F. AA, Sullivan County C.C., Loch Sheldrake, N.Y., 1973; BA, SUNY, Utica/Rome, 1977; Cert. in Basic Electronics, Cleve. Inst. Electronics, 1994; JD, Pace U., 1996. Bar: Conn. 1996, Mass. 1997, N.Y. 1997. Prin. office asst. New Rochelle (N.Y.) City Ct., 1986-92; ct. asst. Mt. Vernon (N.Y.) City Ct., 1992-94; sole practitioner Mt. Vernon, 1996—. Mem. IEEE, ABA, N.Y. State Bar Assn., Am. Mensa, Golden Key, Alpha Beta Kappa. Avocations: fitness activities, running, bodybuilding, electronics, music performance. General practice. Home: 539 New Rochelle Rd Mount Vernon NY 10552-1520

**FISCHEL, ROBERT OSCAR,** lawyer, judge; b. San Antonio, Nov. 5, 1961; s. Edgar and Olga Fischel; m. Janet Anne Belcher, July 18, 1987; children: Courtney Kilgore, Robert Oscar, Alexa Daniels. BS, U. Tex., San Antonio, 1985; JD, St. Mary's U., 1990. Assoc. McGuire & Levy, Irving, Tex., 1990-94; ptnr. Coleman & Fischel, Denton, Tex., 1994-95; owner Law Office of Robert O. Fischel, Ft. Worth, 1995—. Mcpl. judge City of Watauga, Tex., 1998—. Avocations: swimming, bowling, softball, skiing. Personal injury, General practice, Family and matrimonial. Home: 4904 Hot Springs Trl Fort Worth TX 76137-4162 Office: PO Box 162536 Fort Worth TX 76161-2536

**FISCHER, CAREY MICHAEL,** lawyer; b. Cleve., Apr. 4, 1950; s. Ernest and Kitty (Lehrer) F.; m. Ellen Schoenfeld, Aug. 17, 1975; children: Jordan, Douglas. BA, Tulane U., 1972; JD, U. Miami, 1975. Bar: Fla. 1975, U.S. Dist. Ct. (so. dist.) Fla. 1976, U.S. Ct. Appeals (5th and 11th cirs.) 1981, U.S. Supreme Ct. 1986. Assoc. Ferrero, Middlebrooks & Houston, Ft. Lauderdale, Fla., 1975-77; assoc. Ferrero, Middlebrooks & Strickland, Ft. Lauderdale, 1977-82, ptnr., 1983-85; ptnr. Ferrero, Middlebrooks, Strickland & Fischer, Ft. Lauderdale, 1985-90; pvt. practice Ft. Lauderdale, 1990—. Mem. long range planning and budget Jewish Fedn. of Ft. Lauderdale, 1989-90; bd. dirs. Jewish Community Ctr., 1987; pres. Temple Emanu El of Greater Ft. Lauderdale, 1987; exec. bd. Temple Bat Yam, East Ft. Lauderdale, 1996—; Broward trustee Performing Arts for Community Edn., 1992-94. Named Legal Exec. of Yr. Broward County Legal Secs. Assn., 1983. Mem. Fla. Bar (jud. selection and tenure com.), Broward County Bar Assn. (co-chmn. pub. rels. com. 1989-90, co-chmn. trial lawyers sect. 1990-92), Broward County Trial Lawyers Assn. (bd. dirs. 1985—, pres.-elect 1990, pres. 1991), U. Miami Sch. Law Alumnae Assn. (bd. dirs. 1990-94), Adopt-A-Family of Fla., Inc. (bd. dirs. Broward County chpt. 1990), Am. Bd. Trial Advocates. Avocations: music, coaching youth soccer, writing. General civil litigation, Personal injury, Product liability. Address: 750 SE 3rd Ave Ste 300 Fort Lauderdale FL 33316-1153

**FISCHER, DAVID CHARLES,** lawyer; b. Columbia, S.C., Oct. 10, 1952; s. Emeric and Bernice (Cooper) F.; m. Vicki Joyce Stoller, Nov. 9, 1985; children: Adam, Jeremy. BA, Vanderbilt U., 1975; JD, Coll. William & Mary, 1978. Bar: Mich. 1978, N.Y. 1980. Lawyer GM, Detroit, 1978-79, N.Y.C., 1979-80; assoc. Finley Kumble Wagner Heine Underberg & Casey, N.Y.C., 1980-82, Burns Summit Rovins & Feldesman, N.Y.C., 1982-86; ptnr. Summit Rovins & Feldesman, N.Y.C., 1986-90, Loeb & Loeb, LLP, N.Y.C., 1990—. General corporate, Mergers and acquisitions, Securities.

**FISCHER, DAVID JON,** lawyer; b. Danville, Ill., July 27, 1952; s. Oscar Ralph and Sarah Pauline (Pomerantz) F. BA, U. Miami, 1974, JD, 1977. Bar: Fla. 1977, Iowa 1978, (mid. dist.) Fla. 1993, U.S. Ct. Appeals (8th cir.) 1978, U.S. Ct. Appeals (D.C. cir.) 1979, U.S. Ct. Appeals (llth cir.) 1984, U.S. Tax Ct. 1987, Ga. 1989, U.S. Dist. Ct. (no. dist.) Ga. 1990, U.S. Supreme Ct. 1990, U.S. Dist. Ct. (mid. dist.) Fla., 1993. Atty. Iowa Dept. Social Svcs., Des Moines, 1978; assoc. Parrish & Del Gallo P.C., Des Moines, 1978-79, Donald M. Murtha & Assocs., Washington, 1979-80; assoc. editor Lawyers Coop. Pub. Co., Washington, 1980-82; pvt. practice law Washington, 1982-83, Des Moines, 1983-84, Atlanta, 1984-93; pvt. practice Tampa, Fla., 1993; asst. dist. legal counsel Fla. Dept. Health and Rehab. Svcs., Largo, 1993-95; pvt. practice law Atlanta, 1995—; part-time atty. Fla. Dept. of Children and Families, 1996—; prof. John Marshall Law Sch., Atlanta, 1986-88; instr. legal studies program dept. ins. and risk mgmt. Ga. State U., 1988-93, instr. aviation adminstrn. program Coll. Pub. and Urban Affairs, 1989-93; apptd. gen. counsel Techwerks, Inc., Mo., 1990-92; instr. Bridge the Gap seminar, Inst. CLE in Ga., 1993; presenter State of Fla. Dept. Health and Rehabilitative Svcs. Dist. Legal Counsel Workshop, 1994, 96, 97; spkr. Clearwater Bar Assn., 1993, 94, 95. Author: The Aeronaut's Law Handbook, 1986, (with others) Georgia Corporate Practice Forms for the Small Business Attorney, 1992; contbg. editor Balloon Life mag., 1986-96; editor: (suppl.) Georgia Corporate Forms, 1993—, Florida Criminal Sentencing, 1997—; editor: Georgia Corporate Forms, rev. edit., 1999. Vol. liaison Atlanta Com. for the Olympic Games, 1991-92. Mem. ABA (sect. com. 1980-82), Fed. Bar Assn., Iowa Bar Assn., State Bar Ga., Atlanta Bar Assn., Fla. Bar Assn., D.C. Bar Assn., Polk County Bar Assn., Pros. Attys.

Coun. Ga. (tech. editor Computer Crime Jour.), U. of Miami Alumni Assn., Balloon Fedn. Am. (chmn. com. 1986-91), Carolinas Balloon Assn., Ga. Balloon Assn. (chmn. com. 1985-90), Chesapeake Balloon Assn., Great Ea. Balloon Assn., Alpha Epsilon Pi (hon., faculty advisor). Jewish. Avocations: hot air balloon pilot, writing, competetive sports. General civil litigation, General corporate, Computer.

**FISCHER, ERIC ROBERT,** lawyer, educator; b. N.Y.C., Aug. 22, 1945; s. Maurice and Pauline (Pilcer) F.; m. Anita Ellen Cohen, July 31, 1977; children: Joshua, Lauren. BA, U. Pa., 1967; MBA, JD, Stanford U., 1971; LLM in Taxation, Boston U., 1982. Bar: N.Y. 1975, Mass. 1977. Assoc. Fried, Frank, Harris, Shriver & Jacobson, N.Y.C., 1971-76; v.p., asst. gen. counsel, asst. sec. First Nat. Bank of Boston, 1976-86; exec. v.p., gen. counsel, corp. sec. UST Corp., Boston, 1986—; lectr. on law Boston U. Law Sch., 1984—. Trustee Boston Lyric Opera, Inc., 1989—; bd. dirs. Boston Area Youth Soccer, 1989-90, Spirit of Mass. Boys Soccer Club, 1991-97. Mem. ABA (banking law com., vice chmn. cmty. banking subcom., banking law com.), Bank Capital Markets Assn. (chmn. banking law subcom. 1984-90), UN Assn. Boston (treas. 1978-91), New Eng. Legal Found. (bd. dirs. 1990-92). Jewish. Banking, General corporate, Securities. Home: 205 Waban Ave Waban MA 02468-2101 Office: UST Corp 40 Court St Boston MA 02108-2202 *The pursuit of an objective which you believe is meaningful and constructive (whether you are right or wrong) gives definition to your life and allows you to accept your own limitations.*

**FISCHER, MARK ALAN,** lawyer, law educator; b. Evanston, Ill., Sept. 28, 1950; s. Lee Earle and Zelda (Dlugo) F. BA magna cum laude, Emerson Coll., 1975; JD, Boston Coll., 1980. Bar: Mass. 1980, U.S. Dist. Ct. Mass. 1980, U.S. Ct. Appeals (1st cir.) Mass. 1985. Sole practice Cambridge, Mass., 1980-83; mem. Cohen & Burg, Boston, 1983-86; ptnr. Wolf, Greenfield & Sacks, Boston, 1986-96, Palmer & Dodge, Boston, 1996—; co-chair Pub. & Entertainment Group, Intellectual Property Group; lectr. copyright and trademark law Boston Coll. Law Sch., 1985-87, entertainment law New Eng. Sch. Law, Boston, 1983-93; assoc. prof. music law Berklee Coll. of Music, 1989-90, 94-95, lectr. intellectual property Northeastern Sch. Law, Boston, 1986; mem. adj. faculty advanced copyright law Suffolk U., 1999—. Contbr. articles to profl. jours.; columnist New Eng. Entertainment Digest, 1982-90; co-editor: Perle & Williams on Publishing Law, (3rd edit.). Mem. ABA, Mass. Bar Assn., Boston Patent Law Assn. (chmn. copyright law com., 1985-96), Copyright Soc. U.S.A. (trustee 1997—), Copyright Soc. New Eng. (co-founder). Entertainment, Trademark and copyright, Computer. Office: Palmer & Dodge 1 Beacon St Ste 22 Boston MA 02108-3190

**FISCHER, MARTIN ALAN,** lawyer, former state insurance government commissioner; b. N.Y.C., Jan. 8, 1937; s. Paul and Frances (Hollander) F.; m. Susan Glatzer, Nov. 20, 1960; children: Nancy, Elizabeth, Michael. BA, Clark U., 1958; LLB, Bklyn Law Sch., 1964; postgrad., NYU. Bar: N.Y. 1964, U.S. Dist. Ct. (so. and ea. dists.) N.Y. 1965, U.S. Ct. Appeals (2d cir.) 1965. Assoc. Otterbourg, Steindler, Houston & Rosen, N.Y.C., 1964-67; assoc. gen. counsel, asst. sec. Warner Communications, Inc., N.Y.C., 1967-77; past pres., dir. Kinney System, Inc., N.Y.C.; chmn. bd. commrs. State Ins. Fund, N.Y.C., 1977-95; with W. Ctr. Assocs., Long Island City, 1995—; bd. dirs. Winston Resources, Inc., The Berkshire Bank, N.Y.C. Mem. Assn. for Better N.Y. Mem. ABA, N.Y. Bar Assn., Bklyn. Bar Assn. Office: W Ctr Assocs 31-00 47 Ave Long Island City NY 11101

**FISCHLER, SHIRLEY BALTER,** retired lawyer; b. Oct. 9, 1926; d. David and Rose (Shapiro) Balter; m. Abraham Saul Fischler, Apr. 9, 1949; children: Bruce Evan, Michael Alan, Lori Faye. BA, Bklyn. Coll., 1947, MA, 1951; JD, Nova U., 1977. Bar: Fla. 1977, D.C. 1980, U.S. Ct. Appeals (D.C. cir.) 1980. Tchr. N.Y.C. Bd. Edn., 1948-50, Richmond (Calif.) Pub. Schs., 1965-66; assoc. Panza, Maurer, Maynard, Platow & Neel, Ft. Lauderdale, Fla., 1977-95; pro bono atty. Broward Lawyers Care, 1982-86. V.p. Gold Cir. Nova Southeastern U., 1995-97, treas., 1997—; bd. govs. Nova U. Law Ctr., 1982-99; mem. Commn. on Status of Women, Broward County, Fla., 1982-87, vice chair, 1983-84, Entourage, Broward Ctr. for Performing Arts. Mem. Fla. Bar Assn., D.C. Bar Assn., Broward County Bar Assn., Bklyn. Coll. Alumni Assn. (sec.-treas. So. Fla. chpt. 1997—), Close Encounters with Music (bd. dirs. 1998—). Family and matrimonial, Probate, Real property. Home: 5000 Taylor St Hollywood FL 33021-5839

**FISCHOFF, GARY CHARLES,** lawyer; b. Manhasset, N.Y., Nov. 23, 1954; s. Harold and Ann (Yablon) F.; m. Linda Lee Sacca, Nov. 22, 1985; 1 child, Lisa Frances. BA, U. Buffalo, 1976; JD, St. John's U., Jamaica, N.Y., 1983. Bar: N.J. 1983, U.S. Dist. Ct. N.J. 1983, N.Y. 1984, U.S. Dist. Ct. (so. and ea. dists.) N.Y. 1985, U.S. Dist. Ct. (no. and we. dist.) N.Y., U.S. Ct. Appeals (2d cir.) 1988. Asst. treas. IAP, Inc., Lyndhurst, N.J., 1980-82; assoc. Hannoch Weisman, Roseland, N.J., 1983-85; ptnr. Fischoff Gelberg & Director, Garden City, N.Y., 1985-96, Fischoff & Assocs., Garden City, 1996—; lectr. seminar Nat. Bus. Inst., Westbury, N.Y., 1990, 91, Practicing Law Inst., 1992, 93, N.Y. State Bar Assn., 1995. Rep. Greentree Homeowners Assn., Northport, N.Y., 1988-89; trustee Suffolk County Vanderbilt Mus., 1994—, corp. sec., 1995-97, treas. 1997-99, 1st v.p., 1999—. Mem. Am. Bankruptcy Bd. Cert. (cert. bus. bankruptcy and consumer bankruptcy), N.Y. State Bar Assn. (real property sect., seminar lectr. 1995, Practicing Law Inst., continuing legal edn. lectr. 1992, 93), Nassau County Bar Assn. (mem. bankruptcy com., jud. liaison 1988-89). Jewish. Avocation: bicycling. Bankruptcy, General civil litigation, Real property. Office: Fischoff & Assocs 600 Old Country Rd Garden City NY 11530-2001

**FISH, A. JOE,** federal judge; b. L.A., Nov. 12, 1942; s. John Allen and Mary Magdalene (Martin) F.; m. Betty Fish, Jan. 23, 1971; children: Abigail, Stephen. B.A., Yale U., 1965, LL.B., 1968. Bar: Tex. Assoc. firm McKenzie & Baer, Dallas, 1968-80; judge Tex. Dist. Ct., 1980-81; assoc. judge Tex. Appeals Ct., 1981-83; judge U.S. Dist Ct. (no. dist.) Tex., Dallas, 1983—. Mem. ABA, State Bar Assn. Tex., Dallas Bar Assn. Office: US District Court US Courthouse 1100 Commerce St Ste 15d6L Dallas TX 75242-1027

**FISH, EDMUND JEROME,** lawyer; b. Washington, Aug. 18, 1962; s. Paul Waring and Jacquelyn Ann (Shea) F.; m. Elizabeth Anne Peacock, Mar. 26, 1988; children: Alexandra Shea, Patrick Eamon, Owen Christopher. BS, Marquette U., 1984; JD, Wayne State U., 1987. Bar: D.C. 1987, U.S. Ct. Appeals (fed. cir.) 1987, Calif. 1994. Law clk. to Chief Judge Howard Markey U.S. Ct. Appeals (fed. cir.), Washington, 1987-89; assoc. Weil, Gotshal & Manges, Washington/Silicon Valley, 1989-95; sr. v.p. corp. devel., gen. counsel InterTrust Techs. Corp., Sunnyvale, Calif., 1995—; patent counsel Assn. Biotech. Cos., 1991—. Mem. Am. Intellectual Property Assn. Office: InterTrust Techs Corp 460 Oakmead Pkwy Sunnyvale CA 94086-4708

**FISH, PAUL MATHEW,** lawyer; b. N.Y.C., Sept. 27, 1947; s. Louis and Shirley (Aaronowitz) F.; m. Patrice Ellen Schooley, Nov. 27, 1976. BA, Drake U., 1969; JD, Harvey U., 1972. Bar: N.Mex. 1972, U.S. Dist. Ct. N.Mex. 1972, U.S. Ct. Appeals (10th cir.) 1972, U.S. Ct. Appeals 1999, U.S. Supreme Ct. 1993,. Assoc. Cotter, Atkinson, Campbell, Kelsey & Hanna, Albuquerque, 1972-74; ptnr. Modrall, Sperling, Roehl, Harris & Sisk, P.A., Albuquerque, 1974—; chmn. Chpt. 11 Local Rules Com., Albuquerque, 1981, bankruptcy law sect. N.Mex. State Bar, Albuquerque, 1983. Mem. ABA (com. on loan practices and lender liabiltiy), N.Mex. Bar Assn., Albuquerque Bar Assn., Am. Coll. Bankruptcy. Avocation: raising wine grapes. Federal civil litigation, Bankruptcy, Construction. Home: PO Box 7 50 Tunnel Springs Rd Placitas NM 87043-8831 Office: Modrall Law Firm PO Box 2168 Albuquerque NM 87103-2168

**FISHBERG, GERARD,** lawyer; b. Bronx, N.Y., May 23, 1946; s. Alfred and Sarah (Goldberg) F.; m. Eileen Taubman, Dec. 23, 1972; children: David, Dana. BA, Hofstra U., 1968; JD, St. John's U., Bklyn., 1971. Bar: N.Y. 1972, U.S. Dist. Ct. (ea. and so. dists.) N.Y. 1973, U.S. Ct. Appeals (2d cir.) 1975, U.S. Supreme Ct. 1976. Assoc. Cullen & Dykman, Garden City, N.Y., 1972-79, ptnr., 1980—. Assoc. editor St. John's U. Law Rev., 1970-71. Mem. legis. com. N.Y. Conf. of Mayors and Mcpl. Ofcls., Albany, 1976—; bd. dirs. Am. Heart Assn. L.I. region, 1995—, treas. 1997-98, exec. com., 1997—, vice chair, 1998—; bd. dirs. Heritage Affiliate 1999—. Capt. USAR, 1968-77. St. Thomas Moore scholar St. John's U. Sch. Law, 1969-71. Mem. N.Y. State Bar Assn. (mcpl. law and labor law sects., sec. 1985-87, 1st vice chmn. 1989-91, chmn. 1991-93, mem. ho. of dels. 1993-95, mem. exec. com. 1978—), Nassau County Bar Assn. (chmn. mcpl. law com. 1981-83, 85-87, chmn. labor law com. 1991-92, bd. dirs. 1999—), Garden City C. of C., Rotary (bd. dirs. 1988-94, treas. 1990-91, pres. 1992-93), Rotacare (bd. dirs. 1992—, pres. 1993-99). Jewish. Labor. Home: 1 Bucknell Dr Plainview NY 11803-1801 Office: Cullen & Dykman 100 Quentin Roosevelt Bvld Garden City NY 11530

**FISHBURNE, BENJAMIN P., III,** lawyer; b. South Bend, Ind., Nov. 14, 1943; s. Benjamin Postell and Peggy (Gahan) F.; m. Edith E., Aug. 5, 1983. BA cum laude, U. Notre Dame, 1965; JD, U. Va., 1968. Bar: Va. 1968, U.S. Ct. Mil. Appeals 1968, U.S. Army Ct. Mil. Rev. 1968, D.C. 1972. Capt. Judge Advocate gen's. corps. US Army, 1968-72; atty. Surrey & Morse, Washington, 1968; ptnr. Surrey & Morse, 1975; mng. ptnr. Surrey & Morse, Washington, 1981-84; ptnr. Jones, Day, Reavis & Pogue, 1986, ptnr.-in-charge Hong Kong office, 1986-91, ptnr., 1991-93; ptnr. Winston & Strawn, Washington, 1993—; gen. counsel. Nat. Coun. U.S.-China Trade, 1981-87, assoc. coun. 1987-89, chmn. legal com. 1994—; mem. nat. coun. U.S.-China Trade Investment Delegation to China, 1986; alt. mem. U. Assn's. Nat. Policy panel study U.S.-China Rels., 1979; spkr. in field. Contbr. articles to profl. jours. Co-chmn. Am. C. of C. Hong Kong legal com., 1990, mem. bd. govs., 1991; mem. bd. advisors Johns Hopkins Nanjing Ctr., 1986-97. Mem. ABA (mem. Mid. East law com. internat. sect. 1979-81), Am. Arbitration Assn. (mem. China-U.S. Conciliation Ctr. adv. com. 1993—, mem. spl. corp. com. East-West trade arbitration 1973-79), Chartered Inst. Arbitrators (assoc.), Order of Coif. Private international, Mergers and acquisitions, Alternative dispute resolution. Home: 5535 Nevada Ave NW Washington DC 20015-1768 Office: Winston & Strawn 1400 L St NW Ste 800 Washington DC 20005-3508

**FISHER, ANN BAILEN,** lawyer; b. N.Y.C., Oct. 15, 1951; d. Eliot and Elise (Thompson) Bailen; m. John C. Fisher, Apr. 6, 1980. BA magna cum laude, Radcliffe Coll., 1973; JD, Harvard U., 1976. Bar: N.Y. 1977. Assoc. Sullivan & Cromwell, N.Y.C., 1976-80, 82-84, ptnr., 1984—; assoc. Sullivan & Cromwell, Paris, 1980-82. Mem. ABA, N.Y. State Bar Assn. Episcopalian. Clubs: Cosmopolitan, Harvard (N.Y.C.). Securities, General corporate. Office: Sullivan & Cromwell 125 Broad St Fl 28 New York NY 10004-2489

**FISHER, ANN L.,** pro tem judge; b. Reading, Pa., Mar. 31, 1948; d. William E. and Florence (Makowiecki) Lewis; m. Donald E. Fisher, Dec. 27, 1965 (div. July 1986); children: Caroline E., Catherine E., John Michael (dec.); m. David H. DeBlasio, May 28, 1988; 1 child, Michael Joseph DeBlasio. BS in Liberal Studies, Oreg. State U., 1975; JD, Willamette U., 1983. Bar: Oreg. 1984, U.S. Dist. Ct. Oreg. 1984, U.S. Ct. Appeals (9th cir.) 1984, Wash. 1987, U.S. Dist. Ct. (we. dist.) Wash. 1987, U.S. Dist. Ct. (ea. dist.) Wash. 1996, U.S. Ct. Appeals (fed. cir.) 1996. Atty. Spears, Lubersky, Portland, Oreg., 1983-85, Greene & Markley, Portland, Oreg., 1985-89; asst. gen. counsel Portland GE, 1989-94; atty. Schwabe, Williamson & Wyatt, Portland, 1994-96; founder Ann L. Fisher Legal and Consulting Svcs., Portland, 1996—; pro tem judge Multnomah County Cir. Ct., Portland, 1995—; spkr. on energy ethics, 1993-95; spkr. on energy issues, 1997—. Contbg. author: (treatise) ABA Year in Review, 1994, 95, Fed. Energy Bar Yr. Rev., 1997. Mem. ABA, Wash. State Bar Assn., Oreg. State Bar Assn. (ins. and bar sponsored program com. 1985-87, sec. 1986-87, chmn. 1987-88, MCLE bd. 1991-94, sec. 1992-93, chmn. 1993-94, Disciplinary Bd. Region 5 1991-97, chair 1996, 97, ethics com. 1998—), Multnomah Bar Assn. (membership com. 1987-91, The Multnomah Lawyer publ. com. 1994-96, chair 1995-96, professionalism com. 1997—), Fed. Energy Bar Assn. (electric utility regulation com. 1996—), Fed. Bar Assn., Sect. of Natural Resources, Energy and Environ. Law (vice chair electric power com., vice chair gas pipelines com. 1994-96), Gus Solomon Inns of Ct. Avocations: reading, writing, family activities. E-mail: energlaw@aol.com. Fax: (503) 223-2305. Office: Ann L Fisher Legal and Cons Svcs 1425 SW 20th Ave Ste 202 Portland OR 97201-2485

**FISHER, BART STEVEN,** lawyer, educator, investment banker; b. St. Louis, Feb. 16, 1943; s. Irvin and Orene (Moskow) F.; m. Margaret Cottony, Mar. 1, 1969; 1 child, Ross Alan. AB, Washington U., 1963; MA, Johns Hopkins Sch. Advanced Internat. Studies, 1967, PhD, 1970; JD, Harvard U., 1972. Bar: D.C. 1972. Assoc. Patton, Boggs & Blow, Washington, 1972-78, ptnr., 1978-94; ptnr. Arent Fox Kintner Plotkin & Kahn, Washington, 1994-95; mng. ptnr. Capital House, LLC, 1995—; of counsel Porter, Wright, Morris & Arthur, 1996—; adj. prof. internat. rels. Georgetown U. Sch. Fgn. Svc., Washington, 1974-82, 97; profl. lectr. internat. rels. Johns Hopkins U. Sch. Advanced Internat. Studies, 1993—, George Mason U., 1991, 93; bd. dirs., CitX Corp., exec. br. Webcasting Corp. Author: The International Coffee Agreement, 1972, (with John H. Barton) International Trade and Investment: Regulating International Business, 1986; editor: Regulating the Multinational Enterprise, 1983, Barter in the World Economy, 1985. Pres. Aplastic Anemia Found. Am. Inc., Balt., 1983-92, pres. emeritus, 1993; bd. dirs. Nat. Marrow Donor Program, Marrow Found., Aplastic Anemia Found., The Inst. at Mars Hill Coll.; program com. Georgetown Leadership Sem., Washington, 1981—; pres. Capital Baseball, Inc.; ex-officio bd. govs. Internat. Practice sect. Bar Va.; participating mem. Pres. Coun. on Year 2000 Conversion. Recipient Dean's Cert. Appreciation Georgetown U. Sch. Fgn. Svc., Washington, 1984. Mem. ABA, Internat. Bar Assn., Am. Soc. Internat. Law (rapporteur, panel trade policy and insts. 1974-77), Va. State Bar (bd. govs. internat. law sect.), Wash. Fgn. Law Soc., Parkville Post Am. Legion, Great Falls Swim and Tennis Club Va. Jewish. Private international, Public international, Administrative and regulatory. Home: 9009 Potomac Forest Dr Great Falls VA 22066-4110 Office: Porter Wright Morris & Arthur 1667 K St NW Ste 1100 Washington DC 20006-1660

**FISHER, BENJAMIN CHATBURN,** lawyer; b. Coos Bay, Oreg., Feb. 6, 1923; s. Benjamin S. and Catherine Selina (Chatburn) F.; m. Jean L. Whiting, June 30, 1951; children: John, Richard, Robert. AB with honors, U. Ill., 1948; JD magna cum laude, Harvard U., 1951. Bar: D.C. 1951. Law clk. to Judge Learned Hand, 2d cir., N.Y.C., 1951-52; mem. firm Fisher, Wayland, Cooper, Leader & Zaragoza, Washington, 1952—; mem. edn. appeal bd. U.S. Office Edn., 1973-83; mem. Adminstrv. Con. U.S., 1970-76; U.S. del. Plenipotentiary Conf. Internat. Telecomm. Union, Nice, France, 1989, Geneva, 1992, Kyoto, Japan, 1994, Mpls., 1998; mem. U.S. del. World Radio Conf., Torremolinos, Spain, 1992, Geneva, 1995, 97; mem. nat. com. radio comm. sect., 1989—; chmn. bd. dirs. Ctr. Adminstrv. Justice, Washington, 1972-77; gen. counsel Commn. Population Growth and Am. Future, 1970-72. Bd. dirs., v.p. Boys and Girls Clubs of Greater Washington, 1990—; bd. govs. Sigma Chi Found., 1991—. Mem. ABA (chmn. sect. adminstrv. law 1968-69, mem. ho. of dels. 1970-72, 73-75), Fed. Commn. Bar Assn. (pres. 1967-68), D.C. Bar Assn., Am. Law Inst., Soc. Satellite Profls. (chmn. 1983-85, bd. dirs. 1986-93, gen. counsel 1993—), Rotary (bd. dirs. Washington Club 1980-85, pres. 1983-84), Phi Beta Kappa, Phi Kappa Phi. Administrative and regulatory. Home: 5118 Cammack Dr Bethesda MD 20816-2902 Office: 2001 Pennsylvania Ave NW Washington DC 20006-1850

**FISHER, D. MICHAEL,** state attorney general; b. Pitts., Nov. 7, 1944; s. C. Francis and Dolores (Darby) F.; m. Carol Hudak, Aug. 9, 1973; children: Michelle Lynn, Brett Michael. AB, Georgetown U., 1966; JD, Georgetown Law Ctr., 1969. Bar: Pa. 1970. Asst. dist. atty. Allegheny County, Pitts., 1970-74; rep. Pa. Ho. of Reps., Harrisburg, 1974-80; mem. Pa. Senate, Harrisburg, 1980-97; ptnr. Houston Harbaugh, Pitts., 1984-97; atty. gen. Commonwealth of Pa., Harrisburg, 1997—; chmn. House Subcom. on Crime and Corrections, 1979-80, Senate Environ. Resources & Energy, 1981-90, Senate Majority Policy Com., 1988-90, Senate Rep. Caucus, 1992—; vice-chmn. Senate Jud. Com., 1981-90; Majority Whip, 1990-96. Author numerous reports. Rep. candidate for lt. gov. Pa., 1986; mem. Pa. Gov.'s Energy Coun., 1981-86, Pa. Energy Devel. Authority, 1984-86, Environ. Quality Bd., 1980-90, Pa. Commn. on Crime and Delinquency, 1979—; del. Rep. Nat. Conv., 1988, 92. Named Man of Yr. Upper St. Clair Rep. Club, 1980, Outstanding Young Man Am., 1977-79, Man of Yr. Vector's Law & Govt., 1991. Mem. Pa. Bar Assn., Elks, Am. Legion, Bethel Park Chamber, Rotary. Roman Catholic. Avocations: golf, hockey, football. Office: Atty Gen 16 Strawberry Sq Harrisburg PA 17101-1800

**FISHER, DAVID HUGH,** lawyer; b. Topeka, Kans., Dec. 5, 1914; s. Hugh Thomas and Helen B. (Smith) F.; m. Ferne Forman (dec. Jan. 1980); m. Mary Frances Martin, Feb. 14, 1986; children: David Hugh Jr., Gwendolyn House. AB, Kans. U., 1936, LLB, 1938, JD, 1968. Bar: Kans. 1938, U.S. Dist. Ct. Kans. 1942, U.S. Ct. Appeals (10th cir.) 1952, U.S. Supreme Ct. 1979. Assoc. Fisher, Snattinger & Smith, Topeka, 1938-43; ptnr. Fisher, Patterson, Sayler & Smith, Topeka, 1946—; chmn. state membership Internat. Assn. Ins. Counsel, 1975-85, Kans. Def. Counsel. Mem. Gov.'s Health Care Providers Study Commn. Lt. USNR, 1943-46, Pacific. Mem. ABA, Kans. Bar Assn. (chmn. legal-med. com., profl. reations, cert. appreciation 1986), Am. Judicature Soc., Topeka Bar Assn. (pres. 1979-80, cert. appreciation 1980), Knife & Fork Club (pres. 1979-80), Topeka Country Club, Mason, Media Grotto, Sigma Phi Epsilon, Phi Delta Phi. Republican. Methodist. Avocations: boating, fishing, travel. Estate planning, Probate. Office: Fisher Patterson Sayler & Smith 3550 SW Fifth St PO Box 949 Topeka KS 66601-0949

**FISHER, DONALD ELTON, JR.,** lawyer, mediator; b. Dec. 18, 1923. BS in Mining Engring., U. Pitts., 1949, M in Letters, 1952; JD, So. Methodist U., 1958. Bar: Tex., 1957, U.S. Dist. Ct. (so. dist.) Tex., 1961, U.S. Ct. Appeals (5th, 11th cirs.), 1981; lic. comml. pilot. Head jr. varsity football coach U. Pitts., asst. athletic dir., asst. varsity football coach; trust officer Nat. Trust Co.; divisn. counsel Plymouth Oil Corp.; labor negotiator Gulf Oil Corp., petroleum engr.; pvt. practice, pvt. practice mediator/arbitrator; mediator Nat. Assn. Securities Dealers. Co-chmn. small bus. group Greater Houston Partnership, mem. regional mobility com., mem. banking and fin. com., mem. steering com. Capt. USMC, group legal officer; Naval aviator USN, squadron legal officer. Decorated Disting. Flying Cross, 5 Air Medals. Mem. Inst. TRANSNATIONAL Arbitration (supporting assoc., mem. adv. bd.), Assn. Atty.-Mediators, Inc., Soc. Profl. In Dispute Resolution, Am. Arbitration Assn., Naval Aviators Assn., Marine Corps Reserve Officers Assn., Tex. Bar Found., Tex. Assn. Mediators, Galleria C. of C., Toastmaster (past president). Alternative dispute resolution, General corporate, Contracts commercial. Office: 3033 Chimney Rock Rd Ste 600 Houston TX 77056-6248

**FISHER, ELIZABETH BLAIR,** paralegal; b. Little Rock, Dec. 3, 1960; d. Benjamen P. and Sharon (Blair) Aiken; m. Patrick P. Roe, Dec. 31, 1979 (div. 1994); children: Patrick E. Roe, Jennifer D. Roe; m. John Eric Fisher, Jan. 18, 1997. Dental asst. and sectarial grad., Va. Inst. Tech., 1984; paralegal grad., La. State U., 1997. Lic. notary pub. Exec. sec. Tift (Ga.) County Tax Assessor, 1992-93; adminstrv. asst. Hibernia, Shreveport, 1994-95, United Way, Shreveport, 1995; paralegal Gregory J. Barro, PLC, Shreveport, 1995-97; paralegal office of atty. gen. dept. justice State of La., Shreveport, 1997—. Mem. N.W. La. Paralegal Assn. Democrat. Lutheran. Avocations: computers, music, reading, collecting angels and stamps. E-mail fishere@ag.state.la.us. Office: Office of Atty GenC Dept of Justice 330 Marshall St Ste 777 Shreveport LA 71101-3016

**FISHER, ERIC A.,** lawyer; b. Columbus, Ind., Apr. 18, 1968; s. Larry S. Fisher and Linda M. Tarry; m. Lauren Maria Dyck, July 27, 1991; 1 child, John Stanton. BS, Tex. A&M U., 1990; JD, U. Tex., 1995. Bar: Tex. 1995. Petroleum acct. Exxon Co., USA, Midland, Tex., 1990-92; assoc. Fulbright & Jaworski LLP, San Antonio, 1995-97; corp. counsel Valero Energy Corp., San Antonio, 1997—. Bd. dirs. Human Soc. Bexar County, San Antonio, 1998. Mem. Order of the Coif. General corporate, Contracts commercial. Office: Valero Energy Corp One Valero Pl San Antonio TX 78205

**FISHER, GUY G.,** lawyer; b. Austin, Tex., June 12, 1965; s. Guy Cade and Syd Hodgin Fisher; m. Stacy Ann, July 1, 1995. BBA, Southwestern U., 1987; JD, U. Houston, 1990. Assoc. Bracewell & Patterson, Houston, 1990-93, Gary Riebschlager & Assoc., Houston, 1993-95, Williams Bailey, LLP, Houston, 1995—. Mem. Tex. Bar Assn., Tex. Trial Lawyers Assn., Houston Bar Assn. Democrat. Episcopalian. Avocations: golf, hunting, fishing, snow skiing, softball. Personal injury, Product liability, Toxic tort. Home: 2211 Villa Rose Dr Houston TX 77062-4721 Office: Williams Bailey 8441 Gulf Fwy Houston TX 77017-5000

**FISHER, JAMES A.,** lawyer; b. Pitts., May 25, 1942; s. David H.W. and Jean K. (Crum) F.; m. Judy Trosper Giefel, aug. 13, 1966; 1 child, Steven Frederick. BA, U. Mich., 1964; JD, Wayne State U., 1968. Bar: Mich. 1968. Pres., atty. Vandervoort, Christ & Fisher, PC, Battle Creek, Mich., 1968—. Past dir. Battle Creek Cmty. Concert Assn.; founder, dir. Silent Observer, Battle Creek, 1970—; past dir. Jr. Achievement, Battle Creek. Paul Harris fellow Rotary Club, 1989. Mem. ABA, Mich. Bar Assn., Calhoun County Bar Assn. (pres. 1971-73), Battle Creek Area C. of C. (chmn. bd. 1981-82), Rotary (pres., dir. 1987-88), Battle Creek Country Club. Avocations: golf, racquetball, biking, reading. E-mail: jfisher@vandervoortlaw.com. General practice, Estate planning, Family and matrimonial. Home: 53 Minges Rd W Battle Creek MI 49015-7903 Office: Vandervoort Christ et al 312 Old Kent Bank Bldg Battle Creek MI 49017-7016

**FISHER, LAWRENCE N.,** lawyer. BA, U. So. Calif., 1965, JD, 1968. Bar: Calif. 1969. Assoc. ptnr. Hahn & Han, 1969-74; tax counsel Fluor Corp., Irvine, Calif., 1974-76; sr. tax counsel Flour Corp., Irvine, Calif., 1976-78; v.p. adminstrn. Fluor Arabia Ltd., 1978-79; v.p., corp. law and asst. sec. Fluor Corp., Irvine, 1984—. Office: Fluor Corp 3333 Michelson Dr Irvine CA 92612-0625*

**FISHER, MARCIA ANN,** legal administrator; b. Geneva, Ill., Feb. 28, 1957; d. Robert L. and Beverly J. (Hopp) F. Student, Moser Bus. Sch., 1975; student, U. Ill., 1975-76; BS, U. Iowa, 1978, BS in Indsl. Relations, 1980. Paralegal Rate, Nolan, Moen & Parsons, Iowa City, 1980-82, legal adminstr., 1982—. Appointed Iowa State Foster Care Review Bd., 1987; del. Citizen Ambassador Program to People's Republic of China, 1988, to USSR, 1990. Rotary scholar, 1975. Mem. Nat. Assn. Legal Adminstrs., Iowa Assn. Legal Adminstrs., Iowa Assn. Legal Assts. (treas. 1984). Avocations: gourmet cooking, tennis, photography, swimming, reading. Office: 8307 Spanish Rd Cedar Rapids IA 52404-9036

**FISHER, MARTIN LOUIS,** lawyer; b. Adair, Iowa, May 3, 1952; s. William Louis and Laura Louise (Matousek) F.; m. Linda Sue Hemminger, Dec. 27, 1981. BA, Augustana Coll., Sioux Falls, S.D., 1974; JD, U. Calif., San Diego, 1979. Bar: Iowa 1979. Ptnr. Fisher, Fisher & Fisher, Adair, Iowa, 1979—; magistrate State of Iowa, 1979—. Personal injury, Family and matrimonial. Office: Fisher Fisher & Fisher PO Box 158 Adair IA 50002-0158

**FISHER, MICHAEL BRUCE,** lawyer; b. Montgomery, Ala., Jan. 2, 1945; s. Philip and Rita (Joss) F.; m. Noreen Rene Zidel, June 25, 1967; children: Anne Elizabeth, Alex Nicholas. BA, U. Minn., 1967; JD, U. Calif.-Berkeley, 1970. Bar: N.Y. 1971, Minn. 1972, U.S. Dist. Ct. Minn. 1972. Assoc. Rosenman, Colin, et al, N.Y.C., 1970-71, Mullin, Swirnoff & Weinberg, P.A., Mpls., 1972-73; staff atty. Fingerhut Corp., Mpls., 1974, assoc. gen. counsel, 1975-80, gen. counsel, 1980-83, v.p., gen. counsel, sec., 1983-90; of counsel Oppenheimer, Wolff & Donnelly, 1990; pres. Warshawsky & Co., Chgo., 1990-91; v.p., gen. counsel Allied Mktg. Group, Inc., Dallas, 1992-93; pvt. practice Mpls., 1993-97; gen. mgr. sys., dir. mktg. Sun Harvest, Ft. Myers, Fla., 1998—; bd. advisors Automated Comms. Inc., 1991-96. Mem. exec. com., dir. Big Sisters Mpls., Inc., 1976-83, Big Bros./Big Sisters Mpls., Inc. 1984-90; v.p., bd. dirs., pres. Herzl Camp Assn., Inc., Mpls., 1971—; vol. Minn. Pub. TV, St. Paul, gen. auction chmn., 1988-89; bd. dirs. Minn. Pub. Lobby, 1989-95. Mem. ABA, Minn. Bar Assn., Am. Corp. Counsel Assn. Minn., Minn. Retail Mchts. Assn. (trustee 1983-89, exec. com. 1988-89), Direct Mktg. Assn. (govt. affairs com. 1980-92), Flying Golf Club, Inc. (v.p. 1998—), 3d Class Mail Assn. (bd. dirs. 1979-89, sec. 1981-86, exec. vice chmn. 1987-88, chmn. bd. dirs. 1988-89), Parcel Shippers Assn. (v.p., bd. dirs. 1980-86, pres. 1987, chmn. bd. dirs. 1988-90). Jewish. Office: 14810 Metro Pkwy Fort Myers FL 33912-4307

**FISHER, MICHAEL ERNEST,** lawyer; b. Heidelberg, Germany, Jan. 23, 1960; came to U.S., 1960; s. Ernest Ebenezer and Linda Arlene (Berg) F.; m. Deborah Elizabeth Matthews, Aug. 9, 1986; children: Carter, Grace. BA, Spring Arbor Coll., 1981; JD, Harvard U., 1984. Bar: Mich. 1984. Assoc. Miller Canfield Paddock and Stone, Detroit, 1984-87; v.p. Hibbs and Fisher, P.C., Detroit, 1988-94; asst. city attorney City of Livonia, Mich., 1994—;

coop. attorney Fair Housing Ctr. Metropolitan Detroit, 1991-95. Author: Mike's Guide to the Motor City, 1993. Recipient Spirit of Detroit award Mayor Coleman A. Young, Detroit, 1992, Christian Man of Yr. award Trinity Faith United Meth. Ch., Detroit, 1992. Democrat. Avocations: studying, teaching the Bible. Office: City of Livonia 33000 Civic Center Dr Livonia MI 48154-3097

**FISHER, MICHAEL MATTHEW,** lawyer; b. Charleston, W.Va., Sept. 24, 1961; s. Matt C. and Betty Jane (Dawson) F.; m. Terri Sue Tawney, July 23, 1983; children: Samuel Dawson, Sarah Michael. BSBA, W.Va. U., 1983; JD cum laude, N.Y. Law Sch., 1986. Bar: W.Va. 1986, U.S. Dist. Ct. (so. dist.) W.Va. 1986, U.S. Ct. Appeals (4th cir.) 1990; diploma Nat. Inst. Trial Advocacy, Phila., 1989. Assoc. Jenkins, Fenstermaker, Krieger, Kayes & Farrell, Huntington, W.Va., 1986-90; asst. U.S. Atty. U.S. Atty.'s Office, Charleston, W.Va., 1990-93; ptnr. Offutt, Fisher & Nord, Charleston, 1993—. Mem. ABA, Def. Rsch. Inst., Def. Trial Counsel W.Va., Cabell County Bar Assn. Republican. Methodist. Avocations: all sports, music, travel. General civil litigation, Insurance, Professional liability. Home: 208 Shellar Dr Charleston WV 25314-1060 Office: Offutt Fisher & Nord PO Box 2833 Charleston WV 25330-2833

**FISHER, MORTON POE, JR.,** lawyer; b. Balt., Aug. 17, 1936; s. Morton Poe Sr. and Adelaide (Block) F.; m. Ann P. Fisher, Aug. 12, 1962; children: Stephen N., Marjorie P. AB, Dartmouth Coll., Hanover, N.H., 1958; LLB, Yale U., 1961. Bar: Md. 1961, D.C. 1961. Law clk. to presiding justice U.S. Dist. Ct. Md., Balt., 1961-62; assoc. Piper & Marbury, 1962-68; asst. gen. counsel Rouse Co., 1968-73; ptnr. Frank, Bernstein, Conaway & Goldman, Balt., 1973-92; mng. ptnr. Balt. office Ballard Spahr Andrews & Ingersoll, Balt., 1992—; faculty mem. U. Md. Law Sch., 1978-87. Mem. Balt. County Econ. Devel. Commn., 1988-90, Mayor's Adv. Commn., Balt. City, Risk Mgmt. Com. Balto City, 1999; bd. dirs. Balt. Downtown Partnership, 1998; dean U. of Shopping ctrs., 1998-99. Mem. ABA (vice chmn. real property divsn 1990-92, chmn. sect. real property, probate and trust law 1993-94), Am. Coll. Real Estate Lawyers (pres. 1988-89), Am. Coll. Constrn. Lawyers, Am. Law Inst., Anglo-Am. Real Property Inst., Internat. Coun. Shopping Ctrs. (co-chmn. law conf. 1995-97, co-dean U. Shopping Ctr. 1998—). Real property, Environmental. Office: Ballard Spahr Andrews & Ingersoll 300 E Lombard St Ste 1900 Baltimore MD 21202-6739

**FISHER, MYRON R.,** lawyer; b. Chgo., Aug. 13, 1935. B.A., Calif. State U., Long Beach, 1964; J.D., Southwestern U., 1969. Bar: Calif. 1970, U.S. Dist. Ct. (cen. dist.) Calif. 1970, U.S. Supreme Ct. 1974. Dep. pub. defender San Bernardino County (Calif.), 1970-71; assoc. Anderson, Adams & Bacon, Rosemead, Calif., 1971-74; sole practice, San Clemente, Calif., 1974—; judge pro tem South Orange County Mcpl. Ct., 1978—. Served with U.S. Army, 1955-57. Mem. State Bar Calif., South Orange County Bar Assn. (dir. 1978-83), Orange County Bar Assn., Los Angeles Trial Lawyers Assn., Orange County Trial Lawyers Assn., Calif. Trial Lawyers Assn., Assn. Trial Lawyers Am. Insurance, Personal injury, Probate. Office: Fisher Profl Bldg 630 S El Camino Real San Clemente CA 92672-4200

**FISHER, RANDALL EUGENE,** lawyer, educator; b. Wichita, Kans., June 3, 1949; s. George Allen Fisher and LaVonna (Brooks) Jackson; m. Arlena L. Eveleigh, May 20, 1970 (div. 1976); 1 child, Scott N.; m. Kathy R. Vetter, July 21, 1978 (div. 1985); m. Deena M. Bolton, Aug. 2, 1986; children: Anthony Michael, Nicholas Wade. BA, Wesleyan U., Salina, Kans., 1971; JD, Washburn U., 1976. Bar: Kans. 1976, U.S. Dist. Ct. Kans. 1976, U.S. Ct. Appeals (10th cir.) 1981, U.S. Supreme Ct. 1981. Law clk. to assoc. justice Kans. Supreme Ct., Topeka, 1976-78; assoc. Barta & Barta, Salina, 1978-80; staff atty. Legal Aid of Wichita, 1980-81; ptnr. McDonald, Tinker, Skaer, Quinn & Herrington PA, Wichita, 1981-87, also bd. dirs.; judge U.S. Dist. Ct. Kans., 1987-89; assoc. Michaud, Hutton & Bradshaw, Wichita, 1989—; adj. prof. Wichita State U., 1982—; trustee, vice chmn. Wichita Legal Aid, 1983—, now chmn.; faculty mem. Nat. Inst. Trial Advocacy, 1985—. Author: (with others) Settling Personal Injury Cases in Kansas, 1986, KBA KS Worker's Compensation Practice Manual, 1985-88, Kansas Uninsured and Underinsured Motorist Issues, 1987, (with others) Current Issues in Kansas Auto Insurance, 1988; ann. supplements. Advisor Law Explorer Post, Wichita, 1985-86. Recipient Dist. Advocacy Internat. Trial Lawyers Assn., 1975. Mem. ABA, Kans. Bar Assn., Wichita Bar Assn., Assn. Trial Lawyers Am., Kans. Trial Lawyers Assn. (bd. editors 1978-80), Internat. Trial Lawyers Assn., Am. Judge's Assn., Kans. Dist. Judge's Assn., Order of Barristers, Am. Judicature Soc. Methodist. Avocations: photography, writing, computers, conservation. Workers' compensation, Personal injury, Federal civil litigation. Address: Michaud Hutton Fisher Hutton PO Box 638 Wichita KS 67201-0638

**FISHER, RAYMOND CORLEY,** lawyer; b. Oakland, Calif., July 12, 1939; s. Raymond Henry and Mary Elizabeth (Corley) F.; m. Nancy Leigh Fairchilds, Jan. 22, 1961; children: Jeffrey Scott, Amy Fisher Ahlers. BA, U. Calif., Santa Barbara, 1961; LLB, Stanford U., 1966. Bar: Calif. 1967, U.S. Ct. Appeals (9th cir.) 1967, U.S. Dist. Ct. (no. and cen. dists.) Calif. 1967, U.S. Ct. Claims 1967, U.S. Supreme Ct. 1967. Law clk. to Hon. J. Skelly Wright U.S. Ct. Appeals (D.C. cir.), Washington, 1966-67; law clk. to Hon. William J. Brennan U.S. Supreme Ct., Washington, 1967-68; ptnr. Tuttle & Taylor, L.A., L.A., 1968-88; sr. litigation ptnr. Heller, Ehrman, White & McAuliffe, L.A., 1988-97; assoc. atty. gen. U.S. Dept. of Justice, Washington, 1997—; exec. com. 9th Cir. Jud. Conf., 1989-91; mem. Am. Law Inst., So. Calif. ADR Panel, CPR Inst. for Dispute Resolution. Pres. Stanford Law Rev., 1965-66. Spl. asst. to Gov. of Calif., Sacramento and L.A., 1978—; dir. Constl. Rights Found., L.A., 1978-97, pres., 1983-87; pres. L.A. City Bd. Civil Svc. Commn., 1987-88; dep. gen. counsel Christopher Commn., L.A., 1991-92; pres. L.A. City Bd. Police Commrs., 1996-97. With USAR, 1957. Fellow Am. Coll. Trial Lawyers, Am. Bar Found.; mem. ABA, Fed. Bar Assn. (exec. com. 1990-96), Calif. State Bar, L.A. County Bar Assn., Chancery Club, Order of Coif. Federal civil litigation, General civil litigation, State civil litigation. Office: U S Dept of Justice Office of Assoc Atty Gen 950 Pennsylvania Ave N W Washington DC 20530

**FISHER, ROBERT SCOTT,** lawyer; b. Detroit, July 16, 1960; s. Alvin Fisher and Beverly (Raider) Levin. BA, U. Mich., 1982; JD, U. Colo., 1985. Bar: Colo. 1985, U.S. Dist. Ct. Colo. 1985, Mich. 1987, U.S. Ct. Appeals (10th cir.) 1989, U.S. Supreme Ct. 1989, U.S. Ct. Appeals (D.C. cir.) 1999. Prin. Law Office of Robert S. Fisher, Colorado Springs, Colo., 1985—. Mem. Colo. Bar Assn., El Paso County Bar Assn., Phi Delta Phi. Avocations: scuba diving, ice hockey, skiing, racquetball. Family and matrimonial, Criminal, Personal injury. Home: 508 N Sheridan Ave Colorado Springs CO 80909-4518 Office: 502 W Weber Colorado Springs CO 80903

**FISHER, ROGER DUMMER,** lawyer, educator, negotiation expert; b. Winnetka, Ill., May 28, 1922; s. Walter Taylor and Katharine (Dummer) F.; m. Caroline Speer, Sept. 18, 1948; children: Elliott Speer, Peter Ryerson. AB, Harvard U., 1943, LLB magna cum laude, 1948; LHD, Conn. Coll., 1994; DHL, Bay Path Coll., 1999. Bar: Mass. 1948, D.C. 1950. Asst. to gen. counsel, then asst. to dep. U.S. spl. rep. ECA, Paris, 1948-49; with firm Covington & Burling, Washington, 1950-56; asst. to solicitor gen. U.S., 1956-58; lectr. law Harvard Law Sch., Cambridge, Mass., 1958-60, prof. law, 1960-76, Samuel Williston prof. law, 1976-92; prof. emeritus Harvard Law Sch., 1992—; dir. Harvard negotiation project Harvard Law Sch., Cambridge, Mass., 1980—; vis. prof. internat. rels. dept. London Sch. Econs., 1965-66; cons. pub. affairs editor WGBH-TV, Cambridge, 1969; tech. adivsor Found. for Internat. Conciliation, Geneva, 1984-87. Originator, 1st exec. editor: (pub. TV series) The Advocates, 1969-70, moderator, 1970-71; co-originator, exec. editor: (pub. TV series) Arabs and Israelis, 1975; author: International Conflict for Beginners, 1969, Dear Israelis, Dear Arabs, 1972, International Mediation: A Working Guide, 1978, International Crises and the Role of Law: Points of Choice, 1978, Improving Compliance with International Law, 1981; co-author: Getting to Yes: Negotiating Agreement Withoug Giving In, 1981, 2d edit., 1991, Getting Together: Building Relationships as We Negotiate, 1988, Beyond Machiavelli: Tools for Coping with Conflict, 1994, Getting Ready to Negotiate: The Getting to Yes Workbook, 1995, Coping with International Conflict: A Systematic Approach to Influence in International Negotiation, 1997, Getting It Done: How to Lead When You're Not in Charge, 1998; co-author, editor: International Conflict and Behavioral Science--The Craigville Papers, 1964; lectr., contbr. articles on internat. rels., negotiation, internat. law and TV. Bd. dirs. Coun. for Livable World; trustee Hudson Inst., 1962-95. 1st lt. USAF, 1942-46. Recipient Sziland Peace award 1981, Peace Advocate award Lawyers Alliance for Nuclear Arms Control, 1988, Spl. Contbn. award Ctr. Pub. Resources, 1993, Steve Brutschè award Assn. Atty. Mediators, 1994, D'Alemberte-Raven Outstanding Achievements and Contributions to Dispute Resolution award, 1995, Honorato Vasquez Nat. Order Insignia Great Cross Republic Ecuador, 1999, Lifetime Achievement award Am. Coll. Civil Trial Mediators, 1999, Pioneer award New Eng. Soc. Profls. Dispute Reolution, 1999, St. Thomas More award St. Mary's U. Law Sch., 1999; named Guggenheim fellow 1965-66. Fellow Am. Acad. Arts and Scis.; mem. ABA (sect. dispute resolution), Am. Soc. Internat. Law (exec. coun. 1961-64, 66-69, v.p. 1982-84), Mass. Bar Assn., Commn. to Study Orgn. of Peace, Coun. Fgn. Rels., Phi Beta Kappa. Clubs: Metropolitan (Washington); Harvard (N.Y.C.). Office: Harvard U Law Sch Harvard Negotiation Project Pound Hall # 524 Cambridge MA 02138 also: Conflict Mgmt Group 9 Waterhouse St Cambridge MA 02138-3607

**FISHER, SOLOMON,** lawyer; b. Phila., Apr. 4, 1935; s. Samuel and Ethel (Chernicoff) F.; m. Alice M. Rosenthal, June 30, 1963; children: Emil Eric, Suzanne Ruth. BS, Temple U., 1957, JD, 1960. Bar: Pa. 1960, D.C. 1964, U.S. Ct. Fed. Claims 1963, U.S. Tax Ct. 1964, U.S. Supreme Ct. 1964. Trial atty. tax divsn. U.S. Dept. Justice, Washington, 1960-64; assoc. Dilworth, Paxson, Kalish & Kauffman, Phila., 1964-68, ptnr., 1968-84; ptnr. Horvitz, Fisher, Miller & Sedlack, Phila., 1984-93, Reed Smith Shaw & McClay, Phila., 1993—; lectr. tax practice Grad. Tax Law program Temple U., Phila., 1976—; lectr. civil and criminal penalties, 1986-93; adj. assoc. prof. Grad. Sch. Mgmt., Widener U., 1993. Pres. Phila. chpt. Am. Jewish Com., 1970-72, chmn. 1972-74, nat. bd. govs. 1976-83, nat. bd. trustees, nat. exec. coun.; pres. Jewish Cmty. Rels. Coun. Phila., 1977-79, mem. exec. com. adv. coun. 1978-81; bd. trustees Fedn. Jewish Agys. 1976-84, 86-95; pres. Congregation Adath Jeshurun, 1983-86, Auerbach Ctrl. Agy. for Jewish Edn., 1996-98. Mem. ABA, Pa. Bar Assn., Fed. Bar Assn., Phila. Bar Assn., (former sec.-treas. tax sect.), Am. Coll. Tax Counsel, Locust Club, Tau Epsilon Rho (main chancellor Phila. chpt. 1983-84, chancellor 1985-86). Taxation, general, Personal income taxation, Corporate taxation. Office: Reed Smith Shaw & McClay 2500 One Liberty Pl 1650 Market St Fl 25 Philadelphia PA 19103-7394

**FISHER, STEWART WAYNE,** lawyer; b. Phila., Mar. 5, 1950; s. Frederick and Evalyn (Wilson) F.; m. Melinda Ruley, Oct. 1, 1994; 1 child, Henry J.; children from previous marriage: Kira H., Amos N., Emily E. BA magna cum laude, Duke U., 1972; MA, Yale U., 1974; JD with honors, U. N.C., 1982. Bar: N.C. 1982, U.S. Dist. Ct. (ea. and mid. dists.) N.C. 1982, U.S. Ct. Appeals (4th cir.) 1993, U.S. Dist. Ct. (west dist.) N.C. 1997, U.S. Supreme Ct. 1997; bd. cert. Civil Trial Advocate Nat. Bd. Trial Advocavy, 1998. Atty. Haywood, Denny & Miller, Durham, N.C., 1982-85; ptnr. Glenn, Mills & Fisher, PA, Durham, 1985—; faculty Nat. Inst. for Trial Advocacy, Durham, 1988—. Coop. atty. ACLU, Raleigh, 1992—. Mem. ABA, ATLA, Nat. Employment Lawyers, N.C. Acad. Trial Lawyers, N.C. Bar Assn., Phi Beta Kappa. Democrat. Avocations: fishing, gardening. Civil rights, Labor, Personal injury. Office: Glenn Mills & Fisher PA PO Box 3865 Durham NC 27702-3865

**FISHER, THOMAS EDWARD,** lawyer; b. Cleve., Sept. 29, 1926; s. McArthur and Ruth Morgan (Dissette) F.; m. Virginia Moore, June 29, 1957; children: Laura, Linda, John. BS in Naval Sci. and Tactics, Purdue U., 1947, BS in Engring. Law, 1950; JD, Ind. U., 1950. Bar: Ohio 1951, U.S. Dist. Ct. (no. dist.) Ohio 1954, U.S. Supreme Ct. 1955, U.S. Ct. Appeals (Fed. cir.) 1973. Asst. to v.p. Lempco Products, Bedford, Ohio, 1950-51; house counsel Willard Storage Battery Co., Cleve., 1951-54; assoc. Schram & Knowles, Cleve., 1954-55; ptnr. Watts, Hoffmann, Fisher & Heinke Co. (predecessor firms), Cleve., 1955—. Councilman Mentor (Ohio) on the Lake, 1955-57; chmn. ARC, Painesville, Ohio, 1956. Lt. USN, 1944. Mem. ABA (divsn. chair), Cleve. Bar Assn. (trustee), Am. Intellectual Property Law Assn. (chair com., bd. dirs.), Cleve. Intellectual Property Law Assn. (pres.), Cleve. World Trade Assn., Nat. Inventors Hall of Fame (pres.), Nat. Coun. Patent Law Assns. (chair). Avocations: woodworking, fishing, travel, gardening. Patent, Trademark and copyright, Federal civil litigation. Home: 617 Falls Rd Chagrin Falls OH 44022-2560 Office: Watts Hoffmann Fisher & Heinke Co 1100 Superior Ave Cleveland OH 44114-2518

**FISHER, THOMAS GEORGE,** lawyer, retired media company executive; b. Debrecen, Hungary, Oct. 2, 1931; came to U.S., 1951; s. Eugene J. and Viola Elizabeth (Rittersporn) F.; m. Rita Knisley, Feb. 14, 1960; children: Thomas G. Jr., Katherine F. Vaaler. B.S., Am. U., 1957, J.D., 1959; postgrad., Harvard U., 1956. Bar: D.C. 1959, Iowa 1977. Atty. FCC, Washington, 1959-61, 65-66; pvt. law practice Washington, 1961-65, 66-69; asst. counsel Meredith Corp., N.Y.C., 1969-72; assoc. gen. counsel Meredith Corp., Des Moines, 1972-76, gen. counsel, 1976-80, v.p. gen. counsel, 1980-94, corp. sec., 1988-94; comml. law liaison ABA Ctr. and East European Law Initiative, Krakow, Poland, 1994-95; atty. Legal Aid Soc. Polk County, 1996—. Contbr. articles to profl. jours. Bd. dirs. Des Moines Met. Opera Co., Indianola, 1980-94, pres., 1990-91; bd. dirs. Civic Music Assn., Des Moines, 1982-92, pres., 1987-88; chmn. legis. com. Greater Des Moines C. of C., 1976-77; bd. dirs. Legal Aid Soc. Polk County, 1986-93, pres., 1993; bd. dirs., sec. Friends of Benedictine Edn. in Hungary Found., 1999—. With U.S. Army, 1952-54. Mem. ABA, Iowa State Bar Assn. (chmn. corp. counsel subcom. 1979-82), Polk County Bar Assn., Embassy Club. Communications, Intellectual property. Office: Legal Aid Assn Polk County 1111 9th St Ste 380 Des Moines IA 50314-2527

**FISHER, THOMAS GEORGE, JR.,** lawyer; b. Washington, June 1, 1961; s. Thomas George and Rita (Knisley) F.; m. Susan Jane Koenig, June 23, 1990. BA, Iowa State U., 1983; JD with high distinction, U. Iowa, 1986. Bar: Iowa 1986, U.S. Dist. Ct. (so. dist.) Iowa 1987, U.S. Ct. Appeals (8th cir.) 1987, U.S. Dist. Ct. (no. dist.) Iowa 1993. Jud. clk. Iowa Supreme Ct., Davenport, 1986-87; assoc. Duncan, Jones, Riley & Finley, P.C., Des Moines, 1987-91; asst. atty. gen. State of Iowa, Justice Dept., Des Moines, 1991-95; counsel Am. Mut. Life Ins. Co., Des Moines, 1995-96; ptnr. Hogan & Fisher, PLC, Des Moines, 1997—. Precinct chair Polk County Dem. Party, Des Moines, 1988-90, 94-96, 98—; candidate Iowa Ho. of Reps. Dists. 73, 1994; mem. Twenty-First Century Forum, Des Moines Leadership Inst.; bd. dirs., vice chair Anawim Housing. Mem. Blackstone Inn of Ct. Democrat. Roman Catholic. Criminal, Constitutional, Immigration, naturalization, and customs. Office: Hogan & Fisher PLC 3101 Ingersoll Ave Des Moines IA 50312-3918

**FISHER, THOMAS GRAHAM,** judge; b. Flint, Mich., May 15, 1940; s. John Corwin and Bonnie Decou (Graham) F.; m. Barbara Alden Molnar, June 2, 1963; children: Anne Corwin, Thomas Molnar. AB, Earlham Coll., 1962; JD, Ind. U., 1965. Bar: Ind. 1965, U.S. Dist. Ct. (no. dist.) Ind. 1965, U.S. Sup. Ct. 1969. Assoc., John R. Nesbitt, Remington and Rensselaer, Ind., 1965-68; ptnr. Nesbitt & Fisher, Remington and Rensselaer, 1968-73, Nesbitt, Fisher & Daugherty, Rensselaer, Remington, 1973-78, Nesbitt, Fisher, Daugherty & Nesbitt, 1978-82, Nesbitt, Fisher & Nesbitt, 1982-83, Fisher & Nesbitt, 1983-86, judge, Ind. Tax Ct., Indpls., 1986—; pros. atty. Jasper County, Ind., 1967-86; lectr. bus. law St. Joseph's Coll., Rensselaer, 1970-86; trustee Earlham Coll., 1995—. Recipient Eugene Feller award Ind. Pros. Attys. Assn., Indpls., 1986. Mem. ABA, Ind. Bar Assn., Jasper County Bar Assn., Nat. Conf. State Tax Judges, Ind. Soc. Chgo., Columbia Club (bd. dirs. 1991-99, sec. 1992, treas. 1993, pres. 1997), Rotary of Indpls. (v.p. 1998-99, pres.-elect 1999-00), Jaycees (Outstanding Young Man of Am. award 1975). Republican. Mem. Soc. of Friends. Home: 4702 Mallard View Dr Indianapolis IN 46226-2187 Office: Ind Tax Ct 115 W Washington St Ste 1160S Indianapolis IN 46204-3418

**FISHER, WAYNE,** lawyer; b. Cameron, Tex.. BBA cum laude, Baylor U., 1959, LLB, 1961. Bar: Tex. 1961, U.S. Dist. Ct. (so. dist.) Tex. 1961, U.S. Ct. Appeals (5th and 11th cirs.) 1982, U.S. Supreme Ct. 1982, U.S. Dist. Ct. (ea. and we. dists.) 1983, U.S. Dist. Ct. (no. dist.) Tex. 1988, U.S. Dist. Ct. Ariz. 1990, U.S. Claims Ct. 1990; cert. personal injury trial law specialist Tex. Bd. Legal Specialization. Assoc. Fulbright & Jaworski, Houston, 1961-66; founder, ptnr. Fisher, Boyd, Brown, Boudreaux & Huguenard, LLP, Houston, 1966—; mem. dist. ct. adv. group U.S. Dist. Ct. (so. dist.) Tex. 1991; spkr. in field. Contbr. articles to profl. jours. Bd. dirs. South Tex. Coll. Law, 1986—, Houston Symphony Orch., 1987—; state membership chair The Supreme Ct. Hist. Soc., 1992. Recipient Disting. Alumni award Baylor U., 1991. Fellow Am. Coll. Trial Lawyers (complex litigation com., spl. problems in the adminstrn. justice com., regent 1993—), Internat. Acad. Trial Lawyers (bd. dirs. 1985—, admissions com. 1985-86, sec.-treas. 1989-91, dean of acad. 1991-92, pres. 1993), Am. Bd. Trial Advs., Inner Circle Advs., Tex. Bar Found. (sec., bd. dirs. 1973-74); mem. ATLA, ABA (tort and ins. practice sect., trial techniques com., aviation and space law com., professionalism com., chmn. task force on the size of civil juries in fed. cts.), Am. Judicature Soc., State Bar Tex. (dir. 1972-75, spl. com. to study disciplinary procedures 1973-74, chmn. adminstrn. justice com. 1975-76, personal injury trial law adv. commn. 1978-80, com. on fed. laws and regulations affecting the bar 1990—, pres.-elect 1980-81, pres. 1981-82), Tex. Trial Lawyers Assn. (pres. 1974-75), Houston Trial Lawyers Assn. (pres. 1971-72), Houston Bar Assn., Internat. Acad. Trial Lawyers (pres. 1993-95), Supreme Ct. Hist. Soc. Found. (state chair La., Miss. and Tex.). Personal injury. Office: Fisher Boyd Brown Boudreaux & Huguenard LLP Wells Fargo Plaza 70th Fl 1000 Louisiana St Houston TX 77002-5000

**FISHMAN, BARRY STUART,** lawyer; b. Chgo., June 14, 1943; s. Jacob M. and Anita (Epstein) F.; B.A., U. Wis., 1965; J.D., DePaul U., 1968; m. Meredith Porte, Mar. 27, 1976; 1 child, Janna. Admitted to Ill. bar, 1968, Fla., Calif. bars, 1969; partner firm Fishman & Fishman, Chgo., 1968-72; counsel real estate fin. dept. Baird & Warner, Inc., Chgo., 1972-75; gen. counsel Biscayne Fed. Savs. & Loan Assn., Miami, Fla., 1976-79; mem. firm, Ea. regional council Logs Nationwide Representation of Lenders; mem. firm Pallot, Poppell, Goodman & Slotnick, Miami, 1977-80; sr. ptnr. Shapiro & Fishman, North Miami Beach, Tampa, Jacksonville, Orlando and Deerfield Beach, Fla., 1984—; dir. investment div. Cushman and Wakefield of Fla., 1978—. Mem. big gifts com. Greater Miami Jewish Fedn., 1977—; dir. Neighborhood Housing Services, Dade County, Fla., 1977—. Mem. Fla., Calif., Ill., Chgo., Dade County bar assns., Nat. Assn. Realtors, Real Estate Securities and Syndication Inst., Mortgage Bankers Assn., Fla. Mortgage Bankers Assn., Comml. Law League. Jewish. Clubs: Turnberry Isle Yacht & Racquet, Turnberry C.C. Home: 1025 NE 203rd Ln Miami FL 33179-2529 Office: 20803 Biscayne Blvd Ste 300 Aventura FL 33180-1429

**FISHMAN, EDWARD MARC,** lawyer; b. Cambridge, Mass., Apr. 28, 1946; s. Eli Manuel and Marian (Goldberg) F.; m. Barbara Ellen Stern, June 29, 1969 (div. Sept. 1982); children: Andrea Stern, Bradley Craig; m. Tracy Ann Lind, July 13, 1985; children: Alison Leigh, Kendall Paige. AB, Bowdoin Coll., 1968; JD, Columbia U., 1972. Bar: Tex. 1972. Assoc. Akin, Gump, Strauss, Hauer & Feld, Dallas, 1972-73, Luce, Hennessy, Smith & Castle, Dallas, 1973-76; corp. counsel Centex Corp., Dallas, 1976-78; from assoc. to ptnr. Brice & Barron, Dallas, 1978-82; v.p. Baker, Smith & Mills, Dallas, 1982-86; pres. Fishman, Jones, Walsh & Gray, Dallas, 1986-99; v.p. Clements, Allen, Fishman, Woods & Walsh, P.C., Dallas, 1999—. Bd. dirs. Space Found. Roundtable, Dallas, 1985-87, Hope Cottage, Dallas, 1990-96; officer local pub. TV sta., Dallas, 1976—. Mem. ABA, Tex. Bar Assn., Dallas Bar Assn. Avocations: reading, bicycling, swimming, running, skiing. Real property, General corporate, Landlord-tenant. Home: 6103 Alpha Rd Dallas TX 75240-3532 Office: Clements Allen Fishman Woods & Walsh PC 15303 Dallas Pkwy Ste 750 Dallas TX 75001

**FISHMAN, FRED NORMAN,** lawyer; b. N.Y.C., Aug. 21, 1925; s. Arthur Elihu and Frederica (Greenspan) F.; m. Claire S. Powsner, Sept. 19, 1948; children: Robert J., Nancy K. S.B. summa cum laude, Harvard U., 1946, LL.B. magna cum laude, 1948; postgrad., Yale U., 1945-46. Bar: N.Y. State 1950, U.S. Supreme Ct. 1954. Law clk. to Chief Judge Calvert Magruder, U.S. Ct. Appeals, 1st Circuit, Boston, 1948-49; to Asso. Justice Felix Frankfurter, Supreme Ct. U.S., 1949-50; asso. firm Dewey, Ballantine, Bushby, Palmer & Wood (and predecessors), N.Y.C., 1950-57; with Freeport Minerals Co., N.Y.C., 1957-61; asst. sec. Freeport Minerals Co., 1958-59, asst. v.p., 1959-61; partner firm Kaye, Scholer, Fierman, Hays & Handler, N.Y.C., 1962-92, mem. exec. com., 1970-87, chmn. exec. com., 1981-83, spl. counsel, 1993-95. Editor, officer: Harvard Law Rev. chmn. Harvard Law Sch. Fund, 1977-79; mem. bd. overseers' com. to visit Harvard Law Sch., 1975-81, 88-94; chmn. com. Harvard Law Sch. Class of 1948 Twenty-Fifth Anniversary Gift, Forty-Fifth Anniversary Gift; mem. bd. overseers' com. to visit Grad. Sch. Edn., Harvard U., 1971-77, bd. overseers' Com. on Univ. Resources, 1991—, permanent class com. Harvard Coll. Class of 1946; bd. overseers' com. to visit Med. Sch. and Sch. of Dental Medicine Harvard U., 1997—; trustee Public Edn. Assn., N.Y.C., 1956-73, chmn. bd., 1970-71; dir. Harvard Alumni Assn., 1981-83; trustee Hosp. for Joint Diseases and Med. Center, N.Y.C., 1971-73; trustee Lawyers' Com. for Civil Rights under Law, 1979—, bd. dirs., 1983—, co-chmn., 1983-85; mem. steering com. Campaign for Harvard Law Sch., 1991-95. Fellow Am. Bar Found.; mem. ABA, Assn. of Bar of City of N.Y. (chmn. com. fed. legis. 1963-66, exec. com. 1966-70, chmn. com. corp. law 1980-82, treas. 1993-94), N.Y. State Bar Assn., Am. Law Inst. (adviser corp. governance project 1980-92), Legal Aid Soc. (bd. dirs. 1991-94), Harvard Law Sch. Assn. (pres. 1986-88, 1st v.p. 1984-86, coun. 1978-82, exec. com. 1980-82, 88-90, trustee N.Y.C. assn. 1966-69, v.p. N.Y.C. assn. 1974-75, pres. 1988-89), Phi Beta Kappa, Harvard Club N.Y.C. General corporate, Mergers and acquisitions, Finance. Home: 650 Park Ave Apt 3D New York NY 10021-6115 Office: Kaye Scholer Fierman Hays & Handler LLP 425 Park Ave New York NY 10022-3506

**FISHMAN, KENNETH JAY,** lawyer; b. Roslyn, N.Y., Nov. 12, 1950; s. George Norman and Eudys Sonia (Goldstein) F.; m. Barbara Dalton, June 1973 (div. 1977); m. Nancy Ellen Santos, Sept. 22, 1984; children: Jason Edward, Hayley Alissa. BS in Econs., U. Pa., 1972; JD cum laude, Suffolk U., 1976. Bar: Mass. 1977, U.S. Dist. Ct. Mass. 1977, U.S. Dist. Ct. (no. dist.) Calif. 1982, U.S. Ct. Appeals (4th and 3rd cirs.) 1980, (6th cir.) 1982, (1st cir.) 1983, (5th and 10th cirs.) 1985, (8th cir.) 1985, U.S. Tax Ct. 1981, U.S. Ct. Mil. Appeals 1981, U.S. Dist. Ct. (ea. dist.) Wis. 1991, U.S. Ct. Appeals (2d cir.) 1993, U.S. Fed. Claims Ct. 1997, U.S. Supreme Ct. 1980. Assoc. Law Offices F. Lee Bailey, Boston, 1976-84; ptnr. Law Offices Bailey & Fishman, Boston, 1984-91, Law Offices Bailey, Fishman & Leonard, Boston, 1991-97, Law Offices Fishman, Ankner & Horstmann, Boston, 1997—; former instr. Met. Coll., Boston U. Note editor Suffolk U. Law Rev., 1975-76; author: (with F. Lee Bailey) Bailey/Rothblatt Criminal Law Series, 1986—. Mem. ABA, ATLA, NACDL, Mass. Assn. Criminal Def. Lawyers (treas.), Mass. Bar Assn. Democrat. Jewish. Criminal, General civil litigation, Personal injury. Office: Law Offices Fishman Ankner & Horstmann 66 Long Wharf Boston MA 02110-3605

**FISHMAN, LEWIS WARREN,** lawyer, educator; b. Bklyn., Dec. 19, 1951. BA in Polit. Sci., Syracuse U., 1972; MPA, Maxwell-Syracuse U., 1973; JD, U. Miami, 1976. Bar: Fla. 1976, U.S. Dist. Ct. (so. dist.) Fla. 1977, U.S. Dist. Ct. D.C. 1978, U.S. Ct. Appeals (5th and 11th cirs.) 1981. Assoc. Simons & Fishman P.A. (and predecessor firm), Miami, 1976-80; ptnr., 1980-81; assoc. Wood, Lucksinger & Epstein, Miami, 1982—; adj. prof. law Fla. Internat. U., 1981, 83, 84, 91; mem. bd. legal specialization and edn. Fla. Bar, 1999—. Mem. Fla. Acad. Healthcare Attys. (bd. dirs., sec. 1986-88, pres. 1990-92), Nat. Health Lawyers Assn. (lectr. 1983, 88-89), Fla. Hosp. Assn. (lectr. 1983, 88-89), Fla. Hosp. Assn. (lectr.), Fla.Med. Record Assn. (lectr. 1982, 83, 84), Am. Acad. Hosp. Attys. (lectr. 1989, 90, 91), Nat. Health Lawyers Assn., Cath. Health Assn., Fla. Bar Assn. (mem. exec. coun. health law sect. 1988-97, chmn. health law sect. 1988-97, chmn. health law sect. 1995-96, cert. health law atty., mem. health law cert. com. 1994-99, vice chmn. 1995-96, chmn. 1996-98, bd. legal specialization and edn. 1999—). Jewish. Health, General corporate, Insurance. Home: 14140 SW 104th Ave Miami FL 33176-7064 Office: 9130 S Dadeland Blvd Miami FL 33156-7818

**FISHMAN, RICHARD GLENN,** lawyer, accountant; b. Orange, N.J., June 2, 1952; s. Irving and Eleanor (Tanenbaum) F.; m. Jean Goldhammer, Aug. 11, 1974; children: Neil Samuel, Peter Lawrence, Ellen Melissa. BA in Econs. with highest honors and highest distinction, Rutgers U., 1974; JD, Yale U., 1977; LLM in Taxation, NYU, 1980. Bar: N.Y. 1978, N.J. 1978, U.S. Dist. Ct. N.J. 1978, U.S. Ct. Claims 1978, U.S. Tax Ct. 1978, U.S. Dist. Ct. (so. dist.) N.Y. 1979, U.S. Ct. Appeals (3d cir.) 1994. Assoc. Stroock & Stroock & Lavan, N.Y.C., 1977-80, Roberts & Holland, N.Y.C., 1980-85; tax mgr. Spicer & Oppenheim (formerly Oppenheim, Appel, Dixon & Co.), N.Y.C., 1985-87, ptnr., 1987-88; sr. tax. counsel AlliedSignal Inc., Morristown, N.J., 1988-94; dir. internat. taxes and sr. tax counsel AlliedSignal Inc., Morristown, 1994-96, sector tax dir., engineered materials sector, 1996-97, assoc. gen. tax counsel, 1997—. Contbr. articles to profl. jours. Mem. ABA, AICPA, N.Y. State Bar Assn., N.J. State Bar Assn. Corporate taxation, Taxation, general, Public international. Home: 6 Tilden Ct Livingston NJ 07039-2419 Office: Allied Signal PO Box 1057 Morristown NJ 07962-1057

**FISK, MERLIN EDGAR,** judge; b. Great Falls, Mont., Mar. 18, 1921; s. Edgar Anson and Eleanor Sybil (Worden) F.; m. Margery Anne Hall, May 27, 1942; children: Mary Dana, Catherine, Anne, Elizabeth. BSChemE, Mont. State U., 1942. Tech. adminstr. Lago Oil & Transport Co., Ltd. subsidiary Exxon Corp., Aruba, Aruba Netherlands Antilles, 1942-62; v.p., gen. mgr. Antilles Chem. Co. subsidiary Exxon Corp., 1962-64; dir. mfg. Esso Pappas Indsl. Co., Athens, Greece, 1964-67; gen. mgr. Essochem, S.A. subsidiary Exxon Corp., Madrid, 1967-69; mgr. ops. and planning Essochem, S.A. subsidiary Exxon Corp., Brussels, 1969-71, ret., 1971; judge probate div. State of Conn., Newtown, 1979-91; ret., 1991; pres. judge Conn. Probate Assembly, 1990-91. Mem. Commn. on Aging, Newtown, 1987-99; trustee Cyrenius H. Booth Libr., Newtown, 1975-95, 97—; bd. dirs. Newtown Meals on Wheels, Inc., 1974-93, Recording for the Blind, Inc. Conn. chpt., New Haven, 1975-92, Waterbury (Conn.) Ballet Co., 1987-97. Mem. Am. Arbitration Assn. (comml. panel 1991-98), Men's Literary and Social Club of Newtown (pres. 1984-85). Republican. Episcopalian. Avocations: golf, gardening, reading.

**FISKE, ROBERT BISHOP, JR.,** lawyer; b. N.Y.C., Dec. 28, 1930; s. Robert Bishop and Lenore (Seymour) F.; m. Janet Tinsley, Aug. 21, 1954; children: Linda Goucher, Robert Bishop, Susan Williams. BA, Yale U., 1952; JD, U. Mich., 1955, LLD (hon.), 1997. Bar: Mich. 1955, N.Y. 1956, U.S. Ct. Appeals ( 2nd cir.) 1957, U.S. Supreme Ct. 1961. Assoc. Davis, Polk, Wardwell, Sunderland & Kiendl, 1955-57; asst. U.S. atty. So. Dist. N.Y., 1957-61; assoc. Davis, Polk & Wardwell, 1961-64, ptnr., 1964-76, 80-99; U.S. atty. So. Dist. N.Y., N.Y.C., 1976-80; ind. counsel for Whitewater, Little Rock, 1994. Fellow Am. Coll. Trial Lawyers (pres. 1991-92); mem. ABA (chmn. standing com. on fed. judiciary 1984-87), Assn. of Bar of City of N.Y., Fed. Bar Coun. (pres. 1982-84), N.Y. State Bar Assn., Noroton Yacht Club, Wee Burn Country Club. Republican. Congregationalist. Federal civil litigation, State civil litigation, Criminal. Home: 19 Juniper Rd Darien CT 06820-5707 Office: 450 Lexington Ave New York NY 10017-3911

**FISS, OWEN M.,** law educator; b. 1938. BA, Dartmouth Coll., 1959; BPhil, Oxford U., 1961; LLB, Harvard U., 1964. Bar: N.Y. 1965. Law clk. to Judge Thurgood Marshall, U.S. Ct. Appeals 2d Cir., 1964-65, to Justice Brennan, U.S. Supreme Ct., 1965; spl. asst. to asst. atty. gen., civil rights div. U.S. Dept. Justice, Washington, 1966-67, acting dir. Office of Planning Coordination, 1968; prof. U. Chgo. Law Sch., 1968-74; prof. Yale U. Law Sch., New Haven, 1974-84, Alexander M. Bickel prof. pub. law, 1984-92, Sterling prof., 1992—; vis. prof. Stanford U., 1973. Mem. Harvard Law Rev.; author: Injunctions, 1972; The Civil Rights Injunction, 1978; (with R.M. Cover) The Structure of Procedure, 1979; (with D. Rendleman) Injunctions, 2d edit., 1984; (with Cover and J. Resnik) Procedure, 1988; (with Cover and Resnik) The Federal Procedural System, 1988, 3d edit., 1991, Holmes Devise History of the Supreme Ct. :Troubled Beginnings of the Modern State, 1888-1910, 1993, Liberalism Divided, 1996, The Irony of Free Speech, 1996, A Community of Equals, 1999; mem. editl. bd. Philosophy and Pub. Affairs and Found. Press, Yale Jour. Criticism, Yale Jour. Law and Humanities, Law, Econs. and Orgns. Office: Yale Law Sch PO Box 401A New Haven CT 06520

**FITCH, BRENT E.,** lawyer; b. Balt., Dec. 19, 1969; s. Larry W. and Linda W. Fitch; m. Anita J. Schroeder, Nov. 7, 1998. BA in History, U. Okla., 1993.; JD, Oklahoma City U., 1997. Bar: Okla., U.S. Dist. Ct. (we. dist.) Okla. Intern Foliart Huff Ottaway & Caldwell, Oklahoma City, 1995-97; atty. Holloway Dobson Hudson Bachman Alden Jennings & Holloway, Oklahoma City, 1997—. Mem. adv. bd. Delta Upsilon Corp., Oklahoma City, 1997—. Mem. Okla. Bar Assn. Product liability, General civil litigation, Personal injury. Office: Holloway Dobson et al 211 N Robinson Ave Ste 900 Oklahoma City OK 73102-7105

**FITCH, RAYMOND WILLIAM,** lawyer, musician; b. Mpls., Apr. 10, 1931; s. Ray W. and Eleanor (Fleetham) F.; m. Antoinette C. Suwalsky, May 31, 1958; children: Albert, Robert, Michael, Anne. B.S.L., U. Minn., 1953, JD, 1955. Bar: Minn. 1955, U.S. Supreme Ct. 1988. Assoc. Tyrrell, Jardine, St. Paul, 1957-65, Robb & Van Eps, Mpls., 1965-68; ptnr. Fitch, Johnson & Larson & Walsh, Mpls., 1968—; advisor Minn. Legislature, 1970-84; tchr. legal affairs Mpls. pub. schs., 1975-82; tchr., advisor, musician Basilica St. Mary, Mpls., 1968-96; musician St. Mary's, Waverly, Minn., 1996—. Served to lst lt. U.S. Army, 1955-57. Mem. Minn. Bar Assn., Hennepin County Bar Assn., Am. Arbitration Assn. (arbitrator 1980—), Delta Tau Delta. Roman Catholic. Lodge: Knight of Holy Sepulchre. Workers' compensation, Insurance, Personal injury. Office: Fitch & Johnson 100 Washington Ave S Ste 648 Minneapolis MN 55401-2121

**FITTERER, RICHARD CLARENCE,** judge; b. Ellensburg, Wash., Jan. 22, 1946; s. L. George and Margeret H. (Lewis) F.; m. Janice M. Ivey, Feb. 14, 1968 (dec.); children: Christian C. (dec.), Zane I., Aaron G. BCS, Seattle U., 1968; JD, U. Puget Sound, 1975. Bar: Wash. 1976, U.S. Dist. Ct. (we. dist.) Wash. 1976, U.S. Dist. Ct. (ea. dist.) Wash. 1977. Assoc. Patrick R. Acres, Moses Lake, Wash., 1977; sole practice Moses Lake, 1977-79, 83-95; ptnr. Milne, Lemargie & Fitterer, Ephrata, Wash., 1979-1983; judge Grant County Dist. Ct., 1995—; instr. Wash. State Jud. Coll. Bd. dirs. Columbia Basin Rodeo Assn. Moses Lake Roundup, 1984-91, United Way, Moses Lake, 1978-81, Moses Lake C. of C., 1979-83, 87-88. Mem. ATLA, ABA, Am. Judges Assn., Wash. State Dist. Judges Assn. (chair rules com. 1999—), Grant County Bar Assn. (pres. 1993), Wash. State Trial Lawyers Assn., Moses Lake Golf and Country Club (bd. dirs. 1989-92, pres. 1991-92), Elks (bd. dirs. 1984). Roman Catholic. Avocations: skiing, boating, golfing, photography. Home: 322 N Crestview Dr Moses Lake WA 98837-1412 Office: PO Box 37 Ephrata WA 98823-0037

**FITZGERALD, GEOFFREY M.,** lawyer; b. Torrington, Conn., May 14, 1958; s. Robert M. and Jeanne M. (McCormick) F.; m. Ellen W. Starr, Aug. 3, 1985; children: Emmett Starr, Tatum Starr. BA cum laude, Middlebury (Vt.) Coll., 1980; JD cum laude, U. Maine, 1985. Law clk. Vt. Supreme Ct., Montpelier, 1985-86; assoc. Sylvester & Maley Inc., Burlington, Vt., 1986-96, Brian J. Grearson P.C., Barre, Vt., 1996—. Youth soccer, basketball, and baseball coach Montpelier Recreation Dept., 1994—. Mem. Am. Trial Lawyers Assn., Vt. Bar Assn., Vt. Trial Lawyers Assn. Avocations: hiking, golf, skiing, tennis. Personal injury, Workers' compensation. Office: Brian J Greason PC Airport Rd RR 3 Box 6688 Barre VT 05641-8606

**FITZGERALD, JAMES MICHAEL,** federal judge; b. Portland, Oreg., Oct. 7, 1920; s. Thomas and Florence (Linderman) F.; m. Karin Rose Benton, Jan. 19, 1950; children: Dennis James, Denise Lyn, Debra Jo, Kevin Thomas. BA, Willamette U., 1950, LLB, 1951; postgrad., U. Wash., 1952. Bar: Alaska 1953. Asst. U.S. atty. Ketchikan and Anchorage, Alaska, 1952-56; city atty. City of Anchorage, 1956-59; legal counsel to Gov. Alaska, Anchorage, 1959; commr. pub. safety State of Alaska, 1959; judge Alaska Superior Ct., 3d Jud. Dist., 1959-69, presiding judge, 1969-72; assoc. justice Alaska Supreme Ct., Anchorage, 1972-75; judge U.S. Dist. Ct. for Alaska, Anchorage, from 1975, formerly chief judge, now sr. judge. Mem. advisory bd. Salvation Army, Anchorage, 1962—, chmn., 1965-66; mem. Anchorage Parks and Recreation Bd., 1965-77, chmn., 1966. Served with AUS, 1940-41; Served with USMCR, 1942-46. Office: US Dist Ct 222 W 7th Ave Box 50 Anchorage AK 99513-7564

**FITZGERALD, JAMES PATRICK,** lawyer; b. Omaha, Nebr., Nov. 30, 1946; s. James Joseph and Lorraine (Hickey) F.; m. Dianne Fager, Dec. 17, 1968; 1 child, James Timothy. BA, U. Nebr., 1968; JD, Creighton U., 1974. Bar: Nebr. 1974, U.S. Dist. Ct. Nebr. 1974, U.S. Ct. Appeals (8th cir.) 1974. Law clk. U.S. Dist. Ct. Nebr., Omaha, 1974-76.; atty. McGrath, North, Mullin & Kratz, P.C., Omaha, 1976—. Sgt. U.S. Army, 1968-71. Mem. ABA, Nebr. Bar Assn., Assn. Trial Lawyers Am., Nebr. Assn. Trial Attys., Def. Rsch. Inst. General civil litigation, Contracts commercial. Home: 16728 Jones Cir Omaha NE 68118-2711 Office: McGrath North Mullin & Kratz 1 Central Park Plz Ste 1400 Omaha NE 68102-1680

**FITZGERALD, JOHN EDWARD, III,** lawyer; b. Cambridge, Mass., Jan. 12, 1945; s. John Edward Jr. and Kathleen (Sullivan) FitzG. BCE, U.S. Mil. Acad., West Point, N.Y., 1969; JD, M in Pub. Policy Analysis, U. Pa., 1975. Bar: Pa. 1975, N.Y. 1978, Calif. 1983, U.S. Supreme Ct. 1991. Commd. 2d lt. U.S. Army, 1969, advanced through grades to capt., 1971, resigned, 1972; assoc. Saul Ewing Remick & Saul, Phila., 1975-77, Shearman & Sterling, N.Y.C., 1977-78; atty., dir. govt. rels. and pub. affairs Pepsico, Inc., Purchase, N.Y., 1978-82; sr. v.p., dept. head Security Pacific Corp., Los Angeles, 1982-83; ptnr. Schlesinger, FitzGerald & Johnson, Palm Springs, Calif., 1983-87; mng. ptnr. FitzGerald & Assocs., Palm Springs, 1987—; judge pro tem Desert Jud. Dist.; lectr. Calif. Continuing Edn. of the Bar; trustee Nat. Coun. Freedom Found., Valley Forge, Pa.; lectr. Calif. Employment Lawyers Assn. Bd. dirs., chmn.-elect Desert Hosp. Found.; bd. dirs., chmn. Palm Sprngs Boys and Girls Club, Desert Youth Found.; chmn. United Way of the Desert; mem. Com. of 25, Palm Springs; trustee, v.p., Palm Springs Desert Mus. Named Palm Springs Disting. Citizen of Yr., 1999. Mem. ABA, Calif. Bar Assn., Desert Bar Assn. (trustee, chmn. cmty. law sch.), Riverside County Bar Assn., Orange County Bar Assn., Assn. Trial Lawyers Am., Calif. Trial Lawyers Assn. (lectr.), Am. Arbitration Assn. (arbitrator), O'Donnell Golf Club, Desert Bus. Roundtable, World Affairs Coun., Lincoln Club of the Coachella Valley (bd. dirs., jud. nomination com.). Labor, Contracts commercial, General civil litigation. Office: Ste 105 3001 Tahquitz Canyon Way Palm Springs CA 92262-6900

**FITZGERALD, JOSEPH MICHAEL, JR.,** lawyer; b. Norfolk, Va., Oct. 9, 1943; s. Joseph Michael and Grace Elizabeth (Finegan) F.; m. Lynne Marie Leslie, May 3, 1973; children: Joseph Glenn, Leslie Marie. BS, Mt. St. Mary's Coll., 1965; JD, Cath. U. Am., 1970; LLM, U. Miami, 1973; JCL, St. Thomas Aquinas, 1986; MA, St. Thomas U., 1988; D of Ministry, Grad. Theol. Found., 1983. Bar: Fla. 1970, D.C. 1991, Va. 1993, U.S. Dist. Ct. (so. dist.) Fla. 1971, U.S. Dist. Ct. (we. dist.) Va. 1998, U.S. Ct. Appeals (11th cir.) 1973, U.S. Supreme Ct. 1980; cert. mediator. Investigator Retail Credit Co., Miami, 1965-66; intelligence analyst Def. Intelligence Agy., Washington, 1966-70; ptnr. Fitzgerald & Fitzgerald, Miami, 1970-79, McDermott, Will & Emery, Miami, 1979-84, Wood, Lucksinger & Epstein, Miami, 1984-88, Fitzgerald, Portela & Portuondo, Miami, 1989-92, Fitzgerald, Charlip, Delgado, Befeler & Portuondo, P.A., Miami, 1992-94, Fitzgerald & Portuondo, Miami, 1994-96, Fitzgerald & Assocs., Miami, 1996—; adj. faculty Sch. of Law and Inst. of Pastoral Ministry St. Thomas U., 1989—; bd. dirs. Security Bank, Ft. Lauderdale, Fla.; lectr. environ. law and health law various symposia and univs.; advisor to Office Environ. Affairs Fla. Dept. State, 1971; spl. counsel Broward County Environ. Quality Control Bd., 1975-82; spl. asst. state's atty. for environ. crimes Broward County, Fla., 1974-76; appeals judge Met. Tribunal of Archdiocese of Miami, 1986-96. Contbr. articles to profl. jours. Trustee Fla. Ind. Coll. and Univs. Found., 1977-79, Inst. on Man and Oceans, 1976-81, Boystown of Fla., 1978-83, Kiwanis Youth Found., 1980-81, Seton Shrine Ctr., 1980-81, St. Francis Hosp. Found., 1981-85, Legal Svcs. Miami, 1985-87, 89-94; chmn. Mediation Ministries, 1990—, Ctr. for Law and Ministry, 1990—, Charlottesville Housing Found., 1995—. Mem. ABA, Fla. Bar Assn. (award of merit 1975, 76), Cath. Lawyers Guild (pres. 1984), Serra Internat. (trustee 1979-80, pres. 1984-85), Kiwanis, Knights of Malta, Knights of St. Gregory. Avocations: skiing, fishing, bicycling, reading, sailing. General civil litigation, Constitutional. Home: 5710 S Le Jeune Rd Coral Gables FL 33146-2816 also: 700 Harris St Ste 201 Charlottesville VA 22903-4584 Office: 2665 S Bayshore Dr Ste M-103 Miami FL 33133-5402

**FITZGERALD, JUDITH KLASWICK,** federal judge; b. Spangler, Pa., May 10, 1948; d. Julius Francis and Regina Marie (Pregno) Klaswick; m. June 5, 1971 (div. Dec. 1982); 1 child; m. Barry Robert Fitzgerald, Sept. 20, 1986; 1 child. BSBA, U. Pitts., 1970, JD, 1973. Legal rschr. Assocs. Fin., Pitts., 1972-73; law clk. to pres. judge Beaver County (Pa.) Ct. Common Pleas, 1973-74; law clk. to judge Pa. Superior Ct., Pitts., 1974-75; asst. U.S. atty. U.S. Dist. Ct. (we. dist.) Pa., Pitts. and Erie, 1976-87; U.S. bankruptcy judge U.S. Dist. Ct. (we. dist.) Pa., Pitts., Erie and Johnstown, 1987—. Co-author: Bankruptcy and Divorce, Support and Property Division, 1991; editor: Pennsylvania Law of Juvenile Delinquency and Deprivation, 1976; contbr. articles to profl. jours. Mem. Pitts. Camerata, 1978-80, Allegheny County Polit.-Legal Edn. Project, 1980, West Pa. Conservancy, 1990—, Mendelssohn Choir Pitts., 1982—; mem. coun. Program to Aid Citizen Enterprise, 1985-87. Recipient Spl. Achievement awards Dept. Justice, Spl. Recognition award Pittsburgh mag., Operation Exodus Outstanding Performance award Dept. Commerce, 1986. Mem. Allegheny County Bar Assn., Women's Bar Assn. of Western Pa., Nat. Conf. Bankruptcy Judges, Am. Bankruptcy Inst., Nat. Conf. Bankruptcy Clks., Comml. Law League of Am., Fed. Criminal Investigators Assn. (Spl. Svc. award 1988), Zonta. Republican. Lutheran. Avocations: singing, reading, traveling. Office: US Bankruptcy Ct 600 Grant St Ste 5490 Pittsburgh PA 15219-2702

**FITZGERALD, KEVIN GERARD,** lawyer; b. Milw., Aug. 1, 1963; s. Raymond E. and Virginia L. Fitzgerald; m. Jill Ann Hussinger, 1997; 1 child, Zachary J. Mitschrich. BS, Marquette U., 1984; JD, U. Wis., 1987. Bar: Wis. 1987, Fla. 1994, U.S. Dist. Ct. (ea. and we. dists.) Wis. Ptnr. Foley & Lardner, Milw., 1987—; bd. dirs. T.E. Brennan Co., Milw. Contbr. articles to profl. jours. Mem. ABA, Fedn. Regulatory Counsel, Milw. Bar Assn. Insurance, Administrative and regulatory. Office: Foley and Lardner 777 E Wisconsin Ave Milwaukee WI 53202-5367

**FITZGERALD, KEVIN MICHAEL,** lawyer, mediator; b. Kansas City, Kans., May 10, 1956; s. Thomas Francis and Theresa Ann (Grosdidier) FitzG.; m. Susan Patricia Parker, June 21, 1980; children: Kathryn Ann, Shannon Elizabeth, Erin Parker. BBA, U. Tex., Arlington, 1981; JD, U. Ark., 1985. Bar: Mo. 1985, U.S. Dist. Ct. Mo. 1985, U.S. Ct. Appeals (8th cir.) 1985. Assoc. Taylor, Stafford, Woody, Cowherd and Clithero, Springfield, Mo., 1985-90; ptnr. Taylor, Stafford, Woody, Clithero and FitzGerald, Springfield, 1990—. Mem. Mo. Bar Assn., Springfield Met. Bar Assn. (sec. 1997), Legal Aid Southwest Mo. (bd. dirs. 1993-96). General civil litigation, Personal injury, Product liability. Office: Taylor Stafford Woody Clithero & FitzGerald 3315 E Ridgeview St Ste 1000 Springfield MO 65804-4083

**FITZ-GERALD, ROGER MILLER,** lawyer; b. N.Y.C., July 13, 1935; s. Gerald Hartpence and Rovenia Francis (Miller) F.-G.; m. Martha Ann Odell, 1967 (div. 1985); children: Kathleen Odell, Maureen Roxanne, Arthur Thomas; m. Janice Evens, 1993. B.S. with honors, U. Ill., 1957, J.D. with honors, 1961. Bar: Ill. 1961, U.S. Dist. Ct. (no. dist.) 1961, U.S. Patent and Trademark Office, 1965, U.S. Ct. Customs and Patent Appeals, 1978, U.S. Ct. Appeals (fed. cir.) 1982, U.S. Dist. Ct. (so. dist.) Ill. 1992, U.S. Dist. Ct. (cen. dist.) Ill. 1994. Assoc. Kirkland, Ellis, Hodson, Chaffetz & Masters, Chgo., 1961-64; assoc. specializing in fgn. patent law Fitch, Even, Tabin & Luedeka, Chgo., 1964-72; patent atty. Bell & Howell Co., Chgo., 1972-74, sr. patent atty., 1974-75, group patent atty., 1975-76, group patent counsel, 1976-82, sr. patent counsel, 1982-85, sr. tech. law counsel, 1985-86, chief tech. law counsel, 1986-90; pvt. practice Urbana, Wilmette, Belleville, Ill., 1990—, St. Louis, 1990—. Author: (with Ferdinand J. Zeni) Precinct Captain's Guide, 1968; contbg. author: Materials on Legislation (Read, MacDonald, Fordham and Pierce), 1973. Constl. revision chmn. Ill. Young Republican Orgn., 1968-70. Served with AUS, 1957. Mem. ABA, Ill. Bar Assn., Chgo. Bar Assn., Champaign County Ill. Bar Assn., Intellectual Property Law Assn. Chgo., Am. Intellectual Property Law Assn., Assn. Corp. Patent Counsel, Computer Law Assn., Order of Coif, Phi Beta Kappa, Phi Eta Sigma, Phi Delta Phi, Delta Upsilon (province gov. 1969-75). Patent, Trademark and copyright, Computer. Home: 906B E Colorado Ave Urbana IL 61801-6305 Office: 1104 S Orchard St Urbana IL 61801-4852

**FITZGERALD, TIMOTHY JOHN,** lawyer; b. Lakewood, Ohio, Dec. 26, 1962; s. Edward Redmond and Margaret Therese F.; m. Tamela Jo Bacino, Jan. 9, 1988; children: Brendan, Sean, Claire. BSBA, Marquette U., 1986; JD, Cleve. State U., 1989. Bar: Ohio 1989, U.S. Dist. Ct. (no. dist.) Ohio 1990, U.S. Ct. Appeals (6th cir.) 1990, U.S. Dist. Ct. Ariz. 1997. Ptnr. Gallagher, Sharp, Fulton & Norman, Cleve., 1989—; del. 8th Jud. Dist. Conf., Cleve., 1997-98. Co-author: Bad Faith Litigation in Ohio, 1995. Bd. dirs. St. Raphael Sch. Bd., Bay Village, Ohio, 1998. Mem. Ohio State Bar Assn., Cleve. Bar Assn. (trial counsel, cert. grievance com. 1994—, com. on homeless 1996-97, profl. ethics com. 1996—), Cleve. Area Civil Trial Attys. Republican. Roman Catholic. Avocations: jogging, Am. Civil War, equestrian sports. General civil litigation, Appellate, Professional liability. Office: Gallagher Sharp Fulton & Norman 1501 Euclid Ave Cleveland OH 44115-2108

**FITZGERALD, WILLIAM EMIL,** lawyer; b. Seoul, Korea, Nov. 1, 1955; s. William Eberhart and Nova Boydetta (Longtain) F.; m. Kathryn Lee Jerman, Aug. 13, 1983; children: Jacqueline Leigh, Neiland Bennett. BS, U.S. Mil. Acad., 1977; JD, Duke U., 1985. Bar: Oreg., N.C., U.S. Dist. Ct. Oreg., U.S. Ct. Appeals (9th cir.), U.S. Supreme Ct. Trial atty. Tax divsn. U.S. Dept. Justice, Washington, 1991-95; asst. U.S. atty. U.S. Atty.'s Office, Eugene, Oreg., 1995—. Capt. JAG, U.S. Army, 1985-91. Mem. Nat. Assn. Asst. U.S. Attys. Office: Office US Atty 701 High St Eugene OR 97401-2713

**FITZGERALD, WILLIAM TERRY,** lawyer; b. Burlington, Iowa, July 6, 1951; s. William Lewis and Mary Lou (Curran) F.; m. Patricia Eileen Hunziker, May 19, 1973; 1 child, Mollie M. BA, U. Mo., 1973; JD, U. Mo., Kansas City, 1975. Bar: Kans. 1976, U.S. Dist. Ct. Kans. 1976, Mo. 1988, Tex. 1992, U.S. Ct. Appeals (10th cir.) 1992, U.S. Dist. Ct. (so. dist.) Tex. 1993, U.S. Ct. Appeals (5th cir.) 19698, U.S. Dist. Ct. (ea. dist.) Tex. 1999. Atty. McAnany, Van Cleave & Phillips, P.A., Kansas City, Kans., 1974-86; atty. Niewald, Waldeck & Brown, Houston, 1986-94, Fitzgerald & Gartner L.L.P., Houston, 1994—. Mem. Tex. Assn. Def. Counsel, Tex. Bar Assn., Mo. Bar Assn., Kans. Bar Assn., Kans. Trial Lawyers Assn. Avocations: golf, fishing. Personal injury, Environmental, Product liability. Office: Fitgerald & Gartner LLP 1200 Smith St Ste 1150 Houston TX 77002-4369

**FITZHUGH, DAVID MICHAEL,** lawyer; b. San Francisco, Nov. 24, 1946; s. William DeHart and Betty Jean (Jeffries) F.; m. Jenny Lu Conner, Dec. 22, 1967; children: Ross DeHart, Cameron Hyatt, Michael Jeffries. Student Carleton Coll., 1964-67; B.A., Coll. William and Mary, 1972; J.D., U. Va., 1975. Bar: D.C. 1975, U.S. Dist. Ct. D.C. 1979, U.S. Dist. Ct. Md. 1987, U.S. Ct. Claims 1980, U.S. Ct. Appeals (fed. cir.) 1982, U.S. Ct. Appeals (D.C. cir.) 1987, U.S. Ct. Appeals (4th cir.) 1989, U.S. Supreme Ct. 1982. Assoc. McKenna & Cuneo, Washington, 1975-80, ptnr., 1980-98, chmn. litigation dept., 1984-94; assoc. counsel Office of Counsel, Naval Air Systems Command, 1999—. Mem. editl. bd. Nat. Contract Mgmt. Assn. Jour., 1975—. Contbr. articles to legal publs. Capt. USMC, 1967-71, Vietnam. Mem. ABA (litigation sect., discovery com. pub. contracts sect.). Federal civil litigation, Government contracts and claims. Home: 13261 Clipper Cir Solomons MD 20688-3022 Office: Office of Counsel AIR 7.7 Bldg 2272 Ste 257 47123 Buse Rd Unit IPT Patuxent River MD 20670-1547

**FITZMAURICE, EDWARD JOSEPH, JR.,** lawyer; b. Stamford, Conn., Apr. 10, 1940; s. Edward Joseph and Elizabeth Ann F.; m. Marcia Ann Kirstein, Dec. 3, 1966; children: Carey Elizabeth, Evan Edward. BA, Villanova U., 1962; JD, So. Meth. U., 1971. Bar: Tex., U.S. Dist. Ct. (no. and ea. dists.) Tex. Capt. Braniff Internat., Dallas, 1966-82; assoc. Kern Wooley & Maloney, Dallas, 1983; of counsel Hicks James & Preston PC, Dallas, 1984-96; solo practice Dallas, 1996—. Capt. USMC, 1962-66. Decorated 11 Air medals; recipient Presdl. Unit Citation, 1966. Avocation: aviation. Aviation, Family and matrimonial, Criminal. Home: 4036 Candlenut Ln Dallas TX 75244-6608 Office: 1341 W Mockingbird Ln Ste 718E Dallas TX 75247-4939

**FITZPATRICK, DUROSS,** federal judge; b. Macon, Ga., Oct. 19, 1934; s. Mark W. and Jane L. (Duross) F.; m. Beverly O'Connor, Mar. 17, 1963; children: Mark O'Connor, Devon Hart. B.S. in Forestry, U. Ga., 1961, LL.B., 1966. Bar: Ga. 1965. Assoc. Elliott & Davis, Macon, 1966-67; sole practice, Cochran, Ga., 1967-83; ptnr. Fitzpatrick & Mullis, Cochran, 1983-86; judge U.S. Dist. Ct. (mid. dist.) Ga., Macon, 1986-95, chief judge, 1995—; bd. govs. State Bar Ga., 1976-83, mem. exec. com., 1979-84, pres., 1984-85; mem. Ga. Chief Justice's Commn. on Professionalism. Legal counsel Republican del. Gen. Assembly Ga., 1969. Served with USMC, 1954-57. Fellow Am. Bar Found., Ga. Bar Found.; mem. Oconee Bar Assn. pres. 1970), Am. Inns Ct. (master of the Bench, Joseph Henry Lumpkin chpt.), Macon Bar Assn. Republican. Episcopalian. Home: RR 1 Box 1525 Jeffersonville GA 31044-9768 Office: US Dist Ct PO Box 1014 425 Mulberry St Macon GA 31202

**FITZPATRICK, HAROLD FRANCIS,** lawyer; b. Jersey City, Oct. 16, 1947; s. Harold G. and Anne Marie F.; m. Joanne M. Merry, Sept. 22, 1973; children: Elizabeth, Kevin, Matthew, Christopher. AB, Boston Coll., 1969; MBA, NYU, 1971; JD, Harvard U., 1974. Bar: N.J. 1974, U.S. Dist. Ct. N.J. 1974, U.S. Ct. Internat. Trade, 1986, U.S. Supreme Ct. 1994. Securities analyst Chase Manhattan Bank, N.Y.C., 1970-71, Brown Bros., Harriman & Co., N.Y.C., 1971; staff asst. U.S. Senate, Washington, 1972; law clk. to assoc. justice N.J. Supreme Ct., Trenton, 1974-75; assoc. Cleary, Gottlieb, Steen & Hamilton, N.Y.C., 1975-78; mng. ptnr. Fitzpatrick & Waterman, Secaucus, N.J., 1978—, Bayonne, N.J., 1978—, Hackettstown, N.J., 1996—; gen. counsel Housing Authority City of Bayonne, 1976—, Color Pigments Mfrs. Assn., Alexandria, Va., 1978—, N.J. Assn. Housing and Redevel. Authorities, Brick, N.J., 1979—, Housing Authority Town of Secaucus, N.J., 1980-88, Rahway (N.J.) Geriatrics Ctr. Inc., 1981-92, Housing Authority City of Englewood, N.J., 1985-91, Housing Authority City of Rahway, 1986—, Edgewater Mcpl. Utilities Authority, 1986-93, Housing Authority City of Woodbridge, N.J., 1988-94, Housing Authority City of Asbury Pk., N.J., 1991-94, Bd. Edn. City of Rahway, 1994-97, N.J. Pub. Housing Authority Joint Ins. Fund, 1995—. Mem. ABA, N.J. Bar Assn., Hudson County Bar Assn. (trustee, officer 1984-92, pres. 1993), Beta Gamma Sigma. General corporate, Environmental, Municipal (including bonds). Office: Fitzpatrick & Waterman 400 Plaza Dr Secaucus NJ 07094-3605

**FITZPATRICK, JAMES DAVID,** lawyer; b. Syracuse, N.Y., Oct. 21, 1938; s. William Francis and Margaret Mary (Shortt) F. *Mr. Fitzpatrick's twin brothers, Francis and William, have courageously worked to overcome their affliction of cerebral palsy. They have been great examples and inspirations to him to become all that he can be in order to serve God and others and to be a true world citizen.* BS, Holy Cross Coll., Worcester, Mass., 1960; JD, Syracuse U., 1963. Bar: N.Y. 1963, U.S. Dist. Ct. (no. dist.) N.Y. 1965. Assoc. Bond, Schoeneck & King, Syracuse, N.Y., 1963-76, mem., 1976-88, ptnr., 1988—; pres. Hiscock Legal Aid Soc., Syracuse, 1975-76; faculty Nat. Bus. Inst., Eau Claire, Wis., 1990—; del. Russian Conf. on Banking-The Kremlin, Moscow, 1992, 93. Mem. presdl. Roundtable, Washington, 1991-92; founding mem. pres.'s task force Nat. Coalition Against Pornography, Common Cause; chmn. adv. bd. Rep. Nat. Coms., 1994; mem. The Studio Mus. in Harlem, Am. Mus. Nat. History; founding mem. Am. Air Mus.; nat. adv. coun. USN Meml. Found. Recipient Afghanistan Freedom Fighter award Afghan Mercy Fund, 1989, Rep. Senatorial Medal of Freedom, Honored Friend of El Savador award, 1991, Wisdom award of Honor, Wisdom Soc. for Advancement of Knowledge, Learning and Rsch. in Edn., named to Wisdom Hall of Fame, 1999. Mem. ABA, NAACP, N.Y. State Bar Assn., Onondaga County Bar Assn. (chmn. real estate com. 1990-96), Internat. Bar Assn., Am. Land Title Assn., UN Assn. of U.S.A., Habitat for Humanity Internat., Amnesty Internat. U.S.A., Nat. Audubon Soc., Ctr. for Nat. Independence in Politics, Smithsonian Nat. Assocs., Nat. Trust for Hist. Preservation, Navy League U.S., World Future Soc., Ams. Guild, Internat. Platform Assn. (spkr. Internat. Youth Ctr., New Delhi), Inst. Global Ethics. Republican. Roman Catholic. Avocations: housing education, reading, walking. Real property, Private international. Home: 201 Croyden Rd Syracuse NY 13224-1917 Office: Bond Schoeneck & King 1 Lincoln Ctr Fl 18 Syracuse NY 13202-1355

**FITZPATRICK, JOSEPH MARK,** lawyer; b. Jersey City, May 27, 1925; s. Joseph Francis Stephen and Meave (Wilson) F.; m. Elizabeth Anne Keane, June 18, 1949; children: Elizabeth A., Susan E., Christopher M., Stephen R. ME, Stevens Inst. Tech., 1945; JD, Georgetown U., 1951. Bar: Va. 1950, U.S. Patent Office 1950, N.Y. 1954. Trial atty. anti-trust divsn. Dept. Justice, 1951-53; mem. firm Ward, McElhannon, Brooks & Fitzpatrick, N.Y.C., 1954-70, Fitzpatrick, Cella, Harper & Scinto, N.Y.C., 1970—. With USNR, 1943-46. Fellow Am. Coll. Trial Lawyers; mem. ABA, Va. Bar Assn., N.Y. Bar Assn., Assn. of Bar of City of N.Y., Am. Intellectual Property Law Assn., N.Y. Intellectual Property Law Assn., Manasquan River Yacht Club. Federal civil litigation, Patent, Trademark and copyright. Home: 17 Oak Ln Scarsdale NY 10583-1628 Office: Fitzpatrick Cella Harper Scinto 30 Rockefeller Plz New York NY 10112-0002

**FITZPATRICK, LAUREN ELAINE,** lawyer; b. Canton, Ohio, Aug. 25, 1957; d. William J. and Olive Elaine (Stover) F.; m. David Francis DePasquale, Sept. 10, 1988; children: Ryan Noelle, Alexandra Lauren. BS in Law Enforcement Criminal Justice, Kent State U., 1979; JD, Akron State U., 1982. Bar: U.S. Dist. Ct. (no. dist.) Ohio 1983; U.S. Ct. Appeals (6th cir.) 1984. Assoc. Ferruccio & Reinbold, Canton, Ohio, 1983-84; asst. prosecutor Stark County Prosecutor, Canton, Ohio, 1984-85, 1984-85; asst. law dir. City of Canton Law Dept., Canton, Ohio, 1985-88; magistrate City of Massillon, Ohio, 1988-89; pvt. practice Canton, Ohio, 1989—; legal cons. Grand Oaks Montessori Sch., Canton, 1995—; ptnr. Fitzpatrick Enterprises, Canton, 1972—. Campaign chmn. Mariella Mestel for Judge, Canton, 1995; vol. W. Scott Gwin for law Dir., Canton, 1986; Harry Klide for Judge, Canton, 1984. Recipient Excellent Achievement Study of Remedies II award Lawyers Coop. Pub., 1983. Mem. Stark County Bar Assn., Glenmoor Country Club. Avocations: reading, swimming, weight training, gardening. Real property, Contracts commercial. Office: 4942 Higbee Ave NW Ste A Canton OH 44718-2554

**FITZPATRICK, WILLIAM JOHN,** lawyer; b. N.Y.C., Oct. 13, 1952; s. William and Ann F.; m. Diane Langenmayr; children: Daniel, Sara, Sean. JD, Syracuse U. Bar: N.Y. 1977. Asst. dist. atty. Onondaga County Dist. Attys. Office, Syracuse, N.Y., 1977-87; pvt. practice pvt. practice, Syracuse, N.Y., 1987-91; dist. atty. Onondaga County, Syracuse, N.Y., 1992—. Mem. N.Y. State Dist. Attys. Assn. (pres. 1998-99). Avocation: collecting baseball memorabilia. Office: Onondaga County Dist Atty 421 Montgomery St Ste 12 Syracuse NY 13202-2923

**FITZSIMMONS, BRADY MICHAEL,** judge; b. New Orleans, July 17, 1941; s. Huyet Walter and Henrietta Fitzsimmons; m. Aurelia Geraldine Mannion, Oct. 5, 1968; children: Brendan, Ian, Cavan, Devin. BA in English, Spring Hill Coll., 1967; MA in English, La. State U., 1969; JD, Loyola U., 1975. Instr. English Southeastern La. U., Hammond, 1969-72, Loyola U., New Orleans, 1972-75; pub. defender State of La., Office of Pub. Defender, Covington, 1978-79; ptnr. LeGardeur & Fitzsimmons, Covington, 1979-83; asst. dist. atty. State of La., Office of Dist. Atty., Covington, 1986-88; judge 22d Jud. Dist. Ct., Covington, 1988-95, 1st Cir. Ct. Appeals, Baton Rouge, La., 1995—; adj. faculty Loyola U. Sch. Law, New Orleans, 1975; faculty advisor Nat. Jud. Coll., Reno, 1992; lectr. La. Assn. Def. Counsel, 1998, La. State Police Acad., La. State Bar Assn. Fellow La. Bar Found.; mem. ABA, La. Bar Assn., Am. Judges Assn., Thomas More Inn of Ct., Wex Malone Inn of Ct. Avocations: golf, sailing. Office: 1st Cir Ct Appeal 832 E Boston St Covington LA 70433-2985

**FITZSIMMONS, ELLEN MARIE,** lawyer. Sr. gen. counsel CSX Corp., Richmond, asst. gen. counsel, 1995-97, gen. counsel, 1997—. Office: CSX Corp One James Ctr PO Box 85629 901 E Cary St Richmond VA 23285-5629

**FITZWATER, SIDNEY ALLEN,** federal judge; b. Olney, Md., Sept. 22, 1953; s. Ivan Welton and Kathleen Elizabeth (Schroeder) F.; B.A., Baylor U., 1975, J.D., 1976; m. Nancy Jane Ware, Aug. 6, 1976; children—John Welton, Joseph Leon, James Sidney. Bar: Tex. 1977, U.S. Supreme Ct. 1981. Assoc. Vinson & Elkins, Houston, 1976-78, Rain Harrell Emery Young & Doke, Dallas, 1978-82; judge 298th Jud. Dist. Tex., Dallas, 1982-86; judge U.S. Dist Ct. (no. dist.) Tex., 1986—. Bd. dirs. Dallas Services for Visually Impaired Children, 1980-85; mem. exec. com. Dallas County Reps., 1981-82; state del. Tex. Rep. Conv., 1980, 82, 84; mem. exec. com. Tex. Young Reps., 1981-82; bd. dirs. Dallas County Rep. Men's Club, 1984-85. Recipient Baylor U. award of merit, 1983, Ft. Worth Ind. Sch. Dist. Disting. Alumni award, 1986; named Outstanding Young Alumnus, Baylor U., 1985. Fellow Tex. Bar Found.; mem. State Bar Tex., Dallas Bar Assn., Nat. Order of Barristers, Phi Alpha Delta, Omicron Delta Kappa. Office: US Courthouse 1100 Commerce St Ste 15a3A Dallas TX 75242-1027

**FIX, PATRICIA SOWINSKI,** lawyer; b. Sept. 11, 1966; d. Gene Anthony and Josephine Sowinski; m. Gregory Fix. BA, U. Ill., 1988; JD, Loyola U., 1991. Bar: Ill. Asst. state's atty., chief traffic divsn. Lake County State's Atty., Waukegan, Ill., 1991—. Office: Lake County State's Atty 18 N County St Waukegan IL 60085-4304

**FLADUNG, RICHARD DENIS,** lawyer; b. Kansas City, Mo., Aug. 1, 1953; s. Jerome Francis and Rosemary (Voeste) F.; m. Leslie Lynn Cox, June 1, 1985; children: Daniel Edwin, Erica Anne, Derek Richard. BSCE, U. Kans., 1976, postgrad., 1977; JD, Washburn U., 1980. Bar: Kans. 1980, U.S. Dist. Ct. Kans. 1980, Ind. 1981, U.S. Dist. Ct. (so. dist.) Ind. 1981, U.S. Patent and Trademark Office 1982, Mo. 1983, Tex. 1984, U.S. Dist. Ct. (we. dist.) Mo. 1983, U.S. Dist. Ct. (so. dist.) Tex. 1984, U.S. Ct. Appeals (fed. cir.) 1984, U.S. Ct. Appeals (5th cir.) 1987, U.S. Supreme Ct. 1987, U.S. Dist. Ct. (we. dist.) Tex. 1988. Engr. Black and Veatch Cons. Engrs., Kansas City, 1975-80; corp. counsel CTB Inc., Milford, Ind., 1980-82; patent atty. Chase & Yakimo and predecessor firm, Kansas City, 1982-83, Bush, Moseley, Riddle and Jackson and predecessor firm, Houston, 1983-87, Pravel, Hewitt & Kimball, Houston, 1987-98, Akin, Gump, Strauss, Hauer & Feld, Houston, 1999—. Contbr. articles on patent matters and ins. coverage for intellectual property matters to profl. edn. programs. Legal aide to spkr. of Kans. Ho. of Reps., Topeka, 1980. Named One of Outstanding Young Men of Am., 1985. Mem. ABA (vice chmn. patent, trademark sect. young lawyer div. 1988-89), ASCE, Houston Bar Assn. (ex officio bd. dirs. 1987-88, vice chmn. profl. responsibility com. 1991—), Am. Intellectual Property Law Assn., Tex. Young Lawyers Assn. (bd. dirs. 1988), Mo. Bar Assn., Ind. Bar Assn., Houston Young Lawyers Assn. (pres. 1987-88, exec. mem. bd. dirs. 1987-88, Outstanding Com. Chmn. award 1984-86), Kansas City Bar Assn., Houston Intellectual Property Law Assn., Pi Alpha Kappa (treas. 1974-75). Roman Catholic. Avocations: tennis, jogging, biking, golf. Patent, Intellectual property, Federal civil litigation. Office: Akin Gump Strauss Hauer & Feld 1900 Pennzoil Pl S Tower 711 Louisiana St Houston TX 77002-2716

**FLAGG, BARBARA JEAN,** law educator; b. San Diego, Jan. 30, 1947; d. Durlin James Flagg and Mary Barbara (Weins) Lehto. AB, U. Calif., Riverside, 1967, MA, 1971; JD, U. Calif., Berkeley, 1987. Law clk. Cir. Judge Ruth Bader Ginsburg, Washington, 1987-88; asst. prof. law Washington U., St. Louis, 1988-93, assoc. prof. law, 1993-95, prof. law, 1995—. Author: Was Blind, But Now I See, 1997; contbr. articles to profl. jours. Mem. Order of Coif. Office: Washington U Sch of Law Campus Box 1120 One Brookings Dr Saint Louis MO 63130

**FLAGG, RONALD SIMON,** lawyer; b. Milw., Dec. 3, 1953; s. Arnold and Marian (Levy) F.; m. Patricia Sharin, June 20, 1982; children: Laura Sharon, Emily Rachel, Naomi Erica. AB, U. Chgo., 1975; JD, Harvard U., 1978. Bar: Wis. 1978, U.S. Dist. Ct. (ea. dist.) Wis. 1978, U.S. Ct. Appeals (7th cir.) 1979, D.C. 1980, U.S. Dist. Ct. D.C. 1980, U.S. Ct. Appeals (D.C. cir.) 1980, U.S. Ct. Appeals (3d cir.) 1984, U.S. Supreme Ct. 1986, U.S. Ct. Appeals (5th cir.) 1987, U.S. Ct. Appeals (8th cir.) 1989. Law clk. to presiding judge U.S. Dist. Ct. (ea. dist.) Wis., Milw., 1978-80; atty., adv. office of intelligence policy and rev. U.S. Dept. Justice, Washington, 1980-82; assoc. Sidley & Austin, Washington, 1982-85, ptnr., 1986—. Bd. dirs. Nat. Vets. Legal Svcs. Program. Mem. ABA, D.C. Bar Assn. (pub. svc. activities com). Administrative and regulatory, Federal civil litigation, Securities. Home: 3909 Garrison St NW Washington DC 20016-4219 Office: Sidley & Austin 1722 I St NW Fl 7 Washington DC 20006-3795

**FLAHERTY, DANIEL LEE,** prosecutor; b. Des Moines, Apr. 6, 1955; s. Jerry A. and Mary A. (Durlacher) F.; m. Kathleen L. Harrington, Aug. 10, 1980; children: Scott D., Amy J., Lacy A. BA, N.W. Mo. State U., 1978; JD, South Tex. Coll. Law, 1982. Bar: Tex. 1982, U.S. Dist. Ct. (so. dist.) Tex. 1983, U.S. Dist. Ct. (ea. dist.) Tex. 1985, U.S. Ct. Appeals (5th cir.) 1985, Iowa 1989, U.S. Dist. Ct. (no. dist.) Iowa 1991, U.S. Dist. Ct. (so. dist.) Iowa 1992, U.S. Ct. Appeals (8th cir.) 1992. Assoc. Newton Schwartz, P.C., Houston, 1982-83, George Chandler & Assocs., Baytown, Tex., 1983-85, Brack & Brack, Baytown, 1985-87, Margolin, Gildmeister, Willia, Mugan & Keane, Sioux City, Iowa, 1989-91; ptnr. Daniel L. Flaherty, Highlands, Tex., 1987-89; asst. county atty. Polk County Atty.'s Office, Des Moines, 1991—; lectr. Iowa Judges Conf., Des Moines, 1993; panelist Iowa Magistrates Conf., Des Moines, 1997, Iowa Clks. Conf., Des Moines, 1997. Contbr. articles to legal publs. Com. mem. troop 81 Boy Scouts Am., Baytown, 1983-89, chmn. membership com. Raven dist., 1987-89, scoutmaster troop 204, Sioux City, 1989-91, com. mem. troop 17, Des Moines, 1991-92, cubmaster pack 17, 1992-96, Webelos den leader 1993-96, scoutmaster troop 17, 1997—, commr. Hawkeye dist. Mid-Iowa coun., 1994-96, asst. dist. commr., 1997—, mem. com., chmn. roundtable, 1990-92; precinct chmn. Iowa Dem. Com., Des Moines, 1993—; mem., elder Christian Ch. (Disciples of Christ). Recipient Scouters award Prairie Gold coun. Boy Scouts Am., 1990, dist. award, 1991, merit cubmaster's award, 1996, Webelos den leader award, 1996, Commr.'s Key, Hawkeye dist., 1997, Arrowhead award, 1997. Avocations: jogging, swimming, boy scouting. Office: Polk County Atty's Office 111 Court Ave Rm 340 Des Moines IA 50309-2218

**FLAHERTY, DAVID THOMAS, JR.,** lawyer; b. Boston, June 17, 1953; S. David Thomas Sr. and Nancy Ann (Hamill) F.; children: Alexandra Lynn, David Thomas III. BS in Math., German, U. N.C., 1974, JD, 1978. Bar: Mass. 1979, N.C. 1979, U.S. Dist. Ct. (we. dist.) N.C. 1979, U.S. Dist. Ct. (mid. dist.) N.C. 1981, U.S. Ct. Appeals (4th cir.) 1981, U.S. Tax Ct. 1982, U.S. Supreme Ct., 1987, U.S. Ct. Fed. Claims, 1992. Assoc. Wilson & Palmer, Lenoir, N.C., 1979-80, Ted West P.A., Lenoir, 1980-82; ptnr. Robbins, Flaherty & Lackey, Lenoir, 1982-85, Robbins & Flaherty, Lenoir, 1985-88, Delk, Flaherty, Swanson & Hartshorn, P.A., Lenoir, 1988-89, Delk, Flaherty, Robbins, Swanson & Hartshorn, P.A., Lenoir, 1989-90, Flaherty, Robbins, Swanson & Hartshorn, P.A., 1990-95; dist. atty. 25th prosecutorial dist. Office Dist. Atty., Lenoir, 1995—; mem. N.C. Ho. of Reps., Raleigh, 1988-94, N.C. Cts. Commn., 1989—, N.C. Jud. Adv. Commn., 1997—. Mem. exec. com. Caldwell County Reps., Lenoir, 1985-86, 88—. Mem. N.C. Bar Assn., N.C. Conf. Dist. Attys., 25th Judicial Dist. Bar Assn. (mem. exec. com. 1987-88), Reps. Men's Club, Blue Key. Methodist. Avocations: water and snow skiing, motorcycling. Home: 228 Pennton Ave SW Lenoir NC 28645-4316 Office: Office of Dist Atty Caldwell County Courthouse PO Box 718 Lenoir NC 28645-0718

**FLAHERTY, JOHN PAUL, JR.,** state supreme court chief justice; b. Pitts., Nov. 19, 1931; s. John Paul and Mary G. (McLaughlin) F.; m. Linet Flaherty; 7 children, 2 stepchildren. BA, Duquesne U., 1953; JD, U. Pitts., 1958; LLD (hon.), Widener U., 1993. Bar: Pa. 1958. Pvt. practice Pitts., 1958-73; mem. faculty Carnegie-Mellon U., 1958-73; judge Ct. Common Pleas Allegheny County, 1973-79, pres. judge civil div., 1978-79; justice Supreme Ct. Pa., 1979-96, chief justice, 1996—; USIA speaker in Far East, 1985-86. Mem. Pa. Hist. Soc.; bd. visitors U. Pitts. Sch. Law; chair Pa. County Records Com. Recipient Medallion of Distinction U. Pitts., 1987; named Man of Yr. in law and govt., Greater Pitts. Jaycees, 1978, named to Century Club of Disting. Alumni, Duquesne U., 1994; recipient Judicial award Pa. Bar Assn., 1993. Mem. Pa. Acad. Sci. (chmn. hon. exec. bd. 1978-89, Disting. Alumnus award 1977), Am. Law Inst., Pa. Soc., Mil. History Soc. Ireland, Friendly Sons St. Patrick, Am. Legion. Office: Pa Supreme Ct 6 Gateway Ctr Pittsburgh PA 15222-1318 *The law is the energy of the living world, and although developed and defined by the judiciary in our Anglo-American society, it is applied and is derived by and from the people. It exists only to protect one person from being hurt, physically or economically, by another. Serious problems face our age. In the final analysis, the judiciary must accomodate the various solutions which will be forthcoming. I hope that my brothers have the foresight and the stamina to accomodate what might be quite novel innovations in the law, which is the living energy, to make this world a place in which it's worth living, since that is the function of the law. Every case involves people. There is no such thing as a small case.*

**FLAHERTY, KAREN JANET,** lawyer; b. Milw., May 17, 1956; d. Theodore Daniel and Barbara Jean Gabos; m. Michael Francis Flaherty, Sept. 3, 1983; children: Michael Francis, Timothy Daniel, Katherine Ann. BA, Mt. Mary Coll., Milw., 1977; JD, Marquette U., 1980. Bar: Wis., 1980, U.S. Dist. Ct. (ea., we. dists.) Wis., 1980, U.S. Ct. Appeals (7th cir.), 1994. Assoc. Levy & Levy S.C., Cedarburg, Wis., 1980-83; asst. city atty. City of Wauwatosa, Wis., 1983-85; assoc. Houseman & Feind, S.C., Grafton, Wis., 1989-93; asst. city atty. City of Brookfield, Wis., 1994—; adj. prof. Concordia U., Mequon, Wis., 1993. V.p. bd. dirs. Brookfield Soccer Assn., 1998. Recipient Svc. award Am. Legion, 1993. Mem. Assn. Women Lawyers, Wis. Bar Assn. (women in the bar com. 1988-95, membership com.), Waukesha Bar Assn. Avocations: travel, youth sports coach. Office: City of Brookfield 2000 N Calhoun Rd Brookfield WI 53005-5095

**FLAHERTY, ROBERT PATRICK,** lawyer; b. Louisville, Sept. 28, 1971; s. Verlin E. and Frances M. Flaherty. BA magna cum laude, U. Louisville, 1993; JD, Washington & Lee U., 1996. Bar: Ky. 1996, U.S. Dist. Ct. (we. dist.) Ky. 1998. Asst. ct. atty. Jefferson County Attys. Office, Louisville, 1996-97; assoc. O'Koon, Manifee & Gray, Louisville, 1997-98, Sholar & Assocs., Shepherdsville, Ky., 1998—. General practice. Home: 8841 Deer Path Cir Louisville KY 40220-1615 Office: Sholar & Assocs 129 W Fourth St Shepherdsville KY 40165

**FLAME, ANDREW JAY,** lawyer; b. Phila., Apr. 4, 1968; s. Sheldon Paul and Rita Ann Flame; m. Lori Jill Bolno, Nov. 17, 1996. BS in Mktg., Pa. State U., 1990; JD, Temple U., 1993. Bar: Pa. 1993, N.J. 1993, U.S. Dist. Ct. N.J. 1993, U.S. Dist. Ct. (ea. dist.) Pa. 1993, D.C. 1994, U.S. Dist. Ct. (mid. dist.) Pa. 1994. Law clk. to Hon. Louis Pollack U.S. Dist. Ct. (ea. dist.) Pa., Phila., 1992-93, law clk. to Hon. Stuart Dalzell, 1994; assoc. Drinker Biddle & Reath LLP, Phila., 1993—. Founder, Camp 4 Happy Days, Phila., 1985-86; trainer Youth Implemented Programs, San Francisco, 1988; trustee Reform Congregation Keneseth Israel, Phila., 1994—; mem. Golden Slipper Club Charity, Phila., 1994—; mem. com. Cheltenham Twp. (Pa.) Drug/Alcohol Bd., 1979-86, 91-93. Avocations: sports, travel. Bankruptcy, General civil litigation, Consumer commercial. Home: 148 Green Valley Cir Dresher PA 19025-1515 Office: Drinker Biddle & Reath LLP One Logan Square Philadelphia PA 19103

**FLAMM, ANNE LEDERMAN,** lawyer, bioethicist; b. N.Y.C., May 22, 1967; d. Richard J. and Barbara W. Lederman; m. Scott D. Flamm, Mar. 22, 1997. AB, Princeton U., 1989; JD, Case Western Res. U., 1995. Bar: Ohio 1995, U.S. Dist. Ct. (no. dist.) Ohio 1995. Credit trainee, analyst Chem. Bank, N.Y.C., 1989-90, account officer, 1990-91; pricing assoc. Progressive Ins. Co., Cleve., 1991-92; instr. The Princeton Rev., Cleve., 1991-94; assoc. Kahn, Kleinman, Yanowitz & Arnson, LPA, Cleve., 1995-98; bioethics fellow Cleve. Clinic Found., 1998—. Contbr. articles to profl. jours. Vice chair, mem. Cleve. Play House Crew, 1995—. Mem. Princeton Alumni Assn. No. Ohio (chair young alumni). Jewish.

**FLAMM, LEONARD N(ATHAN),** lawyer; b. Newark, May 23, 1943; s. Sydney Lewis and Lillian (Schreiber) F. Cert., London Sch. Econs., 1964; BA, Dartmouth Coll., 1965; JD, Harvard U., 1968. Bar: N.J. 1968, N.Y. 1970, U.S. Ct. Appeals (2d cir.) 1970, Fla. 1976, U.S. Dist. Ct. (so. and ea. dists.) N.Y. 1976, U.S. Ct. Appeals (7th cir.) 1986, U.S. Ct. Appeals (3d cir.) 1987, U.S. Supreme Ct. 1989. Assoc. Marshall, Bratter, Greene, Allison & Tucker, N.Y.C., 1968-70, Donovan, Leisure, Newton & Irvine, N.Y.C., 1970-72, Glass, Greenberg & Irwin, N.Y.C., 1972-75; ptnr. Hockert & Flamm, N.Y.C., 1975-90; pvt. practice N.Y.C., 1990—. Contbg. author Employee Rights Litigation: Pleadings and Practice, 1991. Named one of Best Lawyers in U.S., Town & Country Mag., 1985. Mem. Assn. Bar City N.Y. (legal referral panel 1975—), Nat. Employment Lawyers Assn. (v.p. N.Y. chpt., nat. co-chmn. Age Discrimination in Employment Act com.). Federal civil litigation, Labor, Civil rights. Home: 80 Roosevelt St Closter NJ 07624-2711 Office: 880 3rd Ave Ste 1300 New York NY 10022-4730

**FLANAGAN, JAMES HENRY, JR.,** lawyer; b. San Francisco, Sept. 11, 1934; s. James Henry Sr. and Mary Patricia (Gleason) F.; m. Charlotte Anne Nevins, June 11, 1960; children: Nancy, Christopher, Christina, Alexis, Victoria, Grace. AB in Polit. Sci., Stanford U., 1956, JD, 1961. Bar: Calif. 1962, U.S. Dist. Ct. (no. dist.) Calif. 1962, U.S. Ct. Appeals (9th cir.) 1962, U.S. Dist. Co. (so. dist.) Calif. 1964, U.S. Dist. Ct. (ea. dist.) Calif. 1967, Oreg. 1984. Assoc. Creede, Dawson & McElrath, Fresno, Calif., 1962-64; ptnr. Pettitt, Blumberg & Sherr and successor firms, Fresno, 1964-75; pvt. practice Clovis, Calif., 1975-92, North Fork, Calif., 1992—; instr. Humprey's Coll. Law, Fresno, 1964-69, bus. Calif. State U., Fresno, 1986—, Coll. of Notre Dame MPA prog., Belmont, 1990-91, Nat. U., 1991—, Emerson Inst., 1998—; judge pro tem Fresno County Superior Ct., 1974-77; gen. counsel Kings River Water Assn., 1976-79. Author: California Water District Laws, 1962. Mem. exec. com. parish coun. St. Helen's Ch., 1982-85, chmn. exec. com., 1985; pres. parish coun. St. John's Cathedral, 1974-82; pres. bd. dirs. 3d Fl. Ctrl. Calif.; bd. dirs. Fresno Facts Found., 1969-70, Fresno Dance Repertory Assn., St. Anthony's Retreat Ctr., Three Rivers, Calif.; pres. Inst. for Interactive Edn., Inc. (formerly Dispute Resolution Ctr. Ctrl. Calif.), 1988—; pres. Am. Benefit Devel. Corp., 1995-98; co-founder Am. Benefit Trust; active Clovis Big Dry Creek Hist. Soc. Recipient President award Fresno Jaycees, 1964. Mem. ATLA, Calif. Bar Assn., Fresno County Bar Assn., Calif. Trial Lawyers Assn. (chpt. pres. 1975, 83, mem. state bd. govs. 1990-94), Fresno Trial Lawyers Assn., Am. Arbitration Assn., Stanford Alumni Assn. (life, svc. award), Fresno Region Stanford Club (pres. 1979-80), Celtic Cultural Soc. Ctrl. Calif. (pres. 1977-78), Fresno county and City C. of C. (chmn. natural resources com. 1977-78), Clovis C. of C., North Fork C. of C. (pres. 1993-96, sec. 1998—), Serra Club (pres. Fresno chpt. 1980-81, v.p. 1986-87), Rotary, Elks. Republican. Roman Catholic. Avocations: writing, music, gardening, sailing, fishing. E-mail: jayflanagan@netptc.net. Alternative dispute resolution, General practice, Estate planning. Office: PO Box 1555 North Fork CA 93643-1555

**FLANAGAN, JOHN ANTHONY,** lawyer, educator; b. Sioux City, Iowa, Nov. 29, 1942; s. J. Maurice and Lorna K. (Fowler) F.; m. Martha Lang, May 8, 1982; children: Sean, Kathryn, Molly. BA, State U. of Iowa, 1964; JD, Georgetown U., 1968. Bar: Iowa 1968, D.C. 1975, Ohio 1977. Law clk. to judge U.S. Tax Ct., Washington, 1968-70; trial atty. U.S. Dept. Justice, Washington, 1970-74; prof. law U. Cin., 1974-78; sr. tax ptnr. Graydon, Head & Ritchey, Cin., 1978—; adj. prof. U. Cin., 1978--. Contbr. articles to profl. jours. Corp. mgr. United Way, Cin., 1988; head lawyers' div. Fine Arts Fund, Cin., 1987-88; mem. Downtown Cin. Inc. Mem. D.C. Bar Assn., Cin. Bar Assn., Order of Coif. Roman Catholic. Avocations: gardening, golf, fly fishing. Corporate taxation, Taxation, general, General corporate. Home: 5 Walsh Ln Cincinnati OH 45208-3435 Office: Graydon Head & Ritchey 1900 Fifth-Third Ctr PO Box 6464 Cincinnati OH 45202

**FLANAGAN, JOSEPH PATRICK, JR.,** lawyer; b. Wilkes-Barre, Pa., Sept. 18, 1924; s. Joseph P. and Grace B. F.; m. Mary Elizabeth Mayock, Aug. 5, 1950; children: Maureen Elizabeth, Joseph P. III. B.S., U.S. Naval Acad., 1947; J.D., U. Pa., 1952. Bar: Pa. 1953, U.S. Dist. Ct. (ea. dist.) Pa. 1953, U.S. Ct. Appeals (3d cir.) 1953, U.S. Supreme Ct. 1997. Assoc. Saul, Ewing, Remick & Saul, Phila., 1952-56; ptnr. Ballard, Spahr, Andrews & Ingersoll, Phila., 1956-94, chmn. pub. fin. dept., 1961-90. Editor: Practicing Law Inst., Health Facilities Financing, 1976; co-author: In Search of Capital-A Trustee's Guide to Hospital Financing; reviewing editor Disclosure Roles of Counsel in State and Local Government Securities Offerings. editor-in-chief: U. Pa. Law Rev., 1951-52; contbr. articles to profl. jours. Bd. dirs. Phila. Com. of 70, 1952-56; former trustee Wyoming Sem., Kingston, Pa.; former mem. bd. visitors U. Pa. Law Sch.; bd. dirs. John Bartram Assn.; adv. coun. of federalism Nat. Govs. Assn., 1988. Served to lt. (j.g.) USN, 1946-49. Fellow Am. Bar Found.; mem. NASD (regulation arbitrator 1998—), ABA (past chmn. urban, state and local govt. sect.), Phila. Bar Assn. (past chmn. bus. law sect., bd. govs., past founding chmn. tax exempt fin. com., past chmn. profl. edn. com., client's security fund com., fee disputes com.), Pa. Bar Assn., Pa. Bar Inst. (pres. 1983, chmn. curriculum and course planning com. 1976-88), Phila. Club, Racquet Club, Phila. Cricket Club, Corinthian Yacht Club, Chesapeake Bay Yacht Club, Army Navy Country Club of Va. Republican. Roman Catholic. Finance, Health. Home: 401 E Mill Rd Flourtown PA 19031-1631 Office: Ballard Spahr Andrews & Ingersoll 1735 Market St Fl 49 Philadelphia PA 19103-7501

**FLANAGAN, L. MARTIN,** lawyer; b. Greenville, S.C., Jan. 22, 1932; s. Leon Smith and Eloise (Martin) F.; m. Mary Georgie deSaussure, Feb. 5, 1955; children: Patrick B.; Michael C., Georgiana M., M. Kathleen. AB, The Citadel, 1953; LLB, U. Va., 1958, JD, 1970. Bar: S.C. 1958, Fla. 1959, U.S. Supreme Ct. 1971, U.S. Dist. Ct. S.C. 1958, U.S. Dist. Ct. (so. dist.) Fla. 1959, U.S. dist. Ct. (mid. dist.) Fla. 1989, U.S. Ct. Appeals (5th cir.) 1965, U.S. Ct. Appeals (11th cir.) 1988; cert. circuit ct. mediator. Clerk Jones, Adams, Paine & Foster, West Palm Beach, Fla., 1958-59, assoc., 1959-64, partner, 1964-75; shareholder Jones, Paine & Foster, P.A., West Palm Beach, 1975-80, Jones & Foster, P.A., West Palm Beach, 1980-89; shareholder Jones, Foster, Johnston & Stubbs P.A., West Palm Beach, 1989-91, of counsel, 1991—; of counsel Flanagan & Maniotis P.A., 1993—. Founder: Trial Advocate Quarterly, 1982, editorial bd. mem., 1982-91. Judge Palm Springs (Fla.) Municipality, 1960-65, Lake Clarke Shores (Fla.) Municipality, 1967; councilman Lake Clarke Shores, 1964-66; committeeman Rep. Exec. Com., Palm Beach County, 1964-74. Capt. U.S. Army, 1953-55. Recipient Execptional Performance citation Def. Rsch. Inst., 1982. Mem. ABA, Am. Bd. Trial Advocates (diplomate 1981-92). Fedn. Ins. and Corp. Counsel, Product Liability Adv. Coun., Fla. Def. Lawyers Assn. (pres. 1982), Fla. Bar, Palm Beach County Bar Assn., The Acad. of Fla. Trial Lawyers, Assn. Trial Lawyer Am. Republican. Presbyterian. Avocations: presidential political buttons, vintage fountain pens, vintage autos. Product liability, Personal injury. Home: 115 Russlyn Dr West Palm Beach FL 33405-3355 Office: Flanagan & Maniotis 2586 Forest Hill Blvd West Palm Beach FL 33406-5994

**FLANAGAN, LEO M., JR.,** lawyer; b. Chgo., Oct. 4, 1942; s. Leo Michael and Alice Corrine F.; m. Carol M. Tusek, Aug. 27, 1966; children: Keri Ann Castoro, Sean P. Flanagan. BA, Lewis U., 1965; JD, DePaul U., 1969. Bar: Ill. 1969, U.S. Dist. Ct. (no. dist.) 1969, U.S. Dist. Ct. (no. dist.) Ill. 1970. Lawyer Brittain & Ketcham P.C., Elgin, Ill., 1970—; bank dir. Elgin Fin. Savings Bank, 1982—; mediation judge No. Ill. U., De Kalb, 1998; v.p., dir. Accumation, Inc., Crystal Lake, Ill., 1971—. Mem. Kane County Bar Assn. (mem. Kane mediation panel 1997—). Avocations: coaching youth baseball and basketball. State civil litigation, General corporate, Family and matrimonial. Home: 196 Oakmont Dr Elgin IL 60123-4931 Office: Brittain & Ketcham PC 85 Market St Elgin IL 60123-5083

**FLANAGAN, MARI JO FLORIO,** lawyer; b. N.Y.C.; d. Michael and Josephine M. Florio; m. John F. Flanagan, Oct. 9, 1992; 1 child, Nathan C. Scopac. AB, Douglass Coll., 1970; JD, U. N.C., 1976. Counsel Olin Corp., Stamford, Conn., 1977-86; assoc. gen. counsel Savin Corp., Stamford, 1986-89; gen. counsel Lex Svc., Inc., Stamford, 1989-92; asst. gen. counsel VNU, USA, Inc., N.Y.C., 1992-97; v.p., gen. counsel, sec. Brink's, Inc., Darien, Conn., 1997—. Campaign counsel Flanagan for Congress, Westchester County, N.Y., 1992. Mem. Am. Corp. Counsel Assn., Corp. Bar, Conn. Women's Forum. Contracts commercial, Private international, Mergers and acquisitions. Office: Brink's Inc 1 Thorndal Cir Darien CT 06820-5425

**FLANAGAN, MICHAEL CHARLES,** lawyer; b. Walters, Okla., July 1, 1954; s. Funston Pershing and Frances Rita (Novotny) F.; children: Sarah, Bridget, Kristin, Jennifer, Brian. BS in Bus. and Acctg., Okla. State U., 1976; JD, Oklahoma City U., 1979. Bar: Okla. 1980, Colo. 1993. Acct. Hunter, Towe & Talbot, Oklahoma City, 1976-80; pvt. practice Walters, Okla., 1980—; pres. bd. dirs. Cotton County Law Libr., Walters, 1980—. Bd. dirs. Nat. Wheat Harvest Festival, Walters, 1985, 99; del. Cotton County Dem. Com., 1985; treas. Miss Walters Pageant, Inc., 1989—; pres. Walters Theatre Guild, 1985-90. Mem. Okla. Bar Assn. (probate code com. 1991—), Colo. Bar Assn., Cotton County Bar Assn. (pres. 1984-91, 98. Roman Catholic. Avocations: golf, chess, reading, computers. Contracts commercial, Probate, Real property. Home: PO Box 5 Lawton OK 73572-0005 Office: 217 N Broadway St Walters OK 73572-1225

**FLANAGAN, MICHAEL PERKINS,** lawyer; b. Kinston, N.C., Aug. 2, 1944; s. Roy Chetwynd and Beatrice (Murrey) F.; m. Mary Northup, Nov. 4, 1967 (div. June 1986); m. Louise Wood, June 23, 1990; 1 child, Katherine Gillie. BA, U. N.C., 1968, JD, 1971. Bar: Fla. 1971, N.C. 1972, U.S. Dist. Ct. (ea., mid., we. dists.) N.C., U.S. Ct. Appeals (4th cir.). Assoc. Granville Alley, Atty., Tampa, Fla., 1971, Ward, Tucker, Ward & Smith, New Bern, N.C., 1972-75; dir., shareholder Ward and Smith, P.A., New Bern, N.C., 1975—. Campaign chmn. Crave County Cancer Crusade, New Bern, 1973; active United Way, Greenville, N.C., 1988. Mem. N.C. Bar Assn. (bankruptcy sec., chmn. 1988-89), Ea. Carolina Yacht Club (commodore), New Bern Country Club. Bankruptcy. Office: Ward & Smith PA PO Box 8088 Greenville NC 27835-8088

**FLANARY, JAMES LEE,** lawyer; b. Kingsport, Tenn., Dec. 9, 1955; s. Charles K. and Ruth Imogene (Evans) F.; m. Carol Rawlins, Aug. 29, 1993; children: Paul William, Joshua Carl, Haley Michelle. BS, E. Tenn. State U., 1979; JD, U. Tenn., 1986. Bar: Tenn. 1986, U.S. Dist. Ct. (ea. dist.) Tenn. 1986. Assoc. Fogelsong, Cruze, Shope & Kerr, Knoxville, Tenn., 1986-87; ptnr. Hagood & Flanary, Knoxville, 1987-90; capt. USAF Judge Advocate Gen. Corps, 1990—; spl. judge Knox County Gen. Sessions Ct., Knoxville, 1987—. Capt. U.S. Army, 1979-83; maj. USAF, 1990—, Lt. Col., USAF, 1999; staff judge advocate, Air Forces Iceland, 1997-99; Military Judge, USAF (Wash. D.C.) 1999—. Mem. ABA, Tenn. Trial Lawyer's Assn., Knoxville Bar Assn. (One of Outstanding Young Men in Am.). Avocations: camping, golf, fishing, hiking. Contracts commercial, Criminal, Personal injury. Address: 508 Kincaid St Kingsport TN 37660-1424

**FLANDERS, ROBERT G., JR.,** state supreme court justice; b. Freeport, N.Y., July 9, 1949; m. Ann I. Walls, May 29, 1971; children: Danielle, Heather, Zachary. AB magna cum laude, Brown U., 1971; JD, Harvard Law Sch., 1974. Bar: N.Y. 1975, Mass. 1976, R.I. 1976, U.S. Ct. of Appeals (1st and 2d. cir.), U.S. Dist. Ct. (so. dist., ea. dist.) N.Y., R.I., Mass. Assoc. Paul, Weiss, Rifkind, Wharton & Garrison, N.Y.C., 1974-75; ptnr., chmn. litig. dept. Edwards & Angell, Providence, 1975-87; founding ptnr. Flanders & Medeiros Inc., 1987-96; assoc. justice R.I. Supreme Ct., 1996—. Contbr. articles to profl. publ. Bd. dirs. R.I. Pre-paid Legal Svcs. Corp., 1983—, Rsch. Engring. and Mfg. Inc., 1990—, Dunes Club, 1992-98, R. I. Bar Found., 1994—, Greater Providence YMCA, 1995—, Providence Performing Arts Ctr., 1997—. Mem. ABA. avocations: tennis, clarinet, jazz, poetry, cigars. Office: Rhode Island Supreme Ct 250 Benefit St Providence RI 02903-2719

**FLANNAGAN, BENJAMIN COLLINS, IV,** lawyer; b. Richmond, Va., Sept. 7, 1927; s. Benjamin Collins and Virginia Carolyn (Gay) F.; B.A., U. Va., 1947, M.A. in Econs., 1948, J.D., 1951; LL.M., Georgetown U., 1956. Admitted to Va. bar, 1951; trial atty. Justice Dept., Washington, 1955—, chief civil litigation unit, appellate and civil litigation sect., internal security div., 1971-73, spl. asst. internal security sect. criminal div., 1973-74, sr. trial atty. spl. litigation sect., 1974-79, sr. legal adv. gen. litigation and legal advice sect., 1979-93; retired 1993. Mem. editorial bd. Va. Law Rev., 1949-50, book rev. editor, 1950-51. Served to 1st lt. U.S. Army, 1952-55. Recipient Sustained Superior Service award Justice Dept., 1964, 74, 82, Spl. Commendation for Outstanding Service award criminal div., 1976, 84. Mem. Va. Bar Assn., Beta Gamma Sigma. Episcopalian. Clubs: Country of Va. (Richmond), Deep Run Hunt (Manakin-Sabot). Home: 210 Nottingham Rd Richmond VA 23221-3115

**FLANNERY, ELLEN JOANNE,** lawyer; b. Bklyn., Dec. 13, 1951; d. William Rowan and Mary Jane (Hamilla) Flannery. AB cum laude, Mount Holyoke Coll., 1973; JD cum laude, Boston U., 1978. Bar: Mass. 1978, D.C. 1979, U.S. Ct. Appeals (D.C. cir.) 1979, U.S. Ct. Appeals (4th cir.) 1981, U.S. Ct. Appeals (6th cir.) 1983, U.S. Ct. Appeals (3d cir.) 1987, U.S. Dist. Ct. D.C. 1980, U.S. Dist. Ct. Md. 1985, U.S. Supreme Ct. 1983. Spl. asst. to commr. of health Mass. Dept. Pub. Health, Boston, 1973-75; law clk. U.S. Ct. Appeals D.C. cir., Washington, 1978-79; assoc. Covington & Burling, Washington, 1979-86, ptnr., 1986—; lectr. ins. U. Va. Sch. Law, 1984-90, Boston U. Sch. Law, 1993, U. Md. Sch. Law, 1994; mem. Nat. Conf. Lawyers and Scientists, AAAS-ABA, 1989-92. Contbr. to articles to profl. jours. Fellow Am. Bar Found.; mem. ABA (chmn. com. med. practice 1987-88, chmn. life scis div. 1982-84, 88-91, vice chair food and drug law com. 1991-97, chmn. sect. sci. and tech. 1992-93, del. of sci. and tech. sect. to ho. of dels. 1993—, chmn. coordinating group on bioethics and the law 1998—). Product liability, Health, Administrative and regulatory. Office: Covington & Burling PO Box 7566 1201 Pennsylvania Ave NW Washington DC 20044

**FLANNERY, HARRY AUDLEY,** lawyer; b. New Castle, Pa., June 11, 1947; s. Wilbur Eugene and Ruth (Donaldson) F.; m. Maureen Louise Flaherty, June 28, 1969; children: Preston Wilbur, Courtney Lilyan. BA, Wesleyan U., 1969; JD, Ohio No. U., 1972; LLM in Taxation, Boston U., 1973. Bar: Pa. 1972, U.S. Tax Ct. 1973, U.S. Dist. Ct. (we. dist.) Pa. 1975, U.S. Supreme Ct. 1976, U.S. Ct. Appeals 1984. Sr. gen. svcs. specialist Pitts. Nat. Bank, 1973, asst. trust officer, 1974-75, trust legal officer, 1976; atty. Pa. Power Co., New Castle, 1977-98, FirstEnergy Corp., 1998—; sec. fed. and state polit. coms. Pa. Power Co., New Castle, 1983—; v.p. Euclid Manor Corp.; mem. panel arbitrators Bur. Mediation Dept. Labor and Industry. Assoc. editor Pitts. Legal Jour., 1981—; contbr. numerous articles to legal publs. Bd. dirs. Lawrence County chpt. Pa. Assn. for Blind, 1st v.p., 1994-96, pres. 1996-98; mem. Highland Presbyn. Ch., New Castle, Estate Planning Coun. of Pitts., 1975-77; sec. Lil Maur Found., 1989—; elected mem. sch. bd. dirs. Neshannock Twp. Sch. Bd., Pa., 1993—; mem. Pearson Park Commn., 1993-95; v.p. Neshannock Twp. Sch. Bd., Lawrence County, Pa., 1998—. Mem. ABA (labor and employment law sect. com. on labor arbitration and law of collective bargaining agreements, tax sect. 1973-92, com. excise and employment taxes, subcom. payroll tax issues 1978-80), Pa. Bar Assn. (workmen's compensation sect., adminstrv. law sect., labor and employment law sect., pub. utility law sect., in house counsel com. 1995-98, 99—, dispute resolution com. 1989-91, 99—), Allegheny County Bar Assn. (coun., taxation sect. 1975-77, labor law sect., workmen's compensation sect.), Pitts. Legal Jour. Com., Lawrence County Bar Assn., Allegheny Tax Soc., Pennsylvania Soc. (life), Am. Arbitration Assn., The Supreme Ct. Pa. Hist. Soc. (life, trustee 1994—, sec. 1995—, v.p. 1999—), Pa. Sch. Bd. Assn., Duquesne Club, Lawrence Club, New Castle Country Club, Lions (bd. dirs. 1982-91, tailtwister 1983-84, 3rd v.p. 1984-85, 2nd v.p. 1985, 1st v.p. 1986-87, pres. 1987-88), New Castle Lions Charities, Inc. (Lion of Yr. 1988-89), Phi Alpha Delta (life). Republican. Avocations: family, writing, tennis, boating. Workers' compensation, Public utilities, Labor. Home: 116 Valhalla Dr New Castle PA 16105-1037 Office: Pa Power Co 1 E Washington St New Castle PA 16101-3814

**FLANNERY, JOHN PHILIP,** lawyer; b. N.Y.C., May 15, 1946; s. John Philip and Agnes Geraldine (Applegate) F.; m. Bettina Gregory, Nov. 14, 1981. BS in Physics, Fordham Coll., 1967; BS in Engring., Columbia U., 1969, JD, 1972; student Art Students League, 1972-73. 1 child, Diana Elizabeth. Bar: N.Y. 1973, U.S. Dist. Ct. (so. dist.) N.Y. 1973, U.S. Ct. Appeals (2d cir.) 1973. Mem. staff Ford Found. Project to Restructure Columbia U., 1968; news rep. nat. press relations IBM, 1970; law clk. Adminstrv. Conf. U.S., 1971; law clk. U.S. Ct. Appeals 2d cir., 1972-74; asst. U.S. atty. Narcotics and Ofcl. Corruption units So. Dist. N.Y., 1974-79; sr. assoc. Poletti Freidin Prashker Feldman & Gartner, N.Y.C., 1979-82; spl. counsel U.S. Senate Judiciary Com., 1982; spl. counsel U.S. Senate Labor Com., 1982-83; Dem. candidate for U.S. Congress from Va. 10th Dist., 1983-84; sole practice in civil and criminal litigation, 1984—; spl. counsel Sen. Howard Metzenbaum, 1985-87; asst. dist. atty., Bronx, N.Y., 1986-87; counsel, bd. dirs. Washington Internat. Horse Show Assn., 1989-91; legal expert "Crime in D.C.", Fox-TV, 1993, "Crime Bill", Wis. Pub. Radio, 1994, "People vs. O.J. Simpson", ABC Network Radio, 1994-95, "Va.'s No Parole" Larry King Live CNN, 1994, "Imprisonment" CBS Morning Show, 1994, Habeas Reform Court T.V., 1996, Terrorism, 1996; spl. counsel U.S. House Judiciary Com., 1996-97; project dir., spl. counsel U.S. Edn. and Work Force Com., 1997-98; spl. coun. (impeachment proceedings) U.S. Rep. Zoe Lofgren, 1998—, lectr. in field. Committeeman Dem. Party N.Y. County, 1979-80; mem. legis. commn. Citizen's Union, 1971-72; mem. Arlington Transp. Commn., 1983-85; chmn. bus. coun. Va. Gov.'s War on Drugs Task Force, 1983-84; committeeman Dem. Party Arlington County, 1983-84; coord. N.Y. State Lawyers Com. for Senator Edward M. Kennedy, 1979-80; dir. Citizens for Senator M. Kennedy, 1980; pres. Franklin Soc., 1979-80; del. Dem. Nat. Conv., 1988, Va. Assembly U. W.Va., 1990; committeeman Loudoun County Dem. Com., 1995—, sec. 1995—, chmn., 1995-97; del. 10th Congress and Dist. Com., 1997—; mem. Ctrl. State (Va.) Com., 1997—. Recipient U.S. Justice Dept. award for Outstanding Contbns. in the Field of Drug Law Enforcement 1977; U.S. Atty. Gen.'s Spl. Commendation for Outstanding Svc., 1979, FLEOA Award, Fed. Law Enforcement Officer's Assn., 1984, NACDL's Marshall Stern Award Outstanding Legis. Achievement, 1997; Mem. ABA, Bar Assn. of City of N.Y., N.Y. County Lawyers Assn., Arlington County Bar Assn., Loudon County Bar Assn., Nat. Assn. Criminal Def. Lawyers (chair briefbank com. 1990-91, legis. co-chair 1991—, dir. 1993—, President's commendation 1991, 92, 95), Acad. Polit. Sci., Va. Coll. Criminal Def. Attys. (bd. dirs. 1993-96). Democrat. Author: Commercial Information Brokers, 1973; Habeas Corpus Bores Hole in Prisoners' Civil Rights Action, 1975; Pro Se Litigation, 1975; Prison Corruption: A Mockery of Justice, 1980; Conspiracy: A Primer, 1988, Is Innocence Relevant to Execution? If Not, Isn't that Murder?, 1994, Equal Justice For All, 1995, Virginia Governor Allen's No-Parole Plan: A Billion Dollar Wasteland of Prisons, 1995. Home: Shamrock Farm 38138 Forest Mills Rd Leesburg VA 20175-9146 Office: Rep Zoe Lofgren 318 Cannon House Off Bldg Washington DC 20515-0001

**FLANNERY, THOMAS AQUINAS,** federal judge; b. Washington, May 10, 1918; s. John J. and Mary (Sullivan) C.; m. Rita Sullivan, Mar. 3, 1951; children: Thomas Aquinas, Irene M. LL.B., Cath. U., 1940. Bar: D.C. 1940. Practice in Washington, 1940-42, 45-48; trial atty. Dept. Justice, Washington, 1948-50; asst. U.S. Atty. Washington, 1950-62; ptnr. Hamilton and Hamilton Washington, 1962-69; U.S. atty for D.C. Washington, 1969-71; U.S. dist. judge for D.C., 1971-85; now sr. judge U.S. Dist. Ct. for D.C., 1985-99. Served as combat intelligence officer USAF, 1942-45, ETO. Fellow Am. Coll. Trial Lawyers; Mem. Am., D.C. bar assns. Office: US Dist Ct US Courthouse 333 Constitution Ave NW Washington DC 20001-2802

**FLASTER, RICHARD JOEL,** lawyer; b. N.Y.C., Jan. 7, 1943; s. Charles and Sylvia (Moss) F.; m. Esther S. Stomel; children: Kiva Moss, Eben Scott. BS in Econs., U. Pa., 1963; JD, Harvard U., 1966. Bar: N.Y. 1967, U.S. Tax Ct. 1971, N.J. 1972, D.C. 1972. Law clk. to judge U.S. Dist Ct. (ea. dist.), N.Y., 1966-68; Reginald Heber Smith fellow U. Pa., 1968-69; assoc. Stroock & Stroock & Lavan, N.Y.C., 1969-72; pres. Liebman & Flaster, P.C., Cherry Hill, N.J., 1972-86, Flaster, Greenberg et. al., Cherry Hill, N.J., 1986—; bd. dirs. Jefferson Bank, N.J.; mem. adv. bd. Living Arts Repertory Theatre; frequent lectr. on various tax subjects ABA, N.J. Inst. Continuing Legal Edn.$d, Harvard U., 1966. Bar: N.Y. 1967, U.S. Tax Ct. 1971, N.J. 1972, D.C. 1972. Law clk. to judge U.S. Dist. Ct. (ea. dist.) N.Y., 1966-68; Reginald Heber Smith fellow U. Pa., 1968-69; assoc. Stroock & Stroock & Lavan, N.Y.C., 1969-72; pres. Liebman & Flaster, P.C., Cherry Hill, N.J., 1972-86; pres. Flaster, Greenberg, Wallenstein, Roderick, Spirgel, Zuckerman, Skinner & Kirchner P.C., Cherry Hill, N.J., 1986—; bd. dirs. Jefferson Bank, N.J.; mem. bd. advisors Living Arts Repertory Theatre; frequent lectr. on various tax subjects ABA, N.J. Inst. Continuing Legal Edn. Mem. N.J. State Bar Assn., N.Y. State Bar Assn., Washington D.C. Bar Assn. Beta Gamma Sigma, Beta Alpha Psi, Pi Gamma Mu. Author: Basic Federal Tax Aspects of Real Estate Transactions, 1976, Tax Aspects of Separation and Divorce, 1982; tax editor N.J. Family Lawyer, 1982-92; editor Tax & Business Report, 1987—. Author: Basic Federal Tax Aspects of Real Estate Transactions, 1976, Tax Aspects of Separation and Divorce, 1982; tax editor N.J. Family Lawyer, 1982-92; editor Tax & Business Report, 1987—. Mem. N.J. State Bar Assn., Washington D.C. Bar Assn., Beta Gamma Sigma, Beta Alpha Psi, Pi Gamma Mu. Corporate taxation, Estate taxation. Office: Flaster Greenberg et al 1735 Market St 3 Mellon Bank Ctr Fl 39 Philadelphia PA 19103

**FLATTERY, THOMAS LONG,** lawyer, legal administrator; b. Detroit, Nov. 14, 1922; s. Thomas J. and Rosemary (Long) F.; m. Gloria M. Hughes, June 10, 1947 (dec.); children: Constance Marie, Carol Dianne Lee, Michael Patrick, Thomas Hughes, Dennis Jerome, Betsy Ann Sprecher; m. Barbara J. Balfour, Oct. 4, 1986. BS, U.S. Mil. Acad., 1947; JD, UCLA, 1955; LLM, U. So. Calif., 1965. Bar: Calif. 1955, U.S. Patent and Trademark Office 1957, U.S. Customs Ct. 1968, U.S. Supreme Ct. 1974, Conn. 1983, N.Y. 1984. With Motor Products Corp., Detroit, 1950, Equitable Life Assurance Soc., Detroit, 1951, Bohn Aluminum & Brass Co., Hamtramck, Mich., 1952; mem. legal staff, asst. contract adminstr. Radioplane Co. (divsn. Northrop Corp.), Van Nuys, Calif., 1955-57; successively corp. counsel, gen. counsel, asst. sec. McCulloch Corp., L.A., 1957-64; sec., corp. counsel Technicolor, Inc., Hollywood, Calif., 1964-70; successively corp. counsel, asst. sec., v.p., sec. and gen. counsel Amcord, Inc., Newport Beach, Calif., 1970-72; v.p., sec., gen. counsel Schick Inc., L.A., 1972-75; counsel, asst. sec. C.F. Braun & Co., Alhambra, Calif., 1975-76; sr. v.p., sec., gen. counsel Automation Industries, Inc. (now PCC Tech. Industries Inc. a unit of Penn Cen. Corp.), Greenwich, Conn., 1976-86; v.p., gen. counsel G&H Tech., Inc. (a unit of Penn Cen. Corp.), Santa Monica, Calif., 1986-93; temp. judge Mcpl. Ct. Calif. L.A. Jud. Dist. and Santa Monica Unified Cts., 1987—; settlement officer L.A. Superior and Mcpl. Cts., 1991—; pvt. practice, 1993—; panelist Am. Arbitration Assn., 1991—; jud. arbitrator and mediator Alternative Dispute Resolution Programs L.A. Superior and Mcpl. Cts, 1993—, Calif. Ct. Appeals 2d Appellate Dist., 1999—. Contbr. articles to various legal jours. Served to 1st lt. AUS, 1942-50. Mem. ABA, Nat. Assn. Secs. Dealers, Inc (bd. arbitrators 1996, mediators 1997), State Bar Calif. (co-chmn. corp. law dept. com. 1978-79, lectr. continuing legal edn. program), L.A. County Bar Assn. (chmn. corp. law dept. com. 1966-67), Century City Bar Assn. (chmn. corp. law dept. com. 1979-80), Conn. Bar Assn., Santa Monica Bar Assn., N.Y. State Bar Assn., Am. Soc. Corp. Secs. (L.A. regional group pres. 1973-74), L.A. Intellectual Property Law Assn., Am. Ednl. League (trustee 1988—, sec. 1998—), L.A. West Am. Inn of Ct., West Point Alumni Assn., Army Athletic Assn., L.A. West Am. Inn of Ct., Friendly Sons St. Patrick, Jonathan Club (dir. 1996—), Braemar Country Club, Phi Alpha Delta. Roman Catholic. Alternative dispute resolution, General corporate, Intellectual property. Home and Office: 439 Via De La Paz Pacific Palisades CA 90272-4633

**FLAUM, JOEL MARTIN,** federal judge; b. Hudson, N.Y., Nov. 26, 1936; s. Louis and Sally (Berger) F.; m. Delilah Brummet, June 4, 1989; children from previous marriage: Jonathan, Alison. BA, Union Coll., Schenectady, 1958; JD, Northwestern U., 1963, LLM, 1964. Bar: Ill. 1963. Asst. state's atty. Cook County, Ill., 1965-69, 1st asst. atty. gen. Ill., 1969-72; 1st asst. U.S. atty. Chgo., 1972-75; judge U.S. Dist. Ct. (no. dist.) Ill., Chgo., 1975-83, U.S. Ct. Appeals (7th cir.), 1983—; adj. prof. Northwestern U. Sch. Law, 1993—; lectr. DePaul U. Coll. of Law, 1987-88; mem. Ill. Law Enforcement Commn., 1970-72; cons. U.S. Dept. Justice, Law Enforcement Assistance Adminstrn., 1970-71. Mem.: Northwestern U. Law Rev., 1962-63; contbr. articles to legal jours. Mem. vis. com. U. Chgo. Law Sch., 1983-86, Northwestern U. Sch. Law, 1983—; mem. adv. com. USCG Acad., 1990-93. Lt. comdr. JAGC, USNR, 1981-92. Ford Found. fellow, 1963-64. Fellow Am. Bar Found. (life); mem. ABA, Fed. Bar Assn., Ill. Bar Assn., Chgo. Bar Found. (life), 7th Cir. Bar Assn., Chgo. Inn of Ct., Chgo. Bar Assn., Maritime Law Assn., Navy-Marine Corps Ret. Judge Advs. Assn., Am. Judicature Soc., Naval Res. Assn., Legal Club Chgo., Law Club Chgo. Jewish. Office: US Ct Appeals 7th Ct 219 S Dearborn St Chicago IL 60604-1702

**FLAXMAN, KENNETH N.,** lawyer; b. N.Y.C., Apr. 30, 1948; s. Abraham A. and Muriel (Sussman) F.; m. Judith G. Safran, May 30, 1968; children: Abie, Joel, Seth. BE in Elec. Engring., CUNY, 1968; JD, Ill. Inst. Tech., 1972. Bar: Ill. 1972, N.C. 1978, U.S. Supreme Ct. 1975, U.S. Ct. Appeals (7th cir.) 1972, U.S. Ct. Appeals (D.C. cir.) 1973, U.S. Ct. Appeals (4th cir.) 1975, U.S. Ct. Appeals (3d cir.) 1976, U.S. Dist. Ct. (no. dist.) Ill. 1972. Staff atty. Bus. and Profl. People for the Pub. Interest, Chgo., 1972-73; pvt. practice law Chgo., 1973—. Civil rights, Federal civil litigation, Constitutional. Home: 2310 Grant St Evanston IL 60201-2109 Office: 122 S Michigan Ave Chicago IL 60603-6191

**FLAYHART, MARTIN ALBERT,** lawyer; b. Williamsport, Pa., Mar. 1, 1950; s. William Henry and Naomi (Laux) F. BA with hons., U. Va., 1971; JD, U. Pa., 1974. Bar: Pa. 1974, U.S. Dist. Ct. (mid. dist.) Pa. 1976, U.S. Ct. Appeals (3rd cir.) 1985, U.S. Supreme Ct. 1986. Assoc. Smith & Williamson, Lock Haven, Pa., 1974-76; ptnr. Saxton & Flayhart, Lock Haven, 1977-83; dist. atty. Clinton County, Lock Haven, 1979; pvt. practice Jersey Shore, Pa., 1983-84; ptnr. Carpenter, Harris & Flayhart, Jersey Shore, 1984—; lectr. Lock Haven U., 1981-85, 90, Lycoming Coll., Williamsport, Pa., 1993-94, State U. of Chernivtsi Law Sch., Ukraine, 1993. Pres. Jersey Shore Area C. of C., Pa., 1990; com. Lycoming County Dem. Party, 1988-98. Mem. ABA, Fed. Bar Assn., Lycoming County Bar Assn., Pa. Bar Assn., Rotary (pres. Lock Haven club 1991, Rotarian of Yr. 1990), Phi Beta Kappa. Methodist. Avocation: rare book collecting. General practice. Office: Carpenter Harris & Flayhart PO Box 505 128 S Main St Jersey Shore PA 17740-1810

**FLECK, JOHN R.,** lawyer; b. Huntington, Ind., Oct. 9, 1944; s. Ford Bloom and Deloris (Morrison) F.; m. Susan E., Dec. 31, 1975; children: Todd., Heather Fleck Erekson, Jeremy W. BA, Purdue U., 1966; JD, Ind. U., 1971. Bar: Ind. 1971, U.S. Supreme Ct. 1976, U.S. Dist. Ct. (no. and so. dists.) Ind. 1971. Law clk. Allen Superior Ct., Ft. Wayne, Ind., 1971-72; pvt. practice law Ft. Wayne, 1972—; adj. prof. Ind. U., Ft. Wayne, 1972-75; assoc. city atty. City of Ft. Wayne, 1972-75; atty. Town of Markle, Ind., 1975-80; city atty. City of New Haven, 1998—. Bd. dirs. Canterbury Sch., Ft. Wayne, 1988—; pres., bd. dirs. United Cerebral Palsy, Ft. Wayne, 1972—. Criminal. Office: 625 Lincoln Tower Fort Wayne IN 46802

**FLECK, (KEVIN) SEAN,** lawyer; b. Noblesville, Ind., July 13, 1956; s. Albert James and Mary Ellen (Rossman) F.; m. Cynthia Jo Allen, Aug. 11, 1979 (div. 1988); 1 child, Erin Marie; m. Donna Jean Early, Nov. 23, 1989; children: Colin Patrick, Mary Kathleen, John Reilly (Jack), Michael McNeely. BS, Purdue U., 1977; JD, Ind. U., 1980. Bar: Ind. 1981, U.S. Dist. Ct. (so. dist.) Ind. 1981. Farmer Noblesville, 1969-78; ptnr. Holt, Fleck & Free, Noblesville, 1981—. Del. Ind. Rep. State Conv., Indpls., 1982—; bd. dirs. Hamilton County ARC, Noblesville, 1984-90, Hamilton County Coun. on Aging, 1991-92; precinct committeeman Hamilton County Rep. Party, 1990—; mem. Hamilton County Alcoholic Beverage Commn., 1992—, chmn., 1993—. Recipient Award of Appreciation Hamilton County ARC, 1988-89, Disaster Relief award, 1990-91, pro bono award Ind. bar Found., 1991. Mem. Ind. State Bar Assn., Hamilton County Bar Assn. (legal aid adminstr. 1981-94, pres. 1998—), Noblesville Midday Rotary, Noblesville Elks, Noblesville C. of C., Fishers C. of C., KC. Roman Catholic. Avocations: reading, music. Probate, General corporate, Estate planning. Office: Holt Fleck & Free 83 S 9th St Noblesville IN 46060-2610

**FLEEMAN, MARY GRACE,** lawyer, librarian; b. Morgantown, W.Va., Aug. 24, 1947; d. George Ellis and Mary Jane (Stackpole) Moore; m. Keith Patrick Fleeman, Oct. 25, 1980. B.S., Allegheny Coll., 1969; M.S. in L.S., U. N.C., 1971; M.S.M., Frostburg State Coll., 1979; J.D. with highest honors, George Washington U., 1985. Library fellow U. N.C., Chapel Hill, 1970-71; asst. exchange and gift librarian U.S. Geol. Survey, Reston, Va., 1971-73, serials cataloger, 1973-74; cataloger Frostburg State Coll. (Md.), 1974-79; serials cataloger U. Okla., Norman, 1979-80; head cataloger George Washington U. Law Library, Washington, 1980-85; assoc. Arnold & Porter, Washington, 1985-92, spl. counsel, 1993—. Mem. ABA, Md. State Bar Assn., D.C. Bar Assn., Order of Coif. Beta Phi Mu, Alpha Xi Delta. Taxation, general, Pension, profit-sharing, and employee benefits, Corporate taxation. Office: Arnold & Porter 555 12th St NW Washington DC 20004-1206

**FLEISCHER, ARTHUR, JR.,** lawyer; b. Hartford, Conn., Jan. 27, 1933; s. Arthur and Clare Lillian (Katzenstein) F.; m. Susan Abby Levin, July 6, 1958; children: Elizabeth, Katherine. BA, Yale U., 1953, LLB, 1958. Bar: N.Y. 1959. Assoc. Strasser, Spiegelberg, Fried & Frank, N.Y.C., 1958-61; legal asst. SEC, Washington, 1961-62; exec. asst. to chmn. SEC, 1962-64; assoc. Fried, Frank, Harris, Shriver & Jacobson, N.Y.C., 1964-67, ptnr., 1967—, chmn., 1989-97, sr. ptnr., 1997—; vis. lectr. law Columbia U., N.Y.C., 1972-73; adviser to adv. com. Fed. Securities Code Project, Am. Law Inst., 1970-78; adviser to com. to consider new issue proposals Nat. Assn. Securities Dealers, 1973-75, mem. com. corp. financing, 1976-80; bd. dirs. Haleakala, Inc. (The Kitchen), N.Y.; chmn. Ann. Inst. on Securities Regulation, Practising Law Inst., 1969-81; mem. indsl. issuers adv. com. SEC, 1972-73; mem. adv. com. corp. disclosure, 1976-77; bd. govs. Am. Stock Exch., 1977-83; legal adv. com, bd. dirs. N.Y. Stock Exch., 1987-91; mem. adv. bd. J. Ira Harris Ctr. Mich. Bus. Sch. Co-author: Tender Offers, 1978, 5th edit., 1995, Board Games, 1988; co-editor: Annual Institute on Securities Regulation, 1970-81; contbr. articles to profl. jours. Mem. adv. coun. Ctr. for study of fin. instns. U. Pa., 1969—; trustee, mem. photography com. of Whitney Mus.; trustee Ind. Curators, Internat. Recipient Disting. Cmty. Svc. award Brandeis U., 1983, Judge Learned Hand Human Rels. award Am. Jewish Com., 1983, Harold P. Seligson award Practicing Law Inst., 1988, Judge Joseph W. Proskauer award UJA Fedn., 1994. Mem. ABA (mem. com. on fed. regulation of securities regulation 1969—), Assn. Bar City N.Y. (mem. spl. com. on lawyers role in securities transactions 1973-77, chmn. com. securities regulation 1972-74), Century Country Club (N.Y.C.). Home: 1050 Park Ave New York NY 10028-1031 Office: Fried Frank Harris 1 New York Plz Fl 22 New York NY 10004-1980

**FLEISCHER, ELIZABETH B.,** lawyer; b. Washington, Sept. 30, 1962. BA, Yale U., 1984; JD, NYU, 1987. Bar: N.Y. 1988, Washington, 1989. Assoc. Shereff, Friedman, Hoffman & Goodman, N.Y.C., Cadwalader, Wickersham & Taft, N.Y.C.; atty. Paine Webber Inc., Weehawken, N.J., 1994—. Securities, General corporate. Office: Paine Webber Inc 1000 Harbor Blvd Fl 8 Weehawken NJ 07087-6790

**FLEISCHER, HUGH WILLIAM,** lawyer; b. Riverside, Calif., Aug. 14, 1938; s. Frederick John and Helen Marie (Bendorf) F.; m. Lanie Lacey, May 31, 1960; children: Robin, Erin, Ian. BA, Washington U., St. Louis, 1961; JD, U. Denver, 1964. Bar: Colo. 1964, U.S. Supreme Ct. 1970, Alaska, 1971, Mo. 1972. Atty. U.S. Dept. Justice, Washington, 1964-70, Alaska Legal Svcs. Corp., Anchorage, 1971-72; atty., adviser St. Louis Legal Aid Soc., 1972; ptnr. Hedland, Fleischer, Friedman, Brennan & Cooke, Anchorage, 1972-96. Co-dir., McGovern for Pres. campaign, Anchorage, 1972; pres. Bartlett Dem. Club, Anchorage, 1987; bd. dirs. Alaska Pub. Interest Group, 1974—, Out North Theater, 1988-94; pres. Anchorage Friends of Library, 1989-92. Avocations: reading, mountain climbing. Criminal, Labor, Personal injury. Home: 1401 W 11th Ave Anchorage AK 99501-4248 Office: 310 K St Ste 200 Anchorage AK 99501-2064

**FLEISCHER, STEVEN H.,** lawyer; b. Somerville, N.J., Dec. 6, 1956; s. Paul and Ruth F.; m. Judith A. Latourette, July 25, 1987; 1 child, Arielle N. JD, Capital U., 1983. Bar: N.J. 1983. Ptnr. Fleischer, Fleischer & Lainer, Somerville, 1983—. Mem. Somerset County Bar Assn. (sec. young lawyers div. 1993). Civil rights, Family and matrimonial, Personal injury. Office: Fleischer Fleischer & Lainer 25 N Bridge St Ste 1 Somerville NJ 08876-2178

**FLEISCHLI, GEORGE ROBERT,** lawyer; b. Springfield, Ill., Aug. 23, 1940; s. Edward Constantine and Margaret Dorothy (Troesch) F.; m. Ann Elizabeth Malmer, Nov. 5, 1966; children: Mary Elizabeth, Margaret Ann. BS, U. Ill., 1962, JD with honors, 1965, MA in Labor Rels., 1970. Bar: Ill. 1965, Wis. 1971. Rsch. asst. U. Ill., Urbana, 1965-66, 69-70; mediator, examiner employee rels. commn. State of Wis., Madison, 1970-75, gen. counsel employee rels. commn., 1976-81; pvt. practice Madison, 1981—; instr., guest speaker U. Wis., Madison. Contbr. articles to profl. jours. Capt. USAF, 1966-69. Mem. Ill. Bar Assn., Wis. Bar Assn., Nat. Acad. Arbitrators (chmn. legal affairs com. 1978-90, bd. govs. 1990-93, chmn. com. profl. responsibility and grievance 1994-97, v.p. 1997-99), Order of Coif. Labor, Administrative and regulatory. Office: 131 W Wilson St Ste 1100 Madison WI 53703-3245

**FLEISCHMAN, EDWARD HIRSH,** lawyer; b. Cambridge, Mass., June 25, 1932; s. Louis Isaac and Jean (Grossman) F.; m. Joan Barbara Walden, Dec. 27, 1953 (dec. 1993), m. Judy Vernon, Sept. 27, 1998. BA, Harvard U.; LLB, Columbia U., 1959. Bar: N.Y. 1959, U.S. Supreme Ct. 1980. Assoc. Beekman & Bogue, N.Y.C., 1959-67, ptnr., 1968-86; commr. SEC, Washington, 1986-92; ptnr. Rosenman & Colin, 1992-94; sr. counsel Linklaters & Paines, N.Y.C., 1994—; adj. prof. NYU Law Sch., 1976—; bd. dirs. Wit Capital Group, Inc. Served with U.S. Army, 1952-55. Mem. ABA (chmn. internat. law com. on internat. securities transactions 1999—, bus. law com. on counsel responsibility 1995-99, com. on devels. in bus. financing 1987-91, subcom. model simplified indenture 1980-83, adminstrv. law com. on securities, commodities and exchs. 1981-84, bus. law subcom. broker-dealer matters 1973-78, subcom. rule 144 1970-72), Am. Law Inst., Am. Coll. Investment Counsel (pres. 1990-91), Am. Soc. Corp. Secs., Internat. Bar Assn., Internat. Law Assn. (chmn. com. on internat. securities regulation 1998—), Security Traders Assn. (bd. govs.). Republican. Jewish. Securities, Administrative and regulatory, Private international. Office: Linklaters 1345 6th Ave New York NY 10105-0302 Home: 897 Franklin Lake Rd Franklin Lakes NJ 07417-2115

**FLEISCHMAN, HERMAN ISRAEL,** lawyer; b. Bklyn., Aug. 30, 1950; s. Boris and Bella (Weisbrot) F.; m. Francine Moskowitz, Feb. 3, 1973; children: Meredith, Brandon, Gary. BA, Bklyn. Coll., 1972; JD, Bklyn. Sch. Law, 1976; MPA, NYU, 1974. Bar: N.Y. 1977, U.S. Dist. Ct. (ea., so., we. and no. dists.) N.Y. 1977, U.S. Ct. Appeals (D.C. cir.) 1979, U.S. Tax Ct. 1982. Asst. counsel Amalgamated Ins. Co., N.Y.C., 1976; asst. spl. atty. gen. State of N.Y., N.Y.C., 1977-79; asst. counsel N.Y. State Dept. Mental

Hygiene, Staten Island, N.Y., 1979; assoc. Ackerman, Salwen & Glass, N.Y.C., 1979-80; sole practice N.Y.C., 1980—. Mem. Thomas Jefferson Dem. Club, Bklyn., 1983-85; chmn. B'nai Brith Youth Orgn., 1980-82; bd. dirs. Big Apple Region, vice chmn., 1986-88, bd. dirs. Nassau and Suffolk Counties, N.Y., 1990-98. Recipient Citation, Town of Hempstead, 1986, Dist. Key award, B'nai B'rith Youth Org., 1979, Man of Yr. award, B'nai B'rith Youth Org., 1980; named Coach of Yr., North Merrick-North Bellmore Basketball League, 1998. Mem. ABA, ATLA, N.Y. State Bar Assn., Bklyn. Bar Assn., United Mut. Industries, Inc. (pres. 1983—). General practice, General civil litigation, Personal injury.

**FLEISCHMAN, KEITH MARTIN,** lawyer; b. Newark, June 13, 1958. BA, U. Vt., 1980; JD, Calif. Western U., 1984. Bar: N.Y. 1985, U.S. Dist. Ct. (so. dist.) N.Y. 1986, U.S. Ct. Appeals (2d cir.) 1989, U.S. Ct. Appeals (11th cir.) 1995. Asst. dist. atty. Bronx (N.Y.) County Dist. Atty., Rackets and Maj. Offense, 1984-88; trial atty. U.S. Dept. Justice, Dallas Bank Fraud Task Force, Washington, 1988-90; asst. U.S. atty. U.S. Atty. Office, Dist. Conn., 1990-92; trial lawyer, ptnr. Milberg Weiss Bershad Hynes & Lerach LLP, N.Y.C., 1992—; inst., lectr. trial practice U.S. Dept. Justice, Washington, 1990-91. Coord. com. mem. New England Bank Fraud Task Force, Dist. Conn., 1990-92. Avocations: skiing, climbing. Securities, Civil rights, General civil litigation. Office: Milberg Weiss Bershad Hynes & Lerach LLP One Pennsylvania Plaza New York NY 10119

**FLEISCHMANN, ROGER JUSTICE,** lawyer; b. Buffalo, Sept. 23, 1934; s. Edwin and Clover Fleischmann; m. Martha Ann Stennis, June 27, 1959; children: Roger J. Jr., Susan. BA magna cum laude, Harvard U., 1956, LLB, 1959. Bar: Calif. 1960, U.S. Dist. Ct. (no. dist.) Calif. 1960, U.S. Supreme Ct. 1967. Assoc. Bledsoe E. Smith, San Francisco, 1960-62; assoc. Graham & James, San Francisco, 1962-68, ptnr., 1968-69, pvt. practice, 1969-79, 98—; ptnr. Fleischmann & Fleischmann, San Francisco, 1979-98; lectr. Golden Gate U. Sch. Law, 1973. Co-author: Countertrade: International Trade Without Cash, 1983. Mem. Mayor's Task Force on Fgn. Investment, San Francisco, 1985-86; commr. Asian Art Mus., 1986-92. With U.S. Army, 1959-64. Mem. Calif. State Bar Assn., San Francisco Bar Assn., Japan Soc. (pres. 1979-80, bd. dirs. 1976-99). Avocations: golf, tennis, travel, hiking. E-mail: rjf@rjflawoffices.com. Contracts commercial, Private international, Product liability. Home: 12 Lower Dr Mill Valley CA 94941-1418 Office: 1 Maritime Plz Fl 4 San Francisco CA 94111-3404

**FLEISCHMANN, THOMAS JOSEPH,** lawyer; b. Saginaw, Mich., Oct. 6, 1947; s. Clarence W. and Catherine L. (Byrne) F.; m. Mary E. Walker, Dec. 29, 1973. BS, U. Dayton, 1969; JD, Boston U., 1972. Bar: Ohio, 1972, Mich., 1972, U.S. Dist. Ct. (ea. dist.) Mich. 1973, Ill. 1979, U.S. Ct. Appeals (6th and 7th cir.) 1980, U.S. Dist. Ct. (no. dist.) Ill. 1982, U.S. Supreme Ct. 1985. Asst. Prosecuting Atty., Jackson, Mich., 1972-73; atty. Adams, Goler & Boham, Jackson, Mich., 1973-75, Aymond, Sullivan & Schwartz, Jackson, Mich., 1975-78; spl. atty. criminal divsn. U.S. Dept. Justice, Chgo., 1978-80; ptnr. Rooks, Pitts & Poust, Chgo., 1980-85; atty., founding owner Gessler, Flynn, Fleischman, Hughes & Socol, Ltd., Chgo., 1985-95; pvt. practice Chgo., 1995—; lectr. Ill. Inst. Continuing Edn.; spl. teaching faculty, lectr. Jackson (Ill.) C.C., 1972-74. Bd. dirs. Fox River chpt. ARC, 1995—. Recipient Meritorious award U.S. Dept. Justice, 1979. Mem. ABA, Kane County Bar Assn., Abraham Lincoln Marovitz Inn of Ct. (founding officer, recording officer 1994-95). Federal civil litigation, Personal injury, Professional liability. Office: 35 E Wacker Dr Ste 1212 Chicago IL 60601-2109

**FLEISHER, STEVEN M.,** lawyer; b. Chgo., Feb. 5, 1945; s. Max M. and Meta J. (Shifris) F.; m. Marilyn J. Eto, Sept. 2, 1984. AB cum laude, Yale U., 1966; JD cum laude, Harvard U., 1969. Bar: Calif. 1970, U.S. Ct. Appeals (9th cir.) 1970, U.S. Dist. Ct. (no. dist.) Calif. 1970, D.C. 1973, U.S. Ct. Appeals (D.C. cir.) 1973, U.S. Supreme Ct. 1973. Law clk. U.S. Dist. Ct., San Francisco, 1969-70; atty. Calif. Rural Legal Assistance, Gilroy, 1970-72; gen. counsel Food Advocates, Davis, Calif., 1973-74; dir. Drew Health Rights Project, San Francisco, 1974-76; counsel Calif. Dept. Consumer Affairs, Sacramento, 1976-78; ptnr. Fleisher & Neckritz, Oakland, Calif., 1978-82; shareholder Burnhill, Morehouse, Burford, Schofied & Schiller, Walnut Creek, Calif., 1982-87; ptnr. McNichols, McCann & Inderbitzen, Pleasanton, Calif., 1987-91, Hallgrimson, McNichols, McCann & Inderbitzen, Pleasonton, Calif., 1991-95; assoc. gen. counsel Calif. Med. Assn., San Francisco, 1995—; cons. Western Consortium for Health Edn., San Francisco, 1974-78; bd. dirs. Nat. Health Law Program, L.A., 1988-94; arbitrator U.S. Dist. Ct., San Francisco, 1984-91; judge protem Contra Costa County Superior Ct., Martinez, Calif., 1984-88. Contbg. author Advising California Partnerships, 1988, California Sole Proprietorships & Partnerships, 1992; contbg. editor Calif. Ltd. Liability Cos. Reginald H. Smith fellow Office Legal Svcs., Calif., 1970-72. Mem. ABA (bus. law sect. partnership and unicorp. assns. com. 1991—, vice chair corp. counsel com. Torts & Ins. Practice Sect. 1996-98), Am. Soc. Med. Assn. Counsel (sec., treas. 1999—), D.C. Bar Assn., Calif. State Bar Partnership (com. 1989-94, exec. com. bus. law sect. 1993-96, nonprofits orgn. com. bus. law sect. 1996—). Health, General corporate, Non-profit and tax-exempt organizations. Office: Calif Med Assn 221 Main St San Francisco CA 94105-1906

**FLEMING, DAWN DEANN,** lawyer; b. East Chgo., Ind., Oct. 14, 1961; d. Harry Dean and Glenda Lee Fleming; m. Jon Forrest Chaffee, June 25, 1983 (div. Oct. 1993). BA, Univ. Minn., 1986; JD, Western State U., 1995. Bar: Calif. Loan officer Knutson Mort. Corp., Bloomington, Minn., 1986-88; property mgr. Property Mgmt., Inc., Mpls., 1988-89; mortgage counselor Columbia Mort. Corp., Fullerton, Calif., 1989-93; law clerk Law Offices of Theodore Anderson, Fullerton, Calif., 1994-96; lawyer Frank B. Myers & Assocs., Newport Beach, Calif., 1996-98; ptnr. Myers & Fleming LLP, Newport Beach, Calif., 1998—. Co-author: Liability Limitation in Service and Consulting Contracts, 1998. Recipient Am. Ind. award Lawyers Coop. Pub., 1993. Mem. ABA, Internat. Mktg. Assn. (dir. 1998—), Legal Mktg. Assn. (dir. 1997—), Am. Soc. Internat. Law., Soc. Am. Inst. Mining, Metallurgical and Petroleum Engrs., Western State Univ. Alumni Assn. (dir. 1997—), Orange County Bar Assn. (bus. & corp. sect., internat. law sect.), Am. Soc. Internat. Law. Private international, Construction, General corporate. Office: Myers & Fleming LLP 20301 SW Acacia St Ste 150 Newport Beach CA 92660-1741

**FLEMING, GEORGE MATTHEWS,** lawyer; b. Houston, Mar. 26, 1946; s. George McMillian and Mary Kathryn (Matthews) F.; children: Matthew Joseph, Kathryn Nicole, Tyler James. BBA, U. Tex., Austin, 1968; JD, U. Tex., 1971. Bar: Tex. 1971, U.S. Dist. Ct. (so., no., we. and ea. dists.) Tex. 1976, U.S. Dist. D.C. 1973, U.S. Ct. Appeals (5th cir.) 1976, U.S. Ct. Appeals (7th cir.) 1979, U.S. Ct. Appeals (11th cir.) 1982, U.S. Ct. Appeals (D.C. cir.) 1974, U.S. Supreme Ct. 1974. Trial atty. torts sect. U.S. Dept. Justice, Washington, 1972-76; ptnr. Byrd, Davis & Eisenberg, Austin, 1976-82, Fleming, Betts & Cooke, Houston, 1982-86; prin. Fleming & Assocs., L.L.P., Houston, 1986—; lectr. South Tex. Coll. Law, Houston, Embry-Riddle Aero. U.,Orlando, Fla., So. Meth. U. Air Law Symposium; lectr. aviation accident law litigation N.Y. Law Jour. Seminar, N.Y.C. Contbr. articles to profl. jours. Served to lt. U.S. Army, 1972. Mem. D.C. Bar Assn., ABA (ins. and compensation law com., chmn. mil. aviation com.), Houston Bar Assn., Assn. Trial Lawyers Am., Tex. Trial Lawyers Assn., Fed. Bar Assn., Lawyer Pilots Bar Assn., Internat. Soc. Air Safety Investigators. Democrat. Roman Catholic. Federal civil litigation, State civil litigation, Personal injury. Home: 30 W Rivercrest Dr Houston TX 77042-2127 Office: 1330 Post Oak Blvd Suite 3030 Houston TX 77056

**FLEMING, JOSEPH CLIFTON, JR.,** dean, law educator; b. Atlanta, July 24, 1942; s. Joseph Clifton Sr. and Claudia Leola (Duncan) F.; m. Linda Wightman, May 27, 1964; children: Allison, Erin, Anne, Matthew Clifton, Stephen Joseph, Michael Grant. BS, Brigham Young U., 1964; JD, George Washington U., 1967. Bar: Wash. 1967, U.S. Dist. Ct. (we. dist.) Wash. 1967, U.S. Tax Ct. 1969, U.S. Ct. Appeals (9th cir.) 1970, Utah 1979. Assoc. Bogle & Gates, Seattle, 1967-73; assoc. prof. Law Sch. U. of Puget Sound, Tacoma, 1973-74; assoc. prof. Law Sch. Brigham Young U., Provo, Utah, 1974-76, prof. Law sch., 1976-98, assoc. dean Law Sch., 1986—; Ernest L. Wilkinson prof. Law Sch. Brigham Young U., Provo, 1998—; Fulbright prof. faculty law U. Nairobi, Kenya, 1977-78; prof. in residence Office of Chief Counsel IRS, Washington, 1985-86; vis. prof. U. Queensland, Brisbane, Australia, 1997. Author: Estate and Gift Tax, 1975, Tax Aspects of Buying and Selling Corporate Businesses, 1984, Tax Aspects of Forming and Operating Closely Held Corporations, 1992, Federal Income Tax: Doctrine, Structure and Policy, 1995, 2nd edit., 1999; notes editor George Washington U. Law Rev., 1966-67; contbr. numerous articles to profl. jours. Bishop Ch. of Jesus Christ of LDS, Orem, Utah, 1981-85. Mem. ABA (subcom. chair tax sect. corp. tax com. 1979-83, chair tax sect. com. on teaching taxation 1992-94), Am. Law Inst. (tax adv. group 1988-94, 98—). Office: Brigham Young U J Reuben Clark Law Sch PO Box 28000 Provo UT 84602-8000

**FLEMING, JOSEPH Z.,** lawyer; b. Miami, Fla., Jan. 30, 1941; s. Richard Marion and Lenore C. Fleming; m. Betty Corcoran, Feb. 12, 1947; 1 child, Katherine Anne. BA in English, U. Fla., 1958; postgrad., U. Chgo., 1959, Hague Acad. Internat. Law, 1966; JD, U. Va., 1965; LLM in Labor Law, NYU, 1966. Bar: fla. 1965, D.C. 1981. Assoc. Paul & Thomson, Miami, 1966-72, ptnr., 1972-74; ptnr. fleming & Neuman, 1974-81, Fleming & Huck, Miami, 1981-86; sole practice Miami, 1986-87, Fleming & Klink, 1987-88; pvt. practice, 1988-96, 96—, Ford & Harrison; lectr. profl. programs, seminars. Author: Airline and Railroad Labor Law, 1981-99, 10th edit., 1999; editor, contbg. author Environmental Regulation and Litigation in Florida, 1980, 82, 84, 85, 87, 88, 90, 91, 93, 94, 95, 97, 99; contbg. author: Environmental Pollution and Individual Rights, 1978, Reporter's Handbook, 1979—, Historic Preservation Law, 1984, 85, 86, 87, 89, 99, Entertainment Arts and Sports Law, 1989, 90, 91, 97, 98, 99. Trustee Met. Dade County Ctr. for Fine Arts, 1982-86; mem. Bidcayne Bay Environ. Task Force Subcom., 1982-83, well field protection adv. com. Dade County Task Force, 1984-87; mem. Noguchi-Bayfront Park Trust, Miami, 1983-89; pres., bd. dirs. Fla. Rural Legal Svcs., 1967-78, Pres.'s Water Policy Implementation Workshops, Dept. of Interior Water Task Force, 1979; bd. dirs. Miami chpt. Am. Jewish Com. Recipient conservation award Fla. Audubon Soc., 1981, 89, Tropical Audubon Soc., 1979, award Dade County Mental Health Assn., 1974, award Miami Design Preservation League, 1982, 83, award Progressive Architecture, 1982, Am. Jewish Com. award. Mem. Am. Law Inst., ABA (continuing profl. edn. com. 1985—), Fla. Bar Assn. (past chmn. environ. and land use law sect., labor law and employment descrimination law sect., entertainment, arts and sports law sect.). Labor, Environmental, Administrative and regulatory. Home: 34 LaGorce Cir Miami Beach FL 33141-4520 Office: 516 Ingraham Bldg 25 SE 2nd Ave Miami FL 33131-1506

**FLEMING, JULIAN DENVER, JR.,** lawyer; b. Rome, Ga., Jan. 12, 1934; s. Julian D. and Margaret Madison (Mangham) F.; m. Sidney Howell, June 28, 1960; 1 dau., Julie Adrianne. Student, U. Pa., 1951-53; BChemE, Ga. Inst. Tech., 1955, PhD, 1959; JD, Emory U., 1967. Bar: Ga. 1966, D.C. 1967; registered profl. engr., Ga., Calif. Rsch. engr., prof. chem. engring. Ga. Inst. Tech., 1955-67; ptnr. Sutherland, Asbill & Brennan, Atlanta, 1967—. Contbr. articles to profl. jours.; patentee in field. Bd. dirs. Mental Health Assn. Ga., 1970-80; bd. dirs. Mental Health Assn. Met. Atlanta, 1970-80, pres., 1974-75; mem. coun. legal advisors Rep. Nat. Com., 1981-85. Fellow Am. Inst. Chemists, Am. Coll. Trial Lawyers, Am. Bar Found.; mem. AAAS, ABA (coun. sect. sci. and tech. 1980-82, vice chmn. 1982-84, chmn. 1985-86, ho. dels. 1990, 94-96, bd. govs. 1994-95, chmn. spl. citation issues com. 1995-96, coord. commn. on legal tech. 1995-97, standing com. on tech. and info. sys. 1997—), AIChE, Nat. Conf. Lawyers and Scientists (chmn. ABA del. 1988-90, ABA liaison 1990-93, standing com. on nat. conf. groups 1990, chmn. 1992-93), Bleckley Inn of Ct. (master of bench). Achievements include patent for data apparatus. Federal civil litigation, State civil litigation, Intellectual property. Home: 1248 Oxford Rd NE Atlanta GA 30306-2610 Office: Sutherland Asbill & Brennan 999 Peachtree St NE Ste 2300 Atlanta GA 30309-3996

**FLEMING, LISA L.,** lawyer; b. Louisville, Nov. 14, 1961; d. Joseph D. Ware. BA cum laude, Hanover (Ind.) Coll., 1982; JD, U. Louisville, 1985. Bar: Ind., Ohio, U.S. Dist. Ct. (so. and no. dists.) Ind.; cert. mediator pursuant to Ind. Trial Rules. Assoc. gen. counsel Midland Enterprises, Inc., Cin.; career cons. Hanover Coll. Mem. Leadership So. Ind., 1990-98, v.p. programming, 1996-97; bd. dirs. Comty. Youth Leadership Collaborative, 1995—. Mem. NAFE, ABA (admiralty and corp. counsel coms.), Ind. State Bar Assn. (articles and by-laws com.), Clark County Bar Assn., Cin. Bar Assn., Am. Corp. Counsel Assn. (bd. dirs., chpt. treas. 1992-95), River City Bus. and Profl. Women, Ky. Women Advs., Focus Louisville, Hanover Coll. Alumni Assn. (bd. dirs. 1990-96, pres. elect 1991-92, pres. bd. dirs. 1992-93, past pres. 1993-94), So. Ind. C. of C. (chair govt. affairs debate subcom. 1991-95, women's bus. coun., 1991-95, chair political skill workshop subcom. 1993-95), Phi Mu (alumnae pres. Louisville chpt. 1985-91, nat. risk mgmt. educator 1996-98, Sigma area collegiate dir. 1996-97, nat. extentsion dir. 1998—). General corporate, Admiralty, Transportation. Office: Midland Enterprises 300 Pike St Cincinnati OH 45202-4222

**FLEMING, MACK GERALD,** lawyer; b. Hartwell, Ga., May 3, 1932; s. Mack Judson and Dessie Leola (Vickery) F.; m. Elizabeth McClellan, Mar. 30, 1963; children: Katharine Lee, John McClellan. B.S., Clemson (S.C.) U., 1956; J.D., Am. U., Washington, 1966. Asst. dir. prodn. control Woodside Mills, Simpsonville, S.C., 1959-60; adminstrv. asst. to mem. Congress, 1960-64; dir. Congressional Liaison Office, VA, Washington, 1965-68; spl. asst. to adminstr. Congressional Liaison Office, VA, 1968-69; adminstrv. asst., counsel to mem. congress, 1969-70; pvt. practice law Washington, 1970-74; chief counsel Com. on Vets. Affairs, U.S. Ho. of Reps., 1974-80, staff dir. and chief counsel, 1980-95; pvt. practice Seneca, S.C., 1997—. Served to 1st lt. U.S. Army, 1956-58. Mem. D.C., S.C. bar assns. Democrat. Methodist. Home: 3023 Lake Keowee Ln Seneca SC 29672-6747

**FLEMING, MACKLIN,** judge, author; b. Chgo., Sept. 6, 1911; s. Ingram Macklin Stainback and Hazel (Caldwell) Fleming; m. Polly Naething, May 17, 1941; children: Penelope, Frances, Ingram. BA, Yale U., 1934, LLB, 1937; LLD, Pepperdine U., 1968. Bar: N.Y. 1938, Calif. 1946. Assoc. Sullivan & Cromwell, N.Y.C., 1937-39; atty. Bituminous Coal divsn. U.S. Govt., Washington, 1939-41; pvt. practice San Francisco, 1946-49; asst. U.S. atty. U.S. Atty.'s Office, San Francisco, 1949-53; assoc. Mitchell, Silberberg & Knupp, L.A., 1954-59; judge Superior Ct., L.A., 1959-64; justice Calif. Ct. Appeal, L.A., 1964-81; of counsel Troy and Gould, L.A., 1981-91, 98—; assigned judge Superior Ct., L.A., 1992-98. Author: The Price of Perfect Justice, 1974, Of Crimes and Rights, 1978, Lawyers, Money, & Success, 1997. Chmn. Far Eastern Art Coun., L.A. County Mus., 1967-69; v.p. Ctr. Theater Group, L.A., 1970. Capt. U.S. Army, 1941-46. Fellow Am. Bar Found.; mem. ABA, L.A. County Bar Assn., Bar of City of N.Y., Inst. of Jud. Adminstrn., Selden Soc. Democrat. Episcopalian. Avocations: skiing, tennis, gardening. Home: 331 N Carmelina Ave Los Angeles CA 90049-2701 Office: Troy & Gould 1801 Century Park E Ste 1600 Los Angeles CA 90067-2318

**FLEMING, MICHAEL PAUL,** lawyer; b. Orlando, Fla., June 25, 1963; s. Joseph Patrick and Therese (Eccles); m. Natalie Jackson, Oct. 15, 1988; children: Shannon Isabel, Nicholas Patrick, Patrick Edward, Michael Paul, Eamon John. BA, U. St. Thomas, 1984; JD, U. Houston, 1987. Bar: Tex. 1987; U.S. Dist. Ct. (so. dist.) Tex. 1988; U.S. Ct. Appeals (5th cir.) 1988, U.S. Supreme Ct. 1991; cert. personal injury. Ptnr. Fleming & Fleming, Houston, 1987-91; asst. county atty. Harris County, Houston, 1991-96; elected Harris county atty. Harris County atty., 1996—. Mem. State Bar of Tex., Houston Bar Assn., Ancient Order of Hibernians, KC, Phi Delta Phi. Roman Catholic. Avocation: genealogy. Home: 6106 Lymbar Dr Houston TX 77096-4619 Office: Harris County Atty 1019 Congress St # 15 Houston TX 77002-1700

**FLEMING, RICHARD ALFRED,** lawyer; b. Amityville, N.Y., Oct. 23, 1953; s. Alfred Joseph and Rose Theresa Fleming; m. Catherine Campbell Shepstone, July 16, 1988; 1 child, Maureen Frances. BA, SUNY, Plattsburgh, 1975; JD, Western State Coll. Law, 1978. Bar: Calif. 1979, U.S. Dist. Ct. (ctrl. dist.) Calif. 1980; cert. instr. Calif. C.Cs., 1980. Assoc. Law Office R.A. Bender, Huntington Beach, Calif., 1979-82; mng. atty. Jacoby & Myers Law Office, Fullerton, Calif., 1982-86; assoc. Law Office Elaine K. Bunzel, Anaheim, Calif., 1986—; tchr. legal rsch. Coastline C.C., Huntington Beach, 1980-83. Co-chmn. Santiago de Compostela Cath. Ch. Parish Coun., 1997—. Democrat. Roman Catholic. Avocations: sports, jogging. Family and matrimonial, Bankruptcy, Probate. Home: 22902 Springwater Lake Forest CA 92630-5417 Office: Law Office Elaine K Bunzel 101 E Lincoln Ave Ste 250 Anaheim CA 92805-3206

**FLEMING, TOMMY WAYNE,** lawyer; b. Canyon, Tex., Nov. 13, 1941; s. Benjamin Dalby and Willie Mildred (Vineyard) F.; m. Sally Ann Moore, Nov. 30, 1968; children: Benjamin Dalby II, Hunter Leah. Student, West Tex. State U., 1960-61; BBA, U. Tex., 1964, JD, 1966. Bar: Tex. 1969, U.S. Dist. Ct. (so. dist.) Tex. 1971, U.S. Supreme Ct. 1978, U.S. Ct. Appeals (5th cir.) 1983. Asst. dist. atty. Office Dist. Atty., Amarillo, Tex., 1969-70; asst. criminal dist. atty. Cameron County Criminal Dist. Atty.'s Office, Brownsville, Tex., 1970-72; ptnr. Wiech, Lewis & Fleming, Brownsville, 1972-74, Wiech, Fleming, Hamilton & Uribe, Brownsville, 1974-82, Wiech & Black, Brownsville, 1982-89, Atlas & Hall, Brownsville, 1989-94, Fleming, Hewitt & Olvera, Brownsville, 1994-98, Fleming & Olvera, Brownsville, 1998—; mem. State Grievance Oversight Com., 1983—. Chmn. Brownsville Cmty. Health Clinci, 1978-79. 1st lt. U.S. Army, 1966-69. Fellow Tex. Bar Found. (life, bd. dirs. 1984-87); mem. Tex. Assn. Bank Counsel, State Bar Tex. (bd. dirs. 1981-84), Cameron County bar Assn. (bd. dirs. 1972-79, pres. 1979-80), Brownsville Hist. Assn. (bd. dirs. 1977-80). Banking, Contracts commercial, General practice. Home: 915 Santa Ana Ave Rancho Viejo TX 78575-9749 Office: Fleming & Olvera 1650 Paredes Line Rd Ste 102 Brownsville TX 78521-1602

**FLESCHNER, G. STEVEN,** lawyer; b. Terre Haute, Ind., July 4, 1949; s. George Harold and Irene (Morris) F.; m. C. Kathleen O'Brien, Aug. 10, 1973; children: paul S., Kristin A., Kathryn E., Timothy J. BS, Ind. State U., 1971; JD, Washburn U., 1974; LLM, U. Mo., 1977. Bar: Mo. 1974, U.S. Dist. Ct. (so. dist.) Ind. 1977, U.S. Supreme Ct. 1977, U.S. Dist. Ct. (we. dist.) Mo. 1978. Assoc. Jackson & Sherman, Kansas City, Mo., 1974-78; pvt. practice Terre Haute, 1978; ptnr. Fleschner & Fleschner, Terre Haute, 1979-86, Fleschner, Fleschner & Newlin, Terre Haute, 1986; sr. ptnr. Fleschner,Fleschner, Stark, Tanoos & Newlin, Terre Haute, 1987—; civil mediator, 1994-97. Bd. dirs., pres. Terre Haute YMCA, 1991-96. Mem. ABA, ATLA, Ind. Bar Assn., Ind. Trial Lawyers Assn., Terre Haute Bar Assn. Personal injury. Office: Fleschner Fleschner Stark Tanoos & Newlin 201 Ohio St Terre Haute IN 47807-3420

**FLETCHER, ANTHONY L.,** lawyer; b. Washington, Dec. 12, 1935; s. Robert J. and Lyndell (Pickett) F.; m. Juliana Schump, Sept. 3, 1960 (div. 1977); children: Leigh Anne Grinstead, Kristine Marie Giffin, Julie Bowen Cimino; m. Zelda L. Fletcher, Mar. 30, 1986. BA, Princeton U., 1957; JD, Harvard U., 1962. Bar: N.Y. 1963, U.S. Ct. Appeals (2d cir.) 1966, U.S. Ct. Appeals (7th cir.) 1966, U.S. Supreme Ct. 1966, U.S. Ct. Appeals (3d cir.) 1969, U.S. Ct. Appeals (5th cir.) 1973, U.S. Ct. Appeals (1st cir.) 1981, U.S. Ct. Appeals (9th cir.) 1983. Assoc. Simpson,Thacher & Bartlett, N.Y.C., 1962-71; assoc. Conboy, Hewitt, O-Brien & Boardman, N.Y.C., 1971-74, ptnr., 1974-86; ptnr. Hunton & Williams, N.Y.C., 1986-97; prin. Fish & Richardson P.C., N.Y.C., 1997—. Editor-in-chief Trademark Reporter, 1982-84; contbr. articles to profl. jours. With U.S. Army, 1957-59. Mem. Internat. Trademark Assn. (bd. dirs. N.Y.C. 1983-85), Princeton Club. Episcopalian. Trademark and copyright, Federal civil litigation, State civil litigation. Office: Fish & Richardson PC 45 Rockefeller Plz Fl 28 New York NY 10111-2889

**FLETCHER, BETTY B.,** federal judge; b. Tacoma, Mar. 29, 1923. B.A., Stanford U., 1943; LL.B., U. Wash., 1956. Bar: Wash. 1956. Mem. firm Preston, Thorgrimson, Ellis, Holman & Fletcher, Seattle, 1956-1979; judge U.S. Ct. Appeals (9th cir.), Seattle, 1979—, sr. judge, 1998-. Mem. ABA (Margaret Brent award 1992), Wash. State Bar Assn., Am. Law Inst., Fed. Judges Assn. (past pres.), Order of Coif, Phi Beta Kappa. Office: US Ct Appeals 9th Cir 1010 5th Ave Ste 1000 Seattle WA 98104-1196

**FLETCHER, DOUGLAS CHARLES,** lawyer; b. Rockford, Ill., Mar. 5, 1943; s. Fred Leland and Dorothy Ann Fletcher; m. Adele Ann Pinkerton, Aug. 20, 1964 (div. Apr. 1985); children: Adrian, Lauren, Robin. BA in Econs. and Engring., U. Nev., Reno, 1969, MBA in Fin. cum laude, 1972; JD, U. of Pacific, 1975; postgrad., Colo. State U., 1976. Bar: Nev. 1975, U.S. Ct. Appeals (9th cir.) 1976. Design engr. Nev. Bell, 1967-70; economist Sierra Pacific Power Co., 1970-72, gen. counsel, 1975-78; operating trustee Lear Motors Co., 1978-79; ptnr. Leslie Gray & Assocs., 1979-81; oper. trustee Horseshoe Club Casinos, 1981-82, Mapes Hotel and Money Tree Casinos, 1982-85; owner, ptnr. Douglas C. Fletcher, Ltd., 1985—; advisor U. Nev. Grad. Bus. Sch., Reno, 1976-85; mem. U.S. Trustee Panel, 1978-95; judge pro tem Reno Mcpl. Ct., 1980-82. Author: Bond Reverse Yield Gaps of Public Utilities, 1972. Mem. ctrl. planning com. Republican Party of Washoe County, 1978-82; bd. dirs. Washoe County Youth Found., Reno, 1983-92, Eagles Nest Assn., Reno, 1998; founder, bd. dirs. Sierra League, Reno, 1989-99; bd. dirs., pres. ski team advisors U. Nev., Reno, 1982-99. Mem. No. Nev. Bankruptcy Bar Assn. (founding mem.), Washoe County Bar Assn., State Bur. Nev. (environ. law com. 1975—), Reno Tennis Club (pres., bd. dirs.), U.S. Ski Coaches Assn. (cert.), Reno Ski and Recreation Club (bd. dirs., pres.), Prospectors Club (bd. dirs. 1978-79), Sigma Nu, Phi Kappa Phi, Beta Gamma Sigma. Bankruptcy, General corporate, Real property. Office: 20 Sharps Cir Reno NV 89509-8009

**FLETCHER, JAMES HARRY,** lawyer; b. Jan. 31, 1928; s. Ira Donald and Helen (Burdick) F.; m. Marilyn G. Manley, July 12, 1952; children—Sandra G., Karen L., Leslie A., Cherri. J.D., Columbia U., 1952. BAR: D.C. 1952, U.S. Dist. Ct. D.C. 1952, N.Y. 1953, U.S. Dist. Ct. (so. and ea. dists.) N.Y. 1957, U.S. Ct. Mil. Appeals 1956, U.S. Tax Ct. 1964. Ptnr. Fletcher, Sibell and Migatz, P.C. and predecessor firms, Manhasset, NY, 1955—; sec., dir. Micro Contacts, Inc., Hicksville, N.Y., Micro Pneumatic Logic, Inc., Ft. Lauderdale, Fla., Roslyn, N.Y. Contbr. articles to Columbia Law Rev., 1950-52. Mem. Manhasset Pub. Schs. Citizens Adv. Com. for Vocat. Guidance; village justice Village of Plandome Heights. Served with USAF, 1952-55. Mem. L.I. Tax and Estate Planning Council, Tax Inst. C. W. Post Coll., Nassau County Bar Assn., N.Y. State Bar Assn., ABA. Republican. Congregationalist. Clubs: Nassau Country (past pres.), Rotary (past pres., Paul Harris fellow 1982). Lodge: Masons (past master). General corporate, Probate, Estate taxation. Home: 46 Brookwold Dr Manhasset NY 11030-1935 Office: Fletcher Sibell and Migatz 22 Bayview Ave Manhasset NY 11030-1804

**FLETCHER, MICHAEL S.,** lawyer; b. Winchester, Va., Nov. 23, 1961; s. James William and Patty Jo (Stotler) F. BS, U. Tenn., Knoxville, 1984; JD, Seton Hall U., Newark, 1988. Bar: N.J. 1988, Pa. 1988, U.S. Dist. Ct. N.J. 1988, U.S. Dist. Ct. (ea. dist.) Pa. 1989. Law sec. to Hon. Donald G. Collester Jr. Superior Ct. N.J., Morristown, 1988-89; assoc. LaBrum and Doak, P.C., Phila., 1989-90; asst. dep. pub. defender State of N.J., Morristown, 1990—. Assoc. editor Seton Hall Law Rev., 1988. Shop steward Comms. Workers Am. Local 1037, Newark, 1991—; treas. Cornerstone Evang. Free Ch., 1994—. Office: Office of Pub Defender 25 Washington St Morristown NJ 07960-3950

**FLETCHER, NORMAN S.,** state supreme court justice; b. July 10, 1934; s. Frank Pickett and Hattie Sears Fletcher; m. Dorothy Johnson, 1957; children: Mary Kiker, Elizabeth Coan. BA, U. Ga., 1956, LLB, 1958; LLM, U. Va., 1995. Assoc. Matthews, Maddox, Walton and Smith, Rome, Ga., 1958-63; pvt. practice LaFayette, Ga., 1963-90; city atty. City of LaFayette, 1965-89; county atty. County of Walker, 1973-88; spl. asst. atty. gen. State of Ga., Atlanta, 1979-89; justice Supreme Ct. of Ga., Atlanta, 1990—, now presiding justice; mem. State Disciplinary Bd., 1984-87, chair investigative panel, 1986-87. Ruling elder Peachtree Presbyn. Ch., Atlanta; former officer First Presbyn. Ch. of Rome, Ga., LaFayette Presbyn. Ch., Cherokee Presbytery; former commr. Presbyn. Ch. USA Gen. Assembly, 1984, 85; bd. visitors U. Ga. Sch. Law, 1992-95, chmn., 1994-95. Master Joseph Henry Lumpkin Inn of Ct.; fellow Am. Bar Found., Ga. Bar Found.; mem. State Bar Ga. (chair local govt. sect. 1977-78), U. Ga. Law Sch. Alumni Assn. (pres. 1977), Rotary. Office: Supreme Ct Ga 244 Washington St SW Rm 572 Atlanta GA 30334-9007

**FLETCHER, PAUL GERALD,** lawyer; b. Boston, Mar. 20, 1945; m. Susan Mary Beckerman, Aug. 11, 1968; children: Lynne, Michael, Allison. BAE, U. Fla., 1967; JD, U. Miami, 1970. Bar: Fla. 1970, U.S. Dist. Ct. (so. dist.) Fla. 1970, U.S. Ct. Mil. Appeals 1971, U.S. Supreme Ct. 1973, U.S. Ct. Appeals (11th cir.) 1982. Judge adv. USAF, 1970-74; ptnr. Peskoe, Fletcher & Cahan, Homestead, Fla., 1974-77, Fletcher & Langer, Homestead, 1977-84; sr. ptnr. Paul G. Fletcher, P.A., Coral Gables, Fla., 1984—; instr. bus. law No. Mich. U., Marquette, 1970-72; mem. adv. bd. Amerifirst Fla. Trust

Co., 1987-91. Pres. Homestead ARC, 1975. Capt. USAF, 1970-74. Recipient Service award ARC, 1977, Leadership award Jewish Fedn., 1980; named in Leading Am. Attys. in Family Law, Fla., 1997—. Mem. Fla. Bar Assn. (family law, real properties coms.), Homestead Bar Assn. (pres. 1980-81), ATLA, Am. Arbitration Assn. (arbitrator), Kendall-South Dade Bar Assn., Coral Gables Bar Assn., First Family Law Inns of Ct. (master 1993—), Attys. Real Property Coun., Kiwanis (v.p. 1980, pres. 1983), B'nai B'rith (adv. bd. 1974-81, v.p. 1979-80), Tau Epsilon Phi. Democrat. Avocations: tennis, racquetball, photography, World War II history, baseball cards. Fax #: 305-661-6197. Family and matrimonial, Real property, Probate. Office: 1500 S Dixie Hwy Ste 200 Coral Gables FL 33146-3033

**FLETCHER, RICHARD ROYCE,** lawyer; b. Garden City, Kans., Aug. 3, 1959; s. Dick Royce and Betty Sue (Rabun) F.; m. Rhonda Denise Pacanowski, Aug. 10, 1979; children: Chelsie N., Christin D., Catherine M. BS, Lubbock Christian U., 1981; MBA, Abilene Christian U., 1985; JD, Tex. Tech. U., 1989. Bar: Tex. 1989, N.Mex. 1990, U.S. Dist. Ct. (we. dist.) Tex. 1991, U.S. Ct. Appeals (5th cir.) 1992, U.S. Dist. Ct. (so. dist.) Tex. 1993, U.S. Supreme Ct. 1993, U.S. Dist. Ct. N.Mex. 1995, U.S. Ct. Appeals (10th cir.) 1996, U.S. Dist. Ct. (no. dist.) Tex. 1997; cert. personal injury law, Tex. Bd. Legal Specialization. Ptnr., shareholder Cotton, Bledsoe, Tighe & Dawson, Midland, Tex., 1996—. Mem. Tex. Assn. of Def. Counsel, Order of Barristers, Midland County Bar Assn., Phi Delta Phi. Mem. Church of Christ. Avocations: backpacking, fly fishing, racquetball. General civil litigation, Insurance, Personal injury. Office: Cotton Bledsoe Tighe & Dawson 500 W Illinois Ave Ste 300 Midland TX 79701-4337

**FLETCHER, ROBERT,** retired lawyer, horologist; b. Birmingham, Ala., May 4, 1920; s. Robert Hall and Beatrice (Skelding) Jones; m. Florence K. Szuba, Sept. 12, 1942; children—Andrew R., William Alan. B.F.A., Ohio U., Athens, 1943; LL.B., J.D., Case Western Res U., 1948. Bar: Ohio bar 1948. Asst. gen. counsel Cleve. Transit System, 1951-56; with firm Jamison, Ulrich, Johnson & Burt, Cleve., 1956-59, Meyers, Stevens & Rea, Cleve., 1959-61; pvt. practice Cleve., 1961-82; horologist Parma, Ohio, 1982—; Lectr. Am. Heart Assn. Served with AUS, World War II, Korea. Recipient Speakers Bur. award Am. Heart Assn., 1973-76. Republican. Presbyterian. Club: Rosicrucian Order. Home: 5801 Hollywood Dr Cleveland OH 44129-5220

**FLEUR, MARY LOUISE,** legal administrator; b. Rochester, N.Y., Dec. 30, 1951; d. John James and Mary (Cisterna) Schwartz; m. Jeffrey P. Guinan, Dec. 20, 1975 (div. Dec. 1977); m. Edward R. Fleur, Mary 25, 1991; children: James Carter, Edna Louise. BA with honors, Manhattanville Coll., 1973. Legal asst. Milbank Tweed Hadley & McCloy, N.Y.C., 1975-77, managerial asst., 1978-80; office adminstr. Burlingham Underwood & Lord, N.Y.C., 1980-84; dir. adminstrn. Demov Morris & Hammerling, N.Y.C., 1984-87; dir. fin. and adminstrn. Spengler, Carlson, Gubar, Brodsky & Frischling, N.Y.C., 1987-92; dir. billings and collections Reid & Priest, N.Y.C., 1992-94, exec. dir., 1995-98; v.p. EFFE Corp., Greenwich, Conn., 1998—. Contbr. articles to profl. jours. Mem. ABA (assoc., advisor com. on legal assts. 1978-80), Assn. Legal Adminstrs., N.Y.C. Paralegal Assn. (dir. 1977-79). Avocations: reading, computers. Office: EFFE Corporation 176 Bedford Rd Greenwich CT 06831-2536

**FLEURY, RONALD J.,** editor. Editor-in-chief N.J. Law Jour., Newark. Office: Am Lawyer Media LLP PO Box 20081 Newark NJ 07101-6081

**FLICKER, HOWARD,** lawyer; b. Phila., May 10, 1947; s. Jack Flicker and Sylvia Williamson; m. Frances Terry Gittleman, June 15, 1975; children: Jacqueline, Benjamin, Robert. Bar: U.S. Supreme Ct. 1975, Colo. 1978, U.S. Dist. Ct. Colo. 1980, U.S. Ct. Appeals (10th cir.) 1995. Lawyer U.S. Small Bus. Adminstrn., L.A., 1972-73; ptnr. Wyman & Flicker, Beverly Hills, Calif., 1973-78; lawyer The Frickey Law Firm, Lakewood, Colo., 1978—. Chmn. Arapahoe County Rep. Mens Club, Englewood, Colo., 1983-86. Mem. CTLAWPAC (v.p. 1994-98), Colo. Trial Lawyers Assn., Million Dollar Advs. Forum. Republican. Jewish. Avocations: golf, skiing. FAX: 303-671-2667. Personal injury, State civil litigation, Federal civil litigation. Office: The Frickey Law Firm PC 1450 S Havana St Ste 704 Aurora CO 80012-4034

**FLICKINGER, DON JACOB,** patent agent; b. Massillon, Ohio, Dec. 31, 1933; s. John Jacob and Elizabeth Ann (Slinger) F.; m. Sonja Loy Jersild (dec. Aug. 1987); 1 child, Packy J. Flickinger. Student, Kent (Ohio) State U., 1951-54, U. Ariz., 1958; BA, Ariz. State U., 1963, MA, 1964. Bar: U.S. Patent and Trademark Office, 1973. Apprentice tool and die maker Spun Steel Corp., Canton, Ohio, 1951-54; staff Ariz. State U., Tempe, 1963-65; law clerk, paralegal Drummond, Cahill & Phillips, Phoenix, 1966-73; reg. patent agent Drummond, Nelson & Ptak, Phoenix, 1973-77, self employed, Phoenix, 1977-94; counsel Parsons & Goltry, Phoenix, 1995—; lectr., instr. Patent Seminars & Courses, Phoenix, 1977—; staff Rio Salado C.C., Phoenix, 1982-84. Patentee Collapsible Dust Pan, Hort. Growing Unit. Comdg. officer Poolee Enrichment Program, Family Marine Force, Poolee Assistance Co., Phoenix; sponsor Thunderbird Little League, Phoenix, 1985, 86, 87; big brother Valley Big Brothers, Phoenix, 1968-70; participant, staff Valley Big Bros./Big Sisters Fish-a-Ree, 1984-87; judge Crown Royal Kinetic Contraption Compeition, 1990. With USMC, 1954-57. Am. Soc. Tool. scholar, Tucson, 1960; recipient Disting. Svc. cert. Valley Big Brothers, Phoenix,1970, Honor award Westside Area Career Project, Glendale, 1981. Mem. BBB, NRA (endowment), Nat. Wildlife Fedn. (leaders club), Am. Legion, Ariz. Heritage Alliance, Phoenix Symphony Guild, Sundome Performing Arts Assn., Wilderness Soc., Nature Conservancy, Sea Shepard Conservation Soc., Legal Defense Fund, Defenders of Wildlife, Am. Legion, Mensa, Kappa Delta Pi. Republican. Buddhist. Avocations: philosophy, reading, woodworking, arts & crafts, fishing. Patent. Office: Parsons & Assocs 340 E Palm Ln Ste 260 Phoenix AZ 85004-4530

**FLICKINGER, HARRY HARNER,** organization and business executive, management consultant; b. Hanover, Pa., July 27, 1936; s. Harry Roosevelt and Goldie Anna (Harner) F.; m. Hsin Yang, May 30, 1961; children: Audrey Mae, Deborah Lynn. B.S. in Psychology, U. Md., 1958. Investigator U.S. Civil Service Commn., Washington, 1962-64; personnel specialist U.S. Naval Ordinance Lab., Silver Spring., Md., 1964-66; from asst. dir. to dir. personnel U.S. OMB, Washington, 1966-73; asst. dir. personnel AEC and Dept. Energy, Washington, 1973-78; dir. personnel U.S. Dept. Justice, Washington, 1978-79, dep. asst. atty. gen. adminstrn., 1979-85, assoc. asst. atty. gen., 1985-87, asst. atty. gen., 1987-92; exec. dir. Am. Consortium for Internat. Pub. Adminstrn., Washington, 1993; pres. Flickinger Enterprises, Gaithersburg, Md., 1994—. Recipient Presdl. Disting. Exec. Rank award, 1988. Office: 8730 Lochaven Dr Gaithersburg MD 20882-4464

**FLINTOFT, GERALD JAMES,** lawyer; b. White Plains, N.Y., Jan. 29, 1935; s. Gerald Vincent and Edith Mary (O'Shaughnessy) F.; divorced; children: Gerald Patrick, Thomas Moore; married; 1 child, Mark. BS in Chemistry magna cum laude, St. John's U., 1957; JD, Georgetown U., 1964. Bar: N.Y. 1965, U.S. Ct. Appeals (fed. cir.) 1982. New product, patent devel. Ciba-Geigy Corp., Ardsley, N.Y., 1957-58; instr., chemistry U.S. Naval Acad., Annapolis, Md., 1960-62; assoc. Reavis & McGrath, N.Y.C., 1964-65, Fish & Neave, N.Y.C., 1965-69; assoc. Pennie & Edmonds LLP, N.Y.C., 1969-72, ptnr., 1972-78, sr. ptnr., 1978—. Contbr. chpts. to various profl. publ.; bd. editors Georgetown Law Jour., 1964. Lt. U.S. Navy, 1958-62. Recipient 4 Am. Jurisprudence awards Bancroft-Whitney Co., 1960-64. Mem. N.Y. Intellectual Property Law Assn., Assn. Bar N.Y.C., Am. Intellectual Property Law Assn., Assn. Trial Lawyers Am., N.Y. Athletic Club. Roman Catholic. Avocations: basketball player & coach, golf, walking, photography. Intellectual property, Patent, Federal civil litigation. Office: Pennie & Edmonds 1155 Avenue Of The Americas New York NY 10036-2711

**FLIPPEN, EDWARD L.,** lawyer; b. Richmond, Va., Dec. 2, 1939; s. Hannie Thomas Flippen; m. Pearcy light, Feb. 14, 1970; children: Elizabeth Hunter, Margaret Harlan. BS, Va. Commonwealth U., 1965; MBA, Coll. of William and Mary, 1967, JD, 1974. Bar: Va. 1974, N.C. 1981. Gen. atty. Va. State Corp. Commn., Richmond, 1975-78, assoc. gen. counsel, 1978-80, dep. gen. counsel, 1979-80; asst. gen. counsel Duke Power Co., Charlotte, N.C., 1980-81; assoc., 1981-83; ptnr. Mays & Valentine, L.L.P., Richmond, 1983-99, McGuire, Woods, Battle & Boothe L.L.P., Richmond, 1999—; adj. law prof. Coll. of William and Mary, 1996—, Washington & Lee U., 1997—; vis. fellow U. London, 1998-99; chmn. Gov's. Blue Ribbon Commn. Higher Edn., 1998—. Author: How Friends Can Help You With Jobs, 1999. bd. visitors Va. Commonwealth U., Richmond, 1994—; mem. adv. bd. Va. Ctr. on Aging, Richmond, 1994—; trustee River Rd. United Meth. ch., Richmond, 1995-98. With U.S. Army, 1958-61. Mem. Va. State Bar (chmn. adminstrv. law sect., 1986-87), Soc. for Advanced Legal Studies (assoc. fellow). Republican. Avocations: writing, skeet and trap, assisting others in job placements. Public utilities. Office: McGuire Woods Battle & Boothe LLP One James Ctr 901 E Cary St Richmond VA 23219-4057

**FLITZ, JAMES HENRY,** lawyer; b. Munich, Germany, Mar. 8, 1956; m. Suzanne Summerwill. BS, U. Iowa, 1978, MS, 1980, JD, 1982. Bar: Iowa. Sole practice law Cedar Rapids, Iowa, 1982-86; asst. city atty. City of Cedar Rapids, 1986-98, city atty., 1998—. Office: City Atty's Office 7th Fl City Hall Cedar Rapids IA 52401

**FLOM, JOSEPH HAROLD,** lawyer; b. Balt., Dec. 20, 1923; s. Isadore and Fannie (Fishman) F.; m. Claire Cohen, Nov. 14, 1958; children: Peter Leslie, Jason Robert. Student, Coll. City N.Y.; LLB cum laude, Harvard U., 1948; LHD (hon.), Queens Coll., 1984; LLD (hon.), Fordham U., 1990. Practice of law N.Y.C., 1949—; bd. dirs. Warnaco, Inc., Am.-Israel Friendship League; spl. counsel subcom. on adminstrn. of internal revenue laws House Ways and Means Com., 1951-52; mem. com. on tender offers SEC, 1983. Editor Harvard Law Rev., 1947-48; co-editor: Disclosure Requirements of Public Corporations and Insiders, 1967, Texas Gulf Sulphur-Insider Disclosure Problems, 1968, Lawyer's Conflicts-The Evolving Case Law, 1991. Mem. N.Y.C. Mayor's Commn. on Status of Women, 1976-77; mem. Mayor's Coun. Econ. Advisors, 1990-93; co-chmn. task force on capital fin. and constrn. N.Y.C. Bd. Edn., 1987-89; co-chmn. N.Y.C. Operation Welcome Home Commn., 1991; chmn. N.Y.C. Commn. on Bicentennial of Constn., 1986-89; trustee Fedn. Jewish Philanthropies N.Y., 1977-86, Barnard Coll., 1983-93, N.Y. Hist. Soc., 1989-94; chair adv. com. Export-Import Bank of U.S., 1995; trustee Mt. Sinai-NYU Health Sys., 1978-99; trustee Petrie Stores Liquidating Trust; mem. Archdiocesan Task Force on Crime Prevention and Youth, 1982-87; trustee Skadden Fellowship Found., Constl. Edn. Found., 1989-93, United Way N.Y.C., 1991-97; mayor's rep. Met. Mus. of Art, 1990-93; mem. Mayor's Mgmt. Adv. Task Force, 1991-93; chair Woodrow Wilson Internat. Ctr. for Scholars, 1994-98. Fellow ABA; mem. Assn. Bar City N.Y. Office: Skadden Arps Slate 919 3rd Ave Fl 35 New York NY 10022-3902

**FLOM, KATHERINE S.,** lawyer; b. Mpls., Aug. 15, 1955; d. Floyd and Eleanore F.; m. Malcolm D. Reid. BA in Econs., Bates Coll., 1977; JD, Hamline U. Sch. Law, 1982. Bar: Minn. 1982, U.S. Dist. Ct. Minn. 1990, U.S. Ct. Appeals (8th cir.) 1995. Law clk. Judge Charles Porter Dist. Ct. Hennepin County, Mpls., 1983; asst. pub. defender Hennepin County, Mpls., 1984-90; from assoc. to ptnr. Meshbesher & Spence, Mpls., 1990—. Pres. Minn. Consumer Alliance, Mpls., 1997-98; bd. dirs. Am. Lung Assn.-Hennepin County, 1994-97, Working Opportunities for Women, St. Paul, 1991-94. Mem. Minn. Trial Lawyers Assn. (bd. govs. 1992—, trial PAC co-chair 1998—), Minn. State Bar Assn., Minn. Women Lawyers. Personal injury, Product liability. Office: Meshbesher & Spence 9950 Wayata Blvd Saint Louis Park MN 55426

**FLOOD, JAMES J(OSEPH), JR.,** retired lawyer; b. Oceanside, N.Y., June 16, 1931; s. James Joseph and Marguerite Elinor (Datz) F.; m. Dorothy Eleanor Lehrfeld, Aug. 13, 1955; children: James J. III, Maureen, Sharon Marie, Jean Ann, Kathleen E., Thomas E. BA, U. Notre Dame, 1953; JD, George Washington U., 1958. Bar: Va. 1958, D.C. 1960. Atty. U.S. Dept. Justice, Washington, 1958-60, asst. U.S. atty., 1960-61; atty. Texaco, Inc., N.Y.C., 1961-67; ptnr. Farmer, Shibley, McGuinn & Flood, Washington, 1967-80; ptnr. Flood & Ward, Washington, 1980-96, retired, 1996—. Lt. comdr. USN, 1953-58, Korea. Mem. ABA, Fed. Energy Bar Assn. (chmn. natural resources law sect. 1978, pres. 1982-83), Columbia Country Club, Mid-Ocean Club, Jupiter Hills Club. Republican. Roman Catholic. Avocation: golf. Administrative and regulatory, FERC practice.

**FLOOD, JOAN MOORE,** paralegal; b. Hampton, Va., Oct. 10, 1941; d. Harold W. and Estalena (Fancher) M.; 1 child by former marriage, Angelique. B.Mus., North Tex. State U., 1963, postgrad., 1977; postgrad. So. Meth. U., 1967-68, Tex. Women's U., 1978-79, U. Dallas, 1985-86. Clk. Criminal Dist. Ct. Number 2, Dallas County, Tex., 1972-75; reins. libr. Scor Reins. Co., Dallas, 1975-80; corp. ins. paralegal Assocs. Ins. Group, 1980-83; corp. securities paralegal Akin, Gump, Strauss, Hauer & Feld, 1983-89; asst. sec. Knoll Internat. Holdings Inc., Saddle Brook, N.J., 1989-90, 21 Internat. Holdings, Inc., N.Y.C., 1990-92; dir. compliance Am. Svc. Life Ins. Co., Ft. Worth., 1992-93; v.p., sec. Express Comm., Inc., Dallas, 1993-94; fin. transactions paralegal Thompson & Knight, Dallas, 1994-96; corp. transactions paralegal Jones, Day, Reavis & Pogue, Dallas, 1996-97, Weil, Gotshal & Manges, LLPú, 1998—. Mem. ABA, Tex. Bar Assn. Home: PO Box 190165 Dallas TX 75219-0165

**FLOR, PATRICK JOHN,** lawyer; b. Elizabeth, N.J., Dec. 14, 1963; s. Donald Walter and Romaine Alice Flor; m. Catherine Theodoracopoulos, Aug. 7, 1994; 1 child, Christopher Patrick. BA, Rutgers Coll., 1986, MA, 1987, JD, 1990; LLM, Temple Law Sch., 1997. Bar: Pa. 1990, N.J. 1991, U.S. Dist. Ct. N.J. 1991, U.S. Ct. Appeals for Armed Forces 1991, N.J. 1998. Sr. def. counsel USN JAG Corps, Jacksonville/S.I., Fla./N.Y., 1991-92; staff judge advocate USN JAG Corps, Naval Station, N.Y., 1992-94; assoc. Law Office of Kevin Lynch, East Brunswick, N.J., 1994-95, Fein Such Karin & Shepard, Parsippany, N.J., 1995-97, Deutsch, Resnick, Green & Kiernan, Hackensack, N.J., 1997—; judge mock trial NITA Tournament of Champions, Phila., 1997, 98. Lt. comdr. USN, 1990-94. Mem. ATLA, Naval Res. Assn. General civil litigation, Criminal, Labor. Office: Deutsch Resnick Green & Kiernan 1 University Plz Ste 305 Hackensack NJ 07601-6205

**FLORENCE, HENRY JOHN,** lawyer; b. Rockville Centre, N.Y., Dec. 11, 1934; s. Henry Dulap and Mary (Hanley) F.; m. A. Jean Butler, June 13, 1959; 1 child, Henry John Jr. BS in Econs., Villanova U., 1956; JD, Fordham U., 1961. Bar: N.Y. 1962, Ariz. 1963, U.S. Dist. Ct. Ariz. 1967, U.S. Ct. Appeals (9th cir.) 1970, U.S. Supreme Ct. 1970. Advisor legal aid Navajo Indian Tribe, Window Rock, Ariz., 1962-63; asst. atty. Maricopa County, Phoenix, 1964-65, chief civil dep., 1965-67; ptnr. Stewart & Florence Ltd., Phoenix, 1967-73; sole practice Phoenix, 1973—. Pres. Ariz. Family, Phoenix, 1972-78. Served to lt. (j.g.) USN, 1956-58. Mem. Ariz. Bar Assn. (atty.), Nat. Assn. Criminal Def. Lawyers, Assn. Trial Lawyers Am., Calif. Attys. for Criminal Justice, Ariz. Attys. for Criminal Justice. Democrat. Roman Catholic. Avocation: philatelist. Criminal. Office: 45 W Jefferson St Phoenix AZ 85003-2307

**FLORENCE, KENNETH JAMES,** lawyer; b. Hanford, Calif., July 31, 1943; s. Ivy Owen and louella (Dobson) F.; m. Verena Magdalena Demuth, Dec. 10, 1967. BA, Whittier Coll., 1965; JD, Hastings Coll. Law U. Calif., San Francisco, 1974. Bar: Calif. 1974, U.S. Dist. Ct. (ctrl. dist.) Calif. 1974, U.S. Dist. Ct. (ea. and so. dists.) Calif. 1976, U.S. Dist. Ct. (no. dist.) Calif. 1980, U.S. Ct. Appeals (9th cir.) 1975, U.S. Supreme Ct. 1984. Dist. mgr. Pacific T&T, Calif., 1969-71; assoc. Parker, Milliken, et al, L.A., 1974-78; ptnr. Dern, Mason, et al, 1978-84, Swerdlow Florence Sanchez & Rathbun A Law Corp., Beverly Hills, 1984—; pres. Westside Legal Services, Inc., Santa Monica, Calif., 1982-83. Served to lt. USNR, 1966-69, Vietnam. Col. J.G. Boswell scholar, 1961. Mem. ABA (co-chmn. state labor law com. 1988-91). Democrat. Labor. Office: Swerdlow Florence Sanchez & Rathbun 9401 Wilshire Blvd Ste 828 Beverly Hills CA 90212-2921

**FLORY, JUDITH A.,** lawyer; b. Rutland, Vt.; d. John D. Jr. and Louise G. Flory. BA in Polit Sci., Siena Coll., 1982; JD, Albany Law Sch., 1985. Bar: N.Y., 1986, U.S. Dist. Ct. (no. dist.) N.Y., 1986, U.S. Dist. Ct. (so. dist.) N.Y., 1989, U.S. Dist. Ct. (we. dist.) N.Y., 1991, U.S. Tax Ct., 1991. Atty. Richard V. D'Alessandro Profl. Corp., Albany, N.Y., 1985. Mem. ABA, N.Y. State Bar Assn. Pension, profit-sharing, and employee benefits, Estate planning, Estate taxation. Office: Richard V D'Alessandro Profl Corp 69 Columbia St Albany NY 12210-2708

**FLOWE, BENJAMIN HUGH, JR.,** lawyer; b. Durham, N.C., Feb. 8, 1956; s. Benjamin H. and Dorothy Amelia (Bell) F.; children: Samantha Kathleen, Andrew Benjamin. AB in Sociology and Psychology cum laude, Duke U., 1978; JD with high honors, N.C. U., 1981. Bar: U.S. Ct. Appeals (D.C. cir.) 1981, U.S. Supreme Ct. 1990. Assoc. Arent, Fox et al, Washington, 1981-84, Bowman, Conner & Touhey P.C., Washington, 1984-87; assoc. Verner, Liipfert, Bernhard, McPherson & Hand, Washington, 1987-89, ptnr., 1990-96; pvt. practice, Washington, 1996-97; ptnr. Berliner, Corcoran & Rowe, L.L.P., Washington, 1997—; contbr. congrl. testimony on export controls Ctr. for Strategic and Internat. Studies; mem. tech. adv. com. Commerce Dept. Author: Export Compliance Guide, 1995; contbr. articles to profl. jours. Mem. ABA (vice chair export controls and econ. sanctions com.), Am. Electronics Assn., Am. Soc. Internat. Law, Order of the Coif. Democrat. Presbyterian. Avocations: skiing, writing, golf, tennis. Private international, Admiralty, Contracts commercial. Home: 8120 Paisley Pl Potomac MD 20854-2748 Office: Berliner Corcoran & Rowe LLP 1101 17th St NW Ste 1100 Washington DC 20036-4798

**FLOWE, CAROL CONNOR,** lawyer; b. Owensboro, Ky., Jan. 3, 1950; d. Marvin C. Connor and Ethel Marie (Thorn) Smith; children: Samantha Kathleen, Andrew Benjamin. BME magna cum laude, Murray State U., 1972; JD summa cum laude, Ind. U., 1976. Bar: Ohio 1977, D.C. 1981, U.S. Dist. Ct. (so. dist.) Ohio 1977, U.S. Dist. Ct. Md. 1983, U.S. Dist. Ct. D.C. 1981, U.S. Supreme Ct. 1987, U.S. Ct. Appeals (2d, 4th, 5th, 7th and D.C. cirs.). Assoc. Baker & Hostetler, Columbus, Ohio, 1976-80, Arent Fox Kintner Plotkin & Kahn, Washington, 1980-87; deputy gen. counsel Pension Benefit Guaranty Corp., Washington, 1987-89, gen. counsel, 1989-95; ptnr. Arent, Fox, Kintner, Plotkin & Kahn, 1995—. Mem. ABA, D.C. Bar Assn., Order of Coif, Alpha Chi, Phi Alpha Delta. Avocations: computers, reading. Federal civil litigation, Pension, profit-sharing, and employee benefits, Labor. Home: 8608 Aqueduct Rd Potomac MD 20854-6249 Office: Arent Fox Kintner Plotkin & Kahn 1050 Connecticut Ave NW Ste 500 Washington DC 20036-5339

**FLOYD, KIMBERLY HAYES,** lawyer; b. Greensboro, N.C., Jan. 10, 1958; d. Joe Don and Bonita Jean (Hayes) F. BS, Campbell U., 1980, JD, 1983; postgrad., London Sch. Econs., 1982. Bar: N.C. 1985, U.S. Dist. Ct. (mid. dist.) N.C. 1986, U.S. Dist. Ct. (ea. dist.) N.C. 1994, U.S. Supreme Ct. 1991. Ptnr. Joe D. Floyd, PA, Law Firm, High Point, N.C., 1985—. Co-chmn. Guilford County Dole for Pres. Campaign, N.C., 1995-96; del. Rep. Nat. Convention, 1996; mem. Jr. League of High Point, 1990—; pub. spkr. childwatch com. in coop. with Guilford County Dept. Social Svcs., 1992-94, mem. legis. action/pub. policy com., 1994-98, asst. chmn., 1996-97, chmn., 1997-98; del. N.C. Pub. Affairs Com., 1996-98; spkr. Green St. Bapt. Ch. Women's Conf., 1995. Named one of Outstanding Young Women of Am., 1988, 91; recipient Disting. Alumna award Campbell U., 1997. Mem. N.C. Bar Assn., N.C. Acad. Trial Lawyers, N.C. Assn. Women Attys. (gov. bd. dirs. 1992-94), Guilford County Bar Assn. (sec.-treas. 1992-93), High Point Bar Assn. Republican. Baptist. Personal injury, Workers' compensation, General civil litigation. Office: Joe D Floyd PA Law Firm 401 S Main St High Point NC 27260-6634

**FLOYD, WALTER LEO,** lawyer; b. St. Louis, May 29, 1933; s. Walter L. Sr. and Estelle E. (Kiess) F.; children: Michael W., Mary Ann, Mark L.; m. Patricia A. Knapko, Sept. 3, 1994. BS, St. Louis U., 1955, LLD, 1959. Bar: Mo. 1959, Ill. 1959, U.S. Dist. (ea. dist.) Mo. 1959. Owner The Floyd Law Firm P.C., St. Louis, 1959—. Contbr. articles to profl. jours. Fellow: Orgn. Nat. Bd. Trial Advocacy; mem. Mo. Assn. Trial Attys. (sec. 1961, v.p. 1962, 85), Am. Trial Lawyers Assn. (lectr.), Mo. Bar Assn., Ill. Assn., Phi Delta Phi. Democrat. Unitarian. Federal civil litigation, General civil litigation, State civil litigation. Address: Floyd Law Firm 8151 Clayton Rd # 202 Saint Louis MO 63117-1103

**FLUHR, STEVEN SOLOMON,** lawyer; b. N.Y.C., Mar. 31, 1959; s. Irving Fluhr and Rita Shain; m. Elizabeth Ann Koehr, Oct. 1, 1988; children: Katherine Michelle, Alexandra Sophia. AB, Vassar Coll., 1981; JD, St. Louis U., 1984. Bar: Mo. 1984, Ill. 1985, U.S. Ct. Appeals (8th cir.) 1990, U.S. Dist. Ct. (ea. dist.) Mo. 1986. Staff atty. legal svcs. plan United Auto Workers, St. Louis, 1984-87; assoc. Dubail Judge P.C., Creve Coeur, Mo., 1987-89; ptnr. Rekowsi & Collins, Collinsville, Ill., 1989-90, Gourley Sallerson & Fluhr, St. Louis, 1990-95; atty. Fluhr & Moore L.L.C., Clayton, Mo., 1995—; city atty., prosecuting atty., Hanley Hills, Mo., 1989—; prosecuting atty. Olivette, Mo., 1990—. Mem. Bar Assn. Metro. St. Louis, Lawyers Assn. St. Louis. Municipal (including bonds), Personal injury, General civil litigation. Home: 18 Friese Dr Olivette MO 63132-3108 Office: Fluhr & Moore LLC 225 S Meramec Ave Ste 532T Clayton MO 63105-3598

**FLUM, JOSEPH,** lawyer; b. June 13, 1924. BS in Pre-Law, Temple U., 1947; cert. in fgn. svc., Georgetown U., 1949; JD, Temple U., 1951; PhD, Pacific Western U., 1977. Bar: Pa. Owner, operator Flum's Dept. Store, Newtown, Pa., 1950—; pvt. practice law Newtown, 1961—; lectr. law-related edn., world travel, exploration, and cultures; author, lectr., prof. worldwide anthropol. film documentaries and travel logs; sch. bd. rep. from U.S. to mainland China. Author: The Weave and The Woven, 1989, The Flum Atlas, 1989. Bd. dirs. Council Rock Sch. Dist., Pa., 1967-79, pres., 1971-73; chmn. legis. com. Bucks County Sch. Dirs., 1967-79, chmn. Bucks County Sch.'s legis. com., 1972—; mem. com. revision state sch. code, mem. com. on law-related edn. Pa. Dept. Edn., 1974—, mem. global edn. adv. com., 1978—, apptd. to com. for revision of state sch. code, 1974—; others. Recipient Chapel of Four Chaplains Legion of Honor award, commendation Coun. Rock Edn. Assn., 1980. Fellow Explorers Club; mem. Pa. Bar Assn. (youth-edn. com.), Bucks County Bar Assn., ABA, Northeastern Bar Assn., Phila. Anthropol. Assn., Am. Anthropol. Assn., Smithsonian Instn., Am. Legion, Newtown Hist. Assn., others. Avocations: anthropology, archeology, international travel and exploration. Office: State St at Centre Ave Newtown PA 18940

**FLYNN, BRENDAN THOMAS,** lawyer; b. Hartford, Conn., Feb. 22, 1964; s. John Thomas Jr. and Abigail Cecelia (Moriarty) F.; m. Nancy Gail Stedman. BA in History, Swarthmore Coll., 1986; postgrad., U. Exeter, Eng., 1988; JD with honors, U. Conn., 1989. Bar: Conn. 1989, U.S. Dist. Ct. Conn. 1990. Law clk. to Judge O'Connell Conn. Appellate Ct., Hartford, 1989-90; assoc. Rogin, Nassau, Caplan, Lassman & Hirtle, Hartford, 1990—. Assoc. editor and contbr. Conn. Jour. Internat. Law, 1988-89. Vol. Pub. TV stas.; mem. Wethersfield (Conn.) Dem. Town Com., 1992—, mem. Wethersfield Town Coun., 1995—. Mem. ABA, Hartford County Bar Assn., Conn. Bar Assn., Conn. Trial Lawyers Assn. Avocations: soccer, politics. Contracts commercial, Consumer commercial, Administrative and regulatory. Office: Rogin Nassau Caplan Lassman & Hirtle 185 Asylum St Hartford CT 06103-3408

**FLYNN, CHARLES P.,** lawyer; b. Chgo., Apr. 17, 1943. BA, Willamette U., 1965; LLB, Harvard U., 1968. Bar: Alaska 1968, U.S. Dist. Ct. Alaska 1968, U.S. Ct. Appeals (9th cir.) 1968. Lawyer Burr Pease & Kurtz, Anchorage, 1968-70, shareholder, 1970—. General civil litigation, Environmental, Labor. Office: Burr Pease & Kurtz 810 N St Ste 220 Anchorage AK 99501-3293

**FLYNN, PETER ANTHONY,** judge; b. Bronxville, N.Y., July 23, 1942; s. Ralph Harold and Caroline (Lindberg) F. BA magna cum laude, Harvard U., 1963; LLB, Yale U., 1966. Bar: Ill. 1969, U.S. Dist. Ct. (no. and so. dists.) Ill. 1969, U.S. Ct. Appeals (7th cir.) 1969, U.S. Supreme Ct. 1976, U.S. Dist. Ct. (ea. dist.) Wis. 1980, U.S. Ct. Appeals (2d and 5th cirs.) 1980, U.S. Ct. Appeals (9th cir.) 1987. Asst. lect. law U. Ife, 1967-69; assoc. Jenner & Block, Chgo., 1969-75; ptnr. Cherry & Flynn, Chgo., 1976-99; judge Cir. Ct. of Cook County, Chgo., 1999—. Mem. Olympia Fields Plan Commn., Ill., 1979-83, chmn., 1983-85; trustee Village of Olympia Fields, 1985-89; pres. Touchstone Theatre, 1990-93; active U.S. Peace Corps, 1967-69. Mem. ABA, Ill. Bar Assn., Am. Law Inst., Atticus Finch Inn of Ct. Roman Catholic. Avocations: theater, piano, poetry, guitar, choral music, sailing.

**FLYNN, WALTER ANDREW,** lawyer; b. Bridgeport, Conn., Aug. 2, 1943; s. Walter Andrew and Irene G. (Finnerly) F.; m. Kathleen C. Morris, Aug. 24, 1976; children: Meghan, Erin, Caitlin. BS, Boston Coll., 1965; JD, Georgetown U., 1968; LLM in Tax, NYU, 1971. Bar: Conn. 1968, U.S. Dist.

Ct. Conn. 1971, U.S. Ct. Appeals (2d cir.) 1971, U.S. Supreme Ct. 1973. Ptnr. Goldstein & Peck P.C., Bridgeport, 1971—. Town atty. Weston, Conn., 1981-87. Capt. U.S. Army, 1968-70, Vietnam. Mem. ABA, Con. Bar Assn. (exec. com. estates and probate sect. 1987—), Westport Bar Assn., Greater Bridgeport Bar Assn. (pres. 1987-88). Avocation: golf. Estate planning, Taxation, general. Office: Goldstein & Peck PC 1087 Broad St Bridgeport CT 06604-4261

**FOBE, NICHOLAS M(ATTHEW),** lawyer; b. Ghent, Belgium, Jan. 13, 1961; came to U.S., 1979; s. Matthieu and Françoise (DeSchryver) F.; m. Rachelle Tetenbaum, June 12, 1986; children: Irene, Lennie. BM, Jacksonville U., 1982; MM, Ind. U., 1986; JD, Fordham U., 1992, Georgetown U., 1992. Bar: N.Y. 1993, D.C. 1993, Md. 1994, U.S. Dist. Ct. (so. and no. dists.) Md., U.S. Dist. Ct. (so. and ea. dists.) N.Y. 1993, U.S. Supreme Ct. 1996. Ptnr. Verstegen & Fobe, Washington, 1997—; notary public State of Md., Montgomery County, 1995—, D.C., 1998—. Mem. Milbrook Chamber Orch. Named Disting. Citizen State of Md., 1993. Mem. Belgian-Am. Assn., Union Francophone des Belges à l'Étranger, Nederlandse Vereniging, Washington Flanders Club (co-founder, bd. dirs., v.p. 1994—, author legal column newsletter 1994—), Amateur Chamber Music Players. Avocation: violist in string quartet, chamber ensembles. Estate planning, Probate, Private international. Home: 19316 Dimona Dr Brookeville MD 20833-2627

**FOBES, RONALD L.,** prosecutor; b. Indpls., Oct. 17, 1938; s. George R. Fobes and Virginia R. Cunix; m. Betty J. Fobes, Oct. 24, 1984; 1 child, Pamela L. Ames. BA, U. Dayton, 1963; JD, U. Kans., 1966. Bar: Ohio. Asst. law dir. Springfield, Ohio, 1966-67; asst. pros. atty. Montgomery, Ohio, 1967-79; pvt. practice atty. Dayton/Troy, Ohio, 1979-85; prosecutor Mcpl., Miamisburg, Ohio, 1985—. Mem. Nat. Dist. Atty. Assn., Ohio State Bar, Dayton Bar Assn., Masons, Scottish Rite, Antioch Shrine. Avocations: hunting, flying pilot. Office: 10 N 1st St Miamisburg OH 45342-2305

**FOCHT, MICHAEL HARRISON, JR.,** lawyer; b. Reading, Pa., Jan. 5, 1965; s. Michael Harrison Sr. and Sandra Lee (Scholwin) F.; m. Michele Billera, Sept. 5, 1992; 1 child, Samantha. BA in Econs., Bus. Adminstrn., Vanderbilt U., 1987; JD, St. Mary's U., 1990. Bar: Tex. 1990, Fla. 1991, U.S. Dist. Ct. (mid. dist.) Fla. 1991, U.S. Ct. Appeals (5th and 11th cirs.) 1991. Summer assoc. Fulbright & Jaworski, Washington, 1989; assoc. Metzger, Sonneborn & Rutter, PA, West Palm Beach, Fla., 1990-92; assoc. counsel Nat. Med. Enterprises, Santa Monica, Calif., 1992—. Founder, chpt. pres. Federalist Soc. for Laws and Pub. Policy, San Antonio, 1987-90; mem. The Heritage Found., Washington, 1987—; vol. Project Literacy, West Palm Beach, 1991. Mem. ABA (forum on health law), Assn. Trial Lawyers Am., Am. Acad. Hosp. Attys., State Bar Tex. (health law sect.), Fla. Bar Assn. (health law sect.), Nat. Health Lawyers Assn. Republican. Roman Catholic. Health, General corporate. Office: Nat Med Enterprises 2700 Colorado Ave Santa Monica CA 90404-3553

**FOCHT, THEODORE HAROLD,** lawyer, educator; b. Reading, Pa., Aug. 20, 1934; s. Harold Edwin and Ruth Naomi (Boyer) F.; m. Joyce Gundy, Aug. 11, 1956; children: David Scott, Eric Steven. AB in Philosophy, Franklin and Marshall Coll., 1956; JD, Coll. of William and Mary, 1959. Bar: Va. 1959. Teaching assoc. Columbia U. Sch. Law, N.Y.C., 1959-60; atty. Office of Gen. Counsel SEC, Washington, 1960-61, legal asst. to Commr., Washington, 1961-63; mem. faculty U. Conn. Sch. Law, Hartford, 1963-71 (leave of absence, 1969-71); spl. counsel on securities legislation Interstate and Fgn. Commerce Com., U.S. Ho. of Reps., Washington, 1969-71; gen. counsel Securities Investor Protection Corp., Washington, 1971-94, pres., 1984-94; adj. prof. law American U. Sch. Law, Washington, 1979-84; mem. Fla. State Comptroller's Task Force on Regulatory DeCoupling, 1995. Mem. Va. State Bar, Phi Beta Kappa. General corporate, Bankruptcy, Securities. Home: 8436 Pinafore Dr New Port Richey FL 34653-6739

**FODEN, MARIA LUISA DE CASTRO,** lawyer; b. Santiago, Chile, Mar. 4, 1947; came to U.S., 1967; d. Diego F. De Castro Reyes and Ana Eguigueren-Rozas; m. Edward Foden, Jan. 27, 1969; children: Edward, Mary, Ann. BA, Rutgers U., 1971; JD, U. Conn., 1978. Bar: Conn. 1980, U.S. Dist. Ct. Conn. 1980. Pvt. practice, Hartford, Conn., 1980—. Roman Catholic. General practice, Criminal, Family and matrimonial. Office: 107 Oak St Hartford CT 06106-1515

**FODERA, LEONARD V.,** lawyer; b. Bklyn., Sept. 9, 1956; s. Vito Leonard and Nancy Rose (Calderola) F.; m. Kathleen M. Scanlon, Sept. 4, 1981; children: Leonard, Nancy. BA, LaSalle Coll., Phila., 1978; JD, Temple U., Phila., 1989. Bar: Pa. 1989, U.S. Dist. Ct. (ea. dist.) Pa. 1989. Gen. counsel Plymouth Risk Mgmt., Plymouth Meeting, Pa., 1990-92; assoc. Sheller Ludwig & Badey, Phila., 1992-95; ptnr. Monheit, Monheit, Silverman & Fodera, PC, Phila., 1995—. Legal counsel Roosevelt Adv. Counsel, 1989—; mem. Cinnaminson Curriculum Com., N.J., 1992-93, Cinnaminson planning bd., 1998—; advisor Com. of 70, Phila., 1986—. Mem. ABA, Assn. Trial Lawyers Am., Phila. Bar Assn., Million Dollar Advocates Forum, Phila. Trial Lawyers Assn. Roman Catholic. E-mail: civil@civilrights.com. Professional liability, State civil litigation, Civil rights. Office: Mongheit Monheit Silverman Fodera 2010 Chestnut St Philadelphia PA 19103-4411

**FOGARTY, JAMES ROBERT,** lawyer; b. Norwalk, Conn., Jan. 24, 1943; s. James R. and Alice (Henshon) F.; m. Frances Sclafani, Dec. 12, 1975; children—Brendan John, Brian Henshon. B.A., Fordham U., 1964, LL.B., 1967; LL.M., NYU, 1972. Bar: N.Y. 1967, Conn. 1968, U.S. Supreme Ct. 1973, U.S. Ct. Appeals (2d cir.) 1975. Law clk. Honorable Howard Alcorn, Conn. Supreme Ct., Hartford, Conn., 1968-69; ptnr. Durey & Pierson, Stamford, Conn., 1969-79, Epstein & Fogarty, Stamford, 1969-95; prin. Fogarty, Cohen, Selby & Nemiroff, LLC, 1995—. Editor Conn. Bar Jour., 1976-82. Mem. Rep. Town Meeting, Greenwich, Conn., 1969-73; mem. Inland Wetlands and Water Courses Agy., Greenwich, 1973-80; bd. dirs. YMCA, Stamford, Conn., 1982-84. Mem. Conn. Bar Assn., Am. Coll. Trial Lawyers, Am. Bd. Trial Advocates (assoc.). Roman Catholic. Clubs: Greenwich Country, Indian Harbor Yacht (Greenwich, Conn.). State civil litigation, Federal civil litigation. Office: Fogarty Cohen Selby & Nemiroff LLC 88 Field Point Rd Greenwich CT 06830-6468

**FOGARTY, JANET E.,** lawyer; b. Cambridge, Mass., June 16, 1950; d. Frederick A. and Joan Burgess; m. William L. Fogarty, June 7, 1969; 1 child, William P., II. BS, U. San Francisco, 1985, JD, 1991. Bar: Calif. Real estate salesperson Westborough Realty, South San Francisco, 1977-81; v.p., office mgr. Real Vest Realtors, Millbrae, Calif., 1985-87; real estate broker Real Vest Realtors, Millbrae, 1981-90; assoc. Lillick & Charles, San Francisco, 1991-93; of counsel Lakin Spears, Palo Alto, Calif., 1993-96, Deborah Wilder & Assocs., Burlingame, Calif., 1996-98, Fogarty & Watson LLP, Burlingame, 1998—; city rep., dir. City/County Assn. Govts., 1991-94; chmn. Growth Mgmt. Policy Com., 1992-95; instr. San Jose (Calif.) State U., 1999. Mayor City of Millbrae, 1990-91, 93-94, mem. City Coun., 1987-95; bd. dirs. Bay Area Air Quality Mgmt. Dist., San Francisco, 1992-96; bd. dirs., chmn. San Mateo Transit Dist., San Carlos, Calif., 1975-85, chmn., 1980-81; bd. dirs. Multi-City TSM Agy., South San Francisco, 1993-95, chmn., 1993-95. Mem. Soroptimist (pres. 1990-91, Woman Distinction award 1995), Rep. Women's Fedn., Calif. Elected Women's Assn., Calif. Women Lawyers, Millbrae C. of C. (chmn. 1999), Visiting Nurses Assn. Hospice (chmn. 1997—). Republican. Roman Catholic. Avocations: reading, politics, travel. Real property, Land use and zoning (including planning), Landlord-tenant. Home: 1126 Hillcrest Blvd Millbrae CA 94030-2235 Office: Fogarty & Watson LLP 1633 Bayshore Hwy Ste 329 Burlingame CA 94010-1515

**FOGARTY, JOHN PATRICK CODY,** lawyer; b. Washington, Sept. 12, 1958; m. Sarah Shiffert, Jan. 20, 1989. BA, George Washington U., 1981; JD cum laude, New Eng. Sch. Law, 1984; postgrad., Georgetown U., 1985-87. Bar: Mass. 1985, D.C. 1985. Sr. atty. NLRG, Inc., Charlottesville, Va., 1984-85; atty., editor Environ. Law Inst., Washington, 1985-87; atty. office of toxic substances EPA, Washington, 1987-89, atty. office of enforcement, 1989-91, sr. atty. office of enforcement, 1991-92, asst. enforcement counsel Superfund, 1992-94; assoc. dir. RCRA Enforcement Divsn., Washington, 1995-98; dep. dir. Office of Planning and Policy Analysis, Washington, 1998—; cons. in field; speaker on environ. issues. Co-author: The Clean Water Desk Book, 1988, Environmental Law and Practice, 1992, 94; editor, co-author: Law of Environment Protection, 1987, 90-91, 95-97; contbr. articles to profl. publs. Bd. trustees Sandy Spring Friends Sch., 1998—. New Eng. scholar, 1982. Mem. D.C. Bar Assn., Environ. Law Inst. (assoc.). Mem. Soc. of Friends. Home: 4408 Fairfield Dr Bethesda MD 20814-4743 Office: EPA 1200 Pennsylvania Ave NW Washington DC 20004-2403

**FOGEL, ADELAIDE FORST,** lawyer; b. N.Y.C., July 26, 1915; d. Leon and Antoinette (Hahn) Forst; BA, Washington Sq. Coll., 1936; LLB, N.Y. U., 1939; m. David Fogel, June 2, 1940; children: Ann Fogel Vivell, Susan Lee Fogel Lloyd. Admitted to N.Y. State bar; individual practice law, N.Y.C., 1940—. Patron N.Y. Philharmonic; trustee Temple Israel, N.Y.C., past pres. Sisterhood. Mem. Met. Mus. Art, Mus. Natural History, NYU Law Alumni Assn. (pres's. coun.). Estate planning, Real property.

**FOGEL, J(OAN) CATHY,** lawyer; b. Chgo., Mar. 18, 1943; d. Norman Jack and Esther Lois (Grobstein) Friedman; m. Jay Bernard Lichtenberg, June 29, 1968 (dec. Apr. 1981); 1 child, Ian Robert; m. Donald Benjamin Fogel, Sept. 27, 1987; children: Alexis Jill, D. Brandon. BS, U. Wis., 1964; JD, Cath. U., 1977. Bar: U.S. Ct.Appeals (D.C. cir.) 1977, D.C. 1978, U.S. Ct. Appeals (7th cir.) 1979, U.S. Ct. Appeals (2d cir.) 1979, U.S. Supreme Ct. 1981, U.S. Ct. Appeals (3d cir.) 1984. Research librarian Library Congress, Washington, 1964-66; legislative research specialist Am. Pub. Power Assn., Washington, 1966-71; assoc. Duncan, Miller & Pembroke, Washington, 1977-83, ptnr., 1983-88; ptnr. Verner, Liipfert, Bernhard, McPherson and Hand, Washington, 1989—; spl. asst. atty. gen. State of N.D., 1979-86. Contbr. articles to profl. jours. Mem. ABA, Women's Bar Assn., D.C. Bar Assn., Fed. Energy Bar Assn. (chmn. fed. power act parts I & II 1985-86, vice-chmn. power mktg. agys. 1988-89, chmn. power mktg. agys. 1989-90). Democrat. Jewish. Avocations: oenophile, travel. Antitrust, Federal civil litigation, FERC practice. Home: 3804 Woodbine St Chevy Chase MD 20815-4957 Office: Verner Liipfert Bernhard McPherson & Hand 901 15th St NW Ste 700 Washington DC 20005-2327

**FOGEL, JOSEPH LEWIS,** lawyer; b. Berkeley, Calif., Feb. 12, 1961; s. David and Muriel F.; m. Renate A. Stolzer, Aug. 14, 1994. BA, U. Calif., San Diego, 1983; JD, DePaul U., 1986. Bar: Ill. 1986, U.S. Dist. Ct. (no. dist.) Ill. 1986, U.S. Ct. Appeals (7th cir.) 1986. Assoc. Jenner & Block, Chgo., 1986-89, Skadden, Arps, Chgo., 1989-94; ptnr. Freeborn & Peters, Chgo., 1994—; barrister Abraham Lincoln Marovitz Am. Inn Cts., 1998. Avocations: basketball, golf, reading, hockey. General civil litigation, Antitrust, Professional liability. Office: Freeborn & Peters 311 S Wacker Dr Ste 3000 Chicago IL 60606-6679

**FOGEL, LARK HOUSE,** lawyer; b. El Paso, Tex., Feb. 19, 1961; d. Robert M. and Sara E. (Harris) House; divorced; 1 child, Leo Francis. BA, U. Colo., 1983, JD, 1988. Bar: Tex., 1989; U.S. Dist. Ct. (we. dist.) 1990. Assoc. Law Office James Scherr, El Paso, 1989-92, ptnr., 1992-93; pvt. practice El Paso, 1993—. Mem. ABA, Am. Trial Lawyers Assn., El Paso Bar Assn. Personal injury, Workers' compensation. Home: 8105 E Lakeshore Dr Parker CO 80134-5817 Office: 109 N Oregon St Ste 1314 El Paso TX 79901-1148

**FOGEL, RICHARD,** lawyer; b. Bklyn.; m. Sheila Feldman; children: Bruce, Lori Ellen. BA, York Coll., CUNY, 1971; JD, N.Y. Law Sch., 1974. Bar: N.J. 1976, U.S. Dist. Ct. N.J. 1976, N.Y. 1981, U.S. Tax Ct. 1977. Tax law specialist IRS, Newark, 1975-77; sr. pension cons., atty. N.Y. Life, N.Y.C., 1977-81; pvt. practice, Franklin, N.J., 1981-85, Wayne, N.J., 1985-88, McAfee, N.J., 1988—; lectr. Inst. for Continuing Legal Edn., Newark, 1977—; mem. adj. faculty Upsala Coll., East Orange, N.J., 1978-88; presenter 34th ann. meeting. Internat. Soc. for Systems Scis., Portland State U., 1990. Recipient Certs. of Appreciation, IRS, Newark, 1977, Inst. Continuing Legal Edn., Newark, 1981-82, 84, Cert. in Recognition of Accomplishments, Coop. Extension Cook Coll., Rutgers U., 1982, Disting. Grad. award York Coll., 1984, Founder's Day Dist. Alumni award, 1992. Pension, profit-sharing, and employee benefits, Estate planning, Real property. Home: 28 Elizabeth Dr Sussex NJ 07461-3402 Office: Vernon Colonial Pla PO Box 737 Rt 94 Mc Afee NJ 07428

**FOGELNEST, ROBERT,** lawyer; b. Phila., Aug. 29, 1946; s. Phillip Harold and Charlotte (Wolkov) F.; m. M.J. Wolf, Jan. 21, 1972 (div. 1980); 1 child, B. Jacob; m. Susan W. Van Dusen, Mar. 27, 1991. BA, Temple U., 1973; JD, Rutgers U., 1976. Bar: Pa. 1976, N.Y. 1987, U.S. Dist. Ct. (ea. dist.) Pa. 1976, U.S. Dist. Ct. (ea. and so. dists.) N.Y. 1987, U.S. Dist. Ct. (we. dist.) Pa. 1988, U.S. Tax Ct. 1984, U.S. Ct. Appeals (3d cir.) 1985. Asst. dist. atty. Phila., 1976-79; ptnr. Ellis, Fogelnest & Newman, P.C., Phila., 1979-85; pvt. practice, N.Y.C., 1985—; mem. bd. regents Nat. Criminal Def. Coll. Editorial adviser Inside Drug Law, 1984-89. Fellow Am. Bd. Criminal Lawyers (gov.), Pa. Assn. Crimininal Def. Lawyers, N.Y. Assn. Criminal Def. Lawyers (dir.); mem. Nat. Assn. Criminal Def. Lawyers (pres. 1995-96). Criminal, Private international. Office: 475 Park Ave S Ste 3300 New York NY 10016-6901

**FOGG, BLAINE VILES,** lawyer; b. Boston, Mar. 29, 1940; s. Sanford L. and Dorothy (Viles) F.; m. Diane Abitbol, June 22, 1964; children: William, Matthew, Katherine. AB, Williams Coll., 1962; JD, Harvard U., 1965. Bar: N.Y. 1966. Assoc. Skadden, Arps, Slate, Meagher & Flom, N.Y.C., 1966-71, ptnr., 1971—. Mergers and acquisitions. Office: Skadden Arps Slate 919 3rd Ave New York NY 10022-3902

**FOGLEMAN, CHRISTOPHER CURTIS,** lawyer; b. Williamsport, Pa., Sept. 20, 1959; s. Paul Arthur and Cecelia Eleanor (Smith) F.; m. Karen Arline Hayes, July 18, 1981; children: Matthew Warren, Nicholas Paul, Kevin Christopher, Danielle Elizabeth, Alexander Michael. BA, King's Coll., Wilkes-Barre, Pa., 1981; JD, Am. U., 1984. Bar: Md. 1985, D.C. 1989, Va. 1990. Jud. law clk. Montgomery County Cir. Ct., Rockville, Md., 1984-85; asst. pub. defender Montgomery County Office Pub. Defender, Rockville, 1985-88; ptnr. Gleason, Flynn and Emig, Chartered, Rockville, 1988—. Mem. Montgomery County Bar Assn., Md. Bar Assn., Nat. Assn. Criminal Defense Lawyers, Md. Criminal Defense Attys. Assn. Democrat. Roman Catholic. Contracts commercial, General civil litigation, Personal injury. Office: Gleason Flynn and Emig Chartered 451 Hungerford Dr Ste 600 Rockville MD 20850-5105

**FOGLEMAN, JOHN NELSON,** lawyer; b. Memphis, Jan. 2, 1956; s. Julian Barton and Margaret (Henderson) F.; m. Nancy Darlene Norris, Aug. 14, 1976; children: John Nelson Jr., Adam Barrett. BS in Edn., Ark. State U., 1978; JD, U. Ark., 1981. Bar: Ark. 1981, U.S. Dist. Ct. (ea. dist.) Ark. 1981. Assoc. Hale, Fogleman & Rogers, West Memphis, Ark., 1981-85, ptnr., 1985-94; cir. judge 2d Jud. Dist. Ark., 1995—; city atty. City of Marion, 1982-94; dep. pros. atty. 2d jud. dist. Crittenden County, Marion, Ark., 1983-94. Mem. sch. bd. Marion Sch. Dist., 1985-94; pres. Marion C. of C., 1982-83. Mem. ABA, Ark. Bar Assn., Assn. Trial Lawyers Am., Ark. Trial Lawyers Assn. (mem. Ark. sentencing commn. 1998—, chair jud. resources assessment com. 1998—). Methodist. Avocations: jogging, reading, gardening. General practice, Personal injury, Criminal. Home: 206 Rivertrace Dr Marion AR 72364-2602 Office: 116 Military Rd Marion AR 72364-1753

**FOHRMAN, DARRYL,** lawyer; b. Chgo., Dec. 11, 1940; s. Irving and Betty Fohrman; m. Gail Solrr, May 4, 1966 (div. July 1984); children: Lisa Fohrman Becker, Julie. BA with honors, U. Mich., 1961; JD, U. Chgo., 1964. Bar: Ill. 1964, Fla. 1990. Clk. to Hon. Justice Arthur Murphy Ill. Appellate Ct., 1964; assoc. Goldberg, Weigle, Mallen & Revlon, Chgo., 1965; founder, mng. ptnr. Fohrman Lurie, Chgo., 1965-84; pvt. practice Key West, Fla., 1990—; pres., CEO Dunhill Fin. Corp., Chgo., 1984-89. Author: (screenplay) Lake Shore Drive, 1983. Mem. Ill. Bar Assn., Fla. Bar Assn. Avocations: bicycle riding, swimming. Probate, General practice, Estate planning. Home and Office: 322 Elizabeth St Key West FL 33040-6805

**FOLBERG, HAROLD JAY,** lawyer, mediator, educator, university dean; b. East St. Louis, Ill., July 7, 1941; s. Louis and Matilda (Ross) F.; m. Diana L. Taylor, May 1, 1983; children: Lisa, Rachel, Ross. BA, San Francisco State U., 1963; JD, U. Calif., Berkeley, 1968. Bar: Oreg. 1968. Assoc. Rives & Schwab, Portland, Oreg., 1968-69; dir. Legal Aid Service, Portland, 1970-72; exec. dir. Assn. Family and Conciliation Cts., Portland, 1974-80; prof. law Lewis and Clark Law Sch., Portland, 1972-89; clin. asst. prof. child psychiatry U. Oreg. Med. Sch., 1976-89; judge pro-tem Oreg. Trial Cts., 1974-89; dean, prof. U. San Francisco Sch. Law, 1989—; chair jud. coun. Calif. Task Force on Alternative Dispute Resolution and the Jud. Sys., 1998—; Rockefeller Found. scholar in residence Bellagio, Italy, 1996; vis. prof. U. Wash. Sch. Law, 1985-86; mem. vis. faculty Nat. Jud. Coll., 1975—; mem. Nat. Commn. on Accreditation for Marriage and Family Therapists, 1984-90; cons. Calif. Jud. Coun., U.S. Dist. Ct. (no. dist.) Calif. Author: Joint Custody and Shared Parenting, 1984, 2d edit., 1991; (with Taylor) Mediation-A Comprehensive Guide to Resolving Conflicts without Litigation, 1984; (with Milne) Divorce Mediation-Theory and Practice, 1988; mem. editorial bd. Conciliation Cts. Rev., Jour. of Divorce, Mediation Quar.; contbr. articles to profl. jours. Bd. dirs. Internat. Bioethics Inst., 1989-95, Oreg. Dispute Resolution Adv. Coun., 1988-89. Mem. ABA (chmn. mediation and arbitration com. family law sect. 1980-82), Oreg. State Bar Assn. (chmn. family and juvenile law sect. 1979-80), Am. Bd. Trial Advs., Multnomah Bar Assn. (chmn. bd. dirs. legal aid svc. 1973-76), Am. Arbitration Assn. (mem. panel of arbitrators), Internat. Soc. Family Law, Assn. Family and Conciliation Cts. (pres. 1983-84), Assn. Marriage and Family Therapists (disting. mem.), Am. Assn. Law Schs. (chmn. alternative dispute resolution sect. 1988), Acad. Family Mediators (bd. dirs., pres. 1988), Soc. Profls. in Dispute Resolution, World Assn. Law Profs. (sec.-gen. 1995—). Office: U San Francisco Sch Law 2130 Fulton St San Francisco CA 94117-1080

**FOLEY, DAVID N.,** lawyer, former social studies educator; b. Washington, Feb. 6, 1960; s. William Edward and Marguerite Pratt F.; m. Denise Amy Riley, Sept. 17, 1994. BA, U. N.H., 1982, MAT, 1986; JD, Franklin Pierce Law Ctr., 1991. Bar: N.H. 1991, Maine 1993, U.S. Dist. Ct. N.H. 1997. Social studies tchr. Wilmington (Vt.) H.S., 1986-88; staff atty. N.H. Pub. Defender, Dover/Keene, 1992-96; pvt. practice, Henniker, N.H., 1996-97; assoc. Robert Howard Law Office, Henniker, N.H., 1997-98, ptnr., 1998—. Mem. N.H. Bar Assn. (law-related edn. adv. bd. 1993—), Rotary (sec. 1998, pres. 1999—). Avocations: hiking, traveling, Gemutlichkeit. Criminal, Family and matrimonial, General civil litigation. Office: Robert Howard Law Office 10 Main St PO Box 900 Henniker NH 03242-0900

**FOLEY, MARTIN JAMES,** lawyer; b. Nebr., Nov. 7, 1946; s. James Gleason and Mary Elizabeth (O'Brien) F.; m. Linda Sivyer; children: James Gleason II, Daniel Patrick, Ryan Edward, Michelle Sivyer. Cert. Completion, Cambridge U., 1967; BA in Philosophy, U. So. Calif., 1968, JD, 1974, MBA, 1975. Bar: Calif. 1975, U.S. Dist. Ct. (cen. dist.) Calif. 1975, U.S. Dist. Ct. (ea., so. and no. dists.) Calif. 1980, U.S. Ct. Appeals (9th cir.) 1980, U.S. Ct. Fed. Claims, U.S. Supreme Ct. Acct. Ford Motor Co., San Jose, Calif., 1968, cost analyst, 1970-71; assoc. Adams, Duque & Hazeltine, 1975-80; sr. ptnr. Bryan, Cave, McPheeters & McRoberts, L.A., 1980-89, Sonnenschein Nath & Rosenthal, L.A., 1990—; mem. bd. govs. Gen. Alumni Assn., U. So. Calif., 1982-84, ct. appt. settlement officer Calif. State, 1992-94, U.S. Dist. Ct. (cen. dist.), 1998—; lectr. groups and profl. confs. Contbr. articles to profl. jours. Served to lt. (j.g.) USNR, 1968-70. Mem. ABA (numerous coms.), Calif. Bar Assn. (conf. of dels. 1979-93), L.A. County Bar Assn., Jonathan Club (L.A.), Annandale Golf Club (Pasadena, Calif.). Republican. Roman Catholic. Intellectual property, Aviation, Labor. Office: Sonnenschein Nath Rosenthal 601 S Figueroa St Ste 1500 Los Angeles CA 90017-5720

**FOLEY, SALLY LEE,** lawyer; b. Elko, Nev., Aug. 23, 1948; d. Arthur Lee II and Edith Louise (Butler) F.; m. Richard Allan Solomon, Dec. 21, 1975 (div. Oct. 1987); 1 child, Jennifer Lee. AB in History/Polit. Sci., Ind. U., 1970; JD, Georgetown U., 1973. Bar: Mich. 1973, U.S. Dist. Ct. (ea. dist.) Mich. 1974, D.C. 1975, U.S. Ct. Appeals (D.C. cir.) 1975, U.S. Dist. Ct. (we. dist.) Mich. 1976, U.S. Ct. Appeals (6th cir.) 1977. Law clk. Mich. Atty. Gen. Consumer Protection and Antitrust Divsn., Lansing, summer 1972; asst. atty. gen. State of Mich., Lansing, 1973-75; ptnr. Solomon and Foley, Detroit, 1975-87; sr. assoc. atty. Barbier & Tolleson, Detroit and Troy, 1988-89; counsel Harness, Dickey & Pierce, P.L.C., Troy, 1989-95; shareholder Howard & Howard, Bloofield Hills, Mich., 1995-97; atty. Plunkett & Cooney, Bloomfield Hills, Mich., 1997—; mem. State of Mich. Atty. Gen.'s Adv. Com.; mem. Mich. Franchise Adv. Com., 1975—;mem. Mich. Consumer Protection Act Adv. Com., 1977—; comml. arbitrator Am. Arbitration Assn., 1990—. Mem. Christ Ch. Cranbrook, Bloomfield Hills, Mich., 1980—; patron Founders' Soc./Detroit Inst. Arts, 1980—; bd. dirs. South Oakland County Shelter, 1988-91; host Internat. Visitors Coun. Met. Detroit, 1993—. Mem. ABA (mem. sect. of antitrust law state antitrust enforcement com. 1977—, franchising com. 1977—, mem. sect. bus. law, litigation sect. 1986—, sect. patent, trademark and copyright law 1989—, sect. antitrust law franchise registration and regulation task force 1993-94, assoc. editor Jour. of the Forum Com. on Franchising 1978-82, editor, 1982-85, governing bd. forum com. on franchising 1984-87), Internat. Franchise Assn. (legal/legis. com. 1988—), Internat. Bar Assn. (sect. on bus. law 1985—, coun. of dels. 1992—, internat. franchising com. 1987—, sect. on gen. practice, mem. profl. program com. 1994—, indigenous peoples and devel. law com. 1994—), Internat. Trademark Assn. (licensing com. 1989-91, membership com. 1991-94, task force on licensing 1991-93, L.Am. and Caribbean licensing com. 1993-94, planning com. 1995-96, alt. dispute resolution, 1996—), Nat. Assn. Women Lawyers (bd. dirs. 1993-94, v.p. 1994-95, pres. elect 1995-96, pres. 1996-97, immediate past pres.), Women Lawyers Assn. Mich. (pub. adv. com. 1977—, bd. dirs. 1979-82, 83-84, historian 1979-85, ), Detroit Bar Assn., Detroit Econ. Club, Kappa Alpha Theta, Southeastern Mich. Alumni Assn., Georgetown U. Alumni Club Mich. (bd. dirs. 1979-80). Democrat. Episcopalian. Avocations: art, political party activities. Franchising, Intellectual property, Trademark and copyright. Office: Plunkett & Cooney PC 505 N Woodward Ave Ste 3000 Bloomfield Hills MI 48304-2967

**FOLEY, STEPHEN PATRICK,** lawyer; b. Milwaukee, Jan. 19, 1964; s. John F. and Patricia M. F.; married, Aug. 3, 1991; 1 child, Daniel Ryan. BA, Monterey Inst. Internat. Studies, Monterey, Calif., MA, 1987; JD, U. Wisc., Madison, 1990. Mng. ptnr. Foley & Casey, L.L.C., Milw., 1995—. Assn. Trial Lawyers Am., State Bar Wis. Personal injury. Office: Foley & Casey LLC 611 E Wells St Fl 3 Milwaukee WI 53202-3816

**FOLEY, THOMAS JOHN,** lawyer; b. Detroit, July 3, 1954; s. Thomas John and Mary Catherine (Gluekert) F.; m. Virginia Lee, Aug. 20, 1977; 1 child, Kaitlin Shea. BA, Mich. State U., 1976, JD, 1979. Bar: Mich. 1980, Ohio 1992, U.S. Dist. Ct. (ea. and we. dists.) Mich. 1980, U.S.Ct. Appeals (6th cir.) 1980. Assoc. Kitch, Drutchas, Wagner, Denardis & Valitutti, Detroit, 1980-84, assoc. prin., 1984-87, prin., shareholder, 1987—. Contbr. articles to profl. jours. Mem. FBA, Internat. Assn. Def. Counsel, Def. Rsch. Inst., Food and Drug Law Inst., Greater Detroit C. of C. Avocations: swimming, private pilot. General civil litigation, Personal injury, Product liability. Office: Kitch Drutchas et al 1 Woodward Ave Fl 10 Detroit MI 48226-3402

**FOLKENFLIK, MAX,** lawyer; b. Phila., Sept. 9, 1948; s. Bernard Folkenflik and Florence (Rogosin) Field; m. Margaret A. McGerity, Apr., 3, 1971; children: Alexander, Andrew. BS, Cornell U., 1970; JD, Georgetown U., 1975. Bar: N.Y. 1976, U.S. Dist. Ct. (so. dist.) N.Y. 1976, (ea. dist.) N.Y. 1976, U.S. Tax Ct. 1977, U.S. Ct. Appeals (2d cir.) 1994, U.S. Ct. Appeals (3d cir.) 1997. Assoc. Kronish, Lieb, Shainswit, Weiner & Hellman, N.Y.C., 1975-79, Cravath, Swaine & Moore, N.Y.C., 1979-83; ptnr. Morrison, Paul & Beiley, N.Y.C., 1983-84, Morrison, Cohen & Singer, N.Y.C., 1984-85, Wistendahl & Folkenflik, N.Y.C., 1985-88, Folkenflik & McGerity, N.Y.C., 1988—. Mem. staff Georgetown U. Law Review, 1973-74, editor 1974-75. Mem. ABA, Assn. of Bar of City of N.Y. Democrat. Jewish. Avocation: photography. Federal civil litigation, State civil litigation, Securities. Home: 261 W 90th St New York NY 10024-1119 Office: Folkenflik & McGerity 1370 Ave Of The Americas New York NY 10019-4602

**FOLLICK, EDWIN DUANE,** law educator, chiropractic physician; b. Glendale, Calif., Feb. 4, 1935; s. Edwin Fulfford and Esther Agnes (Catherwood) F.; m. Marilyn K. Sherk, Mar. 24, 1986. BA, Calif. State U., L.A., 1956, MA, 1961; MA, Pepperdine U., 1957, MPA, 1977; PhD, DTh, St. Andrews Theol. Coll., Sem. of Free Prot. Episc. Ch., London, 1958; MS in Libr. Sci., U. So. Calif., 1963, MEd in Instructional Materials, 1964, AdvMEd in Edn. Adminstrn., 1969; postgrad., Calif. Coll. Law, 1965; LLB, Blackstone Law Sch., 1966, JD, 1967; DC, Cleve. Chiropractic Coll., L.A.,

1972; PhD, Academia Theatina, Pescara, 1978; MA in Organizational Mgmt., Antioch U., L.A., 1990. Tchr., libr. adminstr. L.A. City Schs., 1957-68; law librarian Glendale U. Coll. Law, 1968-69; coll. librarian Cleve. Chiropractic Coll., L.A., 1969-74, dir. edn. and admissions, 1974-84, prof. jurisprudence, 1975—, dean student affairs, 1976-92, chaplain, 1985—, dean of edn., 1989—; assoc. prof. Newport U., 1982; extern prof. St. Andrews Theol. Coll., London, 1961; dir. West Valley Chiropractic Health Ctr., 1972—. Contbr. articles to profl. jours. Chaplain's asst. U.S. Army, 1958-60. Decorated cavaliere Internat. Order Legion of Honor of Immaculata (Italy); Knight of Malta, Sovereign Order of St. John of Jerusalem; Knight Grand Prelate, comdr. with star, Order of Signum Fidei; comdr. chevalier Byzantine Imperial Order of Constantine the Gt.; comdr. ritter Order St. Gereon; chevalier Mil. and Hospitaller Order of St. Lazarus of Jerusalem (Malta); numerous others. Mem. ALA, NEA, Am. Assn. Sch. Librarians, L.A. Sch. Libr. Assn., Calif. Sch. Libr. Assn., Assn. Coll. and Rsch. Librarians, Am. Assn. Law Librarians, Am. Chiropractic Assn., Internat. Chiropractors Assn., Nat. Geog. Soc., Internat. Platform Assn., Phi Delta Kappa, Sigma Chi Psi, Delta Tau Alpha. Democrat. Episcopalian. Home: 6435 Jumilla Ave Woodland Hills CA 91367-2833 Office: 590 N Vermont Ave Los Angeles CA 90004-2115 also: 7022 Owensmouth Ave Canoga Park CA 91303-2005

**FOLMAR, LARRY JOHN,** lawyer; b. Philipsburg, Pa., Aug. 3, 1942; s. Loyal Arden and Gertrude Beatrice (Sankey) F. BA, Pa. State U., 1964; JD, Dickinson Sch. Law, Carlisle, Pa., 1971. Bar: Pa. 1971, U.S. Dist. Ct. (ea. dist.) Pa. 1977, U.S. Ct. Appeals (3d cir.) 1979, U.S. Supreme Ct. 1991. Assoc. McQuaide, Blasko, Brown & Geiser, State College, Pa., 1971-73, Henderson, Wetherill, O'Hey & Horsey, Norristown, Pa., 1973-84; asst. pub. defender County of Montgomery, Norristown, 1984, asst. dist. atty., 1984-85, asst. county solicitor, 1985—; pvt. practice Norristown, 1985—. 1st lt. U.S. Army, 1966-68, Vietnam. Mem. Pa. Bar Assn., Montgomery Bar Assn. (chmn. mcpl. law com. 1980-81, bd. dirs. 1991-93, chmn. law reporter com. 1995), Masons, Tall Cedars of Lebanon, Shriners. General civil litigation, Land use and zoning (including planning), Probate. Office: PO Box 751 Norristown PA 19404-0751

**FOLS, STACY ALISON,** lawyer, law educator; b. Dec. 31, 1961. MA, Johns Hopkins U., 1989; BA, Rutgers U., 1987, JD, 1995. Bar: N.J. 1995, Pa. 1995, U.S. Dist. Ct. N.J. 1995, U.S. Dist. Ct. (ea. dist.) Pa. 1996, U.S. Ct. Appeals (3d cir.) 1997, U.S. Supreme Ct. 1999. Law clk. Hon. M.P. King, Westmont, N.J., 1995-96; assoc. Montgomery, McCracken, Walker & Rhoads LLP, Cherry Hill, N.J., 1996—; adj. prof. English, Rutgers U., Camden, 1989-95, adj. prof. law, 1997—. Mem. Nat. Assn. Women Lawyers, N.J. Assn. Women Bus. Owners. Appellate, Libel, General civil litigation. Office: Montgomery McCracken Walker & Rhoads 457 Haddonfield Rd Ste 600 Cherry Hill NJ 08002-2220

**FOLSOM, DAVID,** judge; b. 1947. Student, So. State Coll., 1965-67; BA, U. Ark., 1969, JD, 1974. Assoc. Young & Patton, 1974-76; ptnr. Young, Patton & Folsom, 1974-90; dep. prosecuting atty. Lafayette County, 1978-81; pvt. practice, 1990-95; dist. judge U.S. Dist. Ct. (ea. dist.) Tex., 1995—; tchr. Arks. Sr. H.S., 1969-71. Mem. Ark. Bar Assn., Tex. Bar Assn., Ark. Trial Lawyers Assn., Texarkana Bar Asn., Tex. Trial Lawyers Assn., Northeast Tex. Bar Assn., Assn. of Trial Lawyers of Am., Southwest Ark. Bar Assn., Delta Theta Phi. Office: US Dist Ct 309 US Courthouse 500 Stateline Ave Texarkana TX 75501

**FONG, LESLIE KALEIOPU WAH CHEONG,** lawyer; b. Honolulu, May 24, 1946; s. Harold K.W. and Beatrice (Wong) F.; m. Bernice San Nicolas Furukawa, Dec. 17, 1988; children: Alina K., Andrew K., Nicolas K.F., Christian K. Student, Ch. Coll. of Hawaii, Laie, 1965, U. Hawaii, 1966; BA, Brigham Young U., 1973; JD, U. of the Pacific, Sacramento, 1979. Bar: Hawaii 1979, U.S. Dist. Ct. Hawaii 1979, U.S. Ct. Appeals 1979. Ptnr. Lam, Holzer & Fong, Honolulu, 1979-81; atty. Law Offices of Leslie Fong, Honolulu, 1981-83, Huang & Assocs., Taipei, Taiwan, 1983-84, Law Offices of Paul Tomar, Honolulu, 1985; pvt. practice Honolulu, 1985—. Mem. Manoa Neighborhood Bd., Honolulu, 1989-90; bd. dirs. Child Abuse and Neglect Secondary Prevention Adv. Com., Honolulu, 1992—; pres. Child and Parent Advocates, 1992—. With U.S. Army, 1971-74. Mem. Hawaii State Bar Assn., McGeorge Alumni Assn. Personal injury, Workers' compensation, Family and matrimonial. Home: 1456 Thurston Ave Apt 252 Honolulu HI 96822-3633 Office: 210 Ward Ave Ste 328 Honolulu HI 96814-4012

**FONG, PETER C. K.,** lawyer, judge, company executive; b. Honolulu, Oct. 28, 1955; s. Arthur S.K. and Victoria K.Y. (Chun) F. BBA with honors, U. Hawaii, 1977; JD, Boston Coll., 1980. Bar: Hawaii 1980, U.S. Dist. Ct. Hawaii 1980, U.S. Ct. Appeals (9th cir.) 1980, U.S. Supreme Ct. 1983. Law clk. to presiding justice Supreme Ct. Hawaii, Honolulu, 1980-81; dep. pros. atty. Pros. Atty.'s Office, Honolulu, 1981-84; with Davis, Reid & Richards, Honolulu, 1984-89; chief legal counsel, chief clk. Senate jud. com. Hawaii State Legislature, 1989—; judge per diem Dist./Family Ct., Hawaii, 1989—; ptnr. Hong, Kwock & Fong, Honolulu, 1990-91, Fong & Fong, Honolulu, 1989—; pres., CEO, dir. Chun Kim Chow, Ltd., Honolulu, 1998—; gen. legal counsel Hawaii Jr. C. of C., 1983-84; pres., bd. dirs. Legal Aid Soc. Hawaii, 1984-90; pres., 1986-87; arbitrator Hawaiian Cir. Ct., 1986—, Am. Arbitration Assn., 1989—; mediator Arbitration Forums, Inc., 1989—. Editorial staff Boston Coll. Internat. and Comp. Law Rev., 1978-80. Mem. City and County Honolulu Neighborhood Bd., 1981-83; campaign treas. for Hawaii state senator, 1981-89; mem. aux. admissions com. Boston Coll. Law Sch., 1982—, major gifts com. and sustaining membership fundraising drive com. YMCA, 1988; del. Gov.'s Congress on Hawaii's internat. role, 1988; del. Hawaii Jud. Forsight Congress, 1991; mem. hearings com. Hawaii State Atty.'s Disciplinary Bd., 1991—. Recipient Pres.'s award Hawaii Jr. C. of C., 1984; named one of ten Outstanding Persons of Hawaii, 1990, 92. Mem. ABA, ATLA, Hawaii State Bar Assn. (co-chmn. and vice-chmn., jud. salary com., mem. legis. com., coord. legis. resource bank, mem. task force on disciplinary counsel), Hawaii Developer's Coun., Am. Judicature Soc., Hawaii Supreme Ct. Hist. Soc., Hawaii Trial Judges Assn., Nat. Coun. Juvenile and Family Ct. Judges, Rsch. Bd. of Advisors, Nat. Assn. Dist. Attys., U.S. Supreme Ct. Hist. Soc., Mortar Bd., Tu Chiang Shen (past pres.), Waialae Country Club. General practice, General civil litigation, Insurance. Home: 5255 Makalena St Honolulu HI 96821-1808 Office: Fong & Fong Grosvener Ctr Makai Tower 733 Bishop St Ste 1550 Honolulu HI 96813-4003

**FONG, PHYLLIS KAMOI,** lawyer; b. Phila., Oct. 16, 1953; d. Bernard W.D. and Roberta (Wat) F.; m. Paul E. Tellier, Nov. 25, 1978. BA, Pomona Coll., 1975; JD, Vanderbilt U., 1978. Bar: Tenn. 1978, D.C. 1982. Atty. U.S. Commn. on Civil Rights, Washington, 1978-81; asst. gen. counsel Legal Svcs. Corp., Washington, 1981-83; assoc. counsel to the insp. gen. Office of Insp. Gen, U.S. Small Bus. Adminstrn., Washington, 1983-88, asst. insp. gen. for mgmt. and policy, 1988-94, asst. insp. gen. for mgmt. and legal counsel, 1994—. Mem. ABA, Tenn. Bar Assn., D.C. Bar Assn. Office: 409 3rd St SW Ste 7 Washington DC 20024-3212

**FONTES, J. MARIO F., JR.,** lawyer; b. São Paulo, Brazil, Jan. 17, 1964; m. Gladys Fontes, Jan. 7, 1995. BA cum laude in Econs. and Internat. Studies, Am. U., Washington, 1987; JD, Cath. U., Washington, 1992. Bar: Pa. 1993, Fla. 1995, U.S. Ct. Claims 1993, U.S. Ct. Internat. Trade 1993. Assoc. Porter, Wright, Morris & Arthur, Washington, 1992-93, Hughes Hubbard & Reed, Miami, Fla., 1993-96, Baker & McKenzie, Miami, 1996—. Mem. ABA, Inter-Am. Bar Assn., Pa. Bar Assn., Brazilian-Am. Chamber (mem. program com. 1994-95), Phi Kappa Phi. General corporate, Securities, Private international. Office: Baker & McKenzie 1200 Brickell Ave Miami FL 33131-3214

**FONTHEIM, CLAUDE G.B.,** lawyer, advisor; b. Bethlehem, Pa., Aug. 24, 1955; s. Ernest G. and Margot (Hass) F.; m. Orit Frenkel, Dec. 7, 1985. BA in Polit. Sci. & Near East Studies with high distinction and high honors, U. Mich., M in Pub. Policy, 1981, JD, 1981. Bar: D.C. 1981. Assoc. Ginsburg, Feldman & Bress, Washington, 1981-82, Akin, Gump, Strauss, Hauer & Feld, Washington, 1983-87; Crowell & Moring, Washington, 1988-90; mng. dir. IBECS, Inc., Washington, 1990—; CEO Fontheim Internat., Washington, 1990—; lectr. internat. trade and investment; chmn. Dem. Leadership Council Project on Am., the New Global Economy and Trade; gen. counsel Internat. Bus. & Econs. Cons. Svcs., Inc., 1985-88, Export Coun. Renewable Energy, Washington, 1985-87; mem. adv. bd. internat. law study Renewable Energy Inst. Mng. editor Mich. Yearbook Internat. Legal Studies, 1980-81; contbr. articles to legal jours. Policy advisor nat. polit. candidates. Mem. ABA (sec. com. internat. trade 1981-83, steering com. 1983-85, former exec. dir. study internat. trade laws), Phi Beta Kappa. Democrat. Jewish. Private international, Legislative, General corporate. Office: Fontheim Internat LLC 888 16th St NW Ste 300 Washington DC 20006-4103

**FONVIELLE, CHARLES DAVID,** lawyer; b. Melbourne, Fla., Dec. 28, 1944; s. Charles David Fonvielle Jr. and Margaret Jordan Palmer; m. Deborah Konas, July 25, 1970; children: C. Caulley, D. Jordan. BA, U. Fla., 1968; JD, Fla. State U., 1972. Bar: Fla. 1972, U.S. Dist. Ct. (no., mid. and so. dists.) Fla. Asst. pub. defender Fla. Pub. Defender Assn., Tallahassee, 1972-74; pvt. practice Tallahassee, 1974-77; ptnr. Thompson, Wadsworth, Messer, Turner & Rhodes, Tallahassee, 1977-80, Green & Fonvielle, Tallahassee, 1980-84, Green, Fonvielle & Hinkle, Tallahassee, 1984-85, Fonvielle Hinkle & Lewis, Tallahassee, 1985—. Bd. dirs. Fla. State U. Coll. of Law, endowed prof. litigation. Mem. ALTA (sustaining), Tallahassee Bar Assn. (bd. dirs. 1978-79), Acad. Fla. Trial Lawyers (Eagle sponsor 1990—), Nat. Bd. Trial Advocacy (cert.), Fla. Bar Assn. (bd. legal specialization and edn. 1991—), Fla. State U. Pres.'s Club (bd. visitors). Avocations: physical fitness, flying, spearfishing, sports cars. Personal injury, Product liability, Professional liability. Office: Fonvielle Hinkle & Lewis 3375 Capital Cir NE Ste A Tallahassee FL 32308-3778

**FONVILLE, HAROLD WAYNE, II,** lawyer; b. Humboldt, Tenn., June 27, 1968; s. H. Wayne and Johnnie (Bryant) F. JD, U. Memphis, 1994. Bar: Tenn. 1994, U.S. Dist. Ct. (we. dist.) Tenn. 1994. Assoc. Farris, Mathews, Branan & Hellen, Memphis, 1994—; chmn. Nat. Conf. Law Revs., Memphis, 1993-94, advisor, 1994—; asst. city atty. Town of Collierville, Tenn., 1996—. Capt. U.S. Army N.G., 1985—. Mem. Tenn. Trial Lawyers Assn., Memphis Bar Assn., N.G. Assn. U.S., N.G. Assn. Tenn., U. Memphis Law Alumni Assn. (bd. dirs. 1994—). General civil litigation, Municipal (including bonds), Contracts commercial. Home: 4981 Cole Rd Memphis TN 38117-4201 Office: Farris Mathews Branan Et Al One Commerce Sq Ste 2000 Memphis TN 38103

**FOOTE, RICHARD CHARLES,** lawyer; b. Bay Village, Ohio, July 4, 1951; s. George Harry and Arlene Marie Foote; 1 child, Elizabeth Ann. BA, Harvard U., 1973; JD, Case Western Res. U., 1976. Bar: Ohio 1976, U.S. Dist. Ct. (no. dist.) Ohio 1976, U.S. Ct. Appeals (6th cir.) 1982. Ptnr. Law Offices of Mark L. Hoffman and Richard C. Foote, Shaker Heights, Ohio, 1983—. Mem. Cuyahoga County Bar Assn., Bar Assn. Greater Cleve. Methodist. Bankruptcy, Probate. Office: Ohio Savs Bldg 20133 Farnsleigh Rd Cleveland OH 44122-3613

**FORBES, ARTHUR LEE, III,** lawyer; b. Houston, Sept. 3, 1928; s. Arthur Lee Jr. and Corinne (Mayfield) F.; m. Nita R. Harrison, Mar. 25, 1957; children—Tricia, Kim, Arthur Lee. B.S.C.E., U. Tex.-Austin, 1952; J.D., S. Tex. Coll. Law, 1959. Bar: Tex. 1959, U.S. Ct. Appeals (5th cir.) 1960, U.S. Supreme Ct. 1967. Ptnr. firm Lee & Forbes, Houston, 1960-73, Shapiro, Forbes & Cox, Houston, 1974-88; gen. counsel Bay Houston Towing Co., 1989—. Served to lt. USMC, 1952-54. Mem. ABA, Tex. Bar Assn., Houston Bar Assn., Assn. Trial Lawyers Am., Houston Trial Lawyers Assn., Sigma Chi, Phi Delta Phi, Unitarian. Club: Houston Racquet. General corporate, General practice, Environmental. Home: 5 Leisure Ln Houston TX 77024-5123 Office: Three Riverway Ste 450 Houston TX 77056

**FORBES, FRANKLIN SIM,** lawyer, educator; b. Kingsport, Tenn., Sept. 21, 1936; s. Harvey Sim and Virginia Smith (Pooler) F.; m. Suzanne Marie Willard, June 30, 1962; children—Franklin Sim, Anne Marie. BA, U. Hawaii, 1959; JD, U. Iowa, 1963. Bar: Hawaii 1963, Nebr. 1964. Law clk. Hawaii Supreme Ct., 1963; mem. faculty U. Nebr. Coll. Bus. Adminstrn., Omaha, 1965—, prof. law, 1965—, chmn. dept. law and society, 1970-97, acting chmn. dept. profl. acctg., 1986-87, Peter Keweit disting. prof. law, 1987-93; pvt. practice, Omaha, 1964—. Author: Going Into Business in Nebraska: The Legal Aspects, 1983, Instructor's Resource Guide-Business Law, 1983-88, Starting and Operating a Business in Nebraska, 1995, Debtors and Creditors Rights, 1988, Legal Environment of Telemarketing, 1991; contbr. articles to legal publs. Mem. integration com. Omaha Sch. Bd., 1974; mem. St. James Bd. Edn., Omaha, 1974; pres. parish coun. St. James Roman Cath. Ch., 1975, St. Elizabeth Ann Ch., 1983-84, 90-91. Recipient Real Dean award U. Hawaii, 1959, Gt. Tchr. award U. Nebr., 1978, 81, Chancellor's medal U. Nebr., 1977, Outstanding Achievement award U. Nebr. Coll. Bus. Adminstrn., 1983, 84, 85, 87, 88; Rotary Found. grantee Australia, 1972. Mem. ABA, Am. Arbitration Assn., Am. Judicature Soc., Midwest Bus. Adminstrs. Assn., Midwest Bus. Law Assn. (pres. 1975), Nebr. Bar Assn., Omaha Bar Assn. (del. conf. Future Law 1979), Hawaii Bar Assn., Nat. Golden Key Soc., Alpha Phi Omega, Phi Alpha Delta, Beta Gamma Sigma, Phi Theta Chi. Democrat. Club: Rotary. Office: Univ Nebr Coll Bus Adminstrn Omaha NE 68182-0001

**FORBES, MORTON GERALD,** lawyer; b. Atlanta, July 12, 1938; s. Arthur Mark and Mary Dean (Power) F.; m. Eunice Lee Haynsworth, Jan. 25, 1963; children: John, Ashley, Sarah. AB, Wofford Coll., 1962; JD, U. Ga., 1965. Bar: Ga. 1965, U.S. Dist. Ct. (mid. dist.) Ga. 1965, U.S. Dist. Ct. (so. dist.) Ga. 1968, U.S. Dist. Ct. (no. dist.) Ga. 1993, U.S. Ct. Appeals (5th cir.) 1974, U.S. Ct. Appeals (4th cir.) 1972, U.S. Ct. Appeals (11th cir.) 1981. Assoc. Pierce, Ranitz, Lee, Berry & Mahoney, 1967-70; ptnr. Pierce, Ranitz, Berry, Mahoney & Forbes, 1970-76, Pierce, Ranitz, Mahoney, Forbes & Coolidge, 1976-81; ptnr., sec. Ranitz, Mahoney, Forbes & Coolidge, P.C., 1981-91, Forbes & Bowman, 1991—; gen. counsel Ga. Fen. Young Rep. Clubs, 1971-72; guest lectr. dept. dental hygiene Armstrong State Coll., 1970-72. Mem. Savannah Port Authority, 1973—, chmn., 1979-81; mem. Chatham County Devel. Authority, 1973-80; mem. nat. com. Nat. Fedn. Young Reps., 1973; mem. econ. adv. coun. Coastal Area Planning and Devel. Authority, 1980—; bd. dirs. Savannah Symphony Soc., 1971-75; Ga. del. to Japan/Southeast Trade Mission, Kyoto, Japan, 1983, S.E. U.S.A./Japan Assn. meeting, Birmingham, Ala., 1984. Served with USN, 1965-67. Recipient Outstanding Service award Savannah Port Authority, 1981. Mem. ABA, State Bar Ga., Am. Judicature Soc., Nat. Assn. Bond Counsel, Ga. Def. Lawyers Assn. (v.p. 1987—, mem. exec. com. 1988, bd. dirs., exec. v.p. 1990-91, pres. 1991-92), Savannah Bar Assn. (exec. com. 1989-94, pres. 1992-93), Libel Def. Resource Ctr., Def. Rsch. Inst. (state chmn. 1992—), Savannah Econ. Devel. Action Council (founding), Savannah Area Wofford Coll. Alumni Club (past pres.), Soc. of the Cincinnati (Va.), St. Andrews Soc., Soc. Colonial Wars, Sons of Revolution (sec. 1988-92). Republican. Presbyterian. Clubs: Chatham, Savannah Yacht, 1st City, The Landings Club. Product liability, Insurance, Federal civil litigation. Office: Forbes & Bowman PO Box 13929 Savannah GA 31416-0929

**FORCADE, BILLY STUART,** lawyer; b. Lincoln, Nebr., Jan. 22, 1946; s. Billy Wesley and Pearl Marguritte (Stewart) F.; m. Emily Kukula Forcade, Sept. 28, 1985; 1 child, William Michael. BS, U. Ill., 1971; JD, John Marshall Law Sch., Chgo., 1976. Bar: Ill. 1976, Wis. 1977, U.S. Ct. Appeals (7th cir.) 1978, U.S. Dist. Ct. 1979, U.S. Supreme Ct. 1982. Lab. tech. Stepan Chem., Joliet, Ill., 1967; petroleum analyst U.S. Army, 1968-70; rsch. chemist Witco Chem. Co., Chgo., 1971-76; gen. counsel Citizens for a Better Environ., Chgo., 1976-83; instr. part time Northeastern Ill. U., Chgo., 1982, 84; bd. mem. Ill. Polution Control Bd., Chgo., 1983—. Author: Hazardous Waste Management, 1984. Mem. 42nd Ward Regular Dem. Orgn., Chgo., 1981—. Mem. Chgo. Bar Assn. Democrat. Environmental, Administrative and regulatory, State civil litigation. Home: 9223 Keeler Ave Skokie IL 60076-1627 Office: Illinois Pollution Control 100 W Randolph St Ste 11-500 Chicago IL 60601-3233

**FORD, BERNADETTE K.,** lawyer; b. Queens, N.Y., July 11, 1960; d. Alexander Stanley and Ita Angela F.; m. Michael G. Brisson, Apr. 19, 1986; 1 child. BA, St. John's U., 1981, JD, 1985. Bar: N.Y. 1986, N.J. 1987, U.S. Dist. Ct. (ea. dist.) N.Y. 1988. Asst. dist. atty. Queens Dist. Attys. Office, 1985—, dep. bur. chief, 1994—; instr. Practicing Law Inst., N.Y.C., 1997; panelist St. John's U. Law Homecoming, 1997. Mem. N.Y. Bar Assn., Nassau County Bar Assn. Roman Catholic. Office: Queens Dist Ct Attys Office 12501 Queens Blvd Kew Gardens NY 11415-1514

**FORD, BYRON TODD,** lawyer; b. Sheffield, Ala., Apr. 16, 1965; s. William Henry and Vivian (Hallman) F. BS, U. N. Ala., 1990; JD, U. Ala., Montgomery, 1994. Bar: U.S. Dist. Ct. (mid. dist.) Ala. 1996, U.S. Dist. Ct. (no. dist.) Ala. 1998, U.S. Dist. Ct. (so. dist.) Ala. 1998. Pvt. practice Eutaw, Ala., 1996—; asst. dist. atty. State of Ala., Office of Dist. Atty., Demopolis, 1996—. Mem. Ala. Dist. Attys. Assn. Democrat. Baptist. State civil litigation, General civil litigation, Personal injury. Office: 104 Main St Eutaw AL 35462-1104

**FORD, GARY MANNING,** lawyer; b. Lawton, Okla., Apr. 18, 1950; s. Joe Manning Ford and Jessie Glyn Walker; m. Nancy Elizabeth Ebb, July 21, 1979; children: Michael, Daniel. AB, Harvard Coll., 1972; JD, Boston U., 1977. Bar: Mass. 1978, U.S. Dist. Ct. D.C. 1979, U.S. Ct. Appeals (D.C. cir.) 1985, U.S. Supreme Ct. 1987, U.S. Ct. Appeals (2nd cir.) 1988, U.S. Ct. Appeals (11th cir.) 1991, U.S. Ct. Appeals (10th cir.) 1992. Staff atty. Pension Benefit Guaranty Corp., Washington, 1977-79; Employee Retirement Income Security Act counsel U.S. Senate Com. on Labor and Human Resources, Washington, 1980-81; assoc. Groom and Nordberg, Chartered, Washington, 1981-84, prin., 1984-87; gen. counsel Pension Benefit Guaranty Corp., Washington, 1987-89; prin. Groom Law Group, Chartered, Washington, 1989—; first v.p., bd. dirs. CPC Health Corp., Rockville, Md., 1995—. Mem. editl. bd. Jour. Employee Benefits Taxation, 1994—. Pack leader Boy Scouts Am., Bethesda, Md., 1988-94. Mem. ABA, Employee Retirement Income Security Act Roundtable. Democrat. Unitarian. Avocations: cycling, swimming, travel, reading. Pension, profit-sharing, and employee benefits, Bankruptcy, Health. Office: Groom Law Group Chartered Ste 1200 1701 Pennsylvania Ave NW Washington DC 20006-5805

**FORD, MARK L.,** lawyer; b. Lexington, Ky., Nov. 7, 1960; s. Thomas Robert and Harriet (Lowrey) F.; m. Sue Thomas, May 17, 1986; children: Darian, Thomas. BA, Ind. U., 1982; JD, U. Ky., 1985. Bar: Ky. 1985, U.S. Dist. Ct. (ea. dist.) Ky. 1987, U.S. Ct. Appeals (6th cir.) 1990, Ct. Vet. Appeals 1990, U. Supreme Ct. 1997. Rschr. Coun. State Govts., Lexington, 1984-85; assoc. Forester & Forester, Harlan, Ky., 1985-88; ptnr. Smith & Ford, Harlan, 1988-90; pvt. practice law Harlan, 1990—; pres. Eas. Broadcasting Co., 1998—;. Co-author: Emergency Management in the States, 1984. Trustee Harlan (Ky.) County Pub. Libr. Bd. Trustees, 1990-94. Mem. Harlan County Bar Assn. (treas. 1990-97). Office: 105 Central St Harlan KY 40831

**FORD, MARK WILLIAM,** lawyer; b. Pa., Nov. 11, 1956; s. Floyd Filmore and Ruth (Campbell) F.; divorced; 1 child, Marc Anthony; m. Ellen Irene Young, Jan. 2, 1993. BA, Ursinus Coll., 1979; JD, Rutgers U., Camden, N.J., 1982. Assoc. Lee & McFarland, Camden, 1983-88, Sue Ellen Johnson, Marlton, N.J., 1988-89, Console, Marmero, Berlin, N.J., 1989-92; pvt. practice Gloucester, N.J., 1992—. Pres., bd. dirs. Metro Camden Habitat, 1986—; chmn. publicity com. Gloucester City Dem. club, 1992—; mem. human rels. com. City of Gloucester, 1998. Mem. Gloucester City Small Bus. Assn., Gloucester City C. of C., Lions (bd. dirs. Gloucester chpt., 3d v.p. 1998—), Rotary (v.p. 1998—). Baptist. Avocation: running. Bankruptcy, Personal injury, Workers' compensation. Home: 217A New Broadway Brooklawn NJ 08030-2547 Office: 4 1/2 N Broadway Gloucester City NJ 08030-1507

**FORD, MICHAEL W.,** lawyer; b. Peoria, Ill., Dec. 9, 1938; s. Benjamin W. and Charlene (Oder) F.; m. Kristine L. Ford; children from a previous marriage: Sarah, Scott, Amy, Michael B. BA, U. Chgo., 1960; JD, Loyola U., 1965. Bar: Ill. 1965, U.S. Dist. Ct. (no. dist.) Ill. 1965, U.S. Dist. Ct. (ea. dist.) Wis. 1974, U.S. Dist. Ct. (mid. dist.) Ill. 1986, U.S. Dist. Ct. Nebr. 1987, U.S. Ct. Appeals (7th cir.) 1965, U.S. Ct. Appeals (3d cir.) 1988, U.S. Ct. Appeals (6th dist.) 1989, U.S. Supreme Ct. 1977. Mng. ptnr., sr. ptnr. in charge of gen. and corp. litigation Chapman and Cutler, Chgo., 1965—. Contbr. numerous articles to profl. jours.; spkr. many seminars for legal or ednl. groups. Mem. nominating com. Riverwoods, Ill. Caucus, 1992-93. Mem. ABA (mem. trial evidence com. and other coms.), Chgo. Bar Assn. General civil litigation, Environmental, Toxic tort. Home: 4 Timberwood Ln Deerfield IL 60015-2400 Office: Bayko Gibson Carnegie Hagan Schoenmaker & Meyer LLP Three 1st Nat Plz Ste 3700 Chicago IL 60602

**FORD, NANCY L.,** lawyer, university administrator; b. Ft. Wayne, Ind., Jan. 28, 1947; d. Edward H. and Betty L. Heck; children: Ninette, Jerome, Pasha. BA in English and Edn., Ind. U., 1970; JD, Temple U., 1975. Bar: Pa. 1975, Ill. 1982, U.S. Dist. Ct. (ea. dist.) Pa. 1975. Adminstr. Free Law Sch. Phila., 1973-79; atty. Bomsteiin and Ford, Phila., 1975-76; sole practitioner Phila., 1976-79; from asst. prof. to assoc. prof. legal studies U. Ill. at Springfield (formerly Sangamon State U.), 1979—, dir. Ctr. for Legal Studies, 1984-93, assoc. v.p. for acad. affairs, 1989-93, exec. dir. Inst. for Pub. Affairs, 1993—; atty. Family Svc. Ctr. of Sangamon County, Springfield, 1982—; bd. dirs. Ill. Issues mag., U. Ill. at Springfield, 1993—. Contbr. chpt. to book, articles and revs. to profl. jours. Bd. dirs. Springfield Urban League, 1998—; bd. dirs. Sangamon County Pvt. Industry Coun., chmn. program and planning com., 1983—; mem. Ill. Authority on Residential Care, State of Ill., 1993-97; mem. adv. bd. The Lincoln Legal Papers Project, Springfield, 1990-94. Recipient grants in field. Mem. Am. Soc. for Pub. Adminstrn. (conf. planning com. 1997-98), Govt. Bar Assn., Am. legal Studies Assn. Avocations: reading, swimming, boating, antique collecting, making stained glass windows, lamps, objects. Email: ford.nancy@uis.edu. Home: 619 S Glenwood Ave Springfield IL 62704-2440 Office: U Ill at Springfield Inst for Pub Affairs PO Box 19243 Springfield IL 62794-9243

**FORD, ROBERT DAVID,** lawyer; b. New Orleans, Oct. 30, 1956; s. Thomas Paul and Inez Mary (Rodriguez) F.; m. Jean Ann Burg, May 5, 1979; children: Robert David Jr., Charlene Elizabeth, Timothy Michael. BA, U. New Orleans, 1978; JD, Loyola U., 1983. Bar: La. 1983, U.S. Dist. Ct. (ea. dist.) La. 1983, U.S. Dist. Ct. (mid. dist.) La. 1997, U.S. Ct. Appeals (5th cir.) 1985. Claims rep. State Farm Mut. Auto Ins. Co., Metairie, La., 1978-80; assoc. Hammett, Leake & Hammett, New Orleans, 1983-86; ptnr. Thomas, Hayes, Beahm & Buckley, New Orleans, 1986-95; mem. Chehardy, Sherman, Ellis, Breslin & Murray, Metairie, La., 1995-96; with Hailey, McNamara, Hall, Larmann & Papale, Metairie, 1996—. Mem. ABA (coms. on health law, profl. liability and products liability litigation 1992, subcoms. on hosp. and clinic med. devices and med. malpractice liability 1992), La. Bar Assn., La. Assn. Def. Counsel, Am. Soc. Law and Medicine, La. Soc. Hosp. Attys. of La. Hosp. Assn., Def. Rsch. Inst., Phi Kappa Theta, Pi Alpha Delta. Republican. Roman Catholic. Avocations: golf, softball. Health, Product liability, Insurance. Home: 8 Caney Ct Kenner LA 70065-3944 Office: Hailey McNamara Hall Larmann & Papale 1 Galleria Blvd Ste 1400 Metairie LA 70001-7543

**FOREMAN, EDWARD RAWSON,** lawyer; b. Atlanta, May 15, 1939; s. Robert Langdon and Mary (Shedden) F.; m. Margaret Reeves, Oct. 19, 1968; children: Margaret Langdon, Mary Rawson. BA, Washington & Lee U., 1962; JD, Emory U., 1965. Bar: Ga. 1965. Assoc. Jones, Bird & Howell, Atlanta, 1965-70, ptnr., 1970-82; ptnr. Alston & Bird, Atlanta, 1982—; chmn. McAliley Endowment Trust, 1978—; lectr. Inst. for Continuing Legal Edn. in Ga., 1989; panelist, moderator Bus. Atlanta's Office Leasing and Tenant Opportunities in 1990s. Bd. editors Comml. Leasing Law and Strategy, 1996—. Bd. dirs. Ansley Park Beautification Found., Atlanta, 1984—; bd. dirs. Midtown Alliance, Atlanta, 1988-96, sec., chmn. fundraising com., 1989-91, v.p., 1991, pres., 1992; trustee Paidela Sch. Endowment Fund, Atlanta, 1980—, Woodruff Arts Ctr., Atlanta, 1985-90; chmn. Emory U. Law Fund, Atlanta, 1981; chmn. legal divsn. United Way Met. Atlanta, 1984; chmn. strategic planning com. High Mus. Art, 1986-95, chmn., bd. dirs. 1998—, chmn. nominating com., 1993-95; vestryman, sr. warden St. Luke's Episc. Ch., 1975, 94, mem. com., 1975—; pres. Atlanta Legal Aid Soc., 1975-76, Atlanta Preservation Ctr., 1986-91; trustee Miss Hall's Sch., Pittsfield, Mass., 1990—. Recipient Cmty. Svc. award Martin Luther King Jr. Ctr. Nonviolent Social Change, 1980, Outstanding Svc. award Atlanta Preservation Ctr., Inc., 1983. Mem. ABA (mem. comml. leasing com. 1987—), State Bar Ga. (chmn., panelist, moderator comml. leasing seminars 1979-86), Atlanta Bar Assn. (chmn., panelist, moderator leasing seminars 1979-86, chmn. hdqrs. search com. 1988-96), Lawyers Club Atlanta (chmn. long-range planning com. 1989-90), Atlanta Bar Found. (bd. dirs.), Old War Horse Lawyers Club, Nine O'Clocks Club (mem. centennial com. 1983), Highlands Country Club N.C. Democrat. Episcopalian. Landlord-tenant, Real property. Home: 238 15th St NE House 16 Atlanta GA

30309-3594 Office: Alston & Bird 4200 One Atlantic Ctr 1201 W Peachtree St NW Atlanta GA 30309-3424

**FOREMAN, JAMES LOUIS,** retired judge; b. Metropolis, Ill., May 12, 1927; s. James C. and Anna Elizabeth (Henne) F.; m. Mabel Inez Dunn, June 16, 1948; children: Beth Foreman Banks, Rhonda Foreman Riepe, Nanette Foreman Love. BS in Commerce and Law, U. Ill., 1950, JD, 1952. Bar: Ill. Ind. practice law Metropolis, Ill.; ptnr. Chase and Foreman, Metropolis, until 1972; state's atty. State of Ill., Massac County; asst. atty. gen. State of Ill.; chief judge U.S. Dist. Ct. (so. dist.) Ill., Benton, 1979-92, sr. status, 1992—. Pres. Bd. of Edn., Metropolis. With USN, 1945-46. Mem. Ill. State Bar Assn., Metropolic C. of C. (past pres.). Republican. Home: 38 Hilanoa-East Dr Metropolis IL 62960-2533 Office: US Dist Ct 301 W Main St Benton IL 62812-1362

**FOREMAN, LEE DAVID,** lawyer; b. Tacoma, July 6, 1946; s. Lee Alfred and Shirley Alma (Stone) F.; m. Susan Lynn Hinke, Apr. 2, 1978; children: Seth Lee, Emily Park. AB with distinction, Stanford U., 1968, JD, 1972. Bar: Colo. 1972, U.S. Dist. Ct. Colo. 1972, U.S. Ct. Appeals (10th cir.) 1977. Dep. state pub. defender Colo. State Pub. Defender's Office, Denver, 1972-77; ptnr. Haddon, Morgan & Foreman, P.C., Denver, 1978—. Fellow Am. Coll. Trial Lawyers; mem. ABA, Denver Bar Assn. (vol. lawyer of yr. 1988), Boulder Bar Assn., Colo. Bar Assn., Colo. Criminal Def. Bar (pres. 1981-82, bd. dirs. 1982—), Nat. Assn. Criminal Def. Lawyers. Democrat. Avocations: skiing, golf, trout fishing. Criminal, General civil litigation, Administrative and regulatory.

**FORESTER, KARL S.,** federal judge; b. 1940. BA, U. Ky., 1962, JD, 1966. With Eugene Goss Esp., 1966-68; mem. firm Goss & Forester, 1968-75, Forester, Forester, Buttermore & Turner, P.S.C., 1975-88; judge U.S. Dist. Ct. (ea. dist.) Ky., Lexington, 1988—. Mem. Ky. Bar Assn., Harlan County Bar Assn., Fayette County Bar Assn. Office: US Dist Ct PO Box 2165 Lexington KY 40588-2165

**FORINO, ALFRED PAUL,** lawyer, consultant; b. Waterbury, Conn., July 17, 1957; s. Bernard A. Forino and Margaret A. Mandino. BS in Commerce, Rider U., 1979; JD, George Washington U., 1982. Bar: Conn. 1982, U.S. Dist. Ct. Conn. 1982, U.S. Ct. Appeals (2nd cir.) 1986, U.S. Supreme Ct. 1986. Law clerk State of Conn. Trial Bench, New Haven, 1982-84; assoc. Pinney, Payne, VanLenten et al., Danbury, Conn., 1984-88; sr. trial attorney Naab & Danforth, New Haven, Conn., 1988-94, Sizemore, Forino & Griffin, New Haven, Conn., 1994-98; mng. attorney Forino & Griffin, New Haven, Conn., 1998—; founder, mem. HIVed, LLC, Wallingford, Conn., 1998—. Author Conn. Lawyer, 1988. Mem. Conn. Defense Lawyer's Assn., Stonewall Speakers Assn., Omicron Delta Epsilon. Insurance, Personal injury, Professional liability. Home: 273 S Main St Wallingford CT 06492-4602 Office: Forino & Griffin 265 Church St New Haven CT 06510-7013

**FORLANO, FREDERICK PETER,** lawyer; b. N.Y.C., July 12, 1947; s. Pasquale Genaro and Theresa Susan (Hartmann) F.; children: Christopher S., Jason D., Jennifer R.; m. Sharon S. Guinnup, 1995. AS, Suffolk Community Coll., 1968; BA in Math., Adelphi U., 1969; JD, U. Houston, 1975. Bar: Tex. 1975, U.S. Dist. Ct. (so. dist.) Tex. 1976, U.S. Ct. Appeals (5th cir.) 1976, U.S. Ct. Appeals (11th cir.) 1981, U.S. Tax Ct. 1977. Commd. 2nd lt. USAF, 1970, advanced through grades to maj., 1984; ptnr. Finger, Small, Cohen & Forlano, Houston, 1975-88; pvt. practice law Houston, 1988—. Advisor, legal v.p. Meadows Civic Assn., Stafford, Tex., 1977, pres., 1978-79; advisor Parents Without Ptnrs., Houston, 1987—; trustee The Wilhelm Schole, 1977—. With USAFR (ret.), 1970-92. Mem. Tex. Bar Assn., Houston Bar Assn., Ft. Bend Bar Assn., Res. Officers Assn. Republican. Roman Catholic. Avocations: golf, tennis, horses. State civil litigation, Federal civil litigation, Probate. Office: 1170 Phoenix Tower 3200 Southwest Fwy Houston TX 77027-7528

**FORMAN, JAMES DOUGLAS,** lawyer; b. Mineola, N.Y., Nov. 12, 1932; s. Leo and Kathryn F.; m. Marcia Fore; children: Karli, Elizabeth. AB, Princeton U., 1954; LLB, Columbia U., 1957. Bar: N.Y. 1958. Pvt. practice Mineola, 1957—. Author: Cry Havoc, 1988, The Big Bang, 1989, The Scottish Dirk: Reality and Romance, 1991, Prince Charlie's Year, 1991, Becca's Story, 1992, The Blunderbuss 1500-1900, 1994, about 40 others. Bd. mem. Landmarks com., Sands Point, N.Y., 1987—. Mem. Ky. Rifle Assn., Co. Mil. Historians. Avocations: portrait painting, woodworking. Home: 2 Glen Rd Port Washington NY 11050-1207 Office: 131 Mineola Blvd Mineola NY 11501-3919

**FORMAN, KENNETH ALAN,** lawyer; b. Montclair, N.J., Oct. 9, 1954; s. David and Arline Forman; m. Deborah Monchek; children: Beth, Rafaela, Ilysa, Davita. BA, Syracuse U., 1977; JD, U. Miami, 1981. Bar: Fla., U.S. Dist. Ct. (so. dist.) Fla., U.S. Ct. Appeals (11th cir.). Atty. Law Office of George Raman, Miami, 1982, Frank Murray PA, Miami, 1982-89; sole practice Kenneth Alan Forman P.A., Miami, 1989—; lectr. Barry U., Miami Shores, Fla., 1994, Miami Dade C.C., Miami, 1994. Co-author: Immigration Law Update, 1984; columnist Caribbean Today, 1991. Mem. ABA, Nat. Assn. Consumer Bankruptcy Attys., Am. Immigration Lawyers Assn., Assn. Fla. Trial Lawyers. Avocations: painting, writing, fishing. Bankruptcy, Immigration, naturalization, and customs. Office: 1175 NE 125th St Ste 607 North Miami FL 33161-5013

**FORMAN, WILLIAM HARPER, JR.,** lawyer; b. Houston, Aug. 13, 1936; s. William Harper and Ermaleen (Lukas) F.; m. Olive Goodwill Roberts, June 17, 1967; 1 child, William Harper III. BA, Tulane U., 1958, JD, 1961; postgrad., Coll. of William and Mary, 1965; MA in Govt., La. State U., 1970. Bar: La. 1961, U.S. Dist. Ct. (ea. dist.) La. 1982, U.S. Ct. Mil. Appeals 1989. Commd. 1st lt. USAF, 1961, advanced through grades to capt., 1967; judge adv. USAF, Philippines, Vietnam, Thailand, 1961-63, resigned, 1967; lt. col. USAFR, 1981; project leader Gulf South Rsch. Inst., La., 1968-69; atty. FTC, New Orleans, 1969-72, sec. consumer adv. bd., 1970-72, pub. info. officer, 1971-72, vice-chmn. consumer adv. bd., 1972-73; atty. City of New Orleans, Community Improvement Agy., 1972-79; pvt. practice New Orleans, 1977—; of counsel Law Office of Robert C. Evans, 1986-88; assoc. Law Offices of Inabnett, Suthon, Forman and Justrabo, New Orleans, 1989-95; adj. prof. dept. polit. sci. Tulane U., New Orleans, 1995—; lectr. mil. criminal law Tulane U., U. New Orleans, 1972-91; lectr. internat. law of war, mil. criminal law Tulane U., 1978-85. Author texts for La. State Hist. Markers, Calumet Plantation and Jefferson City in New Orleans, 1971, 79; contbr. articles to profl. jours. Counsel Downtown Devel. Dist., New Orleans, 1975-80; mem. La. State Consumer Adv. Bd., 1975-81; notary pub., 1975—; bd. dirs. La. Consumers' League, 1970-72, pres. 1972-73; bd. dirs. Ecology Ctr. of La., Inc., 1974-75, vice chmn. 1975-76; bd. dirs. Jefferson City Improvement Assn. of New Orleans, 1977-78, pres. 1975-77, 78-79; incorporator Preservation Resource Ctr. of New Orleans, 1974, treas. 1974-76; trustee La. Landmarks Soc., 1978-79, 81-83, corr. sec. 1979-81; v.p. La. SAR, 1981-87, 97—, chmn. ROTC awards com. 1975-87, chpt. chmn. 1987—, chpt. pres. 1995-96, chmn. ceremony commemorating the birthday of George Washington 1995-96; treas. La. Assn. of Soc. of Cin., 1983-85, v.p. 1985-87, pres. 1987-89. Decorated Meritorious Svc. medal USAF, 1990; recipient Meritorious Svc. medals SAR, 1981, 87, 95, Patriot medal 1990, Bronz Good Citizenship medal, 1996; George Washington Disting. Prof. La. Assn. Soc. Cincinnati. Mem. ABA, La. State Bar Assn. (pub. rels. com. 1970-72, chmn. consumer protection com. 1972-78). Consumer commercial, Military, Real property. Home: 5301 Camp St New Orleans LA 70115-3035 Office: Norman Mayer Bldg Tulane Univ New Orleans LA 70118-5698

**FORMELLER, DANIEL RICHARD,** lawyer; b. Chgo., Aug. 15, 1949; s. Vernon Richard and Shirley Mae (Gruber) F.; m. Ann M. Paa, Aug. 17, 1974; children: Matthew Daniel, Kathryn Ann, Christina Marie. BA with honors, U. Ill., 1970; JD cum laude, DePaul U., 1976. Bar: Ill. 1976, U.S. Dist. Ct. (no. and cen. dists.) Ill. 1976, U.S. Ct. Appeals (7th cir.) 1976, U.S. Ct. Appeals (D.C. cir.) 1995. Assoc. McKenna, Storer, Rowe, White & Farrug, Chgo., 1976-82, ptnr., 1982-86; ptnr. Tressler, Soderstrom, Maloney & Priess, Chgo., 1986—. Exec. editor DePaul U. Law Rev., 1975-76. With USN, 1970-72, Vietnam. Mem. ABA, Ill. Bar Assn., Ill. Assn. Def. Trial Counsel (pres. 1994-95), Chgo. Bar Assn., Assn. Def. Trial Attys. General civil litigation, Federal civil litigation, Product liability. Office: Tressler Soderstrom et al 233 S Wacker Dr Chicago IL 60606-6306

**FORMOSO, MARIKA GULYAS,** lawyer; b. London, May 22, 1965; d. Imre Gulyas and Joan K.M. Rixon; m. Hector Formoso-Murias, Jan. 6, 1990; children: Helen, Hector, Harry. BS, Georgetown U., 1987; MA, U. London, 1988; JD, U. Miami, 1993. Bar: Fla. Assoc. Zimble Formoso-Murias, Miami, Fla., 1990-96, Zimble Formoso-Murias, P.A., Miami, 1996—. Dean's Law scholar U. Miami, 1991, 92. Mem. Gables by the Sea Homeowners Assn. (v.p. 1996-97, pres. 1997-98), Georgetown Club Miami (bd. dirs.). Real property, Probate. Office: Formoso-Murias PA One Unity Sq 401 SW 27th Ave Miami FL 33135-2903

**FORREST, BRADLEY ALBERT,** lawyer; b. Mpls., July 15, 1956; s. Vincent Clarence and Beverly (Malmrose) F.; m. Arlene Terry Clementson, Aug. 19, 1978; children: Kelsey, Whitney, Dylan. B in Elec. Engring., U. Minn., 1978, JD, 1981. Bar: Minn. 1981, U.S. Patent and Trademark Office, U.S. Ct. Appeals (fed. cir.) 1982, U.S. Supreme Ct. 1982. Atty. Rosemount Inc., Eden Prairie, Minn., 1981-84, IBM Corp., Rochester, Minn., 1981-93; trademark and copyright counsel IBM Corp., Thornwood, N.Y., 1993-95; ptnr. Schwegman, Lundberg, Woessner & Kluth, P.A., Mpls., 1995—. Mem. Am. Intellectual Property Law Assn. (chair subcom. 1996-99), Minn. Intellectual Property Law Assn. (treas. 1996-97, sec. 1999-00). Intellectual property, Contracts commercial, Patent. Office: Schwegman Lundberg Woessner & Kluth PA 1600 TCF Tower 121 S 8th St Minneapolis MN 55402-2810

**FORREST, HERBERT EMERSON,** lawyer; b. N.Y.C., Sept. 20, 1923; s. Jacob K. and Rose (Fried) F.; m. Marilyn Lefsky, Jan. 12, 1952; children: Glenn Clifford, Andrew Matthew. Student, CCNY, 1941, Ohio U., 1943-44; BA with distinction, George Washington U., 1948, JD with highest honors, 1952. Bar: Va. 1952, D.C. 1952, U.S. Supreme Ct. 1956, Md. 1959, U.S. Ct. Appeals (D.C. cir.) 1953, (1st cir.) 1992, (2d cir.) 1971, (3d cir.) 1957, (4th cir.) 1956, (5th cir.) 1981, (7th cir.) 1996, (8th cir.) 1991, (9th cir.) 1994, (11th cir.) 1981. Plate printer Bur. Engraving and Printing, Washington, 1942-43, 1946-52; law clk. to chief judge Bolitha J. Laws U.S. Dist. Ct., Washington, 1952-55; pvt. practice Washington, 1952-87; with Welch & Morgan, 1955-65; with Steptoe & Johnson, 1965-85, of counsel, 1986-87; trial atty. fed. programs br. civil divsn. U.S. Dept. Justice, Washington, 1987—; chmn. adv. bd. D.C. Criminal Justice Act, 1971-74; sec. com. admissions and grievances U.S. Ct. Appeals, D.C., 1973-79; title-1 audit hearing bd. U.S. Office Edn. HEW, 1976-79; edn. appeals bd. U.S. Dept. Edn., 1979-82; mem. Lawyer's Support Com. for Visitors Service Center, 1975-87. Contbr. articles to legal jours.; advisory bd.: Duke Law Jour, 1969-75. Pres. Whittier Woods PTA, 1970-71. Served with F.A., Signal Corps U.S. Army, 1943-46. Recipient Walsh award in Irish history, 1952, Goddard award in commerce, 1952. Fellow Am. Bar Found. (life); mem. George Washington Law Assn., Am. Judicature Soc., ABA (council 1972-75, 1981-84, budget officer 1985-88, vice chmn. task force on sect. devel. 1987-89, chmn. com. on agy. rule making 1968-72, 1976-81, chmn. membership com. 1984-85, editor ann. reports 1973-88, adminstrv. law sect., mem. comm. com. public utilities law sect., vice chmn. industry regulation com. 1985-86, chmn. comm. subcom. 1983-85, antitrust law sect., internat. law sect., sec. judicial adminstrn., sect. sci. and tech., comm. forum), Va. State Bar Assn., Fed. Bar Assn. (chmn. jud. rev. com. 1981-85, vice chmn. adminstrv. law sect. 1985-87), Fed. Comm. Bar Assn. (del. to ABA Ho. Dels. 1979-81, exec. com. 1967-71, 76-84, v.p. 1981-82, pres. 1982-83, chmn. telecomm. com. 1983-87), D.C. Bar Assn. (past sec., exec. com.), NAM, Nat. Conf. Bar Pres., Washington Council Lawyers, Legal Aid and Pub. Defender Assn., Am. Arbitration Assn. (comml. panel 1976-87), D.C. Unified Bar (bd. govs. 1976-79, chmn. com. on employment discrimination complaint service 1973-79, chmn. task force on services to public 1974-78, chmn. com. on appointment counsel in criminal cases 1978-88, co-chmn. com. on participation govt. employees in pro bono activities 1977-79), Broadcast Pioneers, Order of Coif, Phi Beta Kappa, Pi Gamma Mu., Artus, Phi Eta Sigma, Phi Delta Phi. Democrat. Lodge: B'nai Brith. Home: 8706 Bellwood Rd Bethesda MD 20817-3033 Office: US Dept Justice 901 E St NW Rm 1050 Fed Washington DC 20004-2037

**FORREST, ROBERT EDWIN,** lawyer; b. Washington, July 31, 1949; s. Henry Smith and Jane (Witt) F.; m. Deirdre Loretto McGahey, Sept. 23, 1978; children: Matthew Henry, John Robert, Caitlin. BA, Northwestern U., 1971; JD, Georgetown U., 1974. Bar: D.C. 1975, Md. 1984, U.S. Ct. Appeals (D.C. cir.) 1976, U.S. Ct. Appeals (6th cir.) 1985, U.S. Ct. Appeals (11th cir.) 1991, U.S. Dist. Ct. D.C. 1976, U.S. Supreme Ct. 1980, U.S. Dist. Ct. (ea. and we. dists.) Mich. 1981. Law clk. to Hon. June L. Green U.S. Dist. Ct. D.C, Washington, 1974-75; tax div. trial atty. U.S. Dept. Justice, Washington, 1975-81; prin. ptnr. Raymond & Prokop, P.C., Detroit, 1981—; adj. prof. U. Detroit/Mercy Sch. of Law, 1987—. Mem. Fed. Bar Assn. (exec. bd. 1984-90, pres. 1989-90). Methodist. Taxation, general, Federal civil litigation, Criminal. Home: 4861 Malibu Dr Bloomfield Hills MI 48302-2252 Office: Raymond & Prokop 2000 Town Ctr Ste 2400 Southfield MI 48075-1315

**FORRESTER, J. OWEN,** federal judge; b. 1939. B.S., Ga. Inst. Tech., 1961; LL.B., Emory U., 1966. Bar: Ga. 1966. Staff atty. Ga. gubernatorial candidate, 1966-67; assoc. Fisher & Phillips, Atlanta, 1967-69; magistrate U.S. Dist. Ct. (no. dist.) Ga., Atlanta, 1976-81, judge, 1981—. Office: US Dist Ct 1921 US Courthouse 75 Spring St SW Atlanta GA 30303-3309

**FORRESTER, KEVIN KREG,** lawyer; b. Beaver Dam, Wis., June 14, 1957; s. Roger Eugene and Gretchen Adeline (Yungclas) F.; m. Cheryl Kim Bahde, June 6, 1981; children: Courtney Kristine, Christopher Cody. BA, U. Calif., San Diego, 1980; JD, U. San Diego, 1986. Bar: U.S. Supreme Ct. Sales assoc. Century 21, Solana Beach, Calif., 1980-81; broker, assoc. Rand & Stewart Realtors, Rancho Santa Fe, Calif., 1981-83; law clk. Shernoff & Levine, San Diego, 1983-85; asst. to gen. counsel Pacific Scene, Inc., San Diego, 1985-87; atty. pvt. practice, Encinitas, Calif., 1987—; ct. appointed mediator, bd. of arbitrators NASD Regulation, Inc.; San Diego County Superior Ct. pro tem judge. Pres. Colony of Olivenhain (Calif.) Town Coun., 1990, 91. Mem. Internat. Acad. Mediators, Soc. Profls. Dispute Resolution, State Bar Calif., Calif. Assn. Realtors, San Diego County Bar Assn., North San Diego County Assn. Realtors, So. Calif. Mediation Assn., U. Calif. San Diego Alumni Assn. (gen. counsel 1992—, dir. 1985-92), William B. Enright Am. Inn of Ct. Republican. Avocation: running. Real property, Alternative dispute resolution, Sports. Office: 4403 Manchester Ave Ste 205 Encinitas CA 92024-7903

**FORRY, JOHN INGRAM,** lawyer; b. Washington, Feb. 9, 1945; s. John Emerson and Marion Carlotta (MacArthur) F.; m. Carol Ann Micken, Jan. 12, 1980; children: Alicia Ann, Camilla Lorraine. BA, Amherst Coll., 1966; JD, Harvard U., 1969. Bar: Calif. 1970, D.C. 1998, N.Y. 1998, U.S. Tax Ct. 1977, U.S. Supreme Ct. 1975. Founding ptnr. Forry Golbert Singer & Gelles, L.A., 1973-80; sr. ptnr. Morgan, Lewis & Bockius, L.A., 1980-97, McDermott, Will & Emery, N.Y.C., 1997-98, Ernst & Young LLP, N.Y.C., 1999—. Co-author, editor: A Practical Guide to Foreign Investment in the United States, 1979, 3d edit., 1989, 4 other books; contbr. over 40 articles to profl. jours. Co-founder Forry Fund in Philosophy and Sci., Amherst (Mass.) Coll., 1984—; mem. adv. group to U.S. Commr. of Internal Revenue, Washington, 1985-86. Mem. ABA. Republican. Roman Catholic. Avocations: philosophical implications of scientific developments, automobile racing, mountain climbing, scuba diving. Fax: 212-773-5604. Finance, Private international, Corporate taxation. Office: Ernst & Young LLP 787 7th Ave Fl 14 New York NY 10019-6085

**FORSGREN, F. LESLIE,** lawyer; b. Aug. 13, 1921; s. Evald Herman Forsgren and Caroline Ryan; m. Joy Ann Mullis, Aug. 12, 1948 (dec.); children: Frank Mullis, Caroline June. AA, N.D. Sch. Forestry, 1940; LLB, N.D. State U., 1945. Pvt. practice law Hazen, N.D., 1946-50, Crosby, N.C., 1950—; states atty. Divide County, Crosby, 1951-55, vets. svc. officer, 1954-94, judge, 1976-82; city atty. Crosby, 1955-94; nat. v.p. Lawyer Pilot Bar Assn., Crosby, 1971-72; bank atty. Farmers State Bank, Crosby. With USMC, 1945-46. Mem. Kiwanis Internat. (pres. 1974-75). Avocations: horse husbandry and sales. Oil, gas, and mineral, Aviation, Probate. Home: 707 1st St SW Crosby ND 58730 Office: 112 S Main St Crosby ND 58730

**FORSHEY, TIMOTHY ALLAN,** lawyer; b. Urbana, Ill., Apr. 25, 1961; s. Thomas Collins Forshey and Paula Jean (Upp) Baker; m. Shannon Marie Gillham, May 11, 1996. BA, Ill. Wesleyan U., 1983; MS, N.E. Mo. State U., 1986; JD, U. Ill., 1989. Bar: Ariz. 1990, Ill. 1990, Colo. 1999. Student prosecutor Champaign County State's Atty. Office, Champaign, Ill., 1987-89; atty. Jones, Skelton and Hochuli, Phoenix, 1989-91, Goldstein, Kingsley & McGroder, Phoenix, 1991-93, Matz & Rubin, Phoenix, 1993-95, Timothy A. Forshey P.C., Phoenix, 1995-97, Davis, McKee & Forshey P.C., Phoenix, 1997—. Vol. Am. Kidney Found., Phoenix, 1989—, March of Dimes, Phoenix, 1989—; approved atty. NRA, Washington, 1995—; head coach, mem. adv. bd. Pop Warner Football, Phoenix, 1990. Mem. ATLA, U.S. Practical Shooting Assn., Ariz. State Bar Assn., Ill. State Bar Assn., Maricopa County Bar Assn., Mensa. Republican. Avocations: target shooting, hunting, camping, reading, theater. General civil litigation, General corporate, Criminal. Office: Davis McKee & Forshey 5333 N 7th St Ste A201 Phoenix AZ 85014-2821

**FORSMAN, ALPHEUS EDWIN,** lawyer; b. Montgomery, Ala., May 12, 1941; m. Greta Friedman, July 5, 1964; children: Ellen E., Jennifer Ann. BA with distinction, George Washington U., 1963, JD, 1967. Bar: Va. 1968, D.C. 1969, U.S. Supreme Ct. 1973, Mo. 1979; cert. trade mark agt. Can. Trademark examiner U.S. Patent Office, Washington, 1967-69; atty. Marriott Corp., Washington, 1969-72; assoc. Roylance, Abrams, Berdo and Kaul, Washington, 1972-75, ptnr., 1975-78; trademark atty. Ralston Purina Co., St. Louis, 1978-81, trademark counsel, 1981-91, v.p., sr. trademark counsel, 1991-96; asst. v.p. Eveready Battery Co., Inc., St. Louis, 1986-98; asst. sec. Ralston Purina Co., St. Louis, 1990—, v.p., sr. counsel, 1996—; v.p. Eveready Battery Co., 1998—; asst. sec. Continental Baking Co., 1990-95. Mem. ABA, Bar. Assn. Met. St. Louis, Inst. Trade Mark Attys., London. Trademark and copyright. Home: 417 Glan Tai Dr Manchester MO 63011-4067 Office: Ralston Purina Co Checkerboard Sq Saint Louis MO 63164-0001

**FORST, JOHN KELLY,** bank holding company executive; b. Summit, N.J., Mar. 22, 1960; s. John Jerry and Jean (Kelly) F. BBA, George Washington U., 1984; JD, Capital U., 1991; LLM, Georgetown U., 1997. Bar: Fla. 1991; cert. fin. planner. Congl. aide U.S. House of Reps., Washington, 1981-85; v.p. mktg. MAP Fin. Group, Sarasota, Fla., 1985-86; asst. v.p., trust officer First Union Nat. Bank, St Petersburg, Fla., 1987-88; v.p., counsel Huntington Trust Co., Columbus, Ohio, 1989-92; v.p. domestic & internat. fiduciary svcs. 1st Union Nat. Bank, Miami, Fla., 1992-94; v.p. and counsel, regulatory affairs Allied Irish Banks and 1st Md. Bancorp., Balt., 1994-96; sr. v.p., counsel regulatory affairs Allied Irish Bank & 1st Md. Bancorp., Balt., 1996-97; atty., advisor U.S. Securities and Exch. Commn., Washington, 1997—. Editor-in-chief Capital U. Law Rev., 1990-91. Mem. ABA, Fla. Bar Assn., Nat. Assn. Securities Dealers (registered prin.), Internat. Bd. Cert. Fin. Planners, Delta Theta Phi, Sigma Chi. Republican. Lutheran. Banking, Securities, Administrative and regulatory.

**FORSTER, CLIFFORD,** lawyer; b. N.Y.C., July 6, 1913; s. Charles Von Foerster and Margaret (Ruckwild) F.; m. Helene Gaubert, Sept. 9, 1972 (dec. 1976); m. Joan Smith, Sept. 20, 1981. BA, Yale U., 1935, LLB, 1938. Bar: N.Y. 1939, U.S. Dist. Ct. (so. dist.) N.Y. 1956, U.S. Ct. Appeals (2d cir.) 1973, U.S. Supreme Ct. 1980. Staff and spl. counsel ACLU, N.Y.C., 1940-54; counsel Internat. League Rights of Man, N.Y.C., 1955-65; assoc. Fitelson, Lasky, Aslan, Couture, N.Y.C., 1960-90; bd. dirs. Internat. Rescue Com., N.Y.C., 1971—. Recipient Commdr. Order of Merit West German Gov., 1972. Mem. Assn. of Bar of City of N.Y. Roman Catholic. Avocation: assisting Hispanic baseball teams and leagues in N.Y.C. Civil rights, General civil litigation, Trademark and copyright.

**FORSTER, JONATHAN SHAWN,** lawyer; b. L.A., Nov. 28, 1970; s. Eric Gad Forster and Sally Forster Jones. BA, UCLA, 1992; JD, Loyola U., L.A., 1995. Bar: Calif. 1995, U.S. Dist. Ct. (ctrl. and so. dists.) Calif. 1995. Atty. Roquemore, Pringle & Moore, L.A., 1995-98, Jones, Kaufman & Ackerman LLP, L.A., 1998—. Mem. ABA, L.A. County Bar Assn. Avocations: ice hockey, skiing. Contracts commercial, Mergers and acquisitions, Real property. Office: Jones Kaufman & Ackerman LLP 10960 Wilshire Blvd Ste 1225 Los Angeles CA 90024-3703

**FORSYTH, ANDREW WATSON, III,** lawyer; b. Pitts., Oct. 19, 1953; s. Andrew Watson Jr. and Margo Evans (Thompson) F.; m. Margaret Eugenia Hodgdon, Sept. 30, 1989. BA in Polit. Sci., Allegheny Coll., 1976; JD, Duke U., 1979; LLM in Taxation, George Washington U., 1986. Bar: D.C. 1979, Pa. 1980. Rsch. cons. Internat. Energy Assocs., Ltd., Washington, 1979-80; litigation atty. NLRB, Washington, 1980-83; legis. asst. to Senator John Heinz, U.S. Senate, Washington, 1983-85; pvt. practice, Washington, 1985-86, Pitts., 1986—; lectr. continuing profl. edn. for CPAs. Author CLE manuals. Ruling elder Presbyn. Ch.-Sewickley, Pa., 1994—. Mem. Allegheny County Bar Assn., Rotary. Republican. Avocations: golf, hiking, reading. Federal civil litigation, Estate planning, Taxation, general. Home: 307 Timber Ln Sewickley PA 15143-8952 Office: PO Box 23214 Pittsburgh PA 15222-6214

**FORSYTHE, JANET WINIFRED,** lawyer; b. L.A., May 12, 1957; d. John Winston and Madeleine S. (Henry) F. BA, George Washington U., 1979; JD, Georgetown U., 1982. Bar: Calif. 1983. Head atty. City and County of San Francisco, 1983-97; criminal law specialist, 1988-98. Bd. dirs. No. Calif. Svc. League, San Francisco, 1985-87, Black Coalition on AIDS, v.p., 1996—; founding mem. Women Across Generations, 1997—. Coro Found. City Focus fellow, 1989-90. Mem. Bar Assn. San Francisco (chmn. community law week 1988, jud. evaluation com. 1989-91, bd. dirs. Barristers Club 1987-88, Barrister of Yr. 1988, bd. dirs., 1992-93, criminal justice adv. com., 1992-96), Calif. Women Lawyers, Lawyers Club San Francisco. Democrat. Judeo-Christian. Avocations: biking, weight training, embroidery, crocheting. Criminal, Trademark and copyright, Mergers and acquisitions. Office: PO Box 320115 San Francisco CA 94132

**FORSYTHE, RANDALL NEWMAN,** paralegal, educator; b. Hammond, Ind., Mar. 24, 1959; s. Perry Newman and Elwanda (Cox) F.; children: Kenneth Newman, Keith Randall. AA in Law Enforcement, Calumet Coll., Whiting, Ind., 1979, BA in Criminal Justice magna cum laude, 1982, BS in Mgmt. magna cum laude, 1982; Lawyer's Asst. Cert., Roosevelt U., Chgo., 1986. Labor leader/painter Inland Steel Co., East Chicago, Ind., 1978-86; ins. and securities rep. Primerica, Portage, Ind., 1984-91; paralegal Katz, Brenman & Angel, Merrillville, Ind., 1987-91, Komyatte & Freeland, P.C., Highland, Ind., 1991—; coord. paralegal divsn. Sawyer Coll., Merrillville, 1989-92, paralegal instr., 1989—; ct. apptd. spl. advocate Juvenile divsn. Lake County Superior Ct., Gary, Ind., 1987—. Manuscript/book reviewer West Pub. Co., St. Paul, 1991—. Parliamentarian Orchard Dr. Bapt. Ch., Hammond, Ind., 1981-91. Mem. Assn. Trial Lawyers Am., Nat. Assn. Legal Assts., Ind. Legal Assts. (Ind. Legal Asst. of Yr. 1990, liaison to nat. orgn. 1989-92, 97). Avocations: coaching children's Little League baseball, basketball, football teams, adult softball, hunting, fishing, camping. Office: Komyatte & Freeland PC 9650 Gordon Dr Highland IN 46322-2909

**FORTAIN, RENEE THERESE,** lawyer; b. Pomona, Calif., Aug. 14, 1965; d. Roger Auguste Fortain and Denise Marie-Ange Sarrazin; m. David Martin Godosky, July 3, 1998. BS in Psychology, Willamette U., 1987; JD, Loyola U., 1991. Bar: Calif. 1991, N.J. 1992, N.Y. 1992, U.S. Supreme Ct. 1998. Asst. dist. atty. Bronx Dist. Atty.'s Office, 1992-97; agy. atty. N.Y.C. Police Dept., 1997—; vol. arbitrator N.Y. Small Claims Ct., 1997—. Team leader N.Y. Cares Soup Kitchen, 1997—. Mem. Bar Assn. of City of N.Y. (corrections com. 1997—), Assn. of Arbitrators. Roman Catholic. Avocations: running, travel, reading. Office: NYC Police Dept Office of Advocate 1 Police Plz New York NY 10038-1403

**FORTENBAUGH, SAMUEL BYROD, III,** lawyer; b. Phila., Nov. 6, 1933; s. Samuel Byrod Jr. and Katherine Francisca (Wall) F.; children: Samuel Byrod IV, Cristina Fortenbaugh Alemany, Katherine Dooley, Francesca Cowden. BA, Williams Coll., 1955; LLB, Harvard U., 1960. Bar: N.Y. 1961, U.S. Dist. Ct. (so. dist.) N.Y. 1961. Assoc. Kelley Drye & Warren, N.Y.C., 1960-69, ptnr., 1970-79; ptnr. Morgan, Lewis & Bockius, N.Y.C., 1980—; bd. dirs. Baldwin Tech. Co., Inc., Norwalk, Conn., Goodman Equipment Corp., Chgo.; bd. dirs., sec. Furgueson Capital Mgmt. Inc., N.Y.C.; chmn. bd. dirs., sec. Wall Industries, Inc., Kannapolis, N.C.; chmn. bd. dirs. Knight Textile Corp, Saluda, S.C.; trustee Patroni Scholastici, New Brunswick, N.J., 1978—, sec. 1985—; lectr. profl. seminars. Contbr. articles to profl. jours. Mem. ABA, Assn. of Bar of City of N.Y. (mem. Young

Lawyers com. 1962-65, corp. law com. 1976-79, com. on securities regulation 1982-85, chmn. com. on issue distbn. of securities 1984-85), Racquet and Tennis Club, Univ. Club. (N.Y.C.), Bay Head (N.J.) Yacht Club, Indian Harbor Yacht Club (Greenwich, Conn.), Phi Beta Kappa. Mergers and acquisitions, Securities, General corporate. Office: Morgan Lewis & Bockius LLP 101 Park Ave Fl 45 New York NY 10178-0002

**FORTIER, ROBERT FREDERIC,** lawyer; b. Chgo., Sept. 5, 1949; m. Mardelle LaDonna Eide, July 27, 1974. BA with honors, U. Ill., 1971, JD, 1974. Bar: Ill. 1975, U.S. Dist. Ct. (no. dist.) Ill. 1975. Atty. Liberty Mut. Ins. Co., Chgo., 1975-76; assoc. Tews, Abbey & Theisen, Chgo., 1976-77; assoc. gen. counsel Alliance of Am. Insurer, Chgo., 1977-83; sole practice Lisle, Ill., 1983—; free-lance writer Lisle, 1988—; cons. govt. affairs Fortier Mangerial Systems Inc., Lisle, 1984-86. Author: (with Mardelle Fortier) St. Thomas More's Theme of Utopia in Literature, 1992; contbr. articles to Chgo. Sun-Times and Chgo. Tribune, 1983—, The Ligourian mag. Served with USAR, 1971-76. Mem. ABA, CATO Inst., Heritage Found., Knights of Immaculata. Roman Catholic. Avocations: history, nature. Estate planning, Taxation, general, Labor. Home and Office: 5515 E Lake Dr Ste A Lisle IL 60532-2664

**FORTIER, SAMUEL JOHN,** lawyer; b. Spokane, Wash., Mar. 30, 1952; s. Charles Henry and Mary (Petersen) F.; m. Dagmar Christine Mikko, Sept. 15, 1983; children: Nova Marie, Matthew Theodore. BA cum laude, Boston U., 1974; JD magna cum laude, Gonzaga U., 1982. Bar: Alaska 1982, U.S. Dist. Ct. Alaska 1983, U.S. Ct. Appeals (9th cir.) 1987. Acting exec. dir. Bristol Bay Native Assn., Dillingham, Alaska, 1974-76; fin. analyst Alaska Fedn. of Natives, Anchorage, Alaska, 1976-78; loan analyst State of Alaska, Anchorage, 1978-79; law clk. consumer protection div., atty. gen.'s office State of Wash., Spokane, 1980-82; assoc. Cummings & Routh P.C., Anchorage, 1982-84; ptnr. Fortier & Mikko, Anchorage, 1984—; adj. prof. U. Alaska, Anchorage, 1982-85; speaker workshop Small Bus. Adminstrn., Anchorage, 1982-85; manpower dir. VISTA. Mem. ABA, Alaska Bar Assn. (native law sect.), Anchorage Bar Assn. Democrat. Avocations: reading, writing, camping, skiing. General corporate, Native American, Federal civil litigation. Home: 6800 Sequoia Cir Anchorage AK 99516-3755 Office: Fortier & Mikko 2550 Denali St Ste 1500 Anchorage AK 99503-2753

**FORTIN, RAYMOND D.,** lawyer. BA, U. Fla., 1974, JD, 1977. Bar: Ga. 1977. Pvt. practice, 1977-81; staff counsel The Citizens & So. Corp., 1981-89; mng. atty. SunTrust Banks, Inc., Atlanta, 1989-91, sr. v.p., 1991—. General corporate. Office: SunTrust Banks Inc 303 Peachtree St NE Fl 30 Atlanta GA 30308-3201

**FORTMAN, MARVIN,** law educator, consultant; b. Bklyn., Oct. 20, 1930; s. Herman and Bess (Smith) F.; m. Sorale Esther Elpern, Aug. 3, 1958; children: Brian E., Anita J., Deborah J. BS in Acctg., U. Ariz., 1957, JD magna cum laude, 1960; LLM, NYU, 1961. Bar: Ariz. 1960, N.Y. 1961, U.S. Tax Ct. 1962, U.S. Ct. Appeals 1962, U.S. Supreme Ct. 1962. Assoc. Aranow, Brodsky, Bolinger, Einhorn & Dann, N.Y.C., 1961-63, O'Connor, Cavanaugh, Anderson, Westover & Beshears, Phoenix, Ariz., 1963-65; prof. bus. law, bus. and pub. adminstrn. U. Ariz., Tucson, 1965—; legal cons. various corps., 1963—. Author: Legal Aspects of Doing Business in Arizona, 1970; contbr. articles to profl. jours. Mem. legal com. Ariz. Coun. on Econ. Edn., Tucson, 1975—, Sabbar Shrine Temple, Tucson, 1978—, legal advisor, chmn. wills and gifts, 1981-84, 1990—. With U.S. Army, 1951-53; ETO. Kenneson fellow NYU, 1960-61. Mem. N.Y. State Bar Assn., Ariz. Bar Assn. (wills, trusts, estates sect.), Phi Kappa Phi, Beta Gamma Sigma (v.p., treas. 1972—), Beta Alpha Psi, Alpha Kappa Psi. Home: 5844 E 15th St Tucson AZ 85711-4508 Office: U Ariz Coll Of Bus And Pub Adminstr Tucson AZ 85721-0001

**FORTSON, JAMES LEON, JR.,** lawyer; b. Shreveport, La., May 5, 1949; s. James Leon and Hellon Mildred (Atkins) F.; children: Stephen Christopher, Travis Leon, Heather Helaine. BS, La. State U., 1971, JD, 1974. Bar: La. 1974, U.S. Dist. Ct. (we. dist.) La. 1974, U.S. Ct. Appeals (5th cir.) 1976. Pvt. practice Shreveport, 1974—. Mem. Am. Bd. Trial Advocates, La. Trial Lawyers Assn. (bd. govs. 1986-93, emeritus mem. bd. govs. 1993—), La. State Bar Assn. (mem. ho. of dels. 1990—, bd. cert. family law bd. legal specialization 1995—), La. Bd. Legal Specialization (family law adv. com.), N.W. La. Trial Lawyers Assn. (founding mem.), Lawyer-Pilots Bar Assn. Democrat. Avocation: pilot. Family and matrimonial, Personal injury, General civil litigation. Office: PO Box 7691 151 Freestate Blvd Shreveport LA 71107-6511

**FORTUNE, JOANNE C.,** accountant, appraiser, lawyer; b. N.Y.C., Jan. 24, 1941; d. Joseph A. and Mary C. Fortune; BS summa cum laude in Acctg. and Psychology, Syracuse (N.Y.) U., 1961; postgrad. London Sch. Econs.; LLB, NYU, 1967; real estate appraisal studies Pace U., 1978; m. Carl Postighone, Sept. 24, 1960; children: Renee, Carl, Joseph. Account mgr. Cherry-Burrell Co., Cedar Rapids, Iowa, 1961-63; acct. Sperduto, Priskie, Greenhut & Futterman, N.Y.C., 1968-70; acct., fin. adv. City Club, Yonkers, N.Y., 1970-77; pvt. practice Westchester County, Bronxville, N.Y., 1977—; real estate developer West Coast Fla. Mem. Caretta Found.; head youth counseling Teens in Trouble; mem. U.S. Congressional Adv. Bd., Am. Security Coun., Internat. Biog. Ctr. Recipient Sponsers award McLean Heights Youth Assn., 1978, 79, 80, 81, 82, 86, East Yonkers Boys Club, 1990; citation Am. Wildlife Assn. Mem. Real Estate Appraisers Assn., Builders Inst., N.Y. State Assessors Assn., N.Y. State Accts. Assn., Western Assn. Women, Am. Mgrs. Assn., N.Y. Bar Assn., West County Bar Assn., Gulf-Life Ecology Assn. to Preserve Sea Life (pres.). Roman Catholic. Home: 105 Bajart Pl Yonkers NY 10705-2725 Office: 55 Pondfield Rd Bronxville NY 10708-3703 also: 18 E 81st St New York NY 10028-0231

**FORTUNO, VICTOR M.,** lawyer; b. N.Y.C., Jan. 24, 1952; s. Victor M. Fortuno and Ceda Aguayo; m. Vicki Ann Clark; children: Adam R., Victor III, Scott, Erica, Bryce. AB in Econs., Columbia U., 1974, JD, 1977. Bar: Pa. 1977, U.S. Dist. Ct. (ea. dist.) Pa. 1977, U.S. Ct. Appeals (3d cir.) 1977, U.S. Supreme Ct. 1980, U.S. Ct. Appeals (D.C. cir.) 1987, D.C. 1988, U.S. Dist. Ct. D.C. 1988, U.S. Ct. Appeals (4th cir.) 1988, U.S. Dist. Ct. Ariz. 1991. Staff atty. Community Legal Svcs., Inc., Phila., 1977-78; asst. dist. atty. Office Dist. Atty., Phila., 1978-83; staff atty. Legal Svcs. Corp., Washington, 1983-85, acting dir. compliance div., 1985-86, asst. gen. counsel, 1986, sr. litigation counsel, 1986-88, acting gen. counsel, 1987, 91, dep. gen. counsel, 1988-91, gen. counsel, 1991—, corp. sec., 1995—, v.p., 1999—. Dir. Columbia Coll. Alumni Assn., 1981-83, Phila. Health Plan, 1980-83. Pulitzer Found. scholar, 1970-74, Assn. of Bar of City of N.Y. C. Bainbridge Smith scholar, 1974-77. Mem. ABA, D.C. Bar Assn.. E-mail: fortuno@netscape.net. Fax:(202) 336 8954. Home: 7479 Thorncliff Ln Springfield VA 22153-2153 Office: Legal Svcs Corp 750 1st St NE Ste 1000 Washington DC 20002-4241

**FORWARD, DOROTHY ELIZABETH,** legal assistant; b. Medford, Mass., Oct. 12, 1919; d. Roy Clifford and Julia (Lane) Hurd; m. Winston W. Forward, Sept. 29, 1942. Student, UCLA, 1964. Sec. nat. dir. fund raising ARC, Washington, 1943-46; legal sec. William W. Waters, Esq., L.A., 1953-56; office mgr. Winston W. Forward, Ins. Adjuster, Arcadia, Calif., 1956-64; legal asst. John M. Podlech, Esq., Pasadena, 1964-79; dir. Calif. Probate Insts., Arcadia, 1970—; ind. probate legal asst., 1979—; condr. workshops in probate procedures, 1967-92; vol. lectr. to sr. citizens in estate planning; vol. sec. All-Ch. Coun. United Meth. Ch., Arcadia, 1998, 99; pres. Philathea (women's club), Arcadia, 1999, 2nd v.p., Arcadia Travelers, 2000, Arcadia, Calif. Vol., 2d v.p. program Arcadia Travelers. Recipient ARC Meritorious Svc. award, 1945. Office: PO Box 660311 Arcadia CA 91066-0311

**FORZANI, RINALDO, III,** lawyer; b. N.Y.C., Mar. 7, 1958; s. Rinaldo Jr. and Geraldine (Scarpinati) F.; m. Lorraine Susan Lionetti, July 3, 1982; 1 child, Benjamin Rinaldo. BA Politics wih honors, NYU, 1979; JD, Hofstra U., 1982. Bar: N.J. 1982, U.S. Dist. Ct. N.J. 1982. Assoc. Harry R. Howard, P.A., Florham Park, N.J., 1982-83, Howard and Gendel, Edqs., Paterson, N.J., 1984; ptnr. Harry R. Howard, P.A., Parsippany, N.J., 1985-91; prin. Rinaldo Forzani III, Esq., Bernardsville, N.J., 1991—. Mem. Morris County Bar Assn., Adams Village Condominium Assn. (treas. 1990-94, pres. 1995-98), Spring Ridge Condominium Assn. (v.p. 1990-97, pres. 1997-98). Avocations: skiing, hiking, tennis, jazz piano, reading. General civil litigation, Insurance, Personal injury. Home: 76 Commonwealth Dr Basking Ridge NJ 07920-3094 Office: Rinaldo Forzani III Esq 61 Claremont Rd Bernardsville NJ 07924-2232

**FOSHEE, DEBORAH CUNNINGHAM,** lawyer, educator; b. Tampa, Fla., Sept. 16, 1958; d. Mark and Gloria Plymale Cunningham; m. David Julian Foshee, Oct. 30, 1986 (div. Mar. 1999); 1 child, Hank. BA, Tulane U., 1980, JD cum laude, 1983. Bar: La. 1983, U.S. Dist. Ct. (ea. dist.) La. 1983, U.S. Dist. Ct. (we. dist.) La. 1985, U.S. Cir. Ct. (5th cir.) 1985. Assoc. Hammett, Leake & Hammett, New Orleans, 1983-86, Lemle & Kelleher, New Orleans, 1986-90; ptnr. Gordon, Arata, McCollum & Duplantis, New Orleans, 1990-95, Adams & Reese, New Orleans, 1995—; team leader, tchr. Nat. Inst. Trial Advocacy, 1990—, trial program La. State U., Baton Rouge, 1994—; tchr. La. Assn. Def. Counsel, 1994—, Emory Sch. Law, Atlanta, 1995; mem. Med. Legal Interprofl. Com., 1994—. Bd. dirs. Youth Svcs. Bur., Covington, La., 1996—, St. Tammany Art Assn., Covington, 1998—; commr. Home Rule Charter Commn., St. Tammany Parish, La., 1997-98; mem. steering com. Vision St. Tammany, 1997—; mem. land use com. New Direction 2025, ST. Tammany Parish, 1998—. Recipient Appreciation award La. State Bar Assn., 1988. Mem. Am. Health Lawyers Assn. (mem. healthcare fraud abuse subcom. 1997—, false claims working group 1999—), St. Tammany Hist. Soc., Inns of Ct. Episcopalian. Avocations: historic preservation, gardening, computers. Home: 201 Carroll St Mandeville LA 70448-5707 Office: Adams & Reese 4500 One Shell Sq New Orleans LA 70139-7755

**FOSS, GEORGE B., JR.,** lawyer, correspondent; b. Birmingham, Ala., Sept. 21, 1924; s. George Bridges Foss and Mary Gladys (Gardien) Corn; m. Luz Maria Peña; children: Daphne E. Holldorff, Anne K. Vazquez, Brian G., Holly T. AB, Birmingham (Ala.) So. Coll., 1949; JD, Duke U., 1951; postgrad., Ga. Tech. U., 1955, U. Miami, 1983. Bar: Ala., 1951, U.S. Supreme Ct., 1955, Fla., 1958. Asst. city atty. City of Birmingham, 1951-55, planning dir., 1955-57; ptnr. Beasley & Foss law firm, Birmingham, 1957; sr. planner, atty. City of St. Petersburg, Fla., 1957-59; assoc. Fowler, White, Gillen, Yancey and Humkey, Tampa, Fla., 1959; assoc. atty. Zewadski, DiVito & Charwick, St. Petersburg, 1959-60; ptnr. Fowler, White, Gillen, Humkey & Trenam, St. Petersburg, 1960-67, Fowler, White, Burnett, Hurley & Strickroot, Miami, 1967-83; pvt. practice Miami, 1984—, Cuernavaca, Mex., 1986—; legal adv. (Miami chpt.) English Speaking U., 1985-86; lectr. in field. Contbr. articles to profl. jours. Pres. Miami chpt. Soc. So. Families, 1983-84. Mem. ABA, Ala. State Bar, Fla. Bar (chmn. regulation of land use com., real property sect. 1975-80), Birmingham Bar Assn., St. Petersburg Bar Assn., Dade County Bar Assn., Assn. to Unite the Democracies, Fla. Planning and Zoning Assn. (pres. So. Fla. chpt.), Miami, Lakewood Estates Property Owners Assn. (pres.), St. Petersburg, Navy League, Sigma Alpha Epsilon (pres. 1946), Phi Delta Phi (v.p. 1950-51), Omicron Delta Kappa. Democrat. Episcopalian. Avocations: skin diving, snorkeling, record collecting, leading discussion groups. General civil litigation, General practice, Land use and zoning (including planning). Home and Office: Francisco Villa 111, Colonial Rancho Cortes, Cuernavaca Mexico 62120

**FOSTER, ARTHUR KEY, JR.,** lawyer; b. Birmingham, Ala., Nov. 22, 1933; s. Arthur Key and Vonceil (Oden) F.; m. Jean Lyles Foster, Jan. 7, 1967; children: Arthur Key III, Brooke Oden. B.S.E., Princeton U., 1955; JD, U. Va., 1960. Bar: Ala. 1960. Ptnr. Balch & Bingham, Birmingham, 1965—. Trustee Episcopal Found. Jefferson County; bd. dirs. Met. YMCA, Downtown Club, Highlands Day Sch., Altamont Sch. Served to lt., USN, 1955-60. Mem. ABA, Ala. Bar Assn., B'ham Bar Assn., Estate Planning Council of Birmingham, Nat. Assn. Bond Lawyers, Newcomen Soc. of U.S. Republican. Episcopalian. Club: Kiwanis (bd. dirs.). Estate planning, Probate, Municipal (including bonds). Office: Balch & Bingham PO Box 306 Birmingham AL 35201-0306

**FOSTER, C(HARLES) ALLEN,** lawyer; b. Aug. 26, 1941; s. Charles Shearer and Bessie Lea (Long) F.; m. Susan Coomes; children: Charles, Shearer Sanders II, Susan Elizabeth Coomes, Charles Henry Edward. BA summa cum laude, Princeton U., 1963; BA in Jurisprudence 1st class honors, Oxford (Eng.) U., 1965, MA in Jurisprudence, 1971; JD magna cum laude, Harvard U., 1967. Bar: N.C. 1967, U.S. Dist. Ct. (mid. dist.) 1968, U.S. Dist. Ct. (we. dist.) 1968, U.S. Dist. Ct. (ea. dist.) 1968, U.S. Tax Ct. 1970, U.S. Ct. Appeals (4th cir.), U.S. Ct. Appeals (5th cir.) 1970, U.S. Ct. Appeals (11th cir.) 1991, U.S. Ct. Appeals (10th cir.) 1993, U.S. Ct. Appeals (fed. cir.) 1995, U.S. Supreme Ct. 1971, D.C. 1984, U.S. Dist. Ct. D.C. 1985, U.S. Dist. Ct. (no. dist.) Tex. 1990, U.S. Dist. Ct. (so. dist.) Tex. 1991, U.S. Ct. Fed. Claims 1994. Assoc. McLendon, Brim, Brooks, Pierce & Daniels, Greensboro, N.C., 1967-72, ptnr., 1972-73; sec., dir., gen. counsel Spanco Industries, Inc., Greensboro and Sanford, N.C., 1973-75, Conestee, S.C., 1973-75; ptnr. Turner, Enochs, Foster, Sparrow & Burnley, Greensboro, 1975-81, Foster, Conner & Robson, 1983-88, Patton, Boggs LLP, 1988-99, Greenberg Traurig, Washington, 1999—; sr. lectr. law Duke U., 1981-88; arbitrator Am. Arbitration Assn., mem. nat. panels of labor, constrn. and internat. comml. arbitrators; mem. Nat. Acad. Arbitrators; pub. mem. N.C. Tax Rev. Bd., 1972-76; mem. N.C. Judicial Selection Study Commn., 1987-88; U.S. rep. Internat. Energy Agy. Dispute Resolution Ctr., Paris, 1984—; permanent panel arbitrator Martin Marietta and Atomic Trades and Labor Coun.; hearing officer Guilford Tech. Inst., Greensboro, others. Author: Construction and Design Law, 1984—, Construction and Design Law Digest, 1981—, Law and Practice of Commercial Arbitration in North Carolina, 1984; contbr. articles to profl. jours. Co-founder, sec., bd. dirs. Greensboro Day Sch.; bd. dirs. Greensboro Opera Co., 1980-83, Young Women's Christian Assn., 1968-84, atty.; group chmn. United Fund Dr., 1979; alumni coun.; exec. com. Princeton U. Alumni Assn.; exec. com. Harvard Law Sch. Assn. N.C., 1970; group chmn. United Fund Dr., 1969-70; precinct chmn. Guilford County Rep. Exec. Com., 1974-76, 84-92, chmn. fin. com., 1975-76; Rep. candidate for atty.-gen. N.C., 1984; active N.C. Tax Rev. Bd., 1975-79; spl. counsel Rep. Nat. Com., 1989—; spl. litigation counsel N.C. Rep. Cen. Com., 1987—; co. Mem. ABA (litigation sect., labor and employment discrimination law sect., forum com. on constrn. industry), Am. Law Inst., Am. Arbitration Assn. (bd. dirs. 1980-83, nat. panels labor, constrn., internat. comml. arbitrators 1975—, chmn. N.C. regional adv. coun. 1979-83), Am. Coll. Constrn. Arbitrators (pres. 1983-84), Princeton U. Alumni Assn. (pres. alumni coun., exec. com. 1978-79, pres. mid. N.C. chpt. 1968-80), N.C. Bar Assn. (coun. sect. constnl. law), Greensboro Bar Assn., 18th Jud. Dist. Bar Assn., Phi Beta Kappa, Cap and Gown Club. Federal civil litigation, Labor. Home: 3060 Q St NW Washington DC 20007-3080

**FOSTER, CHARLES CRAWFORD,** lawyer, educator; b. Galveston, Tex., Aug. 1, 1941; s. Louie Brown and Helen (Hall) F.; m. Marta Brito, Sept. 7, 1967 (div. Apr. 1986); children: John, Ruth; m. Lily Chen, Jan. 7, 1989; children: Zachary, Anthony. AA, Del Mar Jr. Coll., 1961; BA, U. Tex., 1963, JD, 1967. Bar: Tex. 1967, N.Y. 1969. Assoc. Reid & Priest, N.Y.C., 1967-69, Butler & Binion, Houston, 1969-73; ptnr. Tindall & Foster, Houston, 1973—; hon. consul gen. Kingdom of Thailand, 1996—; adj. prof. immigration law U. Houston, 1985-89; chmn. World Trade Divsn. Greater Houston Partnership, 1997—, bd. dirs.; chmn. Asia Soc.-Tex., bd. trustees, 1990—; bd. dirs. Houston Forum, Houston World Affairs Coun., 1990—; bd. dirs. Houston Forum, Inst. Internat. Edn., The Houston Club, 1999—, Brit. Am. Bus. Assn., Houston Ballet Found., Assn. of Cmty. TV, Houston Holocaust Mus. Contbr. articles to profl. jours. Chmn. Immigration Reform Gov.'s Task Force on Tex., 1984-87; mem. exec. coun. Houston chpt. Drug Abuse Reinstated Edn. Corp., 1996—. Rotary Internat. fellow U. Concepción, Chile, 1964; recipient Houston Internat. Svc. award Houston Jaycees, 1996; Hon. Consul Gen. of Kingdom of Thailand, 1997; honoree Am. Immigration Law Found., 1998. Mem. ABA (chmn. immigration com. internat. law and practice sect. 1982-90, chmn. coordinating com. on immigration and law 1987-89), Am. Immigration Lawyers Assn. (pres. 1981-82, Outstanding Svc. award 1985), Tex. Bar Assn. (chmn. com. law on immigration and nationality 1984-86), Tex. Bd. Legal Specialization (chmn. immigration adv. commn. 1979—), Houston Bar Assn., Asia Soc. (trustee 1992—, chmn. Houston Ctr. 1992—), Rotary. Methodist. Avocations: mountain climbing, photography, travel. Immigration, naturalization, and customs. Home: 17 Courtlandt Pl Houston TX 77006-4013 Office: Tindall & Foster 2800 Chase Tower 600 Travis St Houston TX 77002-3094

**FOSTER, CINDY COOPER,** lawyer; b. Knoxville, Tenn., Feb. 23, 1970; d. Lawrence Edward Cooper and Donna Eileen (Petree) Lunsford; m. Ralph Thomas Foster, Aug. 13, 1988; 1 child, Chloe Larissa. BS cum laude, U. Tenn., 1991, JD magna cum laude, 1994. Bar: Tenn. 1995. Assoc. Sobieski, Messer & Assocs., Knoxville, 1995-98. Recipient Alumni scholarship U. Tenn., Knoxville, 1987, Am. Jurisprudence award Lawyers Coop. Pub., 1992. Mem. Tenn. Lawyers Assn. for Women, Tenn. Bar Assn., East Tenn. Lawyers Assn. for Women, Knoxville Bar Assn. Democrat. General civil litigation, Civil rights, Labor.

**FOSTER, DAVID LEE,** lawyer; b. Des Moines, Dec. 13, 1933; s. Carl Dewitt and Dorothy Jo (Bell) F.; m. Marilyn Lee Bokemeier, Aug. 12, 1957 (div. June 1978); children: Gwendolyn Foster Reed, Cynthia Foster Curry, David Lee Jr.; m. Kathleen Carol Walsh, Mar. 24, 1979; 1 child, John Wickersham. Student, Simpson Coll., 1951-52; BA, U. Iowa, 1954, JD, 1957. Bar: Iowa 1957, N.Y. 1958, Ohio 1964, U.S. Supreme Ct. 1975. Assoc. Cravath, Swaine & Moore, N.Y.C., 1957-63; from assoc. to ptnr. Jones, Day, Cockley & Reavis, Cleve., 1963-72; ptnr. Willkie Farr & Gallagher, N.Y.C., 1972—; lectr. So. Meth. U., 1979-84, U. Pitts., 1984, Practicing Law Inst., N.Y.C., 1984-85; mem. adv. bd. Civil RICO Report LRP Publs., 1988—; bd. govs. N.Y. Ins. Exch., 1987-96. Contbr. chpts. to book, articles to legal jours. Mem., bd. trustees Cardigan Mountain Sch., 1995—. Served with USNR, 1952-60. Fellow Am. Coll. Trial Lawyers, Internat. Acad. Trial Lawyers (bd. dirs. 1987-92); mem. Am. Counsel Assn. (pres. 1994-95, bd. dirs. 1992—), River Club, Order of Coif, Phi Beta Kappa. Avocations: flying; fishing. Antitrust, Insurance, Federal civil litigation. Office: Willkie Farr & Gallagher 787 7th Ave New York NY 10019-6099

**FOSTER, DAVID SCOTT,** lawyer; b. White Plains, N.Y., July 13, 1938; s. William James and Ruth Elizabeth (Seltzer) F.; m. Eleanore Stalker, Dec. 21, 1959; children: David Scott, Robert McEachron. BA, Amherst Coll., 1960; LLB, Harvard U., 1963. Bar: N.Y. 1963, D.C. 1977, Calif. 1978. Jud. law clk. U.S. Dist. Ct. (so. dist.) N.Y., 1963-64; assoc. Debevoise & Plimpton, N.Y.C., 1964-72; internat. tax counsel U.S. Treasury Dept., Washington, 1972-77; ptnr. Brobeck, Phleger & Harrison, San Francisco, 1978-90, Coudert Bros., San Francisco, 1990-91, Thelen, Reid & Priest LLP, San Francisco, 1991—. Mem. ABA, San Francisco Bar Assn., Internat. Fiscal Assn., Western Pension and Benefits Confs., St. Francis Yacht Club (San Francisco). Presbyterian. Pension, profit-sharing, and employee benefits, Taxation, general. Office: Thelen Reid & Priest LLP 2 Embarcadero Ctr San Francisco CA 94111-3823

**FOSTER, DOUGLAS TAYLOR,** lawyer, investor; b. L.A., Oct. 30, 1927; s. James Taylor Foster and Irene Eve Erickson; m. Nita Burt Peterson, July 3, 1951 (div. May, 1975); children: Jane Taylor Dickson, Stephanie Foster Abram. BA in Econs., Bus., U. Wash., 1950; JD, Stanford U., 1956. Bar: Calif. 1957, U.S. Dist. Ct. (so. dist.) Calif. 1957, U.S. Ct. Appeals (9th cir.) 1959, U.S. Dist. Ct. (no. dist.) Calif. 1969, U.S. Supreme Ct. 1971, U.S. Dist. Ct. (ea. dist.) Calif. 1985. From assoc. to ptnr. Farrand, Fisher & Farrand, L.A., 1956-66; legal counsel McClatchy Newspapers and Broadcasting, Sacramento, Calif., 1957-81; ptnr. Diepenbrock, Wulff, Plant & Hannegan, Sacramento, 1981-84; lawyer pvt. practice, Sacramento, 1985—; sec. bus. and corp. sect. L.A. County Bar Assn., 1966. Candidate L.A. County Rep. Ctrl. Com., San Marino, Calif., 1965. Lt. USN, 1950-53, Korean War. Mem. ABA, Calif. State Bar, Sacramento County Bar Assn., Calif. Trial Lawyers Assn., Consumer Attys. of Calif., Capital City Trial Lawyers Corp., Consumer Attys. of Sacramento County, Rotary Club Arden-Arcade, Seattle Yacht Club, Sacramento Yacht Club, Sutter Club. Presbyterian. Achievements include successful defense of cable television license, Lake of the Pines Development, No. Calif., involving first judicial interpretation and ruling under the Cable TV Act of 1984 in U.S. Dist. Ct. (ea. dist.) Calif., 1986. Avocations: boating, tennis, golf, bridge, other sports. General civil litigation, Communications, General corporate. Office: Douglas F Foster Esq 2625 Fair Oaks Blvd Ste 1 Sacramento CA 95864-4936

**FOSTER, ERIK KOEHLER,** lawyer; b. Cin., Oct. 15, 1953; s. Stanley H. and Dorothy K. (Koehler) F. BA, The Colo. Coll., 1976; JD, U. Cin., 1986. Bar: Colo. 1986, U.S. Dist. Ct. Colo. 1986. Musician After Hours Jazz, Colorado Springs, 1972-79; real estate broker Olympic Investment Realty, Colorado Springs, 1979-83; ptnr. Moye Giles O'Keefe Vermeire & Gorrell, Denver, 1986—. Named to Order of the Coif, U. Cin., 1986. Real property. Home: 1025 S Linda Ln Evergreen CO 80439-9528 Office: Moye Giles et al 1225 17th St Fl 29 Denver CO 80202-5534

**FOSTER, GEORGE WILLIAM, JR.,** lawyer, educator; b. Boston, Nov. 23, 1919; s. George William and Marguerite (Werner) F.; m. Jeanette Raymond, May 26, 1950; children—Susan, Bill, Fred. Student, Antioch Coll., 1937-40; B.S. in Chemistry, Stanford U., 1947; LL.B., Georgetown U., 1951; LL.M., Yale U., 1952. Bar: Wis. bar 1972. Exec. asst. to U.S. Senator, 1949-50; spl. asst. to Sec. of State Dean Acheson, 1951; asst. prof. law U. Wis., Madison, 1952-56; assoc. prof. U. Wis., 1956-59, prof., 1959-86, assoc. dean, 1969-72, prof. emeritus, 1986—; reporter Wis. Long-Arm Process Statute, 1955-59; cons. sch. desegregation guidelines HEW, 1965; legal advisor Ministry of Justice, Kabul, Afghanistan, 1976. Served to lt. (j.g.) USN, 1942-46. Mem. Am. Orthithologists Union, Am. Law Inst. Democrat. Home: 5616 Lake Mendota Dr Madison WI 53705-1036 Office: U Wis N Lawn Ave Bldg Madison WI 53704-5034

**FOSTER, J. DON,** prosecutor. BS in Indsl. Mgmt., Ga. Inst. Tech., 1968; postgrad., U. Ala., 1968; JD, U. Ala., Tuscaloosa, 1971. Ptnr. Gallalee, Denniston & Edington, Mobile, 1971-76; pvt. practice Foley and Fairhope, Ala., 1976-95; mcpl. judge City of Foley, 1977-78; U.S. atty. So. Dist. Ala., Mobile, 1995—; vice-chmn. Atty. Gen's. Adv. Subcom. on Health Care Fraud; mem. Atty. Gen's. Adv. Subcom. on Environ. Crimes, Civil Rights, Indian Affairs, Divil Issues and Justice Programs. Capt. U.S. Army, 1971-75. Mem. Ala. Bar Assn., Mobile County Bar Assn., Baldwin County Bar Assn. Office: US Atty's Office 63 S Royal St Ste 600 Mobile AL 36602-3245

**FOSTER, JAMES (JAY) R.,** lawyer; b. Biloxi, Miss., Aug. 10, 1968; m. Sheila M. Bosarge, Nov. 23, 1996. BA, Tulane U., 1991; JD, Miss. Coll., 1994. Law clk. Miss. Supreme Ct., Jackson, Miss. Ct. Appeals, Jackson; lawyer Allen Vaughn Cobb & Hood, Gulfport, Miss.; chmn. Young Lawyers Judiciary Com. Mem. incorporation task force West Jackson County Civic Assn. Insurance, Personal injury, General civil litigation. Office: Allen Vaughn Cobb & Hood PO Box 4108 Gulfport MS 39502-4108

**FOSTER, JOHN ROBERT,** lawyer; b. Long Beach, Calif., Feb. 13, 1940; s. Orlon c. and Catherine Rose (Rhind) F.; m. Nancy Crandall, June 17, 1962; children: John Crandall, Christopher Peter, Blayney Robert, Courtland William. BA in History, San Jose State U., 1961; LLB, U. Calif., Berkeley, 1964. Bar: Calif. 1965, U.S. Dist. Ct. (no. dist.) Calif. 1965, U.S. Ct. Appeals (9th cir.) 1965; cert. specialist in probate, estate planning, and trust law. Dep. legis. counsel State of Calif., Sacramento, 1964-65; pres. Rusconi, Foster, Thomas & Wilson, APC, Morgan Hill, Calif., 1965—; asst. dist. atty. San Benito County, Hollister, Calif., 1967. Mem. Morgan Hill Unified Sch. Dist. Bd. Edn., 1967-74, 79-83, chmn. bd., 1969-71; councilman City of Morgan Hill, 1984-88, 97-98, mayor, 1984. Named Citizen of Yr., City of Morgan Hill. Mem. Calif. State Bar (past state bar exec. com. on estate planning, probate and trusts), Santa Clara County Bar Assn., Gilroy-Morgan Hill Bar Assn. (past pres.), Morgan Hill C. of C. (past pres.), Masons, Rotary (past pres. Morgan Hill). Republican. Methodist. Avocations: skiing, fly fishing, backpacking, camping. E-mail: bob@rftw.com. General corporate, Estate planning, Probate. Home: 17630 Black Oak Ct Morgan Hill CA 95037-9442 Office: Rusconi Foster Thomas & Wilson 30 Keystone Ave Morgan Hill CA 95037-4325

**FOSTER, JULIE IRENE,** lawyer; b. Billings, Mont., June 4, 1955; d. Robert Harrison and Sheila Irene (Dunstan) Asher; m. Craig Richard Foster, June 30, 1979; children: Cheryl Irene, Matthew Thomas, Mark Benjamin. BS magna cum laude, Cen. Conn. State U., 1977; JD, Western New Eng. Coll., 1981; MBA, U. Conn., 1988. Bar: Conn. 1982. Assoc. Jowdy and Jowdy, Danbury, Conn., 1983; pvt. practice Ridgefield, Conn. Mem. Danbury Bar Assn., Danbury Med. Soc. Republican. Methodist. Criminal, Family and matrimonial, Probate. Home and Office: 805 N Salem Rd Ridgefield CT 06877-1714

**FOSTER, M. JOAN,** lawyer; b. Cin.; d. William and Marguerite (DeHaven) Moeller; children: Peter Graf, James DeHaven. BA, Duke U., 1961; JD cum laude, Seton Hall U., 1976. Bar: N.J. 1976, U.S. Dist. Ct. N.J. 1976, U.S. Ct. Appeals (3d cir.) 1980, U.S. Dist. Ct (no. dist.) Calif. 1982. Assoc. Lowenstein, Sandler, Kohl, Fisher & Boylan, Roseland, N.J., 1976-79; assoc. Grotta, Glassman & Hoffman, PA, Roseland, 1980-85, prin., 1986—; adj. prof. Seton Hall Law Sch., Newark, 1978-80. Trustee N.J. Symphony Orch., Newark, 1989—, vice chair, 1997—. Mem. ABA (labor and employment law sect. 1980—, internat. law sect. 1988—), N.J. State Bar Assn. (exec. com. labor and employment sect. 1982—, editor-in-chief 1984-88, sec. 1991-92, vice chair 1992-93, chair 1993-94, health and hosp. law sect. 1988—), N.J. Pub. Employer Labor Rels. Assn. (trustee 1993—), N.J. Network of Bus. and Profl. Women (trustee 1980—, pres. bd. trustees 1991-93), U.S. Dist. Ct. Hist. Soc. (trustee, exec. com. N.J. dist. 1989-92). Labor. Office: Grotta Glassman & Hoffman PA 75 Livingston Ave Ste 13 Roseland NJ 07068-3701

**FOSTER, M. SHANNON,** lawyer, law enforcement educator; b. Ft. Smith, Ark., July 19, 1960; d. James Edward and Susan (Townley) F. BA, U. Calif., Irvine, 1992; JD, Loyola U., 1995. Bar: Ark. 1995, U.S. Dist. Ct. (we. dist.) Ark. 1998. Sales analyst, supr. Alcon Surg., Irvine, 1985-88; sr. fin. analyst Rockwell Internat., Newport Beach, Calif., 1988-92; dep. prosecuting atty. Office of Prosecutor, Little Rock, 1995-96; pvt. practice Ft. Smith, 1997—. Author: Domestic Violence Prosecution, 1996. Bd. dirs. Citizens Police Acad., Little Rock, 1996-97, Ft. Smith, 1998—; vol. Vol. Atty. Program, Ft. Smith, 1998. Mem. AMA, Ark. Bar Assn., Sebastian County Bar Assn., Mensa, Golden Key Honor Soc. Democrat. Family and matrimonial, Bankruptcy, Federal civil litigation. Home: 3306 Hendricks Blvd Fort Smith AR 72903-5464 Office: 703 Rogers Ave Fort Smith AR 72901-2409

**FOSTER, MARK STEPHEN,** lawyer; b. Edgerton, Mo., Feb. 6, 1948; s. George Elliott and Annabel Lee (Bradshaw) F.; m. Camille Pepper, June 27, 1970; children: Natalie Ashley, Stephanie Ann. BS, U. Mo., 1970; JD, Duke U., 1973. Bar: Mo. 1973, U.S. Ct. Mil. Appeals 1974, Hawaii 1975, U.S. Dist. Ct. Hawaii 1975, U.S. Dist. Ct. (we. dist.) Mo. 1977, U.S. Ct. Appeals (8th cir.) 1986, U.S. Supreme Ct. 1994. Assoc. Stinson, Mag & Fizzell, Kansas City, 1977-80, ptnr., 1980—, mng. ptnr., 1987-90, bd. dirs., 1991—, chmn. bd. dirs., 1998—; arbitration panelist Nat. Assn. Securities Dealers, N.Y.C., 1985—, Pvt. Adjudication Found., Durham, N.C., 1988—. Active Citizens Assn., Kansas City, 1982-92; pres. Spelman Med. Found., Smithville, Mo., 1984-88; bd. dirs. Alzheimers Assn. Metro. Kansas City, 1997—, 1st v.p., 1998—, pres., 1999. Lt. comdr. USNR, ret. Mem. ABA, Hawaii Bar Assn., Mo. Bar Assn., Kansas City Met. Bar Assn., Am. Arbitration Assn. (panelist 1990—, large complex case adv. com. 1993—), Carriage Club, Masons. Labor, General civil litigation, Bankruptcy. Home: 1035 W 65th St Kansas City MO 64113-1813 Office: Stinson Mag & Fizzell PC PO Box 419251 1201 Walnut St Ste 2800 Kansas City MO 64106-2117

**FOSTER, MICHAEL THOMAS,** lawyer; b. La Porte, Ind., Feb. 14, 1951; s. Gerald Richard and Dolores (Pinkleman) F.; children: Michelle K., Jeffrey D., Steven T., Paul David Toller, Danielle L. BS, St. John's U., Collegeville, Minn., 1972; JD, U. Nebr., 1974. Bar: Nebr. 1975, Iowa 1978, Ill. 1985, Ind. 1990; CLU. Staff corp. atty. Lincoln (Nebr.) Libertylife Ins. Co., 1973-77; assoc. Qualley, Larson & Jones, Sioux City, Iowa, 1977-79; advanced mktg. specialist Allied Life Ins. Co., Des Moines, 1979-82; pvt. practice estate and bus. planning various locations, 1981—; adv. mktg. specialist Mut. Trust Life Ins. Co., Oakbrook, Ill., 1984-86; dir. adv. mktg. Zurich Am. Life Ins. Co., Schaumburg, Ill., 1986-87; estate and bus. planning specialist Prudential Life Ins. Co., Chgo. and Indpls., 1988-90; chartered fin. cons. Revision author: Estate Planning; contbr. articles to profl. jours. Mem. Chgo. Estate Planning Coun. Fellow Life Mgmt. Inst.; mem. Assn. Life Underwriters, ABA, Ill. Bar Assn., Iowa Bar Assn., Nebr. State Bar Assn., Ind. Bar Assn., Internat. Claims Assn. Fax: 765-526-6062. Address: 1800 Broad St New Castle IN 47362-3925

**FOULKE, EDWIN GERHART, JR.,** lawyer; b. Perkasie, Pa., Oct. 30, 1952; s. Edwin G. and Mary Claire (Keller) F. BA, N.C. State U., 1974; JD, Loyola U., New Orleans, 1978; LLM, Georgetown U., 1993. Bar: S.C. 1979, U.S. Dist. Ct. S.C. 1979, U.S. Ct. Appeals (4th cir.) 1979, Ga. 1986, U.S. Ct. Appeals (11th cir.) 1986, D.C. 1989, U.S. Ct. Appeals (D.C. cir.) 1989, U.S. Supreme Ct. 1990, N.C. 1997. Assoc. Thompson, Mann & Hutson, Greenville, S.C., 1978-83, Rainey, Britton, Gibbes & Clarkson, Greenville, 1983-85; ptnr. Constangy, Brooks & Smith, Columbia, S.C., 1985-90; chmn. Occupational Safety and Health Rev. Commn., Washington, 1990-95; ptnr. Jackson Lewis, Greenville, S.C., 1995—; instr. St. Mary's Dominican Coll., New Orleans, 1977-78. Field rep. Reagan/Bush Campaign, Columbia, 1980, S.C. state coord., 1984; sec., treas. Employment Labor Law Sect., Columbia, 1981-82. Mem. ABA, S.C. Bar Assn., Ga. Bar Assn., Greenville County Bar Assn. (chmn. pub. rels. com. 1984-85), SAR, Rotary. Roman Catholic. Avocations: swimming, tennis, skiing, golf. Office: Jackson Lewis & Krupman 301 N Main St Ste 2100 Greenville SC 29601-2122

**FOURNARIS, THEODORE J.,** lawyer; b. Lancaster, Pa., Apr. 27, 1946; s. James S. and Stella (Petrakis) F.; m. Ana M. Cartaya, Dec. 30, 1979; children: Ana Nicole, Alexander. BA, Franklin and Marshall Coll., 1968; MA, Boston U., 1971; JD, U. Miami, 1973. Bar: Fla. 1974, U.S. Dist. Ct. (so. dist.) Fla. 1986. Staff atty. FPC, Washington, 1974; assoc. Friedman, Britton & Stettin, Miami, Fla., 1975-76; ptnr. Carey Dwyer Cole Selwood & Bernard, Miami, 1977-82; pvt. practice, Miami, 1982—. With U.S. Army, 1968-71. Mem. ATLA, Fla. Acad. Trial Lawyers. Avocations: boating, travel. Personal injury, Product liability, General civil litigation. Office: 145 Almeria Ave Coral Gables FL 33134-6008

**FOURNIE, RAYMOND RICHARD,** lawyer; b. Belleville, Ill., Jan. 3, 1951; s. Raymond Victor and Gladys M. (Muskopf) F.; m. Mary Lindeman, Sept. 2, 1978; children: Sarah Dozier, John David, Anne Gerard, David Raymond. BS, U. Ill., 1973; JD, St. Louis U., 1979. Bar: Mo. 1979, Ill. 1980. Assoc. Moser, Marsalek, et al., St. Louis, 1979-80, Brown, James & Rabbitt, P.C., St. Louis, 1981-82, Shepherd, Sandberg & Phoenix, P.C., St. Louis, 1982-86; shareholder Shepherd, Sandberg & Phoenix, St. Louis, 1986-88; ptnr. Armstrong, Teasdale, Schlafly & Davis, St. Louis, 1988—. U. Ill. fellow, 1974. Mem. Mo. Bar Assn., Ill. Bar Assn., St. Louis Bar Assn. (sec. trial sect.), Lawyers Assn. (v.p. 1987-88, pres. 1990-91), Actors Equity Assn. Roman Catholic. Avocations: professional singer and actor, baseball, golf. General civil litigation, Entertainment, Personal injury. Home: 4 Ridgetop St Saint Louis MO 63117-1021 Office: Armstrong Teasdale LLP One Metropolitan Sq Ste 2600 Saint Louis MO 63102-2740

**FOUSTE, DONNA H.,** association executive; b. N.Y.C., Feb. 26, 1944; d. Donald Lynn and Edna (Parker) Ham; m. James Edward Fouste, Nov. 2, 1980. AA in Mgmt. and Supervision, Coastline Community Coll., Fountain Valley, Calif., 1980; BS in Organizational Behavior, U. San Francisco, 1985, MS in Orgnl. Devel., 1988. Officer mgr., bus. mgr. Fulwider, Patton, Rieber, Lee & Utecht, L.A., 1971-79, 89-91; patent adminstrn. specialist Discovision Assocs., Costa Mesa, Calif., 1979-82; law office mgr. City of Anaheim, Calif., 1982-89; exec. dir. Orange County Bar Assn., Santa Ana, Calif., 1992—; instr. Rancho Santiago Coll., Santa Ana, with legal asst. program, 1987—; instr. U. Calif., Irvine, 1997; mem. adv. bd. Pub. Svc. Inst., Santa Ana, 1986-88. Patron Friends of South Coase Repertory, Costa Mesa, Calif., 1985; mem. applause chpt. Performing Arts Ctr., Costa Mesa, 1986-87. Recipient Silver medal in Chess Corp. Challenge, 1988, Tribute to Women award YWCA, 1997, Spirit of Volunteerism award Vol. Ctr. of Greater Orange County, 1996. Mem. Assn. Legal Adminstrs., Nat. Assn. Bar Execs. (membership chair 1999), State Bar Calif. (minimum continuing legal edn. com.), Am. Soc. Assn. Execs., So. Calif. Soc. Assn. Execs., Execs. of Calif. Law Assns. Avocations: gourmet cooking, skiing, gardening. Office: Orange County Bar Assn PO Box 17777 Irvine CA 92623-7777

**FOUTS, DOUGLAS ROBERT,** lawyer; b. New Philadelphia, Ohio, Jan. 1, 1950; s. Robert V. and Mary F. Fouts; m. Jill Ann Marchbank, Aug. 17, 1975; 1 child, Kristen Hunter Fouts. BA with honors, Muskingum Coll., 1972; JD cum laude, Cleve. Marshall Coll. Law, 1975. Bar: U.S. Dist. Ct. (no. dist.) Ohio 1976. Sole practice Solon, Ohio, 1976—; arbitrator, chmn. Geauga and Cuyahoga County Arbitration, Cleve., Chardon, Ohio, 1977—; ct. apptd. counsel Cuyahoga County Probate, Cleve., 1981—m ct. appraiser, 1986—. Mem. Ohio State Bar Assn., Cleve. Bar Assn. Avocations: reading, golf, baseball. Estate planning, General practice, General corporate. Office: Atty at Law 30575 Bainbridge Rd Ste 160 Solon OH 44139-2275

**FOWLER, DANIEL MCKAY,** lawyer; b. Chgo., Mar. 25, 1950; m. Julia M. Duffy, Apr. 20, 1990; children: Douglas M., Peter M. BA, Monmouth Coll., 1972; JD, U. Denver, 1975. Bar: Colo. 1975, Wyo. 1994, U.S. Dist. Ct. Colo. 1975, U.S. Ct. Appeals (10th cir.) 1975. Shareholder Wood, Ris & Hames, P.C., Denver, 1975-87; pres. Fowler, Schimberg & Flanagan, P.C., Denver, 1987—. Mem. ABA, Colo. Bar Assn., Denver Bar Assn., Def. Rsch. Inst., Fedn. Ins. and Corp. Counsel, Colo. Def. Lawyers Assn., Denver Athletic Club, Lakewood Country Club. Avocations: motorcycle touring, skiing, boating, travel. General civil litigation, Insurance, Personal injury. Office: Fowler Schimberg & Flanagan PC 1640 Grant St Ste 300 Denver CO 80203-1640

**FOWLER, DAVID LUCAS,** corporate lawyer; b. Heidelberg, Germany, Sept. 26, 1952; s. James Daniel and Nannie Romay (Lucas) F.; m. Cynthia Lou Smith, Aug. 19, 1989. BS, U.S. Mil. Acad., 1974; JD, Georgetown U., 1981. Bar: N.J. 1982, Calif. 1990, U.S. Ct. Fed. Claims 1990, U.S. Dist. Ct. (cen. dist.) Calif. 1990. 2d lt. U.S. Army, 1974, advanced through grades to maj.; infantry platoon leader U.S. Army, Berlin, 1975-76, asst. protocol officer, 1976-77, aide-de-campe U.S. Commander, 1977-78; minority augmentation recruit officer U.S. Mil. Acad., 1978; chief adminstrv. law sect. U.S. Army Tng. Ctr., Ft. Dix, N.J., 1983-86; command judge advocate U.S. Army Field Sta., Sinop, Turkey, 1985-86; trial atty. U.S. Army Legal Svcs. Agy., Falls Church, Va., 1986-89; resigned U.S. Army, 1989; corp. staff counsel Hughes Aircraft Co., L.A., 1989-94; sr. staff counsel Electro-Optical Sys. Hughes Aircraft Co., El Segundo, Calif., 1994-95; asst. gen. counsel Hughes Aircraft Co., Arlington, Va., 1996-97; v.p., dep. gen. counsel Raytheon Sys. Co., Arlington, Va., 1998—; asst. sec. Hughes Electronics and Hughes Aircraft Co., 1996—. Bd. dirs. West Point Soc. L.A., 1993. Mem. ABA (public contract law sect.), Armed Svcs. Bds. of Contract Appeals Assn., Army Sci. Bd. Avocations: reading, weightlifting, golf. Government contracts and claims, General corporate, General civil litigation. Office: Raytheon Sys Co 1100 Wilson Blvd Ste 2000 Arlington VA 22209-2297

**FOWLER, DAVID THOMAS,** lawyer; b. Flushing, N.Y., June 16, 1955; s. David Thomas Jr. and Ellen (McGrath) F.; m. Margaret Anne Conway, Apr. 8, 1979; children: Matthew, Elizabeth, Timothy, Jacqueline. BA cum laude, St. John's U., 1977, JD, 1980. Bar: N.Y. 1981, U.S. Dist. Ct. (ea. and so. dists.) N.Y. 1981. Law clk. Richard J. Finamore, Great Neck, N.Y., 1979-80, assoc., 1981-83; assoc. Newman, Schlau, N.Y.C., 1983-86, ptnr., 1986-88; assoc. McCabe & Cozzens, Mineola, N.Y., 1988-92, ptnr., 1992-97; ptnr. McCabe, Collins, McGeough & Fowler, LLP, Mineola, 1998—. Trustee Floral Park (N.Y.) Bellerose Sch. Dist., 1997—; co-v.p. L.I. chpt. Adoptive Parents Com., Bellmore, N.Y., 1996-98; treas., bd. dirs. Floral Park Little League, 1993—, treas., 1994-97. Recipient Disting. Svc. award L.I. chpt. Adoptive Parents Com., 1996, Ken Kramer award Floral Park Little League, 1998. Mem. Nassau-Suffolk Trial Lawyers Assn., Nassau Bar Assn., Southside Civic Assn., Floral Park Indians Athletic Club (coord. basketball divsn. 1993-99, coord. soccer divsn. 1995-97, basketball coach 1992-98, soccer coach 1994-99). Avocations: golf, softball, reading, basketball, traveling. Personal injury, State civil litigation, Insurance. Home: 43 Oak St Floral Park NY 11001-3409 Office: McCabe Collins McGeough Fowler LLP 114 Old Country Rd Mineola NY 11501-4400

**FOWLER, DONALD RAYMOND,** retired lawyer, educator; b. Raton, N.Mex., June 2, 1926; s. Homer F. and Grace B. (Honeyfield) F.; m. Anna M. Averyt, Feb. 6, 1960; children: Mark D., Kelly A. BA, U. N.Mex., 1950; JD, 1951; MA, Claremont Grad. Sch., 1979, PhD, 1983. Bar: N.Mex. 1951, Calif. 1964, U.S. Supreme Ct. 1980. Atty. AEC, Los Alamos and Albuquerque, 1951-61, chief counsel Nev. Ops., 1962-63; pvt. practice, Albuquerque, 1961-62; asst., then dep. staff counsel Calif. Inst. Tech., Pasadena, 1963-72, staff counsel, 1972-75, gen. counsel, 1975-90; lectr. exec. mgmt. program Claremont Grad. Sch., Calif., 1981-84. Contbr. articles to profl. publs. Served with USAAF, 1944-46. Recipient NASA Pub. Svc. award, 1981. Mem. Calif. State Bar Assn., Fed. Bar Assn., Nat. Assn. Coll. and Univ. Attys. (exec. bd. 1979-82, 84-90, chmn. publs. com. 1982-84, pres. 1987-88, chmn. nominations com. 1988-89, chmn. honors and awards com. 1989-90, Life Mem. award 1991, Disting. Svc. award 1992), Calif. Assn. for Rsch. in Astronomy (sec. 1985-90).

**FOWLER, FLORA DAUN,** lawyer; b. Washington, Aug. 11, 1923; d. Herman Hartwell and Flora Elizabeth (Adams) Sanford; m. Kenneth Leo Fowler, Aug. 22, 1941; children: Kenneth Jr., Michael, Kathleen, Daun, Jonathan, Colin, Kevin, James, Shawn, Maureen, Wendelyn, Liam, Tobias, Melanie. Student, Wilson Tchrs. Coll., 1940-41; AA, U. Md., 1973; JD, U. Balt., 1976. Bar: Fla. 1977, U.S. Dist. Ct. (mid. dist.) Fla. 1979, U.S. Ct. Appeals (5th and 11th cirs.) 1981. Staff atty. Cen. Fla. Legal Services Inc., Daytona Beach, 1978-80, mng. atty., 1980-81; pvt. practice, Daytona Beach, 1981-93; ret., 1993. Past editor Seabrook Acres Citizens' League Newsletter; columnist Bowie Express & Community Times; contbr. poems to New Voices in American Poetry, 1974. V.p. Seabrook (Md.) Acres Citizens League, 1970; past v.p. Prince Georges County Civic Fedn., Md.; past unit chmn. League of Women Voters, Prince Georges County; past pres., v.p., publicity chmn. Lanham-Bowie Dem. Club, Seabrook. Recipient Evening Star Trophy award Prince Georges County Civic Fedn., 1969. Mem. Fla. S. Ct. Hist. Soc. Democrat. Roman Catholic. Avocations: swimming, creative writing, Cursillo. State civil litigation, Family and matrimonial, General practice.

**FOWLER, J. EDWARD,** lawyer. AB, Princeton U., 1953; LLB, Yale U., 1959. Bar: N.Y. 1960. Atty. Debevoise, Plimpton, Lyons & Gates, 1959-68; gen. counsel internat. divsn. Mobil Oil Corp., 1974-77, asst. gen. counsel, 1977-78, assoc. gen. counsel, 1979-83, gen. counsel mktg. and refining divsn., 1983-86; gen. counsel Mobil Corp., Fairfax, Va., 1986-95; sr. ptnr. Holland & Knight, Washington, D.C., 1995-98. Bd. editors Yale Law Jour., 1958-59. Bd. dirs. Nat. Symphony Orch. Assn., 1991—, pres., 1995-98; trustee Shakespeare Theatre, 1993—. Fax: 202-797-9546. Office: 10 Kalorama Cir NW Washington DC 20008-1616

**FOWLER, MICHAEL ROSS,** law educator; b. Washington, Apr. 14, 1960; s. James Randlett and Margaret (Williamson) F.; m. Julie Marie Bunck, May 29, 1989. BA in History, Dartmouth Coll., 1982; MA in Fgn. Affairs, U. Va., 1985; JD, Harvard U., 1986. Bar: Mass. 1986, U.S. Dist. Ct. Mass. 1986, D.C. 1988, Md. 1990. Scholar-in-residence The White Burkett Miller Ctr. Pub. Affairs, Charlottesville, Va., 1986; assoc. Mintz, Levin, Cohn, Ferris, Glovsky & Popeo, Boston, 1986-90; vis. lectr. Tufts U., Medford, Mass., 1990; rsch. fellow Inst. for Study of World Politics, Washington, 1990-91; vis. lectr. U. Va., Charlottesville, 1991-92; Fulbright scholar U. Ryukyus, Okinawa, Japan, 1992-93; profl. lectr. Georgetown U., 1993-94; Ford Found. lectr. to Vietnam, Inst. for Internat. Rels. in Hanoi, 1995; vis. asst. prof. U. Louisville, 1996-99; vis. scholar U. Ryukyus, Okinawa, Japan, 1999—. Author: Winston S. Churchill: Philosopher and Statesman, 1985, Thinking About Human Rights, 1987, Law, Power and the Sovereign State, 1995, With Justice For All?: The Nature of the American Legal System, 1998. White House intern Carter Adminstrn., Washington, 1979-80. Democrat. Episcopalian. Office: Patterson Sch Diplomacy U Ky 455 Patterson Tower Ky Lexington KY 40506-0001

**FOX, ANTHONY N.,** lawyer; b. Lynhurst, N.J., Apr. 26, 1958; s. Vincent James and Mary Anne (Garafolo) F.; m. Sandra Leigh Son, Oct. 15, 1983; children: Brittany Amber, Stephanie Nicole. BA in Polit. Sci., Maryville (Tenn.) Coll., 1980; JD cum laude, Cumberland Sch. Law, Birmingham, Ala., 1983. Assoc. Gonce, Young, Howard & Westbrook, Florence, Ala., 1983-86, Clark & Scott P.C., Birmingham, Ala., 1986-91; ptnr. Clark & Scott P.C., Birmingham, 5, 1991-94, mng. ptnr., 1994—; statewide corp. counsel CBS Inc., Cin., 1994—. Sec. Hickory Ridge Homeowners, Birmingham, 1989. Mem. Ala. State Bar Assn., Ala. Claims Assn., Workmen's Compensation Assn. Ala., Phi Alpha Delta (pres. 1982-83). Methodist. Avocation: gardening. Product liability, Insurance, Personal injury. Home: 5008 Longleaf Ln Birmingham AL 35242-3452 Office: Clark & Scott PC PO Box 380548 Birmingham AL 35238-0548

**FOX, AUDREY BRAKER,** lawyer; b. N.Y., Oct. 29, 1964; d. Martin J. and Jacqueline K. Braker; m. Larry A. Fox, Apr. 10, 1994. BA with high distinction, U. Ariz., 1986; JD cum laude, Boston U., 1989. Assoc. Hanson, Bridgett, Marcus, Vlahos & Rudy, San Francisco, 1989-91, Hanson & Norris, San Mateo, Calif., 1991—. Mem. ABA, San Mateo County Bar Assn. (mem. client rels. com. 1994—), Calif. Bar Assn., Phi Beta Kappa. Family and matrimonial, Estate planning, Probate. Office: Hanson & Norris # 575 777 Mariners Island Blvd San Mateo CA 94404-1588

**FOX, BYRON NEAL,** lawyer; b. St. Louis, May 15, 1948; s. Meyer and Thelma (Werber) F.; m. Cynthia Penner, Aug. 25, 1984. BS, Tulane U., 1970; MBA, Boston U., 1974; JD, Kans. U., 1973. Bar: Mo. Pres. Fox & Partee, Kansas City, Mo., 1988-93. Chmn. Kans. City Bd. of Zoning Adjustment, 1993-98. Stockbroker Dain Rauscher, Inc., 1998—. Homestead Commn., 1993—. 1st lt. U.S. Army, 1973. Mem. ABA, Mo. Bar Assn., Kansas City Bar Assn. Jewish, Nat. Assn. Criminal Defense Lawyers, Am. Royal Assn. (bd. govs.), Kans. City Club. Criminal, General civil litigation, Family and matrimonial. Office: Fox & Partee 410 Archibald St Fl 2 Kansas City MO 64111-3001

**FOX, ELAINE SAPHIER,** lawyer; b. Chgo., Nov. 18, 1934; d. Nathan Abraham and Rhoda M. (Schneidman) Saphier; m. Alan A. Fox, Apr. 25, 1954; children: Susan Fox Lorge, Wendy Fox Schneider, Mimi. BS, Northwestern U., 1955; JD, Ill. Inst. Tech., 1975. Bar: Ill., 1975, U.S. Dist. Ct. (no. dist.) Ill., 1975, U.S. Ct. Appeals (7th cir.) 1975, U.S. Ct. Appeals (fed. cir.) 1985. Trial atty. NLRB, Chgo., 1975-80; assoc. Hirsh & Schwartzman, Chgo., 1980-81; assoc. Gottlieb & Schwartz, Chgo., 1981-84, ptnr., 1984-90; ptnr. D'Ancona & Pflaum, Chgo., 1990—. Contbr. articles to profl. jours. and mags. Bd. dirs., exec. com. Am. Cancer Soc., Chgo., 1993—; mem. nat. and local governing coun. Am. Jewish Congress, Chgo., 1991—; bd. dirs. Jewish Vocat. Svc. Mem. ABA (subcom. nat. labor rels. bd. practice and procedures, employment and labor rels. law, labor and employment law com., Women Rainmakers, midwest regional mgmt. chair Nat. Labor Rels. Bd. practice and procedure com.), Women's Bar Assn., Chgo. Bar Assn. (labor and employment rels. vice chmn. 1989-90, chmn. 1990-91, co-chmn. Alliance for Women 1994-95, co-chair bd. mgrs. 1996—), Decalogue Assn. Avocations: swimming, walking, reading, theater, art. Labor, General civil litigation. Office: Dancona and Pflaum 11 E Wacker Dr Ste 2800 Chicago IL 60601-2101

**FOX, GARY DEVENOW,** lawyer; b. Detroit, Sept. 8, 1951; s. Edward J. Fox. BA in Polit. Sci. and Drama, Drury Coll., 1973; JD, U. Fla., 1976. Bar: Fla. 1976, U.S. Dist. Ct. (so. and mid. dists.) Fla. 1977, U.S. Ct. Appeals (5th and 11th cirs.) 1977, U.S. Supreme Ct. 1981. From assoc. to ptnr. Frates, Floyd, Pearson, Stewart, Richman & Greer, Miami, 1976-84; ptnr. Stewart, Tilghman, Fox & Bianchi, PA, Miami, 1984—. Exec. editor U. Fla. Law Rev.; contbr. articles to profl. jours. Mem. ABA, Fla. Bar (cert. civil trial advocacy 1983, chmn. code and rules of evidence com. 1997—, civil procedure rules com.), Fla. Bd. Bar Examiners, Dade County Bar Assn., Assn. Trial Lawyers Am. (substaining, lectr.), Acad. Fla. Trial Lawyers (diplomate, lectr.), Dade County Trial Lawyers Assn. (bd. dirs. 1986-89), Am. Bd. Trial Advocates (pres. Miami chpt. and Fla. fedn.), Bankers Club. Avocations: tennis, skiing. Professional liability, Product liability, Personal injury. Office: 1 SE 3rd Ave Ste 3000 Miami FL 33131-1715

**FOX, GREGORY JOHN,** lawyer; b. Phila., Sept. 27, 1854; s. Robert Joseph and Dora (De Lazzero) F. AB in Econs., Muhlenberg Coll., 1976; JD, Temple U., 1976, LLM in Taxation, 1984. Bar: Pa. 1979, U.S. Dist. Ct. (ea. dist.) Pa. 1979, U.S. Ct. Appeals (3d cir.) 1980. Assoc. Schnader, Harrison, Segal & Lewis, Phila., 1979-86; assoc. Montgomery, McCracken, Walker & Rhoads, Phila., 1986-88, ptnr., 1988—. Mem. pres.'s adv. bd. Archbishop Ryan H.S., Phila., 1996—; mem. Muhlenberg Coll. alumni bd., Allentown, Pa., 1997—; bd. dirs. St. Thomas More Soc., Phila., 1995—. Named one of top benefits lawyers in U.S., Nat. Law Jour., May, 1998. Republican. Roman Catholic. Avocations: biking, exercise, politics. Pension, profit-sharing, and employee benefits, Immigration, naturalization, and customs. Office: Montgomery McCracken Walker & Rhoads LLP 123 S Broad St Fl 24 Philadelphia PA 19109-1099

**FOX, HERB,** lawyer; b. N.Y.C., Aug. 7, 1954; m. Margaret E. Mason, Dec. 4, 1956. BA, CUNY, 1976; JD, Golden Gate U., 1986. Bar: Calif. 1986, U.S. Dist. Ct. (ctrl. dist.) Calif. 1991, U.S. Dist. Ct. (no. dist.) Calif. 1992, U.S. Ct. Appeals (9th cir.) 1998; cert. specialist in appellate law, Calif. Sr. rsch. atty. Ct. of Appeal, Calif., Ventura, 1987-90; assoc. atty. Nichols, Guthrie and Sims, Santa Barbara, Calif., 1993-96, Grokenberger and Wilson, Santa Barbara, 1993-96; ptnr. Kirker and Fox, Santa Barbara, 1996-99. Bd. dirs. DOGPAC, Santa Barbara, 1997—. Mem. Santa Barbara County Bar Assn. Appellate, General civil litigation, Real property. Office: 3 W Carrillo St Ste 203 Santa Barbara CA 93101-3205

**FOX, JAMES CARROLL,** federal judge; b. Atchison, Kans., Nov. 6, 1928; s. Jared Copeland and Ethel (Carroll) F.; m. Katharine deRosset Rhett, Dec. 30, 1950; children: James Carroll, Jr., Jane Fox Brown, Ruth Fox Jordan. BSBA, U. N.C., 1950, JD with honors, 1957. Bar: N.C. 1957. Law clk. U.S. Dist. Ct. (ea. dist.) N.C., Wilmington, 1957-58; assoc. Carter & Murchison, Wilmington, N.C., 1958-59; ptnr. Murchison, Fox & Newton, Wilmington, N.C., 1960-82; judge U.S. Dist. Ct. (ea. dist.) N.C., Wilmington, 1982—; lectr. in field. Contbr. articles to profl. jours. Vestryman, St. James Episcopal Ch., 1973-75, 79-82. Mem. Hew Hanover County Bar Assn. (pres. 1967-68), Fifth Jud. Dist. Bar Assn. (sec. 1960-62), N.C. Bar Assn. Office: US Dist Ct Alton Lennon Fed Bldg PO Box 2143 Wilmington NC 28402-2143

**FOX, JAMES EDWARD, JR.,** government official; b. Columbus, Ohio, Dec. 1, 1948; s. James Edward and Alice Jane (Andrix) F.; m. Julianne Feller, Sept. 12, 1970; children—Abigail, Katharine, James Edward. B.A., Ohio State U., 1972; M.A., George Washington U., 1976. Research asst. U.S. Congress, Washington, 1973-74, legis. asst., 1974-75; minority cons. com. on fgn. affairs U.S. Ho. of Reps., Washington, 1975-83; dep. asst. sec. Dept. State, Washington, 1983-84, prin. dep. asst. sec., 1985; spl. asst. to Pres. White House, Washington, 1985-86; asst. sec. legis. affairs Dept. of State, Washington, DC, 1986—. Republican. Home: 5615 Nebraska Ave NW Washington DC 20015-1257

**FOX, JAMES ERWIN,** lawyer; b. Princeton, Ky., June 15, 1945; s. James William and Gladys Imogene (Smiley) F.;m. Susan Marie Graham, Jan. 28, 1967; children: Graham Hardy, Austin Garrett. BA, Western Ky. U., 1967; JD, Memphis State U., 1970. Bar: Tenn. 1971, U.S.Dist. Ct. (we. dist.) Tenn. 1972, U.S. Ct. Appeals (6th cir.) 1973, U.S. Ct. Appeals (5th cir.) 1975 and 1981, U.S. Supreme Ct. 1977, U.S. Ct. Appeals (10th cir.) 1979, U.S. Ct. Appeals (11th & D.C. cirs.) 1981, U.S. Ct. Appeals (fed. cir.) 1983, U.S. Ct. Appeals (4th cir.) 1984, U.S. Claims Ct. 1987. Law clk. to fed. dist. judge Memphis, 1971-72; atty. Thomason, Crawford & Hendrix, Memphis, 1972-73; staff atty. Tenn. Valley Authority, Knoxville, Tenn., 1973-78; asst. gen. counsel Tenn. Valley Authority, Knoxville, 1978-81, assoc. gen. counsel, 1981-87, dep. gen. counsel, 1987-92, v.p., dep. gen. counsel, 1992—. Author Memphis State U. Law Rev., 1968, 69, 72. Mem. ABA, Assn. Trial Lawyers Am., Tenn. Bar Assn., Fed. Bar Assn. Democrat. Church of Christ. Avocations: tennis, reading, travel. Fax: 423-632-3307. Federal civil litigation, Government contracts and claims, Personal injury. Office: Tenn Valley Authority 400 W Summit Hill Dr Knoxville TN 37902

**FOX, JAN WOODWARD,** lawyer; b. Dallas, Sept. 25, 1950; d. Jackson Spurgeon and Louie (Henry) Woodward; m. Robert Scott Ramsey Feb. 18, 1978 (div.); 1 child, Benjamin Ramsey. Student, U. Paris, 1970-71; BA cum laude, Harvard U., 1972; JD, U. Tex., 1975. Bar: Tex., U.S. Dist. Ct. (so., no., ea. dists.) Tex., U.S. Ct. Appeals (5th cir.), U.S. Supreme Ct.; bd. cert. civil trial and criminal law Tex. Bd. Legal Specialization. Assoc. Mitchell, George & Belt, Austin, Tex., 1975-76; assoc. Haynes & Fullenweider, Houston, 1976-80, shareholder, dir., 1980-89; pvt. practice Houston, 1989—. Contbr. articles to profl. jours. Mem. adv. com. Senate-House Select Com. Judiciary, 1983-84; dir. Homes St. Mark Adoption Agy., 1990-97, mem. planning com., 1991-93; chair Houston Trial Lawyers Found., 1993; mem. alumnae bd. Hockaday Sch., 1994-98, trustee, 1994—. Recipient Cmty. Svc. award Houston chpt. ACLU, 1997. Mem. ABA, ATLA (trustee 1997-98), Nat. Coll. Criminal Def. Lawyers and Pub. Defenders, State Bar Tex. (mem. adminstrn. justice com. 1986-87, adminstrn. rules evidence com. 1985-87), Tex. Trial Lawyers Assn. (pres. 1996), Tex. Criminal Def. Lawyers Assn.

Houston Bar Assn., Houston Trial Lawyers Assn. (pres. 1992). Personal injury, General civil litigation, Criminal. Home: 3402 University Blvd Houston TX 77005-3356 Office: 2444 Times Blvd Ste 316 Houston TX 77005-3243

**FOX, MARY ELLEN,** lawyer; b. Upper Sandusky, Ohio, Aug. 8, 1956; d. Paul Eugene and Anna Marie (Walton) F. BA in Acctg. and Polit. Sci., Ohio No. U., 1978, JD, 1981. Bar: Ohio 1981, U.S. Dist. Ct. (no. dist.) Ohio 1982. Assoc. Stansbery, Schoenberger and Scheck, Upper Sandusky, 1981-85; ptnr. Stansbery, Schoenberger, Scheck & Fox, Upper Sandusky, 1985-90; assoc. Osborn Co., LPA, Upper Sandusky, 1990-92; ptnr. Osborn & Fox Co., LPA, Upper Sandusky, 1993—; bd. dirs. Community 1st Bank, N.A., Forest, Ohio, 1985—; solicitor Village of Nev., Ohio, 1982—; librarian Wyandot County Law Library, Upper Sandusky, 1983—. Bd. dirs. Wyandot County Council on Alcoholism, Upper Sandusky, 1983-86, Pvt. Industry Coun., 1995—, Upper Sandusky C. of C., 1994—. Mem.ABA, Ohio Bar Assn., Wyandot County Bar Assn. (sec., treas. 1982, v.p. 1983, pres. 1984), Alpha Xi Delta (bldg. corp. bd. 1978-91, pledge advisor 1979-89, province sec. 1981-85, province pres. 1986-89, chpt. dir. 1986-91). Republican. Methodist. Avocations: walking, sewing, music, swimming. General practice, Family and matrimonial, Banking. Home: 14370 SH Route 2 # 37 Forest OH 45843 Office: Osborn & Fox Co LPA 116 E Wyandot Ave Upper Sandusky OH 43351-1430

**FOX, SUSAN E.,** legal assistant; b. Uniontown, Pa., June 17, 1955; d. James Ira Sr. and Elizabeth Ann (Kirk) F. BS in Journ., W.Va. U., 1977; Cert. Completion, Nat. Ctr. for Paralegal Tng., Atlanta, 1977. Legal asst. Jackson, Kelly, Holt & O'Farrell, Charleston, W.Va., 1978-79, Dennis, Corry, Webb & Carlock, Atlanta, 1979-84, Dennis, Corry, Porter & Thornton, Atlanta, 1984-89, Ga.-Pacific Corp., Atlanta, 1989-98, Radcliffe, DeHaas & Monaghan, Uniontown, Pa., 1998—. Bd. dirs. Met. Atlanta Coun. on Alcohol and Drugs, 1991-92, treas., 1992-93, pres., 1993-94; bd. dirs. DeKalb Rape Crisis Ctr., 1994-96; bd. dirs. Ga.-Pacific Svc. Force, 1995-96; chmn., mem. devel. Jr. League of DeKalb County, Decatur, Ga., 1989-90, cmty. rsch. chmn., 1990-91, corr. sec., 1991-92, pres.-elect, 1994-95, pres., 1995-96; mem. Leadership DeKalb, 1995; Olympic vol., Equestrian Venue Comm. Ctr., 1996. Republican. Presbyterian. Avocations: needlework, reading, collecting foxes and seashells. Home: 26 Belmont Cir # 2 Uniontown PA 15401-4703 Office: Radcliffe DeHaas & Monaghan 99 E Main St Uniontown PA 15401-3519

**FOXHOVEN, JERRY RAY,** lawyer; b. Yankton, S.D., July 24, 1952; s. Elmer William and Ida Elizabeth (Lubbers) F.; m. Julie Ann Greco, Apr. 6, 1985; children: Anthony Michael, Peter Joseph. BS summa cum laude, Morningside Coll., 1974; JD, Drake U., 1977. Bar: Iowa 1977, U.S. Dist. Ct. (so. and no. dists.) Iowa 1977, U.S. Ct. Appeals (8th cir.) 1977, U.S. Supreme Ct. 1981, Nebr. 1985, U.S. Dist. Ct. Nebr. 1985, Wis. 1986. Assoc. Critelli & Pille, Des Moines, 1977-79; ptnr. Critelli & Foxhoven, Des Moines, 1979-82, Foxhoven & McCann, Des Moines, 1982-88; ptnr. Peddicord, Wharton, Thune, Foxhoven & Spencer, P.C., 1988-91, pvt. practice, 1991—; instr. criminal justice dept. Des Moines Area Community Coll., Ankeny, Iowa, 1978-81, Am. Inst. Banking, 1982-85. Mem. steering com. Culver for U.S. Senate, Des Moines, 1980; chmn. Iowa State Foster Care Rev. Bd.; bd. dirs., nat. pres. Nat. Assn. Foster Care Reviewers; mem. parish council Sacred Heart Roman Cath. Ch., West Des Moines, 1982. Democrat. Lodge: Masons (master 1990). Personal injury, State civil litigation, Criminal. Home: 1155 Prairie View Dr West Des Moines IA 50266-7515 Office: 505 5th Ave Des Moines IA 50309-2324

**FOY, HERBERT MILES, III,** lawyer, educator; b. Statesville, N.C., Mar. 22, 1945; s. Herbert Miles Jr. and Perci Aileen (Lazenby) F.; m. Eleanor Jane Meschan, June 27, 1970; children: Anna Meschan, Sarah Aileen. AB, U. N.C., 1967; MA, Harvard U., 1968; JD, U. Va., 1972. Bar: N.C. 1973, U.S. Dist. Ct. (mid. and we. dists.) N.C., U.S. Ct. Appeals (4th cir.). Jud. clk. U.S. Ct. Appeals (5th cir.), Atlanta, 1972-73; assoc. Smith, Moore, Smith, Schell & Hunter, Greensboro, N.C., 1973-77, 81-83, ptnr., 1983-84; sr. atty. advisor office legal counsel U.S. Dept. Justice, Washington, 1977-81; assoc. prof. Sch. Law Wake Forest U., Winston-Salem, N.C., 1984-87, prof., 1987—; assoc. dean acad. affairs Sch. Law Wake Forest U., Winston-Salem, 1990-95. Contbr. articles to legal jours. Morehead scholar, 1963; Woodrow Wilson fellow, 1968. Mem. ABA, N.C. Bar Assn., N.C. State Bar Assn., Fosythe County Bar Assn., Order of Coif, Phi Beta Kappa. Democrat. Methodist. Avocations: banjo playing, gardening, athletics, poetry. Home: 2328 Oak Ridge Rd Oak Ridge NC 27310-9701 Office: Wake Forest U Sch Law PO Box 7206U Winston Salem NC 27109-7206

**FRAICHE, DONNA DIMARTINO,** lawyer; b. New Orleans, Dec. 8, 1951; d. Anthony and Rose Mary (Batchelona) DiM.; m. John F. Fraiche, Dec. 27, 1974; children: Geoffrey Michael, Ariane Michele. Student, St. Mary's Dominican Coll., New Orleans, 1969, La. State U. and A & M Coll., 1972; JD, Loyola U., 1975. Bar: La. 1975, U.S. Dist. Ct. (ea., we., mid. dists.) La. 1975, U.S. Dist. Ct. (no. dist.) W.Va. 1984, U.S. Dist. Ct. D.C. 1984, U.S. Ct. Appeals (D.C. cir.) 1977, U.S. Ct. Appeals (3d, 4th, 5th, 10th, 11th cirs.) 1975, U.S. Supreme Ct. 1979, U.S. Ct. Claims 1979, U.S. Tax Ct. 1977; diplomate Am. Coll. Healthcare Execs. Mng. ptnr. New Orleans office Locke Liddell & Sapp LLP, 1975—; adj. prof. Joint Commn. on Accreditaitons of Hosps., Sch. Pub. Health Tulane U., advocacy tng. program Sch. Law La. State U., summer sch. for lawyers La. State U. Author: (with others) An Analysis of the Revised Mediacl Staff Standards of the Joint Commission on Accreditation of Hospitals, 1984, New Legal Aspects of Credentialing, 1992; contbr. chpts. to books., numerous articles to profl. jours. Past pres. Loyola U. Alumni; bd. trustees Loyola U., instnl. advancement com. U. Plan. Com.; former vice chair, trustee Our Lady of Holy Cross Coll., New Orleans; past chmn. bd., pres. New Orleans Regional Med. Ctr.; mem. La. State Arts Coun., 1984-89, exec. com.; bd. dirs. ARC; past mem. La. Children's Mus. Bd.; mem. City Bus. Publ. Roundtable, New Orleans, 1992. Recipient Prix d'Elegance award Top 10 Best Dressed Women in New Orleans, Achiever's award Am. Coun. of Career Women, 1990, Role Model award Young Leadership Coun., 1991, Women of Distinction award S.E. La. Girl Scout Coun., 1992. Mem. ABA (health law com. 1980—, chmn. New Orleans health law forum 1982, mem. exec. com. women rainmakers interest group 1996—), Am. Health Lawyers Assn. (bd. dirs. 1982, exec. com. 1984, pres. 1989, com. chmn. 1988-91), La. Healthcare Commn. (chair 1996—), Ne Orleans Regional C. of C. (bd. dirs., com. on govtl. affairs). Roman Catholic. Health, Antitrust. Office: Locke Liddell & Sapp LLP Pan Am Life Ctr 601 Poydras St Ste 2400 New Orleans LA 70130-6029

**FRAIDEN, NORMAN ARTHUR,** lawyer; b. N.Y.C., Mar. 2, 1943; s. Morris and Mollie (Tepper) F.; m. Arlene Joyce Zied, Dec. 24, 1967; children: David Alan, Mark Gerald. BA, Hunter Coll., 1964; LLB, Bklyn. Law Sch., 1967. Bar: N.Y. 1967, U.S. Dist. Ct. (so. dist.) N.Y. 1967. Ptnr. Blumenfeld and Fraiden, N.Y.C., 1970-95, Fraiden & Palen, 1996—. Corr. sec. Jewish Community Ctr. Men's Club, Harrison, N.Y., 1990—. Mem. ATLA, N.Y. State Trial Lawyers Assn., Bronx Bar Assn., N.Y. State Bar Assn. Avocations: tennis, chess, swimming, soccer. Fax: 718-401-3328. Personal injury, Product liability, State civil litigation. Office: Fraiden & Palen 327 E 149th St Bronx NY 10451-5685

**FRAIDIN, STEPHEN,** lawyer; b. Boston, July 29, 1939; s. Morris and Freda (Rozeff) F.; m. Susan Greene, July 4, 1963; children: Matthew, Sam, Sarah. AB, Tufts U., 1961; JD, Yale U., 1964. Bar: N.Y. 1965. Ptnr. Fried, Frank, Harris, Shriver & Jacobson, N.Y.C., 1964—; vis. lectr. Yale U. Law Sch., 1988—, mem. exec. com.; mem. editl. adv. bd. Prentice Hall Law and Bus.; bd. dirs. Selfhelp Cmty. Svcs. Inc. Contbr. numerous articles to profl. jours. Mem. bd. overseers Tufts U. Arts and Scis.; bd. dirs. UJA-Fedn. N.Y. Mem. ABA, Assn. of Bar of City of N.Y. General corporate, Mergers and acquisitions. Office: Fried Frank Harris Shriver & Jacobson 1 New York Plz Fl 22 New York NY 10004-1980

**FRALEY, MARK THOMAS,** lawyer; b. Wilkes-Barre, Pa., Sept. 20, 1952; m. Helen E. Tanner, May, 1987. BA in Philosophy, U. Cin., 1974; JD, Nashville Sch. Law, 1983. Bar: Tenn. 1983, U.S. Dist. Ct. (mid. dist.) Tenn. 1988, U.S. Ct. Appeals (6th cir.) 1995. Dir. pks. and recreation City of Gatlinburg, Tenn., 1975-78, City of Sevierville, Tenn., 1978-79; tech. svc. advisor State of Tenn., Nashville, 1979-83, asst. commr. conservation, 1983-86; asst. commr., dir. Tenn. State Pks., Nashville, 1986-87; pvt. practice Nashville, 1987—; pres. Commn. of Am. Outdoor Legal Issue Task Force, Washington, 1986-87; adj. prof. dept. health, phys. edn. and recreation Mid. Tenn. State U., 1990; instr. social security law Nashville Sch. Law, 1997—. Author: (pamphlet) Pk. Rehab., 1982; contbr. articles to profl. jours. Mem. Tenn. Recreation and Pks. Assn. (v.p. 1982-83, Fellow award 1988), Tenn. Bar Assn., Nashville Bar Assn. Democrat. Avocations: swimming, tennis, gardening. General practice, Administrative and regulatory, Pension, profit-sharing, and employee benefits. Home: 2810 White Oak Dr Nashville TN 37215-1222 Office: 211 3rd Ave N Nashville TN 37201-1603

**FRANCESCHI, ERNEST JOSEPH, JR.,** lawyer; b. L.A., Feb. 1, 1957; s. Ernest Joseph and Doris Cecilia (Beluche) F. BS, U. So. Calif., 1978; JD, Southwestern U., L.A., 1980. Bar: Calif. 1984, U.S. Dist. Ct. (cen. dist.) Calif. 1984, U.S. Dist. Ct. (ea. dist.) Calif. 1986, U.S. Dist. Ct. (no. and so. dists.) Calif. 1987, U.S. Ct. Appeals (9th cir.) 1984, U.S. Supreme Ct. 1989. Pvt. practice law L.A., 1984—. Mem. Assn. Trial Lawyers Am., Calif. Trial Lawyers Assn., L.A. Trial Lawyers Assn., Trial Lawyers for Pub. Justice, Fed. Bar Assn. Personal injury, Federal civil litigation. Office: 445 S Figueroa St Ste 2600 Los Angeles CA 90071-1630

**FRANCH, RICHARD THOMAS,** lawyer; b. Melrose Park, Ill., Sept. 23, 1942; s. Robert and Julia (Martino) F.; m. Patricia Staufenberg, Apr. 18, 1971 (dec. Apr. 1994); children: Richard T. Jr., Katherine J.; m. Susan L. Rice, Sept. 1, 1995. B.A. cum laude, U. Notre Dame, 1964; J.D., U. Chgo., 1967. Bar: Ill. 1967, U.S. Dist. Ct. (no. dist.) Ill. 1967, U.S. Supreme Ct. 1980, U.S. Ct. Appeals (2d cir.) 1984, U.S. Ct. Appeals (3d cir.) 1981, U.S. Ct. Appeals (6th cir.) 1991, U.S. Ct. Appeals (7th cir.) 1971, U.S. Ct. Appeals (8th cir.) 1981, U.S. Ct. Appeals (9th cir.) 1997, U.S. Dist. Ct. (no. dist.) Wis. 1989, U.S. Tax Ct. 1994. Assoc. Jenner & Block, Chgo., 1967-68, 70-74, ptnr., 1975—; former mem. Ill. Supreme Ct. Rules Com. Served to capt. U.S. Army, 1968-70. Decorated Bronze star, Army Commendation medal. Fellow Am. Coll. Trial Lawyers; mem. Am. Law Inst. Federal civil litigation, State civil litigation, Antitrust. Office: Jenner & Block Ste 4700 One IBM Plz Chicago IL 60611

**FRANCHINI, GENE EDWARD,** state supreme court justice; b. Albuquerque, May 19, 1935; s. Mario and Lena (Vaio) F.; m. Glynn Hatchell, Mar. 22, 1969; children: Pamela, Lori (dec.), Gina, Joseph James, Nancy. BBA, Loyola U., 1955; degree in adminstrn., U. N.Mex., 1957; JD, Georgetown U., 1960; LLM, U. Va., 1995. Bar: N.Mex. 1960, U.S. Dist. Ct. N.Mex. 1961, U.S. Ct. Appeals (10th cir.) 1970, U.S. Supreme Ct. 1973. Ptnr. Matteucci, Gutierrez & Franchini, Albuquerque, 1960-70, Matteucci, Franchini & Calkins, Albuquerque, 1970-75; judge State of N.Mex. 2d Jud. Dist., Albuquerque, 1975-81; atty.-at-large Franchini, Wagner, Oliver, Franchini & Curtis, Albuquerque, 1982-90; chief justice N.Mex. Supreme Ct., Santa Fe, 1990-99, justice, 1999—; v.p. bd. dirs. Conf. Chief Justices, 1997-98. Chmn. Albuquerque Pers. Bd., 1972, Albuquerque Labor Rels. Bd., 1972, Albuquerque Interim Bd. Ethics, 1972. Capt. USAF, 1960-66. Recipient Highest award Albuquerque Human Rights Bd., 1999. Mem. Am. Bd. Trial Advocates, N.Mex. Trial Lawyers (pres. 1967-68), N.Mex. Bar Assn. (bd. dirs. 1976-78), Albuquerque Bar Assn. (bd. dirs. 1976-78, Outstanding Judge award 1997). Democrat. Roman Catholic. Avocations: fishing, hunting, golf, mushroom hunting. Home: 4901 Laurene Ct NW Albuquerque NM 87120-1026 Office: NMex Supreme Ct PO Box 848 Santa Fe NM 87504-0848

**FRANCIS, JAMES CLARK, IV,** judge; b. Tulsa, Okla., Oct. 3, 1952; s. James C. and F. Ruth Francis; m. Elizabeth Bradford, Aug. 19, 1978; children: Nathaniel, Jeremy. BA, Yale Coll., 1974, JD, 1978; M of Pub. Policy, Harvard U., 1978. Bar: N.Y. 1979, U.S. Dist. Ct. (so. dist.) N.Y. 1979, U.S. Dist. Ct. (ea. dist.) N.Y. 1980, U.S. Ct. Appeals (2nd cir.) 1980. Law clk. Hon. Robert L. Carter, N.Y.C., 1978-79; staff atty. Legal Aid Soc., N.Y.C., 1979-85; U.S. Magistrate judge U.S. Dist. Ct. (so. dist.) N.Y., N.Y.C., 1985-98, chief U.S. Magistrate judge, 1998—. Author: (chpts.) Moore's Federal Practice, 1997; curator (exhibit) Discreet Persons Learned in Law, 1995. Mem. profl. adv. bd. Epilepsy Inst., N.Y.C.; bd. dirs. Port Washington (N.Y.) Soccer Club. Mem. N.Y. State Bar Assn. (jud. com. 1989—), Assn. Bar of City of N.Y. (fed. cts com. 1995-98). Democrat. Avocations: travel, sports, coaching soccer. Office: US Court 500 Pearl St New York NY 10007-1316

**FRANCIS, MERRILL RICHARD,** lawyer; b. Iowa City, Jan. 28, 1932; m. Mardi Munson, Dec. 22, 1991; children from previous marriage: Kerry L., David M., Robin A. B.A. magna cum laude, Pomona Coll., 1954; J.D., Stanford U., 1959. Bar: Calif. 1960, Supreme Ct. 1970. Ptnr. Sheppard, Mullin, Richter & Hampton, Los Angeles, 1959—. Mem. Fellows of Contemporary Art, 1980—. Served to lt. (j.g.) U.S. Navy, 1954-56. Fellow Am. Bar Found., Am. Coll. Bankruptcy (chmn. 9th cir. admissions coun. 1992-95, bd. dirs. 1995—, chair bd. regents 1995—); mem. ABA Bus. Law Sect. (chmn. secured creditors com. 1981-85, chmn. bus. bankruptcy com. 1986-89, chmn. Task Force on Fed. Ct. Structure 1990-93, mem. Coun. Bus. Law sect. 1991-95, chmn. ad hoc com. on brown bag programs 1994-97), State Bar of Calif. (mem. debtor/creditor and bankruptcy com. of bus. law sect. 1978-79), L.A. County Bar Assn. (mem. real property sect., exec. com. 1970-80, mem. comml. law and bankruptcy sect., sect. chmn. 1976-77), Fin. Lawyers Conf. (bd. govs. 1970—, pres. 1972-73), La Canada-Flintridge C. of C. and Cmty. Assn. (pres. 1971-72), Order of the Coif, Jonathan Club, Phi Beta Kappa. Banking, Bankruptcy, Contracts commercial. Office: Sheppard Mullin Richter & Hampton 333 S Hope St Fl 48 Los Angeles CA 90071-1406

**FRANCIS, PATRICIA ANN,** lawyer; b. Amory, Miss., Apr. 17, 1963; d. Jack Clifford and Mary Lib (Barrett) F.; m. Timothy Sean Griffin, Apr. 7, 1990. BA, Miss. State U., 1984; JD, U. Va., 1988. Assoc. Nixon, Hargrave, Devans & Doyle, N.Y.C., 1988-89, Dewey Ballantine, N.Y.C., 1989-91; assoc. Dow, Lohnes & Albertson, Washington, 1991-96, mem., 1997—. Mergers and acquisitions, Finance, General corporate.

**FRANCIS, SHANNON CLAIRE,** lawyer; b. Buffalo, Mar. 4; d. Malcolm Joseph Jr. and Jo Ann (Mitchell) F. AA, Union Coll., Cranford, N.J., 1988; BS, Rutgers U., Newark, 1990; JD, U. Tenn., 1992. Bar: Tenn. 1993. Asst. pub. defender Pub. Defender Conf., Knoxville, Tenn., 1993—; paralegal instr. Knoxville Bus. Coll., 1995—. Home: 404 Hayworth Dr Knoxville TN 37920-4435 Office: Pub Defender's Office 6th Jud Dist 1209 Euclid Ave Knoxville TN 37921-6732

**FRANCO, RALPH ABRAHAM,** lawyer; b. Montgomery, Ala., Dec. 27, 1921; s. Abraham and Matilda (Habib) F.; m. Lila Keene, June 9, 1974; 1 stepchild, Charles Walton deCelle. BS, U. Ala., 1943; JD, U. Ala., 1948. Bar: Ala. 1948. Assoc. Hill, Hill, Carter, Franco, Cole & Black P.C. and predecessor firms, Montgomery, 1948-53, ptnr., 1953-88, stockholder, 1988—; mem. adv. bd. dirs. internal medicine residency program med. sch. U. Ala., Montgomery. Past pres. Jewish Fedn., Montgomery; bd. dirs., past pres. St. Margaret's Hosp. Found., St. Margaret's Found.; bd. dirs. Cath. Social Svc., Montgomery, pres., 1984-86, dir. emeritus; bd. dirs., pres. U. Ala. Law Sch. A Found.; bd. dirs., past pres. Etz Ahayem Synagogue. Capt. inf. U.S. Army, 1943-52, PTO, JACG, 1952-74, ret. col. Fellow Am. Bar Found.; mem. ABA, Ala. Bar Assn. (past pres. young lawyers, chmn. real property and probate sect. 1985-86), Montgomery County Bar Assn. (bd. dirs.), llth Jud. Cir. Hist. Soc. (bd. dirs. 1985—), Ala. Law Inst., Ret. Officers Assn., Blue and Gray Assn. (bd. dirs.), U. Ala. Law Sch. Alumni Assn. (past pres., bd. dirs.), Chancellors Soc. (Auburn U. Montgomery), Lions (bd. dirs. Montgomery, past pres.), Standard Country Club (bd. dirs. 1970-76). Real property, Landlord-tenant, Probate. Home: 3609 Thomas Ave Montgomery AL 36111-2013 Office: Hill Hill Carter et al 425 S Perry St Montgomery AL 36104-4235

**FRANEY, MARTIN THOMAS,** lawyer; b. Cleve., Nov. 14, 1953; s. Martin Francis and Mary Monica (McMahon) F.; m. Kathleen Moehring, Apr. 22, 1995. BA in History, John Carroll U., 1975; JD, Case Western Res. U., 1978. Bar: Ohio 1978, U.S. Dist Ct. 1984. Asst. county prosecutor Cuyahoga County Prosecutor's Office, Cleve., 1978-84; atty. William J. Coyne & Assoc., Cleve., 1984-94, Gravens & Franey, Cleve., 1994—. Mem. Cleve. Bar Assn., Ohio State Bar Assn. Avocation: golf. General civil litigation. Home: 6866 Westwood Dr Brecksville OH 44141-2616 Office: Gravens & Franey Co LPA 1240 Standard Bldg Cleveland OH 44113

**FRANGES, ANNE KING,** lawyer; b. N.Y.C., Nov. 4, 1938; d. John Francis and Catherine Arnold (Brown) King; children: Alexandra Katherine, Christopher Stephen. AB cum laude, Harvard U./Radcliffe Coll., 1960; JD, Rutgers U., 1976. Bar: N.J. 1976, U.S. Dist. Ct. N.J. 1976. Ptnr. Franges & Thelin, Montclair, N.J., 1976—. Sec. class of 1960, Radcliffe Coll., 1965-75, gift chairwoman for 30th Radcliffe reunion, class agt. 40th reunion, 1996—; trustee Montclair Counseling Ctr., 1980086. Mem. ABA (family law sect.), N.Y. Bar Assn. (family law sect.), Essex County Bar Assn. (exec. com. family law 1995—, ethics com. 1998—). Democrat. Episcopalian. Clubs: Harvard of N.J. (pres. 1984-85), Radcliffe of N.J. (pres. 1973-76. Family and matrimonial, Real property, General corporate. Home: 161 Walnut St Livingston NJ 07039-5005 Office: Franges & Thelin 460 Bloomfield Ave Montclair NJ 07042-3552

**FRANK, ARTHUR J.,** lawyer; b. Chgo., Mar. 18, 1946; s. Maurice A. and Elizabeth H. (Hoffmann) F.; m. Fredrica Frank, Oct. 22, 1969 (div. 1976); m. Mary Kay Dawson, Oct. 16, 1983; 1 child, Rebecca Anne. BSBA, Babson Coll., 1967; JD, U. Ill., 1971. Bar: Ill. 1971, U.S. Dist. Ct. (no. dist.) Ill. 1971, U.S. Dist. Ct. Md. 1989, U.S. Supreme Ct. 1989, D.C. 1989, U.S. Dist. Ct. D.C. 1990, Md. 1990. Mng. ptnr. Frank Assocs., Ltd., Chgo., 1971-86; regional ptnr. Hyatt Legal Svcs., Washington, 1986-90; sr. ptnr. Frank & Breads, Washington, 1990—. Pres. Lawyers for the Creative Arts, Chgo., 1974-75; bd. dirs. Neighborhood Justice of Chgo., 1979-81, Legal Assistance Found., Chgo., 1981-82; chmn. Second City Ballet, Chgo., 1986; mem. Dem. Nat. Com., 1994—, Dem. Congl. Campaign Com., 1994—. Mem. ATLA, ABA, Chgo. Bar Assn. (bd. mgrs., chmn. creative arts com. young lawyers sect. 1974-75, chmn. commn. on profl. responsibility young lawyers sect. 1975-76, bd. dirs. young lawyers sect. 1976-77, chmn.-elect young lawyers sect. 1977-78, chmn. legis. task force 1977, chmn. planning com. young lawyers sect. 1977-79, chmn. young lawyers sect. 1978-79, spl. com. on appointive selection of judges 1979, mem. spl. commn. code profl. responsibility of Supreme Ct. Ill. 1979), Md. Bar Assn. (mem. sect. estates and trusts), D.C. Bar Assn. (chmn. law firm mgmt. com. 1990-91, working group on reform of D.C. courts 1997-98, family law action group 1998—), Montgomery County Bar Assn., Prince George's County Bar Assn. General civil litigation, General corporate, Personal injury. Home: One Tripoli Ter North Potomac MD 20878-2853 Office: Frank & Assocs 1700 K St NW Ste 700 Washington DC 20006-3813

**FRANK, BARRY H.,** lawyer; b. Nov. 19, 1938; s. David and Rose (Pearl) F.; divorced; children: Toby L., S. Kenneth, Gary A. BS, Pa. State U., 1960; LLB, Temple U., 1963. Bar: Pa. 1964. Staff atty. IRS, Phila., 1963-66; tax mgr. Ernst & Whinney, Phila., 1966-74; exec. v.p., gen. counsel Nat. Freight, Inc., Vineland, N.J., 1974-75; ptnr. Pechner, Dorman, Wolffe, Rounick & Cabot, Phila., 1975-87, Mesirov, Gelman, Jaffe, Cramer & Jamieson, LLP, Phila., 1987—; instr. Temple U. Tax Inst., Phila., 1976—. Co-author: Alimony, Child Support and Counsel Fees; mem. editl. bd. The Practical Acct.; contbr. numerous articles to profl. jours. Mem. exec. com. Mayor's Small Bus. Adv. Coun., Phila., 1981-83. Mem. ABA, AICPA, Phila. Bar Assn., Pa. Inst. CPAs, Phila. C. of C. (chmn. small bus. coun. 1977-78, chmn. emeritus 1981-83, bd. dirs. 1977-78, 80-81). Republican. Jewish. Corporate taxation, Taxation, general, Estate taxation. Office: Mesirov Gelman Jaffe Cramer & Jamieson 1735 Market St Ste 3901 Philadelphia PA 19103-7503

**FRANK, BEN W.,** lawyer, administrator; b. Lampasas, Tex., Oct. 23, 1929; s. Hugo C. and Nadine G. (Machen) F.; m. Maymie A. Bowles, July 30, 1961 (dec. June 1994); children: Carl, Rick; m. Eleanor B. Bodenhamer, July 5, 1997. BA, U. Tex., 1956; LLB, Ark. U., 1964, JD, 1979. Bar: Ark. 1964. Claims mgr. CNA, Little Rock, 1958-64, Comml. Union, Little Rock, 1964-79; adminstr. Ark. Workers Compensation Commn., Little Rock, 1979-98; city judge, city atty. Traskwood, Ark., 1971-92; commr. Ark. Worker's Compensation Commn., Little Rock. Staff Sgt. USAF, 1948-54. Mem. Ark. Adjuster Assn. (pres. 1978), Claim Mgrs. Coun. (chmn. 1970), Ins. Arbitration Commn. (chmn. 1972), Ark. Spl. Arbitration Commn. (chmn. 1972-79), Little Rock Power Squadron. Republican. Lutheran. Avocation: boating. Home: 25 Shannon Dr Little Rock AR 72207-5144

**FRANK, BERNARD,** lawyer; b. Wilkes-Barre, Pa., June 11, 1913; s. Abraham and Fanny F.; m. Muriel I. Levy, June 19, 1938; children: Roberta R. Penn, Allan R. PhB, Muhlenberg Coll., Allentown, Pa., 1935, LHD, 1987; JD, U. Pa., 1938; postgrad., NYU, 1940-42. Bar: Pa. 1939. Since practiced in Allentown; asst. U.S. atty. Eastern Dist. Pa., 1950-51; asst. city solicitor Allentown, 1956-60. Author articles on ombudsmen in profl. jours. Vice chmn. B'nai B'rith Nat. Commn. Adult Jewish Edn., 1959-61, chmn., 1961-63; bd. dirs. Muhlenberg Coll., 1987-93. With AUS, 1943-46. Decorated comdr. Order of North Star Sweden; recipient Disting. Service award Internat. Ombudsman Inst., 1980. Mem. ABA (chmn. com. ombudsman 1970-76, vice chmn. com. on pub. advs. and pub. representation adminstrv. law sect. 1984-92), Internat. Bar Assn. (chmn. com. ombudsman 1973-80), Fed. Bar Assn. (chmn. com. ombudsman 1973-80), Pa. Bar Assn., Lehigh Bar Assn., Inter-Am. Bar Assn., World Assn. Lawyers, U.S. Assn. Ombudsmen (hon.), Internat. Ombudsman Inst. (hon. life mem., bd. dirs. 1978-89, pres. 1984-88), Jewish Pub. Soc. Am. (bd. dirs. 1982—, v.p. 1986-89, 94-98), 94th Inf. Div. (pres. 1953-54). General corporate, Estate planning. Home: 3203 W Cedar St Allentown PA 18104-3407 Office: 640 Hamilton Mall Allentown PA 18101-2110

**FRANK, GEORGE ANDREW,** lawyer; b. Budapest, Hungary, Apr. 6, 1938; came to U.S., 1957; s. Alex and Ilona (Weiss) F.; m. Carole Shames, Feb. 14, 1979; children: Cheryl, Charles. BS, Colo. State U., 1960; PhD in Organic Chemistry, MIT, 1965; JD, Temple U., 1977. Bar: Pa. 1977, U.S. Dist. Ct. (ea. dist.) Pa. 1977, D.C. 1980, U.S. Ct. Appeals (fed. cir.) 1982, U.S. Supreme Ct. 1984. Sr. chemist Rohm & Haas Co., Phila., 1965-69; lab. head Borden Chem., Phila., 1969-73; sr. scientist Thiokol Corp., Trenton, N.J., 1973-74; counsel Du Pont Corp., Wilmington, Del., 1974-85, sr. counsel, 1986-92, corp. counsel, 1992—; external adv. com. Colo. State U. Coll. Natural Scis., 1996—. Contbr. articles to profl. jours; patentee in field. Recipient Merck award Merck & Co., 1960; Sun Oil Co. grantee, 1964; fellow NIH. Mem. ABA (chair divsn. biotech. 1993-94, coun. 1994-98, chair chem. practice com. 1998—), Phila. Patent Lawyers Assn. (chair bioscis. com. 1983-87, bd. govs. 1987-92, pres. 1992-93), Am. Intellectual Property Law Assn. (chair task force 1986), Benjamin Franklin Am. Inn of Cts. (v.p. 1996-97, pres. 1997-98). Republican. Avocations: tennis, squash, travel, books, opera. Patent, Intellectual property. Home: 229 Gypsy Ln Wynnewood PA 19096-1112 Office: Du Pont Corp Legal Dept BMP 17-2126 Wilmington DE 19880-0017

**FRANK, JACOB,** lawyer; b. Albany, Apr. 4, 1936; s. Isidore and Sara F.; m. Yoelith Frank, Aug. 26, 1936; children: Eytan, Michael, Adam, Orly. BEE, Rensselaer Poly. Inst., 1957; LLB, Am. U., 1963; postgrad., George Washington U. Coll. Law, 1964-67, NYU Law Sch., 1969-73. Bar: D.C. 1963, Mass. 1979, U.S. Patent Office. V.p., gen. counsel Data Gen. Corp., Westboro, Mass.; chmn. pension com. General corporate. Home: 16 Cakebread Dr Sudbury MA 01776-1206 Office: Data Gen Corp 4400 Computer Dr Westborough MA 01580-0001

**FRANK, JAY ALLAN,** lawyer; b. Chgo., Apr. 6, 1943; s. Roy and Phyllis Frank; m. Feb. 1973; 2 children. BS with honors, U. Ill., 1965, JD, 1968. Bar: Ill. 1969, U.S. Dist. Ct. (no. dist.) Ill. 1970, U.S. Ct. Appeals (7th cir.) 1970, U.S. Supreme Ct. 1970. Assoc. Aaron, Aaron, Schimberg and Hess, Chgo., 1969-73; ptnr. Eisner, Miller and Frank, Chgo., 1973-74, Eisner, Miller, Frank and Melamed, Chgo., 1974-76, Frank and Melamed, Ltd., Chgo., 1976-91, Frank, Miller, Melamed, Tabis & McDonnell, P.C., Chgo., 1991—. Advisor, cons. Salvation Army, Chgo., 1980—. Mem. ABA, Am. Acad. Matrimonial Lawyers, Ill. Bar Assn., Chgo. Bar Assn., N.W. Bar Assn., Ill. Trial Lawyers Assn. Avocation: running. General civil litigation, Family and matrimonial, Contracts commercial. Office: Frank Miller Melamed Tabis & McDonnell PC 200 S Wacker Dr Chicago IL 60606-5829

**FRANK, JEFFREY MICHAEL,** lawyer; b. Cleve., Mar. 4, 1967; s. Dennis Norman and Peggy Ann (Meyer) F.; m. Julie Anne Sturman, Aug. 17, 1997. BA, U. Mich., 1989; JD, Boston U., 1992. Bar: Mich. 1992, U.S.

Dist. Ct. (ea. dist.) Mich. 1992, U.S. Dist. Ct. (we. dist.) Mich. 1998. Atty. Mager, Mercer, Scott & Alber, P.C., Troy, Mich., 1992—; mem. steering com. Def. Rsch. Inst. Fidelity and Surety Com., Chgo., 1998—. Profl. adv. com. Jewish Fedn. Met. Detroit, 1998. Mem. ABA (rep. fidelity and surety law divsn. tort and ins. practice sect. 1995—). General civil litigation, Construction, Probate.

**FRANK, JENNIFER KAREN,** lawyer; b. Watertown, N.Y., Aug. 23, 1971; d. Jon Phillip and Karen Eleanor Constance; m. Patrick Douglas Frank, Aug. 2, 1997. BA in Polit. Sci., LeMoyne Coll., 1993; JD, Union U., 1996. Bar: N.Y. 1997, U.S. Dist. Ct. (no. dist.) N.Y. 1997. Assoc. Thaler & Thaler, Ithaca, N.Y., 1996-97, Hiscock & Barclay, Syracuse, N.Y., 1997—. Mem. ABA, N.Y. State Bar Assn. Republican. Roman Catholic. Contracts commercial, Personal injury, Native American. Office: Hiscock & Barclay PO Box 4878 Syracuse NY 13221-4878

**FRANK, JOHN LEROY,** lawyer, government executive, educator; b. Eau Claire, Wis., Mar. 13, 1952; s. George LeRoy and Frances Elaine (Torgerson) F. BS summa cum laude, U. Wis., Eau Claire, 1974; JD cum laude, U. Wis., Madison, 1977. Bar: Wis. 1977, U.S. Dist. Ct. (we. dist.) Wis. 1977, U.S. Supreme Ct. 1982. Instr. law U. Wis., Madison, 1976-77; assoc. Garvey, Anderson, Kelly & Ryberg, S.C., Eau Claire, 1977-81; legis dir., counsel Congressman Steve Gunderson, Washington, 1981-85, chief of staff, counsel, 1985-89; staff coord. 92 Group, Washington, 1987-89; paralegal instr., program dir. Chippewa Valley Tech. Coll., 1989-93, 97—; pvt. practice Eau Claire, Wis., 1990-93, 97—; counsel, minority cons. House Subcommittee on Livestock, Washington, 1993-95; counsel Congressman Steve Gunderson, Washington, 1993-97; dep. minority counsel House Com. on Agr., Washington, 1993-95, dep. chief counsel, 1995-97; commr. W. Ctrl. Wis. Regional Planning Commn., Eau Claire, 1998—. Named One of Outstanding Young Men in Am., U.S. Jaycees, 1977. Mem. ABA, Fed. Bar Assn., Wis. Bar Assn., U. Wis. Alumni Assn. (outstanding sr. arts & scis. 1974), Phi Delta Phi, Phi Gamma Delta (Durrance award 1978). Republican. Lutheran. Address: 2113 Meadow Ln Eau Claire WI 54701-7965

**FRANK, JULIE ANN,** lawyer; b. Omaha, Aug. 5, 1953; d. Morton Stanley Frank and Elaine Edith (Meyerson) Potts; m. Howard Nathan Kaplan, Oct. 26, 1985; 1 child, Martin Kaplan. BA in Psychology, U. Tex., 1975; JD, Creighton U., 1979. Bar: Nebr. 1979, Tex. 1980. Clk. to justice Nebr. Supreme Ct., Lincoln, 1979-80; assoc. Qualley, Larson & Jones, Omaha, 1980-81; sole practice Omaha, 1981-83; pntr. Pollak, Frank & Hicks, Omaha, 1983-90; ptnr. Frank & Gryva, Omaha, 1990—; instr. Met. Community Coll., Omaha, 1982-84, Buena Vista Coll., Omaha, 1982-84, U. Nebr., 1983. Bd. dirs. Nebr. Civil Liberties Union, 1981-85, Omaha Jewish Family Svcs., 1989—; sec. bd. Jewish Family Svcs., 1991-92, v.p., 1992-93, pres., 1993-96; adminstrv. coord. Douglas County Dems., 1982; del. Douglas County Conv., 1984, 86; mem. cen. com. Nebr. Dem. Com., 1984-86; mem. Nat. Coun. Jewish Women, Omaha; mem. community rels. com. Anti-defamation League, 1987-90, bd. dirs., 1992-94; chmn. Nebr. Women's Polit. Caucus; bd. dirs. Assn. of Jewish Family and Children's Agencies, 1996—. Mem. ABA, Nebr. State Bar Assn. (co-chairperson Women and Law sect. 1987-88, bd. dirs. 1987-89), Omaha Bar Assn. (lawyers referral com., particpant in law day "Meet a Lawyer" program, 1986-88, 97). Bankruptcy, Criminal, Juvenile. Home: 661 N 57th St Omaha NE 68132-2031 Office: Frank & Gryva 1823 Harney St Ste 201 Omaha NE 68102-1913

**FRANK, LLOYD,** lawyer, retired chemical company executive; b. N.Y.C., Aug. 9, 1925; s. Herman and Selma (Lowenstein) F.; m. Beatrice Silverstein, Dec. 26, 1954; children: Margaret Lois, Frederick. B.A., Oberlin Coll., 1947; J.D., Cornell U., 1950. Bar: N.Y. 1950, U.S. Supreme Ct. 1973. Practiced law N.Y.C., 1950—; sr. ptnr, exec. com., chmn. corp. dept. Parker Chapin Flattau & Klimpl LLP; sec., dir. Grow Group, Inc., N.Y.C., 1964-95; bd. dirs. Madison Industries, Inc., N.Y.C., Metro-Tel Corp., Miami, Fla., Pub. Art Fund, Inc., N.Y.C., Park Electrochem. Corp., Lake Success, N.Y., Internat. Longevity Ctr. U.S.A. Ltd.; sec. Esquire Radio & Electronics, Inc., Bklyn.; lectr. Am. Mgmt. Assn., 1967-77, Probe Internat., Inc., 1975-77, Corp. Seminars, Inc., 1968-71. Mem. ABA (com. negotiated acquisitions), Assn. Bar City of N.Y. (com. on internat. environ. law com. on product liability, com. on lawyers in transition, com. on securities law), N.Y. County Lawyers Assn. (com. on corp. law depts.).. General corporate, Public international, Securities. Home: 25 Central Park W Apt 17Q New York NY 10023-7211 Office: Parker Chapin Flattau & Klimpl LLP Ste 1700 1211 Avenue Of The Americas New York NY 10036-8735

**FRANK, MARVIN JAMES,** lawyer, accountant; b. South Bend, Ind., Nov. 19, 1939; s. Maurice N. and Mildred B. F.; 1 child, Phillip B.; m. Susan J. Blickman; children: Brendan M., Brook A., Briton J. BS in Acctg., Ind. U., 1962; JD, Ind. U., Indpls., 1966. Bar: Ind. 1966. CPA, Ind. Acct., tax mgr. Arthur Andersen & Co., Indpls., 1962-67; atty., ptnr. Bamberger & Feibleman, Indpls., 1967-75; sr. prin. Maurer, Garelick, Cohen & Frank, Indpls., 1975-82, Ancel, Miroff & Frank, P.C., Indpls., 1982-90, Frank & Kraft, A Prof. Corp., Indpls., 1990—. Co-author: LEGACY: Plan, Protect & Preserve Your Estate, 1996; contbr. articles to profl. jours. Mem. ABA, Ind. State Bar Assn., Indpls. Bar Assn., Am. Acad. Estate Planning Attys., Nat. Network Estate Planning Attys., Ind. Network Estate Planning Attys., Am. Assn. Attys., Ind. CPA Soc. Office: Frank & Kraft A Profl Corp 135 N Pennsylvania St Indianapolis IN 46204-2400

**FRANK, WILLIAM NELSON,** lawyer, accountant; b. Cin., June 3, 1953; s. Nelson A. and Marion A. (Kirbert) F.; m. Brenda L. Norwood, Sept. 30, 1995. Student, Capital U., 1971-74; BS in Edn., Bowling Green State U., 1975; JD, U. Toledo, 1978; postgrad., U. Cin., 1980-82. Bar: Ohio, 1978, U.S. Dist. Ct., U.S. Tax Ct., U.S. Supreme Ct.; CPA, Ohio; cert. tchr., Ohio.. Asst. city prosecutor City of Columbus, Ohio, 1978-80; asst. pub. defender Hamilton (Ohio) County, 1981-84; sole practice William N. Frank, Columbus, 1978-85; regional fin. mktg. mgr. Primerica Fin. Svcs., Columbus, 1984-90, Cin., 1990-92; atty., acct. Tyirin, Benvie & Co., Cin., 1990-92; atty. Hyatt Legal Svcs., Cin., 1992-93; pvt. practice Cin., 1993—; spl. counsel to Ohio Atty. Gen., 1996—; auditor Phillip Willeke, Inc., Columbus, 1985-87; securities rep. 1st Am. Nat. Securities, Columbus, 1985-92; lectr. in law Hondros Career Ctr., 1993—, special council to the Ohio Attorney Genl., 1996—. Mem. Hamilton County Rep. Club, Cin., 1981—. Named to Hon. Order Ky. Cols. Commonwealth of Ky., 1978. Mem. AICPA, Cin. Bar Assn., Ohio Soc. CPAs, Cheviot Masons (worshipful master), Royal Order of Scotland, Knights Templar, Royal Arch Mason, Order of Eastern Star, Shriners, Cin. Hist. Soc. (tour dir.), Order of DeMolay (chevalier degree 1972, Legion of Honor 1994), Delta Tau Upsilon, Phi Alpha Delta. Republican. Mem. Ch. of Christ. Avocations: tennis, Scottish Bagpipe musician, martial arts. Criminal, Taxation, general, Probate. Home: 3260 Milverton Ct Cincinnati OH 45248-2857 Office: 3050 Harrison Ave Cincinnati OH 45211-5752

**FRANKE, ANN HARRIET,** lawyer; b. Bethesda, Md., Feb. 17, 1952; d. Charles Frederick and Mary (St. John) F. BA, MA, U. Pa., Phila., 1974, JD, 1977; LLM, Georgetown U., 1978. Bar: Pa. 1977, D.C. 1978, U.S. Ct. Appeals (D.C. cir.) 1978. Assoc. Sobol & Trister, Washington, 1978-81; asst. corp. counsel Dist. of Columbia, Washington, 1981-82; asst., assoc., counsel Am. Assn. U. Profs., Washington, 1982-97; dir. employment liability svcs. United Educators Ins., Chevy Chase, Md., 1997—; editorial advisor West Edn. Law Reporter, Mpls., 1990-97; editorial bd. Edn. Law, 1992—; mem. adv. coun. Appleseed Found., 1997—. Speaker various confs. and univs., 1982—. Bd. dirs. Hans Kindler Found., 1992—. Fulbright grantee Coun. for Internat. Exchange of Scholars, Australia, 1990. Mem. Chamber Music Conf. (bd. dirs. 1986-97), D.C. Bar Assn. (steering com., labor law divsn., edn. task force 1999—), Nat. Capital Cello Club (bd. dirs. 1984—). Avocations: chamber music, cello, piano. Education and schools, Civil rights, Labor.

**FRANKE, HARRY FREDERICK,** lawyer; b. Milw., Oct. 13, 1922; s. Harry Frederick and Harriet Constance F.; m. Mary Louise Winkelman; children: Jay, John, Mary Ann, Mark. JD, U. Wis., 1949. Mem. Wis. State Legis., 1950-52, 52-56; ptnr. Cook & Franke. With U.S. Army. Office: Cook & Franke 660 E Mason St Ste 401 Milwaukee WI 53202-3877

**FRANKE, LINDA FREDERICK,** lawyer; b. Mankato, Minn., Aug. 28, 1947; d. Cletus and Valeria (Haefner) Frederick; m. Willis L. Franke, Dec. 17, 1966; children: Paul W., Gregory J. BA, U. Mo., 1981, JD, 1984. Bar: Mo. 1985, U.S. Dist. Ct. (we. dist.) Mo. 1985. Rsch. assoc. Koenigsdorf, Kusnetzky and Wyrsch, Kansas City, Mo., 1984-85; asst. gen. counsel dept. revenue State of Mo., Independence, 1985-86; claims rep. workers' compensation Cigna Ins. Co., Overland Park, Kans., 1986-87; sr. claims rep. workers' compensation Gulf Ins. Co., Kansas City, Mo., 1987-88; worker's compensation atty. Fireman's Fund Ins. Co., Kansas City, 1988—; mem. Mo. Worker's Compensation Com. U. Mo. scholar, 1980, 81. Mem. Platte County Bar Assn., Kansas City Met. Bar Assn. (adv. bd. workers' compensation com.). Insurance, Workers' compensation, Administrative and regulatory. Home: 8117 NW Eastside Dr Weatherby Lake MO 64152 Office: Bren Przybeck & Stotler 1100 Walnut St Kansas City MO 64106-2109

**FRANKE, PATRICK JOSEPH,** lawyer; b. Dallas, July 7, 1968; s. Carl William and Dolores Ann Franke; m. Julie Lynn Pavelich, Aug. 14, 1993; children: Kathryn, Andrew. BS in Polit. Sci., Santa Clara (Calif.) U., 1990; JD, U. Tex., 1993. Bar: Wash. 1993, U.S. Dist. Ct. (we. dist.) Wash. 1993. Atty. Smith & Leary P.L.L.C., Seattle, 1993—. Mem. Fed. Bar Assn. (ethics and practice com. 1997—), King County Bar Assn. (cmty. involvement com. 1997—), Phi Beta Kappa. General civil litigation, Contracts commercial, General corporate. Office: Smith & Leary PLLC 316 Occidental Ave S Ste 500 Seattle WA 98104-2889

**FRANKEL, JAMES BURTON,** lawyer; b. Chgo., Feb. 25, 1924; s. Louis and Thelma (Cohn) F.; m. Louise Untermyer, Jan. 22, 1956; children: Nina, Sara, Simon. Student U. Chgo., 1940-42; BS, U.S. Naval Acad., 1945; LLB, Yale U., 1952; MPA, Harvard U., 1990. Bar: Calif. 1953. Mem. Steinhart, Goldberg, Feigenbaum & Ladar, San Francisco, 1954-72; of counsel Cooper, White & Cooper, San Francisco, 1972-97; sr. fellow, lectr. in law Yale U., 1971-72; lectr. Stanford U. Law Sch., 1973-75; vis. prof. U. Calif. Law Sch., 1975-76, lectr. 1992—; lectr. U. San Francisco Law Sch., 1994—; adj. asst. prof. Hastings Coll. Law, 1996—. Pres. Council Civic Unity of San Francisco Bay Area, 1964-66; chmn. San Francisco Citizens Charter Revision Com., 1968-70; mem. San Francisco Pub. Schs. Commn., 1975-76; trustee Natural Resources Def. Council, 1972-77, 79-92, staff atty., 1977-79, hon. trustee, 1992—; chmn. San Francisco Citizens Energy Policy Adv. Com., 1981-82. Mem. ABA, Calif. Bar Assn., San Francisco Bar Assn. Democrat. General corporate, Probate, Real property.

**FRANKEL, ROGER L.,** lawyer; b. Washington, Apr. 6, 1946; s. Louis Max and Sara Betty (Seltzer) F.; m. Betty Ann Frank, Oct. 15, 1978; children—Jason, Jessica, Jamie. B.A., Brandeis U., 1968; J.D. with honors, George Washington U., 1971. Bar: D.C. 1971, Md., 1972. Ptnr. Swindler, Berlin, Shereff, Friedman, LLP, Washington. Mem. ABA, Md. Bar Assn., Montgomery County Bar Assn. (chmn. bankruptcy sect. 1980-82). Jewish. Club: Woodmont Country (Rockville, Md.) (bd. govs. 1985—). Bankruptcy. Home: 7321 Heatherhill Ct Bethesda MD 20817-4668 Office: Swindler Berlin Shereff Friedman LLP 3000 K St NW Ste 300 Washington DC 20007-5101

**FRANKEL, SANDOR,** lawyer, author; b. N.Y.C., Nov. 16, 1943; s. David and Bessie (Edelson) F. BA, N.Y. U., 1964; LLB, Harvard U., 1967. Bar: N.Y. 1967, D.C. 1968, U.S. Supreme Ct. 1976. Staff mem. White House Task Force on Crime, 1967; counsel Nat. Commn. Reform Fed. Criminal Laws, 1968; asst. U.S. atty. for D.C., 1968-71; pvt. practice N.Y.C., 1971—; lectr. N.Y. U. Inst. on Fed. Taxation, 1976, 77. Author: Beyond a Reasonable Doubt, 1972 (Edgar Allan Poe award), The Aleph Solution, 1978, How to Defend Yourself Against the IRS, 1985, 3d. edit. 1987; contbr. articles to profl. publs. Mem. Phi Beta Kappa. Criminal, Federal civil litigation, State civil litigation. Office: Frankel & Abrams 230 Park Ave New York NY 10169-0005

**FRANKEL, TAMAR,** law educator; b. Tel Aviv, July 4, 1925; came to U.S., 1963; d. Elazar Hofman and Judith Hofman-Ashkenazi; m. Raymond Clifford Atkins; children: Anat Bird, Michael. Diploma, Jerusalem Law Classes, 1948; LLM, Harvard U., 1965, SJD, 1972. Bar: Mass. 1972. Asst. atty. gen. legis. dept. Ministry of Justice State of Israel, 1948-50; pvt. practice Tel Aviv, 1951-62; legal advisor State of Israel Bonds Orgn. Europe, Paris, 1962-63; assoc. Ropes & Gray, Boston, 1964-65, Arnold & Porter, Washington, 1965-66; spl. asst. to commr. of corps. State of Calif., 1966-67; lectr. Boston U. Sch. Law, 1967, asst. prof. law, 1968-70, prof. law, 1971—; vis. prof. law Harvard U., 1979-80, vis. prof. bus. mgmt., 1980; vis. prof. law U. Calif., Berkeley, 1982-83; mem. faculty Grad. Sch. Banking, Madison, Wis., 1985; guest scholar Brookings Inst., Washington, 1986-87; atty. fellow SEC, Washington, 1996-97; vis. prof. Tokyo U. Law Sch., 1997; chair Internat. Forum on the White Paper-Internet Orgn., 1998; faculty fellow Berkman Ctr. Internet and Soc. Law Sch. Harvard U. Author: The Regulation of Money Managers, 1978, 80, Securitization: Structured Financing, Financial Assets Pools, and Asset-Backed Securities, 1991; contbr. chpts. to books, articles to profl. jours. and newspapers. Mem. ABA (com. on fed. regulation of securities, banking com. sect. corp. banking and bus. law), Am. Law Inst. (ad. vom. restatement of trusts), Israel Bar, Boston Bar Assn. Office: Boston U Sch Law 765 Commonwealth Ave Boston MA 02215-1401

**FRANKENHEIM, SAMUEL,** lawyer; b. N.Y.C., Dec. 20, 1932; s. Samuel and Mary Emma (Ward) F.; m. Nina Barbara Mennerich, Sept. 2, 1960; children: Robert Mennerich, John Frederick. BA, Cornell U., 1954, LLB, 1959. Bar: N.Y. 1959, Mass. 1976. Law clk. N.Y. Ct. Appeals, 1959-61; assoc. Shearman & Sterling, attys., N.Y.C., 1961-68, ptnr., 1968-69; sr. v.p., dir. Damon Corp., Needham Heights, Mass., 1969-78; sr. v.p., gen. counsel mem. Office of Chmn. Gen. Cinema Corp., Chestnut Hill, Mass., 1979-92; counsel Ropes & Gray, Boston, 1992—; mem. corp. Ptnrs. Healthcare Sys., Inc., 1999—; trustee Ea. Enterprises. Overseer Newton-Wellesley Hosp., Newton, Mass., 1973-85, pres., 1980-82; bd. givs. Newell Health Care Sys., 1983-93; overseer Wang Ctr. for Performing Arts, Boston, 1985-87, trustee, 1987-97; trustee Huntington Theatre Co., Boston, 1993—; assoc. First Night, Inc., 1988, chmn. bd., 1991-93; chmn. bd. Internat. Alliance of First Night Celebrations, 1994-99, treas., 1999—. 1st lt. USAF, 1955-57. Mem. ABA. General corporate. Home: 115 Shornecliffe Rd Newton MA 02458-2420 Office: Ropes & Gray 1 International Pl Fl 4 Boston MA 02110-2624

**FRANKL, KENNETH RICHARD,** retired lawyer; b. N.Y.C., May 23, 1924; s. Hugo Joseph and Sydney (Miller) F.; m. Jeanne Ritchie Silver, Aug. 6, 1972; 1 child, Kathryn; 1 son by previous marriage, Keith E. AB cum laude, Harvard U., 1945, LLB, 1950. Bar: N.Y. 1951, U.S. Ct. Appeals (2d cir.) 1956. Asst. dist. atty. N.Y. County, 1951-56; assoc. firm Liebman Eulau & Robinson, N.Y.C., 1959-60; asst. gen. atty. CBS, 1960-69; gen. counsel, asst. sec. Bishop Industries, Inc., 1969-70; v.p., gen. counsel, sec. RKO Gen., Inc. and Subs., 1970-84, cons.; ptnr. Law Offices of Ronald Kahn, N.Y.C., 1986; v.p. Charles H. Greenthal Comml. Co., N.Y.C., 1989-91; dir. staff Spl. Com. to Study Defender Sys. of N.Y.C. Assn. of the Bar, 1957-58. Co-author: (report) Equal Justice for the Accused, 1959. Mem. East Hampton Jewish Ctr., Amateur Chamber Music Soc. Served with Signal Corps, U.S. Army, 1943-46, PTO. Mem. Harvard Club N.Y. Home: PO Box 955 67 Old Montauk Hwy Amagansett NY 11930

**FRANKLE, EDWARD ALAN,** lawyer; b. N.Y.C., Dec. 14, 1946; m. Myrna Elaine Friedman, Feb. 22, 1986. BSE, Cath. U. Am., 1968, MSE, 1971; JD, Georgetown U., 1974. Bar: Md. 1974, D.C. 1980, U.S. Ct. Claims, 1976, U.S. Supreme Ct. 1978. Aerospace engr. Naval Ordnance Sta., Indian Head, Md., 1968-71; trial atty. Navy Gen. Counsel, Washington, 1974-78, asst. to gen. counsel, 1978-79, assoc. chief trial atty., 1979-80; assoc. dir. for policy SSS, Washington, 1980-82; chief counsel Goddard Space Flight Ctr., NASA, Greenbelt, Md., 1982-85; dep. gen. counsel NASA, Washington, 1985-88, gen. counsel, 1988—. Recipient Presdl. Rank, Meritorious Exec., 1988, Disting. Exec., 1992, NASA Disting. Svc. medal, 1993. Mem. ABA, AIAA (legal aspects com.), Internat. Inst. Space Law. Office: NASA Gen Counsel 300 E St SW Washington DC 20546-0005

**FRANKLIN, BARRY SCOTT,** lawyer; b. N.Y.C., Feb. 16, 1954; s. Theodore and Bernice Franklin; m. Nicola Louise Harbott, May 27, 1984; children: Jessica, Jeffrey, Daniel. BA, U. Fla., 1976; JD, Nova U., 1979. Bar: Fla. 1979, N.Y. 1984, U.S. Dist. Ct. (so. dist.) Fla., U.S. Ct. Appeals (11th cir.), U.S. Tax Ct.; bd. cert. family law. Assoc. Law Offices Paul Backman, 1981; ptnr. Backman, Franklin & Assocs., 1981-82, Young Stern Tannenbaum PA, 1982-92, Young, Franklin, Berman PA, 1992-94, Franklin & Marbin PA, 1994-96; pvt. practice law, 1996—. Contbr. chpt. to book. Guardian ad litem GAL program, Broward County, Fla. Fellow Am. Acad. Matrimonial Lawyers. Avocations: biking, hiking, camping. Family and matrimonial, Appellate, General civil litigation. Office: 290 NW 165th St North Miami Beach FL 33169

**FRANKLIN, BRUCE WALTER,** lawyer; b. Ellendale, N.D., Feb. 26, 1936; s. Wallace Henry and Frances (Webb) F.; m. Kristy Ann Jones, Feb. 7, 1944; children: Kevin, Monica, Taylor. Student, U. Mich., 1954-56; LLB, Detroit Coll. Law, 1962. Bar: Mich. 1963. Sole practice Troy, Mich., from 1962; mng. ptnr. Franklin, Bigler, Berry & Johnston, P.C., Troy, 1991-98; now mng. ptnr. Bruce Franklin P.C., Troy; pres., CEO Lanward III Devel. Corp. (Arbor Springs Plantation). *Highly successful trial attorney for 35 years. Currently president and CEO of Landward III (Arbor Springs Plantation), a major 2000 acre golf residential development in Metro Atlanta. Also president of Arbor Springs Realty and Alta Vista Properties, a commercial developer. Chairman of the board of the United Methodist Retirement Communities form 1994-1997. UMRC is a multiple CCRC facility with emphasis on dementia care in southeastern Michigan. Accomplishments during his tenure included the implementation of a 15 million dollar state of the art dementia center and the creation of a foundation board for an innovative and highly successful fund raising program.* Past chmn. Mich. Young Reps., United Meth. Retirement Cmtys. Served with U.S. Army. Product liability, Personal injury, State civil litigation. Office: Landward III 250 Arbor Springs Plantation Dr Newnan GA 30265

**FRANKLIN, CHRISTINE CARROLL,** lawyer; b. Glens Falls, N.Y., July 4, 1949. BA cum laude, Newton Coll., 1971; MA, U. Va., 1974; JD, UCLA, 1979. Bar: Calif. 1980, Ill. 1994, D.C. 1995, Colo. 1995, U.S. Dist. Ct. (no., so. and ctrl. dists.) Calif., U.S. Dist. Ct. (no. dist.) Ill. Dep. atty. gen. Office of Calif. Atty. Gen., L.A., 1980-86; assoc. Weissburg & Aronson, L.A., 1987-89; assoc. Thelen, Marrin, Johnson & Bridges, L.A., 1989-94, ptnr., 1995-98; pvt. practice Chgo., 1998—. Mem. ABA (adminstrv. law and regulatory practice sect. coun. 1996-99), Chgo. Bar Assn. Banking, General civil litigation, Insurance. Home and Office: 1366 N Dearborn St Chicago IL 60610-2052

**FRANKLIN, FREDERICK RUSSELL,** retired legal association executive; b. Mar. 20, 1929; s. Ernest James and Frances (Price) F.; m. Barbara Ann Donovan, Jan. 26, 1952; children: Katherine Elizabeth, Frederick Russell. AB, Ind. U., 1951, JD with high distinction, 1956. Bar: Ind. 1956. Trial atty. criminal div. and ct. of claims sect. civil div. U.S. Dept. Justice, Washington, 1956-60; gen. counsel Ind. State Bar Assn., Indpls., 1960-67; dir. continuing legal edn. for Ind., adj. prof. law Ind. U., Indpls., 1965-68; staff dir. profl. standards ABA, Chgo., 1968-70, legal edn. and admissions to the bar, 1972-92, Sr. lawyers divsn., 1988-93; ret., 1993; exec. v.p. Nat. Attys. Title Assurance Fund, Inc., Indpls., 1970-72. Trustee Olympia Fields (Ill.) United Meth. Ch., 1980-84; treas. bd. dirs. Olympia Fields Pub. Libr., 1984-91; mem. Olympia Fields Pub. Safety Bd., 1983-92. Capt. USAF, 1951-53. Named to Honorable Order Ky. Cols., 1967, 74, Adm. Tex. Navy, 1967, Adm. Nebr. Navy, 1972, 74, Sagamore of Wabash, 1972. Fellow Ind. Bar Found. (life); mem. ABA (coun. sr. lawyers divsn. 1993—, mem. com. bar admissions 1993-97, 99—, vice chair affiliate outreach com. divsn. sr. lawyers 1995—, vice-chair membership com. sr. lawyers divsn. 1995—, vice chair pub. com. 1995—, vice-historian 1995-96, historian 1996—, long range planning com. 1995—), Ind. State Bar Assn. (sec.-treas. sr. lawyers sect. 1998—, coun. sr. lawyers sect. 1996—, editor sr. lawyers sect. newsletter 1996-98, vice chair articles and bylaws com. 1994—, legal edn. and bar admissions com. 1990—), Fed. Bar Assn. (officer, found. bd. dirs. 1974—, historian 1979—, life fellow 1976—, treas. sr. lawyers divsn. 1993-95, sec. 1995-97, dep. chair 1997-98, chair 1998—, nat. coun. 1961-93, 97—, nat. v.p 1967-69, chpt. pres. 1965-66, chmn. admission to practice and recert. com. 1980-82, bd. dirs. Chgo. chpt. 1984-93), Nat. Orgn. Bar Counsel (pres. 1967), Ind. U. Air Force ROTC Alumni Assn. (pres. 1997-98), Lakwview Hills Homeowners Assn. (pres. 1997—), Kiwanis, Elks, Order of Coif, Am. Legion (life), Phi Delta Phi. Home: 7788 N Lakeview Dr Unionville IN 47468-9729

**FRANKLIN, GARY LAWRENCE,** lawyer; b. N.Y.C., May 17, 1963; s. Girard Harry and Gloria Blanche (Friedman) F.; m. Shanley M. Hinge, June 12, 1992; children: Natalie, Blanche. BA, Tufts U., 1985; JD, U. Calif., San Francisco, 1987-90. Bar: Calif. 1990, N.Y. 1994, U.S. Dist. Ct. (no. dist.) Calif. 1990, U.S. Dist. Ct. (no., so. and ea. dists.) N.Y. 1994, U.S. Ct. Appeals (9th cir.) 1990. Assoc. McCracken Byers & Martin, Foster City, Calif., 1990-93, Teitlebaum Hiller Rodman Paden & Hibsher, N.Y.C., 1994-95, Farrell Fritz Caemmerer Cleary Barnosky & Armentano, Uniondale, N.Y., 1996-98, Saretsky Katz Dranoff & Glass, N.Y.C., 1998—. Note editor: (jour.) COMM/ENT, 1989-90; contbr. articles to profl. jours. Mem. Bar Assn. of City of N.Y. (mem. environ. law com., chair subcom. on recycling 1995-98). Avocations: skiing, windsurfing, mountain biking, gardening, reading. Environmental, Insurance, General civil litigation. Home: 41 W 94th St New York NY 10025-7113 Office: Saretsky Katz Dranoff & Glass LLP 331 Madison Ave New York NY 10017-5102

**FRANKLIN, JONI JEANETTE,** lawyer; b. Council Grove, Kans., Jan. 26, 1971; d. Jerry P. and Sonja Jeanette F. BA, Kans. State U., 1993; JD, Kans. U., 1996; cert., Nairobi (Kenya) Law Sch., 1994. Bar: Kans. 1996, U.S. Dist. Ct. Kans. 1996. Assoc. Prochaska & Scott, Wichita, Kans., 1996-97, Render Kamas L.C., Wichita, 1998—. Pro bono atty. Wichita Lawyers That Care, 1997—; vol. atty. Sedgwick County Protection from Abuse, Wichita, 1997—; vol. Cystic Fibrosis Assn., 1997-98, Katelyn's Hope, 1998; active East Hts. United Meth. Ch., 1998—. Named Woman of the Yr. Leukemia Soc., 1999. Mem. ABA, Kans. Bar Assn., Wichita Bar Assn., Wichita Young Lawyer's Assn. (pres. elect 1999), Wichita Womens Atty. Assn. Democrat. Avocations: theater, softball, volleyball. Personal injury, Workers' compensation, General civil litigation. Office: Render Kamas LC PO Box 700 Wichita KS 67201-0700

**FRANKLIN, SCOTT BRADLEY,** accountant, lawyer; b. Milw., 1970. BBA in Acctg., U. Wis., 1992; JD, Marquette U., 1995. Bar: Wis. 1995, U.S. Dist. (ea. dist.) Wis. 1995, U.S. Tax Bar 1995; CPA, Wis. Intern Office U.S. Atty., Milw., 1993-94, Milwaukee County Circuit Ct., Milw., 1994; intern Office Dist. Counsel, IRS, Milw., 1994; mgr. Kohler and Franklin, CPA's, Milw., 1995—; instr. Becker C.P.A. Rev. Course, Milw., 1996—. Contbr. articles to profl. jours. Fellow Wis. Inst. CPA's (fed. taxation com. 1997—); mem. ABA, AICPA, Stat Bar Wis. E-mail: SBFranklin@prodigy.com. Office: Kohler and Franklin CPA's 250 W Coventry Ct Ste 211 Milwaukee WI 53217-3966

**FRANKLIN, WEBB,** lawyer; b. Greenwood, Miss., Dec. 13, 1941; s. Webster C. Franklin and Elizabeth Irby Franklin Rankin; m. Edna Green Lott, June 12, 1965; children: Webster C., Melissa Lansdale. BA, Miss. State U., 1963; JD, U. Miss., 1966. Pvt. practice Greenwood, Miss., 1970-78; asst. dist. atty. 4th Cir. Ct., Miss., 1972-78, cir. judge, 1978-82; mem. U.S. Congress, 1983-86; commr. Lower Miss. Delta Study Commn., 1988-90; state bd. atty. State of Miss., 1992—; sr. ptnr. Lott Franklin Fonda & Flanagan, Greenwood, 1989—. Republican. Episcopalian. Home: 613 River Rd Greenwood MS 38930-4214 Office: Lott Franklin Fonda & Flanagan PO Box 1176 Greenwood MS 38935-1176

**FRANKS, HERBERT HOOVER,** lawyer; b. Joliet, Ill., Jan. 25, 1934; s. Carol and Lottie (Dermer) F.; m. Eileen Pepper, June 22, 1957; children: David, Jack, Eli. BS, Roosevelt U., 1954; postgrad., Am. U., 1960. Bar: Ill. 1961, U.S. Dist. Ct. (no. dist.) Ill. 1961, U.S. Supreme Ct. 1967. Ptnr. Franks, Gerkin & McKenna, 1985—; chmn. Wonder Lake State Bank, Ill., 1979—, First Nat. Bank, Marengo, Ill., 1976-84, mem. exec. com., 1976—; vice-chmn. hotel mgmt. orgn. Bricton Group, Park Ridge, Ill., 1992-98. Bus. editor Am. U. Law Rev., 1959, 60. State pres. Young Dems. of Ill., 1970-72; trustee Hebrew Theol. Coll., Skokie, Ill., 1974—; trustee, sec. Forest Inst. Profl. Psychology, Springfield, Mo., 1979-91; chmn. Forest Hosp., Des Plaines, 1980-88. With U.S. Army, 1956-58. Fellow Ill. State Bar (bd. govs. 1994-97, treas. 1996-97, 3d v.p. 1997-98, 2d v.p. 1998-99, pres.-elect 1999—); mem. Ill. Trial Lawyers (mng. bd. 1975-92, treas. 1985-87), Masons, Shriners, Sigma Nu Phi (pres. 1980-82). Workers' compensation, Banking. Home: 19324 E Grant Hwy Marengo IL 60152-9438 Office: Franks Gerkin & McKenna 19333 E Grant Hwy Marengo IL 60152-8234

**FRANKS, HERSCHEL PICKENS,** judge; b. Savannah, Tenn., May 28, 1930; s. Herschel R. and Vada (Pickens) F.; m. Judy Black; 1 child, Ramona. Student U. Tenn.-Martin, U. Md.; JD, U. Tenn.-Knoxville; grad. Nat. Jud. Coll. of U. Nev. Bar: Tenn. 1959, U.S. Supreme Ct. 1968. Claims atty. U.S. Fidelity & Guaranty Co., Knoxville, 1958; ptnr. Harris, Moon, Meacham & Franks, Chattanooga, 1959-70; chancellor 3d Chancery div. of Hamilton County, 1970-78; judge Tenn. Ct. Appeals, Chattanooga, 1978—; spl. justice Tenn. Supreme Ct., 1979, 86, 87; presiding judge Hamilton County Trial Cts., 1977-78; spl. judge Tenn. Ct. of Criminal Appeals, 1990-92; mem. commn. to study appellate cts., 1990-92. Served with USNG, 1949-50, USAF, 1950-54. Mem. ABA (award of merit), Tenn. Bar Assn. (award of merit 1968-69), Tenn. Bar Found., Chattanooga Bar Found., Chattanooga Bar Assn. (pres. 1968-69, Founds. of Freedom award 1986), Am. Judicature Soc., Inst. Jud. Adminstrn., Optimists (pres. 1965-66), Community Service award 1971), Mountain City Club, City Farmers Club, Phi Alpha Delta. Mem. United Ch. of Christ. Address: 540 Mccallie Ave Ste 562 Chattanooga TN 37402-2039

**FRANKS, JON MICHAEL,** lawyer, mediator; b. Marshall, Tex., Sept. 26, 1941; s. Francis William and Clara Bell (Caldwell) F.; m. Sue Powers, May 23, 1987; children: Brian Alan, Michael Shawn. BA, Southwestern U., 1963; LLB, U. Tex., 1966. Bar. Tex. 1966, U.S. Dist. Ct. (no. dist.) Tex.; cert. family lawyer, Tex. Bd. of Legal Specialization. Lawyer Pettigrew and Buckley, Grand Prairie, Tex., 1966-67; pvt. practice Irving, Tex., 1967-68, 71-79, 88—; ptnr. Franks and Vice, Irving, 1968-71, Franks and Luce, Irving, 1979-88; mem. child support and visitation guidelines com. Tex. Supreme Ct., Austin, 1989; mem. Southlake Ct. of Records Com., 1990—. Commr. Irving Planning and Zoning Bd., 1971-74; judge Mcpl. Ct., Irving, 1974-78, Southlake, Tex., 1978-88, Southlake City Coun., 1992—. Fellow Am. Acad. Matrimonial Lawyers; mem. ABA (family law sect.), Tex. Acad. Family Law Specialists (bd. dirs. 1988-90), North Tex. Assn. Family Law Specialists (pres. 1985-87), Tex. Bar Assn. (family law sect.), Dallas Bar Assn. (pres. family law sect. 1989), Tarrant County Family Law Assn., Am. Acad. Atty.-Mediators. Republican. Methodist. Avocations: gun collector, trap shooting, bicycling, tennis. Family and matrimonial. Office: 115 E Worth St Ste 100 Grapevine TX 76051-5357

**FRANKS, WILLIAM J.,** judge; b. Uniontown, Pa., Jan. 6, 1932; m. Lena Franks; 1 child, Regina. BA in Pre-law, U. Pitts., 1953, LLB, 1956, JD, 1968; postgrad., U. Ga., 1958. Bar: Pa. 1956, U.S. Dist. Ct. (we. dist.) Pa. 1961. Pvt. practice, Uniontown, 1956-77; asst. dist. atty. Fayette County, Uniontown, 1960-69; judge Ct. Common Pleas Fayette County, Uniontown, 1978-96, pres. judge, 1996—; instr. bus. law U. Ga., 1958; instr. Am. Inst. Banking, 1960-65; solicitor Fayette County Contr., 1970; counsel Fayette County Child Welfare Svcs., Fayette County Cmty. Action Agy. With JAGC, U.S. Army, 1957-59. Mem. ABA, ATLA, Am. Arbitration Assn., Pa. Bar Assn., Fayette County Bar Assn., AMVETS, Cath. War Vets., Sons of Italy, KC (4th degree), Phi Beta Kappa, Phi Alpha Delta. Roman Catholic. Office: Fayette County Ct Common Pleas 61 E Main St Uniontown PA 15401-3514

**FRANKS, WILLIAM WOOLERY,** lawyer; b. Bryn Mawr, Pa., Dec. 18, 1947; s. Ernest H. and Eleanore W. (Woolery) F.; m. Cat Austin, May 3, 1980; children: Sebastian, Nikolas, Robin. BS in Psychology, Colo. State U., 1970; MEd, Plymouth State Coll., 1974; JD, Franklin Pierce Law Ctr., 1978. Bar: N.H. 1978, U.S. Dist. Ct. N.H. 1978, U.S. Supreme Ct. 1986, U.S. Ct. Appeals (1st cir.) 1981, U.S. Virgin Islands 1997. Assoc. Falardeau, & Mahan, Tilton, N.H., 1978-80; ptnr. Falardeau, Mahan & Franks, Tilton, 1980-83, Falardeau & Franks, Tilton, 1983-86; pres., shareholder Franks & Shepherd PA, Tilton, 1987-95, William W. Franks, PA, Tilton, 1995-97; mng. atty. Legal Svcs. V.I., St. Croix, 1998—; adv. bd. First Deposit Nat. Banks, Tilton, 1986—; investigator 1st Security Svcs. Corp., Boston, 1975-78. Dem. nominee for N.H. Ho. Reps., 1994; bd. dirs. Twin Rivers Cmty. Corp., Tilton; trustee Spaulding Youth Ctr., Northfield, N.H., cottage tchr., trainer, 1970-75; vice chair Town of Sanbornton, N.H. Zoning Bd.; coach Sanbornton Youth Soccer; performer Streetcar Co. Prodns. Office: Christiansted 3017 Estate Orange Grv Christiansted VI 00820-4313

**FRANO, ANDREW JOSEPH,** lawyer, civil engineer; b. Chgo., July 14, 1953; s. Joseph Neil Frano and Lorraine Rose (Jeczalik) Patchett; children: Alaina Marie, Jacqueline Elyse. BSCE, Bradley U., 1975, MSCE, 1976; JD, Ill. Inst. Tech., 1982. Bar: Ill. 1982, Nebr. 1986, U.S. Dist. Ct. (no. dist.) Ill. 1982, U.S. Dist. Ct. Nebr. 1992, Ariz. 1993, Tex. 1997; registered profl. engr., Ill., Ind., Nebr.; lic. gen. engrng. constrn. contractor Fla., Utah. Soils lab. instr. and residence hall dir. Bradley U., Peoria, Ill., 1975-76; civil engr. Harza Engrng. Co., Chgo., 1976-85; pvt. practice Chgo., 1982-85; pres. GEC Engrng. Co. Inc., Chgo., 1985-86; corp. constrn. atty. Peter Kiewit Sons Inc., Omaha, Nebr., 1986-92; asst. gen. counsel Harza Engrng. Co., Chgo., 1992-95; owner The Law and Engring. Office of Andrew J. Frano, 1996—; adj. asst. prof. dept. civil and architectural engring., Ill. Inst. Tech., Chgo., 1993—; corp. atty., civil engr. T.J. Lambrecht Constrn., Inc., Joliet, Ill., 1996-98; prin. engr. Mirza-RSV Engring., Inc., Chgo., 1998—. Chmn. San. Improvement Dist. 111, Sarpy County, Nebr., 1987-92; vol. atty. Chgo. Vol. Legal Svcs., 1983-85; bd. dirs., treas. Trails Assn. Inc., Roselle, Ill., 1983-86. Mem. ASCE, Tau Beta Pi, Chi Epsilon. Republican. Roman Catholic. Avocations: basketball, tennis. Construction, General practice. Home: 2 N Dee Rd Apt 107 Park Ridge IL 60068-2871 Office: Mirza-RSV Engring Inc 7221 W Touhy Ave Chicago IL 60631-4324

**FRANSE, R(ICHARD) NELSON,** lawyer, television broadcaster; b. Clovis, N.Mex., Feb. 5, 1961; s. Roy and Jerie Lou Franse; m. M. Marie McCulloch; 1 child, Colson Brack. B Univ. Studies, U. N.Mex., 1984, JD, 1987. Bar: N.Mex. 1987. Assoc. Rodey Dickason Sloan Akin et al, Albuquerque. Mem. Am. Bd. Profl. Liability Attys. (diplomat 1997). Baptist. Avocation: Monday morning quarterbacking. Professional liability, Sports. Office: Rodey Dickason Sloan Et Al 201 3d St NW Ste 2200 Albuquerque NM 87102

**FRANTZ, DAVID JOSEPH,** lawyer; b. Cleve., Nov. 13, 1948; s. Joseph Clarence and June Marie (Clancey) F.; m. Diahn Case, May 10, 1976; children: Dana, Christopher, Lauren. BSBA, Georgetown U., 1970, LLB, 1974. Bar: Va. 1974, D.C. 1975, U.S. Ct. Appeals (D.C. and 4th cirs.) 1975, U.S. Dist. Ct. Md. 1989, U.S. Supreme Ct. 1999. Assoc. Lamb, Eastman & Keats, Washington, 1974-79; pvt. practice Washington, 1979-82; ptnr. Menler & Lamb, Washington, 1982-85, Conlon, Frantz, Phelan & Pires, Washington, 1985—; lectr. D.C. Bar Continuing Legal Edn. Program, Washington, 1985—. Mem. ABA (litigation sect.), Va. Trial Lawyers Assn., Order of Barristers. Personal injury, Non-profit and tax-exempt organizations, General civil litigation. Office: Conlon Frantz Phelan & Pires 1818 N St NW Washington DC 20036-2406

**FRANTZ, ROBERT WESLEY,** lawyer; b. Long Branch, N.J., Dec. 31, 1950. BS, Rutgers U., New Brunswick, N.J., 1973; JD, Rutgers U., Newark, 1977. Bar: N.J. 1977, U.S. Dist. Ct. N.J. 1977, U.S. Ct. Appeals (4th and 10th cirs.) 1978, U.S. Ct. Appeals (6th, 7th and 8th cirs.) 1979, D.C. 1980, U.S. Ct. Appeals (9th cir.) 1980, U.S. Dist. Ct. D.C. 1981. Trial atty. U.S. Dept. Justice, Washington, 1977-80; assoc. Hamel and Park, Washington, 1980-82; asst. gen. counsel Chem. Mfrs. Assn., Washington, 1982-85; counsel, environ. protection GE, Fairfield, Conn., 1985-88, Pittsfield, Mass., 1988-89; mgr. and counsel Environ. Remediation Program, Fairfield, Conn., 1989-95; mgr., sr. counsel Environ. Ops. Program, Fairfield, 1995-98; gen. mgr., counsel GE Engines Svcs., Cin., 1998—; mem. sci. adv. bd. subcom. on risk reduction options U.S. EPA, 1996—. Contbr. articles to profl. publs.; editorial bd. Rutgers Law Rev., 1976. Mem. Newtown (Conn.) Charter Revision Commn., 1986-87. Mem. ABA (exec. editor Natural Resources and Environment 1986-93, coun. mem. sect. natural resources 1993-96). Avocations: sailing, golf, skiing, bicycling, woodworking. Environmental, Federal civil litigation, General civil litigation. Office: GE Engine Svcs 1 Neumann Way # Md-t164 Cincinnati OH 45215-1915

**FRANTZ, THOMAS RICHARD,** lawyer; b. Waynesboro, Pa., Sept. 10, 1947; s. John Richard and Janet (Donnelly) F.; 1 son, Thomas Richard; m. Dianne Boffa, June 22, 1985; children: Lindsey Amore, Elissa Noel. BA, Coll. William and Mary, 1970, JD, 1973, LLM, 1981. Bar: Va., U.S. Dist. Ct. (ea. dist.) Va. 1974, U.S. Ct. Appeals (4th cir.) 1974, U.S. Supreme Ct. 1978. Supr. tax dept. Peat Marwick, Mitchell & Co., 1973-74; officer, dir. Williams, Mullen, Clark & Dobbins, P.C., Virginia Beach, Va., 1974—; adj. prof. law Coll. William and Mary, 1981-82, trustee tax conf. 1984—; planning com. Old Dominion U. Tax Conf., 1977-81, chmn., 1981. Contbr. articles to profl. jours. King Neptune XXIII, Virginia Beach Neptune Festival, 1996; mem. exec. com. Va. Marine Mus. Sci., 1980—, pres., 1999—; bd. mem. Cape Henry Collegiate Sch., 1986-98, chmn., 1991-92; bd. dirs. Va. Beach Found., 1987—, chmn., 1995-97; bd. dirs. Virginia Beach Vision, 1993—, Hampton Roads Partnership, 1997—. Capt. USAR, 1972-79. Mem. AICPA, ABA (tax, bus. and health law sects.), Am. Coll. Tax Counsel, Am. Coll. Trusts and Estates Counsel, Best Lawyers in Am. (tax, trusts and estates, corp. law), Am. Assn. Attys.-CPAs, Va. Bar Assn., Va. State Bar (bd. govs. trusts and estates sect.), Virginia Beach Bar Assn., Princess Anne Country Club, Cavalier Yacht and Country Club. Lutheran. Corporate taxation, Estate taxation, Personal income taxation. Address: 900 One Columbus Ctr Virginia Beach VA 23462

**FRANTZ, WILLIAM MICHAEL,** lawyer; b. Calgary, Alberta, Canada, Mar. 28, 1965; came to U.S., 1986; s. William John and Magdalen Johanna F.; m. Robin Michelle Dickerson, April 22, 1989. 1 child, William John Frantz IV. BA, U. Alberta, Can., 1986; JD, Calif. Western, San Diego, 1989. Bar: Calif. 1991. Pvt. practice San Diego, 1991-94; assoc. Law Offices Gregory Mutz, San Diego, 1994-97, Frantz & Geraci L.L.P., San Diego, 1997-99; pvt. practice San Diego, 1999—; arbitrator: Nat. Assn. Securities Dealers, Futures Trading Assn. General civil litigation, Securities. Office: 11077 1/2 Camino Playa Carmel San Diego CA 92124-4142

**FRANZ, J. NOLAND,** lawyer; b. Washington, Oct. 1, 1940; s. Jewett Noland and Louise C. (Cies) F.; m. Charline S. Schmelzer, Feb. 25, 1967 (div. Dec. 1988); children: Jason, Wyatt. BA, Kans. U., 1962; JD, U. Mich., 1965; MBA, U. Mo., 1967. Bar: Mo. 1965, Ariz. 1974; cert. estate and trust specialist State Bar Ariz. Assoc. Gage & Tucker, Kansas City, 1967-70; atty. Securities & Exch. Commn., Washington Regional Office, Washington, 1970-73; ptnr. Gray Plant Mooty Mooty & Bennett, Phoenix, 1982-84, O'Connor Cavanaugh Anderson Westover Killingsworth & Besheas, Phoenix, 1984-86, Carson Messinger Elliott Laughlin & Regan, Phoenix, 1973-82, 86-90; atty. pvt. practice, Phoenix, 1990—; dir. Southwest Microwave, Inc., Tempe, Ariz., 1995—. Corp. coun., mem. Desert Foothills Land Trust, Foothills Cmty. Found., Ariz., 1991—; bd. dirs., exec. com., past v.p. Florence Crittenton Svcs. Ariz., Inc., Phoenix; mem. Valley Leadership, Phoenix, 1983-84; bd. dirs., past pres. Wildest Club in Town Ariz. Zool. Soc., Phoenix, 1983-91. Mem. Nat. Network Estate Planning Attys., Nat. Acad. Elder Law Attys., Ariz. Bus. Leadership Assn., Valley Estate Planners, Rotary (pres. 1989-90). Avocations: golf, travel, hiking, reading. Fax: 602-945-9594. E-mail: j.franz@azbar.org. Estate planning, Probate, Estate taxation. Office: 7509 E 1st St Scottsdale AZ 85251-4501

**FRANZ, WILLIAM MANSUR,** lawyer; b. Dayton, Ohio, Dec. 3, 1930; s. Robert and Muriel (Bisbee) F.; m. Jane Speers, May 26, 1962; children: David, Julie, Elizabeth, Susan. BA in Russian Studies, Syracuse U., 1953; LLB, Chgo.-Kent Coll. Law, 1959. Bar: Ill. 1959, U.S. Dist. Ct. (no. dist.) Ill. 1959. Assoc. Righeimer & Righeimer, Chgo., 1959, Corcoran & Corcoran, Evanston, Ill., 1959-61; ptnr. Franz & Franz, Crystal Lake, Ill., 1961-73, Franz, Naughton & Leahy, Crystal Lake, 1974-87, Franz & Kerrick, Crystal Lake, 1987—. Served to 1st lt. USAF, 1951-53. Mem. Ill. Bar Assn., McHenry County Bar Assn. Club: Crystal Lake Country. Lodge: Lions. Construction, Real property, General practice. Home: 623 Leonard Pky Crystal Lake IL 60014-5209 Office: Franz & Kerrick 453 Coventry Green Crystal Lake IL 60014-7504

**FRANZEN, DOUGLAS JOHN,** lawyer; b. Omaha, Oct. 20, 1952; s. Clifford John Franzen and Betty Corrine Satherlie; m. Patricia Lynn Peterson, Sept. 22, 1979; children: Christian, Anna. BA, U. Minn., 1975; JD, William Mitchell Coll. Law, 1979; postgrad., London Sch. Econs., 1989-91. Bar: Minn. 1979, U.S. Dist. Ct. Minn. 1981. Assoc. O'Connor & Hannan, Mpls., 1979-86, ptnr., 1986-89; shareholder McGrann Shea Franzen Carnival Straughn & Lamb, Chartered, Mpls., 1989—. Bd. dirs. Minn. Dance Theater, Mpls., 1996—; mem. adv. bd. Salvation Army ARC, Mpls., 1987-88; chmn. bd. mgmt. Hiawatha YMCA, Mpls., 1986. Recipient Fgn. and Commonwealth Office award Brit. Coun., 1989. Mem. ABA, Minn. State Bar Assn., Minn. Govt. Rels. Coun., Hennepin County Bar Assn. Legislative, Administrative and regulatory. Office: McGrann Shea Franzen Carnival Straughn & Lamb 800 Lasalle Ave Ste 2200 Minneapolis MN 55402-2041

**FRANZKE, RICHARD ALBERT,** lawyer; b. Lewistown, Mont., Mar. 7, 1935; s. Arthur A. and Senta (Clark) F.; divorced; children: Mark, Jean, Robert. BA in Polit. Sci., Willamette U., 1958, JD with honors, 1960. Bar: Oreg. 1960, U.S. Dist. Ct. Oreg., 1960, U.S. Supreme Ct., 1961. Ptnr. Stoel, Rives, Portland, 1960—; bd. dirs., chmn. various coms. Assn. Gen. Contractors Am., Portland, 1972-79; mem. com. on legis. affairs Assn. Builders & Contractors, Portland, 1983—. Author: A Study of the Construct by Contract Issue, 1979. Mem. Gov.'s Task Force on Reform of Worker's Compensation, Salem, Oreg., 1980-81; atty. gen.'s com. on Pub. Contracting. Recipient SIR award Assn. Gen. Contractors, 1979, Nat. Winner Outstanding Oral Argument award U.S. Moot Ct., 1959. Mem. ABA (sect. pub. contract law), Oreg. Bar (law sch. liaison, com. on practice and procedure specialization), Multnomah County Bar Assn. Republican. Avocations: antique autos, antique furniture, boating, water skiing. Construction. Home: 14980 SW 133rd Ave Tigard OR 97224-1646 Office: Stoel Rives 900 SW 5th Ave Ste 2300 Portland OR 97204-1235

**FRASCH, BRIAN BERNARD,** lawyer; b. San Francisco, Apr. 13, 1956; s. Norman Albert Frasch and Elizabeth Louise (Michelfelder) Milsten. BA magna cum laude, U. Calif., Santa Barbara, 1978; JD, U. Calif., Berkeley, 1982. Bar: Calif. 1982, U.S. Dist. Ct. (no. dist.) Calif. 1982, U.S. Dist. Ct. (so. dist.) Calif. 1983. Law clk. to chief judge U.S. Dist. Ct. (so. dist.) Calif., 1983-84; assoc. Graham & James, San Francisco, 1984-86, Lillick & McHose, San Diego, 1986-90; ptnr. Stephenson Prairie & Frasch, San Diego, 1990-96, Hillyer & Irwin, San Diego, 1996—. Assoc. editor: California Law Rev., 1981-82. Mem. ABA (litigation sect.), Calif. Bar Assn. (litigation sect.), San Diego County Bar Assn., San Diego Bldg. Owners and Mgrs. Assn. (bd. dirs. 1990-98, gen. counsel 1995-98), Westside Athletic Club. Landlord-tenant, Real property, General civil litigation. Office: Hillyer & Irwin 550 W C St Ste 1600 San Diego CA 92101-3568

**FRASER, BRIAN SCOTT,** lawyer; b. Bronxville, N.Y., Oct. 14, 1956. BA, Manhattanville Coll., 1978; JD, Fordham U., 1984. Bar: N.Y. 1987, U.S. Dist. Ct. (so. and ea. dists.) N.Y. 1991. Law clk. hon. William H. Timbers U.S. Ct. Appeals 2nd Cir., Bridgeport, Conn., 1984-85; assoc. Cravath, Swaine & Moore, N.Y.C., 1985-91; ptnr. Richard Spears Kibbe & Orbe, N.Y.C., 1991—. Active Scarsdale (N.Y.) Town and Village Civic Assn. Mem. ABA (sects. litigation and intellectual property), Fed. Bar Coun., Bar Assn. City of N.Y. (mem. antitrust com. 1991-94. Federal civil litigation, Securities, Antitrust. Office: Richards Spears Kibbe & Orbe One Chase Manhattan Plaza New York NY 10005

**FRASER, EVERETT MACKAY,** lawyer; b. Mpls., July 20, 1921; s. Everett and Barbara Lois (MacKay) F.; m. Elizabeth Barbara Graves, Mar. 9, 1966; children: Alexander Martin, Margaret Lois. BA in Math. and Physics, U. Minn., 1943; JD, Columbia U., 1948. Bar: Minn. 1949, Mass. 1968. Patent atty. ITT, 1948-50; patent adviser Signal Corps, U.S. Army, Ft. Monmouth, N.J., 1950-51, legal counsel Harlan Bradt Assocs., N.Y.C., 1952-53; patent atty. Burroughs Corp., N.Y.C., 1954-56, mgr. N.Y. patent operation, 1956-59; chief patent counsel LFE Corp., Clinton, Mass., 1959-61, gen. counsel, 1961-88, sec., 1962-88, v.p., 1970-88; spl. counsel Mark IV Industries, Inc., Clinton, 1988—. Mem. town meeting Town of Arlington (Mass.), 1977—, mem. fin. com., 1981—. Served to lt. USNR, 1943-46; ATO, PTO. Mem. ABA, Mass. Bar Assn., Boston Bar Assn., Am. Intellectual Property Law Assn., Boston Patent Law Assn. Democrat. Unitarian-Universalist. General corporate, Patent. Address: LFE Industrial Systems Corp 900 Middlesex Tpke Bldg 6 Billerica MA 01821-3929

**FRASER, ROBERT WILLIAM,** lawyer; b. Seattle, Oct. 5, 1924; s. Phil Gordon and Theta Laura (Furey) F.; children: Jan Marie, Phil Gordon, Patricia Diane. LLB, Northeastern U., 1949. Bar: Mont. 1949, Calif. 1950, U.S. Dist. Ct. (so. dist.) Calif. 1952, U.S. Supreme Ct. 1955, U.S. Ct. Appeals (9th cir.) 1957. Lawyer Santa Ana, Calif., 1950—; breeder Scottish highland cattle, San Juan Capistrano. Candidate dist. atty., Orange County, Calif., 1954, canidate judge, 1980. 1st lt. USMC, 1942-52. Fellow Soc. Antiquaries Scotland; mem. State Bar Calif. (com. adminstrn. justice 1961-63), Calif. Trial Lawyers Assn., Orange County Trial Lawyers Assn., Orange County Bar Assn. (chmn. com. on adminstrn. of justice, pres. 1962-63), Masons, York Rite. Episcopalian. Avocation: Highland Clan Fraser (Scotland). General practice, Criminal, General civil litigation. Office: 1536 E Washington Ave Santa Ana CA 92701-3246

**FRASIER, RALPH KENNEDY,** lawyer, banker; b. Winston-Salem, N.C., Sept. 16, 1938; s. LeRoy Benjamin and Kathryn O. (Kennedy) F.; m. Jeannine Quick, Aug. 1981; children: Karen D. Frasier Alston, Gail S. Frasier Cox, Ralph Kennedy Jr., Keith Lowery, Marie Kennedy, Rochelle Doar. BS, N.C. Cen. U., Durham, 1963, JD, 1965. Bar: N.C. 1965, Ohio 1976. With Wachovia Bank and Trust Co., N.A., Winston-Salem, N.C., 1965-70; v.p., counsel Wachovia Bank and Trust Co., N.A., 1969-70; asst. counsel, v.p. parent co. Wachovia Corp., 1970-75; v.p., gen. counsel Huntington Nat. Bank, Columbus, Ohio, 1975-76; sr. v.p. Huntington Nat. Bank, 1976-83, sec., 1981-98, exec. v.p., 1983-98, cashier, 1983-98; v.p. Huntington Bancshares Inc., 1976-86, gen. counsel, 1976-98, sec., 1981-98; sec., dir. Huntington Mortgage Co., Huntington State Bank, Huntington Leasing Co., Huntington Bancshares Fin. Corp., Huntington Investment Mgmt. Co., Huntington Nat. Life Ins. Co., Huntington Co., 1976-88; v.p., asst. sec. Huntington Bank N.E. Ohio, 1982-84; asst. sec. Huntington Bancshares Ky., 1985-97; sec. Huntington Trust Co., N.A., 1987-97, Huntington Bancshares Ind., Inc., 1986-97, Huntington Fin. Services Co., 1987-98; dir. The Huntington Nat. Bank, Columbus, Ohio, 1998—; of counsel Porter Wright Morris & Arthur LLP, Columbus, 1998—; trustee Online Computer Libr. Ctr., Inc., Columbus, 1999—. Bd. dirs. Family Svcs. Winston-Salem, 1966-74, sec., 1966-71, 74, v.p., 1974; chmn. Winston-Salem Transit Authority, 1974-75; bd. dirs. Rsch. for Advancement of Personalities, 1968-71, Winston-Salem Citizens for Fair Housing, 1970-74, N.C. United Community Svcs., 1970-74; treas. Forsyth County (N.C.) Citizens Com. Adequate Justice Bldg., 1968; trustee Appalachian State U., Boone, N.C., 1973-83, endowment fund, 1973-83, Columbus Drug Edn. and Prevention Fund, Inc., 1989-92; trustee, vice chmn. employment and Edn. Commn. Franklin County, 1982-85; mem. Winston-Salem Forsyth County Sch. Bd. Adv. Coun., 1973-74, Atty. Gen's Ohio Task Force Minorities in Bus., 1977-78; bd. dirs. Inorads Columbus, Inc., 1986-95, Greater Columbus Arts Coun., 1986-94, Columbus Urban League Inc., 1987-94, vice chmn., 1990-94; trustee Riverside Meth. Hosp. Found., 1989-90, Grant Med. Ctr., 1990-95, Grant/Riverside Meth. Hosps., 1995-97; trustee Ohio Health Corp., 1997—; dir. Cmty. Mutual Ins. Co., 1989-92, mem. audit com., 1989-92; trustee N.C. Ctrl. U., Durham, 1993—, vice-chmn., 1993-94, chmn. 1995, chair ednl. planning and acad. affairs com., 1995—, mem. audit devel. coms., 1998—; mem. Ohio Bd. Regents, 1987-96, vice-chmn., 1993-95, chmn., 1995-96; trustee Nat. Jud. Coll., Reno, Nevada, 1996—, fin. and audit com., 1997—, treas. 1998—, Columbus Bar Found., 1998— (fellows com. 1998—, grants com., 1998—); AEFC Pension Adminstrn. Com. defined benefit plan of the ABA, Am. Bar Endowment, Am. Bar Found., and Nat. Jud. Coll., Chgo, Ill., 1998—. With AUS, 1958-60. Mem. ABA, Nat. Bar Assn., Ohio Bar Assn., Columbus Bar Assn. Banking, Consumer commercial, General corporate. Office: Porter Wright Morris & Arthur LLP 41 S High St Ste 3100 Columbus OH 43215-6101

**FRASSETTO, EUGENE A.,** lawyer; b. Salinas, Calif., Feb. 25, 1950; s. Eugene Edward and Dorothy Marguerite F.; m. Deborah D. Bruzda, July 2, 1976; children: Gina Marie, Angela Denise, Anthony Edward. BA, U. Calif., Berkeley, 1971, Oreg. State U., 1976; JD, Willamette U., 1984. Ops. mgr. Beaver State Movers, Covallis, Oreg., 1977-81; law clerk Heltzel Byers Upjohn Shaw, Salem, Oreg., 1982-84; judicial clerk Oreg. Supreme Ct., Salem, Oreg., 1984-86; atty. Stoel Rives LLP, Portland, Oreg., 1986—. Contbr. article to profl. jour. Adv. bd. Autistic Children's Activity Program, Portland, Oreg., 1987—. Mem. Oreg. State Bar (chair land use sect. exec. com. 1990-98, real estate sect. 1996-97). Real property. Office: Stoel Rives LLP 900 SW 5th Ave Ste 2600 Portland OR 97204-1268

**FRAWLEY, MICHAEL K.,** lawyer; b. Reading, Pa., Aug. 2, 1959; s. George Michael and Jolene Merecedes F.; m. Elizabeth A. West, Aug. 19, 1989 (div. Oct. 1997). BA in Econs., U. Notre Dame, 1982; JD, U. of the Pacific, 1987. Bar: Calif. Prosecutor Ventura (Calif.) County Dist. Atty., 1987-92, supr., 1992-93, sr. deputy dist. atty., 1993-98, chief deputy dist. atty., 1998—. Bd. dirs. Habitat for Humanity, Ventura, 1995, 96, 97; lit. tchr. Project Literacy, Ventura, 1991; vol. Alameda County Big Bros./Big Sisters, 1983. Mem. Calif. Bar Assn. Avocations: tennis, swimming, hiking, reading, travel. Office: Ventura County Dist Atty 4245 Market St Ste 209 Ventura CA 93003-8009

**FRAZEN, MITCHELL HALE,** lawyer; b. Great Lakes, Ill., Sept. 19, 1955; s. Sidney Joseph and Norma Ileane (Solomon) F.; m. Mary Elizabeth Huelsbusch, Sept. 14, 1974; children: Daniel Joseph, Christina Elizabeth. BA, U. Ill., 1977; JD, U. Mich., 1980. Bar: Ill. 1980, U.S. Dist. Ct. (no. dist.) Ill. 1980, U.S. Ct. Appeals (7th cir.) 1987, U.S. Dist. Ct. (ea. dist.) Wis. 1994, U.S. Ct. Appeals (8th cir.) 1995, U.S. Dist. Ct. (ea. dist.) Mich. 1995. Assoc. Phelan, Pope & John, Ltd., Chgo., 1980-87; shareholder Burditt & Radzius, Chartered, Chgo., 1987-98, dir., 1989-98; ptnr. Litchfield Cavo, Chgo., 1998—; arbitrator, chairperson mandatory ct.-annexed arbitration program Cook County Cir. Ct., Chgo., 1990—, mediator vol. mediation program, 1992—. Bd. govs. Chgo. Coun. Lawyers, 1992-95; chair State Ct. Practices Com., 1995—. Mem. ABA, Chgo. Bar Assn., Phi Beta Kappa, Order of Coif. Democrat. Lutheran. General civil litigation, Insurance, Personal injury. Home: 4050 Hudson Dr Hoffman Est IL 60195-1717 Office: Litchfield Cavo Ste 200 303 W Madison St Chicago IL 60606-3309

**FRAZER, MARILEE HELEN,** prosecutor, pathologist; b. Wilmington, Del., Nov. 20, 1953; d. August Henry and Christine (Hoover) F. BA in Biol. Scis., U. Del., 1975; MD, Jefferson Med. Coll., 1978; JD, Wayne State U., 1989. Diplomate Am. Bd. Anatomic Pathology, Am. Bd. Forensic Pathology. Dep. coroner Cuyahoga County Coroner's Office, Cleve., 1983-84; asst. med. examiner Wayne County Med. Examiner's Office, Detroit, 1984-89; atty. Mich. Ct. Appeals, Detroit, 1989-90; asst. prosecuting atty. Wayne County Prosecutor's Office, 1990—. Fellow Am. Coll. Pathology; mem. Nat. Assn. Med. Examiners, Am. Acad. Forensic Scis. Office: Wayne County Prosecutor Office 1441 Saint Antoine St Rm 1253 Detroit MI 48226-2311

**FRAZIER, STEVEN CARL,** lawyer; b. Kingsport, Tenn., Jan. 8, 1954; s. Carl Dexter and Jean (Winegar) F.; divorced; children: John Carl, Jacob Steven. BS, U. Tenn., 1976, JD, 1979. Bar: Tenn. 1980. Sole practice Church Hill, Tenn., 1980-82; ptnr. Frazier & Faulk, Church Hill, 1982-83; appeals referee dept. employment sec. State of Tenn., Kingsport, 1983; sole practice Church Hill, Tenn., 1983—; intern Senator Bill Brock, 1975; atty. City of Mt. Carmel, Tenn., 1986-88; chmn. Foster Care Rev. Bd., Rogersville, Tenn., 1981-85; city judge Town of Church Hill, 1988—. Parlimentarian Hawkins County Young Reps., Rogersville, 1986; deacon First Bapt. Ch., Church Hill. Named one of Outstanding Young Men Am., 1982, 84. Mem. ABA, Tenn. Bar Assn., Hawkins County Bar Assn., Kingsport Bar Assn., Church Hill Jaycees (pres. 1984-86), Gideons Internat., Tenn. Capital Club, Kiwanis (pres. 1983-84, 88-89, 96-97), East Hawkins C. of C. (sec. 1994-95). Baptist. Real property, Probate, General practice. Home and Office: PO Box 1208 Church Hill TN 37642-1208

**FRAZIER, WILLIAM SUMPTER,** lawyer, pharmacist; b. Mexia, Tex., Aug. 8, 1941; s. William Sumpter and Johnnie Ione (Archer) F.; m. Carolyn Casey, July 26, 1946; children—Casey Rene, Kelley Shea. A.A. with honors, Nararro Jr. Coll.; B.S. in Pharmacy, U. Tex.; J.D., with honors, South Tex. Coll. Law. Bar: Tex. 1972, U.S. dist. ct. (so. dist.) Fla. 1982, U.S. Supreme Ct. 1973. Pharmacist, Tidelands Hosp., Channelview, Tex., 1967-69; chief pharmacist San Jacinto Meth. Hosp., Baytown, Tex., 1969-71; sole practice, Houston, 1971—. Mem. Intertribal Council of Houston, Gulf Coast Polit. Caucus. Mem. ABA, Tex. Bar Assn., Tex. Pharm. Assn., Am. Pharm. Assn. Mem. Ch. of Christ. Criminal, Personal injury, General civil litigation. Home: 27127 Glencreek Dr Huffman TX 77336-3712 Office: 8030 Fm 1960 Rd E Humble TX 77346-1765

**FRAZZA, GEORGE S.,** lawyer, business executive; b. Paterson, N.J., Jan. 21, 1934; s. Paul T. and Myrtle Mary (Van Riper) F.; m. Marie Pollara, Sept. 17, 1955; children: Caren, Janine, Leslie, Lauren. A.B., Marietta Coll., 1955; LL.B., Columbia U., 1958. Bar: N.Y. 1959. Atty. Rogers & Wells, N.Y.C., 1958-66; atty. Johnson & Johnson, New Brunswick, N.J., 1966, assoc. gen. counsel, 1973, corp. sec., 1975, v.p., gen. counsel, 1978-97; of counsel Patterson, Belknap, Webb & Tyler, N.Y.C., 1997—. Bd. dirs. N.J. Ballet, Morristown, 1983-97. Mem. Assn. Gen. Counsel (pres.), ABA (chair elect bus. sect.), N.Y. State Bar Assn., Assn. of Bar of City of N.Y., Am. Corp. Counsel Assn., Am. Arbitration Assn. (bd. dirs.). Club: Roxiticus. General corporate. Office: Patterson Belknap Webb & Tyler 1133 Avenue of Americas New York NY 10036-6710

**FRECON, ALAIN,** lawyer; b. Casablanca, Morocco, Jan. 27, 1946; came to U.S. 1974; Diploma, Centre Notarial de Formation et D'information Professionnelle and Faculté de Droit-Paris II, 1969; Lic. en Droit, Faculté de Droit-Paris II, 1973; LLM in Internat. Bus., Stanford U., 1976; JD, William Mitchell Coll. Law, 1982. Bar: France 1968, Minn. 1982. Assoc. Ader, Rochelois & Roy, Paris, 1969-74; of counsel Jones, Bell, Simpson, & Abbott, L.A., 1976-81; assoc. Dorsey and Whitney, Mpls., 1981-85; ptnr., chmn. internat. bus. practice Popham, Haik, Schnobrich & Kaufman Ltd., 1985-92; seminar promoter and guest speaker on internat. bus. Author: (handbooks) Negotiation of International Contracts, 1984, Legal Issue of Doing Business in India, 1985, Practical Issues of Doing Business in the United States, 1986, Legal Issues of Doing Business in France, 1986, Practical Considerations in Going International, 1988, Global Markets and The Law, 1988. Reader Nat. Assn. Blind, Paris, 1973; internat. press rels. com. Valery Giscard D'Estaing campaign, Paris, 1974; vol. Stanford, Calif. Legal Aid Soc., 1975; chmn. Minn. French Festival, Mpls., 1985-86; appointed to bd. dirs. Minn. Export Fin. Authority by Gov. Perpich, 1987-91; decreed Conseiller du Commerce Exterieur to France, 1988; appointed French hon. consul for Minn., 1994. Mem. ABA, Internat. Bar Assn., Fed. Bar Assn., Minn. Bar Assn., Hennepin Bar Assn., Am. Arbitration Assn., French Am. C. of C. (bd. dirs. 1984-94, pres. 1987-90), Paris Bar. Private international, Contracts commercial, General corporate. Office: Frecon & Assocs 902 Foshay Tower 150 S 5th St Ste 2300 Minneapolis MN 55402-4223

**FREDERICI, C. CARLETON,** lawyer; b. Sioux City, Iowa, Jan. 17, 1938; s. Cecil Carleton and Lois Alida (Selzer) F.; m. Virginia A. Gregori, Oct. 14, 1961 (div.); m. Susan A. Low, Oct. 1, 1983; children: Gloria M., Carleton J., Charles W., Seth L. Student Iowa State U., 1956. BA, U. Iowa, 1960, JD with high distinction, 1965. Bar: Iowa 1965, N.Y. 1966, U.S. Dist. Ct. (no. dist.) Iowa 1968, U.S. Dist. Ct. (so. dist.) Iowa 1969, U.S. Supreme Ct. 1970, U.S. Ct. Appeals (8th cir.) 1970, U.S. Ct. Appeals (3d cir.) 1973. Assoc. firm Willkie, Farr & Gallagher, N.Y.C., 1965-68, firm Shull, Marshall & Marks, Sioux City, Iowa, 1968-69; assoc. firm Davis, Brown, Koehn, Shors & Roberts, P.C., Des Moines, 1969-71, jr. ptnr., 1971-73, sr. ptnr., 1973-90, shareholder, 1990-95, counsel, 1996—; speaker Supreme Ct. Day, Law Sch. Drake U., 1973. Contbr. articles to legal publs. Vestryman St. Luke's Ch., bd. dirs. 1976-78, 1982-85; mem. Polk County Rep. Cen. Com., 1969-71. Served to 1st lt. U.S. Army, 1961-62. Mem. ABA (chmn. 8th cir. commn. on class actions and derivative suits), Iowa Bar Assn. (chmn. prison reform com., adv. mem. fed. practice commn., litigation sect. bench and bar com.), Polk County Bar Assn. (bench and bar com.), Assn. Bar City N.Y., Am. Judicature Soc. (bd. dirs. Iowa 1990-96), Order of Coif, Wakonda Club (Des Moines). Episcopalian. Federal civil litigation, State civil litigation. Office: Davis Brown Koehn Shors & Roberts PC 666 Walnut St Ste 2500 Des Moines IA 50309-3904

**FREDERICKS, BARRY IRWIN,** lawyer; b. Bklyn., Oct. 3, 1936; m. Beverly Sharon Cohen, June 21, 1987; children from a previous marriage: Elizabeth, Jessica, Amanda, Alexander. AB, Ohio State U., 1958; JD, U. Mich., 1961. Bar: D.C. 1961, N.Y. 1965, N.J. 1972, Colo. 1992, U.S. Dist. Ct. D.C. 1961, U.S. Dist. Ct. (ea. and so. dists.) N.Y. 1965, U.S. Dist. Ct. N.J. 1972, U.S. Dist. Ct. (no. dist.) N.Y. 1985, U.S. Dist. Ct. (we. dist.) N.Y. 1991, U.S. Dist. Ct. (ea. dist.) Wis. 1985, U.S. Dist. Ct. Ariz. 1992, U.S. Dist. Ct. (we. dist.) Wis. 1996, U.S. Ct. Internat. Trade 1985, U.S. Tax Ct. 1974, U.S. Ct. Mil. Appeals, 1961, U.S. Ct. Appeals (D.C. cir.) 1961, U.S. Ct. Appeals (2nd cir.) 1965, U.S. Ct. Appeals (3rd cir.) 1978, U.S. Ct. Appeals (1st cir.) 1994, U.S. Ct. Appeals (7th cir.) 1996, U.S. Supreme Ct. 1965. Asst. chief counsel divsn. corp. fin. SEC, Washington, 1961; trial attyl divsn. civil rights U.S. Dept. Justice, Washington, 1962, asst. U.S. atty., 1962-65, U.S. commr. for D.C., 1965-66; assoc. Robinson, Silverman, Pearce, et al, N.Y.C., 1967-71; ptnr. Harris, Fredericks, et al, N.Y.C., L.A., 1971-77, Goldschmidt, Fredericks & Oshatz, N.Y.C., 1977-85; sr. ptnr. Law Office Barry I. Fredericks, N.Y.C., Englewood Cliffs, N.J., 1987—; counsel Gilberg & Kurent, Englewood Cliffs, N.J., 1996; govs. adv. com. N.J. Criminal Justice Standards and Goals, 1975-77; mem. bd. govs. N.J. State Law Enforcement Agy., 1977-79; pres., chief operating officer Operation Raleigh USA, 1983-87; lectr. on trial advocacy Practicing Law Inst., 1984—, Victorian Bar Coun., Melbourne, Australia, 1990; faculty Univ. Va. Sch. Law Trial Advocacy Inst., 1986—, Univ. Mich. Sch. Law Inst. Continuing Legal Edn., 1988-96, Nat. Inst. for Trial Advocacy, 1992—; sec. Cardoza U. Law Sch. Trial Advocacy Inst., 1993; mediator U.S. Dist. Ct. (so. dist.) N.Y., 1993. Councilman, Ridgewood, N.J., 1980-84; mem. planning bd., Ridgewood, 1980-81. Recipient William S. Brennan Jr. award U. Va. Law Sch., 1994. Mem. ABA, Assn. Trial Lawyers Am., N.Y. County Lawyer's Assn., N.Y. State Trial Lawyers Assn., Fed. Bar Assn. N.Y., N.J. Fed. Bar (v.p. 1981-90), N.J. State Bar Assn., D.C. Bar Assn. General civil litigation, Trademark and copyright, Criminal. Office: 560 Sylvan Ave Englewood Cliffs NJ 07632

**FREDERICKS, HENRY JACOB,** lawyer; b. St. Louis, Dec. 1, 1925; s. Henry Jacob III and Mary Elizabeth (Pieron) F.; m. Marjorie Helen Kiely, 1951 (div. 1962; dec.); children: Joseph Henry, James Andrew, Elizabeth Ann.; m. Susan Kay Brennecke, 1971 (div. 1991); 1 child, William Michael; m. Deborah Jean Rose, 1992; 1 child, Daniel Baptise Jerome. JD, St. Louis U., 1950; postgrad., Sch. Commerce and Fin., 1945-47. Bar: Mo. 1950, U.S. Dist. Ct. (ea. and so. dists.) Mo. 1951, U.S. Ct. Appeals (8th cir.) 1978, U.S. Supreme Ct. 1986. Pvt. practice St. Louis County, 1950-80; assoc. Mark D. Eagleton, St. Louis, 1960, Goldenhersh Fredericks & Newman, St. Louis, 1961-69, Friedman and Fredericks, St. Louis, 1969-81; chief trial atty. for cir. atty. St. Louis, 1955, 1st asst. to cir. atty. Thomas F. Eagleton, 1987, spl. asst. to cir. attys., 1960-81; asst. U.S. atty. Ea. Dist. Mo., Dept. Justice, 1981—; lectr. in field; chmn. bd. Gateway Boxing Promotions, Inc. Mem. Mo. Athletic Commn., 1974-76, boxing chmn. Mo. Athletic Commn. and AAU, 1977. Served with USAAF, 1943-46, ETO. Decorated Air medal with 4 battle stars. Mem. ABA, Mo. Bar Assn., St. Louis County Bar Assn., Am. Trial Lawyers Assn., Internat. Platform Assn., St. Louis Amateur Boxing Assn., Inc. (pres.), Delta Theta Phi. Home: 216 Woodcliffe Place Dr Chesterfield MO 63005-1518 Office: US Ct and Custom House Office US Atty Saint Louis MO 63101

**FREDERICKS, JAMES MATTHEW,** lawyer; b. Mpls., July 21, 1962; s. James Gerard and Catherine Bridget (Woods) F.; m. Barbara Ann Curran, Nov. 3, 1990; children: John G., David J., Catherine M., Bridget A. BA in Fin., U. St. Thomas, 1984; JD, Marquette U., 1987. Bar: Wis. 1987, U.S. Dist. Ct. (ea. and we. dists.) Wis. 1987. Lawyer Borgelt, Powell, Peterson & Frauen, Milw., 1987—. Author: (book chpt.) Wisconsin Trial Practice, 1999; exec. editor law rev. Marquette U., 1986-87. Mem. Def. Rsch. Inst., Wis. Bar Assn., Civil Trial Counsel of Wis. Roman Catholic. General civil litigation, Insurance, Environmental. Home: 22070 W Ridge Rd Waukesha WI 53186-5397 Office: Borgelt Powell Peterson Frauen SC 735 N Water St Ste 1500 Milwaukee WI 53202-4188

**FREDERICKS, WESLEY CHARLES, JR.,** lawyer; b. N.Y.C., Mar. 31, 1948; s. Wesley Charles and Dionysia W. (Bitsanis) F.; m. Jeanne Maria Judson, May 19, 1973; children: Carolyn Anne, Wesley Charles III. BA, Johns Hopkins U., 1970; JD, Columbia U., 1973. Bar: N.Y. 1974, Conn. 1976, U.S. Supreme Ct. 1979. Assoc. Shearman & Sterling, N.Y.C., 1973-83, Cummings & Lockwood, Stamford, Conn., 1976; chmn. bd. Lotus Performance Carps, L.P., Norwood, N.J., 1983-87; group exec. cons. Group Lotus PLC, 1987; automotive industry cons., 1988-90; pres., CEO Mfrs. Products Co., 1990-94; cousnel Gersten, Savage, Kaplowitz & Fredericks, LLP, N.Y.C., 1994, ptnr., 1995-98; ptnr. Dorsey & Whitney LLP, N.Y.C., 1998—; lawyer; b. N.Y.C., Mar. 31, 1948; s. Wesley Charles and Dionysia W. (Bitsanis) F.; m. Jeanne Maria Judson, May 19, 1973; children: Carolyn Anne, Wesley C. III. BA Johns Hopkins U., 1970; JD, Columbia U., 1973. Bar: N.Y. 1974, Conn. 1976, U.S. Supreme Ct. 1979. Assoc. Shearman & Sterling, N.Y.C., 1973-83, Cummings & Lockwood, Stamford, Conn., 1976; chmn. bd. Lotus Performance Cars, L.P., Norwood, N.J., 1983-87; group exec. cons. Group Lotus PLC, 1987; automotive industry cons., 1988-90; pres, CEO Mfrs. Products Co., 1990-94; counsel Gersten, Savage, Kaplowitz & Fredericks, LLP, N.Y.C., 1994, ptnr., 1995-98, Dorsey & Whitney LLP, N.Y.C., 1998—. Mem. Johns Hopkins U. Alumni Schs. Com. With USMC, 1968-69. Mem. ABA (co-chmn. bus. law sect. subcom. multinat. mergers and acquisitions 1996—, mem. com. on negotiated acquisitions 1997—), Mashomack Fish and Game Preserve, Campfire Am. Club (N.Y.), Weston Gun Club (Conn.), Sigma Phi Epsilon. Republican. Congregationalist. Mem. ABA (co-chmn. bus. law sect. subcom. multinat. mergers and acquisitions 1996—, mem. com. on negotiated acquisitions 1997—), Mashomack Fish and Game Preserve, Campfire Am. Club (N.Y.), Weston Golf Club (Conn.), Sigma Phi Epsilon. Republican. Congregationalist. Private international, Mergers and acquisitions, Securities. Home: 221 Benedict Hill Rd New Canaan CT 06840-2913 Office: Dorsey & Whitney LLP 250 Park Ave New York NY 10177

**FREDERICKS, WILLIAM CURTIS,** lawyer; b. Washington, July 3, 1961; s. J. Wayne and Anne Curtis Fredericks; m. Ivy Lindstrom, Jan. 21, 1995; children: Charlotte Lindstrom, Thomas Curtis. BA in Polit. Sci., Swarthmore Coll., 1983; MLitt in Internat. Rels., Oxford (Eng.) U., 1988; JD, Columbia U., 1988. Bar: N.Y. 1990, U.S. Dist. Ct. (so. and ea. dists.) N.Y. 1990, U.S. Ct. Appeals (2nd cir.) 1991, U.S. Ct. Appeals (10th cir.) 1997, U.S. Ct. Appeals (6th cir.) 1998. Law clk. hon. Robert S. Gawthrop U.S. Dist. Ct. Pa., Phila., 1988-89; assoc. Simpson Thacher & Bartlett, N.Y.C., 1989-93, Willkie Farr & Gallagher, N.Y.C., 1993-97; ptnr. Milberg Weiss Bershad Hynes & Lerach LLP, N.Y.C., 1997—; Articles editor Columbia Jour. Transnational Law, 1987-88. V.p. Swarthmore Coll. Alumni Assn., 1988-90. Mem. Assn. of the Bar of the City of N.Y. (chair com. on mil. affairs and justice 1997—). Democrat. Federal civil litigation, General civil litigation, Securities. Office: Milberg Weiss Bershad Hynes & Lerach LLP One Pennsylvania Plaza New York NY 10119-0165

**FREDERICKSEN, SCOTT L.,** lawyer; b. Williston, N.D., Sept. 20, 1952; s. Earl H. and Lillian H. Fredericksen; m. Dana Pugh, May 30, 1987; children: Jason, Anders, Erik. BA, U. N.D., 1974; JD, Boston U., 1977. Bar: Ill. 1977, U.S. Dist. Ct. (no. dist.) Ill. 1977, U.S. Ct. Appeals (7th cir.) 1978, U.S. Ct. Appeals (5th cir.) 1982, D.C. 1985, U.S. Ct. Appeals (D.C.) 1985, U.S. Ct. Appeals (4th cir.) 1989, Va. 1991, Wash. 1994, U.S. Dist. Ct. (we. dist.) Wash. 1994, U.S. Dist. Ct. (ea. dist.) Wash. 1998. Atty. Williams and Montgomery, Chgo., 1977-79, Freeman, Atkins & Coleman, Chgo., 1980-84; asst. U.S. atty. U.S. Atty.'s Office, D.C., Washington, 1984-89, U.S. Atty.'s Office, Ea. Dist. Va., Alexandria, 1989-91; assoc. ind. counsel Office of Ind. Counsel, Washington, 1991-94; ptnr. Stoel Rives LLP, Seattle, 1994—, chair L&E group. 1Mem. ABA (white collar crime, litigation and L&E sects.), AUSA (D.C. chpt.). Federal civil litigation, General civil litigation, Labor. Home: 9524 SE 68th St Mercer Island WA 98040-5119 Office: Stoel Rives LLP 600 University St Ste 3600 Seattle WA 98101-4109

**FREDERICKSON, JOHN DREW,** lawyer; b. Passaic, N.J., Oct. 28, 1956; s. C.M. and Margaret E. (Zechmeister). BS magna cum laude, Seton Hall U., 1978, JD, 1981. Bar: N.J. 1981, D.C. 1981, U.S. Dist. Ct. N.J. 1981, U.S. Supreme Ct. 1985, N.Y. 1989, U.S. Dist. Ct. N.Y. 1989. Ptnr. Carmel, Daub & Frederickson, Ft. Lee, N.J., 1980—. Assoc. editor Seton Hall U. Law Rev., 1980-81. Mem. ABA, NSPE, N.J. Bar Assn., Bergen County Bar Assn., Essex County Bar Assn., Assn. Trial Lawyers Am., N.J. Trial Lawyers Assn., Internat. Soc. Law, Pi Sigma Alpha, Phi Alpha Theta. Republican. Roman Catholic. Avocations: golf, collecting coins, collecting stamps, tennis. Home: 37 Glendale St Nutley NJ 07110-1219 Office: Carmel Daub & Frederickson 2200 Fletcher Ave Fort Lee NJ 07024-5005

**FREDERIKSEN, PAUL ASGER,** lawyer; b. Copenhagen, June 1, 1946; came to U.S., 1954; s. George A. and Valborg (Andersen) F.; m. Brenda Jane Pazaricky; children: Cassandra, Anders. BA, U. Kans., 1970; postgrad., So. Bapt. Sem., Louisville, 1971; JD, U. Colo., 1976. Bar: Colo. 1976. Pvt. practice Boulder and Denver, Colo., 1976-81; assoc. Hemminger & Frederiksen, Englewood, Colo., 1981-82, ptnr., 1982-86, mng. ptnr., 1986-89; pvt. practice Parker, Colo., 1989—. Chmn. tnr. com. Longs Park coun. Boy Scouts Am., Greeley, 1975-77; founder, chmn. bd. Christian Conciliation Svc. Denver, 1980—. Mem. ABA, Colo. Bar Assn. (chmn. tech. com. 1988-89, mem. bd. govs. 1990-92, mem. long-range planning com. 1992), Douglas County Bar Assn. (pres. 1989), Am. Arbitration Assn., Christian Legal Soc. (mem. conciliation com. 1980-86). Avocations: camping, biking, computers. E-mail: maclaw@uswest.net. Fax: 303-841-4564. Family and matrimonial, General practice, Estate planning. also: 250 Steele St Ste 303 Denver CO 80206-5200

**FREDMAN, HOWARD S,** lawyer; b. St. Louis, Feb. 1, 1944; s. Manuel and Sydine Fredman; children: Jocelyn Bly, Amber Alexandra, Cameron Penn. BA, Princeton U., 1966; JD, Columbia U., 1969. Bar: Calif. 1970, U.S. Dist. Ct. (no. dist.) Calif. 1970, U.S. Ct. Appeals (9th cir.) 1970, U.S. Dist. Ct. (so. dist.) Calif. 1974, U.S. Dist. Ct. (ctrl. dist.) Calif. 1975, U.S. Dist. Ct. (ea. dist.) Calif. 1997. Law clk. to Hon. Milton Pollack U.S. Dist. Ct. (so. dist.) N.Y., 1969-70; assoc. McCutchen, Doyle, Brown & Enersen, San Francisco, 1970-75; counsel, sr. atty., atty. legal divsn. Atlantic Richfield Co., L.A., 1975-87; assoc. Frandzel & Share, L.A., 1987-90; ptnr. Frandzel Share Robins & Bloom, L.A., 1991—. Mem. L.A. County Bar Assn. (chmn. antitrust sect. 1986-87, exec. com. antitrust sect. 1982—, nominating com. 1986-87). Democrat. Jewish. General civil litigation, Banking, Antitrust. Office: 1875 Century Park East Ste 2200 Los Angeles CA 90067

**FREDRICKSON, ROBERT ALAN,** lawyer; b. Rockford, Ill., June 1, 1945; s. Robert D. and M. Maxine (Klenner) F.; m. Carol A. Janicki; children: Kristen D., Karen J., Robert S. BBA with honors, U. Wis.-Madison, 1967, JD with honors, 1971. Bar: Wis. 1971, Ill. 1971, U.S. Dist. Ct. (we. dist.) Wis. 1971, U.S. Dist. Ct. (no. dist.) Ill. 1971, U.S. Supreme Ct. 1983. Assoc. Reno, Zahm, Folgate, Lindberg & Powell, Rockford, 1971-74; ptnr. Reno, Zahm, Folgate, Lindberg & Powell, 1974—. Mem. ABA, Am. Arbitration Assn., State Bar Wis., Assn. Trial Lawyers Am., Ill. Trial Lawyers Assn., Winnebago County Bar Assn., Rotary. Congregationalist. Avocations: fishing, outdoor activities, house construction, downhill skiing. General civil litigation, Personal injury, Insurance. Home: 4106 Eaton Dr Rockford IL 61114-6123 Office: Reno Zahm Folgate Lindberg & Powell 1415 E State St Ste 905 Rockford IL 61104-2333

**FREE, E. LEBRON,** lawyer; b. Cleveland, Tenn., Jan. 27, 1940; s. James D. and Mary Kathleen (Hunt) F.; children: Jason LeBron, Ryan Edward. BA, Berea Coll., 1963; ThM, So. Meth. U., 1966; JD, Okla. City U., 1974. Bar: Ga. 1974, Fla. 1975, U.S. Dist. Ct. (mid. dist.) Fla. 1975, U.S. Supreme Ct. 1975. Litigation atty. Jim Walter Corp., Tampa, Fla., 1975-79; prin. E. Lebron Free, P.A., Clearwater, Fla., 1980—. Editor Res. IPSA Loquitur, 1996—. Bd. dirs. Ye Mystice Krewe of Neptune, Pinellas County, Fla., 1980-90, capt., 1984; bd. dirs. Hospice of the Fla. Suncoast, 1981-91; chmn., 1984; mem. Met. Planning Orgn., Pinellas County, 1984, Zoning Bd., Clearwater, 1984; bd. dirs. Family Svc. Ctrs., 1993—. Mem. ABA, ATLA, Canakaris Inns of Ct. (bd. dirs. 1997—), Fla. Bar Assn. (family law sect., chmn. fee arbitration com. 1991), Fla. Acad. Trial Lawyers, Clearwater Bar Assn., Rotary (Paul Harris fellow 1992), Masons. Avocation: sailing. Fax: 727-724-3708. Family and matrimonial, Probate, Personal injury. Office: 2725 Park Dr Ste 3 Clearwater FL 33763-1023

**FREE, ROBERT ALAN,** lawyer; b. San Diego, July 29, 1946; s. Albert Joe and Nelly Fay (Cox) F.; m. Carolyn Corker, Apr. 21, 1970; children: Brian, Tyler, Jay. BA, U. Calif., Berkeley, 1969; MA, Stanford U., 1970; JD, U. Wash., 1975. Bar: Wash. 1975, U.S. Dist. Ct. (we. dist.) Wash. 1975, U.S. Ct. Appeals (9th cir.) 1983, U.S. Dist. Ct. Hawaii, 1993, U.S. Supreme Ct. 1996. Of counsel Damon Key Bocken Leong & Kupchak, Honolulu, 1991-93; ptnr. MacDonald, Hoague & Bayless, Seattle, 1975-91, 93—. Co-author: Visa Processing Guide, 1996; contbr. articles to law jours. Mem. legal com. ACLU, Seattle, 1975-98; pres. Wash. Citizens for Abortion Reform, Seattle, 1978; bd. dirs. Planned Parenthood Seattle-King County, 1988-91; mem. adv. com. Compassion in Dying, Seattle, 1997—. Mem. Am. Immigration Lawyers Assn. (pres. Wash. chpt. 1985-86, nat. bd. dirs. 1988-91), King County Bar Assn. Immigration, naturalization, and customs. Office: MacDonald Hoague & Bayless 705 2nd Ave Ste 1500 Seattle WA 98104-1745

**FREEBERG, ERIC OLAFUR,** lawyer, real estate developer, venture capitalist; b. L.A., Dec. 14, 1951; s. George F. and Inga M. Freeberg; m. Sandra L. Durrett, Aug. 19, 1972; children: Larisa, Kristina, Jon. BA in History, U. Calif., Santa Cruz, 1974; JD, U. Calif., Berkeley, 1979. Ptnr. Luce, Forward, Hamilton & Scripps, San Diego, 1979-92; pvt. practice Rancho Santa Fe, 1992—; real estate developer, 1982—; pres., chmn. various cos. U.S., 1984—; mediator Calif., 1993—. Pro bono counsel, mem. Bethlehem Luth. Ch., Encinitas, Calif., 1982—; mem. fin. com. various Rep. candidates. Mem. Calif. Bar Assn., San Diego County Bar Assn., San Diego Dispute Resolution Forum, Calif. Dispute Resolution Forum, La Jolla Golden Triangle Rotary Club (charter mem. dist. 5340 San Diego County 1986—), La Jolla Beach and Tennis Club. Republican. Lutheran. Avocations: fishing, coaching Little League. Real property. Home: PO Box 8884 Rancho Santa Fe CA 92067-8884 Office: PO Box 9440 Rancho Santa Fe CA 92067-4440

**FREED, DANIEL JOSEF,** law educator; b. New York, May 12, 1927; s. Julius Leon and Sara (Lobel) F.; m. Judith Darrow, June 30, 1967; children: Peter Jacob, Emily Sara; children from previous marriage: Jonathan Michael, Amy. BS, Yale U., 1948, LLB, 1951; LLD (hon.), New England Coll., 1994. Bar: N.Y. 1952, D.C. 1953, U.S. Supreme Ct. 1955. Atty.-investigator, preparedness subcom., com. on armed svcs., U.S. Senate, Washington, 1951-52; assoc. Ford, Bergson, Adams & Borkland, Washington, 1952-59; sr. trial atty. antitrust divsn. U.S. Dept. Justice, Washington, 1959-64, assoc. dir. office of criminal justice, 1964-66, acting dir., 1966-68, dir., 1968-69; prof. law and its adminstrn. Yale U., New Haven, 1969-75, clin. prof., 1975-94, clin. prof. emeritus, profl. lectr. in law, 1994—; dir. clin. program law Yale U., 1969-72, dir. Daniel and Florence Guggenheim program in criminal justice, 1972-87, dir. criminal sentencing program, 1988-96. Co-author: (with Wald) Bail in the United States: 1964, publ.1964; editor (periodical) Fed. Sentencing Reporter, 1988—; contbr. articles to profl. jours. Trustee Vera Inst. Justice, N.Y., 1970—; pres. Yale Law Sch. Assn. Washington, 1968. With USN, 1945-46. Recipient Glenn R. Winters award Am. Judges Assn., 1992. Democrat. Jewish. Avocations: metal sculpture, swimming. Home: 226 Lawrence St New Haven CT 06511-2419 Office: Yale Law Sch 127 Wall St PO Box 208215 New Haven CT 06520-8215

**FREED, EVAN PHILLIP,** lawyer; b. L.A., Sept. 11, 1946; s. Joseph Yale and Miriam Freed. BA, Calif. State U., L.A., 1970; JD, U. West L.A., 1978. Bar: Calif. 1979. Dep. pub. defender L.A. County Pub. Defender, 1982-87; criminal def. atty. Alt. Def. Counsel, L.A., 1987-95; criminal prosecutor City Atty., L.A., 1995-97; pvt. practice law Marina Del Rey, Calif., 1997—. Mem. Calif. Pub. Defenders Assn., L.A. County Bar, Masons. Republican. Jewish. Avocation: computer internet. Fax: (209) 821-5404. Criminal, Immigration, naturalization, and customs. Office: PO Box 11415 Marina Dl Rey CA 90295-7415

**FREED, KENNETH ALAN,** lawyer; b. Buffalo, Apr. 28, 1957; s. Sherwood E. and Renee (Liebesman) F.; m. Odette Ashley Freed; children: David Benjamin, Daniel Lawrence. BA in Econs. magna cum laude, Boston U., 1979; JD, U. Chgo., 1982. Bar: Calif. 1982, U.S. Dist. Ct. (no. dist.) Calif., 1982. Prin., shareholder Feldman, Waldman & Kline, San Francisco, 1982-95; sr. v.p., gen. counsel Sydran Svcs., Inc., San Ramon, Calif., 1995—. Mem. ABA, Calif. Bar Assn. Franchising, Contracts commercial, Mergers and acquisitions. Home: 3291 Blackhawk Meadow Dr Danville CA 94506-5805 Office: 3000 Executive Pkwy Ste 515 San Ramon CA 94583-2399

**FREEDLANDER, BARRETT WALTER,** lawyer; b. Pitts., Oct. 7, 1941; s. Maurice Philip and Leah (Stark) F.; m. Laura Loewenstein, May 21, 1971; children: John, David, Laura. BA, U. Pa., 1962; LLB, U. Md., Balt., 1965. Bar: Md. 1965. Law clk. to Edward S. Northrop U.S. Dist. Ct., Balt., 1965-66; asst. states atty. State of Md., Balt., 1967-68; from assoc. to ptnr. Niles, Barton & Wilmer, Balt., 1969-87; ptnr. Weinberg & Green, Balt., 1988—; gen. counsel Balt. Life Ins., Owings Mills, Md., 1997—. Trustee Balt. Mus. Art, 1993—; bd. dirs.— U.S. Lacrosse, 1993, pres. 1997-98. Served wih U.S. Army, 1965-72. Recipient Alumni award of merit U. Pa., 1996, H. Hunter Lott award, 1993. Mem. ABA, Md. State Bar Assn., Assn. Ski Def. Attys. (pres. 1992), Def. Rsch. Inst., Assn. Life Ins. Counsel, Md. League Life and Health Insurers (bd. dirs. 1997—), Md. Life and Health Guaranty Assn. (bd. dirs. 1997—). Avocations: skiing, squash, fly fishing, reading, U. Pa. activities. Federal civil litigation, General civil litigation, State civil litigation.

**FREEDMAN, BART JOSEPH,** lawyer; b. New Haven, Sept. 27, 1955; s. Lawrence Zelic and Dorothy (Robinson) F.; m. Esme Detweiler, Sept. 28, 1985; children: Luke Edward, Samuel Meade, Benjamin Zelic. BA, Carleton Coll., 1977; JD, U. Pa., 1982. Bar: Wash. 1984, U.S. Dist. Ct. (we. dist.) Wash. 1984, U.S. Ct. Appeals (9th cir.) 1985, U.S. Dist. Ct. (ea. dist.) Wash. 1988. Law clk. to chief justice Samuel Roberts Supreme Ct. Pa., Erie, 1982-83; asst. city solicitor City of Phila., 1984; assoc. Perkins Coie, Seattle, 1984-90; ptnr. Preston Gates & Ellis, Seattle, 1990—. Editor: Natural Resource Damages, 1993. Bd. dirs. Seattle Metrocenter YMCA, 1988-97, chmn. 1993-97; bd. dirs. Leadership Tomorrow, 1996-97; chair Sierra Club Inner City Outings Program, Seattle, 1986-90; chmn. bd. advisors Earth Svc. Corps/YMCA, Seattle, 1990-97. Mem. ABA (com. on corp. counsel 1985—), Wash. State Bar Assn., Seattle-King County Bar Assn. (participant neighborhood legal clinics 1985-94). Environmental, Federal civil litigation, General civil litigation. Office: Preston Gates & Ellis 701 5th Ave Ste 5000 Seattle WA 98104-7078

**FREEDMAN, BERNARD BENJAMIN,** lawyer; b. Buffalo, July 18, 1939; s. Isadore and Clare (Sugarman) F.; m. Lynda Lee Bargman, July 3, 1963; children: Amy, Andrew, Betsy. Student, U. Buffalo, 1957-60; JD, SUNY, Buffalo, 1964. Bar: N.Y. 1964, U.S. Dist. Ct. (we. dist.) N.Y. 1965, U.S. Supreme Ct. 1982. Assoc. Maidy, Donnelly & Manchester, Buffalo, 1964-65, Lesher, Howitt, Manchester & Jenkins, Buffalo, 1965-66, Lippes & Kaminsky, Buffalo, 1966-70; chief civil div. Legal Aid Bur. Inc., Buffalo, 1970-81; pvt. practice Kenmore, N.Y., 1970-82; hearing examiner Erie County Family Ct., Buffalo, 1982; ptnr. Norton Radin Hoover Freedman, Kenmore, 1982-96, sole proprietor, 1996—; pres. Legal Aid Bur., Buffalo, Inc. Past mem. bd. editors Buffalo Law Rev. Past bd. dirs. Temple Shaarey Zedek. Mem. ABA, N.Y. State Bar Assn. (mem. ho. of delegates), Erie County Bar Assn. (past bd. dirs., former pres.), SUNY at Buffalo Law Sch. Alumni Assn. (past mem. bd. dirs., chmn. bd. ethics), Greater Buffalo Track Club. Democrat. Jewish. Avocation: marathon runner. General civil litigation, Family and matrimonial, Personal injury. Home: 74 Heritage Rd W Buffalo NY 14221-2314 Office: Norton Radin Hoover Freedman 2858 Delaware Ave Buffalo NY 14217-2733

**FREEDMAN, FRANK HARLAN,** federal judge; b. Springfield, Mass., Dec. 15, 1924; s. Alvin Samuel and Ida Hilda (Rosenberg) F.; m. Eleanor Labinger, July 26, 1953; children: Joan Robin Goodman, Wendy Beth Greedman Mackler, Barry Alan. LL.B., Boston U., 1949, LL.M., 1950; Ph.D. (hon.), Western New Eng. Coll., Springfield, 1970. Pvt. practice law, 1950-68; mayor City of Springfield, 1968-72; judge U.S. Dist. Ct. Mass., Springfield, 1972-86, chief judge, 1986-92; now sr. judge, 1992—. Chmn. fund raising drs. Muscular Dystrophy, Leukemia Soc.; mem. Susan Auchter Kidney Fund Raising Com.; mem. Springfield City Council, 1960-67, pres., 1962; del. Republican Nat. Conv., 1964, 68; mem. Springfield Rep. Com., 1959-72. Served with USNR, 1943-46. Greenaway Drive Elem. Sch. rededicated as Frank H. Freedman Sch., 1974; recipient Silver Shingle award for disting. service Boston U., 1984. Mem. Hampden County (Mass.) Bar Assn., Lewis Marshall Club on Jurisprudence (pres.). Jewish. Office: US Dist Ct 1550 Main St Rm 525 Springfield MA 01103-1428

**FREEDMAN, HELEN EDELSTEIN,** justice; b. New York, N.Y., Dec. 15, 1942; d. David Simeon and Frances (Fisher) Edelstein; m. Henry A. Freedman, June 7, 1964; children: Katherine Eleanor, Elizabeth Sarah. BA, Smith Coll., 1963; JD, NYU, 1967. Bar: N.Y. 1970, U.S. Dist. Ct. (so. and ea. dists.), U.S. Supreme Ct. 1979. Staff atty. office of gen. counsel Am. Arbitration Assn., N.Y.C., 1967-69; assoc. Hubbel, Cohen & Stiefel, N.Y.C.,

1970-71, Shaw, Bernstein, Scheuer, Boyden & Sarnoff, N.Y.C., 1971-74; law sec. Civil Ct., N.Y.C., 1974-76; sr. atty. housing litigation bur. N.Y.C. Dept. Housing Preservation and Devel., 1976; supervising atty. Dist. Coun. 37 Legal Svcs. Plan, N.Y.C., 1976-78; judge Civil Ct., N.Y.C., 1979-88; acting justice Supreme Ct., N.Y.C., 1984-88, justice, 1989-95; apptd. to appellate term 1st dept. NY Supreme Ct., N.Y.C., 1995—; co-chair State Judges Mass Tort Litigation Com.; mem. pattern jury instrns. com., Supreme Ct. Justices; adj. prof. N.Y. Law Sch., 1999; lectr. in field. Author: New York Objections, 1999; contbr. articles to profl. jours. Fellow Am. Bar Found.; mem. ABA (chair small claims ct. com. 1986-89, bioethics com. nat. conf. spl. ct. judges, N.Y. State Ct. del. to ann. meetings, nat. conf. spl. ct. judges, 1987, 88, Spl. Cts. Conf. award 1987, 88, 93, Jud. Excellence award 1998), Nat. Assn. Women Judges, N.Y. State Bar Assn., N.Y. Women's Bar Assn., N.Y. State Assn. Women Judges (pres. 1995-97), Assn. of Bar of City of N.Y. (mem. various coms., chair com. med. malpractice, v.p. 1994-95). Home: 150 W 96th St New York NY 10025-6469 Office: NY Supreme Ct 60 Centre St Fl 1 New York NY 10007-1488

**FREEDMAN, IRVING MELVIN,** lawyer; b. Aug. 18, 1928; s. Max and Celia (Cooperstock) F.; m. Daryl Nadine Siegel, July 6, 1952; children: Debbie, Wendy. BSEE, Northeastern U., 1954; JD with hons., George Washington U., D.C., 1958. Bar: U.S. Patent and Trademark Office 1957, Mass. 1958, D.C. 1962, U.S. Ct. Appeals (fed. cir.) 1962, U.S. Supreme Ct. 1964, N.C. 1988. Engring. trainee GE, Lynn, Mass., 1953-55; patent atty. trainee GE Patent Operation, Washington, 1955-56; patent atty GE Instruments, Lynn, Mass., 1958-62; patent counsel GE Elec. Aerospace, Utica, N.Y., 1962-81, GE Semiconductor, Rsch. Triangle, N.C., 1981-84; intellectual property counsel GE Indsl. Electronics, Charlottesville, Va., 1984-88; intellectual property lawyer pvt. practice, Chapel Hill, N.C., 1988—; consultant, patent prosecution GE Med. Florence, S.C., 1992—; expert witness, cons., various law firms, N.C., 1996—. With USCG, 1946-49. Mem. Am. Intellectual Property Law Assn. (life), Carolina Intellectual Property Law Assn., Licensing Execs. Soc. (varous coms. 1964—). Avocations: travel, continuing education. Intellectual property, Patent. Home and Office: 33 Wedgewood Rd Chapel Hill NC 27514-9025

**FREEDMAN, MARYANN SACCOMANDO,** lawyer; b. Buffalo, N.Y., Sept. 12, 1934; d. James Vincent and Rosaria (Rizzo) Saccomando; m. Robert Paul Freedman, Apr. 9, 1961; children: Brenda Marie, Donald Vincent. JD, U. Buffalo, 1958. Bar: N.Y. 1959, U.S. Dist. Ct. (we. dist.) N.Y. 1959, U.S. Supreme Ct. 1963. Law clk. Saperston McNaughton & Saperston, Buffalo, 1957-59, assoc., 1959-61; ptnr. Freedman & Freedman, Buffalo, 1961-75; confidential legal rsch. asst. Buffalo City Ct., 1972-75; asst. atty. gen. N.Y. State Dept. Law, Buffalo, 1977-90; spl. counsel Lavin & Kleiman, Buffalo, 1991-95; of counsel Cohen & Lombardo, P.C., Buffalo, 1995—, 1995—; asst. prof. Erie C.C., Buffalo, 1975-76; lectr. Erie County Emergency Med. Technician Program, Buffalo, 1975-83, Buffalo and Erie County Police Acad., 1975-86; referee N.Y. State. Jud. Conduct Commn., 1998—. Bd. editors N.Y. State Bar Jour., 1983-97. Founder, panel mem. Alliance for Dispute Resolution, 1997—; trustee YMCA, Buffalo, 1982-87; chmn. United Way Task Force on Legal Svcs., Buffalo, 1983; chair Buffalo Philharm. Orch. Stabilization Com., 1991-94; mem. dean's adv. coun. sch. law State U. Buffalo, 1991-93; bd. dirs. Downtown Nursing Home, Buffalo, 1982-91, Better Bus. Bur., Buffalo, 1983-92; mem. Gov.'s Departmental and Statewide Jud. Screening coms., 1997—, Jud. Compensation Commn., 1997—; co-host Ask Women radio, 1996-98. Recipient Buffalo Bison award City of Buffalo, 1976, Legal Svcs. for Elderly and Handicapped award, 1986, SUNY Buffalo Disting. Alumni award, 1986, Hilbert Coll. Pres.'s medal, 1987, Wise Woman award Nat. Orgn. Italian-Am. Women, 1987, Barrister award Nat. Columbus Day Com., 1987, Westchester Legal Svcs. award, 1987; named Outstanding Woman in Law, U. Buffalo Cmty. Adv. Coun., 1984, Outstanding Citizen Buffalo News, 1986, Disting. Alumnus, U. Buffalo Law Alumni, 1988, Woman of Yr. Buffalo Philharm. Orch., 1993. Mem. ABA (ho. dels. 1986—), N.Y. State Bar Assn. (pres-elect, chair ho. of dels. 1986-87, pres. 1987-88, Ruth G. Schapiro award 1994), N.Y. State Bar Found. (bd. dirs., v.p. 1994-97, pres. 1997—), Erie County Bar Assn. (pres. 1981-82, Spl. Svc. award 1984, Lawyer of Yr. 1987), Cattaraugus County Bar Assn. (Law Day award 1986), Assn. of Italian-Am. Women of West N.Y. (Lifetime Achievement award 1999), Aid to Indigent Prisoners Soc. (pres. 1981-82), Women Lawyers Assn. Western N.Y. (pres. 1962-64), Buffalo Geol. Soc. (treas. 1999). Clubs: Zonta (pres. 1978-79, area dir. dist. IV 1979-80, 82-83). General practice, General civil litigation, Family and matrimonial. Office: 343 Elmwood Ave Buffalo NY 14222-2203

**FREEDMAN, MONROE HENRY,** lawyer, educator, columnist; b. Mt. Vernon, N.Y., Apr. 10, 1928; s. Chauncey and Dorothea (Kornblum) F.; m. Audrey Willock, Sept. 24, 1950 (dec. 1998); children: Alice Freedman Korngold, Sarah Freedman Izquierdo, Caleb (dec. 1992), Judah. AB cum laude, Harvard U., 1951, LLB, 1954, LLM, 1956. Bar: Mass. 1954, Pa. 1957, D.C. 1960, U.S. Dist. Ct. (ea. dist. N.Y.), U.S. Ct. Appeals (D.C. cir.) 1960, U.S. Supreme Ct. 1960, U.S. Ct. Appeals (2d cir.) 1968, N.Y. 1978, U.S. Ct. Appeals (9th cir.) 1982, U.S. Ct. Appeals (11th cir.) 1986, U.S. Ct. Appeals (Fed. cir.) 1987. Assoc. Wolf, Block, Schorr & Solis-Cohen, Phila., 1956-58; ptnr. Freedman & Temple, Washington, 1969-73; dir. Stern Community Law Firm, Washington, 1970-71; prof. law George Washington U., 1958-73; dean Hofstra Law Sch., Hempstead, N.Y., 1973-77, prof. law, 1973—, Howard Lichtenstein Disting. prof. legal ethics, 1989—; Drinko-Baker & Hostetler chair in law Cleve. State U., 1992; faculty asst. Harvard U. Law Sch., 1954-56, instr. trial advocacy, 1978—; lectr. on lawyers' ethics; exec. dir. U.S. Holocaust Meml. Coun., 1980-82, gen. counsel, 1982-83, sr. adviser to chmn., 1982-87; cons. U.S. Commn. on Civil Rights, 1960-64, Neighborhood Legal Services Program, 1970; legis. cons. to Senator John L. McClellan, 1959; spl. com. on courtroom conduct N.Y.C. Bar Assn., 1972; exec. dir. Criminal Trial Inst., 1965-66; expert witness on legal ethics state and fed. ct. proceedings, U.S. Senate and House Coms., U.S. Dept. Justice, FDIC; spl. investigator Rochester Inst. Tech., 1991; reporter Am. Lawyer's Code of Conduct, 1979-81; mem. Arbitration panel U.S. Dist. Ct. (ea. dist.) N.Y., 1986—; Inaugural Wickwire lectr. Dalhousie Law Sch., N.S., 1992; lectr. S.C. Bar Found., 1993, numerous profl. confs; adv. subgroup on ethics U.S. Dist. Ct. (ea. dist.) N.Y., 1994-96. Author: Contracts, 1973, Lawyers' Ethics in an Adversary System, 1975 (ABA gavel award, cert. of merit 1976), Teacher's Manual Contracts, 1978, American Lawyer's Code of Conduct, 1981, Understanding Lawyers' Ethics, 1990, Group Defamation and Freedom of Speech—The Relationship Between Language and Violence, 1995; co-editor; columnist Cases and Controversies, Am. Lawyer Media, 1990-96, (with Supreme Ct. Justice Ruth Bader Ginsburg) Freedom, Life, & Death: Materials on Comparative Constitutional Law, 1997; television appearances include Donohue, CNN Money Line, CBS 60 Minutes, CNN Late Edition, Court TV, and others; contbr. articles to profl. jours. Recipient Martin Luther King Jr. Humanitarian award, 1987, The Lehman-LaGuardia Award for Civic Achievement, 1996. Fellow Am. Bar Found. (life); mem. ABA (ethics adv. to chair criminal justice sect. 1993—, Michael Franck award 1998), ACLU (nat. bd. dirs. 1970-80, nat. adv. coun. 1980—, spl. litigation counsel 1971-73), Am. Law Inst. (consultative group on the law governing lawyers, 1990-99, consultative group on Uniform Comml. Code art. 2 1990—), Soc. Am. Law Tchrs. (mem. governing bd. 1974-79, exec. com. 1976-79, chmn. com. on profl. responsibility 1974-79, 87-90), ABA (vice chmn. ethical considerations com. criminal justice sect. 1989-90, ethics advisor to chmn. criminal justice sect., 1993-96), N.Y. State Bar Assn. (com. on legal edn. and admission to bar 1988-92, criminal justice sect. com. on profl. responsibility, 1990-92, award for Dedication to Scholarship and pub. svc. 1997), Assn. Bar City N.Y. (com. on profl. responsibility 1987-90, com. on profl. and jud. ethics 1991-92), Fed. Bar Assn. (chmn. com. on profl. disciplinary standards and procedures 1970-71), Am. Jewish Congress (nat. governing coun. 1984-86), Am. Arbitration Assn. (arbitrator, nat. panel arbitrators 1964—, cert. svc. award 1986), Nat. Network on Right to Counsel (exec. bd., exec. com. 1986-90), Nat. Prison Project (steering com. 1970-90), Nat. Assn. Criminal Def. Lawyers (vice chmn. ethics adv. com. 1991-93, co-chmn., 1994). Democrat. Jewish.

**FREEDMAN, RANDALL LEE,** lawyer; b. St. Louis, Mar. 19, 1948; s. Leon Joseph and Hope Delores (Wright) F.; 1 child, Jacqueline Hope. BA, S.E. Mo. State U., 1970; JD, U. Mo., 1973. Bar: Mo. 1973, U.S. Dist. Ct. (ea. dist.) Mo. 1974, Tex. 1975, U.S. Dist. Ct. (no. dist.) Tex. 1976, U.S. Ct. Appeals (5th and 8th cirs.) 1977. Law clk. to Hon. H. Kenneth Wangelin Fed. Dist. Ct. Ea. Dist. Mo., 1973-74; asst. house counsel Nat. Chemsearch Corp., Irving, Tex., 1974-75; assoc. Douglas J. Brooks, Dallas, 1975-76; sole practitioner Dallas, 1977—. Contbr. articles to profl. jours. Regents scholar S.E. Mo. State U., 1966, Gramling scholar, 1969, Ulysses Grant Dubach scholar, 1968. Mem. State Bar Tex., Mo. Bar, Dallas Bar Assn., Phi Alpha Theta. Avocations: tennis, running, reading, writing. Banking, Consumer commercial, Contracts commercial. Office: 4026 Lemmon Ave Dallas TX 75219-3736

**FREEDMAN, WALTER,** lawyer; b. St. Louis, Oct. 30, 1914; s. Sam and Sophie (Gordon) F.; m. Maxine Weil, June 23, 1940; children—Jay W., Sandra Freedman Sabel. A.B., Washington U., 1937, J.D., 1937; LL.M., Harvard, 1938. Bar: Mo. bar, Ill. bar, D.C. bar. Atty. SEC, Washington, 1938-40, U.S. Dept. Interior, Washington, 1940-42; chief counsel Office Export Control, Foreign Econ. Adminstrn., 1942-44, dir., 1944-45; partner Freedman, Levy, Kroll & Simonds (and predecessor firm), Washington, 1946—; Fairchild fellow Harvard U. Law Sch., 1937-38. Editor-in-chief: Washington U. Law Quarterly, 1936-37; Contbr. articles to profl. jours. Decorated chevalier de l'Order de la Couronne (Belgium), 1950; recipient Disting. Alumni award Washington U. Sch. Law, 1995. Mem. Washington Bd. Trade, Am. Law Inst., ABA, Fed. Bar Assn., D.C. Bar Assn., Woodmont country Club (bd. mgrs.), Cosmos Club, Phi Beta Kappa, Omicron Delta Kappa, Phi Sigma Alpha. Jewish (trustee temple). Administrative and regulatory, General corporate, Probate. Home: 4545 W St NW Washington DC 20007-5315 Office: 1050 Connecticut Ave NW Washington DC 20036-5366

**FREEHLING, DANIEL JOSEPH,** law educator, law library director; b. Montgomery, Ala., Nov. 13, 1950; s. Saul Irving and Grace (Lieberman) L. BS, Huntingdon Coll., 1972; JD, U. Ala., 1975, MLS, 1977. Ref. libr., asst. to assoc. dean U. Ala. Sch. Law, Tuscaloosa, 1975-77; assoc. law libr. U. Md., Balt., 1977-79, Cornell U., Ithaca, N.Y., 1979-82; law libr. dir., assoc. prof. U. Maine, Portland, 1982-86; law libr. dir., assoc. prof. law Boston U., 1986-92, prof., 1992—, assoc. dean for adminstrn., 1993-97, 99—; mem. steering com., law program com. Rsch. Librs. Group, 1989-91; treas. New Eng. Law Libr. Consortium, 1989-91; vice chair, chair-elect sect. on law librs. Assn. Am. Law Schs., 1990-91, chair, 1992. Mem. ABA (accreditation com. 1995—), Am. Assn. Law Librs. (chair acad. law librs. spl. interest sect. 1981-82, edn. com. 1982-83, membership com. 1983-84, program chair 1987-88, local arrangements co-chair 1992-93, chair mentoring and retention com. 1995-96). Home: 6 Priscilla Ln Winchester MA 01890-4021 Office: Boston U Law Sch Pappas Law Libr 765 Commonwealth Ave Boston MA 02215-1401

**FREELAND, CHARLES,** lawyer, accountant; b. Balt., July 18, 1940; s. Benjamin and Beatrice (Polakoff) F.; m. Beverly Klaff, July 15, 1965; children—Stephen Jason, Jennifer Jill, Gwen Nicole, Kimberly Suzanne. B.S., U. Md., 1962, LL.B., 1965; diploma U.S. Naval Justice Sch., 1966. Bar: Md. 1965, U.S. Dist. Ct. Md. 1965, U.S. Tax Ct. 1966, U.S. Ct. Mil. Apls. 1966, U.S. Ct. Claims 1968, U.S. Supreme Ct. 1969, U.S. Ct. Appeals (4th cir.) 1974. Fin. v.p. Collins Electronics Mfg. Co.; dir. fin. planning Cellu-Craft, Inc., Stevensville, Md., 1963-65; controller Braun-Crystal Mfg. Co., Inc., Middle Village, N.Y., 1969-70, BCN Design Products, Inc., Bayshore, N.Y., 1969-70; asst. city solicitor City of Balt., 1972-82; pvt. practice law and acctg., Balt., 1971-93; ptnr. Kaplan, Freeland & Schwartz, Balt., 1982-86; pres. Charles Freeland, PC, 1986—. Served to lt. USNR, 1965-68. Mem. Am. Judicature Soc., Am. Assn. Attys.-CPA's, ABA, Md. Bar Assn., Balt. County Bar Assn., Am. Assn. CPA's, Md. Assn. CPA's, Am. Arbitration Assn. (nat. panel 1970—). Democrat. Jewish. Club: Woodholme Country. Corporate taxation, General corporate, Personal income taxation. Home: PO Box 422 4 Timothys Green Ct Brooklandville MD 21022 Office: 1300 York Rd Ste 180 Lutherville Timonium MD 21093-6806

**FREELAND, JAMES M. JACKSON,** lawyer, educator; b. Miami, Fla., Feb. 17, 1927; s. Byron Brazil and Mary Helen (Jackson) F.; m. Valerie; children: Carole Leigh, Thomas Byron, James Jackson Jr. AB, Duke U., 1950; JD, U. Fla., Gainesville, 1954; postgrad. fellow, Yale U. Law Sch., 1960-61. Bar: Fla. 1954. Assoc. firm Dowling & Culverhouse, Jacksonville, 1954-57; mem. faculty Law Sch. U. Fla., Gainesville, 1957-60, 61-62, 65—, prof. law, 1970-95; dir. grad. tax law program U. Fla., 1977-82, disting. svc. prof. law, emeritus, 1995—, prof. emeritus, 1995—; of counsel August & Kulunas, P.A., West Palm Beach, Fla., 1995—; prof. law NYU Law Sch., 1963-65; vis. prof. U. Ariz. Law Sch., Tucson, 1969-70; mem. tax faculty Practicing Law Inst., 1969-76; vis. tax prof. Leiden U., The Netherlands, 1983. Co-author: Federal Income Taxation of Estates, Trusts and Beneficiaries, 1970, 3d edit., 1998, The Florida Will and Trust Manual, 1983, The Tennessee Will and Trust Manual, 1984, Fundamentals of Federal Income Taxation, 1972, 10th edit., 1998; adv. editor Jour. Corp. Taxation, 1977—, S Corp. Tax Jour., 1989—. Served with USNR, 1944-46. Named Outstanding prof. U. Fla., 1968, Outstanding Law Prof., 1970-73, 75; Designated Disting. Service Prof. Law, 1982. Mem. ABA, Am. Law Inst., Am. Coll. Tax Counsel, The Fla. Bar Tax Sect., (Outstanding Tax Lawyer State of Fla. 1982), Am. Judicature Soc., Order of Coif, Fla. Blue Key, Phi Kappa Phi. Republican. Methodist. Home: 7700 NW 41st Ave Gainesville FL 32606-4114 *Always be aware of others, but compete only with yourself.*

**FREELAND, JOHN HALE,** lawyer; b. Oxford, Miss., Dec. 20, 1956; s. Thomas Henry and Judith Lee (Hale) F.; m. Cynthia Rose Strobl, Mar. 21, 1987. BA, U. Miss., 1974, JD, 1986. Bar: Miss., U.S. Dist. Ct. (no. dist.) Miss. 1987. Law clk. Miss. Supreme Ct., Jackson, 1986-87, U.S. Dist. Ct. (no. dist.) Miss., Oxford, 1987-88; ptnr. Freeland & Freeland, Oxford, 1988-95; shareholder Markow, Walker & Reeves, P.A., Oxford, 1995—. Editor MS Lawyer, 1998-99). Elder, fin. sec., Sunday sch. tchr. 1st Presbyn. Ch., Oxford. Lt. USNR, 1979-83. Mem. ABA, Miss. Bar Assn. (dir. young lawyers div. 1993-94), Rotary. Presbyterian. Avocations: sailing, gardening. Bankruptcy, General civil litigation, Workers' compensation. Office: 6007 Harrison Ave Oxford MS 38655

**FREELS, JESSE SAUNDERS, JR.,** lawyer; b. Sherman, Tex., Feb. 8, 1943; s. Jesse Saunders Sr. and Margaret (Stout) F.; m. Valerie Wood, Jan. 16, 1971; children: J.S. "Trey" III, John Andrew. BA, BS, Howard Payne U., 1965; JD, St. Mary's U., San Antonio, 1969. Bar: Tex. 1969, U.S. Dist. Ct. (ea. and we. dists.) Tex. 1971. Asst. county atty. Grayson County, Sherman, 1969-71; ptnr. Doss, Thompson & Freels, Denison, Tex., 1971-78; judge Grayson County, Sherman, 1978-83; ptnr. Freels & Johnston, P.C., Sherman, 1983—; bd. dirs. Am. Bank of Tex., Sherman, 1975—, Tex. Ctr. for the Judiciary, Austin, 1979-83. Mem. Tex. Bar Assn., Grayson County Bar Assn., Tex. Bar Found. (life), Masons (past master Lodge 403, Denison). Banking, Bankruptcy, General civil litigation. Home: 109 Spring Valley Dr Denison TX 75020-3724 Office: Freels & Johnston PC 114 S Crockett St Sherman TX 75090-5906

**FREEMAN, ANTOINETTE ROSEFELDT,** lawyer; b. Atlantic City, Oct. 7, 1937; d. Bernard Paul and Fannie (Levin) Rosefeldt; m. Alan Richard Freeman, June 22, 1958 (div. Apr. 1979); children: Barry David, Robin Lisa. BA, Rutgers U., 1972; JD, Ind. U., 1975; LLM, Temple U., 1979. Bar: Pa. 1975, Wash. 1992, U.S. Dist. Ct. (ea. dist.) Pa. 1976, U.S. Ct. Appeals (3d cir.) 1982. Substitute tchr. Washington Twp. Sch. Dist., Indpls., 1972; dep. prosecutor intern Marion County Prosecutor, Indpls., 1974-75; asst. dist. atty. City of Phila., 1975-76; mgr. EEO Wyeth Labs., Radnor, Pa., 1976-80, SmithKline & French Labs., Phila., 1980-82; sr. counsel SmithKline Beecham Corp., Phila., 1982-91; assoc. gen. counsel Immunex Corp., 1991—; arbitrator Am. Arbitration Assn., 1976—; Counsel Regional Interests Developing Efficient Transp., 1983-85; adv. bd. Family Svc. Phila., 1980-81, Greater Phila. C. of C., 1983; pres. Croskey Ct. Condominium Assn., 1983-87; bd. dirs. Logan Sq. Neighborhood Assn., 1983-91, pres., 1985-87; v.p., sec. Friends of Logan Sq. Found., 1985-91; counsel Hapoel Games USA; chairperson Ctr. City Coalition for Quality of Life; atty. Vol. Lawyers for the Arts, Phila., 1985-91; bd. dirs. Sr. Employment and Ednl. Svc., BathHouse Theater, 1991-99, v.p. 1994-96; bd. dirs. Bellini preview group Seattle Opera Guild, 1994-96 ; mem. Assoc. Corp. Coun. for Arts., 1992-93. Mem. ABA, Pa. Bar Assn., Phila. Bar Assn., Wash. State Bar Assn., Merit Employers Coun. (1st v.p. 1978-79), Phila. Women's Network, Phila. Lawyers Club, Phila. Vol. Lawyers for Arts. Democrat. Jewish. Administrative and regulatory, Government contracts and claims, Labor. Office: Immunex Corp 51 University St Seattle WA 98101-2936

**FREEMAN, CHARLES E.,** state supreme court justice; b. Richmond, Va., Dec. 12, 1933; m. Marylee Voelker; 1 child, Kevin. BA in Liberal Arts, Va. Union U., 1954; JD, John Marshall Law Sch., 1962, LLD (hon.), 1992. Bar: Ill. 1962. Pvt. practice, 1962-76; pvt. practice, Cook County, Chgo., Ill., 1962-76; asst. state's atty. Cook County, 1964; asst. atty. Bd. Election Commrs., Chgo., 1964-65; mem. Ill. Indsl. Commn., Chgo., 1965-73, Ill. Commerce Commn., Chgo., 1973-76; judge law and chancery divsns. Cook County Circuit Ct., Chgo., 1976-86; judge Appellate Ct. Ill., 1986-90; chief justice Ill. Supreme Ct., 1990—. First African-Am. to swear in a Mayor city Chgo., to serve on Ill. Supreme Ct., 1990; leader in case disposition by published opinion, 1988, 89; recipient Cert. Achievement, Internat. Christian Fellowship Missions, Earl B. Dickerson award Chgo. Bar Assn., Merit award Habilative Systems, award Statesmanship, Monarch Awards Found. of Alpha Kappa Alpha, Freedom award John Marshall Law Sch. Mem. ABA (cert. Recognition, task force opportunities minorities in jud. adminstrn. divsn. and coms. opportunities minorities in profession), Am. Judges' Assn., Am. Judicature Soc., Ill. State Bar Assn., Ill. Jud. Coun. (Kenneth Wilson Meml. award, Meritorious Svc. award), Ill. Judges' Assn., Cook County Bar Assn. (Kenneth E. Wilson award, Cert. Merit, Ida Platt award, Presdl. award, Jud. award), Du Page County Bar Assn. Office: Supreme Ct Ill 160 N La Salle St Fl 20 Chicago IL 60601-3103

**FREEMAN, DAVID JOHN,** lawyer; b. N.Y.C., Aug. 9, 1948; s. John L. and Josephine F. (Wilding) F.; m. Ellen Gogolick, Dec. 29, 1974; children: Matthew, Julie. B.A., Harvard U., 1970; J.D., 1975. Bar: Mass. 1975, D.C. 1977, N.Y. 1982, U.S. Dist. Ct. D.C. 1981, N.Y. 1982, U.S. Dist. Ct. D.C. 1981, U.S. Dist. Ct. (so. and ea. dists.) N.Y. 1982, U.S. Ct. Appeals (D.C. cir.) 1979, U.S. Ct. Appeals (2nd cir.) 1982, U.S. Cupreme Ct. 1988. Spl. asst. to U.S. Senator Frank E. Moss, 1970-72; trial atty. FTC, Washington, 1975-77; assoc. Ginsburg, Feldman & Bress, Washington, 1977-81, Holtzmann, Wise & Shepard, N.Y.C., 1981-84; ptnr., 1984-94; ptnr., chmn. environ. dept. Battle Fowler, 1994—; spl. legal counsel N.Am. Environ. Affairs, UN Environ. Programme; co-chair emeritus ISO 14000 Legal Issues Forum, U.S. Tech. Com. to TC-207, Internat. Com. Standardization. Editor-in-chief: Jour. Environ Law Practice (West). Mem. ABA (natural resources sect.), Assn. Bar City of N.Y., Harvard Law Sch. Assn., N.Y. STate Bar Assn. (environ. law sect., co-chair hazardous waste com.). Environmental, Federal civil litigation. Office: Battle Fowler LLP 75 E 55th St New York NY 10022-3205

**FREEMAN, DAVID RALPH,** lawyer; b. Kansas City, Mo., Mar. 10, 1934; m. Marilyn Williams. BA in History, BJ, U. Mo., 1957, JD, 1965. Bar: Mo., U.S. Dist. Ct. (ea. and we. dists.), U.S. Ct. Appeals (7th and 8th cirs.), U.S. Dist. Ct. (so. dist.) Ill. Atty. Freeman & Williamson, Independence, Mo., 1965-68; prosecuting atty. State of Mo., Jackson County, 1967-72; atty. Sheridan, Sanders, Carr & White, Kansas City, 1970-72; fed. pub. defender Adminstrv. Office of U.S. Cts., Kansas City, 1973-79; dir. dept. social svcs. State of Mo., Jefferson City, 1979-81; atty. F. Joe DeLong III, Jefferson City, 1981-82; fed. pub. defender Adminstrv. Office U.S. Cts., St. Louis, 1982-95; ret., 1995; pvt. practice Collinsville, Ill., 1995—. Lt. Col. USMCR, 1957-61. Recipient Lon O. Hocker Meml. Trial Lawyer award Mo. Bar Found., 1969. Criminal. Office: PO Box 975 Collinsville IL 62234-0975

**FREEMAN, DEBORAH LYNN,** lawyer; b. Santa Monica, Calif., Jan. 12, 1955; d. T.L. Gordon and Patricia I. (von Walden) F. BA in History with distinction, Stanford U., 1976; JD with honors, U. Denver, 1982. Bar: Colo. 1982. Ptnr. Saunders, Snyder, Ross & Dickson P.C., Denver, 1982-94, Trout & Raley, P.C., Denver, 1996—. Mem. ABA, Colo. Bar Assn. (chmn. environ. law sect. 1989-90), Denver Bar Assn. (sec. young lawyers div. 1985-86). Environmental, Real property. Office: Trout & Raley PC 1775 Sherman St Ste 1300 Denver CO 80203-4316

**FREEMAN, FRANKLIN EDWARD, JR.,** state supreme court justice; b. Dobson, N.C., May 5, 1945; s. Franklin Edward and Clara E. (Smith) F.; m. Margaret Carson McKnight, 1966 (div. 1974); children: Margaret Elizabeth, Nancy Lorrin; m. Katherine Lynn Lloyd, Aug. 12, 1978; children: Katherine Ann, Franklin Edward III, Alexander Lloyd, May Clare. BA, U. N.C., 1967, JD, 1970. Bar: N.C. 1970. Rsch. asst. Assoc. Justice Dan K. Moore, Raleigh, N.C., 1970-71; asst. dist. atty. 17th jud. dist. N.C. Ct. System, 1971-73; exec. sec. Jud. Coun., 1973-78; asst. dir. Adminstrv. Office of Cts., Raleigh, 1973-78, dir., 1981-93; dist. atty. 17th jud. dist. N.C. Ct. System, 1979-81; sec. N.C. Dept. Correction, Raleigh, 1993-97; chief staff Gov. James B. Hunt, Jr., 1997-99; assoc. justice N.C. Supreme Ct., 1999—. Contbr. articles to profl. jours. tchr. Sunday sch. Main Street United Meth. Ch., Reidsville, 1996—, chmn. every mem. canvas, 1980, chmn. adminstrv. bd., 1981; mem. Hayes Barton Meth. Ch., Raleigh; pres. Raleigh Host Lions Club, 1992—. Recipient Svc. award Conf. Superior Ct. Judges, Svc. award Conf. Dist. Ct. Judges, Svc. award N.C. Clks. Superior Ct. Assn., Svc. award N.C. Magistrates Assn. Mem. N.C. State Bar, N.C. Correctional Assn., Surry County Bar Assn., Rockingham County Bar Assn., 10th Dist. Bar Assn., 17th Dist. Bar Assn., State Correctional Adminstrs., Conf. State Ct. Adminstrs. (pres-elect 1992-93, bd. dirs. 1987-90, 94-95), Lions Club (pres. Raleigh Host club 1994), Delta Upsilon. Democrat. Avocations: horses, history, reading. Office: NC Supreme Ct PO Box 2170 Raleigh NC 27602*

**FREEMAN, GEORGE CLEMON, JR.,** lawyer; b. Birmingham, Ala., Jan. 3, 1929; s. George Clemon and Annie Laura (Gill) F.; m. Anne Colston Hobson, Dec. 6, 1958; children: Anne Colston McEvoy, George Clemon III, Joseph Reid Anderson. BA magna cum laude, Vanderbilt U., 1950; LLB, Yale U., 1956. Bar: Ala. 1956, Va. 1958, D.C. 1974. Law clk. to Justice Hugo L. Black U.S. Supreme Ct., 1956; assoc. Hunton & Williams, Richmond, Va., 1957-63, ptnr., 1963-95, sr. counsel, 1995—. Contbr. articles to profl. jours. Pres. Va. chpt. Nature Conservancy, 1962-63; counsel Va. Outdoors Recreation Study Com. Va. Legis., 1963-65; mem. sect. 301 Superfund Act Study Group Congl. Adv. Com., 1981-82; mem. Falls James Com., 1973-89; chmn. Richmond City Dem. Com., 1969-71; chmn. adv. coun. Energy Policy Studies Ctr. U. Va., 1981-85; chmn. legal adv. com. to Va. Commn. on Transp. in the 21st Century, 1986-87; mem. Va. Gov.'s Commn. to Study Historic Preservation, 1987-88, Va. Coun. on the Environment, 1989-91; chmn. Va. Bd. Hist. Resources, 1989-91; mem. The Atlantic Coun., 1986-95; bd. dirs. Nat. Mus. Am. History, 1997—. Lt. (j.g.) USN, 1951-54. Ctr. for Pub. Resources fellow, 1990—. Fellow Am. Bar Found. (Va. state chmn. 1986-90); mem. ABA (chmn. standing com. on facilities of Law Libr. of Congress 1967-73, coordinating group on regulatory reform 1981-85, nominating com. 1984-87, chmn. civil justice coordinating com. 1990-92, sect. bus. law, sect. coun. 1976-79, chmn. ad hoc com. on Fed. Criminal Code 1979-81, chmn. program com. 1981-82, chmn. ad hoc com. on tort law reform 1986-87, sect. del. to ho. of dels. 1983-87, sec. 1987-88, vice-chmn. and ed. The Business Lawyer 1988-89, chmn.-elect 1989-90, chmn. 1990-91), Richmond Bar Assn., Va. Bar Assn., Am. Law Inst. (coun. 1980—, advisor to coun. on project on compensation and liability for product and process injuries 1986-91, advisor restatement of law, THRD, torts apportionment 1993-97, advisor restatement law THRD torts gen. prins. 1997—), Am. Judicature Soc., Country Club of Va., Knickerbocker Club, Met. Club, Phi Beta Kappa, Phi Delta Phi, Omicron Delta Kappa, Alpha Tau Omega. Democrat. Episcopalian. Avocation: gardening. Environmental, Administrative and regulatory, Constitutional. Home: Oyster Shell Point Farm Oyster Shell Rd Callao VA 22435-0680 Office: Hunton & Williams East Tower Fl 15 PO Box 1535 Richmond VA 23218-1535

**FREEMAN, GERALD RUSSELL,** lawyer; b. Mpls., Feb. 14, 1928; s. Samuel W. Freeman and Mildred Lorraine (Linton) Wofford; m. Ann Leslie Alton; 1 child, Brady Michael; children by previous marriage: Gerald Russell, Jon L., Craig V., Pamela A., Kelley M. BA, U. Minn., 1952; BS in Law, William Mitchell Coll. Law, Mpls., 1958, JD, 1960. Bar: Minn. 1960. Sole practice Mpls., 1960-67; ptnr. Collins, Freeman & Flakne, Mpls., 1967-73, Freeman, Gill, Keating & Ebersold, Mpls., 1973-86, Freeman, Alton, Dodd & Greer, Mpls., 1986-91, Freeman & Alton, Ltd., Mpls., 1991—; lectr. Golden Valley Med. Ctr., Mpls., 1976-81; adj. prof. Hamline Law Sch., St. Paul, 1981; legal counsel, bd. dirs. Vinland Nature Ctr., Mpls., 1984-85. Mem. chm. dependency adv. com. United Hosp., St. Paul, 1988-94. With U.S. Army, 1946-48. Mem. ABA (com. on alcohol and drug abuse), Minn. Bar Assn., Hennepin County Bar Assn., Am. Trial Lawyers Assn., Minn. Trial Lawyers Assn., Am. Judicature Soc., Am. Arbitration Assn. (nat. panel arbitrators), Minn. Bd. Profl. Responsibility, Minn. Hist. Soc., Douglas K.

Amdahl Inn of Ct., Minn. Lawyers Concerned for Lawyers (bd. dirs. 1996—). Fax: 612-475-1214. General civil litigation, Personal injury, General practice. Home: 2105 Xanthus Ln N Minneapolis MN 55447-2055 Office: 12450 Wayzata Blvd Ste 224 Minnetonka MN 55305-1927

**FREEMAN, GILL SHERRYL,** judge; b. N.Y.C., June 24, 1949; d. Norman and Arlene (Vigdor) Jacovitz. BS in Edn. cum laude, Temple U., 1970; student, U. Wis., 1966-68; MEd, U. Miami, Miami, Fla., 1973; JD cum laude, U. Miami, 1977. Bar: Fla. 1977, U.S. Dist. Ct. (so. dist.) 1977, U.S. Dist. Ct. (mid. dist.) Fla. 1984, U.S. Ct. Appeals (5th cir.) 1977. Tchr. Dade County Pub. Schs., Miami, 1970-76; assoc. Walton, Lantaff, Schroeder & Carson, Miami, 1977-82; assoc. Ruden, McClosky, Smith, Schuster & Russell, Miami, 1982-97, ptnr., 1983-97; apptd. cir. ct. judge Dade County Fla., 1997—; vice chair Fla. Supreme Ct. Gender Bias Study Commn., 1987-90; chair Fla. Supreme Ct. Gender Bias Study Implementation Commn. Elected Fellow of the ABA, 1993; Master, Family Law Inns. of Ct., 1992. Mem. Fla. Bar Assn. (pres. 1984-85), Fla. Assn. Women Lawyers, Supreme Ct. Commn. on Fairness. Avocations: alpine skiing, travel, tennis. Office: Courthouse Ctr 175 WW 1st Ave Miami FL 33128

**FREEMAN, JAMES ATTICUS, III,** lawyer, insurance and business consultant; b. Gadsden, Ala., Jan. 27, 1947; s. James Atticus and Dorothy Mae (Watson) F.; m. Judith Gail Davis, June 19, 1970; children: Gwendolyn Gail, James Atticus IV, Laura Marie. BS, Vanderbilt U., 1969, JD, 1972. Bar: Tenn. 1972. Broadcaster, newsman GE Broadcasting, Nashville, 1965-72; atty. The Murray Ohio Mfg. Co., Nashville, 1972-73, legal officer, 1973-81; asst. v.p., legal officer, asst. sec. The Murray Ohio Mfg. Co., Brentwood, Tenn., 1981-86, asst. v.p., legal officer, dir. risk mgmt., 1986-90, sec., 1988-90; of counsel Blackburn, Little, Smith & Slobey, Nashville, 1990-92; atty. Blackburn & Slobey, 1992-94; shareholder Blackburn Slobey Freeman & Happell PC, 1995—; pres. Litigation Mgmt. Specialists, Inc., 1989—; founder Nat. Alternative Dispute Resolution Svcs. Tenn., Inc.; bd. dirs. Some Assembly Required, Inc., Phoenix Property Mgmt. Svcs., Inc., Product Assembly, Inc.; lectr. corp. law, mem. bd. advisers Southeastern Inst. Paralegal Edn., Nashville, 1982-98); guest lectr. U. Wis. Sch. Engring., Madison, 1983—; resource cons. Med Marc Ins., 1992—. Mem. ABA, Tenn. Bar Assn., Nashville Bar Assn. (chmn. membership com. 1984, program chmn. corp. sect. 1985-86), Def. Rsch. Inst., Soc. Metals (mem. adj. faculty Cleve. chpt. 1984-88), Outdoor Power Equipment Inst. (chmn. corp. counsel com. 1976-84), Bicycle Mfrs. Assn. (chmn. legal affairs com. 1978-81), Vanderbilt Alumni Assn., Risk and Ins. Mgmt. Soc. (v.p. Cumberland chpt. 1988, 89, Phi Alpha Delta. Episcopalian. Personal injury, Insurance, General corporate. Office: Litigation Mgmt Specialists One Nat Bank Plaza 414 Union St Ste 2051 Nashville TN 37219-1790 also: Blackburn Slobey Freeman & Happell One Nat Bank Plaza 414 Union St Ste 2050 Nashville TN 37219-1789

**FREEMAN, KATHLEEN JANE,** lawyer; b. Oceanside, N.Y., Oct. 31, 1953; d. Edward John and Anna Pauline (Swana) Chojnowski; m. Eric Alden Freeman, June 29, 1991. BA in Natural Scis., SUNY, Buffalo, 1975; MS in Environ. Engring., Manhattan Coll., 1978; JD, Bklyn. Law Sch., 1984. Bar: N.Y. 1985, N.J. 1986, Mass. 1987. Environ. scientist Holzmacher, McLendon & Murrell, P.C., Melville, N.Y., 1975-76; environ. engr. Nestle Enterprises, Inc., White Plains, N.Y., 1978-79; environ. engr. U.S. EPA, N.Y.C., 1979-84, asst. regional counsel, 1984-86; environ. atty. Foley, Hoag & Eliot, Boston, 1986-95; environ. atty., ptnr. Bowditch & Dewey, Worcester and Framingham, Mass., 1995—; apptd. mem. Legal Adv. Com. to Mass. on Permit Streamlining, Boston, 1994—, Environ. Results Program Design Com. to Mass., Boston, 1995—. Co-author: (book chpt.) Controllers Business Advisor, 1995—. Apptd. mem. Wastewater Mgmt. Com., Wayland, Mass., 1994-97, bd. dirs. Metro West C. of C., 1999—. Mem. Women's Bar Assn., Mass. Bar Assn., Boston Bar Assn., Moot Ct. Honor Soc. (Barristers award 1984), Sigma Xi. Avocations: sailing, hiking, traveling, museums, wine-tasting. Environmental, Administrative and regulatory. Home: 19 Michael Rd Wayland MA 01778-2223 Office: Bowditch & Dewey 161 Worcester Rd Ste 600 Framingham MA 01701-5313

**FREEMAN, LEWIS BERNARD,** forensic accountant, lawyer; b. Cortland, N.Y., May 4, 1949; s. Lawrence Freeman and Doris (Katzmen) Gold.; m. Eddi Ann R. Freeman, Nov. 26, 1976; children: Jaron, Abigail. BBA, U. Miami, Coral Gables, 1971; JD, 1974. Bar: Fla. Pres. Freeman & Ptnrs., Miami, 1992—; CPA Freeman, Dawson & Rosenbaum, CPAs, Miami, 1992—; pres. Epilepsy Found. Fla., 1990-94; bd. mem. U. Miami Law Sch. Alumni, Coral Gables, 1990-98, Miami Children's Mus., 1994-97; com. Fla. Bar on CPA's, Talahassee, 1997. Named Humanitarian of Yr. EPIL Found. of Fla., Miami, 1996, Outstanding Alumnus of Yr., U. Miami, 1994, Outstanding Spkr. of Yr. Fla. Inst. CPAs, Tallahassee, 1982. Democrat. Jewish. General civil litigation, Bankruptcy. Office: Lewis B Freeman & Ptnrs 3250 Mary St Ste 100 Coconut Grove FL 33133-5232

**FREEMAN, MARK ALLAN,** lawyer; b. Tulsa, Oct. 19, 1954; s. Bennie John and Carolyn Jean (Moore) F.; m. Leigh Erin Jones, Aug. 5, 1978; children: Matthew Allan, Sarah Beth. Student, Okla. State U., 1972-74; BS, U. Tulsa, 1976; JD, So. Meth. U., 1980. Bar: Tex. 1980, U.S. Dist. Ct. (ea dist.) Tex. 1981, U.S. Ct. Appeals (5th cir.) 1981, U.S. Supreme Ct. 1984, U.S. Dist. Ct. (so. dist.) Tex. 1985. Assoc. Wells, Peyton, Beard, Greenberg, Hunt & Crawford, Beaumont, Tex., 1980-84, ptnr., 1985-97; ptnr. Stevens, Baldo & Freeman, Beaumont, 1998—. Contbr. articles to profl. jours. Mem. Tex. Bar Assn., Jefferson County Bar Assn., Bar Assn. of the 5th Cir., Maritime Law Assn. (procter 1981). Baptist. Admiralty, Federal civil litigation. Office: Stevens Baldo & Freeman PO Box 4950 Beaumont TX 77704-4950

**FREEMAN, MILTON VICTOR,** lawyer; b. N.Y.C., Nov. 16, 1911; s. Samuel and Celia (Gelfand) F.; m. Phyllis Young, Dec. 19, 1937; children: Nancy Lois (Mrs. Gans), Daniel Martin, Andrew Samuel, Amy Martha (Mrs. Malone). AB, CCNY, 1931; LLB, Columbia U., 1934. Bar: N.Y. 1934, D.C. 1946, U.S. Supreme Ct. 1943. With gen. counsel's office SEC, 1934-42, asst. solicitor, 1942-46; staff securities div. FTC, 1934; with Arnold & Porter (and predecessor firms), Washington, 1946—; adj. prof. Yale U., 1947, Georgetown U. Law Sch., 1952; vis. scholar various univs., 1978-79; mem. adv. bd. Bur. Nat. Affairs, Securities Regulation and Law Report, Washington, Internat. Fin. Law Rev., London. Contbr. articles to profl. jours.; bd. editors Columbia Law Rev., 1933-34 (Ordronaux prize 1934). Mem. adv. bd. Securities Regulation Inst., U. Calif., San Diego. Mem. ABA (chmn. subcom. SEC practice and enforcement 1972-83, exec. com. fed. regulation of securities com. 1983—, ad hoc com. on ALI corp. governance project, ad hoc com. on insider trading), Am. Law Inst. (advisor, corp. governance project), Fed. Bar Assn., D.C. Bar Assn., Internat. Law Inst. (hon. chmn. 1977-81, trustee 1955-86), Anxiety Disorders Assn. Am. (bd. dirs.). General corporate, Securities, Administrative and regulatory. Home: 125 Summer St Lbby 6 Boston MA 02110-1616 Office: 555 12th St NW Washington DC 20004-1200

**FREEMAN, RICHARD CAMERON,** federal judge; b. Atlanta, Dec. 14, 1926. A.B., Emory U., 1950, LL.B., 1952. Bar: Ga. 1953. Since practiced in Atlanta; mem. firm Haas, Holland & Blackshear, 1955-58; ptnr. Haas, Holland, Freeman, Levison & Gibert, 1958-71; judge U.S. Dist. Ct. (no. dist.) Ga., Atlanta, 1971—, sr. judge; alderman City of Atlanta, 1962-71; pres. Atlanta Humane Soc., 1981. Mem. Ga. Bar Assn., Atlanta Bar Assn., Chi Phi, Phi Delta Phi. Office: US Dist Ct 2121 US Courthouse 75 Spring St SW Atlanta GA 30303-3309

**FREEMAN, ROBERT E.,** lawyer; b. Tarrytown, N.Y., June 15, 1968; s. Jack B. and Ellen R. Freeman; m. Philippa J. Smith, Sept. 5, 1998. AB in Politics/Econs., Princeton U., 1990; JD cum laude, Georgetown U., 1993. Bar: N.Y., D.C., U.S. Dist. Ct. (so. dist.) N.Y. Jr. assoc. Morgan, Lewis & Bockius, Washington, 1993-95; assoc. to sr. assoc. Rogers & Wells LLP, N.Y.C., 1995—. Author: Antitrust Law Developments, 4th edit., 1997. Mem. ABA (sports/entertainment divsn.). Democrat. Avocations: golf, running, weight-lifting, music, film. Sports, Antitrust, Federal civil litigation. Home: 170 E 88th St Apt 2C New York NY 10128-2277 Office: Rogers & Wells LLP 200 Park Ave Fl 8E New York NY 10166-0800

**FREEMAN, RUSSELL ADAMS,** lawyer; b. Albany, N.Y., July 22, 1932; s. Russell Marvin and Edith (Adams) F.; m. Elizabeth Frances McHale, June 30, 1956; children: Lynn, James. BA, Amherst Coll., 1954; JD, Albany (N.Y.) Law Sch., 1957; LLM, U. So. Calif., 1966. Bar: N.Y. 1957, Calif. 1960. Practiced in Albany, 1957-59; with Security Pacific Nat. Bank, L.A., 1959-92, v.p., 1968-72, counsel, 1968-74, head legal dept., 1968-74; sr. v.p. Security Pacific Corp., L.A., 1972-81, exec. v.p., 1981-92, gen. counsel, 1972-92; sr. counsel O'Melveny & Myers, L.A., 1992-94; bd. govs. Fin. Lawyers Conf., 1972-74; faculty Pacific Coast Banking Sch., 1980-81; lectr. in field, 1965-94. Contbr. articles to profl. publns. Trustee Flintridge Prep. Sch., La Canada, Calif., 1978-80. Mem. ABA (mem. banking com.), Am. Bankers Assn. (mem. govt. rels. com. 1981-84, del. to Leadership Conf. 1984-86, 90-92), Assn. Banking Holding Cos., Calif. Bankers Assn. (dir., chmn. govt. rels. group 1979-81, 86-88, dir. and chmn. fed. govt. rels. 1985-86, Almon B. McCallum award for disting. and meritorious legal svc. 1986), Calif. Bankers Clearing House Assn. (chmn. pub. policy adv. com. 1980-81, 88-89), Calif. State Bar, L.A. County Bar Assn. past chmn. comml. law and bankruptcy sect., Outstanding Corp. Counsel award 1989, corp. law dept. sect., Constl. Rights Found. (bd. dirs. 1986-94). Banking.

**FREEMAN, TODD IRA,** lawyer; b. Mpls., Nov. 24, 1953; s. Earl Stanley and Gretta Lois (Rudick) F.; m. Judy Lynn Sigel, June 15, 1975; children: Jennifer, Katie, Zachary. BS in Mktg., U. Colo., 1974; JD, U. Minn., 1978. Bar: Minn. 1978, U.S. Dist. Ct. Minn. 1978, U.S. Tax Ct. 1980; CPA, Minn. Acct. Coopers & Lybrand, Mpls., 1978-80; shareholder Larkin, Hoffman, Daly & Lindgren, Mpls., 1980—, treas., 1990—, also bd. dirs., 1990-93. Bd. dirs. Temple of Aaron, St. Paul, 1983—, Sholom Home, Inc., St. Paul, 1983-89. Mem. ABA (tax sect., past chmn. personal svc. orgns.), AICPA, Minn. Soc. CPAs (tax conf. com. 1987—), Minn. State Bar Assn., Hennepin County Bar Assn. Avocations: tennis, racquetball, football. Estate planning, General corporate, Pension, profit-sharing, and employee benefits. Office: Larkin Hoffman Daly & Lindgren 7900 Xerxes Ave S Ste 1500 Minneapolis MN 55431-1128

**FREEMAN, TOM M.,** lawyer; b. Wauwatosa, Wis., Oct. 5, 1952; s. Max and Betty J. (Zimmerman) F.; m. Judith Casper, June 23, 1974; children: Sarah Carolyn, Benjamin Robert. BA with honors, U. Wis., 1974; JD cum laude, Harvard U., 1977. Bar: Wis. 1977, Ill. 1978, Calif. 1980, U.S. Dist. Ct. (we. dist.) Wis. 1977, U.S. Ct. Appeals (7th cir.) 1978, U.S. Dist. Ct. (no. dist.) Calif. 1980, U.S. Ct. Appeals (9th cir.) 1982. Law clk. Wis. Supreme Ct., Madison, 1977-78; staff atty. U.S. Ct. Appeals (7th cir.), Chgo., 1978-80; assoc. Brobeck, Phleger, Harrison, LLP, San Francisco, 1980-85. Democrat. Jewish. General civil litigation, Insurance. Office: Brobeck Phleger & Harrison LLP Spear St Tower 1 Market San Francisco CA 94105

**FREEMAN, V(ERNIE) EDWARD, II,** lawyer; b. Cookeville, Tenn., Sept. 4, 1961; s. V. Edward and Shirley (McCulley) F.; m. Suzanne Dotson, June 4, 1983; children: Jared Edward, Brooke-Anne. BS, Samford U., 1983, JD, 1986. Bar. Ala. 1986, U.S. Dist. Ct. (no. dist.) Ala. 1990, U.S. Ct. Appeals (11th cir.) 1990, U.S. Supreme Ct. 1992. Ptnr. Stone, Patton, Kierce & Freeman, Bessemer, Ala., 1986—. Bd. dirs ARC, Bessemer, 1989—, Bessemer YMCA; chmn. bd. dirs. Salvation Army, Bessemer, 1992. Mem. Ala. Bar Assn., Bessemer Bar Assn., Rotary Internat. (bd. dirs.). Baptist. Avocations: bonsai trees, fishing, investments. General civil litigation, Insurance, Personal injury. Office: Stone Patton Kierce & Freeman 118 18th St N Bessemer AL 35020-5000

**FREERS, STEVEN GEORGE,** lawyer; b. Indpls., Jan. 8, 1949; s. Howard P. and Eleanor (Reeder) F.; m. Christine Helena Lamos, Sept. 5, 1970; 4 children. J.D., Wayne State U., 1974. Bar: Mich. 1974. Ptnr. Binkowski & Freers, Warren, Mich., 1979-85 . Lodge: Elks (sec. bldg. corp.) Home: 32749 Rugby Dr Warren MI 48093-6941 Office: 31730 Hoover Rd Ste C Warren MI 48093-1700

**FREIJE, PHILIP CHARLES,** lawyer; b. Princeton, N.J., July 27, 1944; s. Brahim K. and Evelyn M. (Haddad) F.; m. Karen Mae Janovic, Oct. 18, 1969; children: Michael P., James C., Christine L. BA, U. Conn., 1966, JD, 1969; LLM, George Washington U., 1972. Bar: Conn. 1970, D.C. 1970, U.S. Supreme Ct. 1973. Assoc. Conway, Londregan, Leuba & McNamara, New London, Conn., 1969; atty.-advisor Office of Fgn. Direct Investment, U.S. Dept. Commerce, Washington, 1970-73, asst. dir. litigation, 1974; legal advisor Social & Econ. Statistics Adminstrn., U.S. Dept. Commerce, Washington, 1974-75; dep. asst. gen. counsel adminstrn./econ. affairs Office of Gen. Counsel, U.S. Dept. Commerce, Washington, 1975-81, dep. asst. gen. counsel econ. affairs/regulation, 1981-85, dep. chief counsel for econ. affairs, 1985-92, chief counsel for econ. affairs, 1992-98; bureau coun. U.S. Census Bureau U.S. Dept. Commerce, 1998—. Dir. Lake Barcroft Community Assn., Falls Church, Va., 1980-82. Mem. ABA, Fed. Bar Assn., Conn. Bar Assn., D.C. Bar Assn., Am. Judicature Soc. Home: 6212 Beachway Dr Falls Church VA 22041-1423 Office: US Dept Commerce 14th & Constitution Ave NW Washington DC 20230-0001

**FREILING, DON RYNN,** lawyer; b. San Antonio, July 22, 1966; s. Don Russell and Laura Jeanette Freiling. BBA, Abilene Christian U., 1988; JD, St. Mary's U., San Antonio, 1992. Bar: Tex. 1992, U.S. Dist. Ct. (no., so., we. and ea. dist.) Tex., U.S. Ct. Appeals (5th cir.). Law clk. Hon. David O. Belew, Jr., Ft. Worth, 1992-94, Hon. Jer Kendall, Dallas, 1994-96; assoc. Maloney Bean & Horn, P.C., Irving, Tex., 1997—. Mem. ABA (litigation sect.). Federal civil litigation, General civil litigation, State civil litigation. Office: Maloney Bean & Horn PC 102 Decker Ct Ste 200 Irving TX 75062-2740

**FREIMUND, JEFFREY A. O.,** lawyer; b. Portland, Oreg., July 29, 1960; s. Justus H.G. and Joann E. F.; m. Teresa L. Weaver, July 7, 1990; children: Gabriel C.J. BA in Philosophy, We. Wash. U., 1982; JD, Willamette U., 1987. Bar: Wash. 1987, U.S. Dist. Ct. (we. and ea. dists.) Wash. 1987, U.S. Ct. Appeals (9th cir.) 1987. Asst. atty. gen. Wash. Atty. Gen.'s Office, Olympia, 1987—. Author, editor Willamette Law Rev., 1986-87. Vol. Olympia Dem. Com., 1994. Recipient Sec.'s award Wash. Dept. Social and Health Svcs., 1998. Mem. Wash. State Bar Assn. Avocations: basketball, fishing, boating, gardening. Office: Wash State Atty General's Office PO Box 40126 629 Woodland Sq Loop Olympia WA 98504-0126

**FREITAS, DAVID PRINCE,** lawyer; b. San Francisco, Oct. 21, 1940; s. Walter Francis and Marno Catherine (Prince) F.; m. Alice Urrutia, June 24, 1961 (div. 1972); children: Diane Phillips, Nancy Freitas, Megan Neale; m. Patricia Garbarino, June 20, 1996. BS, U. San Franciso, 1964; JD, San Francisco Law Sch., 1968. Bar: Calif. 1969. Atty. Freitas Law Firm, San Rafael, Calif., 1969-96, Ragghianti, Freitas, Montobbio & Wallace LLP, San Rafael, 1996—; bd. dirs. St. Vincent's Sch.; lectr. in field; judge pro tempore San Francisco and Marin Counties; spl. master Superior Cts. of Marin and Sonoma. Contbr. articles to profl. jours. Bd. dirs. Guide Dogs for the Blind, San Rafal, 1994-95, Marin Agrl. Land Trust, 1991-92, Marin County Humane Soc., 1967-71. Fellow Am. Coll. Trial Lawyers, Internat. Acad. Trial Lawyers, Internat. Soc. Barristers; mem. Internat. Assn. Def. Counsel, Am. Bd. Trial Adv. (San Francisco chpt., pres. 1993, nat. bd. dirs. 1992—, exec. com. 1990—), Nat. Bd. Trial Adv. (diplomate), Assn. Def. Counsel N.C. (pres. 1985, bd. dirs. 1977-86), Calif. State Bar Assn. (adminstrn. justice com. 1982, jury instrns. com. 1977), Calif. Def. Counsel (bd. dirs. 1984), Marin County Bar Assn. (secr. 1987, treas. 1984), Def. Rsch. Inst. (Nat. Execptional Performance award 1985), Cal-ABOTA (bd. chair 1995), Edward J. McFetridge Am. Inn Ct. (pres. 1993, exec. com. 1990—), San Rafal C. of C. (bd. dirs. 1995—). General civil litigation, Personal injury. Home: 19 Palm Ave San Rafael CA 94901-2221 Office: Ragghianti Freitas Montobbio Wallace LLP 874 4th St San Rafael CA 94901-3246

**FRELS, KELLY,** lawyer; b. Lolita, Tex., Dec. 28, 1943; s. Leon A. and Aileen K. Frels; m. Carmela Madden, Sept. 10, 1970; children: Jonathan, Catherine. BS in Edn., S.W. Tex. State U., San Marcos, 1966; JD, U. Tex., 1970. Bar: Tex., U.S. Dist. Ct. (so., no., we. and ea. dists.), U.S. Ct. Appeals (5th and 11th cirs.), U.S. Supreme Ct. Atty. Bracewell & Patterson, Houston, 1976-95, mng. ptnr., 1995—. Mem. bd. experts Lawyers Alert, 1984-88; mem. adv. bd. Edn. Law Reporter, 1981-88; contbr. numerous articles to profl. jours. Bd. dirs., mem. exec. com. Greater Houston Partnership, 1998—, chair govt. rels. com., 1998—. Mem. ABA (pub. edn. com. 1985-86), Houston Bar Assn. (bd. dirs. 1988-91, 95-96, treas. 1990, 2d v.p. 1991, 1st v.p. 1992, pres. 1994), State Bar Tex. (bd. dirs. 1995-98, chmn. sch. law sect. 1973-76, chair long range planning com. 1997-98, chair legal svcs. com. 1997-98, chair lawyer referral com. 1998—, vice chair nominating com. 1997-98), S.W. Tex. U. Alumni Assn. (pres. 1973), Houston Club (pres. 1999—). Roman Catholic. Education and schools, General civil litigation, Labor. Home: 5607 Bordley Dr Houston TX 77056-2329 Office: Bracewell & Patterson LLP 711 Louisiana St Ste 2900 Houston TX 77002-2781

**FRENCH, COLIN VAL,** lawyer; b. Phila., July 20, 1957; s. Calvin Valdean and Ella LaVon (Crum) F.; m. Amanda Mitchell, June 16, 1984. BS magna cum laude, Graceland Coll., 1979; JD, Drake U., 1982; LLM in Tax, So. Meth. U., 1983. Bar: Iowa 1982, Tex. 1983. Nat. atty. Boy Scouts Am., Irving, Tex., 1984-86; atty. So. Meth. U., Dallas, 1986-88, Boy Scouts Am. Nat. Office, Irving, Tex., 1988—; mem. Legal Ethics and Sports Law Coms., Dallas, 1985—; bd. dirs. Charitable Accord, 1997—; chmn., bd. dirs. Hillcrest Acad., 1997—. Editor newspaper The Gavel, 1981-82, newsletter Finance Update, 1985-86, Tax and Issues Newsletter, 1998—. Mem. ABA, Dallas Bar Assn. (entertainment law com., 1986—), Rotary (trustee Dallas found.). Republican. Mem. Reorganized Ch. of Jesus Christ of Latter Day Saints. Avocations: music writing and performance, golf, tennis. General corporate, Taxation, general, Entertainment. Home: 6215 Meadow Rd Dallas TX 75230-5138 Office: Boy Scouts Am 1325 W Walnut Hill Ln Irving TX 75038-3096

**FRENCH, DANIEL J.,** prosecutor. JD, Syracuse U. Law clk. Judge Rosemary Pooler, former aide to U.S. Sen. Daniel Patrick Moynihan; interim U.S. atty. no. dist. N.Y. U.S. Dept. Justice, 1999—. Democrat. Office: 100 S Clinton St Syracuse NY 13261-7198*

**FRENCH, JOHN, III,** lawyer; b. Boston, July 12, 1932; s. John and Rhoda (Walker) F.; m. Leslie Ten Eyck, Jan. 11, 1957 (div. 1961); children: John B., Lawrence C.; m. Anne Hubbell, Jan. 9, 1965 (div. 1983); children: Daniel J., Susanna H.; m. Marina Kellen, Nov. 21, 1987. BA, Dartmouth Coll., 1955; JD, Harvard U., 1958. Bar: N.Y. 1959, D.C. 1988. Assoc. Milbank, Tweed, Hadley & McCloy, N.Y.C., 1961-68, Satterlee & Stephens, N.Y.C., 1968-73; asst. gen. counsel Continental Group, Inc., Stamford, Conn., 1973-81; v.p., gen. counsel, sec. Peabody Internat. Corp., Stamford, Conn., 1981-82; ptnr. Appleton, Rice & Perrin, N.Y.C., 1982-84; ptnr. Beveridge and Diamond, N.Y.C., 1985-93, counsel, 1993-99; chmn. Tudor Assocs., LLC, N.Y.C., 1999—; exec. v.p., gen. counsel The Nat. Urban Tech. Ctr., MC; lectr. Practising Law Inst., 1979-83, Am. Law Inst., 1978; bd. dirs. Resorts Mgmt., Inc., Tudor Assocs., LLC, N.Y.C. Contbr. articles to profl. jours. Trustee Hudson River Found., YMCA-YWCA Camping Svcs. of Greater N.Y., Inc.; bd. dirs. Third St. Music Sch. Settlement House, Inc., N.Y.C., Internat. House, Inc., N.Y.C., Young Concert Artists, Inc., 33 E. 70th St. Corp., Teatro alla Scala Found.; mem. Westchester County Planning Bd., 1974-85; mem. N.Y. State Environ. Bd., 1976-88. Capt. JAGC, USAF, 1958-61. Mem. ABA, N.Y. State Bar Assn. (lectr.), Assn. of Bar of City of N.Y. (lectr.), Environ. Law Inst., Am. Soc. Corp. Secs., Met. Opera, Soc. Mayflower Descs., River Club, Harvard Club, Knickerbocker Club, The Pilgrims, Century Assn. Republican. General corporate, Environmental. Home: 33 E 70th St New York NY 10021-4941 Office: Tudor Assocs LLC 33 E 70th St New York NY 10021-4941

**FRENCH, JOHN DWYER,** lawyer; b. Berkeley, Calif., June 26, 1933; s. Horton Irving and Gertrude Margery (Ritzen) F.; m. Annette Richard, 1955; m. Berna Jo Mahling, 1986. BA summa cum laude, U. Minn., 1955; postgrad, Oxford U., Eng., 1955-56; LLB magna cum laude, Harvard U., 1960. Bar: D.C. 1960, Minn. 1963. Law clk. Justice Felix Frankfurter, U.S. Supreme Ct., 1960-61; legal asst. to commr. FTC, 1961-62; assoc. Ropes & Gray, Boston, 1962-63; assoc. Faegre & Benson, Mpls., 1963-66, ptnr., 1967-75, mng. ptnr., 1975-94, chmn. mgmt. com., 1989-94; mem. adj. faculty Law Sch. U. Minn., 1965-70, mem. search com. for dean of Coll. of Liberal Arts, 1996; mem. exec. com. Lawyers Com. for Civil Rights Under Law, 1978—; co-chmn. U.S. Dist. Judge Nominating Commn., 1979; vice chmn. adv. com., mem. dir. search com., chmn. devel. office search com. Hubert Humphrey Inst., 1979-87. Contbr. numerous articles and revs. to legal jours. Chmn. or co-chmn. Minn. State Dem. Farm Labor Party Conv., 1970-90, 94, chmn. Mondale Vol. Com., 1972, treas., 1974; assoc. chmn. Minn. Dem.-Farmer-Labor Party, 1985-86; mem. Dem. Nat. Com., 1985-86; mem. Dem. Nat. Conv., 1976, 78, 80, 84, 88; trustee Twin Cities Public TV, Inc., 1980-86, mem. overseers com. to visit Harvard U. Law Sch., 1970-75, 77-82; chmn. Minn. steering com. Dukakis for Pres., 1987-88; mem. Sec. of State's Commn. on Electoral Reform, Minn., 1994; mem. Mayor's Commn. on Regulatory Reform, Mpls., 1995. With U.S. Army, 1955-56. Rotary Found. fellow, 1955-56. Mem. ABA (editorial bd. jour. 1976-79, commn. to study fed. trade 1969—), Minn. Bar Assn., Hennepin County Bar Assn., Jud. Coun. Minn., Lawyers Alliance for Nuclear Arms Control (nat. bd. dirs. 1982-84), U. Minn. Alumni Assn. (exec. com. 1985-87, v.p. 1989-91, pres. 1991-92, Vol. of Yr. award 1988), Phi Beta Kappa. Episcopalian. Antitrust, Administrative and regulatory, Federal civil litigation. Office: Faegre & Benson 2200 Norwest Ctr 90 S 7th St Ste 2200 Minneapolis MN 55402-3901

**FRENCH, TIMOTHY A.,** lawyer; b. New Britain, Conn., Aug. 22, 1959; s. George William and Joan (Stanley) F.; m. Jo Lynn Haley, Dec. 20, 1986; children: George William, Lindley Claire, Charles Stanley. AB, Harvard U., 1982; JD, Northwestern U., 1985. Bar: Ill. 1985, U.S. Dist. Ct. (no. dist.) Ill. 1985, U.S. Ct. Appeals (7th and D.C. cirs.), U.S. Ct. Claims. Assoc. Gardner, Carton & Douglas, Chgo., 1986-89; ptnr. Neal, Gerber & Eisenberg, Chgo., 1989—. Contbr. articles to profl. jours. Mem. vestry St. Chrysostom's Ch., Chgo., 1996-97. Avocations; tennis, running, golf, scouting, piano. Bankruptcy, Contracts commercial, General civil litigation. Office: Neal Gerber & Eisenberg 2 N Lasalle St Ste 2200 Chicago IL 60602-3702

**FRENTHEWAY, JOHN E.,** lawyer; b. Cheyenne, Wyo., Apr. 6, 1949; s. Charles Jake and Gladys (Lauver) F.; m. Erma Kay Pace, Aug. 15, 1970; children: Marcus John, Jarad Scott, Rebecca Kay, Seth Paul, Joshua Elias, Zachary Jason. BS in Animal Sci., U. Wyo., 1973, BS in Edn., 1976, JD, 1981. Bar: Wyo. U.S. Dist. Ct. Wyo. Assoc. Graves, Hacker and Phalen, Cheyenne, 1981-83; asst. state pub. defender State Pub. Defenders Office Wyo., Cheyenne, 1982—; guardian ad litem Juvenile Ct. First Jud. Dist. Ct. Wyo., Cheyenne, 1982—; pvt. practice Cheyenne, 1983—; apptd. mem. Wyo. Juvenile Commn., Cheyenne, 1991-95, Wyo. Juvenile Adv. Coun., 1997—. V.p., coach Cheyenne Soccer Assn., 1982-93; unit commr. Boy Scouts Am., Cheyenne, 1984-86, roundtable commr., 1984-88. Mem. Wyo. Bar Assn. (Pres. Select award 1998), Laramie County Bar Assn. (cert. exemplary svc. 1998). Juvenile, Family and matrimonial. Home: 1878 Horse Creek Rd Cheyenne WY 82009-9342 Office: PO Box 181 Cheyenne WY 82003-0181

**FRENZEL, JAMES CHARLES,** lawyer; b. Ft. Monmouth, N.J., Dec. 12, 1945; s. Charles H. and Virginia L. Frenzel; m. Susan B. Frenzel, Sept. 29, 1979; 1 chld, Charles J. BA in History, Duke U., 1967, JD, 1970. Bar: Ga., N.C., U.S. Supreme Ct., U.S. Ct. Appeals (4th, 6th and 11th cirs.). Assoc. Womble, Carlyle, Sandridge & Rice, Winston-Salem, N.C., 1970-77, ptnr., 1977-90; ptnr. Smith, Gambrell & Russell, Atlanta, 1990-91, Greene, Buckley, Jones & McQueen, Atlanta, 1991-95; prin. James C. Frenzel, P.C., Atlanta, 1995—; vis. prof. Wake Forest U. Sch. Law, Winston-Salem, 1985-87; dir. Southeastern Bankruptcy Law Inst., Atlanta. Author: Problem Loans in N.C., 1985, Secured Lending in Georgia, 1992; editor: How to Start a Pro Bono Bankruptcy Program, 1996. Bd. dirs. Continuing Legal Edn. in Ga., Athens, 1993; speaker Ctrl. Eastern European Initiative-U.S. Aid, Romania, 1996. Mem. ABA (mem. bus. sect. ethics com. 1996-99), Ga. Bar Assn. (chmn. bankruptcy sect. 1994-95), N.C. Bar Assn. (chmn. bankruptcy sect. 1989-90). Bankruptcy. Home: 8985 Huntcliff Trce Atlanta GA 30350-1733 Office: 3343 Peachtree Rd NE Ste 750 Atlanta GA 30326-1429

**FRERICKS, TIMOTHY MATTHEW,** lawyer; b. Marion, Ohio, June 5, 1949; s. Theodore Paul and Dorothy Jane (Fetter) F.; BA, Notre Dame U., 1971; JD, Ohio No. U., 1974. Bar: Ohio 1974. Ptnr. Frericks and Howard, Marion, 1974—. Contbr. articles to local newspaper. Bd. dirs. Marion Catholic High Sch., 1982-85, Columbus Diocesan Schs., 1982-85, Marion Cadets Drum and Bugle Corps, 1978-88, sec., 1986—; trustee Marion H.A.N.D., Inc., 1989, Marion Shelter Program, Inc., 1988—; rep. precinct capt., 1980—; founder Citizens for Responsible Govt., Marion, 1983—. Mem. Ohio Bar Assn., Marion County Bar Assn. (pres. 1993), Kiwanis (v.p. 1981, pres. 1991), Optimists (chmn. cmty. svc. 1975-82), KC.

Home: 2916 Neidhart Rd Marion OH 43302-8463 Office: Frericks & Howard 152 E Center Marion OH 43302

**FREUD, JOHN SIGMUND,** lawyer; b. Johnstown, Pa., Dec. 11, 1956; s. Fred and Betty (Kapuloff) F.; m. Deborah Elizabeth O'Connor, May 25, 1986; children: Jessica Shaye, Alyxandra Jacqueline. Student, Harvard U., 1975; BA magna cum laude, Brandeis U., 1978; JD, U. Miami (Fla.), 1981. Bar: Fla. 1981, Mass. 1982, U.S. Dist. Ct. (so., no. and mid. dists.) Fla. 1982, U.S. Ct. Appeals (5th and 11th cirs.) 1982, U.S. Supreme Ct. 1985. Assoc. Braod and Cassel, Bay Harbor Islands, Fla., 1980-82; assoc. Guren, Merritt, Udell, Sogg & Cohen, Miami, Fla., 1982-84, Blank, Rome, Comisky & McCauley, Miami, 1984-86; ptnr. Levine, Geiger, Kuperstein & Freud P.A., Miami, 1986-90; pvt. practice Miami, 1990—. Recipient Antitrust Book award U. Miami Sch. Law. Mem. ABA, Am. Arbitration Assn., Fla. Bar Assn., Dade County Bar Assn. (young lawyers sect.), Mass. Bar Assn., Greater Miami C. of C. Democrat. Jewish. Avocations: tennis, basketball. General civil litigation, Insurance, Consumer commercial. Office: John S Freud P A 2699 S Bayshore Dr Ste 300 Miami FL 33133-5408

**FREUD, NICHOLAS S.,** lawyer; b. N.Y.C., Feb. 6, 1942; s. Frederick and Fredericka (von Rothenburg) F.; m. Elsa Doskow, July 23, 1966; 1 child, Christopher. AB, Yale U., 1963, JD, 1966. Bar: N.Y. 1968, Calif. 1970, U.S. Tax Ct. 1973. Ptnr. Chickering & Gregory, San Francisco, 1978-85, Russin & Vecchi, San Francisco, 1986-93, Jeffer, Mangels, Butler & Marmaro, LLP, San Francisco, 1993—; Mem. joint adv. bd. Calif. Continuing Edn. of Bar, chair taxation subcom. 1987-87; mem. fgn. income adv. bd. Tax Management Internat. Jour., mem. bd. advs. The Jour. of Internat. Taxation; mem. adv. bd. NYU Inst. on Fed. Taxation. Author: (with Charles G. Stephenson and K. Bruce Friedman) International Estate Planning, rev. edit., 1997; contbr. articles to profl. jours. Fellow Am. Coll. of Tax Counsel (cert. specialist in taxation law) mem. ABA (tax sect. coun. dir. 1995-97, chair com. on U.S. activities of foreigners and tax treaties 1989-91, vice chair 1987-89, chair subcom. on tax treaties 1981-87), Calif. State Bar Assn. (taxation sect. exec. com. 1981-85, vice chair 1982-83, chair 1983-84, vice chair income tax com. 1981-82, chair 1982-83, vice chair personal income tax subcom. 1979-80, chair 1980-81, co-chair fgn. tax subcom. 1978-79), N.Y. State Bar Assn. (taxation sect., mem. com. on U.S. activities of fgn. taxpayers and fgn. activities of U.S. taxpayers), Bar Assn. of San Francisco, Bar Assn. of City of N.Y., San Francisco Tax Club (pres. 1988), San Francisco Internat. Tax Group. Taxation, general, Private international. Office: Jeffer Mangels Butler & Marmaro LLP 1 Sansome St Fl 12 San Francisco CA 94104-4430

**FREUDENTHAL, DAVID D.,** prosecutor. U.S. atty. for Wyo. U.S. Dept. Justice, Cheyenne, 1994—. Office: US Atty Dist Wyo 2120 Capitol Ave Rm 4002 Cheyenne WY 82001-3633

**FREUND, FRED A.,** retired lawyer; b. N.Y.C., June 18, 1928; s. Sidney J. and Cora (Strasser) F.; m. Rosalie Sampo, Nov. 18, 1975 (div. Apr. 1983); m. Patricia A. Gardner, Mar. 13, 1957 (div. Jan. 1967); children: Gregory G., K. Bailey. A.B., Columbia U., 1948, J.D., 1949. Bar: N.Y. 1949, U.S. Supreme Ct. 1968. Law clk. to chief judge U.S. Dist. Ct. So. Dist. N.Y., N.Y.C., 1949-51; assoc. Kaye, Scholer, Fierman, Hays & Handler, N.Y.C., 1953-58, ptnr., 1959-93, ret., 1993. Served to 1st lt. USAF, 1951-53. Mem. ABA, Assn. Bar City N.Y., Phi Beta Kappa. Home: 1085 Park Ave Apt 4C New York NY 10128-1179 *Balancing the quest for excellence with humility and humor.*

**FREW, STEPHEN B.,** lawyer; b. Painesville, Ohio, Mar. 8, 1951; s. Ralph K. and Eleanor Frew; m. Jacqueline Frew. Mng. ptnr. Kiesler & Berman, Chgo. Federal civil litigation, General civil litigation. Office: Kiesler & Berman 188 W Randolph St Ste 1300 Chicago IL 60601-2970

**FREY, ANDREW LEWIS,** lawyer; b. N.Y.C., Aug. 11, 1938; s. Daniel B. and Ruth J. Frey; children: Matthew S., Alexandra S. BA with high honors, Swarthmore Coll., 1959; LLB, Columbia U., 1962. Bar: N.Y. 1962, D.C. 1966, U.S. Supreme Ct. 1972. Law clk. to judge U.S. Ct. Appeals (D.C. cir.), 1962-63; spl. counsel to Gov. U.S. V.I., 1963-65; assoc. Koteen & Burt, Washington, 1965-70; ptnr. Dutton, Gwirtzman, Zumas, Wise & Frey, Washington, 1970-72; dep. solicitor gen. Office U.S. Solicitor Gen., Washington, 1972-86; ptnr. Mayer Brown & Platt, Washington, N.Y.C., 1986—. Recipient John Marshall award Dept. Justice, 1975, Disting. Service award Atty. Gen., 1980, Presdl. award for Meritorious Service, 1985. Mem. Am. Law Inst., Am. Acad. Appellate Lawyers, D.C. Bar Assn., Phi Beta Kappa. Notes editor Columbia Law Rev., 1961-62. Office: Mayer Brown & Platt 1675 Broadway Fl 19 New York NY 10019-5820

**FREYER, DANA HARTMAN,** lawyer; b. Pitts., Apr. 17, 1944; m. Bruce M. Freyer, Dec. 21, 1969. Student, L' Institut De Hautes Etudes Internationales, Geneva, 1963-64; BA, Conn. Coll., 1965; postgrad., Columbia U., 1968, JD, 1971. Bar: N.Y. 1972, Ill. 1974, U.S. Dist. Ct. (no. dist.) Ill. 1974, U.S. Ct. Appeals (7th cir.) 1976, U.S. Supreme Ct. 1977, U.S. Dist. Ct. (so. dist.) N.Y. 1978, U.S. Dist. Ct. (ea. dist.) N.Y. 1981, U.S. Ct. Appeals (2d cir.) 1982. Staff atty. Legal Aid Soc. Westchester County, Mt. Vernon, N.Y., 1971-72; assoc. Friedman & Koven, Chgo., 1973-77, Skadden, Arps, Slate, Meagher & Flom, LLP, N.Y.C., 1977-88; spl. counsel Skadden, Arps, Slate, Meagher & Flom, N.Y.C., 1988-93, ptnr., 1994—; pres. Westchester Legal Services, Inc., White Plains, N.Y., 1985-87, bd. dirs., 1978-98; mem. governing coun. Comml. Arbitration and Mediation Ctr. for Ams., rules rev. task force; U.S. Coun. for Internat. Bus. Arbitration Com.; London Ct. of Internat. Arbitration; adv. bd. World Arbitration and Mediation Report. Mem. editl. bd. ADR Currents. Mem. ABA, Bar Assn. of City of N.Y., Internat. Bar Assn. General civil litigation, Alternative dispute resolution, Private international. Office: Skadden Arps Slate Meagher & Flom LLP 919 3rd Ave New York NY 10022-3902

**FREYTAG, SHARON NELSON,** lawyer; b. Larned, Kans., May 11, 1943; d. John Seldon and Ruth Marie (Herbel) Nelson; children: Kurt David, Hillary Lee. BS with highest distinction, U. Kans., Lawrence, 1965; MA, U. Mich., 1966; JD cum laude, So. Meth. U., 1981. Bar: Tex. 1981, U.S. Dist. Ct. (no. dist.) Tex. 1981, U.S. Ct. Appeals (5th cir.) 1982, U.S. Supreme Ct. 1993; cert. civil appellate law. Tchr. English, Gaithersburg (Md.) H.S., 1966-70; instr. English, Eastfield Coll., 1974-78; law clk. U.S. Dist. Ct. for No. Dist. Tex., 1981-82, U.S. Ct. Appeals 5th Cir., 1982; ptnr. appellate sect. Haynes and Boone, Dallas, 1983—, vis. prof. law Southern Meth. U., 1985-86; bd. dirs. State Bar Tex.; faculty Appellate Adv. program NITA. Editor-in-chief Southwestern Law Jour., 1980-81; contbr. articles to law jours. Woodrow Wilson fellow. Recipient John Marshall Constl. Law award, Baird Cmty. Spirit award, 1995. Mem. ABA (mem. litigation sect., chair subcom. on local rules), Fed. Bar Assn. (co-chmn. appellate practice and advocacy sect. 1990-91), Tex. Bar Assn. (mem. appellate coun. 1995-98), State Bar Tex. (bd. dirs. 1997—), Dallas Bar Assn. (mem. appellate coun.), Higginbotham Inn of Ct., Barristers, Order of Coif, Phi Beta Kappa. Lutheran. Federal civil litigation, State civil litigation, Appellate. Office: Haynes & Boone 3100 NationsBank Plz Dallas TX 75202

**FRICK, BENJAMIN CHARLES,** lawyer; b. Overbrook, Pa., Feb. 23, 1960; s. Sidney Wanning and Marie Pauline (Strickler) F.; m. Stephanie Ann Sears, June 1, 1991; children: Sarah Marie, Anna Elizabeth. BA, Cornell U., 1982; JD, U. Richmond, 1985; LLM in Taxation, Villanova U., 1994. Bar: Pa. 1985. Clerk to Hon. John B. Hannum U.S. dist. court, 1984; trust officer Provident Nat. Bank, Phila., 1985-89; sole practice Haverford, Pa., 1989—. Mem. ABA, S.R. (bd. dirs. Pa. Soc. 1987—, sec. 1991-95, treas. 1995-97, v.p. 1997—), Ardmore Presbyn. Ch. (deacon), Pa. Bar Assn., Phila. Bar Assn., Soc. Mayflower Descendants, Colonial Soc. Pa., Soc. Colonial Wars, Mil. Order Loyal Legion U.S. (sec. 1993-95, v.p. 1995-97, pres. 1997—), The Racquet Club, The Union League of Phila., The Phila. Club, Phi Alpha Delta (pres. local chpt. 1984-85), Alpha Delta Phi. Republican. Presbyterian. Estate planning, Probate, Estate taxation. Office: 355 Lancaster Ave Haverford PA 19041-1547

**FRICK, JOHN MICHAEL,** lawyer, mediator; b. Dallas, June 2, 1963; s. Leroy Norwood and Rose Marie (Trock) F.; m. Jennifer Anne Wall, Oct. 13, 1989 (div. Nov. 1992); 1 child, Chelsea Lauren; m. Brandelynn Rader, May 21, 1994; children: Nicholas Rader Galvan, Riley Halston Frick. BA, So. Meth. U., 1985, BS, 1985, JD, 1988. Bar: Tex., U.S. Dist. Ct. (no. dist.) Tex. 1989, U.S. Dist. Ct. (we., ea. and so. dists.) Tex. 1992, U.S. Ct. Appeals (5th cir.) 1992. Briefing atty. Ct. Appeals (5th dist.) Tex., Dallas, 1988-89; assoc. Godwin & Carlton, P.C., Dallas, 1989-95; ptnr. Mills Presby and Assocs., L.L.P., Dallas, 1995—; adj. prof. law So. Meth. U., Dallas, 1997; summary jury trial judge Dallas County Soft Tissue Summary Jury Trial Pilot Program. Mem. Dallas Bar Assn., Collin County Bar Assn. Roman Catholic. State civil litigation, Federal civil litigation, Alternative dispute resolution. Office: Mills Presby and Assocs LLP 5910 N Central Ewy Ste 900 Dallas TX 75206-5141

**FRICK, ROBERT HATHAWAY,** lawyer; b. Cleve., June 28, 1924; s. Claude Oates and Urshal May (Hathaway) F.; m. Lenore M. Maurin, Aug. 16, 1947 (dec. Sept. 1993); children: Elaine D. Frick , Barbara A. Frick Bundick, Catherine L. Frick Cayer. BBA, U. Mich., 1948, JD, 1950; postgrad. Harvard Bus. Sch., 1965. Bar: Mich. 1951, Ill. 1951, Ohio 1952, N.Y. 1962, U.S. Supreme Ct. 1981. Atty., Amoco Corp. (formerly Standard Oil Co. Ind.), Chgo., 1950, 52-60, Paris, 1960-62, N.Y.C., 1962-68, Chgo., 1968-71, assoc. gen. counsel, Chgo., 1972-87; pvt. practice, Cleve., 1951-52. Served with USAAF, 1943-46. Mem. ABA, Am. Soc. Internat. Law, Assn. of Bar of City of N.Y., Ill. Bar Assn., Chgo. Bar Assn., Order of Coif, Westmoreland Country Club, Meadows Country Club, Univ. Club Chgo., Mid Am. Club, Sigma Phi Epsilon. Republican. General corporate, Administrative and regulatory, Oil, gas, and mineral. Home: 921 Westerfield Dr Wilmette IL 60091-1810

**FRICKE, DAVID ROBERT,** lawyer; b. Bloomfield Hills, Mich., Apr. 7, 1961; s. Richard I. and Jeanne Fricke; m. Geri M. Matusiak, June 30, 1984; children: Sarah P., Ryan D., Grace J. BA, U. Vt., 1983; JD, Wake Forest U., 1986. Bar: N.C. 1986, U.S. Dist. Ct. (ea. dist.) N.C. 1986. Assoc. LeBoeuf, Lamb, Leiby & MacRae, Raleigh, N.C., 1986-93; ptnr. Hunton & Williams, Raleigh, 1994—; adj. faculty mem. Meredith Coll., Raleigh, 1993-96. Mem. ABA, N.C. State Bar, Nat. Assn. Bond Lawyers. Democrat. Avocations: golf, reading, traveling. Municipal (including bonds), Real property, Finance. Office: Hunton & Williams One Hannover Sq Fayetteville St Mall Raleigh NC 27602

**FRICKE, RICHARD JOHN,** lawyer; b. Ithaca, N.Y., Apr. 17, 1945; s. Richard I. and Jeanne L. (Hines) F.; m. Carol A. Borelli, June 17, 1967 (div. 1990); children: Laura, Richard, Amanda; m. Penny Yrizarry, Dec. 29, 1990 (div. 1999); children: Stephanie, Matthew, Tyler. BA, Cornell U., 1967, JD, 1970. Bar: Conn. 1970. Assoc. Gregory & Adams, Wilton, Conn., 1970-73; ptnr. Crehan & Fricke, Ridgefield, Conn., 1973-90; gen. counsel Connex Internat. Inc.; corp. counsel, pres. Safe Alternatives Corp. of Am., Inc.; pres., gen. counsel, dir. T.F.I. Industries, Inc.; gen. counsel Gold Mustache Pub. Corp., Inc.; sec., dir. DXTC.COM, Inc.; dir. Village Bank & Trust Co.; town atty. Town of Ridgefield, 1973-81. Co-patentee low reactive pressure foam, polyurethane foam for cellulostic products. Bd. dirs. Ridgefield Community Ctr., Ridgefield Montessori, Ridgefield Community Kindergarten; founder, pres. Ridgefield Lacross League; constable Town of Wilton, Conn.; mem. Conn. Bar Commn. on Women, 1976. Mem. ABA, Conn. Bar Assn., Danbury Bar Assn. Democrat. Roman Catholic. Family and matrimonial, Real property, General practice. Address: 440 Main St Ridgefield CT 06877-4525

**FRIDKIN, JEFFREY DAVID,** lawyer; b. Kansas City, Kans., Dec. 16, 1953; s. Harold Lozar and Lucille Ann (Smith) F.; m. Lucy June Wilson, June 8, 1974; children: Dustin Jacob, Elysia Dawn. BA, U. Mo., 1977, JD, 1980. Bar: Mo. 1980, U.S. Dist. Ct. (we. dist.) Mo. 1980, U.S. Ct. Appeals (8th cir.) 1980, Fla. 1985, U.S. Dist. Ct. (so. and mid. dists.) Fla. 1986. From assoc. to ptnr. Linde, Thompson, Fairchild, Langworthy, Kohn & Van Dyke, Kansas City, 1979-85; assoc. Mershon, Sawyer, Johnston, Dunwody & Cole, Naples, Fla., 1985-88, ptnr., 1988—. Mem. Centurions, Kansas City, 1984-85. Mem. Collier County Econ. Devel. Counsel. Democrat. Federal civil litigation, State civil litigation.

**FRIEBERT, ROBERT HOWARD,** lawyer; b. Milw., Aug. 24, 1938; s. Lewis and Erna F.; m. Susan Frances Sweed, Aug. 11, 1968; children: Jonathan, Ellen, Leslie. BBA, U. Wis., 1962, LLB, 1962. Bar: Wis. 1962, U.S. Dist. Ct. (we. dist.) Wis. 1962, U.S. Ct. Appeals (7th cir.) 1964, U.S. Supreme Ct. 1967, U.S. Dist. Ct. (ea. dist.) Wis. 1968, U.S. Ct. Appeals (9th cir.) 1977, U.S. Ct. Appeals (D.C. cir.) 1998. Asst. U.S. atty. U.S. Justice Dept., Madison, Wis., 1962-64; assoc. LaFollette, Sinykin, Doyle & Abrahamson, Madison, Wis., 1964-66; state pub. defender Wis. Supreme Ct., Madison, 1966-68; assoc. Shellow, Shellow & Coffey, Milw., 1968-71; ptnr. Friebert, Finerty & St. John, Milw., 1971—. treas. campaign fund Wis. Gov. Pat Lucey, 1971; co-chair Pres. Carter Re-election Campaign, Wis., 1980, Gary Hart Campaign for Pres., Wis., 1984; chair Al Gore Campaign for Pres., Wis., 1988; trustee Med. Coll. Wis., 1993—. Recipient Human Rels. award, Am. Jewish Com., Milw., 1996. Fellow Am Acad. Appellate Lawyers; mem. Wis. Bar Assn. Administrative and regulatory, General civil litigation, General practice. Office: Friebert Finerty & St John 330 E Kilbourn Ave Ste 1250 Milwaukee WI 53202-3158

**FRIED, ARTHUR,** lawyer; m. Kym Vanderbilt. JD magna cum laude, Cornell U., 1975. Bar: N.Y. Law clk. to Hon. John M. Cannella U.S. Dist. Ct. (so. dist.) N.Y., 1975-77; with The Legal Aid Soc. N.Y.C., 1977-90; acting gen. counsel, dep. gen. counsel N.Y.C. Human Resources Adminstrn.; gen. counsel N.Y.C. Dept. Housing Preservation and Devel., to 1995, Social Security Adminstrn., Balt., 1995—. Mem. Order of Coif. Office: Social Security Adminstrn Altmeyer Bldg 6401 Security Blvd Baltimore MD 21235-0001

**FRIED, CHARLES,** law educator; b. Prague, Czechoslovakia, Apr. 15, 1935; came to U.S., 1941, naturalized, 1948; s. Anthony and Marta (Winterstein) F.; m. Anne Sumerscale, June 13, 1959; children: Gregory, Antonia. AB, Princeton U., 1956; BA, Oxford (Eng.) U., 1958, MA, 1961; LLB, Columbia U., 1960; LLD (hon.), New Eng. Sch. of Law, 1987, Pepperdine U., 1994, Suffolk U., 1996. Bar: D.C. 1961, Mass. 1966. Law clk. to Hon. John M. Harlan U.S. Supreme Ct., 1960; from asst. prof. to prof. law Harvard U., Cambridge, 1961-85, Carter prof. gen. jurisprudence, 1981-85, 89-95, Carter prof. emeritus, disting. lectr. Law Sch., 1995—, Beneficial prof. law, 1999—; assoc. justice Supreme Jud. Ct. Mass., Boston, 1995-99; spl. cons. Treasury Dept., 1961-62; cons. White House office Policy Devel., 1982, Dept. Transp., 1081-82, Dept. Justice, 1983; solicitor gen. U.S., 1985-89. Author: An Anatomy of Values, 1970, Medical Experimentation: Personal Integrity and Social Policy, 1974, Right and Wrong, 1978, Contract as Promise: A Theory of Contractual Obligation, 1981, Order and Law: Arguing the Reagan Revolution, 1991; contbr. legal and philos. jours. Guggenheim fellow, 1971-72. Fellow Am. Acad. Arts and Scis.; mem. Inst. Medicine, Am. Law Inst., Century Assn., Mass. Hist. Soc., Phi Beta Kappa. Office: Harvard Law Sch 1300 New Courthouse Cambridge MA 02138

**FRIED, DAVID M.,** lawyer; b. Perth Amboy, N.J., Aug. 14, 1956; s. Lawrence and Florence Ruth Fried; m. Ellie June Kesselman, Aug. 22, 1982; children: Danielle Jill, Holly Stephanie, Sarah Jenny. BA, Rutgers U., New Brunswick, N.J., 1978; JD, Rutgers U., Camden, N.J., 1981. Bar: N.J. 1981. Assoc. Parker, McCay & Crisendo, Mt. Laurel, N.J., 1981-83, Napodano & Raffo, Edison, N.J., 1983-84; ptnr. Blume, Goldfaden, Berkowitz et al, Chatham, N.J., 1984—. Mem. ATLA (bd. govs. N.J. chpt. 1990-98), ABOTA, N.J. Bar Assn. (civil trial com. 1996—). Avocations: tennis, golf. Personal injury, Product liability, Professional liability. Office: Blume Goldfaden Et Al 1 Main St Chatham NJ 07928-2426

**FRIED, DONALD DAVID,** lawyer; b. N.Y.C., Feb. 28, 1936; s. Fred and Sylvia (Falk) F.; m. Joan Hilbert, Sept. 15, 1963; children: Neil, Derek. BA, CCNY, 1956; JD, Harvard U., 1959. Bar: N.Y. 1959. Assoc. Conboy, Hewitt, O'Brien & Boardman, N.Y.C., 1960-68, ptnr., 1968-86; ptnr. Hunton & Williams, N.Y.C., 1986-88, 92-96; sr. counsel, 1996—; v.p., sec., assoc. gen. counsel Philip Morris Cos., Inc., N.Y.C., 1988-91. General corporate, Mergers and acquisitions, Securities. Home: 37 W 12th St New York NY 10011-8502 Office: Hunton & Williams 200 Park Ave Rm 4400 New York NY 10166-0091

**FRIED, RICHARD F.,** lawyer; b. S.I., N.Y., Apr. 13, 1961; s. Lawrence M. and Regina Fried; m. Gay L. Lieberman, Nov. 26, 1989; children: Aaron Morris, Dina Michele, Lawrence Mayer. BA, Rutgers U., 1983; JD, Western New Eng. Coll., Springfield, Mass., 1991. Bar: Conn. 1991, Mass. 1992, N.J. 1997, N.Y. 1998. Pvt. practice Springfield 1993-96; assoc. Morisi, O'Connel & Brighenti, Springfield, 1996-98, Hall & Hall, 1998-99; contract atty. East Brunswick, N.J., 1999—. Pres. Springfield Symphony Chorus, 1995-97. Mem. Mass. Bar Assn., Hampden County Bar Assn., Mass. Conveyancers Assn. Real property, Family and matrimonial. Office: 7 Green Hills Rd East Brunswick NJ 08816-2877

**FRIED, SAMUEL,** lawyer; b. Bklyn., Aug. 16, 1951; s. Zoltan and Helen (Katina) F.; m. Gigi Panush, Dec. 27, 1981; children: Eva M., Orly Z., Jacob J., Molly R., Susanna R. AB, Washington U., St. Louis, 1971; JD, Boston U., 1974, LLM, 1997. Bar: Mass. 1974, Ill. 1983, Mich. 1989; ordained rabbi, 1971. Assoc. Warner & Stackpole, Boston, 1974-77; staff atty. The Bendix Corp., Southfield, Mich., 1977-79, sr. atty., 1979-80, asst. treas., 1980-81; v.p., corp. counsel Clevite Industries, Inc., Glenview, Ill., 1981-83, v.p., sec., gen. counsel, 1983-87; v.p., sec. gen. counsel Exide Corp., Troy, Mich., 1987-91; v.p., gen. counsel The Limited Inc., 1991-99, sr. v.p., gen. counsel, sec., 1999—. Editor: Psychosurgery, 1974. Mem. ABA, Am. Corp. Counsel Assn., Mich. Gen. Counsels Assn., Phi Beta Kappa. Jewish. Avocations: music, reading. General corporate, Securities, Corporate taxation. Office: The Limited Inc PO Box 16000 3 Limited Pky Columbus OH 43216

**FRIEDEMANN, GLENN R.,** lawyer; b. Warwick, R.I., Sept. 22, 1958; s. Zygmunt J. and Ruth B. F.; m. Marilyn J. Woloohojian; 1 child, Alexander. BA, Providence Coll., 1980; JD, Suffolk U. Law Sch., 1983. Legal counsel R.I. Joint Com. Legis. Affairs, Providence, 1983-88, R.I. Office of Gen. Treasurer, Providence, 1988-92, Tillinghast, Licht & Semonoff, Providence, 1992—. Mem. ABA (computer litigation com. 1990-94), R.I. Bar Assn. (technology com. 1998—). Avocations: computer programming, skiing, sailing. Office: Tillinghast Licht & Semonoff One Park Row Providence RI 02903

**FRIEDEN, CLIFFORD E.,** lawyer; b. L.A., Mar. 8, 1949; s. Sidney S. and Norma (Stern) F.; m. Dinah S. Baumring, June 20, 1971; children: Jamie, Kari, Curtis. BA, UCLA, 1971; JD, U. Calif., Berkeley, 1974. Bar: Calif. 1974, U.S. Dist. Ct. (so. dist.) Calif. 1974, U.S. Dist. Ct. (cen. dist.) Calif. 1977. Ptnr. Rutan & Tucker, Costa Mesa, Calif., 1974—. Active Med. Disaster Response, Newport Beach, Calif., 1990-91, Orange County chpt. ARC, 1995—. Mem. Orange County Bar Assn. (del. state conv. 1983-95, chair judiciary com. 1987-88, bd. dirs. 1989-91), Phi Beta Kappa. Avocations: basketball, jogging. State civil litigation, Real property, Consumer commercial. Office: Rutan & Tucker PO Box 1950 611 Anton Blvd Ste 1400 Costa Mesa CA 92626-1998

**FRIEDENTHAL, JACK H.,** dean, educator, lawyer; b. Denver, Sept. 22, 1931; m. Jo Anne Marder; 3 children. A.B., Stanford U., 1953; J.D., Harvard U., 1958. Bar: Calif. 1959, D.C. 1990. Sole practice, 1959—; from asst. prof. to assoc. prof. Stanford (Calif.) U., 1958-64, prof., 1964-88, George E. Osborne prof. law, 1980-88, assoc. dean, 1985-87; dean, prof. George Washington U. Nat. Law Ctr., Washington, 1988-98, Freda H. Alverson prof. law, 1998—; vis. prof. U. Mich. Law Sch., Ann Arbor, 1965, 71, Harvard Law Sch., 1976-77; cons. Law Revision Commn., 1964. Co-author: Introduction to Evidence, 1985, Civil Procedure (text), 2d edit., 1993, 6th edit. 1993, Civil Procedure (casebook) 7th edit., 1997, 1993 Civil Procedure Supplement, Pleading Joinder Discovery, 1968, Gilbert Law Summaries: Civil Procedure & Practice, 1992-93; contbr. articles to profl. jours. Office: George Washington U Law Sch 2000 H St NW Washington DC 20006-4234*

**FRIEDL, RICK,** lawyer, former academic administrator; b. Berwyn, Ill., Aug. 31, 1947; s. Raymond J. and Ione L. (Anderson) F.; m. Dawn Friedl; children: Richard, Angela, Ryan, Ariana. BA, Calif. State U., Northridge, 1969; MA, UCLA, 1976; postgrad. UCLA, 1984; JD Western State U., 1987. Bar: Calif. 1988, U.S. Dist. Ct. (ctrl. dist.) Calif., 1992. Dept. mgr. Calif. Dept. Indsl. Rels., 1973-78; mem. faculty dept. polit. sci. U. So. Calif., 1978-80; pres. Pacific Coll. Law, 1981-86; staff counsel state fund, Calif., 1988-89; prin. Law Offices of Rick Friedl, 1989—. Author: The Political Economy of Cuban Dependency, 1982; tech. editor Glendale Law Rev., 1984; contbr. articles to profl. jours. Calif. State Grad. fellow, 1970-72. Mem. ABA, Calif. State Bar Assn., Los Angeles County Bar Assn., Am. Polit. Sci. Assn., Latin Am. Studies Assn., Acad. Polit. Sci., Pacific Coast Council Latin Am. Studies, Calif. Trial Lawyers Assn. Workers' compensation, Real property, Government contracts and claims. Home: PO Box 2095 California City CA 93504-0095

**FRIEDLAND, MICHAEL KEITH,** lawyer, educator; b. Fontana, Calif., Nov. 11, 1966; s. Melvin L. and Carole J. F.; m. Jennifer M. Yuan, July 18, 1993; children: Robert, Steven. BA, U. Calif., Berkeley, 1988; JD, Harvard U., 1991. Bar: Calif. 1991, U.S. Supreme Ct. 1995, U.S. Ct. Appeals (fed. cir.) 1997. Assoc. Irell & Manella, LLP, Newport Beach, Calif., 1991-96, Knobbe, Martens, Olson & Bear, LLP, Newport Beach, 1996—; adj. prof. Whittier Law Sch., Costa Mesa, Calif., 1997—. Traffic commr. City of Redlands, Calif., 1984. Mem. Fed. Bar Assn., Federalist Soc., Orange County Law Assn. Republican. Jewish. Avocations: tennis, theme parks. Intellectual property, Federal civil litigation. Office: Knobbe Martins Olson & Bear 620 Newport Center Dr Fl 16 Newport Beach CA 92660-6420

**FRIEDLAND, SHELLY LEAH,** lawyer; b. Orange, N.J., Apr. 15, 1965; d. Bernard and Zita Isa F. AB, Columbia U., 1987; JD, Harvard U., 1997. Bar: N.Y. 1998. Assoc. Paul, Weiss, Rifkind, Wharton & Garrison, N.Y.C., 1998—. General civil litigation. Office: Paul Weiss Rifkind Wharton & Garrison 1285 Ave of the Americas New York NY 10019

**FRIEDLANDER, D. GILBERT,** lawyer; b. Hazleton, Pa., Sept. 10, 1946. BA, U. Tex., 1968, JD, 1971. Bar: Tex. 1972, N.Y. 1973. Sr. shareholder, bd. dirs. Johnson & Gibbs, 1973-91; gen. counsel Electronic Data Systems Corp., Plano, Tex., 1991—; sr. v.p., corp. sec., CSU for legal affairs Electronic Data Systems Corp., Plano. Mem. ABA, N.Y. State Bar Assn., State Bar Tex. (corp. com., corp. banking and bus. law sect. 1980—, chmn. com. for rev. corp. tax law 1983-85), Dallas Bar Assn., Dallas Assn. Young Lawyers. Office: Electronic Data Systems Corp Mail Stop H3-3A-05 5400 Legacy Dr Plano TX 75024-3199*

**FRIEDLANDER, JEROME PEYSER, II,** lawyer; b. Washington, Feb. 7, 1944; s. Mark Peyser and Helen (Finkel) F.; m. Irene Bluethenthal, Apr. 23, 1972; children: Jennifer R., Tyler Weil. BS, Georgetown U., 1965; LLB, U. Va., 1968. Bar: Va. 1968, U.S. Dist. Ct. (ea. dist.) Va. 1968, U.S. Ct. Appeals (4th and D.C. cirs.) 1978, U.S. Supreme Ct. 1978. Ptnr. Friedlander & Friedlander, P.C., Arlington, Va., 1976—; substitute judge Arlington (Va.) Gen. Dist. Ct. Author: Virginia Landlord-Tenant Law, 1992, 2nd edit., 1998, The Limited Liability Company, 1994; co-author: Legal Aspects of Doing Business in North America, 1987; contbr. articles to profl. jours. With U.S. Army, 1969-71. Mem. ABA, FBA (past pres. No. Va. chpt.). Personal injury, Contracts commercial, General practice. Office: Friedlander & Friedlander PC 1364 Beverly Rd Ste 201 Mc Lean VA 22101-3627

**FRIEDLANDER, LISA L.,** lawyer; b. Washington, Apr. 23, 1969; d. Norman P. and Illeene Leventhal; m. Scott W. Friedlander, June 27, 1998. BA in Econs., U. Pa., 1991; JD, Am. U., 1995. Bar: Md. 1996, D.C. 1997, U.S. Ct. Appeals (D.C. cir.) 1997. Assoc. Cole, Raywid & Braverman, Washington, 1996-98, Preston, Gates, Ellis & Rouvelas Meeds LLP, Washington, 1998—; atty. vol. Washington Legal Clinic Homeless, 1997—. Vol. Hand to Hand, Potomac, Md., 1991—, Anti Defamation League, Washington, 1995—. Mem. ABA, Fed. Comm. Bar Assn. (vol.). Communications, General civil litigation. Office: Preston Gates Ellis & Rouvelas Meeds Llp Ste 500 1735 New York Ave NW Washington DC 20006-5209

**FRIEDLANDER, MARK,** lawyer, commissioner; b. Bklyn., Oct. 19, 1945; s. Rabbi J.W. and Jennie E. Friedlander; m. Frances M. Wahrsager, July 12, 1970 (dec. Jan. 1995); children: Eric, Robert, Sima; m. Mindy H. Greene, May 21, 1996. BA, Bklyn. Coll., 1965; JD, Harvard U., 1968; LLM, NYU, 1974. Bar: N.Y. 1969, U.S. Tax Ct. 1977, U.S. Ct. Appeals (2d cir.) 1977,

U.S. Supreme Ct. 1982. Asst. dir. adminstrn. N.Y. State 2d Judicial Dept., Bklyn., 1973-76; trial lawyer Herzfeld & Rubin P.C., N.Y.C., 1976-81; tax commr. N.Y. State Tax Commn., N.Y.C., 1981-87; assoc. commr. N.Y. State Dept. Tax and Fin., N.Y.C., 1987-89; tax commr., pres. N.Y. City Tax Appeals Tribunal, 1989—. Pres. Riverdale Jewish Cmty. Coun., Bronx, 1980—. Capt. USAF, 1969-72; col. USAFR, 1991—. Mem. Phi Beta Kappa. Avocations: historical research, opera, Jewish music, astronomy, politics. Office: NYC Tax Appeals Tribunal One Centre St Rm 2400 New York NY 10007

**FRIEDLI, HELEN RUSSELL,** lawyer; b. Indpls., July 8, 1956; d. William F. and Helen F. Russell; m. E. Kipp Friedli, May 19; children: Katherine, Laura. BS, Purdue U., 1977; JD, Ind. U., 1980. Bar: Ill. 1980. Ptnr. McDermott, Will & Emery, Chgo., 1980—. Mergers and acquisitions, General corporate, Securities. Office: McDermott Will & Emery 227 W Monroe St Ste 3100 Chicago IL 60606-5096

**FRIEDMAN, AVERY S.,** lawyer; b. Walla Walla, Wash., Aug. 5, 1945; s. Joseph H. and Marjorie (Greenbaum) F.; m. Betsey Nims, Dec. 28, 1968; children: Erika Grace, Jorey Nims, Tyler Joseph. BA, U. Louisville, 1968; JD, Cleve. State U., 1973. Bar: U.S. Ct. Appeals (6th cir.) 1974, U.S. Ct. Appeals (4th cir.) 1986, U.S. Ct. Appeals (1st cir.) 1987, U.S. Supreme Ct. 1977. Assoc. dir. Lawyers for Housing, 1972-75; chief counsel The Housing Advocates, Inc., 1975-82, Fair Housing Coun. N.E. Ohio, 1990—; atty. Friedman & Assocs., Cleve.; adj. law faculty Cleve. State U., 1973-75, asst. adj. prof. urban affairs, 1975—; vis. lectr. U. Mich., Stanford U., Duke U., U. Calif., Berkeley, U. Tex., U. N.C., U. Hawaii, U. Wis., numerous others; cons. to HUD, EEOC, City of Kansas City, Mo., State of Tex., also various human rights commns. and couns. on civil rights, others; legal cons. Office of Gen. Counsel, Nat. NAACP, 1986; spl. counsel State of Tex. Atty. Gen. and Commn. on Human Rights, 1992—; spl. counsel to pres. Internat. Assn. Office Human Rights Agys., 1996—. Civil rights. Office: 701 Citizens Bldg Cleveland OH 44114

**FRIEDMAN, BART,** lawyer; b. N.Y.C., Dec. 5, 1944; s. Philip and Florence (Beckerman) F.; m. Wendy Alpern Stein, Jan. 11, 1986; children: Benjamin Alpern, Jacob Stein. AB, L.I. U., 1966; JD, Harvard U., 1969. Bar: N.Y. 1970, Mass. 1972. Rsch. fellow Harvard U. Bus. Sch., Cambridge, Mass., 1969-70; assoc. Cahill, Gordon & Reindel, N.Y.C., 1970-72, 77-80, ptnr., 1980—; spl. counsel SEC, Washington, 1974-75, asst. dir., 1975-77; lectr. internat. tax program, Harvard U. Sch. Law, 1971, 85. Mem. vis. com. Harvard U. Grad. Sch. Edn., 1995—, com. on univ. resources, 1996—; trustee Julliard Sch., 1988—, vice chmn., 1994—; trustee Brookings Inst., 1997—, chmn. N.Y. adv. com., 1997—, coun. fgn. rels., 1995—, jt. task force on resources for fgn. affairs; mem. ind. task force on non-lethal weapons; mem., del. to NATO Hdqrs. and Field, 1998; mem. adv. bd. Remarque Inst. NYU, 1997—. Mem. Assn. Bar City of N.Y., Coun. Fgn. Rels., Explorers Club, Down Town Assn. (N.Y.C.), The River Club, City Tavern Club (Washington), The Tuxedo Club, Century Assn. Securities, General corporate. Home: 1172 Park Ave Apt 5B New York NY 10128-1213 Office: Cahill Gordon & Reindel 80 Pine St Fl 17 New York NY 10005-1790

**FRIEDMAN, BERNARD ALVIN,** federal judge; b. Detroit, Sept. 23, 1943; s. David and Rae (Garber) F.; m. Rozanne Golston, Aug. 16, 1970; children: Matthew, Megan. Student, Detroit Inst. Tech., 1962-65; JD, Detroit Coll. Law, 1968. Bar: Mich. 1968, Fla. 1968, U.S. Dist. Ct. (ea. dist.) Mich. 1968, U.S. Ct. Mil. Appeals 1972. Asst. prosecutor Wayne County, Detroit, 1968-71; ptnr. Harrison & Friedman, Southfield, Mich., 1971-78, Lippitt, Harrison, Friedman & Whitefield, Southfield, 1978-82; judge Mich. Dist. Ct. 48th dist., Bloomfield Hills, 1982-88; U.S. dist. judge Ea. Dist. Mich., Detroit, 1988—. Lt. U.S. Army, 1967-74. Recipient Disting. Service award Oakland County Bar Assn., 1986. Avocation: running. Office: US Dist Ct US Courthouse Rm 238 231 W Lafayette Blvd Detroit MI 48226-2700

**FRIEDMAN, DANIEL MORTIMER,** federal judge; b. N.Y.C., Feb. 8, 1916; s. Henry Michael F. and Julia (Freedman) Friedman; m. Leah Lipson, Jan. 16, 1955 (dec. Dec. 1969), m. Elizabeth Ellis, Oct. 18, 1975. AB, Columbia U., 1937, LLB, 1940. Bar: N.Y. 1941. Practice law N.Y.C., 1940-42; with SEC, Washington, 1942-51; with Justice Dept., Washington, 1951-78, asst. to solicitor gen., 1959-62, 2d asst. to solicitor gen., 1962-68, 1st dep. solicitor gen., 1968-78; chief judge Ct. Claims and U.S. Ct. Appeals, Washington, 1978-89, sr. judge, 1989—. Served with AUS, 1942-46. Recipient Exceptional Service award Atty. Gen., 1969. Office: US Ct Appeals Federal Circuit 717 Madison Pl NW Washington DC 20439-0002

**FRIEDMAN, ELAINE FLORENCE,** lawyer; b. N.Y.C., Aug. 22, 1924; d. Henry J. and Charlotte Leah (Youdelman) F.; m. Louis Schwartz, Apr. 10, 1949; 1 child, James Evan. BA, Hunter Coll., 1944; JD, Columbia U., 1946. Bar: N.Y. 1947, U.S. Dist. Ct. (so. and ea. dists.) N.Y., U.S. Ct. Appeals (2d cir.), U.S. Supreme Ct. 1954. Assoc. Oseas, Pepper & Siegel, N.Y.C., 1947-48, Bernstein & Benton, N.Y.C., 1948-51, Copeland & Elkins, N.Y.C., 1951-53; sole practice N.Y.C., 1953—; bd. dirs. Health Ins. Plan of Greater N.Y. Mem Fedn. Internat. des Femmes Juristes (v.p. U.S. chpt. 1993-95), N.Y. Bar Assn., Hunter Coll. Alumni Assn., Columbia Law School Assn. Jewish. Avocation: poetry. Family and matrimonial, General practice, Probate. Home: 2 Agnes Cir Ardsley NY 10502-1709 Office: 60 E 42nd St New York NY 10165-0006

**FRIEDMAN, ERIC S.,** lawyer. BA, George Washington U., 1979; JD, George Mason U., 1986. Bar: Md. 1987, D.C. 1990. Atty./investigator Montgomery County Consumer Affairs, Rockville, Md., 1980—. Office: 100 Maryland Ave Ste 330 Rockville MD 20850-2322

**FRIEDMAN, EUGENE STUART,** lawyer; b. N.Y.C., Apr. 5, 1941; s. Abe and Etta (Fischer) F.; m. Karin L. Mehlem, Feb. 3, 1968; children: Gabrielle, Douglas, Jason. AB, NYU, 1961; LLB, Columbia U., 1964. Bar: N.Y. 1965, U.S. Supreme Ct. 1979. Atty. NLRB, San Francisco, 1965-67; assoc., ptnr. Cohen, Weiss & Simon, N.Y.C., 1968-86; sr. ptnr. Friedman & Levine, N.Y.C., 1987—; lectr. Ill. Inst. Continuing Legal Edn., Chgo., 1982-84, NYU Conf. Labor & Practicing Law Inst., N.Y.C., 1983-85. Contbr. articles to profl. jours. Active N.Y. State Task Force Plant Closings, N.Y.C., 1984. With USN, 1964-65. Mem. N.Y. State Bar Assn., Assn. of Bar of City of N.Y. (chmn. labor & employment law com. 1987-90), Am. Arbitration Assn. (law com.). Democrat. Jewish. Avocations: scuba diving, tennis. Labor, Pension, profit-sharing, and employee benefits. Home: 277 W End Ave New York NY 10023-2604 Office: Friedman & Levine 1500 Broadway New York NY 10036-4015

**FRIEDMAN, HAL DANIEL,** lawyer; b. N.Y.C., Dec. 13, 1965; s. Malcom and Joyce (Danin) F. BA, U. Ky., 1989; JD, Brandies Sch. Law, Louisville, 1992. Bar: Ky. 1992, U.S. Dist. Ct. (we. and ea. dists.) Ky., U.S. Ct. Appeals (6th cir.). Assoc. Morgan & Pottinger, P.S.C., Louisville, 1992-95, supervising atty. creditors' rights divsn., 1995-98, shareholder, dir. legal practice, 1998—; adj. prof. bus. law U. Ky. Jefferson C.C., 1996-97; frequent spkr. CLE seminars. Co-author: (monograph) Consumer Bankruptcy in Kentucky: Chapter 7 Practice, 1996, 98; editor U. Louisvllle Law Rev., 1991-92; contbr. articles to law jours. Mem. ACCEPT counseling com. adv. bd. ARC, 1997—. Mem. Ky. Bar Assn. (alternative dispute resolution com. 1992—, publs. com. 1993—), Louisville Bar Assn., Sigma Chi. Consumer commercial, Bankruptcy, Contracts commercial. Office: Morgan & Pottinger PSC 601 W Main St Louisville KY 40202-2976

**FRIEDMAN, J. KENT,** lawyer; b. Columbia, S.C., Feb. 12, 1944; s. Earl B. and Rose (Frolich) F.; m. Barbara Robins, July 25, 1965 (div. Dec. 1989); children: Elizabeth, Alison, Brent, Andrew; m. Ann Loretson, Oct. 11, 1992; 1 child, Ryan. BBA, Tulane U., 1966, LLB, 1967; LLM, Boston U., 1968. Bar: Tex. 1968. Assoc. Sullivan & Worcester, Boston, 1967-68; assoc. Butler, Binion, Rice, Cook & Knapp, Houston, 1968-74, ptnr., 1974-82; mng. ptnr. Mayor, Day, Caldwell & Keeton, Houston, 1982-92, sr. ptnr., 1992—; bd. dirs. Sam Houston Race Park. Bd. govs. Am. Jewish Com., N.Y.C., 1984-94; mem. exec. com. bd. dirs. Houston Symphony, 1985—; bd. regents Tex. So. U., Houston, 1987-90; chmn. cmty. rels. coun. Jewish Fedn. Greater Houston, 1988-89; co-pres. Found. for Jones Hall, Houston, 1988-97; pres. Friends of Hermann Park, Houston, 1996-97; co-chair Greater Houston Inner City Games, 1997—. Recipient Max Nathan award Am. Jewish Com., Houston, 1990, Leon Jaworski award Houston Bar Assn. Auxilliary, 1999. Mem. Houston Club, Houston City Club. Estate planning, Estate taxation, Administrative and regulatory. Office: Mayor Day Caldwell & Keeton 700 Louisiana St Ste 1900 Houston TX 77002

**FRIEDMAN, JAMES DENNIS,** lawyer; b. Dubuque, Iowa, Jan. 11, 1947; s. Elmer J. and Rosemary Catherine (Stillmunkes) F.; m. Kathleen Marie Maersch, Aug. 16, 1969; children: Scott, Ryan, Andrea, Sean. AB in Polit. Sci., Marquette U., 1969; JD, U. Notre Dame, 1972. Bar: Wis. 1972, U.S. Supreme Ct. 1978, U.S. Ct. Appeals (D.C. cir.) 1973, U.S. Ct. Appeals (7th cir.) 1976, U.S. Ct. Appeals (6th cir.) 1989, Ill. 1996, U.S. Tax Ct. 1997. Pvt. practice Milw., 1972-81; ptnr. Quarles & Brady, Milw., 1981—; presenter in field; mem. legis. coun. spl. study com. on regulation of fin. instns. State of Wis., 1986-87; bd. dirs. Am. Paper and Packaging Corp., Concours Motors, Inc., Equal Justice Coalition, Inc. Mng. Editor: Notre Dame Law Review, 1971-72; contbr. articles to profl. jours. Alderman 4th and 7th dists. Mequon, Wis., 1979-85, pres. common coun., 1980-82, bd. ethics 1996-98, chair blue ribbon visioning com. 1998—; bd. dirs. Weyenrg, Pub. Libr. Found. Inc., 1983—, pres., 1984—; bd. dirs. Ptnrs. Advancing Values in Edn. Inc., 1987—, Wis. Law Found., 1998—; bd. visitors Marquette U. Ctr. for Study of Entrepreneurship, Milw., 1987-95; bd. dirs. Ozaukee Family Svcs., 1983—, sec., 1993-98; bd. dirs. Notre Dame Club of Milw., 1984-88, sec., 1978, v.p., 1986-88; bd. dirs. Marquette Club of Milw., 1987-88; chair attys. unit United Way Fund Dr. Greater Milw., 1987; mem. St. James Ch., Mequon. Named Outstanding Sr., Coll. of Liberal Arts, Marquette U. Mem. ABA (banking law com. sect. bus. law), State Bar Wis. (chair bd. govs. 1999—, chair exec. com. 1999—, fin. com. 1997-98, strategic planning task force 1997-98, bd. govs. 1996—, exec. com. 1998—, internat. transactions sect. bd. dirs. 1984—, sec. and chair-elect 1988-89, chair 1989-90, del. to ABA Ho. of Dels. 1980-82, standing com. on adminstrn. justice and judiciary 1979-81, legal edn. and bar admissions com. 1984-89, com. on minority lawyers 1992—, chmn. 1997—, bd. dirs. young lawyers divsn. 1978-82, chmn. divsn. bar admission stds. and requirements com. 1979, So. Regional chair 1998-99), Milw. Bar Assn., Wis. Acad. Trial Lawyers (bd. dirs. 1980-82), Wis. Bankers Assn., Milw. Country Club, Sigma Phi Epsilon. Roman Catholic. Avocations: tennis, golf. Banking, Health, General corporate. Office: Quarles & Brady 411 E Wisconsin Ave Ste 2550 Milwaukee WI 53202-4497

**FRIEDMAN, JEFFREY LAWRENCE,** lawyer; b. N.Y.C., Apr. 20, 1960; s. Alan Jay and Joan Elizabeth Friedman; m. Donna Sue Bailenson, June 24, 1990; children: Samuel Ben, Jessica Leigh. BA in Psychology, Boston U., 1982; JD, Bklyn. Law Sch., 1985. Bar: N.Y. 1985. Legal asst. Shearson Lehman Bros., N.Y.C., 1983-85, atty., 1985-93; atty. Smith Barney, N.Y.C., 1993-97, Salomon Smith Barney, N.Y.C., 1997—. Securities, Labor, General corporate. Home: 20 Hampton Ct Woodbury NY 11797-2424 Office: Salomon Smith Barney 388 Greenwich St Fl 19 New York NY 10013-2339

**FRIEDMAN, JON GEORGE,** lawyer; b. N.Y.C., Sept. 2, 1951; s. George Alexander and Viola Elizabeth (Elson) F. BBA, Adelphi U., 1972; MBA, Golden Gate U., 1972; MPA, NYU, 1974; JD, Hofstra U., 1977; MA, NYU, 1978. Bar: N.Y. 1978, U.S. Dist. Ct. (ea. and so. dists.) N.Y. 1978, U.S. Ct. Appeals (2d cir.) 1981, U.S. Supreme Ct. 1984, U.S. Dist. Ct. P.R. 1982. V.p., gen. counsel Allou Distbrs., Inc., Brentwood, N.Y., 1978-82; bus. cons. internat. trade, fin. Long Island, N.Y., 1982—; v.p., bus. editor Caribbean Bus., San Juan, P.R., 1983-84; sole practice Long Island, 1984—, P.R., 1984—. Contbr. articles to profl. jours. Mem. ABA, N.Y. State Bar Assn., Assn. of Bar of City of N.Y. Avocations: flying airplanes, parachuting, water skiing, reading, traveling. Federal civil litigation, Criminal, Private international. Home and Office: 82-52 259th St Floral Park NY 11004

**FRIEDMAN, LESLEY M.,** consultant; b. Dayton, OH, Dec. 1, 1953; d. Howard and Wilma Friedman. BA, Mt. Holyoke Coll., S. Hadley, Mass., 1975; JD, NYU, 1985. Pres., CEO Spl. Counsel Internat., N.Y.C., 1987-96; cons. West Palm Beach, Fla., 1996—. Office: 222 Lakeview Ave Ste 160-257 West Palm Beach FL 33401-6145

**FRIEDMAN, MARVIN ROSS,** lawyer; b. Mpls., July 13, 1941; s. H. W. and Katherine F.; widowed; children: Natasha E., Chloe J. BBA, U. Miami, 1966, JD, 1969. Bar: Fla. 1969. Pvt. practice, Coral Cables, Fla., 1970—. Hon. trustee Mus. Contemporary Art, Miami, 1997—, Diabetes Rsch. Found., Miami, 1997—, Mus. Modern Art, Miami, 1997—. Mem. ATLA, Fla. Acad. Trial Lawyers, Dade County Trial Lawyers Assn. Personal injury, Product liability. Office: Friedman & Friedman 2600 S Douglas Rd Ste 1011 Coral Gables FL 33134-6142

**FRIEDMAN, NICHOLAS R.,** lawyer; b. Bogata, Colombia, Nov. 13, 1946; came to U.S., 1952; s. Max and Ingrid (Rosenthal) F.; m. Mary F. Brooks, July 14, 1967; 1 child, Nicholas David. BA, Fla. State U., 1968. Bar: Fla. 1975, U.S. Dist. Ct. (so. dist.) Fla. 1975, U.S. Ct. Appeals (5th cir.) 1975. Asst. staff counsel The Fla. Bar, Miami, 1975-77; br. staff counsel The Fla. Bar, Ft. Lauderdale, Fla., 1977-78; pvt. practice Miami, 1978-80; ptnr. Rubin & Friedman, Miami, 1980-82, Bassett, Miller, Friedman & Baur, P.A., Miami, 1982-83, Bassett, Friedman & MIller, P.A., Miami, 1983-84; sr. ptnr. Friedman, Baur & Langen, P.A., Miami, 1984-86, Friedman & Baur, P.A., Miami, 1986-88, Friedman, Baur, Miller & Webner, P.A., Miami, 1988—; bd. dirs. Coll. Law Fla. State U., Tallahassee, 1982—; mem. profl. ethics com. Fla. Bar, 1987—; pres. German Am. Trade Coun., 1989—; lectr. on legal ethics. Contbg. author Fla. Reporter's Handbook, 1978—. Capt. U.S. Army, Vietnam. Decorated Bronze Star; recipient German-Am. Friendship award, German ambassador, Miami, 1986. Mem. Fla. BaR (profl. ethics com. 1987—), Phi Delta Phi, Rotary (Paul Harris fellow 1988). Real property, General corporate. Office: Friedman Baur Miller & Webner PA 100 N Biscayne Blvd 21st Fl New World Tower Miami FL 33132

**FRIEDMAN, RALPH DAVID,** lawyer; b. Phila., June 14, 1942; s. Albert H. and Reba (Goldstein) F.; m. Sandra Scott, July 11, 1965; children: Jennifer Amy, Susanne Jill. BSBA, Pa. State U., 1963; JD, Temple U., 1967. Bar: Pa. 1967, U.S. Dist. Ct. (ea. dist.) Pa. 1967, U.S. Tax Ct. 1978. Former jud. law clk. to presiding judge Ct. Common Pleas, Phila., 1968-70; ptnr. Friedman & Friedman, Jenkintown, Pa., 1970-98, Kramer & Friedman, 1998—; bd. dirs., chmn. Chase Savs. and Loan Assn., Phila.; bd. dirs. Fred Waring Enterprises, Inc., Del. Water Gap. Author: (pamphlet) What You Should Know About Real Estate, 1978. Ward leader Cheltenham Twp. Regular Rep. Orgn., Glenside, Pa., 1987-92. Paul Harris fellow Rotary. Mem. Pa. Bar Assn., Rotary (pres. Elkins Park, Pa. club 1982-83, pres. 1989-90), Gundaker Found., Montgomery County Bar Assn., Rydal Country Club, Philmont Country Club. Republican. Jewish. Avocations: golf, fountain pen collecting, tennis, O Gange model trains. General practice, Real property, Personal injury. Office: Kramer & Friedman 1077 Rydal Rd Ste 100 Rydal PA 19046-1712

**FRIEDMAN, RICHARD I(RWIN),** public defender; b. Newark, Oct. 2, 1947; s. Irving R. and Esther Friedman; m. Harriet Bronfeld, Sept. 23, 1982; children: Rebecca Friedman, Natasha Murphy. BA in Polit. Sci., Rutgers U., Newark, 1969; MSW in Cmty. Practice, U. Mich., 1971; JD, Rutgers U., Newark, 1980. Bar: N.J. 1980, U.S. Dist. Ct. N.J. 1980, N.Y. 1989, U.S. Supreme Ct. 1991, U.S. Ct. Appeals (3rd cir.) 1996; cert. in staff tng., behavior modification, school social worker, N.J. Caseworker Essex County (N.J.) Welfare Bd., 1969; cmty. organizer N.W. Interfaith Ctrs. for Racial Justice, Detroit, 1969-70; rschr., analyst legal svcs. bail project N.J. Adminstrv. Office of Cts., 1970; rschr. cmty. action program UAW, Mich., 1970-71; tchr. secondary sch., Newark, 1971-72; social worker South Orange-Maplewood Bd. Edn., 1972; program coord. North Essex (N.J.) Drug Abuse Coun., Inc., 1973-74; field rep. div. mental health advocacy N.J. Dept. Pub. Adv., 1971-81, asst. dep. pub. adv., 1981-94; atty. divsn. mental health and guardianship advocacy N.J. Office Pub. Defender, Newark, 1994-95, spl. counsel, 1995-96, asst. dep. pub. defender, 1996-98; deputy pub. defender., mng. atty. Newark, 1998—; prodr., host Sta. WFMU, East Orange, N.J., 1971-72; rschr. N.J. ACLU, 1971-72, cons. to dir. N.J. Coun. Chs., 1973; Krol coord., 1992-98; mem. adj. prof. Rutgers U. Law Sch., Newark, 1994, 97—; adj. prof. Seton Hall Law Sch., 1996—. Mem. N.J. State com. SANE, 1972-80, legal advisor, 1980-85; pres. Orange Tenants Assn., 1976; bd. govs. N.J. Fedn. YM-YWCA's Camps, 1981-97. Mem. ABA (ethics com. divsn. govt. and pub. sector lawyers 1994-96), ATLA, N.J. Bar Assn., N.Y. Bar Assn., Essex County Bar Assn. Home: 43 Green Pl North Caldwell NJ 07006-4545

**FRIEDMAN, RICHARD NATHAN,** lawyer; b. Phila., June 13, 1941; s. Martin Harry Friedman and Caroline (Fruchtman) Shaines; m. Catherine Helen Gulotta, Nov. 7, 1970; 1 child, Melissa Danielle. BA, U. Miami, 1962, JD, 1965; LLM in Taxation, Georgetown U., 1967. Bar: Fla. 1965. Staff atty. SEC, Washington, 1965-66; pvt. practice Washington, 1966-67; individual practice law, Miami, Fla., 1968—; CEO All-Star Sports Agts., Inc., 1996—; player agt. NBPA, 1996—; adj. prof. U. Miami, 1972-76; arbitrator N.Y. Stock Exch., 1973—, AMEX, NASD, 1988—, AAA, 1996—. Founder, pres. Am. Stockholders Assn., Inc., 1971-74, Stop Transit-Over People, Inc., 1975-87; chmn. Sales Taxes Oppressing People, Fla., 1987-97; mem. endowment com. U. Miami, 1970—; mem. Soc. Univ. Founders, U. Miami, 1980; co-chmn. sports com. Fla. Bar. Recipient Merit cert. Dade County Bar Assn., 1972-73; numerous certs. of appreciation Rotary Internat., Kiwanis and other service orgns., 1970—; Richard N. Friedman Week held in his honor City of Homestead, Fla., Apr. 1978; named Hon. Citizen State of Tenn., 1970, Citizen of Day Dade County (Fla.), Radio Sta. WINZ, 1980; recipient Leaders award Sunrise Community, 1986. Mem. Unified Bar D.C., Columnist Community Newspapers, Miami, 1989—; featured performer motion picture Lenny, 1974, other TV and theatrical films; rec. artist The Singing Attorney. Securities, Mergers and acquisitions, Entertainment. Office: 9655 S Dixie Hwy Ste 209 Miami FL 33156-2813

**FRIEDMAN, ROBERT MICHAEL,** lawyer; b. Memphis, June 19, 1950; s. Harold Samuel and Margaret (Siegel) F.; m. Elaine Freda Burson, Dec. 21, 1975; children: Daniel Justin, Jonathan Aaron. B.S., U. Tenn., 1973, J.D., 1975; postgrad., Exeter U., Eng., 1974, Nat. Coll. Trial Advocacy, 1985. Bar: Tenn. 1976, U.S. Dist. Ct. (we. dist.) Tenn. 1977, U.S. Dist Ct. (no. dist.) Miss. 1979, U.S. Ct. Appeals (5th cir.) 1979, U.S. Supreme Ct. 1983, U.S. Dist. Ct. (so. dist.) Tex. 1986, U.S. Ct. Appeals (6th cir.) 1986. Assoc. Cassell & Fink, Memphis, 1976-78; pres., sr. ptnr. Friedman & Sissman, P.C., Memphis, 1978-91, Friedman, Sissman & Heaton, P.C., Memphis, 1991—; commr. State of Tenn. Jud. Selection Commn., 1994—; corp. legal/litigation counsel, dir. Tenn. Interpreting Svc. for Deaf, Memphis, 1981-89, Mid-South Hospitality Mgmt. Ctr., Inc., Memphis, 1984-88; legal counsel Moss Hotel Co., Inc., 1986-89, Helena Hotel Co., 1986-89, Charlestown Hotel Co., 1986-89, Jackson Hotel Co., 1986-89, Murfreesboro Hotel Co., 1986-89, Santee Hotel Co., 1986-89, Kingsport Hotel Co., 1986-89, Raleigh Hotel Assocs., Ltd., 1986-89, Ozark Regional Eye Ctr., 1986-90, Brookfield Mortgage Co., Inc., 1987—, Mt. Pleasant Hotel Co., 1987-89, Hattiesburg Hotel Assocs. Ltd., 1987-89, Wright and Assocs. Constrn. Co. Inc., 1987-90, Pro Billiards Tour Assn. Inc., 1996—; legal counsel, pres. Biloxi Hotel Co., Inc., 1986-89; litigation counsel Independence Fed. Bank Batesville, Ark., 1987-88; legal counsel Autorama, Inc., 1988—; bd. dirs./legal counsel Evan R. Harwood Day Tng. Ctr., 1989—; legal/litigation counsel Super D Drugs, Inc., 1989-93, So. Comm. Vols., Inc., WEVL FM Cmty. Radio, 1990-92; mem. staff, contbr. Tenn. Law Rev., 1974-75, recipient cert., 1975; corp. gen., litigation counsel U.S. for Inversiones Tesmo, Sociedad Anonima, Republic of Costa Rica, 1990—; rep. of Tenn. Bar Assn. and State of Tenn. to Nat. Summit Crime and Violence, 1994; legal counsel Pro Billiards Tour Assn., Inc., 1996—. Bd. dirs. Project 1st Offenders, Shelby County, Tenn., 1976-78; bd. dirs., legal counsel Memphis Community Ctr. for Deaf and Hearing Impaired, 1980-81; bd. dirs. Eagle Scout Day, Chickasaw coun. Boy Scouts Am., 1978—, Ea. Dist. committeeman, 1991-93, mem. adv. bd., 1993—, chmn. Eagle Scout recognition day, 1993-98, chaair Silver Beaver Com., 1999; scoutmaster Boy Scouts Am., Memphis, 1991—, mem. nat. bd. dirs. Nat. Eagle Scout Assn., 1998—; mem. U. Tenn. Coll. Law Alumni Adv. Coun., Dean's Cir., 1992—; rep. of Tenn. Bar Assn. and State of Tenn. Nat. Summit Crime and Violence, 1994. With USCG, 1971-77. James E. West fellow, 1996; A.S. Graves Meml. scholar, 1974-75; recipient Outstanding Svc. award and Key, Alpha Phi Omega, 1972, Am. Jurisprudence award Lawyers Co-op. Pub. Co. and Bancroft-Whitney Co., 1973-74, Chancellor's Honor award George C. Taylor Sch. Law, U. Tenn., 1975, Robert W. Richie Outstanding Svc. award Tenn. Assn. Criminal Def. Lawyers, 1993, Order of Arrow, Vigil of Honor, 1994, Nat. award Boy Scouts Am., 1996, Silver Beaver award, 1998. Mem. ABA, ATLA, Tenn. Bar Assn. (ho. dels. 1991-94, bd. dirs. criminal justice sect. 1998—, chmn. criminal justice sect. 1991-94, exec. bd. criminal justice sect. 1998-99, atty./solicitor Tenn Supreme Ct. 1994), Tenn. Jud. Selection Commn. (Tenn. state commr. 1994—), Tenn. Trial Lawyers Assn., Tenn. Assn. Criminal Defense Lawyers (bd. dirs. 1994), Nat. Assn. Criminal Def. Lawyers (vice chmn. law practice mgmt. com. 1990-93, co-chmn. forfeiture abuse task force 1991-93), Memphis and Shelby County Bar Assn., Fed. Bar Assn., Nat. Criminal Justice Assn. (charter 1984—), Alpha Phi Omega, Delta Theta Phi. Democrat. Jewish. Fax: 901-527-3633. Criminal, Personal injury, General corporate. Home: 3303 Spencer Dr Memphis TN 38115-3000 Office: Friedman Sissman & Heaton PC 100 N Main St Ste 3400 Memphis TN 38103-0534 *If we fail to vigilantly and aggressively fight to maintain each of our personal rights and liberties, we shall soon have none. If we withhold the full bounty of our individual freedoms from even the most heinous individual, by so doing we shall thereby become enslaved.*

**FRIEDMAN, RONALD MICHAEL,** judge; b. Miami, Fla., June 11, 1942; s. Milton and Sylvia S. (Stern) F.; m. Janyce L. Friedmann, May 23, 1981; stepchildren: Lisa, David. BSBA, U. N.C., 1964; JD, U. Miami, 1967; LLM in Taxation, NYU, 1969. Bar: Fla. 1967, Calif. 1969; CPA, Fla. Assoc. Wyman, Bautzer, Rothman & Kuchel, L.A., 1968-71, Lederer & Jacobs, Beverly Hills, Calif., 1971-73; ptnr. Sankary & Friedman, L.A., 1973-76, Freidin, Silber & Friedman, Miami, 1976-77; pvt. practice law Coral Gables, Fla., 1977-85; cir. ct. judge State of Fla., Miami, 1985—; instr. law sch. Northrop U., 1975-76. Author: How to Prove a Profit Motive in Horse Breeding, 1976; contbr. articles to profl. jours. Past bd. dirs. South Fla. Epilepsy Found.; past bd. dirs. Greater Miami Jewish Fedn., leadership coun.; past chmn. tax com. L.A. Bar Assn., Beverly Hills Bar Assn.; past mem. bd. dirs. Jewish Family and Children's Svcs.; past trustee U. Miami Alumni Assn.; others. Mem. Dade County Bar Assn., B'nai Brith (past pres., couns., South Dade chpt., past pres., state v.p. youth adult bd., past pres. Bench and Bar South Dade adult bd., past nat. youth commr., Outstanding Man of Yr. award Koach chpt. 1981), Fla. Bar (bd. govs., cir. com.), U. Miami Law Alumni Assn. (judicial dir., Thomas Davison III Svc. award, 1993). Democrat. Office: 1304 Dade County Courthouse 73 W Flagler St Miami FL 33130-1731

**FRIEDMAN, SAMUEL SELIG,** lawyer; b. N.Y.C., July 25, 1935; s. Nathan and Anne M. (Sobel) F.; m. Maxine E. Goldfarb, Jan. 7, 1961; 1 child, Alison J. BS, MIT, 1956; MBA, U. Pa., 1959; LLB, Columbia U., 1965. Bar: N.Y. 1965, U.S. Dist. Ct. (so. and ea. dists.) N.Y. 1967, U.S. Supreme Ct. 1984. Assoc. Lord, Day & Lord, N.Y.C., 1965-72; ptnr., mem. exec. com. Lord Day & Lord, Barrett Smith and predecessor firm, N.Y.C., 1972-94; ptnr. Morgan, Lewis & Bockius, N.Y.C., 1994—. Vice chmn., dir., mem. exec. com. Times Square Bus. Improvement Dist., 1992-95. 1st lt. U.S. Army, 1959-62. Mem. ABA, N.Y. State Bar Assn., Assn. of Bar of City of N.Y., MIT Club N.Y., The Penn Club, Phi Delta Phi. Avocations: travel, wine, sports. General corporate, Securities, Mergers and acquisitions. Office: Morgan Lewis & Bockius 101 Park Ave New York NY 10178-0060

**FRIEDMAN, SARI MARTIN,** lawyer; b. Bklyn., Nov. 17, 1956; d. David and Sylvia (Friedman) Martin; m. Kenneth L. Friedman, Aug. 10, 1980; children: Andrea, Deborah. BA, Hofstra U., N.Y., 1977; JD, Hofstra Law Sch., 1980. Bar: U.S. Dist. Ct. (ea. and so. dists.) N.Y., 1981, U.S. Supreme Ct. 1993. Law clk. appellate divsn. Supreme Ct., Bklyn., 1980-84; atty. pvt. practice, Garden City, N.Y., 1985—; gen. counsel Father's Rights Assn. N.Y., L.I., 1990—; counsel. Nat. Ctr. for Men, 1994—, Dad's Advocacy Group, Bklyn., 1993—. Author: Monthly Father's Rights Newsletter; mem. Hofstra U. Law Rev. Mem. Nassau Bar Assn. Office: 585 Stewart Ave Garden City NY 11530-4783

**FRIEDMAN, SCOTT EDWARD,** lawyer; b. Salt Lake City, Sept. 17, 1958. BA, Trinity Coll., Hartford, Conn., 1980; JD, Washington U., St. Louis, 1983; LLM, U. Pa., 1984. Bar: N.Y. 1984, Pa. 1984. Ptnr. Lippes Silverstein Mathias & Wexler, LLP, Buffalo, 1994—. Author: Sex Law, 1991, The Law of Parent-Child Relationships, 1992, How to Run a Family Business, 1993, How to Profit by Forming Your Own Limited Liability Company, 1995, The Successful Family Business, 1998; contbr. articles to profl. jours. Mem. ABA, N.Y. Bar Assn., Erie County Bar Assn. General corporate. Office: Lippes Silverstein Mathias & Wexler 28 Church St Buffalo NY 14202-3908

**FRIEDMAN, SIMON,** lawyer; b. Novosibirsk, USSR, Aug. 30, 1945; came to U.S., 1954; s. Ozjasz and Luba (Zinkowskaya) F.; m. Linda S. Mandeville, Feb. 25, 1984; children: Scott L. M., Lisa G. M. BA, Columbia U., N.Y.C., 1965, King's Coll., Cambridge, Eng., 1967; PHD, Yale U., 1971, JD, 1980. Bar: N.Y. 1981, Calif. 1998; U.S. Dist. Ct. (so. dist.) N.Y. 1989. Asst. prof. English Reed Coll., Portland, Oreg., 1971-77; assoc. Cravath, Swaine & Moore, N.Y.C., 1980-88; assoc. Milbank, Tweed, Hadley & McCloy, N.Y.C., 1988-93, of counsel, 1993-97; ptnr. Milbank, Tweed, Hadley & McCloy, L.A., 1997—. Corporate taxation, Taxation, general. Home: 3841 Keswick Rd La Canada CA 91011-3945 Office: Milbank Tweed Hadley McCloy 601 S Figueroa St Los Angeles CA 90017-5704

**FRIEDMAN, STEPHEN JAMES,** lawyer; b. Mar. 19, 1938; s. A.E. Robert and Janice Clara (Miller) F.; m. Fredrica L. Schwab, June 25, 1961; children: Vanessa V., Alexander S. AB magna cum laude, Princeton U., 1959; LLB magna cum laude, Harvard U., 1962. Bar: N.Y. 1962, D.C. 1982. Law clk. to justice William J. Brennan Jr. U.S. Supreme Ct., 1963-64; spl. asst. to maritime adminstr. Maritime Adminstrn., Dept. Commerce, 1964-65; assoc. Debevoise & Plimpton, N.Y.C., 1965-70, ptnr., 1970-77, 81-86, 93—; dep. asst. sec. for capital markets policy Dept. Treasury, Washington, 1977-79; commr. SEC, 1980-81; exec. v.p., gen. counsel E.F. Hutton Group Inc., N.Y.C., 1986-88, Equitable Life Assurance Soc., N.Y.C., 1988-93; lectr. law Columbia U., N.Y.C., 1974-77, 82-85. Author: An Affair With Freedom, the Opinions and Speeches of William J. Brennan, Jr., 1967; contbr. articles on legal and policy aspects of fin. inst. to profl. jours. Active Coun. on Fgn. Rels.; trustee, chmn. emeritus Am. Ballet Theatre, N.Y.C.; vice chmn. Overseas Devel. Coun.; dir. United Way N.Y.C.; mem. bd. govs. NASD, 1991-94, Chgo. Bd. Options Exch., 1982-88. With USAR, 1962-68. Mem. ABA, Assn. of Bar of the City of N.Y. (chmn. com. on securities regulation), Univ. Club. Office: Debevoise & Plimpton 875 3rd Ave Fl 23 New York NY 10022-6256

**FRIEDMAN, TOD H.,** lawyer; b. Columbus, Ohio, Sept. 6, 1962; s. Bernard and Katherine F.; married, Aug. 11, 1985; children: Rachel, Ross, Kara. BA in Journalism, Ohio State U., 1984; MS, Syracuse U., 1988, JB, 1988. Bar: Ohio 1989, U.S. Dist. Ct. (so. dist.) Ohio 1989. With U.S. Atty., Syracuse, N.Y., 1985-88; assoc. Bricker & Eckler, Columbus, 1988-94; asst. gen. counsel Schottenstein Stores Corp., Columbus, 1994—. Mem. legal and tax adv. Columbus Jewish Found., 1989—. Mem. ABA, Columbus Bar Assn. (admissions com. 1989—), Ohio Bar Assn. Real property, General corporate.

**FRIES, KENNETH EUGENE,** lawyer; m. Janet Martin; 1 child, Clint. BA, Stanford U., 1963; JD, U. Calif., Berkeley, 1966; M in Comparative Lit., U. Chgo., 1968. Atty. adviser U.S. Agy. for Internat. Devel., Washington, 1969-77, asst. gen. counsel for contract and commodity mgmt., 1977-93, dep. gen. counsel, 1994; gen. counsel U.S. Trade and Devel. Agy., Washington, 1995—; vis. instr. Internat. Devel. Law Inst., Rome; negotiation adviser Internat. Law Inst., Washington; U.S. del. devel. assistance com./fin. aspects Orgn. for Econ. Coop. and Devel., Paris; U.S. del. UN Commn. on Internat. Trade Law, Model Procurement Law. Office: 1621 N Kent St Ste 300 Arlington VA 22209-2131

**FRIEZE, H(AROLD) DELBERT,** lawyer; b. Tulsa, Feb. 15, 1943; s. Harold William and Violet Izenna (Schnelle) F.; m. Connie Dixon, Dec. 28, 1966; 1 child, Todd William. BBA, U. Okla., 1966; JD, U. Tulsa, 1975. Bar: Okla. 1975, U.S. Dist. Ct. (no. dist.) Okla. 1975, U.S. Dist. Ct. (ea. dist.) Okla. 1976. Ptnr. Petrik & Frieze, Broken Arrow, Okla., 1975—; bd. dirs. 1st Nat. Bank & Trust Co., Broken Arrow. Bd. mem. Broken Arrow Bd. Adjustment, 1976-78; asst. city atty. City Broken Arrow, 1978-81; charter mem., bd. dirs. Broken Arrow Citizens Crime Commn., 1983—; atty. Broken Arrow Bd. of Edn., 1992—. Mem. Tulsa County Bar Assn. Republican. Methodist. Lodge: Rotary (past pres. Broken Arrow club, Paul Harris fellow 1983). State civil litigation, Contracts commercial, Real property. Office: Petrik & Frieze 121 E College St Broken Arrow OK 74012-3910

**FRIGERIO, CHARLES STRAITH,** lawyer; b. Detroit, Mar. 8, 1957; s. Louie John and LaVern (Straith) F.; m. Annette Angela Russo, Oct. 18, 1985; 1 child, Charles Anthony. BA, St. Mary's U., 1979, JD, 1982. Bar: Tex. 1982, U.S. Ct. Appeals (5th cir.) 1987, U.S. Supreme Ct. 1987; cert. in personal injury trial law. Pros. atty. City Attys. Office, San Antonio, 1982-84; trial atty. City Atty's. Office, San Antonio, 1984—; litigation chief and chief prosecutor City Atty.'s Office, San Antonio, 1995; pvt. practice law enforcement litigation San Antonio, 1995—. Mem. Dem. Nat. Com., San Antonio, 1976; asst. mgr. local campaigns, San Antonio, 1976-84. Mem. ABA, Tex. Bar Assn., Fed. Bar Assn., San Antonio Bar Assn., Assn. Trial Lawyers Am., Cath. Lawyers Assn., Delta Epsilom Sigma. Democrat. Roman Catholic. Home: 317 Cleveland Ct San Antonio TX 78209-5862 Office: Riverview Towers 111 Soledad St Ste 840 San Antonio TX 78205-2219

**FRISBIE, CHARLES,** lawyer; b. Kansas City, Mo., June 1, 1939; s. A.C. Jr. and Florence (Waddell) F.; m. Julia Louise Ross, June 28, 1969; children: Ross Waddell, Andrew James Louis. AB, Princeton U., 1961; JD, U. Mich., 1964. Bar: Mo. 1964, U.S. Supreme Ct. 1968. Assoc. Lathrop Righter Gordon & Parker, Kansas City, Mo., 1964-70; ptnr. Lathrop & Norquist, Kansas City, Mo., 1971-94; mem. Lathrop & Gage L.C., Kansas City, Mo., 1994—. Lt. USAFR, 1964-70. Mem. ABA, Mo. Bar Assn. (chmn. internat. law com. 1995-97), The River Club (dir. 1993—, sec. 1995-98), Kansas City Country Club (sec., bd. dirs. 1981-84). Republican. Episcopalian. Avocations: golf, reading. Banking, Contracts commercial, Real property. Home: 808 Romany Rd Kansas City MO 64113-2013 Office: Lathrop & Gage LC 2345 Grand Blvd Ste 2600 Kansas City MO 64108-2617

**FRISBIE, CURTIS LYNN, JR.,** lawyer; b. Greenville, Miss., Sept. 13, 1943; s. Curtis Lynn and Edith L. (Brantley) F.; m. Gena F. Johnson, May 30, 1965; children: Curtis L. III, Mark A. BSBA, U. Ala., 1966; JD, St. Mary's U., San Antonio, 1971. Bar: Tex. 1971; U.S. Dist. Ct. (no. dist.) Ga. 1974, U.S. Dist. Ct. (no. dist.) Tex. 1978, U.S. Dist. Ct. (we. dist.) Tex. 1985, U.S. Dist. Ct. (ea. and so. dists.) Tex. 1986, U.S. Dist. Ct. (ea. dist.) Wis. 1986; U.S. Tax Ct. 1986; U.S. Ct. Appeals (5th cir.) 1975, U.S. Ct. Appeals (10th cir.) 1982, U.S. Ct. Appeals (8th cir.) 1987; U.S. Supreme Ct. 1977. Trial atty. Antitrust divsn. U.S. Dept. Justice, Atlanta, 1971-73; assoc. King & Spalding, Atlanta, 1974-77; ptnr. Gardere & Wynne LLP, Dallas, 1978—. Assoc. editor St. Mary's Law Jour., 1970-71. Capt. USMC, 1966-69, Vietnam. Fellow Tex. Bar Found.; mem. ABA (antitrust sect.), Tex. Bar Assn. (antitrust sect., coun. mem. 1995—), Dallas Bar Assn. (pres. antitrust and trade regulation sect.), Phi Alpha Delta. Avocations: scuba diving, racquetball, hunting. Antitrust, Federal civil litigation, Trademark and copyright. Home: 5605 Palomar Ln Dallas TX 75229-6417 Office: Gardere & Wynne LLP 3000 Thanksgiving Tower 1601 Elm St Dallas TX 75201-4761

**FRISCH, DAVID BRUCE,** lawyer; b. Bryn Mawr, Pa., Nov. 14, 1955; s. Frederick Bolte and Betty Gilmour (Roulston) F. BS in Biology with high honors, Rutgers U., 1977; MBA, U. Miami, 1978; JD, Villanova U., 1983. Bar: N.J. 1983, Pa. 1984, Fla. 1991, U.S. Dist. Ct. (N.J.) 1983. Assoc. Kirkman, Mulligan, Bell et al, Atlantic City, N.J., 1983-85; assoc. Levine, Staller, Sklar et al, Atlantic City, 1985-92, ptnr., 1992-94; prin. Law Offices David B. Frisch, Linwood, N.J., 1994—. Mem. Villanova Law Rev., 1982-83. Chmn. bd. dirs. Miss American Orgn. George H. Cook Honors scholar, 1976-77. Presbyterian. Fax: 609-926-2223. Real property, Contracts commercial, Banking. Office: 650 New Rd Linwood NJ 08221-1239

**FRISCH, HARRY DAVID,** lawyer, consultant; b. N.Y.C., June 5, 1954; s. Isaac and Regina (Rottenberg) F.; m. Sherry Beth Bannerman, 1992; children:, Rachel Michele, Michael Elliot. BS, CCNY, 1976; postgrad., Rutgers U., 1976-77; JD, Pace U., 1980. Bar: N.Y 1981, U.S. Dist. Ct. (so. and ea. dists.) N.Y. 1981, U.S. Ct. Appeals (2d cir.) 1984, U.S. Supreme Ct. 1986, U.S. Ct. Appeals (5th cir.) 1987. Law clk. Shearson Hayden Stone, Inc., N.Y.C., 1977-80; assoc. gen. counsel Shearson Loeb Rhoades, Inc., N.Y.C., 1980-82; asst. v.p., asst. corp. sec., assoc. gen. counsel Shearson/Am. Express, Inc., N.Y.C., 1982-85; v.p., sr. litigator, assoc. gen. counsel Shearson Lehman Bros., Inc., N.Y.C., 1985-88; 1st v.p., sr. litigator, assoc. gen. counsel Shearson Lehman Hutton, Inc., N.Y.C., 1988-90, Shearson Lehman Bros., Inc., N.Y.C., 1990-93; 1st v.p., sr. litigator, asst. gen. counsel Smith Barney Shearson Inc., N.Y.C., 1993-94; asst. gen. counsel Gruntal & Co. Inc., N.Y.C., 1994-97, Gruntal & Co., L.L.C., N.Y.C., 1997-99; spl. counsel Lubiner & Schmidt, N.Y.C., 1999—. Contbr. articles to profl. jours. Mem. ABA, N.Y. State Bar Assn., Assn. of Bar of City of N.Y., N.Y. County Lawyers Assn., Fed. Bar Council. Democrat. Jewish. Federal civil litigation, Securities. Home: 49 Hudson Watch Dr Ossining NY 10562-2442 Office: Lubiner & Schmidt 111 Broadway Fl 13 New York NY 10006-1901

**FRISS, WARREN EDWARD,** lawyer; b. Bklyn., Dec. 10, 1963; s. Irving and Corinne F.; m. Amanda J. Scope, May 28, 1988; children: Zachary, Taylor. BS, SUNY, 1985; JD, U. Pa., 1988. Bar: N.Y., N.J. Atty. Shea & Gould, N.Y.C., 1988-89, Hutten, Ingram, N.Y.C., 1989-95; deputy counsel gen. The Topps Co., Inc., N.Y.C., 1995—. Sports, General corporate, Intellectual property. Office: The Topps Co Inc New York NY 10004

**FRITH, DOUGLAS KYLE,** lawyer; b. Henry County, Va., Sept. 2, 1931; s. Jacob and Sally Ada (Nunn) F.; m. Ella Margaret Tuck, Sept. 10, 1960; children—Margaret Frith Ringers, Susan Elaine Lonkevich. A.B., Roanoke Coll., 1952; J.D., Washington and Lee U., 1957. Bar: Va. 1957. Sole practice, 1957-58; assoc. Taylor & Young, Martinsville, Va., 1957-58; ptnr. Young, Kiser & Frith, 1960-71, Frith, Gardner & Gardner, 1973-78; pres. Douglas K. Frith & Assocs., P.C., Martinsville, 1979—; bd. dirs. Frith Constrn. Co., Inc., Frith Equipment Corp.; substitute judge 21st Gen. Dist. Ct., 21st Juvenile and Domestic Relations Dist. Ct., 1969-80. Chmn., March of Dimes, 1960, Brotherhood Week, 1960; capt. profl. div. United Fund, 1971. Served with U.S. Army, 1952-54. Mem. ABA, Am. Bd. Trial Advocates, Va. Bar Assn., Martinsville-Henry Count Bar Assn. (pres. 1970-71), Va. Trial Lawyers Assn. (dist. v.p. 1970-71, del. at large 1971-77). Republican. Baptist. Club: Kiwanis. Personal injury, Estate planning, Real property. Address: PO Box 591 58 W Church St Martinsville VA 24112-6210

**FRITZ, COLLIN MARTIN,** lawyer; b. Des Moines, June 8, 1947; s. Collin Wilburn and Jeanne (Wills) F.; m. Susyn Miller; children: Courtney, Skylar. BA, U. Iowa, 1969, JD, 1973. Bar: Iowa 1974, Hawaii, 1977, U.S. Dist. Ct. Hawaii 1976, U.S. Ct. Appeals (9th cir.) 1980. Ptnr. Trecker Rosenberg & Fritz, Kailua, Hawaii, 1976-79, Trecker & Fritz, Kailua, 1979-80, McKenzie, Trecker & Fritz, Honolulu, 1980-93, Trecker & Fritz, 1994—. Bd. dirs. ARC, Honolulu, 1979-82, ACLU, Honolulu, 1977-83; pres. Consumer Lawyers Hawaii. Fellow Hawaii Acad. Plaintiffs Attys.; mem. Legal Aid Soc., Am. Trial Lawyers Assn., Hawaii Bar Assn. Club: Honolulu. Personal injury. Office: McKenzie Trecker and Fritz 820 Mililani St Ste 701 Honolulu HI 96813-2986

**FRITZ, MARTIN ANDREW,** lawyer; b. Pitts., May 2, 1964; s. George Richard and Margaret Jean Fritz; m. Mary Ellen Bolish, June 3, 1989; children: McKenzie B., Madison K. BA summa cum laude, U. Pitts., 1986; JD cum laude, Pa. State U., 1992. Bar: Pa. 1993. Sr. staff acct. Ernst & Young, Pitts., 1986-89; atty., CPA Duane, Morris and Heckscher, Harrisburg, Pa., 1991—; NFL agt. NFL Players Assn., Washington, 1997—; CFL agt. CFL Players Assn., Toronto, Can., 1997—; spkr. in field. Editor Dickinson Sch. of Law, Pa. State U., 1990-92. Mem. atty. adv. com. United Way of Capital Region, Harrisburg, 1996—; membership chmn. Highlands Civic Assn., Mechanicsburg, Pa., 1997; ch. coun. Grace Evang. Luth. Ch., Camp Hill, Pa., 1998—. Presdl. scholar U. Pitts., 1983-86. Mem. AICPA, Am. Assn. of Attys.-CPAs, Ctrl. Pa. Estate Planning Coun., Pa. Bar Assn. (vice-chairperson sports, entertainment, and art law com.), Sports Lawyers Assn. Republican. Lutheran. Avocations: weight lifting, running, golfing, traveling, music. Sports, Real property, General corporate. Office: Duane Morris and Heckscher PO Box 1003 Harrisburg PA 17108-1003

**FRIX, PAIGE LANE,** lawyer, accountant; b. Washington, Apr. 13, 1961; d. William Elza Smith Jr. and Janet Helen (Peoples) Davis; m. Kemmy Deane Frix, July 29, 1993; 1 child, Avery Karlin. BBA, U. Okla., 1984, JD, 1987. Bar: Okla. 1987; CPA, Okla. Pvt. practice Muskogee, Okla., 1987—; instr. Becker CPA Rev. Course, Tulsa, 1988—; cons. Frix & Foster Constrn. Co., Inc., Muskogee, 1990—. Sunday sch. tchr. Honor Heights Meth. Ch., Muskogee, 1996—; trustee Steve Yaffe Charitable Trust, Muskogee; bd. dirs. Promoting Animal Welfare Soc., Inc., Muskogee, 1992—; mem. Five Civilized Tribes Mus. Aux., 1997—. Mem. Okla. Bar Assn., Muskogee County Bar Assn. Democrat. Corporate taxation, Real property, Estate planning. Home and Office: PO Box 284 Muskogee OK 74402-0284

**FRIZELL, DAVID J.,** lawyer; b. National Park, N.J., Sept. 13, 1948; s. Robert E. and Kathleen S. (Ford) F.; m. Aurelia M. Watson, Aug. 5, 1989; children: Brigid, St. John, Catherine. AB, Rutgers U., 1970, JD (with honors), 1973. Bar: N.J. 1973, U.S. Dist. Ct. N.J. 1973, U.S. Supreme Ct. 1986. Assoc. Moss & Inglese, Metuchen, N.J., 1973-75; counsel Levin Affiliates, Plainfield, N.J., 1975-77; ptnr. Frizell & Pozycki, Metuchen, 1977-93, Frizell Goldman & Jaffe, 1993—; mem. Urban Land Inst., Washington, 1979-86, N.J. Legislature Adv. Com. Land Use Law Revisions; mem., cons. N.J. Fedn. of Planning Ofcls., Scotch Plains, 1981; lectr. Inst. for Continuing Legal Edn. Author: New Jersey Land Use Law; contbr. articles to profl. jours.; editor Land Use Law Newsletter, 1983-92. Mem. ABA, N.J. State Bar Assn. (dir. housing & urban affairs com. 1980-82, chmn. land use sect. 1983, dir. 1984—, Outstanding Service award 1983), Middlesex County Bar Assn. (chmn. real estate com. 1984), Metuchen C. of C. Dem. Roman Catholic. Avocations: sailing, running, football, basketball. E-mail: fgjlaw@aol.com. Real property, State civil litigation, Health. Office: PO Box 474 Metuchen NJ 08840

**FRIZELL, SAMUEL,** law educator; b. Buena Vista, Colo., Aug. 30, 1933; s. Franklin Guy and Ruth Wilma (Noel) F.; m. Donna Mae Knowlton, Dec. 26, 1955 (div. June 1973); children: Franklin Guy III, LaVerne Anne; m. Linda Moncure, Jul. 3, 1973 (div. June 1996); m. Jeannette Graham, Jan. 1997. AA cum laude, Ft. Lewis Coll., 1957; BA cum laude, Adams State Coll., 1959, EdM, 1960; JD, Hastings U. Calif., 1964. Bar: Calif. 1965. Assoc. atty. McCutcheon, Black, Verleger & Shea, L.A., 1964-67; atty. Law Offices Samuel Frizell, Santa Ana, Calif., 1967-82; adj. prof. Cerritos Coll., Norwalk, Calif., 1977-81; adj. prof. Western State U., Fullerton, Calif., 1982-84, assoc. prof., 1984-90, prof., 1990-98; prof. emeritus Western State U., Fullerton, 1998—; cons. Law Offices Samuel Frizell, Mira Loma, Calif., 1982—. Author: Frizell's Torts Tips, 1992; contbr. articles to profl. jours.; editor law jour. Mem. Main St. Adv. Panel, Garden Grove, Calif., 1975-76; judge pro-tem Orange County Superior Ct., Santa Ana, 1979-80; chair, com. atty. advertising Orange County Bar Assn., 1975; bd. dirs. Orange County Trial Lawyers Assn., 1972-75; adv. panel to legal assts. Cerritos Coll., Norwalk, 1982-86. Fellow Soc. Antiquaries; mem. Order of the Coif. Avocations: polo, history, horse breeding & training, saddle making. Office: Western State U 1111 N State College Blvd Fullerton CA 92831-3000

**FRIZZELL, GREGORY KENT,** judge; b. Wichita, Kans., Dec. 13, 1956; s. D. Kent and Shirley Elaine (Piatt) F.; m. Kelly Susan Nash, Mar. 9, 1991; children: Benjamin Newcomb, Hannah Kirsten, Robert Nash, David Gregory, Elizabeth Piatt, Jubilee Kathryn. BA, U. Tulsa, 1981; JD, U. Mich., 1984. Bar: Okla. 1985, U.S. Dist. Ct. (no., ea. and we. dists.) Okla. 1985, U.S. Ct. Appeals (10th cir.) 1985, U.S. Supreme Ct. 1990. Jud. clk. to judge U.S. Dist. Ct. for No. Dist. Okla., Tulsa, 1984-86; pvt. practice Tulsa, 1986-95; gen. counsel Okla. Tax Commn., 1995-97; dist. judge Tulsa County, 1997—. Counsel bd. dirs. Tulsa Speech and Hearing Assn., 1987-95, pres., 1994-95. Mem. Okla. Bar Assn. (young lawyers rep. to client security fund com. 1990-92), Am. Inns of Ct., Rotary. Avocations: duck hunting, flying. Office: Tulsa County Courthouse 500 S Denver Ave Tulsa OK 74103-3838

**FROEBE, GERALD ALLEN,** lawyer; b. The Dalles, Oreg., Feb. 16, 1935; s. Earl Wayne and Ethelene Alvina (Ogle) F.; m. Olivia Ann Tharaldson, Aug. 31, 1958; children: Dana Lynn, Heidi Ann. BBA, U. Oreg., 1956, LLB, 1961; LLM, NYU, 1962. Bar: N.Y. 1962, Oreg. 1962, U.S. Dist. Ct. Oreg. 1962. Auditor Arthur Andersen & Co., Seattle, 1956-58; lawyer, ptnr. Miller, Nash, Wiener, Hager & Carlsen, Portland, Oreg., 1962—. Editor-in-chief Oreg. Law Rev., Eugene, 1960-61. Republican. Christian. Avocations: hiking, travel. Pension, profit-sharing, and employee benefits, Taxation, general, Estate planning. Home: 1109 SW Ardmore Ave Portland OR 97205-1004 Office: Miller Nash 111 SW 5th Ave Ste 3500 Portland OR 97204-3699

**FROEHLICH, DALE EDWARD,** lawyer, air transportation executive; b. Nov. 11, 1947; m. Ann C. Grauvogl; children: Addy Johanna, Edward Michael. BA, St. Mary's Coll., Winona, Minn., 1969; JD, George Washington U., 1975, MBA, 1976; postgrad., Ctrl. Mich. U., 1978-80, Purdue U., 1978-80. Bar: S.D. 1975, D.C. 1975. Counsel, legis. asst. to Congressman Badillo (N.Y.) U.S. Ho. Reps., Washington, 1975-76; asst. prof. Sch. Bus. Adminstrn., cir Law Ctr. Ctrl. Mich. U., Mount Pleasant, Mich., 1976-79; acad. bus. adminstr. schs. of chem., material, nuc. engring. Purdue U., West Lafayette, Ind., 1979-80; dep. states atty. Minnehaha County Courtho., Sioux Falls, S.D., 1981-83; adminstrv. asst. Minnehaha County Commn., Sioux Falls, 1984-89; in-ho. corp. counsel Midco Comm., Inc., Sioux Falls, 1989-93; pres., CEO Daedalus Inc. and BAC, Inc., Sioux Falls, 1990—; part-time pres. Action Carriers/Brokers, Inc. and Total Transp. Svcs., Inc., Sioux Falls, 1994—. Bd. dirs., mem. capital improvements/bldg. com. Sioux Empire Fair; mem. Men Againt Violence and Citizens Against Rape and Domestic Violence endeavors of Domestic Violence Project; pres., bd. dirs. Vol. Info. Ctr., Youth Enrichment Svcs.; mem. judging panel Golden Rule awards JC Penney and Vol. Info. Ctr., 1996; mem. S.D. Juvenile Justice Project Task Force, Sioux Falls City Charter Revision Commn.; 1st v.p., bd. dirs., mem. outcome based study task force, mem. planning divsn./needs assessment com., mem. medium firms divsn., unit 1 campaign, mem. allocations/assessment rev. task force Sioux Empire United Way; judge ann. leadership luncheon YWCA, 1989; judge ann. contest Jr. Achievement; mem. cmty. issues com. Minn. Pub. Radio; vol. March of Dimes/Birth Defects Found., Sioux Falls Banquet, Hugh O'Brien Found./Youth Leadership; vol. arts auction, sidewalk arts festival Civic Fine Arts Ctr.; vol. Partners program Turn-About (now Turning Point); vol. capital campaign Kilian Coll.; vol. mem. Lincoln Day com., mem. Rep. Forum Elephant Club, mem. hdqrs. club, mem. state party exec. com. region IX, mem. state party point com., chmn. Minnehaha County Rep. Party; mem. adminstrv. svcs. coun., co-chairperson Cath. schs. capital fund drive St. Michael's Cath. Parish; mem. Unified Cath. Schs. Fin. Com.; chairperson budget and fin. com. Cath. Edn. Coordination Com. Bush Found. Summer Leadership fellow Harvard U., 1987. Mem. S.D. State Bar Assn. (chmn. state bar pub. info. com.), 2nd Jud. Cir. Bar Assn., Nat. Air Transp. Assn. (mem. aircraft sales com.), Nat. Bus. Aircraft Assn., Assn. Air Med. Svcs., Am. Trucking Assn., Exptl. Aircraft Assn. (local and nat. chpts.), Air Force Assn. (Dakotah chpt.), S.D. Pilots Assn., S.D. Fixed Base Operators Assn. (sec./treas.), S.D. Truckers Assn. (bd. dirs.), Sioux Falls Area C. of C. (mem. transp. com., mem. tax coun., mem. pub. affairs com., chairperson sch. budget rev. task force, presenter leadership seminar series), Sales and Mktg. Execs. (mem. membership retention com., mem. program com., mem. ann. golf outing com.), Toastmasters (v.p. Talk of the Town chpt. 1187), Lions, Rotary (bd. dirs. Downtown club, mem. spl. events com., mem. program com. 1989, 93, mem. youth exch. com.), Sioux Empire Fed. Credit Union (bd. dirs.), Refereral Ptnrs. Meeting (Downtown Club), Eta Sigma Phi (pres.), Sigma Delta Epsilon. Home: 1111 S 2nd Ave Sioux Falls SD 57105-0809

**FROHLICH, ANTHONY WILLIAM,** lawyer, master commissioner; b. Covington, Ky., Dec. 8, 1954; s. Kenneth Raymond and Joan Jude (Laake) F.; m. Candace Powell Robbins, May 31, 1975; children: Kenneth Zane, Matthew Andrew. BS, No. Ky. U., 1976, JD, 1980. Bar: Ky. 1980, U.S. Dist. Ct. (ea. dist.) Ky. 1981. Staff atty. Boone County (Ky.) Child Support Program, 1980-97; city atty. City of Walton, 1980-89; master commr. Boone County Cir. Ct., Burlington, Ky., 1989—; asst. commonwealth atty. 54th Jud. Dist., Burlington, Ky., 1984-89; ptnr. Mathis, Dallas & Frohlich, Florence, Ky., 1980-96, Law Office of Anthony W. Frohlich, Florence, Ky., 1996—; pres. Soccer Tech., Union, Ky., 1994. Bd. dirs. No. Ky. Soccer Club, Florence, 1994, Consumer Credit Counseling Svcs. Greater Cin., 1999; state coach Ky. Youth Soccer, 1994-96; coaching dir. Ky. Olympic Devel. Program Dist. One, Florence, 1992-94; active Union Town Plan Steering Com., 1999. Named Coach of Yr., No. Ky. Soccer Club, 1992. Mem. ABA, ATLA, Ky. Bar Assn., Boone County Bar Assn. (treas. 1980), Ky. Acad. Trial Lawyers. Roman Catholic. Avocations: coaching soccer, basketball. General practice. Home: 9253 Us Highway 42 Union KY 41091-7410 Office: Law Office Anthony Frohlich PO Box 396 Florence KY 41022-0396

**FROHMADER, FREDERICK OLIVER,** lawyer; b. Tacoma, Wash., Mar. 12, 1930; s. Frederick William and Elizabeth May (Farrell) F.; m. Brenda Frohmader (dec.); children: Fred Albert Aubert, Frederick William, Lisa Kim. BCS, Seattle U., 1953; LLB, Gonzaga U., 1960, JD, 1967. Bar: Wash. Lawyer in pvt. practice, Tacoma, 1960—; with Pierce County Prosecutor, Tacoma, 1961-62; represented various Wash. Indians and Indian tribes in their fishing and hunting rights under various treaties signed with U.S., 1962-83. Served to 1st lt. U.S. Army, 1953-56. Mem. Wash. State Bar Assn., Wash. State Trial Lawyers Assn., Elks. Christian. Avocations: history, military history and military science, western history, western art. Home: 629 S Winnifred St Tacoma WA 98465-2538 Office: 1130 S 11th St Tacoma WA 98405-4017

**FROHNMAYER, DAVID BRADEN,** academic administrator; b. Medford, Oreg., July 9, 1940; s. Otto J. and MarAbel (Fisher) B. F.; m. Lynn Diane Johnson, Dec. 30, 1970; children: Kirsten (dec.), Mark, Kathryn (dec.), Jonathan, Amy. AB magna cum laude, Harvard U., 1962; BA, Oxford (Eng.) U., 1964, MA (Rhodes scholar), 1971; JD, U. Calif., Berkeley, 1967; LLD (hon.), Willamette U., 1988; D Pub. Svc. (hon.), U. Portland, 1989. Bar: Calif. 1967, U.S. Dist. Ct. (no. dist.) Calif. 1967, Oreg. 1971, U.S. Dist. Ct. Oreg. 1971, U.S. Supreme Ct. 1981. Assoc. Pillsbury, Madison & Sutro, San Francisco, 1967-69; asst. to sec. Dept. HEW, 1969-70; prof. law U. Oreg., 1971-81, spl. asst. to univ. pres., 1971-79; atty. gen. State of Oreg., 1981-91; dean Sch. Law U. Oreg., 1992-94, pres., 1994—; chmn. Conf. Western Attys. Gen., 1985-86; chmn. Am. Coun. Edn. Govtl. Rels. commn, 1996-98; bd. dirs. South Umpqua Bank. Mem. Oreg. Ho. of Reps, 1975-81; mem. coun. pub. reps. NIH, 1999—; bd. dirs. Fred Hutchinson Cancer Rsch. Ctr., Nat. Marrow Donor Program, Fanconi Anemia Rsch. Fund, Inc., Tax Free Trust of Oreg. Fund; active Oreg. Progress Bd. Recipient awards Weaver Constl. Law Essay competition Am. Bar Found., 1972, 74; Rhodes scholar, 1962. Mem. ABA (Ross essay winner 1980), Oreg. Bar Assn., Calif. Bar Assn., Nat. Assn. Attys. Gen. (pres. 1987, Wyman award 1987), Round Table Eugene, Order of Coif, Phi Beta Kappa, Rotary. Republican. Presbyterian. Home: 2315 McMorran St Eugene OR 97403-1750 Office: U Oreg Johnson Hall Office of Pres Eugene OR 97403

**FROLIK, LAWRENCE ANTON,** law educator, lawyer, consultant; b. Lincoln, Nebr., Jan. 10, 1944; s. Elvin F. and Rita K. (Haley) F.; m. Ellen M. Doyle, Sept. 25, 1973; children: Winnefred, Cornelius. BA with distinction, U. Nebr., 1966; JD cum laude, Harvard U., 1969, LLM cum laude, 1972. Asst. prof. U. Pitts., 1975-78, assoc. prof., 1978-81, prof., 1981—; dir. Pitts. office programing Grater Inst. for Law & Behavioral Rsch.; bd. dirs. Kendal Corp. Author: Federal Tax Aspects of Injury, 1993, Loss and Damage, 1987; co-author: Pennsylvania Elder Law Manual, 1988, Advising the Elderly and Disabled Client, 1991, 2d edit., 1999, The Elderly and the Law: Cases and Materials, 1991, Elder Law in a Nutshell, 1995, 2d edit., 1998, Residence Options for Older or Disabled Clients, 1997, Aging and the Law: An Interdisciplinary Reader, 1999. Mem. exec. com. Gruter Inst. Law and Behavioral Rsch. Capt. U.S. Army, 1969-71. Fellow Am. Bar Found., Am. Coll. Trust and Estate Counsel; mem. Phi Beta Kappa. Home: 4345 Schenley Farms Ter Pittsburgh PA 15213-1206 Office: U Pitts Sch Law Pittsburgh PA 15260

**FROMM, EVA MARIA,** lawyer; b. Herne, Germany, May 6, 1956; came to U.S., 1959; d. Georg and Eva (Aust) F. BS in Chem. Engring., Syracuse U., 1978; JD, U. Houston, 1985. Bar: Tex. 1985, U.S. Dist. Ct. (so. dist.) Tex. 1987, U.S. Ct. Appeals (5th cir.) 1997. Engr. Chrysler Corp., Deer Park, Mich., 1978-79; process engr. Mobay Chem. Co., Baytown, Tex., 1980, ETI Engrs. Inc., Houston, 1981-82; engr. Petromas Inc., Houston, 1982-83; sr. chem. engr. NUS Corp., Houston, 1983-84; briefing clk., assoc. Hill Parker Franklin Cardwell & Jones, Houston, 1985-86; assoc. Fulbright & Jaworski LLP, Houston, 1986-93, ptnr., 1994—. Author, editor: Texas Environmental Law Handbook, 1989, 4th edit., 1996, (book chpt.) Environmental Aspects of Real Estate Transactions, 1997. Mem. ABA (co-chair real estate and probate sect., underground storage tank and RCRA com. 1994-95), Houston

Bar Assn. (co-chair legal line com. 1988-90; sec. environ. law sect. 1991, vice-chair 1992, chair 1993). Environmental, Toxic tort, Personal injury. Home: 19 Serenity Woods Pl The Woodlands TX 77382-1262 Office: Fulbright & Jaworski LLP 1301 Mckinney St Ste 5100 Houston TX 77010-3031

**FROMM, JEFFERY BERNARD,** lawyer; b. Washington, Oct. 9, 1947; s. Seymour Morris and Frances Sylvia (Goldstein) F.; m. Mary Ellen Sommer, Sept. 11, 1971; children: Aaron M., David P. BS in Elec. Engring., BA in Physics, U. Pa., 1970; JD, Widener U., 1981. Bar: Pa. 1982, Calif. 1982, U.S. Ct. Appeals (9th and fed. cirs.) 1982, Colo. 1988. Patent atty. Hewlett-Packard Co., Palo Alto, Calif., 1981-83; sr. patent atty. Hewlett-Packard Co., Palo Alto, 1983-85; mng. patent counsel Hewlett-Packard Co., Andover, Mass., 1985-87; sr. mng. counsel intellectual property Hewlett-Packard Co., Ft. Collins, Colo., 1987—. Asst. scout master Boy Scouts Am., Ft. Collins, 1988-96; asst. coach-umpire Little League, Andover and San Jose, Calif., 1983-87. Mem. ABA, Pa. Bar Assn., Calif. Bar Assn., Colo. Bar Assn., Denver Bar Assn., IEEE, Am. Corp. Counsel Assn. Avocations: skiing, golf. Computer, Patent, Trademark and copyright. Office: Hewlett-Packard Co 3404 E Harmony Rd Fort Collins CO 80528-9599

**FRONEBERGER, JOEL DOUGLAS,** lawyer; b. Sulphur Springs, Tex., Sept. 5, 1962; s. Murry E. and Johnnie M. (Inman) F.; m. Alison King, July 27, 1996. BBA, Tex. A&M U., 1987-89; JD, Okla. City U., 1992. Bar: Tex., U.S. Ct. Appeals (5th cir.), U.S. Dist. Ct. (no. dist.) Tex., U.S. Dist. Ct. (ea. dist.) Tex. Instr. LEXIS/NEXIS Mead Data Corp., Oklahoma City, 1990-92; owner Doug's Jewelers, Sulphur Springs, 1983-88; asst. atty. Law Offices of Robert B. Ardis, Sulphur Springs, 1992-93; pvt. practice Sulphur Springs, 1993-97; collections atty. Hopkins Meml. Hosp., Sulphur Springs, 1996—; mem. faculty N.E. Tex. C.C., 1997. Polio Plus campaign dir. Rotary, Sulphur Springs, 1987-88; active League Street Ch. of Christ. Mem. Hopkins County Bar Assn. (v.p.). Democratic. Avocations: flying helicopters, stained glass, music, movies, camping. Personal injury, Bankruptcy, Criminal. Office: 517 Main St Sulphur Springs TX 75482-2711

**FROST, BARRY WARREN,** lawyer; b. Glen Ridge, N.J., Aug. 17, 1947; m. Nancy Teich, Aug. 16, 1970; children: Benjamin, Alison. BS, Bradley U., 1969; JD, N.Y. Law Sch., 1976. Bar: N.J. 1976, U.S. Dist. Ct. N.J. 1976, U.S. Dist. Ct. (so. and ea. dists.) N.Y. 1977, N.Y. 1977. Assoc. Gladstein & Isaac, N.Y.C., 1972-77; ptnr. Teich, Groh & Frost, Trenton, N.J., 1977—. Bankruptcy, Contracts commercial, Banking. Office: Teich Groh & Frost 691 Highway 33 Trenton NJ 08619-4407

**FROST, BRIAN STANDISH,** lawyer; b. Kansas City, Mo., Feb. 24, 1958; s. Hugh Lathan and Sharon Duayne Frost; m. Kathy L. Whittington, Mar. 7, 1992. Student, Okla. State U., 1978-80; BBA, Washburn U., 1982, JD, 1985. Bar: Kans. 1985, U.S. Dist. Ct. Kans. 1985, U.S. Ct. Appeals (10th cir.) 1986. Assoc. Law Office Brock R. Snyder, Topeka, 1985-90, Florez and Frost, Topeka, 1990-98; Brian Frost, Atty. at Law, 1998—; counsel CASA of Shawnee County; guardian ad litem Domestic Divsn., Shawnee County; Family Law Com., Shawnee County. Mem. Topeka Bar Assn., Kans. Trial Lawyers Assn., Sigma Phi Epsilon. Democrat. Methodist. Avocations: music, computers, golf. General civil litigation, Family and matrimonial, General corporate. Home: 8001 SW 21st Ter Topeka KS 66614-4832 Office: Florez and Frost 933 S Kansas Ave Topeka KS 66612-1210

**FROST, EDMUND BOWEN,** lawyer; b. Pueblo, Colo., Dec. 5, 1942; s. Hildreth and Doris (Bowen) F.; m. Molly Spitzer; children: Julia A., Elizabeth E., Edmund N., Luette S. BA, Dartmouth Coll., 1964; JD magna cum laude, U. Mich., 1967. Bar: Colo. 1967, D.C. 1970, U.S. Supreme Ct. 1980. Assoc. Steptoe & Johnson, Washington, 1969-75; chief legal advisor to commr. ICC, Washington, 1975-76; asst. dir. for gen. litigation Bur. Competition, FTC, Washington, 1976-77; v.p., gen. counsel Chem. Mfrs. Assn., Washington, 1978-82; ptnr. Kirland & Ellis, Washington, 1982-88, Davis, Graham & Stubbs, Washington, 1988-94; sr. v.p. and gen. counsel Clean Sites, Inc., Alexandria, Va., 1994-99; bd. dirs., exec. dir., sec. Ctr. for Land Renewal, Inc., Alexandria, 1996—; shareholder, dir. Leonard Hurt Frost & Lilly, P.C., Washington, 1998—; adv. coun. Environtl. Law Inst., 1998—; bd. dirs., exec. com., sec. Comty. Coun. for Homeless, Washington, 1993—. Contbr. articles to profl. jours. Participant pub. policy dialogs on environ. issues Keystone (Colo.) Ctr., 1980—;guest artisan Washington Nat. Cathedral, 1997—. Capt. U.S. Army, 1967-69. Mem. Cosmos Club Washington. Avocations: sculpture and stone carving, skiing, mountain climbing, tuba and euphonium. Environmental, Federal civil litigation, Non-profit and tax-exempt organizations. Home: 3309 35th St NW Washington DC 20016-3141

**FROST, JEROME KENNETH,** lawyer; b. July 4, 1939; s. Carl Kenneth and Madeline May (Michel) F.; m. Carol Ann Brown, May 16, 1967; children: Arthur, Carl, Anya, Jonah, Jerome. BA, Siena Coll., 1962; JD, Boston Coll., 1965. Bar: N.Y. 1965, U.S. Dist. Ct. (no. dist.) N.Y. 1965, U.S. Ct. Appeals (2d cir.) 1982. Assoc. Wagar, Taylor, Howd & Brearton, Troy, N.Y., 1965-66; ptnr. Lee, LeForestier & Frost, Troy, N.Y., 1967-75; sole practice Troy, N.Y., 1976—; asst. corp. counsel City of Troy, 1970-73, Rensselaer County Pub. Defender, 1995. Editor Boston Coll. Law Rev., 1965. Player, agt. Lansingburgh Little League, 1982—. Presdl. scholar Boston Coll., 1965. Mem. Rensselaer County Bar Assn., Order of Coif, Alpha Sigma Nu, Delta Epsilon Sigma, Alpha Kappa Alpha, Alpha Mu Gamma. Roman Catholic. Personal injury, Family and matrimonial, Criminal. Home: 20 Deepkill Ln Troy NY 12182-9738 Office: 105 Jordan Rd Troy NY 12180-8376

**FROST, WAYNE N.,** lawyer; b. Winters, Tex., Nov. 24, 1953; s. J.F. and Dorothy (Martin) F.; m. Susan Amini, Aug. 15, 1981; children: Daniel Morgan, Charlotte Nicole. BA in Criminal Justice, U. Tex., Odessa, 1976; M Criminal Justice Adminstrn., Oklahoma City U., 1978; JD, Detroit Coll. Law, 1984; postgrad., U. Houston, 1987. Bar: Tex. 1986, U.S. Dist. Ct. (we. dist.) Tex. 1990. Law clk. U.S. Atty.'s Office, Detroit, 1984; tchg. fellow, dir. moot ct. program Detroit Coll. Law, 1984; asst. dist. atty. Midland County Dist. Atty.'s Office, Midland, Tex., 1984—, chief narcotics prosecutor, 1992—, sr. staff atty., 1986—; pvt. practice Midland, 1986—; guest lectr. Tex. Crime-Stoppers, West Tex. Area Peace Officers Assn.; instr. Tex. Narcotics Control Program. Contbr. articles to legal mag. Sunday sch. tchr. 1st Baptist Ch., Midland; hon. dep. Ector County Sheriff's Dept., Odessa, Tex., 1974—; bd. dirs. MADD, Midland, 1993—. Mem. Nat. Dist. Attys. Assn., Tex. Dist. and County Attys. Assn., Tex. Narcotics Officers Assn. (guest lectr., counsel gen.), Sheriffs Assn. Tex., Midland Scottish Rite Assn. (past pres., trustee scholarship found.), U. Tex. Alumni Assn. (life), Masons (32d degree), DeMolay (Legion of Honor), Phi Theta Kappa. Republican. Baptist. Avocations: jogging, hunting, antiques, classical music. Criminal, General practice, Family and matrimonial. Home: 4503 Teakwood Trce Midland TX 79707-1626 Office: Midland County Dist Atty's Office 200 W Wall St Ste 201 Midland TX 79701-4512 also: PO Box 2233 214 W Texas Ave Ste 815 Midland TX 79701-4600

**FROST, WINSTON LYLE,** lawyer, educator; b. Washington, June 26, 1958; s. Lyle Gooden and Elizabeth Caddell (McLennan) F. BA in Social Sci., U. Calif., Irvine, 1979; JD, O.W. Coburn Sch. of Law, 1982; MBA, Pepperdine U., 1989; LLM in Taxation, Washington U., 1993; MA in Internat. Human Rights, Simon Greenleaf U., 1994; Diplomé Internat. Human Rights, Internat. Human Rights Inst., Strasbourg, France, 1995; MA in Faith and Culture, Trinity Internat. U., 1998; postgrad., Claremont Grad. Schs., 1996—. Bar: Ill. 1982, Calif. 1986, U.S. Dist. Ct. (cen. dist.) Calif. 1987, U.S. Supreme Ct. 1987, D.C. 1989. Pvt. practice Carthage, Ill., 1982-84; adjunct faculty Carl Sandburg Coll., Carthage, Ill., 1982-84; legal editor James Pub. Co., Costa Mesa, Calif., 1985-86; assoc. Law Offices of John Ford, Irvine, Calif., 1986-89, Hunt and Colaw, Inc., Santa Ana, Calif., 1989, Cassidy, Warner, Brown, Combs and Thurber, Santa Ana, Calif., 1989-90; ptnr. Harbin and Frost, Santa Ana, 1990—; prof. Simon Greenleaf U., Anaheim, Calif., 1987-97, asst. dean Sch. Internat. Human Rights, 1994-96; acad. dean Trinity Sch. Law, 1996-97, dean 1998—; arbitrator Orange County Superior Ct., 1992—; judge pro tem Orange County Mcpl. Ct., 1992—; mediator Christian Conciliation Svc., 1995—; columnist Brokers and Agents mag., 1997—. Editor Jour. Christian Juris, 1980-81; editorial staff Athletes in Action mag., 1986-87; columnist Orange County Reporter, 1989-91; editor Orange County Bar Jour., 1991-93. Mem. campaign staff Reagan for Pres., 1980. Recipient Outstanding Achievement award The Travelers, 1987, 88. Mem. ABA, Orange County Bar Assn. (bd. dir. 1988-90, 92-95), Orange County Bar Found. (bd. dirs. 1992-95), Orange County Trial Lawyers Assn., Orange County Barristers (bd. dirs. 1988, pres. 1990), Orange County Ins. Def. Assn. (pres. 1991), Christian Legal Soc., Calif. Trial Lawyers Assn., Peter M. Elliot Inn of Ct., Kiwanis, Toastmasters. Republican. Avocations: collecting books, poetry, community theater, travel. General civil litigation, Real property. Office: Trinity Law Sch 2200 N Grand Ave Santa Ana CA 92705-7016

**FRUE, WILLIAM CALHOUN,** lawyer; b. Pontiac, Mich., Dec. 29, 1934; s. William Calhoun and Evelyn Laura Frue; m. Eloise Saunders, June 22, 1956 (div. Dec. 1989); m. Jane Torres Fletcher, Dec. 30, 1989; children: William C. III, John C., Michael C., Victoria. BA, Washington & Lee U., 1956; LLB, U. N.C., 1960. Bar: N.C. 1960, U.S. Dist. Ct. (we. dist.) N.C. 1961, U.S. Tax Ct. 1968, U.S. Ct. Appeals (4th cir.) 1988. Rsch. asst. Inst. of Govt., Chapel Hill, N.C., 1958-60; assoc. Wright & Shuford, Asheville, N.C., 1961-69; ptnr. Shuford, Frue & Sluder, Asheville, 1969-72, Shuford, Frue & Best, Asheville, 1973-84, The Frue Law Firm, Asheville, 1984—. Editor Popular Govt. mag., 1958-60. Chmn. Asheville Police Retirement Fund, 1973-83, Morehead Scholarship Selectincom., 1965-90, Asheville Planning and Zoning Commn., 1982-92. Mem. N.C. Bar Assn., Burcombe County Bar Assn., (sec., v.p. 1978-92), Trout Unltd. (N.C. coun. 1965). Democrat. Episcopalian. Avocations: fishing, camping. Real property, Probate, State civil litigation. Office: PO Box 7627 Asheville NC 28802-7627

**FRUIN, ROGER JOSEPH,** lawyer; b. El Paso, Ill., July 27, 1915; s. William Mark and Ella (Hayes) F.; m. Mary Frances Barth, June 18, 1940; children: Nancy Fluss, Karen Todd, Jeanne Cooper. AB, U. Ill., 1936, JD, 1938. Bar: Ill. 1938, U.S. Dist. Ct. (ea. dist.) Ill. 1943. Assoc. Hannah & Figenbaum, Mattoon, Ill., 1938-41; pvt. practice Paris, Ill., 1941-43, 46; ptnr. Lauher & Fruin, Paris, 1947-63; pvt. practice Paris, 1963-66; ptnr. Fruin & Lund, Paris, 1967-72; pvt. practice Paris, 1972-75; ptnr. Fruin, Andrews & Hoff, Paris, 1975-87, Fruin & Garst, Paris, 1987-91, 93-97, Fruin Garst Piper, Paris, Paris, 1991-93; ptnr. Fruin, Garst & Kash, Paris, 1997, of counsel, 1997—; asst. atty. gen. State of Ill., Paris, 1946-70; chmn. Inst. on Continuing Legal Edn., Ill. Bar Assn., Springfield, 1973-74. Contbr. articles to profl. jours. Bd. dirs. Paris Community YMCA, 1987-93; sec., treas. Paris YMCA Spl. Endowment Trust, 1982—; mem. St. Mary's Cath. Ch., Paris, former mem. ch. sch. bldg. com.; former mem. deanery and diocesan bds. Confraternity of Christian Doctrine, Diocese of Springfield, Ill. Sgt. U.S. Army, 1943-46, ETO. Recipient Addis E. Hull award IICLE, 1990; named Ill. Tree Farmer of Yr., 1994. Fellow Am. Coll. Trust & Estate Counsel; mem. ABA, Ill. State Bar Assn. (life), Paris C. of C. (bd. dirs.), U. Ill. Alumni Assn. (life), KC (grand knight 1942-43), VFW, Elks, Am. Legion. Democrat. Roman Catholic. Avocations: American Walnut Council, Illinois Walnut Council. Estate planning, Probate. Office: Fruin Garst & Kash 129 N Central Ave Paris IL 61944-1704

**FRUMER, RICHARD J.,** lawyer; b. Phila., Feb. 2, 1966; s. Marshall and Hilda F. BA in Sociology, Pa. State U., 1988; JD, Villanova Law Sch., 1991. Sole practice law Wayne, Pa., 1993—. General civil litigation, Criminal. Office: 2 S Bryn Mawr Ave Bryn Mawr PA 19010-3214

**FRY, MORTON HARRISON, II,** lawyer; b. N.Y.C., May 15, 1946; s. George Thomas Clark and Louise Magdalen (Cronin) F.; m. Patricia Laylin Coffin, May 29, 1971. AB, Princeton U., 1968; JD, Yale U., 1971. Bar: N.Y. 1973, U.S. Ct. Mil. Appeals 1973, U.S. Dsit. Ct. (so. and ea. dists.) N.Y. 1975, U.S. Ct. Appeals (2d cir.) 1975. Assoc. Cravath, Swaine & Moore, N.Y.C., 1971-72, 75-79; dep. gen. counsel Columbia Pictures Industries, Inc., N.Y.C., 1979-81; v.p., gen. cousnel Warner Home Video Inc., N.Y.C., 1982-83; exec.v.p. Wanrer Electronic Home Svcs., N.Y.C., 1983-84; sr. counsel corp. and new techs. Warner Comms. Inc., N.Y.C., 1984-85; pres., CEO, bd. dirs. The Congress Video Group, Inc., 1985-87; pres., cons. Fry Assocs., 1987-89; ptnr. Marshall, Morris, Bomser & Fry, N.Y.C., 1990-94; rubin, Bailin, Ortoli, Mayer, Baker & Fry, N.Y.C., 1995—. Mem. Dem. Nat. Fin. Com. Capt. USMC, 1966-75. Democrat. Congregationalist. Entertainment, Communications, Public international. Home: 382 Lafayette St Apt 4 New York NY 10003-6944

**FRYE, HELEN JACKSON,** judge; b. Klamath Falls, Oreg., Dec. 10, 1930; d. Earl and Elizabeth (Kirkpatrick) Jackson; m. William Frye, Sept. 7, 1952; children: Eric, Karen, Heidi; 1 adopted child, Hedy; m. Perry Holloman, July 10, 1980 (dec. Sept. 1991). BA in English with honors, U. Oreg., 1953, MA, 1960, JD, 1966. Bar: Oreg. 1966. Public sch. tchr. Oreg., 1956-63; with Riddlesberger, Pederson, Brownhill & Young, 1966-67, Husband & Johnson, Eugene, 1968-71; trial judge State of Oreg., 1971-80; U.S. dist judge Dist. Oreg. Portland, 1980-95; sr. judge U.S. Dist. Ct., Portland, 1995—. Office: 1107 US Courthouse 1000 SW 3rd Ave Portland OR 97204-2930

**FRYE, HENRY E.,** state supreme court justice; b. Ellerbe, N.C., Aug. 1, 1932; s. Walter A. and Pearl Alma (Motley) F.; m. Edith Shirley Taylor, Aug. 25, 1956; children: Henry Eric, Harlan Elbert. BS in Biol. Scis., A & T U., N.C., 1953; JD with honors, U. N.C., 1959. Bar: N.C. 1959. Asst. U.S. atty. (middle dist.), N.C., 1963-65; prof. law N.C. Central U., Durham, 1965-67; practice law Greensboro, N.C., 1967-83; rep. N.C. Gen. Assembly, 1969-80, N.C. Senate, 1980-82; assoc. justice N.C. Supreme Ct., Raleigh, 1983—; organizer, pres. Greensboro Nat. Bank, 1971-80. Deacon Providence Baptist Ch. Capt. USAF, 1953-55. Mem. ABA, N.C. Bar Assn., Greensboro Bar Assn., Nat. Bar Assn., Am. Judicature Soc. (chair bd. dirs. 1995-97), Kappa Alpha Psi. Office: NC Supreme Ct PO Box 1841 Raleigh NC 27602-1841

**FRYE, MARY CATHERINE,** prosecutor; b. Amarillo, Tex., Feb. 9, 1950; d. John Gristy and Estelle Angelina (Ashton) F.; m. Irwin Allen Popowsky, Dec. 18, 1977; children: Matthew Frye, Rebecca Susan. AB, Oberlin Coll., 1972; JD, U. Pa., 1977. Bar: Pa. 1977. Law clk. Phila. Orphans' Ct., 1977-79; assoc. Reager, Selkowitz & Adler, Harrisburg, Pa., 1980-89; staff atty. Pa. State Edn. Assn., Harrisburg, 1989-92; chief counsel Pa. Assn. Elem. and Secondary Sch. Prins., Harrisburg, 1992-94; chief civil divsn./asst. U.S. atty. U.S. Atty.'s Office (mid. dist.) Pa., Harrisburg, 1994—; adj. prof. law Widener U., Harrisburg, 1994-94. Author: Sexual Harassment: A Guide for Administrators, 1993. Democrat. Home: 4218 Kirkwood Rd Harrisburg PA 17110-3122 Office: US Atty's Office 228 Walnut St Harrisburg PA 17101-1714

**FRYE, RICHARD ARTHUR,** lawyer; b. Akron, Ohio, Sept. 3, 1948; s. Virgil Arthur and Margaret (Mullen) F.; children: Kathleen, Emily, Abigail. BA, Wittenberg U., 1970; JD, Ohio State U., 1973. Bar: Ohio 1973, U.S. Ct. Mil. Appeals, 1974, U.S. Dist. Ct. (so. dist.) Ohio 1974, U.S. Ct. Appeals (6th cir.) 1978, U.S. Supreme Ct. 1980, U.S. Ct. Appeals (fed. cir.) 1987, U.S. Ct. Appeals (9th cir.) 1998. Ptnr. Chester, Willcox & Saxbe LLP, Columbus, 1996—. Co-author: Ohio Eminent Domain Practice, 1977, Personal Injury Litigation in Ohio, 1985. Bd. dirs. Am. Heart Assn., Franklin County, Ohio, 1985-87, Legal Aid Soc. Columbus, 1996—, J. Ashburn Youth Ctr., 1996—; chmn. adv. com. on local rules U.S. Dist. Ct. for So. Dist. Ohio, 1990—; reporter adv. group Civil Justice Reform Act, 1992-97, mem. adv. group 1991-95. Fellow Columbus Bar Found., Ohio State Bar Found.; mem. Fed. Bar assn. (pres. Columbus chpt. 1991), Ohio State Bar Assn. (chmn. fed. cts. and practice com. 1988-90), Columbus Bar Assn. (chmn. fed. ct. com. 1988-91). Democrat. Methodist. Federal civil litigation, General civil litigation. Office: Chester Willcox & Saxbe LLP 17 S High St Ste 900 Columbus OH 43215-3442

**FRYE, ROLAND MUSHAT, JR.,** lawyer; b. Princeton, N.J., Feb. 8, 1950; s. Roland Mushat and Jean (Steiner) F.; m. Susan Marie Pettey, Jan. 23, 1988. AB cum laude, Princeton U., 1972; JD, Cornell U., 1975. Bar: Pa. 1975, D.C. 1978, U.S. Ct. Appeals (D.C. cir.) 1991, U.S. Supreme Ct. 1991. Litigation assoc. White and Williams, Phila., 1975-77; litigation atty. U.S. Dept. Energy, Washington, 1977-79, asst. solicitor, 1979-80; presiding officer Fed. Energy Regulatory Commn., Washington, 1980-83, chief presiding officer, 1983-85, supervisory atty., 1985-88, adv. atty., 1988-91; energy atty. Pepper, Hamilton & Scheetz, Washington, 1991-92; sr. atty. Office Commn. Appellate Adjudication U.S. Nuclear Regulatory Commn., Washington, 1992—; mediator Ctr. for Community Justice, D.C. Superior Ct., 1984-86; bd. editors alumni mag. Sidwell Friends Sch., 1994—. Editor Cornell Law Rev., 1974-75; contbr. articles to profl. jours. Mem. schs. and ann. giving coms. Princeton U., Washington and Phila., 1978-91; arbitrator Better Bus. Bur. Greater Washington, 1983-86, Phila. Ct. Common Pleas, 1975-77. Capt. USAR. Recipient Outstanding Young Man Am. award U.S. Jaycees, 1979. Mem. ABA, D.C. Bar Assn. (fee arbitration panel 1983-89, com. on alt. dispute resolution 1983-87), Fed. Bar Assn., Fed. Energy Bar Assn. (adminstrv. practice com. 1991-92), Sidwell Friends Sch. Alumni Assn. (exec. com. 1985-93, 94—, v.p. 1987-89, pres. 1989-93, Newmyer award), Soc. Cin., St. Andrews Soc., Prettyman-Leventhal Am. Inn of Ct. (barrister 1989-92, master 1992-99, exec. com. 1992-99, program chmn. 1993-95, counsellor 1995-96, pres.-elect 1996-97, pres. 1997-98, nat./emeritus mem. 1999—). Democrat. Presbyterian. Avocations: trout fishing, singing, travel. Home: 207 S Royal St Alexandria VA 22314-3329 Office: US Nuclear Regulatory Commn 11555 Rockville Pike Rockville MD 20852-2739

**FRYEFIELD, PETER JAY,** judge; b. Brookline, Mass., Feb. 27, 1949; s. Warren Baer and Ann (Steinhouse) F.; m. Diane Michelle Buerger, June 4, 1978; children: Arden Whitney, Warren Buerger, Branham Laine. BS, U Fla., 1971, JD, 1974. Bar: Fla. 1975, U.S. Dist. Ct. (mid. dist.) Fla. 1975, U.S. Ct. Appeals (5th cir.) 1978, U.S. Supreme Ct. 1980, U.S. Ct. Appeals (11th and fed. cirs.) 1983; cert. in civil trial law 1995. Pub. defender 4th Jud. Cir., State of Fla., Jacksonville, 1974-77; ptnr. Allen, Margol & Fryefield, Jacksonville, 1977-85, Margol, Fryefield & Pennington, Jacksonville, 1985-87; pvt. practice Jacksonville, 1987-91; ptnr. Fryefield & Whitman, Jacksonville, 1992-95; cir. ct. judge 4th Jud. Cir. of Fla., Jacksonville, 1995—. Pres. Blackhawk Bluff Civic Assn., Jacksonville, 1983, Kids in Concert, 1990; treas. Aslam House Inc.; bd. dirs. N.W. Mental Health Svcs. Inc. Mem. Jacksonville Bar Assn. (mem. ethics com.), Assn. Trial Lawyers Am., Acad. Fla. Trial Lawyers, DPT Litigation Group, Aquatic Injury Safety Group. Jewish. Avocations: golf, guitar, biking, skiing. Office: Duval County Courthouse 330 E Bay St Jacksonville FL 32202-2921

**FRYMAN, VIRGIL THOMAS, JR.,** lawyer; b. Maysville, Ky., Apr. 9, 1940; s. Virgil Thomas and Elizabeth Louis (Marshall) F. AB cum laude, Harvard U., 1962, LLB, 1966. Bar: N.Y. 1967, U.S. Ct. Appeals (2d cir.) 1967, U.S. Dist. Ct. (so. and ea. dists.) N.Y. 1968, U.S. Supreme Ct. 1970, U.S. Ct. Appeals (6th cir.) 1988, U.S. Dist. Ct. (ea. and we. dist.) Ky. 1988. Assoc. Cravath, Swaine & Moore, N.Y.C., 1966-73; asst. U.S. atty. U.S. Dist. Ct. (so. dist) N.Y., N.Y.C., 1973-78; assoc. gen. counsel Price Waterhouse, N.Y.C., 1978-86; staff counsel U.S. Ho. of Reps. select com. to investigate covert arms transactions with Iran, 1987; mem. Greenebaum Doll & McDonald P.L.L.C., Lexington, Ky., 1988—. Contbr. to Proving Federal Crimes, 6th edit., 1976. Mem. ABA, Assn. Bar City of N.Y., Ky. Bar Assn., Fayette County Bar Assn., Harvard Club, Idle Hour Country Club. Democrat. Episcopalian. Federal civil litigation, State civil litigation, Criminal. Home: Fed Hill Washington KY 41096-0173 Office: Greenebaum Doll & McDonald PLLC 1400 Vine Center Tower PO Box 1808 Lexington KY 40588-1808

**FRYT, MICHAEL DAVID,** lawyer; b. Colorado Springs, Colo., May 11, 1955; s. Monte Stanislaus and Dorothy Antoinette (Fischman) F. BS in Acctg. magna cum laude, U. Colo., Colorado Springs, 1977; JD, U. Colo., Boulder, 1980. Bar: Tex 1980. Tax atty. Exxon Co. U.S.A., Houston, 1980-83, Esso Eastern, Inc., Houston, 1983-85; U.S. tax atty Esso Australia Ltd., Sydney, 1985-86; sr. tax atty Exxon Chem. Internat. Inc., Brussels, 1986-88; sr tax counsel TRW Inc., Cleve., 1988—. Co-author: Planning For Belgian Coordination Centers After U.S. Tax Reform, 1987. Basketball referee, Little League baseball coach Brussels Sports Assn., 1988. Mem. ABA, State Bar Tex. Republican. Roman Catholic. Avocations: mountain climbing, tennis, basketball, baseball, golf. Corporate taxation, Mergers and acquisitions, Private international. Home: 8933 Fern Valley Cv Cordova TN 38018-7661 Office: TRW Inc 1900 Richmond Rd Cleveland OH 44124-3760

**FUCCI, RICK JAMES,** lawyer; b. Jersey City, May 19, 1968; s. James R. and Mary Jane Fucci. BA, U. Mich., 1990; JD, Boston U., 1994. Bar: Fla. 1995, Mass. 1995, U.S. Dist. Ct. (so. dist.) Fla. 1997. Assoc. Lucio, Mandler, Croland, Bronstein & Steele, P.A., Miami, Fla., 1995-96, Steele & Hanson, P.A., Miami, 1996-98, Akerman, Senterfitt & Eidson, P.A., Miami, 1998—. General corporate. Office: Akerman Senterfitt & Eidson One SE 3rd Ave Miami FL 33131

**FUCHS, JACK FREDERICK,** lawyer; b. Cin., Aug. 21, 1952; Bar: Ohio 1982, U.S. Dist. Ct. (so. dist.) Ohio 1984, U.S. Ct. Appeals (6th cir.) 1984, U.S. Ct. Appeals (4th cir.) 1989, Ky. 1992, U.S. Dist. Ct. (we. and ea. dists.) Ky. 1992. BA, U. Chgo., 1974; MA, U. Cin., 1976, JD, 1982. Bar: Ohio 1982, U.S. Dist. Ct. (so. dist.) Ohio 1984, U.S. Ct. Appeals (6th cir.) 1984, U.S. Ct. Appeals (4th cir.) 1989, Ky. 1992, U.S. Dist. Ct. (ea. and we. dists.) Ky. 1992, U.S. Ct. Appeals (3d cir.) 1995, U.S. Ct. Appeals (5th cir.) 1995. Jud. clk. to hon. John W. Peck U.S. Ct. Appeals (6th cir.), Cin., 1982-84; assoc. Paxton & Seasongood, Cin., 1984-88; assoc. Thompson, Hine and Flory, Cin., 1988-90, ptnr., 1991—. Trustee, vol. Lawyers for the Poor Found. Mem. ABA, Ohio Bar Assn., Fed. Bar Assn., Cin. Bar Assn. Democrat. Roman Catholic. Avocation: computers. Federal civil litigation, State civil litigation, General civil litigation. Home: 7700 Ashley View Dr Cincinnati OH 45227-3948 Office: Thompson Hine and Flory 312 Walnut St Ste 1400 Cincinnati OH 45202-4089

**FUCHS, OLIVIA ANNE MORRIS,** lawyer; b. Louisville, Ky., May 2, 1949; d. H.H. Morris Jr. and Betty Jean Wills Saltkill; m. Robet Edward Fuchs, Dec. 27, 1969. BA, U. Louisville, 1977; JD cum laude, 1980. Bar: Ky. 1980, Ind. 1987, U.S. Dist. Ct. (we. dist.) Ky. 1985, U.S. Tax Ct. 1987. Assoc. Brown, Todd & Heyburn, Louisville, 1981-87; mem. Conliffe, Sandmann & Sullivan PLLC, Louisville, 1987-97; pvt. practice Louisville, 1997—. Notes editor Jour. Family Law, 1979-80. Vol. advocate R.A.P.E. Relief Ctr. YWCA, Louisville, 1981-87. Mem. ABA, Ind. Bar Assn., Ky. Bar Assn., Louisville Bar Assn. (probate sect. chmn. 1990, profl. responsibility com., com. chmn. 1988), U. Louisville Law Alumni Coun. (bd. dirs., pres. 1997—), Exec. Club Louisville (pres. 1996-97), Jefferson Club, Citizens for Better Judges, Phi Alpha Delta. Democrat. Presbyterian. Estate taxation, Probate, Family and matrimonial. Office: 745 W Main St Ste 250 Louisville KY 40202-2647

**FUDGE, EDWARD WILLIAM,** lawyer; b. Lester, Ala., July 13, 1944; s. Benjamin Lee and Sybil Belle (Short) F.; m. Sara Faye Locke, June 23, 1967; children: Melanie, Jeremy. AA, Fla. Coll., Tampa, 1965; BA, Abilene Christian U., 1967, MA, 1968; JD, U. Houston, 1988. Bar: Tex. 1988, U.S. Ct. Appeals (5th cir.), U.S. Dist. Ct. (so. dist.) Tex. Minister Ch. of Christ, Kirkwood, Mo., 1968-72; editor-in-chief The C.E.I. Pub. Co., Athens, Ala., 1972-75; editor The Good Newspaper, Houston, 1982-85; propr. Providential Press, Houston, 1982—; assoc. Jenkens & Gilchrist, Houston, 1988-91, Simmons, Fletcher & Fudge, Houston, 1991-97, Lanier, Parker & Sullivan, P.C., Houston, 1997—. Author numerous books; contbr. articles to profl. jours. Elder Bering Dr. Ch. of Christ, Houston, 1983-90, 92—; bd. dirs. Christian Conciliation Svc., Houston, 1983-85, Christ's Prison Fellowship, 1993-96. Mem. ABA, Houston Bar Assn., Tex. Bar Assn., Evang. Theol. Soc. (past regional officer). Avocations: writing, publishing, lecturing, teaching. Personal injury. Home: 21442 Park Royale Dr Katy TX 77450-4723

**FUENTES-CID, PEDRO JOSE,** lawyer, lobbyist; b. Holguin, Cuba, Jan. 6, 1939; came to U.S., 1953; s. Leopoldo Bartolome and Dolores Esther Fuentes; m. Lucy Artiles, Sept. 24, 1991 (div. Jan. 1994); 1 child, Pedro B. Licentiate, U. Havana, 1961; MA, U. Miami, 1981, JD, 1987. Bar: Fla. 1989. Sole practitioner Miami, Fla., 1989—. Contbr. articles to profl. jours. Mem. ABA, ATLA, Cuban-Am. Bar Assn., Phi Alpha Theta. Republican. Roman Catholic. Avocations: sailing, camping, softball, weight lifting. State civil litigation, Admiralty, Personal injury. Office: 3727 SW 8th St Ste 106 Coral Gables FL 33134-3158

**FUFIDIO, GEORGE E.,** lawyer; b. Bronx, N.Y., May 8, 1957; s. George E., Sr. and Eleanor F.; m. Jean Marie Costa, Nov. 11, 1984; children: Maria, Michele, Andrea. BS, Fordham U., 1979; JD, U. Miami, 1982. Bar: N.Y. 1983, Fla. 1983, U.S. Dist. Ct. (so. and ea. dists.) N.Y. 1985, U.S. Supreme Ct. 1998, U.S. Ct. Appeals (2d cir.) 1997. Asst. dist. atty., dep. bur. chief, homocide bur. West Chester County Dist. Atty.'s Office, White Plains, N.Y., 1982-88; ptnr. Mancuso, Ruben & Fufidio, White Plains, 1988—. Mem. Columbia Lawyers Assn. of West Chester County (pres. 1997-98), N.Y. State

Bar Assn., N.Y. State Assn. Criminal Def. Lawyers. Criminal, Personal injury. Office: Mancuso Rubin & Fufidio Ste 1502 One North Broadway White Plains NY 10601

**FUGATE, WILBUR LINDSAY,** lawyer; b. Pulaski, Va., Mar. 27, 1913; s. Jesse Honaker and Elizabeth Gertrude (Brown) F.; m. Barbara Louise Brown, Sept. 19, 1942; m. Cornelia Wolfolk Alfriend, Jan. 2, 1971; children—William, Richard, Barbara, Elizabeth. B.A. cum. laude, Davidson Coll., 1934; LL.B., U. Va., 1937; LL.M., George Washington U., 1951, S.J.D., 1954. Bar: Va. 1937, W.Va. 1938, U.S. Supreme Ct. 1949, D.C. 1971, U.S. Dist. Ct. D.C. 1971, U.S. Ct. Appeals (D.C. cir.) 1971, U.S. Dist. Ct. (ea. dist.) Va. 1979, U.S. Ct. Appeals (5th and 8th cirs.) 1980. Assoc. Campbell & McNeer, Huntington, W.Va., 1937-38; counsel Kanawha Banking & Trust Co., Charleston, W.Va., 1938-42; with antitrust div. Dept. Justice, 1947-73; asst. chief trial sect. Dept. Justice, Washington, 1951-53; chief Honolulu office Dept. Justice, 1960-61; chief fgn. commerce sect. Dept. Justice, Washington, 1962-73; of counsel Glassie, Pewitt, Beebe & Shanks, Washington, 1974-77, Baker & Hostetler, Washington, 1977—; U.S. del. OECD Restrictive Bus. Practices Commn., 1962-73. Author: Foreign Commerce and the Antitrust Laws, 1958, 5th edit., 1997; contbr. articles to legal jours., chpts. to books; bd. advisors Va. Jour. Internat. Law, 1976—. Served to lt. USCG, 1942-45. Mem. ABA (chmn. Antitrust com. internat. law sect. 1975-76, chmn. subcoms. in patents, fgn. antitrust laws sect. antitrust law 1971-77), Fed. Bar Assn., Internat. Bar Assn., Inter-Am. Bar Assn., Cosmos Club, Univ. Club, Army-Navy Country Club. Democrat. Presbyterian. Antitrust, Private international, Administrative and regulatory. Home: 4800 Fillmore Ave Apt 1152 Alexandria VA 22311-5054 Office: 437 N Lee St Alexandria VA 22314-2301

**FUJIYAMA, RODNEY MICHIO,** lawyer; b. Honolulu, Aug. 1, 1945; s. Wallace Sachio Fujiyama and Jean (Osumi) Shin; m. Vicki Ann Yamaguchi, Dec. 28, 1968; children—Christopher, Laurie, Sandra, Jonathan, Shannon. Student Oberlin Coll., 1963-64; B.A. with high honors, U. Hawaii, 1967; J.D., U. Calif.-San Francisco, 1970. Bar: Hawaii 1970, U.S. Dist. Ct. Hawaii 1970, U.S. Ct. Appeals (9th cir.) 1971. Assoc., Chuck & Fujiyama, Honolulu, 1970-74; assoc. Law Offices of Wallace S. Fujiyama, Honolulu, 1974; ptnr. Fujiyama, Duffy, Fujiyama, Honolulu, 1975-78, Fujiyama, Duffy, Fujiyama & Koshiba, Honolulu, 1979, Fujiyama, Duffy & Fujiyama, Honolulu, 1979—; per diem judge Dist. Ct. of 1st Cir., State of Hawaii, Honolulu, 1979-85. Mem. ABA, Hawaii State Bar Assn., Assn. Trial Lawyers Am., Phi Beta Kappa. General corporate, Administrative and regulatory, Real property. Office: Fujiyama Duffy & Fujiyama 1001 Bishop St 2700 Pauahi Tower Honolulu HI 96813

**FUKUMOTO, LESLIE SATSUKI,** lawyer; b. L.A., Mar. 10, 1955; parents: Robert Fukumoto and Florence Teruko Kodama Kuroda. BA, U. Hawaii, 1977; JD, William S. Richard Sch. Law, 1980. Bar: Hawaii 1980, U.S. Dist. Ct. Hawaii 1980, U.S. Ct. Appeals (9th cir.) 1981. Dep. pub. defender State of Hawaii, Honolulu, 1980-81; assoc. Pyun, Kim & Okimoto, Honolulu, 1981-83; ptnr. Pyun, Okimoto & Fukumoto, Honolulu, 1983-84; sole practice Honolulu, 1984-85; ptnr. Fukumoto & Wong, Honolulu, 1985-93, Tanaka & Fukumoto, Honolulu, 1993-94; prin. Fukumoto Law Corp., Honolulu, 1994—; bd. dirs. Ichiryo Enterprises, Inc., Honolulu. Assoc. editor U. Hawaii Law Rev., 1979-80. Mem. ATLA, Honolulu Club. Personal injury, State civil litigation, Federal civil litigation. Office: 1001 Bishop St Ste 2760 Honolulu HI 96813-3407

**FULFREE, RICHARD W.,** lawyer; b. May 14, 1933; s. George Mitchell and Theresa (Amicucci) F.; m. Regina M. Malek, Oct. 17, 1954 (div.); children: Peter, David; m. Ellen P. Kratz, Apr. 20, 1985; children: Linda, Robert. BA, Iona Coll., 1954; LLB, JD, N.Y. Law Sch., 1959. Trial examiner N.Y. State Liquor Auth., N.Y.C., 1960-63; from trial atty. to acting corp. counsel City of Yonkers, N.Y., 1963-69; ptnr. Wekstein, Friedman & Fulfree, 1969-73, Wekstein & Fulfree, 1973-89; pvt. practice, 1989—. Avocations: racing and training standard bred horses, fishing, football, baseball, driving racehorses. Home: 115 Bennett Ave Yonkers NY 10701-6309

**FULL, ROBERT WITMER,** lawyer; b. Parkersburg, W.Va., Aug. 8, 1949; s. Donald Davis and Mary Alberta (Witmer) F.; m. Sharon Lynn Barcic, June 21, 1975; children: Robbie, Amy, Ryan, Eric. BA, W.Va. U., 1971, JD, 1974. Bar: W.Va. 1974, U.S. Dist. Ct. (so. dist.) W.Va. 1974, U.S. Ct. Appeals (4th cir.) 1990. Asst. prosecuting atty. Wood County Prosecutor's Office, Parkersburg, 1974-76; assoc. Ronning & Brown, Parkersburg, 1974-77, Ronning, Wilson & Brown, Parkersburg, 1982-84; ptnr. Ronning, Brown & Full, Parkersburg, 1977-82; assoc. Goodwin & Goodwin, Parkersburg, 1984-87, ptnr., 1988—; asst. city atty. City of Parkersburg, 1978-79. Bd. dirs. Mid Ohio Valley United Way, campaign chmn., 1999. Mem. ABA, Wood County Bar Assn. (pres. 1983-84), W.Va. State Bar Assn., Def. Trial counsel W.Va., W.Va. Bar Assn., Mid-Ohio Valley C. of C., Rotary (pres. 1993-94), ELks, Sigma Chi. Republican. Roman Catholic. General practice, General civil litigation, Contracts commercial. Home: Lakeview Estates 824 Lakeview Dr Apt 306-c Parkersburg WV 26104-1649 Office: Goodwin & Goodwin Towne Square 201 3rd St Parkersburg WV 26101-5355

**FULLAM, JOHN P.,** federal judge; b. Gardenville, Pa., Dec. 10, 1921; s. Thomas L. and Mary Nolan F.; m. Alice Hilliar Freiheit, Apr. 15, 1950; children: Nancy, Sally, Thomas, Jeffrey. B.S., Villanova U., 1942; J.D., Harvard U., 1948. Atty. Bristol, Pa., 1948-60; judge Pa. Ct. Common Pleas, 7th Jud. Dist., 1960-66; judge U.S. Dist. Ct. (ea. dist.) Pa., Phila., 1966—, chief judge, 1986-90; now sr. judge; lectr. in law U. Pa. Law Sch., Phila., Temple U. Law Sch., Phila.; mem. adv. com. Codes of Conduct of Jud. Conf. U.S., mem. adminstrn. magistrates sys., mem. com. to rev. jud. coun. disciplinary and disability orders. Democratic candidate for U.S. Congress, 1954, 56. Mem. Am. Law Inst., Pa. Bar Assn., Bucks County Bar Assn., Phila. Bar Assn. Office: 15614 US Courthouse Ind Mall W 601 Market St Philadelphia PA 19106-1713

**FULLER, DAVID OTIS, JR.,** lawyer; b. Grand Rapids, Mich., May 28, 1939; s. David Otis and Virginia Chapin (Emery) F.; m. Isabelle Patrice Gigout, July 5, 1968; children: Thomas Andrew, Christian Scott, Pierre Emery, Margaret Isabelle. BA, Wheaton Coll., 1961; JD, Harvard U., 1964; postgrad. George Washington U., 1963, U. Paris, 1966. Bar: Mich 1964, N.Y. 1967, U.S. Sup. Ct. 1968. Law clk. U.S. Ho. of Reps. Judiciary Com., 1963; assoc. Amberg, Law & Fallon, Grand Rapids, 1964-65; asst. dist. atty. N.Y. County, 1966-72, law sec. to justice, 1972-73; corp. atty. Pan Am. World Airways, Inc., 1973-74; dep. gen. counsel Reader's Digest Assn., Inc., 1974-84; pvt. practice, N.Y.C., 1984-87; ptnr. Baker, Nelson & Williams, N.Y.C., 1987-94, Bosworth, Gray & Fuller, Bronxville, N.Y., 1994—; justice Tuckahoe Village, N.Y., 1986—; lectr. Am. Bar Assn., Practicing Law Inst., Bronx C.C. Warden Episc. Ch., 1991-97. Editor Harvard Jour. on Legislation, 1962-64; contbr. articles to profl. jours. Mem. ABA, Internat. Bar Assn., N.Y. State Bar Assn. (chmn. privacy com. 1982-84), Assn. Bar City N.Y. (communications law com. 1984-87), Am. Arbitration Assn. (arbitrator 1983-96), N.Y. State Magistrates Assn. (dir. 1998—), Westchester County Bar Assn., Westchester County Magistrates Assn. (pres. 1993-94). Republican. Club: Harvard (N.Y.C.). Avocations: fishing, skiing, coins, racquet sports, French. General practice, Intellectual property, General civil litigation. Office: Bosworth Gray & Fuller 116 Kraft Ave Bronxville NY 10708-3810

**FULLER, DAVID RALPH,** lawyer; b. Pittsfield, Mass., Feb. 12, 1932; s. Everett Joseph and Myrtle Thankfull (Bellinger) F.; m. Joanne Morris, Aug. 15, 1953; children: Susan Anne, Thomas Edward, Mary Elizabeth. AB, U. Calif., Berkeley, 1953, JD, 1956. Bar: Calif. 1956, U.S. Ct. Appeals (9th cir.) 1956, U.S. Supreme Ct. 1972. Atty. Pacific Gas and Electric, San Francisco, 1956-62, Peters, Fuller, Rush et al, Chico, Calif., 1962-97; retired, 1997. Pres. Chico C. of C., 1968; trustee Chico Unified Sch. Dist., 1967-71, Butte Community Coll., Chico, 1976-90. Recipient Disting. Svc. award Chico Jr. C. of C., 1970. Mem. No. Calif. Def. Counsel Assn. (bd. dirs. 1980—), Assn. Def. Trial Lawyers, Am. Bd. Trial Advs. (assoc.), Rotary (Chico club pres. 1978, Paul Harris fellow 19660. Republican. Presbyterian. Avocations: skiing, gardening, hiking. General civil litigation. Home: 5 Canterbury Cir Chico CA 95926-2411

**FULLER, DIANNA LYNN,** lawyer; b. Glen Ridge, N.J., June 28, 1963; d. Alice E. (Middleton) F. BA, Heidelberg Coll., 1985; JD, Rutgers U., 1988. Bar: N.J. 1990, U.S. Dist. Ct. N.J. 1990. Law clk. to justices Alvin Weiss and Thomas P. Zampino Superior Ct. of N.J., Newark, 1988-89; staff atty. Essex-Newark Legal Svcs., Newark, 1989—. Mem. N.J. State Bar Assn., Essex County Bar Assn., Suburban Athletic Club. Family and matrimonial. Office: Essex-Newark Legal Svcs 106 Halsey St Fl 2 Newark NJ 07102-3018

**FULLER, HENRY CHESTER, JR.,** patent lawyer; b. Milw., Sept. 11, 1935; s. Henry Chester and Mary Levina (Caldwell) F.; m. Diane Natalie Achatz, June 13, 1964; children—Christine, Richard. B.S., U. Wis., 1957; J.D., Marquette U., 1962. Bar: Wis. 1962. Geophysicist, Chevron Oil Co., Calif., 1957-59; assoc. Affeldt & Lichtsinn, Milw., 1962-66; patent atty. Wheeler, House, Fuller & Hohenfeldt, Milw., 1966-83; pres. Fuller, House & Hohenfeldt, Milw., 1983—. Recipient 1st place award NSF, 1953. Mem. ABA, Wis. Bar Assn., Milw. Bar Assn., Am. Patent Law Assn. Lutheran. Clubs: Wis., Lions (pres. 1980) (Milw.). Patentee safety brake for chain saw. Patent, Trademark and copyright, Federal civil litigation. Office: 633 W Wisconsin Ave Milwaukee WI 53203-1918

**FULLER, JACK A.,** lawyer; b. San Pedro, Calif., May 26, 1952; s. Donald E. and Jeanne W. F. BA, U. Calif., Santa Barbara, 1975; JD, McGeorge Sch. Law, Sacramento, 1978. Dep. dist. atty. L.A. County, L.A., 1979-83; pvt. practice Long Beach, Calif., 1983—. Mem. L.A. County Bar Assn., Long Beach Bar Assn. (spkr. domestic violence def. 1994, bd. govs. 1995-96), Calif. Attys. for Criminal Justice. Avocation: golf. Office: Law Offices of Jack A Fuller 111 W Ocean Blvd Ste 625 Long Beach CA 90802-4685

**FULLER, KENNETH T.,** lawyer; b. New Brockton, Ala., Apr. 17, 1931; s. Everett Carlisle and Pauline (Boyett) F.; m. Rebecca Phillips, Mar. 28, 1953; 1 son; Mark Everett. B.S. in Commerce and Bus. Adminstrn., U. Ala., 1952, LL.B., 1957. Bar: Ala. 1957. Law clk. to justice Ala. Supreme Ct., Montgomery, 1957-58; dist. atty. 12th Jud. Cir. Ct., 1958-62; sole practice law, Enterprise, Ala., 1962-70; ptnr. Cassady, Fuller & Marsh, Enterprise, 1970—. Served to lt. col. Ala. N.G., 1952-74. Mem. ABA, Ala. Bar Assn., Ala. Def. Lawyers Assn. (dir. 1979-81, 1984-86, pres. 1998-99), Coffee County Bar Assn. (pres. 1970-72, 1978-80). Baptist. General practice, Insurance, General corporate. Office: Cassady Fuller & Marsh PO Box 780 Enterprise AL 36331-0910

**FULLER, LAWRENCE ARTHUR,** lawyer; b. Miami Beach, Fla., Mar. 8, 1949; s. Bernard Charles and Ruth (Katz) F.; m. Hope Kourland, May 26, 1974; children: Allison, Andrew. BS, Boston U., 1971; JD, U. Miami, 1974. Bar: Fla. 1974, U.S. Dist. Ct. (so. and no. dists.) Fla. 1975, U.S. Dist. Ct. (mdi. dist.) Fla. 1985, U.S. Ct. Appeals (5th cir.) 1978, U.S. Ct. Appeals (11th cir.) 1981. Law clk. Fla. Supreme Ct., Tallahassee, 1974-75; mem. Stephens, Thornton, Magill & Sevier, Miami, 1975-76; ptnr. Fuller, Feingold & Mallah, Miami Beach, 1976-90, Fuller, Mallah & Assocs., Miami Beach, 1990—. Mem. Miami Beach Budget Adv. Bd., 1980-85; mem. Miami Beach Youth Adv. Bd., 1985-91; mem. com. City of Miami Beach Young Profls., Miami Beach Tourist and Conv. Ctr. Expansion Authority, 1992-95; mem. Dade County Equal Opportunity Bd. Mem. Miami Beach Bar Assn. (bd. dirs. 1984-90), Dade County Bar Assn., Assn. Trial Lawyers Am., Acad. Fla. Trial Lawyers, Miami Beach C. of C., Am. Arbitration Assn. (arbitrator). Avocations: golf, boating, waterskiing. Fax: (305) 534-9894. E-mail: fma@fullermallah.com. General civil litigation, Insurance, Personal injury. Home: 925 N Shore Dr Miami Beach FL 33141-2439 Office: Fuller Mallah & Assocs 1111 Lincoln Rd Ste 802 Miami Beach FL 33139-2451

**FULLER, MARK EVERETT,** lawyer; b. Ala., Dec. 27, 1958; s. Kenneth T. and Rebecca (Phillips) F.; m. Mary Elisa Boyd; children: Kailin, Meredith, Everett. BS in Chem. Engring., U. Ala., Tuscaloosa, 1982, JD, 1985. Bar: Ala. 1985, U.S. Dist. Ct. Ala. 1985, U.S. Ct. Appeals (11th cir.) 1985. CEO, chmn. bd. Doss Aviation, Inc., Colorado Springs, Colo., 1989—; dist. atty. 12th Jud. Cir. Ct., 1997—. Mem. Ala. State Rep. Exec. Com. Mem. ABA, Ala. Bar Assn., Coffee County Bar Assn., Ala. Def. Lawyers Assn., Lions, Ducks Unltd., Bench and Bar. Republican. Baptist. General civil litigation, Government contracts and claims, Personal injury. Office: PO Box 311102 Enterprise AL 36331-1102

**FULLER, ROBERT E., JR.,** lawyer; b. Raleigh, N.C., Mar. 5, 1949; s. Robert E. and Ethell (Strickland) F.; 1 child, Zachary Lee. BA, Wake Forest U., 1971, JD, 1974. Bar: N.C. 1974, U.S. Dist. Ct. (ea. dist.) N.C. 1975, U.S. Supreme Ct. 1996. Assoc. Cecil P. Merritt, Atty., Goldsboro, N.C., 1974-75, Thomas E. Strickland, P.A., Goldsboro, 1975-81; atty. Robert E. Fuller, Jr., Goldsboro, 1981—; legal advisor N.C. Paralegal Assn., 1991-93, Wayne County AIDS Network, N.C., 1994—. Editor Wake Forest Jurist, 1973. Chmn. Crossroads to Understanding, Goldsboro, 1995—; bd. dirs. We Can, Goldsboro, 1995—. Mem. N.C. Bar Assn., Internat. Order Odd Fellows (Lodge 6). Democrat. Baptist. Avocations: reading John Gresham books. Pension, profit-sharing, and employee benefits, Probate. Office: 109 N William St Goldsboro NC 27530-3703

**FULLER, ROBERT L(EANDER),** lawyer; b. N.Y.C., Sept. 8, 1943; s. Robert L. and Elsie V. Fuller; m. Barbara Braverman, Dec. 5, 1973. BS cum laude, SUNY, Stony Brook, 1971; MBA, Columbia U., 1972; JD, Cath. U., Washington, 1977; M. Laws in Taxation, Georgetown U., 1981. Bar: Md. 1977, D.C. 1978; CPA: N.Y. 1974, D.C. 1975; Acct. Ernst & Ernst, N.Y.C., 1972-74; controller Warner-Jenkinson East Inc., N.Y.C., 1974-75, Atomic Indsl. Forum, Inc., N.Y.C., Washington, 1975-76; tax analyst So. Rwy. Co., Washington, 1976-78; asst. tax counsel CACI, Inc., Arlington, Va., 1978-84; tax counsel, mgr. VSE Corp., Alexandria, Va., 1984-87; exec. dir. taxes Ciba Corning Diagnostics Corp., Medfield, Mass., 1988-96; sr. mgr. KPMG Peat Marwick, LLP, Boston, 1997-98; dir. taxes Instron Corp., Canton, Mass., 1998—. With USN, 1961-67. Mem. ABA (tax sect.), AICPA, Mayflower Descendants, SAR, Sigma Pi Sigma. Corporate taxation, State and local taxation, Private international. Home: 151 Grove St Wellesley MA 02482-7001 Office: 100 Royall St Canton MA 02021-1009

**FULLER, RODNEY CHARLES,** lawyer; b. Niles, Mich., Sept. 27, 1965; s. Charles Lewis and Gwendolyn Sue (Tittle) F. BA, U. Mich., 1988; JD, Valparaiso U., 1992. Bar: Mich. 1992, U.S. Dist. Ct. (we. dist.) Mich. 1993. Staff atty. Berrien County Legal Svcs., St. Joseph, Mich., 1992-94; assoc. Jancha Law Office, St. Joseph, Mich., 1994-97; atty. pvt. practice, 1997—. Cadet Army ROTC, Ann Arbor, Mich., 1984-87. Recipient Eagle Scout award Boy Scouts Am., 1982, Order of the Arrow award (ordeal mem.), 1982. Mem. Phi Kappa Tau. Home: 915 Michigan Ave # 3 Saint Joseph MI 49085-1518 Office: Jancha Law Office 807 Myrtle Ave Saint Joseph MI 49085-2001

**FULLER, SAMUEL ASHBY,** lawyer, mining company executive; b. Indpls., Sept. 2, 1924; s. John L.H. and Mary (Ashby) F.; m. Betty Winn Hamilton, June 10, 1948; children—Mary Cheryl Fuller Hargrove, Karen E. Fuller Wolfe, Deborah R. BS in Gen. Engring. U. Cin., 1946, JD, 1947; cert. fin. planner, Coll. for Fin. Planning, 1989. Bar: Ohio 1948, Ind. 1951, Fla. 1984; cert. fin. planner, 1989. Cleve. claims rep. Mfrs. and Mchts. Indemnity Co., 1947-48; claims supr. Indemnity Ins. Co. N.Am., 1948-50; with firm Stewart, Irwin, Gilliom, Fuller & Meyer (formerly Murray, Mannon, Fairchild & Stewart), Indpls., 1950-85; with firm Lewis Kappes Fuller & Eads (name changed to Lewis & Kappes), Indpls., 1985-89, of counsel, 1990—; pres., dir. Irsugo Consol. Mines, Ltd., 1953-80; dir. Ind. Pub. Health Found., Inc., 1972-84; staff instr. Purdue U. Life Ins. and Mktg. Inst., 1954-61; instr. Am. Coll. Life Underwriters, Indpls., 1964-74; mem. Ind. State Bd. Law Examiners, 1984-96, treas. 1987-88. Bd. dirs. Southwest Social Centre, Inc., 1965-70; pres., dir. Westminster Village North, Inc., 1981-89. Fellow Indpls. Bar Found.; mem. Ind. State Bar Assn. (bd. mgrs. 1986-88), 7th Cir. Bar Assn., Fla. Bar, Sun City Ctr. Golf and Racquet Club, Lincoln Hills Golf Club, Caloosa Golf and Country Club, Masons, Beta Theta Pi. Republican. Roman Catholic. Probate, General civil litigation, General corporate. Home: 306 Thornhill Pl Sun City Center FL 33573-5842 Office: Lewis & Kappes 1700 One American Sq PO Box 82053 Indianapolis IN 46282-0003

**FULLER, VINCENT J.,** lawyer; b. Ossining, N.Y., June 21, 1931. BA, Williams Coll., 1952; LLB, Georgetown U., 1956, LLD, 1988. Bar: D.C. 1956, N.Y. 1957, U.S. Dist. Ct. (so. dist.) N.Y. 1964, U.S. Ct. Appeals D.C. 1956, U.S. Ct. Appeals (2d cir.) 1965, U.S. Ct. Appeals (5th cir.) 1967, U.S. Ct. Appeals (6th cir.) 1969, U.S. Ct. Appeals (7th cir.) 1977, U.S. Supreme Ct. 1962. Ptnr. Williams & Connolly, Washington. Mem. ABA. E-mail: vinful81@msn.com. General civil litigation, Criminal. Office: Williams & Connolly 725 12th St NW Washington DC 20005-5901

**FULLERTON, STUART LATIMER,** corporate lawyer; b. Washington, July 13, 1960; s. George Latimer and Dorothy H. (Mallan) F.; m. Shelby Lynn Haverson, June 18, 1989; children: Maisie Haverson, Sallie Mallan. BA, U. Calif., Berkeley, 1983; JD, Georgetown U., 1987. Bar: N.Y. 1988, D.C. 1990, Pa. 1994. Assoc. Curtis, Mallet-Prevost, Colt & Mosle, N.Y.C., 1987-88, O'Melveny & Myers, Washington, 1988-90; trial atty. U.S. Dept. of Justice, Washington, 1990-93; assoc. Harkins Cunningham, Phila., 1993-95; counsel Zeneca Inc., Wilmington, Del., 1995—. Democrat. Episcopalian. Home: 358 Valley Rd Merion Station PA 19066-1520 Office: Zeneca Inc 1800 Concord Pike Wilmington DE 19803-2910

**FULSHER, ALLAN ARTHUR,** lawyer; b. Portland, Oreg., July 5, 1952; s. Rémy Walter and Barbara Lee (French) F.; m. Karen Louise Schmid, Dec. 28, 1974 (dec. Sept. 1990); children: Brian Rémy, Louise Katherine, Elizabeth Alane. BA in Biology, U. Oreg., 1974, BA in Econs., 1976; JD, U. of Pacific, 1979. Bar: Oreg. 1979, Calif. 1980, U.S. Dist. Ct. Oreg. 1980, U.S. Dist. Ct. (ea. dist.) Calif. 1981, U.S. Ct. Appeals (9th cir.) 1982, U.S. Dist. Ct. (no. dist.) Calif. 1985, U.S. Dist. Ct. (so. dist.) Calif. 1986. Assoc. Law Offices of Jacques B. Nichols PC, Portland, 1979-82, Ragen, Roberts, O'Scannlain, Robertson & Neill, Portland, 1982-83; shareholder Bauer, Hermann, Fountain & Rhoades PC, Portland, 1983-87, v.p., 1984-87; shareholder, v.p. Fulsher and Weatherhead PC, Portland, 1987-88, pres., 1988—; gen. counsel Peregrine Holdings, Ltd., Beaverton, Oreg., 1993-97, Peregrine Capital, Inc., Beaverton, 1993—; mgr. Stamford Bridge, LLC, 1995—; pres., mgr. Portland Profl. Soccer, L.L.C., Tigard, Oreg., 1998—; gen. counsel Premier Soccer Alliance, L.L.C., Dallas, 1998—. Mem. Audi Quattro Club U.S.A. Republican. Roman Catholic. Avocations: basketball, automobile racing and restoration, coaching youth and adult sports. Finance, Mergers and acquisitions, Communications. Home: 16399 SE Sager Rd Portland OR 97236-5509 Office: Peregrine Capital Inc 9725 SW Beaverton Hillsdale Hw Beaverton OR 97005-3305

**FULTON, ROBERT MAURICE,** lawyer; b. Boynton Beach, Fla., Oct. 23, 1968; s. Kimberly Farrel and Joyce Myrtle Fulton; m. Tonya Daniels, Aug. 7, 1993; 1 child, Kimberly Clara. BS, U. Fla., 1991; JD with honors, Duke U., 1994. Bar: Fla. 1994, U.S. Dist. Ct. (mid., so., and no. dists.) Fla. 1994. Assoc. Hill, Ward & Henderson PA, Tampa, 1994—. Big Brother Big Brothers, Big Sisters of Tampa Bay, Tampa, 1995—. Mem. ABA (vice-chair products, consumer, gen. liability sects. 1998-99), Def. Rsch. Inst. (com. mem. 1997—), Fla. Def. Lawyers Assn. Republican. Roman Catholic. Avocations: basketball, scuba diving, hiking, cooking, college football. Product liability, General civil litigation, Federal civil litigation. Office: Hill Ward & Henderson PA 101 E Kennedy Blvd Ste 3700 Tampa FL 33602-5156

**FULTZ, ROBERT EDWARD,** lawyer; b. Columbus, Ohio, May 24, 1941; s. Clair Ervin and Isabelle (Eichelberger) F.; m. Judith Ann McClannan, June 15, 1963; children: Cynthia, Jennifer, Stephen. BA cum laude, Ohio State U., 1963; JD with distinction, U. Mich., 1965. Ohio 1966, U.S. Supreme Ct. 1970. Assoc. Porter, Wright, Morris & Arthur, Columbus, 1966-70, ptnr., 1971—. Past trustee Columbus Symphony Orch. and Ballet; past trustee, sec. United Cerebral Palsy of Columbus; past trustee, treas. Goodwill Industries; past trustee, pres. Cen. Community House; former advisor, bd. dirs. United Negro Coll. Fund; trustee Columbus Assn. for Performing Arts, Columbus Law Libr. Assn. Mem. Ohio State Bar Assn., Columbus Bar Assn., Phi Beta Kappa, Delta Upsilon (treas.). Real property, Banking, Contracts commercial. Home: 4630 Burbank Dr Columbus OH 43220-2806

**FUNDERBURK, RAYMOND,** judge; b. Phila., Mar. 2, 1944; s. Walter and Inez (Prince) F.; m. Alfreida Livingston. AA, Olive-Harvey Coll., 1972; BA, U. Ill., 1974; MPA, Roosevelt U., 1975; JD, U. Ill., 1978. Bar: Ill. 1979, U.S. Dist. Ct. (no. dist.) Ill. 1979, U.S. Ct. Appeals (7th and fed. cirs.) 1983, U.S. Supreme Ct. 1983. Staff atty. Cook County Legal Assistance, Harvey, Ill., 1978-80; mng. atty. Cook County Legal Assistance, Harvey, 1980-82; assoc. O. Kenneth Thomas Ltd., Harvey, 1982-83, Jones, Ware & Grenard, Chgo., 1983-88, Earl L. Neal and Assocs., Chgo., 1988-93; judge Cir. Ct. of Cook County, Chgo., Ill., 1993—; bd. dirs. Cook County Legal Assistance Found., Oak Park, Ill., chmn. 1985-87; active legal adv. bd. Thornton Community Coll., South Holland, Ill., 1982—, Aunt Martha's Service, Park Forest, Ill., 1981-83. Chmn. Zoning Bd. of Appeals, Park Forest, 1988—, Housing Bd. of Appeals, Park Forest, 1988—, Equal Employment Opportunity Bd., Park Forest, 1988—, Housing Rev. Bd., Park Forest, 1988—; bd. dirs. Park Forest Pub. Library, 1982. Served with U.S. Army, 1965-67. Recipient Cert. of Appreciation Aunt Martha's Youth Svc., 1980, Thornton Community Coll., 1985, Wendell Phillips High Sch., 1985, South Suburban YMCA, 1986, 1987. Mem. ABA, Chgo. Bar Assn., Cook County Bar Assn., Ill. Jud. Coun., Phi Alpha Delta, Alpha Phi Alpha. Democrat. Avocations: running, chess, tennis. Home: 25 Monee Rd Park Forest IL 60466-2106 Office: Cir Ct of Cook County Ill Rm 2600 Richard J Daley Ctr Dearborn & Randolph Sts Chicago IL 60602

**FUNK, DAVID ALBERT,** retired law educator; b. Wooster, Ohio, Apr. 22, 1927; s. Daniel Coyle and Elizabeth Mary (Reese) F.; children—Beverly Joan, Susan Elizabeth, John Ross, Carolyn Louise; m. Sandra Nadine Henselmeier, Oct. 2, 1976. Student, U. Mo., 1945-46, Harvard Coll., 1946; BA in Econs., Coll. of Wooster, 1949; MA, Ohio State U., 1968; JD, Case Western Res. U., 1951, LLM, 1972; LLM, Columbia U., 1973. Bar: Ohio 1951, U.S. Dist. Ct. (no. dist.) Ohio 1962, U.S. Tax Ct. 1963, U.S. Ct. Appeals (6th cir.) 1970, U.S. Supreme Ct. 1971. Ptnr. Funk, Funk & Eberhart, Wooster, Ohio, 1951-72; assoc. prof. law Ind. U. Sch. Law, Indpls., 1973-76, prof., 1976-97, prof. emeritus, 1997—; vis. lectr. Coll. of Wooster, 1962-63; dir. Juridical Sci. Inst., Indpls., 1982—. Author: Oriental Jurisprudence, 1974, Group Dynamic Law, 1982; (with others) Rechtsgeschichte und Rechtssoziologie, 1985, Group Dynamic Law: Exposition and Practice, 1988; contbr. articles to profl. jours. Chmn. bd. trustees Wayne County Law Library Assn., 1956-71; mem. Permanent Jud. Commn., Synod of Ohio, United Presbyn. Ch. in the U.S., 1968. Served to seaman 1st class USNR, 1945-46. Harlan Fiske Stone fellow Columbia U., 1973; recipient Am. Jurisprudence award in Comparative Law, Case Western Res. U., 1970. Mem. Assn. Am. Law Schs. (sec. comparative law sect. 1977-79, chmn. law and religion sect. 1977-81, sec.-treas. law and social sci. sect. 1983-86), Am. Soc. for Legal History, Pi Sigma Alpha. Republican. Home: 6208 N Delaware St Indianapolis IN 46220-1824

**FUNKHOUSER, ROBERT BRUCE,** lawyer; b. Calgary, Alta., Can., Jan. 3, 1959. AB, Harvard U., 1981; JD, Fordham U., 1987. Bar: N.Y. 1988, D.C. 1993. Law clk. Hon. Lloyd F. MacMahon, N.Y.C., 1987-88; assoc. Hughes Hubbard & Reed, N.Y.C., 1988-92; assoc. Hughes Hubbard & Reed, Washington, 1992-97, counsel, 1997—. Editor Fordham Law Rev., 1986-87. Mem. ABA (antitrust sect.). Antitrust, Insurance, General civil litigation. Office: Hughes Hubbard & Reed LLP 1775 I St NW Washington DC 20006-2402

**FUNNELL, KEVIN JOSEPH,** lawyer; b. Schenectady, Sept. 25, 1949; s. Joseph Edwin and Marjorie Arlene (Rogers) F.; m. Janis L. Weide, Mar. 6, 1976. BA, U. Kans., 1971; JD, U. Denver, 1974. Bar: Colo. 1974, Tex. 1986. Denver county counsel Transam. Title Ins. Co., Denver, 1975-77; assoc. resident counsel Midland Fed. Savs. & Loan Assn., Denver, 1977-81; assoc. Calkins, Kramer, Grimshaw & Harring, Denver, 1981-84, ptnr., 1984-86; ptnr. Winstead, McGuire, Sechrest & Minick, Dallas, 1986-88, McKenna, Conner & Cuneo, Denver, 1988-90, McKenna & Cuneo, Denver, 1990-91; of counsel Popham, Haik et al, Denver, 1991-92; pvt. practice Denver and Dallas, 1992-96; ptnr. Parsons & Funnell, L.L.P., 1996—. Fellow Am. Coll. Mortgage Attys.; mem. ABA, Colo. Bar Assn., Tex. Bar Assn., Denver Bar Assn. Banking, Contracts commercial, Real property.

**FUOCO, PHILIP STEPHEN,** lawyer; b. Riverside, N.J., Oct. 28, 1946; s. Francis and Mary Helen Fuoco; m. Carol Freeman, June 7, 1969; 1 child. BA in Philosophy, U. Notre Dame, 1968; JD, Villanova (Pa.) U., 1971. Bar: N.J. 1972, U.S. Dist. Ct. N.J. 1972, Pa. 1973, U.S. Dist. Ct. (ea. dist.) Pa. 1975, U.S. Ct. Appeals (3d cir.) 1977, U.S. Supreme Ct. 1980; cert.

criminal trial atty. N.J. Supreme Ct. Trial atty. civil rights div. U.S. Dept. Justice, Washington, 1971-75; asst. U.S. atty. U.S. Dist. Ct. (ea. dist.) Pa., Phila., 1975; pvt. practice N.J., 1975—; adj. prof. law Rutgers U., Camden, 1997—. Contbr. articles to profl. jours. and law revs. Bd. dirs. Steininger Ctr., 1990-92, Haddonfield Zoning Bd., 1984-88; mem. Haddonfield Environ. Commn., 1991-93; apptd. mem. com. on model jury charges-criminal N.J. Supreme Ct., 1996, apptd. mem. dist. IV ethics com., 1997, steering com. First Night Haddonfield, 1999—. Fellow NEH, 1978. Mem. ABA, ACLU, Nat. Assn. Dist. Attys., Nat. Assn. Criminal Def. Lawyers, Camden County Bar Assn. (trustee 1986-89), Assn. Criminal Def. Lawyers N.J., N.J. Bar Assn., Camden County Inns of Ct., Lions (Haddonfield pres. 1986-87). Criminal, Civil rights, Federal civil litigation. Office: 24 Wilkins Ave Haddonfield NJ 08033-2406

**FURBER, PHILIP CRAIG,** lawyer; b. Grand Rapids, Mich., Sept. 21, 1943; s. Robert W. and Elinor J. (Hutchison) F.; m. Lydia Suthard, Nov. 11, 1995; children: Michele L., Bradley C. BS, Ind. U., 1967; JD, Cleve. State U., 1975. Bar: Ohio 1975, U.S. Tax Ct. 1976, U.S. Ct. Appeals (6th cir.) 1978, U.S. Ct. Claims 1979; CPA, Ohio. Staff acct. Arthur Andersen & Co., Chgo., 1967-68; adminstrn. asst. trust dept. Soc. Nat. Bank, Cleve., 1968-69; staff acct. John Dobson & Co., South Bend, Ind., 1969-72; prin. atty. McCarthy, Lebit, Crystal & Haiman Co., LPA, Cleve., 1975-86; sole practice Cleve., 1986-87; adminstrv. ptnr. Selker, Furber & Spotts, Cleve., 1987-98; sole practice Selker & Furber Ltd., Cleve., 1998—; of counsel Timothy A. Shimko & Assocs., Cleve., 1998—; asst. to spl. master Cleve. Sch. Desegregation U.S. Dist. Ct., 1976-80. Bd. dirs. Lakewood Luth. Sch., Cleve. Luth. High Sch., Fairview Park, Ohio, 1979-81. Mem. ABA, Ohio Soc. CPA's, Cleve. Bar Assn. General corporate, Probate, Estate planning. Home: 3330 Cannon Rd Twinsburg OH 44087-1816 Office: 2010 Huntington Bldg 925 Euclid Ave Cleveland OH 44115-1408

**FURBUSH, DAVID MALCOLM,** lawyer; b. Palo Alto, Calif., Mar. 25, 1954; s. Malcolm Harvey and Margaret (McKittrick) F. BA, Harvard U., 1975, JD, 1978. Bar: Calif. 1978, U.S. Dist. Ct. (no. dist.) Calif. 1978, U.S. Ct. Appeals (9th cir.) 1987, U.S. Supreme Ct. 1990. Assoc. Chickering & Gregory, San Francisco, 1978-81, Brobeck, Phleger & Harrison, San Francisco, 1981-85; ptnr. Brobeck, Phleger & Harrison, Palo Alto, Calif., 1985—. Federal civil litigation, Securities, Patent. Office: Brobeck Phleger & Harrison Two Embarcadero Pl 2200 Geng Rd Palo Alto CA 94303-3322

**FUREY, JAMES MICHAEL,** lawyer; b. East Rockaway, N.Y., May 2, 1927; s. Francis Leo and Loretta (Kenney) F.; m. Dolores Solosky, Aug. 4, 1956; children: James, Dennis, Kathleen Furey Tran, Sheila Furey O'Malley. BA, St. John's U., 1951, JD, 1957. Bar: N.Y. 1957, U.S. Dist. Ct. (so. and ea. dists.) N.Y. 1958, U.S. Ct. Appeals (2d cir.) 1975. Atty. Lawless & Lynch, N.Y.C., 1956-61; ptnr. Schaffner & Furey, N.Y.C., 1961-64, Clune & Furey, Mineola, N.Y., 1964-68, Furey & Mooney, Hempstead, N.Y., 1968-80; atty. Furey & Furey, Hempstead, N.Y., 1980—; lectr. numerous med. orgns., 1975-84. Candidate Mayor, Village of Mineola, 1974. With USN, 1945-46. Mem. Am. Bd. Profl. Liability (treas. 1990—), Nassau Suffolk Trial Lawyers (pres. 1980-81), Nassau County Bar Assn. (bd. dirs. 1986-89), N.Y. State Bar Trial Lawyers (chmn. malpractice sect. 1990—, spokesman legis. com. 1973, spokesman legis. hearing 1986), North Hills Country Club (bd. govs. 1992), Bay View Oaks Assn. (pres. 1972). General civil litigation, Insurance, Personal injury. Home: 220 Cherry Valley Ave Garden City NY 11530-1528 Office: Furey & Furey 600 Front St Hempstead NY 11550-4494

**FUREY, JOHN J.,** lawyer; b. Coaldale, Pa., Nov. 3, 1949; s. James J. and Georgene C. (Young) F.; m. Jill A. Luscombe, Nov. 23, 1975; children: Matthew J., Andrew S. BS, Villanova U., 1971, JD, 1975, LLM, 1984. Bar: Pa. 1975, Fla. 1994; CPA, Pa. VISTA vol. Vols. in Service to Am., Rose Hill, N.C., 1971-72; staff atty. Legal Services N.E. Pa., Wilkes-Barre, 1975-77; atty. Legal Services Corp., Phila., 1977-80, dep. regional dir., 1980-81; assoc. corp. counsel Mrs. Paul's Kitchen's, Phila., 1981-82; asst. counsel, asst. sec. Campbell Soup Co., Camden, N.J., 1982-85, assoc. counsel, asst. sec., 1985-89, assoc. counsel, dep. corp. sec., 1989-90; corp. counsel, dep. corp. sec., 1990-92; corp. sec., corp. counsel Campbell Soup Co., Camden, N.J., 1992-97; corp. sec. Campbell Soup Co., Camden, 1997—. Pension, profit-sharing, and employee benefits, General corporate, Securities. Home: 1508 Spring Mill Ln Villanova PA 19085-2016 Office: Campbell Soup Co Campbell Pl Camden NJ 08103

**FUREY, PATRICK DENNIS,** lawyer; b. Salmon, Idaho, June 7, 1954; s. Jack Bartlett and Nancy June (Stafford) F.; children: Rex Taylor, Jackson Bradford. BA in English, U. Idaho, 1976, JD, 1979. Bar: Idaho 1979, U.S. Dist. Ct. Idaho 1979, U.S. Ct. Appeals (9th cir.) 1984. Law clk. to chief justice Idaho Supreme Ct., Boise, 1979-80; law clk. to sr. dist. judge U.S. Dist. Ct. Idaho, Boise, 1980-81; lectr. Boise area Legal Secs. Assn., 1989, Idaho plaintiff and def. attys., ins. profls. Nat. Bus. Inst., Inc., Boise, 1991. Recipient cert. of appreciation Idaho Supreme Ct., 1980, cert. of merit Idaho Law Found., 1990, 91; named to Outstanding Young Men Am., U.S. Jaycees, 1982, 84. Mem. Am. Judicature Soc., Idaho State Bar, Boise Bar Assn. (lectr. 1986), Idaho Assn. Ins. Def. Counsel, Phi Alpha Delta. Republican. Methodist. General civil litigation, Aviation, Product liability. Office: Ringert Clark Chartered PO Box 2773 Boise ID 83701-2773

**FURGESON, WILLIAM ROYAL,** federal judge; b. Lubbock, Tex., Dec. 9, 1941; s. W. Royal and Mary Alyene (Hardwick) F.; m. Marion McElroy, Aug. 15, 1964 (div.); m. Juli Ann Bernat, July 29, 1973; children—Kelly Lynn, Houston, Joshua, Seth, Jill. B.A. in English, Tex. Tech Coll., 1964; J.D. with honors, U. Tex., 1967. Bar: Tex. 1969, U.S. Dist. Ct. (we. dist.) Tex. 1971, U.S. Ct. Appeals (5th cir.) 1974, U.S. Supreme Ct. 1976. Law clk. to presiding judge U.S. Dist. Ct. for No. Dist. Tex., 1969-70; ptnr. Kemp, Smith, Duncan & Hammond, El Paso, Tex., 1970-94; judge U.S. Dist. Ct. (we. dist.) Tex., Midland/Odessa, 1994—. Gen. campaign chmn. El Paso United Way, 1979, 1st v.p., 1980, pres., 1981; mem. Jewish Fedn., El Paso, 1980-86; trustee Baylor U. Coll. Dentistry, 1982-86; chmn. YWCA Capital Devel. Campaign, 1986-87. Served to capt. U.S. Army, 1967-69. Decorated Bronze Star; recipient Service award Social Workers of El Paso, 1982, Faculty award U. Tex. Law Sch., 1983. Mem. El Paso Bar Assn. (pres. 1982-83, Outstanding Young Lawyer award 1972), Am. Law Inst., U. Tex. Law Sch. Assn. (pres. 1978), U. Tex. Law Rev. Assn. (pres. 1982-83), El Paso Legal Assistance Soc. (bd. dirs. 1972-78), NCCJ (chmn. El Paso region 1980), ABA, Fed. Bar Assn. (pres. West Tex. chpt. 1987), Am. Law Inst., Tex. Bar Assn. (sec., treas., chair anti-trust and trade regulation sect. 1985-86), Am. Bar Found., Tex. Bar Found. Democrat. Jewish. Office: US Dist Ct 200 E Wall St Ste 301 Midland TX 79701-5248

**FURMAN, C. DEAN,** lawyer; b. Alexandria, Va., Feb. 18, 1968; s. Clifford Dean and Diane Bell Furman; m. Christian Davis, May 29, 1993. BA in Philosophy & Polit. Sci., U. Miami, 1990; JD, U. Va., 1993. Bar: Ky., 1993, U.S. Dist. Ct. (we. dist.) Ky., 1994, U.S. Ct. Appeals (6th cir.), 1994, Fla., 1995. Assoc. Woodward, Hobson & Fulton, Louisville, 1993-98; asst. U.S. atty.; adj. prof. U. Louisville Sch. Law, 1996-97, 99. Gen. counsel, bd. dirs. Louisville Jaycees, 1994-96. Mem. ABA, Ky. Bar Assn., Louisville Bar Assn. Democrat. Avocations: photography, raquetball. General civil litigation, General corporate, Insurance. Office: US Attys Office 510 W Broadway Louisville KY 40202-2237

**FURMAN, HEZEKIAH WYNDOL CARROLL,** lawyer; b. Bennettsville, S.C., Jan. 13, 1922; s. Rickey Laurence and Nell McColl (Carroll) F.; m. Nola Emily Harrington, June 21, 1946 (dec. Mar. 5, 1999); children: H. Wyndol C., Duncan F., Margaret Alexa Furman Stuart. BS, The Citadel the Mil. Coll. of. S.C., Med. U. S.C., 1943; postgrad., U. So. Wales, Swansea Coll., 1945; JD, U. Mich., 1954; postgrad., Acad. Internat. Law, The Hague, 1963. Bar: Mich. 1954, S.C. 1965, U.S. Dist. Ct. S.C. 1965, U.S. Ct. Appeals (4th cir.) 1966, U.S. Ct. Mil. Appeals 1954, U.S. Supreme Ct. 1959, Republic Korea 1956, Ryukyu Islands 1958. Commd. 2d lt AUS, 1942; advanced through grades to lt. col. U.S. Army, 1964, atty., 1954-65, retired, 1965; assoc. Murchison and West, Camden, S.C., 1965-70; ptnr. Holland and Furman, Camden, 1970-72; owner Law Offices of Furman, Camden, 1975-80; sr. ptnr. Furman, Speedy and Stegner, Camden, 1980—; judge Republic of Korea, 1956, Ryukyu Islands, 1958; bd. dirs. S.C. Pacific R.R.; Master in Equity, 5th cir., S.C., 1982; resigned commn. enlisted 2d lit. AUS, 1942, promoted to cpl., recommissioned 2d lt. inf., 1944, 1st lt., 1945; commd. U.S. Army, 1946, lt. col. 1965; col. S.C. Militia, 1989. Author: (handbook) Dope for Drags, 1942; designer: (log book) Parachutists Log, 1948; lectr. Univ. Md., 1963-64. Decorated Bronze Star, Purple Heart, 3 Battle Stars, Army Commendation medal, Combat Infantry badge, Gilderman's badge, Parachutists's badges for USA, rep. of China, Israel, Guatemala, El Salvador, South Africa, East Germany, People's Republic of China, Soviet Union, Poland, Hungary, Dominican Republic, Mex., Thailand, Myanmar, Philippines, Slovakia; recipient Order of The Palmetto award, 1994; inducted Officer's Candidate Sch., Hall of Fame, Ft. Benning, 1994. Mem. Kershaw County Bar Assn. (pres. 1968-69), Am. Trial Lawyers Assn., S.C. Trial Lawyers Assn. Avocation: skydiving, military parachuting, travel, adventure writing. General practice, Criminal, General civil litigation. Office: Furman Speedy and Stegner 1 Lafayette Ct Camden SC 29020

**FURMAN, HOWARD,** mediator, arbitrator, lawyer; b. Newark, Nov. 30, 1938; s. Emanuel and Lilyan (Feldman) F.; m. Elaine Sheitleman, June 12, 1960 (div. 1982); children: Deborah Toby, Naomi N'chama, David Seth; m. 2d Janice Wheeler, Jan. 14, 1984. BA in Econs., Rutgers U., 1966; JD cum laude, Birmingham Sch. Law, 1985. Bar: Ala. 1985, U.S. Dist. Ct. (no. dist.) Ala. 1986, U.S. Dist. Ct. (so. dist.) Ala. 1996. Designer/draftsman ITT, Nutley, N.J., 1957-61; pers. mgr. Computer Products Inc., Belmar, N.J., 1962-64, Arde Engring. Co., Newark, 1964-66; econs. instr. Rutgers U., New Brunswick, N.J., 1966-74; dir. indsl. rels. Harvard Ind. Frequency Engring. Labs. Divsn., Farmingdale, N.J., 1966-74; commr. Fed. Mediation and Conciliation Service, Birmingham, Ala., 1974-96; pvt. practice, Birmingham, 1985—; instr. bus. law Jefferson State C.C., 1989-95; instr. human resources mgmt. Nova U., 1993; prof. personal property, adminstrv. law, sales and alternative dispute resolution Birmingham Sch. Law, 1993—. Pres. Ocean Twp. Police Res. (N.J.), 1968. Recipient ofcl. commendation Fed. Mediation and Conciliation Svc., 1979, 81-82, 88. Mem. ABA, Ala. Bar Assn., Birmingham Bar Assn., Soc. Profls. in Dispute Resolution, Fed. Soc. Labor Rels. Profls., Indsl. Rels. Rsch. Assn., Sigma Delta Kappa. Jewish. Home: 900 Kathryne Cir Birmingham AL 35235-1722

**FURMAN, JAMES HOUSLEY,** lawyer; b. Charlotte, N.C., Oct. 9, 1946; s. Henry Jones and Nell (Housley) F.; m. Susan Marie Barnett, Mar. 12, 1969; children: James Housley Jr., Jason Haynsworth. BS in Aero. Sci., Embry-Riddle Aero. U., 1972; MBA, U. North Fla., 1977; JD, U. Tex., 1980. Bar: Tex. 1981, U.S. Dist. Ct. (we. and so. dists.) Tex. 1983, U.S. Ct. Appeals (5th cir.) 1984, U.S. Dist. Ct. (no. dist.) Tex. 1993; bd. cert. personal injury trial law Tex. Bd. Legal Specialization. Briefing atty. Supreme Ct. Tex., Austin, 1981-82; assoc. Byrd, Davis & Eisenberg, Austin, 1982-87, ptnr., 1988—. Mem. coun. Boy Scouts Am., Austin. With U.S. Army, 1966-71, Viet Nam; with USAR, ARNG, 1971-87. Decorated Bronze Star, Army Commendation medal, Purple Heart. Mem. Coll. State Bar Tex. (coun. mem. aviation sect.), Lawyer Pilots Bar Assn., Am. Trial Lawyers Assn. (chair, vice chmn. aviation sect., sec.), Tex. Trial Lawyers Assn. Presbyterian. E-mail: jamesfurman@compuserve.com. Aviation, General civil litigation, Personal injury. Home: 6301 Royal Birkdale Overloo Austin TX 78746-6141 Office: Byrd Davis & Eisenberg LLP 707 W 34th St Austin TX 78705-1204

**FURNARI, DOREEN S.,** lawyer; b. Tallahassee, Nov. 24, 1962; m. Gerald D. Furnari. BS, Fla. State U., 1984; MBA, U. Miami, 1986, JD, 1989. Bar: Fla. 1989. Assoc. Mershon, Sawyer, Johnston, Dunwody & Cole, Miami, Fla., 1989-95; asst. gen. counsel Carnival Corp., Miami, 1995—. Securities, Contracts commercial, General corporate. Office: Carnival Corp 3655 NW 87th Ave Miami FL 33178-2418

**FURNESS, CATHERINE BROWN,** lawyer; b. Cedar Rapids, Iowa, June 11, 1953; d. Clifford Charles and Opal M. Brown; children: Mariah, Brennan, Colin. BA, U. Iowa, 1974, JD, 1979. Bar: Minn. 1979, U.S. Dist. Ct. Minn. 1979. With So. Minn. Legal Svcs., 1979-81, Walbran, Walbran & Walbran, Owatonna, Minn., 1981-83; pvt. practice Owatonna, 1983—. Mem. Golden Retriever Club. Family and matrimonial. Address: PO Box 603 Owatonna MN 55060-0603

**FURNESS, PETER JOHN,** lawyer; b. Providence, Jan. 30, 1956; s. Robert I. and Elsie R. (Mooradian) F.; m. Anne Marie Tommasiello, June 7, 1981; children: Lindsey Elizabeth, Jonathan Peter. BA, U. R.I., 1979; JD, U. Pitts., 1982. Bar: Pa. 1982, U.S. Dist. Ct. (we. dist.) Pa. 1982, R.I. 1987, Mass. 1989, U.S. Dist. Ct. Mass. 1989. Atty. Mazzotta & Winters, Pitts., 1984-86, Hinckley, Allen, Snyder & Comen, Providence, 1986-91; ptnr. Nixon Peabody LLP, Boston/Providence, 1991—; lectr. Nat. Bus. Inst., Inc., 1986—. Author: (seminar books) NBI Foreclosure in Rhode Island, 1986, NBI Basic Bankruptcy in Rhode Island, 1988, NBI Protection of Secured Interests in Bankruptcy, 1989. Bd. dirs. R.I. Chpt. for Prevention of Child Abuse. Mem. ABA, Am. Bankruptcy Inst., Fed. Bar Assn., Pa. Bar Assn., R.I. Bar Assn., Mass. Bar Assn., Comml. Law League, Phi Beta Kappa, Phi Kappa Phi. Avocations: photography, golf, fishing, vol. work with nonprofit orgns. Banking, Contracts commercial, Bankruptcy. Office: Nixon Peabody LLP 1 Citizens Plz Providence RI 02903-1344

**FURNISS, PETER GLENN,** lawyer; b. N.Y.C., June 15, 1967; s. George M. and Ruth G. (Christensen) F.; m. Gillian Joyce McLoughlin, Mar. 10, 1996. AB in Classics summa cum laude, Columbia U., 1989, MA in Classics, 1992; JD magna cum laude, Harvard U., 1995. Bar: Mass. 1996, N.Y. 1996. Editl. asst. Cambridge U. Press, N.Y.C., 1989-90; mem. devel. staff Environ. Def. Fund, N.Y.C., 1991-92; assoc. Debevoise & Plimpton, N.Y.C., 1995—. Contbr. articles to profl. jours. Mem. Phi Beta Kappa. Finance, Private international, Aviation. Office: Debevoise & Plimpton 875 3rd Ave Fl 23 New York NY 10022-6256

**FURRY, RICHARD LOGAN,** lawyer; b. Chgo., Jan. 14, 1926; s. Logan Steele and Mary Catherine (Keehan) F.; m. Catherine Virginia Carey, Apr. 14, 1956; children: Carmel F. Klein, Claire F. Miley, Celia F. Meholic, Camela M. Furry. PhB, U. Chgo., 1944, JD, 1950. Bar: Ohio 1964, Ill. 1950, U.S. Dist. Ct. (so. dist.) Ohio 1966, U.S. Ct. Appeals (6th cir.) 1966, U.S. Supreme Ct., 1966. Pvt. practice Chgo., 1950-64; corp. counsel Springfield, Ohio, 1964-65; pvt. practice Dayton, Ohio, 1966-84; shareholder, dir. Dunlevey, Mahan & Furry, Dayton, 1985—; pres. Dayton Council Navy League of U.S., 1986-87. With USNR, 1944-46, PTO. Recipient Award of Merit Ohio Legal Ctr. Inst., 1971, Lincoln award Ill. State Bar Assn., 1960. Mem. Ohio State Bar Assn., Dayton Bar Assn., Fed. Bar Assn.(pres. Dayton chpt. 1993-94). Mergers and acquisitions, Securities, General corporate. Home: 3480 Governors Trl Kettering OH 45409-1105 Office: Dunlevey Mahan & Furry 110 N Main St Ste 1000 Dayton OH 45402-1738

**FURST, WILLIAM,** lawyer; b. Newark; s. Sigmund and Minnie Furst; m. Estee Baime, Jan. 7, 1943; children: Stan, Alan, Joel. LLB, Rutgers U., 1936. Ptnr. Furst and Gelfond, PA, Roseland, N.J. Trustee Twp. So. Orange, N.J., 1972. Capt. U.S. Army, 1943-46. Mem. ABA, N.J. State Bar Assn., Essex County Bar Assn. Jewish. Home: 42 N Hillside Ave Livingston NJ 07039-1923 Office: Furst & Gelfond PA 5 Becker Farm Rd Roseland NJ 07068-1727

**FURTH, DOUGLAS LAYTON,** lawyer; b. July 16, 1957; s. John Lewis and Hope Layton Furth; married, Apr. 22, 1989; children: John, Mary, Sarah. AB, Dartmouth Coll., 1979; JD, Georgetown U., 1982. Assoc. Fabian & Clendenin, Salt Lake City, 1982-86, Weil, Gotshal & Manges, N.Y.C., 1986-88; ptnr. Battle Fowler LLP, N.Y.C., 1988—. Bankruptcy. Office: Battle Fowler LLP 75 E 55th St New York NY 10022-3205

**FURTON, JOSEPH RAE, JR.,** lawyer; b. Mt. Clemens, Mich., Dec. 21, 1967; s. Joseph Rae and Sandra Kay Furton. AB, U. Mich., 1990, JD, 1993. Bar: Mich. 1995, U.S. Dist. Ct. (ea. dist.) Mich. 1995, U.S. Dist. Ct. (we. dist.) Mich. 1996, U.S. Ct. Appeals (6th cir.) 1996. Law clk. Alaska Superior Ct., Ketchikan, 1994-95; atty. Keller, Thoma, Schwarze, Schwarze, DuBay & Katz, Detroit, 1995—. Columnist, Labor and Employment Notes, 1997—. Mem. ABA, Mich. Bar Assn. Labor, Constitutional, Education and schools. Office: Keller Thoma et al 440 E Congress St Detroit MI 48226-2917

**FUSCO, ANDREW G.,** lawyer; b. Punxsutawney, Pa., Jan. 11, 1948; s. Albert G. and Virginia N. (Whitesell) F.; m. Deborah K. Lucas; children: Matthew, Geoffrey, David. BS in Bus. Adminstrn. and Fin., W.Va. U., 1970, JD, 1973. Bar: W.Va. 1973, U.S. Ct. Appeals (4th cir.) 1974, U.S. Supreme Ct. 1977, U.S. Ct. Appeals (fed. cir.) 1985, U.S. Tax Ct. 1995. Pvt. practice Morgantown, W.Va., 1973-85; prin. The Fusco Legal Group, L.C., Morgantown, 1998—; pros. atty. Monongalia County, W.Va., 1977-81, 1977-81; instr. Coll. Bus. and Econs., Law Ctr., W.Va. U., 1975-76, sch. journalism, 1997—; dir. Pitts. Environ. Systems Inc., 1983-86. Author: Antitrust Law (West Virginia Practice Handbook), 1991; editor, contbg. author: Twenty Feet From Glory (John R. Goodwin), 1970, Business Law (John R. Goodwin), 1972, Beyond Baker Street (Michael Harrison), 1976. Bd. dirs. W.Va. Career Colls., 1971-76; mem. profl. adv. bd. Childbirth and Parent Edn. Assn., 1975-82, Rape and Domestic Violence Info. Ctr., 1977-81; mem. W.Va. Sec. State's Tribunal on Election Reform, 1977-81; chmn. Monongalia County Drug Edn. Task Force, 1978-80; mem. bd. advisors Nat. Smokers Alliance, 1998—. Recipient Am. Jurisprudence award Bancroft-Whitney Publ. Co., 1971; named Outstanding Young Man of Morgantown, 1979. Mem. ABA (civic rico com., antitrust law sect.), ATLA, Monongalia County Bar Assn., Am. Judicature Soc., W.Va. Bar Assn., Baker St. Irregulars of N.Y., Sherlock Holmes Soc. London, Nat. Dist. Attys. Assn., Son of Italy, W.Va. Law Sch. Assn., Monongalia Arts Ctr. (pres., treas., trustee). Democrat. Roman Catholic. E-mail: andyfusco@aol.com. Fax: 304-594-1181. General corporate, General civil litigation, Antitrust. Home: 20 Harewood Mnr Morgantown WV 26508-9108 Office: The Fusco Legal Group LC 2400 Cranberry Sq Morgantown WV 26508-9209

**FUSELIER, LOUIS ALFRED,** lawyer; b. New Orleans, Mar. 26, 1932; s. Robert Howe and Monica (Hanemann) F.; m. Eveline Gasquet Fenner, Dec. 27, 1956; children: Louis Alfred, Henri de la Claire, Elizabeth Fenner. B.S., La. State U., 1953; LL.B., Tulane U., 1959. Bar: La. 1959, Miss. 1964, U.S. Supreme Ct. 1965. Trial atty. NLRB, New Orleans, 1959-62; pres., ptnr. Fuselier, Hector, Robertson & Ott and successor firms, 1969-94; v.p., ptnr. Young, Williams, Henderson & Fuselier, P.A., Jackson, Miss., 1994—. Capt. USAF, 1953-56. Fellow Am. Acad. Hosp. Attys., Am. Coll. Labor and Employment Lawyers, The Am. Employment Laws Coun., Am. Law Inst.; mem. ABA (practice and procedure com. of labor law sect.), La. Bar Assn. (past chmn. labor law sect.), Miss. Bar Assn., Hinds County Bar Assn., Miss. Bar Found., Miss. Def. Lawyers, Miss. Wildlife Fedn. (pres. 1975-76), Newcomen Soc., Soc. Human Resource Mgmt. (accredited pers. diplomate), Miss. Econ. Coun. (dir. 1996-97), Miss. Mfrs. Assn., Boston Club (New Orleans), Country Club of Jackson, Univ. Club (Jackson), Rotary (Paul Harris fellow). Administrative and regulatory, Civil rights, Labor. Home: 3804 Old Canton Rd Jackson MS 39216-3521

**FUSTÉ, JOSÉ ANTONIO,** federal judge; b. San Juan, Puerto Rico, Nov. 3, 1943. BBA, U. P.R., San Juan, 1965, LLB, 1968. Ptnr. Jimenez & Fuste, Hato Rey, P.R., 1968-85; judge U.S. Dist. Ct. P.R., San Juan, 1985—; prof. U. P.R., 1972-85. Roman Catholic. Office: US Courthouse CH-133 150 Ave Carlos Chardon Hato Rey San Juan PR 00918-1703

**FUSTER, JAIME B.,** supreme court justice; b. Guayama, P.R., Jan. 12, 1941; s. Jaime L. and Maria Luisa (Berlingeri) F.; m. Mary Jo Fuster, Dec. 19, 1966; children: Maria Luisa, Jaime. BA, Notre Dame U., 1962; JD, U. P.R., 1965; LLM, Columbia U., 1966; SJD, Harvard U., 1974; LLD(hon.), Temple U., 1985. Bar: P.R. Prof. law U. P.R., 1966-73, 78-80, project dir. Study on Legal Profession of P.R., Ctr. Social Research, 1970-73, dean Law Sch., 1974-78; ednl. cons. Office of Cts. Adminstrn. Govt. of P.R., 1978-80; dep. asst. atty. gen. U.S. Dept. Justice, Washington, 1980-81; pres. Cath. U. P.R., 1981-84; mem. Congress from P.R., Washington, 1984-92; resident commr. Commonwealth of P.R., 1984-92; assoc. justice P.R. Supreme Ct., 1992—; cons., lectr. in field. Author: Political and Civil Rights in Puerto Rico, 1968, The Duties of Citizens, 1973, The Lawyers of Puerto Rico: A Sociological Study, 1974, Law and Problems of Elderly People, 1978; editor-in-chief U. P.R. Law Rev., 1964-65; contbr. chpts. to books, articles to profl. jours. Named One of Outstanding Young Men of Am., U.S. Jr. C. of C., 1978. Mem. Assn. Am. Colls. (adv. bd. 1980-84), Interam. Bar Found. (bd. dirs. 1975-79). Democrat. Roman Catholic. Avocation: tennis. Office: PO Box 2392 San Juan PR 00902-2392

**FUTCH, LYNN,** lawyer; b. St. Petersburg, Fla., Apr. 22, 1961; d. M. Daniel Jr. and Florence Corrine (Coe) Futch. Student, Broward C.C., 1978-79; BS in Mktg. cum laude, Fla. State U., 1982, JD with honors, 1984. Bar: Fla. 1985, U.D. Dist. Ct. (so. dist.) Fla. 1985. Intern Broward County State's Atty., Ft. Lauderdale, Fla., 1984; with Pyszka, Kessler, Massey, Weldon, Catri, Holton, & Douberley, P.A., Ft. Lauderdale, 1985-89; assoc. Conrad, Scherer & Jenne, Ft. Lauderdale, 1989-95; ptnr. Conrad, Scherer & Jenne, P.A., Ft. Lauderdale, 1995-98; dir. dept. legal affairs Broward Sheriff's Office, Ft. Lauderdale, 1998—. Bd. dirs. Friends of Ft. Lauderdale Librs., 1987-94, Jr. League Ft. Lauderdale, 1988-93, Legal Aid Svcs., Broward, 1996-98; mem jud. selection, adminstrn. and tenure com. Fla. Bar, 1990-93, joint presdl. advt. task force, 1995-97, bd. govs. young lawyers divsn., 1993-99. Mem. Broward County Bar Assn. (bd. dirs. 1990-99, sec.-treas. 1995-96, pres.-elect 1996-97, pres. 1998-99, young lawyers sect., exec. com., sec.-treas. 1989-90, pres.-elect 1990-91, pres. 1991-92), Fed. Bar Assn. (Broward County chpt., exec. com. 1988-90, sec. 1990-91, pres.-elect 1991-92, pres. 1992-93), Broward Lawyers Care (adv. com.), Zeta Tau Alpha. Republican. Roman Catholic. General civil litigation, Government contracts and claims, Labor. Office: Broward Sheriff's Office 2601 W Broward Blvd Fort Lauderdale FL 33312-1308

**FUTRELL, JOHN MAURICE,** lawyer; b. Bryan, Tex., Jan. 12, 1956; s. Maurice Chilton and Mary Dean (Feltner) F.; m. Ingrid Elizabeth Jones, May 9, 1981; children: Richard Landy Jones, Cathryn Grace. BS, Miss. State U., 1978; JD, U. Miss., 1981; LLM, Tulane U., 1982. Bar: Miss. 1981, La. 1981, U.S. Dist. Ct. (ea. dist.) La. 1982, U.S. Ct. Appeals (5th cir.) 1983, U.S. Ct. Appeals (11th cir.) 1990, U.S. Dist. Ct. (we. dist.) La. 1991, Tex. 1994. Assoc. Faris, Ellis, Cutrone & Gilmore, New Orleans, 1982-91, ptnr., 1991-93; ptnr. Lee, Futrell & Perles, L.L.P., New Orleans, 1993—; lectr. U. New Orleans Paralegal Inst., 1983, Hattiesburg (Miss.) Legal Secs. Assn. Continuing Legal Edn. Seminar, 1993; judge Tulane Moot Ct. Bd., 1983—. Editor: Miss. Law Jour., 1980. Co-founder Maurice Futrell Social Svcs. Ctr. and Michael Futrell Orphanage, Banglor, India, Global Outreach, Tupelo, Miss., 1979, 1991; vestry mem., lay eucharistic min. St. Andrew's Episcopal Ch.; v.p. state Palmer and Calhoun Neighborhood Assn., 1995-97; den leader Pack 108 New Orleans Coun. Boy Scouts Am. Mem. ABA (regional reporter Excess, Reinsurance and Surplus Lines Com. Tort and Insurance Practice Sect.), U.S. Maritime Law Assn., 5th Fed. Cir. Bar Assn., Lambda Chi Alpha, Omicron Delta Kappa. Episcopalian. Avocation: running. Admiralty, Insurance, Appellate. Office: Lee Futrell & Perles LLP 201 Saint Charles Ave Ste 2409 New Orleans LA 70170-2409

**FUTRELL, STEPHAN RAY,** lawyer; b. Rockingham, N.C., Jan. 1, 1956; s. Wilton Ray and Bettie Ann (Horton) F. BA, Wake Forest U., 1978; JD, Georgetown U., 1981. Bar: N.C. 1981, U.S. Dist. Ct. (mid. dist.) N.C. 1981, U.S. Dist. Ct. (we. dist.) N.C. Assoc. Womble Carlyle Sandridge & Rice, Winston-Salem, N.C., 1981-83, Allman Spry Humphreys & Armentrout, Winston-Salem, 1984-85; ptnr. Kitchin Neal Webb Webb & Futrell, PA, Rockingham, 1985—; city atty. City Hamlet, N.C., 1997—; county atty. Richmond County, N.C., 1999—. Pres. Richmond County Young Democrats, Rockingham, 1987-88; mem. Rockingham Civitans, 1986-89, sec. 1987-89; mem. Richmond County Arts Coun., 1995—, v.p., 1996-98, pres., 1998—. Mem. ABA, N.C. Def. Lawyers Assn., N.C. Bar Assn., Richmond County Bar Assn. Democrat. General civil litigation, Personal injury, Insurance. Home: 701 Hillcrest Dr Rockingham NC 28379-2561 Office: Leath Bynum Kitchin & Neal 111 Washington Sq Rockingham NC 28379

**FUTTER, VICTOR,** lawyer; b. N.Y.C., Jan. 22, 1919; s. Leon Nathan and Merle Caroline (Allison) F.; m. Joan Babette Feinberg, Jan. 26, 1943; children: Jeffrey Leesam, Ellen Victoria Futter Shutkin, Deborah Gail Futter Cohan. AB in Govt. and English with honors, Columbia U., 1939, JD, 1942. Bar: N.Y. 1942, U.S. Supreme Ct 1948. Assoc. firm Sullivan & Cromwell, 1946-52; with Allied Corp. (now Allied Signal Inc.), Morristown, N.J., 1952-84, assoc. gen. counsel, 1976-78, v.p., sec., 1978-84; dir. Allied Chem. Nuclear Products, 1977-84; gen. counsel, sec. to bd. trustees Fairleigh Dickinson U., 1984-85; spl. prof. law Hofstra Law Sch., 1976-78, 88-89, 94—, spl. cons. to the dean, 1997—; lectr., seminar on corp. in modern soc. Columbia U. Law Sch., 1986-98. Editor: Columbia Law Rev; gen. editor Nonprofit Governance: An Executive's Guide, 1997; contbr. articles to profl.

jours. Trustee, dep. mayor Village of Flower Hill, N.Y., 1974-76; mem. senate Columbia U., 1969-75; chmn. bd. Columbia Coll. Fund, 1970-72; pres. parents and friends com. Mt. Holyoke Coll., 1978-80; pres. Flower Hill Assn., 1968-70; bd. dirs. N.Y. Young Dems., 1948-52, Nat. Exec. Svc. Corps, 1997—, Soc. Columbia Grads., 1998—; co-chmn. fund drive Port Washington Cmty. Chest, 1965-66, bd. dirs., 1965-75; mem. coun. overseers C.W. Post, 1984-85; bd. dirs. Acad. Polit. Sci., 1986-94; bd. dirs. Greenwich House, 1985—, sr. vice chair, 1991—; bd. dirs. Nat. Assn. Local Arts Agys.-Arts for Am., 1989-91, Am. Soc. Corp. Secs., 1987-90, pres. N.Y. chpt., 1983-84; chmn. Com. on Nonprofits, 1992-97; bd. dirs. Justice Resource Ctr., 1992-97; chair ad hoc Lunch Group for Nonprofits, 1993—. Maj. AUS. Recipient Alumni medal Columbia U., 1970, Disting. Svc. award Am. Soc. Corp. Secs., 1994; James Kent scholar. Fellow Am. Bar Found.; mem. ABA (bd. govs. 1999—, coun. sr. lawyers divsn. 1989-97, chair 1995-96, chair Editl. Bd. Experience, 1989-95, liaison to ABA CEELI program 1990—, sec. on bus. law, corp. laws com., com. on non-profit corps., com. on corp. govs., sect. on internat. law and practice 1990—), Assn. of Bar of City of N.Y. (com. on internat. human rights 1983-85, com. on 2d century 1985-89, sr. lawyers com. 1989—, chair 1992-95, nonprofit com. 1995-96, Disting. Svc. award Individual Mentor Program 1995), Am. Law Inst. (consultative group for restatement of law governing lawyers 1987-98), Nat. Assn. Corp. Dirs. (pres. N.Y. chpt. 1988-89), Nat. Assn. Coll. Univ. Attys. (sec. on personal rels., tenure and retirement programs 1984-86), Am. Judicature Soc., N.Y. Lawyers Alliance for World Security, Columbia Coll. Alumni Assn. (pres. 1972-74), The Supreme Ct. Hist. Soc., Dramatists Guild, Playwrights First, U.S. Lawn Tennis Assn., Am. Philatelic Soc., Univ. Club (coun. 1996-99, chair spl. events com. 1993—, chair club activities com. 1996-99), Manhasset Bay Yacht Club, Cold Spring Harbor Beach Club, Village Club of Sands Point, Phi Beta Kappa. General corporate, Federal civil litigation, Securities.

**FUTTERMAN, STANLEY NORMAN,** lawyer; b. N.Y.C., Aug. 18, 1940; s. Louis and Mildred (Friedman) F.; Linda Roth, Aug. 26, 1962; children: David, Daniel, Matthew. AB, Columbia U., 1961; LLB, Harvard U., 1964, MPA, 1969. Bar: N.Y. 1966, U.S. Dist. Ct. (so. and ea. dists.) N.Y. 1976, U.S. Ct. Apls. (2d cir.) 1977, U.S. Sup. Ct. 1977, U.S. Ct. Apls. (5th cir.) 1978. Law clk. to chief judge U.S. Ct. Appeals (1st cir.), Boston, 1964-65; spl. asst. to legal adviser U.S. Dept. State, Washington, 1965-67; asst. legal adviser for spl. polit. affairs, 1967-68, asst. legal adviser for East Asian and Pacific affairs, 1969-71; assoc. prof. law NYU, 1971-75; assoc. Poletti Freidin Prashker Feldman & Gartner, N.Y.C., 1976-78, ptnr., 1978-85; ptnr. Epstein Becker Borsody & Green, 1985-87, founding ptnr. Eikenberry, Futtermen & Herbert, 1987—; vis. prof. law U. Wis., Madison, 1975. Chmn. spl. com. on campaign financing ACLU, mem. com. on free speech and assn., 1972-84; treas. Larchmont (N.Y.) Dem. Com., 1974-77; trustee Beth Emeth Synagogue, Larchmont, N.Y. Mem. ABA, N.Y. State Bar Assn. (chmn. com. excessive litigiousness), Am. Arbitration Assn. (panel comml. arbitrators), Assn. of Bar of City of N.Y., Fed. Bar Council, Supreme Ct. Hist. Soc. Club: Harvard (N.Y.C.). Contbg. author: None of Your Business, 1974, The Constitution and the Conduct of Foreign Policy, 1976; contbr. articles to law revs. Labor, State civil litigation, Federal civil litigation. Office: Eikenberry Futtermen & Herbert 99 Wall St New York NY 10005-4301

**GAAL, JOHN,** lawyer; b. Flushing, N.Y., Oct. 10, 1952; s. Stephen Alfred and Marjorie (Lappin) G.; m. Barbara Jeanne Zacher, Aug. 5, 1973; children: Bryan A., Adam C., Benjamin Z. BA cum laude, U. Notre Dame, 1974, JD magna cum laude, 1977. Bar: N.Y. 1978, U.S. Ct. Appeals (D.C. cir.) 1978, U.S. Dist. Ct. (no. dist.) N.Y. 1979, U.S. Supreme Ct. 1986. Law clk. to judge U.S. Ct. Appeals (D.C. cir.), Washington, 1977-78; assoc. Bond, Schoeneck & King, Syracuse, N.Y., 1978-85, ptnr., 1986—; bd. dirs. Legal Svcs. of Ctrl. N.Y., Syracuse, 1981-87, 94—, pres. 1999—; adj. prof. Syracuse U., 1989-92. Editor: Senior Citizens Handbook, 1988; contbg. author: Public Sector Labor and Employment Law, 1988; mem. editl. bd. Jour. Coll. and Univ. Law, 1998—; columnist The Bus. Jour., 1998—; contbr. articles to profl. publs. Fellow Am. Bar Found.; mem. ABA (labor and employment law sect.), N.Y. State Bar Assn. (labor and employment law sect., chair young lawyer sect. 1989-90, spl. com. on AIDS and the law 1988, spl. com. on mandatory pro bono svc. 1989, ho. of dels. 1987-89, 90-91, co-chair adhoc com. ethics 1999—). Democrat. Roman Catholic. Labor. Home: 6732 Serah Ln Jamesville NY 13078-9690 Office: Bond Schoeneck & King 1 Lincoln Ctr Fl 18 Syracuse NY 13202-1324

**GAAR, NORMAN EDWARD,** lawyer, former state senator; b. Kansas City, Mo., Sept. 29, 1929; s. William Edward and Lola Eugene (McKain) G.; student Baker U., 1947-49; A.B., U. Mich., 1955, J.D., 1956; children: Anne, James, William, John; m. Marilyn A. Wiegraffe, Apr. 12, 1986. Bar: Mo. 1957, Kans. 1962, U.S. Supreme Ct. 1969. Assoc. Stinson, Mag, Thomson, McEvers & Fizzell, Kansas City, 1956-59; ptnr. Stinson, Mag & Fizzell, Kansas City, 1959-79; mng. ptnr. Gaar & Bell, Kansas City and St. Louis, Mo., Overland Park and Wichita, Kans., 1979-87, ptnr. Burke, Williams, Sorensen & Gaar, Overland Park, Kans., L.A., Camarillo, Fresno and Costa Mesa, Calif., 1987-96; shareholder McDowell, Rice, Smith & Gaar, Kansas City, Mo., Kansas City and Overland Park, Kans., 1996—; mem. Kans. Senate, 1965-84, majority leader, 1976-80; mem. faculty N.Y. Practising Law Inst., 1969-74; adv. dir. Panel Pubs., Inc., N.Y.C. Mcpl. judge City of Westwood, Kans., 1959-63, mayor, 1963-65. Served with U.S. Navy, 1949-53. Decorated Air medal (2); named State of Kans. Disting. Citizen, 1962. Fellow Am. Coll. Bd. Counsel; mem. ABA, Am. Radio Relay League, Nat. Assn. Bond Lawyers, Calif. Assn. Bond Lawyers (charter), Flying Midshipmen Assn., Assn. Naval Aviators, Antique Airplane Assn., Exptl. Aircraft Assn., People to People. Republican. Episcopalian. Club: Woodside Racquet. Securities, Municipal (including bonds). Office: 40 Executive Hills Overland Park KS 66210-1891

**GABBARD, (JAMES) DOUGLAS, II,** judge; b. Lindsay, Okla., Mar. 27, 1952; s. James Douglas and Mona Dean (Dodd) G.; m. Connie Sue Mace, Dec. 30, 1977 (div. Feb. 1979); m. Robyn Marie Kohlhaas, June 18, 1981; children: Resa Marie, David Ryan, James Douglas III, Michael Drew. BS, Okla. U., 1974, JD, 1977; grad., Nat. Jud. Coll., 1987; U. Kans. Law Orgnl. Econs., 1997. Bar: Okla. 1978. Ptnr. Stubblefeild & Gabbard, Atoka, Okla., 1978; sole practice Atoka, 1979; asst. dist. atty. State of Okla., Atoka, 1979-82; 1st asst. dist. atty. State of Okla., Atoka, Durant and Coalgate, 1982-85; dist. judge 25th Jud. Dist. State of Okla., Atoka and Coalgate, 1985—; presiding judge South East Adminstrn. Dist., Okla., 1992—, State Ct. Tax Review, Okla., 1992—; presiding judge of emergency panel of State Ct. Criminal Appeals, State Ct. on Judiciary (Trial divsn.), 1997—; dir. Okla. Trial Judges Assn., 1996—; mcpl. judge City of Atoka, 1978-79;. Mem. Bryan County/Durant Arbitration Com., 1984; negotiator Bryan Meml. Hosp. Bd., Durant, 1984-85. Mem. Okla. Bar Assn. (legal ethics com. 1988-90, jud. adminstrv. com. 1988-90, resolutions com., 1998—, long range planning com. 1999—, bench and bar com. 1999—), Okla. Jud. Conf., Am. Judges Assn., Masons. Democrat. Methodist. Avocations: painting, tennis, reading, jogging. Home: 1401 S Walker Dr Atoka OK 74525-3611 Office: County Ct House Atoka OK 74525

**GABEL, GEORGE DESAUSSURE, JR.,** lawyer; b. Jacksonville, Fla., Feb. 14, 1940; s. George DeSaussure and Juanita (Brittain) G.; m. Judith Kay Adams, July 21, 1962; children: Laura Gabel Hartman, Meredith Gabel Harris. AB, Davidson Coll., 1961; JD, U. Fla., 1964. Bar: Fla. 1964, D.C. 1972. With Toole, Taylor, Moseley, Gabel & Milton, Jacksonville, 1966-74, Gabel & Hair (formerly Wahl & Gabel), Jacksonville, 1974-98, Holland & Knight, 1998—; mem. Fla. Jud. Nominating Commn., 4th Circuit, 1982-86. Pres. Willing Hands, Inc., 1971-72; chmn. N.E. Fla. March of Dimes, 1974-75; mem. budget com. United Way, 1972-74, chmn. rev. com., 1976; bd. dirs. Central and South brs. YMCA, 1973-79, Camp Immokalee, 1982-86; elder Riverside Presbyterian Ch., 1970-77, 80-86, 90-92, 97—, clk. session, 1975-76, 85-86, trustee, 1988-91; pres. Riverside Presbyn. Day Sch., 1977-79; chmn. Nat. Eagle Scout Assn., 1974-75; pres. Boy Scouts Am., North Fla. Coun. 1993-96, Silver Beaver award, 1978; trustee Davidson Coll., 1984-95; Norwegian Consul, 1989—; pres. Jacksonville Consular Corps., 1992-93, 96—. Capt. U.S. Army, 1964-66. Fellow Am. Coll. Trial Lawyers, Am. Bar Found.; mem. ABA (chmn. admiralty and maritime law com. 1980-81, chmn. media law and defamation torts com. 1988-89, tort and ins. practice sect.), Am. Counsel Assn. (bd. dirs. 1980-82, pres. 1992-93), Assn. Trial Lawyers Am., Maritime Law Assn. U.S. (bd. dirs. 1994-97), Assn. Average Adjusters (overseas subsriber), Fla. Bar (chmn. grievance com. 1973-75, chmn. admiralty law com. 1978-79, chmn. media and communications law com. 1990-91), Southeastern Admiralty Law Inst. (bd. govs. 1973-75), Duval County Legal Aid Assn. (bd. dirs. 1971-74, 81-84), Am. Inn of Ct. (master of bench, sec.-treas. 1990-95), Rotary of Jacksonville (bd. mem. 1982-84, 1988-89, pres. 1987-88). Democrat. Admiralty, Federal civil litigation, State civil litigation. Home: 1850 Shadowlawn St Jacksonville FL 32205-9430 Office: Holland & Knight 50 N Laura St Ste 3900 Jacksonville FL 32202-3622

**GABEL, MICHAEL WAYNE,** lawyer; b. N.Y.C., Jan. 5, 1951; s. Stanley Harvey and Sheila F. (Goldberg) G.; m. Wendee Warren, Nov. 8, 1986; children: Joshua Addison. BA in Psychology cum laude, Queens Coll., CUNY, 1978; JD cum laude, N.Y. Law Sch., 1981. Bar: N.Y. 1982, N.J. 1988, Fla. 1990, Nev. 1990, U.S. Dist. Ct. (ea. and so. dists.) N.Y. 1982, U.S. Dist. Ct. (no. dist.) Calif. 1987, U.S. Dist. Ct. N.J. 1988, U.S. Dist. Ct. Nev. 1990, U.S. Dist. Ct. (cen. dist.) Fla. 1991. Sr. atty. Mcpl. Employees Legal Svcs., N.Y.C., 1981-83; sole practitioner N.Y.C., 1983-87; sr. atty. Kantrowitz & Goldhamer P.C., New City, N.Y., Bergen, N.J., 1987-90; pvt. practice Law Offices of Michael W. Gabel, P.A., Orlando and Daytona, Fla., 1990—; with Am. States Ins. Co., 1990-98; mng. atty. SAFECO Ins. Co., 1998—. Mem. ABA, Fla. Bar. Avocations: writing short stories and poetry, guitar, physical fitness. Personal injury, Insurance, Criminal. Office: 2201 Lucien Way Fl 4 Maitland FL 32751-7003

**GABERINO, JOHN ANTHONY, JR.,** lawyer; b. Tulsa, Aug. 6, 1941; s. John A. Sr. and Elizabeth (McCafferty) G.; m. Marjory Ann Diamond, Aug. 21, 1965; children: Christina M., Megan E., Courtney L., John A. III, Kathleen A. AB cum laude, Georgetown U., 1963, JD, 1966. Bar: Okla. 1966, U.S. Dist. Co. (no. and we. dists.) Okla. 1968, U.S. Ct. Appeals (10th cir.) 1968, U.S. Tax Ct. 1968, U.S. Supreme Ct. 1994. Assoc. Huffman, Arrington & Kihle, Tulsa, 1968-75; ptnr. Arrington, Kihle, Gaberino & Dunn, Tulsa, 1975-87, also bd. dirs., 1987-97; sr. v.p., gen. counsel ONEOK, Inc., 1998—; counsel, bd. dirs. St. Francis Health Sys., Inc., Tulsa, 1989-97. Chmn. Georgetown U. Law Ctr. Alumni Bd., 1990-92; bd. govs. Georgetown U., 1990—; pres. Georgetown U. Club Okla.; chmn. Georgetown U. AAP for Okla.; past chmn. Christ the King Bd. Edn.; past pres. bd. trustees Monte Cassino Sch.; chmn. bd. trustees Monte Cassino Sch. Endowment Fund; bd. dirs. W.K. Warren Found., Tulsa Area United Way; chmn. bd. dirs. Operation Aware, Inc., 1991. Capt. U.S. Army, 1966-68. Recipient John Carroll medal Georgetown U., 1993. Fellow ABA; mem. NCCJ (bd. dirs. Tulsa chpt., pres. 1993-95), Okla. Bar Assn. (mem. bd. govs. 1990-92, 95, 97-99, v.p. 1995, pres. 1998), Tulsa Bar Assn. (chmn. constrn. and bylaws com., bd. dirs. 1989, 91-94, sec. 1988, pres. 1993), Tulsa County Bar Found. (bd. dirs. 1993—, pres. 1994), Knights Holy Sepulchre (hon. soc. Cath. ch.), So. Hills Country Club (mem. bd. govs. 1990-95, 1st v.p. 1991-93, pres. 1994), Met. Tulsa C. of C. (bd. dirs. 1996—), Phi Beta Kappa. Democrat. Roman Catholic. Avocations: golf, tennis. General corporate, Health, Public utilities. Office: ONEOK Inc 100 W 5th St Tulsa OK 74103-4240

**GABERMAN, HARRY,** lawyer, economic analyst; b. Springfield, Mass., May 6, 1913; s. Nathan and Elizabeth (Binder) G.; m. Ingeborg Luise Gruda, Sept. 24, 1953; children: Claudia, Natalie Gaberman Razzook, Victor Lucius. JD, George Washington U., 1941; LLM, Cath. U. Am., 1954. Bar: D.C. 1942. Atty.-investigator, atty-advisor U.S. Mil. Govt. and U.S. High Commn. for Germany, Berlin, Frankfurt, Bonn; indsl. specialist, bus. economist U.S. Mil. Govt. and U.S. High Commn. for Germany, Berlin, Frankfort, Bonn; dep. U.S. agt. before Italian-U.S. Conciliation Commn.; legal and intercorp. rels. analyst U.S. Mil. Govt. and U.S. High Commn. for Germany, Berlin, Frankfort, Bonn, 1945-53, asst. chief industry control sect., 1945-53; asst. legal advisor, attache Am. Embassy, Rome, 1953; pvt. practice Washington, 1953-55; intelligence analyst Army Transp. Intelligence Agy., Gravelly Point, Va., 1955-56; supervisory atty.-advisor, atty.-advisor Air Force Sys. Command, Andrews AFB, Md., 1956-75; asst. to U.S. mem. Four-power liquidation of German War Potential Com., Berlin, 1946; chief deconcentration br. U.S. High Commn., Frankfurt, 1949; acting dep. U.S. mem. law com. Allied Kommandatura, Berlin, 1951; U.S. mem. 3-power Film Reorgn. Com., Bonn, 1949-50. *Mr. Gaberman's responsibilities include overseeing 14 substantive law councils containing 83 constituent comittees.* Contbr. articles to profl. jours. Recipient Profl. Achievement award George Washington U. Law Alumni, 1983. Mem. Fed. Bar Assn. (dep. coun. and com. coord. 1982, coun. and com. coord. overseeing 14 substantive law couns. containing 83 constituent coms. 1983, chmn. coun. on govt. contracts 1970-75, 80-81, chmn. internat. procurement com. 1977-79, dep. chmn. sect. on internat. law and its newsletter editor 1984-97, dep. chmn. sect. on internat. law and its newsletter contbg. editor 1998-99, numerous Disting. Svc. awards, others), D.C. Bar Assn. (chmn. govt. contracts com. 1964-66), Diplomatic and Consular Officers Ret. (charter mem.), Am. Fgn. Svcs. Assn., Air Force Assn. Avocations: walking, reading, listening to classic and semi-classic music. Government contracts and claims, Private international, Public international. Address: 5117 Overlook Park Annandale VA 22003-4361

**GABINET, SARAH JOAN,** lawyer; b. Salem, Oreg., Dec. 19, 1953; d. Leon and Laille Gabinet; m. John M. Siegel, Jan. 5, 1986; 1 child, Nathan. BA, Oberlin Coll., 1975; MS, Ind. U., 1977; JD, Case Western Res. U., 1982. Bar: Ohio 1982, U.S. Dist. Ct. (no. dist.) Ohio, U.S. Ct. Appeals (6th cir.). Judicial clk. Ohio Ct. Appeals (8th dist.), Cleve., 1982-83; ptnr. Kohrman, Jackson & Krantz PLL, Cleve., 1983—. Author: (book chpt.) Civil Discovery Practice, 1995. Mem. bd. trustees Temple Tifereth Israel, Cleve., 1995—. Mem. FBA, Ohio State Bar Assn., Cleve. Bar Assn. Avocations: golf, ice hockey. General civil litigation, Family and matrimonial. Office: Kohrman Jackson & Krantz 1375 E 9th St Cleveland OH 44114-1724

**GABLE, EDWARD BRENNAN, JR.,** lawyer; b. Shamokin, Pa., Mar. 15, 1929; s. Edward Brennan and Kathleen (Welsh) G. B.S., Villanova U., 1953; J.D., Georgetown U., 1957; m. Judy Lipshy July 17, 1981; children by previous marriage: Karen Lynn, Kimberly Ann, Katherine Rebel; stepchildren: Steven H., Karen Sue, Scott Michael. Bar: D.C. 1957, U.S. Dist. Ct. D.C. 1957, U.S. Ct. Appeals (D.C. cir.) 1957, U.S. Ct. Customs and Patent Appeals, 1959, U.S. Customs Ct. , 1961, U.S. Ct. Mil. Appeals, 1966, U.S. Supreme Ct., 1967, U.S. Ct. Appeals (fed. cir.) 1982. With U.S. Customs Svc., Treasury Dept., Washington, 1958-88, chief documentation br., 1965-66, chief carrier rulings br., 1966-76, chief penalties br., 1976-78, spl. asst. to asst. commr. Office of Regulations and Rulings, 1978-82, dir. carriers, drawback and bonds div., 1983-88, legal cons. in maritime law, Washington, 1988—; mem. U.S. del. Intergovtl. Maritime Cons. Orgn., London, 1972-75, U.S. rep., inter-sessional meeting, Hamburg, Fed. Republic Germany, 1973. Pres., Customs Fed. Credit Union, 1967-69. Recipient Superior Performance award Treasury Dept., 1962, commendation letter from asst. sec. treasury, 1964, Customs Outstanding Performance award, 1983, Customs Cash Performance award, 1984, 85. Mem. Customs Lawyers Assn. (pres. 1965-66), Fed. Bar Assn., Propeller Club U.S., United Seamen's Svc. (council of trustees 1986-88), Nat. Lawyers Club, Elks, Delta Pi Epsilon, Delta Theta Phi. Roman Catholic. Home and Office: 955 26th St NW Washington DC 20037-2009

**GABOVITCH, STEVEN ALAN,** lawyer, accountant; b. Newton, Mass., Feb. 7, 1953; s. William and Annette (Richman) G.; m. Rhonda Merle Kitover, Aug. 6, 1978; childre: Daniel J., Lindsey D. BS in Acctg., Boston Coll., 1975, JD, 1978; LLM in Taxation, Boston U., 1982. Bar: Mass. 1978, R.I. 1979, U.S. Dist. Ct. R.I. 1979, U.S. Tax Ct. 1980, U.S. Ct. Appeals (1st cir.) 1980, U.S. Dist. Ct. Mass. 1981, U.S. Ct. Appeals (fed. cir.) 1982, U.S. Supreme Ct. 1983; CPA. Tax specialist Peat, Marwick, Mitchell & Co., Providence, 1978-80; prin. William Gabovitch & Co., Boston, 1980-97; pvt. practice Stoughton, Mass., 1998—; lectr. on bankruptcy taxation. Contbr. articles to profl. jours. Mem. Am. Bankruptcy Inst., Nat. Soc. Tax Preparers, R.I. Bar Assn., Mass. Bar Assn., Boston Bar Assn., Beta Gamma Sigma. Estate taxation, Bankruptcy, Personal income taxation. Office: 378 Page St 3 Deerfield Corp Ctr Stoughton MA 02072

**GABOVITCH, WILLIAM,** lawyer, accountant; b. Boston, June 18, 1922; s. Ezra and Lena Ruth (Elkins) G.; m. Annette Richman, Sept. 19, 1925; children: Steven A., Ellis. BSBA, Boston U., 1943; JD, Boston Coll., 1949; LLM in Taxation NYU, 1950. Bar: Mass. 1949, U.S. Dist. Ct. Mass., U.S. Dist. Ct. R.I., U.S. Ct. Appeals (1st cir.), U.S. Tax Ct., U.S. Ct. Claims, U.S. Ct. Appeals (fed. cir.), U.S. Supreme Ct.; C.P.A., Mass. Sr. ptnr. William Gabovitch & Co., C.P.A.s, Boston, 1962—; lectr. in legal acctg. and taxation Boston Coll. Law Sch., 1959-70; examiner and trustee in bankruptcy, state ct. receiver. Campaign treas. Congressman Robert F. Drinan, 1970-84. Lt. (s.g.) USNR, 1943-46. Mem. ABA, Am. Inst. CPA's, Mass. Soc. CPA's, Mass. Bar Assn., Boston Bar Assn., Mensa, Masons. Corporate taxation, Bankruptcy, Appellate. Home: 33 Old Nugent Farm Rd Gloucester MA 01930-3169 Office: 148 State St Boston MA 02109-2506

**GABRIEL, BRIAN PIERCE,** lawyer; b. Pitts., Aug. 19, 1969; s. John Edward and Sharon Ann Gabriel. Student, Allegheny Coll., Meadville, Pa., 1987-89; BA, Indiana U. Pa., 1991; JD, U. Pitts., 1994. BAr: Pa. 1994, U.S. Dist. Ct. (we. dist.) Pa. 1994, U.S. Ct. Appeals (3d cir.) 1995. Asst. city solicitor City of Pitts., 1995—. Mem. Young Dems. of Allegheny County, Pitts., 1998—. Mem. ATLA, Fed. Bar Assn., Pa. Bar Assn., Allegheny County Bar Assn. Democrat. Office: City of Pitts Dept Law 313 City-County Bldg 414 Grant St Pittsburgh PA 15219-2409

**GABRIEL, EBERHARD JOHN,** lawyer; b. Bucharest, Rumania, Mar. 22, 1942; came to U.S., 1952, naturalized, 1955; s. William and Margaret (Eberhart) Krzyzewski; m. Janice Josephine Jedrzejewski, Aug. 21, 1965; children: John, Stephanie, Christopher. BA in English, St. Joseph's Coll. of Ind., 1963; JD, Georgetown U., 1966. Bar: Md. 1966, U.S. Supreme Ct. 1972, Minn. 1993. Staff atty. Fgn. Claims Settlement Commn., Washington, 1966-68; corp. atty. Govt. Employees Ins. Co./GEICO, Washington, 1968-70; sr. v.p., gen. counsel Govt. Employees Fin. Corp., Denver, 1970-87; pres., chief exec. officer MNC Am. Corp./Am. Indsl. Banks, Denver, 1987-89; v.p., asst. gen. counsel and compliance officer ITT Consumer Fin. Corp., Mpls., 1989-94; pvt. practice, 1994-95; coun. Comml. Credit Co., 1995-99; sec., v.p., gen. counsel Travelers Bank, 1998—; fellow St. Joseph's Coll.; pres. Indsl. Bankers Assn. Colo., 1985-86, 87-89; bd. dirs., sec., treas. Indsl. Bank Savs. Guaranty Corp. Colo., 1973-83, pres., 1983-87; lectr. Am. Fin. Svcs. Assn., Advanced Mgmt. Program, 1974-81, 85, 87; mem. law com., 1978-89, bd. dirs., 1988-89. Bd. dirs. Jeffco/Lakewood (Colo.) C. of C., 1974-80, 82-86, chmn., 1984-85; mem. Jefferson County DA Adult Diversion Coun., 1985-89; mem. Jefferson Found., 1985-87; mem. adv. coun. Colo. Office Regulatory Reform, Colo. Dept. Regulatory Agys., 1984-89; trustee Lakewood Polit. Action Com., 1978-89, chmn. 1986-87, Lakewood on Parade, 1980, chmn. bd. govs., 1982; vice chmn. fin. div. United Way Metro Denver, 1982. Mem. ABA, Md. Bar Assn., Phi Alpha Delta. Roman Catholic. General corporate, Banking, Consumer commercial. Home: 6178 Mississippi Ln New Market MD 21774-6247

**GABRIEL, RICHARD WEISNER,** lawyer; b. Greensboro, N.C., Nov. 2, 1949; s. George Deeb and Lillian (Weisner) G.; m. Elizabeth Diane Burton, June 23, 1979; children: Margaret Elizabeth, Richard Weisner Jr. AB, Duke U., 1971; MBA, U. N.C., Greensboro, 1977; JD, Wake Forest U., 1975. Bar: N.C. 1975, U.S. Supreme Ct. 1978, U.S. Tax Ct. 1981, U.S. Dist. Ct. (mid. dist.) N.C. 1975. Pvt. practice Greensboro, 1975-77; mng. ptnr. Gabriel, Berry & Weston LLP, Greensboro, 1978—; vis. lectr. Guilford Coll., Greensboro, 1977-81; counsel Internat. Home Furnishings Reps. Assn., High Point, N.C., 1988—. Co-author: (manuals) Proving Damages in North Carolina, 1989, Trial Advocacy in North Carolina, 1990, Trying the Automobile Injury Case in North Carolina, 1992, 93, 95, Counseling the Small Business Client in North Carolina, 1996, Negotiating and Drafting Acquisition Agreements in North Carolina, 1999; contbg. author Contact Mag., 1988—; editor-in-chief Wake Forest Jurist, 1975. With N.C. Army N.G., 1971-77. Recipient award for exemplary svc. Upjohn Health Care Svcs., 1988, Presdl. Citation, IHFRA, 1991. Personal injury, General corporate, Probate. Office: Gabriel Berry & Weston LLP 214 Commerce Pl Greensboro NC 27401-2427

**GADDIS, LARRY ROY,** lawyer; b. Pratt, Kans., Nov. 8, 1941; s. Wade G. and Lorena (Pearce) G.; m. Barbara Ann Law, June 14, 1972; children: Jeffrey Wade, Aaron Paul. BA, U. Colo., Boulder, 1963; J.D., U. Colo., 1969. Bar: Colo. 1969, U.S. Dist. Ct. Colo. 1969, U.S. Ct. Appeals (10th cir.) 1969. Staff atty. Pikes Peak Legal Services, Colorado Springs, Colo., 1969-71; dir. Pikes Peak Legal Services, 1971-73; ptnr. Gaddis, Kin & Herd, P.C., Colorado Springs, 1973—; vis. prof. U. Colo.-Colorado Springs, 1971-74; mem. Colorado Springs Estate Planning Coun., 1983—, pres., 1991. Bd. dirs. Colorado Springs Sch., 1973-96, pres., 1987-91, trustee emeritus, jud. performance commn., 1993—, cmty. trust, 1992—; Colo. Springs community trust; Pikes Peak Community Found., 1997—; chmn. profl. adv. coun. Cath. Diocese of Colorado Springs, 1996-99. Mem. El Paso County Bar Assn. (probate sect. 1982—, pres. 1988), Colo. Bar Assn. (exec. council 1978), ABA, Phi Kappa Alpha. Democrat. Episcopalian. Probate, General corporate, Real property. Office: 118 S Wahsatch Ave Colorado Springs CO 80903-3677

**GADDY, MAUREEN,** lawyer; b. Franklin, Ind., Aug. 10, 1955; d. Robert E. and Marie E. (Minnemeyer) Hughes; m. Charles P. Gaddy, Oct. 3, 1981; children: Ross J. Christopher J. BS, Ball State U., 1976; JD, Ind. U., 1979. Bar: Ind., U.S. Dist. Ct. (so. dist.) Ind., U.S. Ct. Appeals (7th cir.). Assoc. Clark & Clark, Indpls., 1979-82; atty. pvt. practice, Indpls., 1982-85; ptnr. Gaddy & Gaddy, Indpls., 1985—; spkr. in field. Master commr. Marion Superior Ct., Indpls., 1985-97; mem. campaign staff Conrad for Gov. Commn., Indpls., 1976, various campaign coms., Indpls., 1976-89. Mem. Ind. State Bar Assn., Indpls. Bar Assn. Democrat. Avocations: parenting, reading, piano, crafts. Family and matrimonial, Juvenile. Office: Gaddy & Gaddy 1010 N High School Rd Indianapolis IN 46224-6100

**GADDY, WILLIAM BRIAN,** lawyer; b. Lebanon, Mo., Sept. 7, 1968; s. William Jerry and Carolyn Faye Gaddy; m. Sarah Schulz, May 25, 1991. BS in Accountancy, U. Mo., Columbia, 1991; JD, U. Mo., Kansas City, 1994. Bar: Mo. 1994, U.S. Dist. Ct. (we. dist.) Mo. 1994, U.S. Ct. Appeals (8th cir.) 1994, Kans. 1995, U.S. Dist. Ct. Kans. 1996, U.S. Dist. Ct. Ariz. 1997. Assoc. Wyrsch Hobbs Mirakian & Lee, Kansas City, Mo., 1994—; adj. prof. Sch. of Law U. Mo., Kansas City, 1997—; mem. Vol. Atty. Project, Kansas City, 1994—. Staff mem., tech. editor U. Mo.-Kansas City Law Rev., 1992-94; author, lectr. CLE seminars, 1997, 98. Mem. Nat. Assn. Criminal Def. Lawyers, Mo. Assn. Criminal Def. Lawyers, Kansas City Met. Bar Assn. Criminal, Appellate, General civil litigation. Home: 8383 N Britt Ct Kansas City MO 64151-1856 Office: Wyrsch Hobbs Mirakian & Lee PC 1300 Mercantile Tower 1101 Walnut St Kansas City MO 64106-2134

**GADOLA, PAUL V.,** federal judge; b. 1929. AB, Mich. State U., 1951; JD, U. Mich., 1953. Diplomate Nat. Bd. Trial Advocacy; Bar: Mich. Atty. Hoffman and Rubenstein, Flint, Mich., 1955-60; pvt. practice Flint, 1960-88; judge U.S. Dist. Ct. (ea. dist.) Mich., Detroit, 1988—; mem. bd. dirs. Mackinac Ctr. for Pub. Policy Rsch.; past trustee, chmn. bd. dirs. Mott Coll. With U.S. Army, 1953-55. Fellow Am. Trial Lawyers Found. (life), Roscoe Pound Found. (life), Mich. State Bar Found.; mem. Mich. State Bar Assn., U. Mich. Alumni Assn., Mich. State U. Alumni Assn., Soc. Irish/Am. Lawyers (pres.), Hannah Soc. and Pres.'s Club of Mich. State U., Federalist Soc., Flint Coll. and Cultural Fund Committed of Sponsors, Phila. Soc., Econ. Club of Detroit. Address: Federal Building 600 Church St Rm #140 Flint MI 48502-1214

**GADON, STEVEN FRANKLIN,** lawyer; b. Roxbury, Mass., Oct. 27, 1931; s. Sydney A. and Sarah G. (Feinstein) G.; m. Barbara Kaminsky, Sept. 5, 1954; children: Richard, Susan, Amy, Beth. BS, U. Pa., 1954; LLB, Temple U., 1959; LLM, NYU, 1964. Bar: Pa. 1963; CPA, Pa. Acct. Main, Lafrentz & Co., Phila., 1956-62; ptnr. MacCoy, Evans & Lewis, Phila., 1962-66, Meltzer & Schiffrin, Phila., 1966-76, Spector, Gadon & Rosen, Phila., 1976—; sec., bd. dirs. Simkins Industries, Inc., New Haven. Mem. Am. Assn. Attys.-CPA's, AICPA, Pa. Inst. CPA's. Jewish. Avocations: running, opera. General corporate, Pension, profit-sharing, and employee benefits, Corporate taxation. Home: 535 Broad Acres Rd Narberth PA 19072-1508 Office: Spector Gadon & Rosen 1635 Market St Fl 7 Philadelphia PA 19103-2217

**GADRE, ANIRUDDHA RUDY,** lawyer; b. Seattle, July 15, 1970; s. Sharadchandra and Shailaja S. Gadre. BA, Franklin A. Marshall Coll., Lancaster, Pa., 1991; JD, U. Wash., 1994. Assoc. Perkins Coie LLP, Seattle, 1994—. Computer, Entertainment, Intellectual property. Office: Perkins Coie LLP 411 108th Ave NE Ste 1800 Bellevue WA 98004-5584

**GADSDEN, CHRISTOPHER HENRY,** lawyer; b. Bryn Mawr, Pa., Aug. 7, 1946; s. Henry White and Patricia (Parker) G.; m. Eleanore R.B. Hoeffel, July 27, 1968; children: William C., Eleanore P., Patricia C. BS, Yale U., 1968, JD, 1973. Bar: Pa. 1973, U.S. Dist. Ct. (ea. dist.) Pa. 1973. Assoc. Drinker Biddle & Reath, Phila., 1973-80, ptnr., 1980-98; mng. ptnr. Drinker Biddle & Reath, 1998—; lectr. law U. Pa. Law Sch., Phila., 1986-89, 93. Author: Pennsylvania Estate Planning, 1996; contbg. author: Local Public Finance and the Fiscal Squeeze, 1977; co-editor: Administration of Estates, 1983. Mem. vestry St. Thomas Ch., Whitemarsh, Ft. Washington, Pa., 1980-82; trustee Abington (Pa.) Meml. Hosp., 1980—, chair bd. trustees, 1994-98; pres. bd. trustees Germantown Acad., Ft. Washington, 1987-90. With U.S. Army, 1968-70. Fellow Am. Coll. Trust and Estate Counsel; mem. Phila. Bar Assn. (probate and trust law sect., chair 1994), Phila. Cricket Club. Democrat. Avocations: squash, tennis, gardening. Probate, Estate planning, Non-profit and tax-exempt organizations. Home: 140 W Chestnut Hill Ave Philadelphia PA 19118-3702 Office: Drinker Biddle & Reath 1000 Westlakes Dr Ste 300 Berwyn PA 19312-2409

**GADSDEN, JAMES,** lawyer; b. Bryn Mawr, Pa., July 5, 1949; s. Charles C. and Marie Ella (Dittmann) G.; children: Hilary DuBois Nieukirk, Courtney Dittmann; m. Barbara Chase Howard, May 4, 1991. BA in Polit. Sci. with distinction, U. Rochester, 1971; JD, Columbia U., 1974. Bar: U.S. Dist. Ct. (ea. dist., so. dist.) N.Y. 1975, N.Y. 1975, U.S. Ct. Appeals (2d cir.) 1975. Assoc. Carter, Ledyard & Milburn, N.Y.C., 1974-83, ptnr., 1984—. Vestry Christ Ch., Rye, N.Y., 1998—. Fellow Am. Bar Found.; mem. ABA (bus. law sect., vice chair trust indentures and indenture trustees), Assn. of Bar of City of N.Y. (bankruptcy law com. 1999—), Fed. Bar Coun., Down Town Assn. Democrat. Episcopalian. Bankruptcy, Contracts commercial, General civil litigation. Home: 24 Central Ave Rye NY 10580-2816 Office: Carter Ledyard & Milburn 2 Wall St Fl 13 New York NY 10005-2072

**GAERTNER, GARY M.,** judge; b. St. Louis; m. Maureen; children—Gary M., Lisa, Mark. Student in polit. sci. St. Louis U., JD, Sch. Law; grad. Nat. Jud. Coll., U. Nev., Mo. Trial Judges Coll., Am. Acad. Jud. Edn., U. N.H., Sch. Law U. Va., Stanford U. Law Sch., Harvard U. Sch. Law; attended Oxford (Eng.) U. Bar: Mo., Ill., U.S. dist. ct., U.S. Ct. Appeals, U.S. Supreme Ct. After pvt. practice law, served as asst. city counselor City of St. Louis, until 1964, assoc. city counsel, 1964-67, city counselor, 1967-69; former judge 22d Jud. Cir. Mo., 1969-85, including presiding judge criminal divs., juvenile judge, asst. presiding judge and presiding judge and chief adminstrv. officer 22d Jud. Cir. Mo.; chief judge Ct. Appeals (ea. dist.) Mo., 1985; past pres. Mo. Council Juvenile Ct. Judges; former chmn., former chmn. juvenile subcom. Mo. Council Criminal Justice, region 5; former mem. St. Louis Commn. on Crime and Law Enforcement. Bd. dirs. Boys Town Mo.; v.p. Khoury Internat. Leagues, Policeman and Fireman's Fund of St. Louis, Shared Resource Enterprises Inc.; former dist. chmn., now dist. vice-chmn. Tomahawk dist. Boy Scouts Am.; past mem. exec. bd. St. Louis Area council Boy Scouts Am. Served with USCG. Recipient awards, including Judiciary award St. Louis Grand Jury Assn., Man of Yr. award George Khoury Internat. Assn., Spl. Act. award U.S. Assn. Fed. Investigators; named an Outstanding Young St. Louisian, St. Louis Jaycees; recipient diploma Jud. Skills Am. Acad. Jud. Edn. Mem. ABA, Mo. Bar Assn., Mo. Assn. Trial Attys., Bar Assn. Met. St. Louis, Lawyers Assn. Met. St. Louis, Am. Judicature Soc., Phi Delta Phi. Office: 111 N 7th St Saint Louis MO 63101-2100

**GAFFIN, GERALD ELIOT,** lawyer; b. Worcester, Mass., Apr. 28, 1932; m. Joan Rockoff; children: Lisa M. Brown, David M. JD, Boston U., 1956. Bar: Mass. 1956. Assoc. Wasserman & Salter, Boston, 1956-58; pvt. practice Boston, 1958-59; ptnr. Gaffin & Waldstein, Framingham, Mass., 1959—; asst. dist. atty. Middlesex County, 1961-62. Counsel Danforth Art Mus., Framingham, 1988—; counsel, bd. dirs. Metrowest United Way, 1980—; gen. counsel, bd. dirs. Metrowest C. of C., Framingham, 1976—. Mem. Am. Trial Lawyers Assn., Mass. Assn. Trial Attys.,Middlesex County Bar Assn. (pres. 1991-92), South Middlesex County Bar Assn. (pres. 1974-75). State civil litigation, Criminal, Personal injury. Office: Gaffin & Waldstein PO Box 886 Framingham MA 01701-0886

**GAFFNER, DAVID LEWIS,** lawyer; b. Bronx, Sept. 15, 1954; s. Martin and Sydel Esther (Waltzer) G.; m. Michele B. Levinson, May 13, 1955; 1 child, Sheryl Renee. BA, Queens Coll., 1976; JD, Bklyn. Law Sch., 1979. Bar: N.Y. 1980, U.S. Dist. Ct. (ea. and so. dists.) N.Y. 1980. Editor Matthew Bender & Co., N.Y.C., 1979-83; ptnr. Gaffner, Zanini & Smith, Kew Gardens, N.Y., 1981-83; assoc. Barbara & Barbara, Carle Place, N.Y., 1983-85; mng. atty. Law Offices of Richard Hartman, Little Neck, N.Y., 1985-88; ptnr. Marsh & Gaffner, P.C., Great Neck, N.Y., 1988—. Author: Benders Civil Practice-Matrimonial, 1981, (with others) NYCP-Equitable Distribution, 1981, Custody & Visitation, 1983; editor book Disputed Paternity Actions Proceedings, 1982. Mem. ABA, N.Y. State Bar Assn., Nassau County Bar Assn., Phi Beta Kappa. Avocations: baseball, softball, football. Family and matrimonial, Real property. Office: Marsh & Gaffner PC 25301 Northern Blvd Little Neck NY 11362-1458

**GAFFNEY, MARK WILLIAM,** lawyer; b. Spokane, Wash., July 3, 1951; s. William Joseph and Anne Veronica (McGovern) G.; m. Jean Elizabeth O'Leary, Oct. 8, 1988. BA, U. Notre Dame, 1973, JD, George Washington U., 1976. Bar: Wash. 1976, N.Y. 1982, D.C. 1984, Conn. 1984. Law clk. antitrust div. U.S. Dept. Justice, Washington, 1974-76, trial atty., N.Y.C., 1976-81; assoc. Solin & Breindel, P.C., N.Y.C., 1982-83; ptnr. Chapman, Moran & Gaffney, Stamford, Conn., 1984-85; of counsel Kaplan & Kilsheimer, N.Y.C., 1985-93; corp. counsel Sta. WLNY-TV, Inc., Melville, N.Y., 1993-95. Recipient Spl. Achievement award U.S. Dept. Justice, 1978, 1979. Mem. ABA, Assn. of Bar of City of N.Y., Conn. Bar Assn., N.Y. Athletic Club. Republican. Roman Catholic. Antitrust, Federal civil litigation, State civil litigation. Home: 1395 Roosevelt Ave Pelham NY 10803-3605 Office: 34 Audrey Ave Oyster Bay NY 11771-1548

**GAGE, GASTON HEMPHILL,** lawyer; b. Charlotte, N.C., June 16, 1930; s. Lucius Gaston and Margaret (White) G.; m. Jane Basinger, July 11, 1959; children: Gaston Hemphill Jr., John Robert, Stephen Matheson. BA, Duke U., 1953; LLB, U. N.C., 1958. Bar: N.C. 1958, U.S. Ct. Appeals (4th cir.) 1964, U.S. Ct. Appeals (7th and fed. cirs.) 1983, U.S. Supreme Ct. 1965, U.S. Ct. Fed. Claims. Ptnr. Grier, Parker, Poe, Thompson, Bernstein, Gage & Preston, Charlotte, 1964-84, Parker, Poe, Thompson, Bernstein, Gage & Preston, Charlotte, 1984-90, Parker, Poe, Adams & Bernstein, Charlotte, 1990—. Dir. Elon Homes for Children, Elon Coll., N.C., 1986—, vice chair, 1995-96, chair, 1996-97; pres. Boys Town of N.C., Charlotte, 1974-78, A.G. Jr. High PTA, Charlotte, 1974-75, Mecklenburg Kiwanis, Charlotte, 1968; sec., ofcl. bd. Myers Park United Meth. Ch., Charlotte, 1970-72. Mem. ABA, N.C. Bar Assn., N.C. State Bar Assn., Mecklenburg County Bar Assn., Kiwanis (lt. gov. Carolinas dist. 1995-96). Methodist. General civil litigation, General corporate, Product liability. Home: 324 Lockley Dr Charlotte NC 28207-2330 Office: Parker Poe Adams & Bernstein 201 S College St Ste 2500 Charlotte NC 28244-4468

**GAGE, JOHN CUTTER,** lawyer, farmer, cattle breeder; b. Kansas City, Mo., July 4, 1923; s. John Bailey and Marjorie (Hires) G.; m. Eleanor Jane Pack, June 16, 1950; children: John B., Claudia Anne, David F. Assoc. Gage, Hodges, Moore & Park, Kansas City, 1952-55; pvt. practice Lawrence, Kans., 1955-57; ptnr. James B. Pearson, Mission, Kans., 1957-58, Gage & Tucker, Kansas City, 1958-90; pvt. practice Lawrence, Kans., 1990—. Contbr. articles to profl. jours. Pres. Am. Milking Shorthorn Soc., 1960-62, Am. Royal Livestock Show, 1970-71. Lt. U.S. Army, 1945-49. Mem. ABA, Mo. Bar Assn., Kans. Bar Assn., Am. Arbitration Assn., Am. Agrl. Law Assn. Alternative dispute resolution, Estate planning, Probate. Office: 1009 New Hampshire St Ste A Lawrence KS 66044-3045

**GAGLIARDI, LEE PARSONS,** federal judge; b. Larchmont, N.Y., July 17, 1918; s. Frank M. and Mary F. (DeCicco) G.; m. Marian Hope Selden, Aug. 5, 1943; children: Elizabeth G. (Mrs. Charles J. Tobin III) Marian S. (dec.). Grad., Phillips Exeter Acad.; B.A., Williams Coll., 1941; J.D., Columbia U., 1947. Bar: N.Y. 1948. Asst. to gen. atty. N.Y. Central R.R. Co., N.Y.C., 1948-55; partner Clark, Gagliardi, Gallagher & Smyth, N.Y.C., 1955-72; judge U.S. Dist. Ct. (so. dist.) N.Y., 1972—, now sr. judge. Chmn. Bd. Police Commrs., Mamaroneck, N.Y., 1970-72; sec. Westchester County Caddie Scholarship Com., 1964-72; bd. govs. New Rochelle Hosp. Med. Ctr., N.Y., 1975-85; bd. dirs. Sherman Fairchild Found., Inc., 1979-93. Mem. Dorset (Vt.) Field Club, Wilderness Country Club (Naples, Fla.). Office: US Dist Ct So Dist PO Box 768 Historic Rt 7A Manchester VT 05254-0768

**GAGLIARDO, THOMAS JAMES,** lawyer; b. Cleve., June 13, 1947. BA, John Carroll U., 1968; JD, Cath. U. Am., 1974. Bar: Md., D.C., Ohio, U.S. Ct. Appeals (4th, D.C. and 6th cirs.), U.S. Supreme Ct. Ptnr. Gagliardo & Zipin, Silver Spring, Md. Labor, Civil rights, Federal civil litigation. Office: Gagliardo & Zipin Atrium At Station Square 1010 Wayne Ave Ste 500 Silver Spring MD 20910-5600

**GAGNE, WILLIAM RODERICK,** lawyer; b. Phila., Jan. 6, 1955; s. William Richard G. and Mary Elizabeth (Bast) Brennan; m. Pamela Jean Bashore, Aug. 26, 1978; children: Roderick Bashore, Evan Rhodes, Brenton Lower. BA, Ithaca Coll., 1976; JD, Dickinson Sch. Law, 1980; LLM, Georgetown U., 1983. Bar: Pa. 1980, U.S. Dist. Ct. (we. dist.) Pa. 1980, Fla. 1982, U.S. Tax Ct. 1982, U.S. Dist. Ct. (ea. dist.) Pa. 1985. Assoc. Wayman, Irvin & McAuley, Pitts., 1980-81, McClure & Watkins, P.C., Pitts., 1981-83, Pelino & Lentz, Phila., 1985-89; assoc. Clark, Ladner, Fortenbaugh and Young, Phila., 1989-90, ptnr., 1991-96; ptnr. Pepper Hamilton LLP, Phila., 1996—; bd. dirs. Edwin L. Heim Co., Harrisburg, Pa., Hamburg Industries, Inc. Contbr. articles to profl. jours. Mem. ABA (sec. com. on S corps. sect. taxation 1988-90, chmn. subcom. on 589 publs. 1986-90, subcom. on publs. 1990-92, subcom. on newly enacted legislation 1992-94, chmn. subcom. on legis. devels. 1992-94), Pa. Bar Assn., Phila. Bar Assn. (chmn. fed. tax com. of taxation sect.), Phila. Cricket Club, Phi Alpha Delta. Republican. Episcopalian. Avocations: golf, travel, tennis. General corporate, Estate planning. Home: 515 Cresheim Valley Rd Glenside PA 19038-8408 Office: Pepper Hamilton LLP 300 Two Logan Sq 18th and Arch St Philadelphia PA 19103

**GAGNON, PAUL MICHAEL,** lawyer; b. Manchester, N.H., July 9, 1949; s. Raymond Charles, Sr. and Mary Elizabeth (Mullen) G.; m. Catherine Mary McBride, June 5, 1976; children—Nicole Marie, Amy Catherine. B.A., U. N.H., 1971; J.D., Suffolk U., 1977. Bar: N.H. 1977, U.S. Dist. Ct. N.H. 1977, U.S. Supreme Ct. 1984. Asst. county atty. Hillsborough County, Manchester, 1977-79, county atty., 1982-86; assoc. Malloy & Sullivan, 1979-81; sole practice, Manchester, 1981—; now U.S. atty. N.H. Dept. Justice, Concord; criminal law instr. St. Anselm's Coll., 1985-86. Bd. dirs. Hillsborough County Task Force Crimes Against Children, 1984-86; advisor Law Explorer post Boy Scouts Am., Manchester, 1981; committeeman Nat. State Democratic Com., 1984-86; Dem. candidate for gov., N.H., 1986. Served to 1st lt. USAF, 1971-74, N.H. Air N.G., 1975—. Mem. N.H. Bar Assn. (chmn. com. 1981-83), Manchester Bar Assn., ABA, Am. Trial Lawyers Assn., N.H. Assn. County Prosecutors. Democrat. Roman Catholic. Office: US Atty's Office James C Cleveland Fed Bldg 55 Pleasant St Rm 352 Concord NH 03301-3939*

**GAGNON, STEWART WALTER,** lawyer; b. Beaumont, Tex., Jan. 29, 1949; s. Stewart Paul and Helen Anne (Payne) G.; m. Lynn Bass, July 29, 1972; children—Ashley Lynn, Jason Stewart. Student, Trinity U., 1967-69; B.A., U. Houston, 1971; J.D., S. Tex. Coll. Law, 1974. Bar: Tex. 19—, U.S. Dist. Ct. (so. dist.) Tex. 1975, U.S. Ct. Apls. (5th cir.) 1975, U.S. Supreme Ct. 1976. Assoc. firm Fulbright & Jaworski, Houston, 1974-83, participating assoc., 1983—, ptnr., 1987—; mem. family & law coun. State Bar of Tex., 1990—, Supreme Ct. Commn. on Child Support Guidelines; master/referee Harris County Dist. Cts., Houston, 1977—. Asst. scoutmaster Boy Scouts Am., Troop 642, Houston, 1970—; mem. State Dem. Exec. Com., Tex., 1984-90; mem. Houston Found. Bd. Pub. Trust, 1982-90; lectr. Spring Branch Ind. Sch. Dist., 1976—; mem., bd. dirs. Sam Houston Area coun. Boy Scouts Am. Recipient Award of Merit, Boy Scouts Am., 1982, Silver Beaver award, 1983, Dan R. Price award for Outstanding Contbns. to Family Law in the State of Tex., 1994. Fellow Am. Acad. Matrimonial Lawyers; mem. Houston Bar Assn., Tex. Bar Assn. (dist. 4 com. on admissions), Gulf Coast Family Law Specialists Assn. (dir., pres. 1986—), Tex. Acad. Family Law Lawyers (v.p., pres. 1988), Gulf Coast Legal Found. (bd. dirs., pres. 1991), Houston Volunteer Lawyers Program, 1987-88; Presbyterian. Family and matrimonial. Home: 11610 Mockingbird Ln Houston TX 77024-6320 Office: Fulbright & Jaworski 1301 Mckinney St Houston TX 77010-3031

**GAILLIARD, ROBERT LEE,** lawyer; b. Charleston, S.C., Aug. 6, 1950; s. Julius and Phyllis (Bryan) G.; m. Sylvia L. Barnes; children: Lee Allyson, Christian Bethany, Julius Joshua. B.A. in History, U. Pa., 1973; J.D., NYU, 1977. Bar: S.C. 1977, D.C. 1980, U.S. Ct. Appeals (4th cir.) 1980. Mng. atty. Neighborhood Legal Assistance Program, Charleston, S.C., 1977-81; sole practice, Charleston, 1981—; adminstrv. law judge Pub. Service Commn. (S.C.), 1984-86. Bd. dirs. Charleston Meml. Hosp., 1984-85, Charleston Aviation Authority, 1985-95, Peninsula Optimist Club, Charleston, 1983-84; exec. com. Charleston Dem. party, 1984. Recipient Vanderbilt medal NYU Law Sch., 1977, Thomas Corn award Neighborhood Legal Assistance Program, Charleston, 1983. Mem. S.C. Bar Assn., NBA. Democrat. African Methodist Episcopalian. Club: Owls Whist (Charleston). Lodge: Nehemiah. General practice. Home: 763 Sterling Dr Charleston SC 29412-9178 Office: 1071 King St Charleston SC 29403-3760

**GAINES, HOWARD CLARKE,** retired lawyer; b. Washington, Sept. 6, 1909; s. Howard Wright and Ruth Adeline-Clarke Thomas Gaines; m. Audrey Allen, July 18, 1936; children: Clarke Allen, Margaret Anne. J.D., Cath. U. Am., 1936. Bar: D.C. bar 1936, U.S. Supreme Ct. bar 1946, U.S. Ct. Claims bar 1947, Calif. bar 1948. Individual practice law Washington, 1938-43, 46-47, Santa Barbara, Calif., 1948-51; asso. firm Price, Postel & Parma, Santa Barbara, 1951-54; partner Price, Postel & Parma, 1954-88; of counsel, 1989-94, ret., 1994; chmn. Santa Barbara Bench and Bar Com., 1972-74. Chmn. Santa Barbara Police and Fire Commn., 1948-52; mem. adv. bd. Santa Barbara Com. on Alcoholism, 1956-67; bd. dirs. Santa Barbara Humane Soc., 1958-69, 85-92; bd. trustees Santa Barbara Botanic Garden, 1960—, v.p., 1967-69; bd. trustees Cancer Found. Santa Barbara, 1960-77; dir. Santa Barbara Mental Health Assn., 1957-59, v.p., 1959; pres. Santa Barbara Found., 1976-79, trustee, 1979—. Fellow Am. Bar Found.; mem. ABA, Bar Assn. D.C., State Bar Calif. (gov. 1969-72, v.p. 1971-72, tres. 1971-72), Santa Barbara County Bar Assn. (pres. 1957-58), Am. Judicature Soc., Santa Barbara Club. Republican. Episcopalian. Home: 1306 Las Alturas Rd Santa Barbara CA 93103-1600 *Strive for a career in productive work you truly enjoy. Give due respect to others and their opinions. Learn to listen before voicing criticism or giving constructive advice. Season your life with a little humor.*

**GAINES, IRVING DAVID,** lawyer; b. Milw., Oct. 14, 1923; s. Harry and Anna (Finkelman) Ginsburg; m. Ruth Rudolph, May 22, 1947 (dec. Apr. 5, 1979); children: Jeffrey S., Howard R., Mindy S. Gaines Pearce; m. Lois Shier, Nov. 25, 1979. BA, U. Wis., Madison, 1943; JD, 1947; postgrad., U. Pa., 1943-44. Bar: Wis. 1947, Fla. 1971, U.S. Dist. Ct. (ea. dist.) Wis. 1947, U.S. Dist. Ct. (we. dist.) Wis. 1970, U.S. Dist. Ct. (so. dist.) Fla. 1972, U.S. Dist. Ct. (mid. dist.) Fla. 1976, U.S. Ct. Appeals (7th cir.) 1954, U.S. Ct. Appeals (11th cir.) 1981, U.S. Supreme Ct. 1954. Sole practice Milw., 1947-72; ptnr. Gaines & Saichek, S.C. (and predecessor firm), Milw., 1972-78; sr. ptnr. Gaines Law Offices, S.C., Milw., 1979—; arbitrator N.Y. Stock Exchange, Nat. Assn. Securities Dealers, Am. Stock Exchange, Am. Arbitration Assn. 1988—. Mem. bd. visitor U. Wis. Law Sch., 1987-96, Cir. Ct. Commn., 1997—. Served with AUS, 1943-46. Mem. ABA (various coms.), Fla. Bar Assn. (past mem. exec. com., cts. com., econs. law com., past chn. unauthorized practice of law com., past chmn. negligence sect., lectr. programs, seminars), State Bar Assn. Wis. (bd. govs. 1982-85, comms. com. 1981-85, 88-91), 7th Fed. Cir. Bar Assn., Wis. Acad. Trial Lawyers (pres. 1958-59, 70-71). Insurance, Real property, State civil litigation. Home: 7821 N Mohawk Rd Milwaukee WI 53217-3123 Office: 312 E Wisconsin Ave Ste 208 Milwaukee WI 53202-4305

**GAINES, RALPH DEWAR, JR.,** lawyer, farmer; b. Cartersville, Ga., July 10, 1925; s. Raphh Dewar Gaines and Bessis Ellen Shaw; m. Mary Sue Pafford, July 21, 1951; children: Ralph Dewar III, Charles P., Mary Susannah, Priscilla Shaw, L. Shaw. BBA, Tulane U., 1946; JD, U. Ala. Sch. Law, 1949. Bar: Ala. 1949, U. S. Dist. Ct. (no. dist.) Ala. 1958, U. S. Supreme Ct. 1978. Sr. ptnr. Gaines, Gaines, Rasco & Little P.C., Talladega, Ala., 1949—; pres. Talladega County Bar Assn., 1973, Ala. Def. Lawyers Assn., 1973-74; moderator, spkr. Ala. Civil Justice Reform Com., 1986-87; chmn. Farrah Law Soc. U. Ala., 1990-92; pres. Law Sch. Alumni Assn. U. Ala., 1994. Pres. Talladega Kiwanis Club, 1954, Talladega C. of C., 1959, Talladega United Fund, 1963. Lt. USN, 1943-46. Fellow ABA, Am. Coll. Trial Lawyers, Ala. Law Found. Democrat. Baptist. Avocation: raising Polled Hereford cows. Federal civil litigation, State civil litigation, Insurance. Office: Gaines Gaines Rasco & Little PC PO Box 275 Talladega AL 35161-0275

**GAINES, ROBERT DARRYL,** lawyer, food services executive; b. Kansas City, Mo., May 27, 1951; s. Ralph Robert and Betty June (Crawford) G.; m. Shanette Carrol Kirch, Aug. 14, 1977; 1 child, Ariel Kirch. BA, U. Ariz., 1972; MBA, Mich. State U., 1973; JD, U. Mo., Kansas City, 1983. Bar: Mo. 1983, Ariz. 1983. Pvt. practice law Kansas City, 1983—; pres. Colony Lobster Pot Co., Kansas City, 1984—, Colony Pla Co., Kansas City, 1985—. Mem. ABA, Mo. Bar Assn., Ariz. Bar Assn., Kansas City Bar Assn., Nat. Restaurant Assn., Mo. Restaurant Assn., Phi Delta Phi (treas. 1982-83). Avocations: flying, racquetball. General corporate, Contracts commercial. Home: 11201 Madison Ave Kansas City MO 64114-5238 also: 8821 State Line Rd Kansas City MO 64114-2704

**GAINES, ROBERT MARTIN,** lawyer; b. Hartford, Conn., Nov. 27, 1931; s. Charles Edward and Ellen Marie (Hammerstrom) G.; m. Joan Isabel Sanderson, May 20, 1961 (div. Oct. 1983); children: Todd, Dayna; m. Julie Ann Ramsdell, May 11, 1985. AB, U. Conn., 1953, JD, 1956. Bar: Conn. 1956, U.S. Ct. Mil. Appeals 1959, U.S. Dist. Ct. Conn. 1961, U.S. Tax Ct., 1994. Assoc. Regnier & Moller, Hartford, 1960-62; asst. counsel Pratt & Whitney, East Hartford, Conn., 1962—. Mem. Somers (Conn.) Bd. Edn., 1968-70. With USAF, 1957-60. Mem. Am. Corp. Counsel Assn. Republican. Roman Catholic. Avocations: sports, music. Contracts commercial, Government contracts and claims, Administrative and regulatory. Home: 44163 S Main St Manchester CT 06040

**GAINES, ROBERT PENDLETON,** lawyer; b. Daytona Beach, Fla., Apr. 6, 1927; s. Marion Toulmin and Marion (Howie) G.; m. Doris Bolton, July 8, 1961; children: Jennifer, Amante, Edmund. BA, U. Fla., 1950, LLB, 1956. Bar: Fla. 1956, U.S. Dist. Ct. (no. dist.) Fla. 1956, U.S. Ct. Appeals (5th cir.) 1958, U.S. Ct. Appeals (11th cir.) 1982, U.S. Supreme Ct. 1988. From assoc. to ptnr. Beggs & Lane and predecessor firms, Pensacola, Fla., 1956—. Mem. Fla. Commn. on Local Govt., Tallahassee, 1973-74. Lt. U.S. Army, 1945-47, 1950-53, Korea. Mem. ABA, Fla. Def. Lawyers Assn. (prs. 1974-75), Internat. Assn. Def. Counsel, Maritime Law Assn. U.S., Southeastern Admiralty Inst., Pensacola C. of C. (pres. 1969), Pensacola Jaycees (pres. 1961), Rotary (bd. dirs.), Order of Coif, Phi Beta Kappa. Democrat. Episcopalian. Avocation: fishing. Federal civil litigation, State civil litigation, Admiralty. Home: 8839 Burning Tree Rd Pensacola FL 32514-5606 Office: Beggs & Lane PO Box 12950 Pensacola FL 32576-2950

**GAINES, TYLER BELT,** lawyer; b. Omaha, Oct. 21, 1924; s. Francis S. and Dorothy Tyler (Belt) G.; m. Elizabeth Bush Caldwell, Feb. 24, 1951; children: Katherine C., Elizabeth D., David T., Sarah B., Mary C.; m. Agneta Margareta Anderhagen, Nov. 27, 1977; stepchildren: Anna C., Anders C. Student Yale U., 1942-43, U. Omaha, 1946; LLB, Nebr. U., 1949. Bar: Nebr. 1949, U.S. Supreme Ct. 1964, U.S. Ct. Appeals (8th cir.) 1953, U.S. Dist. Ct. Nebr. 1949, U.S. Tax Ct. 1970. Ptnr., Gaines, Mullen, Pansing & Hogan and predecessor firms, Omaha, 1960—. Bd. dirs. Gilbert and Martha Hitchcock Found., 1970—, Kirkpatrick Charity Found., 1991—, Brownell Talbot Sch. Found., 1994—, Forest Lawn Cemetary, 1960—. Served with USNR, 1943-45. Mem. Am. Coll. Probate Counsel, Nebr. Bar Assn., Omaha Bar Assn. (pres. 1982-83). Republican. Episcopalian. Clubs: Omaha Country, Omaha. Probate, Taxation, general, General civil litigation. Office: Gaines Mullen Pansing & Hogan 10050 Regency Cir Ste 200 Omaha NE 68114-3721

**GAINES, WEAVER HENDERSON,** lawyer; b. Ft. Meade, S.D., Aug. 31, 1943; s. Weaver Henderson and Bertha Louise (Harris) G. AB in Philosophy, Dartmouth Coll., 1965; LLB, U. Va., 1968. Bar: N.Y. 1969, Pa. 1979, U.S. Dist. Ct. (so. dist.) N.Y. 1973, U.S. Dist. Ct. (ea. dist.) N.Y. 1975, U.S. Ct. Appeals (2d cir.) 1975. Assoc. Dewey, Ballantine, Bushby, Palmer & Wood, N.Y.C., 1970-79; sr. staff counsel INA Corp., Phila., 1979; asst. gen. counsel, sec. Thyssen-Bornemisza Inc., N.Y.C., 1979-82, v.p. strategic projects, 1982-85; v.p., dep. gen. counsel Mut. of N.Y., N.Y.C., 1985-86, sr. v.p., gen. counsel, 1986-90, exec. v.p., gen. counsel, 1990-92; pres. Unified Mgmt. Corp., 1989-90; chmn., CEO Ixion Biotechnology, Inc., Alachua, Fla., 1993—; bd. dirs. First ING Life Ins. Co. of N.Y., Unified Fin. Svcs., Inc., Voyetra Turtle Beach, Inc., Ixion Biotechnology, Inc., BIO Fla. Inc., North Fla. Tech. Inovation Corp., Dance Alive!. Bd. dirs. N.Y. Lawyers for Nixon, 1972; sr. advisor Bush/Quayle '92. Capt. U.S. Army, 1968-70, Vietnam. Decorated Bronze Star. Mem. ABA, Assn. of Bar of City of N.Y., Am. Corp. Counsel Assn., Assn. Life Ins. Counsel, N.Y. Athletic Club, Haile Plantation Golf and Country Club. Republican. Episcopalian. Antitrust, General corporate, Insurance. Office: Ixion Biotechnology Inc 13709 Progress Blvd # 13 Alachua FL 32615-9544

**GAITAN, FERNANDO J., JR.,** federal judge; b. 1948. Student, Kansas City (Kans.) C.C., 1966-67, Donnelly Coll., 1967-68, Pittsburg State U., 1968-70; JD, U. Mo., Kansas City, 1974. Atty. Southwestern Bell Telephone Co., 1974-80; judge 16th jud. cir. Jackson County Cir. Ct., 1980-86; judge Mo. Ct. Appeals (we. dist.), 1986-91; fed. judge U.S. Dist. Ct. (we. dist.) Mo., Kansas City, 1991—. Past pres. bd. dirs. De La Salle Edn. Ctr., Inc., 1985-87, active, 1983—; active Kansas City Mus., 1988—, St. Luke's Hosp., Kansas City, 1984—, NAACP, 1982—, NCCJ, 1984—. Mem. ABA, Mo. Bar Assn., Kansas City Met. Bar Assn., Lawyers' Assn., Jackson County Bar Assn., Univ. Club, Hillcrest Country Club, U. Mo. Kansas City Law Found., KCMC Child Devel. Corp., Kappa Alpha Psi. Office: US Dist Ct 7952 US Cthouse 400 E 9th St Kansas City MO 64106-2607

**GAITHER, JOHN F.,** lawyer; b. Evansville, Ind., Mar. 31, 1949; s. John F. and Marjilee G.; m. Christine Luby, Nov. 26, 1971; children: John F. III, Maria Theresa. BA in Acctg., U. Notre Dame, 1971, JD, 1974. Bar: Ind. 1974, Ill. 1975, U.S. Ct. Appeals (7th cir.) 1975, U.S. Ct. Mil. Appeals 1977. CPA, Ind. Law clk. to Hon. Wilbur F. Pell, Jr. Ct. of Appeals 7th Cir., Chgo., 1974-76; assoc. atty. Bell, Boyd & Lloyd, Chgo., 1979-82; sr. atty. Baxter Healthcare Corp., Deerfield, Ill., 1982-83, asst. sec., sr. atty., 1983-84, asst. sec., asst. gen. counsel, 1984-85; sec., assoc. gen. counsel Baxter Internat. Inc., Deerfield, 1985-87, sec., dep. gen. counsel, 1987-91; v.p. law/devel. Baxter Diagnostics Inc., Deerfield, 1991-92; v.p. law, strategic planning Baxter Global Businesses, Deerfield, 1992-93; dep. gen. counsel, v.p. strategic planning Baxter Internat. Inc., Deerfield, 1993-94, corp. v.p., corp. devel., 1994—. Editor-in-chief Notre Dame Lawyer, 1973-74; contbr. articles to profl. jours. Lt. comdr. USNR, 1976-79. Mem. ABA, Ill. Bar Assn., Ind. Bar Assn., Chgo. Bar Assn., Ind. Assn. CPAs. Avocations: sailing, skiing. General corporate, Securities, Mergers and acquisitions. Office: Baxter Internat Inc 1 Baxter Pkwy Deerfield IL 60015-4625

**GAJARSA, ARTHUR J.,** judge; b. Norcia, Italy, Mar. 1, 1941; came to U.S., 1949; m. Melanie E. Martinelli. BSEE, Rensselaer Polytech Inst, 1962; JD, Georgetown U., 1967; MA in Econs., Cath. U., 1968. Bar: U.S. Patent Office 1963, D.C. 1968, U.S. Dist. Ct. D.C. 1968, U.S. Ct. Appeals (D.C. cir.) 1968, Conn. 1969, U.S. Supreme Ct. 1971, U.S. Superior Ct. 1972, U.S. Ct. Appeals (D.C. cir.) 1972, U.S. Ct. Appeals (9th cir.) 1974, U.S. Dist. Ct. (no. dist.) N.Y. 1980. Patent examiner U.S. Patent Office, Dept. Commerce, 1962-63; patent adviser USAF, Dept. Def., 1963-64, Cushman, Darby & Cushman, 1964-67; law clk. to Judge Joseph C. McGarraghy U.S. Dist. Ct. (D.C.), Washington, 1967-68; atty. office gen. counsel Aetna Life and Casualty Co., 1968-69; spl. counsel, asst. to commr. Indian affairs Bur. Indian Affairs, Dept. Interior, 1969-71; assoc. Duncan and Brown, 1971-72; ptnr. Gajarsa, Liss & Sterenbuch, 1972-78, Gajarsa, Liss & Conroy, 1978-80, Wender, Murase & White, 1980-86; ptnr., officer Joseph, Gajarsa, McDermott & Reiner, P.C., 1987-97; judge U.S. Ct. Appeals Fed. Cir., Washington, 1997—; bd. dirs. Eyring Corp., 1992-96. Contbr. articles to profl. jours. Trustee Rensselaer Neuman Found., 1973—, Found. Improving Understanding of Arts, 1982-96, Outward Bound, 1987-96, Rensselaer Polytech Inst., 1994—; gov. John Carroll Soc., 1992—; regent Georgetown U., 1995—. Recipient Sun and Balance medal Rensselaer Polytech Inst.,

1990, Rensselaer Key Alumni award, 1992, Gigi Pieri award Camp Hale Assn., 1992, 125th Anniversary medal Georgetown U. Law Ctr., 1995, Order of Commendatore, Republic Italy, 1995, Alumni Fellows award Rensselaer Alumni Assn., 1996. Mem. FBA, ABA, Fed. Cir. Bar Assn., Nat. Italian Am. Found. (bd. dirs. 1976-99, gen. counsel 1976-89, pres. 1989-92, vice-chair 1993-96), D.C. Bar Assn., Am. Judicature Assn. Office: US Ct Appeals Fed Cir 717 Madison Pl NW Washington DC 20439-0002

**GALANE, MORTON ROBERT,** lawyer; b. N.Y.C., Mar. 15, 1926; s. Harry J. and Sylvia (Schenkelbach) G.; children: Suzanne Galane Ash, Jonathan A. B.E.E., CCNY, 1946; LL.B., George Washington U., 1950. Bar: D.C. 1950, Nev. 1955, Calif. 1975. Patent examiner U.S. Patent Office, Washington, 1948-50; spl. partner firm Roberts & McInnis, Washington, 1950-54; practice as Morton R. Galane, P.C., Las Vegas, Nev., 1955—; spl. counsel to Gov. Nev., 1967-70. Contbr. articles to profl. jours. Chmn. Gov.'s Com. on Future of Nev., 1979-80. Fellow Am. Coll. Trial Lawyers; mem. IEEE, ABA (council litigation sect. 1977-83), Am. Law Inst., State Bar Nev., State Bar Calif., D.C. Bar. Federal civil litigation, Libel. Home: 2019 Bannie Ave Las Vegas NV 89102-2208 Office: 302 Carson Ave Ste 1100 Las Vegas NV 89101-5909

**GALANIS, JOHN WILLIAM,** lawyer; b. Milw., May 9, 1937; s. William and Angeline (Koroniou) G.; m. Patricia Caro, Nov. 29, 1969; children: Lia, William, Charles, John. BBA cum laude, U. Wis., 1959; JD, U. Mich., 1963; postgrad. (Ford Found. grantee), London Sch. Econs., 1964. Bar: Wis. 1965; CPA, Wis. Assoc. firm Whyte & Hirschboeck S.C., Milw., 1964-68; sr. v.p., gen. counsel, sec. MGIC Investment Corp. and Mortgage Guaranty Ins. Corp., Milw., 1968-88; ptnr. Galanis, Pollack & Jacobs, S.C., Milw., 1988—. Assoc. editor: Mich. Law Rev, 1962-63. Bd. visitors Law Sch. U. Mich., Sch. Bus. U. Wis.; past chmn. Milw. Found.; bd. dirs., past pres. Milw. Boys' and Girls' Club; bd. dirs. Milw. Heart Found.; pres. Family Svc. Milw.; trustee Milw. Pub. Mus. Friends. Recipient Disting. Svc. award Internat. Inst., Hope Chest award Nat. MS Soc., Disting. Alumni award Milw. Boys' Club, Disting. Svc. award Milw. Civic Alliance Club, 1989. Mem. ABA, Wis. Bar Assn., Milw. Bar Assn., Am. Hellenic Ednl. Progessive Assn., Order of Coif, Milw. Athletic Club, Western Racquet Club. Greek Orthodox. General corporate, Insurance, Finance. Home: 1200 Woodlawn Cir Elm Grove WI 53122-1639 Office: MGIC Pl Milwaukee WI 53201

**GALANTE, JOYCE MILDRED,** lawyer; d. Nicholas T. and Violet A. Galante. BA, Marymount Coll., 1962; LLB, Union U., 1965. Bar: N.Y. 1966. Pvt. practice Troy, N.Y., 1966—; trustee Supreme Ct. Library, Troy, 1976-93; mem. Capital Regional Econ. Coun., Albany, N.Y., 1984; mem. Law Guardian Panel Rensselaer County Family, 1966—; mem. com. profl. standards for 3rd Jud. Dist., 1994—, chmn., 1997-98, mem. com. on character and fitness, 1992-94. Trustee, officer, Rensselaer County Hist. Soc., Troy, 1989-95; pres., officer Sunnyside Ctr., Inc., Troy, 1970-85. Named Vol. of Yr. Jr. League of Troy, 1986. Mem. ABA, N.Y. State Bar Assn. (Rensselaer County del. 1977-79, ho. of dels. 1977-79), Rensselaer County Bar Assn. (pres. 1976-77). Democrat. Roman Catholic. Family and matrimonial. Office: PO Box 605 Troy NY 12181-0605

**GALATI, VITO,** lawyer; b. Phila., Feb. 25, 1953; s. Nick and Gemma (Pasquini) G.; m. Rayna K. Bramer, May 28, 1988; 1 child, Alexandra. BA, Grove City (Pa.) Coll., 1975; JD, Western New Eng. Coll., Springfield, Mass., 1978; LLM in Taxation, Georgetown U., 1979. Bar: Pa. 1979, Hawaii 1980, U.S. Dist. Ct. Hawaii 1980, U.S. Tax Ct. 1981. Assoc. Cades Schutte Fleming & Wright, Honolulu, 1979-85, ptnr., 1985—; mem. Tax Found. Hawaii, Honolulu, 1997—; mem. tax group State of Hawaii, Econ. Revitalization Task Force; spkr. in field. Contbr. articles to profl. jours. Mem. ABA, Hawaii Bar Assn. (chair Hawaii tax sect.: partnerships and S corps. 1983-84). Taxation, general, Corporate taxation, State and local taxation. Home: 608 Kahiau Loop Honolulu HI 96821-2540 Office: Cades Schutte Fleming & Wright 1000 Bishop St Ste 1400 Honolulu HI 96813-4298

**GALATZ, HENRY FRANCIS,** lawyer; b. N.Y.C., Feb. 5, 1947; s. Julius D. and Dorothy (Kirschen) G.; m. Colleen Prager, Aug. 19, 1973; children: Benjamin Chase, Brandon Kyle. BA, U. Ariz., 1970, MEd, MA with honors, 1973; JD, U. the Pacific, 1979. Bar: Ill. 1981, U.S. Dist. Ct. (no. dist.) Ill. 1982, U.S. Dist. Ct. (ea. dist.) Mich. 1982, U.S. Dist. Ct. (ea. dist.) Mo. 1985, U.S. Dist. Ct. Mont. 1986, U.S. Dist. Ct. (we. dist.) Tex. 1987, U.S. Ct. Appeals (7th cir.) 1981, U.S. Ct. Appeals (6th cir.) 1982, U.S. Supreme Ct. 1985, U.S. Dist. Ct. (no. dist.) Calif. 1992, U.S. Dist. Ct. Nebr. 1993, U.S. Dist. Ct. (no. dist.) Ohio 1997; cert. coach and referee U.S. Soccer Fedn. Cons. labor rels. Phoenix Closures, Chgo., 1974-75, Galatz Elec. Corp., Las Vegas, Nev., 1975-80; labor counsel W.W. Grainger, Inc., Skokie, Ill., 1980—; pvt. practice Olympia Fields, Ill., 1981—; hearing officer Ill. State Bd. Edn., Chgo., 1982—; atty. Chgo. Legal Svcs. Found., 1983—, Ill. Inst. for Dispute Resolution, 1992—; mem. com. Employment Law Inst., Northwestern U., Evanston, Ill. Pres., coach Homewood-Flossmoor (Ill.) Soccer Club, 1985—, Intercollegiate Varsity Athletics (soccer and lacrosse); co-chair soccer Ill. Prairie State Games, 1992; pres. P.O.P.S. Homewood-Flossmoor H.S., 1996—; mem. bd. edn., pers. com. Homewood-Flossmoor H.S., 1998—. Recipient Judge Mason Rothwell Award, 1979, Cert. of Merit Chgo. Legal Services Found., 1983. Mem. ABA, ATLA, Am. Corp. Counsel Assn. (labor and employment sect.), Ill. Bar Assn., Chgo. Bar Assn., Am. Arbitrators Assn. (arbitrator), Am. Judicature Soc., Ill. Trial Lawyers Assn., North Shore (Ill.) Labor Counsel Assn., Phi Delta Phi, Alpha Epsilon Pi. Democrat. Jewish. Avocations: soccer, lacrosse. Labor, Federal civil litigation, Education and schools. Home: PO Box 374 Flossmoor IL 60422-0374 Office: W W Grainger Inc 455 Knightsbridge Pkwy Lincolnshire IL 60069-3620

**GALATZ, NEIL GILBERT,** lawyer; b. N.Y.C., Jan. 22, 1933; s. Julius D. and Dorothy (Kirschen) G.; m. Elaine Bricker, Aug. 20, 1961; children—Leesa, Lara. B.A., Adelphi U., 1953; J.D., Columbia U., 1956. Bar: N.Y. 1957, Nev. 1958, U.S. Dist. Ct. Nev. 1958, U.S. Ct. Appeals (9th cir.) 1959, Ariz. 1961, U.S. Dist. Ct. Ariz. 1961, U.S. Supreme Ct. 1976. Sr. trial dep. dist. atty. Clark County Dist. Attys. Office, Las Vegas, 1959-61; assoc. Langerman, Begam & Lewis, Phoenix, 1961-62; sole practice, Las Vegas, 1962-66; ptnr. Wiener, Goldwater & Galatz, Las Vegas, 1967-76; sr. ptnr. Galatz, Earl & Assocs., Las Vegas, 1976—; mem. Nev. Gov.'s Com. on No-Fault Ins., 1971-72; mem. com. on alt. dispute resolution Nev. Supreme Ct., 1983-84; chmn. Nev. Bd. Chinese Medicine, 1973-75; lectr. numerous legal assns., med. socs., also other instns., 1963—; mem. nat. adv. council, mem. seminar faculty Practicing Law Inst., 1968-72. Contbr. articles to legal jours., chpts. to books and manuals. Bd. dirs. Combined Jewish Appeal, 1975-92; campaign chmn. Harry Reid Senatorial Campaign, 1982. Fellow Internat. Acad. Trial Lawyers (bd. dirs.), Internat. Soc. Barristers; mem. ABA (sect. on negligence law), Nev. Bar Assn. (bd. bar examiners 1972-74, bd. govs. 1990—), Ariz. Bar Assn., N.Y. State Bar Assn., Clark County Bar Assn. (chmn. legal-med. relations 1966-67), Assn. Trial Lawyers Am. (citation for outstanding leadership 1971), Western Trial Lawyers Assn. (pres. 1964-65, sec. 1967-68, bd. govs. 1968-74), Nev. Trial Lawyers Assn. (v.p. 1967-68, pres. 1968-69, bd. dirs. 1970-81, pres. So. chpt. 1963-65), Am. Morgan Horse Assn. (pres. region VII, 1984-85). Democrat. Personal injury, Product liability. Office: Galatz Earl & Assocs 710 S 4th St Las Vegas NV 89101-6707

**GALBRAITH, ROBERT LYELL, JR.,** lawyer; b. Rochester, N.Y., May 18, 1960; s. Robert Lyell and Barbara Williams Galbraith; m. Debra Lee Dastyck, June 25, 1985; children: Taylor, Mary. BA, Hamilton Coll., 1982; JD, U. Buffalo, 1986. Bar: N.Y. 1987, U.S. Dist. Ct. (we. dist.) N.Y. 1987. Assoc. Osborn, Reed, VandeVate & Burke, Rochester, N.Y., 1986-88; assoc. Saperston & Day, P.C., Rochester, 1989-92, ptnr., 1992-98, chmn. R.E. practice group, 1994-98; ptnr. Davidson, Fink, Cook, Kelly & Galbraith LLP., Rochester, 1998—; adv. bd. mem. Ticor/Chgo. Title Ins. Co., Rochester, 1991—; assoc. mem. N.Y. State Econ. Devel. Coun., Rochester, 1991—; adv. bd. dirs. Rochester Binding and Finishing, Rochester, 1993-96. Bd. mem., pres. Mental Health Assn., Rochester, 1991—; coach Brighton (N.Y.) Town Soccer, 1996—. Named Vol. of the Yr., Mental Health Assn., Rochester, 1995, one of 40 under 40 Rochester Bus. Jour., 1996. Mem. N.Y. State Bar Assn. (exec. com. for young lawyers sect., liason to real property exec. 1992-97), Monroe County Bar Assn. (real estate sect., pres. 1992-98). Avocations: skiing, reading, soccer, football. Banking, Contracts commercial, Real property. Office: Davidson Fink Cook Kelly & Galbraith LLP 28 E Main St Ste 900 Rochester NY 14614-1916

**GALBUT, MARTIN RICHARD,** lawyer; b. Miami Beach, Fla., June 27, 1946; s. Paul A. and Ethel (Kolnick) G.; m. Cynthia Ann Slaughter, June 4, 1972; children: Keith Richard, Lindsay Anne. BS in Speech, Northwestern U., 1968, JD cum laude, 1971. Bar: Ariz. 1972, U.S. Dist. Ct. Ariz. 1972, U.S. Ct. Appeals (9th cir.) 1972. Assoc. Brown, Vlassis & Bain P.A., Phoenix, 1971-75; founder, ptnr. McLoone, Theobald & Galbut P.C., Phoenix, 1975-86; of counsel Furth, Fahrner, Bluemle & Mason, 1986-89; ptnr. Galbut & Conant, P.C., Phoenix, 1989—; presenter guest "Law Talk" Cable TV; judge pro tem Maricopa County Superior Ct.; lectr. comml. real estate litigation, arbitration, mediation and intellectual property Lorman Bus. Seminars. Contbr. articles to profl. jours. Chmn., law rev. Ariz. State Air Pollution Control Hearing Bd., 1984-89; mem. Govs. Task Force on Urban Air Quality, 1986, City Phoenix Environ. Quality Commn., 1987-88; bd. dirs. Men's Art Council Phoenix Art Mus.; bd. dirs. founder Ariz. Asthma Found. Clarion de Witt Hardy scholar, Kosmerl scholar; Russel Sage grantee. Mem. ABA, Ariz. State Bar Assn. (lectr., securities law and litigation com. and sect.), Am. Arbitration Assn. (arbitrator), Nat. Assn. Securities Dealers (arbitrator, trainer and lectr.). Democrat. Jewish. Avocations: painting, collecting antiques and fine art, travel, golf. General civil litigation, Securities, Antitrust. Office: Galbut & Conant PC 2425 E Camelback Rd Ste 1020 Phoenix AZ 85016-4216

**GALE, CONNIE R(UTH),** lawyer; b. Cleve., July 15, 1946; m. Curtis S. Gale, Dec. 20, 1967. Student, Miami U., Oxford, Ohio, 1964-66; BA with distinction, U. Mich., 1967, JD, 1971; MBA, Mich. State U., 1981. Bar: mich. 1971. Law clk. to presiding justice Mich. Supreme Ct., Lansing, 1971-72; asst. atty. gen. State of Mich., Lansing, 1973; corp. counsel Chrysler Corp., Highland Park, Mich., 1973-81; assoc. gen. counsel Fed.-Mogul Corp., Southfield, Mich., 1981-86; v.p., gen. counsel, sec. Allnet Communication Svcs., Inc. (subs. ALC), Bingham Farms, Mich., 1987-95, ALC Communications Corp., Bingham Farms, 1987-95; of counsel Raymond & Prokop PC, Southfield, 1995-96. Mem. ABA (meetings com. bus. law sect.), Mich. Bar Assn. (chmn. in-house counsel com. 1984-93, chair bus. law sect. 1991, alt. dispute resolution com. 1986-89), Am. Corp. Counsel Assn. (chmn. securities law com. Detroit chpt. 1990, chmn. membership 1991, treas. 1992, sec. 1993, v.p. 1994, pres. 1995), Phi Kappa Phi. Contracts commercial, General corporate, Securities.

**GALE, FOURNIER JOSEPH, III,** lawyer; b. Mobile, Ala., Aug. 3, 1944; s. Fournier J. Jr. and Clara (Beckham) G.; m. Louise Smith, Aug. 7, 1965; children: Carolyn, Jeanette. BA, U. Ala., 1966, JD, 1969; postgrad., Oxford U., summer 1968. Bar: Ala. 1969. From assoc. to ptnr. Cabaniss, Johnston, Gardner, Dumas & O'Neal, Birmingham, Ala., 1969-84; ptnr. Maynard, Cooper & Gale, PC, Birmingham, 1984—; bd. dirs. McWane, Inc., Birmingham; gen. counsel, bd. dirs. Bus. Coun. Ala., Birmingham, 1977—; mem. Ala. Permanent Study Commn. on Judiciary, 1977-83; mem. Jefferson County Jud. Nominating Commn., 1993—; chmn. Ala. Commn. on Higher Edn., 1998—; spl. counsel to Gov. Don Siegelman, 1999—. Mem. Leadership Birmingham, 1986-87; pres. U. Ala. Law Sch. Found., 1987—. Mem. ABA (standing com. on environ. law, standing com. on fed. judiciary), Birmingham Bar Assn. (pres. 1989), Ala. Young Lawyers Assn. (pres. 1976-77), Am. Judicature Soc. (bd. dirs. 1980-85), Jud. Conf. Ala., Am. Bar Found., Kiwanis. Roman Catholic. Environmental, General civil litigation, Administrative and regulatory. Home: 2937 Southwood Rd Birmingham AL 35223-1232 Office: Maynard Cooper & Gale PC 2400 Amsouth Harbert Plz Birmingham AL 35203

**GALE, JOHN QUENTIN,** lawyer; b. Hartford, Conn., June 16, 1951; s. John J. and Doris A. (Boissoneault) G.; m. Tracy Thompson, Sept. 23, 1978; children: Adrienne Hope, Calabria T., Aurelia D., Nathaniel J. BSEE, U. Pa., 1973; JD, U. Conn., 1977. Bar: Conn. 1977, U.S. Dist. Ct. 1978. Engr. GE, Valley Force, Pa., 1972-74; staff atty., corp. counsel City of Hartford, 1977; ptnr. Calvocoressi & Gale, Hartford, 1977—; bd. dirs. New Horizons, Inc., pres., 1998—; bd. dirs. Farmington, Conn. Vision Svcs., Inc., Hartford, Immanuel House, Inc. Founder, editor Professional Discipline Digest, 1991. Trustee Bloomfield (Conn.) United Meth. Ch., 1991—; treas. Hartford Dem. Town Com., 1994—. Recipient Salutation for Improving City award Hartford Courant Columnist-Tom Condon, 1993. Mem. Conn. Bar Assn. (mem. profl. discipline com. 1987—, chmn. profl. discipline com. 1994—), Greater Hartford C. of C. (govt. affairs com. 1988—), Lions Club (dir. 1980—), Phi Delta Phi (hon.). Avocations: recreational sports, bluegrass mandolin, 1941 Oldsmobile, golf, 1897 house. General practice, Personal injury, Probate. Office: Calvocoressi & Gale 363 Main St Hartford CT 06106-1885

**GALE, ROBERT HARRISON, JR.,** lawyer; b. Syracuse, Kans., Feb. 21, 1953; s. Robert H. and Avonne (Gould) G.; m. Linda C. Reitz, June 18, 1978; children: Joshua Robert, Zachary Tyler. BS, U. Kans., 1975, JD, 1978. Bar: Kans. 1978, U.S. Dist. Ct. Kans. 1978, U.S. Ct. Appeals (10th cir.) 1978. Asst. dist. atty. Johnson County, Olathe, Kans., 1978-79; Hamilton County atty. Syracuse, Kans., 1979-85; ptnr. Gale & Gale, Syracuse, 1983-88; city atty. Syracuse, 1988—; dir. First Nat. Bank, Syracuse, 1980-82; dir., pres. S.C.A.T., Inc., Syracuse, 1982-84. Precinct committeeman Dem. Party, Johnson and Hamilton Counties, Kans.; county chmn. Dem. party; elder First Presbyn. Ch., Syracuse; pres. Sch. Bd. Unified Sch. Dist. 494. Mem. Kans. Bar Assn., Kans. County and Dist. Attys. Assn., Nat. Dist. Attys. Assn., ABA, Hamilton C. of C. (bd. dirs. 1983-84), Rotary, Moose. General practice. Home: 507 N Hamilton Syracuse KS 67878 Office: Gale & Gale 211 N Main St PO Box 906 Syracuse KS 67878-0906

**GALELLA, JOSEPH PETER,** lawyer; b. N.Y.C., Oct. 19, 1956; s. Joseph Anthony and Stella Agnes (McKee) G.; m. Elaine Fowler, Aug. 15, 1981; 1 child, Joseph George. BA, Franklin & Marshall Coll., 1978; JD, U. Miami, 1981. Bar: Fla. 1981, N.Y. 1982, U.S. Dist. Ct. (so. dist.) Fla. 1982, U.S. Ct. Appeals (11th cir.) 1982. Assoc. Karsch & Meyer, N.Y.C., 1981-82; sole practice Peekskill, N.Y., 1983—; title atty. Kenneth Pregno Agy., Ltd., Peekskill, 1984—; of counsel Hersh & Hersh, Peekskill, 1994—. Rep. Franklin & Marshall Coll. Alumni Admissions Program, 1979-90; bd. dirs. Peekskill Field Library, 1985—, pres. 1998—. Mem. Fla. Bar, Westchester County Bar Assn., Peekskill Bar Assn. (pres. 1993-94), Ossing Bar Assn. Democrat. Roman Catholic. Avocations: swimming, racquetball, tennis, reading. Real property, Probate. Home: 110 Mountain View Rd Cortlandt Mnr NY 10567-6238

**GALES, ROBERT ROBINSON,** judge; b. N.Y.C., Feb. 15, 1941; s. Arthur S. and Gertrude L. (Robinson) G.; m. Karen A. Terry, Nov. 25, 1986; children: Laurie Ann, Thomas Michael, Robert Robinson II, Brian Timothy, Victoria Marie. BA in History and Geography, Ohio Wesleyan U., 1962; JD, Syracuse U., 1965; LLM, George Washington U., 1966; postgrad. U. Philippines, 1969, Indsl. Coll. Armed Forces, 1971, Air U., 1977, 89. Bar: N.Y. 1966, U.S. Dist. Ct. (so. and ea. dists.) N.Y. 1967, U.S. Dist. Ct. (we. dist.) Wash. 1967, U.S. Ct. Appeals Armed Forces 1967, U.S. Ct. Claims 1967, U.S. Ct. Appeals (9th cir.) 1968, D.C. 1973, U.S. Dist. Ct. (ea. dist.) Va. 1973, U.S. Ct. Appeals (4th cir.) 1973, U.S. Ct. Appeals (2d cir.) 1975, U.S. Customs Ct. 1977, U.S. Ct. Customs and Patent Appeals 1978, Ill. 1978, U.S. Ct. Internat. Trade, 1980, U.S. Ct. Appeals (Fed. cir.) 1982, U.S. Ct. Appeals (7th cir.) 1983, U.S. Dist. Ct. (no. dist.) Ill. 1983, U.S. Dist. Ct. (so. dist.) Ill. 1984. Travel cons. ESSO Touring Svc., N.Y.C., 1960; dep. dir. internat. law 13th Air Force, Philippines, 1969-71; asst. legal advisor U.S. del. Renegotiation of Philippines-U.S. Status of Forces Agreement, 1969-71; chief civil law Tactical Air Command, USAF, Hampton, Va., 1971-72, chief adminstrv. law, 1972-73; assoc. Herzfeld & Rubin, P.C., N.Y.C., 1973-77; task force coord. Volkswagen of Am., Inc., Englewood Cliffs, N.J., 1977; sr. atty. Velsicol Chem. Corp., sec. fgn. subsidiaries, 1977-80; asst. atty. gen. Consumer Protection div. Office of Ill. Atty. Gen., Bensenville and Joliet, 1981-83; chief utility and Acquisition Law, 375th Air Base Group, Scott AFB, Dept. Air Force, Belleville, Ill., 1984-87; dept. counsel Def. Legal Services Agy., Directorate for Indsl. Security Clearance Rev., Arlington, Va., 1987-88, mem. appeal bd., 1988-90, chief adminstrv. judge, 1990-94; chief adminstrv. judge Def. Legal Svcs. Agy., Def. Office Hearings and Appeals, 1994—; mobilization asst. to dir. Judiciary USAF, 1987-89; dir. Civil Law Office of Judge Adv. Gen., 1989-91; sr. res. advisor to staff judge adv. Air Force Dist. of Wash., 1991-92; vis. adj. lectr. Manhattan Coll., 1973-77, N.J. Inst. Tech., 1975-77, Ill. Inst. Tech., 1978-84, So. Ill. Univ., Carbondale, 1984-86. Contbg. editor, writer to newspapers. Mem. Wash. State Soccer Commn., 1967-68; chmn. exploring com. Far East council Philippine dist. Boy Scouts Am., 1969-71; dist. judge adv. Va. VFW, 1972-73; pres., chmn. exec. com. Briarcliff Citizens for Responsive Govt., 1973-74; bd. dirs. Ossining (N.Y.) Area Jaycees, 1973-74, sec., 1974-75; pres. Ossining Hist. Soc., 1974-76; Rep. dist. leader Town of Ossining, 1974-78; dir. Soc. Prevention of Cruelty to Animals of Westchester, 1974-77; bd. dir. Briarcliff-Ossining-Scarborough br. ARC, 1975-76; mem. Westchester County Rep. Com., 1975-78; commr. Wayne Twp. (Ill.) Soccer, 1979-83; Rep. precinct committeeman Wayne Twp., 1979-82; adv. bd. Elgin (Ill.) High Sch., 1979-83; trustee Wayne Twp., 1979-85; pres. Melstone neighborhood bd. Little Rocky Run Homeowners Assn., 1987-92. Ret. col. USAFR, Vietnam. Decorated Legion of Merit, Bronze Star, Meritorious Service medal with 3 oak leaf clusters, Air Force Commendation medal with 3 oak leaf clusters, Air Force Achievement medal (U.S.) Air Force Recognition Ribbon; various medals Republic of Vietnam, Outstanding Contribution to Contracting award USAF, 1986, N.Y. State Conspicuous Svc. Cross with 2 silver devices, 1997; Master of the Bench and mem. Prettyman-Leventhal Am. inn of Court, 1996—. Mem. Am. Judges Assn., Nat. Assn. Adminstrv. Law Judges, mem. bd. advs. to the Journal of The Nat. Assn. of Adminstn. Law Judges, 1995—. Vietnam Vets. Bar Assn. (air force judge adv.), Arnold Air Soc., Delta Phi Epsilon, Phi Alpha Delta. Republican. Contbr. articles to profl. jours. Avocations: sports, travel, collecting model soldiers, dining, writing. Home: 6638 Rockland Dr Clifton VA 20124-2501

**GALGANSKI, TERRY JAMES,** lawyer; b. Wausau, Wis., Nov. 4, 1954; s. Richard Thomas and Eunice Mary (Fahl) G.; m. Martha Hensley, May 23, 1981; children; Sara Alynne, Daniel Thomas. BA, Northwestern U., 1977; JD, St. Louis U., 1980. Bar: Mo. 1980, Ill. 1981. Assoc. Whaley & McAuliffe, Clayton, Mo., 1980-87, McAuliffe & Assocs., Clayton, 1987-88; asst. group counsel Sverdrup Corp., St. Louis, 1988-90, atty. corp. legal dept., 1990-93; atty. Sverdrup Environ., Inc., St. Louis, 1991—; sr. atty. Sverdrup Civil, Inc., St. Louis, 1993—; atty. Sverdrup So. Constructors, Inc., Orlando, Fla., 1992—. Active Hazardous Waste Action Coalition. Mem. ABA (the forum on the constrn. industry, pub. contracts, torts and ins. pvt. sect., contracts and subcontracts subcom., chmn. ins. and bond subcom. 1993—), Mo. Bar Assn. (constrn. law com.), Corp. Counsel Assn. Construction, Environmental, Insurance. Home: 119 W Cedar Ave Saint Louis MO 63119-2905

**GALIARDO, JOHN WILLIAM,** lawyer; b. Elizabeth, N.J., Dec. 28, 1933; s. Joseph A. and Genevieve A. (Luxich) G.; m. Joan A. DeTurk, Aug. 26, 1961; children: Richard C., Christopher D., Elizabeth A. BS, U. Md., 1956; LLB, Columbia U., 1962. Bar: N.Y. 1962. Assoc. Dewey, Ballantine, Bushby, Palmer & Wood, N.Y.C., 1962-71; asst. gen. counsel E.R. Squibb & Sons, Inc., Princeton, N.J., 1971-77; v.p., gen. counsel Becton Dickinson and Co., Franklin Lakes, N.J., 1977-94, vice chmn. bd. dirs., gen. counsel, 1994—; trustee Com. for Econ. Devel., 1994—, HealthCare Inst. N.J., 1998—; mem. Healthcare Leadership Coun., 1994, trustee, 1995—; bd. dirs. VISX, Inc., N.J. Mfrs. Inst. Cos., Gynetics, Inc. Treas. Charter Study Commn., Scotch Plains, N.J., 1970-71; mem. Joint Consol. Com., Princeton, N.J., 1973-76; mem. legal adv. coun. Atlantic Legal Found., N.Y.C., 1986-92, trustee, 1992—; trustee Ind. Coll. Fund N.J., Summit, 1986-93, chmn., 1992; trustee Fairleigh Dickinson U., 1993—; bd. dirs. Project Hope, 1995—. Mem. ABA, N.Y. State Bar Assn., Assn. Bar of City of N.Y., Health Industry Mfrs. Assn. (bd. dirs. 1995—, chmn. 1998—), N.J. Bus. & Industry Assn. (trustee 1995—). General corporate. Home: 56 Crooked Tree Ln Princeton NJ 08540-2950 Office: Becton Dickinson & Co 1 Becton Dr Franklin Lakes NJ 07417-1880

**GALIHER, RICHARD WILKINSON, JR.,** lawyer; b. Washington, D.C., June 6, 1942; s. Richard Wilkinson and Phyllis (Jacobson) G.; m. Louise J. Galiher, Feb. 12, 1972; children: Richard Wilkinson III, Louise J. BA, U. Notre Dame, 1964; JD, Cath. U. Law Sch., 1968. Bar: D.C. 1968, Md. 1969. Assoc. Galiher, Clarke, Mantell & Donally, 1968-75, ptnr., 1975-83; ptnr. Galiher, Clarke & Galiher, Rockville, Md., 1983-95, prin., 1995—. With USCG, 1966-72. Named Alumni Yr. Notre Dame Alumni Assn. Mem. Am. Legion, Knights of Columbus, Columbia Country Club, Lawyers Club. Workers' compensation. Office: Galiher Clarke & Galiher 401 E Jefferson St Ste 101 Rockville MD 20850-2617

**GALIP, RONALD GEORGE,** lawyer; b. Youngstown, Ohio, Feb. 28, 1934; s. George A. and Agnes A. (Ellis) G.; m. Eileen E. Bott, 1955; children: Rochelle D. Galip Root, Kathleen A. Galip Mootz. BA, Youngstown (Ohio) State U., 1955; JD, Ohio State U., 1957. Gen. counsel Cafaro Co., Youngstown, 1957-78; ptnr. Galip & Manos, Youngstown, 1978-83; sole practice Youngstown, 1983—; counsel, bd. dirs. Youngstown Devel. Co. Mem. Ohio Bar Assn., Mahoning County Bar Assn., Internat. Council Shopping Ctrs. Roman Catholic. Avocations: golf, tennis, travel. Real property, Landlord-tenant. Home: 3445 Logan Way Youngstown OH 44505-2260 Office: 721 Boardman Poland Rd Youngstown OH 44512-5107

**GALISON, EDWARD,** lawyer; b. N.Y.C., Aug. 29, 1941; s. Philip and Marcella Galison; m. Barbara Boyar (div. 1984); m. Barbara C. Glazier, Apr. 1, 1988; children: Laura, David, Marni. BA, Adelphi U., 1962; JD, Albany Law U., 1969. Bar: N.Y. 1969, Fla. 1973, U.S. Dist. Ct. (ea. dist.) N.Y. 1973. Criminal, Family and matrimonial, Real property. Office: 1539 Franklin Ave Mineola NY 11501-4806

**GALKA, LAWRENCE S.,** lawyer; b. Mpls., Aug. 11, 1933; s. Frank R. and Stella A. Galka; married; children: Lawrence Stefan, Renee Ann. BCE, Marquette U., 1955, JD, 1958. Chief trial deputy Colo. Pub. Defender, Colorado Springs, 1977-80; pvt. practice Colorado Springs, 1980—. Named 3 time Master Nat. Cycling Champion, 1989-93. Criminal. Office: 102 S Tejon St Ste 1100 Colorado Springs CO 80903-2253

**GALL, ROBERT JAY,** lawyer; b. Athens, Ohio, Jan. 18, 1957; s. Homer B. Jr. and Jean Elliott Gall; m. Cherie Hill, Dec. 4, 1982; 1 child, Anna Claire. AB, Miami U., 1979; JD, Coll. of William and Mary, 1982. Bar: Ohio 1982, U.S. Ct. Appeals (6th cir.) 1982, U.S. Dist. Ct. (so. dist.) Ohio 1983, U.S. Supreme Ct. 1985. Atty. Mollica, Gall, Sloan & Sillery, Athens, 1982—; bd. dirs. Bank One, Athens. Bd. dirs., vice-chair Ohio U. Coll. Osteo. Medicine, Athens; bd. dirs., chair Sheltering Arms Hosp. Found., Athens; vice chmn. Athens County Port Authority. Mem. ABA, Ohio State Bar Assn. (bd. govs. sect. for estate planning probate and trust law), Athens County Bar Assn. (pres.). Estate planning, Probate, General corporate. Office: Mollica Gall Sloan & Sillery Co LPA 35 N College St Athens OH 45701-2529

**GALLAGHER, BRIAN JOHN,** lawyer; b. Bklyn., Oct. 24, 1939; s. John Joseph and Margaret R. (Smith) G.; m. Mary Loughney, Sept. 10, 1966; children—Amanda, Ian. B.S.S., Fairfield U., 1961; J.D., Fordham U., 1964; postgrad. NYU Law Sch., 1969-70. Bar: N.Y. 1965, U.S. Dist. Ct. (so. dist.) N.Y. 1967, U.S. Dist. Ct. (ea. dist.) N.Y. 1974, U.S. Ct. Appeals (2d cir.) 1971, U.S. Ct. Appeals (11th cir.) 1982, U.S. Ct. Appeals (D.C. cir.) 1986. Ptnr., Kronish, Lieb, Weiner & Hellman, LLP, N.Y.C., 1976—; asst. U.S. Atty. So. Dist. N.Y., 1967-71. Mayor, Village of Pelham Manor, N.Y., 1995-97, trustee, 1989-95. Mem. ABA, N.Y. State Bar Assn., Assn. Bar City N.Y., Fed. Bar Coun., Larchmont (N.Y.) Yacht Club. Antitrust, Federal civil litigation, Private international. Office: 1114 Avenue Of The Americas New York NY 10036-7703

**GALLAGHER, BYRON PATRICK, JR.,** lawyer; b. Bay City, Mich., Feb. 29, 1964; s. Byron Patrick and Ethel Jean (Gebowski) G.; m. Michelle Francis Burdick, May 21, 1994; 1 child, Byron Patrick III. AB, Kenyon Coll., Gambier, Ohio, 1986; JD, Washington U., St. Louis, 1989. Bar: Mich. 1989, U.S. Dist. Ct. (we. dist.) Mich. 1990, U.S. Dist. Ct. (ea. dist.) Mich. 1995. Ptnr. Gallagher Duby, PLC, East Lansing, 1998—. Bd. dirs. Ingham County Social Svc. Bd., Mason, Mich., 1991-92, Ingham County Commn., Mason, 1993-97, Mich. Underground Storage Tank Fin. Assurance Authority, 1996—; Rep. cand. Mich. State Senate, 1998. Mem. Ingham County Bar Assn. (bd. dirs. 1996—), County Club of Lansing, Mich. Athletic Club. Republican. Avocations: flying, golf. General corporate, Probate, Real property. Home: 1203 Hillgate Way Lansing MI 48912-5014 Office: Gallagher Duby PLC 2510 Kerry St Ste 210 Lansing MI 48912-3671

**GALLAGHER, DONALD AVERY, JR.,** lawyer; b. Corvallis, Oreg., Sept. 13, 1946; s. Donald A. Sr. and Rachel A. (McColm) G.; m. Janet K. Kerr, Dec. 21, 1968; children: Brandon, Cameron. BS, Oreg. State U., 1968; JD, U. Oreg., 1974. Bar: Oreg. 1974, U.S. Dist. Ct. Oreg. 1975. Ptnr. Arnold, Gallagher, Saydack, Percell & Roberts, Eugene, Oreg., 1993—; sec. Bowerman Found., Eugene, 1983-92. Bd. dirs. Eugene Family YMCA, 1984-90; chmn. OSB ethics com., 1988-89. Mem. Oreg. Stae Bar Assn. (ethics com. 1987-90). Republican. General corporate, Mergers and acquisitions, Real property. Office: Arnold Gallagher Saydach Percell & Roberts 800 Willamette St Ste 800 Eugene OR 97401-2996

**GALLAGHER, GEORGE R.,** judge. Sr. judge D.C. Ct. Appeals. Office: 500 Indiana Ave NW Ste 6000 Washington DC 20001-2131

**GALLAGHER, JEROME FRANCIS, JR.,** lawyer; b. Passaic, N.J., Sept. 16, 1958; s. Jerome F. and Iris (Torres) G.; m. Deirdre O. Stewart, Sept. 27, 1992; children: Nicholas, Colin, Caroline. BS in Man and Tech. with distinction, N.J. Inst. Tech., Newark, 1980; JD, Rutgers U., Newark, 1983. Bar: N.J. 1983, U.S. Dist. Ct. N.J. 1983, U.S. Ct. Appeals (3d cir.) 1994. Assoc. Shanley & Fisher, P.C., Morristown, N.J., 1983-84, Dunn, Pashman, Sponzilli, Swick & Finnerty, Esq., Hackensack, N.J., 1984-90; ptnr. Baron, Gallagher & Perzley, Esq., Parsippany, N.J., 1990-98, Gallagher, Cavanaugh & Perzley, L.C.C., Parsippany, 1998—. Pres. St. Mary's H.S. Assn., Wharton, N.J., 1993-95. Mem. N.J. State Bar Assn., Bergen County Bar Assn., Comml. Law League Am. Avocations: skiing, model trains, civic organizations. Bankruptcy, State civil litigation, Consumer commercial. Office: Gallagher Cavanaugh & Perzley LLC 2001 Route 46 Ste 202 Parsippany NJ 07054-1315

**GALLAGHER, TIMOTHY D.,** lawyer; b. Garfield Heights, Ohio, Feb. 1, 1964; s. William D. and Anne Higgins G.; m. Claire Mary Donahue, Oct. 29, 1994; children: Madeline Anne, William Barry. BA, U. Notre Dame, 1986; JD, Georgetown U., 1990. Bar: N.Y. State 1991, U.S. Dist. Ct. (so. dist.) N.Y. 1994, U.S. Dist. Ct. (ea. dist.) N.Y. 1994, U.S. Ct. Appeals (2d cir.) 1996. Law clk. to Hon. Thomas A. Flannery U.S. Dist. Ct. D.C., 1990-91; assoc. While & Case, N.Y.C., 1991-93; assoc. McMahon, Martine & Gallagher, N.Y.C., 1993-97, ptnr., 1998—. Mem. N.Y. State Bar Assn. (mem. com. on professionalism, fed. and comml. section 1997—, mem. faculty legal edn. course 1998). Roman Catholic. State civil litigation, Insurance, Personal injury. Office: McMahon Martine & Gallagher 90 Broad St New York NY 10004-2205

**GALLAGHER, WILLIAM F.,** lawyer; b. New Haven, Conn., June 28, 1937. BBS, Fairfield U., 1959; LLB, U. Conn., 1963. Bar: Conn. 1963, U.S. Dist. Ct. Conn. 1964, U.S. Ct. Appeals (2d cir.) 1966, U.S. Supreme Ct. 1969. Asst. corp. counsel West Haven, Conn., 1969-72; spl. asst. state's atty. New Haven County, 1974-82; ptnr. Gallagher Gallagher & Calistro, New Haven, Conn., 1982—; lectr. Conn. Bar Assn. Trial Advocacy Program, 1976-90, Advanced Civil Procedure, 1993—, Conn. Trial Lawyers Assn., Coll. Evidence 1987-97, Supreme and Appellate Ct. Rev., 1987—, Tort Reform, 1988-90, Advocacy Seminars, 1983—; Conn. State Trial referee, 1984—. Mem. editl. bd. Conn. Law Tribune, 1986—; editor Conn. Trial Lawyres Assn. Foru, 1993—. Fellow Am. Bar Found., Am. Coll. Trial Lawyers; mem. ABA (family law sect. 1979—, tort and ins. practice sect. 1989—, litig. sect. 1989—), ATLA, Conn. Bar Assn. (pres.-elect 1998-99), Am. Acad. Appellate Lawyers, Conn. Bar Found., Nat. Panel Arbitrators, Am. Arbitration Assn., Roscoe Pound Found., New Haven County Bar Assn. (pres. 1993-94), Conn. Trial Lawyers Assn. (bd. govs. 1983—, pres. 1990-91), Am. Judicature Soc., Trial Lawyers for Pub. Justice. E-mail: wfg@gallaghergc-law.com. General civil litigation, Personal injury. Office: Gallagher Gallagher & Calistro PO Box 1925 1377 Boulevard New Haven CT 06509*

**GALLANIS, KATHRYN ANN,** prosecutor; b. Evanston, Ill., June 10, 1960; d. Thomas Constantine and Helen K. (Karkazis) G. BBA, So. Meth. U., 1982. Bar: Ill. 1985. Asst. states atty. Cook County States Attys. Office, Chgo., 1985-98; atty. Bruce Farrel Dorn & Assocs., 1998—; prof. criminal justice dept. Lewis U., Romeoville, Ill. Bd. dirs. Greek Orthodox Basketball Tournament, Glenview, Ill., 1988—, Nat. Hellenic Invitational Basketball, Chgo., 1994—, Chgo. Coun. Fgn. Rels.; mem. (life) Art Inst., New Trier Citizens League. Mem. ABA, Chgo. Bar Assn. (jud. evaluation com.), New Trier Rep. Orgn., Profl. Soc. for Abused Children, So. Meth. Alumni Assn., LWV (bd. dirs.), Hellenic Am. Police Assn., Hellenic Bar Assn., Jr. League of Chgo., Found. for Women. Avocations: skiing, reading, piano. Home: 136 Melrose Ave Kenilworth IL 60043-1249 Office: Bruce Farrel Dorn & Assocs 120 N Lasalle St Chicago IL 60602-2412

**GALLANT, GARY,** lawyer; b. Camden, N.J., Apr. 5, 1967; s. Gary G. and Barbara (Burdick) G. BA, Rutgers U., 1989, JD, 1992. Bar: N.J., Pa., D.C. Campaign mgr. U.S. Rep. Jim Saxton, Mt. Holly, N.J., 1992, dist. rep., 1993-94; chief staff U.S. Rep. Jim Saxton, Washington, 1996—; asst. prosecutor Burlington County Prosecutor's Office, Mt. Holly, 1992-93; chief counsel Congress' Joint Econ. Comm., Washington, 1994-96; Bd. trustees N.J. Dept. Corrections, Trenton, 1994—. Republican. Roman Catholic. Avocations: boating, baseball, water skiing. Office: Swidler Berlin Shereff Friedman LLP 3000 K St NW Ste 300 Washington DC 20007-5116

**GALLANT, JEFFREY ANDREW,** lawyer; b. Saginaw, Mich., Feb. 25, 1965; s. Thomas John and Betty Jane Gallant; m. Angelina Renee Vega, May 25, 1996. BA in Philosophy, U. Mich., 1986, JD, 1990. Bar: Mich. 1990. Trial atty. Dept. Justice, Washington, 1990-96; assoc. Feeney, Kellett, Bloomfield Hills, Mich., 1996-98; asst. U.S. atty. U.S. Dist. Ct. for Ea. Dist. Okla., Muskogee, 1998—. Candidate state rep. Rep. Orgn., Clarkston, Mich., 1996; mem. Friends of Libr. Mem. Optimist Club, KC, Phi Beta Kappa. Roman Catholic. Avocations: reading, volunteering. Office: US Atty Office 1200 W Okmulgee St Muskogee OK 74401-6848

**GALLEGOS, ESTEBAN GUILLERMO,** lawyer; b. Valparaiso, Chile, Dec. 26, 1956. AS, Santa Barbara (Calif.) City Coll., 1982, JD, 1987. Bar: Calif. 1987, U.S. Dist. Ct. (cen. dist.) Calif. 1988, U.S. Supreme Ct. 1994, U.S. Ct. Appeals (9th cir.) 1994. Assoc. Law Offices of McKay & French, Santa Monica, Calif., 1987-89, Roxborough & Assocs., L.A., 1989-96; ptnr. Roxborough, Pomerance, Gallegos & Nye, L.A., 1998—. Sgt. USMC, 1974-78. Recipient Specialized Law Enforcement Cert., Calif. State Dept. Justice, 1987. Mem. ATLA, Calif. Bar Assn., Beverly Hills Bar Assn. (co-chair community access cable TV com. 1989—, bd. govs., prodn. chair com. for arts), ABA (bus. law sect., intellectual property sect., entertainment law sect.), Calif. Lawyers for the Arts (bd. dirs.), Latin Bus. Assn., Nat. Bd. Trial Advocacy (cert. civil trial advocate). Trademark and copyright, General civil litigation, Entertainment. Office: Roxborough Pomerance Gallegos & Nye 10866 Wilshire Blvd Ste 1200 Los Angeles CA 90024-4358

**GALLEGOS, LARRY DUAYNE,** lawyer; b. Cheverly, Md., Mar. 23, 1951; s. Belarmino R. and Helen (Schlotthauer) G.; m. Claudia M. King, Oct. 1, 1994; 1 child, Will Adam. BS summa cum laude, U. Puget Sound, 1978; JD, Harvard U., 1981. Bar: Colo. 1981, U.S. Dist. Ct. Colo. 1981, U.S. Tax Ct. 1989. Assoc. Pendleton & Sabian, Denver, 1981-83; assoc. O'Connor & Hannan, Denver, 1983-86, ptnr., 1986-89; ptnr. Rossi & Judd, P.C., Denver, 1989-92, Berliner Zisser Walter & Gallegos, P.C., Denver, 1992—. Served with U.S. Army (ARCOM), 1972-74. Mem. ABA (real property, probate and trust law sect.), Colo. Bar Assn., Colo. Trial Lawyers Assn., Denver Bar Assn., U.S. Golf Assn. Avocations: tennis, golf. General civil litigation, Contracts commercial, Finance. Office: Berliner Zisser Walter & Gallegos PC 1700 Lincoln St Ste 4700 Denver CO 80203-4547

**GALLEN, JAMES MICHAEL,** lawyer; b. East St. Louis, Ill., Jan. 29, 1952; s. James V. and Catherine Ellen (English) G.; m. JoAnn Bundschuh, July 26, 1980; children: James W., Katherine Ann. BS in Commerce magna cum laude, St. Louis U., 1973, JD, 1976. Bar: Mo. 1976, U.S. Dist. Ct. (ea. dist.) Mo. 1976, Ill. 1977. Assoc. Evans & Dixon, St. Louis, 1976-83, ptnr., 1984—. Author: When Workers Lie to Get a Job, 1991, (with others), Injuries in the Workplace: The Missouri Workers' Compensation Claims Process, 1992, Injuries in the Workplace: The Illinois Workers' Compensation Claims Process, 1992, Workers' Compensation in Illinois, 1995, Defending a Heart Case: Don't Let Your Company Skip a Beat, 1995; contbg. author: Workers' Compensation and Occupational Medicine, 1992, History of St. Clair County, Vol. II, 1992, Worker's Compensation Defense and Occupational Medicine, 1995, contbg. author, 17th Annual Worker's Compensation and Occupational Medicine Seminar Handbook - Repetitive Motion Injuries: Proof and Defense; Heart Claims; Proof and Defense, 1997; contbr. numerous articles to profl. publs. Mem. adv. bd. SSM. Rehab. Inst., St. Louis, 1986—, v.p. external affairs, 1989-90, v.p. for program svcs., 1990-94; chair organizing com. Bus Review of Ams. with Disabilities Act (vice pres., 1997, pres., 1998; past pres., 1999), 1991, Ams. with Disabilities Act, Practical Applications for Your Bus., 1992; del. Mo. Rep. Conv., 1992. Recipient St. Louis Success award Mo. Mchts. and Mfrs. Assn., 1991. Mem. ABA (workers' compensation and employers' liability law com., liability law vice chair, torts and ins. practice sect.), Ill. State Bar Assn., Met. St. Louis Bar Assn., St. Louis U. Law Alumni Assn. (v.p. 1987-91, pres. 1991-98), mem. Dean's Adv. Couns., St. Louis U. Law Sch., 1998—, Mo. Athletic Club (nominating com. 1990), Alpha Sigma Nu, Beta Gamma Sigma. Republican. Roman Catholic. Workers' compensation. Office: Evans & Dixon 200 N Broadway Ste 1200 Saint Louis MO 63102-2749

**GALLIAN, RUSSELL JOSEPH,** lawyer; b. San Mateo, Calif., Apr. 24, 1948; s. Phillip Hugh and Betty Jane (Boulton) G.; m. Marian Barbara Howard, Sept. 21, 1969; children: Lisa, Cherie, Joseph, Russell, Yvette, Jason, Ryan. BS, U. San Francisco, 1969, JD with honors, 1974. Bar: Calif. 1974, Utah 1975, U.S. Ct. Appeals (10th cir.) 1975, U.S. Supreme Ct. 1990; CPA, Calif. Staff acct. Arthur Andersen & Co., CPAs, San Francisco, 1969-71; treas., contr. N.Am. Reassurance Life Svc. Co., Palo Alto, Calif., 1972-74; assoc. VanCott Bagley Cornwell & McCarthy, Salt Lake City, 1975-77; sr. ptnr. Gallian & Westfall, Wilcox & Wright LC, St. George, Utah, 1977—; chmn. bd. dirs. Dixie Title Co., St. George. Chmn. Tooele (Utah) City Planning Commn., 1978; atty. City of Tooele, 1978-80, Town of Ivins, Utah, 1982—, Town of Springdale, Utah, 1987-90, Town of Rockville, Utah, 1987, Town of Virgin, 1995—; commr. Washington County, 1993-96; chmn. Washington County Econ. Devel. Coun., 1993-96; bd. dirs. Dixie Ctr., 1993-96; active Habitat Conservation Plan Steering Com. Mem. ABA, Utah State Bar Assn., Tooele County Bar Assn. (pres. 1978-79), So. Utah Bar Assn. (pres. 1986-87). Republican. Mormon. Real property, Banking. Office: Gallian & Westfall Wilcox & Wright LC 59 S 100 E Saint George UT 84770-3422

**GALLIGAN, MATTHEW G.,** lawyer; b. New Haven, Sept. 1, 1923; s. Matthew J. and Mary J. (Gordon) G.; m. Anne Elizabeth Reynolds, Apr. 10, 1950. BS, Fordham U., 1947; JD, Georgetown U., 1950. Bar: Conn. 1951. Sole practice Wallingford, Conn., 1952—; asst. pros. atty. Town of Wallingford, 1953-55, town atty., 1956-57, 1960-69; counsel joint senate ho. judiciary com. Conn. Gen. Assembly, 1971; mem. adv. bd. Am. Nat. Bank, 1979. Corporator Meriden-Wallingford (Conn.) Hosp., 1975. Mem. Conn. Bar Assn., New Haven County Bar Assn., Meriden-Wallingford Bar Assn. Roman Catholic. Lodge: Elks, Rotary. Fax: 203-269-1401. General practice, Probate, Real property. Office: 300 Long Hill Rd Wallingford CT 06492-4948

**GALLIGAN, THOMAS C., JR.,** dean, law educator. AB, Stanford U., 1977; JD, U. Puget Sound, 1981; LLM, Columbia U., 1986. With Lane Powell Moss & Miller, Seattle; prof. law Paul Hebert Law Ctr. La. State U., Dale E. Bennett prof. law, 1997, exec. dir. La. Jud. Coll., 1996-98; dean, prof. law U. Tenn., Knoxville, 1998—; spkr. on legal topics to various groups, 1987—. Co-author: (books) Legislation and Jurisprudence on Maritime Personal Injury Law, 1997, Louisiana Tort Law, 1996, supplemented 1997; contbr. articles to law revs. and acad. jours. Recipient John Minor Wisdom award for acad. excellence in legal scholarship Tulane Law Rev., 1996-97. Fax: 423-974-6595. Office: Ste 278 1505 W Cumberland Ave Knoxville TN 37996-1810*

**GALLINGER, LORRAINE D.,** prosecutor; b. Sept. 2, 1948. BS, U. Wyo., 1970; JD, Cath. U. Am., 1975. Bar: D.C., Mont. 1st asst. U.S. atty. Dept. Justice, Billings, Mont., 1976-85, 91, sr. litigation counsel, chief civil divsn., 1985-91, acting U.S. atty., 1991-93; first asst. U.S. Attys. Office, Billings, Mont., 1993—; instr. Atty. Gen. Advocacy Inst. Recipient Dir.'s Superior Performance award AUSA, 1988. Office: US Attys Office PO Box 1478 Billings MT 59103-1478

**GALLIVAN, HENRY MILLS,** lawyer; b. Greenville, S.C., May 17, 1951; s. Harold Francis and Genevieve (Mills) G.; m. Carol Anne Provence, June 9, 1973; children—Anne Genevieve, Henry Mills, Harriet Provence. B.A., Vanderbilt U., 1973; J.D., U. S.C., 1976. Bar: S.C. 1976, U.S. Dist. Ct. S.C. 1976, U.S. Supreme Ct. 1989. Mem. Gibbes, Gallivan, White & Boyd, P.A., Greenville, 1976—, prin., 1979—. Bd. dirs. Birthright of Greenville, Inc., 1980-87, Eastern Seal Soc. Greenville, 1984-87; trustee St. Mary's Sch. Trust Fund, Greenville, 1984; mem. Greenville County Health Planning Council, 1979-84, St. Francis Hosp. Found., 1996-98; pres. Mardi Gras Charity Ball, 1996. Mem. ABA, S.C. Bar Assn., S.C. Def. Trial Attys. Assn. (exec. com. 1990-98, sec. 1999), Def. Research Inst., Am. Judicature Soc. Roman Catholic. Lodge: Rotary. Federal civil litigation, State civil litigation, Workers' compensation. Office: Rainey Britton Gibbes & Clarkson PA 330 E Coffee St Greenville SC 29603

**GALLMAN, RYAN LANCE,** lawyer; b. Buffalo, Dec. 27, 1967; s. Stuart Allen and Hynda (Jacobson) G. BS, U. Pa., 1989; JD, SUNY, Buffalo, 1993, MBA, 1994. Bar: N.Y., Fla., U.S. Dist. Ct. (we. and no. dists.) N.Y. From law clk. to assoc. Law Office Joseph A. Ables, Buffalo, N.Y., 1992-95; assoc. Block & Colucci P.C., Buffalo, 1995—. Bd. dirs. Am. Jewish Com., Buffalo-Niagra chpt., 1995—. General civil litigation. Home: 939 Delaware Ave Apt 205 Buffalo NY 14209-1841 Office: Block & Colucci PC 2000 Liberty Bldg 424 Main Buffalo NY 14202

**GALLO, A. ANDREW,** lawyer; b. Rockville Centre, N.Y., May 6, 1960; s. Adam Anthony and Jane Gwendolyn Gallo; m. Margaret Mary Fitzpatrick, July 4, 1987; children: Grant Edward, Anna Gabrielle. BA, Hofstra U., 1982; JD, Coll. William and Mary, 1985. Bar: Tex. 1985, Mo. 1993, U.S. Dist. Ct. (so. and we. dists.) Tex. 1986. Atty. Exxon Corp., Houston, 1985-86, Ryan & Shoss, Houston, 1986-87, Amoco Corp., Houston, 1987-99; of counsel McElroy, Sullivan, Ryan & Miller, L.L.P., Austin, Tex., 1999—. Recipient AmJur award remedies, Am. Jurisprudence, Williamsburg, Va., 1984, AmJur award Trusts and estates Am. Jurisprudence, Williamsburg, 1985. Mem. Tex. Bar Assn., Mo. Bar Assn., Order of the Coif. Avocations: running, choir. Fax: 512-327-6566. E-mail: aagallo@msrm.com. Administrative and regulatory, General civil litigation, Oil, gas, and mineral. Office: McElroy Sullivan Ryan Et Al 1201 Spyglass Dr Austin TX 78746-6924

**GALLO, JON JOSEPH,** lawyer; b. Santa Monica, Calif., Apr. 19, 1942; s. Philip S. and Josephine (Sarazan) G.; m. Jo Ann Broome, June 13, 1964 (div. 1984); children: Valerie Ann, Donald Philip; m. Eileen Florence, July 4, 1985; 1 child, Kevin Jon. BA, Occidental Coll., 1964; JD, UCLA, 1967. Bar: Calif. 1968, U.S. Ct. Appeals (9th cir.) 1968, U.S. Tax Ct. 1969. Assoc. Greenberg, Glusker, Fields, Claman & Machtinger, L.A., 1967-75, ptnr., 1975—; bd. dirs. USC Probate and Trust Conf., L.A., 1980—, UCLA Estate Planning Inst., chmn. 1992—. Contbr. articles to profl. jours. Fellow Am. Coll. Trust and Estate Counsel; mem. ABA (chair Generation Skipping Taxation com. 1992-95, co-chair life ins. com. 1995—), Internat. Acad. Estate and Trust Law, Assn. for Advanced Life Underwriting (assoc. mem.). Avocation: photography. Estate planning, Probate, Estate taxation. Office: Greenberg Glusker Fields Claman & Machtinger LLP Ste 2100 1900 Avenue Of The Stars Los Angeles CA 90067-4502

**GALLOWAY, HUNTER HENDERSON, III,** lawyer, small business owner; b. Abingdon, Va., Nov. 16, 1945; s. Hunter Henderson Jr. and Katherine Cosby (Hines) G.; m. Linda Sharlene Alley, June 20, 1971 (div. Feb. 1975); m. Deborah Lynn Brannon, Dec. 18, 1977; children: Andrew Michael, Hunter Henderson IV, Patrick B., Thomas J. BBA, U. N.C., 1968, JD, 1972. Bar: N.C. 1972, U.S. Dist. Ct. (mid. dist.) 1974, U.S. Tax Ct. 1976, U.S. Ct. Appeals (4th cir.) 1979, U.S. Supreme Ct. 1983. Assoc. Hoyle, Hoyle & Boone, Greensboro, 1972-78; sole practice Greensboro, 1978—; tchr. U. N.C., Greensboro, 1974-82; dealer Galloway Buick Co., Greensboro, 1978—. Served with N.C. N.G., 1968-74. Recipient Wall Street Jour. award, U. N.C., 1968. Mem. ABA, N.C. Bar Assn., Greensboro Bar Assn., N.C. Acad. Trial Lawyers. Democrat. Presbyterian. Club: Greensboro Country. Lodge: Rotary. Avocations: trap shooting, hunting, camping. Real property, Consumer commercial. Home: 1815 Nottingham Rd Greensboro NC 27408-5612 Office: Galloway Buick Co 401 N Murrow Blvd Greensboro NC 27401-3009

**GALLOWAY, JOHN W., JR.,** lawyer; b. Rockwood, Tenn., Mar. 4, 1954; s. John W. and Avilee (Garrett) G.; m. Pamela A. Kissel, June 5, 1980; children: Laura K., Amanda K. BS, Tenn. Tech. U., 1975; JD, U. Tenn., 1978. Bar: Tenn. 1978. Asst. dist. atty. gen. 8th Jud. Dist., Huntsville, Tenn., 1982—. Capt. U.S. Army, 1978-82. Democrat. Methodist. Avocations: farming. Office: Dist Atty Gen Office PO Box 10 Huntsville TN 37756-0010

**GALLOWAY, NEWTON MONROE,** lawyer; b. Griffin, Ga., Nov. 21, 1957; s. Newton Kalor and Dorothy Elizabeth (Smith) G.; m. Teri Lynn Race, Mar. 31, 1984 (div. 1996). BA, Mercer U., 1978, JD, 1981. Bar: U.S. Ct. Appeals (11th cir.), U.S. Dist. Ct. (no., mid. and so. dists.) Ga., Ga 1981. Assoc. Greene, Buckley, DeRieux & Jones, Atlanta, 1981-88; ptnr. Mullins & Whalen, Griffin, Ga., 1988-93, Hendrix & Smith, 1993-96; pvt. practice Newton M. Galloway & Assocs., 1996—; legal counsel Ga. Pub. Comm. Assn. Mng. editor staff, jud. com. Mercerr Law Rev.; contbr. articles to profl. jours. Mem. Griffing Downtown Counsel/Main St. Exec. Coun.; bd. dirs. Arts Clayton, 1988-90. Named Outstanding Young Men in Am., 1984. Mem. ABA, Am. Cancer Soc. (South Fulton unit bd. dirs.), Ga. Trust Hist. Prescervation (ways and means fundraising com.), Ga. Bar Assn. (exec. counsel, alt. 1989-92), Atlanta Bar Assn., Atlanata Hist. Soc., Griffin-Spalding County Bar Assn., Griffin-Spalding County C. of C., Griffin Community Concerts Assn. (pres. 1990-91), Pike County C. of C., Mercer U. Alumni Assn. (v.p. Atlanta area 1984-85), Lambda Chi Alpha (pres. 1985-86), Phi Eta Sigma, Sigma Mu. Public utilities, General civil litigation, Construction. Office: Newton M Galloway & Assocs 113 Concord St Zebulon GA 30295

**GALLUCCI, MICHAEL A.,** lawyer; b. Jersey City, Nov. 26, 1966; s. Michael J. and Marilyn A. (Christiano) G.; m. Catherine Jane Branch, June 17, 1995. BA, Catholic U., 1988, JD, 1991. Bar: N.J. 1991, U.S. Dist. Ct. N.J. 1991. Legis. aide Bergen County Freeholders, Hackensack, N.J., 1992-93; assoc. Nowell Amoroso, Hackensack, 1996—. Sec. Teaneck (N.J.) Hist. Preservation, 1992-95; coun. liaison Teaneck Econ. Devel. Corp., 1996-97, Teaneck Planning Bd., 1997—; nominating com. chmn. Bergen County (N.J.) Boy Scouts, 1997—; dep. mayor Teaneck, 1996—, coun., 1995—. Mem. N.J. State Bar Assn., Bergen County Bar Assn. Avocations: golf, travel, skiing. General civil litigation, General practice, Consumer commercial. Home: 112 Johnson Ave Teaneck NJ 07666-4216 Office: Nowell Amoroso 155 Polifly Rd Hackensack NJ 07601-1749

**GALLUP, DAVID M.,** lawyer. AB in French & History, Washington U., St. Louis, 1988; JD, Am. U., 1991. Bar: Md. 1992. Gen. counsel World Svc. Authority, Washington, 1992—; sec. World Citizen Found.; pres. World Svc. Authority, 1999—. Legal columnist World Citizen News. Mem. ABA, Md. State Bar Assn. Avocations: photography, drawing, painting, international cultural activities. Office: World Service Authority 1012 14th St NW Washington DC 20005-3406

**GALSO, ERNEST PETER GABRIEL,** lawyer; b. South Bend, Ind., Sept. 5, 1964. BA in History, U. Notre Dame, 1986; JD, Ind. U., 1989. Bar: Ill. 1989, Ind. 1991. Asst. state's atty. Vermilion County State's Atty., Danville, Ill., 1990-91; assoc. Noell & Assocs. Law Office, South Bend, Ind., 1991-96; pvt. practice South Bend, 1996—; bd. dirs. Legal Svcs. Program of Northern Ind., South Bend. Mem. Saint Joseph County Bar Assn., Ind. State Bar Assn. Avocation: running. Family and matrimonial, Personal injury, Criminal. Office: 618 E Colfax Ave South Bend IN 46617-2827

**GALVIN, CHARLES O'NEILL,** law educator; b. Wilmington, N.C., Sept. 29, 1919; s. George Patrick and Marie (O'Neill) G.; m. Margaret Edna Gillespie, June 29, 1946; children: Katherine Marie, George Patrick, Paul Edward, Charles O'Neill, Elizabeth Genevieve. BSc, So. Meth. U., 1940; MBA, Northwestern U., 1941, JD, 1947; SJD, Harvard U., 1961; LLD, Capital, 1990. Bar: Ill. 1947, Tex. 1948, U.S. Dist. Ct. (no. dist.) Tex. 1948, U.S. Tax Ct. 1949; CPA, Tex. Pvt. practice Dallas, 1947-52; from asst. to assoc. prof. So. Meth. U., Dallas, 1952-55, prof., 1955-82, dean Sch. Law, 1963-78; Centennial prof. law Vanderbilt U., Nashville, 1983-90, Centennial prof. emeritus, 1990—, exec. in residence, 1990-93; of counsel Haynes and Boone, LLP, Dallas, 1994—; Thayer tchg. fellow Harvard U., 1956-57; vis. prof. U. Mich., 1957, Duke U., 1979, Pepperdine U., 1980; Raymond Rice Disting. vis. prof. U. Kans., 1990; adj. prof. law U. Tex., 1995-97, So. Meth. U., 1996—; bd. dirs. State Farm Ins., Bloomington, Ill., 1980-95; trustee Am. Tax Policy Inst., 1992-97. Author: Estate Planning Manual, 1987; tax editor Oil and Gas Reporter; co-editor: Texas Will Manual, 1972—. Chmn. Dallas County Community Action, Dallas 1970-72; pres. Cath. Found., Dallas, 1963-67. Served to lt. comdr. USNR, 1942-46. Recipient Disting. Alumnus award So. Meth. U., 1984, Disting. Alumnus award Northwestern U., Chgo., 1993, John Rogers award Southwestern Legal Found., Dallas, 1997, McGill award Cath. Found., 1997. Fellow Am. Bar. Found., Tex. Bar Found.; mem. ABA, Tex. Bar Assn., Dallas Bar Assn., Am. Law Inst. (life), Am. Judicature Soc., Tex. Soc. CPA's, Am. Inst. CPA's, Order of Coif, Am. Tax Policy Inst., Phi Delta Theta, Beta Gamma Sigma. Roman Catholic. Home: 4240 Twin Post Rd Dallas TX 75244-6741 Office: Haynes and Boone LLP 3200 Nations Bank Plz 901 Main St Dallas TX 75202-3789

**GALVIN, CHRISTINE M.,** lawyer; b. Rochester, N.Y., Apr. 17, 1954; d. Willard Harold and Shirley (Oster) G.; m. Raphael E. Rettig, Aug. 14, 1982. BS cum laude, U. N.H., 1976; JD, Albany Law Sch., Albany, 1982. Bar: N.Y. 1983, U.S. Dist. Ct. (no. dist.) N.Y., 1983. Assoc. Kouray & Kouray, Schenectady, N.Y., 1982-88; pvt. practice Schenectady, 1988-89; assoc. Gordon, Siegel, Mastro, Mullaney, Gordon & Galvin, PC, Schenectady, 1989-91; ptnr. Gordon, Siegel, Mastro, Mullaney, Gordon & Galvin, Schenectady, 1991—. Chmn. planning bd. Town of Wright, N.Y., 1990-94, mem. master plan com., 1991-98, zoning bd. appeals, 1997—; bd. dirs. Hispanic Outreach Svcs., 1998—. Mem. N.Y. State Bar Assn., N.Y. State Trial Lawyers Assn., Capital Dist. Trial Lawyers Assn. (bd. dirs. 1998—), Schenectady County Bar Assn. (bd. dirs. 1993-96), Capital Dist. Women's Bar Assn. (bd. dirs. 1994-98). Personal injury, Product liability, General civil litigation. Office: Gordon Siegel Mastro Mullaney Gordon & Galvin PC 670 Franklin St Schenectady NY 12305-2113

**GALVIN, DANIEL LEO,** lawyer; b. Hammond, Ind., May 25, 1951; s. Francis Joseph and Mary (McGraw) G.; m. Barbara Joan Patterson, Dec. 31, 1992. BBA in Mgmt., U. Notre Dame, 1973; JD, John Marshall Law Sch., Chgo., 1976; LLM in Estate Planning, U. Miami, 1985. Bar: Ind. 1977, Fla. 1986. Assoc. Galvin, Galvin & Leeney, Hammond, 1977-84; sr. trust real estate officer Sun Bank/South Fla., Ft. Lauderdale, 1986-89; ptnr. Galvin Stalmack & Kirschner, Ft. Lauderdale, 1989-91; pvt. practice Law Office of Daniel L. Galvin, Ft. Lauderdale and Naples, 1991-98; assoc. Wollman, Strauss & Assocs., Naples, 1998—. Pres. St. Joseph Ch. Parish Coun., Hammond, 1982-83; dir., treas. Archdiocesan Edn. Found., Miami, 1991—; sec. Can. Am. Internat. Bus. Coun., Naples, 1996-97. Recipient Disting. Svc. award Hammond Jaycees, 1985. Mem. Hammond Bar Assn. (treas. 1983-84). Republican. Roman Catholic. Estate planning. Office: Wollman Strauss & Assocs 5129 Castello Dr Ste 1 Naples FL 34103-1926

**GALVIN, MADELINE SHEILA,** lawyer; b. N.Y.C., Jan. 31, 1948; d. Rod Sheil and Madeline (Twiss) G.; m. James E. Morgan, July 25, 1993. BA cum laude with highest honors, Russell Sage Coll., 1970; JD, Albany Law Sch., 1973. Bar: N.Y. 1974, U.S. Dist. Ct. (no. dist.) N.Y. 1974, U.S. Ct. Appeals (2d cir.), U.S. Supreme Ct. 1978; cert. parliamentarian, lic. real estate broker. Atty. N.Y. State Dept. Law, Albany, 1973-74; sr. atty. Dormitory Authority State of N.Y., Elsmere, 1974-78; sole practice, Delmar, N.Y., 1974—. Bd. dirs., mem. endowment com., mem. exec. bd. YMCA, Albany, 1980-86; bd. dirs. Mercy House, 1980-83, v.p., 1981-82; mem. fin. com. Ronald McDonald House, 1981-83; mem. alumni bd. Doane Stuart Sch., 1988-92; mem. Bethlehem Zoning Bd. Appeals, to 1990; elected Town Bethlehem Town Coun., 1990-93; rep. committeeman 15th dist. Town of Bethlehem, vice chmn. land use mgmt. adv. com., 1989-90. Kellas scholar, 1967-70. Mem. AAUW (recognition cert. Albany br., pres. 1983-84), Nat. Assn. Parliamentarians, ABA, N.Y. State Bar Assn. (numerous coms.), Albany

County Bar Assn., N.Y. State Trial Lawyers Assn., Am. Trial Lawyers Assn., Albany Claims Assn., Albany Law Sch. Alumni Assn., N.Y. Geneal. and Biog. Soc., Strafford Hist. Soc., Russell Sage Coll. Alumni Assn. (pres. 1983-87, pres. bd. dirs., 1987-88), Albany Inst. History and Art, DAR (regent 1980-82, bd. dirs.), Bethlehem C. of C., Capital Dist. Trial Lawyers Assn., Am. Trial Lawyers Assn., Athenian Honor Soc., Russell Sage Coll. Alumni Assn. (pres. 1983-87, bd. dirs. 1987-90, past pres.), Zonta (Albany 1980-92), Doane Stuart Sch. Alumni Assn. (bd. dirs. 1988-92), Phi Alpha Theta. Roman Catholic. General practice, Probate, General civil litigation. Office: 217 Delaware Ave Delmar NY 12054-1205

**GALVIN, ROBERT J.**, lawyer; b. New Haven, Dec. 10, 1938; s. Herman I. and Freda (Helfand) G.; m. Susan I. Goldstein, Oct. 15, 1960 (div.); children: David B., Peter J. AB, Union Coll., Schenectady, N.Y., 1961; JD, Suffolk U., Boston, 1967. Bar: Mass. 1967, U.S. Dist. Ct. Mass. 1967, U.S. Supreme Ct. 1988. Pvt. practice law Boston, 1967-78; ptnr. Lippman & Galvin, Boston, 1978-84; of counsel Gage, Tucker & Vom Baur, Boston, 1984-86; ptnr. Davis, Malm & D'Agostine, Boston, 1986—; lectr. Boston Ctr. Adult Edn., 1972-89, Northeastern U., Boston, 1977-78. Real estate columnist Boston Ledger, 1981; co-author, editor Massachusetts Condominium Law, 1988, 91, 93, 96, 97, 98; contbg. author: Crocker's Notes on Common Forms, 1995-96, 99; contbr. numerous articles to profl. jours. Bd. dirs., v.p. Rental Housing Assn. divsn. Greater Boston Real Estate Bd., 1974, Boston Ctr. Adult Edn., 1979—, chmn. fin. com. 1985-86, pres. 1987-91; bd. dirs. Thoreau Soc., Inc., 1993—, chmn. fin. com., chmn. exec. com.; bd. dirs. Beech Hill Found., Inc., 1989—, pres. 1989—. Fellow Mass. Bar Found. (life mem. Greater Boston 3 grantmaking adv. com. 1997, 98, 99); mem. Mass. Bar Assn. (coun. mem. property law sect. 1977-80, chmn. condominium com. 1979-91), Mass. Continuing Legal Edn. (real estate curriculum adv. com. 1983-87), Am. Arbitration Assn. (comml. arbitration panel), Mass. Conveyancer's Assn., Cmty. Assns. Inst. (atty.'s com. New Eng. chpt.), Soc. for Censure, Reproof and Arraignment of Pub. Error. Real property. Home: 344 Pond St Jamaica Plain MA 02130-2447 Office: Davis Malm & D'Agostine PC One Boston Pl Ste # 3700 Boston MA 02108

**GALVIS, SERGIO J.**, lawyer; b. Cali, Colombia, 1958. BA, William & Mary, 1980; JD, Harvard U., 1983. Bar: N.Y. 1984. Ptnr. Sullivan & Cromwell, N.Y.C. Office: Sullivan & Cromwell 125 Broad St New York NY 10004-2489

**GAMA, J. RICHARD**, lawyer; b. Phoenix, June 13, 1946; s. Joe Rito and Angelita (Santoyas) G.; m. Sylvia M. Rodriguez, Aug. 12, 1972 (div. Dec. 1997); children: Richard G., Marisa A. BS in Bus. Mgmt., Ariz. State U., 1968, JD, 1972. Bar: Ariz., U.S. Dist. Ct. Ariz. Ptnr. Wyles & Gama, Phoenix, 1972-75, Gama & Guerrero, Phoenix, 1975-83; pvt. practice Phoenix, 1988-97; ptnr. Roush, McCracken, Gama, Guerrero & Miller, Phoenix, 1998—. Bd. dirs. Phoenix Meml. Hosp., 1979-89, Friendly House, Phoenix, 1985-88. Personal injury, Professional liability. Home: 209 W Frier Dr Phoenix AZ 85021-7232 Office: Roush McCracken Gama Guerrero & Miller 650 N 3rd Ave Phoenix AZ 85003-1523

**GAMBLE, JOSEPH GRAHAM, JR.**, lawyer; b. Des Moines, June 12, 1926; s. Joseph Graham and Ella Theolian (Hildreth) G.; m. Jane Elizabeth Wilkinson, Sept. 20, 1974. AB, U. Fla., 1948; LLB, U. Ala., 1950. Bar: Ala. 1950, U.S. Dist. Ct. (no. dist.) Ala. 1951, U.S. Ct. Appeals (5th cir.) 1955-81, U.S. Ct. Appeals (11th cir.) 1981, U.S. Supreme Ct. 1960. Assoc. Spain, Gillon & Young, Birmingham, Ala., 1950-60; with Liberty Nat. Life Ins. Co., Birmingham, Ala., 1960-83, asst. gen. counsel, 1973-83; sec. Torchmark Corp., Birmingham, Ala., 1980-86, asst. gen. counsel, 1983-86; sole practice Birmingham, Ala., 1987—; ret., 1998. Bd. dirs. Travelers Aid Soc., Birmingham, 1976-95. Fellow Life Office Mgmt. Assn.; mem. ABA, Ala. Bar Assn., Birmingham Bar Assn., Phi Alpha Delta. Republican. Episcopalian. Insurance, General corporate, Probate. Home: 3333 Spring Valley Ct Birmingham AL 35223-2006 Office: 6 Office Park Cir Ste 318 Birmingham AL 35223-2542

**GAMBRO, MICHAEL S.**, lawyer; b. N.Y.C., July 15, 1954; s. A. John and Rose A. (Grandinetti) G.; m. Joan L. Thurneyssen, Aug. 9, 1980; children: Dana E., Merrill R., Christopher J. BS summa cum laude, Tufts U., 1976; JD, Columbia U., 1980. Bar: N.Y. 1981, U.S. Dist. Ct. (so. dist.) N.Y. 1981, U.S. Dist. Ct. N.J. 1981, N.J. 1983, Calif. 1988. Assoc. Cadwalader, Wickersham & Taft, N.Y.C., 1980-86, ptnr., 1987-88; ptnr. Cadwalader, Wickersham & Taft, L.A., 1988-94, N.Y.C., 1994—. Harlan Fiske Stone scholar, 1978-79, 1979-80. Mem. ABA, Phi Beta Kappa, Psi Chi. General corporate, Securities. Office: Cadwalader Wickersham & Taft 100 Maiden Ln New York NY 10038-4818

**GAMM, GORDON JULIUS**, lawyer; b. Shreveport, La., July 14, 1939; s. Sylvian Willer Gamm and Leona (Gordon) Windes. BA, Drake U., 1963; JD, Tulane U., 1970. Bar: La. 1970, Mo. 1971, Colo. 1993. Atty. pvt. practice, Kansas City, 1977-93, Boulder, Colo., 1993—. Founder Bragg's Symposium, 1980—. Mem. Colo. Bar Assn., Boulder Bar Assn., Boulder Valley Rotary. Estate planning, Probate. Office: 4450 Arapahoe Ave Ste 106 Boulder CO 80303-9102

**GAMMAGE, ROBERT ALTON (BOB GAMMAGE)**, lawyer; b. Houston, Mar. 13, 1938; s. Paul and Sara Ella (Marshall) G.; m. Judy Ann Adcock, Aug. 3, 1962 (div. 1979); children: Terry Lynne, Sara Noel, Robert Alton Jr.; m. Lynda Ray Hallmark, July 4, 1980; 1 child, Samuel Paul. AA, Del Mar Coll., Corpus Christi, Tex., 1958; BS, U. Corpus Christi, (now Tex. A&M U.), 1963; MA, Sam Houston State U., 1965; JD, U. Tex., 1969; LLM, U. Va., 1986. Bar: Tex. 1969, U.S. Dist. Ct. (so. dist.) Tex. 1970, U.S. Ct. Appeals (5th cir.) 1970, U.S. Supreme Ct. 1973, U.S. Ct. Appeals (11th cir.) 1981, U.S. Dist. Ct. (we. dist.) Tex. 1983, U.S. Ct. Mil. Appeals 1986, U.S. Ct. Appeals (D.C. cir. 1993). Tchg. fellow, dir. fraternities Sam Houston State U., Huntsville, Tex., 1963-65; dean of men, dir. student activities U. Corpus Christi, 1965-66; property mgr. Harrison-Wilson-Pearson, Austin, Tex., 1966-69; pvt. practice law Houston, 1969-79; mem. Tex. House of Reps., Austin, 1971-73, Tex. Senate, Austin, 1973-76; del. Tex. Constl. Conv., Austin, 1974; mem. U.S. House of Reps., Washington, 1977-79; asst. atty. gen. State of Tex., Austin, 1979-80; pvt. practice Austin, 1980-82; spl. cons. U.S. Dept. of Energy, 1980; justice Tex. Ct. Appeals, Austin, 1982-91, TX State Supreme Ct, Austin, TX, 1991-95; pvt. practice Austin, 1995—; of counsel Steven E. Rogers, Dallas, Gammage, Hampton, Marcin & Ray, Austin; mem. Tex. Jud. Budget Bd., Austin, 1983-88, Supreme Ct. Jud. Edn. Exec. Com., 1985-93, Tex. Jud. Coun., Austin, 1986-93, Jud. Com. on Ct. Funding, Austin, 1988-91; instr. govt. San Jacinto Coll., Pasadena, Tex., 1969-70; adj. prof. South Tex. Coll. Law, Houston, 1971-73; vis. prof. polit. sci. Sam Houston State U., Huntsville, Tex., 1996-97; vis. prof. pub. adminstrn. Tex. A&M U., Corpus Christi, 1997. With U.S. Army, 1959-60, USAR, 1960-64, USNR, 1965-95. Named Outstanding Sen. Tex. Intercollegiate Students Assn., 1973; recipient Disting. Svc. award Alcoholism Coun. Tex., 1976. Mem. ABA, State Bar Tex. (Disting. Svc. award 1975, vice chmn. funding judiciary com. 1988-91), Am. Judicature Soc., Inst. Jud. Adminstrn., Tex. Ctr. Legal Ethics and Professionalism. Democrat. Baptist. Avocations: skiing, water sports, teaching, writing, jogging. Alternative dispute resolution, Appellate, General civil litigation. Office: 611 W 15th St Austin TX 78701-1513 also: PO Box 400 Llano TX 78643-0400

**GAMS, AARON JOSEPH**, lawyer; b. N.Y.C., Apr. 5, 1959; s. Theodore Charles and Alma Raphel (Gianea) G.; m. Zinora Ann Koven; children: Theodore Cameron, Brennan, Megan Ann Khan Karen; 1 step child, Megan Ann. BA, Boston Coll., 1980; JD, Boston U., 1983, MBA, 1983; PhD, Columbia State U., 1997. Bar: N.Y. Ptnr. The Ogden Group Inc., Northbrook, Ill., 1984-95; sr. ptnr. Davis Gams and Peterson Inc., N.Y.C., 1995—; sr. advisor Legal Aide for Disadvantaged, N.Y.C. Author: A Dangerous Year, 1997. Vol. Neon Light Shelter for the Homeless, Chgo., 1991-95, Amnesty Internat., London, 1991—; asst. dir. Habitat for Humanity Internat., 1997—. British Formula Ford champion Royal Auto. Club, 1982; recipient Winfield award Ecole Pilotage Winfield, Toulon, France, 1984. Mem. ABA, ATLA, N.Y. Bar Assn., N.Y. Trial Law Assn., Conn. Bar Assn., Pa. Bar Assn., Fed. Bar Assn., Atlanta Bar Assn., Univ. Club. Avocations: motor racing, blue-water sailing, skeet shooting, tennis. E-Mail: welitagate@aol.com. Office: March Grp Inc 244 5th Ave New York NY 10001-7604

**GANDARA, DANIEL**, lawyer; b. L.A., July 7, 1948; s. Henry and Cecilia (Contreras) G.; m. Juleann Cottini, Aug. 26, 1972; children: Mario, Enrico. BA, UCLA, 1970; JD, Harvard U., 1974. Bar: Calif. 1974, Wash. 1978. Asst. city atty. City of L.A., 1974-77; staff atty. FTC, Seattle, 1977-79; ptnr. Lane, Powell, Moss & Miller, Seattle, 1979-87, Graham & Dunn, Seattle, 1987-93, Vandeberg, Johnson & Gandara, Seattle, 1993—. Mem. ABA, Wash. State Bar Assn., King County Bar Assn., Hispanic Nat. Bar Assn., Wash. State Hispanic C. of C., Seattle Athletic Club. Democrat. Roman Catholic. State civil litigation, Federal civil litigation, Antitrust. Home: 2010 E Lynn St Seattle WA 98112-2620 Office: Vandeberg Johnson & Gandara 600 Union St Seattle WA 98101

**GANDER, DEBORAH J.**, lawyer, educator; b. Port St. Joe, Fla., Dec. 12, 1971; d. Charles and JoAnn Gander. BS, U. Miami, 1991, JD magna cum laude, 1994. Bar: Fla. 1994, U.S. Ct. Appeals (11th cir.) 1994, U.S. Dist. Ct. (so. dist.) Fla. 1995. Judicial law clk. U.S. Ct. of Appeals (11th cir.), Miami, 1994-95; assoc. Russo & Culmo, P.A., Miami, 1995-96, Robles & Gonzalez, Miami, 1996—. Personal injury, State civil litigation. Office: Robles & Gonzalez 100 S Biscayne Blvd Ste 900 Miami FL 33131-2026

**GANDY, HOKE CONWAY**, judge, state official; b. Washington, Nov. 3, 1934; s. Hoke and Anne B. (Conway) G.; m. Carol Anderson, Aug. 29, 1965; children: Jennifer, Constance, Margaret. *Earliest ancestor, Edwin Conway, came to Virginia circa 1640, as the recipient of a colonial land grant. His grandson, also name Edwin, married Anne Ball whose sister, Mary Ball, was the mother of George Washington. A great granddaughter of the first Edwin Conway was Eleanor Rose Conway, mothe rof President James Madison, who was born at the Conway family plantation, Belle Grove, Port Conway, Virginia. Great Grandfather, Robert Moncure Conway, served in the Confederate Army during the Civil War with Terry's Texas Rangers, while his brother, Moncure Daniel Conway, was an abolitionist whose biography is entitled Southern Emancipator.* BA, Colo. State U., 1962; JD, U. Denver, 1968. Bar: Colo. 1969, U.S. Dist. Ct. Colo. 1969. Pvt. practice Ft. Collins, Colo., 1969-81; adminstrv. law judge divsn. adminstrv. hearings State of Colo., Denver, 1981—. Bd. dirs. Foothills-Gateway Rehab. Ctr., 1970-80, Colo. State Bd. Dental Examiners, 1976-81; Dem. candidate for Colo. Senate, 1974, dist. atty., 1976; trustee Internat. Bluegrass Music Assn. Trust Fund, 1990—. With USN, 1954-58. Mem. Nat. Assn. Adminstrv. Law Judges (pres. Colo. chpt. 1985-86), Sertoma (Centurion award 1973, Tribune award 1975, Senator award 1977, 79, sec. Honor club 1977-78, pres. Ft. Collins club 1978-79, pres. Front Range club 1988-89). Home: 724 Winchester Dr Fort Collins CO 80526-2636

**GANDY, PAUL DWAYNE**, lawyer; b. Castle AFB, Calif., June 10, 1956; s. Lynell Wesley and Alice Marquette (Cross) G. BA, Harvard U., 1978; JD, U. Tex., 1984. Bar: Iowa 1987, U.S. Dist. Ct. (so. dist.) Iowa 1991, U.S. Ct. Appeals (8th cir.) 1995, U.S. Supreme Ct. 1997; cert. in consumer bankruptcy. Pvt. practice Fairfield, Iowa, 1991—. Mem. ABA, Am. Bankruptcy Inst., Iowa State Bar Assn., Nat. Assn. Consumer Bankruptcy Attys. Office: 104 1/2 N Main St Ste 2 Fairfield IA 52556-2802

**GANGLE, MARGARET ELLEN**, lawyer, educator; b. St. Louis, Nov. 8, 1949; d. William Tidwell and Catharine Marie Gangle; m. Jim Casinger, May 11, 1968; children: Jennifer Cook, Stephen Casinger. BA, U. Ark., 1980; JD, Washington U., St. Louis, 1983. Bar: Mo. 1983, U.S. Dist. Ct. (ea. dist.) Mo. 1984, U.S. Ct. Appeals (8th cir.) 1984. Assoc. J.B. Carter & Assoc., St. Louis, 1983-86; pvt. practice St. Louis, 1986-92; staff atty. 22d Jud. Cir. Ct., St. Louis, 1992—; adj. prof. Webster U., St. Louis, 1991—. Mem. Nat. Assn. Counsel for Children, Mo. Juvenile Justice Assn. (regional rep. 1993—). Office: Family Ct Juvenile Divsn 920 N Vandeventer Ave Saint Louis MO 63108-3530

**GANGLE, SANDRA SMITH**, lawyer, arbitrator, mediator; b. Brockton, Mass., Jan. 11, 1943; d. Milton and Irene M. (Powers) Smith; m. Eugene M. Gangle, Dec. 21, 1968; children: Melanie Jean, Jonathan Rocco. BA, Coll. New Rochelle, 1964; MA, U. Oreg.; JD, Willamette U., 1980. Bar: Oreg. 1980. Instr. French Oreg. State U., Corvallis, 1968-71, Wiliamette U., Salem, Oreg., 1971-74; instr. ESL Chemeketa C.C., Salem, 1975-79; labor arbitrator Salem, 1980—, pvt. practice, 1980-86, 96—; ptnr. Depenbrock, Gangle & Greer, 1986-96; mem. Oreg., Idaho, Wash., Mont. Arbitration Panels; mem. NASD securities arbitration panel, mediator employment & bus. disputes; clin. prof. Portland State U., 1981-84; cons. State Oreg., 1981. Contbr. articles to profl. jours. Land-use chmn. Faye Wright Neighborhood Assn., Salem, 1983-84; mem. Civil Svc. Commn., Marion County Fire Dist., Salem, 1983-89; mem. U.S. Postal Svc. Expedited Arbitration Panel, 1984-91; mem. Salem Neighbor-to-Neighbor Mediation Panel, 1986-91; mem. panel Fed. Mediation & Conciliation Svc., 1986—; ct. apptd. arbitrator, mediator Marion, Polk & Yamhill Counties, 1996—; mem. Marion County Cir. Ct. Dispute Resolution Commn., 1993-95; trustee Salem Peace Plaza, 1985-97; convenor Salem Peace Roundtable, 1995; bd. dirs. Salem YWCA, 1997—; chair planning com. joint conf. between oreg. Women Lawyers & Assn. Women Solicitors, 1998. NDEA fellow, 1967. Fellow Chartered Inst. Arbitrators (London); mem. Am. Arbitration Assn. (arbitrator/mediator), Soc. Profls. in Dispute Resolution (chpt. co-pres. 1993-94), Oreg. State Bar Assn. Alternative dispute resolution. Office: Sandra Smith Gangle PC 117 Commercial St NE Ste 310 Salem OR 97301-3406

**GANGSTAD, JOHN ERIK**, lawyer; b. New Brunswick, N.J., May 16, 1948; s. Edward Otis and Ruth Margaret (Fletcher) G.; m. Cynthia Diane Coffman, July 5, 1974; children: Allison, Erik, Amy. BA, U. Tex., 1970, JD, 1974. Bar: Tex. 1974, U.S. Dist. Ct. (no. dist.) Tex. 1974. Assoc. Turner, Hitchins, McInnery, Webb & Hartnett, Dallas, 1974-76, ptnr., 1977-81; ptnr. Brown McCarroll & Oaks Hartline, L.L.P., Austin, Tex., 1982—; partnership com. State Bar Tex., 1981-98. Bd. dirs. Found. for the Homeless, Austin, 1988—. With USNG. Mem. ABA, Tex. Bar Assn., Order of Coif. Presbyterian. Avocations: golf, reading. General corporate, Mergers and acquisitions, Securities. Home: 3106 Eaneswood Dr Austin TX 78746-6717 Office: Brown McCarroll & Oaks Hartline LLP 1400 Franklin Pla 111 Congress Ave Ste 1200 Austin TX 78701-4049

**GANN, PAMELA BROOKS**, academic administrator; b. 1948. BA, U. N.C., 1970; JD, Duke U., 1973. Bar: Ga. 1973, N.C. 1974. Assoc. King & Spalding, Atlanta, 1973, Robinson, Bradshaw & Hinson, P.A., Charlotte, N.C., 1974-75; asst. prof. Duke U. Sch. Law, Durham, N.C., 1975-78, assoc. prof., 1978-80, prof., 1980-99, dean, 1988-99; pres. Claremont McKenna Coll., Claremont, Calif., 1999—; vis. asst. prof. U. Mich. Law Sch., 1977; vis. assoc. prof. U. Va., 1980. Author: (with D. Kahn) Corporate Taxation and Taxation of Partnerships and Partners, 1979, 83, 89; article editor Duke Law Jour. Mem. Am. Law Inst., Coun. Fgn. Rels., Order of Coif, Phi Beta Kappa. Office: Claremont McKenna Coll Office of the Pres 500 E 9th St Claremont CA 91711-5903

**GANNAM, MICHAEL JOSEPH**, lawyer; b. Savannah, Ga., Nov. 10, 1922; s. Karam George and Annie (Abraham) G.; m. Marion Collins DeFrank, June 11, 1949; children: James, Ann, Elizabeth, Jsoeph. JD, 1948; MA, U. N.C., 1950. Bar: Ga. 1948, U.S. Dist. Ct. (so. dist.) Ga. 1950, U.S. Supreme Ct. 1971, U.S. Ct. Appeals (11th cir.) 1971. Assoc. Bouhan, Lawrence, Williams & Levy, Savannah, Ga., 1950-59; ptnr. Findley, Shea, Friedman, Gannam, Head & Buchsbaum, Savannah, Ga., 1959-70, atty. pvt. practice, 1970-81; sr. ptnr. Gannam and Gnann, Savannah, Ga., 1981—; instr. bus. law polit. sci. and history Armstrong State coll., 1951-62. Bd. dirs. Historic Savannah Found.; bd. dirs., legal counsel Telfair Acad. Arts & Scis.; past pres. Legal Aid Soc. Savannah; mem. Savannah-Chatham Bd. Zoning Appeals, 1961-63, Savannah Arts Com., 1982-85; chmn. Gilmer Lectr. Series Fund, 1980—; bd. dirs. Savannah Coun. World Affairs, 1983-87; pres. Savannah Bar Assn.; bd. govs. State Bar Ga., 1968-99. General practice, General civil litigation, Probate. Home: 235 E Gordon St Savannah GA 31401-5003 Office: Gannam & Gnann 130 W Bay St Savannah GA 31401-1109

**GANNON, CHRISTOPHER J. I.**, lawyer; b. Pitts., Mar. 13, 1962; s. Edward J. I. and Mary Jane (Burns) G. BBA, St. Bonaventure U., 1984; JD, Duquesne U., 1987. Bar: Pa. 1987, N.C. 1997; U.S. Dist. Ct. (we. dist.) Pa. 1987. Assoc. Hazlett, Gannon & Jacobs, Pitts., 1987-88; corp. atty. Lord Corp., Erie, Pa., Cary, N.C., Pa., 1988—. Treas. Met. Erie County Advs., Inc./United Cerebral Palsy, 1990-92, bd. dirs. 1989-95, pres., 1992-95. Mem. Pa. Bar Assn. (zone chmn. young lawyers divsn. 1992-95, 96-97, exec. com. 1992-95, 96-97), Allegheny County Bar Assn., Erie County Bar Assn. (chmn. young lawyers com. 1991-92), Erie County Bar Found. (trustee 1993-94), N.C. Bar Assn. Republican. Roman Catholic. General corporate, Environmental, Private international. Home: 106 Robbins Reef Way Cary NC 27513-2244 Office: Lord Corp PO Box 8012 111 Lord Dr Cary NC 27512-8012

**GANNON, JOHN SEXTON**, lawyer, management consultant, arbitrator/mediator; b. East Orange, N.J., Apr. 7, 1927; s. John Joseph and Agnes (Sexton) G.; m. Diane Ditchy, Aug. 11, 1951; children: Mary Catherine, John, Lanie Elizabeth, James. BA, U. Mich., 1951; JD, Wayne State U., Detroit, 1961. Bar: Mich. 1962, Tenn. 1971, U.S. Ct. Appeals (6th cir.) 1977, U.S. Dist. Ct. (mid. dist.) 1989; approved mediator Tenn. Supreme Ct. Labor negotiator, mgr. employee rels. Chrysler Corp., Highland Park, Mich., 1951-61; labor counsel, mgr. employee rels. Ex-Cell-O Corp., Highland Park, 1961-65; assoc. Constangy & Powell, Atlanta, 1966; v.p. employee rels., labor counsel Werthan Industries, Nashville, 1967-80; ptnr. Dearborn & Ewing, Nashville, 1980-90; pvt. practice Nashville, 1991—; mem. adj. faculty Owens Sch., Vanderbilt U., Nashville, 1975-85; instr. Soc. Human Resource Mgmt. Profl. cert. program Mid. Tenn. State U., 1993—; pres. Employee Rels. Svcs., Inc., Nashville, 1987—. Contbr. articles to profl. jours. Mem. Birmingham (Mich.) Bd. Zoning Appeals, 1963-66; mem. Human Rels. Commn., Nashville, 1979-89; chmn. Tenn. Citizens for Ct. Modernization, Nashville, 1979-80; mem. Pvt. Industry Coun., Nashville, 1986-95. With USN, 1945-47. Mem. ABA, FBA (chmn. sr. lawyers divsn. mediatin and arbitration com.), Tenn. Bar Assn., Mich. Bar Assn., Nashville Bar Assn., Soc. Human Resource Mgmt., Am. Arbitration Assn. (panel employment mediators and arbitrators), Univ. Club, Hillwood Country Club, Kiwanis. Alternative dispute resolution, Labor, Pension, profit-sharing, and employee benefits. Home: 216 Jackson Blvd Nashville TN 37205-3300

**GANNON, MARK STEPHEN**, lawyer; b. Stuttgart, Fed. Republic Germany, Mar. 2, 1950; (parents Am. citizens); s. Vincent de Paul and Denise (Heinle) G.; m. Kathryn Ennis, Aug. 14, 1971; children: Mark Stephen II, Matthew Christopher. BA cum laude, Marquette U., 1971; JD, Emory U., 1976. Bar: Ga. 1976, U.S. Dist. Ct. (no. dist.) Ga. 1976. Assoc. Savell, Williams, Cox & Angel, Atlanta, 1976-80; ptnr. Savell & Williams, Atlanta, 1980—; mem. faculty Workers' Compensation Law Inst., St. Simons, Ga., 1989, 95, 98. Bd. dirs. Hillside Cottages, Inc., Atlanta, 1978-86, Briarcliff Community Sports, Inc., Atlanta, 1986-88; co-chmn. Immaculate Heart of Mary Bd. Edn., 1990-91, chmn., 1991-92. Mem. Ga. Def. Lawyers assn., Def. Rsch. Inst., Atlanta Bar Assn. (chmn. workers' compensation sect. 1989-90), State Bar of Ga. (legis. com. 1989-90, exec. com. 1995—, mem. rules and mediation com. gov.'s adv. coun. 1994—), Lawyers Club Atlanta. Roman Catholic. Workers' compensation, Personal injury, Insurance. Home: 1052 Clifton Rd NE Atlanta GA 30307-1228 Office: Savell & Williams 245 Peachtree Center Ave NE Atlanta GA 30303-1222

**GANO, KENNETH REDMAN, JR.**, lawyer; b. Charleston, Ill., Mar. 11, 1952; s. Kenneth Redman Gano and Melba Maxine Gano Brown; m. Charlotte Amelia Carlet, May 21, 1983; children: Jacob Redman, James Alexander Greer, Benjamin Isaac. BA, Ea. Ill. U., 1977; JD, No. Ill. U., 1980. Bar: Ill. 1980, U.S. Dist. Ct. (ctrl. dist.) Ill. 1980, U.S. Dist. Ct. (so. dist.) Ill. 1989, U.S. Ct. Appeals (7th cir.) 1991. Assoc. Ron Tulin, Ltd., Charleston, 1980-82; ptnr. Newton & Gano, Charleston, 1982-84; pvt. practice, 1989—; instr. Lakeland Coll., Mattoon, Ill., 1980-82, Eastern Ill. U., Charleston, 1983. Mem. Ill. Bar Assn. Office: Crossroads Law Ctr 1901 S 4th St # 215 Effingham IL 62401-4187

**GANS, NANCY FREEMAN**, lawyer; b. Phila., Nov. 26, 1943; d. Milton V. and Phyllis Freeman; m. Jerome S. Gans, June 21, 1964; children: Lisa Michelle, Rachel Marie, Shira Jeanne. BA, U. Rochester, 1965; postgrad., Georgetown U., 1967-68; JD, Harvard U., 1970. Bar: Mass., U.S. Dist. Ct. Mass., U.S. Supreme Ct. Assoc. Sullivan & Worcester, Boston, 1970-73, Law Offices of Richard A. Glaser, Natick, Mass., 1983-84; ptnr. Gans & Stedman, Wellesley, Mass., 1985-92, Moulton & Welburn, Boston, 1993-97, Moulton & Gans, LLP, Boston, 1997—; lectr., tchg. asst. Harvard Law Sch., Harvard Med. Sch., Mass. Mental Health Ctr., Emmanuel Coll., Boston Inst. for Psychotherapy, 1970-75. v.p., trustee, chmn. ednl. policy com., chmn. nominating com., chmn. recruitment com., chmn. by-law revision com., chmn. negotiation com., mem. exec. com., mem. long range plan steering com., mem. budget com., mem. Purim ball host com. Solomon Schechter Day Sch., 1982-96; legal cons. confidentiality in group psychotherapy task force Northeastern Soc. for Group Psychotherapy, 1991; dir. Boston Inst. for Psychotherapy, 1992-96. Sr. Kennedy fellow Harvard U., 1973-75. mem. Mass. Bar Assn., Mass. Bar Found. Antitrust, General civil litigation, Securities. Office: Moulton & Gans 133 Federal St Boston MA 02110-1703

**GANS, STEVEN H.**, lawyer; b. Boston, June 14, 1960; s. Werner J. and Florence (Kalis) G.; m. Lori B. Gans, Oct. 30, 1988; 1 child, Noah Henry. Student, Cornell U., 1978-79; BA, Brandeis U., 1982; postgrad., Harvard U., 1988-89; JD, U. Pa., 1989. Bar: Mass. 1989. Front office exec., player Balt. Blast Profl. Soccer Team, 1982-84; assoc. Goulston & Storrs, P.C., Boston, 1989-93; of counsel Broude & Hochberg, L.L.P., Boston, 1993—; pres., gen. counsel Biscuit Books, Inc., Newton, Mass., 1993—; COO, gen. counsel New Eng. Mobile Book Fair, Inc., Newton, 1993—. Mem. Mass. Gov.'s Subcommn. on Phys. Fitness, Boston, 1992—; bd. dirs., mem. exec. com., chmn. health and phys. edn. Leventhal-Sidman Jewish Cmty. Ctr., Newton, 1993—; chmn. pet care assistance fund Angell Meml. Hosp.-Mass. SPCA, Boston, 1995-97; mem. adv. bd. Sta. WBUR-FM, nat. pub. radio, Boston, 1995—. Mem. ABA, Mass. Bar Assn. Democrat. Jewish. Avocations: soccer, animals, reading, writing, animal welfare issues. General corporate, Sports, Contracts commercial. Home: 46 Oakvale Rd Waban MA 02468-1117 Office: New Eng Mobile Book Fair Inc 82-84 Needham St Newton Highlands MA 02161

**GANS, WALTER GIDEON**, lawyer; b. Trutnov, Czechoslovakia, Jan. 11, 1936; came to U.S., 1949, naturalized, 1957; s. Frederick and Erna (Mueller) G.; m. Harriet Arlene Goldhagen, Oct. 6, 1938 (dec.); children: David Ian, Erik Anthony. BA, Bowdoin Coll., 1957; JD, NYU, 1961, LLM in Comparative Law, 1967. Bar: N.Y. 1961. Assoc. Fried, Frank, harris, Shriver & Jacobson, N.Y.C., 1961-63; internat. atty. Latex Corp., N.Y.C., 1963-67; assoc. counsel Olin Corp., New Haven and Stamford, Conn., 1967-71; counsel Olin Corp., New Haven and Stamford, 1972-75, sr. counsel internat., 1975-79; v.p., gen. counsel and sec. Siemens Corp., N.Y.C., 1979—; active CPR Inst. for Dispute Resolution, mem. exec. com. 1995—; active European Am. Gen. Counsel Group; dir. Food and Drug Law Inst.; mem. Conf. Bd. Coun. of Chief Legal Officers; mem. lawyers com. Human Rights' Internat. Rule Coun. Mem. ABA (mem. antitrust, bus. law, dispute resolution, litigation, internat. law and practice sects.), Am. Arbitration Assn. (internat. panel arbitrators, corp. counsel com.), Am. Fgn. Law Assn., Am. Corp. Counsel Assn. (N.Y.C. chpt. bd. dirs.), N.Y. State Bar Assn., Assn. Bar City of N.Y. (fgn. and comparative law com. 1973-75, 82-85, com. corp. law depts. 1986-89, fed. cts. com. 1992-95, adv. com. corp. lawyers 1992-95, 125th anniversary campaign com.), Internat. Bar Assn., The Corp. Bar. Alternative dispute resolution, Private international, General corporate. Office: Siemens Corp 1301 Avenue Of The Americas New York NY 10019-6022

**GANSKE, VICKI SMITH**, lawyer; b. Lubbock, Tex., Sept. 16, 1947; d. Richard Claire Smith and Virginia (Collier) Frances; m. Frederick C. Ganske, Dec. 27, 1969; children: Richard F., Charles D. BA in Speech, Tex. Tech. U., 1969, JD, 1977. Bar: Tex. 1977; cert. residential real estate Tex. Bd. Legal Specialization. Tchr. English J.F. Kennedy H.S., Agana, Guam, 1973-74; briefing atty. Ct. of Civil Appeals, Ft. Worth, 1978-80; staff atty. Tandy Corp., 1980-82; sole practice Ft. Worth, 1982-87; v.p., corp. counsel Foster Mortgage Corp., 1987-92; of counsel Hunter & Cameron, Ft. Worth, 1992—. Author, editor: Residential Loan Origination State Disclosures & Regulations, 1994. Mem. Tarrant County Young Lawyers (pres. 1982), Tarrant County Women's Bar Assn. (pres., archivist), Tarrant County Bar Assn., Consumer Credit Counseling Svc. Greater Ft. Worth (chair). Home: 2225 Goldenrod Ave Fort Worth TX 76111-1610 Office: Hunter & Cameron 1701 River Run Ste 1115 Fort Worth TX 76107-6557

**GANT, HORACE ZED,** lawyer; b. Van Buren, Ark., Apr. 1, 1914; s. George Washington and Ida Elizabeth (Stephenson) G.; m. Edith Imogene Farabough, Oct. 10, 1937; children: Alice Margaret, Linda Beth, Zed George, Paul David. LLB, U. Ark., 1936, JD, 1969. Bar: Ark. 1936, U.S. Dist. Ct. (we. dist.) Ark. 1937, U.S. Supreme Ct. 1943. Asst. pros. atty., Van Buren, 1936-41; sole practice, Van Buren, 1941-43; atty. War Relocation Authority, Washington, 1943, U.S. Dept. Interior, Washington, 1947; field atty. VA, Little Rock, 1947-73; chancery judge Ark. 15th Jud. Dist., Van Buren, 1973-75; ptnr. Gant & Gant, Van Buren, 1975—; chmn. bd. dirs. Western Ark. Legal Svcs., Ft. Smith, 1991, pres. bd. dirs., 1991-92; chancery ct. master Ark. 12th Jud. Dist., Ft. Smith, 1976-91. Bd. dirs. Harbor House and Gateway House, Ft. Smith, Ark., 1974-84; chmn. Western Ark. Adv. Council, Ft. Smith, 1976-81; pres. Mental Health Assn., Ft. Smith, 1978; trustee Boggan Edn. Scholarship Trust Fund, chmn., 1979—; deacon 1st Baptist Ch., Van Buren. Lt. comdr. USN, 1943-46. Mem. Ark. Bar Assn., Masons (master 1942-43). Democrat. Probate, Family and matrimonial, General practice. Home: 403 S 7th St Van Buren AR 72956-5813 Office: Gant & Gant PO Box 416 Van Buren AR 72957-0416

**GANT, JESSE, III,** lawyer, playwright; b. Chattanooga, June 8, 1959; s. Jesse Jr. and Bernice Thompson; m. Petra Gant, Nov. 3, 1980 (div.); children: Jesse IV, Petra B.I.; m. Susan Loveridge, Dec. 3, 1997. AA, Ctrl. Tex. Coll., Killeen, 1980; BS in Sociology, U. Md., 1984; JD, William Mitchell Coll., 1989; grad. with honors, Non-commn. Officer's Acad. Bar: Minn. 1990. Sgt. U.S. Army, Killeen, Tex., Berlin, Germany, 1978-86; intern to Hon. Charles Porter; pres., writer, inventor Gant's Creative Creativity Unltd., St. Paul, 1986—; pres. Gant Law Office, Mpls., 1990—, Sharp Law Firm, Mpls., 1997—. Inventor various toys; dir. (play) Sexual Personality Complex, Once Upon a Time; writer (screenplays) The Diet King, Hypnotized, Protect the Children, Make It Funky, Broken Hearts, Narcotic Nation, (teleplay) Glad to Be Me (You), Being a Parent is Love and Confusion, (manuscript) Rooker: Save the Children, several proposed TV series; actor (indsl. movies) Retention: Key to Survival, Abbott Northwestern Hosp., commls., plays; singer Jefferson Ch. Choir, Detlev Kuhn Band; contbr. articles to various newspapers; speaker on legal issues. Vol. atty. Urban League, pres. People United for Progress. Mem. Minn. State Bar Assn. Democrat. Avocations: writing, acting, exercise, movies. Civil rights, General civil litigation, Insurance. Office: Gant Law Office 301 4th Ave S Ste 670 Minneapolis MN 55415-1019

**GANTT, DAVID,** lawyer; b. Winston-Salem, N.C., Oct. 2, 1956; s. Charles Heman and Augusta Pharr G.; m. Charise Lowery, Aug. 11, 1979; children: Brett Daniel, Carrie Michelle. BA in Econs., U. N.C., 1978; JD, Campbell U., 1981. Atty. pvt. practice, Asheville, N.C.; spkr. in field. Commr. Buncombe County N.C., 1996—. Democrat. Methodist. Avocations: hiking, camping. Personal injury, Workers' compensation, Pension, profit-sharing, and employee benefits. Office: 82 Church St Asheville NC 28801-3622

**GANZ, CHARLES DAVID,** lawyer; b. N.Y.C., Oct. 1, 1946; s. Harold Leonard and Mimi (Platzker) G.; m. Carol Susan Fisher, June 5, 1969; children: Jonathan, Adam, Melissa. AB, Franklin and Marshall Coll., 1968; JD, Duke U., 1972; LLM in Taxation, NYU, 1976. Bar: N.Y. 1973, U.S. Ct. Appeals (2d cir.) 1973, Ga. 1976, U.S. Dist. Ct. (so. and ea. dists.) N.Y. 1973, U.S. Ct. Appeals (11th cir) 1979, U.S. Dist. Ct. (no. dist.) Ga. 1979. Assoc. Cahill Gordon & Reindel, N.Y.C., 1972-76; assoc. Gambrell & Russell, Atlanta, 1976-77, ptnr., 1978-81; ptnr. Branch, Pike & Ganz, Atlanta, 1982-95, Sutherland, Asbill & Brennan, Atlanta, 1998—; trustee, pres. Ga. Fed. Tax Conf., 1985-87; bd. dirs. Rentokil Holdings, Inc.; trustee The Davis Acad., Japan Am. Soc. Ga., 1999—. Trustee Atlanta Ballet, 1980-82. Served to staff sgt. USAR, 1968-74. Mem. ABA, Ga. Bar Assn., N.Y. Bar Assn., Atlanta Bar Assn., Atlanta Tax Forum. Jewish. General corporate, Securities, Corporate taxation. Home: 160 Hidden Falls Ln NW Atlanta GA 30328-1960

**GANZ, DAVID L.,** lawyer; b. N.Y.C., July 28, 1951; s. Daniel M. and Beverlee (Kaufman) G.; m. Barbara Bondanza, Nov. 3, 1974 (div. 1978); m. Sharon Ruth Lamnin, Oct. 30, 1981 (div. 1996); children: Scott Harry, Elyse Toby, Pamela Rebecca; m. Kathleen Ann Gotsch, Dec. 28, 1996. BS in Fgn. Svc., Georgetown U., 1973; JD, St. John's U., 1976. Bar: N.Y. 1977, D.C. 1980, N.J. 1985. Assoc. Regan, Dorsey & De Riso, Flushing, N.Y., 1977-79; ptnr. Durst & Ganz, N.Y.C., 1979-80; mng. ptnr. Ganz, Hollinger & Towe, N.Y.C., 1981-98, Ganz & Hollinger, N.Y.C., 1999—; exec. com. Industry Coun. Tangible Assets, Washington, 1983—, bd. dirs.; cons. in field. Author: A Critical Guide to the Anthologies of African Literature, 1973, A Legal and Legislative History of 31 USC Sec 342d-324i, 1976, The World of Coin Collecting, 1980, 3d edit., 1998, The 90 Second Lawyer, 1996, The 90 Second Lawyer's Guide to Selling Real Estate, 1997, How to Get an Instant Mortgage, 1997, Planning Your Rare Coin Retirement, 1998, Guide Commemorative Coin Values, 1999; corr. Numis. News Weekly, 1969-73, asst. editor, 1973-74, spl. corr., 1974-75, columnist, 1969-76, 96—; contbg. editor, columnist COINage Mag., 1974—; columnist Coin World, 1974-96, COINS Mag., 1973-83; contbr. articles to profl. jours. Mem. U.S. Assay Commn., 1974; bd. dirs. Georgetown Libr. Assocs., Washington, 1982—; mem. N.Y. County Draft Bd., 1984, Bergen County, N.J., 1985—, vice chair, 1996—; sec., mem. Zoning and Adjustment Bd., Fair Lawn, N.J., 1988-92, chmn., 1993-97; elected mem. Dem. County Com. Bergen County, 1988-96, borough coun. Borough of Fair Lawn, 1998—, mayor, 1999—. Decorated Order of St. Agatha (Republic of San Marino). Fellow Am. Numis. Soc. (life); mem. Am. Numis. Assn. (life, legis. coun. 1978-81, 83-95, elected bd. govs. 1985-95, v.p. 1991-93, pres. 1993-95), Assn. of Bar of City of N.Y. (com. on state legis. 1987-90), N.Y. State Bar Assn. (mem. civil practice com., chmn. subcom. 1978-84), Profl. Numis. Guild Inc. affiliated mem. 1989—, gen. coun. 1981-92), Am. Soc. Internat. Law, Nat. Assn. Coin and Precious Metals Dealers (asoc. mem., gen. coun. 1981-85), Flushing Lawyers Club (pres. 1982-83). Democrat. Jewish. Avocation: numismatic. Legislative, Private international, Contracts commercial. Office: Ganz & Hollinger 1394 3rd Ave New York NY 10021-0404

**GANZ, HOWARD LAURENCE,** lawyer; b. N.Y.C., Apr. 3, 1942; s. Myron and Beatrice (W.) G.; children: Beth, David. BA, Colgate U., 1963; LLB, Columbia U., 1966. Bar: N.Y. 1966, U.S. Dist. Ct. (so. dist.) N.Y. 1968, U.S. Dist. Ct. (ea. dist.) N.Y. 1969, U.S. Dist. Ct. (no. dist.) Calif. 1984, U.S. Ct. Appeals (3d cir.) 1974, U.S. Ct. Appeals (4th cir.) 1985, U.S. Dist. Ct. (9th cir.) 1984, U.S. Dist. Ct. (D.C. cir.) 1986, U.S. Supreme Ct. 1986. Law clk. to Hon. Marvin E. Frankel U.S. Dist. Ct., N.Y.C., 1966-68; assoc., ptnr. Proskauer Rose LLP, N.Y.C., 1968—, assoc. ptnr., mem. exec. com. Named One of 100 Best Lawyers in N.Y., N.Y. Mag., 1995, One of Best Lawyers in America, 1997. Mem. Fed. Bar Coun., N.Y. State Bar Assn., N.Y. County Lawyers Assn., Assn. of Bar of City of N.Y. General civil litigation, Labor, Sports. Office: Proskauer Rose LLP 1585 Broadway New York NY 10036-8200

**GANZ, MARC DAVID,** lawyer; b. N.Y.C., Oct. 10, 1969; s. Melvin and Bette Carol G.; m. Jodi Berlin, June 15, 1996. BA in History and Polit. Sci., U. Wis., 1991; JD, Washington U., St. Louis, 1994; LLM in Taxation, NYU, 1995. Bar: N.Y. 1995, U.S. Tax Ct. 1995, U.S. Dist. Ct. (so. dist.) N.Y. 1995. Law clk. U.S. Tax Ct., Washington, 1995-96; internat. tax cons. Price Waterhouse Cooper, LLP, N.Y.C., 1996-98; tax assoc. Kelley, Drye & Warren, N.Y.C., 1998—. Contbr. articles to profl. jours. Mem. N.Y. Cares, 1998—, Children's Hearing Inst., N.Y.C., 1997—, Cure For Lymphona, N.Y.C., 1996—. With U.S. Army, 1987-89. Mem. ABA, N.Y. State Bar Assn., NYU Tax Soc. Corporate taxation, Taxation, general, Public international. Office: Kelley Drye & Warren LLP 101 Park Ave New York NY 10178-0002

**GANZ, MARY KEOHAN,** lawyer; b. Weymouth, Mass., Nov. 17, 1954; d. Francis and Margaret (Quinn) Keohan; m. Alan H. Ganz, Sept. 7, 1980. BA magna cum laude, Emmanuel Coll., 1976; JD, Suffolk U., 1979. Bar: Mass. 1979, U.S. Dist. Ct. Mass. 1979, N.H. 1981, U.S. Dist. Ct. N.H. 1981. Pvt. practice, Seabrook, N.H., 1981—. Bd. dirs. My Greatest Dream Inc., Seabrook, 1985—. Mem. ABA, N.H. Bar Assn., Rockingham County Bar Assn., Seabrook Bus. and Profl. Assn. (pres. 1986-87), Seacoast Vis. Nurses Assn. (bd. dirs. 1994—, sec. 1997-98, v.p. 1998-99, pres. 1999—), Phi Delta Phi, Kappa Gamma Pi. Roman Catholic. General practice. Office: 779 Lafayette Rd Seabrook NH 03874-4215

**GANZ, ROBERT E.,** lawyer; b. Trenton, N.J., Mar. 31, 1951; s. Richard S. and Corrine M. Ganz; m. Dorothy Avalon Brociner, Sept. 6, 1992; children: Joel R., Miriam L., Kayla S. BA magna cum laude, U. Rochester, 1973; JD, Cath. U. Am., 1975. Bar: N.Y. 1976. Assoc. atty. Woods, Oviatt, Gilman, Sturman & Clarke, Rochester, N.Y., 1975-78, O'Connell & Aronowitz P.C., Albany, N.Y., 1978-80; atty. Law Offices of Robert Ganz, Albany, 1981-87; founding and mng. ptnr., atty. Ganz & Wolkenbreit, Albany, 1988—; exec. dir. Empire State Foodsvc. Assocs., Albany, 1992-97. Assoc. editor Cath. U. Law Rev., 1974-75; mem. bd. editors Computer Law Strategist, 1992-97, Bankruptcy and Comml. Law Advisor, 1990-95. Chair bldg. fund, v.p. Interfaith Chapel House, Albany, 1986-88; bd. dirs., sec. Bone Marrow Found. N.E., Albany, 1992-96; pres. Congregation Ohav Shalom, 1996-98. Mem. N.Y. State Bar Assn. (exec. com. bus. law sect. 1985-95), Albany County Bar Assn. Jewish. Avocations: reading, theater, travel. General civil litigation, Computer, Labor. Office: Ganz & Wolkenbreit LLP 1 Columbia Cir Ste 7 Albany NY 12203-6381

**GAON, SLOAN DANIEL,** lawyer; b. N.Y.C., Apr. 29, 1969; s. Don and Renee (Fox) G. BA, Clark U., 1991; JD, Syracuse U., 1995. Bar: N.Y. 1995. Atty. Turbochef, N.Y.C., 1996—. Bd. dirs. Eastward Bound, Boston, 1993—. Mem. ABA. Office: Turbochef 745 5th Ave New York NY 10151-0099

**GARBARINO, ROBERT PAUL,** retired administrative dean, lawyer; b. Wanaque, N.J., Oct. 6, 1929; s. Attillio and Theresa (Napello) G.; m. Joyce A. Sullivan, June 29, 1957; children: Lynn, Lisa, Mark, Steven. BBA cum laude, St. Bonaventure U., 1951; JD with highest class honors, Villanova U., 1956. Bar: Pa. 1956, U.S. Dist. Ct. (ea. dist.) Pa. 1956, U.S. Ct. Appeals (3d cir.) 1962, U.S. Supreme Ct. 1962, U.S. Tax Ct. 1966, U.S. Ct. Internat. Trade 1966. Law clk. U.S. Dist. Ct. (ea. dist.) Pa., Phila., 1956-57; asst. counsel Phila. Electric Co., Phila., 1957-60, asst. gen. counsel, 1960-62; ptnr. Kania & Garbarino & predecessor firm, Phila. and Bala Cynwyd, Pa., 1962-81; assoc. dean adminstrn. Sch. Law Villanova (Pa.) U., 1981-96; right-of-way cons. Edison Electric Inst., N.Y.C., 1960-62; trustee reorgn. Tele-Tronics Co., Phila., 1962-64; mem. bd. consultors Law Sch. Villanova U., 1967-81, chmn., vice chmn. bd. consultors, 1971-96, chmn. Profl. Sports Career Counseling Panel Villanova U.; mem pres.'s adv. coun. St. Bonaventure U., N.Y., 1975-86, chmn., 1976-78. Contbr. articles to profl. jours. Mem. community leadership seminar Fels Inst. Local and State Govt., 1961. Staff sgt. USMC, 1951-53. Mem. ABA, Phila. Bar Assn., Order of Coif. Home: 120 Ladderback Ln Devon PA 19333-1815

**GARBER, ALBERT CAESAR,** lawyer; b. N.Y.C., Aug. 24, 1920; s. Nathan and Katie Garber; m. Elysee Bacher, Dec. 23, 1945; children: Leonard, Carol. BA, NYU, 1940; JD, U. So. Calif., 1948. Bar: Calif., U.S. Dist. Ct. (ctrl. dist.) Calif., U.S. Supreme Ct. Ptnr. Minsky & Garber, L.A., 1949-55, Minsky, Garber & Rudof, L.A., 1956-76, Garber & Rudof, L.A., 1976-80, Garber & Garber, L.A., 1980—. Contbr. articles to profl. jours. Mem. Dem. Orgn., 1941-98, People for the Am. Way, 1978-98, So. Poverty Law Ctr., 1985-98. Mem. State Bar of Calif. (Certs. of Appreciation 1973—), Criminal Cts. Bar Assn. (pres. 1959-60, Jerry Giesler Meml. award 1970, Joseph Rosen Justice award 1986), Calif. Attys. for Criminal Justice (v.p. 1974-77). Jewish. Avocations: home in the desert, sporting activities, reading, cruises. Criminal, Probate, Personal injury. Home: 2783 Angelo Dr Los Angeles CA 90077-2135 Office: Garber & Garber PLC 3660 Wilshire Blvd Los Angeles CA 90010-2756

**GARBER, KEVIN JOHN,** lawyer; b. Bellefonte, Pa., Feb. 23, 1956; s. Richard John and Marlyn Jean Garber; m. Suzanne Elizabeth Weiland, July 29, 1978; children: Sarah K., John G. BS, Pa. State U., 1978; MS, U. Wis., 1981; PhD, U. Pitts., 1983; JD, Duquesne U., 1987. Bar: Pa. 1987, U.S. Patent Office 1990. Assoc. Reed Smith Shaw & McClay, Pitts., 1986-88, 89-96; atty. H.J. Heinz Co., Pitts., 1988-89; ptnr. Babst Calland Clements & Zomnir, Pitts., 1996—; adj. prof. environtl. law Duquesne U. Law Sch., Pitts., 1995—; adj. faculty nat. scis. Point Park Coll., Pitts., 1993—. Author: (with others) Allegheny Watershed Network, 1998; contbr. articles to profl. publs. Mem. ABA, Pa. Bar Assn., Allegheny County Bar Assn. Republican. Roman Catholic. Environmental, Oil, gas, and mineral, Patent. Office: Babst Calland Clements & Zomnir Two Gateway Ctr Pittsburgh PA 15222

**GARBER, ROBERT EDWARD,** lawyer, insurance company executive; b. N.Y.C., Jan. 4, 1949; s. Edward Robert and Estelle (Rosenberg) G.; m. Mary Ellen Roche, Jan. 17, 1981; 1 child, Edward Thomas. A.B., Princeton U., 1970; J.D., Columbia U., 1973. Bar: N.Y. 1974. Law clk. U.S. Dist. Ct. (so. dist.), N.Y.C., 1973-75; assoc. Debevoise, Plimpton, Lyons & Gates, N.Y.C., 1976-79; assoc. counsel, v.p. Irving Trust, N.Y.C., 1979-82, sr. v.p., 1982-87; gen. counsel Irving Bank Corp. and Irving Trust Co., N.Y.C., 1987-89; sr. v.p., dep. gen. counsel Equitable Life Assurance Soc. U.S., N.Y.C., 1989-93; sr. v.p., gen. counsel Equitable Cos., Inc. and Equitable Life Assurance Soc. U.S., 1993-94, exec. v.p., gen. counsel, 1994—; dir. Am. Arbitration Assn. Served to capt. USAR, 1970-78. Mem. Assn. of Bar of City of N.Y. Banking, General corporate, Insurance. Home: 45 Sturgis Rd Bronxville NY 10708-5012 Office: Equitable Life Assurance Soc US Rm 203 1290 Avenue Of The Americas Fl Conc2 New York NY 10104-1472

**GARBER, YALE,** lawyer, consultant; b. N.Y.C., Nov. 22, 1925; s. Harry and Lillian (Gillule) G.; m. Frances Karlit, Jan. 29, 1949; 1 child, Sherry Wittenstein. BA, Bklyn. Coll., 1949; LLB, N.Y. Law Sch., 1952; LLM, Bklyn. Law Sch., 1957. Bar: N.Y., U.S. Dist. Ct. (ea. and so. dists.) N.Y., U.S. Supreme Ct. Fed. atty. N.Y.C.; exec. dir. Apparel Mfg. Assn., N.Y.C.; cons. Garment Mfrs. Adv. Bd., N.Y.C., 1985—. Mem. Am. Legion (comdr. 1954-59, judge adv. 1959-65). Avocations: auto racing, sponsoring and promoting auto racing. Home: 6006 Royal Poinciana Ln Tamarac FL 33319-6107

**GARBIS, MARVIN JOSEPH,** judge; b. Balt., June 14, 1936; s. Samuel and Adele E. (Warshaw) G.; m. Phyllis Lorraine Zaroff, Aug. 27, 1961; children: Kendall Rose, Jason Anders, Kerri Jill. BES., Johns Hopkins U., 1958; JD, Harvard U., 1961; LLM, Georgetown U., 1962. Bar: D.C. 1961, Md. 1962. Trial atty. Tax Div., Dept. Justice, Washington, 1962-67; sole practice Balt., 1967-71; ptnr. Garbis, Marvel & Junghans, Balt., 1971-86, Melnicove, Kaufman, Weiner, Smouse & Garbis, Balt., 1986-88, Johnson & Gibbs, Washington, 1988-89; judge U.S. Dist. Ct. Md., 1989—; lectr. U. Md. Law Sch., 1970-85, NYU Fed. Tax Inst., 1970, 74, 79, 87-88; adj. prof. Georgetown U. Law Sch., 1978-80, U. Balt. Law Sch., 1982—; adviser on tax procedure study, jud. com. U.S. Senate, 1969-70; mem. adv. commr. to commr. IRS, 1982; mem. adv. coun. U.S. Claims Ct., 1982—; mem. Md. Inst. for Continuing Profl. Edn. for Lawyers, 1978-80, pres., 1980-82. Author: (with Frome) Procedures in Federal Tax Controversy, 1968, (with Schwait) Tax Refund Litigation, 1971, Tax Court Practice, 1974, (with Struntz) Cases and Materials on Federal Tax Procedure, Civil and Criminal, 1981, (with Junghans and Struntz) Federal Tax Litigation, 1985, (with Struntz and Rubin) Cases and Materials on Tax Procedure and Tax Fraud, 2d edit., 1987, (with Rubin and Morgan) Cases and Material on Tax Procedure and Tax Fraud, 3d edit., 1991; contbr. articles to profl. jours. Recipient Jules Ritholz Meml. Merit award, 1996; E. Barrett Prettyman fellow Georgetown Law Sch., 1961-62; named hon. justice Fed. Ct. Australia, 1998. Mem. Fed. Bar Assn. (pres. Balt. chpt. 1972-73, nat. vice chmn. tax com. 1974-76), Md. Bar Assn. (chmn. tax sect. 1970-71, chmn. continuing legal edn. 1973-80), ABA (chmn. ct. procedure com., tax sect. 1975-77), Balt. Bar Assn. (bd. govs. 1974-79), Fed. Cir. Bar Assn. (bd. dirs. 1985—). Am. Law Inst., Md. Inst. Continuing Profl. Education Lawyers (pres. 1981-82). Office: US Dist Ct 101 W Lombard St Ste 404 Baltimore MD 21201-2626

**GARBRECHT, LOUIS,** lawyer; b. Tulsa, Jan. 21, 1949; s. Louis and Amy (Harris) G.; m. Sandra Kuchta, July 15, 1978 (div. 1980); m. Susan Kay Adams, July 1982; children: Kenneth, Douglas, Steven, Ursala, Heidi. BA, U. Wash., 1971; JD, U. Denver, 1975. Bar: Idaho 1975, U.S. Dist. Ct. Idaho 1975, U.S. Supreme Ct. 1980. Mng. atty. Idaho Legal Aid Svcs., Twin Falls, 1975-80; pvt. practice Twin Falls, 1980-82, Coeur D'Alene, Idaho, 1982—. Mem. Idaho State Bar (bankruptcy sect., worker's compensation). Democrat. Avocations: snow skiing, sailboarding, raquetball. Workers' compensation, Pension, profit-sharing, and employee benefits, Bankruptcy. Home and Office: PO Box 974 Coeur D Alene ID 83816-0974

**GARCETTI, GILBERT I.,** prosecutor. BS, U. So. Calif., L.A.; JD, UCLA, 1968. Dist. atty. County of Los Angeles, 1983—. Office: County of Los Angeles Dist Attys Office 210 W Temple St Rm 18-709 Los Angeles CA 90012-3210

**GARCIA, ADOLFO RAMON,** lawyer; b. Havana, Cuba, Nov. 5, 1948; came to U.S., 1961; s. Adolfo Damian and Luz I. (Garcia) G.; m. Elizabeth Ensor, July 17, 1971; children: Andrew, Laurence. AB magna cum laude, Harvard U., 1971; JD, Georgetown U., 1974. Bar: N.Y. 1975, Mass. 1981. Assoc. Cahill Gordon & Reindel, N.Y.C., 1974-79, Choate, Hall & Stewart, Boston, 1979-82; sr. ptnr. McDermott, Will & Emery, Boston, 1982—, mem. mgmt. coms., 1993—, sr. coord. Spanish-speaking countries/transactions area, 1991—; bd. dirs. Carboclor Industrias. Sec., co-chmn. legal affairs com., bd. dirs. Internat. Bus. Ctr. New Eng. Inc., Boston, 1983-87; past chmn. and pres., bd. dirs. Boston Ctr. for Internat. Visitors, 1981-86; mem. Mass. Internat. Trade Coun., Boston, 1984-86; v.p., dir. New Eng.-Latin Am. Bus. Coun. Mem. Internat. Bar Assn., Boston Bar Assn. (co-chmn. pvt. internat. law sect. 1982-86), InterAm. Bar Assn., Essex County Club, Manchester (Mass.) Yacht Club. Republican. General corporate, Securities, Private international. Home: October Hill Prides Crossing MA 01965 Office: McDermott Will & Emery 28 State St 33rd Flr Boston MA 02109-1775

**GARCIA, ANTHONY J.,** lawyer; b. Santa Fe, Jan. 19, 1956. BUS, U. N.Mex., 1986; JD, U. Calif., San Francisco, 1993. Bar: Calif. 1994, N.Mex. 1994, Colo. 1995, U.S. Ct. Appeals (10th cir.) 1995. Contbg. editor Barclays Pub., San Francisco, 1993-94; contract atty. Law Office of Robert Bruce Collins, Albuquerque, 1994-95; pvt. practice Denver, 1995-96; atty. Riggs Abney et al, Denver, 1996—. Mem. Hispanic Bar Assn. of Colo. Democrat. Avocation: blues guitarist. State civil litigation, Criminal. Office: Riggs Abney Turpen Orbison & Lewis 621 17th St Ste 600 Denver CO 80293-0601

**GARCIA, CASTELAR MEDARDO,** lawyer; b. Conejos, Colo., June 3, 1942; s. Castelar M. Sr. and Anna (Vigil) G.; m. Mary Elizabeth Miller, Apr. 1, 1967; 1 child, Victoria Elisabeth. BA, Adams State Coll., 1965; JD, U. Colo., 1976. Bar: Colo. 1977, U.S. Dist. Ct. Colo. 1977, U.S. Ct. Appeals (10th cir.) 1983, U.S. Ct. Appeals (4th cir.) 1988, U.S. Supreme Ct. 1984. Human resources counselor State of Oreg., Klamath Falls, 1966-68; regional dir. Colo. Civil Rights Com., Alamosa, 1970-73; dep. dist. atty. Denver, 1977-80, chief dep. dist. atty., 1980-84; pvt. practice Alamosa, Colo., 1984—; owner Cumbres Ranch; town atty., Romeo, Colo., Antonito, Colo., Sanford, Colo., 1984—; commr. Colo. Dept. Hwys., 1991, Colo. Dept. Transp., 1991—; chmn. Colo. Transp. Commn., 1996—; chmn. Colo. Dept. Transp. Commn. Mem. Colo. delegation to Cam Real Trade Corridor Consortium between U.S., Can. and Mex. With U.S. Army, 1968-70, Vietnam. Decorated Purple Heart. Mem. Colo. Bar Assn., Hispanic Bar Assn., San Luis Valley Bar Assn. Republican. Roman Catholic. General civil litigation, Criminal, Personal injury. Home: PO Box 90 Alamosa CO 81101-0090 Office: 714 S St Manassa CO 81141

**GARCIA, EDWARD J.,** federal judge; b. 1928. AA, Sacramento City Coll., 1951; LLB, U. Pacific, 1958. Dep. dist. atty. Sacramento County, 1959-64, supervising dep. dist. atty., 1964-69, chief dep. dist. atty., 1969-72; judge Sacramento Mcpl. Ct., 1972-84; judge U.S. Dist. Ct. (ea. dist.) Calif., Sacramento, 1984-96, sr. judge, 1996—. Served with U.S. Army Air Corps, 1946-49. Office: US Dist Ct US Courthouse Clerk Office 501 I St Rm 4-200 Sacramento CA 95814-7300

**GARCIA, HIPOLITO FRANK (HIPPO GARCIA),** federal judge; b. San Antonio, Dec. 4, 1925; s. Hipolito and Francisca G. LLB, St. Mary's U., San Antonio, 1951. Bar: Tex. 1952. Dep. dist. clk. Bexar County, Tex., 1950-52; asst. criminal dist. atty. Dist. Atty's Office, San Antonio, 1952-63; with Garcia, Chavarria & Reeder, 1963-64; judge County Ct. at Law, 1964-74, Tex. Dist. Ct. Dist. 144, 1975-79, U.S. Dist. Ct. (we. dist.) Tex., San Antonio, 1980—. Served U.S. Army, 1943-45. Recipient cert. of Merit Am. Legion. Mem. San Antonio Bar Assn., Am. Bar Assn., Delta Theta Phi. Democrat. Office: US Courthouse 1st Fl 655 E Durango Blvd San Antonio TX 78206-1102

**GARCIA, ORLANDO LUIS,** judge; b. 1952. BA, U. Tex., 1975, JD, 1978. Legis. aide to Hon. Matt Garcia and Ernestine Glossbrenner Tex. Ho. of Reps., 1974-83; atty. Law Offices of Matt Garcia, 1978-85; mem. Tex. Ho. of Reps., 1983-91; atty. Heard, Goggan, Blair & Williams, 1985-90; judge 4th Ct. of Appeals, San Antonio, 1991-94, U.S. Dist. Ct. (we. dist.) Tex., San Antonio, 1994—. Vol. San Antonio State Hosp. Vol. Coun., San Antonio Pro Bono Project. Named One of Ten Best Legislators of 70th Tex. Legislature, State Bar Tex., 1987, Outstanding State Rep. of Yr., Tex. Youth Commn., 1990, Legislator of Yr., Tex. Pub. Employees Assn., 1989, Tex. Alliance for Mentally Ill., 1990,. Mem. State Bar Tex., Tex. Bar Found., San Antonio Bar Assn., Tex. Jud. Coun. Office: US Dist Ct US Courthouse 1st Fl 655 E Durango Blvd San Antonio TX 78206-1102

**GARCIA, RAYMOND ARTHUR,** lawyer; b. Chgo., Sept. 30, 1930; s. Raymond and Evelyn (Rathbun) G.; m. Yvonne Emily Garcia, July 7, 1955; children: Gregory Arthur, Curt Jonathan. BA, U. Ill., 1952; JD, Southwestern U., L.A., 1966. Bar: Calif. 1967, U.S. Dist. Ct. (ctrl. dist.) 1967, U.S. Ct. Appeals (9th cir.) 1967, U.S. Supreme Ct. 1974. Statistician Quaker Oats, L.A., 1953-55; asst. to pres. J.J. Haggarty's Stores, Beverly Hills, Calif., 1955-63; asst. contr. Seibu Dept. Stores, L.A., 1963-64; contr. Gourmet Concessions, L.A., 1964-65; audit rev. spl. U.S. Dept. Def., Bklyn., 1966; contr. Child Bros., L.A., 1967; dep. pub. defender Los Angeles County, L.A., 1967; sr. house counsel Baskin Robbins, Inc., Burbank, Calif., 1970-71; atty. Cohen England Whitfiled, Oxnard, Calif., 1975-79; atty. in pvt. practice Thousand Oaks, Calif., 1968-70, 72—. Mayor, councilman City of Thousand Oaks, 1968-72; mem. So. Calif. Assn. Govt., L.A., 1968-72; pres. Thousand Oaks Sister City, 1994-97; bd. dirs. Conejo Youth Employment, pres., 1993-94; bd. dirs. ARC, pres., Ventura, 1993. Named Man of Yr. Conejo C. of C., 1972. Republican. Lutheran. Avocations: bowling, golf. Probate, Bankruptcy, Family and matrimonial. Office: 100 E Thousand Oaks Blvd Thousand Oaks CA 91360-5713

**GARCIA, RUDOLPH,** lawyer; b. Phila., June 22, 1951; s. Rudolph Sr. and Assunta Rita (Marrara) G.; m. Randi Ellen Pastor, Aug. 3, 1980; 1 child, Jonathan P. BA magna cum laude, Temple U., 1974, JD cum laude, 1977. Bar: Pa. 1977, U.S. Dist. Ct. (ea. dist.) Pa. 1977, U.S. Ct. Appeals (3d cir.) 1982, U.S. Supreme Ct. 1982. Assoc. Wright, Thistle & Gibbons, Phila., 1977-78; assoc. Saul, Ewing, Remick & Saul, Phila., 1978-84, ptnr., 1984—. Judge pro tem Phila. Ct. Common Pleas. Fellow Acad. of Adv.; mem. ABA, Pa. Bar Assn., Phila. Bar Assn. (chmn. local rules subcom. 1988-92, chmn. state civil com. 1999), Phila. Assn. Def. Counsel, Justinian Soc., Phi Beta Kappa. Avocations: computers, photography, golf. Federal civil litigation, State civil litigation, Insurance. Home: 235 Lloyd Ln Wynnewood PA 19096-3323 Office: Saul Ewing Remick & Saul 3800 Centre Sq W Philadelphia PA 19102-2174

**GARCIA-BARRON, GERARD LIONEL,** lawyer; b. L.A., Nov. 29, 1965; s. Jose Sergio and Maria (de Jesus) Barron; m. Irene Silva Garcia, May 16, 1992; children: Nicolas, Tomas. BA, U. So. Calif., 1987, JD, 1990. Bar: Calif. 1992, U.S. Dist. Ct. (ctrl. dist.) Calif. 1992. Assoc. Seals & Tenenbaum, Anaheim, Calif., 1990-92, Mazura & Arguelles, Newport Beach, Calif., 1992-95, Parker Stanbury, LLP, L.A., 1995—. Mem. L.A. Trial Lawyers Assn., Mex.-Am. Bar Assn. Democrat. Roman Catholic. Avocations: running, golf. Criminal, General civil litigation, Personal injury. Office: Parker Stanbury LLP 611 W 6th St Fl 33 Los Angeles CA 90017-3101

**GARCIA BARRON, RAMIRO,** lawyer; b. H. Matamoros, Mexico, Aug. 18, 1966; s. Ramiro Garcia Jimenez and Lourdes Barron Schoellkopf; m. Cecilia Garcia Moreno, Mar. 5, 1994; 1 child, Ramiro A. Garcia. BBA, U. Monterrey, Mexico, 1989; MBA, U. Dallas, 1992; JD, So. Meth. U., 1993. Bar: U.S. Dist. Ct. (no. dist.) Tex. 1995, U.S. Ct. Internat. Trade 1997, U.S. Ct. Appeals (5th cir.) 1997, U.S. Supreme Ct. 1998. Accts. aide investigational divsn. edn. dept. U. Monterrey, 1988-89; rsch. asst. Banco Nacional de Comercio Exterior, Dallas, 1993, Trade Commn. Mexico, Dallas, 1993; assoc. Roberts Cunningham & Stripling, Dallas, 1995—; cons. in field; spkr. in field. Mem. ABA, Am. Soc. Internat. Law, Dallas Bar Assn. Avocations: swimming, cycling, hunting, fishing, triathlons. Private international,

General corporate, General civil litigation. Office: Roberts Cunningham & Stripling LLP 800 Preston Commons West 8117 Preston Rd Dallas TX 75225-6332

**GARDE, JOHN CHARLES,** lawyer; b. Lyndhurst, N.J., Aug. 17, 1961; s. John Charles and Jean (Sheperd) G.; m. L. Allison Ghenn, Aug. 9, 1986. BA, Drew U., 1983; JD, William and Mary, 1986. Bar: N.J. 1986, U.S. Ct. N.J. 1986, U.S. Ct. Appeals (2nd, 3rd and 7th cirs.) 1990. Law sec. to presiding judge Superior Ct Appellate div., Hackensack, N.J., 1986-87; assoc. McCarter & English, Newark, 1987-94, ptnr., 1995—. Contbr. William and Mary Law Rev. Warden St. Thomas Epis. Ch., 1987—; trustee St. Phillip's Acad., 1996—. Mem. ABA, N.J. State Bar Assn., Essex County Bar Assn., Order of the Coif, Phi Beta Kappa. Republican. Episcopalian. General civil litigation, Insurance, Product liability. Office: McCarter & English 100 Mulberry St Newark NJ 07102-4004

**GARDEBRING, SANDRA S.,** academic administrator. Grad., Luther Coll., Decorah, Iowa; JD, U. Minn. Dir. Region 5 U.S. EPA; commr. Minn. Pollution Control Agy., Minn. Dept. Human Svcs.; judge Minn. Ct. Appeals; assoc. justice Minn. Supreme Ct., 1991-98; v.p. U. Minn., 1998—; chmn. bd. regional planning agy. Met. Coun. Mem. Ctr. Victims of Torture; mem. Minn. Advocates, LWV; past bd. dirs. St. Paul United Way, Camp DuNord, Project Environment Found., Clean Sites. Office: U Minn 11 Morris Hall 100 Church St SE Minneapolis MN 55455-0110

**GARDILL, JAMES CLARK,** lawyer; b. Glendale, W.Va., Sept. 29, 1946; s. James B. and Agnes T. (Clark) G.; m. Linda Ann Truban, Aug. 12, 1972; children: James Christopher, Catherine T., Rebecca Ann. Student, Wheeling Coll., 1964-65; AB, West Liberty State Coll., 1968; JD, W.Va. U., 1973. Bar: W.Va. 1973, U.S. Dist. Ct. (no. and so. dists.) W.Va. 1973, U.S. Ct. Appeals (4th cir.). Ptnr. Phillips, Gardill, Kaiser & Altmeyer, Wheeling, W.Va., 1973—; mcpl. judge City of Glendale, 1982—; mem. W.Va. Workmen's Compensation Adv. Bd., Charleston, 1979-92 ; dir. Wesbanco Inc., Wheeling, Wheeling Hosp., Easter Seal Rehab. Ctr., Wheeling, Wesbanco Bank Wheeling; adj. lectr. Coll. Law, W.Va. U., 1998; lectr. estate planning and tax issues. Bd. dirs. Wheeling Soc. for Crippled Children. With U.S. Army, 1968-70. Mem. Estate Planning Coun., W.Va. Bar Assn., Ohio County Bar Assn. (pres. 1984-85). Democrat. E-mail: jamesgardill@PBKA.com. Banking, General corporate, Estate planning. Home: 408 Jefferson Ave Glen Dale WV 26038-1323 Office: Phillips Gardill Kaiser & Altmeyer 61 14th St Wheeling WV 26003-3411

**GARDINER, BARRY LEE,** tax lawyer; b. N.Y.C., May 16, 1940; s. Arthur A. and Dorothy (Williams) G.; m. Ronni Susan Decter, Oct. 20, 1968; children—Beth, Jill. B.S. in Bus., Bucknell U., 1962; J.D., Rutgers U., 1965; LL.M. in Taxation, NYU, 1971. Bar: N.Y., N.J. Assoc. Stein & Stein, Esqs., Newark, 1965-67, Bennett & Bennett, Esqs., Newark, 1967-68, Lynton Klein Opton & Saslow, Esqs., N.Y.C., 1968-72; ptnr. Rosen & Reade, Esqs., N.Y.C., 1972—. Trustee, v.p. Jewish Documentation Ctr., N.Y.C., 1978—; committeeman United Jewish Community, Bergen County, N.J., 1984—. Mem. N.Y. State Bar Assn., N.J. Bar Assn., Bergen County Bar Assn. Democrat. Jewish. Avocations: running; golf. Home: 36 Feather Ln Westwood NJ 07675-7107 Office: Rosen & Reade 666 5th Ave New York NY 10103-0001

**GARDINER, LESTER RAYMOND, JR.,** lawyer; b. Salt Lake City, Aug. 20, 1931; s. Lester Raymond and Sarah Lucille (Kener) G.; m. Janet Ruth Thatcher, Apr. 11, 1955; children: Allison Gardiner Bigelow, John Alfred, Annette Gardiner Weed, Leslie Gardiner Crandall, Robert Thatcher, Lisa Gardiner West, James Raymond, Elizabeth Gardiner Smith, David William, Sarah Janet. BS with honors, U. Utah, 1954; JD, U. Mich., 1959. Bar: Utah 1959, U.S. Dist. Ct. Utah 1959, U.S. Ct. Appeals (10th cir.) 1960. Law clk. U.S. Dist. Ct., 1959; assoc. then ptnr. Van Cott, Bagley, Cornwall & McCarthy, Salt Lake City, 1960-67; ptnr. Gardiner & Johnson, Salt Lake City, 1967-72, Christensen, Gardiner, Jensen & Evans, 1972-78, Fox, Edwards, Gardiner & Brown, Salt Lake City, 1978-87, Chapman & Cutler, 1987-89, Gardiner & Hintze, 1990-92; CEO and pres. Snowbird Ski and Summer Resort, Snowbird Corp., 1993-97; prin., mgmt. cons. Ray Gardiner Assocs., 1998—; reporter, mem. Utah Sup. Ct. Com. on Adoption of Uniform Rules of Evidence, 1970-73, mem. com. on revision of criminal code, 1975-78; master of the bench Am. Inn of Ct. I, 1980-90; mem. com. bar examiners Utah State Bar, 1973; instr. bus. law U. Utah, 1965-66; adj. prof. law Brigham Young U., 1984-85. Mem. Republican State Central Com. Utah, 1967-72, mem. exec. com. Utah Rep. Party, 1975-78, chmn. state convs., 1980, 81; mem. Salt Lake City Bd. Edn., 1971-72; bd. dirs. Salt Lake City Pub. Library, 1974-75; trustee Utah Sports Found., 1987-91; bd. dirs. and exec. com. Salt Lake City Visitors and Conv. Bur., 1988-91, 93-98. Served to 1st lt. USAF, 1954-56. Mem. Utah State Bar Assn., Sons of Utah Pioneers, Utah Ski Assn. (bd. dirs. 1994-97), Nat. Ski Areas Assn. (mem. pub. lands com. 1994-97, gov. affairs com. 1994-97), Rotary. Mormon. Office: Ray Gardiner Assocs 93 Laurel St Salt Lake City UT 84103-4349

**GARDNER, BRIAN E.,** lawyer; b. Des Moines, July 13, 1952; s. Lawrence E. and Sarah I. (Hill) G.; m. Rondi L. Veland, Aug. 7, 1976; children: Meredith Anne, Stephanie Lynn, John Clinton. BS, Iowa State U., 1974; JD, U. Iowa, 1978. Bar: Iowa 1978, Mo. 1978, Kans. 1979, U.S. Ct. Appeals (10th cir.) 1980, U.S. Dist. Ct. Kans. 1979, U.S. Dist. Ct. (we. dist.) Mo. 1978. Assoc. Morrison, Hecker, Curtis, Kuder & Parrish, Kansas City, Mo., 1978-80, Parker & Handsaker, Nevada, Iowa, 1980-81, Morrison, Hecker, Curtis, Kuder & Parrish, Overland Park, Kans., 1981-83; ptnr. Morrison & Hecker, Kansas City, Mo., 1983—, mng. ptnr., 1990-93, 96—; city atty. Mission Hills, Kans., 1992—. Bd. dirs. Overland Park Conv. and Visitors Bur., 1985-97, chmn., 1988-90; dir., mem. exec. com. Johnson County C.C. Found., Overland Park, 1990—, pres., 1997—; bd. dirs. KCPT, 1993—, chmn., 1997-98; active Kansas City Area Devel. Coun., 1992—, Civic Coun. Greater Kansas City, 1998—. Mem. Kans. Bar Assn., Kans. Assn. Def. Counsel, Kansas City Met. Bar Assn., Mo. Bar Assn., Johnson County Bar Assn., Blue Hills Country Club, Cardinal Key, Phi Beta Kappa. Lutheran. Avocation: golf. Environmental, Land use and zoning (including planning). Office: Morrison & Hecker LLP 2600 Grand Blvd Kansas City MO 64108-4606

**GARDNER, CARYN SUE,** lawyer; b. Queens, N.Y., Mar. 9, 1960; d. Louis Arthur and Rhoda (Madonick) G. BA in Environ. Sci. and Urban Planning, SUNY, Binghamton, 1982; JD, DePaul U., 1985. Bar: Ill. 1985, U.S. Dist. Ct. (no. dist.) Ill. 1987, U.S. Ct. Appeals (7th cir.) 1987. Assoc. Rivkin, Radler, Dunne & Bayh, Chgo., 1985-86, Rudd & Kim, Schaumburg, Ill., 1986-87, Schain, Firsel & Burney, Schaumburg, 1987-92, Bickley & Bickley, Schaumburg, 1992-93, Bickley, Hart & Gardner, Schaumburg, 1993—; asst. instr. Harper Coll., Palatine, Ill., 1987-92, prof., 1992—; atty. Assn. Condominium, Townhouse and Homeowners Assns., Schaumburg, 1987, Assn. Condominium Edn., South Barrington, Ill., 1990—. Mem. ABA, Chgo. Bar Assn. Avocations: tennis, swimming, reading, movies. Real property, Nonprofit and tax-exempt organizations, General civil litigation. Office: Bickley Hart & Gardner 117 E Schaumburg Rd Schaumburg IL 60194-3518

**GARDNER, D. MAX,** lawyer; b. Glendale, Calif., June 11, 1961; s. Max C. and Velma (Goldman) G.; m. L. Jenifer Wollum, July 7, 1983; children: Ben, Brad, Mallory. BA, Brigham Young U., 1984, JD. Assoc. Young-Wooldridge, Bakersfield, Calif., 1987-91, Noriega & Alexander, Bakersfield, Calif., 1991-94; pvt. practice Law Office of D. Max Gardner, Bakersfield, Calif., 1995—. Mem. Ctrl. Calif. Bankruptcy Assn. Bankruptcy. Office: 5500 Ming Ave Ste 257 Bakersfield CA 93309-4625

**GARDNER, DALE RAY,** lawyer; b. Broken Arrow, Okla., May 8, 1946; s. Edward Dale and Dahlia Faye (McKeen) G.; m. Phyllis Ann Weinschrott, Dec. 27, 1969. BA in History, So. Ill. U., 1968; MA in History, St. Mary's U., San Antonio, 1975; JD, Tulsa U., 1979. Bar: Okla. 1979, Colo. 1986, Tex. 1991, U.S. Ct. Mil. Appeals 1988, U.S. Ct. Claims 1989, U.S. Dist. Ct. (no. dist.) Okla. 1981, U.S. Dist. Ct. Colo. 1986, U.S. Dist. Ct. (so. dist.) Tex. 1992, U.S. Ct. Appeals (10th cir.) 1986. Pvt. practice Sapulpa, Okla., 1979-80, 94—; asst. dist. atty. child support enforcement unit 24th Dist. Oklahoma, Sapulpa, 1980-86, 94-95; pvt. practice Aurora, Colo., 1986-91, Houston, 1991-94; mng. atty. Hyatt Legal Svcs., Aurora, 1988-89; city atty. City of Sapulpa, Okla., 1996—. Author: Immigration Act of 1965: The Preliminary Results, 1974, Teapot Dome: Civil Legal Cases that Closed the Scandal, 1989. Mem. Child Support Enforcement, Sapulpa, 1980-86, 94-96; trustee United Way, Sapulpa, 1985, 95; Domestic Violence Counsel, Sapulpa, 1985; chmn. bd. trustees 1st Presbyn. Ch., Sapulpa, 1985. Capt. U.S. Army, 1969-75, Vietnam., lt. col Res., judge adv. Mem. Okla. Bar Assn., Tex. Bar Assn., Creek County Bar, Gold Coat Club (pres.), Sertoma (pres. Sapulpa 1985, pres. Collumbine 1988, 90, Sertoman of Yr. 1985). Democrat. Avocations: fishing, post card collecting. Home: 1533 Terrill Cir Sapulpa OK 74066-2567 Office: 7 S Park St Sapulpa OK 74066-4219

**GARDNER, DAVID CHRISTOPHER,** lawyer; b. Paragould, Ark., Nov. 10, 1968; s. Franklin Edward and Rayetta Faye Gardner; m. Shelly Renee Chronister, Sept. 10, 1994; 1 child, Evan. BA in Polit. Sci., Ark. State U., 1991; JD, U. Ark., Little Rock, 1994. Bar: Ark. 1994. Assoc. counsel Entergy Power Group, Little Rock, 1994-95; assoc. Womack, Landis, Phelps, McNeill and McDaniel, PA, Jonesboro, Ark., 1995—; dir., pres. Better Life Counseling Ctr., Jonesboro, 1998-99. Recipient Pro Bono Atty. for the Quarter award Ark. Vol. Lawyers for the Elderly, Jonesboro, 1997. Mem. ABA, Ark. Bar Assn., Craighead County Bar Assn., Federalist Soc., Greater Jonesboro C. of C. Avocations: golf, horseback riding. Fax: 870-932-2553. E-mail: cgardner@wlpmm-firm.com. Office: Womack Landis Phelps McNeil & McDaniel PA 301 W Washington Ave Jonesboro AR 72401-2778

**GARDNER, ERIC RAYMOND,** lawyer; b. Derry, N.H., Nov. 13, 1946; s. William Rudolph and Lois Brooks (Wilson) G.; m. Kathleen Linda Chertok, June 14, 1969 (div. Mar. 1985); children: Matthew Eric, Thomas Martin; m. Melissa Rae Hastings, Oct. 21, 1988. BA in Polit. Sci., U. N.H., 1969; JD, Boston U., 1972. Bar: N.H. 1972, Mass. 1972, U.S. Dist. Ct. Vt., 1987, U.S. Supreme Ct. 1979. Law clk. N.H. Supreme Ct., Concord, 1972-73; assoc. Goodnow, Arwe, Ayer & Prigge, Keene, N.H., 1973-76; ptnr. Goodnow, Arwe, Ayer, Prigge & Gardner, Keene, 1977-81; pvt. practice Keene, 1981—; appointee N.H. Supreme Ct. Profl. Conduct Com., Concord, 1984-93. Editor Boston U. Law Rev., 1971-72. Clk., dir. Monodnock United Way, Keene, 1975-80; dir. Keene Family YMCA, 1974-82; chair Cheshire County Crimestoppers, Inc., 1997-98. Fellow N.H. Bar Found.; mem. ABA, ATLA, Am. Bd. Trial Advocates, Nat. Bd. Trial Advocacy, N.H. Trial Lawyers Assn., Greater Keene C. of C. (clk./dir. 1975-80). Avocations: flying, golf, tennis, skiing, travel. Personal injury, Product liability, Professional liability. Office: PO Box C 222 West St Keene NH 03431-2455

**GARDNER, GARY EDWARD,** lawyer; b. Windsor, Ont., Can., Oct. 21, 1952; s. Edward Thomas and Antonionette Ursla (Urbanski) G.; m. Sheila Mary Hand, Oct. 5, 1984. BA, Mich. State U., 1975; JD, U. Detroit, 1981. Mktg. officer Ford Motor Co. Australia, Melbourne, 1975-77; analyst Ford Motor Co., Dearborn, Mich., 1977-79; asst. to gen. counsel Ford Motor Co. Australia, Melbourne, 1979-80; assoc. James R. Shively, P.C., Detroit, 1980-82; instr. law Detroit Coll. of Bus., Dearborn, Mich., 1982-84; ptnr. Shively, McCloskey, Corriveau & Gardner, Mich., 1984-86; pvt. practice Dearborn, 1986-90; ptnr. Gardner & Doyle, 1990-94, Gary Edward Gardner, P.C., Dearborn, Mich., 1995—; atty. pvt. practice, Dearborn, Mich., 1995—. Candidate Judge of Ct. of Appeals S.E. Mich., 1988; candidate Judge 19th Dist. Ct., 1992, 94, Judge Wayne County Cir. Ct., 1998; bench-bar liaison com. Wayne County Cir. Ct., 1999. Mem. ABA, Mich. Bar Assn. (com. domestic violence 1993-99), Dearborn Bar Assn. (pres. 1996-97), Wayne County Family Law Bar Assn. (founding mem., pres. 1997-99), Fairlane Club, Detroit Coll. Rugby Club, Kiwanis Club Dearborn. Republican. Roman Catholic. Family and matrimonial, Criminal, Real property. Home: 246 River Ln Dearborn MI 48124-1047 Office: 25121 Ford Rd Dearborn MI 48128-1058

**GARDNER, J. STEPHEN,** lawyer; b. Dayton, Ohio, May 10, 1944; s. David L. and Mary (Webb) Gardner; m. Sandra Ellen Ott, Dec. 23, 1967; children: Stephen, Truett, P.J. BA in Math., U. Fla., 1966, JD, 1969. Bar: Fla. 1969, U.S. Dist Ct. (mid. dist.) Fla. 1971. Co-founder, ptnr. Ott & Gardner, Tampa, Fla., 1971-72, Bucklew, Ramsey, Ott & Gardner, Tampa, 1972-75; ptnr. Trinkle & Redman, Brandon, 1976-81; co-founder, shareholder Bush, Ross, Gardner, Warren & Rudy, P.A., Tampa, 1981—; mem. adv. bd. SouthTrust Bank, 1986, South Hillsborough Cmty. Bank, 1988-92. Past chmn. Tampa Downtown Partnrship; past pres. Davis Islands Civic Assn.; bd. dirs. Young Life Tampa, 1972, 88; bd. dirs. F.L.O.A.T., Inc., 1986-87, v.p. 1987; mem. Leadership Tampa Class of 1980; mem. bd. counelors U. Tampa, 1976-84; chmn. pastor-parish com. Hyde Park United Meth. Ch., 1982, chmn. ch. and society com., 1975, chmn. budget raisning com., 1984, lay leader, 1985, Sunday sch. supt., 1986-87, Sunday sch. tchr., 1973-86, mem. adminstrv. bd., 1974-87, chmn., 1976, co-chmn. capital campaign com., 1997. 1st lt. U.S. Army, 1969-71, Vietnam; capt. USAR, 1972-75. Decorated Bronze star with oak leaf cluster. Mem. AMA, Fla. Bar Assn. (probate rules com. 1985-87), Hillsborough County Bar Assn., Tampa Tennis Assn. (past pres.), Ye Mystic Krewe Gasparilla, Tampa Yacht and Country Club (past commodore), Exch. Club (past pres. Tampa ), Univ. Club Tampa (bd. dirs., past pres.). Methodist. Real property, Banking, Probate. Office: Bush Ross Gardner Warren & Rudy PA 220 S Franklin St Tampa FL 33602-5330

**GARDNER, KATHLEEN D.,** gas company executive, lawyer; b. Fayetteville, Ark., July 14, 1947; d. Harold Andrew and Bess (Gunn) Dulan; m. Robert Gardner, June 7, 1969 (dec. Sept. 1974); m. Cecil Alexander, Feb. 4, 1995; 1 child, Christina Ann. BS, U. Ark., 1969, JD, 1978; MA, U. Ala., 1972. Atty., corp. officer SW Energy Co., Fayetteville, 1978-85; asst. gen. counsel, asst. v.p. Reliant Energy Akrla a divsn. of Reliant Energy Resources, Little Rock, 1985-86, gen. counsel, v.p., 1986—; chmn. Regional Tng. Program, Birmingham, Ala., 1972-75. Bd. dirs. the New Sch. Fayetteville, 1978-79, Robert K. Gardner Meml. Fund, Fayetteville; past bd. dirs. Keep Ark. Beautiful Commn., Ballet Ark., Ark. Mus. Sci. and History, Vis. Nurse Corp. Named Outstanding Young woman Fayetteville Jaycettes, Ark. Jaycettes, recipient Woman of Achievement in Energy award, 1990; named to Top 100 Women in Ark., Ark. Bus. Newspaper, 1995, 96, 97, 98, 99. Mem. ABA, Ark. Bar Assn. (sec. natural resources sect. 1981), Pulaski County Bar Assn., Am. Gas Assn., DAR, Ark. Assn. Def. Counsel, Am. Arbitration Assn. (Ark. adv. coun.), Alpha Delta Pi. Episcopal. Office: Reliant Energy 400 E Capitol Ave Little Rock AR 72202-2465

**GARDNER, RUSSELL MENESE,** lawyer; b. High Point, N.C., July 14, 1920; s. Joseph Hayes and Clara Emma-Lee (Flynn) G.; m. Joyce Thresher, Mar. 7, 1946; children: Winthrop G., Page Stansbury, June Thresher. AB, Duke U., 1942, JD, 1948. Bar: Fla. 1948, U.S. Ct. Appeals (5th cir.) 1949, U.S. Tax Ct. 1949, U.S. Supreme Ct. 1985. Ptnr. McCune, Hiaasen, Crum, Gardner & Duke and predecessor firms, Ft. Lauderdale, Fla., 1948-90, Gunster, Yoakley, Valdes-Fauli & Stewart, 1990—; bd. govs. Shepard Broad Law Ctr. Nova S.E. U. Trustee Mus. of Art, Inc., Ft. Lauderdale, pres., 1964-67; bd. dirs. Stranahan House, Inc., 1981—, pres. 1983-85; bd. dirs. Ft. Laud Hist. Soc., 1962—, pres. 1975-85, pres. emeritus, 1985—; mem. estate planning council, Duke U. Sch. Law; bd. dirs., vice chmn. Broward Performing Arts Found., Inc., 1985—. Served to lt. USNR, 1943-49. Fellow Am. Coll. Trust and Estate Counsel; mem. Am. Judicature Soc., ABA (real property, probate, trust sect.), Fla. Bar Assn. (probate, guardianship rules com.), Broward County Bar Assn. (estate planning council), Coral Ridge Country Club, Lauderdale Yacht Club, Tower Club. Democrat. Presbyterian. Probate, Real property, Estate taxation. Home: PO Box 14636 Fort Lauderdale FL 33302-4636

**GARDNER, STEPHEN DAVID,** lawyer, law educator; b. Newark, N.J., Dec. 3, 1939; s. Henry and Florence (Temeles) G.; m. Mary Francis Voce, Sept. 19, 1973; children: Benjamin Voce-Gardner, Daniel Voce-Gardner. BA, U. Fla., 1961, LLB, 1964; LLM in Taxation, NYU, 1965. Bar: Fla. 1964, N.Y. 1967, U.S. Supreme Ct. 1980. Assoc. Maguire Voorhis & Wells, Orlando, Fla., 1965-66; assoc. prof. law NYU Sch. Law, N.Y.C., 1966-68, adj. prof. law, 1969—; assoc. Hughes Hubbard & Reed, N.Y.C., 1968-71; ptnr. Kronish Lieb Weiner & Hellman, N.Y.C., 1971—, mng. ptnr., 1980—; dir. Safra Nat. Bank, N.Y.C., 1987—, David Schwartz Found., N.Y.C., 1980—. Contbr. articles and revs. to profl. jours. Sgt., USAR, 1969-72. Mem. N.Y. State Bar Assn., Fla. Bar, Assn. Bar of City of New York, Tax Club of N.Y., Order of Coif. Jewish. Avocations: skiing, swimming, gardening. Corporate taxation, Taxation, general. Office: Kronish Lieb Weiner & Hellman 1114 Ave of Americas New York NY 10036

**GARDNER, SUE SHAFFER,** lawyer; b. Buffalo, Jan. 19, 1931; d. Harvey Jay Shaffer and Freda (Ballotin) Harris; m. Arnold B. Gardner, Aug. 24, 1952; children: Jonathan H., Diane R. BA, Smith Coll., Northampton, Mass., 1952; JD, SUNY, Buffalo, 1976. Bar: N.Y. 1977, U.S. Dist. Ct. (we. dist.) N.Y. 1977. Assoc. Kavinoky & Cook, Buffalo, 1976-81, ptnr., 1981—; chmn. tax and legal com. Found. for Jewish Philanthropies, Buffalo, 1981-84; mem. dean's adv. com. SUNY Law Sch., Buffalo, 1995—. Bd. dirs. City of Buffalo Landmark and Preservation Bd., 1985-89, chair, 1986; bd. mgrs. Buffalo and Erie County Hist. Soc., 1988—; bd. dirs. SUNY-Buffalo Law Sch. Alumni Assn., 1984-86; bd. dirs. ARC, Buffalo, 1978-94, chairperson, 1984-86, mem. eastern ops. adv. coun., Washington, 1983-86, chmn., 1985-86; trustee Cmty. Found. of Greater Buffalo, N.Y., 1999—. Recipient Leadership award YWCA, Buffalo, 1987, ann. citation NCCJ, Buffalo, 1988, Disting. Alumni award SUNY-Buffalo, 1989, Outstanding Women award, 1992, Citizen of Yr. award YMCA, 1991. Fellow Am. Coll. Estate and Trust Counsel; mem. N.Y. State Bar Assn., N.Y. State Women's Bar Assn., Estate Analysts Western N.Y., N.Y. State Interest in Lawyers Accounts Fund (bd. dirs. 1991—), Erie County Bar Assn. (chmn. surrogate's ct. com. 1987-89, bd. dirs. 1989-93), Am. Jewish Com. (nat. legal com. 1988—). Estate planning, Probate, Estate taxation. Home: 89 Middlesex Rd Buffalo NY 14216-3617 Office: Kavinoky & Cook 120 Delaware Ave Rm 600 Buffalo NY 14202-2793

**GARDNER, WILLIAM F.,** lawyer; b. Birmingham, Ala., Apr. 24, 1934; s. Lucien D. and Amy Y. (Young) G.; m. Melanie Terrell, Oct. 20, 1961; children; John L., Robert T. BA, U. Ala., 1956; LLB, U. Va., 1959. Bar: Ala. 1959, U.S. Dist. Cts. (no., mid., so. dists.) Ala., U.S. Ct. Appeals (5th cir, 11th cir.); Supreme Ct. Ala. Assoc. Cabaniss Johnston, Birmingham, Ala., 1959-65; ptnr. Cabaniss, Johnston, Gardner, Dumas & O'Neal, Birmingham, 1965—; chmn. Equal Employment Opportunity Com. Defense, Rsch. and Trial Lawyers Assn., 1974-75. Contbr. articles to legal jours. Fellow Am. Coll. Trial Lawyers. Episcopalian. Labor, Federal civil litigation. Home: 3706 Mountain Park Cir Birmingham AL 35213-4424 Office: Cabaniss Johnston Gardner Dumas & O'Neal PO Box 830612 Birmingham AL 35283-0612

**GARDNER, WOODFORD LLOYD, JR.,** lawyer; b. Pryor, Okla., Feb. 4, 1945; s. Woodford Lloyd Sr. and Capitola Overstreet (Arterburn) G.; m. Sandra Kaye Bishop, Aug. 7, 1966; children: Allison Wood, John Bishop. BS, Western Ky. U., 1967; JD, U. Ky., 1969. Bar: Ky. 1969, U.S. Dist. Ct. (ea. dist.) Ky. 1969, U.S. Dist. Ct. (we. dist.) Ky. 1979. Law clk. to presiding justice U.S. Dist. Ct. (ea. dist.) Ky., Lexington, 1969; ptnr. Redford, Redford & Gardner, Glasgow, Ky., 1971-91, Richardson, Gardner & Barrickman, Glasgow, Ky., 1991—; bd. dirs. South Ctrl. Bank of Barren County, Inc., Nat. Park Concessions, INc., Mammoth Cave, Ky.; judge, exec. Barren County, Glasgow, 1982-94; atty. Commonwealth of Ky., 1975-76. Mng. editor Ky. Law Jour., 1968-69; co-editor: Barren County Heritage; contbr. articles to profl. jours. With U.S. Army, 1969-71. Recipient Ernie award Glasgow-Barren County C. of C., 1988. Mem. Ky. Bar Assn. (ho. of dels. 1978-85), Barren County Bar Assn. (pres. 1978-79). Banking, General civil litigation, General practice. Office: Richardson Gardner & Barrickman 117 E Washington St Ste 1 Glasgow KY 42141-2696

**GARFIELD, MARTIN RICHARD,** lawyer; b. N.Y.C., Feb. 19, 1935; s. Harry and Sarah (Spielman) G.; m. Susan Scher, July 20, 1978 (div. Oct. 1990); 1 child, Robin. BA, Hunter Coll., 1957; JD, Bklyn. Law Sch., 1964. Bar: N.Y. 1965, U.S. Dist. Ct. (ea. and so. dists.) N.Y. 1979, U.S. Supreme Ct. 1996. Assoc. Figueroa & Madow, N.Y.C., 1965-68, Schneider Kleinick & Weitz, N.Y.C., 1968-70; ptnr. Breadbar Garfield & Solomon, N.Y.C., 1970-86; sr. ptnr. Breadbar Garfield & Schmelkin, N.Y.C., 1986—; arbitrator Civil Ct. N.Y. County, 1986—; mgr. N.Y. State Athletic Commn., 1996—. Mem. Am. Trial Lawyers Assn., N.Y. State Bar Assn. (torts, ins. sect.), N.Y. Trials Lawyers Assn. Avocations: tennis, basketball, boxing analysis, body building. State civil litigation, Personal injury, Product liability. Office: Breadbar Garfield & Schmelkin 11 Park Pl Fl 10 New York NY 10007-2895

**GARFINKEL, BARRY HERBERT,** lawyer; b. Bklyn., June 19, 1928; s. Abraham and Shirley (Siegel) G.; m. Gloria Lorenz, Feb. 16, 1969; children—David, James, Paul. BSS, CCNY, 1950; LLB, Yale U., 1955. Bar: N.Y. State 1955, U.S. Supreme Ct. 1959. Law clk. to Hon. Edward Weinfeld U.S. Dist. Ct., N.Y.C., 1955-56; assoc. Skadden, Arps, Slate, Meagher & Flom, N.Y.C., 1956-61; ptnr. Skadden, Arps, Slate, Meagher & Flom, 1961—; trustee, chmn. Practising Law Inst., Law Ctr. Found. of N.Y. U. Sch. Law Aperture Fedn., program com. 2d. Cir. Jud. Conf. Mng. editor: Yale Law Jour. Bd. dirs., former dir. Jewish Mus., Legal Aid Soc.; dir. Aperture Found.; trustee N.Y. Community Trust; pres. coun. Mus. City of N.Y.; chmn. lawyers' div., spl. gifts campaign United Jewish Appeal/Fedn. Jewish Philanthropies, 1979-81; mem. print com. Whitney Mus., Com. on Rsch. Libraries N.Y. Pub. Lib. Recipient Torch of Learning award Am. Friends of Hebrew U., 1983, Brandeis Distingish. Community Svc. award Brandeis U., 1985. Fellow Am. Coll. Trial Lawyers, Am. Bar Found.; mem. ABA, Am. Arbitration Assn., Assn. of Bar of City of N.Y. (exec. com., judiciary com., past chmn. fed. cts. com.), N.Y. State Bar Assn., Am. Law Inst. Club: Yale (N.Y.C.). Federal civil litigation, State civil litigation, Private international. Home: 211 Central Park W New York NY 10024-6020 Office: Skadden Arps Slate Meagher & Flom 919 3rd Ave New York NY 10022-3902

**GARFINKEL, NEIL B.,** lawyer; b. New Hyde Park, N.Y., Jan. 29, 1964; s. Elliot Z. and Diana (Fein) G.; m. Shari Chaitin, Aug. 14, 1988; children: Alyssa Hope, Joshua Phillip. BA summa cum laude, SUNY, Albany, 1986; JD, Cornell U., 1989. Bar: N.Y. 1990. Assoc. Proskauer, Rose, Goetz & Mendelsohn, N.Y.C., 1989-91, Bank & Bank, Garden City, N.Y., 1992-94; pntr. Abrams, Garfinkel & Rosen, LLP, N.Y.C., 1994—. Mem. N.Y. State Bar Assn., Phi Beta Kappa. Real property, Banking. Office: Abrams Garfinkel & Rosen LLP 370 Lexington Ave Rm 802 New York NY 10017-6503 also: 12301 Wilshire Blvd Ste 402 Los Angeles CA 90025-1000

**GARFUNKEL, ALAN J.,** lawyer; b. Savannah, Ga., Oct. 26, 1947; s. Sylvan Adler Garfunkel and Eve D. (Darmstadter) Goldmann; m. Lori A. Corsun, June 27, 1993; children: S. Jonathan, Michael J., Danielle A., Joshua B. A.B., NYU, 1968, LL.M. in Taxation, 1975; J.D., Columbia U., 1972. Bar: N.Y. 1972, U.S. Dist. Ct. (so. and ea. dists.) N.Y. 1974, U.S. Ct. Appeals (2d cir.) 1975, U.S. Tax Ct. 1975. Sr. trial atty. Office of Chief Counsel, IRS, N.Y.C., 1972-77; assoc. firm Proskauer Rose Geotz & Mendelsohn, N.Y.C., 1977-80; atty. pvt. practice, N.Y.C., 1980—. Served with USAR, 1969-74. Mem. N.Y. State Bar Assn. (tax sect.), New York County Lawyers Assn., Bar Assn. of City of N.Y., Omicron Delta Epsilon. Personal income taxation, Corporate taxation, State and local taxation. Home: 63 Lincoln Rd Scarsdale NY 10583-7533 Office: 477 Madison Ave New York NY 10022-5802

**GARGANO, FRANCINE ANN,** lawyer; b. Plainfield, N.J., Feb. 10, 1957; d. Rosalie Janice Gargano. B.A. Seton Hall U., 1980; J.D. cum laude, Detroit Coll. of Law, 1983. Bar: N.J. 1983, U.S. Supreme Ct. 1986. Sole practice North Plainfield, N.J., 1983—; dir. YWCA Legal Clinic, Plainfield, 1983—; Union County coordinator Haitian Pro Bono Projects, ABA, Plainfield, 1983—; rsch. asst. prof. Detroit Coll. Law, Detroit, 1980-83. Author: Homosexual Marriages Are Not Possible. Trustee Plainfield Area YWCA, 1983-84; bd. dirs. Haitian Advancement Assn., Elizabeth, N.J., 1983-84; mem. N. Plainfield Bd. Adjustment; mem. Historic Preservation commn., Youth Svcs. commn., Mcpl. Alliance. Recipient Internat. Legal Scholar award Detroit Coll. Law Internat. Law Soc., 1980-82, Jessup Internat. Law Competition award, 1982, H. Rakol Scholarship award Detroit Bar Assn., 1982, Vol. of Yr. Congl. award, 1995. Mem. ABA, Union County Bar Assn., N.J. Bar Assn., Plainfield Bar Assn., Am. Immigration Lawyers Assn., Detroit Coll. Law Internat. Law Soc. (pres. 1980-82), Vicinage 13 Women's Bar Assn. (pres.), Somerset County Bar Assn. (chmn. ADR com.). Democrat. Roman Catholic.. Civil rights, Constitutional, Public international. Office: 53 Mountain Blvd Warren NJ 07059

**GARGIULO, ANDREA W.,** lawyer; b. Hartford, Conn., Apr. 26, 1946; d. Charles M. and Irma S. (Rubin) Weiner; m. Richard A. Gargiulo, Nov. 26, 1975; 1 child, John K. BA, Smith Coll., 1968; JD cum laude, Suffolk U., 1972. Bar: Mass. 1972, U.S. Dist. Ct. Mass. 1975, U.S. Ct. Appeals (11th cir.) 1981, U.S. Supreme Ct. 1983. Asst. dist. atty. Middlesex County, Mass., 1972-75; chmn. Boston Fin. Commn., 1975-77; counsel Gargiulo,

Rudnick, & Gargiulo, Boston, 1976—; chmn. Boston Licensing Bd., 1977-89; lectr. Northeastern U. Coll. Criminal Justice, Boston, 1978, 80; bd. dirs. Arbella Mut. Ins. Co.; host (TV show) Women Today, 1994-96. Mem. Mass. Ethics Commn., 1985-88; mem. bd. overseers Children's Hosp., Boston, 1983—; chmn. Mass. Bd. Overseers, 1996. Mem. Bay Club, Beacon Hill Garden Club, Harvard Mus. Assn., Wianno Yacht Club, Univ. Club. Democrat. Avocation: sailing, acting. Administrative and regulatory, General practice, General civil litigation. Home: 13 W Cedar St Boston MA 02108-1211 Office: Gargiulo Rudnick & Gargiulo 66 Long Wharf Boston MA 02110-3605

**GARIBALDI, MARIE LOUISE,** state supreme court justice; b. Jersey City, Nov. 26, 1934; d. Louis J. and Marie (Serventi) G. BA, Conn. Coll., 1956; LLB, Columbia U., 1959; LLM in Tax. Law, NYU, 1963. Atty. Office of Regional Counsel, IRS, N.Y.C., 1960-66; assoc. McCarter & English, Newark, 1966-69; ptnr. Riker, Danzig, Scherer, Hyland & Perrutti, Newark, 1969-82; assoc. justice N.J. Supreme Court, Newark, 1982—. Contbr. articles to profl. jours. Trustee St. Peter's Coll.; co-chmn. Thomas Kean's campaign for Gov. of N.J., 1981, mem. transition team, 1981; mem. Gov. Byrne's Commn. on Dept. of Commerce, 1981. Recipient Disting. Alumni award NYU Law Alumni of N.J., 1982; recipient Disting. Alumni award Columbia U., 1982. Fellow Am. Bar Found.; mem. N.J. Bar Assn. (pres. 1982), Columbia U. Sch. Law Alumni Assn. (bd. dirs.). Roman Catholic.

**GARLAND, JAMES BOYCE,** lawyer; b. Gastonia, N.C., June 16, 1920; s. Peter Woods and Kathleen (Boyce) G.; m. Elizabeth Matthews, Nov. 9, 1951 (dec.); children: Elizabeth Garland Wren, Woods Garland Potts, James Boyce Jr., Rebecca Garland Morris. BS, U. N.C., 1941, LLB, 1946. Bar: N.C. 1946, U.S. Ct. Appeals (4th cir) 1981, U.S. Supreme Ct. 1989. Ptnr. Garland & Garland, Gastonia, 1946-59, Garland & Eck, Gastonia, 1961-62, Garland & Alala, Gastonia, 1962-80, chmn. bd. dirs., 1980-88, Garland & Wren, 1988-93; mem. N.C. House of Reps., 1949-51; campaign chmn. United Way of Gaston County, Inc., 1988, pres., 1990; chmn. bd. trustees Lees McRae Coll., 1984-86; vice-chmn. bd. trustees Gaston Coll., 1988-90; chmn., bd. visitors Lineberger Comprehensive Cancer Ctr. U. N.C., Chapel Hill, 1988-92; pres. U. N.C. Law Alumni Assoc., 1971-72, U. N.C. Gen. Alumni Assoc., 1973-74; vice-chmn. bd. visitors U. N.C., Chapel Hill; mem. N.C. Local Govt. Commn., 1970-75, Gastonia City Council, 1985-87; Mayor City of Gastonia, 1987—; bd. dirs. N.C. League of Municipalities, 1992-94, commissioned 2nd Lt. Field Artillery, 1942, ; sec. bd. trustees U. N.C., Charlotte, 1993—; pres. Schiele Mus. Natural History and Planetarium, 1984-85. Served to capt. N.C. N.G., 1942-59. Decorated Bronze Star; named Citizen of the Year Gastonia Civitan Club Fellow Am. Bar Found; mem. ABA, N.C. Bar Assn. (chmn. edn. law com., v.p. 1984-85, N.C. Soc. Cin., Gen. Practice Hall of Fame 1995), Gaston County Bar Assn. (pres.), N.C. State Bar, Gaston County C. of C. (pres. 1980-81), N.C. Jr. C. of C. (v.p. 1953-54), Gastonia Jr. C. of C. (pres. 1952-53), Disting. Service award 1955), Daniel Jonathan Stowe Botanical Garden (pres. 1991-96, vice chmn. bd. 1996—), Jaycees (W. Duke Kimbrell Life-time Achievement award 1998), Gaston Country Club, Biltmore Forest Country Club, Rotary (pres. 1960-61, dist. gov. 1966-67), Phi Delta Phi. Presbyterian. Democrat. General practice, Estate planning, Education and schools. Home: 1339 Covenant Dr Gastonia NC 28054-3861 Office: Garland & Drum PA PO Box 1657 Gastonia NC 28053-1657

**GARLAND, MERRICK BRIAN,** federal judge; b. Chgo., Nov. 13, 1952; s. Cyril and Shirley Garland. AB summa cum laude, Harvard U., 1974, JD magna cum laude, 1977. Bar: D.C. 1979, U.S. Dist. Ct. D.C. 1980, U.S. Ct. Appeals (D.C. and 9th cirs.) 1980, U.S. Ct. Appeals (4th cir.) 1983, U.S. Supreme Ct. 1983. Law clk. to judge U.S. Ct. Appeals (2d cir.), N.Y.C., 1977-78; law clk. to justice U.S. Supreme Ct., Washington, 1978-79; spl. asst. to U.S. atty. gen. Dept. Justice, Washington, 1979-81; from assoc. to ptnr. Arnold & Porter, Washington, 1981-89; asst. U.S. atty. Dept. Justice, Washington, 1989-92; ptnr. Arnold & Porter, Washington, 1992-93; dep. asst. atty. gen., criminal divsn. Dept. Justice, Washington, 1993-94, prin. assoc. dep. atty. gen., 1994-97; circuit judge U.S. Ct. Appeals, Washington, 1997—; assoc. ind. counsel, 1987-88; lectr. on law Harvard U. Law Sch., 1985-86. Author: Antitrust and State Action Yale Law Jour., 1983, Deregulation and Jud. Rev., Harvard Law Rev., 1985. Mem. Phi Beta Kappa. Office: US Courthouse 333 Constitution Ave NW Washington DC 20001-2802

**GARLAND, RICHARD ROGER,** lawyer; b. Princeton, Ill., Aug. 20, 1958; s. Louis Roger and Irene Marie (Tonozzi) G. BA in Polit. Sci. summa cum laude, U. S. Fla., 1979; JD with honors, U. Fla., 1982. Bar: Fla. 1982, U.S. Dist. Ct. (mid. dist.) Fla. 1983, U.S. Ct. Appeals (11th cir.) 1987, U.S. Supreme Ct. 1988, U.S. Ct. Appeals (fed. cir.) 1995; Fla. Bar cert. in appellate practice, 1995. Instr., supr. appellate advocacy U. Fla., Gainesville, 1981-82; assoc. Dickinson, O'Riorden, Gibbons, Quale, Shields & Carlton, Venice, Fla., 1983-85, Sarasota, Fla., 1986-90; ptnr., sr. atty. Dickinson & Gibbons, Sarasota, Fla., 1991—. Pres. parish coun. San Pedro Cath. Ch., North Port, Fla., 1986-92; mem. Sarasota County Libr. Adv. Bd., 1999-2001. Mem. ABA, Fla. Bar Assn., Sarasota County Bar Assn. (editor newsletter 1991-93, bd. dirs. 1994-96, treas. 1996-97, sec. 1997-98, v.p. 1998-99, pres.-elect 1999—), Judge John M. Scheb Am. Inn of Ct. (treas. 1998-99, counselor 1999—, master), U. South Fla. Alumni Assn., Phi Kappa Phi, Pi Sigma Alpha. Democrat. Roman Catholic. General civil litigation, Health, Appellate. Office: Dickinson & Gibbons PA 1750 Ringling Blvd Sarasota FL 34236-6836

**GARLAND, SYLVIA DILLOF,** lawyer; b. N.Y.C., June 4, 1919; d. Morris and Frieda (Gassner) Dillof; m. Albert Garland, May 4, 1942; children: Margaret Garland Clunie, Paul B. BA, Bklyn. Coll., 1939; JD cum laude, N.Y. Law Sch., 1960. Bar: N.Y. 1960, U.S. Ct. Appeals (2d cir.) 1965, U.S. Ct. Claims 1965, U.S. Supreme Ct. 1967, U.S. Customs Ct. 1972, U.S. Ct. Appeals (5th cir.), 1979. Assoc. Borden, Skidell, Fleck and Steindler, Jamaica, N.Y., 1960-61, Fields, Zimmerman, Skodnick & Segall, Jamaica, 1961-65, Marshall, Brater, Greene, Allison & Tucker, N.Y.C., 1965-68; law sec. to N.Y. Supreme Ct. justice Suffolk County, 1968-70; ptnr. Hofheimer, Gartlir & Gross, N.Y.C., 1970—; asst. adj. prof. N.Y. Law Sch., 1974-79; mem. com. on character and fitness N.Y. State Supreme Ct., 1st Jud. Dept., 1985—, vice chmn., 1991—Judge Charles W. Foressel award N.Y. Law Sch., 1997. Author: Workman's Compensation, 1957, Labor Law, 1959, Wills, 1962; contbg. author: Guardians and Custodians, 1970; editor-in-chief Law Rev. Jour., N.Y. Law Forum, 1959-60 (svc. award 1960); contbr. articles to mag. Trustee N.Y. Law Sch., 1979-90, trustee emeritus, 1991—; pres. Oakland chpt. B'nai Brith, Bayside, N.Y., 1955-57. Recipient Disting. Alumnus award N.Y. Law Sch., 1978, Judge Charles W. Foressel award N.Y. Law Sch., 1997. Mem. ABA (litigation sect.), N.Y. State Bar Assn., Queen's County Bar Assn. (sec. civil practice 1960-79), N.Y. Law Sch. Alumni Assn. (pres. 1976-77), N.Y. Law Forum Alumni Assn. (pres. 1963-65). Jewish. Family and matrimonial, General civil litigation, State civil litigation. Home: 425 E 58th St New York NY 10022-2300

**GARLIN, ALEXANDER,** lawyer; b. N.Y.C., Feb. 17, 1949; s. Alexander and Martha M. G.; m. Virginia Louise Chavez; 1 child, Annelise Chavez. BA in English, SUNY, Stony Brook, 1973; JD, U. Colo., 1976. Bar: Colo. 1976, U.S. Dist. Ct. Colo. 1977. Dep. state pub. defender Colo. State Pub. Defender, Denver, 1977-78; office head Colo. State Pub. Defender, Golden, 1978-83; atty. Chavez & Garlin, Boulder, 1983-86; pvt. practice Boulder, 1986-91; atty. Hult Garlin Driscoll & Murray, Boulder and Denver, 1991—. Mem. Colo. Bar Assn., Colo. Trial Lawyers Assn., Boulder Bar Assn., Boulder County Bar Assn. (sec. and treas. 1997-99, pres.-elect 1999—). Avocations: computers, music, inventions. Personal injury, Criminal, General civil litigation. Office: Hult Garlin Driscoll & Murray 2338 Broadway St # 100 Boulder CO 80304-4107

**GARLING, SCIPIO,** editor. Editor Immigration Report, Washington. Office: Fedn Am Immigration Reform 1666 Connecticut Ave NW Ste 400 Washington DC 20009-1039

**GARLOW, BETTE JO,** lawyer, nonprofit organization worker; b. Kearney, Nebr., Aug. 8, 1954; d. Richard Ellis and Gwendolyn (Burton) Darby; m. William Cody Garlow, Nov. 20, 1982 (div. Nov. 1989); children: Lindsay Jo, Ivy Mae. BS, U. Nebr., Kearney, 1976; JD, U. Mont., 1995, postgrad. Bar: Mont., 1995, Wyo. 1997. Exec. dir. Crisis Intervention Svcs., Cody, Wyo., 1985-87, 1995-97; project atty. civil law program Pa. Coalition Against Domestic Violence, Harrisburg, 1997—; mem. State of Wyo Domestic Violence STOP com., Cheyenne, 1996-97. Vol. grant writer Wyo. Coalition against Domestic Violence, 1997. Recipient Mae Carvel award Venture Clubs Am., Cody, 1988, Fran Elge award women's sect. Mont. Bar, 1995; Erasmus scholar U. Mont., 1993-94, 95. Mem. AAUW, Edna Rankin Law Soc., Soroptomists. Avocations: horseback riding, skiing, antiquing, art museums. Office: Pa Coalition Against DV 6500 Flank Dr Harrisburg PA 17112

**GARMER, WILLIAM ROBERT,** lawyer; b. Balt., May 8, 1946; s. William M. and Grace (DeLane) G.; 1 child, Lindsey DeLane; m. Kimberly Nichols. BA, U. Ky., 1968, JD, 1975. Bar: Ky. 1975, U.S. Dist. Ct. (ea. dist.) Ky. 1977, U.S. Ct. Appeals (6th cir.) 1980, U.S. Supreme Ct. 1979. Law clk. to chief judge U.S. Dist. Ct. (ea. dist.) Ky., Lexington, 1975-76; assoc. prof. law litigation skills U. Ky. Law Sch., Lexington, 1981—; ptnr. Savage, Garmer & Elliott, P.S.C., Lexington, 1984—. Casenote editor St. Mary's Law Jour., 1975; contbr. articles to profl. jours. Elder Presbyn. Ch. With USAF, 1969-73. Fellow Am. Coll. Trial Lawyers; mem. ABA, ATLA, (bd. govs., chair coun. state pres.), Ky. Bar Assn. (com. on specialization and cert. 1982—, litigation com. 1989—), Fayette County Bar Assn., Ky. Acad. Trial Attys. (bd. govs. 1984-89, treas. 1990, sec. 1991, v.p. 1992, pres. 1994, named Trail Lawyer of Yr. 1998), Phi Delta Phi (named One of Best Lawyers in Am. 1989-99). Democrat. General civil litigation, Product liability, Personal injury. Office: Savage Garmer & Elliot PSC 141 N Broadway St Lexington KY 40507-1230

**GARNER, BRYAN ANDREW,** law educator; b. Lubbock, Tex., Nov. 17, 1958; s. Gary Thomas and Mariellen (Griffin) G.; m. Pan Anurugsa, May 26, 1984; children: Caroline Beatrix, Alexandra Bess. BA, U. Tex., 1980, JD, 1984. Bar: Tex. 1984, U.S. Ct. Appeals (5th cir.) 1985, U.S. Dist. Ct. (no. dist.) Tex. 1986. Law clk. to judge U.S. Ct. Appeals (5th cir.), Austin, Tex., 1984-85; assoc. Carrington, Coleman, Sloman & Blumenthal, Dallas, 1985-88; dir. Tex./Oxford Ctr. for Legal Lexicography, U. Tex. Sch. Law, Austin, 1988-90; adj. prof. law Sch. Meth. U., 1990—; vis. assoc. prof. law U. Tex., 1988-90; pres. LawProse, Inc., 1990—; lectr. legal and scholarly orgns; cons. U.S. Judicial Conf. Style Com., 1992—. Author: A Dictionary of Modern Legal Usage, 1987; The Elements of Legal Style, 1991; editor Texas, Our Texas: Remembrances of the University, 1984, Scribes Jour. Legal Writing, 1989—; assoc. editor Tex. Law Rev., 1983-84; contbr. articles to profl. jours. Fellow Tex. Bar Found.; mem. ABA, Am. Law Inst., Tex. Bar Assn. (chmn. plain lang. com. 1990—), Dallas Bar Assn., 5th Cir. Bar Assn., Am. Judicature Soc., Am. Dialect Soc., Dictionary Soc. N.Am., Henry Sweet Soc., Scribes (exec. bd. 1990—), Friars, Phi Beta Kappa. Republican. Episcopalian. Avocation: golf. Home: 6478 Lakehurst Ave Dallas TX 75230-5131

**GARNER, MARY MARTIN,** lawyer; b. Little Rock; d. Jared Owen and Mary Augusta (Conery) Martin; m. Meryl Everett Garner, Aug. 24, 1943 (dec.). JD, George Washington U., 1942. Bar: D.C. 1942, U.S. Supreme Ct. 1973. Atty. Office of Gen. Counsel, Div. Natural Resources, USDA, Washington, 1944-72, dep. dir., 1972-74; sole practice, Washington, 1975—; legal counsel Nat. Assn. Soil Conservation Dists., Washington, 1975—; mem. adv. task force on pollution in Great Lakes, U.S.-Can. Joint Commn., Windsor, Ont., Can., 1976-79; bd. dirs. Inter-Am. Bar Found., Washington, 1976—, Fed. Bar Bldg. Corp., 1983—. Pres. Wash. Club Preservation Fund, 1991—. Recipient Citation for Outstanding Contbn. to Advancement of Human Rights, Capital Area div. UN Assn. of U.S., Washington, 1983, Nat. Assn. Conservation Dists. Disting. Service award, 1972. Mem. ABA (vice chmn. com. on agr., adminstrv. law sect. 1979-81), Fed. Bar Assn. (chmn. internat. law sect. 1981-82, Outstanding Leadership award 1982), Internat. Bar Assn. (mem. governing council 1976-91), Washington Fgn. Law Soc., Inter-Am. Bar Assn. (asst. sec. 1978-85, mem. governing council 1985—), Bar Assn. D.C. (chmn. Inter-Am. relations com. 1976-77, Superior Service award 1977), Zonta Internat. Found. (bd. dirs. 1988-93), Women's Bar Assn. of D.C. (pres. 1957-58), Phi Alpha Delta, Soil Conservation Soc. Am. Democrat. Roman Catholic. Clubs: Nat. Lawyers (bd. govs.), The Washington Club Preservation Fund (dir.). Contbr. articles to profl. jours., chpt. to books, papers. Real property, Environmental, Private international.

**GARNER, W. MICHAEL,** lawyer; b. Huntington, W.Va., Sept. 28, 1949; s. William Max Garner and Celeste (Eichling) Neuffer; m. Christine Ann McElligott, Aug. 18, 1997. AB, Columbia U., 1971; JD, NYU, 1975. Bar: N.Y. 1976, N.J. 1994, Minn. 1997, U.S. Dist. Ct. (so. dist.) N.Y. 1977, U.S. Dist. Ct. (ea. dist.) N.Y. 1980, U.S. Dist. Ct. N.J. 1994, U.S. Dist. Ct. Minn. 1998, U.S. Ct. Appeals (2d cir.) 1980, U.S. Ct. Appeals (11th cir.) 1985, U.S. Ct. Appeals (7th cir.) 1993. Assoc. Hughes Hubbard & Reed, N.Y.C., 1976-80, Rivkin, Sherman & Levy, N.Y.C., 1980-84; ptnr. Schnader, Harrison, Segal & Lewis, N.Y.C., 1985-97, Dady & Garner, P.A., Mpls., 1997—. Author: Franchise and Distribution Law and Practice, 1990; editor Franchise Law Jour., 1988-93; contbr. articles to pubis. Fellow Am. Bar Found.; mem. ABA, Assn. of Bar of City of N.Y. Home: 1815 Summit Ave Saint Paul MN 55105-1835 Office: Dady & Garner PA 4000 IDS Ctr 80 S 8th St Minneapolis MN 55402-2100

**GARNES-THOMAS, TERRI DIANA,** paralegal; b. Washington, Dec. 11, 1962; d. Leander Randolph and Doris Marie (Beale) Garnes; m. Michael Alexander Thomas, Nov. 18, 1989; children: Christopher Lee, Jamil Alexander. Student, U. Albuquerque, 1980-82, Albuquerque Tech. Vocat. Inst., 1983; Cert./Legal Sec., Parks Bus. Coll., 1984; Cert. Paralegal, Prince George's C.C., Largo, Md., 1988. Legal sec. property and narcotics dept. Office of the Dist. Atty., Albuquerque, 1984-85, grand jury sec., 1985-86; temporary receptionist, law libr., legal sec. Roberts & Holland, P.A., Washington, 1986; legal sec. Securities Investor Protector Corp., Washington, 1986-87; legal sec. Am. Ins. Assn., Washington, 1987-89, temporary exec. sec., 1988-89; legal sec. Blum, Yumkas, Mailman, Gutman & Denick, P.A., Balt., 1989; legal sec., legal typist Semmes, Bowen & Semmes, Balt., 1989-92; ind. paralegal Md., 1988—; ind. sales assoc. Pre-Paid Legal Svcs., Inc., Ada, Okla., 1995—; lobbyist Home-Sch. Legal Def. Assn. Congrl. Action Program, 1998; hist. interpreter, tour guide Three Centuries Tours Annapolis. Asst. editor: (book) American Insurance Association Insurance Termination Statutes Handbook, 1988, AIA Insurance Termination Statutes Handbook, 1989; asst. proofer: (brief) Brief of Securities Investor Protection Corporation, Appellee, 1986. Mem., docent Balt. Symphony Assocs., 1995; homesch. parent/tchr. Bittersweet Acad. Recipient cert. of appreciation Nat. Mus. of Women in the Arts, Washington, 1997. Mem. Trinidad and Tobago Assn. of Balt., Christian Home Educators Network. Avocations: music appreciation, showhome docent, tea etiquette, comm. svc. programs. Home: 4008 Walrad St Baltimore MD 21229-4139

**GARNETT, STANLEY IREDALE, II,** lawyer, utility company executive; b. Petersburg, Va., Aug. 11, 1943; s. Stanley Arthur and Edith (Keirstead) G.; children: Matthew S.A., Andrew F.W. BA, Colby Coll., 1965; MBA, U. Pa., 1967; JD, NYU, 1973. Bar: N.Y. 1974. Sr. fin. analyst Standard Oil Co. of N.J., N.Y.C., 1967-70; assoc. Milbank, Tweed, Hadley & McCloy, N.Y.C., 1973-81; v.p.-legal and regulatory Allegheny Power Sys., Inc., N.Y.C., 1981-90, v.p. fin., 1990-94, sr. v.p. fin., 1994-95; sr. advisor Putnam, Hayes & Bartlett, 1996-97, 98—; exec. v.p. Fla. Progress Corp., St. Petersburg, 1997-98; bd. dirs. Bay Corp Holdings, Inc. Vice chmn. Episcopal Ch. Bldg. Fund; trustee, sec. I(CB Internat. Ctr. for Disabled. Joseph P. Wharton scholar, 1965-67. Mem. ABA, N.Y. State Bar Assn. Republican. Episcopalian. Real property. Home: PO Box 67390 Saint Pete Beach FL 33736

**GARRELS, SHERRY ANN,** lawyer; b. Chgo., Feb. 5, 1956; d. William Henry and Jacqueline Ann G.; m. Timothy Anthony Marion, Aug. 1, 1987 (div. June 1988); 1 child, William Garrels-Marion; 1 child, Georgianna Garrels-Rogers. BA, Barat Coll., 1980; certificate, Trinity Coll., 1989; JD, Western State U., 1990. Bar: Calif. 1992, U.S. Dist. Ct. (ctrl. dist.) Calif. 1992, U.S. Dist. Ct. (no. dist.) Calif. 1993, U.S. Dist. Ct. (so. dist.) Calif. 1996, U.S. Ct. Appeals (9th cir.) 1994, U.S. Tax Ct. 1996. Pvt. practice Huntington Beach, Calif., 1992—; arbitrator Nat. Panel Consumer Arbitrators, Huntington Beach, 1996, State Panel Consumer Arbitrators, Huntington Beach, 1996, Better Bus. Bureau, 1996—, U.S. C. of C., 1996, Huntington Beach C. of C., 1996. Editor The Dictum, 1989. Active 4th of July Exec. Bd., Huntington Beach, 1996—. Mem. Assn. Trial Lawyers, L.A. Trial Assn., Orange County Bar Assn., St. Bonny Golf Classic (dir. 1991-97), Delta Theta Phi. Republican. Presbyterian. Avocations: swimming, golf, scuba diving. Fax: 714-374-0104. Criminal, State civil litigation, Real property. Office: 5942 Edinger Ave Ste 113-702 Huntington Beach CA 92649-1763

**GARRETT, DEBORRA ELIZABETH,** lawyer; b. Cambridge, Mass., June 6, 1951; d. Joseph Francis and Joan Kathryn (Nauheimer) G.; children: Francis, Joan. BA in Polit. Sci., Pa. State U., 1972; JD, George Washington U., 1976. Bar: Pa. 1976, U.S. Dist. Ct. (ea. dist.) Pa. 1977, Wash. 1979, U.S. Dist. Ct. (we. dist.) Wash. 1979, U.S. Ct. Appeals (9th cir.) 1987, U.S. Supreme Ct. 1990. Staff atty. NLRB, Phila., 1976-79, Evergreen Legal Svcs., Bellingham, Wash., 1979-81; pvt. practice Bellingham, 1981-83; ptnr. Raas, Johnsen, Garrett & Stuen, Bellingham, 1983-93, The Simonarson Law Firm, Bellingham, 1993—. Mem. Bellingham Planning Commn., 1986-93. Mem. Wash. State Bar Assn. (hearing officer 1991—), Whatcom County Bar Assn., Wash. Women Lawyers, Wash. State Trial Lawyers Assn., Nat. Employment Lawyers Assn., Trial Lawyers for Pub. Justice. Democrat. Avocations: mountain hiking and climbing, textiles, llamas. Labor, Personal injury. Office: The Simonarson Law Firm 1700 D St Bellingham WA 98225-3101

**GARRETT, GORDON HENDERSON,** lawyer; b. Charleston, S.C., Aug. 26, 1937; s. Gordon Hughes and Oleda (Henderson) G.; m. Margaret Moore Wilcox, Nov. 2, 1969; children: Elizabeth Wilcox, Caroline Henderson, Gordon Hughes. BS in Commerce, The Citadel, 1959; JD, U. S.C., 1966. Bar: S.C. 1966, U.S. Supreme Ct. 1966, U.S. Ct. Appeals (4th cir.) 1979. Law clk to chief judge U.S. Dist. Ct., Charleston, S.C., 1965-67; pvt. practice Charleston, S.C., 1967—. Mnging. editor, survey editor, mem. editorial bd. S.C. Law Rev., 1965-66. Mem. S.C. Senate, 1969-72; chmn. Charleston, Berkeley and Dorchester Coun. on Alcohol and Drug Abuse, 1973-74; past bd. dirs. Legal Aid Soc., Charleston; mem. S.C. Gov's. Task Force on Corrections. Capt. AGC, U.S. Army, 1959-62. Mem. ABA, S.C. Bar (real estate sect.), Assn. Citadel Men (life). Democrat. Episcopalian. General practice, Real property, Workers' compensation. Home: 87 Rutledge Ave Charleston SC 29401-1724 Office: 1075 E Montague Ave Charleston SC 29405-4825

**GARRETT, KAREN ANN,** lawyer; b. Franklin, N.H., June 10, 1959; d. Richard Joseph and Ann Marie (Murray) S. BA, U. N.C., 1981; MA, Bowling Green (Ohio) State U., 1985; JD cum laude, Suffolk U., 1988. Bar: Mass. 1988, U.S. Dist. Ct. Mass. 1989. Residence dir. Franklin Pierce Coll., Rindge, N.H., 1981-83; law clk. Community Coll. Counsel's Office Commonwealth of Mass., Bedford, 1987-88; assoc. Sullivan & Hayes, Springfield, Mass., 1988-93, Jackson, Lewis, Schnitzler & Krupman, Boston, 1993—; instr. human resources program Teikyo Post U., Waterbury, Conn., 1989-92. Bd. dirs. Friends of Hamden Law Libr., 1991-93: bd. dirs., exec. com. Springfield chpt. Am. Cancer Soc., 1990-93. Mem. Mass. Bar Assn. (labor and employment law sect.). Avocations: skiing, biking, hiking, woodworking, writing. Labor, Education and schools. Office: Jackson Lewis Schnitzler & Krupman One Beacon St # 3300 Boston MA 02108-2003

**GARRETT, RICHARD G.,** lawyer; b. N.Y.C., Oct. 16, 1948. BA magna cum laude, Emory U., 1970, JD, 1973. Bar: Ga. 1973, Fla 1979; U.S. Dist. Ct. (no. dist.) Ga. 1973, (so. dist.) Fla. 1979, U.S. Dist. Ct. (so. dist. trial bar) Fla. 1979; U.S. Ct. Appeals (5th cir.) 1974; U.S. Ct. Appeals (9th. cir., 11 cir.) 1981; U.S. Supreme Ct. 1981. Program dir., instr. rsch., writing and advocacy Emory U., Sch. of Law, 1972-73; chmn. litigation dept., exec. com. bd. dirs. Greenberg, Traurig, Miami, Fla. Editor: Emory Law Journal, 1972-73. Recipient 1st place and Best Brief award Region V Nat. Moot Ct. Competition, 1972. Mem. ABA, The Fla. Bar Assn., State Bar Ga., Omicron Delta Kappa, Order of the Barristers. Securities, Banking, Real property. Office: Greenberg Traurig 1221 Brickell Ave Miami FL 33131-3224

**GARRIGLE, WILLIAM ALOYSIUS,** lawyer; b. Camden, N.J., Aug. 6, 1941; s. John Michael and Catherine Agnes (Ebeling) G.; m. Jeannette R. Regan, Aug. 15, 1965 (div.); children: Maeve Regan, Emily Way; m. Rosalind Chadwick, Feb. 17, 1984; 1 child, Susan Chadwick. BS, LaSalle U., 1963; LLB, Boston Coll., 1966. Bar: N.J. 1966, U.S. Dist. Ct. N.J., U.S. Ct. Appeals (3rd cir.) 1973, U.S. Supreme Ct., 1973; cert. civil trial atty., N.J.; cert. civil trial adv., Nat. Bd. Trial Advocacy; diplomate Am. Bd. Profl. Liability Attys. Assoc. Taylor, Bischoff, Neutze & Williams, Camden, 1966-67, Moss & Powell, Camden, 1967-70; ptnr. Garrigle Palm & Thomasson, Cherry Hill, N.J., 1970—. With USAR, 1959-67. Mem. ABA, N.J. State Bar Assn., Burlington County Bar Assn., Camden County Bar Assn., Internat. Assn. Def. Counsel, Def. Rsch. Inst., N.J. Def. Assn., Am. Bd. Trial Advs. (diplomate), Fedn. of Ins. and Corp. Counsel, Trial Attys. N.J., Camden County Inn of Ct. (master of the bench, chmn. 1989-96, treas. 1996—), Tavistock Country Club. Federal civil litigation, State civil litigation, Insurance. Home: 223 E Main St Moorestown NJ 08057-2905 Office: Garrigle Palm & Thomasson 1415 Route 70 E Ste 204 Cherry Hill NJ 08034-2237

**GARRISON, DAVID ALEXANDER,** lawyer; b. Charlottesville, Va., July 28, 1964; s. Samuel Alexander Garrison and Mary Christine Wilkinson; m. Maureen Horesh, Oct. 16, 1993; children: Adam, Jacob, Marlo. BS, Old Dominion U., 1986; JD, U. Richmond, 1989. Bar: Va. 1990, Pa. 1996. Asst. regional counsel U.S. EPA, Phila., 1989-94; spl. asst. U.S. atty. ea. dist. Office of U.S. Atty., Phila., 1993; atty. Stevens & Lee, Wayne, Pa., 1995—; mem. Chester County (Pa.) Agrl. Development Council, 1998. Mem. exec. com. Chester County Dem. Party, 1998; mem. Delaware Valley Environ. Inn of Ct., Phila., 1998. Mem. ABA, Pa. Bar Assn., Chester County Bar Assn. (co-founder), Phila. Bar Assn. Avocations: scuba diving, hiking, raquetball, reading. Environmental. Office: 1275 Drummers Ln Ste 202 Wayne PA 19087-1582

**GARRISON, MELISSA LYN,** lawyer; b. San Rafael, Calif., May 21, 1958; d. Jack Lee Garrison and Linda Elizabeth (Evans) Rigney. BA, U. Calif., Santa Cruz, 1981; JD, U. San Francisco, 1992. Bar: Calif. 1993, U.S. Dist. Ct. (no. dist.) Calif. 1993, U.S. Ct. Appeals (9th cir.) 1993. Assoc. Davis & Schroeder, Monterey, Calif., 1993—. Mem. ABA, State Bar of Calif., Monterey County Barristers Assn., Monterey County Women Lawyers Assn. Avocation: travel. State civil litigation, Federal civil litigation, Intellectual property. Office: 9083 Soquel Dr Ste 1 Aptos CA 95003-4001

**GARRISON, PITSER HARDEMAN,** lawyer, mayor emeritus; b. Lufkin, Tex., Mar. 7, 1912; s. Homer and Mattie (Milam) G.; m. Berneice Jones, Dec. 3, 1936 (dec. Apr. 1992); m. Reba Brent, Sept. 29, 1993. Student Lon Morris Jr. Coll., 1929-30, student Stephen F. Austin State U., 1930-32; LL.B., U. Tex., 1935. Bar: Tex. 1935; U.S. Dist. Ct. (ea. dist.) Tex. 1936, U.S. Dist. Ct. (so. dist.) Tex. 1938, U.S. Ct. Appeals (5th cir.) 1939. Ptnr. Garrison, Renfrow, Zeleskey, Cornelius & Rogers, Lufkin, 1935-52, sr. ptnr., 1952-68; chmn., gen. counsel Lufkin Nat. Bank, 1968-81; sole practice, Lufkin, 1981—. Mayor City of Lufkin, 1970-88, mayor emeritus, 1988—; past bd. dirs., past pres. Angelina and Neches River Authority, Lufkin; past pres. Deep East Tex. Council of Govts., Jasper; past bd. dirs., past chmn. Angelina County Tax Appraisal Dist., Lufkin; bd. dirs. Meml. Hosp., Lufkin, 1975-91 . Served to maj. U.S. Army, 1942-46. Recipient Disting. Alumnus award Lon Morris Jr. Coll., 1974; Disting. Alumnus award Stephen F. Austin State U., 1976; named East Texan of the Month, East Tex. C. of C., 1966, East Texan of the Yr., East Tex. C. of C., 1981, East Texan of Yr., Deep East Tex. Council of Govts., 1980. Fellow Am. Coll. Trial Lawyers, Tex. Bar Found. (charter); mem. Angelina County Bar Assn. (past pres.), Tex. Bar Assn., ABA, Phi Delta Phi. Democrat. Methodist. Lodges: Rotary (past pres.), Masons, Shriners. General practice, Probate, State civil litigation. Home: Apt 302 Tom Temple Dr Apt 302 Lufkin TX 75904-5592 Office: PO Box 150537 515 S 1st St Lufkin TX 75901-3867

**GARRITY, WENDELL ARTHUR, JR.,** federal judge; b. Worcester, Mass., June 20, 1920; s. W. Arthur and Mary B. (Kennedy) G.; m. Barbara A. Mullins, May 24, 1952; children: W. Arthur III, Charles A., Anne M. Singleton, Jean M. Garrity Kennedy. A.B., Holy Cross Coll., 1941; LL.B., Harvard U., 1946; LLD (hon.), Coll. of Holy Cross, 1976, U. Mass., 1978, Northeastern U. Law. Sch., 1986; JD (hon.), New Eng. Law Sch., 1978; HLD (hon.), Simmons Coll., 1982, Worcester State Coll., 1986. Bar: Mass. 1946, U.S. Dist. Ct. Mass. 1948, U.S. Supreme Ct. 1954. Law clk. to presiding justice U.S. Dist. Ct. Mass., 1946-47, asst. U.S. atty., 1948-50, U.S.

atty., 1961-66, judge, 1966-85, sr. judge, 1985—; ptnr. Maguire, Roche & Leen, 1950-61; lectr. in field. Contbr. articles to profl. jours. Treas. Dem. Party, Wellesley, 1952-55; town coord. Kennedy Congl. Campaigns, 1952-60; coord. Wis. hdqrs. Kennedy Presdl. Campaign, 1960. Sgt. U.S. Army ETO. Recipient Rabb Human Rels. award Am. Jewish Community, 1979, Roger Baldwin award Mass. CLU Found., 1986, Meml. award 16th Ann. Martin Luther Breakfast, 1986. Mem. ABA. Mass. Bar Assn., Boston Bar Assn. (v.p. 1965-66), Harvard Club, Knights of Malta, Wellesley Club. Democrat. Roman Catholic. Avocation: swimming, cycling. Office: US Dist Ct 1 Courthouse Way Ste 4120 Boston MA 02210-3006

**GARROD, JEFFREY MEAD,** lawyer; b. Newark, Dec. 20, 1947; s. E. Henry and Roslyn Garrod; m. Elaine Terry Chasen, July 4, 1970; children: Justin M., Seth M., Danielle J. BS, Cornell U., 1969; JD, Am. U., 1972. Bar: N.J. 1972, U.S. Dist. Ct. N.J. 1972, N.Y. 1981, U.S. Ct. Appeals (3rd cir.) 1981, U.S. Tax Ct. 1982, U.S. Dist. Ct. (so. dist.) N.Y. 1983, U.S. Ct. Appeals (9th cir.) 1992, U.S. Dist. Ct. (ea. dist.) Mich. 1993, U.S. Dist. Ct. (ea. dist.) N.Y. 1997, U.S. Ct. Appeals (8th cir.) 1998. Law clk. N.J. Superior Ct. Chancery, Morristown, 1972-73; lawyer Hannolm, Weisman, Newark, 1973-75; lawyer, ptnr. Orloff, Lowenbach, Stifelman & Siegel, P.A., Roseland, N.J., 1975—; chmn., mem. com. for atty. client fee arbitration N.J. Supreme Ct., Newark, 1990-95. Mem. ABA, N.J. State Bar Assn., N.Y. State Bar Assn., Essex County Bar Assn. (mem. jud. selection com. 1995—). Avocations: golf, skiing. Federal civil litigation, State civil litigation, Intellectual property. Home: 71 Glenview Rd South Orange NJ 07079-1060 Office: Orloff Lowenbach Stifelman & Siegel PA 101 Eisenhower Pkwy Ste 29 Roseland NJ 07068-1082

**GARRY, JOHN THOMAS, II,** lawyer; b. Albany, N.Y., Dec. 12, 1923; s. Joseph A. II and Jean Theresa (Cramond) G.; m. Mary Regina Hoffman (dec.); children: John, Michael, Regina, Maureen, Suzanne, Patricia; m. Claire Bogne Guy, 1989. Student, Cornell U., 1942-43; BA, St. Bernadine of Siena Coll., 1949; LLB, JD, Union U., 1952. Bar: N.Y. 1952, U.S. Supreme Ct. 1952. Asst. corp. counsel City of Albany, 1953-55, asst. dist. atty., 1955-58, dist. atty., 1958-68; sr. ptnr. Garry & Cahill, Albany, 1968—. Exec. chmn. Dem. Cen. Com., Albany, Albany Big Bros./Big Sisters Am., 1971; trustee Siena Coll., Loudonville, N.Y., 1987-97; mem. Empire State Art Commn., 1990-95, N.Y. State Plz. Art Commn. Served with USAAF, 1943. Decorated Air medal. Mem. ABA, N.Y. State Bar Assn. (character com. admission), Albany County Bar Assn., Am. Judicature Soc., Internat. Narcotic Enforcement Officers Assn., N.Y. State Dist. Attys. Assn. (v.p. 1967), St. Bernadine of Siena Coll. Alumni Assn. (pres. 1964, trustee 1989-97), Am. Legion, VFW, KC (Grand Knight 1956). Club: Wolfert's Roost Country. Lodges: K.C. (past grand knight), Elks. Criminal, Estate planning, General practice.

**GARTEN, DAVID BURTON,** lawyer; b. Iowa City, Mar. 23, 1952; s. William B. and Linda (Laird) G.; m. Anita Wallner, Mar. 12, 1983. BA summa cum laude, honors in Econs., Yale U., 1974, JD, 1977. Law clk. to Hon. Anthony M. Kennedy U.S. Ct. Appeals (9th cir.), Sacramento, 1977-78; assoc. Kirkland & Ellis, Chgo., 1979-84, ptnr., 1984-90; v.p., gen. counsel NL Industries Inc., Houston, 1990—. Mem. Phi Beta Kappa. Avocations: skiing, golf. General civil litigation, Antitrust, Securities. Office: NL Industries Inc 16825 Northchase Dr Ste 1200 Houston TX 77060-6012

**GARTH, BRYANT GEOFFREY,** law educator, foundation executive; b. San Diego, Dec. 9, 1949; s. William and Patricia (Feild) G.; children: Heather, Andrew, Daniela. BA magna cum laude, Yale U., 1972; JD, Stanford U., 1975; PhD, European U. Inst., Florence, Italy, 1979. Bar: Calif. 1975, Ind. 1988. Law clk. to judge U.S. Dist. Ct. (no. dist.) Calif., San Francisco, 1978-79; asst. prof. Ind. U., Bloomington, 1979-82, assoc. prof., 1982-85, prof., 1985-92, dean Law Sch., 1986-90; dir. Am. Bar Found., Chgo., 1990—; cons. Ont. Law Reform Commn., 1984-85, 94, World Bank Argentina Project, 1993-94, World Bank Peru Project, 1996; vis. assoc. prof. U. Mich., Ann Arbor, 1983-84; bd. dirs. Internat. Human Rights Law Inst.; mem. bd. visitors Stanford U. Law Sch., 1993—. Author: Neighborhood Law Firms for the Poor, 1980; co-editor: Access to Justice: A World Survey, 1978, Access to Justice: Emerging Issues and Perspectives, 1979, Dealing in Virtue, 1996; contbr. articles to profl. jours. V.p. H.G. & K.F. Montgomery Found. Rsch. grantee NSF, 1982, 91, 92, 95, 99, Nat. Inst. Dispute Resolution, 1985, Ind. Supreme Ct., 1989, Italian Coun. Rsch., 1989, Keck, 1995, MacArthur, 1997. Mem. Am. Law Inst. (exec. com.), Law and Soc. Assn., Internat. Assn. Procedural Law. Democrat. Office: Am Bar Found 750 N Lake Shore Dr Chicago IL 60611-4403

**GARTH, LEONARD I.,** federal judge; b. Bklyn., Apr. 7, 1921; s. Frank A. and Anne F. (Jacobs) Goldstein; m. Sarah Miriam Kaufman, Sept. 6, 1942; 1 child, Tobie Gail Garth Meisel. BA, Columbia U., 1942; postgrad., Nat. Inst. Pub. Affairs, 1942-43; LLB, Harvard U., 1952. Bar: N.J. 1952. Mem. firm Cole, Berman & Garth (and predecessors), Paterson, N.J., 1952-70; judge U.S. Dist. Ct. for Dist. N.J., Newark, 1970-73; U.S. cir. judge Ct. Appeals for 3d Cir., 1973—; lectr. Inst. Continuing Legal Edn.; lectr., coadj. mem. faculty Rutgers U. Law Sch., 1978-98, Seton Hall Law Sch., 1980-95; mem. N.J. Bd. Bar Examiners, 1964-68; mem. com. on revision gen. and admiralty rules Fed. Dist. Ct. N.J.; former mem. com. on fin. disclosure Jud. Conf. U.S.; adv. bd. Fed. Cts. Study Com. Pres., trustee Harvard Law Sch. Assn. N.J., 1958-63; adv. bd. Law and Soc. Major of Ramapo Coll.; Served as 1st lt. AUS, 1943-46. Mem. ABA (N.J. fellows, appellate judges conf.), Fed. Bar Assn., Passaic County (N.J.) Bar Assn. (pres. 1967-68), Am. Law Inst. Office: Ct Appeals ML King Jr Fed Bldg 50 Walnut St Rm 5040 Newark NJ 07102-3506 also: 20613 US Courthouse Philadelphia PA 19106

**GARTNER, HAROLD HENRY, III,** lawyer; b. L.A., June 23, 1948; s. Harold Henry Jr. and Frances Mildred (Evans) G.; m. Denise Helene Young, June 7, 1975; children: Patrick Christopher, Matthew Alexander. Student, Pasadena City Coll., 1966-67, George Williams Coll., 1967-68, Calif. State U., Los Angeles, 1969; JD cum laude, Loyola U., Los Angeles, 1972. Bar: Calif. 1972, U.S. Dist. Ct. (cen. dist.) Calif. 1973, U.S. Ct. Appeals (9th cir.) 1973. Assoc. Hitt, Murray & Caffray, Long Beach, Calif., 1972; dep. city atty. City of L.A., 1972-73; assoc. Patterson, Ritner & Lockwood, L.A., 1973-79; mng. ptnr. all offices Patterson, Ritner, Lockwood, Gartner & Jurich, L.A., Ventura, Bakersfield, and San Bernardino, Calif., 1991—; instr. law Ventura Coll., 1981. Recipient Am. Jurisprudence award Trusts and Equity, 1971. Mem. ABA, Calif. Bar Assn., Ventura County Bar Assn., Nat. Assn. Def. Counsel, Assn. So. Calif. Def. Counsel, Ventura County Trial Lawyers Assn., Direct Relief Internat. (bd. trustees). Republican. Club: Pacific Corinthian Yacht. Avocations: sailing, scuba diving, skiing. State civil litigation, Insurance, Personal injury. Home: 6900 Via Alba Camarillo CA 93012-8279 Office: Patterson Ritner Lockwood Gartner & Jurich 260 Maple Ct Ste 231 Ventura CA 93003-3570

**GARTRELL, P. GARTH,** lawyer; b. Norwalk, Ohio, Mar. 13, 1954; s. Samuel Kenneth and Ella Glee Gartrell; m. Paula Elke Gartrell, Sept. 6, 1975; children: Heather, Laurie. AB, Capital U., 1976; JD, Ohio State U., 1981; LLM, Harvard U., 1992. Bar: Ohio 1981, Calif. 1986, Pa. 1987. Lawyer Vorys, Sater, Seymour et al, Columbus, Ohio, 1982-84; cons. Wyatt Co., San Diego, 1984-86; lawyer Pepper, Hamilton, Phila., 1986-87, Luce, Forward, San Diego, 1987-92, Pillsbury Madison & Sutro, San Diego, 1992—; nat. practice chair Pillsbury Compensation and Benefits Practice. Author: Retirement Plans, 1989; editor Calif. Tax Lawyer, 199-92. Chair equity com. San Diego County Employees Pension, 1996-98; bd. dirs. San Diego Mus. Art, 1996-98, chmn. nominations com.; bd. dirs. ProKids Golf Acad., treas., 1994-97; bd. dirs. Crimestoppers, 1994-96. Named Role Model of Yr., Mayor of San Diego, 1995. Mem. Calif. Bar Assn. (chair sect. of tax 1989-93). General corporate, Pension, profit-sharing, and employee benefits. Office: Pillsbury Madison & Sutro 101 W Broadway Ste 1800 San Diego CA 92101-8298

**GARTS, JAMES RUFUS, JR.,** lawyer; b. Meadville, Pa., Mar. 22, 1949; s. James Rufus and Priscilla Jane (Greer) G.; m. Susan Damian Hord, June 3, 1971; children: Katherine Elizabeth, James Rufus III, Emily Alice. BA, Tulane U., 1971; JD, 1974. Bar: Tenn. 1974, U.S. Dist. Ct. (we. dist.) Tenn. 1983, U.S. Ct. Appeals (6th cir.) 1984. Assoc., Chandler, Manire, Harris and Shelton, Memphis, 1974-76; asst. dist. atty. gen. State of Tenn., Memphis, 1976-79; ptnr. Harris, Shelton, Dunlap and Cobb, Memphis, 1979—; spl. judge Shelby County, 1984; lectr. continuing edn. Memphis State U., 1988—. Pres. Lakewood Hills Property Owners Assn., 1989-93. Fellow Am. Coll. Trial Lawyers; mem. ABA, Tenn. Bar Assn., Memphis Bar Assn. (bd. dirs. 1989-90), Phi Beta Kappa. Republican. Roman Catholic. Federal civil litigation, State civil litigation, Criminal. Home: 3200 Homewood Dr Memphis TN 38128-4408 Office: Harris Shelton Dunlap & Cobb 1 Commerce Sq Ste 2700 Memphis TN 38103

**GARVERT, MELINDA LEE,** lawyer; b. Manhattan, Kans., Dec. 17, 1954; d. Asel W. and Joanne L. (Cribbs) Harder; m. Thomas L. Garvert, June 28, 1986; children: Luke, Michael, Alex, Rachel. BS, Kans. State U., 1976; JD, Washburn Sch. Law, 1980. Bar: Kans. 1980, Colo. 1988. Assoc. McDonald, Tinker, Skaer, Quinn & Herington, Wichita, Kans., 1980-86; pvt. practice Garden City, Kans., 1986—, Colorado Springs, Colo., 1988—; adv. bd. mem. Covenant Internat., Colorado Springs, 1994—. Mem. ABA, Kans. Bar Assn., Colo. Bar Assn., Am. Acad. Adoption Attys., Garden City C. of C., Better Bus. Bur. (Colorado Springs). Family and matrimonial, Private international. Office: 3021 N Hancock Ave Ste 220 Colorado Springs CO 80907-5797

**GARVEY, CHRISTOPHER JOHN,** lawyer; b. Bronx, N.Y., Dec. 7, 1968; s. Joseph Paul and Carol Concetta Garvey; m. Sara Rose Smithken, Sept. 6, 1998. BS cum laude in Mgmt., Rensselaer Poly. Inst., 1990; JD cum laude, Union U., 1992. Bar: Mass. N.Y., U.S. Dist. Ct. (ea., so., and no. dists.) N.Y. Assoc. DeGraff Foy Holt-Harris & Mealey, Albany, N.Y., 1991-94, Feltman Karesh Major & Farbman, N.Y.C., 1994-96, Graubard Mollen & Miller, N.Y.C., 1996-97, Schneck Weltman & Hashmall, LLP, N.Y.C., 1997—. Campaign worker Com. to Draft Mario Cuomo, Albany, 1992, Paul Tsongas Presdl. campaign, Nashua, N.H., 1992; mem. Comty. Free Dems., N.Y.C., 1996—. Mem. N.Y. State Bar Assn. (mem. com. on professionalism 1996-97, com. on CPLR 1998—, com. on fed. litigation 1998—), Assn. of Bar of N.Y.C. (com. on young lawyers 1996—), N.Y. Athletic Club. Roman Catholic. Avocations: tennis, downhill skiing, fiction writing. Federal civil litigation, State civil litigation, Product liability. Office: Schneck Weltman & Hashmall LLP 1285 Avenue Of The Americas New York NY 10019-6028

**GARVEY, JAMES ANTHONY,** lawyer; b. Buffalo, Jan. 26, 1923; s. Michael Joseph and Cecelia Catherine (Haar) G.; m. Marie Joanna Molloy, Aug. 24, 1948; children: Michael J., James A. Jr., Joseph T., Neil E., Dennis J., Matthew J., Daniel P. BA in Latin, Canisius Coll., 1943; postgrad., Coll. of William and Mary, 1945; JD, U. Buffalo, 1949. Bar: N.Y. 1950, U.S. Dist. Ct. (we. dist.) N.Y. 1951, U.S. Ct. Appeals (2d cir.) 1960, Fla. 1982. Assoc. Mortimer Allan Sullivan, Buffalo, 1950-55; founding ptnr. Gaughan, Magner & Garvey (and successive firms), Buffalo, 1955-86, Garvey & Garvey, Buffalo, 1986—. Counsel, bd. dirs. Alexander Sik Hungarian Boy Scouts Am. Meml. Camp, 1966-81; Mt. Calvary Cemetery, 1976—; counsel, bd. trustees Calasanctius Preparatory Sch., 1964-78. Lt. USNR, 1943-46, ETO. Mem. Assn. Trial Lawyers Am., Am. Bd. Profl. Liability Attys. (charter mem.), N.Y. State Bar Assn., N.Y. State Trial Lawyers Assn. (gov. 8th dist. 1963-65, lectr.), Western N.Y. Trial Lawyers Assn. (bd. govs. 1970-74, v.p. 1972, pres. 1973-74), Erie County Bar Assn. (chmn. com. to study integrated bar 1963-65, judiciary com. 1971-76), St. Thomas Moore Guild (treas. 1963-64, sec. 1965), Am. Legion, VFW, Navy League (v.p. 1992—), NRA, Buffalo Yacht Club, Di Gamma. Democrat. Roman Catholic. Avocations: boating, fishing, hunting. General civil litigation, Personal injury. Home: 1250 E Main St East Aurora NY 14052-2030 Office: Garvey & Garvey 416 Pearl St Buffalo NY 14202-1904

**GARVEY, JANE ROBERTS,** lawyer; b. N.Y.C., Oct. 21, 1919; d. George Alexander and Helen Hickson (Hernon) Roberts; m. Francis Bernard Garvey, June 1, 1946; children: Ellen, Jane, Francis B. Jr. BA, Coll. New Rochelle (N.Y.), 1938; LLB, Columbia U., 1941. Bar: N.Y. 1942, U.S. Bd. Immigration Appeals 1957, U.S. Immigration and Naturalization Svc. 1957, U.S. Supreme Ct. 1958. Jr. assoc. Wikes, Riddel, Bloomer, Jacobi & Maguire, N.Y.C., 1942-44; assoc. Jackson, Nash, Brophy, Barringer & Brooks, N.Y.C., 1944-46; ptnr. Francis B. Garvey Esq., Babylon, N.Y., 1946—. Gov., internat. dir. Zonta Internat., Chgo., 1982-86; dir. planned giving Am. Heart Assn., 1984-87. Recipient spl. commendation USN, 1946, hon. commendation Suffolk County (N.Y.) Legislature, 1983, Angela Merici award for achievement in profl. and civic activities, Ursula Lauris citation for Disting. Svc. to Coll. of New Rochelle, 1978; named Hon. Big Sister of Yr., Big Sister/Big Bros., Washington, 1977, named to LAdy Comdr. Equestrian Order of the Holy Sepulchre granted by Pope John XXIII, named Woman of Yr., Zonta Internat., Suffolk County, 1991. Mem. ABA, N.Y. Bar Assn., Babylon Yacht Club, Southward Ho Golf Club (hon.), Zonta Internat. Found. (pres. 1998—). Republican. Roman Catholic. Avocations: sailing, travel. Probate, Estate taxation, Personal income taxation. Home: 64 W Islip Rd West Islip NY 11795-4536 Office: Francis B Garvey PO Box 788 Babylon NY 11702-0788

**GARVEY, JOHN HUGH,** dean, law educator; b. Sharon, Pa., Sept. 28, 1948; s. Cyril T. and Claudia C. (Evans) G.; m. Jeanne Barnes Walter, Aug. 30, 1975; children: Kevin, Elizabeth, Katherine, Michael, Clare. AB, U. Notre Dame, 1970; JD, Harvard U., 1974. Bar: Ky. 1976, U.S. Supreme Ct. 1982. Law clk. to chief judge U.S. Ct. Appeals (2d cir.), N.Y.C., 1974-75; assoc. Morrison & Foerster, San Francisco, 1975-76; asst. prof. Coll. Law U. Ky., Lexington, 1976-79, assoc. prof. Coll. Law, 1979-80, prof. Coll. Law, 1981-94; univ. rsch. prof. Coll. Law, 1989-90, Ashland prof., 1990-94; prof. Notre Dame Law Sch., South Bend, Ind., 1994—; now dean Boston Coll. Law Sch., Chestnut Hill; asst. to solicitor gen. U.S. Dept. Justice, Washington, 1981-84; vis. prof. law sch. U. Mich., Ann Arbor, 1985-86; chmn. constl. law sect. Assn. Am. Law Schs., Washington, 1991-93. Author: Modern Constitutional Theory, 1989, 3d edit., 1994, The First Amendment, 1992, 2d edit., 1995, What Are Freedoms For?, 1996. Fellow Danforth Found., 1970. Mem. Am. Law Inst., Inst. for Jud. Adminstrn. Office: Boston Coll Law Sch Chestnut Hill MA 02167*

**GARVEY, RICHARD ANTHONY,** lawyer; b. N.Y.C., Jan. 10, 1950; s. James Joseph Garvey and Janet Mary (Mooney) Rowse. AB, Boston Coll., 1972; JD, Harvard U., 1975. Bar: N.Y. 1976. Assoc. Simpson Thacher & Bartlett, N.Y.C., 1975-82, ptnr., 1982-93, 97—. Mem. ABA, N.Y. State Bar Assn., Assn. Bar City N.Y., Phi Beta Kappa. General corporate, Mergers and acquisitions, Securities. Home: 330 E 38th St Apt 44N New York NY 10016-2783 Office: Simpson Thacher & Bartlett 425 Lexington Ave Fl 15 New York NY 10017-3954

**GARWOOD, CYNTHIA LYNN,** lawyer; b. Lafayette, Ind., July 3, 1957; d. Robert and Norma Jean (Wesley) Phillips; m. Douglas Vernon Garwood, Oct. 20, 1979. BA, Purdue U., 1981; JD, Washington U., St. Louis, 1986. Bar: Mo. 1986, Ind. 1987, U.S. Dist. Ct. (no. dist.) Ind. 1987, U.S. Dist. Ct. (so. dist.) Ind. 1987, U.S. Ct. of Appeals (7th cir.) 1990. Mem. ops. staff computing ctr. Purdue U., West Lafayette, Ind., 1975-83; assoc. Schultz, Ewan, Burns & Heid, Lafayette, 1987-89, Bartlett, Robb & Sabol, Lafayette, 1989-91, Cooke, Laszynski & Moore, Lafayette, 1991-94; pvt. practice Lafayette, 1994—; mem. credit com. Purdue U. Fed. Employee Credit Union, 1988-92. Mem. adv. bd. Alt. Cmty. Based Svcs., Tippecanoe County, 1994-98; bd. dirs. Cmty. Ventures in Living, Inc., Ctisis Ctr. of Tippecanoe County, Tippecanoe County Coun. for Child Abuse Prevention. Mem. ABA, Ind. Bar Assn., Mo. Bar Assn., Tippecanoe County Bar Assn. Avocation: swimming. Juvenile, General civil litigation, Family and matrimonial. Office: 324 Main St Lafayette IN 47901-1316

**GARWOOD, WILLIAM LOCKHART,** federal judge; b. Houston, Tex., Oct. 29, 1931; s. Wilmer St. John and Ellen Burdine (Clayton) G.; m. Merle Castlyn Haffler, Aug. 12, 1955; children: William Lockhart, Mary Elliott. BA, Princeton U., 1952; LLB with honors, U. Tex., 1955. Bar: Tex. 1955, U.S. Supreme Ct. 1959. Law clk. to judge U.S. Ct. Appeals (5th cir.), 1955-56; mem. Graves, Dougherty, Hearon, Moody & Garwood (and predecessor firms), Austin, Tex., 1959-79, 81; justice Supreme Ct. Tex., Austin, 1979-80; judge U.S. Ct. Appeals (5th cir.), 1981-97, sr. judge, 1999-; dir. Anderson, Clayton & Co., 1976-79, 81, exec. com., 1977-79, 81; mem. adv. com. on appellate rules U.S. Cts., 1994—, chair 1997—. Pres. Child and Family Service of Austin, 1970-71, St. Andrew's Episcopal Sch., Austin, 1972; bd. dirs. Community Council Austin and Travis County, 1968-72, Human Opportunities Corp. Austin and Travis County, 1966-70, Mental Health and Mental Retardation Ctr. Austin and Travis County, 1966-69, United Fund Austin and Travis County, 1971-73; mem. adv. bd. Salvation Army, Austin, 1972—. Served with U.S. Army, 1956-59. Fellow Tex. Bar Found. (life); mem. Tex. Law Rev. Assn. (pres. 1990-91, dir. 1986-96), Am. Law Inst. (life), Am. Judicature Soc., Order of Coif, Chancellors, Phi Delta Phi. Episcopalian. Office: US Ct Appeals Homer Thornberry Jud Bldg 903 San Jacinto Blvd Austin TX 78701-2450

**GARY, THOMAS,** lawyer; b. Englewood, N.J., Apr. 29, 1950; s. Alfred and Gloria Gary; m. Deborahann Theresa Berko (div.); 1 child, Jordan Ian; m. Olga C. Puerto, Nov. 23, 1994. BA, Oberlin Coll., 1972; JD, Emory U., 1975; LLM in Taxation, U. Miami, 1984, MBA, 1997. Bar: Pa. 1975, Mo. 1980, U.S. Supreme Ct. 1980, Fla. 1983, U.S. Dist. Ct. (so. dist.) Fla. 1986, U.S. Ct. Appeals (11th cir.) 1986. Law clk. to Hon. Caleb R. Layton III Wilmington, Del., 1975-76; assoc. in contract litigation White and Williams, Phila., 1976-78; assoc. in comml. litigation Morgan, Lewis & Bockius, Phila., 1978-80; ptnr. in labor litigation Elliot, Kaiser & Freeman, kansas City, Mo., 1980-82; assoc. in contract and comml. litigation Niewald, Waldeck, Norris & Brown, kansas City, 1982-83; dir. tax practice Beasley, Olle & Downs, Miami, Fla., 1984-85; prin. Thomas Gary & Assocs., P.A., Coral Gables, Fla., 1985—. Bd. editors The Matrimonial Strategist, 1998—. Mem. oversight com. Put Something Back, 1996—; mem. Coral Gables City/H.S. Rels. Com., 1995—. Mem. Coral Gables Bar Assn. (pres. 1998-99), Dade County Bar Assn. (bd. dirs. 1997—), Rotary Club of Coral Gables (bd. dirs., program chair 1998—). Family and matrimonial. Home: 4114 Palmarito St Coral Gables FL 33146-1314 Office: Thomas Gary & Assocs PA 301 Almeria Ave Ste 3 Coral Gables FL 33134-5822

**GARZA, EMILIO M(ILLER),** federal judge; b. San Antonio, Tex., Aug. 1, 1947; s. Antonio Peña and Dionisia (Miller) G. BA, U. Notre Dame, 1969, MA, 1970; JD, U. Tex., 1976. Assoc. Clemens, Spencer, Welmaker & Finck, San Antonio, 1976-82; ptnr. Clemens, Spencer, Welmaker & Finck, San Antonio, Tex., 1982-87; dist. judge 225th Dist. Ct., Bexar County, San Antonio, 1987-88; U.S. dist. judge U.S. Dist. Ct. (we. dist.) Tex., San Antonio, 1988-91; U.S. cir. judge U.S. Ct. Appeals (5th cir.), San Antonio, 1991—. Bd. dirs. Symphony Soc. San Antonio, 1987-89; mem. Century Club San Antonio, 1987-88; adv. coun. U. Tex. San Antonio Coll. Fine Arts and Humanities, 1992-98; adv. bd. Phoenix Inst., 1992—; bd. advisors Hispanic Law Jour. U. Tex. at Austin Sch. Law, 1992-96; adv. com. Notre Dame Law Sch., 1998—. Capt. USMCR, 1970-79, active duty, 1970-73. Mem. State Bar Tex., San Antonio Bar Assn. Office: 8200 I-10 W Ste 501 San Antonio TX 78230

**GASCH, OLIVER,** judge; b. 1906. AB, Princeton U., 1928; LLB, George Washington U., 1932. Ast. corp. counsel, 1937-53, prin. U.S. atty., 1953-56; U.S. atty. D.C., 1956-61; ptnr. Craighill, Aiello, Gasch & Craighill, 1961-65; dist. judge U.S. Dist. Ct., Washington, 1965-99. With U.S. Army, 1942-46, PTO. Fellow Am. Bar Found., Am. Coll. of Trial Lawyers, mem. ABA, Bar Assn D.C. (pres. 1964-65), Fed. Bar Assn. (chmn. com. of gen. counsel 1960-61), Fed. Bar Assn., Am. Law Inst. (life), Barristers D.C. (pres. 1963). Office: US Dist Ct US Courthouse 3d & Constitution Ave NW Washington DC 20001 *Died July 1999.*

**GASIORKIEWICZ, EUGENE ANTHONY,** lawyer; b. Milw., Jan. 7, 1950; s. Eugene Constantine and Loretta Ann (Kasprzak) G.; m. Jana Jamieson, Jan. 12, 1980; children: Suzanne A., Alexei E. AB, Regis Coll., 1971; JD, U. Miss., 1974. Bar: Wis. 1974, U.S. Supreme Ct. 1986. Law clk. to presiding justice Miss. Supreme Ct., Jackson, 1974-75; assoc. Schoone, McManus & Hanson S.C., Racine, Wis., 1975-79; ptnr. Hanson & Gasiorkiewicz S.C., Racine, Wis., 1979-90; pres., shareholder Hanson, Gasiorkiewicz & Weber, S.C., Racine, 1990-96, Hanson & Gasiorkiewicz, S.C., Racine, 1997—; lectr. labor law U. Wis., Racine, 1975-76, worker's comp., State Bar Wis., 1984-86, med. malpractice, Wis. Acad. Trial Lawyers, 1986. Mcpl. judge Village of Wind Point, Wis., 1983-85; moot ct. instr., The Prairie Sch., Racine, 1986-87. Mem. State Bar Wis., Assn. Trial Lawyers Am., Am. Arbitration Assn., Wis. Acad. Trial Lawyers, Nat. Bd. Trial Advocacy (cert. civil trial advocate). Roman Catholic. Avocation: tennis. Personal injury, Federal civil litigation. Home: 3929 S Brook Rd Franksville WI 53126-9303 Office: Hanson & Gasiorkiewicz SC 2932 Northwestern Ave Racine WI 53404-2249

**GASKINS, EURA DUVAL, JR.,** lawyer; b. New Bern, N.C., May 15, 1941; s. Eura Duval Sr. and Arleigh (Skinner) G.; m. Ann Beal, Aug. 29, 1965; children: Natalie Ann, Meredith Nicole. BA, Wake Forest U., 1963; JD, Duke U., 1966. Bar: N.C. 1966, U.S. Ct. Appeals (4th cir.) 1971, U.S. Dist. Ct. (mid. and ea. dists.) N.C. 1973, U.S. Dist. Ct. (we. dist.) 1979, U.S. Ct. Appeals (D.C. cir.) 1981, U.S. Dist. Ct. (D.C. dist.) 1981, U.S. Ct. Claims, 1981, U.S. Supreme Ct., 1983, U.S. Ct. Appeals (fed. cir.) 1983. Assoc. Sanford & Cannon, Raleigh, N.C., 1966, Sanford, Cannon, Adams & McCullough, Raleigh, 1969-71; ptnr. Adams, McCullough & Beard, Raleigh, 1971-90; mng. ptnr. Everett, Gaskins, Hancock & Stevens, Raleigh, 1990—. Chmn. bd. Life Enrichment Counseling Ctr., Raleigh, 1977-78, Theatre in the Park, Raleigh, 1984; me. Sch. Bd. Adv. Coun., 1987—; deacon Hayes Barton Bapt. Ch., 1980—; trustee Raleigh Bapt. Assn., 1981—. Named Boss of Yr. Wake County Legal Secs. Assn., 1989. Mem. Greater Raleigh C. of C. (Svc. award 1989). Democrat. Avocations: running, tennis. Contracts commercial, General civil litigation, Construction. Office: PO Box 911 Raleigh NC 27602-0911

**GASPER, ROBERT W.,** judge, lawyer; b. Long Beach, Calif., Jan. 18, 1955; s. John Stephen Gasper and Patsy Joann Cassaday; m. Carol Ann McKinney, Feb. 22, 1987; children: Christina Gasper, Colin Val Gasper, Wesley Von Gasper. BA, UCLA, 1977; JD, U. San Diego, 1979. Bar: Calif. 1979, U.S. Dsit. Ct. (no., ctrl. and so. dists.) Calif. 1980. Judge protem L.A. and Orange County Superior Ct., 1984—; family law mediator L.A. County Superior Ct., 1984—; court appointed counsel for minors L.A. & Orange County Superior Cts., 1986—; pvt. practice Long Beach, Calif. Mem. Long Beach Bar Assn. (bd. governors 1982—), L.A. County Bar Assn. (mem. family law sect. 1984—). Avocations: history, basketball, youth diversion activities, surfing, gardening. Office: 110 Pine Ave Ste 810 Long Beach CA 90802-4425

**GASS, RAYMOND WILLIAM,** lawyer, consumer products company executive; b. Chgo., Apr. 6, 1937; s. William Frederick and Clara Gertrude (Grotman) G.; m. Patricia Ann Thomas, Apr. 20, 1968; children: Elizabeth Ann, Katharine Patricia, Christina Susanne. BS, Purdue U., 1959; LLB, U. Ill., 1962. Bar: Ill. Patent examiner U.S. Patent Office, Washington, 1962-63; atty. Armour and Co., Chgo., 1963-70; sr. atty. Greyhound Corp., Chgo., 1970-71; sr. v.p., gen. counsel, sec. John Morrell & Co., Chgo., 1971-89; v.p., gen. counsel Alberto-Culver Co., Melrose Park, Ill., 1989-98; bd. dirs. Am. Chemet Corp., Columbia Paint and Coating Co. Mem. ABA, Chgo. Bar Assn. (chmn. com. corp. law depts. 1975-77). General corporate, Labor, Antitrust.

**GAST, RICHARD SHAEFFER,** lawyer; b. Pueblo, Colo., Aug. 1, 1956; s. Robert Shaeffer and Ann (Day) G.; m. Beverly Paterson, Aug. 22, 1981; children: Charles Edward, Robert Shaeffer. BA, Stanford U., 1978; JD, U. Colo., 1981. Bar: Colo. 1981, U.S. Dist. Ct. Colo. 1981. Assoc. March, Myatt, Korb, Carroll & Brandes, Ft. Collins, Colo., 1981-85; shareholder, officer, dir. March & Myatt, P.C., Ft. Collins, Colo., 1985-97, Myatt Brandes & Gast PC, Ft. Collins, 1998—; bd. dirs. Elk Falls Ranch Co.; mem. Jud. Performance Commn., 1992-94. Contbg. editor U. Colo. Law Rev., 1980-81. Organizer local fundraising Am. Cancer Soc., Ft. Collins, 1985-86; mem. Larimer County Land Use Plan Citizens' Rev. Com., Ft. Collins, 1986; mem. choices 95 com., Ft. Collins, 1988; dir. Colo. Lawyers Trust Account Found., 1990-96, chair, grants com., 1990-96, pres., 1995-96; bd. dirs. Ft. Collins Area United Way, 1991-98, pres., 1996-97; bd. dirs. Neighbor to Neighbor, Inc., 1988-91; hearing officer Poudre Sch. Dist., 1995-97. Mem. ABA (corps., bus. and banking law sect.), Colo. Bar Assn. (mem. exec. coun. young lawyers divsn. 1988-91, chmn. 1990-91, bd. govs. 1990-91, 97-98, v.p. 1997-98, exec. coun. 1997-98, budget com. 1997—, real estate sect. coun. 1998—, bd. govs. 1990-91, 97-98, named Outstanding Young Lawyer 1987), Larimer County Bar Assn. (chmn. legal aid program 1986, chmn.-elect young lawyers sect. 1986-87, chmn. 1987-88), Ft. Collins C. of C. (legis. affairs commn. 1988-92). Democrat. Episcopalian. Avocations: skiing, running, soccer, backpacking, mountain biking. Banking, General corporate, Real property. Home: 1129 Oakmont Ct Fort Collins CO 80525-2855 Office: Myatt Brandes & Gast PC 323 S College Ave Ste 1 Fort Collins CO 80524-2845

**GASTL, EUGENE FRANCIS,** lawyer; b. Shawnee, Kans., Apr. 28, 1932; s. Bert J. and Bessie C. (Bell) G.; m. Deanna J. Cordon, June 7, 1959 (div. May 1978); children: Philip E., Catherine L., David B., Brenda M.; m. Arline Blackwood, June 15, 1979. BA, U. Kans., 1954, BL, 1956, JD, 1968. Bar: Kans. 1956, U.S. Dist. Ct. Kans. 1956. Sole practice Shawnee, 1959—. State rep. Kans. Legislature, Topeka, 1961-65, 71-79, senator, 1965-69. Served to specialist grade 3 U.S. Army, 1956-58. Mem. ABA, Kans. Bar Assn., Johnson County Bar Assn., Assn. Trial Lawyers Am., Shawnee C. of C. (v.p. 1965-67). Democrat. Methodist. Lodge: Optimist (bd. dirs. 1961-63). Avocation: reading. Probate, Family and matrimonial, Workers' compensation. Home: 5420 Bluejacket St Shawnee Mission KS 66203-1924 Office: 5811 Nieman Rd Shawnee Mission KS 66203-2855

**GASTWIRTH, STUART LAWRENCE,** lawyer; b. N.Y.C., Feb. 26, 1939; s. Jack Keith and Lillian (Gurchinsky) G.; m. Norma Blechman, June 13, 1965; children—Andrew Evan, David Eric, Jason Marc. B.A., Hofstra U., 1959; J.D., Cornell U., 1962. Bar: N.Y. 1963. Assoc., Cole & Deitz, N.Y.C., 1962-67; atty. Central State Bank, N.Y.C., 1967-69; ptnr. Semon & Gastwirth, Jericho, N.Y., 1969-75; sole practice, Jericho, 1975-81; ptnr. Gastwirth, Mirsky & Heller, Manhasset, N.Y., predecessor firm Gastwirth & Mirsky, 1981-97; ptnr. Gastwirth & Mirsky, 1997—. Bd. dirs. Kings Point Civic Assn., pres. Chmn. Adult Edn. Adv. Com., Great Neck, 1982; mem. exec. com. PTA North High Sch., Great Neck, 1983-85, pres., 1984-86, corr. sec., 1992, 93, 2d v.p., 1994, 1st v.p., 1995. Mem. Nassau County Bar Assn., N.Y. State Bar Assn., Bank Lawyers Conf. of N.Y. Jewish. Clubs: Exchange of North Shore (pres. 1972-73) (L.I., N.Y.), Great Neck Community Fund. Real property, Probate, General corporate. Home: 12 Creek Rd Great Neck NY 11024-1104

**GATES, GREGORY ANSEL,** lawyer; b. Cortland, N.Y., Sept. 25, 1953; s. Herbert Ansel and Mary (O'Connor) G.; m. Margaret Anne Schell, Aug. 9, 1975; children: Ryan Mary, Connor Ansel. BA, SUNY, Oswego, 1975; JD, Albany Law Sch. Union U., 1978. Bar: N.Y. 1979, U.S. Dist. Ct. (no. dist.) N.Y. 1979, U.S. Dist. Ct. (no. dist.) Calif. 1985, U.S. Ct. Appeals (2d cir.) 1993, U.S. Supreme Ct. 1994. Assoc. Levene Gouldin and Thompson, Binghamton, N.Y., 1979-84, ptnr., 1984-85; ptnr. Hickey, Sheehan and Gates, Binghamton, N.Y., 1985—; mem. Continuing Edn. Adv. Com., Binghamton, 1982-87. Commn. of Elections Broome County Gov., Binghamton, 1984-97, town justice, 1997—; dir. Binghamton Whalers Found., 1987--; counsel Broome County Democratic Com., 1984-87. Mem. ABA, N.Y. Bar Assn., Assn. Trial Lawyers Am., Broome County Bar Assn. (dir. 1988-91). Democrat. Roman Catholic. Avocations: hockey, golf, travel. General civil litigation, Personal injury, Criminal. Office: Hickey Sheehan and Gates PO Box 2124 Binghamton NY 13902-2124

**GATES, MARSHALL L.,** lawyer; b. Oakland, Calif., Aug. 3, 1947; s. Edward S. and Florence G.; m. Linda B. Chait, Sept. 3, 1972; children: Andrea, Jennifer, Jeffrey. BA, Rutgers U., 1969; JD, N.Y. Law Sch., 1972. Bar: N.J. 1973, U.S. Dist. Ct. N.J. 1973, U.S. Supreme Ct. 1983; cert. civil and criminal trial atty., 1982. Atty. Johnson & Johnson, Dover, N.J., 1973-76; pvt. practice Succasunna, N.J., 1976—. Coun. mem. Roxbury Twp., Succasunna, 1990—; criminal justice study commn. Morris County, Morristown, N.J., 1974-76. Avocations: family, sports, sports memorabilia. General civil litigation, Personal injury, Criminal. Office: 164 Route 10 W Succasunna NJ 07876-1434

**GATES, PAMELA SUE,** lawyer; b. Anamosa, Iowa, June 28, 1971; d. John Francis and Diane Kay Frasher; m. William Shane Gates, May 25, 1996. BA, Drake U., 1993; JD, U. Iowa, 1996. Bar: Ariz. 1996, U.S. Dist. Ct. Ariz. 1996. Lawyer Bryan Cave LLP, Phoenix, 1996—. Vol. Sojourner Ctr., Phoenix, 1998. Republican. Roman Catholic. Avocations: running, golf, community involvement. Environmental, General civil litigation, Toxic tort.

**GATES, PETER P.,** lawyer; b. N.Y.C., Dec. 27, 1934; s. John Monteith Gates and Ellen (Crenshaw) Houghton; m. Joan Bryan, Oct. 10, 1957; children: Peter NcNair, Courtlandt Dixon, Katharine Lansing. BA, Harvard U., 1956; LLB, Columbia U., 1963. Bar: N.Y. 1963, U.S. Ct. Appeals (2nd cir.) 1966, U.S. Dist. Ct. (so. dist.) N.Y. 1973. Assoc. Carter, Ledyard & Milburn, N.Y.C., 1963-71, ptnr., 1971—. With U.S. Army, 1957-60. em. ABA, N.Y. State Bar Assn., N.Y. County Bar Assn., Assn. of Bar of City of N.Y., Downtown Assn. (pres. 1991-97). Non-profit and tax-exempt organizations, Contracts commercial, General corporate. Home: 325 E 57th St New York NY 10022-2935 Office: Carter Ledyard & Milburn 2 Wall St New York NY 10005-2072

**GATES, STEPHEN FRYE,** lawyer, business executive; b. Clearwater, Fla., May 20, 1946; s. Orris Allison and Olga Betty (Frye) G.; m. Laura Daignault, June 10,, 1972. BA in Econs., Yale U., 1968; JD, Harvard U., 1972, MBA, 1972. Bar: Fla. 1972, Mass. 1973, Ill. 1977, Colo. 1986. Assoc. Choate Hall & Stewart, Boston, 1973-77; atty. Amoco Corp., Chgo., 1977-82; gen. atty. Amoco Corp., 1982-86; regional atty. Amoco Prodn. Co., Denver, 1987-88; asst. treas. Amoco Corp., Chgo., 1988-91, assoc. gen. counsel, corp. sec., 1991-92; v.p. Amoco Chem. Co., 1993-95; v.p., gen. counsel Amoco Corp., Chgo., 1995-98; exec. v.p., group chief of staff BP Amoco p.l.c., London, 1999—; bd. dirs. Nat. Legal Ctr. Pub. Interest, Wash., 1999—. Nat. trustee Newberry Libr., Chgo., 1998—; bd. dirs. Chgo. Sister Cities Internat. Program, Inc., Friends of Prentice Hosp.; mem. adv. coun. Chgo. Schweitzer Urban Fellows Program, 1996—; mem. adv. bd. Chgo. Vol. Legal Svcs., Found., 1996-98; mem. Chgo. Crime Commn., 1997-98. Knox fellow, 1972-73. Mem. ABA, Am. Soc. Corp. Secs., Univ. Club, Mid-Am. Club, Yale Club. Securities, General corporate. Office: BP Amoco PLC, 1 Finsbury Circus, London EC2M 7BA, England

**GATEWOOD, TELA LYNNE,** lawyer; b. Cedar Rapids, Iowa, Mar. 23; d. Chester Russell and Cecilia Mae (McFarland) Weber. BA with distinction, Cornell Coll., Mt. Vernon, Iowa, 1970; JD with distinction, U. Iowa, 1972. Bar: Iowa 1973, Calif. 1974, U.S. Supreme Ct. 1984. Instr. LaVerne Coll., Pt. Mugu, Calif., 1973; asst. city atty. City of Des Moines, 1973-78; sr. trial atty. and supervisory atty. EEOC, Dallas, Phila., 1978-91, acting regional atty. Dallas Dist., 1987-89; adminstrv. judge EEOC, Dallas, 1991-94; adminstrv. law judge Social Security Adminstrn., Oklahoma City, 1994—. Bd. dirs. Day Care Inc., Des Moines, 1975-78, sec., 1977, pres., 1978. Mem. ABA (labor law, litigation, govt. svc., judiciary sects.), NAFE, Nat. Assn. Female Judges, Fed. Bar Assn., U.S. Supreme Ct. Bar Assn., Calif. Bar Assn. Office: Social Security Adminstrn Office of Hearings and Appeals 420 W Main St Ste 400 Oklahoma City OK 73102-4435

**GATHRIGHT, HOWARD T.,** lawyer; b. Phila., May 3, 1935; s. Howard W. and Rose (McGurk) G.; m. Natalie Acquaviva, June 22, 1963 (div. May 1991); children: Donna Marie, Gary Thomas. BA, U. Pa., 1957; JD, Temple U., 1963. Bar: Pa. 1964, U.S. Dist. Ct. Pa. 1964, U.S. Supreme Ct. 1968. Ptnr. Pratt, Gathright & Brett, P.C., Doylestown, Pa., 1964—; with Gathright & Leonard, Doylestown, Pa., 1990—; asst. dist. atty. of Bucks County, Pa., 1966-69; solicitor Doylestown Twp., Pa., 1970-75, New Hope Sewage Project of Bucks County Water and Sewer Authority, 1971-76; bd. dirs. Bean, Mason & Eyer, Doylestown. Bd. dirs. Am. Lung Assn., 1970—; pres. Bucks County Estate Planning Coun., 1972; active Bucks County Emergency Health Coun., Inc., 1977-79; apptd. by gov. to Bucks County Spl. Trial Ct. Nominating Commn., 1987. Served in U.S. Army, 1957, USAR, 1958-63. Mem. ABA, Phila. Bar Assn., Pa. Bar Assn., Bucks County Bar Assn. (pres. 1986-87), Assn. Trial Lawyers Am., Pa. Trial Lawyers Assn., Cen. Bucks C. of C. (pres. 1975, chmn. bd. dirs. 1976, Man of Yr. 1975). Democrat. Roman Catholic. Avocations: sports, tennis. Fax: 215-230-7736. E-mail: gathrightg@aol.com. State civil litigation, Estate planning, Real property. Office: PO Box 310 Doylestown PA 18901-0310

**GATLIN, MICHAEL GERARD,** lawyer, educator; b. Kittery, Maine, May 9, 1956; s. James Patrick and Florence (Lesperance) G.; m. Judith E. Ziman, Nov. 7, 1987; children: Vanessa Marie, Alexandra Elizabeth. BA, Framingham State Coll., 1978; JD, New Eng. Sch. Law, 1982. Bar: Mass. 1982, U.S. Dist. Ct. Mass. 1983, U.S. Ct. Appeals (1st cir.) 1983. Mem. adj. faculty dept. law Dean Jr. Coll., Franklin, Mass., 1986-92; ptnr. Gaynor & Gatlin, Framingham, Mass., 1988—. Bd. dirs., pres. Wayside Cmty. Programs, Inc., Framingham, 1978—; bd. dirs. South Middlesex Consumer Assistance Office-Metrowest, Inc., Framingham; mem. Framingham Planning Bd., 1992-93; chmn. Metrowest AIDS Consortium, 1993—. Recipient citation Mass. Ho. of Reps., 1984. Mem. Mass. Bar Assn., South Middlesex Bar Assn. (pres. 1991-92). Democrat. Contracts commercial, Banking, Labor. Home: 727 Salem End Rd Framingham MA 01702-5542 Office: Gaynor & Gatlin 14 Vernon St Ste 108 Framingham MA 01701-4733

**GATTERMEYER, DANIEL J.,** lawyer; b. Hamilton, Ohio, May 4, 1958; s. Eugene and Mary L. (Hoelle) G.; m. Pamela J. Sloan; children: Tyler, Todd, John, Morgan. BA, Ohio U., 1980; JD, Case Western Reserve U., 1983. Pvt. practice Hamilton, 1983—; asst. prosecutor Butler County Prosecutor's Office, Hamilton, 1985—. Mem. adv. coun. St. Raphael's Social Svc., Hamilton, 1996—; mem. edn. commn. St. Peter in Chains Ch., Hamilton, 1996—; coach West Side Little League, SAY Soccer, Hamilton. Democrat. Roman Catholic. Avocations: basketball, hockey. Workers' compensation, Pension, profit-sharing, and employee benefits, Personal injury. Office: 2 S 3rd St Ste 405 Hamilton OH 45011-6052

**GATTI, JOHN GABRIEL,** law educator, lawyer; b. Bklyn., Oct. 16, 1955; s. Gabriel John and Gloria Bonano Gatti; m. Barbara Scalici, May 15, 1983 (div. Oct. 1998); 1 child, Laura Elizabeth. BA in History and Polit. Sci., Fordham U., 1977; JD, Boston Coll., 1981. Bar: N.Y. 1986, U.S. Supreme Ct. 1990. Tchr., asst. dir. student activities Monsignor Farrell H.S., S.I., N.Y., 1982-86, 89-96; assoc. Law Office of Peter J. Napolitano, S.I., 1986-87, Lee & Antis, S.I., 1987-89; tchr., dir. Performing Arts Inst. Moore Cath. H.S., S.I., 1996-98; tchr. law, English, social studies Bd. of Edn., N.Y.C., 1998—; dir. youth program Richmond County Country Club, S.I., summers 1997, 98; adj. instr. dept. bus. Wagner Coll., S.I., summers, 1989, 90; bd. dirs., artistic cons., dir., performer Seaview Playwright's Theatre, S.I., 1986—; bd. dirs., v.p., performer, dir. S.I. Civic Theatre, 1981-95. Performer in numerous comty. theater prodns., 1977— (20-Yr. Achievement award 1997); dir., prodr. numerous comty. theater prodns., 1977— (20-Yr. Achievement award 1997). Vol. Dem. Party, S.I., 1990—, Campaign of Vito Fossella, S.I., 1996, Campaign of Lou Tobacco, S.I., 1996. Recipient Performer's award S.I. Register, 1985, Achievement award S.I. Civic Theatre, 1990. Mem. Nat. Assn. English Tchrs., N.Y. State Bar Assn., Richmond County Bar Assn., S.I. Rotary (Fundraising Effort award). Democrat. Roman Catholic. Avocations: theater, music, running, boxing, film. Home: 200 Westervelt Ave Staten Island NY 10301-1406

**GATTUSO, DINA,** lawyer; b. Phila.; d. Paul John and Erminia C. Gattuso. BA, Monmouth Coll., West Long Branch, N.J., 1989; JD, Ohio No. U., 1994. Assoc. atty. Law Offices of Franc J.H. Marmero, P.C., Berlin, N.J., 1995—; pub. defender Hi-Nella (N.J.) Boro Mcpl. Ct., 1997—; spl. prosecutor Winslow Twp. Mcpl. Ct., 1998—. Mem. ABA, Camden County Bar Assn. Family and matrimonial, Municipal (including bonds). Office: Law Offices Franc JH Marmero 1040 S Route 73 Berlin NJ 08009-2600

**GAUBY, KARL MARTIN,** lawyer, educator; b. Dayton, Ohio, Apr. 15, 1958; s. Carl William and Georgetta (Hulett) G.; m. Lola David, June 20, 1986; children: Stephanie, Brandon. BA, Berea Coll., 1980; BS, Eastern Ky. U., 1983, MS, 1984; MS, Golden Gate U., 1987; JD, Ariz. State U., 1990, PhD, 1998. Bar: Ariz. 1992, D.C. 1992, U.S. Dist. Ct. Ariz. 1992. Lab. dir. U.S. Pub. Health Svc., Fort Defiance, Ariz., 1983-84, USAF, Luke AFB, Ariz., 1984-88; lawyer Cates & Holloway, Scottsdale, Ariz., 1990-95; sr. counsel U. Phoenix, 1995—. Co-author: (with others) State Trademark and Unfair Competition Law, 1991-95; lectr. in field. Referee Am. Youth Soccer Assn., Phoenix, 1995—; active Phoenix Boys Choir, 1995—, Phoenix Indian Medical Ctr., 1993—. Lt. Col. USAF, 1997—. Recipient Alumni award Ariz. State U., 1997. Mem. Nat. Cert. Agy. (lab. mgmt. exam. writer 1988-90), Am. Soc. Clinical Pathologists (state adv., southwest region 1988-90), Sigma Xi, Phi Sigma, Phi Kappa Phi. Republican. Protestant. Avocations: scuba, skiing, travel, music. E-mail: karl@phoenix.edu. Fax: (602) 968-1159. Home: 3839 E Cathedral Rock Dr Phoenix AZ 85044-6626 Office: Univ Phoenix 4615 E Elwood St Phoenix AZ 85040-1908

**GAUGHAN, DENNIS CHARLES,** lawyer; b. Buffalo, July 3, 1955; s. Charles Joseph Gaughan and Mary Lynn Rucker; m. Mary Rose DeBergalis, Sept. 22, 1989; children: Charles Joseph, Dennis Charles Jr., Joseph Rocco. BA, Syracuse U., 1978; JD, N.Y. Law Sch., 1982. Bar: N.Y. 1984, U.S. Dist. Ct. (we. dist.) N.Y. 1984, U.S. Ct. Appeals (2d cir.) 1984, U.S. Supreme Ct. 1988. Counsel Erie County Dept. Social Svcs., Buffalo, 1984-89; pvt. practice, Hamburg, N.Y., 1989—; asst. town atty. Town of Hamburg, 1995—; prosecutor Village of Blasdell, N.Y. Chmn. Hamburg Rep. Ctrl. Com. 1988-90. Served with USAR, 1983-89. Mem. Nat. Assn. Criminal Lawyers, N.Y. Trial Lawyers Assn., Erie County Bar Assn., KC, Am. Legion, Am. Vets. Roman Catholic. Criminal, Bankruptcy, Family and matrimonial. Home: 5156 Pebble Beach Dr Hamburg NY 14075-5860 Office: 6161 S Park Ave Hamburg NY 14075-3837

**GAUGHAN, JOHN STEPHEN,** lawyer; b. Chgo., Dec. 26, 1932; s. James Joseph and Margaret (Mohaghan) G.; m. Barbara L. Jansen, Aug. 10, 1959; children: Brian, Dennis, Kevin. BS, DePaul U., 1954, JD, 1962. Bar: Ill. 1962, Calif. 1969. Supr. rules and regulations State of Ill. Dept. Revenue, Chgo., 1962-67; supr. charitable trust Ill. Atty. Gen., Chgo., 1967-68; sole practice Santa Ana, Calif., 1969—. Served with U.S. Army, 1954-56. Mem. ABA, Calif. Bar Assn., Ill. Bar Assn. Lodge: Elks. General civil litigation, Consumer commercial, Probate. Home: 4 Rue Chateau Royal Newport Beach CA 92660-5904 Office: 17291 Irvine Blvd Ste 411 Tustin CA 92780-2932

**GAUNT, JANET LOIS,** arbitrator, mediator; b. Lawrence, Mass., Aug. 23, 1947; d. Donald Walter and Lois (Neuhart) Bacon; m. Frank Peyton Gaunt, Dec. 21, 1969; children: Cory C., Andrew D. BA, Oberlin Coll., 1969; JD, Wash. U., St. Louis, 1974. Bar: Wash. 1974, U.S. Dist. Ct. (we. dist.) Wash. 1974, U.S. Ct. Appeals (9th cir.) 1978. Assoc. Davis, Wright, Todd, Riese & Jones, Seattle, 1974-80; arbitrator/mediator Seattle, 1981—; ldir. Seattle King County Labor Law Sect., 1976-77; mem. Pacific Coast Labor Law Planning Com., 1977-83; com. vice chmn. Wash. State Task Force on Gender and Justice on the Cts., 1987-89; chmn. Wash. Pub. Employment Rels. Commn., Olympia, 1989-96. Author, editor: Alternative Dispute Resolution, 1989; author: Public Sector Labor Mediation and Arbitration, Arbitration and Mediation in Washington, 2d edit., 1995. Pres. State Bd. of Wash. Women Lawyers, 1986. Mem. Nat. Acad. Arbitrators (dir. rsch. and edn. found. 1991-96, bd. govs. 1998—), Am. Arbitration Assn., Wash. State Bar Assn.

**GAUNTLETT, DAVID ALLAN,** lawyer; b. Long Beach, Calif., May 16, 1954; s. Allan Leonard Gauntlett and Nelly (Brown) Mayne. BA in History magna cum laude, U. Calif., Irvine, 1976; JD, U. Calif., Berkeley, 1979. Bar: Calif. 1980, U.S. Dist. Ct. (cen. dist.) Calif. 1982, U.S. Dist. Ct. (ea., no. and so. dists.) Calif. 1980, U.S. Ct. Appeals (9th cir.) 1987, U.S. Ct. Appeals (4th cir.) 1993, U.S. Supreme Ct. 1994. Assoc. Paul, Hastings, Janofsky & Walker, L.A., 1979-81, Vitti, Miles & Robinson, Newport Beach, Calif., 1981-83, Burkley, Moore, Greenberg & Lyman, Torrance, Calif., 1983-86; ptnr. Callahan & Gauntlett, Irvine, Calif., 1986-95, Gauntlett & Assocs., Irvine, 1995—. Prodn. mgr. U. Calif. Law Rev., 1978-79. Calif. state scholar. Mem. ABA (chmn. emeritus intellectual property com. torts and ins. practice sect. 1995-96, mem. emerging issues com. 1995—, chmn. com. on ins. intellectual property sect. 1995—, vice chmn. ins. coverage com. litigation sect. 1995-96), Calif. State Bar, Orange County Bar Assn., Assn. Bus. Trial Lawyers. Republican. Episcopalian. Avocations: bicycling, art collection, cooking, sailing, tennis. Federal civil litigation, Patent, Insurance. Office: Gauntlett & Assocs 18400 Von Karman Ave Ste 300 Irvine CA 92612-0505

**GAUS EHNING, MICHELE B.,** lawyer; b. Chgo., July 17, 1964; d. Edward and Gloria Jean (Pope) Gaus; m. Achim R.M. Ehning, Oct. 19, 1997. Student, U. Mich., 1982-83; BA, DePauw U., 1986; JD, John Marshall Law Sch., 1992. Bar: Ill. 1993, U.S. Dist. Ct. (no. dist.) Ill. 1993, U.S. Ct. Appeals (fed. and 7th cirs.) 1993, U.S. Ct. Internat. Trade 1993. Assoc. Riggle and Craven, Chgo., 1991-94; atty. Komatsu Am. Internat. Co., Vernon Hills, Ill., 1994—. Mem. ABA, Chgo. Bar Assn., Nat. Pks. and Conservation Assn. Avocations: musician playing flute and piano, hiking, skiing, snowshoe hiking, traveling. Environmental, General corporate, Real property. Home: 192 E Ranney Ave Vernon Hills IL 60061-4129 Office: Komatsu Am Internat Co 440 N Fairway Dr Vernon Hills IL 60061-1836

**GAUTHIER, CELESTE ANNE,** lawyer; b. New Orleans, Oct. 25, 1969; d. Wendell Haynes and Anne (Barrios) G.; 1 child, Trenton Michael. BA in Sociology, U. New Orleans, 1992; JD, Loyola U., New Orleans, 1995. Bar: La. 1996, U.S. Dist. Ct. (ea. dist.) La. 1996, U.S. Ct. Appeals (5th cir.) 1996. Law clk. Gauthier & Murphy, Metairie, La., 1992-95; law clk. to Hon. Judge Burns 24th Jud. Dist. Ct., Gretna, La., 1996, law clk. to Hon. Judge Sullivan, 1997-98; assoc. Gauthier, Downing, LaBarre, Beiser & Dean, Metairie, La., 1998—; advocate Jeff 25, Jefferson, La., 1997—. Mem. Country Day Parents Assn., Metairie, 1996—, St. Catherine of Siena Parish, Metairie, 1994—, Young Dems. Am., 1995—. Mem. ATLA, La. State Bar Assn. (young lawyers dist. 2 rep. 1998—), Jefferson Bar Assn. (treas. young lawyers sect. 1998, chair-elect 1999), New Orleans Bar Assn., La. Trial Lawyers Assn., Young Leadership Coun. Democrat. Roman Catholic. Avocations: spending time with my son, skiing, reading, walking, culinary interests. Personal injury, Product liability, General civil litigation. Office: Gauthier Downing LaBarre Beiser & Dean 3500 N Hullen St Metairie LA 70002-3420

**GAUTIER, AGNES M.,** lawyer; b. N.Y.C., Aug. 27, 1939; d. Paul and Lucrezia (Spano) Mercurio; m. Emilio P. Gautier, Jan. 19, 1974. BA, Barnard Coll., 1961; JD, NYU, 1964. V.p., gen. counsel J.H. Heineman, Inc., N.Y.C., 1964-73; v.p. N.Y. Stock Exch., N.Y.C., 1973—. Home: 706 E 18th St Brooklyn NY 11230-1801

**GAVER, FRANCES ROUSE,** lawyer; b. Lexington, Ky., Mar. 13, 1929; d. Colvin P. Rouse and Elizabeth Turner Sympson; m. Donald Paul Gaver, Jan. 24, 1953; children: Elizabeth, Donald, William. BA, Wellesley Coll., 1950; MA, U. Pitts., 1968; JD, Monterey (Calif.) Coll. of Law, 1986. Bar: Calif. 1986, U.S. Dist. Ct. (no. dist.) Calif. 1986; cert. specialist in probate, estate planing and trust law, Calif. Assoc. Hoge, Fenton, Jones & Appel, Monterey, 1986-93, Fenton & Keller, Monterey, 1993-97; ptnr. Johnson, Gaver & Leach, Monterey, 1997—. Bd. dirs. Carmel (Calif.) Unified Sch. Dist., 1973-81, Monterey Coll. of Law, 1991-97, Legal Svcs. for Srs., Pacific Grove, Calif., 1994—. Mem. Monterey County Bar Assn. Avocations: playing recorder, swimming. Probate, Estate planning, Estate taxation. Office: Johnson Gaver & Leach LLP 2801 Monterey Salinas Hwy Monterey CA 93940-6401

**GAVIGAN, JAMES COPLEY,** lawyer; b. N.Y.C., Dec. 11, 1946; s. William M. and Gail Lucinda (McCarthy) G.; m. Valerie Viator, Mar. 15, 1980; children: James, John. Diploma, Georgetown U., 1969, JD, 1972. Bar: Fla., 1973; U.S. Dist. Ct. (so. dist.) Fla. 1973. Asst. state atty. 15th Jud. Cir. Ct., Fla., 1973-76; assoc. Walton, Lantaff, Schroeder, Carson & Wohl, West Palm Beach, Fla., 1976-78; ptnr. Hoadley & Gavigan, Fla., 1978-88; pvt. practice Palm Beach, Fla., 1988—. Personal injury, Insurance. Home: 1510 N Ocean Blvd Palm Beach FL 33480-3068 Office: 400 Royal Palm Way Ste 214 Palm Beach FL 33480-4117

**GAWALT, GERARD W(ILFRED),** law historian, writer; b. Boston, Feb. 10, 1943; s. John R. and Regina M. (Chaloux) G.; m. Jane F. Cavanaugh, Aug. 6, 1966; children: Susan, Ann, Ellen. BA, Northeastern U., 1965; MA, Clark U., 1968, Ph.D., 1969. Reporter Milford Daily News, Mass., 1961-63, Worcester Telegram, Mass., 1963-65; instr. Assumption Coll., 1967-68, Clark U., 1968-69; hist. specialist Libr. of Congress, Washington, 1969—, specialist in legal history, 1969—; adj. prof. George Mason U., 1972, Cath. U. Am., 1981; guest lectr. George Washington U., Smithsonian Instn., Salem (Mass.) State U., Coll. of W.Va.; bd. dirs. on publ. of papers of James Monroe Ash Lawn-Highland (James Monroe's Plantation); cons. James Monroe Mus., Fredericksburg, Va.; mem. editl. bd. James Monroe's Papers. Author: Manuscript Sources in the Library of Congress for Research on the American Revolution, 1975, The Promise of Power: The Emergence of the Massachusetts Legal Profession 1760-1840, 1979 (Choice Outstanding Acad. Book of 1980), James Monroe: Presidential Planter, 1993, Roads to Relocation and Renewal: James Monroe and Native Americans, 1996, Gathering History: The American Collection of Marian S. Carson, 1999; also papers in legal and social history; editor: Journal of Gideon Olmsted, Adventures of a Revolutionary War Sea Captain, 1978, John Paul Jones' Memoir of the American Revolution, 1979, The New High Priests: Lawyers in Modern Industrial America, 1984, Narrative of William A. Burwell, 1993; assoc. editor Letters of Dels. to Congress, 1774-1789, 20 vols., 1976—, Political Writings of John J. Beckley, 1995, Jefferson's Slaves: Crop Accounts at Monticello, 1805-1808, 1994, Evolution of the Text of the Declaration of Independence, 1999, Gathering History: The Marian S. Carson Collection, 1999. Mem. publs. bd. Ash Lawn-Highland former home of James Monroe. Alumni scholar Northeastern U., 1960-61; fellow NDEA, 1965-68, Am. Coun. Learned Socs., 1979-80. Mem. Am. Soc. Legal History, Libr. of Congress Profl. Guild (treas. 1977-78, pres. 1978-79). Democrat. Roman Catholic. Home: 8805 Eagle Rock Ln Springfield VA 22153-1726

**GAWTHROP, ROBERT SMITH, III,** federal judge; b. 1942. BA, Amherst Coll., 1964; JD, Dickinson Sch. Law, 1970. Law clk. to Ho. Lee F. Swope Harrisburg, Pa., 1969-70; mem. firm Gawthrop & Greenwood, West Chester, Pa., 1970-78; asst. dist. atty. Office Dist. Atty., West Chester, 1971-78, Wayne County, Pa., 1976-77; judge Ct. Common Pleas, Chester County, 1978-88; dist. judge U.S. Dist. Ct. (ea. dist.) Pa., 1988—; adj. prof. trial advocacy Dickinson Sch. Law, Carlisle, Pa., 1981-82. Contbr. articles to profl. jours. Mem. Berks Grand Opera. 1st lt. Artillery OCS, 1965-67. Mem. ABA, Am. Judicature Soc., Federalist Soc. Law & Pub. Policy Studies, Pa. Bar Assn., Fed. Judges Assn., Fed. Bar Assn., The Savoy Co., The Ardensingers, Gilbert and Sullivan Players, Chester County Gilbert and Sullivan Soc., Orpheus Club, Quarry Club, Appalachian Mountain Club, Delta Kappa Epsilon, Phi Mu Alpha. Office: US Dist Ct 7613 US Courthouse 601 Market St Philadelphia PA 19106-1713

**GAY, BONNIE LEWIS,** lawyer; b. Newton Grove, N.C., Jan. 20, 1942; d. Clarence Henry and Patricia Lucile (Brock) Lewis; m. William Jan Gay, Mar. 10, 1962 (div. 1976); 1 child, Heather Laurie. BA, Am. U., 1962, LLB, 1964. Bar: Va. 1964, D.C. 1966, U.S. Supreme Ct., 1972, N.J. 1978. Law clk. to presiding justice U.S. Dist. Ct. D.C., 1964-66; pvt. practice law, McLean, Va., 1966-68; project dir. Computer Retrieval Systems, Bethesda, Md., 1968-70; atty. opinion sect. office gen. counsel Dept. Treasury, Washington, 1970-73, tech. asst. to asst. gen. counsel, 1974-77; legal counsel Bur. Engraving and Printing, Washington, 1977-80; of counsel office chief counsel Office Revenue Sharing, Washington, 1980-84; asst. dir. Legal Edn. Inst., Dept. Justice, Washington, 1984-89; atty. in charge FOIA/PA unit Exec. Office for U.S. Attys., 1989—; mem. faculty U. Md., 1980—. Contbr. articles to profl. jours.; editorial bd. Fed. Bar News and Jour., 1986-89. Bd. dirs., legal counsel Treasury Hist. Assn., 1973-76, 79-80, 81-83, 85—; sec. Cleve. Terr. Owners Assn., 1981-82; mem. Treasury Women's Adv. Com., 1974-76; trustee Universalist Nat. Meml. Ch., 1969-75, chmn. music, 1969-71, chmn. fin., 1971-75; bd. dirs. Treasury Dept. Fedn. Credit Union, 1975-77; mem. Dean's Adv. Coun. Washington Coll. Law, 1982-85. Mem. ABA (corp. and banking subcom., freedom of info. act and privacy, adminstr. law, vice chmn., continuing legal edn. com. 1988—), Fed. Bar Assn. (treas. D.C. chpt. 1982-83, bd. dirs. 1980-89, rec. sec. 1983-84, corr. sec. 1984-85, 2nd v.p. 1985-86, 1st v.p. 1986-87, pres. elect 1987-88, pres. 1988-89), D.C. Bar Assn. (sec. medico-legal com. 1973-75, mem. continuing legal edn. com. 1986-88—), Va. State Bar, Women's Bar Assn. D.C., Fed. Am. Inn of Ct., Kappa Beta Pi (province pres. 1972-74). Home: 7008 Benjamin St Mc Lean VA 22101-1549 Office: FOIA/PA Unit 601 D St NW Washington DC 20530-0001

**GAY, CARL LLOYD,** lawyer; b. Seattle, Nov. 11, 1950; s. James and Elizabeth Anne (Rogers) G.; m. Robin Ann Winston, Aug. 23, 1975; children: Patrick, Joel, Alexander, Samuel, Nora. Student, U. of Puget Sound, 1969-70; BS in Forestry cum laude, Wash. State U., 1974; JD, Willamette U., 1979. Bar: Wash. 1979, U.S. Dist. Ct. (we. dist.) Wash. 1979. With Taylor & Taylor, 1979-82, Taylor, Taylor & Gay, 1982-85; prin. Greenaway & Gay, Port Angeles, Wash., 1985-91, Greenaway, Gay & Tassie, Port Angeles, 1991-96, Greenaway, Gay & Angier, Port Angeles, 1996—; judge pro tem Clallam County, Port Angeles, 1981-85; commr. superior Ct., 1985-91; judge Juvenile Ct., 1985-87; instr. Guardian Ad Litem Program, Port Angeles, 1985—, Peoples Law Sch., 1989—. Bd. dirs. Cmty. Concert Assn., Port Angeles, 1982-85, 94—, pres., 1984-85, 88-89, 99—; bd. dirs. Am. Heart Assn., 1987—, Clallam County YMCA, 1988—, exec. com., 1995—; mem. adv. bd. Salvation Army, Port Angeles, 1982—; subdivsn. chmn., bd. dirs.

United Way Clallam County, 1987—; bd. dirs., pres. Friends of Libr., Port Angeles, 1983-91; trustee Fisher Cove, 1988—; advisor youth in govt. program YMCA, 1986—; advisor United Meth. Youth Coun., 1987—, trustee, 1989—; chmn. long-range planning com. Port Angeles Sch. Dist. Mem. ABA (real property, probate and trust and gen. practice sects.), ATLA, Wash. Bar Assn. (real property, probate, elder law and trust sects.), Clallam County Bar Assn. (pres. 1995), Nat. Coun. Juvenile and Family Ct. Judges, Superior Ct. Judges Assn. (com.), Wash. State Trial Lawyers Assn., Kiwanis (local bd. dirs. 1982-84, pres. 1986-87, Kiwanian of Yr. 1983-84), Elks. Lutheran. Avocations: backpacking, cross country skiing, raquetball, sailing. Probate, Real property, Contracts commercial. Home: 3220 Mcdougal St Port Angeles WA 98362-6738 Office: Greenaway Gay & Angier 829 E 8th St Ste A Port Angeles WA 98362-6418

**GAY, E(MIL) LAURENCE,** lawyer; b. Bridgeport, Conn., Aug. 10, 1923; s. Emil D. and Helen L. (Mihalich) G.; m. Harriet A. Ripley, Aug. 2, 1952; children: Noel L., Peter C., Marguerite S., Georgette A. BS, Yale U., 1947; JD magna cum laude, Harvard U., 1949. Bar: N.Y. 1950, Conn. 1960, Calif. 1981, Hawaii 1988. Assoc. Root, Ballantine, Harlan, Bushby & Palmer, N.Y.C., 1949-51; mem. legal staff U.S. High Commr. for Germany, Bad Godesberg, 1951-52; law sec., presiding justice appellate div. 1st dept. N.Y. Supreme Ct., N.Y.C., 1953-54; assoc. Debevoise, Plimpton & McLean, N.Y.C., 1954-58; v.p., sec.-treas., gen. counsel Hewitt-Robins, Inc., Stamford, Conn., 1958-65; pres. Litton Gt. Lakes Corp., N.Y.C., 1965-67; sr. v.p. finance AMFAC, Inc., Honolulu, 1967-73; vice chmn. AMFAC, Inc., 1974-78; fin. cons. Burlingame, Calif., 1979-82; of counsel Pettit & Martin, San Francisco, 1982-88, Goodsill, Anderson, Quinn & Stifel, Honolulu, 1988—. Editor Harvard Law Rev., 1948-49. Pres. Honolulu Symphony Soc., 1974-78; trustee Loyola Marymount U., 1977-80, San Francisco Chamber Soloists, 1981-86, Honolulu Chamber Music Series, 1988—; officer, dir. numerous arts and ednl. orgns. 2d lt. AUS, 1943-46. Mem. ABA, State Bar of Hawaii, Pacific Club (Honolulu), Nat. Assn. of Securities Dealers, Am. Arbitration Assn. (mem. arbitration panels), Phi Beta Kappa. Republican. Roman Catholic. Avocations: music, arts. General corporate, Securities, Contracts commercial. Home: 1159 Maunawili Rd Kailua HI 96734-4641 Office: Goodsill Anderson Quinn & Stifel PO Box 3196 Honolulu HI 96801-3196

**GAY, ESMOND PHELPS,** lawyer; b. New Orleans, Sept. 15, 1952; s. Charles Fenner and Harriott (Phelps) G.; m. Marian Enochs, June 6, 1981; children: Jacqueline Elinor, Marian Phelps. AB, Princeton (N.J.) U., 1975; JD, Tulane U., 1979. Bar: La. 1979, U.S. Dist. Ct. (ea. dist.) La. 1979, U.S. Ct. Appeals (5th cir.) 1986. Assoc. Christovich & Kearney, New Orleans, 1979-84, ptnr., 1985—. Mem. Met. Area Com., New Orleans, 1989—; elected participant Met. Leadership Forum, New Orleans, 1988. Mem. ABA, State Bar Tex., Internat. Bar Assn., Fed. Bar Assn., La. Bar Assn. (Ho. of Dels., pres.-elect 1999—), New Orleans Bar Assn. (bd. dirs. 1997—), Fed. Ins. and Corp. Counsel (chmn. maritime law com.), La. Assn. Def. Coun., Def. Rsch. Inst. Admiralty, Product liability, Personal injury. Home: 237 Hector Ave Metairie LA 70005-4117 Office: Christovich & Kearney 601 Poydras St Ste 2300 New Orleans LA 70130-6078*

**GAY, WILLIAM TOLIN,** lawyer; b. Everett, Wash., July 4, 1957; s. Warren Truman and Mary Margaret (McDonald) G.; m. Lori Rika Inano, May 14, 1988; 1 child, Christopher Tolin. JD, U. Wash., 1982, MBA, 1983, LLM, 1984. Bar: Wash. 1983, Calif. 1989, U.S. Dist. Ct. (we. dist.) Wash. 1983, U.S. Ct. Appeals (9th cir.) 1983, U.S. Dist. Ct. (so. dist.) Calif. 1989. Assoc. Blakemore & Mitsuki, Tokyo, 1984-87, Baker & McKenzie, Tokyo, 1987-88, Graham & James, L.A., 1988-91, Bryan Cave, Irvine, Calif., 1991-95; ptnr. McIntyre Burns & Gay, Costa Mesa, Calif., 1996-97, Snell & Wilmer, Irvine, 1998—; mem. Tech. Coast Adv. Group, Calif., 1996. Mergers and acquisitions, General corporate, Private international. Office: Snell & Wilmer LLP 1920 Main St Ste 1200 Irvine CA 92614-7230

**GAYLOR, WILLIAM E., III,** lawyer; b. Sarasota, Fla., Jan. 16, 1964; s. William E. Jr. and Phyllis F. Gaylor. BA, Asbury Coll., 1986; JD, Am. U., 1989; LLM, U. Miami, 1990. Bar: Fla. 1989. Assoc. Isphorphing Korp & Payne, Venice, Fla., 1990-92; ptnr., shareholder Muirhead, Gaylor & Steves LLP, Venice, 1992—; adj. prof. Manatee C.C., 1996—; active Cmty. Found. of Sarasota County, Sarasota, 1997—. Past pres., bd. mem. Cmty. Found. Sarasota County, 1993—; v.p. New Coll. Libr. Assn., Sarasota, 1998—. Mem. ABA, Fla. Bar Assn., Sarasota County Bar Assn. (pres. probate and trust law sect. 1997-98). Avocations: scuba diving, traveling. Estate planning, Probate, Estate taxation. Office: Muirhead Gaylor & Steves LLP 901 Ridgewood Ave Venice FL 34292-1938

**GAYNOR, MARTIN F., III,** lawyer; b. Dorchester, Mass., Feb. 12, 1967; s. Martin F. Jr. and Pamela Gaynor; m. Robin Stewart, July 4, 1968. BA in Econs. with honors, U. Chgo., 1988; JD, Boston Coll., 1993. Bar: Mass. 1993, U.S. Dist. Ct. Mass. 1993, U.S. Ct. Appeals (1st cir.) 1997. Assoc. Hanify & King, Boston, 1993-95; atty. Colley Manion Jones LLP, Boston, 1995—. Mem. Mass. Bar Assn., Boston Bar Assn. State civil litigation, Federal civil litigation, Appellate. Office: Colley Manion Jones LLP 21 Custom House St Boston MA 02110-3507

**GAZERRO, G. JOHN, JR.,** lawyer; b. West Warwick, R.I., Sept. 11, 1940; s. G. John and Lucy (Petrarca) G.; m. Carolyn M. DiPippo, Nov. 22, 1969; children: John Francis, Kerra Lynn. BA, Providence Coll., 1962; JD, Boston U., 1965. Bar: R.I. 1965, U.S. Dist. Ct. R.I. 1969, U.S. Supreme Ct. 1972. Chief inheritance tax, divsn. of taxation State of R.I., 1966-69; asst. atty. gen. State of R.I., Providence, 1969-73; town solicitor Town of West Warwick, R.I., 1978-80, 88-92, Town of Coventry, R.I., 1980-86; ptnr. Gazerro & Richardson, Warwick, 1984—; mem. bd. incorporators, gen. counsel Centreville Savs. Bank, West Warwick, 1984. Mem., treas. Rep. Town Com., West Warwick, 1969-77, legal counsel, 1977-88; mem. exec. com. Rep. State Com., Providence, 1968-82; bd. dirs. Kent County Mental Health, Warwick, 1976-78; mem. bd. incorporators Kent County Hosp., Warwick, 1984-90. Mem. R.I. Bar Assn. Avocations: skeet shooting, trap shooting, hunting. State civil litigation, Banking, Probate. Home: 15 Magnolia Ln Coventry RI 02816-6634 Office: Gazerro & Richardson 1551 Centerville Rd Warwick RI 02886-4251

**GEARHEART, MARK EDWIN,** lawyer; b. Wichita, Kans., July 20, 1955. BS, U. No. Colo., 1977; JD, U. Calif., San Francisco, 1980. Bar: Calif. 1980, U.S. Dist. Ct. (no. dist.) Calif. 1980; cert. specialist in workers compensation, Calif. Assoc. Ury and Goldstein, Vallejo, Calif., 1980-83; mng. atty. Boxer, Ury & Gearheart, Pleasant Hill, Calif., 1983-92; pvt. practice, Pleasant Hill, 1992-93; ptnr. Gearheart & Otis, Pleasant Hill, 1993—. ATLA, Nat. Workplace Injury Litigation Group, Calif. Applicants Attys. Assn. (pres. Walnut Creek chpt. 1998). Democrat. Workers' compensation. Office: Gearheart & Otis 367 Civic Dr Ste 17 Pleasant Hill CA 94523-1935

**GEARIN, KENT FARRELL,** lawyer; b. Union City, Tenn., July 20, 1962; s. Clyde Farrell and Patsy Angeline (Johnson) G.; m. Mary Ann Jackson, Sept. 11, 1983; children: Maxwell Kent, Miles Jackson. Grad. in Criminal Justice, U. Tenn., Martin, 1984; JD, Nashville Sch. Law, 1989. Bar: Tenn., U.S. Dist. Ct. (we. and mid. dists.) Tenn. Atty. Norman Law Office, Nashville, 1989-92, Gearin, Parham & Collins, Martin, 1992-98; bd. dirs. Martin Primary Sch., 1997—. Mem. Rotary. Mem. ABA, Tenn. Bar Assn., Weakley County Bar Assn. (pres. 1992—). Republican. Mem. Ch. of Christ. Avocations: waterfowling, sports car enthusiast, travel, golf, snow skiing. State civil litigation, Criminal, Family and matrimonial. Home: 122 Oakwood Dr Martin TN 38237-3636 Office: Gearin Parham and Collins 317 S Lindell St Martin TN 38237-2440

**GEARY, JOSEPH WILLIAM,** lawyer; b. Dallas, Feb. 2, 1924; s. Joseph William G. and Lucille Paillet; m. Charlotte Walters, June 5, 1948; children: Kelley Lucille, Kathleen, Michael Patrick, Charlotte Colleen. BA, Southern Meth. U., 1946, LLB, 1948. Bar: Tex. 1947, U.S. Dist. Ct. (no. dist.) Tex., U.S. Dist. Ct. (ea. dist.) Tex., U.S. Dist. Ct. (we. dist.) Tex., U.S. Dist. Ct. (so. dist.), U.S. Ct. Appeals, U.S. Supreme Ct. 1957, U.S. Ct. Internat. Trade 1991. Asst. county DA Dist. Atty. Office, Dallas, 1947-51; ptnr. Geary Brice Bamm Staht, Dallas, 1951-56; shareholder Geary Porter & Donovan PC, Dallas, 1956—; bd. dirs. Guardian Savings, Dallas, Trinity Nat. Bank. Advisory dir. Communities Found.; councilman Dallas City Coun., 1959-61. Capt. USAF, 1942-45. Decorated Disting. Flying Cross USAF, 1944, 4 Air Medals, 1944, 45. Republican. Methodist. Avocations: golf, reading. Family and matrimonial, Probate, State civil litigation. Office: Geary Porter & Donovan PC 16475 Dallas Pkwy Ste 500 Addison TX 75001-6837

**GEARY, MICHAEL PHILIP,** lawyer; b. Harvey, Ill., Dec. 19, 1954; s. John Thomas and Patricia Ann (Carpenter) G. BA, Georgetown U., 1977; JD, St. Mary's U., San Antonio, 1980. Bar: Tex. 1980, D.C. 1986, Ohio 1989. Asst. legis. counsel Office of Legis. Counsel, U.S. Senate, Washington, 1980-90; sole practitioner Westlake, Ohio, 1990-94; exec. dir. Ashtabula County Legal Aid Corp., Jefferson, Ohio, 1994—. Trustee Contact-Ashtabula County, 1995-96, Ashtabula County Cmty. Housing Devel. Orgn., Inc., 1998—; mem. Leadership Ashtabula County, Jefferson, Ohio, 1994—. Mem. Ohio State Bar Assn., Ashtabula County Bar Assn. Republican. Roman Catholic. General practice, Family and matrimonial, State civil litigation. Office: Ashtabula County Legal Aid Corp 121 E Walnut St Jefferson OH 44047-1121

**GEBHARDT, ROBERT CHARLES,** lawyer; b. Old Forge, N.Y., Nov. 23, 1937; s. Charles R. and Marcelle M. (Jovet) G.; m. Carolyn A. Searle, Dec. 18, 1968 (div. June 1977); children: Carolyn G., Marcelle C.; m. Johnnie L. Watts, Aug. 29, 1988. AB, SUNY, Albany, 1961; JD, Georgetown U., 1967. Bar: N.Y. 1968, Fla. 1981. Atty. Harris, Beach & Wilcox, Rochester, N.Y., 1967-70; sr. v.p., gen. counsel Lincoln 1st Banks, Inc., Rochester, 1970-81; ptnr. Goldstein, Goldman, Kessler & Underberg, Miami, Fla., 1981-84; sr. v.p. Asset Mgmt. & Disposition, Inc., Naples, Fla., 1986-89; ptnr. Gebhardt & White, P.A., Naples, 1989—. Chmn. Com. of Bank Holding Co. Attys., Rochester, 1978-81. Mem. Fla. Bar, N.Y. Bar, Collier County Bar Assn. Republican. Roman Catholic. Banking, State civil litigation, Real property. Home: 114 Amblewood Ln Naples FL 34105-7103 Office: Gebhardt & White PA 2500 Tamiami Trl N Ste 112 Naples FL 34103-4421

**GEDDIE, ROWLAND HILL, III,** lawyer; b. Tuscaloosa, Ala., Jan. 7, 1954; s. Rowland Hill Jr. and Mary Martha (McGaughy) G.; m. Peggy O'Neal Emmons, Aug. 13, 1977; children: Mary Catherine, Virginia Jane. BA, U. Miss., 1976, JD, 1978. Bar: Miss. 1978, U.S. Dist. Ct. (no. dist.) Miss. 1978, Tex. 1979, Mo. 1995. Assoc. Baker & Botts, Houston, 1978-87; assoc. gen. counsel Lower Colo. River Authority, Austin, Tex., 1987-88; sr. counsel Houston Industries Inc./Houston Lighting & Power Co., 1988-92; contract atty. Tandy Corp./TE Electronics Inc., Ft. Worth, 1993; v.p., gen. counsel, sec. O'Sullivan Industries Holdings Inc., Lamar, Mo., 1993—. Treas. Southgate Civic Club, Houston, 1991-92. Presdl. scholar U.S. Govt., Washington, 1972. Mem. ABA, Am. Corp. Counsel Assn. (co-chair EDGAR issues practice group of corp. and securities law com. 1997-98, chair ann. meeting shareholders and proxy statement issues practice group corp. and securities, 1999), Rotary. Methodist. Avocations: personal computers, cycling, scuba diving. General corporate, Securities. Home: 1503 Gulf St Lamar MO 64759-1830 Office: O'Sullivan Industries Inc 1900 Gulf St Lamar MO 64759-1899

**GEE, PAULINE W.,** public defender; b. Marysville, Calif., June 2, 1949; d. Sun Mee and Gim Ong (Yee) Gee. BS in Sociology, U. Calif., Berkeley, 1971; JD, U. Calif., San Francsico, 1976. Bar: Calif. 1977, U.S. Dist. Ct. (no. dist.) Calif. 1977, U.S. Ct. Appeals (9th cir.) 1977, U.S. Dist. Ct. (so. dist.) Calif. 1990, U.S. Dist. Ct. (ea. dist.) Calif. 1982, U.S. Supreme Ct. 1993. Staff atty. Legal Aid Soc. Clameda County, Oakland, Calif., 1977-80, mng. atty., 1980-82; dist. atty. Calif. Rural Legal Assistance, Marysville, 1982-88, regional counsel, 1988-96, dir. litigation, advocacy and tng., 1996—; adj. profl. Boalt Hall, U. Calif., Berkeley, 1989—; trainer, lectr. in field. Contbr. articles to profl. jours. Mem. Victim Witness Assistance Program of Sutter County, 1987-88; group facilitator Yuba Sutter Partnership in Youth Success, 1990-92; co-founder Alameda Cunty Coalition Against Domestic Violence, 1978—, chair, 1979-80; bd. dirs., treas. YWCA, Oakland, 1978-79; vol. trainer/cons. to battered women's shelters, Oakland, 1976-82, Chico, Calif., 1982, Yuba City, 1982—; mem. legis. com. Calif. Coalition Against Domestic Violence, 1978—; mem. East Dist. Judg. Adv. Com. to Senator Barbara Boxer, 1993-95. Recipient Reginald Heber Smith award Nat. Legal Aid and Defenders Assn., 1991. Mem. ABA (standing com. on legal assts. 1996—), LWV, Calif. State Bar (liaison exec. com. conf. dels., mem. ADR task force, legal svcs. com., cts. and legis. com., legal com. 1991-93, pro per task force 1993-94, budget rev. com. 1993-94, chair legal tech. task force 1992-93, vice chair cts. and legislation 1993-94, vice chair bd. com. on legal svcs. 1992-93, chair 1993-94, women and law com. 1990, del. chair conf. 1992-93, 95-96, pvt. involvement com. 1987-90, chair 1990, exec. com. conf. dels. 1989-91, bd. govs. 1991-94, v.p. 1994), Yuba Sutter Bar Assn. (exec. com. 1995—, pres. 1987, organizer, chair women's com. 1983-86), Calif. Orgn. Small Bars (chair conf. dels. resolution com., chair fast track survey, pres. 1990-92, bd. dirs. 1988-91), Nat. Women and Law Assn. (bd. govs., vice chair 1983-90), Calif. Women Lawyers Assn. (bd. govs., pub. interest com. chair, jud. evaluations com. 1984-86, Fay Stender award 1991), Asian Am. Bar Assn. Sacramento, Calif. Women in Legal Svcs., So. Calif. Chinese Lawyers Assn. (Disting. Svc. award 1992), Nat. Ctr. for Women and Family Law (bd. dirs. 1982-89, 95-96), Calif. State Bar Found. (bd. govs., exec. com. 1991—), San Francisco Women's Alliance, Calif. Jud. Coun. (gender bias com. 1987), Yuba Sutter Women's Profl. Network, Phi Beta Kappa. Avocations: fishing, camping, rockhounding. Home: 7726 Kent Ave Live Oak CA 95953-9633 Office: Calif Rural Legal Assistance 818 D St Marysville CA 95901-5321

**GEE, ROBERT NEIL,** law librarian; b. Miami, Okla., June 22, 1956; s. Robert Sanford and Nancy Ann (Neil) G. AA, Tulsa Jr. Coll., 1976; BA, U. Okla., 1978, JD, 1981; LLM, George Washington U., 1984. Bar: Okla. 1981, U.S. Suprem Ct. 1986, D.C. 1989. Legal reference specialist Library of Congress, Washington, 1984-94; chief law libr. pub. svcs. Law Libr. of Congress, Washington, 1994—. Mem. ABA (recipient Silver Key cert. 1981), Fed. Bar Assn., Okla. Bar Assn., Am. Judicature Soc., D.C. Bar Assn., Phi Delta Phi. Avocations: reading, bowling, travel, current events.

**GEESEMAN, ROBERT GEORGE,** lawyer; b. Shreveport, La., Oct. 23, 1944; s. George Robert and Cora (Hamilton) Glasgow; m. Rosemary Monahan, Aug. 19, 1967; 1 child, Regan Glasgow. B.A., Yale U., 1966; J.D., U. Mich., 1969. Bar: Pa. 1969, U.S. Dist. Ct. (we. dist.) Pa. 1969, U.S. Supreme Ct., 1973, U.S. Tax Ct. 1979. Assoc. Blaxter, O'Neill, Houston & Nash, Pitts., 1969-75; ptnr. Lynch, Lynch, Carr & Kabala, Pitts., 1975-81, Lynch, Kabala & Geeseman, Pitts., 1981, Kabala & Geeseman, Pitts., 1981—; lectr. on tax law and employee benefits; legal adv. bd. Small Bus. Council Am. Mem. ABA (mem. profl. service corps. com. sect. on taxation, chmn. profl. corp. com. sect. econs.; bd. editors Withdrawal Retirement and Disputes, What You and Your Firm Should Know), Pa. Bar Assn., Allegheny County Bar Assn., Pitts. Inst. Legal Medicine, Phi Delta Phi. ClubsL Rosslyn Farms Country, Rivers, Chartiers Country; Moy's (New Haven, Conn.); John's Island Country (Vero Beach, FLa.). Health, Pension, profit-sharing, and employee benefits, Taxation, general. Office: Kabala & Geeseman 200 1st Ave Pittsburgh PA 15222-1575

**GEESLIN, GARY LLOYD,** lawyer; b. Grenada, Miss., Oct. 31, 1940. BA, Miss. State U., 1962; JD, U. Miss., 1968. Bar: Miss. 1968, U.S. Dist. Ct. (no. dist.) Miss. 1968, U.S. Dist. Ct. (so. dist.) Miss. 1972, U.S. Ct. Appeals (5th cir.) 1974, U.S. Ct. Appeals (fed. cir.) 1987. Assoc. Threadgill & Smith, Columbus, Miss., 1968-79; ptnr. Lipscomb, Geeslin & McClanahan, Columbus, 1991-94; pvt. practice, Columbus, 1979-91, 94—. Mem. Old Waverly Golf Club, Rotary (pres. Columbus 1976). General civil litigation, Family and matrimonial, General practice. Office: 107 Merle Dr Columbus MS 39702-7205

**GEFFE, KENT LYNDON,** lawyer, educator; b. Charles City, Iowa, Jan. 29, 1957; s. Herbert Frederick and Clarice Ona (Wood) G.; m. Susan Kay Leise, Aug. 12, 1978 (div. July 1986) 1 child, Jeremiah Kevin; m. Barbara Ann Cox, July 3, 1987; 1 child, Anastasia Catherine. BA, Cornell Coll., Mt. Vernon, Iowa, 1975; JD, U. Iowa, 1981. Bar: Iowa 1981, U.S. Dist. Ct. (no. and so. dists.) Iowa 1982. Intern U.S. Congressman, Washington, 1978, Prisoner Assistance Clinic, Iowa City, 1980-81; jud. magistrate State of Iowa, Marshalltown, 1983-87; city atty. City of Melbourne, Iowa, 1982—; ptnr. Welp & Geffe, Marshalltown, 1981—; adj. faculty Marshalltown C.C., 1981—; adv. bd. consumer credit counseling svcs. Northea. Iowa, Inc., 1998—. Bd. dirs. Runaway and Youth Svcs. Ctr., Marshalltown, 1985-86, Mid-Iowa Workshops, Inc., Marshalltown, 1985-91; mem. adv. coun. Iowa Valley Continuing Edn., Marshalltown, 1992; state legal counsel Iowa Jaycees, 1982-85; grad. Iowa Valley Leadership, Marshalltown, 1990; mem. Mid-Iowa coun. Boy Scouts Am., Des Moines, 1990-95. Named one of Outstanding Young Men of Am., 1984, 85. Mem. Iowa State Bar Assn., Iowa Jaycees, Marshalltown Jaycees (pres. 1985-86), Kiwanis, Nebr.-Iowa Kiwanis Found. (life), Phi Beta Kappa. Avocations: sailing, carpentry, reading. General practice, Taxation, general, Personal injury. Office: Welp & Geffe Law Offices 110 W Southridge Rd PO Box 555 Marshalltown IA 50158-0555

**GEFREH, PAUL THOMAS,** lawyer; b. Scranton, Pa., Apr. 17, 1953; s. Adam and Florence (Ksiazek) G.; m. Nanette Neudeck, July 16, 1983; children: Mark, Tasha. BA, N.D. State U., 1974; JD, U. Neb., 1977. Bar: Colo. 1977, U.S. Dist. Ct. Colo. 1977. Computer programmer U.S. Dept Transp., Washington, 1974-75; ptnr. Lebel & Gefreh, Colorado Springs, Colo., 1977-78; assoc. Murray, Baker & Wendelken, Colorado Springs, 1978-81, Hendricks & Hendricks P.C., Colorado Springs, 1981-84; sole practice Colorado Springs, 1984—; trustee U.S. Bankruptcy Ct., Denver, 1984—. Officer Pikes Peak Children's Advs., Colorado Springs, 1978-84. Mem. ABA, Colo. Bar Assn., El Paso Bar Assn., Colorado Springs Jaycees (officer 1978-84). Roman Catholic. Avocations: hiking, gardening. Consumer commercial, Construction, Bankruptcy. Office: 2125 N Academy Blvd Colorado Springs CO 80909-1507

**GEGEN, THERESA MARY,** lawyer; b. Hastings, Minn., Dec. 29, 1963; d. Charles Francis Gegen and Margaret Ann Thiel. BS in Chemistry, Winona State U., 1987; JD, Baylor U., 1995. Bar: Tex., U.S. Dist. Ct. (no. and ea. dists.) Tex. Law clk. to justice Baker Tex. Supreme Ct., Austin, 1995-96; assoc. Clark, West, Keller, Butler & Ellis, LLP, Dallas, 1996—. Capt. U.S. Army, 1987-92. Mem. Dallas Assn. Young Lawyers, Attys. Serving Cmty., Employment Law Outreach. Labor, Appellate. Office: Clark West Keller Butler & Ellis LLP 1201 Elm St Dallas TX 75270-2102

**GEHAN, MARK WILLIAM,** lawyer; b. St. Paul, Dec. 19, 1946; s. Mark William and Jean Elizabeth (McGee) G.; m. Lucy Lyman Harrison, Aug. 25, 1971; children: Hark Harrison, Alice McGee. BA, U. Notre Dame, 1968; JD, U. Minn., 1971. Asst. county atty. Ramsey County Atty.'s Office, St. Paul, 1972-76; prosecutor, Met. Area Dist. Urban County Attys. Bd., St. Paul, 1976-77; ptnr. Collins Buckley Sauntry & Haugh, St. Paul, 1978—; bd. dirs. Minn. State Bd. Pub. Def., St. Paul, 1982-90. Pres. St. Paul Charter Commn., 1986-94. Mem. Minn. State Bar Assn. (sec. 1995-96, treas. 1996-97), Ramsey County Bar Assn. (pres. 1990-91). Avocations: scuba diving, tennis, guitar. State civil litigation. Office: Collins Buckley Sauntry & Haugh First Nat Bank Bldg 332 Minnesota St Ste W1100 Saint Paul MN 55101-1379

**GEHRES, JAMES,** lawyer; b. Akron, Ohio, July 19, 1932; s. Edwin Jacob and Cleora Mary (Yoakam) G.; m. Eleanor Agnew Mount, July 23, 1960. B.S. in Acctg., U. Utah, 1954; M.B.A., U. Calif.-Berkeley, 1959; J.D., U. Denver, 1970, LL.M. in Taxation, 1977. Bar: Colo. 1970, U.S. Dist. Ct. Colo. 1970, U.S. Tax Ct. 1970, U.S. Supreme Ct. 1973, U.S. Ct. Appeals (10th cir.) 1978, U.S. Ct. Claims 1992. Atty. IRS, Denver, 1965-80, atty. chief counsel's office, 1980—. Served with USAF, 1955-58, capt. Res. ret. Mem. ABA, Colo. Bar Assn., Am. Inst. C.P.A.s, Colo. Soc. C.P.A.s, Am. Assn. Atty.-C.P.A.s, Am. Judicature Soc., Am. Acctg. Assn., Order St. Ives, The Explorers Club, Am. Alpine Club, Colo. Mountain Club (bd. dirs.), Colo. Mountain Club Found. (bd. dirs.), Beta Gamma Sigma, Beta Alpha Psi. Democrat. Contbr. articles to profl. jours. Office: 935 Pennsylvania St Denver CO 80203-3145

**GEHRIG, MICHAEL FORD,** lawyer; b. Cin., Jan. 25, 1947; s. John Richard and Mary Bonita (Ford) G.; m. Barbara Jane Rigg, June 16, 1973; children: Michael Ford, Caroline Cristina, Angela Victoria. BA, Ohio State U., 1970; JD, Chase Coll. Law, Cin., 1974. Bar: Ohio 1974, U.S. Dist. Ct. (so. dist.) Ohio 1974, U.S. Dist. Ct. (ea. dist.) Ky. 1983, U.S. Supreme Ct., 1985. Assoc. Beall, Hermanies & Bortz, Cin., 1974-76; mem. firm Gehrig & Gehrig, Cin., 1976-79, Gehrig, Parker & Baldwin, Cin., 1979-88, Fingerman, Guckenberger & Gehrig, 1988-96, Gehrig, Gelwicks & Eynon, 1996—; lectr. various legal seminars. Contbr. articles to jours., chpts. to books. Recipient book awards Chase Coll. Law, 1971, 73, 74. Mem. ABA, Ohio State Bar Assn., Cin. Bar Assn., Assn. Trial Lawyers Am. (sustaining), Am. Bd. Trial Advocates, Ohio Acad. Trial Lawyers (sustaining), Cin. Hist. Soc., English Speaking Union, Cin. Athletic Club, Univ. Club, Hyde Park Golf & Country Club, Phi Gamma Delta. Episcopalian. Personal injury. Office: Gehrig Gelwicks & Eynon 1140 Bartlett Bldg 36 E 4th St Ste 1140 Cincinnati OH 45202-3809

**GEHRING, RONALD KENT,** lawyer; b. Ft. Wayne, Ind., Feb. 5, 1941; s. Ronald G. and Beverly M. (Failor) G.; m. Teresa L. Eyer, June 18, 1966; children—Gregory D., Douglas K., Suzanne C. AB, Ind. U., 1963, JD, 1967. Bar: Ind. 1967, U.S. Dist. Ct. (no. dist.) Ind. 1967, U.S. Dist. Ct. (so. dist.) Ind. 1967, U.S. Ct. Appeals (7th cir.) 1975. Assoc., Peters, McHie, Enslen & Hand, Hammond, Ind., 1967-70; ptnr. Tourkow, Danehy, Crell, Hood & Gehring, Ft. Wayne, 1971-79, Grossman, Boeglin & Gehring and predecessor, Ft. Wayne, 1980-84; pvt. practice, Ft. Wayne, 1984—; panelist Ind. Collection Law Seminar, 1982-83; bd dir. Concordia Cemetery Assn., 1982-83, Luth. Assn. Broadcasting, Inc.; atty. Ind. Dist. Luthern Church. Mem. ABA, Ind. Trial Lawyers, Comml. Law League, Ind. Bar Assn., Allen County Bar Assn., Phi Delta Phi. Consumer commercial, Probate, Real property. Office: 202 W Berry St Ste 321 Fort Wayne IN 46802-2242

**GEIBELSON, MICHAEL AARON,** lawyer; b. Van Nuys, Calif., Dec. 25, 1970. BA, U. Calif., Berkeley, 1991; JD, Loyola U., L.A., 1995. Bar: Calif. 1995, U.S. Dist. Ct. (ctrl. dist.) Calif. 1995, U.S. Dist. Ct. (so. dist.) Calif. 1996), U.S. Dist. Ct. (ea. dist.) Calif. 1998. Assoc. atty. Robins, Kaplan, Miller & Ciresi LLP, L.A., 1995—. Contbr. articles to profl. jours. Mem. CAALA, Trial Bar Inn of Ct., L.A. County Bar Assn. General civil litigation, Professional liability. Office: Robins Kaplan Miller & Ciresi LLP 2049 Century Park E Ste 3700 Los Angeles CA 90067-3211

**GEIGER, ALEXANDER,** lawyer; b. Kosice, Czechoslovakia, May 21, 1950; came to U.S., 1965; s. Emil and Alice (Brickmann) G.; m. Helene R. Mortar, May 28, 1972; children: Theodore, Aviva. AB, Princeton U., 1972; JD, Cornell U., 1975. Bar: N.Y. 1976, U.S. Dist. Ct. (we. dist.) N.Y. 1976, U.S. Supreme Ct. 1980, U.S. Ct. Appeals (2d cir.) 1985, U.S. Tax Ct. 1986. Assoc. Nixon, Hargrave, Devans & Doyle, Rochester, N.Y., 1975-82; sr. ptnr. Geiger & Rothenberg, Rochester, 1982—; adj. asst. prof. St. John Fisher Coll., Rochester, 1977-78. Mem. N.Y. State Bar Assn., Monroe County Bar Assn., Assn. Trial Lawyers Am., Rochester Inns of Ct. (master). Jewish. Federal civil litigation, State civil litigation, Personal injury. Home: 194 Edgemoor Rd Rochester NY 14618-1230 Office: Geiger & Rothenberg 45 Exchange Blvd Ste 800 Rochester NY 14614-2093

**GEIGER, JAMES NORMAN,** lawyer; b. Mansfield, Ohio, Apr. 5, 1932; s. Ernest R. and Margaret L. (Bauman) G.; m. Paula Hunt, May 11, 1957; children: Nancy G., John W. Student Wabash Coll., Crawfordsville, Ind., 1950-51; BA, Ohio Wesleyan U., 1954; JD, Emory U., 1962, LLD, 1970. Bar: Ga. 1961, U.. Dist. Ct. (mid. dist.) Ga. 1966, U.S. Ct. Appeals (5th and 11th cirs.) 1980, U.S. Dist. Ct. (so. dist.) Ga. 1983. Ptnr. Henderson, Kaley, Geiger and Thurmond, Marietta, Ga., 1962-64, Nunn, Geiger and Hunt, Perry, Ga., 1964-72, Geiger & Geiger, P.C. and predecessors, 1972—. Trustee Westfield (Ga.) Schs., 1970-74; mem. civilian adv. bd. Warner Robins AFB, 1976; chmn. coun. ministries Perry United Meth. Ch., 1970-71, mem. adminstrv. bd., 1968—. Capt. USAF, 1954-57. Mem. ABA, Ga. Bar Assn., Houston County Bar Assn., South Ga. C. of C. (bd. dirs.) Perry C. of C. (pres. 1976, 90), Perry Kiwanis (pres. 1968, Man of Yr. 1968), Perry Club Coun. (pres. 1967), Phi Delta Phi, Pi Sigma Alpha. Methodist. General practice, Contracts commercial, Real property. Home: 1910 Northside Rd Perry GA 31069-2223 Office: Geiger & Geiger 1007 Jernigan St Perry GA 31069-3325

**GEIGER, ROY STEPHEN,** lawyer; b. June 8, 1950; s. Roy Dean and Mary Gertrude (Morett) G.; m. Beth Kelly, Nov. 21, 1984. BA, UCLA, 1972; JD,

U. Calif., Berkeley, 1979. Bar: Calif. 1979. Assoc. Hetland & Wilson, Berkeley, 1979-81, Drummy, Garret, King & Harrison, Costa Mesa, Calif., 1981-83; assoc. Irell & Manella LLP, L.A., 1983-86, ptnr., 1986—. Assoc. editor Calif. Real Property Jour., 1988-89; contbr. articles to profl. jours. Mem. ABA, Calif. State Bar Assn. (co-chair of joint com. on legal opinions in Calif. real estate 1996—, advisor to exec. com. 1993, co-chair exec. com. 1990-92, exec. com. 1990-92, co-chair real estate fin. 1987-89, advisor internat. law section, 1997-98), Am. Coll. of Real Estate Lawyers, L.A. County Bar Assn., State Bar of Calif., Phi Beta Kappa. Real property, Banking, Contracts commercial. Office: Irell & Manella LLP 333 S Hope St Ste 3300 Los Angeles CA 90071-3042

**GEIHS, FREDERICK SIEGFRIED,** lawyer; b. Omaha, Nebr., Oct. 16, 1935; s. Friederich Siegfried Sr. and Dorothy Pauline (Getzschman) G.; m. Janelle J. Jeffrey, Oct. 22, 1966; children: Jeffrey J., Danielle Desiree. BS in Bus. Adminstrn., U. Nebr., Omaha, 1957; JD, Creighton U., 1962. Bar: Nebr. 1962, U.S. Dist. Ct. Nebr. 1962, U.S. Supreme Ct. 1965, Mich. 1975, Minn. 1978, U.S. Ct. Appeals (9th cir.) 1980, Nev. 1981, U.S. Dist. Ct. Nev. 1981. Atty. City Omaha (Nebr.) Law Dept., 1962-65; pvt. practice law Omaha, 1965-71, Edina, Minn., 1978-80; asst. gen., atty. Upland Industries, Omaha, 1971-75; corp. counsel Detroit and No. Savs. and Loan, Houghton, Mich., 1975-77, Knutson Cos., Inc., Mpls., 1977-78; mng. atty. Legal Assistance N.D., Bismark, 1980; dir. litigation Clark County Legal Svcs., Las Vegas, 1980-82; atty. Bell & Young, Las Vegas, 1982-83, Harding & Dawson, Las Vegas; of counsel Hilbrecht & Assocs., Las Vegas; pvt. practice Las Vegas, 1991—. Sec. Young Reps., Omaha, 1965-66; treas. Forgotten Ams., Omaha, 1968-70. Mem. ABA, Minn. State Bar Assn., Nebr. State Bar Assn., Nev. Trial Lawyers Assn., Assn. Trial Lawyers Am., Western State Trial Lawyers Assn., Theta Chi, Phi Alpha Delta. Lutheran. Avocations: skiing, jogging, travel. General civil litigation, General corporate, Personal injury. Office: 3376 S Eastern Ave Ste 148 Las Vegas NV 89109-3367

**GEIL, JOHN CLINTON,** lawyer; b. San Antonio, Oct. 27, 1951; s. William Clinton and Frances E. (Coverdale) G. BA, Occidental Coll., 1972; JD, Lewis and Clark Coll., 1976. Bar: Oreg. 1976, U.S. Dist. Ct. Oreg. 1977, U.S. Ct. Appeals (9th cir.) 1977, U.S. Supreme Ct. 1981, U.S. Ct. Fed. Claims 1995. Pvt. practice, Portland, Oreg., 1976-97. Named to Outstanding Young Men Am., U.S. Jaycees, 1979, 81; recipient Frances Durrell award 1996. Mem. Oreg. Yount Attys. Assn. (pres. 1983-84), ABA (bd. dirs. law student div. 1975-76, assembly speaker young lawyers div. 1987-88, ho. of dels. 1997-98), Multnomah Bar Assn. (bd. dirs. 1994-97, award of merit 1994), Cornelius Honor Soc. Administrative and regulatory, General civil litigation, Native American. Office: 722 SW 2nd Ave Ste 200 Portland OR 97204-3129

**GEIL, JOHN MCINTOSH,** lawyer, business consultant; b. Orange, Tex., Oct. 10, 1948. BA in History, U. N.C., 1970, JD, 1973. Bar: N.C., 1973, U.S. Tax Ct., 1973, U.S. Dist. Ct. (ea. dist.) N.C., 1975, U.S. Ct. Appeals (4th cir.), 1979, U.S. Supreme Ct., 1979, U.S. Dist. Ct. (mid. dist.) N.C., 1991. Ptnr. Poyner & Spruill, Raleigh, N.C., 1973-84, Dolphin Assocs., Raleigh, 1984-88; pres. Caro-Syn Inc., Raleigh, 1984-88; ptnr. Anderson, Rutherford & Geil, Raleigh, 1988-94; of counsel Wilson & Waller, Raleigh, 1994—. With U. S. Army, 1970-76. Mergers and acquisitions, Corporate taxation, General corporate. Office: Wilson & Waller 4600 Marriott Dr Ste 400 Raleigh NC 27612-3305

**GEILER, JANE BUCHANAN,** lawyer, educator; b. Oklahoma City, May 19, 1946; d. Francis Harvey and Louise Adeline (Ewalt) Buchanan; m. Gordon Leigh Phillips II, June 21, 1969 (div. June 1982); m. Hugh Joseph Geiler, Apr. 25, 1987. Student, U. Chgo. McCormick Theol. Sem., 1968-69; BA, U. Okla., 1968; MSW, U. N.C., 1974; JD, St. Louis U., 1980. Bar: Mo. 1980, U.S. Dist. Ct. (we. dist.) Mo. 1980. Asst. pub. defender St. Louis City and County, 1980-82, spl. pub. defender, 1983-94; asst. cir. atty. St. Louis Cir. Atty., 1985—; instr. law for social workers Washington U., St. Louis, 1993-96, 98; mem. child fatality rev. bd., chmn. STAT of Dept. Family Svcs., 1993—; bd. dirs. Family Violence Coun. St. Louis, 1993-96. Contbr. articles to local newspaper. Bd. dirs. Skinker-DeBalivere Cmty. Coun., St. Louis, 1996—; pres. Rosedale Neighborhood Assn., St. Louis, 1996—. Named Child Advocate of Yr., St. Louis Coun. on Child Abuse and Neglect, 1989. Mem. Mo. Bar, St. Louis Met. Bar (exec. bd. 1987-88), Women Lawyers Assn. (exec. com. 1991-92), Nat. Assn. Drug Ct. Profls. Avocations: jet skiing, gardening, reading, drawing, writing articles for neighborhood newspaper. Home: 6151 Washington Blvd Saint Louis MO 63112-1207

**GEIMAN, J. ROBERT,** lawyer; b. Evanston, Ill., Mar. 5, 1931; s. Louis H. and Nancy O'Connell-Crowe G.; m. Ann L. Fitzgerald, July 29, 1972; children: J. Robert, William Patrick, Timothy Michael. BS, Northwestern U., 1953; JD, Notre Dame U., 1956. Bar: Ill. 1956, U.S. Ct. Appeals (7th cir.) 1956, U.S. Supreme Ct. 1969. Assoc. Eckert, Peterson & Lowry, Chgo., 1956-64; ptnr. Peterson, Lowry, Rall, Barber & Ross, Chgo., 1964-70; ptnr. Peterson & Ross, Chgo., 1970-96, of counsel, 1996—; mem. com. on civil jury instructions Ill. Supreme Ct., 1979-81. Case editor Notre Dame Law Rev., 1956. Bd. advisors Cath. Charities of Archdiocese of Chgo., 1973-96. Fellow Internat. Acad. Trial Lawyers, Am. Coll. Trial Lawyers, Ill. Bar Found.; mem. ABA (aviation com., tort and ins. practice sect. 1980-90), Ill. Bar Assn. (sec. 1969-70, sec. bd. govs. 1969-71), Chgo. Bar Assn. (aviation law com. 1970-73), Bar Assn. of 7th Fed. Ct. (meetings com. 1968-70, vice chmn. membership com. 1973-75), Soc. Trial Lawyers, Cath. Lawyers Guild of Chgo. (bd. advisors 1973-96), Law Club Chgo., Chgo. Athletic Assn. (pres. 1973). Republican. Aviation, Health, Federal civil litigation. Home: 900 SW Bay Point Cir Palm City FL 34990-1758 Office: Peterson & Ross 200 E Randolph St Ste 7300 Chicago IL 60601-7012

**GEIS, JEROME ARTHUR,** lawyer, legal educator; b. Shakopee, Minn., May 28, 1946; s. Arthur Adam and Emma Mary (Boegemann) G.; m. Beth Marie Bruger, Aug. 11, 1979; children: Jennifer, Jason, Joan, Janice. BA in History, Govt. magna cum laude, St. John's U., Collegeville, Minn., 1968; JD cum laude, U. Notre Dame, 1973; LLM in Taxation, NYU, 1975. Bar: Minn. 1973, U.S. Dist. Ct. Minn. 1973, U.S. Tax Ct. 1973, U.S. Ct. Appeals (8th cir.) 1973. Law clk. to presiding justice Minn. Supreme Ct., St. Paul, 1973-74; assoc. Dudley & Smith, St. Paul, 1975-76; assoc. Briggs & Morgan P.A., St. Paul, 1976-79, chief tax dept., 1983-95; prof. tax law William Mitchell Coll. of Law, St. Paul, 1976—. Columnist Minn. Law Jour., 1986-89, Bench & Bar, 1990—; editorial cons.: Sales and Use Tax Alert; reviewer Summary Reporter: Finance and Commerce, Minnesota State Bar Assn.; corr. State Tax Notes. Bd. dirs. Western Townhouse Assn., West St. Paul, 1979, St. Matthews Cath. Ch., West St. Paul, 1981; adv. bd. Minn. Inst. of Legal Edn., 1984—. Served to specialist 4th class U.S. Army, 1969-71. Fellow Am. Coll. Tax Counsel; mem. ABA, Am. Law Inst., Tax Inst. Am. (chmn. sales and use tax comm. 1988-90), Nat. Tax Assn., Am. Judicature Soc., Minn. Bar Assn. (bd. dirs. tax coun. sect. 1984-93, chmn. 1990-91), Ramsey County Bar Assn., Minn. Taxpayers Assn. (bd. dirs. 1988—), Inst. Property Taxation, Supreme Ct. Hist. Soc., Nat. Assn. of State Bar Tax Sections (exec. com. 1993—), Minn. Club (bd. dirs. 1997—), KC, Kiwanis (bd. dirs. 1997—). Corporate taxation, Personal income taxation, State and local taxation. Home: 1116 Dodd Rd Saint Paul MN 55118-1821 Office: Briggs & Morgan PA 2200 1st St N Saint Paul MN 55109-3210

**GEISEL, HENRY JULES,** lawyer; b. Cin., Oct. 3, 1947; s. Albert and Else Geisel; m. Ellyn Anne Levy, Sept. 1, 1975; children: Noah L., Gideon L. BS in Econs., U. Pa., 1969; JD, U. Cin., 1972. Bar: Colo. 1972, U.S. Dist. Ct. Colo. 1972. Dep. dist. atty. 20th Jud. Dist., Boulder, Colo., 1973-74, 10th Jud. Dist., Pueblo, Colo., 1974-76; assoc. John R. Naylor, Pueblo, 1976-82, Naylor & Geisel P.C., Pueblo, 1982—. Pres. Temple Emanuel, Pueblo, 1981-82, 85-88; bd. dirs. Pueblo Youth Svcs. Bur., 1978-93, sec., 1989-93; bd. dirs. Pueblo Intensive Phonics Literacy Ctr., Inc., 1989-96, Parkview Hosp. Found., Pueblo, 1986-93, chmn., 1988. Mem. ABA, Colo. Bar Assn., Pueblo County Bar Assn., Colo. Trial Lawyers Assn. Avocations: tennis, bicycling, web-surfing, travel. General practice, Family and matrimonial, State civil litigation. Office: Naylor & Geisel PC 1123 N Elizabeth St Pueblo CO 81003-2233

**GEISLER, THOMAS MILTON, JR.,** lawyer; b. Orange, N.J., Jan. 16, 1943; s. Thomas M. and Helen K. (Thomas) G.; m. Sarah Ann Farrell Geisler, Aug. 6, 1977; children: Sarah C., Ann. C. AB in Math. (cum laude), Harvard Coll., Cambridge, Mass., 1965; JD, Harvard Law Sch., Cambridge, Mass., 1968. Bar: N.J., N.Y., Conn., U.S. Dist. Cts. (2nd cir.), U.S. Supreme Ct. Asst., base legal officer U.S. Naval Submarine Base, New London, Conn., 1969-71; appellate def. counsel Naval Appellate Review Activity, Washington, 1971-72; assoc. Shearman & Sterling, N.Y.C., 1973-80, ptnr., 1980-91; pvt. practice N.Y.C., 1991-96, New Haven, Conn., 1994—; dir., bd. dirs. Friends of Harvard Law Record, Cambridge, Mass., 1997—. Author: Am. Jur. Proof of Facts 3d, 1995, 96, 98, 99; editor: Trial Practice Newsletter, 1986—. Lt., USNR, 1969-72. Recipient Litigation Star ABA Litigation Sect., 1997, Navy Achievement award USN, Washington, 1971. Mem. ABA (trial practice com.), Conn. Bar Assn., Harvard Club of So. Conn., Harvard Club of N.Y.C., Quinnipack Club, Madison Beach Club. Presbyterian. Avocations: tennis. squash, theater, concerts. Federal civil litigation, State civil litigation, Appellate. Office: 205 Church St Ste 305 New Haven CT 06510-1805

**GEISMER, ALAN STEARN, JR.,** lawyer; b. Cleve., June 23, 1948; s. Alan S. and Barbara (Peck) G.; m. Susan Dangel, Oct. 17, 1976; children: Lily, Sarah. AB magna cum laude, Harvard U., 1970, JD, 1975; cert., Cambridge U., 1972. Bar: Mass. 1975, U.S. Dist. Ct. Mass. 1975, U.S. Ct. Appeals (1st cir.) 1979. Assoc. Dangel & Smith, Boston, 1975-77, Mason & Martin, Boston, 1977-79, Goldstein & Manello, Boston, 1979-80; ptnr. Berlin, Clarey & Green, Boston, 1980-86, Kassler & Feuer P.C., Boston, 1986—. pres. Concert Dance Co., Boston, 1985-91; bd. dirs. Jewish Family and Children's Svc., Boston, 1986—, clk., 1989-90, v.p., 1990-93, pres. 1993-96; bd. dirs. Dance Umbrella, Boston, 1991-95; bd. dirs. World Music, Boston, 1995—; vol. Lawyers for the Arts, 1994—. Fellow Am. Acad. Matrimonial Lawyers (bd. mgrs. Mass. chpt. 1995-98); mem. ABA, Mass. Bar Assn., Boston Bar Assn., Longwood Cricket Club (Chestnut Hill, Mass.), Badminton and Tennis Club. Democrat. Avocations: tennis, hiking. Family and matrimonial, Entertainment. Home: 61 Lexington Ave Cambridge MA 02138-3320 Office: Kassler & Feuer PC 101 Arch St Boston MA 02110-1130

**GELB, JOSEPH DONALD,** lawyer; b. Wilkes-Barre, Pa., Dec. 13, 1923; s. Edward and Esther (Fierman) G. m. Anne Mirman, July 3, 1955; children: Adam, Roger. Student, Pa. State Coll., 1943; BS, U. Scranton, 1950; LLB, George Washington U., 1952. Bar: D.C. 1954, Md. 1963, U.S. Supreme Ct. 1972. Adjudicator War Claims Commn., 1952-54; pvt. practice Washington and Md., 1954-69; ptnr. Gelb & Pitsenberger, Washington, 1969-74; prin. Joseph D. Gelb Chartered, Washington, 1974-80, Gelb, Abelson & Siegel, P.C., Washington, 1980-82, Gelb & Siegel, P.C., Washington, 1982-85, Joseph D. Gelb, Chartered, Washington, 1985-93, Gelb & Gelb, P.C., Washington, 1994—. Served with USAAF, 1943-46. Mem. Md. Bar Assn., D.C. Bar Assn., Bethesda Country Club, B'nai B'rith, Masons. General civil litigation, Personal injury, Product liability. Home: 9620 Annlee Ter Bethesda MD 20817-1410 also: 525 N Ocean Blvd Pompano Beach FL 33062-4640 Office: Gelb & Gelb PC 1120 Connecticut Ave NW Washington DC 20036-3902

**GELB, JUDITH ANNE,** lawyer; b. N.Y.C., Apr. 5, 1935; d. Joseph and Sarah (Stein) G.; m. Howard S. Vogel, June 30, 1962; 1 child, Michael S. B.A., Bklyn. Coll., 1955; J.D., Columbia U., 1958. Bar: N.Y. 1959, U.S. Dist. Ct. (so. dist. and ea. dist.) N.Y. 1960, U.S. Ct. Appeals (2d cir.) 1960, U.S. Ct. Mil. Appeals 1962. Asst. to editor N.Y. Law Jour., N.Y.C., 1958-59; confidential asst. to U.S. atty. ea. dist. N.Y., Bklyn., 1959-61; assoc. Whitman & Ransom, N.Y.C., 1961-70, ptnr., 1971-93; ptnr. Whitman Breed Abbott & Morgan LLP, N.Y.C., 1993—. Mem. ABA (individual rights sect., real property & trust law sect.), Fed. Bar Counsel, N.Y. State Bar Assn. (trusts and estates com.), N.Y. State Dist. Attys. Assn., Assn. of Bar of City of N.Y., Columbia Law Sch. Alumni Assn. (bd. dirs.), Girls, Inc. (resources com.), Princeton Club. Estate planning, Probate, Estate taxation. Home: 169 E 69th St New York NY 10021-5163 Office: Whitman Breed Abbott & Morgan LLP 200 Park Ave New York NY 10166-0005

**GELB, RICHARD MARK,** lawyer; b. N.Y.C., June 12, 1947; s. Harold Seymour and Sylvia Mildred (Miller) G.; m. Gail Kleven, July 29, 1973; 1 child, Daniel Kleven. BA, NYU, 1969; JD, Boston Coll., 1973. Bar: Mass. 1973, N.Y. 1975, D.C. 1975, U.S. Dist. Ct. (so. and ea. dists.) N.Y. 1975, U.S. Ct. Appeals (2d cir.) 1975, U.S. Dist. Ct. Conn. 1977, U.S. Ct. Appeals (1st cir.) 1978, U.S. Dist. Ct. Mass. 1978, U.S. Supreme Ct. 1980. Assoc. Proskauer, Rose, Goetz & Mendelsohn, LLP, N.Y.C., 1975-77; ptnr. Gelb & Gelb, LLP, Boston, 1987—. Contbr. articles to profl. publs. Mem. Mass. Bar Assn. (ethics com. 1991-96, civil litig. coun. 1994-96, chmn. bus. litig. com. 1992-94, assoc. editor Mass. Law Rev. 1982-87), Am. Inn of Ct. Found. (trustee 1994-98), Boston Inn of Ct. (pres. 1993-94), Boston Coll. Law Sch. Intellectual Property Am. Inns of Ct. (pres. 1998—), Pi Sigma Alpha. Democrat. Jewish. Federal civil litigation, State civil litigation. Home: 60 Pine Hill Rd Swampscott MA 01907-2240 Office: Gelb & Gelb LLP 20 Custom House St Ste 1030 Boston MA 02110-3559

**GELB, ROGER KENNETH,** lawyer; b. Washington, Nov. 21, 1965; s. Joseph Donald and Anne (Mirman) G.; m. Linda Blinkhorn, 1996. BA, U. S.C., 1987; JD, Nova Southeastern U., Ft. Lauderdale, Fla., 1991. Bar: Pa. 1992, D.C. 1993, U.S. Dist. Ct. D.C. 1994, U.S. Ct. Appeals (D.C. cir.) 1995, U.S. Supreme Ct., 1996. Assoc. Joseph D. Gelb, Chartered, Washington, 1992-93; ptnr. Gelb & Gelb P.C., Washington, 1993—. Vice pres. Crestberry Homeowner's Assn., Bethesda, Md., 1993-95. Mem. ATLA, ABA, Internat. Assn. Jewish Lawyers and Jurists, Bethesda Country Club. Personal injury. Office: Gelb & Gelb PC 1120 Connecticut Ave NW Washington DC 20036-3902

**GELBER, DON JEFFREY,** lawyer; b. L.A., Mar. 10, 1940; s. Oscar and Betty Sheila (Chernitsky) G.; m. Jessica Jeasun Song, May 15, 1967; children: Victoria, Jonathan, Rebecca, Robert. Student UCLA, 1957-58, Reed Coll., 1958-59; AB, Stanford U., 1961, JD, 1963. Bar: Calif. 1964, Hawaii 1964, U.S. Dist. Ct. (cen. and no. dists. Calif.) 1964, U.S. Dist. Ct. Hawaii 1964, U.S. Ct. Appeals (9th cir.) 1964, U.S. Supreme Ct. 1991. Assoc. Greenstein, Yamane & Cowan, Honolulu, 1964-67; reporter Penal Law Revision Project, Hawaii Jud. Council, Honolulu, 1967-69; assoc. H. William Burgess, Honolulu, 1969-72; ptnr. Burgess & Gelber, Honolulu, 1972-73; prin. Law Offices of Don Jeffrey Gelber, Honolulu, 1974-77; pres. Gelber & Wagner, Honolulu, 1978-83, Gelber & Gelber, Honolulu, 1984-89, Gelber, Gelber, Ingersoll, Klevansky & Faris, Honolulu, 1990—; legal counsel Hawaii State Senate Judiciary Com., 1965; adminstrv. asst. to majority floor leader Hawaii State Senate, 1966, legal csl. Edn. Com., 1967, 68; majority counsel Hawaii Ho. of Reps., 1974; spl. counsel Hawaii State Senate, 1983. Contbr. articles to legal publs. Mem. State Bar Calif., ABA (sect. bus. law), Am. Bankruptcy Inst., Hawaii State Bar Assn. (sect. bankruptcy law, bd. dirs. 1991-93, pres. 1993). Clubs: Pacific, Plaza (Honolulu). Bankruptcy, Federal civil litigation, Real property. Office: Gelber Gelber Ingersoll Klevansky & Faris 745 Fort Street Mall Ste 1400 Honolulu HI 96813-3877

**GELBER, ROBERT CARY,** law librarian; b. N.Y.C., Dec. 21, 1951; s. Louis and Dora (Zimmerman) G.; m. Cathy Lynne Domin, Mar. 24, 1974; 1 child, Cari. BA, Pace U., 1973; MLS, Pratt Inst., 1974. Asst. cataloger N.Y. County Lawyer's Assn., N.Y.C., 1969-74; librarian Office Spl. State Prosecutor, N.Y.C., 1974; asst. libr. N.Y. State Appellate Div., N.Y.C., 1974-97, sr. ct. analyst, 1997—; instr. legal rsch., adult edn. program Baruch Coll., SUNY, 1990-91. Mem. Law Librarians Assn. Greater N.Y. Office: NY State Appellate Div 27 Madison Ave New York NY 10010-2201

**GELFMAN, PETER TRUSTMAN,** lawyer; b. New Rochelle, N.Y., Oct. 3, 1963; s. Robert William and Phyllis (Trustman) G.; m. Marguerite Gabrielle Dreyfuss, Sept. 6, 1992; children: Justine Caroline, Max Sokoloff. AB magna cum laude, Harvard Coll., 1986; JD, Yale U., 1989. Bar: N.Y. 1989, D.C. 1990, U.S. Dist. Ct. (so. and ea. dists.) N.Y. 1990, U.S. Ct. Appeals (2nd cir.) 1991. Assoc. Cravath, Swaine & Moore, N.Y.C., 1989-91; asst. U.S. Atty. U.S. Dist. Ct. (so. dist.), N.Y.C., 1992-96; sr. atty. Westvaco Corp., N.Y.C., 1996-99; sr. assoc. gen. counsel Sequa Corp., N.Y.C., 1999—. Active Town Village Civic Club, Scarsdale, N.Y., 1998—; bd. edn. Mt. Pleasant Cottage UFSD, Pleasantville, N.Y., 1999—; bd. ethics Scarsdale (N.Y.) Village, 1999—. Mem. ABA, Am. Corp. Counsel Assn., Assn. Bar City of N.Y. General corporate, Contracts commercial. Office: Sequa Corp 200 Park Ave Rm 4401 New York NY 10166-4400

**GELFMAN, RICHARD DAVID,** lawyer, television journalist; b. Northampton, Mass., Oct. 26, 1947; s. Harold and Lena (August) G.; m. Lenore R. Greenberg, July 27, 1969; children: Hillary, Joanna, Victoria. BS, U. Mass., 1969; JD, U. Md., 1972. Bar: Md. 1973, U.S. Dist. Ct. Md. 1973, D.C. 1974. Chief atty. Legal Aid Bur., Balt., 1973-74; ptnr. Gelfman & Gelfman, P.A., Columbia, Md., 1974—; anchor, reporter Sta. WBAL-TV, Balt., 1974-89; ptnr. Gelfman & Spahn, Columbia, 1989—; reporter various documentaries and investigative reports Sta. WBAL-TV, 1978-89, Sta. WJZ-TV, 1989—. Recipient George Polk award L.I. U., 1982, Unity award Lincoln U., 1983, award UPI, 1986, Alexander Hamilton award Commn. on Bicentennial of U.S. Constn., 1988, Emmy award D.C. region Nat. Assn. TV Arts & Scis., 1991, 92, 93, award Special Reporting AP Broadcasters Assn., 1992, award Excellence in Journalism SPJ, 1994. Mem. ABA (gavel awards 1981, 82), Assn. Trial Lawyers Am., Md. State Bar Assn. (gavel award 1983, 85, 88), Md. Trial Lawyers Assn. General practice, General corporate, Real property. Office: Gelfman & Spahn 5401 Twin Knolls Rd Ste 7 Columbia MD 21045-3257

**GELFMAN, STUART G.,** lawyer; b. Chgo., May 22, 1959; s. Paul M. and Florine Gelfman; m. Wendy Shorr, Sept. 4, 1988; children: William, Noah, Phoebe. BSBA, U. Ill., 1981; JD, John Marshall Law Sch., 1984. Bar: U.S. Dist. Ct. (no. dist.) Ill. 1984. Assoc. Gelfman and Goldberg, Glenview, Ill., 1984-88, ptnr., 1988-97; ptnr. Gelfman and Gelfman, Northfield, Ill., 1997—; real estate broker Gelfman Realty, Northfield. Mem. Chgo. Bar Assn. Family and matrimonial, Real property, Probate. Office: Gelfman and Gelfman 550 W Frontage Rd Ste 2720 Northfield IL 60093-1259

**GELHAUS, ROBERT JOSEPH,** lawyer, publisher; b. Missoula, Mont., Oct. 17, 1941; s. Francis Joseph and Bonnie Una (Mundhenk) G. A.B. magna cum laude, Harvard Coll., 1963; LL.B., Stanford U., 1968. Bar: Calif. 1970, U.S. Dist. Ct., U.S. Ct. Appeals 1970. Assoc. firm Howard, Prim, Rice, Nemerovski, Canady & Pollak, San Francisco, 1970-74; sole practice, San Francisco, 1974—; editor in chief Harcourt Brace Jovanovich Legal & Profl. Publs., Inc., 1974-78; pres. Robert J. Gelhaus, A Profl. Corp., 1978—; instr. econs. U. Wash., 1964-65; instr. law Stanford Law Sch., 1968-69; cons. FCC, 1968-69; asst. Calif. Law Revision Commn., 1967-68. Mem. Calif. Bar Assn., Omicron Delta Epsilon, Order Coif. Club: Harvard of San Francisco. Author: (with James C. Oldham) Summary of Labor Law, 11th edit., 1972. Antitrust, Federal civil litigation, Labor. Home: 1756 Broadway San Francisco CA 94109-2458

**GELINAS, ROBERT ALBERT,** lawyer; b. Springfield, Mass., May 28, 1930; s. Albert Edward and Alvena Loretta Gelinas; m. Judith Ann Marcure, Jan. 30, 1954; children: Lyn Ann, John, William, Michele. BS, St. Michael's Coll., 1951; LLB, Boston U., 1953. Bar: Mass. 1953, U.S. Dist. Ct. Mass. 1959, U.S. Ct. Appeals (1st cir.) 1965. Ptnr. Bulkley, Richardson and Gelinas LLP, Springfield, Mass., 1957—; spl. asst. atty. gen., Mass., 1964-70; mem. faculty trial advocacy program Mass. CLE, trustee Holyoke C.C., 1992—. Mem. Mass. Rep. Com., 1964-72; chmn. profl. unit United Way, Springfield, 1996; mem. com. Nat. Conf. Chicopee Cmty. Ctr., past pres. Recipient Tree of Life award Jewish Nat. Fund, 1997. Mem. ATLA, Mass. Acad. Trial Attys., Mass. Bar Assn., Hampden County Bar Assn. (exec. com., medico-legal com. 1992—). Roman Catholic. Avocations: outdoor activities. Administrative and regulatory, Corporate taxation, Personal injury. Office: Bulkley Richardson and Gelinas LLP 1500 Main St Ste 2700 Springfield MA 01115-0001

**GELLHORN, ERNEST ALBERT EUGENE,** lawyer; b. Oak Park, Ill., Mar. 30, 1935; s. Ernst and Hilde Betty (Obermeier) G.; m. Jaquelin Ann Silker, Feb. 1, 1958; children: Thomas Ernest, Ann Lois. BA cum laude, U. Minn., 1956, LLB magna cum laude, 1962. Bar: Ohio 1962, Va. 1975, Ariz. 1976, D.C. 1986, Calif. 1990. Assoc. Jones, Day, Reavis & Pogue, Cleve., Washington, L.A., 1962-66; prof. law Duke U. Law Sch., 1966-70, U. Va. Law Sch., 1970-75; dean Coll. Law, Ariz. State U., Tempe, 1975-78, Law Sch., U. Wash., Seattle, 1978-79; T. Munford Boyd prof. U. Va. Law Sch., Charlottesville, 1979-82; dean, Galen J. Roush prof. Case Western Res. U. Sch. Law, Cleve., 1982-86; ptnr. Jones, Day, Reavis & Pogue, L.A., Washington, 1986-94; George Mason U. Found. Prof. Law, 1995—; sr. counsel Commn. CIA Activities Within U.S., 1975. Co-author: Antitrust Law and Economics, 4th edit., 1994, Administrative Law and Process, 4th edit., 1997, The Administrative Process, 4th edit., 1993. Lt. USNR, 1956-59. Mem. ABA, Ariz. Bar Assn., Va. Bar Assn., Ohio Bar Assn., D.C. Bar Assn., Calif. Bar Assn., Phi Beta Kappa, Order of Coif. Administrative and regulatory, Antitrust, Appellate. Home: 2907 Normanstone Ln NW Washington DC 20008-2725

**GELLMAN, SUSAN BETH,** lawyer; b. Milw., July 25, 1957; d. Edward Nathan and Rosalie Ivy (Schlitz) G.; m. Jack Steven Chomsky, July 4, 1982; children: Benjamin, Addie. AB magna cum laude, Brandeis U., 1978; MS in Social Work, Columbia U., 1980; JD, Ohio State U., 1986. Bar: Ohio 1986, U.S. Dist. Ct. (so. dist.) Ohio, U.S. Dist. Ct. (no. dist.) Ohio, U.S. Ct. Appeals (6th cir.), U.S. Supreme Ct. 1992. Exec. dir. New Eng. Dist. Women's Am. ORT, Boston, 1980-82; law clk. to Hon. Max Rosenn, U.S. Ct. Appeals for 3d Cir., Wilkes-Barre, Pa., 1986-87; law clk. Hon. John Holschuh, U.S. Dist. Ct. for So. Dist. Ohio, Columbus, 1987-88; asst. pub. defender Ohio State Pub. Defender's Office, Columbus, 1990-96; ptnr. Wolman, Genshaft & Gellman, Columbus, 1996—; adj. prof. Capital U., Columbus, 1989; cons. to various state legislatures and univ. ofcls. on first amendment questions regarding proposed statutes and campus speech codes; cons. to numerous govts., practitioners, scholars, and writers internat. on hate crime and hate speech issues; participation in litig. in several state and fed. Supreme Ct. cases; cons. Assn. for Civil Rights in Israel, Soc. for Religious Pluralism in various Israeli Supreme Ct. and lower ct. cases; expert testimony before Congress on fed. hate crime bill. Mng. editor Ohio State Law Jour.; contbr. articles to profl. jours., including Sticks and Stones. Mem. legal com. Anti-Defamation League. Mem. ABA (vice chmn. first amendment rights com.), Ohio Bar Assn., Columbus Bar Assn. (profl. ethics com.), ACLU (co-chmn. Ctrl. Ohio chpt. 1990-95, legal com.), Order of Coif, Phi Beta Kappa. Democrat. Jewish. Civil rights, Constitutional, Labor. Office: Wolman Genshaft & Gellman 341 S 3d St Ste 301 Columbus OH 43215

**GELMAN, ANDREW RICHARD,** lawyer; b. Chgo., June 20, 1946; s. Sidney S. and Beverly (Burg) G.; m. Amy Herfort, Sept. 1, 1985; children: Stephen S., Adam P., Elizabeth F. BA, U. Pa., 1967; JD, U. Va., 1970. Bar: Va. 1970, Ill. 1971. Assoc. Roan & Grossman Law Firm, Chgo., 1971-74; assoc. McBride, Baker & Coles Law Firm, Chgo., 1974-77, ptnr., 1978—; mem. com. on character and fitness of Ill. Supreme Ct., Chgo., 1979-95. Bd. dirs. Scholarship and Guidance Assn., Chgo., 1979—, Inst. for Edn. and Rsch. of Children's Meml. Hosp., Chgo., 1991—, vice-chair, 1998—; chmn. Med. Rsch. Inst. Coun., 1983-86, 91-92; trustee Michael Reese Hosp. and Med. Ctr., Chgo., 1987-91. Recipient Weigle award Chgo. Bar Found., 1980. Mem. ABA (pub. understanding about the law com. 1987-91, chair probate and estate planning com. gen. practice sect. 1994-97, commn. on mental and phys. disability law 1995-97), Chgo. Bar Assn. (past chmn. divsn. probate practice com., bd. mgrs. 1978-80, chmn. young lawyers sect. 1976-77), Chgo. Estate Planning Coun. Probate, Estate planning, Estate taxation. Office: McBride Baker & Coles 500 W Madison St Fl 40 Chicago IL 60661-2511

**GELMAN, JON LEONARD,** lawyer; b. Paterson, N.J., Mar. 14, 1946; s. Carl and Gussie (Weiss) G.; m. Nancy R. Sugarman, Oct. 2, 1971; children: Michael A., Jason L. BA, Rutgers U., 1967; JD, John Marshall Law Sch., 1971. Bar: N.J. 1971, U.S. Dist. Ct. N.J. 1971, U.S. Tax Ct. 1973, U.S. Ct. Appeals (D.C. cir.) 1973, U.S. Supreme Ct. 1974, U.S. Ct. Appeals (3d cir.) 1980, N.Y. 1985. Pvt. practice Wayne, N.J., 1979—. Author: Workers' Compensation Law, 1999; contbg. columnist N.J. Law Jour.; contbr. articles to profl. jours. Mem. ATLA, Nat. Orgn. Social Security Claimants Rep., Asbestos Litigation Group, Trial Attys. N.J., D.C. Bar Assn., N.J. Bar Assn. (workers' compensation sect.), Passaic County Bar Assn., Workplace Litig. Group (trustee). E-mail: jon@gelmans.com. Workers' compensation, Personal injury, Product liability. Office: 1455 Valley Rd 3rd Flr PO Box 934 Wayne NJ 07474-0934

**GELPI, C. JAMES (JIM GELPI),** lawyer; b. New Orleans, Sept. 2, 1940; s. Sidney L. and Althea Estelle (Moffet) G.; m. Brenda Taylor, Sept. 2, 1989; 1 child, C. Scott. BA, La. State U., 1962; JD, Loyola U. of the South, New Orleans, 1966. Bar: La. 1966, U.S. Dist. Ct. (ea. and mid. dists.) La. 1966,

U.S. Ct. Appeals (5th cir.) 1966, U.S. Supreme Ct. 1981, U.S. Tax Ct. 1982, U.S. Dist. Ct. (we. dist.) La. 1985. Assoc. Badeaux & Discon, New Orleans, 1966-68, McBreen, Tobin & Gelpi, Chgo. and New Orleans, 1968-73; exec. asst. atty. gen. Atty. Gen.'s Office, Baton Rouge, 1973-76; sr. atty. Gelpi and Assocs., New Orleans, 1976—; mem. skills faculty Loyola Sch. of Law, New Orleans, 1989—; mgr. River Ridge Energy, L.L.C. Author instructional brochures Preparing Your Case for Trial in Five Easy and Logical Steps, Opening Statements Do's and Don'ts, Preparing Your Witness. Founder Alliance for Good Govt., New Orleans; bd. dirs. River Ridge (La.) Community Assn. Roman Catholic. Avocation: chess. Administrative and regulatory, General civil litigation, General practice. Home: 250 Bendler Dr River Ridge LA 70123-2602 Office: Gelpi & Assocs PLC 203 Carondelet St Ste 907 New Orleans LA 70130-3087

**GELT, THEODORE ZVI,** lawyer, director; b. Denver, Jan. 29, 1950; s. Louis Eleazar and Betty Goldie (Hellerstein) G.; (div. Apr. 1987); children: Timothy, Sarah; m. Sharon Gelt, July 30, 1993. BA, U. Colo., 1972; JD, U. Denver, 1975; LLM, NYU, 1976. Bar: U.S. Tax Ct. Assoc. Atler, Zall & Haligman, P.C., Denver, 1975-77, Head, Moye, Carver & Ray, Denver, 1977; mem., dir. Silver and Gelt, Denver, 1977-81, Theodore Z. Gelt, P.C., Denver, 1981-82, Roath & Brega, Denver, 1982-88, Gelt, Fleishman & Sterling, Denver, 1989-99, Gelt, Paddison & Assocs. P.C., Denver, 1999—; adj. prof. grad. tax program U. Denver, asst. prof., 1978. Mem. ABA (partnership com. of tax sect.), Nebr. Bar Assn., Colo. Bar Assn. (exec. coun. of tax sect., sec., treas. 1980-81, vice chmn. 1981-82, chmn. 1982-83), Denver Bar Assn. Estate taxation, Estate planning. Office: Gelt Paddison & Assocs PC 1600 Broadway Ste 2600 Denver CO 80202-4989

**GEMBACZ, GILBERT THADDEUS,** judge; b. Lexington, Miss., Aug. 1, 1947; s. Stanley Thaddeus and Mary Dillahunt (Sanders) G.; m. Camille Frances Giraldi, June 27, 1976. BA, Southwestern State Coll., Weatherford, Okla., 1969; JD, Southwestern U., L.A., 1979; MBA in Taxation, Golden Gate U., 1984. Bar: Calif. 1980, U.S. Ct. Appeals (9th cir.) 1980, U.S. Dist. Ct. (cen. dist.) Calif. 1980, U.S. Tax Ct. 1985, U.S. Supreme Ct. 1990. Pvt. practice L.A., 1980-83; staff counsel Calif. State Bd. Equalization, Sacramento, 1983-85; litigation atty. IRS Office of Chief Counsel, L.A., 1985-90; asst. dist. counsel immigration and naturalization svc. U.S. Dept. Justice, L.A., 1990-96; judge U.S. Immigration Ct., L.A., 1996—. Mem. Emergency Preparedness Staff, La Canada, Calif., 1991—. Capt. U.S. Army, 1969-76, col. U.S. Army Res., 1995. Mem. ABA, Calif. Bar Assn., Los Angeles County Bar Assn., Italian Am. Bar Assn. Avocations: sailing, golf. Office: US Immigration Ct 606 S Olive St Fl 15 Los Angeles CA 90014-1604

**GENBERG, IRA,** lawyer; b. Newark, July 27, 1947; s. Jack and Ann (Lerman) G.; m. Rosemary Lawlor, Jan. 15, 1981; children: Jack Michael, Anne Rebecca. AB magna cum laude, Rutgers U., 1969; JD, U. Pa., 1972. Bar: Ga. 1972, D.C. 1978. Assoc. Haas, Holland, Levison & Gibert, Atlanta, 1972-75; ptnr. Stokes, Shapiro, Fussell & Genberg, Atlanta, 1975-87; ptnr., head litigation sect. Smith, Gambrell & Russell LLP, Atlanta, 1987—; spkr. Seminar on Constrn. Litigation, Atlanta, 1985, Seminar on Constrn. Law, Atlanta, 1986; co-chmn. Seminar on Trying A Complex Constrn. Case, 1994. Contbr. articles to Constrn. Bus. Review Mag. Mem. ABA, Ga. Bar Assn., Atlanta Bar Assn., D.C. Bar Assn. Antitrust, General civil litigation, Construction. Office: Smith Gambrell & Russell LLP 1230 Peachtree St NE Atlanta GA 30309-3592

**GENEGO, WILLIAM JOSEPH,** lawyer; b. Albany, Mar. 27, 1950; s. William Joseph and Olga Alice (Sultan) G. BS in Bus. and Pub. Adminstrn. magna cum laude, NYU, 1972; JD, Yale U., 1975; LLM, Georgetown U., 1977. Bar: D.C. 1975, Calif. 1982, U.S. Supreme Ct. 1984, other dist. and appellate cts. Spl. asst. state's atty. Cir. and Dist. Cts. Montgomery County, Md., 1975-77; staff atty. legal intern program Georgetown U. Law Ctr., Washington, 1975-77, adj. prof., dep. dir. legal intern program, 1977-79; cons., vis. supervising atty. Yale Legal Svcs. Orgn., Law Sch. Yale U., New Haven, 1977; with Baker & Fine, Cambridge, Mass., 1980-81; asst. clin. prof. Law Ctr. U. So. Calif., L.A., 1981-83, assoc. clin. prof., 1983-86, clin. prof., 1986-89, adj. prof., 1990-92; vis. prof. law Boston U., 1990, UCLA, 1991-92; pvt. practice Law Offices of William J. Genego, Santa Monica, Calif., 1990—; mem. practitioners' adv. group U.S. Sentencing Commn., 1989—; presenter in field. Mem. adv. bd. Criminal Practice Manual, Bur. Nat. Affairs, 1987—; editor Yale Law Jour., 1974-75; contbr. articles to legal publs. Bd. dirs. Nat. Network for Right to Counsel, 1986-88. Recipient Ann. Humanitarian award inmate rep. com. Fed. Correctional Instn., Danbury, Conn., 1974. Mem. NACDL (chairperson com. on rules of practice and procedure 1991—, Pres.'s award 1988), ABA (mem. ad hoc com. on U.S. Sentencing Commn. 1986—, chairperson competency com. sect. criminal justice 1983-85), Nat. Legal Aid and Defender Assn. (chairperson def. counsel competency com. 1984-87), Calif. Pub. Defenders Assn., Calif. Attys. for Criminal Justice. Criminal, Appellate. Office: Main St Law Bldg 2115 Main St Santa Monica CA 90405-2215

**GENESON, DAVID FRANKLIN,** lawyer; b. N.Y.C., Aug. 29, 1947; s. Jerome and Rose Wall Geneson; m. Mary Elizabeth Thornton, Sept. 5, 1987; children: Jesse Thornton, Arianna Chastain. BS, Rensselaer Poly. Inst., 1969; JD, U. Miami, 1973. Bar: Fla. 1974, U.S. Dist. Ct. (so. dist.) Fla. 1975, U.S. Ct. Appeals (5th cir.) 1975, D.C. 1979, U.S. Supreme Ct. 1985, U.S. Dist. Ct. D.C. 1989, U.S. Dist. Ct. (we. and ea. dists.) Va. 1994, Va. 1995, U.S. Ct. Appeals (4th and 11th cirs.) 1997, U.S. Dist. Ct. (so. dist.) Tx. 1998. Civil engr. N.Y. State Dept. Transp., Albany, 1969; sys. and programming supr. Dade County Schs., Miami, Fla., 1969-74; atty. Adminstrv. Divsn. U.S. Dept. Justice, Washington, 1974-75; asst. U.S. atty. So. Dist. Fla., Miami, 1975-78; sr. trial atty. fraud sect. criminal divsn. U.S. Dept. Justice, Washington, 1978-84; asst. U.S. atty. U.S. Attys. Office, Washington, 1984-90; ptnr. Hunter & Williams, Washington, 1990—; team leader, instr. Nat. Inst. Trial Advocacy, N.Y.C. and Boulder, 1981—; instr. Harvard Law Sch., Cambridge, Mass., Emory Law Sch., Atlanta, Weidner Law Sch., Wilmington, Del., 1988—. Editor, contbr.: Law and Psychiatry, 1973; contbr. articles to profl. jours. Pres. Riverview Civic Assn., Fairfax County, Va., 1995—; bd. dirs. Fairfax County Wetlands Bd., 1995—. Criminal, Environmental, Federal civil litigation. Office: Hunton & Williams 1900 K St NW Washington DC 20006-1110

**GENG, THOMAS W.,** lawyer; b. St. Paul, Dec. 6, 1958; s. Donald Francis and Patricia (Barry) G.; m. Nancy Ferrell, May 16, 1998; 1 child, Stephanie Lynn Ferrell. BA, St. Mary's Coll. of Calif., Moraga, 1981; JD, U. Minn., 1991. Bar: Minn. 1991, U.S. Ct. Appeals (8th cir.) 1992. Mem. staff U.S. Rep. James H. Scheuer, Washington, 1982-86, chief of staff, 1986-88; law clk. Judge Ann Montgomery, Mpls., 1991-92, Judge Gary Larson, Mpls., 1993; atty. Doshan & Bremseth, Wayzata, Minn., 1994—. Recipient Appreciation award St. Paul Optimists Club, 1977. Personal injury, Appellate. Home: 1001 Wildhurst Trl Mound MN 55364-9640 Office: Doshan & Bremseth 810 Lake St E Wayzata MN 55391-1837

**GENGA, JOHN MICHAEL,** lawyer; b. Detroit, Apr. 28, 1962. BA, Stanford U., 1983; JD, U. Mich., 1986. Bar: Calif. 1986, U.S. Dist. Ct. (ctrl. and ea. dists.) Calif. 1987, U.S. Dist. Ct. (no. and so. dists.) Calif. 1988, U.S. Ct. Appeals (9th cir.) 1988, U.S. Supreme Ct. 1993, U.S. Ct. Appeals (10th cir.) 1997. Assoc. Jones, Day, Reavis & Pogue, L.A., 1986-88, Hill Wynne Troop & Meisinger, L.A., 1988-93; ptnr. Troop Steuber Pasich Reddick & Tobey, LLP, L.A., 1994—. Mem. ABA, State Bar Calif., L.A. County Bar Assn. General civil litigation, Entertainment, Intellectual property. Office: Reddick & Tobey LLP 2029 Century Park E Ste 2400 Los Angeles CA 90067-3010

**GENIA, JAMES MICHAEL,** lawyer; b. Chgo., Sept. 16, 1964; s. Anthony Leo and Anne Louise (Hawley) G. BA, Augsburg Coll., 1987; JD, William Mitchell Coll. Law, 1990. Bar: Minn. 1990, U.S. Dist. Ct. Minn. 1992, U.S. Ct. Appeals (8th cir.) 1994, U.S. Supreme Ct. 1999. Judicial law clk. State Minn., Duluth, 1990-92; dep. solicitor gen. Mille Lacs Band of Ojibwe Indians, Onamia, Minn., 1992-93, solicitor gen., 1993-99; atty. Lockridge Grindal Nauen, Mpls., 1999—; bd. dirs. Woodlands Nat. Bank, Onamia, 1996—, chmn., 1997—; vice-chmn. bd. dirs. Anishinabe O.I.C., Onamia, 1992—; bd. dirs. Johnson Inst. Found., 1998—; lectr. Am. Indian sovereignty and treaty rights various univs., cntinuing edn. seminars, civic groups, 1992—; adj. prof. St. Cloud State U., 1999—. Actor Mille Lacs Cmty. Theater, Onamia, 1996—. Bd. dirs. Johnson Inst. Found., 1998—. Mem. ABA, Am. Trial Lawyers Assn., Minn. Am. Indian Bar Assn., Minn. State Bar Assn., William Mitchell Coll. Law Alumni Assn. (bd. dirs. 1996-99). Avocations: softball, golf, jogging, reading, acting. Office: Lockridge Grindal Nauen Ste 2200 100 Washington Ave S Minneapolis MN 55401

**GENIESSE, ROBERT JOHN,** lawyer; b. Appleton, Wis., Sept. 16, 1929; s. Arthur John and Rhoda (Miller) G.; m. Jane Elizabeth Fletcher, June 10, 1961; children: Julia Forrest, Thomas Guy. BA magna cum laude, Williams Coll., 1951; LLB cum laude, Harvard U., 1957. Bar: N.Y. 1958, D.C. 1982. Assoc. Debevoise and Plimpton, N.Y.C., 1957-61, 64-66, ptnr., 1966-94; asst. U.S. atty. So. Dist. N.Y., 1962-63, chief appellate atty., 1963-64. Editor Harvard Law Rev., 1955-57. Bd. dirs. Legal Action Ctr., N.Y., 1973-78, Environ. Def. Fund, 1974-82; trustee Williams Coll., 1974-87; trustee World Monuments Fund, 1993—, sec., gen. counsel, 1995—; trustee Nat. Bldg. Mus., 1994—; trustee Sterling and Francine Clark Art Inst., Williamstown, Mass., 1974—, pres., 1987-98. 1st lt. Inf. U.S. Army, 1952-54. Mem. N.Y. State Bar Assn., D.C. Bar ASsn., Soc. Alumni of Williams Coll. (pres. 1973-74), Phi Beta Kappa. Federal civil litigation, Criminal, Private international. Home: PO Box 516 Boca Grande FL 33921-0516 Office: Devevoise & Plimpton 555 13th St NW Ste 1100E Washington DC 20004-1163

**GENKIN, BARRY HOWARD,** lawyer; b. Phila., Aug. 8, 1949; s. Paul and Pearl (Rosenfeld) G.; m. Marian Block, Aug. 15, 1975; children: Matthew Todd, Kimberly Beth. BS cum laude, Pa. State U., 1971; JD cum laude, U. Balt., 1974; LLM in Taxation, Georgetown U., 1977. Bar: Pa. 1975, Wash. 1977, N.Y. 1995. Spl. counsel div. corp. fin. SEC, Washington, 1975-78; ptnr. Blank Rome Comisky & McCauly LLP, Phila., 1979-93, co-chmn. corp. dept., dist. com., mgmt. com., chmn. budget com.; bd. dirs. Smeal Bus. Sch., Pa. State U.; lectr. various orgns. Contbr. U. Balt. Law Rev., 1991—; lectr. various orgns. Mem. ABA, Pa. Bar Assn., Savs. Insts., Pa. Savs. League, N.J. Savs. League, Meadowlands Country Club, Heuisler Honor Soc., Omicron Delta Kappa. Mergers and acquisitions, Securities, Banking. Home: 544 Howe Rd Merion Station PA 19066-1129 Office: Blank Rome Comisky & McCauley LLP One Logan Sq Philadelphia PA 19103

**GENOVA, DIANE MELISANO,** lawyer; b. Aug. 8, 1948; d. Joseph Louis and Ines (Fiumana) Melisano; m. Joseph Steven Genova, Jan. 15, 1983; children: Anthony Robert, Matthew Edward. AB, Barnard Coll., 1970; postgrad., Harvard U., 1970-71; JD, Columbia U., 1975. Assoc. Milbank, Tweed, Hadley & McCloy, N.Y.C., 1975-80, Tung, Drabkin & Boynton, N.Y.C., 1980-81; v.p., asst. resident counsel Morgan Guaranty Trust Co. N.Y., N.Y.C., 1981-90, mng. dir., assoc. gen. counsel, 1990—. Harlan Fiske Stone scholar, 1972-75. Mem. Assn. of Bar of City of N.Y., N.Y. State Bar Assn. Roman Catholic. Banking, Finance. Office: J P Morgan & Co Inc 60 Wall St New York NY 10260-0001

**GENRICH, WILLARD ADOLPH,** lawyer; b. Buffalo, Feb. 19, 1915; s. John E. and Emma P. (Luescher) G.; m. Eleanor M. Merrill, Mar. 15, 1941; children: Willa Genrich Long, Ellen Genrich Rusling, Willard A., Jeffrey M. LLB, U. Buffalo, 1938; LHD, Medaille Coll., 1973, N.Y. Med. Coll., 1981, Hofstra U., 1985, SUNY, 1986; LLD, Canisius Coll., 1975, L.I. U., 1979, Hobart Coll., 1981, Fordham U., 1984, N.Y. Inst. Tech., 1979; D in Comml. Sci., Niagara U., 1980; D in Civil Law, Mercy Coll., 1981; D in Chiropractic Sci., N.Y. Chiropractic Coll., 1983; LLD, D'Youville Coll., 1987. Bar: N.Y. 1939. Spl. agt. FBI, 1942-46; pvt. practice Amherst, N.Y., 1946—; pres. Genrich Builders, Inc., Buffalo, 1966—; owner, operator 2 hotels; dir. real estate corps.; bd. dirs. N.Y. State Higher Edn. Assistance Corp., 1962-73; bd. regents U. State N.Y., 1973-95, vice chancellor bd. regents, 1977-79, chancellor, 1980-85, chancellor emeritus, 1986—; del. N.Y. State Constl. Conv., 1967. Past trustee N.E. br. YMCA; trustee First Presbyn. Ch. Recipient Pres.'s award Daemen Coll., 1975; Disting. Citizen's award DeVeaux Sch., 1975; Disting. Alumni award U. Buffalo Law Sch., 1978; Disting. Alumni award Alumni Assn. SUNY-Buffalo, 1980; Disting. Citizen's Achievement award Canisius Coll. Bd. Regents, 1980; Citation of Appreciation, Commn. of Ind. Colls. and U. Western N.Y. Consortium of Higher Edn., 1978; Pres.'s award Hilbert Coll., 1983; John Jay award Commn. Ind. Colls. and Univs., 1984; Svc. award Daemen Coll., 1984, Bernard E. Hughes Recognition award N.Y. State Assn. Health, Phys. Edn. Recreation and Dance, 1986; Disting. Svc. award N.Y. State 4201 Schs. Assn., 1986, Merit award N.Y. State Assn. of Two Yr. Colls., 1986; 1st Disting. Alumnus award Benett High Sch., 1990; Friend of Children award N.Y. Assn. Sch. Psychologists, 1991; Community Svc. award Amherst GOP, 1991. Hon.life membership award, N.Y. State, Parent Tchr. Assn.,1993, Daemen Coll. Pres. award, 1994, Park Sch. award, Disting. Edn. Svc., award 1995, Home Economic Tchr. Assn. Corning award, hon. mem. of bd. of visitors of Batavia School for the Blind, hon. mem. Amherst So. Rotary Club. Mem. ABA, N.Y. State Bar Assn., Erie County Bar Assn., Am. Judicature Soc., N.Y. Hon. State PTA (life), Rotary. Real property, Landlord-tenant, General corporate. Home: 66 Getzville Rd Buffalo NY 14226-3514 Office: 4287 Main St Snyder NY 14226-3504

**GENS, RICHARD HOWARD,** lawyer, consultant; b. Lynn, Mass., Jan. 29, 1929; s. Aaron Leonard and Doris L. (Damsky) G.; m. Helen Diane Pransky, June 10, 1952; children—William, Sara Lee, Julie Ann, James, Cory, Noah. B.A., Ohio State, 1949; J.D. cum laude, Boston U., 1952. Bar: Mass. 1952, U.S. Dist. Ct. Mass. 1953, U.S. Ct. Claims 1953, U.S. Ct. Appeals (1st cir.) 1954, U.S. Ct. Appeals (5th cir.) 1975, U.S. Ct. Appeals (7th cir.) 1980, U.S. Supreme Ct. 1956. Atty., Isadore H.Y. Muchnick, Boston, 1952-54; mem. firm Sheff & Gens, Boston, 1954-58, Richard H. Gens, Boston, 1958-73, Leppo & Gens, Boston, 1973-77, Gens & Gens, Sherborn, Mass., 1978—; dir. Voice, Inc., Bellingham; asst. atty. gen. Commonwealth of Mass., 1958-61. Bd. dirs. of pub. charities Commonwealth of Mass., 1959-61. Republican. Jewish. State civil litigation, Criminal, Health. Home and Office: 345 Camp St Apt 602 West Yarmouth MA 02673-2474

**GENTILE, PAULA C.,** lawyer. BA, UCLA, 1971; JD, Southwestern Law Sch., L.A., 1977. Bar: Calif. 1977. Atty. Hill, Genson, Even, L.A.; law prof. U. West Los Angeles, L.A.; judge pro tem L.A. Mcpl. Ct.; hearing officer City of Las Vegas; judge pro tem Justice Ct., Las Vegas; litigation atty. Mirage Resorts, Las Vegas. Trustee Police Civil Svc. Bd., Las Vetas; v.p. Women's Polit. Caucus, Las Vegas. Mem. Italian Lawyers Assn. (pres.). Office: Mirage Resorts Inc 3250 Industrial Rd Las Vegas NV 89109-1132

**GENTINO, ROBERT E.,** lawyer; b. Hartford, Conn., Dec. 9, 1954; s. Edward Joseph and Marjorie Jean (Kissinger) G. BA summa cum laude, U. Conn., 1976; JD, Cornell U., 1980. Bar: Calif. 1980, U.S. Dist. Ct. (ctrl. dist.) Calif. 1980, U.S. Ct. Appeals (9th cir.) 1986. Congl. intern U.S. Rep. William Cotter, Washington, 1975; assoc. Wyman, Bautzer, Rothman, Kuchel & Silbert, L.A., 1980-83; pvt. practice L.A., 1984—; judge pro tem Mcpl. Ct. L.A. County, 1990—; pro bono pub. counsel; law sch. moot ct. judge. Trustee Hollywood United Meth. Ch. General civil litigation, Contracts commercial. Office: 10 Universal City Plz Ste 2000 Universal Cty CA 91608-1074

**GENTRY, FRED DEE,** lawyer; b. Yakia, Wash., Apr. 26, 1940; s. Dee Frederick and Dorthy Marie (Dunne) G.; m. Mary Elizabeth Gladhart, Aug. 21, 1965; 1 child, Katherine. B.A., U. Wash., 1962; J.D., U. Idaho, 1965. Bar: Wash. 1966. U.S. Supreme Ct. 1977. Dep. pros. atty. Thurston County, Olympia, Wash., 1966-68, pros. atty., 1968-69; ptnr. Bean & Gentry, Olympia, 1969—; prof. law St. Martins Coll., Lacey, Wash., 1981-84. Mem. Wash. Def. Counsel, Wash. Trial Lawyers Assn. Personal injury, Insurance, State civil litigation. Home: 516 Dover Pt NE Olympia WA 98506-9726 Office: Bean & Gentry 320 Columbia St NW Olympia WA 98501-1031

**GENTRY, GAVIN MILLER,** lawyer; b. N.Y.C., Oct. 5, 1930; s. Curtis Gavin and Grace (Wattenbarger) G.; m. Mary Jane Coleman, Sept. 28, 1963; children—Janie Coleman, Grace Eleanor. B.S., U. Tenn., 1954, J.D., 1954. Bar: Tenn. 1954, U.S. Dist. Ct. (we. dist.) Tenn. 1956, U.S. Supreme Ct. 1978. Trial counsel U.S. Army, 1954-56; with Armstrong, Allen, Prewitt, Gentry, Johnston & Holmes, Memphis, 1956—, sr. ptnr., 1976—; mem. redrafting com. Tenn. Corp. Law; guest lectr. Memphis State U., U. Tenn. Ctr. Health Scis.; dir. corps. Author: Great Destinations in the Smokies, 1995. Mem. Pres.'s coun. Rhodes Coll., 1970—; bd. dirs. Girl Scouts U.S.A., 1973-75; pres. Memphis Tennis Assn., 1960-66, Tenn. Tennis Assn., 1960-61; treas. Tenn. br. Maureen Connelly Brinker Tennis Found., 1972-79; pres. Les Passees Rehab. Ctr., 1977, Lausanne Sch., 1975-78; elder Idlewild Presbyn. Ch. 1st lt. AUS, 1954-56. Recipient Faculty prize U. Tenn., 1953, 1st prize will writing U. Tenn., 1954; numerous awards and prizes for tennis, 1947—. Mem. ABA, Memphis and Shelby County Bar Assn. (bd. dirs. 1989-90), Tenn. Bar Assn., Am. Soc. Hosp. Attys., Tenn. Hosp. Assn., Nat. Health Lawyers Assn., Am. Soc. Law and Medicine. Club: Univ. (Memphis). Health, General corporate, General civil litigation. Office: Armstrong Allen Prewitt Gentry Johnston & Holmes Brinkley Plz 80 Monroe Ave Ste 700 Memphis TN 38103-2467

**GENTRY, MACK A.,** lawyer; b. Knoxville, Tenn., July 18, 1944; s. Edgar C. and Elizabeth (Cates) G.; m. Cheryl T. Gentry; children: Tucker J., Carter L., Cates E. BSBA, U. Tenn., 1966, JD, 1968; LLM in Taxation, NYU, 1976. Bar: Tenn. 1969, U.S. Dist. Ct. (ea. dist.) Tenn. 1983, U.S. Tax Ct. 1983, U.S. Claims Ct. 1985, U.S. Ct. Appeals (6th cir.) 1986, U.S. Ctl. Appeals (fed. cir.) 1986. Assoc. Kramer, Johnson, Rayson, Greenwood & McVeigh, Knoxville, 1972-75; pres. Gentry, Tipton, Kizer & McLemore, P.C., Knoxville, 1976—; bd. dirs. First & Farmers Bank, Somerset, Ky. Trustee Tenn. Fed. Tax Inst.; bd. dirs. Met. YMCA; bd. dirs., treas. Asbury Ctrs., Inc., U. Tenn. Coll. Law Alumni Adv. Coun. Mem. Tenn. Bar Assn., Knoxville Bar Assn. (chmn. tax sect. 1978-79), Beta Alpha Psi, Phi Delta Phi (v.p. 1966). Taxation, general, Estate planning. Office: Gentry Tipton Kizer & McLemore PC 800 S Gay St Ste 2610 Knoxville TN 37929-2610

**GENZ, MICHAEL ANDREW,** lawyer; b. N.Y.C., Jan. 24, 1947; s. Leonard Francis and Martha Virginia (Tidwell) G.; m. Patricia Ann Hayes, July 8, 1972; children: Andrew, Daniel. BS in Fgn. Svc., Georgetown U., 1969; MA in Tchg., Yale U., 1970; JD, Cath. U., 1980. Police officer New Haven Police Dept., 1971-73; program analyst Nat. Planning Assn., Washington, 1974-76; staff atty. Client Centered Legal Svcs. S.W. Va., Inc., Castlewood, 1980-83; chief atty. So. Md. office Legal Aid Bur., Inc., Hughesville, 1983-95; program officer Legal Svcs. Corp., Washington, 1995-98, dir. office of program performance, 1999—; atty. mem. Md. Trial Ct. Jud. Selection Com. Dist. 12, Charles County, Md., 1986-95; mem. bd. govs. ACLU of Md., Balt., 1986-91. Contbr. articles to profl. jours. Bd. mem. Campaign for Human Devel., Washington, 1986-91; pres. Charles County Human Svcs. Coun., La Plata, Md., 1987-88. Mem. ABA, Va. State Bar Assn., Md. State Bar Assn., Charles County Bar Assn. Landlord-tenant, Juvenile, Consumer commercial. Home: 7706 Spring Oak Dr La Plata MD 20646-3984 Office: Legal Svcs Corp 750 1st St NE Washington DC 20002-4241

**GEOGHAN, JOSEPH EDWARD,** lawyer, chemical company executive; b. N.Y.C., May 26, 1937; s. Joseph Edward and Margaret Anne (Degnan) G.; m. Kathleen Mary Normile, July 15, 1961; children: Margaret, Johanna, Mary, Joseph Edward III, Daniel. BBA, St. John's U., Jamaica, N.Y., 1959; JD, Fordham U., 1964. Bar: N.Y., 1964. Staff asst., various positions law dept. Union Carbide Corp., N.Y.C., 1957-71, area atty., 1971-73, chief internat. counsel, 1973-76, sr. group counsel, 1976-80; asst. gen. counsel Union Carbide Corp., N.Y.C., Danbury, Conn., 1980-85; dep. gen. counsel Union Carbide Corp., Danbury, 1985-87, v.p., gen. counsel, 1987—, sec., 1990—, also bd. dirs. Mem. ABA, N.Y. State Bar Assn., Assn. Bar City N.Y., Corp. Bar Assn. Westchester and Fairfield (bd. dirs., pres. 1996), Assn. Gen. Counsel, Univ. Club (N.Y.C.). Roman Catholic. Avocations: reading, deep sea fishing, golf. General corporate. Office: Union Carbide Corp 39 Old Ridgebury Rd Danbury CT 06810-5108

**GEORGE, ALAN BARRY,** lawyer; b. Lorain, Ohio, Apr. 2, 1942; s. Alson Button and Mary Elizabeth (Bock) G.; m. Corinne Ann Roberts Ludy, Aug. 29, 1964 (div. 1978); m. Susan Lynn Morale, Aug. 21, 1993; 1 child, Sarah. BA, Kent State U., 1965; JD, Case Western Res. U., 1968. Assoc. Ryan, Smith & Carbine, Rutland, Vt., 1968-74; ptnr. Smith, Hansen, Carroll & George, Rutland, 1974-75, Carroll, George, Hill & Anderson, Rutland, 1975-80, Carroll, George & Pratt, Rutland, 1981-98, Keyser, Crowley, Carroll, George & Meub, Rutland, 1998—; gen. counsel Vt. Yankee Nuclear Power Corp., 1978-85, Vt. Elec. Power Corp., 1980-82; chmn. regional bd. Vt. Nat. Bank, 1973-88. Trustee Vt. Legal Aid, 1970-80; mem. Vt. Human Svcs. Bd., 1986-92. Mem. ABA, Vt. Bar Assn., Rutland County Bar Assn. Administrative and regulatory, Mergers and acquisitions, Public utilities. Home: RR 1 Box 873 Pittsford VT 05763-9801 Office: Keyser Crowley Carroll George & Meub 27 S Main St # 29 Rutland VT 05701-5014

**GEORGE, ALEXANDER ANDREW,** lawyer; b. Missoula, Mont., Apr. 26, 1938; s. Andrew Miltiadin and Eleni (Efstathiou) G.; m. Penelope Mitchell, Sept. 29, 1968; children: Andrew A., Stephen A. BBA honors, U. Mont., 1960, JD, 1962; postgrad., John Marshall U., 1964-66. Bar: Mont. 1962, U.S. Ct. Mil. Appeals 1964, U.S. Tax Ct. 1970. Sole practice Missoula, 1966—; mem. adv. com. U. Mont. Tax Inst., 1973-76; adj. lectr. U. Montana Law Sch. Corp. Taxation. Pres. Missoula Civic Symphony, 1973; nat. dir. Assn. Urban and Cmty. Symphony Orch., 1974, Mont. Eye Endowment Found.; pres. Greek Orthodox Ch., 1978, 91. Served to capt. JAG U.S. Army, 1962-66. Recipient Jaycee Disting. Svc. award, 1973. Mem. State Bar Mont. (pres. 1981), Western Mont. Bar Assn. (pres. 1971, lifetime achievement award 1998), Mont. Law Found. (treas. 1986-92), Mont. Soc. CPA, Phi Delta Phi, Alpha Kappa Psi, Sigma Nu (alumni trustee 1966-71), Rotary (pres. 1972, state chmn. found. 1977, membership com. chmn. 1978), Ahepa (pres. 1967, state gov. 1968). Probate, Corporate taxation, General corporate. Home: 4 Greenbrier Ct Missoula MT 59802-3342 Office: 210 N Higgins Ave Ste 234 Missoula MT 59802-4497

**GEORGE, JOHN MARTIN, JR.,** lawyer; b. Normal, Ill., Dec. 17, 1947; s. John and Ada George; m. Judy Ann Watts; children: Sarah, Michael. AB with high honors, U. Ill., 1970, AM, 1971; PhD, Columbia U., 1976; JD cum laude, Harvard U., 1982. Bar: Mass. 1982, U.S. Dist. Ct. Mass. 1983, Ill. 1984, U.S. Dist. Ct. (no. dist.) Ill. 1984, U.S. Ct. Appeals (11th cir.) 1987, U.S. Ct. Appeals (9th cir.) 1988, U.S. Ct. Appeals (7th cir.) 1992. Assoc. Hill & Barlow, Boston, 1982-84; assoc. Sidley & Austin, Chgo., 1984-89, ptnr., 1989—. Editor Harvard U. Law Rev., 1980-82. Mem. ABA, Chgo. Bar Assn., Mid-Day Club, Phi Beta Kappa. Democrat. Episcopalian. Federal civil litigation, Securities, Professional liability. Office: Sidley & Austin 1 First Natl Plz Chicago IL 60603-2003

**GEORGE, KATIE,** lawyer; b. Chillicothe, Ohio, Sept. 4, 1953; d. Harry Paul and Tina Lillian George; m. Nov. 25, 1972 (div. Nov. 1983); 1 child, Alison; m. Timothy John Nusser, June 30, 1985. BBA, U. Toledo, 1983, JD, 1986, MBA, 1989. Bar: Ohio 1987, U.S. Dist. Ct. (no. dist.) Ohio 1993, Fla. 1994. Law clk. Allotta, Singer & Farley, Co., LPA, Toledo, 1985-86; mgmt. specialist Dept. Pub. Utilities City of Toledo, 1987-91, acting commr. Dept. Health, 1992-93, acting mgr. Dept. Pub. Safety, 1991-94; pvt. practice Toledo, 1987-96, Pensacola, Fla., 1996—; asst. dist. legal counsel State of Fla., 1996-97, chief legal counsel, 1997—; part-time instr. U. Toledo, 1987-88, U. West Fla., 1997. Bd. dirs. Toledo BlockWatch, 1993, Ohio Pub. Employers Labor Rels. Assn., 1991-92; mem. Missing and Exploited Children Comprehensive Action Program, 1997-99. Mem. Fla. Bar Assn., Escambia Santa Rosa Bar Assn. Avocations: photography, scuba diving. Office: 160 Governmental Ctr Ste 601 Pensacola FL 32501

**GEORGE, LARRY WAYNE,** lawyer; b. Cin., Oct. 31, 1954. BS in Civil Engring., Va. Poly. Inst. and State U., 1979; JD, W.Va. U., 1982. Bar: W.Va. 1982, U.S. Ct. Appeals (4th cir.) 1983, D.C. 1992, Va. 1993. Assoc. Baer & Colburn, L.C., Huntington, W.Va., 1982-85; pvt. practice Charleston, W.Va., 1985-89; dep. dir. W.Va. Dept. Natural Resources, Charleston, 1989-90; commr. W.Va. Dept. Energy, Charleston, 1990; pvt. practice law Charleston, 1991-93; ptnr. Barth, Thompson & George, 1993—; majority counsel W.Va. Senate, 1984-85. Mem. W.Va. Water Resources Bd., 1978-82; mem. nat. coal coun. U.S. Dept. Energy, 1985-89; mem. coun. on energy and environment Nat. Govs. Assn., 1989-90; chmn. Environ. Transition com. for Gov. Cecil Underwood, 1996-97; chmn. econ. com. Govs. Mining Task Force, 1998. Mem. ABA, W.Va. State Bar (com. on environ. law 1986—, com. on bus., banking and corp. law 1996—), ASCE (energy, environ. and water resources divs.), Ea. Mineral Law Inst., W.Va. Highlands Conservancy (pres. 1983-86). Environmental, Land use and zoning (including planning), General corporate. Home: 3 Birch Tree Ln Charleston WV 25314-2275 Office: Barth Thompson & George 202 Berkeley St Charleston WV 25302-2239

**GEORGE, LESLIE P.,** lawyer; b. Atlanta, Sept. 22, 1948. BA, U. Mo., Kansas City, 1971; JD, John Marshall Law Sch., 1975. Bar: Ga. Sr. staff atty. Ga. Power Co., Atlanta. Greek Orthodox. Avocations: computing, Internet. E-mail: Les.P. George@gpc.com. Fax: 404-506-1599. Office: Ga Power Co BIN 10180 241 Ralph Mcgill Blvd NE Atlanta GA 30308-3374

**GEORGE, LLOYD D.,** federal judge; b. Montpelier, Idaho, Feb. 22, 1930; s. William Ross and Myrtle (Nield) G.; m. LaPrele Badouin, Aug. 6, 1956; children: Douglas Ralph, Michele, Cherie Suzanne, Stephen Lloyd. BS, Brigham Young U., 1955; JD, U. Calif., Berkeley, 1961. Ptnr. Albright, George, Johnson & Steffen, 1969-71, George, Steffen & Simmons, 1971-74; judge U.S. Bankruptcy Ct. (Nev. dist.), 1974-84, U.S. Dist. Ct. Nev., 1984—, chief judge, sr. judge, 1997—; justice of peace Clark County, Nev., 1962-69. Served with USAF, 1955-58. Office: US Dist Ct Foley Fed Bldg Rm 316 300 Las Vegas Blvd S Fl 3 Las Vegas NV 89101-5833

**GEORGE, MICHAEL JOSEPH,** lawyer; b. Great Falls, Mont., Sept. 12, 1961; s. Mitchell A. and Marie C. George; m. Sydne Kolstad, July 20, 1996. BSBA, U. Mont., 1983, JD, 1986. Bar: Mont. 1986, U.S. Dist. Ct. Mont. 1986, U.S. Ct. Appeals (9th cir.) 1988. Assoc. Hoyt & Blewett, Great Falls, Mont., 1986-96; ptnr. Lucero & George, LLP, Great Falls, 1997—. Bd. dirs. Charlie's Friends of CM Russell Mus., Great Falls, 1992-96, Big Bros. and Big Sisters of Great Falls, 1998—. Mem. ATLA, Mont. Trial Lawyers Assn., State Bar Mont., Cascade County Bar Assn. Personal injury, Insurance, Product liability. Office: Lucero & George LLP 410 Central Ave Ste 517 Great Falls MT 59401-3128

**GEORGE, NICHOLAS,** lawyer, entrepreneur; b. Seattle, July 11, 1952; s. Harry and Mary (Courounes) G.; children: Harry Nicholas, James Michael. BA in Polit. Sci. cum laude, Whitman Coll., 1974; MBA in Mktg. and Corp. Planning, U. Chgo., 1979; JD, U. Puget Sound, 1989. Bar: Wash. 1991, U.S. Dist. Ct. (we. dist.) Wash. 1991, U.S. Ct. Appeals (9th cir.) 1991, U.S. Tax Ct. 1992, U.S. Dist. Ct. (ea. dist.) Wash. 1994, U.S. Supreme Ct. 1994. Fin. cons. Pacific Western Investment Co., Lynnwood, Wash., 1975-77; planning dir. Clinton Capital Ventures, Seattle, 1979-81; corp. planning mgr. Tacoma Boatbldg., 1981-83; pres. MegaProf Investors, Bellevue, Wash., 1983-89; practice trial-settlement law bus., Seattle, 1989—; free-lance coll. counselor, Seattle, 1980—. Author: Legitimacy in Government: Ideal, Goal, or Myth? 1974. Bd. auditor St. Demetrios Greek Orthodox Ch., Seattle, 1982-83; bd. dirs. Hellenic Golfers Assn., Seattle, 1981-83. Mem. ABA, Assn. Trial Lawyers Am., Wash. State Bar Assn., Wash. Assn. Criminal Def. Lawyers, Wash. State Trial Lawyers Assn., Fed. Bar Assn., Nat. Assn. Criminal Def. Lawyers, Tacoma-Pierce County Bar Assn., Seattle-King County Bar Assn., Wash. Defender Assn., Wash. State Hist. Soc., Am. Inst. Archeol., Phi Alpha Delta. Greek Orthodox. Avocations: weightlifting, travel, family history, football coaching, writing. Home: 5007 80th St SW Lakewood WA 98499-4077 Office: 1201 Pacific Ave Ste 1502 Tacoma WA 98402-4322

**GEORGE, RICHARD NEILL,** lawyer; b. Watertown, N.Y., Apr. 6, 1933; s. Wendell Dow and Frances Laura (Small) G.; m. Patricia Harman Jackson, June 21, 1958; children—Frances Harman, Richard Neill, Mary Elizabeth. A.B., Yale U., 1955; J.D., Cornell U., 1962. Bar: N.Y. 1962. Assoc. Nixon Peabody, LLP (formerly Nixon, Hargave, Devans & Doyle), Rochester, N.Y., 1962-70, ptnr., 1970—. Committeeman, Brighton Town Republican Com., Rochester, 1966-78; ruling elder Twelve Corners Presbyn. Ch., Rochester, 1977-79, 84-87; mem. permanent jud. commn. Presbytery of Genesee Valley, 1988-94, also moderator. Capt. USAF, 1956-59. Mem. ABA, N.Y. State Bar Assn., Monroe County Bar Assn., Fed. Energy Bar Assn., Exeter Alumni Assn. of Rochester (pres. 1970—). Republican. Clubs: Country of Rochester, Yale of N.Y.C., Amelia Island. Avocations: golf; reading. Administrative and regulatory, Public utilities, FERC practice. Home: 90 Oak Ln Rochester NY 14610-3135 Office: Nixon Peabody LLP PO Box 1051 Clinton Sq Rochester NY 14604-1729

**GEORGE, RONALD M.,** state supreme court chief justice; b. L.A., Mar. 11, 1940. AB, Princeton U., 1961; JD, Stanford U., 1964. Bar: Calif. 1965. Dep. atty. gen. Calif. Dept. Justice, 1965-72; judge L.A. Mcpl. Ct., L.A. County, 1972-77; judge Superior Ct. Calif., L.A. County, 1977-87, supervising judge criminal divsn., 1983-84; assoc. justice 2d dist., divsn. 4 Calif. Ct. Appeal, L.A., 1987-91; assoc. justice Calif. Supreme Ct., San Francisco, 1991-96, chief justice, 1996—. Mem. Calif. Judges Assn. (pres. 1982-83). Avocations: hiking, skiing, running. Office: Calif Supreme Court 350 Mcallister St Fl 5 San Francisco CA 94102-4712

**GEORGE, SAMUEL MILLS,** lawyer; b. Tyler, Tex., Jan. 25, 1950; s. Lloyd Woodrow and Winifred (Kirby) G.; m. Patricia Lee Clayton, Aug. 22, 1970; children—Jennifer Lee, Jessica Lynn, Jacquelyn Dyann. B.A., U. Tex., 1972; J.D., S. Tex. Coll. of Law, 1976. Assoc. Hitner & Cezeaux, Houston, 1976; briefing atty. 12th Ct. Appeals, Tyler, 1977; assoc. Loftis, Rowan, Files, Bain & Clayton, Tyler, 1978-79; ptnr. Loftis, Rowan & George, Tyler, 1979-81, Rowan & George, Tyler, 1981-87; pvt. practice atty, Tyler, 1987—. Lead articles editor S. Tex. Law Jour., 1976. Treas. Brad Burger Dist. Clk. Campaign, Tyler, 1980, Ruth Blake Jud. Campaign, Tyler, 1984. Mem. Tex. Trial Lawyers Assn., Smith County Bar Assn. (sec. 1981). Lodges: Masons, Shriners. Federal civil litigation, State civil litigation, Family and matrimonial. Home: 15578 Mcelroy Rd Whitehouse TX 75791-8330 Office: 400 Troup Hwy Tyler TX 75701-5501

**GEORGE, STEVE DANIEL,** lawyer; b. Muskogee, Okla., Nov. 22, 1941; s. Monroe Jerome and Nadine Elizabeth (Yarbrough) G.; m. Dorothy Ruth George, July, 1966 (div. June 1991); children: Kristin Nicole, Jillanna Elizabeth, Matthew Daniel. BS, Okla. U., 1963, JD, 1966. Bar: Okla. 1966, Mo. 1968. PVT. PRACTICE sALLISAW, oKLA., 1969—. Sgt. Okla. N.G., 1957-63. Mem. Sallisaw C. of C. Democrat. Roman Catholic. Criminal. Office: 1015 E Redwood St Sallisaw OK 74955-3209

**GEORGES, PETER JOHN,** lawyer; b. Wilmington, Del., Sept. 8, 1940; s. John Peter and Olga Demetrius (Kazitoris) G. BS in Chemistry, U. Del., 1962; JD, John Marshall Law Sch., 1970; LLM in Patent and Trade Regulations, George Washington U., 1973. Bar: Ill. 1970, U.S. Ct. Appeals (fed. cir.) 1972, D.C. 1973, U.S. Supreme Ct. 1973, Del. 1977. Chemist engring. labs Bell & Howell Co., Chgo., 1966; patent coordinator Armour & Co., Chgo., 1967; patent agt., atty. UOP Inc., Chgo., 1968-71; Washington counsel UOP Inc., Arlington, Va., 1972-77; ptnr. Kile, Gholz, Bernstein & Georges, Arlington, 1977-78; assoc., then ptnr. Law Office Sidney W. Russell, Arlington, 1978-83; mng. officer Breneman & Georges (and predecessor law firms), Alexandria, 1983—; founding ptnr. Lenastri Properties and Joanastri Properties, Alexandria, Va. Served to 1st lt. USMC, 1963-65, Vietnam. Mem. ABA, Ill. Bar Assn., D.C. Bar Assn., Del. Bar Assn., Fed. Cir. Bar Assn., Assn. Trial Lawyers Am., Am. Intellectual Property Law Assn., Am. Hellenic Lawyers Soc. Trademark and copyright, Patent, Federal civil litigation. Home: 1637 13th St NW Washington DC 20009-4302 Office: Breneman & Georges 3150 Commonwealth Ave Alexandria VA 22305-2712

**GEORGES, RICHARD MARTIN,** lawyer, educator; b. St. Louis, Nov. 17, 1947; s. Martin Mahlon Georges and Josephine (Cipolla) Rice. AB cum laude, Loyola U., New Orleans, 1969; JD cum laude, Stetson Coll. Law, 1972. Bar: 1972, U.S. Dist. Ct. (mid. dist.) Fla. 1973, U.S. Ct. Appeals (11th cir.) 1981, U.S. Supreme Ct. 1982. Ptnr. Kieffer & Georges, St. Petersburg, Fla., 1973-80, Kieffer, Georges & Rahter, St. Petersburg, 1980-85; pvt. practice St. Petersburg, 1985—; adj. prof. Fla. Inst. Tech., Melbourne, 1977-86, Stetson Coll. Law, 1985-90; adj. prof. Eckerd Coll., St. Petersburg, 1986-89. Contbg. author: Florida Law of Trusts, 1983. Arbitrator United Steelworkers Union, Continental Can Co., 1975-80; hearing examiner City of St. Petersburg, 1982—; mem. citizen's adv. com. Pinellas County Met. Planning Orgn., 1986-87; exec. committeeman Pinellas County Rep. Party, Clearwater, Fla., 1981-82. 1st lt. U.S. Army, 1972. Recipient Rafael Steinhardt award Stetson Coll. Law, 1972, Clint Green award, 1972. Mem. ABA, Fla. Bar, St. Petersburg Bar Assn. (chmn. computer com.), Fla. Camera Club Coun. (pres. 1985), Suncoast Camera (Clearwater, v.p. 1982-84, pres. 1985), Phi Alpha Delta. Roman Catholic. General corporate, Insurance, Real property. Office: 3656 1st Ave N Saint Petersburg FL 33713-8407

**GEORGESON, ADAMONT NICHOLAS,** lawyer; b. Albuquerque, Aug. 21, 1946; s. Agamemnon James and Frances (Dellas) G.; m. Tracy Denise McDonald, July 1, 1984. BA, U. Mich., 1968, JD, 1972. Bar: Calif., Mich. Atty. Monterey County Dist. Atty., Monterey, Calif., 1974-76; assoc. Hancock Rothert & Bunshoft, San Francisco, 1977-80; pvt. practice law Mill Valley, Calif., 1981—. Mem. Marin County Bar Assn. (bd. dirs. 1987-89, sec. 1998-99), Kentfield Schs. Found. (v.p.), Olympic Club. Avocations: skiing, running, photography, Scuba diving, sailing. State civil litigation, Contracts commercial, Real property. Office: 591 Redwood Hwy Ste 2275 Mill Valley CA 94941-6025

**GEPPERT, JOHN GUSTAVE,** lawyer; b. DuBois, Pa., July 1, 1956; s. John Gustave and Patricia C. (Greenland) G.; m. Karen M. Platt, Jan. 30, 1988. BBA, U. Notre Dame, 1978; JD, Seton Hall U., 1983. Bar: N.J. 1983, U.S. Dist. Ct. N.J. 1983, U.S. Ct. Appeals (3d cir.) 1984. Law clk. to judge U.S. Ct. Appeals for 3d Cir., Newark, 1983-84; assoc. Pitney, Hardin, Kipp & Szuch, Morristown, N.J., 1984-86; assoc. Wiley, Malehorn & Sirota, Morristown, 1986-88, ptnr., 1988—. Editor-in-chief Seton Hall Law Rev., 1982-83. Mem. Rockaway Twp. (N.J.) City Coun., 1980-83, Rockaway Twp. Planning Bd., 1982;trustee N.J. Tchrs. Pension and Annuity Fund, Trenton, 1981-83; analyst United Way Morris County, 1983—; pres., bd. dirs. Literacy Vols. Am., Morris County, 1997—. Mem. ABA, N.J. Bar Assn., Morris County Bar Assn., Lions (bd. dirs. Rockaway 1983-88). Democrat. Avocations: sports, travel, reading. General civil litigation, General practice. Home: 6 Florie Farm Rd Mendham NJ 07945-1708 Office: Wiley Malehorn & Sirota 250 Madison Ave Morristown NJ 07960-6108

**GERALDSON, RAYMOND I., JR.,** lawyer; b. Racine, Wis., Oct. 19, 1940; s. Raymond I. Sr. and Evelyn (Thorpe) G.; m. Melinda Paine, June 13, 1964; children: Amy, Raymond I. III. BA, DePauw U., 1962; JD, Northwestern U., 1965. Bar: Ill. 1965, D.C. 1966, U.S. Dist. Ct. (no. dist. ) Ill. 1967. Ptnr. Pattishall, McAuliffe, Newbury, Hilliard & Geraldson, Washington, 1965-67, Chgo., 1967—; adj. prof. John Marshall Law Sch. 1978—; lectr. in field. Contbr. articles on trademark law to profl. jours. Trustee Kendall Coll., 1985—, chmn., 1990—. Mem. ABA, Ill. State Bar Assn. (coun. sect. intellectual property law 1978-82, chmn. 1980-81), Chgo. Bar Assn., 7th Crct. Intellectual Property Law Assn. Chgo. (bd. dirs. 1984-86, 92-93, pres. 1991-92), Internat. Trademark Assn. (bd. dirs. 1985-87), Am. Intellectual Property Law Assn., Lawyers for Creative Arts (hons. coun. 1994—, bd. dirs. 1974-94, pres. 1976-78), Legal Club Chgo., Law Club Chgo., Econ. Club Chgo., Sunset Ridge Country Club, Union League Club of Chgo., Sigma Chi. Trademark and copyright, General civil litigation, Intellectual property. Office: Pattishall McAuliffe Newbury Hilliard & Geraldson 311 S Wacker Dr Ste 5000 Chicago IL 60606-6631

**GERARD, STEPHEN STANLEY,** lawyer; b. N.Y.C., June 2, 1936; m. Nancy Mercer Keith, Apr. 25, 1969; children: Robert, Lillian, Stephen. BS, NYU, 1958, JD, 1963; cert. in employee relations law, Inst. for Applied Mgmt. and Law, Newport Beach, Calif., 1983. Bar: N.Y. 1964, U.S. Dist. Ct. (so. and ea. dists.) N.Y. 1967, U.S. Ct. Appeals (2d cir.) 1968. Commd. 2d lt. U.S. Army, 1954, advanced through grades to capt. M.I. Corps, 1966, ret., 1974; assoc. Haight, Gardner, Poor & Havens, N.Y.C., 1965-72; counsel Am. Hoechst Corp., Somerville, N.J., 1972-77, asst. sec., sr. counsel, 1977-87; assoc. gen. counsel Hoechst Celanese Corp., Somerville, 1987—. Patron Colonial Symphony, 1988—; mem. Am. Mus. Natural History. Mem. ABA, Am. Corp. Counsel Assn., Am. Counsel Internat. Personnel, Am. Immigration Lawyers Assn., N.J. World Trade Council, N.J. Assn. Corp. Counsel, Smithsonian Inst. Nat. Assocs. Labor, Pension, profit-sharing, and employee benefits, Immigration, naturalization, and customs. Office: Hoechst Corp PO Box 4915 Warren NJ 07059-0915

**GERBER, ALBERT B.,** lawyer, former legal association executive; b. Phila., July 10, 1913; s. Jacob and Jennie (Suffrin) G.; m. Rhona C. Posner, Nov. 22, 1939; children—Jack J., Gail, Lynne. BS in Edn., U. Pa., 1934, JD, 1937, LLM, 1941; MA in Govt., George Washington U., Washington, 1940. Bar: Pa. 1938. Chief opinion unit Dept. Agr., Washington, 1938-42; ptnr. Gerber & Gafand, Phila., 1946-72; adminstrv. dir. 1st Amendment Lawyers Assn., Phila., 1970-87; pres. Assn. for Research, Inc., Phila., 1972-84; of counsel Galfand, Berger Lurie & March, Phila., 1984-94; counsel United Nat. Ins. Co., Phila., 1972—. Author: Bashful Billionaire, 1967, The Lawyer, 1972, Book of Sex Lists, 1981, Miracles on Park Avenue, 1985; also numerous articles; editor Tax Sense, 1980-83, Internat. Intelligence, 1981-84. Democratic committeeman, Phila., 1950-60, Montgomery County, Pa., 1979-81. Served to sgt. inf. U.S. Army, 1942-45, PTO. Recipient Best Novel award Pa. Assn. Writers, 1980. Mem. ABA, Phila. Bar Assn., Order of Coif. Jewish. Avocations: handball; tennis; volleyball. Office: United Nat Ins Co 3 Bala Plz Ste 300 Bala Cynwyd PA 19004-3481

**GERBER, DAVID A.,** lawyer; b. N.Y.C., Dec. 4, 1944. AB, U. Rochester, 1966; PhD, U. Tex., 1970; JD, UCLA, 1977. Bar: Calif. 1977, U.S. Dist. Ct. (ctrl. dist.) Calif. 1978, U.S. Dist. Ct. (no., ea. and so. dists.) Calif. 1982, U.S. Ct. Appeals (9th cir.) 1978, U.S. Ct. Appeals (1st cir.) 1981, U.S. Ct. Appeals (3d cir.) 1985, U.S. Supreme Ct. 1986. Litig. atty. Loeb & Loeb, L.A., 1977-93, Nordman, Cormany, Hair & Compton, Oxnard, CA, 1993-95, D. Gerber Law Offices, Channel Islands, CA, 1995—. Contbr. articles to profl. jours. Trustee L.A. Copyrigt Soc., 1991-94. Mem. State Bar Calif. (exec. com. of intellectual property sect. 1988-91). Trademark and copyright, Federal civil litigation, General civil litigation. Office: 3600 Harbor Blvd Ste 226 Oxnard CA 93035-4184

**GERBER, EDWARD F.,** lawyer, educator; b. Houston, Oct. 10, 1932; s. Edward F. and Lucille (Beaver) G.; m. Eileen Healy, Sept. 1, 1956; children: Gretchen, Eric, Nils. BS, Syracuse U., 1957, LLB, 1960, JD, 1968. Bar: N.Y. 1960, U.S. Dist. Ct. (no. dist.) N.Y. 1960. Pvt. practice law, Syracuse, N.Y., 1960-64; first asst. dist. atty. Onondaga County, Syracuse, N.Y., 1964-67; spl. prosecutor Onondaga County, 1976; pvt. practice law, Syracuse, 1977—; lectr. Coll. of Law Syracuse U., 1968—; counsel Onondaga County Sheriff, 1978-94, N.Y. State Police Benevolent Assn., 1983—, N.Y. State Police Investigators Assn.; faculty Criminal Law Services Syracuse U. Trial Practice Sessions. Bd. dirs. Onondaga County Young Rep. Club, 1964-66. With USN, 1951-54. Named one of Best Lawyers in Am., 1989. Fellow Am. Coll. Trial Lawyers; mem. ATLA, N.Y. State Bar Assn. (lectr.), Upstate Trial Lawyers Assn. (pres. 1978-79), Onondaga County Bar Assn. (dir. 1969-71), Onondaga Bar Found. (pres. 1983). Criminal, Federal civil litigation, State civil litigation. Home: 21 Drumlins Ter Syracuse NY 13224-2217 Office: 224 Harrison St Ste 500 Syracuse NY 13202-3060

**GERBER, JOEL,** federal judge; b. Chgo., July 16, 1940; s. Peter H. and Marcia L. (Weber) G.; m. Judith R. Smilgoff, Aug. 18, 1963; children—Jay Lawrence, Jeffrey Mark, Jon Victor. B.S.B.A., Roosevelt U., Chgo., 1962; J.D., DePaul U., Chgo., 1965; LL.M., Boston U., 1968. Bar: Ill. 1965, Ga. 1974, Tenn. 1978. Trial atty. IRS, Boston, 1965-72; staff asst. to regional counsel IRS, Atlanta, 1972-76; dist. counsel IRS, Nashville, 1976-80; dep. chief counsel IRS, Washington, 1980-83, acting chief counsel, 1983-84; judge U.S. Tax Ct., Washington, 1984—; gen. counsel ATF Credit Union, Boston, 1968-70; lectr. Vanderbilt U. Sch. Law, Nashville, 1976-80; lectr. U. Miami Grad. Law Sch., 1986-90. Recipient awards U.S. Treasury Dept., 1979, 81, 82; Presdl. Meritorious Exec. Rank award, 1983. Mem. ABA (chmn. spl. com. for lawyers in govt. 1986-90). Office: US Tax Ct 400 2nd St NW Rm 432 Washington DC 20217-0002

**GERBER, LAWRENCE,** lawyer; b. Chgo., Oct. 2, 1940. BBA, Loyola U. Chgo., 1962; JD, Northwestern U., 1965. Bar: Ill. 1965; CPA Ill. Ptnr. McDermott, Will & Emery, Chgo., mng. ptnr., 1991—. Author: Hospital Restructuring: Why, When and How, 1983. Mem. Am. Acad. Hosp. Attys., Ill. Assn. Hosp. Attys. Office: McDermott Will & Emery 227 W Monroe St Ste 3100 Chicago IL 60606-5096

**GERBER, ROBERT EVAN,** lawyer; b. N.Y.C., Feb. 12, 1947; s. Milton M. and Miriam (Simon) G.; m. Jane Flanagan, Nov. 10, 1996. BS with high honors, Rutgers U., 1967; JD magna cum laude, Columbia U., 1970. Bar: N.Y. 1971, U.S. Dist. Ct. (so. and ea. dists.) N.Y. 1972, U.S. Ct. Appeals (2d cir.) 1973, U.S. Ct. Appeals (9th cir.) 1974, U.S. Ct. Appeals (10th cir.) 1975, U.S. Ct. Appeals (11th cir.) 1983, U.S. Supreme Ct. 1983, U.S. Ct. Appeals (5th cir.) 1987, U.S. Ct. Appeals (6th cir.) 1989, U.S. Ct. Appeals (3d cir.) 1997. Assoc. Fried, Frank, Harris, Shriver & Jacobson, N.Y.C., 1970-71, 72-78, ptnr., 1978—. Served to 1st lt. USAF, 1971-72. James Kent scholar, 1970, Harlan Fiske Stone scholar, 1969. Mem. ABA, Assn. Bar City N.Y. (sec. spl. com. on energy 1974-79), Fed. Bar Coun., Am. Bankruptcy Inst., Tau Beta Pi. Bankruptcy, Federal civil litigation, State civil litigation. Home: 13 Colt Rd Summit NJ 07901-3002 Office: Fried Frank Harris Shriver & Jacobson 1 New York Plz Fl 22 New York NY 10004-1980

**GERBERDING COWART, GRETA ELAINE,** lawyer; b. Ft. Wayne, Ind., Aug. 17, 1960; d. Miles Carston G. and Ruth (Hostrup) G., stepmother Joanie Wyatt Gerberding; m. T. David Cowart, Aug. 12, 1995. BS with high distinction, Ind. U., 1982; JD cum laude, 1985. Bar: Ind. 1985, U.S. Dist. Ct. (so. dist.) Ind., CPA, Ind., CEBS. Sr. tax cons. Ernst & Whinney, Indpls., 1985-87; assoc. Klineman, Rose, Wolf and Wallack P.C., Indpls., 1987-89, Hall Render Killian Heath & Lyman P.C., Indpls., 1989-95; ptnr. Haynes and Boone, L.L.P., Dallas, 1996—; presenter at seminars. Author: (with G.P. Gooch) Trust and Estate Income Tax Reporting and Planning, 1985; contbr. chpts. to books, articles to profl. jours. including Jour. Deferred Compensation, 403(b) Answer Book, Benefits Law Jour. Chmn. hospitality area Virginia Slims Tennis Tournament, Indpls., 1987-89; vol. Jello Tennis Classic Tennis Tournament, Indpls., 1990-91; coord. Hospitality and Ball Kids, 1990, Jr. Jamboree GTE Tennis Tournament, Indpls., 1990; vol. Ctr. for Exploration The Children's Mus., Indpls., 1991-94; mem. com. on funding Vision 2002 Luth. Camp Assn., Inc., 1993-94, bd. dirs., 1997—; mem. women's retreat com. King of Glory Lutheran Ch., 1997—; active Brianwood Retreat Ctr., 1998—. Glen Peters fellow Ind. U., 1984. Fellow Ind. Bar Found.; mem. ABA (com. marital deduction legis. real property and probate sect. 1986-87, tax section, gen. income tax com. 1987-89, employee benefits com. 1988—, subcom. health plan design and state regulation 1993—, health care task force 1994—, chmn. COBRA subcom. 1997—), Ind. Bar Assn. (acct.-lawyers com. 1986-89, co-chmn. com. on legis. 1988-92, coun. tax sect. 1988-96, sec.-treas. 1991-92, vice chmn. tax sect. 1992-93, chair elect 1993-94, chair 1994-95), Indpls. Bar Assn., Indpls. Jaycees (treas. 4th Festival 1987 monthly dinner meetings 1988), West Indy Racquet Club (USTA Volvo Tennis Team 1986-87, RCA tounament credentials com. 1993-94), Indpls. Racquet Club (USTA Volvo tennis team 1988-91, 96). Avocations: tennis, sailing, golf, skiing, swimming, artwork. Pension, profit-sharing, and employee benefits, Taxation, general, Health. Office: Haynes and Boone LLP 901 Main St Ste 3100 Dallas TX 75202-3789

**GERDE, CARLYLE NOYES (CY GERDE),** lawyer; b. Long Beach, Calif., Oct. 22, 1946; m. Priscilla A. Murphy, July 4, 1976. BA in Am. Studies, Purdue U., 1967; JD, Ind. U., 1970. Bar: Ind. 1971, U.S. Supreme Ct. 1976, U.S. Tax Ct. 1980. Ptnr. Hanna & Gerde, Lafayette, Ind., 1972-86; registered lobbyist Ind. Twp. Assn., 1975-86; spl. counsel Nat. Assn. Towns and Twps., Washington, 1976-86; adj. prof. indsl. engring. Purdue U., 1972-96; participant White House Conf. Rural Policy, 1978, White House Conf. on Block Grants, 1981, White House Conf. on Liability Ins., 1986; mem. Ind. Gen. Assembly Study Commn. Bd. of govs. Tippecanoe County Hist. Assn., Lafayette, 1976—, Ams. for Nuclear Energy, Washington (co-founder, v.p. 1977—); pres. Battle Ground (Ind.) Hist. Corp., 1986; del. State of Ind. GOP Conventions. Mem. Ind. State Bar Assn., Tippecanoe County Bar Assn., Assn. Trial Lawyers Am., Nat. Assn. Town and Twp. Attys. (co-founder, v.p. 1985-88), Am. Agrl. Lawyers Assn., Lafayette Country Club, Skyline Club, Columbia Club. Office: Hanna & Gerde PO Box 1098 Lafayette IN 47902-1098

**GERDES, DAVID ALAN,** lawyer; b. Aberdeen, S.D., Aug. 10, 1942; s. Cyril Frederick and Lorraine Mary (Boyle) G.; m. Karen Ann Hassinger, Aug. 3, 1968; children: Amy Renee Gerdes-Barse, James David. BS, No. State Coll., Aberdeen, 1965; JD cum laude, U. S.D., 1968. Bar: S.D. 1968, U.S. Dist. Ct. S.D., 1968, U.S. Ct. Appeals (8th cir.) 1973, U.S. Supreme Ct. 1973. Assoc., Martens, Goldsmith, May, Porter & Adam, Pierre, S.D., 1968-73; ptnr. successor firm May, Adam, Gerdes & Thompson, Pierre, 1973—; chmn. disciplinary bd. S.D. Bar, 1980-81, mem. fed. practice com. U.S. Dist. Ct., S.D., 1986-91, 94—; mem. fed. adv. com. U.S. Ct. Appeals (8th cir.), 1989-93; bd. dirs. U.S.D. Law Sch. Found., 1973-84, pres., 1979-84. Mng. editor U. S.D. Law Rev., 1967-68. Chmn. Hughes County Republican Central Com., 1979-81; del. Rep. State Conv., co-chair platform com., 1988, 90; state cen. committeeman, 1985-91. Served to lt. Signal Corps, AUS, 1965-68. Mem. ABA, Nat. Coun. Bar Pres., Internat. Assn. Def. Counsel, Assn. Def. Trial Attys., Am. Judicature Soc., Am. Bd. Trial Advocates, State Bar S.D. (chmn. professionalism com. 1989-90, pres. 1992-93), Pierre Area C. of C. (pres. 1980-81), S.D. C. of C. (bd. dirs. 1998—), Lawyer-Pilots Bar Assn., Def. Research Inst., Am. Soc. Med. Assn. Counsel, Kiwanis, Elks. Republican. Methodist. Author: Physician's Guide to South Dakota Law, 1982. Insurance, Federal civil litigation, Health. Office: May Adam Gerdes & Thompson PO Box 160 503 S Pierre St Pierre SD 57501-4522

**GERDING, RICHARD LOUIS,** lawyer; b. Denver, July 8, 1939; s. Louis C. and Claribel Douglas Gerding; m. Carol Eileen Hutchison, June 14, 1960; children: Christine Marie, David Douglas. BBA, U. N.Mex., 1961, JD, 1964. Bar: N.Mex. 1965, Colo. 1988, U.S. Dist. Ct. Colo. 1978, U.S. Dist. Ct. N.Mex. 1966, U.S. Ct. Appeals (10th cir.) 1968. Law clk. N.Mex. Supreme Ct., Santa Fe, 1964-65; assoc. Tansey, Wood, Rosebrough & Roberts, Farmington, N.Mex., 1965-68; ptnr. Tansey, Rosebrough & Gerding, Farmington, N.Mex., 1968-97, Gerding & O'Loughlin, Farmington, N.Mex., 1997—; mem. rules of evidence com. N.Mex. Supreme Ct., Santa Fe, 1988-94, chmn. disciplinary bd., 1994—; mem. civil trial specialty com. N.Mex. State, 1990—. Chmn. United Way, Farmington, 1986; bd. dirs. Farmington Found. for Performing Arts, 1996—. With U.S. Army, 1956-59. Fellow Am. Coll. Trial Lawyers; mem. Am. Bd. Trial Advs., Best Lawyers Am. Democrat. Methodist. Avocation: fly fishing guide (San Juan River). Office: Gerding & O'Loughlin 304 N Behrend Ave #1020 Farmington NM 87401-5843

**GEREN, GERALD S.,** lawyer; b. Chgo., Nov. 10, 1939; s. Ben and Sara (Block) G.; m. Phyllis Freeman, Feb. 11, 1962; children: Suzanne, Gregory, Bradley. BSMetE, Ill. Inst. Tech., 1961; JD, DePaul U., 1966. Bar: Ill. Supreme Ct. 1966, U.S. Ct. Customs and Patent Appeals 1967, U.S. Patent and Trademark Office 1967, U.S. Dist Ct. (no. dist.) Ill. 1969, U.S. Supreme Ct. 1972, U.S. Ct. Appeals (7th cir.) 1972, U.S. Ct. Appeals (fed. cir.) 1982. Engr. Internat. Harvester, Chgo., 1961-64; atty. Corning Glass Works, Corning, N.Y., 1966-69; assoc. Silverman & Cass, Chgo., 1969-70, Siegal & Geren, Chgo., 1970-71; ptnr. Epton, Mullin & Druth, Chgo., 1971-84, Hill, Steadman & Simpson, Chgo., 1984-94, Gerald S. Geren Ltd., Chgo., 1994-96, Lee, Mann, Smith, McWilliams, Sweeney & Ohlson, 1997—. Contbr. articles to Indsl. Rsch. and Devel., Design News mags. Pres. Chgo. High Tech. Assn., 1981-86, v.p., 1986-87; mem. strategic planning com. Econ. Devel. Commn., Chgo., 1986-91; mem. Ill. Ctr. for Indsl. Tech., 1984-90, Ill. Mfg. Tech. Network, Chgo., 1986-91; mem. pres.' coun., rsch. coun., alumni bd. Ill. Inst. Tech., 1991—, The Leukemia Soc. Am. (Ill. chpt. bd. mem. 1988-90). Mem. ABA, Ill. Bar Assn., Chgo. Bar Assn., Patent Law Assn. Chgo., Am. Intellectual Property Law Assn., Execs. Club, Chgo. Econ. Club, Comml. Club Chgo. (small bus. com. 1985—), Met. Club Chgo. Patent, Trademark and copyright, Federal civil litigation. Office: Lee Mann Smith McWilliams Sweeney & Ohlson 209 S La Salle St Ste 410 Chicago IL 60604-1203

**GERHART, EUGENE CLIFTON,** lawyer; b. Bklyn., Apr. 7, 1912; s. Herman Eugene and Mary Elizabeth (Hamilton) G.; m. Mary Richardson Schreiber, Mar. 30, 1939; children: Catherine Gerhart Landon, Virginia Gerhart Mason. AB, Princeton U., 1934; LLB, Harvard U., 1937. Bar: N.J. 1938, N.Y. 1945. Practiced in Newark, 1938-43, Binghamton, N.Y., 1946—; counsel firm Coughlin & Gerhart, Binghamton; sec. to Judge Manley O. Hudson, Secretariat/League of Nations, Geneva, 1934; lectr. bus. law U. Newark, 1942-43, Triple Cities Coll., 1946-48, Harpur Coll., Endicott, N.Y., 1953-55; lectr. indsl. and labor relations Cornell U., Ithaca, N.Y., 1946; dir., gen. counsel Columbian Mut. Life Ins. Co., 1949-83, acting pres., 1969-70, chmn. bd., 1970-82; mem. coun. SUNY, Cortland, 1967-77, chmn., 1971-77; mem. Select Task Force on Ct. Reorgn. N.Y. State Senate; mem. jud. nominating com. 3d Jud. Dept., State of N.Y.; mem. N.Y. Unified Ct. Sys. Judicial Records Disposition and Archives Devel. Com. Author: American Liberty and Natural Law, America's Advocate: Robert H. Jackson, Robert H. Jackson: Lawyer's Judge, Arthur T. Vanderbilt: The Compleat Counsellor, Quote It!, Quote It II, The Lawyer's Treasury, Quote It Completely!, 1998, World Reference Guide to more than 5500 Memorable Quotations from Law and Literature, 1998; spl. contbg. author: Law Office Econs. and Mgmt, 1962—; mem. editl. bd. Quar. Report of Conf. on Personal Fin. Law, 1965; contbr. articles to legal, other publs. Chmn. Harpur Forum SUNY, Binghamton, 1983-84. Lt. USNR, 1943-46. Fellow Am. Bar Found., Am. Coll. Probate Counsel; mem. ABA (editor Jour. 1946-67, Ross Essay award 1946), Internat. Assn. Ins. Counsel, Assn. Life Ins. Counsel, Am. Judicature Soc., Am. Law Inst., N.Y. State Bar Assn. (editor-in-chief jour. 1961-97, editor-in-chief emeritus 1997—, Disting. Svc. award 1998), Assn. Bar City N.Y., Broome County Bar Assn. (pres. 1961-62, Lifetime Achievement award 1995), Selden Soc., Broome County Princeton Alumni Assn., Harvard Law Sch. Assn. Upstate N.Y. (pres. 1955-57), Scribes (pres., dir. 1966-67), St. Andrew's Soc. Republican. Clubs: Rotary (pres. 1969-70), Cosmos, Oteyokwa Lake (pres. 1971-73), Nassau, Harvard of N.Y., Princeton of N.Y. General corporate, Estate planning, Insurance. Home: 34 W End Ave Binghamton NY 13905-4026 Office: 20 Hawley St Binghamton NY 13902

**GERITY, MICHAEL E.,** lawyer; b. Poplar Bluff, Mo., Aug. 27, 1968; s. Carlton E. and Jacklynn K. Gerity. BS in Biol. Sci., Colo. State U., 1990; JD, Ariz. State U., 1994. Bar: Ariz. 1994, Colo. 1998, U.S. Patent and Trademark Office 1998. Clk. to Judge Thomas C. Kleinschmidt U.S. Ct. Appeals Ariz., Phoenix, 1995; dep. pub. defender Maricopa County Pub. Defender's Office, Phoenix, 1995-97; assoc. Jones, Skelton & Hochuli, Phoenix, 1997—. Mem. Ariz. Assn. Def. Counsel, Ariz. State Bar (sect. on patents and trademarks). Avocations: sports, music. General civil litigation, Intellectual property, Product liability. Office: Jones Skelton & Hochuli 2901 N Central Ave Ste 800 Phoenix AZ 85012-2798

**GERLACH, FRANKLIN THEODORE,** lawyer; b. Portsmouth, Ohio, Apr. 11, 1935; s. Albert T. and Nora Alice (Hayes), G.; m. Cynthia Ann Koehler, Aug. 1, 1958; children—Valarie, Philipp. B.B.A., U. Cin., 1958; M.P.A., Syracuse U., 1959; J.D., U. Cin., 1961. Bar: Ohio 1961, U.S. Dist. Ct. (so. dist.) Ohio 1969, U.S. Supreme Ct. 1971. Dir. Purchasing, Planning and Renewal, City of Portsmouth, 1961-62, city mgr., 1962-66, mayor, 1990-98; asst. dir. Ohio U., Portsmouth, 1966-68; sole practice, Portsmouth, 1968—; solicitor Village New Boston, Ohio, 1968-70; trustee Ohio Acad. Trial Lawyers, Columbus, Ohio, 1984-85. Recipient Outstanding Young Man of Ohio award (1 of 5) Portsmouth Jaycees, 1968, Ohio Jaycees, 1969. Mem. Portsmouth Bar and Law Libr. Assn. (pres. 1986). Democrat. Avocation: antiques. Administrative and regulatory, Personal injury, Workers' compensation. Home: 1221 20th St Portsmouth OH 45662-2924 Office: 814 7th St Portsmouth OH 45662-4128

**GERLACK, LISA MARIE,** lawyer; b. Lakewood, Ohio, Oct. 4, 1964; d. Julius R. and Janet K. (Crevoise) G. BA in English and Spanish, Wittenberg U., 1986; JD, Cleve. State U., 1989. Bar: Ohio 1989, U.S. Dist. Ct. (no. dist.) Ohio 1989, U.S. Ct. Appeals (6th cir.) 1991. Assoc. Friedman, Domiano & Smith Co. LPA, Cleve., 1989—; prosecutor Village of Bentleyville, Bedford, Ohio, 1990-92. Editor (county bar jour.) Law and Fact, 1992—. Mem. Ohio State Bar Assn. (coun. of dels. 1996—), Cuyahoga County Bar Assn., Cleve. Bar Assn., Assn. Trial Lawyers Am. (Ohio gov. new lawyers divsn. 1994), Cleve. Acad. Trial Attys. (bd. dirs. 1994—), Harold H. Burton-Am. Inns of Ct. (barrister 1992—). Avocations: sailing, snow skiing, running, traveling. Personal injury, Product liability, General civil litigation. Office: Friedman Domiano & Smith 600 Standard Bldg 1370 Ontario St Cleveland OH 44113-1701

**GERLANC, GLENN MARC,** lawyer; b. N.Y.C., Jan. 25, 1950. BA, Harvard U., 1972; JD, Hofstra U., 1977; LLM, NYU, 1987. Bar: N.J. 1977, N.Y. 1989. Asst. prosecutor Bergen County Prosecutor's Office, Hackensack, N.J., 1977-80; assoc. atty. Beattie & Padovano, Montvale, N.J., 1980-81; atty. pvt. practice, Hackensack, 1981-90; ptnr. Parisi, Gerlanc & Greenfield P.A., Hackensack, 1991-93, Parisi & Gerlanc P.A., 1993—. Mem. ATLA, N.J. Bar Assn., Bergen County Bar Assn. Personal injury, Workers' compensation, Product liability. Office: Parisi & Gerlanc PA 190 Moore St Hackensack NJ 07601-7418

**GERLT, WAYNE CHRISTOPHER,** lawyer; b. Hartford, Conn., Mar. 7, 1948; m. Elaine Della Barnarda, Feb. 27, 1970; 3 children. BA, U. Conn., 1970; JD, Capital U., 1975. Bar: Ohio 1975, Conn. 1976, U.S. Dist. Ct. Conn. 1976, U.S. Supreme Ct. 1979. Sole practice South Windsor, Conn., 1984—; bd. dirs. new Eng. Cmty. Bankcorp. Mem. ABA, Conn. Bar Assn., Order of Curia. Roman Catholic. General practice, Real property, Family and matrimonial. Home: 10 Robins Wood Way South Windsor CT 06074-2207 Office: 435 Buckland Rd PO Box 559 South Windsor CT 06074-0559

**GERMAIN, REGINA,** lawyer; b. Bath, Maine, Mar. 19, 1961; d. Peter Daniel and Regina Germain. BSFS, Georgetown U., 1983; JD, U. Pitts., 1989. Bar: Pa. 1989, Ariz. 1994, U.S. Supreme Ct. 1997. Sr. legal counselor UN's High Commr. for Refugees, Washington, 1995—. Author: AILA's Asylum Primer: A Practical Guide to U.S. Asylum Law and Procedure, 1998. Immigration, naturalization, and customs, Civil rights, Public international. Office: UNHCR Refugees Office 1775 K St NW Ste 300 Washington DC 20006-1502

**GERMAN, EDWARD CECIL,** lawyer; b. Phila., Dec. 28, 1921; s. Samuel Edward and Reba (Trimble) G.; m. Jane Harlos, Sept. 2, 1950; 1 child, Jeffrey Neal. JD, Temple U., 1950. Bar: Pa. 1951. Ptnr. LaBrum & Doak, Phila., 1953-80, German, Gallagher & Murtagh, Phila., 1980—; cons., lectr. to law schools including Harvard U., U. Pa., Syracuse U., others; bd. dirs., mem. products liability, def. research coms. Def. Research Inst., Def. Research Regional Library Inst.; instr. Practicing Law Inst. Contbr. chpts. to books, articles to profl. jours. Dist. dir. United Fund Campaign, 1960; solicitor-counsel Civic Assns. Delaware County, 1955-60; sec. Haven Beach Assn., 1962-63, v.p., 1963-64; trustee Pop Warner's Little Scholars, 1968—; sec., treas. Henryville Conservation Club. Served with USAAF, 1942-46, with USAF, 1950-51. Mem. ABA (chmn. trial techniques com. 1969, mem. profl. and officers and dirs. liability law com. ins. sect. 1974—, pvt. antitrust litigation com. litigation sect. 1974—, subcom. miscellaneous malpractice re accts., bankers, etc. 1976—), Pa. Bar Assn. (com. unauthorized practice 1976—), Phila. Bar Assn. (mem. Pa. rules of civil procedure com. 1963-71, unauthorized practice law com. 1965—, common pleas ct. com. 1964-71, com. antitrust laws corp. sect., mem. Federal bench-bar conf.), Am. Law Firm Assn. (chmn. bd. 1985-86), Fedn. Ins. Counsel (bd. govs. 1960-62, v.p. 1962-63, sec.-treas. 1963-65, exec. v.p. 1965-66, pres. 1966-67, chmn. bd. 1967-68), Maritime Law Assn., U.S. Am. Legion, 40 and 8, Internat. Assn. Ins. Counsel (def. research com., profl. liability and malpractice com.), Internat. Assn. Humble Humbugs, Pa. C. of C., Phila. Def. Counsel Assn., Scribes, Phi Delta Phi. Lodges: Masons, Shriners. Clubs: Union League, Down Town, Maxwell Meml. Football, Union League (Phila.), Beach Haven (N.J.) Yacht, Little Egg Harbor Yacht, Urban (pres. 1987-88) (Phila.), Little Mill Country, Belleplain Farms Shooting Preserve. Insurance, Personal injury, Environmental. Home: 129 The Mews Haddonfield NJ 08033-1344 Office: German Gallagher & Murtagh 200 S Broad St Philadelphia PA 19102-3803

**GERMAN, JUNE RESNICK,** lawyer; b. N.Y.C., Feb. 24, 1946; d. Irving and Stella (Weintraub) Resnick; m. Harold Jacob German, May 31, 1974; children: Beth Melissa, Heather Alice, Bret. BA, U. Pa., 1965; JD, NYU, 1968. Bar: N.Y. 1968, U.S. Dist. Ct. (ea. and so. dists.) N.Y. 1974, U.S. Ct. Appeals (2d cir.) 1973, U.S. Supreme Ct. 1973. Atty., sr. atty., supervising atty. Mental Health Info. Svc., N.Y.C., 1968-77; atty./advisor Course in Human Behavior Mems. of N.Y. State Judiciary, Nassau and Suffolk County, 1980; pvt. practice, Huntington, N.Y., 1985—. *June Resnick German brought several test cases which guaranteed rights to mentally disabled persons in the civil and criminal justice system, including a landmark case which established that, in New York State, civil involuntary patients have (a) a right to treatment, (b) a right to be treated in a facility that is least restrictive of their liberty, and (c) a right not to be transferred to a correctional facility. She has written several articles pertaining to the rights of the mentally disabled and has prepared amicus curiae briefs to the United States Supreme Court in the fields of mental health and environmental law.* Contbg. author: Bioethics and Human Rights, 1978, Mental Illness, Due Process and the Acquitted Defendant, 1979; contbr. chpts. to books, articles to profl. jours. Chmn. Citizen's Ad Hoc Com. Constrn. of the Dix Hills Water Adminstrn. Bldg., Huntington, N.Y., 1985-90; mem. Citizens Adv. Com. for Dix Hills Water Dist., Huntington, 1992—; dir. House Beautiful Assn. at Dix Hills, 1986—; dir. Citizens for a Livable Environment and Recycling, Huntington, 1989-93; mem. Suffolk County (N.Y.) Dem. Com., 1986—; mem. Deer Park Avenue Task Force, Town of Huntington, 1997-98; mem. Dix Hills Revitalization Com., 1999—. Mem. Suffolk County Bar Assn. Jewish. Avocations: tennis, hiking, travel. General practice, Federal civil litigation, Civil rights. Office: 150 Main St Huntington NY 11743-6908

**GERMANI, ELIA,** lawyer; b. Providence, Feb. 5, 1935; s. Gaetano and Antonia Maria (D'Aguanno) G.; m. Barbara Marie Lanzi, June 22, 1959 (div. 1973); m. Margaret Mary Mulvey, Feb. 12, 1977. AB magna cum laude, U. R.I., 1957; JD, Harvard U., 1961. Bar: R.I. 1962, U.S. Dist. Ct. R.I. 1963. Assoc. Graham, Reid, Ewing & Stapleton, Providence, 1961-67; atty. The Narragansett Elec. Co., Providence, 1968-76; ptnr. Tillinghast, Collins & Graham, Providence, 1976-79; gen. counsel Blue Cross & Blus Shield R.I., Providence, 1979—; gen. counsel, sec. Bus. Systems Corp. Am., Chgo., 1982—. Vice chmn. bd. regents Elem. & Secondary Edn. R.I., 1987-97; bd. govs. Boys & Girls Clubs Providence, 1994—. 2d lt. U.S. Army, 1957-58. Mem. Univ. Club, Aurora Civic Assn. Roman Catholic. Avocations: walking, reading, writing on educational issues. Health, Administrative and regulatory, Juvenile. Office: Blue Cross/Blue Shield RI 444 Westminster St Dept 1 Providence RI 02903-3279

**GERMANI, ELIZABETH A.,** lawyer; b. Portland, Maine, Aug. 19, 1963. BA, Boston Coll., 1985; JD, U. Maine, Portland, 1988. Bar: N.H. 1988, Maine 1989. Assoc. atty. Sulloway & Hollis, Concord, N.H., 1988-92, Friedman & Babcock, Portland, 1992-96; ptnr. Friedman Babcock & Gaythwaite, Portland, 1996—. Federal civil litigation, State civil litigation, Insurance. Office: Friedman Babcock & Gaythwaite 6 City Ctr Portland ME 04101-4081

**GERMANN, GARY STEPHEN,** lawyer; b. Evansville, Ind., Sept. 12, 1948; s. Henry Luther and Esther Louise (Gerichs) G.; m. Beth Coppel, Dec. 27, 1971; children: Mark, David, Matthew, Sarah. BA, Purdue U., 1970; JD, Valparaiso U., 1973. Bar: Iowa 1973, Ind. 1973, U.S. Dist. Ct. (no. dist.) Ind. 1977, U.. Ct. Appeals (7th cir.) 1989, U.S. Supreme Ct. 1989. Dep. pros. atty. Prosecutor's Office, Valparaiso, Ind., 1973-74, chief dep. pros. atty., 1974-77; assoc. Harris and Welsh, Chesterton, Ind., 1977-78; pros. atty. Porter County, Valparaiso, 1978-82; pvt. practice, Portage, Ind., 1982—; assoc. prof. Valparaiso U., 1977. High sch. tchr., elder-trustee 1st Presbyn. Ch., Valparaiso, 1977—; bd. dirs. YMCA, Valparaiso, 1976-80; vol. Am. Cancer Soc., Valparaiso, 1987—; mem. Cmty. Sys. Wide Response Team, Valparaiso, 1994—. Mem. Ind. Bar Assn., Ind. Pub. Defender Coun., Porter County Bar Assn. (pres. 1986). Avocations: basketball, soccer. Personal injury, Criminal, Family and matrimonial. Office: 3437 Airport Rd Portage IN 46368-5107

**GERMANY, GARVIN HOLT, JR.,** retired judge, lawyer; b. Dallas, May 16, 1926; s. Garvin Holt G. and Vera Emily Terry; m. Jerry Ann McSpadden, Aug. 13, 1950; (div. Oct., 1981); children: Cindy Lou Beswick, Terri Germany; m. Joyce ann Proske Welch, Feb. 20, 1982. Bar: Tex. 1955, U.S. Dist. Ct. (no. dist.), U.S. Dist. Ct. (ea. dist.), U.S. Dist. Ct. (so. dist.), U.S. Ct. Appeals (New Orleans), Mil. Ct. Appeals. Assoc. Perry & Wilson, Wichita Falls, Tex., 1955-56, Renfro & Johnson, Dallas, 1956-60; lawyer Joint Claims Com., Dallas, 1960-62; ptnr. Holder Kenyon Germany & Shaw, Freeport, Tex., 1962-90; judge CCL # 2 and probate Brazoria County, Tex., 1991-98; ret. Bd. dirs. Brazoria Cmty. Hist. Mus., Brazoria, 1986—, Brazoria County Hist. Mus., Angleton, Tex., 1991—. Served with USN, 1944-46; 1st lt. USAF, 1951-53. Mem. Dallas Jr. Bar Assn. (pres., lesser offices 1956-96), Masons (past master 1968-69, dist. dep. grand master 22/A grand lodge 1981-82, bd. dirs. 1986—), Rotary, Kiwanis (pres. 1968-69). Methodist. Avocations: flying, model building, restoring, airplanes, genealogy. Home: RT # 9 Smit Estates Brazoria TX 77422

**GERRARD, JOHN M.,** state supreme court justice; b. Schuyler, Nebr., Nov. 2, 1953. BS, Nebr. Wesleyan U., 1976; MPA, U. Ariz., 1977; JD, U. of Pacific, 1981. Pvt. practice Norfolk, 1981-95; city atty. City of Battle Creek, Nebr., 1982-95; justice Nebr. Supreme Ct., Lincoln, 1995—. Office: Nebr Supreme Ct 2214 State Capitol Lincoln NE 68509-8910*

**GERSCH, CHARLES FRANT,** lawyer; b. N.Y.C., Oct. 30, 1942. BA, NYU, 1964; MA, New Sch. for Social Rsch., 1969; JD, U. Puget Sound, 1986. Bar: Wash. 1987, U.S. Dist. Ct. (we. dist.) Wash. 1988. Vol. VISTA Housing Code Enforcement, South Bronx, N.Y., 1967-68; editorial rsch. mgr. Fawcett Pubs., N.Y.C., 1969-71; instr. sociology William Woods Coll., 1972-74, Chapman Coll., 1974-81; vol. law clk. Thurston County Wash. Superior Ct., 1986; pvt. practice Tacoma, 1988—. Mem. Wash. State Bar Assn., Tacoma/Pierce County Bar Assn. Criminal, Constitutional. Office: 170 Old City Hall 625 Commerce St Tacoma WA 98402-4618

**GERSH, JUDAH M.,** lawyer; b. Dayton, Ohio; s. Robert J. and Kathryn F. Gersh; m. Tanya N. Rosenstein. BA magna cum laude, U. Ariz., 1991; JD, U. Mich., 1996. Bar: Mont. 1996, Colo. 1997, U.S. Dist. Ct. Mont. 1997, U.S. Ct. Appeals (9th cir.) 1998, Salish-Kootenai Tribal Ct. 1998, Chippewa-Cree Tribal Ct. 1998. Sole practice Gersh Law Offices, Whitefish, Mont., 1996—. Treas. Alpine II Homeowners Assn., Whitefish, 1996-99, Bet Harim, Flathead Valley, Mont., 1996-98. Mem. ATLA, Mont. Trial Lawyers Assn., N.W. Mont. Bar Assn. (treas. 1997, pres. 1998). Avocations: skiing, climbing. Native American, Insurance, Labor. Office: 236 Wisconsin Ave Whitefish MT 59937-2305

**GERSON, MERVYN STUART,** lawyer; b. Cleve., Nov. 1, 1936; s. Philip Gerson and Rena (Friedman) Davis; m. Linda Hanff, Feb. 14, 1965; children: Laurie Jean Powazek, Philip Stuart, Michael Craig. AB, U. Mich., 1957; JD, 1960. Atty. advisor U.S. Tax Ct., Washington, 1960-62; atty. Gerson, Grekin & Wynhoff, Honolulu, 1981—. Fellow Am. Coll. Trust and Estate Counsel (regent 1995—), Am. Coll. Tax Counsel. Estate planning, Probate, Estate taxation. Office: Gerson Grekin & Wynhoff 1001 Bishop St Honolulu HI 96813-3429

**GERSON, NANCY L.,** lawyer; b. Bronx, Oct. 20, 1957. JD, St. John's Law Sch., Queens, N.Y., 1983. Bar: N.Y. 1983. Pvt. practice law Queens, 1983—. Personal injury, Family and matrimonial, Juvenile. Office: 14633 Hawthorne Ave Flushing NY 11355-2239

**GERSON, STUART MICHAEL,** lawyer; b. N.Y.C., Jan. 16, 1944; s. James and Ethel (Cherney) G.; m. Pamela Somers, July 28, 1979; children: James Barker, Somers Elizabeth, Lindsey Dakota. BA in Polit. Sci., Pa. State U., 1964; JD, Georgetown U., 1967. Bar: D.C. 1968, N.Y. 1999, U.S. Supreme Ct. 1974, U.S. Ct. Appeals (DC cir.) 1972, U.S. Ct. Appeals (5th cir.) 1972, 81, U.S. Ct. Appeals (9th cir.) 1978, U.S. Ct. Appeals (2d cir.) 1979, U.S. Ct. Appeals (11th cir.) 1981, U.S. Ct. Appeals (6th cir.) 1982, U.S. Ct. Appeals (4th cir.) 1984, U.S. Ct. Appeals (3d cir.) 1985, U.S. Ct. Appeals (8th cir.) 1986, U.S. Ct. Appeals (1st, 7th, 10th, fed. cirs.) 1989. Asst. U.S. atty. City of Washington, 1972-75; assoc., then ptnr. Reed Smith Shaw & McClay, Washington, 1975-80; pvt. practice; ptnr. in charge litigation Epstein, Becker & Green, Washington, N.Y.C., 1980-89; adj. prof. of law Georgetown U., 1991; asst. atty. gen. in charge civil div. U.S. Dept. Justice, Washington, 1989-93; acting Atty. Gen. U.S., 1993; atty. and head of litigation Epstein, Becker & Green, P.C., Washington and N.Y.C.; bd. dirs. CHANGE-All Souls Housing Corp., Washington. Contbr. articles to profl. jours. Gen. counsel Nat. Rep. Senatorial Com., Washington, 1985-86; sr. advisor presdl. campaign George Bush, 1988; leader transition team Office Pres. Elect, 1988. Capt. USAF, 1967-72. Decorated Meritorious Svc. Medal. Mem. ABA, D.C. Bar Assn. (steering com. litigation 1985-93), The Barristers (pres.), Nat. Health Lawyers Assn., Am. Inns of Ct., Metro. Club, Lawyers Club. Unitarian. Avocations: competitive running, national track and field official, sailing, reading history. Office: Epstein Becker & Green PC 1227 25th St NW Ste 700 Washington DC 20037-1175 also: 250 Park Ave New York NY 10177-0001

**GERSOVITZ, JEREMY,** lawyer; b. Montreal, Que., Can., July 28, 1956; came to U.S., 1984; s. Benjamin and Sarah Valerie Gersovitz; 1 child, Alexander Samuel. BA in Polit. Sci., Columbia Coll., 1980; MS in Journalism, Northwestern U., Chgo., 1985; JD, U. Mont., 1992. Bar: Mont. 1992, U.S. Dist. Ct. Mont. 1992. Law clk. to Judge T.C. Honzel, 1st Jud. Dist., Helena, Mont., 1992-94; pvt. practice Townsend, Mont., 1994-95; part-time pub. defender Broadwater County, Townsend, Mont., 1994-95; pvt. practice Helena, 1995-97; part-time pub. defender Lewis & Clark County, Helena, 1995-97, pub. defender, 1997—. Mem. bd. editors The Mont. Lawyer., 1996—. Mem. ABA, State Bar Mont., 1st Jud. Dist. Bar Assn. Jewish. Home and Office: 532 N Warren St Helena MT 59601-4014

**GERSTEIN, JOE WILLIE,** lawyer; b. Atlanta, July 29, 1927; s. Arthur and Tena (Hartman) G.; m. Doris Renate Florsheim, May 20, 1956; children: Ellen Claire Gerstein Crooke, Kim Carol Gerstein Wainer. AB, Duke U., 1949, JD, 1952. Bar: Ga. 1953, U.S. Tax Ct., U.S. Ct. Appeals (fed. cir.) 1965, U.S. Supreme Ct. 1967. Sr. ptnr. Gerstein, Carter & Chestnut and predecessor firm Gerstein & Carter, Atlanta and Doraville, Ga., 1957-76; sole practice Doraville, 1976—; former city atty, Doraville; lectr. on taxes, wills, trust and estates at various civic, profl. and ch. orgns.; bd. dirs. Atlanta Estate Planning Council. Contbg. editor Duke U. Law Rev. Past dir. Social Service Fedn. Atlanta. Served with USN, 1944-47. Fellow Am. Coll. Trust and Estate Counsel; mem. ABA, Ga. Bar Assn., Atlanta Bar Assn., Decatur-DeKalb Bar Assn., Met. Atlanta Council Rotary Club Pres. (past chmn.), Comml. Law League Am. (past nat. recording sec.), Atlanta Tax Forum, Big Canoe Men's Golf Assn. (golf com.), Zeta Beta Tau (v.p. AU chpt.), Phi Delta Phi. Jewish. Club: Standard (Atlanta) (legal and golf coms.). Lodges: Rotary (North DeKalb past pres.), Masons (past offices), B'nai B'rith (Gate City past v.p.). Estate planning, Taxation, general, Probate. Home: 2010 Riverside Rd Roswell GA 30076-4026 Office: 6485 Peachtree Industrial Blvd Doraville GA 30360-2112

**GERSTEIN, MARK DOUGLAS,** lawyer; b. Chgo., Nov. 16, 1959; s. Robert Henry and Helene Roberta Gerstein; m. Julia Sara Wolf, Apr. 13, 1986; children: Allison Ruth, Evan Benjamin. BA, U. Mich., 1981; JD, U. Chgo., 1984. Bar: Ill., U.S. Dist. Ct. (no. dist.) Ill. Ptnr., assoc. Katten Muchin & Zavis, Chgo., 1984-96; equity ptnr. Lathan & Watkins, Chgo., 1996—. Dir. Assocs. Ravinia Festival, Chgo., 1996—, Youth Guidance, Chgo., 1995—. Mem. Chgo. Bar Assn. (chmn. com. on corp. control 1998—), Std. Club. Avocations: sailing, cycling. Mergers and acquisitions, General corporate, Securities. Office: Latham & Watkins 233 S Wacker Dr Ste 5800 Chicago IL 60606-6362

**GERSTMANN, ELAN,** lawyer; b. N.Y.C., July 17, 1960; s. Kurt E. and Ethel (Cohen) G.; m. Carol Verdirame, Sept. 22, 1991. BA, Columbia U., 1982; JD, SUNY, Buffalo, 1987. Bar: N.Y. 1988, U.S. Dist. Court (so. and ea. dist.) N.Y. 1988, U.S. Ct. Appeals (2d cir.) 1988, N.J. 1990, D.C. 1990, U.S. Dist. Ct. N.J. 1990, U.S. Ct. Claims 1992, U.S. Supreme Ct. 1993. Assoc. appellate counsel Criminal Appeals Bur., Legal Aid Soc. N.Y., N.Y.C., 1987-88; assoc. Law Office Lionel R. Saporta, N.Y.C., 1988-91; pvt. practice N.Y.C., 1991-92, 95—; assoc. Law Office Laura A. Brevetti, N.Y.C., 1993-95. Contbr. articles to profl. publs. Mem. Am. Soc. Law, Medicine and Ethics, N.Y. State Bar Assn., N.Y. County Lawyer's Assn., Assn. Bar City N.Y. Criminal, General civil litigation. Office: 230 Park Ave Rm 625 New York NY 10169-0699

**GERTLER, MEYER H.,** lawyer; b. New Orleans, Oct. 28, 1945; s. David and Sadie (Redman) G.; m. Marcia Raye Goldstein, Aug. 23, 1967; children—Louis, Danielle, Joshua. B.A., Tulane U., 1967, J.D. 1969. Bar: La. 1970, U.S. Dist. Ct. (ea. and mid. dists.) 1970, U.S. Ct. Apppeals (5th cir.) 1970, U.S. Supreme Ct. 1970. Ptnr. Uddo & Gertler, New Orleans, 1970-76, Gertler & Gertler, New Orleans, 1977-86, Gertler, Gertler & Vincent, New Orleans, 1986—; mem. Asbestos Litigation Group. Mem. La. Trial Lawyers Assn., Am. Trial Lawyers Assn., ABA, Sup. Ct. Hist. Soc., Am. Judicature Soc. Democrat. Jewish. Clubs: B'nai B'rith, Masons. Product liability, Federal civil litigation, State civil litigation. Home: 5462 Bellaire Dr New Orleans LA 70124-1035 Office: Gertler Gertler & Vincent 127129 Carondelet New Orleans LA 70130

**GERTNER, NANCY,** federal judge, educator; b. May 22, 1946; d. Morris and Sadie Gertner; m. John C. Reinstein, Apr. 27, 1985; 3 children. BA cum laude with honors, Columbia U., 1967; MA, JD, Yale U., 1971; degree (hon.), New England Sch. Law, 1979, Suffolk U., 1997. Bar: Mass., U.S. Dist. Ct., U.S. Ct. Appeals (1st and 3rd cirs.), U.S. Supreme Ct. Law clerk to Hon. Luther M. Swygert U.S. Ct. Appeals (7th cir.), Chgo., 1971-72; ptnr. Silverglate, Gertner, Fine & Good, 1973-90, Dwyer, Collora & Gertner, 1990-94; judge U.S. Dist. Ct. Mass., Boston, 1994—; instr. Sch. Law Boston U., 1972-86, 87-90, 94-95; vis. prof. Law Sch. Harvard U., 1985-86, Yale Law Sch., 1997—; instr. Boston Coll. Law Sch., 1995-98; mem. civic justice adv. com. to U.S. Dist. Ct., 1991; mem. adv. com. U.S. Ct. Appeals (1st cir.), 1991-92. Co-author: The Law of Juries; contbr. articles to legal jours. Bd. dirs. Women's Rights Com. Recipient Mass. Choice award, 1987, Black Educator's Alliance award Profl. Svc. to Edn., 1983, New England Hadassah award, 1992, Abigail Adams award Mass. Women's Polit. Caucus Edn. Fund., 1994; voted Best Fed. Judge in Mass., 1999. Mem. ATLA (basic trial advocacy course com., vice chair 1985-86), Mass. Acad. Trial Lawyers, Mass. Civil Liberties Union (bd. dirs., Abraham T. Alper award for Excellence in Civil Liberties, 1980), Boston Bar Assn. (lawyers com. for civil rights under law, steering com. 1979—), Women Judges Hon. Assn. Fax: 617-204-5821. E-mail: honorablenancyugertner@mad.uscourts.gov. Office: US Dist Ct 1 Courthouse Way Boston MA 02210-3002

**GERTZ, THEODORE GERSON,** lawyer; b. Chgo., Sept. 8, 1936; s. Elmer and Ceretta (Samuels) G.; m. Suzanne C., June 19, 1960; children: Craig M., Candace C., Scott W. BA, U. Chgo., 1958; JD, Northwestern U., 1962. Bar: Ill. 1962, U.S. Dist. Ct. (no. dist.) Ill. 1962. Assoc. Marks, Marks & Kaplan, Chgo., 1962-64; assoc. Lowitz, Vihons & Stone, Chgo., 1964-66, ptnr., 1966-71; ptnr. Pretzel & Stouffer, Chgo., 1971-94, Shefsky, Froelich, Chgo., 1995—; gen. counsel Hull House Assn., Chgo., 1977—, Blind Svc. Assn., Chgo., 1987—, Citizens Against Suburban Sprawl, Mettawa, Ill., 1995—, Am. Student Dental Assn., Chgo., 1977—. Author: A Guide to Estate Planning, Illinois Advance Estate Planning. Dir., treas. Mettawa Open Lands, 1987—; former trustee Village of Mettawa, 1994—, Pub. Interest Law Initiative, Chgo. With U.S. Army, 1962-64. Fellow Ill. Bar Found., Ill. Bar Assn., Chgo. Bar Assn., Law Club. Democrat. Jewish. Avocations: reading, nature, working out, dancing, traveling. Estate planning. Home: 950 Benson Ln Libertyville IL 60048-2406 Office: Shefsky and Froelich 444 N Michigan Ave Ste 2600B Chicago IL 60611-3998

**GERWIN, LESLIE ELLEN,** lawyer, public affairs and community relations executive; b. L.A., May 18, 1950; d. Nathan and Beverly Adele (Wilson) G.; m. Bruce Robert Leslie, July 3, 1978; 1 child, Jonathan Gerwin Leslie. BA, Prescott Coll., 1972; JD, Antioch Sch. Law, 1975; MPH, Tulane U., 1988. Bar: D.C. 1975, N.Y. 1981, U.S. Dist. Ct. D.C. 1977, U.S. Dist. Ct. (so. dist.) N.Y. 1980. Staff asst. U.S. Congress, Washington, 1970-72; cons. Congl. Subcom., Washington, 1972-73; instr. U. Miami Law Sch., Coral Gables, Fla., 1975-76; assoc. prof. law Yeshiva U., N.Y.C., 1976-86; vis. assoc. prof. law Tulane Law Sch., New Orleans, 1983-84; pub. policy cons. New Orleans, 1987—; pres. Ariadne Cons., New Orleans, 1994—; dir. devel. and community rels. Planned Parenthood La., Inc., New Orleans, 1989-90; legal advisor La. Coalition for Reproductive Freedom, 1990-92; exec. v.p. Met. Area Com., New Orleans, 1992-94; exec. dir. Met. Area Com. Edn. Fund, New Orleans, 1992-94; bd. dirs. Inst. for Phys. Fitness Rsch., N.Y.C., 1982-86, Challenge/Discovery, Crested Butte, Colo., 1977-80; cons. FDA, Washington, 1977-78, U. Judaism, L.A., 1974-75; mem. Met. Area Com. Leadership Forum, New Orleans, 1988; adj. asst. prof. La. State U. Sch. Medicine, 1996—, La. State U. Med. Sch., Dept. of Public Health and Preventive Medicine. Contbr. articles to profl. jours. Mem. Ind. Dem. Jud. Screening Panel, N.Y.C., 1980; bd. dirs. New Orleans Food Bank for Emergencies, 1987-89; profl. adv. com. MAZON-A Jewish Response to Hunger, L.A., 1986-89; bd. dirs. Second Harvesters Food Bank Greater New Orleans, 1989-94, La. State LWV, 1990-91, Anti-Defamation League, New Orleans, 1989-95, Jewish Endowment Found., 1987-93; trustee Jewish Fedn. Greater New Orleans, 1989-95, 97—; mem. exec. com. Fed. Emergency Mgmt. Agy. Bd., 1997—; trustee Emergency Food and Shelter Program, S.E. La., 1988—; v.p. Tulane U. B'nai B'rith Hillel Found., 1987-90; steering com. Citizens for Pers. Freedom, 1989-91; steering com. Metro 2000, 1989-90; sec. New Orleans sect. Nat. Coun. Jewish Women, 1990-91, state pub. affairs chmn., 1992-96; bd. Contemporary Arts Ctr., 1993-97; chair, bd. advocates Planned Parenthood La., 1995—; v.p. Edn. Tikvat Shalom Conservative Congregation, 1995-97, chair New Orleans Isrel Bonds, 1996-98;

mem. Cmty. Rels. Com., 1986—, vice chair, 1995-97, chair 1997—; adminstr. Area Tng. Ctr., USTA, New Orleans, 1996—. Fellow Inst. of Politics, 1990-91; scholar Xerox Found., 1972-75; Decorated Order of Barristers; named One of Ten Outstanding Young Women of Am., 1987; recipient Herbert J. Garon Young Leadership award Jewish Fedn. Greater New Orleans, 1990; named YWCA Role Model, 1992. Mem. ABA, N.Y. Bar Assn., N.Y. Acad. Scis., Am. Pub. Health Assn., D.C. Bar Assn., Nat. Moot Ct. Honor Soc., Pub. Health Honor Soc., Calif. State Dem. Club (Key Svc. award 1988), Delta Omega. Environmental, Health, Administrative and regulatory.

**GESKE, JANINE PATRICIA,** law educator, former state supreme court justice; b. Port Washington, Wis., May 12, 1949; d. Richard Braem and Georgette (Paulissen) Geske; m. Michael Julian Hogan, Jan. 2, 1982; children: Mia Geske Berman, Sarah Geske Hogan, Kevin Geske Hogan. Student, U. Grenoble, U. Rennes; BA, MA in Tchg., Beloit Coll., 1971; JD, Marquette U., 1975, LLD, 1998. Bar: Wis. 1975, U.S. Dist. Ct. (ea. & we. dists.) Wis. 1975, U.S. Supreme Ct. 1978. Tchr. elem. sch. Lake Zurich, Ill., 1970-72; staff atty., chief staff atty. Legal Aid Soc., Milw., 1975-78; asst. prof. law, clin. dir. Law Sch. Marquette U., Milw., 1978-81; hearing examiner Milw. County CETA, Milw., 1980-81; judge Milw. County Circuit Ct., Milw., 1981-93; justice Supreme Ct. Wis., 1993-98; disting. prof. law Marquette U. Law Sch., Milw., 1998—; dean Wis. Jud. Coll.; mem. faculty Nat. Jud. Coll.; instr. various jud. tng. programs, continuing legal edn. Fellow ABA, mem. Am. Law Inst., Am. Arbitration Assn., Soc. Profls. in Dispute Resolution, Wis. Bar Assn., Wis. Assn. Mediators, Milw. Bar Assn., Dane County Bar Assn., Nat. Women Judges Assn., 7th Cir. Bar Assn., Alpha Sigma Nu. Roman Catholic. Office: Marquette U Law Sch PO Box 1881 Milwaukee WI 53201-1881

**GESLER, ALAN EDWARD,** lawyer; b. Milw., Aug. 25, 1945; s. Paul and Caroline Gesler; m. Judith A. Joy, May 6, 1967; children: Amy, Molly, Joshua. BS cum laude, U. Wis., Milw., 1967; JD, U. Wis., Madison, 1970. Bar: Wis. 1970, U.S. Dist. Ct. (ea. dist.) Wis. 1971, U.S. Supreme Ct. 1974. Mem. Warshafsky, Rotter, Tarnoff, Gesler, Reinhardt & Bloch, S.C., Milw., 1970-94; of counsel Slattery & Hausman, Ltd., Waukesha, Wis., 1994—. Assoc. editor Litigation News, 1978-80. Vice chmn. County Task Force on Mental Retardation, Milw., 1974; active health adv. subcom. Milw. County Suprs., 1975. Fellow Internat. Acad. Trial Lawyers; mem. ABA, Wis. Bar Assn., Assn. Trial Lawyers Am. (bd. govs. 1985-88), Wis. Acad. Trial Lawyers (bd. govs. 1979—, pres. 1983), Am. Bd. Trial Advs. (pres. Wis. chpt. 1991, nat. bd. rep. 1992-95). E-mail: agesler@execpc.com. Personal injury, General civil litigation, Product liability. Office: Slattery & Hausman Ltd N240 W1221 Pewaukee Rd Waukesha WI 53187

**GESMER, ELLEN FRANCES,** lawyer; b. Boston, Sept. 6, 1950; d. Henry and Bessie (Nathanson) G.; m. Alan Stuart Hyde, May 23, 1976; children: Toby Matthew, Laura Zoe. BA summa cum laude, Radcliffe, 1972; JD, Yale U. Law Sch., 1976. Bar: Mass. 1977, N.Y. 1979, Mich. 1983. Law clk. to Hon. Joseph L. Tauro Boston, 1976-77; dir. litigation Bed-Stuy Community Legal Svcs., Bklyn., 1977-83; clin. asst. prof. U. Mich. Law Sch., Ann Arbor, Mich., 1983-84; assoc. Teitelbaum & Hiller, P.C., N.Y., 1985-87; ptnr. Gulielmetti & Gesmer, P.C., N.Y., 1987—. Bd. dirs. Legal Svcs. Alumni Assn., 1985-90, Keystone Dance Found., Inc., 1993-98, Hispanic Housing Coalition, 1982-83; pub. mem. Rent Guidelines Bd., 1990-92. Mem. Am. Arbitration Assn. (comml. panel mem.), Assn. of City of Bar of N.Y. (com. on rights of crime victims 1990-93, com. profl. responsibility 1998—), Women's Bar Assn. (com. jud. 1998—, family law com. 1997—). Family and matrimonial, General civil litigation, Landlord-tenant. Office: Gulielmetti & Gesmer PC 401 Broadway Ste 1901 New York NY 10013-3005

**GETLER, JANINE A.,** lawyer; b. Forest Hills, N.Y., Jan. 2, 1961; d. Joseph John and Camille Francine Getler; m. David M. Stern, Nov. 2, 1986; children: Joseph Jacob, Emily Bora. BA, St. Michael's Coll., Winooski, Vt., 1983; JD, Bklyn. Law Sch., 1991. Rschr. Stad. & Poor's Corp., N.Y.C., 1984-85; legal asst. Merrill Lynch, N.Y.C., 1985-89; rsch. asst. Bklyn. Law Sch., 1989-90; assoc. Beattie Padovano, Montvale, N.J., 1991-94, Price, Meese, Shulman & D'Arminio, P.C., Woodcliff Lake, N.J., 1994—. Bd. dirs. Ramapo Soccer League, Suffern, N.Y., 1997-98; v.p. Montebello Elem. PTA, Suffern, 1998—. Mem. ABA, N.J. State Bar Assn., Bergen County Bar Assn., Nat. Bus. Inst. General practice, FERC practice, Probate. Home: 6 Haskell Ave Airmont NY 10901-6418 Office: Price Meese Shulman & D'Arminio PC 50 Tice Blvd Woodcliff Lake NJ 07675-7654

**GETMAN, WILLARD ETHERIDGE,** lawyer, mediator; b. Cin., Jan. 31, 1949; s. Frank Newton and Dorothy Dill (Etheridge) G. BA, U. N.C., 1971; JD, Stetson U., 1974. Bar: Fla. 1974, N.Y. 1985, U.S. Dist. Ct. (so. dist.) Fla. 1975, U.S. Dist. Ct. (mid. dist.) Fla. 1996, U.S. Supreme Ct. 1997; County Ct. cert. mediator. Assoc., Law Offices John M. Callaway, Lake Worth, Fla., 1974-75; sole practice, West Palm Beach, Fla., 1976-80, Boynton Beach, Fla., 1980-93, Jacksonville, Fla., 1993—. mem./agt. Attys' Title Ins. Fund, Inc., Fla., Atty's. Real Property Coun. NE Fla., Inc. Mem. ABA, N.Y. State Bar Assn., Assn. Trial Lawyers Am., Fla. Bar (trust law com. 1975-76, summary rules com. 1980-84, probate and guardianship rules com. 1981-82), Jacksonville Bar Assn., Estate Planning Coun. N.E. Fla., Cedar Lake Club (Clayville, N.Y.), Trailside Lions, Elks, Moose, Masons, Shriners, Delta Theta Phi. Republican. Presbyterian. Estate planning, Probate, Real property. Home and Office: 567 Lazy Meadow Dr E Jacksonville FL 32225-3428 also: 38 Morgan St PO Box 477 Ilion NY 13357-0477

**GETNICK, NEIL VICTOR,** lawyer; b. Bklyn., Oct. 28, 1953; s. Irving Murray and Zita (Ellman) G.; m. Margaret Joan Finerty, May 21, 1978. BA in Govt. magna cum laude, Cornell U., 1975, JD, 1978. Bar: N.Y. 1979, U.S. Dist. Ct. (so. and ea. dists.) N.Y. 1983. Asst. dist. atty. trial div. N.Y. County, N.Y.C., 1978-81, asst. dist. atty. frauds bur., 1981-82; ptnr. Getnick & Getnick, N.Y., 1983—; mem. Criminal Justice Act panel U.S. Dist. Ct. for So. Dist. N.Y., N.Y.C., 1984-89. Editor-in-chief: Civil Prosecution News, 1994-96. Recipient Pub. Citizenship award N.Y. Pub. Interest Rsch. Group, 1977. Mem. ABA (litigation and criminal law sects.), N.Y. State Bar Assn. (exec. com. comml. and fed. litigation sect., chair com. on civil prosecution), Assn. of Bar of City of N.Y., N.Y. County Lawyers Assn., Internat. Assn. Ind. Pvt. Sector Inspectors Gen. (pres. 1994—), Internat. Assn. of Ind. Pvt. Sector Inspectors Gen. (pres. 1994—). General civil litigation, General corporate, Criminal. Office: Getnick & Getnick Rockefeller Ctr 630 5th Ave Fl 27 New York NY 10111-0100

**GETTLEMAN, ROBERT WILLIAM,** judge; b. Atlantic City, May 5, 1943; s. Charles Edward and Beulah (Oppenheim) G.; m. Joyce Reinitz, Dec. 23, 1964; children: Lynn Katheryn, Jeffrey Alan. BSBA cum laude, Boston U., 1965; JD cum laude, Northwestern U., 1968. Bar: Ill. 1968, U.S. Dist. Ct. (no. dist.) Ill. 1968, U.S. Ct. Appeals (7th cir.) 1968, U.S. Dist. Ct. (ea. dist.) Wis. 1972, U.S. Supreme Ct. 1973. Law clk. to presiding justice U.S. Ct. Appeals, Chgo., 1968-70; assoc. D'Ancona & Pflaum, Chgo., 1970-74, ptnr., 1974-94; judge U.S. Dist. Ct., Ill., 1994—; bd. dirs. John Howard Assn., Chgo., 1973-94, pres., 1978-81, chmn. legal and policy coms.; commr., chmn. devel. disabilities and individual rights coms. Gov.'s Commn. to Revise Mental Health Code of Ill., 1973-77; chmn. steering com. Chgo. Project on Residential Alternatives, 1984-85; mem. Cook County State's Atty.'s Profl. Adv. Com., 1984—; treas. Ill. Guardianship and Advocacy Commn., 1984, vice chmn., 1985, chmn., 1986; bd. dirs., chmn. legal com. Pact, Inc., 1985—; mem. mcpl. officers election bd. Village of Lyons, Ill., 1985. Contbr. articles to law revs. Bd. dirs. Ill. div. ACLU, 1973-78. Recipient August W. Christmann award Mayor of Chgo., 1994. Fellow Am. Bar Found.; mem. ABA, Ill. Bar Assn., Chgo. Bar Assn., 7th Fed. Cir. Bar Assn., Chgo. Council Lawyers. Office: US Dist Ct 1788 Dirksen Bldg 219 S Dearborn St Fl 17 Chicago IL 60604-1702

**GETTNER, ALAN FREDERICK,** lawyer; b. N.Y.C., Dec. 25, 1941; s. Victor Salomon and Henriette Seldner (Herrmann) G.; m. Monah Lawrence, Jan. 19, 1969. BA, Yale U., 1963; MA, U. Chgo., 1964; PhD, Columbia U., 1971, JD, 1979. Bar: N.Y. 1980. Assoc. Debevoise & Plimpton, N.Y.C. and Paris, 1979-84; assoc. Holtzmann, Wise & Shepard, N.Y.C., 1984-85, ptnr., 1986-95, mem. exec. com., 1992-94; ptnr. Patterson, Belknap, Webb & Tyler, LLP., N.Y.C., 1995—. Mem. ABA, Assn. Bar City N.Y., Internat. Bar Assn., Internat. Law Assn., The Lotos Club. Mergers and acquisitions, General corporate, Private international. Office: Patterson Belknap Webb & Tyler LLP 1133 Ave Americas New York NY 10036-6710

**GETTY, CHARLES A.,** judge; b. Johnstown, Pa., July 3, 1939; s. Charles H. and Julia D. G.; m. Sally Hare, Apr. 16, 1998; children: Colleen, Thomas. Degree in bus., U. Pitts., 1961; JD, Duquesne Law Sch., 1972. Bar: Penn. 1972, U.S. Dist. Ct. (we. dist.) Penn. 1975, U.S. Supreme Ct. 1980. Pvt. practice Cambria County Bar Assn., Johnstown, Pa., 1972-95; worker compensation judge Commonwealth of Pa., Johnstown, 1995—. With USNR, 1962-82. Mem. VFW, Am. Legion, Elks. Republican. Avocation: British sport cars. Home: 325 Diamond Blvd Johnstown PA 15905-2713 Office: Commonwealth of Pa 609 Main St Johnstown PA 15901-2111

**GETTY, GERALD WINKLER,** lawyer; b. Chgo., June 17, 1913; s. Oliver and Pearl (Winkler) G.; m. Helen Brennan, Oct. 2, 1938 (dec. 1966); children: Michael, Muriel, Marie; m. Gracia Gibbs, June 3, 1967. JD, DePaul U., 1938, JD (hon.), 1972. Bar: Ill. 1938, Ind. 1938, U.S. Supreme Ct. 1960. Lawyer U.S. Govt., Chgo., 1938-42; pub. defender Cook County, Chgo., 1942-72; ptnr. Getty and Getty, Dolton, Ill., 1972-83; prin. Gerald W. Getty and Assocs., Dolton, 1983—. Author: Public Defender, 1972, Theory of Condominium and Cooperative Apartment Law, 1993. Mem. Calumet Country Club, Elks, Moose. Criminal, Personal injury, Real property. Home and Office: 18430 Kedzie Ave Homewood IL 60430-2723

**GETZ, DAVID H.,** lawyer; b. L.A., Feb. 16, 1960; s. Leon S. and Marianne (Marks) G.; m. Katherine C. Getz, July 22, 1989; children: Nicholas, Taylor. BA, U. Calif., Santa Barbara, 1982; JD, U. San Diego, 1986. Bar: Calif. 1986, U.S. Dist. Ct. (so. dist.) Calif., U.S. Ct. Appeals (9th cir.). Ptnr. Hilman & Getz, San Diego, 1986-91; pvt. practice, San Diego, 1991-93; ptnr. Rudick, Platt, Glatt & Getz, San Diego, 1993—. General civil litigation, Environmental, Construction. Office: Rudick Platt Glatt & Getz 600 B St Ste 1500 San Diego CA 92101-4596

**GETZ, HERBERT A.,** lawyer. BA, Ill. Wesleyan U., 1977; JD, Harvard U., 1980. Bar: Ill. 1980. Assoc. Bell, Boyd & Lloyd, Chgo., 1980-83; gen. counsel Waste Mgmt. Ptnrs., Inc. (now Waste Mgmt., Inc.), Oak Brook, Ill., 1983-85; asst. gen. counsel Waste Mgmt., Inc., Oak Brook, 1985-88; sec., asst. gen. counsel WMX Techs., Inc., Oak Brook, 1988-92, sr. v.p., gen. counsel, sec., 1992—. General corporate, Securities. Office: WMX Techs Inc 3003 Butterfield Rd Oak Brook IL 60523-1100

**GETZENDANNER, SUSAN,** lawyer, former federal judge; b. Chgo., July 24, 1939; d. William B. and Carole S. (Muehling) O'Meara; children—Alexandra, Paul. B.B.A., Loyola U., 1966, J.D., 1966. Bar: Ill. bar 1966. Law clk. U.S. Dist. Ct., Chgo., 1966-68; assoc. Mayer, Brown & Platt, Chgo., 1968-74, ptnr., 1974-80; judge U.S. Dist. Ct., Chgo., 1980-87; ptnr. Skadden, Arps, Slate, Meagher & Flom, Chgo., 1987—. Recipient medal of excellence Loyola U. Law Alumni Assn., 1981. Mem. ABA, Chgo. Council Lawyers. Office: Skadden Arps Slate Meagher Flom 333 W Wacker Dr # 2100 Chicago IL 60606*

**GETZOFF, STEVEN B.,** lawyer; b. N.Y.C., July 24, 1957; s. Stanley S. and Marilyn S. Getoff; m. Lisa Sharon Abrams; children: Corey Michael, Marc David. BA in Polit. Sci., SUNY, Albany, 1979; JD, SUNY, Buffalo, 1982. Bar: N.Y. 1982. Assoc. Lester Schwab Katz & Dwyer, N.Y.C., 1982-89, ptnr., 1990—. Contbr. chpt. to book, articles to profl. jours. Mem. ABA, N.Y. State Bar Assn. Product liability, Antitrust, Contracts commercial. Home: 33 Mountainview Ave Ardsley NY 10502-2009 Office: Lester Schwab Katz & Dwyer 120 Broadway Fl 38 New York NY 10271-0071

**GEVERS, MARCIA BONITA,** lawyer, lecturer, mediator, consultant; b. Mpls., Oct. 11, 1946; d. Sam and Bessie (Gottlieb) Fleisher; m. Michael A. Gevers, Sept. 13, 1970; children: Sarah Nichole, David Seth. BA, Nat. Coll. Edn., 1968; MA, Northea. Ill. U., 1973; JD, DePaul U., 1980. Bar: Ill. 1980, U.S. Dist. Ct. (no. dist.) Ill. 1980, U.S. Supreme Ct. 1985. Tchr. The Harris Sch., Chgo. Bd. Edn., N. Suburban Spl. Edn. Dist., Highland Park, Ill., 1968-73; legis. asst., campaign mgr. Ill. State Rep., Dolton, 1974-79; sole practice Park Forest, Dolton, Ill., 1980-83; ptnr. Getty and Gevers, Dolton, 1983-87; pvt. practice Marica B. Gevers & Assocs., Flossmoor, Ill., 1987—; adj. prof. Gov.'s State U., University Park, 1986-87. Contbr. articles to profl. jours.; producer, host cable TV show, The Law and You, 1982-83. Bd. dirs. Park Forest Zoning Bd. Appeals, Fair Housing Rev. Bd., Housing Bd. Appeals, EEO Rev. Bd., 1975-88; pres. bd. dirs. South Suburban Cmty. Hebrew Day Sch., Olympia Fields, Ill., 1982-86; bd. dirs. Congregation Beth Sholom Ch., Park Forest, 1980-82, Congregation Beth Sholom Ch., Park Forest, 1980-82, Anita M. Stone Jewish Cmty. Ctr., 1996—; pres. Ill. Women's Polit. Caucus; mem. steering com. Nat. Women's Polit. Caucus, Washington; pres., founder Metro South Women's Polit. Caucus, Chgo. suburbs; alt. del. Dem. Nat. Conv., N.Y.C., 1980. Mem. ABA (family law sect.,juvenile, stepfamilies and pub. rels. coms.), Ill. State Bar Assn., Chgo. Bar Assn. (matrimonial law com., Guardian Ad Litem subcom.), Am. Arbitration Assn. (arbitrator), Lodges: Hadassah, B'nai B'rith Women. General civil litigation, Family and matrimonial, Real property. Office: Marcia B Gevers & Assocs 19710 Governors Hwy Flossmoor IL 60422-2040

**GEWERTZ, MARTIN ANSON,** lawyer; b. Dallas, Dec. 3, 1948; s. Irving David and Anita Rose (Indin) G.; m. Sharon Gay Abelman, Mar. 11, 1973; 1 child, Nevin Merrill. BA, U. Tex., 1970; JD, U. Houston, 1972. Bar: Tex. 1973, U.S. Dist. Ct. (we. dist.) Tex. 1976, U.S. Ct. Appeals (5th cir.) 1976, U.S. Supreme Ct. 1976. Pvt. practice San Antonio, 1973—; prof. Law San Antonio Coll., San Antonio, 1980—; 2d asst. city prosecutor City of Leon Valley, Tex., 1980-81. Mem. editorial bd. The Houston Law Review, U. Houston, 1971-72. Mem. Leon Valley Zoning Bd., 1979-80. Recipient Am. Jurisprudence award Bancroft Whitney Co., 1971. Mem. San Antonio Subrogation Assn., Comml. Law League Am., Bankruptcy Bar Assn., San Antonio Bar Assn., Order of the Barons, Phi Delta Phi, Zeta Beta Tau. Jewish. Avocations: karate blackbelt, travel, snow skiing, photography, swimming. Bankruptcy, Consumer commercial, Contracts commercial.

**GEWIRTZ, JEFFREY BRIAN,** lawyer; b. Baldwin Harbor, N.Y., Feb. 26, 1969; s. Arnold David and Clara (Lisogurski) G. BA, Tufts U., 1991; JD, Bklyn. Law Sch., 1994. Bar: N.J. 1994, U.S. Dist. Ct. N.J. 1994, N.Y. 1995, U.S. Dist. Ct. (so. and ea. dists.) N.Y. 1995. Assoc. Dunnington Bartholow & Miller,LLP, N.Y.C., 1994-96; atty. WTA TOUR, Stamford, Conn., 1996-98; pro bono gen. counsel Eastern Tennis Assn., Inc., 1997—; gen. counsel Ladies Profl. Golf Assn., Daytona Beach, Fla., 1998—; adj. prof. sports law N.Y. Law Sch., N.Y.C., 1996-98; adj. asst. prof. sports law Bklyn. Law Sch., 1998. Contbr. articles on sports law to profl. jours. Bklyn. Law Sch. Admissions Merit scholar, 1991-94. Mem. ABA (forum on entertainment and sports industries 1992—), Nat. Sports Law Inst., Soc. for Study of Legal Aspects of Sport and Phys. Activity, N.Y. State Bar Assn. (chair profl. sports com. 1995—), Assn. of Bar of City of N.Y. (com. sports law 1995—). Sports. Office: LPGA 100 International Golf Dr Daytona Beach FL 32124-1092

**GEYSER, LYNNE M.,** lawyer, writer; b. Queens, N.Y., Mar. 28, 1938; d. Henry and Shirley Dannenberg; m. Lewis P. Geyser, 1956 (div. 1974); 1 child, Russell B. Geyser. BA, Queens Coll., 1960; JD, UCLA, 1968. Bar: Calif. 1969. Atty. Zagon, Schiff, Hirsch & Levine, Beverly Hills, Calif., 1969-70; atty., registered legis. advocate Beverly Hills, Malibu, Calif., 1973-75; atty. Freshman, Marantz, Comsky & Deutsch, Beverly Hills, Malibu, Calif., 1971-74; prof. law Glendale (Calif.) U. Law, 1974-76, U. Iowa Sch. Law, Iowa City, 1976-77, Pepperdine U., Malibu, 1977-78; pvt. practice Newport Beach, Calif., 1978-81, San Clemente, 1978—; part-time prof. law Western State Law Sch., Fullerton, Calif., 1978; cons. atty. The Irvine Co., Newport Beach, 1981-86, Std. Mgmt. Co., L.A., 1987-88; instr. Saddleback Coll., Mission Viejo, Calif., early 1990's; lectr., instr. Calif. Assn. Realtors Grad. Realty Inst., 1972-78, U. So. Calif. brokers tng. courses, L.A., 1978-80, UCLA real estate and corp. courses for paralegals, 1973-76; creator and lectr. course on disclosure for licensees, L.A., San Diego and Orange Counties, Calif., 1978-81; faculty advisor, rev. advisor Glendale U. Coll. Law, 1975-76. Chief articles editor UCLA Law Rev., 1967; adv. bd. The Rsch. Jour., 1976; contbr. poetry and short stories to jours. Mem. exec. bd. L.A. County Art Mus. Contemporary Art Coun., L.A., 1971-73; bd. trustees Westwood (L.A.) Art Assn., 1974; bd. govs. La Costa Beach Homeowners Assn., Malibu, 1975; pres. Dana Point (Calif.) Coastal Arts Coun., 1989-90; teaching participant Jr. Achievement, Newport Beach, 1985. Recipient 6 Am. Jurisprudence awards, 1966-68, 2 West Hornbook awards, 1967; nom. Douglas Law Clk. UCLA Law Sch., 1967. Fellow The Legal Inst.; mem. AALS (chair-elect environ. law sect. 1977), San Clemente Sunrise Rotary, Order of Coif. Avocations: world travel, fine arts, writing, computers, performing arts, graphics. Real property, Contracts commercial, General corporate. Office: PO Box 4715 San Clemente CA 92674-4715

**GHERLEIN, GERALD LEE,** lawyer, diversified manufacturing company executive; b. Warren, Ohio, Feb. 16, 1938; s. Jacob A. and Ruth (Matthews) G.; m. Joycelyn Hardin, June 18, 1960; children: David, Christy. Student, Ohio Wesleyan U., 1956-58; B.S. in Bus. Adminstrn, Ohio State U., 1960; J.D., U. Mich., 1963. Bar: Ohio 1963. Assoc. Taft Stettinius & Hollister, Cin., 1963-66; corp. atty. Eaton Corp., Cleve., 1966-68; European legal counsel Eaton Corp., Zug, Switzerland, 1968-71; asst. sec., asso. counsel Eaton Corp., Cleve., 1971-76, v.p., gen. counsel, 1976-91, exec. v.p., gen. counsel, 1991—. Pres. Citizens League Greater Cleve., 1979-81; trustee Cleve. Ballet, 1983-88, vice chmn. 1985-87; trustee WVIZ Pub. Television, 1990—, Armada Funds, 1997—. Mem. ABA, Greater Cleve. Bar Assn. (pres. 1989, trustee), Ohio Bar Assn., Am. Soc. Corp. Secs. (pres. Ohio regional group 1977), Pepper Pike Country Club. Clubs: Union, Tavern, Mayfield Country. General corporate. Home: 3679 Greenwood Dr Cleveland OH 44124-5502 Office: Eaton Corp 1111 Superior Ave E Cleveland OH 44114-2507

**GHETTI, MICHELLE WARD,** law educator; b. Baton Rouge, La., Aug. 8, 1953; d. John Forrest Jr. and Ellen Joy (Dupuis) Ward; children: Jonathan Beau, Christine Michelle, John Scott Jr. BS, La. State U., 1978, JD, 1983. Bar: Tex. 1983, La. 1988, U.S. Dist. Ct. (no. and so. dists.) Tex., U.S. Dist. Ct. (no. dist.) N.Y., U.S. Dist. Ct. (ea, we. and mid. dist.) La. Law clk. Locke, Purnell, Dallas, 1982; assoc. Akin, Gump, Strauss, Hauer, Feld, Dallas, 1983-87, Anderson, Holliday, Jones, Baton Rouge, 1987-88; asst. v.p., atty. Hibernia Nat. Bank, Baton Rouge, 1988-89; owner, atty. Law Offices of Michelle LaBorde, Baton Rouge, 1989-91; asst. prof. So. U. Law Ctr., Baton Rouge, 1991-97, assoc. prof., 1997—; lectr. law, 1985—; instr. La. State U. Office of Govt. Programs, Baton Rouge, 1997, U.S. Dept. of State ATAP Program, Baton Rouge, 1992. Co-editor: Report on the Conclave on Legal Education and Professional Development, 1995; contbr. articles to profl. publs. Vol. Jr. Olympics, Baton Rouge, 1993, Spl. Olympics, Baton Rouge, 1989; mem. Task Force on Violent Crime Office of Gov. of La., Baton Rouge, 1993-96, conclave on legal edn., 1994; mem. St. Thomas Moore Cath. Ch., 1987—, Parkview Baptist Ch., 1995—, La. Indigent Def. Assistance Bd., 1997—; dir. La. chpt. Rutherford Inst., 1989—, Bethany Christian Svcs., Baton Rouge, 1997. Recipient Women of Achievement award YWCA, 1994; named to Hall of Fame La. State U. Law Ctr., 1988—. Master Am. Inns of Ct.; mem. La. State Bar Assn. (lawyer resource com. 1995—), La. Bar Found. (Scholar in Residence 1997-99, bd. dirs. 1997—, chair conclave implementation com. 1997—, acad. fellow), Baton Rouge Bar Assn., So. Student Trial Lawyers Assn. (advisor), So. U. Assn. Criminal Def. Attys. (advisor), La. Law Inst. (coms. on evidence, criminal law and procedure), Moot Ct. Bd. (advisor). Republican. Baptist. Avocations: reading, softball, rollerblading, gardening, refinishing furniture. E-mail: mghetti@sus.edu. Office: So Univ Law Ctr Swan St Baton Rouge LA 70813-0001

**GHOLSON, HUNTER MAURICE,** lawyer; b. Columbus, Miss., Feb. 19, 1933; s. Leonidas Carter and Hunter Marie (McDonell) G.; m. Hortense Jones, June 3, 1961; children: Emily Gholson Bailey, William Webster. BA, U. Miss., 1954, LLB, 1955, JD, 1955. Bar: Miss. 1955, U.S. Ct. Appeals (5th and 11th cirs.) 1955, D.C. 1975, U.S. Supreme Ct. 1975. Ptnr. Gholson, Hicks & Nichols, Columbus, Miss., 1959—; sec., dir. Columbus Marble Works, Inc., 1970—, NBC Capital Corp., Starkville, Miss., 1984—; dir. Gulf States Mfr., Starkville, 1968-94. Sr. warden St. Paul's Ch., Columbus, 1990-93. Lt. USNR, 1955-59. Mem. Old Waverly Golf Club. Episcopalian. Estate planning, Estate taxation, General corporate. Home: 1100 6th St N Columbus MS 39701-3412 Office: Gholson Hicks & Nichols 605 2nd Ave N Columbus MS 39701-4567

**GHOLSTON, ROBERT M.,** lawyer; b. Amarillo, Tex., May 17, 1936; s. John Edward Thurman Gholston and Lora Hodges; m. Sharon E. Crull Brunemmer, July 4, 1958 (div. Apr. 1982); children: Kevin M., Curtis M., Deborah A.; m. Bettie J. Wright, Apr. 28, 1983. AA, Amarillo Jr. Coll., 1956; BA, U. North Tex., 1958; JD, Ind. U., 1964. Bar: Ind., U.S. Dist. Ct. (so. dist.) Ind. 1965, U. S. Ct. Appeals (7th cir.) 1972, U.S. Supreme Ct. 1972. Assoc. Acher & Young, Franklin, Ind., 1965-66; ptnr. Acher & Gholston, Franklin, Ind., 1967-78, Young, Gholston & Young, Franklin, 1979-88; pvt. practice Franklin, 1988—. State legal counsel Ind. Jaycees, 1970-74; treas., v.p. and bd. dirs. local coun. Boy Scouts Am., 1978-88, dist. chmn., 1978-80; bd. dirs. Greenwood (Ind.) C. of C., 1978-80. Republican. Lutheran. Avocations: reading, coin and stamp collecting, biking, hiking, camping. Criminal, Family and matrimonial, General practice. Home: 528 Delbrook Dr New Whiteland IN 46184-1302 Office: 120 W Madison St Franklin IN 46131-2126

**GIALLANZA, CHARLES PHILIP,** lawyer; b. Hornell, N.Y., Nov. 18, 1950; s. Charles Joseph Jr. and Rena Eugena (Foster) G.; children: Charles Edward, Juleah Marie. AS in Aerospace Sci., U. Albuquerque, 1977; BA in Polit. Sci. and English, U. South Fla., 1979; JD, John Marshall Law Sch., 1982. Bar: Ga. 1983, U.S. Dist. Ct. (no. dist.) Ga. 1983; cert. air traffic contr. FAA. With USAF, 1971-79; air traffic contr. USAF Res., Tampa, 1977-79, Dobbins AFB, 1980-81; air traffic contr. USN Res., Dobbins AFB; assoc. James B. Pilcher, Atlanta, 1982-83; pvt. practice Snellville, Ga., 1983—. Advocate assisting Cubans detained in Atlanta prison, 1985, 86; capt. Ga. Def. Force, 1985-86. Recipient photography awards USAF, 1975. Mem. Ga. Bar Assn., Atlanta Bar Assn., Gwinnet Bar Assn. (law day com. 1987-88). Avocations: cross-training, running, weightlifting. Fax: 770-978-4450. State civil litigation, Personal injury, Family and matrimonial. Office: 3881 Stone Mountain Hwy Ste 5 Snellville GA 30039-3978

**GIAMPIETRO, WAYNE BRUCE,** lawyer; b. Chgo., Jan. 20, 1942; s. Joseph Anthony and Jeannette Marie (Zeller) G.; B.A., Purdue U., 1963; J.D., Northwestern U., 1966; m. Mary E. Fordeck, June 15, 1963; children—Joseph, Anthony, Marcus. Bar: Ill. 1966, U.S. Dist. (no. dist.) Ill. 1966, U.S. Tax Ct. 1977, U.S. Ct. Appeals (7th cir.) 1967, U.S. Supreme Ct. 1971. Assoc. Elmer Gertz, Chgo., 1966-73; mem. firm Gertz & Giampietro, Chgo., 1974-75; sole practice, 1975-76; ptnr. Poltrock & Giampietro, 1976-87, ptnr. Witwer, Burlage, Poltrock and Giampietro, 1987-94, Witwer, Poltrock & Giampietro, 1995—. Former cons. atty. Looking Glass div. Traveler's Aid Soc. Contbr. articles to profl. jours. Pres. Chgo. 47th Ward Young Republicans, 1968. Bd. dirs. Ravenswood Conservation Commn. Mem. Ill. Bar Assn. (chmn. sect. on Individual Rights and Responsibilities, 1986-87, 2d pl. Lincoln award 1975), Chgo. Bar Assn., Ill. Bar Assn., First Amendment Lawyers Assn. (sec. 1982, treas. 1983, pres. 1986, nat. chmn. 1987), Chgo. Coun. of Lawyers (mem. ethics com. 1992—), Order of Coif, Phi Alpha Delta. Lutheran. Avocation: stamp collecting. General civil litigation, Constitutional, Labor. Home: 23 Windsor Dr Lincolnshire IL 60069-3410 Office: Witwer Poltrock & Giampietro 125 S Wacker Dr Ste 2700 Chicago IL 60606-4402

**GIANCARLO, J. CHRISTOPHER,** lawyer; b. Jersey City, May 12; s. Hector R. and Ella Jane (Keegan) G.; m. Regina Marie Beyel, June 21, 1959; children: Emma Mary, Luke Christopher, James Henry. BA, Skidmore Coll., 1981; JD, Vanderbilt U., 1984. Bar: N.Y. 1985, N.J. 1986. Assoc. Mudge Rose et al, N.Y.C., 1984-85, Curtis, Mallet-Prevost et al, N.Y.C. and London, 1985-91; ptnr. Giancarlo & Gleiberman, N.Y.C. and London, 1991-97, Brown, Raysman Millstein Felder & Steiner LLP, N.Y.C. and London, 1997—. Contbr. articles to profl. jours. Co-chair N.Y. Profls. for Zimmer, N.Y.C., 1996; mem. Bergen County (N.J.) Hist. Soc., 1994-98. Mem. N.J. State Bar Assn. (del. gen. coun. 1996-98), Assn. of Bar of City of N.Y., Federalist Soc., Brit. Am. C. of C. Republican. Roman Catholic. Avocations: music, music composition, skiing, literature, sailing. Private international, General corporate, Mergers and acquisitions. Office: Brown Raysman Millstein et al 120 W 45th St New York NY 10036-4041

**GIANFRANCESCO, ANTHONY JOSEPH,** lawyer; b. Providence, R.I., Dec. 28, 1956; s. Domenic Michael Gianfrancesco and Italia Petrarca; m. Linda P. Gianfrancesco, Aug. 1, 1981; children: Domenic, Milena, Daniella, Anthony. BS, BA, Brown U., 1979; JD, Case Western Res. U., 1982. Bar: R.I. 1982. Ptnr. Baluch, Gianfrancesco, Mathieu & Szerlag, Providence, 1982—. Bd. dirs. North Providence (R.I.) Youth Soccer, 1995—, Thomas Beckett Found., Providence; mem. Mayor Youth Sports Coun., North Providence, 1996—. Mem. Nat. Italian Am. Bar Assn. (bd. dirs., sec. 1996—), Justinian Law Soc. R.I. (pres. 1995-97), R.I. Trial Lawyers Assn., Sons of Italy. General civil litigation, General practice, Personal injury. Home: 1612 Smith St North Providence RI 02911 Office: Baluch Gianfrancesco Mathieu & Szerlag 155 S Main St Providence RI 02903-2963

**GIANOTTI, ERNEST F.,** lawyer; b. Price, Utah, Nov. 28, 1925; s. Ernest F. and Elizabeth (Crockett) G.; m. Alice Chambers, Oct. 31, 1960 (div. Apr. 1976); m. Rebecca Steinlicht, May 16, 1982; children: Stefani Knoeller, Christine, Lisa. JD, U. of Pacific, 1955. Bar: Mont. 1960, U.S. Dist. Ct. Mont. 1961, High Ct. Am. Samoa 1971, U.S. Ct. Appeals (9th cir.) 1972, High Ct. Trust Ter. 1977, U.S. Supreme Ct. 1977, Commonwealth, No. Marianas 1978, High Ct. Marshall Islands 1983, U.S. Dist. Ct. No. Marianas 1983, Hawaii 1985, U.S. Dist. Ct. Hawaii 1985. Sole practice Great Falls, Mont., 1960-77; assoc. judge High Ct., Trust Territory, Pacific Islands, 1977-85; sole practice Kona, Hawaii, 1985—; del. S. Pacific Judge's Conf., Australia, Saipan, 1982-84. Eastern chmn. State of Mont. Carter for Pres., 1976. Served with USN, 1943-46. Mem. AM. Trial Lawyers Assn., Mont. Bar Assn., Hawaii Bar Assn., VFW. Democrat. Clubs: Marshall Island Yacht, Kona Billiken (bd. dirs. 1986). Lodges: Shriners, Elks. Avocations: skiing, sailing, scuba diving. Criminal, Private international.

**GIANOULAKIS, JOHN LOUIS,** lawyer; b. St. Louis, Nov. 22, 1938; s. Louis John and Marie (Pappas) G.; m. Louise Marotta, Jan. 1961 (dec. 1970); children: Christopher Louis, Kia Louise, Candlin Hamilton Dobbs; m. Dora Rodliff Deady, Sept. 2, 1972. AB, Wash. U., 1960; JD, Harvard U., 1963. Bar: Mo. 1963, U.S. Dist. Ct. (ea. dist.) Mo. 1963, U.S. Ct. Appeals (8th cir.) 1974, U.S. Supreme Ct. 1975, U.S. Ct. Appeals (7th cir.) 1982, U.S. Ct. Appeals (6th cir.) 1987. From assoc. to ptnr. Thompson, Walther & Shewmaker, St. Louis, 1963-70; ptnr. Kohn, Shands & Gianoulakis, St. Louis, 1971-73, Kohn, Shands, Elbert, Gianoulakis & Giljum, St. Louis, 1973—; mem., pres. bd. dirs. Legal Svcs. of Ea. Mo., Inc., St. Louis, 1972-81; mem. bar com. 22d Jud. Cir., St. Louis, 1977-85. Mem., v.p., pres. University City (Mo.) Sch. Bd., 1970-76. Fellow Am. Coll. Trial Lawyers; mem. ABA, Mo. Bar Assn., Bar Assn. Met. St. Louis, Norwood Hills Country Club, Noon Day Club. Democrat. E-mail: jgianoulakis@K-SEGG.com. Labor, Education and schools, Federal civil litigation. Home: 44 Clearview Park Saint Louis MO 63138-3302 Office: Kohn Shands Elbert Gianoulakis & Giljum One Mercantile Ctr 24th Fl Saint Louis MO 63101

**GIANTONIO, CLIFFORD JOHN,** lawyer; b. Englewood, N.J., July 12, 1964; s. John Paul and Patricia (Philips) G. BS, U. Scranton, 1989; JD, Ohio No. U., 1992. Bar: N.J. 1992, U.S. Dist. Ct. N.J. 1992. Law clk. Hon. Robert E. Hamer, 1992-93; assoc. Mortenson & Pomeroy, Springfield, N.J., 1993-95; pvt. practice Paramus, N.J., 1995-97. mem. ABA, N.J. Bar Assn., Bergen County Bar Assn., Bergen County Young Reps. General civil litigation, Insurance, Personal injury. Home: 57 Rafkind Rd Bloomingdale NJ 07403-1515 Office: West 115 Century Rd Paramus NJ 07652

**GIBBES, WILLIAM HOLMAN,** lawyer; b. Hartsville, S.C., Feb. 25, 1930; s. Ernest Lawrence and Nancy (Watson) G.; m. Frances Hagood, May 1, 1954; children: Richard H., William H. Jr., Lynn. BS, U. S.C., 1952, LLB, 1953. Bar: S.C. 1953, U.S. Ct. Mil. Appeals 1954, U.S. Dist. Ct. S.C. 1956, U.S. Supreme Ct. 1959, U.S. Ct. Appeals (4th cir.) 1965. Asst. atty. gen. Columbia, S.C., 1957-62; ptnr. Berry & Gibbes, Columbia, 1962-68, Berry, Lightsey, Gibbes, Columbia, 1968-72; mem. Gibbes Law Firm, P.A., Columbia, 1972—; house of dels. S.C. Bar, 1994-96; chief judge U.S. Army Legal Svcs. Agy., 1980-83. Author: Control of Highway Access - Its Prospects and Problems, Legal Dimensions of Community Health Planning, 1969, Manual for Fee Appraisors, 1960; contbr. articles to S.C. Law Review, Law Rev. Digest, 1960. Chmn. bd. dirs. U. S.C. YMCA, 1956-60. Brig. gen. JAGC, USAR 1980-83. Recipient Legion of Merit, U.S. Army, 1983. Mem. ABA (mil. laws com. 1984-90, meml. com.), S.C. Bar Assn. (exec. com. 1961-62), Am. Bd. Trial Advocates (sec.-treas. 1994-95, pres-elect 1995-96, pres. 1996-97), Judge Advs. Assn. (pres. 1982-83), Richland County Bar Assn., S.C. Credit Ins. Assn. (gen. counsel 1963-94), Tarantella Club, Caprician Club, Summit Club, Forest Lake Country Club, Kiawah Island Club, Kappa Sigma Kappa, Omicron Delta Kappa. Episcopalian. Estate planning, Probate, General civil litigation. Home: 287 Windward Point Rd Columbia SC 29212-8417 Office: PO Box 8265 Columbia SC 29202-8265

**GIBBINS, BOB,** lawyer; b. Seminole, Okla., Feb. 27, 1936; s. Robert Lee and La-Ceile Rene (Shackelford) G.; m. Suzanne K. Gibbins (div. Oct. 1975); children: Bob Jr., Steven, Jenny Durbin, Kyndall Krebs; m. Pam Reed, Feb. 26, 1982. BBA, U. Tex., 1958, LLB, 1961. Bar: Tex. 1961, U.S. Dist. Ct. (no. dist.) Tex. 1961, U.S. Ct. Appeals (5th cir.) 1971, U.S. Supreme Ct. 1974, Colo. 1991; diplomate Am. Bd. Trial Advs., Am. Bd. Profl. Liability Attys. Assoc. Morehead, Sharpe, Tisdale & Gibbins, Plainview, Tex., 1961-71; ptnr. Gibbins & Spivey, Austin, Tex., 1971-76; pvt. practice, Austin, 1976-78; sr. ptnr. Gibbins, Wash and Bratton, Austin, 1978-79, Gibbins, Burrow, Wash & Bratton, Austin, 1979-81, Gibbins, Burrow & Bratton, Austin, 1981-86, Gibbins & Bratton, Austin, 1986-89, Gibbins, Winckler & Bayer, Austin, 1989-91, Gibbins, Winckler & Harvey, Austin, 1991-97; pvt. practice law Austin, 1997—. Co-author: Texas Practical Guide: Personal Injury, 1988, Products Liability Litigation: Trial Strategy, 1988. Recipient War Horse award So. Trial Lawyers Assn., 1991, Faculty Svc. award, Univ. Tex. Sch. of Law, 1992; Bob Gibbins endowed presdl. scholarship named in his honor U. Tex. Sch. of Law, Austin, 1991. Fellow Internat. Acad. Trial Lawyers (bd. dirs. 1993-97), Internat. Soc. Barristers, State Bar Tex., Coll. of the State Bar Tex.; mem. Assn. Trial Lawyers Am. (pres. 1991-92, Lifetime Achievement award 1998, Champion of Justice award 1999), Nat. Bd. Trial Advocacy (civil trial adv.), Am. Bd. Trial Advocates (pres. Austin chpt. 1981), Trial Lawyers for Pub. Justice (bd. dirs 1993), Tex. Trial Lawyers Assn. (dir. emeritus). Personal injury, Product liability, Aviation. Office: 500 W 13th St Austin TX 78701-1827

**GIBBONS, JULIA SMITH,** federal judge; b. Pulaski, Tenn., Dec. 23, 1950; d. John Floyd and Julia Jackson (Abernathy) Smith; m. William Lockhart Gibbons, Aug. 11, 1973; children: Rebecca Carey, William Lockhart Jr. B.A., Vanderbilt U., 1972; J.D., U. Va., 1975. Bar: Tenn. 1975. Law clk. to judge U.S. Ct. Appeals, 1975-76; assoc. Farris, Hancock, Gilman, Branan, Lanier & Hellen, Memphis, 1976-79; legal advisor Gov. Lamar Alexander, Nashville, 1979-81; judge 15th Jud. Cir., Memphis, 1981-83; judge U.S. Dist. Ct. (we. dist.) Tenn., Memphis, 1983-94, chief judge, 1994—. Fellow Am. Bar Found., Tenn. Bar Found.; mem. Tenn. Bar Assn., Memphis Bar Assn., Order of Coif, Phi Beta Kappa. Presbyterian. Office: US Dist Ct 1157 Federal Bldg 167 N Main St Memphis TN 38103-1816

**GIBBONS, STEVEN VAN,** lawyer; b. Bremerton, Wash., May 5, 1955; s. John Farrell and Catherine Gennette (Cooper) G.; m. Darla Denise Recknagle, Oct. 20, 1976; children: Heather, Garrett Wesley, Morgan Rhys, John Weylin. BA with high honors, Brigham Young U., 1980; JD, George Washington U., 1983. Bar: Wash. 1984, U.S. Dist. Ct. (we. dist.) Wash. 1984, U.S. Ct. Appeals (9th cir.) 1984. Assoc. Diamond & Sylvester, Seattle, 1984-85, Lane, Powell, Spears Lubersky, Seattle, 1985—. Mem. Maritime Law Assn. U.S., Seattle King County Bar Assn. (chmn. maritime and fisheries 1986-87), Asia-Pacific Lawyers Assn. Democrat. Mormon. Avocations: sailing, mountaineering. Admiralty, Contracts commercial, Federal civil litigation. Home: 15011 Skogen Ln NE Bainbridge Island WA 98110 Office: Gibbons & Associates PS 1201 3rd Ave Ste 2800 Seattle WA 98101-3029

**GIBBS, DEBORAH P.,** lawyer; b. Baton Rouge, July 4, 1957; d. Joseph Peyton and Ilene (Byrne) Parker; m. Vance A. Gibbs, May 5, 1984; children: Elisa, Parker, Martha. BA, Sweet Briar Coll., 1979; JD, La. State U., 1982. Bar: La. 1982. Sole practitioner Baton Rouge, 1983—. Avocations: gardening, canoeing, walking. Family and matrimonial, General practice, Personal injury. Office: 1111 S Foster Dr Baton Rouge LA 70806-7238

**GIBBS, FREDERICK WINFIELD,** lawyer, communications company executive; b. Buffalo, Mar. 22, 1932; s. Walter L. M. and Elizabeth Mari (Georgi) G.; m. Josephine Janice Jarvis, Dec. 20, 1954; children: Michael, Mathew, Robyn. BA cum laude, Alfred U., 1954; JD with Tax honors, Rutgers U., 1989. Bar: Pa. 1989, N.J. 1989, U.S. Dist. Ct. N.J. 1989. With N.Y. Tel. Co., 1954-65, ITT, 1965-86; mng. dir. ITT Standard Electrica, S.A., 1971-75; chief exec. officer ITT Standard Electrica, Brazil, 1975-77; exec. dir. ops. ITT Communications Ops. Group ITT Communications Ops. Group, 1977; corp. v.p. ITT, 1977-80; pres. U.S. Tel. and Tel. Corp., 1977-79, exec. dir., sr. group exec., 1980-86; dir. System 12, ITT, 1979-80; exec. v.p. ITT, 1980-86, ITT Telecommunications Corp., 1983-86; pvt. practice law Pemberton, N.J., 1989-95; founding ptnr. Gibbs & Gregory Attys. at Law, Pemberton, 1995—; cons. ITT, 1986-89, The World Bank/IFC, 1989—; pres. Mulberry Hill Enterprises, 1989—; bd. dirs. CMC Ind. Trustee Alfred U., 1981—, Whitesbog Found., 1996—; mem. planning bd. Barnegat Light, N.J.; elected Borough Coun., Barnegat Light, 1992, re-elected, 1995, 98. Named Hon. Citizen of Rio de Janeiro, 1973; inducted to Alfred Univ. Athletic Hall of Fame, 1993. Mem. ABA, N.J. Bar Assn., Pa. Bar Assn., Burlington County Bar Assn., Barnegat Light Taxpayers Assn. (v.p. 1989-90, pres. 1990-92), Rotary Internat. (bd. dirs. Pemberton club 1996-97, v.p. 1997-98, pres. 1999-00, Pemberton Rotarian of Yr. 1996-97). Home: 12 E 17th Street Rd Barnegat Light NJ 08006

**GIBBS, LENDON DAVID,** lawyer; b. Eldorado, Ga., June 29, 1942; s. James P. and Helen (Crumley) G.; m. Martha Elaine Maret, Mar. 22, 1969; children: Vickie Lynn, Constance Diane. BBA in Econs., U. Ga., 1969; JD, Woodrow Wilson Coll. Law, Atlanta, 1978. Bar: Ga. 1978, U.S. Dist. Ct. (no. dist.) Ga. 1978. Supr. group ins. human resources dept. Ga. Power Co., Atlanta, 1974-78, employment supr., 1978-80, mgr. employee benefits, 1980-81, asst. to v.p. for risk mgmt., 1981-85, mgr. claims and corp. ins., 1985-90, mgr. risk mgmt., 1990-92, dir. risk mgmt., 1992—. Bd. dirs. Kids' Chance, Valdosta, Ga., 1993—, Ga. Sheriff's Youth Homes, Stockbridge, 1994—. Master sgt. Ga. Air N.G., 1965-81. Mem. ATLA, Ga. Def. Lawyers Assn., Def. Rsch. Inst. (industry wide litigation com. 1995—), Edison Electric Inst. (pres. claims com. 1997-99), Ga. Self Insurers Assn. (bd. dirs. 1992—). Baptist. Avocations: hunting, fishing, woodworking. Home: 1641 Courtleigh Dr Dunwoody GA 30338-4902 Office: Ga Power Co Bin 10180 241 Ralph Mcgill Blvd NE Atlanta GA 30308-3374

**GIBBS, L(IPPMAN) MARTIN,** lawyer; b. Merrick, N.Y., Feb. 27, 1938; s. Harold and Shirley (Marks) G.; m. Dona Lynn Fagg, May 2, 1968; 1 child, Bradford M. BA, Brown U., 1959; JD, Columbia U., 1962. Bar: N.Y. 1963, D.C. 1982. Atty. Port of N.Y. Authority, 1963-64; assoc. Weiner, Neuberger & Sive, N.Y.C., 1964-65, Spear & Hill, N.Y.C., 1966-69; assoc. Finley, Kumble, Wagner, Heine & Underberg, N.Y.C., 1969-72, ptnr., 1972-78; pres. L. Martin Gibbs, P.C., N.Y.C., 1981-87; ptnr. Rogers & Wells, N.Y.C., 1987—; bd. dirs. First Republic Bank, San Francisco. Regional dir. United Fund Drive of Rye, N.Y., 1979; trustee South St. Seaport Mus., 1995—. With USAR, 1962-68. Mem. ABA, NY. State Bar Assn., Assn. Bar City N.Y., Am. Arbitration Assn. (arbitrator 1967—). Avocations: sailing, golf. General corporate, Contracts commercial. Office: Rogers & Wells 200 Park Ave Fl 8E New York NY 10166-0800

**GIBSON, CALVIN ROE,** lawyer; b. Waukegan, Ill., June 13, 1962; s. Herman C. and Alma I. (Poyner) G.; m. Phyllis J. Thomas, June 13, 1995; children: Clayton Alexander, Benjamin Andrew. BA, U. Ark., Little Rock, 1985, U. Ark., Little Rock, 1987; JD, U. Ark., Little Rock, 1989, MPA, 1997. Bar: Ark. 1989, U.S. Ct. Appeals (8th cir.) 1989, U.S. Supreme Ct. 1992. Staff atty. Ark. Hwy. Commn., Little Rock, 1992—; pvt. practice Little Rock, 1. Republican. Methodist. Avocation: flying. Administrative and regulatory, Real property, Labor. Office: AHTD-Legal Divsn 10324 Interstate 30 Little Rock AR 72209-4206

**GIBSON, CHARLES CLIFFORD, III,** lawyer; b. Greenville, Miss., Sept. 14, 1954; s. Charles Clifford and Helen Elizabeth (Shultz) G.; m. Lisa Joy Hartness, May 14, 1978; children: Joy O'Neil, Charles Clifford IV. BS, Miss. State U., Starkville, 1977; JD, U. Ark., 1981. Bar: Ark. 1981, U.S. Dist. Ct. (ea. dist.) Ark. 1982, U.S. Ct. Appeals (8th cir.) 1985, U.S. Supreme Ct. 1990; lic. abstracter, Ark., 1981. Ptnr. Gibson & Hashem, Monticello, Ark., 1981—; pres., dir. Drew County Abstract & Title Co., Monticello, 1981—; bd. dirs. Comml. Bank & Trust Co., Monticello; deputy prosecuting atty. Drew County Ark., Monticello, 1987-95. Editorial bd. Univ. Ark. Law Rev. Law Jour., 1980; contbr. articles to profl. jours. Pres., dir. Drew County C. of C., Monticello, 1985-86 (leadership award 1985-86); pres. S.E. Ark. Legal Inst., 1985-87, Monticello Econ. Devel. Commn., 1997—. Recipient Disting. Svc. award City of Monticello, 1989, scholarship Wall Street Jour., Starkville, Miss., 1976. Mem. Ark. Bar Assn., Ark. Trial Lawyers Assn., Assn. Trial Lawyers Am., Ark. Land Title Assn., Lions Club. Democrat. Methodist. Avocations: fishing, hunting. General civil litigation, Personal injury, Real property. Office: Gibson & Hashem 119 S Main St Monticello AR 71655-4727

**GIBSON, ERNEST WILLARD, III,** retired state supreme court justice; b. Brattleboro, Vt., Sept. 23, 1927; s. Ernest William and Dorothy Pearl (Switzer) G.; m. Charlotte Elaine Hungerford, Sept. 10, 1960; children: Margaret, Mary, John. BA, Yale U., 1951; LLB, Harvard U., 1956. Bar: Vt. State's atty. Windham County, Vt., 1957-61; mem. Vt. Ho. of Reps., 1961-63, chmn. judiciary com., 1963; chmn. Vt. Pub. Svc. Bd., 1963-72; judge Vt. Superior Ct., 1972-83; assoc. justice Vt. Supreme Ct., 1983-97, ret., 1997. Chancellor Episcopal Diocese Vt., 1977-98. trustee, 1973-99, pres. bd. trustees, 1991-99, dep. to gen. conv., 1976-94. Served in U.S. Army, 1945-46, 51-53, Vt. Army Nat. Guard, 1956-71. Mem. Vt. Bar Assn. Avocations: bridge, tennis. Home: 11 Baldwin St Montpelier VT 05602-2110

**GIBSON, FLOYD ROBERT,** federal judge; b. Prescott, Ariz., Mar. 3, 1910; s. Van Robert and Katheryn Ida G.; m. Gertrude Lee Walker, Apr. 23, 1935; children: Charles R., John M., Catherine L. A.B., U. Mo., 1931, LL.B., 1933. Bar: Mo. 1932. Practiced law Independence, 1933-37, Kansas City, 1937-61; mem. firm Johnson, Lucas, Bush & Gibson (and predecessor), 1954-61; county counselor Jackson County, 1943-44; judge U.S. Dist. Ct. (we. dist.) Mo., 1961-65, chief judge, until 1965; judge U.S. Ct. Appeals (8th cir.), Kansas City, Mo., 1965-79, sr. judge, 1979—, chief judge, 1974-80; former chmn. bd. Mfrs. & Mechanics Bank, Kansas City, Mo., Blue Valley Fed. Savs. & Loan Assn.; mem. Nat. Conf. Commrs. Uniform State Laws, 1957—, Jud. Conf. U.S., 1974-80; chmn. Chief Judges Conf., 1977-78; bd. mgrs. Coun. State Govts., 1960-61; pres. Nat. Legis. Conf., 1960-61. Mem. Mo. Gen. Assembly from 7th Dist., 1940-46; mem. Mo. Senate, 1946-61, majority floor leader, 1952-56, pres. pro tem, 1956-60; del. Nat. Democratic Conv., 1956, 60; Mem. Mo. N.G. Named 2d most valuable mem. Mo. Legislature Globe Democrat, 1958, most valuable, 1960; recipient Faculty-Alumni award U. Mo., 1968; citation of merit Mo. Law Sch. Alumni, 1975; Spurgeon Smithson award Mo. Bar Found., 1978. Fellow ABA (adv. bd. editors Jour., chmn. jud. adminstrn. div. 1979-80, chmn. conf. sect. 1980-81, chmn. appellate judges conf. 1973-74, mem. ho. of dels.); mem. Fed. Bar Assn., Mo. Bar, Kansas City Bar Assn. (Ann. Achievement award 1980), Lawyers Assn. Kansas City (past v.p., Charles Evans Whittaker award 1985), Mo. Law Sch. Found. (life), Mo. Acad. Squires, Order of Coif, Phi Delta Phi, Phi Kappa Psi (Man of Yr. 1974). Democrat. Roman Catholic. Clubs: University, Carriage, Mercury. Office: US Ct Appeals 8th Cir 10-20 US Courthouse 400 E 9th St Kansas City MO 64106-2607

**GIBSON, FRANK BYRON, JR.,** lawyer, farmer, small business owner; b. Wilson, N.C., Sept. 9, 1945; s. Frank Byron and Charlotte (Fleming) G.; m. Judith Rogers, Aug. 2, 1969; children: Frank Byron III, Faison Boineau. BA, Dartmouth Coll., 1967; JD, Vanderbilt U. Law Sch., 1975. Assoc. Murchison, Fox & Newton, Wilmington, N.C., 1975-77, ptnr., 1977-80; mng. ptnr. Murchison, Taylor, Kendrick, Gibson & Davenport, Wilmington, 1980-91; pres. Island Earthworks, Inc., Wilmington, 1985—, Gibson Farms, Inc., N.C., 1996—; ptnr. RAMCO Investments, 1992—; bd. dirs. Legal Aid Soc. of Lower Cape Fear, Wilmington; lectr. on aviation law, FAA safety seminars; mem. 4th Cir. Jud. Conf., 1983—. Contbg. writer, mem. editl. bd. The Southern Aviator, 1988-98. Bd. dirs., v.p. St. John's Mus. Art, Wilmington, 1979-84; bd. dirs. Cape Fear Cmty. Found., 1987-92, Cape Fear Hosp. Health Resources Found., 1991-94; bd. dirs., pres. Child Advocacy Commn., Wilmington, 1977-81; vestry, sr. and jr. warden St. John's Episcopal Ch., Wilmington, 1976-82, St. James Episcopal Ch., Wilmington, vestry, 1984-87, 92-95, 99—, sr. warden, 1995; bd. dirs. Found. of the Diocese of Eastern N.C., 1992-95, pres., 1995, trustee Diocese of Ea. N.C., 1996-99; bd. dirs. New Hanover County United Way, 1999—. Capt. USMCR, 1968-73. Recipient Cert. Merit N.C. Dept. Human Resources, 1979, Special award Child Advocacy Commn., 1979, Pro Bono Svc. award New Hanover County Bar Assn., 1995. Mem. ABA, N.C. Bar Assn., Lawyer-Pilots Bar Assn., Airplane Owners and Pilots Assn., Greater Wilmington C. of C. (Spl. award 1979, 89, bd. dirs. 1989-95, v.p. 1992, pres. 1994), Tailhook Assn., Cape Fear Country Club, Cape Fear Club, Cape Fear Rowing Club (bd. dirs.), Carolina Yacht Club, Wrightsville Beach N.C. (bd. govs. 1990-95, fleet capt. 1996, commodore 1997), Carolina Yacht Club (Charleston, S.C.). Republican. Avocations: aviation, boating. Fax: 910-763-6561. E-mail: MTKG@Wilmington.net./FBG31@Juno.com. General corporate, Estate planning, Intellectual property. Home: 2220 Parham Dr Wilmington NC 28403-6034 Office: Murchison Taylor & Gibson LLP 16 N 5th St Wilmington NC 28401-4537

**GIBSON, JOHN ROBERT,** federal judge; b. Springfield, Mo., Dec. 20, 1925; s. Harry B. and Edna (Kerr) G.; m. Mary Elizabeth Vaughn, Sept. 20, 1952 (dec. Aug. 1985); children: Jeanne, John Robert; m. Diane Allen Larrison, Oct. 1, 1986; stepchildren: Holly, Catherine. AB, U. Mo., 1949, JD, 1952. Bar: Mo. 1952. Assoc. Morrison, Hecker, Curtis, Kuder & Parrish, Kansas City, Mo., 1952-58, ptnr., 1958-81; judge U.S. Dist. Ct. (we. dist.) Mo., 1981-82; judge U.S. Ct. Appeals (8th cir.), Kansas City, 1982-94, sr. judge, 1994—. mem. Mo. Press-Bar Commn., 1979-81; mem. com. on adminstrn. of magistrate sys. Jud. Conf. U.S., 1987-91, mem. security and facilities com., 1995—. Vice chmn. Jackson County Charter Transition Com., 1971-72; mem. Jackson County Charter Commn., 1970; v.p. Police Commrs. Bd., Kansas City, 1973-77. Served with AUS, 1944-46. Recipient Citation of Merit award U. Mo. at Columbia Sch. of Law, 1994. Fellow Am. Bar Found.; mem. ABA, Mo. State Bar (gov. 1972-79, pres. 1977-78; Pres.' award 1974, Smithson award 1984), Kansas City Bar Assn. (pres. 1970-71), Lawyers Assn. Kansas City (Charles Evan Whittaker award 1980), Fed. Judges Assn. (bd. dirs. 1991-97), Phi Beta Kappa, Omicron Delta Kappa. Presbyterian. Office: US Ct Appeals 8th Cir 400 E 9th St Ste 1040 Kansas City MO 64106-2695

**GIBSON, JOHN WHEAT,** lawyer; b. Waco, Tex., June 27, 1946; s. John Wheat and Dorothy (Carpenter) G.; m. Melanie McGarrahan Gibson; children: Madeleine, Ruth, Abigail, Jack. BA, U. Tex., 1969, MA, 1976; cert., Casa Nicaraguense, 1986; JD, Baylor U., 1986. Bar: Tex. 1986, U.S. Dist. Ct. (no. dist.) Tex. 1987, U.S. Dist. Ct. (ea. dist.) Tex. 1997; U.S. Ct. Appeals (5th cir.) 1988. Copy editor Waco Tribune Herald, 1976-78; editor Clifton (Tex.) Record, 1978; instr. Temple (Tex.) Jr. Coll., 1978-82, Ea. Ill. U., Charleston, 1982-83; paralegal McLennan County Jail, Waco, 1985-86; staff atty. Proyecto Adelante, Dallas, 1986-87; assoc. Natkin & Flores-Saldivar, Ft. Worth, 1987; pvt. practice law Dallas, 1988—; ponente Primera Jornada Internacional de Juristas, San Salvador, El Salvador, 1990; reporter Sta. KWTX, Waco, 1981-82. Cons. Com. in Solidarity with People El Salvador, 1986-88, adviser, 1988; cons. Cooperativo Refugiados Centroamericanos, 1986-88, Centro Social Hispanico, 1997—; bd. dirs. Am.-Arab Anti-Defamation Com., 1998—. Recipient Friend of Youth award Optimist Club, Temple, 1980, Adviser of Yr. award Tex. Intercollegiate Press Assn., 1980. Mem. Tex. Bar Assn., Nat. Lawyer's Guild (pres. student chpt. 1985-86), Tex. Trial Lawyers Assn. (pres. student chpt. spring 1985), Am. Immigration Lawyers Assn., ACLU. Socialist. Episcopalian. Avocations: bicycling, camping. General civil litigation, Constitutional, Immigration, naturalization, and customs. Office: 701 Commerce St Ste 110 Dallas TX 75202-4521

**GIBSON, KEITH RUSSELL,** lawyer, educator; b. Fulton, N.Y., Feb. 24, 1954; s. Keith Melvin and Retha (Thatcher) G.; m. Victoria Jean Carroll, Mar. 21, 1986; children: Emily Michelle, Robin Bethany, Kyle Russell. BA, Lycoming Coll., 1976; paralegal cert., Adelphi U., 1977; JD, Oklahoma City U., 1984. Bar: Okla. 1984, U.S. Dist. Ct. (no., we., ea. dists.) Okla. 1984. Paralegal Thatcher & Miller, Lewistown, Pa., 1978-81; law clk. Chief Justice Don Barnes Okla. Supreme Ct., Oklahoma City, 1983-84; assoc. Pate & Payne, Oklahoma City, 1984-91; sr. atty. Williams, Box, Forshee & Bullard, P.C., Oklahoma City, 1991—; instr. Oklahoma City U. Legal Asst. Program, 1990-98, officer Sch. of Law Alumni Assn., 1994-96; lectr. Okla. Foreclosure and Repossession Nat. Bus. Inst.; paralegal issues instr. Inst. for Paralegal Edn.; legal advisor Okla. Just Compensation Act. Originator and participant Met. Ch. Legal Clearinghouse, Oklahoma City, 1995. Mem. Oklahoma City U. Law Alumni Assn. (officer 1994-96, participant fundraising 1996), North Oklahoma City Rotary (bd. dirs. 1994-95, sec. 1995-96, Newcomer of Yr. 1991, Pres.'s award 1993-94, Benefactor award Rotary Found. 1993), Citizen's League of Oklahoma City, Friends of the Oklahoma City Libr. Assn., Federalist Soc. (Okla. chpt.), Conf. Consumer Fin. Law. Republican. Bankruptcy, General civil litigation, Consumer commercial. Home: 2713 NW 158th St Edmond OK 73013-8819 Office: Williams Box Forshee & Bullard PC 522 Colcord Dr Oklahoma City OK 73102-2202

**GIBSON, K(ENNETH) WILLIAM,** lawyer, writer; b. Salem, Oreg., Apr. 9, 1949; s. Kenneth Lester and Elsie M. G.; m. Mary B. Alvey, June 18, 1980; children: Kenneth C., John. BA, U. Oreg., 1970, MA, 1972; JD, Lewis & Clark U., 1979. Bar: Oreg. 1979; U.S. Dist. Ct. Oreg. 1980. Ptnr. Duffy, Gibson & Hicks, Portland, Oreg., 1980-84; pvt. practice Portland, 1984-89; ptnr. Gibson & Duffy, Portland, 1989—. Author: (book) How to Build and Manage a Personal Injury Practice, 1997, (Best Legal Publ 1997, Lawyers' Weekly). Mem. ABA (sec. sect. law practice mgmt., coun. mem. 1992-98). Avocation: flying. Personal injury, State civil litigation. Office: Gibson & Duffy 10121 SE Sunnyside Rd Clackamas OR 97015-9765

**GIBSON, KUMIKI S.,** lawyer; b. Buffalo, N.Y., May 24, 1959; d. Will and Kazumi (Tamori) G. AB, Harvard U., 1985; JD, Northeastern U., 1988. Bar: D.C., Mass., N.Y. Law clk. Hon. Clifford Scott Green U.S. Dist. Ct. (ea. dist.) Pa., Phila., 1988-89; assoc. Arnold & Porter, Washington, 1989-91; trial atty. Dept. Justice, Washington, 1992-93, assoc. counsel to V.P. Al Gore, 1993-95, counsel, 1995-97; of counsel Williams & Connolly, Washington, 1997—; mem. Adminstrv. Conf. of U.S., Washington, 1996. Mem. Nat. Coun. Negro Women, Nat. Trust for Hist. Preservation. Federal civil litigation, General civil litigation, State civil litigation. Office: Williams & Connolly 725 12th St NW Washington DC 20005-5901

**GIBSON, LANDON MACK, III,** lawyer; b. Gainesville, Ga., May 8, 1957; s. Landon M. Gibson Jr. and Verba Autrey; m. M. Irene Eggerman, July 16, 1983; children: Landon M. IV, Blair Marie, George Lyle. BS in Psychology, U. Wash., 1979; JD, Seattle U., 1982. Bar: Wash. 1982, U.S. Dist. Ct. (we. dist.) Wash. 1983. Assoc. Tuell, Anderson & Fisher, Tacoma, 1982, Lyle R. Schneider & Assoc., Auburn, Wash., 1982-86; ptnr. Schneider, Gibson & Jarvey, Auburn, 1986—. Mem. Auburn Area C. of C. (bd. dirs. 1996—), KC (grand knight 1985-86), Phi Beta Kappa. Roman Catholic. Avocations: skiing, camping, restoring British sports cars. Family and matrimonial, General civil litigation. Office: Schneider Gibson & Jarvey 901 E Main St Auburn WA 98002-5629

**GIBSON, LORI LYNN,** lawyer; b. Detroit, Mar. 16, 1965; d. Leo Jay and Elizabeth Jane Oeffner; m. Joel Matthew Gibson, Aug. 14, 1993; children: Joshua Davis, James Marshall. BS, Wheaton Coll., 1986; MS, U. Mich., 1987; JD, U. Minn., 1993. Bar: Mich. 1993, U.S. Dist. Ct. (we. dist.) Mich. 1993, U.S. Dist. Ct. (ea. dist.) Mich. 1995, U.S. Ct. Appeals (6th cir.) 1995. Atty. Warner Norcross & Judd LLP, Grand Rapids, Mich., 1993—. Bd. dirs. ARC West Ctrl. Mich., Grand Rapids, 1995-98. Mem. Grand Rapids Bar Assn. Avocations: golf, gardening, reading. General civil litigation, Civil rights, Labor. Office: Warner Norcross & Judd LLP 111 Lyon St NW Ste 900 Grand Rapids MI 49503-2487

**GIBSON, PAULA LAUREN,** lawyer; b. Denver, 1956. BA, UCLA, 1978; JD, Southwestern U., 1981. Bar: Calif. 1981. Assoc. Potter, Bradish and Ellinghouse, Encino, Calif., 1981-82; sr. corps. counsel Calif. Dept. of Corps., Los Angeles, 1982-84; dep. atty. gen. State of Calif., Los Angeles, 1984—; gen. counsel Twilight Films div. Neferiti Entertainment Group, Beverly Hills, Calif., 1985-93. Recipient Outstanding Achievement in civil litigation award Atty. Gen., 1994. Mem. L.A. County Bar Assn. Avocations: underwater photography, snorkeling, bicycling, computers.

**GIBSON, REGINALD WALKER,** federal judge; b. Lynchburg, Va., July 31, 1927; s. McCoy and Julia Ann (Butler) G.; 1 child, Reginald S. B.S., Va. Union U., 1952; postgrad., Wharton Grad. Sch. Bus. Adminstrn., U. Pa., 1952-53; LL.B., Howard U., 1956. Bar: D.C. 1957, Ill. 1972. Agt. IRS, Washington, 1957-61; trial atty. tax div. U.S. Dept. Justice, Washington, 1961-71; sr. tax atty. Internat. Harvester Co., Chgo., 1971-76, gen. tax atty., 1976-82; judge U.S. Ct. of Fed. Claims, Washington, 1982-95; sr. judge U.S. Ct. Fed. Claims, Washington, 1995—. Mem. bus. adbv. council Chgo. Urban League, 1974-82. Served with AUS, 1946-47. Recipient cert. award U.S. Dept. Justice Atty. Gen., 1969, recipient spl. commendation U.S. Dept. Justice Atty. Gen., 1970, Wall St. Jour. award, 1952, Am. Jurisprudence award, 1956; named Alumni of Yr. Howard U. Sch. Law, 1984. Mem. D.C. Bar Assn., Chgo. Bar Assn., Fed. Bar Assn., Nat. Bar Assn., Claims Ct. Bar Assn., J. Edgar Murdock Am. Inn of Ct. (taxation com.). Baptist. Club: Nat. Lawyers (Washington). Home: 6305 Chaucer View Cir Alexandria VA 22304-3548 Office: US Ct Fed Claims 717 Madison Pl NW Washington DC 20005-1011

**GIBSON, VIRGINIA LEE,** lawyer; b. Independence, Mo., Mar. 5, 1946. BA, U. Calif., Berkeley, 1972; JD, U. Calif., San Francisco, 1977. Bar: Calif. 1981. Assoc. Pillsbury, Madison & Sutro, San Francisco, 1980-83; ptnr. Chickering & Gregory, San Francisco, 1983-85, Baker & McKenzie, San Francisco, 1985—. Mem. ABA (employee benefits subcom. tax sect.), Internat. Found. Employee Benefit Plans, Am. Compensation Assn. (internat. compensation and benefits com.), Calif. Bar Assn. (exec. com. tax sect. 1985-88), San Francisco Bar Assn. (internat. and comparative law taxation sects.), Western Pension and Benefits Conf. (pres. San Francisco chpt. 1989-91, program com. 1984-88). Pension, profit-sharing, and employee benefits, Fiduciary. Office: Baker & McKenzie 2 Embarcadero Ctr Ste 2400 San Francisco CA 94111-3909

**GIDEON, KYLE LINEY,** lawyer; b. Arnaudville, La., Jan. 27, 1958; s. Rees Joseph and Elizabeta (Latiolais) G.; m. Monique Giroir, Oct. 10, 1987; 1 child, Rees Douglas. BA, U. Southwestern La., 1980; JD, La. State U., 1984. Bar: La. 1984, U.S. Dist. Ct. (we., mid. and ea. dists.) La., U.S. Ct. Appeals (5th cir.). Law clk. La. 3d Circuit Ct. Appeals, Lafayette, 1984-86; assoc. Davidson, Meaux, Sonnier, McElligott & Swift, Lafayette, 1986-89, ptnr., 1989—. Bd. dirs. Lafayette chpt. ARC, 1989-91. Mem. Coastal Conservation Assn., (pres. La. Acadiana chpt. 1998-99), Ducks Unltd., Inns of Ct. Roman Catholic. Transportation, Insurance, Government contracts and claims. Home: 203 N Anita St Lafayette LA 70501-3216 Office: Davidson Meaux Sonnier McElligott & Swift 810 S Buchanan St Lafayette LA 70501-6882

**GIERBOLINI-ORTIZ, GILBERTO,** federal judge; b. 1926. B.A., U. P.R., 1951, LL.B., 1961. Asst. U.S. atty. Commonwealth P.R., 1961-66; judge Superior Ct. Bayamon, P.R., 1966-67, Superior Ct. Caguas, P.R., 1967-69; solicitor P.R., 1969-72, asst. atty. gen. for antitrust, 1970-72; pvt. practice Jose H. Pico, 1973-74, Arias Cestero, Gierbolini & Garcia Soto, 1974-75, Nido, Berrios, Menendez & Gierbolini, 1975-77, Dubon, Gonzalez & Berrios, 1977-80; judge U.S. Dist. Ct. P.R., San Juan, 1980—; chief judge U.S. Dist. Ct. P.R., 1991-93; sr. judge, 1993—; prof. U. P.R., Cath. U. Law Sch. Chmn. State Elections Bd., P.R., 1972. Capt. U.S. Army, 1951-57. Office: BBV Tower 254 Ave Munoz Rivera Fl 121200-b Hato Rey San Juan PR 00918-1900

**GIERE, JOHN PATRICK,** lawyer; b. Ft. Dodge, Iowa, Mar. 16, 1956; s. Norbert Edward G. and Ruth Ann Backs; m. Lorraine T. Kremer, Aug. 29, 1992. BPhil, Miami U., 1978; JD, Franklin Pierce Law Ctr., 1985; LLM, Boston U., 1992. Bar: N.H. 1986, U.S. Dist. Ct. N.H. 1985. Ptnr. Wescott, Millham & Dyer, Laconia, N.H., 1986—. Sitting mem. Zoning Bd. Adjustment, Belmont, N.H., 1995—. Mem. N.H. Bar Assn. (bd. govs. 1996-98, fin. com. 1991—, prevention & funding com. 1997—), Belknap County Bar Assn. (sec. 1993-95), Rotary. Avocation: woodworking. Real property, Taxation, general, Land use and zoning (including planning). Office: Wescott Millham & Dyer PO Box 1700 28 Bowman St Laconia NH 03247-1700

**GIERINGER, RAYMOND E.,** retired judge; b. Oct. 31, 1925; m. Marion L. Severson, Nov. 20, 1948; children: Mark, Jill, Susan, Kris. B of Mech. Engrng., Marquette U., 1946, LLB, 1948. Pvt. practice Milw., 1948-50; atty. Dunn & Gieringer, Milw., 1950-51; pvt. practice Adams County, Wis., 1959-72; county judge Adams County, Wis., 1972-78, cir. judge, 1978-91; ret., 1991—; pres. Giant Grip Mfg. Co., Oshkosh, 1951-59; pres., founder 1st Wis. Land Corp F/K/A Sand Land Devel. Corp., 1963-72, Cen. Sands Agy., Inc., 1963-72; sec., treas., founder Omro (Wis.) Gear and Machine, Inc. (now Wis. Ordinance Works Ltd.), 1965-72; part-time dist. atty., 1960-66; city atty. City of Adams, 1962-70; exec. com., legis. com., nominating com. Wis. Jud. Conf.; former rep. Jud. Coun.; mem. Criminal Justice Planning Coun., N.E. Dist., Region II. With USN, 1946-54. Mem. ABA (jud. adminstrn. divsn.), Wis. Bar Assn. (media law rels. com.), Wis. Dist. Atty.'s Assn. (1st v.p.), Vol. Assn. Trial Judges of Wis., Shriners, Masons, Pi Tau Sigma, Sigma Phi Delta. Avocations: pilot, hunting, fishing, boating.

**GIERKE, HERMAN FREDRICK, III,** federal judge; b. Williston, N.D., Mar. 13, 1943; s. Herman Fredrick Jr. and Mary (Kelly) G.; m. Jeanine Gierke; children: Todd H.F., Scott H.F., Craig H.F., Michelle Lynn. B.A., U. N.D., 1964, J.D., 1966; attended, JAG Sch., U. Va., 1967, 69. Bar: N.D. 1966, U.S. Dist. Ct. N.D., U.S. Supreme Ct. Practice law Watford City, N.D., 1971-83; state's atty. McKenzie County, 1974-82; city atty. City of Watford, 1974-83; justice N.D. Supreme Ct., Bismarck, 1983-91; judge, then assoc. judge U.S. Ct. Appeals for the Armed Forces, Washington, DC, 1991—; adj. prof. George Washington U. Nat. Law Ctr., Cath. U. Am., Columbus Sch. Law. Served as capt. JAGC, U.S. Army, 1967-71. Recipient Outstanding Service award Gov. of N.D., 1984. Fellow Am. Bar Found., Am. Coll. Estate and Trust Counsel; mem. ABA, N.D. Trial Lawyers Assn. (bd. govs. 1977-83), N.D. State Attys. Assn. (pres. 1979-80), N.D. Council Sch. Attys. (charter), NW Jud. Dist. Bar Assn. (pres. 1977-79), State Bar Assn. N.D. (pres. 1982-83), Am. Judicature Soc., Assn. Trial Lawyers Am., Nat. Dist. Attys. Assn., Aircraft Owners and Pilots Assn., Am. Legion (N.D. comdr. 1984, judge adv. state assn., nat. vice comdr. 1985-86, comdr. 1988-89), Blue Key, Phi Delta Phi. Lutheran. Avocations: racquetball; golf; tennis; raising horses. Office: US Ct Appeals for the Armed Forces 450 E St NW Washington DC 20442-0001

**GIESE, HEINER,** lawyer, real estate investor; b. Passau, Germany, Apr. 16, 1944; came to U.S., 1950, naturalized, 1957; s. Heinz Emil and Wilma Maria (Dunner) G.; m. Barbara Ann Kent, June 28, 1969; children: Anna, Peter. BS in Internat. Affairs, Georgetown U., 1966; JD, U. Wis., 1969. Bar: Wis. 1969, U.S. Dist. Ct. (ea. and we. dists.) Wis. 1969, U.S. Ct. Appeals (7th cir.) 1974, U.S. Supreme Ct. 1974. Law clk. U.S. Dist. Ct., Madison, 1969-70; assoc. Cannon, McLaughlin, Herbon & Staudenmeier, Milw., 1969-74; ptnr. Levin & Giese, Milw., 1974-85, Giese & Weden Law Offices, Milw., 1985—. Bd. dirs. German Fest Milw., 1981-84, legal counsel, 1981—; bd. dirs. German Lang. and Sch. Soc., 1976—, pres., 1982—; bd. dirs. Goethe House, Milw., 1982—, sec., 1997—; Wis. gov.'s rep. Presdl. Commn. for German-Am. Tricentennial, 1983. Recipient Outstanding Young Lawyer award, 1979, Order of Merit, Fed. Republic Germany, 1993. Mem. ABA (young lawyers divsn., regional vice chmn. membership com. 1979-81), Wis. Bar Assn., Milw. Bar Assn. (chmn. lawyer referral svc. 1980-83, 91-93, bd. dirs. 1993-96), Milw. Young Lawyers Assn. (pres. 1978-79), Milw. Apt. Assn., Wis. State Bar (mem. lawyer referral com.). Democrat. Lutheran. General practice, Real property, Private international. Home: 2022 N 72nd St Wauwatosa WI 53213-1828 Office: Giese & Weden 1216 N Prospect Ave Milwaukee WI 53202-3014

**GIEVERS, KAREN A.,** lawyer; b. Culver City, Calif., Apr. 27, 1949; d. Ernest Conrad and Josephine Theresa (Passolt) Prevost; m. Joseph R. Gievers, Nov. 16, 1968 (dec. Feb. 1987); children: Daniel Steven, Donna Ann; m. Frank J. Bach, Nov. 23, 1997. AA, Miami Dade C.C., 1974; BA, Fla. Internat. U., 1975; JD cum laude, U. Miami, 1978. Bar: Fla. 1978, U.S. Dist. Ct. (so. dist.) Fla. 1978, U.S. Dist. Ct. (mid. and no. dist.) Fla. 1979, U.S. Ct. Appeals (5th cir.) 1979, U.S. Ct. Appeals (11th cir.) 1981, U.S. Ct. Claims 1980, U.S. Supreme Ct. 1982; cert. civil trial atty Fla. Bd. Legal Specialties, 1985, Nat. Bd. Trial Advocacy, 1992. Assoc. Sams, Anderson, Gerstein & Ward, P.A., Miami, 1978, Anderson, Moss, Russo & Gievers, P.A., Miami, 1979-83; ptnr., 1983-89; pvt. practice Karen A. Gievers, P.A., 1989—. Bd. editors: So. Dist. Digest, 1981-85. Lectr. FACT, Miami, 1984; pres. Operation SafeDrive, 1987—; mem. MADD, 1986; bd. trustees We Will Rebuild, 1992-93; candidate treas., ins. commr. State of Fla., 1994, candidate sec., 1998. Mem. Fla. Bar Assn. (mem. trial lawyers exec. coun. 1985-88, editor trial lawyers sect. 1984, vice-chmn. evidence com. 1985-88, chmn. 1988-89), Acad. Fla. Trial Lawyers (chmn. pub. com. 1984-86, bd. dirs. 1985-87, treas. 1988-89, sec. 1987-88, pres. elect 1989-90, pres. 1990-91, recipient Pres.'s award 1986, 90), Assn. Trial Lawyers Am., Dade County Bar Assn. (bd. dirs. 1981-84, 85-87, treas. 1987-88, sec. 1988-89, 2nd v.p. 1989-90, 1st v.p. 1990-91, pres.-elect 1991-92, pres. 1992-93), Dade County Trial Lawyers Assn. (sec. 1984, treas. 1985, pres. 1987), Fed. Bar Assn., Fla. Assn. Women Lawyers, Zool. Soc. Fla., Fla. Consumer Fedn. (bd. dirs. 1985-87), Lions Internat., Gray Panthers, Banker's, Gov.'s. Democrat. Personal injury, Federal civil litigation, State civil litigation. Office: Karen A Gievers PA 524 E College Ave Tallahassee FL 32301-2529

**GIFFORD, DONALD ARTHUR,** lawyer; b. Derry, N.H., Nov. 21, 1945; s. George Donald and Bertha Margaret (Gibbs) G.; m. Sandra Louise Robaldo, July 25, 1964; children: Adriana, Roy, Stacy. BA, U. South Fla., 1967; JD with high honors, Fla. State U., 1970. Bar: Fla. 1970, U.S. Dist. Ct. (mid. dist.) Fla. 1970, U.S. Dist. Ct. (no. dist.) Fla. 1981, U.S. Dist. Ct. (so. dist.) Fla. 1982, U.S. Ct. Appeals (5th cir.) 1975, U.S. Ct. Appeals (11th cir.) 1981. U.S. Supreme Ct. 1980. Assoc. Raymond, Wilson, Karl, Conway & Barr, Daytona Beach, Fla., 1972; law clk. U.S. Dist. Ct. (mid. dist.) Fla., Tampa, 1972-73; with Shackleford, Farrior, Stallings & Evans, P.A., Tampa, 1973—. Chair divsn. allocations United Way Greater Tampa, 1987-94, treas., 1991-93, pres., 1994-96; mem., trustee U.S. Fla. Found., 1986—, New Coll. Found., 1990-93. Fellow ABA (ho. of dels 1991-92), Am. Judicature Soc., Am. Bar Found.; mem. Fed. Bar Assn., Fla. Bar (bd. govs. 1989-95, mem. exec. com. 1993-94, chair legis. com. 1993-94, legis. com. 1995-98, mem. bd. legal specialization and edn.), Fla. Bar Found. (bd. dirs. 1996—, chair AOJ com.), Hillsborough County Bar Assn. (bd. dirs. 1981-90, pres. 1988-89), U. South Fla. Nat. Alumni Assn. (pres. 1976, bd. dirs. 1970-92, Outstanding Alumnus 1976, Outstanding Svc. award 1996), Fla. State U. Coll. Law Alumni Assn. (bd. dirs. 1982-96, pres. 1987-88), Greater Tampa C. of C. (gen. counsel, mem. exec. com., bd. govs.), Fla. State U. Alumni Assn. (bd. dirs. 1987—, chmn. 1992-94), F.L.A. Inc. (bd. dirs. 1995-98), Outback Bowl (mem. team rels. com. 1986-95), Tiger Bay Club (bd. dirs. 1988-92). Antitrust, Federal civil litigation. Office: Shackleford Farrior Stallings & Evans PA PO Box 3324 Tampa FL 33601-3324

**GIFFORD, JANET LYNN,** lawyer; b. Coral Gables, Fla., Jan. 21, 1960; d. Paul Edward and Marilyn June (Younger) G. BA, U. Fla., 1981; postgrad., Georgetown U., 1984, U.S. Fla.; JD, Am. U., 1984. Bar: Fla. 1985, U.S. Dist. Ct. (mid. dist.) Fla., U.S. Ct. Appeals (11th cir.). Assoc. Hogg, Allen, Ryce, Norton & Blue, P.A., Tampa, Fla., 1985-86; asst. city atty. City of St. Petersburg, Fla., 1986-90; assoc. Robbins, Gaynor & Bronstein, P.A., 1990-92; gen. cousel Real Estate Devel., Checkers Drive-In Restaurants, Inc., 1992—. Big Bros./Big Sisters, Tampa, 1986—; mem. Sunshine City Jaycees, 1987—, sec. 1988, v.p., 1989. Mem. ABA, St. Petersburg Bar Assn. (Law Week com. 1987-89), Fla. Bar Assn. (govt. law sect.), Fla. Assn. Women Lawyers, Phi Alpha Delta, Omicron Delta Kappa. Avocations: bicycling, tennis, art collecting, reading. Real property, General corporate, Labor. Office: Checkers Drive-In Restaurants Inc 14255 49th St N #1 Clearwater FL 33755-2813

**GIGLER, DANIEL RICHARD,** lawyer; b. Pitts., Apr. 21, 1951; s. Raymond Francis and Dolores Cecelia (Stinson) G.; m. Dorothy Louise Dodson, Sept. 3, 1971. Student, Duquesne U., 1969-70; BA, U. Maryland, 1973; JD, Dickinson Coll., 1976. Bar: Pa. 1976, U.S. Dist. Ct. (we. dist.) Pa. 1978, U.S. Ct. Appeals (3d cir.) 1985, U.S. Ct. Claims 1981, U.S. Supreme Ct. 1989. Law clk. Lycoming County (Pa.) Ct. Common Pleas, Williamsport, Pa., 1976-78; assoc. John A. Knorr, P.C., Pitts., 1978-79; assoc. Robb, Leonard & Mulvihill, Pitts., 1979-84, ptnr., 1984-94, mng. ptnr., 1989-92; sr. litigation counsel Westinghouse Electric Corp., Pitts., 1994—; spl. master Allegheny County (Pa.) Ct. Common Pleas, Pitts., 1989—; panelist U.S. Arbitration and Mediation, Pitts., 1992—, Am. Arbitration Assn. Mem. ABA, Pa. Bar Assn., Allegheny County Bar Assn., Pa. Def. Inst., Am. Inns Ct (Pitts. chpt.). Democrat. Roman Catholic. Personal injury, Product liability, Toxic tort. Office: Westinghouse Electric Corp Law Dept 11 Stanwix St Pittsburgh PA 15222-1312

**GIGLIO, STEVEN RENE,** lawyer; b. Denver, Feb. 13, 1952; s. Dominic Mark and Ruth (Strain) G.; m. Susan Dale Carver, Feb. 12, 1987. BA in Russian Studies, La. State U., 1973, JD, 1976. Bar: La. 1976, U.S. Dist. Ct. (ea., mid. and we. dists.) La. 1979, U.S. Ct. Claims 1990, U.S. Ct. Appeals (5th cir.) 1979, U.S. Supreme Ct. 1981. Pvt. practice Baton Rouge, 1976-79, 93—; asst. gen. counsel La. Dept. Health, Baton Rouge, 1979-87; ptnr. Olds & Giglio, Baton Rouge, 1987-88, Kleinpeter, Schwatzberg & Stevens, Baton Rouge, 1988-93. Patentee in field. Mem. La. Bar Assn. Roman Catholic. General civil litigation, Environmental, Personal injury. Office: 2900 Westfork Dr Ste 200 Baton Rouge LA 70827-0004

**GIGUIERE, MICHELE LOUISE,** lawyer; b. Spokane, Feb. 11, 1944; d. Karl Earl and Mildred Elaine (Phillips) G.; BA, U. Pacific, 1965; MS, U. So. Calif., 1969; JD, Lincoln Law Sch., 1980. Exec. trainee J.W. Robinson Co., Los Angeles, 1965-66; tchr. Novato (Calif.) Unified Sch. Dist., 1967-78; asst. dept. mgr. Emporium, San Rafael, Calif., 1970-74; admitted to Calif. bar, 1980, pvt. practice, Fair Oaks and Sacramento, Calif. 1980—. Mem. ABA, State Bar Calif., Sacramento County Bar Assn., Calif. Women Lawyers, Women Lawyers Sacramento, LWV. Democrat. Presbyterian. Clubs: Network. Landlord-tenant, Real property, General practice. Office: 4811 Chippendale Dr Ste 901 Sacramento CA 95841-2554

**GIL, GUILLERMO,** prosecutor. U.S. atty. Dept. Justice, Hato Rey, P.R., 1993—. Office: US Attys Office Fed Bldg Rm 452 Carlos E Chardon Ave Hato Rey San Juan PR 00918*

**GILBERG, KENNETH ROY,** lawyer; b. Phila., Feb. 2, 1951; s. Leonard David and Roslyn (Tennis) G.; m. Nanci Jane Schwartz, Sept. 7, 1974. BA, Lebanon Valley Coll., 1973; JD, Widener U., 1976. Bar: Pa. 1976. Assoc. Pechner, Dorfman et. al., Phila., 1976-84, ptnr., 1984-87; ptnr. Myerson & Kuhn, Phila., 1988-89; prin. Kenneth R. Gilberg and Assocs., Bala Cynwyd, Pa., 1989-90; ptnr. Mesirov, Gelman, Jaffe, Cramer & Jamieson LLP, Phila., 1990—. Contbr. articles to profl. jours. Past pres. Golden Slipper Camp. Recipient Meritorious Achievement award Pa. Sports Hall of Fame, 1974; named Most Valuable Player Mid-Atlantic Conf., 1973. Mem. Phi Alpha Delta (charter). Republican. Avocations: lacrosse, racquetball, photography, golf, tennis. Labor, Pension, profit-sharing, and employee benefits. Office: Mesirov Gelman Jaffe Cramer & Jamieson 1735 Market St Ste 3901 Philadelphia PA 19103-7598

**GILBERT, BLAINE LOUIS,** lawyer; b. Phila., Aug. 26, 1940; s. Arthur I. and Marcia R. (Kaufman) G.; m. Sondra Gilbert; children: Beth M., Kimberly J. AA, Balt. Jr. Coll., 1961; postgrad., Am. U., 1962; JD, U. Balt., 1965. Bar: Md. 1966, U.S. Dist. Ct. Md. 1968, U.S. Supreme Ct. 1974. Exec. asst. ins. commr. State of Md., Balt., 1965-66; assoc. Polovoy & Polovoy, Balt., 1966-72; ptnr. Angeletti & Gilbert, Balt., 1972-79, Gilbert & Levin, Balt., 1979-92, Blaine L. Gilbert and Assocs. P.A., Balt., 1993—. Mem. ABA, Balt. Bar Assn., Am. Immigration Lawyers Assn., Am. Judicature Soc., Md. Trial Lawyers Assn. Avocations: music, screenwriting. Entertainment, State civil litigation, Immigration, naturalization, and customs. Home: 2B Dorsett Hills Ct Owings Mills MD 21117-1131 Office: Blaine L Gilbert & Assocs PA Lower Level 200 E Lexington St Baltimore MD 21202-3530

**GILBERT, CHARLES E., III,** lawyer; b. Boston, Apr. 17, 1949; s. Charles and Margaret (Perkins) G.; m. Linda P. Gilbert, Dec. 22, 1974 (div. 1986); children: Stacey, Meredith; m. Peggy Bragdon, Oct. 12, 1986; children: Seth, Sean; stepchildren: Rachelle Dixon, Vanessa Dixon. BA, Harvard U., 1972; JD, Boston Coll., 1977. Bar: Maine 1977, Mass. 1977, U.S. Dist. Ct. Maine 1978, U. S. Ct. Appeals (1st cir.) 1987. Law clk. Maine Supreme Jud. Ct., Rockland, 1977-78; assoc., then ptnr. Vafiades, Brountas & Kominsky, Bangor, Maine, 1978-88; ptnr. Gilbert & Heitmann, Bangor, ME, 1988-90; prin. Gilbert Law Offices, P.A., Bangor, ME, 1990—. Trustee Hampden Congl. Ch., 1988-91, pres. 1991-95. Mem. Maine Bar Assn. (mem. pub. affairs com. 1984—), Maine Trial Lawyers Assn., Am. Jud. Soc., Nat. Bd. Trial Advocacy (cert. civil trial practice 1995), Penobscot County Bar Assn., John Waldo Ballow Am. Inn Ct., Harvard Club (chmn. schs. and scholarships com. East Maine chpt.), Spee Club. Republican. E-mail: gil-law@mint.net. Fax: 207-941-9871. General practice, General civil litigation, Personal injury. Office: Gilbert Law Offices PA PO Box 2339 82 Columbia St Bangor ME 04402-2339

**GILBERT, HOWARD E.,** lawyer; b. Chgo., Apr. 3, 1947. BS, U. Ill., 1969; JD, DePaul U., 1972. Bar: Ill. 1972, U.S. Dist. Ct. (no. dist.) Ill. 1972, U.S. Tax Ct. 1973, U.S. Ct. Appeals (7th cir.) 1974, U.S. Supreme Ct. 1979, Fla. 1993. Atty. Altheimer & Gray, Chgo., 1972-74, Panter, Nelson & Bernfield, Chgo., 1974-75, Herman, Tannebaum, Levine & Gilbert, Chgo., 1975-82, Gilbert, Shapiro & Richman, Chgo., 1982-85, Howard E. Gilbert & Assocs., Skokie, Ill., 1986—. Mem. ATLA, ABA, Ill. Trial Lawyers Assn., Ill. State Bar Assn., Chgo. Bar Assn., North Suburban Bar Assn., Aircraft Owners and Pilots Assn. Avocations: flying, boating. E-mail: justiceb@aol.com. General practice, Estate planning, Personal injury. Home: 219 Beech St Highland Park IL 60035-4103 Office: 5420 Old Orchard Rd Ste A205 Skokie IL 60077-1053

**GILBERT, J. PHIL,** federal judge; b. 1949. BS, U. Ill., 1971; JD, Loyola U., Chgo., 1974. Ptnr. Gilbert & Gilbert, Carbondale, Ill., 1974-83, Gilbert, Kimmel, Huffman & Prosser, Carbondale, 1983-88; circuit judge First Jud. Circuit, Ill., 1988-92; fed. judge U.S. Dist. Ct. (so. dist.) Ill., Benton, 1992—, chief judge, 1993—; spl. asst. atty. gen. Pub. Aid Enforcement Divsn., 1974-75; asst. city atty. City of Carbondale, 1975-78; active Nat. Coun. Govt. Ethics Laws, 1988—; mem. Ill. State Bd. Elections, 1982, vice chmn., chmn., 1983-85. Bd. dirs. Friends of Morris Libr., 1988—; active Edn. Coun. 100, 1989—, Boy Scouts Am. Mem. Ill. State Bar, Jackson County Bar Assn., Ill. Judges Assn. (mem. com. jud. retention), Phi Alpha Delta. Office: US Dist Ct 301 W Main St Benton IL 62812-1362

**GILBERT, KEITH THOMAS,** lawyer, consultant; b. Harlingen, Tex., Jan. 29, 1959. BBA, Baylor U., 1982; JD, South Tex. Coll. Law, Tex. A & M U., 1989. Bar: Tex. 1990, U.S. Dist. Ct. (so. dist.) Tex. 1992. Ptnr. Gilbert & Mestemaker, Houston, 1991-96; pvt. practice Houston, 1996—; legal rep., cons. North Channel Tribune Newspaper, Galena Park, Tex., Sandy Ridge Vineyards, Safeco, Colonial Gen., 1997—. Editor: World Trade Policy, 1979. Avocations: chess, muscle cars, stamp collecting, wine. Appellate, State civil litigation, Election. Office: PO Box 1984 Houston TX 77251-1984

**GILBERT, RONALD RHEA,** lawyer; b. Sandusky, Ohio, Dec. 29, 1942; s. Corvin and Mildred (Millikin) G.; m. Jane Johnson, Jan. 24, 1998; children: Elizabeth, Lynne, Lisa. BA, Wittenberg U., 1964; JD, U. Mich., 1967, postgrad., 1967-68; postgrad., Wayne State U., 1973-74. Bar: Mich. 1968, U.S. Dist. Ct. (ea. and we. dists.) Mich. 1968, U.S. Ct. Appeals (6th cir.) 1968, U.S. Ct. Appeals (9th cir.) 1977, U.S. Ct. Appeals (7th cir.) 1984, U.S. Ct. Appeals (3d cir.) 1988, U.S. Ct. Appeals (4th cir.) 1989, U.S. Ct. Appeals (8th cir.) 1990, U.S. Ct. Appeals (10th cir.) 1991, U.S. Ct. Appeals (11th cir.) 1992, U.S. Ct. Appeals (2nd cir.), 1992. Assoc. prosecutor Wayne County, Mich., 1969; assoc. Rouse, Selby, Dickinson, Shaw & Pike, Detroit, 1969-72; ptnr. Charfoos, Christensen, Gilbert & Archer, P.C., Detroit, 1972-84; sole practice, 1984—; instr. Madonna Coll., Detroit, 1977-81; mem. faculty Inst. Continuing Legal Edn., 1977—; speaker symposium on social security law Detroit Coll. Law, 1984; state bar grievance investigator; vol. chmn. Aquatic Injury Safety Found. Co-author: Social Security Disability Claims, 1983; contbr. articles to legal jours. Founder, chmn. Aquatic Injury Safety Group, 1982, chmn., 1982-89; founder, chmn. Found. for Aquatic Injury Prevention, 1988, Found. for Spinal Cord Injury Prevention, 1988; chmn. aquatic safety com. Nat. Safety Coun., 1987; mem. data collection subcom. of Nat. Swimming Safety Com. for Consumer Products Safety Commn.; bd. dirs. Nat. Coordinating Coun. on Spinal Cord Injuries; patron Detroit Art Inst., Detroit Zool. Soc.; mem. Pres.' Club U. Mich.; mem. Detroit Council on World Affairs, 1968-73, Council for Nat. Coop. in Aquatics; mem. combined fed. campaign Nat. Health Agy. Mich.; founder Spinal Cord Injury Traumatic Brain Injury Adv. Com. Mich. Pub. Health Chronic Adv. Com.; co-founder Safe Kids Coalition Southeastern Mich.; mem. Nat. Safe Kids Coalition. Mem. Assn. Trial Lawyers Am., Mich. Trial Lawyers Assn., System Safety Soc., ABA, Mich Bar Assn., Detroit Bar Assn., Am. Arbitration Assn., Am. Judicature Soc., Nat. Spinal Cord Injury Assn. (sec. 1988, bd. dirs., exec. com., chmn. prevention com.), Nat. Head Injury Assn., Mich. Head Injury Assn., Am. Standards and Testing Materials (com. F-24 on water parks and playgrounds, mem. com. F-8), World Water Parks Assn., Nat. Environ. Health Assn., Nat. Pub. Health Assn., Nat. Eagle Scout Assn. (alumni), Blue Key, Pi Kappa Alpha, Pi Sigma Alpha, Pi Delta Epsilon. Clubs: Detroit Athletic, U. Mich. Personal injury, State civil litigation, Insurance. Office: 1310 Ford Bldg Detroit MI 49226

**GILBERT, THEODORE,** lawyer; b. N.Y.C., Jan. 8, 1928; s. Isadore and Rose (Miller) G.; m. Mindy Fajardo, Dec. 22, 1965; children—Michael Jason, Adam Seth. BS, L.I. U., 1948; LLB, Bklyn. Law Sch., 1951. Bar: N.Y. 1951, U.S. Dist. Ct. (so. dist.) N.Y., U.S. Dist. Ct. (ea. dist.) N.Y. 1953, U.S. Supreme Ct. 1964. Chief contracts div., law dept. City of N.Y., 1968-78; sole practice, Flushing, N.Y., 1978—. Adviser Explorer Post 122, Boy Scouts Am., 1983-84. Mem. N.Y. County Lawyers Assn., Nassau County Bar Assn. Democrat. State civil litigation, Construction, General practice. Office: 98 Cuttermill Rd Great Neck NY 11021-3006

**GILBERTSON, DAVID,** state supreme court justice. Former judge S.D. Cir. Ct. (5th jud. cir.), Pierre; assoc. justice S.D. Supreme Ct., Pierre, 1995—. Office: 500 E Capitol Ave Pierre SD 57501-5070

**GILBERTSON, JOEL WARREN,** lawyer; b. Valley City, N.D., Nov. 9, 1949; s. Roy W. and Gwen D. (Haugen) G.; m. Jan Erikson, June 11, 1972; children: David, Lisa. BA, Concordia Coll., Moorhead, Minn., 1972; JD, U. N.D., 1975. Bar: N.D. 1976, U.S. Dist. Ct. N.D. 1976. Ptnr. Binek & Gilbertson, Bowman, N.D., 1976; atty. N.D. Supreme Ct., Bismarck, 1976-78; exec. dir. N.D. Bar Assn., Bismarck, 1978-81; ptnr. Pearce & Durick, Bismarck, 1981-97; exec. v.p., gen. counsel Ind. Cmty. Banks of N.D., 1997—. Served with U.S. Army N.G., 1972-78. Mem. N.D. Bar Assn. (bd. govs. 1989-95, pres. 1992-93), N.D. Bar Found. (vice chmn. 1982-84, chmn. bd. dirs. 1986-89), South Cen. Dist. Bar Assn. (pres. 1987-89). Republican. Lutheran. Avocations: piano, softball. Federal civil litigation, Personal injury, Insurance. Home: 1025 Crescent Ln Bismarck ND 58501-2463 Office: Ind Comty Banks ND PO Box 6128 Bismarck ND 58506-6128

**GILDAN, PHILLIP CLARKE,** lawyer; b. West Palm Beach, Fla., July 17, 1959; s. Herbert Leonard and Kathleen (Yeager) G.; m. Laurie Beth Leinwand, Aug. 25,1985; children: Tyler Ross, Jacob Lee. AB magna cum laude, Dartmouth Coll., 1981; JD cum laude, Harvard U., 1984. Bar: Fla. 1984, U.S. Ct. Appeals (11th cir.) 1986, U.S. Supreme Ct. 1989. Assoc. Nason, Gildan, Yeager, Gerson & White, P.A., West Palm Beach, 1984-89, shareholder, 1989-96; shareholder Greenberg Traurig PA, West Palm Beach, 1997—; lectr. Reinventing Govt. Symposium, Hollywood, Fla., 1994, Risk Mgmt. State Conf., Deerfield Beach, Fla., 1995. Contbr. articles to profl. jours. Dir. Com. for Good Govt., Palm Beach, Fla., 1990-94. Mem. Fla. Bar Assn., Palm Beach County Bar Assn., Am. Inns of Ct. LIV (exec. com. 1991-94), Phi Beta Kappa. General civil litigation, General corporate, Public utilities. Office: Greenberg Traurig Hoffman Lipoff Rosen & Quentel PA 777 S Flagler Dr Ste 300 West Palm Beach FL 33401-6161

**GILDEA, BRIAN MICHAEL,** lawyer; b. New Haven, Nov. 1, 1939; s. Thomas Michael and Lillian Frances (Reilly) G.; children: Larysa Albina, Stefan Bohdan. AS, New Haven U., 1964; BA, Providence Coll., 1967; JD, Suffolk U., 1970. Bar: Conn. 1970, U.S. Dist. Ct. Conn. 1971, U.S. Ct. Appeals (2d cir.) 1975, U.S. Ct. Appeals (3d cir.) 1979, U.S. Ct. Appeals (5th cir.) 1984, U.S. Supreme Ct. 1975. Legal adviser City of Boston, 1969-70; assoc. Celentano, Ivey & Gery, New Haven, 1970-73; ptnr. Celentano & Gildea, New Haven, 1973-74; pvt. practice New Haven, 1974—. Bd. dirs. St. Mary's High Sch., New Haven, 1975-77; mem. Bethany (Conn.) Town Charter Commn., 1976; del. U.S./Japan Bilateral Session, 1988, U.S./China Joint Session on Trade and Econ. Law, 1987. With USAF, 1958-62. Recipient Svc. award Providence Coll., New Haven, 1979, Friar award St. Mary's Alumni Assn., 1980. Mem. ABA, Def. Rsch. Inst., Conn. Bar Assn., New Haven County Bar Assn., Am. Lawyers Assn. Democrat. Roman

Catholic. Avocations: bicycling, tennis, skiing, photography. Federal civil litigation, Immigration, naturalization, and customs, Insurance. Office: 512 Blake St New Haven CT 06515-1287

**GILDEN, JAMES WILLIAM,** lawyer; b. Waterbury, Conn., June 3, 1939; s. Samuel Michael and Adele Gilden; m. Sheila A. Garbus, Nov. 18, 1962 (div. Aug. 1979); 1 child, David; m. Lois J. Anderson, Aug. 9, 1980; 1 child, Heidi Anderson-Gilden; 1 stepchild, Eric Anderson. BA, U. Conn., 1961; JD, New Eng. Sch. Law, 1965. Atty. Office of Robert A. Stanziani, Boston, 1965-67, Gilden & Dowd, Boston, 1968-70, Gilden & Aronson, Boston, 1970-78; pvt. practice Boston/Sharon, Mass., 1978-80; atty. Beacon Hill Law Assocs., Boston, 1980-87; pvt. practice Boston, 1987—. Pres. Ocean State Lyric Opera Co., Providence, R.I., 1994-98, Sharon Jaycees, 1970-71, Cottage St. Sch. PTO, Sharon, 1980, Sharon Operation Serve, 1970-75. Avocations: boating, reading, firearms. Criminal, State civil litigation, Family and matrimonial. Office: 2001 Beacon St Brighton MA 02135-7786

**GILES, EDWARD LEE,** lawyer; b. West Palm Beach, Fla., Nov. 18, 1950; s. Elmer Lee and Dorothy (Hicks) G.; m. Melissa Louise Agnew, Apr. 19, 1981; children: Lara, Scott. BA, Stetson U., 1972; JD, St. Thomas U., 1990. Bar: Fla. 1991, U.S. Dist. Ct. (so. dist.) Fla. 1992. Legal asst. Wagner, Nugent, Johnson, P.A., West Palm Beach, 1977-90, atty., 1991-92; asst. atty. gen. Dept. Legal Affairs, State of Fla., West Palm Beach, 1992—. Mem. ABA, Assn. Trial Lawyers Am., Palm Beach County Bar Assn., Fla. Assn. for Women Lawyers, Delta Theta Phi. Democrat. Methodist. Home: 1827 N D St Lake Worth FL 33460-6413 Office: Dept of Legal Affairs State of Fla Ste 300 1655 Palm Beach Lakes Blvd West Palm Beach FL 33401-2299

**GILES, JAMES T.,** federal judge; b. 1943. B.A., Amherst Coll., 1964; LL.B., Yale U., 1967. Mem. Nat. Labor Relations Bd., Phila., 1967-68; assoc. Pepper, Hamilton & Scheetz, 1968-79; judge U.S. Dist. Ct. (ea. dist.) Pa., Phila., 1979—. Mem. Fed. Bar Assn., Phila. Bar Assn. Office: US Dist Ct 8613 US Courthouse Ind Mall W 601 Market St Philadelphia PA 19106-1713

**GILES, WILLIAM JEFFERSON, III,** lawyer; b. Manila, The Philippines, Apr. 10, 1936; came to U.S., 1938; s. William Jefferson and Gardner (Anderson) G.; m. Nancy Gifford Seff, May 9, 1957; children: William Jefferson IV, Gregory Gifford. BS, U. Calif., Berkeley, 1957; postgrad., Golden Gate Coll., 1958-59, Stanford U., 1960; JD, U. S.D., 1961. Bar: Iowa 1961, U.S. Dist. Ct. Iowa 1961, U.S. Ct. Appeals (8th cir.) 1971, U.S. Supreme Ct. 1971, Nebr. 1982, U.S. Ct. Appeals (9th cir.) 1988. Pvt. practice Sioux City, Iowa, 1961—; of counsel Whicher & Whicher, Sioux City, 1966-75, Whicher & Hart, Sioux City, 1975-77; lectr. in field. Contbr. articles to profl. jours. Bd. dirs. Sioux City Mus. and Hist. Soc., 1976-79, Sioux City Cmty. Theatre, 1974-76. Capt. USAR, 1957-68. Recipient Gold Seal award Phi Beta Kappa, 1953. Fellow Am. Acad. Matrimonial Lawyers (chmn. bankruptcy com. 1992—), Internat. Acad. Matrimonial Lawyers; mem. ABA, ATLA, Iowa Bar Assn., Iowa Assn. Trial Lawyers, Comml. Law League Am., Sioux City Country Club, Phi Delta Phi, Phi Phi. Republican. Family and matrimonial, Personal injury, Bankruptcy. Home: 3827 Country Club Blvd Sioux City IA 51104-1327 Office: 322 Frances Bldg 505 5th St Sioux City IA 51101 also: 3940 Hideaway Acres Crofton NE 68730-0088

**GILFIX, SUZANNE GLICK,** lawyer; b. Worcester, Mass., Sept. 26, 1966; d. Edward Malcolm and Carol Seder Glick; m. Ronald Joseph Gilfix, July 25, 1993; children: Adam William, Zachary Samuel. BA, Harvard U., 1988; JD, Boston U., 1991. Bar: Mass. 1991. Litigation assoc. Bingham, Dana & Gould, Boston, 1991-93; asst. atty. gen. Mass. Office Atty. Gen., Boston, 1994—. Bd. dirs., mem. civil rights exec. com. Anti-Defamation League, Boston, 1996—; bd. dirs. Local Jewish Cmty. Ctr., Westborough, Mass., 1997—. Avocations: walking, hiking, writing, singing, balancing children, husband, career and community activism and still smiling. Office: Office Atty Gen 1 Ashburton Pl Boston MA 02108-1518

**GILFORD, STEVEN ROSS,** lawyer; b. Chgo., Dec. 2, 1952; s. Ronald M. and Adele (Miller) G.; m. Anne Christine Johnson, Jan. 2, 1974; children: Sarah Julia, Zachary Michael, Eliza Rebecca. BA, Dartmouth Coll., 1974; JD, Duke U., 1978, M of Pub. Policy Scis., 1978. Bar: Ill. 1978, U.S. Dist. Ct. (no. dist.) Ill. 1978, U.S. Ct. Appeals (7th cir.) 1981, U.S. Ct. Appeals (D.C. cir.) 1984, U.S. Ct. Appeals (5th cir.) 1988, U.S. Dist. Ct. (ea. dist.) Mich. 1995. Assoc. Isham, Lincoln & Beale, Chgo., 1978-85, ptnr., 1985-87; ptnr. Mayer Brown & Platt, Chgo., 1987—. Adminstrv. law editor Duke Law Jour., 1976-77. Bd. dirs. Evanston (Ill.) YMCA, 1982-92, sec., 1985, vice chmn., 1986-92; patricipating atty. ACLU, 1983—, bd. dirs. Ill., 1991-96, v.p. devel., 1993-96; bd. dirs. Roger Bawldwin Found., 1993-96; elected mem. bd. edn. dist. 202 Evanston Twp. H.S., 1993—, v.p., 1995-96, pres., 1996-98, mem. joint task force on safety, 1995-96; mem. Met. Family Svcs., Evanston Skokie Valley Cmty. Adv. Bd., 1997-98; mem., bd. dirs. Met. Family Svcs., 1998—. Mem. ABA, Ill. Bar Assn., Chgo. Bar Assn. General civil litigation, Insurance, Libel. Home: 2728 Harrison St Evanston IL 60201-1216 Office: Mayer Brown & Platt 190 S La Salle St Ste 3100 Chicago IL 60603-3441

**GILHOUSEN, BRENT JAMES,** lawyer; b. Anacortes, Wash., Sept. 24, 1946; s. Darrell J. and Jean Sarah (Sabatine) G.; m. Sandra M. King, Aug. 13, 1983; 2 children: Lindsay Elizabeth, Shane Shroeder. BA, Wash. State U., 1968; JD, U. Oreg., 1973. Bar: Wash. 1973, U.S. Dist. Ct. (we. dist.) Wash. 1973, U.S. Ct. Appeals (9th cir.) 1973, U.S. Supreme Ct. 1980, Mo. 1981, U.S. Ct. Appeals (4th cir.) 1986. From atty.-advisor to sr. atty. U.S. EPA, Seattle, 1973-80; from environ. atty. to asst. gen. counsel-environ. Monsanto Co., St. Louis, 1980-97; asst. gen. counsel-environ. Solutia Inc., St. Louis, 1997—; mem. Superfund Settlements Project, Washington, 1988-95; legal com. Chem. Industry Inst. Toxicology, Rsch. Triangle Park, N.C., 1986-99; mem. environ. law adv. com. Nat. Chamber Litigation Ctr., Washington, 1992-97. Mem. editl. bd. Hazardous Waste Strategies Update, 1994—. With USAR, 1968-74. Mem. ABA (sect. natural resources, energy and environ. law, chair corp. counsel com. 1994-96, vice-chair hazardous waste com. 1991—), Chem. Mfrs. Assn. (enforcement subcom. 1995—), Def. Rsch. Inst., Forest Hills Country Club, Am. Legion. Republican. Avocations: skiing, golf, boating. Administrative and regulatory, Federal civil litigation, Environmental. Home: 1 Peakmont Ln Chesterfield MO 63005-6806 Office: Solutia Inc 10300 Olive Blvd Saint Louis MO 63141-7893

**GILHULY, PETER MARTIN,** lawyer; b. Stamford, Conn., Aug. 20, 1961; s. Robert T. and Anne (Kilby) G.; m. Namhee Han, Aug. 20, 1988; children: Emma, Thompson Young, John Daniel. BA with honors, Wesleyan U., Middletown, Conn., 1983; JD cum laude, Harvard U., 1990. Bar: Calif. 1990, U.S. Dist. Ct. (ctrl. dist.) Calif. 1990. Vol. U.S. Peace Corps, Argali, Nepal, 1983-86; assoc. Latham & Watkins, L.A., 1990-98, ptnr., 1998—; mem. adv. bd. Pacific Gemini LLC, L.A., 1995-97. Contbr. articles to law jours. Bd. dirs. Pub. Counsel, L.A., 1995-96. Recipient President's award Los Angeles County Barristers, 1998. Avocations: skiing, running, tennis. Bankruptcy, Consumer commercial, General corporate. Office: Latham & Watkins 633 W 5th St Ste 4000 Los Angeles CA 90071-2005

**GILIOLI, ERIC LAWRENCE,** lawyer; b. Cin., Sept. 9, 1957; s. Daniel Ettore and Helen Marie (Tiersch) G.; m. Vivia J. Chen. AB, Harvard Coll., 1979; JD, Fordham U., 1983; Giurisprudenza, U. Milan, 1996. Bar: N.Y. 1984, D.C. 1985, U.S. Dist. Ct. (so. and ea. dists.) N.Y., U.S. Ct. Internat. Trade. Assoc. Marks & Murase, N.Y.C., 1983-91, spl. counsel, 1992-97; ptnr. Studio Legale Gilioli, Milan, Italy, 1986-97; internat. counsel Curtis, Mallet-Prevost, Colt & Musle, 1997-98, ptnr., 1998—; ptnr. Curtis, Mallet-Prevost & Gilioli, Milan, 1998—. Mem. Fordham Law Sch. Alumni Assn. (dir. 1985-94), Fordham Internat. Law Jour. Alumni Assn. (assoc. dir. 1985—), Italy- Am. C. of C., Swedish C. of C., Norwegian C. of C., Havard Club (N.Y.C.). Private international, General corporate, Mergers and acquisitions. Office: Curtis Mallet-Prevost Colt & Mosle 101 Park Ave Fl 34 New York NY 10178-0061

**GILKES, ARTHUR GWYER,** lawyer; b. Bronxville, N.Y., Feb. 6, 1915; s. Arthur Burton and Frances (Gwyer) G.; m. Ann Fullan, Feb. 26, 1942; children: Arthur Gwyer Jr., Ann Colwell Gilkes Liu, Judith Porter Gilkes Benson, Jane Scott Gilkes Strassgütl. A.B., Princeton U., 1939; LL.B. cum laude, NYU, 1947. Of counsel Leydig, Voit & Mayor, Ltd., Chgo.; mem. Comité Privé of European Experts of Intellectual Property. Patent. Home: 6 Country Rd E Village Of Golf FL 33436 *Died July 25, 1999.*

**GILL, AMBER MCLAUGHLIN,** lawyer; b. Houston, Dec. 12, 1960; d. Donald Buford and Wanda Jo (Windham) McLaughlin; m. Raymond Penn Gill, Aug. 16, 1997. BSc cum laude, Sam Houston State U., 1982; JD, Tex. Tech. Sch. Law, 1986. Bar: Tex. 1986, Okla. 1987, U.S. Dist. Ct. (western dist.) Tex. 1989, U.S. Ct. Appeals (5th cir.) 1989, U.S. Dist. Ct. (we. dist.) Okla. 1996, U.S. Ct. Appeals (10th cir.) 1996, U.S. Supreme Ct. 1998. Attorney Jones, Bryant & Nigh, Enid, Okla., 1986-88; trust dept. mgr. Travis Bank & Trust, Austin, Tex., 1988; attorney White & Allison, Austin, Tex., 1988-89; asst. county attorney Travis County Attorney's Office, Austin, Tex., 1989-91, asst. dist. attorney, 1992-95; pvt. practice Enid, Okla., 1995—; contract labor attorney Jones & Wyatt, Enid, 1995-97. Treas., bd. dirs. Garfield County Child Advocacy Coun., 1997-99. Avocations: snow skiing, tennis, jogging, horse back riding. Criminal, Family and matrimonial, Juvenile. Office: PO Box 3802 Enid OK 73702-3802

**GILL, HERBERT COGBILL,** judge; b. Petersburg, Va., Aug. 8, 1943; s. Herbert Cogbill and Olive Lorraine (Stewart) G.; m. Judith Blick, Jan. 25, 1965; children: Sherry Lynn, Rachel Elizabeth. BA, Hampden-Sydney Coll., 1965; JD, U. Richmond, 1971. Asst. commonwealth atty. State of Va., Chesterfield, 1971-80; ptnr. Rudy & Gill, Chesterfield, 1975-87; judge 12th Jud. Cir., Chesterfield, 1987—. V.p. Red Cross, Chesterfield, 1979; dist. dir. Boy Scouts Am., Chesterfield, 1993; trustee Belmont Meth. Ch., Richmond, 1996. Office: Law Libr PO Box 297 Chesterfield VA 23832-0004

**GILL, LYLE BENNETT,** lawyer; b. Lincoln, Nebr., May 11, 1916; s. George Orville and Ruth (Bennett) G.; BA, Swarthmore Coll., 1937; LLB, Nebr. Coll. Law, 1940; m. Rita M. Cronin, Aug. 28, 1975; children by previous marriage: George, Valerie, Marguerite. Bar: Nebr. 1940. Practice law, Fremont, 1945-98; city atty. Fremont, 1959-62, 67-94. Vice chmn. ARC, Dodge County, 1953-59; chmn., Dodge County Republican Com., 1945-51. Served with USNR, 1942-45, 1951-52; lt. comdr. (ret.). Mem. ABA, Nebr. Bar Assn., Dodge County Bar Assn. (pres. 1962), VFW, Am. Legion. Episcopalian. Home: PO Box 642 Fremont NE 68026-0642

**GILL, PATRICK DAVID,** lawyer; b. N.Y., Apr. 27, 1944; s. Patrick John and Ellen A. Gill; m. Ann Brooke, May 13, 1972; children: Elizabeth, Kimberly, Roger. BA, CUNY Queens, 1965; JD, NYU Sch. Law, 1968. Bar: N.Y. 1968, U.S. Ct. Internat. Trade 1968, U.S. Ct. Appeals (2nd cir.) 1969, U.S. Dist. Ct. (so. and ea. dists.) N.Y. 1977, D.C. 1980, U.S. Ct. Appeals (fed. cir.) 1982, U.S. Supreme Ct. 1990. Trial atty. U.S. Dept. Justice, N.Y., 1968-73; assoc. Sharretts, Paley, Carter & Blannelt, N.Y., 1973-77; ptnr. Rode & Qualey, N.Y., 1977—. With USAR, 1968-74. Bd. dirs. Customs and Internat. Bar Assn. (chmn. adminstrn. practice com., 1981-90, sec. 1990-92, v.p. 1992-94, pres. 1994-96). Avocations: tennis, boating. Immigration, naturalization, and customs, Private international. Office: Rode & Qualey 295 Madison Ave New York NY 10017-6304

**GILL, RICHARD LAWRENCE,** lawyer; b. Chgo., Jan. 8, 1946; s. Joseph Richard and Dolores Ann (Powers) G.; m. Mary Helen Walker, July 14, 1990; children: Kyla Marie, Matthew Joseph. BA, Coll. of St. Thomas, St. Paul, 1968; JD, U. Minn., 1971. Bar: Minn. 1971, U.S. Dist. Ct. Minn. 1971, U.S. Supreme Ct. 1979, U.S. Ct. Appeals (8th cir.) 1983, U.S. Ct. Appeals (4th cir.) 1990, Ill. 1992. Spl. asst. atty. gen. State of Minn., St. Paul, 1971-73; assoc. Maun, Hazel, Green, Hayes, Simon & Aretz, St. Paul, 1974-77; ptnr. Gill & Brinkman, St. Paul, 1978-84, Robins, Kaplan, Miller & Ciresi, Mpls., 1984—. Vol. Courage Ctr., Golden Valley, Minn., 1981—; youth football coach Maplewood (Minn.) Athletic Assn., 1978-80. Mem. ABA, Minn. Bar Assn., Hennepin County Bar Assn., Ramsey County Bar Assn., Assn. Trial Lawyers Am., Minn. Trial Lawyers Assn., Town and Country Club. Avocations: skiing, tennis, golf. General civil litigation, Product liability, Patent. Office: Robins Kaplan Miller & Ciresi 800 Lasalle Ave Ste 2800 Minneapolis MN 55402-2015

**GILL, W(ALTER) BRENT,** lawyer; b. Bedford, Ind., May 23, 1950; s. Jim and Barbara Dean (Medlock) G.; m. Marina Mae Floyd, May 18, 1974; children: Keenan Shane, Trevor Floyd, Bryce Bennett. BS in Edn., Ind. U., 1976; postgrad., Ohio No. U., 1976-77; JD cum laude, Ind. U., Indpls., 1979; diploma, Nat. Inst. for Trial Advocacy, Boulder, Colo., 1983. Bar: Ind. 1980, U.S. Dist. Ct. (so. dist.) Ind. 1980, U.S. Dist. Ct. (no. dist.) Ind. 1990, U.S. Ct. Appeals (7th cir.) 1992; cert. civil trial advocate. Law clk. Ind. Jud. Ctr., Indpls., 1977-78, Ind. Ct. Appeals, Indpls., 1978-80; atty. Goebel & Gill, Indpls., 1980-82, Montgomery, Elsner & Pardieck, Seymour, Ind., 1982-85, Pardieck, Gill & Vargo, Seymour, 1985—. With U.S. Navy, 1969-71. Fellow Roscoe Pound Found., Ind. Coll. of Trial Lawyers; mem. ABA, Ind. Bar Assn., Jackson County Bar Assn. (pres. 1987-88), Assn. Trial Lawyers Am. (in state del. 1996—), Ind. Trial Lawyers Assn. (bd. dirs. 1988—, exec. com. 1995—). Personal injury, Product liability. Home: 2993 N County Rd 400 E Seymour IN 47274 Office: Pardieck Gill & Vargo 100 N Chestnut St Seymour IN 47274-2102

**GILLAN, KAYLA J.,** lawyer. JD, U. Calif., Davis, 1984. Gen. counsel Calif. Pub. Employees Ret. Sys., Sacramento, 1996—. Named one of Top 50 Women Lawyers Nat. Law Jour., 1998. Pension, profit-sharing, and employee benefits, Labor. Office: Calif Pub Employees Ret Sys Lincoln Plz 400 P St Sacramento CA 95814-5345*

**GILLECE, JAMES PATRICK, JR.,** lawyer; b. Annapolis, Md., May 26, 1944; s. James Patrick and Erna Virginia (Barling) G.; m. Jane C. Szczepaniak, Apr. 24, 1971 (div. 1998); children: Jessica K., Jocelyn J., Jillian N., James P. III, Juliette A., John M. Szczepaniak -Gillece; m. Rosa Beza, Feb. 12, 1999. BA, LaSalle U., 1966; JD, U. Notre Dame, 1969. Bar: Md. 1969, U.S. Dist. Ct. Md. 1969, U.S. Ct. Appeals (4th cir.) 1972, U.S. Supreme Ct. 1974, U.S. Ct. Appeals (7th cir.) 1992, U.S. Ct. Appeals (8th and 11th cir.) 1995. Assoc. Piper & Marbury, Balt., 1969-77, ptnr., 1977-92, dir. poverty law program, 1971-72; ptnr. Miles & Stockbridge, Balt., 1992-93; prin. Miles and Stockbridge, Balt., 1994-98; ptnr. McGuire, Woods, Battle & Boothe, Balt., 1998—; cons. Mercy Hosp. Dietitians Program, Balt., 1986—. Bd. dirs. Balt. City Fair, 1984-88, Legal Aid Soc. Balt., 1984, Family Cirsis Ctr. Baltimore County, Inc., 1992-97, Everyman Theatre, 1995—; mem. law adv. coun. U. Notre Dame, 1983—; mem. Com. to Keep Supreme Bench Judges, Com. for Mayor Kurt Schmoke, 1987, Lawyers Com. for Jerry Brown, 1976; bd. trustees Everyman Theatre, 1996—. Mem. ABA, FBA, Am. Judicature Soc. (bd. dirs. 1988-90), Md. State Bar Assn. (Disting. Svc. award), Balt. Bar Assn., Notre Dame Law Assn. (pres. 1983-99, bd. dirs. 1977—, exec. coun., life mem.), U. Notre Dame Law Adv. Coun., Internat. Childbirth Edn. Assn. (cons. 1987-97). Democrat. Roman Catholic. E-mail: jpgillec@mwbb.com. FAX: 410-659-4484. General civil litigation, Labor, Criminal. Home: 3809 Greenway Baltimore MD 21218-1826 Office: McGuire Woods Battle & Boothe 7 Saint Paul St Ste 1000 Baltimore MD 21202-1671

**GILLEN, ARTHUR FITZPATRICK,** retired lawyer; b. So. St. Paul, Minn., Oct. 10, 1919; s. Leonard Peter and Cecelia (Koppy) G.; m. Louise Rosemary Powers, April 28, 1945; children: Robert, Anne Marie, Theodore, Janice, Peter, Mary. BS, U. Minn., 1941, JD, 1943. Bar: Minn., 1943. Sr. partner LeVander Gillen & Miller, PA Attys., So. St. Paul, Minn., 1943-95, LeVander Gillen & Miller PA Attys., So. St. Paul, 1943-95; bd. dirs., pres. Jr. C. of C., C. of C., and Kiwanis; bd. dirs. Gemstone Products Co. and Twin City Concrete, So. St. Paul, 1982—. State rep Minn. Legislature, 1943-51; state senator, Minn. Legislature, 1951-59. Named Man of Year, So. St. Paul Jr. C. of C., 1951. Named to hall of fame, So. St. Paul (Minn.) C. of C., 1992. Republican. Roman Catholic. Avocations: photography, computers, travel, autos. Home: 21043 N 124th Ave Sun City West AZ 85375-1953

**GILLEN, JAMES ROBERT,** lawyer, insurance company executive; b. N.Y.C., Nov. 14, 1937; s. James Matthew and Katharine Isabel (Fritz) G.; m. Rita Marie Wahleithner, June 15, 1963 (div. 1992); children: Jennifer Elaine, Nancy Louise, Paula Anne; m. Edda Lya Pacheco, Dec. 10, 1994. AB magna cum laude, Harvard U., 1959, LLB cum laude, 1965. Bar: N.Y. 1966, N.J. 1975. Assoc. firm White & Case, N.Y.C., 1965-72; v.p., assoc. gen. counsel Prudential Ins. Co. Am., Newark, 1972-77, sr. v.p., assoc. gen. counsel, 1977-80, sr. v.p. pub. affairs, 1980-84, sr. v.p., gen. counsel, 1984-98; mem. bd. trustees Columbia Inst. Investor Project, 1991-97; legal adv. com. New York Stock Exch., 1986-89. Trustee United Way Essex and West Hudson Counties, 1981-90, pres., 1986-88; mem. Mendham Twp. (N.J.) Bd. Edn., 1981-82; trustee N.J. Shakespeare Festival, 1991-99, Mendham Twp. Libr., 1979-82; dir., chmn. Neurol. Inst. N.J., 1998—. Lt. (j.g.) USN, 1959-62. Mem. ABA, N.J. Bar Assn., Assn. Life Ins. Counsel, Harvard Club (N.Y.C.), Morris Country Golf Club. General corporate, Finance, Insurance. Home: 72 Washington Valley Rd Morristown NJ 07960-3332

**GILLESPIE, GEORGE JOSEPH, III,** lawyer; b. N.Y.C., May 18, 1930; s. George Joseph Jr. and Dorothy Elizabeth (McKenna) G.; m. Eileen Tracy Dealy, July 27, 1955; children: Gail Gillespie Garcia, John D., Myles D., Eileen G. Fahey. A.B. magna cum laude, Georgetown U., 1952; LL.B. magna cum laude, Harvard U., 1955. Bar: N.Y. 1957. Assoc. Cravath, Swaine & Moore, N.Y.C., 1956-62; ptnr. Cravath, Swaine & Moore, 1963—; bd. dirs. Washington Post Co., White Mountains Holdings Inc. Trustee, treas., John M. Olin Found.; pres., trustee Pinkerton Found., Arthur Ross Found., William S. Paley Found., ; bd. dirs., sec. Mus. TV and Radio; trustee Mt. Sinai/NYU Med. Ctr., chmn. bd. dirs. Madison Square Boys and Girls Club; bd. dirs., chmn. emeritus Nat. Multiple Sclerosis Soc. Frederick Sheldon traveling fellow Harvard U., 1955-56. Century Assn., Winged Foot Golf Club, Prouts Neck Country Club, Falmouth Country Club, Double Eagle Club, Am. Yacht Club, Portland Country Club. Republican. Roman Catholic. Office: Cravath Swaine & Moore Worldwide Pla 825 8th Ave Fl 38 New York NY 10019-7475

**GILLESPIE, SAMUEL H., III,** lawyer, oil company executive. BA, Middlebury Coll., 1966; JD, Vanderbilt U., 1972. Bar: N.Y. 1973. Assoc. Milbank, Tweed, Hadley & McCloy, 1972-82, counsel, 1982-85; asst. gen. counsel Mobil Corp., Mobil South, 1985-87; asst. gen. counsel M&R divsn. Mobil Corp., 1987-89, asst. gen. counsel Exploration and Producing divsn., 1990-94; v.p., gen. cousnel Mobil Oil Corp., Fairfax, Va., 1994—, now sr. v.p., gen. counsel. Office: Mobil Oil Corp 3225 Gallows Rd Fairfax VA 22037-0002*

**GILLETTE, W. MICHAEL,** state supreme court justice; b. Seattle, Dec. 29, 1941; s. Elton George and Hazel Irene (Hand) G.; m. Susan Dandy Marmaduke, 1989; children: Kevin, Saima, Ali, Quinton. AB cum laude in German, Polit. Sci., Whitman Coll., 1963; LLB, Harvard U., 1966. Bar: Oreg. 1966, U.S. Dist. Ct. Oreg. 1966, U.S. Ct. Appeals (9th cir.) 1966, Samoa 1969, U.S. Supreme Ct. 1970, U.S. Dist. Ct. Vt. 1973. Assoc. Rives & Rogers, Portland, Oreg., 1966-67; dep. dist. atty. Multnomah County, Portland, 1967-69; asst. atty. gen. Govt. of Am. Samoa, 1969-71, State of Oreg., Salem, 1971-77; judge Oreg. Ct. Appeals, Salem, 1977-86; assoc. justice Oreg. Supreme Ct., Salem, 1986—. Avocation: officiating basketball. *

**GILLIAM, EARL B.,** federal judge; b. Clovis, N.Mex., Aug. 17, 1931; s. James Earl and Lula Mae G.; m. Rebecca L. Prater; children: Earl Kenneth, Derrick James. B.A., Calif. State U., San Diego, 1953; J.D., Hastings Coll. Law, 1957. Bar: Calif. 1957. Dep. dist. atty. San Diego, 1957-62; judge San Diego Mcpl. Ct., 1963-74, Superior Ct. Calif., San Diego County, 1975-80; judge U.S. Dist. Ct. (so. dist.) Calif., San Diego, 1980-93, sr. judge, 1993—; head Trial Practice Dept. Western State U. Law Sch., San Diego, 1969—. Recipient Trial Judge of Yr. award San Diego County Trial Lawyers Assn., 1981. Office: US Dist Ct 5195 US Cthouse 940 Front St San Diego CA 92101-8994

**GILLIAM, STEVEN PHILIP, SR.,** lawyer; b. L.A., Feb. 5, 1949; s. Robert Walter Gilliam and Carlene (Fincher) Durkee; m. Susan Lynch, Nov. 7, 1971; children: Steven Philip Jr., Laney Evelyn. BBA in Econs., U. Ga., 1971, JD cum laude, 1974. Bar: Ga. 1974, U.S. Dist. Ct. Ga., U.S. Ct. Appeals (5th and 11th cirs.) 1974, U.S. Supreme Ct. 1980. Ptnr. Smith, Smith & Frost, Gainesville, Ga., 1974-83, Smith, Frost. Gilliam & Williams, 1983-86, Smith, Gilliam & Williams, 1986-97; vice-chair Gainesville Hall '96, 1993—; mem. U.S. Dist. Ct. Magistrate Selection Com., 1998. Pres. United Way of Hall County, Gainesville, 1984; chmn. Gainesville Coll. Found., 1987, Rehab. Industries of N.E. Ga., Gainesville, 1988-90, Hall County Needs Assessment, 1990-91; bd. visitors Raban Gap Nacoochee Sch. Named Hall County Young Man of Yr., 1985, 96, Olympic Cmty. Hero Torchbearer, 1996, Man of Yr. Rotary, 1996. Fellow Lawyers Found. Ga., Atlanta Lawyers Club; mem. ABA, Ga. Bar Assn. (chairperson professionalism com. 1996—), Northeastern Bar Assn. (pres. 1982), Def. Rsch. Inst., Assn. Def. Trial Attys., Gainesville-Hall C. of C. (v.p. 1987-89, chmn. 1998-99, Silver Shovel award 1986), Leadership Ga. (trustee 1989-91), Chattahoochee Country Club (pres. 1989), Ga. Bulldog Club, Gridiron Secret Soc. Presbyterian. Avocations: backpacking, hunting, Kayaking, golf, flyfishing. Banking, Workers' compensation, Personal injury. Home: 1450 Heritage Rd Gainesville GA 30501-1247 Office: Smith Gilliam & Williams 301 Green St NE Ste 200 Gainesville GA 30501-3362

**GILLIG, JOHN STEPHENSON,** lawyer; b. Lexington, Ky., May 27, 1951. Bar: Ky. 1976, U.S. Dist. Ct. (ea. and we. dist.) Ky. 1984, U.S. Ct. Appeals (6th cir.) 1984, U.S. Supreme Ct. 1984. Law clk. Ky. Supreme Ct., Frankfort, 1976-77; policy analyst Congl. Sunbelt Coun., U.S. Ho. of Reps., Washington, 1981-83; asst. atty. gen. Ky. Atty. Gen., Frankfort, 1984-95, environ. spl. coun., 1992-95; counsel to spkr. Spkr.'s Office, Ky. Ho. of Reps., Frankfort, 1995—; mem. criminal rules adv. com. Ky. Supreme Ct., Frankfort, Ky., 1988-92, task force on ethics, 1989-91; mem. legis. task force on sentencing Legis. Rsch. Commn., Frankfort, 1990-91; commr. Ky. Emergency Response Commn., Frankfort, 1995, Nat. Conf. of Commissioners on Uniform Senate Laws, 1997—. Author: Kentucky Post-Conviction Manual, 1990; contbr. articles to profl. jours. Officer, bd. dirs. Ky. YMCA Youth Assn., Frankfort, 1987-94, 96—. Paul Harris fellow Rotary Internat., 1990; recipient Disting. Svc. award Ky. Commonwealth Attys. Assn., 1992. Methodist. Avocations: state and local history, naval history. Office: Office Spkr of the House State Capitol 700 Capitol Ave Ste 309 Frankfort KY 40601-3415

**GILLIGAN, KEVIN MICHAEL,** lawyer; b. Glens Falls, N.Y., Mar. 12, 1950; s. Stephen V. and Joan Marie (Rogers) G.; m. Eileen Dombroski, Dec. 23, 1953; children: Adeline, Louis, Min. BA, Hobart Coll., Geneva, N.Y., 1972; JD, Syracuse U., 1979. Bar: N.Y. 1980, U.S. Dist. Ct. (no. and we. dists.) N.Y. 1980, U.S. Supreme Ct. 1991. Ins. underwriter Gen. Accident Ins., Syracuse, N.Y., 1972-76; ptnr. Costello, Cooney & Fearon, Syracuse, 1979—. Onondaga County legislator, Syracuse, 1992-93; chair grievance rev. bd. Town of LaFayette, N.Y., 1996-98; mem. Air Force Acad. Adv. Com., Hon. James T. Walsh, M.C., 25th Congl. Dist., N.Y., 1988—; dir. Vietnam Vets. Leadership Program, 1990—; mem. Onodaga County (N.Y.) Planning Fedn., 1985—. Mem. Ancient Order of Hibernians in Am. Republicn. Roman Catholic. Environmental, Municipal (including bonds), Land use and zoning (including planning). Home: 2739 Summer Ridge Rd La Fayette NY 13084-9727 Office: Costello Cooney & Fearon Salina Pl 205 S Salina St Ste 400 Syracuse NY 13202-1327

**GILLIGAN, MARY ANN,** law librarian; b. Elizabeth, N.J., June 20, 1956; d. John Francis and Margaret Mary (Boyle) G. BA, Park Coll., 1977; MLS, Rutgers U., 1980. Asst. Time Inc., N.Y.C., 1981-83; law libr. Chubb & Son, Inc., Warren, N.J., 1985, Pennie & Edmonds LLP, N.Y.C., 1985—. Mem. ABA, Am. Assn. Law Librs., Spl. Librs. Assn., Law Libr. Assn. Greater N.Y. (bd. dirs. 1998—). Democrat. Roman Catholic. Avocations: crafts, singing. Office: Pennie & Edmonds LLP 1155 Ave Of The Americas New York NY 10036-2711

**GILLIKIN, VIRGINIA,** lawyer; b. Providence, July 30, 1952; d. Durwood Earl and Theresa Marie (Goushakjian) G. BA cum laude, Providence Coll., 1974; MA, MEd, Columbia U., 1976; JD, Bklyn. Law Sch., 1982. Bar: N.Y. 1983, U.S. Dist. Ct. (so. and ea. dists.) N.Y. 1988. Assoc. Newman, Tannenbaum, Helpern, Syracuse & Hirschtritt, N.Y.C., 1982-83; assoc. Martin, Clearwater & Bell, N.Y.C., 1983-86, Berman, Paley, Goldstein & Berman, N.Y.C., 1987-88, Brody & Fabiani, N.Y.C., 1988-89; pvt. practice N.Y.C., 1989—. Mem. N.Y. State Bar Assn., N.Y.C. Lawyers Assn. Avocations: body building, sports, nutrition. General civil litigation, Personal injury. Office: 200 E 27th St Ste 6T New York NY 10016-9224

**GILLILAND, JOHN CAMPBELL, II,** lawyer; b. Bellefonte, Pa., June 4, 1945; s. John Campbell and Miriam Ruth (Forsythe) G.; m. Karen Gardner, Nov. 2, 1997; children: Jennifer, John, David. BA, Pa. State U., 1967; JD Georgetown U., 1971. Bar: Pa. 1971, Ind. 1979, Ky. 1991, Ohio 1992. Ptnr., McQuaide, Blasko & Brown, Inc., State College, Pa., 1974-79, DeFur, Voran, Hanley, Radcliff & Reed, Muncie, Ind., 1979-90; prin. Gilliland & Assocs., Covington, Ky., 1991—; lectr. econs. dept. Ball State U., Muncie. Bd. dirs. United Way Delaware County, v.p., 1983-85; bd. dirs. Vis. Nurses Assn.; v.p. Muncie chpt. ARC, 1983-85; bd. govs. Friends of Bracken Library. Served to capt. U.S. Army, 1971-72. Fellow, Rotary Found., Queens Coll., Belfast, Ireland, 1968-69. Mem. ABA, Ind. Bar Assn., Ky. Bar Assn., Ohio Bar Assn., Am. Heath Lawyers Assn., Ind. Soc. Hosp. Attys. (chmn. 1989), Pa. Soc. Hosp. Attys. (pres. 1978-79), East Central Ind. Pers. Assn. (bd. dirs.). Republican. Presbyterian. Health, Labor, General corporate. Home: 38 Kathryn Ave Florence KY 41042-1536 Office: 211 Grandview Dr Ste 205 Covington KY 41017-2726

**GILLIN, MALVIN JAMES, JR.,** lawyer; b. Norfolk, Va., Apr. 28, 1946; s. Malvin James Gillin and Jacqueline A. (Howell) Kyslowsky; m. Arleen Elizabeth Gillin: children: Christine Lynn, Malvin James III, Craig Dean. BA, U. Hawaii, 1969; JD, U. Denver, 1974. Bar: Hawaii 1975, U.S. Dist. Ct. Hawaii 1975, U.S. Ct. Appeals (9th cir.) 1983, U.S. Supreme Ct. 1983, Colo. 1984. Dep. atty. gen. State of Hawaii, Honolulu, 1975-76; pvt. practice law Honolulu, 1976—. Mem. ATLA, Hawaii Bar Assn., Hawaii Assn. Criminal Def. Lawyers (pres. 1998—), Nat. Assn. Criminal Def. Lawyers. Roman Catholic. Avocations: scuba diving, sailing, marathon running. Personal injury, Criminal. Office: 733 Bishop St Ste 1290 Honolulu HI 96813-4002

**GILLINGHAM, STEPHEN THOMAS,** financial planner; b. St. Paul, May 30, 1944; s. Thomas Elmwood and Barbara Alice (Sickles) G.; m. Carolyn Jean Alvey, June 5, 1976; children: Kenneth, Brett. BA, Juniata Coll., 1966; JD, The George Washington U., 1969. Bar: Va. 1971; CFP. Tax specialist Price Waterhouse, Washington, 1969-71; tax law specialist IRS, Washington, 1971-77; sr. tax lawyer Internat. Paper Co., N.Y.C., 1977-83; dir. tax rsch. and planning The Singer Co., Stanford, Conn., 1983-88; tax counsel Am. Cyanamid Co., Wayne, N.J., 1988-95; fin. planner The Thompson Group, Inc., White Plains, N.Y., 1995—; lectr. World Trade Inst., 1980-90. Contbg. editor Tax Lawyer, 1984-88. Trustees coun. Juniata Coll. With U.S. Army, 1970-75. Named one of Outstanding Young Men in Am., Jaycees, 1979. Mem. Va. Bar Assn., N.J. Tax Group (chmn. 1991-95), Tax Execs. Inst., Inst. Cert. Fin. Planners. Avocations: golf, swimming, hiking. Home: 4 Northway Hartsdale NY 10530-2109 Office: The Thompson Group Inc 244 Westchester Ave White Plains NY 10604-2907

**GILLIO, VICKIE ANN,** lawyer; b. Chgo., May 8, 1948; d. Rocco Robert and Viva Gene (Sherover) G. BA cum laude, St. Norbert Coll., 1969; JD, U. Ill., 1972. Bar: Pa. 1974, Ill. 1975, U.S. Dist. Ct. (southeast dist.) Pa. 1975, U.S. Dist. Ct. (no. dist.) Ill. 1978. Atty. Lehigh Valley Legal Svcs., Easton, Pa., 1974-78; with office of spl. counsel U.S. Merit Sys. Protection Bd., 1983-85; atty. in charge Chgo. field office Ill. Civil Svc. Commn., 1983-85, adminstrv. hearing officer; gen. counsel Waubonsee C.C., Sugar Grove, Ill., 1985-88, Kusper & Raucci, Chartered, Chgo., 1988-92; prin. Kusper & Raucci, Chartered, 1990-92, Gillio & Assocs., Chgo., 1992—; adj. prof. negotiations Chgo. Kent Coll. Law-Ill. Inst. Tech., 1987—; adj. prof. pub. law MPA program at Ill. Inst. Tech. Editor Newsletter of the Community College Consortium, 1990-92. Mem. ABA (state and local govt. collective bargaining and employment sect.), Ill. State Bar Assn. (co-editor newsletter edn.-law sect. 1994-95, labor employment law com., vice-chair edn. law sect.), Chgo. Bar Assn., Nat. Assn. Coll. and Univ. Attys. Administrative and regulatory, Education and schools, Civil rights. Office: Gillio & Assocs Willoughby Towers 8 S Michigan Ave Ste 810 Chicago IL 60603-3309

**GILLIS, GEOFFREY LAWRENCE,** lawyer; b. Grand Rapids, MI, July 23, 1944; s. Lawrence Robert and Marie (Beyne) G.; m. Susan Stephanie Koss, May 2, 1970; children: Margaret Elizabeth, Elizabeth Anne. BA, U. Mich., 1966, JD, 1969. Bar: Mich. 1969, U.S. Dist. Ct. (ea. and we. dists.) Mich., U.S. Ct. Appeals (6th cir.). Ptnr. Wheeler, Upham, Bryant & Uhl, Grand Rapids, 1975-82; v.p. Wheeler Upham, P.C., Grand Rapids, 1982—; lectr. Inst. for CLE, 1993, 95, 98. V.p. Ryerson Libr. Found., Grand Rapids; pres. Grand Rapids Montessori Soc., 1985-91; dir., v.p. Heritage Hill Assn., Grand Rapids, 1970-83; dir. Grand Rapids Hist. Soc., 1983. Avocations: sailing, bird hunting, history. General civil litigation, Contracts commercial, Transportation. Home: 33 College Ave SE Grand Rapids MI 49503-4401 Office: Wheeler Upham PC 40 Pearl St NW Ste 200 Grand Rapids MI 49503-3028

**GILLIS, JOHN LAMB, JR.,** lawyer; b. St. Louis, June 13, 1939. Student, Brown U.; AB, Washington U., 1965; LLB, Stanford U., 1968. Bar: Mo. 1968. Ptnr., chmn. securities dept. Armstrong Teasdale LLP, St. Louis. Securities, Finance, Mergers and acquisitions. Address: Armstrong Teasdale LLP 1 Metropolitan Sq Saint Louis MO 63102-2733

**GILLIS, RICHARD MOFFITT, JR.,** lawyer; b. Phila., Oct. 30, 1934; s. Richard Moffitt Gillis and Amy Weise; m. Carol Ann Dickens, July 25, 1964 (div. May 1994); children: Richard M. III, Andrew D., Alison E. BA in English, Wesleyan U., Middletown, Conn., 1956; postgrad., GM Inst. Tech., Flint, Mich., 1957; LLB, U. Pa., 1967. Bar: Pa. 1967, U.S. Dist. Ct. Pa. 1967, U.S. Tax Ct. 1967. Ptnr. Harris, Gillis & Davis, Phila., 1967-79; assoc. Strong, Barnett, Hayes & Hamilton, Phila., 1979-85; sr. clk. Phila. Orphans' Ct., Ct. of Common Pleas, Phila., 1980-85; pvt. practice Phila., 1985—. Co-author: Fiduciary Accounting Pennsylvania Bar Institute, 1989, 93. With U.S. Army, 1957-60. Mem. Phila. Estate Planning Coun. (dir.), Nat. Counter Intelligence Corps Assn. (v.p. mil. liaison 1989-98) Phila. Bar Assn. (environ. law com. 1996—), Rotary. Republican. Avocations: photography, tennis, swimming, sailing, biking. Estate planning, Probate, Personal income taxation. Home: 870 N 28th St Apt 203 Philadelphia PA 19130-1729 Office: 42 S 15th St Philadelphia PA 19102-2218

**GILLMAR, STANLEY FRANK,** lawyer; b. Honolulu, Aug. 17, 1935; s. Stanley Eric and Ruth (Scudder) g.; m. Constance Joan Sedgwick; children: Sara Tamsin, Amy Katherine. AB cum laude with high honors, Brown U., 1957; LLB, Harvard U., 1963. Bar: Calif. 1963. Ptnr. Graham & James, San Francisco, 1970-92; of counsel Mackenzie & Albritton, 1993—. Co-author: How To Be An Importer and Pay For Youth World Travels, 1979; co-pub.: Travelers Guide to Importing, 1980. Sec. Calif. Coun. Internat. Trade, 1973-92; mem. Mayor San Francisco Adv. Coun. Econ. Devel., 1976-82; mem. Title IX Loan Bd., 1982-96, sec. 1986-92; dir. The San Francisco Ministry to Nursing Homes, 1992-94, treas., 1992-94; dir. Inverness Found., 1995—, pres., 1996—; dir. Marin Agrl. Land Trust, 1999—. Served with USNR, 1957-60. Mem. ABA, Calif. State Bar, Bar Assn. San Francisco, Bankers Club (San Francisco), Villa Taverna Club, Inverness Yacht Club. Real property, Private international, Contracts commercial. Office: One Post St Ste 500 San Francisco CA 94104

**GILMAN, DEREK,** lawyer; b. Springfield, Mass., Sept. 24, 1961; s. John Richard and Julia Ann (Streeter) G.; m. Deborah Jane Furletti, May 1, 1987; 1 child, Julian Philip. BS, U.S. Mil. Acad., 1983; MA, Cambridge U., 1990; JD, U. Conn., 1992; LLM, NYU, 1997. Bar: Conn. 1992. Assoc. Curtis Brinckerhoff & Barrett P.C., Stamford, Conn., 1993—. Assoc. editor Conn. Law Rev., 1991-92. Capt. U.S. Army, 1983-88. Estate planning, Taxation, general, Probate. Office: Curtis Brinckerhoff Barrett 666 Summer St Ste 4 Stamford CT 06901-1416

**GILMAN, RONALD LEE,** judge; b. Memphis, Oct. 16, 1942; s. Seymour and Rosalind (Kuzin) G.; m. Betsy Dunn, June 11, 1966; children: Laura M., Sherry I. BS, MIT, 1964; JD cum laude, Harvard U., 1967. Bar: Tenn. 1967, U.S. Supreme Ct. 1971. Mem. Farris, Mathews, Gilman, Branan & Hellen, Memphis, 1967-97; judge U.S. Ct. Appeals (6th cir.), 1997—; judge Tenn. Ct. of Judiciary, 1979-87; lectr. trial advocacy U. Memphis Law Sch., 1980-97. Contbr. articles to profl. jours. Regional chmn. ednl. coun. MIT, 1968-88; bd. dirs. Memphis Jewish Home, 1984-87, Chickasaw coun. Boy Scouts Am., 1993—; mem. Leadership Memphis. Recipient Sam A. Myar Jr. Meml. award for outstanding svc.scs to legal profession and cmty., 1981. Mem. ABA (ho. of dels. 1990-97), Am. Law Inst., Am. Judicature Soc., Am. Coll. Trust and Estate Counsel, Memphis Bar Assn. (pres. 1987), Tenn. Bar Assn. (spkr. ho. of dels. 1985-87, pres. 1990-91), 6th Cir. Jud. Conf. (life), Am. Arbitration Assn. (mem. large, complex case panel 1993-97). Democrat. Jewish. Office: Fed Bldg Ste 1176 167 N Main St Memphis TN 38103-1816

**GILMAN, SCOTT,** lawyer; b. Lake Success, N.Y., Oct. 17, 1960; m. Robin Lisa Green, Oct. 26, 1997. BBA, Hofstra U., 1983; JD, Touro Law Sch., Huntington, N.Y., 1988. Bar: N.Y. 1989, N.J. 1989, Fla. 1994, U.S. Dist. Ct. N.J. 1989, U.S. Dist. Ct. (ea. and so. dists.) N.Y. 1993, U.S. Ct. Appeals 1994, U.S. Mil. Ct. Appeals 1994, U.S. Supreme Ct. 1994. Mng. atty. Friedlander, Gaines, Cohen & Rosenberg, N.Y.C., 1989-90; trial atty. DC 37 MELS, N.Y.C., 1990—; bd. dirs., counsel Rapid Abstract, Inc., Levittown, N.Y., 1996—; exec. sec. FFR/MELSSA-AFSCME, N.Y.C., 1990—; arbitrator Small Claims Ct. of City of N.Y., 1996—; hearing officer, tax assessment rev. Supreme Ct. of State of N.Y. Vol., Project HOPE, 1995—. Recipient Pro Bono award N.Y. County Lawyers Assn., 1997. Avocation: travel. Personal injury, Bankruptcy, General civil litigation. Office: 225 Broadway Rm 1201 New York NY 10007-3001

**GILMAN, SHELDON GLENN,** lawyer; b. Cleve., July 20, 1943. BBA, Ohio U., 1965; JD, Case Western Res. U., 1967. Bar: Ohio 1967, Ky. 1971, Ind. 1982, Fla. 1984, D.C. 1985, Tenn. 1985, U.S. Supreme Ct., 1987. Mem. staff accts. tax dept. Arthur Andersen & Co., Cleve., 1967-68; assoc. Handmaker, Weber & Meyer, Louisville, 1971-74, ptnr., 1974-83; ptnr. Barnett & Alagia, Louisville, 1984-87; ptnr. Lynch, Cox, Gilman & Mahan, P.S.C., 1987—; gen. counsel Louisville Assn. Life Underwriters, 1977, 78, 90; adj. prof. law U. of Louisville Sch. of Law. Bd. dirs., chmn. Louisville Minority Bus. Resource Ctr., 1975-80; pres. Congregation Adath Jeshurun, 1986-88; bd. dirs., v.p., sec. Louisville Orch., 1982-85; bd. dirs. City of Devondale (Ky.), 1976, United Synagogue of Cons. Judaism, N.Y., 1989—, also pres. Ohio Valley region. With JAGC, AUS, 1968-71. Mem. Ky. Bar Assn. (ethics com. 1982—, ethics hotline com. 1990), Louisville Employee Benefit Council (pres. 1980). Pension, profit-sharing, and employee benefits, Probate, Corporate taxation. Office: Lynch Cox Gilman & Mahan 500 Meidinger Tower Louisville KY 40202-3473

**GILMOOR, RICHARD H.,** judge; b. Sacramento, Sept. 7, 1941; m. Janet Ann Walker, June 15, 1963; children: Dana, Donald. BA, U. Calif., Berkeley, 1963; JD, Hastings Coll. Law, San Francisco, 1968. Supervising dep. dist. atty. Dist. Atty.'s Office, Sacramento, 1970-92; mcpl. ct. judge Sacramento Cts., 1992-94, superior ct. judge, 1994—; adj. prof. U. of the Pacific, Sacramento, 1986-91. Judge peer ct. Sacramento Juvenile Ct., 1998—. Lt. (j.g.) USN, 1963-65. Named Pros. of the Yr. Calif. Dist. Atty.'s Assn., 1991. Mem. Anthony M. Kennedy Inn of Ct. (mem. emeritus 1995—). Office: Sacramento Cts 720 9th St Sacramento CA 95814-1311

**GILMORE, HORACE WELDON,** federal judge; b. Columbus, Ohio, Apr. 4, 1918; s. Charles Thomas and Lucille (Weldon) G.; m. Mary Hays, June 20, 1942; children—Lindsay Gilmore Feinberg. A.B., U. Mich., 1939, J.D., 1942. Bar: Mich. bar 1946. Law clk. U.S. Ct. Appeals, 1946-47; practiced in Detroit, 1947-51; spl. asst. U.S. atty., Detroit, 1951-52; mem. Mich. Bd. Tax Appeals, 1954; dep. atty. gen. State of Mich., 1955-56; circuit judge 3d Jud. Circuit, Detroit, 1956-80; judge U.S. Dist. Ct. (ea. dist.) Mich., 1980—; now sr. judge U.S. Dist. Ct. (ea. dist.) Mich., Detroit; adj. prof. law Wayne State U. Law Sch., 1966-82; lectr. law U. Mich. Law Sch., 1969-90; faculty Nat. Coll. State Judiciary, 1966-83; mem. Mich. Jud. Tenure Commn., 1969-76; chmn. Mich. Com. to Revise Criminal Code, 1965-82, Mich. Com. to Revise Criminal Procedure, 1971-79; trustee Inst. for Ct. Mgmt. Author: Michigan Civil Procedure Before Trial, 2d edit, 1975; contbr. numerous articles to legal jours. Served with USNR, 1942-46. Mem. ABA, State Bar Mich., Am. Judicature Soc., Am. Law Inst., Nat. Conf. State Trial Judges. Office: US Dist Ct 867 US Courthouse 231 W Lafayette Blvd Detroit MI 48226-2700

**GILMORE, JAMES STUART, III,** governor; b. Richmond, Va., Oct. 6, 1949; s. James Stuart, Jr. and Margaret Kandle G. BA, U. Va., 1971, JD, 1977. Atty. Harris, Tuck, Freasier & Johnson, 1977-80, Benedetti, Gilmore, Warthen & Dalton, 1984-87; commonwealth's atty. Henrico County, Va., 1987-93; atty. gen. Commonwealth of Va., 1993-97; pntr. LeClair Ryan, Richmond, Va., 1997; gov. Commonwealth of Va., 1998—; alt. del. Rep. Nat. Conv., 1976; chmn. Henrico County Rep. Com., 1982-85. With U.S. Army, 1971-74. Mem. Nat. Dist. Atty. Assn., Va. Bar Assn., Va. Trial Lawyers Assn., Va. Commonwealt Attys. Assn. Methodist. Office: Office of Gov State Capitol Bldg 3rd Fl Richmond VA 23219

**GILMORE, JEAN LINDA,** court administrator; b. Jersey City, Mar. 13, 1948; d. John Paul and Jean Claire (Bushman) Doffont; m. Bruce Martin Gilmore, Sept. 6, 1969 (div. Sept. 1990); 1 child, Robert B. Grad. high sch., Kearny, N.J. Cert. mcpl. ct. adminstr., N.J. Loan clk. First Nat. Bank, Kearny, 1974-81; mcpl. ct. adminstr. Town of Harrison, N.J., 1981—. Charter mem., past officer Harrison Cancer League, 1973—. Mem. NAFE, Nat. Assn. Ct. Mgmt., N.J. Ct. Adminstrs. Assn. N.J., Nat. Notary Assn. Avocation: travel. Office: Harrison Mcpl Ct 318 Harrison Ave Harrison NJ 07029-1752

**GILMORE, VANESSA D.,** federal judge; b. St. Albans, N.Y., Oct. 26, 1956. BS, Hampton U., 1977; JD, U. Houston, 1981. Bar: Tex. 1982, U.S. Ct. Appeals (5th cir.), U.S. Dist. Ct. (so. dist.) Tex. Fashion buyer Foley's Dept. Store, 1977-79; ptnr. Vickery, Kilbride, Gilmore & Vickery, Houston, 1981-85, 86-94; atty. Sue Schecter & Assocs., Houston, 1985-86; judge U.S. Dist. Ct. (So. dist.) Tex., Houston, 1994—; spkr. ATLA, San Diego, 1990, ABA, Atlanta, 1991, N.Y.C., 1993, Legislative Tex., Austin, 1992, Hampton U. Alumni Assn., Dallas, 1992, Laredo Bus. and Profl. Women's Assn., 1993, XI Ann. Border Gov.'s Conf., Monterrey, Mex., 1993, Gov.'s Bus. Devel. Coun., Ausitn, 1993, Tex. A&M U., 1993, State Bar of Tex., Austin, 1993, Houston Bus. Coun., 1993, Minority Enterprise Devel. Week, Houston, 1993, Holman St. Bapt. Ch., 1994, Greater Houston Women's Found., 1994, The Kinkaid Sch., 1995, So. Meth. U., Dallas, 1996, South Tex. Coll. of Law, 1996, among others. Contbr. articles to profl. jours. Bd. dirs. Houston Ballet, Tex. So. Univ. Found., Neighborhood Recovery Community Redevel. Corp., 1992-95; chair African Am. Art Adv. Assn., Mus. Fine Arts; mem. scv. acad. nominations bd. Rep. Jack Fields, Tex., 1993, 94; active Texans for NAFTA; mem. Tex. Dept. Commerce, 1991-94, chairperson, 1992-94; mem. adv. bd. St. Joseph's Hosp.; mem. Leadership Tex. Named One of Houston's Black Achievers, Human Enrichment of Life Program, 1989; recipient Citizen of the Month award Houston Defender, 1990, YWCA award, 1991, Austin Met. Resource Bus. Ctr. award, 1991, Houston Bus. and Profl. Men's Club award, 1992, Disting. Svc. award Nat. Black MBA Assn., 1994, Cmty. Svc. award Holman St. Bapt. Ch., 1994. Mem. ABA, NAACP (chair chs. and orgns. com. Freedom Fund banquets 1989-93), ATLA, Am. Leadership Forum, Tex. Trial Lawyers Assn., Tex. Lyceum Assn., Houston Bar Assn., Houston Lawyers Assn., U. Houston Law Alumni (bd. dirs. 1993—), W.J. Durham Legal Soc., Links, Inc. (Mo. chpt., chair LEAD substance abuse and teen pregnancy prevention program 1990-91). Office: US Courthouse 515 Rusk Ave Rm 9513 Houston TX 77002-2605

**GILROY, TRACY ANNE HUNSAKER,** lawyer; b. St. Louis, Aug. 13, 1959; d. Raymond Thomas Hunsaker and Dorothy Jayne (Hickman) Hunsaker Reilly. BA, U. Dayton, 1981; JD, St. Louis U., 1984. Bar: Mo. 1984, Ill. 1985. Atty. Mo. State Hwy. and Transp. Dept., St. Louis, 1984-89; of counsel Draheim & Pranschke, St. Louis, 1989-94; pvt. practice The Gilroy Law Firm, St. Louis, 1994—. Mem. ABA (bar svcs. standing com., reporter The Affiliate, bd. dirs. LPM solo divsn.), Mo. Bar Assn. (chair eminent domain com., legis. com., bd. govs. 1998—), St. Louis Bar Found. (pres. 1998-99), St. Louis Met. Bar Assn. (pres. 1997-98, chair young lawyers sect. 1993, chair legis. com. 1985-87, chair, vice-chair, chair trial sect., chair social com., chair auction com., media com.), Woman Lawyers Assn. (mem.-at-large, chair legis. com. 1984-87, sec. 1987), Lawyers Assn., Assn. Trial Lawyers Am. Avocations: golf, skiing, bicycling, writing, painting. General civil litigation, Condemnation, Real property. Office: Gilroy Law Firm 1610 Des Peres Rd # 300 Saint Louis MO 63131-1813

**GILSTER, PETER STUART,** lawyer; b. Carbondale, Ill., Dec. 10, 1939; s. John Sprigg and Ruth E. (Robinson) G.; m. Carol Clevenger, June 30, 1968; children: John F., Thomas B. BS, U. Ill., 1962, JD, 1965. Bar: Ill. 1965, Mo. 1968, U.S. Dist. Ct. (ea. dist.) Mo. 1969, U.S. Patent Office 1970, U.S. Ct. Appeals (8th cir.) 1978, U.S. Supreme Ct. 1978, U.S. Ct. Customs and Patent Appeals 1980, U.S. Ct. Appeals (fed. cir.) 1983. Assoc. Koenig, Senniger, Powers & Leavitt, St. Louis, 1967-71, ptnr., 1971-72; patent atty. Monsanto Co., St. Louis, 1972-77; ptnr. Kalish & Glister, St. Louis, 1977-96, Peper, Martin, Jensen, Michael and Hetiage, St. Louis, 1997-98, Blackwell, Sanders, Peper Martin, LLC, St. Louis, 1998-99; head patent sect., chair internat. practice group Kalish & Gilster Intellectual Property Group, St. Louis; officer Greensfelder, Hemker & Gale, P.C. Intellectual Property Grp., 1999—; seminar lectr. U. Mo.-St. Louis, 1976-83. Capt. USAR, 1966-67. Decorated Army Commendation medal. Mem. ABA, IEEE, AAAS, Am. Intellectual Property Law Assn., Ill. Bar Assn., Mo. Bar Assn. (patent, trademark, and copyright com.), Lawyer Pilots Bar Assn., Fed. Cir. Bar Assn., Bar Assn. Met. St. Louis (chmn. patent sect. 1975-76), Assoc. Pilots St. Louis (v.p. 1977-83, bd. dirs. 1975-87), World Affairs Coun. St. Louis, Soc. Hispano-Am. St. Louis (bd. dirs. 1993-96, treas. 1994-96), Media Club St. Louis, Phi Delta Phi. Patent, Trademark and copyright, Federal civil litigation.

**GILSTRAP, JAMES RODNEY,** lawyer, judge; b. Pensacola, Fla., May 1, 1957; s. Joseph C. and Wynona Frances (James) G.; m. Sherry Sullivan, June 18, 1977; children: Lauren Gray, Stephen Sullivan. BA magna cum laude, Baylor U., 1978, JD, 1981. Bar: Tex. 1981, U.S. Dist. Ct. (ea. dist.) Tex. 1982, U.S. Ct. Appeals (5th cir.) 1982). Atty., assoc. Abney, Baldwin & Searcy, Marshall, Tex., 1981-84; ptnr. Smith & Gilstrap, Marshall, 1984—; county judge Harrison County, Tex., 1989—; instr. East Tex. Bapt. U., Marshall, 1982-86; bd. dirs. Smith Steel Casting Co., Marshall, 1992—. Pres. Trinity Episcopal Sch., Marshall, 1991-92; trustee The Davidson Found., Marshall, 1992—. Recipient Pres.'s award Harrison County Hist. Soc., 1990. Mem. ABA, N.E. Tex. Bar Assn., Harrison County Bar Assn., Masons, Phi Beta Kappa. Democrat. Baptist. Avocations: water sports, tree farming, reading. Real property, Probate, Banking. Office: Smith & Gilstrap 100 W Houston St Marshall TX 75670-4038

**GIMBEL, FRANKLYN M.,** lawyer; b. Milw., Mar. 18, 1936; s. Virginia Grace Pivar; m. Barbara Posner, Aug. 3, 1958 (div. May 1969); children: Tod, Joshua; m. Martha Anne Knewtson, July 24, 1982; children: Rachel, Noah. BBA, U. Wis., 1958; JD, Marquette U., 1960. Bar: Wis. 1960, U.S. Dist. Ct. (ea. dist.) Wis. 1960, U.S. Supreme Ct. 1966. Staff atty. U.S. Atty. Dept. Justice, Milw., 1963-68; ptnr. Gimbel, Reilly, Guerin and Brown, Milw., 1968—. Vice chairperson Milw. Fire and Police Commn., 1977-82; bd. dirs. Milw. Expn. and Conv. Ctr. and Arena, 1982-94. Fellow Am. Bar Found., Am. Coll. Trial Lawyers; mem. Wis. State Bar Assn. (pres. 1986-87), Milw. Bar Assn. (pres. 1976-77, Greater Milw. Com. Lawyer of the Yr. 1989, 98), Rotary (dir., chmn. Wis. Ctr. dist., v.p. 1999-00). Jewish. Criminal, Labor, General civil litigation. Home: 3075 N Lake Dr Milwaukee WI 53211-3403 Office: Gimbel Reilly Guerlin and Brown 111 E Kilbourn Ave Milwaukee WI 53202-6611

**GINART, MICHAEL CHARLES, JR.,** lawyer; b. New Orleans, Sept. 10, 1961; s. Michael Charles Ginart and Celcia (Kirchem) Ginart Tanet; m. Alice Rose Johnson, Feb. 14, 1987; 1 child, John Claude. BS in Bus. and Distributive Edn., Northwest State U., Natchitoches, La., 1984; JD, Loyola U., New Orleans, 1988. Bar: La. 1988. Atty. Kelly, Davenport & Hogg, New Orleans, 1988-89, Law Office of Richard A. Tonry, Chalmette, La., 1989-90; ptnr., atty. Law Office of Tonry and Ginart, Chalmette, 1990—. Bd. dirs. St. Bernard Youth Found., Chalmette. Mem. ABA, ATLA, La. Bar Assn., St. Bernard Bar Assn. (pres. 1997—), Chalmette Alumni Assn. (bd. dirs.). Personal injury, Criminal. Office: Law Office Tonry & Ginart 8651 W Judge Perez Dr Chalmette LA 70043-1619

**GINDER, PETER CRAIG,** lawyer; b. West Point, N.Y., Aug. 25, 1946; s. Allen Woodrow and Ruth Cameron (Paulsen) G.; m. Julia Kathleen Montgomery, June 21, 1969; children: Jonathon, Brian. AB, Dartmouth Coll., 1968; JD, U. Denver, 1974. Bar: Alaska 1974, U.S. Dist. Ct. Alaska 1974, U.S. Ct. Appeals (9th cir.) 1974. Assoc. Ely, Guess & Rudd, Anchorage, 1974-76; assoc. Kemppel & Huffman, Anchorage, 1977-78; asst. mcpl. atty. Municipality of Anchorage, 1976-77; ptnr. Kemppel, Huffman & Ginder, P.C., Anchorage, 1977-96; pvt. practice Anchorage, 1996—. Co-author: Estate Planning and Probate in Alaska, 1986. Ambassador Anchorage Olympic Com., 1986-89; chmn. Gt. Alaska Shootout Com., 1988, Anchorage Sister Cities Commn., 1996—. Fellow Am. Coll. Trust & Estate Counsel; mem. ABA, Alaska Bar Assn., Anchorage Bar Assn., Anchorage Estate Planning Council (pres. 1984). Avocations: reading, downhill skiing, family activities. Fax: 907-258-6009. E-mail: pglaw@alaska.net. Probate, Contracts commercial, Real property. Office: Kemppel Huffman & Ginder PC 601 W 5th Ave Ste 901 Anchorage AK 99501-2226

**GINDIN, WILLIAM HOWARD,** judge; b. Perth Amboy, N.J., Sept. 1, 1931; s. Jac Paul and Belle Ruth (Steinberg) G.; m. Jane Hersh, June 24, 1954; children: Thomas L., Suzanne Hinsdale; m. Emily Shimkin, Dec. 25, 1965; children: Geoffrey A. Drucker, Janine Drucker Gordon. A.B., Brown U., 1953; J.D., Yale U., 1956. Bar: N.J. 1956, U.S. Supreme Ct. 1965, U.S. Ct. Appeals (3d cir.) 1980. Assoc., Gindin & Gindin, Plainfield, N.J., 1956-62, ptnr., Plainfield and Bridgewater, N.J., 1962-82; adminstrv. law judge, Newark, 1982-85; U.S. bankruptcy judge, Trenton, 1985-90, chief judge, 1990-98; adj. prof. Rutgers Camden Law Sch., 1988-93; lectr. Inst. Continuing Legal Edn., Profl. Edn. Systems, Inc.; bd. govs. Nat. Conf. Bankruptcy Judges (3d cir.), 1989-92, Am. Judicature Soc. Mem. bd. editors N.J. Bar Assn. Jour., 1962-72. Mem. Plainfield (N.J.) Human Relations Commn., 1965-72, chmn., 1968-72; pres. Temple Sholom, Plainfield, 1979-81; regional v.p. Union Am. Hebrew Congregations, 1983-86; trustee Princeton Jewish Ctr.; vice chair Opera Festival of N.J. Fellow Am. Bar Found., Assn. Fed. Bar (adv. bd.), Bankruptcy Inn of Ct. N.J. (pres.); mem. ABA, Plainfield Bar Assn., Union County Bar Assn., Mercer County Bar Assn., N.J. Bar Assn., Am. Judicature Soc., Plainfield Rotary (pres. 1974-75). Home: 30 James Ct Princeton NJ 08540-2633 Office: US Bankruptcy Ct 402 E State St Trenton NJ 08608-1507

**GINGOLD, DENNIS MARC,** lawyer; b. Plainfield, N.J., June 23, 1949; s. Michael Richard and Sally (Weiss) G.; m. Anne Carol Pearson, Sept. 4, 1970; children: Stacy Michele, Samantha Anne. BA, Rollins Coll., 1971; JD, Seton Hall U., 1974; postgrad., Princeton U., NYU, 1974-75; LLM in Internat. Legal Studies, NYU, 1975; postgrad., SUNY, Buffalo, 1975-76. Bar: N.J. 1974, U.S. Dist. Ct. N.J. 1974, Colo. 1981, U.S. Dist. Ct. Colo. 1981, U.S. Ct. Appeals (10th cir.) 1984, U.S. Supreme Ct. 1985, D.C. 1989, U.S. Dist. Ct. D.C. 1989, U.S. Ct. Appeals (9th cir.) 1991. Atty.-advisor U.S. Compt. Currency, Washington, 1976-79; regional counsel 12th Nat. Bank Region U.S. Compt. Currency, Denver, 1979-80; ptnr. Gorsuch, Kirgis, Campbell, Walker & Grover, Denver, 1980-82, Kirkland & Ellis, Denver and Washington, 1982-85; lead banking ptnr. Squire, Sanders & Dempsey, Washington, 1985-88; ptnr. Foley, Hoag & Eliot, Washington, 1988-90, Ross and Hardies, Washington, 1990-91, Dickstein, Shapiro & Morin, Washington, 1991—; adj. prof. law U. Denver, 1981-82. Sr. mem. Seton Hall U. Law Jour., 1972-73. Named one of the Top 20 Banking Lawyers in U.S. Nat. Law Jour., 1983; Reginald Heber Smith fellow, 1975-76. Mem. D.C. Bar Assn., Colo. Bar Assn., N.J. Bar Assn., Denver Bar Assn., Banking Law Inst. (adv. coun. 1983-86), Denver Athletic Club, Bethesda Country Club. Banking, General corporate. Home: 8712 Crider Brook Way Potomac MD 20854-4547

**GINGOLD, HARLAN BRUCE,** lawyer; b. Syracuse, N.Y., Jan. 3, 1946; s. Eli and Sarle (Greenhouse) G.; m. Diane Port, Dec. 20, 1970; children: Alan R., Brian M., Eric R. BA, Syracuse U., 1967, JD, 1970. Bar: N.Y. 1971, U.S. Dist. Ct. (no. dist.) N.Y. 1971, U.S. Supreme Ct. 1977. Assoc. Primo & Marino, Syracuse, 1971-72, Driscoll, Mathews, Gingold and Cass, Syracuse, 1972-73; ptnr. Gingold & Gingold, Syracuse, 1973-85; ptnr., v.p., sec. Macht, Brenizer & Gingold, P.C., Syracuse, 1985—; pub. adv. coun. N.Y.S. Ethics Com., 1998—. Bd. visitors Syracuse U. Coll. Law, 1982-84; bd. dirs. Temple Adath Yeshurun, Syracuse, 1984-90, Am. Diabetes Assn., Syracuse, 1989-96, Hiscock Legal Aid Soc., 1998—. Mem. ABA, N.Y. State Bar Assn. (ho. dels. 1994-96, 98—, com. on profl. discipline 1999), N.Y. State Bar Leaders(exec. counsel 1994—), Onondaga County Bar Assn. (bd. dirs. 1990-97, past pres., officer 1990-97), N.Y. State Supreme Ct. (appellate div. 4th dept., 5th dist. grievance com. 1995—). Avocation: golf. Family and matrimonial, Consumer commercial. Office: Macht Brenizer & Gingold PC State Tower Bldg Lbby Fl Syracuse NY 13202-1798

**GINGRAS, JOHN RICHARD,** lawyer, consultant; b. Paterson, N.J., May 1, 1949; s. Louis Donah and Carol Gilmore (Doyle) G.; m. Nancy Margaret Conway, Aug. 29, 1970; 2 children. BS, St. Joseph's U., 1971, MBA, 1979; MS in Fin. Svcs., Am. Coll., 1980; JD, Widener U., 1983. Bar: Pa. 1984. Trust acct. Girard Bank, Phila., 1969-71; sales mgr. Equitable Life Assurance Soc., Wayne, Pa., 1971-76; pvt. practice fin. planner Newtown Square, Pa., 1976-80; assoc. Huver & Assocs., Villanova, Pa., 1980-86; pres. Settlement Funding, Inc., Broomall, Pa., 1986-95. Pres. bd. dirs. MNJ Community Svcs. Found., 1976-90; bd. dirs. Jaycees; active Cradle of Liberty coun. Boy Scouts Am. Recipient Silver Beaver award Boy Scouts Am., God and Svc. award; named one of Outstanding Young Pennsylvanian, Pa. Jaycees, 1976. Mem. ABA, ATLA, Pa. Bar Assn., Am. Soc. CLUs/ChFC, SAR, Sigma Phi Epsilon (alumni bd.), Delta Theta Phi. Republican. Presbyterian. Avocations: art collector, antiques, golf, skiing. Personal injury, Insurance, Product liability.

**GINSBERG, ALAN,** lawyer; b. Bellmore, N.Y., July 4, 1959; s. Samuel Ginsberg and Helen Rosenfield; m. Darby McCauliffe, Nov. 19, 1965. BS in Criminal Justice, Fla. Internat. U., 1981; JD, Nova Law Sch., 1984. Bar: Fla. 1984, U.S. Dist. Ct. (so. dist.) Fla. 1991. Attorney Cohen & Cohen PA, Hollywood, Fla., 1985-90; pvt. practice Miami, Fla., 1991—. Active Rep. Party, Washington, 1997-98. Recipient Pro Bono award Broward (Fla.) Lawyers Care, 1996, Certificate of Appreciation Dade (Fla.) County Pub. Schs., 1998, Certificate of Appreciation GreaterMiami Legal Svcs., Dade, 1995. Mem. Nat. Orgn. Socoil (security claims rep. 1994—), Fla. Trial Lawyers Assn. Democrat. Jewish. Avocations: golf, basketball, reading, scuba diving. Criminal, Personal injury, Pension, profit-sharing, and employee benefits. Home: 5980 N Bayshore Dr Miami FL 33137-2306 Office: 13899 Biscayne Blvd Ste 401 North Miami Beach FL 33181-1652

**GINSBERG, BARRY,** lawyer; b. Bklyn., June 23, 1952; s. Samuel and Helen (Rosenfeld) G.; m. Linda Mary Wagner, Nov. 29, 1979; children: Nathan W., Joanna W. BA cum laude, SUNY Buffalo, 1975, JD cum laude, 1980. Bar: Ill. 1980, N.Y. 1987; cert. fraud examiner. Counsel U.S. Ct. Appeals 7th cir., Chgo., 1980-82; assoc. Isham Lincoln & Beale, Chgo., 1982-87; asst. dist. atty. N.Y. County Dist. Atty., N.Y.C., 1987-94; ptnr. Arthur Andersen, N.Y.C., 1994-98; prin. Barry Ginsberg, Atty.-at-Law, N.Y.C., 1998-99; assoc. gen. counsel, mng. dir. Decision Strategies/Fairfax Internat., N.Y.C., Stanford, Conn., 1999—. Coach Am. Youth Soccer Orgn., Dobbs Ferry, N.Y., 1992—. Mem. ABA (white collar crim com.), Internat. Assn. Ind. Pvt. Sector Inspectors Gen. (bd. dirs.), N.Y. State Bar Assn. (civil prosecuting com.), Assn. CFE's, Assn. of Bar of City of N.Y., N.Y. County Lawyers Assn. Avocations: running, weight lifting, kayaking, biking. Home: 15 Hollywood Dr Dobbs Ferry NY 10522-3008 Office: 595 Summer St Ste 2 Stamford CT 06901-1407

**GINSBERG, DAVID M.,** lawyer; b. Phila.. BA, U. Pa., 1984, BS, 1984, JD, 1987. Bar: Pa. 1987, N.J. 1987, U.S. Dist. Ct. N.J. 1987, U.S. Dist. Ct. (ea. dist.) Pa. 1988, U.S. Dist. Ct. Pa. 1995, U.S. Ct. Appeals (3d cir.) 1991. Ptnr. Sidney Ginsberg PC, Phila., 1987—. Mem. ABA, Phila. Bar Assn., Pa. Bar Assn., Am. Trial Lawyers Assn., N.J. State Bar Assn., Pa. Trial Lawyers Assn., Phila. Trial Lawyers Assn. General civil litigation, Contracts commercial, Personal injury. Office: Sidney Ginsberg PC 1420 Walnut St Ste 1006 Philadelphia PA 19102-4010

**GINSBERG, ERNEST,** lawyer, banker; b. Syracuse, N.Y., Feb. 14, 1931; s. Morris Henry and Mildred Florence (Slive) G.; m. Harriet Gay Scharf, Dec. 20, 1959; children: Alan Justin, Robert Daniel. BA, Syracuse U., 1953, JD, 1955; LLM, Georgetown U., 1963. Bar: N.Y. 1955, U.S. Supreme Ct. 1964. Pvt. practice law Syracuse, 1957-61; mem. staff, office chief counsel IRS, Washington, 1961-63; tax counsel Comptr. of Currency, Washington, 1964-65, assoc. chief counsel, 1965-68; v.p. legal affairs, sec. Republic Nat. Bank N.Y., N.Y.C., 1968-74; sr. v.p. legal affairs, sec. Republic Nat. Bank, N.Y.C., 1975-86, exec. v.p., gen. counsel, sec., 1984-86, vice chmn. bd., gen. counsel, 1986-94, vice chmn. bd., 1990—; sr. v.p., sec. legal affairs Republic N.Y. Corp., N.Y.C., 1974-84, exec. v.p., gen. counsel, sec., 1984-86, vice chmn. bd., gen. counsel, sec., 1984-86, vice chmn. bd., gen. counsel, sec., 1986-94, vice chmn. bd., 1986-99, also bd. dirs.; bd. visitors Syracuse U. Coll. Law. Chmn. emeritus Roundabout Theatre Co., N.Y.C. With U.S. Army, 1955-57. Mem. Am. Bankers Assn. (bd. dirs. 1995-97), Am. Bankers Coun. (co-chmn. 1992-94), N.Y. State Bankers Assn. (pres. 1993-94), Bankers Roundtable (bd. dirs. 1995-97), Phi Sigma Delta, Phi Delta Phi. Banking, General corporate, Administrative and regulatory. Office: Republic NY Corp 452 5th Ave New York NY 10018-2706

**GINSBERG, JEROME MAURICE,** lawyer; b. Bklyn., May 8, 1939; s. Frank Ralph and Minnie (Altwerger) G.; m. Carol Elaine Cordover, Aug. 9, 1964; children: Andrew Ian, Lynn Ellen, Peter Ross. BA, CCNY, 1960; JD, NYU, 1963. Bar: N.Y. 1963, U.S. Dist. Ct. (so. and ea. dists.) N.Y. 1969, U.S. Supreme Ct. 1967. Assoc. Panken & Panken, N.Y.C., 1963-64; ptnr. Sakona, Ginsberg & Katsorhis, N.Y.C., 1964-83, Ginsberg & Katsorhis, N.Y.C., 1983—; lectr. U. Md., 1980, Criminal Cts. Bar Assn., Queens, N.Y., 1983; profl law Korea U., 1993. Author: Prepaid Legal Plan Primer, 1980, False Arrest, Malicious Prosecution and Police Misconduct, 1992; editor Queens Bar Bull., 1966-74; contbr. articles to profl. jours. Pres. Young Dems. Queens County, N.Y., 1959, independence Dem. Club, Jamaica, N.Y., 1974; v.p. Plainview Jewish Ctr., 1984, pres., 1986. With U.S. Army, 1956-61. Recipient award of Honor, Queens Lawyers Club, 1981; Fulbright scholar, 1993. Mem. ABA (ho. of dels. 1992—), Queens County Bar Assn. (pres. 1980-81, award of Meritorious Svc. 1982), Brandies Assn. (pres. 1979-80), Network Bar Leaders (chmn. 1984-86), N.Y. State Bar Assn. (ho. of dels. 1987-94), N.Y. State Trial Lawyers (bd. dirs. 1994—), Network of Bar Leaders (pres. 1984-86), KP. Jewish. State civil litigation, Family and matrimonial, Personal injury. Office: Ginsberg & Katsorhis 77-53 Main St Flushing NY 11367-3442

**GINSBERG, MARC ROBERT,** lawyer, mediator; b. N.Y.C., Mar. 31, 1958; s. Irwin and Lilyan (Zinn) G.; m. Tali Welkovitz, Apr. 16, 1989; children: Sami Heather, Michael Jay. BA, U. Fla., 1979, JD, 1981. Bar: Fla. 1981, U.S. Dist. Ct. (so. dist.) Fla. 1982; cert. civil trial atty., Fla. 1994. Mediator Dade County Cir. Ct., Miami, Fla., 1989-91; gen. counsel Underwriters Guarantee Ins. Co., Miami, 1990—. Mem. Assn. Trial Lawyers Am., Fla. Acad. Trial Lawyers. Personal injury. Office: Mandina & Ginsberg PA 1110 Brickell Ave Ste 805 Miami FL 33131-3138

**GINSBERG, ROBERT MICHAEL,** lawyer; b. N.Y.C., June 25, 1935; s. David A. and Paula (Daniels) G.; m. Judy Ann Haworth, Dec. 19, 1969 (div. Dec. 1978); 1 child, Simon; m. Annette Elizabeth Hult, June 6, 1982; children: Elizabeth, David. B.A., U. Mich., 1956; LL.D., Yale U., 1959. Bar: N.Y. 1961, U.S. Dist. Ct. (so. dist.) N.Y. 1963, U.S. Dist. Ct. (ea. dist.) N.Y., 1974, U.S. Ct. Appeals (2d cir.) 1974, U.S. Supreme Ct. 1983. Sole practice, N.Y.C., 1963-68, 79-84; ptnr. Fuchsberg & Fuchsberg, 1968-79; ptnr. Ginsberg & Broome, N.Y.C., 1984—. Democratic State committeeman, N.Y.C., 1969-71, state committeeman, 1974—. Served with U.S. Army, 1959. Mem. Am. Trial Lawyers Assn., N.Y. State Trial Lawyers Assn., N.Y. County Bar Assn. Democrat. Jewish. Personal injury. Home: 275 W 96th St New York NY 10025-6200 Office: Ginsberg & Broome 225 Broadway New York NY 10007-3001

**GINSBURG, CHARLES DAVID,** lawyer; b. N.Y.C., Apr. 20, 1912; s. Nathan and Rae (Lewis) G.; m. Marianne Laïs; children by previous marriage: Jonathan, Susan, Mark. AB, W.Va. U., 1932; LLB, Harvard U., 1935. Bar: W. Va. 1935, U.S. Supreme Ct. 1940, D.C. 1946, U.S. Ct. Appeals (2d, 3rd, 4th, 7th, and Fed. cirs.) 1946, U.S. Claims Ct. 1960, U.S. Tax Ct. 1961. Atty. for public utilities div. and office of gen. counsel SEC, 1935-39; law sec. to Justice William O. Douglas, 1939; asst. to commr. SEC, 1939-40; legal adviser Price Stblzn. Div., Nat. Def. Adv. Com., 1940-41; gen. counsel Office Price Adminstrn. and Civilian Supply, 1941-42, OPA, 1942-43; pvt. practice law Ginsburg, Feldman and Bress, Washington, 1946-98; founding ptnr. Ginsburg, Feldman & Bress, 1946-98; sr. counsel, firm Powell, Goldstein, Frazer & Murphy, LLP, 1998; adminstrv. asst. to Senator M.M. Neely, W.Va., 1950; adj. prof. internat. law Georgetown U. (Grad. Sch. Law), 1959-67; Dep. commr. U.S. del. Austrian Treaty Commn., Vienna, 1947; adviser U.S. del. Council Fgn. Ministers, London, 1947; Mem. Presdl. Emergency Bd. 166 (Airlines), 1966; mem. Pres.'s Commn. on Postal Orgn., 1967; chmn. Presdl. Emergency Bd. 169 (Railroads), 1969; exec. dir. Nat. Adv. Commn. Civil Disorders, 1967. Author: The Future of German Reparations; Contbr. to legal jours. Bd. mem., chmn. exec. com. Nat. Symphony Orch. Assn., 1960-69; bd. govs. Weizmann Inst., 1965 (hon. fellow 1972); mem. vis. com. Harvard-Mass. Inst. Tech. Joint Ctr. on Urban Studies, 1969; trustee St. John's Coll., 1969-76, chmn. bd., 1974-76; overseers com. Kennedy Sch. Govt. Harvard, 1971—; mem. coun. Nat. Harvard Law Sch. Assn., 1972—, gen. counsel Dem. Nat. Com., 1968-70. Served from pvt. to capt. AUS, 1942-46; dep. dir. econs. div. Office Mil. Govt., 1945-46, Germany. Decorated Bronze Star, Legion of Merit; recipient Presdl. Cert. of Merit. Mem. ABA, Fed. Bar Assn, Am. Law Inst., Coun. on Fgn. Rels., Met. Club, Army and Navy Club, Phi Beta Kappa. Democrat. Administrative and regulatory, General corporate, Federal civil litigation. Home: 619 S Lee St Alexandria VA 22314-3819 Office: 1001 Pennsylvania Ave NW Washington DC 20004-2505

**GINSBURG, DOUGLAS HOWARD,** federal judge, educator; b. Chgo., May 25, 1946; s. Maurice and Katherine (Goodmont) G.; m. Claudia De Secundy, May 31, 1968 (div. Sept. 1980); 1 child, Jessica DeSecundy; m. Hallee Perkins Morgan, May 9, 1981; children: Hallee Katherine Morgan, Hannah Maurice Morgan. Diploma, Latin Sch. Chgo., 1963; BS, Cornell U., 1970; JD, U. Chgo., 1973. Bar: Ill. 1973, Mass. 1982, U.S. Supreme Ct. 1984, U.S. Ct. Appeals (9th cir.) 1986. Assoc. Covington & Burling, Washington, 1972; law clk. U.S. Ct. Appeals, Washington, 1973-74, U.S. Supreme Ct., Washington, 1974-75; prof. Harvard U., 1975-83; dep. asst. atty. gen. for regulatory affairs antitrust divsn U.S. Dept. Justice, Washington, 1983-84, asst. atty. gen. antitrust divsn., 1985-86; adminstr. for info. and regulatory affairs Exec. Office Pres., Office Mgmt. and Budget, Washington, 1984-85; judge U.S. Ct. Appeals (D.C. cir.), 1986—; vis. prof. law Columbia U., N.Y.C., 1987-88; lectr. law Harvard U., Cambridge, Mass., 1987-91; disting. prof. law George Mason U., Arlington, Va., 1988—; Charles J. Merriam vis. scholar, sr. lectr. U. Chgo., 1990—. Author: Regulation of Broadcasting: Law and Policy Towards Radio, Television and Cable Communications, 1979, Antitrust, Uncertainty, and Technological Innovation, 1980; co-author: Regulation of the Electronic Mass Media, 1991; editor: (with W. Abernathy) Government, Technology and the Future of the Automobile, 1980; contbr. articles to profl. jours. Mecham scholar U. Chgo. Law Sch., 1970-73; recipient Casper Platt award U. Chgo. Law Sch., 1972. Mem. Am. Econ. Assn., Am. Law and Econs. Assn., Mont Pelerin Soc., Order of Coif, Phi Kappa Phi. Avocations: historic preservation, antiques, fox hunting. Office: US Ct Appeals 333 Constitution Ave NW Washington DC 20001-2866

**GINSBURG, MARTIN DAVID,** lawyer, educator; b. N.Y.C., June 10, 1932; s. Morris and Evelyn (Bayer) G.; m. Ruth Bader, June 23, 1954; children: Jane, James. AB, Cornell U., 1953; JD, Harvard U., 1958; LLD (hon.), Lewis and Clark Coll., 1992, Wheaton Coll., 1997. Bar: N.Y. 1959, D.C. 1980. Practiced in N.Y.C., 1959-79; mem. firm Weil, Gotshal & Manges, N.Y.C., 1963-79; of counsel firm Fried, Frank, Harris, Shriver and Jacobson, Washington, 1980—; Charles Keller Beekman prof. law Columbia U. Law Sch., N.Y.C., 1979-80; prof. law Georgetown U. Law Center, Washington, 1980—; lectr. U. Leiden, The Netherlands, 1982; lectr. Salzburg Seminar Austria, 1984; mem. tax div. adv. group Dept. Justice, 1980-81; mem. adv. group to Commr. Internal Revenue, 1978-80; mem. adv. bd. U. Calif. Securities Regulation Inst., 1973-91; adj. prof. law NYU, 1967-79; vis. prof. law Stanford (Calif.) U., 1978, Harvard U., Cambridge, Mass., 1986, U. Chgo., 1990, NYU, 1993; cons. joint com. on taxation U.S. Congress, 1979-80; chmn. tax adv. bd. Commerce Clearing House, 1982-94; mem. bd. advisors NYU/IRS Continuing Profl. Edn. Program, 1983-88, co-chmn., 1986-88; sub coun. on capital allocation, co-chmn. taxation expert group Competitiveness Policy Coun., 1993-95; chmn. tax adv. bd. Little, Brown, 1994-96; bd. dirs. Millennium Chems., Inc., Chgo. Classical Rec. Found.; lectr. various tax insts. Co-author, editor: Tax Consequences of Investments, 1969; co-author: Mergers, Acquisitions and Leverage Buyouts, 1989; contbr. articles to legal jours. Mem. vis. com. Harvard Law Sch., 1994-98. 1st lt., arty. U.S. Army, 1954-56. Chair in taxation named in his honor, Georgetown U. Law Ctr., 1986; recipient Marshall-Wythe Medallion, Coll. of William and Mary Sch. Law, 1996, Outstanding achievemnt award Tax Soc. of NYU, 1993. Fellow Am. Coll. Tax Counsel, Am. Bar Found.; mem. Am. Law Inst. (cons. Fed. Income Tax Project 1974-93), N.Y. State Bar Assn. (mem. tax sect. exec. com. 1969—, chmn. tax sect. 1975, ho. of dels. 1976-77), Assn. Bar City N.Y. (chmn. com. taxation 1977-79, mem. audit com. 1980-81), ABA (mem. com. corp. taxation, tax sect. 1973—, chmn. com. simplification 1979-81, mem. tax sect. coun. 1984-87). Corporate taxation, Personal income taxation. Office: 600 New Jersey Ave NW Washington DC 20001-2022

**GINSBURG, NANCY LISA,** lawyer; b. N.Y.C., May 23, 1965; d. Monte and Laura Ginsburg. BA, U. Pa., 1987; JD, Union U., 1991. Bar: Conn. 1991, N.Y. 1992, D.C. 1993. Staff atty. The Legal Aid Soc., N.Y.C., 1991—. Mem. Bar Assn. of City of N.Y. Office: The Legal Aid Soc 49 Thomas St New York NY 10013-3821

**GINSBURG, RUTH BADER,** United States supreme court justice; b. Bklyn., Mar. 15, 1933; d. Nathan and Celia (Amster) Bader; m. Martin David Ginsburg, June 23, 1954; children: Jane Carol, James Steven. AB, Cornell U., 1954; postgrad., Harvard Law Sch., 1956-58; LLB Kent scholar, Columbia Law Sch., 1959; LLD (hon.), Lund (Sweden) U., 1969, Am. U., 1981, Vt. Law Sch., 1984, Georgetown U., 1985, DePaul U., 1985, Bklyn. Law Sch., 1987, Amherst Coll., 1991, Rutgers U., 1991, Lewis and Clark Coll., 1992, Radcliffe Coll., 1994, NYU, 1994, Columbia U., 1994, Smith Coll., 1994, L.I. U., 1994, U. Ill., 1995, Brandeis U., 1996, Wheaton Coll., 1997, Jewish Theol. Sem. of Am., 1997, George Washington U. Law Sch., 1997; DHL (hon.), Hebrew Union Coll., 1988. Bar: N.Y. 1959, D.C. 1975, U.S. Supreme Ct. 1967. Law sec. to judge U.S. Dist. Ct. (so. dist.) N.Y., 1959-61; rsch. assoc. Columbia Law Sch., N.Y.C., 1961-62, assoc. dir. project internat. procedure, 1962-63; asst. prof. Rutgers U. Sch. Law, Newark, 1963-66, assoc. prof., 1966-69, prof., 1969-72; prof. Columbia U. Sch. Law, N.Y.C., 1972-80; U.S. Cir. judge U.S. Ct. Appeals, D.C. Cir., Washington, 1980-93; assoc. justice U.S. Supreme Ct., Washington, 1993—; Phi Beta Kappa vis. scholar, 1973-74; fellow Ctr. for Advanced Study in Behavioral Scis., Stanford, Calif., 1977-78; lectr. Aspen (Colo.) Inst., 1990, Salzburg Seminar, Austria, 1984; gen. counsel ACLU, 1973-80, bd. dirs., 1974-80. Author: (with Anders Bruzelius) Civil Procedure in Sweden, 1965; Swedish Code ofJudicial Procedure, 1968; (with others) Sex-Based Discrimination, 1974, supplement, 1978; contbr. numerous articles to books and jours. Fellow Am. Bar Found.; mem. AAAS, Am. Law Inst. (coun. mem. 1978-93), Coun. Fgn. Rels. Office: US Supreme Ct One First St NE Washington DC 20543

**GINTLING, KAREN JANETTE,** lawyer; b. Balt., Oct. 7, 1955; d. Nevin John and Pearl Louise G. AA, Essex C.C., Balt., 1975; BA, U. Balt., 1977, LLD, 1980. Bar: Md. 1982, U.S. Dist. Ct. Md. 1982, U.S. Bankruptcy Ct. 1982. Sr. assoc. Lentz, Hooper, Jacobs & Blevins, Belair, Md., 1982-93; pvt. practice Belair and Cambridge, Md., 1993—; legal advisor Midshore Coun. on Domestic Violence, Cambridge, Md., 1997-98. Mem. Md. State Bar Assn., Harford County Bar Assn. Family and matrimonial, Workers' compensation, Personal injury. Office: 321 Fulford Ave Bel Air MD 21014-3815 also: 539 Poplar St Cambridge MD 21613-1833

**GIOFFRE, BRUNO JOSEPH,** lawyer; b. Port Chester, N.Y., June 27, 1934; s. Anthony B. and Louise (Giorno) G.; m. Kathleen M. Bartlik, Nov. 14, 1959; children: Kathleen, Lisa, Michael, Christopher, B. Scott, David, Kerry. BA, Cornell U., 1956, JD, 1958. Bar: N.Y. 1958, U.S. Dist. Ct. (so. dist.) N.Y. 1973. Sr. mem. Gioffre & Gioffre, P.C., Purchase, N.Y., 1958—; justice Town of Rye (N.Y.), 1965—; chmn. bd. dirs. Sound Fed. Savs. & Loan Assn. Trustee United Hosp.; counsel Port Chester Pub. Library. Mem. Port Chester-Rye Bar Assn., Westchester Bar Assn., N.Y. Bar Assn., ABA, Westchester County Magistrate's Assn., N.Y. Magistrate's Assn. Clubs: Elks, KC. Real property, Probate. Home and Office: 2900 Westchester Ave Purchase NY 10577-2552

**GIOFFREDI, JOHN M.,** lawyer; b. Des Moines, Jan. 30, 1956; s. Gualtiero Giovanni and Margarett Mary Gioffredi. BS, Iowa State U., 1978; JD, Creighton U., 1981. Bar: Tex. 1982. With Gioffredi and Assocs., Dallas, 1983—. Criminal. Office: Gioffredi and Assocs 6500 Greenville Ave Ste 700 Dallas TX 75206-1017

**GIOIA, DANIEL AUGUST,** lawyer; b. Bellerose, N.Y., Dec. 23, 1950; s. Joseph Daniel G. and Concetta P. Della Femina; m. Helen Dumas, June 30, 1973; children: Martha Dumas, Thomas Joseph, David Albert, Carl Daniel. BA in Govt., Georgetown U., 1972; JD, Am. U., 1975. Ptnr. Spangler, Jennings & Dougherty, Merrillville, Ind., 1975—. Mem. Lake County Bar Assn. (bd. mgrs. 1987-91), Valpo Soccer Club (pres. 1992-98). Roman Catholic. Avocation: soccer referee and coach. General civil litigation, Personal injury, Family and matrimonial. Home and office: 4204 Hemlock St Valparaiso IN 46383-1820

**GIOIELLA, RUSSELL MICHAEL,** lawyer; b. Camden, N.J., Mar. 10, 1954; s. Michael S. and Mildred (Leonardo) G.; m. Nerissa M. Radell, June 28, 1980; 1 child, Natalya. BA summa cum laude, Cath. U., 1976; JD, NYU, 1979, MA, 1980. Bar: N.Y. 1980, U.S. Dist. Ct. (so. and ea. dists.) N.Y. 1980, U.S. Ct. Appeals (2nd and 3rd cirs.) 1980, U.S. Dist. Ct. (no. dist.) N.Y. 1982, U.S. Supreme Ct. 1984. Assoc. Litman, Kaufman and Asche, N.Y.C., 1979-84; ptnr. Litman, Kaufman, Asche and Lupkin, N.Y.C., 1985, Litman, Asche, Lupkin & Gioiella, N.Y.C., 1986-93, Litman, Asche, Lupkin, Gioiella & Bassin, N.Y.C., 1994-96, Litman, Asche & Gioiella LLP, N.Y.C., 1996—; mem. First Jud. Dept. Assigned Counsel Screening Panel, 1998—. Mem. steering com. N.Y. State Coalition to Abolish the Death Penalty, 1992. Mem. ABA, NACDL, Assn. of Bar of City of N.Y. (mem. com. on product liability 1988-91, mem. criminal cts. com. 1992-94), N.Y. Criminal Bar Assn. (pres. 1997-98), N.Y. State Assn. Criminal Def. Lawyers (treas. 1995-97, v.p. 1999—), Columbia Lawyers, Phi Beta Kappa. Democrat. Avocations: fatherhood, music, biking, wine, Russian literature. Criminal, General civil litigation, Personal injury. Office: Litman Asche & Gioiella 45 Broadway New York NY 10006-3007

**GIORDANO, LAWRENCE FRANCIS,** lawyer; b. Buffalo, Feb. 17, 1953; s. Anthony Jerome and Martha Ann (Taylor) G.; m. Elaine Kristie Thomas, May 29, 1976; children: Bradley Thomas, Evan Taylor. BS with highest honors in Psychology, Denison U., 1975; JD, Georgetown U., 1978. Bar: Tenn. 1978, U.S. Dist. Ct. (ea. dist.) Tenn. 1979, U.S. Ct. Appeals (6th cir.) 1980, U.S. Supreme Ct. 1983. Assoc. Stone & Hinds, P.C., Knoxville, Tenn., 1978-81, ptnr., 1981-88; ptnr. Thomforde & Giordano, P.C., Knoxville, 1988-90, McCampbell & Young, P.C., Knoxville, 1990-91, London, Amburn & Giordano, Knoxville, 1991-92, Susano, Sheppeard & Giordano, Knoxville, 1993-94; spl. counsel Lewis, King, Krieg, Waldrop & Catron, P.C., Knoxville, 1994-97, shareholder, 1997—; spl. judge Knox County Gen. Sessions Ct., 1988—; adminstrv. law judge State of Tenn. Dept. Edn., 1994-96; adj. prof. U. Tenn. Coll. Law, 1993—; instr. Knoxville Police Acad., 1989. Mem. exec. bd. Knoxville Metro Soccer League, 1980-85; mem. community network Knox County Youth Alcohol Hwy. Safety Project, Knoxville, 1987-90. Nat. Merit scholar, 1971-75, Kenneth I. Brown scholar, 1974. Mem. ABA, Tenn. Bar Assn., Knoxville Bar Assn. (bd. govs. 1986-92, treas. 1986-90, sec. 1991-92), Def. Rsch. Inst., Am. Inns of Ct. (master of the bench 1991—, pres. 1994-95), Sertoma (v.p. chpt. 1987-89, pres. 1989-90), Phi Beta Kappa, Omicron Delta Kappa. Democrat. Roman Catholic. Avocations: soccer, gardening, reading, theater. General civil litigation, General practice, Criminal. Home: 1822 Nantasket Rd Knoxville TN 37922-5769 Office: Lewis King Krieg Waldrop & Catron PC 620 Market St Fl 5 Knoxville TN 37902-2231

**GIORZA, JOHN C.,** lawyer; b. Lexington, Mo., May 25, 1950; s. Alphonso Ceno and Iris (Polla) G.; m. Jane Ray Dempsy, Sept. 5, 1981. BA, Westminster Coll., 1972; MBA, U. Mo. 1974, 1974; JD, U. Mo., 1978. Bar: U.S. Dist. Ct. (we. dist.) Mo. 1978. Assoc. Aull, Sherman & Worthington, Lexington, 1978-83; ptnr. Aull, Sherman, Worthington, Giorza & Hamilton, Lexington, 1983—; bd. dirs. Bank Midwest Lexington, N.A. Mem. ABA, Mo. Bar Assn., Mo. Assn. Trial Attys., Kansas City Bar Assn., Lafayette County Bar Assn. (pres. 1979-80), U. Mo. Alumni Assn. (bd. dirs. Lafayette county chpt.). Clubs: Shirkey Golf (Richmond, Mo.) (pres. 1982-85); Lexington Investors. Lodge: Lions (v.p. local chpt. 1983, 88). Avocations: travel, golf, sporting events. General practice, Probate, Consumer commercial. Home: 66 Lakeview Dr Lexington MO 64067-2101 Office: Aull Sherman Worthington Giorza & Hamilton PO Box 280 Lexington MO 64067-0280

**GIOVANNIELLO, JOSEPH, JR.,** lawyer; b. Bklyn., Aug. 4, 1958; s. Joseph and Margaret Montgomery (Torr) G.; m. Deborah Kesselman, June 25, 1988. BA, Yale U., 1980; JD, U. Va., 1983. Bar: N.Y. 1984, D.C. 1984, Hawaii 1984, U.S. Dist. Ct. (so. and ea. dists.) 1985, U.S. Ct. Appeals (2d and 3d cirs.) 1988. Law clk. U.S. Dist. Ct., Honolulu, 1983-84; assoc. Paul, Weiss, Rifkind, N.Y.C., 1984-86, Shereff, Friedman, Hoffman & Goodman, N.Y.C., 1986-91, Kornstein Weisz & Wexler, 1991-96; asst. gen. counsel Ladenburg Thalmann & Co. Inc., 1996-98, gen. counsel, 1998—. Mem. N.Y. State Bar Assn., Assn. of Bar of City of N.Y. Securities, General civil litigation, General corporate.

**GIPSTEIN, MILTON FIVENSON,** lawyer, psychiatrist; b. Schenectady, N.Y., Aug. 31, 1951; s. Milton and Evelyn G.; m. Carol Grace Zippin, July 21, 1974; children: Steven Mark, Richard Seth. BA, Columbia U., 1972; MD, SUNY, Syracuse, 1976; JD, U. N.C., 1981. Bar: Mass., 1982; diplomate Am. Bd. Psychiatry and Neurology. Resident psychiat. U. N.C., Chapel Hill, 1976-79; practice medicine specializing in psychiat. Dept. Corrections N.C., Raleigh, 1979-81; med. dir. Brockton (Mass.) Dist. Ct. Clinic, 1981-86, Bridgewater (Mass.) St. Hosp., 1986-87, Charter Hosp. of Aurora, Colo., 1988-97; med. dir. of forensic svcs. Columbine Psychiatric Hosp., Littleton, Colo., 1991-98; med. dir. forensic psychiatry divsn. Marvin Foote Youth Detention Facility, Englewood, Colo., 1997—; cons. med.-legal N.C. Legal Aid Soc., Raleigh, 1976-81, forensic Mass. Treatment Ctr. Sexually Dangerous, Bridgewater, 1981-88, psychiat. La. Gov.'s Task Force Mental Health, Baton Rouge, 1982, Jefferson Ctr. Mental Health, 1996—; med.-legal cons. Med. Evaluators, Inc., Denver, 1991—, SAFE HOUSE adolescent residental treatment ctr., Denver, 1997—; legal counsel indigent clients mental health Com. Pub. Counsel Svcs., Boston, 1982-88; lectr. mental health legal advisors com. Law and Mental Health for Mass. Supreme Ct., Boston, 1982-88. Cons. Pub. Health Adv. Com. Town of Sharon, Mass., 1983-84, Mental Health Legal Advisors Com. Mass. Supreme Ct., Boston, 1985-88; v.p. community affairs Heights Elem. Sch. PTA, Sharon, 1983-84; adv. com. gifted and talented Cherry Creek H.S., 1992-97, Campus Middle Sch., 1993-96. Mem. ABA, Mass. Bar Assn., Am. Profl. Practice Assn. Avocation: boating, antique documents, swimming. Health, Personal injury, Professional liability. Office: 4660 S Yosemite St # 9062 Englewood CO 80111-1227

**GIRARD, NETTABELL,** lawyer; b. Pocatello, Idaho, Feb. 24, 1938; d. George and Arranetta (Bell) Girard. Student, Idaho State U., 1957-58; BS, U. Wyo., 1959, JD, 1961. Bar: Wyo. 1961, D.C. 1969, U.S. Supreme Ct. 1969. Practiced in Riverton, 1963-69; atty.-adviser on gen. counsel's staff HUD; assigned Office Interstate Land Sales Registration, Washington, 1969-70; sect. chief interstate land sales Office Gen. Counsel, 1970-73; ptnr. Larson & Larson, Riverton, 1973-85; pvt. practice Riverton, 1985—; guest lectr. at high schs.; condr. seminar on law for layman Riverton br. A.A.U.W., 1965; condr. course on women and law; lectr. equal rights, job discrimination, land use planning. Editor Wyoming Clubwoman, 1966-68; bd. editors Wyo. Law Jour., 1959-61; writer Obiter Dictum column Women Lawyers Jour., Dear Legal Advisor column Solutions for Seniors, 1988-94; featured in Riverton Ranger, 1994; also articles in legal jours. Chmn. fund dr. Wind River chpt. ARC, 1965; chmn. Citizens Com. for Better Hosp. Improvement, 1965; chmn. subcom. on polit. legal rights and responsibilities Gov.'s Commn. on Status Women, 1965-69, mem. adv. com., 1973-93; rep. Nat. Conf. G ovs. Commn., Washington, 1966; local chmn. Law Day, 1966, 67, county chmn. Law Day, 1994, 95, 96, 97; mem. state bd. Wyo. Girl Scouts USA, sec. 1974-89, mem. nat. bd., 1978-81; state vol. adv. Nat. Found., March of Dimes, 1967-69; legal counsel Wyo. Women's Conf., 1977; gov. apptd. State Wyo. Indsl. Siting Coun., 1995—. Recipient Spl. Achievement award HUD, 1972, Disting. Leadership award Girl Scouts U.S.A., 1973, Franklin D. Roosevelt award Wyo. chpt. March of Dimes, 1985, Thanks Badge award Girl Scout Coun., 1987, Women Helping Women award in recognition of effective advancement status of women Riverton Club of Soroptimist Internat., 1990, Spl. award plaque in appreciation and recognition of 27 yrs. of svc. to State of Wyo., Wyo. Commn. for Women, 1964-92, Appreciation award Wyo. Sr. Citizens and Solutions for Srs., 1994, Arts in Action Pierrot award for outstanding musician, 1998. Mem. AAUW (br. pres.), Wyo. Bar Assn., Fremont County Bar Assn. (Spl. Recognition cert. 1997), D.C. Bar Assn., Women's Bar Assn. D.C., Internat. Fedn. Women Lawyers, Am. Judicature Soc., Assn. Trial Lawyers Am., Wyo. Trial Lawyers Assn., Nat. Assn. Women Lawyers (del. Wyo., nat. sec. 1969-70, v.p. 1970-71, pres. 1972-73), Wyo. Fedn. Women's Clubs (state editor, pres.-elect 1968-69, treas. 1974-76), Prog. Women's Club (pres.-elect. 1994-95), Riverton Chautauqua Club (pres. 1965-67), Riverton Civic League (pres. 1987-89), Kappa Delta, Delta Kappa Gamma (state chpt. hon.). Bankruptcy, Contracts commercial, General practice. Home: PO Box 687 Riverton WY 82501-0687 Office: 513 E Main St Riverton WY 82501-4440 *I believe first and foremost in the freedom of the individual: the right of the individual to be different, to be unique, and to pursue his or her particular heart's desire so long as that pursuit does not endanger the life or freedom of another. Perhaps because as a woman lawyer in predominately a man's profession, I have experienced the bitterness and dissolutionment of discrimination, I have actively worked through the equal rights movement toward the realization of individual freedom for all people. I support equality, not in the sense of "sameness," but in the realization of greater opportunities for individual development and differentiation.*

**GIRARD, ROBERT DAVID,** lawyer; b. Pitts., Aug. 2, 1946; s. Oscar L. and Ruth (Alpern) G. AB, UCLA, 1967; LLB, Yale U., 1970. Bar: Calif. 1971, U.S. Dist. Ct. (cen. dist.) Calif. 1971. Ptnr. Musick, Peeler & Garrett, L.A., 1970-85, Girard, Ellingsen, Christensen & West, L.A., 1985-88, Jones, Day, Reavis & Pogue, L.A., 1988-92, Musick Peeler & Garrett, L.A., 1992-98; with Sonnenschein Nath & Rosenthal, L.A., 1998—. Bd. dirs. Calif. Pediatric Ctr., L.A., 1980—, chmn., 1998—. Mem. ABA, L.A. County Bar Assn., Am. Acad. Hosp. Attys., Nat. Health Lawyers Assn., Calif. Health Care Lawyers Assn. (bd. dirs. 1982-85), Jonathan, Phi Beta Kappa. Administrative and regulatory, General corporate, Health. Office: Sonnenschein Nath & Rosenthal 601 S Figueroa St Ste 1500 Los Angeles CA 90017-5720

**GIRARDS, JAMES EDWARD,** lawyer; b. Manhasset, N.Y., Aug. 16, 1963; s. H.V. and Barbara (Davis) G.; m. Julie Ann Calame, June 27, 1987; children: Jessica Lauren, James Edward. BS, Baylor U., 1986; JD, St. Mary's Law Sch., 1989. Bar: Tex. 1989, U.S. Dist. Ct. (no., so. and ea. dists.) Tex. 1991. Assoc. Law Offices Windle Turley, P.C., Dallas, 1989-94; prin. Tracy & Girards, Dallas, 1994-97, The Girards Law Firm, Dallas, 1997—. Contbr. articles to profl. jours. Recipient Am. Jurisprudence Contracts award AmJur Pub. Co., 1986. Mem. ABA, ATLA (pres.'s club 1999), Tex. Trial Lawyers Assn. (assoc. dir. 1999—), Dallas Trial Lawyers Assn. (dir. 1998—), Dallas Bar Assn., Dallas Assn. Young Lawyers, State Bar Tex., Coll. of State Bar of Tex., Am. Mensa, Ltd., Million Dollar Advocates Forum. Personal injury. Office: La Sierra Bldg 5445 La Sierra Dr Ste 250 Dallas TX 75231-4137

**GIRDWOOD, DERIK RENARD,** lawyer; b. Cliftonville, Mich., England, Feb. 14, 1952; s. George Renard and Else M. G.; m. Biserka Girdwood; children: John, Laura, Christopher, David. BS in Bus., Wayne State U., Detroit, 1974; JD, Detroit Coll. Law, 1992. Bar: Mich. 1992; U.S. Fed. Ct. (ea. dist.) 1998. Atty. pvt. practice, Sterling Heights, Mich., 1992—. Author: Law Review, 1990, 92. Mem. Macomb County Bar, Oakland County Bar. Criminal, Labor, Juvenile. Office: PO Box 754 Sterling Heights MI 48311-0754

**GIRVIN, JAMES EDWARD,** lawyer; b. Albany, N.Y., Dec. 7, 1955; s. James Joseph and Joan (Haggerty) G.; m. Theresa Kelly, Dec. 12, 1981; children: James P., Kevin P., Kelly M. BA in Polit. Sci. cum laude, Siena Coll., Loudonville, N.Y., 1978; JD, Albany Law Sch., 1981. Bar: N.Y., Mass., U.S. Dist. Ct. (no. dist.) N.Y., U.S. Ct. Appeals (2d cir.), U.S. Supreme Ct., U.S. Ct. Mil. Appeals. From assoc. to profl. O'Connell and Aronowitz, PC, Albany, 1986-91; ptnr. Ruberti, Girvin & Ferlazzo, PC, Albany, 1991—; instr. bus. law McKendrie Coll., Radcliffe, Ky., 1993. Author: Interview/Selection Procedures for Shared Decision Making Teams and Advisory Committees, 1995. Counsel, Albany Sports Found., 1995—; bd. dirs. St. Catherine's Home for Children, Albany, 1996—. Capt. U.S. Army, 1982-85. Recipient VIP award Capital Dist. Ctr. for the Disabled, 1994. Mem. N.Y. State Bar Assn., Albany County Bar Assn., KC, Siena Coll. Alumni Assn. (trustee scholarship com. 1996—). Education and schools, Labor, Municipal (including bonds). Home: 2723 Doellner Cir Castleton On Hudson NY 12033-9752 Office: Ruberti Girvin & Ferlazzo 120 State St Albany NY 12207-1606

**GISSER, SHELDON M.,** lawyer; b. Cleve., June 8, 1938; s. Morris S. and Esther (Zelikow) G.; m. Nan S. Schwab, June 26, 1960; children: Marilyn R., Daniel J. AB, Dartmouth Coll., 1960; JD, U. Chgo., 1963. Bar: Ohio 1963, U.S. Dist. Ct. (no. dist.) Ohio 1963, U.S. Ct. Appeals (6th cir.) 1965. Assoc. Bernard S. Goldfarb, Cleve., 1963-66; sole practitioner Cleve., 1967-69; assoc. Selker, Patchan & Einbund, Cleve., 1970-73; ptnr. Zipkin, Turoff & Gisser, Cleve., 1973-76, Shapiro, Turoff & Gisser, Cleve., 1977-92, Zamore & Gisser, Cleve., 1992-95, Zamore, Luria & Belkin, Shaker Heights, Ohio, 1995-98, Turoff & Sprague, Shaker Heights, 1998—; bd. dirs., v.p., sec. Cleve. Coin Machine Exch., Inc., Cleve., 1966—, Entertainment Resource Corp., Cleve., 1970—; ptnr. The Fayerweather Co., Cleve., 1970—. Bd. trustees, sec. Alzheimers Assn. Cleve., 1986-94; mem. cmty. adv. coun., pres. Mental Devel. Ctr. of Case Western Res., Cleve., 1980-93. Mem. Ohio State Bar Assn., Cleve. Bar Assn. Jewish. Avocations: photography, cross-country skiing, travel, reading. Office: Zamore Turoff & Sprague 20600 Chagrin Blvd Shaker Heights OH 44122

**GITLEN, PHILIP H.,** lawyer, law educator; b. N.Y.C., Nov. 27, 1947; s. A. Robert and Martha G.; m. Melody A. Mackenzie; children: Laurel, Max, Hillary. BA magna cum laude, Lehigh U., 1969; JD, NYU, 1972. Bar: N.Y. 1972. Gen. counsel N.Y. State Dept. Environ. Conservation, Albany, 1974-78; ptnr. Whiteman Osterman & Hanna, Albany, 1981—; adj. prof. Albany Law Sch., 1994—. Fax: 518-487-7777. E-mail: phg@woh.com. Office: Whiteman Osterman & Hanna One Commerce Plz Albany NY 12260

**GITLIN, RICHARD ALAN,** lawyer; b. Hartford, Conn., May 26, 1942; s. Max and Mary (Kaminsky) G.; m. Nancy Bobrow, Aug. 22, 1964; children: Jeffrey, David, Michael. B.A., U. Conn., 1964, J.D., 1967. Bar: Conn. 1967. Founding mem. Hebb & Gitlin, Hartford, 1973-99; ptnr. Bingham Dana, LLP, Hartford, 1999—; pres. INSOL Internat., 1991-93; mem. Bankruptcy and Creditors' Rights Adv. Com., Practising Law Inst., 1981—; chmn., panelist, moderator, lectr. seminars. Author, co-author outlines for Practicing Law Inst. Book, 1980-81, also articles. Mem. ABA (bus. bankruptcy com. of corp., banking and bus. law sect. 1981—). Bankruptcy, Finance. Office: Bingham Dana LLP One State St Hartford CT 06103-3178

**GITTER, MAX,** lawyer; b. Samarkand, Uzbekistan, Nov. 17, 1943; came to U.S., 1950; s. Wolf and Paula (Nissenbaum) G.; m. Elisabeth Karla Gesmer, June 22, 1969; children: Emily F., Michael A. AB, Harvard U., 1965; LLB, Yale U., 1968. Bar: N.Y., D.C., U.S. Dist. Ct. (so. and ea. dists.) N.Y., U.S. Ct. Appeals (2d, D.C., 4th and 9th cirs.), U.S. Supreme Ct. Instr. U. Chgo. Law Sch., 1968-69; assoc. Paul, Weiss, Rifkind, Wharton & Garrison, N.Y.C., 1969-76, ptnr., 1976—; vis. lectr. law Yale U., 1986-88; mem. Internat. Steering Com. on Free Trade with Israel; vice chmn., Yivo Inst. for Jewish Rsch. Spl. counsel Mayor of N.Y.C. to Investigate Office of Chief Medical Examiner, 1985. Mem. Fed. Bar Coun., Assn. Bar City of N.Y. (vice chmn. com. on profl. and jud. ethics 1985-86), Am. Law Inst. (spkr., panelist 1985-89), Practicing Law Inst. (spkr., panelist 1983-92), N.Y. State Bar Assn. (exec. com. sect. on comml. and fed. litigation 1994—). Federal civil litigation, State civil litigation. Office: Paul Weiss Rifkind Wharton & Garrison Rm 200 1285 Ave Of The Americas Fl 21 New York NY 10019-6028

**GITTES, FREDERICK M.,** lawyer; b. Hampton, Va., June 4, 1947; s. Hymam R. and Pearl (Levin) G. Cert. achievement, U. Oslo, Norway, 1967; BA with honors, Rollins Coll., 1968; JD cum laude, Ohio State U., 1975. Bar: Ohio 1975, U.S. Supreme Ct., U.S. Ct. Appeals (6th cir.), U.S. Dist. Ct. (so. dist.) Ohio. Ptnr. Spater, Gittes, Schulte, Kolman, Columbus, Ohio, 1975—. Contbr. articles to profl. jours. Bd. dirs., founder Columbus Tenants Union, 1970-74; bd. dirs. Columbus Recycling Ctr., 1987-90, Columbus Legal Aid Soc., 1989-97. Walter J. Black Teaching fellow L.I. U., 1968-69. Fellow Columbus Bar Found., Coll. Labor and Employment Lawyers; mem. Nat. Employment Lawyers Assn. (bd. dirs. 1990, v.p. 1998—), Ohio Employment Lawyers Assn. (state chair 1988—), Ohio State Bar Assn. (chair civil rights com., v.p. labor/employment law sect.), Columbus Bar Assn. General civil litigation, Civil rights, Labor. Office: Spater Gittes Schulte Kolman 723 Oak St Columbus OH 43205-1011

**GIUFFRÉ, JOHN JOSEPH,** lawyer; b. Bklyn., Nov. 30, 1963; s. John B. and Marilyn N. G.; m. Lauren P. Dippel, Sept. 1, 1990; 1 child, John Paul. BA, Columbia Coll., 1984; JD cum laude, U. Pa., 1987. Bar: N.J. 1987, N.Y. 1988, Conn. 1988, Pa. 1988, U.S. Dist. Ct. (so. and ea. dists.) N.Y. 1989. Assoc. labor and employment law sect. Morgan, Lewis & Bockius, N.Y.C., 1987-88; assoc. McLaughlin & McLaughlin, Bklyn., 1988-93; founding ptnr. Giuffré & Kaplan, PC, Hicksville, N.Y., 1994—. Editor: U. Pa. Jour. Comparative Bus. and Capital Market Law, 1985-86; sr. editor: U. Pa. Jour. Internat. Bus. Law, 1986-87. Vol. lawyer Bklyn. Bar Assn. Vol. Lawyer Project, 1992-93; trustee 1st Presbyn. Ch., Flushing, N.Y., 1991-92, pres. bd. trustees, 1993, elder, 1996—; bd. dirs. Flushing Christian Sch., 1994—. Mem. Nassau County Bar Assn., Phi Beta Kappa. Avocations: reading, studying history, ice hockey. General civil litigation, Personal injury, Probate. Office: Giuffré & Kaplan PC 28 E Old Country Rd Hicksville NY 11801-4207

**GIUFFRIDA, NOEL PETER,** lawyer; b. N.Y.C., Jan. 10, 1932; s. Natale Angelo Giuffrida and Margaret Francis Alpino; m. Jacklynn Sally Montgomery, June 4, 1956 (div. Sept. 1966); children: Michele F. Harris, Charles M. BA, USL, 1957; JD, Tulane U., 1960; grad., U. Va., 1967. Bar: La. 1960, Miss. 1971, U.S. Dist. Ct. (no. dist.) Miss., U.S. Ct. Mil. Appeals. Col. U.S. Army, 1940-53, 66-70. Decorated Disting. Svc. cross U.S. Army, Vietnam, 1967, two Silver stars U.S. Army, Korea-Vietnam, 1968. Republican. Avocations: boating, golf, working out, yard work. Criminal, General civil litigation, General practice. Home and Office: 919A Glastonbury Cir Ridgeland MS 39157-1210

**GIULITTO, PAULA CHRISTINE,** lawyer; b. Ravenna, Ohio, June 20, 1967; d. Joseph and F. Jean G.; m. Lawrence A. Sutter III, Nov. 22, 1997. BS, Miami (Ohio) U., 1989; JD, U. Akron Sch. Law, 1992. Bar. Ohio 1992. Assoc. Giulitto & Berger Attys. at Law, Ravenna, 1992—. bd. dirs. ARC, Ravenna, 1994—, chmn. bd. 1997—; mem. bd. dirs. Boys and Girls Club, Ravenna, 1996—. Mem. ABA, ATLA, Portage County Bar Assn. Personal injury, State civil litigation, Family and matrimonial. Office: Giulitto & Berger 222 W Main St PO Box 350 Ravenna OH 44266-0350

**GIVAN, RICHARD MARTIN,** retired state supreme court justice; b. Indpls., June 7, 1921; s. Clinton Hodell and Glee (Bowen) G.; m. Pauline Marie Haggart, Feb. 28, 1945; children: Madalyn Givan Hesson, Sandra Givan Chenoweth, Patricia Givan Smith, Elizabeth Givan Whipple. LL.B., Ind. U., 1951. Bar: Ind. 1952. Partner firm Bowen, Myers, Northam & Givan, 1960-69; justice Ind. Supreme Ct., 1969-74, chief justice, 1974-87, assoc. justice, 1987-95; ret.; dep. pub. defender Ind., 1952-53; dep. atty. gen., 1953-54; dep. pros. atty. Marion County, 1965-66; ret., 1995; mem. Ind. Ho. Reps., 1967-68. Served to 2d lt. USAAF, 1942-45. Mem. Ind. Bar Assn., Indpls. Bar Assn., Ind. Soc. Chgo., Newcomen Soc. N.Am., Internat. Arabian Horse Assn. (past dir., chmn. ethical practices rev. bd.), Ind. Arabian Horse Club (pres. 1971-72), Lions, Sigma Delta Kappa. Mem. Soc. of Friends. Home: 6690 S County Road 1025 E Indianapolis IN 46231-2495

**GIVAS, THOMAS PETER,** lawyer; b. Poughkeepsie, N.Y., July 10, 1957; s. Peter Thomas and Maria (Bay) G.; m. Lynn Marie Kimball, May 22, 1982; children: Stephanie Fay, Peter Thomas, Nicholas James. BA, Dartmouth Coll., 1979; JD, Syracuse U., 1982. Bar: N.Y. 1983, U.S. Dist. Ct. (no. dist.) N.Y. 1983, U.S. Dist. Ct. (we. dist.) N.Y. 1985. Lawyer Ali, Pappas & Cox, P.C., Syracuse, N.Y., 1983—. Mem. Onondaga County Bar Assn., N.Y. State Bar Assn., Comml. Law League. Republican. Greek Orthodox. Avocations: skiing, golf. Consumer commercial, Contracts commercial, State civil litigation. Home: 3917 Sandpiper Ln Liverpool NY 13090-1528 Office: Ali Pappas & Cox 500 Syracuse Bldg 224 Harrison St Ste 500 Syracuse NY 13202-3035

**GIVENS, EDWIN D.,** lawyer; b. Charleston, S.C., Sept. 4, 1963; s. Willie E. and Juanita H. Givens; m. Kelly Ann Seabrook, Nov. 26, 1994. BS in Computer Sci., S.C. State U., Orangeburg, 1985; JD, U. S.C., 1994. Bar: S.C. 1994, U.S. Dist. Ct. S.C. 1994. With Offices of Franchot Brown, Columbia, S.C., 1991-92, S.C. House Jud. Com., Columbia, 1992-94; assoc. Rosen, Rosen & Hagood, Charleston, 1993, Newmam & Sabb, P.A., Charleston, 1994-97; atty. S.C. Commr. for the Blind, Charleston, 1997-98; assoc. McNair Law Firm, Charleston, 1998—. Bd. dirs. 100 Black Men of Am., 1995—, S.C. Philharm., Columbia, 1998; trustee S.C. State U., Orangeburg, 1995—. Named to Outstanding Young of Am., 1996; S.C. State U. Presdl. schoalr, 1985. Mem. ABA (vice chair minorities in the profession 1996-97). Democrat. Baptist. Avocations: golf, running. Legislative, General civil litigation, Administrative and regulatory. Office: McNair Law Firm PO Box 11290 1301 Gervais St Columbia SC 29201-3326

**GIVENS, GEORGE FRANKLIN,** lawyer; b. Roanoke, Va., Sept. 18, 1946; s. Irvin Carlile and Alice Daniel (McCallum) G.; m. Mary Ann Barnack, Sept. 14, 1973; children: Gregory Franklin, Meredith McCallum, Andrew Ryan. BA in History, Va. Commonwealth U., 1970; MA in Ednl. Adminstrn., East Carolina U., 1979; JD, N.C. Ctrl. U., 1, 1983. Bar: N.C. 1983, Va. 1984. Tchr., asst. prin., coach Gaston (N.C.) Jr./Sr. H.S. Northampton County Schs., 1970-79; prin. Murfreesboro (N.C.) Mid. Sch. Hertford County Schs., 1979-80; staff atty., sr. staff atty., prin. legis. analyst Gen. Assembly N.C., Raleigh, 1985—; counsel environ. rev. com. Gen. Assembly N.C., 1986—; counsel House Environ. Com., Senate Agr./Environ./Natural Resources Com., 1987—. Episcopalian. Avocation: flying. Home: PO Box 85 Raleigh NC 27602-0085 Office: Gen Assembly NC 545 Legis Office Bldg 300 N Salisbury St Raleigh NC 27603-5925

**GIVENS, RICHARD AYRES,** lawyer; b. N.Y.C., June 16, 1932; s. Meredith Bruner and Ruth Wheelock (Ayres) G.; m. Janet Eaton, Aug. 24, 1957; children: Susan Ruth, Jane Lucile. AB, Columbia U., 1953; MS in Econs., U. Wis., 1954; LLB, Columbia U., 1959. Bar: N.Y. 1959, U.S. Dist. Ctr. (so. and ea. dists.) N.Y. 1960, U.S. Ct. Appeals (2d cir.) 1962, U.S. Supreme Ct. 1966, U.S. Ct. Claims 1980, U.S. Ct. Appeals (4th cir.) 1981. Assoc. Hughes, Hubbard & Reed, N.Y.C., 1959-61; asst. U.S. atty. So. Dist. N.Y., 1961-71; regional dir. FTC, N.Y.C., 1971-77; counsel Botein, Hays & Sklar, N.Y.C., 1977-89; law clk. to Hon. Vincent L. Broderick U.S. Dist. Ct. (so. dist.) N.Y., White Plains, 1992-95; law sec. to Hon. Jay Gold acting Supreme Ct. Justice N.Y., 1995-96; chmn. program on drafting documents in plain lang., 1981. Author: Manual of Federal Practice, 5th edit., 1998, Advocacy: The Art of Pleading a Cause, 1980, 3d rev. edit., 1992, Legal Strategies for Industrial Innovation (Best Law Book of 1982 award Assn. Am. Pubs.), 1982; Antitrust: An Economic Approach, 1983; contbr. articles to profl. jours. With U.S. Army, 1954-56. Mem. ABA, N.Y. State Bar Assn. (chmn. task force on simplification 1985-89, legis. com., antitrust sect. 1980-83), Assn. of Bar of City of N.Y. Democrat. Unitarian.

**GIVENS, RICHARD DONALD,** lawyer; b. Yosemite, Calif., July 4, 1939; s. Frank Raymond and Violet Gladis (Von Glahn) G.; m. Marsha Jean Leahy Artunian, June 19, 1965 (div. Jan. 1982); children: Leslie, Amy, Katie. BA, Stanford U., 1962; LLB, JD, U. Calif., San Francisco, 1965. Bar: Calif. 1966, U.S. Dist. Ct. (no. dist.) Calif. 1966, U.S. Ct. Appeals (9th cir.) 1966. Assoc. Ropers, Majeski, Phelps, Redwood City, Calif., 1966-69; assoc. gen. counsel Boise Cascade Corp., Palo Alto, Calif., 1969-73; gen. counsel Boise Cascade Bldg. Co., L.A., 1969-73; prin. Leahy, O'Dea & Givens, San Francisco, 1973-86; pvt. practice Redwood City, 1986—; arbitrator Am. Arbitration Assn., San Francisco, 1994-95. Contbr. articles to profl. jours. Chmn. bd. dirs. Bay Area Lupus Found., San Jose, Calif., 1994—; spl. master San Mateo Superior Ct., Redwood City, 1995. Mem. ABA, San Francisco Bar Assn. (various coms.), San Mateo Bar Assn. (various coms.), Stanford Jr. Alumni (pres. 1967-68). Avocations: duck hunting, fishing, sailing. General civil litigation, Environmental, Real property. Home: 1394 Sequoia Tahoe City CA Address: 617 Veterans Blvd Ste 106 Redwood City CA 94063-1404

**GIVENS, STANN WILLIAM,** lawyer; b. Appleton, Wis., Feb. 20, 1950; s. Paul Ronald and Leona (Janssen) G.; m. Bonnie MacGregor, Aug. 28, 1971; children: Christian MacGregor, Emily Kate. BS, Bucknell U., 1971; JD, The Fla. State U., 1973. Bar: Fla. 1974, U.S. Ct. Appeals (5th cir.) 1974, U.S. Dist. Ct. (mid. dist.) Fla. 1974. Asst. state atty. Hillsborough State Atty.'s Office, Tampa, Fla., 1973-75; asst. city atty. City of Tampa, 1975-77; atty. Stann W. Givens, P.A., Tampa, 1977-93, Knox and Givens, P.A., 1993—. Race dir. Gasparilla Distance Classic, Tampa, 1980-81, dir., 1977-85; elder Temple Terrace (Fla.) Presbyn. Ch., 1976—; moderator permanent jud. commn. Synod of South Atlantic of Presbyn. Ch., 1977-88. Recipient Outstanding Young Men Am. award, 1980, 77, Outstanding Community Svc. award Boys Club Tampa, 1981. Fellow Am. Acad. Matrimonial Lawyers; mem. Fla. Bar (cert. in marital and family law, chair marital and family law bd. cert. com., chair 13th jud. cir. grievance com.), Hillsborough County Bar Assn. (chair family law sect. 1988-89). Presbyterian. Avocations: youth sports, golf. Family and matrimonial, Personal injury, Criminal. Office: Knox and Givens PA 607 W Horatio St Tampa FL 33606-2272

**GIVHAN, ROBERT MARCUS,** lawyer; b. Mineral Wells, Tex., May 10, 1959; s. Walter Houston Givhan and Marion Blackwell Callen Stothart; m. Janet Lee Dothard, May 6, 1989; children: Vivian Lee, Charlotte Ann, Virginia Mae. BA, U. Ala., Tuscaloosa, 1981; JD, Cumberland Sch. Law, Birmingham, Ala., 1986. Bar: Ala. 1987, D.C. 1989, U.S. Supreme Ct. 1989, U.S. Ct. Appeals (D.C. and 11th cirs.), U.S. Dist. Ct. (so., mid. and no. dists.) Ala. 1987. Assoc. Perry and Russell, Montgomery, Ala., 1987-88; dep. dist. atty. 15th Jud. Cir. of Ala., Montgomery, 1988-91; dep. atty. gen. Office of Atty. Gen. of Ala., Montgomery, 1991-95; ptnr. Johnston Barton Proctor & Powell LLP, Birmingham, 1995—. Fellow Am. Coll. Pros. Attys.; mem. ABA (vice chmn. antitrust competition and trade regulation com. of adminstrv. law sect. 1994—), Ala. State Bar Assn., Birmingham Bar Assn. (co-chmn. econs. of law practice com. 1998, 99), Am. Health Lawyers Assn. Episcopalian. Avocations: whitewater rafting, hiking, music collecting, book collecting. General civil litigation, Antitrust, Health. Home: 427 Cliff Pl Birmingham AL 35209-5201 Office: 2900 AmSouth/Harbert Plz 1901 6th Ave N Birmingham AL 35203-2618

**GIVHAN, THOMAS BARTRAM,** lawyer; b. Lexington, Ky., Sept. 24, 1926; s. Thomas Holman and Eva Mae (Beck) G.; m. Sharon Rose Richard, June 10, 1949 (dec.); children: Elisè Charles, Ellen Foster, Aaron Todd. JD, U. Ky., 1951. Bar: Ky. 1957, U.S. Dist. Ct. (ea. dist.) Ky. 1951, U.S. Dist. Ct. (we. dist.) Ky. 1957, U.S. Supreme Ct. 1972. City atty. City of Shepherdsville, Ky., 1953-57; county atty. Bullitt County, Shepherdsville, 1958-61, 66-73, 1982-89; mem. Ky. Ho. of Reps., Frankfort, 1974-78, chmn. judiciary com., 1976-78; ptnr. Givhan & Spainhour, P.S.C., Shepherdsville, 1979—; mem. Ky. Gov.'s Ad Hoc Com. on Jud. Reform, Frankfort, 1976. Chmn. Bullitt County Dem. Reform, 1968-71; mem. Bullitt County Planning Commn., 1995—. With USMC, 1945-46, PTO. Mem. ABA, Ky. Bar Assn. (ho. of dels. 1964-68, character and fitness com. 1968-74, CLE award 1981), Ky. Acad. Trial Attys. (gov. 1978-86), Bullitt County Bar Assn. (sec./treas. 1956-61). General civil litigation, General practice, Personal injury. Office: Givhan & Spainhour PSC Profl Bldg Shepherdsville KY 40165

**GIZA, DAVID ALAN,** lawyer; b. Chgo., May 16, 1958; s. Bruno Frank and Marianne Theresa (Mozdren) G.; m. Karen Ann Van Maldegiam, Nov. 5, 1988. BS, DePaul U., 1981; JD, John Marshall U., 1984. Bar: Ill. 1985, U.S. Dist. Ct. (no. dist.) Ill. 1985. Atty. pvt. practice, Chgo., 1985-86; assoc. Larry Karchmar, Ltd., Chgo., 1986-87, Kovitz, Shifrin & Waitzman, Chgo., 1987; atty. W.W. Grainger, Inc., Skokie, Ill., 1987-91; atty. W.W. Grainger, Inc., Lincolnshire, Ill., 1991—, divsn. atty., 1993-96, sr. atty., 1996-98, asst. gen. counsel, 1998—. Trustee Village of Libertyville, Ill., 1995—; chmn. Camp Lake (Wis.)/Ctr. Lake Rehab. Dist., 1990—. Mem. Am. Trial Lawyers Assn., Am. Corp. Counsel Assn., Ill. State Bar Assn., Chgo. Bar Assn., Lake County Bar Assn. Republican. Roman Catholic. Avocations: politics, water sports, reading, travel, cooking. Fax: 847-913-7584. E-mail: giza.d@grainger.com.. General corporate, Contracts commercial, General civil litigation. Office: W W Grainger Inc 333 Knightsbridge Pkwy Lincolnshire IL 60069-3639

**GJERTSEN, O. GERARD,** lawyer; b. Bklyn., June 24, 1932; s. Ole Gerhard and Hilma (Jorgensen) G.; m. Carol Ann Jurkops, June 2, 1962; children: Gerard, Gary, Krista, Karen. BA, Columbia Coll., 1954; JD, NYU, 1958. Bar: N.Y. 1958, U.S. Dist. Ct. (so. dist.) N.Y. 1960. Ptnr. Thacher Proffitt & Wood, N.Y.C., 1964—. Vice chmn. Tuckahoe (N.Y.) Urban Renewal Agy. With U.S. Army, 1954-55. Mem. ABA, N.Y. State Bar Assn., Assn. of Bar of City of N.Y., Westchester County Bar Assn., White Plains Bar Assn., Scarsdale Golf Club. Avocations: music, sports. Estate planning, Real property. Home: 262 Dante Ave Tuckahoe NY 10707-3015 Office: Thacher Proffitt & Wood 11 Martine Ave Fl 8 White Plains NY 10606-1934

**GLADDEN, JOSEPH RHEA, JR.,** lawyer; b. Atlanta, Oct. 5, 1942; s. Joseph Rhea Sr. and Frances (Baker) G.; m. Sarah Elizabeth Bynum, Aug. 21, 1965; children: Joseph III, Elizabeth. AB, Emory U., 1964; LLB, U. Va., 1967. Bar: Ga. 1968, U.S. Dist. Ct. (no. dist.) Ga. 1968, U.S. Ct. Appeals (5th cir.) 1968, U.S. Ct. Appeals (11th cir.) 1985. Assoc. King & Spalding, Atlanta, 1967-73, ptnr., 1973-85; v.p., sr. staff counsel The Coca-Cola Co., Atlanta, 1985-87, v.p. dep. gen. counsel, 1987-90, v.p., gen. counsel, 1990-91, sr. v.p., gen. counsel, 1991—; bd. dirs. Coca-Cola Enterprises, Emory Healthcarere; chmn. bd. dirs. Wesley Woods Ctr. of Emory U., Inc., oca-Cola Amatil. Chmn. bd. trustees Agnes Scott Coll..; bd. dirs. Atlanta Ballet; trustee Lovett Sch., Acad. Search Cons. Svc. Mem. ABA (com. corp. law gen. counsel), Am Corp. Counsel Assn., Ga. Bar Assn., State Bar Ga., Assn. Gen. Counsel, Atlanta Bar Assn., Commerce Club, Piedmont Driving Club. Antitrust, Federal civil litigation, General corporate. Office: The Coca-Cola Co PO Drawer 1734 Atlanta GA 30301-1734

**GLADISH, DAVID STEPHEN,** lawyer; b. Cedar Rapids, Iowa, Apr. 20, 1969; s. Allen and Michelle Gladish. BA in Criminal Justice cum laude, Calumet Coll. of St. Joseph, Hammond, Ind., 1991; JD, Valparaiso U., 1995. Bar: Ind. 1995, Ill. 1995, U.S. Dist. Ct. (no. and so. dists.) Ind. 1998, U.S. Dist. Ct. (no. dist.) Ill. 1998, U.S. Ct. Appeals (7th cir.) 1998. Probation officer Hammond City Ct., 1992-96; assoc. Smith & DeBonis, Highland, Ind., 1995—. Office: Smith & DeBonis 9696 Gordon Dr Highland IN 46322-2909

**GLADSTONE, RICHARD WILTON, II,** lawyer; b. Pitts., May 21, 1945; s. Richard Wilton and Doris (Whitehill) G.; m. Virginia Long Gladstone, Dec. 28, 1973; children: Chase Whitehill, Sheppard Heatherington. BS in Engring., Lehigh U., Bethlehem, Pa., 1967; JD, U. Pitts., 1970. Ptnr. Eckert, Seamans, Cherin & Mellott, Pitts., 1970—. Bd. mem. Animal Rescue League, Pitts., 1985-90, Sdopted Family Found., Pitts., 1990-98. Mem. Rolling Rock Club, Duquesne Club. Republican. Presbyterian. Avocations: tennis, squash. Office: Eckert Seamans Cherin & Mellott 42nd Fl 600 Grant St Pittsburgh PA 15219

**GLADSTONE, ROBERT ALBERT,** lawyer; b. Phila., June 2, 1942; s. Albert Frederick and Elizabeth (O'Neill) G.; m. Barbara M. Cranmer, June 21, 1964; children: Frederick Robert, Elizabeth Rose. BA, Ursinus Coll., Collegeville, Pa., 1964; JD, Rutgers U., Newark, 1968. Bar: N.J. 1968, U.S. Dist. Ct. N.J. 1968, U.S. Ct. Claims 1992. Assoc. Pellettieri & Rabstein, Trenton, N.J., 1968-71; ptnr. Brener & Gladstone, Trenton, 1971-74, Warren Goldberg & Berman, Princeton, N.J., 1975-82, Schaff, Motiuk, Gladstone & Reed, Flemington, N.J., 1982-90; city atty. City of Trenton, 1971-75; ptnr., shareholder Shanley & Fisher, P.C., Morristown, N.J., 1990—; twp. atty. Twp. of Lawrence, Lawrenceville, N.J., 1985-88; mem. com. on tax ct. N.J. Supreme Ct., 1982-86; chmn. D'Imperio Property Superfund Site Group, Hamilton Twp., N.J., 1994—. Contbr. articles to law jours. Chmn. Mercer County Rep. Com., Trenton, 1977-80; chmn. bd. trustees Coll. of N.J., Ewing, 1977; mem. devel. bd. Prevention Edn., Lawrenceville, 1992—, Greater Trenton C.M.H.C., 1994—. Mem. ABA, N.J. Bar Assn. (chmn. local govt. law sect. 1981-84), Trial Attys. N.J. Avocations: golf, outdoor activities. General civil litigation, Environmental, Condemnation. Home: 297 River Rd Belle Mead NJ 08502-5607 Office: Shanley & Fisher 131 Madison Ave Morristown NJ 07960-6097

**GLANSTEIN, ELEANOR ELOVICH,** lawyer; b. Bklyn., Feb. 23, 1944; d. Sol Herman and Fanny (Berglas) Elovich; m. Joel Charles Glanstein, July 2, 1966; children: David, Stacey. BA, Bklyn. Coll., 1964; MA, NYU, 1965; JD, Hofstra U., 1975. Bar: N.Y. 1976, U.S. Dist. Ct. (so. and ea. dists.) N.Y. 1976, U.S. Supreme Ct. 1978. Tchr. Lafayette High Sch., Bklyn., 1965-70; assoc. Markowitz & Glanstein, N.Y.C., 1975-80; pvt. practice N.Y.C., 1980—; adj. faculty N.Y. Law Sch., 1989—. Mem. ABA, Indsl. Relations Rsch. Assn., N.Y. State Bar Assn., N.Y. County Lawyers Assn., Soc. Profls. in Dispute Resolution. General practice. Office: 880 3rd Ave New York NY 10022-4730

**GLANSTEIN, JOEL CHARLES,** lawyer; b. Jersey City, May 16, 1940; s. Harry I. and Katherine G.; m. Eleanor Elovich, July 2, 1966; children: David Michael, Stacey Alison. BA with honors, Lehigh U., 1962; LLB, NYU, 1965, LLM in Labor Law, 1969. Bar: N.Y. 1967, D.C. 1975, U. S. Ct. Appeals (2d cir.) 1970, U.S. Supreme Ct. 1971, U.S. Ct. Appeals (1st cir.) 1972, U.S. Ct. Appeals (3d cir.) 1978, U.S. Ct. Appeals (11th and 9th cirs.) 1981, U.S. Ct. Appeals (5th cir.) 1982, U.S. Ct. Appeals (6th cir.) 1984, U.S. Ct. Appeals (7th cir.) 1999. Assoc. Pressman & Scribner, N.Y.C., 1968-69; ptnr. Scribner, Glanstein & Klein, N.Y.C., 1970-72, Markowitz & Glanstein, LLP, N.Y.C., 1972-79, O'Donnell & Schwartz, N.Y.C., 1980-90; O'Donnell, Schwartz, Glanstein & Rosen, N.Y.C., 1991—; adj. assoc. prof. N.Y. Law Sch., N.Y.C., 1980-95. Mem. ABA (labor and employment law sect., com. on internat. labor law 1976, com. on law of alternative dispute resolution 1976), N.Y. State Bar Assn. (labor and employment law sect., chmn. 1987-88), N.Y. County Lawyers Assn., D.C. Bar Assn., Maritime Law Assn. U.S., Downtown Athletic Club. Labor, Pension, profit-sharing, and employee benefits, Admiralty. Office: O'Donnell Schwartz Glanstein & Rosen LLP 305 Madison Ave Rm 1022 New York NY 10165-0100

**GLANTZ, WENDY NEWMAN,** lawyer; b. L.I., N.Y., Dec. 16, 1956; d. Sidney and Sarah (Rudnitsky) Newman; m. Ronald Paul Glantz, Dec. 29, 1983. BS, SUNY, Stonybrook, 1978; JD, Nova Law Ctr., 1982. Bar: Fla., 1983. Assoc. Glazer & Glazer, Hallandale, Fla., 1983-85; ptnr. Pasin & Glantz, Lauderhill, Fla., 1985-86; ptnr. Glantz & Glantz, Lauderhill and Plantation, Fla., 1985-86, Plantation and Miami, Fla., 1986—; seminar leader Marital Strategies, Ft. Lauderdale, 1985—. Editor Pipeline, 1985-86; contbr. articles to profl. mags. Co-chairperson, editor Parents Anonymous, 1986—, mem. adv. bd.; chairperson Bus. Profl. Group of Sunrise Jewish Ctr., 1988—; sponsor Jewish Community Ctr., mem. fund raising com.; mem. South Fla. Symphony, Women of Fine Arts. Mem. ABA (family law sect.), NAFE (pres. S.E. chpt. 1985—), Fla. Bar Assn. (family law sect.), Assn. Trial Lawyers Am., Broward County Bar Assn. (program coord. continuing legal edn. family law sect.), West Broward Bar Assn. (pres. 1989-90), Fla. Assn. Women Lawyers (bd. dirs.), Broward County Women Lawyers Assn. (pres. 1988-90), Nat. Assn. Women Bus. Owners (Broward chpt.), Plantation C. of C. Family and matrimonial. Office: Glantz & Glantz 7951 SW 6th St Ste 200 Fort Lauderdale FL 33324-3223

**GLANZER, MONA NAOMI,** lawyer; b. N.Y.C., July 29, 1931; d. David and Henrietta (Schweitzer) Sorcher; m. Murray A. Glanzer, Sept. 20, 1953; children: Michael John, Marla Curtis, James S. LLB, Bklyn. Law Sch., 1953. Bar: N.Y. 1954, U.S. Dist. Ct. (so. and ea. dists.) N.Y. 1965, U.S. Supreme Ct. 1976, U.S. Ct. Appeals (2d cir.) 1981. Editor CCH Pension Plan Guide, Chgo., 1953-54; assoc. Harry H. Rains, Rains, Pogrebin & Scher, Mineola, N.Y., 1965-71; ptnr. Rains & Pogrebin, P.C., Mineola, 1971—; arbitrator small claims U.S. Dist Ct., N.Y., 1985—. Contbr. articles to profl. jours. Mem. adv. com. Recodification N.Y. State Workers' Compensation Law Project, 1985-87. Recipient Presdl. Pvt. Sector Initiative Commendation citation. Fellow ABA Found.; mem. Am. Arbitration Assn. (panel 1987—, arbitrator), Coun. Lic. Physiotherapists N.Y. (hon.), N.Y. State Assn. Profl. Land Surveyors (hon.), N.Y. State Bar Assn. (chair labor and employment law sect. 1988-89, chair com. pension, welfare and related plans 1983-86, chair com. labor standards legis. 1986-87), Nassau-Suffolk Women's Bar Assn. (pres. 1986-87). Alternative dispute resolution, Labor, Pension, profit-sharing, and employee benefits.

**GLASER, ARTHUR HENRY,** lawyer; b. Jersey City, May 1, 1947; s. Ned C. and Lorraine I. (Neil) G.; m. Waynelia Potter, Mar. 19, 1994; children: Kimberly N., Kevin M., Daniel J. BS, Hampden-Sydney Coll., 1968; JD, U. Va., 1973. Bar: Ga. 1973, U.S. Dist. Ct. (no. and mid. dists.) Ga., U.S. Ct. Appeals (11th cir.). Assoc. Swift, Currie, McGhee & Hiers, Atlanta, 1973-78, ptnr., 1978-83; ptnr. Drew, Eckl & Farnham, Atlanta, 1983-98, Self, Glaser & Davis, LLP, Atlanta, 1999—. Mem. ABA, Ga. Bar Assn., Atlanta Bar Assn. Presbyterian. Insurance, Libel, Personal injury. Home: 1540 Burnt Hickory Rd NW Marietta GA 30064-1308 Office: Self Glaser & Davis LLP Ste 1650 400 Interstate North Pkwy SE Atlanta GA 30339-5029

**GLASER, HOWARD B.,** lawyer; b. 1958; m. Julia Glaser; children: Sarah, Erica. BA, SUNY, 1980; JD cum laude, Harvard U., 1994. Asst. to dir. polit. action and legislation Dist. Coun. 37 Am. Fedn. State, County and Mcpl. Employees, 1981-82; dep. dir. pub. info. N.Y. State Dept. Taxation and Fin., 1983-86; spl. asst. N.Y. Gov. Mario Cuomo, 1986-91; gen. dep. asst. sec. for cmty. planning and devel. U.S. Dept. Housing and Urban Devel., Washington, 1994-97, dep. gen. counsel for programs and regulation, 1997—. Office: Dept Housing & Urban Devel 451 7th St SW Washington DC 20410-0002

**GLASER, LENORE MERYL,** lawyer; b. Harvey, Ill., Aug. 4, 1950. BA, Reed Coll., 1973; JD, Northeastern U., 1980. Bar: Mass. 1980, U.S. Dist. Ct. Mass. 1980, U.S. Ct. Appeals (1st cir.) 1980. Housing atty. Western Mass. Legal Svcs., Holyoke, 1980-83; staff atty. Inquilinos Boriqus en Accion, Boston, 1983-85; assoc. Johnson & Somberg, Boston, 1985-87, ptnr., 1987-90; pvt. practice Boston, 1990-96; of counsel Stern, Shapiro, Weissberg & Garin, Boston, 1996—; adj. prof. Suffolk U. Law Sch., Boston, 1985-87, U. Mass., Boston, 1985, 87, 90. Contbr. articles to profl. jours. Curi-clk. La Alianza Hispana, Boston, 1994—. Mem. Am. Immigration Lawyers Assn., Mass. Bar Assn. Criminal, Immigration, naturalization, and customs, Appellate. Office: 90 Canal St Fl 5 Boston MA 02114-2018

**GLASER, STEVEN JAY,** lawyer; b. Tacoma, Dec. 5, 1957; s. Ernest Stanley and Janice Fern (Stone) G.; 1 child, Jacob Andrew. Student, Oxford (Eng.) U., 1979; BSBA, Georgetown U., 1980; JD, John Marshall Law Sch., 1983. ABar: Ill. 1983, Ariz. 1984, U.S. Dist. Ct. Ariz. 1984, U.S. Ct. Appeals (9th and D.C. cirs.) 1984. Law clk. to judge Maricopa County Superior Ct., Phoenix, 1983-84; asst. atty. gen. State of Ariz., Phoenix, 1984-85; staff atty. Ariz. Corp. Commn., Phoenix, 1985-90; sr. atty. regulatory affairs Tucson Electric Power Co., 1990-92, mgr. legal dept., 1992-94, mgr. contracts and wholesale mktg., 1994, v.p. wholesale/retail pricing and system planning, 1994—; v.p. Energy Svcs., 1996—. Mem. ABA, Ariz. Bar Assn., Ill. Bar Assn., Pima County Bar Assn., So. Ariz. Water Resources Assn. (bd. dirs. 1991-93), Tuscon Parks Found., Georgetown U. Alumni Assn., Phi Delta Phi. Republican. Jewish. Avocations: golf, tennis. Administrative and regulatory, General corporate, Public utilities. Office: Tucson Electric Power Co PO Box 711 220 W 6th St Tucson AZ 85701-1093

**GLASGOW, NORMAN MILTON,** lawyer; b. Washington, Aug. 14, 1922; children—Norman M., Heather Glasgow Harris, Glenn. BS, U. Md., 1943; LLB, JD George Washington U., 1949. Bar: D.C. 1949, U.S. Supreme Ct. 1956, Md. 1960. Assoc. Wilkes, McGarraghy & Artis, Washington, 1949-55; ptnr. Wilkes & Artis, Washington, 1955-82; pres. Wilkes, Artis, Hedrick & Lane, Washington, 1982-86, sr. prin., 1988—. Bd. dirs., gen. counsel Greater Washington Bd. Trade, 1986, 87, 88; mem., chmn. Md. PAC, 1981-93; bd. govs. Washington Bldg. Congress; mem. Citizens Tech. Adv. Com. for Drafting Bldg. Code and Zoning Regulations, Washington, Commrs. Citizens Adv. Com. on Zoning, Washington, Balt. Conv. Ctr. Authority Transp. Revenue Com., Gov's. Salary Commn., Gov's. Special Com. on Vehicle Emissions Inspection Program, Gov.'s Adv. Redistricting Com.; chmn. Govs. Task Force Statewide Bldg. Performance Standards, Md. Stadium Authority, 1993-97, Md. Economic Growth, Resource Protection and Planning Comm., co-chair subcom. for updating state planning and zoning laws, 1993-97; chmn. Md. Econ. Growth Task Force; mem. Gov.'s Western. Md. Econ. Devel. Strategies Task Force, 1998—. Served to 1st lt. U.S. Army, 1942-46, ETO. Recipient Outstanding Alumni award George Washington U., 1985, Outstanding Service award D.C. Real Estate, Greater Washington Bd. Trade, 1978. Mem. Supreme Ct. Bar Assn., D.C. Bar Assn., Md. Bar Assn., Urban Land Inst., Am. Soc. Planning Ofcls., Washington Bldg. Congress, Nat. Assn. Bus. Economists, Nat. Conf. of States on Bldg. Codes and Standards, Lambda Alpha. Avocation: gardening. Land use and zoning (including planning), Real property. Home: 9012 Brickyard Rd Potomac MD 20854-1634 Office: Wilkes Artis Hedrick & Lane 1666 K St NW Ste 1100 Washington DC 20006-2897

**GLASS, BENJAMIN PHILIP,** lawyer; b. Belfast, Maine, July 4, 1966; s. Steven G. and Harriet H. Glass; m. Janice Kirby, Oct. 2, 1993; children: Joshua Aaron, Kirby Kathryn. BA, Coll. Charleston, 1988; JD, U. S.C., 1993. Bar: S.C. 1993, U.S. Dist. Ct. S.C. 1995, U.S. Ct. Appeals (4th cir.) 1995, U.S. Ct. Appeals (6th cir.) 1996, U.S. Ct. Appeals (11th cir.) 1997. Law clk. hon. Henry M. Herlong Jr. U.S. Dist. Judge Dist. S.C., Greenville, 1993-95; assoc. Ogletree, Deakins, Nash, Smoak & Stewart, P.C., Greenville, 1995-98, Moore & Van Allen, PLLC, Charleston, S.C., 1998—. V.p. edn. Congregation Beth Israel, Greenville, 1996-98. Mem. ABA. Jewish. Avocations: fishing, camping. Labor, Federal civil litigation, State civil litigation. Office: Moore & Van Allen PLLC 40 Calhoun St Ste 300 Charleston SC 29401-3535

**GLASS, FRED STEPHEN,** lawyer; b. Asheboro, N.C., Oct. 17, 1940; s. Emmett Frederick and Colene F. (Foust) G.; m. Gloria A. Grant, June 12, 1964; 1 child, Elizabeth Foust; m. Martha G. Daughtry, June 9, 1982. BA, Wake Forest U., 1963, JD, 1966. Bar: N.C. 1966, U.S. Dist Ct. (ea. dist.) N.C. 1966, (mid. dist.) N.C., (we. dist.) N.C.; U.S. Ct. Appeals (4th cir.), U.S. Supreme Ct. Research asst. presiding justice N.C. Supreme Ct., 1966-67; ptnr. Miller, Beck, O'Briant and Glass, Asheboro, N.C., 1971-77; exec. dir. and legal counsel N.C. Democratic Party, 1977-78; dep. commr. N.C. Indsl. Commn., 1978; spl. Congl. asst. 4th Congl. Dist. N.C., 1979; ptnr. Harris, Cheshire, Leager and Southern, Raleigh, N.C., 1979-86; ptnr. Poyner and Spruill, Raleigh, 1987-94; Brooks, Stevens & Pope, P.A., Cary, 1994-98; mng. ptnr. Glass & Vining, LLC, 1998—; prof. law and govt. Asheboro Jr. Coll. Bus., 1973-76. Author: Legal Guide for Reserve Commanding Officers; contbg. editor: N.C. Will Drafting and Probate Practice Handbook, 1983; contbr. articles to profl. jours. Basketball coach and fitness instr. Randolph County YMCA; pub. chmn., United Appeal; bd. dirs., Randolph County Emergency Med. Technician Bd., Capital Bank; mem. adv. bd. Naval War Coll. operations law; active Dem. campaigns, Boy Scouts Am., council commr. for Roundtables, 1980-89, asst. dist. commr. 1979-84, asst. scoutmaster; mem. nat. com. Boy Scouts of Am., council ex. bd., council commr., chancellor, council commrs. coll., 1980-83, Boy Scouts Am. Nat. Com., 1987-90, coun. pres. 1994-96; force judge adv. COMRNCF, 1985-89; v.p. Healthcare Bus. Mgmt., LLC. Rear adm. JAGC, USNR. Disting. Svc. Medal award, 1996. Meritorious Svc. medal with gold star, Meritorious Unit Commendation, Nat. Meritorious Svc. award USNR, 1995, Navy Commendation medal with Gold Star, Nat. Defense Svc. medal with Bronze Star, Seabee Combat Warfare Specialist Cert.; recipient numerous Scouters Tng. award Boy Scouts Am., Disting. Eagle Scout award, 1991, Young Man of Yr. award City Asheboro. Mem. ABA (standing com. on armed forces law), Randolph County Bar Assn. (pres. 1971-74), 19th Jud. Dist. Bar Assn. (pres. 1974-75), N.C. Bar Assn. (chmn. young lawyer sect. Randolph County), Dist. Criminal Law Symposium (chmn. 1976), N.C. Def. Lawyers Assn. (computer in litigation support 1989), N.C. Bar Assn. (computers in law office 1995), N.C. Coun. Entrepreneurial Devel., N.C. Bar Found., Cary C. of C. (bd. dirs.), Rotary, Sovereign Mil. Order Temple Jerusalem, Naval Order U.S. Democrat. Methodist. Fax: 919-233-7151. Health, Nuclear power, General civil litigation. Home: 113 Whispering Pines Ct Cary NC 27511-4059 Office: PO Box 5894 Cary NC 27512-5894

**GLASS, GEOFFREY THEODORE,** lawyer; b. Washington, June 17, 1954; s. C. Edwin and Irene Glass; m. Deborah Anne Bodeson, Nov. 11, 1989; children: Hannah Irene, Elliott Edwin. BA, Amherst Coll., 1976; JD, U. Va., 1980. Bar: Minn. 1980, U.S. Dist. Ct. Minn. 1981, Calif. 1982, U.S. Dist. Ct. (cen. dist.) Calif. 1983, (no. and ea. dist.) Calif. 1984, (so. dist.) Calif. 1985, U.S. Ct. Appeals (9th cir.) 1985. Assoc. Robins, Kaplan, Miller & Ciresi, Mnpls. & Newport Beach, Calif., 1980-86; ptnr. Robins, Kaplan, Miller & Cires, Newport Beach, Calif., 1986-97; judge Orange County Mcpl. Ct., 1997-98, Orange County Superior Ct., 1998—. Avocation: jazz music. Insurance, General civil litigation. Office: Harbor Justice Ctr 4601 Jamboree Rd Newport Beach CA 92660-2527

**GLASS, ROBERT DAVIS,** judge; b. Wetumpka, Ala., Nov. 28, 1922; s. Isaiah and M.E. (Davis) G.; m. Doris E. Powell, Dec. 9, 1951; children: Robert Jr., Roberta Diane, Rosalyn Doris. BA, N.C. Cen. U., 1949, JD, 1951, LLD (hon.), 1988; LLD (hon.), U. Bridgeport, 1990. Bar: N.C. 1951, Conn. 1962. Pvt. practice Charlotte, N.C., 1951-53, New Bern, N.C., 1953-60; claims examiner Hartford, Conn., 1961-62; pvt. practice Waterbury, Conn., 1962-66; asst. U.S. atty. U.S. Dist. Ct. Conn., New Haven, 1966-67; judge Conn. Juvenile Ct., 1967-78, Conn. Superior Ct., 1978-84; adminstrv. judge, superior ct. Conn. Jud. Dist., Waterbury, 1984-87; assoc. justice Conn. Supreme Ct., Hartford, 1987-92, judge trial referee, 1992—. Pres. Conn. Fedn. Black Dem. Clubs, 1965-66; former mem. Appeals Bd. Conn. Justice Commn.; bd. dirs. Pearl Street Neighborhood House, Waterbury, 1965-66, pres. 1966; trustee Post Coll., Waterbury, 1986; bd. of visitors Law Sch. N.C. Cen. U., 1988. Served with U.S. Army, 1943-46. Fellow Am. Bar Found.; mem. ABA, Nat. Bar Assn. (life), Nat. Bar Assn. Jud. Coun., Am. Judicature Soc., Conn. Bar Assn., Waterbury Bar Assn., Omega Psi Phi. Baptist. Lodges: Elks, Masons. Avocation: golf. Office: Conn Superior Ct 300 Grand St Waterbury CT 06702-1900

**GLASS, ROY LEONARD,** lawyer; b. Littleton, N.H., Jan. 27, 1947; s. Jack Irving and Noreen (Leithwait) Kline; m. Suzanne Schmidt Goldstein, May 20, 1967 (div. Oct. 1978); 1 child, Shannon Renee; m. Patricia Lee Wimbish, Dec. 9, 1978 (div. 1988); 1 child, Ashley Leigh; m. Lauren Rachel Adams, Aug. 8, 1998. AA with honors, St. Petersburg Jr. Coll., Fla., 1971; BA, U. South Fla., 1972; JD, Fla. State U., 1975. Bar: Fla. 1976, U.S. Dist. Ct. (mid. dist.) Fla. 1977, U.S. Dist. Ct. (no. dist.) Fla. 1978, U.S. Supreme Ct. 1979, U.S. Ct. Appeals (11th cir.) 1983. Assoc. Meyers, Mooney & Adler, Orlando, Fla., 1976-78, Barrett, Boyd & Bajoczky, Tallahassee, 1978-79; sole practice Tallahassee, 1979-81; ptnr. Deserio & Glass, St. Petersburg, Fla., 1981-82; assoc. Battaglia, Ross, Hastings, Dicus & Andrews, St. Petersburg, 1982-85; sole practice St. Petersburg, 1985—; lectr. Floridians Against Constl. Tampering, Fla., 1984. Capt. U.S. Army, 1966-70, Vietnam. Mem. ABA, ATLA, Am. Arbitration Assn., Fla. Trial Lawyers (mem. spkrs. bur.), Fla. Bar Assn. (health law com. 1984-85, chmn. health care profls. subcom. 1984-85, mem. exec. coun. health care sect. 1986-94, mem. spkrs. bur.), St. Petersburg Bar Assn. (legis. com. 1983-85, liaison med. soc., med. rels. com. 1985—, trial lawyers 1987—, mem. spkrs. bur.), Pinellas County Trial Lawyers Assn., St. Petersburg C. of C. (urban solutions task force 1983-84), Phi Delta Phi, Phi Kappa Phi, Beta Gamma Sigma. Clubs: Suncoast Tiger Bay (St. Petersburg, Fang & Claw award 1983), Breakfast Sertoma (Cert. of Appreciation 1984), Westgate High Twelve (Cert. of Appreciation 1987), Fla. Bar Health Law Sect. (Meritorious Svc. award 1994). Personal injury, State civil litigation, Administrative and regulatory. Office: 3131 66th St N Ste A Saint Petersburg FL 33710-3115

**GLASSEN, JAMES WARREN,** lawyer; b. Moberly, Mo., Dec. 16, 1954; s. Benjamin Marshall and Geraldine (Butts) G.; m. Mary Anne Davis, Dec. 26, 1987; children: Benjamin Marshall II, Meghan Anne Shon. BSBA, Georgetown U., 1977; JD, U. Mo., Kansas City, 1982. Bar: U.S. Dist. Ct. D.C. 1983, N.Y. 1989, N.J. 1989, U.S. Dist. Ct. N.J., U.S. Ct. Appeals (D.C. cir.), U.S. Dist. Ct. (ea. and so. dists.) N.Y., U.S. Ct. Appeals (3d cir.). Legis. dir. to U.S. Congressman Harold L. Volkmer Washington, 1976-83; assoc. Lipsen, Hamberger, Whitten & Hamberger, Washington, 1983-88, Postner & Rubin, N.Y.C., 1988-89; dep. atty. gen. N.J. Atty. Gen.'s Office, Trenton, 1989-94; ptnr. Roth & Glassen, Summit, N.J., 1994-97; of counsel Scarinci & Hollenbeck, Secaucus, N.J., 1997—; chair Union County (N.J.) Commn. Human Rels., 1998; mem. N.J. DEP Task Force on County Environ. Health Act, Trenton, 1994-95. Revisor: New Jersey State Grand Jury Manual, 1993. Mem. D.C. Bar Assn., U.S. Tax Ct., N.J. Bar Assn. Democrat. Roman Catholic. Avocation: golf. Environmental, General civil litigation, Criminal. Office: Scarinci & Hollenbeck PO Box 3189 500 Plaza Dr Secaucus NJ 07096-3189

**GLASSER, IRA SAUL,** civil liberties organization executive; b. Bklyn., Apr. 18, 1938; s. Sidney and Anne (Goldstein) G.; m. Trude Maria Robinson, June 28, 1959; children: David, Andrew, Peter, Sally. BS in Math., Queens Coll., 1959; MA in Math., Ohio State U., 1960. Instr. math. Queens Coll., N.Y.C., 1960-63; lectr. math. Sarah Lawrence Coll., Bronxville, N.Y., 1962-65; assoc. editor Current Mag., N.Y.C., 1962-64, editor, 1964-67; assoc. dir. N.Y. Civil Liberties Union, N.Y.C., 1967-70, exec. dir., 1970-78; exec. dir. ACLU, 1978—; cons. U. Ill.-Champaign-Urbana, 1964-65; dir. Asian Am. Legal Def. and Edn. Fund., N.Y.C., 1974—; dir. Drug Policy Found., Washington, 1991—. Author: Visions of Liberty: The Bill of Rights for All Americans, 1991; co-author: Doing Good: The Limits of Benevolence, 1978; contbr. articles to profl. jours. Chmn. St. Vincents Hosp, N.Y.C., Community Adv. Bd., N.Y.C., 1970-72. Recipient Martin Luther King, Jr. award N.Y. Assn. Black Sch. Suprs., 1971, Gavel award ABA, 1972, Allard K. Lowenstein award Park River Ind. Dem., 1981, Malcolm, Martin, Mandela award Greater Bapt. Trinity Ch., 1993. Avocation: sports.

**GLASSER, ISRAEL LEO,** federal judge; b. N.Y.C., Apr. 6, 1924; s. David and Sadie (Krupp) G.; m. Grace Gribetz, Aug. 24, 1952; children—Dorothy, David, James, Marjorie. LL.B., Bklyn. Law Sch., 1948; B.A., CUNY, 1976. Bar: N.Y. 1948. Fellow Bklyn. Law Sch., 1948-49, instr., 1950-52, asst. prof. law, 1952-53, asso. prof., 1953-55, prof., 1955-69, adj. prof., 1969-77, dean, 1977-81; judge U.S. Dist. Ct. N.Y., 1981—; judge N.Y. State Family Ct., N.Y.C., 1969-77. Mem. ABA, Assn. of Bar of City of N.Y. Office: US Dist Ct 225 Cadman Plz E Brooklyn NY 11201-1818

**GLASSER, PHILIP RUSSELL,** lawyer; b. Braddock, Pa., Dec. 7, 1948; s. Russell Clement and Mary Louise (Smith) G.; m. E. Joyce Gottardi, Nov. 13, 1970; children: Kimberly, Peter. BA, Indiana U. Pa., 1970; JD, U. Pitts., 1975. Bar: Pa. 1975, U.S. Dist. Ct. (we. dist.) Pa. 1975, U.S. Ct. Criminal Appeals/Armed Forces 1976, Mo. 1994, U.S. Dist. Ct. (we. dist.) Mo. 1994, Kans. 1995, U.S. Dist. Ct. Kans. 1995. Atty. Johnstown (Pa.) Savs. Bank, 1980-81, Westinghouse Elec. Corp., Pitts., 1981-87; mgr. loan adminstrn. Westinghouse Credit Co., Pitts., 1987-88, US West Fin. Svc., Kansas City, Mo., 1988-91; loan officer Boatmen's 1st Nat. Bank, Kansas City, 1991-94; pvt. practice, Overland Park, Kans., 1994—. Maj. USAR (ret.), Saudi Arabia, Iraq. Contracts commercial, General corporate, General practice. Office: 12980 Metcalf Ave Ste 180 Overland Park KS 66213-2646

**GLASSMAN, CAROLINE DUBY,** state supreme court justice; b. Baker, Oreg., Sept. 13, 1922; d. Charles Ferdinand and Caroline Marie (Colton) Duby; m. Harry Paul Glassman, May 21, 1953; 1 son, Max Avon. LLB summa cum laude, Williamette U., 1944. Bar: Oreg. 1944, Calif. 1952, Maine 1969. Atty. Title Ins. & Trust Co., Salem, Oreg., 1944-46; assoc. Belli, Ashe, Pinney & Melvin Belli, San Francisco, 1952-58; ptnr. Glassman & Potter, Portland, Maine, 1973-78, Glassman, Beagle & Ridge, Portland, 1978-83; justice Maine Supreme Judicial Ct., Portland, 1983-97; lectr. Sch. Law, U. Maine, 1967-68, 80. Author: Legal Status of Homemakers in State of Maine, 1977. Mem. Am. Law Inst., Oreg. Bar Assn., Calif. Bar Assn., Maine Bar Assn., Maine Trial Law Assn. Roman Catholic. Home: 56 Thomas St Portland ME 04102-3639

**GLASSMAN, JEROLD ERWIN,** lawyer; b. Newark, Oct. 12, 1935; s. Morris and Leah (Katz) G.; m. Joan Kay, June 15, 1957; children: Sherri, Steven, Jill. BS, Rutgers U., 1957; JD, Seton Hall U., 1966. Bar: N.J. 1966, Calif. 1977. Dir. labor rels. El Al Israel Airlines, N.Y.C., 1967; assoc. Grotta & Oberwager, Newark, 1967-70; ptnr. Grotta, Oberwager & Glassman, Newark, 1970-75; mng. ptnr. Grotta, Glassman & Hoffman, Newark, 1975-77, Roseland, N.J., 1977—; bd. dirs. Essex Valley Healthcare, Inc., East Orange, N.J., Theresa Grotta Ctr., West Orange, N.J.; mem. ethics com. N.J. Supreme Ct. part V-C. Spl. labor counsel Gov. Christine Todd Whitman, 1992—, N.J. Sports Authority, 1981—, N.J. Transit, 1984. With USNR, 1953-61. Mem. ABA (labor and econs. sects.), N.J. Bar Assn. (labor and casino law sects.), Greenbrook Club, Boca West Club. Republican. Jewish. Avocation: golfing. Labor. Office: Grotta Glassman & Hoffman PA 75 Livingston Ave Ste 13 Roseland NJ 07068-3701

**GLASSMOYER, THOMAS PARVIN,** lawyer; b. Reading, Pa., Sept. 4, 1915; s. James Arthur and Margaretha (Parvin) G.; m. Frances Helen Thierolf, May 9, 1942; children—Deborah Jane Beck, Nancy Parvin Brittingham, Wendy Jean Barber. AB, Ursinus Coll., 1936, LLB (hon.), 1972; LLB, U. Pa., 1939. Bar: Pa. 1940. Law clk. Common Pleas Ct. 6, Phila., 1939-40; assoc. Murdoch, Paxson, Kalish & Green, Phila., 1940-42; atty. Dept. Justice and Office Price Adminstrn., 1942-43; assoc. Schnader, Harrison, Segal & Lewis, Phila., 1946-50, ptnr., 1950-87, retired ptnr., 1988—, chmn. pension com., 1969-84, chmn. tax dept., 1972-84, chmn. investment com., 1984-86, chmn. bd. trustees of Retirement Trust, 1986-89; sec. The Lawrewnce McFadden Co., Phila., 1992, dir., 1994—; lectr. NYU Inst. Fed. Taxation; adv. bd. U. Pa. Tax Conf., 1968-88. Author: (with Sherwin T. McDowell) Legal Problems in Tax Returns, 1949; editor-in-chief U. Pa. Law Rev., 1938-39. Past pres. Upper Dublin Twp. PTA Council; mem. Zoning Bd. Adjustment Upper Dublin Twp., Montgomery County, Pa., 1957-59, bd. commrs., 1959-71, pres., 1968-69; mem. Upper Dublin Environ. Control Bd., 1972-82; bd. dirs. Ursinus Coll., Collegeville, Pa., 1956—, 1st v.p., 1978-81, pres., 1981-90, chmn. exec. com., 1981-97; bd. dirs. Wissahickon Valley Watershed Assn., 1974-76; trustee Bernard G. Segal Found., Phila., 1969—, Charlotte W. Newcombe Found., Princeton, N.J., 1982—. Served to 1st lt. JAG Dept., AUS, 1943-46. Recipient Eagle Scout award, Boy Scouts Am. Fellow Pa. Bar Found. (life, sec. 1993—); mem. ABA, FBA, Pa. Bar Assn. (ho. of dels. 1982-88, membership com., by-laws com.), Phila. Bar Assn., Judge Advs. Assn., Pa. Folklife Soc. (bd. dirs., sec.), Nat. Assn. Coll. and Univ. Attys., 1939 Code Club, Lawyers Club Phila., Manorlu Club, Mfrs. Golf and Country Club, Union League of Phila., Order of Coif, Order of Arrow. Republican. Lutheran. Avocation: golf, philately. Pension, profit-sharing, and employee benefits, Taxation, general, Estate taxation. Home: 1648 N Hills Ave Willow Grove PA 19090-4231 Office: Schnader Harrison Segal & Lewis 1600 Market St Ste 3600 Philadelphia PA 19103-7240

**GLAVIN, A. RITA CHANDELLIER (MRS. JAMES HENRY GLAVIN, III),** lawyer; b. Schenectady, N.Y., May 11, 1937; d. Pierre Charles and Helen C. (Fox) Chandellier; m. James H. Glavin, III, June 1, 1963; children: Helene, James, Rita, Henry. AB cum laude, Middlebury Coll., 1958; JD, Union U., 1961. Bar: N.Y. 1961, U.S. Dist. Ct. (no. dist.) N.Y. 1961, U.S. Tax Ct. 1965, U.S. Supreme Ct. 1978. Assoc. Eugene Steiner, Albany, N.Y., 1961-64, Helen Fox Chandellier, Schenectady, 1965-76; mem. Glavin and Glavin, Waterford, Schenectady, 1965-86, 87—, Albany, 1965-86, 87—; del. 4th Jud. Dist. Nominating Conv., 1966-67; confidential law clk. presiding justices N.Y. State Ct. Claims, 1968-71; surrogate judge Saratoga County, 1986. Mem. editl. bd. Albany Law Rev., 1960-61. Bd. dirs., chmn. fin. com. Schenectady YWCA, 1979-81; mem. Univ. Coun. SUNY, Albany, 1985—; tech. advisor HSA of Northeastern N.Y. Maternity and Pediat. Com., 1976; bd. dirs. Schenectady Jr. League, 1974, 76; assn. coun. mem., coll. trustees SUNY, 1991—, sec., 1996—; del. N.Y. State Jr. League Pub. Affairs Com., 1976; sec. Bellevue Maternity Hosp., Inc., 1966—, bd. dirs. 1966-83, bd. advisors, 1984—; trustee Middlebury Coll., 1978-88, chmn. law com., 1982-88, vice chmn. bd. dirs., 1986-87. Mem. N.Y. State Bar Assn. (mem. ho. of dels. 1987-88, nominating com. 1988-90), Saratoga County Bar Assn. (exec. com. 1981—, v.p. 1985, pres. 1986), Schenectady County Bar Assn., Phi Beta Kappa, Kappa Kappa Gamma. General practice. Office: Glavin & Glavin PO Box 40 69 2nd St Waterford NY 12188-2422

**GLAVIN, JAMES HENRY, III,** lawyer; b. Albany, N.Y., Oct. 6, 1931; s. James Henry, Jr. and Elizabeth Mary (Gibbons) G.; m. A. Rita Chandellier, June 1, 1963; children—Helene Elizabeth, James C., Rita Marie, James Henry IV. A.B., Villanova U., 1953; J.D., Albany Law Sch., 1956. Bar: N.Y. 1956, U.S. Dist. Ct. (no. dist.) N.Y. 1957, U.S. Supreme Ct. 1959, U.S. Dist. Ct. (mid. dist.) Tenn. 1959, U.S. Ct. Appeals (D.C. cir.) 1976, U.S. Ct. Mil. Appeals 1959. Mem. Glavin and Glavin, Waterford, N.Y., 1960—; chmn. regional bd. Key Bank, N.A., 1968-93. County chmn. Democratic Party, Saratoga County, N.Y., 1964-68; bd. dirs. Bellevue Maternity Hosp., 1968—, Waterford Central Catholic Sch., 1969—; trustee St. Mary's Ch., Waterford, 1974—, Waterford Rural Cemetery. Served to capt. JAGC, USAF, 1957-60. Mem. ABA, Assn. Trial Lawyers Am., Am. Soc. Law and Medicine, Am. Acad. Polit. and Social Sci., ICC Practitioners Assn., Am. Psychology-Law Soc., N.Y. Trial Lawyers Assn., Am. Acad. Hosp. Attys., Transp. Lawyers Assn., Nat. Health Lawyers Assn., Fed. Bar Assn., N.Y. State Bar Assn., Estate Planning Coun. Eastern N.Y., Saratoga County Bar Assn., Albany County Bar Assn., Rensselaer County Bar Assn., Internat. Soc. Gen. Semantics, Mystery Writers Am., Soc. Am. Baseball Rsch. Roman Catholic. Clubs: Nat. Lawyers, Air Force Assn.; Lions (past pres.), KC. Author: The Tour Broker and the Interstate Commerce Commission, 1977; editor: Administrative Law Practice in New York, 1988. General practice. Home: 66 Saratoga Ave Waterford NY 12188-2640 Office: Glavin & Glavin 69 2nd St Waterford NY 12188-2422

**GLAVIN, KEVIN CHARLES,** lawyer, educator; b. Providence, R.I., Aug. 1, 1949; s. Charles Francis and Lola Glavin; m. Donna Bettencourt, Aug. 23, 1980. AB, Providence Coll., 1971; JD, Suffolk Law Sch., 1974. Bar: R.I. 1975, Mass. 1984, U.S. Dist. Ct. R.I. 1975, U.S. Supreme Ct. 1979. Spl. asst. atty. gen. R.I. Dept. Atty. Gen., Providence, 1975-79; mng. atty. Kemper Ins. Co., Providence, 1979-94; arbitrator R.I. Superior Ct., Providence, 1989—; ptnr. Murray, Cutcliffe & Glavin, Providence, 1994—; adj. faculty Roger Williams U., Bristol, R.I., 1986—. V.P. Kent Heights PTA, East Providence, 1989; treas. Colt Andrews PTA, Bristol, 1993. Recipient Order of the Gavel, Newport Ski Club, 1982. Mem. R.I. Superior Ct. (bench bar com. 1992—), Pawtucket Bar Assn. Avocations: tennis, skiing, sailing. General civil litigation, Product liability, Personal injury. Office: Murray Cutcliffe and Glavin 155 S Main St Providence RI 02903-2963

**GLAVIN, WILLIAM PATRICK, IV,** lawyer; b. LaFayette, Ind., June 26, 1965; s. William Patrick III and Rosemary (Stair) G.; m. Carrie Lynn Stack, Apr. 19, 1997. BA, North Ctrl. Coll., Naperville, Ill., 1985; JD, Pepperdine U., Malibu, Calif., 1988. Bar: Calif. 1988. Assoc. Fain, Kaufman & Young, Beverly Hills, Calif., 1988-94, Kolodny & Anteau, LLP, Beverly Hills, 1994-98; ptnr. Glavin & Kolter, LLP, L.A., 1998—; pro bono atty. South Bay Free Clinic, Manhattan Beach, Calif., 1997—. Expert advice columnist So. Calif. Divorce Mag.; contbr. numerous articles to profl. jours. Mem. Beverly Hills Bar Assn., Los Angeles County Bar assn., Kiwanis Club. Republican. Avocations: whitewater rafting, scuba diving. Family and matrimonial, Juvenile. Office: Law Offices Glavin & Kolter 12424 Wilshire Blvd Ste 1120 Los Angeles CA 90025-1071

**GLAZE, THOMAS A.,** state supreme court justice; b. Jan. 14, 1938; s. Phyllis Laser; children: Steve, Mike, Julie, Amy, Ashley. BSBA, U. Ark., 1960, JD, 1964. Exec. dir. Election Research Council Inc., 1964-65; legal advisor, 1965-66; staff atty. Pulaski County Legal Aid, 1966-67, asst. then dep. atty. gen., 1967-70; pvt. practice law, 1970-79; chancellor Ark. Chancery Ct., 6th Jud. Cir., 1979-80; judge Ark. Ct. Appeals, 1981-86; assoc. justice Ark. Supreme Ct., 1987—; co-author Ark. Election Act, 1969, Ark. Consumer Act; lectr. U. Ark. Bd. dirs. Vis. Nurses Corp., Youth Home Inc. Office: Ark Supreme Ct Justice Building 625 Marshall St Little Rock AR 72201-1054*

**GLAZER, DONALD WAYNE,** lawyer, business executive, educator; b. Cleve., July 26, 1944; s. Julius and Ethel (Goldstein) G.; children: Elizabeth M., Mollie S. AB summa cum laude, Dartmouth Coll., 1966; JD magna cum laude, Harvard U., 1969; LLM, U. Pa., 1970. Bar: Mass. 1970. Assoc. Ropes & Gray, Boston, 1970-78, ptnr., 1978-92, counsel, 1992-96; ptnr. Am. Bus. Ptnrs. LLC, Boston, 1996-98; pres. Mugar/Glazer Holdings, Inc., Boston, 1992-95; vice chmn. fin. New Eng. TV Corp. and WHDH-TV, Inc., Boston, 1992-93; adv. counsel Goodwin Procter & Hoar, Boston, 1997—; co-founder Provant, Inc., Boston, 1998—; instr. corp. fin. Boston U. Law Sch., 1975; lectr. law Harvard U., Cambridge, Mass., 1978-91. Co-author: Massachusetts Corporation Law and Practice, 1991, Fitzgibbon and Glazer on Legal Opinions, 1992; co-editor First Ann. Inst. on Securities Regulation, 1970; contbr. articles to legal jours. Past chmn., trustee Cowen Slavin Found.; past trustee Santa Fe Neuroscis. Inst.; dir. Newton Girls Soccer League, past co-chmn. intramural com.; past trustee, past treas. Hillel Founds. of Greater Boston Inc.; trustee Program for Young Negotiators. Fellow Salzburg Seminar in Am. Studies, 1975. Mem. ABA (chmn. legal opinions com., co-reporter Legal Opinion Prins., past chmn. subcom. on employee benefits and exec. compensation, fed. securities law com., past co-chmn. task force on sec. 16 devels.), Boston Bar Assn. (past chmn., corp. sec., past chmn. securities law com., past co-chmn. legal opinions com.), Am. Law Inst., Tri-Bar Legal Opinions Com. (co-reporter Third-party Closing Opinions). Jewish. General corporate, Securities, Finance. Home: 225 Kenrick St Newton MA 02458-2731

**GLAZER, JACK HENRY,** lawyer; b. Paterson, N.J., Jan. 14, 1928; s. Samuel and Martha (Merkin) G.; m. Zelda d'Angleterre, 1979. BA, Duke U., 1950; JD, Georgetown U., 1956; postgrad. U. Frankfurt (W.Ger.), 1956-57; S.J.D. U. Calif.-Berkeley, 1977. Bar: D.C. 1957, Calif. 1968. Atty., GAO and NASA, 1958-60; mem. maritime div. UN Internat. Labour Office, Geneva, Switzerland, 1960; spl. legal adv. UN Internat. Telecommunication Union, Geneva, 1960-62; atty. NASA Washington, 1963-66; chief counsel NASA-Ames Research Center, Moffett Field, Calif., 1966-88; gov. Calif. Maritime Acad., 1975-78; asst. prof. Hastings Coll. Law, 1985-87; prof., assoc. dean bus. sch. San Francisco State U., 1988-92. Dir. San Francisco Palace of Fine Arts, 1995. Comdr. Calif. Naval Militia, ret. Capt. JAGC, USNR, ret. Mem. Calif. Bar Assn., D.C. Bar Assn., White's Inn (reader). Contbr. articles on internat. law to profl. jours. Office: White's Inn 37 White St San Francisco CA 94109-2609

**GLAZER, RACHELLE HOFFMAN,** lawyer; b. Dallas, Aug. 18, 1958; married; 4 children. BA, U. N.C., 1980; JD, So. Meth. U., 1983. Bar: Tex. 1983, U.S. Dist. Ct. (no. dist.) Tex. 1983, U.S. Dist. Ct. (so. dist.) Tex. 1987, U.S. Ct. Appeals (5th cir.) 1988, U.S. Dist. Ct. (we. dist.) Tex. 1994, U.S. Dist. Ct. (ea. dist.) Tex. 1995. Assoc. Thompson & Knight, Dallas, 1983-89; shareholder Thompson & Knight, P.C., Dallas, 1989—. Mng. editor Southwestern Law Rev., So. Meth. U., 1982-83. Mem. Phi Beta Kappa. General civil litigation, Insurance, Personal injury. Office: Thompson & Knight 1700 Pacific Ave Ste 3300 Dallas TX 75201-4693

**GLEASON, JAMES MULLANEY,** lawyer, insurance executive; b. Sioux City, Iowa, Sept. 27, 1948; s. Harry H. and Dorothy (Mullaney) G; m. Margaret McGuire. BA, Briar Cliff Coll., Sioux City, 1973; JD, Creighton U., 1976. Bar: Iowa 1976, Nebr. 1976. Asst. counsel Woodmen of the World, Omaha, 1976-80, asst. gen. counsel, 1980-96, assoc. gen. counsel, 1996—, asst. v.p., 1993—. With U.S. Army, 1968-69. Fellow Life Office Mgmt. Assn. (master), Life Mgmt. Inst.; mem. Assn. Fraternal Benefit Counsel, Internat. Claim Assn. (exec. com.), Nebr. Fraternal Congress (pres. 1993-94). Democrat. Roman Catholic. Insurance, Civil rights, Personal injury. Office: Woodmen of World Life Ins Soc 1700 Farnam St Ste 2200 Omaha NE 68102-2007

**GLEASON, JAMES PATRICK,** lawyer; b. Pitts., July 7, 1953; s. James Edwin and Beatrice Frances G.; m. Virginia Mary Wahlgren, May 21, 1982; children: Calvin, Dixon, Liam. BA, U. Pitts., 1979; JD, Santa Clara U., 1982. Bar: Calif. 1983. Supr. trial atty. Office Pub. Defender, San Jose, Calif., 1984—. Office: Office Pub Defender 120 W Mission St San Jose CA 95110-1722

**GLEDHILL, KAREN ABLE,** lawyer; b. Greenwood, S.C., Sept. 29, 1960; d. Carlos Hobson Able and Blanche Robertson; m. John W. Gledhill, Oct. 18, 1987; children: Douglas, Sarah, Julia. BA in Journalism, U. S.C., 1980, MBA, 1985; JD, Columbia U., 1988. Bar: Mass. 1988, N.C. 1991, S.C. 1993. Assoc. Goulston & Storrs, Boston, 1988-91; shareholder Robinson, Bradshaw & Hinson, Charlotte, N.C., 1992—. Mem. ABA, Am. Health Lawyers Assn., N.C. Bar Assn. (Lawyer of Yr. 1998), Health Law Coun. of N.C. Bar Assn. Office: Robinson Bradshaw & Henson PA 101 N Tryon St Charlotte NC 28246-0100

**GLEESON, JOHN,** judge, educator; b. 1953. BA, Georgetown U., 1975; JD, U. Va., 1980. Bar: N.Y. Law clk. to Hon. Boyce F. Martin Jr. U.S. Cir. Ct., 1980-81; assoc. Cravath, Swaine & Moore, N.Y.C., 1981-85; asst. U.S. atty. for ea. dist. N.Y. Dept. Justice, N.Y.C., 1985-94; judge U.S. Dist. Ct. (ea. dist.) N.Y., Bklyn., 1994—; adj. prof. law Bklyn. Sch. Law, 1990-97, NYU Law Sch., 1995—; vis. prof. law U. Va. Sch. Law, 1994. Office: US Dist Ct 225 Cadman Plz W Brooklyn NY 11201-2741

**GLEESON, PAUL FRANCIS,** lawyer; b. Bronx, June 20, 1941; s. William Francis and Julia Anne (Dargis) G.; children: Kevin F., Sean W., Brendan J., Colleen J. AB in History, Fordham U., 1963; JD, U. Chgo., 1966. Bar: Ill. 1966, Fed. Trial Bar Ill. 1969, U.S. Ct. Appeals (6th cir.) 1972, U.S. Ct. Appeals (7th cir.) 1973, U.S. Ct. Appeals (8th cir.) 1997. Assoc. Vedder, Price, Kaufman & Kammholz, Chgo., 1966-73, ptnr., 1973—; adj. prof. DePaul U. Sch. of Law, 1991. Co-author (with Day, Green & Cleveland) The Equal Employment Opportunity Compliance Manual, 1978; columnist: (with B. Alper) Gleeson and Alper on Employment Law, Merrill's Illinois Legal Times, 1988-90. Capt. U.S. Army, 1966-68, Vietnam. Decorated Bronze Star; Floyd Russell Mechem scholar, 1963-66. Mem. Chgo. Bar Assn., Ill. Assn. Hosp. Attys., Am. Legion, VFW (post comdr. Northbrook, Ill.), Order of Coif, Phi Beta Kappa. Roman Catholic. Labor. Office: Vedder Price Kaufman & Kammholz 222 N La Salle St Ste 2600 Chicago IL 60601-1003

**GLEICHMAN, NORMAN M.,** lawyer. Gen. counsel Fed. Mine Safety and Health Review Commn., Washington. Office: Fed Mine Safety & Health Rev Commn 1730 K St NW Fl 6 Washington DC 20006-3868

**GLEISS, HENRY WESTON,** lawyer; b. Detroit, Nov. 22, 1928; s. George Herman and Mary Elizabeth (Weston) G.; m. Joan Bette Christopher, July 23, 1955; children—Kent G., Keith W. B.A., Denison U., 1951; J.D., U. Mich., 1954. Bar: Mich. 1955, U.S. Dist. Ct. (ea. dist.) Mich. 1955, U.S. Dist. Ct. (we. dist.) Mich. 1960, U.S. Ct. Appeals (6th cir.) 1964, U.S. Supreme Ct. 1967. Sole practice, Benton Harbor, Mich., 1957-61; ptnr. Globensky, Gleiss, Bittner & Hyrns, P.C., St. Joseph, 1961—; spl. asst. atty. gen. Mich., 1960—. Officer Jaycees, Mich.; bd. dirs. United Fund. Served with U.S. Army, 1955-57. Mem. ABA, Mich. Bar Assn., Berrien County Bar Assn. (pres. 1974), Assn. Trial Lawyers Am., Twin Cities C. of C. (v.p. 1975). Congregationalist. Clubs: Kiwanis, Moose (Benton Harbor); Economic of S.W. Mich.; Elks (St. Joseph). Condemnation, State civil litigation, Personal injury. Home: 2409 Langley Ave Saint Joseph MI 49085-2150 Office: 610 Ship St Saint Joseph MI 49085-1120

**GLEKEL, JEFFREY IVES,** lawyer; b. N.Y.C., Apr. 8, 1947; s. Newton and Gertrude (Burr) G.; m. Cynthia R. Leder, June 18, 1988; 1 child, David L. AB, Columbia U., 1969; JD, Yale U., 1972. Bar: N.Y. 1973, U.S. Supreme Ct. 1981, U.S. Ct. Appeals (2d cir.) 1974, U.S. Dist. Ct. (so. dist.) N.Y. 1974. Law clk. to judge U.S. Dist. Ct. (so. dist.) N.Y., 1972-73; asst. U.S. atty. So. Dist. N.Y., 1973-77; law clk. to justice Byron R. White, U.S. Supreme Ct., Washington, 1977-78; ptnr. Skadden, Arps, Slate, Meagher and Flom, N.Y.C., 1980—; Editor, contbr.: Civil Litigation Practice, 1990; Business Crimes, 1982; note and comment editor Yale Law Jour., 1971-72. Contbr. articles to law jours. Mem. Assn. Bar City of N.Y. (chmn. com. fed. legislation 1984-87), ABA. Federal civil litigation, Criminal, Constitutional. Office: Skadden Arps Slate Meagher & Flom 919 3rd Ave New York NY 10022-3902

**GLENDENNING, DON MARK,** lawyer; b. Dallas, Dec. 24, 1953; s. Don Thomas and Nancy (Malloy) G.; m. Carol Peterson, Dec. 30, 1979. BA, Rice U., 1976; JD, Stanford U., 1979. Bar: Tex. 1979. Assoc. Rain Harrell Emery Young & Doke, Dallas, 1979-85; ptnr. Rain, Harrell, Emery, Young & Doke, Dallas, 1985-87; shareholder Locke Liddell & Sapp (formerly Locke Purnell Rain Harrell, P.C.), Dallas, 1987-98; ptnr. Locke Liddell & Sapp LLP, Dallas, 1999—. Vol. legal counsel, dir. The Nat. Tree Trust; bd. dirs. Dallas Trees and Park Found.; vol. legal counsel Dallas Zool. Soc.; vol. legal counsel Quality Tex. Fedn. Republican. Presbyterian. General corporate, Securities. Office: Locke Liddell & Sapp LLP 2200 Ross Ave Ste 2200 Dallas TX 75201-2748

**GLENDON, MARY ANN,** law educator; b. 1938. BA, U. Chgo., 1959, JD, 1961, M Comparative Law, 1963. Bar: Ill. 1964, Mass. 1980. Legal intern. EEC, Brussels, Belgium, 1963; assoc. Mayer, Brown & Platt, Chgo., 1963-68; prof. Boston Coll., 1968-86; vis. prof. Harvard U., 1974-75, prof., 1986—; vis. prof. U. Chgo., 1983, 84, 86. Author: Rights Talk, 1991, A Nation Under Lawyers, 1994. Foreign Law fellow U. Libre de Bruxelles, 1962-63, Ford Found. fellow, 1975-76. Mem. Am. Acad. Arts & Scis. Office: Harvard U Law Sch Cambridge MA 02138

**GLENN, CLETA MAE,** lawyer; b. Clinton, Ill., Sept. 24, 1921; d. John and Mattie Sylvester (Anderson) G.; m. Rex Eugene Loggans, Sept. 3, 1948 (div.); 1 child, Susan. BS, U. Ill., 1947; JD, DePaul U. Coll. Law, 1976. Bar: Ill. 1977. Real estate builder, developer, 1959-69; comm. dir. Transp. Rsch. Ctr., Northwestern U., Evanston, Ill., 1969-72; pvt. practice law Chgo., 1977—; lectr. Assn. Trial Lawyers Am., John Marshall Law Sch. Editor: Collective Bargaining and Technological Change in American Transportation, 1979; contbr. articles to profl. publs. With USN, 1943-59. Recipient Real Estate Humanitarian award Kislak Co., Miami, Fla., 1962. Mem. ATLA, ABA, Ill. Bar Assn. (assembly rep., mem. standing com. on traffic, family law sect. coun.), Chgo. Bar Assn., Ill. Trial Lawyers Assn., Lex Leggio, Phi Alpha Delta. Personal injury. Home: 200 E Delaware Pl Chicago IL 60611-1757 Office: 200 W Madison St Ste 2850 Chicago IL 60606-3498

**GLENN, DANIEL O.,** lawyer; b. Elma, Wash., Aug. 1, 1942; m. Carleen Glenn. BA, Cen. Wash. U., 1963; JD, U. Wash., 1972. Bar: Wash., 1972, U.S. Dist. Ct. (W. dist.) Wash., 1972, U.S. Supreme Ct., 1974. Instr. Olympia (Wash.) Schs., 1963-69; ptnr. Buzzard, Brown & Glenn, Olympia, 1972-74, Buzzard & Glenn, Olympia, 1974-76, Buzzard, Glenn & Henderson, Olympia, 1976-77, 85-89, Buzzard, Glenn, Henderson & Morris, Olympia, 1977-85, Glenn, Henderson & Hoffman, Olympia, 1989-92, Glenn & Hoffman, Olympia, 1992—. Mem. ABA, Wash. State Trial Lawyers Assn., Wash. State Bar Assn., Am. Trial Lawyers Assn. Office: Glenn & Hoffman PS 2424 Evergreen Park Dr SW Olympia WA 98502-6041

**GLENN, DAVID MILTON,** lawyer; b. Myrtle Beach, S.C., Nov. 18, 1956; s. James Milton and Doris Jean (Baker) G.; m. Mary Ruth Boss, Apr. 22, 1989; children: Jacob David, Madeline Margaret. BS in Econs., Okla. State U., 1979; JD, Baylor U., 1981. Bar: Tex. 1982. Assoc. Frank Jelinek, Inc., Arlington, Tex., 1981-83; pvt. practice Dallas, 1983-85, Irving, Tex., 1989—; assoc. Smith, Miller & Carlton, Dallas, 1985-87, Law offices of Judson Francis, Dallas, 1987-89; pvt. practice Irving, Tex., 1989—, Grapevine, Tex., 1999—. Pres. Trolley For Toys, Irving, Tex., 1993—. Baptist. Avocations: golf, baseball, running. Personal injury, Professional liability, Product liability. Office: 1020 S Main St Grapevine TX 76051-5541

**GLENN, ROBERT EASTWOOD,** lawyer; b. Catlettsburg, Ky., Dec. 24, 1929; s. Albert Sidney and Pauline Elizabeth (Eastwood) G.; m. Clydenne Reinhard, Mar. 16, 1956; children: Pauline Glenn O'Brien, Robert Eastwood Jr. BS cum laude, Washington and Lee U., 1951, JD cum laude, 1953. Bar: Va. 1952, U.S. Dist. Ct. (we. dist.) Va. 1958, U.S. Ct. Appeals (4th cir.) 1974, U.S. Supreme Ct. 1975, U.S. Tax Ct. 1994. Assoc. Eggleston & Holton, Roanoke, Va., 1957-60; ptnr. Glenn, Feldmann, Darby & Goodlatte, Roanoke, 1960—; mem. Va. Bd. Bar Examiners, Richmond, 1982—, pres., 1993—. Mem. State Coun. for Higher Edn. for Va., 1980-84; rector Radford (Va.) U., 1975-79, bd. visitors, 1972-79; chmn. Roanoke City Rep. Com., 1968-70, Roanoke Valley ARC, 1974-76; mem. Va. Found. for Humanities, 1995—. Fellow ABA Found., Va. Bar Found.; mem. ABA, Roanoke Bar Assn. (res. 1980-81), Roanoke Regional C. of C. (pres. 1988), Roanoke Country Club, Shenandoah Club (v.p. 1981-82, 97—), Beta Gamma Sigma, Order of the Coif. Roman Catholic. General corporate, Communications, Real property. Home: 3101 Allendale St SW Roanoke VA 24014-3118 Office: Glenn Feldmann Darby & Goodlatte 210 1st St SW Ste 200 Roanoke VA 24011-1607

**GLENNON, CHARLES EDWARD,** judge, lawyer; b. Monticello, Ill., Apr. 5, 1942; s. William Edward and Beatrice Jane (Pierson) G.; m. Sylvia Ann McClintock, Aug. 24, 1965 (div. Aug. 1972); children: David, Caroline; m. Victoria Louise Pearre, Oct. 26, 1974; 1 child, Andrew. BA, U. Ill., 1964, JD, 1966. Bar: Ill. 1966, U.S. Supreme Ct. 1974. Assoc. Fellheimer & Fellheimer, Pontiac, Ill., 1968-73; ptnr. Gomien & Glennon Ltd., Dwight, Ill., 1973-75; cir. judge State of Ill., Pontiac, 1976-98; chief judge 11th cir., 1991-95; lectr., author criminal law Ill. Village atty., Dwight, 1973-75; chmn. Salvation Army Adv. Bd., Pontiac, 1976; chmn. criminal law com. Ill. Jud. Conf., 1989-99, del., mem. exec. com., 1993-98; former mem. Regional Youth Planning Commn., Livingston County Commn. on Children and Youth; bd. dirs. Nat. Arts Found., 1998—. With U.S. Army, 1966-68. Fellow Ill. Bar Found.; mem. Livingston County Bar Assn. (pres. 1991-93), Ill. Bar Assn., Ill. Judges Assn., Am. Assn. Juvenile and Family Ct. Judges, Lions, Rotary, Elks. Republican. Episcopalian. Home: 10521 E 1700 North Rd Pontiac IL 61764-3113

**GLENNON, MICHAEL JOHN,** law educator; b. Chgo., Dec. 19, 1947; s. William John and Catherine (Feil) G. BA summa cum laude, St. Thomas Coll., 1970; JD, U. Minn., 1973. Asst. counsel Office Legis. Coun., Washington, 1973-77; legal counsel Senate Fgn. Rels. Com., Washington, 1977-80; atty. Busby Rehm & Leonard, Washington, 1980-81; assoc. prof. law U. Cinn., 1981-83; prof. law U. Cinn. Coll. Law, 1983-86, U. Calif., Davis, 1987—; cons. Internat. Atomic Energy Agy., Vienna, 1998. Author: Constitutional Diplomacy, 1990, When No Majority Rules, 1992; co-author: U.S. Foreign Relations and National Security Law, 1987; mem. bd. editors Am. Jour. Internat. Law, 1986-99. Fulbright scholar, Lithuania, 1998; recipient Cert. merit Am. Soc. Internat. Law, 1981. Mem. Am. Law Inst., D.C. Bar Assn., Minn. Bar. Assn. Democrat. Avocation: fly fishing. Home: PO Box 130 Applegate CA 95703-0130 Office: U Calif Davis CA 95616

**GLESSNER, THOMAS ALLEN,** lawyer; b. Portland, Oreg., July 15, 1952; s. Ronald Walter and Marian Edna (Brannan) G.; m. Laura Lynn Braendlein, Aug. 27, 1977; children: Joshua Thomas, SaraLynn Joy, Brannan Timothy, Jefferson Samuel. AA, Highline C.C., Midway, Wash., 1972; BA, U. Wash., 1974, JD, 1977. Bar: Wash. 1977, Va. 1998, U.S. Dist. Ct. (we. dist.) 1977, U.S. Supreme Ct. 1989. Assoc. Holm, Glessner, Mogren & Glessner PS, Renton, Wash., 1977-87; instr. law Highline C.C., Midway, 1984-87; pres., gen. counsel Nat. Inst. Family and Life Advocates, 1987—. Rep. precinct committeeman, Renton, 1984-87; mem. state steering comm., Jack Kemp for Pres., Seattle, 1988; nat. co-chmn. Families for Bush/Quayle '92; bd. dirs., Crisis Pregnancy Ctr., King County, Wash., pres., 1987; pres. Christian Action Coun., 1987-93; mem. Coun. Nat. Policy. Recipient Humanitarian award Human Life of Wash., 1987. Mem. ABA, Wash. State Bar Assn., U.S. Supreme Ct. Bar, King County Bar Assn., Christian Legal Soc., Kiwanis (local pres. 1983, local bd. dirs. 1982-85), Phi Beta Kappa, Sigma Nu. Presbyterian. Constitutional, Legislative, Family and matrimonial. Home: 6708 Farmstead Ln Fredericksburg VA 22407-1700

**GLICKER, BRIAN IRVING,** lawyer; b. Cardiff, Wales, July 12, 1958; came to U.S., 1985; s. David Arnold and Renee Barbara (Goldblatt) G.; m. Karen Adele Eshel, Nov. 22, 1987; children: Hayley Samantha, Daniel Joseph. BA, U. Judaism, L.A., 1989; JD, U. Calif., San Francisco, 1992. Bar: Calif. 1992, U.S. Dist. Ct. (ctrl., no. and ea. dists.) Calif. 1993, U.S. Ct. Appeals (9th cir.) 1993. Dir. Pasadena (Calif.) Jewish Cmty. Ctr., 1987-89; vice prin. Sinai Sch., L.A., 1989-91; assoc. Abend, Lepper, Jacobson, Walnut Creek, Calif., 1991—, Knopfler & Robertson, Woodland Hills, Calif., 1994—; spkr., advisor Calif. Assn. Cmty. Mgrs., 1994—; mem., spkr. Cmty. Assn. Inst., Calif., 1994—; lectr. U. Judaism, 1996. Mem. Brit.-Am. C. of C. Jewish. Avocations: golf, gastronomy. General civil litigation, Construction, Personal injury. Office: Knopfler & Robertson 21650 Oxnard St Ste 500 Woodland Hills CA 91367-4911

**GLICKMAN, FRED ELLIOTT,** lawyer; b. N.Y.C., Sept. 1, 1946; s. Stanley and Anita (Lipow) G.; m. Margery Feinschreiber, Apr. 24, 1977; children—David, Michael, Laura. B.A., Dartmouth Coll., 1968; M.B.A., U. Chgo., 1971; J.D., Columbia U., 1974. Bar: Ill. 1974, Fla. 1982, U.S. Dist. Ct. (no. dist.) Ill. 1974, U.S. Dist. Ct. (so. dist.) Fla. 1983, U.S. Tax Ct. 1978. Assoc. Sonnenschein, Carlin, Nath & Rosenthal, Chgo., 1974-75; atty. Allied Van Lines, Broadview, Ill., 1975-76; assoc. Fishel and Kahn, Chgo., 1976-77, Laser Schostok, Kolman & Flank, Chgo., 1977-81; ptnr. Feinschreiber & Assocs., Key Biscayne and Miami, Fla., 1981-85; sole practice, Miami, 1985—. Contbr. articles to profl jours. Mem. S. Miami Kendall Bar Assn (bd. dirs. 1996—). Estate planning, State civil litigation, General corporate. Home: 13740 SW 78th Ct Miami FL 33158-1108 Office: Ste 508 9200 S Dadeland Blvd Miami FL 33156-2713

**GLICKMAN, GLADYS,** lawyer, writer; b. N.Y.C., Feb. 28, 1920; d. Reuben and Sadie (Levy) Glickman. BA, Bklyn. Coll., 1939; JD, DePaul U., 1959. Bar: Ill. 1959, N.Y. 1961. Editor Bur. Nat. Affairs, Inc., Washington, 1942-44, Research Inst. Am., N.Y.C., 1944-48; asst. dir., labor rels. rsch. Continental Can Co., N.Y.C., 1948-51; supr. Wage Stabilization Bd., N.Y.C., 1951-53; writer, editor Matthew Bender and Co., N.Y.C., 1959—; corp. counsel Parents Magazine Enterprises, Inc., N.Y.C., 1961-78; v.p. legal Gruner and Jahr, USA Pub., N.Y.C., 1978-93. Author: Franchising, 1969, (with others) Warrens Forms of Agreement, 1964. Mem. ABA, N.Y. County Lawyers Assn. (com. mem.), Ill. State Bar Assn. Jewish. Franchising, Pension, profit-sharing, and employee benefits, Trademark and copyright.

**GLICKMAN, PHILIP S.,** lawyer; b. Rochester, N.Y., Aug. 22, 1948. BA in History and Polit. Sci., George Washington U., 1970; JD, New Eng. Sch. Law, 1974. Bar: N.Y. 1975, U.S. Dist. Ct. (we. dist.) N.Y. 1975, U.S. Ct. Appeals (2d cir.) 1976, U.S. Ct. Appeals (D.C. cir.) 1991, U.S. Ct. Appeals (fed. cir.) 1992), U.S. Ct. Appeals (11th cir.) 1995, U.S. Ct. Appeals (3d and 4th cirs.) 1996, U.S. Supreme Ct. 1980. Intern U.S. Ho. of Reps., Washington, 1967; clk. U.S. Senate, Washington, 1970; assoc. Robert F. Wood, P.C., Rochester, 1974-75, Friedman & Greenfield, P.C., Rochester, 1976-78; gen. practice, counsel for other attys., Rochester, 1975-76; asst. atty. gen. Rochester Regional Office, N.Y. State Dept. Law, 1978-80; pvt. practice, Rochester,, 1980—. Founding orgn. New Eng. Jour. on Prison Law, 1973-74; contbr. numerous articles on criminal appeals to Daily Record, Rochester, also columns N.Y. Times and Rochester Democrat & Chronicle. Mem. Monroe County Bar Assn. (sec. criminal justice sect. 1992-95). Fax: 716-232-2802. E-mail: glickman@frontiernet.net. Appellate. Office: 450 Reynolds Arcade Bldg Rochester NY 14614

**GLICKMAN, STEPHEN,** judge. Ptnr. Zuckerman, Spaeder, Goldstein, Taylor & Kolker, 1980-99; judge D.C. Ct. Appeals, 1999—. Office: DC Ct Appeals 6th Pl 500 Indiana Ave NW Washington DC 20001*

**GLICKSMAN, EUGENE JAY,** lawyer; b. N.Y.C., Aug. 10, 1954; s. David and Elsie (Lerner) G.; m. Patricia Cardoso, Sept. 23, 1984; 1 child, Elizabeth Ann. BA in Polit. Sci., CUNY, 1975, JD, 1978. Bar: N.Y. 1980, U.S. Dist. Ct. (so. and ea. dists.) N.Y. 1980, U.S. Supreme Ct. 1992. Immigration inspector U.S. Dept. Justice, Immigration and Naturalization Svc., N.Y.C., 1976-80; assoc. Antonio C. Martinez, N.Y.C., 1980-81, Harry Spar, N.Y.C., 1981-83; atty. pvt. practice, N.Y.C., 1983-93; ptnr. Glicksman & Cardoso, N.Y.C., 1993—. Arbitrator N.Y.C. Civil Cts., 1982-91; adminstrv. law judge N.Y.C. Taxi & Limousine Commn., 1991-98; aux. police officer N.Y.C. Police Dept., 1972-75. Mem. Am. Immigration Lawyers Assn. (N.Y. chpt. treas. 1993-94), N.Y. State Bar Assn., N.Y. County Lawyers Assn. (chair com. immigration and nationality law 1994-97). Immigration, naturalization, and customs. Office: Glicksman & Cardoso 150 Broadway Rm 1115 New York NY 10038-4302

**GLIEGE, JOHN GERHARDT,** lawyer; b. Chgo., Aug. 3, 1948; s. Gerhardt John Gliege and Jane Heidke; children: Gerhardt, Stephanie, Kristine. BA, Ariz. State U., 1969, MPA, 1970, JD, 1974. Bar: Ariz. 1974. Pvt. practice Scottsdale, Ariz., 1974-81, Flagstaff, Ariz., 1981-94, 98—, Sedona, Ariz., 1994-97, Williams, Ariz., 1997-98; prof. paralegal studies No. Ariz. U., Flagstaff, 1981-83, prof. urban planning and cmty. devel., 1984—; prof. paralegal studies Yavapai Cmty. Coll., Prescott, Ariz., 1995-97. Municipal (including bonds), Administrative and regulatory, Environmental. Address: PO Box 1388 Flagstaff AZ 86002-1388

**GLINSEK, GERALD JOHN,** lawyer; b. Akron, Ohio, Jan. 16, 1939; s. Rudolph Paul and Angela Louise (Stanger) G.; m. Karen Rosemary Mehen, Oct. 17, 1968 (div. Aug. 1990); children: Kelli, Daniel; m. Maureen Louise Nuosce, May 7, 1994 (dec. Aug. 1998); 1 child from previous marriage, Rebecca Ann. BA, U. Akron, 1963, JD, 1967. Bar: Ohio 1967, U.S. Dist. Ct. (no. dist.) Ohio 1969, U.S. Ct. Appeals (6th cir. 1986), U.S. Supreme Ct. 1986. Asst. pros. atty. Summit County Prosecutors Office, Akron, 1967-71; pvt. practice Akron, 1971—. With U.S. Army, 1957. Mem. ABA, Ohio Bar Assn., Akron Bar Assn. (treas. 1981), Summit County Legal Aid Soc. (pres. 1978-82), Phi Kappa Tau (advisor 1982—). Democrat. Roman Catholic. Avocations: travel, skiing. Family and matrimonial, Personal injury,

Criminal. Home: 1861 Wiltshire Rd Akron OH 44313-6101 Office: 88 S Portage Path Akron OH 44303-1023

**GLITZENSTEIN, ERIC ROBERT,** lawyer; b. N.Y.C., July 29, 1957; s. Irving and Gertrude (Weinstein) G. BA, Johns Hopkins U., 1978; JD magna cum laude, Georgetown U., 1981. Bar: D.C. 1982, U.S. Ct. Appeals (D.C. cir.) 1982, U.S. Supreme Ct. 1988. Law clk. to Judge Thomas Flannery, U.S. Dist. Ct. for D.C., Washington, 1981-82; dir. Freedom of Info. Clearinghouse, Washington, 1982-83; staff atty. Pub. Citizen Litigation Group, Washington, 1983-89; of counsel Harmon, Curran, Gallagher & Spielberg, Washington, 1989—; mng. ptnr. Meyer & Glitzenstein, Washington, 1993-99; adj. prof. Georgetown U. Law Ctr., 1993-99. Co-author: Judicial Record of Robert Bork, 1987, Litigation under FOIA and Privacy Act 1985-91; contbr. articles to profl. jours. Recipient First Amendment award Playboy Found., 1989. Mem. ABA (vice chmn. com. on govt. info. 1990-93), Fed. Bar Assn. (chmn. com. on govt. info. 1989—, mem. exec. com. on adminstrv. law 1989-90), D.C. Bar. Administrative and regulatory, Environmental, Federal civil litigation. Office: Meyer & Glitzenstein 1601 Connecticut Ave NW Washington DC 20009-1035

**GLOBER, GEORGE EDWARD, JR.,** lawyer; b. Edwards AFB, Calif., Aug. 10, 1944; s. George Edward and Catharine (Crain) G.; m. Deirdre Denman, May 22, 1971; children—Denman, Nancy King. A.B., Cornell U., 1966; J.D., Harvard U., 1969. Bar: Tex. 1969, U.S. Sup. Ct. 1976. tchg. fellow natural scis. Harvard U., 1967-69; assoc., Vinson & Elkins, Houston, 1969-77; dir. Houston Dept. Pub. Service, 1977-78; mem. law dept. Exxon Corp. and Affiliates, 1978—, counsel Exxon Corp., 1995—, asst. gen. counsel Exxon Chem. Co., 1991-94; chief atty. refining, environ. and health Exxon Co. USA, 1988-91; gen. counsel Exxon Prodn. Rsch. Co., 1982-88. With Air N.G., 1969-75. Fellow Houston Bar Assn.; mem. ABA, Am. Intellectual Property Law Assn., Internat. Law Assn., Tex. Bar Assn., Dallas Bar Assn., Assn. Corp. Patent Counsel. General corporate, Patent, Environmental. Office: Exxon Corp 5959 Las Colinas Blvd Irving TX 75039-2298

**GLOCK, EARL FERDINAND,** lawyer; b. Johnstown, Pa., July 21, 1924; s. Earl F. and Claire (McNeelis) G.; m. Margaret Mary Kohler, Dec. 29, 1950; children: Margretta, Earl F. III, Karl, Christine, Catherine, Jeanette, Mary Rose. BA, Harvard U., 1948, JD, 1951. Bar: Pa. 1952, U.S. Dist. Ct. (we. dist.) U.S. Tax. Ct. 1980, U.S. Ct. Appeals (3d cir.) 1981, U.S. Supreme Ct. 1985. Pvt. practice Johnstown, 1952—. Bd. dirs. Johnstown Symphony Orch., 1960-81; bd. dirs. Mercy Hosp. Johnstown, 1962-90, pres., chmn., 1980-88; trustee Ebensburg (Pa.) Ctr., state sch., 1985—. With AUS, 1943-45, CBI. Mem. Pa. Bar Assn. (bd. govs. 1980-83), Cambria County Bar Assn. (bd. mgrs. 1987-90, pres. 1990-91), Citizens Cemetery Assn. (trustee 1971—), Sunnehanna Country Club, Elks. Republican. Roman Catholic. Avocation: travel. Office: 243 Adams St Johnstown PA 15901-2002

**GLOGOFF, DAVID LOUIS,** lawyer; b. Long Branch, NJ, Dec. 27, 1968; s. Michael Russ and Sally Ann (Gothelf) G. Student, Oxford (Eng.) U., 1989-90; BA, Hobart Coll., Geneva, N.Y., 1991; JD, Tulane U., New Orleans, 1994. Bar: N.J. 1994, N.Y. 1995, U.S. Dist. Ct. (ea. dist.) N.Y. 1996, U.S. Dist. Ct. (so. dist.) N.Y. 1996, U.S. Dist. Ct. N.J. 1998. Assoc. Keane & Marlowe, N.Y.C., 1994, Flood Johnston & McShane, N.Y.C., 1995-98, Smith, Stratton, Wise, Heher, Brennan, Princeton, N.J., 1998—. Trustee Princeton Friends of Open Space. Mem. ABA, N.Y. Bar Assn., Assn. Bar City N.Y. (com. internat. trade 1994), Princeton Bar Assn., Cornell Club. Avocations: tennis, skiing, squash, travel. General corporate, Securities, Private international. Office: Smith Stratton Wise Heher and Brennan 600 College Rd E Princeton NJ 08540-6636

**GLOSBAND, DANIEL MARTIN,** lawyer; b. Salem, Mass., July 3, 1944; s. Leon Glosband and Ruth Pauline (Wentworth) Glosband School; m. Merrily Cotton, Dec. 23, 1967; children: Alexander, Gabriel, Oliver. BA, U. Mass., 1966; JD, Cornell, U., 1969. Bar: Mass. 1969, U.S. Dist. Ct. Mass. 1970, U.S. Ct. Appeals (1st cir.) 1971, U.S. Dist. Ct. Conn. 1971, U.S. Dist. Ct. Vt. 1974, U.S. Supreme Ct. 1982. Assoc., then ptnr. firm Widett & Widett, Boston, 1969-75; ptnr. Goldstein & Manello, Boston, 1976-87, Goodwin, Procter and Hoar, Boston, 1988—; adviser Am. Law Inst. Transnat. Insolvency Project, 1994—. Contbr. numerous articles on bankruptcy to profl. jours. Fellow Am. Coll. Bankruptcy (dir. 1999—), Am. Bar Found., Mass. Bar Found.; mem. Mass. Bar Assn. (chmn. bankruptcy com. 1980-83), Boston Bar Assn. (chmn. bankruptcy com. 1977-80), ABA (sect. on corps., chmn. internat. bankruptcy com. 1990-95), Internat. Bar Assn. (sect. bus. law, vice chmn. insolvency and creditors rights com. 1997—, del. UN Commn. Internat. Trade Law). Democrat. Jewish. Bankruptcy. Home: 34 Atlantic Ave Swampscott MA 01907-2404 Office: Goodwin Procter & Hoar Exchange Pl Boston MA 02109-2803

**GLOSE, HERBERT JAMES,** lawyer, educator; b. Buffalo, N.Y., Nov. 17, 1957; s. Herbert John and Bernadine Margaret Glose; m. Anne Glose, Mar. 20, 1982; children: Herbie, Lauren, Patrick. Student, U. Rochester, 1975-76; BA magna cum laude, U. Notre Dame, 1979; JD cum laude, SUNY, Amherst, 1982. Bar: N.Y. 1983, U.S. Dist. Ct. (we. dist.) N.Y. 1983. Ptnr. Moot & Sprague, Buffalo, N.Y., 1983-90, Giardino & Schober, LLP, Buffalo, 1990-97, Harris Beach & Wilcox, LLP, Hamburg, N.Y., 1997—; counsel to bd. United Way Buffalo and Erie County, 1990—; mem. adv. bd. Kids Voting N.Y., Buffalo, 1996—. Dir. Taste of Buffalo, 1990—, chair, 1994; dir., v.p. Buffalo Jr. C. of C., 1985-90. Named Torchbearer 1996 Olympic Torch Run, U.S. Olympic Com./United Way, Atlanta, 1996. Mem. N.Y. State Bar Assn., Bar Assn. Erie County (corp. law com. 1983—, chair 1996—), St. Benadicts Golf League, Amherst (N.Y.) C. of C. Avocations: golf, coaching Little League baseball, hockey dad. General corporate, Finance, Non-profit and tax-exempt organizations. Office: Harris Beach & Wilcox LLP One Grimsby Dr Hamburg NY 14075

**GLOSSER, HARRY JOHN, JR.,** lawyer; b. Pottsville, Pa., Jan. 13, 1946; s. Harry Joseph and Anne (Rosenberger) G.; m. Lorraine D. Wanner, Jan. 28, 1995. BS in Acctg., Rider U., 1967; JD, Dickinson Sch. Law, 1970. Bar: Pa. 1970, U.S. Dist. Ct. (ea. dist.) Pa. 1974. Law clk., assoc. Curtin and Heefner, Morrisville, Pa., 1970-71; assoc. Timby & Godwin, Newton, Pa., 1970-74; ptnr. Godwin & Glosser, Newton, 1975; pvt. practice Morrisville, Pa., 1975-81, 85—; ptnr. Donahue & Glosser, Morrisville, 1981-85; solicitor Bristol-Bensalem Human Svcs. Ctr., Bristol Twp., Pa., 1978-87, Morrisville Sch. Dist., 1985-88. Mem. sch. bd. Morrisville Sch. Dist., 1974; pres. Morrisville Sch. Bd. Dirs., 1975-78; sec. Palmer Farm Homeowners Assn., Inc. Mem. Pa. Bar Assn., Bucks County Bar Assn. (chmn. Orphans Ct. sect.). General practice, Bankruptcy, General civil litigation. Home: 1988 Satter Ct Yardley PA 19067-7218 Office: 331 W Bridge St Morrisville PA 19067-2342

**GLOSSER, WILLIAM LOUIS,** lawyer; b. Johnstown, Pa., Aug. 30, 1929; s. Saul I. and Eva (Hurwitz) G.; m. Patricia Freeman, Feb. 5, 1932; children: Alix Paul, Jill P., Jonathan. BS Temple U., 1951; LLB, U. Pa., 1954. Bar: Pa. 1954, Fla. 1956, U.S. Dist. Ct. (we. dist.) Pa. 1956, U.S. Dist. Ct. (so. dist.) Fla. 1957. Assoc. Broad and Cassel, Miami Beach, Fla., 1956-57; sole practice, Coral Gables, Fla., 1957-61, Johnstown, Pa., 1962—; magistrate judge U.S. Dist. Ct. (we. dist.) Pa., 1972-93; corp. sec., dir. Glosser Bros., Inc., Johnstown, 1969-85; of counsel Smorto, Persio, Webb & McGill, Johnstown, 1988—. Bd. dirs. Lee Hosp., Johnstown, Greater Johnstown (Pa.) Cmty. Found., ret.; mem. Johnstown adv. council Pa. Human Relations Commn.; pres. United Jewish Fedn. Johnstown, 1970-75; chmn. fund drive United Way, 1985, pres., 1987-88; bd. dirs. Mt. Aloysius Coll., 1980-84, Cmty. Found. Greater Johnstown, Pa., 1990—. Served with U.S. Army, 1954-56. Mem. Pa. Bar Assn., Fla. Bar Assn., Cambria County Bar Assn., Pa. Bar Assn., Greater Johnstown C. of C. (pres. 1985), Rotary (pres. 1990); B'nai B'rith (pres. lodge 1965-67, 83-84). Jewish. General corporate, General practice, Personal injury. Home: 521 Luzerne St Johnstown PA 15905-2324 Office: Smorto Persio Webb & McGill 430 Main St Johnstown PA 15901-1823

**GLOTTA, RONALD DELON,** lawyer; b. Lajunta, Colo., Mar. 18, 1941; s. John Wallace and Marian (Kisner) G.; m. Sharon S. Glotta, Aug. 27, 1961 (div. Mar. 1986); children: Holly Ann, Jeffrey Delon; m. Marietta Lynn Baba, June 23, 1990 (div. Oct. 1998). BA with honors, U. Kans., 1963; JD, U. Mich., 1966. Bar: Mich. 1966. Atty. Marcus, McCroskey, Libner, Reamon, Williams & Dilley, Muskegon, Mich., 1966-68; ptnr. Philo, Maki, Moore, Pitts, Ravitz, Glotta, Cockrel & Robb, Detroit, 1968-70; prin. Glotta & Adelman, Detroit, 1970-85, Glotta, Rawlings & Skutt, Detroit, 1985-96, Glotta, Skutt & Assts, Detroit, 1996—. Mem. Phi Beta Kappa. Workers' compensation, Personal injury, Labor. Home: 2065 Hyde Park Rd Detroit MI 48207-3885

**GLOVER, DURANT MURRELL,** lawyer; b. Wilmington, N.C., Mar. 6, 1951; s. Murrell Kelso and Erma Elizabeth (Williams) G.; m. Carol Ann Marquett, Dec. 16, 1978. AB, Duke U., 1973; JD with honors, U. N.C., 1976. Bar: N.C. 1976, U.S. Dist. Ct. (mid. dist.) N.C. 1976, U.S. Ct. Appeals (4th cir.) 1977, U.S. Supreme Ct. 1980. Assoc. Frassineti & Shaw, Greensboro, N.C., 1976-77; ptnr. Frassineti & Glover, Greensboro, 1977—. Mem., counsel Tarheel Triad Girl Scout Council Inc., Colfax, N.C., 1980—. Mem. N.C. Bar Assn., Greensboro Bar Assn. (editor Greensboro Bar News 1983-87, bd. dirs. 1987-89), Order of Coif. Republican. Presbyterian. Probate, Real property, Consumer commercial. Home: 405 Staunton Dr Greensboro NC 27410-6070 Office: Frassineti & Glover PO Box 1799 Greensboro NC 27402-1799

**GLOVSKY, SUSAN G. L.,** lawyer; b. Boston, Apr. 16, 1955; d. Leonard B. and Marilyn S. (Shapiro) Loitherstein; m. Steven M. Glovsky, May 25, 1980; 1 child, Lowell Eliott. BS in Chemistry, U. Vt., 1977; JD, Boston U., 1980. Bar: Mass. 1980, Mich. 1980, U.S. Dist. Ct. (ea. dist.) Mich. 1980, U.S. Patent Office 1981, N.Y. 1982, U.S. Dist. Ct. Mass. 1982, U.S. Ct. Appeals (1st cir.) 1982, U.S. Ct. Appeals (fed. cir.) 1991, U.S. Supreme Ct. 1995. Assoc. Levin, Levin, Garvett & Dill, Southfield, Mich., 1980-81, Ladas & Parry, N.Y.C., 1981-82, Dahlen & Gatewood, Boston, 1982-83; ptnr. Dahlen & Glovsky, Boston, 1983-85; pvt. practice Boston and Salem, Mass., 1985-93; of counsel Hamilton, Brook, Smith & Reynolds, Lexington, Mass., 1993-98; prin. Hamilton, Brook, Smith & Reynolds, Lexington, 1998—; adj. prof. Suffolk U. Law Sch. Mem. ABA (litigation sect.), Mass. Bar Assn., Boston Bar Assn., Boston Patent Law Assn. (past pres., chmn. litigation com. 1989—), Am. Arbitration Assn. (panel arbitrators 1985—, co-chair IP adv. com. 1999—). Jewish. Avocations: swimming, skiing. Federal civil litigation, Trademark and copyright, Patent. Home: 131 Federal St Salem MA 01970-3242 Office: Hamilton Brook Smith & Reynolds 2 Militia Dr Lexington MA 02421-4799

**GLUCK, MARSHALL J.,** lawyer; b. N.Y.C., Nov. 12, 1943; s. Benjamin I. and Gertrude (Trichter) G.; m. Ruth Rubin, July 5, 1970; children: Abbe R., Simon A. BA, Lafayette Coll., 1965; JD, NYU, 1968, LLM in Taxation, 1970. Bar: N.Y. 1968, U.S. Tax Ct. 1970, U.S. Ct. Appeals (2d cir.) 1971, U.S. Dist. Ct. (so. and ea. dists.) N.Y. 1972, U.S. Supreme Ct. 1973. Contbr. articles to profl. jours. With U.S. Army, 1969. Mem. ABA, N.Y. State Bar Assn., Nat. Health Lawyers Assn., East Hampton Tennis Club (gov. 1990-93), City Athletic Club, Pi Lambda Phi. Avocations: travel, theater, sports. General corporate, Health, General practice. Office: Robinson Brog Leinwand Greene Genovese & Gluck PC Ste 31L 1345 Avenue Of The Americas New York NY 10105-0144

**GLUSBAND, STEVEN JOSEPH,** lawyer; b. Berlin, Jan. 15, 1947; came to U.S., 1949; s. Morris and Docia (Waitman) G.; m. Roberta Gail Jacobs, Nov. 22, 1981; children: Ilana, Jonathan. BBA, CCNY, 1969; JD, Fordham U., 1973; LLM, NYU, 1978. Bar: N.Y. 1974, U.S. Dist. Ct. (so. dist.) N.Y. 1974, U.S. Ct. Appeals (2nd cir.) 1974. Trial atty. SEC, N.Y.C., 1974-75, spl. trial counsel, 1976-77; assoc. Sage Gray Todd & Sims, N.Y.C., 1977-80, ptnr., 1981-87; ptnr. Carter, Ledyard & Milburn, N.Y.C., 1987—; dir. MER Telemanagement Solutions Ltd. Mem. ABA (com. fed. regulation of securities, securities litigation), Assn. of Bar of N.Y.C. (com. on futures regulation 1986-88). General corporate, Securities, Commodities. Home: 343 E 30th St New York NY 10016-6417 Office: Carter Ledyard & Milburn 2 Wall St Fl 13 New York NY 10005-2072

**GLYNN, JAMES MARTIN,** lawyer; b. Bronx, N.Y., June 4, 1962. BA, CUNY, 1986; JD, Pace U., 1992. Bar: N.Y. 1993, Conn. 1993. Pvt. practice, Bronx, 1993—. General practice, Family and matrimonial. Office: 1845 Hunt Ave Ste 2 Bronx NY 10462-3622

**GLYNN, MARILYN,** lawyer. Gen. counsel Office of Govt. Ethics, Washington. Office: Office of Govt Ethics 1201 New York Ave NW Ste 500 Washington DC 20005-3968*

**GNICHTEL, WILLIAM VAN ORDEN,** lawyer; b. Summit, N.J., Jan. 11, 1934; s. William Stone and Edith Parrot (Van Orden) G.; m. Emily Hopkins Martenet, July 11, 1959 (dec.); children: William Van Orden Jr., Edwin Martenet; m. Mary B. Gayley, June 7, 1996. BA, Trinity Coll., 1956; LLB, Columbia U., 1959. Bar: N.Y. 1961, Mass. 1997. Ptnr. Whitman & Ransom, N.Y.C., 1968-88; resident ptnr. Whitman & Ransom, Saudi Arabia, 1980-85; ptnr. Chadbourne & Parke, N.Y.C., 1988-92; spl. counsel Law Firm of Salah Al-Hejailan, Riyadh, Saudi Arabia, Saudi Arabia, 1986-95; lectr. in field. Contbr. articles to profl. jours. Mem. ABA, Assn. of Bar of City of N.Y., Union Club, Knickerbocker Club (N.Y.C.), Somerset Club (Boston), Onteora Club (Tannersville, N.Y.; exec. vp. 1974-75, pres. 1976-77, bd. dirs. 1970-77), Masons, Phi Delta Phi. Episcopalian. Banking, Finance, Private international. Address: PO Box 431 Lincoln MA 01773-0431

**GOAD, FRANK ROARK,** lawyer; b. Scottsville, Ky., Apr. 14, 1915; s. Frank R. and Anna Laura (Kemp) G.; m. Pat Howell, Apr. 16, 1982; children by previous marriage—Margaret, Hutchins, Frank. J.D., U. Louisville, 1942. Bar: Ky. 1942. County atty. Commonwealth of Ky., Scottsville, 1950-53, commonwealth atty., Bowling Green and Scottsville, 1953-56; city atty. City of Scottsville, 1957-58; chmn. Ky. workers compensation bd. Commonwealth of Ky., Frankfort, 1960-70; Circuit judge 49th Jud. Circuit, Simpson and Allen Counties, Ky., 1970-80; dir. Farmers Nat. Bank, Scottsville, 1956—, chmn. bd., 1984—; mem. firm Cole, Moore & Baker, Bowling Green, 1984—; v.p. Mid South Life Ins., Co., Nashville, 1964-65. Served with U.S. Army, 1944-46. Mem. Am. Trial Lawyers Assn., Ky. Bar Assn., Bowling Green Bar Assn. Democrat. Methodist. Lodges: Elks, Rotary. Insurance, Workers' compensation, Banking. Office: Cole Moore & Baker 921 College St Bowling Green KY 42101-2134

**GOANS, JUDY WINEGAR,** lawyer; b. Knoxville, Tenn., Sept. 27, 1949; d. Robert Henry and Lula Mae (Myers) Winegar; m. Ronald Earl Goans, June 18, 1971; children: Robert Henson, Ronald Earl Jr. Student, Sam Houston State U., 1967-68; BS in Engring. Physics, U. Tenn., 1971, postgrad., 1971-74, JD, 1978. Bar: Tenn. 1978, U.S. Dist. Ct. (ea. dist.) Tenn. 1979, U.S. Patent Office 1980, U.S. Ct. Appeals (Fed. cir.) 1980, U.S. Supreme Ct. 1983. Instr. legal rights Knoxville Women's Ctr., 1977-78; patent analyst nuclear div. Union Carbide Corp., Oak Ridge, Tenn., 1978-79; patent atty. U.S. Dept. Energy, Washington, 1979-82; legis. and internat. intellectual property specialist Patent and Trademark Office, Washington, 1982-89; pvt. practice law Clinton, Tenn., 1990-96; cons. internat. intellectual property law Clinton and Washington, 1993—; judge Rich Moot Ct. competition, Washington, 1984, Knoxville, 1991; head U.S. Del. 13th session World Intellectual Property Orgn. Permanent Com. for Devel. Cooperation Related to Intellectual Property, 1989; mem. hearing com. Bd. Responsibility of the Supreme Ct. Tenn., 1992—; dir. and chief of party SIPRE Project, Cairo. Del. Nat. Women's Conf., Houston, 1977; bd. dirs. Nat. Orgn. for Women, Washington, 1977-79, Good Shepherd Kingergarten, 1987, Knoxville Women Ctr. 1992-93; legal adv. bd. Knoxville Rape Crisis Ctr., 1979. Mem. ABA, Tenn. Bar Assn., Am. Intellectual Property Law Assn., Govt. Patent Lawyers Assn. (sec. 1981-83), Patent and Trademark Office Soc. (bd. dir. 1986-88), East Tenn. Laywers Assn. for Women (pres. elect 1990-91, pres. 1992, bd. dirs.), Knoxville Assn. Women Execs. (bd. dirs.), Greater Knoxville Lions Club, Tau Beta Pi (bd. dirs. Greater Smoky Mountain Alumni Chpt. 1991—), Sigma Pi Sigma, (sec. U. Tenn. chpt. 1970-71). Episcopalian. Home: 1422 Eagle Bend Dr Clinton TN 37716-4029 Office: SIPRE Project-Cairo care Janice Dance 2021 Wilson Blvd Ste 1200 Arlington VA 22201-3006

**GODBEY, ROBERT CARSON,** lawyer; b. Houston, June 7, 1953; s. Charles Perry and Bobbye Lee Godbey; m. Ellen Carson, June 2, 1979. BS, BSEE, So. Meth. U., 1975; JD, Harvard U., 1980. Bar: D.C. 1980, U.S. Patent Office, 1981, Hawaii 1988. Telecommunications engr. Southwestern Bell, Dallas, 1975-76, Tex. Instruments, Dallas, 1976-77; assoc. Peabody, Lambert & Meyers, Washington, 1980-84; asst. U.S. atty. U.S. Dept. of Justice, Washington, 1984-87, Honolulu, 1987-91; ptnr. Jackson & Godbey, 1991—. Mem. ABA, IEEE, Hawaii State Bar Assn. (past chmn. intellectual property sect. 1994-96, past chmn. tech. com., 1995-97). General civil litigation, Intellectual property. Office: 2300 Pauahi Tower 1001 Bishop St Honolulu HI 96813-3429

**GODBOLD, JOHN COOPER,** federal judge; b. Coy, Ala., Mar. 24, 1920; s. Edwin Condie and Elsie (Williamson) G.; m. Elizabeth Showalter, July 18, 1942; children: Susan, Richard, John C., Cornelia, Sally. BS, Auburn U., 1940; JD, Harvard U., 1948; LLD (hon.), Samford U., 1981, Auburn U., 1988, Stetson U., 1994. Bar: Ala. 1948. With firm Richard T. Rives, Montgomery, 1948-49; ptnr. Godbold & Hobbs and successor firms, 1949-66; cir. judge U.S. Ct. Appeals (5th cir.), 1966-81, chief judge, 1981; chief judge U.S. Ct. Appeals (11th cir.), 1981-86, sr. judge, 1987—; dir. Fed. Jud. Ctr., Washington, 1987-90. Mem. Fed. Jud. Ctr. Bd., 1976-81. With field arty. AUS, 1941-46. Mem. ABA, Fed. Bar Assn., Ala. Bar Assn., Montgomery County Bar Assn., Alpha Tau Omega, Omicron Delta Kappa, Phi Kappa Phi. Episcopalian. Office: US Ct Appeals 11th Circuit PO Box 1589 Montgomery AL 36102-1589

**GODBOUT, ARTHUR RICHARD, JR.,** lawyer; b. Hartford, Conn., Oct. 7, 1957; s. Arthur Richard and Elizabeth Anne (Desmond) G. BSBA, Georgetown U., 1979, JD, 1986. Bar: Conn. 1987. Pvt. practice Avon, Conn., 1987—. Real property. Home: 272 Griswold Rd Wethersfield CT 06109-3625 Office: PO Box 1175 Avon CT 06001-1175

**GODDARD, CLAUDE PHILIP, JR.,** lawyer; b. Long Beach, Calif., Oct. 31, 1952; s. Claude Philip and Doris Marian (Dow) G.; m. Ellen Kohn, May 23, 1981; children: Marian Laura, Nora Margaret. BS with distinction, U.S. Naval Acad., 1974; JD cum laude, U. Pa., 1979. Bar: N.H. 1979, D.C. 1985, U.S. Dist. Ct. D.C. 1989, U.S. Ct. Appeals (9th cir.) 1985, U.S. Ct. Appeals (fed. cir.) 1991. Ensign U.S. Navy, 1974, advanced through grades to lt. comdr., 1987, atty., 1979-87, resigned, 1987; assoc. Keck, Mahin & Cate, Washington, 1987-89, ptnr., 1990; ptnr. Jenner & Block, Washington, 1990-95; shareholder Kilcullen, Wilson and Kilcullen, Chartered, Washington, 1995-99, Wickwire Gavin, P.C., Vienna, Va., 1999—. Government contracts and claims, Federal civil litigation, General civil litigation.

**GODDARD, RAY,** lawyer; b. Cin., Nov. 6, 1925; s. Paul and Christine (Quinton) G.; m. Betty Ainsworth, July 21, 1946 (div. 1973); children: Ray Q. Stephen, Denise; m. Carmella J. Pino, Sept. 14, 1973. LLB cum laude, U. Balt., 1954. Bar: Md. 1954, U.S. Supreme Ct. 1958, U.S. Ct. Claims 1962. Dep. dist. counsel U.S. Army C.E., Balt., 1955-64; spl. trial counsel U.S. Dept. Justice, Washington, 1964-81; fed. adminstrv. law judge HHS, Portland, Maine, 1981-84; sr. assoc. Max E. Greenberg, Cantor & Reiss, N.Y.C., 1984-88; ptnr. Blodnick, Pomeranz, Reiss, Shultz & Abramowitz, N.Y.C., 1988-89; sr. ptnr. Goddard & Blum, N.Y.C., 1989-92, Goddard, Ronan & Dineen, N.Y.C., 1992—; lectr. profl. orgns. and ednl. instns. Author monographs on constrn. contract law. Recipient U.S. Dept. Justice award, 1980. Mem. ABA. Avocation: photography. Construction. Office: Goddard Ronan & Dineen 201 E 42nd St New York NY 10017-5704

**GODDARD, RICHARD PATRICK,** lawyer; b. South Bend, Ind., Sept. 29, 1952; s. Melvin and Barbara Louise (Dosmann) G.; m. Anne Unverzagt, Nov. 24, 1979; children: Timothy, Kathryn, Elizabeth, Margaret. BA, Oberlin Coll., 1974; JD magna cum laude, Washington and Lee U., 1979. Bar: Ohio 1979, U.S. Dist. Ct. (no. dist.) Ohio 1979, U.S. Ct. Appeals (6th cir.) 1981, U.S. Supreme Ct. 1983, U.S. Dist. Ct. (so. dist.) Ohio 1999. Assoc. Calfee, Halter & Griswold, Cleve., 1978-87, ptnr., 1987—. Mem. ABA, Ohio Bar Assn., Cleve. Bar Assn., Cleve. Athletic Club, Shaker Heights Country Club, Omicron Delta Kappa. Construction, Labor, Civil rights. Home: 3065 Fairfax Rd Cleveland OH 44118-4057 Office: Calfee Halter Griswold LLP 800 Superior Ave E Ste 1400 Cleveland OH 44114-2688

**GODDARD, ROSS MILLARD, JR.,** lawyer; b. Macon, Ga., June 16, 1927; s. Ross Millard and Susie Mae (Collins) G.; 1 adopted child, Matthew Kristen. Student, Vanderbilt U., 1944-45; AB in Econs., Emory U., 1949, JD, 1953; diploma, The Judge Advocate Gen.'s Sch., 1962. Bar: Ga. 1953, U.S. Dist. Ct. (no. dist.) Ga. 1954, U.S. Ct. Appeals (5th and 11th cirs.) 1954, U.S. Ct. Mil. Appeals 1955, U.S. Supreme Ct. 1962. Commd. 1st lt. U.S. Army, 1955, advanced through grades to col., 1973; airborne inf. U.S. Army, various locations, 1958-61; ret. U.S. Army, 1978; pvt. practice Decatur, Ga., 1978-98; vis. instr. JAG Sch., Charlottesville, Va., 1968-73, FBI Nat. Police Acad., Quantico, Va., 1971-72. Mem. Ga. Rail Passenger Authority, 1994—; scoutmaster Decatur area Boy Scouts Am., 1983—; mem. exec. com. DeKalb Rep. Party, 1993—. Decorated Legion of Merit (2). Mem. Assn. U.S. Army, Nat. Assn. RR Passengers (bd. dirs. 1981—, pres. Ga. chpt. 1980-94, dir. 1994—, newsletter editor 1983-94, co-author Ga. statute on rail passenger authority 1985), Ret. Officers Assn., Am. Legion, Nat. RR Hist. Soc. Republican. Baptist. Avocations: hiking, photography, camping, railroads. General practice, Criminal, Military. Office: 700 Wachovia Bldg 315 W Ponce De Leon Ave Decatur GA 30030-2441

**GODFREY, CULLEN MICHAEL,** lawyer; b. Ft. Worth, Apr. 8, 1945; s. Cullen Aubrey and Agnes (Eiland) G.; m. Melinda McDonald, Aug. 29, 1970. BA, U. Tex., 1968, JD, 1970. Bar: Tex. 1969, U.S. Dist. Ct. (we. dist.) Tex. 1971, U.S. Ct. appeals (5th cir.) 1979, U.S. Ct. Appeals (11th cir.) 1981. Ptnr. Sloan, Muller & Godfrey, Austin, Tex., 1969-72; staff atty. Hunt Oil Co., Dallas, 1972-74; staff atty. Tesoro Petroleum Corp., San Antonio, 1974-75, sr. atty., 1975-78, asst. gen. counsel, 1978-82; asst. gen. counsel Am. Petrofina, Inc. (now FINA, Inc.), Dallas, 1982-88, gen. counsel, 1988-90, v.p., sec., gen. counsel, 1990-95, sr. v.p., sec., gen. counsel, 1995—; Bd. dirs. Normandy Life Ins. Co., Fina Oil & Chem. Co., Trust pipe Line Co., River Pipeline Co. Author: Legal Aspects of the Purchase and Sale of Oil and Gas Properties, 1992; contbr. articles to profl. jours. Bd. trustees Dallas Mus. Art, 1993-95, 98—, chmn. corp. com., 1993-95; bd. dirs. United Way MEt. Dallas, Inc., 1999—, gen. campaign chmn., 1999; bd. dirs. Dallas County Heritage Soc., 1998—. With Tex. N.G., 1968-74. Recipient Anti-Defamation League Jurispirdence award, 1999. Fellow Tex. Bar Found., Dallas Bar Found.; mem. ABA (chmn. subcom. on fgn. investment reporting, internat. law sect. 1984-87), State Bar Tex. (coun. oil gas and mineral law sect. 1992-95, coun. bus. law sect. 1998—, coll. mem. 1989—, com. on continuing legal edn. 1997—, com. legal aspect arts 1998—), Dallas Bar Assn., Tex. Bd. Legal Specialization (bd. cert. oil, gas. and mineral law), Am. Petroleum Inst. (bd. dirs. 1998—, gen. com. law 1989—, chmn. 1997—, gen. com. comms. 1995-97), Tex. Bus. Law Found. 9bd. dirs. 1990—, chmn. 1995-98), Greater Dallas Crime Commn. (dir. 1991—, chmn. 1997-98), Southwestern Legal Found. (rsch. fellow, adv. bd. internat. oil 7 gas edn. ctr., co-chmn. 44th-45th inst. on oil & gas law and taxation). General corporate, Oil, gas, and mineral, Private international. Office: FINA Inc PO Box 2159 Dallas TX 75221-2159

**GODFREY, PAUL BARD,** lawyer; b. Denver, Jan. 10, 1927; s. Thurman A. and Florence B. (Bard) G.; children: Brett, Scott. BA, U. Wyo., 1949, JD, 1955. Bar: Wyo. 1955, U.S. Ct. Appeals (10th cir.) 1955, U.S. Dist. Ct. Wyo. 1955, Colo. 1987, Ariz., 1995. Ptnr. Henderson, Thomson & Godfrey, 1955-60, Cheyenne, Wyo., ptnr., Henderson & Godfrey, 1960-67; ptnr. Godfrey & Sundahl, 1975-91, of counsel, Gallo & Godfrey, 1993-96, of counsel, Godfrey & Assoc., 1996—. bd. dir. Black Hills Corp., 1977-92. Chmn. Young Republicans, 1957-58; Rep. committeeman, 1964-66. Served with U.S. Army, 1945-46. Mem. ABA, Internat. Acad. Trail Lawyers, Bd. Trial Advs., Wyo. Bar Assn., Laramie County Bar Assn., Am. Legion, C. of C. (pres. 1961-62), Elks, Shriners, Masons. Episcopalian. State civil litigation, Public utilities, Environmental. Home: PO Box 2756 Cheyenne WY 82003-2756

**GODINO, MARC LAWRENCE,** lawyer, musician; b. N.Y.C., Sept. 10, 1961; s. Rino L. and Dolores E. Godino. BS, Susquehanna U., 1983; JD, 1995. Assoc. Law Offices of Bruce R. Safran, Tarzana, Calif., 1996—. Mem. ABA, L.A. County Bar Assn., Soc. Am. Magicians. Avocations: golf, gennis, music, fitness. Securities, Entertainment, Personal injury. Office: Law Offices of Bruce R Safran 5195 Lindley Ave Tarzana CA 91356-4349

**GODONE-MARESCA, LILLIAN,** lawyer; b. Buenos Aires, June 9, 1958; came to the U.S., 1991; d. Armand C.E. Godone-Signanini and E. Nydia

Soracco-Godone; m. Paul Alexander Maresca-Lowell (dec.); children: Catherine Victoria, Gerard Frank, Warren Paul. BA, Cath. U. Buenos Aires, 1975, MA, 1977, JD summa cum laude, 1979, advanced tchg. degree in jud. sci., 1981. Bar: Dist. Ct. Buenos Aires 1980, Calif. 1995, U.S. Dist. Ct. (ea. dist.) Calif. 1995, U.S. Dist. Ct. (so. dist.) Calif. 1998; lic. real estate broker, Calif. Advisor Sub-Sec. of State for Fgn. Trade, Buenos Aires, 1982; pvt. practice law Buenos Aires, 1982-86; therapist Ocean Pkwy. Developmental Ctr., N.Y., 1992; pvt. practice law Sacramento, 1995-96, San Diego, 1997—; asst. instr. Cath. U., Buenos Aires, 1983-86; adj. instr. U.S. Internat. U., San Diego, spring 1998. Contbr. articles to profl. jours.; author of poetry. Vol. San Diego Vol. Lawyer Program, 1993-94, Legal Svcs. No. Calif., Sacramento, 1995-96; catechist St. Ignatius, Sacramento, 1995-96, St. Michael's, Poway, Calif., 1997-98. Mem. Internat. Soc. Poets (disting.), State Bar Calif., Mothers Twins Club. Republican. Roman Catholic. Avocations: spending time with her children, the right to life, writing. Bankruptcy, Family and matrimonial, Personal injury. Home: 11551 Avenida Sivrita San Diego CA 92128-4519 Office: 6920 Miramar Rd Ste 301 San Diego CA 92121-2643

**GODWIN, DAVID,** prosecutor. U.S. atty. no. dist. W.Va. U.S. Dept. Justice, 1999—. Office: Ste 200 1100 Main St Wheeling WV 26003-0011*

**GODWIN, KIMBERLY ANN,** federal agency administrator, lawyer; b. Fargo, N.D., July 18, 1960; d. Robert Chandler and Kathryn Marie (Haney) G. BA in Polit. Sci., U. N.H., 1980; MS in Mass Comm., Boston U., 1984, JD, 1984. Bar: D.C. 1984, U.S. Supreme Ct. 1990. Legal intern Army Corps of Engrs., Waltham, Mass., 1983-84; assoc. Booz, Allen & Hamilton, Inc., Bethesda, Md., 1986-88; cons. Dept. State, Washington, 1984-86, asst. dir. comm. interagy. affairs, 1988-92, chief of policy diplomatic telecom. svc., 1992-96, dir. external affairs, 1997—; cons. Elton Assocs., Inc., Arlington, Va., 1984—. Mem. ABA (vice chmn. internat. comm. com. 1989—), Phi Beta Kappa, Pi Sigma Alpha. Avocations: flying, tennis, skiing. Home: 6215 Walhonding Rd Bethesda MD 20816-2138 Office: Dept State IRM/EA Rm 4428 2201 C St NW Washington DC 20520-0001

**GODWIN, RICHARD JEFFREY,** lawyer; b. Richland, Wash., Sept. 25, 1951; s. Richard P. and Reatha (Trumble) G.; m. Georgette Walsh, May 22, 1982; children: R. Christopher, Ross E., Hillary W. BA, Yale U., 1973; JD, Columbia U., 1977. Bar: CAlif. 1977, D.C. 1980. Honors atty. U.S. Dept. Transp., Washington, 1977-78; atty., advisor Fed. R.R. Adminstrn., Washington, 1978-83; counsel Bechtel Corp., San Francisco, 1983-88; sr. counsel Bechtel Corp., Gaithersburg, Md., 1988-93; prin. coun. Bechtel Power Corp., Gaithersburg, 1993—. Mem. ABA, D.C. Computer Law Forum. Presbyterian. Contracts commercial, Construction, Nuclear power. Home: 10304 Cavanaugh Ct Rockville MD 20850-5401 Office: Bechtel Power Corp 9801 Washingtonian Blvd Gaithersburg MD 20878-5356

**GODWIN, ROBERT ANTHONY,** lawyer; b. Phila., Apr. 24, 1938; s. Robert Anthony and Mary (MacElderry) G.; m. Isabel A. Tumelty, Jan. 20, 1941; children: Cara G., Marisa A., Elise D. B.S., Villanova U., 1960, J.D., 1963. Bar: Pa. 1964, U.S. dist. ct. (ea. dist.) Pa. 1964, U.S. Ct. Appeals (3d cir.) 1964, U.S. Supreme Ct. 1981. Vol. defender, Phila., 1964; assoc. Eastburn & Gray, Doylestown, Pa., 1968-70; asst. pub. defender Bucks County (Pa.), 1969-71; sole practice Newtown, 1971-73; ptnr. Timby & Godwin, Newtown, 1973-75; owner Robert A. Godwin & Assocs., Newtown, 1975—. Served with JAG, USMC, 1964-68; col. USMCR, ret. Mem. Pa. Bar Assn., Pa. Trial Lawyers Assn., Bucks County Bar Assn. Club: Rotary. General practice, Federal civil litigation, State civil litigation. Office: Box 450 110 S State St Newtown PA 18940-3508

**GOEBEL, WILLIAM HORN,** lawyer; b. N.Y.C., Dec. 7, 1941; s. Harry H. and Maxine (Hamburger) G.; m. Barbara Golden, July 30, 1966; children: Jason, Pamela. AB, Columbia U., 1963; JD, NYU, 1966. Bar: N.Y. 1966. Assoc. Bernard Trencher, N.Y.C., 1966-69; real estate atty. J.C. Penney Co., Inc., N.Y.C., 1969-71; assoc. gen. counsel N.K. Winston Corp., N.Y.C., 1971-72, Teachers Ins. and Annuity Assn. Am./Coll. Retirement Equities Fund, N.Y.C., 1972—; lectr. NYU Sch. Continuing Edn., 1985—; sr. coun. Team Leader, 1991—; mem. adv. bd. Commonwealth Land Title/Transamerica Title Ins. Co., 1992—; v.p. M.O.A. Enterprises, Inc./M.O.A Holdings, Inc., 1992—. Mem. Assn. of Bar of City of N.Y., N.Y. State Bar Assn. (fin. subcom. of real estate sect. 1998—). Real property, Contracts commercial. Office: Tchrs Ins & Annuity Assn Am 730 3rd Ave New York NY 10017-3206

**GOELTZ, THOMAS A.,** lawyer. BA in Econs. summa cum laude, DePauw U., 1969; JD magna cum laude, Mich. U., 1973. Assoc. Riddell, Williams, Ivie, Bullitt & Walkinshaw, Seattle, 1973-75; dep. prosecuting atty. civil divsn. King County Prosecuting Atty.'s Office, Seattle, 1976-79; prin. Cohen, Keegan & Goeltz, Seattle, 1979-86; ptnr. Davis Wright Tremaine, Seattle, 1986—; cons. state and local govt. agencies on environ. land use issues; adv. shoreline mgmt. City of Seattle; part-time lectr. Law Sch. U. Wash., Seattle, 1976-79. Editor Mich. Law Rev. Active Gov. Task Force on Regulatory Reform, 1993-95. Mem. ABA (urban, state & local govt. law sect.), Wash. State Bar Assn. (real property sect., past chair land use and environ. law sect.), Seattle-King County Bar Assn., Am. Coll. Real Estate Lawyers, Nat. Assn. Indsl. and Office Park, ICSC, Order of Coif. Land use and zoning (including planning), Real property, Environmental. Office: Davis Wright Tremaine 2600 Century Sq 1501 4th Ave Seattle WA 98101-1688

**GOELZ, ROBERT DEAN,** lawyer; b. Passaic, N.J., July 3, 1951; s. Robert M. and Catherine (Witte) G.; m. Pamela A. Wahrer, Oct. 18, 1975. BA in Econs., U. Dayton, 1973, JD, 1978. Bar: Ohio 1978, U.S. Dist. Ct. (so. dist.) Ohio 1978, U.S. Ct. Appeals (6th cir.) 1980, U.S. Supreme Ct. 1982. Asst. pros. atty. Montgomery County, Dayton, Ohio, 1979-84; assoc. Flanagan, Lieberman, Hoffman & Swaim, Dayton, 1984-89, ptnr., 1990—. Mem. ABA, Ohio State Bar Assn., Dayton Bar Assn. Republican. Roman Catholic. Avocations: gourmet cook, oenophile. Family and matrimonial. Office: Flanagan Lieberman Hoffman & Swaim 318 W 4th St Dayton OH 45402-1437

**GOERGEN, MICHAEL JAMES,** lawyer; b. Buffalo, Sept. 23, 1952; s. John Joseph and Mary Carol (Buchert) G.; m. Betsy Haynes Jenkins, Mar. 10, 1973; 1 child, Elizabeth Haynes. BA, George Washington U., 1973, JD, 1979. Bar: D.C. Ct. Appeals 1979, U.S. Dist. Ct. D.C. 1980, U.S. Ct. Appeals (D.C. cir.) 1981, U.S. Claims Ct. 1981, U.S. Ct. Appeals Md. 1984, U.S. Dist. Ct. Md. 1984, Va. 1985, U.S. Ct. Appeals (4th cir.) 1985, U.S. Dist. Ct. (ea. dist.) Va. 1985, U.S. Bankruptcy Ct. (ea. dist.) Va. 1990. Law clk. The Washington Post, 1977-79; assoc. Faulkner Shands & Stupar, Washington, 1979-81, Walstad, Kasimer, Tansey & Ittig, Washington, 1981-83; pvt. practice law Washington, 1983—; of counsel Sims Walker & Steinfeld, Washington, 1985-93. Construction, Contracts commercial. Office: #223 4910 Massachusetts Ave NW Washington DC 20016-4300

**GOETHEL, STEPHEN B.,** lawyer; b. Grand Rapids, Mich., Apr. 10, 1953; S. Warren B. Goethel and Beverly (Hendrick) Barrett; m. Lisa B. Chapple, July 29, 1978; children: Dana, Erica, Matthew. BA, Mich. State U., 1975; JD, Detroit Coll. Law, 1979. Bar: Mich. 1979, U.S. Dist. Ct. (ea. dist.) Mich. 1979. Asst. prosecutor Oakland County, Mich., 1979-80; assoc. Carlin, Ranno & Goethel, Southfield, Mich., 1980-83; pvt. practice Pontiac, Mich., 1983; ptnr. Stein, Moran & Westerman, Ann Arbor, Mich., 1983—. Bd. dirs. Old West Side Assn., Ann Arbor, 1984-86. Mem. ATLA, Mich. Trial Lawyers Assn., State Bar of Mich., Washtenaw County Bar Assn. Personal injury, Insurance. Office: 320 N Main St Ann Arbor MI 48104-1127

**GOETTEL, GERARD LOUIS,** federal judge; b. N.Y.C., Aug. 5, 1928; s. Louis and Agnes Beatrice (White) G.; m. Elinor Praeger, June 4, 1951; children: Sheryl, Glenn, James. Student, The Citadel, 1946-48; B.A., Duke U., 1950; J.D. (Harlan Fiske Stone scholar), Columbia U., 1955. Bar: N.Y. 1955. Asst. U.S. atty. So. Dist. N.Y., N.Y.C., 1955-58; dep. chief atty. gen.'s spl. group on organized crime Dept. Justice, N.Y.C., 1958-59; asso. firm Lowenstein, Pitcher, Hotchkiss, Amann & Parr, N.Y.C., 1959-62; counsel N.Y. Life Ins. Co., N.Y.C., 1962-68; with Natanson & Reich, N.Y.C., 1968-69; asso. gen. counsel Overmyer Co., N.Y.C., 1969-71; asst. counsel N.Y. Ct. on the Judiciary, 1971; U.S. magistrate U.S. Dist. Ct., So. Dist. N.Y., 1971-76, U.S. dist. judge, 1976—; now sr. judge; adj. prof. law Fordham U. Law Sch., 1978-87, Pace U. Law Sch., 1988-91; mem. com. on criminal justice act Jud. Conf. U.S., 1981-87, mem. cir. com. on pretrial phase of civil litigation, chmn. dist. coms. on discovery and criminal justice act 1982-85. Mem. council Fresh Air Fund, N.Y.C., 1961-64; bd. dirs. Community Action Program, Yonkers, N.Y., 1964-66. Served to lt. (j.g.) USCG, 1951-53. Club: Greenwoods Country (Winsted, Conn.). Office: 14 Cottage Pl Waterbury CT 06702-1904

**GOETZ, CLARENCE EDWARD,** retired judge, retired chief magistrate judge; b. Balt., Feb. 4, 1932. AA, U. Balt., 1961, LLB, 1964. Bar: Md. 1964. Assoc. Hackney & Yourtee, Anne Arundel County, Md., 1965-66; asst. U.S. atty. for Md., 1966-70; U.S. magistrate judge for Md. Balt., 1970-97; asst. prof. U. Balt., 1975, Towson State Coll., 1976; cons., arbitrator, mediator. Mem. Fed. Magistrate Judges Assn. Office: 400 E Pratt St Ste 800 Baltimore MD 21202-3122

**GOETZ, PETER,** lawyer; b. N.Y.C., Dec. 8, 1934; s. Robert L. and Lucy (Dunaif) G.; children: Andrew, Lucy, Jane. BCE, Rensselaer Poly. Inst., 1956; JD, Bklyn. Law Sch., 1960. Bar: N.Y. 1960, U.S. Dist. Ct. (so. and ea. dist.) N.Y. 1962, U. S. Dist. Ct. St. Thomas, U.S. Ct. of Appeals (2nd, 3rd and 5th cir.), U.S. Supreme Ct. 1969. Assoc. Maxe Greenberg, N.Y.C., 1962-64; sr. ptnr. Goetz, Fitzpatrick & Flynn, N.Y.C., 1967—; adv. bd. Metro Mediation Svcs., N.Y.C., 1988—. Author: (with others) Construction Litigation Representing the Contractor, 1991, Strategies of Construction Litigation, 1992, ADR A Practical Guide to Construction Disputes, 1994. Mem. ABA (arbitration com. 1960—), N.Y. State Bar Assn., Bar Assn. of City of N.Y. (constrn. law com. 1967), N.Y. County Bar Assn. (constrn. law com.), Am. Arbitration Assn. (coml. practice com. 1989—). Avocations: aircraft pilot instructor, skiing, tennis. Construction, Federal civil litigation, General civil litigation. Office: Goetz Fitzpatrick & Flynn 1 Penn Plz Ste 4401 New York NY 10119-0196

**GOETZINGER, ROBERT HERSCHEL,** lawyer, prosecuter; b. Beaver, Okla., Jan. 16, 1934; s. Willis Herschel Edward and Hassie Belle G.; m. Janice M. Goetzinger, Feb. 28, 1967; children: David Willis, Monica, Whitney. BBA, Okla. U., 1956; LLB, U. Okla. Law Sch., 1959. Commd. 2d lt. U.S. Army, 1956, advanced through grades to maj., 1973; atty. Ellis County, Arnett, Okla., 1959-62, Beaver County, Beaver, Okla., 1962-63; ptnr. Lansden, Drum & Goetzinger, Beaver, Okla., 1962-74; pvt. practice Beaver, Okla., 1974-92; asst. dist. atty. Okla. 1st Dist., Beaver, Okla., 1992—; part-time asst. dist. atty. Okla. 1st Dist., Beaver, 1968-92. Beaver City Atty. (pro bono), 1962-89. Mem. Am. Legion, Masonic Lodge #269. Office: District Attys Office 111 W 2nd St Beaver OK 73932

**GOFF, ROBERT WILLIAM, JR.,** lawyer; b. Houston, Apr. 22, 1946; s. Robert William and Emma Kate (Richey) G.; m. Donna M. Davidson, Dec. 22, 1968 (div. 1971); m. Sandra Kaye Chenault, June 22, 1974; 1 child, Melinda Kaye. BBA, Tex. Tech U., 1968; JD, U. Tex., Austin, 1971. Bar: Tex. 1971, U.S. Dist. Ct. (no. dist.) Tex.; cert. in estate planning and probate law. Atty. Sherrill, Crosnoe & Goff, Wichita Falls, Tex., 1971—; bd. dirs. United Regional Health Care Sys. Bd. dirs. Bethania Regional Health Care Found., Wichita Falls, 1988-98, North Tex. Rehab. Ctr., Inc., 1994-98, United Regional Health Care Found., 1998-99; trustee Bethania Regional Health Care Ctr., Wichita Falls, 1994-97, United Regional Health Care Found., 1998—. Mem. ABA, Wichita County Bar Assn. (pres. 1980-81), Wichita Club (pres., bd. dirs. 1981-85), Wichita Falls Country Club (bd. dirs. 1987-90). Avocations: golf, hunting, fly fishing. Estate planning, Probate, Estate taxation. Home: 2503 Elmwood Cir N Wichita Falls TX 76308-3915 Office: Sherrill Crosnoe & Goff 2301 Kell Blvd Ste 200 Wichita Falls TX 76308-1042

**GOGGIN, WENDY,** prosecutor. Acting U.S. atty. ea. dist. Tenn. U.S. Dept. Justice. Office: PO Box 872 Knoxville TN 37901*

**GOGLIA, CHARLES A., JR.,** lawyer; b. Phila., Aug. 26, 1931; s. Charles and Marie A. (Beckman) G.; m. Patricia A. Morrissey, July 26, 1958; children: Philip L., Catherine A. BS, St. Joseph's U., Phila., 1953; LLB, Boston Coll., 1958. Bar: Mass. 1958, U.S. Dist. Ct. Mass. 1959, U.S. Ct. Appeals (1st cir.) 1964, U.S. Tax Ct. 1977, U.S. Supreme Ct. 1993. Atty. Sheff & Gens, Boston, 1958-61, Foley, Hoag & Eliot, Boston, 1961-68; ptnr. Foley, Hoag & Eliot, 1968-74; pvt. practice Wellesley, Mass., 1974—; corporator, trustee, mem. bd. investment, exec. com. Bank Five for Savings, Burlington, Mass., 1974-92; mem. hearing com. Bd. Bar Overseers, Boston, 1984-86. Counsel Town of Nantucket, Mass., 1970-82, spl. counsel, 1982-85, Town of Weston, Mass., 1974-85, town counsel, 1986-92, spl. counsel, 1992—, mem. zoning bd. appeals, 1964-66, 74-85, mem. planning bd., 1973-74; spl. counsel Mass. Cable TV Commn., Boston, 1973-74. With USNAR, 1951-59. Mem. Wellesley Country Club (past pres.). Avocations: golf, travel. State civil litigation, General corporate, Real property. Home: 1 Hopewell Farm Rd Natick MA 01760-5570 Office: Wellesley Office Pk 65 William St Wellesley MA 02481-3802

**GOGNAT, RICHARD J.,** lawyer; b. Vincennes, Ind., May 4, 1958; m. Helena Morales; children: Remi, Tori. BS in Bus., Regis U., 1982; JD with honors, U. Tulsa, 1989. Bar: Colo. 1989. Div. landman Global Nat. Resources Corp., Houston, 1984-86; assoc. Calkins, Kramer, Grimshaw & Harring, Denver, 1989-93, Clanahan, Tanner, Downing & Knowlton, Denver, 1993-94; atty. Duke Energy, Denver, 1994-96, sr. atty., 1997-98; v.p., gen. counsel TEPPCO Crude Oil, LLC, Denver, 1998—. General corporate, Mergers and acquisitions, Contracts commercial. Office: TEPPCO Crude Oil LLC Ste 300N 6312 S Fiddlers Green Cir Englewood CO 80111-4927

**GOGO, GREGORY,** lawyer; b. Varos, Lemnos, Greece, Oct. 6, 1943; s. Soterio and Christina (Choleva) G.; m. Paraskevi Vivi Batzaka, July 15, 1989; 1 child, Chloe. BA, U. Chgo., 1966; MA, Rutgers U., 1972; JD, Seton Hall U., 1980. Bar: N.J. 1980, U.S. Dist. Ct. N.J. 1980. Reporter The Trentonian, Trenton, N.J., 1968-69; asst. project dir. Trenton Health Ctr., 1969-71; dir. planning UPI, Trenton, 1973-77; instr. sociology Trenton State Coll., 1973-77; assoc. Merlino, Rottkamp, Trenton, 1980-83; pvt. practice Trenton, 1983—; corp. counsel Coronis Bldg. Sys. Exec. bd. dirs. ARC, Trenton, 1972-77; spl. advisor to Pres. NAACP, Trenton, 1973-74; mem. parish coun. St. George Orthodox Ch., Hamilton Twp., N.J., 1984-88, atty. for St. George, 1995—. Recipient Archon Politis award Am. Hellenic Ednl. Prog. Assn., 1981, Cert. Merit, ARC, Trenton, 1977. Mem. N.J. Bar Assn., Mercer County Bar Assn., N.J. Assn. Trial Lawyers, Hellenic Vision (founding mem. 1992, pres. 1999—). Democrat. Workers' compensation, Personal injury, State civil litigation. Home: 14 Carla Way Lawrenceville NJ 08648-1500 Office: 1542 Kuser Rd Ste 1B Trenton NJ 08619-3829

**GOLAY, FRANK H., JR.,** lawyer; b. Chgo., 1948. BA, Cornell U., 1970, MAT, 1972, JD, 1977. Bar: N.Y. 1978. Ptnr. Sullivan & Cromwell, L.A. Securities, General corporate. Office: Sullivan & Cromwell 1888 Century Park E Los Angeles CA 90067-1702

**GOLD, ALAN STEPHEN,** federal judge; b. N.Y.C., Jan. 8, 1944; s. Frank and Geraldine (Guenzberg) G.; m. Susan Fine, May 28, 1965; children: Carol, Natalie. BA with high honors, U. Fla., 1966; JD, Duke U., 1969; M in Taxation, U. Miami, Fla., 1974. Bar: Fla., 1969, Dade County, Fla. (11th judicial cir.), 1992. Law clk. to Hon. Charles Carrol Fla. 3d Dist Ct. Appeal, Miami, 1969-71; asst. atty. Met. Dade County Atty's Office, Miami, 1971-75; ptnr. Greenberg, Traurig, Hoffman, Lipoff, Rosen & Quentel, P.A., Miami, 1975-92; apptd. judge 11th Circuit Ct., Dade County, Fla., 1992-98; appt. judge U.S. Dist. Ct. (so. dist.) Fla., Miami, 1998—. Contbr. articles to legal jours. Co-gen. counsel Fla. High Speed Rail Transp. Commn., 1985—; city atty. Village of Bal Harbour, Fla., 1976-82; spl. counsel Broward County, Fla., 1984-88; trustee Palmer Sch., Miami, 1987-88; bd. dirs. Actor's Playhouse, Miami, 1989—, South Dade Jewish Community Ctr., Miami, 1985-85; apptd. Fla. Environ. Land Mgmt. Com., 1987. Disting. scholar Fla. State U., 1990; recipient award for outstanding contbn. in field of legis. affairs South Fla. Bldrs. Assn., 1989. Mem. ABA, Fla. Bar. Assn. (com. on environment and land use law 1983-84, Disting. Svc. award 1984), Urban Land Inst. (nat. policy coun. 1988—), Greater Miami C. of C. (chmn. land use com. 1989-90), Am. Coll. Real Estate Attys. Democrat. Jewish. Avocations: trekking, vacationing, raising horses, sail fishing, reading. Office: US Dist Ct Fla 301 N Miami Ave Fl 10 Miami FL 33128-7702

**GOLD, EDWARD DAVID,** lawyer; b. Detroit, Jan. 17, 1941; s. Morris and Hilda (Robinson) G.; m. Francine Sheila Kamin, Jan. 8, 1967; children: Lorne Brian, Karen Beth. Student, Wayne State U., 1958-61; JD, Detroit Coll. Law, 1964. Bar: Mich. 1965, U.S. Dist. Ct. (ea. dist.) Mich. 1965, U.S. Ct. Appeals (6th cir.) 1965, D.C. 1966. Atty. gen. counsel FCC, Washington, 1965-66; ptnr. Conn, Conn & Gold, Detroit, 1966-67, May, Conn, Conn & Gold, Livonia, Mich., 1967-69, Hyman, Gurwin, Nachman, Gold & Alterman, Southfield, Mich., 1971-88, Butzel Long, Birmingham, Mich., 1988—; chmn. Friend of Ct. Adv. Com., Lansing, Mich., 1982-88; mem. Oakland County Criminal Justice Coordinating Coun., 1976-77; contbr. lectr. Inst. Continuing Legal Edn., Ann Arbor, Mich., 1981—, Mich. Trial Lawyers Assn. Author: Michigan Family Law, 1988; contbr. articles to legal jours. Mem. Southfield Transp. Commn., 1975-77; chmn. attys.' divsn. Jewish Welfare Fedn., Detroit, chairperson atty. disp. bd. Tri-County Hearing Panel 71, 1994-98; mem. nat. young leadership cabinet United Jewish Appeal, N.Y.C., 1978-80; bd. dirs. Oakland County Legal Aid Soc., 1979-84; pres. Jewish Family Svc., Detroit, 1988-90. Tau Epsilon Rho scholar, 1963. Fellow Am. Coll. Family Trial Lawyers, Am. Acad. Matrimonial Lawyers (bd. dirs. 1986—, pres. Mich. chpt. 1992-93, nat. bd. govs. 1998—); mem. Mich. Bar Assn. (coun. real property law sect. 1973-81, coun. family law sect. 1974-75, 77-82, chmn. family law sect. 1981-82, rep. assembly 1978-82), Oakland County Bar Assn. (bd. dirs. 1984-93, pres. 1992-93), Southfield Bar Assn. (pres. 1975-76), Bar Assn. D.C., Am. Arbitration Assn., Alpha Epsilon Pi (nat. pres. 1976-77, Order of Lion award 1986). Avocation: golf. Real property, Family and matrimonial, General corporate. Office: Butzel Long 32270 Telegraph Rd Ste 200 Birmingham MI 48025-2457

**GOLD, GEORGE MYRON,** lawyer, editor, writer, consultant; b. Bklyn., June 28, 1935; s. Harry and Rose Miriam (Meyerson) G.; m. Bunny Winters, Dec. 24, 1960; 1 child, Seth Harris. A.B., U. Rochester, 1956; J.D., NYU, 1959. Bar: N.Y. 1960. Practice N.Y.C., 1960-64, 67-78; legal editor Prentice-Hall, Inc., Englewood Cliffs, N.J., 1960-62; assoc. Speiser, Shumate, Geoghan & Law, N.Y.C., 1962-64; assoc. editor Rsch. and Rev. Svc. Am., Inc., Indpls., 1964-67; dir. publs., mng. editor Estate Planners Quar., Farnsworth Pub. Co., Inc., Rockville Centre, N.Y., 1967-69; editor-in-chief Trusts & Estates, N.Y.C., 1969-76; mng. editor Trust News, N.Y.C., 1976-78; dir. news publs. and info. ABA, Chgo., 1978-83; sr. assoc. editor and dir. book divsn. ABA Jour., Chgo., 1984-87; dir. publs. and editor Trial Mag. Assn. Trial Lawyers Am., 1988-89; cons. North Potomac, Md., 1989-90; exec. sr. law editor Mead Data Cen., Dayton, 1990-93; exec. editor Stevens Pub., Washington, 1993-94; corp. editl. dir. Stevens Pub., 1994-95, v.p. editorial, 1995; cons., Ashburn, Va., 1995—. Author: The Propriety, Procedure and Evidentiary Effect of a Jury View, 1959, Investments by Trustees, Executors and Administrators, 1961, What You Should Know About Intestacy, 1962, What You Should Know About the Common Disaster, 1962, The Powers of Your Trustee, 1962, What You Should Know About the Antenuptial Agreement, 1963, Who May Be the Beneficiary of Your Will, 1963, What You Should Know About The Spendthrift Trust, 1963, Comprehensive Estate Analysis, 1966, You're Worth More Than You Think, 1966, Medicare Handbook, 1966, The ABCs of Administering Your Estate, 1966, The Will: An Instrument for Service and Sales, 1966, A Tax-Sheltered Pension Plan for the Close-Corporation Stockholder, 1968, Social Security Law in Nutshell, 1968, What You Should Know About Custodial Gifts to Minors, 1968, The Short-Term Trust and Estate Planning, 1976, The Importance of a Will, 1976, The Need for an Experienced Executor, 1976, Tax Tips-99 Ways to Reduce the Bite, 1976, Investment Management: No Job for the Amateur, 1971, Who Manages Your Securities, 1972, A Woman's Need for Financial Planning, 1972, The Lawyer's Role in the Search for Peace, 1982, True Counselors: Helping Clients Deal with Loss, 1983, Evaluating and Settling Personal Injury Claims, 1991, Cite Checking: A Guide to Validating Legal Research, 1992, The Compliance Pak for HR Managers-Book I (Hiring, Evaluation & Separation), Book II (Severance), 1993, Selling Life Insurance: Overcoming Objections, 1996; editor: Fundamentals of Federal Income Estate and Gift Taxes, 1965-67, The R & R Tax Handbook, 1965-67, Tax-Free Reorganizations, 1968, Guide to Pension and Profit Sharing Plans, 1968, A Life Underwriter's Guide to Equity Investments, 1968, The Tired Tirade, 1968, A Handbook of Personal Insurance Terminology, 1968, The 15th Anniversary Edition of Estate Planners Quar., 1968, You, Your Heirs and Your Estate, 1968, The Farnsworth Letter for Estate Planners, 1968-69, How to Use Life Insurance in Business and Estate Planning, 1969, Human Drama in Death and Taxes, 1970, Don't Bank on It, 1970, The Feldman Method, 1970, Directory of Trust Instns. (ann.), LawTalk, 1986-87, The Supreme Court and Its Justices, 1987, Aaron J. Broder on Trial: Reflections of a Famous Litigator. Mem. Soc. Law Writers (dir. 1972-75), ABA, Am. Law Inst., N.Y. State Bar Assn., Assn. Bar City N.Y., Estate Planning Council N.Y.C., Nat. Press Club, Soc. Bus. Press Editors, Soc. Human Resources Mgmt., Newsletter Publishers Assn., Washington Independent Writers, Kappa Nu, Pi Alpha Lambda. Club: KP. Probate, Estate planning, Personal injury. Office: 43325 Dovetail Pl Ashburn VA 20147-5312

**GOLD, GORDON STANFORD,** lawyer; b. Detroit, Apr. 24, 1946; s. Norman Nelson and Beverly Ruth (Wolfson) G. BA, U. Mich., 1968, JD, 1971. Bar: Mich. 1971, U.S. Dist. Ct. Mich. 1971, U.S. Ct. Appeals (6th cir.) 1972. Asst. U.S. atty. Detroit, 1972-78; ptnr. Evans & Luptak, Detroit, 1978-87, Seyburn, Kahn, Ginn, Southfield, Mich., 1987—; mem. Oakland County Cir. Ct. Author: Primer on Federal Criminal Procedure, 1986. Chmn. Oakland County Mediation Com., 1995-96; mem. Oakland County Cir. Ct. Com., 1998—. Mem. Fed. Bar Assn. (dir. 1983-85), State Bar mich. (litigation sect. 1997—, jud. candidate rev. com. 1995-97), B'nai B'rith Barristers (pres. 1984-86). General civil litigation, Family and matrimonial, Criminal. Office: Seyburn Kahn Ginn 2000 Town Ctr Ste 1500 Southfield MI 48075-1148

**GOLD, HAROLD,** retired lawyer, accountant; b. N.Y.C., Jan. 14, 1916; s. Samuel and Freida (Swedlow) G.; m. Ellen Facundus, June 18, 1946; children: Sandra L. Gold Brasier, Fred L. Gold. BS in Acctg., UCLA, 1938; JD, U. Minn., 1948. CPA, Minn., Calif. Lectr. income taxation U. Minn., Mpls., 1946-48; pvt. practice Mpls., L.A., 1946-51; regional counsel Western Regional Renegotiation Bd., L.A., 1951-57; mem. adv. bd. federal contracts reports Bur. Nat. Affairs, Washington, 1969-81. Contbr. articles to profl. jours. Capt. U.S. Army Engrs., 1942-46. Fellow ABA (chmn. Pub. Contract Law sect. 1973-74, mem. coun. sect. on Pub. Contract Law (hon.), Nat. Contracts Mgmt. Assn.

**GOLD, HAROLD ARTHUR,** lawyer; b. Pitts., Jan. 13, 1929; m. Anita Hubert, Aug. 18, 1937; children: Howard, Bradley. BBA, U. Pitts., 1952; JD, Georgetown U., 1956. Bar: Pa. 1956, D.C. 1956. Sole practice law Pitts., 1956-64; atty. City of Pitts., 1960-69; ptnr. Baskin and Sears, Pitts., 1965-84, Reed, Smith, Shaw & McClay, Pitts., 1985-93; pres., chief exec. officer Coventry Care, Inc., Monongahela, Pa., 1970-86, chmn. bd., chief exec. officer, 1986-87; adj. prof. law Duquesne U. Pres. Young Dem. Club of Pitts., 1960-66; presdl. elector Pa., 1960; chmn. bd. Mayview State Hosp., Pitts., 1971-75. Served to lt. U.S. Army, 1948-49, 52-53. Mem. ABA, Pa. Bar Assn., Allegheny County Bar Assn. (real property council 1983-86). Real property, Banking, Finance. Office: The Pitt Bldg 213 Smithfield St Pittsburgh PA 15222-2224

**GOLD, I. RANDALL,** lawyer; b. Chgo., Nov. 2, 1951; Albert Samuel and Lois (Rodrick) G.; m. Marcey Dale Miller, Nov. 18, 1978; children: Eric Matthew, Brian David. BS with high honors, U. Ill., 1973, JD, 1976. Bar: Ill. 1976, U.S. Dist. Ct. (no. dist.) Ill. 1976, Fla. 1979, U.S. Dist. Ct. (so. dist.) Fla. 1979, U.S. Ct. Appeals (5th and 7th cirs.) 1979, U.S. Tax Ct. 1979, U.S. Ct. Appeals (11th cir.) 1981, U.S. Supreme Ct. 1982, U.S. Dist. Ct. (mid. dist.) Fla. 1987; CPA, Ill., Fla. Tax staff Ernst & Ernst, Chgo., 1976-77; asst. state atty. Cook County, Ill., 1977-78, Dade County, Miami, Fla., 1978-82; spl. atty. Miami Strike Force U.S. Dept. Justice, Fla., 1982-87; pvt. practice Miami, 1987-92; asst. U.S. atty. U.S. Dist. Ct. (mid. dist.) Fla., 1992—; lectr. Roosevelt U., Chgo., 1976-77; vice chmn. fed. practice com. on criminal sect. Fla. Bar, 1986-88, profl. ethics com., 1992—; instr. Rollins Coll. paralegal program, 1992-97; adj. prof. criminal justice program U. Ctrl. Fla., 1994—; adj. prof. law U. Orlando, 1998-99. Co-chmn. Greater Oviedo Cmty. Devel. Program, 1992-93; adviser Jr. Achievement, Chgo., 1976-78,

Miami, 1982-84; coach, judge Nat. Trial Competition, U. Miami Law Sch., 1983-86, 88, 90; mentor Seminole County Sch., 1994—; coach mock trial program legal project Dade County Pub. Schs., 1985-89, 91-92, ptnr. program, 1989-92. Mem. ABA (govt. litigation counsel com., complex crimes com. litigation sect.), FBA, AICPA, ATLA, Fla. Bar, Ill. Bar Assn., Ill. Soc. CPAs, Fla. Inst. CPAs (com. on rels. with Fla. Bar 1985-86, bd. dirs. South Dade chpt. 1987-92), Orange County Bar Assn. (professionalism com., bankruptcy com.), Seminole County Bar Assn., Am. Assn. Atty. CPAs, Am. Inns of Ct. (master), U. Ill. Alumni Club (v.p.), Delta Sigma Pi. Jewish. Office: 80 N Hughey Ave Ste 201 Orlando FL 32801-2224

**GOLD, KENNETH CRAIG,** lawyer; b. N.Y.C., Jan. 30, 1961; m. Linda Stein. BS, Rutgers U., 1983; JD, U. Pa., 1987. Bar: Pa. 1987, N.J. 1988, Mich. 1990. Assoc. Wolf, Block, Schorr & Solis, Phila., 1987-89, Manko, Gold & Katcher, Bala Cynwyd, Pa., 1989-90; ptnr. Honigman, Miller, Schwartz & Cohn, Detroit, 1990—. Co-author: Michigan Environmental Law Handbook, 1994. Bd. dirs. Am. Jewish Com., Detroit, 1990—. Mem. Mich. Assn. Environ. Profls. Environmental, Administrative and regulatory. Office: Honigman Miller Schwartz & Cohn 2290 1st Nat Bldg Detroit MI 48226

**GOLD, MITCHELL M.,** retired lawyer; b. L.A., Nov. 22, 1931; s. J. George and Jennie (Rothblatt) G.; m. Geraldine Adele Turk, Aug. 30, 1953; children: Barry P., Danna B. BA, UCLA, 1953, LLB, 1958. Bar: Calif. 1959, U.S. Dist. Ct. (cen. dist.) Calif. 1959, U.S. Dist. Ct. (so. dist.) 1982. Assoc. Gold, Needleman & Fain, L.A., 1959-60; partner Gold, Sturman & Gold, L.A., 1960-70, Gold & Gold, L.A., 1971-82; pvt. practice L.A., 1982—, retired. With U.S. Army, 1954-56. Mem. ABA, Beverly Hills Bar Assn. Avocations: stamp collecting, travel. Consumer commercial.

**GOLD, PETER FREDERICK,** lawyer; b. N.Y.C., Nov. 10, 1945; s. John and Dolores (Soyer) G.; m. Dee Crafferty, June 6, 1982; children: Joshua, Katharine. BA, Cornell U., 1967; MSc, London Sch. Econs., 1968; JD, NYU, 1971. Bar: D.C. 1988, N.Y. 1972, U.S. Dist. Ct. (so. dist.) N.Y. 1972, U.S. Dist. Ct. (ea. dist.) N.Y. 1972. Assoc. atty. Paul, Weiss, Rifkind, Wharton & Garrison, N.Y.C., 1971-75; legis. dir. Senator Gary Hart, Washington, 1975-81; ptnr. Wellford, Wegman, Krulwich, Gold & Hoff, Washington, 1981-84, Winthrop, Stimson, Putnam & Roberts, Washington, 1984-94; pres. The Gold Group, Chartered, Washington, 1994—, C.G. Sloan & Co., Inc., 1995-97. Editor in chief Review of Law and Social Change, 1970. Nat. policy dir. Hart for Pres. Campaign, Washington, 1984; chmn., founder First Book, Washington, 1992—; dir. Share Our Strength, Washington, 1990—; mem. Clinton-Gore Transition Team, Washington, 1992. Recipient Disting. Visitor Program European Econ. Community, Brussels, Belgium, 1982. Mem. D.C. Bar Assn., Fed. Bar Assn., N.Y.C. Bar Assn., Kenwood Golf & Country Club, Four Streams Golf Club. Democrat. Jewish. Avocation: tennis, golf. Legislative, Private international, Antitrust. Home: 13640 Glenhurst Rd North Potomac MD 20878-3921 Office: The Gold Group Chartered 1319 F St NW Ste 500 Washington DC 20004-1106

**GOLD, RICHARD L.,** lawyer; b. N.Y.C., Feb. 23, 1950; s. Murray and Ruth Lillian (Nesselson) G.; m. Mary Laroe, Mar. 15, 1975; 1 child, Scott. BA, SUNY, Binghamton, 1972; student, Columbia U., 1972-73; JD, NYU, 1976. Bar: N.Y. 1976. From assoc. to ptnr. Bandler & Kass, N.Y.C., 1976-85; ptnr. Sylvor, Schneer, Gold & Morelli, N.Y.C., 1985—, Morelli & Gold, LLP, N.Y.C., 1996—. Contbr: You and the Law, 1984. Coach baseball Stamford (Conn.) Am. Little League, 1994-97, Stamford Babe Ruth, 1998. Mem. ABA, N.Y. State Bar Assn., Bar Assn. City of N.Y., Phi Beta Kappa. Avocation: sports. Federal civil litigation, General civil litigation, Family and matrimonial. Office: 605 3d Ave New York NY 10158

**GOLD, STEVEN BRUCE,** lawyer; b. Longbeach, Calif., Dec. 12, 1962; s. Larry and Ruth (Geller) G.; m. Anne Denise Markus, Dec. 23, 1984; children: Shannon Ilea, Erica Beth. BA in Environ. Studies with high honors, U. Calif., Santa Barbara, 1985; JD, U. Calif., Davis, 1988; cert. in hazardous materials mgmt, U. Calif., San Diego, 1992, OSHA HAZWOPER cert., 1999. Bar: Calif. 1988, U.S. Dist. Ct. (so. dist.) 1988. Dep. city atty. San Diego City Atty's. Office, 1989—, spl. dep. dist. atty., 1990-95, 97—; instr. Office Spl. Investigations USAF, 1992-96, Univ. San Diego, 1992-95, Calif. Dist. Atty's. Assn., 1990-99. Co-author: The Complete Guide to Hazardous Material Enforcement and Liability, 1987. Bd. dirs. Kids on the Block, San Diego, 1996—, pres. 1999; reviewer Boy Scouts Am., 1994—. Recipient Gov.'s Restitution award, 1998. Mem. State Bar Calif. (environ. law sect.), Air and Waste Mgmt. Assn. (chair pub. rels. 1997-98), Eagle Scout Alumni Assn. Office: San Diego City Atty Office Consumer Environ Prot Unit 1200 3rd Ave Ste 700 San Diego CA 92101-4103

**GOLD, STEVEN MICHAEL,** lawyer; b. Bklyn., Sept. 19, 1953; s. Joseph and Gladys (Guss) G.; m. Susan Schwartz, Jan. 9, 1977; children: Rachel, David, Hannah. BA, Hobart Coll., 1975; JD, Cornell U., 1978. Bar: Conn. 1979, N.Y. 1979, U.S. Dist. Ct. Conn. 1979, U.S. Dist. Ct. (no. dist.) N.Y. 1979. Confidential law asst. 3d dept. appellate div. N.Y. Supreme Ct., Albany, 1978-79; assoc. Schatz & Schatz, Ribicoff & Kotkin, Hartford & Stamford, Conn., 1979-86; ptnr. Schatz & Schatz, Ribicoff & Kotkin, Stamford, 1987-96, Shipman & Goodwin, LLP, Stamford, 1996—. Treas. Cmty. Coun. Westport/Weston, Conn., 1985, 1st v.p., 1987, bd. dirs., 1985-87; bd. dirs., counsel Urban League Greater Bridgeport, 1987-92; bd. dirs., v.p. Stamford Symphony Soc., 1990-95, counsel, 1994-95; bd. dirs. Nursing & Home Care, 1996-97. Mem. ABA, N.Y. State Bar Assn., Conn. Bar Assn., Stamford/Norwalk Regional Bar Assn., Assn. Comml. Fin. Attys., Nat. Assn. Transp. Practitioners (treas. Conn. chpt. 1983-85), Entrepreneurship Inst. (adv. bd. 1989-91), Phi Delta Phi, Pi Gamma Mu. Democrat. Jewish. Avocation: squash. General corporate, Contracts commercial, Computer. Office: Shipman & Goodwin LLP One Landmark Sq Stamford CT 06901

**GOLDBERG, AUBREY,** lawyer; b. Suffolk, Va., Dec. 2, 1940; s. Meyer R. and Miriam (Pearl) G.; m. Joanne Holland, Aug. 25, 1963; children: Devon Jon, Jennifer Jonine. BA, Coll. William & Mary, 1963, JD, 1966. Bar: Va. 1966, Nev. 1968, U.S. Dist. Ct. Nev. 1968, U.S. Ct. Appeals (9th cir.) 1985. Ptnr. Greenman, Goldberg, Raby & Martinez, Las Vegas, 1970—; settlement judge Nev. Supreme Ct., 1997—. Served to capt. USAF, 1966-70 Vietnam; lt. col. USAFR. Mem. ABA, Nev. Bar Assn. (bd. govs. 1986-93, pres. 1992-93), Clark County Bar Assn. (pres. 1978, 1st annual pres. award 1985), Las Vegas C. of C., Assn. Trial Lawyers Am., Nev. Trial Lawyers Assn. Democrat. Jewish. Avocations: tennis, weight lifting, jogging. General practice, Personal injury, Workers' compensation. Office: Greenman Goldberg Raby & Martinez 601 S 9th St Las Vegas NV 89101-7012

**GOLDBERG, DAVID,** lawyer, law educator; b. N.Y.C., Dec. 31, 1934; s. Philip and Esther (Dobbs) G.; m. Emily Ruth Messing, Aug. 17, 1958; children: Sara, Ari. BA, CUNY, 1956; LLB, Yale U., 1959. Bar: N.Y. 1960. Law clerk to judge U.S. Dist. Ct., N.Y.C., 1960-62; assoc. Kaye, Scholer, Fierman, Hays and Handler, N.Y.C., 1962-68, ptnr., 1969-83; ptnr. Cowan, Liebowitz and Latman, N.Y.C., 1983—; adj. prof. law NYU, 1976-96. Contbr. articles on copyright and trademark law to N.Y. Law Jour., other profl. jours. Pres. Hillcrest Jewish Ctr., Jamaica Estates, N.Y., 1987-89. Served as sgt. U.S. Army, 1959-60. Mem. ABA (fin. officer sect. intellectual property law 1986-89, spkr. on copyright devels. 1984, 85, 87, 90), Copright Soc. USA (pres. 1978-80, hon. trustee 1980—, spkr. on copyright devels. annually 1984—), U.S. Trademark Assn. (spkr. on trademarks and copyright overlap 1987). Democrat. Avocation: fishing. Entertainment, Trademark and copyright. Office: Cowan Liebowitz and Latman 1133 Avenue Of The Americas New York NY 10036-6710

**GOLDBERG, GLENN D.,** lawyer; b. Washington, Apr. 27, 1942; s. Milton J. and Maude Dresden Goldberg; m. Florence F. Goldberg, Dec. 4, 1989. BA, Rutgers U., 1964; JD, Rutgers U., Camden, 1967. Bar: N.J. 1967, N.Y. 1982, U.S. Supreme Ct. 1982. Trial atty. Morgan, Melhuish, Newark, 1968-73; chief trial atty. Essex County Prosecutors Office, Newark, 1973—; dir. spl. prosecutions Essex County Prosecutors Office, Newark. Bd. dirs. Congregation Ohr Torah, West Orange, N.J., 1997—. Mem. ABA, N.J. Bar Assn., Essex County Bar Assn. Jewish. Avocations: astronomy, science fiction, public speaking, hypnosis. Home: 40 Howell Dr Verona NJ 07044-1032 Office: Essex County Prosecutors Office Essex County Cts Bldg Newark NJ 07102

**GOLDBERG, GREGORY EBAN,** lawyer; b. Denver, Oct. 9, 1967; s. Charles and Honey Goldberg. BA, Dartmouth Coll., 1990; JD, Columbia Law Sch., 1995. Bar: Colo. 1995, U.S. Dist. Ct. Colo. 1995, U.S. Ct. Appeals (10th cir.) 1995. Law clk. to Judge Paul J. Kelly Jr. U.S. Ct. Appeals (10th cir.), Santa Fe, N.Mex., 1995-96; assoc. Arnold & Porter, Denver, 1996-99; asst. U.S. atty. Maj. Crimes divsn., Denver, 1999—. Ptnr. in Leadership Anti-Defamation League, Denver, 1998—. Mem. ABA, Colo. Bar Assn., Dartmouth Alumni Assn. (bd. dirs.), Graland Alumni Assn. (bd. dirs. 1995—). Avocations: snowshoeing, mountain biking, backpacking, home renovations. Environmental, Administrative and regulatory, General corporate. Office: Office of the US Atty 1961 Stout St Ste 1300 Denver CO 80294

**GOLDBERG, JAMES R.,** lawyer; b. East Cleveland, Ohio, Aug. 12, 1938; s. William and Celia (Schwartz) G.; m. Marilyn A. Goldberg; children: Bonnie Kraus, Laura Hudak. BS, Ohio State U., 1960; JD, Case Western Res. U., 1964. Bar: Ohio 1964, U.S. Dist. Ct. (no. dist.) Ohio, U.S. Claims Ct. V.p. Weisman, Goldberg & Weisman Co., Clev., 1964—. With U.S. Army, 1961. General civil litigation, Personal injury, Product liability. Office: Weisman Goldberg & Weisman Co 1600 Midland Bldg Cleveland OH 44115

**GOLDBERG, JAY,** lawyer; b. N.Y.C., Jan. 2, 1933; s. Joseph and Lillian (Adler) G.; m. Rema, Dec. 27, 1959; children: Justin, Julie. BA, Bklyn. Coll., 1954; JD, Harvard U., 1957. Bar: N.Y. 1957, U.S. Ct. Appeals (2d, 4th and 9th cirs.) 1971, U.S. Supreme Ct. 1961. Asst. dist. atty. N.Y. County Dist. Atty. Office, N.Y.C., 1957-61; spl. asst. to atty. gen. Washington, 1961-63; spl. asst. to U.S. Atty. no. dist. Hammond, Ind., 1961-67; lawyer, sole practice N.Y.C., 1963—; lectr. trial practice Harvard Law Sch., 1976-88; com. on grievances U.S. Dist. Ct. (so. dist.) N.Y., 1989—. Editorial mgr. White Collar Crime Law Reporter, 1989—; contbr. articles to profl. jours. Recipient Merit award for Advocacy of Individual Rights for Persons Advised, N.Y. Criminal Bar Assn., 1989. Mem. Friars Club (gov. 1988-92). Federal civil litigation, Criminal, Family and matrimonial. Home: 200 E 65th St New York NY 10021-6603 Office: 250 Park Ave New York NY 10177-0001

**GOLDBERG, JOEL HENRY,** lawyer; b. Lewiston, Maine, Feb. 7, 1945; s. George and Evelyn Anne (Mackin) G.; m. Allyne Ross; 1 child, Ross Lewis. BA, Brandeis U., 1967; JD, Columbia U., 1970. Bar: N.Y. 1971, D.C. 1980. Atty. CAB, Washington, 1970-73; atty. SEC, Washington, 1973-77, assoc. dir. div. investment mgmt., 1979-81; dir. div. investment mgmt. SEC, 1981-83; ptnr. Swidler Berlin Shereff Friedman, LLP, N.Y.C., 1985—. Mem. ABA (com. on securities regulation). Democrat. Jewish. Securities.

**GOLDBERG, JOHN A.,** lawyer; b. Cin., July 15, 1941; s. Abe A. and June E. Goldberg; m. Barbara Schilling, May 15, 1976; children: Sarah, Mark. BA, Loyola U., 1964; MEd, Xavier U., 1966; JD, No. Ky. U., 1972. Atty. Lindhorst & Dreidame, Cin., 1972—. Mem. Ohio State Bar Assn., Cin. Bar Assn. Personal injury. Office: Lindhorst & Dreidame Co LPA 312 Walnut St Ste 2300 Cincinnati OH 45202-4091

**GOLDBERG, JOLANDE ELISABETH,** law librarian, lawyer; b. Pforzheim, Germany, Aug. 11, 1931; came to U.S., 1967; d. Eugen and Luise Rosa (Thorwarth) Haas; m. Lawrence Spencer Goldberg, Sept. 7, 1969; children: Daniel Scott, Elisa Miriam, Clarissa Anna. Referendar, U. Heidelberg, 1957, PhD, 1963; postdoctoral, U. London, 1976-77. Bar: Germany 1961. Mem. rsch. staff Acad. Scis. and Humanities, Heidelberg, 1961-67; rsch. assoc. U. Heidelberg, 1964-67; cataloger, law specialist Libr. of Congress, Washington, 1967-72, asst. law classification specialist, 1972-80, law classification specialist, 1980—, sr. cataloging policy specialist, 1997; sculptor, potter Torpedo Factory Art Ctr., Alexandria, Va., 1974—; lectr. Smithsonian Inst., Washington, 1988—. Author: Probschlag & Meistersignatur, 1963; contbr. articles to profl. jours. Exec. bd. dirs. Friends Torpedo Factory Art Ctr., Alexandria, 1987—. Volkswagenwerk Found. rsch. fellow, Fed. Republic of Germany, 1964-65, German Rsch. Assn. fellow, 1966, German Libr. Inst. grantee, 1981, Robbins Collection sr. rsch. fellow U. Calif. Berkeley, 1995. Mem. ALA (Marta Lange award for disting. librarianship in law and polit. sci. 1999, Assn. Coll. and Rsch. Librs. divsn. Marta Lange Congl. Quarterly award 1999), Internat. Waterlily Soc., Internat. Soc. for Knowledge Orgn., Am. Assn. Law Librs. (Tech. Svcs. Spl. Interest sect. exec. bd. dirs. 1987-91, citation for exceptional contbn. 1992, Reneé Chapman Meml. award 1999), Torpedo Factory Artist Assn., The Art League, Friends of Nat. Arboretum, Corcoran Gallery of Art. Democrat. Jewish. Office: Libr Of Congress Washington DC 20540-0001

**GOLDBERG, JOSEPH,** lawyer; b. Washington, Aug. 21, 1950; s. Morris and Rose (Levin) G.; m. Christine Marie Riggott, Mar. 29, 1980; children: Benjamin R., Louis E. BS, Ohio U., 1972; JD, U. Pa., 1975. Bar: Pa. 1975, N.J. 1981, D.C. 1980, U.S. Ct. Appeals (3d cir.) 1980, U.S. Dist.Ct. (mid. dist.) Pa. 1987, U.S. Supreme Ct. 1989. Assoc. Margolis, Edelstein & Scherlis, Phila., 1975-81; ptnr. Margolis Edelstein, Phila., 1982—. Author: State and Local Government Immunity to Tort Claims, 1992, 2d edit., 1997. Mem. ABA, Pa. Def. Rsch. Inst., Pa. Jud. Rules Com., Phila. Assn. Def. Counsel, Phila. Bar Assn. Avocation: scuba diving. Civil rights, Personal injury, General civil litigation. Office: Margolis Edelstein The Curtis Ctr 4th Fl Independence Sq West Philadelphia PA 19106

**GOLDBERG, LEONARD MARVIN,** lawyer; b. Jersey City, Mar. 21, 1937; s. Jack Geddy and Ida Reva (Steinberg) G.; m. Susan Lee Horstein, Aug. 7, 1960; children: Mark Jay, Philip Seth. A.B. magna cum laude, Tufts U., 1957; J.D. magna cum laude, Harvard U., 1960. Bar: N.J. 1960, U.S. Tax Ct. 1964, N.Y. 1966. Trial atty. tax div. Dept. Justice, Washington, 1960-64; assoc. Roberts & Holland, N.Y.C., 1964-70; ptnr. Clapp & Eisenberg, Newark, N.J., 1970-79; sr. ptnr. Goldberg, Mufson & Spar (formerly Goldberg & Stark), West Orange, N.J., 1979—; lectr. Practicing Law Inst., ABA Taxation Soc., ABA Ctr. for Continuing Edn., N.J. Inst. Continuing Legal Edn., Tenn. Federal Tax Inst., Fairleigh Dickinson U. Tax Inst., Seton Hall U. Tax Inst., Estate Planning Couns.; N.J. del. to lawyers' liaison com. Mid-Atlantic region IRS, 1973-76. Chmn. West Orange pub. edn. com., 1976-77, mem. Am. Jewish Com.; co-chmn. lawyers div., trustee Met. N.J. State of Israel Bonds, 1989-92; v.p., trustee Congl. Oheb Shalom, So. Orange, N.J., 1990-92; pres. Oheb Shalom Hebrew Free Loan Soc., 1990-96. Fellow Am. Coll. Trust and Estate Counsel; mem. (exec. counc., 1999—) ABA, N.J. Bar Assn. (chmn. taxation sect. 1973-75, chmn. small law firms comm. taxation sect.), N.Y. State Bar Assn., Essex County Bar Assn. (chmn. tax com. 1988-89), Estate Planning Coun. No. N.J., Internat. Assn. Jewish Lawyers and Jurists. Contbr. articles to profl. jours. Taxation, general, General corporate, Probate. Home: 6 Huntington Rd Livingston NJ 07039-5112 Office: 200 Executive Dr West Orange NJ 07052-3388

**GOLDBERG, MARK JOEL,** lawyer; b. Pitts., June 2, 1941; s. Charles J. and Eleanore (Letwin) G.; m. Wendy Witt, Dec. 23, 1988; children: Michael, Wendy, Josh, Jamie. BA, Washington and Jefferson Coll., 1963; JD, Case Western Res. U., 1966. Bar: Pa. 1966, Ohio 1966, U.S. Tax Ct. 1969, U.S. Supreme Ct. 1972. Assoc. Jerome Silver, Cleve., 1966-67; pvt. practice, Pitts., 1967-69; ptnr. Goldberg & Wedner, Pitts., 1969-80; ptnr., shareholder Gillotti Goldberg & Capristo, Pitts., 1981-91, Goldberg Gentile & Voelker, Pitts., 1991-92, Goldberg, Gruener, Gentile, Horoho & Avalli, P.C., Pitts., 1992—; mem. drafting com. Pa. Divorce Code, 1978-80, 88; frequent lectr. Pa. Bar Inst., Pa. Trial Lawyers Assn., Am. Acad. Matrimonial Lawyers. Contbr. articles to profl. jours. Committeeman Dem. Party, Pitts., 1970's; pres. bd. dirs. Parent and Child Guidance Ctr., Pitts., 1984-86. Fellow Am. Acad. Matrimonial Lawyers (pres. Pa. chpt. 1988-90, nat. bd. govs. 1991-95); mem. Am. Coll. Family Trial Lawyers (diplomate, officer), Allegheny County Bar Assn. (coun. mem. family law sect. 1972—, chmn. 1982-84), Pa. Bar Assn. (family law sect. chmn. 1986-88), Westmoreland Country Club, Rivers Club. Jewish. Avocations: golf, travel. Family and matrimonial. Home: 14 Carmel Ct Pittsburgh PA 15221-3618 Office: Goldberg Gruener Et Al 1320 Grant Bldg Pittsburgh PA 15219-2200

**GOLDBERG, MARVIN ALLEN,** lawyer, business consultant; b. Phila., Jan. 9, 1943; s. Daniel and Elizabeth (Katz) G.; m. Kathryn Elizabeth Balotsky, Apr. 27, 1974; children: Robert Andrew, MaryBeth Anne. BS, Temple U., 1964, JD, 1967. Bar: Pa. 1968, U.S. Dist. Ct. (ea. dist.) Pa. 1980, U.S. Supreme Ct. 1976. Estate tax atty. IRS, Phila., 1967-68; staff atty. Legal Aid Soc. Northampton County, Easton, Pa., 1969-70, Northampton County Pub. Defender, Easton, Pa., 1969-70; pvt. practice law Phila., 1970-76; tchr. Inst. for Paralegal Tng., Phila., 1973; staff atty. Legal Aid Soc. Phila., 1974-76; CEO Goldberg & Assocs., P.C., Phila., 1976—; cons. Butcher Trade Exchange, Ft. Washington, Pa., 1982-92; dir. North Am. Resources, Phila.; pres. MAGCO, Inc., Mt. Laurel, N.J., 1989-92. Mem. Chestnut St. Assn., Phila; dir. Sr. Citizen Judicare Project, Phila., 1977. With USAF, 1967-73. Mem. ABA, Phila. Bar Assn., Phila. Trial Lawyers Assn., Assn. Trial Lawyers Am., Pa. Trial Lawyers Assn., Attys. Across Am. (founding mem.), Jewish War Vets, Beta Gamma Sigma, Phi Alpha Delta. Avocations: running, sailing, chess, Algebra, 19th century physics. General corporate, Insurance, Personal injury. Office: Goldberg & Assocs PC 1334 Walnut St Fl 5 Philadelphia PA 19107-5311

**GOLDBERG, MAUREEN MCKENNA,** state supreme court justice; b. Pawtucket, R.I., Feb. 11, 1951; m. Robert D. Goldberg. Grad., St. Mary's Acad., 1969; AB cum laude, Providence Coll., 1973; JD cum laude, Suffolk U., 1978. Bar: R.I. 1978, Mass. 1978, U.S. Ct. of Appeals (1st cir.) 1979. Asst. atty. gen. Adminstr. of the Criminal Divsn., 1978-84; town solicitor South Kingstown, 1985-87; town solicitor Town of Westerly, 1987-90, acting town mgr., 1990; spl. legal counsel R.I. State Police; apptd. assoc. justice Superior Ct., 1990-96; assoc. justice R.I. Supreme Ct., 1997—. Mem. ABA, R.I. Bar Assn., R.I. Trial Judges Assn., Pawtucket Bar Assn. Office: Rhode Island Supreme Ct 250 Benefit St Providence RI 02903-2719*

**GOLDBERG, MICHAEL EDWARD,** lawyer; b. Paterson, N.J., May 30, 1955; s. Boris Sheldon and Rita G.; m. Robin L. Stapley, Dec. 21, 1980; children: Aaron, Jordan, Rachel. BS in Econs., Georgetown U., 1977; JD, George Washington Nat. Law Ctr, 1981. Corp. assoc. Strooch, Strooch & Lavar, N.Y.C., 1981-83; corp. assoc. Parker, Chapin, Flattau & Klimpl, N.Y.C., 1983-86; 1st v.p. Lehman Bros., N.Y.C., 1986-94; dep. gen. counsel Nomura Securities Internat., Inc., N.Y.C., 1994—; also bd. dirs. Nomura Securities Internat., Inc. Mem. Bond Market Assn. (various coms.), Securities Industry Assn. (legal and compliance com.). General corporate, Securities. Office: Nomura Securities Internat Inc 18th Fl 2 World Fin Ctr Bldg B New York NY 10281-1008

**GOLDBERG, NEIL A.,** lawyer; b. N.Y.C., Dec. 24, 1947; s. Bernard G.; children: Jane Hana, Robert Saul. BA cum laude, SUNY, Stony Brook, 1969; JD cum laude, SUNY, Buffalo, 1973. Bar: N.Y. 1974, U.S. Dist. Ct. (we. dist.) N.Y. 1974. Sr. ptnr. Saperston & Day P.C., Buffalo, 1974—, also bd. dirs. Editor Products Liaility in New York, 1997; co-editor in chief Preparing for and Trying the Civil Lawsuit. Mem. ABA, Internat. Assn. Def. Counsel, Def. Rsch. Inst. (com. mem., 1st v.p.), Am. Arbitration Assn. (bd. dirs. 1985—, product liability adv. coun.), N.Y. State Bar Assn. (chmn. product liability com. torts, ins. and compensation law sect. 1986—), Erie County Bar Assn. State civil litigation, Insurance, Personal injury. Office: Saperston & Day PC Three Fountain Plz 1100 M & T Ctr Buffalo NY 14203-1486

**GOLDBERG, RICHARD ROBERT,** lawyer; b. New York, Apr. 27, 1941; s. Joseph and Anne (Blumfield) G.; m. Rita Ann Zieve, June 30, 1963; 1 child, Andrew Louis. BA, Pa. State U., 1961; LLB, U. Md., 1964. Bar: Md. 1964, U.S. Ct. Appeals (4th cir.) 1970, U.S. Supreme Ct. 1974, U.S. Ct. Appeals (5th cir.) 1978, U.S. Ct. Appeals (D.C. cir.) 1992, Pa. 1994, N.J. 1994. Asst. city solicitor to Mayor and City Coun. City of Balt., 1965-70; atty. The Rouse Co., Columbia, Md., 1970-78, v.p., assoc. gen. counsel, 1978-94; ptnr. Ballard, Spahr, Andrews & Ingersoll, Phila., 1994—. Author: Real Estate Development of Downtown Projects, 1981; author and editor: (handbooks) Commercial Real Estate Leasing, Commercial Real Estate Financing; contbr. numerous articles to profl. publs. Chmn. Jewish Coun. of Howard County, Md., 1975-77, chmn. ann. campaign, 1978, 80, 87; pres. Temple Isaiah, Columbia, 1978-79; bd. trustees Jewish Fedn. Howard County, 1993-94. Mem. ABA (sec. real property, probate and trust law, chmn. prohibited transactions com. 1983-85, chmn. mgmt. property com. 1985-87, chmn. nat. insts. and satellite programs 1987-89, advisor UCC drafting com. article 1, article 9), Md. State Bar Assn., Pa. Bar Assn., Phila. Bar Assn., Am. Law Inst. (advisor restatement of the law of mortgages), Anglo-Am. Real Property Inst. (sec. 1990-92, chair-elect 1994, chair 1995), Am. Coll. Real Estate Lawyers (v.p. 1989-90, pres.-elect 1990-91, pres. 1991-92), Urban Land Inst., Am. Coll. of Mortgage Attys. Real property. Home: 325 S 2nd St Philadelphia PA 19106-4317 Office: Ballard Spahr Andrews & Ingersoll 1735 Market St Ste 5100 Philadelphia PA 19103-7599

**GOLDBERG, ROBERT M.,** lawyer; b. Chgo., Jan. 23, 1941; s. Arthur Joseph and Dorothy (Kurgans) G.; m. Barbara Sproston, Feb. 13, 1966; children: Esther Fiona, Angus Ephraim, Duncan Abraham. BA with honors, Amherst Coll., 1963; postgrad. London Sch. Econs., 1964; JD, Harvard U., 1967. Bar: Alaska 1969, Ill. 1969, U.S. Ct. Appeals (9th cir.) 1973, U.S. Ct. Appeals D.C. Cir. 1978, U.S. Sup. Ct. 1978, D.C. 1979. Law clk. U.S. Ct. Appeals for D.C., 1967-68; assoc. Kay, Miller & Libby, Anchorage, 1969-70; assoc. prof. law sea grant program U. Alaska, 1970-72, adj. prof., 1980—; ptnr. Goldberg & Elliott, Anchorage, 1976-78, Goldberg, Breckberg, & Gottstein, Anchorage, 1978-80, Goldberg & Gottstein, Anchorage, 1980-82, Robert M. Goldberg & Assocs., Anchorage, 1982—; adj. prof. law U. Denver, 1973-75; adj. prof. govt. and econs. Alaska Pacific U., Anchorage, 1970-73. Chmn. State of Alaska Labor Rels. Bd., 1990-91; trustee, Alaska Pacific U., 1975-90; pres. Anchorage Community Theater, 1987-90; del. Democratic Nat. Conv., 1974, 76; chmn. Alaska Assn. for Hist. Preservation, 1981-85. Recipient Best Non-Fiction Book award Alaska Press Club, 1970. Mem. ABA, Ill. State Bar Assn., D.C. Bar Assn., Alaska Bar Assn., Fed. Bar Assn., Am. Soc. Internat. Law. Jewish. Editor: Alaska Survey & Report, Vols. I and II, 1970-72. Civil rights, Labor, General practice. Office: 810 N St Anchorage AK 99501-3279 also: 11320 Random Hills Rd Ste 600 Fairfax VA 22030-6001

**GOLDBERG, SCOT DALE,** lawyer; b. Fort Myers, Fla., Jan. 25, 1966; s. Morton A. and Gennie M. Goldberg; m. Suzanne McKenna, Sept. 19, 1990; children: Logan Anthony, Lexi Rae. BA, U. South Fla., 1990; JD, Thomas M. Cooley, 1994. Prosecutor State Atty.'s Office, Fort Myers, 1994-96; civil/criminal litigation Goldstein, Buckley Cechman, Fort Myers, 1996—. Charter rev. com. Charter Rev. Com., Cape Coral, Fla., 1997; lobbiest at large Young Reps., 1987-89. Mem. Fla. Acad. of Trial Lawyers, Assn. of Trial Lawyers of Am., Fla. Bar Assn., U.S. Middle Dist. Fed. Ct. Avocations: fishing charter captain, sport fishing, spending time with children. Personal injury, Criminal, Civil rights.

**GOLDBERG, SHERMAN I.,** banking company executive, lawyer; b. 1942. BA, Miami U., 1964; JD, U. Cin., 1968. Bar: Ill. 1969. With First Chgo. Corp., 1968—, gen. counsel, sec., 1988—, also v.p., 1990—, exec. v.p., gen. counsel; gen. counsel, sec. Bank One, Chgo., 1998—. Office: Bank One 1 First Natl Plz Chicago IL 60603-2003*

**GOLDBERG, STANLEY JOSHUA,** federal judge; b. Balt., Feb. 16, 1939; s. Isidore and Lillian Frances (Kravatz) G.; m. Susan Jane Coplin, July 1, 1962; Rachel Hilary, David Mark. BS, U. Md., 1960, LLB, 1964; postgrad., NYU, 1966-69. Bar: Md. 1964, U.S. Dist. Ct. Md. 1964, N.J. 1967, U.S. Dist. Ct. N.J. 1967, U.S. Tax Ct. 1968. Tax trial atty. office of chief counsel IRS, N.Y.C., 1965-69, 1971-76, spl. trial atty., 1976-84, asst. dist. counsel, 1984-85; assoc. Buckmaster, White, Mindel & Clarke, Balt., 1970; spl. trial judge U.S. Tax Ct., Washington, 1985—. Mem. Md. Bar Assn., D.C. Bar Assn. (hon.). Office: US Tax Ct 400 2nd St NW Washington DC 20217-0002

**GOLDBERG, SUZANNE BETH,** lawyer; b. N.Y.C., Jan. 4, 1964; d. Richard L. and Judith S. Goldberg; life ptnr. Paula L. Ettelbrick; 1 child, Adam B.G. Ettelbrick. AB, Brown U., 1985; JD, Harvard U., 1990. Bar: Mass. 1990, N.Y. 1991. Jud. clk. N.J. Supreme Ct., Jersey City, 1990-91; staff atty. Lambda Legal Def. and Edn. Fund, N.Y.C., 1991—. Co-author: Strangers to the Law: Gay People on Trial, 1998; contbr. articles to profl. jours. Co-founder, bd. dirs. Lesbian and Gay Immigration Rights Task Force, N.Y.C., 1993—. Fellow Skadden Found., 1991; Fulbright fellow, 1985. Mem. Assn. of Bar of City of N.Y. (civil rights com. 1995-98), Phi Beta Kappa. Civil rights. Office: Lambda Legal Def and Edn Fund 120 Wall St Ste 1500 New York NY 10005-3904

**GOLDBERGER, FRANKLIN HENRY,** lawyer; b. Schenectady, N.Y., Oct. 22, 1943; s. Jesse J. and Sarah (Atlas) G.; children: Steven E., Amy L. BA, U. Pitts., 1965; JD, Suffolk U., 1969. Bar: D.C. 1970, N.Y. 1972. Counsel Nat. Labor Rels. Bd., Washington, 1969-73; ptnr. Novak and Goldberger, Schenectady, 1973-78; pvt. practice Schenectady, 1978-82; of counsel Ogletree, Deakins, Nash, Smoak and Stewart, Schenectady, Washington, 1982-89; ptnr., shareholder Ogletree, Deakins, Nash, Smoak and Stewart, Albany, N.Y., 1989—; cons. Saratoga (N.Y.) Performing Arts Ctr., 1996—; bd. dirs. Daus. Sarah Nursing Ctr., Albany. Mem. D.C. Bar Assn. Republican. Jewish. Avocations: acting, music. Labor. Home: 56 Union Ave Saratoga Springs NY 12866-4362

**GOLDBLATT, STEVEN HARRIS,** law educator; b. Bklyn., Apr. 30, 1947; s. J. Irving and Ethel (Epstein) G.; m. Irene P. Burns, June 12, 1981; children: Sarah P., Elizabeth G.B. BA, Franklin & Marshall Coll., 1967; JD, Georgetown U., 1970. Bar: Pa. 1970, D.C. 1981. With Phila. Dist. Atty.'s Office, 1970-81; dir. Appellate Litigation Program Georgetown U. Law Ctr., Washington, 1981-83, prof. law, dir. Appellate Litigation Progam, 1983—; chair rules adv. com. U.S. Ct. Appeals for Armed Forces. Co-author: Analysis and Commentary to the Pennsylvania Crime Code, 1973, Three Prosecutors Look at the Crimes Code, 1974, Ineffective Assistance of Counsel: Attempts to Establish Minimum Standards for Criminal Cases, 1983; reporter Criminal Justice in Crisis, 1988, Achieving Justice in a Diverse America, 1992, An Agenda for Justice: ABA Perspectives on Criminal and Civil Justice Issues, 1996. Mem. ABA (criminal justice sect. chmn. amicus curiae briefs com. 1981-99, crisis in criminal justice com. 1990-91). Office: Georgetown U Law Ctr 600 New Jersey Ave NW Washington DC 20001-2075

**GOLDEN, CHRISTOPHER ANTHONY,** lawyer; b. N.Y.C., Sept. 24, 1937; s. Christopher A. and Helen (Foley) G.; m. Maureen A. Fitzpatrick, May 30, 1964; children: Colleen, Laureen. BA, St. John's Coll., Jamaica, N.Y., 1955; LLB, St. John's Sch. Law, Jamaica, 1967; MBA, St. John's U., 1977. Bar: N.Y. 1967, U.S. Dist. Ct. (so. and ea. dists.) N.Y. 1969, U.S. Ct. Appeals (2d cir.) 1969, U.S. Supreme Ct. 1974, U.S. Ct. Appeals (D.C. cir.) 1982. Mem. firm Flood, Conway, Walsh, Stahl & Farrell, N.Y.C., 1964-77; asst. gen. counsel Dry Dock Savs. Bank, N.Y.C., 1977-82; ptnr. Golden, Wexler & Sarnese, P.C., Garden City, N.Y., 1982—; trustee Dry Dock Savs. Bank, 1982-83; bd. advisors First Am. Title Ins. Co., Chgo. Title Ins. Co. Served with U.S. Army, 1960-61. Mem. ABA, N.Y. State Bar Assn., Nassau County Bar Assn., Am. Coll. Mortgage Attys. (regent), Nat. Mortgage Inst. (trustee 1986—). Banking, Real property, Consumer commercial. Office: Golden Wexler & Sarnese PC 377 Oak St Ste 202 Garden City NY 11530-6547

**GOLDEN, DANIEL LEWIS,** lawyer; b. N.Y.C., May 7, 1913; s. Louis and Rose (Rosen) G.; m. Evelyn Shayevitz, July 9, 1941 (dec.); children: Roger M., Leslie Rosemary. BS, Lafayette Coll., 1934; JD, Rutgers U., 1938; LLD (hon.) Lafayette Coll., 1993. Bar: N.J. 1939, D.C. 1976, U.S. Supreme Ct. 1957. Practice, South River, 1940—; now of counsel Greenbaum, Rowe, Smith, Ravin, Davis & Himmell LLP. dir. Mt. Holly Water Co.; active survey legal systems USSR, East Europe for State Dept. Exchanges Programs, also for ABA, N.J. Bar Assn., 1961-75. Chmn. ethics Com., 1967; mem. N.J. Gov.'s Commn. on Individual Liberty and Personal Privacy, 1977-84; chmn. lawyers sect. March of Dimes, 1961-81; trustee Lafayette Coll., 1975-80. Lt. USAAF, 1942-45. Recipient Kidd hon. citation for law Lafayette Coll., 1970, Bell Disting. Svc. Alumni award Lafayette Coll., 1985, Rutgers Law award, 1971, Edison award Boy Scouts Am., Lawyer of the Year award N.J. Commission on Professionalism, 1998. Fellow Am. Bar Found. (state chmn. 1985-90, nat. sec., vice chmn. 1990-92, nat. chmn. 1992-93), Am. Acad. Matrimonial Lawyers; mem. ABA (ho. of dels. 1972—, chmn. adv. commn. on election law), N.J. Bar Assn. (pres. 1970-71, editorial bd. jour. 1969—), Middlesex County Bar Assn. (pres. 1960-61), Assn. Trial Lawyers Am., Trial Attys. N.J. (trustee 1969—, Lifetime Achievement award 1986), N.J. Bar Found. (Medal of Honor award 1991), Am. Judicature Soc., Pi Lambda Phi. Contbr. articles to profl. jours. Private international, Family and matrimonial, General civil litigation. Office: Greenbaum Rowe Smith Ravin Davis & Himmel LLP PO Box 5600 Metro Corp Campus One Woodbridge NJ 07095

**GOLDEN, E(DWARD) SCOTT,** lawyer; b. Miami, Fla., Sept. 25, 1955; s. Alvan Leonard and Fay Betty (Gray) G.; m. Jane Eileen DeKlavon, June 9, 1979; children: Daniel Bryan, Kimberly Michelle. Student, So. Fla. Christian Coll., 1975-76; BS, MIT, 1978; JD, Harvard U., 1981. Bar: Fla. 1981, U.S. Dist. Ct. (so. dist.) Fla. 1982, U.S. Tax Ct. 1982, U.S. Supreme Ct. 1991, U.S. Dist. Ct. (mid. dist.) Fla. 1993. Assoc. Roberts and Holland, Miami, 1981-82, Valdes-Fauli, Richardson, Cobb & Petrey, P.A., Miami, 1982-83; v.p. Buck and Golden, P.A., Ft. Lauderdale, Fla., 1983-88; sole practice Ft. Lauderdale, Fla., 1988—; judge negotiations competition Nova Southeastern U. Editor-in-chief Harvard Jour. of Law and Pub. Policy, 1980-81; contbr. articles to profl. jours. Mem. West Lauderdale Bapt. Ch., Broward County, Fla., 1982-98, chmn. deacons, 1984-86, 87-88, elder, 1994-98; mem. MIT Ednl. Coun., 1995—; del. Fla. Rep. Conv., 1987, 90; mem. Rep. Exec. Com., Broward County, 1984-94. Named one of Outstanding Young Men of Am., 1986; nominee Order of Silver Knight; Western Electric grantee, 1972-74. Mem. Christian Legal Soc., Zeta Beta Tau. Lodge: Optimists (treas. Dade County Carol City High Sch., 1971-72). Avocations: sports, politics, Bible study. General corporate, Real property, Estate planning. Home: 5410 Buchanan St Hollywood FL 33021-5708 Office: 644 SE 4th Ave Fort Lauderdale FL 33301-3102

**GOLDEN, ELLIOTT,** judge; b. Bklyn., June 28, 1926; s. Barnet David and Rose (Fistel) G.; m. Ana Valbuena, July 8, 1990; children: Jeffrey Stephen, Marjorie Ruth, Peter Michael (dec.); stepchildren: Robert, Elizabeth, William, John. Student, Maritime Acad., 1944-46, NYU, 1947-48; LLB, Bklyn. Law Sch., 1951. Bar: N.Y. 1952, U.S. Dist. Ct. (ea. dist.) N.Y. 1953, U.S. Tax Ct., U.S. Dist. Ct. (so. dist.) N.Y. 1953, U.S. Supreme Ct. 1961. Assoc. Golden & Golden, 1952-64; asst. dist. atty. Kings County, N.Y., 1956-64; chief asst. dist. atty. Kings County, 1964-76; acting dist. atty. Kings County, N.Y., 1968; judge Civil Ct. of City of N.Y., 1977-78; justice Supreme Ct. State of N.Y., 1979-98, jud. hearing officer, 1998—; adj. assoc. prof. N.Y.C. Tech. Coll., 1987-93; arbitrator, mediator Nat. Arbitration & Mediation, 1998—; cons. in field. Contbr. articles to profl. jours. Bd. trustees Greater N.Y. coun. Boy Scouts Am.; hon. vice chmn. March of Dimes; bd. dirs. Bklyn. Philharmonia; mem. adv. bd. Bklyn. PAL; chmn. Bklyn. Lawyers div. Fedn. Jewish Philanthropies; co-chmn. Bklyn. Lawyers div. State of Israel Bonds; assoc. trustee Temple Beth Emeth of Flatbush; mem. exec. com. Lawyers div. United Jewish Appeal; past pres. counsel Hosp. Relief Assn.; bd. dirs. Kings Bay YM-YMHA of Bklyn.; bd. dirs. Bklyn. ARC, Archway Sch. for Spl. Children, Bklyn. Sch. for Spl. Children. Recipient Cert. of Merit, Hosp. Relief Assn., numerous plaques, awards and certs. of appreciation various civic orgns. Mem. Nat. Dist. Attys. Assn. (dir. 1976-77, Disting. Svc. award), Combined Coun. Law Enforcement Ofcls. State N.Y., N.Y. State Dist. Attys. Assn. (sec. 1965-77), K.P. (supreme coun.). Avocations: golf, fishing, computers.

**GOLDEN, GREGG HANNAN STEWART,** lawyer; b. N.Y.C., Nov. 24, 1953; s. Edmond Jerome and Alvia Grace (Weinberger) G.; m. Laura Jean George, Apr. 26, 1992. Grad., Phillips Exeter Acad., 1971; AB with honors, Grinnell Coll., 1975; JD cum laude, Georgetown U., 1980. Bar: Pa. 1980, U.S. Dist. Ct. (mid. dist.) Pa. 1980, U.S. Ct. Appeals (3d and D.C. cirs.) 1981, Calif. 1982, N.J. 1983, D.C. 1984, U.S. Supreme Ct. 1984. Dep. atty. gen. State of Pa., Harrisburg, 1980-83; assoc. Hogan & Hartson, Washington, 1983-86; atty. Office of Enforcement Fed. Home Loan Bank Bd., Washington, 1986-88, assoc. dep. dir., 1988-89; assoc. dep. dir. enforcement Office Thrift Supervision U.S. Dept. Treasury, Washington, 1989-91, dist. counsel 12th Dist., 1990-91; counsel Resolution Trust Corp., Washington, 1991-94, sr. counsel, 1994-95; sr. counsel corp. affairs FDIC, Washington, 1996-99, counsel receivership ops. and litigation, 1999—; trustee, sec. InterFuture, N.Y.C., 1979-89, chairing officer bd. of trustees, 1989—. Rsch. editor: American Criminal Law Review, 1979-80. Lectr. YWCA Rape Crisis Svcs. div., Harrisburg; spl. counsel Pa. State Ethics Commn., Harrisburg, 1981-82; competition judge moot ct. bd. Cath. U. of Am., Washington, 1988-89. Fellow Johnson Found., 1972, Thomas J. Watson Found., 1975. Mem. ABA, D.C. Bar (com. on ct. rules 1985—, co-chmn. com. 1987-90, com. on representation for needy civil litigants 1985-88), Fed. Bar Assn., Pa. Bar Assn. Democrat. Jewish. Federal civil litigation, Administrative and regulatory, Labor. Office: FDIC 550 17th St NW Washington DC 20429-0001

**GOLDEN, HOWARD IRA,** lawyer, financial consultant; b. Chgo., Mar. 7, 1946; s. Alex and Mollie Ann (Brod) G.; m. Emily Weiss, Sept. 12, 1976; children: Molly Iris, Dani Rachel, Benjamin Abraham. BA in Econs., U. Wis., 1968, JD, 1972, MBA in Internat. Mktg., 1972. Bar: Wis. 1972, Ill. 1972, Israel 1976, N.Y. 1981. Assoc. Berger, Newmark & Fenchel, Chgo., 1972-74; asst. city atty. Municipality of Jerusalem, 1977-79; ptnr. Daniel Laitman, P.C., N.Y.C., 1980-85, Dimas, Golden & Johnston, N.Y.C., 1985-86; exec. v.p. Guaranty Acceptance Credit Corp., N.Y.C., 1986-87; ptnr. Eisenberger & Golden, N.Y.C., 1987-89, Howard I. Golden, P.C., N.Y.C., 1989—; mng. dir. Manhattan Equity Ptnrs., L.P., Scarsdale, N.Y., 1991—; mem. Supervisory Bd. Restitution Investment Fund of the Czech Republic, Supervisory Bd. Restitution Investment Fund Slovak Republic; bd. dirs. Khazakstan Investment Fund. Contbr. to profl. publs. Mem. Am. Jewish Congress (com. on law and social action 1983—). Jewish. Avocation: collecting antique maps. General corporate, Real property, Trademark and copyright. Office: 305 Madison Ave Fl 46 New York NY 10165-0006

**GOLDEN, JOHN DENNIS,** lawyer; b. Providence, May 18, 1954; s. Edward J. and Ann V. (Cahill) G.; m. Olga Iglesias, Aug. 2, 1980; children: Jennifer, Jackelyn, John. BA, Providence Coll., 1976; JD, Thomas M. Cooley, 1980. Bar: Mich. 1980, Fla. 1981. Assoc. Harvey Kruse & Weston, Detroit, 1980-82, Blackwell & Walker, Miami, Fla., 1982-83; ptnr. Rumburger Kirk et al, Miami, 1983-89; mng. ptnr. Roth, Edwards & Smith, Miami, 1989-91; shareholder Popham, Haik, Schnobrich & Kaufman, Ltd., Miami, 1991-95; shareholder Carlton, Fields, Ward, Emmanuel, Smith & Cutler, Miami, 1996—, also bd. dirs.; sustaining mem. Product Liability Adv. Coun. Mem. ABA (sustaining, mem. products liability adv. coun.), Mich. Bar Assn., Fla. Bar Assn., Dade County Bar Assn. Republican. Roman Catholic. Avocations: golf, snow skiing. Product liability, Insurance. Office: Carlton Fields Ward Emmanuel Smith & Cutler PO Box 01901 4000 International Pl Miami FL 33131-9101

**GOLDEN, T. MICHAEL,** state supreme court justice; b. 1942. BA in History, U. Wyo., 1964, JD, 1967; LLM, U. Va., 1992. Bar: Wyo. 1967, U.S. Dist. Ct. 1967, U.S. Ct. Appeals (10th cir.) 1967, U.S. Supreme Ct. 1970. Mem. firm Brimmer, MacPherson & Golden, Rawlins, Wyo., 1971-83, Williams, Porter, Day & Neville, Casper, Wyo., 1983-88; justice Wyo. Supreme Ct., Cheyenne, 1988—, chief justice, 1994—, assoc. justice; mem. Wyo. State Bd. Law Examiners, 1977-82, 86-88. Capt. U.S. Army 1967-71. Office: Wyo Supreme Ct Bldg PO Box 1737 2301 Capitol Ave Cheyenne WY 82002*

**GOLDEN, WILSON,** lawyer; b. Holly Springs, Miss., Feb. 15, 1948; s. Woodrow Wilson and Constance Annette (Harris) G.; children: Wilson Harris, Lewis Hamilton, Pamela Camille. BPA, U. Miss., 1970, JD, 1977. Bar: Miss. 1977, U.S. Dist. Ct. (no. and so. dists.) Miss. 1977, U.S. Ct. Appeals (5th cir.) 1977,. Pub. affairs journalist Miss. Authority for Ednl. TV, Jackson, 1970-72; asst. sec. Miss. State Senate, Jackson, 1972-76; ptnr. Lane & Henderson, Greenville, Miss., 1977-80, Watkins Ludlam & Stennis, Jackson, 1980-89, Levanway & Golden, Jackson, 1990-92; v.p. govt. rels. Kaiser Internat., Inc., Fairfax, Va., 1996. Mem. Dem. State Exec. Com., 1976-84, 88-96; mem. Miss. Gov.'s Constl. Study Commn., 1988; mem. Dem. Nat. Com., 1990-92; charter mem. Dem. Leadership Coun. NETWORK, 1988. Major USAR, 1970-90. Recipient Disting. Reporting award Am. Polit. Sci. Assn. 1971, U.S. Law Week award Bur. Nat. Affairs, Inc., Washington, 1978. Mem. ABA, Miss. Bar Assn. Democrat. Presbyterian. Legislative. Home: 3001 Saint Regents Dr Fairfax VA 22031-1236

**GOLDENBERG, EVA J.,** lawyer; b. Nürnberg, Germany, Nov. 24, 1961; came to U.S., 1968; d. David M. Goldenberg and Hildegard (Grünbaum) Katz; m. Benjamin P. Michel. BA, U. Chgo., 1984; JD, Benjamin N. Cardozo Law Sch., N.Y.C., 1987. Bar: N.Y., N.J. Assoc. Riker, Danzig, Scherer, Hyland & Perretti, Morristown, N.J., 1987-90, Kelley, Drye & Warren, N.Y.C., 1990-94; assoc. gen. counsel Russ Berrie & Co., Inc., Oakland, N.J., 1994—. General corporate, General practice, Intellectual property. Office: 111 Bauer Dr Oakland NJ 07436-3123

**GOLDENBERG, STEPHEN BERNARD,** lawyer; b. Cambridge, Mass., Feb. 10, 1943; s. Alexander M. and Gertrude (Perlmutter) G. AB, Kenyon Coll., 1964; postgrad., Georgetown U. Law Sch., 1964-65; JD, Boston Coll., 1967. Bar: Mass. 1967, Fla. 1990. Assoc. Myer Israel, Boston, 1968-74; ptnr. Israel & Goldenberg, Boston, 1974-91, Goldenberg, Walters & Lipson, Brookline, Mass., 1991—. Chmn. rent control bd., Brookline, 1972-75; mem. Brookline Bd. Selectmen, 1976-85, chmn., 1983-84. Mem. ABA, Mass. Bar Assn., Mass. Conveyancers Assn., Brookline C. of C. (pres.). Democrat. Real property, General corporate, Probate. Office: Goldenberg Walters et al 7 Harvard St Brookline MA 02445-7370

**GOLDENBERG, STEVEN SAUL,** lawyer; b. Monticello, N.Y., Apr. 11, 1952; s. Joseph and Lillian (Stone) G.; m. Barbra Ellen Tucker, June 27, 1976; children: Matthew, Jenna, Alycia. BA cum laude, SUNY, Oneonta, 1974; MPA cum laude, NYU, 1976; JD, Benjamin N. Cardozo Sch. Law, 1980. Bar: N.J., N.Y., U.S. Dist. Ct. N.J., U.S. Dist. Ct. (so. dist.) N.Y. Law sec. Hon. David B. Follender, Hackensack, N.J., 1980-81; atty. Saiber Schlesinger Satz & Goldstein, Newark, 1981-94; atty., legis. agt. Buchanan Ingersoll, Princeton, N.J., 1994-95, Greenbaum Rowe Smith Ravin Davis & Himmel, Woodbridge, N.J., 1995—; spl. counsel N.J. Bd. Pub. Utilities, Dept. Environ. Protection, Newark, 1984-91; N.J. Legislature Agt., Trenton, 1996—; counsel to competitors of N.J.'s investor-owned elec. utilities in electric industry restructuring hearings N.J. Bd. Pub. Utilities. Named one of Top 10 N.J. Lawyer/Lobbyists N.J. Law Jour., Newark, 1997-98. Mem. N.J. Bar Assn., N.Y. Bar Assn., N.J. Bus. and Industry Assn. (legal affairs com. 1995—). Avocations: karate, physical fitness, computers, music. E-Mail: sgoldenberg@greenbaumlaw.com. Public utilities, Administrative and regulatory, General civil litigation. Office: Greenbaum Rowe Smith Ravin Davis & Himmel PO Box 5600 Woodbridge NJ 07095-0988

**GOLDENHERSH, ROBERT STANLEY,** lawyer; b. St. Louis, July 23, 1922; s. Boris and Sarah (Lapushin) G.; m. Jeanne Waldman, June 18, 1950; children: Lawrence E., Margaret J., Louise E. JD, Washington U., 1947; LLM in Taxation, NYU, 1948. Bar: Mo. 1947, U.S. Dist. Ct. (ea. dist.) Mo., U.S. Ct. Appeals (8th cir.). Sr. ptnr. Rosenblum, Goldenhersh, Silverstein & Zafft P.C., St. Louis, 1953—. Pres. Congregation Temple Israel, St. Louis, 1975-76; chmn. law sch. div. Elliot Soc. of Washington U., St. Louis, 1984; charter mem. Creve Couer Squires (Mo.), 1980—. Mem. ABA, Mo. Bar Assn., St. Louis Co. Bar Assn., Bar Assn. City of St. Louis, Order of the Coif. Democrat. Jewish. Club: Westwood Country. Avocations: tennis, golf, fishing. Real property, Taxation, general, Contracts commercial. Home: 211 Rondelay Ct Saint Louis MO 63141-7702 Office: Rosenblum Goldenhersh et al 4th Fl Pierre Laclede Ctr 7733 Forsyth Blvd Ste 400 Saint Louis MO 63105-1812

**GOLDER, FREDERICK THOMAS,** lawyer, educator; b. Brookline, Mass., July 5, 1943; s. Michael and Ida Shirley (Gropman) G.; Caron Sue Cohen, Oct. 8, 1966; children: Rachel Beth, David Ross, Naomi Lea. BA in English, U. Mass., 1965; JD, Suffolk Sch. Law, 1968; spl. student, Harvard U., 1968; LLM in Labor, NYU, 1969. Bar: Mass. 1968, U.S. Dist. Ct. Mass. 1969, U.S. Ct. Appeals (1st cir.) 1970, U.S. Supreme Ct. 1972. Formerly ptnr. Bernstein, Golder & Field, P.A., Boston; adj. faculty Northeastern U., Boston, 1972—, Suffolk U. Law Sch.; faculty Mass. Sch. Law, 1988—; writer, Wilmette, Ill., 1982—; labor arbitrator and mediator. Author: Fair Employment Law, 1979, Wage and Hour Law, 1983, Health, Safety, etc., 1984, Legal Compliance Checkups: Business Clients, 1985, Labor and Employment Law: Compliance and Litigation, 1986, Uncivil Rights: Protecting and Preserving Your Job Rights, 1999. Fellow Mass. Bar Found.; mem. Fed. Bar Assn. (disting. service award 1984), Mass. Bar Assn., Assn. Trial Lawyers Am., Mass. Acad. Trial Attys. (disting. faculty award 1984, 86), Plaintiff Employment Lawyers Assn. (bd. dirs. 1986—). Labor, Civil rights, Federal civil litigation.

**GOLDER, LEONARD HOWARD,** lawyer, writer; b. Boston, June 6, 1950; s. Hershel and Pauline (Glass) G.; 1 child, Robert. BA, Clark U., 1972; JD, New Eng. Sch. Law, 1980. Bar: Mass. 1981, U.S. Dist. Ct. Mass. 1981, U.S. Ct. Appeals (1st cir.) Mass. 1981, U.S. Supreme Ct. 1984; lic. notary pub., Mass.; lic. real estate broker, Mass. Assoc. Law Offices Jacob Shair, West Roxbury, Mass., 1982-85; dir. collections unit Mass. Dept. Pub. Welfare, Boston, 1985-87; pvt. practice Stow, Mass., 1987—. Creator: (polit. game) Compromise, 1987; contbr. articles to profl. jours. Social worker Tufts Mental Health, Boston, 1973-81; selectman Town of Stow, Mass., 1997, chmn. Stow Bd. Selectmen, 1994; chmn. Stow Dem. Com., 1994—; adv. mem. Stow Master Plan, 1997; chmn. Stow Dem. Com., 1997; mem. Middlesex County adv. bd., Cambridge, Mass., 1997. Mem. Boston Bar Assn. Avocations: collecting sports and polit. memorabilia, reading, travel. Personal injury, Alternative dispute resolution, Legislative. Home and Office: 67 Old Bolton Rd Stow MA 01775-1212

**GOLDEY, MARK H.,** lawyer; b. N.Y.C., Aug. 28, 1969; s. Michael J. and Gail J. Goldey; m. Lisa S. Goldey, Mar. 28, 1998. BA, Columbia U., 1991; JD, U. Pa., 1996. Bar: Conn. 1996, N.Y. 1997, U.S. Dist. Ct. (so. and ea. dists.) N.Y. 1997. Mem. Anderson Kill & Olick, P.C., N.Y.C., 1996-97; law clk. to Hon. Thomas P. Griesa U.S. Dist. Ct. (so. dist.) N.Y., N.Y.C., 1997-98; assoc. O'Sullivan Graev & Karabell, N.Y.C., 1998—. Mem. N.Y. County Am. Inns of Ct. General practice, Antitrust, General civil litigation. Office: O'Sullivan Graev & Karabell 30 Rockefeller Plz Fl 41 New York NY 10112-0198

**GOLDFARB, BERNARD SANFORD,** lawyer; b. Cleve., Apr. 15, 1917; s. Harry and Esther (Lenson) G.; m. Barbara Brofman, Jan. 4, 1966; children—Meredith Stacey, Lauren Beth. A.B., Case Western Res. U., 1938, J.D., 1940. Bar: Ohio bar 1940. Since practiced in Cleve.; sr. ptnr. firm Goldfarb & Reznick, 1967-95; pvt. practice Cleve., 1997—; spl. counsel to atty. gen. Ohio, 1950, 71-74; mem. Ohio Commn. Uniform Traffic Rules, 1973—. Contbr. legal jours. Served with USAAF, 1942-45. Mem. Am., Ohio, Greater Cleve. bar assns. General practice, Federal civil litigation, Labor. Home: 39 Pepper Creek Dr Pepper Pike OH 44124-5279 Office: 55 Public Sq Ste 1500 Cleveland OH 44113-1998

**GOLDFARB, RONALD LAWRENCE,** lawyer; b. Jersey City, N.J., Oct. 16, 1933; s. Robert S. and Aida J. (Weintraub) G.; m. Joanne Jacob, June 9, 1957; children: Jody, Nicholas, Maximilian Goldfarb. AB, Syracuse U., 1954, LLB, 1956; LLM, Yale, 1960, JSD, 1962. Bar: N.Y. 1956, Calif. 1959, D.C. 1962, U.S. Supreme Ct. 1965. Spl. asst. to U.S. atty. gen. (organized crime sect.), 1961-64; ptnr. Goldfarb and Assocs. and predecessor law firms, 1966—; Dir. Brookings Instn. program on cts. and adminstrn. Justice, 1966-67; mem. staff counsel com. on law and social action Am. Jewish Congress, 1960-61; cons. Pres.'s Poverty Program, 1964, Riots Commn., 1967-68. Author: The Contempt Power, 1963, Ransom: A Critique of the American Bail Systems, 1965, (with Alfred Friendly) Crime and Publicity, 1967, (with Linda Singer) After Conviction--A Review of the American Correction System, 1973, Jails: The Ultimate Ghetto, 1975, Migrant Farm Workers: A Caste of Despair, 1981, (with James Raymond) Clear Understandings: A Guide to Legal Writing, 1983, (with Gail Ross) The Writer's Lawyer: Essential Legal Advice for Writers and Editors in All Media, 1989, Perfect Villains, Imperfect Heroes: Robert F. Kennedy's War Against Organized Crime, 1995, TV or Not TV: Courts, Television and Justice, 1998. Served to capt. JAG Corps USAF, 1957-60. Arthur Garfield Hays fellow N.Y.U., 1960-61; Woodrow Wilson fellow. Mem. ACLU, ABA, D.C. Bar Assn., N.Y. Bar Assn., Calif. Bar Assn., Sigma Alpha Mu., Phi Delta Phi. General civil litigation, Criminal. Office: 1501 M St NW Washington DC 20005-1700

**GOLDFEIN, SHEPARD,** lawyer; b. Englewood, N.J., 1948. AB, Rutgers U., 1970, JD, 1975; MA, U. Chgo., 1977. Bar: N.Y. 1976, N.J. 1977. With Skadden, Arps, Slate, Meagher & Flom LLP, N.Y.C. Editor: Rutgers Law Rev., 1974-75. Mem. Phi Beta Kappa, Pi Sigma Alpha. Office: Skadden Arps Slate Meagher & Flom LLP 919 3rd Ave New York NY 10022-3902

**GOLDIE, RAY ROBERT,** lawyer; b. Dayton, Ohio, Apr. 1, 1920; s. Albert S. and Lillian (Hayman) G.; m. Dorothy Roberta Zafman, Dec. 2, 1941; children: Marilyn, Deanne, Dayle, Ron R. Student, U. So. Calif., 1943-44, JD magna cum laude, 1957; student, San Bernardino Valley Coll., 1950-51. Bar: Calif. 1957; cert. specialist estate planning, trusts and probate law, Calif. Bd. Legal Specialization. Elec. appliance dealer various locations, 1944-54; dep. atty. gen. State Bar of Calif., L.A., 1957-58, 1957-58; pvt. practice San Bernardino, Calif., 1958-87, Rancho Mirage, Calif., 1987—; pres. Trinity Acceptance Corp., 1948-53. Mem. World Peace Through Law Ctr., 1962—; regional dir. Legion Lex U. So. Calif. Sch. Law 1959-75; chmn. San Bernardino United Jewish Appeal, 1963; v.p. United Jewish Welfare Fund, San Bernardino, 1964-66; Santa Anita Hosp., Lake Arrowhead, 1966-69; bd. dirs. San Bernardino Med. Arts Corp.; trustee McCallum Theater, Bob Hope Cultural Ctr., 1996-99, Friends of Cultural Ctr. Found.; bd. dirs. Palm Canyon Theater, 1998—; legal counsel Lake Arrowhead Skating Found., 1998. Fellow Internat. Acad. Law and Sci.; mem. ABA, Assn. Naval Aviation Desert Storm Sqdn. (adminstrv. officer, sec.), San Bernardino County Bar Assn., Riverside County Bar Assn., State Bar Calif. (cert. specialist estate planning, probate and trust law), Am. Judicature Soc., Am. Soc. Hosp. Attys., Calif. Trial Lawyers Assn. (v.p. chpt. 1965-67, pres. 1967-68), Am. Arbitration Assn. (nat. panel arbitrators), Coachella Valley Desert Bar Assn. (chmn. taxation and estate planning, trusts, wills and probate com. 1992-94), Order of the Coif, Lake Arrowhead Country Club (pres. 1972-73, 80-81), Lake Arrowhead Yacht Club, Club at Morningside (CFO 1992-93, sec. 1993-94), Nu Beta Epsilon (pres. 1956-57). General corporate, Nonprofit and tax-exempt organizations, Real property. Home and Office: 1 Hampton Ct Rancho Mirage CA 92270-2585

**GOLDIE, RON ROBERT,** lawyer; b. San Bernardino, Calif., Apr. 6, 1951; s. Ray R. and Dorothy R. (Zafman) G.; m. Betty J. Cooper, June 13, 1983; children: Meghan Ann, Rand R., R. Cooper. Diploma, U. Paris, 1970; BA, U. So. Calif., 1972, MBA, JD, 1975. Bar: Calif. 1975, U.S. Dist. Ct. (cen., no. and so. dists.) Calif., U.S. Tax Ct., U.S. Ct. Appeals (2d, 9th and 11th cirs.). Atty. Goldie Law Corp., Los Angeles and San Bernardino, 1975-82; sole practice Los Angeles, 1982-86; prin. Law Offices of Ron R. Goldie, Los Angeles, 1986-88; sr. ptnr., chmn. bus. dept. Rosen, Wachtell & Gilbert, L.A., 1988-90; sr. ptnr. Jeffer, Mangels, Butler & Marmaro, L.A., 1990—. Republican. Jewish. Avocations: skiing, racquetball. Real property, General corporate, State civil litigation. Home: 11968 Brentridge Dr Los Angeles CA 90049-1552 Office: Jeffer Mangels Butler & Marmaro 2121 Avenue Of The Stars Los Angeles CA 90067-5010

**GOLDING, GILBERT JAMES,** lawyer; b. Phila., July 24, 1950. BS, LaSalle U., 1972; JD, Penn State U., 1975; LLM in Taxation, Temple U., 1983. Bar: Pa. 1975, U.S. Dist. Ct. (we. dist.) Pa. 1975, U.S. Dist. Ct. (ea. dist.) Pa. 1979, U.S. Ct. Appeals (3rd cir.) 1979, U.S. Supreme Ct. 1979. Law clk. The Superior Ct. Pa., 1975-78; assoc. Curtin & Heefner, LLP, Morrisville, Pa., 1978—; dir. Bucks County Bar Assn., Pa., 1982-84; mem. steering com. U.S. Dist. Ct. Pa. Bankruptcy Conf., 1993—. Banking, Bankruptcy. Office: Curtin & Heefner LLP 250 N Pennsylvania Ave Morrisville PA 19067-1104

**GOLDKIND, LEONARD DOUGLAS,** lawyer, educator; b. Laytonville, Calif., Dec. 26, 1953; s. Abe and Rose Lotte Goldkind; m. Victoria Workman Goldkind, Oct. 9, 1982; 1 child, George Simon. BA magna cum laude, San Francisco State U., 1974; JD, San Francisco Law Sch., 1978. Bar: Calif. 1978, U.S. Dist. Ct. (ea. dist.) Calif. 1978. Pvt. practice, Chico and Oroville, Calif., 1978-83; dep. dist. atty. Office Colusa County Dist. Atty., Colusa, Calif., 1987-89, Office Butte County Dist. Atty., Oroville, 1983-87, 89—; vice chmn. Serious Habitual Offender Program, Oroville, 1993—; mem. student acad. rev. bd. Butte County Office Edn., 1994—. V. Recipient recognition Calif. Probation, Parole and Correctional Assn., 1995, Chico Unified Sch. Dist., 1998, Disting. Svc. award Continuing Edn. Assn., 1998. Mem. Calif. Dist. Atty.'s Assn. Democrat. Jewish. Avocations: weight training, reading. Fax: 530-538-7071. Office: Office Butte County Dist Atty 25 County Center Dr Oroville CA 95965-3316

**GOLDMAN, ALAN BARRY,** lawyer, accountant; b. Bklyn., July 9, 1954; s. Lester and Sonya Goldman; m. June Marie Bohling, Sept. 15, 1979; children: Tanya, Zachary. BS, SUNY, Albany, 1976; JD, St. John's U., Jamaica, N.Y., 1983. Bar: N.Y. 1984, U.S. Dist. Ct. (ea. dist.) N.Y. 1984, U.S. Tax Ct. 1984, U.S. Ct. Mil. Appeals 1988, U.S. Supreme Ct. 1988; CPA, N.Y.,

Fla.; diplomate Am. Bd. Forensic Accts. Pvt. practice, Floral Park, N.Y.; ptnr. Kimmel Blau & Goldman, CPA's, Rockville Centre, N.Y. Bd. dirs. Child Care Coun. Nassau County, Franklin Square, N.Y. Mem. ABA, AICPA, Am. Assn. Attorneys-CPAs, N.Y. State Bar Assn., N.Y. State Soc. CPA's, Fla. Inst. CPA's. Taxation, general, Probate, Real property. Home: 31 Vanderbilt Way N Woodmere NY 11581-2333 Office: 16 Verbena Ave Floral Park NY 11001-2712

**GOLDMAN, ELISABETH PARIS,** lawyer; b. Pittsburgh, Pa., Jan. 11, 1939; d. Harold H. and Silvia F. (Koenigsberg) Paris; m. Alvin Lee Goldman, Nov. 23, 1956; children: Polly, Douglas. BA, Queens Coll., 1964; JD, U. Ky., 1975. Bar: Ky. 1975, Calif. 1977. Chief law clk. Supreme Ct. Ky., Frankfort, 1975-76; pvt. practice Elisabeth Goldman PSC, Lexington, Ky., 1977—. Mem. ACLU Louisville, Ky., 1987-90, Hadassah, Chamber Music Soc., Fayette County Health Care Bd.; pres. Ctrl. Ky. Jewish Fedn., 1993-95, Ctrl. Ky. Civil Liberties Union, 1988-90, James Lane Allen PTA, Lexington, Ky., 1971-72. Recipient Pro-Bono Svc. award Ky. Bar Assn., Frankfort, 1994, 95, 96, 97, 98. Mem. Am. Acad. Adoption Attys., Order of Coif, Phi Beta Kappa. Democrat. Avocations: skiing, hiking, dog training. Family and matrimonial. Office: Elisabeth Goldman PSC 118 Old Lafayette Ave Lexington KY 40502-1704

**GOLDMAN, ERIC SCOT,** lawyer; b. Quincy, Mass., Mar. 5, 1957; s. Terry and Harriet (Goldstein) G.; m. Lora Anderson, June 18, 1983; children: William, Daniel, Leigh. BA, Boston Coll., 1979; MSc in Criminal Justice, Northeastern U., 1980; JD, Suffolk U., 1987. Bar: Mass. 1987, U.S. Dist. Ct. Mass. 1987, U.S. Mil. Ct. Appeals. Adminstr. McLean Hosp., Belmont, Mass.; caseworker Norfolk County Dist. Atty.'s Office, Dedham, Mass.; atty. McDermott & Padis, Milton, Mass., 1983-93; assoc. Lynch & Lynch, South Easton, Mass., 1993-98, Lang & Morgera, Boston, 1998-99; pvt. practice Duxbury, Mass., 1999—; mediator Norfolk-Plymouth County; bd. dirs. Criminal Justice Scis. Inst., Washington. Recipient Cert. of Recognition, Norfolk County Dist. Atty., Commonwealth of Mass. Dist. Ct. Mem. Mass Acad. Trial Attys., Norfolk, Plymouth and Bristol County Bar Assn., Braintree Rifle and Pistol Club (pres. 1988—). Avocations: scuba diving, karate, music, firearms training. General civil litigation, Criminal, Insurance. Home: 36 Forge Way Duxbury MA 02332-4743 Office: PO Box 2295 Duxbury MA 02332

**GOLDMAN, GARY CRAIG,** lawyer; b. Phila., Dec. 28, 1951; s. Ronald Walter and Connie Sylvia (Stein) G.; m. Diane Rose Lane, Oct. 1, 1977; children: Justin Edward, Gregory David. BA magna cum laude, Temple U., 1973; JD, Villanova U., 1976. Bar: Pa. 1976, U.S. Dist. Ct. (ea. dist.) Pa. 1981. Jud. law clk. Common Pleas Ct., Northampton County, Pa., 1976-77; asst. atty. gen. office of legal counsel Pa. Dept. Pub. Welfare, Phila., 1977-81, asst. counsel, 1981-84; staff counsel CDI Corp., Phila., 1984-86, v.p., assoc. gen. counsel, 1986—; mem. faculty, planning chmn. Nationwide Comml. Real Estate Leasing Programs. Author: Drafting a Fair Office Lease, 1989, 2d edit., 1999; contbg. author: The Commercial Real Estate Tenant's Handbook, 1987, The Practical Real Estate Lawyer's Manual, 1987, Commercial Tenants' Leasing Transactions Guide, 1991, Office Planning and Design Desk Reference, 1992, Negotiating and Drafting Office Leases; assoc. editor: Villanova Law Rev., 1974-76; contbr. articles to legal jours. Mem. Am. Corp. Counsel Assn., ABA, Phila. Bar Assn. Republican. Jewish. Avocations: golf, coaching little league. General corporate, Labor, Landlord-tenant. Home: 210 Fox Hollow Dr Langhorne PA 19053-2477 Office: CDI Corp 1717 Arch St Fl 35 Philadelphia PA 19103-2713

**GOLDMAN, JEFFREY E.,** lawyer; b. Ft. Worth, Tex., Feb. 11, 1962; s. Murry Mores and Fran Ethel (Eddy) G. BS in Pharmacy, Phila. Coll Pharmacy & Sci., 1985; JD, Temple U , 1992. Assoc. Parker, McCauer, Criscoulu, Marlton, N.J., 1991-93; lawyer pvt. practice, Phila. and Cherry Hill, Pa., N.J., 1993—. Contbg. author National Employment Lawyers Annua., 1998. Bd. dirs. Phila. Gay and Lesbian Comty Ctr. 1996—, chmn. 1996-98. Mem. Nat. Employment Lawyers Assn. (v.p.). Democrat. Jewish. Labor. Office: 210 W Washington Sq Philadelphia PA 19106-3514

**GOLDMAN, JERRY STEPHEN,** lawyer; b. Bklyn., Sept. 7, 1951; s. Bernard I. and Charlotte (Emerling) G.; children by previous marriage: Rachel Dawn, Samantha. BA with honors, NYU 1973; JD, Boston U., 1976; LLM in Taxation, Temple U., 1983. Bar: Mass. 1977, N.Y. 1977, U.S. Dist. Ct. (ea. and so. dists.) N.Y. 1980, U.S. Dsit. Ct. (Mass.) 1997, U.S. Supreme Ct. 1981, Pa. 1982, U.S. Tax Ct. 1983, U.S. Ct. Appeals (3d cir.) 1983, U.S. Dist. Ct. (ea. dist.) Pa. 1983, U.S. Ct. Appeals (2d cir.) 1996, U.S. Ct. Appeals (1st cir.) 1997, U.S. Dist. Ct. Mass. 1997. Sr. asst. dist. atty. Kings County Dist. Atty.'s Office, Bklyn., 1976-82; pvt. practice, N.Y.C. and Phila., 1982—; dir., pres. Huntingdon Brook Community Assn., Bucks Co, Pa., 1985-89. Mem. bd., counsel Citizen's Crime Commn., Phila., 1983-95; atty. Phila. Vol. Lawyers for the Arts, 1983—; chmn. Upper Southampton Planning Commn., 1984-90. Mem. ABA, N.Y. State Bar Assn., Mass. Bar Assn., Pa. Bar Assn., Phila. Bar Assn. Jewish. Avocations: cross-country skiing, music. Taxation, general, Estate planning, General corporate. Office: 1520 Locust St Philadelphia PA 19102-4403 also: 111 Bronty 13th Fl New York NY 10006

**GOLDMAN, JOEL J.,** retired lawyer; b. N.Y.C., Sept. 7, 1940; s. Myron and Pearl (Jacobs) G.; m. Jane I. Stalker, July 23, 1973; children: Elizabeth Ann, Rebecca Lynn. BS, U. Va., 1962, JD, Syracuse U., 1965. Bar: N.Y. 1966, U.S. Dist. Ct. (we. dist.) N.Y. 1966. Law clk. Myron Goldman, N.Y.C., 1965; staff atty., chief trial counsel Legal Aid Soc. Rochester, N.Y., 1966-73; ptnr. Kaman, Berlove, Marafioti, Jacobstein & Goldman, Rochester, 1973-97; ret., 1997; lectr. family law; spl. investigator N.Y. State Spl. Commn. on Attica, 1972; mem. panel arbitrators Am. Arbitration Assn.; mem. faculty Nat. Bus. Inst., 1985-97. Referee, Ea. Assn. Inter-Collegiate Football Ofcls., 1974-95, v.p. Empire chpt., 1988, pres. 1989, Observer, Ea. Coll. Athletic Conf., 1996—, Inductee Jewish Athletes Sports Hall of Fame, 1996. Fellow Am. Acad. Matrimonial Lawyers (ret.); mem. ABA, N.Y. State Bar Assn. (exec. com. family law sect. 1982, mem. exec. com. 1981-97), Monroe County Bar Assn. (chmn. family law sect. 1982, exec. com. 1981-86), Assn. Trial Lawyers Am. Jewish. Author continuing edn. materials. Contbg. editor Bender's Forms for Civil Practice, 1986, Medina's Bostwick, 1986. Family and matrimonial. Home: 67 Mountain Rd Rochester NY 14625-1816 also: 21 Bluebill Ave Apt 1005B Naples FL 34108-1765

**GOLDMAN, LAWRENCE SAUL,** lawyer; b. Phila., Mar. 25, 1942; s. Ephraim Lederer and Belle Joan (Finkelstein) G.; m. Kathi Sue Schleifer, June 20, 1965; children: Carolyn, Jonathan. BA, Brandeis U., 1963; JD, Harvard U., 1966. Bar: N.Y. 1966. Asst. dist. atty. New York County, N.Y.C., 1966-71; asst. gen. counsel N.Y. State Commn. To Investigate N.Y.C., 1971-72; ptnr. Goldman & Hafetz, N.Y.C., 1972—; cons. N.Y.C. Commn. on Police Corruption, 1972. Contbg. author: Criminal Trial Advocacy, 1980—. Trustee Congregation Rodeph Sholom, N.Y.C., 1983-92; bd. dirs. William F. Ryan Comty. Health Ctr., N.Y.C., 1986-88, Bronx Defenders, 1997—; mem. N.Y. State Commn. on Jud. Conduct, 1990—, mem. adv. com. on the criminal law, 1992—. Recipient Man of Yr. award Hogan Assocs., 1984. Mem. NACDL (chmn. ethics adv. com. 1988-92, white collar com. 1992-97, Robert C. Heeney award 1998, v.p. 1999—), N.Y. State Assn. Criminal Def. Lawyers (pres. 1987-89, Thurgood Marshall award 1999), N.Y. Criminal Bar Assn. (pres. 1982-85, Outstanding Practitioner award 1994), N.Y. State Bar Assn. (Outstanding Practitioner award criminal justice sect. 1996), Harvard Club. Democrat. Criminal. Office: 500 Fifth Ave New York NY 10110-0002

**GOLDMAN, MARA KAPELOVITZ,** lawyer; b. Denver, July 12, 1967; d. Leonard H. and Abbey Poze Kapelovitz; m. Adam Goldman, May 30, 1999. BA, Wesleyan U., 1989; JD, Stanford U., 1995. Bar: Calif. 1996. Clk. hon. Pamela Ann Rymer U.S. Ct. Appeals (9th cir.), Pasadena, Calif., 1995-96; assoc. Latham & Watkins, San Francisco, 1996-97, Nolan & Armstrong (now Nolan, Armstron & Barton, LLP), Palo Alto, Calif., 1997—; fellow Stanford Ctr. on Conflict and Negotiation, 1995-96; lectr. law Stanford U., 1999—. Sr. note editor Stanford Law Rev., 1994-95. Mem. Calif. Attys. for Criminal Justice, Santa Clara County Bar Assn. Criminal. Office: Nolan Armstrong & Barton LLP 600 University Ave Palo Alto CA 94301-2019

**GOLDMAN, MICHAEL DAVID,** lawyer; b. Jersey City, Oct. 16, 1942; s. Nathaniel J. and Ruth Goldman; m. Faith I. Frankel, June 5, 1966; children: Leigh S., Amy P. AB, Pa. State U., 1964; JD, Villanova (Pa.) U., 1967. Bar: Del. 1968. Law clk. to presiding judge Ct. Chancery, Wilmington, Del.; ptnr. Potter Anderson & Corroon, Wilmington, 1974—, chmn., 1999—; chmn. bd. Bar Examiners State of Del., 1988-90, vice chmn., 1986-87; spkr., planning com. Tulane Corp. Law Inst., 1988—. Contbr. articles in field to profl. jours. Mem. state exec. bd. Muscular Dystrophy Assn., 1974-76; chmn. atty. div. United Way, Del., 1977, chmn. profl. div., 1978, 80-81; chmn. Am. Jewish Com., Del., 1981-82; chmn. Jewish Community Rels. Com., 1982; bd. dirs. Jewish Fedn. Del., 1982-85. Mem. ABA (bus. sect., corp. laws com. 1995—), Del. Bar Assn. (chmn. sect. on Del. corp. law 1990-92, chmn. subcom. bus. combination statute). General corporate, General civil litigation, Mergers and acquisitions. Office: Potter Anderson & Corroon Hercules Plz PO Box 951 Wilmington DE 19899-0951

**GOLDMAN, MICHAEL P.,** lawyer; b. Chgo., June 10, 1960; s. William J. and Judith Ann (Holleb) G.; m. Karla Sue Berman, June 26, 1983; children: Joshua, Adam, David. BS in Accountancy, U. Ill., 1982; JD cum laude, Loyola U. Chgo., 1985. Bar: Ill. 1985, U.S. Dist. Ct. (no. dist.) Ill. 1985; CPA, Ill. Acct. L. Karp & Sons Inc., Elk Grove Vill., Ill., 1979-81; tax analyst Beatrice Foods Corp., Chgo., 1981-84; ptnr. Katten Muchin & Zavis, Chgo., 1984—; lectr. in field. contbr. articles to profl. jours. Bd. dirs. K.I.D.S.S. for Kids (auxiliary of Children's Meml. Hosp., Chgo.), 1993—. Mem. ABA (tort and ins. and bus. law sects.), Chgo. Bar Assn.(ins. and corp. lawcoms.), Ill. CPA Soc. (chmn ins. co. com.), Soc. Fin. Ins. Examiners. Republican. Jewish. Avocations: skiing, handball. Insurance, General corporate, Securities. Office: Katten Muchin & Zavis 525 W Monroe St Ste 1600 Chicago IL 60661-3693

**GOLDMAN, NATHAN CARLINER,** lawyer, educator; b. Charleston, S.C., Mar. 19, 1950; s. Reuben and Hilda Alta (Carliner) G.; m. Judith Tova Feigon, Oct. 28, 1984; children: Michael Reuben, Miriam Esther. BA, U. S.C., 1972; JD, Duke U., 1975; MA, Johns Hopkins U., 1978, PhD, 1980. Bar: N.C. 1975, Tex. 1985, U.S. Dist. Ct. (mid. dist.) N.C. 1975. Paralegal City Atty.'s Office, Durham, N.C., 1975-76; asst. prof. govt. dept. U. Tex., Austin, Tex., 1980-85; pvt. practice Houston, 1985-86; assoc. Liddell, Sapp, Zivley, Hill & LaBoon, Houston, 1986-88; pvt. practice Houston, 1988—; adj. prof. space law U. Houston, 1985-88; rsch. assoc. Rice U. Inst. Policy Analysis, 1986—; lectr. bus. law, 1988-95; mem. coordinating bd. Space Architecture, U. Houston, 1985—; v.p. Internat. Design in Extreme Environments Assn., U. Houston, 1991—; vis. asst. prof. U. Houston-Clear Lake, 1989-91; adj. prof. South Tex. Coll. Law, 1994-95; gen. counsel Internat. Space Enterprises, 1993—, Globus Ltd. Co., 1994—; info. officer Israel Consulate, 1996-97. Author: Space Commerce, 1985, American Space Law, 1988, 2d edit., 1996, Space Policy: A Primer, 1992; editor: Space and Society, 1984; assoc. editor Jour. Space Commerce, 1990-91; exec. editor Space Governance, 1996—; also articles. Mem. com. on governance of space U.S. Bicentennial Commn., 1986-88, Clear Lake (Tex.) Area Econ. Devel. Found., 1987, Space Collegium, Houston Area Rsch. Ctr., 1987; pres. Windermere Civic Assn., 1990-92; bd. dirs. Hebrew Acad., 1994-96, Men's Club United Orthodox Synagogues, 1994—, pres., 1999—. U.S. Dept. Justice grantee, 1979-80, U. Tex. Inst. for Constructive Capitalism U. grantee, 1983; E.D. Walker Centennial fellow, 1984; NASA Summer fellow U. Calif., 1984. Fellow Internat. Inst. Space Law; mem. ABA, Tex. Bar Assn., Nat. Space Soc. (v.p. 1989-91), Inst. for Social Sci. Study Space (mem. adv. bd. 1990, editor Space Humanization Jour. 1993—), Am. Astrronautical Soc., Inst. for Design in Extreme Environment Assn. (v.p. 1991-96), Space Bus. Roundtable. Avocations: reading, hiking, baseball, softball. General corporate, Private international. Home: 2328 Dryden Rd Houston TX 77030-1104 Office: Rice U PO Box 1892 Houston TX 77251-1892

**GOLDMAN, RICHARD HARRIS,** lawyer; b. Boston, June 17, 1936; s. Charles M. and Irene M. (Marks) G.; m. Patricia Grollman, June 21, 1959; children: Elaine, Stephen. BA, Wesleyan U., 1958; LLB, NYU, 1961. Bar: Mass. 1961, U.S. Dist. Ct. Mass. 1961. Mem. Slater & Goldman, Boston, 1961-76, Widett, Slater & Goldman, PC, Boston, 1976-93; Sullivan & Worcester LLP, 1993—; past trustee, chmn. audit com. Grove Bank. Co-author: The Ritual Dance Between Lessee and Lender; contbr. articles to profl. jours. Trustee, v.p. Temple Israel; former chmn. Newton (Mass.) Human Rights Commn. Mem. ABA, Mass. Bar Assn., Boston Bar Assn. (chmn. leasing com. 1996-97, lectr., chmn. seminar comml. real estate fin. 1997, real estate steering com. 1997—, co-chair real estate sect. 1999—), Mass. Conveyancers Assn., Belmont Country Club (past v.p., sec.). Real property, General corporate, Probate. Home: 47 Vaughn Ave Newton MA 02461-1038 Office: Sullivan & Worcester LLP 1 Post Office Sq Ste 2300 Boston MA 02109-2129

**GOLDMAN, RICHARD LURIE,** lawyer; b. N.Y.C., May 3, 1925; s. Samuel and Harriet (Lurie) G.; m. Priscilla Dilks, Apr. 23, 1960; children: Robert Prescott, Sally Dilks. B.A., Bklyn. Coll., 1948; LL.B., Columbia U., 1951. Bar: N.Y. 1952, U.S. Tax Ct. 1952, D.C. 1961, U.S. Supreme Ct. 1961. Assoc. in Law Columbia Law Sch., N.Y.C., 1951-52; assoc. Cravath, Swaine & Moore, N.Y.C., 1952-57; atty.-advisor Chief Counsel's Office, IRS, Washington, 1957-61; ptnr. Valicenti Leighton Reid & Pine, N.Y.C., 1963-70, Goldman & Gladstone, N.Y.C., 1981—. U.S.A. nat. reporter to Internat. Fiscal Congress, 1975; chmn. Reporters to Congress, 1985. Contbr. articles to legal jours. Exec. bd. Westchester-Putnam Coun. Boy Scouts Am., White Plains, N.Y., 1982—. Served to capt. AUS, 1943-46, 61-62. Harlan Fiske Stone scholar, 1949-51. Mem. Internat. Fiscal Assn. (U.S.A. br., mem. nat. council 1978—, v.p. N.Y. region 1986-90, exec. v.p. 1990-92, pres. 1992-94, pres. emeritus 1994—), ABA (chmn. personal holding co. subcom. 1969-72, corp.-stockholder relationships com. 1955-77, 80—, com. on U.S. activities of foreigners and tax treaties 1976—), N.Y. State Bar Assn. (chmn. fgn. portfolio sales corp. subcom., com. on internat. fin. and investment 1973-75, coms. on tax policy 1974, 87, 89-91, reorgns. 1976, 89, 92-94, U.S. activities of fgn. taxpayers 1976—, fgn. activities of U.S. taxpayers 1976-84, 96—, com. on internat. investment 1993—, com. on internat. estates 1987—, internat. law and practices sect., trusts and estates law sect. 1987—), Assn. Bar City N.Y. Republican. Fax: 914-725-6864. Corporate taxation, Private international, Probate. Home: 200 Old Army Rd Scarsdale NY 10583-2613 Office: Goldman & Gladstone 880 3rd Ave New York NY 10022-4730

**GOLDMAN, STEVEN JASON,** lawyer, accountant; b. Boston, Nov. 11, 1947; s. Philip Charles and Selma Laura (Goldblatt) G. BSBA, Northeastern U., Boston, 1970, MBA, 1974; JD, New Eng. Sch. Law, 1987. Bar: R.I., 1987, U.S. Dist. Ct. R.I. 1988, U.S. Tax Ct. 1987; CPA, R.I. Staff auditor CPA firms, Boston and Providence, 1970-72; sr. accountant Peat, Marwick, Mitchell & Co., Providence, 1972-73; contr. Warwick Fed. Savs. & Loan Assn. (R.I.), 1974, v.p., 1975-79, exec. v.p., 1980-82; pres. Fin. Adv. Svcs., Unltd., 1982-87; pvt. practice, Warwick, 1987—. Fellow AICPA; mem. ABA (taxation div.), Nat. Soc. Tax Profls., R.I. Soc. CPAs, R.I. Bar Assn. (taxation com.), Turk's Head Club, Aircraft Owners and Pilots Assn., Edgewood Yacht Club. Jewish. Avocations: flying, sailing, tennis. Estate planning, Probate, Taxation, general. Office: 1009 Post Rd Warwick RI 02888-3362

**GOLDMAN, WILLIAM LEWIS, SR.,** lawyer; b. Phila., May 13, 1919; s. Samuel and Grace Sunderland (Rice) G.; m. Jean Beneski, July 5, 1947; children: William Lewis Jr., Robert Edward, Jan Grace, Lee Ann, Jeanne. BS, Temple U., 1947, JD, 1951. Bar: Pa. 1951, U.S. Dist. Ct. (ea. dist.) Pa. 1951, D.C. 1951. Prin. Law Offices of William L. Goldman, Doylestown, Pa., 1951—. Lt. comdr. USN, 1943-47, CBI. Fellow Am. Acad. Matrimonial Lawyers, Internat. Acad. Matrimonial Lawyers; mem. Pa. Bar Assn. (chairperson family law sect. 1989-90), Pa. chpt. Am. Acad. Matrimonial Lawyers (bd. mgrs.). Republican. Roman Catholic. Avocation: travel. Family and matrimonial, Consumer commercial, General practice. Office: 90 E State St Doylestown PA 18901-4362

**GOLDNER, LEONARD HOWARD,** lawyer; b. N.Y.C., June 18, 1947; s. Adolph and Florence (Cohen) G.; m. Jacqueline Slotnik, Apr. 1, 1969; children: Claudia Mara, Benjamin Micah. BA, U. Wis., 1969; JD, Harvard U., 1972. Bar: N.Y. 1974, U.S. Dist. Ct. (so. dist.) N.Y. 1974, U.S. Ct. Appeals (2d cir.) 1975. Law clk. U.S. Ct. Appeals (9th cir.) Honolulu, 1972-73; assoc. Simpson Thacher & Bartlett, N.Y.C., 1973-76; assoc. Shereff, Friedman, Hoffman & Goodman, N.Y.C., 1976-79, ptnr., 1979-90; sr. v.p., gen. counsel Symbol Techs., Inc., Holtsville, N.Y., 1990—. Trustee Soc. for Advancement of Judaism, N.Y.C., 1974-85; chmn. West End Synagogue, N.Y.C., 1985-87. Trustee West End Synagogue, N.Y.C., 1985-90, Reconstructionist Rabbinical Coll., Phila., 1988—, bd. govs. Securities, General corporate. Office: One Symbol Plz Holtsville NY 11742

**GOLDROSEN, DONALD NORMAN,** lawyer; b. Glen Ridge, N.J., Jan. 5, 1956; s. Leonard Martin and Joan Goldrosen; m. Suzanne Marie Bardgett, Aug. 2, 1986; children: Bruce, Melissa. BS in Acctg., U. Del., 1978; JD, Villanova U., 1982. Bar: Tex. 1982, Va. 1986. Staff acct. Mironov, Goldman & Wortzel, East Brunswick, N.J., 1979; assoc. Childs, Fortenbach, Beck and Guyton, Houston, 1982-85; assoc., ptnr. Hazel & Thomas, P.C., Fairfax, Va., 1985—; real estate sect. chmn. Hazel & Thomas, P.C., Fairfax, 1996—; mem. law sch. com. George Mason U. Century Club, Fairfax, 1994-97. Mem. staff Villanova Law Rev., 1981, lead articles editor, 1982. Coach youth soccer and basketball Annandale (Va.) Boys and Girls Club, 1994—. Mem. Beta Alpha Psi. Avocations: golf, skiing, tennis. Real property. Office: Hazel & Thomas PC 3110 Fairview Park Dr Ste 1400 Falls Church VA 22042-4503

**GOLDSAMT, BONNIE BLUME,** lawyer; b. N.Y.C., July 31, 1946; d. Frank and Evelyn (Tobias) Blume; m. Jay S. Goldsamt, June 25, 1967; children: Seth, Kathryn, Deborah. BA, Sarah Lawrence Coll., 1967; MA, NYU, 1971; JD, Rutgers U., 1979. Bar: N.J. 1979, N.Y. 1990, U.S. Dist. Ct. N.J. 1979, U.S. Supreme Ct. 1987. Law sec. to judge Superior Ct. N.J. Chancery Family Part, Newark, 1979-80; assoc. Cole, Schotz, Bernstein, Meisel and Forman, Rochelle Park, N.J., 1980-82; asst. county counsel govtl. affairs Essex County, Newark, 1982-84; assoc. Rose & DeFuccio, Hackensack, N.J., 1984-87; sr. assoc. Steven Morey Greenberg, Hackensack, 1987-89; pvt. practice Hackensack, 1989—, Verona, 1992—; speaker Women Bankers Assn., Hackensack, 1982, Seton Hall Law Sch., Newark, 1983; appointed mem. family practice com. N.J. Supreme Ct., 1990-92, ct. apptd. contract arbitrator, Essex County, 1996—, Task Force on Alternative Work Arrangements, State Bar Assn. Dispute Resolution Com.; asst. clin. prof. law Seton Hall Law Sch. Bd. dirs. Downtown Bklyn. Planning Bd., 1974-75; committeeperson Essex County Com., 1987-96; ward co-chair Dem. County Com., Montclair, 1988-91, ward chair, 1993-96; fundraiser, speaker, chair women's issues No. N.J. Clinton Campaign; fin. com. Clinton/Gore campaign; chair women's issues Women's Coalition for Clinton/Gore; surrogate speaker Clinton for Pres. campaign; active Dem. Nat. Conv., Women's Leadership Forum. Named one of Bklyns. Women of the Yr., Bklyn. NOW, 1974. Mem. ABA, Am. Arbitration Assn. (arbitrator 1990—), Essex and Bergen County Comml. Bar Assns. (trustee Bergen County 1988-97, com. mem.), N.J. State Bar Assn. (chair dispute resolution sect. 1999—, family law exec. com., chair child abuse protocol com., elder law com., state bar family law exec. com., exec. com., judicial adminstrn. programming, pro bono com., sec. gen. coun. 1996-97), N.J. Assn. of Profl. Mediators (2nd vice-chair), Women Lawyers in Bergen County (pres. 1985-87, trustee Jean Robertson Found. 1987-88, dir. at large 1987-88, Merit award 1987), N.J. Assn. Profl. Mediators (sec. bd. dirs. 1997-98), Bergen County Bar Found. (trustee 1990-95), Nat. Acad. Elder Law Attys., Acad. of Family Mediators (practitioner mem.), Hadassah. Democrat. Jewish. Avocations: reading, travel. General practice, Family and matrimonial, Alternative dispute resolution. Office: Ste 14 1 University Plaza Dr Hackensack NJ 07601-6207 also: 25 Pompton Ave Verona NJ 07044-2934

**GOLDSCHMID, HARVEY JEROME,** law educator; b. N.Y.C., May 6, 1940; s. Bernard and Rose (Braiker) G.; m. Mary Tait Seibert, Dec. 22, 1973; children: Charles Maxwell, Paul MacNeil, Joseph Tait. AB, Columbia U., 1962, JD, 1965. Bar: N.Y. 1965, U.S. Supreme Ct. 1970. Law clk. to judge 2d Circuit Ct. Appeals, N.Y.C., 1965-66; assoc. firm Debevoise & Plimpton, N.Y.C., 1966-70; asst. prof. law Columbia U., 1970-71, assoc. prof., 1971-73, prof., 1973-84, Dwight prof. law, 1984—, founding dir. Ctr. for Law and Econ. Studies, 1975-78; of counsel Arnold & Porter, N.Y.C., 1995-98; cons. in field to pub. and pvt. orgns.; mem. planning and program com. 2d Cir. Jud. Conf., 1982-85; reporter 2d Cir. Jud. Conf. Evaluation Com., 1980-82, 88-89; mem. legal adv. com. N.Y.S.E., 1997-98, chmn. subcom. on corp. governance; gen. counsel Securities and Exch. Commn., 1998—. Author( with others) Cases and Materials on Trade Regulation, 1975, 4th edit., 1997; editor: (with others) Industrial Concentration: The New Learning, 1974, Business Disclosure: Government's Need to Know, 1979, The Impact of the Modern Corporation, 1984. Chmn. bd. advisors program on philanthropy and the law NYU Sch. Law, 1992-94; bd. dirs. Nat. Ctr. on Philanthropy and the Law, 1996—; nat. bd. visitors U. Ariz. Coll. Law, 1996—; bd. dirs. Greenwall Found., 1996—, vice chair, 1999—. Fellow Am. Bar Found.; mem. ABA (task force on lawyers polit. contbrns. 1997-98), Am. Law Inst. (reporter part IV, duty of care and the bus. judgment rule, corp. governance project 1980-93), N.Y. State Bar Assn., Assn. Bar City N.Y. (v.p. 1985-86, chmn. exec. com. 1984-85, chmn. com. on antitrust and trade regulation 1971-74, nominating com. 1986-87, com. on the 2d century, chmn. com. on securities regulation 1992-95, chmn. audit com. 1988-96, chmn. com. on corp. takeover legislation 1985-86, 88-92, treas., mem. exec. com. 1996-98), Assn. Am. Law Schs. (chmn. sect. antitrust and econ. regulation 1976-78), Am. Assn. Internat. Commn. Jurists (sec.-treas., bd. dirs.), Century Assn., Riverdale Yacht Club (bd. dirs. 1987-90), Phi Beta Kappa. Office: Securities and Exch 450 5th St NW Washington DC 20001-2739

**GOLDSMITH, GERALD P.,** lawyer; b. N.Y.C., Feb. 28, 1930; s. Lazarus A. and Sylvia Lila (Goldfarb) G.; m. Leda Carroll, Aug. 2, 1957; children: Leslie Sara, Nicole. Student, Bradley U., 1948-52; LLB, N.Y. Law Sch., 1958. Bar: N.Y. 1959, U.S. Dist. Ct. (so. and ea. dists.) N.Y. 1963, U.S. Supreme Ct. 1970, U.S. Ct. Appeals (2d cir.) 1984. Pvt. practice, N.Y.C., 1959—. Author: BOATFIXIT, 1959. Pres. young men's divsn. Grand St. Boys Assn., 1954-59; group leader Univ. Settlement House, 1954-59; chmn. Anti-Defamation League, Bronx County, N.Y., 1962-64, co-chmn. met. coun., 1964-66; founder, former mem. exec. com., former chmn. legal and comty. affairs Benjamin Franklin Reform Dem. Club, Bronx County; founder Riverdale YM-YWHA, Bronx, 1967; chmn., v.p. bd. trustees, former sec., chmn. various coms., pro bono atty.; candidate for Bronx County Civil Ct., 1974, 75; campaign chmn., organizer, legal advisor to local, city, state and nat. elections; bd. dirs., pro bono legal advisor Children's Day Treatment Ctr. and Sch., 1980; com. chmn. Assn. Bronx Comty. Orgns. Mem. ATLA, Jewish Trial Lawyers Assn., N.Y. State Trial Lawyers Assn., Bronx County Bar Assn., Rotary Club of Chinatown (pres. 1995-96, exec. com., chmn. various coms., Paul Harris fellow). Democrat. Avocations: boating, jazz. Admiralty, Personal injury, Election. Office: 299 Broadway Rm 1820 New York NY 10007-1901

**GOLDSMITH, HOWARD MICHAEL,** lawyer; b. Atlantic City, Mar. 22, 1942; s. Leonard M. and Annette (Rothenberg) G.; m. Molly Hartman, Dec. 17, 1943; 1 child, Michael Stephen. BS in Bus., Rider Coll., 1965; JD, Dickinson Sch. Law, 1968. Bar: Pa. 1968, U.S. Dist. Ct. (ea. dist.) Pa. 1969, U.S. Supreme Ct. 1973, U.S. Ct. Claims 1980, U.S. Ct. Appeals (3d cir.) 1982, U.S. Ct. Appeals (fed. cir.) 1988. Prin. Howard M. Goldsmith, P.C., Phila., 1968—; apptd. custody rules com., divorce code rev. com., support guidelines com. Phila. county Ct. Common Pleas, Phila.; procedural rules com. Pa. Supreme Ct., 1997—. apptd. master pro tem to hear custody and support cases Phila. County; lectr. in family law. Bd. dirs. Jewish Cmty. Ctr., Klein Br., press., 1987-90. Fellow Am. Acad. Matrimonial Lawyers, Internat. Acad. Matrimonial Lawyers; mem. ABA (family law sect.), ATLA, Pa. Bar Assn. (family law sect., chair 1997-98), Phila. Bar Assn. (chmn. 1987, past chmn. adoption com., commr. jud. selection and retention commn. 1987), Am. Arbitration Assn., Vidocq Soc., B'nai B'rith. Jewish. Home: 9234 Burbank Rd Philadelphia PA 19115-3414 Office: 7716 Castor Ave Philadelphia PA 19152-3607

**GOLDSMITH, KAREN LEE,** lawyer; b. Bridgeport, Conn., Jan. 10, 1946; d. James Joseph and Marjorie (Crowley) Minto; m. Michael Goldsmith, Oct. 12, 1968 (dec. May 1979); children: Susan Chapman, Pamela S., Neil J.; m. Jeffery S. Hooie, June 13, 1980. AA summa cum laude, Seminole Jr. Coll., 1969; BA summa cum laude, U. Cen. Fla., 1975; JD cum laude, U. Fla., 1978. Bar: Fla. 1979, U.S. Dist. Ct. (mid. dist.) Fla. 1979, U.S. Dist. Ct. (so. and no. dists.) Fla. 1981, U.S. Ct. Appeals (11th cir.) 1981. Assoc. Pitts, Eubanks & Ross P.A., Orlando, Fla., 1978-80; assoc. Dempsey & Slaughter P.A., Orlando, 1980-83, ptnr., 1983; ptnr. Dempsey & Goldsmith P.A., Orlando, 1984-90, Goldsmith & Grout, P.A., Winter Park, Fla., 1990—;

lectr. Interhome '86, Ft. Lauderdale, Fla., 1986—, health care related legal issues various orgns., 1978—; speaker profl. meetings, 1982—; speaker Harborside Healthcare Annual Convention, 1992, 94. Author: Advance Directives in Florida, 1993; sr. editor U. Fla. Law Rev., 1978; contbr. articles to profl. jours. Mem. ABA, Am. Health Care Assn. (legal subcom. 1991-95, chair 1998—, regulatory subcom. 1997—, lectr. ann. symposium), Fla. Bar Assn. (chmn. state law week 1985, 86), Orange County Bar Assn. (Outstanding Chmn. 1982), Nat. Health Lawyers Assn. (speaker), Nat. Conv. Med. Dirs. Assn. (speaker 1992), Fla. Assn. Dirs. Nursing (speaker 1992, 96), Fla. Health Care Assn. (various seminars), U. Ctrl. Fla. Alumni Assn. (bd. dirs., exec. com., sec. 1988), Am. Soc. Assn. Execs., Order of Coif, Phi Kappa Phi. Roman Catholic. Administrative and regulatory, General civil litigation, General corporate. Office: Goldsmith & Grout PA 2180 N Park Ave Ste 100 Winter Park FL 32789-2358

**GOLDSMITH, KENNETH JAMES,** lawyer; b. Pasadena, Calif., Nov. 14, 1967; s. John Vincent Sr. and Kathleen McDonald Goldsmith. BA in English, U. Md., 1990, cert. East Asian studies, 1990; JD, U. Balt., 1993. Bar: Md. Legal intern hon. James S. MacAuliffe Jr. Montgomery County Cir. Ct., Rockville, Md., 1991; law clk. Md. State Pub. Defender, Towson, 1992; clin. prosecutor Howard County State's Attys. Office, Ellicott City, Md., 1992-93; staff counsel ABA Criminal Justice Sect., Washington, 1993—; advisor Goldsmith & Assocs., Inc., Bethesda, Md., 1995-98. Editor U. Balt. Law Forum, 1991-93; contbr. articles to profl. jours. leader Appalachia Relief Effort, St. Columba's Episcopal Ch., Washington, 1996, 97, 98; bd. dirs. Transitional Housing Corp., Inc., Washington, 1996-97, Samaritan Ministry Greater Washington, 1998—; mem.-at-large Montgomery County Criminal Justice Coordinating Commn., Rockville, 1998—. Mem. ABA, Montgomery County Bar Assn. Democrat. Episcopalian. Avocations: sailing, martial arts, writing, culinary arts. E-mail: AuSmithEsq@aol.com and goldsmith@staff.abanet.org. Fax: 202-662-1501. Office: ABA Criminal Justice Sect 740 15th St NW Fl 10 Washington DC 20005-1022

**GOLDSMITH, MICHAEL LAWRENCE,** lawyer; b. N.Y.C., Dec. 10, 1962; s. Sheldon and Roslyn Goldsmith; m. Lorraine Bondi, Au. 31, 1986; children: Alexandra, Gavin. BA, NYU, 1983; JD, George Washington U., 1986. Bar: N.Y. 1987, U.S. Dist. Ct. (ea. and so. dists.) N.Y. 1992. Ptnr. Scheich Goldsmith & Drieshpoon, P.C., Richmond Hill, Hicksville, N.Y., 1989—; arbitrator Civil Ct. Queens County, 1993—. Asst. editor Queens County Bar Bull., 1995—; contbr. articles to profl. jours. Mem. Bethpage (N.Y.) State Park Trail Users Com., 1995—; tchr. martial arts Hicksville Sch. Dist., 1997—; student martial arts Twelve Towns YMCA, 1989—. Rudin scholar NYU, 1981-82. Mem. Queens County Bar Assn., John Marshall Lawyers Assn. (bd. dirs. 1993—, sec. 1993-96), South Shore Audubon Soc. (bd. dirs. 1998-99, v.p. 1999—), Kiwanis Club. Avocations: martial arts, birding. General practice, Personal injury, Probate. Office: Scheich Goldsmith et al 10342 Lefferts Blvd S Richmond Hl NY 11419-2012 also: 109 Newbridge Rd Hicksville NY 11801-3908

**GOLDSMITH, RICHARD ELSINGER,** lawyer; b. L.A., Dec. 17, 1933; s. Nat and Ruth (Elsinger) G.; m. Antonia Elisabeth Kunz, Nov. 17, 1967; children: Ruth Elisabeth, Joan Margaret. BA, Harvard U., 1955, JD, 1958; LLM in Tax, NYU, 1965. Bar: Tex. 1958, U.S. Dist. Ct. (we. dist.) Tex. 1961, U.S. Tax Ct. 1967. Mem. Matthews & Branscomb (formerly Matthews, Nowlin, MacFarlane & Barrett), San Antonio, 1960—. Founder, chmn. San Antonio Area Found., 1964, pres., 76-79; pres. Cmty. Guidance Ctr., 1964, 80; pres. United Way San Antonio and Bexar County, 1970-71; co-founder, 1st pres. Half Way House of San Antonio; pres. Jewish Fedn., San Antonio, 1978-79; co-founder Combined Charities Investment Group, 1987, chmn., 1990-99; co-founder, pres. Temple Beth-El Permanent Charities Found., 1988-99. Recipient Donated Legal Svcs. award bus. law section. Tex. Bar Assn. Estate taxation, Estate planning, Taxation, general. Office: Matthews & Branscomb 106 S Saint Marys St Ste 700 San Antonio TX 78205-3692

**GOLDSMITH, STANLEY ALAN,** lawyer; b. N.Y.C., Oct. 18, 1956. AB magna cum laude, Dartmouth Coll., Hanover, N.H., 1977; JD, Vanderbilt U., 1980. Bar: Ohio 1980, U.S. Dist. Ct. (so. dist.) Ohio 1980, Fla. 1983, U.S. Ct. Appeals (6th cir.) 1983, U.S. Dist. Ct. (mid. dist.) Fla. 1984, U.S. Ct. Appeals (11th cir.) 1984, U.S. Supreme Ct. 1990. Assoc. Porter, Wright, Morris & Arthur, Dayton, Ohio, 1980-83; pvt. practice, Sarasota, Fla., 1983—. Mem. ABA, Fla. Bar, Sarasota County Bar Assn. Avocations: swimming, bicycling, travel, cooking. General civil litigation, Contracts commercial, Real property. Office: 1605 Main St Ste 1001 Sarasota FL 34236-5861

**GOLDSMITH, WILLIS JAY,** lawyer; b. Paris, Feb. 21, 1947; came to U.S., 1949; s. Irving and Alice (Rosenfeld) G.; m. Marilynn Jacobson, Aug. 12, 1973; children: Andrew Edward, Helene Sara. AB, Brown U., 1969; JD, NYU, 1972. Bar: N.Y. 1973, U.S. Ct. Appeals (2d cir.) 1975, D.C. 1978, U.S. Ct. Appeals (4th cir.) 1979, U.S. Ct. Appeals (D.C. cir.) 1979, U.S. Supreme Ct. 1980, U.S. Ct. Appeals (6th cir.) 1985, U.S. Ct. Appeals (7th cir.) 1989, U.S. Ct. Appeals (3d cir.) 1991, U.S. Ct. Appeals (5th cir.) 1998. Atty. Dept. Labor, Washington, 1972-74; assoc. Guggenheimer & Untermyer, N.Y.C., 1974-77; assoc. Seyfarth, Shaw, Fairweather & Geraldson, Washington, 1977-79, ptnr., 1979-83; ptnr. Jones, Day, Reavis & Pogue, Washington, 1983—, chmn. labor and employment law practice, 1991—; adj. prof. law Georgetown U., 1988-91; fellow Coll. Labor and Employment Law, 1997—. Contbg. editor Employee Rels. Law Jour., 1983-91; assoc. editor Occupl. Safety and Health Law; mem. editl. adv. bd. Benefits Law Jour., 1991—. Mem. ABA (sect. labor and employment law com. on employee benefits, com. on occupl. safety and health), NYU Ctr. for Labor and Employment Law (bd dirs. 1997—), D.C. Bar Assn., Met. Club (Washington), Kenwood Golf and Country Club (Bethesda, Md.). Democrat. Jewish. Labor, Pension, profit-sharing, and employee benefits. Home: 6409 Elmwood Rd Chevy Chase MD 20815-6621 Office: Jones Day Reavis & Pogue 51 Louisiana Ave NW Washington DC 20001-2113

**GOLDSON, AMY ROBERTSON,** lawyer; b. Boston, Jan. 16, 1953; d. Irving Edgar and E. Emily (Lippman) Robertson; m. Alfred Lloyd Goldson, June 29, 1974. BA magna cum laude, Smith Coll., 1973; JD, Cath. U., 1976. Bar: D.C. 1976, U.S. Dist. Ct. D.C. 1976, U.S. Ct. Appeals (D.C. and 4th cirs.) 1976. Atty. office of chief counsel, tax ct. litigation div. IRS, Washington, 1976-77; assoc. Smothers, Douple, Gayton & Long, Washington, 1977-82; sole practice Washington, 1982—. Gen counsel Congl. Black Caucus Found., Inc., Washington, 1977—. Mem. ABA, Nat. Bar Assn., Washington Bar Assn., D.C. Bar Assn., Phi Beta Kappa. Democrat. Roman Catholic. Club: Links (Washington). Avocations: swimming, skiing, tennis. General practice, Entertainment, General corporate. Home and Office: 4015 28th Pl NW Washington DC 20008-3801

**GOLDSTEIN, ABRAHAM SAMUEL,** lawyer, educator; b. N.Y.C., July 27, 1925; s. Isidore and Yetta (Crystal) G.; m. Ruth Tessler, Aug. 31, 1947 (dec. Feb. 1989); children: William Ira, Marianne Susan; m. Sarah Feidelson, May 7, 1995. B.B.A., CCNY, 1946; LL.B., Yale U., 1949, M.A. (hon.), 1961; M.A. (hon.), Cambridge (Eng.) U., 1964; LL.D. (hon.), N.Y. Law Sch., 1979, DePaul U., 1987. Bar: D.C. bar 1949. Law clk. to judge U.S. Ct. Appeals, 1949-51; partner firm Donohue & Kaufmann, Washington, 1951-56; mem. faculty Yale Law Sch., 1956—, prof. law, 1961—, dean, 1970-75, Sterling prof. law, 1975—; vis. prof. law Stanford Law Sch., summer 1963; vis. fellow Inst. Criminology, fellow Christ's Coll. Cambridge U., 1964-65; faculty Salzburg Seminar in Am. Studies, 1969, Inst. on Social Sci. Methods on Legal Edn., U. Denver, 1970-72; vis. prof. Hebrew U., Jerusalem, 1976, UN Asia and Far East Inst. for Prevention Crime, Tokyo, 1983, Tel Aviv U., 1986; cons. Pres.'s Com. Law Enforcement, 1967; mem. Conn. Bd. of Parole, 1967-69, Conn. Commn. Revise Criminal Code, 1966-70; mem. of the Conn. Planning Com. on Criminal Adminstrn., 1967-71; sr. v.p. Am. Jewish Congress, 1977-84, mem. exec. com., 1977-89, gov. coun., 1989-94. Author: The Insanity Defense, 1967, The Passive Judiciary, 1981, (with L. Orland) Criminal Procedure, 1974, (with J. Goldstein) Crime, Law and Society, 1971; contbr. numerous articles and revs to profl. jours. Served with AUS, 1943- 46. Guggenheim fellow, 1964-65, 75-76, Am. Acad. Arts & Scis., 1975—. Office: Yale Law Sch PO Box 208215 New Haven CT 06520-8215

**GOLDSTEIN, BENJAMIN,** lawyer, law educator; b. Phila., Dec. 2, 1949; s. Harry and Bella (Hochman) G. BS in Education, Temple U., 1971; JD, John Marshall U., Chgo., 1975. Bar: Ill. 1975, N.J. 1976, U.S. Ct. Appeals (7th cir.) 1975, (3rd cir.) 1978; U.S. Supreme Ct. 1978. Law clerk Cir. Ct. Cook County, Chgo., 1973-75; pvt. practice Chgo., 1975-76, Voorhees, N.J., 1976-80; atty., shareholder Maressa, Goldstein, Birsner, Patterson, Drinkwater & Oddo, Berlin, N.J., 1980—; solicitor Zoning Bd., Waterford, N.J., 1987-90, Township Com., Winslow, N.J., 1987-90; solicitor for mayor and coun. City of Lavallette (N.J.), 1995—; adj. prof. law Camden County Coll., Blackwood, N.J., 1984—; arbitrator Superior Ct. N.J., Camden, 1990—; cons. Camden County Dem. Com., Runnemede, N.J., 1988-89; solicitor Kennedy Hosp. Sys., Stratford, N.J., 1994—. Author: (chpt.) Opening Statements, 1995; speaker in field. Mem. ATLA, N.J. Trial Lawyers Assn., ABA, N.J. State Bar Assn. (mock trial judge 1994—). Avocations: flying, scuba diving, boating, horseback riding, piano. Personal injury, Health, Professional liability. Office: Maressa Goldstein Birsner Patterson Drinkwater & Oddo 191 W White Horse Pike Berlin NJ 08009-2021

**GOLDSTEIN, BRIAN ALAN,** lawyer, physician; b. Bronx, N.Y., Oct. 24, 1959; s. Stanley Irving and Hortense (Silverstein) G.; m. Eva Rubinstein, June 19, 1988; children: Ariel Petra, Adam Izak. MD, Ctr. Tech. U., Santo Domingo, Dominican Republic, 1980; JD magna cum laude, SUNY Buffalo, 1995. Diplomate Am. Bd. Surgery; bar: N.Y. 1996, U.S. Dist. Ct. (we. dist.) N.Y., U.S. Dist. Ct. (ea. dist.) Mich., 1997 (we. dist.) 1999. Resident N.Y. Meth. Hosp., Bklyn., 1981-86; surgeon Hadassah Med. Ctr., Jerusalem, 1988-91; cardiothoracic surgeon Tygerburg Hosp., Capetown, South Africa, 1992; assoc. Michael Doran & Assocs., Buffalo, 1994—; instr. surgery Hebrew U., Jerusalem, 1989-91, U. Stellenbosch, South Africa, 1992. Contbr. articles to profl. jours. Fellow Interam. Coll. Physicians and Surgeons; mem. ABA, Internat. Soc. Cardiothoracic Surgeons, Assn. Trial Lawyers Am., N.Y. State Bar Assn., Erie County Bar Assn. (health law com. 1996). Personal injury, Federal civil litigation. Office: Michael Doran & Assocs 1234 Delaware Ave Buffalo NY 14209-1430

**GOLDSTEIN, BRUCE A.,** lawyer; b. Buffalo, May 19, 1945; s. Lew and Sally (Freedman) G.; m. Betsy S. Robins, May 30, 1968; children: Lisa, Dena. BS, SUNY, Buffalo, 1967; JD, U. Mich., 1972. Bar: N.Y. 1973, U.S. Dist. Ct. (we. dist.) N.Y. 1973, U.S. Claims Ct., U.S. Ct. Appeals (2d cir.), U.S. Supreme Ct. 1980. Asst. county atty. Erie County Atty.'s Office, Buffalo, 1973-75; asst. dist. atty. Erie County Dist. Atty., Buffalo, 1975-77; assoc. Lipsitz, Green et. al., Buffalo, 1977-80; ptnr. Serotte, Reich & Goldstein, Buffalo, 1980-85, Bouvier, O'Connor, Buffalo, 1985—; assoc. prof. law SUNY, Buffalo, 1987—. Author: Legal Rights of Persons with Disabilities: An Analysis of Federal Law, 1989—. Mem. Leadership Buffalo, N.Y. State Developmental Disabilities Planning Coun., Albany, 1986-96; bd. dirs. Alexander Graham Bell Assn. for the Deaf, pres., 1994-96. Named Citizen of the Yr., Buffalo News, 1989, Lifetime Membership award Nat. PTA, Brotherhood/Sisterhood award NCCJ, 1993. Mem. N.Y. State Bar Assn., Erie County Bar Assn. Education and schools, Health, Personal injury. Office: Bouvier O'Connor 350 Main St 1400 Main Place Tower Buffalo NY 14202-3714

**GOLDSTEIN, CHARLES ARTHUR,** lawyer; b. N.Y.C., Nov. 20, 1936; s. Murray and Evelyn V. Goldstein; m. Judith Stein, Sept. 29, 1962 (div. 1982); 1 child, Deborah Ruth; m. Carol Sager, Nov. 10, 1990 (div. 1995). A.B., Columbia U., 1958; J.D. cum laude, Harvard U., 1961. Bar: N.Y. 1962. Law clk. U.S. Ct. Appeals (2d cir.), 1961-62; assoc. Fried, Frank, Harris, Shriver & Jacobson, N.Y.C., 1962-69; ptnr. Schulte Roth & Zabel, N.Y.C., 1969-79; ptnr. Weil, Gotshal & Manges, N.Y.C., 1979-83, counsel, 1983-85; ptnr. Shea & Gould, N.Y.C., 1985-94, Sutherland, Asbill & Brennan, N.Y.C., 1994-95; counsel Squire, Sanders & Dempsey, N.Y.C., 1996—; lectr. Columbia U. Law Sch. Gen. counsel to Citizens Budget Commn., 1980-87; mem. Temp. Commn. on City Fins., 1975-77; mem. Gov.'s Task Force on World Trade Ctr. Mem. Am. Coll. Real Estate Lawyers. Republican. Real property. Home: 220 E 65th St New York NY 10021-6620 Office: Squire Sanders & Dempsey 350 Park Ave New York NY 10022-6022

**GOLDSTEIN, DEBRA HOLLY,** judge; b. Newark, Mar. 11, 1953; d. Aaron and Erica (Schreier) Green; m. Joel Ray Goldstein, Aug. 14, 1983; children: Stephen Michael, Jennifer Ann. BA, U. Mich., 1973; JD, Emory U., 1977. Bar: Ga. 1977, Mich. 1978, D.C. 1978, Ala. 1984. Tax analyst atty. Gen. Motors Corp., Detroit, 1977-78; trial atty. U.S. Dept. Labor, Birmingham, Ala., 1978-90; U.S. adminstrv. law judge office hearing and appeals Social Security Adminstrn., Birmingham, 1990—; new judge faculty U.S. adminstrv. law judges Social Security Adminstrn., 1991, 93—; co-chair Pluralism Think Tank, 1999. Mem. editorial bd. The Ala. Lawyer, 1994—, The Addendum, 1995—. Chairperson Women's Coordinating Bur., Birmingham, 1983-85; active United Way, Birmingham, 1983, 87, 90, 98, mem. vis. allocation team, 1998, active adult edn. Temple Beth-El, bd. dirs., 1993-94, co-chair workshop initiative group, 1993-94; program chmn. Sisterhood, 1987-88, adminstrv. v.p., 1989-90, 90-92; scholarship chairperson Nat. Coun. Jewish Women, 1986; mem. steering com. Birmingham Bus. and Profl. Women Fedn., 1987-88, 95—; leader Brownie Troop, 1992—, bd. dirs. Cahaba Girl Scout Coun., 1996—; mem. Cherokee Bend Sch. Com., 1992-98; mem. edn. com. Temple Emanu-El, 1995-97; mem. Leadership for Diversity Initiative, 1995-96, Leadership Birmingham, 1997-98, Women's Network, 1997—. Mem. ABA, Ga. Bar Assn., D.C. Bar Assn., Mich. Bar Assn., Birmingham Bar Assn. (mem. law day com., scholarship com. 1994—, mem. women's liaison and project coms. 1998-99, bd. dirs. women's sect. 1999—, chmn. Long Range Planning com. 1999—), Ala. Bar Assn., Zonta (v.p. 1983-84, bd. dirs. 1988-89, 90-92, intercity chmn. 1995, co-pres. 1996-98), B'nai B'rith Women (chair S.E. region 1984-86, counselor 1986-88, Women's Humanitarian award 1981), Hadassah (local bd. dirs. 1979-83, adminstrv. v.p. 1989-90, 90-92). Jewish. Office: Social Security Adminstrn 1910 3rd Ave N Birmingham AL 35203-3585

**GOLDSTEIN, GLENN ALAN,** lawyer; b. Albany, N.Y., Feb. 12, 1954; s. Martin Arthur and Luisa (Bike) G.; m. Susan Feign, May 27, 1984; children: Lewis Aaron, Daniel Maurice. BS, Cornell U., 1976; JD, Villanova U., 1979. Bar: Pa. 1979. Asst. exec. dir., counsel AFTRA, SAG, Phila., 1979-80, exec. dir., counsel, 1980-87; pvt. practice Phila., 1987—; guest lectr. Cornell Law Sch., 1992-95. Bd. govs. Phila. Music Alliance, 1996—. Named one of Best Lawyers in Phila., Phila. Mag., 1999. Mem. NATAS (bd. dirs. Phila. chpt. 1980-87, treas. 1988-90, counsel Phila. chpt. 1995—, pres. Phila. chpt. 1997-99), NARAS. Jewish. Avocations: music, travel. Entertainment.

**GOLDSTEIN, HOWARD SHELDON,** lawyer; b. Apr. 22, 1952; s. Jerome Harold and Goldie G.; m. Amy Ruth, 1980. BA, CUNY, 1974; JD, Bklyn. Law Sch., 1977. Bar: N.Y. 1978, U.S. Dist. Ct. (so. and ea. dists.) N.Y. 1978. Assoc. Loew & Cohen, Esquires, N.Y.C., 1976-82, ptnr., 1982-87; ptnr. Cohen & Goldstein, N.Y.C., 1988—. Contbr. articles to profl. jours. Mem. N.Y. State Bar Assn. (family law com., legis. com.), N.Y. County Lawyers Assn., Nassau County Bar Assn., N.Y.C. Bar Assn. (legal referral svcs.). Republican. Jewish. Family and matrimonial, General corporate, General civil litigation. Office: Cohen & Goldstein Esqs LLP 32 Broadway Rm 1700 New York NY 10004-1670

**GOLDSTEIN, IRWIN MELVIN,** lawyer; b. Bklyn., Oct. 17, 1944; s. Oscar D. Goldstein and Berdie (Grossman) Schames; m. Maxine B. Herzog, June 14, 1970; children: Oliver M., Evan D., Shawn M. BA, Bklyn. Coll., 1964; JD, St. John's U., Bklyn., 1967; LLM, NYU, 1968. Bar: N.Y. 1968, Fla. 1978. Ptnr. Reynolds, Richards, LaVenture, Hadley & Davis, N.Y.C., 1970-81; mgr. Ira Sarinsky & Co., P.C., N.Y.C., 1982-84, M. Sternlieb & Co., P.C., Hackensack, N.J., 1984-85; ptnr. Edward Isaacs & Co., N.Y.C., 1985—. Personal income taxation, Estate taxation, Probate. Home: 96 Margaret Ave Lawrence NY 11559-1826

**GOLDSTEIN, JACK CHARLES,** lawyer; b. Ft. Worth, May 11, 1942; s. Bennie Harrison and Rae (Shanblum) G.; m. Leslie P. Silber, July 3, 1965; children: Jason Brent, Jill Paige. BSME, Purdue U., 1964; JD with honors, George Washington U., 1968. Bar: Ill. 1968, Tex. 1968, D.C. 1969, U.S. Dist. Ct. D.C. 1969, U.S. Dist. Ct. (no. and so. dists.) Tex. 1971, U.S. Dist. Ct. (we. dist.) Tex. 1974, U.S. Dist. Ct. (ea. dist.) Tex. 1975, U.S. Dist. Ct. (no. dist.) Miss. 1980, U.S. Dist. Ct. (no. dist.) Calif. 1992, U.S. Dist. Ct. (so. dist.) Calif. 1993, U.S. Ct. Appeals (5th cir.) 1970, U.S. Ct. Appeals (7th cir.) 1974, U.S. Ct. Appeals (2d cir.) 1975, U.S. Ct. Appeals (11th cir.) 1981, U.S. Ct. Appeals (fed. cir.) 1982, U.S. Patent and Trademark Office 1968, U.S. Supreme Ct. 1972. Patent examiner U.S. Patent and Trademark Office, Washington, 1964-67; patent advisor Office Naval Rsch., Silver Spring, Md., 1967-68; law clk. to judge U.S. Ct. Customs and Patent Appeals, Washington, 1968-69; adj. prof. S. Tex. Coll. of Law, Houston, 1974-84; atty. Arnold, White & Durkee, Houston, 1969-97; v.p. The Whitaker Corp., Wilmington, Del., 1998, pres., 1998—; mem. intellectual property adv. bd. U. Houston Law Ctr., 1991—; mem. adv. com. U.S. Ct. Appeals for Fed. Cir., Washington, 1984-92; copyright adv. com. Libr. of Congress, Washington, 1981-82; mem. adv. bd. Patent, Trademark & Copyright Jour., Washington, 1978—. Bd. editors The Intellectual Property Law Strategist, 1994—; contbr. articles to profl. publs. Bd. dirs. Found. For A Creative Am., Washington, 1989-94. Recipient Alumni Svc. award George Washington U., 1985, G. Rose Meml. Comp. award John Marshall Law Sch., 1986, Jour. Finalist award Tex. Bar Found., 1981; Jacob Burns award for extraordinary svc. to the Law Sch., George Washington U., 1996. Fellow Tex. Bar Found. (life), Houston Bar Found. (charter life); mem. ABA (chair, sect. intellectual property law 1992-93), FBA, Am. Intellectual Property Law Assn. (pres. 1988-89), Fed. Cir. Bar Assn. (pres. 1987-88), Copyright Soc. U.S.A. (trustee 1979-82), Bar Assn. D.C., D.C. Bar, Houston Intellectual Property Law Assn. (pres. 1979-80, Pres.'s award 1988), State Bar Tex. (chair intellectual property law sect. 1988-89, Chair's award 1992), Coll. State Bar Tex., Internat. Assn. Protection Indsl. Property, Intellectual Property Owners Assn. (bd. dirs. 1998—), Internat. Intellectual Property Assn. (exec. com. 1996—), Assn. Former CAFC Law Clks. and Tech. Advisors (pres. 1979-80), George Washington Law Alumni Assn. (bd. dirs. 1980-84, 93—), Patent and Trademark Office Soc., Order of Coif, Pi Tau Sigma. Patent, Trademark and copyright, Intellectual property. Home: 116 Yardley Pl Hockessin DE 19707-8917 Office: The Whitaker Corp Ste 450 4550 New Linden Hill Rd Wilmington DE 19808-2952

**GOLDSTEIN, JAMES BRUCE,** lawyer; b. Boston, May 16, 1968; s. Robert J. and Barbara A. (Amdur) G.; m. Dawn L. Koren, Oct. 13, 1996. BA, Cornell U., 1990; JD, Boston U., 1993. Bar: Mass. 1994, D.C. 1996, U.S. Dist. Ct. Mass. 1995. Legal intern Tobacco Products Liability Project, Boston, 1991, U.S. House Subcom. on Telecom., Washington, 1992; assoc. atty. Spicer Buchbinder & Assocs., Waltham, Mass., 1994-95; contract atty. Jones, Day, Reavis & Pogue, Washington, 1995, Reed, Smith, Shaw & McClay, McLean, Va., 1995-96; asst. regulatory counsel Nextel Comm., Reston, Va., 1996—; mem. cable TV adv. com. Town of Burlington (Mass.), 1993-94. Mem. Fed. Comm. Bar Assn. Democrat. Jewish. Avocations: baseball, basketball, Harry S. Truman. Communications, Administrative and regulatory, Labor. Home: 9214 Chanute Dr Bethesda MD 20814-3943

**GOLDSTEIN, JOSEPH,** law educator; b. Springfield, Mass., May 7, 1923; s. Nathan E. and Anna (Ginsberg) G.; m. Sonja Lambek, Aug. 3, 1947; children: Joshua, Anne, Jeremiah, Daniel. AB, Dartmouth Coll., 1943; PhD, London Sch. Econs., 1950; LLB, Yale U., 1952, postgrad., 1968. Bar: Va. 1953. Law clk. to judge U.S. Ct. Appeals D.C., 1952-53; acting asst. prof. Stanford Law Sch., 1954-56; Russell Sage resident, vis. scholar Harvard Law Sch., 1955-56; assoc. prof. Yale Law Sch., 1956-59, prof., 1959—, Justus S. Hotchkiss prof. law, 1968, Walton Hale Hamilton prof. law, sci. and social policy, 1970, prof. Child Study Center, Med. Sch., 1976—, Sterling prof. law, 1978-93, Sterling prof. law emeritus, 1993—, Ruttenberg profl. lectr. in law, 1993—; exec. sec., research dir. Gov. Conn. Prison Study Com., 1956-57; cons. devel. neighborhood legal service Community Progress, Inc., New Haven, 1963-64; mem. U.S. atty. gen. com. poverty and adminstrn. criminal justice, 1962-63; cons. Legal Assistance Assos., Inc., New Haven, 1964-73; pres., bd. dirs. Friends of Legal Services South Central Conn., 1981—; bd. dirs. Vera Inst. Justice, 1966—, Sigmund Freud Archives, 1968—; mem. life scis. and social policy com. NRC, 1968; on legal services Office Econ. Opportunity, 1965, Council on Biology in Human Affairs, Salk Inst., 1969. Author: The Government of a British Trade Union, 1953, (with others) Criminal Law, 2d edit., 1962, The Family and the Law, 1965, Psychoanalysis, Psychiatry and Law, 1967, Crime, Law and Society, 1971, (with Anna Freud and Albert J. Solnit) Beyond the Best Interests of the Child, 1973, 2d edit., 1979, Criminal Law-Theory and Process, 1974, Before the Best Interests of the Child, 1979, (with Burke Marshall and Jack Schwartz) The My Lai Massacre and Its Coverup: Beyond the Reach of Law, 1976, (with Anna Freud, Albert J. Solnit and Sonja Goldstein) In the Best Interests of the Child, 1986, The Intelligible Constitution, 1992, (with Albert J. Solnit and Sonja Goldstein) The Best Interest of the Child-The Least Detrimental Alternative, 1996. Served with AUS, 1943-46. Fulbright scholar, 1949-50; law fellow U. Wis., 1958; Fulbright sr. lectr., 1973; Guggenheim fellow, 1982. Fellow Am. Acad. Arts and Scis.; mem. New Haven Legal Assistance Assn.

**GOLDSTEIN, KENNETH B.,** lawyer; b. Bklyn., Sept. 16, 1949; s. Nathan and Isabella (Solow) G. BA, Tulane U., 1973, JD, 1974; postdoctoral, Fordham U., 1979. Bar: N.Y. 1977, U.S. Dist. Ct. (so. and ea. dist.) N.Y. 1980, U.S. Ct. Appeals (D.C. cir.) 1981. Gen. mgr., v.p. Middletown (N.Y.) Window Cleaning Co., Inc., 1974; tchr. various schs., Middletown and Chester, N.Y., 1975-77; asst. sr. v.p., dir. mktg. Saks Fifth Ave, N.Y.C., 1977-79; sr. asst. dist. atty. Orange County, Goshen, N.Y., 1979-81; assoc. Zola & Zola, N.Y.C., 1981-83, Freedman, Weisbein & Samuelson P.C., Garden City, N.Y., 1983-85, Jaffe & Asher, N.Y.C., 1985-91, Raoul Lionel Felder P.C., N.Y.C., 1991—; bd. dirs. Middletown Window Cleaning Co., Inc. Bd. dirs. New Orleans Jazz and Heritage Found., 1972-74. Named one of Outstanding Young Men in Am., 1980. Mem. ABA, N.Y. State Bar Assn., Middletown Bar Assn., Orange County Bar Assn., Order of DeMolay. Republican. Jewish. Avocations: swimming, art, dance, opera. Family and matrimonial, Landlord-tenant, State civil litigation. Home: 145 E 35th St Apt 2me New York NY 10016-4121 Office: Raoul Lionel Felder PC 437 Madison Ave New York NY 10022-7001

**GOLDSTEIN, MARTIN EDWARD,** lawyer; b. St. Louis, Nov. 23, 1934; s. Jack L. and Lillian M. (Rich) G.; m. Judith Braunstein, July 12, 1959; children: Sue Ellen, Jay A. BSChemE, U. Ill., 1955; JD with honors, George Washington U., 1964. Bar: N.Y. 1965, D.C. 1965, U.S. Ct. Appeals (2d cir.) 1967. Chem. engr. GE, Waterford, N.Y., 1955-60; patent trainee GE, Washington, 1960-64; ptnr. Kane, Dalsimer, Kane, Sullivan, Kurucz & Goldstein, N.Y.C., 1965-73, McAulay, Fields, Fisher, Goldstein & Nissen, N.Y.C., 1973-89, Darby & Darby, N.Y.C., 1989—. Contbr. articles to profl. jours. Adv. bd. United Homes for Aged Hebrews, New Rochelle, N.Y., 1984-94; active New Rochelle Planning Bd., 1985-94. 2d lt. U.S. Army, 1956. Mem. ABA, N.Y. Patent, Trademark and Copyright Law Assn. (bd. dirs. 1989-92, pres. 1996-97), Am. Intellectual Property Law Assn. (chmn. antitrust com. 1988-94, chmn. publ. com. 1994-96), Assn. of Bar of City of N.Y. (com. on patents 1971-76, 82-85), New Rochelle Bar Assn., Masons (bd. dirs. med. rsch. lab. 1983-91, pres. 1994-97), Order of Coif. Republican. Jewish. Patent, Trademark and copyright, Intellectual property. Office: Darby & Darby 805 3rd Ave Fl 27 New York NY 10022-7557

**GOLDSTEIN, MARVIN MARK,** lawyer; b. Bklyn., Jan. 24, 1944; s. Abraham and Regina (Winkler) G.; m. Linda Ann Sinkoff, Aug. 4, 1969; 1 child, Randal Ian. BS, Cornell U., 1966; JD, Boston U., 1969. Bar: N.Y. 1969, N.J. 1972. Corp. labor counsel Gen. Cable Corp., N.Y.C., 1970-72; assoc. Grotta, Oberwager & Glassman, Newark, N.J., 1972-76; ptnr. Grotta, Glassman & Hoffman P.A., Roseland, N.J., 1976-98; resident, ptnr. Proskauer Rose LLP, Newark, N.J., 1999—. Asst. sec. Hackensack (N.J.) Med. Ctr., 1987-93, mem. exec. com., 1987-96; bd. trustees United Jewish Community Bergen County, N.J., 1984-90. Mem. ABA (chmn. subcom. fair labor standards act labor law sect.), N.J. Bar Assn. (chmn. adminstrv. law sect. 1987-89, legis. liaison labor law sect. 1986). Labor. Office: Proskauer Rose LLP 1 Newark Ctr Fl 18 Newark NJ 07102-5283

**GOLDSTEIN, MICHAEL B.,** lawyer; b. N.Y.C., Sept. 29, 1943; s. Isaac and Betty (Friedman) G.; m. Jinny M. Loewenthal, Dec. 18, 1966; 1 child, Eric Loren. BA in Govt., Cornell U., 1964; JD, NYU, 1967. Bar: N.Y. 1967, Ill. 1974, D.C 1978. Spl. asst., dep. mayor Office of Mayor, N.Y.C., 1965-66, asst. city adminstr., dir. univ. rels., 1969-72; dir. N.Y.C. Urban Corps, 1966-69; assoc. vice chancellor for urban and govtl. affairs, assoc. prof. urban scis. U. Ill., Chgo., 1972-78; mem. Dow, Lohnes & Albertson PLLC, Washington, 1978—; practice leader Edn. Inst. Pub. Policy and Govt. Rels.; chmn. task force on pub. policy Commn. on Higher Edn. and Adult Learner Am. Coun. on Edn.; mem. bd. advisors Stanford Forum for Coll.

Financing. Contbr. articles to profl. texts and jours. Pres. Nat. Ctr. for Pub. Svc. Internship Programs, 1975-77; bd. dirs., officer Washington Ctr. Internships and Acad. Seminars, 1977—; bd. dirs. and gen. counsel Washington Ballet, 1978—; bd. dirs. Greater Washington Rsch. Ctr., 1982-96, Chgo. Urban Corps, 1972-75, Am. Assoc. Higher Edn., 1998—; trustee Fielding Inst., 1989-94, 98—; trustee, chmn. fin. com. Mt. Vernon Coll., 1991-96; dir. Am.-Russian Cultural Cooperation Found., 1995—; bd. visitors Mt. Vernon Coll., 1996-98, WETA, 1997—, bd. dirs. Am. Assn. Higher Edn., 1998—. Wall St. Jour. Newspaper Fund fellow, 1963, Loeb fellow Harvard U., 1972. Mem. ABA (chmn. edn. law com. 1991-92), Edn. Task Force, D.C. Bar, 1999—, FBA (co-chmn. edn. grants com. 1985-86, 91-92), Edn. Task Force, D.C. Bar, 1999—, Nat. Assn. Coll. and Univ. Attys. (mem. ctrl. office com. 1986-88, vice chmn. pvt. bar com. 1989-90), Nat. Soc. Internships and Exptl. Edn. (pres. 1972), Am. Assn. Higher Edn. (dir. 1997—). Democrat. Jewish. Education and schools, Administrative and regulatory, Legislative. Office: Dow Lohnes & Albertson 1200 New Hampshire Ave NW Washington DC 20036-6802

**GOLDSTEIN, MICHAEL GERALD,** lawyer; b. St. Louis, Sept. 21, 1946; s. Joseph and Sara G. (Findelstein) G.; m. Ilene Marcia Ballin, July 19, 1970; children: Stephen Eric, Rebecca Leigh. BA, Tulane U., 1968; JD, U. Mo., 1971; LLM in Taxation, Washington U., 1972. Bar: Mo. 1971, U.S. Dist. Ct. (ea. dist.) Mo. 1972, U.S. Tax Ct. 1972, U.S. Ct. Appeals (8th cir.) 1974, U.S. Supreme Ct. 1976. Atty. Morris A. Shenker, St. Louis, 1972-78; ptnr. Lashly, Caruthers, Baer & Hamel and predecessor, St. Louis, 1979-84, Suelthaus & Kaplan, P.C. and predecessors, St. Louis, 1974-91; pres., CEO 1st Fin. Resources, 1999—; ptnr., chmn. dept. tax & estate planning Husch & Eppenberger; adj. prof. tax law Washington U. Sch. Law; bd. dirs. Anchor Floor Co., Maritz Inc., 1986-89, Connector Castings Inc., 1971-96; mem. planning com. Mid-Am. Tax Confs., chmn. ALI/ABA Tax Seminar; lectr. taxation field. Author: BNA Tax Mgmt. Portfolios; contbr. numerous articles to profl. jours. and publs. Bd. dirs. Jewish Family and Children's Svc. St. Louis, 1980—, pres., 1986-88; bd. dirs. Jewish Fedn. of St. Louis; trustee United Hebrew Temple, 1986-88; grad. Jwish Fedn. St. Louis Leadership Devel. Coun.; co-chmn. lawyers divsn. Jewish Fedn. St. Louis Campaign, 1981-82, Leadership St. Louis, 1988-89. Capt. USAR, 1970-78. Fellow Am. Coll. Tax Counsel, Am. Coll. Trust and Estate Counsel; mem. ABA (chmn. tax seminar, group editor newsletter for taxation sect.), Am. Law Inst., Mo. Bar Assn., Bar Assn. Met. St. Louis, St. Louis county Bar Assn. Corporate taxation, Estate taxation, State and local taxation. Home: 201 Yacht Mischief Newport Beach CA 92660 Office: 695 Town Center Dr Fl 7 Costa Mesa CA 92626-1924

**GOLDSTEIN, PETER DOBKIN,** lawyer; b. Bklyn., Apr. 12, 1953; s. Louis B. and Martha (Dobkin) G.; m. Marge W. Lilienthal, Aug. 28, 1982; children: Jenna Lilienthal, Daniel Reid. BA cum laude, Brandeis U., 1974; MS, Harvard U., 1977; JD magna cum laude, Boston Coll., 1980. Bar: Conn. 1980, N.Y. 1981, U.S. Dist. Ct. Conn. 1981, U.S. Dist. Ct. (so. and ea. dists.) N.Y. 1983, U.S. Ct. Appeals (2d cir.) 1982, U.S. Ct. Appeals (3d cir.) 1990, U.S. Supreme Ct. 1990. Assoc. Cummings & Lockwood, Stamford, Conn., 1980-82, Bond and Camhi, N.Y.C., 1982-84; ptnr. Dorsey & Whitney, N.Y.C., 1988-92; br. chief divsn. enforcement SEC, N.Y.C., 1992-97; dep. gen. counsel Gabelli Asset Mgmt. Inc., Rye, 1997—. Editor Am. Jour. Law and Medicine, 1979-80. Federal civil litigation, Securities, State civil litigation. Office: One Corporate Ctr Rye NY 10580

**GOLDSTEIN, ROBIN,** lawyer; b. Bklyn., Sept. 23, 1957; s. Jerome and Edna (Cohen) G. SB, MIT, 1979, M of City Planning, 1980; JD, Union U., 1983. Bar: N.Y. 1984, U.S. Patent Office 1984, U.S. Dist. Ct. (ea. and so. dists.) N.Y. 1985, Mass. 1992, U.S. Supreme Ct. 1992, Ct. of Appeals for Fed. Cir. 1992. Patent clk. Internat. Paper Co., N.Y.C., 1982; assoc. Blum, Kaplan, Friedman, Silberman & Beran, N.Y.C., 1983; patent atty. Digital Equipment Corp, Maynard, Mass., 1984-86; patent counsel SONY Corp Am., Park Ridge, N.J., 1986-91; of counsel Schiller & Kusmer, Boston, 1991-93; pvt. practice Palo Alto, Calif., 1993-95, 97—; sr. counsel Apple Computer, Inc., Cupertino, Calif., 1995-97; gen. counsel Newton, Inc., 1997; talk show host Stas. KSCO-KOMY, 1998—. Mem. ABA, Am. Intellectual Property Law Assn. (mem. group 220 oversight com.), N.Y. Patent Law Assn., Sigma Phi Epsilon. Patent, Trademark and copyright, Computer. Home: 4842 National Ave San Jose CA 95124-4919

**GOLDSTEIN, SHELDON MARK,** lawyer; b. Brookline, Mass., Mar. 29, 1943; s. Morris Joseph and Adele (Bulian) G.; 1 child, Brooke Osinoff. BA in History, Syracuse U., 1964; LLB, Boston U., 1967. Bar: Mass. 1968, N.Y. 1970. Assoc. Winer, Abrams & Hershfang, Boston, 1967-68; asst. counsel Israel Discount Bank Ltd., N.Y.C., 1969-70; assoc. Finley, Kumble, Underberg et al, 1970-76; sr. ptnr. Meltzer, Lippe, Goldstein & Schlissel, P.C., Mineola, N.Y., 1976—; lectr. in law Adelphi U., Garden City, 1975-77. V.p. bd. trustees North Shore Synagogue, Syosset, N.Y., 1985-92; bd. dirs. Friends of the Arts, 1992—; v.p. Greater N.Y. Bd. Dirs., Jewish Nat. Fund, 1998—. Mem. Mass. Bar Assn., N.Y. State Bar Assn., Assn. of Bar of City of N.Y., Nassau County Bar Assn. Avocations: tennis, snow skiing, classical music, golf. Real property, Land use and zoning (including planning). Office: Meltzer Lippe Goldstein & Schlissel PC 190 Willis Ave Mineola NY 11501-2693

**GOLDSTEIN, STUART WOLF,** lawyer; b. Buffalo, N.Y., Sept. 9, 1931; s. Joseph and Esther (Wolf) G.; m. Myra Saft Stuart, June 1960 (dec. Aug. 1981); children: Jeffrey, Jonathan, Meryl; m. Nancy Baynes Lux, 1993. Student, U. Buffalo, 1949-52, JD, 1955; postgrad., U. Va., 1956. Bar: N.Y. 1956, Fla. 1974, Ariz. 1977, U.S. Supreme Ct. 1960, U.S Dist. Ct. (we. dist.) N.Y. 1956, U.S. Ct. Mil. Appeals 1957, U.S. Ct. Appeals (2d cir.) N.Y., 1978, U.S. Dist. Ct. Ariz. 1981. Sole practice Buffalo, 1960-79, 82-85, Phoenix, 1980-82, 85—. Pres., founder Cystic Fibrosis Found., Buffalo, 1960; fund-raiser United Fund, United Jewish Appeal; pres. Boys League; active Erie County Spl. Task Force on Energy, Buffalo, 1978. 1st lt. JAG, U.S. Army, 1956-60. Fellow Ariz. Bar Found.; mem. ATLA, Ariz. State Bar Assn., N.Y. Trial Lawyers Assn., Erie County Trial Lawyers, Ariz. Trial Lawyers Assn. (Ariz. real property sect.), N.Y. State Bar Assn., Fla. Bar Assn., Am. Arbitration Assn., Maricopa County Bar Assn., Buffalo Skating Club, Curling Skating Club (legal counsel). Avocations: swimming, jogging. General practice, Personal injury, General civil litigation. Office: 2700 N 3rd St Ste 2010 Phoenix AZ 85004-4602

**GOLDSTEIN, SUSAN TERRY,** lawyer, writer; b. N.Y.C., Jan. 6, 1954; d. Frank and Henriette Goldstein; m. Gerald Michael Panter, June 23, 1989 (div. 1993). BA, U. Conn., 1975; JD, U. Toledo, 1977. Bar: Ohio, 1978, Calif., 1979. Assoc. atty. Harold Rostow, Beverly Hills, Calif., 1979-82, Simon Taub, Beverly Hills, 1982-89; pvt. practice Beverly Hills, 1989—. Author: The Smart Divorce, 1998, Coming Out, 1998. Mem. L.A. County Bar Assn., Beverly Hills Bar Assn. Avocations: tennis, travel, writing. Home: 2650 Bronholly Dr Los Angeles CA 90068-2331 Office: 9401 Wilshire Blvd Ste 1100 Beverly Hills CA 90212-2924

**GOLDSTEN, ROBERT EMANUEL,** lawyer, investor; b. Charlottesville, Va., Oct. 8, 1916; s. Joseph and Rebecca S. (Shapero) B.; m. Janice F. Wasserman, Nov. 30, 1979; children by previous marriage: Douglas Kahn, Ina Lee. BS in Commerce, U. Va., 1937, LLB, 1940. Bar: Va. 1938, D.C. 1941. Ptnr. Goldsten Bros. Developers & Builders, Washington, 1941-72; pres. Gen. Mortgage Corp., Washington, 1948-66, Vero Beach (Fla.) Yacht Basin, Inc., 1957-71, Devel. Funding Corp., Washington, 1972-74; v.p. Allied Fin. Corp., Silver Spring, Md., 1950-58, World Wide Airlines, Burbank, Calif., 1960-62; pres., CEO McLean (Va.) Savs. & Loan Assn., 1977-80; dir. McLean Fin. Corp., 1981-87; chmn. U.S. Mortgage Credit Corp., 1983-87, Allied Protective Sys. Inc., 1981-88; pres. Gen. Funding Corp., Washington, 1998—; vis. lectr. real estate mgmt. Am. U., 1950-57. Pres., Brotherhood, Washington Hebrew Congregation, 1955-56; treas., bd. dirs. Washington Area Coun. on Alcoholism and Drug Abuse, 1971-77, Carl G. Jung Fund of Washington, 1976-79; co-founder Washington Inst. Natural Medicine, 1998. Recipient award for outstanding contbn. to success of Home Builders Met. Washington, 1966, Spl. Beautification award City of Alexandria (Va.), Disting. Svc. award Washington Area Coun. Alcoholism and Drug Abuse, 1977. Mem. U. Va. Alumni Club Washington, Indian Spring Club, Woodmont Country Club, Tower Club, Boca Rio Golf Club, Univ. Club, B'nai B'rith. Democrat. Home and Office: 2561 Del Lago Dr Fort Lauderdale FL 33316-2303 also: 3134 Ellicott St NW Washington DC 20008-2025

**GOLDSTON, DAVID B.,** lawyer; b. Oakland, Calif., Oct. 28, 1951. AB, U. Chgo., 1973; JD, George Washington U., 1977. Bar: D.C. 1977, Ohio 1982. Assoc. Arent, Fox, Kintner, Plotkin & Kahn, Washington, 1977-82; with TRW, Inc., Cleve., 1982-91, v.p., asst. gen. counsel, 1991—. Trustee Rainbow Children's Mus., Cleve., 1997—, Cleve. Scholarship Program, Inc., 1985—, Citizens League Rsch. Inst., Cleve., 1993—. Office: TRW Inc 1900 Richmond Rd Cleveland OH 44124-3760

**GOLDSTONE, MARK LEWIS,** lawyer; b. Phila., Apr. 12, 1959; s. George Ronald and Jacqueline Suzanne (Yentis) G.; m. Mindy Ann Lieberman, Nov. 10, 1984. BA, Lafayette Coll., 1981; postgrad., Tel Aviv (Israel) U., 1982; JD, Temple U., 1984. Bar: Pa. 1985, D.C. 1985, Md. 1991. Fgn. affairs and def. researcher Mondale-Ferraro Campaign, Washington, 1984; legal intern Senator Joseph R. Biden Jr., Washington, 1985; pvt. practice Washington, 1985—; gen. counsel London Fog Corp., Eldersburg, Md., 1990-94; corp. counsel, asst. sec. London Fog Corp., Eldersburg, 1994-95; instr. Inst. for Legal Studies, Arlington, Va., 1988. Contbg. author: Almanac of the Unelected, 1988; contbr. articles to profl. jours. and mags. Pro bono lawyer various peace, justice and social welfare orgns., Washington, 1985—; vol. lawyer Ams. for Harkin, 1991-92. Mem. ABA, Pa. Bar Assn., Nat. Lawyers Guild (bd. dirs. D.C. chpt.), D.C. Bar Assn., Md. Bar Assn., Supreme Ct. Bar Assn. Criminal, General corporate, Constitutional. Home and Office: 9419 Spruce Tree Cir Bethesda MD 20814-1654

**GOLDWEITZ, JULIE,** lawyer. Assoc. counsel Reed Publishing USA. Office: 275 Washington St Newton MA 02458-1646

**GOLEMON, RONALD KINNAN,** lawyer; b. Atlanta, Tex., Nov. 22, 1938; s. William Layton and Avis (Bogle) G.; m. Jacqueline Alice Burst, Sept. 2, 1966; children: Donald Brent, Jennifer Alice. BS in Indsl. Mgmt. Engring., U. Okla., 1961; LLB, U. Tex., 1967. Bar: Tex. 1967, U.S. Ct. Appeals (5th cir.) 1970, U.S. Dist. Ct. (so. dist.) Tex. 1968, U.S. Dist. Ct. (we. dist.) Tex. 1981, U.S. Dist. Ct. (no. dist.) 1986. Engr. asst. Tex. Water Pollution Control Bd., Austin, 1964-67; assoc. Keys, Russell, Watson & Seaman, Corpus Christi, Tex., 1967-71; ptnr. Keys, Russell, Watson & Seaman, 1971-73, Brown McCarroll & Oaks Hartline, Austin, 1974—; mng. ptnr. Brown McCarroll & Oaks Hartline, 1989-94. Contbg. author The Southwestern Legal Foundation, 40th Annual Institute on Oil and Gas Law and Taxation, 1989, The Southwestern Legal Foundation, 43rd Annual Institute on Oil and Gas Law and Taxation, 1992; contbr articles to profl. jours. Alt. mem. RCRA permit adv. com. U.S. EPA, 1983; mem. Gov.'s Hazardous Waste Task Force, 1984-85; v.p. St. Stephen's Sch. PTA, 1985-86, pres., 1986-87; mem. cmty. adv. bd. Ronald McDonald House, Austin, 1990—. Mem. ABA (mem. standing com. membership & liaison 1997—, mem. market rsch. task force 1995-96, chmn. sect. natural resources, energy and environ. law 1994-95, chmn.-elect 1993-94, vice-chmn. 1992-93, mem. coun. liaison environ. group 1989-91, chmn. air quality com. 1986-89, vice chmn. 1982-86), State Bar Tex. (chmn. environ. law sect. 1971-72), Tex. Mining and Reclamation Assn. (dir. 1988—), Travis County Bar Assn., U. Tex. Law Alumni Assn. (pres. 1984-85, mem. exec. bd. 1984-86). Avocations: hunting, skiing, golf. Environmental, Administrative and regulatory. Office: Brown McCarroll & Oaks Hartline 111 Congress Ave Ste 1400 Austin TX 78701-4043

**GOLICK, TOBY,** law educator, legal services administrator; b. Boston, Apr. 9, 1945; d. Albert David and Sara (Sharaf) G.; widower; children: Benjamin Taylor, Samuel Taylor. BA, Columbia U., 1966, JD, 1969. Bar: N.Y. 1969. Mng. atty. Queens (N.Y.) Legal Svcs., 1969-70; atty. Columbia Ctr. on Social Welfare Policy, N.Y.C., 1970-71; sr. atty. Legal Svcs. for Elderly, N.Y.C., 1972-74, 76-85; clin. prof. Yeshiva U. Cardozo Law Sch., N.Y.C., 1985—; dir. Cardozo Bet Tzedek Legal Svcs., N.Y.C., 1985—. Recipient Eleanor Roosevelt award State of N.Y., 1986, Disting. Svc. award Brookdale Ctr. on Aging, N.Y.C., 1998. Mem. N.Y. State Bar Assn., Assn. Bar City N.Y. Home: 54 Morningside Dr New York NY 10025-1740 Office: Yeshiva U Cardozo Law Sch 55 5th Ave New York NY 10003-4301

**GOLIN, CHARLES,** lawyer; b. Phila., Mar. 3, 1924; s. Harry and Mazie Golin; m. Edith Grace Yoffe, June 18, 1950; children: Jonathan L., David W. BS in Bus. Adminstrn., Ohio State U., 1947; JD, Widener Coll., 1976. Bar: Pa., Fla. From gen. mgr. to pres. Lancaster (Pa.) Packing Co., 1947-80; ptnr. Golin, Haefner & Bacher, Lancaster, 1972—. With U.S. Army, 1943-46. Mem. Elks. Republican. Jewish. Avocation: boating. General civil litigation, General corporate, Probate. Office: Golin Haefner & Bacher 135 E King St Lancaster PA 17602-2803

**GOLIS, PAUL ROBERT,** lawyer; b. San Francisco, Sept. 25, 1954. BA with high distinction, Calif. State U., Long Beach, 1977; JD, Syracuse U., 1981. Bar: Fla. 1984, U.S. Dist. Ct. (so. dist.) Fla. 1985. Assoc. Russell L. Forkey, P.A., Ft. Lauderdale, Fla., 1984-85, Josias & Goren, P.A., Ft. Lauderdale, 1985-88; sr. trial atty. State of Fla. Dept. Transp., Ft. Lauderdale, 1988-90; asst. county atty. Palm Beach County, West Palm Beach, Fla., 1990-91; assoc. Scott, Royce, Harris, Bryan & Hyland, Palm Beach Gardens, Fla., 1991-93, Watterson, Hyland & Klett, Palm Beach Gardens, 1993-98; sole practice, Boca Raton, Fla., 1998—; featured spkr. on ethics Nat. Bus. Inst., West Palm Beach, 1999. Bd. dirs. Aid to Victims of Domestic Assault, Inc., 1990-99, v.p., 1993-97, pres. 1997-99, mem. adv. bd., 1999—. Mem. ABA, Fla. Bar Assn. (eminent domain com. 1989—), Palm Beach County Bar Assn. (vice chmn. environ., land use and eminent domain CLE com. 1993-95, chmn. 1995-99, jud. rels. com. 1996—). State civil litigation, Condemnation. Office: 1200 N Federal Hwy Ste 200 Boca Raton FL 33432-2813

**GOLLAHER, MERTON G,** lawyer; b. New London, Conn., Dec. 31, 1962; s. Merton G. Sr. and Jane I. G.; m. Diane Hessinger, Nov. 6, 1993. BA, Amherst Coll., Amherst, Mass., 1984; JD with honors, U. Conn., Hartford, 1991. Bar: Conn. Assoc. scientist Pfizer Ctrl. Rsch., Groton, Conn., 1984-91; atty. Wiggin & Dana, New Haven, Conn., 1991—; dir., officer Manatech, Inc., New Haven, Conn., 1994—. Mem. ABA, NHLA/AAHA, Conn. Health Lawyers Assn. Republican. Roman Catholic. Avocations: golf, sailing. Health, General corporate, Mergers and acquisitions. Office: Wiggin & Dana 1 Century Tower New Haven CT 06510-7013

**GOLLINGER, STUART HOWARD,** lawyer, tax consultant; b. New Haven, Conn., Feb. 3, 1942; s. David and Gertrude (Laginsky) G.; m. Irva Stahl, Feb. 20, 1966 (div. Mar. 1977); children: Geri Lynn, Brad Cory; m. Jeri F. McNamara, June 28, 1998. BA, Colby Coll., 1963; JD, Suffolk U., 1966; ML in Taxation, U. Miami, Coral Gables, Fla., 1968. Bar: Conn. 1966, U.S. Tax Ct. 1983, U.S. Dist. Ct. Conn. 1984. Legis. intern Congressman Giaimo, Washington, 1965; ct. clk. New Haven County Ct., 1968; tax acct. Price, Waterhouse & Co., N.Y.C., 1969; tax atty. Olin Corp., Stamford, Conn., 1969-79, assoc. tax counsel, 1979-83; sole practice Westport, Conn., 1983—; bd. dirs. Westport Ctr. for the Arts, 1984—; lectr. various orgns. on taxation and pension planning, 1984—. contbr. several articles to profl. jours. Mem. Rep. Town Meeting, Westport, 1985. Mem. Conn. Bar Assn. Tax Com., Westport Bar Assn., Westport C. of C. Jewish. Lodge: Rotary. Avocations: photography, weight training, oil painting. Home: 11 Branford Ct Avon CT 06001-4505 Office: State Conn Dept Revenue Svcs 25 Sigourney St Hartford CT 06106-5001

**GOLOMB, BARRY,** lawyer; b. N.Y.C., Sept. 28, 1924; s. Joseph and Rose (Sigal) G.; m. Barbara G. Meisner, June 17, 1948 (dec. 1991); children: Wesley, Ruth.; m. Adeline Jacobowitz Forleiter, Sept. 19, 1992. AB, Harvard U., 1948, JD cum laude, 1951. Bar: N.Y. 1951, U.S. Supreme Ct. 1957, Claims Ct. 1952, U.S. Ct. Appeals (2d cir.) 1953, U.S. Dist. Ct. (so. dist.) N.Y. 1952, U.S. Dist. Ct. (ea. dist.) N.Y. 1967, U.S. Dist. Ct. (no. dist.) N.Y. 1992, Tax Ct. 1956. Assoc. Wasserman Behr & Shagan, N.Y.C., 1951-55; ptnr. Wasserman & Shagan, N.Y.C., 1956-62, Shagan, Edwinn & Golomb, N.Y.C., 1962-79; sr. litigator Otterbourg, Steindler, Houston & Rosen, N.Y.C., 1979-81, Max E. Greenberg, Cantor & Reiss, N.Y.C., 1981-87, Blodnick, Pomeranz, Reiss, Schultz & Abramowitz, N.Y.C., 1988; ptnr. Goddard & Blum, N.Y.C., 1989—; village atty., corp. counsel, Village Ardsley, N.Y., 1959-64, acting village justice, 1977-83; asst. dist. atty. Westchester County, N.Y., 1959-64. Chmn. N.Y. State Boating Adv. Coun., Albany, 1992—, mem. 1980—; past pres., exec. com. man, counsel Nat. Boating Fedn., 1975—; past pres. Ardsley Rep. Club; former dist. leader Greenburgh Town Rep. Orgn., Ardsley, 1960-75. Jewish. Avocations: boating, music. General civil litigation, Construction, General corporate. Home: 62 Yorkshire Dr # B Cranbury NJ 08512-4725 Office: Goddard & Blum 675 3rd Ave New York NY 10017-5704

**GOLOMB, GEORGE EDWIN,** lawyer; b. Newark, Jan. 28, 1947; s. Max and Elizabeth G.; m. Cynthia Lifson, June 3, 1984. BA, Yale U., 1968; JD, U. Pa., 1972. Bar: N.Y. 1974, N.J. 1977, D.C. 1985, Md. 1985. Law clk. to judge U.S. Dist. Ct. (ea. dist.) N.Y., Bklyn., 1974-76; trial atty. civil div. U.S. Dept. Justice, Washington, 1980-84, 1980-84; sole practice Balt., 1986—. Contbr. articles to profl. jours.; co-author: Federal Trial Guide, Federal Evidence Practice Guide, 1989. Fellow, Hague Acad., 1971, Phelps Assn. fellow, 1967. Mem. Balt. City Bar Assn. (exec. com. mem. 1986-96, 99—), Md. State Bar Assn. (bd. govs. 1995-97, labor and employment law), Md. Inst. for Continuing Profl. (lectr.). Federal civil litigation, State civil litigation. Office: Legg Mason Tower 111 S Calvert St Ste 2700 Baltimore MD 21202-6184

**GOMEZ, ALIRIO,** law and business librarian; b. Bogota, Aug. 28, 1960; s. Uriel and Eduvina Gomez; m. Doris Gomez, Dec. 21, 1985; children: Katherine, Daniel, David. BA in Lib. Sci., javeriana U., 1985; MLS, St. John's U., 1991. Tech. libr. Ministry of Health, Bogota, 1979-86; sys. libr. Narcotics and Drug Rsch., N.Y.C., 1989-91; sys. libr. Milbank, Tweed, Hadley & McCloy, N.Y.C., 1991-96, dir. libr. svcs., 1996—; mktg. cons. Lexis-Nexis, N.Y.C., 1998—. Mem. Law Libr. Assn. N.Y., Law Librs. Assn. of N.Y. (chmn. tech. com. 1993-95). Home: 1423 Rose Ln East Meadow NY 11554-3617 Office: Milbank Tweed Hadley & McCloy 1 Chase Plaza New York NY 10003

**GOMEZ, DAVID FREDERICK,** lawyer; b. Los Angeles, Nov. 19, 1940; s. Fred and Jennie (Fujier) G.; m. Kathleen Holt, Oct. 18, 1977. BA in Philosophy, St. Paul's Coll., Washington, 1965, MA in Theology, 1968; JD, U. So. Calif., 1974. Bar: Calif. 1975, U.S. Dist. Ct. (cen. dist.) Calif. 1975, U.S. Dist. Ct. (ea. dist.) Calif. 1977, Ariz. 1981, US. Dist. Ct. Ariz. 1981, U.S. Ct. Claims 1981, U.S. Ct. Appeals (9th cir.) 1981, U.S. Supreme Ct. 1981; ordained priest Roman Cath. Ch., 1969. Staff atty. Nat. Labor Relations Bd., Los Angeles, 1974-75; ptnr. Gomez, Paz, Rodriguez & Sanora, Los Angeles, 1975-77, Garrett, Bourdette & Williams, San Francisco, 1977-80, Van O'Steen & Ptnrs., Phoenix, 1981-85; pres. David F. Gomez, PC, Phoenix, 1985—; faculty Practicing Law Inst., 1989; instr. contracts law Peoples Coll. Law., L.A., 1975-76, Nat. Lawyers Guild; mem. Missionary Soc. St. Paul the Apostle (Paulist Fathers), 1963-75. Author: Somos Chicanos: Strangers in Our Own Land, 1973; co-author: Advanced Strategies in Employment Law, 1988, Arizona Employment Law Handbook, Vol. 2, 1995. Fellow Ariz. Bar Found.; mem. ABA, Maricopa County Bar Assn., Los Abogados Hispanic Bar Assn., Nat. Employment Lawyer's Assn., Calif. State Bar Assn., Ariz. Employment Lawyers Assn. (bd. dirs. 1996—), Ariz. State Bar Assn. (com. on rules of profl. conduct 1991-97, civil jury instructions com. 1992-94, peer rev. com. 1992—). Democrat. Labor, Federal civil litigation, State civil litigation.

**GOMEZ, IVAN A.,** lawyer; b. Cuba, Sept. 13, 1955; s. Severino and Adelina Gomez. BBA in Acctg., Fla. Internat. U., 1977; JD, Loyola U., 1980; LLM in Taxation, U. Miami, 1984. Bar: Fla. 1980, U.S. Dist. Ct. (so. dist.) Fla. 1980, U.S. Tax Ct. 1980, U.S. Ct. Claims 1980, U.S. Ct. Appeals (5th and 11th cirs.) 1980; CPA, Fla.; bd. cert. tax atty. Trial atty., dist. counsel IRS, 1979; assoc. Wood, Lucksinger & Epstein, Miami, Fla., 1984-86, English, McCaughan & O'Bryan, Fort Lauderdale, Fla., 1986-89; pvt. practice Miami, 1989—. Mem. Cuban Am. Bar Assn., Fla. Bar Assn. (co-chair tax sect. com. on internat. tax, gratuitous transfers 1994-95), South Fla. Tax Litigation Assn., Cuban Am. CPA., Greater Miami C. of C., Latin C. of C. Broward County (past pres.), Interam. Businessmen's Assn. Broward County, Inc. Taxation, general, Contracts commercial, Estate planning. Office: 601 Brickell Key Dr Ste 507 Miami FL 33131-2652

**GOMPERS, JOSEPH ALAN,** lawyer; b. Wheeling, W.Va., Jan. 21, 1924; s. William J. and Rose M. (Wilhelm) G.; m. Patricia Ann Nicholl, Mar. 27, 1951; children: Joseph, John, Ann, Patricia, Timothy, Thomas, James, Matthew, Edward, Mary, Eric. AB, Mount St. Mary's Coll., 1944; JD, U. Va., 1948. Bar: W.Va. 1948, U.S. Dist. Ct. (no. dist.) W.Va. 1948, U.S. Ct. Appeals (4th cir.) 1948. Sr. ptnr. Gompers, McCarthy, Hill & McClure, Wheeling, W.Va., 1948—; pros. atty. Ohio County W.Va., Wheeling, 1953-57; mem. W.Va. House of Dels., 1951-52; fiduciary commr. Ohio County, W.Va., 1961-91. Bd. dirs. 12th St. Garage; past bd. dirs. Am. Legion Home Corp., Wheeling Post #1, Ohio Valley Indsl. and Bus. Devel. Corp., Oglebay Inst., YMCA, Vis. Nursing Assn., Boy Scouts Am., W.Va., W.Va. Alcohol Beverage Control Commn.; mem. athletic com. Cen. Cath. High Sch.; mem. parish coun. St. Michael's Cath. Ch. Mem. ATLA, Nat. Lawyers Guild, W.Va. Trial Lawyers Assn., W.Va. Bar Assn., W.Va. State Bar Assn. (former mem. bd. govs.), Ohio County Bar Assn., Elks, K.C., Am. Legion, VFW, Kiwanis, Cave Club. Republican. Avocation: woodworking. General practice, Probate, Estate planning. Office: Gompers McCarthy & McClure 60 14th St Wheeling WV 26003-3430

**GONDEK, DIANA STASIA,** lawyer; b. Waltham, Mass., Jan. 27, 1948; d. Adolph Joseph and Stasia (Czekanski) G. BA, Duke U., 1970; JD, Boston U., 1973. Bar: Mass. 1973, N.Y. 1974, U.S. Dist. Ct. Mass. 1976, U.S. Supreme Ct. 1978, U.S. Ct. Appeals (1st cir.) 1979. Staff atty. Mass. Dept. Edn., Boston, 1973-75; pvt. practice Boston, 1975—. Author: General Laws of Education Relating to School Committees as of January 1, 1984, Issues and Concerns of Importance to Public School Officials, Vol. 1, 1986, Vol. 2, 1988, Legal Status of Professional Personnel in the Public Schools, 1986; writer The Mass. School Law Digest, 1993—. Mem. ABA, Nat. Sch. Bds. Assn., Coun. Sch. Attys., Mass. Bar Assn. Education and schools. Home: 46 Falconer Ave Brockton MA 02301-5831 Office: 121 Mount Vernon St Boston MA 02108-1104

**GONICK, PETER B.,** lawyer; b. N.Y.C., Aug. 22, 1966; s. Paul and Angela Mary Gonick; m. Edie Anne Adams, Sept. 14, 1996; 1 child, Elena Adams. BS in Econ., U. Pa., 1988; JD, U. Wash., 1995. Bar: Wash. 1995, U.S. Dist. Ct. (we. dist.) Wash. 1998. Legal asst. Ballard Spahr Andrews & Ingersoll, Phila., 1988-89; law clk. justice Rosselle Pekelis Wash. State Supreme Ct., Olympia, 1995-96; staff atty. Pub. Defenders Assn., Seattle, 1996-97; assoc. McKay Chadwell, PLLC, Seattle, 1998—. Notes and comments editor Wash. Law Rev., 1995. Agrl. vol. U.S. Peace Corps, Mbeya II, Zaire, 1990-91; pro bono atty. N.W. Immigration Rights Project, Seattle, 1998. Recipient Judge Lawless Meml. award King County Judges, Seattle, 1993, Criminal Law and Contracts Law award Am. Jurisprudence, 1993. Mem. Wash. State Bar Assn., Wash. Assn. Criminal Def. Lawyers, King County Bar Assn., Delta Theta Phi. Avocations: hiking, running, literature. Criminal. Office: McKay Chadwell PLLC 7201 Columbia Ctr 701 5th Ave Seattle WA 98104-7097

**GONICK, RICHARD S.,** lawyer; b. Phila., Jan. 13, 1948; s. Herman William and Rosalyn (Levick) G.; m. Susan Bogosian, Aug. 26, 1973; children: Sean, Melanie. BA, Pa. State U.; JD, Villanova U. Bar: Mass., Pa., U.S. Dist. Ct. Mass. pres. Salem (Mass.) Bar Assn., 1983-86, Ipswich (Mass.) Bar Assn., 1994-96. With USAR. Mem. Historical Soc. Jewish. Avocations: walking, biking, skiing, hiking, poetry. Bankruptcy, Criminal, Personal injury. Home: 38 Chattanooga Rd Ipswich MA 01938-1510

**GONSON, S. DONALD,** lawyer; b. Buffalo, June 13, 1936; s. Samuel and Laura Rose (Greenspan) G.; m. Dorothy Rose, Aug. 28, 1960; children: Julia, Claudia. A.B., Columbia U., 1958; J.D., Harvard U., 1961; postgrad., U. Bombay, India, 1961-62. Bar: Mass. 1962. With Hale and Dorr, Boston, 1962—, sr. ptnr., 1972—; lectr. Fin. Times (U.K.), Instl. Investors, New Eng. Law Inst., Mass. Soc. C.P.A.s; adj. prof. internat. law Fletcher Sch. Law and Diplomacy Tufts U., 1999—; co-chmn. Speech-Tech., N.Y.C., 1987; instr. in law Boston U., 1963-65, bd. trustees Boston Five Cents Savs. Bank, 1978-83, bd. advisors, 1983-88; adj. prof. internat. law Tufts U. Fletcher Sch. Law and Diplomacy. Chmn. Mass. Comty. Devel. Fin. Corp., 1976-82; pres. Cambridge Ctr. for Adult Edn., 1985-88; bd. dirs. Boston Psychoanalytic Soc. and Inst., 1994—, chair Internat. Law Sect. Boston Bar Assn., Fellow, Am. Bar. Found., 1998—. Fulbright scholar, 1961-62. Mem. ABA, Internat. Bar Assn., Mass. Bar Assn., Boston Bar Assn. (chmn. internat. law sect. 1998—), Harvard Club. General corporate, Mergers and acquisitions,

Private international. Home: 32 Hubbard Park Rd Cambridge MA 02138-4731

**GONYNOR, FRANCIS JAMES,** lawyer; b. Cambridge, Mass., Nov. 6, 1959; s. James Francis and Beverly Joan (Lintz) G.; m. Deborah Lynn Snyder, July 25, 1981; children: Brian Christopher, Caroline Jane, Madeline Marie. AA, U. Fla., 1978, BA, 1980; JD, U. Houston, 1983. Bar: Tex. 1983, U.S. Dist. Ct. (so. dist.) Tex. 1983, U.S. Ct. Appeals (5th cir.) 1983. Assoc. Eastham Watson Dale & Forney, Houston, 1983-88, ptnr., 1988—; mediator Am. Arbitration Assn., 1992. Contbr. articles to profl. jours. Mem. Maritime Law Assn., Houston Bar Assn., Coll. of the State Bar of Tex., Galveston Bay Found. Admiralty, Environmental, Federal civil litigation. Home: 3327 Spring Trail Dr Sugar Land TX 77479-3050 Office: Eastham Watson Dale Forney 808 Travis St Fl 20 Houston TX 77002-5706

**GONYO, JEFFREY MYRON,** lawyer; b. Milw., Mar. 30, 1963; s. Russell Myron and Bonedine Kay (Paulson) G. BBA in Acctg., U. Wis., Milw., 1985; MAcc. in Taxation, U. Wis., Madison, 1987, JD, 1989. Bar: Wis. 1990, U.S. Dist. Ct. (we. and ea. dist.) Wis. 1990, U.S. Tax Ct. 1990, U.S. Claims Ct. 1990, U.S. Ct. Internat. Trade 1990, U.S. Ct. Appeals (7th and Fed. cirs.) 1990; CPA, Ill.; accredited tax adv. Pvt. practice tax law Slinger, Wis., 1990—; teaching asst. acctg. U. Wis., Madison, 1986-87; examination reviewer Continuing Profl. Edn., 1992—. Contbr. articles to profl. jours. Founding mem. United We Stand America, mem. We the People, political campaign cons. and coord., 1994-96; ind. candidate U.S. Congress, 1998. Recipient Am. Jurisprudence award, 1989. Mem. ABA, State Bar of Wis., Wis. Soc. CPAs, Order of the Coif. Independent. Roman Catholic. Private international, Corporate taxation, Personal income taxation. Home and Office: 2668 State Rd 164 Slinger WI 53086-9719

**GONZALES, ALBERTO R.,** state supreme court justice, former secretary of state; b. San Antonio, Tex., Aug. 4, 1955. Student, U.S. Air Force Acad., 1975-77; BA, Rice U., 1979; JD, Harvard U., 1982. Bar: Tex. Ptnr. Vinson & Elkins, LLP, Houston, 1982-95; gen. counsel Gov. George W. Bush, 1995-97; sec. of state State of Tex., 1997-98; justice Supreme Ct of Texas, Austin, TX, 1999—. Trustee Tex. Bar Found., 1996—; mem. Tex. Jud. Dists. Bd., 1996-97; bd. dirs. United Way of Tex. Gulf Coast, 1993-94; pres. Leadership Houston, 1993-94; chair Commn. for Dist. Decentralization of Houston Ind. Sch. Dist., 1994; mem. com. on undergrad. admissions Rice U., 1994; chair Rep. Nat. Hispanic Assembly of Houston, 1992-94; pres. Houston Hispanic Forum, 1990-92; chair adv. com. Tex. Real Estae Ctr., 1989-90; bd. dirs. Big Bros. and sisters, Houston, 1985-91, Cath. Charities, Houston, 1989-93, others. Recipient Commitment to Leadership award United Way, 1993, Hispanic Salute award Houston Metro Ford Dealers, 1989, others; named one of Five Outstanding Young Texans, Tex. Jaycess, 1994, Outstanding Young Lawyer of Tex., Tex. Young Lawyers Assn., 1992. Mem. Houston Bar Assn., State Bar Tex. (bd. dirs. 1992-94). Republican. Office: Supreme Court of Texas PO Box 12248 Austin TX 78711-2248

**GONZALES, DANIEL S.,** lawyer; b. San Antonio, Nov. 10, 1959; s. Sam and Mary Louise (Stewart) G.; m. Mary David McCauley, May 16, 1980 (div. 1983); m. Devon Elaine Cattell, Jan. 1, 1988. BA, U. Notre Dame, 1981; JD, Stanford U., 1984. Bar: Calif. 1986, U.S. Dist. Ct. (no. dist.) Calif. 1986, U.S. Tax Ct. 1987, U.S. Ct. Appeals (9th cir.) 1988, U.S. Dist. Ct. (ea. dist.) Calif. 1990. Trivia game writer Axlon Games, Sunnyvale, Calif., 1984; legal writer Matthew Bender & Co., San Francisco, 1984-86; assoc. Carey & Carey, Palo Alto, Calif., 1986-96, Ferrari, Olsen, Ottoboni & Bebb, San Jose, Calif., 1996-97, Bryant, Clohan, Eller, Maines & Baruh, San Jose, 1997—. Mng. editor Stanford Jour. Internat. Law, 1983-84. Candidate Menlo Park (Calif.) City Coun., 1988; bd. dirs. Page Mill YMCA, Palo Alto, 1993-99, YMCA of the Midpeninsula, 1999—, Project Match, San Jose, 1997—, pres., 1998-99; pres. Menlo Park Dispute Resolution Svc., 1994-95. U. Notre Dame scholar, 1977, Nat. Merit scholar, 1977, scholar Nat. Hispanic Scholarship Bd., 1980. Mem. ABA, San Mateo County La Raza Lawyers (pres. 1994), Santa Clara County Bar Assn. (chmn. minority access com. 1994, chmn. judiciary com. 1995), San Mateo County Bar Assn., Palo Alto Area Bar Assn. Democrat. Avocations: guitar, college football. Real property, Land use and zoning (including planning), General corporate. Office: Bryant Clohan Eller Maines & Baruh 101 Park Center Plz Ste 400 San Jose CA 95113-2218

**GONZALES, EDWARD JOSEPH, III,** lawyer; b. Baton Rouge, Aug. 15, 1950; s. Edward Joseph Jr. and Ruth (Attaway) G.; m. Marear Ann Hathorn, Aug. 20, 1977; 1 child, Edward J. IV. BA, Southeastern La. U., 1975; JD, La. State U., 1982. Bar: La. 1982, U.S. Dist. Ct. (mid. dist.) La. 1985, U.S. Ct. Appeals (5th cir.) 1985, U.S. Ct. Appeals (11th cir.) 1997. Law clk. La. 19th Jud. Dist., Baton Rouge, 1982-83; pvt. practice Baton Rouge, 1983-84; asst. U.S. att. Dept. Justice, Baton Rouge, 1985-95; spl. master La. Ins. Receiverships Office, Baton Rouge, 1995-96; assoc. Shows, Cali & Burns, Baton Rouge, 1997—. Recipient commendations FBI, 1989, 94, U.S. Atty. Gen., 1994, Spl. Achievement awards U.S. Dept. Justice, 1988, 89, 90. Criminal, Administrative and regulatory, General civil litigation. Office: Shows Cali & Burns PO Box 4425 Baton Rouge LA 70821-4425

**GONZALES, RICHARD JOSEPH,** lawyer; b. Tucson, Mar. 5, 1950; s. Diego D. and Helen O. (Olivas) G.; divorced; children: Adrianne, Laura. BA, U. Ariz., 1972, JD, 1975. Bar: Ariz. 1976, U.S. Dist. Ct. Ariz. 1976, U.S. Ct. Appeals 1976, U.S. Supreme Ct. 1993. Asst. pub. defender Pima County Pub. Defenders Office, Tucson, 1976-77; dep. atty. criminal div. Pima County Atty.'s Office, Tucson, 1977-80; ptnr. Gonzales & Villarreal, P.C., Tucson, 1980-96, The Gonzales Law Firm, Tucson, 1997—; assoc. instr. bus. law Pima Community Coll.,Tucson, 1977, criminal law, 1978-80; judge pro tem Pima County Superior Ct., 1983—; magistrate City of South Tucson, 1982-85; spl. magistrate City of Tucson, 1982-85; comn. appellate ct. appointments, 1991-95. Mem. Tucson Tomorrow, 1984-87, Citizen's adv. coun. Sunnyside Sch. Dist., 1986-88; chmn. com. Udall for Congress 2d Congl. Dist., United Way Hispanic Leadership Devel. Program, 1984-85, vice-chmn., 1983-84, chmn., 1984-85; bd. dirs. Girls Club of Tucson, Inc., 1980-81, Teatro Carmen, Inc., 1981-85, Sunnyside Devilaides, Inc., 1982-83, Alcoholism Coun. Tucson, 1982-83, Crime Resisters, 1984-85, La Frontera Ctr., Inc., 1985—, Crime Prevention League, 1985; gen. counsel U. Ariz. Hispanic Alumni; bd. dirs. U. aAriz. Law Coll. Assn., 1984-95, Am.-Israel Friendship League, 1990—, Tucson Internat. Mariachi Conf., 1990—. Named one of Outstanding Young Men of Am. U.S. Jaycee's, 1980; recipient Vol. of Yr. award United Way Greater Tucson, 1985, Cmty. Svc. award Ariz. Minority Bar Assn., 1992, Citizen Svc. award U. Ariz. Hispanic Alumni, 1995. Fellow Ariz. Bar Found.; mem. ABA, Ariz. Bar Assn., Pima County Bar Assn., Assn. Trial Lawyers Am., Ariz. Trial Lawyers Assn. (bd. dirs.), Nat. Orgn. on Legal Problems of Edn., Supreme Ct. Hist. Soc., Univ. Ariz. Alumni Assn. (bd. dirs. 1988-91), Tucson 30, Phi Delta Phi. Democrat. Roman Catholic. Lodge: Optimists (Optimist of Yr. 1981). Personal injury, Criminal, General practice. Office: The Gonzales Law Firm 3501 N Campbell Ave Ste 102 Tucson AZ 85719-2032

**GONZALEZ, ALAN FRANCIS,** lawyer; b. Tampa, Fla., Nov. 28, 1951; s. Frank R. and Marina (Font) G.; m. Hilda Martinez, July 28, 1973 (div. May 1982); 1 child, Adria; m. Yolanda Alvarez, Mar. 28, 1986; 1 child, Carly. BA in Mktg., U. South Fla., 1973; MBA, Samford U., Birmingham, Ala., 1977; JD, Samford U., 1977; LLM, U. Fla., 1978. Bar: Fla. 1977, U.S. Tax Ct. 1977, U.S. Ct. Claims 1978, U.S. Dist. Ct. (mid. dist.) 1977, U.S. Ct. Appeals (5th cir.) 1977, U.S. Ct. Appeals (11th cir.) 1995. Assoc. Salem, Salem, Musial & Morse P.A., Tampa, Fla., 1978-79; ptnr. Gonzalez & Scaglione, Attys. at Law, Tampa, 1979-90; pvt. practice Tampa, 1990-92; ptnr. Sierra, Gustafson & Gonzalez, Tampa, 1992-95; pvt. practice Tampa, 1995—; instr. Royalton Coll., South Royalton, Vt., 1973-74, Rollin Coll., 1993; adj. prof. Ala. Christian Coll., Birmingham, 1975-76, Hillsborough C.C., Tampa, 1978-81; asst. prof. U. Ctrl. fla., 1990-92. Author: (Fla. student pocket accompaniment text) Civil Litigation for the Paralegal, 1992; contbr. articles to profl. jours. Mem. ABA, Fla. Acad. Trial Lawyers, Hillsborough County Bar Assn. Avocations: weight training, tennis. Estate planning, Estate taxation. Home: 10243 Woodford Bridge St Tampa FL 33626-1819

**GONZÁLEZ, CARLOS A.,** lawyer; b. Havana, Cuba, July 24, 1960; s. Jorge A. and Ondina (Santos) G.; m. Marilyn Marvin, Aug. 22, 1988; children: Matthew M., Jordan R. BS, Fla. State U., 1983; MA in Religion, Yale U., 1986; JD, Vanderbilt U., 1989. Bar: Ga. 1989, U.S. Dist. Ct. (no. dist.) Ga. 1991, U.S. Ct. Appeals (11th cir.) 1992, U.S. Dist. Ct. (mid. dist.) Ga. 1993. Law clk. to Judge Harold L. Murphy U.S. Dist. Ct. (no. dist.) Ga., Rome, 1989-91; fed. ct. monitor, spl. master U.S. Dist. Ct. (no. dist.) Ga., Atlanta, 1993—; assoc. Rogers & Hardin, Atlanta, 1992-93; pvt. practice Atlanta, 1993—; ptnr. Evans & Gonzalez, Atlanta, 1997—; cons. in higher edn., 1994—, civil rights, 1996. Fellow Inst. for Ministry, Law and Ethics, Salt Lake City. Mem. ABA, Am. Judicature Soc., Atlanta Bar Assn., Fed. Bar Assn., Phi Delta Phi. Methodist. Federal civil litigation, Civil rights, Education and schools. Home: 3087 Belingham Dr NE Atlanta GA 30345-1574 Office: PO Box 450888 Atlanta GA 31145-0888

**GONZALEZ, EDWARD,** lawyer; b. Rio Piedras, P.R., Dec. 30, 1953; s. Eduardo Gonzalez and Casimira Sanchez. BA, U. Colo., 1976; JD, Georgetown U., 1988, LLM in Taxation, 1991. Bar: D.C., Va., U.S. Tax Ct. 1996, U.S. Dist. Ct. D.C. 1997, U.S. Dist. Ct. (ea. dist.) Va. 1997, U.S. Dist. Ct. Md. 1998. Atty. IRS, Washington, 1988-93, Martinez and Sandoval, Arlington, Va., 1993-94, Grossman and Sandoval, McLean, Va., 1994-96; pvt. practice, Washington and McLean, 1996—; atty. IRS, Washington, 1993-98. Mem. Georgetown U. Jour. Legal Ethics, 1987-88; contbr. articles to profl. jours. Mem. ABA, D.C. Bar Assn., Bar Assn. D.C., Va. State Bar Assn., Hispanic Bar Assn. Taxation, general, Estate planning, Banking. Office: 1400 16th St NW Ste 500 Washington DC 20036-2219 also: 1420 Spring Hill Rd Ste 600 Mc Lean VA 22102-3030

**GONZALEZ, FRANCISCO JAVIER,** lawyer; b. Orlando, Fla., July 19, 1969; s. Ernesto J. and Elvira M. Gonzalez; m. Christina M. Morrissee, Apr. 29, 1995; 1 child, Nicholas Matthew. BS in Journalism and Comm., U. Fla., 1991; JD, Cath. U. Am., 1994. Bar: Fla. Law clk. Legal Svcs. Greater Miami (Fla.), Inc., summer 1995, U.S. Dept. Commerce, Office of Chief Counsel, NTIA, Washington, fall 1995; assoc. atty. J. Patrick Fitzgerald, P.A., Coral Gables, Fla., 1994-97; in-house counsel U.S. Sugar Corp., Clewiston, Fla., 1997—. Dir. bd. Jr. Achievement Palm Beaches, West Palm Beach, Fla., 1997—. Real property, General corporate, Contracts commercial. Office: US Sugar Corp PO Box 1207 Clewiston FL 33440-1207

**GONZALEZ, IRMA ELSA,** federal judge; b. 1948. BA, Stanford U., 1970; JD, U. Ariz., 1973. Law clk. to Hon. William C. Frey U.S. Dist. Ct. (Ariz. dist.), 1973-75; asst. U.S. atty. U.S. Attys. Office Ariz., 1975-79, U.S. Attys. Office (ctrl. dist.) Calif., 1979-81; trial atty. antitrust divsn. U.S. Dept. Justice, 1979; assoc. Seltzer Caplan Wilkins & McMahon, San Diego, 1981-84; judge U.S. Magistrate Ct. (so. dist.) Calif., 1984-91; ct. judge San Diego County Superior Ct., 1991-92; dist. judge U.S. Dist. Ct. (so. dist.) Calif., San Diego, 1992—; adj. prof. U. San Diego, 1992; trustee Calif. Western Sch. Law; bd. visitors Sch. Law U. Ariz. Mem. Girl Scout Women's Adv. Cabinet. Mem. Lawyers' Club San Diego, Thomas More Soc., Inns of Ct. Office: Edward J Schwartz US Courthouse 940 Front St Ste 5135 San Diego CA 92101-8911

**GONZALEZ, JOE MANUEL,** lawyer; b. N.Y.C., Aug. 18, 1950; s. Reinaldo Fabregas and Mary Louise (Cermeno) G.; m. Ruia Jane Whiteside, Dec. 30, 1977; children: Matthew Ray, Jane Marie, Jeffrey Joseph, Joseph Manuel. BA, U. South Fla., 1972; JD, Gonzaga U., 1980; LLM in Taxation, Georgetown U., 1981. Bar: Fla. 1981, U.S. Tax Ct. 1983, U.S. Dist. Ct. (mid. dist.) Fla. 1984, U.S. Ct. Appeals (11th cir.) 1984, U.S. Supreme Ct. 1985. Atty. Gonzaga U. Legal Services, Spokane, Wash., 1980; mng. ptnr. Cotterill, Gonzalez, Hayes & Grantham, Fla., 1981-88, Cotterill & Grantham, Pa., 1982-92, Cotterill, Gonzalez & Grantham, Pa., Pa., 1992-93; prin. Joe M. Gonzalez, P.A., 1993—; atty. Hispanic Def. League, Tampa, Fla., 1982-90. Assoc. editor Gonzaga Law Rev. Spl. Report: Pub. Sector Labor Law, 1980. Mem. Sheriff's Hispanic Adv. Coun., Hillsborough County, Fla., 1982-93, City of Tampa Hispanic Adv. Coun., 1983-93, chmn. 1993—; chmn. citizens adv. com. Hillsborough County Planning Commn., 1988-90; pres. Tampa Hispanic Heritage, Inc., 1985-93; founder Carnavale En Tampa, Inc., 1986-90; master of ceremonies Gasparilla Sidewalk Art Festival, 1988; mem. police chief's adv. com., 1988-93; sec. Hispanic Bus. Inst. Fla., Inc., 1988-93. Mem. ABA, Fla. Bar Assn. (jud. nominating prodedures com. 1988-89), Hillsborough County Bar Assn., Assn. Trial Lawyers Am., Nat. Inst. for Trial Advocacy, Complete Census Count Com., Rotary, Phi Delta Phi. Democrat. Presbyterian. Home: 1708 W Richardson Pl Tampa FL 33606-3227 Office: 304 S Willow Ave Tampa FL 33606-2147

**GONZALEZ, JOSE ALEJANDRO, JR.,** federal judge; b. Tampa, Fla., Nov. 26, 1931; s. Jose A. and Luisa Secundina (Collia) G.; m. Frances Frierson, Aug. 22, 1956 (dec. Aug. 1981); children—Margaret Ann, Mary Frances; m. Mary Sue Copeland, Sept. 24, 1983. B.A., U. Fla., 1952, J.D., 1957; LLD, Nova Southeastern U., 1998. Bar: Fla. 1958, U.S. Dist. Ct. (so. dist.) Fla. 1959, U.S. Ct. Appeals 1959, U.S. Supreme Ct. 1963. Practice in Ft. Lauderdale, 1958-64; claim rep. State Farm Mut., Lakeland, Fla., 1957-58; assoc. firm Watson, Hubert and Sousley, 1958-61, ptnr., 1961-64; asst. state atty. 15th Cir. Fla., 1961-64; cir. judge 17th Cir. Ft. Lauderdale, 1964-78, chief judge, 1969-70; assoc. judge 4th Dist. Ct. Appeals, West Palm Beach; U.S. dist. judge So. Dist. Fla., 1978—, sr. judge, 1996—. Bd. dirs. Arthritis Found., 1962-72; bd. dirs. Henderson Clinic Broward County, 1964-68, v.p., 1967-68. Served to 1st lt. AUS, 1952-54. Recipient Kupferman award Laymen's Nat. Bible Assn., 1991; named Broward County Outstanding Young Man, 1967, one of Fla.'s Five Outstanding Young Men, Fla. Jaycees, 1967, Broward Legal Exec. of Yr., 1978. Mem. ABA, Am. Judicature Soc., Fed. Bar Assn., Fla. Bar Assn., Broward County Bar, Ft. Lauderdale Jaycees (dir. 1960-61), Fla. Blue Key, Sigma Chi (Significant Sig), Phi Alpha Delta. Democrat. Club: Kiwanian (pres. 1971-72). Home: 631 Intracoastal Dr Fort Lauderdale FL 33304-3618 Office: US Dist Ct 205 US Courthouse 299 E Broward Blvd Fort Lauderdale FL 33301-1944

**GONZALEZ, RAUL A.,** state supreme court justice; b. Weslaco, Tex., Mar. 22, 1940; s. Raul G. and Paula (Hernandez) G.; m. Dora Blanca Champion, Dec. 22, 1963; children—Celeste, Jaime, Marco, Sonia. BA in Govt., U. Tex., Austin, 1963; JD, U. Houston, 1966; LLM, U. Va., 1986. Bar: Tex. 1966. Asst. U.S. atty. U.S. Dist. Ct. (so. dist.) Tex., Brownsville, 1969-73; atty. Gonzalez & Hamilton, Brownsville, 1973-78; judge 103d Dist. Ct. Tex., Brownsville, 1978-81, U.S. Dist. Ct. Appeals (13th cir.), Corpus Christi, Tex., 1981-84; justice Tex. Supreme Ct., Austin, 1984-99; of counsel Locke Liddell & Sapp LLP. Bd. dirs. Brownsville Boy's Club, Brownsville Community Devel. Corp., So. Tex. Rehab. Ind. Sch. Dist.; U.S. Recipient Outstanding Performance Rating award Dept. Justice, 1972, Toll fellow, 1987. Mem. Christian Legal Soc., Christian Conciliation Service, ABA, Tex. Bar Found. Lodge: Rotary. Avocations: jogging; racquetball. Home: 10511 River Plantation Dr Austin TX 78747-1125 Office: Locke Liddell & Sapp LLP 100 Congress Ave Ste 300 Austin TX 78701-4042

**GONZALEZ-LECAROZ, J.A.,** lawyer; b. San Juan, P.R., Apr. 13, 1955; s. Juan A. Gonzalez and Josefita A. Lecaroz; m. Iris E. Guzman, Nov. 26, 1980; 1 child, Alanna. AA, U. P.R., Arecibo, 1975; BBA, U. P.R., Rio Piedras, 1977, JD, 1980; LLM, U. Houston, 1994. Bar: P.R. 1980, U.S. Ct. Appeals (1st cir.) 1981, Tex. 1990, U.S. Dist. Ct. (so. and no. dists.) Tex. 1992, U.S. Ct. Appeals (5th cir.) 1992. Assoc. Fiddler, Gonzalez & Rodriguez, San Juan, 1980-81; ind. adjuster Franks & Assocs., Houston, 1982-84; sr. claims examiner Ranger Ins. Co., Houston, 1984-88; atty., claims negotiator Makris, Warren & Brockway, Houston, 1988-92; pvt. practice, Houston, 1992—; instr. Alvin (Tex.) C.C., part-time 1984-88; host radio show on legal affairs Sta. KLVL, Houston. Mem. ABA, ATLA, Am. Translators Assn., Houston Bar Assn. Avocations: researching American film history, reading, travel. Personal injury. Office: 6006 Bellaire Blvd Ste 206 Houston TX 77081-5439

**GONZALEZ-PEREZ, RAMON HORACIO,** lawyer, diplomat; b. San Pedro de Macoris, Dominican Republic, May 13, 1949; parents Am. citizens; s. Ramon Horacio and Mercedes Luisa (Perez) G.; m. Gloria Maria Hernandez, June 27, 1986; children: Ramon Horacio, Maria de Fatima, Patricia Antonia, David Rafael. Licenciate Internat. Scis., U. Nacional Pedro Henriquez, 1972, JD magna cum laude, 1977; LLD magna cum laude, U. Autonoma de Santo Domingo, 1977, PhD, 1977; postgrad., Hague Acad. Internat. Law, 1981. Bar: Dominican Republic 1977, N.Y. 1991. Dist. atty. Judicary, Santo Domingo, Dominican Republic, 1978-80, criminal judge, 1980-83; legal advisor Nat. Coun. for Higher Edn., Santo Domingo, Dominican Republic, 1985-86; resident coord. U.S. Embassy, Santo Domingo, Dominican Republic, 1986-89; assoc. Ortiz, Hernandez & Assocs., Santo Domingo, Dominican Republic, 1989-92; legal cons. Ortiz, Hernandez & Assocs., Albertson, N.Y., 1991—; dir. law sch. Universidad Nacional Pedro Henriquez Urena, Santo Domingo, 1983-85, dean law faculty, 1984-85; legal advisor to nat. lottery administr. Santo Domingo, 1994-95; criminal judge Santo Domingo, 1997—. Author: La Nacionalidad, 1972, La Revocabilidad del Acto Administrativo, 1977, El Estado Como Primera Persona de Derecho Internacional, 1977. Pres. Latin Am. Young Leaders meeting Govt. of Republic of China, Taipei, 1985; participant State Dept. Visitor Program, Washington, 1986. Italian Govt. fellow, 1973, Human Rights Inst. fellow, 1984; UN High Comm. for Refugees internship, Geneva, 1984. Mem. ABA, N.Y. State Trial Lawyers Assn., N.Y. State Bar Assn., Dominican Bar Assn., Club Naco, Masons. Republican. Roman Catholic. Avocations: horse riding, swimming, classical music. General practice, General corporate, Private international. Home: 31 Miles Ave Albertson NY 11507-1607 Office: Ortiz Hernandez & Assocs 15834 90th St Jamaica NY 11414-3112

**GOOCH, ANTHONY CUSHING,** lawyer; b. Amarillo, Tex., Dec. 3, 1937; s. Cornelius Skinner and Sidney Seale (Crawford) G.; m. Elizabeth Melissa Ivanoff, May 27, 1963 (div. Nov. 1983); children: Katherine C., Jennifer C., Melissa G., Andrew E.; m. Linda B. Klein, Nov. 7, 1987. BA, U. of South, 1959; diploma, Coll. of Europe, 1960; JD, NYU, 1963, M in Comparative Law, 1964. Bar: N.Y. 1963. Assoc. Cleary, Gottlieb, Steen & Hamilton, N.Y.C., Paris, Brussels, 1963-72; ptnr. Cleary, Gottlieb, Steen & Hamilton, Rio de Janeiro, 1973-78, N.Y.C., 1978—. Co-author: Loan Agreement Documentation, 1982, 2d edit., 1991, Swap Apreement Documentation, 1987, 2d edit., 1988, Documentation for Derivatives, 1993, Credit Support Supplement, 1995, Documentation for Loans, Assignments and Participations, 1996; articles editor NYU Law Rev., 1962-63. Mem. ABA, Inter-Am. Bar Assn., N.Y. State Bar Assn., Assn. Bar City N.Y., New York County Lawyers Assn., Down Town Assn. Democrat. Episcopalian. Private international, Banking, Contracts commercial. Home: Seven Mine Hill Rd Redding CT 06896-2701 Office: 1 Liberty Plz New York NY 10006-1404

**GOOCH, ROBERT FRANCIS,** lawyer; b. San Bernardino, Calif., May 1, 1918; s. Elmer Nicholas and Genevieve Agnes (Rodczweicz) G.; m. Virginia M. Gerardi, July 26, 1947; children—Patrick, Mary Gooch-Wallis, Teresa Gooch Ross, Melissa Gooch-Stevens. B.A., UCLA, 1939; LL.B., Stanford U., 1942. Bar: Calif. 1946. Sole practice, Hawthorne, Calif., 1946-54, Los Angeles, 1968-84; sr. ptnr. Gooch & Barrett, Hawthorne, 1954-64, Gooch & Jones, Hawthorne, 1965-68, sole practitioner, 1968-83, Gooch & Feingold, Los Angeles, 1984-92; mem. adv. com. Los Angeles Dist. Atty. Office, 1964; mem. arbitration panel Am. Arbitration Assn., Los Angeles, Bd. dirs. St. Anne's Found., Los Angeles, 1951-83, pres., 1971-72. With USAF, 1942-45. Mem. Am. Judicature Soc., ABA, Los Angeles County Bar Assn., Calif. State Bar Assn., Jonathan Club. Republican. Roman Catholic. Estate taxation, Probate, Real property.

**GOODART, NAN L.,** lawyer, educator; b. San Francisco, Apr. 4, 1938. BA, San Jose State U., 1959, MA, 1965; JD, U. of the Pacific, 1980. Bar: Calif. 1980, U.S. Dist. Ct. (ea. dist.) Calif. 1981. Tchr. Eastside Union High Sch., San Jose, Calif., 1960-65; counselor San Jose City Coll., 1965-75; atty. Sacramento, 1981—; speaker numerous seminars throughout no. Calif. and other western states, 1988—. Author: Who Will It Hurt When I Die? A Primer on the Living Trust, 1992 (Nat. Mature Media award 1993), The Truth About Living Trusts, 1995 (Nat. Mature Media award 1996). Judge pro tem Sacramento County Small Claims Ct., 1988-96; instr. continuing edn. of bar Am.'s Legal Ctr., Sacramento, 1992—. Mem. Nat. Acad. Elder Law Attys., Calif. State Bar Assn., Sacramento County Bar Assn. Estate planning, Probate, Estate taxation. Office: 7230 S Land Park Dr Ste 121 Sacramento CA 95831-3658

**GOODE, BARRY PAUL,** lawyer; b. N.Y.C., Apr. 11, 1948; s. Hy and Charlotte (Langer) G.; m. Erica Tucker, Sept. 1, 1974; children: Adam, Aaron. AB magna cum laude, Kenyon Coll., 1969; JD cum laude, Harvard U., 1972. Bar: Mass. 1972, Calif. 1975, Hawaii 1995, U.S. Dist. Ct. Mass. 1972, U.S. Dist. Ct. (no. dist.) Calif. 1975, U.S. Dist. Ct. (ctrl. dist.) Calif. 1983, U.S. Ct. Appeals (9th cir.) 1976, U.S. Ct. Appeals (6th cir.) 1999, U.S. Supreme Ct. 1986. Spl. asst. Sen Adlai E. Stevenson III, Washington, 1972-74; assoc. McCutchen, Doyle, Brown & Enersen, San Francisco, 1974-80, ptnr., 1980—. Co-author: Federal Litigation Guide, 1985. Advisor Gov.'s Com. to Review Water Law, San Francisco, 1979; bd. dirs. Stanford Pub. Interest Law Found., 1979-82; bd. dirs. Coro No. Calif., 1997—. Mem. San Francisco Bar Assn. (exec. com. environ. law sect. 1989-91). Environmental, Federal civil litigation, State civil litigation. Office: McCutchen Doyle Brown & Enersen 3 Embarcadero Ctr San Francisco CA 94111-4003

**GOODE, KENNETH GEORGE,** lawyer; b. Winnsboro, S.C., Aug. 7, 1950; s. Marshall Smith and Doris M. (LeGrand) G.; m. Betty Gail Massey, Dec. 19, 1970; children: Marshall, Taylor, Kenneth Jr. BA in Econs., Bus. Adminstrn., Furman U., 1973; JD, U. S.C., 1976. Bar: S.C. 1976. Assoc. Hyatt & Elliott, Columbia, S.C., 1976-78; sole practice Winnsboro, 1978-85; ptnr. Goode & Mueller, Winnsboro, 1985-93, Kenneth G. Goode & Assoc., Winnsboro, 1993—; atty. Fairfield County, 1980—. Bd. dirs. Council Child Abuse and Neglect, 1981-83, U.S. Selective Service, 1984—, Winnsboro Downtown Devel. Assn., 1986—. Named Boss of Yr., Bus. and Profl. Women Assn., 1981; recipient Merit award Nat. Child Safety Council, 1983. Mem. ABA, S.C. Bar Assn., Assn. Trial Lawyers Am., S.C. Trial Lawyers Assn. Democrat. Clubs: Winnsboro Pine Tree Players (v.p. 1984-86). Lodge: Masons. Avocations: reading, trail riding, sports cars. Personal injury, Criminal, Workers' compensation. Home: 309 Old Camden Rd Winnsboro SC 29180-2306 Office: Goode & Assoc 229 S Congress St Winnsboro SC 29180-1105

**GOODEN, PAMELA JOYCE,** lawyer; b. Tuscaloosa, Ala., Nov. 21, 1954; d. Robert Joseph and Betty Jo (Bullock) G.; m. Johnnie Wade Hope, Apr. 26, 1980 (div. Feb. 1984); m. James Douglas Cook, Aug. 3, 1985; children: Cullen, Connor. BA, Judson Coll., 1975; JD, U. Ala., 1978. Bar: Ala. 1978, U.S. Dist. Ct. (mid. dist.) Ala. 1980, U.S. Dist. Ct. (so. dist.) Ala. 1999, U.S. Ct. Appeals (11th cir.) 1993. Staff atty. Legal Svcs. of Ala., Montgomery, 1978-80; assoc. Segrest & Pilgrim, Montgomery, 1980-82; ptnr. Pilgrim & Gooden, Montgomery, 1983-92; pvt. practice Montgomery, 1992—. Mem. ABA, Ala. Bar Assn., Soroptimist Internat. (2d v.p. 1981-82, 1st v.p. 1984-85, pres. 1985-86, corr. sec. 1989-90), So. States Llama Assn., Alpaca and Llama Show Assn. Baptist. Avocations: camping, hiking, fishing, travel, gourmet cooking, llama farming. Fax: (334) 834-5331. E-mail: gooden@earthlink.net. Family and matrimonial, Administrative and regulatory, General civil litigation. Home: 1510 Meriwether Cir Montgomery AL 36117-3423 Office: 1138 S McDonough St Montgomery AL 36104-5044

**GOODHARTZ, GERALD,** law librarian; b. N.Y.C., Oct. 23, 1938; s. Jack and Anna (Sperling) G.; m. Carol Scialli, Aug. 18, 1969; children: Joanna, Allison. BSCE, CCNY, 1961; MLS, U. So. Calif., 1970. Night reference asst. Assn. Bar of City of N.Y., 1956-61; libr. asst. Cravath, Swaine & Moore, N.Y.C., 1961-65; head libr. Rosenman, Colin, Freund, Lewis & Cohen, N.Y.C., 1965-69, Keatinge & Sterling, L.A., 1969-70, Kaye, Scholer, Fierman, Hays & Handler, N.Y.C., 1970-98; mgr. info. svcs. Broad and Cassel, Orlando, 1998-99; head libr. Brown Raysman Millstein Felder & Steiner LLP, N.Y.C., 1999—; libr. planning cons. Olympic Towers, N.Y.C., 1975; lectr. in field. Mem. ABA, ALA, Am. Assn. Law Librs. (cert.), Law Libr. Assn. Greater N.Y., Assn. Law Librs. of Upstate N.Y., Spl. Librs. Assn., Am. Soc. Info. Scientists, Am. Mgmt. Assn., Assn. Info. Mgrs., Nat. Micrographics Assn. Office: Brown Raysman Millstein Felder & Steiner LLP 120 W 45th St New York NY 10036-4041

**GOODING, DAVID MICHAEL,** lawyer, mediator; b. Jacksonville, Fla., June 10, 1952; s. Marion William and Eunice (Drawdy) G.; m. Cathy Rhoden, Aug. 3, 1974; chidlren: Sara Lynn, John Thomas Gooding. BA, U. Fla., 1974; JD, U. Miami, 1988. Asst. state atty. Office of State Atty., Jacksonville, Fla., 1988-89; assoc. Penland & Penland, P.A., Jacksonville, 1989-92; shareholder Kent, Ridge & Crawford, Jacksonville, 1992-97, Kent, Crawford & Gooding, Jacksonville, 1997—; bd. dirs. Anastasia Advertising Art, Inc., St. Augustine, Fla., 1990-97, Samaritan Counseling Ctr., Jacksonville, 1990-94. Bd. dirs. Girls, Inc., Jacksonville, 1997—, Southside

United Meth. Preschool, Jacksonville, 1995-97; adult tchr. Christ Ch., 1994-96—, nursery vol., 1991-94; elder South Jacksoville Presbyn. Ch., 1991-94. Mem. ABA, Fla. Bar, Fla. Trial Lawyers Assn., Jacksonville Trail Lawyers Assn., Masons, Scottish Rite of Freemasonery, Royal Order of Jesters, Shriners (1998 imperial conv. com. counsel 1995—), Christian Legal Soc. (trustee 1997—). Democrat. Presbyerian. Avocations: running. Personal injury, Contracts commercial, Family and matrimonial. Office: Kent Crawford & Gooding 225 Water St Ste 900 Jacksonville FL 32202-5142

**GOODKIND, E. ROBERT,** lawyer; b. Rockville Center, N.Y., May 1, 1932; s. Louis W. and Bertha K. Goodkind; m. Barbara Rosen, Dec. 20, 1956; children: Elisa Goodkind Mandelbaum, John, Peter. BA, Princeton U., 1954; JD, Harvard U., 1959. Ptnr. Goodkind, Labaton, Rudoff & Sucharow, LLP, N.Y.C., 1963—; trustee Am. Acad. Dramatic Arts, N.Y.C., 1973—, chmn. bd. 1983-88; dir. Geraghty & Miller, Inc., Plainview, N.Y., 1986-93. Chmn. bd. The Jewish Mus., N.Y.C., 1994-97; chmn. nat. coun. Am. Jewish Com., N.Y.C., 1998—. Lt. (j.g.) USN, 1954-66. Contracts commercial, General corporate, Estate planning. Home: 9 Douglas Cir Rye NY 10580-2205 Office: Goodkind Labaton Rudoff and Sucharow LLP 100 Park Ave New York NY 10017-5516

**GOODMAN, ALFRED NELSON,** lawyer; b. N.Y.C., Jan. 21, 1945; s. Bernard R. and Mildred (Schlanger) G. BS in Mech. and Aerospace Scis., U. Rochester, 1966; JD, Georgetown U., 1969. Bar: N.Y. 1970, D.C. 1971, U.S. Supreme Ct. 1974. Patent examiner U.S. Patent Office, Washington, 1969-71; assoc. Roylance, Abrams, Berdo & Goodman, Washington, 1971-74, ptnr., 1975—. Mem. Am. Patent Law Assn., ABA, Bar Assn. of D.C. (chmn. patent, trademark and copyright law sect. 1984-85, bd. dirs. 1985-86). Patent, Trademark and copyright, Antitrust. Home: 4948 Sentinel Dr Bethesda MD 20816-3510 Office: Roylance Abrams Berdo & Goodman 1225 Connecticut Ave NW Ste 315 Washington DC 20036-2626

**GOODMAN, ANN PATON,** lawyer; b. Winchester, Mass., Aug. 16, 1957; d. Thomas Paton and Sara Kriner Goodman; m. Donald Smith II, June 15, 1996. AB, Wellesley Coll., 1979; JD, Vanderbilt U., 1984. Bar: Ill. 1984, U.S. Dist. Ct. (no. dist.) Ill. 1984, U.S. Ct. Appeals (7th cir.) 1989, U.S. Supreme Ct. 1995. Assoc. Peterson, Ross, Schloerb & Seidel, Chgo., 1984-87; assoc. McCullough, Campbell & Lane, Chgo., 1987-93, ptnr., 1993—. V.p. Newberry Plz. Condo. Assn., Chgo., 1992—; bd. dirs. Chgo. Wellesley Club, 1986-90. Mem. ABA, Internat. Aviation Women's Assn. (sec. 1998—), Chgo. Bar Assn., Fortnightly of Chgo. Avocations: travel, kayaking, bicycling, golf. Aviation, General civil litigation, Insurance. Office: McCullough Campbell & Lane 401 N Michigan Ave Ste 1300 Chicago IL 60611-4224

**GOODMAN, BARRY JOEL,** lawyer; b. N.Y.C., May 28, 1953; s. Walter Louis and Shirley (Lenzer) G.; m. Nicole Goodman; children: Aaron, Rebecca. BA, Bradley U., 1974; JD with honors, Stetson U., 1977. Bar: Fla. 1977, U.S. Ct. Appeals 1978, Mich. 1979, U.S. Dist. Ct. (we. dist.) Fla., U.S. Dist. Ct. (ea. dist.) Mich. With Diecidue, Ferlita & Prieto, Tampa, Fla., 1977-78; assoc. Provizer, Eisenberg et al, Southfield, Mich., 1979-82; assoc. Thurswell, Chayet & Weiner, Southfield, 1982-87, ptnr., 1987-93; owner Gordon, Goodman & Acker, Southfield, 1993-98, Goodman Acker, Southfield, 1998—; lectr. Inst. Continuing Legal Edn., Ann Arbor, Mich., Mich. Trial Lawyer's Assn., State Bar of Mich. Pres., bd. dirs. West Bloomfield (Mich.) Woods Homeowners Assn., 1980-83; bd. dirs., v.p. Anti-Defamation League, Mich., 1983—; bd. dirs. B'nai B'rith Youth Orgn., Mich., 1995-97. Mem. Mich. Trial Lawyers Assn. (bd. dirs. 1985—, treas. 1995, sec. 1996, v.p. 1997, pres.-elect 1998, pres. 1999—), Oakland County Bar Assn., Oakland County Trial Lawyers Assn. Democrat. Jewish. Avocations: tennis, golf, reading, theater. Personal injury. Office: Goodman Acker PC 17000 W 10 Mile Rd 2d Fl Southfield MI 48075-2945

**GOODMAN, BARRY S.,** lawyer; b. Jersey City, June 7, 1951; s. Milton and Margaret Goodman; m. Emily J. Reynolds, Dec. 5, 1982. BA cum laude, Rutgers Coll., 1973; JD, Rutgers U., Newark, 1977. Bar: N.J., U.S. Dist. Ct. N.J., U.S. Ct. Appeals (3rd cir.), U.S. Supreme Ct. Jud. law clk. hon. Eugene L. Lora Superior Ct. N.J. Appellate Divsn., Hackensack, 1977-78; atty. Essex-Newark Legal Svcs., Orange, N.J., 1978-79, Crummy, Del Deo, Dolan & Purcell, Newark, 1979-84, Greenbaum, Rowe, Smith, Ravin, Davis & Himmel LLP, Woodbridge, N.J., 1984—. Author: (manual) New Jersey Students' Rights, 1977; mem. editl. bd. Rutgers Law Rev., 1976-77; contbr. articles to profl. jours. Vol. atty. Essex-Newark Legal Svcs., 1979-81; mem. Kinoy Fellowship Adv. Com., Newark, 1991-96; mem. 20th reunion conf. com. Rutgers Constnl. Litigation Clinic, Newark, 1991; co-chairperson Hunterdon County Dems. for Clinton Com., Flemington, N.J., 1992; mem. Hunterdon County Dem. Com., Flemington, 1994—, mem. exec. com., 1996—; mem. funds allocation com. United Way Hunterdon County, Clinton, 1995—, agy. admissions com., 1996, trustee, 1997—, treas. 1998-99, exec. com., 1998—, spl. gifts com., 1998—, cmty. rels. com., 1998—, v.p., 1999—; mem. Hunterdon County Health and Human Svcs. Adv. Coun., Flemington, 1998. Mem. ABA (litigation sect., antitrust sect.), Fed. Bar Assn. N.J., N.J. State Bar Assn. (civil trial sect., antitrust sect., real property and probate sect.), Trial Attys. N.J. (trustee 1996—), Middlesex County Bar Assn., Hunterdon County Bar Assn., Rutgers-Newark Sch. Law Alumni Assn. (annual reunion dinner com. 1992, co-chair 1999, annual spring dinner com. 1995-98, treas. 1999—), Phi Beta Kappa, Phi Kappa Phi. Antitrust, General civil litigation, Professional liability. Office: Greenbaum Rowe Smith Ravin Davis & Himmel LLP 99 Wood Ave S Iselin NJ 08830-2715

**GOODMAN, GARY A.,** lawyer; b. N.Y.C., Mar. 8, 1948; s. Nathaniel and Edith (Rosen) G.; m. Susan Schachter, Aug. 13, 1972; children: Max, Jonah, William, Zachary, Holden. AB in History summa cum laude, Economics with honors, U. Rochester, 1970; JD, NYU, 1973. Bar: N.Y. 1974, U.S. Dist. Ct. (so. dist. and ea. dist.) N.Y. 1974, U.S. Dist. Ct. Guam, 1975, U.S. Ct. Appeals (2d cir.) 1975, Calif. 1996, Tex. 1996. Ptnr. Akin, Gump, Strauss, Hauer & Feld, L.L.P., N.Y.C., 1996—, co-head estate practice group. Contbr. numerous articles to profl. jours.. Mem. bd. edn. Locust Valley (N.Y.) Ctrl. Sch. Dist., 1995-96, v.p., 1996-97, pres., 1997-98. Mem. ABA (vice chmn. internat. investment in real estate com. 1983-90, chmn. Pacific Rim trans. subcom. real estate financing com. 1987-88), N.Y. State Bar Assn. (chmn. fgn. investment in U.S. real estate com. 1987-88), Assn. of Bar of City of N.Y. (uniform state laws com. 1978-80, real property law com. 1991-94, 97—, land use com. 1994-97), Internat. Coun. Shopping Ctrs. (task force environ. issues 1987-90, law com. 1991-94), Real Estate Bd. N.Y. Office: Akin Gump Strauss Hauer & Feld LLP 590 Madison Ave New York NY 10022-2524

**GOODMAN, LEWIS ELTON, JR.,** lawyer; b. Lynchburg, Va., Jan. 27, 1936; s. Lewis Elton and Mary (Oliver) G.; m. Elizabeth Shumaker, July 10, 1960; children: William L., Lee E. JD, U. Richmond, 1973. Bar: Va. 1973, U.S. Dist. Ct. (we. dist.) Va. 1973, U.S. Ct. Appeals (4th cir.) 1979, U.S. Supreme Ct. 1986. Pvt. practice Danville, Va., 1973—. Bankruptcy, Real property, Probate. Office: 540 Piney Forest Rd Danville VA 24540-3352

**GOODMAN, LOUIS J.,** prosecuter; b. Newark, July 14, 1953. BA, U. Rochester, 1975; JD, U. Calif., San Francisco, 1980. Dep. dist. atty. Alameda County, Oakland, Calif., 1981-87. Mem. Hayward South Rotary (past pres.). Office: 1290 B St Ste 307 Hayward CA 94541-2996

**GOODMAN, MARK N.,** lawyer; b. Phoenix, Jan. 16, 1952; s. Daniel H. and Joanne Goodman; m. Gwendolyn A. Langfeldt, Oct. 24, 1982; children: Zachary A., Alexander D. BA, Prescott Coll., 1973; JD summa cum laude, Calif. Western Sch. Law, 1977; LLM, U. Calif., Berkeley, 1978. Bar: Ariz. 1977, U.S. Dist. Ct. Ariz. 1978, U.S. Ct. Appeals (9th cir.) 1978, U.S. Supreme Ct. 1981. Practice Law Offices Mark N. Goodman, Prescott, Ariz., 1978-79, 81-82, Mark N. Goodman, Ltd., Prescott, 1983-86; ptnr. alward and Goodman, Ltd., Prescott, 1979-81, Perry, Goodman, Drutz & Musgrove, Prescott, 1986-87, Goodman, Drutz & Musgrove, Prescott, 1987-88, Sears & Goodman, P.C., Prescott, 1988-92, Goodman Law Firm, P.C., Prescott, 1992—. Author: The Ninth Amendment, 1981; contbr. articles to profl. jours.; notes and comments editor Calif. Western Law Rev., 1976. Bd. dirs. Yavapai Symphony Assn., Prescott, 1981-84, N. Ariz. chpt. Alzheimer's Assn., 1995-97. Mem. ABA, Def. Rsch. Inst., State Bar Ariz. (fee arbitration com. vice chmn. 1988—), Yavapai County Bar Assn. (v.p. 1981-82). E-mail: mng@goodmanlaw.com. State civil litigation, Consumer commercial, Real property. Office: Goodman Law Firm PC PO Box 2489 Prescott AZ 86302-2489

**GOODMAN, OSCAR BAYLIN,** mayor, lawyer; b. Phila., July 26, 1939; s. A. Allan and Laura (Baylin) G.; m. Carolyn Goldmark, June 6, 1962; children: Oscar B. Jr., Ross C., Eric A., Cara Lee. BA, Haverford Coll., 1961; JD, U. Pa., 1964. Bar: Nev., U.S. Ct. Appeals. Ptnr. Goodman, Chesnoff and Keach, Las Vegas, 1965—; mayor City of Las Vegas, 1998—. Mem. Nat. Assn. Criminal Def. Lawyers (pres. 1983). Jewish. Office: Off of the Mayor 400 E Stewart Ave Las Vegas NV 89101 also: Goodman Chesnoff and Keach 520 S 4th St Las Vegas NV 89101-6524

**GOODMAN, STEPHEN MURRY,** lawyer; b. Phila., Oct. 8, 1940; s. Edward and Jean (Landau) G.; m. Janis Freeman, Jan. 8, 1983; children: Carl, Rachel. BS cum laude, U. Pa., 1962, LLB magna cum laude, 1965. Bar: D.C. 1967, Pa. 1969. Law clerk to Hon. David Bazelon U.S. Ct. Appeals (D.C. cir.), Washington, 1965-66; law clk. to Hon. William J. Brennan Jr. U.S. Supreme Ct., Washington, 1966-67; ptnr. Goodman & Ewing, Phila., 1970-83, Wolf, Block, Schorr & Solis-Cohen, Phila., 1983-94, Morgan, Lewis & Bockius LLP. Mem. Order of Coif. Democrat. Jewish. Avocation: profl. jazz pianist. Office: Morgan Lewis & Bockius LLP 1701 Market St Philadelphia PA 19103-2903

**GOODNIGHT, DAVID R.,** lawyer; b. Seattle, Sept. 22, 1960; s. Glen Russell and Miriam (O'Dell) G.; m. Shelly Lynn Goodnight, July 30, 1983; children: Audra, Ethan, Laura. JD, Valparaiso (Ind.) U., 1986; LLM, Yale U., 1990. Bar: Ind. 1986, U.S. Ct. Appeals (10th cir. 1989), Wash. 1990, U.S. Dist. Ct. (we. and ea. dist.) Wash. 1990. Law clk. U.S. Dist. Ct., Ft. Wayne, Ind., 1986-88, U.S. Ct. Appeals, 10th Cir., Oklahoma City, 1988-89; ptnr. Dorsey & Whitney, LLP, Seattle, 1990—. Contbr. articles to profl. jours.; editl. adv. bd. De Novo, 1991-95. Recipient Robert Graham award for outstanding pro bono work, 1994. Mem. ABA, Wash. State Bar Assn., King County Bar Assn. Avocations: mountain climbing, bicycling, skiing. Appellate, General civil litigation. Home: 4911 228th St SE Bothell WA 98021-8041 Office: Dorsey & Whitney LLP 1420 5th Ave Seattle WA 98101-4087

**GOODPASTURE, PHILIP HENRY,** lawyer; b. Lisbon, Portugal, Sept. 16, 1960; s. Henry McKennie and Ellen Ingabor (Moller) G.; m. Paige Everett Hargroves, June 25, 1994. BA with high distinction, U. Va., 1982, JD, 1985. Bar: Va. 1985, U.S. Dist. Ct. (ea. dist.) Va. 1985. Assoc. Christian & Barton and predecessor firm, Richmond, Va., 1985-92, ptnr., 1993—, vice-chmn. corp. team, 1994-97, mem. exec. com., 1998. Dir. Downtown Presents Inc., Richmond, 1993—, Va. League for Planned Parenthood, Richmond, 1989-95, Vol. Emergency Families for Children, Richmond, 1998—; dir. Parliament City of Richmond, 1997-98; mem. Leadership Metro Richmond, 1994; mem. leadership devel. coun. ARC, 1995. Mem. Va. Bar Assn., Richmond Bar Assn. Mergers and acquisitions, General corporate, Entertainment. Office: Christian & Barton 909 E Main St Ste 1200 Richmond VA 23219-3013

**GOODRICH, JEFFREY MARK,** lawyer, researcher; b. Jenkintown, Pa., Mar. 19, 1958; s. John Gale and Ruth Elizabeth Goodrich; m. Montserrat Aurora Fragueiro, Dec. 17, 1988. BA in Philosophy, U. N.H., 1983; JD, Franklin Pierce U., 1994. Bar: N.H. 1994, U.S. Dist. Ct. N.H. 1994. Ct. and legal interpreter L.Am. Ctr., Manchester, N.H., 1988-91; pvt. practice Manchester, N.H., 1995-97; ptnr. Moody & Goodrich, P.A., Manchester, N.H., 1997—; mem. adv. bd. L.Am. Ctr., Manchester, 1998—. Mem. N.H. Bar Assn. (law practice mgmt. com. 1995-96). General practice.

**GOODRICH, NATHANIEL HERMAN,** lawyer, former government official; b. N.Y.C., June 30, 1914; m. Marjorie A. Rosenthal, Oct. 4, 1954; children: Robert Dunbar, Thomas Neil. Student, Townsend Harris Hall, 1927-30; AB, Cornell U., 1934, LLB, 1936; grad., Command and Gen. Staff Coll., 1945; sr. officers tng. course, Air Force Sch. Applied Tactics, 1944. Bar: N.Y. 1936, D.C. 1954, U.S. Supreme Ct. 1948; lic. pvt. pilot, FAA. Pvt. practice, 1936-41; counsel Am. Jewish Com., 1938-41; asst. to chief tax amortization div. Office Undersec. War, Washington, 1941-42; legal advisor sci. div. Office War Moblzn. and Reconversion, 1946; counsel Pres.'s Sci. Rsch. Bd., 1947; exec. sec., counsel Pres.'s Spl. Bd. Inquiry Air Safety, 1947-48; counsel to comptroller Dept. Def., 1948, asst. gen. counsel, 1949, dep. gen. counsel, 1952-53, spl. asst. to sec. def., 1956; pvt. practice Washington, 1954-59; gen. counsel FAA, Washington, 1962-70; designated adminstrv. law judge U.S. Civil Svc. Commn., 1971; chief adminstrv. judge Atomic Safety and Licensing Bd. Panel Nuclear Regulatory Commn., 1971-75; v.p., gen. counsel Nat. R.R. Passenger Corp. (Amtrak), Washington, 1975-79; chmn. bd. Chgo. Union Sta. Co., 1977-79; pvt. practice Washington, 1979—; of counsel Seyfarth, Shaw, Fairweather & Geraldson, Washington, 1986—. Served to lt. col. USAAF, 1941-46; Office Asst. Chief of Air Staff Intelligence. Decorated Soldier's medal; recipient FAA award for Disting. Service, 1970. Mem. ABA. Clubs: Metropolitan; Army and Navy; Cosmos, Woodmont Country. Home: 4705 Drummond Ave Chevy Chase MD 20815-5430 Office: Seyfarth Shaw Fairweather et al 815 Connecticut Ave NW Washington DC 20006-4004

**GOODRICH, ROBERT FORESTER,** lawyer; b. London, Nov. 14, 1958; came to U.S., 1959; s. Stanley and Marie G.; m. Karen Goodrich, Aug. 23, 1986; children: Brian, Michael. BA, U. Fla., 1980, JD, 1982. Bar: Fla., U.S. Dist. Ct. (mid. dist.) Fla., U.S. Dist. Ct. (so. dist.) Fla.; cert. civil trial practice. Assoc. Barton, Cox & Davis, Gainesville, Fla., 1983-84, Law Offices Wayne Pomeroy, Ft. Lauderdale, Fla., 1984; ptnr. Pomeroy & Goodrich, Ft. Lauderdale, 1984; assoc. Pomeroy, Betts Pomeroy, Ft. Lauderdale, 1994-96; trial atty. Law Offices Alan Landsberg, Hollywood, Fla., 1997—. Democrat. Avocations: photography, music, literature. Federal civil litigation, General civil litigation, Insurance. Office: Law Offices Alan Landsberg 4000 Hollywood Blvd Ste 501S Hollywood FL 33021-6791

**GOODRICH, THOMAS MICHAEL,** lawyer, engineering and construction executive; b. Milan, Tenn., Apr. 28, 1945; s. Henry Calvin and Billie Grace (Walker) G.; m. Gillian Comer White, Dec. 28, 1968; children: Michael, Braxton, Charles, Grace. BSCE, Tulane U., 1968; JD, U. Ala., 1971. Bar: Ala. 1971. Adminstrv. asst. Supreme Ct. Ala., Montgomery, 1971-72; various mgmt. positions BE & K, Inc., Birmingham, Ala., 1989-95, pres., CEO, 1995—, also bd. dirs.; bd. dirs. First Comml. Bank, Birmingham. Bd. dirs. Birmingham Civil Rights Inst., Constrn. Industry Inst., Birmingham Area coun. Boy Scouts Am., U. Ala. Health System; trustee Nat. Bldg. Mus., Elsenhowen Exchg. Fellow. Capt. U.S Army, 1970-72. Mem. TAPPI, ABA, Ala. State Bar Assn., Assn. Builders and Contractors (pres. 1990), Constrn. Industry Roundtable. Presbyterian. Avocations: hunting, jogging. Construction, General corporate. Office: B E & K Inc PO Box 2332 2000 Internat Park Dr Birmingham AL 35243

**GOODSON, HARLAN WAYNE,** state regulator, educator; b. Newhall, Calif., Mar. 9, 1947; s. Robert Thurman Goodson and Margeret Loraine Underwood; m. Darla Kay Hinderks, (div. Feb. 1987); children: Kimberly, Marc. BA, Golden Gate U., 1976; JD, John F. Kennedy U., 1995; MPA, Golden Gate U., 1999. Sgt. of police Oakland (Calif.) Police Dept., 1971-92; cons. to pres. pro tempore Calif. State Senate, Sacramento, 1994-99; dir. Divsn. of Gambling Control Office of the Atty. Gen., Sacramento; adj. prof. law John F. Kennedy U. Sch. Law, Orinda, Calif., 1996—; mem. gov.'s adv. panel Calif. Earthquake Authority, Sacramento, 1996, 97, mem. governing bd., 1996, 97. Del. Dem. Conv., Sacramento, 1997, L.A., 1998. With USN, 1967-71. Mem. ABA, Calif. State Bar, Oakland Police Activities League (founder, exec. dir. 1982-85, Wish Upon a Star Spl. Recognition 1988), Sigma Chi (charter Zeta Omicron chpt.). Democrat. Avocations: reading, golfing. E-mail: hgoodson@hdcdojnet.state.ca.us. Home: 1208 Grand River Dr Sacramento CA 95831-4420 Office: Office of the Atty Gen 1435 River Park Dr Fl 2D Sacramento CA 95815-4509

**GOODSTEIN, ROBERT I.,** lawyer; b. Hollywood, Fla., Jan. 12, 1952. BS, U. Fla., 1973, JD, 1976; LLM, U. Wash., 1987. Asst. pub. defender Felony divsn. CHEIF, Jacksonville, Fla., 1976-80; pvt. practice Greenspan, Goodstein & Link, Jacksonville, 1980-86; asst. regional coun. U.S. EPA, Seattle, 1987-89; assoc. Short, Cressman & Burgess, Seattle, 1989-90; gen. counsel Port of Tacoma, Wash., 1991—; ptnr. Eisenhower & Carlson, Tacoma, 1995-99, Goodstein Law Group PLLC, Tacoma, 1999—. Environmental, Real property. Office: Goodstein Law Group PLLC 625 Commerce St Ste 340 Tacoma WA 98402-4632

**GOODWIN, ALFRED THEODORE,** federal judge; b. Bellingham, Wash., June 29, 1923; s. Alonzo Theodore and Miriam Hazel (Williams) G.; m. Marjorie Elizabeth Major, Dec. 23, 1943 (div. 1948); 1 son, Michael Theodore; m. Mary Ellin Handelin, Dec. 23, 1949; children: Karl Alfred, Margaret Ellen, Sara Jane, James Paul. B.A., U. Oreg., 1947; J.D., 1951. Bar: Oreg. 1951. Newspaper reporter Eugene (Oreg.) Register-Guard, 1947-50; practiced in Eugene until, 1955; circuit judge Oreg. 2d. Jud. Dist., 1955-60; assoc. justice Oreg. Supreme Ct., 1960-69; judge U.S. Dist. Ct. Oreg., 1969-71; judge U.S. Ct. Appeals for (9th cir.), Pasadena, Calif., 1971-88, chief judge, 1988-91, sr. judge, 1991—. Editor Oreg. Law Rev., 1950-51. Bd. dirs. Central Lane YMCA, Eugene, 1956-60, Salem (Oreg.) Art Assn., 1960-69; adv. bd. Eugene Salvation Army, 1956-60, chmn., 1959. Served to capt., inf. AUS, 1942-46, ETO. Mem. Am. Judicature Soc., Am. Law Inst., ABA (ho. of dels. 1986-87), Order of Coif, Phi Delta Phi, Sigma Delta Chi, Alpha Tau Omega. Republican. Presbyn. Club: Multnomah Athletic (Portland, (Oreg.). Office: US Ct Appeals 9th Cir PO Box 91510 125 S Grand Ave Pasadena CA 91105-1621

**GOODWIN, JOHN ROBERT,** law educator, author; b. Morgantown, W.Va., Nov. 3, 1929; s. John Emory and Ruby Iona G.; m. Betty Lou Wilson, June 2, 1952; children: John R., Elizabeth Ann Paugh, Mark Edward, Luke Jackson, Matthew Emory. B.S., W.Va. U., 1952, LLB, 1964, J.D., 1970. Bar: W.Va., U.S. Supreme Ct. Formerly city atty., county commr., spl. pros. atty., then mayor City of Morgantown; prof. bus. law W.Va. U.; prof. hotel and casino law U. Nev., Las Vegas; Author: Legal Primer for Artists, Craftspersons, 1987, Hotel Law, Principles and Cases, 1987. Served with U.S. Army, Korea. Recipient Bancroft-Whitney award in Constl. Law'; named Outstanding West Virginian, State of West Virginia. Democrat. Author: Twenty Feet From Glory; Business Law, 3d edit.; High Points of Legal History; Travel and Lodging Law; Desert Adventure; Gaming Control Law; editor Hotel and Casino Letter; past editor Bus. Law Rev., Bus. Law Letter. Home: Casa Linda 48 5250 E Lake Mead Blvd Las Vegas NV 89156-6751

**GOODWIN, JOSEPH R.,** judge; b. 1942. BS, W.Va. U., 1965, JD, 1970. Ptnr. Goodwin & Goodwin, 1970-95; judge U.S. Dist. Ct. (so. dist.) W.Va., Charleston, 1995—. Editor W.Va. Law Rev. Mem. W.Va. U. Bd. Advisors, 1981-86; bd. visitors W.Va. U. Coll. Law, 1995-98, chmn., 1998. With USAR, 1965-67. Mem. ABA, W.Va. State Bar Assn., Jackson County Bar Assn., 4th Cir. Jud. Conf. Office: US Dist Ct So Dist WVa PO Box 2546 Charleston WV 25329-2546

**GOODWIN, R. BRAD,** lawyer; b. Waco, Tex., Mar. 5, 1967; s. Ronald Ray and Sharon Tripp Goodwin; m. Julie Reecer, June 12, 1998. BBA, Baylor U., 1989; JD, U. Tulsa, 1992. Bar: Tex. 1992, U.S. Dist. Ct. 1996, U.S. Dist. Ct. (no., so., ea. and we. dists.) Tex. Felony prosecutor El Paso (Tex.) Dist. Atty. Office, 1993-95; divsn. chief Lubbock County Criminal Dist. Atty. Office, Lubbock, 1995-96; assoc. Craig, Terrill & Hale, LLP, Lubbock, 1996-98, McDonald, Clay, Crow & McGartland, Dallas, 1998—. Mem. Tulsa Law Rev., 1990-92. Bd. dirsx. El Paso County Young Lawyers Assn., 1993-95. Mem. ATLA, Tex. Trial Lawyers Assn., Dallas Trial Lawyers Assn., Dallas Bar Assn., Dallas Young Lawyers Assn., North Dallas Bar Assn. Avocations: golf, softball, hunting, fishing. General civil litigation, Personal injury, Insurance. Office: McDonald Clay Crow & McGartland 12222 Merit Dr Ste 1490 Dallas TX 75251-3296

**GOODWIN, ROBERT CRONIN,** lawyer; b. Cleve., Mar. 17, 1941; s. Robert Clifford and Marion (Schmadel) G.; m. Judith Mary Baxter, June 7, 1968; children: Anne, Helen, Sharon, Katherine. AB, Fordham U., 1963; JD, Georgetown U., 1969. Bar: D.C. 1970, Md. 1990. Vol. Peace Corps, Thailand, 1964-65; asst. cmty. devel. advisor AID, Thailand, 1965-66; atty. advisor Office Gen. Coun., Dept. Commerce, 1969-74; dep. asst. gen. coun. internat. & resouce devel. programs Fed. Energy Adminstrn., Washington, 1974-77, asst. gen. coun. internat. conservation & resource devel., 1977; asst. gen. coun. internat. trade & emergency preparedness Dept. Energy, Washington, 1977-79; ptnr. Thompson, Hine & Flory, 1979-82; v.p., gen. coun. China Energy Ventures, Washington, 1982-86; ptnr. Goodwin & Soble, 1986-90; pvt. practice, 1990-92; exec. v.p., gen. coun., dir. U.S.-China Indsl. Exch., Inc., 1992—; guest lectr. internat. petroleum contracts East China Petroleum Inst. Beijing, 1985; frequent lectr. on internat. contracts and Chineses legal and bus. issues; adj. assoc. prof. internat. mgmt. progam, U. Md., 1990—. Editor-in-chief Law and Policy in International Business, 1968-69; co-editor Legal Environ. for Fgn. Direct Investment in U.S., 1994; contbr. articles to profl. jours. Mem. bd. sch. bd., 1980-83. Recipient cert. of Merit Fed. Energy Adminstrn., 1974, cert. Spl. Acheivement, 1974, 76. Mem. ABA, D.C. Bar Assn., Thai-Am. Assn. (chmn. bus. com. 1991, pres. 1995), Nat. Coun. U.S. China Trade (chmn. legal com. 1987), Am. Corp. Counsel Assn., Md.-China Bus. Coun. (bd. dirs., v.p. 1999—). Contracts commercial, Administrative and regulatory, Private international. Home: 3710 Bradley Ln Chevy Chase MD 20815-4257 Office: 7201 Wisconsin Ave Ste 703 Bethesda MD 20814-4850

**GOODWIN, ROLF ERVINE,** lawyer; b. Bethlehem, Pa., May 2, 1956; s. Francis Black and Grethe Julie (Andresen) G.; m. Nancy Elsbeth Sarstedt, Feb. 2, 1991. AB, Harvard Coll., 1978; JD, NYU, 1982. Bar: N.H. 1982. Assoc. Hamblett & Kerrigan P.A., Nashua, N.H., 1982-87; ptnr. Deasy & Dwyer P.A., Nashua, N.H., 1988-98, McLane Graf Raulerson & Middleton PA, 1998—. Pres., trustee Community Music Sch., Nashua, 1984-95; trustee Nashua Symphony Assn., 1983-93; bd. dirs. Harvard Pierian Found., Inc., Cambridge, Mass., 1990—, pres., 1993-97; admissions chmn. Harvard-Radcliffe Club N.H., 1983—. Mem. Nashua Bar Assn., N.H. Bar Assn. (ethics com. 1987—, vice-chair 1993-97, chair 1997—, com. on revision of rules of profl. conduct), Greater Nashua C. of C. (Leadershp. Greater Nashua, Edn. Comm., Local Affairs Comm.). Avocations: classical music, back-country skiing, sailing, hiking, swimming. Contracts commercial, Real property, General corporate. Office: McLane Graf Raulerson & Middleton PA 400 Amherst St PO Box 6180 Nashua NH 03063-6180

**GOODY, WILLIAM KEITH,** lawyer; b. Milw., June 7, 1948; s. James W. and Marjorie (Ferguson) G.; m. Mary C. Costanzi, Aug. 4, 1995; children: Grant, Greyson, Elliott, James. BA, U. Calif., Berkeley, 1970; postgrad., Duke U., 1970-71; JD, U. Wyo., 1975. Bar: Wyo. 1975. Pvt. practice Jackson, Wyo., 1975—; sr. asst. pub. defender State of Wyo., Jackson, 1978-99; lectr. on mental health and criminal law and other subjects. Avocations: mountaineering, skiing, kayaking. Criminal. Home and Office: PO Box 2488 Jackson WY 83001-2488

**GOOGASIAN, GEORGE ARA,** lawyer; b. Pontiac, Mich., Feb. 22, 1936; s. Peter and Lucy (Chobanian) G.; m. Phyllis Elaine Law, June 27, 1959; children—Karen Ann, Steven George, Dean Michael. B.A., U. Mich., 1958; J.D., Northwestern U., 1961. Bar: Mich. 1961. Assoc. Marentay, Rouse, Selby, Fischer & Webber, Detroit, 1961-62; asst. U.S. Atty. U.S. Dept. Justice, Detroit, 1962-64; assoc. Howlett, Hartman & Beier, Pontiac and Bloomfield Hills, Mich., 1964-81; ptnr. Googasian Hopkins Hohauser & Forhan, Bloomfield Hills, Mich., 1981-96, The Googasian Firm, Bloomfield Hills, 1996—; bd. law examiners State of Mich., 1997—. Author: Trial Advocacy Manual, 1984, West Groups Michigan Practice Torts, vols. 14, 15, 1998. Pres. Oakland Parks Found., Pontiac, 1984-89; chmn. Oakland County Dem. party, Pontiac, 1964-70; state campaign chmn. U.S. Senator Philip A. Hart, Detroit, 1970; bd. dirs. Big Bros. Oakland County. 1968-73. Fellow Am. Bar Found., Am. Coll. Trial Lawyers, Internat. Acad. Trial Lawyers; mem. ABA (del. 1992-93, exec. coun. nat. conf. bar pres. 1993-96), ATLA, Am. Bd. Trial Advocates, State Bar Mich. (pres. elect 1991-92, pres. 1992—), Oakland County Bar Assn. (pres. 1985-86), Mich. State Bar Found., Oakland Bar Found. (pres. 1990-92). Presbyterian. Club: U. Mich. Club Greater Detroit. Personal injury, Federal civil litigation, State civil litigation. Home: 3750 Orion Rd Oakland MI 48363-3029 Office: 6895 Telegraph Rd Bloomfield Hills MI 48301-3138

**GOOLRICK, ROBERT MASON,** lawyer; b. Fredericksburg, Va., Mar. 25, 1934; s. John T. and Olive E. (JOnes) G.; m. Audrey J. Dippo (div.);

children: Stephanie M., Meade A. BA with distinction, U. Va., 1956, JD, 1959. BAr: Va. 1959, D.C. 1959, U.S. Dist. Ct. D.C. 1961, U.S. Ct. Appeals (D.C. cir.) 1961. Assoc. Steptoe & Johnson, Washington, 1959-65, ptnr., 1965-79; sole practice Alexandria, Va., 1979-83; cons. bus., oil and gas fin.; instr. U. Va. Law Sch. Author: Public Policy Toward Corporate Growth, 1978, Corporate Mergers and Acquisitions under Federal Securities Laws, 1978. Mem. ABA (corps. sect.), Jefferson Soc., Raven Soc., Order of Coif, Phi Beta Kappa. General corporate, Contracts commercial. Home: 3320 Woodburn Vill Dr No 22 Annandale VA 22003-6860 Office: PO Box 1233 Mc Lean VA 22101-1233

**GOORLEY, RICHARD CARL,** lawyer; b. Buenos Aires, Aug. 19, 1949; came to U.S., 1955; s. John Theodore and Ethel Louise (Coleman) G.; m. Margaret Ellen Osetinsky, Sept. 1, 1984; children: Matthew, Roger, Elliot, Gina. BA, N.E. La. U., 1972; JD, Loyola U. of the South, 1975. Bar: La. 1975, Tex. 1986. Assoc. Law Offices of Lewis Weinstein, Shreveport, La., 1975-77; asst. pub. defender Caddo Parish Pub. Defender's Office, Shreveport, 1977-79; chief asst. pub. defender Caddo Parish Pub. Defender's Office, Shreveport, La., 1981-87; pvt. practice Monroe, La., 1979-81, Shreveport, 1987—; lectr. La. Criminal Def. Lawyers. With USNR, 1968-72. Mem. N.W. La. Criminal Def. Bar (pres. 1995-96), L.A. Assn. Criminal Def. Lawyers (bd. dirs. 1996), Shreveport Futbol Club (v.p. 1997—). Criminal. Office: 509 Marshall St Ste 705 Shreveport LA 71101-3557

**GOPMAN, HOWARD Z.,** lawyer; b. Kansas City, Mo., Oct. 29, 1940; s. Norman S. and Rose E. (Goodman) G.; m. Carol Ann Levin, Mar. 25, 1979; children: James, William. BS, U. Wis., 1962, JD, 1965, MBA, 1967. Cert. Wis. 1965, Ill. 1969, U.S. Dist. Ct. (no. dist.) Ill. 1969. Trial atty. FTC, Washington, 1967-69; assoc. Quinn, Jacobs & Barry, Chgo., 1969-71, Katz, Karacic & Mansfield, Chgo., 1971-73, Michaelson & Marder, Chgo., 1973-74; prin. Howard Z. Gopman & Assocs., Skokie, Ill., 1974—; pres., dir. Am. Realty & Mgmt., Ltd., Skokie, 1977—; comml. arbitrator Am. Arbitration Assn., Chgo., 1977—; arbitrator Nat. Assn. Securities Dealers, Inc., N.Y. Stock Exch., Inc., Am. Stock Exch., Nat. Futures Assn., Cir. Cts. Cook and Lake Counties, Ill. Contbr. articles to profl. jours. Hearing officer Ill. Office Edn., Chgo., 1977—. Mem. ABA, Ill. State Bar Assn., Wis. Bar Assn. Securities, Real property, General corporate. Office: 5225 Old Orchard Rd Ste 24B Skokie IL 60077-1027

**GORA, DANIEL MARTIN,** lawyer; b. Chgo., Oct. 27, 1969; s. Martin O. and Jacqueline K. (Lancaster) G. BS, No. Ill. U., 1992; JD, Hamline U., 1995; MBA, U. St. Thomas, Mpls., 1996, MSS, 1999. Bar: Minn. 1995, Ill. 1996. Assoc. Spence, Ricke & Thurmer, St. Paul, 1992-96; ptnr. Weatherman, Wolters & Gora, Roseville, Minn., 1995-96; pvt. practice Gora Law Offices, St. Paul, 1997-98; info. counsel Dayton-Hudson Corp., 1998; counsel Carlson Cos. Inc., Mpls., 1998—; mem. faculty Minn. Sch. Bus., Brooklyn Center, 1996—, Met. State U., Mpls., 1997—; counsel N.E. Metro Bus. Network, Maplewood, Minn., 1997. Judge Am. Mock Trial Assn., Minn., 1994-99. Dean's Law scholar Hamline U., 1992, Ill. Gen. Assembly scholar, 1988. Mem. ABA, Minn. Bar Assn., Ill. Bar Assn., Fed. Bar Assn., Chgo. Bar Assn., Acad. Polit. Sci., Golden Key Nat. Honor Soc., Phi Sigma Alpha. Avocations: golf, basketball, reading, theater. Contracts commercial, Estate planning, Labor.

**GORDESKY, MORTON,** lawyer; b. Egg Harbor, N.J., Apr. 11, 1929; s. Benjamin and Rose (Suskin) G.; m. Marcelline D. Fallick, June 8, 1952 (div. 1982); children: Benjamin Todd, Nancy Hope Hafuta. BS, Temple U., 1950; JD, Rutgers U., 1954. Bar: Pa. 1955, U.S. Dist. Ct. (ea. dist.) Pa. 1958, U.S. Dist. Ct. Md. 1991, U.S. Ct. Appeals (3rd cir.) 1983, U.S. Ct. Appeals (4th cir.) 1990, U.S. Supreme Ct. 1983. Sole practice, Phila., 1954—. Active Dem. Nat. Com., B'nai Brith. Served with U.S. Army, 1954-56. Mem. Phila. Bar Assn., Amvets (judge adv. 1961-64), Am. Legion. Bankruptcy, Federal civil litigation, State civil litigation. Office: Carlton Bus Ctr 1819 John F Kennedy Blvd Philadelphia PA 19103-1733

**GORDON, ARNOLD MARK,** arbitrator, lawyer; b. Norwich, Conn., Oct. 2, 1937; s. Barney and Rose (Bilsky) G.; m. Carolyn. BSBA, Wayne State U., Detroit, 1959, JD, 1962. Bar: Mich. 1962. With Gordon & Gordon P.C. and predecessor firms, Southfield, Mich.; arbitrator Am. Arbitration Assn., 1969—; lectr. in field. Mem. Am. Coll. Trial Lawyers, State Bar Mich. (chmn. med.-legal com. 1976—, negligence sect. 1977-78, pub. negligence sect. bull.), Detroit Bar Assn. (co-chmn. trial advocacy program continguing legal edn. 1972—), Assn. Trial Lawyers Am. (exec. bd. Mich. 1967—), Mich., Detroit trial lawyers assns., Tau Epsilon Rho. Club: Masons. Office: Gordon & Gordon PC 18411 W 12 Mile Rd Ste 200 Southfield MI 48076-2663

**GORDON, CAREY NATHANIEL,** lawyer, federal agency administrator; b. Cleve., Mar. 11, 1950; s. Murray Byron and Pearl Miriam (Jackson) G.; m. Lois Elizabeth Bradshaw, Nov. 28, 1981. BA, Ohio State U., 1972; MA, U. London, 1973; postgrad., Cambridge (Eng.) U., 1973-74; JD, Cleve. State U., 1977. Bar: Ohio 1977, D.C. 1978, U.S. Supreme Ct. 1983. Assoc. Rippner Schwartz & Carlin, Cleve., 1977-80, ptnr., 1980-84; spl. advisor Atty. Gen.'s Chambers, Khartoum, Sudan, 1984-85; contract advisor U.S. Agy. for Internat. Devel., Khartoum, Cairo, Kinshasa, Islamabad, 1986-94; contracting officer U.S. Agy. for Internat. Devel., Abidjan, Ivory Coast, 1995-97, Phnom Penh, Cambodia, 1997—; vis. lectr. U. Khartoum, 1984-85. Mem. Fed. Bar Assn., Am. Soc. Internat. Law, Cleve. Bar Assn., African Studies Assn. Government contracts and claims, Public international. Office: USAID Cambodia Box P APO AP 96546

**GORDON, DAVID STOTT,** lawyer; b. Atlanta, Mar. 10, 1951; s. Alexander Stott and Kathleen Marie (Maxwell) G.; m. Melodye Anne Vanoy, Oct. 25, 1991. AB in Psychology with honors, U. Ga., 1972; MA, Trinity Evang. Div. Sch., 1995; JD, U. Ga., 1977; postgrad., Judge Adv. Gen. Sch., 1982-83, Georgetown U., 1984-86, U. N.C., 1991; MA in History, Trinity Evang. Div. Sch., 1995. Bar: Ga. 1977, U.S. Supreme Ct. 1983, U.S. Ct. Internat. Trade 1985, Md. 1986, N.C. 1989. Legal assistance officer 1 Armored Divsn., U.S. Army, Grafenwoehr, Germany, 1978; officer in charge Grafenwoehr Law Ctr., U.S. Army, 1979; chief legal instr. Combined Arms Tng. Ctr., U.S. Army, Vilseck, Germany, 1979-80; atty. internat. law Hqrs. U.S. Army Europe, Heidelberg, 1980-82; legal advisor 1st U.S. Army Recruiting Brigade, Ft. Meade, Md., 1983-86; corp. counsel Caldwell Aircraft Trading Co., Charlotte, N.C., 1987-90; sr. v.p., gen. counsel Caldwell Aircraft Trading Co., Charlotte, 1990—, bd. dirs.; ops. officer HQ XVIII Airborne Corps., U.S. Army, Rafha, Saudi Arabia, 1991; internat. law officer 360th Civil Afffairs Brigade, USAR, Columbia, S.C., 1987—. Contbr. articles to profl. jours. Active mem. Christ Ch. (Episcopal), Charlotte, 1991—. Major U.S. Army, 1977-86, 91; lt. col. Res. Decorated Army Commendation medal with two oak leaf clusters, Army Achievement medal. Mem. ABA, N.C. State Bar Assn. (sect. internat. law), Civil Affairs Assn., Robert Burns Soc. Charlotte, S.E. Renaissance Conf., Renaissance Soc. Am., Phi Beta Kappa. Republican. Avocations: history, fencing, music, languages. Private international, Aviation, Military. Home: 2916 Forest Park Dr Charlotte NC 28209-1402 Office: Caldwell Aircraft Trading Ste 1011 4801 E Independence Blvd Charlotte NC 28212-5403

**GORDON, DAVID ZEVI,** retired lawyer; b. Bklyn., Mar. 2, 1943; s. Isidore and Yaffa S. (Stern) G.; m. Karen Baranker, Apr. 25, 1971; children: Ilana, Naomi. BA magna cum laude, Yeshiva U., 1964; JD cum laude, MBA, Columbia U., 1969. Bar: N.Y. 1970, U.S. Dist. Ct. (so. dist.) N.Y. 1973, U.S. Ct. Appeals (2d cir.) 1973. Assoc. Spear and Hill, N.Y.C., 1969-71; sr. assoc. LeBoeuf Lamb Lieby & McRae, N.Y.C., 1971-77; ptnr. Finley Kumble Heine & Underburg, N.Y.C., 1977-78, David Z. Gordon and Assocs., N.Y.C., 1978-81; mng. ptnr. Moroze Sherman Gordon & Gordon, P.C., N.Y.C., 1981-96. Trustee, exec. com. Stern Coll. for Women, 1990-96; co-chmn. United Jewish Appeal, Operation Exodus, 1991-96, Project Renewal, 1987-96, exec. com. Israel econ. devel.; chmn. Israel Bonds, Bronx, 1988-96. Recipient Heritage award Yeshiva U., 1988. Mem. ABA, N.Y. State Bar Assn., N.Y.C. Bar Assn. (mem. com. condemnation and tax certiorari), Real Estate Tax Bar Assn. Democrat. General corporate, Real property, Securities.

**GORDON, DEBORAH LEIGH,** lawyer; b. Washington, Mar. 14, 1950; d. Lou and Dana (Nelson) G. BA, U. Mich., 1972; JD, U. Detroit, 1976. Bar: Mich. 1977, U.S. Dist. Ct. (ea. and we. dists.) Mich. 1977, U.S. Ct. Appeals (6th cir.) 1983, U.S. Supreme Ct. 1985. Asst. atty. gen. civil rights div. State of Mich., Detroit, 1977-78; trial atty. EEOC, Detroit, 1979-80; with Law Office of Sheldon J. Stark, Detroit, 1980-83; ptnr. Stark and Gordon, Detroit, 1983—; cooperating atty. ACLU, Detroit, 1984—. Author: Employment Discrimination Law in Michigan, 1986; co-editor: Sexual Harrassment Law and Practice, 1995. Fellow Am. Coll. Trial Lawyers; mem. Mich. Trial Lawyers Assn. (bd. dirs. 1985-88), Am. Inn of Ct. (bd. dirs. 1984—), Women Lawyers Assn. Mich., Fed. Bar Assn., Detroit Bar Assn. Labor, Civil rights, Personal injury. Office: 26862 Woodward Ave Unit 202 Royal Oak MI 48067-0959

**GORDON, EDGAR GEORGE,** lawyer; b. Detroit, Feb. 27, 1924; s. Edgar George and Verna Florence (Hay) G.; m. Alice Irwin, Feb. 4, 1967; children: David A., J. Scott. A.B., Princeton U., 1947; J.D., Harvard U., 1950. Bar: Mich. 1951, U.S. Supreme Ct. 1953. Assoc., Poole, Warren & Littell, Detroit, 1950-54; ptnr. Poole, Warren, Littell & Gordon, Detroit, 1953-63; gen. counsel Hygrade Food Products Corp., Detroit, 1963-69, sec., 1966-69, v.p., 1968-69; v.p., sec., counsel City Nat. Bank of Detroit, 1969-81; v.p., sec., gen. counsel No. States Bancorp., 1970-81; v.p., sec., counsel First of Am. Bank Corp., Kalamazoo, 1981-84, also ptnr. Howard & Howard, Kalamazoo, 1981—; dir. First Citizens Bank, Troy, Mich., 1973-81, First Nat. Bank, Plymouth, Mich., 1974-81; pres., chmn. bd. First of Am. Mortgage Co., Kalamazoo, 1978-84. Commr., City of Kalamazoo, 1995—. Lt. (j.g.), USNR, 1943-46. Mem. ABA, Mich. Bar Assn., Kalamazoo Bar Assn. Republican. Presbyterian. Clubs: Country of Detroit (Grosse Pointe, Mich.). General corporate, Banking, Probate. Home: 4339 Lakeside Dr Kalamazoo MI 49008-2802 Office: Howard & Howard 400 Kalamazoo Kalamazoo MI 49007

**GORDON, EUGENE ANDREW,** judge; b. Guilford County, N.C., July 10, 1917; s. Charles Robert and Carrie (Scott) G.; m. Virginia Stoner, Jan. 1, 1943; children: Eugene Andrew, Rosemary Anne. AB, Elon Coll., 1938, LLD (hon.), 1982; LLB, Duke U., 1941. Bar: N.C. 1941. Practiced law, 1946-64; mem. firm Young, Young & Gordon, Burlington, 1947-64; solicitor Alamance Gen. County Ct., 1947-54; county atty. Alamance County, 1954-64; U.S. judge Middle Dist. N.C., 1964-82, sr. judge, 1982—; instr. U.S. Atty. Gen.'s Sch. Former chmn. adv. bd. Salvation Army.; Former nat. committeeman N.C. Young Democrats; former pres. Alamance County Young Democrats; chmn. Alamance County Dem. Exec. Com., 1954-64; mem. U.S. Jud. Conf. Adv. Com. on Criminal Rules, 1976-84. Capt. AUS, 1942-46, N.C. Army N.G., 1946-47. Mem. Greensboro Bar Assn., Assn. U.S. Dist. Judges (past pres.). Office: Middle Dist Ct PO Box 3285 US Post Office & Ct House Greensboro NC 27402

**GORDON, EVAN L.,** lawyer; b. N.Y.C., July 10, 1941; s. Myron P. and Henrietta (Lediger) Gordon. AB, Columbia U., 1963, LLB, 1966. Bar: N.Y. 1966, U.S. Dist. Ct. (so. and ea. dists.) N.Y. 1968, U.S. Dist. Ct. (no. and we. dists.) N.Y. 1985, U.S. Ct. Appeals (2nd cir.) 1967, U.S. Ct. Appeals (8th cir.) 1988, U.S. Ct. Appeals (11th cir.) 1986, U.S. Supreme Ct. 1976. Ptnr. Delson & Gordon, N.Y.C., 1968-78, Wofsey, Certilman et al, N.Y.C., 1978-85, Bangser & Weiss, N.Y.C., 1986-89; pvt. practice N.Y.C., 1990—. Contbg. author: The Law of Gray and Counterfeit Goods, 1987. Mem. corp. and security del. to Ea. Europe through People to People Internat., 1990. Mem. ABA (securities litigation com. 1977—), N.Y. State Bar Assn., Assn. of Bar of City of N.Y., Fed. Bar Council. General civil litigation. Home: 400 E 56th St New York NY 10022-4147 Office: 230 Park Ave New York NY 10169-0005

**GORDON, GAIL KIMBERLY,** lawyer; b. Glens Falls, N.Y., Oct. 17, 1962. BA, Wheaton Coll., 1983; JD, Boston U., 1988. Bar: Mass. 1989, N.Y. 1989. Assoc. Skadden, Arps, Slate, Meagher & Flom, N.Y.C., 1988-91, Hickock & Barclay, Syracuse, 1992-93; atty. Student Loan Mktg. Assn., Washington, 1994-97; asst. gen. counsel UUNET, Washington, 1997—. Computer. Office: UUNET an MCI Worldcom Co 3060 Williams Dr Fairfax VA 22031-4648

**GORDON, GILBERT WAYNE,** lawyer; b. Chgo., Feb. 14, 1949; s. Philip and Dorothy (Pollack) G.; m. Bobbie Rosenthaler Gordon, Jan. 26, 1949; children: Richard, Jamie. BS, Bradley U., 1971; JD, Loyola U., Chgo., 1974. Bar: Ill. 1974, U.S. Dist. Ct. (no. dist.) Ill. 1974, U.S. Supreme Ct. 1980. Assoc. Gordon & Brustin, Ltd., Chgo., 1974-77; ptnr. Gordon & Gordon, Ltd., Chgo., 1977-86, Marks, Marks & Kaplan Ltd., Chgo., 1986—; panel of attys. NFL Players Assn., 1984—. Mem. ABA, Ill. Bar Assn., Chgo. Bar Assn., Am. Trial Lawyers Assn., Ill. Trial Lawyers Assn. General civil litigation, Personal injury, Sports. Office: Marks Marks & Kaplan Ltd 120 N La Salle St Chicago IL 60602-2412

**GORDON, GLEN FRANK,** lawyer; b. Wuerzburg, Germany, Apr. 7, 1965; s. Thomas Jon and Catherin Ann (Fillinger) G.; m. Christine Marie Johnson, Apr. 21, 1992. BA with honors, U. Mich., 1987; JD, U. Colo., 1990. Bar: Colo. 1990, U.S. Dist. Ct. Colo. 1990, U.S. Ct. Appeals (10th cir.) 1990. Summer assoc. Latham & Watkins, L.A., 1988; assoc. Buchanan, Gray, Purvis & Schuetze, Boulder, Colo., 1990-94; ptnr. Purvis, Gray & Gordon LLP, Boulder, 1994—. Mem. Boulder Bar Assn. (chmn. civil litigation sect., med.-legal sect.), Am. Inns. of Ct. E-mail: ggordon@pgglaw.com. Fax: 303-440-3688. General civil litigation, Product liability, Personal injury. Office: Purvis Gray & Gordon LLP Schuetze & Gordon 1050 Walnut St Ste 501 Boulder CO 80302-5144 also: 303 E 17th Ave Ste 700 Denver CO 80203-1260

**GORDON, HARRISON J.,** lawyer; b. Newark, Aug. 21, 1950; s. Carl and Rose (Katz) G.; children by previous marriage: Caryn Rachel, Robert Jonathan. BS, U. Bridgeport, 1972; JD, U. Miami, 1975. Bar: N.J. 1976, D.C. 1995, U.S. Dist. Ct. N.J. 1976, U.S. Supreme Ct. 1980. Sole practice West Orange, N.J., 1976-78, Montclair, N.J., 1978-83; ptnr. Gordon & Gordon, West Orange, 1983-87, Gordon, Gordon & Haley, West Orange, 1987-90, Gordon & Gordon, PC, West Orange, 1990—; adj. prof. Montclair State Coll., Upper Montclair, N.J., 1979. Mem. N.J. State Bar Assn. (exec. com. young lawyers div. 1981-83), Assn. Trial Lawyers Am. (chmn. automobile and premises liability sect.), N.J. Trial Lawyers Assn. (bd. govs. 1987-90, sec. 1990-91, treas. 1991-92, 3d v.p. 1992-93, 2d v.p. 1993-94, 1st v.p. 1994-95, pres.-elect 1995—, assoc. editor mag. 1987—, pres. 1996-97), Am. Arbitration Assn. (arbitrator), Soc. Bar and Gavel, Optimists Club (pres. 1981-82), Psi Chi, Phi Alpha Theta. Democrat. Personal injury, Federal civil litigation, State civil litigation. Office: Gordon & Gordon PC 80 Main St West Orange NJ 07052-5460

**GORDON, HOWARD W.,** lawyer; b. Bklyn., June 30, 1942; s. Bernard R. and Lillian Gordon; m. Jeanie C. Gordon, Aug. 17, 1964; children: Joshua, Caren. BBA, Tulane U., 1964; JD, U. Fla., 1966; LLM in Taxation, NYU, 1972. Atty. IRS, Phila., 1968-77, Finley Kumble et al, Miami, Fla., 1978-81, Semet, Lichstein et al, Coral Gables, Fla., 1982-97, Fowler, White, Burnett, Hurley, Banick & Strickroot, Miami, 1997—. Contbr. articles to profl. jours. Col., JAG, U.S. Army, 1968-69, Res., 1969-95. Estate taxation, Estate planning, Probate. Office: Fowler White et al 100 SE 2nd Ave Fl D17 Miami FL 33131-1502

**GORDON, JAMES S.,** lawyer; b. N.Y.C., Feb. 15, 1941; s. George S. and Sylvia A. (Wolfson) G.; m. Marcia G. Gordon, Dec. 22, 1968 (dec.); children: Daniel, Sarah; m. Debbie S. Pase, June 15, 1996. BA with high honors, U. Fla., 1962; LLB, Yale U., 1965. Bar: Ill. 1965, Fla. 1966, U.S. Supreme Ct. 1974. Asst. prof. Ind. U. Sch. Law, Bloomington, 1967-68, assoc. prof., 1969; ptnr. Feiwell, Galper & Gordon, Chgo., 1970-72; sole practice Chgo., 1972-80; pres. James S. Gordon, Ltd., Chgo., 1981-93; chmn. Gordon, Glickman, Flesch & Woody, 1994—. Editor Yale Law Jour., 1963-65; contbr. articles to profl. jours. Mem. Winnetka Caucus, 1981-82. Ford Found. grantee, 1965-66. Mem. Chgo. Bar Assn., Yale U. Law Alumni Assn. (exec. com. 1987-94), Order of Coif, Phi Beta Kappa, Phi Alpha Delta, Legal Club, Birchwood Club (Highland Park, Ill.). Federal civil litigation, Antitrust, Administrative and regulatory. Office: 140 S Dearborn St Ste 404 Chicago IL 60603-5202

**GORDON, JEFFREY,** lawyer; b. Boston, Sept. 6, 1964. BA, Tulane U., 1986, JD, 1989. Bar: Fla. 1990, U.S. Dist. Ct. (mid. dist.) Fla. 1995. Law clk. intern 1st dist. Ct. Appeal Fla., Tallahassee, 1989; spl. asst. pub. defender Dade County, Miami, Fla., 1990-92; cert. cir. ct. arbitrator Palm Beach County, West Palm Beach, Fla., 1990-92; ptnr. Maney & Gordon, P.A., Tampa, Fla., 1992—. Teen ct. judge pro bono Hillsborough County, Tampa, 1992-98. Mem. ATLA, Acad. Fla. Trial Attys., Animal Legal Def. Fund. General civil litigation, Personal injury. Office: Maney & Gordon PA 101 E Kennedy Blvd Ste 3170 Tampa FL 33602-5151

**GORDON, JEROME,** lawyer; b. Chgo., Jan. 27, 1923; s. Charles Harry and Ethel Edith (Teplitz) G.; m. Sylvia Kresner, Aug. 24, 1947; children: Cheryl Diane, Mark Allen, David Steven. BA, Roosevelt U., 1949; MS in Edn., U. So. Calif., 1951; JD, Southwestern U., 1968. Bar: Calif. 1981, U.S. Dist. Ct. (cen. dist.) Calif. 1981, (ea. dist.) 1988. Unemployment ins. specialist M & M Assn., L.A., 1972-79; pvt. practice Woodland Hills, Calif., 1981-86; mng. atty., staff atty. Tulare-Kings Counties Legal Svcs., Inc., Hanford, Calif., 1986-94; pvt. practice Canoga Park, Calif., 1994—. Democrat. Avocations: reading, history, fishing. General civil litigation, Landlord-tenant, General practice. Office: 7657 Winnetka Ave Ste 411 Canoga Park CA 91306-2677

**GORDON, JOAN IRMA,** lawyer; b. N.Y.C., Nov. 1, 1945; d. Morris and Dora (Mittman) G. BA in Polit. Sci., Vassar Coll., 1967; MA in Polit. Sci., Brown U., 1969; JD, Am. U., 1974. Bar: Md. 1974, D.C. 1975, U.S. Dist. Ct. Md., 1976, U.S. Supreme Ct. 1978, N.Y. 1981. Intern N.Y. State Pub. Adminstrn., Albany, 1969-70; adminstrv. asst. to asst. commr. N.Y. State Health Dept., Albany, 1970-71; staff counsel Washington Suburban San. Commn., Hyattsville, Md., 1975-80; legal counsel and govt. affairs officer Montgomery C.C., Rockville, Md., 1980-84, gen. counsel, 1984—; rsch. cons. Inst. Studies in Justice and Soc. Behavior, Am. U. Law Sch., Washington, 1974. Contbr. Maryland Criminal Jury Instructions and Commentary, 1975. Mem. prospective students com. Vassar Coll., Washington, 1975-83; vice-chmn. precinct Dem. Com. Montgomery County, 1976-82, Montgomery County coun. Task Force on Problems of Homeowners Assn., Condominiums and Cooperatives, 1989; mem. archtl control com. Redland Crossing Homeowners Assn., Derwood, Md., 1982-84, bd. dirs., 1984-88, pres. bd. dirs. 1986-87, v.p. 1987-88; mem. Montgomery County Commn. on Common Ownership Communities, 1992-95. Recipient Am. Jurisprudence award, 1972, 73. Mem. ABA, Am. Corp. Counsel Assocs., Nat. Assn. Coll. and Univ. Attys. (chair continuing legal edn. com. 1989-91, bd. dirs. 1987-90), Md. Bar Assn., N.Y. State Bar Assn., Montgomery County Bar Assn. Jewish. Education and schools. Home: 15909 Yukon Ln Rockville MD 20855-2632 Office: Montgomery CC 900 Hungerford Dr Rockville MD 20850-1740

**GORDON, KENNETH IRA,** lawyer; b. Boston, Nov. 4, 1959; s. Henry Jerry and Susan Myrna (Silverman) Levine; m. Wendy Iris Schlosberg, Aug. 5, 1989. BA, Northeastern U., 1982; JD, Suffolk U., 1990. Bar: Mass. 1990, U.S. Dist. Ct. Mass. 1991. Sports writer Palm Beach Post & Evening Times, West Palm Beach, Fla., 1982-85; sports editor North Shore: Sunday, Danvers, Mass., 1985-87; sports copy editor The Boston Globe, 1987-90; assoc. Parker, Coulter, Daley & White, Boston, 1990-94, Perkins, Smith & Cohen, 1994-96; of counsel Rosen & Assoc., 1996—; legal asst. Sportserve, Inc., Boston, 1987-90, counsel, 1990-95, cons., officer, 1991—; corp. counsel Legends and Heroes, Inc., 1995—. Contbr. articles to book and profl. jours. Publicity dir. celebrity all star hockey challenge Boston Garden, 1989, co-chmn. Raytheon gold medal all star challenge, 1991. Recipient AP Sports Editors Assn. Investigative Reporting award, 1983; Travelli scholar, 1980-82. Mem. Sports Lawyers Assn., Phi Delta Phi. Entertainment, Securities, Pension, profit-sharing, and employee benefits.

**GORDON, KEVIN DELL,** lawyer; b. Oklahoma City, June 23, 1958; s. James Dell and Mary Lurana (Tracewell) G.; m. Janice Linn Mathews, Aug. 4, 1979; children: Tracewell, Elise. BA cum laude, Westminster Coll., 1981; JD, Washington U., 1984. Bar: Okla. 1984, U.S. Dist. Ct. (we., no. and ea. dists.) Okla. 1984, U.S. Ct. Appeals (10th cir.) 1985, U.S. Supreme Ct. Shareholder, dir. Crowe & Dunlevy, Oklahoma City, 1984—; adj. prof. health law U. Okla. Law Sch., 1997—. Editor Washington U. Law Quarterly, 1982-84. Trustee, past pres. Youth Svcs. Oklahoma County, 1986—; chair adv. com. Okla. Assn. Youth Svcs., 1994-98. Mem. ABA (ins. coverage com. 1990—), Okla. Bar Assn. (uniform laws com. 1994—, membership com. 1999—, coord./moderator ann. ins. law update 1999—), Assn. Trial Lawyers Am., Am. Health Lawyers Assn., Oklahoma County Bar Assn. (legal aid com. 1990-98, comty. svc. com. 1997—), Ruth Bader Ginsberg Am. Inn of Ct. (chair mentoring com. 1996-99, chair membership com. 1999—, Master of Yr. 1998), Order of Coif. Avocations: sports, gardening, guitar, reading. Health, Insurance, General civil litigation. Home: 8309 Glenwood Ave Oklahoma City OK 73114-1111 Office: Crowe & Dunlevy 20 N Broadway Ave Ste 1800 Oklahoma City OK 73102-8273

**GORDON, LEONARD STEPHEN,** retired lawyer, consultant; b. N.Y.C., Sept. 19, 1933; s. Alexander Ell and Etta Gordon; m. Lillian Robbins; children: Mark Forrest, Alan, Bryan, Scott. Student, Bklyn. Coll., 1954, NYU, 1955. Bar: N.Y., U.S. Dist. Ct. (so. and ea. dists.) N.Y. Atty. Traft & Steinback, Bronx, N.Y., 1954, Joseph Kelner, N.Y.C., 1959-60, Gordon, Jackson & Simon, N.Y.C., 1960—. Lt. col. U.S. Army N.G., 1950-94. Avocations: stamps, coins, antiques. Immigration, naturalization, and customs. Home: 51 Valley Ln E North Woodmere NY 11581-3614

**GORDON, LOUIS,** lawyer; b. Detroit, May 10, 1933; s. Isador and Esther (Kraizman) G.; m. Patricia Janis, Nov. 25, 1973 (div. Mar. 1986); children: Aaron, Marla; m. Johanna C. Gordon, Aug. 15, 1987; children: Susan, Laurie. BSBA, Wayne State U ., 1955, JD, 1958. Sole practitioner Detroit, 1959-75; owner Louis Gordon, P.C., Southfield, Mich., 1976—; spl. asst. atty. gen. State of Mich., Lansing, 1975—. Mem. ABA, Mich. Trial Lawyers Assn., Oakland Bar Assn. Avocations: tennis, golf, sailing, skiing, power boating. Fax: 248 395 4101. Personal injury, Insurance, Product liability. Office: Gordon & Pont PC 21700 Northwestern Hwy Ste 1100 Southfield MI 48075-4923

**GORDON, MYRON L.,** federal judge; b. Kenosha, Wis., Feb. 11, 1918; m. Peggy Gordon, Aug. 16, 1942 (dec. Mar. 1973); children: Wendy, John, Polly; m. Myra Gordon, Mar. 30, 1979. BA, MA, U. Wis., 1939; LLB, Harvard U., 1942. Judge U.S. Ct. Appeals, Milw., 1951-62, Wis. State Supreme Ct., Madison, 1966-67, U.S. Dist. Ct., Milw., 1967—; now sr. judge. Office: US Dist Ct 271 US Courthouse 517 E Wisconsin Ave Milwaukee WI 53202-4500

**GORDON, NORMAN JAMES,** lawyer; b. Dec. 24, 1945; s. Meyer and Alice (Vetzner) G.; m. Cheryl Bisk, June 8, 1969; children: David Benjamin, Joshua. BA, U. Ill., 1967, JD, 1970. Bar: Ill. 1970, Tex. 1974, U.S. Dist. Ct. (we. dist.) Tex. 1974, U.S. Ct. Appeals (5th cir.) 1974, U.S. Supreme Ct. 1974. Asst. states atty. McLean County, Ill., 1970; assoc. Diamond, Rash, Gordon & Jackson P.C. (formerly Diamond, Rash, Leslie & Smith), El Paso, Tex., 1974-76; shareholder Diamond, Rash, Gordon & Jackson P.C., El Paso, Tex., 1976—. V.p. El Paso Comty. Ctr., 1980-82, pres., 1983-86; sec. El Paso Jewish Fedn., 1986-88, v.p., 1988-94, pres., 1994-96; treas. Hospice of El Paso, 1982-83; bd. dirs. Congregation B'nai Zion, El Paso. Capt. JAGC, U.S. Army, 1970-74. Recipient New Leadership award Nat. Jewish Welfare Bd., 1982. Mem. ABA, Ill. Bar Assn., State Bar Tex., Assn. Trial Lawyers Am., Tex. Bd. Legal Specialization (cert. civil trial law), Tex. Trial Lawyers Assn., El Paso Bar Assn. Federal civil litigation, State civil litigation, Personal injury. Office: 7th Fl 300 E Main Dr El Paso TX 79901-1372

**GORDON, ROBERT E.,** lawyer; b. Pensacola, Fla., Feb. 15, 1953; s. Earle Elmer Jr. and Clarice Evelyn (Watson) G.; m. Leesa Brown, Feb. 14, 1980; children: Trevor M., Julia E. BS, U. Fla., 1975, JD, 1978. Bar: Fla. 1978, U.S. Dist. Ct. (so. dist.) Fla. 1979, U.S. Dist. Ct. (mid. dist.) Fla. 1990; bd. cert. civil trial lawyer Fla. Bar Bd. Cert. Assoc. Farish, Farish & Romani, West Palm Beach, Fla., 1978-82, McGee, Jordan, Shuey, Koons & Schroeder, Lake Worth, Fla., 1982-84; shareholder McGee, Jordan, et al, Lake Worth, 1984-92, Davis, Gordon & Doner, West Palm Beach, 1993—; mem. U. Fla. Appellate Adv. Bd. Editors, Gainesville, 1977-78. Contbr. articles to profl. jours. Pres. Young Dems. Palm Beach County, West Palm Beach, 1981-82; mem. Land Use Adv. Bd., Palm Beach County, 1986-87; participant Leadership Palm Beach County, West Palm Beach, 1990. Mem. Assn. Trial Lawyers Am., Acad. Fla. Trial Lawyers, Palm Beach County Bar Assn., Palm Beach County Trial Lawyers Assn. (pres. 1997-98). Avocation:

golf. Personal injury, General civil litigation. Office: Davis Gordon & Doner PA 515 N Flagler Dr Ste 700 West Palm Beach FL 33401-4324

**GORDON, ROBERT M.,** lawyer; b. Lafayette, calif., Dec. 29, 1966; s. Marshall Hewitt and Eleanor (Everall) G. BA, U. Calif., Berkeley, 1986; MBA, Claremont (Calif.) Grad. Sch., 1987; JD, Georgetown U., 1990. Bar: D.C. 1991, Calif. 1992; CFP. Assoc. Myerson & Kuhn, N.Y.C., 1989; atty. Wiley, Rein & Fielding, Washington, 1990-92; counsel Office of Rep. Dreier, Washington, 1992-94, Com. on Commerce, U.S. Ho. of Reps., Washington, 1994—. Office: US Ho of Reps Com on Commerce 316 Ford House Office Bldg Washington DC 20515-0001

**GORDON, SCOTT R.,** lawyer; b. Riverside, Calif., Feb. 17, 1959; s. Keith A. and Sandra R. Gordon; m. Betsey P. Pheeney, Aug. 9, 1986; children: Michael, Hunter, Conner, Rachel. BBA, U. Miss., 1981; JD, Capital U., 1988, MBA, 1988. Bar: W.Va. 1988, Ohio 1989, U.S. Dist. Ct. (no. dist.) Ohio 1991, U.S. Dist. Ct. (so. dist.) Ohio 1992. Assoc. Kay, Casto & Cheeney, Charleston, W.Va., 1988-90; asst. atty. gen. State of Ohio Atty. Gen., Columbus, 1991-93; assoc. Law Offices of Donald Johnson, Van Wert, Ohio, 1993-96; pvt. practice law Van Wert, 1996—; solicitor Village Ohio City, Ohio, 1997—, Village Haviland, Ohio, 1997—. Pres. bd. dirs. First Presbyn. Ch., Van Wert, 1995; coach Van Wert YMCA, 1995—; mem. ctrl. com. Van Wert County Rep., 1998—. Mem. Van Wert Area C. of C. (pres. 1997-98). Avocations: coaching youth sports, swimming, running, biking. Family and matrimonial, General practice. Home: 10442 Wildwood Dr Van Wert OH 45891-9051 Office: 116 W Main St Van Wert OH 45891-1704

**GORDON, THEODORA,** lawyer; b. N.Y.C., Nov. 4, 1923; d. Samuel and Rose (Perlstein) G. BA, Hunter Coll., 1945; JD, U. Chgo., 1947. Bar: Ill. 1948. Collection atty. Chgo. Assn. Credit Men, 1949-51, Spiegel, Inc., Chgo., 1951-53; product liability atty. Toni Co. div. Gillette Co., Chgo., 1953-74; sole practice Chgo., 1974—; cons. Gillette Co., Boston, 1974-85; arbitrator Am. Arbitration Assn., Chgo., 1985—; instr. Keller Grad. Sch. of Mgmt. Contbr. articles to profl. jours. Pres. Elaine Settler Found., 1960-62, bd. dirs., 1960—; bd. dirs. Levinson Ctr. for Mentally Handicapped, 1975-81. Mem. Women's Bar Ill. (pres. 1964-65), Chgo. Bar Assn., Decalogue Soc. (first woman pres.), Ill. State Bar Assn., Am. Assn. Trial Lawyers. Democrat. Jewish. Avocations: reading, knitting, theater, opera. General practice, Personal injury, Probate. Home: 6033 N Sheridan Rd Apt 16K Chicago IL 60660-3024 Office: 8 S Michigan Ave Chicago IL 60603-3357

**GORDON, WENDY JANE,** law educator; b. N.Y.C.. BA with distinction, Cornell U., 1971; postgrad., Yale U., 1974-75; JD, U. Pa., 1975. Bar: Conn. 1985, D.C. 1986, U.S. Ct. Appeals (2d cir.). Assoc. Pierson, Ball and Dowd, Washington, 1976-79; from asst. prof. to assoc. prof. law Western New England Coll. Sch. of Law, Springfield, Mass., 1979-84; assoc. prof. Rutgers U. Law Sch., Newark, 1985-91, prof., 1991-93; prof. Boston U., 1993—, Paul Liacos scholar in law, 1995—; vis. lit. property Weil, Gotshal & Manges, N.Y.C., 1982-83; vis. assoc. prof. Georgetown U. Law Ctr., Washington, 1983-84, Law Sch., U. Mich., Ann Arbor, 1984-85; vis. prof. Law Sch., U. Chgo., 1991-92; lectr. in law Law Sch., Yale U., 1993; Disting. Vis. faculty U. Toronto Faculty of Law, 1997; vis. scholar Griffith U., Australia, summer 1997; mem. consultative group project on drafting a restatement on unfair competition Am. Law Inst., Phila., 1988-94. Mem. editl. bd. Comm. Law and Policy; bd. dirs. Ency. of Law and Econs.; contbr. articles to profl. jours. Grantee for newly apptd. profs. Rutgers U., 1985-86, Rsch. Coun. summer fellowship award, 1986, Fulbright Scholar, 1999—, vis. sr. rsch. fellow St. John's Coll., Oxford, U.K., 1999—; recipient L. L. Fuller prize in jurisprudence Inst. for Humane Studies, 1988, N.J. Gov.'s fellowship in humanities N.J. Higher Edn. Dept., 1990, Rockefeller Found. residency at Bellagio, 1993. Mem. Am. Soc. for Polit. and Legal Philosophy, Law and Humanities Inst., Assn. Am. Law Schs. (chair-elect sect. on intellectual property 1996-97); hon. mem. Sr. Common Rm. St. Peter's Coll., Oxford. Avocation: rowing. Office: Boston U Sch of Law 765 Commonwealth Ave Boston MA 02215-1401

**GORE, WEAVER ELLIS, JR.,** lawyer; b. Marks, Miss., Nov. 27, 1925; s. Weaver Ellis Gore and Bessie Elizah Griffin; m. Ernestine Thompson, Dec. 6, 1950 (dec. July 1969); children: Rebecca Susan, Kathryn Dell; m. Edythe Smith Williams, Dec. 17, 1970. BA, Millsaps Coll., 1949; LLB, Jackson Law Sch., 1949. Bar: Miss. 1951, U.S. Dist. Ct. Miss., U.S. Ct. Appeals (5th cir.) 1956, U.S. Supreme Ct. Pvt. practice Jackson, Miss. Mem. Civil Svc. Commn., Jackson, 1976-80. With U.S. Army, 1943-46. Mem. Masons. Republican. Methodist. Avocations: fishing, woodworking, stock car racing. Office: 120 N Congress St Jackson MS 39201-2606

**GORELICK, JAMIE SHONA,** lawyer; b. N.Y.C., May 6, 1950; d. Leonard and Shirley (Fishman) G.; m. Richard E. Waldhorn, Sept. 28, 1975; children: Daniel H., Dana E. BA, Radcliffe Coll., 1972; JD, Harvard U., 1975. Bar: D.C. 1975, U.S. Dist. Ct. D.C. 1976, U.S. Tax Ct. 1976, U.S. Ct. Claims 1976, U.S. Ct. Appeals (D.C. cir.) 1976, U.S. Ct. Appeals (5th cir.) 1977, U.S. Supreme Ct. 1979, U.S. Ct. Appeals (Fed. cir.) 1982, U.S. Ct. Internat. Trade 1984, U.S. Dist. Ct. Md. 1985, U.S. Ct. Appeals (4th cir.) 1986, U.S. Ct. Appeals (3d. cir.) 1988. With Miller, Cassidy, Larroca & Lewin, Washington, 1975-79, 81-93; asst. to sec., counselor to dep. sec. U.S. Dept. Energy, Washington, 1979-80; gen. counsel Dept. Def., Washington, 1993-94; dep. atty. gen. Dept. Justice, Washington, 1994-97; vice chair Fannie Mae, Washington, 1997—; mem. chmn.'s adv. coun. U.S. Senate Jud. Com., 1988-93; tchg. mem. trial advocacy workshop Harvard Law Sch., Cambridge, Mass., 1982, 84; vice chair task force evaluation of audit investigative inspection components Dept. Def., Washington, 1979-80; mem. sec.'s transition team Dept. Energy, Washington, 1979; bd. dirs. Fannie Mae, Fannie Mae Found., D.C. Coll. Access, Am.'s Promise-Alliance for Youth, Nat. Park Found., Carnegie Endowment, Nat. Women's Law Ctr., Bazelon Ctr. Mental Health Law, Washington Legal Clinic for Homeless, Local Initiatives Support Corp., Nat. Legal Ctr. for the Pub. Interest; coun. mem. Am. Law Inst., D.C. Bar Found.; co-chair adv. com. Presdl. Commn. on Critical Infrastructure Protection; mem. Nat. Commn. Support Law Enforcement, Washington, 1995—; mem. nat. security adv. panel CIA; mem. threat reduction adv. com. Dept. Def. Mem. editl. bd. Corp. Criminal Liability Reporter, 1986-93, Destruction of Evidence, 1989; contbr. articles to profl. jours. Mem. bd. overseers Harvard Coll., 1989-93. Fellow Am. Bar Found.; mem. ABA (chair complex crimes litigation com. litigation sect. 1984-87, vice-chair complex crimes litigation com. 1983-84, Nat. Commn. to Support Law Enforcement, 1995—, sec. litigation sect. 1988-90, coun. mem. 1990-93, com. on profl. discipline, ho. of dels. 1991-93, 97—), D.C. Bar (pres. 1992-93, bd. govs. 1982-88, sec. bd. govs. 1981-82, bar found. advisors 1985-93, legal ethics com.), Womens Bar Assn., Am. Law Inst. (coun.), Coun. on Fgn. Rels. Office: Fannie Mae 3900 Wisconsin Ave NW Washington DC 20016-2892

**GOREN, JOHN ALAN,** lawyer; b. Houston, June 9, 1948; s. Jack and Leah Sakowitz (Nathan) G. BS in Econs., U. Pa., Phila., 1970; JD cum laude, U. Ga., 1974. Bar: Ga. 1974, Tex. 1977, U.S. Supreme Ct. 1979, U.S. Ct. Appeals (5th and 11th cirs.) 1984, U. S. Ct. Appeals (fed. cir.) 1984, U.S. Dist. Ct. (no. dist.) Tex. 1983; bd. cert. Civil Appellate Law, Tex. Bd. Legal Specialization, 1987. Sole practitioner Dallas. Developer For Kid's Sake Seminar, Collin County, Tex., 1992—; mem. worship com. Temple Emanu-El, Dallas, 1990-96, sustentation campaign com., 1994—; former dir. Dallas chpt. Am. Jewish Com.; pres. Wharton Alumni Club Dallas, 1980; active worker Dallas County Rep. Party and numerous Rep. campaigns, including chmn. ballot security, senatorial spl. election, 1992, v.p. Metrocrest Rep. Club, 1997-98, treas., 1995-96, 93-94, mem. Dallas County Rep. Assembly, Dallas County Rep. Forum, other sustaining orgns.; del. Rep. Party State Conv., 1996, alternate, 1990, 92, 94. Mem. Dallas Bar Assn. (founder, chmn. appellate law sect. 1990-91, chmn. Dallas Ct. Appeals centennial celebration com. 1993, member various other coms. and subcoms., Most Outstanding Sect. Chair award 1992), Plano (Tex.) Bar Assn. (pres. 1994-95), State Bar of Tex. (mandatory continuing legal edn. com. 1995—). Appellate. Home: 11308 Park Central Pl Apt D Dallas TX 75230-3311 Office: 4655 N Central Expy Dallas TX 75205-4022

**GOREN, STEVEN ELIOT,** lawyer; b. Detroit, Apr. 9, 1960; s. Robert and Judith A. (Wise) G.; m. Eva Calmidis, Sept. 25, 1980; children: Robert C., Sophia J. BA with high distinction, U. Mich., 1981, JD cum laude, 1984. Bar: Mich. 1984, U.S. Dist. Ct. (ea. dist.) Mich. 1984. Atty. Dickinson, Wright, Moon, VanDusen & Freeman, Bloomfield Hills, Mich., 1984-86, pvt. practice, Birmingham, Mich., 1986—; adjunct prof. U. Detroit Law Sch., 1989-95; med. malpractice task force Mich. Trial lawyers, 1989. Contbr. articles to profl. jours. Precinct Del. Democratic Party, Beverly Hills, Mich., 1990-91. Personal injury, Product liability. Office: 30400 Telegraph Rd Ste 470 Bingham Farms MI 48025-4541

**GORENFELD, WILLIAM ROGERS,** lawyer; b. L.A., Dec. 16, 1942; s. Abraham and Clara Gorenfeld; m. Suzanne Stein, Apr. 12, 1970; children: John W., Louis B. BA in Sociology, Calif. State U., Northridge, 1965; JD, Loyola U., L.A., 1969. Bar: Calif. 1970. Staff atty. San Gabriel Legal Aid, El Monte, Calif., 1970-72, Indian Legal Svcs., Ukiah, Calif., 1975-77; adj. prof. Loyola U., 1972-75; exec. dir. Marin Legal Aid, San Rafael, Calif., 1977-82; rsch. atty. Calif. Ct. Appeal, Ventura, 1982—. Contbr. articles to mag. Treas. Hist. Ft. Tejon Found., 1997—. Mem. Calif. State Bar (chmn. com. on history 1990-91). Avocations: jogging, military history, baseball. Office: Calif Ct Appeal 200 E Santa Clara St Ventura CA 93001-2718

**GORENSTEIN, CHARLES,** lawyer; b. Phila., Nov. 25, 1950; s. Samuel and Ethel (Gershman) G.; m. Gail Barbara Newman, July 8, 1973; children: Jeremy L., Heather M. BS in Engring. Mechanics, Pa. State U., 1972; JD, Am. U., 1980. Bar: D.C. 1981, Va. 1988, U.S. Patent and Trademark Office 1979, U.S. Dist. Ct. (D.C. dist.) 1982, U.S. Dist. Ct. (ea. dist.) Va. 1989, U.S. Dist. Ct. (ea. dist.) Mich. 1995, U.S. Dist. Ct. (ea. dist.) Wis. 1995, U.S. Ct. Appeals (D.C. and fed. cirs.) 1982, U.S. Ct. Appeals (4th cir.) 1989. Examiner U.S. Patent & Trademark Office, Washington, 1972-79; patent advisor U.S. Army Electronics Rsch. & Devel. Command, Adelphi, Md., 1979-81; assoc. Finnegan, Henderson, Farabow, Garrett & Dunner, Washington, 1981; ptnr. Birch, Stewart, Kolasch & Birch, Falls Church, Va., 1982—. Indsl. and profl. adv. coun. Coll. Engring./Pa. State U., University Park, Pa., 1988-93. Mem. ABA, U.S. Trademark Assn., Am. Intellectual Property Law Assn., Md. Patent Law Assn., Am. Internat. Soc. Indsl. Property. Avocations: skiing, golf. Trademark and copyright, Patent, Federal civil litigation. Home: 1718 Crestview Dr Potomac MD 20854-2630 Office: 8110 Gatehouse Rd Ste 500 E Falls Church VA 22042-1210

**GORES, THOMAS C.,** lawyer; b. Milw., Sept. 24, 1948; s. Kenneth W. and Carolyn (Camblin) G.; m. Ann P. Pacelli, June 13, 1970; children: Lauren, Jake, Kathryn. BA, U. Notre Dame, 1970, JD, 1973; LLM, U. Miami, 1977. Bar: Wash. 1973, U.S. Tax Ct. 1973. Assoc., then ptnr. Bogle & Gates, Seattle, 1973-78, ptnr., 1978-93; ptnr. Gores & Blais, Seattle, 1993—. Fellow Am. Coll. Trust and Estate Counsel; mem. Wash. State Bar Assn., Seattle Estate Planning Coun. (pres.). Estate planning, Probate, Estate taxation. Office: Gores & Blais 1420 5th Ave Ste 2600 Seattle WA 98101-1357

**GORMAN, CHRIS,** lawyer; b. Frankfort, Ky., Jan. 22, 1943; m. Vicki Lynn Beekman; two sons. Grad., U. Ky. Bar: Ky., 1967. Former ptnr. Conliffe, Sandman, Gorman, and Sullivan, Louisville; former dir. civil div. Jefferson County Attys. Office; atty. gen. Ky., 1992-95; gen. counsel Taylor Bldg. Corp. Am., Louisville, 1996—; ptnr. Sheffer, Hutchinson, Kinney, Louisville. Address: Nat City Tower 101 S 5th St Ste 1600 Louisville KY 40202-3107

**GORMAN, DEIRDRE A.,** lawyer; b. Newark, Dec. 19, 1955; d. Francis William and Doris Katherine (Daniels) G., m. Lane C. Hoyt, Dec. 28, 1986; children: Liam Quinn O'Gorman-Hoyt, Dylan Francis O'Gorman-Hoyt. BS in Police Sci., Weber State U., Ogden, Utah, 1978; JD, Pepperdine U., 1982. Bar: Calif. 1983, Utah 1982; U.S. Ct. Appeals (10th cir.), 1993; qualified for death penalty representation. Atty. Utah Legal Svcs., Ogden, 1984, Weber County Pub. Defender, Ogden, 1987; atty., assoc. Farr, Kaufman, Hamilton, Ogden, 1984-88, ptnr., 1988—; com. mem. Criminal Justice Act Adv. Com., U.S. Dist. Ct., Salt Lake City, 1995; criminal justice act panel atty. U.S. Dist. Ct. Utah. Mem. Nat. Assn. Criminal Def. Attys., Utah Criminal Defense Lawyer's Assn., Weber County Pub. Defenders Assn. (trustee 1995). Democrat. Roman Catholic. Criminal, Personal injury. Office: Farr Kaufman et al 205 26th St Ste 34 Ogden UT 84401-3119

**GORMAN, GERALD WARNER,** lawyer; b. North Kansas City, Mo., May 30, 1933; s. William Shelton and Bessie (Warner) G.; m. Anita Belle McPike, June 26, 1954; children: Guinevere Eve, Victoria Rose. AB cum laude, Harvard U., 1954, LLB magna cum laude, 1956. Bar: Mo. 1956. Assoc. firm Dietrich, Tyler, Davis, Burrell & Dicus, Kansas City, 1956-62; ptnr. Dietrich, Davis, Dicus, Rowlands, Schmitt & Gorman, 1963-90; dir. Slagle, Bernard & Gorman, P.C., 1990—; bd.dirs. Musser-Davis Land Co., Curry Investment Co. Bd. govs. Citizens Assn. Kansas City, 1962—; trustee Harvard/Radcliffe Club Kansas City Endowment Fund, chmn. bd. trustees, 1977-83; trustee Kansas City Mus., 1967-82; chmn. bd. trustees Avondale Meth. Ch., 1969-92; mem. Citizens Bond Com. of Kansas City, 1973—, chmn. 7th jud. cir. citizens com., 1982-84; chmn. Downtown Coun. Allis Plaza Reconstrn., 1983-85; bd. dirs. Spofford Home for Children, 1972-77, Clay County Econ. Devel. Commn., 1989-94, mem. exec. com., 1991-93. With U.S. Army, 1956-58; capt. USAR, 1958-64. Mem. Lawyers Assn. Kansas City (exec. com. 1968-71), ABA, Mo. Bar Assn., Kansas City Bar Assn., Clay County Bar Assn., Harvard Law Sch. Assn. Mo. (pres. 1973), Harvard Club (pres. 1966), Univ. Club (bd. dirs. 1983-86, 88-93, pres. 1990-91), Kansas City Club (bd. dirs. 1993-97), 611 Club (bd. dirs. 1987-91, pres. 1990), Kansas City Country Club, Old Pike Country Club, River Club. Republican. General corporate, Taxation, general, Probate. Home: 917 NE Vivion Rd Kansas City MO 64118-5317 Office: 4600 Madison Ave Ste 600 Kansas City MO 64112-3031

**GORMAN, JAMES EDWARD,** lawyer; b. Summit, Ill., Nov. 11, 1930; s. James Edward and Mae Catherine (Kiracek) G.; m. Beverly Ann Fink; children: Gregory, Stephen, Robert, William Mudge, Ann, James, Mary. BA, St. Ambrose Coll., 1952; JD, U. Ill., 1955. Bar: Ill. 1956, U.S. Dist. Ct. (so. dist.) Ill. 1958, U.S. Ct. Appeals 1979, U.S. Supreme Ct. 1980. Assoc. Heyl, Royster, Voelker and Allen, Peoria, Ill., 1957-59, Bernard, Gorman, Davidson, Edwardsville, Granite City, Ill., 1959-61; ptnr. Reed, Armstrong, Gorman, Coffey, Thomson, Gilbert & Mudge, Edwardsville, Ill., 1961—. With U.S. Army, 1955-57. Mem. ABA, Ill. Bar Assn., Am. Coll. Trial Lawyers, Ill. Trial Lawyers Assn., Am. Trial Lawyers Assn., Madison County Bar Assn., KC. Roman Catholic. Insurance, Personal injury. Office: Reed Armstrong Gorman Coffey Gilbert & Mudge PC 101 W Vandalia St Ste 300 Edwardsville IL 62025-1949

**GORMAN, ROBERT DENNIS,** lawyer; b. Santa Fe, N.Mex., Nov. 3, 1955; s. Robert D. and Virginia M. Gorman; m. Cathy M. Sanchez, Sept. 9, 1978; children: Sarah, Lillian, Stephanie. BBA, U. N.Mex., 1977, JD, 1983. Bar: N.Mex. 1983, U.S. Dist. Ct. N.Mex. 1983, U.S. Tax Ct. 1983, U.S. Ct. Appeals (10th cir.) 1983, U.S. Ct. Claims 1993, U.S. Supreme Ct. 1993. CPA, N.Mex. Auditor, rsch. adminstr. N.Mex. State Auditor, Santa Fe, 1977-84; pvt. practice acctg., Santa Fe and Albuquerque, 1978-83; assoc. Eaves, Darling & Porter, Albuquerque, 1983-89; pvt. practice, Albuquerque, 1989—; mem. supervisory com. First Fin. Credit Union, Albuquerque, 1990-92; instr. bus. law U. Phoenix, 1991. Parish and fin. coun. mem. Holy Rosary Parish, Albuquerque, 1988—. Mem. ABA, AICPA, N.Mex. State Bar (dir. tax sect. 1984-95), N.Mex. Soc. CPAs (ethics com. 1998). Democrat. Roman Catholic. Avocations: skiing, running. Taxation, general, Probate, Real property. Office: 1201 Lomas Blvd NW Albuquerque NM 87102-1855

**GORMAN, THOMAS O(RLO),** lawyer; b. Elyria, Ohio, June 13, 1948; s. John M. and Dorothy (Bogart) G.; 1 son, John. AB, John Carroll U., 1970; JD cum laude, Cleve. State U., 1973; LLM, Georgetown U., 1982. Bar: Ohio 1973, D.C. 1981, N.Y. 1990. Atty. Pub. Defenders Office, Cleve., 1973-75; ptnr. Gorman, Bakeman & Benjamin, Cleve., 1975-78; atty., sr. counsel Divsn. of Enforcement, SEC, Washington, 1978-82; spl. trial counsel Office of Gen. Counsel, 1982-85; adj. prof. law Cleve. State U., 1974-76. Editor Cleve. State Law Review. Mem. ABA. Office: Porter Wright Morris & Arthur 1667 K St NW Washington DC 20006-1605

**GORNBEIN, HENRY SEIDEL,** lawyer; b. Detroit, May 27, 1943; s. Abe Siedel and Lillian (Westerman) G.; m. Debra Marilyn Gornbein, June 13, 1993; children: Jonathan David and Laurie Beth. B Philosophy, Montieth Coll., Wayne State, 1965; JD, Univ. of Mich.-Ann Arbor, 1968. Bar: Mich. 1968. Law clk. Wayne County Cir. Ct., Detroit, 1968-69; assoc. Gage & Brukoff, Southfield, Mich., 1969-70, Coleman, Goodman & Schifman, Southfield, 1970-71; ptnr. Bayer, Goren, Gornbein, Gropman & Kaplan, P.C., Southfield, 1979-81; sole practice and ptnr. in various entities, 1971-81; assoc. Baskin, Feldstein & Gornbein, Birmingham, Mich., 1982-85; pvt. practice, Birmingham, 1985-95; ptnr. Bookholder, Bassett, Gornbein, Solomon & Cohen, PLLC, 1995-98; creator, host (cable TV show) Practical Law; pres. Am. Divorce Info. Network, Inc., pub. Divorce Online (internet). Family and matrimonial. Home and Office: 4190 Telegraph Rd Ste 3000 Bloomfield Hills MI 48302-2082

**GORRIN, EUGENE,** lawyer; b. Irvington, N.J., Apr. 22, 1956; s. Harry and Ruth (Goldberg) G. BA, Rutgers U., 1978; JD, George Washington U., 1981; LLM in Taxation, NYU, 1982. Bar: N.J. 1981, U.S. Dist. Ct. N.J. 1981, U.S. Tax Ct. 1982, U.S. Supreme Ct. 1985. Assoc. Ozzard, Rizzolo, Klein, Mauro & Savo, Somerville, N.J., 1982-83; Assoc. Levine, Furman & Davis, East Brunswick, N.J., 1984-88; ptnr. Cole, Schotz, Meisel, Forman & Leonard, P.A., Hackensack, N.J., 1988-98; corp. adv. specialist Family Office Group Merrill Lynch Trust Co., Plainsboro, N.J., 1999—. Contbr. articles to profl. pubs. Mem. ABA (taxation sect.), N.J. Bar Assn. (taxation sect.), U.S. Supreme Ct. Hist. Soc., Phi Alpha Delta. Estate planning, Corporate taxation, Personal income taxation. Home: 2607 Frederick Ter Union NJ 07083-5603 Office: Merrill Lynch Trust Co Family Office Group 800 Scudders Mill Rd # 1F Plainsboro NJ 08536-1606

**GORRY, JAMES A., III,** lawyer; b. Wilmington, Del., Mar. 1, 1939; s. James A. Jr. and Carolyn Allmond Gorry; m. Anne Evans, May 7, 1975; children: Scott Baker, Katherine Gorry Lawson. BA, U. Del., 1961; JD, Washington & Lee U., 1964. Bar: Va. 1964, U.S. Dist. Ct. (ea. dist.) Va. 1968, U.S. Ct. Appeals (4th cir.) 1982, U.S. Supreme Ct. 1982. Atty. U.S. Army-Judge Adv. Gen. Corps, Virginia Beach, Va., 1965-68, Murphy, Bennett & Gorry, Virginia Beach, 1968-72, Broyles, Gorry, Moore & Brydges, Virginia Beach, 1972-82, Taylor & Walker, P.C., Norfolk, Va., 1982-99; ptnr. DMZ Law Group, L.L.P., Norfolk, 1999—; commr. in chancery Virginia Beach Cir. Ct., 1985—. Capt. U.S. Army, 1964-68. Mem. Va. State Bar (bd. govs. civil litigation sect. 1994—), Va. Assn. Def. Attys. (dir. 1993-96), Va. Trial Lawyers' Assn., Va. Bar Assn., Virginia Beach Bar Assn. (pres. 1980), Norfolk-Portsmouth Bar Assn. Avocations: scuba diving, golfing, running. Fax: 757-624-3479. Product liability, Toxic tort, Personal injury. Home: 40 Rader St Apt 310 Norfolk VA 23510-1036 Office: DMZ Law Group LLP 300 E Main St Fl 13 Norfolk VA 23510-1753

**GORSKE, ROBERT HERMAN,** retired lawyer; b. Milw., June 8, 1932; s. Herman Albert and Lorraine (McDermott) G.; m. Antonette Dujick, Aug. 28, 1954; 1 child, Judith Mary (Mrs. Charles H. McMullen). Student, U. Wis., Milw., 1949-50; B.A. cum laude, Marquette U., 1953, J.D. magna cum laude, 1955, MS in Clin. Psychology, 1996; LL.M. (W.W. Cook fellow), U. Mich., 1959; student, Hague Acad. Internat. Law, The Netherlands, 1981. Bar: Wis. bar 1955, D.C. bar 1975, U.S. Supreme Ct. bar 1970. Assoc. firm Quarles, Spence & Quarles, Milw., 1955-56; atty. Allis-Chalmers Mfg. Co., West Allis, Wis., 1956-62; instr. law U. Mich. Law Sch., Ann Arbor, 1958-59; lectr. law Marquette U. Law Sch., Milw., 1963; assoc. firm Quarles, Herriott & Clemons, Milw., 1962-64; atty. Wis. Electric Power Co., Milw., 1964-67, gen. counsel, 1967-94, v.p., 1970-72, 76-94, dir., 1991-94; mem. firm Quarles & Brady, Milw., 1972-76; gen. counsel Wis. Energy Corp., Milw., 1981-94; tutor in psychiatry Med. Coll. Wis., 1995. Contbr. articles to profl. jours.; Editor-in-chief: Marquette Law Rev, 1954-55. Bd. dirs. Guadalupe Children's Med. Dental Clinic, Inc., Milw., 1976-86; bd. dirs. Milw. Urban League, 1991-94, treas., 1993-94; trustee Ronald McDonald House, Wauwatosa, Wis., 1987-94. Mem. State Bar Wis., Edison Electric Inst. (vice chmn. legal com. 1975-77, chmn. 1977-79), Am. Arbitration Assn. (panelist comml. arbitrators 1985—), Ctr. for Pub. Resources (com. on alt. dispute resolution 1985-94, exec. com. 1991-94, panel disting. neutrals 1991-94). Alternative dispute resolution, General corporate, Public utilities. Home: 12700 Stephen Pl Elm Grove WI 53122-1964

**GORSKI, JAMES MICHAEL,** lawyer; b. Coupeville, Wash.; s. Leonard George and Mildred Reuble Gorski; m. Susan Elizabeth Erchinger, Dec. 28, 1974; children: James L., Tristan F. BA, U. Wash., 1974; JD, Willamette U., 1977. Bar: Alaska 1977, U.S. Dist. Ct. Alaska 1977, U.S. Ct. Appeals (9th cir.) 1979, U.S. Supreme Ct. 1984. Atty. Hughes Thorsness Powell Huddleston & Bauman LLC, Anchorage, Alaska, 1977—; bd. dirs., officer Anchorage Econ. Devel. Corp. Bd. dirs. 2001 Special Olympics World Winter Games, Anchorage, 1998—; v.p., bd. dirs. 1996 Chugiak Eagle River Arctic Winter Games, 1993-97; bd. dirs. Eagle River Found., 1996—, Eagle River Nature Ctr., 1996—, Alaska Moving Arts Ctr., 1996—. Roman Catholic. Contracts commercial, Real property, Mergers and acquisitions. Home: 10243 Stewart Dr Eagle River AK 99577-9514 Office: Hughes Thorsness Powell Huddleston & Bauman 550 W 7th Ave Ste 1100 Anchorage AK 99501-3563

**GORSKI, RONALD WILLIAM,** lawyer; b. Cambridge, Mass., Feb. 15, 1962; s. Marian and Kazimiera Gorski; m. Ronda Marie Gibbons, May 21, 1988; 1 child, Brittany Katherine. BA, Boston Coll., 1984; JD, Suffolk Law Sch., Boston, 1987. Bar: Mass. 1987, U.S. Dist. Ct. Mass. 1988. Atty. Electric Mut., Beverly, Mass., 1987-92; litigation supr. Arkwright Mut., Waltham, Mass., 1992-94; assoc. gen. counsel Factory Mut. Engring. and Rsch. Corp., Norwood, Mass., 1994—. Mem. Am. Corp. Counsel Assn., KC (recorder 1997—). General corporate, Insurance, General civil litigation. Office: Factory Mutual 1151 Boston Providence Hwy Norwood MA 02062-5082

**GORSUCH, SANDRA CARDO,** lawyer; b. Friendship, Wis., Dec. 6, 1962; d. Gerald A. Cardo and Judith M. Flott; m. Andrew H. Gorsuch, June 17, 1989; children: Rachel Mary, Abel James. BS, U. Wis., 1985; JD, Hamline U., 1990. Bar: Wis. 1990, U.S. Dist. Ct. (ea. and we. dists.) Wis. 1990. Assoc. Chiquoine & Krueger, S.C., Reedsburg, Wis., 1990-95; pvt. practice Reedsburg, 1995—. Bd. dirs. Sauk County Health Care Ctr.-Benefit Club Found., Reedsburg, 1997—. Family and matrimonial, Probate, Real property. Office: 212 N Walnut St Reedsburg WI 53959-1658

**GORTON, NATHANIEL M.,** federal judge; b. 1938; m. Jodi Linnell; children: Kerry, Craig, Nan. AB, Dartmouth Coll., 1960; LLB, Columbia U., 1966. Bar: Mass. 1966, U.S. Dist. Ct. Mass. 1967, U.S. Ct. Appeals (5th cir.) 1975, U.S. Ct. Appeals (9th cir.) 1977, U.S. Ct. Appeals (1st cir.) 1979, U.S. Ct. Appeals (11th cir.) 1990. Assoc. Nutter, McClennen & Fish, Boston, 1966-69; assoc. Powers & Hall, P.C., Boston, 1970-74, ptnr., dir., 1975-92; district judge Mass., 1992—. Trustee Buckingham Browne & Nichols Sch., Cambridge, Mass., 1984-93, chmn., 1989-93; mem. corp. Boston Children's Svcs., 1991—; mem. Wellesley Town Meeting, 1971-86; sr. warden All Saints Episcopal Ch., Brookline, Mass., 1975-80; apptd. Mass. Citizens Commn. on Gen. Ct., 1976; mem. com. Modern Legis., 1967-69; coach Wellesley Little League and Youth Hockey, 1983-87; bd. dirs. Rep. Club Mass., 1991-92; mem. fin. com. Citizens for Joe Malone, 1989-90; mem. Weld/Cellucci Com., 1989-90; program chmn. Boston chpt. Ripon Soc., 1967-68. (Lt. (j.g.) USN, 1960-62. Mem. Boston Bar Assn. (law day classroom program, 1987-93, litigation, adminstrn. justice sect.). Avocations: hockey, tennis, skiing, sailing, mem. Boston Atoms Hockey N.Am.- (nat. finalist 1988, 91). Office: Dist Judge Mass US Dist Ct 595 Main St Worcester MA 01608-2025

**GORUP, GEARY N.,** lawyer; b. Feb. 6; s. Ted J. and Thelma (Ihle) G.; m. Sylvia Gorup, Aug. 3, 1974; children: Geoffrey K., Genee Bree. ABA, Kansas City (Kans.) Comm. Col., 1969; BA in Polit. Sci., Kans. State U., 1971; JD, U. Kans., 1974. Prosecutor City of Wichita, Kans., 1974-75; dep. county atty. Butler County Atty.'s Office, El Dorado, Kans., 1975-76, county atty., 1976-80; trial divsn. atty. Sedgwick County Dist. Atty.'s Office, Wichita, 1980-82, chief appellate divsn., 1982-87, asst. dist. atty., 1980-87; of counsel Moore & Rapp, P.A., Wichita, 1987-88, Law Office of Leslie F. Hulnick, Wichita, 1988-91; pvt. practice Wichita, 1987-93, 97-99; mcpl. ct. judge City of Wichita, 1993-97; of counsel Render, Kamas, L.C., Wichita, 1997—. Contbr. articles to profl. jours.; author/editor: The Defense Never Rests, 1989-92; author/lectr. seminars/books and materials. Pres. Am. Youth Soccer Orgn., Hawthorne, Calif., 1998-99, nat. sec., 1997—, nat. bd. dirs., 1997—, sect. 4 dir., 1991-92, area dir., Kans.-Okla., 1991-92, regional commr., 1988-90. Mem. Kans. Assn. Criminal Def. Lawyers (bd. dirs., newsletter editor), Kans. County and Dist. Atty. Assn. (bd. dirs. 1978-80,

Prosecutor of the Yr. 1980), Kans. Bar Assn. (chmn. criminal law sect. 1991-92), Wichita Bar Assn. (continuing legal edn. 1988-92, criminal law com. 1986-92), Kans. Trial Lawyers Assn. (chmn. criminal law com. 1990-92), Nat. Assn. Criminal Def. Lawyers. Office: 11108 W 14th St N Wichita KS 67212-1137

**GOSAIN, VINEET,** lawyer; b. Kansas City, Mo., Apr. 21, 1969; s. Jagan N. and Poonam Gosain; m. Rebecca Jane Reese, May 23, 1998. BS, U. Ill., 1991; JD, Chgo.-Kent Coll. of Law, 1994. Bar: Ill. 1994, U.S. Dist. Ct. (no. dist.) Ill. 1994, U.S. Ct. Appeals (7th cir.) 1997. Assoc. Baker & Enright, Chgo., 1994-96, Oppenheimer Wolff & Donnelly, Chgo., 1996—. Insurance, Labor. Office: Oppenheimer Wolff & Donnelly 180 N Stetson Ave Fl 45 Chicago IL 60601-6710

**GOSANKO, GARY NICOLAS,** lawyer; b. Seattle, Mar. 28, 1954; s. Clarence N. and Louella Mae Gosanko; m. Ann Valarie Rice, May 23, 1992. BA in Econs. cum laude, Wash. State U., 1977; JD magna cum laude, U. Puget Sound, 1983. Bar: Wash. Law clk. Honorable Herbert Swanson, Wash. State Ct. Appeals, Seattle, 1983-85; pvt. practice Seattle, 1985—. Mem. Assn. Trial Lawyers Am., Wash. State Trial Lawyers. Avocations: skiing, sailing, golf. Personal injury, Insurance. Office: 7513 SE 27th St Ste A Mercer Island WA 98040-2836

**GOSCINAK, VIRGINIA CASEY,** lawyer; b. Boston, July 29, 1948; d. James D. and Virgina (Burke) Casey. BS in Biology, Simmons Coll., 1970; MAT, Suffolk U., 1976, JD, 1981. Bar: Mass. 1981, U.S. Dist. Ct. Mass. 1982, U.S. Ct. Appeals (1st cir.) 1982. Assoc. Bingham, Dana & Gould, Boston, 1982-85; ptnr. Kilburn, Casey Goscinak & Coombs, Boston, 1985—; arbitrator Am. Arbitration Assn., Boston, 1987—. North Area Task Force mem. Charlestown (Mass.) Preservation Soc., 1983—; mediator Cambridge Mediation Group; mem. Friends of City Sq., 1988—. Mem. Internat. Assn. Def. Counsel, Mass. Bar Assn., Boston Bar Assn., Mass. Assn. Women Lawyers. General civil litigation, Product liability, Personal injury. Office: Kilburn Casey et al One Washington Mall Boston MA 02108

**GOSDECK, THOMAS JOSEPH,** lawyer; b. Buffalo, Oct. 10, 1951; s. Kermit Ronald and Mary Jane (O'Brien) G.; m. Catherine E. Schuth, July 31, 1982. BA, SUNY, 1973, JD, 1976. Bar: N.Y. 1979. Counsel environ. conservation com. N.Y. State Senate, Albany, 1980-82, counsel agr. com., 1982-85, counsel consumer protection com., 1985-88; ptnr. Newman, Kehoe et al., Lyons, N.Y., 1985-88, Steinhaus Assocs., Albany, 1988-90, DeGraff, Foy, Holt-Harris & Mealey, Albany, 1991-92, Hill & Gosdeck, Albany, 1993—. Counsel Webster (N.Y.) Republican Com., 1987-88. Recipient Teddi award Camp Good Day & Spl. Times, Rochester, N.Y., 1982. Mem. Normanside Country Club, Ft. Orange Club. Roman Catholic. Avocations: golf, reading, travel, photography. Legislative, Real property, General corporate. Office: Hill & Gosdeck 99 Washington Ave Ste 1950 Albany NY 12210-2823

**GOSE, RICHARD VERNIE,** lawyer; b. Hot Springs, S.D., Aug. 3, 1927. MS in Engring., Northwestern U., 1955; LLB, George Washington U., 1967; JD, George Washington U., 1968. Bar: N.Mex. 1967, U.S. Supreme Ct. 1976, Wyo. 1979; registered prof. engr., Wyo.; children: Beverly Marie, Donald Paul, Celeste Marlene. Exec. asst. to U.S. Senator Hickey, Washington, 1960-62; mgr. E.G. & G., Inc., Washington, 1964-66; asst. atty. gen. State of N.Mex., Santa Fe, 1967-70; pvt. practice law, Santa Fe, 1967—, Santa Fe/Prescott, 1989—; assoc. prof. engring. U. Wyo., 1957-60; owner, mgr. Gose & Assocs., Santa Fe, 1967-78; pvt. practice law, Casper, Wyo., 1978-83; pres. Argosy Internat., Inc., 1994—; ranch mgr., foreman, 1945-49; mem. Phoenix com. on fgn. rels., 1980—; co-chmn. Henry Jackson for Pres., M.Mex., 1976, Wyo. Johnson for Pres., 1960. With U.S. Army, 1950-52. Mem. N.Mex. Bar Assn., Wyo. Bar Assn., Yavapai County Bar Assn., Masons, High Country Hounds, Phoenix Com. Foreign Rels., High Country Hounds, Phi Delta Theta, Pi Tau Sigma, Sigma Tau. Methodist. General civil litigation, Real property, Oil, gas, and mineral. Home and Office: PO Box 3998 Prescott AZ 86302-3998

**GOSLINER, MICHAEL L.,** lawyer; b. 1953. AB, U. Calif.; JD, U. Calif., San Francisco. Gen. counsel Marine Mammal Commn., Washington, DC. Office: Marine Mammal Commn 4340 East West Hwy Ste 905 Bethesda MD 20814-4447*

**GOSS, J. BRADFORD,** lawyer; b. Carbondale, Ill., Aug. 18, 1956; s. Charles Thomas and Mary (Kovach) G.; m. Deborah Bennett Goss, Aug. 8, 1981; children: Andrew Thomas, Julia Elizabeth, Margaret Katherine, John Charles Bennett. BA in Pol. Sci. magna cum laude, Vanderbilt U., 1978; JD magna cum laude, U. Ill., 1983. Bar: Minn. 1983, Mo. 1987, Ill. 1988. Assoc. Leonard, Street & Deinard, Mpls., 1983-87; assoc. Husch, Eppenberger, et al, St. Louis, 1987-90, partner, 1991-94; v.p., gen. counsel Whittaker Construction, Inc., St. Peters, Mo., 1994—. Editor (with others): U. Ill. Law Review, 1982-83. Bd. trustees Webster Groves (Mo.) Presbyn. Ch., 1993—. Mem. ABA, (real property sec.), Home Builders Assn. (bd. dirs., legislative policy com., chmn. polit. action com. 1998). Presbyn. Avocations: bicycling, wine collecting. Real property, Contracts commercial, Environmental. Office: Whittaker Construction Inc 355 Mid Rivers Mall Dr # A Saint Peters MO 63376-1593

**GOSS, JAMES WILLIAM,** lawyer; b. London, Ont., Can., Mar. 10, 1941; s. Joseph Allen and Virginia Ruth (Farrah) G.; m. Rita Meyer, Aug. 2, 1969; children: Anne Candace, Jennette Courtney. BBA, West Mich. U., 1966; MS, U. Ill., 1972; JD, Georgetown U., 1974. Bar: Mich. 1974, U.S. Dist. Ct. (ea. dist.) Mich. 1974, U.S. Ct. Appeals (6th cir.) 1974. Sr. acct. Price Waterhouse & Co., Washington, 1969-71; assoc. Miller, Canfield, Paddock & Stone, Detroit, 1974-82, James W. Goss P.C., Southfield, Mich., 1982-88; ptnr. Dean & Fulkerson, Troy, Mich., 1988-95, James W. Goss P.C., Grosse Pointe Farms, Mich., 1995—; adj. lectr. U. Mich. Law, Ann Arbor, 1978-82. Bd. dirs. Old Newsboys Goodfellow Fund of Detroit, 1990-96, Adrian Coll., 1991-96; bd. dirs., v.p. Svc. to Older Citizens, Grosse Pointe, Mich., 1997—; bd. dirs. Grosse Pointe Hist. Soc., 1998-99; bd. govs. William L. Clements Libr., U. Mich., 1998—. Named Outstanding Goodfellow, Old Newsboys Goodfellows of Detroit, 1991; recipient Disting. Alumni award Western Mich. U., 1995. Mem. ABA, Mich. Bar Assn., Assn. Def. Trial Attys., Georgetown U. Law Alumni Assn., Grosse Pointe Yacht Club, Georgetown Club of Mich., Old Club, Commanderie de Bordeaux, Hundred Club, Rotary, Masons. Presbyterian. Avocations: philately, wine collecting, cartographic collecting. Taxation, general, Estate planning, General civil litigation. Home: 398 Rivard Blvd Grosse Pointe MI 48230-1629 Office: 230 Punch and Judy Bldg 21 Kercheval Ave Grosse Pointe MI 48236-3698

**GOSS, JAY BRYAN,** lawyer, accountant; b. Texarkana, Ark., Jan. 8, 1955; s. James Bryan and Betty Jean (Vance) G.; m. Jeannie Crumpler, June 4, 1977 (div. May 1989); children: Jason, Justin, Calli; m. Cathy Hill, July 1, 1990. BBA in Acctg., West Tex. State U., 1977; JD, Tex. Tech. Sch. of Law, 1980. Bar: Tex 1980, U.S. Dist. Ct. (no. dist.) Tex. 1981, (so. dist.) Tex. 1983; cert. civil trial specialist Nat. Bd. Trial Advocacy. Tax acct. Peat Marwick, Mitchell, Dallas, 1980-82; ptnr. Vance Bruchez & Goss, Bryan, Tex., 1982-90, Bruchez, Goss, Thornton, Meronoff, Michel & Hathorne, Bryan, 1991—; dir. Bd. Legal Specialization. Bd. dirs. Brazos Valley Coun. for Alcohol and Drug Abuse; mem. Leadership Brazos, Bryan, Tex., 1989. Fellow Tex. Bar Found. (dir. bd. of legal specialization 1998—), State Bar Tex. (bd. dirs. 1992-95), Coll. of the State Bar (dir. 1996—). Baptist. Construction, Personal injury. Address: 4343 Carter Creek Pkwy Ste 100 Bryan TX 77802-4455

**GOSS, REBECCA O.,** lawyer, pharmaceutical company executive. BS, Ind. U., 1970, JD, 1975. Bar: Ind. 1975. Lectr. Ind. U. Sch. Bus., 1979-80; counsel Nat. Ins. Assn., 1980-81; atty. Eli Lilly and Co., Indpls., 1981-83, sec., gen. counsel Elanco Products co. divsn., 1983-88, sec., gen. counsel Pharm. divsn., 1988-93, dep. gen. counsel, asst. sec., 1993-95, v.p., gen. counsel, 1995-98, now sr. v.p., gen. counsel, 1998—. Office: Eli Lilly and Co Lilly Corp Ctr Indianapolis IN 46285-0001

**GOSS, STEVEN BRYANT,** lawyer; b. Laconia, N.H., Jan. 13, 1948; s. Arnold Shirley and Mary Elizabeth Goss; m. Lora Florence Smith; children: Tyon, Rowen, Joslin, Cathrin. BA in Math., Dartmouth Coll., 1970; JD, Franklin Pierce Law Ctr., 1992. Bar: N.H. Pvt. practice Loudon, N.H., 1992-94; assoc. Martin, Lord & Osman, Lancaster, N.H., 1994—. Dir. Farm Bur. Grafton Com., Haverhill, N.H., 1998—; mem. N.H. and Maine Ayrshire Clubs, Haverhill, 1985—. Mem. N.H. Bar Assn. (elder law sect. 1992—, estate planning-probate sect. 1992—). Avocations: skiing, water sports. Estate planning, Probate, Real property. Home: RR 2 Box 167D Pike NH 03780-9704 Office: Martin Lord & Osman PA 149 Main St Lancaster NH 03584-3032

**GOSS, SUSAN J.,** law librarian; b. Cleve., June 29, 1944; d. Harry S. and Judith M. Gilman; m. Gary L. Goss, Sept. 16, 1965; children: Sarah, Maggie. BA, UCLA, 1966; MLS, C.W. Post Coll., Greenvale, N.Y., 1985. Acquisitions libr. Touro Law Libr., Huntington, N.Y., 1985—. Mem. ALA, ACLU, Assn. Am. Law Librs., Amnesty Internat. Democrat. Avocations: reading, bird watching. Office: Touro Law Libr 300 Nassau Rd Huntington NY 11743-4346

**GOSSELS, CLAUS PETER ROLF,** lawyer; b. Berlin, Aug. 11, 1930; came to U.S., 1941; s. Max and Charlotte (Lewy) G.; m. Nancy Lee Tuber, June 29, 1958; children: Lisa Rae, Amy Devra, Daniel Joshua. AB, Harvard U., 1951, LLB, 1954. Bar: Mass. 1955, U.S. Dist. Ct. Mass. 1957, U.S. Ct. Appeals (1st cir.) 1957, U.S. Supreme Ct. 1965. Assoc. Sullivan & Worcester, Boston, 1956-65; mem. Zelman, Gossels & Alexander, Boston, 1965-72, Weston, Patrick, Willard & Redding, Boston, 1972—; master Superior Ct., Mass., 1984—. Co-author, editor: Vetaher Libenu, 1980, Chadesh Yameynu, 1997. Moderator Town of Wayland, Mass., 1982—. With U.S. Army, 1954-56. Mem. Mass. Bar Assn., Boston Bar Assn., Mass. Moderators Assn., Mass. Acad. Trial Lawyers. Jewish. Avocations: reading, tennis, travel, gardening, theatre. General civil litigation, Family and matrimonial, Education and schools. Home: 32 Hampshire Rd Wayland MA 01778-1021 Office: Weston Patrick Willard & Redding 84 State St Boston MA 02109-2299

**GOSTIN, LAWRENCE,** lawyer, educator; b. N.Y.C., Oct. 19, 1949; s. Joseph and Sylvia (Berkman) G.; m. Jean Catherine Allison, July 30, 1977; children: Bryn Gareth, Kieran Gavin. JD, Duke U., 1974; BA summa cum laude, SUNY-Brockport, 1971, LLD (hon.). Bar: N.Y., Council Europe. Fulbright fellow U. Oxford, 1974-75; vis. prof. social policy McMaster U., Hamilton, Ont., Can. 1978-79; legal dir. Nat. Assn. Mental Health, London, 1975-82; vis. fellow U. Oxford Ctr. for Criminological Research, 1982-83; gen. sec. Nat. Council Civil Liberties, London, 1983-85; sr. fellow in health law Harvard U. Sch. Public Health, 1985—; exec. dir. Am. Soc. Law, Medicine, and Ethics, Boston, 1987-94; adj. assoc. prof. Sch. Pub. Health Harvard U., 1988—, lectr. Law Sch., 1990—; adj. prof. Sch. Pub. Health Harvard U., 1990—; vis. prof. Georgetown U. Law Ctr., 1993-94, assoc. prof., 1994-95, prof., 1996—; prof. Johns Hopkins Sch. Hygiene and Pub. Health, 1994—; co-dir. Georgetown/Johns Hopkins Program on Law and Pub. Health; legis. council U.S. Senate Labor and Human Resources Com., Washington, 1987, 88; bd. dirs., nat. exec. com. Am. Civil Liberties Union, 1987—; assoc dir. Harvard U. WHO Internat. Collaborating Ctr. on Health Legis., 1989—. Mem. legal affairs com. Internat. League Socs. for Mentally Handicapped, Brussels, 1980—. Western European editor Internat. Jour. Law and Psychiatry, London, 1978-81; editor in chief: Law Medicine & Health Care; exec. editor: Am. Jour. Law and Medicine; sect. editor Jour. Am. Med. Assn.; editor: Secure Provision, 1985, AIDS and the Health Care System, 1990, Surrogate Motherhood: Politics and Privacy, 1990, Implementing the Americans with Disabilities Act, 1993; co-editor: Law, Science and Medicine 2d edit., 1996; author: Human Rights and Public Health in the AIDS Pandemic, 1997, The Rights of Persons with HIV Disease, 1996, Mental Health Services: Law and Practice, 1986; Institutions Observed, 1986; Mental Health: Tribunal Procedure, 1984, 2nd edit., 1992; A Human Condition, 1975, 2d vol., 1977, Civil Liberties in Conflict, 1988. Trustee, Cobden Trust, London, 1983-85; chmn. Advocacy Alliance, London, 1981-84; sec. All Party Parliamentary Civil Liberties Group, London, 1984-85; bd. dirs. ACLU, 1986—, exec. com. 1988—; mem. com. experts drafting conventions on human experientation UN, Siracusa, Italy 1980-82. Recipient Rosemary Deldridge Meml. award Nat. Consumer Council U.K., 1983; fellow Kennedy Inst. of Ethics, 1994—. Avocations: climbing; vegetable growing. Home: 10413 Masters Ter Potomac MD 20854-3862 Office: Georgetown U Law Ctr 600 New Jersey Ave NW Washington DC 20001-2075

**GOSTYLA, JEFFREY F.,** lawyer; b. New Britian, Conn., Oct. 7, 1958; s. Edward Peter Gostyla and Barbara Marion Wierbicka; m. Heidi Lee Hoffman, July 18, 1998. BA, Villanova U., 1990; JD, Quinnipiac Coll., 1994. Bar: Conn., U.S. Dist. Ct. Conn., U.S. Ct. Appeals (2nd cir.). Atty. Eisenberg, Anderson, Michalik & Lynch, New Britain, 1994—. Editor-in-chief Conn. Probate Law Jour., 1993-94. Corporator New Britain YMCA, 1998; com. mem. Berlin (Conn.) Dem. Town Com., 1998. Mem. New Britain Bar Assn. (exec. com. 1997—), Berlin Lions Club, Timberlin Golf Club, Inc. (pres. 1996—), Ctrl. Conn. Chpt. Villanova Alumni (pres. 1997—), Italian Polit. Ind. Club. Democrat. Roman Catholic. Avocation: golf. Office: Eisenberg Anderson Michalik & Lynch 136 W Main St New Britain CT 06052-1315

**GOTANDA, BRENDA HUSTIS,** lawyer; b. Poughkeepsie, N.Y., Feb. 16, 1968; d. W. Bruce and Barbara (Powles) Hustis; m. John Yukio Gotanda, June 18, 1994. BA, Boston Coll., 1990; postgrad., U. London, 1992; JD, U. Tex., 1993. Bar: Mass. 1993, Pa. 1994, N.J. 1994, D.C. 1994. Assoc. atty. Goodwin, Procter & Hoar, Boston, 1993-94, Manko Gold & Katcher, Bala Cynwyd, Pa., 1994—. Co-author: The Law of Hazardous Waste, 1993, OSHA Handbook, 1997; assoc. editor Tex. Internat. Law Jour., Austin, 1992-93; contbr. articles to profl. jours. Vol. atty. Homeless Advocacy Project, Phila., 1995-98. Robert S. Strauss Endowed Presdl. scholar U. Tex., 1991. Mem. ABA, Pa. Bar Assn., Phila. Bar Assn. (chair pub. svc. law com. 1995-96, environ. law com. 1997-98), Soc. Women Environ. Profls. (co-chair 1998—). Avocations: swimming, sailing, travel. Environmental, Administrative and regulatory, Labor. Office: Manko Gold & Katcher 401 E City Ave Ste 500 Bala Cynwyd PA 19004-1167

**GOTCHER, JAMES RONALD,** lawyer; b. Dallas, Jan. 18, 1947; s. James Bentley and Elga Audra (Dyess) G.; m. Satoko Hata, June 20, 1970; 1 son, James Kensuke. BA in History magna cum laude, Calif. State U., Long Beach, 1972; postgrad., U. Hawaii, 1972-73; JD, Loyola U., L.A., 1976. Bar: Calif. 1976 (cert. legal specialist immigration and nationality law), U.S. Supreme Ct. 1980. Assoc. Gruber & Kelman, 1976-77; ptnr. Gotcher & Shapiro, 1977-81, Aberson, Lynes & Gotcher, 1982-89; counsel Coudert Brothers, 1989-93; prin. Law Offices of James R. Gotcher, 1993—; lawyer; b. Dallas, Jan. 18, 1947; s. James Bentley and Elga Audra (Dyess) G.; m. Satoko Hata, June 20, 1970; 1 son, James Kensuke. B.A. magna cum laude in History, Calif. State U.-Long Beach, 1972; postgrad. U. Hawaii, 1972-73; J.D., Loyola U., Los Angeles, 1976. Bar: Calif. 1976 (cert. legal specialist immigration & nationality law), U.S. Supreme Ct. 1980. Assoc. Gruber & Kelman, 1976-77; ptnr. Gotcher & Shapiro, 1977-81; ptnr. Aberson, Lynes & Gotcher, 1982-89; counsel Coudert Brothers, 1989-93; prin. Law Offices of James R. Gotcher, 1993—. Mem. Town Hall of Los Angeles. Served with USAF, 1965-68. Decorated Bronze Star. Mem. Los Angeles County Bar Assn. (chmn. immigration law sect. 1983-84), Am. Immigration Lawyers Assn., ABA. Clubs: University (Los Angeles). Author: Comprehensive guide to U.S. Nonimmigrant Visas, 1983; contbr. articles to legal jours. Author: Comprehensive Guide to U.S. Nonimmigrant Visas, 1983; contbr. articles to legal jours. Mem. Town Hall of L.A. With USAF, 1965-68. Decorated Bronze Star. Mem. ABA, Los Angeles County Bar Assn. (chmn. immigration law sect. 1983-84), Am. Immigration Lawyers Assn., Univ. Club (L.A.). Immigration, naturalization, and customs. Address: 15300 Ventura Blvd Ste 507 Sherman Oaks CA 91403-5844

**GOTO, BRUCE T.,** lawyer; b. Honolulu, Jan. 20, 1961; s. George T. and Nobuko K. Goto; m. Dawn R. Pelowski, Dec. 29, 1990. BA, U. Calif., Davis, 1983; JD, U. Calif., Berkeley, 1986; postgrad., Keio U., Tokyo, 1991-92. Bar: Hawaii 1986, Calif. 1993, Wash. 1993. Assoc. Goodsill Anderson Quinn & Stifel, Honolulu, 1986-88; fgn. atty. Braun Moriya Hoashi & Kubota, Tokyo, 1989-91; in-house counsel Marubeni Hytech Corp., Tokyo, 1991-93; assoc., ptnr. Riddell Williams Bullitt & Walkinshaw, Seattle, 1993-95; prin. Graham & James/Riddell Williams, Seattle, 1996—. Contbr. articles to profl. jours. Bd. dirs., exec. com. A Contemporary Theatre, Seattle; legal counsel Asian Counseling and Referral Svc., Seattle. Mem. Licensing Execs. Soc., Wash. Software Alliance. Computer, Intellectual property, Private international. Office: Graham & James/Riddell Williams 1001 4th Ave Ste 4500 Seattle WA 98154-1065

**GOTTHELF, BETH,** lawyer; b. Detroit, Mar. 24, 1958. BS in Pub. Adminstrn., Oakland U., 1980; JD, U. Detroit, 1985. Bar: Mich. 1986, U.S. Dist. Ct. (ea. dist.) Mich. 1986. Claims rep. Social Security Adminstrn., Pontiac, Mich., 1979-82; law clk. U.S. Atty.'s Office, Detroit, 1984-85; asst. prof. law Clemont-Ferrand U. de Droit, France, 1985-86; jud. law clk. Mich. Ct. Appeals, Detroit, 1986-87; assoc. firm Philip G. Tannian P.C., Detroit, 1987-89, Honingman, Miller, Schwartz and Cohn, Detroit, 1989-91; from assoc. to ptnr. Seyburn, Kahn, Ginn, Bess, Deitch and Serlin P.C., Southfield, Mich., 1991—. Bd. dirs. Nat. Multiple Sclerosis Soc. Mem. ABA (solid and hazardous waste com., chmn. water and wetlands, natural resources, energy and environ. law sect., mem. fed. adv. com. on storm water), Am. Electroplaters and Surface Finishers Assn., Oakland County Bar Assn. (chair environ. law sec.), Mich. State Bar Assn. (environ. law sect., past chair, coun. mem., program com., solid waste/hazardous waste/ins. com., superfund com., past sec., treas.), S.E. Mich. Coun. Govts. (environ. policy adv. coun.), Greater Detroit C. of C. (chair task force on water & sewer issues). Jewish. E-mail: bgotthelf@seyburn.com. Environmental, Natural resources, Real property. Office: Seyburn Kahn Ginn Bess Deitch and Serlin PC 2000 Town Ctr Ste 1500 Southfield MI 48075-1148

**GOTTLIEB, DANIEL SETH,** lawyer; b. Los Angeles, Sept. 19, 1954; s. Seymour and Blanche Joyce (Kaufman) G.; m. Marilynn Jeanne Payne, July 21, 1985; children: Gwendolyn Z., Rebecca Lucinda. BA summa cum laude, Columbia U., 1976; JD, Harvard U., 1980. Bar: Wash. 1980, U.S. Dist. Ct. (we. dist.) Wash. 1980. Assoc. Riddell, Williams, Bullitt & Walkinshaw, Seattle, 1980-86, ptnr., 1986-95; prin. Graham & James LLP/Riddell Williams P.S., Seattle, 1996-97; mem. Gottlieb, Fisher & Andrews, PLLC, Seattle, 1997—; coord. S.E. Legal Clinic, Seattle, 1984-86. Mem. Seattle Fremont Adv. Com. Recipient Achievement award Seattle-King County Econ. Devel. Coun., 1990. Mem. ABA, Nat. Assn. Bond Lawyers, Wash. State Bar Assn., King County Bar Assn. (treas. 1993-95, 2d v.p. 1995-96, 1st v.p. 1996-97, pres. 1997-98, bd. dirs. young lawyers divsn. 1987-90, treas. 1987-88, vice-chmn. 1988-89, chmn. 1989-90, chmn. legal info. and referral cliics com. 1986-87), Wash. State Assn. Mcpl. Attys., Wash. Coun. Sch. Attys., Wash. State Soc. Hosp. Attys., Bainbridge Island-North Kitsap Jewish Chavurah (v.p. and sec. 1993-95). Jewish. Avocations: tuba, hiking, bicycling. Municipal (including bonds). Home: 4880 NE North Tolo Rd Bainbridge Is WA 98110-3461 Office: Gottlieb Fisher & Andrews PLLC 1325 Fourth Ave Ste 1200 Seattle WA 98101-2531

**GOTTLIEB, IRA LEONARD,** lawyer; b. N.Y.C., Sept. 3, 1938; s. Joseph S. and Jaye (Rice) G.; m. Jane Mallory Snyder Campbell, Aug. 24, 1965 (div. 1971); 1 child, Katherine; m. Julie Carol Keller, Oct. 11, 1974; children: Justin, Anne. BA, CCNY, 1960; JD, U. Wis., 1968. Bar: Oreg. 1969, U.S. Dist. Ct. Oreg. 1970, U.S. Supreme Ct. 1976. Sales Peter Pan Inc., Boston, 1963-65; clk. Oreg. Supreme Ct., Salem, 1968; atty. Multnomah County Legal Aid, Portland, Oreg., 1968-71; adj. prof. law Lewis & Clark Coll., Portland, 1971-81; pvt. practice Portland, 1971-81, 95—; ptnr. Keller, Gottlieb & Gorin, Portland, 1981-95. Contbr. articles to profl. jours. 1st lt. U.S. Army, 1960-62. Fellow Am. Acad. Matrimonial Lawyers. Jewish. Family and matrimonial, Appellate. Office: 621 SW Morrison St Ste 350 Portland OR 97205-3806

**GOTTLIEB, JAMES RUBEL,** federal agency administrator, lawyer; b. N.Y.C., July 2, 1947; s. Robert J. Gottlieb and Mildred C. Blaufox; m. Roberta James, 1974; children: Zoe, Zachary. BA, Mich. State U., 1969; MA, NYU, 1970; JD, N.Y. Law Sch., 1974. Bar: N.Y. 1974, D.C. 1983. Trial asst. Fuchsberg & Fuchsberg, 1971-74, assoc., 1974-77; adminstrv. asst., legis. dir., counsel for rep. Ted Weiss U.S. House of Reps., 1977-83, staff dir., chief counsel Human Resources & Intergovt. Rels. Subcom., 1983-93; chief counsel, staff dir. Senate Com. on Vets. Affairs, Washington, 1993-94; minority chief counsel, staff dir. Senate Com. Vets. Affairs, Washington, 1995—. Office: Senate Com on Vets Affairs 202 Hart Senate Ofc Washington DC 20510-0001

**GOTTLIEB, JONATHAN W.,** lawyer; b. Washington, June 24, 1959; s. Julius Judah and Charlotte (Papernick) G.; m. Deborah Jo Levine, June 28, 1987; 1 child, Maya Lane. BA with honors, DePaul U., 1982; student, Am. U., 1984-85; JD, N.Y. Law Sch., 1985. Bar: Pa. 1986, D.C. 1989, U.S. Ct. Appeals (D.C. cir.) 1990. Assoc. Ginsburg, Feldman & Bress, Washington, 1986; trial atty. FERC, Washington, 1987-88; assoc. Wickwire, Gavin & Gibbs, Washington, 1988-89, Ballard Spahr Andrews & Ingersoll, Washington, 1990-92; ptnr. Reid & Priest, Washington, 1992—; chmn. legal affairs task force Nat. Hydropower Assn.; counsel Mid-Atlantic Ind. Power Producers; gen. counsel Power Markets Devel. Co., 1995—. Contbg. editor Project Fin. Monthly; editor Competitive Utility, 1995—. Donor mem. Corning Mus. Glass. Mem. ABA, Fed. Energy Bar Assn., Pa. Bar Assn., D.C. Bar Assn. Republican. Avocations: glass collecting, stained glass making, gardening. Finance, Public utilities. Home: 9317 W Parkhill Dr Bethesda MD 20814-3966

**GOTTLIEB, PAUL MITCHEL,** lawyer; b. N.Y.C., Mar. 30, 1954; s. Henry Gottlieb and Thelma Ethel (Friedman) Miller; m. Helene Manya Roiter, Apr. 3, 1982; children: Jordan Seth, Zachary Michael. BA, Hobart Coll., 1976; JD, MBA, Washington U., St. Louis, 1980. Bar: Ill. 1980, U.S. Dist. Ct. (no. dist.) Ill. 1980, N.Y. 1988. Assoc. Rudnick & Wolfe, Chgo., 1980-81; ind. trader Chgo. Bd. of Trade, 1981-83; staff atty. Chgo. Merc. Exch., 1983-84; v.p. market regulation Chgo. Merc. Exchange, 1984-87; commodity counsel Morgan Stanley and Co. Inc., N.Y.C., 1987-89; spl. counsel commodities, futures and derivative products Skadden, Arps, Slate, Meagher & Flom, N.Y.C., 1989-92; ptnr., chair derivative products practice group Seward & Kissel, N.Y.C., 1992-96; dir., sr. counsel structured products & commodities Union Bank of Switzerland, N.Y.C., 1996-98; sr. v.p., dep. gen. counsel PaineWebber Inc., N.Y.C., 1998—; Eisenhower Exch. fellow to New Zealand, 1992; adj. prof. Ctr. for Tech. & Fin. Svcs. Polytechnic U.; adviser risk mgmt. adv. bd. Stern Sch. of Bus., NYU. Contbr. chpts. to books, articles to profl. jours. Mem. Futures Industry Assn. (law and compliance divsn.), Securities Industry Assn. (law and compliance divsn.), Bond Market Assn. Jewish. Avocations: coaching youth hockey and lacrosse, tennis, golf. Administrative and regulatory, Securities. Home: 11 Highpoint Pl West Windsor NJ 08550-5238 Office: PaineWebber Inc 1285 Avenue Of The Americas New York NY 10019-6028

**GOTTS, ILENE KNABLE,** lawyer; b. Phila., Nov. 25, 1959; d. Harry Lee and Ethel Beatrice (Teitelman) Knable; m. Michael D. Gotts, May 25, 1986; children: Isaac, Samuel. BA magna cum laude with hon., U. Md., 1980; JD cum laude, Georgetown U., 1984. Bar: D.C. 1984, N.Y., 1997, U.S. Dist. Ct. D.C. 1986, U.S. Ct. Appeals (D.C. cir.) 1985, U.S. Dist. Ct. Md. 1987, U.S. Ct. Appeals (fed. cir.) 1989, U.S. Supreme Ct. 1988. Staff atty. FTC, 1984-86; assoc. Foley & Lardner, Washington, 1986-92, ptnr., head legis./adminstrv. group, antitrust practice group, 1992-96; ptnr. Wachtell, Lipton, Rosen & Katz, N.Y.C., 1996—; adj. prof. George Washington U. Law Ctr., 1995-96. Mem. editorial bd. The Practical Lawyer, 1994—; mem. editorial adv. bd. The Antitrust Counselor, 1995—; contbr. articles to profl. jours. Recipient Sklar award; Mary Elizabeth Robey scholar. Mem. ABA (health care com. antitrust sect. 1988—, vice chair intellectual property com. 1994-97, consumer protection com. 1994—, vice chair Clayton Act com. 1997-98, chmn. 1998—), FBA (chair health care com. of antitrust sect. 1991-95, chair antitrust and trade regulation sect. 1995-97), D.C. Bar (steering com., antitrust and trade regulation com. 1994-95), N.Y. Bar Assn. (task force of women and the law), Am. Law Inst., Washington Coun. Lawyers (exec. com. and bd. dirs. 1988-97, pres. 1994-95), Mortar Board, Phi Beta Kappa, Phi Kappa Phi, Pi Sigma Alpha, Phi Alpha Theta. Democrat. Jewish. Antitrust, Administrative and regulatory. Office: Wachtell Lipton Rosen & Katz 51 W 52d St New York NY 10019

**GOTTSCHALK, THOMAS A.,** lawyer; b. Decatur, Ind., July 5, 1942; s. John Simson and Edith (Liechty) G.; m. Barbara J. Risen, Aug. 28, 1965; children: Deborah, Diane. AB, Earlham Coll., 1964; JD, U. Chgo., 1967. Bar: Ill. 1967, D.C. 1986, U.S. Supreme Ct. Assoc. Kirkland & Ellis, Chgo., 1967-73, ptnr., 1973-94; sr. v.p., gen. counsel Gen. Motors Corp., 1994—. Trustee Earlham Coll., Richmond, Ind., 1972—, chmn., 1985-91. Mem.

ABA (mem. litigation, antitrust and criminal law sects.), D.C. Bar Assn., Chgo. Coun. of Lawyers, Conf. Bd. Coun. of Chief Legal Officers. General civil litigation, Antitrust, Administrative and regulatory. Office: Gen Motors Corp PO Box 33122 Detroit MI 48232-5122

**GOTWALS, CHARLES PLACE, JR.**, lawyer; b. Muskogee, Okla., May 19, 1917; s. Charles Place and Anna M. (Koehler) G.; m. Mary Frances Brownlee, Jan. 31, 1948 (dec. Mar. 1982); children: Charles William, James Robert, Frances Ann, Virginia Hunt; m. Marion Miller, Jan. 6, 1984. A.B., U. Okla., 1938, J.D., 1940. Bar: Okla. 1940. Pvt. practice Tulsa, 1940—; ptnr. Gable & Gotwals, until 1990; of counsel, 1990—. Sr. warden Trinity Episcopal Ch., Tulsa, 1984-87, also former vestryman and jr. warden. Served to maj. AUS, 1942-46, ETO. Decorated Bronze Star. Mem. ABA, Tulsa County Bar Assn. (sec. 1949), Okla. Bar Assn., Am. Judicature Soc., Order of Coif, Phi Beta Kappa, Phi Delta Phi, Beta Theta Pi. Clubs: Kiwanian (pres. 1961), Tulsa, Summit. Office: 2000 Nationsbank Ctr 15 W 6th St Tulsa OK 74119-5415

**GOUDE, CHARLES REUBEN**, lawyer, public defender; b. Hemingway, S.C., Apr. 17, 1950; s. Bethel Oliver and Miriam Helena (Joye) G. BA in History magna cum laude, U. S.C., 1975, JD, 1979. Bar: S.C. 1979, U.S. Ct. Mil. Appeals 1980, U.S. Dist. Ct. S.C. 1984. Sole practice Georgetown, S.C., 1984—; dep. pub. defender Georgetown County, 1984-85, pub. defender, 1985—; adj. faculty Horry Georgetown Tech. Coll., 1986—. Served to sgt. USMC, 1968-72; served to capt. JAG USAF, 1980-84. Mem. Am. Trial Lawyers Assn., S.C. Bar Assn., Georgetown County Bar Assn., Phi Beta Kappa. General practice, State civil litigation, Family and matrimonial. Home: RR 3 Box 269A Hemingway SC 29554-9803 Office: PO Box 706 Georgetown SC 29442-0706

**GOUGH, JOHN FRANCIS**, lawyer; b. Phila., Nov. 28, 1934; s. John Joseph and Honora Veronica (Garrity) G.; m. Natalie Smith, Mar. 8, 1964; children: David, Robert, J. Joseph II, Richard, Jonathan, Kristin. AB cum laude, St. Joseph's U., 1957; JD, Yale Law Sch., 1960. Bar: Pa. 1961, N.J. 1994, U.S. Dist. Ct. (ea. dist.) Pa. 1961, U.S. Ct. Appeals (3d cir.) 1966, U.S. Supreme Ct. 1967. Assoc. Erskine, Barbieri & Sheer, Phila., 1960-65, White and Williams, Phila., 1965-68; ptnr. White and Williams, 1968-80, Toll, Ebby & Gough, Phila., 1980-87; ptnr., chmn. corp. dept. Abrahams & Loewenstein, Phila., 1987-88; ptnr. Hoyle, Morris & Kerr, Phila., 1988-92; ptnr. Montgomery, Mccracken, Walker & Rhoads, LLP, Phila., 1992-98, co-chair bus. bankruptcy sect., 1998; ptnr. Hoyle, Morris & Kerr LLP, Phila., 1998—; exec. com. Ea. Dist Bankruptcy Conf., 1989—; faculty co-chmn. and lectr. Temple Grad. Sch. Law C.L.E. Program, 1989-92; lectr. U. Pa. Grad. Sch., Temple Law Sch., 1990—. Contbr. to Temple Law Quar.; author course materials for profl. and ednl. orgns. Pres. Highfield Sch. PTA, Plymouth, Pa., 1966-68, Greene Towne Montessori Sch., Phila., 1979-80; v.p., exec. com. Schuylkill River Devel. Coun. Mem. ABA, Am. Law Inst., Phila. Bar Assn. (pres. Jr. Bar Assn. 1964-65), Hosp. Attys. S.E. Pa. (pres. 1977-79), Am. Bankruptcy Inst. (bd. cert. in bus. bankruptcy), Yale Club Phila. Avocations: tennis, fitness. Bankruptcy, General corporate, Mergers and acquisitions. Office: Hoyle Morris and Kerr LLP One Liberty Pl Ste 4900 Philadelphia PA 19103

**GOUGH, KEVIN ROBERT**, lawyer; b. N.Y.C., June 13, 1962; s. James Patrick and Noreen (O'Sullivan) G. BA, Coll. William and Mary, 1984; JD, U. Ga., 1987. Bar: Ga. 1987, U.S. Dist Ct. (no., so. and mid. dists.) Ga., U.S. Ct. Appeals (11th cir.), U.S. Supreme Ct. Law clk. to Hon. Myron H. Thompson U.S. Dist. Ct. (mid. dist.) Ala., Montgomery, 1987-88; assoc. Blasingame, Burch, Garrard & Bryant, Athens, Ga., 1988-89; asst. dist. atty. Brunswick (Ga.) Jud. Cir., 1989-93; pvt. practice Brunswick, 1993—. Mem. editorial staff Ga. Law Rev., 1985-87. Mem. ABA, State Bar Ga., Brunswick-Glynn County Bar Assn. (pres. 1993), Golden Isles C. of C., Brunswick Jaycees, Order of Barristers. Roman Catholic. Criminal, Family and matrimonial, Insurance. Home: 174 Saint Clair Dr Saint Simons Is GA 31522-1041 Office: PO Box 898 Brunswick GA 31521-0898

**GOULD, ALAN I.**, lawyer; b. Phila., Jan. 4, 1940; s. Louis and Yvette (Balasny) G.; m. Joyce P. Feinstein, Sept. 19, 1965; 1 child, Traci Eve. BBA, U. Miami, Fla., 1961, JD, 1964. Bar: Fla. 1964, N.J. 1966, U.S. Dist. Ct. N.J. 1966, U.S. Supreme Ct. 1983, U.S. Ct. Appeals (3rd cir.) 1985. Assoc. George M. James Esq., Wildwood, N.J., 1966-70; pvt. practice Wildwood, 1970-75; ptnr. Gould & Neidig, Wildwood, 1975-80, Alan I. Gould, Wildwood, 1980-82, Valore, McAllister, Westmoreland, Gould, Vesper & Schwartz, Wildwood and Northfield, 1982-87, Mairone, Biel, Gould, Zlotnick, Feinberg & Griffith, Wildwood and Atlantic City, 1988, Cooper, Perskie, April, Niedelman, Wagenheim & Levenson, Wildwood, Northfield and Atlantic City, 1989-95; prin. Alan I. Gould, P.C., Wildwood, 1996—; chmn. N.J. Lawyers Fund for Clients Protection, 1987-91, chmn. 1991; lectr. in field. Mem. editl. bd. N.J. Lawyer, Weekly Newspaper. Solicitor Lower Twp. Pub. Schs., 1980-85, Wildwood Crest Pub. Schs., 1985-95, Cape May County Drug Abuse Coun., Parking Authority, City of Wildwood, 1973-87, Cape May County br. Am. Cancer Soc., Cape Ednl. Fund Inc.; trustee in bankruptcy U.S. Trustee of N.J.; mem. Supreme Ct. N.J. Task Force on Spl. Civil Part, 1986-88; Supreme Ct. apptd. trustee Interest on Lawyers Trust Accts. (IOLTA) Fund, 1993-97, chair, 1997; chmn. bd. govs. Burdette Tomlin Meml. Hosp., 1985-89, mem., 1976-79, pres., 1979-84. Recipient Profl. Lawyer of Yr. award N.J. Commn. on Professionalism in the Law and Cape May County Bar Assn., 1997, N.J. State Bar Found. medal of honor, 1998. Mem. ABA, Cape May County Bar Assn (pres. 1982), N.J. Bar Assn. (trustee 1982-89, chair jud. and prosecutor appts. com., mem. jud adminstrn. com.), N.J. Bar Found. (trustee), Fla. Bar Assn., Fed. Bar Assn., Assn. Trial Lawyers Am., Am. Judicature Soc., Assn. Criminal Def. Lawyers, Navy League of U.S., Lions (pres. 1974), N.J. Lawyer (editl. bd. weekly newspaper), N.J. Fund for Interest on Lawyers Trust Acount (chmn. 1997). Avocations: running, golf, tennis, basketball. Bankruptcy, State civil litigation, Contracts commercial. Office: 3000 Pacific Ave Wildwood NJ 08260-4945

**GOULD, BRET ADAM**, lawyer; b. Miami Beach, Feb. 21, 1964; s. Donald B. and Carol (Friedman) G. BS, Fla. Internat. U., 1986; JD, U. Miss., 1989. Bar: Fla. Atty. 12th Cir. Pub. Defender, Bradenton, Fla., 1989-90, 12th Cir. State's Atty., Bradenton, 1990—. Democrat. Jewish. Avocation: pistol target shooting. Home: 5411 Lindburg St Riverview FL 33569-3796 Office: Office of State's Atty 12th Cir 1112 Manatee Ave W Fl 6 Bradenton FL 34205-7804

**GOULD, EDWARD WARD**, lawyer; b. Warwick, R.I., Jan. 3, 1957; s. Whitney and Shirley (Willis) G.; m. Lynn Frances O'Rourke, May 30, 1981; children: Kathryn, Andrew, Matthew, Kelly. AB, Brown U., 1979; JD, Boston U., 1982. Bar: Maine 1982, U.S. Dist. Ct. Maine 1982, U.S. Ct. Appeals (1st cir.) 1985. With Gross, Minsky, Mogul & Singal, P.A., Bangor, Maine, 1982—; pres. Bangor Area Vis. Nurses, 1998—. Bd. dirs. Penobscot Area Housing Devel. Corp., Bangor, 1986—; YMCA, Bangor, 1998—. Mem. Maine Trial Lawyers Assn. (bd. govs.). General civil litigation, Personal injury, Workers' compensation. Office: Gross Minsky Mogul & Singal 23 Water St Ste 400 Bangor ME 04401-6372

**GOULD, HOWARD NEAL**, lawyer; b. Omaha, Dec. 27, 1951; s. Arthur S. and Helen Gould; m. Patricia Marie Murray, May 29, 1984. Student, Washington U., 1970-71; AB in Physics, Columbia Coll., 1973; JD, Georgetown U., 1977. Bar: Neb. 1977, Calif. 1978. Assoc. Kutak, Rock & Campbell, Omaha, 1977-79; ptnr. Doland & Gould, L.A., 1979-98, Doland, Gould & Fingerman, 1999—; judge pro tem small claims divsn. Santa Monica (Calif.) Mcpl. Ct., 1989—. Coord. coun. Palisades Charter Sch., Pacfic Palisades, Calif., 1995—, Goving. Coun. Palisadas Elem. Charter Sch., 1993-96; mem. Cmty. Coun. Pacfic Palisades, 1994-98, support group Amnesty Internat. U.S.A., 1980-85, bioethics com. Daniel Freeman Marina Hosp., Marina del Rey, Calif. 1988—; bd. mgrs. Palisades-Malibu YMCA, 1993-99; coun. Infectious Diseas Assn. Calif., 1989-95;. Mem. ABA (real estate sect.), Calif. Bar Assn., Beverly Hills Bar Assn., Nebr. Bar Assn., Am. Arbitration Assn. (arbitrator, comml. law & constrn. law panels 1993—), Columbia Univ. Alumni Assn. (bd. dirs. 1982-95). Avocations: golf, camping, sailing. General civil litigation, Real property, Contracts commercial. Office: Doland Gould & Fingerman 10866 Wilshire Blvd Ste 300 Los Angeles CA 90024-4354

**GOULD, JULIAN SAUL**, lawyer; b. L.A., Apr. 15, 1924; s. David H. and Jeanette (Palm) G.; m. Norma Patricia Gould; 1 child, Paul Julian. Student, U. So. Calif., 1946-48; JD, Southwestern U., L.A., 1950. Bar: Calif. 1950. Lawyer in pvt. practice L.A., 1950—. Named Alumnus of Yr., Southwestern U., 1972. Mem. Hollywood Bar Assn. (pres. 1978), Am. Legion (comdr. 24th Dist. 1960), Southwestern U. Alumni Assn. (pres. 1972), Masons (32 deg., Shriners. Democrat. Family and matrimonial, General civil litigation, Probate. Office: 1741 Ivar Ave Ste 213 Los Angeles CA 90028-5115

**GOULD, MICHAEL ALAN**, lawyer; b. St. Louis, Sept. 6, 1954; s. Alan K. and Clara Marcille (Smoot) G.; m. Melissa Gay Jones, Aug. 4, 1979; children: Kerry Anne, Hunter Charles. BA in Polit. Sci., U. Mo., Kansas City, 1975, JD, 1981. Bar: Mo. 1982, U.S. Dist. Ct. (we. and ea. dists.) Mo. 1982. Law clk., staff atty. U.S. EPA, Kansas City, Mo., 1979-82; atty., ptnr. Bowen & Gould, North Kansas City, 1982-91, Bowen, Gould & Kanan, North Kansas City, 1991-92, Gould & Assocs., North Kansas City, 1992—. Pres. St. Luke Presbyn. Men's Group, Kansas City, 1989-94. 1st lt. USMC, 1975-78. Mem. Clay County Bar Assn., Platte County Bar Assn., Kansas City Met. Bar Assn., Mo. Assn. Trial Attys. Republican. Avocations: scuba diving, basketball, horseback riding. General civil litigation, Consumer commercial, Bankruptcy. Office: 2700 Commerce Tower 911 Main St Kansas City MO 64105-2007 Address: PO Box 13446 Kansas City MO 64199-3446

**GOULD, ROBERT P.**, lawyer; b. Drumright, Okla., July 22, 1919; s. Clyde Frederick Gould and Rexy Lee Moore; m. Kathleen Curnutt; children: Sheryl Kay, Robert Craig. BA, Wichita State U., 1949; JD, Washburn U. Law Sch., 1958. Bar: Kans., Mo., U.S. Dist. Ct. Kans. Feature writer, reporter Wichita Beacon, Wall St. Jour., 1949-52; from claims adjuster to claims mgr. Farmers Ins. Group., Topeka, Kansas City, Mo., 1952-74; chair personal injury dept. Ross and Houghland, Overland Park, Kans., 1975-79; of counsel Perry and Hammil, Overland Park, 1979-88; sole practice law Lenexa, Kans., 1988—. Bd. dirs. Legal Assistance to the Elderly, Mission, Kans., 1979-80; precinct com. Rep. Party, Topeka, 1957. Served in U.S. Navy, 1942-45. Mem. Mo. Bar Assn., Kans. Bar Assn., Kans. Trial Lawyers Assn., Mo. Trial Lawyers Assn., Johnson County Kans. Bar Assn. Baptist. Avocations: reading, travel, boating, writing. Workers' compensation, Personal injury, General civil litigation. Office: 9728 Rosehill Rd Lenexa KS 66215-1414

**GOULD, RODNEY ELLIOTT**, lawyer, university dean, professor; b. Boston, June 3, 1943; s. Samuel H. and Sylvia (Gerrish) G.; m. Nancy Lund, Sept. 10, 1968; children: Jody R., Amy L. Student, London Sch. Econs., 1963-64; AB, Colby Coll., 1965; JD, Columbia U., 1968. Bar: D.C. 1969, N.Y. 1969, U.S. Dist Ct. (so. dist.) N.Y. 1969, U.S. Dist. Ct. D.C. 1969, U.S. Ct. Appeals (2nd cir.) 1969, U.S. Ct. Appeals (D.C. cir.) 1970, Mass. 1975, U.S. Dist. Ct. Mass. 1975, U.S. Ct. Appeals (3d and 8th cirs.) 1981, U.S. Ct. Appeals (1st cir.) 1989, U.S. Supreme Ct. 1989, U.S. Ct. Appeals (6th cir.) 1990, U.S. Ct. Appeals (4th cir.) 1998. Law clk. to judge U.S. Dist. Ct. for So. Dist. N.Y., 1968-69; assoc. Covington & Burling, Washington, 1969-75, Rosenman Colin Freund Lewis & Cohen, N.Y.C., 1979-82; assoc. dir. FTC, Boston, 1975-78; antitrust counsel Digital Equipment Co., Maynard, Mass., 1983-84; gen. counsel Internat. Weekends, Boston, 1985-86; ptnr. Rubin Hay & Gould, Framingham, Mass., 1986—; adj. prof. Law Sch., Western New Eng. U., Springfield, Mass., 1980-82, Northeastern U., Boston, 1983—, Boston U., 1985—; lectr. in field. Editor Columbia Law Rev., 1967-68. Bd. dirs. Mass. Aububon Soc., 1996—. Mem. ABA, Mass. Bar Assn., N.Y. Bar Assn., D.C. Bar Assn., Phi Beta Kappa. Antitrust, Travel. Home: 84 Gordon Rd Newton MA 02168 Office: Rubin Hay & Gould 205 Newbury St Framingham MA 01701-4581

**GOULD, RONALD MURRAY**, lawyer; b. St. Louis, Oct. 17, 1946; s. Harry H. and Sylvia C. (Sadofsky) G.; m. Suzanne H. Goldblatt, Dec. 1, 1968; children: Daniel, Rebecca. BS in Econs., U. Pa., 1968; JD, U. Mich., 1973. Bar: Wash. 1975, U.S. Dist. Ct. (we. dist.) Wash. 1976, U.S. Ct. Appeals (9th cir.) 1980, U.S. Supreme Ct. 1981, U.S. Dist. Ct. (ea. dist.) Wash. 1982, U.S. Ct. Appeals (fed. cir.) 1986. Law clk. to hon. Wade H. McCree Jr. U.S. Ct. Appeals (6th cir.), Detroit, 1973-74; law clk. to hon. justice Potter Stewart U.S. Supreme Ct., Washington, 1974-75; assoc. Perkins Coie, Seattle, 1975-80, ptnr., 1981—. Editor-in-chief Mich. Law Rev., 1972-73; editor: Washington Civil Procedure Deskbook, 1981, author with others, 1986, 92. Exec. bd. chief Seattle coun. Boy Scouts Am., Seattle, 1984—; mem. cmty. rels. coun. Jewish Fedn. of Greater Seattle, 1985-88; bd. dirs. econ. devel. coun. Seattle and King County, 1991-94; citizens cabinet mem. Gov. Mike Lowry, Seattle, 1993-96; bd. trustees Bellevue Cmty. Coll., 1993—, chair bd. 1995-96. Fellow ABA (antitrust sect., litigation sect.); mem. Wash. State Bar Assn. (bd. govs. 1988-91, pres. 1994-95), King County Bar Assn. (Award for Disting. Svc. 1987), Supreme Ct. Hist. Soc., 9th Jud. Cir. Hist. Soc. (bd. dirs. 1994—). Democrat. Jewish. Avocations: reading, chess. Antitrust, Federal civil litigation, Professional liability. Office: Perkins Coie 1201 3rd Ave Fl 40 Seattle WA 98101-3029

**GOULDER, DIANE KESSLER**, lawyer; b. Columbus, Ohio, Apr. 27, 1950; d. Berry Lester and Shirley Lorraine (Goldstein) Kessler; m. Eric Alan Goulder, June 30, 1974; children: Jeremy, Joel, Anna Lisa. BA, Ohio State U., 1972; JD, Cornell U., 1975. Bar: Ohio 1975. Assoc. Mayer Terakedis & Weed, Columbus, 1975-76, Mayer, Terakedis & Blue Co. L.P.A., Columbus, 1976-79; pvt. practice Worthington, Ohio, 1979-85; prin. Martin, Eichenberger & Baxter Co., L.P.A., 1985-87, Martin & Eichenberger Co., L.P.A., 1987-89; ptnr. Porter, Wright, Morris & Arthur, 1989—; of counsel James J. Tansey & Assocs., Worthington, 1984-85. Active Twig 173, Women's Aux. of Children's Hosp., Worthington, 1980-85; trustee Goodwill Rehab. Ctr., 1993—, immediate past chair, 1999. Mem. ABA (adj. mem. taxation com. 1979—), Ohio Bar Assn., Ohio Women's Bar Assn., Columbus Bar Assn. (employee benefits com. 1984—), Women Lawyers Franklin County, Mortar Bd. E-mail: dgoulder@porterwright.com. Pension, profit-sharing, and employee benefits, Estate planning, Corporate taxation. Office: Porter Wright Morris & Arthur 41 S High St Ste 2800 Columbus OH 43215-6194

**GOULDIN, DAVID MILLEN**, lawyer; b. Binghamton, N.Y., Mar. 8, 1941; s. Paul C. and Virginia M. G.; m. Deborah A., Aug. 20, 1966; children—Robert, Michael, Lauryn, Derek. A.B., Princeton U., 1963; J.D., Cornell U., 1966. Bar: N.Y., U.S. Dist. Ct. N.Y. Ptnr. Levene, Gouldin & Thompson, Binghamton, 1966—. Pres., Broome County (N.Y.) Arena, 1979; chmn. Broome County Health Fair, 1986-87; gen. chmn. ministry endowment campaign Broome County Council of Chs., 1986-87, United Way Broome County, 1980, pres., 1982-84; chmn. United Way N.Y. State, 1992; chancellor Wyo. Conf. of United Meth. Ch., 1987—; bd. dirs. Roberson Ctr. for Arts, 1983-89, United Health Svcs. Hosps., 1991—, Broome County Urban League, 1993—, sec. 1993; trustee Wyo. Sem., 1973-88. Recipient Sertoma Svc. to Mankind Dist. award, 1988, Dist. Citizen award Baden-Powell Coun. of Boy Scouts, 1996; named to Sect. Four Hall of Fame, 1977, Outstanding Young Men Am., U.S. Jaycees, 1975. Mem. Broome County Bar Assn. (pres. 1989), N.Y. State Bar Assn. (chmn. TICL sect. 1993, Root-Stimson award 1987, John Lech award, 1999), Fedn. Bar 6th Dist. (pres. 1975), Rotary. Republican. State civil litigation, Personal injury, Federal civil litigation. Home: 85 Highland Ave Binghamton NY 13905-4039 Office: PO Box F1706 Binghamton NY 13902-0106

**GOUNLEY, DENNIS JOSEPH**, lawyer; b. Phila., Jan. 29, 1950; s. George Gerard and Elizabeth Mary (Maggioncalda) G.; m. Martha Ann Zatezalo, Sept. 25, 1976. B.A., St. Joseph's Coll., Phila., 1971; J.D., Dickinson Sch. Law, 1974. Bar: Pa. 1974, U.S. Dist. Ct. (we. dist.) Pa. 1995, U.S. Ct. Appeals (3d cir.) 1976, U.S. Supreme Ct. 1977. Sole practice, Greensburg, Pa., 1974-83, 1990—; ptnr. Gounley & O'Halloran, Greensburg, 1984-90; Westmoreland County mental health rev. officer, 1991—. Council mem. Franklin Towne Condominium Assn., Murrysville, Pa., 1976-79. Mem. Pa. Bar Assn., Westmoreland Bar Assn., Rotary. Republican. Roman Catholic. General civil litigation, Real property, Probate. Home: 3590 N Hills Rd Murrysville PA 15668-1438 Office: 15 E Otterman St Greensburg PA 15601-2543

**GOURAIGE, HERVÉ**, lawyer; b. Port-au-Prince, Haiti, Feb. 12, 1950; came to U.S., 1962; s. Frantz and Altagracia (Rodriguez) G.; m. Carla J. Edwards, Oct. 21, 1989; 1 child, Sophia India. BA, Boston U., 1972, Oxford (Eng.) U., 1974; MA, Oxford (Eng.) U., 1982; JD, Harvard U., 1977. Bar: N.Y. 1978, U.S. Dist. Ct. (ea. and so. dists.) N.Y. 1978, U.S. Ct. Appeals (2d, 3d and 9th cirs.) 1982, U.S. Supreme Ct. 1982, N.J. 1991, U.S. Dist. Ct. N.J. 1991. Assoc. Mudge Rose Guthrie Alexander & Ferdon, N.Y.C., 1977-84; asst. U.S. atty. for so. dist. N.Y. U.S. Dept. Justice, N.Y.C., 1984-91; of counsel Crummy, Del Deo, Dolan, Newark, 1991-94, Latham & Watkins, Newark, N.J., 1994—. Trustee Newark Community Sch. Arts, 1992—. Rhodes scholar, 1972. Mem. ABA, Am. Law Inst., Assn. Bar City N.Y. Democrat. Roman Catholic. Avocations: tennis, soccer, reading. Criminal, General civil litigation, Health. Office: Latham & Watkins One Newark Center Newark NJ 07101-3174

**GOURAS, MARK STEVEN**, lawyer; b. Seattle, Apr. 21, 1961; s. Robert N. and Suzanne Marie Gouras; m. Elvira Pilar Lipio, July 27, 1984. BA in English, U. Wash., 1983; JD, U. Puget Sound, 1986. Bar: Wash. 1986, U.S. Dist. Ct. (we. dist.) Wash. Assoc. Albert & Slater, P.S., Federal Way, Wash., 1986-88, Taylor, Kiefer & Bartlett, Seattle, 1988-93; pvt. practice Seattle, 1993-96; ptnr. Hillman & Gouras, LLP, Tukwila, Wash., 1997—. Mem. ABA, Wash. State Bar Assn., Seattle-King County Bar Assn. Republican. State civil litigation, Family and matrimonial, Real property. Office: 16040 Christensen Rd Ste 215 Tukwila WA 98188-2966

**GOURDINE, SIMON PETER**, lawyer; b. Jersey City, July 30, 1940; s. Simon Samuel and Laura Emily (Rembert) G.; m. Patricia Campbell, Aug. 1, 1964; children: David Laurence, Peter Christopher, Laura Allison. B.A., City Coll. N.Y., 1962; J.D., Fordham U., 1965; P.M.D., Harvard Bus. Sch., 1979. Bar: N.Y. 1966, U.S. Dist. Ct. (so. dist.) N.Y. 1967, U.S. Supreme Ct. 1976. Asst. U.S. atty. So. Dist. N.Y., 1967-69; atty. Celanese Corp., 1969-70; asst. to commr. Nat. Basketball Assn., N.Y.C., 1970-72, v.p. adminstrn., 1973-74, dep. commr., 1974-81; commr. N.Y.C. Dept. Consumer Affairs, 1982-84; sec. The Rockefeller Found., 1984-86; dir. labor rels. Met. Transp. Authority, 1986-90; exec. dir., gen. counsel Nat. Basketball Players Assn., N.Y.C., 1990-96; gen. ptnr. TCS TV Ptnrs., LP, 1990-93; gen. counsel to chancellor N.Y.C. Bd. Edn., 1996-98; mem. N.Y. State Banking Bd., 1979-90; mem. N.Y.C. Charter Revision Commn., 1988-89. Bd. dirs. Police Athletic League, 1974—, Fresh Air Fund, 1985—, Fund for City of N.Y., 1990-94, Fleet Bank N.Y., 1993—; mem. N.Y.C. Civil Svc. Commn., 1981-82, Gov.'s Exec. Adv. Commn. on Adminstrn. Justice, 1981-82, Mayor's Com. on Taxi Regulatory Issues., 1981-82. Served to capt. U.S. Army, 1965-67. Decorated Army Commendation medal, South Vietnam, 1967. Mem. 100 Black Men Inc. Home: 5251 Fieldston Rd Bronx NY 10471-2911

**GOURVITZ, ELLIOT HOWARD**, lawyer; b. Lewistown, Pa., Sept. 21, 1945; s. Louis and Irene (Brass) G.; m. Bonnie S. Hirsch; children: Evan, Amy, Ross, Ari. BA, Rutgers U., 1966, JD, 1969. Bar: N.J. 1969, N.Y. 1985, U.S. Dist. Ct. N.J. 1969, U.S. Tax Ct. 1970, U.S. Ct. Claims 1970, U.S. Ct. Appeals (3d cir.) 1972, U.S. Supreme Ct. 1973, U.S. Ct. Appeals (2d, 4th, 5th, 7th, 8th, 9th, 10th, and fed. cirs.) 1982, U.S. Dist. Ct. (ea. dist.) Wis. 1985, U.S. Ct. Internat. Trade 1985; cert. matrimonial atty., N.J. Pvt. practice, Springfield, N.J. Contbr. articles to jours. on matrimonial law and taxation. Chmn. Early Settlement Panel of Union County, panelist Essex and Middlesex Counties. Named Man of Yr., United Cerebral Palsy League Union County, 1980. Fellow Am. Acad. Matrimonial Attys. (pres. N.J.), Internat. Acad. Matrimonial Lawyers; mem. Am. Coll. Trial Lawyers (diplomate), N.J. Bar Assn., N.Y. State Bar Assn. Family and matrimonial.

**GOUTTIERE, JOHN P.**, lawyer; b. Toledo, Mar. 18, 1949. BA in American Studies, Bowling Green State U., 1971; JD, Ohio No. U., 1974. Bar: Ohio 1974, U.S. Dist. Ct. (no. dist.) Ohio 1975, U.S. Supreme Ct. 1997. Ptnr. Ferstle & Gouttiere, Toledo, 1975-85; pres. John P Gouttiere Co. LPA, Toledo, 1985—; adj. prof. U. Toledo Coll. Law. Pres. Corp. for Legal Svcs. and Assistance to the Poor, 1996—, Toledo Legal Aid Soc., 1994-96, bd. trustees, 1987—. Mem. Comml. Law League Am., Ohio State Bar Assn., Lucas County Bar Assn. (pres. 1986), Toledo Bar Assn. Contracts commercial, Probate, Real property. Office: John P Gouttiere Co LPA 310 Bell Bldg 709 Madison Ave Toledo OH 43624-1637

**GOVER, ALAN SHORE**, lawyer; b. Lyons, N.Y., Sept. 5, 1948; s. Norman Marvin and Beatrice L. (Shore) G.; m. Ellen Rae Ross, Dec. 4, 1976; children: Maxwell Ross, Mary Trace. AB, Tufts U., 1970; JD, Georgetown U., 1973. Bar: Tex. 1973, D.C. 1980, U.S. Dist. Ct. (so. dist.) Tex. 1974, U.S. Dist. Ct. (we. dist.) Tex. 1976, U.S Dist. Ct. (no. dist.) Tex. 1988, U.S. Dist. Ct. (ea. dist.) Tex. 1990, U.S. Ct. Appeals (5th cir.) 1974, U.S. Ct. Appeals (D.C. cir.) 1977, U.S. Dist. Ct. (we. dist.) 1979, U.S. Ct. Appeals (2d cir.) 1979, D.C. 1980, U.S. Ct. Appeals (9th and 11th cirs.) 1981, U.S. Ct. Appeals (8th cir.) 1981, U.S. Supreme Ct. 1976. Assoc. Baker & Botts, Houston, 1973-80, ptnr., 1981-85; ptnr. Weil, Gotshal & Manges, Houston, 1985—. Co-author: The Texas Nonjudicial Foreclosure Process, 1990; editor, chmn. editorial bd. P.L.I. Oil and Gas and Bankruptcy Laws, 1985. Trustee Congregation Beth Israel, Houston, 1980-86, v.p., 1996—; trustee Houston Ballet, 1986—, v.p., 1993-96; chmn. ann. fund St. John's Sch., Houston, 1993-95; trustee Retina Rsch. Found., Houston, St. John's Sch., Houston, 1996—. Fellow Tex. Bar Found.; mem. ABA, Coronado Club, N.Y. Athletic Club, The Argyle (San Antonio). Jewish. Public utilities, Mergers and acquisitions, Finance. Office: Weil Gotshal & Manges 700 Louisiana St Ste 1600 Houston TX 77002-2784

**GOVERN, KEVIN HUGH**, lawyer; b. Indpls., Oct. 12, 1962; s. Francis Whitton and Liane Elisabeth (Wittek) G.; m. Karen Lynne Karwoski, May 30, 1992. BA in History, Marquette U., Milw., 1984, JD, 1987; LLM, The Judge Advocate Gen.'s Sch. U.S. Army, Charlottesville, Va., 1995. Bar: Wis. 1987, U.S. Dist. Ct. (ea. and we. dist.) Wis. 1987, U.S. Ct. Mil. Appeals 1993. Commd. 2d lt. U.S. Army, 1984, advanced through grades to maj., 1994; adminstrv. law officer XVIII Airborne Corps, Ft. Bragg, N.C., 1987-88, trial counsel, 1988-89, chief ops. law, 1989-90; group judge advocate 10th Spl. Forces Group, Ft. Devens, Mass., 1990-92; sr. def. counsel U.S. Army TDS, Ft. Benning, Ga., 1992-94; field screening officer U.S. Army JAGC, 1990-94; chief mil. and civil law 1st Armored Divsn., Bad Kreuznach, Germany, 1995-97; legal advisor command ops. rev. bd. Hdqrs. USSOCOM, MacDill AFB, Fla., 1997—. Decorated Meritorious Svc. medals (2), Army Commendation medals (3). Mem. ABA, Phi Alpha Theta (sec. 1983-84), Phi Delta Phi (asst. province pres. 1991-92, acting province pres. 1992-94). Roman Catholic. Office: Mac Dill AFB Hdqrs USSOCOM Attn: SOOR PSC Box 3500 Tampa FL 33621

**GOVETT, BRETT CHRISTOPHER**, lawyer; b. Corpus Christi, Tex., May 17, 1965; s. Raymond Weston and Martha Lenora (Barton) G.; m. Cynthia Lynn Rowell, June 5, 1993. BA in Chemistry cum laude, The Citadel, 1987; JD cum laude, Tex. Tech U., 1990. Bar: Tex. 1990, U.S. Ct. Appeals (5th cir.) 1990, U.S. Dist. Ct. (so. dist.) Tex. 1990, U.S. Dist. Ct. (no. dist.) Tex. 1991, U.S. Supreme Ct. 1998. Jud. clk. for Judge Reynaldo G. Garza U.S. Ct. Appeals (5th cir.), Brownsville, Tex., 1990-91; assoc. Fulbright & Jaworski L.L.P., Dallas, 1991-98, ptnr., 1999—. Note editor Tex. Tech. Law Rev., 1989-90, contbr. articles. Mem. Southwestern Legal Found. Mem. ABA, Tex. Bar Assn., Dallas Bar Assn., Order of Coif. Federal civil litigation, State civil litigation, Professional liability. Office: Fulbright & Jaworski LLP 2200 Ross Ave Ste 2800 Dallas TX 75201-2784

**GOWIN, RICHARD BRYAN**, lawyer; b. Louisville, Oct. 16, 1969; s. Charles R. and Sherrin M. Gowin; m. Lisa M. Gowin, Dec. 19, 1998. BS, U. Ky., 1992, JD, 1996. Bar: Ky. 1997. Law clk. U.S. Army Corps Engrs., Louisville, 1992, Ky. Local Governance Project, Lexington, Ky., 1993-96; atty. Hoge & Assocs., Louisville, 1997—. Mem. ABA, Ky. Bar Assn., Louisville Bar Assn. (family law sect.). Family and matrimonial. Home: 3312 Eagle Pass Louisville KY 40213-1216 Office: Hoge & Assocs Ste 400 Starks Bldg Louisville KY 40202

**GOZZI, JOANNA**, lawyer; b. Syracuse, N.Y., Sept. 5, 1954; d. Ernest John Sr. and Grace (Barletta) G.; m. John Joseph Trombetta, Sept. 27, 1980; children: Jessica Grace, Justin Nicholas. Bar: N.Y. 1980, U.S. Dist. Ct. (no. dist.) N.Y. 1981, U.S. Dist. Ct. (we. dist.) N.Y. 1995, U.S. Ct. Appeals 1998. Assoc. Lischak Law Firm, Syracuse, 1979-81; dep. county atty. mcpl. unit Onondaga County Law Dept., Syracuse, 1981-84, dep. county atty. family ct. unit, 1985-89, sr. dep. county atty. mcpl. unit, 1990—. Pres. Women's Polit. Action Coalition, 1991—; mem. Foster Care Adv. Bd., Syracuse, 1987-90, Child Abuse Mgmt. Com., Syracuse, 1988-90, Permanency Planning Com.,

1988-90; bd. dirs. Greater East Syracuse Day Care Ctr., Syracuse, 1990-92, Humane Assn. Cen. N.Y., 1992. Republican. Roman Catholic. Home: 102 Kathleen Ter Camillus NY 13031-1252 Office: Onondaga County Law Dept 10th Fl Civic Center Syracuse NY 13202

**GRAB, FREDERICK CHARLES,** lawyer; b. N.Y.C., Aug. 1, 1946; s. Daniel Justin and Elizabeth (Kam) G. BS in Aerospace Engring., Polytech U. N.Y., 1967; JD, U. So. Calif., 1977. Bar: Calif. 1978, U.S. Dist. Ct. (cen. dist.) Calif. 1978, U.S. Supreme Ct. 1988, U.S. Ct. Appeals (9th cir.) 1989. Deputy atty. gen. Calif. Atty. Gen., L.A., 1977—. Contbr. articles to profl. jours. Avocations: playwright, author, composer, musican.

**GRABER, PATRICK MATTHEW,** lawyer; b. Chgo., Mar. 1, 1950; s. William Allen and Loretta Jane (Stapleton) G.; m. Patricia Ann Brown, June 6, 1981; children: Kelly, Ryan, Terrence. BSAE, Purdue U., 1972; JD, U. Notre Dame, 1979. Bar: Ill. 1979. Assoc. Peterson, Ross, Schloerby & Seidel, Chgo., 1979-87, ptnr., 1987; founding ptnr. McCullough, Campbell & Lane, Chgo., 1987—. Active Chgo. area coun. Boy Scouts Am.; mem. Lake View Citizens Coun., Chgo., 1986-90. Capt. USMC, 1971-76, comdr. USNR, 1979-98, ret. Mem. Def. Rsch. Inst., Ill. Assn. of Def. Trial Coun., Trial Lawyers Club of Chgo., Irish Fellowship Club of Chgo. Roman Catholic. Avocation: flying. Aviation, General civil litigation, Insurance. Home: 9750 S Longwood Dr Chicago IL 60643-1610 Office: McCullough Campbell & Lane 401 N Michigan Ave Ste 1300 Chicago IL 60611-4224

**GRABER, SUSAN P.,** judge; b. Oklahoma City, July 5, 1949; d. Julius A. and Bertha (Fenyves) G.; m. William June, May 3, 1981; 1 child, Rachel June-Graber. BA, Wellesley Coll., 1969; JD, Yale U., 1972. Bar: N.Mex. 1972, Ohio 1977, Oreg. 1978. Asst. atty. gen. Bur. of Revenue, Santa Fe, 1972-74; assoc. Jones Gallegos Snead & Wertheim, Santa Fe, 1974-75, Taft Stettinius & Hollister, Cin., 1975-78; assoc., then ptnr. Stoel Rives Boley Jones & Grey, Portland, Oreg., 1978-88; judge, then presiding judge Oreg. Ct. Appeals, Salem, 1988-90; assoc. justice Oreg. Supreme Ct., Salem, 1990-98; judge U.S. Ct. Appeals (9th cir.), Portland, 1998—. Mem. Gov.'s Adv. Coun. on Legal Svcs., 1979-88; bd. dirs. U.S. Dist. Ct. of Oreg. Hist. Soc., 1985—, Oreg. Law Found., 1990-91; mem. bd. visitors Sch. Law, U. Oreg., 1986-93. Mem. Oreg. State Bar (jud. adminstrn. com. 1985-87, pro bono com. 1988-90), Ninth Cir. Jud. Conf. (chair exec. com. 1987-88), Oreg. Jud. Conf. (edn. com. 1988-91, program chair 1990), Oreg. Appellate Judges Assn. (sec.-treas. 1990-91, vice chair 1991-92, chair 1992-93), Am. Inns of Ct. (master), Phi Beta Kappa. Office: US Ct Appeals 9th Cir Pioneer Courthouse 555 SW Yamhill St Portland OR 97204-1336

**GRABOW, RAYMOND JOHN,** mayor, lawyer; b. Cleve., Jan. 27, 1932; s. Joseph Stanley and Frances (Kalata) G.; m. Margaret Jean Knoll, Nov. 27, 1969; children: Rachel Jean, Ryan Joseph. BSBA, Kent State U., 1953; JD, Western Res. U., 1958. Bar: Ohio 1958. Counsel No. Ohio Petroleum Retailers Assn., Cleve., 1965-78; counsel, trustee Alliance of Poles Fed. Credit Union, 1972; also gen. counsel Alliance of Poles of Am.; councilman City of Warrensville Heights (Ohio), 1962-68, mayor, 1968-98; sec. Space Comfort Co., S.S.K., Inc.; fed. panelist U.S. Dist. Ct.; active Dem. Exec. Com., Cuyahoga County, 1966-98, precinct com., 1966-80; trustee Brentwood Hosp., Nat. League Cities, Brentwood Found.; bd. govs. Meridia Southpoint Hosp., 1996-99; pres. West Harbor Lagoons Assn. Mem. Ohio Jud. Conf. (life), Ohio State Bar Assn., Cuyahoga County Bar Assn., Cleve. Bar Assn., U.S. Conf. of Mayors, Am. Legion, PLAV Vets, Cleve. Soc., Warrensville Heights C. of C. (trustee 1989-98), Ohio Assn. Pub. Safety Dirs., Ohio Mcpl. League, Mcpl. Treas. Assn., Order of Alhambra, Fraternal Order of Eagles. Home: 20114 Gladstone Rd Cleveland OH 44122-6644 Office: 5005 Rockside Rd Cleveland OH 44131-2194

**GRACE, BRIAN GUILES,** lawyer; b. Lawrence, Kans., Dec. 26, 1942; s. Bernard and Theola Avida (Guiles) G.; m. Carol Diane Seaver, June 9, 1967; children: Kevin A., Jeff S., Brady A. BBA, U. Kans., 1964, JD, 1967. Bar: Kans. 1967, U.S. Dist. Ct. Kans. 1967, U.S. Ct. Appeals (10th cir.) 1974, U.S. Supreme Ct. 1991. Assoc., ptnr. Curfman, Harris, Stallings, Grace & Snow and predecessor firm, Wichita, Kans., 1967-84; ptnr. Grace Unruh & Pratt and predecessor firms, Wichita, 1984—; mem. Fed. Bench and Bar Comm., 1992-96. Bd. dirs. Leukemia Soc. Kans. Inc., Wichita, 1974-77; chmn. bd. edn. Desegretion Com., 1990-95. Mem. ABA (vice chmn. constn. litigation com. 1974-76), Assn. of Trial Lawyers of Am., Kans. Bar Assn. (bench and bar com. 1991—, chmn. 1993-96), Kans. Trial Lawyers Assn. (editor jour. 1989-91). Avocations: golf, tennis, bridge. Personal injury, General civil litigation, Labor. Home: 36 Stratford Rd Wichita KS 67206-2029 Office: 501 N Market St Wichita KS 67214-3513

**GRACE, BRIAN VINCENT,** lawyer; b. San Diego, Aug. 26, 1959; s. Philip Henry and Marie Larkin Grace; m. Carol Anne Schilling, Apr. 5, 1980; children: Laura Anne, Melissa Anne. AA, Mesa Coll., San Diego, 1985; B Gen Studies, U. Kans., 1991, JD, 1994. Bar: Kas. 1994, U.S. Dist. Ct. Kans. 1994. Dep. sheriff San Diego Sheriff's Dept., 1982-86; legal intern Jackson County Prosecutor's Office, Kansas City, Mo., 1993-94; asst. county atty. Republic County, Belleville, Kans., 1994-97, county atty., 1997—. Mem. Cmty. Corrections Bd., Salina, Kans., 1996—. With USAF, 1977-81, U.S. Army, 1986-89. Mem. Kans. Bar Assn., VFW (judge adv. post 3722 1995—). Republican. Lutheran. Avocations: hiking, camping, canoeing, hunting. Office: Republic County Atty's Office PO Box 466 Belleville KS 66935-0466

**GRACE, (WALTER) CHARLES,** prosecutor; b. Elmira, N.Y., Mar. 4, 1947; s. Claude Henry and Grace Anne (Richardson) G.; m. Barbbara Lynn Eaglen, Oct. 3, 1981; children: Katherine Anne, Charles Brigham. BA History, Duke U., 1969; JD, U. Tenn., 1972. Bar: Ill., 1972; U.S. Dist. Ct. (ea. and so. dists.) Ill., 1972. Asst. state's atty. Jackson County, Murphysboro, Ill., 1972-73; assoc. Donald R. Mitchell Law Office, Carbondale, Ill., 1973-74; atty. Jackson County Pub. Defender, Murphysboro, 1974-77; ptnr. Lockwood & Grace, Carbondale, 1977-78; pvt. practice Lockwood & Grace, 1978-79; ptnr. Hendricks, Watt & Grace, Murphysboro, 1979-82; assoc. Feirich, Schone, Mager, Green & Assocs., Carbondale, 1982-83, Feirich, Schoen, Mager, Green & Assocs., Carbondale, 1983-88; state's atty. Jackson County State's Atty., Murphysboro, 1988-93; U.S. Atty. U.S. Atty.'s Office, Fairview Heights, Ill., 1993—; chmn. Jackson County Child Advocacy Adv. Bd., 1988-93; adv. bd. Ill. State Violent Crime Victim's Adv. Bd., 1988-90; com. mem. Jackson County Juv. Justice Task Force, 1988-93; exec. com. Ill. State's Atty.'s Assn., 1991-93; legis. com. Ill. Sate's Atty.'s Assn., 1992-93; co-chmn. Jackson County SAFE Policy/Gang Policy Interagy. Steering Com. Adv. Bd., 1991-93; master So. Ill. Am. Inn. of Ct., 1992—; others. Active NAACP,, Carbondale; mem. Jackson County Heart Fund Campaign, 1976-77; bd. dirs. Carbondale United Way, 1978-80, capt. campaign drive, profl. div., 1980; mem. planning com. John A. Logan Coll.-Jackson County Bar Assn. Continuing Edn. Programs; mem. adv. com. to Corrections and Law Enforcment Programs, So. Ill. U. Sch. of Tech. Careers, 1978-89; mem. Hill House Board, Inc., 1979-84; pres. 1980-82; lector St. Francis Xavier Ch., Carbondale. Mem. Jackson County Bar Assn. (sec. 1978-79, pres. 1980-81), Ill. State Bar Assn. (mem. criminal law sect., family law sect., tort law sect.), ABA (family law and criminal law sects.), Assn. Trial Lawyers of Am., Nat. Legal Aid and Defender Assn., Ill. Pub. Defenders Assn., So. Ill. Am. Inns of Ct. (barrister 1993-95). Democrat. Roman Catholic. Avocations: golf, swimming, cooking, enology. Home: 431 Phillips Rd Carbondale IL 62901-7459 Office: US Attys Office 9 Executive Dr Ste 300 Fairview Heights IL 62208-1344*

**GRACE, JAMES MARTIN, JR.,** lawyer; b. Columbus, Ohio, Sept. 6, 1967; s. James Martin and Letitia Jean (Stively) G.; m. Michèle Lee Sirna, June 22, 1991. BA, U. Notre Dame, 1989; JD cum laude, U. Houston, 1992. Bar: Tex. Law clk. to Hon. Samuel B. Kent U.S. Dist. Ct. (so. dist.) Tex., Galveston, 1992-93; assoc. Baker & Botts, LLP, Houston, 1993—. Author tchr.'s guide: Copyright Law, 1992. Adv. coun. Local Initiatives Support Corp.; pres. R Club PAC; mem. Tex. Accts. and Lawyers for the Arts, 1998—. Mem. State Bar Tex., Houston Bar Assn., Houston Young Lawyers Assn., Houston Jaycees (dir. edn. 1993-94, legal counsel 1994, Outstanding Leadership award 1993, Silver Key award 1994), Notre Dame Alumni Assn. (treas. Class of '89), Notre Dame Club of Houston (bd. dirs.), Order of the Barons, Phi Delta Phi. Republican. Roman Catholic. Avocations: soccer, football, reading. Securities, Mergers and acquisitions. Office: Baker & Botts LLP 910 Louisiana St Ste 3000 Houston TX 77002-4991

**GRACE, THOMAS EDWARD,** lawyer; b. Carlinville, Ill., Sept. 14, 1954; s. Fredrick R. and Julia M. (Link) G.; m. Julia A. Stone, Oct. 30, 1982; children: Alexander Wade, Victoria Ruth. BA, Ill. State U., 1976; JD, John Marshall Law Sch., 1979; MBA, Northwestern U., 1989. Bar: Ill. 1979, U.S. Dist. Ct. (no. dist.) Ill. 1982. Sr. atty. Montgomery Ward & Co., Chgo., 1979-86; atty. Ameritech Services, Inc., Schaumburg, Ill., 1986-90; sr. atty. Bellcore, Livingston, N.J., 1990—. Editor law rev. John Marshall Law Sch., 1977-79. Mem. assoc. bd. Chgo. Lung Assn., Chgo., 1982-84; mem. jr. bd. Lawrence Hall Sch. for Boys, Chgo., 1982-86. Mem. ABA, Ill. Bar Assn. Republican. Episcopalian. Avocations: golf, hunting, trap and skeet shooting. Antitrust, Communications, General corporate. Office: Bellcore Bldg C 290 W Mount Pleasant Ave # 2b330 Livingston NJ 07039-2729

**GRACEFFA, JOHN PHILIP,** lawyer; b. Boston, Aug. 4, 1953; s. Anthony Joseph and Ruth Elizabeth (Nudd) G.; m. Elaine Marie Margeson, June 17, 1978; 1 child, Victoria Rose. BA magna cum laude, Ea. Nazarene Coll., Quincy, Mass., 1975; JD cum laude, Suffolk U., 1979. Bar: Mass. 1979, U.S. Dist. Ct. Mass. 1980, U.S. Ct. Appeals (1st cir.) 1981, R.I. 1994, U.S. Supreme Ct. 1994, U.S. Dist. Ct. R.I. 1995; CPCU. Asst. atty. gen. Mass. Office of the Atty. Gen., Boston, 1979-84; lawyer Gallagher and Gallagher, P.C., Boston, 1984-89, mgr. litigation, 1990-95; lawyer Morrison, Mahoney & Miller, Boston and Providence, Mass., 1995—; former mem. adj. faculty Northea. U. Sch. Continuing Edn., Boston, 1994-95. Contbr. articles to profl. jours. Spl. asst. atty. gen. Office of the Atty. Gen., Boston, 1992. Mem. FBA, Mass. Bar Assn., R.I. Bar Assn., Mass. Def. Lawyers Assn., Boston Bar Assn., Hingham Yacht Club. Avocations: yacht cruising and racing, bicycling, reading, skiing, travel. Insurance, Administrative and regulatory, Toxic tort. Office: Morrison Mahoney & Miller 250 Summer St Fl 1 Boston MA 02210-1181

**GRACIN, HANK,** lawyer; b. Massapequa Park, N.Y., Jan. 27, 1957; s. Bernard Tobias and Ada (Rosenberg) G.; m. Marisol L. Perez, Sept. 9, 1990. BA with honors, SUNY, Binghamton, 1978; JD cum laude, NYU, 1981. Bar: N.Y. 1982, U.S. Dist. Ct. (so. dist.) N.Y. 1982. Assoc. Sullivan & Cromwell, N.Y.C., 1981-83, Schulte Roth & Zabel, N.Y.C., 1983-86, Fulbright Jaworski & Reavis McGrath, N.Y.C., 1986-90; corp. counsel Computer Assocs. Internat., Inc., 1990-94; counsel Lehman & Eilen, 1994—. Editor: Private Placements and Restricted Securities, 1981. Mem. Nassau County Bar Assn., Order of Coif (NYU chpt.). Avocations: bicycling, reading, piano. Computer, Intellectual property, Securities. Office: Lehman & Eilen Ste 505 50 Charles Lindbergh Blvd Uniondale NY 11553-3612

**GRAD, FRANK PAUL,** law educator, lawyer; b. Vienna, May 2, 1924; came to U.S., 1939, naturalized, 1943; s. Morris and Clara Sophie (Scher) G.; m. Lisa Szilagyi, Dec. 6, 1946; children: David Anthony, Catharine Ann. B.A. magna cum laude, Bklyn. Coll., 1947; LL.B., Columbia U., 1949. Bar: N.Y. 1949. Assoc. in law Columbia U. Law Sch., N.Y.C., 1949-50, asst. dir. Legis. Drafting Research Fund, 1953-55, assoc. dir., 1956-68, dir., 1969-95, mem. faculty, 1954—, prof., 1969—, Joseph P. Chamberlain prof. legis., 1982-95, Joseph P. Chamberlain prof. emeritus legis. and spl. lectr., 1995—; mem. legal adv. com. U.S. Council Environ. Quality, 1970-73; mem. N.Y. Deptl. Com. Ct. Adminstrn., Appellate Div., 1st Dept., 1970-74; counsel N.Y. State Spl. Adv. Panel Med. Malpractice, 1975; legal counsel Nat. Mcpl. League, 1967-88; cons. in field, 1955—; reporter U.S. Superfund Study group, 1981-82; dir. rsch. N.Y.C. Charter Revision Commn., 1982-83, N.Y. State-City Commn. on Integrity in Govt., 1986. Author: Public Health Law Manual, 1st edit., 1965, 2d rev. edit., 1990, The Drafting of State Constitutions, 1963, Environmental law: Sources and Problems, 3d edit., 1985, Treatise on Environemntal Law, 8 vols., 1973-99; co-author other legal reports; contbr. legal jours.; draftsman mcpl. codes and state legislation. Served with AUS, 1943-46. 10th Horace E. Read Meml. lectr. Dalhousie Law Sch., 1984. Mem. ABA, APHA, Assn. of Bar of City of N.Y., N.Y. Bar Assn., Am. Law Inst., Am. Soc. Law and Medicine, World Conservation Union (commn. on environ. law 1991—), Human Genome Orgn., Internat. Coun. Environ. Law, N.Y.. Soc. Med. Jurisprudence. Office: Columbia U Sch Law 435 W 116th St New York NY 10027-7297

**GRADER, SCOTT PAUL,** lawyer; b. Bklyn., June 25, 1956; s. Jack and Bernice Grader; m. Patricia Lande, Feb. 11, 1995. BA with honors, CUNY, 1977; JD with honors, Rutgers U., 1980; LLM, U. London, 1983. Bar: N.Y. 1981. Asst. gen. counsel N.Y.C. Office of Econ. Devel., 1981-82; assoc. Cahill, Gordon & Reindel, N.Y.C., 1984-86; assoc. Paul, Weiss, Rifkind, Wharton & Garrison, N.Y.C., 1986-97, counsel, 1998—. Assoc. editor Rutgers-Camden Law Rev., 1978-80. Hague Acad. Internat. scholar, The Hague, The Netherlands, 1983. Mem. Assn. of Bar of City of N.Y. General corporate, Mergers and acquisitions, Securities. Home: 670 W End Ave Apt 14C New York NY 10025-7328 Office: Paul Weiss Rifkind Wharton & Garrison 1285 Ave of the Ams New York NY 10019

**GRADOVILLE, ROBERT THOMAS,** lawyer; b. Des Moines, May 16, 1946. BA, Loras Coll., 1968; MBA, Ind. U., 1970; JD, Duke U., 1973; LLM in Taxation, NYU, 1976. Bar: N.Y. 1975, Conn. 1979. Mgr. Coopers & Lybrand, N.Y.C., 1974-78; assoc. Bergman, Horowitz & Reynolds, New Haven, 1978-81; mem. Kleban, Samor, Perles, etc., Southport, Conn., 1981-92, DeSarbo, Reichert & Gradoville, P.C., North Haven, Conn., 1992—. Pres. Farmington Canal Rail to Trail Assn., 1991. Recipient Silver medal N.C. CPA, 1973. Mem. ABA (tax sect.), AICPA, Conn. Bar Assn. (tax sect.), Conn. Soc. CPAs (mem. fed. tax. com. 1984-95, mem. personal fin. planning com. 1996—, mem. employee benefit plan com. 1998—, Disting. Author award 1990), High Lane Club (pres. 1995-96). Taxation, general, Pension, profit-sharing, and employee benefits, Estate planning. Office: DeSarbo Reichert & Gradoville PC 250 State St North Haven CT 06473-2193

**GRADY, FRANCIS XAVIER,** lawyer; b. Cleve., Nov. 17, 1957; s. John J. and Mary Veronica (Carey) G.; m. Donita Marie Labas. BS in Internat. Politics magna cum laude, Georgetown U., 1980; cert. advanced European studies, Coll. Europe, 1981; JD, Ohio State U., 1984. Bar: Ohio 1984, D.C. 1985. Atty. FDIC, Washington, 1984-86; assoc. Muldoon, Murphy & Faucette, Washington, 1986-87, Hahn, Loeser & Parks, Cleve., 1987-90; of counsel Seeley, Savidge & Aussem, Cleve., 1990-94; ptnr. Grady & Assocs., Cleve., 1994—. Author: The New CRA: A Practical Guide to Compliance, 1997; contbr. articles to profl. jours. Mem. Am.'s Cmty. Bankers. Roman Catholic. Banking, General corporate, Mergers and acquisitions. Office: Grady & Assocs 116 Center Ridge Rd Rocky River OH 44116-4306

**GRADY, GREGORY,** lawyer, banker; b. Takoma Park, Md., Oct. 10, 1945; s. Francis Joseph Grady and Deane (McGehee) Black; m. Carol Love Harrison, Feb. 25, 1978; children: Olivia Love, Blake McGregor, Harrison Edwards. BA in Econs., U. Va., 1969; JD, Tulane U., 1972. Bar: D.C. 1973, U.S. Ct. Appeals (D.C. cir.) 1973, U.S. Ct. Appeals (4th cir.) 1975, U.S. Supreme Ct. 1976, U.S. Ct. Appeals (5th cir.) 1977, U.S. Ct. Appeals (10th cir.) 1979, U.S. Ct. Appeals (11th cir.) 1981, U.S. Ct. Appeals (6th cir.) 1982, U.S. Dist. Ct. 1988. Staff atty., supervisory atty. FPC, Washington, 1972-74; assoc. Littman, Richter, Wright & Talisman, P.C., Washington, 1974-79; mem. Wright & Talisman, P.C., Washington, 1979—, pres., chmn. bd. dirs., chmn. exec. com., 1997-98, mng. mem., 1999—; bd. dirs. Bank of Franklin, Miss., D.R. McGehee Ins. Agy., Inc., Miss. Mem. Fed. Energy Bar Assn., D.C. Bar Assn., Congl. Country Club. Republican. Episcopalian. FERC practice, Administrative and regulatory, Federal civil litigation. Home: 666 Live Oak Dr Mc Lean VA 22101-1569 Office: Wright & Talisman PC 1200 G St NW Ste 600 Washington DC 20005-3838

**GRADY, JOHN F.,** federal judge; b. Chgo., May 23, 1929; s. John F. and Lucille F. (Shroder) G.; m. Patsy Grady, Aug. 10, 1968; 1 child, John F. BS, Northwestern U., 1952, JD, 1954. Bar: Ill. 1955. Assoc. Sonnenschein, Berkson, Lautmann, Levinson & Morse, Chgo., 1954-56; asst. U.S. atty. No. Dist. Ill., 1956-61, chief criminal divsn., 1960-61; assoc. Snyder, Clarke, Dalziel, Holmquist & Johnson, Waukegan, Ill., 1961-63; practice law Waukegan, 1963-76; judge U.S. Dist. Ct. (no. dist.) Ill., Chgo., 1976-86, chief judge, 1986-90, sr. judge, 1994—; mem. com. criminal law U.S. Jud. Conf., 1982-87, adv. com. civil rules, 1984-90, chair, 1987-90; mem. bench book com. Fed. Jud. Ctr., 1988-93; mem. Nat. State-Fed. Jud. Coun., 1990-92, Jud. Panel on Multidist. Litigation, 1992—. Assoc. editor: Northwestern U. Law Rev. Mem. Phi Beta Kappa. Office: US Dist Ct 2286 Dirksen Bldg 219 S Dearborn St Chicago IL 60604-1702

**GRADY, KEVIN E.,** lawyer; b. Charlotte, N.C., Jan. 19, 1948; s. Thomas F. and Rosemary (Loughran) G.; m. Mary Beth O'Brien, Dec. 27, 1975; children: Martin E., Donald F. BA, Vanderbilt U., 1969; JD, Harvard U., 1974. Bar: Ga. 1974, U.S. Dist. Ct. (no. dist.) Ga. 1975, U.S. Ct. Appeals (11th cir.) 1981, U.S. Supreme Ct. 1990. Assoc. Jones, Bird & Howell, Atlanta, 1974-76; trial atty. Antitrust divsn. U.S. Dept. Justice, Atlanta, 1976-77; ptnr. Alston & Bird, Atlanta, 1977—. Editor: Georgia Hospital Law Manual, 1997. Mem. bd. trust Vanderbilt U., 1995-97. Recipient Top Hat award St. Vincent de Paul Soc., 1995. Mem. ABA (mem. coun. antitrust sect. 1995-98, publs. officer 1998—), Ga. Acad. Healthcare Attys. (pres. 1997-98), Am. Health Lawyers Assn. (vice chair antitrust program 1992-99, chair 1999—), Am. Counsel Assn. (dir. 1991—, pres. 1995), State Bar Ga. (vice chair health law sect. 1998-99). Democrat. Roman Catholic. Avocations: running, racketball, reading. Antitrust, Federal civil litigation, Health. Office: Alston & Bird 1201 W Peachtree St NW Ste 4200 Atlanta GA 30309-3424

**GRADY, MAUREEN FRANCES,** lawyer; b. N.Y.C., Oct. 6, 1960; d. Frank J. and Pauline (Laberge) G. BA, Manhattan Coll., 1982; JD, Georgetown U., 1985. Bar: N.Y. 1986, U.S. Dist. Ct. (so. and ea. dists.) N.Y. 1987, U.S. Ct. Appeals (2d cir.) 1990. Assoc. Griffin, Scully & Savona, N.Y.C., 1985-87, Morris & Duffy, N.Y.C., 1987-88, Summit, Rovins & Feldesman, N.Y.C., 1988-89; asst. gen. counsel N.Y.C. Transit Authority, 1989-92; trial atty. Fireman's Fund Ins. Co., N.Y.C., 1992-97; sr. assoc. DeCicco Gibbons & McNamara, P.C., N.Y.C., 1998-99; assoc. Kral Clerkin Redmond Ryan Perry & Girvan, N.Y.C., 1999—. Recipient Bur. Nat. Affairs award. Mem. Assn. of Bar of City of N.Y. (young lawyers com. 1987-90, constrn. law com. 1991-92, spl. com. on alcoholism and substance abuse 1994-97, sec. spl. com. on alcoholism and substance abuse 1995-97, product liability com. 1995-98), Phi Beta Kappa, Epsilon Sigma Pi, Phi Alpha Theta. Personal injury, Insurance, Product liability.

**GRADY, THOMAS MICHAEL,** lawyer; b. Boston, Nov. 10, 1952; s. John C. and Jean M. (Harvey) G.; m. Jacquelyn Roberts, May 15, 1982; children: David R., Caroline M. AB, Harvard U., 1975; JD, Suffolk U., 1981. Bar: Ill. 1981, Pa. 1987. Atty. Container Corp. Am., Chgo., 1981-84; regional atty. Container Corp. Am., Carol Stream, Ill., 1984-86; sr. regional atty. Container Corp. Am., Valley Forge, Pa., 1986; sr. counsel Rohm & Haas Co., Phila., 1986—. Mem. Am. Corp. Counsel Assn., Nat. Agrl. Chems. Assn. (law com. 1990-93). General corporate, Antitrust, Mergers and acquisitions. Home: 537 Beaumont Cir West Chester PA 19380-6437 Office: Rohm and Haas Co Independence Mall Philadelphia PA 19105

**GRAF, BAYARD MAYHEW,** lawyer; b. West Grove, Pa., Jan. 17, 1926; s. Charles Earl and Elisabeth Helen (Mayhew) G.; m. Ruthann Hemphill, June 17, 1950; children—Bayard H., Evan M., Beverly R. B.S., Northwestern U., 1946; M.A., U. Pa., 1949; LL.B., Temple U., 1953. Bar: Pa. 1953, U.S. Dist. Ct. (ea. dist.) Pa. 1955, U.S. Ct. Appeals (3d cir.) 1955, U.S. Ct. Appeals (7th cir.) 1965, U.S. Ct. Appeals (D.C. cir.) 1976, U.S. Tax Ct. 1974, ICC bar 1971, U.S. Supreme Ct. 1967. Law clk. to justice Pa. Supreme Ct., 1953-55; assoc. Rawle & Henderson, 1955-57, J. Willison Smith, Jr., 1957-71, Harold E. Kohn, P.A., 1971-76; asst. v.p. Kohn, Savett, Klein & Graf, P.C., Phila., 1976-91; sole practice law, Devon, Pa., 1991—; lectr. fin. Temple U.; sec., dir. Melmark Home, Inc.; sec. Eden Charitable Found., Melmork Charitable Found.; former dir., sec.-treas. Arronson Found., Lavine Found. Past bd. dirs. ; mem. pres.'s council USO Phila.; mgr. championship Little League baseball team, former treas. USN League Phila. Coun. Served to capt. Supply Corps, USNR, 1973-78. Mem. ABA, Pa. Bar Assn., Phila. Bar Assn., Chester County Bar Assn., Lawyers Club Phila., D.C. Bar Assn., Am. Acad. Hosp. Attys., Nat. Health Lawyers Assn., Presbyn. Social Union (past pres.), l), Phi Kappa Psi (former atty gen., sec. 1988-90), Phi Alpha Delta (former justice). Republican. Presbyterian (ruling elder, clk. of session). Clubs: Union League (Phila.); Waynesborough Country. Probate, General corporate, Family and matrimonial. Home and Office: 162 Beaumont Rd Devon PA 19333-1849

**GRAF, GREGORY C.,** lawyer; b. Forest Hills, N.Y., Aug. 25, 1958; s. George H. and Gloria G.; m. Lisa K. Carpenter, Aug. 14, 1982; children: Jennifer, Erica. BA, Ind. State U., 1980; JD, U. Tulsa, 1983. Asst. prosecutor City Atty.'s Office, Tulsa, 1982-83; assoc. Cogswell & Wiehale, Denver, 1983; asst. U.S. atty. U.S. Atty.'s Office, Denver, 1991-97; ptnr. Seawell, Gilbertson & Graf, Denver, 1997—. Editor Tulsa Law Jour., 1981-83. Lt. Col. USAFR, 1984—, judge advocate. Master Masons. Criminal, Estate planning, Family and matrimonial. Home: 9441 S Chesapeake St Highlands Ranch CO 80126 Office: 999 18th St Ste 3200 Denver CO 80202-2432

**GRAF, SHERYL SUSAN,** lawyer; b. Auburn, Wash., Feb. 23, 1959; d. Lawrence S. and Joyce May Graf; widowed, 1983; m. Gerald Cox, Feb. 14, 1987. AA, Grossmont Coll., El Cajon, Calif., 1977; JD, Thomas Jefferson Sch. Law, San Diego, 1994. Bar: Calif. 1995, U.S. Dist. Ct. (so. dist.) Calif. 1995. Exec. adminstr. Anacomp, Inc., San Diego, 1980-91; lawyer Law Offices of Sheryl S. Graf, El Cajon, Calif., 1995—. Contbr. articles to law revs. Mem. San Diego County Bar Assn. (chair solo and small firm sect. 1996-97), Calif. Attys. for Criminal Justice, Lawyers Club East County (bd. dirs. 1997—), Delta Theta Phi. Avocation: skiing. Criminal, Family and matrimonial, Bankruptcy. Office: 275 E Douglas Ave Ste 115 El Cajon CA 92020-4548

**GRAFF, DOUGLAS ERIC,** lawyer; b. Cleve., Apr. 7, 1953; s. Richard Alison and Lois Marie (Boehmer) G.; m. Jean Stevens, Jan. 20, 1989; children: Jenna Leigh, Joel Douglas. BA, Capital U., 1974; MPA, Am. U., 1981; JD, Ohio State U., 1984. Bar: Ohio 1985, U.S. Dist. Ct. (so. dist.) Ohio 1986, U.S. Ct. Appeals (6th cir.) 1995, U.S. Supreme Ct. 1997. Program analyst Nat. Adv. Coun. Edn. Disadvantaged Children, Washington, 1975-76; v.p. ops. Royal Gen. Co., Cleve., 1976-80; pvt. practice law Columbus, OH, 1985—; assoc. counsel, dir. hosp. med. staff svcs. Ohio State Med. Assn., 1985-91; mng. ptnr. Graff & Assocs., L.P.A., 1991-98; ptnr., mem. exec. com. Robins Preston Beckett Graff et al., Columbus, 1998—; adj. faculty dept. health and human svcs. Columbus State U., 1993—; bd. dirs. Columbus Blue Cross/Blue Shield Fed. Credit Union, 1986-95, pres., 1988-94; speaker in field. Author: Physician's Guide to Ohio Law, 1989, Ohio Model Medical Staff By-laws, 1990, Law of Massage Therapy in Ohio, 1992, Medical Records and the Law in Ohio, 1993; contbr. articles to profl. jours. Mem. ABA, Am. Soc. Assn. Execs., Nat. Health Lawyers Assn., Ohio State Bar Assn., Ohio Soc. Assn. Execs., Columbus Bar Assn., Delta Sigma Rho, Tau Kappa Alpha, Phi Alpha Delta. Health, Administrative and regulatory, Real property. Home: 13391 Havens Corners Rd SW Pataskala OH 43062-7784 Office: 1328 Dublin Rd Columbus OH 43215-1054

**GRAFT, WILLIAM CHRISTOPHER,** lawyer; b. Barrington, Ill., Aug. 22, 1961; s. Michael Joseph and Patricia Louise (Cassin) G.; m. Mary Cecilia Fitzpatrick, Sept. 8, 1990. BA in Philosophy, Creighton U., 1982; JD, DePaul U., 1986. Bar: Ill. 1986. Assoc. Gardner, Carton & Douglas, Chgo., 1986-88, Holleb & Coff, Chgo., 1988-89, Keck, Mahin & Cate, Schaumburg, Ill., 1989—. Editor DePaul Law Rev., 1985-86. Vol. atty. Legal Clinic for Disabled, Chgo., 1990—; mem. DePaul Law Alumni Bd., Chgo., 1986-90; bd. dirs. Preservation of Human Dignity Women's Counseling Ctr., Palatine, Ill., 1988-92, Barrington Area Arts Coun., 1993—. Mem. ABA, Ill. Bar Assn. Roman Catholic. Avocations: golf, literature, art. Real property, General corporate, Estate planning. Home: 22 Stone Ridge Dr Barrington IL 60010-9593 Office: Keck Mahin & Cate 1515 E Woodfield Rd Schaumburg IL 60173-6046

**GRAHAM, ARNOLD HAROLD,** lawyer, educator; b. N.Y.C., Dec. 29, 1917; s. Julius E. and Rose Goldstein; m. Roselle Lesser, Dec. 23, 1939; children: Stuart R., Joel M., Jul E. B.S. with honors, NYU, 1945; LL.B., J.D. with honors, N.Y. Law Sch., 1952. Bar: N.Y. 1952, U.S. Supreme Ct. 1959, also U.S. Internat. Trade 1959, U.S. Tax Ct. 1959, U.S. Ct. Appeals for 2d Circuit 1959, U.S. Dist. Ct. for Hawaii 1959; C.P.A., N.Y. Practice pub. acctg. N.Y.C., 1945-52, individual practice law, 1952-76; dep. atty. gen. N.Y., 1952-54; cons. N.Y. Law Sch., N.Y.C., 1952-76; asst. dean, prof., treas. N.Y. Law Sch., 1976-77, vice dean, prof., treas., 1977-85, cons., 1985—; cons., arbitrator Am. Arbitration Assn., 1952—; examiner of attys., N.Y.C.; law cons. exam. div. Am. Inst. C.P.A.s, 1976—; bd. visitors Appellate div., 1st dept. Supreme Ct. N.Y.; mem. jud. screening panel bankruptcy div. U.S. Dist. Ct. for So. Dist. N.Y., 1983-84; numerous guardianship appointments N.Y. State Supreme Ct., Surrogate's Ct.; mem. ind. screening panel Civil Ct. of City of N.Y., 1984. Trustee Ave R Temple, Kings Hwy. Bd. Trade; bd. advisers United Jewish Appeal; mem. exec. com. trusts and estates div. United Jewish Appeal-Fedn. Jewish Philanthropies. Recipient Ira Stone award for prof. of yr. N.Y. Law Sch., 1981; John Marshall Harlan fellow. Fellow Am. Bar Found.; mem. ABA, Am. Law Inst., Am. Assn. Attys.-C.P.A.s (founder), Am. Trial Lawyers Assn., N.Y. Trial Lawyers Assn., Consular Law Soc., Fed. Bar Assn., Am. Bar Assn., Inst. Jud. Adminstrn., N.Y. State C.P.A. Soc., Fed. Bar Council, N.Y. County Lawyers Assn., Am. Arbitration Assn., Jewish Lawyers' Guild, Phi Delta Phi (hon., Disting. Alumnus award Dwight Inn). Jewish. Club: Merchants. Office: 2223 Avenue T Brooklyn NY 11229-3635

**GRAHAM, CHRISTOPHER,** lawyer; b. Dayton, Ohio, Jan. 28, 1946; s. Thomas D. and Christine (Wood) G.; m. Marsha Carol Gum, Aug. 24, 1968; children: Christiana, Elizabeth, Margaret. BSBA, U. Mo., 1968, JD, 1971; LLM in Taxation, Georgetown U., 1973. Law clk. Mo. Supreme Court, Jefferson City, Mo., 1971-72; ptnr. Graham and Graham, Jefferson City, 1975-97; adminstrv. law judge State of Mo., Jefferson City, 1997—. City atty. City of Jefferson, 1977-81, state rep. Gen. Assembly, 1983-91; bd. dirs. Capital Region Med. Ctr.; mem. Cole County Hist. Soc., bd. dirs.; exec. bd. Great Rivers Coun. Boy Scouts Am. Col. JAGC U.S. Army Res. Mem. ABA, Mo. Bar Assn., Fla. Bar Assn., Lions, Arts Council (pres. 1976-77). Democrat. Administrative and regulatory, Transportation, Military. Home: 1204 Major Dr Jefferson City MO 65101-3660 Office: Adminstrv Law Judge PO Box 1216 Jefferson City MO 65102-1216

**GRAHAM, CHRISTOPHER FRANCIS,** lawyer; b. Darby, Pa., June 21, 1957; s. Thomas Francis Graham and Margaret Veronica Kerr; m. Theresa Elizabeth Smith, Mar. 10, 1984 (dec. Apr. 1996); 1 child, Christopher F. Jr. Student, London U., 1978-79; BS in Bus. Adminstrn. magna cum laude, Georgetown U., 1979; JD, Pa. U., 1982. Bar: Hawaii 1997, U.S. Dist. Ct. (so. and ea. dist.) N.Y. 1983, U.S. Ct. Appeals (2d and 5th cirs.) 1991, U.S. Tax Ct. 1987, U.S. Supreme Ct. 1991. Assoc. Weil Gotshal & Manges, N.Y.C., 1982-84, Cadwalader Wickersham & Taft, N.Y.C., 1984-89; ptnr. Thacher Proffitt & Wood, N.Y.C., 1989—; mem. exec. com. Thacher Proffitt & Wood, 1997—; mem. bd. advisors, adj. prof. St. John's U. Sch. Law. Trustee Georgetown Dean's Coun., Washington, 1986-91; co-chmn. Save Our Aging Religious, N.Y.C., 1994—; head coach Eastchester (N.Y.) Youth Soccer, 1996—. Mem. ABA, Am. Bankruptcy Inst. (chmn. real estate com. 1996—, dir. law sch. medal program 1997—), Alpha Sigma Nu. Bankruptcy, Real property, General corporate. Home: 3 Hillside Rd Bronxville NY 10708-5116 Office: Thacher Proffitt & Wood 2 World Trade Ctr New York NY 10048-0203

**GRAHAM, DAVID ANTONY,** lawyer; b. N.Y.C., Feb. 3, 1953; s. Lorenz Bell Jr. and Adele (Hersher) G.; children: Xochitl, Joaquin, Esmeralda, Erica, Julian, Miguel. AA, Community Coll., Denver, 1976; BA in Econs., U. Denver, 1978; JD, U. N.Mex., 1981. Bar: Colo. 1981, N.Mex. 1982, Alaska 1997, U.S. Dist. Ct. Colo. 1981, U.S. Ct. Appeals (10th cir.) 1981, U.S. Dist. Ct. N.Mex. 1982. Ptnr. Graham & Graham, Denver, 1981-82, San Luis, Colo., 1982-85; ptnr. Lopez, Chavez & Graham, Taos, N.Mex., 1985-88; pvt. practice Taos, 1988—; city atty. Municipality of San Luis, 1983-94. Capt. CAP. Fellow HEW, 1978-81; grantee U. Denver, 1976-78. Mem. Assn. Trial Lawyers Am., N.Mex. Trial Lawyers Assn., Aircraft Owners and Pilots Assn. State civil litigation, Criminal, Personal injury. Office: 315 Seward St Sitka AK 99835-7524

**GRAHAM, DONALD LYNN,** federal judge; b. Salisbury, N.C., Dec. 15, 1948; s. Ernest Jethro and Mildred (Donald) G.; m. Brenda Joyce Savage, Sept. 27, 1969; 1 child, Sherrian Lynne. BA magna cum laude, W.Va. State Coll., 1971; JD, Ohio State U., 1974. Bar: Ohio 1974, U.S. Ct. Mil. Appeals, 1974, Fla. 1980, U.S. Dist. Ct. (so. dist.) Fla. 1980, Supreme Ct. 1980, U.S. Ct. Appeals (5th and 11th cirs.) 1981. Asst. U.S. atty. U.S. Dist. Ct. (so. dist.) Fla., Miami, 1979-84; ptnr. Raskin & Graham, Miami, 1984-91; judge U.S. Dist. Ct. (so. dist.) Fla., 1991—; instr. U. Md., Hanau, Fed. Republic Germany, 1977-78, Embry Riddle U., Homestead, Fla., 1978-79. Served to Maj., asst. staff judge adv. U.S. Army, 1974-79. Recipient Arthur S. Fleming award Washington Jaycees, 1982, Superior Performance award U.S. Dept. Justice; named One of Outstanding Young Men of Am., 1984. Mem. Assn. Trial Lawyers Am., Nat. Bar Assn., Fed. Bar Assn. (so. Fla. pres. 1984-85, treas. 1982-83), Fla. Bar Assn., N.Y. Bar Assn., Ohio Bar Assn., NAACP, Alpha Phi Alpha. Democrat. Baptist. Avocation: fishing, reading. Office: US Courthouse 99 NE 4th St Rm 1067 Miami FL 33132-2138

**GRAHAM, HARDY MOORE,** lawyer; b. Meridian, Miss., Oct. 21, 1912; s. Sanford Martin and Mary Emma (Hardy) G.; Cora Lee Poindexter, Oct. 26, 1938; children: Hardy Poindexter, Richard Newell. Student, U. So. Calif., 1932; BA, LLB, U. Miss., 1934. Bar: Miss. 1934, Tenn. 1946, U.S. Ct. Appeals (D.C. cir.) 1943, U.S. Dist. Ct. Miss. 1934, U.S. Supreme Ct. 1943, U.S. Dist. Ct. (we. dist.) Tenn. 1952. Ptnr. Graham & Graham, Meridian, 1934-43; atty. FTC, Washington, 1943-44; pvt. practice Union City, Tenn., 1946—; city judge City of Union City, 1950-58; bd. dirs., 1st v.p. Meridian Coca-Cola Bottling Co., 1964-97; ptnr. Union City Coca-Cola Bottling Co.; v.p. Coca-Cola Coin Caterers Corp. 7-Up Bottler; pres. Tenn. Soft Drink Assn., 1963-65. Mayor City of Union City, 1950-58; pres. Union City C. of C., 1948-50, bd. dirs.; chmn. March of Dimes, Obion County Tenn., 1947; mem. Union City Sch. Bd., 1958-66, vice chmn., 1958-60, chmn., 1964-66; chmn. indsl. bd. Union City, 1968-97; bd. dirs. Tenn. Mcpl. League, 1950-58, pres., 1956-57; former trustee Union U., Jackson, Tenn., 1st Bapt. Ch., Union City; pres. U. Tenn. Martin Devel. Com., 1970-72; mem. U. Tenn., Knoxville Devel. Coun., 1970-75, 82-85, bd. dirs. U. Miss. Found., 1987-93. Lt. USNR, 1944-46, ETO. Named Law Alumnus of Yr., U. Miss. Law Sch., 1984, Young Man of Yr., Union City, 1948; recipient Disting. Svc. award U. Tenn., Martin, 1989, U. Miss. Hall of Fame Disting. Alumnus award, 1989; Union City named Graham Park in his honor, 1986. Mem. ABA, Tenn. Bar Assn., Miss. Bar Assn., Union City-Obion County Bar Assn., (pres. 1948-49, past. bd. dirs.), Meridian Country Club, Union City Country Club, Rotary (pres. Union City 1963-64, Paul Harris fellow). Republican. Baptist. Avocation: international travel. Probate, Real property, Estate taxation. Home: 630 E Main St Union City TN 38261-3515 Office: 1915 E Reelfoot Ave Union City TN 38261-6007

**GRAHAM, HAROLD STEVEN,** lawyer; b. Kansas City, Mo., Feb. 1, 1950; s. Martie Sydney and Elsie Helen (Bradford) G.; m. Deborah Ruth Glick, Apr. 8, 1973; children: Elizabeth, Jonathan, Joshua, Lauren. BS with distinction, U. Wis., 1972; JD, U. Chgo., 1976. Bar: Mo. 1976. Assoc. Lathrop, Koontz & Norquist, Kansas City, 1976-81; mem. Lathrop & Norquist, L.C., Kansas City, 1982-95, Lathrop & Gage L.C., Kansas City, 1996—. Active Kansas City Tomorrow Alumni Assn. Year X; bd. dirs. Hyman Brand Hebrew Acad., Kansas City, 1985—, Beth Shalom Synagogue, Kansas City, 1983-88, Jewish Community Campus, 1992-98. Mem. ABA (sect. on real property and trust law, mem. Forum on Affordable Housing), Mo. Bar Assn. (property law com.), Kansas City Met. Bar Assn. Avocations: tennis, running. Banking, Finance, General corporate. Office: Lathrop & Gage LC 2345 Grand Blvd Ste 2600 Kansas City MO 64108-2617

**GRAHAM, JAMES LOWELL,** federal judge; b. 1939. BA, JD summa cum laude, Ohio State U., 1962. Pvt. practice law Crabbe, Brown, Jones, Potts & Schmidt, Columbus, Ohio, 1962-69, Graham, Dutro, Nemeth, and predecessors, Columbus, 1969-86; judge U.S. Dist. Ct. (so. dist.) Ohio, Columbus, 1986—; faculty Ohio Jud. Coll., Ohio Legal Inst. Chmn. Ohio Bar Examiners, 1974, Devel. Commn. City of Columbus, 1976-77; mem. legal svcs. Salvation Army of columbus, 1967-77, legal sect. United Way Campaign, 1976-80. Fellow Am. Coll. Trial Lawyers; mem. Capital U. Coll. of Law Assn. (dean's coun.), Ohio State U. A;umni Assn. Office: US Dist Ct 169 US Courthouse 85 Marconi Blvd Columbus OH 43215-2823

**GRAHAM, JAN,** state attorney general; b. Salt Lake City. BS in Psychology, Clark U., Worcester, Mass., 1973; MS in Psychology, U. Utah, 1977, JD, 1980. Bar: Utah. Ptnr. Jones, Waldo, Holbrook & McDonough, Salt Lake City, 1979-89; soliciter gen. Utah Atty. Gen.'s Office, Salt Lake City, 1989-93; atty. gen. State of Utah, 1993—; adj. prof. law U. Utah Law Sch.; bar commr. Utah State Bar, 1991; master of bench Utah Inns Ct. VII; mem. Utah Commn. on Justice in 21st Century; bd. dirs. Jones, Waldo, Holbrook & McDonough; bd. trustees Coll. Law U. Utah (pres.). Fin. devel. chair YWCA; chair Ctrl. Bus. Improvement Dist.; mem. Salt Lake City Olympic Bid Com. 1988 Games. Named Woman Lawyer Yr. Utah, 1987. Mem. Am. Arbitration Assn. (nat. panel arbitrators), Women Lawyers Utah (co-founder, mem. exec. com.). Office: Office of Attorney General 236 State Capitol Building Salt Lake City UT 84114-1202*

**GRAHAM, JESSE JAPHET, II,** lawyer; b. Kingston, N.Y., May 16, 1950; s. Kelsey D. and Florence M. (Smith) G.; m. Margaret Mary Breuer, Aug. 18, 1973; children: Courtney E., Michael B., Peter A. BA, Rider Coll., 1972; JD, Bklyn. Law Sch., 1975; LLM, George Washington U., 1979. Bar: N.Y. 1976, D.C. 1978, U.S. Ct. Mil. Appeals 1978, U.S. Customs Ct. 1979, U.S. Ct. Claims 1979, U.S. Ct. Customs and Patent Appeals 1979, U.S. Tax Ct. 1979, U.S. Supreme Ct. 1979. Assoc. Campbell, Currior & C'Connor, Eastcester, N.Y., 1979-80; ptnr. Bower & Gardner, N.Y.C., 1980-94, Parker Chapin Flattau & Klimpl LLP, N.Y.C., 1994—; mem. faculty various seminars in field; mem. faculty Practising Law Inst., N.Y.C., 1986-95. Contbg. author: Hospital Liability, 1980-94; guest commentator Court TV, NewsTalk TV and radio stas., including CNN, FOX 5, and FOX News, 1994—. Lt. USNR, Judge Advs. Gen. Corps., 1976-79. Personal injury, Insurance. Home: 4 Pine Glen Dr Blauvelt NY 10913-1150 Office: Parker Chapin et al Ste 1700 1211 Avenue Of The Americas New York NY 10036-8735

**GRAHAM, JOHN JOSEPH,** lawyer, economics educator; b. New Haven, Sept. 12, 1920; s. Hugh Munson and Alice W. (Cummings) G. BA in Econs., Yale U., 1942, MA, 1943; JD, Boston Coll., 1946; MA, Boston U., 1949; DHL (hon.), Am. Coll. Greece, 1997. Bar: Mass. 1946, U.S. Dist. Ct. Mass. 1947, U.S. Dist. Ct. Conn. 1949, U.S. Cir. Ct. Appeals (1st cir.) 1947, U.S. Cir. Ct. Appeals (2d cir.) 1953, U.S. Supreme Ct. 1952. Pvt. practice Boston, 1946—; asst. commerce counsel New Haven R.R., 1947-49; atty. Rwy. Express Agy., Northeastern U.S., 1949-53; arbitrator fed. med. and conciliation svc. Am. Arbitration Assn., N.Y.C. and Washington, 1953—; lectr. in econs. Northeastern U. Grad. Sch. Bus. Adminstrn., Boston, 1953-68; vis. prof. econs. Am. Coll. of Greece, Athens, 1981—. Spl. asst. atty. gen. Commonwealth of Mass., 1961; pres. Mass. Consumer Assn., 1961; fin. trustee Met. Transit Authority, Boston, 1957-61; commr. State Dept. Pub. Utilities, Mass., 1957. Mem. World Peace Through Law Ctr. (founding mem.), Nat. Economists Club (founding mem.), Acad. Polit. Sci. (life), Am. Econ. Assn., Mansfield Law Soc. U.K., Fed. Bar Assn., Yale Club. Roman Catholic. General practice, General civil litigation, Private international. Home and Office: PO Box 1962 Boston MA 02105-1962

**GRAHAM, JUL ELIOT,** lawyer, educator; b. Bklyn., June 14, 1953; s. Arnold Harold and Roselle (Lesser) G.; m. Sherry Robin Goldberg, Nov. 2, 1980. BA in Polit. Sci. cum laude, NYU, 1975; JD magna cum laude, N.Y. Law Sch., 1978. Bar: N.Y. 1979, U.S. Supreme Ct. 1984. Cons. Consumer Law Tng. Ctr., N.Y. Law Sch., 1976, mem. adj. faculty, 1980—; prin. appellate law rsch. asst. appellate div. 1st Dept., Supreme Ct. of State of N.Y., N.Y.C., 1978-79, staff atty., 1979-82, assoc. atty., 1982-83, law asst. to the justices, 1983-88, exec. sec. deptl. adv. com. to family ct., 1979-82, editor criminal trial advocacy handbook, 1980—, prin. appellate ct. atty. to the justices, 1988—, 1st Dept., 1990—; Assoc. editor N.Y. Law Sch. Law Rev., 1976-78, contbg. author, 1975. Guest lectr. Joe Franklin Show, WOR-TV, 1982—. Mem. N.Y. County Lawyers Assn. (com. on communications and entertainment law 1980—, com. on penal and correctional reform 1980— , spl. com. on practical legal edn. 1979—), Am. Arbitration Assn. (arbitrator 1985—), Internat. Radio and TV Soc., Am. Film Inst., Phi Delta Phi, Phi Sigma Alpha. Home: 249 Adelaide Ave Staten Island NY 10306-3949 Office: NY State Supreme Ct Appellate Div 1st Jud Dept 27 Madison Ave New York NY 10010-2201

**GRAHAM, MARJORIE GADARIAN,** lawyer; b. San Antonio, Tex., Mar. 13, 1947; d. Ardzvig Vartan and Dorothy Marie Gadarian; m. Stuart M. Graham, Jr., Apr. 17, 1982. BA in German, Northwestern U., 1969; JD, U. Fla., 1972. Bar: Fla. 1972, U.S. Dist. Ct. (so. dist.) Fla. 1973, U.S. Ct. Appeals (5th cir.) 1974, U.S. Supreme Ct. 1978. Rsch. aide to Hon. James H. Walden Fourth Dist. Ct. of Appeal, 1972-73; shareholder Jones & Foster, P.A., 1974-87; sole practitioner Palm Beach Gardens, Fla., 1987—. Contbr. articles to profl. jours. Mem. citizens involvement roundtable Martin County Met. Planing Orgn., 1997-99. Mem. ABA, Palm Beach County Bar Assn., Def. Rsch. Inst., Fedn. Ins. and Corp. Counsel, Fla. Def. Lawyers (bd. dirs. 1982-83, 88-90), past chair Amicus Curiae com.), Am. Law Inst. Appellate. Office: Ste D129 11211 Prosperity Farms Rd Palm Beach Gardens FL 33410

**GRAHAM, ROBERT CHASE,** lawyer; b. Tucson, Nov. 14, 1964; s. John Howard and Sandra Lee (Chase) G.; m. Linda Marie Grimes, Aug. 29, 1986. Student, Mesa Coll., 1986; BA, Brigham Young U., 1989, JD, 1992. Bar: Nev. 1992, U.S. Ct. Appeals (9th cir.) 1992. R&D team leader IBM, Provo, Utah, 1988; systems programmer Novell, Inc., Provo, Utah, 1989; assoc. Jimmerson, Davis & Santoro, Las Vegas, 1991-93; sr. shareholder Kerr & Graham, P.C., Las Vegas, 1993-95; sr. ptnr. Hoskin & Graham, Las Vegas, Nev., 1995—. Editor-in-chief Nevada Federal Reporter, 1993, The Communiqué, 1994-96; pub. Finance and Business Report, 1987-88. Chmn. trial adv. bd. Moot Ct. Brigham Young U., 1991-92. Recipient Faculty award of achievement, Brigham Young U., 1990, Outstanding Cmty. Scv. award Las Vegas Met. Police Dept., 1995. Mem. ABA, Fed. Bar Assn., Clark County Bar Assn. (Outstanding Svc. award 1994), State Bar of Nev. (exec. com. bus. law sect. 1993), Am. and Nev. Inns of Ct., Phi Delta Phi. Republican. Mormon. Avocations: music composition, volleyball, aviation, travel. Federal civil litigation, Contracts commercial, Probate. Office: Hoskin & Graham 211 N Buffalo Dr Ste A Las Vegas NV 89145-0373

**GRAHAM, ROBERT CLARE, III,** lawyer; b. Albuquerque, Mar. 24, 1955; s. Robert C. Jr. and Helen (Hoagland) G.; children: Jennifer, Jessica, Kourtney, Kate. BA, DePauw U., 1977; JD magna cum laude, Pepperdine U., 1980. Bar: Mo. 1980, Ill. 1981, U.S. Dist. Ct. (ea. dist.) Mo. 1981. Assoc. Shephard, Sandberg & Phoenix, St. Louis, 1980-82, Suelthaus & Kaplan, PC and predecessors, St. Louis, 1982-91, Armstrong, Teasdale, Schlafly & Davis, St. Louis, 1991—. Chmn. Kirkwood (Mo.) Greentree Festival, 1985. Named one of Outstanding Young Men in Am. Jaycees, 1981; recipient Outstanding Service to the Community of Kirkwood award. Mem. ABA, Ill. Bar Assn., Mo. Bar Assn., Bar Assn. Met. St. Louis, St. Louis County Bar Assn. Republican. Presbyterian. Banking, General corporate, Real property. Office: Armstrong Teasdale Schlafly & Davis 1 Metropolitan Sq Ste 2600 Saint Louis MO 63102-2740

**GRAHAM, SAMUEL R.,** lawyer, mediator; b. Mercedes, Tex., Oct. 14, 1944; s. Leon Roy and Mary (Norrod) G.; m. Mary Louise Graham III. BA, U. Tex., 1969, JD, 1983. Bar: Tex. 1983, U.S. Dist. Ct. (we. dist.) Tex., U.S. Ct. Appeals (5th cir.). Asst. atty. gen. State of Tex., Austin, 1975-79; ptnr. Walks graham Chapman & Moore, Austin, 1979-80; owner Samuel R. Graham & Assocs., Austin, 1980-82; ptnr. Barron & Graham, Austin, 1982-86, Barron, Graham & Adler, Austin, 1986-90; pvt. practice Austin, 1990—. Chmn. Austin Elec. Utility Commn., 1977-82. Probate, Alternative dispute resolution. Office: 114 W 7th St Austin TX 78701-3000

**GRAHAM, SELDON BAIN, JR.,** lawyer, engineer; b. Franklin, Tex., Apr. 14, 1926; s. Seldon Bain and Lillian Emma (Struwe) G.; m. Patricia Gene Noah, Feb. 14, 1953; children—Seldon Bain, Kyle, Laurie. B.S., U.S. Mil. Acad., 1951; J.D., U. Tex., 1970. Registered profl. engr., Tex. Bar: Tex. 1970, U.S. Dist. Ct. (so. dist.) Tex. 1980, U.S. Ct. Appeals (5th cir.) 1983; cert. in oil, gas and mineral law Tex. Bd. Legal Specialization. Commd. 2d lt. U.S. Army, 1946; advanced through grades to col., 1979; with Office of Dep. Chief of Staff for Personnel, 1979; ret., 1979; area reservoir engr. ARCO, Okla., 1954-60; div. regulatory engr. Mobil Oil Co., Corpus Christi, 1961-67; counsel Exxon Co. USA, Houston, 1970-85. Decorated Legion of Merit. Mem. Soc. Petroleum Engrs. Methodist. Oil, gas, and mineral. Home and Office: 4713 Palisade Dr Austin TX 78731-4516

**GRAHAM, STEPHEN MICHAEL,** lawyer; b. Houston, May 1, 1951; s. Frederick Mitchell and Lillian Louise (Miller) G.; m. Joanne Marie Sealock, Aug. 24, 1974; children: Aimee Elizabeth, Joseph Sealock, Jessica Anne. BS, Iowa State U., 1973; JD, Yale U., 1976. Bar: Wash. 1977. Assoc. Perkins Coie, Seattle, 1976-83, ptnr., 1983. Bd. dirs. Wash. Spl. Olympics, Seattle, 1979-83, pres., 1983; mem. Seattle Bd. Ethics, 1982-88, chmn., 1983-88; mem. Seattle Fair Campaign Practices Commn., 1982-88; trustee Cornish Coll. Arts, 1986-91, mem. exec. com., 1989-91; trustee Arboretum Found., 1994-96; mem. exec. com. Sch. Law, Yale U., 1988-92, 93-97; bd. dirs. Perkins Coie Cmty. Svc. Found., 1988-91; trustee Seattle Repertory Theatre, 1993-95; trustee Seattle Children's Theatre, 1996-98, mem. exec. com., 1997-98; bd. dirs. Wash. Biotech. and Biomed. Assn., 1996—, mem. exec. com., 1997—; trustee Fred Hutchinson Cancer Rsch. Ctr., 1999—. Mem. ABA, Wash. State Bar ASsn., Seattle-King County Bar Assn., Wash. Athletic Club, Rainier Club. Episcopalian. General corporate, Securities, Contracts commercial. Office: Perkins Coie 1201 3rd Ave Fl 48 Seattle WA 98101-3029

**GRAHAM, WILLIAM EDGAR, JR.,** lawyer, retired utility company executive; b. Jackson Springs, N.C., Dec. 31, 1929; s. William Edgar and Minnie Blanch (Autry) G.; m. Jean Dixon McLaurin, Nov. 24, 1962; children: William McLaurin, John McMillan, Sally Faircloth. AB, U. N.C., 1952, JD with honors, 1956. Bar: N.C. bar. Law clk. U.S. Ct. Appeals 4th Circuit, 1956-57; individual practice law Charlotte, N.C., 1957-69; judge N.C. Ct. Appeals, 1969-73; sr. v.p., gen. counsel Carolina Power & Light Co., Raleigh, N.C., 1973-81, exec. v.p., 1981-85, vice chmn., 1985-93; counsel Hunton & Williams, 1994—. Served with USAF, 1952-54. Mem. ABA, N.C. Bar Assn., Wake County Bar Assn. Presbyterian. General corporate. Home: 761 Bishops Park Dr Raleigh NC 27605-3234 Office: Hunton & Williams PO Box 109 Raleigh NC 27602-0109

**GRAIFMAN, BRIAN DALE,** lawyer; b. N.Y.C., Feb. 26, 1955; s. Julius and Ruth (Deutsch) G.; m. Lori Beth Graber, Nov. 28, 1992; 3 children. MusB in Music Theory, Manhattan Sch. Music, 1978; JD, N.Y. Law Sch., 1988. Bar: N.Y. 1988, Conn. 1988, U.S. Dist. Ct. (so. and ea. dists.) N.Y. 1990, U.S. Ct. Appeals (2d cir.) 1990, U.S. Dist. Ct. Conn. 1992, U.S. Supreme Ct. 1992. Assoc. Skadden Arps Slate Meagher & Flom, N.Y.C., 1988, 89-92; law clk. to Judge Roger J. Miner U.S. Ct. Appeals (2d cir.), N.Y.C., 1988-89; assoc. Schreiber, Simmons, Mac Knight & Tweedy, N.Y.C., 1992-94; ptnr. Caro & Graifman, P.C., N.Y.C., 1994-97; sr. assoc. Gusrae, Kaplan & Bruno, N.Y.C., 1998—. Co-author instnl. video Ten Tough Times, 1991; producer music album Barbie Allen Dance/Exercise # 2, 1983 (Gold Album); Research Editor, N.Y.L. Sch.L.Rev.; contbr. articles to profl. publs. Mem. ABA, N.Y. State Bar Assn., Assn. Bar City N.Y., Conn. Bar Assn., N.Y. County Lawyers Assn. (mem. appellate cts. com. 1992—, mem. fed. cts. com. 1994—). General civil litigation. Home: 128 Perth Ave New Rochelle NY 10804-3528 Office: Gusrae Kaplan & Bruno 120 Wall St Ste 1102 New York NY 10005-3977

**GRAIFMAN, GARY STEVEN,** lawyer; b. N.Y.C., Feb. 19, 1952; m. Deborah Eigen, Sept. 25, 1982. BA, SUNY, New Paltz, 1974; JD, N.Y. Law Sch., 1980. Bar: N.Y. 1981, U.S. Dist. Ct. (so. dist.) N.Y. 1981, U.S. Ct. Appeals (2d cir.) 1982, U.S. Ct. Appeals (8th cir.) 1990, N.J. 1994. Dir. bus. Overseas Tele Video Corp., N.Y.C., 1980-82; ptnr. Atlas & Graifman, N.Y.C., 1982-89, Kantrowitz & Goldhamer, Chestnut Ridge, N.Y., 1989—; Dir., legal counsel Pvt. Art Dealers Assn., N.Y.C., 1990—. Assoc. editor Circus Mag., 1977-80. Dir. Rockland Ctr. for the Arts, West Nyack, N.Y., 1991—. Mem. Assn. of Bar of City of N.Y. (mem. computer law com. 1989-91). General corporate, Real property, Trademark and copyright. Office: Kantrowitz & Goldhamer 747 Chestnut Ridge Rd Ste 200 Spring Valley NY 10977-6216

**GRAINEY, PHILIP J.,** lawyer; b. Helena, Mont., Apr. 6, 1950; s. Bernard and Elizabeth (Roche) G.; m. Marilyn Rose Marron, Aug. 12, 1972; children: Heather Lynn, Kate Elizabeth, Brennin Patrick. BA in Psychology, U. Mont., 1972, JD, 1975. Bar: Mont., U.S. Dist. Ct. Mont. Ptnr. French & Grainey, Ronan, Mont., 1975-81, French, Grainey & Duckworth, Ronan, Mont., 1981-85, French, Mercer, Grainey & Duckworth, Ronan and Polson, Mont., 1985-86, French, Mercer & Grainey, Ronan and Polson, Mont., 1986-95; French, Mercer, Grainey & O'Neill, 1995—; lawyer St. Luke Cmty. Hosp., Ronan, 1976—, chmn. bd., 1982-86; atty. City of Ronan, 1980-84, City of Polson, Mont., 1986-94. Bd. dirs. Big. Bros. and Sisters, Ronan, 1979-82; mem. Ronan Vol. Fire Dept., 1978-84. Mem. Mont. Bar Assn., Ronan C. of C. (pres.), Mission Mountain Country Club (bd. dirs. 1982-92), Elks. Avocations: golf, music, tennis, hunting, fishing. Real property, Probate, Banking. Office: French Mercer Grainey & O'Neill 324 Main St SW Ronan MT 59864-2707 Also: PO Box 460 Polson MT 59860-0460

**GRAMMIG, ROBERT JAMES,** lawyer; b. Oceanside, Calif., June 15, 1956; s. Richard Adolf and Mary Elizabeth (Spisak) G.; m. Laurel Jean Lenfestey, Aug. 10, 1996. BA, U. Pa., 1978, MA, 1978; JD, Harvard U., 1981. Bar: Fla. 1982, D.C. 1986, U.S. Dist. Ct. (mid. dist.) Fla. 1982, U.S. Ct. Appeals (11th and 5th cirs.) 1982, U.S. Supreme Ct. 1985. Law clk. to Hon. Thomas A. Clark U.S. Ct. Appeals (5th and 11th cirs.), Atlanta, 1981-82; assoc. Holland & Knight, Tampa, Fla., 1982-88, ptnr., 1989—. Bd. dirs. Child Abuse Coun., Tampa, 1993-97; mem. Leadership Tampa, 1994-95; Sec. Tampa Bay Internat. Trade Coun., 1994, vice chmn., 1995. Mem. Tampa Bay Coun. on Fgn. Rels., German Am. C. of C., U.S.-Austrian C. of C., Phi Beta Kappa. Republican. Roman Catholic. General corporate, Securities, Private international. Home: 21 Bahama Cir Tampa FL 33606-3317 Office: Holland & Knight 400 N Ashley Dr Ste 2300 Tampa FL 33602-4322

**GRANADE, GINNY SMITH,** lawyer; b. Lexington, Va., Mar. 7, 1950; d. Milton Hannibal and Callie Rives Smith; m. Fred K. Granade, Oct. 9, 1976; children: Taylor Rives Granade, Milton Smith Granade, Joseph Kee Granade. BA, Hollins Coll., 1972; JD, U. Tex., 1975. Bar: Tex. 1975, Ala. 1976, U.S. Dist. Ct. (mid. dist.) Ala. 1976, U.S. Ct. Appeals (5th cir.) 1976, U.S. Dist. Ct. (so. dist.) Ala. 1977, U.S. Supreme Ct. 1980, U.S. Ct. Appeals (11th cir.) 1981. Judicial law clk. U.S. Ct. Appeals 5th Cir., Montgomery, Ala., 1975-76; asst. U.S. atty. U.S. Atty.'s Office so. dist. Ala., Mobile, 1977-89, asst. U.S. atty. chief criminal divsn., 1990-97, 1st asst. U.S. atty., 1997—; mem. adv. com. on rules U.S. Dist. Ct. So. Dist., 1990—; mem. com. lawyer qualifications and conduct U.S. Ct. Appeals 11th cir., 1992—; mem. IOLTA grants com. AIA Bar Found., Montgomery, 1997—. Fellow Am. Coll. Trial Lawyers; mem. ABA, Brock Am. Inn of Ct. Presbyterian. Office: US Attys Office 63 S Royal St Ste 600 Mobile AL 36602-3245

**GRANAT, RICHARD STUART,** lawyer, educator; b. N.Y.C., Nov. 11, 1940; s. George and Judith G.; m. Nancy Ruth Wruble, Dec. 23, 1962; children: Lisa, Hilary, Peter, David. BA, Lehigh U., 1962; JD (Harlan Fiske Stone scholar), Columbia U., 1965. Bar: Md. 1966, D.C. 1977. Asst. counsel U.S. OEO, Washington, 1965-67, dir. housing programs 1967-78; asst. dir. Model Cities Agy., Office of Mayor, Balt., 1968-69; dir. Community Planning and Evaluation Inst. 1970-71; pres. Univ. Rsch. Corp. Mgmt. Svcs. Corp., 1970-77; pvt. practice, Washington and Md., 1969—; pres. Automated Legal Systems, Inc., Phila., 1984-89; dir. M.A. in Legal Studies Program, Antioch Sch. Law, 1979-83; pres., chmn. bd. Ctr. for Legal Studies, Washington, 1979-89; chmn bd. dirs. Ctr. Sch., Rockville, Md.; pres. Inst. Paralegal Tng., Inc., Phila., 1982-89, The Phila. Inst. 1987-89; pres. Nat. Ctr. for Edn. Testing Inc., 1986-89, Inst. for Employee Benefits Tng., 1986-89; pres. The Inst. for Law and Tech., Phila., 1990-92; pres. Interactive Legal Media, Inc., 1992—; instr. Rutgers Sch. Law, Camden, N.J., 1992-94, Sch. Lang., U. Balt., 1995—; adj. prof. Sch. Law U. Md., 1994—, dir. Ctr. for Law Practice Tech., 1994—, Peoples Law Libr. of Md., 1996—, dir. Ctr. for On-Line Mediation, Inc., 1996—. Mem. ABA, Md. Bar Assn., D.C. Bar Assn. Civil rights. Home: 320 Morgause Pl N Baltimore MD 21208-1430 Office: 9141 Reisentown Rd Owings Mills MD 21117

**GRANATA, LINDA M.,** lawyer; b. Montreal, June 9, 1951; d. Albert Joseph and Marylka (Aksamit) G. BS in Broadcasting, U. Fla., 1974; JD, Nova U., 1988. Bar: Fla. 1988, U.S. Dist. Ct. (so. dist.) Fla. 1989, U.S. Ct. Appeals (11th cir.) 1990, U.S. Tax Ct. 1990. Pres. Mkt. Makers, Inc., Miami, Fla., 1978-88, Ethylene Eaters, Inc., North Miami, Fla., 1981-88, 92—; law clk. to Hon. Paul M. Marko III 17th Cir. Ct., Ft. Lauderdale, Fla., 1986-87; corp. counsel Quantum Assocs., Inc., Miami Beach, 1988-89; assoc. Richard C. Fox, P.A., Boca Raton, Fla., 1989-90; pvt. practice North Miami, 1990-93; corp. counsel World Trade Consortium, Inc., Miami, 1993-99; arbitrator Nat. Assn. Securities Dealers, Ft. Lauderdale, 1990—, Nat. Futures Assn., Ft. Lauderdale, 1990-95; guardian ad litum 17th Cir. Ct. Broward County, 1996-99. Mem. Am. Arbitration Assn., Nat. Panel Consumer Arbitrators. General corporate, Securities, Contracts commercial. Office: 20101 NE 16th Pl Ste 200 Miami FL 33179-2720

**GRANDE, THOMAS ROBERT,** lawyer; b. Providence, Dec. 27, 1952; s. Albert and Gloria (Palmieri) G. Student, U. Copenhagen, 1975; BA in Govt., Bates Coll., Lewiston, Maine, 1976; JD, U. Hawaii, 1985. Bar: Hawaii, 1985, U.S. Dist. Ct. Hawaii 1985, U.S. Ct. Appeals (9th cir.) 1985. Exec. dir. Common Cause Hawaii, Honolulu, 1979-82; law clk. to chief justice Federated States Micronesia Supreme Ct., Pohnpei, Caroline Islands, 1985; ptnr. Davis Levin Livingston Grande, Honolulu, 1985—. Contbr. articles to profl. jours. Vista Vol. Waimanalo Coun. Community Orgns., 1978; candidate for nat. governing bd. Common Cause, Washington, 1983; vol. ACLU, Honolulu, 1983-84; organizer Com. to Keep Waimanalo Rural, 1984; bd. dirs. Hawaii's Thousand Friends, Honolulu, 1987, Hawaii Lawyers Care, 1988. Recipient Outstanding Contbn. to the Delivery of Legal Svcs. award Hawaii Lawyers Care, 1994. Mem. ABA (sec. litig., chair state law subcom. of com. on class actions, co-editor State Survey of Class Actions Rules 1999), ATLA, Hawaii Bar Assn. (chmn. lawyer referral com. 1991-94), Consumer Lawyers Hawaii (mem. bd. govs. 1993—, parliamentarian 1993-94, sec. 1994-95, v.p. 1995-96), Am. Inns of Ct. (barrister 1989-90). Avocations: hiking, reading, martial arts, gardening. Fax: 808545-7802. E-mail: tgrande@davislevin.com. General civil litigation, Personal injury, Construction. Office: Davis Levin Livingston Grande Merchant Square 10 Marin Ln Honolulu HI 96817-5112

**GRANGE, JANET LENORE,** lawyer, accountant, consultant; b. Chgo., Sept. 5, 1958; d. Albert Edward and Marie Loretta (Hart) G. BS in Acctg., U. Ill., Chgo., 1980; JD, U. Ill., 1983. Bar: Ill. 1983; CPA, Ill. Sr. tax cons. Grant Thornton, Chgo., 1983-85, Deloitte, Haskins & Sells, Chgo., 1985-86, Kraft, Inc., Glenview, Ill., 1986-88; assoc. prof. acctg. Chgo. State U., 1989—; sole practitioner of law; Nissan HBCU fellow, 1992; mem. hearing bd. Ill. Atty. Registration and Disciplinary Com., 1994—. Mem. Ill. State Bar Assn., Beta Gamma Sigma. Avocations: tennis, aerobics. Corporate taxation, Taxation, general, Personal income taxation.

**GRANGER, DAVID IRELAND,** lawyer; b. Washington, Sept. 4, 1932. AB, Princeton U., 1954; LLB, Harvard U., 1959. Bar: D.C. 1959. Atty. Dept. Justice, Washington, 1961-65; pvt. practice Washington, 1959-61, 65—. Trustee Landon Sch., Washington, 1967-70, Potomac Sch., McLean, Va., 1971-78, chmn., 1974-76; bd. dirs. Peirce Warwick Adoption Svc., Washington, 1968-72, pres. 1970-72. With U.S. Army, 1954-56. Mem. ABA, D.C. Bar. General practice, Antitrust, General corporate. Office: Ste 600 1800 Massachusetts Ave NW Washington DC 20036-1222

**GRANHOLM, JENNIFER MULHERN,** state attorney general; b. Vancouver, B.C., Can., Feb. 5, 1959; came to U.S., 1962; d. Civtor Ivar and Shirley Alfreda (Dowden) G.; m. Daniel Granholm Mulhern, May 23, 1986; children: Kathryn, Cecelia, Jack. BA, U. Calif., Berkeley, 1984; JD, Harvard U., 1987. Bar: Mich. 1987, U.S. Dist. Ct. (ea. dist.) Mich. 1987, U.S. Ct. Appeals (6th cir.) 1987. Jud. law clk. 6th Cir Ct. Appeals, Detroit, 1987-88; exec. asst. Wayne County Exec., Detroit, 1988-89; asst. U.S. atty. Dept. Justice, Detroit, 1990-94; corp. counsel Wayne County, Detroit, 1994—; elected atty. gen., 1999; gen. counsel Detroit/Wayne County Stadium Authority, 1996—. Contbr. articles to profl. jours. V.p., bd.dirs. YWCA, Inkster, Mich., 1995—; del. Dem. Nat. Conv., Chgo., 1996; chair sel. com. U.S. Sen., Detroit, 1997; mem. LEadership DEtroit, 1990—. Mem. Detrout Bar Assn., Women's Law Assn., Inc. Soc. Irish Lawyers. Roman Catholic. Avocations: running, family, laughing. Office: Atty Gen PO Box 30212 Lansing MI 48909-7712

**GRANOFF, GARY CHARLES,** lawyer, investment company executive; b. N.Y.C., Feb. 2, 1948; s. N. Henry and Jeannette (Trum) G.; m. Leslie Barbara Resnick, Dec. 21, 1969; children: Stephen, Robert, Joshua. BBA in Acctg., George Washington U., 1970, JD with honors, 1973. Bar: N.Y., 1974, Fla., 1974, U.S. Dist. Ct. (so. dist.) N.Y., 1976. Assoc. Dreyer & Traub, N.Y.C., 1973-75; ptnr. Ezon, Langberg & Granoff, N.Y.C., 1975-78, Granoff & Walker, N.Y.C., 1982-92, Granoff, Walker & Forlenza P.C., N.Y.C., 1993—; pvt. practice N.Y.C., 1978-81; pres., also bd. dirs. Elk Assocs. Funding Corp., N.Y.C., 1979—, GCG Assocs., Inc., N.Y.C., 1982—; pres., dir. Gemini Capital Corp., 1996—; atty. del. to U.S.-China Joint Session on Trade, Investment and Econ. Law, Beijing, 1987; mem. dean's adv. bd. George Washington U. Law Sch., 1993-. Campaign vol. Mondale for Pres., N.Y.C., 1984; fundraiser Robert Garcia for Congress, N.Y.C., Dem. Senatorial Campaign Com., N.Y.C., 1987-88; active N.Y. Lawyers for Dukakis com., 1988; chmn. N.Y.C. chpt. George Washington U. Nat. Law Ctr. Leadership Gifts Com.; mem. dean's adv. bd. Law Sch. George Washington U., 1994—; bd. trustees George Washington U., 1998. Mem. ABA, N.Y. State Bar Assn., Fla. Bar Assn., Assn. of Bar of City of N.Y., People to People Internat., Nat. Assn. Investment Cos. (legis com.), George Washington U. Alumni Assn. (chmn. N.Y.C. chpt., bd. dirs. law sch. alumni assn., alumni com. 21 century, bd. trustees), bd. trustees George Washington U., North Shore Country Club (chmn. legal com., bd. govs. 1994-96, 98-99). Avocations: golf, tennis, skiing. Contracts commercial, Finance, Real property. Office: Granoff Walker & Forlenza 747 3rd Ave Fl 4 New York NY 10017-2803

**GRANT, ARTHUR GORDON, JR.,** lawyer; b. New Orleans, May 16, 1945; s. Arthur Gordon and Martha (McCutchon) G.; children: Arthur Gordon III, Kathryn S., Douglas M. BA, U. N.C., 1967; JD, Tulane U., 1970. Bar: La. 1970, U.S. Ct. Appeals (5th cir.) 1970, U.S. Dist. Ct. (ea. and mid. dists.) La. 1970, U.S. Dist. Ct. (we. dist.) La. 1970, U.S. Dist. Ct. (11th cir.) 1981, U.S. Supreme Ct. 1990, U.S. Dist. Ct. (so. dist.) Tex. 1998. Assoc. Montgomery, Barnett, Brown, Read, Hammond & Mintz, New Orleans, 1970-73, ptnr., 1973—; law instr. U. New Orleans Sch. Naval Architecture, 1990—; bd. dirs. Am. Boat and Yacht Coun., Millersville, Md., 1990-98. Author: Recreational Craft, Jurisdiction, Claims and Coverage, 1989; contbg. author: Recreational Boating Law, 1992, Benedict on Admiralty, Vol. 8, 7th edit., 1995. Bd. govs. Propellor Club Port of New Orleans, 1989-90, 92-94. Mem. La. Bar Assn., Soc. Naval Architects and Marine Engrs., Maritime Law Assn. U.S. (vice chmn. recreational boating com. 1990-94), Bar Assn. of the Fifth Fed. Cir., Southeastern Admiralty Law Inst. Avocations: hunting, fishing, boating, civil war history. E-mail: ggrant@monbar.com. Admiralty, Product liability, Federal civil litigation. Office: Montgomery Barnett Brown Read Hammond & Mintz 3200 Energy Ctr New Orleans LA 70163

**GRANT, BURTON FRED,** lawyer; b. Chgo., Mar. 16, 1938; s. Louis Z. and Ruth (Kaplan) G.; m. Joan Carolyn Friedman, July 11, 1965; children: Robin, Steven, Lauren. BA, De Paul U., 1959, JD, 1962; LLM, John Marshall U., 1965. Bar: Ill. 1963, U.S. Dist. Ct. (no. dist.) Ill. 1963. Sole practice Chgo., 1963-73; ptnr. Grant, Kaplan & Grant, Chgo., 1973-76, Grant, Grant & Stein, Chgo., 1977-81; prin. Grant & Grant, Chgo., 1981—; adj. prof. De Paul U. Sch. Law, Chgo., 1979-83. Contbr. articles to profl. jours. Named one of Leading Attorneys at Law in Family Law in State of Ill., (pub.) Law and Leading Attorneys, one of 20 Top Divorce Lawyers North Shore Mag., 1997. Fellow Am. Acad. Matrimonial Lawyers (cert.); mem. ABA, Ill. Bar Assn., Chgo. Bar Assn., N.W. Suburban Bar Assn. (cert. appreciation 1986), North Suburban Bar ASsn. (bd. mgrs. 1992—), Lake County Bar Assn., Phi Alpha Delta. Avocations: travel, photography. Family and matrimonial. Office: Grant & Grant 180 N La Salle St Ste 2400 Chicago IL 60601-2787 also: 707 Skokie Blvd Ste 600 Northbrook IL 60062-2841

**GRANT, CHARLES JOSEPH,** lawyer; b. Wheeling, W.Va., Feb. 28, 1948; s. Joseph H. Grant and Gloria Hargrave Carter; children: Erin Nicole. BA, Ohio U., 1971; JD, Georgetown U., 1974. Dep. fed. pub. defender Fed. Pub. Def., St. Croix, Virgin Islands, 1975-77; dep. dist. atty. L.A. Dist. Atty. Office, 1978-81; asst. dist. atty. Phila. Dist. Atty. Office, 1982-89, chief major trials unit, felony trials unit, 1991-93, chief homicide, 1994-95; assoc. Law Office of Joseph D. Shein, P.C., Phila., 1989-91; sr. assoc. Ronald A. White, P.C., Phila., 1996—; adj. prof. Temple U., Phila., 1993-94. Mem. Alpha Phi Alpha. Office: Ronald A White PC 1401 Walnut St Fl 2D Philadelphia PA 19102-3128

**GRANT, DEANDRA MICHELLE,** lawyer; b. Denton, Tex., July 28, 1968; d. Robert and Ginger Grant. BSBA, Trinity U., 1990; JD, So. Meth. U., 1993. Bar: Tex. 1993. Atty. Dallas County Dist. Atty.'s Office, Dallas, 1993-94; ptnr. Dueno & Grant, Dallas, 1995—. Bd. dirs. White Rock Rep. Women, Dallas, 1997-98. Mem. Dallas Criminal Def. Lawyers Assn., Tex. Criminal Def. Lawyers Assn. Roman Catholic. Criminal. Office: 2401 Turtle Creek Blvd Dallas TX 75219-4712

**GRANT, GEORGE CLARENCE,** lawyer; b. Monroe County, Ga., Oct. 16, 1917; s. Joseph Clarence and Nannie (Smarr) G.; m. Frances Barnes, Nov. 16, 1947; children: Fran B., Martha Grant Clark. JD, Mercer U., 1938. Bar: Ga. 1938, U.S. Dist. Ct. (mid. dist.) Ga., U.S. Ct. Appeals (11th cir.), U.S. Supreme Ct. Assoc. Martin, Martin & Snow, Macon, Ga., 1938-48; ptnr. Martin, Snow, Grant and Martin, Snow, Grant & Napier, Macon, Ga., 1948-92; retired Martin, Snow, Grant & Napier, 1992. Pres. Macon Jr. C. of C., 1948-49. Lt. comdr. USN, 1941-46. Fellow Am. Coll. Trial Lawyers, Am. Bar Found., Ga. Def. Lawyers Assn. (pres. 1983-84, bd. dirs. 1981-99). Independent. Baptist. General civil litigation, Personal injury, Product liability. Home: 1830 Waverland Cir Macon GA 31211-1116 Office: Martin Snow Grant & Napier PO Box 1606 Macon GA 31202-1606

**GRANT, ISABELLA HORTON,** retired judge; b. L.A., Sept. 24, 1924; d. John Daniel and Hannabelle (Horton) Grant. BA, Swarthmore Coll., 1944; MA, UCLA, 1946; JD, Columbia U., 1950; LLD (hon.), Molloy Coll., 1976. Jr. profl. asst. OSS, Washington, 1944-45; economist Inst. Indsl. Relations, UCLA, 1946-47, Office Price Stblzn., Los Angeles, 1951-52; ptnr. Livingston, Grant, Stone & Kay, San Francisco, 1953-79; judge Mcpl. Ct., San Francisco, 1979-82, Superior Ct., San Francisco, 1982-97; ret. 1997. Bd. dirs. Kid Turn, Pocket Opera. Fellow ABA; mem. Am. Arbitration Assn., San Francisco Ethics Commn., San Francisco Bar Assn. (bd. dirs. 1978-79), Acad. Matrimonial Lawyers (pres. No. Calif. chpt. 1976), Assn. Family and Conciliation Cts. (pres. Calif. chpt. 1987-89), Nat. Coll. Probate Judges, Queen's Bench (pres. 1964), Calif. Tennis Club, Phi Beta Kappa.

**GRANT, JOAN CAROLYN,** lawyer; b. Chgo., Sept. 2, 1943; d. Leo and Fay (Silverstein) Friedman; m. Burton F. Grant, July 11, 1965; children: Robin, Steven, Lauren. AB with distinction, U. Mich., 1965; JD, DePaul U., 1980. Bar: Ill. 1980, U.S. Dist. Ct. (no. dist.) Ill. 1980, Fla. 1982. Atty. Grant and Grant, Chgo., 1980—. Author: Family Law Litigation in Illinois, 1993; cntbr. articles to profl. jours. Mem. ABA, Women's Bar Assn. (lectr.), Assn. Women Atty. (lectr.), Ill. State Bar Assn. (family law sect. coun. 1994-99, lectr., chair custody com., co-chair bar and bench com. 1998-99, bar and bench sect. coun. 1999—), North Suburban Bar Assn. (lectr.), Lake County Bar Assn. (family law com.), Chgo. Bar Assn. (vice-chair, sec. 1988-92, chair matrimonial law com. 1992-93, bd. mgrs. 1994-96, lectr.). Family and matrimonial. Office: Grant and Grant 180 N La Salle St Ste 2400 Chicago IL 60601-2787 also: 707 Skokie Blvd Ste 600 Northbrook IL 60062

**GRANT, MERWIN DARWIN,** lawyer; b. Safford, Ariz., May 7, 1944; s. Darwin Dewey and Erma (Whiting) G.; m. Charlotte Richey, June 27, 1969; children: Brandon, Taggart, Christian, Brittany. BA in Econs., Brigham Young U., 1968; JD, Duke U., 1971. Bar: Ariz. 1971, U.S. Dist. Ct. Ariz., U.S. Dist. Ct. (we. dist.) Tex., U.S. Ct. Appeals (5th, 7th, 8th, 9th and 10th cirs.), U.S. Tax Ct., U.S. Supreme Ct. Pres. Merwin D. Grant, P.C., Phoenix, 1977—; ptnr. Beus, Gilbert & Morrill, Phoenix, 1984-93, Grant, Williams, Lake & Dangerfield P.C., Phoenix, 1994—. Guest condr. Phoenix Symphony Orch., 1989. Bd. dirs. Grand Canyon coun. Boy Scouts Am., Phoenix, 1974-76, Maricopa Hosp., Health Sys. Bd., 1997—; pres., bd. dirs. Golden Gate Settlement, Phoenix, 1975-80, 84-88; charter mem. Rep. Presl. Task Force, Washington, 1984—. Fellow Ariz. Bar Found.; mem. ABA (litigation sect.), Assn. Trial Lawyers Am., Kiwanis (bd. dirs. Phoenix chpt. 1972-79). Federal civil litigation, State civil litigation, Private international. Office: Grant Williams Lake & Dangerfield 302 N 1st Ave Phoenix AZ 85003-1500

**GRANT, PATRICK ALEXANDER,** lawyer, association administrator; b. Denver, Nov. 14, 1945; s. Edwin Hendrie and Mary Belle (McIntyre) G.; m. Carla Clyde Yancey, Aug. 16, 1975; children: Mary Cameron, Sara Mansur, Alexis Hendrie. BA with honors, Colgate U., 1967; MBA, Denver U., 1973; JD, Drake U., 1976. Bar: Colo. 1977. Law clk. to Judge Donald P. Smith, Jr. Colo. Ct. Appeals, Denver, 1976-77; assoc. Grant, McHendrie, Haines & Crouse, PC, Denver, 1977-83, ptnr., v.p., 1984-91, also bd. dirs.; state rep. Colo. Gen. Assembly, Denver, 1984-92, vice-chmn. fin. com., 1987-88, chmn. audit com., 1989-90, chmn. judiciary com., 1988-92, chmn. legal svcs. com., 1988-89; mem. Colo. Coun. Elected Ofcls. for Soviet Jewry, Denver, 1985-92, Colo. Spl. Task Force Tort Liability and Ins., Denver, 1985; bd. dirs. Colo. Sports Hall of Fame, 1999, Colo. State U. Livestock Leader Coun. Upper sch. chmn. parents divsn. Kent Denver Leadership Fund, 1996-97; mem. Denver Cmty. Mental Health Commn., 1985-86; mem. exec. coun., planning com. St. Joseph Hosp., Denver, 1985-88; mem. Denver Bd. for Developmentally Disabled, 1987-88; vestryman, jr. warden St. Barnabas Parish, Denver, 1979-84; mem. adv. com. Nat. Ctr. Preventive Law, 1987-90; bd. dirs. Colo. Jud. Inst., 1990-96; mem. exec. bd. Parents Assn., Gettysburg (Pa.) Coll.; exec. bd. Denver coun. Boy Scouts Am., 1997—; scout show chmn. Roundup Riders of Rockies, 1999—. Gates Found. fellow John F. Kennedy Sch. Govt. Harvard U., 1985, Toll Fellow Coun. of State Govts., 1987; recipient Outstanding Alumni award Kent Denver Country Day Sch., 1986, Colo. Wildlife Fedn. Appreciation award, 1987, Disting. Svc. to Higher Edn. award U. Denver, 1988, Bus. Legis. of Yr., award Colo. Pub. Affairs Coun., 1989, Outstanding Achievement award EPA, 1989, award of honor Hist. Denver, 1989, Stephen H. Hart award Colo. Hist. Soc., 1990, Spl. Recognition award AIA; named one of Outstanding Young Men in Am., U.S. Jaycees, 1980, Legislator of Yr. Associated Builders and Contractors, 1991, Gen. Heritage award for Former Legislator, 1997. Mem. Colo. Med. Soc. Found. (bd. dirs., pres. 1997-99, pres. emeritus 1999—), Western Stock Show Assn. (exec. com., bd. dirs. 1984—, exec. v.p. and CEO 1990-91, pres. and CEO 1991—), Metro Denver C. of C. (chmn. econ. devel. coun. 1995-96, chmn. pub. affairs coun. 1999—). Republican. Episcopalian. Avocation: wood chopping, horseback riding. Environmental, Real property, Transportation. Home: 5 Parkway Ln Englewood CO 80110-4228 Office: 4655 Humboldt St Denver CO 80216-2818

**GRANT, RUSSELL PORTER, JR.,** lawyer; b. Ft. Sill, Okla., Nov. 5, 1943; s. Russell Porter and Jimmie (Bell) G.; m. Janice Rae Lockley, Nov. 19, 1966; 1 child, Russell Porter III. BS, U.S. Mil. Acad., 1966; JD, U. Miss., 1974. Bar: Miss. 1974, U.S. Dist. Ct. (no. dist.) Miss. 1974, U.S. Ct. Appeals (5th cir.) 1980, U.S. Dist. Ct. (so. dist.) Miss. 1992. Ptnr. Patterson & Patterson, Aberdeen, Miss., 1974-80; petroleum landman Aberdeen, 1980-81; ops. landman Hughes & Hughes Oil and Gas, Jackson, Miss., 1981-84; mgr. gas contracts Hughes Ea. Petroleum, Ltd., Jackson, 1984-88; corp. counsel Hughes Ea. Petroleum, Inc., Jackson, 1988-89; pvt. practice Jackson, 1989-90, 91; assoc. Overstreet & Kuykendall, Jackson, 1990-91; ptnr. McKibben, Grant & Assocs., Jackson, 1991-95; mem. legal com. Interstate Oil and Gas Compact Commn., Oklahoma City, 1992—; speaker Oil and Gas Inst., U. Ala., 1990, natural gas seminar Miss. Natural Gas Assn., 1986. Co-chair exec. com. Monroe County Rep. Party, Aberdeen, 1980; pres. Aberdeen Exch. Club, 1978-79; mem. Monroe County (Miss.) Port Authority, 1979-80. Capt. U.S. Army, 1966-72. Named Outstanding Com. Chair, Aberdeen C. of C., 1979. Mem. Miss. Oil and Gas Lawyers (pres. 1986-87, Miss. Assn. Petroleum Landmen (v.p. 1987-88, pres. 1994-95), Miss. Bar (chmn. natural resources sect. 1988-89), Am. Assn. Profl. Landmen (cert. profl. landman), The Federalist Soc., Nat. Lawyers Assn. Episcopalian. Avocations: art, architecture, gardening, music, history. Oil, gas, and mineral, Contracts commercial, Real property. Home and Office: 1818 Aztec Dr Jackson MS 39211-6503

**GRANT, STEPHEN ALLEN,** lawyer; b. N.Y.C., Nov. 4, 1938; s. Benton H. and Irene A. Grant; m. Anne. K. Bagley, Feb. 11, 1961 (div. Nov. 1975); children: Stephen, Katharine, Michael; m. Anne-Marie Laignel, Dec. 8, 1975; children: Natalie, Elizabeth, Alexandra. AB, Yale U., 1960; LLB, Columbia U., 1965. Bar: N.Y. 1965, U.S. Supreme Ct. 1969. Law clk. to judge U.S. Ct. Appeals (2d cir.), N.Y.C., 1965-66; assoc. Sullivan & Cromwell, N.Y.C., 1966-73, ptnr., 1973—. Mem. Japan-U.S. Friendship Commn., U.S.-Japan Conf. on Cultural and Ednl. Interchange, 1989-92. Lt. (j.g.) USNR, 1960-62. Mem. ABA, N.Y. State Bar Assn., Assn. of Bar of City of N.Y., Coun. Fgn. Rels. Clubs: Down Town, Links. Private international, Securities, General corporate. Home: 200 E 66th St # C2103 New York NY 10021-6728 Office: Sullivan & Cromwell 125 Broad St Fl 28 New York NY 10004-2489

**GRANT, WALTER MATTHEWS,** lawyer, corporate executive; b. Winchester, Ky., Mar. 30, 1945; s. Raymond Russell and Mary Mitchell (Rees) G.; m. Ann Carol Straus, Aug. 5, 1967; children—Walter Matthews II, Jean Ann, Raymond Russell II. ABJ, U. Ky., Lexington, 1967; JD, Vanderbilt U., 1971. Bar: Ga. 1971, Tenn. 1992. Assoc. Alston & Bird, Atlanta, 1971-76, ptnr., 1976-83; v.p., gen. counsel, sec. Contel Corp., Atlanta, 1983-91; sr. v.p., gen. counsel Smith & Nephew N.Am., Memphis, 1991-93; sr. v.p., gen. counsel, sec. The Actava Group Inc., Atlanta, 1993-96, Bruno's Inc., Birmingham, Ala., 1996—. Editor in chief Vanderbilt Law Rev., 1970-71, Ga. State Bar Jour., 1979-82. Baptist. General corporate, Mergers and acquisitions. Home: 23 Rose Gate Dr NE Atlanta GA 30342-4161 Office: Bruno's Inc PO Box 2486 Birmingham AL 35201-2486

**GRANT BRUCE, DARLENE CAMILLE,** lawyer; b. Jackson Heights, N.Y., Apr. 25, 1959; d. Leonard DaCosta and Lucille Eleanor Grant; m. Raymond Lloyd Bruce, Nov. 30, 1996. BA, Brandeis U., 1981; JD, Georgetown U., 1986. Bar: N.Y. 1987, U.S. Dist. Ct. (ea. dist.) N.Y., U.S. Ct. Appeals (D.C. cir.) 1995, U.S. Supreme Ct.; cert. tng., Nat. Inst. Corrections. Jud. clk., Judge Mary Johnson Lowe U.S. Dist. Ct. N.Y., N.Y.C., 1984; jud. clk., Judge Paul Webber Superior Ct., Washington, 1985; assoc. Cullen & Dykman, Garden City, N.Y., 1986-87, Law Offic Lee H. Bostic, Queens Village, N.Y., 1987-89; asst. atty. gen. V.I. Dept. Justice, Solicitor Gen. divsn., U.S. V.I., 1989-94; asst. gen. counsel Coun. for D.C., Office of Gen. Counsel, 1994; gen. counsel for prison litigation Nat. Coun. on Crime and Delinquency, Washington, 1994-98; spl. master U.S. Dist. Ct. V.I., 1996—; assoc. counsel N.Y. State Assembly, Albany, 1998—; instr. Charles Hamilton Houston Inst., Georgetown U. Law Ctr., Washington, 1994. Chair Brandeis U. alumni admissions coun., 1990—; chair St. Thomas Interagy. Coun. on Homeless, 1992-94; legal advisor V.I. Inst. Performing Arts, 1993-94; bd. trustees, Corona-East Elmhurst Civic Assn., 1987-89. Recipient awards Nat. Assn. Atty. Gens. appellate advocacy program, Am. Trial Lawyers Assn. Mem. ABA, Nat. Bar Assn., Am. Correctional Assn. (legal affairs com. 1997—), N.Y. State Bar Assn., Met. Black Bar Assn. (bd. dirs. 1997—), Macon B. Allen Bar Assn., D.C. Bar Assn., V.I. Bar Assn., Phi Delta Phi, Delta Sigma Theta, Inc. (legal advisor 1992-94, v.p. 1990-92). Office: Office of Special Master 210 W 137th St Apt 1 New York NY 10030-2429

**GRANTHAM, GENE M.,** lawyer; b. Seattle, Apr. 4, 1945. BS, U. Wash., 1968; JD, Willamette U., 1974. Bar: Wash. 1974. Pvt. practice law Seattle. Personal injury, Criminal. Office: #500 119 First Ave S Seattle WA 93104

**GRANTHAM, KIRK PINKERTON,** lawyer, insurance company executive; b. Tupelo, Miss., Oct. 12, 1941; s. Homer Kirk and Lucile (Pinkerton) G.; m. Damaris Falkner, Aug. 25, 1964 (div. 1980); 1 child, Dodson Kirk; m. Cheryl Mellinger, Apr. 25, 1983; 1 child, Tyler Kirk. B in Pub. Adminstrn., U. Miss., 1963, JD, 1966. Bar: Miss. 1966, Fla. 1971; cert. real property law and wills, trusts and estate planning. Estate tax atty. IRS, W. Palm Beach, Fla., 1966-72; ptnr. Day, Grantham & Hess, Lake Worth, Fla., 1972-81; assoc. Shutts & Bowen, Lake Worth, 1981-86; pvt. practice, West Palm Beach, 1986—; pres. Std. Title Ins. Agy., Inc., West Palm Beach. Pres. Palm Beach County Heart Assn., 1991. Sgt. USAR, 1966-72. Recipient Leadership award YMCA, 1987. Mem. Fla. Bar Assn., ABA, Miss. Bar Assn., Lake Worth Bar Assn. (pres. 1978), Tuskawillow Club. Republican. Episcopalian. Estate planning, Probate, Real property. Office: 1860 Forest Hill Blvd West Palm Beach FL 33406-6022

**GRANTHAM, ROBERT EDWARD,** lawyer, educator; b. Rosedale, Miss., Apr. 18, 1944; s. Robert Oliver and Edith Evelyn (Lott) G.; m. Toni Lorraine Ray, Nov. 24, 1982; children: Heather, Robert Kendal. AA, U. Md., 1974; BS, U. Albuquerque, 1975; JD, U. Okla., 1978. Bar: Okla. 1979; cert. secondary social studies tchr. Legal intern U.S. Atty., Oklahoma City, Okla., 1975-76, Moore & Foster, Oklahoma City, Okla., 1976-77; ptnr. Shrader & Grantham, Oklahoma City, Okla., 1978-80; gen. counsel LG Williams Oil Co., Oklahoma City, Okla., 1980-82; dist. counsel Resource Inv. Cirp., Oklahoma City, Okla., 1982-84; staff atty. Stack & Barnes, Oklahoma City, Okla., 1984-86; ptnr. Wheat & Grantham, Oklahoma City, Okla., 1986-90; staff atty. Fogg, Fogg & Handley, El Reno, Okla., 1991—; prof. Redlands C.C., El Reno, Okla., 1991—. Bd. dirs. Youth & Family Svcs., El Reno, 1984-87, ARC, El Reno, 1984-87; mem. acad. achievement com. El Reno Pub. Schs., 1993—, mem. parental involvment com., 1995—, graduation rate com., 1995—; vice chmn. Mcpl. Planning Commn., El Reno, 1992—. With U.S. Army, 1962-74. Mem. Okla. Bar Assn., Okla. Bd. Bar Examiners, Canadian County Bar Assn. Democrat. Roman Catholic. Avocations: tennis, golf, sports cars, coaching little league sports, video games. Family and matrimonial, Real property, Education and schools. Home: 921 SW 24th St El Reno OK 73036-5819 Office: Fogg Fogg & Handley 421 S Rock Island Ave El Reno OK 73036-3753

**GRANTLAND, BRENDA,** lawyer; b. Decatur, Ala., July 3, 1952; d. Everette Clyde and Florence Blanche Grantland. BA, U. Ala., 1974; JD, George Washington U., 1981. Bar: D.C. 1982, Md. 1985, Calif. 1993, U.S. Dist. Ct. (various dists./states), U.S. Ct. Appeals (3d cir.), U.S. Ct. Appeals (5th cir.), U.S. Ct. Appeals (9th cir.), U.S. Ct. Appeals (10th cir.), U.S. Ct. Appeals (D.C. cir.), U.S. Supreme Ct. Pvt. practice Washington, 1982-93, Mill Valley, Calif., 1993-98, Sausalito, Calif., 1998—. Author: Your House is Under Arrest, 1993; co-author: Forfeiture and Double Jeopardy, 1994. Bd. dirs. Forfeiture Endangers Am. Rights, Washington, 1997—, pres., 1994-97. Website named One of Top 5% of All Websites, Lycos, 1996. Appellate, Civil rights, Criminal. Home and Office: 20 Sunnyside Ave Ste A204 Mill Valley CA 94941-1928

**GRANVILLE, WARREN JAMES,** attorney general; b. Flushing, N.Y.; s. Warren Joseph and Joan Patricia (Knox) G.; m. Diana Rae Martin, Aug. 20, 1977; 1 child, Martin James. BA, Fla. State U., 1975; JD, Ariz. State U., 1979. Bar: Ariz., 1979, U.S. Dist. Ct. Ariz., 1980, U.S. Ct. Appeals (9th cir.), 1984, U.S. Supreme Ct., 1984. Law clerk Ariz. Atty. Gen.'s Office, Phoenix, 1978-79, asst. atty. gen., 1980—; adviser Victim's Rights COm., Phoenix, 1988—. Coach State Bar Mock Trial Program Greenway H.S., 1993—. Mem. State Bar Ariz. (Disting. Pub. Lawyer award 1993), Maricopa County Bar Assn. Republican. Office: Ariz Atty Gen's Office 1275 W Washington St Phoenix AZ 85007-2926

**GRASKI, DIANA,** lawyer, educator; b. Detroit, Nov. 7, 1964; m. Henry Felix Graski, Dec. 13, 1997. BA, U. Colo., 1989; JD, Drake U., 1992. Bar: Colo. 1992, U.S. Dist. Ct. Colo. 1992. Pvt. practice Diana Graski, P.C., Colorado Springs, Colo., 1994—; instr. Denver Paralegal Inst., Colorado Springs, 1995—, Pikes Peak C.C., Colorado Springs, 1996—, mem. legal asst. adv. bd., 1998—. Mem. Colo. Bar Assn., El Paso County Bar Assn. General practice, General civil litigation, Family and matrimonial. Office: 330 E Costilla St # 2 Colorado Springs CO 80903-2106

**GRASSI, JOSEPH F.,** lawyer; b. N.Y.C., Dec. 6, 1949. BA, Queens Coll., 1970; JD, NYU, 1974. Bar: N.Y. 1974. Assoc. Milbank, Tweed, Hadley & McCloy, N.Y.C., 1976-79; asst. corp. counsel Corp. Counsel of N.Y.C., 1979-83; pvt. practice N.Y.C., 1983—. Mem. ABA, N.Y. County Lawyers' Assn. General civil litigation, Construction, Government contracts and claims. Home: 7002 Boulevard E Guttenberg NJ 07093-4929 Office: 270 Madison Ave Rm 700 New York NY 10016-0601

**GRASSIA, THOMAS CHARLES,** lawyer; b. Westfield, Mass., Aug. 26, 1946; s. Thomas C. and Assunta (Abatiell) G.; m. Judith Chace Cranshaw, Aug. 15, 1970; children: Susan C., Joseph C. B.A., Boston U., 1968; J.D., Suffolk U., 1974. Bar: Mass. 1974, U.S. Dist. Ct. Mass. 1976, U.S. Supreme Ct. 1980. Asst. v.p. Plymouth Rubber Co., Canton, Mass., 1969-71; ptnr., P.T.S. Computer Svcs., Waltham, Mass., 1971-81; ptnr. D'Angio & Grassia, Waltham, 1974-85, Grassia & Assoc., P.A., Natick, Mass., 1985-98, Grassia, Murphy & Whitney, P.A., Natick, 1998—; agt. Lawyers Title Ins. Co., Richmond, Va., First Am. Title Ins. Co., Fidelity Nat. Title Ins. Co.; bd. dirs. many regional corps; pres., treas., bd. dirs. Lender's Title & Abstract Co., Ltd., Natick. Contbr. articles to profl. publs., lectr. on law, pub. interest subjects. Mem. Bd. Health, Sherborn, Mass., 1976-81, Bd. Selectmen,

Sherborn, 1981-85; trustee Leonard Morse Hosp., Natick, Mass., 1981-84; mem. Met. Boston Hosp. Council, Burlington, Mass., 1983-84; mem., team leader Sherborn Fire and Rescue Dept., 1974—; former mem. Sherborn Sch. Bd. Long Range Planning com., Sherborn Land Maintenance Study com., Sherborn Police Chief Selection com., Sherborn Emergency Med. Study com. Mem. ABA, Mass. Bar Assn., Mass. Conveyances Assn., Am. Arbitration Assn. (comml. arbitration bd.), New Eng. Helicopter Pilots Assn. (immediate past pres., chmn. bd. dirs.). General corporate, Real property, Sports. Home: PO Box 178 Sherborn MA 01770-0178 Office: Grassia Murphy & Whitney PA 5 Commonwealth Rd Natick MA 01760-1526

**GRATTAN, GEORGE GILMER, IV,** lawyer; b. Harrisonburg, Va., Nov. 13, 1933; s. George Gilmer III and Elizabeth (Conover) G.; m. Martha Townes, Aug. 27, 1955; children—Rebecca, Kathleen, G. Stuart, David. B.A., U. Va., 1955, J.D., 1960. Bar: Va. 1960. Ptnr. Christian, Barton, Epps, Brent & Chappell, Richmond, Va., 1960-74; legal adviser U. Va., Charlottesville, 1974-88. Former pres. Big Bros. Richmond; former bd. dirs. Big Bros. Am. Served as 1st lt. U.S Army, 1955-57. Fellow Va. Law Found., Am. Bar Found.; mem. Va. Bar Assn. (pres. 1984-85), SPEBSQSA, Inc. (barbershop Quartet & chorus). Presbyterian. Home and Office: 5250 Advance Mills Rd Earlysville VA 22936-1830

**GRAVEL, JOHN COOK,** lawyer; b. Burlington, Vt., Dec. 8, 1947; s. Clarke Albert and Phyllis Jean (Cook) G.; m. Mary Ann Luchini, June 14, 1969; children: Judson Christopher, Jamie Lee. BA in History, St. Michael's Coll., Winooski, Vt., 1969; JD, Boston Coll., 1972. Bar: Vt. 1972, U.S. Dist. Ct. Vt. 1973, U.S. Ct. Appeals (2d cir.) 1977. Assoc. Gravel, Shea & Wright, Burlington, 1972-79; ptnr. Bauer Anderson & Gravel, Burlington, 1980—, sec., bd. dirs.; sec. Burlington Internat. Games, Inc., 1975-92. Appointee Vt. Statutory Revision Com., Montpelier, 1979—; trustee emeritus Burlington Coll., 1980-83, 90—, chmn. adv. bd., 1988—, past pres.; bd. dirs. Flynn Theatre for Performing Arts, Ltd., Burlington, 1980-91, dir. emeritus, 1991—, past pres.; bd. dirs. Chittenden County United Way, Burlington, 1985-91; bd. dirs. Vt. Cath. Charities, Inc., Burlington, 1976-85, past pres. Lt. U.S. Army, 1970-72. Mem. ABA, Vt. Bar Assn. Republican. Roman Catholic. Avocations: acting, musical theater, writing. Consumer commercial, General corporate, Probate. Home: 50 Prospect Hl Burlington VT 05401-1606 Office: Bauer Anderson & Gravel 40 College St Apt 100 Burlington VT 05401-4436

**GRAVELLE, DOUGLAS ARTHUR,** lawyer; b. San Francisco, Oct. 19, 1967; s. Douglas Norman and Roberta Madelyn (Michel) G.; m. Stephanie Kim, Sept. 17, 1994. BS, U. Calif., Davis, 1989; JD, UCLA, 1993. Bar: Calif. 1993. Atty. Texaco Inc., Universal City, Calif., 1993-98, McCutchen, Doyle, Brown & Enersen, L.A., 1998—. Environmental, General civil litigation, General corporate. Office: McCutchen Doyle et al 355 S Grand Ave Ste 4400 Los Angeles CA 90071-3106

**GRAVES, JAMES CLEMENTS,** lawyer; b. Texarkana, Ark., Sept. 24, 1945; s. Louis Francis Jr. and Wilton Clements G. BA, U. Tex., 1967; JD, U. Ark., 1975. Bar: Ark. 1975, U.S. Dist. Ct. (we. dist.) Ark. 1976; cert. law enforcement instr. Ark. Criminal Justice Sys., 1986. Pvt. practice Murfreesboro, Ark., 1975-82; ptnr. Darling & Graves, Attys., Nashville, Ark., 1982-88; pvt. practice Nashville, Ark., 1988-90; ptnr. Graves & Graves, Attys., Nashville, Ark., 1990—; bd. dirs., v.p. Graves Pub. Co., Inc., Nashville, Ark., 1986—; city atty. Nashville, Ark., 1982—; dep. prosecutor Pike County, Murfreesboro, Ark., 1978-81, Howard County, Nashville, Ark., 1983-93; rep. ho. of dels. Ark. Bar, 1995-97. Contbr. articles to profl. jours. Mem. Dem. ctrl. com. Howard County Dem. Party, Nashville, Ark., 1988—, vice chair, 1992—. Lt. USN, 1967-71, Vietnam. Mem. Ark. City Atty. Assn. (v.p. 1992-94), Ark. Bar Assn. (editl. adv. 1997—), Rotary Internat. (pres. 1992-93). Consumer commercial, Criminal, Family and matrimonial. Office: Graves & Graves Atty 420 N Main St # 1 Nashville AR 71852-2006

**GRAVES, JOHN WILLIAM,** state supreme court justice; b. Paducah, Ky., Oct. 17, 1935; m. Mary Ann Breivo; children: James Anthony, Kevin Andrew. BS, U. Notre Dame, 1957; postgrad., U. Louisville, 1957-58; JD, U. Ky., 1963. Bar: Ky. 1963. Dist. judge, 1984-88; circuit ct. judge McCracken Cir., 1989-95; justice Ky. Supreme Ct., 1995—. Col. U.S. Army Res. Decorated Army Commendation medal, Army Meritorious Svc. medal. Office: State Capitol Capital Bldg Rm 230 700 Capitol Ave Frankfort KY 40601-3410*

**GRAVES, PATRICK LEE,** lawyer; b. Pasadena, Calif., Sept. 16, 1945; s. James Edward and Virginia (Dudley) G.; children: Carrie Kathleen, Michael Patrick. AS, Citrus Jr. Coll., Glendora, Calif., 1969; BS, Calif. State Polytechnic U., 1973; BS in Law, Western State U., 1973, JD, 1975. Bar: Calif. 1975, U.S. Dist. Ct. (cen. dist.) Calif. 1976, U.S. Ct. Appeals (9th cir.) 1978, U.S. Supreme Ct. 1980. Assoc. Lynberg & Watkins, Los Angeles, 1975-80, ptnr., 1981-93; ptnr. Graves & King, Riverside, Calif., 1993—; settlement officer Los Angeles Superior Ct., 1988—, arbitrator, 1981—; arbitrator San Bernardino Superior Ct., 1990—; mediator L.A. Superior Ct., 1993—, Riverside Superior Ct., 1996—, AAA-Inland Empire, 1996—. judge pro tem L.A. Superior Ct., 1992—. Sustaining mem. Rep. Nat. Com., Washington, 1979—; mem. Nat. Rep. Congl. Com., 1980—. Mem. ABA, San Bernardino County Bar Assn., Assn. So. Calif. Def. Counsel (chmn. 1988, bd. dirs. 1996—), Def. Rsch. Inst., Upland (Calif.) C. of C. Avocations: flyfishing, golf. Personal injury, Real property, Government contracts and claims. Home: 424 Monterey Ln # B San Clemente CA 92672-5329 Office: Graves & King 3610 14th St Fl 2D Riverside CA 92501-3843

**GRAVES, RAY REYNOLDS,** judge; b. Tuscumbia, Ala., Jan. 10, 1946; s. Isaac and Olga Ernestine (Wilder) G.; children: Claire Elisë, Reynolds Douglass. BA, Trinity Coll., Hartford, Conn., 1967; JD, Wayne State U., 1970. Bar: Mich. 1971, U.S. Dist. Ct. (ea. dist.) Mich. 1971, U.S. Ct. Appeals (6th cir.) 1972, U.S. Supreme Ct. 1976, D.C. 1977. Defender, Legal Aid and Defender Assn., Detroit, 1970-71; assoc. Liberson, Fink, Feiler, Crystal & Burdick, 1971-72, Patmon, Young & Kirk, 1972-73; ptnr. Lewis, White, Clay & Graves, 1974-81; mem. legal dept. Detroit Edison Co., 1981; judge U.S. Bankruptcy Ct., Eastern Dist. Mich., Detroit, 1982—, chief judge U.S. Bankruptcy Ct., 1991-95; Mem. U.S. Ct. Com., State Bar Mich. bd. dirs. Mich. Cancer Found.; trustee Mich. Opera Theatre, 1986-88; vestry Christ Ch. Episcopal, Grosse Pointe, Mich., 1994-97; del. Diocesan Conv. of the Episcopal Ch., Mich., 1997. Fellow Am. Coll. Bankruptcy, 1993; mem. Nat. Conf. Bankruptcy Judges (bd. govs. 1984-88), World Assn. Judges, World Peace Through Law Conf., Assn. Black Judges Mich., Wolverine Bar Assn., Detroit Bar Assn., D.C. Bar Assn., Delta Kappa Epsilon, Sigma Pi Phi, Iota Boulé. Episcopalian. Office: US Bankruptcy Ct 211 W Fort St Ste 1900 Detroit MI 48226-3228

**GRAVES, ROBERT,** lawyer; b. Portland, Maine, May 26, 1940; s. William W. and Lillian Graves. BS, Boston U., 1963; JD, Suffolk U., Boston, 1969. Bar: Mass. 1969, U.S. Dist. Ct. 1969, U.S. Ct. Appeals 1969, U.S. Mil. Appeals 1974, U.S. Supreme Ct. 1974, U.S. Tax Ct. 1978. Judge advocate gen. USAR, 1968-69; propr. Robert Graves & Assocs., Burlington, Mass. Mem. Corp. Winchester (Mass.) Hosp., 1986—; alumni bd. dirs. Boston U., 1994—. Mem. Mass. Bar Assn., Boston Bar Assn., Masons, Shriners. Family and matrimonial, General civil litigation, State civil litigation. Home: 5 Coolidge Rd Winchester MA 01890-2222 Office: Robert Graves & Assocs 44 Mall Rd Ste 202 Burlington MA 01803-4530

**GRAVING, RICHARD JOHN,** law educator; b. Duluth, Minn., Aug. 24, 1929; s. Lawrence Richard and Laura Magdalene (Loucks) G.; m. Florence Sara Semel; children: Daniel, Sarah. BA, U. Minn., 1950; JD, Harvard U., 1953; postgrad., Nat. U. Mex., 1964-66. Bar: Minn. 1953, N.Y. 1956, U.S. Dist. Ct. (so. dist.) N.Y. 1956, Pa. 1968, U.S. Dist. Ct. (we. dist.) Pa. 1968, Tex. 1982, U.S. Dist. Ct. (so. dist.) Tex. 1982. Assoc. Reid & Priest, N.Y.C., 1955-61, Mexico City, 1961-66; v.p. Am. & Fgn. Power Co., Inc., Mexico City, 1966-68; atty. Gulf Oil Corp., Pitts., 1968-69, Madrid, 1969-73, London, 1973-80, Houston, 1980-82; pvt. practice London, 1982-84; prof. law South Tex. Coll. (affiliated with Tex. A&M U.), Houston, 1983—. With U.S. Army, 1953-55. Mem. Am. Soc. Internat. Law. Home: 8515 Ariel St Houston TX 77074-2806 Office: Inst Transnat Arbitration 1303 San Jacinto St Houston TX 77002-7013

**GRAY, BRIAN MARK,** lawyer; b. Detroit, Dec. 21, 1939; s. Joseph Clay and Mary Jane (Bond) G.; m. Patricia Kay Gillett, Aug. 19, 1967; children: Diana Lisa, Amy Noel. BA, U. Mich., 1961, JD, 1964; postgrad., U. London, 1965, U. Brussels, 1966. Bar: Mich. 1967, U.S. Dist. Ct. Mich. 1967, U.S. Ct. Customs and Patent Appeals 1981, U.S. Ct. Appeals (fed. cir.) 1985, U.S. Supreme Ct. 1974. Assoc. Butzel, Eamon, Long, Gust & Kennedy, Detroit, 1964; sr. rsch. clk., chief judge Mich. Ct. Appeals, Grand Rapids, 1967-68; ptnr. Krueger, Gray & Lesica, Muskegon, Mich., 1967-74; pvt. practice Anchorage, 1975—; of counsel in patent matters; cons. in field. Author: Your Estate Plan, 1980, European Community Corporate Mergers. Del. U.S.-Japan Bilateral Session Legal and Econ. Rels., 1988; del. designate Moscow Conf. Law and Econ. Rels., 1990. Rsch. grantee U. London, 1965. Mem. ABA, Mat-Su Borough Bar Assn., Mich. Bar Assn., Alaska Bar Assn., Soc. Gray's Inn (life), Phi Alpha Delta, Phi Beta Kappa. Lutheran. Avocations: breeding and training Arabian horses, building and flying experimental aircraft. Patent, Trademark and copyright, Estate planning.

**GRAY, CAROL A.,** lawyer; b. Jamaica, W.I., Aug. 31, 1965; 1 child, Dominique. BA, Amherst Coll., 1987; JD, NYU, 1992. Bar: N.Y., N.J. Staff atty. Neighborhood Defender Svc. Harlem, N.Y.C., 1992-96; atty. Bklyn. Defender Svc., 1996—. Mem. ABA, N.Y. Bar Assn. Avocation: tennis. Office: Bklyn Defender Svc 111 Livingston St Brooklyn NY 11201-5078

**GRAY, CHARLES ROBERT,** lawyer; b. Kirksville, Mo., Aug. 22, 1952; s. George Devon and Bettie Louise (McCormick) G.; m. Dana Elizabeth Kehr, June 1, 1974; children: Jennifer, Jessica, Marcus, Gregory, Victoria. BS, N.E. Mo. State U., 1974; JD, U. Mo., Kansas City, 1978. Bar: Mo. 1978, Va. 1993, U.S. Dist. Ct. (we. dist.) Mo. 1978, U.S. Ct. Appeals (fed. cir.) 1992, U.S. Ct. Appeals (4th cir.) 1995, U.S. Supreme Ct. 1981; cert. mediator; cert. hearing officer Va. Supreme Ct., 1997. Pvt. practice Parkville, Mo., 1978-81; asst. pub. defender 5th Judicial Cir. Ct. Mo., St. Joseph, 1978-79; pub. defender 6th Judicial Cir. Ct. Mo., Platte City, 1981; asst. dist. counsel Army Corps of Engrs., Kansas City, 1981-82, Vicksburg, Miss., 1982-83; chief counsel space shuttle, MX missile U.S. Army, Vandenberg AFB, Calif., 1983-85; chief counsel troop support agy. U.S. Army, Ft. Lee, Va., 1985-87; fraud counsel Def. Gen. Supply Ctr. Dept. of Def., Richmond, Va., 1987-93; pvt. practice, Chester, Va., 1993—; owner Pvt. Jud. Svcs., Inc., Chester, 1993—; adj. prof. St. Leo Coll., Ft. Lee, 1986-91, John Tyler Coll., Chester, Va., 1994—. Mem. Selective Svc. Draft Bd., Brookfield, Mo., 1972-74; pres. Old Towne Parkville Assn., 1979-81, Chester (Va.) Youth Sports Boosters, 1989-91; den leader Boy Scouts Am., Chester, 1991—. Victor Wilson honor scholar, 1977; recipient Am. Jurisprudence award Coop-Bancroft-Whitney, 1989. Mem. ATLA, Am. Arbitration Assn. (mem. nat. panel arbitrators 1994—, mem. govt. disputes panel 1995—, mem. constrn. panel 1995—, mem. comml. panel 1995—), Def. Rsch. Inst. (approved mem. panel on mediation and arbitration), Mo. Bar Assn., Va. Bar Assn., Va. Trial Lawyers Assn. Methodist. Avocations: coaching youth sports, cub scouts, softball, tennis, basketball. Construction, General practice, Personal injury. Home: PO Drawer B Chester VA 23831 Office: Pres/Presiding Ofcl Pvt Jud Svcs PO Drawer B Chester VA 23831-0317

**GRAY, EDWARD ANTHONY,** lawyer; b. Phila., May 23, 1952. JD cum laude, Temple U., 1978. Bar: Pa. 1978, U.S. Dist. Ct. (ea. dist.) Pa. 1979, N.J. 1985, U.S. Dist. Ct. N.J. 1987, U.S. Ct. Appeals (3d cir.) 1987, N.Y. Ct. Appeals 1993, U.S. Ct. Appeals (7th cir.) 1994. Assoc. George J. Lavin & Assoc., Phila., 1985-87, shareholder, 1987-90; shareholder Lavin, Coleman, Finarelli & Gray, Phila., 1990—; lectr. Temple U. Trial Advocacy Program, mem. faculty Temple U. Masters of Trial Advocacy; judge pro tem Phila. Ct. Common Pleas. Mem. ABA, Trial Attys. Am., Pa. Bar Assn., N.J. Bar Assn., Def. Rsch. Inst., Products Def. Inst., Pa. Def. Inst. Product liability, General civil litigation, Personal injury. Office: Lavin Coleman Finarelli & Gray Penn Mutual Bldg 510 Walnut St Ste 10 Philadelphia PA 19106-3619

**GRAY, GLENN OLIVER,** lawyer; b. Charleston, S.C., Jan. 23, 1963; s. James Oliver and Julie (Frazier) G.; m. Glenda Faye Coleman, Aug. 26, 1989. BS, U. S.C., 1985, JD, 1989. Bar: S.C. 1989, N.J. 1990, N.Y. 1990, U.S. Dist. Ct. N.J. 1990, U.S. Dist. Ct. (so. and ea. dists.) N.Y. 1991, U.S. Ct. Appeals (2d and 3d cir.) 1993, U.S. Supreme Ct. 1995. Assoc. Dreisman & Gross, N.Y.C., 1989-91, Bower & Gardner, N.Y.C., 1991-94, Aaronson Rappeport Feinstein & Deutsch, N.Y.C., 1994-95; sr. atty. Jones Hirsch Connors & Bull, LLP, N.Y.C., 1995—. Bd. dirs., mem. Fund for City of N.Y., 1992-96; mem. U.S. Supreme Ct. Hist. Found., S.C. Bar Found. Mem. Am. Hosp. Assn., Nat. Bar Assn., Am. Corp. Counsel Assn., N.Y. State Bar Assn., S.C. Bar Assn., N.J. Bar Assn., N.Y. Med. Def. Bar Assn., N.Y. County Lawyers Assn., Charleston County Bar Assn., Masons (King Solomon Grand Lodge), Alpha Phi Alpha. Baptist. Avocations: golf, tennis, basketball, reading, travel. Federal civil litigation, State civil litigation, Health. Office: Jones Hirsch Connors & Bull 101 E 52nd St Fl 22 New York NY 10022-6061

**GRAY, J. CHARLES,** lawyer, cattle rancher; b. Leesburg, Fla., Mar. 26, 1932; s. G. Wayne and Mary Evelyn (Albright) G.; m. Saundra Hagood, Aug. 18, 1955; children: Terese Ren, John Charles Jr., Lee Jerome. BA, U. Fla., 1955, JD, 1958. Bar: Fla. 1958. County atty. Orange County (Fla.), 1978-85; chmn. Gray, Harris & Robinson, P.A.; chmn. Fla. Turnpike Authority, 1965-67; city solicitor City of Orlando (Fla.), 1960-61; pres. Santa Gertrudis Breeders Internat., 1981-83. Chmn. Pres.'s Council Advisors, U. Central Fla., 1978-84; pres. U. Cen. Fla. Found., 1990-91; pres. Orange County U. Fla. Alumni Assn., Pi Kappa Alpha Alumni Assn.; past dist. v.p. U. Fla. Alumni Assn.; mem. U. Fla. Pres.'s Council; mem. Com. of 100; founding bd. dirs. Fla. Epilepsy Found.; chmn. Econ. Devel. Commn. Mid. Fla., 1987-89; mem. Fla. Econ. Devel. Adv. Coun. Mem. U. Fla. Hall of Fame. Mem. ABA, Orange County Bar Assn., Fla. Bar Assn., Fla. Blue Key, Phi Alpha Delta, Pi Kappa Alpha. Republican. Episcopalian. Clubs: University (past dir.), Citrus Club of Orlando (dir.), U. Club of Orlando. Real property. Home: PO Box 3068 Orlando FL 32802-3068 Office: 201 E Pine St Ste 1200 Orlando FL 32801-2725

**GRAY, JAN CHARLES,** lawyer, business owner; b. Des Moines, June 15, 1947; s. Charles Donald and Mary C. Gray; 1 child, Charles Jan. BA in Econs., U. Calif., Berkeley, 1969; MBA, Pepperdine U., 1986; JD, Harvard U., 1972. Bar: Calif. 1972, D.C. 1974, Wyo. 1992. Law clk. Kindel & Anderson, L.A., 1971-72; assoc. Halstead, Baker & Sterling, L.A., 1972-75; sr. v.p., gen. counsel and sec. Ralphs Grocery Co., L.A., 1975-97; pres. Am. Presidents Resorts, Custer, S.D., Casper/Glenrock, Wyo., 1983—; owner Big Bear (Calif.) Cabins-Lakeside, 1988—; pres. Mt. Rushmore Broadcasting, Inc., 1991—; owner Sta. KGOS/KERM, Torrington, Wyo., 1993—, Sta. KRAL/KIQZ, Rawlins, Wyo., 1993—, Sta. KZMX, Hot Springs, S.D., 1993—, Sta. KFCR, Custer, S.D., 1992—, Sta. KQLT-FM, Casper, Wyo., 1994—, Sta. KASS-FM, Casper, 1995—, Sta. KVOC-AM, Casper, 1997—, KAWK-FM, Rapid City, S.D., 1997—, KHOC, Casper, Wyo., 1998—; judge pro tem L.A. Mcpl. Ct., 1977-85; instr. bus. UCLA, 1976-85, Pepperdine MBA Program, 1983-85; arbitrator Am. Arbitration Assn., 1977-97; media spokesman So. Calif. Grocers Assn., 1979-90, Calif. Grocers Assn., 1979-97, Calif. Retailers Assn., 1979-97; real estate broker, Calif., 1973—. Contbg. author: Life or Death, Who Controls?, 1976; contbr. articles to profl. jours. Trustee South Bay U. Coll. Law, 1978-79; mem. bd. visitors Southwestern U. Sch. Law, 1983—; mem. L.A. County Pvt. Industry Coun., 1982-96, exec. com. 1984-88, chmn. econ. devel. task force, 1986-89, chmn. mktg. com. 1991-93; mem. L.A. County Martin Luther King, Jr. Gen. Hosp. Authority, 1984—; mem. L.A. County Aviation Commn, 1986-92, chmn., 1990-91; L.A. Police Crime Prevention Adv. Coun., 1986—; Angelus Plaza Adv. Bd., 1983-85; bd. dirs. RecyCAL of So. Calif., 1983-89; trustee Santa Monica Hosp. Found., 1986-91, adv. bd., 1991—; mem. L.A. County Dem. Cen. Com., 1980-90, L.A. City Employees' Retirement System Comsn., 1993—; del. Dem. Nat. Conv., 1980. Recipient So. Calif. Grocers Assn. award for outstanding contbns. to food industry, 1982, appreciation award for No on 11 Campaign, Calif./Nev. Soft Drink Assn., 1983; Tyler Price Meml. award Mex.-Am. Grocers Assn., 1995, Radio Affiliate of Yr.-Classic Rock ABC, 1998. Mem. ABA, Calif. Bar Assn., L.A. County Bar Assn. (exec. com. corp. law depts. sect. 1974-76, 79—, chmn. 1989-90, exec. com. barristers sect. 1974-75, 79-81, trustee 1991-93, jud. evaluation com. 1993—, nominating com. 1994), San Fernando Valley Bar Assn. (chmn. real property sect. 1975-77, L.A. Pub. Affairs Officers Assn., L.A. World Affairs Coun., Calif. Retailers Assn. (supermarket com.), Food Mktg. Inst. (govt. rels. com. 1977-97, benefits coun. 1993-97, chmn. lawyers and economists 1993-95), So. Calif. Bus. Assn. (bd. dirs. 1981—, mem. exec. com. 1982—, sec. 1986-91, chair 1991—), Town Hall L.A., U. Calif. Alumni Assn., Ephebian Soc. L.A., Harvard Club of So. Calif., L.A. Athletic Club, Petroleum Club, Casper Country Club, Phi Beta Kappa. General corporate. Home: 2793 Creston Dr Los Angeles CA 90068-2209 Office: PO Box 2515 Casper WY 82602-2515 also: PO Box 3328 Hollywood CA 90078-3328

**GRAY, JEFFREY HUGH,** lawyer; b. Danville, Va., June 28, 1956; s. Hugh Alton and Nather (Crutchlow) G.; m. Yvonne Sheri Martin. BA in Polit. Sci., U. S.C., 1977; JD, Wash. & Lee U., 1981. Bar: S.C. 1981, Va. 1982. Atty. Nexsen, Pruet, Jacobs & Pollard, Columbia, S.C., 1981-82; atty. Willcox & Savage, P.C., Norfolk, Va., 1982-97, Va. Beach, Va., 1997—; arbitrator Nat. Assn. Securities Dealers, 1995—;. Bd. dirs. Hampton Roads C. of C. Virginia Beach Divsn., 1997—, chmn. pub. affairs com. 1998—; cabinet mem. United Way of South Hampton Roads, 1997—, vice chair, 1999; mem. Va. Supreme Ct.'s Jury Reform Task Force, 1998—. Mem. ABA, Va. State Bar Assn. (chmn. young lawyers com. 1989-91), bd. govs. litigation sect. 1995—, chmn. 1998-99), Va. Beach Bar Assn. (chmn. mentor program 1998—), Norfolk-Portsmouth Bar Assn., Va. Assn. Def. Attys., Va. Trial Lawyers Assn. Avocations: jazz guitar, mountain biking. Securities, Federal civil litigation, General civil litigation. Office: Willcox & Savage PC Ste 1010 One Columbus Ctr Virginia Beach VA 23462

**GRAY, JERRY CLINTON,** judge; b. Atlanta, Aug. 24, 1952; s. E.H. Ladd and Emma Louise Gray; m. Debra Kay Smith, Sept. 3, 1976; children: Sidney, Daren, Jerri. Bar: Ga. 1979, U.S. Dist. Ct. (no. dist.) Ga. 1979, U.S. Supreme Ct. 1988. Asst. dist. atty. Piedmond Jud. Cir., Jefferson, Ga., 1991-92; pub. defender Jackson County Pub. Defender's Office, Jefferson, 1983-90, Barrow County Pub. Defender's Office, Winder, Ga., 1987-91; judge State Court of Jackson County, Jefferson. Mem. U.S. Chess Fedn. (life). Methodist. Avocation: chess. Home: 3635 US Highway 441 S Commerce GA 30529-6707 Office: State Court Jackson County 66 Washington St Jefferson GA 30549-1002

**GRAY, JOANNE MARIA,** lawyer; b. Worcester, Mass., Dec. 29, 1958; d. Joseph Patrick and Jean Marie (Simonelli) G. AB, Coll. of Holy Cross, 1980; JD, Fordham U., 1983. Bar: N.Y. 1983, U.S. Dist. Ct. (ea. and so. dists.) N.Y., U.S. Ct. Appeals (2d cir.). Assoc. Martin Clearwater & Bell, N.Y.C., 1983-84, Kopff Nardelli & Dopf, N.Y.C., 1984-87, Schneck Weltman & Hashmall, N.Y.C., 1987-90; ptnr. Schneck, Weltman, Hashnall & Mischel, N.Y.C., 1991—. Editor-in-chief: The Superfund and Hazardous Waste Report. Mem. ABA, N.Y. State Bar Assn. Product liability, Environmental. Office: Schneck Weltman & Hashmall 1285 Avenue Of The Americas New York NY 10019-6028

**GRAY, JOHN LEONARD,** lawyer; b. N.Y.C., Feb. 14, 1924; s. James E. and Edna M. Gray; m. Margaret S. Gray, Aug. 23, 1947 (div. Jan. 1976); children: Linda S., James S.; m. Elizabeth Z. Gray, Apr. 24, 1976. BChE, Pratt Inst., N.Y.C., 1943; JD, Albany Law Sch., 1948. Bar: N.Y. 1951, Ohio 1951. Patent counsel, gen. counsel Battelle Meml. Inst., Columbus, Ohio, 1949-72; ptnr. Kegler Brown Hill & Ritter, Columbus, 1972-89, of counsel, 1989—; v.p. Battelle Devel. Corp., Scientific Advances Inc. Lt. (j.g.) USN, 1943-46, PTO, ATO. Mem. Ohio C. of C. (bd. dirs., mem. exec. com. 1994—), Navy League (bd. dir. 1990—), Rotary (pres. 1994-95). Intellectual property, Patent, Trademark and copyright. Office: Kegler Brown Hill & Ritter 65 E State St Ste 1800 Columbus OH 43215-4295

**GRAY, KARLA MARIE,** state supreme court justice. BA, Western Mich. U., MA in African History; JD, Hastings Coll. of Law, San Francisco, 1976. Bar: Mont. 1976, Calif. 1977. Law clk. to Hon. W. D. Murray U.S. Dist. Ct., 1976-77; staff atty. Atlantic Richfield Co., 1977-81; pvt. practice law Butte, Mont., 1981-84; staff atty., legis. lobbyist Mont. Power Co., Butte, 1984-91; justice Supreme Ct. Mont., Helena, 1991—. Mem. Mont. Supreme Ct. Gender Fairness Task Force. Fellow Am. Bar Found., Am. Judicature Soc., Internat. Women's Forum; mem. State Bar Mont., Silver Bow County Bar Assn. (past pres.), Nat. Assn. Women Judges. Avocations: travel, reading, piano, family genealogy, cross-country skiing. Office: Supreme Ct Mont Justice Bldg 215 N Sanders St Helena MT 59601-4522

**GRAY, KIMBERLY S.,** lawyer; b. Waynesboro, Pa., May 25, 1959; d. Harold Richard and Lillian May Null; m. Robert John Gray. BA in Psychology, Shippensburg (Pa.) U., 1989; JD, Dickinson Sch. Law, Carlisle, Pa., 1994. Bar: Pa. 1994, U.S. Dist. Ct. (mid. dist.) Pa. 1995. Shareholder/mng. atty. Martin & Gray, P.C., Chambersburg & Waynesboro, Pa., 1995-98; asst. counsel Highmark Inc., Camp Hill, Pa., 1998—; adj. prof. law The Dickinson Sch. of Law, Carlisle, 1997—. Bd. dirs. Cumberland Valley Mental Health, Chambersburg, 1996-98, Family Health Svcs., Chambersburg, 1995-98, Coyle Free Libr., Chambersburg, 1997-98; mem. Health Cmtys. Partnership Preventive Health Task Force, Chambersburg, 1997-98; mem. adv. bd. Big Bros. Big Sisters Franklin County, 1997-98. Recipient Monroe E. Trout Law and Medicine award Dickinson Sch. Law, 1994, Disting. Alumni award Hagerstown Bus. Coll., 1999. Mem. Nat. Health Lawyers Assn., Pa. Bar Assn. (health law com., legis. subcom. 1995—, chair 1998—, interdisciplinary com. on med. and health related issues 1996-97, zone 3 del. to Ho. of Dels. 1997-2000), Franklin County Bar Assn. (chmn. law and you com. 1996-98, co-chmn. bench/bar conf. com. 1995). Republican. Methodist. Avocations: foreign language, culture and travel, horseback riding, music, art. Health. Office: Highmark Inc 1800 Center St Camp Hill PA 17089-0001

**GRAY, LILLIA ANN,** lawyer; b. Miami, Fla., Aug. 18, 1955; d. Elbert Lewis and Lillia Irene (Aschiero) G. AA, Miami-Dade Community Coll., 1976; BA summa cum laude, Cen. Wesleyan Coll., 1979; JD, U. S.C., 1984. Bar: S.C., Ga. Shareholder Cooper, Coffas, Moore and Gray, P.A. Mem. Girl Scouts of Am. (first class and Marion medal). Mem. ABA, Ga. State Bar Assn., Ga. Trial Lawyers Assn., Comml. Law League, S.C. Bar Assn., S.C. Bankruptcy Law Assn., S.C. Women Lawyers Assn. Home: 279 Thornhill Rd Columbia SC 29212-1836

**GRAY, MARVIN LEE, JR.,** lawyer; b. Pitts., May 9, 1945; s. Marvin L. and Frances (Stringfellow) G.; m. Jill Miller, Aug. 14, 1971; children: Elizabeth Ann, Carolyn Jill. AB, Princeton U., 1966; JD magna cum laude, Harvard U., 1969. Bar: Wash. 1973, U.S. Supreme Ct. 1977, Alaska 1984. Law clk. to judge U.S. Ct. Appeals, N.Y.C., 1969-70; law clk. to justice U.S. Supreme Ct., Washington, 1970-71; asst. U.S. atty. U.S. Dept. Justice, Seattle, 1973-76; ptnr. Davis Wright Tremaine, Seattle, 1976—, mng. ptnr., 1985-88; staff counsel Rockefeller Commn. on CIA Activities in U.S., Washington, 1974; lectr. trial practice U. Wash. Law Sch., Seattle, 1979-80. Lay reader Episcopal Ch. of Ascension, Seattle, 1982-94. Capt. USAF, 1971-73. Fellow Am. Coll. Trial Lawyers; mem. ABA, Am. Law Inst. Antitrust, Federal civil litigation. Office: Davis Wright Tremaine 1501 4th Ave Ste 2600 Seattle WA 98101-1688

**GRAY, PAUL BRYAN,** lawyer, historian, arbitrator; b. L.A., Apr. 10, 1938; s. Sylvester Bryan and Alice Esther (Flick) G.; m. Dorothy Jo Knorpp, Aug. 13, 1963 (div. May 1977); children: Christopher, Mark; m. Felipa Rios, July 31, 1987. JD, Hastings Coll. Law, U. Calif., San Francisco, 1968. Assoc. Unthoff, Gomez Vega and Unthoff, Mexico City, 1968-70; pvt. practice, South El Monte, Calif., 1970-93, Claremont, Calif., 1993—; judge pro tem Mcpl. Ct. L.A., 1975—; arbitrator Superior Ct. L.A., 1990—. Author: Forster v. Pico: The Struggle for the Rancho Santa Margarita, 1997. Reader The Huntington Libr., San Marino, Calif., 1985—. General civil litigation. Office: 250 W 1st St Ste 312 Claremont CA 91711-4740

**GRAY, R. BENTON,** lawyer; b. Cleve., July 5, 1951; s. Roland Benton and Esther (Lockwood) G.; m. Kathleen Maloney, Aug. 9, 1998; children: John David, Michael Stuart. BA, Kenyon Coll., 1973; MA, U. Rochester, 1976; JD, Duke U., 1983. Bar: Ohio, 1983, U.S. Dist. Ct. (no. dist.) Ohio 1986, U.S. Ct. Appeals (6th cir.) 1986, U.S. Ct. Appeals (7th cir.) 1997. Assoc. Thompson, Hine and Flory, Cleve., 1983-92; ptnr. Thompson, Hine and Flory LLP, Cleve., 1993-98. Contbr. articles, treatise to profl. jours. Chmn., vice chmn., mem. Citizens Adv. Com., Cleve., 1984-86. Mem. Ohio Bar Assn., Cleve. Bar Assn. General civil litigation, Professional liability, Labor.

Office: R Benton Gray & Co 3900 Key Ctr 25201 Chagrin Blvd Ste 160 Cleveland OH 44122-5633

**GRAY, RICHARD L.,** lawyer; b. El Cajon, Calif., Dec. 5, 1966; s. Harrell A. and Dorothy M. Gray; m. Tara L. Jensen, Sept. 19, 1998. BA, U. Ark., 1989; JD, Washington U., 1996. Law clk. Mo. Supreme Ct., Jefferson City, 1996-97; assoc. Shook, Hardy & Bacon LLP, Kansas City, Mo., 1997—. Active Big Bros./Big Sisters, 1998-99. Mem. Mo. Bar Assn., Kansas City Met. Bar Assn. (torts com. 1998—). Office: Shook Hardy & Bacon LLP 1200 Main St Ste 2100 Kansas City MO 64105-2118

**GRAY, ROBERT JOSEPH,** lawyer; b. Oak Park, Ill., Feb. 15, 1966; s. Donald Frank and Jane Gray; m. Danalee Jacobson, Sept. 2, 1995; 1 child, Parker Robert. BA, U. Ill., 1988; JD, Marquette U., 1991. Bar: Wis. 1991, U.S. Dist. Ct. (ea. and we. dists.) Wis. 1991. Assoc. Jerome A Maeder Law Office, Wausau, Wis., 1991—. Mem. ABA, ATLA, Wis. Bar Assn., Marathon County Bar Assn., Phi Alpha Delta. Personal injury, Workers' compensation, Pension, profit-sharing, and employee benefits. Office: Jerome A Maeder Law Office 602 Jackson St Wausau WI 54403-5549

**GRAY, SIDNEY,** lawyer; b. Milw., Aug. 14, 1933; s. Morris and Anna (Dubb) Goldberg; m. Eileen Betty Baum, May 31, 1953; children: Jodee Lynn, David Scott. BS, U. Wis., 1965; JD, Marquette U., 1967. Bar: Wis. 1967, U.S. Dist. Ct. (ea. dist.) Wis. 1967, U.S. Supreme Ct. Pvt. practice Sidney Gray & Assocs., Milw., 1967—. Avocations: reading, golf, family. Aviation, Personal injury, Probate. Home: 1404 W De La Warr Cir Mequon WI 53092-5040 Office: Sidney Gray & Assocs 135 W Wells St Ste 340 Milwaukee WI 53203-1807

**GRAY, STEVEN JOSEPH,** lawyer; b. Lincoln, Nebr., Apr. 24, 1957; s. Edward W. Gray and Mary Virginia Rielly; m. Nancy Grant Gray, Nov. 30, 1991; children: Hannah Kathleen, Caroline Grant. BA, U. Notre Dame, 1979, MBA, 1982; JD, Case Western Res. U., 1986. Bar: Ill. 1987. Assoc. Arter & Hadden, Cleve., 1987-91, Washington, 1991-93; assoc. Ritter Eichner & Norris, Washington, 1993-94; ptnr. Vedder Price Kaufman & Kammholz, Chgo., 1994—. Author: The Underwriten Offerings, Securities Law Techniques, 1999. Mem. gov. bd., v.p. Scholarship & Guidance Assn., Chgo., 1994—; mem. adv. bd. The Entrepreneurship Inst., Chgo., 1996—. Mem. ABA (fed. regulation securities com. 1998—), Chgo. Bar Assn. Avocations: writing, travel, symphony, golf, tennis. Securities, General corporate, Municipal (including bonds). Office: Vedder Price Kaufman & Kammholz 222 N Lasalle St Chicago IL 60601-1003

**GRAY, WILLIAM CAMPBELL,** lawyer; b. North Wilkesboro, N.C., Mar. 3, 1951. BA, U. N.C., 1973; JD, Wake Forest U., 1976. Bar: N.C., U.S. Dist. Ct. (we. and mid. dists.) N.C., U.S. Ct. Appeals (4th, 5th and 11th cirs.), U.S. Supreme Ct. Ptnr. Cunningham & Gray, Wilkesboro, N.C., 1976—; Bar: N.C., 1976, U.S. Dist. Ct. (we. dist.) N.C., 1977, (mid. dist.) N.C., 1977, U.S. Supreme Ct., 1980, U.S. Ct. Appeals (4th cir.) 1978, (5th cir.) 1981, (11th cir.) 1981; chmn. 23d Jud. Bar Candidate Com., 1991—. Rep. Town of Wilkesboro, 1988—. Mem. 23d Jud. Bar Assn. (pres. 1987), Wilkes County Bar Assn. (pres. 1985), Elks, local country club. Democrat. Methodist. Criminal. Office: Cunningham & Gray PO Box 520 Wilkesboro NC 28697

**GRAY, WILLIAM J.,** lawyer; b. Albany, Nov. 9, 1930; s. Cornelius W. and Irene C. G.; m. Helen W., Aug. 16, 1958; childre: William J., Robert K., Christine M. Elizabeth A. Richard L. BS, Am. U., 1955; LLB, Albany U., 1958, Jd, 1967. Bar: N.Y., U.S. Supreme Ct., U.S. Dist. Ct. (no. dist.) N.Y., U.S. Ct. Claims, U.S. Ct. Appeals. Asst. corp. counsel City of Albany, 1960-62; asst. dist. atty. County of Albany, 1962-69; atty. pvt. practice, Albany, 1960—; lectr. in field. Bd. dirs. Hope House, Albany, 1990—, Lemerick, Albany, 1960—. Staff sgt. U.S. Army, 1951-55. Mem. N.Y. State Trial Lawyers Assn., Albany County Bar Assn., Bethlehem Bus. & Profl. Assn. (pres. 1965—, bd. dirs. 1990—). Roman Catholic. Avocations: travel, golf, charity work, sports. Criminal, Civil rights, Constitutional. Office: 134 State St Albany NY 12207-1628

**GRAY, WILLIAM R.,** lawyer; b. Peoria, Ill., Aug. 25, 1941; s. John J. and Alverna K. (Kennedy) G.; m. Tiana M. Yeager, June 12, 1982; children: Ann Katherine, Thomas William. BA, U. Colo., 1963, JD, 1966. Bar: Colo. 1966; U.S. Dist. Ct. Colo. 1966; U.S. Ct. Appeals (10th cir.) 1976. Dep. dist. atty. Dist. Atty.'s Office/10th Jud. Dist., Pueblo, Colo., 1967-69, Dist. Atty.'s Office/20th Jud. Dist., Boulder, Colo., 1969-70; dep. state pub. defender Colo. State Pub. Defender, Boulder, 1970-72; ptnr. Miller & Gray, Boulder, 1973-85, Purvis, Gray & Gordon, LLP, Boulder, 1985—; mem./vice chair, chmn., Colo. Supreme Ct. grievance com., 1983-88, mem. criminal rules com., 1982-84; adj. prof. law U. Colo. Sch. of Law, Boulder, 1984. Bd. dirs. Mental Health Ctr. of Boulder County, 1972-78. Fellow Am. Coll. Trial Lawyers (Courageous Advocacy award 1985), Internat. Soc. Barristers, Am. Bar Found., Colo. Bar Foun., Colo. Bar Assn. (Professionalism award 1995), Am. Bd. Trial Advocates. Democrat. Personal injury, Product liability, Environmental. Office: Purvis Gray & Gordon LLP 1050 Walnut St Ste 501 Boulder CO 80302-5144

**GRAY-FUSON, JOAN LORRAINE,** lawyer; b. Glendale, Calif., Mar. 25, 1938; d. Stanley Wayne Brune and Maxine Lorraine (Falconer) Talkin; m. Darrell Herbert Gray, June 26, 1959 (div. 1972); children: Michael Herbert Gray, Thomas Edward Gray; m. Arnold Max Fuson, Dec. 18, 1977; children: Marie Fuson Hudson, Karen Fuson, Gregory J. Fuson. BA in Edn., Calif. State U., 1960; JD, U. of the Pacific, 1978. Bar: Calif. 1978, U.S. Dist. Ct. (ea. dist.) Calif. 1978. Tchr. Rio Linda Union Sch. Dist., Sacramento, Calif., 1960-65; pvt. practice Sacramento, 1978-81; staff counsel State of Calif. Water Resources Control Bd., Sacramento, 1982-91; sr. staff counsel State of Calif. Dept. of Conservation, Sacramento, 1991—. Elder on session Fremont Presbyn. Ch., Sacramento, 1995-97. Avocations: gardening, folk dancing, fitness. Office: Dept of Conservation 801 K St # Ms24-3 Sacramento CA 95814-3500

**GRAYSHAW, JAMES RAYMOND,** judge; b. Cleve., Apr. 3, 1948; s. Thomas J. and Bettie Lee (Griffith) G.; m. Susan Hancher, Oct. 15, 1980; 1 child, John H. BA, L.I. U., Bklyn., 1970; JD, Bklyn. Law Sch., 1975. Legal asst. Cadwalader, Wickersham & Taft, N.Y.C., 1975-77; law asst. Civil Ct., City N.Y., 1977-80; sr. law asst. Supreme Ct., State N.Y., 1980-82; judge housing part Civil Ct., City N.Y., 1983—; judge advocate Cmty. Advocacy Ctr., N.Y.C., 1996. Sgt. U.S. Army, 1970-72. Mem. Queens Bar Assn., Protestant Lawyers N.Y.C. (dir. 1980—), Vietnam Vets. Am., 16th Inf. Reg. Assn., Masons. Democrat. Lutheran. Home: 21107 28th Ave Bayside NY 11360-2508 Office: Civil Ct City NY 89-17 Sutphin Blvd Jamaica NY 11435

**GRAYSON, BETTE RITA,** lawyer; b. Newark, July 10, 1947; d. Sidney and Joan (Rosenman) G.; m. Stanley Noah Kruzweil, Aug. 17, 1975; children: Jeremy, Cynthia. BA, NYU, 1969; JD, Bklyn. Law Sch., 1977. Bar: N.J. 1977. Lawyer sole practice Union and Springfield, N.J., 1977—; former real estate counsel City of Plainfield, N.J.; former spl. real estate counsel City of Orange; former rev. atty. for State Bank South Orange, N.J.; chairperson Fee Arbitration Com. Union County, N.J.; mem. adv. bd. Crown Bank. V.p. Millburn (N.J.) Hadassah, 1985-87, mem. steering com. for planned gifts; trustee Internat. Youth Orgn., 1997-98; treas. Millburn Hoopsters, 1997—. Recipient Trust Bklyn. Law Sch., 1974, Woman of Excellence award Union County, 1998. Mem. Women Lawyers Union County (pres. 1990-92, v.p. 1988-90, sec. 1983-84, treas. 1986-88). Democrat. Real property, Family and matrimonial, Land use and zoning (including planning). Office: 140 Mountain Ave Springfield NJ 07081-1725

**GRAYSON, EDWARD DAVIS,** lawyer, manufacturing company executive; b. Davenport, Iowa, June 20, 1938; s. Charles E. and Isabelle (Davis) G.; m. Alice Ann McLaughlin; children: Alice Anne, Maureen Isabelle, Edward Davis Jr. B.A., U. Iowa, 1960, LLB, 1964. Bar: Iowa 1964, Mass. 1967. Atty. Goodwin, Procter & Hoar, Boston, 1967-74; sr. v.p., gen. counsel Wang Labs., Inc., Lowell, Mass., 1974-92; v.p., gen. counsel Honeywell, Inc., Mpls., 1992—. Trustee U. Lowell, Mas., 1981-87, chmn. bd. trustees, 1982-85, 87; dir. Bus. Econs. Edn. Found., 1992—. Capt. USAF, 1964-67. Mem. ABA (com. corp. law depts.), Mass. Bar Assn. (bd. dels. 1977-80), Greater Mpls. C. of C. (dir. 1992—). General corporate. Office: Honeywell Inc Honeywell Plz PO Box 524 Minneapolis MN 55440-0524

**GRAYSON, JOHN ALLAN,** lawyer; b. Lowell, Ind., Oct. 14, 1930; s. Cecil Alaric and May (Modesitt) G.; m. Barbara Burroughs Merrill, Aug. 28, 1954; children: Merrill Ellis, Heather Hartwell Grayson Blalock. BSS, Northwestern U., 1952; JD, U. Mich., 1955. Bar: Mich. 1955, Ind. 1955, U.S. Dist. Ct. (no. dist., so. dist.) Ind. 1955. Assoc. Ross McCord Ice & Miller, Indpls., 1955-65; ptnr. Ice Miller Donadio & Ryan, Indpls., 1966-96; ind. civil mediator, 1996—; vis. asst. prof. Ind. U., Bloomington, 1957-58, adj. instr. real estate law, Indpls., 1959-66; author, lectr., conductor seminars in field; mem. Comparative Law Study delegation to Japan, People's Republic China, 1986. Contbr. numerous articles to profl. jours. Bd. dirs. Greater Indpls. Progress Com., 1981-86, Ind. Repertory Theatre, Inc., 1979-85, Indpls. Arts Chorale, 1982-87, Bosma Industries for Blind, Inc., 1988—, chmn. bd. dirs. 1988-89, Crossroads Rehab. Ctr., 1972-82, pres. 1974-77; mem. First Congregational Ch. Mem. ABA (ho. of dels. 1988-90, nat. conf. lawyers and realtors 1989-92), Ind. State Bar Assn. (sr. lawyers divsn., v.p. 1988, pres. 1989-90), Indpls. Bar Assn. (bd. mgrs. 1985-87), Indpls. Legal Aid Soc., Am. Coll. Real Estate Lawyers (bd. govs. 1987-90), Am. Bar Found., Ind. Bar Foun., Indpls. Bar Found., Ind. Land Title Assn. (hon. life), Kiwanis Club Indpls. (pres. 1994), Internat. Wine and Food Soc., Confrerie de la Chaine des Rotisseurs, Confrerie des Chevaliers du Tastevin, Ind. Repertory Soc. Avocations: travel, golf. Real property, Landlord-tenant, Alternative dispute resolution. Home: 8540 Olde Mill Run Indianapolis IN 46260-5305 Office: 1 American Sq #82001 Indianapolis IN 46282-0002

**GRAYSON, NEIL ESTRIDGE,** lawyer; b. Aug. 11, 1962; s. Patrick H. Jr. Grayson. BA, Wofford Coll., 1984; JD, U. S.C., 1987. Bar: N.Y. 1987, Ga. 1991. Assoc. Cravath, Swaine & Moore, N.Y.C., 1987-91; ptnr. Nelson Mullins Riley & Scarborough, L.L.P., Atlanta, 1991—. Securities. Home: 400 Sassafras Rd Roswell GA 30076-3629 Office: Nelson Mullins Riley & Scarborough LLP 999 Peachtree St NE Atlanta GA 30309-3915

**GRAYSON, RICHARD A.,** lawyer, educator, consultant; b. St. Paul, Minn., Jan. 23, 1930; s. Ellison Capers and Inez Santos (Carroll) G.; m. Carol Grewe, July 22, 1959; children: Pamela, Peter, R. Jon, Jenifer. AB, U. Rochester, 1952; JD, U. Minn., 1958. Bar: Minn., U.S. Dist. Ct. Minn. Assoc. Berryman, Fisher & Johnson, St. Paul, 1958-64; ptnr. Fisher, Johnson & Grayson, St. Paul, 1964-69, Sanborn & Grayson, St. Paul, 1969—; assoc. prof. U. Minn., 1958-94. Author: Funerals Are Stranger Than Fiction, 1994; editor Mortuary Law and Bus. Quar., 1992-98. Lt. USN, 1952-56. Recipient Humane award Am. Humane Soc., 1969, Outstanding Svc. award Minn. Vision Found., 1995. Mem. Rotary (pres. St. Paul chpt. 1989-90), Gyro Club (pres. 1995-97). Probate. Home: 1805 Eagle Ridge Dr Mendota Heights MN 55118 Office: Sanborn & Grayson 50 5th St E Ste 201 Saint Paul MN 55101-1198

**GRAYSON, RUSSELL WAYNE,** lawyer; b. N.Y.C., Oct. 13, 1953; s. Philip and Pearl (Gefter) G.; 1 child, Rebecca Sarah. BA cum laude, CUNY, 1981; JD, Rutgers U., 1984. Bar: N.J. 1985, U.S. Dist. Ct. N.J. 1985, U.S. Supreme Ct. 1992. Trial atty. James D. Butler, PA, Jersey City, 1985-88, Ravich Koster Tobin Oleckna Reitman & Greenstein, Rahway, N.J., 1988-91; mng. ptnr., trial atty. Garces, Grabler & Grayson, Plainfield, N.J., 1991—. Mem. Assn. Trial Laywers Am., N.J. Trial Lawyers Assn., Assn. Criminal Def. Attys. Democrat. Jewish. Criminal, Product liability, Personal injury. Office: Garces Grabler & Grayson 415 Watchung Ave Plainfield NJ 07060-1718

**GRAYSON, ZACHARY LOUIS,** lawyer; b. Phila., Aug. 18, 1959; s. Harry and Shirley (Bogdanoff) Garfinkel; m. Marcia Caren Anstandig, Aug. 4, 1985; children: Ariel Michal, Avi Tzvi, Alexander Shmuel Yosef. BA, U. Pitts., 1985, JD, 1988. Bar: Pa. 1988, U.S. Dist. Ct. (ea. dist.) Pa. 1988;. Lectr. U. Pitts., 1983-84; speechwriter Israeli cultural rep. to greater Pitts. area, 1984-86; trial atty. spl. ops. unit div. enforcement Commodity Futures Trading Commn., Washington, 1988-89; assoc. Cozen and O'Connor, Phila., 1989-92; assoc. Wolf, Block, Schorr and Solis-Cohen, Phila., 1992-96, ptnr., 1996-97; gen. counsel Atlas Comms., Ltd., Blue Bell, Pa., 1997—; spl. counsel Pa. Ins. Commr., 1992-97. Trustee, sec. Jewish Publ. Soc., 1993—; mem. 71st Precinct Community Coun., Bklyn., 1979, Pitts. Conf. Soviet Jewry, 1981; bd. dirs. Zionist Orgn. Am., Pitts., 1982-83; mem. bd. mng. dirs. Labor Zionist Ednl. Ctr., Pitts., 1986-89; pres. Bnai Brith Justice Lodge, 1996-97, founder, trustee Project Justice, 1996—. Mem. ABA (task force on ins. insolvency 1994—), Pa. Bar Assn., Phila. Bar Assn. Jewish. General civil litigation, Communications, Administrative and regulatory. Office: Atlas Comms Ltd Law Dept 484 Norristown Rd Blue Bell PA 19422-2354

**GRAZIANO, CRAIG FRANK,** lawyer; b. Des Moines, Dec. 7, 1950; s. Charles Dominic and Corrine Rose (Comito) G. BA summa cum laude, Macalester Coll., 1973; JD with honors, Drake U., 1975. Bar: Iowa 1976, U.S. Dist. Ct. (no. and so. dists.) Iowa 1978, U.S. Ct. Appeals (8th cir.) 1977, U.S. Supreme Ct. 1988. Law clk. to Hon. M. D. Van Oosterhout U.S. Ct. Appeals (8th cir.), Sioux City, Iowa, 1976-78; assoc. Dickinson, Mackaman, Tyler & Hagen, P.C., Des Moines, 1978-82, ptnr., 1982-98; with Office of Consumer Advocate Iowa Dept. Justice, Des Moines, 1999—. Mem. Gov.'s Task Force on Adminstrv. Rules and Rule-Making, 1999—. Mem. ABA, Iowa Bar Assn. (chair specialization com. 1993-96, chair adminstrv. law sect. 1996-99), Polk County Bar Assn., Order of Coif, Phi Beta Kappa. Administrative and regulatory, Appellate, Public utilities. Home: 500 44th St Des Moines IA 50312-2408 Office: 310 Maple St Des Moines IA 50319-0063

**GRAZIANO, JOHN ANTHONY,** legal administrator; b. Apr. 22, 1944; s. John B. and Lena L. (Barone) G.; m. Aleda Louise CrowningShield; children: John, Jason, and Jessica. BA in Polit. Sci., Villanova U., 1966; MA, Coll. St. Rose, 1976. Exec. sec. profl. licensing svcs. N.Y. State Edn. Dept., 1969-80; pres. Capitol Hill Mgmt. Svcs., Inc., Albany, N.Y., 1980-97; dep. adminstr. Office Atty. Gen. State N.Y., Albany, 1997—. Trustee Albany Bus. Improvement Dist., St. Anne's Inst., Albany County Hist. Soc. Avocations: boating, hunting, and fishing. Home: 4 Sage Hill Ln N Albany NY 12204-1318 Office: Office Atty Gen Divsn Adminstrn Agy Bldg 4 7th Fl Albany NY 12224-0341

**GREAGAN, WILLIAM JOSEPH,** lawyer; b. Albany, N.Y., Feb. 11, 1963; s. William Joseph Greagan and Dolores Sandra Stiles. BA in Polit. Sci., Siena Coll., 1985; JD, Union U., Albany, 1988. Bar: N.Y. 1989, U.S. Dist. Ct. (no. dist.) N.Y. 1989, U.S. Dist. Ct. (we. dist.) N.Y. 1997. From assoc. to ptnr. Carter, Conboy, Case, Blackmore, Napierski & Maloney, P.C., Albany, 1989—; Mem. Def. Rsch. Inst., N.Y. State Bar Assn. Environmental, Product liability, General civil litigation. Home: 165 S Manning Blvd Albany NY 12208-1811 Office: Carter Conboy Case Blackmore Napierski & Maloney PC 20 Corporate Woods Blvd Ste 8 Albany NY 12211-2362

**GREANEY, JOHN M.,** state supreme court justice; b. Westfield, Mass., Apr. 8, 1939; s. Patrick Joseph and Margaret Irene (Fitzgerald) G.; m. Susan H. Greaney, Nov. 23, 1967. 1 child, Jessica S. BA summa cum laude, Holly Cross Coll., 1960; JD, NYU, 1963; LLD (hon.), Westfield State Coll., 1967, Western New England Coll., 1969; LLD, New England Law Sch., 1991. Bar: Mass., Supreme Judicial Ct., U.S. Dist. Ct., U.S. Supreme Ct. Ptnr. Ely & King, Springfield, Mass., 1963-73; presiding judge Hampden County Housing Ct., Springfield, Mass., 1973-75; assoc. judge Mass. Superior Ct., Boston, 1975-76; assoc. justice Mass. Appeals Ct., Boston, 1976-84, 1976-84, chief justice, 1984-89; assoc. justice Mass. Supreme Judicial Ct., Boston, 1989—; former faculty mem. Western New England Law Sch., Westfield State Coll.; co-chair. Supreme Judicial Ct's Gender Bias Study Commn; mem. bd. Tribunes WGBY-Channel #57. Former assoc. editor Mass. Law Review. Trustee, dir. Westfield Atheneum, participant Child and Family Svcs. Program. Fellow Am. Bar Found.; mem. ABA (litigation, judicial adminstrn. section), Hampden County Bar Assn.(former mem. exec. com., grievance com., treas.), Mass. Bar Assn.(former chmn. Young Lawyers section, bd. delegates, exec. com., grievance com., legal svc. to the poor com., (current) civil litigation, criminal law sections ), Am. Law Inst. Avocations: competitive running, reading. Office: Mass Supreme Jud Court Pemberton Sq 1300 New Courthouse Boston MA 02108*

**GREATHEAD, R. SCOTT,** lawyer, human rights advocate; b. Santa Monica, Calif., May 18, 1946; s. Edwin B. and Carolyn (Craig) G.; m. Christina Pennoyer, Jan. 30, 1982 (div. June 1997); children: Katherine, Frances, Molly. AB, Princeton U., 1968; JD, U. Va., 1972. Assoc. Lord, Day & Lord, N.Y.C., 1972-80; dep. chief asst. atty. gen. N.Y. State Atty. Gen.'s Office, N.Y.C., 1980-82, chief asst. atty. gen., 1982-83, 1st asst. atty. gen., 1984-90; ptnr. Owen & Davis PC, N.Y.C., 1990—. Contbr. articles to profl. jours. Bd. dirs. Lawyers Com. for Human Rights, N.Y.C., 1980—, N.Y. League Conservation Voters, N.Y.C., 1992—; gen. counsel Ctr. for Reproductive Law & Policy, N.Y.C., 1992—; mem. bd. advisors Ctr. for Econ. and Social Rights, N.Y.C., 1995—. Mem. Coun. on Fgn. Rels., Assn. Bar of the City of N.Y. General civil litigation. Office: Owen & Davis PC 805 3rd Ave New York NY 10022-7513

**GREAVES, JOHN ALLEN,** lawyer; b. Kansas City, Mo., Feb. 18, 1948; s. John Allen Greaves and Nancy Lee (Farmer) Greaves-Meltzer; m. Sharon Louise Peace Ventura, Dec. 23, 1967 (div. Mar. 1971); 1 child, Karen Christine Greaves Calogne; m. Jerri Lynn Crawford, Sept. 5, 1981. BA in Polit. Sci., U. Mo., 1976; MPA, JD with honors, Drake U., 1992. Bar: Iowa 1992, U.S. Dist. Ct. (so. dist.) Iowa 1992, Calif. 1994, U.S. Dist. Ct. (no. and cen. dists.) Calif. 1994, U.S. Dist. Ct. (so. and ea. dists.) Calif . 1995, U.S. Dist. Ct. N.Mex. 1995, U.S. Ct. Appeals (9th cir.) 1995, U.S. Dist. Ct. (no. dist.) N.Y. 1996, U.S. Dist. Ct. S.C. 1995, U.S. Ct. Appeals (4th and 10th cirs.) 1996. Pres., CEO VIPilot Svcs., Inc., Kansas City, 1980-83; pilot Air Illinois, Carbondale, Ill., 1983-84, Wright Airlines, Cleve., 1983-84, ComAir Airlines, Cin., 1984-88; jud. law clk. to Hon. Arthur E. Gamble Iowa Dist. Ct., Des Moines, 1990-91; pvt. practice Des Moines, 1992-94; assoc. Baum, Hedlund, Aristei, Guilford & Downey, L.A., 1994—; mem. plaintiffs' steering com. Atlantic S.E. Airlines crash, Carrollton, Ga., 1995. Mem. ABA, ATLA, Airline Pilots Assn., Plaintiff's Steering Com., Atlatnic Southeast Airlines Crash Near Carollton, GA, 1995, (chmn. contract adminstrn. com. 1985-87, Disting. Svc. award 1987), Lawyer/Pilot Bar Assn., State Bar Calif., State Bar Iowa, Iowa Trial Lawyers Assn., Delta Theta Phi. Avocations: aviation, snow and water skiing, boating and sailing, tennis, golf. Aviation, Personal injury, Product liability. Home: 3664 May St Los Angeles CA 90066-3606 Office: Baum Hedlund Aristei Gilford & Downey 12100 Wilshire Blvd Ste 950 Los Angeles CA 90025-7107

**GREBE, MICHAEL W.,** lawyer; b. Peoria, Ill., Oct. 25, 1940. BS, U.S. Mil. Acad., 1962; JD magna cum laude, U. Mich., 1970. Bar: Wis. 1970. Ptnr. Foley & Lardner, Milw. Note and comment editor U. Mich. Law Review, 1969-70. Mem. State Bar Wis., Milw. Bar Assn., Order of Coif. General corporate. Office: Foley & Lardner 777 E Wisconsin Ave Ste 3800 Milwaukee WI 53202-5367*

**GREBOW, ARTHUR JEFFREY,** lawyer; b. N.Y.C., Nov. 17, 1942; s. Karl and Shirley G.; m. Helen M., June 19, 1965; children—Jennifer, Katherine, Matthew. B.A., Columbia U., 1964; J.D., Cornell U., 1967. Bar: Calif. 1968, U.S. Dist. Ct. (cen. and so. dists.) Calif. 1968. Law clk. to judge Calif. Ct. Appeals, 1967-68; assoc. Cruikshank, Antin & Grebow and predecessor, Los Angeles, 1969-75, ptnr., 1975-83, Antin, Stern, Litz& Grebow, Los Angeles, 1983—; judge pro tem Beverly Hills Mcpl. Ct., 1973—, Los Angeles Mcpl. Ct., 1977—; arbitrator Los Angeles Superior Ct., 1980—; lectr. continuing edn. of bar, evaluating and proving damages, 1977. Mem. ABA, State Bar Calif. (hearing referee 1980—), Los Angeles County Bar Assn., Beverly Hills Bar Assn. (gov. 1976-78, editor Jour. 1975), Assn. Bus. Trial Lawyers, Calif. Bus. Trial Lawyers Assn. State civil litigation, Federal civil litigation, Family and matrimonial. Office: 10900 Wilshire Blvd Ste 600 Los Angeles CA 90024-6501

**GRECH, CHRISTOPHER ALAN,** lawyer; b. Richmond, Va., Oct. 5, 1960; s. George Alfred and Stella Mary Grech. BS in Mktg. and Mgmt., Fordham U., 1982; JD, Calif. Western Sch. of Law, San Diego, 1985. Bar: N.J. 1987, U.S. Dist. Ct. N.J. 1987, Md. 1993, D.C. 1994, N.Y. 1995. Solo practitioner Hackensack, N.J., 1988-94, Berlin, Md., 1994—. Mem. ABA, City of Balt. Bar Assn., Bergen County Bar Assn., Internat. Law Soc., Md. Trial Lawyers Assn., Worcester County Bar Assn., Ocean Pines Yacht Club, Ocean Pines Country Club, KC, Phi Alpha Delta. Avocations: fishing, tennis, boating, jogging, bicycling. General civil litigation, General practice, Criminal. Home: 76 Teal Cir Berlin MD 21811-1542 Office: 7200 Coastal Hwy Ste 306 Ocean City MD 21842-2932

**GRECO, GUY BENJAMIN,** lawyer; b. Glen Ridge, N.J., May 28, 1951; s. Benjamin Francis and Dorothy Ann (Smith) G.; m. Marietta Suzanne D'Oro, June 16, 1973 (div. 1984); m. Pamela Ann Beckham McGuire, Feb. 2, 1993. BA, Rutgers U., 1973, JD, 1976. Bar: N.J. 1976, Oreg. 1977, U.S. Dist. Ct. N.J. 1976, Oreg. 1977, U.S. Supreme Ct. 1984. Assoc. Litchfield, MacPherson & Carstens, Newport, Oreg., 1977-81; ptnr. Greco & Escobar, Newport, 1981-89; pvt. practice Newport, 1989—. Chmn. Lincoln County Red Cross, Newport, 1979; pres. Oreg. Coast Coun. for the Arts, 1988-89. Mem. ABA, Oreg. Bar Assn., Lincoln County Bar Assn., Oreg. State Bar (counsel 1985, spl. task force on legal technicians 1991-92, legal assts. com. 1989-92, unlawful practice of law com. 1992-95, disciplinary bd. 1993-99, legal ethics com. 1995-98, client security fund com., 1998—, local profl. responsibility com.). Democrat. Criminal, Personal injury, Workers' compensation. Office: PO Box 1070 Newport OR 97365-0081

**GREEN, BRUCE,** lawyer; b. Sallisaw, Okla.; s. J. Fred and Bulah G.; m. Barbara Ann Green; children: Robert Bruce Green Jr., Catherine A. Green Watson. Grad., Northeastern State Coll., 1955; JD, U. Okla., 1957. With Green, Green, & Green, 1958-61; asst. U.S. atty. U.S. Dist. Ct. (ea. dist.) Okla., 1961, U.S. atty., 1965-69; pvt. practice Muskogee, Okla., 1969-91; asst. U.S. atty. U.S. Dist. Ct. (ea. dist.) Okla., 1991, sr. litig. counsel, 1992-96, civil chief, 1996—; U.S. atty. U.S. Dist. Ct. (ea. dist.) Okla.atty, 1997—. With USAR. Fax: 918-684-5130. Office: US Atty's Office 1200 W Okmulgee St Muskogee OK 74401-6848*

**GREEN, CAROL H.,** lawyer, educator, journalist; b. Seattle, Feb. 18, 1944. BA in History/Journalism summa cum laude, La. Tech. U., 1965; MSL, Yale U., 1977; JD, U. Denver, 1979. Reporter Shreveport (La.) Times, 1965-66, Guam Daily News, 1966-67; city editor Pacific Jour., Agana, Guam, 1967-68, reporter, editl. writer, 1968-76, legal affairs reporter, 1977-79; asst. editor editl. page Denver Post, 1979-81, house counsel, 1980-83, labor rels. mgr., 1981-83; assoc. Holme Roberts & Owen, 1983-85; v.p. human resources and legal affairs Denver Post, 1985-87, mgr. circulation, 1988-90; gen. mgr. Distbn. Systems Am., Inc., 1990-92; dir. labor rels. Newsday, 1992-95, dir. comm. & labor rels., 1996-97; v.p. Weber Mgmt. Cons., 1997-98; v.p. human resources Denver Post, 1998—; 1985 speaker for USIA, India, Egypt; mem. Mailers Tech. Adv. Com. to Postmaster Gen., 1991-92. Recipient McWilliams award for juvenile justice, Denver, 1971, award for interpretive reporting Denver Newspaper Guild, 1979. Mem. ABA (forum on comm. law), Colo. Bar Assn. (bd. govs. 1985-87, chair BAR-press com. 1980), Newspaper Assn. Am. (mem. human resources and labor rels. com.), Denver Bar Assn. (co-chiar jud. sel. and benefits com. 1982-85, 2st v.p. 1986), Colo. and Internat. Women's Dorum, Leadership Denver, Human Resources Planning Soc., Soc. Human Resources Mgmt., Indsl. Rels. Rsch. Assn., Colo. Assn. Human Resources Assn., Huntington Camera Club. Episcopalian.

**GREEN, CAROLYN F.,** lawyer; b. Seattle, July 24, 1953; m. Kenneth Kenneth F. Green, June 11, 1963; children: Leslie, Allison. BA, U. Mass., 1965; JD, Western State U., Fullerton, Calif., 1989. Bar: Calif. 1990. Sole practitioner Orange, Calif., 1990—. Avocations: gardening, reading, music. Family and matrimonial. Office: 1 City Blvd W Ste 1110 Orange CA 92868-3649

**GREEN, CLIFFORD SCOTT,** federal judge; b. Phila., Apr. 2, 1923; s. Robert Lewis and Alice (Robinson) G.; m. Mabel Wood, June 20, 1959. B.S., Temple U., 1948, J.D., 1951. Bar: Pa. 1952. Practiced law Phila., 1952-64; dep. atty. gen. State of Pa., 1954; judge County Ct., Phila., 1964-68, Ct. Common Pleas, 1968-71; judge U.S. Dist. Ct. for Eastern Dist. Pa., Phila., 1971-88, sr. judge, 1988—; former lectr. in law Temple U.

Former bd. dirs. Children's Aid Soc. of Pa.; former bd. mgrs. Children's Hosp., Phila.; trustee Temple U. Served with USAAF, 1943-46. Recipient Judge William Hastie award NAACP Legal Def. Fund, 1985, awards for community service Women's Christian Alliance, awards for community service Health and Welfare Council, awards for community service Opportunities Industrialization Center, J. Austin Norris Barrister's award, 1988, Temple Law Alumni Assn. award 1994, Justice Thurgood Marshall Meml. award Nat. Bar Assn., 1994. Mem. Sigma Pi Phi. Presbyterian. Office: US Courthouse Independence Mall W #15613 601 Market St Philadelphia PA 19106-1713

**GREEN, CUMER L.,** lawyer; b. Moscow, Idaho, Oct. 6, 1941; s. Leon Grant and Gwen Pratt G.; m. JoAnne Ames; children: Scott, Cliff, Holly, Stephen, Chris. BS in Bus., U. Idaho, 1963, MA in Acctg., 1969, JD, 1969. Bar: Idaho 1969; U.S. Dist. Ct. Idaho, 1969, U.S. Ct. Appeals (9th cir.) 1971, U.S. Tax Ct. 1971, U.S. Dist. Ct. (cen. dist.) Calif. 1987; CPA, Idaho. Assoc. Eberle & Berlin, Boise, 1969-71; pvt. practice Boise, 1971-72; ptnr. Green & Bithell, Boise, 1972-75, Green & Frost, Boise, 1973-75, Green & Cantrill, Boise, 1975-80, Green & Sullivan, Boise, 1980-81; owner Green Law Offices, Boise, 1981-88, 90—; ptnr. Green & Nyman, Boise, 1988-90. Treas. Ford for Pres., Boise; chmn. Gov's Task Force on Local Govt. Revenue Problems, 1970; prin. sponser Law Inst., Boise, 1992—. With USMC, 1959-60. Mem. ABA, Nat. Bd. Sch. Attys., Idaho State Bar Assn. (commr. 1995-98, pres. 1998), Idaho State Code Commn. (commr. 1998—), Phi Alpha Delta. Republican. Avocation: jogging, skiing. E-mail: cumer-green@aol.com. General civil litigation, Taxation, general, Education and schools. Office: PO Box 2597 Boise ID 83701-2597*

**GREEN, ERIC HOWARD,** lawyer; b. N.Y.C., Jan. 5, 1950; s. Bernard and Edith Green; m. Mona M. Green, July 10, 1982; children: Zachary Samuel, Shawn Alexander. BA, SUNY, Buffalo, 1972, JD, 1976. Bar: N.Y. 1977, U.S. Dist. Ct. (so. and ea. dist.) N.Y. 1979, U.S. Supreme Ct. 1985. Assoc. Pops & Estrin, N.Y.C., 1976-77, Karp & Silver, Queens, N.Y., 1977-81, Edward Leshaw, Esq., N.Y.C., 1981-82; mng. ptnr. Eric H. Green, Esq., N.Y.C., 1982—; instr. Nat. Inst. of Trial Advocacy, Cardoza Law Sch., N.Y.C., 1987—, U. Buffalo, coll. of Urban Studies, 1974-76; lectr. NYU, Sch. Continuing Edn., N.Y.C., 1986-90; arbitrator Am. Arbitration Assn., 1987—. Mem. N.Y. Dem. Judicial Screening Panel, N.Y.C., 1989; advisor, vol. N.Y.C. Open Doors Edn. Program, 1985-89. Mem. ATLA, N.Y. County Lawyers Assn., N.Y. State Bar Assn., N.Y. State Trial Lawyers Assn. (bd. dirs., speaker cmty. speakers bur. 1988—), N.Y. County Lawyers Assn. (fee dispute com., Supreme Ct. com.), Assn. Bar City N.Y. (tort litigation com., chmn. mediation subcom.). Avocations: sports, theatre, antiques. Personal injury, General civil litigation, General practice. Office: 295 Madison Ave New York NY 10017-6304

**GREEN, EVE MARIE,** lawyer; b. Chgo., Apr. 9, 1964; d. Thomas Francis and Dorothy Marie Spinelle; m. Michael Christopher Green, Nov. 5, 1988; 1 child, Jessica. BSN, Marquette U., 1986; JD, John Marshall Law Sch., 1991. Bar: Ill. 1991, Hawaii 1991, U.S. Dist. Ct. (no. dist.) Ill. 1991, U.S. Dist. Ct. Hawaii 1991. Assoc. Schutter & Glickstein, Honolulu, 1991-94, Bollinger, Ruberry & Garvey, Chgo., 1994-96, Law Office of James Krueger, Wailuku, 1997—. Mem. ATLA, ABA, Am. Assn. of Nurse Attys., Ill. State Bar Assn. General civil litigation, Personal injury, Product liability. Home: 115 Kulalani Dr Kula HI 96790-9611 Office: Law Office of James Krueger 2065 Main St Wailuku HI 96793-1693

**GREEN, HARLAND NORTON,** lawyer, accountant; b. Los Angeles, Feb. 14, 1930; s. William and Lena (Schwimer) G.; m. Melva Nudelman, Dec. 20, 1953. BS in Acctg., UCLA, 1951, JD, 1953; LLM in Taxation, U. S.C., 1962. Bar: Calif. 1955, U.S. Supreme Ct. 1963. Accountant J. Arthur Greenfield & Co., CPA's, Los Angeles, 1956-58; assoc. atty. Rosenthal & Green and predecessors, Beverly Hills, Calif., 1958-61, ptnr., 1961-68; pvt. practice Beverly Hills, 1969-72; pres. Harland N. Green, P.C., Beverly Hills, 1972—. Contbr. articles to UCLA Law Rev. Vice chmn., bd. trustees So. Calif. chpt. Nat. Multiple Sclerosis Soc. Named an Outstanding Trustee So. Calif. chpt. Multiple Sclerosis Soc., 1966, Most Valuable Trustee, 1976. Mem. ABA, Calif. Bar Assn., Beverly Hills Bar Assn., Assn. Attys.-CPA's Los Angeles Copyright Soc., Order of Coif, Phi Beta Kappa, Beta Gamma Sigma. Estate planning, Probate, Estate taxation.

**GREEN, JAMES FRANCIS,** lawyer, consultant; b. Pittsfield, Mass., Oct. 1, 1948; s. Earl Levi and Frances Eleanor (Walshe) G.; m. Eileen Mary Kelly, July 31, 1971; children: Michael Walshe, Maura Kelly, Kelsey Kathryn. BA, St. Anselm Coll., 1970; JD, Suffolk U., 1973. Bar: Mass. 1973, U.S. Dist. Ct. Mass. 1974, U.S. Ct. Appeals (D.C. cir.) 1975, U.S. Dist. Ct. D.C. 1975, U.S. Supreme Ct. 1977, U.S. Ct. Appeals (4th cir.) 1978. Rsch. counsel Joint Com. on Jud. Reform of Joint Jud. Com. of Gen. Ct. Commonwealth of Mass., Boston, 1973-74; ptnr. Drucas, Edgerton & Green, Salem, Mass., 1974; gen. ptnr. Ashcraft & Gerel, Washington, 1975—; presdl. appointment Nat. Ad Hoc Com. on Disability. Mem. Mass. Bar Assn., Boston Bar Assn., Fed. Bar Assn. (bd. dirs. Washington chpt., 1985-86, internat. law com.), Bar Assn. D.C., D.C. Bar Assn., ABA (torts and ins. practice law sections, vice chmn. nat. com. on liaison with the judicial adminstrn.), Assn. Trial Lawyers of Am. (section chmn. nat. com. on workers compensation 1989-90), Am. Soc. Law and Medicine. Democrat. Roman Catholic. Personal injury, Workers' compensation, Federal civil litigation. Home: 6522 Heather Brook Ct Mc Lean VA 22101-1607 Office: Ashcraft & Gerel 4900 Seminary Rd Ste 650 Alexandria VA 22311-1878

**GREEN, JAMES R.,** lawyer; b. Ann Arbor, Mich., Aug. 23, 1943; s. Clarence Raymond and Mary (Steere) G.; m. Harriet Louise Earl, July 5, 1969; children: Elizabeth, James R., Kathryn, Annie, Joe. Student, U. Mich., 1961-63, No. Mich. U., 1964-65, Wayne State U., 1965; BS, Eastern Mich. U., 1968; JD, U. tulsa, 1977. Bar: Fla., U.S. Dist. Ct. (no. dist.) Fla., U.S. Ct. Appeals (11th cir.); bd. cert. trial lawyer, Fla.; cert. Nat. Bd. Trial Advocacy. Ptnr. Levin, Middlebrooks, Thomas, Mitchell, Green, Echsner, Proctor & Papantonio, Pensacola, Fla., 1977—. Lt. comdr. USN, 1968-74. Mem. ABA, ATLA, Excambia-Santa Rosa Bar Assn., Acad. Fla. Trial Lawyers, Am. Judicature Soc. Democrat. Methoist. Avocations: golf, horseback riding. General civil litigation, Personal injury, Product liability. Home: 7050 Luth Rd Molino FL 32577-9437 Office: Levin Middlebrooks et al 316 S Baylen St Pensacola FL 32501-5900

**GREEN, JAMES SAMUEL,** lawyer; b. Berwick, Pa., May 24, 1947; m. Carla Eyer; children: Jennifer, Emily, James Samuel Jr., Jared. AB, Princeton U., 1969; JD, Villanova U., 1972. Bar: Del. 1972, Pa. 1973, U.S. Dist. Ct. Del. 1973, U.S. Ct. Appeals (3d cir.) 1981, U.S. Supreme Ct. 1990. Assoc. Connolly, Bove, Lodge & Hutz, Wilmington, Del., 1972-74, ptnr., 1977-90; dep. atty. gen. State of Del., Wilmington, 1975-76; ptnr. Duane Morris & Heckscher, Wilmington, 1990-99, Seitz, Van Ogtrop & Green, P.A., Wilmington, 1999—. Mem. Del. Bd. Unauthorized Practice of Law, chmn., 1994-99; bd. dirs. Blue-White, Inc., David Wellborn Found. Mem. ABA, ATLA, Am. Bd. Trial Advocates (nat. bd. dirs. 1991—), Del. State Bar Assn. (treas. 1980-81, chmn. litigation sect. 1988-91), Ivy Club (Princeton), Wilmington Country Club. Federal civil litigation, State civil litigation, Libel. Home: 2603 W 17th St Wilmington DE 19806-1108 Office: Seitz Van Ogtrop & Green PA PO Box 68 Wilmington DE 19899-0068

**GREEN, JAY NELSON,** lawyer; b. Kilgore, Tex., Jan. 11, 1958; s. James Perry and Ouida Norris G.; m. Ellen Elizabeth Bradley, Aug. 16, 1980; children: Cullen, Mason, Weston. BBA, Baylor U., 1979, JD, 1982. Bar: Tex.; U.S. Dist. Ct. (ea. dist. Tex.) 1983; U.S. Ct. Appeals (5th cir.) 1983; cert. Tex. Bd. Legal Specialization. Mem. staff Potter, Minton, Roberts, Davis & Jones, Tyler, Tex., 1982—; pres. Tyler Teen Ct, Inc., 1990-91; v.p. Smith County Young Lawyers, Tyler, 1985; instr. Tyler Jr. Coll., 1987. Mem. steering com. Bush Re-election for Smith County, Tyler, 1998; chmn. Smith County, Tom Phillips Campaign, Tyler, 1988. Named Smith County Outstanding Young Lawyer, 1991. Baptist. Avocations: golf, family. Professional liability, Municipal (including bonds), Personal injury. Office: Potter Minton Roberts Davis & Jones PC PO Box 359 Tyler TX 75710-0359

**GREEN, JEFFREY C.,** lawyer; b. Newark, July 6, 1941; s. Albert and Mildred (Rosenberg) G.; m. Iris Landow, Aug. 23, 1964; children: Michelle, Marlene. BA, Rutgers U., 1963, JD, 1966; postgrad., Nat. Coll. State Judiciary, Reno, 1974-75. Bar: N.J. 1966, U.S. Dist. Ct. N.J. 1966. Law clk. to judge N.J. Superior Ct., Middlesex County Ct., New Brunswick, 1966-67; assoc. Toolan, Romond & Burgess, Perth Amboy, N.J., 1967-68; ptnr. Green & Green and predecessors, Somerset, N.J., 1968—; prosecutor Franklin Twp. Mcpl. Ct., Somerset, 1969-70, mcpl. judge, 1970-76, 97—; judge Millstone (N.J.) Mcpl. Ct., 1970-76, Manville (N.J.) Mcpl. Ct., 1972-73; atty. Cranbury (N.J.) Bd. Adjustment, 1978—. Legal counsel Temple Beth El, Somerset, 1974—; bd. dirs. Middlesex County Legal Svcs. Corp., New Brunswick, 1983—. Named Man of Yr., Temple Beth El, 1984; recipient Pro Bono Achievement award Middlesex County Legal Svcs. Corp., 1985, 87. Mem. N.J. State Bar Assn. (trustee 1997—, Gen. Practitioner of Yr. award 1997), Middlesex County Bar Assn. (pres. 1985-86), Middlesex County Bar Found. (trustee 1990—, pres. 1994-95), Franklin Twp. Jaycees (pres. 1970-71), Lions Club. Democrat. Contracts commercial, General corporate, General practice. Home: 3 Denise Ct Somerset NJ 08873-2834 Office: Green & Green PO Box 5321 Somerset NJ 08875-5321

**GREEN, JERSEY MICHAEL-LEE,** lawyer; b. Washington, Feb. 29, 1952; m. Jonelle Sue Burke, May 12, 1988. BA in criminology, U. Md., 1976; JD, Syracuse U., 1983. Bar: Colo. 1983, U.S. Dist. Ct. Colo. 1983, U.S. Ct. Appeals (10th cir.) 1983, U.S. Tax Ct. 1983, U.S. Ct. Appeals (9th cir.) 1987, U.S. Supreme Ct. 1988, U.S. Ct. Appeals (2d cir.) 1990, U.S. Dist. Ct. Ariz. 1994. Atty. Wagner & Waller, P.C., Denver, 1983-86, Waller, Mark & Allen, P.C., Denver, 1986-89, Orten & Hindman P.C., Denver, 1989-90, Elrod, Katz, Preeo, Look, Moison & Silverman, P.C., Denver, 1990-97, Preeo, Silverman & Green, P.C., Denver, 1998—. Mem. exec. com. staff Lawyers for Romer, Denver, 1986; precinct committeeman, 1989-92. Recipient Syracuse (N.Y.) Def. Group scholarship, 1982. Mem. Assn. Trial Lawyers Am., Colo. Trial Lawyers Assn., Arapahoe County Bar Assn., Syracuse U. Alumni Assn. (pres. Colo. 1987-89). Democrat. Avocations: mountaineering, skiing, running. E-mail: Jersey@preeosilv.com. General civil litigation. Office: Preeo Silverman and Green PC 1401 17th St Ste 800 Denver CO 80202-1246

**GREEN, JOSEPH LIBORY,** lawyer; b. St. Louis, Mar. 20, 1960; s. Joseph Richard and Kathleen Ann Green; m. Sherry Michelle Fedder, Oct. 7, 1989; children: Bryan Smith, Samantha Joe Green, Jacob Fedder Green, Jacqueline Michelle Green. BSBA, Truman State U., 1982; JD, St. Louis U., 1987. Bar: Mo. 1988, U.S. Dist. Ct. (ea. dist.) Mo. 1993, U.S. Dist. Ct. (we. dist.) Mo. 1996, U.S. Ct. Appeals (8th cir.) 1998, U.S. Supreme Ct. 1998. Asst. pub. def. St. Joseph (Mo.) Pub. Def.'s Office, 1988; chief trial atty. St. Louis County Pub. Def.'s Office, Clayton, Mo., 1989-90; capital litigation atty. Mo. State Pub. Def.'s Office, St. Louis, 1990-93; assoc. Wittner, Poger, Rosenblum & Spewak, P.C., Clayton, 1993-96; sole practitioner St. Charles, Mo., 1996; ptnr. Baerveldt, Bagsby, Lee & Green, L.L.C., St. Charles, 1996—. Dem. candidate for county prosecutor, St. Charles, 1994, 98. Mem. Nat. Assn. Criminal Def. Lawyers, Mo. Assn. Criminal Def. Lawyers. Criminal, Civil rights, Personal injury. Office: Baerveldt Bagsby Lee & Green LLP 566 1st Capitol Dr Saint Charles MO 63301-2726

**GREEN, JOYCE HENS,** federal judge; b. N.Y.C., Nov. 13, 1928; d. James S. and Hedy (Bucher) Hens; m. Samuel Green, Sept. 25, 1965 (dec.); children: Michael Timothy, June Heather, James Harry. BA, U. Md., 1949; JD, George Washington U., 1951, LLD, 1994. Practice law Washington, 1951-68, Arlington, Va., 1956-68; ptnr. Green & Green, 1966-68; assoc. judge Superior Ct., D.C., 1968-79; judge U.S. Dist. Ct. for D.C., 1979—; judge presiding U.S. Fgn. Intelligence Surveillance Ct., 1988-95; bd. advisors George Washington U. Law Sch. Co-author: Dissolution of Marriage, 1986, supplements, 1987-89; contbr. supplements Marriage and Family Law Agreements, 1985-89. Chair Task Force on Gender, Race and Ethnic Bias for the D.C. Cir. Recipient Alumni Achievement award George Washington U., 1975, Profl. Achievement award, 1978, Outstanding Contbn. to Equal Rights award Women's Legal Def. Fund, 1976, hon. doctor of Laws George Washington U., 1994, U.S. Dept. Justice Edmund J. Randolph award Jud. Conf. of U.S., 1995. Fellow Am. Bar Found.; ABA (jud. adminstrn. divsn., chair nat. conf. fed. trial judges), Fed. Judges Assn., Nat. Assn. Women Judges, Va. Bar Assn., Bar Assn. D.C. (jud. honoree of Yr. 1994), D.C. Bar, D.C. Women's Bar Assn., (pres. 1960-62, women lawyer of yr. 1979), Exec. Women in Govt. (chmn. 1977), Lawyers Club of Washington, Woman's Forum of Washington D.C. Office: US Dist Barrett Prettyman US Courthouse 333 Constitution Ave NW Washington DC 20001-2802

**GREEN, JUNE LAZENBY,** federal judge; b. Arnold, Md., Jan. 23, 1914; d. Eugene H. and Jessie T. (Briggs) Lazenby; m. John Cawley Green, Sept. 5, 1936. JD, Am. U., 1941. Bar: Md. 1943, D.C. 1945. Claims adjuster Lumbermans Mut. Casualty Co., Washington, 1942-43, claims atty., 1943-47; pvt. practice Washington Bldg., Washington, 1947-68; pvt. practice Annapolis (Md.) br. office Washington Bldg., 1950-68; judge U.S. Dist. Ct. D.C., 1968-84, sr. judge, 1984—; mem. spl. ct. Regional Reorganization Railroad Act, 1987-97; examiner bar, Washington, 1963-68. Named Woman Lawyer of Yr., 1965; recipient Lifetime Achievement award Alumni Assn. of Am. U., 1986. Mem. ABA, Md. Bar Assn., Bar Assn. D.C. (bd. dirs. 1966-68, award 1984), Women's Bar Assn. D.C. (pres. 1955-57), Federal Judges Assn., Am. Jud. Soc. Home: 464 W Joyce Ln Arnold MD 21012-2207 also: 550 N St SW Washington DC 20024-4643 Office: US Dist Ct US Courthouse 333 Constitution Ave NW Washington DC 20001-2802

**GREEN, LAWRENCE RODMAN,** lawyer; b. N.Y.C., June 20, 1946; s. Julius and Ethel (Rodman) G.; m. Judith Jaffess, Apr. 7, 1978; children: Douglas, Jeffrey, Emily. BA, Rutgers Coll., 1968; JD, Hofstra U., 1978; MA, New Sch. Social Rsch., 1975. Bar: N.Y. 1979, Fla. 1980. Asst. dist. atty. N.Y. County Dist. Atty.'s Office, N.Y.C., 1978-81; ptnr. Lester Schwab Katz & Dwyer, N.Y.C., 1981—. With U.S. Army, 1968-71. Mem. SAE (affiliate), Am. Boat and Yacht Coun. E-mail: lgreen@lskdnylaw.com. Product liability, General civil litigation. Home: 16 Farview Rd Millburn NJ 07041-1707 Office: Lester Schwab Katz & Dwyer 120 Broadway Fl 39 New York NY 10271-0002

**GREEN, NORMAN HARRY,** lawyer; b. L.A., Nov. 11, 1952; s. Leonard L. and Lily (Merecki) G.; m. Rachel Rubin, Oct. 19, 1980; children: Andrew S., L. Stephen. AB, U. Calif., Irvine, 1974; JD, UCLA, 1979. Bar: Calif. 1979; cert. specialist taxation U.S. Tax Ct. Tax auditor IRS, San Francisco, 1974-76; customs officer U.S. Customs Svc., L.A., 1977; tax acct. Arthur Andersen & Co., L.A., 1979-80; lawyer Barclay & Moskatel, Beverly Hills, Calif., 1980-84; ptnr., tax lawyer Irsfeld, Irsfeld & Younger, Glendale, Calif., 1984—. Dir., gen. counsel June Ebensteiner Hospice Found., Calabasas, Calif., 1990—. Mem. Glendale Bar Assn., L.A. County Bar Assn. (chmn. arbitration com. 1995-97), Glendale C. of C. (chmn. legis. action com. 1986-89), Kiwanis (Hollywood sec. 1990-93, pres. 1993-94). Avocations: hiking, gourmet cooking, singing. Estate planning, Probate, Taxation, general. Office: Irsfeld Irsfeld & Younger LLP 100 W Broadway Ste 900 Glendale CA 91210-1296

**GREEN, PHILIP R.,** lawyer; b. London, Eng.; came to U.S., 1957; m. Beverly Robin Green. BA, UCLA, 1975; JD, Western State U., 1979. Bar: Calif. 1980. Assoc. Herron & Herron Law Offices, San Francisco, 1981-83; founding mem. Law Offices of Green & Green, Marin County, Calif., 1984—; ptnr. Law Offices of Green & Green, San Rafael, San Francisco, 1984—. Author legal texts on intellectual property. Bd. dirs. San Rafael Redevel. Agy. Bus. Improvement Dist., 1987-94, SofTECH-North Bay Software and Info. Tech. Assn., San Rafael, 1997-98. Recipient Cert. Recognition Calif. State Legis., 1987, Resolution of Appreciation City of San Rafael, 1994, Pro Bono Legal Svc. award Calif. State Bar Assn., 1987. Mem. Marin County Bar Assn. (co-chair intellectual property sect. 1998—). Avocations: tennis, winter sports, swimming. Intellectual property, Trademark and copyright, Computer. Office: Law Offices of Green & Green 1700 Montgomery St Ste 111 San Francisco CA 94111-1022 also: Law Offices of Green & Green 1000 4th St Ste 595 San Rafael CA 94901-3136

**GREEN, RICHARD,** lawyer, psychiatrist, educator; b. Bklyn., June 6, 1936; s. Leo Harry and Rose (Ingber) G.; m. Melissa Hines; 1 child, Adam Hines-Green. AB, Syracuse U., 1957; MD, Johns Hopkins U., 1961; JD, Yale U., 1987. Diplomate Am. Bd. Psychiatry and Neurology; bar: Calif. 1987, D.C. 1989. Intern Kings County Hosp., Bklyn., 1962-64; resident in psychiatry UCLA Neuropsychiat. Inst., 1962-64, NIMH, Bethesda, Md., 1965-66; from asst. prof. to prof. dept. psychiatry UCLA, 1968-74; prof. psychiatry and psychology SUNY, Stony Brook, 1974-85; prof. psychiatry UCLA, 1986-94, prof. law, 1988-90, prof. emeritus psychiatry, 1994—; affiliated lectr., faculty of law Cambridge U., 1994—; faculty mem. law sch. UCLA, 1991-92; head dir. of rsch., cons. psychiatrist Gender Identity Clinic Charing Cross Hosp., London; vis. fellow, sr. rsch. fellow Inst. Criminology, Cambridge U., 1994—. Author: Sexual Identity Conflict in Children and Adults, 1974, Impotence, 1981, The Sissy Boy Syndrome and the Development of Homosexuality, 1987, Sexual Science and the Law, 1992; co-editor: Transsexualism and Sex Reassignment, 1969, Sociolegal Control of Homosexuality: A Multination Comparison, 1997; editor: Human Sexuality: A Health Practitioner's Text, 1975, 2d edit., 1979; editor Jour. Archives of Sexual Behavior, 1971—. Vol. atty., ACLU, LA. Vis. scholar U. Cambridge, Eng., 1980-81, Fulbright scholar King's Coll., London, and Univ. Cambridge, 1992; fellow Ctr. Advanced Study in Behavioral Scis., Stanford, Calif., 1982-83. Fellow Royal Coll. Psychiatrists, Soc. Sci. Study of Sex (pres. 1974-77), Internat. Acad. Sex Rsch. (founding pres. 1973, elected pres. 1998—); mem. Calif. Bar Assn., D.C. Bar Assn., Harry Benjamin Internat. Gender Dysphoria Assn. (pres. 1998-99). Avocations: photography, traveling, antiques. Civil rights, Health. Office: Charing Cross Hosp, Gender Identity Clinic Dept Psychiatry, London W6 8RF, England

**GREEN, RICHARD GEORGE,** lawyer; b. N.Y.C., Dec. 13, 1913; s. Louis and Kate G. (Gottler) G.; m. Lynn Estelle Gold, Nov. 15, 1940 (div. 1954); m. Ruth M. Davis, July 2, 1954; children: Anna, Jennifer, Nancy, Richard Jr. BA, CUNY, 1932; LLB, Bklyn. Law Sch., 1936, JD, 1967. Bar: N.Y. 1937, U.S. Dist. Ct. (so. dist.) N.Y. 1940, U.S. Ct. Internat. Trade 1951, U.S. Ct. Appeals (2d cir.) 1951, U.S. Dist. Ct. (ea. dist.) 1964, U.S. Supreme Ct. 1967, U.S. Ct. Appeals (Fed. cir.) 1982. Asst. corp. counsel City of Long Beach, N.Y., 1937; assoc. Irving Ribman Esq., N.Y.C., 1938-39; mng. atty. Hays, St. John, Abramson & Schulman, N.Y.C., 1939-40; house counsel Newspaper PM Inc., N.Y.C., 1940-48; pvt. practice law N.Y.C., 1948-76; ptnr. Green & Hillman, N.Y.C., 1976-93; pvt. practice N.Y.C., 1993—; adj. prof. SUNY, Stony Brook, 1974-75; lectr. Rutgers Law Sch., Newark, 1975-77, NYU Law Sch., N.Y.C., 1975-77; arbitrator Civil Ct., N.Y.C., 1980—; spec master N.Y. Supreme Ct., 1991—, Civil Ct., N.Y.C., 1994—. Editor Jour. Assn. for Psychiat. Treatment Offenders, 1963-66. park commr. Village Lloyd Harbor, N.Y., 1969-73; pres. Cold Spring Harbor Youth Ctr., N.Y., 1969-73; chmn. bd. dirs., trustee Inst. Advancement Med. Communication, N.Y.C. and Phila., 1965-80; bd. dirs., pres. Harry Futterman Fund Inc., N.Y.C., 1950-85. 1st lt., U.S. Army, 1943-46. Mem. ABA (various coms.), Assn. Bar of City of N.Y., N.Y. County Lawyers Assn., Copyright Soc. U.S. (trustee 1982-85, 88-90, editl. bd. 1984-86), ACLU (chmn. free speech and assn. com. 1980-86), Am. Arbitration Assn. (arbitrator 1960—), Nat. Press Club (Washington). Avocations: swimming, fishing, reading. Entertainment, Libel, Trademark and copyright. Home: 37 W 12th St New York NY 10011-8502 Office: Ste 2116 1270 Avenue Of The Americas New York NY 10020-1801

**GREEN, ROBERT ALEXIS, JR.,** lawyer, judge; b. Gainesville, Fla., June 14, 1938; s. Robert Alexis and Lucile (Harris) G.; m. Saundra Marie Jones, June 6, 1959; children: Katherine Marie, Melanie Green Hancock, Robert Alexis III. AB, U. Fla., 1959, BA, 1960, LLB, JD, 1962. Bar: Fla. 1963, U.S. Dist. Ct. (all dists.) Fla. 1970-72, U.S. Supreme Ct. 1967; cert. county, family, cir. civil mediator/arbitrator, Fla. Ptnr. Green & Pierce, Attys. at Law, Gainesville, 1965-69; pub. defender 8th jud. cir. State of Fla., Gainesville, 1963-72, circuit judge 8th jud. cir., 1973-86; ptnr. Green & Hobbs P.A., Starke, Fla., 1986-87; ptnr., pres. R.A. Green, P.A., Starke, 1988—; pres. Fla. Mediation Acad. Inc., Starke, 1995-98. Recipient L. Clayton Nance award Fla. State Pub. Defender Assn., 1973, Reginald Heber Smith award Nat. Legal Aid and Defender Assn., 1973; Ford Found. grantee, 1964-67. Mem. Fla. Acad. Profl. Mediators (diplomate; pres. 1995), Am. Arbitration Assn. (Whitney North Seymour medal 1991). Methodist. Achievements include being youngest public defender appointed/elected in Florida, youngest elected circuit court judge. Alternative dispute resolution. Office: RA Green PA PO Box 1206 Starke FL 32091-1206

**GREEN, SAUL A.,** prosecutor. U.S. atty. Ea. Dist. Mich., Detroit. Office: US Atty for Ea Dist Mich 211 W Fort St Ste 2000 Detroit MI 48226-3202*

**GREEN, SONYA YVETTE,** paralegal; b. Jersey City, N.J., Feb. 18, 1965; d. Clarence and Rachel (Fykes) G. BA, Coll. St. Elizabeth, 1987; AA, U. Bridgeport, 1988. Paralegal Samowitz & Samowitz, Bridgeport, Conn., 1988—. Tchr. Sunday sch. Golden Hill United Meth. Ch., Bridgeport, 1990—, edn. chmn., 1993-94. Methodist. Avocations: collecting sports memorabilia & art. Home: 38 Grove St # 3 Bridgeport CT 06605-1408 Office: Samowitz & Samowitz 851 Clinton Ave Bridgeport CT 06604-2304

**GREEN, TOM E.,** lawyer. BA in English, U. Utah, 1977, JD, 1980. Law clk. to former U.S. Chief Justice Warren Burger; litigation ptnr. Jones, Day, Reavis & Pogue; exec. v.p., gen. counsel Trammell Crow Co., Dallas, Chgo. Title and Trust Co.; with Dell Computer Corp., Austin, Tex., 1994—, gen. counsel, sec., sr. v.p. law and adminstrn., gen. counsel. Office: Dell Computer Corp 1 Dell Way Round Rock TX 78682-0001*

**GREEN, WILLIAM PORTER,** lawyer; b. Jacksonville, Ill., Mar. 19, 1920; s. Hugh Parker and Clara Belle (Hopper) G.; m. Rose Marie Hall, Oct. 1, 1944; children: Hugh Michael, Robert Alan, Richard William. BA, Ill. Coll., 1941; JD, Northwestern U., Evanston, Ill., 1947. Bar: Ill. 1947, Calif. 1948, U.S. Dist. Ct. (so. dist.) Tex. 1986, U.S. Ct. Customs and Patent Appeals, U.S. Patent and Trademark Office 1948, U.S. Ct. Appeals (fed. cir.) 1982, U.S. Ct. Appeals (5th and 9th cir.), U.S. Supreme Ct. 1948, U.S. Dist. Ct. (cen. dist.) Calif. 1949, (so. dist.) Tex.1986. Pvt. practice L.A., 1947—; mem. Wills, Green & Mueth, L.A., 1974-83; of counsel Nilsson, Robbins, Dalgarn, Berliner, Carson & Wurst, L.A., 1984-91; of counsel Nilsson, Wurst & Green L.A., 1992—; del. Calif. State Bar Conv., 1982—, chmn., 1986. Bd. editors Ill. Law Rev., 1946; patentee in field. Mem. L.A. world Affairs Coun., 1975—; deacon local Presbyn. Ch., 1961-63. Mem. ABA, Calif. State Bar, Am. Intellectual Property Law Assn., L.A. Patent Law Assn. (past. sec.-treas., mem. bd. govs.), Lawyers Club L.A. (past treas., past sec., mem. bd. govs., pres. 1985-86), Los Angeles County Bar Assn. (trustee 1986-87), Am. Legion (past post comdr.), Northwestern U. Alumni Club So. Calif., Big Ten Club So. Calif., Town Hall Calif. Club, PGA West Golf Club (La Quinta, Calif.), Phi Beta Kappa, Phi Delta Phi, Phi Alpha. Republican. Patent, Trademark and copyright. Home: 3570 Lombardy Rd Pasadena CA 91107-5627 Office: 707 Wilshire Blvd Ste 3200 Los Angeles CA 90017-3514

**GREENAPPLE, STEVEN BRUCE,** lawyer; b. New Hyde Park, N.Y., Dec. 3, 1958; s. Lawrence and Emily Greenapple; children: Joshua, Benjamin. BS, Cornell U., 1981, JD, 1984. Bar: N.Y. 1985, N.J. 1987, U.S. Dist. Ct. N.J. 1987. Assoc. Drake Sommers Loeb & Tarshis, Newburgh, N.Y., 1984-85, Sills, Cummis, Zuckerman, Radin, Tischman, Epstein & Gross, Newark, 1985-86; assoc. Greenwood & Young Tarshis Dimiero & Sayovitz, West Orange, N.J., 1987-90, ptnr., 1991-94; of counsel Dillon Bitar & Luther, Morristown, N.J., 1994, ptnr., 1995—. Sec. Employee Stock Ownership Plan Assn., N.J., 1992-97. Mem. ABA, N.Y. State Bar Assn., N.J. State Bar Assn., Morris County Bar Assn. General corporate, Mergers and acquisitions, Contracts commercial. Office: Dillon Bitar & Luther 53 Maple Ave # 398 Morristown NJ 07960-5219

**GREENAWALT, ROBERT KENT,** lawyer, law educator; b. Bklyn., June 25, 1936; s. Kenneth William and Martha (Sloan) G.; m. Sanja Milic, July 14, 1968 (dec. Nov. 1988); children: Robert Milic, Alexander Kent Anton, Andrei Milenko Kenneth; m. Elaine Pagels, June 1995; children: Sarah Pagels, David. A.B. with honors, Swarthmore Coll., 1958; Ph.B.; Keasbey fellow, Oxford (Eng.) U., 1960; LL.B.; Kent scholar, Columbia U., 1963. Bar: N.Y. 1963. Law clk. to Justice Harlan, U.S. Supreme Ct., 1963-64; spl. asst. AID, Washington, 1964-65; mem. faculty Columbia U. Law Sch., 1965—, prof. law, 1969—, Cardozo prof., 1979—, Univ. prof., 1990—; dep. solicitor gen. U.S., 1971-72; assoc. dir. N.Y. Inst. Legal Edn., 1969; vis. prof. Stanford U. Law Sch., 1970, Northwestern U. Law Sch., 1983, Marshall-Wythe Sch. Law, 1985, N.Y.U. Law Sch., 1989-90; atty. Lawyers Com. Civil Rights, 1965, trustee, 1992; mem. staff Task Force Law Enforcement N.Y.C., 1965; vis. fellow All Souls Coll. Oxford (Eng.) U., 1979. Co-author: The Sectarian College and The Public Purse, 1970; author: Legal Protections of Privacy, 1976, Discrimination and Reverse Discrimination, 1983, Conflicts of Law and Morality, 1987, Religious Convictions and Political Choice, 1988, Speech, Crime and the Uses of Language, 1989, Law and Objectivity, 1992,

Private Consciences and Public Reasons, 1995, Fighting Words, 1995; editor in chief Columbia U. Law Rev., 1962-63; contbr. articles to legal jours. Recipient Ivy award Swarthmore Coll., 1958; fellow Am. Council Learned Soc., 1972-73. Fellow Am. Acad. Arts and Scis.; mem. Am. Philos. Soc., Am. Law Inst., Am. Soc. Polit. and Legal Philosophy (pres. 1992-93). Office: Columbia U Law Sch 435 W 116th St New York NY 10027-7201

**GREENAWALT, WILLIAM SLOAN,** lawyer; b. Bklyn., Mar. 4, 1934; s. Kenneth William and Martha Frances (Sloan) G.; m. Jane DeLano Plunkett, Aug. 17, 1957 (div. May 1986); m. Peggy Ellen Freed Tomarkin, Oct. 31, 1987; children: John DeLano, David Sloan, Katherine Downs. AB, Cornell U., 1956; LLB, Yale U., 1961. Bar: N.Y. 1962, U.S. Dist. Ct. (so. and ea. dists.) N.Y. 1962, U.S. Ct. Apls. (2d cir.) 1962, U.S. Supreme Ct. 1966. Assoc. Sullivan & Cromwell, N.Y.C., 1961-65; N.E. regional legal svcs. dir. U.S. Office Econ. Opportunity, N.Y.C., 1965-68; assoc. Rogers & Wells, N.Y.C., 1968-69, ptnr., 1969-77, sr. ptnr., 1977-81; sr. ptnr. Halperin, Shivitz, Eisenberg, Schneider & Greenawalt, N.Y.C., 1981-86, Eisenberg Honig Fogler Greenawalt & Davis, N.Y.C., 1986-91, Bangser Klein Rocca & Blum, N.Y.C., 1991-93, Loselle Greenawalt Kaplan Blair & Adler, N.Y.C., 1993-97, Loselle Greenawalt Kaplan & Blair, N.Y.C., 1997—, Meyer Greenawalt Taub & Wild, LLP, N.Y.C., 1999—; lectr. in field. Bd. editors: Yale Law Jour., 1959-61; contbr. articles in field to profl. jours. Chmn. bd. dirs. Applied Resources, Inc., N.Y.C., 1968-70; chmn. Cmty. Aid Employment of Ex-Offenders, Westchester, N.Y., 1971; pres. Westchester Legal Svcs., 1971-74, bd. dirs., 1975-91; mem. N.Y. State Gov.'s Task Force on Elem. and Secondary Edn., 1974-75; mem. Pres. Carter's Task Force on Criminal Justice, 1976; mem. adv. coun. N.Y. State Senate Dems., 1978—; asst. and acting treas. N.Y. State Dem. Party, 1990-96, vice chair, 1996—; chair Greenburgh Dem. Party, 1997—; mem. Greenburgh Recreation Commn., 1976-83, Dem. Statewide Spl. Commn. on Polit. Ethics, 1986-87, Statewide Spl. Commn. on Election Law and Campaign Spending Reform, 1989-95; pres. Westchester Crime Victims Assistance Agy., 1981-82; commr. Taconic State Pks., Recreation and Hist. Preservation Commn., 1984-96, chmn., 1989-96; vice chmn. N.Y. State Coun. on Pks., Recreation and Hist. Preservation, 1989-94; moderator Scarsdale Congl. Ch., 1988-90; mem. Westchester County Parks, Recreation and Conservation Bd., 1998—; mem. Westchester County Execs. Transition Team on Planning, 1997. Lt. comdr. USN, 1956-58, with Res., 1961-68. Fellow N.Y. Bar Found.; mem. ABA, Am. Arbitration Assn. (mem. panel comml. arbitrators 1977—), N.Y. State Bar Assn. (chmn. com. on availability of legal svcs. 1968-70, chmn. action unit 3 1979-81, chmn. spl. commn. on alternatives to jud. resolution of disputes 1981-85), Assn. of Bar of City of N.Y., Nat. Legal Aid and Defenders Assn., Sphinx Head, Aleph Samach, County Tennis Club Westchester (Scarsdale, N.Y., pres. 1979-80), Yale Club. Phi Alpha Delta, Chi Psi. Democrat. Congregationalist. Federal civil litigation, State civil litigation, Securities. Office: Meyer Greenawalt Et Al 230 Park Ave Rm 2525 New York NY 10169-2599

**GREENBAUM, FREDERICK JOEL,** lawyer; b. Kansas City, Mo., Oct. 28, 1952; s. Louis and Anne Greenbaum; m. Christina Marie Rodarte, Oct. 26, 1985; children: Phillip Nathan, Patrice Annette, Joseph Maxwell, Aaron John. BS, Kans. State U., 1974; JD magna cum laude, Washburn U., 1980. Bar: Kans. 1980, Mo. 1987. Pres., mng. ptnr. McAnany, Van Cleave and Phillips, Kansas City, 1980—. Workers' compensation, Labor, Personal injury. Home: 4861 W 90th St Shawnee Mission KS 66207-2205 Office: McAnany Van Cleave & Phillips 707 Minnesota Ave Ste 400 Kansas City KS 66101-2719

**GREENBAUM, JEFFREY ALAN,** lawyer; b. Ft. Benning, Ga., Feb. 9, 1968; s. Thomas L. and Rosalie (Montag) G. BA (summa cum laude), Brandeis U., Waltham, Mass., 1990; JD, Columbia U., N.Y.C., 1993. Bar: N.Y., U.S. Dist. Ct. (so. and ea. dists.) N.Y. Assoc. Paul, Weiss, Rifkind, Wharton & Garrison, N.Y.C., 1993-97, Frankfurt, Garbus, Klein & Selz, N.Y.C., 1997—. Named Harlan Fiske Stone scholar Columbia U., N.Y.C., 1991-93. Mem. ABA, Assn. Bar of City of N.Y., N.Y. New Media Assn., Phi Beta Kappa. Advertising. Office: Frankfurt Garbus Klein & Selz 488 Madison Ave Fl 9 New York NY 10022-5754

**GREENBERG, BRUCE A.,** lawyer; b. L.A., Feb. 6, 1954. BS, U. So. Calif., L.A., 1975; JD, Southwestern U., 1978. Pvt. practice law L.A., 1978—. Mem. L.A. Trial Lawyers Assn. Personal injury, Consumer commercial. Office: Brandon Greenberg & Yarc 200 Oceangate Ste 440 Long Beach CA 90802-4332

**GREENBERG, CATHY ANNE,** lawyer; b. Detroit, Sept. 10, 1955; d. Ralph Albert and Violet G.; m. Daniel W. Klein, Oct. 30, 1981; 1 child, Ryan. BA, Mich. State U., Lansing, 1977; JD, Detroit Coll. Law, 1981. Bar: Mich. 1981, U.S. Ct. Appeals (6th cir.) 1988. Atty. Salbury, Bean & Laritz, Detroit, 1981, pvt. practice, Birmingham, Mich., 1981-83, Legal Aid, Pontiac, Mich., 1983-87, pvt. practice, Sylvan Lake, Mich., 1987—. Family and matrimonial. Office: 2360 Orchard Lake Rd Sylvan Lake MI 48320-1613

**GREENBERG, DANIEL HERBERT,** lawyer; b. N.Y.C., Dec. 30, 1919; s. Moses Bernard and Sadye (Saltzman) G.; m. Jane Marian Frank, Jan. 22, 1943 (div. Apr. 1964); 1 child, Stanley Frank (dec.); m. Patricia Joy Williams, Aug. 29, 1964 (div. Jan. 1975); children: Dale Jeremy, Jason Bernard, Andrea Elizabeth, Nicole Victoria. BA, U. Wis., 1941; JD, Columbia U., 1947. Bar: N.Y. 1947, U.S. Supreme Ct. 1953, D.C. 1957. Asst. U.S. atty. U.S. Dept. Justice, N.Y.C., 1949-53; pvt. practice, N.Y.C., 1953—; spl. commr. in admiralty U.S. Dist. Ct. (so. dist.) N.Y., 1959-64; guest lectr. in trial practice Columbia Law Sch., 1965-66. Lt. col. USAF and Res., 1941-79, World War II, Korea. Decorated Disting. Flying Cross, Air medal with three clusters, eight battle stars, Disting. Unit citation with one cluster, Cert. of Valor, 15th Air Force, Italy, 1944. Democrat. Jewish. Home: 77 Renchy St Fairfield CT 06430-4129 Office: 36 W 44th St Ste 1206 New York NY 10036-8102

**GREENBERG, ELENA LYNN,** lawyer; b. Bklyn., Aug. 30, 1957; s. Jerome S. and Marilyn G. BA, U. Rochester, 1979; JD, St. Johns U., 1982. Assoc. atty. Solewitz, Solewitz & Leeds, Mineola, N.Y., 1982-85, Blondnick Abramovitz & Newmanschultz, Lake Success, N.Y., 1988-91, Chalres McEvily, Mineola, 1985-88, 91-96; ptnr. McEvily & Greenberg LLP, Mineola, 1997-99, Garden City, N.Y., 1999—; Bar: N.Y. 1983. Mem. Am. Inns of Ct., N.Y. State Bar Assn., Nassau County Bar Assn. Family and matrimonial. Office: McEvily & Greenberg 585 Stewart Ave Garden City NY 11530-4783

**GREENBERG, JACK,** lawyer, law educator; b. N.Y.C., Dec. 22, 1924; s. Max and Bertha (Rosenberg) G.; m. Sema Ann Tanzer, 1950 (div. 1970); children: Josiah, David, Sarah, Ezra; m. Deborah M. Cole, 1970; children: Suzanne, William Cole. AB, Columbia U., 1945, LLB, 1948, LLD, 1984; LLD, Morgan State Coll., Central State Coll., 1965, Lincoln U., 1977, John Jay Coll. Criminal Justice, 1983, De Paul U., 1994. Bar: N.Y. 1949. Rsch. asst. N.Y. State Law Revision Commn., 1949; asst. counsel NAACP Legal Def. and Ednl. Fund, 1949-61, dir.-counsel, 1961-84; argued in sch. segregation, sit-in, employment discrimination, poverty, capital punishment, other cases before U.S. Supreme Ct.; adj. prof. Columbia U. Law Sch., 1970-84, prof., vice dean, 1984-89; dean Columbia Coll., 1989-93; prof. Columbia U. Law Sch., 1993—; cons. Ctr. Applied Legal Studies, U. Witwatersrand, 1978; vis. lectr. Yale U. Law Sch., 1971; vis. prof. CCNY, 1977, Tokyo U., 1993-94, 99, St. Louis U. Law Sch., 1994, Lewis and Clark Law Sch., 1994-98, Princeton U., 1995, U. Munich, 1998; lectr. Harvard U. Law Sch., 1983, Shikes fellow, 1981; Disting. lectr. humanities Columbia Coll. Phys. and Surg., 1998. Author: (with H. Hill) Citizens Guide to Desegregation, 1955, Race Relations and American Law, 1959, Judicial Process and Social Change, 1976, (with James Vorenberg) Dean Cuisine or the Liberated Man's Guide to Fine Cooking, 1990, Crusaders in the Courts, 1994; contbg. author: Race, Sex and Religious Discrimination in International Law, 1981; contbr. articles to legal jours. Bd. dirs. N.Y.C. Legal Aid Soc., Internat. League for Human Rights, Mex.-Am. Legal Def. Fund, 1968-75, Asian Am. Legal Def. Fund, 1980—, Human Rights Watch, 1978-98, NAACP Legal Def. and Ednl. Fund. Co-recipient Grenville Clark prize, 1978; hon. fellow U. Pa. Law Sch., 1975. Fellow Am. Coll. Trial Lawyers; mem. ABA (commn. to study FTC, adv. com. to spl. com. on crime prevention, sect. on individual rights and responsibilities, Silver Gavel award, Thurgood Marshall prize), N.Y. State Bar Assn. (exec. dir. spl. com. study state antitrust laws 1956), Am. Law Inst., Bar Assn. City N.Y. (Cardozo lectr. 1973) Adminstrv. Conf. U.S. Home: 118 Riverside Dr New York NY 10024-3708 Office: Columbia Law Sch 435 W 116th St New York NY 10027-7297

**GREENBERG, KAREN ALANE,** lawyer; b. St. Louis, Nov. 20, 1960; d. Burton Marvin and Phyllis Ann (Trugman) Greenberg; m. Andrew Feist Wasserman, Oct. 12, 1991. BA, Washington U., St. Louis, 1983; JD, St. Louis U., 1986. Bar: Mo. 1986, Ill. 1987, U.S. Dist. Ct. (ea. dist.) Mo. 1986, U.S. Dist. Ct. (so. dist.) Ill. 1987. Assoc. Portman, Edwards, Cooper and Singer, Clayton, Mo., 1986-88, Greenberg and Pleban, St. Louis, 1988—. Trustee United Hebrew Congregation, St. Louis, 1994-97; bd. dirs. Delcrest, St. Louis, 1994-98, Women's Self Help Ctr., St. Louis, 1994-98. Mem. ABA, Assn. Trial Lawyers Am., Ill. Bar Assn., Mo. Bar Assn., Bar Assn. Met. St. Louis. Avocations: swimming, walking, music, tennis, reading. General civil litigation, Personal injury, Workers' compensation. Office: Greenberg and Pleban 100 S 4th St Ste 600 Saint Louis MO 63102-1822

**GREENBERG, LAWRENCE ALLAN,** lawyer; b. Bklyn., Nov. 1, 1946; s. Joseph David and Shirley Albert Greenberg; m. Diane Sonia Daniel, Mar. 28, 1976; children: Jason Scott, Michelle Wendy. BA, Duke U., 1968; JD, Columbia U., 1972. Bar: N.Y. 1973, Pa. 1980, N.J. 1980, Fla. 1981. Assoc. Schwartz, Mermelstein, Burns, Lesser & Jacoby, N.Y.C., 1973-76, Marshall, Bratter, Green, Allison & Tucker, N.Y.C., 1976-79, Liebman & Flaster, Cherry Hill, N.J., 1979-80; v.p. Chase Manhattan Pvt. Bank, Palm Beach, Fla., 1980—. V.p., treas. Jewish Arts Found., Palm Beach, 1987—. Mem. N.Y. State Bar Assn., Fla. Bar Assn., N.Y.C. Bar Assn., Palm Beach Bar Assn. Avocations: reading, jogging. Home: 1740 Grantham Dr West Palm Beach FL 33414-8974 Office: Chase Manhattan Pvt Bank 205 Royal Palm Way Palm Beach FL 33480-4396

**GREENBERG, MORTON IRA,** federal judge; b. Philadelphia, Pa., Mar. 20, 1933; s. Harry Arnold and Pauline (Hofkin) G.; m. Barbara-Ann Kissel, May 29, 1987; children from first marriage: Elizabeth, Suzanne, Lawrence. AB, U. Pa., 1954; LLB, Yale U., 1957. Bar: N.J. 1958, U.S. Dist. Ct. N.J. 1958, U.S. Ct. Appeals (3d cir.) 1972, U.S. Supreme Ct. 1973. Law clk.office of atty. gen. State of N.J., Trenton, 1957-58, dep. atty. gen., 1958-60, asst. atty. gen., 1971-73; pvt. practice, Cape May, N.J., 1960-71; judge law div. Superior Ct. N.J., New Brunswick, 1973-76; judge chancery and gen. equity divs. Superior Ct. N.J., Trenton, 1976-80, judge appellate div., 1980-87; judge U.S. Ct. Appeals (3d cir.), Trenton and Phila., 1987—. Office: US Ct Appeals US Courthouse 402 E State St Ste 7050 Trenton NJ 08608-1507*

**GREENBERG, MORTON PAUL,** lawyer, consultant, insurance broker, underwriter; b. Fall River, Mass., June 2, 1946; s. Harry and Sylvia Shirley (Davis) G.; m. Louise Beryl Schindler, Jan. 24, 1970; 1 child, Alexis Lynn. BSBA, NYU, 1968; JD, Bklyn. Law Sch., 1971. Bar: N.Y. 1972; CLU Am. Coll., 1975. Atty. Hanner, Fitzmaurice & Onorato, N.Y.C., 1971-72; dir., counsel, cons. on advanced underwriting The Mfrs. Life Ins. Co., Toronto, Ont., Can., 1972-98; mng. gen. agt. for lifetime settlements Viaticus, Inc., Chgo., 1999—; mng. gen. agt. Coventry Fin., Ft. Washington, Pa., 1999—; mem. sales ideas com. Million Dollar Roundtable, Chgo., 1982-83; 4th ann. George M. Graves meml. lectr., 1991; mem. adv. bd. Keeping Current, 1999—; speaker on law, tax, lifetime settlements, and advanced underwriting to various profl. groups, U.S., Can. Author: (tech. jour.) ManuBriefs. Mem. ABA, N.Y. State Bar Assn., Assn. for Advanced Life Underwriting (mem. bus. ins. and estate planning steering com. 1989-93), Internat. Platform Assn., Nat. Assn. Life Underwriters, Soc. of Fin. Svcs. Profls., NYU Alumni Assn., Stern Sch. Bus. Alumni Assn. Estate planning, Corporate taxation, Personal income taxation. Office: PO Box 183 7617 E Sunrise Trail Parker CO 80134-6915

**GREENBERG, MYRON SILVER,** lawyer; b. L.A., Oct. 17, 1945; s. Earl W. and Geri (Silver) G.; m. Shlomit Gross; children: David, Amy, Sophie, Benjamin. BSBA, UCLA, 1967; JD, 1970. Bar: Calif., 1971, U.S. Dist. Ct. (middle dist.) Calif. 1971, U.S. Tax Ct. 1977; cert. splst. in taxation law bd. legal specialization State Bar Calif.; CPA, Calif. Staff acct. Touche Ross & Co., L.A., 1970-71; assoc. Kaplan, Livingston, Goodwin, Berkowitz, & Selvin, Beverly Hills, Calif., 1971-74; ptnr. Myron S. Greenberg, a Profl. Corp., Larkspur, Calif., 1982—; professorial lectr. tax. Golden Gate U.; instr. U. Calif., Berkeley, 1989—; mem. taxation law adv. commn. Calif. Bd. Legal Specialization, 1998—. Author: California Attorney's Guide to Professional Corporations, 1977, 79; bd. editors UCLA Law Rev., 1969-70. Mem. San Anselmo Planning Commn., 1976-77; mem. adv. bd. cert. program personal fin. planning U. Calif., Berkeley, 1991—. Mem. AHA (bd. dirs. Marin county chpt. 1984-90, pres. 1988-89), ABA, AICPAs, L.A. County Bar Assn., Marin County (Calif.) Bar Assn. (bd. dirs. 1994-2000, pres. 1999), Real Estate Tax Inst. Calif. Cont. Edn. Bar (planning com.), Larkspur C. of C. (bd. dirs. 1985-87). Democrat. Jewish. Corporate taxation, Personal income taxation, Estate taxation. Office: # 205 700 Larkspur Landing Cir Larkspur CA 94939-1711

**GREENBERG, PHILIP ALAN,** lawyer; b. Bklyn., Aug. 2, 1948; s. Harry and Jeannette (Nataf) G. BA cum laude, Bklyn. Coll., 1970; JD, N.Y.U., 1973. Bar: N.Y. 1974, U.S. Dist. Ct. (ea. and so. dists.) N.Y. 1975, U.S. Ct. Appeals (2d cir.) 1975, U.S. Supreme Ct. 1977 N.J. 1988. Assoc. Kamerman & Kamerman, N.Y.C., 1973-78, ptnr., 1978-82; ptnr. Segal, Liling, Erlitz & Greenberg, N.Y.C., 1982, Segal, Liling & Greenberg, N.Y.C., 1982-84, Segal & Greenberg, N.Y.C., 1984; mng. ptnr. Segal, Post, DeMott & Crow, N.Y.C., 1985, Segal, Greenberg, McDonald & Maher, N.Y.C., 1985-86, Segal, Greenberg & McDonald, N.Y.C., 1986-87, Segal & Greenberg, N.Y.C., 1987-93, Bizar & Martin, N.Y.C., 1993-95; ptnr. Wallman Greenberg Gasman & McKnight, N.Y.C., 1995—; mem. faculty para legal Sobelsohn Sch. Trustee Congregation Emunath Israel, 1984—, chmn. law and ins. com., 1987—. Mem. ABA (com. mem., lit. mem.), N.Y. Bar Assn., Assn. of Bar of City of N.Y., Mason (Maimonides-Marshall #739, master), Masters & Wardens Assn. (past pres. 6th Manhattan 1990-91), Internat. Assoc. Tribune, Phi Alpha Delta. Democrat. Jewish. General corporate, General civil litigation, Family and matrimonial. Home: 7 Francisco Ave Little Falls NJ 07424-2316 Office: Wallman Greenberg Gasman & McKnight 350 5th Ave Ste 3000 New York NY 10118-3022

**GREENBERG, ROBERT JAY,** law educator; b. N.Y.C., Nov. 22, 1959; s. Murray Louis and Jeanette (Adams) G. BA, Yeshiva U., 1981, JD, 1984. Bar: N.Y. 1986, U.S. Dist. Ct. (ea. and so. dists.) N.Y. 1986, U.S. Supreme Ct. 1989, U.S. Ct. Appeals (2nd. cir.) 1998. Asst. to judge N.Y.C. Civil Ct., Bklyn., 1982; assoc. Simon, Meyrowitz, Meyrowitz and Schlussel, N.Y.C., 1983-86; instr. Bruriah High Sch. for Girls, Elizabeth, N.J., 1985-87; lectr. Nat. Acad. for Paralegal Studies, Mahwah, N.J., 1987-88; sr. legal editor Matthew Bender and Co., Inc., N.Y.C., 1987-94; adj. asst. prof. bus. law Yeshiva U., N.Y.C., 1994-98, asst. prof., 1998—; lectr. NYU Inst. Paralegal Studies, N.Y.C., 1994—; instr. dept. paralegal studies Queens College CUNY, 1994—. Asst. to author: Judaism and Vegetarianism, Judaism and Global Survival. Lectr. in Jewish law Congregation Beth Yehuda, Staten Island, 1980-93, Young Israel of Forest Hills, Queens, 1993—. Recipient Disting. Svc. award Congregation Beth Yehuda, 1988, Outstanding Svc. award, 1991. Mem. ABA, N.Y. State Bar Assn., N.Y. County Lawyers Assn. Democrat. General corporate, Intellectual property, Probate. Office: 6939 Yellowstone Blvd Apt 508 Forest Hills NY 11375-3734

**GREENBERG, RONALD DAVID,** lawyer, law educator; b. San Antonio, Sept. 9, 1939; s. Benjamin and Sylvia (Ghetlzer) G. BS, U. Tex., 1957; MBA, Harvard U., 1961, JD, 1964. Bar: N.Y., 1966, U.S. Dist. Ct. (ea. and so. dists.) N.Y. 1970, U.S. Ct. Appeals (2d cir.) 1975, U.S. Supreme Ct. 1975. Engring. lab. instr. U. Tex., 1957; engr. Redstone Arsenal, Army Ballistic Missile Agy., 1957; engr., bus. analyst Exxon Corp., N.Y.C., 1957-64; rsch. asst. Harvard Bus. Sch.; with Smithsonian Astrophys. Observatory and Ednl. Testing Svc., N.J., 1961-62; atty., engr. Allied Corp., N.Y.C., 1964-67; assoc. Arthur, Dry, Kalish, Taylor & Wood, N.Y.C., 1967-69, Valicenti, Leighton, Reid & Pine, N.Y.C., 1969-70; instr. faculty Columbia U., N.Y.C., 1972-81, adj. prof. bus. law and taxation, 1970-71, 82-98; of counsel Delson & Gordon, N.Y.C., 1973-87; sole practitioner N.Y.C., 1988—; lectr., cons. AICPA, Inst. Internal Auditors, New Haven C. of C., Citibank, Mfrs. Hanover Trust Co., Harcourt, Brace, Jovanovich, Inc., Prudential-Bache, Drexel, Burnham & Lambert, E.F. Hutton; vol. instr. vol. income tax program, Columbia U., N.Y.C., 1991-92; vis. prof. Stanford U., Palo Alto, Calif., 1978, Harvard U., Boston, 1981. Author: Business Income Tax Materials, 1994; (with others): Business Organizations: Corporations, 1998, General Practice in New York, 1998; editor: The Compleat Lawyer, 1985-88, Tax Lawyer, 1982-95; editor in chief N.Y. Internat. Law Rev., 1988-91, chair adv. bd., 1992—; editor in chief Internat. Law Practicum, 1987-91; contbr. chpts. to books, articles to profl. jours. Cons. coun. City of N.Y., 1971-72, Manhattan C.C., 1974-76. Lt. USNR, 1957-59. Recipient Outstanding Prof. award Columbia U. Grad. Sch. Bus., 1973, MIT Fellowship Mech. Engring. Dept., 1959, Harvard U., Teagle Found., 1959-61; grantee Ford Found., 1977, Columbia U. Ctr. Internat. Studies, Sch. Internat. Pub. Affairs, 1992, Columbia Bus. Sch., 1976, 92, 93, 94. Mem. ABA (chmn. com. on taxation gen. practice sect. 1978-83, chmn. com. on corp. banking and bus. law. gen. practice sect. 1985-87, moderator, chair profl. edn. programs 1986, 87), ASME, NSPE, N.Y. State Bar Assn. (gen. practice sect., chmn. tax law com. 1983-92, chmn. bus. law com. 1985-88, internat. law & practice sect., chmn. pubs. com. 1988-91, coord. study com. on med. malpractice legislation, 1980-82), Assn. of Bar of City of N.Y., N.Y. Acad. Scis., Mensa, Rye Golf Club, Tau Beta Pi, Pi Tau Sigma, Phi Eta Sigma. Private international, Corporate taxation, General corporate.

**GREENBERG, STEVEN MOREY,** lawyer; b. Jersey City, Apr. 9, 1949; s. Joseph and Rhoda (Weisenfeld) G. AB cum laude, Syracuse U., 1971; JD, U. Pa., 1974. Bar: N.J. 1974, U.S. Dist. Ct. N.J. 1974, N.Y. 1980, U.S. Dist. Ct. (so. dist.) N.Y. 1986, U.S. Dist. Ct. (ea. dist.) N.Y. 1986, U.S. Ct. Appeals (3d cir.) 1987, U.S. Ct. Fed. Claims 1989. Assoc. Carpenter, Bennett & Morrissey, Newark, N.J., 1974-77, Cole, Berman & Belsky, Rochelle Park, N.J., 1977-79; pvt. practice Hackensack, N.J., 1979-94; atty. Bergenfield (N.J.) Rent Leveling Bd., 1985-89, 92-93, 1999—; atty. Bergenfield Planning Bd., 1993-96; ptnr. Greenberg & Marmorstein, Hackensack, N.J., 1994-97, Greenberg & Lanz, Hackensack, N.J., 1997—. Trustee, past chmn. youth activities com. Jewish Ctr. of Teaneck, N.J., 1978—, mem. exec. com., 1992-97, v.p., 1992-94, pres., 1994-97; pres. Jewish Inst. of Bioethics, N.Y.C., 1998—; trustee, chmn., com. campus youth svcs., sub-com. planning and allocations United Jewish Appeal Fedn. Bergen County and N. Hudson, 1997—; dir., v.p. JH & RC Sr. Housing, Inc., Jersey City, 1991-94; past v.p., past sec. Sam Gorovoy Group Care Home for Sr. Adults, Bergenfield, N.J., trustee, 1983-96, pres., 1986-90; mem. adv. bd. dirs. Jewish Home and Rehab. Ctr., Jersey City and River Vale, N.J., 1982-90, chmn. pers. com., 1986—, governing body, 1986—, exec. com., 1987—, v.p., 1990—; trustee Jewish Family Svc., Inc., Bergen County, 1986-96, exec. com., 1990-96, treas., 1990-92, v.p., 1992-96; trustee The Solomon Schechter Day Sch. of Bergen County, 1986-87, Bergenfield Mus. Soc., 1989—, Teaneck Jewish Meml. Assn., 1989—, v.p., 1990-92, pres., 1992—; mem. Jewish Community Rels. Coun., 1986-93, 99—; mem. N.J. regional adv. bd. Anti-Defamation League of B'nai B'rith, 1989—, exec. com., 1989—; mem. Jewish Community Coun. Teaneck, 1989-93; mem. cmty. advocacy program UJA (United Jewish Appeal) Fedn. of Bergen County and North Hudson Resource Coun., 1991—, dir., 1995—; dir. Union for Traditional Judaism, 1993-97; trustee UJA Assn. for Developmental Disabilities, 1999—. Recipient Second Century award Jewish Theol. Sem. Am., 1988. Mem. ABA, N.J. Bar Assn., Bergen County Bar Assn., N.Y. State Bar Assn., Assn. Transp. Practitioners, UJA Assn. for Developmental Disabilities, Phi Kappa Phi, Pi Sigma Alpha. State civil litigation, Contracts commercial, General corporate. Home: 96 Westminster Ave Bergenfield NJ 07621-3916 Office: 2 University Plaza Hackensack NJ 07601-6202

**GREENBERG, STEWART GARY,** lawyer; b. Flushing, N.Y., Feb. 2, 1955; s. Herman Leo and Constance Ann G.; m. Wendy L., Dec. 25, 1976; childre: Melissa, Jonathan, Jennifer, Michael. BA, NYU, 1976; JD, U. Miami, 1979. Bar: Fla. 1979, N.Y. 1986. Assoc. Rizzo & Koltun, Miami, Fla., 1976-83; ptnr. Koltun & Greenberg, Miami, Fla., 1983-93; atty. pvt. practice, Miami, Fla., 1993—; CEO, dir. Upscale Techs., Inc., Miami, 1996-97. Pres. Bet Shira Congregation, Miami, 1990-91, v.p., 1984-90; bd. dirs. Jewish Adoption & Foster Care Options, Sunrise, Fla., 1998—. Mem. Assn. Trial Lawyers Am., Acad. Fla. Trial Lawyers, Dade County Trial Lawyers Assn. Avocations: golf, sailing, fishing. Personal injury, Product liability, Insurance. Office: 11440 N Kendall Dr Ste 400 Miami FL 33176-1025

**GREENBERG, SUSAN ELLEN,** lawyer; b. Bklyn., Jan. 5, 1968; d. Kenneth Lloyd and Roberta Lefer (Meschkow) Bates; m. Bryan Scott Greenberg, May 30, 1993. BA, U. Fla., 1989; JD, Cornell Law Sch., 1992. Bar: Fla. 1992, N.J. 1992. Assoc. Friedman Siegelbaum, Roseland, N.J., 1992-95, Caruana, Langan, Lorenzen et al, Miami, Fla., 1995-96, Hunt, Cook, Riggs, Mehr & Miller, P.A., Boca Raton, Fla., 1996—; lectr. Nat. Bus. Inst., West Palm Beach, Fla., 1998. V.p. Temple Solel Hollywood, Fla., 1998. Democrat. Jewish. Avocations: reading, bicycling. Family and matrimonial. Office: Hunt Cook Riggs Mehr and Miller PA 2200 NW Corporate Blvd Ste 401 Boca Raton FL 33431-7369

**GREENBERGER, HOWARD LEROY,** lawyer, educator; b. Pitts., July 16, 1929; s. Abraham Harry and Alice (Levine) G.; m. Bette Jo Bergad, June 15, 1959. BS magna cum laude, U. Pitts., 1951; JD cum laude, NYU, 1954; diploma in law (Fulbright scholar), Oxford (Eng.) U., 1955. Bar: Pa. 1955, D.C. 1954, N.Y. 1969, U.S. Supreme Ct. 1964. Law clk. U.S. Ct. Appeals (3d cir.), 1958-60; assoc. Kaufman & Kaufman, Pitts., 1960-61; assoc. prof. law NYU, 1961-65, prof., 1965—; assoc. dean NYU Sch. Law, 1968-72; dean and dir. Practising Law Inst., 1972-75; senator NYU, 1994—; cons. in field.; v.p. Nat. Ctr. Para-Legal Tng.; pres. Early Am. Industries Assn., 1979-82; chmn. Commn. on Fgn. Grad. Study, AALS. Author: (with G. Cole) The Meriden Experiment, 1973; Study of the Quality of Continuing Legal Education in the U.S, 1980; contbr. articles to legal publs.; chmn. editorial bd. Jour. Legal Edn, 1974-77. Pres. N.Y.C. chpt. Am. Jewish Com., 1977-79, nat. bd. govs., 1979-85; vice chmn., gen. counsel Coalition to Free Soviet Jews, 1977—; trustee Law Ctr. Found., 1973-91, Am. Friends of Hebrew U. Jerusalem, 1986—; chair New Amsterdam dist. Boy Scouts Am., 1990—, Ctr. on Social Welfare Policy and Law, 1991—, Blaustein Inst. on Human Rights, 1992—. Capt. JAGC, U.S. Army, 1955-58. Recipient Alumni Meritorious Svc. award NYU, 1977, Stanley Isaacs award Am. Jewish Com., 1982, Gt. Tchr. award NYU, 1993, Friendship award Govt. of Germany, 1988, Robert B. McKay Disting. Svc. award N.Y.U. Sch. of Law, 1997, Great Tchr. award 1999; Root-Tilden grantee NYU, 1954. Fellow Am. Bar Found.; mem. ABA, Assn. of Bar of City of N.Y., N.Y. County Lawyers Assn. (bd. dirs. 1990—), Am. Law Inst., Assn. Am. Law Schs., NYU Club (pres. 1981-83, Masons, Sojourners, Order of Coif, Phi Epsilon Pi. Democrat. Jewish. Home: 4 Washington Square Vlg Apt 16 New York NY 10012-1936 Office: NYU Sch Law Vand Hall 40 Washington Sq S New York NY 10012-1005

**GREENBERGER, I. MICHAEL,** lawyer; b. Scranton, Pa., Oct. 30, 1945; s. David and Betty (Kabatchnick) G.; m. Marcia Devins, July 19, 1969; children: Sarah Devins, Anne Devins. AB, Lafayette Coll., 1967; JD, U. Pa., 1970. Bar: D.C. 1971, U.S. Dist. Ct. D.C. 1971, U.S. Ct. Appeals (D.C. cir.) 1971, U.S. Supreme Ct. 1975. Law clk. to Judge Carl McGowan U.S. Ct. Appeals for D.C. Circuit, Washington, 1970-71; legis. asst. to U.S. Congresswoman Elizabeth Holtzman, 1972-73; atty., advisor Office of Criminal Justice, Office U.S. Atty. Gen., 1973; assoc. Shea & Gardner, Washington, 1973-77, ptnr., 1977-97; dir. divsn. of trading and markets U.S. Commodity Futures Trading Commn., 1997—; bd. govs. D.C. Bar 1995-98, com. on legal ethics, 1993-95; mem. D.C. Cir. Adv. Com. on Procedures, 1983-89; mem. steering com. D.C. Pro Bono Partnership, 1994-97, Lafayette Coll. Leadership Coun., 1994-99; mediator office of cir. exec. U.S. Cts. for D.C., 1989—; mem. D.C. Cir. Jud. Conf., 1983—; legal cons. Software Engring. Inst., Carnegie-Mellon U., 1986-87; mem. steering com. Pres.'s Working Group on Fin. Mkts., 1997—; mem. hedge fund task force Internat. Orgn. of Secs. Commrs., 1999—. Editor-in-chief U. Pa. Law Rev., 1969-70; contbr. articles to profl. jours. Bd. dirs. Washington Legal Clinic for the Homeless, 1993-98, Am. Rivers, 1993-98, sec., 1995-98; bd. dirs. MIT Enterprise Forum Washington, 1984-87, Advanced Tech. Assn. Md., 1985-87, D.C. Prisoners' Legal Svc. Project, 1997-98. Mem. Am. Law Inst., Phi Beta Kappa. Federal civil litigation, Appellate, Securities. Address: 2757 Brandywine St NW Washington DC 20008-1041

**GREENBLATT, MARTIN ELLIOTT,** lawyer; b. Boston, Apr. 26, 1939; s. Harry J. and Mollie (Brown) G.; m. Linda Rosenbleet, Mar. 5, 1965; children: Robin A., Richard B. BA, Brandeis U., 1960; LLB, Cornell U., 1963.

Bar: Mass. 1963, U.S. Dist. Ct. Mass., U.S. Ct. Appeals (1st cir.), U.S. Supreme Ct. Staff atty. Fed. Communications Commn., Washington, 1964-65; asst. city solicitor City of Newton (Mass.), 1965-70; ptnr. Greenblatt & Greenblatt, Boston, 1970-73, Kaplan, Soshnick, Greenblatt & Goodman, Boston, 1973-78, Tyler & Reynolds, Boston, 1978-81, Casner & Edwards, Boston, 1981—. Bd. dirs. N.E. Regional Bd. Anti-Defamation League, Boston, 1975—. Served as 1st lt. M.I. Corps, U.S. Army, 1968-69. Mem. ABA, Mass. Bar Assn., Phi Alpha Delta. Republican. Jewish. Avocation: amateur radio. General corporate, Mergers and acquisitions, Securities. Home: 551 Boylston St Brookline MA 02445-5738 Office: Casner & Edwards One Federal St Boston MA 02110-2508

**GREENE, ADDISON KENT,** lawyer, accountant; b. Cardston, Alta., Can., Dec. 23, 1941; s. Addison Allen and Amy (Shipley) G.; m. Janice Hanks, Aug. 30, 1967; children: Lisa, Tiffany, Tyler, Darin. BS in Acctg., Brigham Young U., 1968; JD, U. Utah, 1973. Bar: Utah 1973, Nev. 1974, U.S. Tax Ct. 1979. Staff acct. Seidman and Seidman, Las Vegas, Nev., 1968-69, Peat Marwick Mitchell, Los Angeles, 1969-70; atty. Clark Greene & Assocs., Ltd., Las Vegas, 1973—; instr. Nev. Bar Rev., Las Vegas, 1975-78; bd. dirs. Cumorah Credit Union. Mem. Citizen's for Responsible Gov't, Las Vegas, 1979—; asst. dist. com. mem. Boy Scouts Am., Las Vegas, 1985—. Mem. ABA, Utah Bar Assn., Nev. Bar Assn., Nev. Soc. CPA's (assoc.), Am. Assn., Pension Actuaries (assoc.). Republican. Mormon. Avocations: golf, snow skiing. Pension, profit-sharing, and employee benefits, Probate, Estate planning. Office: Clark Greene & Assocs Ltd 3770 Howard Hughes Pkwy Ste 195 Las Vegas NV 89109-0976

**GREENE, ANDREA LEIGH,** lawyer; b. Queens, N.Y., Feb. 5, 1965; d. David A. and Renée (Strum) G.; m. Michael Alan Goldman, June 28, 1992; children: Jonathan, Matthew. BA, Washington U., 1987; JD, Benjamin N. Cardozo Sch. Law, 1990. Bar: N.Y. 1991, U.S. Dist. Ct. (ea. dist.) N.Y. 1991, U.S. Dist. Ct. (so. dist.) N.Y. 1991. Assoc. Squadron Ellenoff Plesent & Sheinfeld LLP, N.Y.C., 1990—. Nat. Merit scholarship, 1983, scholarship Res. Officers Assn., 1983. Mem. Assn. of the Bar of the City of N.Y., Nassau County Bar Assn. Democrat. Avocation: cooking. Real property. Office: Squadron Ellenoff Plesent & Sheinfeld LLP 551 5th Ave Fl 22 New York NY 10176-0049

**GREENE, ARTHUR M.,** lawyer; b. N.Y.C., Aug. 6, 1936; s. William B. and Hazel C. Greene; m. Carol A. Jansen, Apr. 17, 1992; children: Stephanie Bosworth, Andrea. BSc, Cornell U., 1958; LLB, N.Y. Law Sch., 1966. Bar: N.Y. 1967, Fla. 1995, U.S. Dist. Ct. (no. dist.) N.Y. 1975, U.S. Ct. Appeals (2nd cir.) 1971, U.S. Supreme Ct. 1995. House counsel Transamerica Ins. Co., Syracuse, N.Y., 1967-69, Empire Mut. Ins. Co., Syracuse, 1969-78; pvt. practice Syracuse, 1978-82; ptnr. Greene & Reid, Syracuse, 1982—. Co-author: Service of Process: Manual for the Attorney, 1984, Handling The Plaintiff's Personal Injury Case, 1989. Mem. Onondaga County Bar Assn. (chair ins. com. 1976-83, bd. dirs. 1979-86, chair lawyers ref. com. 1986-93). Avocations: sailing, bicycling, kayaking, running, roller blading. Personal injury, General civil litigation, Insurance. Office: Greene & Reid 892 E Brighton Ave Syracuse NY 13205-2538

**GREENE, FREDRICA KERTZ,** lawyer, writer; b. San Francisco. JD, Hastings, 1976. Assoc. Carrow & Forest, Novato, Calif., 1977-79; pvt. practice San Rafael, Calif., 1979—. Mem. Marin County Bar Assn., Paradise Cay Home Owners Assn. (sec., treas. 1980—). Family and matrimonial. Office: PO Box 151475 San Rafael CA 94915-1475

**GREENE, HAROLD H.,** federal judge; b. 1923. B.S., George Washington U., 1949, J.D., 1952; LLD (hon.), Bridgeport U., George Washington U. Asst. U.S. Atty. D.C., 1953-57; with Office Legal Counsel and Civil Rights Div. (Chief of Appeals) Dept. Justice, 1957-65; judge D.C. Ct. Gen. Sessions, 1965-66, chief judge, 1966-71; chief judge Superior Ct. of D.C., 1971-78; judge U.S. Dist. Ct. (D.C. dist.), 1978—; now sr. judge. Mem. ABA, Bar Assn. D.C., Am. Judicature Soc., World Assn. Trial Judges (chmn. 1975-77). Office: US Dist Ct US Courthouse 333 Constitution Ave NW Washington DC 20001-2802

**GREENE, IRA S.,** lawyer; b. N.Y.C., Nov. 21, 1946; s. Melvin and Syd (Semmelman) G.; m. Robin Colin, Dec. 29, 1973; children: Jessica, Alexander. BA, Syracuse U., 1968; postgrad., U. Buffalo, 1968-69; JD, N.Y. U., 1971. Bar: N.Y. 1972, U.S. Dist. Ct. (ea. dist.) N.Y. 1972, U.S. Ct. Appeals (2d cir.) 1974. Counsel Gainsburg, Gottlieb, Levitan & Cole, N.Y.C., 1982-84; ptnr. Gainsburg, Gottlieb, Levitan, Greene & Cole, N.Y.C., 1984-86, Gainsburg, Greene & Hirsch, Purchase, N.Y., 1986-91, Squadron, Ellenoff, Plesent & Sheinfeld, N.Y.C., 1991—; lectr. in field. Mem. Assn. Comml. Fin. Attys., Bank Lawyers Conf., Bankruptcy Lawyers Bar Assn., Assn. of Bar of City of N.Y. Banking, Bankruptcy, Contracts commercial. Office: Squadron Ellenoff Plesent & Sheinfeld 551 5th Ave Fl 22 New York NY 10176-0049

**GREENE, JOHN JOSEPH,** lawyer; b. Marshall, Tex., Jan. 19, 1946; William Henry and Camille Anne (Riley) G.; BA, U. Houston, 1969, MA, 1974; JD, South Tex. Coll., 1978. Bar: Tex. 1978, U.S. Supreme Ct., 1982. Asst. atty. City of Amarillo, Tex., 1978-79; asst. atty. Harris County, Tex., 1979-83; pvt. practice, 1983—; city atty. City of Conroe (Tex.), 1983-89, sr. asst. city atty. City of Austin (Tex.), 1990—. Capt. USAR, 1969-76. Decorated Bronze Star, Air Medal. Roman Catholic. Office: 114 W 7th St Ste 400 Austin TX 78701-3008

**GREENE, JOHN THOMAS,** judge; b. Salt Lake City, Nov. 28, 1929; s. John Thomas and Mary Agnes (Hindley) G.; m. Dorothy Kay Buchanan, Mar. 31, 1955; children: Thomas Buchanan Greene, John Buchanan Greene, Mary Kay Greene Platt. BA in Polit. Sci., U. Utah, 1952, JD, 1955. Bar: Utah 1955, U.S. Dist. Ct. (10th cir.) 1955, U.S. Supreme Ct. 1966. Pvt. practice Salt Lake City, 1955-57, asst. U.S. atty., 1957-59; ptnr. Marr, Wilkins & Cannon (and successor firms), Salt Lake City, 1959-75; ptnr., pres., chmn. bd. dirs. Greene, Callister & Nebeker, Salt Lake City, 1975-85; judge U.S. Dist. Ct., Salt Lake City, 1985—. Author: (manual) American Mining Law, 1960; contbr. articles to profl. jours. Chmn. Salt Lake City Cmty. Coun., 1970-75, Utah State Bldg. Authority, Salt Lake City, 1980-85; Regent Utah State Bd. Higher Edn., Salt Lake City, 1982-86. Recipient Order of Coif U. Utah, 1955, Merit of Honor award, 1994, Utah Fed. Bar Disting. Svc. award, 1997. Fellow ABA Found. (life); ABA ho. of dels. 1972-92, bd. govs. 1987-91; mem. Dist. Judges Assn. (pres. 10th cir. 1998—); Utah Bar Assn. (pres. 1971-72, Judge of Yr. award 1995), Am. Law Inst. (life, panelist and lectr. 1980-85, advisor 1986-98); Phi Beta Kappa. Mormon. Avocations: travel, reading, tennis. Office: US Dist Ct 350 S Main St Ste 150 Salt Lake City UT 84101-2180

**GREENE, KORRY ALDEN,** lawyer; b. Natrona Heights, Pa., Dec. 3, 1960; s. John Shaffer and Mary Adele (Whaley) G. BS in Curriculum/Instrn., U. Md., 1983; JD, Duquesne U., 1988. Bar: Pa. 1989. Assoc. Jones, Gregg, Creehan & Gerace, Pitts., 1989-90, Grogan, Graffam, McGinley & Lucchino, P.C., Pitts., 1991—. Moot ct. competition judge U. Pitts. Sch. Law, 1994—, Duquesne U. Sch. Law, 1990—, mem. alumni bd. govs. selection com., 1991, mem. alumni bd. govs., 1995-97; founder, chmn. bd. New Kensington Summer Youth Programs, 1995—; commr. Gosby "Goose" Pryor Summer Basketball League, 1994—; youth mentor program spkr. YMCA of Pitts., 1993-95; program chmn. Greater Pitts. coun. Boy Scouts Am. Eagle Awards Dinner, 1992-97, mem. pub. rels. com., 1990-94; co-founder A-K Youth Group, 1988, co-chmn., 1989, chairperson, 1990-92; active fundraisers Phi Beta Sigma, 1980-85; Hugh O'Brien Youth Found. panelist, 1997; bd. dirs. Allegheny County Bar Assn. Svcs. Inc., 1998—; bd. dirs. Pa./Del. affil. Am. Heart Assn. Recipient Alle-Kiski Extraordinary Svc. award, 1995, Unity in the Cmty. award Sheraton Broadcasting Co., 1995, Proclamation Pa. State Senate, 1996, Disting. Svc. award Duquesne U. Sch. Law, 1988, 10 Under Forty Leaders of Tomorrow Inaugural award 1999; named to Outstanding Young Men of Am., 1988. Mem. ABA, Nat. Bar Assn., U. Md. African Am. Alumni Assn., U. Md. Alumni Assn., Duquesne U. Law Alumni Assn., Homer S. Brown Law Assn., Allegheny County Bar Assn. (Outstanding Young Atty. 1996). Democrat. Mem. AME Ch. Avocations: working with young people, sports, theater, music. Appellate, Personal injury, General civil litigation. Office: Grogan Graffam McGinley & Lucchino 3 Gateway Ctr Fl 22 Pittsburgh PA 15222-1000

**GREENE, PHILIP JAMES,** lawyer; b. Washington, Nov. 12, 1961; s. Edward Allen and Elizabeth Ann (Love) G.; m. Elise Marie Greene; children: Hannah Marie, Madeleine Dupre, Olivia Ann. BA, Mt. St. Mary's Coll., 1983; JD, Loyola U., New Orleans, 1986. Bar: Md., Pa., D.C. Assoc. McNamee, Hosea & Scott, P.A., Greenbelt, Md., 1986-88; assoc. gen. counsel U.S. Dept. Commerce/Office of Chief Counsel/Tech, Washington, 1988—; bur. counsel Nat. Tech. Info. Svc., Springfield, Va., 1988—. Writer, editor: (mag.) Headliners, 1988-89. Recipient Gen. Counsel's award Outstanding Office Atty., 1992; named to Outstanding Young Men of Am., 1990. Mem. Md. State Bar Assn., D.C. Bar Assn. (intellectual property sect.), Pa. Bar Assn., La. Soc., Loyola U. Alumni Assn. (bd. dirs. 1989—, pres. Washington chpt.), Chestnut Lodge Golf Soc. (bd. dirs. 1987—). Republican. Roman Catholic. Avocations: golf, homebrewing, canoeing, skiing, writing. Home: 3015 Beech St NW Washington DC 20015-2203 Office: US Dept Commerce 14th St NW Rm 4835 Washington DC 20011-4316

**GREENE, RALPH VERNON,** lawyer; b. Cleve., Apr. 5, 1910; s. Charles R. and Pauline J. (Desch) G.; m. Martha F. Burwell, Aug. 12, 1939 (dec. 1994); 1 child, Betsy; m. Irene G. Karls-Benson, Feb. 3, 1995. Student Cleve. Coll., Western Res. U., 1942; JD magna cum laude, John Marshall Law Sch., 1946. Bar: Ohio 1946, U.S. Dist. Ct. (no. dist.) Ohio 1954, U.S. Supreme Ct. 1960. With Cleve. Trust Co., 1929-43, Land Title Guarantee & Trust Co., Painesville, Ohio, 1945-46; sole practice, Willoughby, Ohio, 1946-62, 64-77; ptnr. Greene & Tulley (formerly Greene, Tulley & Jurjans), Willoughby, 1962—; sec., dir. Feedall, Inc., 1947-95. Mem. Willoughby Hills (Ohio) Charter Commn., 1970-71; trustee Lake County Bd. Mental Retardation, 1971-73, Willoughby Sch. Fine Arts, 1967-75; bd. mgrs. YMCA, 1968-79, trustee, 1975-79, mem. devel. com., 1991—; advisor to registrants SSS, 1950-75. Served with U.S. Army, 1943-45; ETO. Recipient Corpus Juris Secundum award, 1945; Am. Jurisprudence award, 1945; award SSS, 1975; named Man of Yr., YMCA, 1975. Mem. Ohio State Bar Assn., Lake County Bar Assn. (pres. 1956), Cleve. State U. Law Sch. Alumni Assn. Republican. Baptist. Probate, Estate planning, Estate taxation. Office: 38021 Euclid Ave Willoughby OH 44094-6101

**GREENE, ROBERT LEE,** lawyer; b. Malden, Mo., Oct. 10, 1965; s. Ira Guy and Joann M. (Chezar) G.; m. Cindy S. Greene, May 25, 1991. BSBA, S.E. Mo. State U., 1988; JD, U. Memphis, 1991. Bar: Tenn. 1991, Mo. 1992, U.S. Dist. Ct. (we. dist.) Mo. 1992. Atty. at law West & Rose, Attys. at Law, Kingsport, Tenn., 1991-92, Martin & Assoc., P.C. Attys. at Law, Springfield, Mo., 1992-96; corp. gen. counsel D.J. Roofing Supply, Inc., Springfield, 1996—. Mem. ABA, Mo. Bar Assn., Springfield Metro Bar Assn. Republican. Avocations: bass fishing, golf, reading novels, attending college sporting events. General corporate, General civil litigation, Workers' compensation. Office: D J Roofing Supply Inc PO Box 8165 2037 W Woodland St Springfield MO 65807-5913

**GREENE, ROBERT MICHAEL,** lawyer; b. Buffalo, Jan. 14, 1945; s. Gerald Henry and Dorothy Louise (Doll) G.; m. Catherine Ellen Ostanski, Sept. 28, 1974; children: Amy, Megan, Timothy, Daniel. BA, Canisius Coll., 1966; JD, U. Notre Dame, 1969; LLM, NYU, 1971. Bar: N.Y. 1970, U.S. Dist. Ct. (we. dist.) N.Y. 1970, U.S. Ct. Appeals (2d cir.) 1970. Atty. VISTA, N.Y.C., 1969-71; assoc. Phillips, Lytle, Hitchcock, Blaine & Huber, Buffalo, 1971-75, ptnr., 1976-81, mng. ptnr., 1982-95, CEO, 1995—; del. White House Conf. on Small Bus., 1986; bd. dirs. Armor Box Corp., Cello Pack Corp., Corson Mfg., Gioia Mgmt., Inc., Niagara Envelope Co., Inc. Author: Managing Partner 101: A Primer on Law Firm Leadership, 1990, Making Partner, A Guide for Law Firm Associates, 1992; co-author: Summary of Land Use Regulation in the State of New York and State Land Use Programs, 1974; editor: The Quality Pursuit: Assuring Standards in the Practice of Law, 1989; bd. editors Law Practice Mgmt. mag., 1989-93, articles editor, 1992-93. Trustee Canisius Coll., 1971-77, 92—, chmn. 1993-97; chmn. Shea's Ctr. for Performing Arts, Buffalo, 1981-85; pres. Zool. Soc. of Buffalo, 1987-92; bd. overseers Buffalo Philharm. Orch., 1987-92, vice chmn., 1997—; pres. bd. Cath. Edn. Diocese of Buffalo, 1987-97; trustee Western N.Y. Pub. Broadcasting Assn., 1984—, chmn. 1993-96; Greater Buffalo Devel. Found., 1992-93; bd. dirs. Greater Buffalo Partnership, 1993—, sec. 1996—. Recipient LaSalle award Canisius Coll., 1980, Bd. Regents Dist. Citizens Achievement award, 1987, Disting. Alumni award 1991, Signum Fidei award St. Joseph's Collegiate Inst., 1990, Golden Marquee award Shea's Buffalo Theatre, 1984, Theodore Roosevelt Exemplary Citizen award, 1993. Mem. N.Y. State Bar Assn., Erie County Bar Assn., U. Notre Dame Law Assn. (bd. dirs. 1988—), Buffalo Club, Country Club Buffalo. Democrat. Roman Catholic. General corporate, Health. Office: Phillips Lytle Hitchcock Blaine & Huber 3400 Marine Midland Ctr Buffalo NY 14203-2887

**GREENE, STEPHEN CRAIG,** lawyer; b. Watertown, N.Y., Apr. 27, 1946; s. Harold Adelbert and Mildred Esther (Baker) G. A.B., Syracuse U., 1967, J.D., 1970; m. Nancy Jean Adams, Mar. 28, 1965; children: Kathryn, Stephen, Hilary. Bar: N.Y., 1971, U.S. Tax Ct., 1977. Asst. to pres. SUNY, Oswego, 1970-73; assoc. firm Leyden E. Brown, Oswego, 1973-75; ptnr. Brown and Greene, 1976-81; pvt. practice law, 1981—; bd. dirs. Found. Corp. Legal Studies, Inc., 1968-70; town atty. Oswego, 1972—; counsel Oswego County Bd. Realtors, 1978—. Mem. Oswego County Rep. Com., 1974-85, counsel, 1980-83; bd. dirs. Oswego Hosp., 1981—, mem. exec. com., 1985—, pres., 1996-98; pres. Oswego Health, Inc., 1997—; bd. dirs. Oswego Health, Inc., 1997—, pres., 1997—; bd. dirs. United Way of Oswego County, Inc., 1985-88; bd. dirs. Campbell's Point Assn., 1994-96; gen counsel Express Abstract Co., 1992-95. Recipient Ins. Counsel Jour. award Internat. Assn. Ins. Counsel, 1970. Mem. ABA, N.Y. Bar Assn., Oswego County Bar Assns., Greater Oswego C. of C. (bd. dir. 1980-87), Phi Delta Phi. Episcopalian. Clubs: Oswego Country (counsel 1977-81). Lodges: Masons, Shriners. General corporate, Probate, Real property. Home: 611 W 1st St Oswego NY 13126-4137 Office: 85 W Bridge St Oswego NY 13126-2011

**GREENE, STEVEN K.,** lawyer; b. Englewood, N.J., Oct. 8, 1960; s. Martin S. G. and Claire McCormick; m. Blair Timothy, Sept. 5, 1956 (div. June 1998); 1 child, Colleen Patricia. BA, George Washington U., 1983; JD, Drake U., 1986. Bar: N.J. 1986, U.S. Dist. Ct. N.J. 1986. Atty. Peak & Parkes, Middlesex, N.J., 1986-88, Leonard & Butler, Morristown, N.J., 1988-92, Bongiovanni, Collins & Warden, Denville, N.J., 1992-96, pvt. practice, Denville, N.J., 1996—. Mem. N.J. Bar Assn., Morris County Bar Assn. Democrat. Jewish. Avocations: marathon running, baseball, family. General civil litigation, Criminal, Personal injury. Office: 94 Diamond Spring Rd Denville NJ 07834-2719

**GREENE, TIMOTHY GEDDES,** lawyer; b. Lewiston, Idaho, May 12, 1939; s. George and Norma (Geddes) G.; m. Patricia Apcar, Sept. 13, 1969; children: Andrew Apcar, Jonathan Apcar. BA cum laude, U. Idaho, 1961; LLB, George Washington U., 1965. Bar: D.C., 1966, Tex., 1990. Exec v.p., gen. counsel Sallie Mae SEC, Washington, 1965-69, exec. asst. to the chmn., 1969-71; spl. asst. to gen. counsel U.S. Treasury Dept., Washington, 1971-73; sec. U.S. Emergency Loan Guarantee Bd., Washington, 1971-73; exec. v.p., gen. counsel Student Loan Mktg. Assn. Sallie Mae, Washington, 1973-79; prin. Eggers & Greene, Dallas, 1979-90, Stuart Mill Capital, Inc., Arlington, Va., 1997—. Bd. dirs. Wolf Trap Found. for the Performing Arts, Vienna, Va., 1991-97, NCCJ, 1993—. Ford Found. fellow Brown U. Grad. Sch. Econs., 1961-62. Republican. Mem. LDS Ch. Avocations: sports, golf, tennis. Legislative, General corporate. Home: 1006 Bellview Rd Mc Lean VA 22102-1102

**GREENEBAUM, LEONARD CHARLES,** lawyer; b. Langgoens, Germany, Feb. 6, 1934; came to U.S. 1937, naturalized, 1952; s. Norbert and Henny Lisa (Greenbaum) G.; m. Barbara Rosendorf, Feb. 10, 1957; children: Beth Lynn, Cathy Sue, Steven I. BS cum laude in Commerce, Washington and Lee U., 1956, JD cum laude, 1959. Bar: D.C. 1959, Va. 1959, Md. 1965. Atty. Sachs, Greenebaum & Tayler and predecessor firms, Washington, 1959-64, ptnr., 1964-75, mng. ptnr., 1975-90; ptnr., D.C. coord. litigation Baker & Hostetler, Washington, 1990-95, firmwide litigation group chair, 1996—; arbitrator Am. Arbitration Assn., Washington, 1975—; mem. Washington and Lee U. Law Coun. Chmn. bd. Davis Meml. Goodwill Industries, Washington, 1979-82; bd. dirs. Coun. for Ct. Excellence. Capt. U.S. Army, 1957. Recipient Svc. to Handicapped People award Davis Meml. Goodwill Industries, 1982. Fellow Am. Bar Found. (life); mem. Am. Bd. Trial Advocates, D.C. Bar Assn., Md. Bar Assn., Internat. Platform Assn., Jud. Conf. D.C. Cir., Supreme Ct. Hist. Soc. (hon.), Univ. Club (Washington), Bethesda (Md.) Country Club, Wild Dunes Club (Isle of Palms S.C.), Dunes West Club (Charleston, S.C.), George Town Club (Washington), Order of Coif, Phi Delta Phi. Jewish. Federal civil litigation, General practice, Criminal. Home: 6121 Shady Oak Ln Bethesda MD 20817-6027 Office: Baker & Hostetler 1050 Connecticut Ave NW Washington DC 20036-5304

**GREENER, RALPH BERTRAM,** lawyer; b. Rahway, N.J., Sept. 23, 1940; s. Ralph Bertram and Mary Ellen (Esch) G.; m. Jean Elizabeth Wilson, Mar. 21, 1964; children: Eric Wilson, Erin Hope, Nicholas Christian. BA, Wheaton Coll., 1962; JD, Duke U., 1968. Bar: Minn. 1969, U.S. Dist. Ct. 1969, U.S. Tax Ct. 1988. With Fredrikson & Byron P.A., Mpls., 1969—; chmn. Minn. Lawyers Mutual Ins. Co., Mpls. 1981—; pres. Nat. Assn. of Bar-Related Ins. Cos., 1989-90. 1st Lt. USMCR, 1962-65. Recipient award of profl. excellence Minn. State Bar Assn., 1993. Mem. Rotary Club. General corporate, Insurance, Non-profit and tax-exempt organizations. Home: 1018 W Minnehaha Pky Minneapolis MN 55419-1161 Office: Fredrikson & Byron PA 1100 International Ctr 900 2nd Ave S Minneapolis MN 55402-3314

**GREENFIELD, JAMES MILTON,** lawyer; b. Meadville, Pa., Feb. 5, 1951; s. Milton H. Greenfield and Alice M. (Mickle) Heald; m. Linda A. Speace, June 5, 1993; 1 child, Amy E. BBA, U. Wis., 1973; JD, U. Pitts., 1977. Bar: Pa. 1977, U.S. Dist. Ct. (we. dist.) Pa. 1981, U.S. Ct. Appeals (3d cir.) 1983, U.S. Tax Ct. 1987; CPA, Ill., Pa. Ptnr. Dale, Woodward, Montgomery, Greenfield & Pemrick, Franklin, Pa., 1977—; solicitor Franklin Indsl. and Comml. Devel. Authority, Franklin, 1985—. Active Vis. Nurses Assn. Mem. ABA, Pa. Bar Assn., Venango County Bar Assn, Franklin Area C. of C. (past chmn.). Republican. Methodist. Club: The Franklin (bd. dirs. 1983-84). Lodge: Elks. Probate, Bankruptcy, Contracts commercial. Home: Rosemont Farm Franklin PA 16323 Office: Dale Woodward Montgomery Greenfield & Pemrick 1030 Liberty St Franklin PA 16323-1243

**GREENFIELD, JAMES ROBERT,** lawyer; b. Phila., Mar. 31, 1926; s. Milton and Katherine E. (Rosenberg) G.; m. Phyllis Chaplowe, Aug. 17, 1947 (dec. May 1978); m. Joyce MacDonald Koehler, Mar. 22, 1980. B.S., Bates Coll., 1947; J.D., Yale U., 1950. Bar: Conn. 1950, U.S. Dist. Ct. Conn. 1951, U.S. Ct. Appeals (2d cir.) 1966, U.S. Supreme Ct. 1959. Atty. Chaplowe & Greenfield, 1950-54, Markle & Greenfield, New Haven, 1954-58; sr. ptnr. Lander, Greenfield & Krick, New Haven, 1958-80, Greenfield, Krick & Jacobs, New Haven, 1980-90, Greenfield & Murphy, New Haven, 1990-98; of counsel Tyler Cooper & Alcorn, New Haven, 1998—; lectr. U. Conn., 1966-67, 71-72, 75-76. Mem. editorial bd. Conn. Bar Jour, 1963-77. Pres. New Haven Symphony, 1976-78, Conn. Bar Found., 1976-77; bd. dirs. Nat. Jud. Coll., 1978-84. With USNR, 1944-46. Fellow Am. Bar Found. (state chmn. 1985-90); mem. ABA (state del. 1975-78, bd. govs. 1978-81, ho. of dels. 1972-83, spl. com. on goverance 1983-84, chmn. various coms.), Conn. Bar Assn. (pres. 1973-74, Disting. Profl. Svc. award 1989), Judicature Soc. (bd. dirs. 1983-87), Am. Acad. Matrimonial Lawyers (pres. Conn. chpt. 1993-94), Internat. Acad. Matrimonial Lawyers, New Haven County Bar Assn. (pres. 1969-70, Lifetime Achievment award 1993), Yale Law Sch. Assn. (sec. 1977-80), Quinnipiack Club. Family and matrimonial. Office: Tyler Cooper & Alcorn 205 Church St New Haven CT 06510-1805

**GREENFIELD, MICHAEL C.,** lawyer; b. Chgo., May 4, 1934. BA, U. Ill., 1955; JD, Northwestern U., 1957. Bar: Ill. 1957, U.S. Supreme Ct. 1974, Ind. 1982. Asst. states atty. Cook County (Ill.), 1957-59; ptnr. Asher, Gittler & Greenfield, Ltd., Chgo., 1959—, Asher, Gittler, Greenfield & D'Alba, Ltd., Chgo.; mem. inquiry bd. Ill. Supreme Ct. Disciplinary Commn., 1973-77, mem. hearing bd., 1978-94, 97—, vice chmn., 1984, chmn., 1985, mem. oversight comm., 1995-96. Mem. ABA, Internat. Found. Employee Benefit Plans (bd. dirs. 1977-80, 85-88, 92-94), Ill. Bar Assn., Chgo. Bar Assn. Pension, profit-sharing, and employee benefits, Labor. Office: Asher Gittler Greenfield & D'Alba Ltd 125 S Wacker Dr Ste 1100 Chicago IL 60606-4397

**GREENFIELD, MILTON, JR.,** lawyer; b. St. Louis, Dec. 13, 1910; s. Milton and Hilda (Loewenstein) G.; m. Jane Elizabeth Stocke, Nov. 8, 1956; children: George W. Beeler Jr., Janet B. Nesin. AB cum laude, Harvard U., 1932, JD, 1935. Bar: Mo. 1935. Ptnr. Greenfield, Davidson, St. Louis, 1983-88; pvt. practice St. Louis, 1989—; mem. part-time faculty St. Louis U. Sch. Law, 1945-63; past chmn. local character com. and mem. 22d cir. bar com. Mo. Supreme Ct.; past chmn. Mo. and St. Louis jr. bar groups. Past chmn. St. Louis Community Found., St. Louis U. Bequest and Gift Coun.; past pres. St. Louis Estate Planning Coun.; past chmn. gift and bequest com. Barnes Hosp.; past chmn. bd. advisors Lang Found.; civilian atty. for Ordnance Dept., 1943-45. Contbr. articles to legal publs. Fellow Am. Coll. Trust and Estate Coun. (past pres.); mem. Internat. Acad. Estate and Trust Law (academician), Bar Assn. St. Louis (former v.p.), St. Louis Bar Found. (past pres.), Bellerive Country Club, Westwood Country Club (past pres.). Estate planning, Probate, Estate taxation. Home: 900 S Hanley Rd Apt 9E Saint Louis MO 63105-2668 Office: 7751 Carondelet Ave Ste 500 Saint Louis MO 63105-3369

**GREENFIELD, SCOTT H.,** lawyer; b. Perth Amboy, N.J., Feb. 9, 1958; s. Edwin S. and Phyllis Joy Greenfield; m. Theresa Anne Amigo, Sept. 16, 1984; children: Rebecca Catherine, Jack Alexander. BS, Cornell U., 1979; JD, N.Y. Law Sch., 1982. Bar: N.Y. 1983, U.S. Dist. Ct. (so. and ea. dists.) N.Y. 1983, U.S. Ct. Appeals (2d cir.) 1985, (3d cir.) 1990, U.S. Supreme Ct. 1987. Ptnr. Meyer & Greenfield, N.Y.C., 1983-93; pvt. practice N.Y.C., 1994—; arbitrator N.Y.C. Civil Ct., 1991—. Mem. Nat. Assn. Criminal Def. Lawyers, N.Y. State Assn. Criminal Def. Lawyers (chair amicus com. 1995, bd. dirs. 1999—), N.Y. State Bar Assn., N.Y. Criminal Bar Assn. Criminal. Office: 233 Broadway Fl 51 New York NY 10279-5199

**GREENHAUS, PHILIP SHERWOOD,** lawyer; b. N.Y.C., Jan. 30, 1943; s. Louis and Claire (Lefrak) G.; m. Anita Fay Bilt, July 5, 1947; children: David, Daniel. BA, NYU, 1965; JD, Bklyn. Law Sch., 1968. Bar: N.Y. 1968, U.S. Dist. Ct. (so. dist.) N.Y., U.S. Ct. Appeals (2d cir.). Assoc. McDonough Schneider & Marcus, N.Y.C., 1968-75, Baller Stoll & Itzler, N.Y.C., 1975-77, Wallman and Kramer, N.Y.C., 1977-81; pvt. practice N.Y.C., 1982—. Contbr. articles to profl. jours. Fellow Am. Acad. Matrimonial Lawyers (bd. mgrs.). Avocations: skiing, automobiles. Family and matrimonial. Office: 501 5th Ave New York NY 10017-6107

**GREENHILL, JONATHAN SETH,** lawyer; b. N.Y.C., Dec. 25, 1953; s. Ira Judd and Elaine Diane (Maltzman) G.; m. Elena Caldera, Sept. 5, 1987; children: Caitlin Jo, Alexander Jared. BA, John Hopkins U., 1976; MPA with distinction, NYU, 1978; JD, U. Denver, 1980. Bar: N.Y., 1981, U.S. Dist. Ct. (ea. and so. dists.) N.Y., 1981, U.S. Ct. Appeals (4th cir.) 1995. Asst. dir. Pub. Affairs Program U. Denver, 1979-80; officer U.S. Fgn. Svc., Washington, Latin Am. and Europe, 1980-90; prin. Greenhill Ptnrs. P.C., N.Y.C., 1990—. Contbr. articles to profl. jours. Mem. ABA, Assn. Bar City N.Y., Johns Hopkins Lawyers Roundtable, Johns Hopkins U. Alumni Assn. (bd. dirs. 1990—), Loss Execs. Assn. (assoc.), The Penn Club of N.Y., Phi Alpha Delta, Delta Phi. Avocations: Spanish and French languages. General practice, Insurance, General civil litigation. Office: Greenhill Ptnrs PC 555 Fifth Ave New York NY 10017-2416

**GREENLAW, DAWN SHARON,** lawyer; b. Lawton, Okla., Oct. 9, 1969; d. Douglas Warren and Linda Ann Greenlaw. BA in Polit. Sci., U. Vt., 1990, MPA, 1991; MA in Polit. Sci., Boston Coll., 1993; JD, U. Conn., Hartford, 1996; postgrad., Boston U., 1997—. Bar: Conn., 1996, Mass., 1997, U.S. Dist. Ct. Conn., 1997. Pvt. practice atty. West Hartford, Conn., 1996-97; sr. corp. atty. Exec. Risk, Inc., Simbury, Conn., 1997—; adj. prof. criminology Cuny Coll., Mass., 1996. Notes and comments editor Conn. Ins. Law Jour., 1994-96; mem. staff Ann. Rev. Banking Law, 1998. Recipient Am. Jurisprudence award, 1994. Republican. Roman Catholic. Insurance, Contracts commercial, General corporate. Home: 45 Cobblestone Rd Glastonbury CT 06033-2505 Office: Exec Risk Inc 82 Hopmeadow St Weatogue CT 06089-9694

**GREENLEAF, JOHN L., JR.,** lawyer; b. Ft. Campbell, Ky., July 27, 1953; s. John L. Sr. and Betty R. G.; m. Carol K. Hood, Dec. 18, 1971; children: Sara E., J. Luke, Danielle H. BS, U. Ill., 1975; JD, John Marshall Law Sch., 1978. Bar: Ill. 1978, U.S. Dist. Ct. (so. and cen. dists.) Ill. 1978, U.S. Supreme Ct. 1982. Assoc. Byers & Byers, Inc., Decatur, Ill., 1978-80; ptnr. Byers, Byers & Greenleaf, Inc., Decatur, 1980-89; pvt. practice Decatur, 1989-98; assoc. Frank H. Byers, Decatur, 1998—. Dir. Decatur Foursquare Broadcasting--WFHL TV 23, 1980-98; adv. dir. New Life Pregnancy Ctr., Decatur, 1994—; treas. Decatur Jaycees, 1982, Com. to Elect Frank H. Byers, II as State's Atty., 1988. Named Leading Ill. Atty., Am. Rsch. Corp., 1996. Mem. Ill. Bar Assn. Avocations: teaching and preaching the Bible, snow skiing, swimming, golfing. Estate planning, Bankruptcy, General corporate. Office: 3795 N Woodford PO Box 2227 Decatur IL 62524-2227

**GREENLEAF, WALTER FRANKLIN,** lawyer; b. Griffin, Ga., Sept. 21, 1946; s. Walter Helmuth and Vida Mildred (Goheen) G. B.A., Mich. State U., 1968; M.A., U. N.C., 1970, J.D., U. Ala., 1973. Bar: Ala. 1973, Fla. 1974, U.S. Dist. Ct. (no. dist.) Ala. 1973, U.S. Ct. Appeals (5th cir.) 1974, U.S. Dist. Ct. (so. dist.) Fla. 1977, U.S. Ct. Appeals (11th cir) 1981. Law clk. U.S. Dist. Ct., Birmingham, Ala., 1973-74; assoc. Sirote, Permutt, et al., Birmingham, Ala., 1975-76; assoc., then ptnr. Welbaum Guernsey, Hingston, Greenleaf, & Gregory, LLP, Miami, Fla., 1976—. Editor, Ala. Law Rev., 1972-73. Mem. ABA, Dade County Bar Assn., Am. Arbitration Assn. (panel of arbitrators), Order Coif, Phi Beta Kappa, Phi Kappa Phi, Phi Delta Phi, Omicron Delta Kappa. Insurance, Construction, Probate. Home: 417 Madeira Ave Miami FL 33134-4234 Office: Welbaum Guernsey Hingston Greenleaf & Gregory LLP 901 Ponce De Leon Blvd Miami FL 33134-3073

**GREENLEY, BEVERLY JANE,** lawyer, educator; b. Cleve., Sept. 24, 1947; d. Gaylord H. and Joan C. (Gurklis) G. BA, Principia Coll., 1969; JD, U. Mo., 1976; LLM, Washington U., 1981. Bar: Mo. 1976, Ill. 1977, U.S. Dist. Ct. (we. dist.) Mo. 1976, U.S. Tax Ct. 1979. Ptnr., McCarter & Greenley, St. Louis, 1976-81, McCarter Snyder & Greenley, St. Louis, 1981-85; assoc. prof. law Stetson U. Coll. Law, St. Petersburg, Fla., 1981-85; ptnr. Gage & Tucker, St. Louis, 1985-87, Husch, Eppenberger, Donohue, Cornfeld & Jenkins, St. Louis, 1987-90, McCarter & Greenley, St. Louis, 1990—; estate planning lectr. for CLE programs, 1997—. Co-author: Missouri Lawyer's Guide, 1984. Mem. Mo. Bar Assn., Ill. Bar Assn. Estate planning, Taxation, general, Probate. Office: 1 Metropolitan Sq Ste 2160 Saint Louis MO 63102-2797

**GREENMAN, FREDERICK F., JR.,** lawyer; b. N.Y.C., Feb. 22, 1933; s. Frederick F. and Mildred G.; m. Angela Lancieri; children: Paul Rudolph, Jodi La Bourene. BA, Harvard U., 1954, LLB, 1961, LLM, 1963. Bar: N.Y. 1962. Assoc. Hays, Sklar & Herzberg, N.Y.C., 1962-66; asst. U.S. atty. So. Dist. N.Y., N.Y.C., 1966-69; assoc. Linden and Deutsch, N.Y.C., 1969-70; ptnr. Deutsch Klagsbrun & Blasband (and predecessor firm), 1971—. Mem. Assn. Bar City N.Y., N.Y. State Bar Assn. Jewish. General civil litigation, Trademark and copyright. Office: Deutsch Klagsbrun & Blasband 800 3rd Ave New York NY 10022-7604

**GREENO, JOHN GORDON,** lawyer, university administrator; b. Mpls., Mar. 30, 1958; m. Patricia Joan Hawk, July 26, 1986; children: Emily, James. BA with distinction, Stanford U., 1980; JD, U. Va., 1983. Bar: Pa. 1983. Assoc. Berkman, Ruslander et al, Pitts., 1983-88; assoc. Doepken, Keevican & Weiss, Pitts., 1988-92, mem., 1993-95; assoc. gen. counsel U. Pitts., 1995-98, asst. vice chancellor, 1998—. Bd. dirs. Vocat. Rehab. Ctr., Pitts., 1995-98, chmn. Projects With Industry, 1994-95; pres. Pitts. Pub. Theater Assn., Pitts., 1993-94; mem. parish coun. Calvary Episcopal Ch., Pitts., 1989-90. Mem. County Bar Assn. (pub. svc. com. 1994-98). Avocations: soccer coaching, ice hockey, soccer. Office: U Pittsburgh 200 S Craig St Pittsburgh PA 15213-3705

**GREENSLADE, GEORGE ALFRED,** lawyer; b. Jan. 20, 1961. BA, SUNY, Albany, 1983; JD, U. Pa., 1987. Bar: N.Y. Assoc. Baker & McKenzie, N.Y.C. General corporate, Securities. Office: Baker & McKenzie 805 3rd Ave New York NY 10022-7513

**GREENSPAN, JEFFREY DOV,** lawyer; b. Chgo., July 19, 1954; s. Philip and Sylvia (Haberman) G.; m. Eleanor Helen Goldman, Aug. 28, 1983. BS in Econs., U. Ill., Urbana, 1976; JD, Ill. Inst. Tech., 1979. Bar: Ill. 1979, U.S. Dist. Ct. (no. dist.) Ill. 1979, U.S. Ct. Appeals (7th cir.) 1979. Atty. Govs. Office Consumer Services, Chgo., 1978-80; asst. pub. defender Cook County Pub. Defenders Office, Chgo., 1980-81; asst. corp. counsel Village of Skokie, Ill., 1981-91; of counsel Fioretti & Des Jardins, 1990-91; with Ancel, Glink, Diamond, Cope & Bush, P.C., 1991—; sec., treas. Polit. Cons., Inc., Skokie, 1984—. Author polit. computer software Master Campaigner, 1984. Mem. Niles (Ill.) Twp. Dem. Orgn., 1976—; chmn. Niles Twp. Com. on Youth, 1982-85, TRY-Citizens for Drug Awareness, Niles, 1983-84; mem. Centereast Bd. Authority, 1998—; bd. dirs. Niles Twp. H.S., 1999—. Mem. Chgo. Bar Assn. (chmn. devel. of law com. 1990-91, chmn. local govt. law com. 1992-93). State civil litigation, Land use and zoning (including planning), Municipal (including bonds). Home: 9445 Keeler Ave Skokie IL 60076-1442

**GREENSPAN, LEON JOSEPH,** lawyer; b. Phila., Feb. 10, 1932; s. Joseph and Minerva (Podolsky) G.; m. Irene Gordon, Nov. 2, 1958; children: Marjorie, David, Michael, Lisa. AB, Temple U., 1955, JD, 1958. Bar: N.Y. 1959, U.S. Supreme Ct. 1969, N.J. 1985, Fla. 1985, Pa. 1986, Conn. 1991. Pvt. practice law White Plains, N.Y., 1959-64; ptnr. Greenspan and Aurnou, White Plains, 1964-77, Greenspan, Jaffe & Rosenblatt, White Plains, 1987-91, Greenspan & Greenspan, White Plains, 1992—; counsel Brown, Boston; lectr. Fla. Bar CLER Program, 1991, 92, 99; atty. Tarrytown (N.Y.) Housing Authority. Pres. Hebrew Inst., White Plains; vice chmn. ann. dinner NCCJ. Recipient Pres.'s award Union Orthodox Synagogues, 1982; honoree Hebrew Inst., White Plains, 1983. Mem. ABA, Westchester County Bar Assn., White Plains Bar Assn., N.Y. State Trial Lawyers Assn., Criminal Cts. Bar Assn. Westchester County. General civil litigation, Criminal, Taxation, general. Home: 14 Pinebrook Dr White Plains NY 10605-4713 Office: Greenspan & Greenspan 34 S Broadway 6th Fl White Plains NY 10601-4400

**GREENSPAN, MICHAEL EVAN,** lawyer; b. White Plains, N.Y., Jan. 18, 1967; s. Leon Joseph and Irene (Gordon) G.; m. Diane Gloria Blum, July 2, 1989; children: Daniel, Marc. BA magna cum laude, Temple U., 1988, JD, 1991. Bar: N.Y. 1992, U.S. Dist. Ct. (so. and ea. dists.) N.Y. 1992, U.S. Dist. Ct. Conn. 1992, U.S. Ct. Appeals (2d cir.) 1993, U.S. Ct. Appeals (11th cir.) 1996. Assoc. Greenspan, Jaffe & Rosenblatt, White Plains, 1991-92; ptnr. Greenspan & Greenspan, White Plains, 1992—; mem. panel of appellate attys. to prosecute indigent criminal appeals, mem. panel of attys. representing indigents accused of misdemeanors State Bar N.Y.; Temple U. del. Symposium on the Presidency, Washington, 1987. Mem. exec. com. Loucks Track & Field Games, White Plains, 1991—. Recipient Lewis F. Powell Jr. medallion Am. Coll. Trial Lawyers Assn., 1991, James J. Manderino award Phila. Trial Lawyers Assn., 1991. Mem. ATLA, N.Y. Trial Lawyers Assn., Barristers Soc., N.Y. State Bar Assn. (contbg. editor ins. and compensation law sect. Automobile Liability Newsletter 1997—), Westchester County Bar Assn., White Plains Bar Assn., Westchester Track and Field and Cross-Country Ofcls. Orgn., Golden Key, Order of Omega, Phi Beta Kappa, Pi Sigma Alpha, Phi Alpha Theta, Delta Tau Delta. Republican. Jewish. Avocations: officiating high school track and field, race walking, basketball. General civil litigation, Family and matrimonial, Criminal. Office: Greenspan & Greenspan 34 S Broadway Ste 605 White Plains NY 10601-4428

**GREENSPON, ROBERT ALAN,** lawyer; b. Hartford, Conn., Apr. 17, 1947; s. George Arthur and Shirley Jean (Shelton) G.; m. Claire Alice Stone, Aug. 21, 1971; children: Colin Haynes, Alison Shelton. AB, Franklin and Marshall, 1969; JD, Columbia U., 1972. Bar: Conn. 1973, N.Y. 1998, U.S. Dist. Conn. 1973, U.S. Ct. Appeals (2d cir.) 1983. Assoc. Robinson & Cole, Hartford, Conn., 1972-78; ptnr. Robinson & Cole, Hartford, 1978-81, Stamford, Conn., 1981-86; sr. v.p., gen. counsel Guinness Peat Aviation Corp., Stamford, N.Y.C., N.Y.C., Shannon, Ireland, 1985-92; ptnr. Latham & Watkins, N.Y.C., 1992—. Contbr. articles to profl. jours. Mem. ABA (comml. fin. services, aircraft fin.), Conn. Bar Assn., N.Y. State Bar Assn., Internat. Bar Assn., Southwestern Legal Found. (bd. advisors internat. and comparative law ctr.). Private international, Contracts commercial, Federal civil litigation. Home: 49 Old Farm Rd Darien CT 06820-6119 Office: Latham & Watkins 885 3rd Ave Fl 10 New York NY 10022-4834

**GREENSPON, SUSAN JEAN,** lawyer; b. Cin., Oct. 28, 1964; d. Charles D. and Barbara E. (Fogelson) Poncher; m. Steven M. Greenspon, May 20, 1991; children: Isaac, Eli. BA, U. Wis., 1986; JD, Loyola U., Chgo., 1989. Bar: Ill. 1989. Assoc. Rosenthal & Schanfield, Chgo., 1989-91, Kovitz, Shifrin & Waitzman, Buffalo Grove, Ill., 1991—; cons. Lawyers for the Creative Arts, Chgo., 1984—, Ill. Assn. Gifted Children, Chgo., 1989—; atty. Buffalo Grove Friends of Parks Found., 1996—. Author, editor Corp. Connection, 1997. Recipient Am. Jurisprudence awards, 1988, 89. Mem. ABA, Chgo. Bar Assn., Ill. State Ba Assn., Northwest Suburban Bar Assn. General corporate, Contracts commercial. Office: Kovitz Shifrin & Waitzman 750 W Lake Cook Rd Ste 350 Buffalo Grove IL 60089-2086

**GREENSTEIN, J. RICHARD,** lawyer; b. Phila., July 29, 1941; s. Daniel S. and Ruth H. Greenstein; m. Susan Sobel, Apr. 7, 1968; 1 child, Jennifer. AB, Cornell U., 1963; LLB, U. Pa., 1966; LLM in Taxation, NYU, 1971. Bar: Pa. 1966, U.S. Dist. Ct. (ea. dist.) Pa., U.S. Tax Ct. Assoc. Greenstein Gorelick Silverman & Price, Phila., 1966-71, ptnr., 1971-89; ptnr. Hepburn Willcox Hamilton & Putnam, Phila., 1989—. Bd. dirs. Haverford Twp. Sch. Dist., Pa., 1987-91. Recipient Merit award Chapel of Four Chaplains, Phila., 1974. Avocations: golf, tennis. General corporate, Taxation, general, Estate planning. Office: Hepburn Willcox Hamilton & Putnam 1100 One Penn Ctr Philadelphia PA 19103

**GREENSTEIN, KAREN ANNE,** lawyer; b. N.Y.C., Jan. 21, 1969; d. Robert Alan and Ericka (Lief) G.; m. Sean Sullivan, May 11, 1996. AB, U. Mich., 1990; JD, NYU, 1995. Assoc. Loeb & Loeb, LLP, N.Y.C., 1995—. Recipient Cornerstone award Lawyers Alliance of N.Y., 1998. Mem. ABA. General corporate, Mergers and acquisitions. Office: Loeb and Loeb LLP 345 Park Ave Fl 18 New York NY 10154-1895

**GREENSTEIN, MARLA NAN,** lawyer; b. Chgo., Jan. 20, 1957; d. Charles Allen and Lenore (Gould) G. Cert., Oxford U., Eng., 1978; AB, Georgetown U., 1979; JD, Loyola U., 1982. Bar: Ill. 1982, Alaska 1997, U.S. Dist. Ct. (no. dist.) Ill. 1982, U.S. Ct. Appeals (7th cir.) 1983. Sr. staff atty. Am. Judicature Soc., Chgo., 1982-85, Alaska Jud. Council, Anchorage, 1985-89; exec. dir. Ala. Commn. Jud. Conduct, Anchorage, 1989—; cons. Com. on Cts. and Justice, Chgo., 1985. Author: Handbook for Judicial Nominating Commissioners, 1984. Mem. ABA (chair lawyers conf. jud. divsn. 1996-97), Assn. Jud. Disciplinary Counsel (bd. dirs. 1992—), Am. Judicature Soc. (bd. dirs. 1992-97, exec. com. 1997—), Pi Sigma Alpha. Avocations: photography, drawing. Office: Commn on Jud Conduct 310 K St Ste 301 Anchorage AK 99501-2064

**GREENSTEIN, RICHARD HENRY,** lawyer; b. Newark, June 29, 1946; s. Jacob Harold and Florence G.; m. Irene Beth Polishuk, July 4, 1973; children: Suzanne Beth, Jonathan Henry. AB, Rutgers Coll., 1968; JD, Boston U., 1971. Bar: N.J. 1971, U.S. Dist. Ct. N.J. 1971, U.S. Supreme Ct. 1985. Law clk. Superior Ct. N.J., Elizabeth, 1971-72; asst. county prosecutor Union County Prosecutor, Elizabeth, 1972-74; assoc. atty. Mandel, Wysoker, Sherman, et al, Perth Amboy, N.J., 1974-77, Fox and Fox, Newark, 1977-83; ptnr. Kein, Pollatschek & Greenstein, Union, N.J., 1983—; atty. Young Astronauts N.J. Inc., 1989—; mem. ethics com. Supreme Ct. Dist. N.J., 1991-95. Lighting dir. Wash. Sch. PTA Show, Westfield, N.J., 1985-94. Mem. Exchange Club Union (pres.-elect, dir. 1983—). Jewish. Avocations: skiing, hiking, reading. Banking, Land use and zoning (including planning), General corporate. Home: 743 Saint Marks Ave Westfield NJ 07090-2035 Office: Kein Pollatschek & Greenstein 2042 Morris Ave Union NJ 07083-6028

**GREENSTONE, ADAM FRANKLIN,** lawyer; b. Washington, Dec. 1, 1963; s. James Paul and Elaine Beatrice (Hurwitz) G. BA, Gettsburg Coll., 1985; MSc, London Sch. Econs., 1986; JD, George Washington U., 1990. Bar: Pa. 1991, D.C. 1993. Law clk. to Hon. Eugene R. Sullivan, U.S. Ct. Mil. Appeals (now Ct. Appeals for Armed Forces), Washington, 1990-92; atty.-advisor Office Gen. Counsel, NASA, Washington, 1992-97; dep. gen. counsel Office Adminstrn., Exec. Office of Pres., Washington, 1997—. Mem. ABA, Am. Soc. Internat. Law, Eisenhower World Affairs Inst. Jewish. Office: Exec Office of Pres Office Adminstrn 725 17th St NW Washington DC 20503-0009

**GREENWALD, ANDREW ERIC,** lawyer; b. N.Y.C., May 31, 1942; s. Harold and Lillian G.; m. Paula S., Aug. 20, 1967; children: Brooke Ellen, Karen Michelle. BS, U. Wis., 1964; JD, Georgetown U., 1967. Bar: D.C. 1968, Md. 1969, U.S. Ct. Appeals Md. 1969. Lawyer Nat. Labor Rels. Bd., Washington, 1967-68; asst. corp. counsel D.C. Govt., 1968-69; shareholder Joseph, Greenwald & Laake PA, Greenbelt, Md., 1969—; past mem. dept. family and cmty. devel. U. Md. *Author of articles in Trial Magazine: Deposing medical Experts, May, 1990; In the Beginning: Examples of Opening Statements, May, 1989; Shattered Dreams: A Look at the Seriously Injured Child, May, 1985; Let Me Ask You This-Some Thoughts on Cross-Examination, June, 1983; Oh, Didn't I Tell You? A Look at Informed Consent, June, 1982; Medical Malpractice Litigation: A Modest Settlement Proposal, May, 1980; Effective Pre-Trial Discovery in Medical Negligence Cases/What You Don't Know Might Hurt You, July, 1979; Contributor to Best of Trial, ATLA, 1990; The Profoundly Injured Child, ATLA, 1986; How to Recognize and Handle Recreational Liability Cases: Sports Torts, ATLA, 1980.* Contbr. articles to profl. jours. Active adv. com. Georgetown U. Continuing Legal Edn., 1991, Georgetown U. Law Ctr. Alumni Bd., 1995. Mem. ATLA (chmn. tort sect. 1985), ABA, Nat. Inst. Trial Advocacy, Am. Bd. Profl. Liability Attys., Am. Bd. Trial Advocates, William B. Bryant Inn, Am. Inns of Ct. Personal injury, Product liability, General civil litigation. Office: Joseph Greenwald & Laake PA 6404 Ivy Ln Ste 400 Greenbelt MD 20770-1407

**GREENWALD, DAVID JEFFREY,** lawyer; b. Newark, Jan. 1, 1959; s. Howard Stanley and Rieva (Forman) G.; m. Beth Ann Sterenfeld, June 10, 1984; children: Hilary Lynn, Emily Sarah. Student, Duke U., 1976-78; BSE, U. Pa., 1980; JD, Columbia U., 1983. Bar: N.Y. 1984, N.J. 1984. Assoc. Fried, Frank, Harris, Shriver & Jacobson, N.Y.C., 1983-90, ptnr., 1990-94; v.p., gen. counsel, prin. investment area Goldman, Sachs & Co., N.Y.C., 1994-98, mng. dir. gen. counsel merchant banking divsn., 1998—. Harlan Fiske Stone scholar, Columbia U., 1983. Mem. Bar Assn. City of N.Y., Beta Gamma Sigma. Mergers and acquisitions, General corporate, Securities. Office: Goldman Sachs & Co 85 Broad St New York NY 10004-2456

**GREENWALD, HAROLD,** lawyer; b. Yonkers, N.Y., Apr. 2, 1907; s. Louis and Rose (Schwartz) G.; m. Dorothy Nass, June 26, 1943 (dec.). LLB, NYU, 1928. Assoc. Law Office Waldo G. Morse, N.Y.C., 1928-34; counsel Coop. Grange League Fedn., 1934-64; ptnr. Greenwald, Kovner, Goldsmith, N.Y.C., 1944-60, Danziger, Bangser, Klipstein, Goldsmith & Greenwald, N.Y.C., 1960-77; of counsel Bangser, Klein, Rocca & Blum, N.Y.C., 1977—; counsel, N.Y.State Prisoners of War Programs, 1943-44; gen. counsel Agway Inc., 1964, Quality Bakers Am. Coop., N.Y.c., 1943-86; me. conf. N.Y. Legis. Com. for Revision of Coop. Corp. Law, 1965. Counsel to Ams. for Energy Independence, Washington, 1975-76; trustee Wall St. Synagogue, 1965—. Mem. ABA, Assn. Bar City of N.Y., Internat. Assn. Jewish Lawyers and Jurists, Zionisi Orgn. Am. (bd. dirs. 1943—, chmn. fin. com. 1945-93). Antitrust, General corporate, Private international. Office: Bangser Klein Rocca & Blum 230 Park Ave Fl 26 New York NY 10169-0178

**GREENWELL, PATRICK BERNARD,** lawyer; b. Martins Ferry, Ohio, Apr. 8, 1954; s. Bernard Thomas and Georgeanne (Edmundson) G.; m. Sandra Nora Hearn, May 9, 1981; children: Erica Ann, James Patrick, Angela Sara, Joshua Jeffrey. Student, U. Hartford, 1974-77, Ohio State U., 1977-79; JD, Western State U., 1985. Bar: Calif. 1986, U.S. Dist. Ct. (so. dist.) Calif. 1986, U.S. Dist. Ct. (ctrl. dist.) Calif. 1993, U.S. Supreme Ct. 1996. Tech. trainer Measurex Corp., Cupertino, Calif., 1977-80; owner Highland's Mktg., South Lake Tahoe, Calif., 1980-83; law clk. McCarty Patterson & Ferguson, San Diego, 1983-85; atty. Law Office of Patrick Greenwell, Encinitas, Calif., 1986-90; dep. dist. atty. County of Stanislaus, Modesto, 1990-91; dep. county counsel County of Tuolumne, Sonora, Calif., 1991-95, county counsel, 1995—; fee arbitrator State Bar Calif., San Francisco, 1994—. Author: Willing to Love Again, 1996. Chmn. Children's Holiday Party, Sonora, 1994, 95, 96; pres. Born Again Marriages, Sonora, 1996, 97. With USN, 1973-77. Mem. Sonora Sunrise Rotary Club (pres. 1994, 95), BPO Elks Club. Republican. Avocations: camping, snow skiing, woodworking, family. Home: 17100 Fitch Ranch Rd Sonora CA 95370-9677 Office: County of Tuolomne 2 S Green St Sonora CA 95370-4618

**GREENWOOD, CHARLES,** lawyer; b. Phila., July 10, 1942; s. Abraham and Lea (Swerdlow) G.; m. Linda Myra Nightingale, Aug. 27, 1971; children: Arin Evan, Lee Abraham. B.A., Temple U., 1964, M.A., 1968; J.D., U. Calif.-Hastings Coll. Law, San Francisco, 1971. Bar: R.I. 1971, Calif. 1971, U.S. Dist. Ct. R.I. 1971, U.S. Supreme Ct. 1980. Sr. atty. R.I. Legal Services, Providence, R.I., 1971-78; sole practice law, Providence, R.I., 1978-81; ptnr. McKenna, Greenwood & Feinstein, Providence, 1981—; mem. faculty Temple U., 1965-67, 78, U. R.I., 1972-74, Am. Paralegal Inst., Newton, Mass., 1982-83. Temple U. scholar, 1964-66, SUNY-Buffalo scholar, 1967-68, U. Calif.-Hastings Law Sch. scholar, 1968-71. Mem. R.I. Bar Assn., Calif. Bar Assn. Family and matrimonial, Federal civil litigation, State civil litigation. Home: 6 Berkeley Rd East Greenwich RI 02818-4110 Office: 333 Westminster St Providence RI 02903-3302

**GREENWOOD, DANN E.,** lawyer; b. Dickinson, N.D., Sept. 21, 1952; s. Lawrence E. and Joyce E. (Henley) G.; m. Debra K. Ableidinger, June 15, 1975; children: Jay, Lindsey, Paige. BSBA magna cum laude, U. N.D., 1974, JD, 1977. Bar: N.D. 1977, U.S. Dist. Ct. N.D. 1980. Ptnr. Greenwood, Greenwood & Greenwood and predecessor firms, Dickinson, 1977—, Greenwood & Ramsey. Mem. N.D. Supreme Ct. Disciplinary Bd., 1984—, Norther Lights Boy Scouts Council, Dickinson, 1985—; bd. dirs. Legal Assistance N.D., Bismarck, 1980-86. Mem. ABA, N.D. Bar Assn. (pres. 1998-99), Stark-Dunn County Bar Assn., N.D. Trial Lawyers Assn. (sec. 1983-84, treas. 1984-85, v.p. 1985-86, pres. 1987-88). Lutheran. Lodges: Kiwanis, Masons, Shriners, Elks. Personal injury, State civil litigation, Family and matrimonial. Home: PO Box 688 Dickinson ND 58602-0688*

**GREENWOOD, MARK LAWRENCE,** lawyer; b. Fargo, N.D., Sept. 14, 1951; s. Lawrence Edward and Joyce Eleanor (Henley) G.; m. Linda Marie Heck, June 5, 1973; children: Dawn Malinda, Jonn Scott, Geoff Michael. BBA, Dickinson State U., 1973; JD, N.D. State U., 1976. Bar: N.D. 1976, U.S. Dist. Ct. N.D. 1976. Ptnr. Greenwood Law Offices, Dickinson, N.D., 1976-79, Greenwood, Greenwood & Greenwood, Dickinson, 1979-91, Greenwood, Greenwood, Greenwood, Selinger and Ramsey, P.C., Dickinson, 1991-98; pvt. practice Dickinson, 1998—. Chmn. Dist. 37 Dem. NPL, Dickinson, 1988-92, treas., 1986-88. Mem. Nat. Assn. Criminal Def. Lawyers, N.D. Trial Lawyers Assn., SW Jud. Dist. Bar Assn. (sec. 1982-84, pres. 1984-86, N.D. Bar Assn. (bd. govs. 1984-86), Dickinson Lodge 32 A.F. & A.M. (master 1984), El Zagel Temple Shrine, El Zagel Frontiersmen (pres. 1985), Dickinson Jaycees (sec. 1976). Methodist. Avocations: firearms and bow hunting, camping, reading. E-mail: mlglaw@pop.ctctel.com. Criminal, Personal injury, General civil litigation. Office: PO Box 327 Dickinson ND 58602-0327

**GREENWOOD, P. NICHOLAS,** lawyer; b. Birmingham, Ala., Aug. 9, 1945. BS, U. N.C., 1967; JD, Vanderbilt U., 1971. Bar: Ala. 1972. Atty. Bradley Arant Rose & White LLP, Birmingham, Ala. Mem. editl. bd. Vanderbilt Law Rev., 1971. Mem. ABA, Ala. State Bar, Birmingham Bar Assn., Order of Coif. Banking, Finance. Office: Bradley Arant Rose & White LLP PO Box 830709 2001 Park Pl Ste 1400 Birmingham AL 35283

**GREER, BERNARD LEWIS, JR.,** lawyer; b. Knoxville, Tenn., Sept. 11, 1940; s. Bernard Lewis and Margaret Strickland (Vinsinger) G.; m. Lynda Lea Kidd, June 11, 1966; children: Andrew Scott, William Vinsinger. BA magna cum laude, U. Tenn., 1962, postgrad., 1964-65; JD, Emory U., 1968. Bar: N.Y. 1969, Ga. 1975; conseil juridique France, 1971. Assoc. Willkie Farr & Gallagher, N.Y.C., 1968-71, 73-74, Willke, Farr & Gallagher, Paris, 1971-73, Shoob, McLain, Merritt & Lyle, Atlanta, 1974-77, O'Callaghan, Saunders & Stumm, 1977-85; ptnr. Alston & Bird, Atlanta, 1985—; mem. adv. bd. Internat. and Comparative Law Ctr., Southwestern Legal Found., 1978—; participant various seminars; lectr. on European bus. instns. and practice Emory U. Law Sch., Atlanta, 1975—, Ga. State U. Law Sch., 1975—. Mem. Emory U. Law Rev., 1967-68; contbr. to legal publs. Counsel, trustee, mem. exec. com. Atlanta Bot. Garden, Inc.; mem. exec. com., bd. dirs. Ga. Coun. for Internat. Visitors, 1986-93, pres., 1989-90; bd. visitors U. Tenn. Coll. Liberal Arts, Knoxville, 1988-91. 1st lt. U.S. Army, 1962-64. Internat. bus. fellow S.E. region, 1988. Mem. ABA, Internat. Bar Assn. (coun. bus. law sect. 1990-94), State Bar Ga. (chmn. internat. law sect. 1982-83, chmn. com. on internationalization of practice of law 1989—), State Bar N.Y., Atlanta Bar Assn., Assn. Bar City N.Y., Soc. Internat. Bus. Fellows, Am. Arbitration Assn. (panel of arbitrators 1987—), Scabbard and Blade, Omicron Delta Kappa, Pi Sigma Alpha, Pi Delta Phi, Phi Eta Sigma. Private international, Securities, General corporate. Office: Alston & Bird 1 Atlantic Ctr 1201 W Peachtree St NW Ste 4200 Atlanta GA 30309-3424

**GREER, CHARLES EUGENE,** company executive, lawyer; b. Columbus, Ohio, Mar. 28, 1945; s. Earl E. Greer and Margaret I. Cavanass; 1 child, Erin Elizabeth. BS, Ind. U., 1972, JD, 1976. Bar: Ind. 1976. Pres. Willoughby Industries, Inc., Indpls., 1976-91, pres., CEO, 1991-93; ptnr. Ice Miller Donadio & Ryan, 1976-91; pres. ECM Corp., Indpls., 1993—; pres. Loggins, Inc., Indpls., 1995—, bus. turnaround specialist, 1995—. Served to sgt. USAF, 1965-68, Vietnam. Mem. Ind. Bar Assn., Order of Coif, Phi Eta Sigma, Beta Gamma Sigma. Office: 5581 Sunset Ln Indianapolis IN 46228-1468

**GREER, GORDON BRUCE,** lawyer; b. Butler, Pa., Feb. 17, 1932; s. Samuel Walker and Winifred (Fletcher) G.; m. Nancy Linda Hannaford, June 14, 1959; children: Gordon Bruce, Alison Clark. BA, Harvard U., 1953, JD cum laude, 1959. Bar: Wis. 1959, Mass. 1961. Assoc. Foley, Sammond & Lardner, Milw., 1959-61; assoc. Bingham Dana LLP, Boston, 1961-67, ptnr., 1967-97, of counsel, 1997—; lectr. Boston U. Sch. Law. Editor Harvard Law Rev. Vos. 71, 72. Maj. USAFR. Mem. Mass. Bar Assn., Boston Bar Assn., Brae Burn Country Club, Harvard Club (Boston). Republican. General corporate, Private international. Home: 45 Fieldmont Rd Belmont MA 02478-2606 Office: Bingham Dana LLP 150 Federal St Boston MA 02110-1713

**GREER, LAWRENCE B.,** lawyer; b. Phoenix, May 25, 1955; s. Charles E. and Nora Maureen (McArdle) G. BBA, So. Meth. U., 1978; JD, Houston Law Ctr., 1981. Bar: Tex. 1981. Briefing atty. U.S. Ct. Appeals (14th cir.), Houston, 1981-82; trial atty. Hudgins, Hudgins & Warrick, Houston, 1981-95, Greer & Martin, L.L.P., Houston, 1995—. Office: Greer & Martin LLP The Esperson Bldg S 815 Walker St Ste 1447 Houston TX 77002-5716

**GREER, RAYMOND WHITE,** lawyer; b. Port Arthur, Tex., July 20, 1954; s. Mervyn Hardy Greer and Eva Nadine (White) Swain; m. Pamela V. Brown; children: Emily Ann, Sarah Kelly, Jonathan Collin. BA magna cum laude, Sam Houston State, 1977; JD, U. Houston, 1981. Assoc. Hoover, Cox & Shearer, Houston, 1980-83, Hinton & Morris, Houston, 1983-85; pvt. practice Houston, 1985-86; prin. Morris & Greer, P.C., Houston, 1986-90, Raymond W. Greer & Assocs., P.C., Houston, 1990-98, Rigg & Greer, Houston, 1998—; lectr. in field; mem. dist. 4 grievance com. State Bar Tex. Former mem. adv. com. Enterprising Girls Scouts Beyond Bars, San Jacinto coun. Recipient Outstanding Alumnus award, Dept. English, Sam Houston U., 1986, Disting. Alumni Alpha Chi. Mem. ABA, State Bar Tex., Houston Bar Assn., Fort Bend County Bar Assn., Rotary (Houston asst. chmn. fresh start com. 1996-97—, chmn. fresh start com. 1997-98, dir. 1998—), Alumni Assn. (2d v.p., chmn. membership com., combined charter and membership com. 1995-96, 1st v.p. 1996-97, pres. 1997-98, immediate past pres. 1998-99), Sam Houston State U. Avocations: golf, reading. General civil litigation, Consumer commercial, Family and matrimonial. Office: Rigg & Greer 13333 Southwest Fwy Ste 100 Sugar Land TX 77478-3545

**GREGG, JOHN PENNYPACKER,** lawyer; b. Phila., May 25, 1947; s. William Pemberton and Sarah E. (High) G. AB, Trinity Coll., 1969; JD, Villanova U., 1974. Bar: Pa. 1974, U.S. Dist. Ct. (ea. dist.) Pa. 1974. Tchr., dir. student activities The Pennington (N.J.) Sch., 1969-71; atty. Pub.

Defenders Office, Norristown, Pa., 1974—, High, Swartz, Roberts & Seidel, Norristown, 1975—; bd. dirs. Rittenhouse Book Distbr. Inc., King of Prussia, Pa. Bd. dirs. Phila. Toboggan Co., Lansdale, 1987-91, Lower Merion Shared Housing Corp., Ardmore, Pa., 1991-95, Lower Merion Affordable Housing, Narberth, Pa., 1995—, The Episcopal Acad., Merion, Pa., 1986-89; ann. giving com. Inglis House, Phila., 1991-92. Recipient Legion of Honor Chapel of the Four Chaplains, Phila., 1980, Harry L. Green Svc. award, 1990, Disting. Svc. award Episcopal Acad., 1990. Mem. Pa. Bar Assn., Montgomery Bar Assn. (com. chmn. 1991-94). Criminal, Family and matrimonial. Home: 635 Walnut Ln Haverford PA 19041-1225 Office: High Swartz Roberts & Seidel 40 E Airy St Norristown PA 19401-4803

**GREGO, SAMUEL ROBERT,** lawyer; b. Pitts., July 23, 1956; s. Samuel Robert and Gertrude Pauline (Franczak) G.; m. Dorothy Anne Yourish, Oct. 2, 1982; children: Nicholas Edward, Derek Samuel. BS in Social Sci. & Bus. Adminstrn., Carnegie Mellon U., 1978; JD, U. Pitts., 1981. Bar: Pa. 1981, U.S. Ct. Appeals (3d cir.) 1988. Assoc. Springer, Bush & Perry, Pitts., 1981-87, ptnr., shareholder, 1988-98; atty. Goldberg, Kamin & Garvin, Pitts., 1998—. Mem. Allegheny County Bar Assn., River Forest Golf Club. Democrat. Roman Catholic. Avocations: golf, softball, current events, movies. Bankruptcy, Contracts commercial, General civil litigation. Office: Goldberg Kamin & Garvin 1806 Frick Bldg Pittsburgh PA 15219

**GREGOIRE, CHRISTINE O.,** state attorney general; b. Auburn, Wash.; m. Michael Gregoire; 2 children. BA, U. Wash.; JD cum laude, Gonzaga U., 1977. Clerk, typist Wash. State Adult Probation/ Parole Office, Seattle, 1969; caseworker Wash. Dept. Social and Health Scis., Everett, 1974; asst. atty. gen. State of Wash., Spokane, 1977-81, sr. asst. atty. gen., 1981-82; dep. atty. gen. State of Wash., Olympia, 1982-88; dir. Wash. State Dept. Ecology, 1988-92; atty. gen. State of Wash., 1992—; dir. Wash. State Dept. Ecology, 1988-92. chair Puget Sound Water Quality Authority, 1990-92, Nat. Com. State Environ. Dirs., 1991-92, States/B.C. Oil Spill Task Force, 1989-92. Mem. Nat. Assn. Attys. Gen. (consumer protection and environment com., energy com., children and the law subcom.). *

**GREGOR, JAMES P.,** lawyer; b. Monongahela, Pa., Sept. 15, 1952; s. Theodore J. and Ann M. Gregor; m. Joyce L. Gregor, Aug. 17, 1974; children: Jamie Lynn, Evan Michael. BSBA, Bucknell U., 1974; JD, U. Pitts., 1977. Bar: Pa. 1977, U.S. Dist. Ct. (mid. dist.) Pa. 1979, U.S. Ct. Appeals (3d cir.) 1995, U.S. Supreme Ct. 1998. Pub. defender Monroe County Pub. Defenders Office, Stroudsburg, Pa., 1977-79, asst. dist. atty., 1979-88; asst county solicitor Monroe County Commrs., Stroudsburg, 1979-91; assoc. Williams, Williams and Gregor, Stroudsburg, 1980-84; pvt. practice, Stroudsburg, 1984-96; dist. atty. Monroe County Dist. Attys. Office, Stroudsburg, 1992-96; legal counsel Pa. State Tae Kwon Do Assn., Stroudsburg, 1996—; assoc. Rosenblum Law Office, Stroudsburg, 1996—; dist. atty. Monroe County, 1991; guest lectr. criminal justice East Stroudsburg U., 1990-95. Author (editl. column) Chgo. Tribune, 1994. Past chmn. Monroe County Victim's Policy Bd., Stroudsburg, 1992-96; mem. aux. bd. Women's Resources, Monroe County, 1992-96; soccer coach Monroe County YMCA, Stroudsburg, 1990—; mem. Monroe County Prison Bd., 1992-96. Recipient Spl. Recognition award Pa. State Tae Kwon Do Assn., 1995. Mem. ATLA, Pa. Bar Assn., Monroe County Bar Assn. Office: Home: 207 Amy Ct Stroudsburg PA 18360-9159 Office: Robert M. Rosenblum Law Office 802 Main St Stroudsburg PA 18360-1602

**GREGORY, LEWIS DEAN,** trust company executive; b. Wichita, Kans., May 13, 1953; s. Harry Samuel III and Virginia Dorothy (Womer) G.; m. Laura Lorraine Davis, March 4, 1978; children: Paul Lewis, Erin Elizabeth. BA in Communications, U. Kans., Lawrence, 1975; MS in Journalism, U. Kans., 1976; JD, Washburn U., 1983. Bar: Kans. 1984, U.S. Dist. Ct. Kans. 1984. Cons. Delta Upsilon Frat., Inc., Indpls., 1975-76; mktg. rep. IBM, Kansas City, Mo., 1976-80; assoc. Hershberger, Patterson, Jones & Roth, Wichita, 1983-84; trust mktg. mgr. Bank IV Wichita, 1984-86; v.p., trust officer, sales mgr. BancOklahoma Trust Co., Tulsa, 1986-88, Boatmen's Trust Co., Kansas City, 1988-97; dist. trust mgr. Merrill Lynch Trust Co., 1997—. Dir. Am. Heart Assn., Wichita, Kans., 1985-86; pres. YMCA Men's Club, Tulsa, 1987-88; del. Rep. Party, Tulsa, 1988; trustee Leukemia Soc., 1992-96. Mem. ABA, Kans. Bar Assn., Johnson County Bar Assn., Kansas City Met. Bar Assn., Estate Planning Soc., Kiwanis, Kans. Univ. Alumni Assn. (pres. Greater Kansas City chpt. 1994-96, nat. bd. dirs. 1997—), Delta Upsilon (Indpls. dir. 1987-90, dir. Kans. chpt. 1977-90). Republican. Methodist. Avocation: running. Home: 12205 Aberdeen Rd Shawnee Mission KS 66209-1208

**GREGORY, MARGARET ELLEN,** lawyer; b. Nebr. City, Nebr., Feb. 26, 1953; d. Edward Fugitt and Marjorie Ann (Elam) Askew; m. Mark Stephen Gregory, May 29, 1976 (div. Nov. 1990); m. John Tyler Makepeace, April 28, 1996; children: Megan, Mark, Scott, Robert. BA in Journalism, Iowa State U., 1974; JD, Coll. William Mary, 1977. Bar: Va. 1977, Colo. 1979. Lawyer U.S. Army, Ft. Carson, Colo., 1977-80, District Atty., Colorado Springs, Colo., 1980-83; pvt. practice Colorado Springs, Colo., 1983—. Editor League Peaks magazine, 1992-93. Chmn. Commn. Children Families (city and county chpts.), Colorado Springs, 1997-98; bd. dirs. Junior League, Colorado Springs, 1991-93, 98—, pres.-elect, 98-99, pres., 1999—. Capt. U.S. Army, 1977-80. Republican. Avocations: reading, volunteer work, travel. Fax: 719-633-0666. Office: 405 S Cascade Ave Ste 103 Colorado Springs CO 80903-3885

**GREGORY, RICK DEAN,** lawyer; b. Edmond, Okla., Feb. 22, 1954; s. Jerry D. and Elaine (Hall) G. BA in History, Cen. State U., 1977; JD, Oklahoma City U., 1981. Bar: Okla. 1982, U.S. Dist. Ct. (ea. and we. dist.) Okla. 1982, U.S. Ct. Appeals (10th cir.) 1982. Juvenile parole officer dept. human services State of Okla., Oklahoma City, 1977-81; law clk. Jess Horn, Inc., Oklahoma City, 1981-82; pvt. practice, Oklahoma City, 1982—. Editor: Policy Options on Political Reform, 1974; author: A Historical, Legal and Moral Analysis of Unauthorized Audio Duplication in the United States, 1975. Mem. ABA, Am. Trial Lawyers Assn., Am. Judicature Soc., Okla. Bar Assn., Okla. Trial Lawyers Assn., Okla. County Bar Assn., Can. County Bar Assn., Okla. Criminal Defense Lawyers Assn. Democrat. Methodist. Avocations: skiing, tennis, swimming. Criminal, Personal injury, Insurance.

**GREGORY, RUSSELL,** lawyer; b. Detroit, Dec. 12, 1960; s. Fred and Nora Gregory. BA in Psychology, U. Mich., 1983; JD cum laude, Detroit Coll. Law, 1986. Bar: Mich. 1986, Fla. 1988, U.S. Dist. Ct. (ea. dist.) Mich. 1987. Assoc. atty. Kitch, Saurbier et al, Detroit, 1987-89, Thurswell, Chayet, Southfield, Mich., 1989-94; prin. The Law Offices of Russell Gregory, Farmington Hills, Mich., 1994-97; ptnr. Gregory & Reiter, Farmington Hills, 1997—; mediator Wayne and Oakland County Mediations Tribunals, 1993—. Mem. ATLA, Mich. Trial Lawyers Assn. Personal injury. Office: Gregory & Reiter Am Baby and Child Law Ctrs 3700 Grand River Ste 210 Farmington Hills MI 48335

**GREGORY, WILLIAM STANLEY,** lawyer; b. Greenwood, Miss., Mar. 12, 1949; s. Carlyle and Charlotte Ruby (Richardson) G.; m. Vicki Sue Lovelady, Aug. 15, 1970. BS in Commerce and Bus. Adminstrn., U. Ala., 1971, MBA, 1973, JD, 1974. Bar: Ala. 1974, U.S. Dist. Ct. (mid. dist.) Ala. 1979, U.S. Ct. Appeals (5th cir.) 1979, U.S. Ct. Appeals (11th cir.) 1980, U.S. Tax Ct. 1979, U.S. Dist. Ct. (no. dist.) Ala. 1991. Assoc. Johnson, Thorington, North, Haskell & Slaughter, Montgomery, Ala., 1974-78; jr. ptnr. Johnson & Thorington, Montgomery, Ala., 1979-90; sr. ptnr. Thorington & Gregory, Montgomery, Ala., 1990—; spl. asst. atty. gen. State of Ala., Montgomery, 1978-82; mem. taxpayer bill of rights drafting com. tax sect. Ala. State Bar, Montgomery, 1990-91. Pres. Montgomery Symphony Assn., 1980, 92, Highland Ave. Adult & Sr. Citizens Ctr., Montgomery, 1986-99; mem. Montgomery Estate Planning Coun. Capt. USAR, 1971-75. Mem. SAR, Kiwanis (v.p. 1989-90). Presbyterian. Avocation: music. Municipal (including bonds), State and local taxation, General corporate. Home: 8218 Wynlakes Blvd Montgomery AL 36117-5101 Office: Thorington & Gregory 504 S Perry St Montgomery AL 36104-4616

**GREIF, ARTHUR JOHN,** lawyer; b. Morristown, N.J., July 16, 1951; s. Charles Elwyn Sr. and Evelyn Alice Greif; m. Donna Mae Karlson, June 21, 1986. BA, Coll. William & Mary, 1973; JD, U. Pitts., 1977. Bar: Pa. 1977, U.S. Dist. Ct. Pa. 1977, Maine 1982, Colo. 1984, U.S. Dist. Ct. Maine 1989, U.S. Ct. Appeals (1st cir.) 1998. Assoc. Reed Smith Shaw McClay, Pitts., 1977-79; asst. gen. counsel Pa. Human Rels. Commn., Pitts., 1979-80; sole practice Portland, Maine, 1982-83; assoc. Branney Hewitt Engels & Barnes, Englewood, Colo., 1983-84; sole practice Readfield, Maine, 1984-88; assoc. Isaacson & Raymond, Lewiston, Maine, 1989-92, Lowry & Assocs., Bangor, Maine, 1992-97; atty., shareholder Gilbert Law Offices, Bangor, 1997—. Democrat. Avocations: bicycle touring and racing, marathon running. Personal injury, Labor, Criminal. Home: 351 Marn Rd N Hampden ME 04444 Office: Gilbert Law Offices PA 82 Columbia St Bangor ME 04401-6357

**GREIF, JOSEPH,** lawyer; b. N.Y.C., June 25, 1943; s. Jacob J. and Dorothy (Harrison) G.; m. Aline Bohm, Jan. 1, 1966; children: Jeffrey, Julie. BBA, U. Pitts., 1964; JD, NYU, 1967. Bar: N.Y. 1967, D.C. 1968, U.S. Tax Ct. 1986; CPA, Md., D.C. Instr. No. Va. C.C., Annandale, 1967-68; mgmt. cons. Computer Sci. Corp., Silver Spring, Md., 1967-70; tax mgr. Arthur Andersen & Co., Washington, 1970-75; sr. assoc. Ginsberg, Feldman & Bress, Washington, 1975-77; ptnr. Touche Ross & Co., Washington, 1977-84, McGuffie, Greif, Whitney & Handal, Washington, 1984-90; of counsel McNeily, Rosenfeld & Rubenstein, Washington, 1991-98, Neimark & Nadel, Washington-Ft. Lauderdale, Fla., 1998—; lectr. George Washington U. Grad. Sch. Bus., Washington, 1993-95. Co-author, editor: Managing Membership Societies, 1979; contbr. articles on taxation, comml. leasing, computer systems contracting, exec. compensation, exec. contracts to profl. jours. Bd. dirs. Nat. Assn. for Mental Health, Washington, 1973-75, Combined Health Appeal, Washington, 1980-81, Assn. Devel. Coun., Washington, 1987-89; task force mem. White House Task Force on Charitable Giving, Washington, 1979-80. Mem. AICPA (chmn. fed. tax divsn. task force on exempt orgns. 1983-86), ABA, D.C. Bar Assn., Am. Soc. Assn. Execs. (mem. govt. affairs and long range planning coms., Outstanding Svc. award, tech. sect. coun. 1996—), D.C. Inst. CPAs, Greater Washington Soc. Assn. Execs. (mem. tech. task force 1994—), Computer Law Assn. Avocations: boating, squash. Corporate taxation, Computer, Contracts commercial. Home: 6108 Wayside Dr North Bethesda MD 20852-3534 Office: Neimark & Nadel 5335 Wisconsin Ave NW Ste 360 Washington DC 20015-2030 also: Neimark & Nadel 800 Corporate Dr Ste 420 Fort Lauderdale FL 33334-3621

**GREIG, BRIAN STROTHER,** lawyer; b. Austin, Tex., Apr. 10, 1950; s. Ben Wayne Greig and Virginia Ann (Strother) Higgins; m. Jane Ann Sentilles, June 17, 1972; children: Travis Darden, Grace Hanna. BA, Washington and Lee U., 1972; JD, U. Tex., 1975. Bar: Tex. 1975, U.S. Dist. Ct. (ea. dist.) Tex. 1976, U.S. Ct. Appeals (5th cir.) 1976, U.S. Dist. Ct. (so. dist.) Tex. 1977, U.S. Dist. Ct. (we. dist.) Tex. 1980, U.S. Supreme Ct. 1980, U.S. DIst. Ct. (no. dist.) Tex. 1984, U.S. Ct. Appeals (11th cir.) 1984. Law clk. to chief judge U.S. Dist. Ct., Beaumont, Tex., 1975-76; ptnr. Fulbright & Jaworski L.L.P., Austin, 1976—; mem. Austin Tomorrow On-Going Goals Assembly Com., 1981; pres. Austin Mgmt. Lawyers Forum, 1987, 93. Editor-in-chief Tex. Assn. Bus. Employment Law Handbook; editorial bd. Tex. Labor Letter. Pres. Austin Lawyers and Accts. for Arts, 1981; trustee Laguna Gloria Art Mus., Austin, 1983-91, pres., 1989-90, chmn., 1990-91; bd. dirs. Zachary Scott Theater Ctr., Austin, 1981; mem. devel. bd. Inst. Texan Cultures, 1991-98; trustee Westminster Manor Health Facilities Corp. of Travis County, Tex., 1991-96, sec., 1995-96; trustee St. Stephan's Episcopal Sch., 1995—; pres. Austin Mus. Art, 1991-92, trustee, 1991-93. Fellow Tex. Bar Found. (life), Am. Coll. Labor and Employment Lawyers; mem. ABA, Am. Arbitration Assn. (employment adv. coun. 1995—), Tex. Bar Assn., Travis County Bar Assn., Tex. Commn. on Human Rights Task Force, Tarry House Club, Headliners Club (trustee 1998—), Met. Club, Admirals Club. Methodist. Avocations: hunting, fishing. Labor, General civil litigation, Construction. Office: Fulbright & Jaworski LLP 600 Congress Ave Ste 2400 Austin TX 78701-3271

**GREIGG, RONALD EDWIN,** lawyer; b. Washington, June 29, 1946; s. Edwin E. and Helen Marie (Marcy) G.; m. Patricia Anne Crowe, June 5, 1968; children: Elizabeth, Rebecca. BBA, Am. U., 1969, MBA in Fin., 1971; JD, Stetson U., 1976. Registered patent atty.; bar: Fla. 1976, D.C. 1978, Va. 1985, U.S. Dist. Ct. (mid. dist.) Fla. 1976, U.S. Dist. Ct. (ea. dist.) Va. 1988, U.S. Ct. Appeals (D.C. cir.) 1979, U.S. Ct. Appeals (fed. cir.) 1982, U.S. Supreme Ct. 1980. Assoc. David E. De Serio, St. Petersburg, Fla., 1977-78, Edwin E. Greigg, Washington, 1979-82, Harris, Barrett & Dew, St. Petersburg, Fla., 1982-84; ptnr. Greigg & Greigg, Arlington, Va., 1984—. Author: A Guide to the FTC Franchise Disclosure Rule, 1979, Patent Infringement Damages, 1988. Mem. ABA, Am. Intellectual property Law Assn., Assn. Internationale pour la Protection de la Propriete Industrielle, Soc. Automotive Engrs., D.C. Bar Assn., Fla. Bar Assn., Va. Bar Assn., Washington Area Lawyers for the Arts, Inst. of Trademark Agts. (London), Internat. Trademark Assn., Phi Alpha Delta. Republican. Episcopalian. Avocations: sailing, classic cars. Trademark and copyright, Patent, Computer. Office: Greigg & Greigg 5203 Leesburg Pike Ste 600 Falls Church VA 22041-3405

**GREILSHEIMER, WILLIAM HENRY,** lawyer; b. N.Y.C., Sept. 28, 1941; s. Jerome Jacob and Lillian (Gans) G.; m. Carol Leslie Horwitz, Sept. 6, 1970; children: Jeffrey Mark, Deborah Lynn. AB, Dartmouth Coll., 1963; JD, Yale U., 1966. Bar: N.Y. 1967, U.S. Ct. Appeals (2d cir.) 1968, U.S. Dist. Ct. (so. and ea. dists.) N.Y. 1968, U.S. Dist. Ct. Conn. 1997, U.S. Supreme Ct. 1970. Ptnr. Delson & Gordon, N.Y.C., 1967-73, Burns, Summit, Rovins & Feldeslman, N.Y.C., 1973-81; ptnr. Ferber, Greilsheimer, Chan & Essner, N.Y.C., 1981-96, counsel, 1997-98; lectr., co-author continuing legal edn. program, 1987. Trustee Stephen Wise Free Synagogue, N.Y.C., 1987-90. Mem. ABA, Assn. of Bar of City of N.Y. (com. on lectures and continuing edn. 1991-93, com. on corp. law 1993-95), N.Y. County Lawyers Assn. (corp. law com., securities and exchanges com.). Democrat. Jewish. Avocations: jogging, tennis, cross-country skiing. General corporate, Securities, Private international. Home: 91 Central Park W New York NY 10023-4600 Office: 420 Lexington Ave New York NY 10170-0002

**GREINER, JAMES RALPH,** lawyer; b. Sacramento, Calif., May 10, 1955; s. Ralph James and Lucille Shirley (Miracle) G. BA, U. Calif., Davis, 1977; JD, McGeorge U., 1983. Extern Calif. Supreme Ct., San Francisco; with Bolling, Walter & Gawthrop, Sacramento, Rodney A. Klein, Sacramento; assoc. Shea & Smith, Sacramento, Montague & Cochrane, Sacramento; pvt. practice law Sacramento, 1990—; mock trial coach Rio Americano H.S., speaker The Amer. Assoc. of Law Libraries 1996 natl. conference, The Amer. Inns of Court 1996 natl. conference; dist. 2 rep. Calif. State Bar Bd. Govs.; CJA panel rep. Fed. Ct. (ea. dist.), Calif. Recipient Edn.-Bus. Partnership award Calif. State U., Sacramento, 1998. Mem. ABA, Assn. Trial Lawyers Am., Assn. Fed. Def. Attys., Sacramento County Bar Assn. (pres. 1998, 1st v.p., 2d v.p., sec./treas., pres.'s award 1994, chair law day com. 1990-97, chair membership com. 1994-97, chair Mardi Gras com. 1994—, chair lawyer referral and info. svc. 1992-93, conf. dels. 1991-97, Sacramento lawyer policy com. 1991-98, cmty. edn. com. 1992-97, membership directory com. 1992-97, judiciary com. 1993—, bench bar media com. 1993-98, chair events com. 1995-97, indigent def. panel 1991—, pictorial dir. 1993-98, mem. bar found. 1994—, Sacramento county bd. of law libr. 1995—), State Bar Calif. (criminal justice sect.), Calif. Pub. Defenders Assn., Consumer Attys. Calif., Capitol City Consumer Attys., Anthony M. Kennedy Am. Inn of Ct., Milton L. Schwartz Inn of Ct. Criminal, General civil litigation. Office: 555 University Ave Ste 290 Sacramento CA 95825-6511

**GREINER, MARK L.,** lawyer; b. Petaluma, Calif., May 6, 1963; s. Gary D. and Joan B. Greiner; m. Laura E. Andersen, May 30, 1992; 1 child, Jacob G. BA in Polit. Sci., Iowa State U., 1990; JD, Drake U., 1994. Bar: Iowa. Asst. atty. gen. State of Iowa, Office of Atty. Gen., Council Bluffs, 1994-97; asst. county atty. Pottawattamie County Office of Atty., Council Bluffs, 1997—; pvt. practice Council Bluffs. Treas. Southwest Iowa Domestic Violence Coalition, 1997—. With U.S. Army, 1983-86. Mem. Iowa State Bar Assn. Republican. Presbyn. Avocations: computers, photography. E-mail: mgreiner@nfinity.com. Home: 3835 Brookdale Ave Ames IA 50010-3905 Office: 229 S Main St Council Bluffs IA 51503-6504

**GREINER, MARY LOUISE,** lawyer; b. St. Louis, Aug. 18, 1949; d. Theodore H. and Dorothy E. (Walters) G.; m. S. Charles Baber. BA, Hamline U., 1971; JD, U. Minn., 1974; MSSW, U. Tex., 1994. Bar: Minn. 1974, U.S. Dist. Ct. Minn. 1974, Hawaii 1976, U.S. Dist. Ct. Hawaii 1976, Tex. 1989. Staff atty. Fed. Res. Bank, Mpls., 1974-75; instr. L.A. Community Coll. Extension, Okinawa, Japan, 1975-76; assoc. Stubenberg Law Firm, Honolulu, 1976-77; spl. counsel State of Hawaii, Honolulu, 1977; counsel Control Data Corp., Mpls., 1978-87; pres. Greiner & Assoc., Bloomington, Minn., 1987-88; assoc. gen. counsel Electronic Data Systems Corp., Plano, Tex., 1989-92; clin. social worker, mediator Pastoral Counseling & Edn. Ctr., Dallas, 1994—. Chair exec. com. Tex. Lawyers Assistance Program. Mem. ABA, State Bar Tex., Dallas Women Lawyers, Tex. Lawyers Concerned for Lawyers (bd. dirs.). Unitarian. Avocations: travel, reading, gardening. Alternative dispute resolution, Health. Office: Pastoral Counseling and Edn Ctr 4525 Lemmon Ave Ste 200 Dallas TX 75219-2100

**GREINER, ROBERT PHILIP,** lawyer, real estate broker; b. Herkimer, N.Y., July 3, 1930; s. Max Henry and Margaret Mary (O'Hara) G. BA, U. Rochester, 1951; MBA, Syracuse U., 1957; LLB, UCLA, 1964. Bar: Calif. 1965; CPA, Calif.; lic. real estate broker, Calif. Pvt. practice acct., CPA, 1962-64; lawyer L.A. (Calif.) Pub. Defenders Office, 1965-87; pvt. practice lawyer and real estate broker Calif., 1987—. Pres. Guide Dog Boosters, Los Alamitos, Calif., 1984. Staff sgt. USAF, 1951-55. Mem. World Affairs Coun. of Sonoma City, Calif. Real property. Home and Office: 730 Natalie Dr Windsor CA 95492-8870

**GREISMANN, ZVI,** lawyer; b. Tel-Aviv, May 29, 1951; came to U.S., 1957; BA, L.I. U., 1973; JD, Antioch U., 1981. Bar: Md. 1982, U.S. Dist. Ct. Md., U.S. Ct. Appeals (4th cir.) 1982. Asst. prof., instr. legal rsch. and writing Columbus Sch. Law, Cath. U. Am., Washington, 1981-83; asst. atty. gen. Office Atty. Gen. Md., Balt., 1983-85; prin. counsel Balt. City Law Dept., 1986-91; sr. atty. Montgomery County Pub. Schs., Rockville, Md., 1991—; asst. prof. Villa Julie Coll., Stevenson, Md., 1984-91, U. Md., College Park, 1993-95. Co-author: Special Education Law and Practice, 1997; editor Antioch Law Jour.; contbg. editor LRP Publs.; contbr. articles to profl. jours. Recipient Citation in Recognition of Svc. to the Law Dept., Mayor Kurt L. Schmoke, Balt., 1991, Citizen Citation in Recognition of Significant and Scholarly Contbn. in the Area of Edn. Law, Mayor Kurt L. Schmoke, Balt., 1991. Fax: 301-279-3819. E-mail: Zvi Greismann@fc.mcps.k12.md.us. Office: Montgomery County Pub Schs 850 Hungerford Dr Rockville MD 20850-1718

**GRENIER, EDWARD JOSEPH, JR.,** lawyer; b. N.Y.C., Nov. 26, 1933; s. Edward Joseph and Jane Veronica (Farrell) G.; m. Patricia J. Cederle, June 22, 1957; children: Victoria-Anne, Edward Joseph III, Peter C. BA summa cum laude, Manhattan Coll., N.Y.C., 1954; LLB magna cum laude, Harvard U., 1959. Bar: D.C. 1959, N.Y. 1983, U.S. Ct. Appeals (D.C. cir.) 1959, U.S. Ct. Mil. Appeals 1960, U.S. Ct. Appeals (3d cir.) 1966, U.S. Supreme Ct. 1966, U.S. Ct. Appeals (9th cir.) 1973, U.S. Ct. Appeals (10th cir.) 1977, U.S. Ct. Appeals (5th cir., 11th cir.) 1982. Law clk. U.S. Ct. Appeals (D.C. cir.), 1959-60; assoc. Covington & Burling, Washington, 1960-68; ptnr. Sutherland, Asbill & Brennan, Washington, 1968—; speaker in field of energy related issues to profl. orgns.; bd. dirs. Found. of Energy Law Jour., 1990-91, 97-98. Contbr. articles in field to legal jours. Chmn. bd. trustees, mem. exec. com. Connelly Sch. Holy Child, Potomac, Md., 1976-85, trustee, 1976-88; bd. dirs. D.C. Recording for the Blind, Washington, 1977-89. 1st lt. USAF, 1954-56. Fellow Am. Bar Found.; mem. ABA (chmn. sec. adminstrv. law 1986-87, sec., del. Ho. of Dels. 1991-97), FBA, D.C. Bar Assn., Fed. Energy Bar Assn. (bd. dirs. 1986-89, 95-99, v.p. 1995-96, pres.-elect 1996-97, pres. 1997-98), Am. Inns of Ct. (master of bench Prettyman-Leventhal Inn of Ct. 1988—, pres. 1991-92, counselor 1997-98), Met. Club, Congl. Country Club. FERC practice. Office: Sutherland Asbill & Brennan 1275 Pennsylvania Ave NW Ste 1 Washington DC 20004-2415

**GRENIG, JAY EDWARD,** law educator; b. Salt Lake City, Apr. 18, 1943; s. Robert Edward and Betty (Gifford) G.; m. Sharon Flanigan, Dec. 22, 1967; children: Robert Jay, Alejandro Edward, Christian Michael. Student, U. Ariz., 1961-63; BA, Willamette U., Salem, Oreg., 1966; postgrad., Ariz. State U., 1968-69; JD, U. Calif.-Hastings Coll. Law, 1971. Bar: Calif. 1972, U.S. Dist. Ct. (no. dist.) Calif. 1973, U.S. Ct. Appeals (9th cir.) 1974, U.S. Ct. Claims 1974, Wis. 1980. Asst. dean Coll. of Law Willamette U., Salem, 1971-72; assoc. firm Johnson & Stanton, San Francisco, 1972-73; sole practice San Mateo, Calif., 1973-77; assoc. prof., dir. Employment Law Inst., Pepperdine U. Sch. Law, Malibu, Calif., 1977-79; prof. law Marquette U. Sch. Law, Milw., 1980—; lectr. U. So. Calif. Grad. Sch. Pub. Adminstrn., L.A., 1978; reporter civil justice reform act adv. group U.S. Dist. Ct. (ea. dist.) Wis., 1991—; pres., bd. dirs. Ctr. Pub. Representation, 1993-97. Author: (with others) Private Sector Labor Law, 1980, West's California Education Code Forms, 1981, California Government Codes Forms with Practice Commentaries, 1985, Labor Arbitration Advocacy, 1989, West's Federal Forms, 1992, Wisconsin Civil Procedure, 1994, Wisconsin Civil Discovery, 1996, Alternative Dispute, 1997; editor Calif. Sch. Law Digest, 1973-84, Wisconsin Civil Discovery, 1996, West's Alternative Dispute Resolution, 1997; contbr. articles to legal publs. Bd. trustees Univ. Lake Sch., 1992-95. With U.S. Army, 1966-68. Mem. Am. Law Inst., Am. Arbitration Assn. (regional adv. bd. L.A. 1979), Assn. Am. Law Schs. (chmn. labor and employment law sect. 1991-92), State Bar Assn. Wis., Nat. Acad. Arbitrators (bd. govs.), Order of Coif, Thurston Soc. Home: 122 Birch Rd Delafield WI 53018-1305 Office: Marquette U Law Sch 1103 W Wisconsin Ave Milwaukee WI 53233-2313

**GREW, ROBERT RALPH,** lawyer; b. Metamora, Ohio, Mar. 25, 1931; m. Anne Gano Bailey, Aug. 2, 1958. AB in Letters and Law, U. Mich., 1953, JD, 1955. Bar: Mich. 1955, N.Y. 1958. Assoc. Carter, Ledyard & Milburn, N.Y.C., 1957-68, ptnr., 1968-98, of counsel, 1999—; lectr. legal problems in banking and in venture capital investments Practising Law Inst. Mem. Pilgrims of U.S., English Speaking Union (nat. v.p. 1989-93), Union Club, Lansdowne Club (London). Republican. E-mail grew@clm.com. Banking, General corporate, Real property. Office: Carter Ledyard & Milburn 2 Wall St New York NY 10005-2001 also: 1350 I St NW Washington DC 20005-3305

**GREY, FRANCIS JOSEPH,** accountant, accounting company executive, educator; b. Yeadon, Pa., Nov. 30, 1931; s. William and Delia (Mullin) G.; m. Marlene M. Ward, June 24, 1961; children: Francis Joseph Jr., Melissa Ann. BS in Econs., Villanova U., 1958. CPA. Tax profl. Coopers & Lybrand, Phila., 1958-64, tax ptnr. in charge, 1964-72, mng. ptnr. tax, 1972—; mem. devel. com. Villanova (Pa.) U., 1972—; bd. dirs. Del. County Hosp., Upper Darby, Pa.; adj. prof. Villanova Law Sch. Author: Tax Planning for Real Estate, 1978, 88, Pa. Taxation of Corporations, 1980; contbr. articles to profl. jours. Adv. com. Wharton Sch. Tax Conf., Phila., 1970-88, Internat. Bus. Forum, Phila., 1980-88. Sgt. U.S. Army, 1952-53, Korea. Mem. AICPAs, Pa. Inst. CPAs (v.p. 1988), Internat. Fiscal Assn. (treas. 1975), Phila. C. of C. (bd. dirs. 1975—), Phila. Country Club (bd. dirs. 1980-84), Union League of Phila., Locust Club, Beta Gamma Sigma. Republican. Roman Catholic. Avocations: golf, tennis, sports.

**GREY, ROBERT J.,** lawyer; b. Richmond, Va., Aug. 5, 1950. BS, Va. Commonwealth U., 1973; JD, Washington & Lee U., 1976. Bar: Va. 1978. Ptnr. LeClair Ryan, Richmond, Va., 1995—. Mem. ABA (chair ho. dels. 1998—, bd. govs., exec. com.), Grtr. Richmond C. of C. (past chair). E-mail: rgrey@leclairryan.com. Legislative, General corporate, Administrative and regulatory. Office: LeClair Ryan 707 E Main St Fl 11 Richmond VA 23219-2814*

**GRIBOUSKI, JAMES JOSEPH,** lawyer; b. Worcester, Mass., Jan. 31, 1954; s. G. Joseph and Elaine E. Gribouski; m. Margaret b. Gribouski, Apr. 25, 1981; children: Shaun, Sarah, Eileen, Jeffrey. BA, Southeastern Mass. U., 1976; JD, Northeastern U., 1980. Bar: Mass., U.S. Dist. Ct. Mass. Asst. dist. atty. State of Mass., Essex County, Salem, 1980-84; assoc. Shannon & Ford, Worcester, 1984-89; pvt. practice Worcester, 1989-97; ptnr. Glickman, Sugarman, Kneeland & Gribouski, Worcester, 1997—; guest lectr. Mass. CLE, Boston, 1992—. Co-author: Trying Drug Cases in Mass., 1994. Coach Sutton (Mass.) Youth Baseball League, 1989—, Basketball League, 1992—. Mem. ATLA, Mass Bar Assn., Mass. Criminal Def. Lawyers Assn., Worcester County Bar Assn. Avocations: skiing, mountain biking, baseball. Personal injury, Criminal. Office: Glickman Sugarman Kneeland & Gribouski 11 Harvard St Worcester MA 01609-2839

**GRIER, PHILLIP MICHAEL,** lawyer, former association executive; b. Quitman, Ga., Aug. 31, 1941; s. Phillip Moore and Helen Dale Parrish

(Cottingham) G. BA, Furman U., 1963; JD, U. S.C., 1969. Bar: S.C. 1969, U.S. Dist. Ct. S.C. 1969, U.S. Ct. Appeals (4th cir.) 1972, U.S. Supreme Ct. 1978, U.S. Ct. Appeals (fed. cir.) 1985. Assoc. Haynsworth, Perry, Bryant, Marion & Johnstone, Greenville, S.C., 1969-70; asst. to pres. U. S.C., Columbia, 1969, staff counsel, 1970-74, gen. counsel, 1974-79; exec. dir., CEO Nat. Assn. Coll. and Univ. Attys., Washington, 1979-96; cons. Fulbright & Jaworski, Washington, 1996—; bd. dirs. Am. Coun. Edn., 1992-94; mem. adv. bd. Ctr. for Constl. Studies, U. Notre Dame and Mercer U., 1981-92; mem. secretariat of nat. higher edn. orgns. Nat. Ctr. for Higher Edn., Washington, 1979-96. Author: (with Joseph P. O'Neill) Financing in a Period of Retrenchment: A Primer for Small Private Colleges, 1984. Editor: The Corporate Counsellors Deskbook (Non-Profit Organizations Supplement), 1983; editor, contbg. author: Legal Deskbook for Administrators of Independent Colleges and Universities, 1982, 83, 84; editor Coll. Law Digest, 1980-96; mem. editorial adv. com. West Pub. Co., St. Paul, 1980-96; editorial bd. Jour. Coll. and Univ. Law, U. Notre Dame, Ind., 1979-96. With U.S. Army, 1963-66, USAR, 1966-74. Mem. Order of St. John, Soc. Colonial Wars, St. Nicholas Soc. of N.Y., Mil. Order Fgn. Wars, Ancient and Honorable Artillery Co., City Tavern Club (bd. govs. 1992—, sec. 1994, v.p. 1996-99), Cosmos Club (legal affairs com. 1986-90, com. reciprocity 1988-90, house com. 1990-95, chmn. 1992-95). General corporate, Administrative and regulatory, Federal civil litigation. Office: 5th Fl 801 Pennsylvania Ave NW Washington DC 20004-2615

**GRIESA, THOMAS POOLE,** federal judge; b. Kansas City, Mo., Oct. 11, 1930; s. Charles Henry and Stella Lusk (Bedell) G.; m. Christine Pollard Meyer, Jan. 5, 1963. A.B. cum laude, Harvard U., 1952; LL.B., Stanford U., 1958. Bar: Wash. 1958, N.Y. 1961. Atty. Justice Dept., 1958-60; with firm Symmers, Fish & Warner, N.Y.C., 1960-61, Davis Polk & Wardwell, N.Y.C., 1961-72; partner Davis Polk & Wardwell, 1970-72; judge U.S. Dist. Ct. So. Dist. N.Y., 1972—, chief judge, 1993—. Mem.: Stanford Law Rev., 1956-58. Bd. visitors Stanford Law Sch., 1982-84. Served to lt. (j.g.) USCGR, 1952-54. Mem. Bar Assn. City N.Y., Union Club N.Y.C. Christian Scientist. Office: US Dist Ct US Courthouse 500 Pearl St New York NY 10007-1316

**GRIFFIN, BRYANT WADE,** retired judge; b. New Brunswick, N.J., Nov. 19, 1915; s. Bryant Wade and Maurine (McPherson) G.; m. Dorothy Thauwald, Sept. 2, 1939; children—Nancy Schaul, Bryant W., Georgia Griffin Peterson. A.B., U. Cin., 1937, LL.B., 1939. Bar: Ohio 1939, N.J. 1940. Assoc. McCarter & English, Newark, 1939-40; with legal dept. Central R.R. N.J., 1940; ptnr. Hauck & Griffin, Clinton, N.J., 1940-43; sr. ptnr., founder Moser, Cooper, Rose & English, 1946-75; judge Superior Ct. N.J., Elibeth, 9785, Flemington, 1985-94; lectr. Practicing Law Inst., N.Y. and N.J. Served to lt. USNR, 1943-46. Mem. ABA, N.J. Bar Assn., Union County Bar Assn. (pres. 1963), Summit Bar Assn. (pres. 1960), Hunterdon County Bar Assn., Retired Judges Assn. N.J. (pres. 1992-94), Citizens Trust Co. (past dir.). Republican. Clubs: Marco Bay Yacht, Port of the Islands Gun, Down Town Assn. (Summit), Amwell Valley Conservancy. Died May 22, 1999. Home: 8115 Fellowship Rd Basking Ridge NJ 07920-3913

**GRIFFIN, CAMPBELL ARTHUR, JR.,** lawyer; b. Joplin, Mo., July 17, 1929; s. Campbell Arthur and Clara M. (Smith) G.; m. Margaret Ann Adams, Oct. 19, 1958; children: Campbell A., Laura Ann. BA, U. Mo., 1951, MA in Acctg., 1952; JD, U. Tex., 1957. Bar: Tex. 1957. Assoc. Vinson & Elkins, L.L.P., Houston, 1957-67, ptnr., 1968-92; mem. mgmt. com. Vinson & Elkins, L.L.P., 1981-90, mng. ptnr. Dallas office, 1986-89; adj. prof. adminstrv. sci. Jones Grad. Sch. Adminstrn., Rice U., 1992-94. Mem. ofcl. bd. Bethany Christian Ch., Houston, 1962-65, 66-69, chmn. bd. elders, 1968; bd. dirs. Houston Pops Orch., 1982-87; councilman City of Hunters Creek Village, Tex., 1993-95; pres. Windcliff Property Owners Assn., Estes Park, Colo., 1995-96; dir. Cornell Corrections, Inc., 1996—; mem. St. Martin's Episcopal Ch., Houston. Mem. ABA, Houston Bar Assn., State Bar Tex. (bus. law sect. chmn. 1974-75), Tex. Bus Law Found. (chmn. 1988-89, dir. 1988—), Houston Racquet Club (dir. 1992-94). General corporate, Securities.

**GRIFFIN, CARL RUSSELL, III,** lawyer; b. Tacoma, Wash., July 24, 1955; m. Denise C. Corten, Aug. 16, 1980; children: Emily Kate, Elizabeth Joan. BA, Bowdoin Coll., 1977; JD, U. Maine, 1980. Pvt. practice Boothbay Harbor, Maine, 1980—. Bd. dirs. Boothbay Harbor YMCA, 1989-95. Mem. Maine State Bar Assn., Boothbay Region Fishermen's Meml. Fund (dir. 1980-99), Rotary (dir., past pres.), Boothbay Region Hist. Soc. (dir. 1990), Phi Beta Kappa. Republican. Avocations: boating, skiing, basketball, Maine history, church. Estate planning, Real property, Estate taxation. Office: 59 Atlantic Ave PO Box 456 Boothbay Harbor ME 04538-0456

**GRIFFIN, HARRY LEIGH,** lawyer; b. Charlotte, N.C., May 1, 1935; s. Harry Leigh and Irma (Waters) G.; m. Brenda Raudenbush, June 6, 1960 (div. 1993), children: Harry L. III, David W., Heather L., Andrea B.; m. Deborah S. Gabbard, Mar. 7, 1997. BA magna cum laude, Harvard Coll., 1957; LLB, Duke U., 1963. Bar; N.C. 1963, Ga. 1964. Law clk. to Hon. J. Spencer Bell U.S. Ct. Appeals (4th cir.), Charlotte, 1963-64; from assoc. to ptnr. Smith, Currie & Hancock, Atlanta, 1964-77; ptnr. Trotter, Bondurant, Griffin, Miller & Hishon, Atlanta, 1977-80, Griffin, Cochrane & Marshall (and predecessor firm), Atlanta, 1980—; mem. human rels. commn. City of Atlanta; mediator Resolution Resoruces, Inc.; lectr. constl. law various ednl. insts. and profl. assns., 1964—; founding fellow Am. Coll. of Constrn. Lawyers. Author: Practical Construction Law, 1976; also articles. Served with U.S. Army, 1960-63. Mem. ABA, Ga. Bar Assn., Atlanta Bar Assn., N.C. Bar Assn. Roman Catholic. Avocations: trout fishing, reading. Construction, General civil litigation, Alternative dispute resolution. Home: 6 Walker Ter NE Atlanta GA 30309-3319

**GRIFFIN, JAMES ALFRED,** lawyer; b. Jamaica, N.Y., Nov. 19, 1954; s. Raymond Lawrence and Helen Griffin. BA, Dowling Coll., 1976; BS, SUNY, Stony Brook, 1979; JD, Touro Law Sch., 1987. Bar: N.Y. 1987. Assoc. Jones, Hirsch, Connors & Bull, N.Y.C., 1987-89; assoc. to ptnr. Frank Mitchell Cosso, P.C., Westbury, N.Y., 1989-91; ptnr. Griffin and Pellicane, Westbury, 1991-93, Griffin Pellicane & Sands, P.C., Westbury, 1993-95; pvt. practice Oyster Bay, N.Y., 1995—; corp. sec. Environtl. Remediation Holding Corp., Oyster Bay, and Lafayette, La., 1996-99. Mem. N.Y. State Bar Assn., Nassau County Bar Assn., Am. Acad. of Physician Assistants (del. 1981-83), N.Y. State Soc. of Physician Assistants (del. 1981-83, corp. counsel 1979). Avocation: sailing. General civil litigation, General practice, Oil, gas, and mineral. Office: 3 Audrey Ave Oyster Bay NY 11771-1503

**GRIFFIN, LAWRENCE JOSEPH,** lawyer; b. Chgo., Dec. 11, 1965; s. Eugen Leo and Elena Rachel (Bruno) G.; m. Elizabeth Griffin, Mar. 18, 1995. BA, Cornell U., 1988; JD, DePaul U., 1991. Bar: Ill. 1991, Calif. 1997, Wis. 1997, U.S. Dist. Ct. (no. dist.) Ill. 1991, U.S. Ct. Appeals (7th cir.) 1992. Assoc. Eugene L. Griffin & Assocs., Ltd., Chgo., 1991—; arbitrator Cook County Manditory Arbitration, Chgo., 1994—. Mem. ATLA, ABA, Ill. Bar Assn., Chgo. Bar Assn. (profl. reponsibility com. 1994—, tort law com. 1994—), Calif. Bar Assn., Wis. Bar Assn., Ill. Trial Lawyers Assn. Personal injury, Product liability, State and local taxation. Office: Eugene L Griffin & Assocs 29 N Wacker Dr Ste 650 Chicago IL 60606-3203

**GRIFFIN, MARILYN OTTEMAN,** lawyer; b. Harlingen, Tex., Dec. 18, 1964; d. DeWayne Gerald and Myrtis Marilyn (Brett) Otteman; m. Michael John Griffin, III, Jan. 12, 1991; children: Michael John IV, Matthew Laurence, Mackenzie Grace, Marilyn Brett. BA in English, Tex. Tech U., 1987; JD, South Tex. Coll. of Law, 1992. Bar: Tex. 1992. Asst. dist. atty. Dist. Atty.'s Office, Houston, 1991-92; staff atty. Eric Carter, P.C., Houston, 1992-93; lawyer, sole practice Law Offices of Marilyn O. Griffin, Houston, 1993-96; ptnr. Griffin & Griffin, Houston, 1997—. Fellow Assn. Women Attys., Houston Young Lawyers Assn. (co-chair substance abuse com. 1992—); mem. Def. Rsch. and Trial Lawyers Assn., Rotary Club. Republican. Roman Catholic. Avocations: scuba diving, golf, public speaking. General civil litigation, Probate, Personal injury. Office: Griffin & Griffin 1314 Texas St Ste 1305 Houston TX 77002-3515

**GRIFFIN, ROBERT GERARD,** lawyer; b. Towanda, Pa., Apr. 10, 1962; s. Francis Laurence and Anne Marie (Bouchard) G.; m. Beth Patten, June 23, 1984; children: Hope Elizabeth, Carly Marie. BA, U. N.C., 1983, JD, 1989. Bar: N.C. 1989, U.S. Dist. Ct. (mid. dist.) N.C. 1990. Sales rep. Procter & Gamble, Cin., 1984-85; legal asst. Golding, Crews, Meekings, Gordon & Gray, Charlotte, N.C., 1985-86; assoc. Fisher Fisher Gayle Clinard & Craig, P.A., High Point, N.C., 1989-93, shareholder, officer, 1994—, also bd. dirs. Mem. KC (advocate 1993-95), Lions (tailtwister 1989), Kiwanis. Roman Catholic. Avocations: golf, tennis. General civil litigation, Probate, Estate planning. Office: Fisher Fisher Gayle et al PO Drawer 1150 101 S Main St Ste 800 High Point NC 27260-5239

**GRIFFIN, ROBERT PAUL,** former United States senator, state supreme court justice; b. Detroit, Nov. 6, 1923; s. J.A. and Beulah M. G.; m. Marjorie J. Anderson, 1947; children—Paul Robert, Richard Allen, James Anderson, Martha Jill. AB, BS, Central Mich. U., 1947, LLD, 1963; JD, U. Mich., 1950, LLD, 1973; LL.D., Eastern Mich. U., 1969, Albion Coll., 1970, Western Mich. U., 1971, Grand Valley State Coll., 1971, Detroit Coll. Bus., 1972, Detroit Coll. Law, 1973; L.H.D., Hillsdale (Mich.) Coll., 1970; J.C.D., Rollins Coll., 1970; Ed.D., No. Mich. U., 1970; D. Pub. Service, Detroit Inst. Tech., 1971. Bar: Mich. 1950. Pvt. practice Traverse City, Mich., 1950-56; mem. 85th-89th congresses from 9th Dist. Mich., Washington, 1957-66; mem. U.S. Senate from Mich., Washington, 1966-79; counsel Miller, Canfield, Paddock & Stone, Traverse City, 1979-86; assoc. justice Mich. Supreme Ct., Lansing, 1987-95. Trustee Gerald R. Ford Found. Served with inf. AUS, World War II, ETO. Named 1 of 10 Outstanding Young Men of Nation U.S. Jaycees, 1959. Mem. ABA, Mich. Bar Assn., D.C. Bar Assn., Kiwanis.

**GRIFFIN, SHARON L.,** lawyer; b. Toledo, June 14, 1939; d. Werner Gustave and Martha Lou (Doyle) Knauf; m. John Anthony Griffin, May 21, 1963 (div. 1975); children: Simone Louise, Matthew Compton. BA, U. Mich., 1961; JD, U. Toledo, 1982. Bar: Ohio 1983, U.S. Dist. Ct. (no. dist.) Ohio 1985, U.S. Ct. Appeals (6th cir.) 1987, U.S. Supreme Ct. 1988. Editorial asst. Am. Jour. Comparative Law, U. Mich. Law Sch., Ann Arbor, 1962-64; adminstrv. asst. dept. edn. U. Melbourne (Australia), 1965; legal sec. Papua New Guinea, 1969-71; office mgr. engring. firm, Papua New Guinea, 1969-71; employment placement counselor Snelling and Snelling Pers., Toledo, 1972-74; adminstrv. asst. to dean U. Toledo Coll. Law, 1974-77; adminstrv. asst. Met. Toledo Consortium, 1977-83, acting program coord., 1983; litter control grant coord. dept. community devel. City of Toledo, 1984-85; pvt. practice Toledo, 1983—; mediator citizens settlement dispute program Toledo Mcpl. Ct. Vol. numerous local polit. campaigns; mem. legal svcs. com. Battered Women's Shelter, YWCA, Toledo; trustee YWCA, Toledo; mem. allocations com. United Way Greater Toledo, also team leader children svcs. panel; v.p. for fund raising, mem. adv. bd., past membership chmn. Democratic Women's Campaign Assn.; precinct chmn. Toledo Dem. Com., 1986—. Mem. ABA (family law com.), Ohio Bar Assn., Lucas County Bar Assn., Toledo Bar Assn. (pro bono program, citizens dispute settlement program com., family law com., cert. of commendation 1986), Toledo Law Assn., Women's Bar Assn. (pub. rels. com., newsletter com.), Ohio Acad. Trial Lawyers, ACLU (bd. dirs., legal com.), NOW (adv. counsel Toledo chpt.). Family and matrimonial, Civil rights, Juvenile. Office: Spitzer Bldg 520 Madison Ave Ste 837 Toledo OH 43604-1355

**GRIFFIN, SHAWN MICHAEL,** lawyer; b. Hornell, N.Y., Jan. 26, 1964; s. James William and Robin G.; m. Amy Jon Rees, Mar. 31, 1966; children: Patrick, Michael, Alexandra. BBA in Finance magna cum laude, St. Bonaventure U., 1986; JD/MBA cum laude, SUNY, Buffalo, 1989. Bar: N.Y.; U.S. Dist. Ct. (we. dist. N.Y.) 1990. Assoc. Harris, Beach & Wilcox LLP, Rochester, N.Y., 1990-96, ptnr., co-chmn. pub. fin./econ. devel. practice group, 1997—; mem., spkr. N.Y. State Econ. Devel. Coun., Albany, 1992—. Author: (book) Transactions Involving Industrial Development Agencies, 1998. Bd. dirs. YMCA Bayview, Rochester, 1993-94. With USAR JAG Svcs. Roman Catholic. Avocations: golf, skiing, travel. Municipal (including bonds), Real property, Contracts commercial. Office: Harris Beach & Wilcox LLP 130 E Main St Rochester NY 14604-1610

**GRIFFIN, WILLIAM MELL, III,** lawyer; b. Tallahassee, Feb. 1, 1957; s. William Mell Jr. and June Winona (Cooper) G.; m. Kathryn Elizabeth Lawson, Dec. 11, 1993; children: William Mell IV, George Lawson. BA, U. Va., 1979; JD, So. Meth. U., 1982. Bar: Ark. 1982, U.S. Dist. Ct. (ea. and we. dists.) Ark. 1982, U.S. Ct. Appeals (8th cir.) 1983. Assoc. Friday, Eldredge & Clark, Little Rock, 1982-87, ptnr., 1987—. Mem. ABA (torts and ins. practice sect.), Ark. Bar Assn., Pulaski County Bar Assn., William R. Overton Inn of Ct., Ark. Def. Counsel, Def. Rsch. Inst., Fedn. Ins. and Corp. Counsel, Leadership Greater Little Rock, Phi Delta Phi. Democrat. Avocations: running, hunting. State civil litigation, Federal civil litigation, Insurance. Home: 420 Midland St Little Rock AR 72205-4177 Office: Friday Eldredge & Clark 2000 1st Commercial Bldg Little Rock AR 72201

**GRIFFITH, C. LAURIE,** lawyer; b. Concord, Calif., Sept. 19, 1964; d. Clyde Edward and Suzanne (Grant) G. BA in Fin. Mgmt., Hood Coll., 1986; JD, U. Louisville, 1995. Bar: Ky. 1996. Lease adminstr. John Akridge Devel., Washington, 1987-88; intern, health and welfare cons. Presbyn. Ch., Louisville, 1988-90; non-ordained pastor Fairview Presbyn. Ch., Princeton, Ind., 1990-91; employment and edn. counselor Coun. of Three Rivers Am. Indian Ctr., Louisville, 1991-94; assoc. Boehl, Stopher & Graves, Louisville, 1996—. Vol. Rape Relief Ctr., Louisville, 1992—; spl. advocate CASA, Louisville, 1994-95; legal advocate, jud. bypass Reproductive Freedom Project, Louisville, 1997—. Mem. Brandeis Inn of Ct. Presbyterian. E-mail: cgriffith@bsg-law.com. General corporate, Non-profit and tax-exempt organizations, Intellectual property. Office: Boehl Stopher & Graves 400 W Market St Louisville KY 40202-3346

**GRIFFITH, DONALD KENDALL,** lawyer; b. Aurora, Ill., Feb. 4, 1933; s. Walter George and Mary Elizabeth Griffith; m. Susan Smykal, Aug. 4, 1962; children: Kay, Kendall. Grad. in History with honors, Culver Mil. Acad., 1951, BA, U. Ill., 1955, JD, 1958. Bar: Ill. 1958, U.S. Supreme Ct. 1973. Assoc. Hinshaw & Culbertson, Chgo., 1959-65, ptnr., 1965-98, of counsel, 1999—; spl. asst. atty. gen. Ill., 1970-72; lectr. Ill. Inst. Continuing Legal Edn., 1970—. Trustee, Lawrence Hall Youth Svcs., 1967—, v.p. for program, 1969-74; bd. dirs. Child Care Assn. Ill., 1970-73; mem. Lake Forest High Sch. Bd. Edn., 1983-84. 2d lt. USAF, 1956. Fellow Am. Acad. Appellate Lawyers; mem. ABA (chmn. appellate advocacy com., tort and ins. practice sect. 1983-84), Ill. Bar Assn., Chgo. Bar Assn., Appellate Lawyers Assn. Ill. (pres. 1973-74), Def. Rsch. Inst., Ill. Def. Counsel, Chgo. Trial Lawyers Club, Alpha Chi Rho (chpt. pres.), Phi Delta Phi. Club: University of Chgo., Knollwood. Mem. editorial bd. Ill. Civil Practice After Trial, 1970; co-editor The Brief, 1975-83; contbg. author Civil Practice After Trial, 1984, 89; contbr. article to legal jour. State civil litigation, Federal civil litigation, Insurance. Office: Hinshaw & Culbertson 222 N La Salle St Ste 300 Chicago IL 60601-1081

**GRIFFITH, EDWARD, II,** lawyer; b. Wilkes-Barre, Pa., Feb. 9, 1948; s. Edward Meredith Griffith and Jane (Randall) Griffith Jones; m. Linda Christine Scribner, Aug. 9, 1969 (div. July 1982); children: Trevor Scribner, Stewart Randall; m. Katherine Greybill, Oct. 24, 1987. BA, Lehigh U., 1970; JD, Dickinson Sch. Law, 1973. Bar: Pa. 1973, U.S. Dist. Ct. (ea. dist.) Pa. 1973, U.S. Ct. Appeal (3rd cir.) 1973, U.S. Supreme Ct. 1978. Ptnr. Duane, Morris & Heckscher, Phila., 1973—; cons. Pa. State Bd. Law Examiners, Phila, 1974-77. Master John E. Stively Inn of Ct.; mem. ABA, Pa. Bar Assn., Chester County Bar Assn., Def. Rsch. Inst., Pa. Def. Inst. Republican. Presbyterian. Avocations: hunting, fishing, gardening. General civil litigation, Insurance, Personal injury. Office: Duane Morris & Heckscher 735 Chesterbrook Blvd Ste 300 Wayne PA 19087-5638

**GRIFFITH, EMLYN IRVING,** lawyer; b. Utica, N.Y., May 13, 1923; s. William A. and Maud A. (Charles) G.; m. Mary L. Kilpatrick, Aug. 13, 1946; children: William L., James R. AB, Colgate U., 1942; JD, Cornell U., 1950; 9 hon. doctorates. Bar: N.Y. 1950, U.S. Supreme Ct. 1954. Pvt. practice law Lockport, N.Y., 1950-52, Rome, N.Y., 1952—; bd. dirs. various corps. and founds.; treas. N.Y. State Photonics Devel. Corp., 1989—. Contbr. articles to profl. jours. in U.S. and U.K. Mem. N.Y. State Bd. Regents, 1973-96, Gov.'s Com. on Librs., 1976-78; co-chmn. State Conf. Professions, 1974-77, 85-90; mem. U.S. Forum Edn. Orgn. Leaders, 1978-80, Intergovtl. Adv. Coun. on Edn., 1982-86; del. to China-U.S. Joint Session on Trade and Law, Beijing, 1987, Soviet-Am. Conf. on Comparative Edn., Moscow, 1988, N.Y. State-USSR Lawyers Conf., Moscow, 1990; pres. Nat. Assn. State Bds. Edn., 1979-80, Nat. Assn. State Bds. Edn. Found., 1997-99; pres. Nat. Welsh-Am. Found., 1981-83; v.p. Hon. Soc. Cymmrodorion, London, 1988—; trustee, bd. pensions United Presbyn. Ch., 1966-72, Aerospace Edn. Found., 1979-96, Erie Canal Mus., 1996—, Cazenovia Coll., 1996—. Maj. USAAC, 1942-46. Recipient Disting. Svc. to Am. Edn. award Nat. Assn. State Bds. Edn., 1995, Conspicuous Svc. award State of N.Y., 1992, Exceptional Svc. citation Air Force Assn., 1980; Doolittle fellow Aerospace Edn. Found., 1988, Welsh Heritage award Nat. Welsh Am. Found., 1997. Fellow Am. Bar Found., N.Y. Bar Found. (recipient Root-Stimson award for pub. svc. 1986, bd. dirs. 1989—); mem. ABA (com. pub. edn. 1974—), N.Y. State Bar assn. (ho. dels. 1974-76, com. lawyer competency 1986-89, co-chmn. com. atty. professionalism, 1989-92, mem. bd. editors Bar Jour. 1986-97), Oneida County Bar Assn. (pres. 1974-75), State Conf. County Bar Officers (chmn. 1974-76), Osgoode Soc. Can., Selden Soc., Eng., Rome Club, Colgate Club N.Y.C, Cornell Club of N.Y., Phi Gamma Delta Internat. (pres. bd. trustees 1982-86, pres. edn. found. 1992-94). General practice, Probate, Real property. Office: 225 N Washington St Rome NY 13440-5724

**GRIFFITH, JAMES D.,** retired lawyer; b. Evanston, Ill., Aug. 28, 1929; s. Wendell Crabtree and Mary Griffith; m. Elizabeth Meyer, Sept. 21, 1957 (div. July 1987); children: Ian Hunt, Alison Gail Griffith; m. Phyllis A. Zaruba Oct. 22, 1994. BA, DePauw U., 1951; JD, Northwestern U., Chgo., 1953. Bar: Ill. 1953, Mich. 1973, Ind. 1980. Assoc. Campbell, Clithero & Fischer, Chgo., 1956-63; ptnr. Graham, Stevenson & Griffith, Chgo., 1963-67; prin. Pauker & Griffith, Ltd., Chgo., 1969-79; pvt. practice, Chgo., 1967-69, 80-95; ret., 1995; magistrate Village of Glenview, Ill., 1961-65. Contbr. articles to profl. jours. Founder, pres. Com. on Lake Michigan Pollution, Wilmette, Ill., 1967-69, Fifty Percent, Chgo., 1991—; active Chgo. Crime Commn., 1967-72; pres. Lake Michigan Fedn., Chgo., 1973-74, 92-94; pres. Glenview Civic Party, 1981; dir. Family Svc. Ctr., Wilmette. With U.S. Army, 1954-56. Mem. Nat. Strategy Forum, Chgo. Coun. on Fgn. Rels., Sheridan Shore Yacht Club (Wilmette, commodore 1970), Rotary Internat. Avocations: sailing, tennis, skiing, canoeing, bridge. General civil litigation, Estate planning, General practice. Home: 1210 Glendenning Rd Wilmette IL 60091-1547

**GRIFFITH, MARY E.,** lawyer, educator; b. North Platte, Nebr., Apr. 4, 1949; d. William Alden and Florene (Henry) G.; 1 child, Este Pearl. BA, Roger Williams Coll., 1974; JD, W.Va. U., 1988. Bar: W.Va. 1988; U.S. Dist. Ct. (so. dist.) W.Va. 1989, U.S. Ct. Appeals (4th cir.) 1990. Staff atty. Appalachian Rsch. and Def. Fund, Princeton, W.Va., 1988-91; atty. in pvt. practice, Princeton, 1991-92; atty., ptnr. Bell & Griffith, L.C., Princeton, 1992—; adj. faculty Bluefield (W.Va.) State coll., 1998—. Mem. Cmty. Connections, Inc., 1993—; pres. Appalachian South Folklife Ctr., 1990—. Mem. Nat. Assn. Counsel for Children, Nat. Assn. Social Security Claimants Reps. Democrat. Personal injury, Family and matrimonial, Juvenile. Office: Bell & Griffith LC 1625 N Walker St Princeton WV 24740-2624

**GRIFFITH, MICHAEL JOHN,** lawyer; b. Altoona, Pa., Feb. 17, 1949; s. William Howard and Patricia Ruth (Carney) G. Student, U. Ga., 1967-69; BA, U. West Fla., 1971; JD, U. Miss., 1974. Bar: Miss. 1974, U.S. Dist. Ct. (no. dist.) Miss. 1974, Fla. 1976, U.S. Dist. Ct. (no. dist.) Fla. 1976, U.S. Ct. Appeals (5th cir.) 1976, U.S. Ct. Appeals (11th cir.) 1981, U.S. Supreme Ct. 1981, Colo. 1993. Staff atty. Fla. Real Estate Commn., Winter Park, Fla., 1974-75; asst. state's atty. Office State's Atty. 20th Jud. Cir., Fla., 1975-76; ptnr. Levin, Middlebrooks, Mabie, Thomas, Mayes & Mitchell, P.A., Pensacola, Fla., 1976-90; pvt. practice law Pensacola, 1990—. Bd. dirs. Fiesta Five Flags, Pensacola, Humane Soc. Pensacola; trustee Pensacola Beach United Ch. of Christ. Mem. Miss. Bar Assn., Assn. Trial Lawyers Am., Colo. Bar Assn., Fla. Bar Assn. (mem. ethics com. criminal law sect.), Escambia-Santa Rosa Bar Assn., Nat. Assn. Criminal Def. Lawyers (life mem.), Fla. Assn. Criminal Def. Lawyers, Acad. Fla. Trial Lawyers, Irish Politicians Club, Exec. Club, Pensacola Yatch Club. Republican. Avocations: scuba diving, fishing, water skiing, snow skiing. Criminal, Family and matrimonial, Personal injury. Home: 240 Sabine Dr Pensacola Beach FL 32561-5223 Office: 304 E Government St Pensacola FL 32501-6021

**GRIFFITH, RICHARD LATTIMORE,** lawyer; b. Abilene, Tex., Feb. 8, 1939; s. Richard Allan and Lorayne (Lattimore) G.; m. Sarah Brewster, Feb. 16, 1963 (dec. 1979); 1 child, Grey; m. Betsy Brooks, Apr. 19, 1980. BA, U. Okla., 1961; LLB, U. Tex., 1963. Bar: Tex. 1965, U.S. Dist. Ct. (no. dist.) Tex. 1966, U.S. Ct. Appeals (5th cir.) 1981, U.S. Dist. Ct. (ea. dist.) Okla. 1976, U.S. Dist. Ct. (we. dist.) Okla. 1967. Ptnr., chmn. health law sect. Cantey & Hanger, Ft. Worth, Tex., 1965—; chmn. Health Law Sect. State Bar of Tex., 1988. Co-author: Texas Hospital Law, 1988, 3d edit., 1998; contbr. articles to profl. jours. 1st lt. U.S. Army, 1963-65. Fellow Am. Coll. Trial Lawyers, Tex. Bar Found. (life); mem. Am. Bd. Trial Advocates (chpt. pres. 1985, state chmn. 1995), Def. Counsel Trial Acad. (faculty), Coll. of State Bar of Tex., Internat. Assn. Def. Counsel, Def. Rsch. Inst. (bd. dirs. S.W. region), Tex. Assn. Def. Counsel (v.p. 1984-85, regional v.p. 1986-88, 92-93), Tarrant County Bar Assn., Tex. Bar Assn. Eldon Mahon Inn of Ct. (emeritus). Avocations: gardening, fishing, hunting, cooking. Health, General civil litigation, Personal injury. Home: 6332 Curzon Ave Fort Worth TX 76116-4604 Office: Cantey & Hanger 2100 Burnett Plaza 801 Cherry St Fort Worth TX 76102-6898

**GRIFFITH, STEVEN FRANKLIN, SR.,** lawyer, real estate title insurance agent and investor; b. New Orleans, July 14, 1948; s. Hugh Franklin and Rose Marie (Teutone) G.; m. Mary Elizabeth McMillan Frank, Dec. 9, 1972; children: Steven Franklin Jr., Jason Franklin. BBA, Loyola U., New Orleans, 1970, JD, 1972. Bar: La. 1972, U.S. Dist. Ct. (ea. dist.) La. 1975, U.S. Ct. Appeals (5th cir.) 1975, U.S. Supreme Ct. 1976. With Law Offices of Senator George T. Oubre, Norco, La., 1971-75; sole practice Destrehan, La., 1975—. Pres. 29th Jud. Dist. Bar Assn., 1999—. Fellow La. State Bar Found.; mem. ABA, ATLA, La. State Bar Assn. (ho. of dels. 1987—), La. Trial Lawyers Assn., New Orleans Trial Lawyers Assn., Fed. Bar Assn., St. Charles Parish Bar Assn. (pres. 1999—), Lions. Democrat. Real property, Personal injury, Insurance.

**GRIGGS, FARRAR O'NEAL,** lawyer; b. Concord, N.C., Jan. 17, 1948; s. Farrar O'Neal Sr. and Katherine Long (Turbyfill) G.; m. Peggy Jane Link, Apr. 27, 1974 (div. Aug. 1991); children: Rebekah Lauren, Emily Farrar, Ethan Link, Eleanor Jane; m. Cynthia Lynn Scott, Dec. 2, 1995. Student, Duke U., 1966-68; BA in English, U. N.C., 1970; JD, John Marshall Law Sch., Chgo., 1977; postgrad., Northwestern U., 1976. Bar: N.C., U.S. Dist. Ct. (we. dist.) N.C., U.S. Tax Ct. Account rep. Cannon Mills, Inc., N.Y.C., 1972-75; owner law practice Farrar Griggs Jr., Atty., Kannapolis, N.C., 1977—; owner Griggs Properties, Kannapolis, 1983—. Mem. Kannapolis Bd. Edn., 1988-92; past. treas., mem. coun. Boy Scouts Am.; coach Youth Soccer, 1991, 92, 96, baseball, 1990; trustee Cabarros Bapt. Assn. Lt. U.S. Navy, 1970-72. Mem. N.C. Bar Assn., Am. Legion, Kannapolis C. of C. (past pres.-elect, bd. dirs.), Kannapolis Rotary Club (past treas., bd. dirs.). Republican. Baptist. Avocations: whitewater rafting, fishing, hiking, cabinetry, antiques. Real property, Probate, General practice. Office: 601 Coach St Kannapolis NC 28083-6023

**GRIGGS, WADE GARNEY, III,** lawyer; b. Houston, May 27, 1970; s. Wade Garney Jr. and Janita Pamela (Frye) G.; m. Blakely Lesesne Dickson, May 28, 1994; 1 child, Wade Garney Griggs IV. BA, Vanderbilt U., 1992; JD, U. Houston, 1995. Bar: Tex. 1995, S.C. 1996, U.S. Dist. Ct. S.C., U.S. Dist. Ct. (we., ea., and so. dists.) Tex. Atty. Littler Mendelson, Houston, 1992, Ogletree Deakins Nash Smoak & Stewart P.C., Greenville, S.C., 1993—. Bd. dirs. Safe Harbor Women's Shelter, Greenville, S.C., 1998. Episcopalian. Labor. Office: Ogletree Deakins Nash Smoak & Stewart PC 300 N Main St Ste 500 Greenville SC 29601-2195

**GRIGSBY, ROBERT S.,** lawyer, educator; b. Mars, Pa., Jan. 26, 1926; s. Jess C. and Elizabeth D. (Shomaker) G.; m. Jean R. Reber, June 16, 1950; 1 child, Pamela S. McCready. BS, U. Pitts., 1950; LLB, Duquesne U., 1955. Bar: Pa. 1956, U.S. Dist. Ct. (we. dist.) Pa. 1955, U.S. Ct. Appeals (3rd cir.) 1957, U.S. Supreme Ct. 1965. From assoc. to ptnr. Dalzel, McFalls, Breden & Martin (and predecessor firms), Pitts., 1958-85; judge Ct. Common Pleas of Allegheny County, Pitts., 1978-79; dir., ptnr. Cohen & Grigsby, P.C., Pitts., 1985—; adj. prof. U. Pitts. Sch. Law, 1981—. Solicitor, contr. Allegheny County, Pitts., 1976-78. With USN, 1944-46. Fellow Am. Coll.

Trial Lawyers; mem. ABA, Internat. Assn. Def. Counsel, Maritime Law Assn., Product Liability Adv. Coun., Pa. Bar Inst., Pa. Bar Assn., Allegheny County Bar Assn., Acad. Trial Lawyers Allegheny County, Fedn. Ins. and Corp. Counsel. Avocations: gardening, golf, fishing. Labor, Personal injury, Product liability. Home: 117 Westholm Dr Sewickley PA 15143-8388

**GRILLER, GORDON MOORE,** court administrator; b. Sioux City, Iowa, Feb. 3, 1944; s.Joseph Edwards and Arlene (Searles) G. m. Helen Mary Friederichs, aug. 20, 1966; children: Heather, Chad. BA in Political Sci., U. Minn., 1966, MA in Pub. Affairs, 1969. Mgnt. analyst Hennepin County Adminstr., Mpls., 1968-72; asst. court adminstr. Hennepin County Municipal Ct., Mpls., 1972-77, ct. adminstr., 1977-78; judicial dist. adminstr. 2nd Dist. Ct. Minn., St. Paul, 1978-87; ct. adminstr. Superior Ct. Ariz., Phoenix, Ariz., 1987—; bd. dirs. Nat. Ctr. State Cts., 1997—. Vice-chmn. Bloomington Sch. Bd., Minn., 1981-87. Sgt. USAAF, 1968-74 Res. Recipient Warren E. Burger award Inst. Ct. Mgnt.,1988, Leadership Fellows award Bush Leadership Program, 1974. Mem. Nat. Assn. Trial Ct. Adminstrs.(pres. 1983-84), Ariz. Ct. Assn., Nat. Assn Ct. Mgmt., Am. Judicature Soc., (bd. dirs. 1997—). Lutheran. Avocations: running, kyaking, racquetball, scuba diving. Home: 8507 E San Jacinto Dr Scottsdale AZ 85258-2576 Office: Superior Ct Ariz 201 W Jefferson St Fl 4 Phoenix AZ 85003-2243

**GRIM, DOUGLAS PAUL,** lawyer; b. Bellingham, Wash., May 12, 1940; s. Paul R. and Vivian I. (McMillen) G.; m. Catherine Powers, Dec. 28, 1968; children: Caryn, Devin. BA, Lawrence Coll., 1962; LLB, Stanford U., 1965; LLM, N.Y.U., 1966. Bar: Calif. 1966, U.S. Supreme Ct. 1985. Assoc. Hanna and Morton, Los Angeles, 1966-72; of counsel Harris, Noble, Uhler & Gallop, Los Angeles, 1972-75; ptnr. Nicholas, Kolliner, Myers, D'Angelo and Givens, Los Angeles, 1975; sole practice, Los Angeles, 1975—; instr. Golden Gate U. Sch. Law, 1975; dir. Am. Internat. Seaview Properties, Inc., 1976—; chmn. bd. Agri-Feeds, Inc., 1981—. Chmn. exec. com. Troop 35 Los Angeles Area Council Boy Scouts Am., 1967-72; v.p., dir. Los Angeles Jaycees, 1966-75. Recipient Michael F. Tobey award Los Angeles Jr. C. of C., 1972; named one of Outstanding Young Men of Am., 1972. Mem. State Bar of Calif., Los Angeles County Bar Assn., ABA. Methodist. Clubs: Jonathan, Riviera Tennis (Los Angeles), Wilshire Kiwanis (bd. dirs.), Uptown Investment (pres. 1978). Author: Drafting a 1244 Plan; Medical Reimbursement Plans. Corporate taxation, Real property, Probate. Home: PO Box 712251 Los Angeles CA 90071-7251 Office: 333 S Hope St 36th Floor Suite 3630 Los Angeles CA 90071

**GRIMES, STEPHEN HENRY,** retired state supreme court justice; b. Peoria, Ill., Nov. 17, 1927; s. Henry Holbrook and June (Kellar) G.; m. Mary Fay Fulghum, Dec. 29, 1951; children: Gay Diane, Mary June, Sue Anne, Sheri Lynn. Student, Fla. So. Coll., 1946-47; BS in Bus. Adminstrn. with honors, U. Fla., 1951, LLB with honors, 1954; LLD (hon.), Stetson U., 1980. Bar: Fla. 1954, U.S. Dist. Ct. (no. and so. dists.) 1954, U.S. Ct. Appeals (5th cir.) 1965, U.S. Supreme Ct. 1972. Since practiced in Bartow, Fla.; ptnr. Holland and Knight and predecessor firm, Tallahassee, 1954-73, 98—; judge Ct. Appeal 2d Dist. Fla., Lakeland, Fla., 1973-87; chief judge Ct. Appeal 2d Dist. Fla., 1978-80; chmn. Conf. Fla. Dist. Cts. Appeal, 1978-80; justice Fla. Supreme Ct., Tallahassee, 1987-97, chief justice, 1994-96; chair Article V Task Force, 1994-96; mem. Fla. Jud. Qualification Commn., 1982-86, vice chmn., 1985-86; chmn. Fla. Jud. Coun., 1989-94. Contbr. articles U. Fla. Law Rev., 1951, 54. Bd. dirs. Bartow Meml. Hosp., 1958-61, Bartow Library, 1968-78; trustee Polk Community Coll., Winter Haven, Fla., 1967-70, chmn., 1969-70; bd. govs. Polk Pub. Mus., 1976—; bd. dirs. Fla. History Assocs. Lt. (j.g.) USN, 1951-53. Fellow Am. Coll. Trial Lawyers; mem. ABA, Fla. Bar Assn. (bd. govs. jr. bar 1956-58, bd. dirs. trial lawyers sect. 1967-69, sec. 1969, vice chmn. appellate rules com. 1976-77, vice chmn. tort litigation rev. commn. 1985-86), 10th Cir. Bar Assn. (pres. 1966), Am. Judicature Soc., Bartow C. of C. (pres. 1964), Rotary (dist. gov. 1960-61). Episcopalian (sr. warden 1964-65, 77). Office: Holland & Knight LLP 315 S Calhoun St Tallahassee FL 32301-1856

**GRIMES, WILLIAM ALVAN,** retired state supreme court chief justice; b. Dover, N.H., July 4, 1911; s. Frank J. and Annie (Ash) G.; m. Barbara Terry Parsons, June 22, 1940; children: Gail Terry, Gordon Francis. BS, U. N.H., 1934, LLD, 1969; JD, Boston U., 1937; LLD, William Mitchell Coll. Law, 1979, Calif. Western Sch. Law, 1981. Bar: N.H. 1937. Assoc. Cooper & Hall, Rochester, N.H., 1937-41; ptnr. Cooper, Hall & Grimes, Rochester, 1941-47; solicitor City of Dover, 1946-47; justice N.H. Superior Ct., Concord, 1947-66; justice Supreme Ct. of N.H., 1966-79, chief justice, 1979-81; mem. faculty Nat. Jud. Coll.; disting. vis. prof. Calif. Western Sch. Law, 1982-85, U. San Diego Sch. Law, 1986, U. Okla. Coll. of Law, 1987—; adj. prof. U. Nev.; mem. exec. com., past chmn. Appellate Judges Conf.; chmn. N.H. Vocat. Rehab. Planning Commn., N.H. Gov.'s Commn. on Crime and Delinquency; mem. council judges Nat. Council Crime and Delinquency; chmn. edn. com. Appellate Judges Conf.; mem. adv. council Nat. Center for State Cts.; mem. Gov.'s Commn. on Laws Affecting Children, Gov.'s Com. on Correctional Tng.; mem. adv. council for Appellate Justice; mem. planning com. Nat. Conf. Standards for Adminstrn. Criminal Justice; del. to White House Conf. on Children, Nat. Conf. on Correctional Manpower and Tng. Author: Criminal Law Outline, annually, 1974—. Mem. N.H. Ho. of Reps., 1933-35, 37-39; mem. adv. council Lincoln Filene Ctr. for Citizenship and Pub. Affairs. Lt. USNR, World War II. Recipient Silver Shingle award, Centennial award Boston U. Sch. Law, Meritorious Svc. award Nat. Rehab. Assn., Archie award N.H. Easter Seal Soc., Irwin Griswold award for teaching excellence Nat. Jud. Coll., 1988, Appellate Judges Conf. Recognition award, 1996, Lifetime Achievement award Student Bar Assn., U. Okla. Coll. Law, 1998; William A. Grimes Fund for Jud. Edn. created by Nation's Appellate Judges; Civil Libertarian award created in his name U. Okla. Coll. Law. Mem. ABA (past chmn. div. jud. adminstrn., chmn. drug abuse com. criminal law sect., pres.'s task force on appellate advocacy, com. to investigate fed. law enforcement agys., Spl. Merit award jud. adminstrn. div.), Stafford County Bar Assn., N.H. Bar Assn. (gavel award, disting. service award, Lifetime Achievement award 1996, William A. Grimes award for jud. professionalism 1999), Am. Judicature Soc. (Herbert Harley award 1988), N.H. Judges Assn. (William A. Grimes lecture fund). Democrat.

**GRIMM, PATRICIA LEE,** lawyer; b. Cleve., Aug. 15, 1949; d. William Albert and Mary Julie (Ziska) Schumann. BS in Edn., Ohio State U., 1971, M.Counseling, 1973; JD, Capital U., Columbus, 1983. Bar: Ohio 1983. Tchr. Columbus City Schs., 1973-79; supr. Night Pros., Newark, Ohio, 1980-83; law clk. Ohio State Med. Bd., Columbus, 1981-83; pvt. practice law Columbus, 1983—; vol. mediator Franklin Cts., Columbus, 1987. Bd. trustes Fathers & Children for Equal Justice, 1988. Mem. Ohio Bar Assn., Columbus Bar Assn., Delta Theta Phi. Home: 6245 Evans Rd New Albany OH 43054-9540 Office: 4937 W Broad St Columbus OH 43228-1646

**GRIMMER, STEPHEN ANDREW,** lawyer; b. St. Louis, June 9, 1953; s. Ralph J. and Rosemary Patricia G.; m. Ruth Ann Gerhart, June 14, 1975 (div. 1997); children: Nick, Alex, Samuel, Anna. BCE, Tex. Tech. U., 1975; JD, U. Tex., 1981. Bar: Tex. 1981, U.S. Dist. Ct. (no. dist.) Tex. 1982, U.S. Dist. Ct. (we. dist.) Tex. 1987, U.S. Ct. Appeals (5th cir.) 1987, U.S. Supreme Ct. 1989, U.S. Patent Office 1983. Assoc. Underwood, Wilson, Berry, Stein & Johnson, Amarillo, Tex., 1981-85; assoc. Haynes & Boone, Dallas, 1985-89; ptnr. Cantey & Hanger, Dallas, 1990-93; shareholder Turner, Dealey, Zimmermann & Grimmer, Dallas, 1993-97; pvt. practice Dallas, 1997—; of counsel Jones, Allen & Fuquay, Dallas, 1997—. Contbr. articles to profl. jours. Troop com. chmn., asst. scoutmaster Boy Scouts Am., Dallas, 1992-97; Little League mgr., Dallas, 1994—. Mem. Dallas Bar Assn. (chmn. judicial evaluation com. 1997—, judicial preference poll com. 1997—), State Bar Tex. (vice chmn. com. 1988), Tex. Pro Bono Coll. Avocations: coaching baseball and soccer, golf, running, church activities. General civil litigation, Construction, Intellectual property. Office: Jones Allen & Fuquay 8828 Greenville Ave Dallas TX 75243-7143

**GRIMSHAW, THOMAS TOLLIN,** lawyer; b. Mpls., Oct. 31, 1932; s. U.L. and Judith (Austrid) G.; children: Scott, Lynn, Steve, Lisa, Shane. Student, Hamline U., 1951; BA, U. Minn., 1953; JD, Northwestern U., 1956. Bar: Ill., Colo. 1956. Assoc. Calkins, Rodden & Kramer, Denver, 1956-62; pvt. practice Denver, 1963-64; ptnr. Calkins, Kramer, Grimshaw & Harring, Denver, 1965-84, of counsel, 1984-94; ptnr. Grimshaw & Harring, 1994—; bd. dirs. Colo. Housing Fin. Authority, Denver; mem. Nat. Conf. Commrs. on Uniform State Laws Com., 1987—; Colo. Coun. on Econ. Edn., 1987—; bd. dirs. Bank of Cherry Creek, Luth. Med. Ctr., Lutheran Hosp., The Edn. Found. State rep. Colo. Gen. Assembly, Denver, 1967-70; mem., chmn. Colo. Housing Bd., Denver, 1970-74; bd. dirs., chmn. State Bd. for Community Colls., and Occupational Edn., Denver, 1979-86; bd. dirs. Cen. Bapt. Theol. Sem., Kansas City, Kans., 1978-88, 94—. Mem. Denver Bar Assn. (chmn. pub. relations com. 1969-70), Colo. Bar Assn. (bd. govs. 1969-70, chmn. pub. relations com. 1970-71, sr. v.p. 1971-72, chmn. legis. com. 1972-77), ABA, Denver Athletic Club (past bd. dirs.), Jacques DeMolay, Colo. Consistory. Republican. Baptist. Land use and zoning (including planning), Municipal (including bonds), Real property. Office: Grimshaw & Harring 1700 Lincoln St Ste 3800 Denver CO 80203-4538

**GRIMWADE, RICHARD LLEWELLYN,** lawyer; b. Chgo., Apr. 26, 1945; s. Eric Illingworth and Pauline J. (Crandall) G.; m. Alexandra M. Galbraith, Feb. 22, 1981; children: Eric Montgomery, Sarah Elizabeth. BA, Lawrence U., 1967; JD cum laude, U. Wis., 1971. Bar: Wis. 1971, N.Y. 1971, Ill. 1978, Calif. 1981, U.S. Dist. Ct. (so. and ea. dists. ) N.Y., 1971, U.S. Dist. Ct. (no. dist.) Wis., 1971, U.S. Dist. Ct. (no. dist.) Ill., 1978, U.S. Dist. Ct. (ctrl. dist.) Calif., 1981, U.S. Ct. Appeals (2d cir.) 1971, U.S. Ct. Appeals (7th cir.) 1978, U.S. Ct. Appeals (9th cir.) 1981. Atty. Davis Polk, N.Y.C., 1971-75; ptnr. Barton Klugman, L.A., 1983-93; pvt. practice L.A., 1993—. Mem. U. Wis. Law Rev., 1969-71. Bd. mgrs. Ketchum Downtown YMCA, L.A., 1991-97; trustee Reform L.A. Pub. Schs. (LEARN), 1993-97. Recipient 3 Am. Jurisprudence awards for evidence, legis., and acctg. and law Bancroft-Whitney, 1970. Mem. State Bar Calif., State Bar Wis., State Bar N.Y., State Bar Ill., Rotary L.A. (bd. dirs. 1991-93, sec. 1994), Toastmasters (Best Spkr. award, Best Performer award 1996, Best Table Topics award 1997), Order of Coif. Avocations: golf, poetry, running, public speaking, history. Professional liability, General civil litigation, Insurance. Office: MCI Center 700 S Flower St Ste 1100 Los Angeles CA 90017-4113

**GRINDSTAFF, EVERETT JAMES,** lawyer; b. Abilene, Tex., May 7, 1931; s. Everett Clinton and Atha Marie (Porter) G.; m. Jeannette, Apr. 3, 1954; children: Jeff, Michelle. BBA, Baylor U., 1954, LLB. Bar: Tex. Ptnr. Grindstaff & Grindstaff, Ballinger, Tex. Dir. State Bar Tex., 1971-74. With U.S. Army Counter Intelligence Corp., 1954-56. Recipient Humanitarian award Juvenile Diabetes Found., 1983, Distinction award Am. Diabetes Assn., 1983, Charles Best award, 1984. Fellow Tex. Bar Found. (life). Real property, Oil, gas, and mineral, Probate. Office: Grindstaff & Grindstaff PO Box 269 707 Hutchins Ave Ballinger TX 76821-5608

**GRINNAN, GLORIA KATHERINE,** lawyer; b. Ohio, July 25, 1961; d. Edward Leonard and Agnes (Vol) G. BS, Miami U., Oxford, Ohio, 1983; JD, Ind. U., Indpls., 1988. Bar: Ind. 1988, U.S. Dist. Ct. (no. and so. dists.) Ind. 1988, U.S. Ct. Appeals (7th cir.) 1994. Assoc. Landwerlen & Rothkopf, Indpls., 1988-90, Pardieck, Gill & Vargo, Indpls., 1990-92; dir. Legal Search, Indpls., 1986-89; pvt. practice, Indpls., 1992—; master commr. Marion Superior Ct., Indpls., 1992—. Precinct committeeman Marion County Dem. Com., 1991. Fellow Indpls. Bar Assn. (Disting. 1995, bd. mgrs. 1992-94, mem. exec. com. family law sect. 1994—, ADR sect. 1995—); mem. Ind. Bar Assn., Nat. Assn. Counsel for Children. Roman Catholic. Avocations: reading writing, travel. Family and matrimonial, State civil litigation, General practice. Office: 244 N College Ave Indianapolis IN 46202-3702

**GRINNELL, JOSEPH FOX,** financial company executive, lawyer; b. Lake Forest, Ill., July 4, 1923; s. Robert L. and Mary King G.; m. Marjorie Volwiler, Aug. 24, 1946; children—Stephen F., Christine K. Burcham, James W. B.A., Yale U., 1945; J.D., Northwestern U., 1949. Bar: Ill. 1949, U.S. Dist. Ct. (no. dist.) Ill. 1949, Minn. 1954, Assoc., Winston-Strawn, Chgo., 1949-54; sr. v.p. law Investors Diversified Services, Mpls., 1954-83; of counsel Pepin Dayton Herman Graham & Getts, Mpls., 1983-87. Bd. dirs. Guthrie Theater, Mpls., 1970-71, Minn. Orch. Assn., Mpls., 1976-78; bd. dirs., chmn. Minn. Pollution Control Agy., Mpls., 1973-81. Served to lt. (j.g.) USN, 1942-46, PTO. Democrat. Presbyterian. Home: 6101 Idylwood Dr Minneapolis MN 55436-1232

**GRINSTED, ALBERT HUGH, III,** lawyer; b. Cocoa, Fla., June 3, 1951; s. Albert Hugh and June Gastineau G.; m. Patricia Speas, March 20, 1976; children: Justin, Evan. AA, Tallahassee Cmty. Coll., 1972; BSc, Fla. State U., 1977, JD, 1979. Bar: Fla. 1980. Asst. state attorney 1st Judicial Cir. Fla., Shalimar, Fla., 1980—; adj. prof. Okaloosa Walton Cmty. Coll., Niceville, Fla., 1983-84; lectr. in field. Mem. Nat. Dist. Attorney's Assn., Fla. Prosecuting Attorney's Assn. (edn. com. 1997-98). Republican. Avocations: golf, camping, skiing, boating, music. Home: PO Box 915 Shalimar FL 32579-0915

**GRISI, JAMES ROBERT,** lawyer; b. Jersey City, Sept. 7, 1953; s. Rudolph and Ruth (Miller) G.; m. Sunday L. DiPalma, Mar. 9, 1991; 1 child, James C. DiPalma-Grisi. BA, Rutgers U., 1983; JD, Rutgers U., Newark, 1988. Bar: N.Y. 1989, N.J. 1989, U.S. Dist. Ct. (ea. and so. dist.) N.Y. 1989, U.S. Dist. Ct. N.J. 1989. Ptnr. Friedman & Levine, N.Y.C., 1989—. Author articles and procs. Mem. Assn. Bar City of N.Y. Labor, Pension, profit-sharing, and employee benefits, Federal civil litigation. Office: Friedman & Levine 1500 Broadway Ste 2300 New York NY 10036-4015

**GROBSTEIN, GENE LAWRENCE,** lawyer; b. Bklyn., July 26, 1950; s. Murray and Florence Grobstein; m. Terry Lee Whitebook, Mar. 17, 1979; children: Kiersha, Samuel, Matthew. BA in Polit. Sci., U. Cin., 1972; JD, Pace U., 1982. Bar: N.Y., U.S. Dist. Ct. (so. and no. dists.) N.Y., U.S. Supreme Ct. Founder sole practice Newburgh, N.Y., 1983—. Mem. N.Y. State Bar Assn., Orange County Bar Assn., Mid-Hudson Bankruptcy Bar Assn. Bankruptcy, Family and matrimonial, Real property. Office: 10 Little Britain Rd Newburgh NY 12550-5100

**GROCE, EWIN PETTY,** lawyer; b. Ft. Worth, Dec. 19, 1953; s. Charles Tillman and Mary Elizabeth (Hill) G.; m. Elisita Bernis Groce, Oct. 29, 1982; children: Tamara Roxanne, Jonathan Paul, Meghan Elizabeth. BA cum laude, U. Tex., 1979; postgrad., Golden Gate Seminary, 1982; JD, Whitter Law Sch., 1989; postgrad., Fuller Seminary. Bar: Kans. Supreme Ct. 1990, Mo. Supreme Ct. 1991, U.S. Dist. Ct. (ea. dist.) Kans. 1990, U.S. Dist. Ct. (we. dist.) Mo. 1991. Paralegal Groce & Groce Law Offices, Ft. Worth, 1979-81, Abraham Liao Law Offices, Monterey Park, Calif., 1987-88; paralegal litigation dept. Charles M. Finkel Law Offices, Beverly Hills, Calif., 1988-90; lawyer Ewin Groce Law Offices, Overland Park, Kans., 1990—; lectr. continuing legal edn. Consiliators Training Workshop, Kansas City, Mo., 1991—. Author numerous poems. Worked with immigrant Chinese for Evang. Formosan Ch., L.A., 1983-90; vol. mediatorChristian Conciliation Svc., L.A., 1989-90, Kansas City, 1990—, bd. dirs., 1990—; First Amendment law advisor Metro Vineyard Fellowship, Kansas City, 1990-92; cons. immigration law Grace Training Ctr., Kansas City, 1991-92. Mem. ABA, Assn. Trial Lawyers Am., Christian Legal Soc., Christian Conciliation Svc, Kansas City (mediators panel). Republican. Avocations: music (drums and orchestral percussion) karate/kung fu, poetry, chinese language. Immigration, naturalization, and customs, Private international, General civil litigation. Office: Law Offices Abraham C Liao 300 S Garfield Ave Monterey Park CA 91754-3336

**GROCE, STEVEN FRED,** lawyer; b. Springfield, Mo., Aug. 6, 1956; s. Robert V. and Celeste (Moon) G. BA in Psychology, S.W. Mo. State U., 1980; JD, U. Mo., Kansas City, 1984. Bar: Mo. 1984, U.S. Dist. Ct. (we. dist.) Mo. 1984, U.S. Supreme Ct., 1990. Ptnr. Grace, Groce & DeArmon, P.C., Springfield, 1984—. Author: Self Defense and the Law, 1982. Mem. ABA, U.S. Supreme Ct. Bar, Mo. Bar Assn., Tex. Bar Assn., Springfield Met. Bar Assn. Criminal, Real property, Personal injury. Office: 1200 E Woodhurst Dr Ste 100B Springfield MO 65804-4261

**GROETZINGER, JON, JR.,** lawyer, consumer products executive; b. N.Y.C., Feb. 12, 1949; s. Jon M. and Elinor Groetzinger; m. Carol Marie O'Connor, Jan. 24, 1981; 3 children. AB magna cum laude, Middlebury Coll., 1971; JD in Internat. Legal Affairs, Cornell U., 1974. Bar: N.H. 1974, N.Y. 1980, Mass. 1980, Fla. 1982, Md. 1985, Ohio 1991, U.S. Supreme Ct. 1980. Assoc. McLane, Graf, Greene, Raulerson and Middleton, P.A., Manchester, N.H., 1974-76; atty. John A. Gray Law Offices, Boston, 1978-81; pvt. practice N.H., Boston, 1977-81; chief internat. counsel Martin Marietta Corp., Bethesda, Md., 1981-88; pres., exec. v.p. Martin Marietta Overseas Corp., Bethesda, 1984-88; sr. v.p., gen. counsel, corp. sec. Am. Greetings Corp., Cleve., 1988—; chmn. internat. adv. bd. Case Western Res. U. Law Sch., 1995—, Disting. vis. lectr., 1997—. Trustee Middlebury (Vt.) Coll., 1974-76, mem. bd. overseers, 1977—; bd. dirs. Cleve. Coun. on World Affairs, 1991-98, 99—; bd. dirs. Can.-U.S. Law Inst.; mem. exec. com. The Conf. Bds. Coun. Chief Legal Officers, 1996—, membership chmn., 1997-98, program chair, 1999—. Mem. ABA, N.H. Bar Assn., Fla. Bar Assn., Ohio Bar Assn., Cleve. Bar Assn., Md. Bar Assn., N.Y. Bar Assn., Mass. Bar Assn., Supreme Ct. Bar Assn., Am. Soc. Corp. Secs. (sec. Ohio chpt. 1995—, v.p. 1996-97, pres. 1997-98), Phi Beta Kappa. E-mail: jgroetzi@yahoo.com. General corporate, Private international, Contracts commercial. Office: Am Greetings Corp 1 American Rd Cleveland OH 44144-2301

**GROFF, DAVID CLARK, JR.,** lawyer; b. Detroit, June 16, 1946; s. David Clark and Marguerite (Lowrie) G.; m. Roslyn Solomon; children: Eric W., Paul D. BA in Polit. Sci., U. Mich., 1968, JD, 1972. Bar: Wash. 1972, U.S. Dist. Ct. (we. dist.) Wash. 1972, U.S. Ct. Appeals (9th cir.) 1972. Assoc. Davis, Wright & Jones, Seattle, 1972-78; ptnr. Davis Wright Tremaine (previously Davis, Wright & Jones), Seattle, 1978-92, Groff & Murphy, Seattle, 1992—. Author: Washington Constrn. Law, 1980-91; mem. editorial bd. Mich. Law Rev., 1971-72; contbr. articles to legal jours. Bd. govs. Wash. Spl. Olympics, 1990-96; trustee Seattle Repertory Theatre, 1992—. Mem. ABA (steering com. on Constrn. Forum 1987-90), Wash. State Bar Assn. (bd. dirs., sect. pub. contracts and pvt. constrn. law 1987-90), Order of Coif. Avocations: bicycling, sailing, fishing, photography. E-mail: dgroff@groff&murphy.com. Construction, Federal civil litigation, Government contracts and claims. Home: 1700 36th Ave Seattle WA 98122-3419 Office: Groff & Murphy 1191 2nd Ave Ste 1900 Seattle WA 98101-2994

**GROFF, JOSEPH HALSEY, III,** lawyer; b. Woodbury, N.J., Aug. 23, 1949; s. Joseph Halsey Jr. and Helen Shallcross G.; m. Christine Ann Maule, May 27, 1978; children: Lindsay, Sarah. BA in Econs. magna cum laude, Tufts U., 1971; JD, Georgetown U., 1976. Bar: U.S. Dist. Ct. N.J. 1976, Maine 1984, U.S. Dist. Ct. Maine 1984, U.S. Ct. Appeals (1st cir.) 1984. Tchr. Delsea Regional H.S., Franklinville, N.J., 1971-72; asst. to comptroller Hecht Co., Silver Spring, Md., 1973; trial atty. tax div. Dept. Justice, Washington, 1976-82; asst. U.S. atty. Dept. Justice, Portland, Maine, 1982-89; chmn. litig., atty. Jensen Baird Gardner & Henry, Portland, 1989-95, pres., mng. ptnr., 1995—; chmn. bd. dirs. Maine Title Co., Portland, 1992-95. Solicitation vol. United Way, Portland, 1994—; chmn. Maine Criminal Justice Commn., Augusta, 1992-95, Town Coun., Cape Elizabeth, Maine, 1997—; sr. warden St. Albans Episc. Ch., Cape Elizabeth, 1988-93. Mem. ABA, Maine Trial Lawyers, Maine Bar Found., Soc. Cin. Avocations: skiing, golfing, basketball. Federal civil litigation, General civil litigation, Criminal. Office: Jensen Baird Gardner & Henry 10 Free St Ste 4 Portland ME 04101-3942

**GROGAN, LYNN LANGLEY,** lawyer; b. Rockingham, N.C., Jan. 16, 1957; d. John Wesley and Hilda Maske Langley; m. Lee Roy Grogan Jr., Oct. 29, 1983; children: Erin Margaret, Hannah Elizabeth, Mary-Stamper. AB, Davidson Coll., 1979; JD, Mercer U., 1983. Counselor Jack Eckerd Found., Tampa, Fla., 1979-80; assoc. Hirsch, Beil & Partin, P.C., Columbus, Ga., 1983-86, ptnr., 1986-89; ptnr. Hirsch, Partin, Grogan & Grogan, P.C., Columbus, 1989—; chmn. Child Fatality/Abuse Protocol, Columbus, 1990-93; lectr. CLE, Atlanta. Bd. dirs. Muscogee Edn. Excellence Found., Columbus, 1994-97; founding bd. dirs. Easter Seal Soc. West Ga., Columbus, 1986; bd. dirs. March of Dimes, Columbus, 1984-86; chmn. State Public Affairs Com., Atlanta, 1991-92. Recipient Leadership award Leadership Columbus, 1995, Woman of Achievement award Concharty Order of Girl Scouts U.S., 1998. Fellow Am. Acad. Matrimonial Lawyers; mem. Ga. State Bar Assn., Columbus Bar Assn., Jr. League of Columbus (pres. 1996-97). Avocations: biking, reading, stitchery. Family and matrimonial. Home: 2715 Lynda Ln Columbus GA 31906-1248 Office: Hirsch Partin Grogan & Grogan PC 1021 3d Ave Columbus GA 31901

**GROGAN, MICHAEL KEVIN,** lawyer, negotiator; b. Chgo., Sept. 26, 1951; s. William P. and Margaret (Campbell) G.; m. Nancy Ann Wilson, July 24, 1974; children: Margaret Lindsay, Kathryn Eileen, Michael Patrick. BS, MacMurray Coll., 1972; JD, Mercer U., 1976. Bar: Fla. 1976, Ga. 1976, U.S. Ct. Appeals (5th cir.) 1976, U.S. Ct. Appeals (11th cir.) 1982; cert. city and local govt. law. Assoc. Coffman, Coleman, Andrews & Grogan P.A. and predecessors, Jacksonville, Fla., 1976-81, ptnr., 1981—; labor law chpt. Specialized Legal Research, Little, Brown & Co., 1987—; superboard Riverside Avondale Preservation, Jacksonville, 1978-90. Mng. editor Mercer Law Rev., Macon, Ga., 1975-76. Mem. Rep. Nat. Com., Washington, 1980—; chmn. Fla. Pub. Employment Labor Rels. Forum, 1985—. Recipient Marsicano award for local govt. work, 1999; Ill. State scholar, 1969-72, Gov.'s intern, 1971. Mem. ABA, Fla. Bar Assn. (exec. coun. bar law and local law govt. sects. 1982—, past chmn. local govt. law sect.), Ga. Bar Assn., River Club, Fla. Yacht Club, Oak Bridge Country Club. Roman Catholic. Labor, Civil rights, Administrative and regulatory. Office: Coffman Coleman Andrews & Grogan PA PO Box 40089 Jacksonville FL 32203-0089

**GROGAN, ROBERT HARRIS,** lawyer; b. Bklyn., Feb. 25, 1933; s. Robert Michael and Nora Howarth (Johnson) G. AB, Harvard U., 1955; LLB, U. Va., 1961; m. Delia Ann Grossi, Dec. 23, 1967 (div. 1982); m. Lynn D. Habian, June 20, 1987. Bar: Va., 1961, N.Y., 1962, Ill., 1977, Fla., 1986; cert. cir. ct. mediator, Fla., 1996—; assoc. Milbank, Tweed, Hadley & McCloy, N.Y.C., 1961-66; counsel Anaconda Co., N.Y.C., 1966-68; assoc. Shearman & Sterling, N.Y.C., 1968-75; v.p., gen. counsel staff Citibank, N.Y.C., 1975-76; ptnr. Mayer, Brown & Platt, Chgo., 1976-81; of counsel Olwine, Connelly, Chase, O'Donnell & Weyher, N.Y.C., 1981-87, sr. v.p., dep. sr. counsel, S.E. Bank, N.A., Miami, Fla., 1987-91; sr. v.p., gen. counsel Republic Nat. Bank of Miami, Fla., 1992-96; ind. bank, bus. and legal cons., 1996—; vice chmn. exec. adv. coun. Andreas Bus. Sch. Barry U., Miami Shores, Fla., 1995-97; lectr. in field. Sec., bd. dirs. 3d Equity Owners Corp., coop. housing corp., 1975-77, pres., bd. dirs., 1982-86. With U.S. Army, 1956-58. Mem. ABA, Fla. Bar, N.Y. Bar, Va. State Bar Assn., Ill. State Bar Assn., Am. Arbitration Assn. (comml. panel neutral arbitrators 1997—), Phi Delta Phi, Harvard Club (N.Y.C), Harvard Faculty Club (Cambridge, Mass.). Contbg. author: The Local Economic Development Corporation, 1970. Banking, Contracts commercial, General corporate. Address: PO Box 666 Palm Beach FL 33480-0666

**GROGAN, VIRGINIA S.,** lawyer; b. Pasadena, Calif., Nov. 19, 1051; d. Bruce Mason and Helen Maude Gorsuch; m. Aug. 17, 1973 (div. June 1975); m. Allen R. Grogan, Jan. 10, 1982; children: Travis, Tess. BS, Occidental Coll., Eagle Rock, Calif., 1973; JD, U. So. Calif. Bar: Calif. 1979. Assoc. Latham & Watkins, L.A., 1979-86, ptnr., 1987-97, chmn. assocs. com., 1995-97; mng. ptnr. Orange County Office Latham & Watkins, Costa Mesa, Calif., 1997—. Mem. exec. roundtable U. Calif., Irvine, 1998—; mem. adv. com. Orange County Performing Arts, Costa Mesa, 1998—,. Mem. ABA, Los Angeles County Bar Assn., Orange County Bar Assn. (judiciary com. 1998—), Legion Lex. Avocations: tennis, classical music. Securities, Consumer commercial. Home: 630 Diamond St Laguna Beach CA 92651-3406 Office: Latham & Watkins 650 Town Center Dr Costa Mesa CA 92626-1989

**GROH, JENNIFER CALFA,** law librarian; b. Patchogue, N.Y., Mar. 28, 1970; d. Anthony Bernard and Mary (Fogerty) C.; m. William Matthew Groh, May 10, 1997. BA in Social Sci., St. Joseph's Coll., 1992; MA in Internat. Edn., NYU, 1993; MSLS, Pratt Inst., Bklyn., 1996. Reference page Patchogue (N.Y.)-Medford Libr., 1986-93; from libr. asst. to asst. libr. Morgan & Finnegan, N.Y.C., 1994—. NYU grad. scholar, 1992, Law Libr. Assn. scholar, N.Y. 1995, Am. Assn. Law Librs. scholar, 1996. Mem. ALA, Spl. Librs. Assn., Law Libr. Assn. Greater N.Y. Home: 2750 Sawmill Rd North Bellmore NY 11710 Office: Morgan & Finnegan 345 Park Ave New York NY 10154-0053

**GRONER, BEVERLY ANNE,** lawyer; b. Des Moines; d. Benjamin L. and Annabelle (Miller) Zavat; m. Jack Davis; children: Morrilou Davis Morell, Lewis A. Davis, Andrew G. Davis; m. Samuel Brian Groner, Dec. 17, 1962. Student, Drake U., 1939-40, Cath. U., 1954-56; JD, Am. U., 1959. Bar: Md. 1959, U.S. Supreme Ct. 1963, D.C. 1965. Pvt. practice Bethesda Md., Washington, 1959—; chmn. Md. Gov.'s Commn. on Domestic Relations Laws 1977-87; exec. com. trustee Montgomery-Prince George's Continuing Legal Edn. Inst., 1983—, pres., 1992-98; lectr. to lay, profl. groups; speaker to Bar Assns. and numerous seminars; participant continuing legal edn. programs, local and nat.; participant, faculty mem. trial demonstration films Am. Law Inst.-ABA Legal Consortium; participant numerous TV, radio programs; seminar leader, expert-in-residence Harvard Law Sch., 1987, Family Law, Georgetown U. Law Ctr., 1988, 89; mem. gov.'s com. ERA, 1978-80; faculty mem. Montgomery County Bar Assn. Law Sch. for the Pub., 1991, Inst. on Professionalism, 1992. Cons. editor Family Law Reporter, 1986-90, MD Family Law Monthly, 1993—; mem. bd. editors Fairshare 1992-97; contbr. numerous articles to profl. jours. Pres. Am. Acad. Matrimonial Lawyers Found., 1994-98. Named One of Leading Matrimonial Practitioners in U.S., Nat. Law Jour., 1979, 87, Best Divorce Lawyer in Md., Washingtonian Mag., 1981, One of Best Matrimonial Lawyers in U.S., Town and Country mag., 1985, Best Lawyers in Am., 1987—; recipient Disting. Svc. award Va. State Bar Assn., 1982, Okla. Bar Assn., 1987, Md. Gubernatorial citation, 1987. Fellow Am. Acad. Matrimonial Lawyers (pres. Md. chpt. 1992-98, pres.-elect found. 1993-94); mem. Bar Assn. Montgomery County (exec. com. chmn. family law sect. 1976, chmn. fee arbitration panel 1974-77, legal ethics com.), Md. State Bar Assn. bd. of govs., (gov., chmn. family law sect. 1975-77, vice chmn. com. continuing legal edn., ethics com. 1991—, mem. inquiry panel and grievance com., 1991—, faculty mem. on Professionalism 1992), ABA (chmn. family law sect. 1986-87, rep. to White House conf. on Yr. of Child 1984, sec. family law sect. 1983-84, vice chmn. 1984-85, chmn. sect. marital property com., assn. adv. to nat. conf. commrs. on uniform marital property act, mem. faculty family law advocacy inst. 1988, 90), Am. Acad. of Matrimonial Lawyers, Md. State Bar Assn. (mem. inquiry panel and grievance com. 1991—), Phi Alpha Delta. Family and matrimonial. Home: 5600 Wisconsin Ave Apt 1602 Chevy Chase MD 20815-4413 Office: Chevy Chase Bldg 5530 Wisconsin Ave Ste 1208 Chevy Chase MD 20815-4301

**GRONER, SAMUEL BRIAN,** lawyer; b. Buffalo, Dec. 27, 1916; s. Louis and Lena (Blinkoff) G.; m. Beverly Anne Groner; children: Jonathan B. (dec. 1962), Morri Lou Morell, Lewis A. Davis, Laurence M., Andrew G. Davis. AB, Cornell U., 1937, JD, 1939; MA in Econs., Am. U., 1950. Bar: N.Y. 1939, D.C. 1952, Md. 1953, U.S. Supreme Ct. 1944. Pvt. practice law Buffalo, 1939-40; atty. U.S. Dept. War and Office Price Adminstrn., 1940-43; atty.-adviser U.S. Dept. Justice, Washington, 1946-53; pvt. practice law Md. and Washington, 1953-63; ptnr. Groner, Stone & Greiger, Washington, 1955-57, Groner & Groner, Silver Spring and Bethesda, Md., 1962—; asst. counsel Naval Ship Systems Command, Washington, 1963-73; trial atty. Office Gen. Counsel, Dept. Navy, Washington, 1973-74, assoc. chief trial atty., 1974-79; adminstrv. law judge and mem. Bd. Contract Appeals U.S. Dept. Labor, Washington, 1979—, acting chmn., 1987, mem. Bd. Alien Labor Certification Appeals, 1990—, acting adminstrv. appeals judge Benefits Rev. Bd., 1988-89; instr. Terrell Law Sch., Washington, 1948; mem. faculty USDA Grad. Sch., 1972—; reporter Md. Gov.'s Commn. on Domestic Rels. Laws, 1977-87; participant in continuing legal and jud. edn. Author: Modern Business Law, 1983, (with others) The Improvement of the Administration of Justice, 6th edit., 1981; assoc. editor Fed. Bar Jour., 1948-55; contbr. articles to profl. jours. Active PTA, civic assns., Jewish Community Coun., Community Chest; mem. Montgomery County Commn. on Handicapped Individuals, 1977-85, vice chmn., 1980-81. 1st lt. inf. and M.I.S., U.S. Army, 1943-46, ETO. Recipient Navy Superior Civilian Service award, 1979. Mem. ABA (liaison commn. on professionalism 1985—, advisor to standing com. on lawyer competence 1986—, family law sect., jud. adminstrn. div., vice chmn. pub. contract law sect., com. on adminstrv. claims and remedies 1976-79, chmn. 1979-80), Fed. Bar Assn., Montgomery County Bar Assn. and Bar Found., Bar Assn. of D.C., Bar Assn. Met. St. Louis, Cornell Law Assn. (pres. D.C. chpt. 1947-54), Am. Law Inst., Inst. for Jud. Adminstrn., Am. Judicature Soc., Supreme Ct. Hist. Soc., Govt. Adminstrv. Trial Lawyers Assn., Nat. Lawyers Club, Cosmos Club, Cornell Club N.Y.C., Officers and Faculty Club (U.S. Naval Acad., Annapolis), Phi Beta Kappa. Government contracts and claims, Workers' compensation. Home: 5600 Wisconsin Ave Apt 1602 Chevy Chase MD 20815-4413 Office: 800 K St NW Ste 400 Washington DC 20001-8000

**GROOM, DAVID A.,** lawyer; b. Evanston, Ill., June 16, 1967; s. John Miller and Carolyn Anderson Groom; m. Tracy Dawn Lilleskau, Aug. 7, 1993. BBA, U. Okla., 1990, JD with distinction, 1993; LLM in Taxation, U. Denver, 1995. CPA, Okla. Assoc. J. Michael Entz & Assocs., Oklahoma City, 1993-94, Antonio Bates Bernard P.C., Denver, 1994-97, Gorsuch Kirgis LLP, Denver, 1997—. Mem. Colo. Bar Assn., Colo. Soc. CPA, Okla. Bar Assn., Denver Bar Assn. Taxation, general, Mergers and acquisitions, General corporate. Office: Gorsuch Kirgis LLP 1515 Arapahoe St Denver CO 80202-3150

**GROPPER, ALLAN LOUIS,** lawyer; b. N.Y.C., Jan. 25, 1944; s. Jerome F. and Susan M. (Weingarten) G.; m. Jane Evangelist, Aug. 10, 1968 (dec. Feb. 1999); 1 child, Andrew. BA, Yale U., 1965; JD, Harvard U., 1969. Bar: N.Y. 1969, U.S. Dist. Ct. (so. and ea. dists.) N.Y. 1971, U.S. Ct. Appeals (2d cir.) 1971, U.S. Supreme Ct. 1974. Atty. Civil Appeals Bur., Legal Aid Soc., N.Y.C., 1969-71; assoc. White & Case, N.Y.C., 1972-77, ptnr., 1978—. Bd. dirs. Browning Sch., 1990—, pres., 1997—; bd. dirs. Legal Aid Soc., 1990—, v.p., 1996—; bd. dirs. N.Y. Lawyers for Pub. Interest, 1990—. Mem. ABA (bus. bankruptcy com.), Assn. of Bar of City of N.Y. (v.p. 1995-96, mem. exec. com. 1991-96, chmn. 1994-95), N.Y. State Bar Assn. (bankruptcy law com. 1984—). Bankruptcy, General civil litigation. Home: 115 Central Park W New York NY 10023-4153 Office: White & Case Bldg Ll 1155 Avenue Of The Americas New York NY 10036-2787

**GROSCHADL, PAUL STEPHEN,** lawyer; b. N.Y.C., Feb. 2, 1951; s. Fred and Kathleen (McGilloway) G.; m. Patricia Lee Pedersen, Apr. 10, 1982. B.A., U. Tampa (Fla.), 1972; J.D., SUNY-Buffalo, 1975. Bar: N.Y. 1976, U.S. Dist. Cts. (no. and we. dists.) N.Y. 1976, U.S. Supreme Ct. 1980. Assoc., Woods, Oviatt, Gilman, Sturman & Clarke, Rochester, N.Y., 1976-83, ptnr., 1983—. Mem. Monroe County Bar Assn. (bankruptcy com. 1980—), N.Y. State Bar Assn. (bankruptcy com. 1979—). Bankruptcy, Banking, General corporate. Office: Woods Oviatt Gilman Sturman & Clarke 700 Crossroads Bldg Rochester NY 14614-2004

**GROSECLOSE, LYNN HUNTER,** lawyer; b. Marion, Va., Apr. 22, 1943; s. Byron Glen and Wilma Comer G.; m. Sharon L. Pair; children: Seth, Zachery, Meredith. BA, Emory & Henry Coll., 1964; postgrad., Emory U., 1964-65; JD, U. Va., 1970. Bar: Fla. 1971, U.S. Dist. Ct. (mid. dist.) Fla. 1972, U.S. Ct. Appeals (5th cir.) 1980, U.S. Ct. Appeals (11th cir.) 1981, Colo. 1993. Prof. Orlando Jr. Coll., Fla., 1965-67; atty. Langston & Massey, Attys., Lakeland, Fla., 1971-75; ptnr. Sprott & Groseclose, Attys., Lakeland, 1975-80, Jacobs, Valentine, Groseclose, Lakeland, 1980-84, Lane, Trohn, Bradenton, Fla., 1984-96, Brown, Clark, Sarasota, Fla., 1996—. Sr., jr. warden St. Davids Episcopal Ch.; pres., bd. dirs. Vols. in Svc. to Elderly, Gulfcoast Legal Svcs., Sarasota Manatee Legal Aide. Mem. Sarasota County Bar Assn., Manatee County Bar Assn., Colo. Bar Assn., Fla. Def. Lawyers Assn., Fedn. Ins. and Corp. Counsel, Fla. Bar Found. (legal assistance to poor com. 1997—). Democrat. Avocations: history, remodeling, golf. Professional liability, Personal injury, Insurance. Home: 7512 Preserves Ct Sarasota FL 34243-3700 Office: Brown Clark Attys 1819 Main St Ste 1100 Sarasota FL 34236-5999

**GROSMAN, ALAN M.,** lawyer; b. Mar. 13, 1935; s. Charles M. and Grace (Fishman) G.; m. Bette Bloomenthal, Dec. 27, 1967; children, Ellen, Carol. BA, Wesleyan U., 1956; MA, Yale U., 1957; JD, N.Y. Law Sch., 1965. Bar: N.J. 1965, U.S. Dist. Ct. N.J. 1965, U.S. Supreme Ct. 1969. Ptnr. Grosman & Grosman and predecessors, Millburn, N.J., 1965—; asst. prosecutor Essex County, N.J., 1968-69; prosecutor Millburn, 1981—; mem. family part practice com. N.J. Supreme Ct., 1984-88, mem. dispute resolution task force, 1987-88, com. on women in the cts., 1991-93; chmn. N.J. World Trade Coun., 1975-77, dir., 1978—; lectr. in field. Reporter New Haven Jour., 1959-60, Newark Evening News, 1961-62; author: New Jersey Family Law, 1999; contbr. articles to profl. jours. Mem. ABA (chmn. alimony, maintenance and support com. family law sect. 1983-87, editor ABA Family Law Quar. 1993—), N.J. State Bar Assn. (exec. editor N.J. Family Lawyer 1980-91, mem. exec. com. family law sect. 1980—, chmn. sect. 1987-88, appellate practice com. 1995—), Am. Acad. Matrimonial Lawyers (pres. N.J. chpt. 1983-85, nat. bd. govs. 1984-88, editor Jour. AAML 1980-90), Essex County Bar Assn. (chmn. family law com. 1970-72), N.Y. Law Sch. Alumni Assn. (bd. dirs. 1988-98), Millburn-Short Hills Rep. Club, Inc. (counsel 1988—), Phi Beta Kappa. Family and matrimonial. Address: 75 Main St Ste 205 Millburn NJ 07041-1322

**GROSS, ALAN MARC,** lawyer; b. Trenton, N.J., June 9, 1960; s. William and Lois G. BBA, Emory U., 1982; JD with honors, U. Fla., 1985. Bar: Fla. 1985, U.S. Dist. Ct. (mid. dist.) Fla. 1986, U.S. Tax Ct. 1988; CPA, Fla. Accountant, tax sr. Arthur Andersen & Co., Tampa, Fla., 1985-87; ptnr. Battaglia, Ross, Dicus & Wein, P.A., St. Petersburg, Fla., 1987-95, Powell, Carney, Hayes & Silverstein, P.A., St. Petersburg, 1995—. Participant Leadership St. Petersburg, 1991, Leadership Tampa Bay, 1994. Mem. Fla. Bar Assn., Fla. Inst. CPA's, Am. Assn. Attys. and CPA's, St. Petersburg Bar Assn. (chmn. tax sect. 1990, Pro Bono award), Suncoast Estate Planning Coun. (charter). Probate, General corporate, Taxation, general. Home: 11346 Heritage Way Largo FL 33778-2901 Office: Powell Carney Hayes & Silverstein PA 1 Progress Plz Ste 1210 Saint Petersburg FL 33701-4335

**GROSS, ARI MICHAEL,** lawyer; b. Champagne, Ill., Aug. 18, 1962; s. Ira and Alice (Dzen) G. BS, U. Mass., 1985; JD, NYLS, 1991. Bar: N.Y. 1992, N.J. 1992, U.S. Dist. Ct. (so. and ea. dists.) N.Y. 1992, U.S. Ct. Appeals (2d cir.) 1992, U.S. Dist. Ct. N.J. 1992. Atty. Law Offices of F. Lee Bailey and Aron Broder, N.Y.C., 1992; trial atty. Fuchsberg & Fuchsberg, N.Y.C., 1992—. Atty. pro bono panel N.Y. County Lawyers Assn., 1992—, Legal Aid Bankruptcy Clinic, 1993—. Rsch. grantee Sigma Xi, 1983, Explorers Club, 1983, Barbour Fund, 1983. Mem. ABA, Am. Trial Lawyers Assn., N.Y. State Trial Lawyers Assn., N.Y. State Bar Assn., N.J. Trial Lawyers Assn., L.I. Head Injury Assn. Avocations: basketball, European and American film, computers, certified open water diver. Personal injury, Civil rights, Product liability. Office: Fuchsberg & Fuchsberg 100 Church St Rm 1800 New York NY 10007-2667

**GROSS, BRYON WILLIAM,** lawyer; b. Rochester, N.Y., Jan. 28, 1964; s. William E. Gross and Diana L. Peets; m. Pamela J. Murray, Feb. 28, 1993; 1 child, Adam M. BA, St. Lawrence U., 1986; JD, We. New Eng. Coll., 1990. Pvt. practice Springfield, Mass., 1993-98; Burke, Albright, Marten & Rzepka, Rochester, N.Y., 1998—. Vol. VITA, 1989-98. Mem. N.Y. State Bar Assn., Mass. Trial Lawyers Assn., Monroe County Bar Assn. (guardian and ct. evaluations com. 1998). General civil litigation, Estate planning, Workers' compensation. Office: Burke Albright Marten & Rzepka 500 East Ave Rochester NY 14607-1912

**GROSS, JOHN H.,** lawyer; b. Cleve., Apr. 2, 1942. BS, U. Pa., 1964; JD, George Washington U., 1967. Bar: N.Y. Asst. U.S. atty. (so. dist.) N.Y., 1969-75, asst. chief criminal divsn., 1974-75; assoc. spl. counsel U.S. Dept. Justice, 1979; ptnr. Anderson, Kill, Olick & Oshinsky, N.Y.; adj. prof. law N.Y.U., 1983-89. Mem. Assn. of the Bar of the City of N.Y. Office: Proskauer Rose LLP 1585 Broadway New York NY 10036-8200

**GROSS, JOHN H.,** lawyer; b. N.Y.C., Apr. 5, 1947; s. Harold Andrew and Eleanor Blanche Gross; m. Judith Ball Anderson, Dec. 31, 1967 (div. Apr. 1982); children: Deborah Anne Zeman, Alexander David, Daniel Jeremy, Alison Caron; m. Hope Matthews, Aug. 21, 1982; stepchildren: Gregory Garn, Jessica Hasapis. BS, Cornell U., 1968, JD, 1971. Bar: U.S. Dist. Ct. (ea. dist.) 1974, U.S. Dist. Ct. (no. dist.) 1971, U.S. Supreme Ct. 1980. Assoc. Ingerman Smith, Northport, N.Y., 1971-76; ptnr. Ingerman Smith, Northport, 1976—; pres. Suffolk County Bar Assn., 1994-95; mem. nominating com. N.Y. State Bar Assn., Albany, 1994-97, chair com. on alternative dispute resolution, 1997-98. Contbr.: Public Sector Labor Law, 1992. Capt. U.S. Army, 1971-76. Recipient Pres. award Suffolk County (N.Y.) Bar Assn., 1993. Fellow N.Y. State Bar Found. Republican. Episcopalian. Avocations: fly fishing, light and tackle saltwater fishing. Education and schools, Labor. Office: Ingerman Smith 167 Main St Northport NY 11768-1746

**GROSS, JOHNNY E.,** lawyer; b. St. Louis, May 14, 1962; s. Everett R. and Ruby J. (Honeycutt) G. BS in Biol. Sci., Ark. Tech. U., 1985; MS in Edn. Secondary Sch. Leadership, U. Ctrl. Ark., 1991; JD, U. Ark., 1995. Bar: Ark. 1995, U.S. Dist. Ct. (ea. and we. dists.) Ark. 1996. Store clk. Ark. Tech. U., Russellville, 1983-85; substitute tchr. Escambia County Schs., Pensacola, Fla., 1986-87; tchr. Little Rock Sch. Dist., 1987-96; atty. Ark. Dept. Human Svcs., Bentonville, 1996—; v.p. Little Rock Classroom Tchrs. Assn., 1991-95. Active New Party, Little Rock, 1995-97. With U.S. Army, 1980-82. Mem. Nat. Assn. Counsel for Children, Am. Profl. Soc. on the Abuse of Children, Ark. Bar Assn. (environ. sect. 1995—, youth edn. com. 1995—). Avocation: running. Home: 300 Moberly Ln Apt J11 Bentonville AR 72712-6169 Office: Ark Dept Human Svcs 1206 SE J St Bentonville AR 72712-6575

**GROSS, LESLIE JAY,** lawyer; b. Coral Gables, Fla., July 24, 1944; s. Bernard Charles and Lillian (Adler) G.; m. Frances L. Londow, June 16, 1968; children: Jonathan Eric, Jason Marc. BA magna cum laude, Harvard U., 1965, JD, 1968. Bar: Fla. 1971, U.S. Dist. Ct. (so. dist.) Fla. 1971, U.S. Ct. Appeals (5th cir.) 1971, U.S. Tax Ct. 1971, U.S. Supreme Ct. 1971; registered real estate broker, registered mortgage broker, registered securities broker. Rsch. aide Fla. 3d Dist. Ct. Appeal, Miami, Fla., 1968-69; prof. social sci. Miami-Dade Community Coll., 1969-70; assoc. Greenberg, Traurig, et al., Miami, 1969-70, Patton, Kanner, et al., Miami, 1970-71, Fromberg, Fromberg, Roth, Miami, 1971-72; ptnr. Fromberg, Fromberg, Gross, et al., Miami, 1973-88; assoc. Thornton, David, Murray, et al., Miami, 1988-94; atty. agt. Atty.'s Title Ins. Fund, First Am. Title, Miami, 1971-94; adj. prof. U. Miami Sch. Law, 1984; lectr. seminar Nat. Aircraft Fin. Assn., 1990. Contbr. articles to profl. jours. Mem. transp. com. Greater Miami C. of C., 1984-85; v.p., pres., bd. dirs. Kendale Homeowners Assn., Miami, 1970-81; vol. Dem. candidates in state and nat. elections, Miami, 1968, 70, 72, 87, 88; mem. Vision Coun. Land Use Task Force, Miami, 1988-89; judge Silver Knight awards Miami Herald, 1987, 92, 93, 94, 95, judge spelling bee, 1987; bd. dirs. Internat. Assn. Fin. Planning, 1983-84; founding mem., bd. dirs. The Actors Playhouse, 1987—, sec., 1990—. Mem. Harvard Law Sch. Assn., Harvard Club of Miami (v.p. 1985-90, pres. 1990-94, dir. 1985-99). Democrat. Jewish. Avocations: gardening, humorous creative writing, photography, aerobics, travel. General corporate, Finance, Real property. Home: 10471 SW 126th St Miami FL 33176-4749

**GROSS, LYNN WESTFALL,** lawyer; b. Detroit, May 6, 1965; d. James Edward and Donalea Joan Westfall; m. Walter Scott Gross III, Mar. 25, 1995; 1 child: Stacey Renee Gross. BS, Oakland U., 1987; JD, Detroit Coll. Law, 1993. Bar: Mich. 1993, U.S. Dist. Ct. (ea. dist.) 1993, U.S. Ct. Appeals (6th cir.) 1993. Asst. branch mgr. Comerica Bank, Troy, Mich., 1987-89; law clerk Mich. Nat. Bank, Farmington Hills, 1989-93; atty. Lewis & Munday, P.C., Detroit, 1993-98, Raymond, Walsh & Accettura, P.C., Farmington Hills, 1998—. Bd. dirs., sec., mem. Oakland U. Alumni Assn., Rochester Hills, Mich., 1995—. Mem. Detroit Met. Bar Assn., Oakland County Bar Assn. Avocations: golfing, skiing, reading. Probate, Estate planning, General civil litigation. Office: Raymond Walsh & Accettura 35055 W 12 Mile Rd Ste 114 Farmington Hills MI 48331

**GROSS, RICHARD BENJAMIN,** lawyer; b. Santa Monica, Calif., Sept. 26, 1947; s. Edward L. and Adele P. Gross; m. Pamela McGovern, June 1, 1985; 1 child, Hannah McGovern. Student, UCLA, 1965-68; BA, U. Calif., Berkeley, 1970; JD, Harvard U., 1973; postgrad., Cambridge (Eng.) U., 1973-74. Bar: N.Y. 1975, U.S. Dist. Ct. (so. dist.) N.Y. 1975, U.S. Ct. Appeals (2d cir.) 1975, Ill. 1987. Assoc. White & Case, N.Y.C., 1974-77; assoc. counsel Am. Express Co., N.Y.C., 1977-82; sr. v.p., gen. counsel and sec. Citicorp Diners Club, Inc., Chgo., 1982-90; sr. v.p., gen. counsel Citicorp Ins. Group, Inc., N.Y.C., 1990-91; sr. v.p., gen. counsel, sec. Ambac Fin. Group, Inc., N.Y.C., 1991-98; mng. dir., gen. counsel U.S. Trust Corp., N.Y.C., 1998—. Bd. dirs. Randall's Island Sports Found., 1999—. Mem. ABA (com. of corp. gen. counsel, com. on fed. regulation of securities, com. on banking), N.Y. State Bar Assn., Assn. of the Bar of the City of N.Y., Am. Soc. Internat. Law, Am. Soc. Corp. Secs., Am. Corp. Counsel Assn., Fin. Svcs. Roundtable (mem. lawyers coun.). Fax: (212) 852-1310. General corporate, Securities, Banking. Office: US Trust Corp 114 W 47th St New York NY 10036-1510

**GROSS, RICHARD WILSON,** lawyer; b. Morgantown, W.Va., May 17, 1948; s. Glem Richard and Margery Jean (Wilson) G.; children: Amy Kathleen, Shawn Patrick, Shannon Christine, Shealy Cathleen. BFA, West Va. U., 1971; JD, U. Miami, 1975; postgrad., Fla. Internat. U., 1977. Bar: Fla. 1975, U.S. Dist. Ct. (so. dist.) Fla. 1989. Dir. econ. and community devel. City of Hialeah, Fla., 1974-81, asst. city atty., 1981-86, dep. city atty., 1986-90; mng ptnr. Wetzel and Gross, Hialeah, Fla., 1990-98; pvt. practice Hialeah, 1998—. Mem. Fla. Bar Assn., Dade County Bar Assn., Hialeah-Miami Springs (Fla.) Bar Assn., Miami Springs C. of C. (pres. 1991-92). Democrat. Roman Catholic. Home: PO Box 111302 Hialeah FL 33011-1302 Office: 39 E 6th St Hialeah FL 33010-4845

**GROSS, STEVEN RONALD,** lawyer; b. Hartford, Conn., Jan. 23, 1955; s. Norman David and Sally Barbara (Dansky) G.; m. Susan Larkey Stonehill, Nov. 13, 1982 (div. May 1991). BA, George Washington U., 1978; JD, Western New Eng. Coll., 1981. Bar: Mass., U.S. Dist. Ct. Mass., U.S. Ct. Appeals (1st cir.). Investigator Conn. Criminal Injuries Compensation Bd., Hartford, 1981; atty. Dean R. Singwald Assoc., New Haven, 1982; real estate mgr. Windsor Locks (Conn.) Office, 1983-84; asst. dir., corp. officer CIGNA Securities, Hartford, 1984-87; corp. svcs./counsel N.A. Holding Co., East Hartford, 1987-89; atty. Bacon, Wilson et al, Springfield, Mass., 1989-90; pvt. practice Springfield, 1990—; instr. legal rsch. writing program Western New Eng. Sch. of Law, 1980. Mem. steering com. and fund raising com. Re-Election of Senator Edward M. Kennedy, Springfield, 1994; Conn. campaign coord. Michael Dukakis for Pres., Hartford, 1988. Mem. ABA (employment and labor law com. 1981—), Conn. Bus. and Industry Assn., C. of C. Democrat. Jewish. Avocations: sailing, cross country skiing. Labor, Securities, Libel. Office: 31 Elm St Ste 616 Springfield MA 01103-1807

**GROSSBERG, DAVID ALAN,** lawyer; b. Evanston, Ill., Oct. 13, 1950; s. Edmund J. and Alice (Kaven) G.; m. Robyn DeKoven, Apr. 11, 1981; children: Jonathan, Samuel. AB, U. Calif., Berkeley, 1972; JD, U. Chgo., 1975. Bar: Ill. 1976; U.S. Dist. Ct. (no. dist.) Ill. 1976; U.S. Ct. Appeals (7th cir.) 1977; U.S. Supreme Ct. 1982. Law clk. to Hon. Lewis R. Morgan U.S. Ct. Appeals (5th cir.), New Orleans, 1975-76; assoc. D'Ancona & Pflaum, Chgo., 1976-81, ptnr., 1982-93; ptnr. Sachnoff & Weaver, Ltd., Chgo., 1993-98, Schiff, Hardin & Waite, Chgo., 1998—. Pres. midwest region Am. Jewish Congress, Chgo., 1987-91, nat. v.p.; chmn. domestic concerns Jewish community rels. coun. Jewish United Fund of Met. Chgo., 1989-91; bd. dirs. Med. Rsch. Inst. coun. Michael Reese Hosp., Chgo., 1988-91, Pub. Interest Law Initiative, Chgo., 1987-90; pres. North Shore Congregation Israel, 1995-97. General corporate, Mergers and acquisitions, Real property. Office: Schiff Hardin & Waite 6600 Sears Tower 233 S Wacker Dr Chicago IL 60606-6473

**GROSSBERG, MARC ELIAS,** lawyer; b. Houston, Dec. 26, 1940; s. Sylvester and Leah (Hochman) G.; m. Eva M. Wolski, Jan. 3, 1981; 1 child, Nicole; children from previous marriage: Lee Ann Krishnan, Toni. BS in Polit. Sci., U. Houston, 1961; JD with honors, U. Tex., 1965. Bar: Tex. 1965, Calif. 1966, Fla. 1980, U.S. Supreme Ct. 1980; bd. cert. fed. income taxation, Tex. Acct. Brochstein Toomin & Co CPAs (now Deloitte Touche), Houston, 1961-62; law clk. hon. Walter Ely U.S. Ct. Appeals (9th cir.), L.A., 1965-66; assoc. Fulbright & Jaworski, Houston, 1966-71; ptnr. Schlanger Mills Mayer & Grossberg, LLP, Houston, 1974—. Advanceman, speech writer 1968 Hubert Humphry Presdl. Campaign; pres. Tex. Bill of Rights Found., Houston, 1971-72, Jewish Family Svc., Houston, 1986-87, U. Tex. Law Rev. Assn.; commr. Housing Authority City of Houston, 1974-78. Mem. ABA (tax sect. and litig. sects.). Democrat. Jewish. Avocations: computers, racquetball. Taxation, general, Personal income taxation, General civil litigation. Home: 9127 Briar Forest Dr Houston TX 77024-7213 Office: Schlanger Mills Mayer & Grossberg 5847 San Felipe St Ste 1700 Houston TX 77057-3009

**GROSSMAN, DEBRA A.,** lawyer, real estate manager, radio talk show host; b. Cleve., July 29, 1951; d. Morris M. and Idelle R. (Bialosky) G. BA, Syracuse U., 1973; JD, Suffolk U., 1976. Bar: Mass. 1977, U.S. Dist. Ct. Mass. 1977. Sole practice Lexington, Mass., 1977-79; ptnr. Kurland & Grossman, P.C., Lowell, Mass., 1979-94; property mgr. KD Mgmt. Co., Lowell, 1983—, Chelmsford, Mass., 1994-98; talk show host "Legal Briefs" WCCM Radio, Lawrence, Mass., 1989-97. Bd. dirs. Downtown Lowell Bus. Assn., 1987; lectr. Greater Lowell Alzheimers Assn., 1987; vice chair Lowell Hist. Bd., 1995-97, chair, 1997—. Mem. Mass. Assn. Women Lawyers (asst. treas. 1981-82, bd. dirs. 1979-81), Mass. Bar Assn. (mem. family law sect.), Mass. Acad. Trial Lawyers, Greater Lowel Bar Assn. (bd. dirs. 1993-96, Lawyer for the Day program dir. 1990-92), Syracuse U. Alumni Club, Greater Boston Club, Assn. Trial Lawyers Am., Mass. Family and Probate Am. Inn Ct. General civil litigation, Family and matrimonial, Personal injury. Office: Kurland & Grossman PC 34 Chelmsford St Chelmsford MA 01824-3060

**GROSSMAN, H. PHILIP,** lawyer; b. Louisville, Oct. 19, 1955; m. Evalyn M. Grossman. BA, Washington U., St. Louis, 1977; JD, U. Louisville, 1980. Bar: Ky. 1980, U.S. Dist. Ct. (we. dist.) Ky. 1980, U.S. Ct. Appeals (6th cir.) 1986, U.S. Dist. Ct. (ea. dist.) Ky. 1987, U.S. Supreme Ct. 1988, Ind. 1989. Assoc. Franklin and King, P.S.C., Louisville, 1980-81, Heideman Law Offices, Louisville, 1981-83; ptnr. Taustine, Post, Sotsky, Berman, Fineman & Kohn, Louisville, 1983-98, Fernandez, Friedman, Grossman & Kohn, Louisville, 1998—. Bd. dirs. Jewish Community Ctr., Louisville; counsel Ky. Head Injury Assn., 1989, 90; sec. Ky. Coalition for People with Handicaps, 1990-92. Mem. ABA, ATLA, Ky. Bar Assn., Louisville Bar Assn. (bd. dirs. 1991—, pres. 1996), Ky. Acad. Trial Attys. (bd. govs. 1989-92, 99), Inn of Ct. (Louis D. Brandeis master, 1997—). Personal injury, General civil litigation. Office: Fernandez Friedman Grossman & Kohn 2400 Nat City Twr 101 S 5th St Louisville KY 40202-3103

**GROSSMAN, JEROME KENT,** lawyer, accountant; b. St. Louis, Apr. 15, 1953; s. Marvin and Myra Lee (Barnholtz) G.; m. Debbie Ada Kogan, Aug. 7, 1977; children: Hannah Felicia, Marni Celeste. AB cum laude, Georgetown U., 1974, JD, 1977. Bar: Mo. 1977, D.C. 1978, U.S. Ct. Claims 1979, U.S. Tax Ct. 1979, Del. 1980, U.S. Dist. Ct. Del. 1982; CPA, Mo. Acct., controller U.S. Dept. State, Washington, 1974-77; acct. Arthur Andersen & Co., St. Louis, 1977-79; mem. firm Bayard, Handelman and Murdoch, P.A., Wilmington, Del., 1979-88; ptnr. Young Conaway Stargatt & Taylor LLP, Wilmington, 1988—. Co-author: ALI-ABA Course of Study on the Reform Act of 1984, 86. V.p. Jewish Cmty. Ctr., Wilmington, 1986-88, 89-90, treas., 1989-90, Congregation Beth Shalom, Wilmington, 1988-90, pres., 1990-92; co-chmn. Del. State Com., State of Israel Bonds, 1992-95, chmn., 1995—; treas. Jewish Fedn. Del., 1989-90; pres. Del. Gratz Hebrew H.S., 1997—; trustee Jewish Com. of Del. Endowment Fund, 1988-95; bd. dirs., trustee Del. Symphony Assn., 1998—. Fellow Am. Coll. Tax Counsel; mem. ABA (tax sect., chmn. inventories subcom. 1982-86, vice chmn. 1986-88, chmn. 1988-90, com. on tax acctg.), Del. Bar Assn. (chair sect. of taxation 1996-97), Del. Tax Inst. (planning com. 1985-86, 94—), Del. Soc. CPAs (chmn. tax com. 1980-85, coun. 1985-87, 93—, ethics com. 1989-92, pres.-elect 1999—), Alpha Sigma Nu. Democrat. Avocations: choir, opera, bridge. Corporate taxation, Estate planning, Taxation, general. Home: 803 Westover Rd Wilmington DE 19807-2978 Office: Young Conaway Stargatt & Taylor LLP PO Box 391 Wilmington DE 19899-0391

**GROSSMAN, RANDY,** lawyer; b. N.Y.C., May 6, 1960; s. Arthur Joshua and Marlyn Grossman; m. Jacqueline Kaye Grossman, Jan. 17, 1988; 1 child, Matthew David. BA, George Washington U., 1982; JD, Touro Coll. Sch. Law, 1985. Bar: N.J. 1986, D.C. 1993, N.Y. 1996. Assoc. Unger & Unger, Newark, 1986, Greenberg, Feiner et al, West New York, N.J., 1987-93; ptnr. Horn, Shechtman & Hirsch, Jersey City, 1993—. Gen. counsel Aztek East Condo. Assn., Hackensack, N.J., 1992—; atty., advisor mock trial team Bayonne (N.J.) H.S., 1994—. Mem. ATLA, N.J. Stat eBar Assn., N.Y. State Bar Assn. Personal injury, Workers' compensation, Toxic tort. Office: Horn Shechtman & Hirsch PO Box 8238 Jersey City NJ 07308-8238

**GROSSMAN, ROBERT LOUIS,** lawyer; b. Cleve., Dec. 20, 1954; s. Sidney and Lillian Belle (Davis) G.; m. Rochelle Carol Shear, Nov. 7, 1987; children: Zachary, Jonathan, David, Andrew. BA with honors, Ohio State U., 1975, JD with honors, 1978, MA with honors, 1979. Bar: Ohio 1978, U.S. Ct. Appeals (5th cir.) 1979, Fla. 1982. Law clk. U.S. Dist. Ct. (so. dist.)

Ohio, Columbus, 1977-78; sr. atty. U.S. Govt. EEOC, Houston, 1979-82; shareholder Greenberg, Traurig, Hoffman, Lipoff, Rosen & Quentel, P.A., Miami, 1982—. Editor: Florida Corporate Practice, 2d edit., 1991. Chmn. South Dade Jewish Leadership Coun., 1997—; bd. dirs. Greater Miami Jewish Fedn. South Dade, Miami, 1987—, campaign chmn., 1995-97; bd. dirs. Greater Miami Jewish Fedn., 1995—, exec. com., 1997-99, Alper Jewish Comm. Ctr., 1997—, exec. com., 1998—. Donald Becker Meml. scholar Ohio State U., 1975, 76, fellow, 1978. Mem. ABA (corp. securities sect.), Fla. Bar Assn., Dade County Bar Assn., Order of Coif. Avocations: sports, reading, travel. Mergers and acquisitions, Securities, General corporate. Office: Greenberg Traurig 1221 Brickell Ave Miami FL 33131-3224

**GROSSMAN, SANFORD,** retired lawyer; b. N.Y.C., July 4, 1929; s. Philip and Irene (Hare) G.; m. Barbara Rothman, May 23, 1951; children: Daniel J., Donna A. Student, NYU, 1947-49; LL.B., Bklyn. Law Sch., 1952. Bar: N.Y. 1953, U.S. Supreme Ct. 1964. Pvt. practice law N.Y.C., 1954-79; ptnr. Simpson Thacher & Bartlett, N.Y.C., 1979-90, of counsel, 1991-93, retired, 1993. Served with U.S. Army, 1952-54. Mem. Assn. Bar City N.Y., N.Y. County Lawyers Assn., Westchester Bar Assn., Am. Coll. Real Estate Lawyers, Princeton Club (N.Y.C.). Real property. Office: Simpson Thacher & Bartlett 425 Lexington Ave Fl 14 New York NY 10017-3903

**GROSSMAN, STACY JILL,** lawyer; b. N.Y.C., Nov. 17, 1970; d. George Joseph and Lois Hope G. BA, Brown U., 1992; JD, Boston U., 1995. Bar: N.J. 1995, N.Y. 1996, U.S. Dist. Ct. (so. dist.) 1997. Assoc. Kenneth David Burrows, N.Y.C., 1995—; owner Legal Fiction, N.Y.C., 1998—. Mem. Bar Assn. City of N.Y., Vol. Lawyers for Arts, The New Group (jr. bd. dirs.). General practice, Entertainment, Family and matrimonial. Office: Kenneth David Burrows 425 Park Ave New York NY 10022-3506

**GROSSMAN, VICTOR G.,** lawyer; b. N.Y.C., Nov. 21, 1951; s. Jacob and Frances (Gaezer) G.; m. Jamie Williams, Apr. 8, 1984; children: Robert William, Sarah Frances. BA in Am. Studies with honors, Brandeis U., 1973; JD, Hofstra U., 1978. Bar: N.Y. 1979, U.S. Dist. Ct. (so. and ea. dist.) N.Y. 1980, U.S. Supreme Ct. 1984. Pvt. practice White Plains, N.Y., 1979-82; atty. Aurnou Kurzman Midler & Friedman, White Plains, 1982-87; pvt. practice Carmel, N.Y., 1987—. Mem. zoning bd. appeals Town of Southeast, Brewster, N.Y., 1989-91; legislator Putnam County Legis., Carmel, 1990-92; dep. supr. Town of Southeast, 1994-96. Criminal, Family and matrimonial, State civil litigation. Home: 40 Seven Oaks Ln Brewster NY 10509-1610 Office: Nine Fair St Carmel NY 10512-1213

**GROSSMANN, RONALD STANYER,** lawyer; b. Chgo., Nov. 9, 1944; s. Andrew Eugene and Gladys M. Grossmann; m. Jo Ellen Hanson, May 11, 1968; children: Kenneth Frederick, Emilie Beth. BA, Northwestern U., 1966; JD, U. Mich., 1969. Bar: Oreg., 1969. Law clk. Oreg. Supreme Ct., Salem, 1969-70; assoc. Stoel Rives Boley Jones & Grey, Portland, Oreg., 1970-76, ptnr., 1976—. Mem. ABA, Oreg. Bar Assn. Office: Stoel Rives LLP 900 SW 5th Ave Ste 2600 Portland OR 97204-1268

**GROSZ, MORTON ERIC,** lawyer; b. N.Y.C., Feb. 1, 1944; s. Armand A. and Gisele (Zucker) G.; m. Judith Harriet Armour, June 15, 1969; children: David, Jeffrey. BS in Econs., U. Pa., 1965; LLB, Boston U., 1968; LLM in Internat. Law, NYU, 1969. Bar: N.Y. 1968. Assoc. Barrett Smith Schapiro Simon & Armstrong, N.Y.C., 1969-76; ptnr. Barett, Smith Schapiro Simon & Armstrong, N.Y.C., 1976-88, Chadbourne & Parke, N.Y.C., 1988—. Mem. Assn. of Bar of City of N.Y. (corp. law com. 1975-77, 89-92). General corporate, Contracts commercial, Finance. Office: Chadbourne & Parke 30 Rockefeller Plz New York NY 10112-0002

**GROTTA, HAROLD EDWARD,** lawyer; b. Newark, July 27, 1911; s. Theodore and Fanny (Matz) G.; m. Jane M. Meyer; children: Toni Wolfman, James. BS, U. Va., 1931, JD, 1933. Assoc. Hannoch & Lasser, Newark, 1934-40; sole practice Newark, 1940-55; ptnr. Grotta & Oberwager, Newark, 1955-61, Grotta, Oberwager & Glassman, Newark, 1961-73; prin. Grotta, Glassman & Hoffman, Newark, 1977—; dir. indsl. relations Continental Copper & Steel, N.Y.C., 1970-76. Editor: Va. Law Review, 1932-33. Pres. Newark Beth Israel Med. Ctr., 1975, trustee, 1960—, Congn. B'Nai Jeshurun, 1973-76, pres.,trustee, 1960—, pres., chmn. of bd. N.J. Symphony Orch., Newark, 1979-81, trustee 1978—; bd. dirs., Paper Mill Playhouse, Millburn, N.J., pres. 1973-78. Mem. ABA, N.J. State Bar Assn., Essex County Bar Assn., Zeta Beta Tau. Clubs: Mountain Ridge (West Caldwell) (bd. govs. 1944—); Mission Hills (Rancho Mirage). Home: Llewellyn Park 5 Elm Court Way West Orange NJ 07052-4927 Office: Grotta Glassman & Hoffman 75 Livingston Ave Ste 13 Roseland NJ 07068-3701

**GRUBB, STEVEN COCHRAN,** lawyer; b. Atlanta, Apr. 17, 1955; s. Alex Caswell and Mary Ellen (Cochran) G. BA, U. Va., 1977; JD, U. Memphis, 1980, MPA, 1984. Bar: Tenn. 1981, U.S. Dist. Ct. (we. dist.) Tenn. 1982, U.S. Ct. Appeals (6th cir.) 1985. Insp. Va. Alcohol Beverage Control Commn., Norfolk, 1977-78; atty. Law Office of Robert L. Dobbs, Memphis, 1981-85; pvt. practice Law Office of Steven C. Grubb, Memphis, 1986-93; ptnr. Norwood, Phillips, Deboo, Howard & Grubb, Memphis, 1993-95, Phillips, Howard & Grubb, Memphis, 1995—. Bd. dirs. Ruth Mackey Cancer Found., 1993—. Mem. U.S. Jr. C. of C. (nat. v.p. 1993-94, pres. Memphis chpt. 1989-90, pres. Tenn. 1992-93, Outstanding Chpt. Pres. 1990, Outstanding State Pres. 1994). Avocations: toy collecting, automobile racing. Personal injury, Workers' compensation, Criminal. Office: Phillips Howard & Grubb 22 N Front St Ste 800 Memphis TN 38103-2179

**GRUBBS, DONALD SHAW, JR.,** retired actuary; b. Bellvue, Pa., Dec. 15, 1929; s. Donald Shaw and Zora Fay (Craven) G.; m. Margaret Helen Crooke, Dec. 27, 1969; children: David, Deborah, Daniel, Dawson, Dwight, Douglas. AB, Tex. A&M U., 1951; postgrad., L.A. State Coll., 1953-54, Fresno State Coll., 1954-55, Boston U., 1955-57, Princeton Theol. Sem., 1959-60, Westminster Theol. Sem., 1960-61; JD, Georgetown U., 1979. Bar: D.C. 1979. Actuarial asst. New Eng. Mut. Life Ins. Co., Boston, 1955-58, Warner Watson, Inc., Boston, 1958-59; cons. actuary John B. St. John, Penllyn, Pa., 1959-65, Grubbs & Co., Phila., 1965-72; v.p. actuary Nat. Health and Welfare Retirement Assn., N.Y.C., 1972-74; dir. actuarial div. IRS, Washington, 1974-76; cons. actuary Buck Cons., Inc., Washington, 1976-86; pres. Grubbs and Co., Inc., Silver Spring, Md., 1986-95, retired, 1995—; chmn. Joint Bd. for Enrollment Actuaries, Washington, 1975-76. Author: (with G.E. Johnson) The Variable Annuity, 1967, (with D.M. McGill) Fundamentals of Private Pensions, 6th edit., 1989. V.p. NAACP, Ambler, Pa., 1961-62; chmn. Warminster (Pa.) Child Day Care Assn., 1962-64. 1st lt. U.S. Army, 1951-53, Korea. Decorated Bronze Star with V U.S. Army, 1953; recipient Employee Benefits Outstanding Achievement award Pension World, 1986. Fellow Soc. of Actuaries (sec. 1983-84), Conf. Consulting Actuaries; mem. ABA, Middle Atlantic Actuarial Club (pres. 1981-82), UN Assn. (v.p. nat. capital area divsn. 1996-98). Democrat. Unitarian. Home: 10216 Royal Rd Silver Spring MD 20903-1613

**GRUBBS, ROBERT HOWARD,** lawyer; b. Wilkinsburg, Pa., Mar. 28, 1946; s. Jack H. and Margaret Charlotte (Weaver) G.; m. Mary Jo Grubbs; 1 child, Margaret Elizabeth. BA, Denison U., 1968; JD, U. S.C., 1977. S.C. 1977, N.C. 1985. Assoc. McKay, Sherill, Walker & Townsend, Columbia, S.C., 1977-81, ptnr., 1981-85; assoc. Womble Carlyle Sandridge & Rice PLLC, Winston-Salem, N.C., 1985-91, mem., 1991—. Sgt. U.S. Army, 1968-71. Environmental, Toxic tort. Home: 5131 Laurel View Dr Winston Salem NC 27104-5101 Office: Womble Carlyle Sandridge & Rice PLLC 200 W 2nd St Winston Salem NC 27101-4019

**GRUBE, KARL BERTRAM,** judge; b. Elmhurst, Ill., Jan. 13, 1946; s. Karl Ludwig and Gerturde (Bertram) G.; m. Mary B. Harr, May 4, 1974 (div. Aug. 1991). BSBA, Elmhurst Coll., 1967; JD, Stetson U., 1970; M in Judicial Studies, U. Nev., 1992. Asst. pub. defender State of Fla., Clearwater, 1970-73; county ct. judge State of Fla., St. Petersburg, 1977—; pvt. practice Seminole, Fla., 1973-76; city atty. City of Redington Beach, Fla., 1975-76; asst. dean Fla. Jud. Coll., Tallahassee, 1984-85; faculty mem., course coord., mem. faculty coun. Nat. Jud. Coll.; mem. Nat. Hwy. Traffic Safety Jud. Tng. Implementation Bd. Contbr. articles to profl. jours. Dir. Pinellas Comprehensive Addiction Svcs., Clearwater, 1982-88. Jud. fellow U.S. Dept. Transp., 1998, Nat. Hwy. Traffic Safety Adminstn., 1999. Mem. ABA (conf. chmn. divsn. jud. adminstrn. 1992, del. to jud. divsn. coun. 1997—, Dedicated Svc. award 1991), Fla. Bar Assn. (civil rule com.), Colo. Bar Assn., Fla. Conf. County Ct. Judges (pers. com. 1984-85), Rolls Royce Owner's Club (editor 1982-84). Lutheran. Avocations: collecting fountain pens, collecting antique watches, auto restoration. Office: Pinellas County Ct 150 5th St N Ste 304 Saint Petersburg FL 33701-3700

**GRUCCIO-THORMAN, LILLIAN JOAN,** lawyer; b. Camden, N.J., Jan. 30, 1927; d. Joseph and Millie Gruccio. grad. Steelman Bus. Sch., 1945; AA, Rutgers U., 1947, LLB, 1951, LLD, 1968. Bar: N.J. 1952, U.S. Dist. Ct. N.J. 1952, U.S. Supreme Ct. 1960. Ptnr., Frank C. Propert, Camden, 1952-55; assoc. Lewis & Hutchinson and successors, Camden, 1956-61; with legal dept. Campbell Soup Co., 1955; sole practice Pennsauken, N.J., 1961-73, Medford, N.J., 1973—. Mem. Camden City Juvenile Conf. Com., 1957-62; mem. Burlington County coun. Girl Scouts USA, 1975, chmn. by-laws com., 1975; bd. dirs. Camden County Health and Welfare Coun., 1957-61, YWCA Camden, 1959-67, chmn. adult program com. 1957-67; mem. budget com. United Fund, 1968; recreation sec. Leisure Towne Civic League, mem. by-laws com. 1975. Mem. ABA, N.J. Bar Assn., Burlington County Bar Assn., Camden County Bar Assn., Rutgers U. Law Sch. Alumni Assn. (chancellor South Jersey div. 1962). Republican. Baptist. Lodge: Zonta. General corporate, Probate, Real property. Home: 802 Cranbury Cross Rd N Brunswick NJ 08902-2204 Office: Cedarbrook Bldg Taunton Blvd Medford NJ 08055

**GRUE, THOMAS ANDREW,** lawyer; b. Plattsburgh, N.Y., Sept. 21, 1959; s. Ellsworth Charles and Emily Ruth (Noseworthy) G.; m. Karen Sue Couch, Apr. 19, 1986; children: Robert Thomas, Rachel Mae. BA, Cornell U., 1981; JD, SUNY, Buffalo, 1984. Bar: N.Y. 1984, U.S. Army Ct. Military Review. Assoc. Couch, White, Brenner, Howard & Fiegenbaum, Albany, N.Y., 1984-88; ptnr. Poissant & Nichols P.C., Malone, N.Y., 1990—; instr. Bus. Law, Kans. State U., Manhattan, 1985-86. Sr. editor Buffalo Law Review, 1982-83. Capt. U.S. Army, 1984-88. Mem. Franklin County Bar Assn. General civil litigation, Personal injury, Family and matrimonial. Home: 21 Morton St Malone NY 12953-1614 Office: Poissant & Nichols PC 55 W Main St Malone NY 12953-1813

**GRUEN, EVELYN JEANETTE,** lawyer, accountant; b. Vancouver, B.C., Can., Oct. 13, 1956; came to U.S., 1960; d. Kurt and Mary Rose (Spörk) G. BS, Calif. State U., Northridge, 1977; MBus in Taxation, U. So. Calif., 1981, MBA, 1981, JD, 1981. Bar: Calif. 1981, U.S. Dist. Ct. (cen. dist.) Calif. 1981, U.S. Ct. Appeals (9th cir.) 1981, U.S. Tax Ct. 1984, U.S. Supreme Ct. 1988. Assoc. Pepper, Hamilton & Scheetz, L.A., 1981-83; mng. atty. L.A. office Raynolds, Hagendorf, Vance & Deason, 1983-84; sole practice Simi Valley, Calif., 1984—. Mem. ABA, Calif. State Bar, Calif. Bar Assn., L.A. County Bar Assn., Phi Alpha Delta, Phi Kappa Phi. General civil litigation, Private international, Estate taxation. Office: PO Box 202 Simi Valley CA 93062-0202

**GRUEN, MICHAEL STEPHAN,** lawyer; b. L.A., Mar. 25, 1942; s. Victor and Elsie Caroline (Krummeck) G.; m. Susanna Lloyd, July 18, 1964; m. Vanessa Elisabeth Ahlfors, Jan. 3, 1976; children: Madeleine, Alexis, Viveca; stepchildren: Stefan, Sebastian. BA cum laude, Harvard U., 1963; LLB, UCLA, 1966. Bar: Calif. 1966, N.Y. 1967, U.S. Ct. Appeals (2d cir.) 1976, U.S. Supreme Ct. 1975, U.S. Dist. Ct. (so. and ea. dists.) N.Y. 1986. Assoc. Paul, Weiss, Rifkind, Wharton & Garrison, N.Y.C., 1966-69, Gilinsky, Stillman & Mishkin, N.Y.C., 1969-70, Wolf, Popper, Ross, Wolf & Jones, N.Y.C., 1970-74; gen. counsel Bio-Med. Scis., Inc., Fairfield, N.J., 1974-75; pvt. practice N.Y.C., 1975-80; mem. Gruen & Muskin, N.Y.C., 1980, Gruen, Muskin & Thau, N.Y.C., 1981-88, Gruen, Gilliatt & Livingston, N.Y.C., 1989-90, Gruen & Livingston, N.Y.C., 1990-97, Gruen & Farrelly LLP, N.Y.C., 1998—. Contbr. articles to legal and gen. publs. Bd. dirs. Boys' Athletic League, 1966-82, Columbia Land Conservancy, 1986—, pres., 1988-91; dir. N.Y. Landmarks Conservancy, 1972-94, adv. coun., 1994-97; chmn. Historic Dists. Coun., 1974-79; bd. advisors Prep. Divsn. Bklyn. Coll. Ctr. for Performing Arts, 1980-83; mem. law com. Mcpl. Art Soc., 1987—; pres. Riverside Dems., N.Y.C., 1971-72. Mem. ABA (litig. sect.), N.Y. State Bar Assn., Assn. of Bar of City of N.Y. Federal civil litigation, State civil litigation, General corporate. Office: 500 5th Ave Ste 5225 New York NY 10110-5299

**GRUENINGER, DANIEL J.,** lawyer; b. Belleville, Ill., Jan. 11, 1962; s. Roy A. and Ethel R. (Peterson) G.; children: Adam D., Catherine A. BS in Polit. Sci., So. Ill. U., 1984, JD, 1987. Bar: Ill. 1987, U.S. Dist. Ct. (so. dist.) Ill. 1988, U.S. Dist. Ct. (ea. dist.) N.C. 1991, Supreme Ct. U.S. 1998. Asst. states atty. Peoria (Ill.) County States Atty., 1987-88; assoc. Bernard & Davidson, Granite CIty, Ill., 1988, Kurowski Law Firm, Swansea, Ill., 1995-96; ptnr. Grueninger & Connors, Belleville, Ill., 1996—. Capt. U.S. Army, 1988-95. Avocation: coin collecting. Family and matrimonial, Juvenile. Office: Grueninger & Connors 424 S High St Belleville IL 62220-2119

**GRUHIN, MICHAEL H.,** lawyer; b. Newark, Sept. 8, 1951; s. Robert C. and Pauline (Rosenblum) G.; m. Gloria S. Gruhin; children: David, Stacey. BA, Ohio State U., 1973; JD, Cleve. Marshall Coll. Law, 1976. Bar: Ohio 1976, Fla. 1977, Ill. 1978, N.J. 1977, U.S. Supreme Ct. 1981, U.S. Dist. Ct. (no. dist.) Ohio 1977, U.S. Dist. Ct. N.J. 1977; cert. workers compensation specialist, Ohio. Ptnr. Levey & Gruhin, Attys., Cleve., 1981—. Mem. ATLA, Ohio State Bar Assn., Cleve. Bar Assn., Cuyahoga County Bar Assn., Ohio Assn. Trial Attys. E-mail: MHG@Ohiolaw.com. Personal injury, Workers' compensation. Office: Levey & Gruhin Attys 1468 W 9th St Ste 750 Cleveland OH 44113-1200

**GRUND, DAVID IRA,** lawyer; b. Feb. 5, 1947; s. Julian and Ethel (Brudner) G.; m. Rachel Reifer, Dec. 16, 1972; 1 child, Melissa. BS, DePaul U., 1968, JD, 1972. Bar: Ill. 1973, U.S. Dist. Ct. (no. dist.) Ill. 1973. Prin. ptnr. Grund & Starkopf, Chgo.; lectr. in field. Bd. dirs. Ill. Holocaust Meml. Found., Skokie, 1989—, U.C.P., Ill. Chgo., 1988—; bd. dirs. Glencoe Social Svcs. Mem. Am. Acad. Matrimonial Lawyers (bd. mgrs. Ill. chpt. 1987—, chmn. admissions com. 1992-97), Ill. Bar Assn., Chgo. Bar Assn. (matrimonial law sect., cts. and legis. subcom.), Ill. Trial Lawyers Assn., Ill. Leading Lawyers, Decalogue Soc. Lawyers, Standard Club (Chgo.). Jewish. Avocations: golf, running, photography. Family and matrimonial. Office: Grund & Starkopf 111 E Wacker Dr Chicago IL 60601-3713

**GRUNDMEYER, DOUGLAS LANAUX,** lawyer, editor; b. New Orleans, Nov. 6, 1948; s. Raymond Wallace and Eva Myrl (Lanaux) G.; m. Elaine Ann Toscano, Jan. 19, 1977; 1 child, Sarah Elaine. BA, Tulane U., 1970, JD, 1976; MA in English, U. New Orleans, 1974. Bar: La. 1976, Calif. 1980, U.S. Dist. Ct. (no. dist.) Calif. 1980, U.S. Dist. Ct. (ea., mid. and we. dists.) La. 1988, U.S. Ct. Appeals (5th cir.) 1988, U.S. Ct. Appeals (11th cir.) 1996, U.S. Supreme Ct. 1989. Sr. law clk. to presiding judge La. State Ct. of Appeal (4th cir.), New Orleans, 1976-78, 80-88; assoc. legal editor Bancroft-Whitney Co., San Francisco, 1978-80, contract editor, 1981-92; assoc. Chaffe, McCall, Phillips, Toler & Sarpy, L.L.P., New Orleans, 1988-91, spl. ptnr., 1992-94, ptnr., 1994—; contract editor Clark Boardman Callaghan, Rochester, N.Y., 1993-96, West Group, Rochester, 1997—. Contbg. editor American Jurisprudence 2d, Criminal Law, 1981; contbg. author La. Appellate Practice Handbook, 1986, Effective Appellate Practice in Louisiana, 1995. Mem. ABA, State Bar Calif., La. Bar Assn., Scribes. Democrat. Roman Catholic. General civil litigation, Admiralty, Appellate. Office: 2300 Energy Ctr 1100 Poydras St New Orleans LA 70163-1101

**GRUNEWALD, MARK HOWARD,** dean. BA, Emory U., 1969; JD with highest honors, George Washington U., 1972. Bar: D.C. 1973, Va. 1979. Assoc. Arent, Fox, Kintner, Plotkin & Kahn, Washington, 1972-73; atty. advisor Office of Legal Counsel U.S. Dept. Justice, 1973-76; from asst. prof. to assoc. prof. law Washington and Lee U., Lexington, Va., 1976-86, prof. law, 1986—, assoc. dean, 1992-96, interim dean, 1999—. Editor-in-chief George Washington Law Rev. Mem. Order of Coif. Office: Washington and Lee U Law Sch Lexington VA 24450-0303*

**GRUNEWALD, RAYMOND BERNHARD,** lawyer; b. N.Y.C., Feb. 10, 1928; s. Ivan Oscar and Verna Allesandria (Lindgren) G.; m. Irma Geiser; children: Peter Bernhard, Iris Elizabeth. BS, Fordham U., 1949, JD, 1952. Bar: N.Y. 1952, U.S. Ct. Mil. Appeals 1956, U.S. Dist. Ct. (so. and ea. dists.) N.Y. 1957, U.S. Ct. Appeals (2d cir.) 1962, U.S. Supreme Ct. 1963, U.S. Tax Ct. 1970, U.S. Ct. Appeals (fed. cir.) 1986. Sole practice law N.Y.C., 1956-60, 70—; asst. U.S. Atty., chief criminal and civil divsns. Dept. Justice, N.Y.C., 1961-70. Candidate for Nassau County Comptroller, 1985, Nassau County Exec., 1987, Nassau County Ct., 1990, N.Y. Supreme Ct., 1991, 92; dep. chmn. Nassau County Dem. Com., Mineola, N.Y. Served to col. JAGC, U.S. Army, 1952-56, Korea, with Res. 1957-83. Decorated Legion of Merit. Mem. ABA, Nassau County Bar Assn., Fed. Bar Council, Assn. Bar City N.Y., N.Y. County Lawyers Assn. Lutheran. Club: Squadron "A". Avocations: politics, reading, art collecting. Criminal, General civil litigation, Personal injury. Home: 1 Hewlett Rd Greenvale NY 11548-1125 Office: 805 3rd Ave Fl 6 New York NY 10022-7509

**GRUSH, JULIUS SIDNEY,** lawyer; b. Los Angeles, Dec. 4, 1937; children: Robin, Randi, Ronna, Rodney. BS, UCLA, 1960; postgrad., U. Calif., San Francisco, 1960-62; LLB, Southwestern U., 1964. Bar: Calif. 1965. Dep. city atty. City of Los Angeles, 1965-67; sole practice Los Angeles, 1967—; prof. Bar-Bri Harcourt Brace Pubs. Bar Course, Los Angeles, 1986—. Pres. Lockhurst Booster Club; mem. City of Hope (past pres.). Mem. ABA, Los Angeles Bar Assn., Beverly Hills Bar Assn., Century City Bar Assn., Phi Alpha Delta. Republican. State civil litigation, General corporate, Real property. Office: 1900 Avenue Of The Stars Fl 25 Los Angeles CA 90067-4301

**GRUTMAN, JEWEL HUMPHREY,** lawyer, writer; b. N.Y.C., Mar. 13, 1931; d. Robert and Gladys Humphrey; m. Robert W. Bjork, June 26, 1954 (div. Apr. 22, 1975); 1 child, Bruce Bjork; m. Roy Grutman, Oct. 30, 1975 (wid. 1994); m. Fredrick Yonkman, July 4, 1998. BA magna cum laude, Mt. Holyoke Coll., 1952; LLB, Columbia U., 1955. Bar: N.Y., U.S. Dist. Ct. (So. Dist.) N.Y. 1971, U.S. Dist. Ct. (ea. dist.) N.Y. 1974, U.S. Dist. Ct. Conn. 1984, U.S. Supreme Ct. 1984. Atty. Debevoise & Plimpton, N.Y.C., 1954-60; ptnr. Eaton Van Winkle, N.Y.C., 1976-79, Grutman Greene & Humphrey, N.Y.C., 1979—. Co-author: (with CD-ROM) The Ledgerbook of Thomas Blue Eagle, 1994 (Christopher award 1995, Internat. Reading Assn. award), (CD-ROM) The Journey of Thomas Blue Eagle, 1995 (Best Project award Intermedia, Asia, 1995, Creative NGee ANN Disting. award 1995, EMMA award best visual content 1996), The Journal of Julia Singing Bear, 1995; asst. prodr., editor (ednl. film on art) Where Time is a River (1st prize Women's Film Festival); contbr. photograph illustrations: The Reforming Power of the Scriptures, 1996; developer series of designs based on Native Am. art; contbr. articles to mags. and newspapers. Dir. Inwood Ho., N.Y.C., 1970-80; past mem. various coms. Mt. Holyoke Coll.; mem. com. sr. advisors N.Y. Commn. for Internat. Bus. and UN, 1997; past chmn. com. to establish Barbara Black Fellowship at Columbia U. Law Sch.; past pres. 85th St. Playground Assn., N.Y.C.; active supporter The Children's Storefront, Harlem, N.Y.C.; active fundraiser N.Y. Jr. League. Mem. Assn. Bar of City of N.Y. (past mem. young lawyers com., admissions com., post-admission edn. com. in field of securities), The River Club (N.Y.C.), The Stanwich Club (Greenwich, Conn.), Sombrero Golf Club (Marathon, Fla.). Avocations: opera, golf, tennis, poetry. General civil litigation, Libel, Constitutional.

**GRUTZ, JAMES ARTHUR,** lawyer; b. Dubuque, Iowa, Oct. 24, 1940; s. Clarence Peter and Edna Evelyn (Nelson) G.; m. Kate Boyle, Aug. 20, 1941; children: Kristin, Rachel, Karrin, Adam, Brendan. BA, Loras Coll., 1963; JD, Northwestern U., 1966. Bar: Wash. 1967, U.S. Dist. Ct. (we. dist.) Wash. 1968, U.S. Ct. Appeals (9th cir.) 1972, U.S. Supreme Ct. 1979. Law clk. Wash. Supreme Ct., Olympia, 1967-68; assoc. Jackson, Ulvestad & Goodwin, Seattle, 1968-74; ptnr. Jackson, Ulvestad, Goodwin & Grutz, Seattle, 1974-81, Goodwin, Grutz & Scott, Seattle, 1981-96, Grutz, Scott & Kinney, Seattle, 1996—. Mem. ABA, Wash. Bar Assn., Seattle-King County Bar Assn., Assn. Trial Lawyers Am., Wash. Trial Lawyers Assn. Roman Catholic. Avocations: baseball, softball. Personal injury, Probate, Workers' compensation.

**GRZECA, MICHAEL (GERARD),** lawyer; b. Milw., Aug. 5, 1949; s. Leonard George and Katherine Anne (Lewis) G.; m. Linda Gail Schultz, Aug. 15, 1970; children—Amy Marie, Laura Elizabeth. B.A., Marquette U., 1971, J.D., 1974. Bar: Wis. 1974, U.S. Dist. Ct. (ea. and we. dists.) Wis. 1974, U.S. Supreme Ct., 1977. Assoc., Everson, Whitney, Everson & Brehm, S.C., Green Bay, Wis., 1974-80, shareholder, 1980-86; prin. Grzeca & Stanton, S.C., 1986-95; pvt. practice, Green Bay, 1995—; spl. counsel Wis. Bd. Attys. Profl. Responsibility, 1983—; cir. ct. commr., 1991—. Editor Wis. Ins. Issues, 1984—. Bd. dirs. Big Bros.-Big Sisters of Northeastern Wis., Green Bay, 1977-86 , pres., 1979-81, 85, legal counsel, 1985—. Served as officer USAR, 1974-80. Mem. ABA, Def. Research Inst., Order of Barristers. Insurance, State civil litigation, Personal injury. Office: Brown County Ct House 100 S Jefferson St Green Bay WI 54301

**GUARINI, FRANK J.,** lawyer, real estate developer; b. Jersey City, N.J., Aug. 20, 1924; s. Frank J. G., Sr. and Caroline Loretta Critelli. BA, Dartmouth Coll., 1946; JD, NYU, 1950, LLM, 1955; LHD (hon.), St. Peter's Coll., 1994; Litt. D. (hon.), N.J. City U., 1993. Bar: N.J., N.Y., D.C., Ct. Internat. Trade. Sr. ptnr. Guarini & Guarini, Jersey City, N.J., 1951—; senator State of N.J., Trenton, 1966-73; mem. Ho. of Reps., Washington, 1979-93. Bd. dirs. John Cabot U., Rome, 1994—; founder Guarini Ctr. for Govtl. Affairs St. Peter's Coll., Jersey City, N.J., 1994—; bd. dirs. Washington Ctr. for Interns, 1993-96, The New Cmty. Found., Newark, 1993-94; pres., chmn. Nat. Italian Am. Found., 1999—; rep. U.S. UN, N.Y.C., 1997-98; alumni trustee Hague (The Netherlands) Acad. Internat. Law, 1956-60. Fellow ABA; mem. Am. Trial Lawyers Assn. (nat. bd. govs. 1975-78), N.J. State Bar Assn. (mem. gen. coun. 1960-63), N.Y. Athletic Club. Democrat. Roman Catholic. Avocations: skiing, tennis, archeology, travel. Fax: 1-908-77-8645. Taxation, general, Real property, Trade. Office: Guarini & Guarini 30 Montgomery St Ste 15 Jersey City NJ 07302-3821

**GUBERMAN, DAVID AARON,** lawyer; b. Brookline, Mass., Nov. 29, 1949; s. Joshua Abram and Mildred (Katz) G.; m. Jayne Kravetz, Aug. 10, 1980; children: Rachel Meira, Dalia Yael. BA, Harvard U., 1971, JD, 1975, MBA, 1975. Bar: Mass. 1975, U.S. Dist. Ct. Mass. 1976, D.C. 1980, U.S. Ct. Appeals (1st cir.) 1986, U.S. Ct. Appeals (3d cir.) 1992. Law clk. Mass. Ct. Appeals, Boston, 1975-76; assoc. Mason & Martin, Boston, 1976-77; spl. asst. U.S. Dept. Commerce, Washington, 1977-81; assoc. Ross & Bogin, Washington, 1982; assoc. Sherin & Lodgen, Boston, 1983-86, ptnr., 1986—. Co-author: U.S.A. and China: Technology and Patents Sale and License, 1981. Sec. Harvard Hillel Found., Cambridge, Mass., 1987-98; mem. Dem. City Com., Newton, Mass., 1972-80, 87—; pres. Am. For Peace Now, 1988-90, treas., 1991-95; mem. Wexner Heritage Found.; mem. exec. com. Jewish Community Rels. Coun. of Greater Boston. Mem. Am. Law Inst. Jewish. Avocations: classical music, sailing, reading, hiking. General civil litigation. Office: Sherin and Lodgen LLP 100 Summer St Ste 2800 Boston MA 02110-2109

**GUBERMAN, TED,** lawyer; b. Cin., Apr. 29, 1940; s. Louis and Betty Rose G. BA, Harvard Coll., 1962; MA, ABD, U. Calif., Berkeley, 1968, 71; JD, Washington U., St. Louis, 1976. Pvt. practitioner Hillsboro, Mo. Criminal, Personal injury, Workers' compensation. Office: 10632 Highway 21 Hillsboro MO 63050-5039

**GUBINSKY, MARK KEVIN,** lawyer; b. Washington, Feb. 19, 1967; s. Louis and Brenda (Marshall) Gubinsky; m. Kathleen Berexa, Sept. 6, 1969. BS in Journalism, U. Md., 1990; JD, U. Pitts., 1994. Bar: Pa. 1994, U.S. Dist. Ct. (we. dist.) Pa. 1994. Atty. Orie & Zivic, Pitts., 1994-96, Frank Bails Kirk Murcko & Toal, Pitts., 1996—. Mem. Pa. Bar Assn. (family law sect.), Allegheny county Bar Assn. (family law sect.). Family and matrimonial. Office: Frank Bails et al Gulf Tower 33d Fl Pittsburgh PA 15219

**GUBITS, DAVID BARRY,** lawyer; b. New Brighton, Pa., July 12, 1941; s. Harry William and Florence Leonore (Weiner) G.; m. Ruth Miriam Farkas, Apr. 11, 1965; children: Jonathan, Daniel. AB, Brown U., 1963; JD, NYU, 1966. Bar: N.Y. 1967, U.S. Dist. Ct. (no. dist.) N.Y. 1967, U.S. Ct. Appeals (2nd cir.) 1969, U.S. Dist. Ct. (so. and ea. dists. ) N.Y. 1977, U.S. Supreme Ct. 1978. Assoc. Appellate Div. 3rd Dept., Albany, N.Y., 1966-68, Gerald N. Jacobowitz, Walden, N.Y., 1967-72; ptnr. Jacobowitz & Gubits, Walden, 1973—. Dep. atty. Village of Washingtonville (N.Y.), 1973—, Village of Highland Falls (N.Y.), 1976—, Village of Maybrook (N.Y.), 1983—; spl. counsel Town of Wawarsing, Ellenville, N.Y., 1983—, Village of New Paltz

(N.Y.), 1984; mem. adv. counsel Stewart Airport Land Authority, New Windsor, N.Y., 1972-81; pres. UJA/Fedn. Rockland County, 1991-92, exec. bd., 1988—. Mem. N.Y. State Bar Assn. (land use control com. 1979-81, real estate devel. com. 1982-84), ABA (fed. grants com. 1979-84), Orange County Bar Assn. (chmn. continuing legal edn. com. 1979-80), North Am. Loon Fund., Audubon Soc. Avocations: wilderness canoeing, history. Real property, General practice, Contracts commercial. Home: 126 W Clarkstown Rd New City NY 10956-1558 Office: Jacobowitz & Gubits 158 Orange Ave PO Box 367 Walden NY 12586-0367

**GUBLER, JOHN GRAY,** lawyer; b. Las Vegas, June 16, 1942; s. V. Gray and Loreta N. (Newton) G.; m. Mollie Boyle, Jan. 10, 1987; 1 child, J. Gray; children from previous marriage: Laura, Matthew. BA, U. Calif.-Berkeley, 1964; JD, U. Utah, 1971; LLM in Taxation, NYU, 1973. Bar: Nev. 1971, U.S. Dist. Ct. Nev. 1973, U.S. Tax Ct. 1974, U.S. Ct. Appeals (9th cir.) 1978. Dep. pub. defender Clark County, Nev., 1973-74; ptnr. Gubler & Gubler, Las Vegas, 1974-88, ptnr. Gubler and Peters, Las Vegas, 1989—; instr. continuing edn. community coll. Served with U.S. Army, 1966-68. Mem. Clark County Bar Assn., ABA, State Bar of Nev. (disciplinary com. 1979-88), Las Vegas-Paradise Rotary (pres. 1981-82), Knife & Fork Club (pres. 1978-80). Ch of Jesus Christ of Latter Day Saints. Estate planning, Probate. Office: Gubler & Peters 302 E Carson Ave Ste 601 Las Vegas NV 89101-5989

**GUBNER, ADAM LANCE,** lawyer; b. L.A., Feb. 14, 1968; s. Michael Paul and Arri Gubner; m. Kimberly Ann Brown, Oct. 14, 1995; 1 child, Jeremy Daniel. BA in Philosophy, U. Calif., Santa Barbara, 1990; JD with distinction, U. of the Pacific, 1993. Assoc. Arter & Hadden, L.A., 1994-97, Stroock & Stroock & Lavan, L.A., 1997—. Bankruptcy, Contracts commercial. Office: Stroock & Stroock & Lavan LLP 2029 Century Park E Fl 16 Los Angeles CA 90067-2901

**GUDEMAN, LEROY DENNIS,** lawyer; b. Francesville, Ind., May 25, 1926; s. Joseph Benjamin and Hulda (Getz) G.; children: Jay, Jerry, Mary Ann, Thomas, Andrew, Susan; m. Kay Crecelius, July 21, 1990. AB, Ind. U., 1950, JD, 1954. Bar: Ind. 1954, U.S. Dist. Ct. (no. and so. dists.) Ind. 1954. Pvt. practice Knox, Ind., 1957—. Pres. Starke County Fine Arts Commn., Knox, 1986—. Cpl. U.S. Army, 1955-57. Mem. ABA, Ind. State Bar Assn., Starke-Pulaski Bar Assn. (pres. 1982-84), Kiwanis (pres. Knox chpt. 1967-68). Republican. Avocations: golf, fishing. Real property, Probate, General civil litigation. Home: 1021 W 50 S Knox IN 46534-9467 Office: 14 E Washington St Knox IN 46534-1147

**GUEDEL, WILLIAM GREGORY,** lawyer; b. Torrance, Calif., Sept. 5, 1969; s. William E. and Aija A. Guedel. BS in Bus. Adminstrn., U. So. Calif., L.A., 1991; JD, U. Wash., 1994. Bar: Wash. 1994, U.S. Dist. Ct. (we. dist.) Wash. 1997, U.S. Ct. Fed. Claims, 1998. Law clk. U. Wash. divsn. Atty. Gen. Wash., Seattle, 1992-93; atty., legal intern Poole and Assocs., P.S.C., Seattle, 1993-95; adminstrv. law atty. U.S. Army Office of the Staff Judge Adv., Ft. Hood, Tex., 1995-96; lawyer Oles Morrison Rinker & Baker LLP, Seattle, 1996—. Capt. U.S. Army, Wash. Army Nat. Guard. Mem. ABA, Wash. State Bar Assn. (chmn. com. for legal svcs. to the armed forces 1998-99), King County Bar Assn., Soc. Am. Mil. Engrs. Avocations: reading, boxing. Construction, Contracts commercial, Government contracts and claims. Office: Oles Morrison Rinker & Baker LLP 701 5th Ave Ste 3300 Seattle WA 98104-7082

**GUENDELSBERGER, ROBERT JOSEPH,** lawyer; b. Jamaica, N.Y., Nov. 13, 1950; s. Harold Guendelsberger and Audrey L. (Mack) Pogonowski; m. Roberta E. Knight, Feb. 3, 1979; children: Rebecca, Gretchen, Kaitlin, Heidi. BA, Alfred U., 1972; JD, Ohio No. U., 1976. Bar: Conn. 1976, U.S. Dist. Ct. Conn. 1977. Ptnr. Guendelsberger & Taylor, New Milford, Conn., 1983—; justice of peace Town of New Milford, 1976—. Chmn. New Milford Rep. Town Com., 1978-88; chmn. New Milford Bd. Edn., 1990-92. Mem. Conn. Bar Assn., Litchfield County Bar Assn., New Milford Bar Assn., Assn. Trial Lawyers Am., Conn. Trial Lawyers Assn. Personal injury, Workers' compensation, General civil litigation. Office: 28 Park Lane Rd New Milford CT 06776-2908

**GUERIN, JOHN JOSEPH,** lawyer; b. L.A., Mar. 24, 1926; s. Joseph Paul Guerin and Margaret E. Jones; m. Nadine Susan Martinez, Nov. 1, 1963; children: Alfred, Teresa, Yvonne, Edward, Arthur, Nina, Jo Jo, Mike, Tom, Kegis. Student, Colo. U., 1944-46; JD, Loyola U., 1949. Bar: Calif. 1949, U.S. Supreme Ct. 1975. With Guerin, McKay & Tendler, L.A., 1949-50, Robinson, Guerin & Powers, L.A., 1950-52; ptnr. Guerin & Guerin, L.A., 1952-62; pvt. practice L.A., 1962-68, Huntington Beach, Calif., 1968—. ROTC Capt. USN, 1944-46; capt. USAF Res., 1950-57. Mem. ATLA, Consumer Attys. Calif., Orange County Bar. Avocations: horse races, poker, exercise. Appellate, Probate, Entertainment. Office: 1118 Ocean Ave Huntington Beach CA 92648-4817

**GUERKE, I. BARRY,** lawyer; b. Wilmington, Del., Oct. 1, 1948; s. Irvin Philip and Lois Eileen (Lynch) G.; m. Carol Ann Smith, July 4, 1970 (div. Jan. 1988); children: Kelly M., Kevin A., Casey R.; m. Eileen K. Phillips, May 10, 1996. BA, U. Del., 1970; JD, Dickinson Sch. of Law, 1973. Bar: Del. 1974, U.S. Dist. Ct. Del. 1974, U.S. Ct. Appeals (3d cir.) 1982. Law clk. Del. Supreme Ct., Wilmington, 1973-74; assoc. Schmittinger & Rodriguez, P.A., Dover, Del., 1974-78; ptnr., prin. Parkowski, Noble & Guerke, P.A., Dover, 1978—; mem. Jud. Nominating Commn., Del., 1987-89, sec., 1989-92; chair Gov.'s Magistrates Screening Com., Del., 1985-87. Contbr. chpt. to book: The Delaware Bar in the Twentieth Century, 1994. Chmn. bd. dirs. Ctrl. Del. YMCA, Dover, 1983-89, 93-94; bd. dirs. YMCA of Del., Inc., Wilmington, 1984-95; campaign bd. dirs. Kent County United Way, Dover, 1985-87. Named Citizen of Yr. Ctrl. Del. YMCA, 1988, Adult Vol. of Yr. Ctrl. Del. YMCA, 1988, 93. Mem. ABA, ATLA, Del. State Bar Assn. (asst. sec. 1981-82, sec. 1982-83, v.p. 1986-87), Kent County Bar Assn. (pres. 1985-86), Del. Trial Lawyers Assn. (bd. govs. 1986-90, 95—). Avocations: scuba diving, sailing, golf, running. Personal injury, General civil litigation. Home: 400 Quail Run Camden Wyoming DE 19934-9550 Office: Parkowski Noble & Guerke PA 116 W Water St Dover DE 19904-6739

**GUERRA, ROLANDO GILBERTO, JR.,** lawyer, mediator, arbitrator; b. Dupo, Ill., Aug. 19, 1960; s. Rolando Gilberto and Maria Esther Guerra; m. Krista Garcia, July 2, 1994; children: Sophia, Isabella. BA cum laude, Tulane U., 1982; JD, Stetson U., St. Petersburg, Fla., 1986. Bar: Fla. 1986, U.S. Dist. Ct. (mid. dist.) Fla. 1986, U.S. Ct. Appeals (11th cir.) 1986; cert. mediator, Fla. Asst. state atty. Office State Atty. for 13th Circuit, Tampa, Fla., 1986-90; assoc. Beltz, Ruth Newman, St. Petersburg, 1990-91, 92-95; ptnr. Gutman & Guerra, P.A., Tampa, 1991; assoc. Law Office Henry Bardi, Tampa, 1995—; faculty adviser Nat. Coll. Dist. Attys., 1989; mem. faculty Fla. Pros. Attys. Assn., 1988; arbitrator on lemon law Office Atty. Gen., Tampa, 1998. Mem. Fla. Bar, Hillsborough County Bar Assn. Republican. Roman Catholic. Avocations: racquetball, scuba diving, travel. State civil litigation, Insurance, Personal injury. Home: 3117 W Hawthorne Rd Tampa FL 33611-2935 Office: Law Office Henry Bardi 500 N Westshore Blvd Tampa FL 33609-5005

**GUERRIERI, JOSEPH, JR.,** lawyer; b. Detroit, June 11, 1947; s. Joseph Guerrieri; m. Ursula Annemarie Koch, Aug. 30, 1969; children: Joseph III, Justin Matthew. BA, U. Mich., 1969; JD with honors, George Washington U., 1972. Bar: D.C. 1973, U.S. Ct. Appeals (2d, 3d, 4th, 5th, 6th, 7th, 8th and D.C. cirs.), U.S. Supreme Ct. Law clk. to Hon. Nicholas S. Nunzio, 1972-73; asst. U.S. atty. D.C., 1973-77; ptnr. Guerrieri Edmond & Clayman, Washington, 1985—. Fellow ABA (co-chmn. railway and airline labor com. 1982-85, union adminstrn. and procedure com. 1988-91, law and employment sect.), Coll. Labor and Employment Law; mem. D.C. Bar Assn. Federal civil litigation, Labor. Office: Guerrieri Edmond & Clayman Ste 700 1625 Massachusetts Ave NW Washington DC 20036-2243

**GUERRY, WILLIAM,** lawyer; b. Norfolk, Va., Apr. 3, 1961; s. William M. and Russell Adelia (Bradford) G.; m. Samantha Semerad, Sept. 8, 1990; 1 child, William. BA, U. Va., 1983, JD, 1986. Bar: Va. 1987, DC 1988, U.S. Ct. Appeals (fed. cir.). Law clk. Justice Russell Supreme Ct. Va., Richmond, 1986-87; from assoc. to ptnr. Collier Shannon, Washington, 1987—. Environmental. Office: Collier Shannon 3050 K St NW Washington DC 20007-5108

**GUESS, JAMES DAVID,** lawyer; b. Lampasas, Tex., Jan. 21, 1941; s. David Ira and Lila Blanch (Reagan) G.; m. Susan Lawyer, Dec. 19, 1981; children: Corey, Stephanie, Casey, Chris. BS in Edn., Southwestern U., 1963; JD, St. Mary's U., 1968. Bar: Tex. 1968, U.S. Dist. Ct. (we. dist.) Tex. 1974, U.S. Ct. Appeals (5th cir.) 1974, U.S. Dist. Ct. (so. dist.) Tex. 1978, U.S. Dist. Ct. (no. dist.) Tex. 1982. Assoc. Groce Locke & Hebdon, San Antonio, 1968-74, ptnr., 1975-86; shareholder Groce Locke & Hebdon P.C., San Antonio, 1986-96, Jenkens & Gilchrist, San Antonio, 1996-99, Law Offices of James D. Guess, San Antonio, 1999—; sustaining mem. Products Liability Adv. Coun.; mem. Am. Bd. Trial Advs. With USN, 1961-67, Vietnam. Mem. Tex. Assn. Def. Coun. (past pres.), Def. Rsch. Inst. (bd. dirs. 1998—), Internat. Assn. Def. Counsel. Avocations: sports, golf, hunting. Aviation, Product liability. Home: 13318 Southwalk St San Antonio TX 78232-4843 Office: Law Offices James D Guess 8620 N New Braunfels Ave San Antonio TX 78217-6361

**GUEST, ABBI TAYLOR,** lawyer, judge, educator; b. Plainview, N.Y., Oct. 28, 1966; d. Leonard and Kelli Taylor; m. John Bradford, June 6, 1998; 1 child, Maryann Nicole. BA, New Coll., Sarasota, Fla., 1988; JD, Mercer U., Macon, Ga., 1991. Bar: Ga. 1991, Fla. 1991, U.S. Ct. Appeals (11th cir.) 1991, U.S. Dist. Ct. (no. dist.) Ga. Atty. Fain Mayor & Wiley, Atlanta, 1991-92, Office of Deklab County Pub. Defender, Decatur, Ga., 1992-95; magistrate judge Dekalb County, Decatur, 1997—; atty. Peters Roberts Borusk & Guest, Decatur, 1995—; adj. prof. law Ga. State U., Atlanta, 1998—. Mem. GACDL (area v.p. 1996—, chmn. membership com. 1997—), Nat. Assn. Criminal Def. Lawyers, Dekalb Bar Assn. (chmn. Law Day 1995), Ga. Trial Practice and Litigation. Criminal, Juvenile, Appellate. Office: Peters Roberts Borusk & Guest 2786 N Decatur Rd Ste 245 Decatur GA 30033-5983

**GUEST, BRIAN MILTON,** lawyer; b. Vineland, N.J., Mar. 18, 1948; s. Edmund James Jr. and Vivian D. Guest. AB in Polit. Sci. with distinction, Rutgers U., 1970; JD, Boston U., 1973. Bar: N.J. 1973, U.S. Dist. Ct. N.J. 1973, U.S. Supreme Ct. 1978, U.S. Ct. Appeals (3d cir.) 1981; diplomate N.J. Mcpl. Govt. Law, 1994. Assoc. Hartman & Schlesinger, Mt. Holly, N.J., 1973-78; ptnr. Hartman & Schlesinger, Mt. Holly, 1978-82, Bookbinder & Guest, Burlington, N.J., 1982-83, Bookbinder, Guest & Domzalski, Burlington, 1983-90, Guest, Domzalski, Kurts & Langraf, Burlington, 1990-91, Guest, Domzalski, Kurts, Landgraf & McNeill, Burlington & Cherry Hill, N.J., 1991-94, Kearns, Vassallo, Guest & Kearns, Willingboro, N.J., 1994—; pres. Raritan Sigma Phi Epsilon Corp., New Brunswick, N.J., 1983-89, trustee, 1982-92. Bd. dirs. Drenk Mental Health Svcs., Inc., 1996—; trustee 1st United Meth. Ch., Moorestown, N.J., 1995-97, Meml. Health Alliance, 1999—. Mem. ABA, Trial Attys. N.J., N.J. Bar Assn. (gen. counsel del. 1983-86), Burlington County Bar Assn. (trustee 1982-84), Burlington County C. of C. (bd. dirs. 1987—, treas. 1989, v.p. 1990, pres. 1991), Masons (worshipful master Mt. Holly club 1982), Rotary, Sigma Phi Epsilon (trustee 1982-91). Land use and zoning (including planning), Probate, Real property. Office: Kearns Vassallo Guest & Kearns 630 Beverly Rancocas Rd Willingboro NJ 08046-3736

**GUETHLEIN, WILLIAM O.,** lawyer; b. Cin., May 4, 1927; s. William O. and Catherine (Sandmann) G.; m. Bette Mivelaz, Aug. 4, 1961 (dec. 1974). LLD, U. Louisville, 1950. Bar: Ky. 1950, U.S. Dist. Ct. Ky. 1954, U.S. Ct. Appeals (6th cir.) 1954. Assoc. Boehl Stopher and Graves, Louisville, 1950-60, sr. ptnr., 1960—. Lt. USAR, 1952-60. Fellow Am. Acad. Trial Lawyers; mem. ABA, Jefferson County Bar Assn., Ky. Bar Assn., Am. Assn. Hosp. Attys. Avocation: tennis. Federal civil litigation, State civil litigation, Environmental. Office: Boehl Stopher & Graves Aegon Ctr 400 W Market St Ste 2300 Louisville KY 40202-3366

**GUEVARA, ROGER,** lawyer; b. San Antonio, Nov. 1, 1954; s. Joe Martinez and Lupe (Zamudio) G.; m. Alma Lou Cuellar, June 13, 1972; children: Roger Anton I, Fennelle Nicole, Brianna Camille. Assoc. degree, San Antonio Coll., 1978; BA, St. Mary's U., San Antonio, 1980; JD, Thurgood Marshall Sch. Law, 1984. Bar: Tex. 1985, U.S. Dist. Ct. (we. dist.) Tex. 1987, U.S. Ct. Appeals (fed. and 5th cirs.) 1986. Pvt. practice San Antonio. Mem. ABA, San Antonio Bar Assn., Tex. Trial Lawyers, Assn. Trial Lawyers Am. Personal injury, Insurance. Office: 3114 W Commerce St San Antonio TX 78207-3722

**GUFFEY, DOUGLAS OLIVER,** lawyer; b. Boise, Nov. 30, 1951; s. Ellsworth Grover and Melba Jane (Roberts) G.; m. Teddylen Alisha Mincks, June 21, 1975; children: L. Bryant, Rhiannon A., Andreana T. BS, Ariz. State U., 1974; MBA, JD, Harvard U., 1978. Bar: Ariz. 1978. From assoc. to ptnr. Streich, Lang, Weeks & Cardon, Phoenix, 1982-94; exec. dir. Sun Med. Mgmt., Mesa, Ariz., 1996—; pvt. practice Mesa, 1994—. Author: (with others) Enforcing Secured Claims in Arizona, 1987. Served to capt. U.S. Army, 1978-82. Republican. Club: Harvard Bus. Sch. (Phoenix). Avocation: reading. Finance, Contracts commercial, Health. Office: Sun Med Management LC 1454 S Dobson Rd Ste 1 Mesa AZ 85202-4707

**GUGGENHEIM, MARTIN FRANKLIN,** law educator, lawyer; b. N.Y.C., May 29, 1946; s. Werner and Fanny (Monatt) G.; m. Denise Silverman, May 29, 1969; children—Jamie, Courtney, Lesley. BA, SUNY-Buffalo, 1968; JD, NYU, 1971. Bar: N.Y. 1972, U.S. Dist. Ct. (so. dist. and ea. dist.) N.Y. 1973, U.S. Ct. Appeals (2d cir.) 1974, U.S. Ct. Appeals (3d cir.) 1979, U.S. Ct. Appeals (6th cir.) 1977, U.S. Supreme Ct. 1976. Staff atty. Legal Aid Soc., N.Y.C., 1971-72, dir. spl. litigation unit, juvenile rights div., 1972-73; clin. instr. NYU Sch. Law, N.Y.C., 1973-75; staff atty. juvenile rights project ACLU, N.Y.C., 1975-79, acting dir., 1976-77; asst. prof. clin. law NYU, N.Y.C., 1975-77, assoc. prof. clin. law, 1977-79, prof. clin. law, 1980—; exec. dir. Washington Sq. Legal Services, Inc., N.Y.C., 1986—; pres., founding dir. Family Def. Law Project, Inc., N.Y.C., 1992—; advisor program for children Edna McConnell Clark Found., 1993—; dir. clin. and advocacy programs, NYU, 1989—; cons. juvenile justice standards project ABA/Inst. Jud. Adminstrn., 1979-81; acting dir. Clin. Advocacy Programs, Sch. of Law N.Y.U., 1988-89. Author: (with Alan Sussman) The Rights of Parents, 1980; Abuse and Neglect Volume, 1982; The Rights of Young People, 2d edit., 1985, (with Anthony G. Amsterdam and Randy Hertz) Trial Manual for Defense Attorneys in Juvenile Court, 1991, (with Alexandra Lowe and Diane Curtis) The Rights of Families, 1996. Dir. William J. Brennan Ctr., NYU, 1995—, adv. bd. N.Y.C. Adminstrn. Children, 1997—. Arthur Garfield Hays Civil Liberties fellow, 1970-71, Criminal Law Edn. and Research fellow, 1969-70. Mem. ABA (juvenile justice sect.), Am. Assn. Law Schs. (clin. legal edn. sect.). Office: NYU Sch Law 249 Sullivan St New York NY 10012-1079

**GUGGENHIME, RICHARD JOHNSON,** lawyer; b. San Francisco, Mar. 6, 1940; s Richard E. and Charlotte G.; m. Emlen Hall, June 5, 1965 (div.); children: Andrew, Lisa, Molly; m. Judith Perry Swift, Oct. 3, 1992. AB in Polit. Sci. with distinction, Stanford U., 1961; JD, Harvard U., 1964. Bar: Calif. 1965, U.S. Dist. Ct. (no. dist.) Calif. 1965, U.S. Ct. Appeals (9th cir.) 1965. Assoc. Heller, Ehrman, White & McAuliffe, 1965-71, ptnr., 1972—; spl. asst. to U.S. Senator Hugh Scott, 1964; bd. dirs. Comml. Bank of San Francisco, 1980-81, Global Savs. Bank, San Francisco, 1984-86, North Am. Trust Co., 1996-99. Mem. San Francisco Bd. Permit Appeals, 1978-86; bd. dirs. Marine World Africa USA, 1980-86; mem. San Francisco Fire Commn., 1986-88, Recreation and Parks Commn., 1988-92; chmn. bd. trustees San Francisco Univ. High Sch., 1987-90; trustee St. Ignatius Prep. Sch., San Francisco, 1987-96. Mem. Am. Coll. Probate Counsel, San Francisco Opera Assn. (bd. dir.), Bohemian Club, Wine and Food Soc. Club, Olympic Club, Chevaliers du Tastevin Club (San Francisco), Thunderbird Country Club (Rancho Mirage, Calif.). Probate, Estate planning. Home: 2621 Larkin St San Francisco CA 94109-1512 Office: Heller Ehrman White & McAuliffe 333 Bush St San Francisco CA 94104-2806

**GUICE, STEPHEN W.,** lawyer; b. Woodbury, N.J., Feb. 18, 1958; s. Marvin Ray and Shirley Guice. BS, Wagner Coll., 1980; JD, Rutgers U., 1984. Bar: N.J. 1984, Pa. 1984, U.S. Ct. Appeals (3d cir.) 1984, U.S. Supreme Ct. 1989. Law clk. Gloucester County Superior Ct., Woodbury, N.J., 1984-85; assoc. Horn, Goldnbery, Gorny, Daniels, Atlantic City, 1985-86, Friedman, Bafundo & Porter, Cherry Hill, N.J., 1986-92; pvt. practice, Barrington, N.J., 1992—. Avocations: volleyball, skiing. Personal injury, Real property, Municipal (including bonds). Office: 413 Clements Bridge Rd Barrington NJ 08007-1809

**GUILD, IRENE LILLIAN,** attorney general; b. Milford, Mass., May 27, 1949; d. Roy Prescott and Sara Lucretia (Snyer) Stone; children: Gregory Howe Jr., Daniel David. BS in Criminal Justice, Westfield State Coll., 1989; JD, Boston U., 1991, MA in Hist. Preservation, 1992. Bar: Mass. 1991, U.S. Supreme Ct. 1996. Asst. Office Atty. Gen., Boston, 1992—. With U.S. Army, 1974-75. Mem. ABA, Mass. Bar Assn. (property law sect. 1995—), Mass. Conveyancer's Assn., Norwood Hist. Soc., Nat. Trust Historic Preservation, N.E. Legal Preservation Network, U.S. Supreme Ct. Hist. Soc. Avocations: writing, mountain biking, hiking, internet. Home: 9 Kimball Ct Natick MA 01760-4461 Office: Office Atty Gen 200 Portland St Boston MA 02114-1722

**GUILFORD, ANDREW JOHN,** lawyer; b. Santa Monica, Calif., Nov. 28, 1950; s. Howard Owens and Elsie Jennette (Hargreaves) G.; m. Loreen Mary Gogain, Dec. 22, 1973; children: Colleen Catherine, Amanda Joy. AB summa cum laude, UCLA, 1972, JD, 1975. Bar: Calif. 1975, U.S. Dist. Ct. (cen. dist.) Calif. 1976, U.S. Ct. Appeals (9th cir.) 1976, U.S. Supreme Ct. 1979, U.S. Dist. Ct. (so. dist.) Calif. 1981, U.S. Dist. Ct. (no. and ea. dists.) Calif. 1990. Assoc. Sheppard, Mullin, Richter & Hampton, L.A. and Orange County, Calif., 1975-82; ptnr. Sheppard, Mullin, Richter & Hampton, Orange County, 1983—; lectr. The Rutter Group, Encino, Calif., 1983—, Continuing Edn. of the Bar, Berkeley, 1978—, Hastings Ctr. for Advocacy, San Francisco, 1988; judge pro tem, arbitrator Calif. Superior Ct., 1983—; mem. commn. future legal profession and state bar. Author UCLA Law Review, 1975. Mem. Amicus Publico, Santa Ana, Calif., 1986; bd. dirs. Constl. Rights Found., 1990, Pub. Law Ctr. Orange County, 1990—, Baroque Music Festival, 1992-96, NCCJ, 1995-99, UCLA Law Alumni Assn., 1992-95; subdeacon, warden, del. Episcopal Ch. Recipient resolution of commendation Calif. Assembly, Outstanding Svc. award Poverty Law Ctr., 1991; co-recipient President's Pro Bono award State Bar; Regents scholar U. Calif., Berkeley, 1968-72. Fellow Am. Coll. Trial Lawyers; mem. ABA, FBA, Assn. Bus. Trial Lawyers (founding officer Orange County chpt.), Am. Arbitration Assn. (arbitrator large complex case program 1993—), Calif. Bar Assn. (pres. 1999—, lectr. continuing edn. of bar 1978—, bd. govs. 1996—), Orange County Bar Assn. (bd. dirs. 1985-87, officer 1988-90, pres. 1991, chmn. bus. litigation sect. 1983, state bar conv. 1986, 87, law-motion com. 1982, standing com. trial ct. delay reduction 1987-93), 9th Cir. Jud. Conf. (rep. 1990-93, 99—), Phi Beta Kappa (sec.-treas. 1978-80, v.p. 1980-84), Pi Gamma Mu, Sigma Pi. Republican. Avocations: theater, photography, sports, gardening, poetry. State civil litigation, Federal civil litigation, Alternative dispute resolution. Home: 23 Via Terracaleta Coto De Caza CA 92679-4016 Office: Sheppard Mullin Richter & Hampton 650 Town Center Dr Fl 4 Costa Mesa CA 92626-1993

**GUILLORY, JEFFERY MICHAEL,** lawyer; b. Kansas City, Mo., July 26, 1966; s. Glenford Lee and Brenda Charlene (Thomas) G.; m. Leanna Carol Rainbolt, Aug. 10, 1991. Student, Mo. So. State Coll., Joplin, 1984-86; BA in Polit. Sci., Ctrl. Meth. Coll., Fayette, Mo., 1988; JD, U. Ark., 1991. Bar: Mo. 1991, U.S. Dist. Ct. (we. dist.) Mo. 1991, U.S. Supreme Ct. 1994. Law clk. Hall, Wright & Baker, P.A., Fayetteville, Ark., 1989-91; assoc. atty. Law Office of Allan C. Wilcox, Joplin, 1991-92; ptnr. Wilcox & Guillory, Joplin, 1992-95; assoc. atty. Roberts, Fleischaker, Williams, Wilson & Powell, Joplin, 1995-97; pvt. practice Law Office Jeffery M. Guillory, Joplin, 1997—; adj. prof. Mo. So. State Coll., 1995—. Bd. dirs., v.p. Habitat for Humanity, 1996—; property trustee United Meth. Ch. Mo. West Conf., 1996—; asst. scoutmaster Boy Scouts Am., Joplin, 1991—; chmn. bd. Discovery Presch., 1996-98. Mem. ABA, ATLA, Am. Immigration Lawyers Assn., Mo. Bar Assn., Mo. Assn. Trial Lawyers, Jasper County Bar Assn., Kiwanis. Avocations: camping, travel, skiing, volleyball, arts and crafts. Personal injury, Workers' compensation, General practice. Office: PO Box 1613 Joplin MO 64802-1613

**GUILLORY, ROBERT E.,** lawyer; b. New Orleans, July 7, 1952; mem. Maureen Kaough. BA, McNeese State U., 1974; JD, La. State U., 1976. Bar: La. 1976. Law clk. to chief judge La. Ct. Appeals (3d cir.), 1976-77; ptnr. Guillory & McCall, Lake Charles, La., 1980—. Bd. dirs. Lake Charles chpt. Coastal Conservation Assn.; mem. La. Wildlife Fedn., Ducks Unltd., Arts and Humanities Coun. S.W. La. Fellow La. Bar Found.; mem. ABA (ho. dels. 1998—), S.W. La. Bar Assn. (pres. 1995-96), La. State Bar Assn. (pres.-elect 1998—, bd. govs. 1996-98, civil law and litig. sects., legal malpractice ins. com., environ. law com., ins. com., negligence compensation and admiralty law com., civil law com., labor and employment law com.), Nat. Conf. Bar Pres., So. Conf. Bar Pres., S.W. La. Assn. Def. Coun., La. Assn. Def. Counsel, Def. Rsch. Inst., La. Bar Found., Phi Kappa Phi, Delta Theta Phi. Avocations: duck hunting, water sports, reading. Office: Guillory & McCall LLC 901 Lake Shore Dr Lake Charles LA 70601-5276*

**GUIMERA, IRENE MERMELSTEIN,** lawyer; b. Bklyn., Dec. 19, 1953; d. Morris and Leona (Silverman) Mermelstein; m. Joseph E. Guimera, Oct. 20, 1976; 1 child, Stephanie. BA, NYU, 1974; JD, Columbia U., 1977. Bar: N.Y. 1978, Calif. 1981, U.S. Dist. Ct. (so. and ea. dists.) N.Y. 1978, U.S. Dist. Ct. (cen. dist.) Calif. 1981, U.S. Dist. Ct. (so. dist.) Calif. 1982; lic. real estate broker, Calif. Assoc. Golenbock & Barell, N.Y.C., 1977-79; atty. Gen. Instrument Corp., N.Y.C., 1979-80, System Devel. Corp., Santa Monica, Calif., 1981-84; ptnr. Guimera & Guimera, Manhattan Beach, Calif., 1984—. Contbr. articles to legal publs. Harlan Fiske Stone scholar Columbia U., 1975-77. Fellow Nat. Contract Mgmt. Assn. (v.p. Calif.-South Bay chpt. 1985-86); mem. ABA, Calif. Bar Assn., L.A. County Bar Assn., Phi Beta Kappa. Government contracts and claims, General corporate, Real property. Office: Guimera & Guimera Ste 200 225 S Sepulveda Blvd Manhattan Beach CA 90266-6865

**GUIN, DON LESTER,** insurance company executive; b. Shreveport, La., Nov. 5, 1940; s. Lester and Ethelyn (Dumas) G.; m. Mary Ann Guin, Feb. 3, 1979. BBA in Ins., U. Ga., 1962; BS in Law, Kensington U., Glendale, Calif., 1987, JD, 1989. Bar: Calif. 1990, U.S. Ct. Appeals (5th and 9th cirs.) 1990, U.S. Dist. Ct. (no. dist.) Calif. 1990, U.S. Ct. Appeals (fed. cir.) 1991, U.S. Dist. Ct. (ea. dist.) Tex. 1991, U.S. Ct. Internat. Trade 1991, U.S. Ct. Fed. Claims 1992, U.S. Supreme Ct. 1994. Adjuster, supr. Lindsey & Newsom, Beaumont, Tex., 1963-71; mgr. Lindsey & Newsom, Port Arthur, Tex., 1968-71; asst. to pres. Lindsey & Newsom, Tyler, Tex., 1971-74, v.p. ops., 1977-84, sr. v.p., 1984—; sr. v.p. adminstrn. and legal Lindsey Morden, 1990—; sr. v.p., corp. sec. Lindsey Morden Claims Svc. Inc., Lindsey Morden Claims Mgmt., 1992-93, sr. v.p., treas. U.S. Ops., 1993—, sr. v.p., corp. treas., chief legal officer, 1995—; sr. v.p., corp. treas. and sec. Vale Nat. Training Ctrs, Inc., 1993—; sr. v.p., corp. treas, corp. sec., chief legal officer, 1995—; bd. dirs. Lindsey Morden Claims Svc., Inc., Lindsey Morden Claims Mgmt., Inc., exec. com., mgmt. com., compensation com., incentive com., Vale Nat. Tng. Ctrs., Lindsey & Newsom Inc.; trustee Lindsey and Newsom Benefit Trusts, 1990-91, plan adminstr. Lindsey Morden Profit Sharing Retirement Trust, 1994, Lindsey & Newsom Retirement Funds, 1990—; sr. v.p., corp. sec., CLO Lindsey Morden Group, Inc., 1996—; mem. adv. bd. Kemper Ins. Group; sr. v.p., corp. sec. Lindsey & Newsom, Vale Nat; bd. dirs. Tyler Mus. Art, chmn. pers. policy com., chair fin. com., 1999. Author: Analysis of Garage Liability, 1972, Dishonesty Claims Handling, 1973, Casualty Reporting Manual, 1975, Sexual Harassment in the Workplace, 1986, (audio cassette) Beating the Bears of Bad Faith, 1991, (video cassette) Bad Faith and Preventing Errors and Omissions Claims, 1987. Trustee Lindsey Morden Benefit Trusts, Lindsey Morden Retirement Trusts, 1992—; dir. assoc. U. Tex Health Ctr., 1995; budget allocation panelist United Way Tyler/Smith County, Tex., 1995; bd. dirs. Tyler Mus. of Art, 1996. Mem. ABA (internat. law sect., corp. law sect.), Can. Bar Assn., Nat. Assn. Def. Counsel, Nat. Assn. Ind. Ins. Adjusters (data processing com. 1976, legis. com. 1990), Bar Assn. D.C., Bar Assn. U.S. Fed. Cir., Defense Inst. Trial Lawyers Assn. (ins. law com.), State Bar Calif. (internat. law sect., tort sect., litigation sect., labor and employment law sect.), Nat. Employee Benefit Found., Def. Rsch. Inst., Alameda County Bar Assn., Inter-Pacific Bar Assn., Italian-Am. Bar Assn., Bar Assn. 5th Fed. Cir., Optimist Club, Kiwanis Club, Sabre Club, Lawyers Club San Francisco, Ins. Soc. U. Ga. (charter mem.), Circle K-Kiwanis. Home: 17389 Hidden Valley Ln Flint TX 75762-9611 Office: Lindsey Morden Claims Svcs Inc 211 Brookside Dr Tyler TX 75711

**GUIN, JUNIUS FOY, JR.,** federal judge; b. Russellville, Ala., Feb. 2, 1924; s. Junius Foy and Ruby (Pace) G.; m. Dorace Jean Caldwell, July 18, 1945; children: Janet Elizabeth Smith, Judith Ann Mullican, Junius Foy III, David Jonathan. Student, Ga. Inst. Tech., 1940-41; AB magna cum laude, U. Ala., JD, 1947; LLD, Magic Valley Christian Coll., 1963. Bar: Ala. 1948. Pvt. practice law Russellville; sr. ptnr. Guin, Guin, Bouldin & Porch, 1948-73; fed. dist. judge U.S. Dist. Ct. (no. dist.) Ala., Birmingham, from 1973, now sr. judge; commr. Ala. Bar, 1965-73, 2d v.p., 1969-70; Pres. Abstract Trust Co., Inc., 1958-73; sec. Iuka TV Cable Co., Inc., Haleyville TV Cable Co., Inc., 1963-73; former dir., gen. counsel First Nat. Bank of Russellville, Franklin Fed. Savs. & Loan Assn. of Russellville.; Lectr. Cumberland-Samford Sch. Law, 1974—, U. Ala. Sch. Law, 1977—. Chmn. Russellville City Planning Com., 1954-57; 1st chmn. Jud. Commn. Ala., 1972-73; mem. Ala. Supreme Ct. Adv. Com. (rules civil procedure), 1971-73; mem. adv. com. on standards of conduct U.S. Jud. Conf., 1980-87, mem. com. on Fed.-State Jurisdiction, 1982-88, mem. ad hoc com. on cameras in the courtroom, 1982-83; Rep. county chmn., 1954-58, 71-72, Rep. state fin. chmn., 1972-73; candidate for U.S. Senator from, Ala., 1954; Ala. Lawyers' Finance chmn. Com. to Re-elect Pres., 1972; former trustee Ala. Christian Coll., Faulkner U., Magic Valley Christian Coll., Childhaven Children's Home; elder Ch. of Christ. Served to 1st lt., inf. AUS, 1943-46. Named Russellville Citizen of Year, 1973; recipient Dean's award U. Ala. Law Sch., 1977. Mem. ABA (mem. spl. com. on resdl. real estate transactions 917-73), Am. Radio Relay League, Ala. Bar Assn. (com. chmn. 1965-73, Award of Merit 1973), Jefferson County Bar Assn., Fed. Bar Assn., Am. Law Inst., Ala. Law Inst. (dir. 1969-73, 76—), Am. Judicature Soc., Farrah Law Soc., Farrah Order Jurisprudence (now Order of Coif), Phi Beta Kappa, Omicron Delta Kappa, Delta Chi. Office: US Dist Ct 619 US Courthouse 1729 5th Ave N Birmingham AL 35203-2000

**GUINN, CHARLES CLIFFORD, JR.,** lawyer; b. Ducktown, Tenn., Oct. 8, 1935; s. Charles Clifford and Rena (Taylor) G.; m. Virginia Julia Barham, June 14, 1985; children: Marcus, Elizabeth, Barry. BA, Tenn. Wesleyan U., 1961; JD, U. Tenn., 1971. Bar: Tenn. 1971, U.S. Dist. Ct. (ea. dist.) Tenn. 1972, U.S. Ct. Appeals (6th cir.) 1976. Pvt. practice, trial lawyer Athens, 1971—; city judge City of Athens, Tenn., 1973-85; gen. sessions judge County of McMinn, Athens, 1985-87; city atty. City of Etowah, Tenn., 1987—; atty. utility bd. Etowah Utilities Dept., 1973—. With USAF, 1955-58. General practice, Municipal (including bonds), Public utilities. Home: Old Madisonville Rd Athens TN 37303 Office: Charles C Guinn Atty PO Box 946 4 W Washington Ave Athens TN 37303-3543

**GUINN, STANLEY WILLIS,** lawyer; b. Detroit, June 9, 1953; s. Willis Hampton and Virginia Mae (Pierson) G.; m. Patricia Shirley Newgord, June 13, 1981; children: Terri Lanae, Scott Stanley. BBA with high distinction, U. Mich., 1979, MBA with distinction, 1981; MS in Taxation with distinction, Walsh Coll., 1987; JD cum laude, U. Mich., 1992. CPA, Mich.; cert. mgmt. acct., Mich. Tax mgr. Coopers & Lybrand, Detroit, 1981-87; tax cons. Upjohn Co., Kalamazoo, 1987-89; litigation atty. Brobeck, Phleger & Harrison, 1992-94, Coughlan, Semmer & Lipman, San Diego, 1994-95; consumer fin. atty. Bank Am. NT & SA, San Francisco, 1995-98, Green Point Credit Corp., San Diego, 1998—. Served with USN, 1974-77. Mem. AICPA, ABA, Calif. State Bar Assn., Inst. Cert. Mgmt. Acctg., Phi Kappa Phi, Beta Gamma Sigma, Beta Alpha Psi, Delta Mu Delta. Republican. Presbyterian. Avocations: tennis, racquetball, running. E-mail: sguinn@gp-credit.com. Consumer commercial, General civil litigation, Taxation, general. Home: 3125 Crystal Ct Escondido CA 92025-7763 Office: Green Pt Credit Corp 10089 Willow Creek Rd San Diego CA 92131-1603

**GUINN, SUSAN LEE,** lawyer; b. Langhorne, Pa., July 22, 1965; d. Walter William and Setsuko (Yamada) G. BSN, U. N.Mex., 1988; JD, U. Denver, 1991. Bar: Calif. 1991, U.S. Dist. Ct. Calif. (so. and cen. dists.) 1991. Ptnr. Robinson, Phillips & Calcagnie, San Diego, 1992—. Mem. ATLA (sustaining mem., polit. action mgmt. com. 1995, publ. com. 1993—, product liability sect. 1997—), Calif. Trial Lawyers Assn. (bd. govs. 1994—, chair women's caucus 1995, edn. com. 1994-95), Attys. Info. Exch. Group, Western Trial Lawyers Assn. (bd. govs., edn. chmn. 1993—), San Diego Trial Lawyers Assn. (sustaining mem.). Avocations: skiing, hiking, reading. General civil litigation, Personal injury, Product liability. Office: Robinson Phillips & Calcagnie 110 Laurel St San Diego CA 92101-1419

**GULDI, REBECCA ELIZABETH,** lawyer; b. Boston, Nov. 26, 1969; d. Richard L. and Sara S. (Pearce) G. BA with distinction, U. Mich., 1992, JD, 1995. Bar: Tex. 1995. Assoc. Locke Liddell & Sapp LLP, Dallas, 1995-99; asst. gen. counsel Software Spectrum, Inc., Garland, Tex., 1999—; dir. Dallas Legal Hospice, 1996—. Mem. Dallas Assn. Young Lawyers (co-chair AIDS Legal Assistance com. 1996—, mock trial com. 1998—), Dallas Bar Assn. General corporate, Securities, Mergers and acquisitions. Office: Software Spectrum Inc 2140 Merrill Dr Garland TX 75041

**GULECAS, JAMES FREDERICK,** lawyer, author; b. Natick, Mass., Jan. 6, 1959; s. Lazarus Harry and Sarah Adeline Gulecas; m. Grace Binlero Orcine, Dec. 26, 1984. BA, Dartmouth Coll., 1981; JD, MBA, U. Calif., Davis, 1994; LLM in Taxation, U. Fla., 1995. Bar: Fla. 1995. Assoc. Alan S. Gassman, P.A., Clearwater, Fla., 1996—. Contbr. articles to profl. jours. Lt. USN, 1982-89. Mem. ABA, Clearwater Bar Assn., Pinellas County Estate Planning Coun., Am. Legion. Estate planning, Estate taxation, Probate. Office: Alan S Gassman PA 1245 Court St Ste 1245 Clearwater FL 33756-5856

**GULICK, PETER VANDYKE,** lawyer; b. Honolulu, Feb. 15, 1930; s. Willard Clark and Harriet (Winch) G.; m. Kathryn Christen, June 23, 1952 (div. Mar. 1987); children: Willard, Sarah, Scott. AB, Princeton U., 1952; postgrad. Stanford U., 1952-53; LLB, U. Wash., 1956. Bar: Wash. 1956, U.S. Dist. Ct. (we. dist.) Wash. 1956, U.S. Ct. Appeals (9th cir.) 1957. Mem. Foster, Pepper & Riviera, Seattle, 1956-78; pvt. practice, Bellevue, Wash., 1979—. Scoutmaster, dist. Round Table commr., chief Seattle coun. Boy Scouts Am., 1971-77; pres. Lake Heights Community Club, 1960; commr. Newport Hills Sewer Dist., 1966-72. Recipient dist. merit award Boy Scouts Am., 1976. Mem. Wash. State Bar Assn., Seattle-King County Bar Assn. Real property, Contracts commercial, General corporate. Office: 1380 112th NE Ste 202 Bellevue WA 98004-3759

**GULINO, FRANK,** lawyer; b. Bklyn., Aug. 14, 1954; s. Frank C. and Frances (Cataldo) G.; m. Donna Regina Cramer, June 30, 1984; children: Frank Regis, Mary Elise. BA, NYU, 1976; JD, Fordham U., 1979. Bar: N.Y. 1980, U.S. Dist. Ct. (no., so. ea. and we. dists.) N.Y. 1980, U.S. Tax Ct. 1980, U.S. Ct. Mil. Appeals 1980, U.S. Ct. Appeals (2d cir.) 1980, U.S. Ct. Internat. Trade 1982, U.S. Supreme Ct. 1983, U.S. Ct. Claims 1985, U.S. Ct. Appeals (8th and fed. cirs.) 1985, D.C. 1986, U.S. Dist. Ct. Nebr. 1986, U.S. Dist. Ct. Hawaii 1986, U.S. Ct. Appeals (3d, 5th, 6th, 7th, 9th, 10th and 11th cirs.) 1986, U.S. Ct. Appeals (D.C. cir.) 1988. Law clk. to U.S. magistrate U.S. Dist. Ct. (so. dist.) N.Y., N.Y.C., 1979-80; assoc. Donovan, Leisure, Newton & Irvine, N.Y.C., 1980-83, Carro, Spanbock, Fass, Geller, Kaster & Cuiffo, N.Y.C., 1984-86; dep. gen. counsel N.Y.C. Housing Authority, 1986-88; assoc. Summit Rovins & Feldesman, N.Y.C., 1988; of counsel Stockfield & Fixler, N.Y.C., 1988-89, ptnr., 1989-91; ptnr. Stockfield, Fixler & Gulino, N.Y.C., 1991-94, Fixler & Gulino, L.L.P., N.Y.C., 1995—; adj. assoc. prof. Fordham U. Sch. Law, N.Y.C., 1983-88. Author: Judgments in Federal Civil Practice, 1989, supplement, 1993. Mem. ABA, Fed. Bar Coun., N.Y. State Bar Assn. (atty. advisor high sch. mock trial program 1980-87), N.Y. State Trial Lawyers Assn., Assn. Trial Lawyers of Am. Insurance, Personal injury, General practice. Office: 222 Broadway New York NY 10038-2510

**GULINSON, GENE GEORGE,** lawyer; b. St. Louis, June 26, 1943; s. Frank Manuel and Lillian G.; m. Francee C. Miller, July 6, 1959; children: Chris, Teri, Tiffany, Scotti Lynn. JD, St. Louis U., 1968. Bar: Mo. 1968, Ariz. 1983, U.S. Dist. Ct. (ea. and we. dist.) Mo. 1968, U.S. Dist. Ct. Ariz. 1985. Asst. prosecuting atty. St. Louis County (Mo.), 1968-71; judge St. George, Mo., 1969-70; pvt. practice Mo., 1971-83, Phoenix, 1983—. Mem. Ariz. Bar Assn., Mo. Bar Assn., Assn. Trial Lawyers Am., 42d Jud. Cir. Bar Assn. (pres. 1971-72), Ariz. Trial Lawyers Assn. (bd. dirs. 1990-91), Personal Injury Trial Lawyers Assn. (pres. 1988-90). Republican. Avocation: baseball. Insurance, Personal injury. Office: 7250 N 16th St Ste 318 Phoenix AZ 85020-5279

**GULLEN, CHRISTOPHER ROY,** lawyer; b. Detroit, Feb. 17, 1950; s. George Edgar and Mary Ruth Gullen; m. Sheila Rae Collins, Aug. 25, 1973; children: Brian Christopher, Katelyn Elizabeth. BA, U. Mich., 1972; JD, Ohio Northern U., 1975. Bar: Mich. 1975, U.S. Dist. Ct. (ea. dist.) Mich. 1975, U.S. Ct. Appeals (6th cir.) 1978. Law clk. Mich. Ct. Appeals, Lansing, 1975-77; ptnr. Gullen & Fitzsimmons, Rochester, Mich., 1977-82, Sarvis, Gullen & Herrmann, Birmingham, Mich., 1982-86; pub. liability atty. Kmart Corp., Troy, Mich., 1986-90; pub. liability counsel Kmart Corp., Troy, 1990—; mediator Oakland County Cir. Ct., 1986—. Author: Rules and Regulations of the Science Court, 1980. Mem. ABA, Mich. Bar Assn. General civil litigation. Office: K Mart Corp 3100 W Big Beaver Rd Troy MI 48084-3163

**GULLY, RUSSELL GEORGE,** lawyer; b. San Angelo, Tex., Feb. 18, 1955; s. Frank Arthur and Dolores Ann (Dierschke) G.; m. Patricia Prost, Aug. 4, 1984; children: Monica, Teresa, Rachel. BA in Math., U. Tex., 1976, MA in Math., 1978, JD, 1984. Bar: Tex. 1984. Computer software instr. Tex. Instruments, Austin, 1978-81; atty. Thompson & Knight, P.C., Dallas, 1984—; state advocate KC, 1996-98. Mem. ABA, S.W. Benefits Assn., Dallas Benefits Soc., Tex. Bar Assn., Dallas Bar Assn. Avocation: Indian princess activities. Pension, profit-sharing, and employee benefits. Office: Thompson & Knight PC 1700 Pacific Ave Ste 330 Dallas TX 75201-7322

**GULOTTA, FRANK ANDREW, JR.,** lawyer; b. N.Y.C., Nov. 2, 1939; s. Frank A. and Josephine M. (Giardina) G.; m. Joanne C. DeLessio, Jan. 29, 1966; children: Lisa, Frank A. BA, Trinity Coll., 1961; JD, Columbia U., 1964. Bar: N.Y. 1965, U.S. Dist. Ct. (ea. dist.) N.Y. 1972, U.S. Supreme Ct. 1970. Asst. dist. atty. Nassau County (N.Y.), 1965-69; prin. Gulotta & Stein, Mineola, N.Y., 1969-95. Dir. Am. Com. Italian Migration; dir. Syosset Little League, 1981-83, Edn. Assistance Corp., 1991-95; mem. Nassau County Police Boys Club; counsel for Sen. Ralph Marino, Com. on Crime, 1979-82. Mem. ABA, Nat. Assn. Criminal Def. Attys., N.Y. State Sheriffs Assn. (grievance com. 10th jud. dist. 1986-95, chmn. 1993-95), N.Y. State Bar Assn., Nassau County Bar Assn. (chmn. grievance com. 1983-85, bd. dirs. 1984—, pres. 1996-97) Criminal Courts Bar Assn., Former Asst. Dist. Attys. Assn. (dir., past pres.), N.Y. State Dist. Atty. Assn., N.Y. State Assn. Criminal Def. Attys., Am. Acad. Profl. Law Enforcement, Nat. Dist. Attys. Assn., Am. Judicature Soc., Columbian Lawyers Assn. (dir.), Am. Diabetes Assn., South Woodbury Civic Assn., Order Sons Itay, Elks, KC. Recipient Frank A. Gullata Criminal Justice award Former Dist. Attys. Assn., Man of Yr. award Middle Earth Crisis Ctr. Roman Catholic. General practice, Criminal, Family and matrimonial. Office: 262 Old Country Rd Mineola NY 11501-4255

**GUMSON, ADAM S.,** laweyr; b. N.Y.C., Mar. 26, 1966; s. Richard P. and Sandra B. Gumson. BA, Duke U., 1988; JD, U. Fla., 1991. Atty. Jupiter (Fla.) Law Ctr. Mem. North Palm Beach Bar Assn. (pres. 1998-99), Palm Beach Bus. Assn. (v.p. 1994-96, pres. 1996-98). General practice. Office: Jupiter Law Ctr 6390 W Indiantown Rd Jupiter FL 33458-4607

**GUNDERSEN, MARK JONATHAN,** lawyer; b. N.Y.C., June 28, 1954; s. Norman George and Dorothy Elaine (Tredge) G.; m. Ellen Janice Tolstuk, Aug. 28, 1982; 1 child, Jeffrey Christopher. BA, Cornell U., 1976; JD, Boston U., 1979. Bar: Mass. 1979, Del. 1980. Sr. counsel E.I. duPont de Nemours & Co., Wilmington, Del., 1979-94; European counsel DuPont Internat. S.A., Geneva, 1984-89; v.p. & gen. counsel DCV Inc., Wilmington, 1994—; atty. Del. Vol. Lawyer Svcs., Wilmington, 1989—. Mem. Pennsbury Twp. Zoning Appeals Bd., Chadds Ford, Pa., 1993—. Mergers and acquisitions, Contracts commercial, General corporate. Office: DCV Inc 3521 Silverside Rd Wilmington DE 19810-4900

**GUNDERSON, BRENT MERRILL,** lawyer; b. Vernal, Utah, Apr. 16, 1960; s. Merrill Ray and Betty Velate (Norton) G.; m. Julie Phillips, Oct. 28, 1983; children: Adam Brent, Jeremy Phillip, Matthew Norton, Hannah, Rachel, Mariah, Kayla. BA, Brigham Young U., 1984; JD, Columbia U., 1987. Bar: Ariz. 1987, U.S. Dist. Ct. Ariz. 1987, U.S. Tax Ct. 1994. Ptnr. Brown & Bain, Phoenix, 1987-96; pvt. practice Mesa, Ariz., 1996—; pres. Ariz. Mgmt. Soc., Phoenix, 1996-97. Asst. dist. commr. Boy Scouts Am., Mesa, Ariz., 1994-97, scoutmaster troop 611, Mesa, 1991-94, troop 761, Mesa, 1999—, chair varsity scout com., 1997-98; precinct capt. Mesa Rep. Precincts 47 & 17, 1988-94; cubmaster pack 761, Boy Scouts Am., 1998-99. Recipient Mesa Dist. award of Merit, 1997, Scoutmaster award of Merit Boy Scouts Am., 1992, named to Scout Leader Hall of Fame, 1993. Mem. Am. Immigration Lawyers Assn. (v.p. Ariz. chpt. 1992-93, Maricopa County Bar Found. (bd. dirs. 1991-95), East Valley Estate Planning Coun. (bd. dirs. 1997-99, pres. 1999—), Am. Immigration Lawyers Assn., Ariz. Mgmt. Soc. (bd. dirs. 1997—). Mem. LDS Ch. Avocations: backpacking, fishing, China. Estate planning, Immigration, naturalization, and customs, Probate. Office: Law Offices Brent M Gunderson PC 123 N Centennial Way Ste 122 Mesa AZ 85201-6747

**GUNDERSON, ELMER MILLARD,** state supreme court justice, law educator; b. Mpls., Aug. 9, 1929; s. Elmer Peter and Carmaleta (Oliver) G.; m. Lupe Gomez, Dec. 29, 1967; 1 son, John Randolph. Student, U. Minn., U. Omaha, 1948-53; LL.B., Creighton U., 1956; LL.M., U. Va., 1982; LL.D., Calif. Western Sch. Law; student appellate judges seminar, N.Y. U., 1971; LL.D., U. Pacific. Bar: Nebr. 1956, Nev. 1958. Atty.-adviser FTC, 1956-57; pvt. practice Las Vegas, 1958-71; justice Nev. Supreme Ct., 1971-89, now sr. justice; instr. bus. law So. regional div. U. Nev.; lectr., author bulls. felony crimes for Clark County Sheriff's Dept.; counsel Sheriff's Protective Assn.; mem. legal staff Clark Council Civil Def. Agy.; legal counsel Nev. Jaycees. Compiler, annotator: Omaha Home Rule Charter; project coordinator: Jud. Orientation Manual, 1974. Chmn. Clark County Child Welfare Bd., Nev. central chpt. Nat. Multiple Sclerosis Soc.; hon. dir. Spring Mountain Youth Camp. Served with U.S. Army. Recipient A.J.S. Herbert Harley award. Mem. Am., Nebr., Nev. bar assns.; Mem. Inst. Jud. Adminstrn., Am. Law Inst., Am. Trial Lawyers Assn., Am. Judicature Soc., Phi Alpha Delta, Alpha Sigma Nu. Office: Nev Supreme Ct 100 N Carson St Carson City NV 89701-4717

**GUNDERSON, ROBERT VERNON, JR.,** lawyer; b. Memphis, Dec. 4, 1951; s. Robert V. and Suzanne (McCarthy) G.; m. Anne Durkheimer, May 15, 1982; children: Katherine Paige, Robert Graham. BA with distinction, U. Kans., 1973; MBA, U. Pa., 1974; MA, Stanford U., 1976; JD, U. Chgo., 1979. Bar: Calif. 1979, U.S. Dist. Ct. (no. dist.) Calif. 1979. Assoc. Cooley, Godward, Castro, Huddleson & Tatum, San Francisco and Palo Alto, Calif., 1979-84, ptnr., 1984-88; ptnr. Brobeck, Phleger & Harrison, Palo Alto, 1988-95, mem. exec. com., 1991-95, chmn. bus. and tech. practice, 1992-95; founder, ptnr. Gunderson Dettmer Stough Villeneuve Franklin & Hachigian, Menlo Park, Calif., 1995—; panelist Venture Capital and Pub. Offering Negotiation, San Francisco and N.Y.C., 1981, 83, 85, 92, Practicing Law Inst., N.Y.C. and San Francisco, 1986; moderator, panelist Third Ann. Securities Law Inst., 1985; dir. Heartport, Inc., Redwood City, Calif.; sec. Dionex Corp., Sunnyvale, Calif., 1983-88, Southwall Techs., Inc., Palo Alto, 1985-88, Conductus, Inc., Sunnyvale, 1992—, Remedy Corp., Mountain View, Calif., 1995-97; vis. lectr. U. Santa Clara Law Sch., 1985, 89. Exec. editor U. Chgo. Law Rev., 1978-79; contbr. articles to profl. jours. Mem. ABA (bus. law sect., various coms.), State Bar Calif. (panelist continuing legal edn. 1984), San Francisco Bar Assn., Am. Fin. Assn., Am. Soc. Corporate Secs., Wharton Club (San Francisco Bay area). Avocations: contemporary art, music, travel. Securities, General corporate. Home: 243 Polhemus Ave Menlo Park CA 94027-5442 Office: Gunderson Dettmer Franklin & Hachigian 155 Constitution Dr Menlo Park CA 94025-1106

**GUNEWARDENE, ROSHANI MALA,** lawyer; b. London, July 30, 1961; d. Swarana L. Gunewardene. BA, Sweet Briar Coll., 1985; JD, U. Conn., 1988; LLM, Columbia U., 1990. Bar: Fla. 1988, U.S. Ct. Appeals (llth cir.) 1988, U.S. Dist. Ct. (mid. and so. dists.) Fla. 1989, U.S. Supreme Ct. 1992. Cert. legal intern Office of Pub. Defender, West Palm Beach, Fla., summer 1987; assoc. Blackwell & Walker, PA, Miami, Fla., 1988-89, George T. Ramani, PA, Coral Gables, Fla., 1990-91, 92-93, Melton & Assocs., PA, Orlando, Fla., 1992; on-call assoc. Leon B. Cheek, III, Esquire, Fern Park, Fla., 1995-98; pvt. practice Altamonte Springs, Fla., 1993—; mem. arbitrator panel U.S. Dist. Ct. for Mid. Dist. Fla., 1996—; cons., assoc. Orange County Bar Assn., Orlando, 1998-99. Contbr. articles to law jours. Mem. Human Rels. Bd., Orlando, Fla., 1993-99, vice chmn., 1995-97, chmn., 1997-98; mem. Seminole County Sheriff's Civilian Rev. Bd., Sanford, Fla., 1998-01; vol. pub. interest law grant chpt. U. Conn. Sch. Law, 1986-87; vol. Ryan's Nursing Home, Amherst, Va., 1983-84; vol. worker braille transl. project Blind Coun., Colombo, Sri Lanka, 1976-78. Scholar Sweet Briar Coll., 1984-85. Mem. Nat. Assn. Securities Dealers (arbitrator), Am. Immigration Lawyers Assn., Fla. Bar (profl. ethics com. 1996-99). Avocations: stamp collecting, music, movies. Immigration, naturalization, and customs, Criminal, Construction. Office: Ste 2213 801 W SR 436 Altamonte Springs FL 32714

**GUNGER, RICHARD WILLIAM,** lawyer; b. Auburn, N.Y., Aug. 7, 1963; s. William Bruce and Lita Patricia G.; m. Barbara Jean Taber, Nov. 24, 1984; children: William Robinson, James Taber. BA magna cum laude, Alfred U., 1985; JD cum laude, Syracuse U., 1988. Bar: N.Y. 1989, U.S. Dist. Ct. (no. dist.) N.Y. 1991, U.S. Dist. Ct. (we. dist.) N.Y. 1993, U.S. Supreme Ct. 1993. Assoc. Albert D. DiGiacomo, Syracuse, N.Y., 1988-89, Cuddy, Durgala & Timian, Auburn, N.Y., 1989-90; atty. pvt. practice, Auburn, N.Y., 1990—; bd. dirs. Cayuga Counseling, Auburn. Alan L. Ponyman scholar, 1985. Mem. ABA, N.Y. State Bar Assn. Cayuga County Bar Assn., KC. General practice, Bankruptcy, Family and matrimonial. Office: 5 Court St Auburn NY 13021-3713

**GUNGOLL, BRADLEY A.,** lawyer; b. Enid, Okla., Jan. 24, 1953; s. Edward O. and Wanda E. Gungoll; m. Leah Webb, Dec. 20, 1975; children: Wade Daniel, William Edward, Wyatt Lee. BS, Okla. State U., 1975; JD, Oklahoma City U., 1979. Bar: Okla., U.S. Dist. Ct. (we., ea. and no. dists.) Okla., U.S. Ct. Appeals (10th cir.). Ptnr. Jones, Gungoll, Jackson, Collins & Dodd, Enid, 1980-83; shareholder Gungoll, Jackson, Collins & Box, P.C., Enid, 1983—. Mem. Okla. Horse Racing Commn., Oklahoma City, 1988-93, chmn., 1993. Fellow Okla. Bar Found.; mem. ATLA, Okla. Bar Assn., Okla. Trial Lawyers Assn., Garfield County Bar Assn., Oakwood Country Club (bd. dirs.). Republican. Roman Catholic. Avocations: hunting, fishing, golf. Federal civil litigation, General civil litigation, State civil litigation. Office: Gungoll Jackson et al 323 W Broadway Ave Enid OK 73701-3837

**GUNN, ALAN,** law educator; b. Syracuse, N.Y., Apr. 8, 1940; s. Albert Dale and Helen Sherwood (Whitnall) G.; m. Bertha Ann Buchwald, 1975; 1 child, William. BS, Rensselaer Poly. Inst., 1961; JD, Cornell U., 1970. Bar: D.C. 1970. Assoc. Hogan & Hartson, Washington, 1970-72; asst. prof. law Washington U., St. Louis, 1972-75, assoc. prof., 1975-76; assoc. prof. law Cornell U., Ithaca, N.Y., 1977-79, prof., 1979-84, J. duPratt White prof., 1984-89; prof. law U. Notre Dame, Ind., 1989-96, John N. Matthews prof., 1996—. Author: Partnership Income Taxation, 1991, 2d edit., 1995; (with Larry D. Ward) Cases, Text and Problems on Federal Income Taxation, 4th edit., 1998; (with Vincent R. Johnson) Studies in American Tort Law, 1994. Methodist. Office: U Notre Dame Law Sch Notre Dame IN 46556

**GUNN, JAMES F.,** lawyer; b. St. Louis, July 11, 1941; s. Donald and Loretto (Hennelly) G.; m. Lee B. Hynek, July 24, 1965; children: James F. Jr., Patrick C., Beth A., Brian D., Matthew A., Sean P. BA, St. Louis U., 1963, JD, 1965. Bar: Mo. 1965, U.S. Dist. Ct. (ea. dist.) Mo. 1965, U.S. Supreme Ct. Ptnr. Gunn & Gunn, St. Louis, 1965-84, The Stolar Partnership, St. Louis, 1984—. Pres., dir. Cystic Fibrosis Assn., St. Louis, 1970s; chmn., dir. Cath. Charities, St. Louis, 1993-98. Mem. Mo. Bar Assn., St. Louis Bar Assn., Mo. Athletic Club. Democrat. Roman Catholic. Avocations: boating, reading. Health, General corporate. Home: Five Troll Ct Manchester MO 63011 Office: The Stolar Partnership 911 Washington Ave Ste 700 Saint Louis MO 63101-1290

**GUNN, LEE DELTON, IV,** lawyer; b. Dearborn, Mich., Sept. 20, 1959; s. Lee Delton Gunn III and Madeline Evelyn (Lorenz) Currier; m. Tracy Raffles, May 12, 1995. BS, U. Fla., 1980, JD, 1982. Bar: Fla. 1983, U.S. Dist. Ct. (mid. dist.) Fla. 1983, U.S. Ct. Appeals (11th cir.) 1983; bd. cert. in civil trial Fla. Bar and Nat. Bd. Trial Advocacy. Assoc. Shackleford, Farrior, Stallings & Evans, P.A., Tampa, Fla., 1983-88, shareholder, 1988-90; founding shareholder Gunn, Ogden & Sullivan, P.A., Tampa, Fla., 1990—; mem. pres.'s coun. U. Fla. Contbr. articles to profl. jours. Mem. Am. Inns of Ct. (barrister 1990—), Def. Rsch. Inst., Fla. Def. Lawyers Assn., Fla. Hosp. Assn. Personal injury, Insurance, Product liability. Home: 336 Blanca Tampa FL 33606 Office: Gunn Ogden & Sullivan PA 100 N Tampa St Ste 2900 Tampa FL 33602-5810

**GUNN, MICHAEL PETER,** lawyer; b. St. Louis, Oct. 18, 1944; s. Donald and Loretto Agnes (Hennelly) G.; m. Carolyn Ormsby Ritter, Nov. 27, 1969; children: Mark Thomas, Christopher Michael, John Ritter, Elizabeth Jane. JD, St. Louis U., 1968. Bar: Mo. 1968, U.S. Dist. Ct. (ea and we. dists.) Mo. 1968, U.S. Tax Ct. 1972. Assoc. Gunn & Gunn, St. Louis, 1968-81; ptnr. Gunn & Lane, St. Louis, 1981-86; pvt. practice Ballwin, Mo., 1986—; rep. ea. dist. Mo. Ct. Appeals. Sgt. U.S. Army, 1969-75. Mem. ABA (del. Ho. of Dels. 1988—), St. Louis Bar Assn., The Mo. Bar (bd. govs. 1990—, exec. com. 1993-94, pres.-elect 1999—), Lawyers Assn. St. Louis (pres. 1981-82), St. Louis Bar Found. (pres. 1988-89), Bar Assn. Met. St. Louis (pres. 1987-88), Nat. Conf. Bar Founds. (trustee 1990—, pres. elect 1993-94). Roman Catholic. Probate, State civil litigation, Estate planning. Home: 2232 Centeroyal Dr Saint Louis MO 63131-1910 Office: Gunn & Rossetes PC Ste 140 13545 Barrett Pkwy Dr Ballwin MO 63021-5896

**GUNNING, FRANCIS PATRICK,** lawyer, insurance association executive; b. Scranton, Pa., Dec. 10, 1923; s. Frank Peter and Mary Loretta (Kelly) G.; m. Nancy C. Hill, Aug. 10, 1951; 1 son, Brian F. Student, City Coll. N.Y., 1941-43; LLB, St. John's U., 1950. Bar: N.Y. 1950. Legal editor Prentice Hall Pub. Co., N.Y.C., 1950-51; legal specialist Tchrs. Ins. & Annuity Assn. Am., Coll. Retirement Equities Fund, N.Y.C., 1951-53, asst. counsel, 1953-57, assoc. counsel, 1957-60, counsel, 1960-65, asst. gen. counsel, 1965-67, assoc. gen. counsel, 1967, v.p., assoc. gen. counsel, 1967-73, sr. v.p., gen. counsel, 1973-74, exec. v.p., gen. counsel, 1974-88, ret., 1988; trustee, mem. exec. and audit coms. Mortgage Growth Investors (now MGI Properties). Contbr. articles on mortgage financing to profl. jours. With USAAF, 1943-46. Mem. ABA, N.Y. State Bar Assn., Am. Land Title Assn., Am. Law Inst., Assn. of Bar of City of N.Y., Assn. Life Ins. Counsel, Nat. Assn. Coll. Univ. Attys., Am. Coll. Real Estate Lawyers. Republican. Roman Catholic. General corporate, Real property, Securities. Home and Office: 32 Kewanee Rd New Rochelle NY 10804-1324

**GUNNISON, MARK STEVEN,** lawyer; b. Chgo., Mar. 29, 1956; s. Gale W. and Catherine E. (Lackland) G.; m. Terese L. Kuhn, Aug. 1, 1980; children: Andrew, Thomas, Billy, Emily, Hannah. BS, U. Kans., 1978, JD, 1981. Bar: Kans. 1981, U.S. Dist. Ct. Kans. 1981, U.S. Ct. Appeals (10th cir.) 1983, U.S. Ct. Appeals (8th cir.) 1994. Ptnr. McDowell, Rice & Smith, Overland Pk., Kans., 1981-96, Payne & Jones, chartered, Overland Pk., 1996—. Avocations: sports, reading, coaching. General civil litigation, Personal injury, Insurance. Office: Payne & Jones chartered PO Box 25625 11000 King St Overland Park KS 66210-1286

**GUNNSTAKS, C. LUKE,** lawyer; b. N.J.; s. Frank and Audrey Gunnstaks; m. Maria Gunnstaks; children: James, Jill, Velvet, Angel. BA, U. Fla., 1973; JD, So. Meth. U., 1990. Bar: Tex. 1991, U.S. Dist. Ct. (ea. dist.) Tex. 1992. Musician, 1970-80, Vince Vance and the Valiants, Dallas, 1980-86, Sgt. Fury and the Valiant Allstars, Dallas, 1986-88; supr. ITI, Inc., Dallas, 1988-91; atty. Gunnstaks Law Office, Dallas, 1991—. Copyright holder. Mem. ABA, Am. Trial Lawyers Assn., Dallas Bar Assn., State Bar of Tex. Avocation: music. Family and matrimonial, Entertainment, Personal injury. Office: Gunnstaks Law Office 15150 Preston Rd Ste 300 Dallas TX 75248-4871

**GUNTER, JOSEPH CLIFFORD, III,** lawyer; b. Ft. Worth, Apr. 26, 1943; s. Joseph Cliford Jr. and Helen (Wright) G.; children: Joseph Clifford IV, Grant Norwood. BA, U. Tex., 1965, JD, 1967. Bar: Tex. 1967. Assoc. McDonald Sanders Ginsberg New Kirk Gibson & Webb, Ft. Worth, 1967-68; ptnr. Bracewell & Patterson, Houston, 1968—. Lt. USNR, 1967-73. Fellow Am. Coll. Trial Lawyers, Tex. Bar Found., Houston Bar Found.; mem. ABA, State Bar Tex., State Bar Colo. Episcopalian. Avocations: golf, tennis, skiing, sailing. Office: Bracewell & Patterson 2900 S Tower Pennzoil Pl 711 Louisiana St Houston TX 77002-2781

**GUNTER, MICHAEL DONWELL,** lawyer; b. Gastonia, N.C., Mar. 26, 1947; s. Daniel Cornelius and DeNorma Joyce (Smith) G.; m. Barbara Jo Benson, June 19, 1970; children: Kimberly Elizabeth, Daniel Cornelius III. BA in History with honors, Wake Forest U., 1969; JD with honors, U. N.C., 1972; MBA with honors, U. Pa., 1973. Bar: N.C. 1972, U.S. Dist. Ct. (mid. dist.) N.C. 1974, U.S. Tax Ct. 1975, U.S. Supreme Ct. 1979, U.S. Claims Ct. 1982, U.S. Ct. Appeals (D.C. cir.) 1985, U.S. Ct. Appeals (4th cir.) 1992. Ptnr. Womble Carlyle Sandridge & Rice PLLC, Winston-Salem, N.C., 1974—; chmn. employee benefits practice group; bd. dirs. G & J Enterprises Inc., Gastonia, Indsl. Belting Inc., Gastonia. Contbr. articles to profl. jours. Coach youth basketball Winston-Salem YMCA, 1981-90; advisor Winston-Salem United Way Christmas Cheer Toy Shop, 1975; fundraiser Deacon Club Wake Forest U., also mem. exec. com., strategic planning com., athletic coun., 1987—, v.p., pres., 1990-92; bd. dirs. Goodwill Industries, Winston-Salem, 1987—, past pres., sec., chmn. fin. com.; bd. dirs. Centenary Meth. Ch., 1980; mem. community problem solving com. United Way, 1988—; mem. Leadership Winston-Salem, Alumni Coun. Wake Forest U., Cert. Com. NCAA, long range planning com. athletic dept. William E. Newcombe scholar U. Pa., 1972-73; selected One of Best Employee Benefits Lawyers in Am., Nat. Law Jour. Mem. ABA, So. Pension Conf., N.C. Bar Assn. (former chmn. tax sect., mem. continuing legal edn. com., sports and entertainment law com.), Forsyth County Bar Assn., Forsyth County Employee Benefit Coun., Winston-Salem Estate Planning Coun. (past bd. dirs.), Profit Sharing Coun. Am., ESOP Assn., Assn. of Pvt. Pension and Welfare, Forsyth Country Club (former pres., bd. dirs.) Piedmont Club, Order of Coif, Rotary (former bd. dirs. Reynolda club). Democrat. Avocations: golf, fishing. Pension, profit-sharing, and employee benefits, Corporate taxation, Mergers and acquisitions. Home: 128 Ballyhoo Dr Lewisville NC 27023-9633 Office: Womble Carlyle Sandridge & Rice PLLC PO Drawer 84 1600 BB&T Financial Ctr Winston Salem NC 27102

**GUNTER, RUSSELL ALLEN,** lawyer; b. Amarillo, Tex., Feb. 21, 1950; s. J.B. and Shirley Ann (Russell) G.; children: Kim, Sarah, Laura, Rachel, Lindsay. BS in Polit. Sci., So. Ark U., 1972; JD, Tex. Tech U., 1975. Bar: Ark., 1975, Tex, 1975, U.S. Dist. Ct. (ea. and we dists.) Ark. 1975, U.S. Supreme Ct. (8th cir.) 1975, U.S. Dist. Ct. (no. dist.) Tex. 1976, U.S. Ct. Appeals (5th cir.), 1980, U.S. Supreme Ct. 1986. Assoc. Gaines N. Houston, Little Rock, 1975-79, Wallace, Dover & Dixon, P.A., Little Rock, 1979-90, McGlinchey Stafford Lang P.L.L.C., Little Rock, 1990-97; Cross, Gunter, Witherspoon & Galchus P.C., Little Rock, 1997—. Mem. ABA (com. on practice and procedure before NLRB labor sect.), Soc. for Human Resource Mgmt. (cert. sr. profl. in human resources), Ark. Bar Assn., Tex. Bar Assn. Labor. Office: 500 E Markham St Ste 200 Little Rock AR 72201-1747

**GUPTA, RAJAT KUMAR,** lawyer, accountant; b. New Delhi, Apr. 22, 1960; came to U.S., 1970; s. Ravindra Kumar and Rama G. BBA, Rutgers Coll., New Brunswick, N.J., 1978-82; JD, Rutgers U., Newark, 1985-88. Bar: N.J. and Pa. 1989, U.S. Tax Ct. 1992; lic. CPA. Staff acct. Borrelli & Assoc's., Highland Park, N.J., 1983-84, S. Kirschenbaum & Co., CPA, East Brunswick, N.J., 1984-85; tax assoc. Coopers & Lybrand, Princeton, N.J., 1988-89; pvt. practice atty. New Brunswick, 1989-98; sr. assoc. Spevack & Cannan, P.A., Iselin, N.J., 1998—; vol. Acct's. for the Public Interest, N.J., 1991—; mentor Rutgers Law Sch., Seton Hall Law Sch., Asian and Pacific Law Students Assn. Prodn. editor Rutgers Computer & Technology Law Jour., 1987-88, Cannonball-One Lap of America, 1988; contbr. articles to profl. jours. Arbitrator Better Bus. Bur., Newark, 1986-87; vol. atty. Rutgers U. Off Campus Housing Ctr., 1996—; mem. com. on character N.J. Supreme Ct., 1997—. Mem. ABA, Asian and Pacific Lawyers Assn. N.J., N.J. State Bar Assn, mem. Middlesex Co. Bar Assn. Hindu. Avocations: tennis, travel, photography, astronomy. Consumer commercial, Real property. Office: Spevack & Cannan PA 525 Green St Iselin NJ 08830-2618

**GUREWITZ, THOMAS MARK,** lawyer; b. Chgo., Nov. 5, 1949; s. Jerome and Miriam (Kass) G.; m. Sarah Ward, Aug. 12, 1972 (div. Apr. 1976). BA, Beloit Coll., 1971; JD, John Marshall Law Sch., Chgo., 1975. Bar: Ill.1975. Staff atty. Legal Svcs. Lake County, Waukegan, Ill., 1976-78; asst. prosecutor City of Waukegan (Ill.), 1977-85; pvt. practice Waukegan, 1978—; dir. Prairie State Legal Svcs., Waukegan, 1981-85. Bd. dirs., founding mem. Lake County Crisis Ctr., Waukegan, 1978-82. Mem. ABA, Ill. Bar Assn. (family law sect. council), Lake County Bar Assn. (sec. 1981-83, 1985-88; chmn. family law com. 1988-89, pres. 1999—), Ill. Trial Lawyers Assn., Am. Assn. Matrimonial Lawyers (bd. dirs.). Family and matrimonial, General practice, Real property. Home: 15245 W Oak Spring Rd Libertyville IL 60048-1619 Office: 20 N Utica St Waukegan IL 60085-4326

**GURFEIN, RICHARD ALAN,** lawyer; b. N.Y.C., Nov. 4, 1946; s. Jack and Ruth (Kronowitz) G.; m. Erica P. Temchin, Oct. 20, 1978; children: Jared L., Amanda, Jessica M., Sarah R. BE, NYU, 1967; JD, Bklyn. Law Sch., 1971. Bar: N.Y. 1972, U.S. Dist. Ct. (so. and ea. dists.) N.Y. 1973, U.S. Supreme Ct. 1976, U.S. Ct. Appeals (2d cir.) 1990. Assoc. Mark B. Wiesen, PC, N.Y.C., 1972-78; ptnr. Wiesen & Gurfein, N.Y.C., 1978-82, Wiesen, Gurfein & Jenkins, N.Y.C., 1982—; pres. Trial1.com, Inc., 1997—; moderator, lectr. Nassau Acad. Law, 1984—, N.Y. State Trial Lawyers Inst., 1985—, treas., 1989-91, pres. 1995-96. Recipient Crown of Good Name award Inst. Jewish Humanities, 1996. Mem. Assn. Trial Lawyers Am., N.Y. State Trial Lawyers Assn. (lectr. continuing legal edn. 1985—, bd. dirs. 1986—, chmn. com. on coms. 1987-88, exec. com. 1987—, dep. treas. 1988-89, treas. 1989-91, sec. 1991-92, v.p. 1992-94, pres. elect 1994-95, pres. 1995-96, past pres. 1996—), N.Y. County Lawyers Assn., Nassau County Bar Assn. (chmn. com. on med. jurisprudence 1983-86), Million Dollar Advocates Forum. Avocations: astronomy, amateur radio, photography, golf, computing. Personal injury, Product liability, State civil litigation. Office: Wiesen Gurfein & Jenkins 11 Park Pl Rm 1100 New York NY 10007-2889

**GURLEY, CURTIS RAYMOND,** lawyer; b. Joplin, Mo., Apr. 5, 1959; s. Carl R. and Glenda (Cummins) G.; m. Rebecca Lynn Miller; 2 children: Jackson M. and Davis C. AB, U. Mo., 1986, JD, 1989. Bar: N.Mex., 1989, U.S. Ct. Appeals (10th cir.) 1989, Mo. 1990, Colo. 1998. Ptnr. Hynes, Hale & Gurley, Farmington, N.Mex. Mem. NACDL, San Juan County Bar (pres. 1993), N.Mex. Trial Lawyers Assn. (bd. dirs.), N.Mex. Criminal Def. Attys. Assn., Elks. Republican. Presbyterian. Administrative and regulatory, Federal civil litigation, State civil litigation. Office: Hynes Hale & Gurley 1000 W Apache St Farmington NM 87401-3805

**GURSTEL, NORMAN KEITH,** lawyer; b. Mpls., Mar. 24, 1939; s. Jules and Etta (Abramowitz) G.; m. Jane Evelyn Golden, Nov. 24, 1984; children: Todd, Dana, Marc. BA, U. Minn., 1960, JD, 1962. Bar: Minn. 1962, U.S. Dist. Ct. Minn. 1963, U.S. Supreme Ct. 1980. Assoc. Robins, Davis & Lyons, Mpls., 1962-67; prin. Gurstel & Gurstel, Mpls., 1967—; arbitrator Hennepin County Dist. Ct., 1988-91; parttime referee family ct. Hennepin County Dist.; lectr. U. Minn. Family Law Seminar. Mem. ABA (corp. banking and bus. law and family law sects.), Minn. Bar Assn. (co-chmn. family ct. com. bankruptcy law sect. 1966-67, family law and bankruptcy law), Hennepin County Bar Assn. (chmn. family law com. 1964-65, vice chmn. 1981-91, fee arbitration bd., creditors remedy com.), Fed. Bar Assn., Assn. Trial Lawyers Am., Minn. Trial Lawyers Assn., Am. Acad. Matrimonial Lawyers, Nat. Council Juvenile and Family Ct. Judges, Comml. Law League Am. (recording sec. 1980-81, bd. govs. 1983-89, pres. 1987-88), Comml. Law League Fund for Pub. Edn. (sec. 1981-83, pres. 1989-92, bd. dirs. 1989-94), Phi Delta Phi. Jewish. Club: Oak Ridge Country (Mpls.). Lodges: Shriners, Masons. Contracts commercial, Bankruptcy, Family and matrimonial. Office: Marc Shawn Inc 3660 Galleria Edina MN 55435-4220

**GUSLER, KATHLEEN MARY,** lawyer; b. West Paterson, N.J., Jan. 27, 1965; d. George and Beverly Ann Gusler. BA, Drew U., 1986; JD, Suffolk U., 1989. Bar: N.J. 1989. Dep. atty. gen. Divsn. Criminal Justice State of N.J., Trenton, 1990—. Office: State of NJ Divsn Criminal Justice CN 086 Trenton NJ 08625

**GUSSIN, ARNOLD MARVIN,** lawyer; b. Bklyn., Nov. 11, 1936; s. Albert and Beatrice (Stutman) G.; m. Leslie Ann Defren, Aug. 22, 1965; children: Randy Alan, Gerri Brooke, Ronni Bara. BA, Queens Coll., 1958; JD, Bklyn. Law Sch., 1961. Bar: N.Y. 1962. Pvt. practice N.Y.C., 1962—; arbitrator Am. Arbitration Assn., N.Y.C., 1967-87. Dir., v.p., pres. Men's Club Temple Israel of Great Neck, N.Y., 1975—, trustee, v.p., 1985-95; dir., v.p. Great Neck Estates Civic Assn., 1990—; chair pub. works adv. com. village Great Neck Estates, 1992-94. Recipient Lion of Judah award State of Israel Bonds, 1989, Chavarim Kol Yisroel award Fedn. Jewish Men's Clubs, N.Y.C., 1992, Burning Bush award Men's Club, Temple Israel, 1992. Mem. N.Y. State Bar Assn. Avocation: skiing. Office: 9 Murray St New York NY 10007-2223

**GUSTAFSON, ALBERT KATSUAKI,** lawyer, engineer; b. Tokyo, Dec. 5, 1949; came to U.S., 1951; s. William A. and Akiko (Osada) G.; m. Helen Melissa Laird, July 31, 1971 (div. 1975); m. Karen Jane Ekblad, Dec. 31, 1978 (div. 1987). BA with distinction, Stanford U., 1972; JD, U. Wash., 1980; LLM, 1988. Bar: Wash. 1981, U.S. Dist. Ct. (we. dist.) Wash. 1981, U.S. Ct. Appeals (9th cir.) 1984, N.Y., 1993. Acoustics analyst Boeing Co., Seattle, 1973-74, material buyer, 1974; legal editor, Book Pub. Co., Seattle, 1975-76; rsch. analyst Batelle Inst., Seattle, 1975-76; legal intern Office of U.S. Atty., Seattle, 1976; engr. U.P.R.R., 1977-85; corp. counsel Dorden, Inc., Centralia, Wash., 1984—, Ansette Fin. Corp., Inc., Seattle, 1987—, Precision Forms, Inc., 1988, Endo and Mamba, 1989—; of counsel Barkats and Assocs., 1991—; prin. Albert K. Gustafson, P.S., Seattle, 1981—; pres. Shomei Corp., 1990—, Shomei, Kokusai, Kabushki, Kaisha, 1991—; v.p. Sierra Capital Mgmt., Inc., 1992—; prof. internat. bus. law. Sch. Internat. Studies Nichibei Kaiwa Gakuen, Tokyo, 1989—, Nippon Tel. & Tel., 1989-90; bd. dirs. Daiki, Inc. Sec. local 117-E, United Transp. Union, 1984, local vice-chmn., 1984; Dem. precinct chmn., 1984. Kraft scholar, 1968; mem. nat. bd. editors Prentice-Hall Rigos CPA Review, 1991—; Calif. State scholar, 1968-72. Mem. ABA, Internat. Bar Assn., Asian Bar Assn., Inter-Pacific Bar Assn., Seattle-King County Bar Assn., Roppongi Bar Assn., Japan-Am. Soc. Democrat. Presbyterian. Clubs: College, City, Century Court. Lodges: Masons, Shriners, Order of DeMolay (master councilor 1968), Rotary. Private international, Immigration, naturalization, and customs, Real property. Address: Green Capital Hiroo # 203, 1-7-17 Hiroo Shibuya-ku, Tokyo 150, Japan Office: 800 3rd Ave Ste 1800 New York NY 10022-7604 also: 75 Shoe Ln, London England EC4 BQ also: 999 3rd Ave Seattle WA 98104-4019 also: 5 Krasnoznamenny By-str, 690000 Vladivostok Russia also: 12111 Wards Ferry Rd Groveland CA 95321-9782

**GUSTAFSON, ALICE FAIRLEIGH,** lawyer; b. Houston, Dec. 1, 1946; d. William H. and Mary Davis (McCord) Bell; m. Charles R. Gustafson, May 30, 1971. BA in Econs., Wellesley (Mass.) Coll., 1968; JD, U. Puget Sound, 1976. Bar: Wash. 1976. Various positions U.S. Dept. HEW, various locations, 1968-75; assoc. Graham & Dunn, Seattle, 1977-83, ptnr., 1983—. Bd. dirs. King County Am. Cancer Soc., Seattle, 1983-85, Women & Bus., Inc., Seattle, 1984-87; mem. nominating com. YWCA Seattle-King County, 1985-88. Mem. ABA, Wash. State Bar Assn. (chair Bench-Bar-Press com. 1988-90), Seattle-King County Bar Assn. (trustee young lawyers divsn. 1980-83, treas. 1985-87), N.W. Comm. Lawyers, Met. Seattle Urban League (bd. dirs. 1991-93). Avocations: sailing, bicycling, skiing. Communications, Labor. Home: 13560 Riviera Pl NE Seattle WA 98125-3845 Office: Graham & Dunn 1420 5th Ave Fl 33 Seattle WA 98101-4087

**GUSTAFSON, JAMES WILLIAM, JR.,** lawyer; b. West Palm Beach Fla., Sept. 14, 1966; s. James William and Barbara Bernheim G. BA with honors, Fla. State U., 1991, JD with honors, 1994. Bar: Fla. 1994, U.S. Dist. Ct. (mid. dist.) Fla. 1994. Lawyer Freeman, Hunter & Malloy, Tampa, Fla., 1994-97, Masterson, Rogers, Woodworth, Masterson & Lopez, St. Petersburg, Fla., 1997—. Bd. dirs. Hillsborough Assn. Retarded Citizens, Tampa, 1996—. With U.S. Army, 1984-87. Mem. Assn. Trial Lawyers Am., Acad. Fla. Trial Lawyers (sec. young lawyers), Masterson Inn Ct. (barrister), Phi Beta Kappa, Phi Delta Phi. Professional liability, Personal injury, Product liability. Office: Masterson Rogers Woodworth Masterson & Lopez 699 1st Ave N Saint Petersburg FL 33701-3601

**GUSTMAN, DAVID CHARLES,** lawyer; b. Yokuska, Japan, Mar. 16, 1954; came to U.S., 1955; s. David C. and Marilyn N. Gustman; m. Lisa S. Seyferth, Mar. 7, 1987; children: Hunter, David, Corrie. BA in Econs., U. Mich., 1975; JD, George Washington U., 1979. Bar: Ill. 1979, U.S. Dist. Ct. (no. dist.) Ill. 1979, U.S. Dist. Ct. (ea. dist.) Wis. 1988, U.S. Dist. Ct. (ctrl. dist.) Ill. 1990, U.S. Dist. Ct. (so. dist.) Ill. 1991, U.S. Ct. Appeals (fed. cir.) 1988, U.S. Ct. Appeals (7th cir.) 1990, U.S. Supreme Ct. 1994, U.S. Ct. Appeals (8th cir.) 1997, U.S. Dist. Ct. (ea. dist.) Mich. 1997. Clk. Arter & Hadden, Washington, 1977-78; assoc. Rooks, Pitts & Poust, Chgo., 1979-84, Freeborn & Peters, Chgo., 1984-86; ptnr. Freeborn & Peters, 1986—, chmn., mng. ptnr., 1996—; operating com. Freeborn & Peters, 1992—. Articles editor: Jour. Internat. Law & Econs., 1978-79. Bd. dirs. Constitutional Rights Found., Chgo., 1982-88. Mem. ABA, Ill. State Bar Assn., Mich. Shores Club. Avocations: skiing, sailing, running. Fax: (312) 360-6571. Antitrust, General civil litigation. Office: Freeborn & Peters 311 S Wacker Dr Ste 3000 Chicago IL 60606-6679

**GUSTUS, STACEY A.,** legal secretary; b. Lakewood, Colo., Sept. 10, 1961; d. Norman Gaylord and Sandra S. (Melton) Holder; m. Wayne A. Gustus, Jr., June 14, 1980; children: Gregory K., Cynthia Jo. Student, U. North Colo., 1979-80. Cert. paralegal. County court tech Adams County DA, Brighton, Colo., 1980-83; legal sec. Peter L. Mattisson, Esq., Westminster, Colo., 1983-85, Hall & Evans, Denver, 1985-90; paralegal Machol & Machol, Denver, 1990-91; legal sec. McKenna & Cuneo, Denver, 1991—. Mem. Nat. Contract Mgmt. Assn. (Denver chpt., sec., treas., newsletter editor, registrar 1994—, sec.). Avocations: sewing, crafts, bowling, sand court volleyball. Office: McKenna & Cuneo LLP 370 17th St Ste 4800 Denver CO 80202-5648

**GUTH, PAUL C.,** lawyer; b. Vienna, Austria, Nov. 8, 1922; came to U.S., 1940; s. Alfred and Margaret (Haas) G.; m. Joan Margaret Totman, Mar. 28, 1962. B.A., Columbia U., 1943, LL.B., 1947. Bar: N.Y. 1948. Assoc. Cleary Gottlieb Friendly & Cox, N.Y.C., 1947-49; assoc. Lauterstein & Lauterstein, N.Y.C., 1950-51, ptnr., 1952-81; ptnr. Kelley Drye & Warren, N.Y.C., 1981—. Mem. editorial bd. Columbia Law Rev. Bd. dirs., officer Robert Lehman Found., Inc., N.Y.C., 1969—, Philip Lehman Found., Inc., N.Y.C., 1972—; pres., bd. dirs. Lutece Found., Inc., N.Y.C., 1983—; mem. fin. adv. bd. Victoria Home for Aged Men and Women, Ossining, N.Y., 1977—; asst. prosecutor war crimes trials Dachau and Mauthausen, 1945-46, chief war crimes investigator 3d Army Intelligence Ctr., 1945. 2d lt. AUS, 1943-46, ETO. Recipient Beck prize Columbia Law Sch., 1943. Mem. Am. Coll. Trust and Estate Counsel, Am. Judicature Soc., Fed. Bar Assn. Republican. Episcopalian. Clubs: Princeton (N.Y.C.), Lake (New Canaan, Conn.), City Club (Lafayette, La.). Avocation: historical studies. Family and matrimonial, Probate, Estate planning. Home: 136 Mariomi Rd New Canaan CT 06840-3311 also: 103 N Lemans St Lafayette LA 70503-4028 Office: Kelley Drye & Warren 101 Park Ave Fl 30 New York NY 10178-0062

**GUTHEINZ, JOSEPH RICHARD,** lawyer, federal agency official; b. Camp Lejune, N.C., Aug. 13, 1955; s. Joseph R. Sr. and Rita A. (O'Leary) G.; m. Lori Ann Bentley, Jan. 16, 1976; children: Joseph, Christopher, Michael, Jim, Bill, Dave. AS, AA, Monterey Peninsula Coll., Calif., 1975; BA, Calif. State U., Sacramento, 1978, MA, 1979; postgrad., U. Calif., Davis, 1979-80; MS in Sys. Mgmt., U. So. Calif., 1985; JD, S. Tex. Coll. Law, 1996. Bar: Tex. 1996, U.S. Dist. Ct. (so. dist.) Tex. 1997, U.S. Vets. Ct. Appeals 1998, U.S. Armed Forces Ct. Appeals 1998, U.S. Ct. Appeals (5th, 10th, 11th cirs.) 1998, U.S. Ct. Appeals (fed. cir.) 1998, U.S. Tax Ct. 1998; lic. FAA comml. pilot; cert. fraud examiner. Officer U.S. Army, Kitzigen, Fed. Rep. Germany, 1980-82; capt., mil. intelligence officer U.S. Army, Stuttgart, Fed. Rep. Germany, 1982-84; capt., aviator U.S. Army, Ft. Polk, La., 1984-86; spl. agt. civil aviation security FAA, Oklahoma City, 1986-87; spl. agt. U.S. Dept. Transp., Denver, 1987-90; sr. spl. agt. Office Insp. Gen. NASA, Houston, 1990—; pvt. practice atty. Houston, 1996—; instr. Ctrl Tex. Coll., Nelligan, Fed. Rep. Germany, 1983; guest spkr. Internat. Bus. Forum, 1995, Assn. Govt. Accts., 1996. Briefed Pres. Yeltsin's econ. advisors, 1995. Named Hon. Lt. Gov. Okla., 1987; Merit scholar S. Tex. Coll. Law. Mem. ATLA, Assn. Certified Fraud Examiners, Tex. Bar Assn. Republican. Roman Catholic. Avocations: reading, pistol shooting, volleyball, chess, weight lifting. General practice. Office: NASA Johnson Space Ctr Crim Invest Code W-Js Bldg 265 2101 Nasa Rd 1 Houston TX 77058-3691 also: 205 Woodcombe Dr Houston TX 77062-2537

**GUTHERY, JOHN M.,** lawyer; b. Broken Bow, Nebr., Nov. 22, 1946; s. John M. and Kay G.; m. Diane Messineo, May 26, 1972; 1 child, Lisa. BS, U. Nebr., 1969, JD, 1972. Bar: Nebr. 1972. Pres. Perry, Guthery, Haase & Gessford, P.C., Lincoln, Nebr., 1972—. Mem. ATLA, ABA (mem. litigation section), Nebr. Bank Attys. Assn. (past pres., 1985-86), Nebr. Assn. Trial Attys., Nebr. State Bar Assn. (pres. 1998-99), Nebr. State Bar Found. (mem. ho. dels. 1979-83, 87-95, exec. coun. 1988-94 pres. elect. 1997-98, pres. 1998-99, chair Nebr. bankruptcy sect.), Lincoln Bar Assn. (bd. trustees, 1985-88, pres. 1990-91). E-mail: jguthery@perrylawfirm.com. General civil litigation, Banking, Personal injury. Office: Perry Guthery Haase & Gessford PC 233 S 13th St Ste 1400 Lincoln NE 68508-2003

**GUTHRIE, JUDITH K.,** federal judge; b. Chgo., July 13, 1948; d. David Curtis and Kathleen McAfee G.; m. John H. Hannah, Jr., May 9, 1992. Student, Ariz. State U., 1966-68; BA, St. Mary's U., 1971; JD cum laude, U. Houston, 1980; postgrad., Harvard U., 1990. Bar: Tex. 1981, U.S. Dist. Ct. (ea. dist.) Tex. 1982, U.S. Ct. Appeals (5th cir.) 1982, U.S. Dist. Ct. (no. dist. ) Tex. 1983, U.S. Dist. Ct. (we. dist.) Tex. 1984. Editor Am. Coun. Edn., Washington, 1972-73; exec. asst. Tex. Ho. Reps., Austin, 1973-75; lobbyist Bracewell & Patterson, Austin, 1975-80; assoc. Bracewell & Patterson, Houston, 1980-81; briefing atty. Tex. Ct. Appeals, Tyler, 1981-82; ptnr. Hannah & Guthrie, Tyler, Tex., 1982-86; magistrate judge U.S. Dist. Ct. (ea. dist.) Tex., Tyler, 1986—; instr. legal asst. program, Tyler Jr. Coll., 1986-87; apptd. Tex. Judicial Coun., 1991-97, gender bias task force, 1991-92; lectr. in field. Contbr. articles to profl. jours. Bd dirs. Found. Women's Resources, Leadership Am., Leadership Tex.; adv. bd. Main St. Project; former Dem. chmn. Smith County; legal asst. adv. bd. Tyler Jr. Coll., 1986—, chmn. of adv. bd. 1996—; mem. Citizens Commn. Tex. Judicial System, 1992-93. Mem. ABA (fed. trial judges legis. com. 1991-93), Am. Judges Assn., Fed. Magistrate Judges Assn., 5th Cir. Bar Assn., State Bar Tex. (dist. 2A grievance com. 1990-96, chmn. 1995-96, coun. mem. women and law sect. 1981-84, bd. dirs. lawyers' credit union 1983-84, citizens and law focused edn. com. 1984-85), Smith County Bar Assn. (chmn. law libr. com. 1985—). Office: US District Court 300 Federal Bldg & US Ct House 211 W Ferguson St Tyler TX 75702-7212

**GUTHRIE, M. EMILY WILLIAMS,** lawyer; b. Joliet, Ill., Feb. 15, 1945; d. Clifford Clarkson and Roberta (Nichols) Williams; m. Richard Young Guthrie, June 28, 1967 (div. Nov. 1995); children: William, Katherine. BA, U. Ill., 1969; MS, Northwestern U., 1977; JD, Chgo.-Kent Coll. Law, 1994. Bar: Ill. 1994, Fed. 1994. Office mgr. Marthaler Architects, Evanston, Ill., 1980-90; pvt. practice Evanston, 1995-97; project mgr. Cyrus Homes, Evanston, 1997—. Alderman, City of Evanston, 1993-97; chmn. Evanston Safety Town, 1984—; founder Warren Cherry Scholarship Fund, Evanston, 1992—. Mem. ABA, Ill. State Bar Assn., Chgo. Bar Assn. Home: 730 Judson Ave Evanston IL 60202-2506 Office: Cyrus Homes Inc 2953 Central St Evanston IL 60201-1245

**GUTIERREZ, LINDA,** lawyer; b. San Antonio, Aug. 11, 1955; d. Frank S. Ill and Adelina (Aguirre) G.; m. Robert J. Lopez. BA, Randolph Macon Women Coll., 1977; JD, U. Tex. Law Sch., 1982. Exec. asst. Mex. Am. Unity Coun., San Antonio, 1979; pvt. practice Law Office of Linda Gutierrez, San Antonio, 1983—. Bd. dirs. Bexar County Women's Bar Assn., Child Advocate San Antonio, Pro Bono Law Project; pres. Mex. Am. Bar Assn., 1987-89; state bar grievance com. Dist. 10B, 1992. Named Outstanding Young Lawyer Bexar County Women's Bar Assn., 1986, Attorney Coach Tex. High Sch. Mock Trial competition., 1985, Outstanding new Attorney Pro Bono Law Project, 1984. Office: EEOC 5410 Fredericksburg Rd Ste 200 San Antonio TX 78229-3555

**GUTIERREZ, MARIA CRISTINA,** lawyer; b. Balt., Feb. 28, 1951; d. Roberto Ignatio and Mary Theresa (Shettle) G.; children: Roberto Santiago, Micajaella Orallia Gabriella. BS, Antioch U., Balt., 1976; JD, U. Balt., 1980. Asst. pub. defender Office of Pub. Def., Balt., 1982-87; ptnr. Rees, Gutierrez & Smearman, Balt., 1985-88; of counsel William H. Murphy, Jr. & Assocs. PA, Balt., 1987-88, ptnr., 1988-93; ptnr. Murphy & Gutierrez PA, Balt., 1993-94; atty. pavt. practice, Balt., 1995-97; ptnr. Redmond, Burgin & Gutierrez, PA, Balt., 1997—; dir. Nat. Assn. Criminal Def. Lawyers, 1993—, Md. Criminal Def. Attys. Assn., 1988—, Pub. Justice Ctr., 1993—; elected sect. mem. MSBA Sect. Criminal Law & Practice, 1995—; treas. Alternative Directions, 1990—; chair CITIPAC, 1980-84. Chairperson Balto. City Polit. Act. Commn., 1979-85; co-founder, treas. Md. Women's Campaign Fund, 1982-83; campaign coord. Balto. Rent Control Campaign, 1979; coord. Peace Action Com., 1971-74; treas., campaign coord., Grassroots McGovern for Pres., 1972. Mem. Nat. Assn. Criminal Def. Lawyers, Md. Criminal Def. Attys. Assn., Md. State Bar Assn. Sect. on Criminal Law and Practice, The Pub. Justice Ctr., The Md. State Bar Assn. Fax: 410-752-1064. E-mail: scarlettRI@aol.com. Criminal, Administrative and regulatory, Personal injury. Office: Redmond Burgin & Gutierrez PA The Fidelity Bldg 210 N Charles St Ste 1301 Baltimore MD 21201-4015

**GUTIERREZ, RENALDY JOSE,** lawyer; b. Masaya, Mas, Nicaragua, July 18, 1947; came to U.S., 1979; s. Felix Eduardo and Natalia (Solano) G.; m. Lourdes M. Montes, Dec. 22, 1974; children: Lourdes Natalia, Renaldy Jose. JD suma cum laude, U. Centroamerican, Managua, Nicaragua, 1971; JD cum laude, U. Miami, Coral Gables, Fla., 1985; LLM, Harvard U., 1988. Bar: Nicaragua 1971, Fla. 1986. Law clk. Ct. of Appeals, Masaya, 1967-69; asst. to legal dept. Banco Nacional, Managua, 1969-74; prof. law Universidad Centroamericana, Managua, 1973-76; gen. counsel Banco de la Vivienda, Managua, 1974-75; legal advisor Banco Nacional, Managua, 1975-77; ptnr. Zuniga & Gutierrez, Managua, 1976-79; gen. counsel Ofvico, Managua, 1977-79, Carmatt Corp. et al., Miami, Fla., 1979-91; of counsel Goytisolo & Saez, Miami, 1991-92; ptnr. Goytisolo, Martinez, De Cordoba & Gutierrez, Miami, 1992—; chmn., gen. counsel Riverdale Farms, Inc., Miami, 1990—; pres. Vision Inc., N.Y.C., 1987—; bd. dirs. Vision Inc., S.A., Panama; pres., bd. dirs. Kira Investments, Inc., Miami, 1989—. Author, coauthor papers. Mem. Republican Presdl. Task Force, Washington, 1984, Republican Senatorial Com., Washington, 1984. Honor scholar Universidad Centroamericana, 1969-71. Mem. ABA, Interamerican Bar Assn., Fla. Bar, Am. Immigration Lawyers Assn., Cuban Am. Bar Assn., Order of Coif. Roman Catholic. Avocations: reading, writing, traveling. General corporate, Contracts commercial, Private international. Home: 556 NW 99th Ct Miami FL 33172-4043 Office: Goytisolo Martinez De Cordoba & Gutierrez 601 Brickell Key Dr Ste 501 Miami FL 33131-2652

**GUTIS, MARK PHILIP,** lawyer; b. Mt. Vernon, N.Y., July 12, 1952; s. David Maxwell Gutis and Shirley (Morris) Queen; m. M. Joyal Guertin, June 2, 1974; 1 child, Sea Helene. BA, Syracuse U., 1974; MS, MLS, So. Conn. State Coll., 1978; JD (with honors), U. Conn., 1987. Bar: Conn. 1987, U.S. Dist. Ct. Conn. 1988. 2d lt. USAF, 1974-77; staff libr. W.Va. U. Med. Ctr., Charleston, W.Va., 1979-80; libr., instr. We. Conn. State Coll., Danbury, Conn., 1980-83; libr. Whiting Forensic Inst., Middletown, Conn., 1983-87; legal asst. Gersten & Gersten, Hartford, Conn., 1987; atty. Brown & Welsh, Meriden, Conn., 1987-88, Green & Kleinman, Hartford, 1988-89; adminstrv. hearing officer Conn. Dept. Motor Vehicles, Wethersfield, Conn., 1989—; atty. Mark P. Gutis, Wethersfield, Conn., 1989—; mediator Conn. Ctr. Mediation, 1998—. Mem. Acad. Family Mediators, Conn. Coun. Divorce Mediation. General practice, Administrative and regulatory. Home and Office: 93 Gilbert Rd Newington CT 06111-2312

**GUTKIN, ARTHUR LEE,** lawyer; b. Elizabeth, N.J., Mar. 29, 1945; s. Joshua Isadore and Rebecca (Dubrow) G.; m. Barbara Ann Schwartz, Aug. 23, 1970; children: Elisa Beth, Ari David. BA, George Washington U., 1967; JD, U. Miami, 1970; postgrad., Temple U., 1988-89. Bar: Fla. 1970, Pa. 1971, U.S. Dist. Ct. (ea. dist.) Pa. 1972, U.S. Dist. Ct. Ariz. 1991, U.S. Ct. Appeals (3d cir.) 1973, U.S. Ct. Appeals (11th cir.) 1993. Asst. dist. atty. Phila. Dist. Atty.'s Office, 1971-72; ptnr. Berkowitz and Gutkin, Attys., Phila., 1972-78; pvt. practice Conshohocken, Pa., 1978—; instr. crim. evidence Montgomery County C.C., Blue Bell, Pa., 1992—, instr. criminal law, 1993—; cons. Coun. Jewish Fedns., N.Y.C., 1990. Commr. Whitemarsh (Pa.) Baseball League, 1991; Dem. candidate Montgomery County Dist. Atty., Norristown, Pa., 1987; fin. dir. Beth Tikvah Temple, Oreland, Pa., 1983. Mem. Am. Trial Lawyers Assn., Pa. Trial Lawyers Assn., Montgomery County Bar Assn. (mem. Woman of Yr. com. 1992, mem. criminal law com. 1993—), Bar and Gavel. Avocations: coaching little league baseball, reading, painting, sponsor Primerica Amateur Cycling Team.

Civil rights, Criminal, Labor. Office: PO Box 610 Conshohocken PA 19428-0610

**GUTKNECHT, TIMOTHY ARTHUR,** lawyer; b. Detroit, Apr. 5, 1968; s. Bruce Arthur and Anita Jane (Thomas) G.; m. Heather Wall, June 9, 1990; 1 child, Andrew Michael. BA, Amherst Coll., 1990; JD, Washington U., St. Louis, 1993. Bar: Ill. 1993, Mo. 1994, U.S. Dist. Ct. (so. dist.) Ill. 1996, U.S. Ct. Appeals (7th cir.) 1997, U.S. Supreme Ct. 1998. Assoc. Crowder & Scoggins, Columbia, Ill., 1993—. Mem. ABA, Ill. State Bar Assn., St. Clair County Bar Assn., Monroe County Bar Assn. (pres. 1998—). General practice, General civil litigation, Appellate. Office: Crowder & Scoggins Ltd 121 W Legion Ave Columbia IL 62236-2341

**GUTMAN, HARRY LARGMAN,** lawyer, educator; b. Phila., Feb. 23, 1942; s. I. Cyrus and Mildred B. (Largman) G.; m. Anne G. Aronsky, Aug. 28, 1971; children: Jonathan, Elizabeth. AB cum laude, Princeton U., 1963; BA, Univ. Coll., Oxford, Eng., 1965; LLB cum laude, Harvard U., 1968; MA (hon.), U. Pa., 1984. Bar: Mass. 1968, Pa. 1989, D.C. 1996, U.S. Tax Ct. 1969. Assoc., Hill & Barlow, Boston, 1968-75, ptnr., 1975-77; clin. assoc. Harvard U. Law Sch., 1971-77; instr. Boston Coll., 1974-77; atty.-advisor Office of Tax Legis. Counsel, U.S. Dept. Treasury, 1977-78, dep. tax legis. counsel, 1978-80; assoc. prof. law U. Va., Charlottesville, 1980-84; prof. U. Pa. Law Sch., 1984-89; ptnr. Drinker Biddle & Reath, Phila., 1989-91; chief of staff joint com. on taxation U.S. Congress, 1991-93; ptnr. King & Spalding, Washington, 1994-99, KPMG LLP, 1999—; cons. Office Tax Policy, U.S. Dept. Treasury, 1980; cons. Am. Law Inst., 1980-84; vis. prof. U. Va. Law Sch., 1985-89, Ill. Inst. Tech., 1986; reporter Am. Law Inst. Generation-Skipping Tax project; Am. Law Inst. Arden House III Conf Recipient Exceptional Service award U.S. Dept. Treasury, 1980. Fellow Am Coll. Tax Counsel. Author: Transactions Between Partners & Partnerships, 1973; Minimizing Estate Taxes: The Effects of Inter Vivos Giving, 1975, (with F. Sander) Tax Aspects of Divorce and Separation, 1985, (with D. Lubick) Treasury's New Views on Carryover Basis, 1979; Effective Federal Tax Rates on Transfers of Wealth, 1979; (with others) Federal Wealth Transfer Taxation: Cases & Materials, 1987, Federal Wealth Transfer Taxes After ERTA, 1983, Reforming Federal Wealth Transfer Taxes After ERTA, 1983, A Comment on the ABA Tax Section Task Force Report on Transfer Tax Restructuring, 1988, Where Does Congress Go From Here? Base Timing and Measurement Issues in the Transfer Tax, 1989. Personal income taxation, Estate taxation, Corporate taxation. Office: KPMG LLP 2001 M St NW Washington DC 20036-3310

**GUTMAN, RICHARD EDWARD,** lawyer; b. New Haven, Apr. 9, 1944; s. Samuel and Marjorie (Leo) G.; m. Jill Leslie Senft, June 8, 1969 (dec.); 1 child, Paul Senft; m. Rosann Seasonwein, Dec. 10, 1987. AB, Harvard U., 1965; JD, Columbia U., 1968. Bar: N.Y. 1969, U.S. Ct. Appeals (2d cir.) 1969, U.S. Dist. Ct. (so. and ea. dists.) N.Y. 1975, U.S. Supreme Ct. 1982, Tex. 1991. Counsel Exxon Corp., N.Y.C., 1978-90; Dallas, 1990-91; asst. gen. counsel Exxon Corp., Dallas, 1992—; pres. 570 Park Ave Apts., Inc., N.Y.C., 1984-89, past bd. dirs. Fellow Am. Bar Found. (life); mem. ABA (fed. regulation securities com., vice chmn. 1995-98), Am. Law Inst., N.Y. State Bar Assn. (exec. com. 1983-86, 93—, securities regulation com. 1980—, chmn. 1993-97, sec. bus. law sec., 1999—), Assn. of Bar of City of N.Y. (securities regulation com. 1980-81, 83-86), Dallas Bar Assn., Coll. of the State Bar of Tex., N.A.M. (corp. fin. and mgmt. com.), Harvard Club (N.Y.C., admissions com. 1983-86, chmn. 1985-86, nominating com. 1986-87, bd. dirs. 1988-91, v.p. 1990-91), Harvard Club (Dallas, bd. dirs. 1998—). Securities, Finance, General corporate.

**GUTNICK, H. YALE,** lawyer; b. Phila., Mar. 20, 1942; s. Abraham L. and Irene (Grosflam) G.; m. Eleanor Stanton, June 10, 1968; m. 2d, Sally Meyers, Oct. 21, 1978 (div. Dec. 1986); children: Todd, Laura, Casey. BA, Ohio Wesleyan U., 1964; JD, U. Pitts., 1967. Bar: Pa. 1967, D.C. 1968, U.S. Dist. Ct. (we. and ea. dists.) Pa. 1967, U.S. Dist. Ct. D.C. 1969, U.S. Ct. Appeals (3d and D.C. cirs.) 1969, U.S. Ct. Appeals (5th cir.) 1976, U.S. Supreme Ct. 1978. Trial atty. U.S. Dept. Justice, Washington, 1967-69; ptnr. Rose, Schmidt, Dixon, Hasley, Whyte & Hardesty, Pitts., 1970-79, Strassburger McKenna Gutnick & Potter, Pitts., 1979—. Mem. ABA, Pa. Bar Assn., D.C. Bar Assn., Am. Trial Lawyers Assn., Pa. Trial Lawyers Assn. Jewish. Antitrust, Federal civil litigation, Entertainment. Office: 322 Blvd of Allies Suite 700 Pittsburgh PA 15222

**GUTOWSKI, MICHAEL FRANCIS,** lawyer; b. Detroit, Oct. 23, 1950; s. John A. and Christine (Militti) G.; m. Susan M. Smith, Nov. 25, 1983; children: Maria C., John C., Jacob S. AB, U. Nebr., 1972; JD, Georgetown U., 1976. Bar: Nebr. 1976, U.S. Dist. Ct. Nebr. 1976. Asst. pub. defender Douglas County, Omaha, 1977-85; pvt. practice Omaha, 1985—. Mem. Nebr. Dem. Cen. Com., 1982-83, 1994—, alt. mem., 1986-88; mem. Douglas County Dem. Cen. Com., 1990-98. Mem. ABA, Nebr. Bar Assn., Omaha Bar Assn. (newsletter com. 1985—), Nebr. Criminal Def. Attys. Assn. Roman Catholic. Criminal, Personal injury, General practice. Office: 209 Solath St 470 Omaha NE 68102-1900

**GUTSTEIN, SOLOMON,** lawyer; b. Newport, R.I., June 18, 1934; s. Morris Aaron and Goldie Leah (Nussbaum) G.; m. Carol Feinhandler, Sept. 3, 1961; children: Jon Eric, David Ethan, Daniel Ari, Joshua Aaron. AB with honors, U. Chgo., 1953, JD, 1956. Bar: Ill. 1956, U.S. Dist. Ct. (no. dist.) Ill. 1957, U.S. Ct. Appeals (7th cir.) 1958, U.S. Ct. Appeals (5th cir.) 1971, U.S. Supreme Ct. 1980; rabbi, 1955. Assoc. Schradzke, Gould & Ratner, Chgo., 1956-60; ptnr. firm Schwartz & Gutstein, Chgo., 1961-65, Gutstein & Cope, Chgo., 1968-72, Gutstein & Schwartz, Chgo., 1980-83, Gutstein & Sherwin, Chgo., 1983-85; ptnr. Arvey, Hodes, Costello & Burman, Chgo., 1991-92, Tenney & Bentley, Chgo., 1992—; spl. asst. atty. gen. State of Ill., 1968-69; adj. prof. law John Marshall Law Sch., 1993—; lectr. bus. law U. Chgo. Grad. Sch. Bus., 1973-82; cons. Ill. Real Property Svc., Bancroft Whitney Co., 1988-89; lectr. in field; real estate broker. Author: Illinois Real Estate, 2 vols., 1983, rev. ann. updates, 1984-95; co-author: Construction Law in Illinois, annually 1980-84, Judaism in Art (The Windows of Shaare Tivkah), 1995, Illinois Real Estate Practice Guide, 2 vols., 1996, rev. annual edit., 1997-99; contbr. chpt. to Commercial Real Estate Transactions, 1962-76; assoc. editor U. Chgo. Law Rev., 1954-56; editl. adviser Basic Real Estate I, also Advanced Real Estate II, 1960s-70s; author: Analysis of the Book of Psalms, 1962; contbr. articles to profl. publs. Mem. Cook County Citizens Fee Rev. Com., 1965; alderman from 40th ward Chgo. City Coun., 1975-79; mem. govt. affairs adv. com. Jewish Fedn., 1984-94. Fuerstenberg scholar U. Chgo., 1950-56; Kosmerl fellow U. Chgo., 1953-56. Mem. Ill. State Bar Assn., Chgo. Bar Assn., Decalogue Soc. Lawyers, B'nai B'rith. Real property, Probate, Health. Office: Tenney & Bentley 111 W Washington St Ste 1900 Chicago IL 60602-2769

**GUTTERMAN, ALAN J.,** lawyer; b. Bklyn., Nov. 21, 1942; s. Hyman and Madeline (Wolfe) G.; m. Emily Scharer, June 23, 1966; children: David, Andrew, Glenn, Jamie. BA with honors, U. Rochester, 1964; JD, Rutgers U., 1967. Bar: N.J. 1967, U.S. Ct. Claims 1970, U.S. Ct. Appeals (3rd cir.) N.J. 1967, U.S. Supreme Ct. 1977. Law clk. U.S. Ct. Appeals 3rd Cir., 1967-68; assoc. Sills, Beck, Summis, Radin & Tischman, Newark, 1968-71; sole practice Union, N.J., 1972-75; ptnr. Gutterman, Wolkstein & Klinger, LLP and predecessor firms, Westfield, N.J., 1975—. Editor: Rutgers Law Rev., 1966-67; contbr. N.J. Law Jour. Councilman, Westfield, N.J., 1975—. Mem. N.J. State Bar Assn., Union County Bar Assn. Republican. Jewish. General corporate, Real property, Probate. Office: Gutterman Wolkstein & Klinger LLP PO Box 2850 240 E Grove St Westfield NJ 07091-2850

**GUTTMAN, EGON,** law educator; b. Neuruppin, Germany, Jan. 27, 1927; came to U.S., 1958, naturalized, 1968; s. Isaac and Blima (Liss) G.; m. Inge Weinberg, June 12, 1966; children: Geoffrey David, Leonard Jay. Student, Cambridge U., 1945-48; LLB, U. London, 1950, LLM, 1952; postgrad., Northwestern U. Sch. Law, 1958-59. Barrister: Eng. 1952. Sole practice Eng., 1952-53; faculty Univ. Coll. and U. Khartoum Sudan, 1953-58, legal advisor to chief justice, 1953-58; founder, editor Sudan Law Jour. & Reports, 1956-57; researcher, lectr. Rutgers U. Sch. Law, Newark, 1959-60; asst. prof. U. Alta., Edmonton, Can., 1960-62; prof. Howard U. Law Sch., Washington, 1962-68, vis. adj. prof., 1968-96; adj. prof. law Washington Coll. Law, Am. U., 1964-68, Levitt Meml. Trust scholar-prof., 1968—; lectr. Practicing Law Inst., 1964—; adj. prof. law Georgetown U. Law Ctr., 1972-74, Johns Hopkins U., Balt., 1973-81; vis. prof. Faculty of Law, U. Cambridge, Wolfson Coll., Eng., 1984; atty.-fellow SEC, 1976-79; cons. to various U.S. agys. and spl. commns.; U.S. rep. to UNCITRAL working groups; mem. various ALI-ABA working groups on the revision of the uniform comml. code; mem. Sec. of State's Adv. Com. on Pvt. Internat. Law. Author: (books) Crime, Cause and Treatment, 1956, (with A. Smith) Cases and Materials on Domestic Relations, 1962, Modern Securities Transfers, 1967, 3d edit. 1987, cumulative supplement, 1998, (with R.G. Vaughn) Cases and Materials on Policy and the Legal Environment, 1973, rev. 1978, 3d edit. 1980, (with R.B. Lubic) Secured Transactions- A Simplified Guide, 1996; (with L.F. Del Duca and A.M. Squilante) Problems and Materials on Secured Transactions Under the Uniform Commercial Code, Commercial Transactions, vol. 1, 1992, (with F. Miller) supplement, 1996-98, Problems and Materials on Sales Under the Uniform Commercial Code and the Convention on International Sale of Goods, Commercial Transactions, vol. 2, 1990, supplement, 1997-98, Problem and Materials on Negotiable Instruments under the Uniform Commerical Code and the U.N. Convention on International Bills of Exchange and International Promissory Notes, Commercial Transactions vol. 3, 1993, supplement, 1997-98, Securities Laws in the United States - A Primer for Foreign Lawyers, 1996-99; contbr. numerous articles, revs., briefs to profl. lit. Howard U. rep. Fund for Edn. in World Order, 1966-68; trustee Silver Spring Jewish Ctr., Md., 1976-79; mem. exec. com. Sha'are Tzedek Hosp., Washington, 1971-72, 97—. Leverhulme scholar, 1948-51; U. London studentship, 1951-52; Ford Found. grad. fellow, 1958-59, NYU summer workshop fellow, 1960, 61, 64; Levitt Meml. Trust scholar-professor 1982; recipient Outstanding Svc. award Student Bar Assn., Am. U., 1970, Law Rev. Outstanding Svc. award, 1981, Washington Coll. of Law Outstanding Contbn. to Acad. Program Devel. award, 1981. Mem. Am. Law Inst., ABA, Fed. Bar Assn. Assn. Trial Lawyers Am., Brit. Inst. Internat. and Comparative Law, Soc. Pub. Tchrs. Law (Eng.), Hon. Soc. Middle Temple, Hardwick Soc. of Inns of Ct., Sudan Philos. Soc., Assn. Can. Law Tchrs., Am. Soc. Internat. Law, Can. Assn. Comparative Law, B'nai Brith Club, Argo Lodge, Phi Alpha Delta (John Sherman Myers award 1972). Fax: (202) 274-4130. E-mail: guttman@wcl.american.edu. Home: 14801 Pennfield Cir Silver Spring MD 20906-1580 Office: Am U Washington Coll Law 4801 Massachusetts Ave NW Washington DC 20016-8196

**GUY, ANDREW A.,** lawyer; b. Kansas City, Mo., May 11, 1952. AB summa cum laude, Princeton U., 1974; JD, U. Va., 1979. Bar: Wash. 1979. With firm Bogle & Gates, P.L.L.C., Seattle, 1979—, ptnr., 1987—. Mem. ABA (litigation sect.), Wash. State Bar Assn. (litigation sect.), King County Bar Assn. (litigation sect., creditors' rights, real property, probate and trust sects.). Contracts commercial, Bankruptcy, General civil litigation. Office: Bogle & Gates PLLC Two Union Sq 601 Union St Ste 4700 Seattle WA 98101-2346

**GUY, GARY EDWARD,** lawyer; b. Washington, Nov. 22, 1952; s. Jack Anthony and Dorothy Elizabeth G.; m. Anita Louise Aidt, July 30, 1983; 1 child, Gary Edward Jr. BA, George Mason U., 1975; JD, Nova U., 1978; LLM, Georgetown U., 1981. Staff atty. Fed. Energy Regulatory Commn., Washington, 1978-81; assoc. Cullen & Dykman, Washington, 1981-87; asst. gen. counsel Equitable Resources, Inc., Pitts., 1987-89; ptnr. Bruder, Gentile & Marcoux, Washington, 1989—. Mem. Masons, KC, Phi Alpha Delta. Roman Catholic. Administrative and regulatory, Appellate, FERC practice. Office: Bruder Gentile & Marcoux 1100 New York Ave NW Ste 510E Washington DC 20005-6188

**GUY, RICHARD P.,** state supreme court justice; b. Coeur d'Alene, Idaho, Oct. 24, 1932; s. Richard H. and Charlotte M. Guy; m. Marilyn K. Guy, Nov. 16, 1963; children: Victoria, Heidi, Emily. JD, Gonzaga U., 1959. Bar: Wash. 1959, Hawaii 1988. Former judge Wash. Superior Ct., Spokane, from 1977; chief justice Wash. Supreme Ct., Olympia, 1998—. Capt. USAS. Mem. Wash. State Bar, Spokane County Bar Assn. Roman Catholic. Office: Wash Supreme Ct Temple of Justice PO Box 40929 Olympia WA 98504-0929

**GUY, STEVE R.,** lawyer; b. Henderson, Tex., July 24, 1957; s. R. H. and Sue Guy; m. Connye T. Poovey, July 29, 1978; 1 child, Chistopher P. AA, Kilgore (Tex.) Coll., 1977; BA, Baylor U., 1980, JD, 1981. Bar: Tex., 1981, U.S. Dist. Ct. (ea. dist.) Tex., U.S. Dist. Ct. (so. dist.) Tex., U.S. Supreme Ct., U.S. Ct. Appeals (5th cir.). Ptnr. Norman, Thrall, Angle & Guy LLP, Rusk, Tex., 1981—. Baptist. General civil litigation, Personal injury, General practice. Office: Norman Thrall Angle & Guy LLP 106 E 5th St Rusk TX 75785-1310

**GUY, WILLIAM LEWIS, III,** lawyer; b. Mpls., Apr. 27, 1946; s. William L. and Elizabeth Jean (Mason) G.; m. Marilyn J. Walter, July 11, 1969; children: Stephanie J., Mark W. BBA, U. N.D., 1968, JD, 1976. Bar: Minn. 1976, N.D. 1976, U.S. Tax Ct. 1976. Ptnr. Gunhus, Grinnell, Klinger, Swenson & Guy, Ltd., Moorhead, Minn., 1976—. Vice chmn. Bd. Pensions Am. Luth. Ch., Mpls., 1980-88. Served to lt. USNR, 1968-73. Mem. Minn. Bar Assn., N.D. Bar Assn. (chaired) chmn. subcom. corp. sect., revised N.D. Bus. Corp. Act 1984), N.D. Soc. CPA's, Minn. Soc. CPA's. Democrat. Avocations: reading, skiing, sailing. Estate planning, Probate, General corporate. Home: 3651 Fairway Rd Fargo ND 58102-1278 Office: Gunhus Grinnell Klinger Swenson & Guy Ltd 215 30th St N Moorhead MN 56560-2546

**GUYNES, VERTA CORINA,** paralegal, business owner; b. San Bernardino, Calif., May 18, 1960; d. Luther C. and Doris Marie (Guynes) G. Student, U. Redlands, 1982. Real estate processor Loren Phillips & Assocs., L.A., 1980-82; corp. legal asst. Ashkenazy Enterprises, Inc., L.A., 1982-83; adminstrv. asst. Dobbins & Assocs., L.A., 1983-84; corp. legal asst. Kindel & Anderson, L.A., 1984-93; proprieter Doris' Christian Books and Gifts, Pasadena, Calif., 1993—; exec. dir., founder Teen Crisis Intervention, Pasadena, 1994—. Recipient Outstanding Contbns. to the Cmty. award Nat. Christian Educator's, L.A., 1996, Outstanding Contbn. to Cmty. Youth award County of Los Angeles, 1996. Mem. Kiwanis Club, Alladena Youth Focus Group. Baptist. Avocations: tennis, racquetball, basketball, cycling. Home: 801 N Garfield Ave Apt 13 Pasadena CA 91104-4267

**GUYNN, RANDALL DAVID,** lawyer; b. L.A., Oct. 13, 1957. BA in Econs. with highest honors, Brigham Young U., 1981; JD, U. Va., 1984. Bar: N.Y. 1987, D.C. 1988. Law clk. to Judge J. Clifford Wallace U.S. Ct. Appeals 9th Cir., San Diego, 1984-85; law clk. to Justice William H. Rehnquist U.S. Supreme Ct., Washington, 1985-86; assoc. Davis Polk & Wardwell, N.Y.C., 1986-93, ptnr., 1993—; co-head Fin. Instns. Group, 1996—. Author: U.S. Disclosure Standards for Banks, 1995, Modernizing Securities Pledging Laws, 1996, Foreign Bank Acquisitions of U.S. Banks, 1998; exec. editor Va. Law Rev., 1983-84; author booklet. Mem. ABA (mem. UCC com. 1993—), Internat. Bar Assn. (chmn. com. on modernizing pledging laws 1994—), Order of Coif. Republican. Mem. LDS Ch. Avocation: photography. Banking, Securities. Office: Davis Polk & Wardwell 405 Lexington Ave New York NY 10017-3906

**GUYTON, ODELL,** lawyer; b. Dublin, Ga., June 3, 1955; s. Clarence and Eleanor Jeanell (Graves) G.; m. Karen Boyer, May 19, 1979; children: Kiley Jeanelle, Dana Laurel, Jeffrey Leonard, Trevor Graves. BA, Moravian Coll., 1977; JD, Am. U., 1981. Bar: Pa. 1981, U.S. Dist. Ct. (ea. dist.) Pa., U.S. Ct. Appeals (3rd cir.). Dep. dist. atty. pre-trial and victim services div. Phila., 1981-88; asst. U.S. atty. U.S. Dist. Ct. (ea. dist.) Pa., 1988-93; of counsel Miller, Alfano & Raspanti, P.C., Phila., 1993—; spl. asst. U.S. Atty. Office/U.S. Dept. Justice, 1993; corp. compliance officer U. Pa., 1997; chmn. Justice Ops. Task Force, Phila., 1986—; co-chmn. Victim Witness Task Force, Phila., 1986—; mem. supervisory bd. Phila. Adult Probation Intensive Supervison Program; mem. bd. dirs. Northwest Victim Svcs. Chmn. Community Safety Program Northwest Interfaith Movement, Phila., 1983-85; mem. exec. com., chmn. acad. program com., bd. trustees Moravian Coll. Named one of Outstanding Young Men of Am., U.S. Jaycees, 1981. Mem. ABA, Pa. Bar, Phila. Bar Assn., Fed. Bar Assn., Pa. Dist. Atty's. Assn.; bd. dirs. Health Care Compliance Assn., Phi Alpha Delta. Avocations: English history, biking, camping. Office: U Pa Office Audit and Compliance St Leonards Ct 3819 Chestnut St Philadelphia PA 19104-3171

**GUZMAN, MATTHEW LOPEZ,** lawyer; b. Joliet, Ill., Apr. 15, 1967; s. Raul and Amelia (Lopez) G.; m. Cynthia Lyn Gendry, Sept. 3, 1994. AA, Joliet (Ill.) Jr. Coll., 1987; BS in Mgmt., So. Ill. U., 1989, JD, 1993. Bar: Ill. 1993, U.S. Dist. Ct. (no. dist.) Ill. 1993. Asst. state's atty. Will County State's Atty.'s Office, Joliet, 1993-95; asst. corp. counsel City of Joliet, 1995-97; asst. states atty., chief misdemeanor divsn. Will County States Atty.'s Office, Joliet, 1997—; prosecutor arson unit Will County States Attys. Office, Joliet, 1994. Mem. Will County Bar Assn. Office: Will County State Atty Office City of Joliet Rm 200 14 W Jefferson St Joliet IL 60432-4300 Address: 1610 Old Oaks Ct Plainfield IL 60544-6553

**GWARTNEY, TORE BEAL,** lawyer; b. St. Maries, Idaho, July 2, 1959; d. James Jergon and Ingrid Ann Beal; m. C. Ryan McCaene (div. May 1991); m. John Michael Gwartney, Dec. 31, 1992. BA, Boise State U., 1982; JD, U. Idaho, 1993. Bar: Idaho 1993. Pvt. practice investment cons., fin. planner Boise, Idaho, 1982-90; assoc. Cosho Humphrey Greener & Welsh, Boise, 1993—, ptnr., shareholder, 1999—. Apptd. mem. Coun. on Domestic Violence, Boise, 1997. Mem. ABA, Idaho State Bar. Lutheran. Avocations: golf, horse back riding. Family and matrimonial, Estate planning. Home: 955 S Tranquil Ln Eagle ID 83616-4366 Office: Cosho Humphrey Greener & Welsh 815 W Washington St Boise ID 83702-5558

**GWINN, D. LEE,** lawyer, mediator; b. May 21, 1960; s. Glenn H. and Sue Gwinn; m. Lynnett Dee Rath, May 21, 1982; children: Grayson, Gibson. BS in Voice Performance, Midwestern State U., Wichita Falls, Tex., 1982; JD, Tex. Tech. U., 1985. Bar: Tex. 1985. Assoc. Chappell & Handy, Ft. Worth, 1985-86, Brown, Herman, Scott, Dean & Miles, Ft. Worth, 1986-92; atty.-mediator in pvt. practice Ft. Worth, 1993—. Mem. Tarrant County Bar Assn. (vice chmn. solo and small firm sect. 1998—, co-chmn. ADR sect.). Ch. of Christ. Avocations: sports, music. Civil rights, Contracts commercial, Estate planning. Office: 6500 W Vickery Blvd Fort Worth TX 76116-9109

**GWYN, WILLIAM BLAIR, JR.,** lawyer; b. North Wilkesboro, N.C., Feb. 14, 1950. BS, Wake Forest U., 1972, MBA, 1975, JD, 1981. Bar: N.C. 1981, U.S. Dist. Ct. N.C. 1981, U.S. Tax Ct. 1982, U.S. Ct. Claims 1986, U.S. Ct. Appeals (fed. cir.) 1986. Mgmt. trainee Wachovia Bank & Trust Co., Winston-Salem, N.C., 1972-73; fin. analyst AMP, Inc., Winston-Salem, 1975-76, product mgr., 1976-78; assoc. Narron Holdford Babb et al, Wilson, N.C., 1981-83; ptnr. Narron Holdford Babb et al, Wilson, 1983-85; assoc. Maupin Taylor Ellis & Adams, Raleigh, N.C., 1985-87; ptnr. Maupin Taylor Ellis & Adams, Raleigh, 1988—. Co-author: Mergers and Acquisitions, 1989, S Corporations, 1990, Corporations and Business Law, 1992. Dir. Am. Heart Assn., Raleigh, 1988—, chmn., 1993-94; dir. Coun. for Entrepreneurial Devel., Research Triangle, 1993—. Mem. ABA, N.C. Bar Assn., Wake County Bar Assn. Presbyterian. Avocations: golf, tennis, sailing. General corporate, Finance, Mergers and acquisitions. Office: Maupin Taylor Ellis & Adams 3200 Beech Leaf Ct Ste 500 Raleigh NC 27604-1064

**GYEMANT, ROBERT ERNEST,** lawyer; b. Managua, Nicaragua, Jan. 17, 1944; s. Emery and Magda (Von Rechnitz) G.; came to U.S., 1949, naturalized, 1954; A.B. magna cum laude, U. Calif. Los Angeles, 1965; J.D., U. Calif. Berkeley, 1968; children from previous marriage: Robert Ernest Jr., Anne Elizabeth; m. Sally Bartch Libhart, Oct. 17, 1992; children: Emily Bartch, Amanda Nancy, Katherine Libhart. Tax accountant Ernst & Ernst, CPAs, Oakland, Calif., 1966-68; CPA, Calif., 1967; admitted to Calif. bar, 1969, N.Y., 1981; asso. atty. Orrick, Herrington, Rowley & Sutcliffe, San Francisco, 1968-69; partner law firm Skornia, Rosenblum & Gyemant, San Francisco, 1969-74; law offices Robert Ernest Gyemant profl. corp., San Francisco, 1975; exec. v.p. finance Topps & Trowsers, San Francisco, 1977-79; cons., pvt. investor, 1979; with ComDial Corp, San Francisco; co-founder Com Vu Corp., N.Y.C., 1979-83; ptnr. Rosen, McCarthy, Gyemant & Babbitts, P.C., San Francisco, 1993-97; prin. Knapp, Petersen & Clarke, P.C., Glendale, Calif., 1997—; instr. U. Calif. at Berkeley, 1968. Mem. Calif. Council Criminal Justice Jud. Process Task Force, 1971-73. Mem. Calif. State Rep. Ctrl. Com.; trustee French-Am. Bilingual Sch., San Francisco, 1978-82; hon. vice consul Republic of Costa Rica, 1981—. Mem. ABA, San Francisco Bar Assn. (co-chmn. sect. on juvenile justice 1971) State Bar Calif. (cert. specialist criminal law 1988-93, com. on unauthorized practice law 1974-76, spl. com. on juvenile justice 1974, commr. San Francisco County juvenile justice comm. 1976—), AICPA, Calif. CPA Soc. (mem. accounting prins. com. 1969), Assn. Def. Counsel, Calif. Trial Lawyers Assn., San Francisco Downtown Assn., San Francisco World Trade Club, N.Y. Athletic Club, Racquet and Tennis Club (N.Y.C.). Author publs. in field; editor: Calif. Law Rev., 1967-68. Email: rgyemant@hfbllp.com. Banking, Bankruptcy, Federal civil litigation. Office: Hill Farrer & Burrill LLP 37th floor 1 California Plz 300 S Grand Ave Los Angeles CA 90071

**GYLLENBORG, SCOTT CHRISTIE,** lawyer; b. Kansas City, Mo., Apr. 3, 1956; s. Richard Eugene Gyllenborg and Anne Marty Aikin. BA in Lit., U. Kans., 1979, JD, 1988. Bar: Kans. 1988, U.S. Dist. Ct. Kans. 1988, U.S. Ct. Appeals (10th cir.) 1997. Asst. dist. atty. Dist. Atty. 10th Jud. Dist., Johnson County, Kans., 1989-91; assoc. Watson and Marshall, L.C., Kansas City, 1991-96; mem. Norton, Hubbard Ruzicka and Kreamer L.C., Olathe, Kans., 1996—; city prosecutor City of Mission Hills, Kans., 1996—. Trustee The Barston Sch., Kansas City, 1998—; dir. Olathe Arts Alliance, 1993-95; mem. Jayhawks for Higher Edn., Lawrence, Kans., 1995—. Named Boss of Yr. Johnson County Legal Profls., 1997-98. Mem. ABA, Nat. Assn. of Criminal Def. Lawyers, Johnson County Bar Assn. (criminal bench/bar com.), Am. Mensa Soc. Avocations: golf, travel, the arts. Office: Norton Hubbard Ruzicka & Kreamer LC 130 N Cherry St Ste 300 Olathe KS 66061-3460

**HAAKH, GILBERT EDWARD,** lawyer; b. Rotterdam, Netherlands, July 25, 1923; came to U.S., 1946; s. Otto and Rose C. (Holder) H. BA, U. Calif., Berkeley, 1947; LLB, Harvard U., 1950. Bar: Calif. 1952, Mass. 1952, U.S. Dist. Ct. (ctrl. dist.) Calif. 1953, U.S. Dist. ct. (so. dist.) Calif. 1972, U.S. Supreme Ct. 1971. Assoc. O'Melveny & Myers, L.A., 1951-61; ptnr. Donnelley, Clark, Chase & Haakh, L.A., 1962-73, MacDonald, Halsted & Laybourne, L.A., 1974-86, Baker & McKenzie, L.A., 1987-93; of counsel Kindel & Anderson, L.A., 1994-96, McKenna & Cuneo, L.A., 1997—; bd. dirs. various corps. Mem. ABA, Los Angeles County Bar Assn., Am. Soc. Corp. Secs., Bond Club of L.A. General corporate, Mergers and acquisitions, Securities. Office: McKenna & Cuneo LLP 444 S Flower St Los Angeles CA 90071-2901

**HAAR, ROBERT THEODORE,** lawyer; b. St. Louis, Apr. 11, 1950; s. Robert Edwin and Mary Ann (Rose) H.; m. Cathleen Annette Sanford, June 21, 1948; children: Alexandra, Matthew, Mark. BS in Elec. Engring., Stanford U., 1972; BPh in Econs., Oxford (Eng.) U., 1974; JD, Yale U., 1977. Law clk. to Hon. Harold Leventhal U.S. Ct. Appeals (D.C. cir.), Washington, 1977-78; law clk. to Justice William H. Rehnquist U.S. Supreme Ct., Washington, 1978-79; atty.-advisor Office of Legal Counsel, U.S. Dept. Justice, Washington, 1979-80; asst. U.S. atty. U.S. Atty.'s Office, St. Louis, 1980-85; ptnr. Kohn, Shands, Elbert, Gianoulakis & Gilsum LLP, St. Louis, 1986-97, Haar & Woods, LLP, St. Louis, 1997—; chair civil justice reform act adv. group U.S. Dist. Ct. (ea. dist.) Mo., 1995-97. Police commr. St. Louis Met. Police Dept., 1994-98. Rhodes scholar, 1972. General civil litigation, Professional liability, Criminal. Home: 3635 Flora Pl Saint Louis MO 63110-3703 Office: Haar & Woods LLP 1010 Market St Ste 1620 Saint Louis MO 63101-2000

**HAARMANN, BRUCE DONALD,** lawyer; b. Milw., Jan. 14, 1952. BA, U. Wis., 1974, JD, 1978. Bar: Wis. 1978; CPCU. Legal counsel Legis. Audit Bur., State of Wis., 1978-84; asst. gen. counsel Wausau (Wis.) Ins. Cos., 1984—. Mem. ABA, Marathon County Bar Assn., Am. Corp. Counsel Assn. Insurance, Contracts commercial, Antitrust. Office: Wausau Ins Cos 2000 Westwood Dr Wausau WI 54401-7802

**HAAS, JACQUELINE CRAWFORD,** lawyer; b. St. Louis, Nov. 9, 1935; d. Ernest Augustus and Nora (Fullard) Crawford; m. Karl Alan Haas, Jan. 27, 1962 (dec. Mar. 1986); children: James Andrew, Susan Jennifer, David Reid, Peter Crawford. AB, Cornell U., 1957; LLB, Harvard U., 1961. Bar: N.Y. 1962, U.S. Dist. Ct. (so. dist.) N.Y. 1963, U.S. Ct. Appeals (2d cir.) 1968, Mass. 1972. Assoc. Lord, Day & Lord, N.Y.C., 1961-63; atty. family ct. div. Legal Aid Soc., Bklyn., 1964-66; exam. atty. N.Y.C. Dept. of Investigation, 1966-68, exec. asst. to commr., 1969-71; pvt. practice Weston, Mass., 1971—; mem. Greater Boston com. Harvard U. Law Sch. Fund, Cambridge, Mass.,

1976—. Del. Mass. Dem. Issues Conv., 1983, 85, 87, 89, 92, 93, 95, 97, 99, Mass. Dem. Nominating Conv., 1984, 86, 94, 96, 98; mem. platform com. Mass. Dem. Com., 1993; mem. Dem. Town Com., Weston, 1984—, vice chmn., 1984-86; chmn. bd. Roxbury-Weston Programs, Inc., 1982-84; mem. family com. METCO, 1973-75, mem. cmty. coord. coun., 1982-85; mem. Weston Housing Needs Com., 1991-93. Mem. ABA (civil practice and procedure of the antitrust sect.), Mass. Bar Assn., Assn. of Bar of N.Y.C., Harvard Law Sch. Assn. Mass. (v.p. 1991—). Democrat. Episcopalian. Avocations: skiing, sailing, literature, travel. General corporate, Federal civil litigation, Criminal. Office: 42 Partridge Hill Rd Weston MA 02493-1750

**HAAS, JOSEPH ALAN,** court administrator, lawyer; b. Riverside, Calif., June 30, 1950; s. Garland August and Pauline (Anderson) H.; m. Barbara Roberts, May 27, 1978; children: Natalie C., Christina R. BA in Econs., U. Wash., 1972, MA in Econs., 1974; JD, U. Puget Sound, 1983. Bar: Wash. 1984, U.S. Dist. Ct. (we. dist.) Wash. 1984, Md. 1986, U.S. Ct. Appeals (4th cir.) 1986. Regional coord. Adminstrv. Office U.S. Cts., Washington, 1975-80; chief dep. clk. U.S. Dist. Ct. for Western Wash., Seattle, 1981-84; clk. U.S. Dist. Ct. Md., Balt., 1984-96, U.S. Dist. Ct. for S.D., Sioux Falls, 1996—. Mem. Nat. Assn. for Ct. Mgmt., Fed. Ct. Clks. Assn. (pres. 1987-88), Fed. Bar Assn. (bd. govs. 1989-96, treas. 1991-95), Wash. State Bar Assn. Office: US Dist Ct 400 S Phillips Ave Rm 128 Sioux Falls SD 57104-6851

**HAAS, MICHAEL WILLIAM,** lawyer; b. Slidell, La., Jan. 21, 1967; s. William E. and Sandra M. (McCreg) H.; m. Brenda A. Burger, May 30, 1992. BSEE, Ohio No. U., 1989; JD, U. Pitts., 1992. Bar: Pa. 1992, D.C. 1994. Assoc. patent atty. Cushman, Darby & Cushman, Washington, 1992-97; intellectual property counsel Respironics Inc., Pitts., 1997—. Intellectual property, Patent. Office: Respironics Inc 1501 Ardmore Blvd Pittsburgh PA 15221-4401

**HAAS, RICHARD,** lawyer; b. Glens Falls, N.Y., Sept. 1, 1924; s. Marc and Henrietta (Vogelsanger) H.; m. Dorothy J. Walz, Aug. 2, 1946; children—Eric, Marco, Gregory. A.B., UCLA, 1946; LL.B., U. Calif.-Berkeley, 1950. Bar: Calif. 1951, U.S. Dist. Ct. (no., cen., ea. and so. dists.) Calif. 1951, U.S. Supreme Ct. 1970. Ptnr. Brobeck, Phleger & Harrison, San Francisco, 1959-79; mem. Lasky, Haas & Cohler, San Francisco, 1979-94. Served to lt. USNR, 1941-46. Fellow Am. Bar Found., Am. Coll. Trial Lawyers; mem. Order of Coif. Republican. Clubs: Claremont Country (Oakland, Calif.); Berkeley Tennis. Antitrust, Federal civil litigation, General practice. Home: 2901 Forest Ave Berkeley CA 94705-1310 Office: Lasky Haas & Cohler 505 Sansome St Fl 12 San Francisco CA 94111-3106

**HABECK, JAMES ROY,** lawyer; b. Berlin, Wis., Aug. 11, 1954; s. Roy J. and Phyllis J. (Hazelwood) H.; m. Penny Ann Gillman. BS, U. Wis., Stevens Point, 1976; JD, Marquette U., 1979. Bar. Wis. 1979, U.S. Dist. Ct. (ea. and we. dists.) Wis. 1979, U.S. Supreme Ct. 1990. Atty. Rutgers Law Office, Sheboygan Falls, Wis., 1979-80; pvt. practice Shawano, Wis., 1980—; family ct. commr. Shawano, Menominee County, 1983—; corp. counsel Shawano County, 1984-87, 90, 93; legal counsel Wis. Towns Assn., Shawano, 1987—. Contbr. newsletter articles Wis. Towns Assn., 1987—. Pres. Big Brothers/Big Sisters, Shawano, 1984-88; v.p. Rep. Ctrl. Com., Shawano County, 1993-99, chmn. 1999—; atty. St. James Lutheran Ch., Shawano, 1983—. Named Friend of 4-H Shawano County 4-H, 1990. Mem. Shawano County Bar Assn. (sec.-treas., pres. 1987-93), Wis. Family Ct. Commrs. Assn. (sec.-treas., pres. 1992-96, dir. 1998—), Shawano County Agrl. Soc., Rotary, White Tails Unlimited, Wild Turkey Fedn. Republican. Lutheran. Avocations: scoring high sch. basketball games. Municipal (including bonds), Family and matrimonial, Probate. Office: Habeck Law Office 141 N Main St Shawano WI 54166-2355

**HABER, JOEL ABBA,** lawyer; b. N.Y.C., Sept. 17, 1943. BS, U. Buffalo, 1964; JD, U. Wis., 1967. Bar: Wis. 1967, Ill. 1968, U.S. Supreme Ct. 1973. Trial atty. SEC, Washington and Chgo., 1967-70; assoc. Schiff, Hardin & Waite, Chgo., 1970-71; ptnr. Chatz, Sugarman, Abrams & Haber, Chgo., 1972-82, Fagel, Haber & Maragos, Chgo., 1982-90, Fagel & Haber, Chgo., 1991—; spl. counsel to Ill. Dept. Ins., 1983—; mem. securities law adv. com. Ill. Sec. of State. Mem. ABA, Wis. Bar Assn., Chgo. Bar Assn., U. Wis. Law Alumni Assn. (pres. 1987-89). General corporate.

**HABER, KARIN DUCHIN,** lawyer; b. Newark, Nov. 5, 1953. BA, Goucher Coll., 1974; JD, Temple U., 1977. Bar: N.J. 1977, U.S. Dist. Ct. 1977, U.S. Supreme Ct. Sole practitioner Union and Florham Park, N.J., 1980-97; ptnr. Haber & Silver, Florham Park, 1997—. Family and matrimonial, Landlord-tenant, General civil litigation. Office: Haber & Silver 123 Columbia Tpke Florham Park NJ 07932-2117

**HABERMANN, TED RICHARD,** lawyer; b. Waupaca, Wis., Nov. 1, 1957; s. Richard Dale and Laura Aleen (Defrates) H. BS, U. Wis., 1980; JD, Valparaiso U., 1983. Bar: Ind. 1983, Tenn. 1989, U.S. Dist. Ct. (no and so. dists.) Ind. 1983, U.S. Dist. Ct. (mid. dist.) Tenn. 1990, U.S. Tax Ct. 1984, U.S. Supreme Ct., 1989. Mng. atty. Davisson & Davisson, P.C., Anderson, Ind., 1984-89; corp. counsel Spectra Distbn./Sound Stage Cos., Nashville, Tenn., 1989-91; gen. counsel, sec. Servpro Industries, Inc., Gallatin, Tenn., 1991-98; asst. gen. counsel, asst. sec. Shoney's Inc., Nashville, 1998—; Contbr. Valparaiso U. Law Rev. Mem. ABA, Ind. Bar Assn. (mem. forum on franchising), Tenn. Bar Assn., Jaycees (v.p. 1987), Exchange Club (dir. 1987), Sigma Phi Epsilon, Delta Theta Phi. Republican. Methodist. Franchising. Home: 4724 Aaron Dr Antioch TN 37013-4218 Office: Shoneys Inc 1717 Elm Hill Pike Nashville TN 37210-3707

**HABIAN, BRUCE GEORGE,** lawyer; b. Rockville Centre, N.Y., Nov. 23, 1947; s. George and Doris Marie (Cipollina) H. A.B., Boston Coll., 1969; J.D., Villanova U., 1972. Bar: N.Y. 1973, N.J. 1974, U.S. Dist. Ct. (so. and ea. dists.) N.Y. 1975, U.S. Ct. Appeals (2d cir.) 1975, U.S. Supreme Ct. 1976. Asst. corp. counsel Office Corp. Counsel N.Y.C., 1972-73; assoc. Martin, Clearwater & Bell, N.Y.C., 1973-79, ptnr., 1979—, sr. ptnr., 1983—; lectr. Practicing Law Inst., N.Y.C., 1981; lectr. in risk mgmt. Hosp. Fin. Mgmt. Assn., Hartford, Conn., 1981; cons. N.Y. State Commr. Health, N.Y.C., 1983; mem. Med. Malpractice Mediation Panel, Nassau County, N.Y., 1983-84. Mem. Assn. Bar City N.Y., ABA (litigation sect.). Republican. Roman Catholic. Club: University (N.Y.C.). Personal injury, Federal civil litigation, State civil litigation. Home: 993 Park Ave Apt 1B New York NY 10028-0809 Office: Martin Clearwater and Bell 220 E 42nd St New York NY 10017-5806

**HABIGER, RICHARD J.,** lawyer; b. Kansas City, Mo., July 25, 1941; s. Albert John and Katherine Delia (McDormott) H.; m. Martha Louise Hauber, Nov. 28, 1964; children: Christine Marie, Timothy Shawn, Brian Paul, Monica Louise, Kathleen Rene. BA, Rockhurst Coll., 1963; JD, U. Mo., Kansas City, 1970. Bar: Mo. 1970, Ill. 1976, U.S. Supreme Ct. 1974, U.S. Ct. Appeals (7th cir.) 1976, U.S. Dist. Ct. (we. dist.) Mo. 1970, U.S. Dist. Ct. (so. dist.) Ill. 1976, U.S. Dist. Ct. (cen. dist.) Ill. 1980, U.S. Tax Ct. 1982. Asst. office mgr. Hudson Oil Co., Kansas City, Kans., 1963-66; claims supr. Blue Cross/Blue Shield, Kansas City, Mo., 1966-68; investigator, clk. Rogers, Field, Gentry, Benjamin & Roberson, Kansas City, Mo., 1968-70; Smith fellow, staff atty. Legal Aid & Defender Soc. of Greater Kansas City, 1970-72; staff atty. Nat. Juvenile Law Ctr., Sch. Law, St. Louis U., 1972-75; sr. staff atty. legal clinic, sch. law So. Ill. U., Carbondale, 1975-80, mng. atty., 1980—. Author: (with others) Law and Tactics in Juvenile Cases, 2nd edit. 1975, Sentencing Problems and Remedies of Sentenced Prisoners, 3d edit. 1987; contbr. articles to profl. jours. Vol. counsel various civic orgns.; co-organizer, instr. High Sch. Legal Edn. Program, Lawyers Com. on Urban Affairs and Sch. Dist. of Kansas City, 1970-71, 71-72; mem. clinic study subcom., curriculum com. Sch. Law, So. Ill. U., 1980-82. Reginald Heber Smith Community Lawyer Fellowship Program fellow, 1970-72. Mem. ABA (sect. criminal justice, criminal appellate issue com. 1979-84, legal edn. and admissions to bar com. 1988—, sect. real property, probate and trust 1988—, spl. needs trusts and other protective vehicles com. 1993—, practice mgmt. com. 1993—), Ill. Bar Assn. (chmn. correctional facilities and svcs. com. 1983-84), Mo. Bar Assn. (juvenile cts. and laws com. 1973-75), Assn. of Am. Law Sch. (clin. legal edn. sect.), Clin. Legal Edn. Assn. (charter), Nat. Acad. Elder Law Attys. Elder, General practice. Home: 54L Meadowood Ln Carbondale IL 62901-1942 Office: So Ill U Sch Law Legal Clinic 104 Lesar Law Bldg Carbondale IL 62901

**HABLUTZEL, NANCY ZIMMERMAN,** lawyer, educator; b. Chgo., Mar. 16, 1940; d. Arnold Fred Zimmerman and Maxine (Lewison) Zimmerman Goodman; m. Philip Norman Hablutzel, July 1, 1980; children: Margo Lynn, Robert Paul. BS, Northwestern U., 1960; MA, Northeastern Ill. U., 1972; JD, Ill. Inst. Tech. Chgo.-Kent Coll. Law, 1980; PhD, Loyola U., Chgo., 1983. Bar: Ill. 1980, U.S. Dist. Ct. (no. dist.) Ill. 1980, U.S. Supreme Ct., 1995. Speech therapist various pub. schs. and hosps., Chgo. and St. Louis, 1960-63, 65-72; audiologist U. Chgo. Hosps., 1963-65; instr. spl. edn. Chgo. State U., 1972-76; asst. prof. Loyola U., Chgo., 1981-87; adj. prof. Ill. Inst. Tech. Chgo.-Kent Coll. Law, 1982—, Lewis U., 1990-92; lectr. Loyola U., Chgo., 1990—; legal dir. Legal Clinic for Disabled, Chgo., 1984-85, exec. dir., 1985-87; of counsel Whitted & Spain P.C., 1987-89; prin. Hablutzel & Assocs., Chgo., 1989-94; hearing officer Circuit Ct. of Cook County, 1994-96, Supervising Hearing Officer, 1995-97; faculty No. Ill. U., 1997—; advisor Ill. Dept. Children and Family Svcs., 1997—. Mem. Ill. Gov.'s Com. on Handicapped, 1972-75; mem. Coun. for Exceptional Children, faculty moderator student div., 1982-87, Ill. Atty. Gen. adv. com. for disabled, 1985—; mem. adv. com. Scouting for People With Disabilities, Chgo. Area Boy Scouts Am., 1988-92. Loyola-Mellon Found. grantee, 1983. Author: (with B. McMahon) Americans With Disabilities Act: Access and Accomodations, 1992; contbg. editor Nat. Disability Law Reporter, 1991-92. Mem. Nat. Coun. of Juvenile and Fam.ly Court Judges, 1995— (Permanency Planning Com. and Continuing Judical Edn. Com.). Fellow Chgo. Bar Found. (life), Ill. Bar Found. (sec. fellows 1992, vice-chair fellows 1993, chair 1994); mem. ABA, Ill. Bar Assn. (assoc., standing com. on juvenile justice, sec. 1986-87, vice chmn. 1987-88, chmn. 1988-89, Inst. Pub. Affairs 1985—, legis. com. 1991—, mem. juvenile justice sect. coun. 1994—), Chgo. Bar Assn. (corp. law com., exec. com. 1984-94, chmn. Div. IV 1988-91, sec. 1991-92, vice chair 1992-93, chair 1993-94), Chgo. Hearing Soc. (Marion Goldman award 1988, bd. dirs. 1992-94). Avocations: sailing, travel, swimming, cooking. Office: 1911 S Indiana Ave Fl 10 Chicago IL 60616-1310

**HABLUTZEL, PHILIP NORMAN,** law educator; b. Flagstaff, Ariz., Aug. 23, 1935; s. Charles Edward and Electa Margaret (Cain) H.; m. Nancy Zimmerman, July 1, 1980; children: Margo Lynn, Robert Paul. BA, La. State U., 1958; postgrad., U. Heidelberg, Fed. Republic Germany, 1959-60, 62-64; MA, U. Chgo., 1960, JD, 1967. Bar: Ill. 1967, U.S. Dist. Ct. (no. dist.) Ill. 1967, U.S. Supreme Ct. 1995. Rsch. atty. Am. Bar Found., Chgo., 1967-68, sr. rsch. atty., 1968-71; asst. prof. law Chgo.-Kent Coll. Law, Ill. Inst. Tech., 1971-73, assoc. prof., 1973-79, prof., 1979—, dir. grad. program in fin. svcs. law, 1985-96; dir. student exch. program with U. Darmstadt, Germany, 1994—; co-dir. Ann. conf. on Not-for-Profit Orgns., Chgo., 1984—; chair Conf. on Derivative Fin. Products, 1995; sr. Fulbright prof. U. Mainz, Germany, 1993; lectr. banking law U. Torcuato di Tella, Buenos Aires, 1995; cons. OEO Legal Svcs. Program, 1967-69; pres., trustee Chgo. Sch. Profl. Psychology, 1979-83; instr. course on profl. responsibility Chgo. Merc. Exch., 1990-93; reporter Ill. sect. state's com. on revision of not-for-profit corp. act, 1984-87; reporter Ill. sect. of state's corp. laws adv. com., 1986-89, mem., 1989—. Author: (with R. Garrett, W. Scott) Model Business Corporation Act Annotated, 2d edit., 3 vols., 1971, (with J. Levi) Model Residential Landlord-Tenant Code, 1969, International Banking Law, 2 vols., 1994. Mem. Adv. com. Scouting for People with Disabilities, Chgo. area Boy Scouts Am., 1988-92. Rotary Found. Advanced Study fellow, 1959-60. Fellow Chgo. Bar Found. (life), Ill. Bar Found.; mem. ABA (chmn. subcom. on adoption of Uniform Trade Secrets Act 1984-86, com. on consumer fin. svcs. 1989—, ad hoc com. on Ctrl. and Ea. European Law Initiative 1991-95), Ill. State Bar Assn. (uniform comml. code revision com. 1989-96, coun., sect. comml. banking and bankruptcy law 1990-96, sec. 1991-92, vice chmn. 1992-93, chmn. 1993-94), Chgo. Bar Assn. (chmn. com. on sci., tech. and law 1971-72, sec. corp. law com. 1986-87, vice-chmn. corp. law com. 1987-88, chmn. corp. law com. 1988-89, task force state takeover legis. 1987-89, joint com. banking act revisions 1988-90, chair ann. seminar on forming and Ill. Corp. 1990—). Republican. Presbyterian. Avocations: travel, opera, classical music, photography. Office: 565 W Adams St Chicago IL 60661-3613

**HABUSH, ROBERT LEE,** lawyer; b. Milw., Mar. 22, 1936; s. Jesse James and Beatrice (Liebenberg) H.; m. Miriam Lee Friedman, Aug. 25, 1957; children: Sherri Ellen, William Scott, Jodi Lynn. BBA, U. Wis., 1959, JD, 1961. Bar: Wis. 1961, U.S. Dist. Ct. (ea. and we. dists.) Wis. 1961, U.S. Ct. Appeals (7th cir.) 1965, U.S. Supreme Ct. 1986. Pres. Habush, Habush, Davis & Rottier, S.C., Milw., 1961—; lectr. U. Wis. Law Sch., Marquette U. Law Sch., State Bar Wis., other legal orgns. Author: Cross Examination of Non Medical Experts, 1981. Contbr. articles to legal jours. Served to capt. U.S. Army, 1959-75. Mem. ABA, Wis. Bar Assn., Wis. Acad. Trial Lawyers (pres. 1968-69), ATLA (bd. govs. 1983-86, pres. 1986-87, mem. Nat. Coll. Advocacy), Internat. Acad. Trial Lawyers (bd. dirs. 1983-87, 91-92), Am. Bd. Trial Advocates, Internat. Soc. Barristers, Inner Circle Advocates, Am. Soc. Writers on Legal Subjects, Nat. Bd. Trial Advocates, Trial Lawyers for Pub. Justice, Roscoe Pound Found. Federal civil litigation, State civil litigation, Personal injury. Office: Habush Habush Davis & Rottier 777 E Wisconsin Ave Ste 2300 Milwaukee WI 53202-5381

**HACHMEISTER, JOHN H.,** lawyer, educator, mediator; b. Chgo., Nov. 24, 1944; s. Howard E. and Leah (Mace) H.; m. Lydia E. McCarver, Jan. 8, 1982; children: Steven, David, Mellissa, Rachel. BA in Polit. Sci., Cen. State U., Edmond, Okla., 1978; postgrad., Oklahoma City U., 1980-82; JD, Southwestern U., L.A., 1984. Bar: Calif. Technician Am. Chain & Cable, Franklin Park, Ill., 1972-76; assoc. Somers, Hall, et al., Gardena, Calif., 1985-90, Spray, Gould & Bowers, L.A., 1990-92, Fiore, Nordberg, et al, Irvine, Calif., 1992-94; pvt. practice Beach Cities Ctr. for Appropriate Dispute Resolution, Redondo Beach, Calif., 1994—; owner Jack's Imagination Enterprises, Redondo Beach, 1988—; former asst. prof. Calif. State U., Northridge; cons., facilitator Oklahoma City Coalition of Neighborhood Assns., 1972-82; spkr. in field. Author: (poetry) Colorado Cowboy Poetry Gathering, 1993; co-inventor solder jig for multi-wire cables, 1992; contbr. articles to profl. jours. Candidate for state sen. Dem. party, Torrance, Calif., 1990, Ho. of Reps., Oklahoma City, 1978; del. Dem. party convs. Okla. and Calif., 1974-92; mem. Mayor's Transp. Task Force, Oklahoma City, 1976-80; lt. gov. Okla. Intercollegiate Legis., 1977-78; judge Southwestern U. Moot Ct. Competition, Santa Ana, Calif., 1993. Named to Outstanding Young Men of Am. Mem. Calif. Bar Assn., Greenpeace, Torrance Area C. of C. (mem. cultural involvement task force, internat. bus. commn.), Human Rels. Found. Torrance. Avocations: hiking, camping, reading, writing, footracing. Product liability, General civil litigation, Construction. Home: 143 Via La Soledad Redondo Beach CA 90277-6625

**HACKETT, BARBARA (KLOKA),** federal judge; b. 1928. B of Philosophy, U. Detroit, 1948, JD, 1950. Bar: Mich. 1951, U.S. Dist. Ct. (ea. dist.) Mich. 1951, U.S. Ct. Appeals (6th cir.) 1951, U.S. Supreme Ct. 1957. Law clk. U.S. Dist. Ct. (ea. dist.) Mich., 1951-52; chief law clk. Mich. Ct. Appeals, 1965-66; asst. pros. atty. Wayne County, Mich., 1967-72; pvt. practice Detroit, 1952-53, 72-73; assoc. Frasco, Hackett & Mills, 1984-86; U.S. magistrate U.S. Dist. Ct. (ea. dist.) Mich., Detroit, 1973-84, judge, 1986—; mem. Interstate Commerce Commn., 1964. Trustee U. Detroit, 1983-89, Mercy High Sch., Farmington Hills, Mich. 1984-86, Detroit Symphony Orch., Orch. Hall Assocs., Detroit Sci. Ctr., United Community Svcs. Recipient Pres.'s Cabinet award U. Detroit Mercy, 1991. Mem. ABA (spl. ct. judge discovery abuse com. 1978-79, com. on cts. in cmty. 1979-84), Am. Judicature Soc., Fed. Bar Assn. (sec. 1981-82), Fed. Judges Assn., Nat. Assn. Women Judges, Nat. Dist. Attys. Assn., Nat. Assn. R.R. Trial Counsel, State Bar Mich., Women Lawyers Assn. Mich. Pros. Attys. Assn. Mich. (Disting. Svc. award 1971), Oakland County Bar Assn., U. Detroit Law Alumni Assn. (officer 1970-75, pres. 1975-77, Alumni Tower award 1976), Washtenaw County Bar Assn., Women's Econ. Club (bd. dirs. 1975-80, pres. 1980-81, named Detroit's Dynamic Women 1992), Econ. Club Detroit (bd. dirs. 1979-85, 88—), Phi Gamma Nu. Office: US Dist Ct Federal Bldg 200 E Liberty St Ste 400 Ann Arbor MI 48104-2121

**HACKETT, STANLEY HAILEY,** lawyer; b. Houston, May 31, 1945; s. Harley Benjamin and Rebecca Easterling (Willis) H.; m. Ann Elaine Aiken, May 29, 1971; children: Elizabeth Ann, Rebecca Aiken. BS in Banking Fin., U. S.C., 1967, JD magna cum laude, 1970; LLM, Harvard U., 1971. Bar: S.C. 1970, D.C. 1975, Ga. 1975. Atty. Office Chief Counsel IRS, Washington, 1971-72, spl. asst. to chief counsel, 1972-73; legis. asst. to Sen. Thurmond U.S. Senate, Washington, 1973-74; assoc. Henkel & Lamon, P.C., Atlanta, 1974-81; ptnr. Henkel, Hackett, Edge & Fleming, Atlanta, 1981-85, Troutman Sanders, Atlanta, 1985—; bd. dirs. Small Bus. Coun. Am., Washington, 1978—; mem. liaison com. S.E. region IRS, 1985—. Contbr. articles on taxation to profl. jours. Mem. Lawyers for Reagan/Bush, 1984; trustee Ga. Fed. Tax Conf.; advisor Ga. State Law Sch. Tax Clinic. Fellow Am. Coll. Tax Counsel; mem. ABA (tax sect.), Ga. Bar Assn. (chmn. tax sect. 1985-86), Phi Delta Theta. Republican. Episcopalian. Taxation, general. Office: Troutman Sanders 5200 Nations Bank Plaza Atlanta GA 30308-2216

**HACKETT, WESLEY PHELPS, JR.,** lawyer; b. Detroit, Jan. 3, 1939; s. Wesley P. and Helen (Decker) H.; children: Kelly D. Hackett Pell, Robin C. BA, Mich. State U., 1960; JD, Wayne State U., 1968. Bar: Mich. 1968, U.S. Dist. Ct. (we. dist.) Mich. 1971, U.S. Ct. Appeals (6th cir.) 1972, U.S. Dist. Ct. (ea. dist.) Mich. 1972, U.S. Supreme Ct. 1972, U.S. Ct. Mil. Appeals 1991. Law clk. Mich. Supreme Ct., Lansing, 1968-70; ptnr. Brown & Hackett, Lansing, 1971-73; pvt. practice Lansing, 1973-84; ptnr. Starr, Bissell & Hackett, Lansing, 1984-87; pvt. practice East Lansing, Mich., 1987-98, Saranac, Mich., 1998—; adj. prof. Thomas M. Cooley Law Sch., Lansing, 1973—; instr. Lansing C.C., 1981-99. Author: Evidence: A Trial Manual for Michigan Lawyers, 1981, Hackett's Evidence: Michigan and Federal, 2d edit., 1995; co-author: Hiring Legal Staff, 1990. Mem. City of East Lansing Planning Commn., 1969-72; bd. dirs. St. Vincent Home for Children, Lansing, 1974-82. 1st lt. USAF, 1961-65. Fellow Coll. Law Practice Mgmt.; mem. ABA (sec. gen. practice sect. 1990-91, vice-chair 1991-92, chair 1993-94, standing com. on lawyer referral and info. svcs. 1997—, sole practitioner of yr. 1994, founders award 1997), State Bar Mich. (chair legal econs. sect. 1990-91). Real property, Estate planning, General corporate.

**HACKNEY, H(IRAM) HAMILTON, III,** lawyer; b. Balt., Feb. 9, 1962; s. H. Hamilton Jr. and Anne King (Bailey) H.; m. Susan Paardecamp, Sept. 14, 1996. BA, Middlebury Coll., 1984; JD, U. Utah, 1990. Bar: Colo. 1990, U.S. Dist. Ct. Colo. 1991, Mass. 1995, U.S. Dist. Ct. Mass. 1995. Assoc. Sherman & Howard, Denver, 1990-91, Holme, Roberts & Owen, Denver, 1991-94, Choate, Hall & Stewart, Boston, 1994—; clk., dir. WasteCap Mass., Boston, 1995—; mem. steering com. environ. law sect. Boston Bar Assn., 1997-99, chair hazardous and solid waste com., 1997-99. Contbr. chpt. to book. Adv. bd. Nature Conservancy Mass., Boston, 1998. Mem. Dedham Country and Polo Club, Luncheon Club Boston (exec. com.). Avocations: golf, tennis. Environmental. Office: Exchange Pl 53 State St Boston MA 02109-2804

**HACKNEY, HUGH EDWARD,** lawyer; b. McGregor, Tex., July 17, 1944. BA, So. Meth. U., 1966, JD, 1969. Bar: Tex. 1970. Mem. Fulbright & Jaworski, LLP, Dallas, 1970-97; lawyer Locke Purnell Rain Harrell, Dallas, 1998-99, Locke Liddell & Sapp LLP, 1999—. Mem. ABA, State Bar Tex., Dallas Bar Assn., Houston Bar Assn., Phi Alpha Delta. General civil litigation, Private international, Labor. Office: Locke Purnell Rain Harrell 2200 Ross Ave Ste 2200 Dallas TX 75201-6776

**HACKWORTH, WILLIAM MICHAEL,** lawyer; b. Richmond, Ky., July 29, 1948; s. William F. and O'Donna F. Hackworth; m. Judith M. McArthur, June 30, 1973; children: William A., Elizabeth M. BA, Ohio State U., 1970; JD, U. Va., 1973, MPA, 1981. Bar: Va. 1973, U.S. Dist. Ct. (we. dist.) Va. 1973, U.S. Supreme Ct. 1977. Trial atty. U.S. Govt., Dept. Justice, Washington, 1974-77; asst. city atty. City of Roanoke, Va., 1978-88; county atty. York County, Yorktown, Va., 1988—. Author: William Hackworth: Revolutionary Soldier, 1995. Capt. U.S. Army, 1974-75. Mem. Va. Local Govt. Attys. (v.p. 1997-98, sec.-treas.), York County Libr. Found., York-Poquoson Bar Assn. (pres. 1995-96). Unitarian-Universalist. Avocations: running, hiking, travel. Office: County of York 224 Ballard St Yorktown VA 23690

**HADDAD, ERNEST MUDARRI,** lawyer; b. Boston, Oct. 30, 1938; s. Abraham and Elaine (Mudarri) H.;m. Kathleen L. Tracy; 1 child, Barton Edward; children from previous marriage: Scott Cochrane, Mark Mudarri. BA, Trinity Coll., Hartford, Conn., 1960; LLB, Boston U., 1964. Bar: Mass. 1964, U.S. Dist. Ct. Mass. 1966, U.S. Supreme Ct., 1981. Asst. dean and mem. faculty sch. law Boston U., 1966-71; asst. sec., gen. counsel Commonwealth of Mass. Exec. Office Human Svcs., Boston, 1971-76; gen. counsel Blue Cross and Blue Shield Mass. Inc., Boston, 1976-80; sec., gen. counsel The Mass. Gen. Hosp., Boston, 1981—, Ptnrs. HealthCare Sys., Inc., Boston, 1995—. Program chmn., mem. exec. com. Boston Study Group, 1979—; bd. commrs. Black Achievers Br. Greater Boston YMCA, 1995—. Recipient Trinity Coll. Alumni medal for Excellence, 1990. Mem. ABA (health law, antitrust law and legal edn.-bar admissions sects.), Am. Corp. Counsel Assn., Am. Health Lawyers Assn., Mass. Bar Assn., Boston Bar Assn. (mem. coun. 1998—, exec. com. 1999—), Boston Bar Found. (trustee, 1998—), Boston U. Law Sch. Alumni Assn. (pres., 1998—). General corporate, Health, Non-profit and tax-exempt organizations. Home: 144 Mount Vernon St Boston MA 02108-1128 Office: Office of Gen Counsel 800 Boylston St Ste 1150 Boston MA 02199-8001

**HADDAD, MARK ANTHONY,** lawyer; b. Paterson, N.J., July 24, 1958; s. William Michael and Marlene Mildred (Morris) H. BS with highest honors, U. Ariz., 1980; JD with honors, Duke U., 1988. Bar: Conn. 1988, N.Y. 1989. CPA Price Waterhouse LLP, Morristown, N.J., 1980-82; v.p. Haas Securities, N.Y.C., 1982-85; assoc. Sullivan & Cromwell, N.Y.C., 1988-92; banking assoc. Goldman Sachs & Co., N.Y.C., 1992-93; mng. ptnr. Afridi & Angell, N.Y.C., 1993—; cons. Cornerstone Group, N.Y.C., 1989—, Elysium Group, N.Y.C., 1992—; bd. dirs. Arab Bankers Assn. N.Am. (ABANA), N.Y.C., 1997—. Editor A & A Newsletter. Mem. N.Y. State Soc. CPAs, Assn. of Bar of City of N.Y. General corporate, Private international, Securities. Home: 96 5th Ave New York NY 10011-7605 Office: Afridi & Angell 230 Park Ave Rm 640 New York NY 10169-0640

**HADDEN, ARTHUR ROBY,** lawyer; b. San Antonio, Feb. 13, 1929; s. Will Alexander and Kathleen (Westerman) H.; m. Marellyn Frances Denton, June 23, 1956; children: Neilson, Lynne, Wesley, Arthur. BBA, U. Tex., 1952, LLB, 1957. Bar: Tex. 1957, U.S. Dist. Ct. (ea. dist.) Tex. 1959, U.S. Ct. Appeals (5th cir.) 1961, U.S. Supreme Ct. 1970, U.S. Dist. Ct. (no. dist.) Tex. 1975. Lawyer Ramey, Brelsford, Hull and Flock, Tyler, Tex., 1957-70; U.S. atty. Ea. Dist. Tex., 1970-77; lawyer, sole practice Law Offices Roby Hadden, Tyler, 1977-94; justice 12th Ct. Appeals, Tex., 1995—; mem. Fed. State Law Enforcement Commn. Tex., Austin, 1976-77. Mem. Human Subjects Investigation Commn. U. Tex. Hosp., Tyler, 1980-90, Mayor's Anti-Crime Task Force, Criminal Justice Div., Tyler, 1986-88. Capt. USAF, 1952-54. Fellow Tex. Bar Found.; mem. Smith County Bar Assn., Nat. Assn. Former U.S. Attys., Downtown Rotary Tyler, Rotary Internat. Republican. Avocations: jogging, mountaineering, snow skiing, tennis, swimming. Oil, gas, and mineral, Probate, Real property. Home: 3335 Heines Dr Tyler TX 75701-9034 Office: 1517 W Front St Tyler TX 75702-7854

**HADDOW, JAMES BUCHANAN,** lawyer; b. Quincy, Mass., June 25, 1959; s. James Edward and Paula Kozodoy Haddow; m. Michelle Ritchie, June 4, 1988; children: Hamish Robert Mackintosh, Max Edward Buchanan Ritchie. BA in Philosophy, Colby Coll., 1982; JD, U. Maine, 1986. Bar: Maine 1986, U.S. Dist. Ct. Maine 1986, U.S. Ct. Appeals (1st cir.) 1990. Assoc. Kelly, Remmel & Zimmerman, Portland, Maine, 1986-87; prin. Profl. Resource Assoc., Portland, 1987-91; assoc. Petruccelli & Martin, Portland, 1991-94, ptnr., 1995—. Mem. Planning Bd., Limington, Maine, 1995-98, chair, 1997-98; mem. Mad Horse Theatre Co. Bd. Trustees, Portland, 1989-93, chair, 1991-93. Mem. ABA, ATLA, Maine State Bar Assn., Cumberland County Bar Assn. Democrat. Avocations: running, hiking, fly fishing. Insurance, General corporate, Antitrust. Office: Petruccelli & Martin LLP PO Box 9733 50 Monument Sq Portland ME 04104-5033

**HADDOW, JON ANDREW,** lawyer; b. Quincy, Mass., Aug. 23, 1960; s. James E. and Paula (Kozodoy) H.; m. Suzanne Ritchie, May 27, 1989; 1 child, Andrew. BA, Colby Coll., 1983; JD, U. Maine, Portland, 1990. Bar: Maine 1990, U.S. Dist. Ct. Maine 1990. Shareholder Farrell, Rosenblatt & Russell, Bangor, Maine, 1996—. Mem. ABA, Maine Bar Assn., Am. Inns of Ct. Avocations: fishing, gardening, hunting, cross-country skiing, canoeing. State civil litigation, Federal civil litigation, Insurance. Office: Farrell Rosenblatt & Russell 61 Main St Bangor ME 04401-6397

**HADEN, CHARLES HAROLD, II,** federal judge; b. Morgantown, W.Va., Apr. 16, 1937; s. Charles H. and Beatrice L. (Costolo) H.; m. Priscilla Ann Miller, June 2, 1956; children: Charles H., Timothy M., Amy Sue. BS, W.Va. U., 1958, JD, 1961. Ptnr. Haden & Haden, Morgantown, W.Va., 1961-69; state tax commr. W.Va., 1969-72; justice Supreme Ct. Appeals W.Va., 1972-75, chief justice, 1975; judge U.S. Dist. Ct. No. and So. Dists. W.Va., Parkersburg, 1975-82; chief judge U.S. Dist. Ct. (so. dist.) W.Va., 1982—; mem. W.Va. Ho. of Dels., 1963-64; asst. prof. Coll. Law, W.Va. U., 1967-68; mem. com. adminstrn. probation system Jud. Conf., 1979-86; mem. 4th Cir. Jud. Coun., 1986-91, 96—, U.S. Jud. Conf., 1997—. Mem. Bd. Edn., Monongalia County, W.Va., 1967-68; bd. dirs. W.Va. U. Found., 1988—; past. mem. vis. coms. W.Va. U. Coll. Law & Sch. Medicine; bd. dirs. W.Va. u. Found.,; mem. U.S. Jud. Conf.; mem. 4th cir. Jud. Coun., 1986-91, 96—. Recipient Outstanding Alumnus award W.Va. U., 1986. Fellow Am. Bar Found.; mem. ABA, W.Va. Bar Assn., W.Va. State Bar Assn., Am. Judicature Soc., 4th Cir. Dist. Judges Assn. (pres. 1993-95), W.Va. U. Alumni Assn. (pres. 1982-83). Office: US Dist Ct PO Box 351 Charleston WV 25322-0351

**HADEN, CHARLES MCINTYRE,** lawyer; b. Timpson, Tex., Aug. 6, 1923; s. Charles Clinton and Cecil Urva (McIntyre) H.; m. Suzanne Tracy, Dec. 20, 1944; children: Sharon Dianne Haden Gabbert, Susan Carol Haden Ince, Charles McIntyre Jr. BA, Rice U., 1949; JD, U. Tex., Austin, 1949. Bar: Tex. 1949, U.S. Dist. Ct. (no., so., ea. and we. dists.) Tex., U.S. Ct. Appeals (5th cir.), U.S. Supreme Ct. Legal counsel Trans Tex. Airways, Houston, 1949; law clk. U.S. Dist. Ct. (so. dist.) Tex., Corpus Christi, 1949-50; asst. dist. atty., prosecutor Capital Docket, Harris County, Houston, 1950-52; assoc. Fulbright & Jaworski, Houston, 1952-63, ptnr., 1963-70; ptnr. Brown & Haden, Houston, 1970-94, Haden & Gabbert, Houston, 1996—; mcpl. judge City of Hunters Creek village, Tex., 1954-56. Contbr. articles to profl. publs. chmn. bd. of Adjustment City of Hunters Creek Village, 1952-54, mayor, 1956-58; chmn. Harris County Reps.; del. to nat. conv., 1964; elder Presbyn. Ch.; moderator Presbyn. Ctrl. South. Lt. (j.g.) USN, 1942-46), PTO. Mem. ABA, Houston Bar Assn., State Bar Tex. (bd. dirs. 1974-76), Houston Trial Lawyers Assn. (pres. 1974-74), Tex. Trial Lawyers Assn. (bd. dirs. 1970-85), Assn. Trial Lawyers Am., Nat. Assn. R.R. Counsel (v.p. 1963-70), Am. Bar Trial Advocacy, Tex. Bar Found., Houstonian Club, Meml. Dr. Country Club. Personal injury. Home: 10709 Old Coach Ln Houston TX 77024-3134 Office: Haden & Gabbert One Riverway Ste 1500 Houston TX 77056-1904

**HADER, CHERYL ELIZABETH,** lawyer; b. Newark, Jan. 8, 1964; d. Aaron Martin and Helen (Friedman) Hader; m. Craig Bruce Brod, May 26, 1991; children: Andrew Blake Brod, Alex William Brod. BA, Yale U., 1985; JD, Harvard U., 1988; LLM, NYU, 1991. Bar: N.Y. 1988, N.J. 1988. Assoc. Cleary, Gottlieb, Steen & Hamilton, N.Y.C., 1988-92; assoc. Paul, Weiss, Rifkind, Wharton & Garrison, N.Y.C., 1992-98, ptnr., 1999—. Asst. editor: Probate and Administration of New York Estates, 1995; contbr. articles to profl. jours. Mem. N.Y. State Bar Assn., Bar Assn. City of N.Y. (estate and gift tax com.). Avocation: skiing. Estate planning, Probate, Estate taxation. Office: Paul Weiss et al Rm 200 1285 Avenue Of The Americas New York NY 10019-6065

**HADLEY, RALPH VINCENT, III,** lawyer; b. Jacksonville, Fla., Aug. 20, 1942; s. Ralph V. and Clare (Cason) H.; m. Carol Fox Hadley, Sept. 18, 1993; children: Graham Kimball, Christopher Bedell, Blair Vincent. BS, U. Fla., 1965, JD, 1968. Bar: Fla. 1968, Calif. 1972. Assoc. Kurz, Toole, Taylor & Moseley, Jacksonville, 1968-69; asst. atty. gen. State of Fla., Orlando, 1972-73; ptnr. Davids, Henson & Hadley, Winter Garden, Fla., 1973-80; sr. ptnr. Hadley & Asma, Winter Garden, 1980-89, Parker, Johnson, Owen, McGuire, Michaud, & Hadley, Orlando, 1989-91, Owen & Hadley, Orlando, 1991-94, Hadley, Gardner & Ornstein, P.A., Winter Park, Fla., 1994-95; Swann, Hadley & Alvarez, P.A., Winter Park, 1995—; vice chmn. bd. dirs. Tucker State Bank, Winter Garden, 1981-88; vice chmn. bd. dirs., sec. Tucker Holding Co., Jacksonville, 1984-88; bd. dirs. BankFIRST, All Sign Products. Bd. dirs. Orange County Dem. Exec. Com., Orlando, 1974-81, Spouse Abuse, Inc., Orlando, 1975-81. Lt. comdr. USN, 1969-72, Vietnam. Recipient award of merit Orange County Legal Aid Soc., 1987, Disting. Svc. award Judge J.C. Jake Stone Legal Aid Soc., 1989, Pres. Pro Bono Svc. award Fla. Bar, 1992. Mem. ABA, Fla. Bar Assn., Calif. Bar Assn., Orange County Bar Assn. (legis. chmn. 1979, 82), Am. Inn of Ct. (master), Winter Park C. of C. (bd. dirs. 1979-80), West Orange C. of C. (bd. dirs. 1979-82), Rotary. Presbyterian. Banking, Contracts commercial, Real property. Office: 1031 W Morse Blvd Winter Park FL 32789-3715

**HADSALL, JOHN D.,** lawyer; b. Ottumwa, Iowa, Nov. 26, 1951; s. Robert C. and Jean (Peak) H.; m. Dinah H. Burnett, May 25, 1996; 1 child, Gregory R. Burnett. BS in Criminology with distinction, Iowa State U., 1975; JD, U. Iowa, 1979. Fingerprint expert Identification divsn. FBI, Washington, 1970-71; pvt. legal aid atty. St. Pete Beach, Fla., 1980—; investigator for abused children Fla. Dept. Health, Sarasota, 1989-90; guardian ad litem Fla. Ct. Sys., Sarasota, 1985-87; civil rights investigator City of Des Moines, 1975-76. Served with U.S. Army, 1971-73. Mem. DAV. Roman Catholic. Avocation: flying. Home: 11455 1st St E Treasure Island FL 33706-4623 Office: JD Hadsall DAV Legal Ctr PO Box 67201 Saint Petersburg FL 33736-7201

**HADWIGER, MICKEY J.,** lawyer; b. Cherokee, Okla., Apr. 20, 1960; s. James A. and Rozella J. Hadwiger; m. Charlotte D. Hadwiger, Sept. 26, 1991; children: Golda Long, Jason Long, Taylor. BS, Okla. State U., 1982; JD, Washburn U., 1986. Bar: Okla. 1986. Assoc. McKnight & Basaway, Enid, Okla., 1987, Elliott, Enabrit, Newgy and Ezzell, Enid, 1987-91, Hadwiger and Hadwiger, Cherokee, 1991-94; pvt. practice, Cherokee, 1995—. Bd. dirs., treas. Okla. Christian Found., Oklahoma City, 1989—. Mem. Okla. Bar Assn., Garfield County Bar Assn., Alfalfa County Bar Assn., Rotary (pres. Cherokee 1998-99). Republican. Mem. Christian Ch. (Disciples of Christ). Avocations: golf, horticulture. Probate, Estate planning, Real property. Office: 202 S Grand Ave Ste 231 Cherokee OK 73728-2030

**HAFER, JOSEPH PAGE,** lawyer; b. Harrisburg, Pa., June 28, 1941; s. George Horace and Betty (Page) H.; children: Bradford G., Susan P., David E. AB, Lafayette Coll., 1963; JD with distinction, U. Mich., 1966. Bar: Pa. 1966, U.S. Dist. Ct. (mid. dist.) Pa. 1966, U.S. Supreme Ct. 1969, U.S. Ct. Appeals (3d cir.) 1976. Assoc. Metzger, Hafer, Keefer, Thomas & Wood, Harrisburg, 1966-77; mng. ptnr. Thomas, Thomas & Hafer, Harrisburg, 1977—; adj. prof. law Dickinson Law Sch., Carlisle, Pa. Pres. Cumberland Valley Sch. Bd., Mechanicsburg, Pa., 1976-85; pres. Hampden Twp. Rep. Assn., Camp Hill, Pa. Fellow Am. Coll. Trial Lawyers; mem. ABA, Pa. Bar Assn., Assn. Trial Lawyers Am., Pa. Trial Lawyers Assn., Dauphin County Bar Assn. (ct. rels. com.). Methodist. Insurance, Personal injury, Workers' compensation. Home: 1530 Waterford Camp Hill PA 17011-1229 Office: Thomas Thomas & Hafer PO Box 999 Harrisburg PA 17108-0999

**HAFETS, RICHARD JAY,** lawyer; b. N.Y.C., Apr. 23, 1951; s. Meyer Hafets and Marilyn (Glanzrock) Bell; m. Claire Margolis, June 18, 1972; children: Brooke, Amy. BS in Bus. summa cum laude, Am. U., Washington, 1973, JD magna cum laude, 1976. Bar: Md. 1976, U. S. Dist. Ct. Md. 1976, U.S. Ct. Appeals (4th cir.) 1976, U.S. Supreme Ct. 1981, D.C. 1997, U.S. Dist. Ct. (D.C.) 1997. Assoc. Piper & Marbury, Balt., 1976-84, ptnr., 1984—, chmn. labor and employment practice, 1990—, chmn. hiring and assoc. coms., 1988-91. Labor atty. Balt. Symphony Orch., 1986-93; bd. dirs., gen. counsel Am. Cancer Soc., Balt., 1983-89; bd. dirs. Md. Ballet, Balt., 1978-80. Mem. ABA, Md. Bar Assn., Balt. City Bar Assn., Order of Coif. Avocations: horses, skiing. Labor, General civil litigation. Home: 7346 Narrow Wind Way Columbia MD 21046-1262 Office: Piper & Marbury 36 S Charles St Baltimore MD 21201-3020

**HAFF, TULA MICHELE,** lawyer; b. Gainesville, Fla., Aug. 16, 1963; d. Manuel George and Mary K. Moshonas; m. Ronald Paul Haff, May 12, 1990; children: Drake Dylan, Mary Nicole. AA in Bus. Adminstrn., Polk C.C., Winter Haven, Fla., 1983; BS in Acctg., U. Fla., 1985, JD, 1988. Bar: Fla. 1989, U.S. Dist. Ct. (mid. and so. dists.) Fla. 1989. Atty. Tripp, Scott, Conklin & Smith, Ft. Lauderdale, Fla., 1988-89, Doyle & McKinley, Bartow, Fla., 1989-91; ptnr. Waddell, Ready, Haff & Pickett, P.A., Auburndale, Fla., 1991—; mem. agt. Attys. Title Ins. Fund, Fla., 1993—. Recipient Spl. Citation of Merit, John Marshall Bar Assn. Mem. Lake Alfred, Winter Haven, Auburndale Bar Assn., 10th Cir. Women Lawyers Assn., Polk County Trial Lawyers Assn., Winter Haven Women's Bar Assn., Real Estate Coun. of Polk County (v.p./treas. 1992-93, pres. 1994-96). Greek Orthodox. General practice, General corporate, Probate. Office: Waddell Ready Haff & Pickett 209 Palmetto St Auburndale FL 33823-3426

**HAFFNER, ALFRED LOVELAND, JR.,** lawyer; b. Bklyn., Sept. 11, 1925; s. Alfred Loveland and Mary Ellen (Myers) H.; m. Mary Dolores Hyland, July 10, 1965; children: Mary Elizabeth, Anne Dolores, Jeanne Marie, Catherine Diane. BS in Engring., U. Mich., 1950, JD, 1956. Bar: N.Y. 1958, U.S. Patent and Trademark Office, 1958, U.S. Dist. Ct. (so. and ea. dists.) N.Y. 1959, U.S. Ct. Claims 1959, U.S. Ct. Appeals (fed. cir.) 1961, U.S. Supreme Ct. 1961, U.S. Ct. Appeals (2d cir.) 1962. Draftsman-engr., indsl. engr., asst. plant engr. Owens-Ill. Glass Co., Bridgeton, N.J., 1950-53, Streator, Ill., 1953-54; since practiced N.Y.C.; assoc. Kenyon & Kenyon, N.Y.C., 1957-60, Ward, McElhannon, Brooks & Fitzpatrick, N.Y.C., 1960-61; ptnr. Ward, McElhannon, Brooks & Fitzpatrick, 1961-71, Brooks Haidt Haffner & Delahunty, N.Y.C., 1971-98, Morgan & Finnegan, LLP, N.Y.C., 1998—; chmn. Nat. Coun. Patent Law Assns., 1973-74, councilman, 1971-88; mem. founding com. Nat. Inventors Hall of Fame Found., 1972, pres., 1973-74, sec., 1980-94, exec. com. 1989-94, endowment trust com., 1991-93, chmn. exhibits com., 1992-95, legal com., 1993-95, 97-98, fin. com., 1993-94, 97—, strategic planning com., 1994-97, chmn., 1995-97, sel. com., 1996-98, bd. dirs. Served with USNR, 1943-46. Mem. ABA, N.Y. State Bar Assn., Am. Intellectual Property Law Assn., N.Y. Intellectual Property Law Assn. (sec. 1964-68, dir. 1968-70, 71-72, pres. 1970-71), Strathmore Assn. Westchester (treas. 1976-79, v.p. 1980-82, pres. 1982-83, exec. com. 1983—), Phi Gamma Delta, Phi Alpha Delta. Patent, Trademark and copyright, Intellectual property. Home: 1 Gainsborough Rd Scarsdale NY 10583-4811 Office: Morgan & Finnegan LLP 345 Park Ave New York NY 10154-0053

**HAFTER, JEROME CHARLES,** lawyer; b. Orlando, Fla., May 16, 1945; s. Jerome Sidney and Mary Margaret (Fugler) H.; m. Jo Cille Dawkins, July 18, 1976; 1 child, Jerome Bryan. BA summa cum laude, Rice U., 1967; BA with first class honours, Oxford U., Eng., 1969, MA, 1976; JD, Yale U., 1972. Bar: Miss. 1974, U.S. Ct. Appeals (5th cir.) 1974, U.S. Dist. Ct. (no. and so. dists.) Miss. 1974. Law clk. to presiding judge U.S. Ct. Appeals (5th cir.), Jackson, Miss., 1972-73; assoc. Lake, Tindall, Hunger & Thackston (now Lake Tindall LLP), Greenville, Miss., 1973-76, ptnr., 1976—; chmn. Miss. Bd. Bar Admissions, Jackson, 1979—; sec., treas. Hafter Realty Inc., Greenville, 1969-92, pres., 1992—; mem. gov.'s constn. commn., Jackson, 1985-87. Author: Family History of Peter Quin, 1964, 2d. rev. edit., 1970. Pres. Downtown Improvement Assn. Greenville, 1980—, Common Cause/Miss., 1976-78; mem. Greenville City Election Commn., 1978—, Greenville Mcpl. Sch. Bd., 1988—, pres., 1995-96, 99—; chmn. com. on tax Miss. Econ. Council, Jackson, 1985, 87, 96-98, Mem. Devel. Found., 1987-88. Served to 1st lt., C.E., U.S. Army, 1972, maj., USAR, 1972-92, ret. Marshall scholar, 1967-69; Leadership Miss. Program fellow, 1976-77. Fellow Miss. Bar Found.; mem. ABA (vice chmn. com. on issues affecting legal profession, young lawyers div., 1980-82, law sch. accreditation com. 1998—), Miss. Bar Assn. (bd. dirs. young lawyers div. 1976-79), Fed. Bar Assn. (v.p. no. Miss. 1977-78, 81-82), Nat. Conf. Bar Examiners (MBE com. 1986-88, trustee 1989—, chmn. 1998-99), Am. Judicature Soc., Greenville C. of C. (bd. dirs. 1976-79, pres. 1992-93), Washington County Hist. Soc. (pres. Greenville chpt. 1981), Miss, Bankruptcy Conf. (chmn. com. on bankruptcy rules 1988), Phi Beta Kappa. Episcopalian. Clubs: Greenville Golf and Country (v.p. 1977-79); Huntercombe Golf (Nuffield, Eng.); Vincents (Oxford, Eng.). Lodge: Kiwanis (Greenville pres. 1978-79, lt. gov. 1982-83). Federal civil litigation, General corporate, Contracts commercial. Home: 316 S Broadway St Greenville MS 38701-4011 Office: Lake Tindall LLP PO Box 918 127 S Poplar St Greenville MS 38701-4026

**HAGAN, ANN P.,** lawyer; b. Mexico, Mo., Oct. 6, 1955; d. Ray J. and Margaret B. H.; m. James M. DeLong, June 4, 1983; children: Shelley, Ross. BA, Rockhurst Coll., 1978; JD, U. Mo., Kansas City, 1981. Bar: Mo. 1981, Ill. 1982, U.S. Dist. Ct. (ea. and we. dists.) Mo., U.S. Ct. Appeals (8th cir.), U.S. Supreme Ct. Assoc. Brown & James, St. Louis, 1981-83; shareholder Seigfreid, Runge et al, Mexico, 1983-93; ptnr. Hagan, Hamlett, Maxwell, L.L.C., Mexico, 1993—. Vice-pres. Altrusa Internat., Mexico, 1984, pres., 1993-94; legal com. chair United Way, Mexico, 1990; pres. St. Brendan sch. bd.; bd. mem. Audrain County Health Care, Inc. Mem. ABA, Mo. Bar Assn., Mo. Def. Lawyers, Def. Rsch. Inst., Audrain County Bar Assn. Avocations: fishing, horses, music. General civil litigation, Personal injury, Insurance. Office: Hagan Hamlett Maxwell LLC 210 E Love St Mexico MO 65265-2880

**HAGAN, JAMES WALTER,** lawyer; b. Hannibal, Mo., Oct. 28, 1963; s. Walter Joseph and Alice Joyce (Evans) H.; m. Stacie Spalding, Aug. 21, 1982; children: Lance Joseph, Whitney McLeod. BA in Govt. summa cum laude, U. Notre Dame, 1986; JD, Yale U., 1989. Bar: Ga. 1989. Law clk. to Hon. James C. Hill, U.S. Ct. Appeals for 11th Cir., Atlanta, 1989-90; assoc. Alston & Bird, Atlanta, 1990-96, ptnr., 1997—. Counselor Atlanta Truancy Project, 1991—; bd. dirs. Atlanta Legal Aid Soc., 1995—. Mem. Ga. Bar Assn. (steering com. trial practice com. younger lawyers sect. 1994—). Product liability, Personal injury, General civil litigation. Office: Alston & Bird One Atlantic Ctr 1201 W Peachtree St NW Ste 4200 Atlanta GA 30309-3424

**HAGAN, MARY ANN,** lawyer; b. Phila., Feb. 18, 1935; d. Harry A. and Marie (Farrell) H. BA, Immaculata (Pa.) Coll., 1956; MA in History, U. Pa., 1958; LLB, Temple U., 1963. Bar: Pa. 1964, U.S. Dist. Ct. Pa. 1972, U.S. Ct. Appeals (3d cir.) 1980, U.S. Tax Ct. 1965, U.S. Ct. Appeals for Federal Cir., 1996. Historian U.S. Dept. Interior, Phila., 1958-60; atty. Urban Renewal Adminstrn., Phila., 1963-65; trial atty. IRS, Office of Chief Counsel, Washington & Phila., 1965-73; supervisory trial atty. U.S. Equal Employment Opportunity Commn., Phila., 1973-77; pvt. practice Phila., 1978—; arbitrator U.S. Dist. Ct., Phila., 1975—, mem. employment panel, 1989—, fed. mediator, 1991—; lectr., Phila. Bar Edn. Ctr., 1997. Author: Working With the Federal Sector Equal Employment Opportunity Regulations, 29 CFR 1614, 1997. Mem. Nat. Employment Lawyers Assn., Phila. Bar Assn. Probate, General civil litigation, Labor. Office: Land Title Bldg 100 S Broad St Ste 1124 Philadelphia PA 19110-1003

**HAGBERG, CHRIS ERIC,** lawyer; b. Steubenville, Ohio, Dec. 19, 1949; s. Rudolf Eric and Sara (Smith) H.; m. Viola Louise Wilgus, Feb. 19, 1978. BS, Duke U., 1975; JD, U. Tulsa, 1978; postgrad., Nat. Law Ctr., George Washington U. Bar: Okla. 1978, Va. 1979, U.S. Ct. Appeals (4th cir.) Calif. 1986. Law clk. to presiding justice U.S. Dist. Ct. (no. dist.) Okla.; asst. counsel ADP Selection Office Dept. Navy, Navy Regional Contracting Ctr., Washington; counsel Naval Supply Ctr., Pearl Harbor, Hawaii; Pacific area counsel Naval Supply Sys. Command, Dept. Navy, Makakilo, Hawaii; assoc. counsel Navy Supply Sys. Command, Washington; atty. Pettit & Martin, L.A., 1985-87, Seyfarth, Shaw, Fairweather and Geraldson, Washington, 1988-91, U.S. Coast Guard HQ, Washington, 1992-93, USN, 1993-95, Dept. Navy OGC/NSWC Carderock, West Bethesda, Md., 1995—. Contbr. articles to legal jours. Lt. USN, 1970-74. Recipient David I. Milsten award, 1978, 7 Am. Jurisprudence awards, 1976-78, First prize Dept. Navy Legal Writing Contest, 1981. Mem. ABA, FBA, Nat. Contract Mgmt. Assn., Order of Coif. Democrat. Presbyterian. Government contracts and claims, Labor, Administrative and regulatory. Home: 9810 Meadow Valley Dr Vienna VA 22181-3215

**HAGBERG, VIOLA WILGUS,** lawyer; b. Salisbury, Md., July 3, 1952; d. William E. and Jean Shelton (Barlow) Wilgus; m. Chris Eric Hagberg, Feb. 19, 1978. BA, Furman U., Greenville, S.C., 1974; JD, U. S.C., 1978, U. Tulsa, 1978; DOD Army Logistics Sch. honor grad. basic mgmt. def. acquisition, def. small purchase, advanced fed. acquisition regulation, Fort Lee, Va., 1981-82. Bar: Okla. 1978, Va. 1979, U.S. Ct. Appeals (4th cir.) 1979. With Lawyers Com. for Civil Rights, Washington, 1979; pub. utility specialist Fed. Energy Regulatory Commn., Washington, 1979-80; contract specialist U.S. Army, C.E., Ft. Shafter, Hawaii, 1980-81; contract officer/supervisory contract specialist Tripler Army Med. Ctr., Hawaii 1981-83; supervisory procurement analyst and chief policy Procurement Div. USCG, Washington, 1983; contracts officer and chief Avionics Engring Contracting Br., 1984; procurement analyst office of sec. Dept. Transp., 1984-85; contracting officer Naval Regional Contracting Ctr., Long Beach, Calif., 1985-87; chief acquisition rev. and policy, Hdqrs. Def. Mapping Agy., Washington, 1987-92, dir. acquisitions, Fairfax, Va., 1992-93, dir. acquisition policy, 1994-96; dir. acquisition polity, tech., and legis. programs Nat. Mapping and Imagery Agy., 1996-97, Office of Gen. Counsel. Mem. ABA (law student div. liaison 1977-78), Nat. Contract Mgmt. Assn., Va. State Bar Assn., Okla. Bar Assn., Phi Alpha Delta, Kappa Delta Epsilon. Government contracts and claims, General corporate, Environmental. Home: 9810 Meadow Valley Dr Vienna VA 22181-3215 Office: Nat Imagery and Mapping Agy Office Gen Counsel 4600 Sangamore (MS-D-10) Bethesda MD 20816

**HAGEN, CATHERINE B.,** lawyer; b. Long Beach, Calif., June 6, 1943; d. Hugh David and Esther Woodward) Burcham; m. Donald R. Hagen, Dec. 21, 1963 (div.); children: Rob, Wes; m. Stephen P. Pepe, Dec. 8, 1991. BA, Occidental Coll., 1964; JD, Loyola U., L.A., 1978. Bar: Calif. 1978, U.S. Dist. Ct. (ctrl. dist.) Calif., U.S. Dist. Ct. (9th cir.), U.S. Supreme Ct. Assoc. O'Melveny & Myers, L.A., 1978-85; ptnr. O'Melveny & Myers, L.A. and Newport Beach, Calif., 1985—. Co-editor in chief: Employment Discrimination Law Supplement, 1998. Mem. L.A. Police Dept. Meml. Fund, 1986—. Labor. Office: O'Melveny & Myers 610 Newport Center Dr Newport Beach CA 92660-6419

**HAGEN, DAVID WARNER,** judge; b. 1931. BBA, U. Wis., 1956; LLB, U. San Francisco, 1959. Bar: Washoe County 1981, Nev. 1992. With Berkley, Randall & Harvey, Berkeley, Calif., 1960-62; pvt. practice Loyalton, Calif., 1962-63; with Guild, Busey & Guild (later Guild, Hagen and Clark Ltd. and Guild & Hagen Ltd.), Reno, 1963-93; judge U.S. Dist. Ct. Nev., Reno, 1993—, chmn. 9th Cir. Art. III, judge edn. com., 1998—; lectr U. Nev., 1968-72; acting dean Nev. Sch. of Law, 1981-83, adj. prof., 1981-87; mem. Nev. Bd. Bar Examiners, 1972-91, chmn., 1989-91; chmn. Nev. Continuing Legal Edn. Com., 1967-75; mem. Nev. Uniform Comml. Code Com. S/sgt. USAF, 1949-52. Fellow Am. Coll. Trial Lawyers (state chmn. 1983-85); mem. VFW, Nev. Bar Assn., Calif. Bar Assn., Washoe County Bar Assn., Am. Bd. Trial Advocates (advocate), Nat. Maritime Hist. Soc., U.S. Sailing Assn. Office: US Dist Ct Fed Bldg & US Courthouse 400 S Virginia St Reno NV 89501-2193

**HAGEN, GLENN W(ILLIAM),** lawyer; b. Detroit, July 8, 1948; s. William A. and Lilian (Abrolat) H.; m. Cynthia Winn, July 21, 1984. BS in Chemistry, U. Ala., 1970; JD, Valparaiso U., 1973. Bar: Mich. 1973, U.S. Dist. Ct. (we. dist.) Mich. 1974, Colo. 1981, U.S. Dist. Ct. Colo. 1982. Ptnr. Peters, Seyburn & Hagen, Kalamazoo, 1973-76; dep. city atty. City of Battle Creek, Mich., 1976-79; staff and regulatory counsel CF&I Steel Corp., Pueblo, Colo., 1979-81; gen. counsel Commonwealth Investment Properties Corp., Littleton, Colo., 1981-82; assoc. Berkowitz & Brady, Denver, 1982-83, Zarlengo, Mott, Zarlengo & Winbourn, Denver, 1983-87; pvt. practice Glenn W. Hagen, P.C., Denver, 1987—; lectr. law office mgmt., small bus. issues, corp. entity and formation issues. Del. Colo. Rep. Com., 1986, 90, 92, 94, 96, 98; referee property tax appeals Douglas and Jefferson Counties; chmn. 18th Jud. Dist., 1999—; small bus. cons. South Met. Denver C. of C., 1994—. Mem. ABA (young lawyers exec. coun. 1978-81, chmn. small bus. enterprises 1986, regional dir. constabars 1992-94, nat. editors conf. 1995, mem. constrn. forum 1996—), Mich. Bar Assn. (young lawyers exec. coun. 1976-80), Colo. Bar Assn. (chmn. long-range planning com. 1983-86, gen. practice exec. coun. 1985—, chmn. small firm sect. 1991-96, law office mgmt. com. 1995—, constrn. law sect. 1996—, chmn. budget com. 1987-89, mem. svcs. com. 1987-89, bus. law sect. 1986-91, alt. dispute resolution com. 1990-94), Denver Bar Assn., Douglas-Elbert County Bar Assn., Colo. Lawyers for Arts, Am. Arbitration Assn. (lectr. law office mgmt.). Lutheran. Avocations: travel, photography, golf. General civil litigation, General corporate, Construction. Home: 2303 E Lansdowne Pl Highlands Ranch CO 80126 Office: Mellon Fin Ctr 1775 Sherman St Ste 2550 Denver CO 80203-4352

**HAGER, JULIE-ANN,** lawyer, educator; b. Kermit, Tex., Aug. 25, 1954; d. Howard Glenn and Marianne Johanne (Ratzer) H. BA magna cum laude, Baylor U., 1976; JD, U. Tex., 1979. Bar: Tex., U.S. Dist. Ct. (we. dist.) Tex., U.S. Ct. Appeals (5th cir.). Assoc. Wilson, Grosen Heider & Burns, Austin, Tex., 1979-83, ptnr., 1983-90; pvt. practice Law Offices of Julie Ann Hager, Austin, 1990—; tchr. U. Tex. Paralegal Inst., Austin, 1990—. Vol. Austin Rape Crisis Hotline, 1988—, Austin Ctr. for Battered Women, Tex. Head Injury Assn., 1987—; vol. mediator Alternative Dispute Resolution, Austin, 1988—; speaker in field. Fellow Tex. Bar Found.; mem. ABA, ATLA, AAUW, Am. Soc. Law and Medicine, Travis County Women's Law Assn., Travis County Bar Assn. Democrat. Avocations: snow skiing, sailing, French horn. Personal injury, Insurance, General civil litigation. Home: 7629 Parkview Cir Austin TX 78731-1127 Office: 111 Congress Ave Ste 1060 Austin TX 78701-4043

**HAGERMAN, JOHN DAVID,** lawyer; b. Houston, Aug. 1, 1941; s. David Angle and Noima L. (Clay) H.; m. Linda J. Lambright, June 25, 1975; children: Clayton Robert, Holly Elizabeth. BBA, So. Meth. U., 1963; JD, U. Tex., Austin, 1966. Bar: Tex. 1966, U.S. Dist. Ct. (so. dist.) Tex. 1967, U.S. Ct. Appeals (5th cir.) 1967, U.S. Supreme Ct. 1969. Pres., ptnr. Hagerman & Seureau, Inc., Spring, Tex., 1966—; condr. bank creditor rights seminars. Contbr. articles to profl. jours. Res. dep. sheriff, Montgomery County, Tex.; bd. dirs. Montgomery County Fair Assn., 1978—. Mem. ABA, Tex. Bar Assn., Houston Bar Assn., Houston Outdoor Advt. Assn., Tex. Assn. Civil Trial Specialists, Tex. Assn. Bank Counsel, Beta Theta Pi. Republican. Club: Petroleum (Houston). Avocations: swimming, tennis, jogging, shooting. Banking, State civil litigation, Contracts commercial. Office: Hagerman & Seureau Inc 24800 Interstate 45 Ste 100 Spring TX 77386-1987

**HAGERMAN, MICHAEL CHARLES,** lawyer, arbitrator, mediator; b. Webster City, Iowa, Aug. 20, 1951; s. Charles Arnold and Jill Hamilton (Son de Regger) H.; children: Kelly, Douglas. BA with honors, U. Iowa, 1973; MBA, U. Utah, 1978; JD, Drake U., 1981; Grad., U.S. Army Command/Gen. Staff, Coll., Ft. Leavenworth, Kans., 1988. Bar: Iowa 1981, Mass. 1995. Clk. Iowa Resources, Legal Aid of Polk County, and State of Iowa, Des Moines, 1978-81; contract atty. Fisher Controls Internat., Inc., Marshalltown, Iowa, 1981-84; contracts mgr. Emerson & Cuming, Inc., Canton, Mass., 1984-85; contract atty. GTE Govt. Sys., Taunton, Mass., 1986-90; v.p., gen. counsel, sec. ISI Sys., Inc., Andover, Mass., 1990-94; legal counsel Swan Tech. Inc., Marlboro, Mass., 1994-95; pvt. practice Franklin, Mass., 1995—; sr. contracts mgr. BankBoston, N.A., 1998—. Contbr. articles to profl. jours. Capt. U.S. Army, 1973-78, Germany; lt. col. U.S. Army Res. ret. Mem. Mass. Bar Assn., Sigma Chi (chpt. Balfour award 1973), Phi Alpha Delta (chpt. pres. 1980-81). Avocations: sailing, writing, travel. Contracts commercial, Computer, Labor.

**HAGGARD, JOEL EDWARD,** lawyer; b. Portland, Oreg., Oct. 10, 1939; s. Henry Edward and Kathryn Shirley (O'Leary) H.; m. Mary Katherine Daley, June 8, 1968; children: Kevin E., Maureen E., Cristin E. BSME, U. Notre Dame, 1961; M in Nuclear Engring., U. Okla., 1963; JD, U. Wash., 1971. Bar: Wash. 1971, U.S. Dist. Ct. (we. dist.) Wash. 1971, U.S. Ct. Appeals (9th cir.) 1971, U.S. Supreme Ct. 1971. Nuclear engr. Westinghouse Corp. Bettis Atomic Power Lab., Pitts., 1963-67; research engr. aerospace div. The Boeing Co., Seattle, 1968; engr., mgmt. cons. King County Dept. Pub. Works, Seattle, 1969-71; assoc. Houghton, Cluck, Coughlin & Riley, Seattle, 1971-74, ptnr., 1975-76; pvt. practice law Seattle, 1977, 85—; ptnr. Haggard, Tousley & Brain, Seattle, 1978-84; judge marriage tribunal, Archdiocese of Seattle, 1975-90; chmn. Columbia River Interstate Compact Commn., 1975—; arbitrator King County Superior Ct., 1986—. Contbr. articles to profl. jours. Past trustee, mem. exec. com., past sec. Seattle Symphony. Mem. ABA, Wash. Bar Assn. (past chmn. environ. law sect., fee arbitration com., past mem. rules of profl. conduct com.), Seattle-King County Bar Assn., Rainier Club, Wash. Athletic Club, Astoria Golf and Country Club, Magnolia Cmty. Club (past pres., bd. dirs.). Land use and zoning (including planning), Real property, Environmental. Office: 1200 5th Ave #1200 Seattle WA 98101-1127

**HAGGARD, WILLIAM ANDREW,** lawyer; b. Miami, Feb. 20, 1942; s. Curtis Andrew and Marjorie (Tumlin) H.; m. Carole Ann Erali; children: Michael Andrew, Rebecca M. BA, Fla. State U., 1964; JD, Mercer U., 1967. Bar: Fla. 1967, U.S. Dist. Ct. (5th cir.) 1972, U.S. Supreme Ct. 1972, U.S. Ct. Appeals 1981. Clk. Fla. State Atty.'s Office, 1967; asst. state atty.

Eleventh Jud. Cir., 1967-68; chief prosecutor, mil. judge, trial counsel USAF, 1968-71; assoc. Frates, Floyd, Pearson & Stewart, 1971-72; ptnr. Rentz, McClellan & Haggard, 1972-79, Rentz & Haggard, 1979-82; sr. ptnr. Haggard & Kirkland, 1982-89, Wm. Andrew Haggard & Assoc., 1989-93, Haggard & Stone, Coral Gables, Fla., 1993—; instr. Fla. bar continuing legal edn., 1977-82; vis. lectr. U. Fla. Law Sch., 1977-82. Commr. Fla. Commn. on Ethics, 1990-91; mem. Mercer U. Alumni Bd.; bd. dirs. Fla. State U. Found.; chmn. Fla. State U. Coll. of Arts and Scis. Leadership Counsel. Fellow Internat. Acad. Trial Lawyers (vice state chair); mem. ATLA, ABA, Am. Bd. Trial Advocates, Dade County Bar Assn., Acad. Fla. Trial Lawyers (bd. dirs. 1995-96), Internat. Soc. Barristers, Phi Delta Phi, Sigma Chi. E-mail: mail@haggardparksstone.com. Home: 330 Alhambra Cir Coral Gables FL 33134-5004

**HAGGERTY, ANCER LEE,** judge; b. 1944. BS, U. Oreg., 1967; JD, Hastings Coll. Law, 1973. Law clk. Metro. Pub. Defender, Portland, 1972, 73, staff atty., 1973-77; assoc. Souther, Spaulding, Kinzey, Williamson and Schwabe, 1977-82, Schwabe, Williamson & Wyatt, 1983-88; judge Multnomah County Dist. Ct., 1989-90, Multnomah County Cir. Ct., 1990-93; dist. judge U.S. Ct. Appeals (9th cir.), Portland, 1994—; Mem. Gov.'s task force evaln.Oreg. Liquor Control Commn., 1978, Jud. Conduct Com., 1989-92; coord. Multnomah County Bar Pro Bono program, 1983-88; mem. Oreg. State Bd. Bar Examiners, 1979-82. Coach, practice judge mock ct. team Jefferson H.S.; asst. coach Whitaker 7th and 8th grade Pop Warner football teams. 1st lt. USMC, 1967-70, Vietnam. Decorated Silver Star medal, Purple Heart; recipient award Alumni Assn. U. Oreg., Local Hero award Martin Luther King, Jr. Elem. Sch. Fifth Grade, 1993. Mem. ABA, Am. Bridge Assn., Oreg. State Bar Assn., Nat. Bar Assn., Lloyd Ctr. Racquet Club, Marine Corps League, Phoenix Bridge Club. Address: US District Ct 100 SW 3rd Ave # 740 Portland OR 97204

**HAGGERTY, WILLIAM FRANCIS,** lawyer; b. Orange, N.J., June 4, 1943; s. Francis Anthony and Grace Agnes (Cullen) H.; m. Emily Catherine Giacobazzi, Sept. 3, 1965; 1 child, Erin Catherine. AB, U. Detroit, 1965, JD, 1979; MA, Eastern Mich. U., 1970. Bar: Mich. 1980, U.S. Dist. Ct. (ea. dist.) Mich. 1980, U.S. Supreme Ct. 1992. Assoc. Greenbaum & Greenbaum, Southfield, Mich., 1979-80; legal editor Mich. Supreme Ct., Lansing, 1980-81, sr. legal editor, 1981-82, asst. reporter of decisions, 1982-84, acting reporter of decisions, 1984-85, reporter of decisions, 1985—; adj. prof. Thomas M. Cooley Law Sch., Lansing, 1983-90; bd. trustees Libr. of Mich., 1990-93. Mem. Assn. Reporters of Jud. Decisions (sec. 1989-90, v.p. 1990-91, pres. 1991-92), Mich. Bar Assn. (adv. bd. Mich. Bar Jour.), Legal Authors Soc., Clarity, Irish Am. Cultural Inst. Office: Mich Supreme Ct PO Box 30052 Lansing MI 48909-7552

**HAGGLUND, CLARANCE EDWARD,** lawyer, publishing company owner; b. Omaha, Feb. 17, 1927; s. Clarance Andrew and Esther May (Kelle) H.; m. Dorothy Souser, Mar. 27, 1953 (div. Aug. 1972); children: Laura, Bret, Katherine; m. Merle Patricia Hagglund, Oct. 28, 1972. BA, U. S.D., 1949; JD, William Mitchell Coll. Law, 1953. Bar: Minn. 1955, U.S. Ct. Appeals (8th cir.) 1974, U.S. Supreme Ct. 1963. Diplomate Am. Bd. Profl. Liability Attys. Ptnr. Hagglund & Johnson and predecessor firms, Mpls., 1973—; mem. Hagglund, Weimer and Speidel, PA; publ., pres. Common Law Publishing Inc., 1991—; pres. Internat. Control Sys., Inc., Mpls., 1979—, Hill River Corp., Mpls., 1976—; gen. counsel Minn. Assn. Profl. Ins. Agts., Inc., Mpls., 1965-86; CFO, Pro-Trac, software for profl. liability ins. industry. Contbr. articles to profl. jours. Served to lt. comdr. USNR, 1945-46, 50-69. Fellow Internat. Soc. Barristers; mem. Lawyers Pilots Bar Assn., U.S. Maritime Law Assn. (proctor), Acad. Cert. Trial Lawyers Minn. (dean 1983-85), Nat. Bd. Trial Advocacy (cert. in civil trial law, bd. dirs.), Douglas Amdahl Inns of Ct. (pres.), Ill. Athletic Club (Chgo.), Edina Country Club (Minn.), Calhoun Beach Club (Mpls.). Roman Catholic. Avocation: flying. Insurance, Federal civil litigation, State civil litigation. Home: 3168 Dean Ct Minneapolis MN 55416-4386 Office: Common Law Publishing Inc. 5101 Olson Memorial Hwy Golden Valley MN 55422-5149

**HAGIN, T. RICHARD,** lawyer; b. Thomasville, Ga., Sept. 13, 1941; s. Wesley R. and Elizabeth (Skinner) H.; m. Deborah Hayes, June 19, 1981; children: Jennifer Bridges, Lori Bridges Greene; children from previous marriage: John Wesley Hagin, Grace Elizabeth Grubbs. AA, North Fla. C.C., Madison, 1961; student, Fla. State U., 1961-62; JD, Stetson U., 1964. Fla. 1964, Oreg. 1992, U.S. Dist. Ct. (mid. dist.) Fla. 1965, U.S. Ct. Appeals (5th cir.) 1965, U.S. Ct. Appeals (11th cir.) 1981, U.S. Ct. Mil. Appeals 1991, U.S. Supreme Ct. 1971. Atty. Law Offices of David A. Davis, Bushnell, Fla., 1964; ptnr. Davis and Hagin, Bushnell, 1965; atty. in pvt. practice Bushnell, 1966-67; ptnr. Hagin, Hughes, Rardon & Rodriguez, Bushnell, 1989-1996, Getzen and Hagin, Bushnell, 1967-71; pres. Getzen & Hagin, P.A., Bushnell, 1971—; local counsel CSX R.R., Bushnell, 1967-87, gen. counsel Tax Collector of Sumter County, Bushnell, 1976-95; forfeiture atty. Sumter County Sheriff Dept., Bushnell, 1983-89; county atty. Sumter County, Fla., 1969-76; city atty. City of Webster, Fla., 1966-87, City of Coleman, Fla., 1969-73; gen. counsel Sumter County Indsl. Authority, Bushnell, 1979-89, Sumter County Hosp. Authority, Bushnell, 1969-85. Mem. City Coun., Bushnell, 1967-69; pros. atty. Sumter County, 1969-73; chmn. Withlacochee Regional Planning Coun., Ocala, Fla., 1973-75; chmn. 5th Jud. Cir. Grievance Com., 1973-76. Mem. ABA, Assn. Trial Lawyers Am., Fla. Bar, Oreg. Bar Assn., Acad. Fla. Trial Lawyers. Democrat. Personal injury, Workers' compensation, Product liability. Office: Getzen and Hagin, P.A. PO Box 248 Bushnell FL 33513-0248

**HAGOOD, LEWIS RUSSELL,** lawyer; b. Persia, Tenn., July 13, 1930; s. Hobart Verlin and Stella Rose (Carter) H.; m. Mary Evelyn Morrisette, Mar. 15, 1952; children: Lewis Russell Jr., Mary Victoria, Paul Gregory. Student, Lincoln Meml. U., Harrogate, Tenn., 1947-49; BS, East Tenn. State U., 1952; JD, U. Tenn., 1963. Bar: Tenn. 1964, U.S. Dist. Ct. (ea. dist.) Tenn. 1964, U.S. Dist. Ct. (ea. dist.) Ky. 1975, U.S. Tax Ct. 1984, U.S. Ct. Appeals (6th cir.) 1968, U.S. Supreme Ct.; cert. fed. mediator for Ea. Dist. Tenn.; cert. mediator Tenn. Supreme Ct. Ptnr. McLellan, Wright, Hagood, Attys., Kingsport, Tenn., 1964-65; assoc. Arnett & Draper, Attys., Knoxville, Tenn., 1965-67; ptnr. Arnett, Draper & Hagood, Knoxville, 1967—; mem., sec. Tenn. Bd. Law Examiners, 1994—; spkr., lectr. in field. Editor-in-chief: Tennessee Law Review, 1963-64; contbr. articles to profl. jours. Bd. dirs. Knoxville Symphony Soc., 1977—; mem. East Tenn. chpt. March of Dimes, 1981-84; bd. dirs. Knoxville Teen Ctr., Inc., 1975-97. With U.S. Army, 1954-56. Fellow Tenn. Bar Found.; mem. ABA, Tenn. Bar Assn. (past chmn. labor law sect.), Knoxville Bar Assn. Republican. Presbyterian. Avocations: golf, fishing, antique autos. Labor, Federal civil litigation, State civil litigation. Office: Arnett Draper & Hagood Plz Towers Ste 2300 Knoxville TN 37929

**HAGOOD, WILLIAM MILLIKEN, III,** lawyer; b. Easley, S.C., Dec. 16, 1938; s. George Cleveland and Mary Louise (Smith) H.; m. Virginia Elizabeth Hays, June 10, 1962; children: William Milliken IV, Virginia Cleveland. BS in Bus. Adminstrn., Presbyn. Coll., Clinton, S.C., 1960; JD, U. S.C., 1963. Bar: S.C. 1963, U.S. Dist. Ct. (we. dist.) S.C. 1963, U.S. Ct. Appeals 1965, U.S. Supreme Ct., 1971. Law clk. Judge Clement F. Haynsworth, Jr., Greenville, S.C., 1964; shareholder Love, Thornton, Arnold & Thomason, P.A., Greenville, 1964—; mem. faculty Trial Acad., Boulder, Colo., 1988. Author: Physician's Guide to Malpractice Law in South Carolina, 1991. Trustee Presbyn. Coll., 1988-94. Recipient Alumni Svc. award Presbyn. Coll., 1991. Fellow Am. Coll. Trial Lawyers; mem. S.C. Bar Assn., Am. Bd. Trial Advocates, Internat. Assn. Def. Counsel, S.C. Def. Trial Lawyers Assn., Phi Beta Kappa. Presbyterian. Avocations: golf, gardening. Personal injury. Office: Love Thornton Arnold & Thomason PA 410 E Washington St Greenville SC 29601-2927

**HAGOORT, THOMAS HENRY,** lawyer; b. Paterson, N.J., May 30, 1932; s. Nicholas Hugh and Rae (Sytsma) H.; m. Lois Ann Bennett, Sept. 6, 1954; children: Nancy Lynn Hagoort Treuhold, Susan Audrey Hagoort Bick. A.B. cum laude, Harvard U., 1954, LL.B. magna cum laude, 1957. Bar: N.Y. 1959. Assoc. firm Cleary, Gottlieb, Steen & Hamilton, N.Y.C., 1957-67, ptnr., 1968-90, of counsel, 1991—; gen. counsel Albany Internat. Corp., 1991—. Note editor, Harvard Law Rev., 1956-57. Pres. Mountainside Hosp., Montclair, N.J., 1983-85, chmn. bd. trustees, 1985-88; pres. Internat. Baccalaureate of N.Am., N.Y.C., 1980-91, Montclair Bd. Edn. 1966-70; mem., Coun. of Found. Internat. Baccalaureate Orgn., Geneva, 1982-96, pres. and chair exec. com., 1990-96. Mem. ABA, N.Y. State Bar Assn., Harvard Club of N.J. (pres. 1977-78), Montclair Golf Club, S.C. Yacht Club. Democrat. General corporate, Finance, Mergers and acquisitions. Home: PO Box 3229 Hilton Head Island SC 29928-0229

**HAGOPIAN, JACOB,** federal judge; b. Providence, July 3, 1927; s. Bedros and Varvar (Leylegian) H.; m. Mary L. Pomoranski, Aug. 14, 1953; children: Mark Jay, Dana Aquinas, Mary Lou, Jan Christian, Jon Gregory. AB, George Washington U., 1957; JD, Am. U., 1960; grad. in Internat. Law, Judge Advocate Gen.'s Sch., 1964; student, Indsl. Coll. Armed Forces, 1967. Bar: Va. 1961, R.I. 1964, U.S. Supreme Ct. 1964, U.S. Dist. Ct. R.I., U.S. Dist. Ct. (ea. dist.) Va., U.S. Ct. Appeals (D.C. cir.), U.S. Ct. Customs and Patent Appeals, U.S. Ct. Claims, U.S. Tax Ct. Enlisted U.S. Army, 1944, advanced through grades to 1st sgt. 11th Airborne Divsn., 2d lt. to 1st lt. 82d Airborne Divsn., 1948-50; capt. U.S. Army Security Agency, Washington, 1950-53, 56-60; with 501st Recon group U.S. Army Security Agency, Korea, 1953, Tokyo, 1954-56; advanced through grades to col. U.S. Army, 1953-68; appellate judge U.S. Ct. Mil. Rev. U.S. Army Ct. Criminal Appeals, Washington, 1968-70; ret. U.S. Army, 1970; appellate judge U.S. Army Judiciary, Washington, 1968-70; dir. law ctr. Roger Williams Coll., Providence, 1970-71; U.S. magistrate judge U.S. Dist. Ct., Providence, 1971—; legal adv. to intelligence cmty. Spl. Ops., Berlin, 1960-63; group supv. def. appellate divsn. USA Judiciary, Washington, 1964-66; dep. and chief criminal law divsn. OTJAG dept. of army The Pentagon, Washington, 1966-68; lectr. Fed. Jud. Ctr., Washington; adj. prof. Am. U., 1971—, Suffolk U. Law Sch.; vis. prof. U.S. Naval War Coll.; mem. hon. faculty fellow AY, 1997—, hon. program, U. R.I. Contbr. articles to profl. jours. Decorated Legion of Merit (2) with first oak leaf cluster; recipient Army Commendation medal with oak leaf cluster. Mem. ABA (former cons. sect. criminal justice, vice chmn. com. on adequate def. and incentives in mil., former sec.-reporter com. mil. law, Houston Justice Assist award 1987), Fed. Bar Assn. (past pres. R.I. chpt., mem. nat. coun., mem. nat. chmn. com. criminal law, chmn. U.S. magistrate judge's com.), Am. Judges Assn., Inst. Jud. Adminstrn., U.S. Naval War Coll. Found., Nat. Def. U. Found. Office: US Dist Ct One Exchange Ter Providence RI 02903

**HAGSTROM, RICHARD MICHAEL,** lawyer; b. Eau Claire, Wis., Feb. 19, 1951; s. Robert James and Edna Marie Hagstrom; m. Deirdre Abbey, Dec. 17, 1977; children: Lindsey Starr, Kevin Ford. BS, U. Minn., 1973; JD, U. Utah, 1976. Bar: Minn. 1976, Utah 1977, U.S. Ct. Appeals (8th cir.) 1981, U.S. Ct. Appeals (10th cir.) 1987, U.S. Ct. Appeals (6th cir.) 1995, U.S. Supreme Ct. 1987, U.S. Dist. Ct. Minn. 1976, U.S. Dist. Ct. Utah 1987, U.S. Dist. Ct. (ea. dist.) Wis. 1989, Ariz. 1994, U.S. Dist. Ct. (ea. dist.) Mich. 1994. Atty. Meagher, Geer, Mpls., 1976-77, Sydney Berde, P.A., St. Paul, 1978-81; shareholder Berde & Hagstrom, P.A., St. Paul, 1981-85; chief antitrust sect. Utah Atty. Gen. Office, Salt Lake City, 1985-88; assoc. Zelle, Hofmann, Voelbel & Grette LLP, Mpls., 1988-91, ptnr., 1992—. Pub. chmn. No. Suburban br. Luth. Brotherhood, St. Paul, 1993-96. Mem. ABA, Minn. Bar Assn., Utah State Bar Assn. Avocations: skiing, water skiing, scuba diving, jet skiing. Antitrust, General civil litigation, Insurance. Office: Zelle Hofmann Voelbel & Grette LLP 33 S 6th St Ste 4400 Minneapolis MN 55402-3710

**HAGUE, ANDREW STUART,** judge; b. Boston, Dec. 2, 1955; s. Harry Michael and Nancy Milroy (Smythe) H.; m. Mary Jane Richards, Aug. 28, 1982; children: Andrew Stuart II, Christopher Michael. BS in Psychology, Tulane U., 1978, JD, 1982. Bar: Fla. 1982; lic. in real estate, Fla. Prosecutor Dade County State Atty.'s Office, Miami, Fla., 1982—, div. chief, chief of gang prosecutions, 1982—, maj. crimes prosecutor, 1995-97; county ct. judge Dade County, Fla., 1997—. Trustee Ransom-Everglades Sch., Miami, 1989—, St. Stephen's Episcopal Sch., Miami, 1992—; mem. N.E. Dade Involved Dems., Miami, 1994—. Mem. NOW. Office: Dade County Richard & Gerstein Justice Bldg 1351 NW 12th St Miami FL 33125-1644

**HAGUE, PAUL CHRISTIAN,** lawyer; b. Cleve., May 6, 1943; s. Joseph Anthony and Virginia Blanche (Galloway) H.; m. Marcia Beth Metz, Sept. 29, 1973; children: Suzanne Elizabeth, John Christian. BA, U. Dayton, 1965; JD, U. Pitts., 1968. Bar: Pa. 1969, Fla. 1983, U.S. Ct. Appeals (3rd cir.) 1970. Assoc. Meyer, Unkovic & Scott, Pitts., 1969-75, ptnr., 1975—. Bd. dirs. Pitts. Jaycees, 1969-72; trustee The Ellis Sch., Pitts. 1986-90. Mem. ABA, Allegheny County Bar Assn. (chmn. young lawyers sect. 1977, bd. govs. 1978, chair civil litigation sect. 1995), Pa. Bar Assn. (ho. of dels. 1995—) , Acad. Trial Lawyers Allegheny County, Pitts. Athletic Assn. (bd. dirs. 1986-89). General civil litigation, Antitrust, Environmental. Office: Meyer Unkovic & Scott 1300 Oliver Building Pittsburgh PA 15222-2300

**HAHN, ELLIOTT JULIUS,** lawyer; b. San Francisco, Dec. 9, 1949; s. Leo Wolf and Sherry Marion (Portnoy) H.; m. Toby Rose Mallen; children: Kara Rebecca, Brittany Atira Mallen, Michael Mallen, Adam Mallen. BA cum laude, U. Pa., 1971, JD, 1974; LLM, Columbia U., 190. Bar: N.J. 1974, Calif. 1976, D.C. 1978, U.S. Dist. Ct. N.J. 1974, U.S. Dist. Ct. (cen. dist.) Calif. 1976, U.S. Supreme Ct. 1980. Assoc. von Malitz, Derenberg, Kunin & Janssen, N.Y.C., 1974-75; law clk. L.A. County Superior Ct., 1975-76; atty. Atlantic Richfield Co., L.A., 1976-79; prof. Summer in Tokyo program Santa Clara Law Sch., 1981-83; assoc. prof. law Calif. Western Coll. Law, San Diego, 1980-85; atty. Morgan, Lewis & Bockius, L.A., 1985-87; assoc. Whitman & Ransom, L.A., 1987-88, ptnr., 1989-93; ptnr. Sonnenschein Nath & Rosenthal, L.A., 1993-97, Hahn & Bolson LLP, 1997—; vis. scholar Nihon U., Tokyo, 1982; vis. lectr. Internat. Christian U., Tokyo, 1982; adj. prof. law Southwestern U. Sch. Law, 1986—, Pepperdine U. law Sch., 1986—, U. So. Calif. Law Sch., 1997—; lectr. U. Calif., Davis, Law Sch. Orientation in U.S.A. Law Program, 1994-97. Author: Japanese Business Law and the Legal System, 1984; contbr. chpt. on Japan to The World Legal Ency.; internat. law editor Calif. Bus. Law Reporter. Vice-chmn. San Diego Internat. Affairs Bd., 1981-85; bd. dirs. San Diego-Yokohama Sister City Soc., 1983-85, L.A.-Nagoya Sister City Soc., 1986—; mem. master planning com. City of Rancho Palos Verdes, Calif., 1989-91; advisor, exec. com. Calif. Internat. Law Sect., 1990-91, 95, appointee exec. com., 1991-94, vice-chmn., 1992-93, chair, 1993-94; appointee, trustee Palos Verdes Libr. Dist., 1993-94; bd. dirs. Internat. Student Ctr. UCLA, 1996—. Mem. ABA, State Bar Calif., L.A. County Bar Assn. (bd. dirs. internat. sect., exec. com. Internat. Legal Sec. 1987—, sec. 1995-96, 2d v.p. 1996-97, 1st v.p. 1997-98, chmn. 1998-99, appointee Pacific rim com. 1990-98, chmn. 1991-92, 95-98, trustee 1997-98), Assn. Asian Studies, U. Pa. Alumni Club (pres. San Diego chpt. 1982, pres. coun. Phila. 1983), Anti Defamation League, Japanese-Am. Soc. (book rev. editor Seattle 1983-85). Jewish. Private international, Contracts commercial, General corporate. Office: Hahn & Bolson LLP 601 S Figueroa St Ste 3700 Los Angeles CA 90017-5742

**HAHN, H. BLAIR,** lawyer; b. Chapel Hill, N.C., Nov. 26, 1958; s. Herbert Ransom and Mary Anna Blair H.; m. Nancy Elizabeth Walker, May 18, 1985; children: Kate, Walker. BA in Bus. Mgmt., N.C. State U., Raleigh, 1980, BA in Econs., 1980; JD, U. S.C., 1992. Bar: S.C. 1992, U.S. Dist. Ct. S.C. 1992, U.S. Ct. Appeals (8th cir.) 1995, U.S. Dist. Ct. Ariz. 1997. Atty. Ness, Motley, Loadholt, Richardson & Poole, Charleston, S.C., 1992—; Bd. dirs. Atlantic Publ. Group, Charleston, 1989—. Editor: S.C. Bar Young Lawyers Newsletter, 1992-93. Product liability, Personal injury. Office: Ness Motley Loadholt Richardson & Poole PO Box 1137 Charleston SC 29402-1137

**HAHN, WILLIAM EDWARD,** lawyer; b. Bklyn., Sept. 3, 1946; s. Ernest Edward and Alice Elizabeth (Moench) H.; m. Elizabeth Weiler Fowles, Mar. 14, 1970; children: Bethany Elyce, Tara Elizabeth, Jillian Lisa. BA, Marietta Coll., 1968; JD, U. Fla., 1972. Bar: Fla. 1972, U.S. Dist. Ct. (mid. dist.) Fla. 1972, U.S. Dist. Ct. (so. and no. dists.) Fla. 1975. Ptnr. MacFarlane, Ferguson, Allison & Kelly, Tampa, Fla., 1972-78; shareholder Newman & Hahn, P.A., Tampa, 1978-79, Shear, Newman & Hahn, P.A., Tampa, 1979-85, Shear, Newman, Hahn & Rosenkranz, P.A., Tampa, 1985—; com. mem. civil jury instructions Fla. Supreme Ct., 1994—. Bd. dirs. Hillsborough County Crisis Ctr., Inc., Tampa, 1975—, indep. day sch., 1985-90. Mem. ABA, Am. Bd. Trial Adv. (officer 1997—), Fla. Bar Assn. (chmn. grievance com. 1992-94), Fla. Supreme Ct. (civil jury instrns. com.), Fedn. Ins. and Corp. Counsel, Hillsborough County Trial Lawyers (com. mem. 1990-94). Democrat. Methodist. Avocations: scuba diving, biking, tennis, swimming. Personal injury, Professional liability, General civil litigation. Home: 11742 Lipsey Rd Tampa FL 33618-3620 Office: Shear Newman Hahn & Rosenkranz PA 201 E Kennedy Blvd Ste 1000 Tampa FL 33602-5173

**HAIG, ROBERT LEIGHTON,** lawyer; b. Plainfield, N.J., July 30, 1947; s. Richard Randall and Edith (Remington) H. AB, Yale U., 1967; JD, Harvard U., 1970. Bar: N.Y. 1971, U.S. Dist. Ct. (so. and ea. dists.) N.Y., U.S. Ct. Appeals (2d cir.). Assoc. Kelley Drye & Warren, N.Y.C., 1970-79, ptnr., 1980—; mem. bd. advisers Law Dept. Mgmt. Adviser, 1995—. Co-author: Preparing for and Trying the Civil Lawsuit, 1987, 91, 94, 97, Federal Civil Practice, 1989, 93, 97, Federal Litigation Guide, 1992, 93, 94, Corporate Counsel's Guide, 1996, 97, Products Liability in New York, 1997; also contbr. chpts. to books, articles to profl. jours.; mem. bd. editors Fed. Litigation Guide Reporter, 1989—, In-House Law Practice Management, 1997—; editor-in-chief Comml. Litigation in N.Y. State Cts., 1995, Bus. and Comml. Litigation in Fed. Cts., 1998. Co-chair Comml. Cts. Task Force, 1995—; mem. legis. com. Com. for Modern Cts., N.Y.C., 1986—, bd. dirs., 1994—; mem. Am. Law Inst., 1998—; mem. N.Y. State Conf. Bar Leaders, exec. coun., 1988-90, dept. disciplinary com. appellate divsn., 1996—, hearing panel chair, 1999—; mem. N.Y. State Jud. Salary Commn., 1997—. Recipient award for excellence in continuing legal edn. Assn. Continuing Legal Edn. Adminstrs., 1991. Fellow Am. Bar Found. (life), N.Y. Bar Found.; mem. ABA (del. 1991—, standing com. on jud. selection, tenure and compensation 1995-96, com. on bus. cts. 1996—, chair subcom. on rels. between inside and outside counsel 1997—), Assn. of Bar of City of N.Y. (mem. jud. com. 1985-88, chmn., 1989-92, mem. coun. on jud. adminstrn. 1989-92, chmn. 1996—), N.Y. County Lawyers Assn. (exec. com. 1986-95, v.p. 1986-92, pres. 1992-94, dir. 1985—, chmn. com. on supreme ct. 1984-86, chmn. fin. com. 1988-90, lectr. 1984—, pres. Found. 1992-94), N.Y. State Bar Assn. (chmn. com. on fed. cts. 1986-88, del. 1988—, chmn. comml. and fed. litig. sect. 1988-90, lectr. 1985—, exec. com. 1991-94, mem. steering com. on commerce and industry 1997—, chair com. on multi-disciplinary practice and the legal profn. 1998—, 1st Ann. award for Disting. Pub. Svc. comml. and fed. litig. sect. 1995). Federal civil litigation, General civil litigation, State civil litigation. Office: Kelley Drye & Warren 101 Park Ave Fl 30 New York NY 10178-0062

**HAIGHT, CHARLES SHERMAN, JR.,** federal judge; b. N.Y.C., Sept. 23, 1930; s. Charles Sherman and Margaret (Edwards) H.; m. Mary Jane Peightal, June 30, 1953; children: Nina E., Susan P. B.A., Yale U., 1952, LL.B., 1955. Bar: N.Y. State 1955. Trial atty., admiralty and shipping dept. Dept. Justice, Washington, 1955-57; assoc. firm Haight, Gardner, Poor & Havens, N.Y.C., 1957-68; ptnr. Haight, Gardner, Poor & Havens, 1968-76; judge U.S. Dist. Ct. for So. Dist. N.Y., 1976—. Bd. dirs. Kennedy Child Study Ctr.; adv. trustee Am.-Scandinavian Found., chmn., 1970-76; bd. mgrs. Havens Fund. Mem. Maritime Law Assn., U.S., N.Y. State Bar Assn., Bar Assn. City N.Y., Fed. Bar Council. Episcopalian. Office: US Dist Ct US Courthouse 500 Pearl St New York NY 10007-1316

**HAIK, RICHARD T., SR.,** federal judge; b. 1950. BS, U. Southwestern La., 1971; JD, Loyola U., New Orleans, 1975. Assoc. Haik & Broussard, 1975-79; ptnr. Haik, Broussard & Haik, 1979-81, Haik, Haik & Minvielle, 1981-84; judge La. State Dist., New Iberia, 1984-91; dist. judge U.S. Dist. Ct. (we. dist.) La., 1991—. With USAR, 1978-81; USNG, 1971-78. Mem. ABA, La. Bar Assn., Iberia Parish Bar Assn., La. Dist. Judge's Assn. (exec. com. 1988-91), Nat. Coun. Juvenile and Family Ct. Judges (steering com. alcohol and substance abuse). Office: US Dist Ct Fed Bldg 705 Jefferson St Ste 213 Lafayette LA 70501-6936

**HAILE, ELSTER SHARON,** lawyer, artist; b. Kingman, Kans., July 16, 1916; s. Elster McClellan and Pauline Shirley Haile; children: Suzanne A., William, Jeanne Edwards Brooks, Stephen McCloud, Michael Forrest, John Patrick. AB, Stanford U., 1938, JD, 1941. Bar: Calif., U.S. Dist. Ct. (no. dist.) Calif. Pvt. practice Palo Alto, Calif.; law prof. San Francisco Law Sch., 1954; judge pro tem Mcpl. Ct. Santa Clara County, San Jose, Calif., 1975-87, Superior Ct. Calif., San Jose, 1990-93; ct. arbitrator Superior Ct. Santa Clara County, 1989-96; arbitrator Am. Arbitration Assn., San Francisco, 1984-89, U.S. Dist. Ct., No. Dist., Calif. Pres. Stanford Law Soc., No. Calif., 1954-55; bd. visitors Stanford Law Sch., 1954-55; bd. dirs. San Mateo County Elem. Sch. Dist., 1957-58; vestry mem. St. Mathews Episcopal Ch., San Mateo, Calif., 1956-59; precinct chmn. Dem. Party, San Mateo County, 1960; co-city atty. Half Moon Bay, Calif., 1961-62; bd. dis. EastPalo Alto Sr. Ctr., East Palo Alto, 1995-98; mem. Kiwanis Club Palo Alto, 1963—. Mem. Calif. Bar Assn., Palo Alto Bar Assn., San Mateo County Bar Assn., Elks. Episcopalian. Avocations: private pilot, watercolorist. General civil litigation, Estate planning, Insurance. Office: 555 Bryant St # 382 Palo Alto CA 94301-1704

**HAILE, JOHN SANDERS,** lawyer; b. Jacksonville, Fla., July 26, 1956; s. John Jr. and Waltress (Sanders) H.; m. Audrey Lee Cryan, Apr. 17, 1982; children: Jay Jon, Jenifer Leigh, Christina Janel, John Christian, Katelyn Elizabeth. AA, Fla. State U., 1975, BS magna cum laude, 1977, JD, 1980. Bar: Fla. 1982, U.S. Tax Ct. 1984. Tax acct. Coopers & Lybrand, Ft. Lauderdale, Fla., 1978-79; tax specialist Peat, Marwick & Mitchell, Ft. Lauderdale, 1980-82; sr. ptnr. Haile & Haile, CPAs, Lake Placid, Fla., 1981—; pres. John Haile, P.A., Lake Placid, Fla., 1982—; trustee City of Deerfield Beach, Fla., 1983-86. Charter mem. Estate Planning Coun., 1984—; elder Trinity Luth. Ch. Bd. of Regents scholar State of Fla., 1974. Mem. ABA, Fla. Bar Assn. (numerous coms.), AICPAs, Am. Assn. Atty.-CPAs, Am. Judicature Soc., Heartland Estate Planning Coun., Tax Practitioners Roundtable, Highlands County Bar Assn., Am. Water Ski Assn., Beta Gamma Sigma, Beta Alpha Psi, Phi Delta Phi. Republican. Avocations: slalom waterskiing, scuba diving, air chair instructing, spearfishing, swimming. Estate planning, Probate, Real property. Office: 119 Us Highway 27 S Lake Placid FL 33852-7918

**HAILE, LAWRENCE BARCLAY,** lawyer; b. Atlanta, Feb. 19, 1938; children: Gretchen Vanderhoof, Eric McKenzie (dec.), Scott McAllister, m. Carole Chimko, Dec.1, 1998. BA in Econs, U. Tex., 1958, LLB, 1961. Bar: Tex. 1961, Calif. 1962. Law clk. to U.S. Judge Joseph M. Ingraham, Houston, 1961-62; pvt. practice law San Francisco, 1962-67, L.A., 1967—; instr. UCLA Civil Trial Clinics, 1974, 76; lectr. law Calif. Continuing Edn. of Bar, 1973-74, 80-89; mem. nat. panel arbitrators Am. Arbitration Assn., 1965—. Assoc. editor: Tex. Law Rev, 1960-61; Contbr. articles profl. publs. Mem. State Bar Calif., Tex., U.S. Supreme Ct. Bar Assn., Internat. Assn. Property Ins. Counsel (founding mem., pres. 1980), Vintage Auto Racing Assn. (bd. dirs.), Vintage Motorsports Coun. (past pres.), Phi Delta Phi, Delta Sigma Rho. Insurance, Federal civil litigation, State civil litigation. Office: 17214 Hemmingway St Van Nuys CA 91406 *Gold is like brass/ Except less crass.*

**HAILEY, HANS RONALD,** lawyer; b. Boston, Feb. 9, 1950; s. William C. and Renate (Weiss) H.; m. Rosalie A. Caprio, May 2, 1981 (div.); 1 child, Alexa Emily. B.A., Boston U., 1973, J.D., 1976. Bar: Mass. 1977, U.S. Dist. Ct. Mass. 1977, U.S. Ct. Appeals (1st cir.) 1978. pvt. practice law, Boston; Bd. dirs. Boston Ctr. for Ind. Living, 1979-88, Easter Seal Soc., 1983—; mem Mass. Archtl. Barriers Bd., 1978-82. Author: So You Think You Have Better Things To Do Than Stay Married, 1991; contbr. articles to profl. jours. Named One of Ten Outstanding Young Leaders Boston Jaycees, 1981. Mem. Mass. Bar Assn., Boston Bar Assn., Mass. Trial Lawyers Assn. (exec. council), Democrat. Roman Catholic. Family and matrimonial, Personal injury. Home: 74 Highview St Westwood MA 02090-3019 Office: 11 Beacon St Ste 1120 Boston MA 02108-3011

**HAIMBAUGH, GEORGE DOW, JR.,** lawyer, educator; b. Rochester, Ind., Nov. 21, 1916; s. George Dow and Agnes Elizabeth (Sharp) H.; m. Katharine Louise Draper, Aug. 20, 1960. A.B., DePauw U., 1938; postgrad., Georgetown U., 1938-40; J.D., Northwestern U., 1952; J.S.D., Yale U., 1962; student, Hague Acad. Internat. Law, 1963. Bar: Ill. 1953, S.C. 1973, U.S. Dist. Ct. (no. dist.) Ohio 1962, U.S. Ct. Appeals (fed. cir.) 1992, U.S. Ct. Internat.Trade 1992, U.S. Supreme Ct. 1969. Asst. prof. U. Akron Coll. Law, 1960-63; assoc. prof. law U. S.C., Columbia, 1963-70, prof., 1970-79, David W. Robinson prof. law, 1979-87, disting. prof. emeritus, 1987—, assoc. Inst. Internat. Studies, 1967—, mem. Byrnes Internat. Ctr. Adv. Council, 1984—; spl. master U.S. Dist. Ct. (no. dist.) Ohio, 1962-63; mem. adv. bd. Nat. Inst. Justice, 1982-85; assoc. Belle W. Baruch Inst. Marine Biology and Coastal Research, 1978—. Mem. Ga.-S.C. Boundary Commn.,

1978—, Columbia's Commn. on Bicentennial of U.S. Constn., 1987-89, co-chmn. bicentennial events com., 1990-95, Global Forum of UN Conf. on Environment and Devel., Rio de Janeiro, 1992; deacon 1st Presbyn Ch., Columbia. Maj. USMC, 1940-46. Recipient Charles Cheney Hyde prize, 1952. Mem. ABA (chmn. adv. com. to standing com. on law and nat. security 1979-82), S.C. Bar Assn. (internat. law com.), Richland County Bar Assn., Am. Law Inst., Am. Soc. Internat. Law, Assn. Am. Law Schs. (chmn. sect. constl. law 1975-77), Order of Coif, Order of Palmetto, Mil. Order World Wars, Soc. Profl. Journalists/Sigma Delta Chi, Phi Gamma Delta, Phi Delta Phi (Dean William L. Prosser award for the 1993-95 Biennium), Delta Phi Epsilon. Republican. Office: U SC Law Sch Columbia SC 29208-0001

**HAINES, TERRY L.,** lawyer, consultant; b. Washington, Pa., Oct. 2, 1957; s. John A. and Ann C. Haines; m. Cathy MacFarlane. BA, Oberlin Coll., 1979; JD, Vt. U., 1982. Bar: Pa. 1983, U.S. Dist. Ct. (we. dist.) Pa. 1983. Legis. asst. com. on judiciary Pa. Assembly, Harrisburg, 1983; sr. staff atty. FCC, Washington, 1983-87; rep. counsel com. on energy and commerce U.S. Ho. of Reps., Washington, 1987-91; chief of staff FCC, Washington, 1991-93; divsn. gen. counsel TCI East, Inc., Bethesda, Md., 1993-94; chief oper. officer, gen. counsel Boland & Madigan, Inc., Washington, 1995—. Avocations: golf, history. Communications, Antitrust, Computer. Office: Boland & Madigan Inc 700 13th St NW Ste 350 Washington DC 20005-3960

**HAINES, THOMAS DAVID, JR.,** lawyer; b. Dallas, Oct. 30, 1956; s. Thomas David Sr. and Carol V. (Mullins) H.; m. Nanette Cluck, Mar. 1, 1986; children: Bennett Ann, Maison Cluck. BS in Polit. Sci., Okla. State U., 1979; JD, U. Okla., 1982. Bar: Okla. 1982, N.Mex. 1983, U.S. Ct. Appeals (10th cir.) 1983, U.S. Dist. Ct. N.Mex. 1983. Assoc. Hinkle, Cox, Eaton, Coffield & Hensley, Roswell, N.Mex., 1982-87, ptnr., 1988—. Contbg. editor N.Mex. Tort and Worker's Compensation Reporter, 1987-90, Employment Law Deskbook for New Mexico Employers, 1997. Youth sponsor First United Meth. Ch., Roswell, 1986-88, chmn. stewardship com. 1990-91, chmn. adminstrv. coun., 1998—; coach Roswell Youth Soccer Assn., 1995—; trustee 1st United Meth. Ch., Roswell, 1996-98. Mem. State Bar Assn. N.Mex. (com. on continuing legal edn., young lawyers divsn. 1989—, mem. med.-legal rev. commn. 1988—), Chaves County Bar Assn., N.Mex. Def. Lawyer's Assn., N.Mex. Trial Lawyer's Assn., Kiwanis (Roswell club, Outstanding Club Sec. award 1993-95, pres. 1998-99, named one Outstanding Young Men in Am. 1990), Phi Delta Phi, Phi Kappa Phi. Republican. Avocations: golf, basketball, music, politics. Workers' compensation, Personal injury, Insurance. Office: Hinkle Cox Eaton Coffield & Hensley 400 N Pennsylvania Ave Ste 700 Roswell NM 88201-4777

**HAINES, THOMAS W. W.,** lawyer; b. Balt., Oct. 10, 1941; s. John Summer and Clara Elizabeth (Ward) H.; m. Vivienne Wilson, Jan. 3, 1981; children: Robert S., Elizabeth E., John M. BA, Cornell U., 1963; LLB, U. Md., 1967. Bar: Md. 1967, U.S. Dist. Ct. Md. 1968, U.S. Ct. Appeals (4th cir.) 1972, U.S. Tax Ct. 1973, U.S. Supreme Ct. 1975. Assoc. Semmes, Bowen & Semmes, Balt., 1968-75, ptnr., 1975-95; ptnr. Venable, Baetjer & Howard, LLP, Balt., 1995—. Fellow Am. Coll. Trust and Estate (counsel); mem. ABA, Md. Bar Assn., Bar Assn. Balt. City, Gibson Island Club, Maryland Club. Episcopalian. Banking, Intellectual property, General corporate. Office: Venable Baetjer & Howard 1800 Mercantile Bank Trust 2 Hopkins Plz Ste 2100 Baltimore MD 21201-2982

**HAIR, MATTOX S.,** mediator, judge, lawyer; b. Coral Gables, Fla., Jan. 18, 1938; s. Henry Horry and Frances Alberta (Strickland) H. BS, Fla. State U., 1960; JD, U. Fla., 1964. Bar: Fla. 1964. Ptnr. Marks, Gray, Conroy & Gibbs, Jacksonville, 1965-88; asst. atty. gen. Fla., 1964-65; mem. Fla. Ho. of Reps. from 22d Dist., 1972-74, Fla. Senate from 9th Dist., 1974-88; cir. judge Duval County Ct., Jacksonville, 1989-92; ptnr. Gabel & Hair, Jacksonville, 1992-97; mediator, arbitrator, pvt. judge. 2d lt. U.S. Army, 1963-64; capt. Fla. N.G., 1955-67. Mem. ABA, Fla. Bar Assn., Jacksonville Bar Assn. (bd. govs. 1968-72), Chester Bedell Inn of Ct. (master of the bench), Rotary Club of Jacksonville, Phi Delta Phi. Baptist. Home: 505 Lancaster St #16 Jacksonville FL 32204-4143 Office: Gabel & Hair 225 Water St Ste 2100 Jacksonville FL 32202-5154

**HAJE, PETER ROBERT,** lawyer; b. N.Y.C., July 31, 1934; s. Arnold John and Edna Marie (Bossert) H.; m. Helen Heineman, Aug. 13, 1943; children: Michael James, Katherine Joy, Lily Elizabeth. BA, Cornell U., 1955; LLB, Harvard U., 1960. Bar: N.Y. 1961, U.S. Dist. Ct. (so. dist.) N.Y. 1965, U.S. Ct. Appeals (2d cir.) 1965, D.C. 1970, U.S. Ct. Appeals (D.C. cir.) 1981. Assoc. Paul, Weiss, Rifkind, Wharton & Garrison, N.Y.C., 1960-68, ptnr., 1969-90; exec. v.p., gen. counsel Time Warner Inc., N.Y.C., 1990—. Securities, Mergers and acquisitions, General corporate. Office: Time Warner Inc 75 Rockefeller Plz New York NY 10019-6990*

**HAJEK, FRANCIS PAUL,** lawyer; b. Hobart, Tasmania, Australia, Oct. 21, 1958; came to U.S., 1966; s. Frank Joseph and Kathleen Beatrice (Blake) H. BA, Yale U., 1980; JD, U. Richmond, 1984. Bar: Va. 1984, U.S. Dist. Ct. (ea. dist.) Va. 1984, U.S. Ct. Appeals (4th cir.) 1986. Law clk. to presiding magistrate U.S. Dist Ct., Norfolk, Va., 1984-85; assoc. Seawell, Dalton, Hughes & Timms, Norfolk, 1985-87, Weinberg & Stein, Norfolk, 1987-89, I'Anson-Hoffman Am. Inn of Ct., 1991-97, Wilson, Hajek & Shapiro, P.C., Virginia Beach, Va., 1989—. Mem. ABA, ATLA, Am. Rail Labor Acad., Va. Bar Assn., Norfolk-Portsmouth Bar Assn. (chmn. exec. com. young lawyer's sect. 1990-91). Roman Catholic. Avocations: squash, tennis. Federal civil litigation, State civil litigation, Personal injury. Home: 2116 Windward Shore Dr Virginia Beach VA 23451-1726 Office: Wilson Hajek & Shapiro PO Box 5369 Virginia Beach VA 23471-0369

**HALAGAO, AVELINO GARABILES,** lawyer; b. Santa Lucia, Ilocos Sur, The Philippines, Nov. 4, 1938; came to U.S., 1972; s. Manuel Habon and Marciana Garabiles H.; m. Concepcion Lorenzana Jimeno, aug. 1, 1962; children: Jesus Michael, Arleen Bernadette, Avelino Jr., Anna Maria, Amanda Marie. LLB, San Beda Coll. Law, Manila, 1962; M in Comparative Law, George Washington U., 1986. Bar: Va. 1987, D.C. 1992, The Philippines 1963. Ptnr. Bello, Halagao & Pimentel, Manila, 1963-65; atty. Commn. on Elections, Manila, 1965-70; judge Republic of The Philippines, Manila, 1970-72; trust officer Nat. Bank Washington, 1973-87; assoc. Coates & Davenport, McLean, Va., 1987-88; mng. ptnr. Avelino G. Halagao & Assocs., Tysons Corner, Va., 1989—; pres., chmn. bd. dirs. Manuel H. Halagao & Sons Transp. Co., Manila, 1968-72; chmn. bd. dirs. QX, Inc., Washington, 1995-97. Mem. Philippine-Am. Bar Assn. (founder, treas. 1976-78, pres. 1984-85, Leadership and Disting. Membership award 1990), Ilocano Soc. Am. (co-founder, pres. 1983-84). Roman Catholic. Avocations: basketball, golfing, fishing, dancing, singing. Immigration, naturalization, and customs, Personal injury, General corporate. Home: 3311 Cullers Ct Woodbridge VA 22192-1086 Office: Avelino G Halagao & Assocs 7799 Leesburg Pike Ste 900N Falls Church VA 22043-2413

**HALASZ, PAUL J.,** lawyer; b. Summit, N.J., Dec. 18, 1964; s. Karoly and Josephine M. (Batchek) H.; m. Kristine Mackenzie Halasz, Nov. 9, 1991; 1 child, Julia. BA, Rutgers, Newark, N.J., 1987; JD, Rutgers, Camden, N.J., 1991. Bar: N.J., 1991; U.S. Dist. Ct. (3rd cir.) 1993. Atty. Pitney, Hardin, Kipp & Szuch, Morristown, N.J., 1991—. Editor-in-chief: Rutgers Law Journal, 1990-91. Com. mem. Morris COunty Dem. Com., Morristown, N.J., 1996—. Mem. ABA, Morris County Bar Assn. Democrat. Roman Catholic. General civil litigation. Office: Pitney Hardin Kipp & Szuch PO Box 1945 Morristown NJ 07962-1945

**HALBER, LORI ELIZABETH,** lawyer; b. Abington, Pa., Feb. 5, 1969; m. Christopher John Halber, Sept. 2, 1995; children: Alexandra Christine, Jacqueline Elizabeth. BS in Econs., U. Pa., 1991; JD, Temple U., 1997. Bar: Pa. 1997, N.J. 1997, U.S. Dist. Ct. Pa. (ea. dist.). Account exec. Waste Mgmt. Inc., Bensalem, Pa., 1992-94; law clk. Advanta Corp., Spring House, Pa., 1995-97; assoc. Obermayer Rebmann Maxwell & Hippel LLP, Phila., 1997—. Labor, Immigration, naturalization, and customs. Office: Obermayer Rebmann Maxwell & Hippel LLP One Penn Ctr 19th Fl 1617 Jfk Blvd Ste 1950 Philadelphia PA 19103-1895

**HALBERT, RICHARD LEWIS,** lawyer; b. Falls City, Nebr., Dec. 10, 1942; s. Chapman and Thelma E. Halbert; m. Esther L. Borcher, Nov. 11, 1972; children: Christopher C., Andrew J. BA, U. Nebr., 1965, JD, 1968. Bar: Nebr., 1968. Dep. county atty. Hall County Atty.'s Office, Grand Island, Nebr., 1968-70; assoc. Wiltse & Halbert, Falls City, Nebr., 1970-71, ptnr., 1971-73; ptnr. Halbert Law Office, Falls City, Nebr., 1973-86; sr. ptnr. Halbert & Dunn, Falls City, Nebr., 1986—; bd. dirs., legal counsel S.E. Nebr. Telephone Co., Falls City, Arck Foods, Inc. Contbr. articles to profl. jours. Bd. govs. Nat. Am. U., Rapid City, S.D., 1996—. Fellow Am. Coll. Trust and Estate Counsel, Nebr. Bar Found.; mem. ABA, Nebr. State Bar Assn., S.E. Nebr. Bar Assn., Falls City C. of C. (pres. 1975), Elks, Lions. Republican. Estate planning, General corporate, General practice. Office: Halbert & Dunn 111 E 17th St Falls City NE 68355-2639

**HALBLEIB, WALTER THOMAS,** lawyer; b. Louisville, Sept. 15, 1964; s. Walter Thomas and Nancy Ellen Halbleib; m. Edith Jean Frick, June 27, 1997. BS cum laude, Miami U., 1987; JD with high distinction, U. Ky., 1991. Bar: Ky. 1991, U.S. Ct. Appeals (6th cir.) 1991. Staff mem. Office of Hon. Sam Nunn, U.S. Senator, Washington, 1987-88; law clk. hon. Bailey Brown U.S. Ct. Appeals (6th cir.), Memphis, 1991-92; lawyer Stites and Harbison, Louisville, 1992—. Editor-in-chief Ky. Law Jour., 1990-91. Vol. instr. Jr. Achievement, Louisville, 1998, 99. Contracts commercial, General corporate, Finance. Office: Stites & Harbison 400 W Market St Ste 1800 Louisville KY 40202-3362

**HALDIN, WILLIAM CARL, JR.,** lawyer; b. Hollywood, Calif., June 24, 1944; s. William Carl and Ruth Irene (Hardesty) H.; m. Zeta Elizabeth Jones, Aug. 5, 1967 (dec. July 1986); 1 child, James William; m. Nancy Kathleen Davidson, Apr. 8, 1990. BA, U. Fla., 1966, MEd, 1968, JD, 1979. Bar: Fla. 1979. Guidance counselor Putnam County Schs., Palatka, Fla., 1967-70; sch. psychologist Marion County Schs., Ocala, Fla., 1971-72, dir. student svcs., 1972-77; ptnr. Matthies, Cross, DeBloisblanc & Haldin, P.A., Ocala, 1982-91, Richard, Blinn & Haldin, P.A., Ocala, 1991—. Contbr. articles to profl. jours. Bd. dirs. Marion County C. of C., Ocala, 1986-89, v.p., 1987; mem. adv. bd. Salvation Army, Ocala, 1988—, chmn., 1993. Mem. Fla. Bar (grievance com. 1984-87), Marion County Bar Assn. General corporate, Real property, Estate planning. Office: Richard Blinn & Haldin PA 808 SE Fort King St Ocala FL 34471-2320

**HALE, DANIEL CUDMORE,** lawyer; b. Denver, Nov. 5, 1944; s. George Ellis and Dorothy Ann (Cudmore) H.; children: Brad, Tessa. BS in Mktg., U. Colo., 1967, JD, 1971. Bar: Colo. 1971, U.S. Dist. Ct. Colo. 1971, U.S. Ct. Appeals (10th cir.) 1971, U.S. Supreme Ct. 1979. Clk. to judge U.S. Dist. Ct., Denver, 1971-72; chief trial dep. Boulder Dist. Atty.'s Office Colo., 1973-76; atty. Miller, Gray & Hale, Boulder, 1976-84; ptnr. Miller, Hale & Harrison, Boulder, 1984—; dist. ct. judge 20th Jud. Dist., 1996—; cert. instr. search and seizure State of Colo., 1980—; instr. trial advocacy U. Colo., 1987—. Bd. dirs. Boulder County Bd. of Developmental Disabilities, Boulder, 1982-88, pres., 1984-85. Mem. ATLA, Boulder County Bar Assn. (sec., treas. 1977-79, bd. govs. 1985-89, 92—, pres.-elect 1989, pres. 1990-91), Colo. Bar Assn., Nat. Assn. Criminal Def. Lawyers, Colo. Criminal Def. Bar. Democrat. Criminal, Personal injury. Home: 1955 Glenwood Dr Boulder CO 80304-2328 Office: 20th Judicial Dist 1777 6th St Boulder CO 80302-5814

**HALE, HARLAND HANNA,** lawyer; b. Toledo, Oct. 22, 1955; s. Harold Harland and Doris Jean H.; m. Janet Lynn Parkhurst, Sept. 16, 1953; 1 child, Harrison Heath. BA, Otterbein Coll., 1976; JD, U. Toledo, 1979. Bar: Ohio, U.S. Dist. Ct. (so. dist.) Ohio, U.S. Ct. Appeals (6th cir.). Asst. pros. atty. Del. County Ohio Pros. Atty., Ohio, 1979-80; in house counsel Ohio Dept. Nat. Resources, Columbus, 1981; pros. atty. Franklin County Pros. Attys. Office, Columbus, 1982—. Mem. Agonis, 1986-96; mem. staff to Congressman Delbert Latta, Washington, 1975-76; mem. com. Perry Twp., Columbus, 1988—. Named Prosecutor of Yr., Advs. for Child Support Enforcement, 1985. Mem. Columbus Bar Assn. (co-chair amnesty week 1986), Ctrl. Ohio Jr. Golf Assn. (bd. dirs. 1987-97), Kiwanis Club. Republican. Avocations: boating, sports, community affairs. Home: 6637 Merwin Rd Columbus OH 43235-2841 Office: Franklin County Prosecutor's Office 373 S High St Columbus OH 43215-4591

**HALE, J. KEVIN,** lawyer; b. Kansas City, Mo., Mar. 7, 1947; s. Jack S. and Mary K. Hale. B of Bus. Adminstrn., U. Notre Dame, 1970; JD, U. Mo., 1973. Ptnr. Hynes Hale & Gurley, Farmington, N.Mex., 1974—; CEO Motor City Inc., Farmington, 1990—, Navajo Dam Enterprises Inc., 1994—. Mem. ABA, Am. Arbitration Assn. (arbitrator 1990—), Navajo Nation Bar Assn., S.J. County Bar Assn., N.Mex. Amigos. General civil litigation, Juvenile, Native American. Office: Hynes Hale & Gurley 1000 W Apache St Farmington NM 87401-3805

**HALE, JAMES THOMAS,** retail company executive, lawyer; b. Mpls., May 14, 1940; s. Thomas Taylor and Alice Louise (Mc Connon) H.; m. Sharon Sue Johnson, Aug. 27, 1960; children: David Scott, Eric James, Kristin Lynn. BA, Dartmouth Coll., 1962; LLB, U. Minn., 1965. Bar: Minn. Law clk. Chief Justice Earl Warren, U.S. Supreme Ct., 1965-66; asso. firm Faegre & Benson, Mpls., 1966-73; ptnr. Faegre & Benson, 1973-79; v.p., dir. corp. growth Gen. Mills, Inc., 1979-80, v.p. fin. and control consumer non-foods, 1981; sr. v.p., gen. counsel, corp. sec. Dayton-Hudson Corp., Mpls., 1981—; adj. prof. U. Minn., 1967-73; dir. N. Atlantic Life Ins. Co.; bd. dirs. Minn. Continuing Legal Edn. Mem. exec. com. Fund Legal Aid Soc., others. Mem. Hennepin County Bar Assn., Order of Coif, Phi Beta Kappa. Office: Dayton-Hudson Corp 777 Nicollet Mall Minneapolis MN 55402-2055*

**HALE, JENNIFER ANSBRO,** lawyer; b. Chgo., Nov. 20, 1961; d. James Michael Ansbro and Margaret Nora Callahan; m. Mark Allen Hale, Feb. 15, 1986; children: Sean Parker, Kevin Garrett. BA, U. Ill., 1984; JD, DePaul U., 1987. Bar: Ill. 1987, U.S. Dist. Ct. Ill. 1987, Trial Bar, 1988. Atty. U.S. Dept. Justice, Chgo., 1987-88; assoc. Mayer, Brown & Platt, Chgo., 1988-95; sr. counsel United Airlines, Chgo., 1995—; bd. dirs. Assn. House Chgo. General civil litigation, Labor, Environmental. Office: United Airlines 1200 E Algonquin Rd Elk Grove IL 60007

**HALE, KATHRYN SCHOLLE,** lawyer; b. Pitts., Dec. 17, 1953; d. Robert Anthony and Audrey T. (Turlick) Scholle; m. Jonathan Bradford Hale, Oct. 5, 1985; children: Jessica Katherine, Benjamin Robert. BA cum laude, Wesleyan U., 1974; JD, NYU, 1977, LLM (Taxation), 1980. Bar: Conn. 1977, N.Y. 1980. Assoc. Tyler, Cooper, Grant, New Haven, Conn., 1977-78, Schoeman Marsh Updike & Welt, N.Y.C., 1980-82, Bergman Horowitz Reynolds & DeSarbo, New Haven, 1982-84; pvt. practice South Windsor, Conn., 1984-91, 97—; adj. prof. Western New Eng. Coll. Sch. Law, 1984-86; cons. mcpl. revenue, 1996; bd. dirs., chair legal com. Citizens Opposed to Radioactive Environment, South Windsor, 1991-96. Grad. editor: (legal periodical) Tax Law Rev., 1979-80; assoc. editor: (legal periodical) Jour. of Internat. Law and Politics, 1976-77. Trustee Adelphic Lit. Soc., Middletown, Conn., 1986-91; mem. Town Coun., Town of South Windsor, 1993—; environ. orgn. rep. Conn. Low Level Radioactive Waste Adv. Com., Hartford, 1991-93; mem. South Windsor Agrl. Land Preservation Adv. Com., 1993; alt. mem. South Windsor Econ. Devel. Commn., 1993; mem. South Windsor Dem. Town Com., 1993—; Girl Scout leader. Mem. People's Action for Clean Energy, Clean Water Action, Alpha Delta Phi Soc. (founding). Democrat. Avocations: softball coach, school classroom volunteer. Family and matrimonial, Estate planning, Real property. Home and Office: 54 Orchard Hill Dr South Windsor CT 06074-3021

**HALE, LANCE MITCHELL,** lawyer; b. Roanoke, Va., Oct. 14, 1956; s. Ralph M. and Ruby A. (Akers) H.; m. Terry Lynn Sprouse; children: Christina Nicole, Laura Michelle, Layna Maribeth, Logan Mitchell. BSBA, U. Va., 1979, MS in Acctg., 1981; JD, N.Y. Law Sch., 1984. Bar: Va. 1984, N.J. 1984; CPA, Va. Staff acct. Robert M. Mussleman, CPA, Atty. at Law, Charlottesville, Va., 1979-81; CPA Schapiro, Wisan & Krassner, P.C., N.Y.C., 1982-84; ptnr. King, Fulghum, Snead & Hale, P.C., Roanoke, 1984-89; pvt. practice Lance M. Hale Esquire, P. C., Roanoke, 1989—. Bd. dirs. estate planning coun. Ferrum Coll., Va., 1988. Mem. Am. Trial Lawyers Assn., Va. Trial Lawyers Assn., Va. Soc. CPAs, First Latvian/Am. Trade Conf., Phi Alpha Delta, Beta Alpha Psi. Avocations: hiking, camping, hunting. General civil litigation, Criminal, Taxation, general. Home: 5 Breezewood Cir Vinton VA 24179-1801 Office: PO Box 1721 Roanoke VA 24008-1721

**HALE, LOUIS DEWITT,** lawyer; b. Caddo Mills, Tex., June 10, 1917; s. Ernest Louis and Ethel M. (Massay) H.; m. Carol Gene Moore, June 8, 1947; children: Janet Sue Hale Wilde, Nancy Carol Hale (dec.). BA, U. Tex., 1937, MA, 1940. Bar: Tex. 1940, U.S. Dist. Ct. (so. dist.) Tex. 1947, U.S. Ct. Appeals (5th cir.) 1974, U.S. Supreme Ct. 1946. Classification analyst Office Emergency Mgmt., Washington, 1941-42; classification officer Office Def. Transp., Washington, 1942-43; pvt. practice Corpus Christi, Tex., 1946-81, Austin, Tex., 1981—; state rep. Tex. Legis., Austin, Tex., 1939-40, 53-62, 1965-78, spkr. pro tempore, 1961-62; chmn. jud. com. Tex. State Legislature 1961-62, 69-74; gen. counsel House Gen. Investigating Com., Austin, 1989-92, Tex. Assn. Builders, Austin, 1978-81; dir. Nueces Invest Corp., Corpus Christi, 1955-98, Ulrich Bros., Inc., Corpus Christi, 1960-69, Tex.-Trans, Inc., Corpus Christi, 1973-78, Dixieland Mfg. Inc. Author: Streamlining Texas Judiciary, 1972; contbr. articles to profl. jours. Mem. Tex. Jud. Coun., Austin, 1961-65, 69-81; chmn. jud. com. Tex. Constnl. Conv., Austin, 1974. Officer. USAF, 1943-46, Res. 1947-73, retired as Lt. col. Recipient Disting. Svc. award Jr. C. of C., 1952. Mem. ABA, State Bar Tex. (Disting. Svc. award 1971, 73, 75), Nat. Assn. Home Builders (hon. life), Tex. State Tchrs. Assn. (hon. life, Disting. Svc. award 1961). Democrat. Baptist. Avocations: public speaking, historical research, coin collecting. Education and schools, Administrative and regulatory, General practice. Home: 7106 Montana Norte Austin TX 78731-2124 Office: 5808 Balcones Dr Ste 101 Austin TX 78731-4276

**HALE, TIMOTHY S.,** lawyer; b. Albuquerque, Mar. 7, 1959; s. Leslie F. and Katherine F. (Danforth) H.; m. Sally Hale; children: Katie, Jackson, Maggie. BA, Boston U., 1981; MA, U. Mass., 1982; JD, U. N.Mex., 1985. Bar: N.Mex. 1986, Colo. 1988, U.S. Dist. Ct. N.Mex. 1989, U.S. Ct. Appeals (10th cir.) 1994. Atty. Wecaus Law Firm, Farmington, N.Mex., 1985-86, Dist. Atty.'s Office, Farmington, N.Mex., 1986-89, Radcliffe, Pdg and Shane, P.A., Albuquerque, 1989-97; Riley, Shane & Hale, P.A. Radcliffe, Pdg and Shane, P.A., 1997—. Civil rights, State civil litigation, Workers' compensation. Office: Riley Shane and Hale PA 6400 Uptown Blvd NE Ste 233 Albuquerque NM 87110-4204

**HALE, ZAN,** editor. Editor Legal Intelligencer Daily Legal Jour., Phila. Office: American Lawyer Media 1617 John F Kennedy Blvd Philadelphia PA 19103-1821

**HALEY, JOHN HARVEY,** lawyer; b. Hot Springs, Ark., May 29, 1931; s. Harvey H. and Anne (Tanner) H.; m. Cynthia Martin, Sept. 7, 1997. AB, Emory U., 1952; LLB, U. Ark., 1955. Bar: Ark. 1955, U.S. Dist. Ct. (we. dist.) Ark. 1955, U.S. Ct. Appeals (8th cir.) 1955, U.S. Supreme Ct. 1971. Clk. Ark. Supreme Ct., Little Rock, 1955-56; ptnr. Rose Law Firm, Little Rock, 1956-71, Haley, Young, Bogard & Gitchell, Little Rock, 1971-73, Laser, Sharp, Haley, Young & Boswell, Little Rock, 1973-82, Haley, Polk & Heister, Little Rock, 1982-86, Arnold, Grobmyer & Haley, Little Rock, 1986-96; owner Haley Law Firm, Little Rock, 1996—; bd. dirs. North Ark. Telephone Co., Flippin, Ark.; Munro and Co., Hot Springs, Ark., Binnacle Industries, Rose Creek Industries, Kappa Realty, Little Rock, Plaza Partnership, Talweg, LLC, Memphis; lectr. U. Ark. Law Sch., Little Rock, 1956-60, CLU instr., 1961-65; spl. counsel liquidation and rehab. Ark. Ins. Dept., 1967-71. Editor Ark. Law Rev., 1954-55. Chmn. Ark. State Bd. Correction, 1967-72, Ark. State Bd. Law Examiners, 1960-63, Election Rsch. Coun., Little Rock, 1961-64; dir. Wildwood Ctr. Performing Arts, Little Rock, 1994—, Florence Crittenden Home, Little Rock, 1994—; scoutmaster Second Presbyn. Ch. Troop, Little Rock, 1962-65. Methodist. Avocations: piloting, sailing, bicycling, underwater photography, skiing. Real property, Taxation, general, General corporate. Home: 3614 Doral Dr Little Rock AR 72212-2920 Office: Haley Law Firm PO Box 3730 Little Rock AR 72203-3730

**HALEY, PETER C.,** lawyer; b. Joliet, Ill., Jan. 3, 1943; s. John P. and Gertrude Blattner H.; m. Ellen Shuck; children: Dylan, Hillary, Michael. AB, U. Calif., Berkeley, 1964, JD, 1967. Bar: Calif., U.S. Dist. Ct. (no. and cen. dists.) Calif., Utah. Assoc. Law Office F.P. Furth, San Francisco, 1971-72; ptnr. Arata, Misuraca, Clement & Haley, Santa Rosa, Calif., 1972-73, Knecht, Haley, Lawrence & Smith, San Francisco, 1973-95, Wright, Robinson, Osthimer & Tatum, San Francisco, 1995—. Author: Calif. and Fidelity Bond Practice, 1996. With U.S. Army, 1967-73. Democrat. Insurance, General civil litigation, Banking. Home: 26 Valley Oak St Portola Vally CA 94028-8048 Office: Wright Robinson Osthimer & Tatum 44 Montgomery St San Francisco CA 94104-4602

**HALFACRE, MICHAEL IAN,** lawyer; b. Niagara Falls, N.Y., July 13, 1966; s. Robert Ernest H. and Elizabeth Van Hekle (Snyder) Haviland; m. Sandra Patton, Aug. 24, 1991. BS, Fla. State U., 1988; JD, U. Dayton, 1991. Bar: N.J. 1991, U.S. Dist. Ct. N.J. 1991. Assoc. Smith, Shaw, Smith & Oxley, West Long Beach, N.J., 1991-93, Bathgate, Wagenen & Wolf, Lakewood, N.J., 1993-95; ptnr. Waldman, Moriarity and Halfacre, Red Bank, N.J., 1995—; trustee Ocean-Monmouth Legal Svcs., Freehold, N.J., 1994—. Mem. Fair Haven (N.J.) Bd. Edn., 1993-94, Young Reps. Monmouth County, 1993—, Fair Haven Borough Coun., 1995—. Mem. N.J. State Bar Assn., Monmouth County Bar Assn. (chair young lawyers com. 1993—, trustee 1995—), N.J. State Bar Found. (trustee 1995—). Presbyterian. Personal injury, General civil litigation, Criminal. Office: Waldman Moriarty & Halfacre 212 Maple Ave Red Bank NJ 07701-1731

**HALICZER, JAMES SOLOMON,** lawyer; b. Ft. Myers, Fla., Oct. 27, 1952; s. Julian and Margaret (Shepard) H.; m. Paula Fleming, Oct. 3, 1987. BA in English Lit., U. So. Fla., 1976, MA in Polit. Sci., 1978; JD, Stetson U., 1981. Bar: Fla. 1982. Assoc. Conrad, Scherer & James, Ft. Lauderdale, Fla., 1982-86, ptnr., 1988-92; assoc. Bernard & Mauro, Ft. Lauderdale, 1985-86; shareholder Cooney, Haliczer, Mattson, Lane, Blackburn, Pettis & Richards, Ft. Lauderdale, 1992-96, Haliczer, Pettis & White, P.A., Ft. Lauderdale, Fla., 1996—. Mem. ABA, Fla. Bar Assn., Broward County Bar Assn., Assn. Trial Lawyers Am., Def. Rsch. Inst., Am. Acad. Healthcare Attys., Phi Kappa Phi, Pi Sigma Alpha, Omicron Delta Kappa. Democrat. Methodist. Avocations: reading, jogging. Personal injury, State civil litigation, Health. Office: Haliczer Pettis & White PA 101 NE 3rd Ave Fort Lauderdale FL 33301-1162

**HALIW, ANDREW JEROME, III,** lawyer, engineer; b. Ansbach, Fed. Republic of Germany, Aug. 8, 1946; came to U.S., 1950; s. Ilko and Sophie (Kindrat) H.; children: Larissa Andrea, Andrea Stephanie. BEE, Wayne State U., 1968, JD, 1972; postgrad. in Fin., U. Mich., 1993—. Bar: Mich. 1973, U.S. Dist. Ct. (ea. dist.) Mich. 1973, U.S. Supreme Ct. 1982, Mich. (6th cir.) 1986; lic. profl. engr., Mich., Fla.; registered patent & trademark atty. Divisional elec. engr. J & L div. LTV, Warren, Mich., 1968-72; ptr. bd. dirs. Sullivan & Leavitt P.C., Northville, Mich., 1972-79, ptnr., 1979-91, also bd. dirs.; ptnr. Haliw, Siciliano & Mychalowych, P.C., Farmington Hills, Mich., 1991—; bd. dirs. Am. Supplier Inst., Dearborn Mich.; chmn. Advanced Systems and Designs, Inc., Dearborn; vice chmn. ASI Internat.; commr. SMART, Oakland County. Atty. Ukrainian Cultural Ctr., Warren, 1984; del., dist. dir. Farmington Hills Reps., 1990—; chair Zoning Bd. Appeals, Farmington Hills. Mem. ABA, Detroit Bar Assn., Oakland County Bar Assn., Detroit Engring. Soc. (dist. bd. dirs.). Republican. Ukrainian Catholic. Contracts commercial, General corporate, Estate planning. Home: 38250 Nine Mile Rd Northville MI 48167-9014 Office: Haliw Siciliano & Mychalowych PC 37000 Grand River Ave Ste 350 Farmington Hills MI 48335

**HALKET, THOMAS D(ANIEL),** lawyer; b. N.Y.C., July 20, 1948. SB in Physics, MIT, 1971, SM in Physics, 1971; JD, Columbia U., 1974. Bar: Mass. 1974, N.Y. 1979, U.S. Dist. Ct. Mass. 1975, U.S. Dist. Ct. (ea. and so. dists.) N.Y. 1979, U.S. Ct. Appeals (1st cir.) 1975, U.S. Ct. Appeals (9th cir.) 1979, U.S. Supreme Ct. 1978. Ptnr. Halket & Pitegoff LLP, White Plains, N.Y., Hughes Hubbard & Reed LLP, N.Y.C. Mem. ABA (chmn. div. aerospace law 1979-83, ventures and entrepreneur divsn. 1986-89, coun. mem. sect. sci. and tech. 1982-85, program chmn. 1981-86, sec. 1985-86, vice-chmn. 1986-87, chmn. 1988-89), AAAS, AIAA (sr.), Am. Arbitration Assn. (chmn. tech. com. 1998—, computer disputes adv. com. 1992-96), Am. Phys. Soc., Bar Assn. City N.Y. (law and sci. com. 1987-90, computer law com. 1993-96, 1997—, tech. in law practice com. 1993-96, chmn. subcom. on software and uniform comml. code 1993-96, 97-99), Computer Law Assn. Fax: (212) 422-4726. E-mail: halket@hugheshubbard.com. General corporate, Private international, Computer. Office: Hughes Hubbard & Reed LLP One Batter Park New York NY 10004

**HALL, ANDREW CLIFFORD,** lawyer; b. Warsaw, Poland, Sept. 16, 1944; s. Edmund and Maria (Hahn) H.; came to U.S., 1949, naturalized, 1954; children: Michael Ian, Adam Stuart, Hilary Meyers Azrael, Katie Meyers; m. Gail Meyers, 1993. BA, U. Fla., 1965, JD with high honors, 1968. Bar: Fla. 1968, U.S. Dist. Ct. (so. dist.) Fla. 1968, U.S. Dist. Ct. (no. dist.) Ga. 1971, U.S. Ct. Appeals (5th cir.) 1971, Ga. 1973, U.S. Supreme Ct. 1974, U.S. Ct. Appeals (D.C. cir.) 1974, U.S. Ct. Appeals (11th cir.) 1981. Law clk. to judge U.S. Dist. Ct.; assoc., Haas, Holland, Levison, Gilbert, Atlanta, 1970-72, Frates, Floyd, Pearson, Stewart, Miami, 1972-75; ptnr. Storace, Hall & Hauser, Miami, 1975-79, Hall & Hauser, 1979-82, Hall & O'Brien, P.A., Miami, 1982-95, Andrew Hall and Assoc., Pa., 1995-99; Hall, David and Joseph, P.A., 1999—; instr. bus. law U. Fla.; Trustee U. Fla., Coll. of Law Found. Bd. dirs. Greater Miami Jewish Fedn.; chmn., bd. trustees, bd. dirs Cen. Agy. Jewish Edn., Ash Ha Torah; mem. coun. of 100 Fla. Internat. U. Mem. ABA, Hebrew Immigrant Aid Assn. (nat. bd. mem.), Fla. State Bar, Am. Judicature Soc., U. Fla. Coll. Law Alumni (coun.), Acad. Fla. Trial Lawyers (diplomate), Assn. Trial Lawyers Am., Phi Kappa Phi, Phi Alpha Delta, Order of Coif. Democrat. Jewish. Antitrust, Federal civil litigation, State civil litigation. Home: 2000 S Bayshore Dr Miami FL 33133-3256 Office: Hall David and Joseph PA Att/Karen Fernandez 1428 Brickell Ave Ph Miami FL 33131-3411

**HALL, CYNTHIA HOLCOMB,** federal judge; b. Los Angeles, Feb. 19, 1929; d. Harold Romeyn and Mildred Gould (Kuck) Holcomb; m. John Harris Hall, June 6, 1970 (dec. Oct. 1980);. A.B., Stanford U., 1951, J.D., 1954; LL.M., NYU, 1960. Bar: Ariz. 1954, Calif. 1956. Law clk. to judge U.S. Ct. Appeals 9th Circuit, 1954-55; trial atty. tax div. Dept. Justice, 1960-64; atty.-adviser Office Tax Legis. Counsel, Treasury Dept., 1964-66; mem. firm Brawerman & Holcomb, Beverly Hills, Calif., 1966-72; judge U.S. Tax Ct., Washington, 1972-81, U.S. Dist. Ct. for central dist. Calif., Los Angeles, 1981-84; cir. judge U.S. Ct. Appeals (9th cir.), Pasadena, Calif., 1984—, sr. judge, 1997—. Served to lt. (j.g.) USNR, 1951-53. Office: US Ct Appeals 9th Cir 125 S Grand Ave Pasadena CA 91105-1621

**HALL, DAVID,** law educator, dean; b. Savannah, May 26, 1950; s. Levi and Ethel H.; m. Marilyn Braithwaite-Hall; children: Sakile, Kiamsha, Rahsaan. BS in Polit. Sci., Kans. State U., 1972; MA in Human Rels., U. Okla., 1975, postgrad., 1975-78, JD, 1978; LLM, Harvard U., 1985, Doctor Juridical Scis., 1988. Bar: Ill., Mass., Okla. Profl. basketball player Spaidero Pallacanestro, Inc., Udine, Italy, 1972-74; grad. asst. human rels. dept. U. Okla., Norman, 1974-75; lawyer Chgo. regional office Fed. Trade Commn., 1978-80; assoc. prof. law Sch. Law U. Okla., Norman, 1983-85; asst. prof. law Sch. Law U. Miss., 1980-83; assoc. dean academic affairs Sch. Law Northeastern U., Boston, 1988-92, prof. law, 1985—, dean Sch. Law, 1993-99, provost, 1999—; instr. ethnic studies dept. and law ctr. U. Okla., Norman, 1975-79; Robert D. Klien U. lectr. Northeastern U.; co-chair legal edn. forum Law Sch. Harvard U., Cambridge, Mass., 1984-85, co-coord. Nat. Symposium on the Constitution and Race, 1987; coord. law student outreach program Barron Assessment Ctr., Boston. Contbr. numerous articles to profl. jours. Mem. bd. Mass. Civil Liberties Union, 1987-88, Inst. Affirmative action, Boston, TransAfrica Forum Scholars Adv. Coun., Washington, commn. on equal justice Mass. Legal Assistance Corp., 1995—, Nat. Consumer Law Ctr., 1993—; pres. African Cultural Soc. St. Paul A.M.E. Ch., Cambridge, Mass.; bd. dirs. Gang Peace Inc., 1995—. named Professor of the Year NAACP, to Savannah Athletic Hall of Fame; honoree African Am. Ist. Oratory Competition; recipient Black Rose award Sigma Gamma Rho., Humanitarian award Nat. Conf. Cmty. and Justice. Fellow Am. Sociol. Assn.; mem. ABA (standing ocm. lawyers' pub. svc. responsibility 1995—), Assn. Law Sch. (diversity in legal edn. 1995-96), Boston Bar Assn., Mass. Bar Assn. (mem. bd. minorities in the profession 1995-96), Okla. Bar Assn. (Outstanding Sr. award), Nat. Conf. Black Lawyers (pres. Mass. chpt. 1986—), Black Faculty and Staff Orgn., Nat. Black Wholistic Soc. (pres. 1993, mem. bd. 1984—), Order of the Coif. Office: Northeastern U Sch Law Provost Office 400 Huntington Ave Boston MA 02115-5005

**HALL, DONALD ORELL,** lawyer, rancher; b. Waco, Tex., Nov. 11, 1926; s. Ernest Orell and Thelma (Day) H.; m. Mary Ann Morgan, Sept. 1, 1951; children: Lisa Don, Brett Clayton. LLB, Baylor U., 1951, JD, 1969. Bar: Tex. 1951, U.S. Dist. Ct. (we. dist.) Tex. 1955, U.S. Ct. Appeals (5th cir.) 1983, U.S. Supreme Ct. 1983. Assoc. Koehne & Fulbright, Waco, 1951-54; judge Waco, 1954-56; dist. atty. Office of Prosecutor, Waco, 1956-67; ptnr. Hall & Kettler, Waco, 1968-87; pvt. practice Waco, 1988—. Guest columnist, newspapers, 1955—. With USN, 1943-46, PTO. Mem. ABA, Waco Bar Assn. (pres. 1955-56), Delta Theta Phi, Masons, Scotish Rite, York Rite. Republican. Baptist. Avocations: outdoors, sports, pilot, hunting, dog breeding, golf. General practice, Family and matrimonial, Personal injury. Home and Office: 8208 Whippoorwill Dr Waco TX 76712-3412

**HALL, FRED WILLIAM, JR.,** lawyer; b. Franklin, N.H., Sept. 22, 1920; s. Fred William and Grace Rachel (Canney) Hall; m. Jane Fell Coe, Sept. 23, 1950; children: Marcella, Susan, John. BS, U. N.H., 1941; JD, U. Mich., 1948; LLD (hon.), U. N.H., 1974. Of counsel Cooper Hall Whittum & Shillaber PC, Rochester, N.H.; bd. dirs. Jarvis Co., Inc., Rochester. Trustee U. N.H., 1966-73, chmn. bd., 1968-72; mem. N.H. Gov.'s Council, 1963-64. Lt. col. U.S. Army, 1941-45, ETO. Decorated Silver Star with oak leaf cluster, Bronze Star with 2 oak leaf cluster; recipient Outstanding Civilian Service medal, Dept. Army, 1979, Civilian Aide award Sec. of the Army, 1970-78, U. N.H. Alumni Meritorious Service award, 1974, Charles Holmes Pettee medal, 1976; Paul Harris fellow, Rotary Found., 1984. Mem. ABA, N.H. Bar Assn. (pres. 1965-66), Rotary. Republican. Episcopalian. Home: 18 Eastern Ave Rochester NH 03867-1400 Office: Cooper Hall Whittum & Shillaber PC 76 Wakefield St Rochester NH 03867-1921

**HALL, GORDON R.,** retired state supreme court chief justice; b. Vernal, Utah, Dec. 14, 1926; s. Roscoe Jefferson and Clara Maud (Freestone) H.; m. Doris Gillespie, Sept. 6, 1947; children: Rick Jefferson, Craig Edwin. B.S., U. Utah, 1949, LL.B., 1951. Bar: Utah 1952. Solo practice Tooele, Utah, 1952-69; county atty. Tooele County, 1958-69; judge 3d Jud. Dist. Utah, 1969-77; assoc. justice Supreme Ct. Utah, 1977-81, chief justice, 1981-94; of counsel Snow, Christensen & Martineau, Salt Lake City, 1994-98; chmn. Utah Jud. Coun., 1983-94; pres. Conf. Chief Justices, 1988-89; chmn. Nat. Ctr. State Cts., 1988-89; pres. Utah Assn. Counties, 1965; mem. Pres.'s Adv. Com. OEO, 1965-66. Served with U.S. Maritime Svc., 1944-46. Mem. ABA, Utah Bar Assn. Office: Snow, Christensen & Martineau 250 N Sandrun Rd Salt Lake City UT 84103-2239

**HALL, GUY CHARLES,** lawyer; b. Chgo., Aug. 11, 1958; s. Marvin Lester and Lorraine (Sorensen) H.; m. Anne Elizabeth Pollard, july 31, 1982; children: Ryan Charles, Tyler John, Abbey Lorraine. BA, U. Ill., 1980; JD, U. Tulsa, 1983. Bar: Ill. 1983, U.S. Dist. Ct. (cen. dist.) Ill. 1984. Prin. Dobbins, Fraker, Tennant, Joy & Perlstein, Champaign, Ill., 1983—. Atty. village of Pesotum (Ill.), 1984—. Mem. Ill. State Bar Assn. (law office econs. sect. coun. 1995, health care sect. coun. 1998—), Champaign County Bar Assn. (v.p. 1993-94, pro bono appreciation award 1986), Ill. Assn. Healthcare Attys., Chi Psi. Avocations: racquetball, softball, weight tng.. General practice, Health, Consumer commercial. Office: Dobbins Fraker Tennant Joy & Perlstein 215 N Neil St Champaign IL 61820-4012

**HALL, HOWARD HARRY,** lawyer; b. Syracuse, N.Y., Jan. 9, 1933; s. Harold Gibner and Mildred E. (Way) H. AB, Syracuse U., 1953, JD, 1959. Bar: N.Y. 1960, U.S. Ct. Appeals (2d cir.) 1960, U.S. Dist. Ct. (we., no., so.dists.) N.Y. 1960, U.S. Supreme Ct. 1963, Calif. 1978, U.S. Ct. Appeals (9th cir.) 1978, U.S. Dist. Ct. (we. dist.) N.Y., U.S. Dist. Ct. (cen. and so. dist.) Calif., 1978. Assoc. Hiscock, Cowie, Bruce, Lee and Mawhinney, Syracuse, N.Y., 1959-61; pvt. practice Syracuse, N.Y., 1961-74, Long Beach, Calif., 1978-82, Paramount, Calif., 1982—. Commr. of edn. Syracuse, N.Y., 1968-72. Capt. USMC, 1953-56. Mem. State Bar of Calif., Calif. Trial Lawyers Assn. Personal injury, Insurance, Criminal. Office: 15559 Paramount Blvd Paramount CA 90723-4330

**HALL, JOAN M.,** lawyer; b. Inman, Nebr., Apr. 13, 1939; d. Warren J. and Delia E. (Allyn) McClurg; m. George J. Cotsirilos, Dec. 4, 1988; children: Colin Michael, Justin Allyn. BA, Nebr. Wesleyan U., 1961; JD, Yale U., 1965. Bar: Ill. 1965, U.S. Dist. Ct. (no. dist.) Ill. 1965, U.S. Ct. Appeals (7th cir.) 1965. Assoc. Jenner & Block, Chgo., 1965-71, sr. ptnr., 1971—; chmn. character and fitness Ill. Supreme Ct., 1988-89; mem. dist. admissions com. U.S. Dist. Ct. (no. dist.) Ill. Mem. exec. com. Yale Law Sch. Assn., 1976-86, treas., 1982-85; bd. dirs. Yale Law Sch. FUnd, 1978—, chmn., 1984-86; bd. dirs. Chgo. Lawyer's Com. Civil Rights Under the Law, 1978—, chmn., 1983-84; bd. dirs. Legal Assistance Found. Chgo., 1979-82; trustee Rush-Presbyn. St. Luke's Hosp., 1984—; mem. Gannon-Proctor Commn., 1982-84; trustee, bd. govs. Nebr. Wesleyan U., 1983—; bd. dirs. Goodman Theatre, Ill. Sports Facility Authority, 1986-96; mem. vis. com. Northwestern U. Sch. Law, 1987-92; mem. adv. coun. De Paul U. Sch. Law, 1987-94; bd. govs. Chgo. Lighthouse for the Blind. Fellow Am. Coll. Trial Lawyers; mem. ABA (chmn. litig. sect. 1982-83, fed. judiciary com. 1985-91, resource devel. coun. 1984-85, Ho. of Dels. 1991-93), Comml. Club (sec. 1995—), Econ. Club (Chgo., dir.). Federal civil litigation, State civil litigation. Office: Jenner & Block 1 E Ibm Plz Fl 4000 Chicago IL 60611-7603

**HALL, JOAN TORRENS,** lawyer; b. Belleville, N.J.; d. Alfred and Margaret (Simpson) Torrens;m. John P. Hall Jr.; children: John P. III, James S. AB, Drew U., 1957; JD, Rutgers U., 1990. Bar: N.J. 1991, D.C. 1991. Tchr. Middletown, R.I., 1958-59; psychology rschr. Princeton U., N.J., 1974-98; pvt. practice, 1990—; vis. lectr. Rutgers Law Sch., Camden, N.J., 1990. Contbr. articles to profl. jours. Bd. dir. League of Women Voters, Hopewell, N.J., 1972-87, 94-97; pres. PTO, Hopewell, 1979-80; chmn. ER Neighborhood Assn., Princeton, 1996-97. Grantee NSF, 1996-97. Mem. ABA, Princeton Bar Assn., Stony Brook Millstone Watershed Assn. (bd. mem.). Avocations: tennis. General practice.

**HALL, JOHN GEORGE,** lawyer; b. S.I., N.Y., Jan. 4, 1936; s. Joseph G. and Estelle (Ahearn) H.; m. Julia Moran, Nov. 21, 1959; children: John, Thomas, Michael, Julia, Mary Elizabeth. BS in Acctg., Villanova U., 1957, LLB, 1960; LLM, Bklyn. Law Sch., 1963. Bar: N.Y. 1961, U.S. Dist. Ct. (ea. and so. dists.) N.Y. 1964, U.S. Dist. Ct. N.J. 1975, U.S. Supreme Ct. 1971, N.J. 1975. Staff atty. Title Guarantee Co., S.I., 1960; atty., bd. counsel Inter-County Title Guarantee and Mortgage Co., S.I., 1961-63; legal rsch. counsel N.Y. State Senate, Albany, 1963, com. counsel, 1964; assoc. counsel Joint Legis. Com. on Alcholic Beverage Control Law, Albany, 1963; assoc. Fach, Sipp & Hall, S.I., 1965-74; pvt. practice, S.I., 1974—. Mng. editor Villanova Law Rev., 1958-60. Sgt. USMCR, 1955-61. Mem. ABA, N.Y. State Bar Assn. (chair real propr. sect. 1997-98), N.J. Bar Assn., Richmond County Bar Assn. (pres. 1974), N.Y. State Trial Lawyers Assn., Richmond County Country Club. Republican. Roman Catholic. Banking, Probate, Real property. Home: 16 Mulberry Ln Colts Neck NJ 07722-1157 Office: 57 Beach St Staten Island NY 10304-2701

**HALL, JOHN HOPKINS,** retired lawyer; b. Dallas, May 10, 1925; s. Albert Brown and Eleanor Pauline (Hopkins) H.; m. Marion Martin, Nov. 23, 1957; children: Ellen Martin, John Hopkins II. Student, U. Tex., 1942, U. of South, Sewanee, Tenn., 1942-43; LL.B., So. Meth. U., 1949. Bar: Tex. bar 1949. Ptnr. Strasburger & Price, Dallas, 1957-93, ret., 1993. Served with U.S. Army, 1943-45. Fellow Tex. Bar Found., Am. Bar Found., Internat. Acad. Trial Lawyers, Am. Coll. Trial Lawyers; mem. Tex. Bar Assn., Tex. Assn. Def. Counsel, Internat. Assn. Def. Counsel, Fin and Feather Club. Episcopalian. Federal civil litigation, State civil litigation, General civil litigation.

**HALL, JOHN THOMAS,** lawyer; b. Phila., May 14, 1938; s. John Thomas and Florence Sara (Robinson) H.; m. Carolyn Park Currie, May 26, 1968; children: Daniel Currie, Kathleen Currie. AB, Dickinson Coll., 1960; MA, U. Md., 1963; JD, U. N.C., 1972. Bar: N.C. 1972. Chmn. dept. speech Mercersburg (Pa.) Acad., 1960-63, U. Balt., 1963-69; research asst. N.C. Ct. Appeals, Raleigh, 1972-73, dir. pre-hearing research staff, 1974-75, asst. clk., marshall, librarian, 1980-81; counsel Dorothea Dix Hosp., Raleigh, 1974; asst. dist. atty. State of N.C., Raleigh, 1975-80, 81-83; pvt. practice Raleigh, 1973-74, 83—; mem. faculty King's Bus. Coll., Raleigh, 1973-75, N.C. Bar Assn., 1987—; undercover inmate Cen. Prison Duke Ctr. on Law and Poverty, Durham, N.C., 1970. Mem. Raleigh Little Theatre, Theatre in the Park, Raleigh; charter mem. Wake County Dem. Men's Club, 1977—. Named Best Actor, Raleigh Little Theatre, 1975, 77, 80, 82, 85, 86, 93, 98. Mem. ABA, N.C. Bar Assn., Wake County Bar Assn. (bd. dirs. 1986-89, vice chmn. exec. com. 1986-87), 10th Jud. Dist. Bar Assn. (bd. dirs. 1986-89, chmn. grievance com. 1987-90), Wake County Acad. Criminal Trial Lawyers (v.p. 1986-87), Scottish Clan Gunn Soc., Neuse River Valley Model R.R. (Raleigh). Roman Catholic. Avocations: model railroading, walking, reading. Criminal, Juvenile. Office: PO Box 1207 Raleigh NC 27602-1207

**HALL, JUDITH DOUGHERTY,** lawyer; b. Pendelton, Oreg., Oct. 24, 1941; d. Norman Madison and Helen Jeanne (Warner) Stringfellow; m. Ralph Clifford Dougherty; children: Erika Pollner, Tara Norick, Deidra; m. Leuvard Wade Hall Jr., Jan. 20, 1998. BA, U. Chgo., 1964; JD, Fla. State U., 1974. Bar: Fla., U.S. Dist. Ct. (no. dist.) Fla., U.S. Ct. Appeals (11th cir.). Asst. pub. defender State of Fla., Talahassee, 1974-80, 96—; atty. pvt. practice, Talahassee, 1981-87, 95-96; asst. capital collateral rep. State of Fla., Talahassee, 1987-95. Mem. Fla. Assn. Criminal Def. Lawyers. Avocation: boating. Home: 2331 Vinkara Dr Tallahassee FL 32303-3723 Office: Pub Defender 2d Jud Cir Ct 301 S Monroe St Ste 401 Tallahassee FL 32301-1803

**HALL, K. MARK,** lawyer; b. Pitts., Nov. 2, 1962; s. Kenneth Bowman and June (Gurke) H.; m. Marilyn Ann Kuhlman, Dec. 30, 1989; children: Geoffrey, Timothy, Christopher. BS in Bus. Adminstrn., Mich. State U., 1984; JD magna cum laude, U. Pitts., 1994. Bar: Pa. 1994, U.S. Dist. Ct. (we. dist.) Pa. 1994, U.S. Ct. Appeals (3d cir.) 1994. Area mgr. PPG Industries, Atlanta and Cin., 1985-91; law clk. to Hon. Joseph F. Weis U.S. Ct. Appeals (3d cir.), Pitts., 1994-96; atty. Babst, Calland, Clements & Zomnir, Pitts., 1996—. Founding mem. New Hope Ch., Pitts., 1994. Nat. Merit scholar, 1979, Alumni Disting. scholar Mich. State U., 1980. Mem. Inns of Ct. Avocations: outdoor recreation, competitive sports. Federal civil litigation, Construction, Environmental. Office: Babst Calland Clements & Zomnir Two Gateway Ctr 8th Fl Pittsburgh PA 15222

**HALL, MICHAEL,** legal decision writer; b. N.Y.C., Sept. 20, 1947; s. Mark and Eva Hall; m. Karen Jane Klein; children: Ian D., Mitchell L. BA, CCNY, 1968; MA in Fgn. Affairs, U. Va., 1970; JD, Fordham U., 1975. Bar: N.Y. 1976, D.C. 1980. Legal decision writer Decision Writing Unit, Jamaica, N.Y. Home: 57 Florida Ave Commack NY 11725-5115 Office: Decision Writing Unit 1 Jamaica Center Plz Jamaica NY 11432-3862

**HALL, MICHAEL WAYNE,** lawyer; b. Walla Walla, Wash., Sept. 13, 1952; s. Charles Wayne and Laura Marie (Le Page) H.; m. Stephanie Francis Uberuaga, Dec. 18; children: Katherine, Alexandra, Annalise, Cameron. BA in Comms., Wash. State U., 1976; JD, Southwestern U., 1987. Bar: U.S. Dist. Ct. Wash. 1988. Founding ptnr. Hall Law Firm, P.S., Edmonds, Wash., 1991—; mediator, v.p. Puget Sound Christian Coll. Bd. dirs. Laser Project Found. Mem. Wash. State Bar Assn. (interprofl. com., mem. alternative dispute resolution sect.), Wash. State Trial Lawyers Assn., Nat. Com. on Planned Giving. Avocation: fly fishing. Office: Hall Law Firm 410 4th Ave N Ste 300B Edmonds WA 98020-3119

**HALL, MILES LEWIS, JR.,** lawyer; b. Fort Lauderdale, Fla., Aug. 14, 1924; s. Miles Lewis and Mary Frances (Dawson) H.; m. Muriel M. Fisher, Nov. 4, 1950; children: Miles Lewis III, Don Thomas. A.B., Princeton U., 1947; J.D., Harvard U., 1950. Bar: Fla. 1951, U.S. Supreme Ct., 1972, U.S. Ct. Appeals (11th cir.), U.S. Dist. Ct. (so. dist.) Fla. Since practiced in Miami; ptnr. Hall & Hedrick, Miami, 1953—; dir. Gen. Portland, Inc., 1974-81. Author: Election of Remedies, Vol. VIII, Fla. Law and Practice, 1958. Pres. Orange Bowl Com., 1964-65, dir., 1950—, sec., treas. 1984-86; vice-chmn., dir. Dade County (Fla.) ARC, 1961-62, chmn., 1963-64, dir., 1967-73; nat. fund cons. ARC, 1963, 66-68, trustee, 1985—; pres. Ransom Sch. Parents Assn., 1966; chmn. South Fla. Gov.'s Scholarship Ball, 1966; mem. exec. bd. South Fla. council Boy Scouts Am., 1966-67; citizens bd. U. Miami, 1961-66; mem. Fla. Council of 100, 1961-97, vice chmn., 1961-62; mem. Coral Gables (Fla.) Biltmore Devel. Com., 1972-73; mem. bd. visitors Coll. Law, Fla. State U., 1974-77; bd. dirs. Coral Gables War Meml. Youth Ctr., 1967—, pres., 1969-72; bd. dirs. Salvation Army, Miami, 1968-83, Fla. Citizens Against Crime 1984-89; bd. dirs. Bok Tower Gardens Found. Inc., 1987—, sec., 1991—; trustee St. Thomas U., 1990-96, vice chmn., 1993-96; trustee Fla. Supreme Ct. Hist. Soc., 1988—, v.p., 1991-92, pres., 1993-95. 2d lt. USAAF, 1943-45. Fellow Am. Bar Found., Fla. Bar Found.; mem. ABA (Fla. c-chmn. membership com. sect. corp. banking and bus. law 1968-72), Dade County Bar Assn. (dir. 1964-65, pres. 1967-68), Fla. Bar Assn., Am. Judicature Soc., Miami-Dade County C. of C. (v.p. 1962-64, dir. 1966-68), Harvard Law Sch. Assn. Fla. (dir. 1964-66), Cottage Club, Harvard Club, The Miami Club (v.p., dir. 1989-91, pres. 1990-91), Princeton Club So. Fla. (past pres.), Alpha Tau Omega. Methodist. State civil litigation, General corporate, Estate planning. Home: 8134 SE Hall Dr Arcadia FL 34266 Office: Hall & Hedrick 25 SE 2nd Ave Ste 1105 Miami FL 33131-1605

**HALL, PETER C.,** lawyer, defender; b. Phila., Dec. 27, 1959; s. Charles Potter and Constance (Nuzum) H.; m. Kristin Anderson, Aug. 4, 1984; children: Charles, Nathan. AB, U. Miami, 1982; JD, Temple U., 1986. Bar: Pa. 1987, U.S. Dist. Ct. (ea. dist.) Pa. 1987. Asst. pub. defender Bucks County Pub. Defender, Doylestown, Pa., 1987-94, chief dep. pub. defender, 1994—. Democrat. Presbyterian. Home: 318 W Durham St Philadelphia PA 19119-2901 Office: Bucks County Pub Defender Courthouse 6th Fl Doylestown PA 18901

**HALL, PIKE, JR.,** lawyer; b. Shreveport, La., May 27, 1931; s. Pike and Hazel (Tucker) H.; m. Anne Oden Hall, Dec. 24, 1951; children: Brevard Hall Knight, Pike III. BA, La. State U., 1951, JD, 1953. Bar: La. 1953. Asst. city atty. City of Shreveport, 1954-58; elected mem. Caddo Prish Sch. Bd., Shreveport, 1964-70; judge 2d Cir. Ct. Appeal, Shreveport, 1971-85, chief judge, 1985-90; assoc. justice Supreme Ct. La., 1990-94; counsel Blanchard, Walker, O'Quin & Roberts, Shreveport, 1994—; past chmn. La. Conf. of Ct. Appeal Judges; past bd. govs., vice chmn. La. Jud. Coll.; chmn. La. Jud. Bugetary Control Bd., 1992-94. Mem. adminstrv. bd. First United Meth. Ch., Shreveport. Mem. ABA, La. State Bar Assn. (past bd. govs., past Ho. of Dels.), Shreveport Bar Assn., Order of Coif. Democrat. Avocations: golf, fishing, hunting. General civil litigation, Alternative dispute resolution, Appellate. Home: 1018 Delaware St Shreveport LA 71106-1402

**HALL, RICHARD EDGAR,** lawyer; b. Boise, Idaho, Feb. 7, 1944; s. Perce and Orpha Hall; m. Tonya Ann McMurtrey; children: Christine, Tara, Michelle, Erin. BA, U. Idaho, 1966; JD, Harvard U., 1969. Bar: Idaho 1970, U.S. Ct. Appeals (9th cir.) 1971. Ptnr. Moffatt, Thomas, Barrett & Blanton, P.C., Boise, 1969-88; pres. Hall, Farley, Oberrecht & Blanton, Boise, 1988—; pres. Idaho chpt. Am. Bd. Trial Advs., 1987-89; vice chmn. bd. dirs. United Heritage Mutual Life Ins. Co. Bd. dirs. Idaho Family Practice Residency, 1981-88. Fellow Am. Coll. Trial Lawyers, Am. Bd. Trial Advs.; mem. Idaho Assn. Def. Counsel (pres.), Fedn. Ins. and Corp. Counsel (chmn. med. malpractice com., regional v.p.), Hillcrest Country Club (pres. 1989), Avid Club, Boise (bd. dirs.), Rotary (pres. Boise 1979). Methodist. E-mail: reh@hallfarley.com. Insurance, Personal injury, General civil litigation. Office: Hall Farley Oberrecht & Blanton PO Box 1271 Boise ID 83701-1271

**HALL, ROBERT TAGGART,** lawyer; b. East Liverpool, Ohio, Sept. 9, 1936; s. Robert Thompson and Olive Jennette (Herbert) H.; m. Sally Wilson, June 18, 1960; children: Robert Jr., Christopher, Thomas. BS, Georgetown U., 1960, JD, 1964. Bar: Va., D.C., U.S. Dist. Ct. (ea. and we. dists.) Va., U.S. Ct. Appeals (4th cir.), U.S. Ct. Appeals (D.C. cir.), U.S. Supreme Ct. Atty. Hall & Sickels, P.C., Reston, Va., 1964—. Fellow Internat. Acad. Trial Lawyers (bd. dirs.), Am. Coll. Trial Lawyers,, Va. Bar Found.; mem. Va. Trial Lawyers Assn. Personal injury, Product liability, Professional liability. Office: Hall and Sickels PC Reston Exec. Ctr. Ste 150 12120 Sunset Hills Rd Reston VA 20190-3231

**HALL, ROBERT TURNBULL, III,** lawyer; b. Norfolk, Va., Aug. 25, 1945; s. Robert Turnbull and Mary Evelyn H.; m. Colleen Coffee, Aug. 17, 1968; children—Meghan, Robert. B.S., Washington and Lee U., 1967; J.D., Georgetown U., 1971. Bar: U.S. Dist. Ct. D.C. 1971, D.C. Ct. Appeals 1971, U.S. Ct. Appeals (D.C. cir.) 1972, U.S. Ct. Appeals (5th cir.) 1972, U.S. Supreme Ct. 1975, U.S. Ct. Appeals (11th cir.) 1981, U.S. Ct. Appeals (9th cir.) 1982, U.S. Ct. Appeals (8th cir.) 1983. Assoc. Thelen, Reid & Priest, N.Y.C., 1971-77, ptnr., 1978—. Mem. ABA, D.C. Bar Assn., Fed. Energy Bar Assn. Administrative and regulatory, FERC practice. Home: 162 Mercer St Princeton NJ 08540-6827 Office: Thelen Reid & Priest 40 W 57th St New York NY 10019-4001

**HALL, STEPHEN CHARLES,** lawyer; b. Carmel, Calif., Sept. 14, 1948; s. Melvin Wiley and Dorothy Louise (Hoyt) H.; m. Kristi Lee Roberts, Feb. 23, 1983; children: Spencer Stephen Rodrigo, Rachel Genevieve Cristina, Trevor Charles. AB, Dickinson Coll., 1971; JD, Vt. Law Sch., 1977. Bar: Pa. 1978, Va. 1979, U.S. Dist. Ct. (ea. dist.) Va. 1982, U.S. Dist. Ct. (we. dist.) Va. 1990, U.S. Ct. Appeals (4th cir.) 1982. Title atty. Chgo. Title Inst. Co., Richmond, 1978-79; assoc. Edward E. Willey Jr., P.C., Richmond, 1979-82; ptnr. Willey & Hall, P.C., Richmond, 1983-88; assoc. Hazel & Thomas, P.C., Richmond, 1988-90, ptnr., 1990-94; ptnr. Keith & Hall, Richmond, 1994—. Contbr. articles to profl. jours. Past chmn. bd. trustees St. Michael's Episcopal Sch. Mem. Richmond Bar Assn. (past chmn. publs. com.), Chesterfield Bar Assn. (chmn. mem. com. 1990-), Bon Air Bus. and Profl. Assn. (past pres.). Episcopalian. Avocations: golf, photography. Federal civil litigation, General civil litigation, State civil litigation. Office: Keith & Hall 2727 Mcrae Rd Richmond VA 23235-3055

**HALL, THOMAS JENNINGS,** lawyer; b. South Bend, Ind., Apr. 30, 1948; s. Waldo J. and Laura E. (Gessinger) H.; m. Janet Barna, Aug. 15, 1970; children: Michael J., Matthew T. AB in Econ., Ind. U., Bloomington, 1971; JD magna cum laude, Ind. U., Indpls., 1974. Bar: Ind. 1974, U.S. Dist. Ct. (no. dist.) Ind. 1974. Law clk. Ind. Ct. Appeals, Indpls., 1973-74; assoc. May Oberfell & Lorber, Ind., 1977-79; ptnr. May & Oberfell & Lorber, South Bend, 1979-97, mng. ptnr., 1984-86, chmn. bus. law sect., 1987-94; ptnr. Thesley & Hall, 1997—. Bd. dirs. Jr. Achievement Michiana, 1988-90. Recipient 1988 Small Bus. Advocate Of Yr. award South Bend Mishawaka and Ind. State C. Of C. 1988. Mem. ABA, Ind. Bar Assn., Michiana Investment Network (chmn. 1988-91), St. Joseph County C. of C. (chmn. small bus. coun. 1983-85, chmn. community progress div. 1990-92, chmn. 1994-95), Rotary (dir. South Bend Chpt. 1988-91). General corporate, Contracts commercial. Office: Tuesley & Hall 340 Columbia Pl PO Box 4136 South Bend IN 46634-4136

**HALL, THOMAS W.,** lawyer; b. Lancaster, Pa., Jan. 12, 1951; s. Denton F. Jr. and Eleanor Lingard H.; m. Peggy Donnelly, Oct. 6, 1984; children: Shane, Jamie, Trevor. BA, Pa. State U., 1972; JD, Villanova U., 1980. Bar: Pa. 1980, U.S. Dist. Ct. (ea. dist.) Pa. 1981. Assoc. Pepper Hamilton & Scheetz, Phila., 1980-85, Law Office William A. Atlee, Lancaster, Pa., 1985-90; ptnr. Atlee & Hall, Lancaster, Pa., 1990-98, Atlee, Hall & Brookhart, Lancaster, Pa., 1998—. William Goldman scholar, Phila., 1977-80. Personal injury, Product liability, Professional liability. Office: Atlee Hall & Brookhart 8 N Queen St Lancaster PA 17603-3878

**HALLANAN, ELIZABETH V.,** federal judge; b. Charleston, W.Va., Jan. 10, 1925; d. Walter Simms and Imogene (Burns) H. U. Charleston, 1946; JD, W.Va. U., 1951; postgrad, U. Mich., 1964. Atty. Crichton & Hallanan, Charleston, 1952-59; mem. W.Va. State Bd. Edn., Charleston, 1955-57, Ho. of Dels., W.Va. Legis., Charleston, 1957-58; asst. commr. pub. instns. Charleston, 1958-59; mem., chmn. W.Va. Pub. Service Commn., Charleston, 1969-75; atty. Lopinsky, Bland, Hallanan, Dodson, Deutsch & Hallanan, Charleston, 1975-84; sr. judge U.S. Dist. Ct. for So. Dist. W.Va., Charleston, 1983—. Recipient Hannah G. Solomon award Nat. Coun. Jewish Women, 1997, Justitia Officium awrd W.Va. U. Coll. Law, 1997; named Woman of Achievement, YWCA, 1997, West Virginian of Yr., Charleston Gazette, 1997. Mem. W.Va. Bar Assn. Office: US Dist Ct PO Box 2546 Charleston WV 25329-2546

**HALL-BARRON, DEBORAH,** lawyer; b. Oakland, Calif., Oct. 7, 1949; d. John Standish Hall and Mary (Swinson) H.; m. Eric Levin Meadow, Feb. 1973 (div. June 1982); 1 child, Jesse Standish Meadow Hall; m. Richie Barron, 1997. Paralegal cert., Sonoma State U., Rohnert Park, Calif., 1984; JD, John F. Kennedy U., Walnut Creek, Calif., 1990. Bar: Calif. 1991. Paralegal Law Offices Marc Libarle/Quentin Kopp, Cotati, Calif., 1983-84,

MacGregor & Buckley, Larkspur, Calif., 1984-86, Law Offices Melvin Belli, San Francisco, 1987-88, Steinhart & Falconer, San Francisco, 1988; mgr. Computerized Litigation Assocs., San Francisco, 1986; law clk. Morton & Lacy, San Francisco, 1989-91, assoc., 1991-96; atty. Law Offices of Charlotte Venner, San Francisco, 1996-97, Plastiras & Terrizzi, San Francisco, San Rafael, Calif., 1998, Bishop, Barry, Howe, Haney & Ryder, San Francisco, Calif., 1998—. Atty. Vol. Legal Svcs., San Francisco, 1991-96; judge San Francisco Youth Ct., 1995-97; com. chmn. Point Richmond (Calif.) coun., 1994-96. Recipient Whiley Manuel Pro Bono award State Bar Calif., 1993. Mem. Nat. Assn. Ins. Women, Def. Rsch. Inst., Bar Assn. San Francisco (del. 4th world conf. on women 1995, chair product liability com.), Internat. Com. Lawyers for Tibet (litigation com. 1991-97, co-chair women's com.), Ins. Claims Assn. (chmn. membership com. 1994-96), Hon. Order of Blue Goose Internat., Queen's Bench (chmn. employment com. 1994-97, bd. dirs. 1996—, newsletter editor and webmaster 1999), BASF intellectual property/entertainment law). Democrat. Avocations: sailing, playing guitar and saxaphone, home brewing, mountain biking, human rights advocate. Intellectual property, Entertainment, Professional liability.

**HALLENBERG, ROBERT LEWIS,** lawyer; b. Oct. 21, 1948; s. Daniel Ward and Anna Mae (Lewis) H.; m. Susan Annette Shaffer, Nov. 29, 1980; children: Shea F., Jonathan E.R., Robert Lewis Jr. BA, U. Ky., 1970, JD, 1973; LLM in Taxation, U. Miami, Fla., 1974. Bar: U. Ky. 1970, U.S. Dist. Ct. (we. dist.) Ky. 1975, U.S. Tax Ct. 1986. Ptnr. Woodward, Hobson & Fulton, Louisville, 1974—; adj. prof. U. Louisville Sch. Law, 1974-80. Bd. dirs. Louisville Theatrical Assocs., 1980-90, v.p., sec., 1985-90; bd. dirs. Goodwill Industries Ky., 1987-93, sec., 1988-91; pres. Louisville Estate Planning Coun., 1979-80; bd. dirs. Louisville Estate Planning Forum, 1986-93, sec., 1992-93; mem. Estate Planning Coun. of Louisville, bd. dirs., 1989-95, pres., 1993-94. Fellow Am. Coll. Trust and Estate Counsel; mem. ABA (subchpt. com. 1974-77, real property, probate and trust com. 1985—), Ky. Bar Assn. (sec. tax com. 1984-85), Owl Creek Country Club (bd. dirs. 1988-91, pres. 1989-90, treas. 1990-91). Republican. Episcopalian. Estate planning, Pension, profit-sharing, and employee benefits, Probate. Office: Woodward Hobson & Fulton 2500 Nat City Tower Louisville KY 40202

**HALLIDAY, STANLEY GRANT,** lawyer; b. Wilmington, Del., Aug. 7, 1948; s. Stanley A. and Grace Marie (Grant) H.; m. Patricia T. Tomory. BA, U. Del., 1970; JD, U. Fla., 1973. Bar. U.S. Dist. Ct. (mid. dist.) Fla. 1974. Asst. pub. defender Office of Pub. Defender, Tampa, Fla., 1976-77; lawyer pvt. practice Tampa, Fla., 1978—. Capt. USAR, 1972-81. Recipient L.E.A.A. fellowship, Gainesville, Fla. Mem. The Fla. Bar Assn., Hillsborough County Bar Assn. Avocations: tennis, skiing. State civil litigation, Family and matrimonial, Criminal. Office: 1906 N Tampa St Tampa FL 33602-2133

**HALLIGAN, BRENDAN PATRICK,** lawyer; b. Tipperary, Ireland, Nov. 19, 1958; came to U.S., 1959; s. Joseph and Christina Ann (O'Connell) H.; m. Bethann Reed, Sept. 17, 1988; children: Katherine, Kevin, Michael. BA, L.I. U., 1980; JD, New Eng. Sch. of Law, 1994. Bar: Mass. 1994, U.S. Dist. Ct. Mass. 1995, U.S. Ct. Appeals (1st cir.) 1996. Asst. money mgr. Securities Settlement Corp., N.Y.C., 1980-82; securities rsch. Chem. Bank, N.Y.C., 1982-84; commodities trader Paine Webber, N.Y.C., 1984-86; instnl. trader Carroll, McEntee & McGinley, N.Y.C., 1986-89, Sanwa-BGK Securities, N.Y.C., 1989; legal asst. Cravath, Swaine & Moore, N.Y.C., 1989-91; asst. counsel Liberty Mut. Ins. Co., Boston, 1994-97, counsel, 1997—. Contbr. chpt. to book in field. Mem. Town of Plymouth (Mass.) Zoning Bd. Appeals, 1992-94; commr. Town of Duxbury (Mass.) Conservation Commn., 1998—; trustee, mem. Worcester Kiltie Pipe Band, 1998—. Mergers and acquisitions, Securities, General corporate. Office: Liberty Mut Ins Co 175 Berkeley St PO Box 140 Boston MA 02117-0140

**HALLIGAN, KEVIN LEO,** lawyer; b. South Orange, N.J., Feb. 1, 1964; s. Kevin Richard and Catherine Ann (Sullivan) H. BA, John Carroll U., 1986; JD, Creighton U., 1989. Bar: Ill. 1989, U.S. Ct. Appeals (7th cir.) 1992, Iowa 1995, U.S. Dist. Ct. (cent. dist.) Ill. 1995, U.S. Dist. Ct. (so. dist.) Iowa 1996. Prosecutor Sangamon County States Attys. Office, Springfield, Ill., 1990-91; assoc. Delano Law Offices, P.C., Springfield, 1991-95, Brooke & O'Brien, P.L.C., Davenport, Iowa, 1995—; corp. dir. H&H Food Sales, Davenport, 1995—. Mem. Dillon Inn of Ct., Kiwanis. Roman Catholic. Avocations: tennis, basketball, fishing, golf. General practice, Personal injury, State civil litigation. Home: 2546 Middle Rd Davenport IA 52803-3640 Office: Brooke & O'Brien PLC 2322 E Kimberly Rd Davenport IA 52807-7205

**HALLIGAN, R. MARK,** lawyer; b. Cleve., Sept. 11, 1953; s. Robert T. and Mary Louise (Sheehan) H.; m. Kathleen Ann Halligan, Aug. 27, 1977; children: Bridget, Kara, Molly. BA summa cum laude, U. Cin., 1975; JD, Northwestern U., 1978. Bar: Ohio, Ill., U.S. Dist. Ct. (no. dist.) Ill., U.S. Dist. Ct. (no. and so. dists. Ohio), U.S. Dist. Ct. (no. dist.) Calif., U.S. Ct. Appeals (6th, 7th and fed. cirs.). Assoc. Vorys, Sater, Seymour & Pease, Columbus, Ohio, 1978-81, Squire, Sanders & Dempsey, Cleve., 1981-88; of counsel Welsh & Katz, Ltd., Chgo., 1989, prin., ptnr., 1990—. Articles editor Jour. Criminal Law and Criminology, 1977-78; contbr. articles to profl. jours. Mem. ABA, Ill. Bar Assn., Chgo. Bar Assn., DuPage Bar Assn., Def. Rsch. Inst., Nat. Assn. R.R. Trial Counsel, Nat. Inst. for Trial Advocacy, Intellectual Property Law Assn Chgo. (chmn. trade secrets and unfair competition com. 1989-92, bd. mgrs. 1992—), Am. Intellectual Property Law Assn., Naperville C. of C., Rotary, Phi Beta Kappa. Home: 1403 Justin Ct Naperville IL 60540-8365 Office: Welsh & Katz Ltd 120 S Riverside Plz # 22 Chicago IL 60606-3913

**HALLINGBY, JO DAVIS,** lawyer, arbitrator; b. N.Y.C.; d. Irwin and Ruth Davis; m. Paul Hallingby Jr., Nov. 17, 1994. BA, Boston U., 1966; JD cum laude, Bklyn. Law Sch., 1973. Bar: N.Y. 1974, U.S. Ct. Appeals (2nd cir.) 1974. Legal intern counsel to chmn. N.Y.C. Planning Commn., summer 1972; law clk. Hon. John R. Bartels U.S. Dist. Judge Ea. Dist. N.Y., 1973; law clk. Hon. William C. Conner U.S. Dist. Judge So. Dist. N.Y., 1974; staff atty. Criminal Appeals Bur., Legal Aid Soc., 1974-77; asst. U.S. atty. Ea. Dist. N.Y., 1978-83; assoc. Kass, Goodkind, Wechsler & Labaton, 1977-78; litigation counsel CBS, Inc., 1983-84; N.Y. counsel Kaye, Scholer, Fierman, Hays & Handler, 1984-93; arbitrator Nat. Assn. Securities Dealers, N.Y. Stock Exch., 1994—; mem. U.S. Commn. on Civil Rights-N.Y. State Adv. Com., 1984-86; jud. com. Assn. of the Bar of the City of N.Y., 1984-90, fed. cts. com., 1990-94; dir. Riverside Park Fund, 1986-93; ct. adv. group com. on civil litigation U.S. Dist. Ct. Ea. Dist. N.Y., 1990-95; dir. Landmarks Preservation Found., 1995—; spkr. in field. Notes editor Bklyn. Law Rev., 1972-73. Office: Nat Assn Securities Dealers NY Stock Exch 1 Sutton Pl S New York NY 10022-2471

**HALLMARK, BRUCE CULLEN, JR.,** lawyer; b. Dallas, Mar. 24, 1958; s. Bruce Cullen and Martha Ann (Rosborough) H.; m. Jone Bergquist, May 10, 1986. BA, St. John's Coll., Santa Fe, 1980; JD, U. Tex., 1984. Bar: N.Mex. 1984, Tex. 1985, U.S. Dist. Ct. N.Mex., U.S. Ct. Appeals (5th, 10th cirs.) 1985. Assoc. Montgomery & Andrews, Santa Fe, 1984; sole practice Santa Fe, 1985-86; atty. Garber and Hallmark P.C., Santa Fe, 1986—. Mem. Tex. Bar Assn., N.Mex. Bar Assn. Democrat. Methodist. Avocations: skiing, bicycling, mountaineering. Estate taxation, General practice, State civil litigation. Home: 2113 Botulph Rd Santa Fe NM 87505-5705 Office: Garber & Hallmark PC 200 W Marcy St Ste 203 Santa Fe NM 87501-2036

**HALLORAN, BRIAN PAUL,** lawyer; b. Covington, Ky., Sept. 22, 1969; s. Kenneth Anthony and Ann Carole (Rymarquis) H. BA in History, Ea. Ky. U., 1990; JD, Salmon P. Chase Coll. Law, 1994. Bar: Ky. 1994, U.S. Dist. Ct. (ea. dist.) Ky. 1996. Pvt. practice, Newport, Ky., 1994—; cons. Globoleochem Cons., Covington, 1994—; counsel Rogue Predator Pictures, LLC, & Rogue Ptnrs., L.P., L.A. Mem. Campell County Rep. Com., Alexandria, Ky., 1996—. Mem. Ky. Bar Assn., Ky. Assn. Trial Attys., No. Ky. Bar Assn., Kenton County Jaycees. Roman Catholic. Avocations: music, golf, soccer, softball, computers. General civil litigation, Criminal, General practice. Office: 300 E 3d St Newport KY 41071-1841

**HALLORAN, JOHN JOSEPH, JR.,** lawyer; b. N.Y.C., July 23, 1959; s. John Joseph and Ellen M. (Shannon) H.; m. Suzanne Halloran, May 31, 1986; children: John J. III, Tyler Matthew, Ashley Elizabeth. BA, SUNY, Albany, 1981; JD, Union U., 1984. Bar: N.Y. 1985, D.C. 1997, U.S. Dist. Ct. (no. dist.) Calif., U.S. Dist. Ct. (so. and ea. dists.) N.Y., U.S. Ct. Appeals (2d cir.), U.S. Supreme Ct., U.S. Dist. Ct. (D.C.), U.S. Ct. Appeals (D.C. cir.). Law clk. to Hon. Matthew J. Jasen N.Y. Ct. Appeals, Buffalo, 1984-85; lawyer Willkie Farr & Gallagher, N.Y.C., 1986-95; lawyer civil divsn., fed. program br. U.S. Dept. Justice, Washington, 1995-98; ptnr. Speiser Krause, N.Y.C., 1998—. Recipient Letter of Commendation, FBI, 1996, Atty. Gen. Spl. Achievement award, 1996, 97, 98. Mem. ABA, N.Y. State Bar Assn. (mem. task force on adminstrv. adjudication 1988-91), Assn. of Bar of City of N.Y. (mem. spl. com. on govt. ethics 1989-95). Office: Speiser Krause Two Grand Ctr Tower 140 E 45th St Fl 34 New York NY 10017-3144 also: 2300 Clarendon Blvd Ste 306 Arlington VA 22201-3367

**HALLORAN, MICHAEL JAMES,** lawyer; b. Berkeley, Calif., May 20, 1941; s. James Joseph and Fern (Ogden) H.; m. Virginia Smedberg, Sept. 6, 1964; children: Pamela, Peter, Shelley. BS, U. Calif., Berkeley, 1962, LLB, 1965. Bar: Calif. 1966, D.C. 1979, Wyo. 1996. Assoc. Keatinge & Sterling, L.A., 1965-67; assoc. Pillsbury, Madison & Sutro, San Francisco, 1967-72, ptnr., 1973-90, 97—; mng. ptnr. Pillsbury, Madison & Sutro, Washington, 1979-82; exec. v.p., gen. counsel BankAm. Corp. and Bank of Am., San Francisco, 1990-96; mem. legal adv. com. N.Y. Stock Exch., 1993-96; bd. overseers Inst. Civil Justice, 1994-98; chair sect. corp. securities banking and emerging cos. Pillsbury Madison & Sutro, 1997—. Editor: Venture Capital and Public Offering Negotiation, 1982—. Mem. corp. governance, shareholder rights and securities transactions com. Calif. Senate Commn., 1986-98; bd. dirs. Am. Conservatory Theater. Mem. ABA (chmn. state regulation of securities com. 1981-84, mem. coun. of sect. of bus. law 1986-90, chmn. banking law com. 1992-96, mem. corp. laws com. 1997—), Bar Assn. San Francisco (bd. dirs. 1993-96), Orinda Country Club. Avocations: skiing, golf, fishing, hiking. Banking, Securities, General corporate. Office: Pillsbury Madison & Sutro LLP 235 Montgomery St Fl 16 San Francisco CA 94104-3074 also: 2550 Hanover St Palo Alto CA 94304-1115

**HALLORAN, MICHAEL JOHN,** lawyer; b. St. Louis, June 4, 1951; s. Edward Anthony Halloran and Helen M. (Kickham) Phillips; m. Gwen V. Carroll, July 25, 1983 (div. Oct. 1984). BS in Commerce, St. Louis U., 1972, JD, 1975. Bar: Ill. 1975, U.S. Dist. Ct. (no. dist.) Ill. 1975, U.S. Ct. Appeals (7th cir.) 1975. Assoc. Seyfarth, Shaw, Fairweather & Geraldson, Chgo., 1975-76, 77-78, Washington, 1976-77; atty. Beinhauer & Rouhana, N.Y.C., 1978-79; assoc. William B. Hanley & Assocs., Chgo., 1979-81; assoc. Bell, Boyd & Lloyd, Chgo., 1981-83, ptnr., 1983-86; pvt. practice, Chgo., 1987—. Federal civil litigation, General civil litigation, State civil litigation. Home: 1017 W Washington St Apt 6F Chicago IL 60607-2112 Office: 53 W Jackson Blvd Ste 319 Chicago IL 60604-3607

**HALLORAN, THOMAS GIULD,** lawyer; b. LaCrosse, Wis., May 1, 1949; s. Roy Daniel and Beverly Jane (McDonald) H. BA, U. Wis., 1971, JD, 1977. Bar; Wis. 1977, U.S. Dist. (we. and ea. dists.) 1977, U.S. Ct. Appeals (7th cir.) 1984, U.S. Supreme Ct. 1984. Assoc. Cook & Franke, Milw., 1977-78; atty. pub. defender office State of Wis., Milw., 1979-80; assoc. Hausmann, McNally & Hupy, Milw., 1981-82; ptnr. Halloran, Burke, Dunn & Henderson S.C., Milw., 1982-86; pvt. practice Milw., 1986—. Mem. ABA, Wis. Bar Assn., Milw. Bar Assn., Nat. Assn. Criminal Def. Lawyers, Phi Delta Phi. Democrat. Roman Catholic. Criminal. Office: 44 E Mifflin St Ste 403 Madison WI 53703-2895

**HALLUIN, ALBERT PRICE,** lawyer; b. Nov. 8, 1939; children: Russell, Marcus. BA, La. State U., 1964; JD, U. Balt., 1969. Bar: Md. 1970, N.Y. 1985, Calif. 1991. Assoc. Jones, Tullar & Cooper, Arlington, Va., 1969-71; sr. patent atty. CPC Internat. Inc., Englewood Cliffs, N.J., 1971-76; counsel Exxon Rsch. & Engring. Co., Florham Park, N.J., 1976-83; v.p., chief intellectual property counsel Cetus Corp., Emeryville, Calif., 1983-90; ptnr. Fleisler, Dubb, Meyer & Lovejoy, San Francisco, 1990-92, Limbach & Limbach, San Francisco, 1992-94, Pennie & Edmonds, Menlo Park, Calif., 1994-97, Howery & Simon, Menlo Park, 1997—; pres., CEO, chmn. Halzyme Tech., Inc., 1995—. Contbr. articles to legal jours. Pres. Belle Roche Homeowners Assn., Redwood City, Calif., 1995—. Named One of Top 20 Intellectual Property Lawyers, Calif. Lawyer's mag., 1993. Mem. ABA, Am. Intellectual Property Law Assn. (chmn. chem. practice com. 1981-83, sec. 1984-85, bd. dirs. 1984-89, founding chmn. biotech. com. 1990-92), Licensing Exec. Soc., Assn. Corp. Patent Counsel, Bar Assn. San Francisco, San Francisco Patent Assn. Republican. Episcopalian. E-mail: HalluinA@Howrey.com. and Halzym@Earthlink.net. FAX: 650-463-8400. Intellectual property. Office: Howrey & Simon 301 Ravenswood Ave Menlo Park CA 94025

**HALLYBURTON, MARGARET D.,** state legislator; b. Peoria, Ill., Oct. 11, 1946; m. John C. Hallyburton. BA, Rivier Coll., 1992; postgrad., Franklin Pierce Law Ctr. Mem. N.H. Ho. of Reps.; mem. judiciary and family law coms. N.H. Ho. of Reps. Mem. ABA (family law sect.), Nat. Assn. of Counsel for Children. Republican.

**HALPENNY, DIANA DORIS,** lawyer; b. San Francisco, Jan. 18, 1951; d. William Frederick and Doris E. Halpenny. BA, Calif. State Coll., 1973; JD Order of Coif, Univ. Pacific, 1980. Bar: Calif. 1980. Bookkeeper, sales clk. Farmers Empire Drugs, Santa Rosa, Calif., 1971-73; activity dir. Beverly Manor Convalescent Hosp., Anaheim, Calif., 1973-74; instructional aide LA County Supt. Schs., Downey, Calif., 1974-76, sub. tchr., 1976-77; assoc. Littler, Mendelson, Fastiff & Tichy, San Jose, Calif., 1980-82, Walters & Shelburne, Sacramento, 1982-84, Kronick Moskovitz Tiedemann & Girard, Sacramento, 1984-85; legal advisor Pub. Employment Rels. Bd., 1985-87; gen. counsel San Juan Unified Sch. Dist., 1987—. Founding mem. In-house Sch. Attys No. Calif.; past pres. no. sect. Sch. Law Study Sect. County Counsels Assn., 1991-92; legal adv. com. Calif. Sch. Bd. Assn. Edn. Legal Alliance; exec. bd. Calif. Edn. Mandated Cost Network, 1987—, chair 1998—. Mem. Calif. Coun. Sch. Attys. (v.p. programs 1993, pres. elect 1994, pres. 1995, exec. bd. dirs. 1993—). Administrative and regulatory, Education and schools, Labor. Office: San Juan Unified Sch Dist 3738 Walnut Ave Carmichael CA 95608-3099

**HALPER, EMANUEL B(ARRY),** real estate lawyer, developer, consultant, author; b. Bronx, N.Y., June 24, 1933; s. Nathan N. and Molly (Rabinowitz) H.; m. Ilona Rubinstein, Mar. 5, 1961; children: Eve Brook, Dan Reed. AB, CCNY, 1954; JD, Columbia U., 1957. Bar: N.Y. 1958, Minn. 1982; real estate broker, N.Y. House counsel Howard Stores Corp., Bklyn., 1960; ptnr. Zissu, Berman, Halper & Gumbinger, N.Y.C., 1965-87, of counsel, 1987—; ptnr. Can. Pacific Realty Co., N.Y.C., 1970—; v.p. devel. Chase Enterprises, Hartford, Conn., 1987-89; pres. Texam. Horizon Ventures, 1989-93, Am. Devel. and Cons. Corp., Greenvale, N.Y., 1989—; adj. prof. real estate NYU, 1973-83; spl. prof. law Hofstra U., 1998—. Author: Wonderful World of Real Estate, 1975 (republished as Conversations in Real Estate, 1990), Shopping Center and Store Leases, 1979, Ground Leases and Land Acqusition Contracts, 1988; columnist N.Y. Law Jour., 1982—; contbg. editor Real Estate Review, N.Y.C., 1973—; chmn. editorial policy com. Internat. Property Investment Jour., Hempstead, N.Y., 1982-87. With USAR, 1957-63. Recipient Disting. Teaching award NYU, 1978, Dean's award Hofstra U. Law Sch., 1987. Mem. ABA (chmn. comml. leasing com. 1986-93, chmn. comml. and indsl. leasing group 1993-94, mem. supervisory coun. of real property, probate and trust law sect. 1994—, mem. standing com. on CLE, 1994-96, mem. standing com. pubs. 1997-98, Gavel award 1977), World Assn. Lawyers (chmn. internat. real estate com. 1982-90), Internat. Inst. for Real Estate Studies (chmn. bd. 1980-87), Am. Coll. Real Estate Lawyers. Jewish. Avocations: writing, painting, gardening, yoga, running. Real property, Construction. Office: PO Box 261 Greenvale NY 11548-0261

**HALPERIN, KYLE MALLARY,** lawyer; b. New Hyde Park, N.Y., Nov. 2, 1965; d. Jerome Roger Halperin and Marleen Wynne Schuss; m. Jeffrey Travis Hellerman, May 30, 1993; 1 child, Cameron P. BA, Haverford Coll., 1987; JD, Yeshiva U., 1990. Bar: N.Y., D.C., U.S. Dist. Ct. (so. and ea. dists.) N.Y. Atty. Halperin Klein & Halperin, N.Y.C., 1990-95; ptnr. The Halperin Law Firm, LLP, N.Y.C., 1996—. Federal civil litigation, State civil litigation, Insurance. Office: The Halperin Law Firm LLP 964 3rd Ave New York NY 10155-0003

**HALPERN, JO-ANNE ORENT,** lawyer; b. Balt., Apr. 13, 1944; d. Max Howard and Marjorie (Ginsburg) Orent; m. M. David Halpern, Aug. 22, 1965; children: Hugh Nathanial, Lee Randall (dec.), Lauren Gail. B.A. Dickinson Coll., 1966; J.D., Dickinson Sch. Law, 1968. Bar: Pa. 1968. Law clk. Daupin County and Commonwealth Ct. Pa., 1965-68; assoc. Hurwitz Klein, Benjamin & Angino, Harrisburg, Pa., 1968-70; sole practice, Hollidaysburg, Pa., 1970—; legal asst. to Blair County Cts., Hollidaysburg, 1974-88; solicitor Blair County Assn. Citizens with Learning Disabilities, 1979—, Family Violence Intervention, Inc., Altoona, Pa., 1980—; lectr., atty. Hospice Program of Home Nursing Agy. Blair County, 1979—. Adviser, bd. dirs. Agudath Achim Sisterhood, 1970—, pres., 1985-88; mem. Fedn. Jewish Philanthropies Bd, 1985—; mem. med. ethics com. Altoona Hosp. Mem. ABA, Pa. Bar Assn. (family law sect., rights of handicapped children sect.), Blair County Bar Assn., Am. Arbitration Assn. (arbitrator), Blair County Assn. Lawyers Wives, Hadassah, Phi Alpha Delta, Phi Mu. Democrat. Jewish. Home: 8 Hickory Hl Hollidaysburg PA 16648-9728 Office: 920 Penn St Hollidaysburg PA 16648-2211

**HALPERN, JOHN (MICHAEL), JR.,** lawyer; b. N.Y.C., June 25, 1945; s. John Michael and Cecelia Halpern; m. Debora Schaeffer, Dec. 29, 1969; children: Jonathan, Lillian, Margaret. BA, U. Calif., Berkeley, 1969; JD, U. Oreg., 1975; student, Dartmouth Coll., 1963-66. Bar: Oreg. 1975, U.S. Dist. Ct. Oreg. 1977, U.S. Ct. Appeals (9th cir.) 1980, U.S. Supreme Ct. 1981. Pvt. practice, Eugene, Oreg., 1975—. Mem. Oreg. Bar Assn., Oreg. Criminal Def. Lawyers Assn. (life), Lane County Bar Assn. Avocations: music, photography, backpacking, family life. Criminal, Personal injury. Office: 130 S Park St Eugene OR 97401-2931

**HALPERN, PHILIP MORGAN,** lawyer; b. Derby, Conn., Apr. 17, 1956; s. Edwin Vincent and Carol Veronica (Gallagher) H.; m. Carolyn G. McElwreath, Mar. 11, 1989. BS magna cum laude, Fordham U., 1977; JD, Pace U., 1980. Bar: N.Y. 1981, U.S. Dist. Ct. (so. and ea. dists.) N.Y. 1981, U.S. Ct. Appeals (2d cir.) 1982, U.S. Tax Ct. 1984, U.S. Supreme Ct. 1985, U.S. Dist. Ct. Conn. 1989, Conn. 1989, U.S. Ct. Appeals (3d cir.) 1991. Law clk. to sr. judge U.S. Dist. Ct. (so. dist.) N.Y., N.Y.C., 1980-82; assoc. litigation dept. Kimmelman, Sexter & Sobel, N.Y.C., 1982-83; ptnr. Pirro, Collier, Cohen, & Halpern LLP, N.Y.C., 1983—; mng. ptnr. Pirro, Collier, Cohen, & Halpern LLP, White Plains, N.Y., 1996—; arbitrator Civil Ct. City N.Y. and Am. Arbitration Assn., 1987-96; adv. coun. Bd. of Judges, So. Dist. of N.Y., 1995—; mediator U.S. Dist. (so. dist.) N.Y., 1998—, mem. adv. com. on civil practice, 1999—. Author: Age Discrimination in Employment Act: Employers Can Enforce Releases Too!, 1992, Fair Value Proceedings: Fixing Fair Value in New York, 1996. Chmn. Young Reps., Tuckahoe, N.Y., 1975-77; chmn. taxi commn. Village of Mamaroneck, N.Y., 1986-87, mem. planning bd., 1987-89. Mem. ABA, N.Y. State Bar Assn. (com. on lawyer competency, com. on fed. judiciary), Assn. of Bar of City of N.Y., Assn. Trial Lawyers Am., N.Y. Trial Lawyers Assn., N.Y. County Lawyers Assn., Fed. Bar Coun., Profl. Golfers Assn. (adv. coun. metro. sect. 1992—), Westchester Country Club. Roman Catholic. Federal civil litigation, State civil litigation, General civil litigation. Office: Pirro Collier Cohen & Halpern One N Lexington Ave White Plains NY 10601 also: 99 Park Ave New York NY 10016-1601

**HALPERN, RALPH LAWRENCE,** lawyer; b. Buffalo, May 12, 1929; s. Julius and Mary C. (Kaminker) H.; m. Harriet Chasin, June 29, 1958; children: Eric B., Steven R., Julie B. LL.B. cum laude, U. Buffalo, 1953. Bar: N.Y. 1953. Teaching assoc. Northwestern U. Law Sch., 1953-54; assoc. firm Jaeckle, Fleischmann, Kelly, Swart & Augspurger, Buffalo, 1957-58; asso. firm Raichle, Banning, Weiss & Halpern (and predecessors), 1958-59, ptnr., 1959-86; ptnr. Jaeckle, Fleischmann & Mugel, Buffalo, 1986—. Pres. Buffalo Coun. World Affairs, 1972-74, Temple Beth Zion, Buffalo, 1981-83; chmn. Buffalo chpt. Am. Jewish Com., 1975-77; bd. govs. United Jewish Fedn., Buffalo, 1972-78, 91-97, v.p., 1992-95. Served to capt. JAGC U.S. Army, 1954-57. Mem. ABA (ho. dels. 1989-95, 97-99), N.Y. State Bar Assn. (chmn. com. profl. ethics 1971-76, chmn. com. jud. election monitoring 1983-86, chmn. spl. com. to consider adoption of ABA model rules of profl. conduct 1983-85, sec. internat. law and practice sect. 1992-93, vice chmn. 1993-95), Erie County Bar Assn., Am. Judicature Soc., Am. Law Inst. Antitrust, Federal civil litigation, General corporate. Home: 88 Middlesex Rd Buffalo NY 14216-3618 Office: Jaeckle Fleischmann & Mugel 800 Fleet Bank Bldg Buffalo NY 14202-2292

**HALPERT, DOUGLAS JOSHUA,** lawyer; b. Bklyn., Nov. 9, 1962; s. Eugene and Miriam (Feigenbaum) H.; m. Yee-Wen Chen, July 22, 1989. BA in English Lit., U. Chgo., 1984; JD, Fordham Law Sch., 1988. Bar: N.Y. 1989, Ohio 1994. Immigration atty. Cohen, Swados, Wright, Hanifin, Bradford & Brett, Buffalo, 1988-94, Frost & Jacobs, Cin., 1994—. Recipient Vol. Lawyer of Yr. award Cin. Bar Assn., 1998. Mem. Am. Immigration Lawyers Assn., Cin. Bar Assn., Alumni Schs. Com. of U. Chgo. Avocations: lit., writing, movies, sports. Office: Frost & Jacobs 2500 PNC Ctr 201 E 5th St Cincinnati OH 45202-4182

**HALPERT, RICHARD LEE,** lawyer; b. Kalamazoo, Mich., Nov. 1, 1947; s. Samuel K. and Rosalie (Zuravel) H.; m. Mary K. Sydlaske, June 24, 1973; children: David, Michael. BA, Kalamazoo Coll., 1969; JD cum laude, Ind. U., 1972. Bar: Mich. 1973, U.S. Dist. Ct. (we. dist.) Mich. 1980, U.S. Supreme Ct. 1985. Trial atty. Van Buren County Pros. Attys. Office, Paw Paw, Mich., 1972-74, Kreis, Enderle, Halpert, Borsos & Ford, Kalamazoo, 1974-82, Halpert & Koning, Kalamazoo, 1982-87, Howard & Howard, Kalamazoo, 1987-95, Halpert, Weston, Wuori & Sawusch, P.C., Kalamazoo, 1996—; lectr. in field. Co-author over 30 manuals for Inst. Continuing Legal Edn.; note editor Ind. Law Jour., 1971-72. Bd. dirs. YMCA, Kalamazoo, 1989-94, bd. trustees, 1998—, Kalamazoo County Rep. Exec. Com., 1975, Kalamazoo County Humane Soc.; trustee Ctrl. Mich. U., Mt. Pleasant, 1981-83. Mem. ATLA, Mich. Trial Lawyers Assn., Am. Burn Assn. (spl. mem. 1984—, rehab. com. 1997—), Internat. Soc. for Burn Injuries (spl. mem.), State Bar Mich. (negligence sect., com. on profl. and jud. ethics 1980-82), Kalamazoo Bar Assn. (chmn. com. on profl. responsibility 1981-83), Phoenix Soc. for Burn Injuries (bd. trustees and exec. com.), Am. Arbitration Assn. Avocations: bicycling, nature photography, hiking. Personal injury. Office: Halpert Weston Wuori and Sawusch PC 136 E Michigan Ave Ste 1050 Kalamazoo MI 49007-3917

**HALPRIN, RICK,** lawyer; b. Chgo., Feb. 28, 1940; s. David Harold and Mary (Stepansky) H.; m. Dale Lawrence, Mar. 17, 1967 (div. June 1970); 1 child, Eden. BA, Roosevelt U., 1964; JD, Massey Coll., 1968. Bar: Mass. 1970, Ill. 1970, U.S. Dist. Ct. (no. dist.) Ill. 1970. Atty. Feldman Posen, Chgo., 1972-73, Oliver & Halprin, Chgo., 1973-79, Halprin & Halprin, Chgo., 1979-82; gen. counsel Chgo. Park Dist., 1982-86; pvt. practice Chgo., 1986—. Capt. USMCR, 1970-72. Mem. Nat. Assn. Criminal Defense Lawyers (advisor), Ill. Bar Assn. (criminal justice com.), Chgo. Bar Assn. Criminal, Civil rights. Office: 542 S Dearborn St Ste 750 Chicago IL 60605-1525

**HALSEY, DOUGLAS MARTIN,** lawyer; b. Warwick, R.I., 1953; s. Donald Post Jr. and Marita H.; m. Amy Klinow, Sept. 5, 1976; children: Mark, Meredith. BA, Columbia U., 1976; JD cum laude, U. Miami, 1979. Bar: Fla. 1979, U.S. Ct. Appeals (11th cir.), U.S. Dist. Ct. (so. dist.) Fla. Assoc. Paul & Thomson, Miami, Fla., 1979-83; ptnr. Thomson, Bohrer, Werth & Razook, Miami, 1985-88, Douglas M. Halsey, P.A., Miami, 1989-97, Halsey & Burns, P.A., Miami, 1997—. Rsch. editor U. Miami Law Review, 1978-79. Mem. Alexis de Tocqueville Soc., United Way of Miami-Dade County, 1995—; chair-elect Children's Home Soc. Fla., 1998-99; bd. dirs. Ctr. for Fla.'s Children, Tallahassee, 1995-99. Mem. Fla. Bar (chmn. environ. and land use law sect. 1993-94, President's Pro Bono Svc. award 1991), Alexis de Tocqueville Soc. Environmental. Office: First Union Fin Ctr 200 S Biscayne Blvd Ste 4980 Miami FL 33131-2310

**HALSTRÖM, FREDERIC NORMAN,** lawyer; b. Boston, Feb. 26, 1944; s. Reginald F. and Margaret M. (Graham) H.; divorced, 1989; children: Ingrid Alexandra, Reginald Frederic II. Student, Northeastern U., 1961-63, USAF Acad., 1963-65; AB, Georgetown U., 1967; JD, Boston Coll., 1970. Bar: Mass. 1970, U.S. Dist. Ct. Mass., 1971, U.S. Dist. Ct. R.I. 1981, U.S. Tax Ct., 1981, U.S. Ct. Appeals (1st cir.) 1971, U.S. Ct. Appeals (11th cir.) 1991. Assoc. Schneider and Reilly, P.C., Boston, 1970-73; ptnr. Parker, Coolter, Daley and White, Boston, 1973-78; prin. Halström Law Office, Boston, 1978—; spl. prosecutor Dist. Atty., Norfolk County, 1969-70; spl. asst. city solicitor City of Quincy, 1980. Editor Mass. Law Quar., 1972; contbr. articles to profl. jours. Fellow Boston Coll. Law Sch., v.p. 1988-91, pres.

1991—, benefactor Frederic N. Halström Nat. Moot Ct. Team. Mem. ABA (chmn. products liability com. gen. practice sect. 1980-85, award of achievement young lawyers divsn. 1978, vice chmn. taxation on ins. cos. sect. 1986-88), Assn. Trial Lawyers Am. (gov. 1981-84, 87—), state del. 1976-78, 86-87, chair various coms.), Mass. Acad. Trial Attys. (co-chmn. tort law sect. 1980—, bd. of govs. 1976—, sec. 1987-88, pres.-elect 1995-96, pres. 1996-97), Mass. Bar Assn. (pres. young lawyers divsn. 1977-78, bd. dels. 1978-80), Middlesex County Bar Assn., Trial Lawyers Pub. Justice (sustaining founder, v.p. 1989—), Thomas F. Lambert Jr. Endowed Chair Trust), Algonquin Club, Univ. Club (Boston). Fax: 617-426-4791. E-mail: FHalstrom@aol.com. Personal injury, Insurance, State civil litigation. Home: 483 River Rd Carlisle MA 01741-1873 Office: 132 Boylston St Boston MA 02116-4616

**HALTOM, B(ILLY) REID,** lawyer; b. Artesia, N. Mex., Sept. 9, 1945; s. Felix Tucker and Shirley Mae (Lucado) H.; m. Elizabeth Ann Berger, Dec. 25, 1964; 1 child, Robb Reid. BA in Philosophy, U. N.Mex, 1969; JD, Tex. Tech U., 1972. Bar: N.Mex. 1973, U.S. Dist. Ct. N.Mex. 1977, U.S. Ct. Appeals (10th cir.) 1980, U.S. Ct. Claims 1980, U.S. Supreme Ct. 1992, U.S. Dist. Ct. Ariz. 1992. Ptnr. Nordhaus, Haltom, Taylor, Taradash & Frye, Albuquerque, 1980—. Fellow ABA, N.Mex. State BAr Assn., Albuquerque Bar Assn., Albuquerque Lawyers Club. Avocations: snow and water skiing, tennis, gourmet cooking. Oil, gas, and mineral, General corporate, Finance. Office: Nordhaus Haltom Taylor Taradash & Frye 500 Marquette Ave NW Ste 1050 Albuquerque NM 87102-5310

**HALTOM, ELBERT BERTRAM, JR.,** retired federal judge; b. Florence, Ala., Dec. 26, 1922; s. Elbert Bertram and Elva Mae (Simpson) H.; m. Constance Boyd Morris, Aug. 19, 1949; 1 dau., Emily Haltom Olsen. Student, Florence State U., 1940-45; JD, U. Ala. Sch. Law, 1948. Practiced in Florence, 1948-80; mem. firm Bradshaw, Barnett & Haltom, 1948-58, Haltom & Patterson, 1959-80; judge U.S. Dist. Ct. (no. dist.) Ala., Birmingham, Huntsville and Florence, 1980-91; sr. judge U.S. Dist. Ct. (no. dist.) Ala., Florence, 1992-98; bar commr. 11th Jud. Cir. Ala., 1976-80. Mem. Ala. Ho. of Reps., 1954-58; mem. Ala. Senate, 1958-62; candidate lt. gov. Ala., 1962; mem. Ala. Democratic Exec. Com., 1966-80. Served with USAAF, 1944-45. Decorated Air medal with four oak leaf clusters. Fellow Internat. Soc. Barristers, Am. Coll. Trial Lawyers; mem. ABA, Ala. Bar Assn., Am. Legion, VFW, Florence Rotary Club, Phi Gamma Delta, Phi Delta Phi. Methodist.

**HALVERSON, STEVEN THOMAS,** lawyer, construction executive; b. Enid, Okla., Aug. 29, 1954; s. Robert James Halverson and Ramona Mae (Ludke) Selenski; m. Diane Mary Schueller, Aug. 21, 1976; children: John Thomas, Anne Kirsten. BA cum laude, St. John's U., 1976; JD, Am. U., 1979. Bar: Va. 1979. Asst. project dir. ABA, Washington, 1977-79; with Briggs & Morgan, St Paul., 1980-83; sr. v.p. M.A. Mortenson Cos., Denver, 1984-99; pres. Haskell Co., Jacksonville, Fla., 1999—; bd. dirs. Ctr. for New West, Rocky Mountain World Trade Ctr., Regis U., Ctrl. City Opera, Lowell Whiteman Sch., Design Build Inst. Am. Co-author: Federal Grant Law, 1982, The Future of Construction, 1997; contbr. articles to profl. jours. Republican. Roman Catholic. Construction, Government contracts and claims, Legislative. Home: 1821 Via Arriba Palos Verdes Peninsula CA 90274-1236 Office: Haskell Co. Haskell Bldg 111 Riverside Ave Jacksonville FL 32202-4921

**HALVORSON, NEWMAN THORBUS, JR.,** lawyer; b. Detroit, Dec. 17, 1936; s. Newman Thorbus and Virginia Westbrook (Markle) H.; m. Sally Clark Stone, May 3, 1969; children: Christina English, Charles Burgess Westbrook. AB, Princeton U., 1958; LLB, Harvard U., 1961. Bar: Ohio 1962, D.C. 1963, U.S. Supreme Ct. 1965. Assoc. Covington & Burling, Washington, 1962-70; asst. U.S. atty. Office of U.S. Atty., Washington, 1983-85; assoc. ind. counsel (spl. prosecutor under Ethics in Govt. Act), 1987-90; ptnr. Covington & Burling, Washington, 1970-83, 85—. Editor, Harvard Law Rev., 1960-61; author: Intermediate Sanctions Regs: Many Questions Remain, Tax Notes, 1998. Sr. warden, Jr. warden, vestryman Christ Ch. Georgetown, Washington, 1983-86, 89-92, chmn. fin. com., 1992-96; bd. dirs. Lupus Found. D.C., 1974-85; mem., bd. dirs. Eugene and Agnes E. Meyer Found., Washington, 1976-91, chmn., 1989-90; bd. mgrs. Hist. Soc. Washington, 1995—; bd. dirs. Coun. for Ct. Excellence, Washington, 1995—; trustee Potomac Sch., McLean, Va., 1980-86, chmn., 1981-83; mem. com. of 100 on Federal City, 1970—, trustee, treas., 1975-79; bd. trustees, mem. exec. com. Greater Washington Rsch. Ctr., 1997—; v.p., trustee Cleveland Park Hist. Soc., 1997—. With USMCR, 1961-67. Mem. ABA, D.C. Bar. Republican. Episcopalian. Clubs: Met. (Washington), Chevy Chase (Md.). General corporate, State and local taxation, Corporate taxation. Home: 3500 Lowell St NW Washington DC 20016-5025 Office: Covington & Burling 1201 Pennsylvania Ave NW PO Box 7566 Washington DC 20044-7566

**HAMANN, CHARLES MARTIN,** lawyer; b. Greenwich, Conn., July 2, 1939; s. Edmund Henry and Mary (Foss) H.; m. Ethel McFarlan, July 11, 1964; children: Charles Franklin, Edmund Tuppan. BA, Yale U., 1961; LLB, Harvard U., 1964. Bar: Mass. 1964. Law clk. Superior Ct., Boston, 1964-65; assoc. Nutter, McClennen & Fish, Boston, 1965-69, Herrick & Smith, Boston, 1969-74; ptnr. Casner & Edwards, LLP, Boston, 1974—. Mem. Belmont Town Meeting, 1970—; mem. Belmont (Mass.) Bd. Appeals, 1974-77; mem. Belmont Warrant (Fin.) Com., 1978-93, also chmn. 3 yrs.; mem. Belmont By-law Rev. Com., 1993—, now chmn. Fellow Am. Coll. Trust and Estate Counsel; mem. Boston Estate Planning Coun. (pres. 1987). Unitarian-Universalist. Avocations: tennis, hiking, swimming, reading. Estate planning, Estate taxation, Probate. Home: 28 Temple St Belmont MA 02478-3545 Office: Casner & Edwards LLP One Federal St Boston MA 02110-2012

**HAMANN, DERYL FREDERICK,** lawyer, bank executive; b. Lehigh, Iowa, Dec. 8, 1932; s. Frederick Carl Hamann and Ada Ellen (Hollingsworth) Hamann Geis; m. Carrie Svea Rosen, Aug. 23, 1954 (dec. 1985); children: Karl E., Daniel A., Esther Hamann Brabec, Julie Hamann Bunderson; m. Eleanor Ramona Nelson Curtis, June 20, 1987. AA, Ft. Dodge Jr. Coll., Iowa, 1953; BS in Law, U. Nebr., 1956, JD cum laude, 1958. Bar: Nebr. 1958, U.S. Dist. Ct. Nebr. 1958, U.S. Ct. Appeals (8th cir.) 1958. Law clk. U.S. Dist. Ct. for Nebr., Lincoln, 1958-59; ptnr. Baird, Holm, McEachen, Pedersen, Hamann & Strasheim, Omaha, 1959—; chmn. adv. com. Supreme Ct. Nebr., Omaha, 1986-95; chmn. bd. or chmn. exec. com. 3 Midwestern Cmty. Banks. Past pres. Omaha Estate Planning Coun. Mem. Nebr. Bar Found. (pres. 1981-86), Nebr. Assn. Bank Attys. (pres. 1985-86). Republican. Lutheran. Avocations: boating, reading. Banking, Estate planning, General corporate. Office: Baird Holm McEachen Pedersen Hamann & Strasheim 1500 Woodmen Tower Omaha NE 68102

**HAMANN, HOWARD EVANS,** lawyer; b. Newport Beach, Calif., Aug. 4, 1957; s. Helge Oscar and Shirley (Evans) H.; m. Kitty Hamann. Student, U.S. Air Force Acad., 1975-77; BA, U. Wyo., 1979; JD, Pepperdine U., 1983. Bar: Calif. 1985, Wyo. 1995, U.S. Dist. Ct. (no., ea., ctrl. and so. dists.) Calif. 1985, U.S. Supreme Ct. 1991. Atty. Mendes & Mount, L.A., 1985-91, Hollins, Schechter & Feinstein, Orange, Calif., 1991-93, Booth, Mitchel & Strange, Costa Mesa, Calif., 1993-96, Kolod, Wager & Gordon, Santa Ana, Calif., 1996-98, Law Offices of Howard E. Hamann, Irvine, Calif., 1998—. Mem. Pepperdine Law Rev., 1983. Mem. Am. Legion. Episcopalian. General civil litigation, Insurance, Product liability. Office: 8 Corporate Park Ste 300 Irvine CA 92606-5196

**HAMBERG, GILBERT LEE,** lawyer; b. Phila., May 29, 1952; s. Marvin and Minnie (Bolnick) H.; m. Elizabeth G. Strulson, Dec. 6, 1981. BA, Wesleyan U., Middletown, Conn., 1974; JD, Temple U., 1977. Bar: Pa. 1977, U.S. Dist. Ct. (we., mid. and ea. dists.) Pa. 1977, U.S. Dist. Ct. (ea. dist.) Mich. 1983, La. 1985, U.S. Dist. Ct. (ea., Mid. and we. dists.) La., N.Y. 1992, U.S. Dist. Ct. (so. dist.) N.Y. 1992. Atty. rates Pa. Pub. Utilities Commn., Harrisburg, 1977-80; asst. gen. counsel Laventhol & Horwath, Phila., 1980-82; counsel AAMCO Transmissions Inc., Bala Cynwyd, Pa., 1982-84; assoc. Monroe & Lemann, New Orleans, 1984-90, Milling, Benson, New Orleans, 1990-92, Bower & Gardner, N.Y.C., 1992-93; pvt. practice Yardley, Pa., 1993—. Mem. Pa. Bar Assn., La. Bar Assn. Avocations: tennis, gardening. Administrative and regulatory, Bankruptcy, Public utilities. Office: 1038 Darby Dr Yardley PA 19067-4519

**HAMBLEN, LAPSLEY WALKER, JR.,** judge; b. Chattanooga, Tenn., Dec. 25, 1926; s. Lapsley Walker Sr. and Libby (Shipley) H.; m. Claudia Royster Terrell, Mar. 20, 1971; children by previous marriage: Lapsley Walker III, Allen M., William Shipley. BA, U. Va., 1949, LLB, 1953. Bar: W.Va. 1954, Ohio 1955, Va. 1957. Trial atty. IRS, Atlanta, 1955; atty. advisor U.S. Tax Ct., 1956; ptnr. Caskie Frost Hobbs & Hamblen and predecessor firms, Lynchburg, Va., 1957-82; dep. asst. atty. gen. tax div. U.S. Dept. Justice, 1982; judge U.S. Tax Ct., Washington, 1982-92, chief judge, 1992-94, 94-96, sr. judge, 1996—; mem. adv. bd. Va. tax rev. U. Va. Law Sch., Charlottesville, 1990—; former trustee So. Fed. Tax Inst.; former co-dir. ann. conf. on fed. taxation U. Va. Served with USN, 1945-46. Fellow Am. Coll. Tax Counsel, Am. Coll. Trust and Estate Counsel, Raven Soc., Order of Coif, Omicron Delta Kappa, Phi Alpha Delta. Presbyterian. Office: US Tax Ct 400 2nd St NW Washington DC 20217-0002

**HAMBRIGHT, ROBERT JOHN,** lawyer; b. Beaumont, Tex., Mar. 28, 1956; s. James William and Edna Ann (Eaheart) H.; children: Rosemary, Phoebe. BBA, BA, So. Methodist U., Dallas, Tex., 1978, JD, 1981. Bar: Tex. 1981, U.S. Dist. Ct. (ea. dist.) Tex. 1982, U.C. Ct. Appeals (5th cir.) 1984, U.S. Tax Ct. 1983, U.S. Supreme Ct. 1986. Assoc. Orgain, Bell & Tucker, L.L.P., Beaumont, Tex., 1981-87, ptnr., 1987—. Contbr. articles to profl. jours. Mem. ABA, State Bar of Tex. (Chmn. Labor and Employment Law Section, 1986-87). Labor. Home: 296 Ridgeland St Beaumont TX 77706-4511 Office: Orgain Bell & Tucker LLP 470 Orleans St Ste 1751 Beaumont TX 77701-3000

**HAMBURG, CHARLES BRUCE,** lawyer; b. Bklyn., June 30, 1939; s. Albert Hamburg and Goldie (Blume) H.; m. Stephanie Barbara Steingesser, June 23, 1962; children: Jeanne M., Louise E. B.Chem. Engring., Poly. Inst. Bklyn., 1960; JD, George Washington U., 1964. Bar: N.Y. 1964. Patent examiner U.S. Patent Office, 1960-63; patent atty. Celanese Corp. Am., N.Y.C., 1963-65; patent atty. Burns, Lobato & Zelnick, N.Y.C., 1965-67; patent atty. Nolte & Nolte, N.Y.C., 1967-75; prin. C. Bruce Hamburg, N.Y.C., 1976-79; ptnr. Jordan & Hamburg, L.L.P., N.Y.C., 1979—. Recipient Superior Service award (2) U.S. Patent Office, 1963, 63. Mem. ABA, Am. Intellectual Property Law Assn., N.Y. Patent Trademark Copyright Law Assn., Internat. Assn. Protection Intellectual Property, Queens Bar Assn., Bklyn. Bar Assn., Licensing Execs. Soc., Internat. Fedn. Intellectual Property Attys. Club: Masons. Author: Patent Fraud and Inequitable Conduct, 1972, 78; Patent Law Handbook, 1983-84, 84-85, 85-86, Doctrine of Equivalents in U.S., 1995 (Japanese), 2d edit., 1998 (Korean); monthly columnist Patent and Trademark Rev., 1976-85; U.S. corr. Patents and Licensing, Japan, 1986—. Patent, Trademark and copyright, Intellectual property. Office: 122 E 42nd St New York NY 10168-0002

**HAMBY, GENE MALCOLM, JR.,** lawyer; b. Florence, Ala., Mar. 23, 1943; s. Gene Malcolm Sr. and Katherine (Koonce) H.; m. Judy Brown, Apr. 10, 1971; children: Mark Clifton, Anne Tyler. BS, U. North Ala., 1965; JD, U. Ala., Tuscaloosa, 1968. Bar: Ala. 1968, U.S. Dist. Ct. (no. dist.) Ala. 1972, U.S. Ct. Appeals (11th cir.) 1981. Assoc. Heflin & Rosser, Attys., Tuscambia, Ala., 1968-70; ptnr. Pitts & Hamby, Sheffield, Ala., 1970-80; pvt. practice Sheffield, 1981-84; ptnr. Hamby & Baker, Attys., Sheffield, 1984-87, Jones, Hamby & Baker, Attys., Sheffield, 1987-89; pvt. practice, Sheffield, 1989—. Bd. dirs. Shoals Indsl. Devel. Authority, Sheffield, 1985-91, Law Sch. Found., U. Ala. Sch. Law, 1985—; past dist. v.p. U. Ala. Alumni, Tuscaloosa; past pres. U. North Ala. Alumni, Florence, Colbert County United Way, Sheffield; chmn. Sheffield Indsl. Devel. Bd., Sheffield, Sheffield Edn. Found., 1992-96; past bd. dirs. United Cerebral Palsy NW Ala., Sheffield, Shoals Indsl. Devel. Authority. With USAR, 1968-74. Recipient Kiwanis Citizen of Yr. award City of Sheffield, 1991. Mem. ABA, Colbert County Bar Assn (past pres.), Ala. State Bar Assn., Ala. Trial Lawyers Assn. (exec. com.), Assn. Trial Lawyers Am., Sheffield Bus. and Profl. Assn. (pres. 1999—), Kiwanis Club (past pres. Sheffield chpt.), Colbert County C. of C. (past-pres.), Phi Kappa Phi. Democrat. Avocation: Indian artifacts. Personal injury, State civil litigation, Real property. Home: PO Box 328 Sheffield AL 35660-0328 Office: 406 N Nashville Ave Sheffield AL 35660-2938

**HAMBY, ROBERT KEVIN,** lawyer; b. Ft. Worth, Aug. 1, 1959; s. Thorton Estill and Ara Lina (Parker) H.; m. Terri Kondik, Jan. 1, 1985; 1 child, Austin Kindred. BA, U. Tex., 1981; JD, Cath. U. of Am., 1993. Pub. affairs specialist Dallas, 1982-87, Tex. Water Commn., Austin, 1987-91; legal clk. U.S. Dept. Justice, Washington, 1991-93; atty. Fulbright & Jaworski L.L.P., Dallas, 1994-98; assoc. gen. counsel, sr. v.p. Tex. Credit Union League, 1998—; law clk. Office of V.P., Washington, 1992, Superior Ct., Washington, 1993; mem. citizens adv. bd. Richardson Ind. Sch. Dist. Former bd. trustees Dallas Mental Health and Mental Retardation Ctr., co-creator Hispanic task force; assoc. mem. Greater Dallas Crime Commn.; mem. youth crime commn., liaison to Washington H.S. crime commn., 1995-96; former chair, mem. Addison Planning and Zoning Commn.; former pres. Valley of Bent Tree Homeowners Assn.; coord. Dallas City Bond Campaign, 1982; mem. Greater Dallas Rep. Forum, Rep. Assembly; mem. citizens rev. bd. Richardson Ind. Sch. Dist. Mem. Dallas Bar Assn. (chair media. rels. com., chair legislation/new laws, tellers com., publns. com., chair judges in cmty. com.), Phi Delta Phi. Republican. Administrative and regulatory, General corporate, Finance. Office: Tex. Credit Union League 4455 Lbj Fwy Ste 1000 Dallas TX 75244-5920

**HAMEL, FRED MEADE,** lawyer; b. Sheridan, Wyo., Nov. 26, 1943; s. Fred Herman and Marie (Kruger) H.; m. Michelle O'Bryan, Dec. 29, 1967; 1 child, Marc Steven. BSBA, U. Denver, 1965; JD, U. Colo., 1968. Bar: Colo. 1968, U.S. Dist. Ct. Colo. 1974, U.S. Ct. Appeals (10th cir.) 1977. Asst. sec. Union Investment Corp., Detroit, 1970-74; v.p. 1st Comml. Corp., Denver, 1970-74; prin. Fred M. Hamel Atty. At Law, Denver, 1974—. Pres. South Cen. Improvment Assn., 1978. Staff sgt. U.S. Army, 1968-70, Vietnam. Mem. Colo. Bar Assn., Denver Bar Assn. Avocation: golf. General civil litigation, Contracts commercial, Real property. Office: 155 S Madison St Ste 206 Denver CO 80209-3013

**HAMEL, LEE,** lawyer; b. N.Y.C., Oct. 1, 1940; s. Herman and Jessie Blanche (Mapes) H.; m. Carole Ann Holmes, Dec. 30, 1965; children: Todd Leland, Stuart Russell. BA, Duke U., 1962; JD, U. Tex., 1967; postgrad., U. Houston, 1997—. Bar: Tex. 1967, U.S. Ct. Appeals (5th and 11th cirs.) 1968, U.S. Ct. Mil. Appeals 1968, U.S. Dist. Ct. (so. dist.) Tex. 1968, U.S. Supreme Ct. 1971, U.S. Tax Ct. 1979, U.S. Dist. Ct. (we. dist.) Tex. 1984, U.S. Dist. Ct. (ea. dist.) Tex. 1994. Asst. U.S. atty. U.S. Dist. Ct. (so. dist.) Tex., Houston, 1968-71, chief Corpus Christi divsn., 1970-71; owner Lee Hamel & Assocs., Houston, 1971-74, 90—; ptnr. Dickerson, Hamel, Early & Pennock, Houston, 1974-88, Hamel & Rouner, Houston, 1988-89; instr. Nat. Inst. for Trial Advocacy, 1986—. Co-editor Nat. Law Jour. Health Care Fraud and Abuse Newsletter, 1998-99. Former trustee St. Luke's Hosp., Houston, St. James Home for Aged, Baytown; former dir. exec. bd. Episcopal Diocese of Tex.; pres. St. Francis Endowment Fund, 1993-94; former councilman Hunters Creek Village, Tex. Comdr. USN, 1962-64, USNR, ret. 1993. Fellow Coll. of State Bar of Tex., Houston Bar Found., State Bar Tex.; mem. ABA (litig. sec., white collar crime com., bus. sec., chair health care fraud subcomittee), FBA, Houston Bar Assn., Houston Vol. Lawyers Assn. (bd. dirs.). Episcopalian. Avocations: backpacking. Federal civil litigation, State civil litigation, Criminal. Office: Lee Hamel & Assocs 1200 Smith St Ste 2900 Houston TX 77002-4502

**HAMEL, RODOLPHE,** lawyer, pharmaceutical company executive; b. Lewiston, Maine, June 3, 1929; s. Rodolphe and Alvina Melanie (Bilodeau) H.; m. Marilyn Vivian Johnsen, June 10, 1957; children: Matthew Edward, Anne Melanie. BA, Yale U., 1950; LLB, Harvard U., 1953. Bar: Maine 1953, D.C. 1953, N.Y. 1957. Assoc. firm Shearman & Sterling, N.Y.C., 1956-66; v.p., corp. sec., gen. counsel Macmillan Inc., N.Y.C., 1972-73; internat. counsel Bristol-Myers Squibb Co. (formerly Bristol-Myers Co.), N.Y.C., 1966-72, 73, v.p., counsel internat. div., 1974-81, assoc. gen. counsel, 1978-89, v.p., 1983-92, gen. counsel, 1989-94, sr. v.p., 1992-94; cons. Bristol-Myers Squibb Co. (formerly Bristol-Myers Co.), 1995—. 1st lt. AUS, 1953-56. Mem. ABA, N.Y. State Bar Assn., Assn. of Bar of City of N.Y., Yale Club. General corporate, Private international. Office: Bristol-Myers Squibb Co 345 Park Ave New York NY 10022-6000

**HAMELBURG, GERALD A.,** lawyer; b. Boston, Apr. 4, 1944; s. Meyer and Mildred H.; m. Barbara Hamelburg, June 16, 1968; children: Eric, Kimberly. BSBA, Boston U., 1967; JD, Boston Coll., 1971. Assoc. Miller, Pierce & Miller, Boston, Widet, Widet, Boston, Widet, Widet, Slater & Goldman, Boston; ptnr. Nix & Wendell, Boston, Hamelburg & Canter, Boston, Greenbaum, Nagel, Fisher & Hamelburg, Boston. Mem. bd. Town of Wellesley, 1977-87, adv. bd. 1985-87. Medic USAR, 1967-73. Mem. ABA, Boston Bar, Mass. Bar, Comml. Law League of Am.. Avocations: skiing, golf, tennis, beach, collecting sports memorabilia. State civil litigation, Personal injury. Office: Greenbaum Nagel Fisher & Hamelburg 185 Devonshire St Ste 400 Boston MA 02110-1407

**HAMER, MARK HARRIS,** lawyer; b. Memphis, July 16, 1966. BA, U. Va., 1988, JD, 1991. Bar: Calif. 1991, U.S. Dist. Ct. (so. dist.) Calif. 1991, U.S. Dist. Ct. (ctrl. and ea. dists.) Calif. 1993, U.S. Dist. Ct. (no. dist.) Calif. 1996. Atty. Gray, Cary, Ware & Freidenrich LLP, San Diego, 1991—. Mem. Fed. Bar Assn., Assn. Bus. Trial Lawyers, Am. Inns Ct. (assoc.), U. Va. Alumni Club (pres. 1991—). Securities, General civil litigation. Office: Gray Cary Ware & Freidenrich LLP 401 B St Ste 1800 San Diego CA 92101-4223

**HAMES, WILLIAM LESTER,** lawyer; b. Pasco, Wash., June 21, 1947; s. Arlie Franklin and Nina Lee (Ryals) H.; m. Pamella Kay Rust, June 3, 1967; children: Robert Alan, Michael Jonathan. *Mr. Hames' father was a blue collar worker. Mr. Hames' mother was a housewife who enrolled her three children in music lessons and enforced three hour per day practice sessions for all three. She instilled a work ethic and discipline which has resulted in Mr. Hames' successful legal career. Brother, Frank, is a partner in a successful music production company in Dallas, Texas. Sister, Gina, is a History Professor at Pacific Lutheran University in Tacoma, Washington. Thanks Mom!.* BS in Psychology, U. Wash., 1974; JD, Willamette U., 1981. Bar: Wash. 1981, U.S. Dist. Ct. (ea. dist.) Wash. 1982, U.S. Ct. Appeals (9th cir.) 1985, U.S. Dist. Ct. (we. dist.) Wash. 1985. Counselor Wash. Juvenile Ct., Walla Walla, Wash., 1974-76; reactor operator control rm. United Nuclear Inc., Richland, Wash., 1976-77; assoc. Sonderman, Egan & Hames, Kennewick, Wash., 1981-84, Timmons & Hames, Kennewick, 1984-86, Sonderman, Timmons & Hames, Kennewick, 1987-88; ptnr. Hames, Anderson & Whitlow, Kennewick, 1988—. *In addition to a thriving personal injury firm, Mr. Hames is the immediate past-President of the Bankruptcy Bar Association for the Eastern District of Washington. He is co-Chairman of the Association's annual seminar and retreat which attracts national caliber speakers. He has been chosen twice as the presenter at the Annual Western and Eastern Washington Bankruptcy Judges Conference.* Mem. Am. Trial Lawyers Assn., Wash. State Bar Assn., Wash. State Trial Lawyers Assn., Benton-Franklin County Bar Assn., Bankruptcy Bar Assn. (bd. dirs.), Fed. Bar Assn. (bd. dirs.). Democrat. Methodist. Bankruptcy, Personal injury, Consumer commercial. Home: 410 W 21st St Kennewick WA 99337 Office: Hames Anderson & Whitlow PO Box 5498 Kennewick WA 99336-0498

**HAMILTON, CLYDE HENRY,** federal judge; b. Edgefield, S.C., Feb. 8, 1934; s. Clyde H. and Edwina (Odom) H.; children: John C., James W. BS, Wofford Coll., 1956; JD with honors, George Washington U., 1961. Bar: S.C. 1961. Assoc. J.R. Folk, Edgefield, 1961-63; assoc., gen. ptnr. Butler, Means, Evins & Browne, Spartanburg, S.C., 1963-81; judge U.S. Dist. Ct. S.C., Columbia, 1981-91, U.S. Ct. Appeals (4th cir.), Richmond, Va., 1991—; reference asst. U.S. Senate Library, Washington, 1958-61; gen. counsel Synalloy Corp., Spartanburg, 1969-80. Mem. editorial staff Cumulative Index of Congl. Com. Hearings, 1935-58; bd. editors George Washington Law Rev., 1959-60. Pres., Spartanburg County Arts Council, 1971-73; pres. Spartanburg Day Sch., 1972-74, sustaining trustee, 1975-81; past mem. steering com. undergrad. merit fellowship program and estate planning council Converse Coll., Spartanburg; trustee Spartanburg Methodist Coll., 1979-84; mem. S.C. Supreme Ct. Bd. Commrs. on Grievances and Discipline, 1980-81; del. Spartanburg County, 4th Congl. Dist. and S.C. Republican Convs., 1976, 80; mem., past chmn. fin. com. and adminstrv. bd. Trinity United Meth. Ch., Spartanburg, trustee, 1980-83. Served to capt. USAR, 1956-62. Recipient Alumni Disting. Svc. award Wofford Coll., 1991. Mem. S.C. Bar Assn., John Belton O'Neall Am. Inn of Ct. (founding mem., past pres. 1987-88), Piedmont Club (bd. govs. 1979-81). Office: US Ct Appeals 4th Cir 1901 Main St Columbia SC 29201-2443

**HAMILTON, CURTIS JAMES, II,** lawyer; b. Huntington, N.Y., Jan. 26, 1969; s. Curtis James II and Mary Margaret H.; m. Emily Christine Weiland, July 7, 1990; children: Victoria, Curtis J. IV, Benjamin, Caroline. BA, Duke U., 1991; JD, U. Cin., 1995. Bar: Ohio 1995, U.S. Ct. Appeals (6th cir.) 1996, U.S. Dist. Ct. (so. dist.) Ohio 1996, Ky. 1998, Ind. 1998, U.S. Dist. Ct. (we. dist.) Ky. 1998, U.S. Dist. Ct. (so. dist.) Ind. 1998. Assoc. Deardorff & Assocs., Cin., 1995-97, Neel, Wilson & Clem, Henderson, Ky., 1997—. Recipient Law Sch. Merit scholar U. Cin., 1992. Mem. Cin. Bar Assn. (com. chair 1997), Ohio Bar Assn., Ky. Bar Assn., Ind. Bar Assn., Henderson, Ky. Lions Club (bd. dirs. 1997—). Mem. Christian Ch. (Disciples of Christ). Avocations: golfing, boating, basketball, coaching. Personal injury, Family and matrimonial, General civil litigation. Home: 2940 N Ridge Path Henderson KY 42420-2237 Office: Neel Wilson & Clem 9 S Main St Henderson KY 42420-3121

**HAMILTON, DAGMAR STRANDBERG,** lawyer, educator; b. Phila., Jan. 10, 1932; d. Eric Wilhelm and Anna Elizabeth (Sjöström) Strandberg; A.B., Swarthmore Coll., 1953; J.D., U. Chgo. Law Sch., 1956; J.D., Am. U., 1961; m. Robert W. Hamilton, June 26, 1953; children: Eric Clark, Robert Andrew Hale, Meredith Hope. Admitted to Tex. bar, 1972; atty., civil rights div. U.S. Dept. Justice, Washington, 1965-66; asst. instr. govt. U. Tex.-Austin, 1966-71; lectr. Law Sch. U. Ariz., Tucson, 1971-72; editor, researcher Assoc. Justice William O. Douglas, U.S. Supreme Ct., 1962-73, 75-76; editor, rschr. Douglas autobiography Random House Co., 1972-73; staff counsel Judiciary Com., U.S. Ho. of Reps., 1973-74; asst. prof. L.B. Johnson Sch. Pub. Affairs, U. Tex., Austin, 1974-77, assoc. prof., 1977-83, prof., 1983—, assoc. dean, 1983-87; interdisciplinary prof. U. Tex. Law Sch., 1983—; vis. prof. Washington U. Law Sch., St. Louis, 1982, U. Maine, Portland, 1992; vis. fellow Univ. London, QMW sch. law, 1987-88, Univ. Oxford Inst European & Comparative Law, 1998. Mem. Tex. Bar Assn., Am. Law Inst., Assn. Pub. Policy Analysis and Mgmt., Swarthmore Coll. Alumni Coun. (rep.), Kappa Beta Phi (hon.), Phi Kappa Phi (hon.). Democrat. Quaker. Contbr. to various publs. Civil rights, Constitutional. Home: 403 Allegro Ln Austin TX 78746-4301 Office: U Tex LBJ Sch Pub Affairs Austin TX 78713

**HAMILTON, DAVID F.,** judge; b. 1957. BA magna cum laude, Haverford Coll., 1979; JD, Yale U., 1983. Law clk. to Hon. Richard D. Cudahy U.S. Ct. Appeals (7th cir.), 1983-84; atty. Barnes & Thornburg, Indpls., 1984-88, 91-94; judge U.S. Dist. Ct. (so. dist.) Ind., Indpls., 1994—; counsel to Gov. of Ind., 1989-91; chair Ind. State Ethics Commn., 1991-94. V.p. for litigation, bd. dirs. Ind. Civil Liberties Union, 1987-88. Fulbright scholar, 1979-80; recipient Sagamore of the Wabash, Gov. Evan Bayh, 1991. Office: US Dist Ct So Dist Ind 46 E Ohio St Rm 330 Indianapolis IN 46204-1921

**HAMILTON, DAVID MICHAEL,** lawyer; b. Lubbock, Tex., Nov. 22, 1952; s. Thomas B. and Mary Kathryn Hamilton; m. Stacy Hamilton, June 24, 1974 (div. Aug. 1987); children: Katie, Jay T. BS cum laude, Tex. Tech. U., 1975, JD, 1978; PhD, Pacific Western U., 1990. Bar: Tex. 1978, U.S. Dist. Ct. (no. and ea. dists.) Tex. 1978, U.S. Dist. Ct. (ea. dist.) Okla. 1978; diplomate Am. Bd. Psychol. Specialities, Am. Coll. Forensic Examiners. Patrol officer Tex. Tech Police Dept. Dispatcher, 1970-73, Levelland Tex. Police Dept., 1973-74, 78; dep. sheriff Hockley County Sheriff's Office, 1974-76; law clk. Allison and Davis Attys., Levelland, 1976-78; briefing atty. Ct. Criminal Appeals, Austin, Tex., 1978-79; pvt. practice law Amarillo, Tex., 1979-82; asst. dist. atty. Potter County Dist. Attys. Office, 1982, Gray, Hemphill, Wheeler, Roberts and Lipscomb, 1984; asst. criminal dist. atty. Lubbock, Tex., 1987; ptnr. Allied Behavior/Forensic Cons., Paris, Tex., 1987, Allied Behavior Cons., Forensic and Wellness, Paris, 1987; pvt. practice law Paris, 1987; govt. mediator Clarington Jr. Coll., 1985—; counseling supr. Allied Psych-Social Counseling Ctr., Paris, 1987—; co-dir. Allied Profls., Paris; presenter in field. Contbr. articles to profl. jours. bd. mem. Tralee Crisis Ctr., Pampa, Tex., 1984, Family Haven Crisis Ctr., Paris, 1988-90, Family Haven Rape Crisis, Paris, 1992; optimist pres. Am. League Baseball, Pampa, 1985, Sunrise Rotary, Pampa, 1986; sec. Big Bros./Big

Sisters, Pampa, 1986; mem. health adv. coun. Paris Ind. Sch. Dist. Recipient Vol. Svc. award Gov.'s Office, 1986; named to Am. Police Hall of Fame, Pampa Police Dept., 1984-85. Fellow Am. Assn. Profl. Hypnotherapists (life, cert.); mem. APA (Am. Psychology Law Soc. divsn. 41), Internat. Soc. for the Study of Multiple Personality and Dissociation (co-chair law and ethics com. 1991-93), Internat. Assn. Counselors and Therapists (life), Am. Coll. Forensic Examiners, Am. Assn. Family Counselors and Mediators (cert.), Nat. Orgn. for Victim's Assistance (mem. legis. and prosecution coms. 1986-87), Victims Initiating Gains in the Legislature (vice chair 1986-87), Tex. Coun. on Family Violence, Tex. Criminal Def. Lawyer's Assn., Tex. Assn. Against Sexual Assault (sec. 1984-85), Tex. Orgn. for Victim's Assistance (charter, 1st pres., chair 1986-87), Tex. Soc. for the Study of Trauma and Dissociation (charter, pres.-elect 1995), Mother's Against Sexual Assault (nat. adv. bd.), Phi Alpha Delta. Office: PO Box 547 Paris TX 75461-0547

**HAMILTON, HARRIET HOMSHER,** lawyer; b. Topeka, Sept. 14, 1956; d. Joseph Anthony and Theresa Ann (Skowyra) Homsher; m. David Scott Hamilton, Oct. 30, 1983; children: Geoffrey Bryce, Mitchell Ross. BA in Polit. Sci., UCLA, 1978; JD, U. Calif., Davis, 1988. Bar: Ill. 1989, U.S. Ct. Appeals (7th cir.) 1990, U.S. Supreme Ct. 1996. Atty. Capell Howard Knabe & Cobb, Montgomery, Ala., 1989; staff atty. U.S. Ct. Appeals (8th cir.), St. Louis, 1989-90; atty. Brauer & Bartholomew Ltd., Belleville, Ill., 1991—; com. mem. summer internship program St. Clair County, 1997. Lt. USN, 1979-85. Mem. Ill. Trial Lawyers Assn., St. Clair County Bar Assn. (bd. dirs. 1996—). Democrat. Avocations: gardening, hiking. Appellate, Personal injury. Office: Cook Shevlin Ysursa Brauer & Bartholomew Ltd 12 W Lincoln St Belleville IL 62220-2018

**HAMILTON, HENRY KERR,** lawyer; b. Toledo, Feb. 27, 1960; s. William Allen and Mary Kerr Hamilton; m. Susan C. Canny, July 11, 1992; 1 child, Caroline. BS in Civil Engring., U. Cin., 1983; JD, U. Toledo, 1986. Bar: Wash. 1986, U.S. Dist. Ct. (we. dist.) Wash. 1986, U.S. Ct. Claims 1987, U.S. Dist. Ct. (ea. dist.) Wash. 1989. Assoc. Ulin, Dann, Elston & Lambe, Seattle, 1986-88; assoc. Stafford Frey Cooper, Seattle, 1988-95, shareholder, 1996—; gen. counsel N.W. Subcontractors Assn., Seattle, 1990-98. Author: (chpt.) Lien and Bond Claims in the 50 States, 1990, (chpt.) 50 State Public Construction Contracting, 1996, (chpt.) The Most Important Questions a Surety Can Ask, 1997. Mem. steering com. Equal Justice Coalition, Seattle, 1995—. Fellow ABA (exec. com. young lawyers divsn. 1994-96, Forum on Constrn. governing com. 1995-97). Avocations: running, skiing, hiking, golf. Construction, Contracts commercial, General civil litigation. Office: Stafford Frey Cooper 1301 5th Ave Ste 2500 Seattle WA 98101-2621

**HAMILTON, JACKSON DOUGLAS,** lawyer; b. Cleve., Feb. 5, 1949; m. Margaret Lawrence Williams, Dec. 19, 1971; children: Jackson Douglas Jr., William Schuyler Lawrence. BA, Colgate U., 1971; JD, U. Pa., 1974. Bar: Calif. 1974, U.S. Dist. Ct. (cen. dist.) Calif. 1974, U.S. Tax Ct. 1978, U.S. Ct. Claims 1984, U.S. Ct. Appeals (6th and 11th cirs.) 1988, N.C. 1991, U.S. Supreme Ct. 1991. Ptnr. Kadison, Pfaelzer, Woodard, Quinn & Rossi, L.A., 1986-87, Spensley, Horn, Jubas & Lubitz, L.A., 1987-91, Roberts & Stevens, Asheville, N.C., 1991—; adj. prof. law U. San Diego, 1981, Golden Gate U., San Francisco, 1981-85, U. N.C., Asheville, 1994; cons. Calif. Continuing Edn. Bar, 1983-84, select com. on sports Calif. Senate, 1983-85. Editor Entertainment Law Reporter, 1979—; contbr. articles to profl. jours. Mem. ABA (tax sect., internat. law sect.), N.C. Bar Assn. (tax. sect. coun.). Republican. Episcopalian. Corporate taxation, General corporate, Taxation, general. Office: Roberts & Stevens BB & T Bldg Asheville NC 28802

**HAMILTON, JEAN CONSTANCE,** judge; b. St. Louis, Nov. 12, 1945; d. Aubrey Bertrand and Rosemary (Crocker) H. A.B., Wellesley Coll., 1968; J.D., Washington U., St. Louis, 1971; LL.M., Yale U., 1982. Bar: Mo. 1971. Atty. Dept. of Justice, Washington, 1971-73, asst. U.S. atty., St. Louis, 1973-78; atty. Southwestern Bell Telephone Co., St. Louis, 1978-81; judge 22d Jud. Circuit, State of Mo., St. Louis, 1982-88; judge Mo. Ct. Appeals (ea. dist.), 1988-90; U.S. dist. judge U.S. Dist. Ct. (ea. dist.) Mo., 1990—, chief judge, 1995—. Mem. ABA, Bar Assn. Met. St. Louis, Women Lawyers Assn. Met. St. Louis, Nat. Assn. Women Judges, Am. Law Inst. Episcopalian. Office: US Court and Custom House 1114 Market St Fl 1 Saint Louis MO 63101-2043

**HAMILTON, JOHN DAYTON, JR.,** lawyer; b. Canandaigua, N.Y., June 11, 1934; s. John Dayton and Faith (Mooney) H.; m. Martha Downey; children: Linda S., John Dayton III. BA cum laude, Princeton U., 1955; JD, Harvard U., 1960. Bar: Mass. 1960. Assoc. Hale and Dorr, Boston, 1960-64, ptnr., 1964—, chmn. dept. real estate, 1976-84, 98—, mng. ptnr., 1984—; treas., dir. Mass. Biomed. Rsch. Corp., 1994—. Gen. counsel, trustee Mus. Sci., Boston, 1976—; mem. Bd. Appeals, Concord, Mass., 1976-78; trustee Beth Israel Hosp., 1989-96, Beth Israel Deaconess Med. Ctr., 1996-98; vice chmn. Boston Adv. Bd. City Yr., Inc., 1995—; mem. adv. coun. Soc. Preservation of New Eng. Antiquities, 1995—. Fellow Am. Bar Found.; mem. ABA, Am. Coll. Real Estate Lawyers, Mass. Conveyancers Assn., Boston Bar Assn. (chmn. real estate sect. 1976-80) Boston Law Firm Group (chmn. 1999—), Concord Country Club., Chappaquoit Yacht Club. Roman Catholic. Avocations: tennis, golf, sailing. Real property, Land use and zoning (including planning), Environmental. Home: 20 Powder Mill Rd Concord MA 01742-4804 Office: Hale and Dorr LLP 60 State St Ste 22 Boston MA 02109-1800

**HAMILTON, JOHN RICHARD,** lawyer; b. El Dorado, Kans., Jan. 8, 1940; s. Silas H. and Ora B. (Barker) H.; m. Shirley A. Tekamp, June 16, 1960 (div. July 1976); children: Michele L., Brian J.; m. Louise Brock, Dec. 22, 1984. BS, Union U., 1962; JD, Washburn Law Sch., 1965. Bar: Kans. 1965, U.S. Dist. Ct. Kans. 1965, U.S. Ct. Appeals (10th cir.) 1969. Ptnr. Crane, Martin, Claussen, Hamilton & Forbes, Topeka, 1965-84; sole practice, Topeka, 1985-87, Hamilton, Gregg, Barker & Johnson, 1988—. Mem. Kans. Bar Assn., Topeka Bar Assn., ABA, Kans. Trial Lawyers Assn. (bd. dirs., v.p. 1982-83). Democrat. Club: Topeka Country. Federal civil litigation, State civil litigation, Condemnation. Home: 2334 SW Mayfair Pl Topeka KS 66611-2054

**HAMILTON, JOHN THOMAS, JR.,** lawyer; b. Delhi, N.Y., Apr. 17, 1951; s. John Thomas and Theresa Anastasia (L'Euyer) H.; m. Julia Ann Whitlow, Sept. 3, 1977; children: John Thomas III, Sara Baer. BS, Hamilton Coll., 1973; JD cum laude, Union U., Albany, N.Y., 1976. Bar: N.Y. 1977, U.S. Dist. Ct. (no., so., ea. and we. dists.) N.Y., U.S. Ct. Appeals (2d cir.). Law clerk Lynn & Lynn, PC, Albany, 1974-75; law clk. Solomon & Solomon, P.C., Albany, 1975-77; assoc. Solomon & Solomon, P.C., 1977, George S. Evans, N.Y.C., 1977-78, Frank E. Maher, Bklyn., 1978-80; pvt. practice, Delhi, 1980—; atty., counsel Sen. Chas. D. Cook, Albany, 1981-98; counsel N.Y.C. Watershed Negotiations, 1990-97; counsel local govt. com. N.Y. Senate, 1983-92, asst. agrl. com., 1981-82, asst. counsel to majority leader, 1999—. Mem. Assn. Retarded Children (life); v.p. Del. County Hist. Assoc., 1985-87, pres. 1988-96; chmn., treas. Cook for Senate, 1978-98; exec. bd. dirs. Otschodela coun. Boy Scouts Am., 1992—. Mem. ATLA, N.Y. State Bar Assn., N.Y. County Lawyers Assn., N.Y. State Trial Lawyers Assn., Delaware County Bar Assn. Republican. General civil litigation, Real property, Personal injury. Home and Office: 145 Main St Delhi NY 13753-1282

**HAMILTON, LAWRENCE JOSEPH,** lawyer; b. Louisville, Oct. 17, 1957; s. Charles Walter and Kathlen Rose Hamilton; m. Alicia Cummings, July 5, 1985; children: Drew, Chase, Parker, Graham. BA in Polit. Sci., U. Louisville, 1978; JD, Vanderbilt U., 1981. Lawyer Smith & Hulsey, Jacksonville, Fla., 1981-83, Gallagher, Baumer, Mikals, Bradford, Cannon and Walters P.A., Jacksonville, Fla., 1983-88, Holland & Knight LLP, Jacksonville, 1988—. Bd. dirs. Leadership Jacksonville, 1997—. Fellow ABA Found., Fla. Bar Found.; mem. ABA, Fla. Bar Assn. (bd. govs. 1993-95, pres. young lawyers divsn. 1994-95, exec. coun. trial lawyers sect. 1997—), Jacksonville Bar Assn. (pres. young lawyers sect. 1987-88). Avocations: travel, golf. General civil litigation, Consumer commercial. Office: Holland & Knight LLP 50 N Laura St Ste 3900 Jacksonville FL 32202-3622

**HAMILTON, MICHAEL ALAN,** lawyer; b. Quakertown, Pa., July 30, 1965; s. Theodore and Helen H.; m. Madeline Caprioli, June 21, 1997. BS, Pa. State U., 1986; JD, Dickinson U., 1993. Bar: Pa. 1993, N.J. 1993, U.S. Dist. Ct. N.J. 1993, U.S. Dist. Ct. (ea. dist.) Pa. 1993. Security investigator Mobil Oil, Farifax, Va., 1987-90; law clk. Rite Aid Corp., Camp Hill, Pa., 1991-93, Pa. State Atty. Gens. Office, Anti-Trust Divsn., Harrisburg, 1992; atty. Cozen & O'Connor, Phila., 1993—. Mem. ABA, Pa. Defense Inst., Defense Rsch. Inst. Insurance, General civil litigation. Office: Cozen & O'Connor 1900 Market St Philadelphia PA 19103-3527

**HAMILTON, PERRIN C.,** lawyer, state official; b. Phila., Oct. 15, 1921; m. Bette J. Shadle; children—Deborah, Maribeth, Perrin Jr. Student Dickinson Coll., 1943, LLB, 1948. Bar: D.C., PA. 1949. Spl. counsel U.S. Senate, 1953; sr. ptnr. Hepburn Willcox Hamilton & Putnam, Phila., 1980—; commr. Crime Victims Bd., Del. River Port Authority; bd. dirs. Valley Forge Mil. Acad., Freedoms Found. Bd. advisors Dickinson Coll., State of Pa. Cabinet Ofcl.; pres., bd. advisors Salvation Army. Lt. USNR, World War II. Decorated Order of Merit, Italy; recipient Freedoms Found. award, 1970. Mem. ABA, Pa. Bar Assn., Phila. Lawyers Club (past pres.), Union League Club (pres.), Merion Cricket Club. Episcopalian. General civil litigation, Constitutional, Probate. Home: 2 Booth Ln Apt 7 Haverford PA 19041-1400 Office: Hepburn Willcox Hamilton & Putnam 1100 One Penn Ctr Plz Philadelphia PA 19103

**HAMILTON, PHILLIP DOUGLAS,** lawyer; b. Pasadena, Calif., Oct. 16, 1954; s. Ivan and Annette O. (Brown) H.; m. Gerry Messner, Sept. 17, 1976 (div. Feb. 1984); m. Janet L. Hester, Apr. 22, 1984; children: Melissa, John, Mark Charles. BA, U. Pa., 1976; JD, Pepperdine U., 1979. Bar: Calif. 1979, U.S. Dist. Ct. (cen. dist.) Calif. 1980. Assoc., Offices of James J. DiCesare, Santa Ana, Calif., 1979-84; sole practice, Newport Beach, Calif., 1984—. Bd. dirs. Juvenile Diabetes Found., Orange County, 1988, pres., 1989, 90, 91. Recipient Am. Jurisprudence award, 1980. Mem. Assn. Trial Lawyers Am., Orange County Trial Lawyers Assn., Calif. Trial Lawyers Assn., Calif. Trial Lawyers Polit. Action Com., Orange County Bar Assn. Presbyterian. Personal injury. Office: 535 Anton Blvd Ste 1150 Costa Mesa CA 92626-1969

**HAMILTON, STEVEN G.,** lawyer; b. 1939. BS, Mont. State U., 1962; JD, UCLA, 1966. Pvt. practice, 1966-68; asst. gen. counsel Garrett Corp., L.A., 1968-80, v.p., gen. counsel, 1980-88; v.p., legal and gen. counsel Alaska Airlines, Inc., Seattle, 1988—. Office: Alaska Airlines PO Box 68900 Seattle WA 98168-0900

**HAMLAR, PORTIA YVONNE TRENHOLM,** lawyer, author; b. Montgomery, Ala.; d. Harper Councill Sr. and Portia Lee (Evans) Trenholm; 1 child, Eric Lafayette. AB, Ala. State U., Montgomery, 1951; MA, Mich. State U., 1953; JD, U. Detroit, 1972; postgrad., U. Mich. Bar: Mich. 1974, Ill. 1988. Atty. Chrysler Corp., Highland Park, Mich., 1973-80; asst. prof. law Widener U., Wilmington, Del., 1980-82; pvt. practice Detroit Metropolitan Area, 1982—; editor DEOC Pub. Co., Rochester, Mich., 1977-81; mem. Orgn. Resources Counselors, Washington, 1974-80; exch. prof. Nat. Urban League, 1976-79. Author: Defending the Employer in OSHA Contests, 1977-81; mem. U. Detroit Law Rev., 1970-73; editor: Mich. Environ. Law Case Digest, 1990—. Mem., v.p. bd. dirs. Rochester Symphony Orch., 1983-86. Mem. ABA (chair subcom. labor law sect. 1975-80, spkr.), Mich. Women's Econ. Club (speaker), Alpha Kappa Mu, Mu Phi Epsilon, Kappa Beta Pi. Avocation: classical piano. Labor, Environmental, Pension, profit-sharing, and employee benefits. Home and office: PO Box 2491 Southfield MI 48037-2491 also: 23605 Riverside Dr Southfield MI 48034-7305

**HAMLIN, JOHN WADSWORTH,** lawyer; b. Buffalo, Aug. 18, 1954; s. Clay Winston Jr. and Elizabeth (Murray) H. BA, Coll. Wooster (Ohio), 1976; MA, U. Conn., 1984, JD, 1988. Bar: Conn. 1989, N.Y. 1998. Law clk. to Hon. B. Avant Edenfield U.S. Dist. Ct. (so. dist.) Ga., Savannah, 1988-89; assoc. Wiggin & Dana, New Haven, Conn., 1989-91; assoc. Paul, Hastings, Janofsky & Walker LLP, Stamford, 1991-97, of counsel, 1997—. Mem. ABA, Conn. Bar Assn. (exec. com. labor and employment sect. 1999—, co-editor Labor and Employment Law Quar. 1999—), U. Conn. Law Sch. Alumni Assn. (bd. dirs. 1990—). Labor, Federal civil litigation. Office: Paul Hastings Janofsky & Walker LLP 1055 Washington Blvd Fl 10 Stamford CT 06901-2216

**HAMMEL, JOHN WINGATE,** lawyer; b. Indpls., Dec. 25, 1943; s. Walter Francis and Mary Vivian (Patterson) H.; m. Linda Ann Yarling, Dec. 22, 1972; children: William Wingate II, Kathryn Christine, Rebecca Ann. BS, Butler U., 1967; postgrad., So. Ill. U., 1967-68; JD, Ind. U., 1975. Bar: Ind. 1975, U.S. Dist. Ct. (so. dist.) Ind. 1975, U.S. Ct. Mil. Appeals 1978, U.S. Ct. Appeals (7th crct.) 1982. Assoc. Yarling, Winter, Tunnell & Robinson, Indpls., 1975-86; ptnr. Yarling & Robinson, Indpls., 1986—. Lt. col. Ind. Army N.G. Mem. ABA, Ind. Bar Assn., Indpls. Bar Assn., 7th Cir. Bar Assn. Republican. Insurance, Consumer commercial, Personal injury. Home: 5242 Rucker Cir Indianapolis IN 46250-2329 Office: Yarling & Robinson 151 N Delaware St Ste 1535 Indianapolis IN 46204-2539

**HAMMER, DAVID LINDLEY,** lawyer, author; b. Newton, Iowa, June 6, 1929; s. Neal paul and Agnes Marilyn (Reece) H.; m. Audrey Lowe, June 20, 1953; children: Julie, Lisa, David. BA, Grinnell Coll., 1951; JD, U. Iowa, 1956. Bar: Iowa 1956, U.S. Dist. Ct. (no. dist.) Iowa 1959, U.S. Dist. Ct. (so. dist.) Iowa 1969, U.S. Ct. Appeals (8th cir.) 1996, U.S. Supreme Ct. 1977. Ptnr. Hammer Simon & Jensen, Galena, Ill. and, Iowa; mem. grievance commn. Iowa Supreme Ct., 1973-85; mem. adv. rules com., 1986-92. Author: Poems from the Ledge, 1980, The Game is Afoot, 1983, For the Sake of the Game, 1986, The 22nd Man, 1989, To Play the Game, 1986, The Quest, 1993, My Dear Watson, 1994, The Before Breakfast Pipe, 1995, A Dangerous Game, 1997, The Vital Essence, 1999. Bd. dirs. Linwood Cemetery Assn., 1973—, pres., 1983-84; bd. dirs., past pres. Finley Hosp., hon. dir.; bd. dirs. Finley Found., 1988-95; past campaign chmn., past pres. United Way; past bd. dirs. Carnegie Stout Pub. Libr. With U.S. Army, 1951-53. Fellow Am. Coll. Trial Lawyers; mem. ABA, Young Lawyers Iowa (past pres.), Iowa Def. Counsel Assn. (pres. 1991-92, del. to Def. Rsch. Inst. 1992-93), Assn. Def. Trial Attys. (exec. coun. 1983-86, past chmn. Iowa chpt.), Iowa State Bar Assn. (past chmn. continuing legal edn. com.), Iowa Acad. Trial Lawyers, Dubuque County Bar Assn. (past pres.), Baker St. Irregulars. Republican. Congregationalist. General civil litigation, Insurance. Office: 700 Locust St Ste 190 Dubuque IA 52001-6824

**HAMMERLE, KURT GEORG,** lawyer; b. Rockford, Ill., May 29, 1965; s. Walter and Charlotte Josefa H. BSME, Va. Poly. Inst. and State U., 1988; JD, Coll. William and Mary, 1991. Bar: Va. 1991, U.S. Dist. Ct. (ea. dist.) Va. 1992, U.S. Ct. Appeals (4th cir.) 1991, U.S. Patent and Trade Office 1993, Ct. Appeals Fed. Cir. 1992. Assoc. Greene & Assocs., Mathews, Va., 1992-94; asst. commonwealth atty. Newport News (Va.) Commonwealth Atty., 1994-98; patent atty. NASA/Langley Rsch. Ctr., Hampton, Va., 1998—; advisor Law Explorer Post, Newport News, Va., 1998. Mem. ABA, Va. Trial Lawyers Assn., Assn. Trial Lawyers Am., James Square Home Owner's Assn. (pres. 1996-99). Roman Catholic. Avocations: tennis, weight-lifting, golf, skiing, rollerblading. Intellectual property, Patent. Office: NASA/Langley Rsch Ctr Mail Stop 212 3 Langley Blvd Stop 212 Hampton VA 23681-0001

**HAMMERLY, MARY LEVERENZ,** lawyer; b. Milw., Apr. 12, 1952; d. Erwin F. and Anna M. (Brehm) Leverenz; children: Aja, Elyse. BM, U. Wis., 1974; JD, U. Puget Sound, 1978. Bar: Wash. 1979, U.S. Dist. Ct. (we. dist.) Wash. 1979, U.S. Ct. of Appeals (9th cir.) 1980. Law clk. to assoc. Johnson & East (now C. Scott East, Inc.), Bellevue, Wash., 1978-82; pvt. practice Redmond, Wash., 1982-83; assoc. Burns & Meyer, Bellevue, 1983-85; ptnr. Burns & Hammerly, Bellevue, 1985-97; pvt. practice Issaquah, Wash., 1997—. Mem. Wash. State Bar Assn. (family law sect.), Seattle King County Bar Assn. (family law sect.). Avocations: downhill skiing, hiking, crafts, wine collecting. Family and matrimonial, Probate, Estate planning. Office: 22525 SE 64th Pl Ste 140 Issaquah WA 98027-8971

**HAMMERMAN, EDWARD SCOTT,** lawyer; b. Washington, Mar. 21, 1969; s. Murray Frederic and Marilyn (Hochberg) H. BA in English, Emory U., 1991; JD, Cath. U. Am., 1994. Bar: Pa. 1994, Fla. 1998, D.C. 1998. Staff atty. Venable Baetjer Howard & Civiletti, Washington, 1994-96; assoc. Leibowitz & Assocs., P.A., Miami, Fla., 1996-98, Collier Shannon Rill & Scott, Washington, 1998—. Editor (newsletter) Broadcasting and the Law, 1996-98. Bd. dirs. Am. Jewish Com., Miami, 1996-98. Mem. Fed. Comms. Bar Assn. (founder, co-chair 1992-94, law studies com.), Assn. Emory Alumni Assn. (exec. com. 1998—), Masons. Democrat. Jewish. Communications, Administrative and regulatory. Office: Collier Shannon Rill & Scott PLLC 3050 K St NW Ste 400 Washington DC 20007-5100

**HAMMERMAN, STEPHEN LAWRENCE,** lawyer, financial services company executive; b. Bklyn., Apr. 18, 1938; s. David S. and Hannah (Chaimowitz) H.; m. Eleanor Draizen; children—Ira, Charles, Michael, Caryn. B.S. in Econs., U. Pa., 1959; LL.B., NYU, 1962. Bar: N.Y. 1962. Assoc. Dewey and Ballantine, N.Y.C., 1962-64; asst. U.S. Attys. U.S. Attys. Office, N.Y.C., 1964-68; assoc. Paul and Weiss, N.Y.C., 1968-69; sr. v.p., gen. counsel White, Weld & Co., N.Y.C., 1969-78; mng. dir., gen. counsel Merrill Lynch-White Weld Capital Markets, N.Y.C., 1978-79; N.Y. regional adminstr. SEC, N.Y.C., 1979-81; asst. to pres., v.p., gen. counsel Merrill, Lynch, Pierce, Fenner & Smith Inc., N.Y.C., 1981-84; sr. v.p., gen. counsel Merrill Lynch & Co. Inc., N.Y.C., 1984-85, exec. v.p., officer, gen. counsel, 1985-92, vice chmn., gen. counsel, 1992—; dir. Merrill Lynch & Co., N.Y.C., 1985—. Author: Securities Law Techniques, 1985. Mem. N.Y. Stock Exchange (legal adv. com.), Securities Industry Assn. (fed. regulation com), N.Y.C. Bar Assn. (investment com. chmn.). Home: 1495 Bay Blvd Atlantic Beach NY 11509-1648 Office: Merrill Lynch & Co Inc World Fin Ctr 250 Vesey St Fl 4 New York NY 10080-0002*

**HAMMERSCHMIDT, BRUCE C.,** lawyer; b. South Bend, Ind., Apr. 26, 1919; s. Louis Martin Hammerschmidt and Emma Katherine Borgerdino; m. Mary Ellen Hammerschmidt, Apr. 24, 1943 (dec. Jan. 1974) 1 child, Kathryn Fuller; m. Carolyn D. Hammerschmidt, Jan. 26, 1975. Bar: ind. 1948, U.S. Dist. Ct. (no. dist.) Ind. 1949, U.S. Ct. Appeals (7th cir.). Ptnr. Hammerschmidt Amaral Jonas, South Bend. Pres., bd. dirs. Family Svc. Inc. of South Bend,1959-65, St. Joseph Coun. Cmty. Svcs., 1960-64; v.p., bd. dirs. United Way, 1964-67; pres., trustee Meml. Hosp., South Bend, 1958-86; emeritus trustee Elmhurst (Ill.) Coll., 1960-89. Lt. USN, 1944-45. Mem. ABA, Ind. State Bar Assn. (bd. mgrs. 1967-70), St. Joseph County Bar Assn. (pres. 1957-58, bd. govs. 1957-60). Republican. Presbyterian. Avocations: skiing, tennis, golf. Estate planning, General practice, Health. Home: 51350 Windsor Manor Ct Granger IN 46530-8307 Office: Hammerschmidt Amaral & Jonas 224 W Jefferson Blvd South Bend IN 46601-1827

**HAMMOND, FRANK JEFFERSON, III,** lawyer; b. Moss Point, Miss., Sept. 18, 1953; s. Frank Jefferson Jr. and Jane (Laird) H.; m. Gale Ray, May 30, 1975; children—Katharine Blakeney, Benjamin Laird. B.B.A., U. Miss., 1974, J.D., 1976; LL.M., U. Fla., 1978. Bar: Miss. 1977, U.S. Dist. Ct. (no. dist.) Miss. 1977, U.S. Dist. Ct. (so. dist.) Miss. 1977, U.S. Ct. Appeals (5th cir.) 1977, U.S. Tax Ct. 1978, U.S. Ct. Appeals (11th cir.) 1980, U.S. Supreme Ct. 1989. Mem. Corlew, Krebs & Hammond, P.A., Pascagoula, Miss., 1978-84; mem. Watkins & Eager, PLLC, Jackson, Miss., 1984—; adj. prof. U. Ala. Sch. Law, Mobile, 1983; adj. faculty U. So. Miss., Gautier, 1983-84; bd. dirs. Merchants and Marine Bank, Pascagoula, Miss. Trustee Dantzler Meml. Meth. Ch., Moss Point, Miss., 1981-84. U. Fla. Grad. Council fellow, 1977; Richard B. Stephens scholar, 1978. Mem. ABA, Miss. State Bar (chmn. sect. estates and trusts 1988-89), Phi Kappa Phi, Beta Alpha Psi, Beta Gamma Sigma, Omicron Delta Kappa. Banking, Real property, Taxation, general. Home: PO Box 650 Jackson MS 39205-0650 Office: Watkins & Eager PLLC 400 E Capitol St Ste 300 Jackson MS 39201-2610

**HAMMOND, GLENN BARRY, SR.,** lawyer, electrical engineer; b. Roanoke, Va., Sept. 3, 1947; s. Howard Reichard and Billie (Cromer) H.; m. Vickie McComb, Dec. 29, 1973 (div.); 1 child, Glenn Barry II. BA, Va. Mil. Inst., 1969; MBA, So. Ill. U., 1974; JD, U. Richmond, 1978; BS elec. engring., Nova Coll., 1995. Bar: Va. 1979, U.S. Dist. Ct. (we. dist.) Va. 1979, U.S. Ct. Appeals (4th cir.) 1981, U.S. Ct. Mil. Appeals 1989, Air Force Ct. Mil. Rev. 1989, U.S. Supreme Ct., 1992. Assoc. Wilson, Hawthorne & Vogel, Roanoke, 1978-79; pvt. practice Roanoke, 1979-80, 86—; atty., advisor to chief adminstrv. law judge Social Security Adminstrn., HHS, Roanoke, 1980-86; ptnr. Wooten & Hart P.C., 1995-98; pres. R.F. Cons., Inc., Roanoke, Va., 1998—; pres. LCH Broadcasting Group, Inc. Roanoke, also bd. dirs. Editor: Psychiatry in Military Law, 1988. Sr. vice comdr. Mil. Order World Wars, Roanoke, 1981. Col. JAGC, USAF, 1969-75, Res. 1975—. Mem. Air Command Assn. (life), DAV (life), VFW (life), AFA (life), Nat. Mil. Intelligence Assn. (life), Armed Forces Comms. Electronics Assn., Nat. Orgn. Social Security Claimants Reps., Masons. Pension, profit-sharing, and employee benefits.

**HAMMOND, HERBERT J.,** lawyer; b. Santa Fe, May 19, 1951. BS magna cum laude, U. N.Mex., 1973; JD, NYU, 1976. Bar: Tex. 1977, U.S. Patent and Trademark Office 1977, U.S. Dist. Ct. (no., so., we. and ea. dists.) Tex. 1977, U.S. Dist. Ct. Nebr. 1985, U.S. Dist. Ct. Wis. (ea. dist.) 1987, U.S. Ct. Appeals (5th and 11th cirs.) Tex. 1981, U.S. Ct. Appeals (fed. cir.) Tex. 1982, U.S. Tax Ct. 1983, U.S. Claims Ct. 1987. Shareholder Thompson & Knight, Dallas. Contbr. to law jours. Mem. State Bar Tex. (vice chmn. com. on computerization of the profession 1989-92, chair computer sect. 1994-95, newsletter editor computer sect.), Am. Intellectual Property Law Assn., Dallas Bar Assn. (chair intellectual property sect. 1998), Phi Beta Kappa, Phi Kappa Phi, Kappa Mu Epsilon. Intellectual property, Computer, Entertainment. Office: Thompson & Knight 1700 Pacific Ave Ste 3300 Dallas TX 75201-4693

**HAMMOND, JANE LAURA,** retired law librarian, lawyer; b. nr. Nashua, Iowa; d. Frank D. and Pauline Hammond. BA, U. Dubuque, 1950; MS, Columbia U., 1952; JD, Villanova U., 1965, LHD, 1993. Bar: Pa. 1965. Cataloguer Harvard Law Libr., 1952-54; asst. libr. Sch. Law Villanova (Pa.) U., 1954-62; libr. Sch. Law, Villanova (Pa.) U., 1962-76; prof. law Sch. Law Villanova (Pa.) U., 1965-76; law libr., prof. law Cornell U., Ithaca, N.Y., 1976-93; adj. prof. Drexel U., 1971-74; mem. depository libr. coun. to pub. printer U.S. Govt. Printing Office, 1975-78; cons. Nat. Law Libr., Monrovia, Liberia, 1989. Fellow ALA; mem. ABA (coun. sect. legal edn. 1984-90, mem. com. on accreditation 1982-87, mem. com. on stds. rev. 1987-95), PEO, Coun. Nat. Libr. Assn. (sec.-treas. 1971-72, chmn. 1979-80), Am. Assn. Law Librs. (sec. 1965-70, pres. 1975-76). Episcopalian. Office: Cornell U Sch Law Myron Taylor Hall Ithaca NY 14853

**HAMMOND, MARGARET,** lawyer; b. Winterville, N.C., June 2, 1949; d. Hoyt and Mary Hammond. BS, N.C. A&T State U., 1971; MA, Atlanta U., 1983; JD, Loyola U., New Orleans, 1984. Bar: La. 1984, U.S. Dist. Ct. (ea. dist.) La. 1987. Instr. polit. sci. N.C. A&T State U., Greensboro, 1973-76, So. U., New Orleans, 1979-82; edn. cons. Edn. Services and Programs Inc., New Orleans, 1982-84, Loyola U., New Orleans, 1982-84; asst. dist. atty. Parish of Orleans, New Orleans, 1984-86; staff atty. Orleans Indigent Defender Program, New Orleans, 1986-92; pvt. practice New Orleans, 1986—. Ford Found. fellow, 1971-73, Earl Warren Found. fellow, 1981-84. Mem. La. Bar Assn., New Orleans Bar Assn., Sorority Inc., Alpha Kappa Alpha. Democrat. Avocations: travel, music. General civil litigation, Criminal, Personal injury. Office: 200 Commercial Sq Slidell LA 70461-5445

**HAMMOND, PATRICIA FLOOD,** lawyer; b. Racine, Wis., Aug. 29, 1948; d. Francis James Flood and Shirley (Osterholt) Erickson; children: Bradley D. Mortensen, Erin N. Mortensen. Student, Wis. State U., Oshkosh, 1966-69, Alverno Coll., West Allis, 1973-74. Bar: Va.1985, U.S. Dist. Ct. (ea. dist.) Va. 1988. Br. dir. Am. Heart Assn., Manassas, Va., 1977-85; attorney Manassas, Va., 1985—; ptnr. Smith, Hudson, Hammond and Alston, Manassas, Va.; mem. VBA-VSB joint com. on alternative dispute resolution. Contbr. articles to newspapers. Mem. ABA, ACLU, ATLA, Nat. Abortion and Reproductive Rights Action League, Va. State Bar Assn., Prince William County Bar Assn. (treas., pres. 1991). Democrat. Episcopalian. Avocation: victorian. Family and matrimonial, Personal injury. Home: 9403 Grant Ave Manassas VA 20110-5509

**HAMMOND, PEIRCE ALDRIDGE, II,** lawyer; b. New Orleans, Apr. 5, 1962; s. John Phelps and Cynthia (Rainold) H. BA, U. Ala., 1984; JD, Tulane U., 1987. Bar: La. 1987, New Orleans, U.S. Dist. Ct. (ea. dist.) La. 1990, U.S. Dist. Ct. (mid. dist.) La. 1990, U.S. Dist. Ct. (we. dist.) La. 1990, U.S. Ct. Appeals (5th cir.) 1990. Asst. DA Orleans Parish DA, New Orleans, 1987-90; assoc. Hebert, Mouledoux & Bland, New Orleans, 1990-93, Cerniglia Law Firm, New Orleans, 1993-94; assoc. Woodley, Williams Fenet et al, New Orleans, 1994-95, of counsel, 1995-97; pvt. practice New Orleans, 1995-98; ptnr. Baus, Hammond & Daly, New Orleans, 1998—.

Mem. La. Assn. Def. Counsel, La. Claims Assn., New Orleans Claims Assn., Maritime Law Assn., Southeastern Admiralty Law Inst. Insurance, General civil litigation, General practice. Office: Baus Hammond & Daly 200 Carondelet St Ste 1600 New Orleans LA 70130-2925

**HAMMOND, STEPHEN VAN,** lawyer; b. Decatur, Ala., Dec. 13, 1948; s. Robert E. and Dorothy O. (Stephenson) H.; m. Shirley Eaken, Aug. 22, 1970; 1 child, Savanne. BA, U. Ala., 1971, JD, 1974. Bar: Ala. 1974, U.S. Dist. Ct. (no. dist.) Ala. 1979, U.S. Ct. Appeals (11th cir.) 1986. Atty. Exxon Co. USA, New Orleans, 1974-79; officer Chenault, Hammond & Hall, P.C., Decatur, 1979—. Pres. Hospice of Morgan County, Decatur, 1988, 96, ARC Morgan County chpt., Decatur, 1985; bd. dirs. Ala. Hospice Orgn. Mem. ABA, Ala. Bar Assn., Morgan County Bar Assn. (pres 1994), Decatur C. of C. (pres. 1989). Episcopalian. Avocation: golf. Insurance, General civil litigation, Oil, gas, and mineral. Office: Chenault Hammond & Hall PC 117 2d Ave NE PO Box 1906 Decatur AL 35602-1906

**HAMNER, LANCE DALTON,** prosecutor; b. Fukuoka, Japan, Sept. 18, 1955; parents Am. citizens; s. Louie D. and Mary Louise (Sloan) H.; m. Karla Jean Cleverly, Sept. 22, 1980; children: Lance Dalton Jr., Nicholas James, Louie Alexander, Samuel Sean, Victoria Jean. BS summa cum laude, Weber State Coll., 1984; JD magna cum laude, Ind. U., 1987. Bar: Ind., U.S. Dist. Ct. (no., so. dist.) Ind. 1988. Atty. Barnes & Thornburg, Indpls., 1988-89; dep. prosecuting atty. Marion County Prosecutor's Office, Indpls., 1989-90; pros. atty. Johnson County, Franklin, Ind., 1990—; legal corr. WGGR Radio News, Indpls., 1995; adj. prof. law Sch. Law Ind. U., In dpls., 1995-96, Bloomington, 1996—; frequent spkr. on legal topics including search and seizure and interrogation law; lectr. Ind. Continuing Legal Edn. Forum, Indpls., 1992; faculty mem. Newly-Elected Pros. Sch., Ind. Pros. Attys. Coun., 1999. Editor Ind. Law Jour., 1987. Asst. scoutmaster Boy Scouts Am., Franklin, Ind., 1995—. Mem. Nat. Dist. Attys. Assn., Ind. Prosecuting Atty.'s Coun., Nat. Eagle Scout Assn., Order of the Coif. Republican. Mormon. Avocations: family, fitness, writing. Office: Prosecutor's Office Courthouse Annex N 18 W Jefferson St Franklin IN 46131-2353

**HAMPAR, ARTHUR EUGENE,** lawyer; b. San Francisco, June 2, 1955; s. Armen and Vivian (Arpimee) H. AB in Philosophy, U. Calif., Berkeley, 1978; JD, U. Santa Clara, 1982. Bar: Calif. 1983. Atty. Boston, Petrivic & Cohen, Bakersfield, Calif., 1984-86; atty. Tulare County Pub. Defender's Office, Visalia, Calif., 1987—. Mem. Congressman Calvin Dooley's Multicultural Commn., 1999. Mem. Tulare County Bar Assn., Tulare County Dep. Attys. Assn. (pres. 1989), Tulare-Kings Hispanic C. of C. Democrat. Roman Catholic/Armenian Orthodox. Office: Tulare County Pub Defenders Office Civic Ctr Rm G 35 Tulare County Courthouse Visalia CA 93291

**HAMPSON, ROBERT GEORGE,** lawyer; b. Elizabeth, N.J., Jan. 28, 1943; s. George Lyle and Barbara (Monkauskas) H.; m. Tamara Davis, Feb. 17, 1979; children: Christopher, Elizabeth, Katharine. BA, Rutgers U., 1968; JD, Seton Hall U., 1971. Bar: N.J. 1972, U.S. Dist. Ct. N.J. 1972. Assoc. Richard F. Plechner, Metuchen, N.J., 1971-73, Burton & Quackenboss, South River, N.J., 1973-74, Robert T. Quackenboss, East Brunswick, N.J., 1974-75; sr. ptnr. Hampson and Millet, Somerset, N.J., 1975—; mcpl. prosecutor Helmetta, N.J., 1972-73, Spotswood, N.J., 1972-73, Madison Twp., N.J., 1972-73, Somerville, N.J., 1975-82. Author: (with others) Industrial Revenue Bond Financing: a supplement, 1968. Served to 1st lt. USAF, 1968-72. Mem. Am. Trial Lawyers Assn., Def. Rsch. Inst., N.J. Bar Assn., N.J. Def. Assn., Middlesex County Trial Lawyers Assn. (past officer), Somerset County Bar Assn. (past trustee), Lawyers Encouraging Govt. and Law (sponsor). Roman Catholic. Avocations: tennis, fishing, golf, skin diving, hi-fi, woodworking. Federal civil litigation, State civil litigation, Environmental.

**HAMPTON, CHARLES EDWIN,** lawyer, mathematician, computer programmer; b. Oct. 22, 1948; s. Roy Mizell and Hazel Lucretia (Cooper) H.; m. Cynthia Torrance, Sept. 14, 1968; children: Charles Edwin Jr., Adam Ethan. Student, Baylor U., 1967, Rice U., 1967-68; BA with highest honors, U. Tex., 1971, JD with high honors, 1977; MA, U. Calif., Berkeley, 1972, Candidate in Philosophy in Math., 1975. Bar: Tex. 1977, U.S. dist. Ct. (we. dist.) Tex. 1979, U.S. Dist. Ct. (no. dist.) Tex. 1980, U.S. Ct. Appeals (5th cir.) 1986. Rsch. asst. U. Calif., 1974-75; briefing atty. to justice Tex. Supreme Ct., 1977-78; assoc. Law Offices Don L. Baker, P.C., Austin, 1981-96; legal counsel Office Ct. Adminstrn., Tex. Jud. Coun., Austin, 1981; staff atty. Supreme Ct. Tex., Austin, 1981-96; assoc. Rinehart & Nugent, 1984-87; mem. vis. com. dept. math. U. Tex. at Austin, 1987-95. NSF fellow, 1971-74; Moody Found. scholar. Mem. ABA, State Bar Tex., Travis County Bar Assn., Chancellors, Order of Coif, Lions, Phi Kappa Phi, Phi Delta Phi. General civil litigation, Bankruptcy, Trademark and copyright. Office: Gammage Hampton Marcin & Ray PO Box 164191 611 W 15th St Ste 200 Austin TX 78701-1513

**HAMPTON, WILLIAM PECK,** lawyer; b. Pontiac, Mich., Jan. 24, 1938. B, Mich. State U., 1960; JD, Wayne State U., 1963. Bar: Mich. 1964. Rep. Mich. Ho. of Reps., 1964-70; cir. judge, presiding judge Oakland County Cir. Ct., 1970-77; sr. ptnr. Secrest, Wardle, Lynch, Hampton, Truex & Morley, Farmington Hills, Mich., 1977—; spl. counsel County of Oakland, Oakland County Drain Commr., Silverdome Stadium Authority; twp. atty. Charter Twp. of Bloomfield, Charter Twp. of West Bloomfield; atty. City of Auburn Hills, City of Bloomfield Hills. Chmn. Mich. State Officers' Compensation Commn., 1994-98; co-chmn. State Bar Com. on Judicial Qualifications, 1990-96. Fellow Am. Coll. Trial Lawyers; mem. State Bar of Mich., Oakland County Bar Assn., Mich. Judges Assn., Mich. Soc. Planning Ofcls. Republican. E-mail: hilld@kohlsecrest.com. General civil litigation, Family and matrimonial, Land use and zoning (including planning). Office: Secrest Wardle Lynch Hampton Truex & Morley 30903 Northwestern Hwy Farmington Hills MI 48334-2556

**HANAS, STEPHEN MICHAEL,** lawyer; b. Hammond, Ind., June 1, 1954; s. Eugene Edward and Laverne Theresa (Carson) H.; m. Carol J. Wedding, Oct. 16, 1976; 1 child, Wesley Preston. BS in Bus Adminstrn., St. Joseph's Coll., 1976; JD, John Marshall Law Sch., 1983. Bar: Ill. 1983, Tex. 1986, U.S. Dist. Ct (no. dist.) Ill., 1983, U.S. Dist. Ct. (so. dist.) Tex. 1987; U.S. Supreme Ct. 1998. Fin. analyst Dun & Bradstreet, Chgo., 1976-78; supr. adminstrn. svcs. E.J. Brach & Sons, Chgo., 1978-79; contracts mgr. Clow Corp., Oakbrook, Ill., 1979-83, corp. counsel, 1983-86; pvt. practice Oak Brook, Ill., 1985-86; managing ptnr. Brooks, Hyatt & Willis, Houston, 1986-89; asst. gen. counsel legal divsn. FDIC, Washington, 1989—; chmn. adminstrv. coun. United Meth., Fairfax Station, 1993—. Trustee archtl. bd. Homeowners Assn., Fairfax Station, Va., 1991—. Mem. ABA (vice chmn. real property 1995—), Ill. State Bar Assn., Water Equipment Mfrs. Assn. (chmn. 1984-85). Republican. Methodist. Contracts commercial, Real property, Banking. Home: 9005 Weatherly Way Lorton VA 22079-3236 Office: FDIC Legal Divsn 550 17th St NW Rm 5038 Washington DC 20429-0001

**HANCHURUCK, STEPHEN PAUL,** lawyer; b. New Haven, Dec. 23, 1955; s. Stephen Adam and Kathleen (Taragowski) H.; m. Laurie Jane Schanely, July 14, 1984; children: Katie Miriam, Yimothy Russell, Timothy Russell, Molly Jeanette. BA, Ricker Coll., 1977; MA, NYU, 1978; JD, Ohio No. U., 1982. Bar: Conn. 1982. Pvt. practice Branford, Conn., 1983—. Mem. ABA, Conn. Bar Assn., New Haven County Bar Assn., New Haven County Young Lawyers' Bar Assn., Jaycees (local pres. 1983—, Jaycee of Yr. award 1984, 85), KC. Democrat. Roman Catholic. Avocations: sports, politics. General practice, Juvenile, Real property. Office: 5 Summit Pl Branford CT 06405-4104

**HANCOCK, ALTON GUY,** lawyer; b. Brunswick County, Va., Oct. 12, 1932; divorced; children: Julie L., Alex G. AA, Bluefield Coll., 1959; JD, U. Richmond, 1965. Bar: Va. 1965, D.C. 1965. Claims rep. State Farm Ins. Co., Falls Church, Va., 1960-67; claim supt. State Farm Ins. Co., Wheaton, Md., 1967-68; def. counsel Ball, McCarthy, Ball & Creigh, Arlington, Va., 1968-69; sr. asst. county atty. County Fairfax, Va., 1968-73; ptnr. Hancock, Brown & Parks, Fairfax, 1972-75; lawyer Dept. Interior, Washington, 1975-80; ptnr. Bowles & Hancock, P.C., Fairfax and Manassas, Va., 1980-88; pvt. practice Fairfax and Manassas, Va., 1988—. Mem. Va. State Bar, Va. Trial Lawyer's Assn., Prince William Couty Bar Assn. Personal injury, Criminal, General civil litigation. Address: 9253 Church St Manassas VA 20110-5542

**HANCOCK, HARRIET DANIELS,** lawyer; b. Columbia, S.C., Sept. 25, 1936; d. Harry Adam and Elizabeth (McCabe) D.; widowed; children: Karen H. Klocko, Jennifer, Gregory. BA in Sociology, U. S.C., Columbia, 1984, JD, 1988. Bar: S.C. 1989, U.S. Dist. Ct. S.C. 1990, U.S. Ct. Appeals (4th cir.) 1992. Law clerk Richland County Pub. Defender, Columbia, 1987-88; assoc. Gregory & Young Law Firm, Columbia, 1988-89, Michael J. Thompson, Esq., P.C., Columbia, 1990—. Adv. Nat. AIDS Network, Washington, 1990—; chair Parents & Friends Lesbians & Gays, 1982—; vol. & bd. chair. Palmetto AIDS Life Support Svcs. S.C., 1985—. Named Outstanding Vol., Nat. AIDS Network, 1987, Outstanding Pub. Citizen, Nat. Assn. So. Workers (S.C. chpt.), 1988, Pro-Bono Lawyer of Yr., S.C. Bar Assn., 1991; recipient president's scholarship Univ. S.C., 1983-84. Mem. ABA, S.C. Bar Assn. (pro-bono program), Phi Beta Kappa. Democrat. Civil rights, Family and matrimonial, General practice. Home: 493 Hickory Hill Dr Columbia SC 29210-4659 Office: Michael J Thompson Esq PC PO Box 1838 Columbia SC 29202-1838

**HANCOCK, JAMES HUGHES,** federal judge; b. 1931. B.S., U. Ala., 1953, LL.B., 1957. Bar: Ala. Ptnr. firm Balch, Bingham, Baker, Hawthorne, Ward & Williams, Birmingham, Ala., 1957-73; judge U.S. Dist. Ct. (no. dist.) Ala., Birmingham, 1973—; now sr. judge. Mem. Ala. Bar Assn. Office: US Dist Ct 681 US Courthouse 1729 5th Ave N Birmingham AL 35203-2000*

**HANCOCK, JONATHAN CROMWELL,** lawyer; b. Paducah, Ky., Apr. 19, 1971; s. William Rowland and Susan Cromwell Hancock. BS, Millsaps Coll., 1993; JD, U. Miss., Oxford, 1996. Bar: Tenn. 1996, U.S. Dist. Ct. Ark. 1998. Law clk. Cir. Ct. Judge John Daughaday, Mayfield, Ky., summer 1994; assoc. McKnight, Hudson, Lewis, Ford & Harrison, Memphis, 1996-97, Glankler Brown PLLC, Memphis, 1998—. Co-editor: Bur. of Nat. Affairs Employment Discrimination Law Chapter 42 Attorneys Fees, 1997. Republican. Methodist. Labor, Federal civil litigation, General civil litigation. Office: Glankler Brown PLLC 1700 One Commerce Sq Memphis TN 38103

**HANCOCK, MARY JANE,** legal assistant; b. Houston, Feb. 16, 1965; d. Lawrence Bartlett and Mary Jane (Muntz) H. BS in Comm., U. Tex., Austin, 1987; MA in Philosophy, U. Houston, 1992. Health underwriter Am. Nat. Ins. Co., Galveston, Tex., 1990-93; legal asst. St. Paul Ins. Co., Houston, 1995—; student. Home: 1416 Sul Ross St Houston TX 77006-4830

**HANCOCK, S. LEE,** lawyer; b. Knoxville, Tenn., Aug. 11, 1955; s. Melton Donald and Alma Helen (McDaniel) H.; m. Kathleen Ann Koll, July 26, 1986. BS summa cum laude, Southwest Mo. State U., 1975; JD cum laude, So. Meth. U., 1979. Bar: Mo. 1979, U.S. Dist. Ct. (we. dist.) Mo. 1979, U.S. Tax Ct. 1982, U.S. Ct. Claims Calif. 1983, Calif. 1988, U.S. Supreme Ct., 1992; CPA, Mo. Assoc. Blackwell, Sanders, Matheny, Weary & Lombardi, Kansas City, Mo., 1979-83, ptnr., 1984-88; ptnr. Allen, Matkins, Leck, Gamble & Mallory, Newport Beach, Calif., 1988-98, of counsel, 1999—; CEO G02 Systems, Inc., Newport Beach, Calif., 1998—; pres., CEO Go2 Systems, Inc. Bd. dirs. U. Calif./Orange County Venture Forum, 1988-95, Orange County Cmty. Found., 1991—, sec. 1994-95, pres. 1995-97. Mem. ABA, Young Execs. Am. (bd. dirs. Orange County chpt. 1992-96, pres. 1994-95), Calif. Bar Assn., Mo. Bar Assn., Orange County Bar Assn., Lawyers Assn. Kansas City (pres. young lawyers sect. 1986-87, bd. dirs. 1986-87), Order of coif, Mensa. Republican. Avocations: flying, sailing, skiing, photography. General corporate, Securities, Contracts commercial. Home: 4 Hampshire Ct Newport Beach CA 92660-4933 Office: G02 Systems, Inc. 18400 Von Karman Fl 4 Newport Beach CA 92715

**HANCOCK, STEWART F., JR.,** law educator, judge; b. Syracuse, N.Y., Feb. 2, 1923; s. Stewart F. and Marion (McLennan) H. BS, U.S. Naval Acad., 1945; LLB, Cornell U., 1950; LLD (hon.), Syracuse U., 1993, Le Moyne Coll., 1999. Corp. counsel, chief legal officer City of Syracuse, 1961-63; justice 5th judicial dist. N.Y. Supreme Ct., 1971-77, assoc. justice appellate divsn. 4th judicial dept., 1977-86; assoc. judge N.Y. Ct. Appeals, Albany, 1986-93; disting. vis. prof. law, jurist in residence Syracuse U., 1994—; counsel Hancock & Estabrook, Syracuse, 1994—; mem. N.Y. State Com. on Profession and the Cts., 1994—. Rep. chmn. Onondaga County, 1964-66; Rep. candidate for Congress, 1966; former mem. Onondaga County Met. Water Bd.; mem. Syracuse Bd. Edn., ARC, Dunbar Ctr., Pebble Hill Sch., Crouse-Irving Meml. Hosp., Syracuse Symphony; mem. First Presbyn. Ch., Cazenovia. Line officer USN, 1945-47, lt. (s.g.) USNR, 1950-51. Fellow Am. Bar Found., New York State Bar Found.; mem. ABA, N.Y. State Bar Assn., Onondaga County Bar Assn. Office: Hancock & Estabrook 1500 Mony Tower 1 PO Box 4976 # 1 Syracuse NY 13221-4976

**HAND, BENNY CHARLES, JR.,** lawyer, judge; b. Valley, Ala., Sept. 12, 1964; s. Benny Charles Sr. and Nelda Lee (Knight) H.; m. Martha Lynne Reynolds, May 29, 1988; 1 child, Hannah Elisabeth. BS in Bus. Mgmt., Auburn U., 1987; JD, Cumberland Sch. Law, 1990. Bar: Ga. 1990, Ala. 1990, U.S. Dist. Ct. (mid. dist.) 1990. Account mgr. Shamrock Rentables, Opelika, Ala., 1984-85; owner, pres. Suburban Pro, Opelika, 1985-87; pres. Premier Car Care, Opelika, 1991-94; pvt. practice Opelika, 1990—; judge Wedowee (Ala.) Mcpl., 1995—; city atty. City of Uniontown, Ala., 1995—; vice chmn. bd. Beacon Coll., Columbus, Ga., 1995—. Bd. dirs. East Ala. Mental Health Human Rights, Opelika, 1994—; deacon Believers Bapt. Ch., Auburn, 1995—; Rep. nominee U.S. Ho. of Reps., 1994; mem. Lee County Rep. Club. Recipient Rutherford Inst. for Outstanding Svc., 1994. Personal injury, Sports, General corporate. Office: 2006 Executive Park Dr Opelika AL 36801-6040

**HAND, BRUCE GEORGE,** lawyer; b. Oak Park, Ill., Apr. 11, 1942; s. Robert David and Dorothy Marie (Riedel) H.; m. Carolyn Jeanne Coleman, July 9, 1966; children: Keith John, Tracey Ellen, Katherine Anne. BA in Liberal Arts & Scis., U. Ill., 1964; JD, U. Oreg., 1969. Bar: Wash. 1969, U.S. Dist. Ct. (we. dist.) Wash. 1970. Assoc. Brumbach & Lamb, Seattle, 1969-74; pvt. practice Bellevue, Wash., 1974—. Trustee St. Thomas Sch., Medina, Wash., 1975-85, pres., 1985; trustee, pres. Hamlin Robinson Sch., Seattle, 1986-87. 1st lt. U.S. Army, 1964-66. Mem. Washington State Bar Assn., King County Bar Assn., East King County Bar Assn., Estate Planning Coun. Seattle. Republican. Episcopalian. Avocations: securities investment, reading. Family and matrimonial, Estate planning, Probate. Home: 2639 82nd Ave NE Medina WA 98039-1507 Office: Ste 301 4122 Factoria Blvd SE Bellevue WA 98006-5259

**HAND, GARY S.,** lawyer; b. Stone Harbor, N.J., July 16, 1967; s. David Walter and Edna V. (Duryea) H. BA, Oglethorpe U., 1989; JD, Ga. State U., 1992. Bar: Ga., Ill. Atty. Hand & Jones P.C., Atlanta, 1994-97, Altheimer & Gray, Chgo., 1997—. Mem. ABA, Am. Bankruptcy Inst. Republican. Episcopalean. Bankruptcy, Finance, General corporate. Office: Altheimer & Gray 10 S Wacker Dr Ste 4000 Chicago IL 60606-7407

**HAND, JAMES STANLEY,** lawyer; b. Mt. Kisco, N.Y., Mar. 14, 1949; m. Gail Stewart; children: Jordan, Alison. BA, UCLA, 1971; JD, U. N.D., 1980. Bar: N.D. 1980, U.S. Dist. Ct. N.D. 1980, U.S. Ct. Appeals (8th cir.) 1983. Assoc. Anderson and Assocs., Grand Forks, N.D., 1980-82; pvt. practice law Grand Forks, 1982-84; ptnr. Hand & Triplett, Grand Forks, 1984-87; state rep. for U.S. Senator Kent Conrad, 1987—; adj. grad. faculty Embry-Riddle Aeronautical U., Grand Forks AFB, 1983; lectr. U. N.D., 1985-86. Pub. mem. N.D. Bd. Nursing, Bismarck, 1986-87; mem. Grand Forks County Child Care Resource and Referral Adv. Bd., 1991-96, Grand Forks Fed. Exec. Assn. Bd., 1996—. Recipient Hammer award Nat. Partnership for Reinventing Govt., 1998. Mem. N.D. Bar Assn., Greater Grand Forks County Bar Assn. Legislative, Government contracts and claims, Immigration, naturalization, and customs. Office: 102 N 4th St Grand Forks ND 58203-3738

**HAND, MATTHEW HENRY,** lawyer; b. McPherson, Kans., June 25, 1962; s. James J. and Helen L. Hand; m. K. Stacy Hand; children: Katharine, Ryan. BA, Washburn U., 1984, JD with honors, 1988. Attty. Phillips Petroleum Co., Amarillo, Tex., 1988-95, Brown & Fortunato P.C., Amarillo, 1995—; spkr. at seminars. Bd. dirs., v.p. Golden Spread coun. Boy Scouts Am., Amarillo, 1998. Mem. Tex. Bar Assn., Okla. Bar Assn., Tex. Assn. Def. Counsel, Def. Rsch. Inst. Avocations: fishing, basketball. General civil litigation, Oil, gas, and mineral, Insurance. Office: Brown & Forunato PC PO Box 9418 905 S Taylor Ste 400 Amarillo TX 79106

**HAND, RANDALL EUGENE,** lawyer; b. Temple, Tex., Oct. 26, 1956; s. Robert E. and Ellen M. (Collier) H.; m. Debra S. Spitzer, Nov. 14, 1982. MPA, JD, So. Meth. U., 1981; BA, U. Notre Dame, 1978. Bar: Tex. 1981, U.S. Dist. Ct. (no. dist.) Tex. 1982, U.S. Ct. Appeals (5th cir.) 1986; cert. civil trial lawyer Tex. Bd. Legal Specialization. Assoc. Brutsche & Clements, Dallas, 1981-82, Weil, Brutsche & Clements, Dallas, 1982, Law Offices of Mark C. Clements, Dallas, 1982-86; shareholder Clements, Allen & Warren, P.C., Dallas, 1986-89; pvt. practice Dallas, 1989-95; bus. svcs. mgr. Tex. Instruments Software, Plano, Tex., 1995-97; contracts mgr. Sterling Software, Plano, 1997—. Author (computer program) mediation document system for WordPerfect 5.0, 1989. Mem. North Dallas C. of C., Dallas, 1989. Mem. ABA, Dallas Bar Assn. (computer use and tech. sect., bus. litigation sect.), Am. Arbitration Assn. Alternative dispute resolution, General civil litigation, Computer. Office: Sterling Software MS 152 5800 Tennyson Pkwy Plano TX 75024-3548

**HAND, STEPHEN BLOCK,** lawyer; b. N.Y.C., Nov. 24, 1942; m. Margaret A. Hand, Oct. 10, 1987; children: Matthew, Alexandra, Gregory. BA, Adelphi U., 1964; JD, St. Johns U., Bklyn., 1967; LLM, NYU, 1973. Estate tax atty. IRS, N.Y.C., 1967-69; assoc. Weisman, Celler et al., N.Y.C., 1969-71, Putney, Twombly et al, N.Y.C., 1971-88, Haskel, Hand and Lancaster, Garden City, N.Y., 1988-96, Jaspan Schlesinger Silverman & Hoffman, Garden City, N.Y., 1996—; bd. dirs. Bruce & Co., N.Y.C.; pub. speaker Nat. Bus. Inst., Mineola, N.Y., 1990. Author: Estate Planning, 1983, Estate Taxation, 1985, Probate and Administration of New York Estates, 1996. Mem. ABA, N.Y. State Bar Assn. (sr. mem. com. on litigation 1989—, mem. exec. com., 1995—, chair CLE, sr. mem. com. on trusts and estates, 1997—, pub. spkr., 1980—, Citations awarded), Tax and Estate Planning Coun. Nassau County, Inc., Nassau County Bar Assn. (chmn. surrogate's ct., trusts and estates com. 1992-94, chmn. com. on CLE, cons. 1988-90). Probate, Estate planning, Estate taxation. Office: Jaspan Schlesinger Silverman & Hoffman Garden City NY 11530

**HAND, WILLIAM BREVARD,** federal judge; b. Mobile, Ala., Jan. 18, 1924; s. Charles C. and Irma W. H.; m. Allison Denby, June 17, 1948; children: Jane Connor Hand Dukes, Virginia Alan Hand Hollis, Allison Hand Peebles. BS in Commerce and Bus. Adminstrn., U. Ala., 1947, JD, 1949; LLD (hon.), U. Mobile, 1990. Bar: Ala. 1949. Assoc. Hand, Arendall, Bedsole, Greaves & Johnston, Mobile, 1949-71; chief judge, then sr. judge U.S. Dist. Ct. (so. dist.) Ala., Mobile, 1971—. Chmn. Mobile County Rep. Exec. Com., 1968-71. Served with U.S. Army, 1943-46. Decorated Bronze Star medal. Mem. Am., Fed., Ala., Mobile bar assns. Methodist. Office: US Dist Ct US Courthouse 113 Saint Joseph St # 7 Mobile AL 36602-3606

**HANDEL, RICHARD CRAIG,** lawyer; b. Hamilton, Ohio, Aug. 11, 1945; s. Alexander F. and Marguerite (Wilks) H.; m. Katharine Jean Carter, Jan. 10, 1970. AB, U. Mich., 1967; MA, Mich. State U., 1968; JD summa cum laude, Ohio State U., 1974; LLM in Taxation, NYU, 1978. Bar: Ohio 1974, S.C. 1983, U.S. Dist. Ct. (so. dist.) Ohio 1975, U.S. Dist. Ct. S.C. 1979, U.S. Tax Ct. 1977, U.S. Ct. Appeals (4th cir.) 1979, U.S. Supreme Ct. 1979; cert. tax specialist. Assoc. Smith & Schnacke, Dayton, Ohio, 1974-77; asst. prof. U. S.C. Sch. Law, Columbia, 1978-83; ptnr. Nexsen, Pruet, Jacobs & Pollard, Columbia, 1983-87, Moore & Van Allen, Columbia, 1987-88, Nexsen Pruet Jacobs & Pollard, Columbia, 1988-89; chief tax policy and appeals S.C. Tax Commn., Columbia, 1989-95; chief coun. Policy S.C. Dept. of Revenue, Columbia, 1995—; adj. prof. U. S.C. Sch. Law, 1990—. Contbr. articles to legal jours. bd. dirs. Friends of Richland County Pub. Libr. Served with U.S. Army, 1969-70, Vietnam. Gerald L. Wallace scholar, 1977-78; recipient Outstanding Law Prof. award, 1980-81. Mem. ABA (com. state and local taxes, chmn. membership com. 1997—, vice-chmn. com. tax procedures 1993-94, com. stds. tax practice), S.C. Bar Assn., Order of Coif. Office: SC Dept Revenue PO Box 125 301 Gervais St Columbia SC 29201-3041

**HANDLER, ALAN B.,** former state supreme court justice; b. Newark, July 20, 1931; m. Rose Marie H.; 5 children. AB, Princeton U., 1953; LLB, Harvard U., 1956. Bar: N.J. 1956. Dep. atty. gen., 1961-64, 1st asst. atty. gen., 1964-68; justice Superior Ct., 1968-73; spl. counsel to gov., 1976-77; assoc. justice N.J. Supreme Ct., Trenton, 1977-99. Mem. Harvard Law Sch. Assn. of N.J. (past pres.), Phi Beta Kappa. *

**HANDLER, ARTHUR M.,** lawyer; b. N.Y.C., Feb. 16, 1937. BS, Queens Coll., 1957; LLB, Columbia U., 1960. Bar: N.Y. 1960, U.S. Dist. Ct. (ea. dist.) N.Y. 1960, U.S. Dist. Ct. (so. dist.) N.Y. 1963, U.S. Tax Ct. 1971, U.S. Ct. Appeals (2d cir.) 1971, U.S. Supreme Ct. 1965. Staff counsel SEC, Washington, 1960-61; law clk. U.S. Dist. Ct. for So. Dist.N.Y., N.Y.C., 1961-62; asst. U.S. atty. So. Dist. N.Y., N.Y.C., 1962-65; assoc. Proskauer, Rose, Goetz & Mendelsohn, N.Y.C., 1965-67; assoc. Golenbock and Barell, N.Y.C., 1967-70, ptnr., 1970-89; ptnr. Whitman & Ransom, N.Y.C., 1990-93, Burns Handler & Burns, N.Y.C., 1993—; arbitrator Am. Stock Exchange, N.Y.C., 1986—. Vol. atty. Pres.'s Com. for Civil Rights under Law, Jackson, Miss., 1966. Mem. ABA, N.Y. State Bar Assn., Bar Assn. of City of N.Y., Fed. Bar Council, Am. Arbitration Assn. (arbitrator 1969—). Clubs: University (N.Y.C.); Lords Valley Country (Hawley, Pa.) (bd. govs. 1977-80). Avocations: golf, skiing, theatre, travel. General civil litigation, Administrative and regulatory. Office: Burns Handler & Burns 220 E 42nd St Rm 3000 New York NY 10017-5806

**HANDLEY, GERALD MATTHEW,** lawyer; b. Phila., Dec. 7, 1942; s. John F. and Helen E. (Gerdelman) H.; m. Sandra I. Martin, June 13, 1970; children: Christopher, Elizabeth. BBA, La Salle Coll., Phila., 1965; JD, U. Mo., Kansas City, 1972. Bar: Mo. 1972, U.S. Dist. Ct. (we. dist.) Mo. 1972, U.S.Supreme Ct., 1976, U.S. Ct. Appeals (8th and 10th cirs.) 1980, U.S Dist. Ct. Kans. 1998. Asst. pub. defender Office Pub. Defender, Kansas City, Mo., 1972-73; 1st asst. pub. defender Office Pub. Defender, Kansas City, 1973-75, interim pub. defender, 1975-76; ptnr. Speck & Handley, Kansas City, 1980-90; pvt. practice Law Offices of G. Handley, 1991; ptnr., 1991—; lectr. Rockhurst Coll., Kansas City, 1976-78; instr. U. Mo. Sch. Law. Contbr. chpts. to law books. Pres., Home Owners Assn., Kansas City, 1980. Served with U.S. Army, 1966-67, Vietnam. Fellow Am. Bd. Criminal Lawyers; mem. ABA, NACDL, Mo. Bar Assn., (Lon Hocker Trial Lawyer award 1977), Mo. Assn. Criminal Def. Lawyers (pres. 1980, hon. bd. dirs.), U.S. Supreme Ct. Bar Assn., Kansas City Met. Bar Assn. Roman Catholic. Avocations: golf, gardening. Criminal. Home: 22 W 54th St Kansas City MO 64112-2816 Office: 1101 Walnut St Ste 1400 Kansas City MO 64106-2182

**HANDLEY, LEON HUNTER,** lawyer; b. Lakeland, Fla., Sept. 9, 1927; s. Driskle Hubert and Mamie (Denmark) H.; m. Mary Virginia Wolfe, May 2, 1953; children: Leon Hunter, Mary Ellen, Laura Catherine, Leann Virginia; BSBA with honors, U. Fla., 1949, JD, 1951. Bar: Fla. 1951, U.S. Dist. Ct. (so. dist.) Fla. 1952, U.S. Dist. Ct. (mid. dist.) Fla. 1962, U.S. Supreme Ct. 1956, U.S. Ct. of Appeals (5th cir.) 1960, U.S. Ct. Appeals (11th cir.) 1981; pres. Gurney & Handley, Orlando, Fla., 1951—; bd. dirs. Beneficial Savs. Bank, chmn.; bd. dirs. Orlando/Tampa, Cracker Groves Inc., Orlando, 1964—; v.p., bd. dirs. So. Indsl. Savs. Bank, Orlando, Mine & Mill Supply Co., Lakeland, 1966—, Claude H. Wolfe, Inc., Orlando, 1969—; gen. counsel, life dir., past pres. Cen. Fla. Fair; chmn. bd. trustees Sta. WMFE-TV. Pres. Chesley Magruder Charitable Trust; elder Presbyn. Ch. Warrant officer U.S. Maritime Svc., 1945-46, ETO; sgt. U.S. Army, 1946-48, Korea; capt. USAFR, 1949-59. Fellow Am. Coll. Trial Lawyers; mem. ABA, Am. Bd. Trial Advocates (Fla. Trial Lawyer of Yr. 1996, advocate), Orange County Bar Assn. (past pres.), Fla. Bar Assn. (past pres. sta. jr. bar sect., bd. govs. 1959-60), Fedn. Ins. and Corp. Counsel, Internat. Assn. Def. Counsel, Assn. Def. Trial Attys., Trial Attys. Am., Am. Judicature Soc. (listed Best Lawyers in Am.), Pres.'s Coun. (founder U. Fla. chpt.), Citrus Club, Orlando Country Club, Univ. Club, Masons (grand orator Fla. 1982, 86) K.T., Shriners, Scottish Rite (33d degree, insp. gen. hon. 1979), Rotary (pres. Orlando chpt. 1984, Paul Harris fellow), Travelers' Century Club, Fla. Blue

Key (pres. 1951), Phi Delta Phi, Alpha Tau Omega (prs. U. of Fla. chpt. 1951), Phi Kappa Phi, Alpha Kappa Psi, Beta Gamma Sigma (U. Fla. Hall of Fame). Republican. Avocations: jogging, handball. Personal injury, General civil litigation. Home: 1621 Spring Lake Dr Orlando FL 32804-7111 Office: Gurney & Handley 225 E Robinson St Ste 450 Orlando FL 32801-1905

**HANDLEY, ROBERT,** lawyer; b. Chgo., 1952; married; 4 children. BA, U. Ill., 1975; JD, No. Ill. U., 1978. Bar: Ill. 1979. Ptnr. Moroni & Handley, Carol Stream, Ill.; adj. prof. Aurora U., 1979-81; mem. inquiry panel and hearing bd. Atty. Registration and Disciplinary Commn. of Supreme Ct. of Ill., 1986-94. Pres. Pre du Chevaux Homeowners Assn., 1989-96; treas. Wayne Cmty. Assn., 1992—; mem. Village of Wayne Plan Commn., 1994—, chair, 1996—; mem. Village of Wayne Zoning Bd. Appeals, 1994, Village of Roselle Zoning Bd. Appeals, 1988-90; mem. St. Patrick Sch. Edn. Commn., 1998—. Mem. Ill. State Bar Assn. (newsletter editor tort law sect. coun. 1995—, Assembly rep. 1983-89, 92-94, chair civil practice and procedure sect. coun. 1993, ins. standing com. 1980-86, pub. rels. com. 1986-90, chair ARDC liaison com. 1998—, com. on membership and bar activities 1994—, seminar spkr./panelist 1986, 89, 92, 94, contbr. trial briefs), Ill. Trial Lawyers Assn. (pub. rels. com. 1984, chair 1986, young lawyers com. 1984, legis. com. 1986-89). Personal injury, Bankruptcy, General civil litigation. Office: Moroni & Handley 373 S Schmale Rd Ste 203 Carol Stream IL 60188-2773

**HANDLIN, JOSEPH JASON,** lawyer; b. N.Y.C., Feb. 21, 1952; s. Nathan and Beatrice (Greenberg) H.; m. Laura Sara Ellin, Aug. 18, 1985. AB magna cum laude, Harvard U., 1973; JD, NYU, 1976. Bar: N.Y. 1977, U.S. Dist. Ct. (so. and ea. dists.) N.Y. 1977. Gen. counsel Muzak Corp., N.Y.C., 1977-78; assoc. Estroff, Frankel & Waldman, N.Y.C., 1978-80, Guggenheimer & Untermyer, N.Y.C., 1980-84, Dahan & Nowick, N.Y.C., 1984-86, Epstein, Becker, Borsody & Green P.C., N.Y.C., 1986-87; ptnr. Surkin & Handlin, N.Y.C., 1987-98; prin. Law Offices of Joseph J. Handlin, N.Y.C., 1998—; adj. instr. Cardozo Law Sch., N.Y.C., 1983-88; asst. prof. NYU, 1988—. Recipient Lewis F. Powell, Jr. Medal for Excellence in Adv. Am. Coll. Trial Lawyers, 1975. Mem. ABA, N.Y. State Bar Assn. (ho. of dels. 1999—), Assn. of Bar of City of N.Y. (sec. com. on small law firm mgmt. 1993-96, chair 1996-99, mem. com. on real property law 1999—), N.Y. County Lawyers Assn., Harvard Club (sec. admissions com. 1986-87, chmn. admissions com. 1990-92, bd. mgrs. 1992-95, sec. club 1996—). Real property. Home: 345 S End Ave Apt 4N New York NY 10280-1064 Office: Law Offices of Joseph J Handlin 75 Maiden Ln Fl 3 New York NY 10038-4810

**HANDSAKER, JERROLD LEE,** lawyer; b. Ames, Iowa, Apr. 12, 1950; s. Vernon Glenn and Hyllis Elenor (Ullestad) H.; m. Janet Marie Gregg, June 25, 1976; children: Melissa Ann, Lori Beth. BS in Indsl. Adminstrn., Iowa State U., 1972; JD, Drake U., 1975. Bar: Iowa 1976, U.S. Tax Ct. 1976, U.S. Dist. Ct. (so. dist.) Iowa 1976, U.S. Dist. Ct. (no. dist.) Iowa 1982, U.S. Supreme Ct. 1987. Assoc. Bloethe Law Firm, Victor, Iowa, 1976-78; lawyer Hattery-Handsaker Law Firm, Nevada, Iowa, 1978-79; ptnr. Parker & Handsaker Law Firm, Nevada, 1979-89; assoc. Buchanan Dotson Buchanan Bibler & Buchanan, Algona, Iowa, 1989-90; ptnr. Buchanan Bibler Buchanan Handsaker & Gabor, Algona, Iowa, 1991-98, of counsel, 1998-99; of counsel Innovative Lighting, Inc., Algona, Iowa, 1999—; pres., CEO Innovative Lighting Inc., Algona, 1993—, Oak Lake Home Owners Assn. Algona, 1990-94; bd. dirs. Mirenco Inc., 1998—. Contbr. article to popular boating mag.; patentee motorized telescopic boat light, 1994, self-concealing landscape lights, 1995. Recipient Maynard Speece award for most popular new invention Minn. Inventors Congress, Redwood Falls, Minn., 1994. Mem. ABA, Nat. Marine Mfrs.'s Assn., Iowa State Bar Assn., Kossuth County Bar Assn. (treas. 1991-98), Am. Boating and Yachting Coun., Kiwanis Club of Algona (bd. dirs., pres. 1997). Republican. Lutheran. Avocations: golf, swimming, volleyball, flying. Probate, Taxation, general, Real property. Home: 62 Smith Cir Algona IA 50511-5004 Office: Innovative Lighting Inc PO Box 494 Algona IA 50511-0494

**HANDY, SETH HOWLAND,** lawyer; b. Providence, July 21, 1967; s. Edward Otis and Susan Eastabrooks Handy; m. Charlotte Crozier Breed, June 15, 1996; 1 child, Benjamin Breed. AB, Harvard U., 1990; JD, Vt. Law Sch., 1996. Bar: R.I. 1996, Mass. 1997, U.S. Dist. Ct. R.I. 1997. Policy analyst Sci. Applications Internat. Corp., Falls Church, Va., 1991-93; assoc. Edwards & Angel, Providence, 1996—. Mem. housing subcom. Mayor's Task Force on Lead Poisoning, Providence, 1998; bd. dirs. San Miguel Sch., Providence, 1996-97, Sandra Geinstein-Gamm Theater, Providence, 1997—; mem. R.I. adv. bd. Conservation Law Found., Providence, 1997—. Mem. R.I. Bar Assn. Unitarian. Avocations: sculpture, squash, hiking, fishing, banjo. Environmental, Municipal (including bonds), General civil litigation. Office: Edwards & Angell 1 Bankboston Plz Ste 2700 Providence RI 02903-2499

**HANDZLIK, JAN LAWRENCE,** lawyer; b. N.Y.C., Sept. 21, 1945; s. Felix Munso and Anna Jean Handzlik; children: Grant, Craig, Anna. BA, U. So. Calif., 1967; JD, UCLA, 1970. Bar: Calif. 1971, U.S. Dist. Ct. (cen. dist.) Calif. 1971, U.S. Ct. Appeals (9th cir.) 1971, U.S. Supreme Ct. 1975, U.S. Tax Ct. 1979, U.S. Dist. Ct. (no. dist.) Calif. 1979, U.S. Dist. Ct. (ea. dist.) Calif. 1981, U.S. Dist. Ct. (so. dist.) Calif. 1982, U.S. Ct. Appeals (2d cir.) 1984, U.S. Ct. Internat. Trade 1984. Law clk. to Hon. Francis C. Whelan, U.S. Dist. Ct. (cen. dist.) Calif., L.A., 1970-71; asst. U.S. atty. fraud and spl. prosecutions unit criminal div. U.S. Dept. Justice, L.A., 1971-76; assoc. Greenberg & Glusker, L.A., 1976-78; ptnr., prin. Stilz, Boyd, Levine & Handzlik, P.C., L.A., 1978-84; prin. Jan Lawrence Handzlik, P.C., L.A., 1984-91; ptnr. Kirkland & Ellis, L.A., 1991—; del. U.S. Ct. Appeals for 9th cir. Jud. Conf., L.A., 1983-85; counsel to ind. Christopher Commn. Study of the L.A. Police Dept., 1991; dep. gen. counsel to Hon. William H. Webster, spl. advisor to L.A. Police Commn. for Investigation of Response to Urban Disorders, 1992; mem. adv. com. for Office of L.A. County Dist. Atty., 1994-96. Mem. editl. adv. bd. DOJ Alert, 1994-95. Bd. dirs. Friends of Child Advs., L.A., 1987-91, Inner City Law Ctr., L.A., 1993—; mem. bd. judges Nat. and Calif. Moot Ct. Competition Teams, UCLA Moot Ct. honors program. Mem. ABA (sect. criminal justice nat. com. on white collar crime 1991—, vice-chair 1998—, co-chair securities fraud subcom. 1994-98, west coast white collar crime com., exec. com. 1993—, vice-chair 1994-96, chair 1996-98, mem. sect. litigation, criminal litigation com. 1989—), Fed. Bar Assn., State Bar Calif. (sects. on criminal law and litigation), L.A. County Bar Assn. (mem. exec. com. criminal justice sect. 1997—, coms. on fed. cts. 1988—, chair criminal practice subcom. 1989-90, fed. appts. evaluation 1989-93, white collar crime com. 1991-97, exec. com. 1991-97). Criminal, Federal civil litigation, State civil litigation. Office: Kirkland & Ellis 300 S Grand Ave Ste 3000 Los Angeles CA 90071-3140

**HANE, JEFFREY W.,** lawyer; b. Brainerd, Minn., Jan. 31, 1963; s. Thomas Loren and Donna Jean Hane; m. Linda Rae Bradseth, Aug. 14, 1993. BA in Polit. Sci., Bemidji State U., 1986; MA in Religion, So. Calif. Coll., 1992; JD, U. N.D., 1993. Bar: Minn. 1993, U.S. Dist. Ct. (no. dist.) Minn. 1993, U.S. Ct. Appeals (8th cir.) 1994. Atty. Brink, Sobolik, Severson, Malm, Hallock, Minn., 1992—; asst. county atty. Kittson County, Minn., Hallock, Minn., 1994—. Mem. Minn. State Bar Assn., N.D. State Bar Assn., Minn. Trial Lawyers Assn., Nat. Lawyers Assn., Christian Legal Soc., Order of the Coif, Order of Barristers. Avocations: carpenter, cross-country skiing. Office: Brink Sobolik Severson Malm 217 S Birch Ave Hallock MN 56728

**HANESIAN, SHAVASP,** lawyer; b. Niagara Falls, N.Y., Sept. 9, 1928; s. Vahan H. and Anna Kabasaklian; m. Laurice A. Campbell, Mar. 17, 1961; children: Brenda, Darrow, Deran, Laurel. BS in Econs. magna cum laude, Niagara U., 1952; JD, SUNY, 1957. Bar: N.Y. 1958, U.S. Dist. Ct. (we. dist.) N.Y. 1963. Instr. econs., money & banking Pa. State Coll., State College, 1952-54; atty. pvt. practice, Niagara Falls, N.Y., 1958—; asst. dist. atty. Niagara County, 1967-91; exec. dir., chief atty. Niagara Falls Legal Aid Soc., 1966-67. Columnist N.Y. Sportsman, 1990-95. With U.S. Army, 1946-48. Mem. N.Y. State Outdoor Writers Assn. (life, legal counsel 1973-98), Fin, Feather, Fur Conservation Soc. (life, pres., legal counsel 1965-67, Recognition award 1983), LaSalle Sportmen's Club (legal counsel 1973—). Avocations: photography, fishing, camping, travel. General practice, Probate, Real property. Home: 5940 S Hewitt Dr Lewiston NY 14092-2217 Office: Niagara County 631 Main St Niagara Falls NY 14301-1739

**HANEY, JAMES KEVIN,** lawyer; b. New Brunswick, N.J., Apr. 11, 1966; s. James Alexander and Caroline Martha (Smolinski) H.; m. Elaine M. (Larsen), June 25, 1995. BA, U. Pa., 1988; JD with honors, St. John's U., 1991; MBA, Seton Hall U., 1998. Bar: N.J. 1991, U.S. Dist. Ct. N.J. 1991, N.Y. 1992, U.S. Ct. Appeals (3d and fed. cirs.) 1998, U.S. Supreme Ct. 1998. Twp. engring. inspector East Brunswick (N.J.) Twp., 1986-89; law clk. to Hon. June Strelecki N.J. Superior Ct., Monmouth County, 1991-92; assoc. Magee, Pagano & Isherwood, Wall, N.J., 1992-93, Zucker, Facher & Zucker, West Orange, N.J., 1993-99, Gilberg & Kiernan, Parsippany, N.J., 1999—. Mem. ABA, Assn. Def. Trial Attys., Def. Rsch. Inst., N.J. Def. Assn., N.J. State Bar Assn., N.Y. State Bar Assn., Ctrl. N.J. Alumni Club U. Pa., St. John's Alumni Assn., Phi Delta Phi. General civil litigation, Toxic tort. Address: Gilberg & Keieknan 140 Littleton Rd Ste 201 Parsippany NJ 07054-1867

**HANGLEY, WILLIAM THOMAS,** lawyer; b. Long Beach, N.Y., Mar. 11, 1941; s. Charles Augustus and Faustine Charmillot H.; m. Mary Dupree Hangley, July 24, 1965; children: Michele Dupree, William Thomas, Katherine Charmillot. BS in Music, SUNY-Coll. at Fredonia, 1963; LLB cum laude, U. Pa., 1966. Bar: Pa. 1966, U.S. Ct. Appeals (3d cir.) 1966, U.S. Dist. Ct. (ea. dist.) Pa. 1966. Assoc. Schnader, Harrison, Segal & Lewis, Phila., 1966-69; mem., CEO, Hangley Connolly Epstein Chicco Foxman & Ewing, Phila, 1969-94, CEO Hangley Aronchick Segal & Pudlin, 1994—; judge protem Phila. Ct. of Common Pleas, 1991—; mem. adv. bd. Pub. Interest Law Ctr. Phila. Contbr. articles to profl. publs. Bd. dirs. Ams. for Dem. Action, 1972-81. Fellow Am. Coll. Trial Lawyers, Am. Bar Found.; mem. ABA (co-chmn. litigation sect. com. on fed. procedure 1990-95—, co-chair task force on merit selection of judges 1995-97, mem. task force on discovery 1997-98, task force on judiciary 1998—), Pa. Bar Assn. (corp. and litigation coms., securities and antitrust subcoms., ho. dels. 1989-92), ACLU, Am. Law Inst., Phila. Bar Assn., Legal Club, Jr. Legal Club, Order of Coif, U. Pa. Inns of Ct. (master of the bench). Roman Catholic. Federal civil litigation, Securities. Office: Hangley Aronchick Segal & Pudlin 1 Logan Sq Fl 12 Philadelphia PA 19103-6995

**HANKIN, MITCHELL ROBERT,** lawyer; b. Phila., May 16, 1949; s. Samuel and Harriet (Cohen) H. BA, Trinity Coll., Hartford, Conn., 1971; JD, Columbia U., 1974. Bar: Pa. 1974, U.S. Dist. Ct. (ea. dist.) Pa. 1975, U.S. Ct. Appeals (3d cir.) 1975. Assoc. Blank, Romeklaus, Comisky, Phila., 1974-75; asst. U.S. atty. U.S. Atty.'s Office, Phila., 1975-76; ptnr. Hankin Enterprises, Willow Grove, Pa., 1976—; bd. dirs. Bank of Old York, Bank of King of Prussia (Pa.), Royal Bank of Pa. Mem. ABA, Pa. Bar Assn., Montgomery County Bar Assn., Phila. Bar Assn., Phi Beta Kappa. State civil litigation, Contracts commercial, Real property. Home: 1115 Barberry Rd Bryn Mawr PA 19010-1907

**HANKIN, SANDRA H.,** lawyer; b. Bklyn., Aug. 15, 1950; d. Alvin and Anita Winegard; m. Joel Hankin, Sept. 3, 1972 (dec. Feb. 1976). BS, SUNY, Stonybrook, 1972; MS, Rutgers U., 1978, PhD, 1979; JD, Suffolk U., 1995. Chemist Dow Chem. Co., Midland, Mich., 1979-84, GTE Labs. Inc., Waltham, Mass., 1984-92; assoc. Jacobson Law Group, Plantation, Fla., 1997, Office Marc A. Ben-Ezra, North Miami Beach, Fla., 1998—; adj. prof. Broward C.C., Dane, Fla., 1996-98. Consumer commercial. Office: Office Marc A Ben-Ezra 951 NE 167th St Ste 102 North Miami Beach FL 33162

**HANKINS, TIMOTHY HOWARD,** lawyer; b. Tazewell, Va., Jan. 25, 1956; s. Ralph Arnold and Phyllis Ann (Belcher) H.; m. Nikki Hankins; children: Tamra Lynn, Amanda Rae. BS in Bus., Va. Commonwealth U., 1978; JD, U. Richmond, 1981. Bar: Va. 1981. Sole practice Newport News, 1981—. Mem. staff U. Richmond Law Rev., 1981. Counsel Gosnold Canal Com., Hampton, Va., 1986, Langley Sch., Hampton, 1986. Mem. ABA, Va. Bar Assn., Newport News Bar Assn., Va. Trial Lawyers Assn., Assn. Trial Lawyers Am., Lawyers Pilots Bar Assn. Republican. Baptist. Personal injury, Criminal, Family and matrimonial. Home: 500 Winston Salem Ave Apt 503 Virginia Beach VA 23451-4790 Office: 306 Main St Newport News VA 23601-3802

**HANKINSON, DEBORAH G.,** state supreme court justice. BS with distinction, Purdue U.; MS, U. Tex., Dallas; JD, So. Meth. U. Bar: Tex., U.S. Ct. Appeals (5th cir.) 1995; cert. civil appellate law Tex. Bd. Legal Specialization. Spl. edn. tchr. Plano (Tex.) Ind. Sch. Dist.; assoc. Thompson and Knight, Dallas, 1983-95; judge U.S. Ct. Appeals (5th cir.), Dallas, 1996, Tex. Supreme Ct., Dallas, 1997—; liaison Gender Bias Reform Implementation Com., family law sect. Dallas Bar. Editor-in-chief Southwestern Law Jour. Fellow Tex. Bar Found., Dallas Bar Found. Mem. ABA (litigation sect., com. appellate practice, judicial sect.), State Bar Tex. (judicial, litigation, appellate sects.), Dallas Bar Assn. (apellate law sect.), 5th Cir. Bar Assn., Coll. of State Bar Tex., Order of the Coif. Office: PO Box 12248 Austin TX 78711-2248*

**HANKS, GEORGE CAROL, JR.,** lawyer; b. Breaux Bridge, La., Sept. 25, 1964; s. George Carol and Quenola Reese Hanks; m. Stacey L. Hanks, Apr. 29, 1995. JD, Harvard U., 1989; BA summa cum laude, La. State U., 1986. Bar: Tex. 1989, U.S. Dist. Ct. (so. dist.) Tex. 1992, U.S. Ct. Appeals (5th cir.) 1993, U.S. Dist. Ct. Ariz. 1994. Judicial law clk. Houston, 1989-91; assoc. atty. Fulbright & Jaworski, Houston, 1991-96, Wickliff & Hall PC, Houston, 1996—; panel chmn. grievance com., spl. disciplinary counsel Tex. State Bar, Houston, 1993—. Contbr. articles to profl. jours. Bd. dirs. Big Bros. and Big Sisters, Houston, 1995-97. Fellow Houston Bar Assn.; mem. Fed. Bar Assn., Tex. Assn. Def. Counsel, Houston Bar Found. Avocations: aviation, ice hockey, scuba diving. General civil litigation. Home: 12035 E Circle Dr Houston TX 77071-3602 Office: Wickliff & Hall 1000 Louisiana St Ste 5400 Houston TX 77002-5006

**HANLEY, WILLIAM STANFORD,** lawyer; b. Chgo., June 4, 1939; s. William Mathias Hanley and Dorothy Elizabeth (Stylinski) Davidson; m. Nancy Fahrnkopf, Nov. 28, 1970; children: William M., Michael J. AB, U. Notre Dame, 1961; JD, U. Chgo., 1964. Bar: Ill. 1964, U.S. Dist. Ct. (ctrl. dist.) Ill. 1964, U.S. Dist. Ct. (no. dist.) Ill. 1965, U.S. Ct. Appeals (7th cir.) 1976, U.S. Tax Ct. 1981, U.S. Supreme Ct. 1992, Maine 1994. Assoc. atty. Arnstein, Gluck, Weitzenfeld and Minow, Chgo., 1965-67; rsch. dir. Ogilvie for Gov. Com., Chgo., 1968; legis. counsel Office of the Gov., Springfield, Ill., 1969-72; with Sorling, Northrup, Hanna, Cullen & Cochran, Ltd., Springfield, 1972—, dir., 1978—, mng. dir., 1982-87, 90-94, pres., 1988; faculty Ill. Inst. for Continuing Legal Edn., 1976; pub. mem. appointee of Gov. James R. Thompson to Gov.'s Task Force on Fin. Svcs., 1985, Gov.'s Human Resources Adv. Coun., 1991-92; chmn. Sec. of State's Adv. Com. on Pub. Records and Privacy, 1992-93. Contbr. articles to profl. jours. and chpts. to books. Ford Found. fellow U. Ill., 1964-65. Mem. ABA (mem. legal econs. and adminstrv. law sect. 1973—), Fed. Regulatory Counsel, Ill. State Bar Assn. (chmn. adminstrv. law sect. coun. 1981-82, adminstrv. law and civil practice sect.), Ill. Appellate Lawyers Assn., Ill. Govt. Bar Assn., Maine Trial Lawyers Assn., Maine State Bar Assn., Greater Springfield C. of C. (chmn. 1995). Administrative and regulatory, General civil litigation, Insurance. Home: 17 Oak Ln Springfield IL 62707-8611 Office: Sorling Northrup Hanna Cullen & Cochran Ltd 800 S Illinois St Springfield IL 62704-2431 also: PO Box 1285 One Perkins Pl Blue Hill ME 04614-1285

**HANLON, LODGE L.,** lawyer, insurance agency executive, accountant; b. Barnesville, Ohio, Apr. 30, 1931; s. Kenneth L. and Sara (Lodge); m. Suzanne Hanlon, July 15, 1961; children: Elizabeth, Thomas, Fred. BSBA in Acctg., Kent (Ohio) State U., 1953; JD, Ohio State U., 1958. Bar: Ohio 1958. Tax acct. Arthur Andersen & Co., Cleve., 1958-63; ptnr. Kinder Kinder & Hanlon, St. Clairsville, Ohio, 1963-84; officer Hanlon Duff & Paleudis Co., St. Clairsville, 1984—; assoc. instr. Ohio U., Belmont County, 1968-84. Founder, sec. Barnesville Area Edn. Found., 1980—; pres. Barnesville Exempted Village Bd. of Edn., 1978, Barnesville C. of C., 1964; chmn. Belmont County Bd. Mental Retardation/Devel. Disabilities, St. Clairsville, 1985-86. Capt. USAF, 1954-56. Mem. Estate Planning Coun. Upper Ohio Valley (bd. dirs., pres. 1991), Am. Legion, Moose, Elks (past exec. ruler Barnesville lodge 1973), Belmont Hills Country Club (trustee, officer 1985-90). Republican. Presbyterian. Avocations: golf, stamp collector. Estate planning, Estate taxation, Probate. Office: Hanlon Duff & Paleudis Co 46457 National Rd W Saint Clairsville OH 43950-9721

**HANNA, HARRY MITCHELL,** lawyer; b. Portland, Oreg., Jan. 13, 1936; s. Joseph John and Amelia Cecelia (Rask) H.; m. Patricia Ann Shelly, Feb. 4, 1967; 1 child, Harry M. Jr. BS, U. Oreg., 1958; JD, Lewis and Clark Coll., 1966. Bar: Oreg. 1966, U.S. Tax Ct. 1967, U.S. Dist. Ct. Oreg. 1970, U.S. Supreme Ct. 1971, U.S. Ct. Appeals (9th cir.) 1973, U.S. Ct. Claims 1973. Airport mgr. Port of Portland, 1964-66; mng. ptnr. Hanna & Purcella, Portland, 1966-80, Niehaus, Hanna, Murphy, Green, Holloway & Connolly, Portland, 1980-88; shareholder, v.p. Hanna, Kerns & Strader, P.C., Portland, 1988—; judge pro-tempore U.S. Dist. Ct. Oreg., 1973-78; adj. prof. N.W. Sch. Law, Lewis and Clark Coll., Portland, 1976-77. Trustee Emanuel Med. Ctr. Found., 1989—; pres. Ctrl. Cath. H.S. Bd., 1992-95; vice chair Life Flight Devel. Bd., 1994-97, chair, 1997—. Mem. ABA, Fed. Bar Assn., Oreg. State Bar Assn., Multnomah Bar Assn., Rotary (pres. East Portland club 1989-90). Avocations: tennis, hunting, fishing, coaching youth athletics. Real property, Taxation, general, General corporate. Office: Hanna Kerns & Strader PC 1300 SW 6th Ave Ste 300 Portland OR 97201-3461

**HANNA, JETT LOWELL,** lawyer; b. Raymondville, Tex., Feb. 28, 1960; s. Thomas Wayne and Wilma Jean (Nowlin) H.; m. Ann Maureen Denkler, Nov. 9, 1991; 1 child, Katharine Mae. BBA, Southern Methodist, 1980; JD, U. Tex., 1983. Bar: Tex. 1983; bd. cert. coml. real estate 1989-94. Nat. closing title officer Stewart Title, Austin, Tex., 1983-87; claims counsel Tex. Lawyers' Ins. Exch., Austin, asst. gen. counsel, v.p. underwriting and adminstrn., 1995—; mem. bd. Travis Ctrl. Appraisal Dist., Austin, 1988-89. Author: The Legal Malpractice Self Audit, 1993; contbr. articles to profl. jours. Fellow State Bar Found., 1994—; chair Ethics Rev. Commn., Austin, 1993-94. Mem.. Profl. Liability Underwriters Soc. Democrat. Professional liability. Home: 7006 Edgefield Dr Austin TX 78731-2926

**HANNA, JOHN, JR.,** lawyer, educator; b. Dec. 27, 1958; m. Jane Merchant, Dec. 27, 1958; children: Elizabeth Hanna Morss, Katharine Hanna Morgan, John M. AB, Princeton U., 1956; LLB, Harvard U., 1959. Bar: N.Y. 1960, Mass. 1964, U.S. Dist. Ct. Mass. 1965, U.S. Dist. Ct. (ea. and so. dists.) N.Y. 1963, U.S. Dist. Ct. (no. dist.) N.Y. 1976, U.S. Dist. Ct. (we. dist.) N.Y. 1963, U.S. Ct. Appeals (1st and 2d cirs.) 1963. Assoc. Root, Barrett, Cohen, Knapp & Smith, N.Y.C., 1959-61; asst. U.S. atty. U.S. Dist. Ct. (so. dist.) N.Y., N.Y.C., 1961-63; assoc. Ropes & Gray, Boston, 1963-69; counsel N.Y. State Officer Employee Rels. Govs. Office, Albany, 1969-73; dep. commr., gen. counsel N.Y. State Dept. Environ. Conservation, Albany, 1973-75; ptnr. Whiteman, Osterman & Hanna, Albany, 1975—; adj. prof. Rensselaer Poly. Inst., Troy, N.Y., 1988—. Co-author: New York State Bar Association Environmental Handbook, 1987, New York Treatise on Environmental Law, 1992. Mem. Town of Chatham (N.Y.) Planning Bd., 1976—; co-chmn. Princeton U. Alumni Schs. Commn. No. N.Y., 1982-94; trustee/treas. Shaker Mus. Found., Old Chatham, N.Y., 1978-96; trustee ea. N.Y. chpt. The Nature Conservancy, 1994, co-chair, 1996—; trustee N.Y. State Archives Partnership Trust, 1995—, chair, 1996—; bd. dirs. Commn. on Environ. Law, Internat. Union for Conservation of Nature, 1999—. Mem. ABA (internat.-comparative law sect.), N.Y. State Bar Assn. (1st vice chmn. 1981-83, chmn. environ. law sect. 1983-84). Environmental, Administrative and regulatory, Private international. Office: Whiteman Osterman & Hanna One Commerce Plz Albany NY 12260

**HANNA, MARTIN SHAD,** lawyer; b. Bowling Green, Ohio, Aug. 4, 1940; s. Martin Lester and Julia Loyal (Moor) H.; m. Ann I. Amos; children: Jennifer Lynn, Jonathan Moor, Katharine Anne. Student, Bowling Green State U.; B.S., Purdue U., 1962; J.D., Am. U., 1965. Bar: Ohio 1965, D.C. 1967, U.S. Supreme Ct. 1969. Ptnr. Hanna, Middleton & Roebke, 1965-70; ptnr. Hanna & Hanna, Bowling Green, 1971—; spl. counsel for atty. gen. Ohio, 1969-71, 82-85, Ohio Bd. Regents, 1974; instr. Bowling Green State U., 1970, Ohio Div. Vocat. Edn., 1970—, Ohio Peace Officer Tng. Council, 1968; legal adviser NW Ohio Vol. Firemen's Assn., 1970—. Contbr. articles to profl. publs. Elder, lay minister Presbyn. Ch.; state chmn. Ohio League Young Republican Clubs, 1972-73; nat. vice chmn. Young Rep. Nat. Fedn., 1973-75, counselor to chmn., 1975-77; cive chmn. Wood County Rep. Exec. Com., Ohio, 1972-80, precinct committeeman, 1968-80; trustee Bowling Green State U., 1976-86; mem. Ohio State Fire Commn., 1979-87; mem. Ohio Rural Fire coun., 1993—. Recipient George Washington honor medal award Freedoms Found. at Valley Forge, 1969, award of merit Ohio Legal Ctr. Inst., 1973, Robert A. Taft Disting. Service award, 1974, James A. Rhodes Leadership award, 1975; named one of 10 Outstanding Young Men, Ohio Jaycees, 1968. Mem. ABA, D.C. Bar Assn., Ohio Bar Assn., Northwest Ohio Bar Assn., Wood County Bar Assn., Toledo Bar Assn., Am. Trauma Soc. (trauma and law com.), Phi Delta Phi, Pi Kappa Delta, Omicron Delta Kappa. State civil litigation, Criminal, Personal injury. Home: PO Box 1137 Bowling Green OH 43402-1137 Office: Hanna & Hanna 700 N Main St Bowling Green OH 43402-1815

**HANNA, ROBERT CECIL,** lawyer; b. Albuquerque, July 28, 1937; s. Samuel Gray and Orvetta (Cecil) H.; BA, U. N.Mex., 1959, JD, 1962. Bar: N.M1962, Hawaii 1974, U.S. Supreme Ct. 1970; practiced in Albuquerque, 1962-70, 72—; organizer, dep. dir. Micronesian Legal Svcs. Corp., Trust Ter. Pacific Islands, 1970-71; practiced in Hilo; Hawaii, 1974; ptnr. Cotter, Atkinson, Kitts, Kelsey & Hanna, Ortega, Snead, Dixon & Hanna, Albuquerque, 1975-77; owner, pres., prin. Robert C. Hanna & Assocs., Albuquerque, 1978-80, 88—; pres. Sedco Internat. USA, Inc., Albuquerque, 1977-79, Suncastle Builders, Inc., Albuquerque, 1978—, Am. Legal Consortium, A Chartered Law Firm, 1984—, The Garden Spa Resort, 1995—; gen. counsel Casas de Sueños The Bed and Breakfast Company, 1991—, Zephyr Mgmt. Co., 1991—; ptnr. Contemporary Devel. Inc., 1989—, N.Mex. Real Estate Consortium Ltd., 1986—; mem. Bd. Bar Commrs., Trust Ter. Pacific Islands, 1971-72. Bd. dirs. Found. for Life Action (nonprofit), L.A., 1990—; founder, pres., bd. dirs. Casa de Sueños Found. (nonprofit), 1993—. Recipient award Rocky Mountain Mineral Law Found., 1962; Pub. Svc. award Micronesian Legal Services Corp. Bd. Dirs., 1972. Mem. Hawaii Bar Assn., N.Mex. Bar Assn., Albuquerque Bar Assn. Private international, Contracts commercial, General civil litigation. Home and Office: 310 Rio Grande Blvd SW Albuquerque NM 87104-1477

**HANNA, TERRY ROSS,** lawyer, small business owner; b. Wadsworth, Ohio, May 17, 1947; s. Harry Ross and Geraldine (Frensley) H.; m. Max Anna Hindes, Jan. 20, 1968; children: Travis, Taylor, Molly. BBA, U. Okla., 1968, JD, 1972; LLM, NYU, 1973; MA in Bibl Studies, Dallas Theol. Sem., 1988. Bar: Okla. 1972, U.S. Tax Ct. 1974, U.S. Ct. Appeals (10th cir.) 1979, U.S. Supreme Ct. 1989; CPA, Okla. Mem. McAfee & Taft, Oklahoma City, 1972-80; pres. P 356 Inc., Oklahoma City, 1980—; of counsel Crowe & Dunlevy, Oklahoma City, 1987—; pres. H.J. Freede, Inc., Oklahoma City, 1998—; owner Mo Jo Video, 1995—; spl. lectr. Oklahoma City U. Sch. Law, 1974-75. Editor Okla. U. Law Rev., 1970-72. Mem. internat. com. Boy Scouts Am., 1988—; dir. U.S. Found. for Internat. Scouting, Irving, 1989—. Baden-Powell fellow World Scout Found., 1988—; recipient Silver Beaver award Boy Scouts Am., 1988. Mem. Okla. Bar Assn. (pres. taxation sect. 1978-79), Sports Lawyers Assn., Order of Arrow (lodge advisor 1989—), Kappa Sigma (chpt. advisor 1974-75), Phi Delta Phi (magister 1972). Republican. Mem. Christian Ch. Avocations: coach, patch collector, fishing, softball, computers. Taxation, general, Health, Entertainment. Home: 2600 W Coffee Creek Rd Edmond OK 73003-3326 Office: Crowe & Dunlevy 1800 Mid America Towers Oklahoma City OK 73102

**HANNAH, LAWRENCE BURLISON,** lawyer; b. Urbana, Ill., Aug. 5, 1943; s. Lawrence Hugh and Margaret Alene (Burlison) H.; m. Kathleen O'Hara, Nov. 8, 1969; 1 child, Scott David. BA, Dartmouth Coll., 1965; JD cum laude, U. Pa., 1968. Bar: Wash. 1971, U.S. Dist. Ct. (we. dist.) Wash. 1971, Ct. of Appeals (9th cir.) 1971, U.S. Supreme Ct. 1990. Analyst U.S. Central Intelligence Agency, Langley, Va., 1969-71; ptnr. Perkins Coie, Bellevue, Wash., 1971—. Contbr. articles to profl. jours. Mem. King County Personnel Bd., Wash., 1984-90; mem. fin. com. Mcpl. Gov. Candidates, King County, 1972—. 1st lt. USAF, 1968-69. Mem. ABA, Wash. State Bar Assn., Seattle-King County Bar Assn., Supreme Ct. Hist. Soc. Methodist. Avocations: jogging, boating, tennis. Labor, Education and schools. Home: 1610 W Lake Sammamish Pky SE Bellevue WA 98008-5229 Office: Perkins Coie 411 108th Ave NE Ste 1800 Bellevue WA 98004-5584

**HANNAH, R. CRAIG,** lawyer; b. Harrison, Ark., Sept. 25, 1964; s. James Robert Hannah and Linda Neal Watson; m. Mitzi Paige Hannah, Aug. 13, 1989; children: Gabrielle, Adrian. BA in Zoology, U. Ark., 1986, JD with honors, 1990. Assoc. Rose Law Firm, Little Rock, Ark., 1990-94; ptnr. Aydelott & Hannah, Searcy, Ark., 1994—; pres. White County Title Co., Searcy, 1997—; atty. White County Bd. of Realtors, Searcy, 1994—. Mem. Kiwanis Club. Contracts commercial, Real property, Personal injury. Office: Aydelott & Hannah 115 W Arch Ave Searcy AR 72143-7701

**HANNAN, DAVID CARROLL,** lawyer; b. Wilmington, Del., Dec. 8, 1945; m. Barbara Lott; children—Leann. Student Emory and Henry Coll., 1964-65; B.A., Auburn U., 1968; J.D., U. Ala.-Tuscaloosa, 1971. Bar: Ala. 1971. Ptnr. Johnstone, Adams, Mobile, Ala., 1971—. Mem. adv. council Mobile Head Start Program, 1972-74; pres. Mobile Track and Field Assn., 1976-77, Mobile Pre-Sch. for Deaf, Inc., 1979-81, Vol. Mobile, Inc., 1982-83; mem. bus. adv. coun. Auburn U. Coll. Bus., 1988-92; fellow Leadership Mobile Program, 1978; vestry St. Paul's Episcopal Ch., 1976-79; mem. nat. coun., exec. adv. bd. S.E. region, coun. pres., coun. commr. and v.p., dist. chmn., dist. fin. chmn., scoutmaster Boy Scouts Am., 1972—, recipient Award of Merit, Silver Beaver; bd. dirs. Leadership Mobile, Inc., 1980-93, Boys Clubs of Mobile, 1979—, Am. Cancer Soc., 1983-84, Mobile Pre-Sch. for Deaf, 1977-83, Vol. Mobile, Inc., 1980-83, Gulf Coast Pub. Broadcasting, Inc., 1988—, United Way of S.W. Ala., Inc., 1989—; mem. adv. bd. Parade Against Drugs, 1984-86; mem. Sr. Bowl Com., 1974—. Mem. ABA, Ala. Bar Assn., Mobile Bar Assn., Def. Rsch. Inst., Ala. Def. Lawyers Assn., Internat. Assn. Def. Counsel (chair accident health and life ins. law com. 1991-93). Episcopalian. Home: 118 Eaton Sq Mobile AL 36608-1936 Office: Johnstone Adams Bailey Gordon & Harris PO Box 1988 Mobile AL 36633-1988

**HANNAN, MYLES,** lawyer, banker; b. Rye, N.Y., Oct. 14, 1936; s. Joseph A. and Rosemary (Edwards) H.; children from previous marriages: Myles Jr., Paul F., Thomas J., Kerry E. BA, Holy Cross Coll., 1958; LLB, Harvard U., 1964. Bar: N.Y. 1964, Mass. 1970, Md. 1994, D.C. 1996, U.S. Dist. Ct. (so. and ea. dists.) N.Y. 1966, U.S. Dist. Ct. Md. 1995. Assoc. Cadwalader, Wickersham & Taft, N.Y.C., 1964-69; v.p., gen. counsel, sec. High Voltage Engring. Corp., Burlington, Mass., 1969-73; v.p., sec. Stop & Shop Cos., Inc., Boston, 1973-79; group v.p. law and adminstrn. Del. North Cos., Inc., Buffalo, 1979-81; v.p., fin., gen. counsel, sec. Anacomp, Inc., Indpls., 1981-84; exec. v.p. Empire of Am. FSB, Buffalo, 1984-89; adminstrv. v.p. Berkeley Group Inc., Buffalo, 1990-91; ptnr. Linowes and Blocher LLP, Washington, 1992—. Trustee Studio Arena Theatre, Buffalo, 1986-89; bd. dirs. Buffalo Philharm. Orch., 1987-89. Lt. USNR, 1958-61. Finance, Landlord-tenant, Real property. Home: 2445 Lyttonsville Rd Apt 1209 Silver Spring MD 20910-1936 Office: Linowes and Blocher LLP 1010 Wayne Ave Ste 1000 Silver Spring MD 20910-5615

**HANNER, KARL TIGER,** lawyer; b. Austin, Tex., Dec. 27, 1964; s. Karl Marion and Lenesse (Harper) H.; m. Amy Michelle Anderson, Oct. 16, 1993; children: Alexandra Marie, Kendall Taylor. Student, Yale U., 1984-86; BA with spl. honors, U. Tex., JD, 1991. Bar: Tex., 1991, U.S. Dist. Ct. (we. dist.), 1991. Assoc. atty. Mullen, MacInnes, Redding & Grove, Austin, 1991-95, Maroney, Crowley & Bankston, Austin, 1995, Brim, Arnett and Robinett, PC, Austin, 1995—. Mem. Tex. Bar Found., Tex. Relays Officials Assn., Austin Young Lawyers Assn., Travis County Bar Assn. Democrat. Roman Catholic. Avocations: athletics, running, gardening. Education and schools, Sports. Office: Brim Arnett and Robinett PC 2525 Wallingwood Dr Bldg 14 Austin TX 78746-6900

**HANNON, LEO FRANCIS,** retired lawyer, educator; b. Boston, June 29, 1926; s. Bernard Francis and Elsie A. (Byrne) H.; m. Marion Ryan, June 7, 1958 (dec.); children: Elizabeth, James, Patricia, Jane. BS, Boston Coll., 1951; LLB, Georgetown U., 1958. Bar: D.C. 1958, U.S. Dist. Ct. D.C. 1958. Spl. agt. Office of Naval Intelligence, Washington, 1953-59; sr. atty. Nat. Labor Rels. Bd., Phila., 1960-69; mng. counsel labor security and benefits E.I. DuPont Co., Wilmington, Del., 1969-90; tchr. U. Del., Newark, 1991-95; mem. Bus. Roundtable Litigation Com., N.Y., Washington, 1980-90. Author: Legal Side of Private Security, 1992; contbr. articles to profl. jours. Bd. mem. Contact USA, Harrisburg, Pa., 1993-96; vol. Seamen's Ctr., Wilmington, Del. With USN, 1944-46, 51-53. Avocations: writing, travel, golf. Home: 1211 Hilltop Ave Wilmington DE 19809-1625

**HANNON, TIMOTHY PATRICK,** lawyer, educator; b. Culver City, Calif., Nov. 29, 1948; s. Justin Aloysius and Ann Elizabeth (Ford) H.; m. Patricia Ann Hanson, May 1, 1976; children: Sean Patrick, James Patrick. Student, U. Vienna, 1968-69, Naval War Coll., 1988; BA, U. Santa Clara, 1970, JD cum laude, 1974. Bar: Calif. 1974, U.S. Dist. Ct. (no. dist.) Calif. 1974, U.S. Dist. Ct. (so. and dists.) Calif. 1978, U.S. Ct. Appeals (9th cir.) 1978, Ct. Appeals Armed Forces 1979, D.C. 1981, U.S. Tax Ct. 1983, U.S. Ct. Claims 1983; cert. trial and def. lawyer Univorm Code Mil. Justice. Assoc. N. Perry Moerdyke, Jr., Palo Alto, Calif., 1975-81; ptnr. Myerdyke & Hannon, Palo Alto, 1982-84, Attwood, Hurst, Knox & Anderson, 1984-86; pvt. practice Campbell, Calif., 1986-97; U.S. Adminstrv. law judge Social Security Adminstrn., 1997—; instr. San Jose State U., 1985-89; instr. De Anza Jr. Coll., Cupertino, Calif., 1987—, instr. extension courses U. Calif., Santa Cruz, 1982-83; lectr. Lincoln Law Sch., San Jose, Calif., 1988—; arbitrator Santa Clara County Superior Ct., Santa Clara County Mcpl. Ct.; sr. mil. mem. expanded Internat. Mil. Edn. Tng., Uganda; judge pro temp Santa Clara County Mcpl Ct. Chmn., Menlo Park Housing Commn., 1979-81; mem. allocations com. vol. United Way Clara County, 1987-90; mem. San Jose Vets. Meml. Com., 1993-99, treas., 1996-99. Admiral Tex. Navy, 1998. With Calif. Army NG, 1970-76, capt., USNR, 1979—. Mem. Santa Clara County Bar Assn. (exec. com.), Santa Clara U. Nat. Alumni, U. Santa Clara Law Alumni Assn. (bd. dirs. 1980-81, sec. 1981-83, v.p. 1983-85, pres. 1985-87), Kiwanis. Roman Catholic. Avocation: flying. State civil litigation, Consumer commercial, General practice. Home: 806 Buckwood Ct San Jose CA 95120-3306 Office: Social Security Adminstrn. 280 S 1st St # 300 San Jose CA 95113-3002

**HANOVER, RICHARD,** lawyer, consultant, physician; b. N.Y.C.. Student, NYU, 1968-71; AB in Psychology, Vassar Coll., 1973; MD, U. Autonoma de Guadalajara, Mexico, 1977; postgrad., N.Y. Med. Coll. Fifth Pathway, 1977-78; JD, Nova U., 1987. Bar: Fla. 1988, N.Y. 1989, U.S. Dist. Ct. (so. and ea. dists.) N.Y. 1990; diplomate Am. Bd. Internal Medicine, Am. Bd. Legal Medicine. Intern internal medicine Met. Hosp., N.Y.C., 1978-79; resident psychiatry CMDNJ-Rutgers, New Brunswick, N.J., 1979-80; pvt. practice medicine with Bernard Hanover M.D., N.Y.C., 1980-92; physician Group/Clinic Med. Practice, Ft. Lauderdale/Miami, Fla., 1984-88; resident in internal medicine N.Y. Downtown Hosp., N.Y.C., 1992-94; attending physician The Mount Sinai Hosp. Employee Health Svc., N.Y.C., 1994-95, Western Queens Cmty. Hosp., L.I., 1995—, Boro Med., P.C., N.Y.C., 1997—; law assoc. Kopff, Nardelli & Dopf, N.Y.C., 1989-90; litigation practice N.Y.C., 1990-92, pvt. cons. legal medicine, 1992—; adj. asst. prof. cmty. and preventive medicine N.Y. Med. Coll., Valhalla, N.Y., 1991-94; clin. instr., preceptor, third yr. internal medicine clerkship/house staff The Mount Sinai Sch. Medicine, N.Y.C., 1994-95; alliance physician The Mount Sinai Hosp., N.Y.C., 1996—; assoc. physician The Mount Sinai Sch. Medicine, 1996—; spkr. in field. Contbr. articles to profl. jours. Fellow Am. Coll. Legal Medicine; mem. AMA, N.Y. State Bar Assn., Assn. of the Bar of the City of N.Y., N.Y. County Lawyers' Assn., Phi Alpha Delta. Personal injury, Health. Office: 320 W 86th St New York NY 10024-3139

**HANRAHAN, MICHAEL G.,** lawyer, business consultant; b. Mount Vernon, N.Y., June 1, 1949; s. G. Michael and Florence M. (Quinn) H.; m. Barbara L. Fluhr, June 11, 1977; children: Thomas M., Elizabeth L. BA, Saint Bonaventure U., 1971; JD, Fordham U., 1974. Bar: N.Y., 1975; U.S. Dist. Ct. (ea. dist.) N.Y. 1975, U.S. Ct. Appeals (2nd cir.) 1975, Supreme Ct. 1997. Ptnr. Hanrahan & Hanrahan, Pelham, N.Y., 1975—, Hanrahan & Curley, Chappaqua, N.Y., 1995—; bd. dirs. John Langenbacher Co., Inc., Bronx, N.Y., U.S. Veneer Co., Inc., 1985—; counsel Entrepreneurial Ctr., Inc., Purchase, N.Y., 1995—. Pres., dir. Pelham (N.Y.) Family Svc., Inc., 1976-80. Mem. Rotary Internat. (pres., dir. 1976—, Paul Harris fellow 1988). General practice, Estate planning, Probate. Office: Hanrahan & Hanrahan 438 5th Ave Pelham NY 10803-1257

**HANSBURY, STEPHAN CHARLES,** lawyer; b. Mt. Holly, N.J., Nov. 3, 1946; s. Charles Clark and Kathryn Irene (Meyer) H.; m. Sharon Buckley; children: Elizabeth Kathryn, Jillian Judith, Stephanie Clark. BA, Allegheny Coll., 1968; MBA, Fairleigh Dickinson U., 1973; JD, Seton Hall U., 1977; cert. civil trial atty., Supreme Ct. N.J., 1989. Bar: N.J. 1977, U.S. Dist. Ct. (no. dist.) N.J. 1977, U.S. Supreme Ct. 1982. Dir. spl. programs Bloomfield (N.J.) Coll., 1968-71; dir. fin. aid Monmouth Coll., West Long Branch, N.J., 1971-72; asst. adminstr. Morris View, Morris Plains, N.J., 1972-78; assoc. Hansbury, Martin & Knapp, Morris Plains, 1978-87, pres., 1987-92; ptnr. Kummer Knox, Naughton & Hansbury, Parsippany, N.J., 1992—, pres., 1996—; mem., gen. counsel Cheshire Home, Florham Park, N.J., 1978—, Ciba-Geigy Corp., Summit, N.J., 1980-92. Legis. aide Assemblyman Arthur Albohn, Morristown, N.J., 1980-83; mem. Morris County Bd. of Social Svcs., 1989-96, chmn. 1992-94. Mem. ABA, N.J. Bar Assn., Morris County Bar Assn. (trustee 1987-90), Rotary (bd. dirs. Morris Plains 1981-83, v.p. 1996-97, pres.-elect 1997-98, pres. 1998—), Morristown Club. Republican. Episcopalian. Avocations: tennis, golf, reading. State civil litigation, Environmental, Real property. Office: Kummer Knox Naughton & Hansbury 299 Cherry Hill Rd Parsippany NJ 07054-1111

**HANSEL, GREGORY PAUL,** lawyer; b. Glen Cove, N.Y., Feb. 21, 1960; s. Paul George and Helen (Stephens) H. BA magna cum laude, Harvard U., 1982; JD, U. Va., 1986. Bar: Fla. 1986, U.S. Ct. Appeals (11th cir.) 1986, U.S. Dist. Ct. (mid. dist.) Fla. 1987, D.C. Ct. Appeals 1988, U.S. Supreme Ct. 1992, Maine 1997. Sr. legis. asst. Atty. Gen. Fla., Tallahassee, 1984; ptnr. Shackleford, Farrior, Stallings & Evans, P.A., Tampa, Fla., 1986-96, Holland & Knight, Tampa, 1996-97; of counsel Preti, Flaherty, Beliveau, Pachios & Haley, LLC, Portland, Maine, 1997—. Co-author: Business Litigation in Florida, 1995. Mem. ABA, Fla. Bar (chmn. Fla. Bar conv. 1995), Maine State Bar Assn. Greek Orthodox. General civil litigation. Office: Preti Flaherty Beliveau Pachios & Haley LLC 1 City Ctr Portland ME 04101-4004

**HANSELMANN, FREDRICK CHARLES,** lawyer; b. Phila., Sept. 1, 1955; s. Helmuth Fredrick and Maria Elizabeth (Dougherty) H.; m. Mary Nina Johnson, May 7, 1983; children: Elizabeth Ryan, Peter Cornelius, Kevin Andrew, Charlotte Mary. BA magna cum laude, La Salle Coll., 1977; JD, U. Notre Dame, 1980. Bar: Pa. 1980, U.S. Dist. Ct. (ea. dist.) Pa. 1981, U.S. Dist. Ct. (mid. dist.) Pa. 1987, U.S. Ct. Appeals (3d cir.) 1981. Assoc. German, Gallagher & Murtagh, P.C., Phila., 1981-85, Wilson, Elser, Moskowitz, Edelman & Dicker, Phila., 1985-90; ptnr. Mylotte David & Fitzpatrick, Phila., 1990—. Mem. ABA, Pa. Bar Assn., Phila. Bar Assn., Def. Rsch. Inst., Profl. Liability Underwriting Soc., Lawyers Club Phila., Notre Dame Club Phila., Avalon Yacht Club, Glen Lake (Mich.) Assn. Republican. Roman Catholic. Insurance, Personal injury, General civil litigation. Home: 118 Azalea Way Flourtown PA 19031-2008 Office: Mylotte David & Fitzpatrick 1635 Market St Fl 9 Philadelphia PA 19103-2217

**HANSEN, CHRISTINA FLORES,** lawyer; b. San Antonio, Nov. 22, 1951; d. Jose and Juanita (Malacara) Flores; m. David Walter Hansen, June 1, 1974; children: Marisa Lee, Nicolas Daniel, Felisa Marie, Esteban Rodriguez, Adam Rodriguez, Sandra Rodriguez, Ricardo Rodriguez. BA, Marquette U., 1973; JD, Drake U., 1986. Bar: Iowa 1987. Counselor Marquette U., Milw., 1973-74; counselor, supr. Iowa Comprehensive Manpower Services, Des Moines, 1976-81, Cen. Iowa Regional Assn. Local Govts., Des Moines, 1981-83; atty. Child Support Recovery Unit, Des Moines, 1987-91; asst. atty. gen. State of Iowa, Des Moines, 1991—; presenter continuing legal edn. seminar on Iowa child support guidelines, 1991, sexual harrassment in the workplace, 1988. Commr. Commn. on Children, Youth & Families, Des Moines 1987-91; chair Hispanic Polit. Caucus, Des Moines, 1987; bd. dirs. Iowa Children & Family Svcs., Des Moines, 1988-91; sec. pres. United Mex. Am. Community Ctr. Bd. Trustees, Des Moines, 1988-90; subcom. cho-chair Mayor's Select Com. on Drug Abuse; bd. dirs. YWCA, 1992-95; mem. Des Moines Chem. Dependency Coun., 1992-93. Mem. ABA, Iowa Bar Assn., Polk County Bar Assn., League of United Latin Am. Citizens, Young Women's Christian Assn. (bd. dirs. 1992), Chem. Dependency Coun., Beta Sigma Phi (treas. Des Moines chpt. 1987-90). Democrat. Roman Catholic. Avocation: reading. Home: 5209 Lower Beaver Rd Des Moines IA 50310-4352 Office: Foster Care Recovery Unit 211 E Maple St Ste 100 Des Moines IA 50309-1858

**HANSEN, CHRISTOPHER AGNEW,** lawyer; b. Yakima, Wash., Dec. 10, 1934; s. Raymond Walter and Christine F.M. (Agnew) H.; m. Sandra Ridgely Pindell, Aug. 4, 1959; children: Anne Ridgely, Christopher Agnew Jr., Eric Bruce. BS, Cornell U., 1957; JD, U. Md., 1963. Bar: Md. 1963, U.S. Supreme Ct. 1973, U.S. Ct. Appeals (4th cir.) D.C. 1978. Law clk. Cir. Ct. for Balt. County, Towson, Md., 1960-63; assoc. Piper & Marbury, Balt., 1963-74; of counsel Casey, Scott, Canfield & Heggestad PC, Washington, 1982-93; ptnr. Constable, Alexander & Skeen, Towson, 1984-86, Parks, Hansen & Ditch, Towson, 1986-94; of counsel Heggestad & Weiss, PC, Washington, 1993—; pvt. practice Towson, 1974-83, 95—. With U.S. Army, 1957-60. Mem. ABA, D.C. Bar, Md. State Bar Assn., Bar Assn. Balt. County, Balt. City Bar Assn., Md. Assn. Def. Trial Counsel, Phi Alpha Delta. Episcopalian. Federal civil litigation, State civil litigation, Insurance. Office: 7313 York Rd Ste 200 Towson MD 21204-7617

**HANSEN, CURTIS LEROY,** federal judge; b. 1933. BS, U. Iowa, 1956; JD, U. N.Mex., 1961. Bar: N.Mex. Law clk. to Hon. Irwin S. Moise N.Mex. Supreme Ct., 1961-62; ptnr. Snead & Hansen, Albuquerque, 1962-64, Richard C. Civerolo, Albuquerque, 1964-71, Civerolo, Hansen & Wolf, P.A., 1971-92; dist. judge U.S. Dist. Ct., N.Mex., 1992—. Mem. State Bar N.Mex., Albuquerque Bar Assn., Am. Coll. Trial Lawyers, Am. Bd. Trial Advocates, Albuquerque Country Club. Office: US Courthouse Chambers 660 333 Lomas Blvd NW Albuquerque NM 87102-2272

**HANSEN, DAVID RASMUSSEN,** federal judge; b. 1938. BA, N.W. Mo. State U., 1960; JD, George Washington U., 1963. Asst. clk. to minority House Appropriations Com. Ho. of Reps., 1960-61; adminstrv. aide 7th Dist. Iowa, 1962-63; pvt. practice law Jones, Cambridge & Carl, Atlantic, Iowa, 1963-64; capt., judge advocate General's Corps U.S. Army, 1964-68; pvt. practice law Barker, Hansen & McNeal, Iowa Falls, Iowa, 1968-76; ptnr. Win-Gin Farms, Iowa Falls, 1971—; judge Police Ct., Iowa, 1969-73, 2d Jud. Dist. Iowa Dist. Ct., 1976-86, U.S. Dist. Ct. (no. dist.) Iowa, Cedar Rapids, 1986-91, U.S. Ct. Appeals (8th cir.), Cedar Rapids, 1991—. Office: US Courthouse 101 1st St SE Cedar Rapids IA 52401-1202*

**HANSEN, H. REESE,** dean, educator; b. Logan, Utah, Apr. 8, 1942; s. Howard F. and Loila Gayle (Reese) H.; m. Kathryn Traveller, June 8, 1962; children: Brian T., Mark T., Dale T., Curtis T. BS, Utah State U., 1964; JD, U. Utah, 1972. Bar: Utah, 1974. Atty. Strong, Poelman & Fox, Salt Lake City, 1972-74; from asst. prof. to assoc. prof. Brigham Young U., Provo, Utah, 1974-79, prof., 1979—, from asst. dean to assoc. dean, 1974-89, dean, 1989—; commr. ex officio Utah State Bar, Salt Lake City, 1989—; commr. Nat. Conf. Commrs. on Uniform State Laws, 1988-95. Co-author: Idaho Probate System, 1977, Utah Probate System, 1977, Cases and Text on Laws of Trusts, 6th edit., 1991; editor: Manual for Justices of Peace--Utah, 1978; contbr. articles to profl. jours. Mem. LDS Ch. Office: Brigham Young U 348A Jrcb Provo UT 84602-1029

**HANSEN, JOHN ALTON,** lawyer; b. La Junta, Colo., May 7, 1933; s. Alton Schow and Ora (Packer) H.; m. Mary C. Williamson, Nov. 9, 1957; children: James P., Julia R., Kathryn M., Steven J. LLB cum laude, Marquette U., 1957. Bar: Wis. 1957, U.S. Dist. Ct. (ea. dist.) Wis. 1957, U.S. Dist. Ct. (we. dist.) Wis. 1961, U.S. Ct. Appeals (7th cir.) 1960. Assoc. Rieser, Stafford, Rosenbaum & Rieser, Madison, Wis., 1960-64; ptnr. Stafford, Rosenbaum, Rieser & Hansen, Madison, Wis., 1964—. Contbr. articles to profl. jours. Bd. dirs. Woolsack Soc., Milw., 1983-89. Lt. USN, 1957-60. Mem. ABA, State Bar Wis., Am. Coll. Trial Lawyers, Dane County Bar Assn., Marquette U. Law Alumni Assn. (bd. dirs. 1975-79). Product liability, General civil litigation, Administrative and regulatory. Office: Stafford Rosenbaum Rieser & Hansen 3 S Pinckney St Madison WI 53703-2866

**HANSEN, JOHN JOSEPH,** lawyer; b. San Anselmo, Calif., Sept. 7, 1961; s. Joseph G. and Barbara M. H.; m. Marjorie Ann Walker, Feb. 18, 1995. BA, Coll. Idaho, 1983; JD, U. Idaho, 1987. Bar: Idaho 1987, U.S. Dist. Ct. Idaho 1987, Wash. 1994. Staff atty. Idaho Legal Aid Svcs., Caldwell, 1987-88; trial atty. Ada County Pub. Defender, Boise, 1988-92; dep. atty. gen. Idaho Atty. Gen., Boise, 1992-93; asst. Open Soc. Fund, Vilnius, Lithuania, 1994; dep. pros. atty. Yakima County Prosecutor, Wash., 1994-97; assoc. Wiebe & Fouser P.A., Caldwell, 1997-98; chief pub. defender Twin Falls County Pub. Defender, Idaho, 1998—. Vol. Ctrl. Wash. chpt. Nat. Multiple Sclerosis Soc., Yakima, 1994-97. Roman Catholic. Avocations: music, books, travel. Office: Twin Falls County Pub Defender PO Box 126 Twin Falls ID 83303-0126

**HANSEN, KENNETH,** lawyer. Gen. counsel Export-Import Bank, Washington. Office: Export-Import Bank 811 Vermont Ave NW Washington DC 20571-0002

**HANSEN, MARK CHARLES,** lawyer; b. N.Y.C., Aug. 13, 1956; s. Charles and Carolyn (Smith) H.; m. Anne Samuels, June 28, 1986; children: Elisabeth Bayard, Caroline Alexandra. AB, Dartmouth Coll., 1978; JD, Harvard U., 1982. Bar: D.C. 1990, Mass. 1983, Md. 1996. Law clk. to hon. William H. Timbers U.S. Ct. Appeals (2d cir.), Bridgeport, Conn., N.Y.C., 1982-83; assoc. Hill & Barlow, Boston, 1983-85; asst. U.S. atty. U.S. Dist. Ct. (so. dist.) N.Y., 1986-89; shareholder Johnson & Gibbs, P.C., Washington, 1990-93; ptnr. Kellogg, Huber, Hansen, Todd & Evans PLLC, Washington, 1993—; faculty Nat. Inst. Trial Advocacy, Georgetown U., Washington, 1991-95. Recipient Spl. Commendation U.S. Dept. of Justice, 1988. Mem. ABA. Federal civil litigation, Criminal, General civil litigation. Office: Kellogg Huber Hansen Todd & Evans PLLC 1301 K St NW Ste 1000 Washington DC 20005-3317

**HANSHAW, A. ALAN,** lawyer; b. Kankakee, Ill., June 23, 1926; s. Armand E. and Deborah Bertine (Sanborn) H.; m. Emma H. Hernandez, Sept. 1, 1951; children: Mark A., John W., David M., Deborah L., A. Andrew. Bar: Ariz. 1955, U.S. Dist. Ct. Ariz. 1956, U.S. Supreme Ct. 1964. Law clk. Ariz. Supreme Ct., 1955-56; asst. city atty. City of Tucson, 1956-58; assoc., then ptnr. Godard, Gin, Hanshaw & Gianas, Tucson, 1958-69; gen. counsel U.S. V.I. Corp., 1964-65; sole practice, Tucson, 1969-72; shareholder, bd. dirs. Waterfall, Economidis, Caldwell, Hanshaw & Villamana, P.C., Tucson, 1972-95; of counsel, 1995-98; retired, 1998—. Pres., United Way of Tucson, 1977; bd. dirs. La Frontera Mental Health Ctr., 1981—, pres., 1983-84. Served with U.S. Mcht. Marine, 1944-46. Mem. Ariz. Bar Assn., State Bar Ariz. (cert. real property specialist), Nat. Health Lawyers Assn. Episcopalian. Clubs: Rotary (Tucson); Mission Bay Yacht (San Diego). General corporate, Health, Real property. Office: Williams Centre 5210 W Williams Circle Suite 800 Tucson AZ 85711

**HANSMANN, HENRY BAETHKE,** law educator; b. Highland Park, Ill., Oct. 5, 1945; s. Elwood Hansmann and Louise Frances (Baethke) Moore; m. Marina Santilli, 1992; 1 child, Lisa Santilli. BA, Brown U., 1967; JD, Yale U., 1974, PhD, 1978. Asst. prof. law U. Pa. Law Sch., Phila., 1975-81, assoc. prof. law, econs. and pub. policy, 1981-83; prof. law Yale U., New Haven, 1983-88, Harris prof., 1988—. Author: The Ownership of Enterprise, 1996. John Simon Guggenheim Found. fellow, 1985-86. Mem. Am. Econ. Assn., Am. Law and Econ. Assn. Home: 340 Livingston St New Haven CT 06511-1336 Office: Yale U Law Sch PO Box 208215 New Haven CT 06520-8215

**HANSON, AVARITA LAUREL,** lawyer; b. N.Y.C., July 21, 1953; d. Earle L. and Gloria (Troupe) H.; m. William A. Alexander, June 14, 1975; children: Justin, Colin. AB, Radcliffe Coll., 1975; JD, U. Pa., 1978. Bar: Tex. 1979, U.S. Ct. Appeals (5th cir.) 1980, U.S. Dist. Ct. (so. dist.) Tex. 1980, U.S. Dist. Ct. (no. dist.) Ga. 1981, U.S. Ct. Appeals (11th cir.) 1981, Ga. 1983. Assoc. Fulbright & Jaworski, Houston, 1978-82; pvt. practice Houston and Atlanta, 1982—; judge Fulton County Juvenile Ct., 1995-97; exec. dir. examining bds. divsn. Ga. Sec. of State, 1997—; ptnr. Secret & Assocs., Atlanta, 1983-84; dir. pro bono project Ga. Bar Assn. and Ga. Legal Svcs. Program, 1985-89; clk. Fulton County Commn., 1990-95; bd. dirs. Atlanta Legal Aid Soc., 1986—, Ga. Legal Svcs. Program, 1995—. Exec. producer TV show Legally Speaking, 1983-90. Candidate coun. City of College Park, Ga., 1985; trustee Ben Hill United Meth. Ch., 1985-88; bd. dirs. YWCA Greater Atlanta, 1989-92. Mem. Ga. Assn. Black Women Attys. (pres. 1985), Atlanta Bar Assn. (adv. bd. 1989—), Gate City Bar Assn. (pres. 1991), Leadership Atlanta, Leadership Ga. (bd. trustees), Radcliffe Coll. Alumnae Assn. (bd. dirs.), Atlanta Women's Network, Ga. Women's Polit Caucus, Harvard Club Ga. (pres. 1994, v.p. 1987-90), Harvard Alumni Assn. (bd. dirs. 1990-93, 95—), Leadership Am. Democrat. Avocation: gourmet cooking. General practice.

**HANSON, BRUCE EUGENE,** lawyer; b. Lincoln, Nebr., Aug. 25, 1942; s. Lester E. and Gladys (Diessner) H.; m. Peggy Pardun, Dec. 25, 1972 (dec. Nov. 1989). BA, U. Minn., 1965, JD, 1966. Bar: Minn. 1966, U.S. Dist. Ct. Minn. 1966, U.S. Tax Ct. 1973, U.S. Ct. Appeals (8th cir.) 1973, U.S. Ct. Appeals (fed. cir.) 1983, U.S. Supreme Ct. 1970. Shareholder Doherty, Rumble & Butler, P.A., St. Paul, 1966-99; ptnr. Oppenheimer, Wolff & Donnelly, LLP, Mpls., 1999—. Dir., sec. Am. Saddlebred Horse Assn.; bd. trustees, chair United Hosp., 1996-98. Mem. ATLA, Ramsey County Bar Assn., Minn. State Bar Assn., Am. Health Lawyers Assn., Minn. Soc. Hosp. Attys., North Oaks Golf Club, Order of Coif, Phi Delta Phi. Health, Federal civil litigation, State civil litigation. Home: 23 Evergreen Rd Saint Paul MN 55127-2077 Office: Oppenheimer Wolff & Donnelly LLP Ste 3400 Plz Vii 45 S 7th St Minneapolis MN 55402

**HANSON, DAVID JAMES,** lawyer; b. Neenah, Wis., July 20, 1943; s. Vernon James and Dorothy O. Hanson; m. Diana G. Severson, Aug. 25, 1965 (div. Sept. 1982); children: Matthew Vernon, Maja Kirsten, Brian Edward; m. Linda Hughes Bochert, May 28, 1983; children: Scott Charles, Sarah Katherine. BS, U. Wis., 1965, JD, 1968. Bar: Wis. 1968, U.S. Dist. Ct. (we. dist.) Wis. 1968, U.S. Dist. Ct. (ea. dist.) Wis. 1969, U.S. Ct. Appeals (7th cir.) 1970, U.S. Supreme Ct. 1976. Asst. atty. gen. State of Wis. Dept. of Justice, Madison, 1968-71, dep. atty. gen., 1976-81; asst. chancellor, chief legal counsel U. Wis., Madison, 1971-76; ptnr. Michael, Best & Friedrich, Madison, 1981—; part-time lectr. Law Sch., U. Wis., Madison, 1972-75; bd. dirs., chair govt. law sect. State Bar Wis., Madison, 1979-88. Author monograph: The Lowered Age of Majority: It's Impact on Higher Education, 1975; contbr. articles to profl. publs. Wis. Epilepsy Assn., Madiso n, 1986—; bd. dirs. Sand County Found., Madison, 1988—, Wis. Ctr. for Academically Talented Youth, Madison, 1991-94, bd. trustees Edgewood Coll., Madison, 1997—. Mem. Madison Club, Amer. Bar Assn. Democrat. Unitarian. Avocations: canoeing, skiing, tennis, biking, hunting. General corporate, Public utilities, Health. Office: Michael Best & Friedrich PO Box 1806 Madison WI 53701-1806

**HANSON, EUGENE PAUL,** laywer; b. Willimantic, Conn., May 22, 1940; s. Jacob Edward Hanson and Virginia Mary Stanford; m. Mary Frances Winston, Oct. 12, 1974; children: Katharine M., Arthur J., Anne E. BA, U. Conn., 1963, MA, 1964; JD, NYU, 1972. Bar: N.Y. 1972, Calif. 1987, N.J. 1995. Instr. English, Tri-State Coll., Angola, Ind., 1967-69; trial aty. antitrust divsn. U.S. Dept. Justice, N.Y.C., 1972-86; assoc. O'Melveny & Myers, L.A. and N.Y.C., 1987-95; pvt. practice, Summit and Chester, N.J., 1996—. Editor, vice chmn.: Sample Jury Instructions in Criminal Antitrust Cases, 1984; editor: Sample Jury Instructions in Civil Antitrust Cases, 1990. With U.S. Army, 1963-65, Vietnam. Mem. N.J. Bar Assn., Morris County Bar Assn. Avocations: literature, music, art. General civil litigation, Antitrust, Securities. Home and Office: 9 Chesterbrook Rd Chester NJ 07930-2016

**HANSON, FRED B.,** lawyer; b. Alexandria, Va.; s. August Theodore and Flora Alice (Kays) H.; m. Jane Roberts, Oct. 24, 1934 (dec. Jan. 1971); m. Lucy Merrick, Dec. 10, 1971 (dec. Nov. 1987); children: Linscott, Per, Marta; m. Marilynn S. Lane, Aug. 12, 1989. Student, DePauw U., 1924-26, Northwestern U., 1927-28; LLB, Ill. Inst. Tech., 1932. Bar: Ind. 1925, Ill. 1932, U.S. Dist. Ct. (no. dist.) Ill. 1932. Ptnr. Ross, Berchem & Hanson, Chgo., 1932-34; sole practice Chgo., 1934-37, 52—; atty. Standard Oil Co., Chgo., 1937-46; ptnr. Hanson & Doyle, Chgo., 1946-52, The Firm of Fred B. Hanson Assocs., Chgo., 1952-86; sole practice Chgo., 1986—; gen. counsel., bd. dirs. various banks and cos. Author: Claim Handling, 1956; contbr. articles to profl. jours. Atty. Village of Glenview, 1950-54, judge, 1946-50; trustee Maryhaven, Glenview, 1946-72. Lt. sgt. USNR, 1943-46; PTO. Mem. ABA, Ill. Bar Assn., Chgo. Bar Assn., Chgo. Yacht Club. Democrat. Avocations: bridge, travel. Banking, General corporate, Probate.

**HANSON, GARY A.,** lawyer, legal educator; b. Santa Fe, Sept. 30, 1954; s. Norman A. Hanson and Mary Gene (Moore) Garrison; m. Tracey J. Tannen, Mar. 11, 1982; children: Paul, Carly, Sean. BS magna cum laude,

U. Utah, 1976; JD, Pepperdine U., 1980. Bar: Calif. 1980, U.S. Dist. Ct. (cen. dist.) Calif. 1980, U.S. Ct. Appeals (9th cir.) 1980. Pvt. practice Westlake Village, Calif., 1980-82; assoc. gen. counsel Pepperdine U., Malibu, Calif., 1982-83, acting gen. counsel, 1983-84, univ. gen. counsel, 1984—; adj. prof. law Pepperdine U., Malibu, 1982—, lectr. bus. law, 1986—; pro bono atty. San Fernando Valley Christian Sch., L.A., 1982-83; mem. Pro Bono Estate Adv. Svc., San Diego, 1983-86; cons. West Ednl. Pub. Co., 1988. Contbr. articles to profl. jours.; pres. Ind. Colls. and Univs. jour., 1989. Recipient Pres.'s award San Diego Christian Found., 1984. Mem. ABA, L.A. County Bar Assn., Nat. Assn. Coll. and Univ. Attys. Republican. General corporate, Education and schools. Office: Pepperdine U Gen Counsel Office TAC 421 24255 Pacific Coast Hwy Malibu CA 90263-0002

**HANSON, JASON DAVID,** lawyer; b. L.A., Feb. 14, 1969; s. William Dean and Merrilyn Ethyl (Coleman) H. BS, Cornell U., 1991; JD, Duke U., 1994. Bar: Md. 1994, D.C. 1995. Assoc. Arnold & Porter, Washington, 1994-97; trial atty. anti trust divsn. U.S. Dept. Justice, Washington, 1997-99; global litigation counsel GE Med. Sys., Milwaukee, Wis., 1999—. Staff editor: Duke Law Jour., 1993-94. Mem. ABA. Office: GE Med Sys 3000 Grandview Blvd # 400 Waukesha WI 53188-1615

**HANSON, JEAN ELIZABETH,** lawyer; b. Alexandria, Minn., June 28, 1949; d. Carroll Melvin and Alice Clarissa (Frykman) H.; m. H. Barndt Hauptfuhrer, May 15, 1982; children: Catherine Jean, Benjamin Colman (twins). BA, Luther Coll., 1971; JD, U. Minn., 1976. Bar: N.Y. 1977, U.S. Dist. Ct. (so. dist.) 1977. Probation officer Hennepin County, Mpls., 1972-73; law clk. Minn. State Pub. Defender, Mpls., 1975-76; assoc. Fried, Frank, Harris, Shriver & Jacobson, N.Y.C., 1976-83, ptnr., 1983-93, 94—; Gen. counsel U.S. Treasury, Washington, 1993-94; mem. bd. regents Luther Coll.; mem. bd. visitors Law Sch. U. Minn. Recipient Disting. Svc. award Luther Coll., 1991, Outstanding Achievement award U. Minn., 1999. Mem. ABA, N.Y. State Bar Assn., Assn. of Bar of City of N.Y. (securities regulation com. 1991-98, mem. task force women in the profession 1995-98), U. Minn. Law Alumni Assn. Democrat. Lutheran. Office: Fried Frank Harris Shriver & Jacobson One New York Plaza New York NY 10004

**HANSON, JERRY CLINTON,** lawyer; b. Freeport, Tex., Aug. 6, 1939; s. C. C. and M. Frances (Richardson) H.; m. Susan S. Hanson, Mar. 27, 1971 (div. 1984); children: Melanie Joy, Blair Clinton. BS with honors, Stephen F. Austin U., 1963; JD with highest honors, South Tex. Coll. of Law, 1969. Bar: Tex. Ptnr. Hanson, Most & Lamson, Houston, 1970-83, Jerry C. Hanson & Assocs., Houston, 1984—; bd. chmn. H.A.S.P., Inc., Houston, 1981-83. Chmn. deed restrictions com. Lakewood Forest Civic Assn., Houston, 1980-82; mem., dir. Simon for Pres. Com., Houston, 1988; mem. Clinton for Pres. Com., Houston, 1992. Mem. ABA, Assn. Trial Lawyers Am., State Bar Tex., Tex. Trial Lawyers Assn., Delta Theta Phi. Democrat. Avocations: tennis, hunting, fishing. General civil litigation, Personal injury, Product liability. Office: Jerry C Hanson & Assocs 12337 Jones Rd Ste 200 Houston TX 77070-4844

**HANSON, JOHN J.,** lawyer; b. Aurora, Nebr., Oct. 22, 1922; s. Peter E. and Hazel Marion (Lounsbury) H.; m. Elizabeth Anne Moss, July 1, 1973; children from their previous marriages—Mark, Eric, Gregory. A.B., U. Denver, 1948; LL.B. cum laude, Harvard U., 1951. Bar: N.Y. bar 1952, Calif. bar 1955. Asso. firm Dewey, Ballantine, Bushby, Palmer & Wood, N.Y.C., 1951-54; ptnr. firm Gibson, Dunn & Crutcher, L.A, 1954—; mem. exec. com. Gibson, Dunn & Crutcher, 1978-87, adv. ptnr., 1991—. Contbr. articles to profl. jours. Trustee Palos Verdes (Calif.) Sch. Dist., 1969-73. Served with U.S. Navy, 1942-45. Fellow Am. Coll. Trial Lawyers; mem. Am. Bar Assn., Los Angeles County Bar Assn. (chmn. antitrust sect. 1979-80), Bel Air Country Club. Antitrust. Home: 953 Linda Flora Dr Los Angeles CA 90049-1630 Office: Gibson Dunn & Crutcher 333 S Grand Ave Ste 4400 Los Angeles CA 90071-3197

**HANSON, KENT BRYAN,** lawyer; b. Litchfield, Minn., Sept. 17, 1954; s. Calvin Bryan and Muriel (Wessman) H.; m. Barbara Jane Elenbaas, Aug. 24, 1974; children: Lindsay Michal, Taylor Jordan, Chase Philip. AA with high honors, Trinity Western Coll., 1974; BA, U. B.C., Vancouver, 1976; JD magna cum laude, U. Minn., 1979. Bar: Minn. 1979, U.S. Dist. Ct. Minn. 1980, U.S. Ct. Appeals (8th cir.) 1980, U.S. Dist. Ct. (we. dist.) Wis. 1983, Wis. 1985, U.S. Ct. Appeals (9th cir.) 1989, U.S. Dist. Ct. Ariz. 1992, Ohio 1993, Calif. 1994. Assoc. Grossman, Karlins, Siegel & Brill, Mpls., 1979-81, Gray, Plant, Mooty, Mooty & Bennett, Mpls., 1981-85; ptnr. Bowman & Brooke, Mpls., 1986-95; CEO Hanson, Marek, Bolkcom & Greene, Ltd., Mpls., 1996—. Bd. dirs. Inner City Boys Club, Ctrl. Free Ch., Mpls., 1979-81; 12th ward del. Mpls. Dem. Farmer Labor Com. Conv., 1982; mem. exec. bd. Ctrl. Free Ch., Mpls., 1986; chair exec. bd. Ctrl. Community Ch., 1993-96. Mem. ABA, State Bar Assn. Wis., Minn. Def. Lawyers Assn., Minn. State Bar Assn., Hennepin County Bar Assn., Calif. State Bar Assn., State Bar of Ohio, Def. Rsch. Inst. Avocations: classical music, golf, tennis, computers, theology. Product liability, Federal civil litigation, State civil litigation. Office: Hanson Marek Bolkcom & Greene Ltd 2200 Rand Tower 527 Marquette Ave Minneapolis MN 55402-1302

**HANSON, NORMAN,** lawyer; b. Roy, Mont., Feb. 12, 1916; s. Peder and Ida S. (Olson) H.; m. Constance Brown, Sept. 5, 1946; children: David, Margaret, Sara. BA with honors, U. Mont., 1937, JD with honors, 1940. Bar: Mont. 1940, U.S. Dist. Ct. Mont. 1940, U.S. Supreme Ct. 1960. Assoc. Brown and Davis, Billings, Mont., 1940; spl. agent FBI, Washington, 1941-42; assoc., ptnr. Brown, Davis and Hanson, Billings, 1946-51; ptnr. Coleman, Jameson and Lamey, Billings, 1952-57; spl asst. to Atty. Gen. of U.S., 1954-55; ptnr. Crowley, Haughey, Hanson, Toole and Dietrich, Billings, 1958-88, of counsel, 1989—; trustee Rocky Mountain Mineral Law Found., Denver, 1969—, pres. 1982-83; lectr. bus. law Montana State U., Billings, 1989. Co-founder, editor: Mont. Law Rev., 1939-40; contbr. articles to profl. jours. Bd. dirs. Mont. Heart Assn., 1956-62, Sch. Dist. 2; numerous cmty. orgns.; com. mem. Gov.'s Com. Edn. Maj. USAF, 1943-46, War Crimes Br., USFET, 1946. Mem. State Bar Mont., Yellowstone County Bar Assn. (pres. 1955-56). Republican. Congregational. Clubs: Rotary (Billings) (pres. 1965-66), Billings Petroleum. Lodge: Masons. Avocations: service with charitable orgns., bridge, golf. Oil, gas, and mineral, General civil litigation, Real property. Home: 2026 Pryor Ln Billings MT 59102-1656 Office: Crowley Haughey Hanson Toole & Dietrich PO Box 2529 Billings MT 59103-2529

**HANSON, RONALD WILLIAM,** lawyer; b. LaCrosse, Wis., Aug. 3, 1950; s. Orlin Eugene and Irene Agnes H.; m. Sandra Kay Cook, Aug. 21, 1971; children: Alec Evan, Corinn Michele. BA summa cum laude, St. Olaf Coll., 1972; JD cum laude, U. Chgo., 1975. Bar: Ill. 1975, U.S. Dist. Ct. (no. dist.) Ill. 1975, U.S. Ct. Appeals (7th cir.) 1978, U.S. Ct. Appeals (10th cir.) 1989. Assoc. Sidley & Austin, Chgo., 1975-83, ptnr., 1983-88, Latham & Watkins, Chgo., 1988—; ofcl. advisor to Nat. Conf. of Commrs. on Uniform State Laws; lectr. Ill. Inst. Continuing Legal Edn., Springfield, 1979—, Am. Bankruptcy Inst., Washington, 1984—, Banking Law Inst., 1985, Practicing Law Inst., 1985—, Am. Law Inst., 1987. Contbr. articles to profl. jours. Mem. ABA, Ill. Bar Assn., Order of Coif, Met. Club, Phi Beta Kappa. Republican. Lutheran. Bankruptcy, Federal civil litigation, Banking. Home: 664 W 58th St Hinsdale IL 60521-5104 Office: Latham & Watkins Sears Tower Ste 5800 Chicago IL 60606-6306

**HANSON, STEPHEN PHILIP,** lawyer; b. Grand Forks, N.D., Mar. 13, 1968; s. Jay D. and Madge N. Hanson. BA in Polit. Sci., George Mason U., 1990; JD, Am. U., 1996. Bar: N.Y. 1996. Assoc. Whitman Breed Abbott & Morgan, LLP, N.Y.C., 1996-97, O'Sullivan Graev & Karabell, LLP, N.Y.C., 1997—. Episcopalian. Avocations: scuba diving, golf, skiing, running, reading. Mergers and acquisitions, Finance, Securities. Office: O'Sullivan Graev & Karabell 30 Rockefeller Plz Fl 41 New York NY 10112-0198

**HANSON, VICTOR G.,** lawyer; b. Detroit, Oct. 26, 1923; s. Ernest A. and Laura Marie (Palmer) H.; m. Laura Ella Udell, Dec. 31, 1971. LLB, Wayne State U., 1949. Bar: Mich. 1949, U.S. Dist. Ct. (ea. dist.) Mich. 1951, U.S. Dist. Ct. (we. dist.) N.Y. 1952, U.S. Supreme Ct. 1952, U.S. Ct. Appeals (7th cir.) 1952, U.S. Ct. Appeals (2d, 6th and 8th cirs.) 1954, U.S. Dist. Ct. (no. and ea. dists.) Ohio 1954, U.S. Dist. Ct. Hawaii, 1957; U.S. Dist. Ct. (so. dist.) N.Y., U.S. Dist. Ct. Minn., U.S. Dist. Ct. (ea. dist.) Wis. Pvt. practice Detroit, 1949—; atty. AFL-CIO, Seafarers Internat. Union, Maritime Trades Dept., Tugmen's Union, Dredgemen's Union, Riggers' Union, Sailors Union Pacific, Marine Engrs. Beneficial Assn. Mem. Mich. Port Commn., Bd. Immigration Appeals, 1954, Immigration and Naturalization Svc., 1954, Gov.'s Spl. Fgn. Trade Expansion Commn., 1962. With USMC, 1945. Mem. ABA (V.P. Labor's Internat. Hall of Fame, com. Am. and maritime law), Am. Arbitration Assn. Labor, Maritime. Office: 19268 Grand River Ave Detroit MI 48223-1798

**HANSON, WILLIAM LEWIS,** lawyer; b. Shanghai, China, Oct. 1, 1924; came to U.S., 1927; s. Victor and Lucia Mae (Parks) H.; m. Elen Stella Hanson, June 26, 1949; children: Raiha Ballard, Victoria Berman, Emily Hanson-McMullen. AB cum laude, high hons., U. Redlands, Calif., 1946; JD, Harvard U., 1950. Bar: Wash., Fed. Tax Ct., 1976, U.S. Supreme Ct., 1983, U.S. Ct. Appeals (9th cir.), 1969. Coll. and peace edn. sec. Am. Friends Svc., Seattle, 1954-59; pvt. practice law Seattle, 1959-70, 73—; tchr. law/history Lakeside Sch., Seattle, 1970-73; arbitrator Arbitration Panel of Superior Ct. of King County. Co-author: A New China Policy, 1965, Uncommon Controversy: Indian Fishing Rights in the Northwest, 1970; author: (booklet) Peace in China, 1958. Bd. dirs., vol. atty. Am. Friends Svc., 1959-69, ACLU, 1965-78; bd. dirs., commentator Jack Straw Found., Seattle, 1972—; bd. dirs. Jack Straw Found., 1985-91, pres. 1991-92; trustee Friends Ednl. Trust, 1992—; bd. dirs. Inst. for Global Security Studies, Seattle, 1991-98; vol., past pres. World Peace Through Law Sect. of Wash. Bar Assn., 1970-91, 96—; planner, chmn. Bar Assn. Conf. on World Law, 1985-96, leader trip to China/Tibet, 1993. Recipient Cmty. Svc. for Peace Ann. award Unitarian Ch., Seattle, 1968. Democrat. Soc. of Friends. Avocations: photography, Chinese art, biking (built titanium bike Seattle Bike Show, 1997). Public international, Non-profit and tax-exempt organizations, Probate. Home and Office: 4819 NE 103rd St Seattle WA 98125-8141

**HANSOTTE, LOUIS BERNARD,** retired lawyer, law educator; b. Atlantic City, Oct. 3, 1927; s. Marcel Alfred and Bertha (Goldsmith) H.; m. Wilma Sleeper, Dec. 29, 1955; children—Beth Marcelle Crandall, Jeffrey Ronal. B.S. in Engring., U.S. Mil. Acad., 1950; LL.B., LaSalle Extension U., 1961. Bar: Calif. 1962, U.S. Dist. Ct. (so. dist.) Calif. 1962; C.L.U. Commd. 2d lt. U.S. Army, 1950, advanced through grades to capt., 1953; served in Korea; resigned, 1955; agt., Supr., then mgr. Pacific Mut. Life and Union Central Life, 1956-64; sr. ptnr. Hansotte, Nostrand & Lange, San Diego, 1964-94; retired, 1994—; instr. bus. law, coordinator real estate program Grossmont Community Coll., El Cajon, Calif., 1964—. Author: Legal Aspects of California Real Estate, 1983; California Probate Real Estate Sales, 1983. Contbr. material to reference books. Mem. Calif. State Bar Assn., San Diego County Bar Assn., Nat. Assn. Life Underwriters, Am. Coll. of Life Underwriters, Calif. Assn. of Real Estate Tchrs., West Point Alumni Assn., Army Athletic Assn., West Point Soc. of San Diego (co-founder, past pres.). E-mail: lhansotte@aol.com. Real property, Probate. Home: PO Box 19324 San Diego CA 92159-0324

**HANWELL, ROBERT MICHAEL,** lawyer; b. Cleve., May 20, 1954; s. Robert James and Nancy Carol (Taylor) H.; 1 child, Jamie Crystal Nichole. BA in Psychology, U. Akron, 1976, JD, 1985. Bar: Ohio 1985, U.S. Dist. Ct. (no. dist.) Ohio 1987. Employment and tng. dir. Medina County Commrs., Medina, Ohio, 1976-86; pvt. practice, Medina, 1985—. Mem. ABA, Medina County Bar Assn., Ohio State Bar Assn., Assn. Trial Lawyers Am., Ohio Assn. Criminal Def. Lawyers, Ohio Acad. Trial Lawyers. Avocations: sports, music. Criminal, Family and matrimonial, General practice. Office: 52 Public Sq Medina OH 44256-2204

**HANZELIK, CARL HAROLD,** lawyer; b. May 5, 1945. AB, Columbia U., 1967; JD, U. Va., 1970. Bar: Pa. 1970, U.S. Dist. Ct. (ea. dist.) Pa. 1970, U.S. Ct. Appeals (3d cir.) 1971 (9th cir.) 1991, U.S. Supreme Ct. 1974. Assoc. Dilworth, Paxson, Kalish & Kauffman, Phila., 1970-75, ptnr., 1975—. Mem. ABA, Pa. Bar Assn., Order of Coif. General civil litigation, Construction. Office: Dilworth Paxson LLP 3200 Mellon Bank Ctr Philadelphia PA 19103

**HANZLIK, RAYBURN DEMARA,** lawyer; b. L.A., June 7, 1938; s. Rayburn Otto and Ethel Winifred (Membery) H.; m. Carolyn Marie Williams; children: Kristina, Rayburn N., Alexander, Geoffrey. BS, Principia Coll., 1960; MA, Woodrow Wilson Sch. Fgn. Affairs, U. Va., 1968; JD, U. Va., 1974. Bar: Va. 1975, D.C. 1977. Staff asst. to Pres. U.S., Washington, 1971-73; assoc. dir. White House Domestic Council, 1975-77; of counsel Danzansky Dickey Tydings Quint & Gordon, Washington, 1977-78, Akin Gump Strauss Hauer & Feld, Washington, 1978-79; pvt. practice L.A., 1979-81; adminstr. Econ. Regulatory Adminstrn., Dept. Energy, Washington, 1981-85; ptnr. Heidrick and Struggles, Inc., 1985-91, McKenna & Hanzlik, Irvine, Calif., 1991-92; chmn. Lanxide Sports Internat., Inc., San Diego, 1992-95, Stealth Propulsion Internat., Ltd., San Diego, Calif. and Melbourne, Australia, 1994-97; exec. v.p. Commodore Corp., N.Y.C. and McLean, Va., 1997-98; mng. dir. Brewer-Hanzlik Nuclear Ptnrs., LLC, 1998—. Contbg. author: Global Politics and Nuclear Energy, 1971, Soviet Foreign Relations and World Communism, 1965. Alt. del. Republican Nat. Conv., 1980; dir. Calif. Rep. Victory Fund, 1980; candidate U.S. Senate, 1980. Served to lt. USN, 1963-68, Vietnam. Mem. ABA, Va. Bar Assn., D.C. Bar Assn. Republican. Christian Scientist. Mergers and acquisitions, Administrative and regulatory, Legislative.

**HAPNER, ELIZABETH LYNN,** lawyer, writer; b. Cleve., May 15, 1957; d. William Ralph Hapner and Anita F. (Thomas) Gillen; 1 child, Kyle William. BA in English, U. Fla., 1978, JD, 1980. Bar: Fla. 1981, U.S. Dist. Ct. (mid. dist.) Fla. 1986. Atty. Pub. Defender's Office, Bartow, Fla., 1981, State Atty.'s Office, Tampa, 1981-86; prin./pres. Elizabeth L. Hapner, P.A., Tampa, 1986-96; judge Hillsborough County, Tampa, 1997—; dir. DUI Counterattack Sch., Tampa, 1985—, pres., 1986-87; dir. Prevention, Rehab., Edn. Program, Inc., Tampa, 1990-98; advisor Children's Bd. Task Force for Judiciary, Tampa, 1991-93. Author: Texas Probate Manual, 1983, Georgia Probate, 1985, Virginia Probate, 1987, Florida Juvenile Procedure, 1986, Florida Civil Procedure, 1990. Mem. Hillsborough County Dem. Adv. Coun., 1988-96, Leadership Tampa, 1997; trustee Carrollwood Recreation Dist., 1989-91; chair sr. pastor nom. com., Forest Hills Presbyn. Ch., 1989-91, 93-94, elder, 1995-96; sustaining mem. Jr. League of Tampa, Inc., Leadership Tampa. Named Victim's Voice, Hillsborough County Victim Assistance Coun., 1991; recipient Pro Bono Svc. award Guardian Ad Litem's Office, Tampa, 1989-96. Mem. ABA, NAFE, Fed. Bar Assn., Internat. Platform Assn., Nat. Assn. Women Judges, Fla. Bar Assn. (juvenile ct. rules com. 1991—, chair 1994-95, family law special needs of children com. 1992—, chair 1996—, bar fee arbitration com., 1989—, family law juvenile com. 1993—, vice chair 1995—), Fla. Acad. Trial Lawyers, Hillsborough County Bar Assn., Mensa. Democrat. Presbyterian. Avocations: swimming, scuba diving, gourmet cooking, sewing. Home: PO Box 272998 Tampa FL 33688-2998

**HAPWARD, CURT MATTHEW,** lawyer, accountant; b. East Orange, N.J., Oct. 27, 1968; s. Richard Carl and Carol Ann Hapward; m. Tara Massey, Aug. 9, 1997. BA, Muhlenberg Coll., 1991; MBA, Seton Hall U., South Orange, N.J., 1997; JD, Seton Hall U., Newark, 1997. Bar: N.J. 1998; CPA, Pa. Auditor, acct. The CIT Group, Livingston, N.J., 1991-94; extern U.S. Bankruptcy Ct. N.J., Newark, 1995; internat. tax cons. Deloitte & Touche LLP, Parsippany, N.J., 1997-98; tax atty. Riker, Danzig, Scherer, Hyland & Perretti LLP, Morristown, N.J., 1998—. N.J. State Bar Found. scholar, 1995-96, 96-97, Essex County Bar Found. scholar, 1995-96. Mem. ABA, AICPA, N.J. State Bar Assn. Estate planning, Estate taxation, Taxation, general. Home: 2819 Rachel Ter Pine Brook NJ 07058-9668 Office: Riker Danzig Scherer Hyland & Perretti LLP One Speedwell Ave Morristown NJ 07962

**HARANTS, STEPHEN JOHN,** lawyer; b. Muncie, Ind., Jan. 15, 1969; s. Albert Agob and Sandra Ann Harants; m. Leslie-Anne Shimkus, Sept. 30, 1995; 1 child, Valerie Anne. BS in Journalism, Franklin Coll., 1991; JD, Ind. U., 1994. Bar: Ind. 1994, U.S. Dist. Ct. (no. and so. dists.) Ind. 1994. Assoc. Steele, Ulmschneider & Eberhard, Ft. Wayne, Ind., 1994-96, Miller, Carson, Boxberger & Murphy, Ft. Wayne, 1997—. Mem. ABA, Def. Rsch. Inst., Ind. Def. Lawyers Assn., Ind. Bar Assn. Federal civil litigation, State civil litigation, Insurance. Office: Miller Carson Boxberger & Murphy 1400 One Summit Sq Fort Wayne IN 46802-3173

**HARAZIN, WILLIAM DENNIS,** lawyer; b. Berwyn, Ill., Aug. 24, 1953; s. Robert John and Mary Ann H.; m. Becky R. French, Mar. 13, 1981. BS, Ill. State U., 1974, postgrad., 1975, JD, 1978. Bar: Ill. 1978, U.S. Dist. Ct. (no. dist.) Ill. 1978, N.C. 1981, U.S. Dist. Ct. (ea. and mid. dists.) N.C. 1981, U.S. Ct. Appeals (4th cir.) 1982. Lectr. So. Ill. U., Carbondale, 1977-78; assoc. Abramson & Fox, Chgo., 1978-79; instr. Durham (N.C.) Tech. Inst., 1979; atty. Ind. Legal Svcs., Raleigh, N.C., 1980-81; ptnr. Barringer, Allen & Pinnix, Raleigh, 1981-88; ptnr. property co. Harazin, French & Pinnix, Raleigh, 1982—; instr. N.C. State U., Raleigh, 1982—; owner Law Office of William D. Harazin, Raleigh, 1988—; mem. legal adv. group. Triangle World Trade Ctr., RTP, N.C., 1990—. Mme. Raleigh Housing Appeals Bd., 1983-86, chmn., 1986-89; mem. Carbondale Fair Housing Bd., 1977-78; exch. mem. to Japan, Rotary Internat., Raleigh, 1986. Mem. ABA (mem. com. internat. bus. law sect. bus. law), Ill. Bar Assn., N.C. Bar Assn. (internat. law com., chair 1998-99, bus. law com.), N.C. World Trade Assn. (pres. 1992-94, Triangle chpt. pres. 1990-92, treas. 1985-90), N.C. Di st. Export Coun., Nat. Assn. Eagle Scouts, Wake County Bar Assn. Contracts commercial, Private international, General corporate. Office: 434 Fayetteville Street Mall Raleigh NC 27601-1701

**HARBAUGH, DANIEL PAUL,** lawyer; b. Wendell, Idaho, May 18, 1948; s. Myron and Manuelita (Garcia) H. BA, Gonzaga U., 1970, JD, 1974. Bar: Washington 1974, U.S. Dist. Ct. (ea. dist.) Wash. 1977, U.S. Ct. Appeals (9th cir.) 1978. Asst. atty. gen. State of Wash., Spokane, 1974-77; ptnr. Richter, Wimberley & Ericson, Spokane, 1977-83, Harbaugh & Bloom, P.S., Spokane, 1983—; bd. dirs. Spokane Legal Svcs., 1982-86; bd. govs. LAWPAC, Seattle, 1980-92. Bd. dirs. Spokane Ballet, 1983-88; chpt. dir. Les Amis du Vin, Spokane, 1985-88; mem. Spokane County Civil Svc. Commn., 1991—, chmn., 1999—, Gonzaga U. Pres'. Coun., 1991—. Mem. ATLA, Wash. State Bar Assn. (spl. dist. counsel 1982-95, mem. com. rules for profl. conduct 1989-92, mem. legis. com. 1995-96), Spokane County Bar Assn. (chair med.-legal com. 1991), Wash. State Trial Lawyers Assn. (v.p. 1988-89, co-chair worker's compensation sect. 1992, 93, spl. select. com. on workers' corp. 1990—, forum 1994—, vice-chmn. 1994-97, mem. legis. com. 1995—), Nat. Orgn. Social Security Claimants Reps., Internat. Wine and Food Soc. (pres. local chpt. 1989-91, cellar master 1994-96), Empire Club, Spokane Club, Spokane Country Club (adminstrv. com. 1995-98, chmn. 1991-98, trustee 1996—, sec.-treas. 1997-98, pres. 1998—), Alpha Sigma Nu, Phi Alpha Delta. Roman Catholic. Workers' compensation, Personal injury. Office: Harbaugh & Bloom PS PO Box 1461 Spokane WA 99210-1461

**HARBECK, DOROTHY ANNE,** lawyer; b. Elizabeth, N.J., Sept. 19, 1962; d. Jay Cleveland and Ella Anne (Phillips) H. BA, Wellesley Coll., 1984; JD, Seton Hall U., 1989. Bar: N.J. 1990, U.S. Dist. Ct. N.J. 1990, U.S. Ct. Appeals (3d cir.) 1992, U.S. Supreme Ct. 1995. Assoc. Drazin & Warshaw, Red Bank, N.J., 1990-94, Donington, Karcher, Salmond, Ronan & Raimone, Tinton Falls, N.J., 1994-95, Graham, Curtin & Sheridan, Trenton, N.J., 1995—. Editor: (jour.) Dictum, 1992; contbr. articles to profl. jours. Bd. dirs. Red Bank Environ. Commn., 1997—. Recipient Nathan Burkan Copyright Law prize ASCAP, 1988, prize Am. Acad. of Poets, 1983; Wellesley Coll. scholar, 1984. Fellow Am. Inns of Ct. Found.; mem. N.J. Bar Assn. General civil litigation, Personal injury, Election. Home: 72 Riverside Ave Apt 50 Red Bank NJ 07701-1084 Office: Graham Curtin & Sheridan 50 W State St Ste 1008 Trenton NJ 08608-1220

**HARBERT, GUY M., III,** lawyer; b. Greenville, S.C., Apr. 17, 1958; s. Guy M. Jr. and Peggy (Simpson) H. BA, Davidson (N.C.) Coll., 1980; JD, Washington and Lee U., 1983. Assoc. Gentry, Locke, Rakes & Moore, Roanoke, Va., 1983-89, ptnr., 1989—. Mem. ABA, Va. Bar Assn., Va. Assn. Def. Attys. General civil litigation, Insurance, Product liability. Office: Gentry Locke Rakes & Moore 800 Crestar Pla PO Box 40013 Roanoke VA 24022-0013

**HARBUS, RICHARD,** arbitrator, mediator; b. N.Y.C., Sept. 15, 1940; children: Jonathan, Alexandra. BA, Columbia U., 1961; JD, Yale U., 1964. Bar: N.Y. 1965. Law clk. U.S. Ct. Appeals (2d cir.), N.Y.C., 1964-66; assoc. Leibman, Eulau, Robinson & Perlman, N.Y.C., 1966-67; atty. Met. Life Ins. Co., N.Y.C., 1967-74; from asst. prof. law to prof. N.Y. Law Sch., N.Y.C., 1974-81; gen. counsel Rsch. Found., CUNY, N.Y.C., 1981-82; prof. law Sch. Law, Touro Coll., Huntington, N.Y., 1982-92; trial officer N.Y.C. Housing Authority, 1992—; hearing officer N.Y. C. Bd. Edn., 1978—; adminstrv. law judge Taxi and Limousine Commn., N.Y.C., 1983-87, Parking Violations Bur., N.Y.C., 1988—; arbitrator N.Y. Civil Ct., N.Y.C., 1975—, Nat. Assn. Securities Dealers, 1992—, N.Y. Stock Exch., 1992—; lectr. Office Ct. Adminstrn., N.Y.C., 1982, Suffolk County Acad. Law, Hauppauge, N.Y., 1987. Contbr. articles to legal publs. Mem. ABA (various coms.), Assn. Arbitrators Civil Ct. N.Y., Am. Arbitration Assn. (comml. mediator). Democrat. Jewish. Avocations: playing piano and cello, reading, travel, photography.

**HARCROW, E. EARL,** lawyer; b. Carrizozo, N.Mex., Mar. 4, 1954; s. James Earl and Nettie (McInnes) H.; m. Julie A., Apr. 16, 1987; children: Ashley Nicole, James Earl. BS, Tex. Tech. U., 1976, JD, 1979. Bar: Tex. 1979, U.S. Dist. Ct. (no. dist.) Tex., U.S. Ct. Appeals (5th cir.) 1979. Asst. dist. atty. Lubbock (Tex.) Dist. Atty. Office, 1979-80, Tarrant Dist. Atty. Office, Ft. Worth, 1980-83; ptnr. Shannon, Gracey, Ratliff & Miller, Ft. Worth, 1983-99; mng. ptnr. Shannon, Gracey, Ratliff & Miller, 1995-96, ptnr. in charge of tech., 1996-99; ptnr. Haynes & Boone, Ft. Worth, 1999—; gen. counsel Dallas Ft. Worth Med. Ctr., 1990—; pres. Tex. Healthcare Resources, 1993—. Dir. Planned Parenthood N. Tex., 1987-92; fellow Tex. Bar Found., 1991—; pres. JAMM Group Inc., 1996—. Health, Personal injury, State civil litigation. Office: Dallas Ft Worth Med Ctr 201 Main St Ste 2200 Fort Worth TX 76102-3126

**HARDCASTLE, HEATH E.,** lawyer; b. Orange, Tex., Sept. 2, 1967; s. F.E. and C.J. (Nunnally) H.; m. Marianne Smith, May 30, 1992. BA in Psychology, U. Ark., 1986, JD, 1990. Bar: Okla. 1990, U.S. Dist. Ct. (no. dist.) Okla. 1990, U.S. Ct. Appeals (10th cir.) 1991, Ark. 1992. Atty. Hall, Estill, Hardwick, Gable, Golden & Nelson, P.C., Tulsa, 1990-92; atty. Albright & Rusher, P.C., Tulsa, 1992—, shareholder, 1996—. Articles editor Ark. Law Rev., 1989-90. Vol., funding panel chair United Way, Tulsa, 1995-99. Mem. Okla. Bar Assn., Ark. Bar Assn., Tulsa County Bar Assn. Avocations: boating, swimming, skiing, reading. General civil litigation, Bankruptcy. Office: Albright & Rusher 2600 Nations Bank Ctr 15 W 6th St Ste 2600 Tulsa OK 74119-5434

**HARDCASTLE, ROBERT THOMAS,** lawyer; b. Modesto, Calif., May 17, 1949; s. Norman Faye and Mary Sue (Lewis) H.; m. Linda Nell Ellis, Nov. 28, 1977; 1 child, Mark Edward. BEd, Colo. State U., 1970; JD, Denver U., 1976; postgrad., Eastern Okla. State Coll., 1977-79. Bar: Okla. 1978, U.S. Dist. Ct. (ea. dist.) Okla. 1978, Colo. 1991. With office civil rights U.S. Govt., Denver, 1972-74; regional planner Kiamichi Econ. Devel. Dist. Okla., Wilburton, 1977-79; pvt. practice Wilburton, 1978-90; gen. counsel, dir. Conception Tech. Inc., Summit Mountain Tours, Inc., City Loan Brokerage. Author: Land Use Study, 1978, Industrial Base Study, 1979. County chmn. Jim Jones for U.S. Senate, 1986; alt. del. Okla. Dem. Com., 1988; city atty. Wilburton, 1984-90, Clayton, Okla., 1987-90. Mem. Lions (v.p. 1984-89, pres. 1990), Rotary. Estate planning, Consumer commercial, General practice.

**HARDEE-THOMAS, MARVA A.,** lawyer; b. Manhattan, N.Y., Mar. 29, 1964; d. Nathaniel Pinckney and Betty (Seabrook) Hardee; m. Michael A. Thomas, July 6, 1996. BA in Polit. Sci., N.C. State U., 1986; JD, Seton Hall U., 1993. Bar: U.S. Dist. Ct. (so. dist.) S.C. 1997. Legal asst. Prudential Securities Inc., Manhattan, 1991-93; law clk. Jersey City Cir. Ct., 1993-94; legal asst. George Sink Attys., Charleston, S.C., 1994; asst. solicitor First Cir. Solicitor's Office, Orangeburg, S.C., 1994-95; pvt. practice Summerville, S.C., 1995—. Republican. Methodist. Criminal, Family and matrimonial, Personal injury. Office: PO Box 50503 Summerville SC 29485-0503

**HARDEN, RICHARD RUSSELL,** lawyer; b. Oak Park, Ill., Apr. 22, 1958; s. James Edward Harden and Patricia Gilkison Murphy; m. Kathryn Diane Knosher, June 21, 1980; childen: Jeffrey Joseph, Colleen Elizabeth. BA, Knox Coll., 1980; JD, U. Ill., 1983. Bar: Ill. 1983. Assoc. Robert P. Moore & Assocs., Champaign, Ill., 1983-86; assoc. Thomas, Mamer & Haughey,

Champaign, 1986-90, ptnr., 1990—; spkr., mem. faculty Ill. Inst. for CLE, Champaign, 1997—, Carle Found., Champaign, 1998. Contbg. author: Medical Evidence, 1997. Various positions, including scoutmaster, cubmaster, asst. scoutmaster, advisor, commr. Boy Scouts Am., Champaign, 1992—, advisor law exploring, learning for life divsn.; elder Westminster Presbyn. Ch., Champaign, 1989-92, 98—. Mem. Ill. Bar Assn., Ill. Assn. Def. Trial Counsel, Champaign County Bar Assn., Phi Beta Kappa. Avocations: camping, hiking, canoeing, golf, climbing. Personal injury, Product liability, General civil litigation. Office: Thomas Mamer & Haughey PO Box 560 30 E Main St Champaign IL 61824-0560

**HARDESTY, W. MARC,** lawyer, educator; b. Daytona Beach, Fla., Sept. 3, 1960; s. Henry Haines and Janet W. H.; m. Margie Gail Boyd; children: Meredith Janet. BA in Polit. Sci., Furman U., 1982; student, U. London, 1981; JD, Mercer U., 1989. Bar: Fla. 1990, U.S. Ct. Appeals (11th cir.) 1990, U.S. Dist. Ct. (mid. dist.) Fla. 1990. Various positions U.S. Army, 1982-89, co. comdr. 345th Combat Support Hosp. Desert Storm, 1990-93; adminstrv. officer U.S. Army, Jacksonville, 1994-95; staff judge adv. officer 143rd Transp. Brigade, Orlando, Fla., 1995-96; maj. USAR, Miami, Fla., 1996—; asst. state atty. State Attys. Office 4th Jud. Cir., Jacksonville, Fla., 1989-94; ptnr. Hardesty & Tyde, P.A., Jacksonville, 1994—; instr. criminal law Am. Inst. Paralegal Studies, Jacksonville U., 1992-93; instr. legal case analysis, criminal law, workers' compensation U. N. Fla., 1993—. Mem. adv. coun. bd. U. Fla., 1994—; explorer post adv. trial team coach Boy Scouts Am.; mem. S. Jacksonville Presbyn. Ch. Decorated Bronze Star; Army ROTC scholar, Rotary scholar. Mem. Fla. Bar Assn. (mem. mil. affairs com. 1998—, mem. jud. evaluation com. 1998—), Jacksonville Bar Assn. (chmn. law explorers com. 1992, 93, numerous others), Acad. Fla. Trial Lawyers, Jacksonville Trial Lawyers Assn., N. Fla. Criminal Def. Lawyers Assn., Rotary, Phi Delta Phi, Alpha Tau Omega. Avocation: offshore sport fishing. Personal injury, Workers' compensation, Criminal. Office: Hardesty & Tyde PA 4004 Atlantic Blvd Jacksonville FL 32207-2037

**HARDIE, JAMES HILLER,** lawyer; b. Pitts., Dec. 1, 1929; s. James H. and Elizabeth Gillespie (Alcorn) H.; m. Frances P. Curtis, Dec. 5, 1953; children: J. Hiller, Janet Hardie Harvey, Andrew G., Michael C., Rachel Hardie Share. A.B., Princeton U., 1951; LL.B., Harvard U., 1954. Bar: Pa. 1955. Assoc. Reed Smith Shaw & McClay, Pitts., 1954-62, ptnr., 1962-99, of counsel, 1999—. Mem. ABA, Am. Law Inst., Pa. Bar Assn. General corporate, Mergers and acquisitions, Securities. Office: Reed Smith Shaw & McClay PO Box 2009 Pittsburgh PA 15230-2009

**HARDIMAN, THERESE ANNE,** lawyer; b. Chestnut Hill, Pa., Mar. 2, 1956; d. Edward Joseph and Grace Joan (Shaw) Hardiman; m. David J.P. Malecki, Feb. 3, 1990; 1 child, Christine Mary; BA in History, BA in Psychology, Mt. St. Mary's Coll., 1978; JD, Thomas M. Cooley Law Sch., 1983. Bar: Pa. 1983. U.S. Dist. Ct. (ea. dist.) Pa. 1983, U.S. Ct. Appeals (3d cir.) 1984, U.S. Dist. Ct. (mid. dist.) Pa. 1989. Staff rsch. asst. Internat. Brotherhood of Teamsters, Washington, 1978-79; law clk. Richard R. Rashid, Atty. at Law, Lansing, Mich., 1981-82; law clk. Pearlstine, Salkin, Hardiman & Robinson, Landsdale, Pa., 1981; staff asst. Employment Rels. Bd., Mich. Dept. Civil Svc., Lansing, 1982; mem. Pearlstine, Salkin, Hardiman & Robinson, Landsdale, 1983-86; v.p. Edward J. Hardiman & Assocs. P.C., 1986-94; sole practitioner, 1995—. Editor-in-chief Pridwin, 1978, layout editor, 1977. Recipient Golden Key award, Delta Theta Phi, 1981; Outstanding Student award Student Bar Assn., Thomas M. Cooley Law Sch., 1982. Mem. ABA, Assn. Trial Lawyers Am., Pa. Assn. Trial Lawyers, Pa. Bar Assn., Monroe County Bar Assn., Montgomery County Bar Assn., Delta Theta Phi. Republican. Roman Catholic. General civil litigation, Municipal (including bonds), Family and matrimonial. Office: PO Box 66 Pocono Pines PA 18350-0066

**HARDIN, ADLAI STEVENSON, JR.,** judge; b. Norwalk, Conn., Sept. 20, 1937; s. Adlai S. and Carol (Moore) H. BA, Princeton U., 1959; LLB, Columbia U., 1962. Bar: N.Y. 1963, U.S. Dist. Ct. (so. and ea. dists.) N.Y. 1965, U.S. Supreme Ct. 1967, U.S. Ct. Appeals (2d cir.) 1965, U.S. Ct. Appeals (5th cir.) 1974, U.S. Ct. Appeals (3d cir.) 1977, U.S. Ct. Appeals (9th cir.) 1982, U.S. Ct. Appeals (4th and D.C. cirs.) 1985, U.S. Ct. Appeals (7th cir.) 1988. Assoc. Milbank, Tweed, Hadley & McCloy, N.Y.C., 1963, ptnr., 1971; judge U.S. Bankruptcy Ct., 1995—. Trustee Spence Sch., 1981-87; former elder, trustee Madison Ave. Presbyn. Ch. With USAR, 1962-68. Mem. ABA (past chmn. N.Y. State membership com., antitrust sect., litigation sect.), Fed. Bar Coun. (trustee 1983-92, v.p. 1986-88, chmn. bd. dirs. 1990-92), Fed. Bar Found. (pres. 1992-94), N.Y. State Bar Assn. (mem. com. on profl. ethics, mem. jud. election monitoring com., mem. internat. litigation com.), Assn. of Bar of City of N.Y. (sec. 1979-82, chmn. com. on profl. and jud. ethics 1970-73, mem. spl. com. on lawyers role in securities transactions, mem. spl. com. to cooperate with ABA in revision of Canons of Ethics, mem. nominating com., mem. com. on membership, mem. com. on profl. discipline), Nat. Conf. Bankruptcy Judges, Am. Bankruptcy Inst. Office: US Bankruptcy Ct US Courthouse 300 Quarropas St White Plains NY 10601-4140

**HARDIN, EDWARD LESTER, JR.,** lawyer; b. Wetumpka, Ala., Mar. 29, 1940; s. Edward Lester and Katherine (Williams) H.; m. Lila Manor, June 10, 1962; children: Leigh Hardin Hancock, Caroline Hardin Butler, Laura Elizabeth, Edward Lester III. BA, Birmingham So. Coll., 1962; JD, U. Ala., 1965. Bar: Ala. 1965, U.S. Dist. Ct. (no., mid. and so. dists.) Ala. 1965, U.S. Ct. Appeals (11th cir.), U.S. Supreme Ct. Assoc., then ptnr. Hare Wynn Newell and Newton, Birmingham, Ala., 1965-71; sr. ptnr. Hardin and Hawkins, Birmingham, 1971-98; exec. v.p., gen. counsel MedPtnrs. Inc., 1998—; bd. dirs. Am. Sports Medicine Inst., Birmingham. Editorial bd. U. Ala. Law Rev., 1964-65; contbr. to profl. publs. Mem. ABA, Am. Bd. Trial Advocates, Assn. Trial Lawyers Am. (bd. govs. 1976), Ala. Bar Assn., Ala. Trial Lawyers Assn. (exec. com., pres. 1975-76), Omicron Delta Kappa, Phi Alpha Delta. Democrat. Methodist. Avocations: Marlin fishing, golf, hunting. General civil litigation, Antitrust, Personal injury. Office: Hardin & Hawkins 2201 Arlington Ave S Birmingham AL 35205-4003

**HARDIN, JAMES CARLISLE, III,** lawyer, educator; b. Charlotte, N.C., Sept. 12, 1948; s. James Carlisle Jr. and Mary Gene (Roberts) H.; m. Sally M. Drennan, June 6, 1968 (div. Dec. 1973); 1 child, Christine M.; m. Caryle Wilson (dec. June 1986); 1 child, James Carlisle IV; m. Katharine C. Harrison, May 2, 1992. AB, Wofford Coll., 1969; MA in History, U. Va., 1970, postgrad., 1970-71; JD, Duke U., 1974. Bar: S.C. 1974, U.S. Dist. Ct. S.C. 1976, N.C. 1989. U.S. Dist. Ct. (we. dist.) N.C. 1989. Ptnr. Roddey, Carpenter & White, P.A., Rock Hill, S.C., 1974-86, Kennedy Covington Lobdell & Hickman, Charlotte & Rock Hill, S.C., 1986—; chmn. specialization adv. bd. S.C. Supreme Ct., 1988-90; mem. S.C. Commn. on Continuing Lawyer Competence and Specialization, 1990-97; instr. Winthrop Univ., Rock Hill, 1979-91; mem. sect. coun. Probate Estate Planning and Trust Sect. S.C. Bar, 1997—, chmn., 1981, 91. Mem. bd. dirs. Rock Hill YMCA, 1986-89, S.C. Meth. Found., 1986—; bd. dirs. St. John's United Meth. Ch., Rock Hill, 1997—; bd. dirs. Piedmont Med. Ctr., 1994—, chmn., 1996. Fellow Am. Coll. Trust and Estate Coun.; mem. Rock Hill C. of C. (bd. dirs. 1991-95), Kiwanis (bd. dirs. Rock Hill 1978-80), Rock Hill Country Club, Phi Beta Kappa. Avocations: golf, swimming. Probate, Estate planning, General corporate. Office: Kennedy Covington Lobdell & Hickman First Union Ctr 113 E Main St Rock Hill SC 29730-4539

**HARDING, CALVIN FREDRICK, JR.,** lawyer; b. Addison, Ill., Aug. 31, 1969; s. Calvin F. Harding Sr. and Linda L. Dedick. BS in Bus. Adminstrn., U. Ctrl. Fla., 1991, MBA, 1992; JD, U. Fla., 1996. Bar: Fla. 1996; CPA, Fla. Gen. counsel United Corp. Mgmt. Corp., Orlando, Fla., 1997-98; pvt. practice Sanford, Fla., 1998—; atty. Bogle & Schulman, P.A., Altamonte Springs, Fla., 1998—. Mem. ABA. Avocations: tennis, golf. General corporate, Real property, Entertainment. Office: Bogle & Schulman PA 706 Turnbull Ave Ste 203 Altamonte Springs FL 32701-6476

**HARDING, JOHN EDWARD,** lawyer; b. San Francisco, Sept. 5, 1963; s. Merle Lewis and Trudy (Evertz) H.; m. Lisa Elliott; children: Jack Joseph, Ryan Elise. BA, St. Mary's Coll., Moraga, Calif., 1986; JD, Golden Gate U., 1989. Bar: Calif. 1989, U.S. Dist. Ct. (no. dist.) Calif. 1989, U.S. Ct. Appeals (9th cir.) 1989, D.C. 1991, Wyo. 1996, U.S. Dist. Ct. (ctrl. dist.) Calif. 1997. Assoc. Law Offices of Merle L. Harding, Pleasanton, Calif., 1989; ptnr. Harding & Harding, Pleasanton, 1990—. Bd. dirs. Tri-Valley br. Am. Heart Assn., Oakland, Calif., 1992-93, Valley Community Health Ctr., Pleasanton, 1992-96. Mem. ABA, ATLA, Consumer Atty. Calif., State Bar Calif., D.C. Bar Assn., Wyo. Bar Assn., Pleasanton C. of C. (bd. dirs. 1993-96, v.p. pub. affairs 1994). Avocations: golf, softball, backpacking, fishing, spectator sports, reading, travel. General practice, General civil litigation, Personal injury. Office: Harding & Harding 78 Mission Dr Ste B Pleasanton CA 94566-7683

**HARDING, MAJOR BEST,** state supreme court chief justice; b. Charlotte, N.C., Oct. 13, 1935; m. Jane Lewis, Dec., 1958; children: Major B. Jr., David L., Alice Harding Sanderson. BS, Wake Forest U., 1957, also LLD; LLM in Jud. Process, U. Va., 1995; LLD, Stetson U., 1991, Fla. Coastal Sch. Law, 1999. Bar: N.C. 1959, Fla. 1960. Staff judge adv. hdqrs. Ft. Gordon, Ga., 1960-62; asst. county solicitor Criminal Ct. of Record, Duval County, Fla., 1962-63; pvt. practice law, 1964-68; judge Juvenile Ct., Duval County, 1968-70; judge 4th Jud. Cir. of Fla., 1970-74, chief judge, 1974-77; justice Supreme Ct. of Fla., Tallahassee, 1991—, chief justice, 1998—; supervisory judge Family Mediation Unit, 1984-90; mem. Matrimonial Law Commn. and Gender Bias Study Commn.; chair Fla. Ct. Edn. Coun., past mem. Jud. Conf.; 1st dean New Judges Coll., 1975, faculty mem. in probate and juvenile areas, until 1979; dean Fla. Jud. Coll., 1984-92, mem. bench-bar commn.; chmn. Supreme Ct. com. on law-related edn., 1997—. Bd. dirs. Legal Aid Assn., Family Consultation Svc., Daniel Meml. Home; past pres. Rotary Club of Riverside, Jacksonville, Fla., Rotary Club of Tallahassee; chmn. U.S. Constn. Bicentennial Commn., Jacksonville; past mem., deacon, elder St. John's Presbyn. Ch.; commr. Gen. Assembly Presbyn. Ch. U.S., 1971; mem. Christ Presbyn. Ch., Tallahassee, clk. of session, elder. Recipient Award for Outstanding Contbn. to Field of Matrimonial Law Am. Acad. Matrimonial Lawyers, 1986, Harry Lee Anstead Professionalism award Dade County Trial Lawyers Assn., 1998. Mem. ABA, The Fla. Bar, N.C. State Bar Assn., Chester Bedell Inn of Ct. (past pres.), Scabbard and Blade, Tallahassee Am. Inn of Ct. (ex officio trustee), Tallahassee Bar Assn., Sigma Chi (Significant Sig award 1997), Phi Delta Phi. Office: Supreme Ct of Fla 500 S Duval St Tallahassee FL 32399-6556

**HARDING, RAY MURRAY, JR.,** judge; b. Logan, Utah, Nov. 23, 1953; s. Ray M. Sr. and Martha (Rasmussen) H.; m. Jeri Lynn; children: Michelle, Nicole, Justin, Skyler. BS, Brigham Young U., 1975; JD, J. Reuben Clark Law Sch., 1978. Bar: Utah 1978. Ptnr. Harding & Harding, American Fork and Pleasant Grove, Utah, 1978-85; owner Harding & Assoc., American Fork and Pleasant Grove, 1986-95; judge 4th Jud. Dist. Ct. Utah County, State of Utah, 1995—; atty. Lindon City and Pleasant Grove City, Utah, 1983-95, Alpine City, 1985-94, American Fork, Utah, 1985-95. Bd. trustees Utah Valley State Coll., 1986-95, chmn., 1991-93. Named Businessman of Yr., Future Bus. Leaders of Am., 1983. Mem. ABA, ATLA, Utah State Bar Assn., Utah Trial Lawyers Assn., Utah County Bar Assn., Pleasant Grove C. of C. (pres. 1983), Kiwanis (local bd. dirs. 1982-83). Avocations: skiing, scuba diving, hiking, hunting, travel. Home: 11165 Yarrow Cir Highland UT 84003-9598 Office: Utah County 4th Judicial Dist Ct 125 N 100 W Provo UT 84601-2849

**HARDING, RONALD EVAN,** lawyer; b. Bronx, N.Y., May 12, 1950; s. Max and Gertrude (Seligman) H.; m. Caryn Miller, Aug. 25, 1973; children: Jarrad MIller, Alison Elisabeth. BA cum laude, SUNY, Albany, 1972; JD cum laude, New Eng. Sch. Law, 1975. Bar: Mass. 1975, U.S. Dist. Ct. Mass. 1976, U.S. Ct. Appeals (1st cir.) 1980, U.S. Supreme Ct. 1982. Law clk. Mass. Superior Ct., Boston, 1976; assoc. Wasserman & Salter, Boston, 1977, Putnam, Bell & Russell, Boston, 1978-79; assoc. Weston, Patrick, Willard & Redding, Boston, 1979-86, ptnr., 1987—. Note & Comment editor New England Law Rev., 1973-75. Avocations: family, carpentry, skiing, hiking. General civil litigation, Personal injury, Environmental. Office: Weston Patrick Willard & Redding 84 State St Ste 11 Boston MA 02109-2299

**HARDISON REISNER, SARAH CASTLE,** lawyer; b. Houston, Sept. 30, 1968; d. Ernest K. III and Lynne (Northcutt) H.; married. BA, U. Richmond, 1991; JD, U. Tenn., 1996. Bar: Tenn. 1996. Assoc. Manier & Herod, Nashville, 1996—. Active Jr. League Nashville, 1997. Mem. Rotary. Republican. Presbyn. Avocations: golf, tennis, horseback riding, quail and dove hunting. Workers' compensation. Office: Manier & Herod 120 4th Ave N Ste 2200 Nashville TN 37219-2402

**HARDT, FREDERICK WILLIAM,** lawyer; b. Riverside, N.J., June 8, 1943; s. Otto Heinrich and Mable Eleanor (Snyder) H.; m. Judith Hildred Laub, Aug. 2, 1968. BA, Franklin & Marshall Coll., 1965; JD, Rutgers U., 1968. Bar: N.J. 1968, U.S. Dist. Ct. N.J. 1968, U.S. Ct. Appeals (3d cir.) 1982; chartered trial atty. Ptnr. Sever & Hardt, Burlington, N.J., 1968-88; pvt. practice Moorestown, N.J., 1988—; asst. counsel N.J. Fedn. Planning Ofcls., 1987-89. Mem. ABA, N.J. Bar Assn. (trustee land use sect. 1997—), Burlington County Bar Assn. Presbyterian. Avocations: reading, wine, food, travel, music. Real property, Land use and zoning (including planning), Condemnation. Office: PO Box 840 300 Chester Ave Moorestown NJ 08057-2512

**HARDT, GERALD EUGENE,** law enforcement administrator; b. Elkhorn, Wis., May 27, 1944; s. David and Elsie Louise Hardt; children: David D., Gerald E. Jr.; m. June Alice Bosetti, July 8, 1973 (div. Dec. 1997); children: Jean Hawkins, Richard Hawkins, Angela Hawkins. AA, Glendale (Ariz.) C.C., 1968; BS, Ariz. State U., 1970, MPA, 1990. Dep. chief Maricopa County Sheriff's Office, Phoenix, 1970-91; release officer Oreg. Ct. Sys., Salem, 1992-95; program mgr. Ariz. Criminal Justice Commn., Phoenix, 1995—; mem. Maricopa Pub. Safety Pers. Retirement Sys. Bd., Phoenix, 1988-91. Pres. Ariz. FBI Nat. Acad. Grads., 1991. Sgt. USAF, 1962-66. Mem. Fraternal Order Police (life), Masons (3rd degree), El Zaribah Temple Shrine, York Rite Freemasonary. Republican. Lutheran. Avocations: travel, reading. E-mail: humbirds@yahoo.com. Fax: 602-728-0752. Home: 7729 W Escuda Dr Glendale AZ 85308-8315 Office: Ariz Criminal Justice Commn 3737 N 7th St Phoenix AZ 85014-5017

**HARDTNER, QUINTIN THEODORE, III,** lawyer; b. Shreveport, La., Mar. 5, 1936; s. Quintin Theodore and Jane (Owen) H.; m. Susan Mayer, June 30, 1962; children: Susan Owen, Quintin Theodore IV, George Jonathan. BBA, Tulane U., 1957, JD 1961. Bar: La. 1961; cert. estate planning and adminstrv. specialist. Assoc. Jones, Walker, Waechter, Poitevent, Carrere & Denegre, New Orleans, 1961-62; ptnr. Hargrove, Guyton, Ramey and Barlow, Shreveport, 1962-94; pres. Barlow & Hardtner L.C., 1994—; regional dir. Bank One, La., N.A., Shreveport Region; dir., chmn. Community Found. Shreveport-Bossier, Sci-Port Discovery Ctr.; past pres. Com. of 100; past dir. Biomed. Rsch. Found. N.W. La. Past mem. adv. bd. Salvation Army; past trustee, past chmn. bd. All Sts. Episcopal Sch., Vicksburg, Miss.; past trustee, past chmn. St. Mark's Day Sch.; past trustee Southfield Sch.; vestryman St. Mark's Episcopal Ch.; past bd. dirs., v.p. Shreveport Assn. for Blind; past bd. dirs. Family and Children's Svcs.; past co-chmn. Centenary Coll. Fund. Served to lt. USMC, 1957-59. Fellow Am. Coll. Trust and Estate Counsel; mem. ABA, La. State Bar Assn. (past mem. ho. of dels., cert. tax atty., cert. estate planning and adminstrn. specialist), Ark.-La.-Tex. Tax Inst. (past bd. dirs.), Shreveport Bar Assn. (past pres.), Estate Planning Council Shreveport (past dir., past pres.), Shreveport Club, Cambridge Club, Rotary (past pres., bd. dirs.). Probate, General corporate, Estate planning. Home: 4142 Fairfield Ave Shreveport LA 71106-1018 Office: 10th Fl Louisiana Tower 501 Edwards St Shreveport LA 71101-3537

**HARDWICK, MARTHA JOSEPHINE,** lawyer; b. Balboa, Canal Zone, Panama, July 30, 1958; '. Charles William and Josephine Reed (Holliman) H. BA, Emory U., 1980, MA, 1980; JD, U. Tex., 1984. Bar: Tex. 1984, U.S. Dist. Ct. (no. dist.) Tex. 1984, U.S. Ct. Appeals (5th cir.) 1986, U.S. Dist. Ct. (so. and ea. dists.) Tex. 1989, U.S. Dist. Ct. (we. dist.) Tex. 1990. Assoc. Rentzel, Wise & Robertson, Dallas, 1984-85, Stinson, Mag & Fizzell, Dallas, 1985-88; ptnr. Bauer, Rentzel, Millard & Hardwick, Dallas, 1988-97, True & Sewell, LLP, Dallas, 1998—. Chmn. com., dir. show Dallas Bar Assn. Ann. Bar None Prodn., 1986—. Mem. Fed. Bar Assn., Jr. League Dallas, Tex. Bar Found., Dallas Bar Found., Altrusa Internat. (legal advisor 1989-91, Altrusan of Yr. 1989-90, 93-94), William Mac Taylor 112th Am. Inn Ct. Republican. Methodist. Avocations: travel, reading, gardening, skiing, theatre. General civil litigation. Office: True & Sewell LLP 8080 N Central Expy Fl 9 Dallas TX 75206-1838

**HARDY, ASHTON RICHARD,** lawyer; b. Gulfport, Miss., Aug. 31, 1935; s. Ashton Maurice and Alice (Baumbach) H.; m. Katherine Ketelsen, Sept. 4, 1959; children: Karin H. Wood, Katherine H. Foster. BBA, Tulane U., 1958, JD, 1962. Bar: La. 1962, FCC, 1976. Ptnr. Jones, Walker, Waechter, Poitevent, Carrere & Denegre, New Orleans, 1962-74, 76-82; gen. counsel FCC, Washington, 1974-76; ptnr. Fawer, Brian, Hardy, Zatzkis, New Orleans, 1982-86, Hardy & Popham, 1986-88, Walker, Bordelon, Hamlin, Theriot & Hardy, New Orleans, 1988-92, Hardy & Carey, New Orleans, 1992—; gen. counsel La. Assn. Broadcasters, 1976-86, Greater New Orleans Assn. Broadcasters, 1976—, La. Assn. Advt. Agys., 1982-86; lectr. in field; advance rep. to Pres. U.S., 1971-74. Bd. dirs. New Orleans Mission, 1989—, Met. Crime Commn. New Orleans, 1993—, vice-chmn., 1997—, United Christian Charities, 1993—. Lt. USN, 1958-60. Mem. La. Bar Assn. (del. ho. of dels. 1987-92), FCC Bar Assn., Nat. Religious Broadcasters (bd. dirs. S.W. chpt. 1994—), Christian Legal Soc., Metairie Country Club (pres. 1986), Comm Club. Administrative and regulatory, Contracts commercial, Communications. Home: 306 Cedar Dr Metairie LA 70005-3902 Office: Hardy & Carey Ste 300 110 Veterans Memorial Blvd Metairie LA 70005-4960

**HARDY, CHARLES LEACH,** federal judge; b. L.A., Jan. 24, 1919; s. Charles Little and Dorothy (Leach) H.; m. Jean McRae, Jan. 26, 1947; children: Charles M., Caroline, Catherine, John L. Julianne, Eileen, Sterling A., Steven W., Janette. BS, U. Ariz., 1947, LLB, 1950. Bar: Ariz. 1949. Pvt. practice Phoenix, 1949-66; dep. county atty. Maricopa County, Ariz., 1952-55; asst. atty. gen. State of Ariz., 1956-59; judge Ariz. Superior Ct., 1966-80; U.S. dist. judge Ariz. Dist., Phoenix, 1980—; now sr. judge. Pres. Young Democratic Clubs Ariz., 1956-57, nat. committeeman, 1957-58; chmn. Maricopa County Dem. Cen. Com., 1958-59; mem. Ariz. Bd. Crippled Children's Services, 1965. Served with F.A. AUS, 1941-45. Decorated Bronze Star. Mem. ABA, Am. Judicature Soc., State Bar Ariz., Maricopa County Bar Assn. Mem. LDS Ch. Office: US Dist Ct US Courthouse & Fed Bldg Rm 7025 3017 US Courthouse Phoenix AZ 85025-0005

**HARDY, DEL,** lawyer; b. Jan. 19, 1954. BA, U. Nev., 1976; JD, U. of the Pacific, 1982. Bar: Calif. 1983, Nev. 1983, U.S. Dist. Ct., U.S. Ct. Appeals (9th cir.), U.S. Tax Ct.; lic. Nev. Gaming Commn. Bd. Dep. atty. gen. State of Nev., Carson City, 1983-86; atty., owner Hardy & Assocs., Reno, 1986—. Mem. ABA, ATLA, Nev. Trial Lawyers. Personal injury, Bankruptcy, General civil litigation. Office: Hardy & Assocs 96 Winter St Reno NV 89503-5605

**HARDY, HARVEY LOUCHARD,** lawyer; b. Dallas, Dec. 2, 1914; s. Nat L. and Winifred H. (Fouraker) H.; m. Edna Vivian Bedell, Feb. 14, 1948; children: Victoria Elizabeth Hardy Pursch, Alice Anne Hardy Gannon. Bar: Tex. 1936, U.S. Dist. Ct. (so. and we. dists.) Tex. 1946, U.S. Ct. Appeals (5th cir.) 1946, U.S. Supreme Ct. 1949. First asst. dist. atty. Bexar County, San Antonio, 1947-50, acting dist. atty., 1950-51; city atty. San Antonio, 1952-53, Castle Hills, Tex., 1959-96, Helotes, Tex., 1984-96, Fair Oaks Ranch, Tex., 1973-96; legal adviser bd. trustees Fireman and Policemen's Pension Fund of San Antonio, 1956-96; of counsel Hardy Jacobson Gazda & Jacobson, San Antonio, 1996—; legal advisor Grey Forest Utilities, 1986-96. Author: A Lifetime at the Bar: A Lawyer's Memoir. 1st lt. inf. U.S. Army, 1941-45. Decorated Bronze Star with cluster. Fellow Tex. Bar Found.; mem. Tex. Bar Assn., San Antonio Bar Found., Tex. Assn. City Atts., San Antonio Bar Assn. Methodist. Home: 215 Atwater Dr San Antonio TX 78213-3321

**HARDY, PAUL DUANE,** lawyer; b. N.Y.C., Nov. 7, 1936; s. Reginald Sayre and Mae Estelle (Sculthorp) H.; m. Jacqueline Hardy, June 8, 1971; children: Valerie, Christopher. BA, U. Pa., 1958; LLB, U. Va., 1961. Bar: Pa. 1963, D.C. 1972, Fla. 1974. Ptnr. Rawle & Henderson Law Firm, Phila., 1963-70, Holland & Knight Law Firm, Tampa, Fla., 1973-86, Stagg Hardy Law Firm, Tampa, 1986-93, Akerman Senterfett Law Firm, 1993—; chief trial counsel U.S. Maritime Adminstrn., Washington, 1970-73. With U.S. Army, 1963-64. Mem. Maritime Law Assn. of U.S. (bd. dirs. 1983-86). Admiralty, Insurance. Office: Akerman Senterfett Law Firm 100 S Ashley Dr Tampa FL 33602-5360

**HARDY, ROBERT PAUL,** lawyer; b. San Francisco, Apr. 30, 1958; s. David John Hardy and Constance Catherine (Parrette) Keenan; m. Mary Louise Stevens, Aug. 6, 1988; children: Nicholas Paul, Jackson Robert. BA, UCLA, 1981; JD, U. So. Calif., 1984. Bar: Calif. 1984, U.S. Dist. Ct. (ctrl. dist.) Calif. 1984, U.S. Ct. Appeals (9th cir.) 1984, N.Y. 1995. Assoc. Kindel & Anderson, L.A., 1984-86; assoc. Jones, Day, Reavis & Pogue, L.A., 1986-91; assoc. Jones, Day, Reavis & Pogue, N.Y., 1991-93, ptnr., 1994-97; ptnr. Brown & Wood, N.Y.C., 1997—. Recipient Am. Jurisprudence award The Lawyers Co-operative Pub. Co. and Bancroft-Whitney Co., 1982. Mem. ABA (employee benefits com. of taxation sect.). Democrat. Episcopalian. Pension, profit-sharing, and employee benefits. Office: Brown & Wood 1 World Trade Ctr Fl 58 New York NY 10048-0557

**HARDYMON, DAVID WAYNE,** lawyer; b. Columbus, Ohio, Aug. 22, 1949; s. Philip Barbour and Margaret Evelyn (Bowers) H.; m. Monica Ella Sleep, Mar. 13, 1982; children: Philip Garnet, Teresa Jeanette. BA in History, Bowling Green State U., 1971; JD, Capital U., Columbus, Ohio, 1976. ssss Ohio 1976, U.S. Dist. Ct. (so. dist.) Ohio 1976; U.S. Supreme Ct. 1980, U.S. Ct. Appeals (6th cir.) 1982, Ky. 1999. Asst. prosecuting atty. Franklin County Prosecutor's Office, Columbus, Ohio, 1976-81; assoc. Vorys, Sater, Seymour & Pease, Columbus, 1981-86, ptnr., 1987—. Mem. Chmn's. Club Franklin Country Rep. Orgn., 1983. Fellow Columbus Bar Found.; mem. Ohio State Bar Assn., Columbus Bar Assn. Avocation: sailing. General civil litigation, Environmental, Product liability. Office: Vorys Sater Seymour & Pease PO Box 1008 52 E Gay St Columbus OH 43215-3161

**HARF, CYNTHIA MINETTE,** lawyer; b. Houston, June 20, 1967. BA, Tulane U., 1989; JD, Calif. Western U., 1993; LLM, U. San Diego, 1998. Bar: Calif. Owner Harf & Assocs., San Diego, 1993—. Mem. ABA, San Diego County Bar Assn. Avocations: step aerobics, spinning classes, yoga, reading, ballroom dancing. Family and matrimonial, Taxation, general, Personal income taxation. Office: Harf & Assocs 7860 Mission Center Ct Ste 103 San Diego CA 92108-1330

**HARFF, CHARLES HENRY,** lawyer, retired diversified industrial company executive; b. Wesel, Germany, Sept. 27, 1929; s. Philip and Stephanie (Dreyfuss) H.; m. Marion Haines MacAfee, July 19, 1958; children—Pamela Haines, John Blair, Todd Philip. B.A., Colgate U., 1951; LL.B., Harvard U., 1954; postgrad., U. Bonn, Fed. Republic Germany, 1955. Bar: N.Y. 1955. Assoc. Chadbourne & Parke, N.Y.C., 1955-64, ptnr., 1964-84; sr. v.p., gen. counsel, sec. Rockwell Internat. Corp., Pitts., 1984-94, sr. v.p., spl. counsel, 1994-96, ret., 1996; cons., 1996—; bd. dirs. Meritor Automotive Inc. Trustee Christian Johnson Endeavor Found., N.Y.C., 1984—; bd. dirs. Atlantic Legal Found., 1989-98, Fulbright Assn., 1995—. Fulbright scholar U. Bonn, Germany, 1955. Mem. ABA, N.Y. State Bar Assn., The Assn. Gen. Counsel, Econ. Club N.Y., Harvard Club, Duquesne Club, Allegheny Country Club, Laurel Valley Golf Club, Farm Neck Golf Club (Martha's Vineyard, Mass.). General corporate, Securities. Home: Blackburn Rd Sewickley PA 15143-8386 Office: Rockwell Internat Corp 625 Liberty Ave Pittsburgh PA 15222-3110

**HARGESHEIMER, ELBERT, III,** lawyer; b. Cleve., Jan. 4, 1944; s. Elbert and Agnes Mary (Heckman) H.; children: Heather Leigh, Elbert IV, Jon-Erik, Piper Elizabeth, Kevin R. Cross, Mark R. Dziob. AB, Cornell U., 1966; JD, SUNY, Buffalo, 1969. Bar: N.Y. 1970, U.S. Dist. Ct. (we. dist.) N.Y. 1971. Assoc. Miller, Bouvier, O'Connor & Cegielski, Buffalo, 1970-73, ptnr., 1973-74; ptnr. Godinho & Hargesheimer, Hamburg, N.Y., 1974-84; pvt. practice law Hamburg, 1984—; chief counsel Joint Legis. Commn. to Revise Bus. and Corp. Law, N.Y. State Assembly and Senate, 1974-75; prosecutor Village of Blasdell (N.Y.), 1978-80, 83-87, village atty. 1980-82; fund chmn. South Towns Hosp. Found., Inc., 1973-76, fin. chmn., bd. dirs., 1976-77, v.p., 1978-82; chmn. Hamburg Town Rep. Com., 1978-88; coord. Erie County Pretrial Svcs. Program, 1987-88; counsel Erie County Rep. Com., 1980-92; mem. Erie County Bd. Ethics, 1979-89, chmn. 1983.; charter mem., counsel S.W. Hamburg Taxpayers Assn. Named Mr. Rep., Town of Hamburg Rep. Club, 1982, Rep. of Yr., Hamburg Twon Rep. Com., 1988. Mem. N.Y. State Bar Assn., Western N.Y. Trial Lawyer's Assn., Theta Chi.

Methodist. General practice, General corporate, Family and matrimonial. Home and Office: 22 Buffalo St Hamburg NY 14075-5002

**HARGRAVE, RUDOLPH,** state supreme court justice; b. Shawnee, Okla., Feb. 15, 1925; s. John Hubert and Daisy (Holmes) H.; m. Madeline Hargrave, May 29, 1949; children: Cindy Lu, John Robert, Jana Sue. LLB, U. Okla., 1949. Bar: Okla. 1949. Pvt. practice Wewoka, Okla., 1949; asst. county atty. Seminole County, 1951-55; judge Seminole County Ct., 1964-67, Seminole County Superior Ct., 1967-69; dist. judge Okla. Dist. Ct., Dist. 22, 1969-79; assoc. justice Okla. Supreme Ct., Oklahoma City, 1979, former vice chief justice, former chief justice, justice, 1979—. Mem. Seminole County Bar Assn., Okla. Bar Assn., ABA. Democrat. Methodist. Lodges: Lions; Masons. Office: Okla Supreme Ct State Capitol Bldg Room 202 Oklahoma City OK 73105*

**HARGRAVES, DIRCK ANTONY,** lawyer; b. Fom Lewis, Wash., Aug. 26, 1966; s. John Charles and Gwendolyn Agnes (Bantum) H. BA, U. Pa., 1988; JD, Am. U., 1993. Bar: Va. 1994, U.S. Dist. Ct. (ea. dist.) 1994, U.S. Ct. Appeals (4th cir.), 1994. Credit analyst 1st Nat. Book Md., Balt., 1988-89, dir. deposit sales team leader, 1989-90; law clerk FDIC, Washington, 1991, staff atty., 1994—. Exec. bd. mem. United Way, 1993-94. Mem. ABA, Nat. Bar Assn., Va. Bar Assn., Aplpha Phi Alpha. Avocations: comic book collecting, jogging, bicycling. Home: 18573 Split Rock Ln Germantown MD 20874-2114 Office: FDIC 550 17th St NW Washington DC 20429-0001

**HARGROVE, WADE HAMPTON,** lawyer; b. Clinton, N.C., Mar. 6, 1940; s. Wade Hampton and Susan (Baker) H.; m. Sandra Dunaway, June 7, 1969; children: Wade Hampton III, Andrew D. AB with honors, U. N.C., 1962, JD, 1965. Bar: N.C. 1965, D.C. 1967. Ptnr. Brooks, Pierce, McLendon, Humphrey, Leonard, Raleigh, N.C.; gen. counsel, exec. dir. N.C. Assn. Broadcasters, 1970—, N.C. CATV Assn., 1980—; chmn. bd. dirs. 1st Union Nat. Bank, Raleigh, 1989-93. Mem. N.C. Gov.'s Council on State Policy, 1974-79; chmn. N.C. News Media Adminstrn. of Justice Coun., 1976, Raleigh, 1976-78; commr. N.C. Milk Commn., 1976-78, chmn. commnr., 1988—, N.C. Agy. for Pub. Telecom., 1979—; spl. advisor to U.S. at Internat. Conf. on Direct Satellite Broadcasts, Geneva, 1983; chair N.C. Ctr. Public Policy Rsch., 1994—; bd. visitors U. N.C., 1991—, U. N.C. Sch. Journalism, 1993—. Recipient Disting. Service award N.C. Assn. Broadcasters, 1973, N.C. CATV Assn., 1985, 88; inducted N.C. Assn. Broadcasters, 1998. Mem. ABA, N.C. State Bar, D.C. Bar, Fed. Comm. Bar Assn., U. N.C. Law Alumni Assn. (pres. 1991—), Capital City Club (bd. govs. 1983-91), Figure Eight Yacht Club, Raleigh Racquet Club, Cardinal Club (bd. govs. 1992—). Presbyterian. Public utilities, Media, General corporate. Home: 1005 Marlowe Rd Raleigh NC 27609-6971 Office: Brooks Pierce McLendon Humphrey Leonard 1600 First Union Bank Capitol Ctr Raleigh NC 27601-1309

**HARIRI, V. M.,** arbitrator, mediator, lawyer, educator. BS, Wayne State U.; JD, Detroit Coll. Law; LLM, London Sch. Econs. and Polit.Sci.; diploma arbitration, Reading (Eng.) U. Pvt. practice internat. and domestic bus. law Detroit; drafting com. Republic of Kazakhstan Code on Arbitration Procedure, Free Econ. Zone Legislation, Republic of Belarus; instr. internat. comml. arbitration Chartered Inst. Arbitrators, Am. Arbitration Assn. Fellow Chartered Inst. Arbitrators (exec. com. N.Am. br., co-founder); mem. ABA, Internat. Bar Assn., Am. Soc. Internat. Law, Am. Arbitration Assn., London Ct. Internat. Arbitration, World Jurist Assn., Mich. Trial Lawyers Assn. Office: 325 N Center St Ste E3 Northville MI 48167-1244

**HARKEY, JOHN D., JR.,** lawyer; b. San Antonio, Sept. 12, 1960; s. John D. Sr. and Lucy Harkey. BBA, U. Tex., 1983, JD, 1985; MBA, Stanford U., 1987. Bar: Tex. 1985. Mng. dir., founder Capstone Capital Corp., Dallas, 1989-92; mng. ptnr. Cracken, Harkey & Payne, LLP, Dallas, 1993—; mgr. Cracken, Harkey, Street & Hartnett, LLC, Dallas, 1998—; vice chmn. El Chico Restaurants, Inc., 1998—; chmn. Consol. Restaurant Cos., Inc., Dallas, 1998—. Author: Collateralized Mortgage Obligations, 1985. Avocations: golf, tennis, downhill skiing, hunting. Personal injury. Home: 4253 Potomac Ave Dallas TX 75205-2626 Office: Cracken & Harkey LLP 5956 Sherry Ln Ste 1401 Dallas TX 75225-8025

**HARKEY, JOHN NORMAN,** judge; b. Russellville, Ark., Feb. 25, 1933; s. Olga John and Margaret (Fleming) H.; m. Willa Moreau Charlton, May 24, 1959; children—John Adam, Sarah Leigh. AS, Marion (Ala.) Inst., 1952; LLB, U. Ark., 1959, BS, BSL, 1959, JD, 1969. Bar: Ark. 1959. Since practiced in Batesville; pros. atty. 3d Jud. Dist. Ark., 1961-65; ins. commr. Ark., 1967-68; chmn. Ark. Commerce Commn., 1968-69; spl. justice Ark. Supreme Ct., 1988; judge juvenile divsn. Ark. 16th Dist., 1989-90; sr. ptnr. Harkey, Walmsley and related firms, Batesville, 1970-92; chancery and probate judge 16th Jud. Dist., Ark., 1993-98, cir., chancery judge, 1999—. 1st lt. USMCR, Korea. Mem. Ark. Bar Assn., Am. Bar Register, U.S. Marine Corps League. Home: 490 Harkey Rd Batesville AR 72501-9294 Office: PO Box 2656 Batesville AR 72503-2656

**HARKEY, ROBERT SHELTON,** lawyer; b. Charlotte, N.C., Dec. 22, 1940; s. Charles Nathan and Josephine Lenora (McKenzie) H.; m. Barbara Carole Payne, Apr. 2, 1983; 1 child, Elizabeth McKenzie. BA, Emory U., 1963, LLB, 1965. Bar: Ga. 1964, U.S. Dist. Ct. (no. dist.) Ga. 1964, U.S. Ct. Appeals (1st, 5th, 7th, 9th and 11th cirs.) 1964-86, U.S. Supreme Ct. Assoc. Swift, Currie, McGhee & Hiers, Atlanta, 1965-68; atty. Delta Air Lines, Atlanta, 1968-74, gen. atty., 1974-79, asst. v.p. law, 1979-85, assoc. gen. counsel, v.p., 1985-88; gen counsel, v.p., 1988-90; gen. counsel, sr. v.p. Delta Air Lines, Atlanta, 1990-94, gen. counsel, sr. v.p., sec., 1994—; mem. coun. Emory U. Law Sch., 1997—. Unit chmn. United Way, Atlanta, 1985; trustee Woodruff Arts Ctr., 1995—; bd. visitors Emory U., 1996—. Mem. ABA (com. gen. counsels), Air Transport Assn. (chmn. law coun. 1996-98), State Bar Ga. (chmn. corp. counsel sect. 1992-93), Atlanta Bar Assn., Corp. Counsel Assn. Greater Atlanta (bd. dirs. 1990), Commerce Club. Presbyterian. Avocations: tennis, reading. Aviation, General corporate, Labor. Office: Delta Air Lines Hartsfield Atlanta Internat Airport Atlanta GA 30320

**HARKINS, DANIEL CONGER,** lawyer; b. Akron, Ohio, Aug. 9, 1960; s. Daniel Drury and Marjorie Helen (Conger) H. BA in Econs., Coll. of Wooster, 1982; JD, Case Western Res. U., 1985; LLM in Taxation, NYU, 1986. Bar: Ohio 1985, D.C. 1986. Assoc. Williams, Zumkehr & Welser, Kent, Ohio, 1985-88; assoc. Martin, Browne, Hull & Harper, Springfield, Ohio, 1988-93, ptnr., 1993-96; pvt. practice Springfield, 1996—. Mem. Bd. Bldg. Appeals, Springfield, 1990-98, vice chmn., 1991-92, chmn., 1995—; trustee Springfield Family YMCA, 1991-95; trustee Springfield Family YMCA, 1991-95, 97—, treas., 1991-94, pres., 1994-96; v.p., sec. Jr. Achievement, 1991-94; trustee Clark County Mental Health Found., 1991-98; chmn. fin. com., mem. ctrl. and exec. coms. Clark County Rep. Com., 1992-97; vice chmn. Clark County Rep. Ctrl. Com., 1994-97; chmn. Clark County Rep. Party, 1997—; coach wrestling team Cath. Ctrl. H.S., Springfield, 1992-93; pres. elect Tecumseh Coun., Boy Scouts Am., 1996—, pres. 1998—, pres.-elect 1996-98; mem. Clark County Bd. of Elections, 1998—. Mem. Ohio State Bar Assn. (chmn. mcpl. income tax com., taxation com. 1995—), D.C. Bar Assn., Clark County Bar Assn. (exec. com. 1991—, treas. 1993—), Clark County Law Libr. Assn. (treas. 1996—). Congregationalist. Avocations: running, swimming, skiing, amateur wrestling. Corporate taxation, Estate taxation, Non-profit and tax-exempt organizations. Office: 333 N Limestone St Ste 104 Springfield OH 45503-4250

**HARKINS, JOHN GRAHAM, JR.,** lawyer; b. Phila., May 9, 1931; s. John Graham and Elizabeth Taylor (Bowers) H.; m. Beatrice Gibson McIlvain, June 30, 1955; children: John Graham III, Alida McIlvain. B.A. with honors, U. Pa., 1953, LL.B. summa cum laude, 1958. Bar: Pa. 1959, U.S. Supreme Ct. 1971. Assoc. firm Pepper, Hamilton & Scheetz, Phila., 1958-63; partner Pepper, Hamilton & Scheetz, 1963-92, co-chmn., 1982-86, chmn., 1986-92; ptnr. Harkins Cunningham, Phila., 1992—; instr. U. Pa., 1956-58, lectr. Law Sch., former bd. overseers-law, 1981-95; mem. adv. com. Inst. Law and Econs., 1981—, com. chmn., 1981-91. Editor-in-chief: U. Pa. Law Rev, 1957-58. Supr. Easttown Twp., Pa., 1972-77; past bd. dirs. Chester County Hosp.; past trustee Curtis Inst. Music; trustee U. Pa., 1987-97, trustee emeritus, 1998—; trustee U. Pa. Health Sys., 1988—, vice chmn., 1991—; mem. bd. overseers U. Pa. Med. Sch., 1990—, chmn., 1991—. With U.S. Army, 1953-55. Fellow Salzburg Seminar in Am. Studies, 1961. Mem. Am. Coll. Trial Lawyers, Am. Law Inst., Am. Bar Assn., Pa. Bar Assn., Phila. Bar Assn., Jud. Conf. U.S. Ct. of Appeals for 3d Circuit, Order of Coif, Phi Beta Kappa. Clubs: Merion Cricket, Radnor Hunt. Antitrust, Federal civil litigation, Securities. Home: Lowbrook PO Box 813 Devon PA 19333-0813 Office: Harkins Cunningham 2800 One Commerce Sq 2005 Market St Ste 1800 Philadelphia PA 19103-7075

**HARLAN, JANE ANN,** lawyer; b. Newton, Iowa, Oct. 8, 1947; d. Ellis and Julia (Blount) H.; m. Adel Zahian Hanna, 1971 (div. 1981); children: Samuel, Laura, Magda. BA, Drake U., 1969; JD, DePaul U., 1974. Bar: Ill. 1975, Wis. 1978, Iowa 1984. Pvt. practice Chgo., 1975-78, Greendale, Wis., 1978-84, Newton, Iowa, 1984-94; adminstrv. asst. Office of State Pub. Defender, Racine, Wis., 1994-95, Milw., 1995-99; atty. Appalachian Rsch. and Defense Fund, Somerset, Ky., 1999—. Cooperating atty. Wis. Civil Liberties Union, Milw., 1978-84; chairperson S.W. Suburban Dems., Milwaukee County, Wis., 1982-83. Recipient Outstanding Svc. plaque, Milw. Dems., 1983, citation for outstanding contbns. Wis. State Assembly, 1984. Mem. NOW, Ky. Bar Assn., Wis. Bar Assn. Avocation: music. Family and matrimonial, General practice. Office: Appalachian Rsch and Def Fund PO Box 1334 Somerset KY 42502-1334

**HARLAN, PETER LLEWELLYN,** lawyer, prosecutor; b. San Diego, Nov. 20, 1953; s. William Lee and Phyllis Gene Harlan; m. Kathleen Sue Cecil. BA, Creighton U., 1975, JD, 1979. Asst. dist. atty., chief of fed. litigation Dallas County Dist. Atty.'s Office, Dallas, 1982—. Office: Dallas County Dist Atty 133 N Industrial Blvd Dallas TX 75207-4300

**HARLAN, WENDY JILL,** lawyer; b. Mpls., Oct. 28, 1968. BA, Wellesley Coll., 1990; JD, Harvard U., 1996. Bar: Maine 1996. Rsch. analyst Cambridge (Mass.) Econ., Inc., 1991-93; assoc. Bernstein, Shur, Sawyer & Nelson, Portland, Maine, 1996—. Mem. Freeport (Maine) Town Com. Mem. ABA, Maine Bar Assn. General corporate, Health. Home: 58 Webster Rd Freeport ME 04032-6228 Office: Bernstein Shur Sawyer and Nelson 100 Middle St Portland ME 04101-4166

**HARLEM, RICHARD ANDREW,** lawyer; b. Oneonta, N.Y., Feb. 9, 1957; s. Robert A. and Ramona A. (Prevost) H.; m. Debra M. Short, June 29, 1985; children: Zachary Andrew, Madeline Ramona, Lesley Marilyn. BA, SUNY, Plattsburgh, 1979; JD, U. Toledo, 1982. Bar: N.Y. 1983, U.S. Dist. Ct. (no. dist.) N.Y. 1983, Fla. 1984, U.S. Supreme Ct. 1988. Assoc. James E. Konstanty, Oneonta, N.Y., 1983; ptnr. Konstanty and Harlem, Oneonta, N.Y., 1984-85; sole practice Oneonta, 1985—; justice of peace Town of Milford, N.Y., 1986—. Pres. Oneonta City Sch. Bd. Edn., Hartwick Coll. Citizen's Bd; bd. dirs. SUCO Day Care Ctr., Oneonta, 1985—, United Way of Greater Oneonta, 1986—; mem. Big Bro./Big Sister, Toledo, 1982—, Newman Bd. Mem. ABA, Otsego County Bar Assn., Del. County Bar Assn., N.Y. State Bar Assn., Fla. Bar Assn., Assn. Trial Lawyers Am., Otsego County C. of C. (mem. govt. affairs com.), Broome County Bar Assn. Republican. Roman Catholic. Lodges: Elks, Kiwanis. Avocations: basketball, racquetball, tennis, swimming. Personal injury, Probate, Real property. Home: 24 Ravine Pkwy N Oneonta NY 13820-4619 Office: 493 Chestnut St PO Box 850 Oneonta NY 13820-0850

**HARLEY, HALVOR LARSON,** banker, lawyer; b. Atlantic City, N.J., Oct. 7, 1948; s. Robison Dooling and Loyde Hazel (Gauchnauer) H. BSc, U. S.C., 1971, MA, 1973; JD, Widener U., 1981. Bar: Pa. 1982, D.C. 1989, U.S. Ct. Appeals (3d cir.) 1987, U.S. Dist. Ct. (ea. dist.) Pa. 1987, U.S. Supreme Ct., 1988, U.S. Ct. Appeals D.C., 1989. Staff psychologist Columbia Area Mental Health Ctr., S.C., 1971-73; dir. Motivational Rsch. Cons., Columbia, 1973-79; psychologist Family Ct. Del., Wilmington, 1979; pvt. practice law Phila., 1982; v.p. investment banking Union Bank, L.A., 1982-88; v.p., mgr. Tokai Bank, Newport Beach., Calif., 1988-94; v.p., mgr. Mellon Pvt. Asset Mgmt., Newport Beach, 1994-97, first v.p., 1994—; regional sales mgr. So. Calif. Pvt. Asset Mgmt., 1994—. Author: Help for Herpes, 1982; contbr. articles to profl. jours. Fundraiser Orange County Performing Art Ctr., 1983-84; trustee, exec. com. Orange County Mus. Arts; vol. Hosp. Ship HOPE, Sri Lanka, 1968-69; bd. dirs., v.p. exec. com. alzheimers Assn. Orange County; bd. dirs. Lido Sands Homeowners Assn., Newport Beach, 1984-85, So. Calif. Entrepreneurship Acad., 1995—; bd. dirs. United Cerebral Palsy of Orange County, chmn. Bastile Day com. Mem. ATLA, Calif. Bankers Assn., Am. Judicature Soc., Indsl. League Orange County (membership com. 1983-84), Am. Bankers Assn., World Trade Ctr. Assocs. Orange County (directing com. 1983-85), Orange County Performing Arts Fraternity (trustee), Psi Chi (chpt. pres. 1971-73). Home: 5015 Lido Sands Dr Newport Beach CA 92663-2403 Office: Mellon Bank 4695 Macarthur Ct Ste 240 Newport Beach CA 92660-8851

**HARLEY, ROBISON DOOLING, JR.,** lawyer, educator; b. Ancon, Panama, July 6, 1946; s. Robison Dooling and Loyde Hazel (Goehenauer) H.; m. Suzanne Purviance Bendel, Aug. 9, 1975; children: Arianne Erin, Lauren Loyde. BA, Brown U., 1968; JD, Temple U., 1971; LLM, U. San Diego, 1985. Bar: Pa. 1971, U.S. Ct. Mil. Appeals 1972, Calif. 1976, U.S. Dist. Ct. (cen. and so. dists) Calif. 1976, N.J. 1977, U.S. Dist. Ct. N.J. 1977, U.S. Supreme Ct. 1980, D.C. 1981, U.S. Ct. Appeals (9th cir.) 1982, U.S. Dist. Ct. (ea. dist.) Pa. 1987, U.S. Ct. Appeals (3rd cir.) 1986. Cert. criminal law specialist Calif. Bd. Legal Specialization, 1981, recertified 1986, 91, 96; cert. criminal trial adv. Nat. Bd. Trial Advocacy, 1982, recertified, 1987, 92, 97. Asst. agy. dir. Safeco Title Ins. Co., L.A., 1975-77; ptnr. Cohen, Stokke & Davis, Santa Ana, Calif., 1977-85; prin. Harley Law Offices, Santa Ana, Calif., 1985—; adj. prof. Orange County Coll. Trial Advocacy, adj. prof., paralegal program U. Calif., trial adv. programs U.S. Army, USN, USAF, USMC; judge pro-tem Orange County Cts. Author: Orange County Trial Lawyers Drunk Driving Syllabus; contbr. articles to profl. jours. and reports. Bd. dirs. Orange County Legal Aid Soc. Served to lt. col. JAGC, USMCR, 1975-94; trial counsel, def. counsel, mil. judge, asst. staff judge adv. USMC, 1971-75, regional def. counsel Western Region, 1986-90, instr., program coord. Army, Navy, Air Force, Marines, Coast Guard Trial Adv. Programs worldwide. Recipient Commendation medal U.S. Navy, Nat. Defense Svc. medal, Reserve medal, 23 Certs. of Commendation and/or Congratulations. Mem. ABA, ATLA, Orange County Bar Assn. (judiciary com., criminal law sect., adminstrn. of justice com.), Orange County Trial Lawyers Assn., Calif. Trial Lawyers Assn., Calif. Attys. for Criminal Justice, Calif. Pub. Defenders Assn., Nat. Assn. for Criminal Def. Attys., Assn. Specialized Criminal Def. Advs., Orange County Criminal Lawyers Assn. (found. com.), Res. Officers Assn., Marine Corps Reserve Officers Assn., Marine Corps Assn. Republican. Avocations: sports, physical fitness, reading. Criminal, Military. Home: 31211 Paseo Miraloma San Juan Capistrano CA 92675-5505 Office: Harley Law Offices 825 N Ross St Santa Ana CA 92701-3419

**HARLOW, ANGELIA DEAN,** lawyer; b. Dallas, Feb. 18, 1964; d. Calvin W. and Judy D. Wesch; m. Steven M. Harlow, Oct. 9, 1993; children: Austin, Travis. BA with honors, U. Tex., 1986; JD, Tex. Tech U., 1989. Bar: Tex. 1989, U.S. Dist. Ct. (so. dist.) Tex. 1991, U.S. Ct. Appeals (5th cir.) 1991, Wash. 1993, U.S. Dist. Ct. (we. dist.) Wash. 1993, Alaska 1996. Atty. Andrews & Kurth, Houston, 1989-93, Stanislaw Ashbaugh LLP, Seattle, 1993-97, Eisenhower & Carlson PLLC, Tacoma, 1997—; pres., bd. dirs. Comml. Real Estate Women-N.W., Seattle. Mem. Wash. State Bar Assn. (environ. and land use sect.), Master Builders Assn. Pierce County. E-mail: aharlow@eisenhowercarlson.com. Real property, Construction, Land use and zoning (including planning). Office: Eisenhower & Carlson PLLC 1201 Pacific Ave Ste 1200 Tacoma WA 98402-4395

**HARLOW, JUDITH LEIGH,** educational institute executive, consultant; b. Denver, Aug. 11, 1943; d. Roy Afton and Virginia Lee (Whitehead) H. BA in Secondary Edn., U. N.Mex., 1966, MA in Counseling, 1973. Cert. in guidance and counseling, ednl. adminstrn., N.Mex.; lic. ednl. diagnostician, mediator. Tchr. Albuquerque Pub. Schs., 1966-79, ednl. diagnostician, 1979-80, adminstr. spl. edn., 1980-87, asst. prin., 1987-95; dir. Inst. for Behavior Intervention in the Schs. Ednl. Assessment Systems, Inc., Albuquerque, 1997—; mem. adv. bd. Desert Hills Residential Treatment Ctr., Albuquerque, 1998—. Vol. N.Mex. Ctr. for Dispute Resolution, Albuquerque. Mem. Coun. for Exceptional Children (Disting. Svc. award N.Mex. 1992). Democrat. Avocations: golf, tennis. Home: 10920 Central Park Dr NE Albuquerque NM 87123-5426 Office: Inst for Behavior Intervention in the Schs 5200 Copper Ave NE Albuquerque NM 87108-1356

**HARMAN, JOHN ROYDEN,** lawyer; b. Elkhart, Ind., June 30, 1921; s. James Lewis and Bessie Bell (Mountjoy) H.; m. Elizabeth Rae Crosier, Dec. 12, 1943 (dec. May 1995); 1 child, James Richard. B.S., U. Ill., 1943; J.D., Ind. U., 1949. Bar: Ind. 1949. Assoc. Proctor & Proctor, Elkhart, 1949-51; pvt. practice, Elkhart, 1952-60; ptnr. Cawley & Harman, 1960-65, Thornburg, McGill, Deahl, Harman, Carey & Murray, 1965-82, Barnes & Thornburg, Elkhart, 1982-89; ret., 1989; atty. City of Elkhart, 1952-60. State del. Ind. Republican Com., 1962-70; pres., bd. dirs. Crippled Childrens Soc.; bd. dirs. United Community Services Elkhart County. 1st lt., F.A., AUS, 1943-46, PTO. Fellow Ind. Bar Found; mem. ABA, Ind. Bar Assn. , Elkhart County Bar Assn. (pres. 1977), Elkhart City Bar Assn. (pres. 1970), Elkhart C. of C. (pres. 1977, bd. dirs. 1972-75), Elcona Country Club (bd. dirs.), Phi Kappa Psi, Alpha Kappa Psi, Phi Delta Phi. Republican. Presbyterian. Avocation: golf. General corporate, Estate planning. Office: NBD Bank Bldg 121 W Franklin St Ste 200 Elkhart IN 46516-3200 *Be honest and forthright—think positively—continually try to enhance the cause of mankind.*

**HARMAN, WALLACE PATRICK,** lawyer; b. El Paso, Tex., Jan. 22, 1949; s. Wallace Irvin and Dorothy Louise (Pearson) H.; m. Gina Marie Ries, Dec. 31, 1988; children: Loren Patrick, Claire Marie. BA, Stanford U., 1972; JD, U. Calif., 1977. Bar: Calif. 1977, U.S. Ct. Appeals (9th cir.) 1977, N.Mex. 1978, U.S. Dist. Ct. N.Mex. 1978, U.S. Ct. Appeals (10th cir.) 1978. Zone adminstrn. mgr. Am. Motors Corp., Burlingame, Calif., 1972-74; atty., shareholder Sutin, Thayer & Browne, APC, Albuquerque, N.Mex., 1977-87, group leader comml. group, 1985-87; atty., shareholder, mng. ptnr., leader bus. group The Payne Law Firm, P.C., Albuquerque, 1987-91; atty., ptnr. Hisey & Wainwright, P.A., Albuquerque, 1991-92; atty., pres., chief exec. officer The Harman Law Firm, P.C., Albuquerque, 1992—; mem. N.Mex. Supreme Ct. Med.-Legal Panel, Albuquerque, 1978-80, 91—; mem. N.Mex. Supreme Ct. Lawyers Assistance Com., Albuquerque, 1991—; area rep. The Taft Sch., Watertown, Conn., 1992—; mem. mentorship program Hatings Coll. Law. Co-author: Recent Developments in Commercial Law, University of New Mexico Law Review, 1989. Bd. advisors Lovelace Med. Ctr., Albuquerque, 1980-89; mem. state bd. trustees The Nature Conservancy, N.Mex., 1984-88; adv. bd. Assistance League Albuquerque, 1982-89, Jr. League Albuquerque, 1984-87, Make-a-Wish Found. of N.Mex., Inc., 1996-97. Recipient AV Rating award Martindale-Hubbell, 1990. Mem. ABA, Albuquerque Bar Assn. Democrat. Avocations: photography, sports, computers, landscaping, writing. E-mail: harman@sandia.net. Banking, General civil litigation, Real property.

**HARMON, GAIL MCGREEVY,** lawyer; b. Kansas City, Kans., Mar. 15, 1943; d. Milton and Barbara (James) McGreevy; m. John W. Harmon, June 11, 1966; children: James, Eve. BA cum laude, Radcliffe Coll., 1965; JD cum laude, Columbia U., 1969. Bar: Mass. 1970, D.C. 1976, U.S. Dist. Ct. D.C. Assoc. Gaston Snow & Ely Bartlett, Boston, 1970-75, Steptoe & Johnson, Washington, 1975-76, Roisman, Kessler & Cashdan, Washington, 1976-77; ptnr. Harmon, Curran & Tousley, Washington, 1977-90, Harmon, Curran, Spielberg & Eisenberg, Washington, 1990—. Pres. Women's Legal Def. Fund, 1982-84; steering com. Emily's List, 1985—; bd. dirs. Population Svcs. Internat., 1998—. Mem. Population Svcs. Internat. (bd. dirs.). Democrat. Episcopalian. Taxation, general, General corporate.

**HARMON, MELINDA FURCHE,** federal judge; b. Port Arthur, Tex., Nov. 1, 1946; d. Frank Cantrell and Wilma (Parish) Furche; m. Frank G. Harmon III, Oct. 16, 1976; children: Mary Elizabeth, Phelps, Francis. AB, Harvard U., 1969; JD, U. Tex., 1972. Bar: Tex. 1973, U.S. Dist. Ct. (so. dist.) Tex. 1974, U.S. Dist. Ct. (no. dist.) Tex. 1975, U.S. Dist. Ct. (ea. dist.) Tex. 1978, U.S. Ct. Appeals (5th and 11th cirs.) 1981, U.S. Supreme Ct. 1982, U.S. Ct. Claims 1987. Law clk. to presiding judge U.S. Dist. Ct. (so. dist.) Tex., Houston, 1973-75; atty. Exxon Co., Houston, 1975-88; judge 280th Jud. Dist. Ct. Tex. State Trial Ct., ctrl. jurisdiction, 1988-89; judge U.S. Dist. Ct. (so. dist.) Tex., Houston, 1989—. Mem. Tex. Bar Assn., Am. Inns of Ct., Houston Bar Assn., Harvard Radcliffe Club. Roman Catholic. Office: US Dist Ct US Courthouse 515 Rusk Ave Ste 9114 Houston TX 77002-2605

**HARMS, ALLAN L.,** patent lawyer; b. Auburn, Nebr., Feb. 14, 1945; m. Sally L. Lucas, Aug. 31, 1968; 2 children. BSEE, U. Nebr., 1968; MBA, U. Iowa, 1973, JD, 1974. Bar: Iowa 1974, U.S. Patent Office 1975. Lawyer White & Wenzel, Cedar Rapids, Iowa, 1974-75; patent lawyer Eells, Blackstock, Affeldt & Harms, Cedar Rapids, 1975-87, Wenzel, Piersall & Harms, P.C., Cedar Rapids, 1987-95, Wenzel & Harms, P.C., Cedar Rapids, 1995—; asst. Linn County Atty., Cedar Rapids, 1975-83. Bd. mem. Invent Iowa, Des Moines, 1998-99. Mem. Iowa Intellectual Property Law Assn. (pres. 1990), SPEBSQSA Internat. (Harmony Hawks Chorus chpt. 1980—, treas. 1986-96, pres. Cedar Rapids chpt. 1997-98), Cedar Rapids Noon Lions Club (pres. 1992-93, Lion of the Yr. 1993). Avocations: barbershop quartet singing, band membership, volunteering. E-mail: wenzelharm@aol.com. Fax: 319-363-8906. Patent. Office: Wenzel & Harms PC 2750 1st Ave NE Cedar Rapids IA 52402-4831

**HARMS, JOHN KEVIN,** lawyer; b. Bittburg Air Base, Germany, Oct. 19, 1960; s. William Robert and Catherine Dorothy (Heslin) H.; m. Panela Tinkham, 1988; children: William Cameron Harms, Wade Devlin Harms. BPA magna cum laude, Loyola U., New Orleans, 1982; JD, Northwestern U., 1985; MBA, Western New Eng. Coll., 1989. Bar: Ill. 1985, U.S. Army Ct. Mil. Rev. 1986, U.S. Ct. Mil. Appeals 1991, Mass. 1994. Commd. 2d lt. USAR, 1982, advance through grades to maj., 1994; aide-de-camp to comdg. gen. 33d Inf. Brigade, Ill. Army Nat. Guard, 1983-85; rsch. asst. Am. Bar Found., Chgo., 1985; legal assistance atty. Office of Staff Judge Advocate, Ft. Devens, Mass., 1986; trial def. counsel U.S. Army Trial Def. Svc., Ft. Devens, Mass., 1986-87, sr. def. counsel, 1987-90; deputy staff judge adv. Office of Staff Judge Adv. Mil. Traffic Mgmt. Command Ea. Area, Bayonne, N.J., 1990-92; internat. ops. law atty. Third Mil. Law Ctr., U.S. Army Res., Boston, 1992-95; adv., environ. law specialist Office of the Staff Judge Adv., 1992-95; chief counsel Devens Res. Forces Tng. Area, Ft. Devens, Mass., 1995-96; gov. contracts atty. Electronic Sys. Ctr., Hanscom AFB, Mass., 1996—; adminstrv. and contract law atty. 94th Regional Support Command, Ft. Devens, 1996—; mem. North Western Law Rev., 1984-85; mem. 1st del. of Am. criminal lawyers to the Peoples Rep. of China as part of Citizen Amb. Program, People to People Internat., 1987. Named Outstanding Young Man Am., 1988. Mem. ABA (spl. com. environ. crimes), Mass. Bar Assn. (mem. environ. law sect.), Boston Bar Assn. (mem. environ. law sect.), Air Force Assn., Armed Forces Comm.-Electronics Assn., Mass. Conveyancers' Assn., Hazardous Waste Site Cleanup Lic. Site Profl. Assn. (mem. steering com.), Bluekey Nat. Honor Fraternity, Alpha Sigma Nu, Delta Sigma Pi, Beta Gamma Sigma. Avocation: mystery writing.

**HARMS, ROBERT WAYNE,** lawyer; b. Stanley, N.D., Aug. 3, 1955; s. Penn Baldwin and Eva Frances (Frisinger) H.; m. Cherie D. Olson, Oct. 11, 1986. BS in Polit. Sci., N.D. State U., 1977; JD, U. N.D., 1980. Bar: N.D. 1980, U.S. Dist. Ct. N.D. 1982, U.S. Ct. Appeals (8th cir.) 1984. Founding ptnr. Harms Law Offices and predecessor firms, Williston, N.D., 1980—; counsel Gov.'s Office, Bismarck, 1994—; mem. Ethics Com., Bismarck, 1984-85, Legal Counsel for Indigents, Bismarck, 1985-89, Law Sch. Com., Grand Forks, N.D., 1989-91. Vice chmn. Rep. Party Dists. 1 and 2, Williston, 1986-91; bd. dirs. Crime Stoppers, Williston, 1989-92; legis. candidate N.D. Rep. Party, Williston, 1988. Scholar Burtness Found., 1978, Blikre scholar Clare T. Blikre, 1976, scholar Nat. Inst. Trial Advocates, 1990; recipient Allan Smith award Allan Smith Co., Grand Forks, 1980. Mem. ABA, ATLA, N.D. Trial Lawyers Assn., Williston Area C. of C. (bd. dirs. 1990-93), Lions, Blue Key Nat. Honor Frat. Avocations: sailing, landscaping, hiking, woodwork. State civil litigation, Family and matrimonial, Personal injury. Home: 815 N Mandan St Bismarck ND 58501-3618 Office: Govs Office State Capitol Bldg 600 E Boulevard Ave Bismarck ND 58505-0660

**HARMS, STEVEN ALAN,** lawyer; b. Detroit, Feb. 15, 1949; s. Herbert Rudolph and Elsa Jane (McClelland) H.; m. Nancy Gayle Banta, June 26, 1971; children: Jennifer Elizabeth, Heather Lynn, Robin Ann. BA, Hope Coll., 1970; JD, Detroit Coll. Law, 1975. Bar: Mich. 1975, U.S. Dist. Ct. (so. dist.) Mich. 1975, U.S. Ct. Appeals (6th cir.) 1982; bd. cert. creditors rights specialist. Ptnr. Muller, Muller, Richmond, Harms, Myers & Sgroi, P.C., Birmingham, Mich.; sec. gen. practice session State Bar Mich., 1982-83;

mediator Oakland County Cir. Ct., 1990—; lectr. in field; adj. prof. Bus. Law Walsh Coll., Troy, Mich., 1990—. Author: Successful Collection of a Judgement, 1981; Rights of Commercial Creditors, 1982, Post Judgement Collection, 1988, Handling the Collection Case in Michigan, 1989, revised edit., 1998; co-author: Atty Fee Agreements, 1995; contbg. editor Michigan Business Formbook, 1997, revised edit., 1998, Michigan Civil Procedure, 1997; editor: General Practitioner, State Bar Mich., 1978-82. Bd. dirs. fin. com. YMCA, North Oakland County, Mich., 1987—, chmn. bd., 1990-91. Republican. Club: Pearson Yacht Owners Assn. (commodore 1988-90), Hunter Sailing Assn. (vice commodore 1985-86, commodore 1987-88). Consumer commercial, Contracts commercial. Office: Muller Muller Richmond Harms Myers & Sgroi PC 33233 Woodward Ave Birmingham MI 48009-0903

**HARNED, PETE,** lawyer; b. Honolulu, May 19, 1959; s. John Joseph Harned and Armenia Carmel Nuccio. AA, Am. River Jr. Coll., Sacramento, 1980; JD, Lincoln Law Sch., 1985. Bar: Calif. 1985, U.S. Dist. Ct. Calif. 1985, U.S. Ct. Appeals (9th cir.) 1985. Dep. dist. atty. Sacramento Dist. Atty., 1985-96; mng. ptnr. Harned & Assocs., Sacramento, 1996—. E-mail: harned@earthlink.net. Personal injury. Office: Harned & Assocs 719 11th St Ste 101 Sacramento CA 95814-0816

**HARNER, TIMOTHY R.,** lawyer; b. Clarkson, N.Y., Sept. 1, 1955; s. Roy Seymour and Helen Belle (Dowden) H.; m. Suzanne Lee Daggs, May 22, 1982; children: Sarah, Andrew. BA, Houghton Coll., 1977; JD cum laude, Harvard Law Sch., 1980. Bar: N.Y., 1981. Law clk. U.S. Ct. Appeals 2nd Cir., N.Y.C., 1980-81; assoc. Nixon, Hargrave, Devans & Doyle, Rochester, N.Y., 1981-85; gen. counsel Upstate Farms Coop., Inc., LeRoy, N.Y., 1985—; dir. Palmer Food Svcs., Rochester. Editor: Harvard Law Rev., 1978-79, devel. officer, 1979-80. Trustee, sec. Roberts Wesleyan Coll., Rochester, 1989. Mem. Am. Corp. Counsel Assn. (past pres. Ctrl. and Western N.Y. chpts. 1997). Republican. Methodist. Avocations: astronomy, golf, jogging. Administrative and regulatory, General corporate, Mergers and acquisitions. Office: Upstate Farms Coop Inc 7115 W Main Rd Le Roy NY 14482-9352

**HARNETT, MATT,** lawyer, educator; b. Bklyn., Aug. 2, 1958; s. Joseph Harnett and Sandra Wohlberg; m. Lorraine Harnett, May 27, 1990; 1 child, Cassie. BS in Polit. Sci., Brockport State Coll., 1980; JD, Vt. Law Sch., 1983. Bar: Vt., U.S. Dist. Ct. Vt. 1986, U.S. Ct. Appeals (2d cir.) 1995. Pub. defender Rutland (Vt.) County Pub. Defender, 1984-87; assoc. atty. Law Office of Peter C. Montagne, P.C., Rutland, 1987-88; pvt. practice Rutland, 1988-90; assoc. Lorentz and Lorentz P.C., Rutland, 1990-91; ptnr. Lorentz, Lorentz and Harnett, Rutland, 1991—; continuing legal edn. presenter Green Mountain Trial Sch., Burlington, Vt., 1994—. On snow coord., ski instr. Killington Jr. Ski Instrn. Program, 1982—. Mem. Vt. Bar Assn. (continuing legal edn. presenter), Rutland County Bar Assn., Killington Ski Club, Rutland Country Club. Criminal, Family and matrimonial, Personal injury. Office: Lorentz Lorentz & Harnett 26 Court St Rutland VT 05701-4003

**HARON, DAVID LAWRENCE,** lawyer; b. Detroit, Sept. 24, 1944; s. Percy Hyman and Bess (Holland) H.; m. Pamela Kay Colburn, May 25, 1969; children: Eric, Andrea. BA, U. Mich., 1966, JD, 1969. Bar: Mich. 1969, U.S. Dist. Ct. (ea. dist.) Mich., 1969, U.S. Supreme Ct. 1974, U.S. Ct. of Appeals (6th cir.) 1996. Law clk. to chief judge Mich. Ct. Appeals, Detroit, 1969-70; assoc. Barris, Sott, Denn & Driker, Detroit, 1970-74; sr. ptnr. Josephson, Tennen, Haron and Bennett, Southfield, Mich., 1974-90; prin., shareholder, sr. v.p. Frank, Stefani, Haron and Hall, Troy, Mich., 1990—; arbitrator Mich. Prudential Securities, Inc. Expedited Arbitrations, 1994-96; cons. Universe Computer Software, 1985; pres., bd. dirs. S&H Licensing Corp., Southfield; panelist Ct. TV Law Ctr. Bar Assn. Mem. editorial bd. Prospectus Jour. Law Reform, 1969, (newsletter) Atty.'s Mktg. Report, 1986-88; contbr. articles to profl. jours. Commr. Farmington Hills Planning Commn., 1996—; vol. handicap parking enforcement officer Farmington Hills Police Dept., 1990-93; bd. dirs. Forest Elem. Sch. PTO, 1983, 87-88; v.p. North Farmington Baseball for Youth, 1984; mem. Sta. WTVS Auction, Detroit, 1985-88; trustee Caring Athletes Team for Children's and Henry Ford Hosps., 1996—, Temple Israel, West Bloomfield, Mich., 1987-93, tchr. Sunday Sch., 1986-88, chmn. Ritual com., 1988-93, advisor youth group, 1987-90; chmn. Farmington Hills Com. to Increase Voter Participation, 1987-89; bd. dirs. Met. Detroit chpt. Zionist Orgn. Am., 1987-90; pres. North Farmington H.S. Parent Club, 1989-95; mem. bd. advisors Farmington Hills Corps.-Salvation Army, 1997—; mem. site selection com. South Oakland County Habitat for Humanity; chair Cardozo Law Soc. of the Jewish Fedn. Met. Detroit, 1999—. Recipient Outstanding Alumnus award Mumford H.S., Detroit, 1985, Cert. recognition City of Farmington Hills, 1986. Fellow The Roscoe Pound Found., Mich. State Bar Found.; mem. ABA (mem. com. on comml. leasing 1987—, real property, probate and trust law sect., mem. bus. law sect. com. on fed. regulation of securities, mem. subcom. on alternative dispute resolution, SEC enforcement matters), ASTM (mem. com. on environ. assessment 1992—), ATLA, Nat. Arbitration Forum (arbitrator), Nat. Health Lawyers Assn. (co-chmn. fraud & abuse SISLC false claims/qui tam working group), Mich. Trial Lawyers Assn., Am. Soc. Writers on Legal Subjects, Internat. Assn. Jewish Lawyers and Jurists, Million Dollar Advocates Forum, State Bar Mich. (mem. pro bono com. real property sect. 1996-98, mem. professionalism com. 1994—, chmn. professionalism com. 1996-98, chmn. unauthorized practice of law com. 1990-92, chmn. Ct. Appeals com. 1977-78, mem. representative assembly 1999—), Nat. Assn. Securities Dealers (mediator 1996—, arbitrator 1997—), Am. Arbitration Assn. (arbitrator, mediator, spkr.), Comml. Law League Am., Detroit Bar Assn., Jewish Fedn., Oakland County Bar Assn. (participant Mich. law-related edn. project 1988-89, real estate com. 1990—, environ. law com. 1992-95, lawyer dispute conciliator, spkr. 1993, chmn. professionalism com. 1995-97, Cir. Ct. facilitator, master Inn of Ct. 1997—), Oakland Bar Adams Pratt Found. (trustee), Jewish Fedn. Met. Detroit, U. Mich. Alumni Assn., U. Mich. Victor's Club, Zionist Orgn. (bd. dirs. Detroit 1987-90), Tau Epsilon Rho, Tau Delta Phi. Jewish. Fax: 248-952-0890. E-mail: dharon@fsh-law.com. General corporate, Real property. Home: 34685 Old Timber Rd Farmington MI 48331-1436 Office: Frank Stefani Haron & Hall 5435 Corporate Dr Ste 225 Troy MI 48098-2624

**HARP, CHADWICK ALLEN,** lawyer; b. Norristown, Pa., Mar. 24, 1969; s. Leroy Allen Jr. and Judith Ann (Beck) H. BA cum laude, George Washington U., 1991; JD, Dickinson Sch. Law, Carlisle, Pa., 1996; postgrad. in estate planning, Temple U., 1999—. Bar: Pa. 1996. Various positions George Washington U. Med. Ctr., 1988-93, asst. to dean, 1990-93; law clk. Breidenbach, Breidenbach & Troncellitti, Norristown, Pa., 1994-96; Atty. Fox, Differ, Callahan, Sheridan & McDevitt, Norristown, Pa., 1999—; adj. prof. Montgomery C.C., 1996—. Bd. dirs. Children's Aid Soc., 1995—. Taxation, general, Estate planning. Office: 3 Penn Ct 325 Swede St Norristown PA 19401-4801

**HARP, JOHN ANDERSON,** lawyer; b. Helena, Ark., Nov. 30, 1950; s. Bert Seth and Mary Eleanor (Jolley) H.; m. Jane Van Cleave, Apr. 26, 1980; children: Anderson, Elizabeth, William, Hamilton. BA, Am. U., Washington, 1973; JD, Mercer U., Macon, Ga., 1980. Bar: Ga., Ala. Ptnr. Taylor, Harp & Callier, Columbus, Ga., 1985—. Co-author: Litigating Head Trauma Cases, 1991; bd. editors Neurolaw Letter, 1991—, IATROGENICS, 1992-93, Topics in Spinal Cord Injury Rehab., 1994—; contbr. articles to profl. jours. Reservist USMCR with Office of Asst. Sec. of Def., The Pentagon, 1996—. Col., USMCR, 1995—. Mem. ABA, ATLA, Ga. Bar Assn., Ala. Bar Assn., Nat. Spinal Cord Assn. (bd. dirs. 1987-95), Marine Corps Res. Officers Assn. (bd. dirs. 1995-98, nat. pres. 1997-98, vice-chmn. bd. dirs. 1998-99, Non Sibi Sed Patriae award), Mercer U. Law Sch. Alumni Assn. (nat. v.p. 1997-98, nat. pres.-elect 1998-99, nat. pres. 1999—). Avocations: running, skiing. Personal injury, General civil litigation, Product liability. Office: Taylor Harp & Callier 233 12th St Ste 900 Columbus GA 31901-2449

**HARPER, CONRAD KENNETH,** lawyer, former government official; b. Detroit, Dec. 2, 1940; s. Archibald Leonard and Georgia Florence (Hall) H.; m. Marsha Louise Wilson, July 17, 1965; children: Warren Wilson, Adam Woodburn. BA, Howard U., 1962; LLB, Harvard U., 1965; LLD (hon.), CUNY, 1990, Vt. Law Sch., 1994. Bar: N.Y. 1966. Law clk. NAACP Legal Def. and Ednl. Fund, N.Y.C., 1965-66, staff lawyer, 1966-70; assoc. Simpson Thacher & Bartlett, N.Y.C., 1971-74, ptnr., 1974-93, 96—; legal adviser U.S. Dept. of State, Washington, 1993-96; lectr. law Rutgers U., 1969-70; vis. lectr. law Yale U., 1977-81; cons. HEW, 1977; chmn. admissions and grievances com. U.S. Ct. Appeals, 2d cir., 1987-93; co-chmn. Lawyers' Com. for Civil Rights Under Law, 1987-89; mem. Permanent Ct. of Arbitration, The Hague, 1993-96, 98—, Adminstrv. Conf. U.S., 1993-95; bd. dirs. N.Y. Life Ins. Co., Pub. Svc. Enterprise Group, Pub. Svc. Electric & Gas. Trustee Inst. Internat. Edn., 1992-93, N.Y. Pub. Libr., chmn. exec. com., 1990-93, vice chmn. bd. trustees, 1991-93; trustee William Nelson Cromwell Found., 1990—, Met. Mus. of Art, 1996—; bd. mgrs. Lewis Walpole Libr., 1989-93; bd. visitors Fordham Law Sch., 1990-93, CUNY, 1989-93; vestryman Ch. of St. Barnabas, Irvington, N.Y., 1982-85; bd. dirs. Phi Beta Kappa Assocs., 1992-93; chancellor The Episc. Diocese of N.Y., 1987-92; mem. bd. legal advisors Martindale-Hubbell, 1990-93. Fellow Am. Bar Found., N.Y. Bar Found., Am. Coll. Trial Lawyers, Am. Acad. Arts and Scis.; mem. ABA (bd. editors jour. 1980-86), Internat. Bar Assn., Nat. Bar Assn., N.Y. State Bar Assn., Assn. of Bar of City of N.Y. (chmn. exec. com. 1979-80, pres. 1990-92), Am. Law Inst. (mem. coun. 1985—, 2nd v.p. 1998—), Am. Assn. for Internat. Commn. Jurists (bd. dirs. 1988-93), Am. Soc. Internat. Law (mem. exec. coun. 1997—, mem. exec. com. 1998—), Met. Black Bar Assn., Internat. Law Assn., N.Y. Law Inst. (mem. exec. com. 1997—), Am. Arbitration Assn. (bd. dirs. 1990-93, 97—, mem. exec. com. 1998—), Acad. Polit. Sci. (bd. dirs. 1998—), Coun. Fgn. Rels., Acad. Am. Poets (bd. dirs. 1990-93), Grolier Club (coun. mem. 1993, 97—), Century Assn., Harvard Club (mem. bd. mgrs. 1993), Yale Club, Phi Beta Kappa. Democrat. Episcopalian. Office: 425 Lexington Ave New York NY 10017-3903

**HARPER, DAVID ALEXANDER,** lawyer; b. Newport, R.I., Apr. 4, 1953; s. Luby Alexander and Westlake Addams H.; m. Linda Gilbert, June 6, 1975 (div. Oct. 1995); children: Mark, Beth, John; m. Deborah Brown, Feb. 10, 1996. AB, Cornell U., 1975; JD, Union U., 1982. Bar: N.Y. 1983, U.S. Dist. Ct. (no. dist.) N.Y. 1983. Assoc. Carusone Toomey & Carusone, Saratoga Springs, N.Y., 1983-86; pvt. practice Saratoga Springs, 1987-90; ptnr. Harper & Pozefsky, Saratoga Springs, 1991—; 1st. asst. dist. atty. Saratoga County, Ballston Spa, N.Y., 1987—. Chmn. Zoning Bd. Appeals, Saratoga Springs, N.Y., 1989—. With U.S. Army, 1975-79. Recipient Disting. Svc. award Legal Aid Soc. N.E. N.Y., 1996. Mem. N.Y. State Bar Assn., N.Y. State Dist. Attys. Assn., Saratoga County Bar Assn., Elks Club. Republican. Episcopalian. Avocation: sailing. Real property, Criminal, State civil litigation. Office: Harper & Pozefsky 25 Walton St Saratoga Springs NY 12866-2051

**HARPER, VESTA TAMORA,** lawyer, paralegal educator; b. Vicksburg, Miss., Sept. 25, 1971; d. Gregory Duwayne and Sara Susette (Jackson) H. BS, Alcorn State U., 1993; MBA, Tex. Tech. U., 1996, JD, 1996. Bar: Tex. 1997. Extern Criminal Dist. Ct. No. 2, Dallas, 1989; legal rsch. asst. West Tex. Legal Svcs., Lubbock, 1995; staff atty. West Tex. Legal Svcs., Ft. Worth, 1998—; contract atty. Exec. Secretariat Sch., Dallas, 1997—; pvt. practice law, Dallas, 1997-98; extern 5th Dist. Ct. Appeals, Dallas, 1997; contract atty. Southeastern Paralegal Inst., Dallas, 1998. Mem. ABA. Home: 9433 Timberleaf Dr Dallas TX 75243-6123 Office: West Tex Legal Svcs 600 E Weatherford St Fort Worth TX 76102-3264

**HARPST, CARLTON LEE,** lawyer; b. Lynwood, Calif., Jan. 15, 1949; m. Lucille Verbal, Aug. 24, 1975; children: Brian, Ashley. BA, U. Calif., Irvine, 1971; JD, Pepperdine U., 1975. Ins. adjustor Transamerica, Costa Mesa, Calif., 1975-76; atty. Law Office of George Chula, Santa Ana, Calif., 1976-78; pvt. practice Santa Ana, 1978-89; supr. civil atty. Ins. Co. N.Am., Orange, Calif., 1989—. With U.S. Army, 1971-77. Insurance. Office: Insurance Co N America Ste 300 725 W Town And Country Rd Orange CA 92868-4707

**HARPSTER, JAMES ERVING,** lawyer; b. Milw., Dec. 24, 1923; s. Philo E. and Pauline (Daanen) H. PhB, Marquette U., 1950, LLB, 1952. Bar: Wis. 1952, Tenn. 1953; dir. info. svcs. Nat. Cotton Council Am., Memphis, 1952-55; dir. public rels. Christian Bros. Coll., 1956; mgr. govt. affairs dept. Memphis C. of C., 1956-62; exec. v.p. Rep. Assn. Memphis and Shelby County, 1962-64; individual practice law, Memphis, 1965; ptnr. Rickey, Shankman, Blanchard, Agee & Harpster, and predecessor firm, Memphis, 1966-80, Harpster & Baird, 1980-83; pvt. practice, Memphis, 1984—. Mem. Shelby County Tax Assessor's Adv. Com., 1960-61; editor, asst. counsel Memphis and Shelby County Charter Com., 1962; mem. Shelby County Election Commn., 1968-70; mem. Tenn. State Bd. Elections, 1970-72, sec., 1972; mem. Tenn. State Election Commn., 1973-83, chmn., 1974, sec., 1975-83; a founder Lions Inst. for Visually Handicapped Children, 1954, chmn. E. H. Crump Meml. Football Game for Blind, 1956; pres. Siena Student Aid Found., 1960; bd. dirs. Memphis Public Affairs Forum; mem. Civic Rsch. Com., Inc., Citizens Assn. Memphis and Shelby County; Republican candidate Tenn. Gen. Assembly, 1964; v.p. Nat. Council Rep. Workshops, 1967-69; pres. Rep. Workshop Shelby County, 1967, 71, 77, 78, Rep. Assn. Memphis and Shelby County, 1966-67; chmn. St. Michael the Defender chpt. Catholics United for the Faith, 1973, 75, 89-92. With USAAF, 1942-46. Mem. Tenn. Bar Assn., Wis. Bar Assn., Navy League U.S., Cardinal Mindszenty Found., Am. Legion, Latin Liturgy Assn. Roman Catholic. Bankruptcy, Immigration, naturalization, and customs, Probate. Home: 3032 E Glengarry Rd Memphis TN 38128-2984 Office: 100 N Main St Ste 3217 Memphis TN 38103-0539

**HARRAL, JOHN MENTEITH,** lawyer; b. Ancon, Panama Canal Zone, June 25, 1948; s. Brooks Jared and Sara (Mumma) H.; m. Marjorie Van Fosson, Aug. 15, 1970; children: Alyse, Jessica. BBA, U. Miss., 1971, JD, 1974. Bar: Miss. 1974, U.S. Dist. Ct. (so. dist.) Miss. 1974, U.S. Ct. Appeals (5th cir.) 1977. Law clk. to Judge J.P. Coleman, U.S. Ct. Appeals (5th cir.), New Orleans, 1978-79; ptnr. White & Morse, Gulfport, Miss., 1979-92, Eaton & Cottrell, P.A., Gulfport, Miss., 1993-97; sole practitioner Gulfport, 1997—; mem. Miss. Gov.'s Jud. Nominating Com., 1990-93; instr. bus. law William Carey Coll. Chmn. Episc. Svcs. for Aging, Mississippi Gulf Coast, 1981-85, also bd. dirs.; bd. dirs. Make-A-Wish Found. Miss.; founder, pres. Gulfport Excellence, 1991—; bd. dirs., exec. com. Christmas in April, Harrison County, 1994—, pres., 1995-96; bd. dirs. Lynn Meadows Discovery Ctr., 1996—, sec., exec. com., 1997—; lay eucharistic min. St. Mark's Episcopal Ch., Gulfport, 1980, vestryman, sr. and jr. warden, Sunday sch. tchr.; pres. Gulfport Downtown Assn., Inc., 1997-98, dir., 1998; founder, v.p. Gulfport Bus. Club, 1999—; mentor Gulfport Schs., 1991—. Lt. JAGC, USNR, 1974-78. Fellow Miss. Bar Found.; mem. ABA, Miss. Bar Assn. (bd. dirs. young lawyers divsn. 1982-84, commr. 1991-94), Harrison County Bar Assn. (pres. young lawyers sect. 1982, pres. 1987-88), Gulf Coast Law Inst. (bd. dirs. 1988-93), Gulfport C. of C. (bd. dirs. 1995-97, pres. 1997), Miss. Coast C. of C. (bd. dirs. 1994-98), Rotary (bd. dirs. 1997-99), Bayou Bluff Tennis Club, Gulfport Yacht Club, Gulfport Bus. Club (v.p. 1999). Republican. Banking, General civil litigation, Insurance. Home: 12 Old Oak Ln Gulfport MS 39503-6210 Office: 1418 20th Ave Gulfport MS 39501-2029

**HARRELL, CHARLES LYDON, JR.,** lawyer; b. Norfolk, Va., Oct. 22, 1916; s. Charles Lydon Sr. and Ethel Theresa (Toone) H.; m. Martha de Weese Guild, Feb. 5, 1943 (dec. March 1991); children: Charles Lydon III, John Morgan, Marshall Guild, deWeese Toone; m. Lynn Aikens Johnson, July 13, 1993. BA, Randolph-Macon Coll., 1938; LLB, U. Richmond, 1941. Bar: Va. 1940, U.S. Dist. Ct. (ea. dist.) Va. 1946, U.S. Bankruptcy Ct. (ea. and we. dist.) Va. 1946, U.S. Ct. Appeals (4th cir.) 1947, U.S. Ct. Internat. Trade 1950, U.S. Supreme Ct. 1952. Ptnr. Harrell & Landrum, Norfolk, 1947-76; pvt. practice, Norfolk, 1987—; commr. in chancery Cir. Ct. Princess Anne County, 1950-76, City of Norfolk, 1955-77; spl. justice Princess Anne County, 1952-65. Mem. health care consumer coun. Naval Hosp., Portsmouth, 1980-90; mem. coun. of ch. Ghent United Meth. Ch., 1950—, tchr. Bible class, 1966—, master, mem. com. Boy Scouts of Am., Sea Scouts; mem. Coun. of Ministries, 1955-88, chmn. commn. on Christian concerns Meth. Ch., 1971-76; co-founder, chmn., pres. bd. dirs. Ghent Venture, Inc.; v.p. Norfolk Seaman's Soc., 1970-80, bd. dirs., 1990—, v.p.; bd. dirs. Handicaps Unltd. of Va., legis. chmn., legal advisor; vol. prayer counsellor Christian Broadcast Network, 1977—; co-founder, bd. dirs. Va. Assn. of Blind, 1981—; dir. Norfolk Interfaith Coalition for the Elderly, Tidewater Christian Outreach Project; pres. Mobility on Wheels, Inc., 1980-83, bd. dirs., 1977—; mem. com. for therapeutic recreation of handicapped people City of Norfolk, 1991—; co-founder, v.p., dir. New Life Devel.; pro bono counsel Tidewater Legal Aid Soc., 1989—. Comdr. USN, to 1962. Decorated 9 campaign medals, 4 combat stars; recipient Cross Mil. Svc., UDC. Mem. ABA, Norfolk-Portsmouth Bar Assn., Va. State Bar Assn. (Lawyers Helping Lawyers), Va. Bar Assn., Jud. Soc., Christian Legal Soc., Am. Legion, VFW (past comdr.), Jr. C. of C., Jesus to the World Evangelistic Assn. (co-founder, bd. dirs., v.p., chmn. bd.), Masons, Shriners, Kiwanis, Ret. Officers Assn., The Fleet Res., Tin Can Sailors Assn., Mine Warfare Assn., The Caine Mutineers, McNeil Law Soc., Phi Beta Kappa, Omicron Delta Kappa (sec. Tidewater Alumni chpt.), Tau Kappa Alpha. Avocations: swimming, scuba diving, spear fishing. General civil litigation, Bankruptcy, Real property. Home and Office: 1302 Westover Ave Norfolk VA 23507-1026

**HARRELL, LIMMIE LEE, JR.,** lawyer; b. Jackson, Tenn., Aug. 15, 1941; s. Limmie Lee Sr. and Mary Benthal (Nowell) H.; m. Betsy D. Harrell; children: Limmie Lee III, Mary Kimberley. BS, Memphis State U., 1963, JD, 1966. Bar: Tenn. 1966, U.S. Dist. Ct. (we. dist.) Tenn. 1968, U.S. Supreme Ct. Ptnr. Harrell & Harrell, Attys., Trenton, Tenn., 1966—; chmn. bd. dirs. Bank of Commerce, Trenton. Pres. Gibson County Young Dems., Trenton, Tenn., 1968. Named one of Outstanding Young Men in Am. Mem. ABA, Tenn. Bar Assn., Gibson County Bar Assn., Assn. Trial Lawyers Am., Tenn. Trial Lawyers Assn., Memphis State Alumni Assn. (pres. 1984-85). Baptist. Club: Pinecrest Country Club (Trenton, Tenn.) (pres. (3) terms). Lodges: Elks (exalted ruler 1971-72), Moose. Avocations: golf, fishing, hunting, water skiing. General practice, Personal injury, Criminal. Home: 300 Rosemont Dr Trenton TN 38382-3116 Office: Harrell & Harrell Attys Court Sq Trenton TN 38382-1862

**HARRELL, MICHAEL P.,** lawyer; b. Plattsburgh, N.Y., Feb. 14, 1960; s. Gerald V. and Carol (Fitzpatrick) H. AB, Dartmouth Coll., 1982; JD, UCLA, 1985. Bar: N.Y. 1986. Assoc. Debevoise & Plimpton, N.Y.C., 1985-91, London, 1991—. Mem. ABA, Internat. Bar Assn., Assn. of Bar of City of N.Y. Mergers and acquisitions, Private international, Contracts commercial. Office: Debevoise & Plimpton, 1 Creed Ct 5 Ludgate Hill, London EC4M 7AA, England

**HARRELL, ROY G., JR.,** lawyer; b. Norfolk, Va., Sept. 14, 1944; s. Roy G. and Winifred B. H. BS with honors, The Citadel; LLB cum laude, Washington & Lee. Bar: Fla.; cert. in real property. Assoc. Jennings, Watts, Clarke & Hamilton, Jacksonville, Fla., 1971-75; assoc. Greene, Mann, Rowe, Stanton, Mastry & Burton, St. Petersburg, Fla., 1975-76, ptnr., 1976-83; founding ptnr. Baynard, Harrell, Ostow & Ulrich (formerly Baynard, Harrell, Mascara & Ostow), St. Petersburg, 1983-94; of counsel Carlton, Fields, Ward, Emmanuel, Smith & Cutler, P.A., St. Petersburg, 1994-98; ptnr. Holland & Knight LLP, St. Petersburg, 1998—; coun. Am. Lawyer's Auxiliary, 1992-93. Notes editor Washington & Lee Law Review. Past chmn. governing bd. S.W. Fla. Water Mgmt. Dist., 1985-98; past co-chair Pinellas Anclote River Basin Bd.; former mem. policy com. Tampa Bay Nat. Estuary Program; former mem. Tampa Bay Water Coordinating Coun.; pres. United Way, Pinella County, 1986; grad. leadership St. Petersburg, 1976, Leadership Tampa Bay; past chmn. campus adv. bd. U. South Fla. Bayboro Campus; former bd. dirs. Bayfront Ctr. Found.; mem. Citizens Vision 2000; former bd. dirs. 1000 Friends of Fla.; immediate past chmn. bd. dirs. St. Anthony's Devel. Found.; former mem. bd. dirs. ARC, Tampa. Capt. U.S. Army, 1969-71. Recipient Leadership award Leadership St. Pete, 1986, Leadership award Nat. Assn. Leadership Orgn., 1986, PACE award Pinellas Emergency Mental Health Svcs. 1986, Human Svcs. award, 1987. Mem. ABA (mem. various coms.), Am. Coll. Mortgage Attys., Va. Bar Assn., Fla. Bar, St. Petersburg Bar Assn., Greater St. Petersburg C. of C. (Mem. of Yr. award 1981, pres. 1986-87), Leadership St. Pete Alumni Assn. (former chair bd. dirs.), Dragon Club, St. Petersburg Yacht Club, Suncoasters, Suncoast Tiger Bay Club, Anthonians (former pres.), Phi Sigma Alpha, Phi Alpha Delta. Real property, Environmental, Banking. Office: Holland & Knight LLP 200 Central Ave Ste 1600 Saint Petersburg FL 33701-3326

**HARRELL, SEARCY WOOD,** lawyer; b. Harrell, Ark., Dec. 16, 1940; s. Searcy Wood and Mary Edith Harrell; m. Ginger Ann Dunn Fisher, Aug. 23, 1960 (div. Aug. 1975); children: Steven, Jonathan, Bennett; m. Peggy Joyce Everett, May 27, 1976. BSBA, U. Ark., 1962, LLB, 1964. Bar: Ark., U.S. Dist. Ct. (ea. and we. dist.) Ark., U.S. Ct. Appeals (8th cir.). Atty. Tompkins, McKenzie, McRae & Harrell, Prescott, Ark., 1965-69, Gaughan, Barnes, Roberts, Harrell & Laney, Camden, Ark., 1969-80, Roberts, Harrell & Lindsey, Camden, 1980-95, Harrell & Lindsey, Camden, 1995—; chmn., CEO Calhoun County Bank, Hampton, 1990—, First Bank of South Ark., Camden, 1995—. Pres. Kiwanis Club, 1973, Camden Boy's Club, 1970; chmn. St. Mark United Meth. Ch., Camden, 1980. Named Disting. Alumnus U. Ark. Sch. of Law, 1988. Methodist. Avocations: golf, scuba, diving, flying. Home: 1516 Edgewood St Camden AR 71701-3210 Office: Harrell & Lindsey 201 Jackson St SW Camden AR 71701-3941

**HARRELL, WALTER HUGH,** lawyer; b. Waco, Tex., May 29, 1924; s. Thomas Walter and Eula Lucille H.; m. Dorothy Marie Harrell, May 27, 1955; children: Gary D. Harrell, Stephen R. Harrell, Deborah K. Wasson. BBA, Baylor U., LLB, JD, 1950. Bar: Tex., U.S. Dist. Ct. (no. dist.) Tex., U.S. Ct. Appeals (5th cir.), U.S. Supreme Ct. Pvt. practice Lubbock, Tex., 1950—. With U.S. Army. Republican. Baptist. Avocation: golf. General civil litigation, Personal injury, Probate. Office: 1708 Metro Tower 1220 Broadway St Lubbock TX 79401-3201

**HARRELSON, F(REDERICK) DANIEL,** lawyer; b. Wayne, Ark., Feb. 23, 1942; s. Frederick Crippen and Martha (Proctor) H.; m. Kathryn Plummer, Aug. 23, 1964; children: Kimberly Anne, Mary Elizabeth. BSBA in Acctg., U. Ark., 1964, LLB, 1967. Bar: Ark. 1967, U.S. Dist. Ct. (ea. dist.) Ark. 1969, U.S. Tax Ct. 1979. Law clk. Ark. Supreme Ct., Little Rock, 1967-68; ptnr. Ramsay, Bridgforth, Harrelson & Starling, Pine Bluff, Ark., 1968—. Mem. Ark. Bar Assn. (chair probate com. 1975), Jefferson County (Ark.) Bar Assn. (pres. 1985). Episcopalian. Avocations: general aviation, golf, fishing. Probate, Estate planning, Estate taxation. Home: 108 Park Pl Pine Bluff AR 71601-6635 Office: Ramsay Bridgforth Harrelson & Starling PO Box 8509 Pine Bluff AR 71611-8509

**HARRIGAN, DANIEL JOSEPH,** lawyer; b. Indpls., Oct. 30, 1937; m. Ann Boersig. BS, Ind. U., 1959, JD, 1962. Bar: Ind. 1963, U.S. Supreme Ct. 1970, U.S. Ct. Appeals (7th cir.) 1965, U.S. Dist. Ct. (no. dist.) 1965, U.S. Dist. Ct. (so. dist.) Ind. 1963. Law clk. to Hon. Dewey Kelley Ind. Appellate Ct., Indpls., 1963; ptnr. Bayliff, Harrigan, Cord & Maugans, Kokomo, Ind., 1966—; lectr. in field. Note editor Ind. Law Jour., 1962. Mem. ATLA (state committeeman 1980-81, bd. govs. 1992-94), Ind. Bar Found., Ind. Bar Assn., Ind. Trial Lawyers Assn. (bd. dirs. 1977—, exec. com, 1977-86, treas. 1978-82, 1st v.p. 1982, 1st v.p. 1983, pres. 1984-85, coll. of fellows 1986—), Howard County Bar Assn. (pres. 1987), Phi Alpha Delta. Transportation, Workers' compensation, Personal injury. Office: Bayliff Harrigan Cord & Maugans PO Box 2249 Kokomo IN 46904-2249

**HARRINGTON, BRUCE MICHAEL,** lawyer, investor; b. Houston, Mar. 12, 1933; s. George Haymond Harrington and Doris (Gladden) Maginnis; m. Anne Griffith Lawhon, Feb. 15, 1958; children: Julia Griffith, Martha Gladden, Susan McIver. B.A., U. Tex., 1960, J.D. with honors, 1961. Bar: Tex. 1961, U.S. Dist. Ct. (so. dist.) Tex. 1962, U.S. Ct. Appeals (5th cir.) 1962, U.S. Supreme Ct. 1973. Assoc. Andrews & Kurth and predecessor firm, Houston, 1961-73, ptnr., 1973-84; dir. Offenhauser Co., Houston, Allied Metals, Inc., Houston. Trustee St. John's Sch., Houston, 1981-92, chmn. bd., CEO, 1986-92; chmn. bd. Covenant House, Tex., 1991-95; trustee St. Luke's Episcopal Hosp., Tex. Med. Ctr., Houston, 1983-86; bd. dirs. YMCA Bd. Mgmt., Am. Cancer Soc., 1992-94, Ctr. for Hearing and Speech, 1993, chmn. bd., 1995-98; vice chmn. Gateway Found., 1993-95; mem. adv. com. Assn. Governing Bds. of Colls. and Univs. Mem. ABA, Nat. Assn. Ind. Schs. (chmn. trustee com.), Ind. Schs. Assn. S.W. (chmn. trustee com., bd. exec. com.), Tex. Bar Assn., Houston Bar Assn., The Mil. and Hosp. Order of St. Lazarus, The Venerable Order of St. John (U.K.), The Order of Saints Maurice and Lazarus (Savoy), Houston Country Club, Petroleum Club, Houston Club, Phi Delta Phi, Order of Coif. Republican. Episcopalian. General corporate. Home: 3608 Overbrook Ln Houston TX 77027-4128

**HARRINGTON, CAROL A.,** lawyer; b. Geneva, Ill., Feb. 13, 1953; d. Eugene P. and M. Ruth (Bowersox) Kloubec; m. Warren J. Harrington, Aug. 19, 1972; children: Jennifer Ruth, Carrie Anne. BS summa cum laude,

U. Ill., 1974, JD magna cum laude, 1977. Bar: Ill. 1977, U.S. Dist. Ct. (no. dist.) Ill. 1977, U.S. Tax Ct. 1979. Assoc. Winston & Strawn, Chgo., 1977-84, ptnr., 1984-88; ptnr. McDermott, Will & Emery, 1988—; speaker in field. Co-author: The New Generation Skipping Tax, 1986, Generation Skipping Tax BNA Management, 1996, Generation-Skipping Transfer Tax, Warren, Gorham & Lamont, 1995; contbr. articles to profl. jours., Trustee and Estate mag. Fellow Am. Coll. Trusts and Estate Coun. (bd. regents 1999—); mem. ABA (chmn. B-1 generation skipping transfer com. 1987-92, coun. real property, probate and trust law sect. 1992-98), Ill. State Bar Assn., Chgo. Bar Assn. (trust law com. divsn. 1), Chgo. Estate Planning Coun. Probate, Estate planning, Estate taxation. Office: McDermott Will & Emery 227 W Monroe St Ste 3100 Chicago IL 60606-5096

**HARRINGTON, CHRISTOPHER MICHAEL,** lawyer; b. Manhattan, N.Y., May 3, 1961; s. Phillip and Joyce Harrington. BA, SUNY, 1990; JD, Western New Eng. Coll., 1994. Bar: Conn. 1995, U.S. Dist. Ct. Conn. 1995. Fed. agt. U.S. Border Patrol, Kingsville, Tex., 1986-87; social worker St. Cabrini Home, Highland, N.Y., 1990-91; atty. Gersten & Clifford, Hartford, Conn., 1994—. General civil litigation, Consumer commercial, Personal injury. Office: Gersten & Clifford 214 Main St Hartford CT 06106-1881

**HARRINGTON, DONALD FRANCIS,** lawyer; b. Cleve., June 24, 1929; s. Willis James and Dorothy Virginia (Hoose) H.; m. Nancy F. Overton, July 26, 1956; 1 child, Donald Francis Jr. BBA, Western Res. U., 1955; LLB, Cleve. State U., 1961, LLM, 1964, JD, 1968. Bar: Fla. 1961, Ohio 1963. Gen. counsel spl. disability fund State of Fla., Tallahassee, 1965-66; indsl. claims judge Dade County, State of Fla., Miami, 1966-70; ptnr. Henry, Stroemer & Harrington, Miami, 1970-76; pvt. practice Coral Gables, Fla., 1976—; sr. trial atty. Fireman's Fund Ins. Co., Miami, 1987-92. With U.S. Army, 1951-53. Mem. VFW, Am. Legion, Fla. Bar Assn. (bd. cert.), Emerald Soc. (past pres.), Elks Club (exalted ruler). Democrat. Roman Catholic. Workers' compensation, Personal injury.

**HARRINGTON, EDWARD F.,** federal judge; b. 1933. AB, Holy Cross Coll., Worcester, Mass., 1955; JD, Boston Coll., 1960. Law clk. to Hon. Paul C. Reardon Mass. Superior Ct., 1960-61; spl. trial atty. criminal div. U.S. Dept. Justice, 1961-65, atty.-in-charge Strike Force Against Organized Crime, 1970-73; asst. U.S. atty. Mass., 1965-69; assoc. Offices of Paul T. Smith, Boston, 1961, Offices of Melvin Louison, Taunton, Mass., 1969; mem. firm Peloquin, McKeon & Reilly, Boston, 1973-75, Gargan, Harrington & Markham, Boston, 1975-77; U.S. atty. Mass., 1977-81; mem. firm Sheridan, Garrahan & Lander, Framingham, Mass., 1981-88; dist. judge Mass., 1988—. Contbr. articles to profl. jours. Chmn. Alcoholic Beverages Control Commn., 1975-77; candidate Dem. Party for Atty. Gen., Mass., 1974; nominee Rep. Party for Atty. Gen., Mass., 1986; campaign chmn. Shriver for Pres. Campaign Com., 1976; advisor Nat. Commn. on Violence, 1968-69; cons. Nat. Commn. on Rev. of Nat. Policy Toward Gambling, 1974-76. Lt. (j.g.) USN, 1955-57; with USNR, 1957-72. Recipient Letter of Commendation FBI Dir. Edgar Hoover, 1968. Office: US Court District US Courthouse 1 Courthouse Way Boston MA 02210-3002

**HARRINGTON, ELLIS JACKSON, JR.,** lawyer; b. Barnesville, Ga., Aug. 10, 1944; s. Ellis Jackson Sr. and Inez (Dixon) H.; m. Elizabeth Gray, Dec. 23, 1965; children: Lisa Jackson, Sara Christine. AB, U. N.C., 1966, JD, 1969. Bar: N.C. 1969, U.S. Ct. Mil. Appeals 1970, U.S. Dist. Ct. (mid. dist.) N.C. 1976. Asst. pub. defender 18th Jud. Dist. of N.C., Greensboro, 1973-75; ptnr. Booth, Fish, Simpson & Harrison, Greensboro, 1975-79, Booth, Harrington Johns & Campbell, Greensboro, 1979-95, Booth, Harrington Johns & Toman, L.L.P., Greensboro, 1995—. Bd. dirs. Child Care Ministries, Greensboro, 1980-86, Greensboro Commn. of Status of Women, 1992-97. Recipient Cert. of Appreciation, ARC, 1987. Mem. ABA, N.C. Bar Assn., Assn. Trial Lawyers Am., 18th Jud. Dist. Bar Assn. (pres. 1986-87), N.C. Acad. Trial Attys., Phi Beta Kappa, Phi Delta Phi. Democrat. Presbyterian. Avocations: travel, fishing, photography. Personal injury, State civil litigation. Office: Booth Harrington Johns & Toman LLP 239 N Edgeworth St Greensboro NC 27401-2217

**HARRINGTON, JAMES JOHN,** lawyer; b. Jersey City, June 10, 1961; s. John and Dorothy Harrington; m. Amy Dykstra, Aug. 23, 1998; 1 child, James. BS in Biology, U. Scranton, 1983; MS in Biochemistry, CUNY, N.Y.C., 1987; JD, cert. environ. law, Pace U., 1991; cert. internat. bus., NYU, 1998. Bar: N.J. 1991, Patent Bar. Sr. scientist N.J. North Regional Forensic Sci. Lab., Little Falls, N.J., 1985-91; assoc. Matthews, Woodbridge & Collins, Princeton, N.J., 1991-93; patent counsel Am. Cyanamid, Wayne, N.J., 1993-95, Novo Nordisk, N.Y.C., 1995-97; sr. atty. Johnson & Johnson, New Brunswick, N.J., 1997—. Editor: Forensic DNA Technology, 1997. Chmn. savs. bond com. Johnson & Johnson, New Brunswick, 1998. Mem. Assn. of the Bar of the City of N.Y. (chair license com. 1998—). Republican. Roman Catholic. Avocations: tennis, golf. Home: 80 Winchester Way Somerset NJ 08873-4902 Office: Johnson & Johnson 1 Johnson And Johnson Plz New Brunswick NJ 08933-0002

**HARRINGTON, JAMES PATRICK,** lawyer; b. Butte, Mont., Jan. 31, 1942; s. James Patrick and Mary Ellen (Harrington) H.; m. Joan Evelyn Lucas, Feb. 1, 1964 (div. Feb. 1977); children: Jeanette, James, Donna, Diana, Laura, Catherine; m. Denise Buckley, Feb. 7, 1992. B.A., Carroll Coll., Helena, Mont., 1964; M.A., U. Wyo., 1967; J.D., Notre Dame, 1970. Bar: Ind. 1970, Mont. 1975, U.. Dist. Ct. (no. dist.) Ind. 1970, U.S. Dist. Ct. (so. dist.) Ind. 1970, U.S. Dist. Ct. Mont. 1975, U.S. Ct. Appeals (7th cir.) 1975, U.S. Ct. Appeals (9th cir.) 1994, U.S. Tax Ct. 1975. Assoc., Thronburg, McGill, Deahl, Harman, Carey & Murray, South Bend, Ind., 1970-75; atty. Mont. Power Co., Butte, 1975-77; ptnr. Poore, Roth & Robinson, Butte, 1977-81; sole practice, Butte, 1981-83, 84—; hearing examiner Mont. Workers Compensation Ct., Helena, 1983-84; sole practice, Butte, 1984—. Mem. Mont. Trial Lawyers Assn., ABA, Silver Bow County Bar Assn. (pres. 1987), Mont. Assn. Def. Counsel, Greys Inn, Delta Epsilon Sigma, Beta Gamma Sigma, Omicron Delta Esilon. Democrat. Roman Catholic. State civil litigation, Workers' compensation, Personal injury. Home and Office: 2900 Lexington Ave Butte MT 59701-1110

**HARRINGTON, JAMES TIMOTHY,** lawyer; b. Chgo., Sept. 4, 1942; s. John Paul and Margaret Rita (Cunneen) H.; m. Roseanne Strupeck, Sept. 4, 1965; children: James Timothy, Roseanne, Maris Zajdela. BA, U. Notre Dame, 1964, JD, 1967. Bar: Ill. 1967, Ind. 1968, U.S. Dist. Ct. (no. dist.) Ill. 1967, U.S. Dist. Ct. (no. and so. dists.) Ind. 1968, U.S. Ct. Appeals (7th cir.) 1969, U.S. Ct. Appeals (4th cir.) 1977, U.S. Ct. Appeals (8th cir.) 1979, U.S. Ct. Appeals (3d cir.) 1981, U.S. Supreme Ct. 1979, U.S. Ct. Appeals (D.C. cir.) 1993. Law clk. U.S. Dist. Ct. (no. dist.) Ind., 1967-69; assoc. Rooks, Pitts & Poust, Chgo., 1969-75, ptnr., 1976-87; ptnr. Ross & Hardies, Chgo., 1987—; lectr. environ. law, fed. procedures, adminstrv. law, 1960—. Vice chmn. Mid Am. Legal Found.; bd. dirs. Ill. Safety Coun. Fellow Am. Bar Found.; mem. Ill. Bar Assn., Ind. Bar Assn., Chgo. Bar Assn. (environ. law com., real estate com.), Indsl. Water Waste and Sewer Group (past chmn.), Air and Waste Mgmt. Assn., Assn. Environ. Law Inst., Ill. Assn. Environ. Profls., Law Club Chgo., Legal Club Chgo., Exec. Club Chgo., Union League Club Chgo. Roman Catholic. Environmental, Federal civil litigation, State civil litigation. Home: 746 Foxdale Ave Winnetka IL 60093-1908 Office: Ross & Hardies 150 N Michigan Ave Ste 2500 Chicago IL 60601-7567

**HARRINGTON, KEVIN PAUL,** lawyer; b. Paterson, N.J., Jan. 1, 1951; s. James John and theresa Elizabeth (Giblin) H. BA, Niagara U., 1973; JD, N. E. Sch. Law, Boston, 1978. Bar: N.J. 1978, U.S. Dist. Ct. N.J. 1978, U.S. Supreme Ct. 1983. Judicial clerkship to hon. Thomas R. Rumana Paterson, N.J., 1978-79; asst. prosecutor Passaic County Prosecutor's Office, Paterson, N.J., 1979-80; assoc. DeYoe & Guiney, Paterson, N.J., 1980-87; ptnr. Catania & Harrington, N. Haledon, N.J., 1987—. Pres., bd. trustees Clinic for Mental Health Svc., Paterson, N.J., 1990—. Recipient Civil Trial Atty. cert., Supreme Ct. N.J., 1986—. Mem. ATLA (bd. govs.), N.J. Def. Assn., N.J. Bar Assn., Passaic County Bar Assn. (trustee), Def. Rsch. Inst. Avocations: sports, golf, scuba diving. Insurance, Personal injury, General civil litigation. Office: Catania & Harrington 909 Belmont Ave Ste 3 North Haledon NJ 07508-2500

**HARRIS, ALLAN MICHAEL,** lawyer, judge; b. N.Y.C., Sept. 30, 1940; s. Lawrence Cecil and Shirley Etta (Jaffe) H.; m. Linda Paula Licker, June 21, 1964 (dec. Oct. 1981); children: Lauren Ivy, Leslie Eden; m. Cheryl Younger, June 23, 1989. BS in Acctg., Temple U., 1965; JD, U. Pa., 1965. Bar: N.J. 1965, N.Y. 1984, U.S. Supreme Ct. 1969. Ptnr. Rubenstein, Albert & Loukedis, Paterson, N.J., 1970, Fontanella, Shashaty, Harris & Lalomia, Paterson, 1971-81; prosecutor City of Fair Lawn, N.J., 1974, judge Mcpl. Ct., 1975-96; counsel Ravin, Greenberg & Marks P.A., Roseland, N.J., 1981—; atty. Paterson Zoning Bd., 1970-72; mem. con. on mcpl. cts. N.J. Supreme Ct., 1983-87. Mem. N.J. Bar Assn., Bergen County Bar Assn., Soc. Photographic Education (counsel), Beta Gamma Sigma. Jewish. E-mail:rgm@ravingreenberg.com. Bankruptcy, Contracts commercial, General corporate. Home: 35 Mercer St Apt 3A New York NY 10013-5808 Office: Ravin Greenberg & Marks 101 Eisenhower Pkwy Ste 27 Roseland NJ 07068-1028

**HARRIS, ALLEN KEITH,** lawyer; b. Amarillo, Tex., Aug. 24, 1941; s. Allen Keith Sr. and Anne Eloise Cronland. AB, George Washington U., 1965; JD, Okla. City U., 1970. Bar: Okla. 1971, U.S. Supreme Ct., U.S. Ct. Appeals (10th cir., D.C. cir.), U.S. Dist. Ct. (no., ea. and we. dists.) Okla. Law clerk U.S. Dist. Ct. (we. dist.) Okla., 1968-70; asst. gen. counsel, asst. oil and gas conservation atty. Okla. Corp. Comm., 1972-74; asst. atty. gen. civil divsn. Okla., 1974-75, asst. atty. gen. energy affairs, 1975-77, special counsel to gov. on Fed. Energy Regulatory Com., 1977-78; utility ratepayer advocate Office of Atty. Gen., Okla., 1978-79; pvt. practice, 1979—; mem. special joint com. on securities industry reform Okla. Legis., 1986-89. Contbr. articles to profl. jours.; editor: Okla. Bar Jour., 1975-78. Fellow Okla. Bar Assn. (life); mem. OBA (Lawyers Helping Lawyers com., Fed. Energy Bar Assn., ABA (adv. coun. ethics 2000 commn.), Mineral Lawyers Soc. Okla. City, Okla. City U. Alumni Assn., Ruth Bader Am. Inn of Ct. (master). Administrative and regulatory, Health, FERC practice. Home: 613 Doe Trl Edmond OK 73003-6467 Office: PO Box 18576 2809 NW Expwy Oklahoma City OK 73154

**HARRIS, ALVIN LOUIS,** lawyer; b. Boston, Jan. 27, 1959; s. Morton Allen and Judye Rose Harris; m. Kathy Lynn Howerton, June 19, 1982; children: Jeffrey Louis, Natalie Rosemary. BA, Vanderbilt U., 1981, JD, 1985. Bar: U.S. Dist. Ct. (mid. dist.) Tenn. 1986, U.S. Ct. Appeals (11th cir.) 1986, U.S. Dist. Ct. (mid. dist.) Ga. 1990. Law clk. hon. R. Lanier Anderson 11th Cir. Ct. Appeals, Macon, Ga., 1985-86; atty. O'Hare, Sherrard & Roe, Nashville, 1986-89, Page, Scrantom, Harris & Chapman, Columbus, Ga., 1990-93, Greene & Greene, Nashville, 1993-97; ptnr. Weed, Hubbard, Berry & Doughty, Nashville, 1997—; adj. bus. law instr. Columbus (Ga.) Coll., 1990-91. Pres. Nashville Chess Ctr., 1996—. Mem. ABA, Tenn. Bar Assn., Cmty. Assn. Inst., Phi Beta Kappa, Order of the Coif. Avocations: chess, running. Contracts commercial, Construction, General civil litigation. Office: Weed Hubbard Berry & Doughty 201 4th Ave N Ste 1420 Nashville TN 37219-2089

**HARRIS, BAYARD EASTER,** lawyer; b. Washington, July 22, 1944; s. Edward Bledsoe and Grace (Childrey) H.; m. Rebecca Bond Jeffress, June 10, 1967; children: Nicholas Bayard, Nathan Bedford (dec. 1989), Ellen Coley. AB in History, U. N.C., 1966; JD cum laude, U. S.C., 1973. Bar: Va. 1974, U.S. Dist. Ct. (we. dist.) Va. 1974, U.S. Ct. Appeals (4th cir.) 1974, U.S. Supreme Ct. 1982. Assoc. Woods, Rogers, Muse, Walker & Thornton, Roanoke, Va., 1973-79, ptnr., 1979-85; ptnr. Woods, Rogers & Hazlegrove, Roanoke, 1985-90; pres. Ctr. for Employment Law, Roanoke, 1991-98; of counsel Woods, Rogers and Hazlegrove, PLC, 1998—; mem. Transp. Safety Bd., 1992-96. Comments and rsch. editor U. S.C. Law Rev., 1972-73. Chpt. chmn. ARC, Roanoke Valley, 1985-87, chmn. ea. ops. hdqrs., 1988-91. Lt. USNR, 1966-70. Recipient Clara Barton award ARC Roanoke Valley chpt., 1986. Mem. ABA (labor and employment sect. 1974—), Va. Bar Assn. (labor and employment com. and sect. 1974—), Rotary. Republican. Episcopalian. Avocations: golf, gardening. Labor, Civil rights, Federal civil litigation. Office: Woods Rogers & Hazlegrove 10 S Jefferson St Ste 1400 Roanoke VA 24011-1314

**HARRIS, BENJAMIN HARTE, JR.,** lawyer; b. Mobile, Ala., Sept. 12, 1937; s. Ben H. and Mary Cade (Aldridge) H.; m. Martha Elliott Lambeth, Aug. 26, 1961; children: Benjamin Harte, Wayt. AB, Davidson Coll., 1959; JD, U. Ala., 1962. Bar: Ala. 1962, U.S. Dist. Ct. (so. dist.) Ala. 1964, U.S. Ct. Appeals (5th cir.) 1981, U.S. Supreme Ct. 1971, U.S. Ct. Appeals (11th cir.) 1981. Assoc. Johnstone, Adams, Bailey, Gordon & Harris (formerly Johnstone, Adams, May, Howard & Hill, L.L.C.), Mobile, Ala., 1964-70, mem., 1971—; chmn. Atty's Ins. Mut. Ala., bd. dirs. Past chmn. bd. dirs. Boys' Club, 1989-95; past chmn., past trustee UMS Prep Sch.; v.p., bd. dirs. Gordon Smith Ctr.; mem. standards com. United Way. Life fellow Am. Bar Found.; fellow Ala. Law Found.; mem. ABA (past ho. of dels., past bd. govs.), Ala. Law Found. (past pres., trustee), Mobile County Bar Assn. (exec. com. 1980-87), Ala. State Bar (bd. commrs. 1978-87, mem. exec. com., trustee bar found., past chmn. disciplinary commn., past pres.), Ala. Law Inst., Ala. Law Sch. Found. (past pres., trustee), Ala. Def. Lawyers Assn., Am. Judicature Soc., Am. Arbitration Assn., Ala. Jud. Commn., 11th Cir Ct. Appeals Hist. Soc. (trustee, v.p.), Nat. Conf. Bar Pres. (past exec. coun.), Brock Inn of Ct. (pres. 1996-98), Mobile Rotary Club (Paul Harris fellow), Athelstan Club. Episcopalian. General civil litigation, Oil, gas, and mineral, Workers' compensation. Office: PO Box 1988 Mobile AL 36633-1988

**HARRIS, BRETT ROSENBERG,** lawyer; b. Livingston, N.J., Nov. 24, 1966; s. Paul Irwin and Edith Rosenberg; m. Mitchell Paul Harris, Nov. 16, 1996. BA, Washington & Jefferson Coll., 1988; JD, NYU, 1991. Summer intern Ctr. for Law and Social Policy, Washington, 1989; summer assoc. Winthrop Stimson Putnam & Roberts, N.Y.C., 1990; assoc. Fox & Fox, Newark, N.J., 1991-95, Wilentz, Goldman & Spitzer, P.A., Woodbridge, N.J., 1995—. Exec. editor: N.Y. Univ. jour. 1990-91. Mem. N.J. State Bar Assn. (mem. computer-related law com. 1995—). Avocation: baseball scorer. General corporate, Computer. Home: 423 Everson Pl Westfield NJ 07090-3229 Office: Wilentz Goldman & Spitzer PA 90 Woodbridge Ctr Dr Ste 901 Woodbridge NJ 07095-1146

**HARRIS, BRIAN CRAIG,** lawyer; b. Newark, Sept. 8, 1941; s. Louis W. and Lillian (Frankel) H.; m. Ellen M. Davis, Aug. 20, 1978; children: Andrea, Keith. BS, boston U., 1963; JD, Rutgers U., 1966. Bar: N.J. 1968, D.C. 1968, U.S. Ct. Appeals (3d cir.) 1968, N.Y. 1984, U.S. Ct. Appeals (2d cir.) 1985. Asst. corp. counsel Newark, 1968-70; assoc. Braff, Litvak & Ertag, East Orange, N.J., 1970-72; ptnr. Braff, Litvak, Ertag, Wortmann & Harris, East Orange, 1972-85, Braff, Ertag, wortmann, Harris & Sukoneck, Livingston, N.J., 1985-91, Braff, Harris & Sukoneck, 1991—; adj. lectr. law and medicine Seton Hall U., South Orange, N.J., 1982-83, trial preparation Rutgers U. Law Sch., 1983, strategy of def. United Tech. Corp., Chgo., 1986. Sustaining mem. Product Liability Adv. Coun., Inc.; contbg. mem. Nat. Ileitis found., N.Y.C., 1983—. Named Master of Inns. of Ct., Arthur J. Vanderbilt Sect., 1988. Mem. ABA (employment law sect., tort and ins. sect.), Internat. Assn. Def. Counsel, Profl. Liability Underwriters Soc., N.Y. State Bar Assn., N.Y. Trial Lawyers Assn., Essex County Trial Lawyers Assn., Middlesex County Trial Lawyers Assn., Def. Rsch. Inst. (mem. com. employment law, mem. com. profl. liability, trustee Hamonie Group), N.J. Trial Lawyers Assn., N.J. Def. Assn., East Hampton Indoor Outdoor Tennis Club, Orange Lawn Tennis Club. Jewish. Avocations: running, basketball, theater, tennis, study of military strategy of land forces in World War II. Personal injury, Product liability, Transportation. Home: Llewellyn Pk West Orange NJ 07052-5402 Office: Braff Harris & Sukoneck 570 W Mount Pleasant Ave Ste 18 Livingston NJ 07039-1678 also: 305 Broadway Fl 7 New York NY 10007-1109

**HARRIS, CHRISTY FRANKLIN,** lawyer; b. Greensboro, N.C., Dec. 8, 1945; s. Luther Franklin and Rebecca Ann (Bluster) H.; children: Stacey Lynn, Aubrey Leigh. AA, Oxford Coll., Emory U.; BA, U. Fla., 1967, JD with honors, 1970. Bar: Fla. 1970, U.S. Dist. Ct. (mid. dist.) Fla. 1970, U.S. Ct. Mil. Appeals 1971, U.S. Ct. Appeals (11th cir.) 1984. Assoc. Holland & Knight, Lakeland, Fla., 1970, 1973-74; pres. Canan & Harris P.A., Lakeland, 1974-76; pres., sr. atty. Harris, Midyette & Clements P.A., Lakeland, 1976-89, Harris & Midyette, P.A., Lakeland, 1989-91, Harris, Midyette, Geary, Darby & Morrell, P.A., Lakeland, Fla., 1991-98, Harris, Midyette & Darby, P.A., Lakeland, Fla., 1998—; mem. 10th cir. Grievance Com., Lakeland, 1976-79, 83-86, chmn. 1979, vice chmn., 1986; mem. Unauthorized Practice of Law Com., 1983-86; bd. dirs. Internat. Speedway Corp., 1986—. Bd. dirs. Program to Aid Drug Abusers, Lakeland, 1975-76, Campfire, 1979-85. Served to capt. USMCR, 1968-73, mil. judge. Named to Hon. Order of Ky. Cols., 1974. Mem. Fla. Bar, Lakeland Bar Assn., Attys. Title Ins. Fund, Order of Coif, Phi Beta Kappa, Phi Kappa Phi. Republican. Avocations: motor sports, sport fishing. Estate planning, Contracts commercial, General corporate. Home: 1335 Longoak Dr N Lakeland FL 33811-2146 Office: Harris Midyette & Darby PA 2012 S Florida Ave PO Box 2451 Lakeland FL 33806-2451

**HARRIS, DALE RAY,** lawyer; b. Crab Orchard, Ill., May 11, 1937; s. Ray B. and Aurelia M. (Davis) H.; m. Toni K. Shapkoff, June 26, 1960; children: Kristen Dee, Julie Diane. BA in Math., U. Colo., 1959; LLB, Harvard U., 1962. Bar: Colo. 1962, U.S. Dist. Ct. Colo. 1962, U.S. Ct. Appeals (10th cir.) 1962, U.S. Supreme Ct. 1981. Assoc. Davis, Graham & Stubbs, Denver, 1962-67, ptnr., 1967—, chmn. mgmt. com., 1982-85; spkr., instr. various antitrust and comml. litig. seminars; bd. dirs. Lend-A-Lawyer, Inc., 1989-94. Mem. campaign cabinet Mile High United Way, 1986-87, chmn., atty. adv. com., 1988, sec., legal counsel, trustee, mem. exec. com., 1989-94, chmn. bd. trustees, 1996, 97; trustee The Spaceship Earth Fund, 1986-89; trustee Legal Aid Found. Colo., 1989-95; mem. devel. coun. U. Colo. Arts and Scis. dept., 1985-93; area chmn. law sch. fund Harvard U., 1978-81; bd. dirs. Colo. Jud. Inst., 1994—, vice chair, 1998—; bd. dirs. Colo. Lawyers Trust Account Found., 1996—; steering com. Youth-At-Work, 1994, School-To-Work, 1995. With USAR, 1962-68. Receipient Williams award, Rocky Mountain Arthritis Found., 1999. Fellow Am. Bar Found. (Colo. state chmn. 1998—); mem. ABA (antitrust and litigation sects.), Colo. Bar Found., Colo. Bar Assn. (chmn. antitrust com. 1980-84, coun. corp. banking and bus. law sect. 1978-83, bd. govs. 1991-95, exec. com. 1993-94, chmn. family violence task force 1996—, pres.-elect 1999), Denver Bar Assn. (chmn. centennial com. 1990-91, pres.-elect 1992-93, pres. 1993-94, bd. trustees 1992-95, Merit award 1997), Colo. Assn. Corp. Counsel (pres. 1973-74), Denver Law Club (pres. 1976-77, Lifetime Achievement award 1997), The Two Percent Club (exec. com. 1994—), Citizens Against Amendment 12 Com. (exec. com. 1994), Phi Beta Kappa, Univ. Club, Rotary (Denver). Antitrust, General civil litigation. Home: 2032 Bellaire St Denver CO 80207-3722 Office: Davis Graham & Stubbs 370 17th St PO Box 185 Denver CO 80201-0185

**HARRIS, GEORGE BRYAN,** lawyer; b. Columbia, S.C., July 8, 1964; s. A. Bryan and Beverly Gaye (Bennett) H. BA, U. Ala., 1986; JD, U. Va., 1989. Bar: Ala. 1989, U.S. Dist. Ct. (no., mid., and so. dists.) Ala. 1990, U.S. Ct. Appeals (11th cir.) 1990, D.C. 1991, U.S. Ct. Appeals (5th cir.) 1992, U.S. Supreme Ct. 1993, London Ct. Internat. Arbitration 1995, U.S. Dist. Ct. (no. dist.) Tex. 1996. Ptnr. Bradley Arant Rose & White LLP, Birmingham, Ala., 1996—; spl. asst. atty. gen. for environment State of Ala., Montgomery, 1990-92. Jr. patron Birmingham Mus. Art. Mem. Birmingham Bar Assn., U. Va. Law Alumni Assn., U. Ala. Alumni Assn., Birmingham Mon. Morning Quarterback Club, Sierra Club, Cahaba River Soc., Delta Tau Delta (v.p., bd. dirs. chpt. 1991-94). Methodist. General civil litigation, State civil litigation, Product liability. Office: Bradley Arant Rose & White 2001 Park Pl Ste 1400 Birmingham AL 35203-2736

**HARRIS, GLENN ANTHONY,** lawyer; b. L.A., May 7, 1951; s. Glenn I. and E. Josephine (Edwards) H.; 1 child, Sarah Fran. BA, U. So. Calif., 1973; MA, Calif. State U., 1976; JD with highest honors, Rutgers U., 1987. Bar: N.J. 1987, Pa. 1987, U.S. Dist. Ct. N.J. 1987, U.S. Dist. Ct. (ea. dist.) Pa. 1988, U.S. Ct. Appeals (3d cir.) 1989. Tchr. Arcadia (Calif.) High Sch., 1973-79; pres. Casablanca Real Estate Investments, San Juan Capistrano, Calif., 1979-84; assoc. Drinker Biddle & Reath, Phila., 1987-90; ptnr. Levin & Hluchan, P.C., Voorhees, N.J., 1990—. Environmental, Insurance, Contracts commercial. Office: Levin & Hluchan PC 1200 Laurel Oak Rd Ste 100 Voorhees NJ 08043-4317

**HARRIS, GORDON H.,** lawyer; b. Atlanta, May 7, 1938; s. Huie H. Harris and Elizabeth (McBrayer) Stroud; m. Dorothy Laing, Dec. 6, 1960; children: Sarah Overmeyer, Bruce McBrayer. BA in Math., U. Fla., 1961, JD with honors, 1965. Bar: Fla. 1966, U.S. Dist. Ct. (mid. dist.) Fla., U.S. Ct. Appeals (5th and 11th cirs.), U.S. Supreme Ct. 1966. Instr. legal writing and research U. Fla. Law Sch., Gainesville, 1965-66; assoc. Holland and Knight, Bartow, Fla., 1966-69; ptnr. Gray, Harris & Robinson, Orlando, Fla., 1969—; asst. atty. Orange County, 1978-84; guest instr. Valencia Community Coll., 1978-80; atty. Tourist Devel. Council, 1977-84; asst. prosecutor Orange County, 1969-71. Exec. editor U. Fla. Law Rev., 1964-65. Mem. East Ctl. Fla. Regional Planning Council, Orlando, 1976-77; sr. warden St. Michael's Episc. Ch., 1980, lay reader 1966—; chmn. bd. trustees Trinity Prep. Sch., 1984—; exec. com. Fla. Citrus Bowl, 1982-85, bd. dirs. 1980-85; bd. dirs. March of Dimes 1977-82, Parents Anonymous of Fla., Inc., 1982-92, Valencia Community Coll. Found., 1978-90. Mem. ABA, Fla. Bar Assn., Orange County Bar Assn., Assn. Trial Lawyers Am., Acad. Fla. Trial Lawyers, U. Fla. Alumni Assn. (nat. pres. 1981, chmn. bd. 1982, dir. Gator boosters 1973-83, province comdr. 1993—), Am. Judicature Soc., Fla. Shrine Assn. (pres. 1982-83), Order of Coif, Fla. Blue Key, Phi Kappa Phi, Phi Delta Pi, Kappa Alpha. Republican. Clubs: Touchdown, Country, University (Orlando); Citrus. Lodge: Shriners (potentate 1983), Masons. Construction, Condemnation, General practice. Office: Gray Harris & Robinson PA PO Box 3068 Orlando FL 32802-3068

**HARRIS, HOWARD DANE, JR.,** lawyer, writer; b. Birmingham, Ala., Aug. 24, 1959; s. Howard Dane Sr. and Mary Constance (Miller) H. BS in Fin., Auburn U., 1982; JD, U. Houston, 1988. Bar: Tex. 1988, U.S. Dist. Ct. (so., no. and we. dists.) Tex., U.S. Ct. Appeals (5th cir.). Comml. banker Capital Bank, N.A., Houston, 1982-84, MBank Houston, N.A., 1984-85; trial lawyer Winstead, Secrest & Minick, Houston, 1988-90; bus. lawyer Nathan, Wood & Summers, Houston, 1990-96, H. Dane Harris, Jr., P.C., Houston, 1996—. Author: Murdered Innocence (a.k.a. Free Fall), 1999. Fundraiser, exec. United Way of Gulf West, Houston, 1989-90; assoc. deacon 2d Bapt. Ch., Houston, 1984-86. Mem. Houston Young Reps. (v.p. 1995-96). Avocations: writing, traveling, sailing. Office: 5850 San Felipe St Ste 500 Houston TX 77057-8003

**HARRIS, HUGH STANLEY, JR.,** lawyer; b. Savannah, Ga., Aug. 6, 1957; s. Hugh Stanley and Nancy Jane (Anderson) H.; m. Stephanie Helen Webster, Aug. 14, 1982 (div. Aug. 1990), m. Nancy Lea Winstead, Aug. 2, 1991; children: Carter Winstead, Alexandra Elizabeth. AB, U. Ga., 1979; JD, U. Tenn., 1982. Bar: Tenn. 1983, N.C. 1984. Assoc. Guess and English, Knoxville, Tenn., 1983, Myers, Hulse & Brown, Charlotte, N.C., 1984-89; ptnr. Myers, Hulse & Harris, Charlotte, 1989-94; pvt. practice Charlotte, 1994—. Chmn. fin. com. Meml. United Meth. Ch. Mem. ATLA, N.C. Acad. Trial Lawyers, Providence Country Club. Democrat. Avocations: scuba diving, skiing, running, hunting, golf. General practice, Personal injury, Insurance. Office: 130 N Mcdowell St Ste A Charlotte NC 28204-2268

**HARRIS, JAMES HAROLD, III,** lawyer, educator; b. Texarkana, Tex., Apr. 26, 1943; s. James Harold Jr. and Mildred (Freeman) H. BA, Dartmouth Coll., 1964; JD, Vanderbilt U., 1967. Bar: Tenn. 1967, U.S. Dist. Ct. (mid. dist.) Tenn. 1972, U.S. Ct. Appeals (6th cir.) 1972. Asst. dean Vanderbilt U. Sch. Law, Nashville, 1971; atty. Met. Govt. Nashville, Nashville, 1972-75; ptnr. Harris & Leach, Nashville, 1975-87, Harris & Baydoun, Nashville, 1987-90; counsel Wyatt, Tarrant, Combs, Gilbert & Milom, Nashville, 1990-93, Gordon, Martin, Jones & Harris, Nashville, 1994—. Capt. USNR, 1967—. Mem. ABA, Tenn. Bar Assn., Nashville Bar Assn., Nashville Entertainment Assn. (legal counsel). Entertainment, Trademark and copyright, Bankruptcy. Home: 103 Burlington Ct Nashville TN 37215-1843 Office: Gordon Martin Jones & Harris 49 Music Sq W Ste 600 Nashville TN 37203-3231

**HARRIS, JAMES T.,** lawyer; b. Chgo., Sept. 13, 1964; s. Walter James and Margaret (Thomas) H. BSME, Tenn. State U., 1989; JD, Chgo.-Kent Coll. Law, 1993. Bar: Ill. 1993, U.S. Dist. Ct. (no. dist.) Ill. 1993, U.S. Ct. Appeals (7th cir.) 1993, U.S. Ct. Appeals (fed. cir.), U.S. Patent Bar 1995. Clk. Office of Civil Rights U.S. Dept. Edn., Chgo., summer 1991; clk. Office of Civil Rights Lee, Mann, Smith, McWilliams, Sweeney & Ohlson, Chgo., 1991-93, assoc., 1993-96; assoc. Isaf, Vaughan and Kerr, Atlanta, 1997—; adj. prof. Columbia Coll.; mem. Supreme Ct. Com. on Character and Fitness. Recipient Bar and Gavel award Chgo.-Kent Coll. Law, 1993, Standish Willis award Black Law Student Assn., Chgo., 1993. Mem. ABA (forum on entertainmentt 1993—), ASME, Am. Corp. Counsel Assn., Am. Intellectual

Property Law Assn., Nat. Acad. Rec. Arts and Scis., Cook County Bar Assn. (co-chair 1994, Presdl. award 1995), Pi Tau Sigma. Avocations: boating, tennis, travel, running, bicycling. Entertainment, Trademark and copyright, Patent.

**HARRIS, JANINE DIANE,** lawyer; b. Akron, Jan. 12, 1948; d. Russell Burton and Ethel Harriett (Smith) H.; m. Robert I. Coward, Sept. 14, 1968 (div. 1977); m. John Richard Ferguson, Feb. 1, 1980; children: Brigit Grace, Rachel Anna. AB, Bryn Mawr Coll., 1970; JD, Georgetown U., 1975. Bar: Va. Supreme Ct. 1975, U.S. Dist. Ct. D.C. 1976, U.S. Ct. Appeals (D.C. cir.) 1976, D.C. Ct. Appeals 1976, U.S. Supreme Ct. 1978, U.S. Ct. Appeals (6th cir.) 1981, U.S. Ct. Appeals (8th cir.) 1981. Assoc. Baker & Hostetler, Washington, 1975-78, Pettit & Martin, Washington, 1978-79, Peabody, Lambert & Meyers, Washington, 1979-82, ptnr., 1983-84; sole practice, Washington, 1984—. pres. bd. trustees Burgundy Farm Country Day Sch., 1993-96; mediator Washington Superior Ct. Multi-Door Dispute Resolution Prog. Contbr. articles to legal jours. Mem. Nat. Conf. Women's Bar Assns. (bd. dirs. 1984-87, pres.-elect 1987-88, v.p. 1986-87, pres. 1988-89), Nat. Found. for Womens' Bar Assn. (pres. 1985-88, dir. 1988—), Women's Bar Assn. D.C. (pres. 1984-85), D.C. Bar (bd. govs. 1984-88), ABA (com. on specialization), Va. Women Attys. Assn. Club: Bryn Mawr. Alternative dispute resolution, Federal civil litigation, General corporate.

**HARRIS, JEFFREY MARK,** lawyer, educator; b. Chgo., Mar. 11, 1946; s. Al J. and Sylvia (Ruskin) H.; m. Laura Elizabeth Fitzgerald, July 13, 1975; children: Michael, Brian, Andrea. BA, So. Ill. U., 1967; JD, DePaul U., 1971. Bar: Ill. 1972, Fla. 1975, U.S. Dist. Ct. (no. dist.) Ill. 1975, U.S. Dist. Ct. (so. dist.) Fla. 1976, U.S. Supreme Ct. Asst. state atty. State Atty.'s Office, Chgo., 1974-76, Ft. Lauderdale, Fla., 1976-78; pvt. practice, Ft. Lauderdale, 1978—; adj. prof. Nova U. Law Ctr., Ft. Lauderdale, 1982-97. Mem. ABA, Fla. Bar Assn. (cert. in criminal law, chmn. grievance com. 1990, mem. law cert. com. 1990-93, evidence com. 1999), Nat. Assn. Criminal Def. Attys., Broward County Criminal Def. Bar Assn. (bd. dirs. 1989—, treas. 1991, v.p. 1992, pres. 1994), Broward County Bar Assn. (vice-chmn. 1998, chmn. bar/bench com. 1999), Fla. Criminal Def. Bar Assn. (bd. dirs. 1992—), B'nai B'rith. Criminal. Office: One E Broward Blvd Fort Lauderdale FL 33301

**HARRIS, JOEL B(RUCE),** lawyer; b. N.Y.C., Oct. 15, 1941; s. Raymond S. and Laura (Greene) H.; m. Barbara J. Rous, June 13, 1965 (div.); 1 child, Clifford S.; m. Deborah Sherman, Apr. 1, 1986 (div.); children: Sydney Anne, Cassidy Raye. AB, Columbia U., 1963; LLB, Harvard U., 1966; LLM, U. London, 1967. Bar: N.Y. 1968, U.S. Dist. Ct. (so. dist.) N.Y. 1970, U.S. Ct. Appeals (2d cir.) 1970, U.S. Dist. Ct. (ea. dist.) N.Y. 1975, U.S. Supreme Ct. 1976, U.S. Ct. Appeals (3d cir.) 1980, U.S. Dist. Ct. (we. dist.) N.Y. 1981. Assoc. Simpson, Thacher & Bartlett, N.Y.C., 1967-70; asst. U.S. atty. So. Dist. N.Y., 1970-74, chief civil rights unit, 1973-74; assoc. Weil, Gotshal & Manges, N.Y.C., 1974-76, ptnr., 1976-86; ptnr. Thacher, Proffitt & Wood, N.Y.C., 1986—; chmn. litigation dept.; speaker, panelist, moderator confs. Contbr. articles to profl. jours. Knox Meml. fellow, 1966-67. Fellow Am. Bar Found.; mem. ABA (chmn. com. internat. litigation 1981-84, chmn. com. personal rights litigation 1984-87), N.Y. State Bar Assn. (mem. internat. law and practice sect., sect. chair 1997-98, mem. exec. com. 1990—, chmn. internat. dispute resolution com. 1990-93, chmn. seasonal meeting 1993), Assn. Bar City N.Y., Inter-Am. Bar Assn., Fed. Bar Coun., Am. Soc. Internat. Law, Internat. Law Assn., Am. Judicature Soc. Federal civil litigation, Private international, State civil litigation. Home: 40 Prince St New York NY 10012-3426 Office: Thacher Proffitt & Wood 2 World Trade Ctr New York NY 10048-0203

**HARRIS, JUDITH A.,** lawyer; b. Allentown, Pa., Aug. 29, 1961; d. Aristides P. and R. Charlotte (Treichler) Harris; m. John P. Servis. AB, Bryn Mawr Coll., 1983; JD, Am. U., 1986; LLM in Taxation, Villanova U., 1991. Bar: Pa., 1986, Va., 1987; U.S. Supreme Ct., 1991; U.S. Tax Ct., 1990. With firm Peil & Egan, P.C., Lehigh Valley, Pa.; instr. Pa. State U., Allentown, 1993—; bd. dirs. Lehigh-Northampton Airport Authority, Allentown, 1997—. Sec. bd. dirs. Allentown Symphony Assn. Mem. Estate Planning Coun. Lehigh Valley (bd. dirs. 1993-98). Estate planning, Taxation, general. Office: Peil & Egan PC PO Box 20467 4510 Bath Pike Lehigh Valley PA 18002-0467

**HARRIS, JUDITH E.,** lawyer; b. Apr. 28, 1945. AB, Mount Holyoke Coll., 1967; JD, Howard U., 1970. Bar: Pa. 1971. City solicitor City of Phila., 1992-93; ptnr. Morgan, Lewis & Bockius LLP, Phila. Office: Morgan Lewis & Bockius LLP 1701 Market St Philadelphia PA 19103-2903

**HARRIS, K. DAVID,** state supreme court justice; b. Jefferson, Iowa, July 29, 1927; s. Orville William and Jessie Heloise (Smart) H.; m. Madonna Theresa Coyne, Sept. 4, 1948; children: Jane, Julia, Frederick. BA, U. Iowa, 1949, JD, 1951. Bar: Iowa 1951, U.S. Dist. Ct (so. dist.) Iowa, 1958. Sole practice Harris & Harris, Jefferson, 1951-62; dist. judge 16th Judicial Dist., Iowa, 1962-72; justice Iowa Supreme Ct., Des Moines, 1972-99, sr. justice, 1999—. Served with U.S. Amry, 1944-46, PTO. Mem. VFW, Am. Legion, Rotary. Roman Catholic. Avocation: writing poetry. Office: Iowa Supreme Ct State Capitol Bldg Des Moines IA 50319-0001

**HARRIS, LINDA CHAPLIK,** lawyer; b. Chgo., May 21, 1949; d. Rubin and Miriam (Lebedow) Chaplik; m. Alan G. Harris, Aug. 7, 1971. Student, Am. U., Washington, 1967-69; BA, U. Mich., 1971; JD, Cath. U. Am., 1974. Bar: Ill. 1974, U.S. Dist. Ct. (no. dist.) Ill. 1974, U.S. Ct. Appeals (7th cir.) 1974. Staff atty. U.S. Ct. Appeals, 7th Cir., Chgo., 1974-76; assoc., then ptnr. Sonnenschein Nath & Rosenthal, Chgo., 1976—, chmn. corp. practice group, 1988-98. Bd. dirs. The Joffrey Ballet of Chgo., 1996—, Anti-Defamation League, 1994—, Women's Bus. Devel. Ctr., 1995—, Women's Issues Network Found., pres., 1994-95. Recipient Women of Achievement award Anti-Defamation League, 1999. Mem. Chgo. Fin. Exch., Internat. Women's Forum, Chicagoland C. of C. (dir. 1994—), Econ. Club, Investor's Cir./Capital Cir. Avocations: film, theater, travel. Mergers and acquisitions, General corporate, Contracts commercial. Office: Sonnenschein Nath & Rosenthal 8000 Sears Tower Chicago IL 60606

**HARRIS, MICALYN SHAFER,** lawyer, educator; b. Chgo., Oct. 31, 1941; d. Erwin and Dorothy (Sampson) Shafer. AB, Wellesley Coll., 1963; JD, U. Chgo., 1966. Bar: Ill. 1966, Mo. 1967, U.S. Dist. Ct. (ea. dist.) Mo. 1967, U.S. Supreme Ct. 1972, U.S. Ct. Appeals (8th cir.), 1974, N.Y. 1981, N.J. 1988, U.S. Dist. Ct. N.J., U.S. Ct. Appeals (3d cir.) 1993. Law clk. U.S. Dist. Ct., Mo., 1967-68; atty. The May Dept. Stores, St. Louis, 1968-70, Ralston-Purina Co., St. Louis, 1970-72; atty., asst. sec. Chromalloy Am. Corp., St. Louis, 1972-76; pvt. practice St. Louis, 1976-78; atty. CPC Internat., Inc., 1978-80; divsn. counsel CPA N.Am., 1980-88, asst. sec., 1981-88; gen. counsel S.B. Thomas, Inc., 1988-87; corp. counsel CPS Internat., Englewood Cliffs, NJ, 1984-88; assoc. counsel Weil, Gotshal & Manges, N.Y.C., 1988-90; pvt. practice, 1991; v.p., sec., gen. counsel Winpro, Inc., 1991—; arbitrator Am., Arbitration Assn., NYSE, NASD, The Aspen Ctr. Conflict Mgmt.; adj. prof. Lubin Sch. Bus. Pace U. Mem. ABA (gov. bd. Ctr. Profl. Responsibility and Ch., publs. com., ABA/BNA Editl. bd., bus. law sect., past chair corp. counsel com., chair corp. comm. subcom., past chair subcom. counseling the mktg. function, mem. securities law com., tender offers and proxy statements subcom., legal bus. ethics com., chair task force on e-mail privacy, vice chair subcom. on computer software contracting, task force on electronic contracting, task force on conflicts of interest, ad hod com. on tech., strategic planning com.), N.Y. State Bar Assn. (securities regulation com., technology law com., chair subcom. on licensing, task force on shrink-wrap licensing), N.J. Bar Assn. (computer law com.), Assn. Bar City N.Y., Bar Assn. Metro St. Louis (past chair TV com.), Mo. Bar Assn. (part chmn. internat. law com.), Ill. Bar Assn., Am. Corp. Counsel Assn. N.Y. (mergers and acquisitions com., corp. law com.), N.J. Gen. Coun., Computer Law Assn., Am. Law Inst. General corporate, Computer, Finance. Address: 625 N Monroe St Ridgewood NJ 07450-1206

**HARRIS, MICHAEL GENE,** optometrist, educator, lawyer; b. San Francisco, Sept. 20, 1942; s. Morry and Gertrude Alice (Epstein) H.; m. Dawn Block; children: Matthew Benjamin, Daniel Evan, Ashley Beth, Lindsay Meredith. BS, U. Calif., 1964, M in Optometry, 1965, D in Optometry, 1966, MS, 1968; JD, John F. Kennedy U., 1985. Bar: Calif., U.S. Dist. Ct. (no. dist.) Calif. Assoc. practice optometry Oakland, Calif., 1965-66, San Francisco, 1966-68; instr., coord. contact lens clinic Ohio State U., 1968-69; asst. clin. prof. optometry U. Calif., Berkeley, 1969-73, dir. contact lens extended care clinic, 1969-83, chief contact lens clinic, 1983—, assoc. clin. prof., 1973-76, asst. chief, then assoc. chief contact lens svc., 1970—, lectr., then sr. lectr., 1978—, vice chmn. faculty Sch. Optometry, 1983-85, 95—, prof. clin. optometry, 1984-86, clin. prof., 1986—, dir. residency program, 1993-95, asst. dean, 1994-95, assoc. dean, 1995—; John de Carle vis. prof. City U., London, 1984; vis. rsch. fellow U. New South Wales, Sydney, Australia, 1989; sr. vis. rsch. scholar U. Melbourne, Victoria, Australia, 1989, 92; pvt. practice optometry, Oakland, 1973-76; mem. ophthalmic devices panel, med. device adv. com. FDA, 1990—, interim chair, 1994; lectr., cons. in field; mem. regulation rev. com. Calif. State Bd. Optometry; cons. hypnosis Calif. Optometric Assn., Am. Optometric Assn.; cons. Nat. Bd. Examiners in Optometry, Soflens divsn. Bausch & Lomb, 1973—, Barnes-Hind Hydrocurve Soft Lenses, Inc., 1974-87, Pilkinton-Barnes Hind, 1987-94, Contact Lens Rsch. Lab., 1976—, Wesley-Jessen Contact Lens Co., 1977—, Palo Alto VA, 1980—, Primarius Corp., Cooper Vision Optics Alcon, 1980—; co-founder Morton D. Sarver Rsch. Lab., 1986. Editor current comments sect. Am. Jour. Optometry, 1974-77; editor Eye Contact, 1984-86; assoc. editor The Video Jour. Clin. Optometry, 1988—; cons. editor Contact Lens Spectrum, 1988—; author: Contact Lenses: Treatment Options for Ocular Disease, Contact Lenses for Pre & Post-Surgery; editor: Problems in Optometry, Special Contact Lens Procedures; Contact Lenses in Ocular Disease, 1990; mem. hon. internat. editl. bd. Contact Lens and Anterior Eye Jour.; contbr. chpts. to books, articles to profl. publs.; author various syllabi. Planning commr. Town of Moraga, Calif., 1986, vice-chmn., 1987-88, chmn., 1988-90; mem. Town Coun., Moraga, 1992—, vice mayor, 1994-95, mem. Medi-Cal. adv. planning commn., 1993-95, chair, 1994—, with Managed Care commn., 1995%, chair, 1996—; with City County Rels. Com., Contra Costa County, Calif.; founding mem. Young Adults divsn. Jewish Welfare Fedn., 1965—, chmn., 1967-68; commr. Sunday Football League, Contra Costa County, 1974-78; chmarer mem. Jewish Cmty. Ctr. Contra Costa County; founding mem. Jewish Cmty. Mus. San Francisco, 1984; Para-Rabbinic, Temple Isaiah, Lafayette, Calif., 1987, bd. dirs., 1990; life mem. Bay Area Coun. for Soviet Jews, 1976; bd. dirs. Jewish Cmty. Rels. Coun. Greater East Bay, 1979—, Campolindo Homeowners Assn., 1981-85; pres. student coun. John F. Kennedy U. Sch. Law, 1984-85; grantor Michael G. Harris Family Endowment Fund, U. Calif., Dr. Michael G. Harris Tchg. award U. Calif. U. Calif. fellow, 1971; Calif. Optometric Assn. scholar, 1965, George Schneider Meml. scholar, 1964, Max Shapero Meml. lectr., 1995. Fellow Am. Acad. Optometry (diplomate cornea and contact lens sect., chmn. contact lens papers, mem. contact lens com. 1974—, vice chmn. contact lens sect. 1980-82, chmn. sect. 1982-84, immediate past chmn. 1984-86, chmn. jud. com. 1989—, chmn. bylaws com. 1989—), Assn. Schs. and Colls. Optometry (coun. on acad. affairs), AAAS, Prentice Soc. (pres.-elect 1994-96, pres. 1996—); mem. ABA, Assn. for Rsch. in Vision and Ophthalmology, Am. Optometric Assn. (proctor 1969—, cons. on hypnosis, mem. contact lens sect., mem. position papers com., mem. com. on ophthalmic stds., subcom. on testing and certification, cons. editor Jour.), Calif. Optometric Assn., Assn. Optometric Contact Lens Educators, Am. Optometric Found., Mexican Soc. Contactology (hon.), Nat. Coun. on Contact Lens Compliance, Internat. Soc. Contact Lens Rsch., Calif. State Bd. Optometry (regulation rev. com.), Calif. Acad. Scis., U. Calif. Optometry Alumni Assn. (life), Calif. Young Lawyers Assn., Contrac Costa Bar Assn., Mus. Soc., JFK U. Sch. Law Alumni Assn., Benjamin Ide Wheeler Soc. U. Calif., B'nai B'rith, Mensa, Robert Gardon Sproul Assn. U. Calif. Democrat. Health, Personal injury, Education and schools. Office: U of Calif Sch Of Optometry Berkeley CA 94720-0001

**HARRIS, MORTON ALLEN,** lawyer; b. Columbus, Ga., Mar. 13, 1934; s. Alvin L. Harris and Harriett (Berman) Wolpin; m. Judye Rose Spielberger, Aug. 11, 1957; children: Alvin L., Wendy, Tracy, Beth. BBA, Emory U., 1956; JD, Harvard U., 1959. Bar: Ga. 1959, U.S. Ct. Appeals (5th and 11th cirs.) 1981, U.S. Tax Ct. 1981, U.S. Supreme Ct. 1981. With Page, Scrantom, Harris & Chapman, Columbus, 1959-93, Hatcher, Stubbs, Land, Hollis & Rothschild, Columbus, 1993—; v.p., bd. dirs. Small Bus. Coun. Am., pres., 1980-86; trustee Ga. Tax Conf., pres., 1988-89; trustee Columbus Pension Bd., 1993—, vice-chair 1996—. Contbg. author: Business Organizations, 1976; dept. editor: The Tax Times, 1986-87; mem. editorial adv. bd. Practical Tax Lawyer, 1986—, Estate Planners Quarterly. Pres. Columbus Estate Planning Coun., Temple Israel, Inc., 1997-99; trustee Inst. for Study Am. Cultures, 1983—, pres. 1997—; spl. advisor Muscogee County Sch. Dist. Health Improvement Program, Columbus, 1983—; trustee Help Found.; bd. dirs. Group Inc., pres., 1999—. Recipient Ann. Vol. award State of Ga., 1985. Fellow Am. Coll. Tax Counsel, Am. Coll. Trust and Estate Counsel; mem. ABA (chmn. tax sect. personal svc. orgn. com. 1978-80, chmn. tax sect. membership com. 1983-86, mem. counsel tax sect. 1989-96, asst. sec. 1989-91, sec. 1991-93), Jaycees (pres. 1966 Columbus chpt., Outstanding Young Man of Yr. 1966), Kiwanis (pres. Columbus chpt. 1971-72). Republican. Jewish. Fax: 706-322-7747. Corporate taxation, Pension, profit-sharing, and employee benefits, Probate.

**HARRIS, PATRICIA ANN,** lawyer; b. Social Circle, Ga., June 5, 1964; d. Willie Paul and Mattie Jane (Roberts) Robinson; m. Barry Harris, July 5, 1987; children: Jazmine, Hayley, Samuel. BA, U. Ga., 1987; JD, Campbell U. Sch. Law, 1992. Bar: Ga. 1992, U.S. Supreme Ct. 1997. Commd. 1st lt. U.S. Army, 1992, advanced through grades to capt.; legal assistance atty., claims judge advocate, prosecutor U.S. Army Judge, Advocate Gen.'s Corps, Augsburg, Germany, 1992-95, def. appellate counsel, 1995-98; chief litigation atty. Nat. Guard Bur., Washington, 1998—. Mem. ABA, Ga. Bar Assn. Avocations: reading, writing. Office: Nat Guard Bur Washington DC 20000

**HARRIS, RAY KENDALL,** lawyer; b. Tucson, July 9, 1957; s. Ray Fisher and Mary Jane (Lewis) H.; m. Patricia Ellen Gallogly, Oct. 10, 1986; children: Ellen Rose, Austin William. BSBA, U. Ariz., 1979, JD, 1982. Bar: Ariz. 1982, U.S. Dist. Ct. Ariz. 1982, U.S. Ct. Appeals (9th cir.) 1985, U.S. Ct. Appeals (10th cir.) 1988. Assoc. Fennemore Craig PC, Phoenix, 1982-88, dir., 1988—; bd. dirs. Ariz. Innovation Network, Phoenix, 1996-98, High Tech. Industry Cluster, Phoenix, 1998—, Ariz. Tech. Incubator, Scottsdale, 1998—. Exec. editor Ariz. Law Rev., 1981-82. Mem. Friends of Sci. and Tech./Ariz. Sci. Ctr., Phoenix, 1994—. Mem. State Bar Ariz. (chair intellectual property sect. 1995-97), Computer Law Assn., Am. Intellectual Property Law Assn., Ariz. Software Assn. (bd. dirs. 1995—). Intellectual property, General civil litigation, Computer. Home: 1410 W Ruth Ave Phoenix AZ 85021-4449 Office: Fennemore Craig PC 3003 N Central Ave Ste 2600 Phoenix AZ 85012-2913

**HARRIS, RICHARD EUGENE VASSAU,** lawyer; b. Detroit, Mar. 16, 1945; s. Joseph S. and Helen Harris; m. Milagros A. Brito; children: Catherine, Byron. AB, Albion Coll., 1967; JD, Harvard U., 1970; postdoctoral, Inst. Advanced Legal Studies, London, 1970-71. Bar: Calif. 1972. Assoc. Orrick, Herrington, Rowley & Sutcliffe, San Francisco, 1972-77; ptnr. Orrick, Herrington & Sutcliffe, San Francisco, 1978-98; pvt. practice Richard E. V. Harris Law Office, Oakland, Ca., 1998—; faculty Calif. Tax Policy Conf., 1987, 95; spkr. univ., govtl. and profl. groups. Mem. Christian Edn. Bd., Piedmont (Calif.) Community Ch., 1983-86. Knox fellow Harvard U., 1970-71. Mem. ABA (urban state and local govt. sect. 1983-88, vice chmn. govt. liability com. 1982-84, antitrust law sect. state action com. 1981—, BOULDER task force 1983-84, internat. com. 1994—, litigation sect. corp. counsel com., subcom. chmn. 1980-82, 83—, vice chmn. 1982-83, tax litigation com. 1992—, co-chmn. Nat. Insts. Antitrust Liability 1983, 85, bus. law sect., SEC investigation atty.-client privilege waiver task force 1988, corp. counsel com., 1995—, conflicts of interest task force 1993-96, conflicts of interest com., 1996—, tax sect., state and local taxes com. 1989—, Ctr. for Profl. Responsibility ABA Ethics 2000 adv. group 1999—), Am. Law Inst. (cons. restatements of law unfair competition 1991-94, governing lawyers 1991-99, torts 1993—, agy. 1996—, trusts 1996—), Bar Assn. San Francisco (ethics com., 1980—). State and local taxation, Professional liability, Antitrust.

**HARRIS, RICHARD FOSTER, III,** lawyer; b. Charlotte, N.C., Apr. 10, 1942; s. Richard Foster and Frances Virginia (McCurdy) H.; m. Jacqueline Kaplan; children—Richard Foster, IV, John Walter Rodney. A.B. in English, Duke U., 1964; J.D., U. N.C., Chapel Hill, 1967. Bar: N.C. 1967, U.S. Dist. Ct. (we. dist.) N.C. 1971, U.S. Ct. Appeals (4th cir.) 1973. Assoc. Eugene C. Hicks III, Charlotte, 1968-70; ptnr. Hicks, Harris & Sterrett and predecessor Hicks & Harris, Charlotte, 1970-81; sole practice, Charlotte, 1982—. Served with Air N.G., 1967-73. Mem. ABA, N.C. State Bar, N.C. Bar Assn. (Outstanding Young Lawyer award 1977, chmn. Young Lawyers Sect. 1977-78), Assn. Trial Lawyers Am., N.C. Acad. Trial Lawyers, Mecklenburg County Bar Assn. (chmn. young lawyers sect. 1976-77). Democrat. Presbyterian. Club: Myers Park Country (Charlotte). General civil litigation, General practice, Workers' compensation. Home: 329 Cherokee Pl Charlotte NC 28207-2301 Office: 757B Providence Rd Charlotte NC 28207-2245

**HARRIS, RONALD DEAN,** lawyer; b. New Albany, Ind., Oct. 7, 1955; s. Robert Eugene and Catherine Louise (Edwards) H.; m. Vivian Benita Land, Sept. 20, 1975; children: Ronald Matthew, John Robert, Dean Jordan. BA in Polit. Sci. with honors, U. Louisville, 1977, JD with honors, 1981. Bar: Ind. 1981, Ky. 1982, U.S. Dist. Ct. (so. and no. dists.) Ind., U.S. Dist. Ct. (we. dist.) Ky., U.S. Ct. Appeals (7th and 6th cirs.). Ptnr. Harris & Harris, Jeffersonville, Ind., 1981-90, sr. ptnr., 1990—; judge pro tem. Jeffersonville City Court, 1994—. Provides pro bono legal svcs. for Clark County (Ind.) Youth Shelter, Clark County Habitat for Humanity and various other local churches and civic orgns.; bd. dirs., sec., treas. Hope Inc., 1993—; chmn. Clark County Election Bd., 1994—; active local politics; co-founder, search and rescue dog handler U.S. Emergency Assistance Command. Maj. staff judge advocate Ind. Air Guard Res., 1993—. Republican. Protestant. Avocations: reading, writing, arboriculture, photography, riflery. General practice, Personal injury, General civil litigation. Home: 9021 Stonemour Way Charlestown IN 47111-9697 Office: Harris & Harris 1407 Youngstown Dr Jeffersonville IN 47130

**HARRIS, RUTH JENSEN,** lawyer; b. Mpls., Mar. 8, 1920; d. Anton and Edith Cecilia (Axtell) J.; m. Reginald Albright Harris, Nov. 25, 1966 (dec. Oct. 1995). BS, U. Minn., 1941, JD, 1943. Bar: Minn. 1944. Democrat. Unitarian. Home: 400 Selby Ave Apt 327 Saint Paul MN 55102-4511

**HARRIS, SCOTT BLAKE,** lawyer; b. N.Y.C., June 18, 1951; s. Stanley Robert and Adele Jean (Ganger) H.; m. Barbara Straughn Harris, Aug. 5, 1978. AB magna cum laude, Brown U., 1973; JD magna cum laude, Harvard U., 1976. Bar: D.C. 1977, U.S. Ct. Appeals (D.C. cir.) 1978, U.S. Supreme Ct. 1983. Law clk. to presiding justice U.S. Dist. Ct., Washington, 1976-77; assoc. Williams & Connolly, Washington, 1977-84, ptnr., 1984-93; chief counsel Bur. Export Adminstrn., U.S. Dept. Commerce, Washington, 1993-94; chief internat. bur. FCC, 1994-96; ptnr. Gibson, Dunn & Crutcher, Washington, 1996-98; mng. ptnr. Harris, Wiltshire & Grannis LLP, Washington, 1998—; mem. adv. bd. Ctr. for Wireless Tech., Va. Tech. U., 1996—, Satellite Comms. Mag., 1996—, Time Domain Sys., Inc., 1999—, Critical Infrastructure Fund LLP, 1999—. Trustee Fed. Comms. Bar Assn. Found., 1997—. Mem. ABA (co-chair telecoms. com., sect. internat. law 1999—), Phi Beta Kappa. Federal civil litigation, Communications, Private international. Home: 3409 Fulton St NW Washington DC 20007-1436 Office: Harris Wiltshire & Grannis LLP 1200 18th St NW Washington DC 20036-2506

**HARRIS, STACY KERNS,** lawyer; b. Detroit, Aug. 16, 1971; m. David Graham Harris. BS, Purdue U., 1993; JD summa cum laude, Ind. U., 1996. Bar: Ind. 1996, U.S. Dist. Ct. (so. and no. dists.) Ind. 1996. Assoc. Sturm, Smith, Parmenter & Feavel, Vincennes, Ind., 1996-98, Bowers, Harrison, Kent & Miller, Evansville, Ind., 1997—. Mem. Ind. Bar Assn., Evansville Bar Assn. Lutheran. Office: Bowers Harrison Kent & Miller 25 NW Riverside Dr Evansville IN 47708-1255

**HARRIS, STANLEY S.,** judge; b. Washington, Oct. 19, 1927; s. Stanley Raymond and Elizabeth (Sutherland) H.; m. Rebecca Ashley, Aug. 1, 1964; children: Scott Sutherland, Todd Ashley, Mark Ashley. BS, U. Va., 1951, JD, 1953. Bar: D.C. 1953, U.S. Supreme Ct. 1964. Assoc., then ptnr. Hogan & Hartson, Washington, 1953-70; judge Superior Ct. D.C., 1971-72, D.C. Ct. Appeals, 1972-82; U.S. atty. for D.C. Dept. Justice, 1982-83; judge U.S. Dist. Ct. D.C., 1983—, sr. judge, 1996—; mem. com. on criminal law Jud. Conf. U.S., 1988-94, chmn. com. intercircuit assignments, 1994—. Served with U.S. Army, 1945-47. Recipient Judiciary award Assn. Fed. Investigators, 1982. Mem. Bar Assn. D.C. (bd. dirs. 1970-72, Lawyer of Yr. award 1982, Disting. Career award 1996), Lawyer's Club of Washington (pres. 1998-99). Republican. Home: 4982 Sentinel Dr # 406 Bethesda MD 20816-3579 Office: US Dist Ct US Courthouse 333 Constitution Ave NW Washington DC 20001-2802

**HARRIS, STEPHEN DONNELL,** lawyer; b. Rochester, N.Y., Sept. 19, 1968; s. Donnell Ray and Norma Ruth Harris. BA, Wake Forest U., 1990, JD, 1993. Bar: N.C., U.S. Dist. Ct. Colo., U.S. Ct. Appeals (10th cir.). Assoc. James I. Merrill, Attys. at Law, Colorado Springs, 1993-98; mng. mem. Merrill, Anderson, King & Harris, LLC, Colorado Springs, 1998—; vis. faculty Colo. Coll., Colorado Springs, 1998—; pres. The Inkera Group, Colorado Springs, 1996—; presenter Pikes Peak Environ. Forum, 1994, 96. Disc jockey reggae show ICRCC 91.5 FM, 1995—. Founder So. Colo. Roots & Culture Fest, 1996—; chair Colorado Springs Open Space Com.; sec. Springs Area Beautiful Assn., Colorado Springs; mem. El Paso County steering com. Legal Aid Found., 1994—. Recipient Organizing award Urban League of Pikes Peak Region, 1996, Svc. to the Environment award Colo. Environ. Coalition, 1996. Mem. Colo. Bar Assn., El Paso County Bar Assn. Environmental, Natural resources, General civil litigation. Home: 1306 E Yampa St Colorado Springs CO 80909-3755 Office: Merrill Anderson King & Harris LLC 20 Boulder Crescent St Ste 100 Colorado Springs CO 80903-3375

**HARRIS, TERRILL JOHNSON,** lawyer; b. Greensboro, N.C., Aug. 15, 1965; d. Wilbur Everette Johnson Jr. and Ann Terrill Appenzeller; m. George Mitchell Harris III, Oct. 10, 1992; 1 child, George Mitchell IV. BA, Wake Forest U., 1987; JD, Duke U., 1990. Bar: N.C. 1990, D.C. 1991, U.S. Dist. Ct. (mid. dist.) N.C. 1990, U.S. Dist. Ct. (ea. dist.) N.C. 1992, U.S. Dist. Ct. (we. dist.) N.C. 1995, U.S. Ct. Appeals (4th cir.) 1994. Assoc. Smith Helms Mulliss & Moore, LLP, Greensboro, 1990-97, ptnr., 1998—. Mem. Am. Health Lawyers Assn., N.C. Bar Assn., N.C. Soc. Health Care Attys., Women's Profl. Forum. Avocations: reading, travel. Health, General civil litigation. Office: Smith Helms Mulliss Moore 300 N Greene St Greensboro NC 27401-2167

**HARRIS, THORNE D., III,** lawyer; b. New Orleans, Nov. 5, 1950; s. Thorne D. and Myra (Banister) H. Jr.; m. Mary Margaret Hattier, June 18, 1971. B.A. in English, U. New Orleans, 1972; J.D., La. State U., 1974. Bar: La. 1974, U.S. Dist. Ct. (ea. dist.) La. 1974, U.S. Dist. Ct. (mid. and we. dists.) La. 1976, U.S. Ct. Appeals (5th cir.) 1974, U.S. Ct. Appeals (11th cir.) 1981. with Sessions, Fishman, et al, New Orleans, 1974-81, Monroe & Lemann, New Orleans, 1981-82, McNulty, O'Conner, et al, New Orleans, 1982-84; sole practice, New Orleans, 1984—; pres. Micro Esq. divsn. Superior Software Inc.; cons. computer law and law office computer systems. Author: Legal Guide to Computer Software Protection: A Practical Handbook on Copyrights, Trademarks, Publishing and Trade Secrets, 1984, The Software Developer's Complete Legal Companion, 1994; contbr. articles to profl. jours. Mem. La. State U. Law Rev. Chmn. U. New Orleans Awards and Scholarship Com., 1980-88; mem. Civitan, New Orleans, 1977-78. Named one of Outstanding Young Men of Am., Jaycees, 1984, 86. Mem. La. State Bar Assn. (sects. on litigation, mineral law, ins., bus. and antitrust 1974—, founder, dir., head Tech. Resource Ctr., founder, 1st chair sole practitioners and small firms sect. 1991-95), New Orleans Bar Assn., ABA (sects. on sci. and tech., patent, copyrights and trademarks, corps. 1975—, chmn. software subcom. of copyright and new technology com. 1984-86, chmn. subcom. piracy, 1986—, chmn. database com. 1987-89), Vol. Lawyers for Arts, Order of Coif, Phi Eta Sigma. Republican. Fax: (504) 822-6102. E-mail: thorne@thornedharris111.com. General practice, Federal civil litigation, Computer. Office: 326 S Broad St New Orleans LA 70119-6416

**HARRIS, WARREN WAYNE,** lawyer; b. Houston, Nov. 5, 1962. BBA, U. Houston, 1985, JD, 1988. Bar: Tex. 1988, U.S. Ct. Appeals (5th cir.) 1989, U.S. Ct. Appeals (fed. cir.) 1995, U.S. Ct. Appeals (8th and 11th cirs.) 1996, U.S. Dist. Ct. (so., no., ea. and we. dists.) Tex. 1990, U.S. Supreme Ct. 1991; bd. cert. civil appellate law Tex. Bd. Legal Specialization. Briefing atty. Tex. Supreme Ct., Austin, 1988-89; ptnr. Porter & Hedges, L.L.P., Houston, 1989-96, Bracewell & Patterson, L.L.P., Houston, 1996—. Editor-in-chief: Houston Lawyer mag., 1991-92; assoc. editor: The Appellate Advocate, 1992-97; editor: Pocket Parts, 1993-95, The Appellate Lawyer, 1994-96. Fellow Tex. Bar Found. (co-chair dist. 4 nominating com. 1994—), Houston Bar Found., Houston Young Lawyers Found. (vice-chair 1996-98); mem. ABA (litigation sect. appellate practice com. 1990—, tort and ins. practice sect. appellate advocacy com. 1990—, chair-elect 1999—), State Bar Tex. (appellate sect. 1988—, coun. 1997—, pro bono com. chair 1997-99), State Bar Coll. (bd. dirs. 1994-95), State Bar Pro Bono Coll., Tex. Young Lawyers Assn. (bd. dirs. 1994-98, outstanding dir. 1995-96, Pres.'s award 1996-97), Houston Bar Assn. (Pres.'s award 1993-94, chair appellate practice sect. 1998-99, coun. appellate practice sect. 1993—), Houston Young Lawyers Assn. (pres. 1999—), Houston Lawyer Referral Svc. (trustee 1994-95), Stages Repertory Theatre (pres. 1994-95, bd. dirs. 1994-96, chair 1994-95, WineFest com. chair 1994-96), Order of Barristers, Order of Barons, Phi Delta Phi (life). Republican. Appellate, Contracts commercial, Personal injury. Office: Bracewell & Patterson LLP 711 Louisiana St Ste 2900 Houston TX 77002-2781

**HARRIS, WAYNE MANLEY,** lawyer; b. Pittsford, N.Y., Dec. 28, 1925; s. George H. and Constance M. Harris; m. Diane C. Quigley, Sept. 30, 1978; children: Wayne, Constance, Karen, Duncan, Claire. LLB, Albany Law Sch., U. Rochester, 1951. Bar: N.Y. 1952, U.S. Supreme Ct. 1958. Ptnr. Harris, Chesworth & O'Brien (and predecessor firms), Rochester, N.Y., 1958—. Pres. Delta Labs., Inc. (non-profit environ. lab.) Adopt-A-Stream program, 1971—, Friends of Bristol Valley Playhouse Found., 1984-87, Monroe County Conservation Coun. Inc., 1956-61, v.p., 1984-87; v.p. Powder Mills Pk. Hatchery Preservation Inc., 1993-95, pres., 1995—. Served with combat inf., Germany, 1944-46. Decorated Bronze Star; recipient Sportsman of Yr. award Genesee Conservation League, Inc., 1960, Conservationist of Yr. award Monroe County Conservation Coun., Inc., 1961, Kiwanian of Yr. award, Kiwanis Club, 1965, Livingston County Fedn. of Sportsmen award, 1966, N.Y. State Conservation Coun. Nat. Wildlife Fedn. Water Conservation Conservationist of Yr. award, 1967, Rochester Acad. Sci. Hon. Fellowship award, 1970, Conservation award Nat. Am. Motors Corp., 1971, Meritorious Leadership in Civic Devel. award Rochester C. of C., 1972, Svc. award Rochester Against Intoxicated Drivers, 1989. Mem. ATLA, N.Y. State Trial Lawyers Assn., AIDA Reins. and Arbitration Soc., Indsl. Mgmt. Coun., Wild Turkey Fedn. Drafter 5 laws passed in N.Y. State. State civil litigation, General corporate, Probate. Home: 60 Mendon Center Rd Honeoye Falls NY 14472-9363 Office: Harris Chesworth & O'Brien 1820 East Ave Rochester NY 14610-1829

**HARRIS, WHITNEY ROBSON,** lawyer, educator; b. Seattle, Aug. 12, 1912; s. Olin Whitney and Lily (Robson) H.; m. Jane Freund Foster, Feb. 14, 1964; 1 child, Eugene Whitney. AB magna cum laude, U. Wash., 1933; JD, U. Calif., 1936; LHD (hon.), McKendree Coll., 1999. Bar: Calif. 1936, U.S. Supreme Ct. 1945, Tex. 1953, U.S. Ct. Mil. Appeals 1955, Mo. 1964. Pvt. practice L.A., 1936-42; trial counsel U.S. Chief of Counsel, Nuremberg, 1945-46; chief legal advice br. U.S. Mil. Govt. for Germany, 1946-48; prof. law So. Meth. U., 1948-54; staff dir. legal service and proc. Com. Orgn. Exec. Br. Govt., 1954; exec. dir. ABA, 1954-55; solicitor for Tex. Southwestern Bell Telephone Co., Dallas, 1955-63; gen. solicitor Southwestern Bell Telephone Co., St. Louis, 1963-65; pvt. practice St. Louis, 1965-89; arbitration judge, 1993—; sr. counselor Mo. Bar Assn., 1987; lectr. UCLA, Stanford U., Washington U., Wellesley Coll., U. Denver, Reed Coll., U. Wash., Claremont Coll., Boston Coll., Williams Coll., So. Meth. U., U. Mo., McKendree Coll. Author: Family Law, 1953, Tyranny On Trial, 1954, 3d edit. 1999, Legal Services and Procedure, 1955; (with others) Law, Culture and Values, 1989; contbr. numerous articles to profl. jours. including Ency. Brit., 1954, The Internat. Lawyer, 1986, Washington U. Law Quar., 1987, U. Toledo Law Rev., 1992. Bd. govs. Winston Churchill Meml. and Libr., 1980—; trustee Nat. Jewish Ctr. Immunol. and Respiratory Medicine, 1980-90. Decorated Legion of Merit, Order of Merit Officer's Class (Germany), Medal of the War Crimes Commn. (Poland); named nat. outstanding fund raising vol. Nat. Soc. Fund Raising Execs., 1985. Mem. ABA (chmn. internat. law sect. 1953-54, chmn. adminstrv. law sect. 1960-61), Japan-Am. Soc. St. Louis (pres. 1978-80, Disting. Svc. award 1995), Naval War Coll. Found. (grad. level), Order of Coif, Phi Beta Kappa, Phi Kappa Psi, Delta Theta Phi. Established Jane and Whitney Harris Rsch. Libr. at Winston Churchill Meml. and Libr., Fulton, Mo., 1980, Jane and Whitney Harris Reading Rooms at St. Louis Country Day Sch., 1980, and at Washington U., 1985, Jane and Whitney Harris Ann. Rsch. Fellowship in Arthritis at Washington U. Sch. Medicine, 1989, Whitney Robson Harris collection on Third Reich at Washington U., 1980, Jane and Whitney Harris Ann. Lecture on Tropical Ecology at U. Mo. St. Louis, 1991, Jane and Whitney Harris Secret Garden at Mo. Botanical Garden, 1993, Jane and Whitney Harris Child Care Facility at Jr. League, St. Louis, 1994, Jane and Whitney Harris Anniversary Garden, Forest Park, St. Louis, 1999. Home: 2 Glen Creek Ln Saint Louis MO 63124-1505 *Tyranny leads to inhumanity, and inhumanity is death. Let us resolve that tyranny shall not extend its sway, nor war become its game—placing our faith in the cause of justice, in the freedom of man, and in the mercy of God.*

**HARRIS, WILLIAM THEODORE, JR.,** lawyer, educator; b. Elizabeth, N.J., Mar. 9, 1949; s. John Clifford Burr and Carolyn Parker; children: Heather, Sherrell; m. Denise Ann Kelley, Oct. 9, 1993. Assocs., Essex County Coll., 1972; BA, Clark U., 1974; JD, Suffolk U., 1979. Bar: Mass. 1980, U.S. Dist. Ct. (1st cir.) 1980. Asst. dist. atty. Dist. Atty.'s Office, Worcester, Mass., 1979-81; instr. Clark U., Worcester, 1990-92; asst. prof. Law Mass. Sch. Law, Andover, Mass., 1992—; atty.-in-charge Com. for Pub. Counsel Svcs., Worcester, 1991-93; with Maynard & Cataldo, Worcester; ptnr. Harris, Ellio H., Rivera-Scozzatava, P.C., Worcester; instr. Nat. Def. Coll., Worcester, 1991—; mem. judicial nominating com., Worcester, 1991—. Vice-chair Human Rights Commn., Worcester, 1991. With U.S. Army, 1968-69, Vietnam. Mem. Nat. Assn. Criminal Def. Lawyers (v.p. Mass. chpt. 1991—), Worcester Bar Assn. Avocations: reading, photography. Home: 183 Moreland St Worcester MA 01609-1049 Office: Harris Ellio H Rivera-Scozzatava PC 40 Southbridge St Worcester MA 01608-2037

**HARRISON, BRYAN GUY,** lawyer; b. Norman, Okla., Nov. 22, 1963; s. Danny Guy and Judith Kay (Dalke) H.; m. Kathleen Hazel Cody, May 8, 1993. BS, Lehigh U., 1986; JD, Emory U., 1989. Bar: Tex. 1989, Ga. 1991. Assoc. Shank, Irwin, Conant, Lipshy & Casterline, Dallas, 1989-90; trial atty. antitrust div. U.S. Dept. Justice, Dallas, 1990-91; assoc. Morris, Manning & Martin, Atlanta, 1991-97, ptnr., 1998—. Computer, Antitrust, General civil litigation. Office: Morris Manning & Martin 3343 Peachtree Rd NE Ste 1600 Atlanta GA 30326-1044

**HARRISON, EARL DAVID,** lawyer, real estate executive; b. Bryn Mawr, Pa., Aug. 25, 1932; divorced; 1 child, H. Jason. BA, Harvard U., 1954; JD, U. Pa., 1960. Bar: D.C. 1960. Pvt. practice Washington; exec. v.p. Washington Real Estate Corp., Washington, 1986-94; pres. EDH Assocs., Inc., 1994—. Capt. U.S. Army, 1954-57. Decorated Order of Rio Branco (Brazil); Order of Merit (Italy). Mem. ABA, Internat. Coun. Shopping Ctrs., D.C. Bar Assn., Washington Assn. Realtors, Greater Washington Comml. Assn. Realtors, Nat. Assn. Realtors, Nat. Restaurant Assn., Met. Washington Restaurant Assn., Coun. Internat. Restaurant Brokers (v.p., gen. coun.), Harvard Club, Nat. Press Club. Real property, Private international, Contracts commercial. Office: 1077 30th St NW Ste 706 Washington DC 20007-3829

**HARRISON, FRANK JOSEPH,** lawyer; b. Streator, Ill., Dec. 5, 1919; s. Frank Joseph and Nell (Webb) H.; m. Shirley Anne Summerhays, Dec. 30, 1950; children: Ellen Harrison Greinacher, Paul, Janice Harrison Tienhaara, Mark. AB, U. Chgo., 1941, JD, 1947; LLM, Harvard U., 1947. Bar: Ill. 1942. Atty. Chgo. Title and Trust Co., 1948-51, Pub. Housing Adminstrn., Chgo., 1951-53; pvt. practice Streator, 1953—; city atty. City of Streator, 1965-71, 73-87; twp. atty., 1990-97; sr. law clk. Ill. Appellate Ct. 3d. Dist., Ottawa, 1971-76; atty. Streator Twp. High. Sch., 1975-83. Compiler, editor: Streator Mcpl. Code of 1968, 1968. Sgt. Signal Intelligence Svc. AUS, 1942-46, PTO, 1st lt. JAGC, 1949. Mem. Ill. Bar Assn., La Salle County Bar Assn., Streator Bar Assn. (pres. 1986-96). Presbyterian. Avocations: tennis, music. Probate, Real property, General practice. Home: 135 W 1st St Streator IL 61364-1241 Office: 114 N Bloomington St Streator IL 61364-2208

**HARRISON, JOHN CONWAY,** state supreme court justice; b. Grand Rapids, Minn., Apr. 28, 1913; s. Francis Randall and Ethlyn (Conway) H.; m. Ethel M. Strict; children—Nina Lyn, Robert Charles, Molly M., Frank R., Virginia Lee. LLD, George Washington U., 1940. Bar: Mont. 1947, U.S. Dist. Ct. 1947. County atty. Lewis and Clark County, Helena, Mont., 1934-60; justice Mont. Supreme Ct., Helena, 1961-98, ret., 1998. Pres. Mont. TB Assn., Helena, 1951-54, Am. Lung Assn., N.Y.C., 1972-73, Mont. coun. Boy Scouts Am., Great Falls, Mont., 1976-78. Col. U.S. Army. Mem. ABA, Mont. Bar Assn., Kiwanis (pres. 1953), Sigma Chi. Home: 215 S Cooke St Helena MT 59601-5143

**HARRISON, JOHN EDWARDS,** lawyer, real estate executive; b. Arlington, Va., Aug. 15, 1946; s. Hunter Creycroft and Margaret (Edwards) H.; m. Sally Hart Jones, July 23, 1969; children—Lucy Love, Sally Hart. Student U. N.C., 1964-66; B.S. in Fgn. Service, Georgetown U., 1971, J.D., 1977. Bar: Va. 1977, U.S. Ct. Appeals (4th cir.) 1977, D.C. 1980, U.S. Ct. Appeals (D.C. cir.). Assoc. Tolbert, Smith Fitzgerald & Ramsey, Arlington, 1977-79, Melrod, Redman & Gartlan, Washington, 1979-81; ptnr. Light & Harrison, P.C., McLean, Va., 1981—; chmn. bd. George H. Rucker Realty, Arlington, 1981—, McLean Fin. Corp., 1981—; dir. McLean Savs. and Loan. Served to 1st lt. U.S. Army, 1966-69, Vietnam. Decorated Silver Star, Bronze Star with V and cluster, Purple Heart. Mem. ABA, Va. Bar Assn., D.C. Bar Assn., Nat. Assn. Realtors. Episcopalian. Clubs: Army Navy (Washington); Farmington Country (Charlottesville, Va.). Federal civil litigation, State civil litigation, Construction. Office: Light & Harrison PC 6849 Old Dominion Dr Mc Lean VA 22101-3705

**HARRISON, JOSEPH GEORGE, JR.,** lawyer; b. Berlin, Md., Aug. 17, 1944; s. Joseph George Sr. and Beatrice (Wyatt) H.; m. Robin Hoddinott, Mar. 12, 1977; children: Brittany, Carrie, Brian, Christopher. BA, U. Md., 1966; JD, U. Balt., 1974. Bar: Md. Ptnr. Williams, Hammond, Moore, Shockley & Harrison, P.A., Ocean City, Md., 1974—. Lt. USN, 1968-71, Vietnam. Mem. Md. Bar Assn. (jud. appointments com. 1987-90, chair litigation sect. 1988, bd. govs. 1997-99), Worcester County Bar Assn. (treas., v.p., pres. 1980-84). Democrat. Methodist. E-mail: whmsh@shore.intercom.net. Real property, General civil litigation, Contracts commercial. Office: Williams Hammond Moore Shockley & Harrison LLP 3509 Coastal Hwy Ocean City MD 21842-3334

**HARRISON, JOSEPH HEAVRIN,** lawyer; b. Evansville, Ind., July 23, 1929; s. Homer William and Lillie Isabelle (Heavrin) H.; m. Sharon Jeanene Miller, June 30, 1957 (div. 1976); children: Joseph Heavrin, Sara Ann; m. Julie Anne Gerard, Dec. 10, 1976; 1 child, Meghann. BA in Econs., U. Notre Dame, Ind., 1952; JD cum laude, U. Notre Dame, 1953. Bar: Ind. 1953, U.S. Dist. Ct. D.C. 1953, U.S. Dist. Ct. (so. dist.) Ind. 1953, U.S. Ct. Appeals (7th cir.) 1968, U.S. Tax Ct. 1984. Mng. ptnr. Bowers, Harrison, Kent & Miller and predecessors, Evansville, Ind., 1955; pres. Sandy's Assocs., Inc. (20 Hardee's franchised restaurants); pres. AHAB, Inc. (Day's Inn, Evansville Airport). Pres. Vanderburgh County Legal Aid Soc., Evansville, 1964-65; Ind. counsel Bush Presdl. campaign, 1988; chmn. Vanderburgh County Election Bd., 1979-90, Vanderburgh Rep. Fin. Com., 1982-89; pres. Evansville Econ. Devel. Commn.; Ind. commr. Ohio River Valley Water Sanitation Commn., 1982—, chmn., 1987; bd. dirs. Arbor Hosp., 1991-94; commr. Vanderburgh County Conv. & Vis. Bur., 1997—. With U.S. Army, 1953-55. Fellow Ind. Bar Found.; mem. ABA, Evansville Bar Assn., Ind. Bar Assn., Am. Judicature Soc., Evansville Country Club (pres. 1976), Oak Meadow Country Club. Republican. Roman Catholic. Avocations: golf, flying. General corporate, Real property, Contracts commercial. Office: Bowers Harrison Kent & Miller PO Box 1287 25 NW Riverside Dr Evansville IN 47708-1255

**HARRISON, MARION EDWYN,** lawyer; b. Phila., Sept. 17, 1931; s. Marion Edwyn and Jessye Beatrice (Cilles) H.; m. Carmelita Ruth Deimel, Sept. 6, 1952; children: Angelique Marie (Mrs. Kevin B. Bounds), Marion Edwyn III, Henry Deimel. BA, U. Va., 1951; LLB, George Washington U., 1954, LLM, 1959. Bar: Va. 1954, D.C. 1958, Supreme Ct. 1958. Spl. asst. to gen. counsel Post Office Dept., 1958-60, assoc. gen. counsel, 1960-61, mem. bd. contract appeals, 1958-61; ptnr. firm Harrison, Lucey & Sagle (and predecessors), Washington, 1961-78, Barnett & Alagia, 1978-84; ptnr. Scott, Harrison & McLeod, 1984-86, Law Offices Marion Edwyn Harrison, Washington, 1986—; mem. coun. Adminstrv. Conf. U.S., 1971-78, sr. conf. fellow, 1984-88; mem. D.C. Law Revision Commn., 1975-92; lectr. Nat. Jud. Coll., Reno, 1979, La. State U. Law Sch., Aix-en-Provence, 1987, 89, Tulane U. Law Sch., Crete, 1997, Hofstra U. Law Sch., Nice, 1999; adv. dir. NationsBank, N.A., 1987-93. Contbr. articles to profl. publs.; editor-in-chief Fed. Bar News, 1960-63; mem. editorial bd. Adminstrv. Law Rev., 1976-89. Trustee AEFC Pension Fund, Chgo., 1986-92; pres. Young Rep. Fedn. Va., 1954-55; mem. Va. Rep. Cen. Com., 1954-55; bd. visitors Judge Adv. Gen. Sch., Charlottesville, Va., 1976-78; chmn. Wolf Trap Assn., 1984-87; bd. dirs. Wolf Trap Found., 1984-88; pub. mem. USIA Insp. Mission, Argentina, 1971. Officer AUS, 1955-58. Decorated Commendation medal. Fellow Am. Bar Found. (life); mem. ABA (chmn. sect. adminstrv. law 1974-75, ho. of dels. 1978-88, bd. govs. 1982-86, chmn. com. on fgn. and internat. orgns. 1986-87, lawyers in govt. com. 1980-82), FBA (nat. coun. 1966-82), Inter-Am. Bar Assn., Bar Assn. D.C. (chmn. adminstrv. law sect. 1970-71, bd. dirs. 1971-72), George Washington U. Law Assn. (pres. 1974-77), Smithsonian Instn. (nat. bd. dirs. 1991-97), Federalist Soc., Soc. Mayflower Desc., Washington Golf and Country Club, Met. Club, Nat. Lawyers Club (Washington), Farmington Country Club (Charlottesville, Va.), Knight of Malta. Republican. Roman Catholic. Administrative and regulatory, General practice, Private international. Home: 4111 N Ridgeview Rd Arlington VA 22207-4617 also: 7222 E Gainey Ranch Rd Scottsdale AZ 85258-1529 Office: 1700 K St NW Ste 700 Washington DC 20006-3813 also: 107 Park Washington Ct Falls Church VA 22046-4519 also: Falkenstrasse 14, 8008 Zurich Switzerland

**HARRISON, MARK ISAAC,** lawyer; b. Pitts., Oct. 17, 1934; s. Coleman and Myrtle (Seidenman) H.; m. Ellen R. Gier, June 15, 1958; children: Lisa, Jill. AB, Antioch Coll., 1957; LLB, Harvard U., 1960. Bar: Ariz. 1961, Colo. 1991. Law clk. to justices Ariz. Supreme Ct., 1960-61; ptnr. Harrison, Harper, Christian & Dichter, Phoenix, 1966-93, Bryan Cave, LLP, Phoenix, 1993—; adj. prof. U. Ariz. Coll. Law, 1995-97; nat. bd. visitors, 1996—. Coauthor: Arizona Appellate Practice, 1966; editorial bd. ABA/BNA Lawyers Manual on Profl. Conduct, 1983-86; contbr. articles to profl. jours. Bd. dirs. Careers for Youth, 1963-67, pres., 1966-67; vice-chmn. Maricopa County Dem. Cen. Com., 1967-68, Ariz. Dem. Com., 1969-70, legal counsel, 1970-72; del. Dem. Nat. Conv., 1968; chmn. Phoenix City bond Adv. Commn., 1976-79; pres. Valley Commerce Assn., 1978; bd. dirs. Planned Parenthood of Cen. and No. Ariz., 1992-98, pres., 1995. Fellow Am. Bar Found., Am. Acad. Appellate Lawyers (pres. 1993-94); mem. ABA (chmn. commn. pub. understanding law 1984-87, standing com. profl. discipline 1976-84, chmn. 1982-84, chmn. coord. com. on professionalism 1987-89, com. on women in the profession, ethics com. 1999—, Michael Franck Profl. Responsibility award 1996), Assn. Profl. Responsibility Lawyers (pres. 1992-93), Maricopa County Bar Assn. (pres. 1970), Am. Bd. Trial Advocates, State Bar Ariz. (bd. govs. 1971-77, pres. 1975-76), Ariz. Bar Found. (pres. 1991), Am. Inns of Ct. (master, pres. Sandra Day O'Connor chpt. 1993-94), Nat. Conf. Bar Pres. (pres. 1977-78), Western States Bar Conf. (pres. 1978-79), Am. Judicature Soc. (exec. com. 1983-86, bd. dirs. 1983-87), Ariz. Civil Liberties Union, Harvard Law Sch. Assn. (nat. exec. oun. 1980-84), Am. Law Inst. (nat. coun., lawyers com. for human rights). General civil litigation, Professional liability. Office: Bryan Cave 2 N Central Ave Ste 2200 Phoenix AZ 85004-4406

**HARRISON, MICHAEL,** lawyer; b. May 27, 1957; s. Michael Sr. and Jane (Venable) H.; m. Nina Lucas Harrison, Oct. 19, 1996. BA with honors, Rutgers Coll., 1982; JD, Harvard, 1985. Bar: U.S. Dist. Ct. N.J. 1986. Atty. Clapp & Eisenberg, N.J., 1985-86, Kesley Drye and Warren, N.Y.C., 1986-87, Schnader, Harrison, Segal & Lewis, Phila., 1987-92; cer. practice, 1992; v.p., gen. counsel Groupe Danone S.A., Stamford, Conn., 1992—; asst. adj. prof. N.Y. U. Mgmt. Inst., 1993—. bd. dirs. Jr. Achievement Southwestern, Conn., 1996—, vice chmn. devel., 1997. Sgt. USMC, 1975-80; capt. USAR, 1997—. Mem. ABA, Nat. Bar. Assn., N.J. State Bar Assn., Westchester County Bar Assn. Mem. Carpatho Rusyn Orthodox Ch. General corporate, Administrative and regulatory, Labor. Office: 208 Harbor Dr Stamford CT 06902-7467 also: 120 White Plains Rd Tarrytown NY 10591-5526

**HARRISON, MICHAEL GREGORY,** judge; b. Lansing, Mich., Aug. 4, 1941; s. Gus and Jean D. (Fuller) H.; m. Deborah L. Dunn, June 17, 1972; children: Abigail Ann, Adam Christopher, Andrew Stephen. AB, Albion (Mich.) Coll., 1963; JD, U. Mich., 1966; postgrad., George Washington U. Bar: Mich. 1966, U.S. Dist. Ct. (ea. and we. dists.) Mich. 1967. Asst. pros. atty. County of Ingham, Lansing, 1968-70, corp. counsel, 1970-76; judge 30th Jud. Cir. State of Mich., Lansing, 1976—; chief judge 30th Jud. Cir. State of Mich., Lansing, 1980-91; judge Ct. of Claims, 1979—; counsel Capital Region Airport Authority, Lansing, 1970-76, Ingham Med. Ctr., Lansing, 1970-76; chmn. Ingham County Bldg. Authority, Mason, Mich., 1971-76; adj. prof. Thomas M. Cooley Law Sch., Lansing, 1976—. Editor Litigation Control, 1996; contbr. chpt. to Michigan Municipal Law, Actions of Governing Bodies, 1980; contbr. articles to profl. jours. Mem. shared vision steering com. United Way-C. of C.; mem. adv. bd. Hospice of Lansing, 1989—; pres. Greater Lansing Urban League, 1974-76, Lansing Symphony Assn., 1974-76; chmn. Mid. Mich. chpt. ARC, Lansing, 1984-86; bd. dirs., sec. St. Lawrence Hosp., Lansing, 1980-88; bd. dirs. ARC Gt. Lakes Regional Blood Svcs., 1991-95, Lansing 2000, 1987—; mem. exec. bd. Chief Okemos coun. Boy Scouts Am.; mem. criminal justice adv. com. Olivet Coll.; hon. bd. dirs. Lansing Area Safety Coun.; mem. State Bar Bd. Commrs., 1993-96; mem. felony sentencing guidelines steering com., mem. caseflow mgmt. coordinating com., mem. juror use and mgmt. task force Mich. Supreme Ct. Recipient Disting. Citizens award Boy Scouts Am., Disting. Vol. award Ingham County Bar Assn., Disting. Alumni award Albion Coll. Fellow Am. Bar Found., Mich. Bar Found. (pres. 1991—); mem. ABA, Am. Judicature Soc. (bd. dirs. 1996—), Mich. Judges Assn. (treas. 1991, sec. 1992, 2d v.p. 1993, 1st v.p. 1994, pres. 1995), Nat. Conf. State Trial Judges (exec. com. 1991-94, vice-chmn. 1995-96, chmn. 1997-98), Country Club Lansing, Rotary. Republican. Congregationalist. Avocations: skiing, golf, tennis, travel, photography. Office: Cir Ct 407 N Cedar St Mason MI 48854-1012

**HARRISON, MOSES W., II,** state supreme court justice; b. Collinsville, Ill., Mar. 30, 1932; m. Sharon Harrison; children: Luke, Clarence. BA, Colo. Coll.; LLB, Washington U., St. Louis. Bar: Ill. 1958, Mo. 1958. Pvt. practice, 1958-73; judge 3d Jud. Cir., Ill., 1973-79, 5th Dist. Appellate Ct., Ill., 1979-92; justice Ill. Supreme Ct., 1992—. Mem. ABA, Am. Judicature Soc., Ill. State Bar Assn. (former bd. govs.), Madison County Bar Assn. (former pres.), Tri-City Bar Assn., Met. St. Louis Bar Assn., Justinian Soc. Office: 333 Salem Pl Ste 170 Fairview Heights IL 62208-1363

**HARRISON, ORRIN LEA, III,** lawyer; b. Dallas, July 1, 1949; s. Orrin Lea Jr. and Annie Bell (Lassig) H.; m. Paula Diane Wagnon, May 29, 1971; children: Orrin IV, Erin, Lindsey. BA cum laude, U. of South; JD with honors, So. Meth. U. Bar: Tex. 1974, U.S. Dist. Ct. (no., so., ea. and we. dists.) Tex., U.S. Ct. Appeals (5th and 11th cirs.), U.S. Supreme Ct. From assoc. to ptnr. Locke, Purnell, Boren, Laney & Neely, Dallas, 1974-87; shareholder Locke, Purnell, Rain & Harrell, Dallas, 1987-92; ptnr. Vinson & Elkins, Dallas, 1992—. Sec. 500 Inc., Dallas, 1981, treas., 1982; chancellor Ch. of Incarnation, Dallas, 1985-97; bd. dirs. Dallas Econ. Devel. Coun., 1986-92; mem. Leadership Dallas, 1988. Lt. JAGC, USN, 1971-75. Fellow Am. Bar Found., Tex. Bar Found. (life); mem. ABA, Tex. Bar Assn. (bd. dirs. 1993—96, Dallas Bar Found. (trustee 1993—), Am. Bd. of Trial Advocates (Dallas pres., 1989), Internat. Soc. of Barristers, Dallas Bar Assn. (bd. dirs. 1983-97, pres. 1992), Tex. Young Lawyers Assn. (bd. dirs. 1981-83), Dallas Young Lawyers Assn. (pres. 1980-81), Tower Club. Republican. Episcopalian. Avocations: skiing, jogging, mountain biking. Federal civil litigation, Antitrust, State civil litigation. Home: 3624 Normandy Ave Dallas TX 75205-2103 Office: Vinson & Elkins 2001 Ross Ave Ste 3700 Dallas TX 75201-2975

**HARRISON, PATRICK WOODS,** lawyer; b. St. Louis, July 14, 1946; s. Charles William and Carolyn (Woods) H.; m. Rebecca Tout, Dec. 23, 1967; children: Heather Ann, Heath Aaron. BS, Ind. U., 1968, JD, 1972. Bar: Ind. 1973, U.S. Dist. Ct. (so. dist.) Ind. 1973, U.S. Dist. Ct. Nebr. 1982, U.S. Supreme Ct. 1977. Assoc. Goltra, Cline, King & Beck, Columbus, Ind., 1972-73; ptnr. Goltra & Harrison, Columbus, 1973-78; pvt. practice Columbus, 1979-80; ptnr. Cline, King, Beck and Harrison, Columbus, 1980-85, Beck, Harrison & Dalmbert, Columbus, 1985—; Ind. Jud. Nominating Commn. nominee Ind. Supreme Ct., 1984. With U.S. Army, 1968-70. Fellow Ind. Trial Lawyers Assn. (bd. dirs. 1984—); mem. Am. Trial Lawyers Assn. Republican. Baptist. Avocation: golf. State civil litigation, Personal injury. Home: 14250 W Mount Healthy Rd Columbus IN 47201-9309 Office: Beck Harrison & Dalmbert 320 Franklin St Columbus IN 47201-6732

**HARRISON, RICHARD EDWARD,** lawyer; b. Oklahoma City, July 7, 1948; s. Charles William and Mary Elizabeth (Pettigrew) H.; m. Edna Lee Hanvey, Aug. 10, 1974; 1 child, Morgan Lee. BA cum laude, Coe Coll., 1970; JD, So. Meth. U., 1973. Bar: Tex. 1974, U.S. Dist Ct. (ea. dist.) Tex. 1974, U.S. Dist. Ct. (no. dist.) Tex. 1977, U.S. Ct. Appeals (5th cir.) 1977; cert. personal injury trial law, civil trial law, Tex. Assoc. Elliott & Nall, Sherman, Tex., 1974-75; assoc. Nall-Harrison-Nall, Sherman, 1975-76, Nall-Kyle-Harrison-Nall, Sherman, 1976-77; ptnr. Nance, Caston & Nall, Sherman, 1977-81, Henderson Bryant & Wolfe, Sherman, 1981-93; Law Office of Richard Harrison, 1993—. Bd. dirs. Texoma Valley council Boy Scouts Am., 1979-84; pres. Dallas Chamber Orch., 1997; trustee Coe Coll., Cedar Rapids, Iowa, 1980-88; pres. Sherman Community Players, 1981; civil trial adv. Nat. Bd. of Trial Advocacy. Fellow Tex. Bar Found.; mem. North Tex. Bar Assn. (pres. 1979-80), Grayson County Bar Assn. (pres. 1978-79), Tex. Young Lawyers Assn. (bd. dirs. 1982-84, Outstanding Young Lawyer of Tex. 1984-85), Sherman Jaycees (pres. 1978, Outstanding Citizen of Sherman award 1983), Rotary (pres. 1989), Nat. Assn. Railroad Trial Attys., Tex. Assn. Def. Counsel (editor Workers Comp. Newsletter, 1988), Episcopalian. Avocations: jogging, reading. State civil litigation, Personal injury, Federal civil litigation. Home: 4839 Allencrest Ln Dallas TX 75244-7710 Office: Law Office of Richard Harrison 307 W Washington St Ste 202 Sherman TX 75090-5883

**HARRISON, SAMUEL HUGHEL,** lawyer; b. Atlanta, Jan. 12, 1956; s. Gresham Hughel and Leslie (Powell) H.; m. Margaret Mary Carew, June 24, 1978; 1 child, Peter James. Student, Mercer U., 1974-75; BA magna cum laude, Washington & Lee U., 1978; JD cum laude, U. Ga., 1981. Bar: Ga. 1981, U.S. Dist. Ct. (no. dist.) Ga. 1981, U.S. Ct. Appeals (11th cir.) 1981, U.S. Dist. Ct. (mid. dist.) Ga. 1985. Ptnr. Harrison & Harrison, Lawrenceville, Ga., 1981-86, 87—; solicitor state ct. Gwinnett County, Lawrenceville, 1986. Vestryman St. Edward the Confessor Episcopal Ch., Lawrenceville, 1983-86; coun. del. Episcopal Diocese of Atlanta, 1986, 88; chancellor St. Matthew's Episcopal Ch., Snellville, Ga., 1998—; mem. Gwinnett County Bd. Registrations and Elections, 1991-96; mem. exec. com. Gwinnett Dems., 1991-96; troop scoutmaster Boy Scouts Am. Mem. Ga. Bar Assn. (mock trial com. young lawyers sect. 1987-88), Ga. Assn. Criminal Def. Lawyers, Nat. Assn. Criminal Def. Lawyers. Avocations: photography, hiking, backpacking, books. Criminal, Family and matrimonial. Office: Harrison & Harrison 151 W Pike St # 88 Lawrenceville GA 30045-4939

**HARRISON, SIMON M.,** lawyer, arbitrator, mediator; b. Miami, Aug. 20, 1954; s. Raymond and Doris (Harris) H.; m. Susan Marie Landefeld, Oct. 20, 1979; 1 child, Robert. BA, U. Fla., 1975, JD, 1978. Bar: Fla. 1978. Ptnr. Perch and Harrison, P.A., Lehigh Acres, Fla., 1978-93; pvt. practice

Ft. Myers, Fla., 1993—; bd. dirs. Gulf Abstract and Title Co., Ft. Myers. Mem. ABA, Fla. State Bar Assn., Colo. Bar Assn., Lee County Bar Assn. Democrat. Jewish. Avocations: scuba diving, golf. Real property, General civil litigation, Banking. Office: Perch and Harrison PA PO Box 7372 Fort Myers FL 33919-0361

**HARRISON, SUE ELLEN,** lawyer; b. Rockville Centre, N.Y., Aug. 2, 1948; d. James Emilin and Audrey (Fenton) H.; m. Michael McCarthy, July 1977 (div. Aug. 1995); children: Brooke, Fenton. BA, U. Colo., 1970, JD, 1974. Atty. VISTA/Nev. Indial Legal Svc., Reno, 1975; asst. atty. gen. Colo. Atty. Gen.'s Office, Denver, 1975-78; pvt. practice Boulder, Colo., 1978-80, 82-84; atty. U.S. EPA, Denver, 1980-82; commr. Colo. Water Quality Control Commn., Denver, 1987-96; asst. city atty. City of Boulder, 1984—. Avocations: hiking, tennis, skiing. Office: City of Boulder PO Box 791 Boulder CO 81306

**HARRISON, WILLIAM ALAN,** judge, arbitrator; b. Detroit, Mar. 13, 1947; s. Roger Holmes and Grace Jane (Campbell) H.; m. Janet Ellan Harrison, May 16, 1970; 1 child, Mark Campbell. BBA, U. Mich., 1969; JD, Wayne State U., 1974. Bar: Wash. 1974. Adminstrv. appeals judge Environ. Hearings Office State of Wash., Olympia, 1975—; arbitrator, 1984—. With USAR, 1970-76. Mem. ABA (exec. com. Nat. Conf. of Adminstrv. Law Judges 1993—), Wash. Athletic Club. Avocations: hunting, fishing. Office: Environmental Hearings Office PO Box 40903 Olympia WA 98504-0903

**HARROD, DANIEL MARK,** lawyer; b. Peoria, Ill., Sept. 23, 1945; s. Samuel Glenn and Dorothe Grace (White) H.; m. Amy Lynn Moore, June 4, 1993; children: Maggie, Emily. BA, Eureka (Ill.) Coll., 1967; JD, John Marshall Law Sch., 1975. Bar: Ill., U.S. Dist. Ct. Ill., U.S. Supreme Ct. Pub. defender Woodford County, Eureka, 1980-90; prin. Harrod Law Firm, Eureka. Chmn., bd. dirs. Peoria Area Civic Chorale, Peoria, 1990—. Lt. col. Ill. Air N.G., 1967-88. Mem. Rotary (sgt. at arms 1985—). Avocations: tennis, racquetball. Real property, Family and matrimonial, Criminal. Home: 206 Moody St Eureka IL 61530-1705 Office: Harrod Law Firm 107 E Eureka Ave Eureka IL 61530-1239

**HARROLD, BERNARD,** lawyer; b. Wells County, Ind., Feb. 5, 1925; s. James Delmer and Marie (Mounsey) H.; m. Kathleen Walker, Nov. 26, 1952; children—Bernard James, Camilla Ruth, Renata Jane. Student, Biarritz Am. U., 1945; A.B., Ind. U., 1949, LL.B., 1951. Bar: Ill. 1951. Since practiced in Chgo.; assoc., then mem. firm Kirkland, Ellis, Hodson, Chaffetz & Masters, 1951-67; sr. ptnr. Wildman, Harrold, Allen & Dixon, 1967—. Note editor: Ind. Law Jour, 1950-51; contbr. articles to profl. jours. Served with AUS, 1944-46, ETO. Fellow Am. Coll. Trial Lawyers, Acad. Law Alumni Fellows Ind. U. Sch. Law; mem. ABA, Ill. Bar Assn. (chmn. evidence program 1970), Chgo. Bar Assn, Law Club, Univ. Club, Order of Coif, Phi Beta Kappa, Phi Eta Sigma. Antitrust, General civil litigation, Environmental. Home: 809 Locust St Winnetka IL 60093-1821 Office: Wildman Harrold Allen & Dixon 225 W Wacker Dr Fl 28 Chicago IL 60606-1228 *I try to see people and events for what they really are, apply my talents, work hard, and pay attention to fairness.*

**HARROLD, DENNIS EDWARD,** lawyer; b. Los Angeles, Nov. 7, 1947; s. Edward Adron and Helen Lucille (Morrison) H.; m. Mary Ann Padgett, Oct. 21, 1972; children: Teresa Lauren, Derek Christopher. BS, Ind. U., 1969; JD, 1972. Bar: Ind. 1972, U.S. Dist. Ct. (so. dist.) Ind. 1972, U.S. Ct. Mil. Appeals 1972, U.S. Ct. Appeals (7th cir.) 1982, U.S. Supreme Ct. 1986. Pub. defender Shelby Superior Ct., Shelbyville, Ind., 1976-77; assoc. Adams & Cramer, Shelbyville, 1976-78; sec. Sosnick, Bate and Harrold, P.C., 1979-85; sec. Bate, Harrold & Bate, P.C., Shelbyville, 1985-96, McNeely, Stephenson Thopy and Harrold, 1996—; sch. bd. atty. Shelbyville Central Schs., Ind., 1978—; atty. Shelby County office of family and children 1987-96; sch. bd. atty. Blue River Career Programs, 1994—. Mem. adv. bd. Salvation Army. Shelbyville, 1982-92. Served to capt. U.S. Army, 1972-76, Korea. Named Hon. Mem. Bar Republic of Korea, Ministry of Justice, Seoul, 1975. Fellow Ind. Bar Found.; mem. ABA, Ind. State Bar Assn. (ho. of dels. 1982-85), Shelby County Bar Assn. (pres. 1990-91), Indpls. Bar Assn., Assn. Trial Lawyers Am., Nat. Sch. Bds. Assn. Council Sch. Attys., Internat. Legal Soc. Korea, Ind. Trial Lawyers Assn., Ind. Pub. Defender Council, dir. Shelby County C. of C., pres. 1996-97, trustee Shelby Rural Elec. Cmty. Fund, Inc. Lions, Elks. Republican. Roman Catholic. Personal injury, Insurance, General practice. Home: 2481 N Richard Dr Shelbyville IN 46176-9487 Office: McNeely Stephenson Thopy and Harrold 30 E Washington St Ste 400 Shelbyville IN 46176-1351

**HART, BROOK,** lawyer; b. N.Y.C., Aug. 24, 1941; s. Walter and Julie H.; m. Barbara Ingersoll, Nov., 1980; children—Morgan M., Lauren L., Ashley I., Ariel J. BA Johns Hopkins U., 1963; LL.B., Columbia U., 1966. Bar: N.Y. 1966, U.S. Ct. Appeals (9th cir.) 1967, Hawaii 1968, U.S. Supreme Ct. 1972, Calif. 1973. Law clk. to chief judge U.S. Dist. Ct. Hawaii, 1966-67; assoc. counsel Legal Aid Soc. Hawaii, 1968; assoc. Greenstein and Cowan, Honolulu, 1968-70; chief pub. defender State of Hawaii, 1970-72; co-founder, ptnr. Hart, Leavitt, Hall and Hunt, Honolulu, 1972-80; co-founder, ptnr. Hart and Wolff, Honolulu, 1980-96; sr. ptnr. Law Offices of Brook Hart, 1996—. instr. course U. Hawaii, 1972-73, lectr. Sch. Law, 1974—; apptd. Nat. Commn. to Study Def. Services, 1974, Planning Group for U.S. Dist. Ct. Hawaii, 1975; spl. counsel City Council of City and County of Honolulu, 1976-77, spl. investigative counsel to trustee in bankruptcy THC Fin. Corp., 1977; mem. Jud. Council State of Hawaii com. on revision state penal codes, 1984—; lectr. schs., profl., civic groups; mem. com. to select Fed. Pub. Defender Dist. of Hawaii, 1981, 95. Recipient Reginald Heber Smith award Nat. Legal Aid and Defender Assn., 1971; named Bencher, Am. Inn of Ct., Hawaii, 1982—. Fellow Am. Bd. Criminal Lawyers; mem. ABA, Hawaii Bar Assn., State Bar Calif., Am. Judicature Soc., Nat. Legal Aid and Defender Assn., Nat. Assn. Criminal Def. Lawyers, Calif. Attys. for Criminal Justice. Contbr. chpts. to books, articles to profl. pubs. Criminal, General civil litigation, Federal civil litigation. Office: 333 Queen St Honolulu HI 96813-4726

**HART, CLIFFORD HARVEY,** lawyer; b. Flint, Mich., Nov. 12, 1935; s. Max S. and Dorothy H. (Fineberg) H.; m. Alice Rosenberg, June 17, 1962; children: Michael F., David E., Steven A. AB, U. Mich., 1957, JD, 1960. Bar: Mich. 1960, U.S. Dist. Ct. (ea. and we. dists.) Mich. 1962; cert. civil trial advocate. Assoc. Stevens & Nelson, Flint, 1960-62; ptnr. White, Newblatt, Nelson & Hart, Flint, 1962-64; with Dean, Dean, Segar & Hart, P.C. and predecessor firms, Flint, 1965-95; pvt. practice Law Offices Clifford H. Hart, 1997—; adj. assoc. prof. Flint Sch. Mgmt., U. Mich., 1972—; lectr. Inst. Continuing Legal Edn., Mich.; lectr.iMIch. Jud. Inst. Pres. Vis. Nurse Assn., Flint, 1967; pres. Temple Beth El, 1973-75; trustee United Way Genesee County, 1981—, chmn. bd., 1990-91, sec., 1988-89, chmn. bd. dirs. Genesee County and Lapeer County, 1990-91; chair corp. adv. bd. U. Mich., Flint, 1988-93; mem. faculty Inst. Continuing Legal Edn., Ann Arbor, Mich., 1984—. Fellow Mich. Bar Found., Roscoe Pound Found.; mem. ABA, ATLA (bd. govs. 1979—, lectr., home budget and office com. 1980-84, 87-89, chair 1989-91, 98—, exec. com. 1984-85, 90-93, chmn. elections com. 1984-87, nat. parliamentarian 1990-91, nat. treas. 1991-92), Mich. State Bar Assn. (chmn. negligence law sect. 1981-82, rep. assembly 1975-81), Mich. Trial Lawyers Assn. (pres. 1977-78, lectr.), Genesee County Bar Assn. (pres. 1975-76), Am. Judicature Soc., Nat. Bd. Trial Advocacy (cert.), B'nai B'rith (past pres.). Democrat. State civil litigation, General civil litigation, Federal civil litigation. Office: Genesee Tower 120 E 1st St Ste 1915 Flint MI 48502-1915

**HART, JOHN CLIFTON,** lawyer; b. Chgo., Apr. 29, 1945; s. Clifton Edwin and Eleanor (Zielinski) H.; m. Dianne Lynn Wenzel, Jan. 18, 1969; children: David Clifton, Steven Philip, Kristin Dianne. BS, Loyola U., 1967; postgrad., Northwestern U., 1967-69; JD, U. N.D., 1972. Bar: Minn. 1973, U.S. Dist. Ct. Minn. 1973, Tex. 1979, U.S. Dist. Ct. (no. dist.) Tex. 1979, U.S. Dist. Ct. we dist.) Tex. 1981, U.S. Dist. Ct. (ea. dist.) Okla. 1981, U.S. Dist. Ct. (ea. dist.) Tex. 1984, U.S. Dist. Ct. (no. dist.) Okla. 1999, U.S. Ct. Appeals (5th and 8th cirs.) 1980. Ptnr. Robins, Zelle, Larson & Kaplan, Mpls., 1973-81; v.p. Gollaher & Hart, Dallas, 1981-84; pres. Hart & Engen, Dallas, 1984-87, Hart & Assocs., Dallas, 1987-88; mng. ptnr. S.W. regional office Robins, Kaplan, Miller & Ciresi, 1988-93; ptnr. Cantey & Hanger L.L.P., 1993-98, Brown, Herman, Dean, Wiseman, Liser & Hart, L.L.P., 1998—; lawyer; b. Chgo., Apr. 29, 1945; s. Clifton Edwin and Eleanor (Zielinski) H.; m. Dianne Lynn Wenzel, Jan. 18, 1969; children: David Clifton, Steven Philip, Kristin Dianne. BS, Loyola U., Chgo., 1967; postgrad. Northwestern U., 1967-69; JD, U. N.D., 1972. Bar: Minn. 1973, U.S. Dist. Ct. Minn. 1973, Tex. 1979, U.S. Dist. Ct. (no. dist.) Tex. 1979, U.S. Ct. Appeals (8th cir.) 1980, U.S. Ct. Appeals (5th cir.) 1980, U.S. Dist. Ct. (we. dist.) Tex. 1981, U.S. Dist. Ct. (ea. dist.) Okla. 1983, U.S. Dist. Ct. (ea. dist.) Tex. 1984, U.S. Supreme Ct., 1997. Ptnr. Robins, Zelle, Larson & Kaplan, Mpls., 1973-81; v.p. Gollaher & Hart, Dallas, 1981-84; pres. Hart & Engen, Dallas, 1984-87, pres. Hart & Assocs., 1987-88, mng. ptnr. S.W. regional office of Robins, Kaplan, Miller & Ciresi, 1988-93; ptnr. Cantey & Hanger, L.L.P., Dallas, 1993-98, ptnr. Brown, Herman, Dean, Wiseman, Liser & Hart, L.L.P., 1998—. Contbr. articles to profl. publs. Maj. USAF, 1969-73. Mem. ABA, State Bar Tex., Tex. Assn. Def. Counsel, Tarrant County Bar Assn., Fedn. Ins. and Corporate Counsel, Def. Rsch. Inst., Loss Exec. Assn. Republican. Lutheran. Contbr. articles to profl. jours. Maj. USAF, 1969-73. Mem. ABA, State Bar Tex., Tex. Assn. Def. Counsel, Tarrant County Bar Assn., Fedn. Ins. and Corporate Counsel, Def. Rsch. Inst., Loss Exec. Assn. Republican. Lutheran. Insurance, Federal civil litigation, State civil litigation. Office: Brown Herman Dean Wiseman Liser & Hart LLP 306 W 7th St Ste 200 Fort Worth TX 76102-4905

**HART, JOHN EDWARD,** lawyer; b. Portland, Oreg., Nov. 21, 1946; s. Wilbur Elmore and Daisy Elizabeth (Bowen) H.; m. Bianca Mannheimer, Mar. 29, 1968 (div. 1985); children: Ashley Rebecca, Rachel Bianca, Eli Jacob; m. Serena Callahan, Nov. 9, 1991; 1 child, Katelyn Elizabeth. Student, Oreg. State U., 1965-66; BS, Portland State U., 1971; JD, Lewis and Clark Coll., 1974. Bar: Oreg. 1974, U.S. Dist. Ct. Oreg. 1974, U.S. Ct. Appeals (9th cir.) 1975. Ptnr. Schwabe, Williamson and Wyatt, Portland, 1973-92, Hoffman, Hart & Wagner, Portland, 1992—; adj. faculty U. Oreg. Dental Sch., 1987—; legal cons. Oreg. Chpt. Obstetricians, Gynecologists, Portland, 1985—, Am. Cancer Soc. Mammography Project, 1987—. Contbr. articles to profl. jours. Co-chmn. Alameda Sch. Fair, Portland, 1983. With U.S. Army, 1967-68. Mem. ABA, Am. Coll. Trial Lawyers, Am. Bd. Trial Advocates (pres. 1995) Am., Inns of Ct., Oreg. State Bar Assn., Oreg. Assn. Def. Counsel (pres. 1989), Multnomah Athletic Club. Democrat. Presbyterian. Avocations: jogging, weight lifting, outdoor activities. General civil litigation, Personal injury, Health. Office: Hoffman Hart & Wagner 1000 SW Broadway Ste 2000 Portland OR 97205-3072

**HART, JOSEPH THOMAS CAMPBELL,** lawyer; b. Orange, N.J., May 23, 1936; s. Maurice I. and Anne G. (Campbell) H. AB, Fordham U., 1958, JD, 1961. Bar: N.Y. 1962, U.S. Dist. Ct. (so. and ea. dists.) N.Y. 1966, U.S. Ct. Appeals (2d cir.) 1974, U.S. Ct. Appeals (5th cir.) 1983. Assoc. Dewey, Ballatine, Bushby, Palmer & Wood, N.Y.C., 1962-65; assoc. Fulton, Rowe, Hart & Coon, N.Y.C., 1965-71, ptnr., 1971—; sec. The G. Unger Vetlesen Found., N.Y.C., 1987, The Ambrose Monell Found., N.Y.C., 1994. Mem. Assn. of the Bar of the City of N.Y. General corporate, General practice, Product liability. Office: Fulton Rowe Hart & Coon One Rockefeller Plaza New York NY 10020

**HART, LAUREN L.,** lawyer; b. Providence, Jan. 30, 1952; d. Giovanni (John) and Ruth Elsie (Schultheis) Luongo. BS in Microbiology, U. R.I., 1975, MS in Food Sci. Tech., 1981; JD, Oklahoma City U., 1998. Bar: Okla. 1998; lic. intellectual property lawyer. Mktg. asst. Agawam Creative Mktg., Rowley, Mass., 1977-79; asst. sales & mktg. Ocean State Jobbers Inc., North Kingstown, R.I., 1979-81; rsch. assoc. U. R.I., Kingston, 1979-81; mktg. rep. lab supply & chem. sales Ea. Scientific Co., Providence, 1981-82; mktg. mgr., v.p. mktg., v.p. corp., ops. officer Alan's Bus. Machines Inc., Barre, Vt., 1983-89; chief exec. officer Continental Resource Group, Ltd., Barre, Vt., 1989—. Mem. U. R.I. Law Rev. Mem. ABA, NAFE, Okla. Bar Assn., Women Bus. Owners Vt., Am. Intellectual Property Lawyers Assn., Soc. Indsl. Microbiology and Biotech., Inst. Food Technologists (Z John Ordahl award 1981), Advt./Image/Mktg. Assn. (pres. 1985-86), Ptnrs. of the Cornell Fine Arts Mus. (founding mem., chmn. pub. rels. 1990-91, pres. 1991-92),. Avocation: black & white darkroom, photography. Intellectual property, Trademark and copyright, Patent. Home: 7629 Hanover Way Oklahoma City OK 73132-6119

**HART, ROBERT CAMILLUS,** lawyer, company executive; b. Milw., July 9, 1934; s. Joseph John and Lorraine Cecilia (Zella) H.; m. Barbara Gormican, May 23, 1959; children: John, Thomas, Anne, Mary. BS, Marquette U., 1956, LLB, 1958. Bar: Wis. 1958. Pvt. practice Milw., 1958-61; atty. Northwestern Mut. Life Ins. Co., Milw., 1961-62; gen. counsel S.C. Johnson & Son, Inc., Racine, Wis., 1962—, now also sr. v.p., sec.; bd. dirs. Johnson Internat. Inc., Johnson Heritage Trust Co., Racine Comml. Airport Corp. Mem. ABA, Wis. Bar Assn., Am. Corp. Counsel Assn. (dir. Wis. chpt. 1985-88), Racine Country Club. Avocations: nature photography, fishing, tennis. General corporate. Home: 13590 N Pima Spring Way Tucson AZ 85737-6872 Office: S C Johnson & Son Inc 1525 Howe St Racine WI 53403-2237

**HART, THOMAS HUGHSON, III,** lawyer; b. Montgomery, Ala., Aug. 19, 1955; s. Thomas H. and Nora A. (McDonald) H.; m. Jane Elizabeth Morgan, Aug. 4, 1979; children: Morgan Elizabeth, Katherine MacDonald, Mary MacQuarrie, Teresa Jane, Thomas MacGregor. BA in Polit. Sci., Furman U., 1977; JD, U. S.C., 1980. Bar: S.C. 1980, U.S. Dist. Ct. S.C. 1981, U.S. Ct. Appeals (4th cir.) 1981, U.S. Ct. Appeals (11th cir.) 1982, U.S. Ct. Appeals (10th cir.) 1985, U.S. Supreme Ct. 1987, U.S. Ct. Appeals (8th cir.) 1990, U.S. Ct. Appeals (3d cir.) 1991, V.I., 1991. Assoc. Blatt and Fales, Barnwell, S.C., 1980-83; ptnr. Ness, Motley, Loadholt, Richardson & Poole, P.A., Barnwell, 1983-90, Brady, Hart & Jacobs, Christiansted, V.I., 1990-93; ptnr. Alkon, Rhea & Hart, Christiansted, 1993—. Editor S.C. Law Rev., 1978-80. Baruch scholar Furman U., Greenville, S.C., 1973-77; James Verner scholar U. S.C. Law Sch., 1978, Paul Cooper scholar, 1979. Mem. ABA, S.C. Trial Lawyers Assn. (bd. govs.), Assn. Trial Lawyers Am., S.C. Bar Assn., V.I. Bar Assn., Barnwell County C. of C. (bd. dirs.). Roman Catholic. Product liability, Environmental, Federal civil litigation. Home: 2 Boetzburg Christiansted VI 00820-4516 Office: 2115 Queen St Christiansted VI 00820-4835

**HART, WILLIAM THOMAS,** federal judge; b. Joliet, Ill., Feb. 4, 1929; s. William Michael and Geraldine (Archambeault) H.; m. Catherine Motta, Nov. 27, 1954; children: Catherine Hart Fornero, Susan Hart DaMario, Julie Hart Boesen, Sally Hart Collins, Nancy Hart McLaughlin. JD, Loyola U., Chgo., 1951. Bar: Ill. 1951, U.S. Dist. Ct. 1951, U.S. Ct. Appeals (7th cir.) 1954, U.S. Ct. Appeals (D.C. cir.) 1977. Asst. U.S. atty. U.S. Dist. Ct. (no. dist.) Ill., Chgo., 1954-56; assoc. Defrees & Fiske, 1956-59; spl. asst. atty. gen. State of Ill., 1957-58; assoc. then ptnr. Schiff, Hardin & Waite, 1959-82; spl. asst. state's atty. Cook County, Ill., 1960; judge U.S. Dist. Ct. Ill., 1982—; now sr. judge; mem. exec. com. U.S. Dist. Ct. (no. dist.) Ill., 1988-92; mem. com. on adminstrn. fed. magistrates sys., Jud. Conf. U.S., 1987-92, 7th cir. Jud. Coun., 1990-92; mem. edn. com. Fed. Jud. Ctr., 1994—. Pres. adv. bd. Mercy Med. Ctr., Aurora, Ill., 1980-81; v.p. Aurora Blood Bank, 1972-77; trustee Rosary H.S., 1981-82, 93-98; bd. dirs. Chgo. Legal Asst. Found., 1974-76. Served with U.S. Army, 1951-53. Decorated Bronze Starl named to Joliet/Will County Hall of Pride, 1992. Mem. 7th Cir. Bar Assn., Law Club, Legal Club, Soc. Trial Lawyers, Union League Club of Aurora, Ill. (hon.), Inn of Ct. Office: US Dist Ct No Dist Ill US Courthouse Rm 2246 219 S Dearborn St Chicago IL 60604-1702

**HARTER, RALPH MILLARD PETER,** lawyer, educator; b. Auburn, N.Y., Mar. 15, 1946; s. Donald Robert and Ruth (Ashdown) H.; m. Robin Ann Bampton, June 29, 1968 (div. Oct. 1994); m. Leslie J. Teague, Sept. 13, 1997; children: Robin Brooke, Donald Bampton. BA, Hobart Coll., 1968; JD, Cornell U., 1972. Bar: Pa. 1972, U.S. Dist. Ct. (ea. dist.) Pa. 1972, N.Y. 1981, U.S. Dist. Ct. (we. dist.) N.Y. 1981. Assoc. Duane, Morris & Heckscher, Phila., 1972-81, Harter, Secrest & Emery, Rochester, N.Y., 1981-83; ptnr. Goldstein, Goldman, Kessler & Underberg, Rochester, 1983-91, Sutton, DeLeeuw, Clark & Darcy, Rochester, 1991-94; mng. ptnr. Burke, Albright, Harter & Rzepka, LLP, Rochester, 1994—; educator elder law issues, right to die, ethics, trusts and estates issues. V.p., gen. counsel, bd. dirs. Otetiana council Inc., Boy Scouts Am., Rochester, 1982—; mem. various coms. Episcopal Diocesen and Ch., Phila. and Rochester, 1972—; chair bd. dirs. Episcopal Ch. Home, 1995—; bd. trustees Colls. of Seneca (Hobart & William Smith Colls.) 1987-96; bd. dirs. Allendale Columbia Sch., 1991-96; trustee Sigma Phi Ednl. Found., N.Y.C., 1990—. Served with USAR, 1969-75. Mem. ABA, N.Y. State Bar Assn. (various sects., lectr.), Pa. Bar Assn., Phila. Bar Assn., Monroe County Bar Assn., Nat. Acad. Elder Law Attys., Rochester Area C. of C. (United Way coms. 1984-96), Alzheimer's Disease and Related Disorders Assn. Inc. (pres., gen. counsel, bd. dirs. 1981—), Assn. of Adirondack Scout Camps (bd. dirs. 1986-93), Cornell U. Law Sch. Assn., Hobart Coll. Alumni Assn. and Alumni Council (pres. 1984-86), Hobart Coll. Statesmen Athletic Assn. (gen. counsel, bd. dirs. 1983—), Hobart Coll. Club of Rochester (pres. 1984—), The Genesse Valley Club (Rochester), Webhannet Golf Club (Kennebunkport, Maine), Delta chpt. Sigma Phi. Republican. Avocations: flyfishing, duck decoy carving, white water rafting, canoeing, golf. Estate planning, Probate, Estate taxation. Home: Tuckaway Farm 98 Canfield Rd Pittsford NY 14534-9709 Office: Burke Albright Harter & Rzepka LLP 500 East Ave Ste 200 Rochester NY 14607-1912

**HARTGLASS, LORI ROBIN,** lawyer; b. Bronxville, N.Y., Oct. 17, 1955. BS in Mgmt., SUNY, Binghamton, 1976; JD, U. Miami, 1984. Bar: Fla. 1984. Atty., ptnr. Holland & Knight LLP, Miami, Fla., 1984-93, Ft. Lauderdale, Fla., 1993—. Chairperson sports challenge Cystic Fibrosis Found., Miami, 1989-96, chairperson Gt. Strides Walk, Ft. Lauderdale, 1997—; trustee Mus. Art, Ft. Lauderdale, 1994-95; mem. leadership coun. Fla. Grand Opera, 1998—. Olympics torchbearer United Way/Atlanta Com. Olympic Games, Ft. Lauderdale, 1996; recipient Golden Rule award J.C. Penney, 1996, VISTA award Nat. Assn. Women Bus. Owners, 1997. Mem. ABA, Internat. Bar Assn. (Fla. rep. women's interest group com.), Fla. Bar Assn., Assn. Comml. Real Estate Women (pres., nat. network del., bd. dirs. 1987-92), Comml. Real Estate Women Ft. Lauderdale/Palm Beach (founding pres., bd. dirs. 1993-98). Office: Holland and Knight LLP 1 E Broward Blvd Fort Lauderdale FL 33301-1804

**HARTIGAN, JOHN DAWSON, JR.,** judge; b. Rochester, Minn., Aug. 4, 1945; s. John D. and Catherine (Fizpatrick) H. Student, U. Notre Dame, 1965; JD, Creighton U., 1978. Assoc. Kennedy Holland DeLacy & Svoboda, Omaha, 1978-85, ptnr., 1985-91; dist. judge Dist. Ct. Nebr., Omaha, 1991—; adj. faculty Sch. of Law Creighton U., 1994—. Mem. ABA, Nebr. Bar Assn., Omaha Bar Assn., Alpha Sigma Nu. Avocation: triathlon. Home: 820 N 38th St Omaha NE 68131-1817 Office: Hall of Justice 1701 Farnam St Omaha NE 68102-2003

**HARTKOP, JEFFREY WELLS,** lawyer; b. Detroit; s. Henry H. and Georgina R. H.; m. Kimberlee June, June 9, 1984; children: Zachary Wells, Nathan Henry, Aaron Nelson. BS, Wayne State U., 1977; JD, U. Detroit, 1987. Atty. Garun Luvow et al, Detroit, 1988-90, Boyer, Churilla & Dawson, Sterling Heights, Mich., 1990—. Mem. State Bar Mich., Mich. Trial Lawyers Assn. (Macomb chpt. pres. 1996-97), Macomb County Bar Assn. (mediator 1995—). Avocation: music. Personal injury, Product liability, Labor. Office: Boyer Churilla & Dawson 43805 Van Dyke Ave Sterling Heights MI 48314-2446

**HARTLEY, CARL WILLIAM, JR.,** lawyer; b. Carthage, Mo., Aug. 12, 1946; s. Carl William and Doris Eillene (Wilcox) H.; m. Martha Anderson Gouch (div. 1991); children: Zach, Jordan. BS, U. Fla., 1968, JD with High Honors, 1976. Bar: Fla. 1976, U.S. Dist. Ct. (so. dist.) Fla. 1976, U.S. Dist. Ct. (mid. dist.) Fla. 1980. Sales rep. Scott Paper Co., Miami, Fla., 1971-73; assoc. Grenbherg, Traurig et al., Miami, 1976-80; ptnr. Thomas Thomas Hartley & Spraker, Orlando, Fla., 1980-83, Holland & Knight, Orlando, 1983-85, Hartley, Wall & Norman, Orlando, 1985—. Editor U. Fla. Law Rev., 1976. Democrat. Methodist. Avocations: fishing, hunting, camping. General civil litigation, Real property, Contracts commercial. Office: Hartley Wall & Norman PO Box 2168 Orlando FL 32802-2168

**HARTLEY, WADE LEON,** lawyer; b. Evergreen, Ala., Oct. 17, 1968; s. Leon and Karen (Kendall) H.; m. Susan Fisher, July 8, 1995. AA, Jefferson Davis Jr. Coll., Brewton, Ala., 1989; BA cum laude, Birmingham-So. U., 1991; JD, U. Ala., Tuscaloosa, 1994. Bar: Ala. 1994, U.S. Dist. Ct. (mid. dist.) Ala. 1994, Poarch Creek Tribal Bar 1996. Pvt. practice, Atmore, Ala.; tribal prosecutor Poarch (Ala.) Creek Indians, 1996—, mem. drug ct. team, 1997—. Vol. Boy Scouts Am., 1986—, Youth Leadership Atmore, 1997—, Am. Reads, 1998. Recipient dist. award of merit Gulf Coast coun. Boy Scouts Am., 1989, Founder's award Yustaga Lodge, 1989. Mem. Lions, Order of Arrow, Sigma Chi (life). Presbyterian. Avocations: collecting scouting memorabilia, antiques, reading. General practice, Criminal, Family and matrimonial. Office: PO Box 25 Atmore AL 36504-0025

**HARTMAN, DOUGLAS COLE,** lawyer; b. Richmond, Va., Jan. 7, 1950; s. Joseph David and Lillian Marie (Gannon) H.; m. Christine C. Coile, May 3, 1980; children: Kimberly, Jonathan, Kelly. BBA, Univ. Miami, Coral Gables, 1972, JD, 1975. Bar: Fla. 1975, U.S. Dist. Ct. (so. dist.) Fla. 1977, U.S. Ct. Appeals (5th and 11th cirs.) 1977. Asst. state atty. State Attys. Office 11th Jud. Cir., Miami, 1974-79; assoc. Offices of Eugene Spellman, Miami, 1979-80; ptnr. Dean & Hartman, P.A., Miami, 1980-90; mng. ptnr. Hartman & Cornely, P.A., Miami, 1990—; bd. dirs. Fla. Assn. Criminal Def. Attys., Miami, 1982-86; mem. Fla. Bar Criminal Rules Com., Tallahassee, 1980-81, Dade County Bar Assn. Criminal Com., Miami 1984-85. Mem. ch. coun. Christ the King Luth. Ch., Miami, 1991-95, pres. ch. found., 1994-96. Hon. mem. Dade County Police Benevolent Assn., Miami, 1980. Avocations: swimming, golf, coaching, football, basketball. Criminal, Administrative and regulatory, Probate. Home: 1000 Pine Branch Dr Weston FL 33326-2840 Office: Hartman & Cornely PA 10680 NW 25th St Ste 200 Miami FL 33172-2108

**HARTMAN, HONEY,** lawyer; b. Columbus, Ohio, July 8, 1939. BS, Ohio State U., 1983; JD, U. Miami, 1987. Criminal. Home: 5618 SW 36th St Hollywood FL 33023-6106

**HARTMAN, RONALD G.,** lawyer; b. Harrisburg, Pa., Aug. 13, 1950; s. Manny and Helene (Levine) H.; m. Leslie Ann Golomb, May 31, 1980; children: Molly, Samuel. BA, U. Pitts., 1972, JD, 1975. Bar: Pa. 1975, U.S. Dist. Ct. (we. dist.) Pa. 1975. Assoc. Baskin & Sears, Pitts., 1975-84; ptnr. Reed Smith Shaw & McClay, Pitts., 1985—. Bd. dirs. Citizens League Southwestern Pa., Pitts., 1988, Am. Cancer Soc.-Allegheny County chpt., Pitts., exec. com., 1990—; bd. dirs. Jewish Family and Children's Svc. of Pitts., pres. 1995-97; bd. dirs. United Jewish Fedn. Greater Pitts., 1995-97, 98—, co-chmn. bus. and profl. divsn., 1989-91, mem. steering com. atty. divsn., 1992—; chair Cardoza Soc., 1999—; bd. dirs. Jewish Chronicle, 1997—. Mem. ABA, Pa. Bar Assn., Allegheny County Bar Assn. Jewish. Avocations: jogging, reading. Real property, Landlord-tenant, Contracts commercial. Home: 500 Glen Arden Dr Pittsburgh PA 15208-2809 Office: Reed Smith Shaw & McClay 435 6th Ave Ste 2 Pittsburgh PA 15219-1886

**HARTMANN, CARL JOSEPH,** lawyer, consultant; b. Rochester, N.Y., Apr. 21, 1954; s. Carl Joseph and Mary (Ercel) H.; m. Kimberly Lynn Japinga, Feb. 15, 1998. JD, Antioch Coll., 1979. Bar: N.Mex. 1980, V.I. 1993, U.S. Dist. Ct. N.Mex. 1981, U.S. Ct. Appeals (10th cir.) 1982, U.S. Ct. Appeals (3d cir.) 1988, D.C. 1994, U.S. Supreme Ct. 1985. Jud. intern U.S. Supreme Ct., Washington, 1979; jud. clk. N.Mex. Ct. Appeals, Santa Fe, 1980-81; asst. prof. law Antioch Coll. Sch. of Law, Washington, 1982-85; ptnr. Law Offices of Carl Hartmann, Albuquerque, 1985-87; assoc. Campbell, Arellano & Rich, St. Thomas, V.I., 1988-89; special counsel Merrill Lynch Pvt. Capital, N.Y.C., 1989-90; ptnr. Law Offices of Carl Hartmann, N.Y.C., 1991—; gen. counsel Emerging Comms., Inc., St. Croix, V.I., 1997-98, Innovative Comms., Corp., St. Croix, 1998—; spl. counsel U.S. Park Svc., Santa Fe, 1987. Author: Legal Analysis for Clinical Students, 1981; co-author: Private Law: An Introduction to Torts, 1980, Clinical Perspectives on Fair Employment, 1979; co-editor-in-chief Antioch Sch. of Law--Law Rev., 1979. Mem. sch. adv. bd. Our Lady of Czestochowa Sch., Paulus Hook, N.J., 1998. Mem. Assn. of the Bar of the City of N.Y., V.I. Bar Assn. Roman Catholic. Avocations: fencing, flying, scuba, skiing, golf. Federal civil litigation, General corporate, Labor. Home: 126 Sussex St Jersey City NJ 07302-6405 Office: 72-08 243rd St New York NY 11363

**HARTMANN, JAMES M.,** lawyer; b. N.Y.C., Mar. 8, 1946; s. Morton Woodrow and Miriam Rose H.; m. Nancy K. Deming, May 20, 1988. BA, St. Lawrence U., 1967; MA, U. Wis., 1968; JD, Bklyn. Law Sch., 1974. Bar:

N.Y. 1975, U.S. Dist. Ct. (so. and ea. dists.) N.Y. 1975, U.S. Ct. Appeals (2d cir.) 1975, U.S. Dist. Ct. (no. and we. dists.) N.Y. 1989, U.S. Supreme Ct. 1991. Gen. atty. U.S. Dept. Justice, N.Y.C., 1975-76, trial atty., 1976-79; pvt. practice N.Y.C., 1979-86, Delhi, N.Y., 1989—; head dept. litig. Frenkel & Hershkowitz, N.Y.C., 1986-89; spl. dist. atty. Del. County, Delhi; mem. libr. com. Supreme Ct., Delhi, 1992—. Mem. N.Y. State Bar Assn., N.Y. Trial Lawyers Assn., N.Y. State Criminal Def. Lawyers Assn., Del. County Bar Assn. (mem. grievance com. 1994—), Pi Sigma Alpha. General civil litigation, Criminal. Office: PO Box 206 Rte 10 Delhi NY 13753

**HARTNETT, DAN DENNIS,** lawyer; b. Houston, Aug. 21, 1946; s. Edgar Douglas Hartnett and Walterine Mary Martindale; m. Lucille Ann Mellen, Dec. 31, 1945; children: D'Anne Hartnett Gloris, Jeffrey Scott Hartnett. BA in Polit. Sci., U. Houston, 1972; JD, U. Tex., 1975. Bar: Tex. 1975, U.S. Dist. Ct. (we. dist.) Tex. 1977. Ptnr. Orsinger & Hartnett, San Antonio, 1975-77; owner Law Offices D.D. Hartnett, San Antonio, 1977-80; sr. atty. Valero Energy Corp., San Antonio, 1980-94; pvt. practice San Antonio, 1994—; bd. dirs. Natural Gas Group Inc., Austin, 1989-94. V.p.-sec. Cath. Consultation Ctr., San Antonio, 1987-93. Sgt. U.S. Army, 1966-70. Mem. Tex. Bar Assn., San Antonio Bar Assn., Tex. Assn. Bus. (life mem.), San Antonio Breakfast Club (pres. 1979—). Roman Catholic. Avocations: golf, travel. Condemnation, Real property, State and local taxation. Office: 8407 Bandera Rd Ste 133-145 San Antonio TX 78250-2570

**HARTNETT, MAURICE A., III,** judge; b. Dover, Del., Jan. 20, 1927; s. Maurice and Anna Louise (Morris) H.; m. Elizabeth Anne Hutchinson, Aug. 21, 1965; 1 child, Anne Elizabeth. *His ancestors, on his mother's side, include John Harris, who in 1720 founded Harris's Ferry, now Harrisburg, Pennsylvania. In 1665 John Winder came to Manokan section of Maryland from Virginia. In 1745 Captain John Morris emigrated to Somerset County, Maryland from Long Island, New York. Colonel Henry Ridgely, about 1657, emigrated to Ann Arundal County, Maryland. William Giles, in 1672, emigrated to Somerset County, Maryland. On his father's side, William Hartnett and Catherine McKinery immigrated from Ireland in 1853 and located in Kent County, Delaware. The Hartnett family engaged in the lumber business in Dover, Delaware for over 100 years* Student, Washington Coll.-Chestertown, Md., 1946-47; BS, U. Del.-Newark, 1951; postgrad. Georgetown U., 1951; JD, George Washington U., 1954; EdM, U. Del., 1956. Bar: Del. 1954, U.S. Dist. Ct. Del. 1957, U.S. Supreme Ct. 1959. Pvt. practice law, Dover, Del., 1955-76; exec. dir. Del. Legis. Ref. Bur., Dover, 1961-69; vice chancellor Del. Ct. Chancery, Dover, 1976-94, justice Del. Supreme Ct., 1994—; code revisor Del. Rev. Code Commn., 1961-72; commr. Nat. Conf. Com. Uniform State Laws, Chgo., 1962—, sec., exec. com., 1977-83; chmn. State Tax Appeal Bd., Wilmington, Del., 1973-76. Served with U.S. Army, 1945-46. Mem. ABA, Del. Bar Assn., Kent County Bar Assn. (pres. 1974), Am. Law Inst. Democrat. Home: 144 Cooper Rd Dover DE 19901-4926 Office: PO Box 476 Dover DE 19903-0476 Office: Del Supreme Court 55 The Green Dover Wilmington DE 19903

**HARTNETT, THOMAS ROBERT, III,** lawyer, author; b. Sioux City, Iowa, July 19, 1920; s. Thomas R. and Florence Mary (Graves) H.; m. Betty Jeanne Dobbins, Mar. 3, 1943; children: Thomas Robert Joseph, Jeanine Elizabeth, Dennis Edward, Glenn Michael. Student, Trinity Coll., 1937-39; LLB, U. So. Calif., 1948. Bar: Tex. 1948, U.S. Dist. Ct. (no. dist.) Tex., 1949, U.S. Ct. Appeasl (5th cir.) 1954, (10th cir.) 1955, (11th cir.) 1983, U.S. Supreme Ct., 1957. Pvt. practice Dallas, 1948-88; of counsel Hartnett Law Firm, Dallas, 1988—. Author: The Root of the Whys on Internet, 1998. With USAAF, 1939-45. Mem. State Bar Tex., Dallas Bar Assn. Republican. Roman Catholic. State civil litigation, Federal civil litigation. Home: 5074 Matilda St Apt 224 Dallas TX 75206-4268 Office: 4900 Thanksgiving Tower 1601 Elm St Dallas TX 75201-7254

**HARTNETT, WILL FORD,** lawyer; b. Austin, Tex., June 3, 1956; s. James Joseph and Emily (High) H.; m. Tammy Lynn Cotton, Dec. 7, 1996; 1 child, Will. BA, Harvard U., 1978; JD, U. Tex., 1981. Bar: Tex. 1981, U.S. Ct. Appeals (5th cir.) 1985, U.S. Supreme Ct. 1985; cert. in Estate Planning and Probate Law Tex. Bd. Legal Specialization. Assoc. Turner & Hitchins, Dallas, 1981-82; ptnr. The Hartnett Law Firm, Dallas, 1982—; bd. dirs. Tex. Guaranteed Student Loan Corp., Austin, 1987-90. Co-author: Annual Survey of Wills and Trusts, 1986. Mem. Tex. Ho. of Reps., 1991—; vice-chmn. House Jud. Affairs Com., 1995—. Fellow Am. Coll. Trust and Estate Coun., Tex. Bar Found.; mem. SAR, Dallas Bar Assn., Mensa, Harvard Club Dallas (bd. dirs., treas. 1983-95), Rotary. Republican. Roman Catholic. Probate, State civil litigation. Home: 4722 Walnut Hill Ln Dallas TX 75229-6354 Office: The Hartnett Law Firm 4900 Thanksgiving Tower Dallas TX 75201

**HARTNICK, ALAN J.,** lawyer, law educator; b. N.Y.C., Feb. 27, 1930; s. Saul and Sally Hartnick; m. Karen L. Hartnick; children: Jonathan (dec.), Kate, Christopher, Maggie. AB magna cum laude, Syracuse U.; JD cum laude, Harvard U. Ptnr. Abelman, Frayne and Schwab, N.Y.C.; adj. prof. Seton Hall U. Sch. Law, Newark, 1976-79, NYU Sch. Law, 1978—; vis. lectr. Yale Law Sch., spring 1979; cons., mem. copyright office adv. com. Libr. Congress, Washington, 1981-84; cons. Registere of Copyrights, 1989; U.S. del. com. govt. experts on the printed work World Intellection Property Orgn., UNESCO, Geneva, 1987. Editor-in-chief Jour. Copyright Soc., 1984-87; contbr. articles to profl. jours. Lt. USNR. Mem. Copyright Soc. USA (pres. 1982-84, hon. trustee 1984—), Mag. Pubs. Assn. (legal affairs com. 1983—), N.Y. State Bar Assn. (com. chair copyright and trademark 1988—), Assn. of the Bar of the City of N.Y. (copyright and literary property com. 1964-67, 78-81, 91-94, 98—, entertainment law com. 1994-97, ad hoc info. superhighway com. 1994-95), Phi Beta Kappa. Entertainment. Home: 168 E 74th St New York NY 10021-3561 Office: Abelman Frayne & Schwab 150 E 42nd St Fl 26 New York NY 10017-5621

**HARTRICK, JANICE KAY,** lawyer; b. Baytown, Tex., Oct. 15, 1952. BA, Rice U., 1974; JD, U. Houston, 1976. Bar: Tex. 1977, La. 1980. With contracts sect. Texaco Corp., Houston, 1977-78; asst. gen. counsel Cities Exploration Co., Watson Oil Corp., Houston, 1978-79; sr. atty. Coastal Corp., Houston, 1979-87; chief counsel, v.p. Seagull Energy Corp., Houston, 1987-97; gen. counsel, sr. v.p. EEX Corp., Houston, 1997—. Contbg. editor Regulation of the Natural Gas Industry, 1980-84. Vice chair adv. bd. Internat. Oil and Gas Ednl. Ctr., Southwestern Legal Found., co-chair 50th Inst. on Oil and Gas Law and Tax. Mem. ABA, Tex. Bar Assn., State Bar of Tex. (oil, gas and mineral law sect. chair 1999—), La. Bar Assn. Avocation: track. General corporate, FERC practice, Public utilities. Office: EEX Corp 2500 Citywest Blvd Ste 1400 Houston TX 77042-3024

**HARTSEL, NORMAN CLYDE,** lawyer; b. San Diego, Sept. 25, 1944; s. Norman E. and Margaret (Vaughan) H.; m. Molly E. Atherholt, June 14, 1969; children—Christian, Bennett. A.B., Kenyon Coll., 1967; J.D., Case Western Res. U., 1970. Bar: Ohio 1970, Mich. 1979, Fla. 1982, U.S. Ct. Appeals (6th cir.) 1984, U.S. Tax Ct. 1982. Assoc. Shumaker, Loop & Kendrick, Toledo, 1971-76, ptnr., 1977-85; pres. Norman C. Hartsel Co. LPA, Toledo, 1985—, ptnr. Watkins & Bates, 1987-88, ptnr. Williams Rd. Devel. Co., 1988—. mgrng. gen. ptnr. T.B. Three Properities, 1984—, H&W Devel. Co, 1987—. Recipient Disting. Alumni award Kenyon Coll., 1981. Mem. ABA, Ohio Bar Assn., Mich. Bar Assn., Fla. Bar Assn., Toledo Bar Assn. Episcopalian. Club: Belmont Country. Estate planning, Probate, Estate taxation. Home: 113 Holly Ln Perrysburg OH 43551-1055

**HARTT, GROVER, III,** lawyer; b. Dallas, Apr. 12, 1948; s. Grover Jr. and Dorothy June (Wilkins) H. BA, So. Meth. U., 1970, LLM in Tax, 1986; JD, Tex. Tech U., 1973. Bar: Tex. 1973, U.S. Dist. Ct. (no. dist.) Tex. 1974, U.S. Dist. Ct. (we. dist.) Tex. 1975, U.S. Ct. Appeals (5th cir.) 1975, U.S. Supreme Ct. 1976. Law clk. to presiding justice Ct. Criminal Appeals Tex., Austin, 1973-75; atty. Hartt and Hartt, Dallas, 1975-79; atty., advisor Office Spl. Counsel U.S. Dept. Energy, Dallas, 1979-80, dep. chief counsel, 1981-83; trial atty. tax divsn. U.S. Dept. Justice, Dallas, 1983-86, dep. atty.-in-charge tax divsn., 1986-95, asst. chief southwestern region civil trial sect. tax divsn., 1995—. Contbg. author: Collier on Bankruptcy. Recipient Atty. Gen's award for disting. svc., 1996. Mem. ABA (mem. ct. procedure com. tax sect., chmn. bankruptcy litigation subcom. 1995—, mem. bus. bankruptcy com. bus. law sect., vice chmn. tax and fed. claims subcom. 1996—), Tex. Bar Assn., Dallas Bar Assn. Office: US Dept Justice Tax Div 717 N Harwood St Ste 400 Dallas TX 75201-6506

**HARTZ, STEVEN EDWARD MARSHALL,** lawyer, educator; b. Cambridge, Mass., July 11, 1948; s. Louis and Stella (Feinberg) H.; m. Janice Lindsay, June 12, 1976. A.B. magna cum laude, Harvard Coll., 1970; J.D. U. Chgo., 1974. Bar: N.Y. 1975, U.S. Dist. Ct. (so. and ea. dists.) N.Y. 1975, Fla. 1979, U.S. Dist. Ct. (so. dist.) Fla. 1979, U.S. Ct. Appeals (2d cir.) 1975, U.S. Tax Ct. 1979, U.S. Ct. Appeals (5th cir.) 1979, U.S. Ct. Appeals (11th cir.) 1981, U.S. Supreme Ct. 1979, U.S. Dist. Ct. (mid. dist.) Fla. 1984. Assoc. Cleary, Gottlieb, Steen & Hamilton, N.Y.C., 1974-79; asst. U.S. atty. U.S. Dept. Justice, Miami, Fla., 1979-82, dep. chief criminal div., chief fraud and pub. corruption sect. 1981-82; sole practice, Miami, Fla., 1982-90; of counsel Akerman, Senterfitt & Eidson, P.A., Miami, 1980, ptnr./shareholder, 1991—; lectr. dept. English, U. Miami 1984, adj. assoc. prof., 1985-86. Co-author: Housing, A Community Handbook, 1973. Vol. atty. M.F.Y. Legal Services, N.Y.C., 1978. Recipient Dirs.' award U.S. Dept. Justice, 1981; Fulbright Hays scholar, 1970. Mem. ABA, Fla. Bar, Assn. Bar City N.Y., N.Y. State Bar Assn., Fed. Bar Assn., Dade County Bar Assn., Nat. Assn. Criminal Def. Lawyers, Phi Beta Kappa. Criminal, Consumer commercial, General civil litigation. Office: One Southeast 3rd Ave 28th Fl Miami FL 33131-4943

**HARTZFELD, HOWARD ALEXANDER, JR.,** lawyer; b. Bartlesville, Okla., July 18, 1966; s. Howard Alexander Sr. and Pearly Faye H. BA in Journalism, U. Okla., 1988; JD, Pepperdine U., 1991; LLM in Transitional Bus., McGeorge Sch. Law, 1993. Bar: Calif. 1992, D.C. 1993, Ariz. 1995, U.S. Dist. Ct. Ariz. 1995. Pvt. practice Washington, 1992, 94-95; stagrere Loeff Claeys Verbeke, Rotterdam, The Netherlands, 1993; pvt. practice Phoenix, 1995-99, Tobin & Louie, 1999—. Mem. ABA (vice chair internat. law com. young lawyers divsn. 1999—), Ariz. State Bar Assn. (mem. exec. bd. young lawyers divsn. 1998-99), Maricopa County Bar (bd. dirs. internat. law sect. 1997-99, treas. 1998-99, chair domestic violence necessities drive 1997). Contracts commercial, General civil litigation, Private international. Office: 13400 Riverside Dr Ste 108 Sherman Oaks CA 91423-2513

**HARTZHEIM, CHARLES JOHN,** lawyer; b. Kaukauna, Wis., May 2, 1941; s. Aloysius A. and Kathryn H. (Hammen) H.; m. Kathy A. Vaughn, March, 1979; children: Steve, Juli M. BSBA, St. Norbert Coll., 1963; JD, Marquette U., 1966. Bar: Wis. 1966, U.S. Dist. Ct. (ea. dist.) Wis. 1966. Assoc. McCarty, Swetz, Curry & Burns, Kaukauna, 1968-71, ptnr., 1971-72; ptnr. Herrling, Clark, Hartzheim & Siddall, Ltd., Appleton, Wis., 1972—; bd. dirs. various client firms. Mem. Fox Valley Estate Planning Coun. Capt. U.S. Army, 1966-68, Vietnam. Mem. Internat. Assn. Fin. Planners, Elks. Republican. Banking, General corporate, Estate planning. Office: Herrling Clark Hartzheim & Siddall Ltd 800 N Lynndale Dr Appleton WI 54914-3017

**HARUTUNIAN, ALBERT T(HEODORE), III,** judge; b. San Diego, May 15, 1955; s. Albert Theodore Jr. and Elsie Ruth Harutunian. BA, Claremont McKenna Coll., 1977; JD, U. Calif., Berkeley, 1980. Bar: Calif. 1980, U.S. Dist. Ct. (so. dist.) Calif. 1980, U.S. Ct. Apppeals (9th cir.) 1982, U.S. Supreme Ct. 1984. Law clk. to judge Howard B. Turrentine U.S. Dist. Ct., San Diego, 1980-81; assoc. Luce, Forward, Hamilton & Scripps, San Diego, 1982-87, ptnr., 1988-95; judge San Diego Mcpl. Ct., 1995-98, San Diego Superior Ct., 1998—; spl. counsel standing com. on discipline U.S. Dist. Ct. Calif., San Diego, 1983-85; chmn. San Diego Bar Labor and Employment Sect., 1988-89; chmn. fed. cts. com. Calif. State Bar, 1989-90. Bd. dirs. ARC San Diego chpt., 1992—, Crime Victims Fund, 1995-97; bd. govs. Muscular Dystrophy Assn., San Diego, 1985; mem. LEAD Inc., San Diego, 1986—; mem. planning com. San Diego United Way, 1986-92. Named one of Outstanding Young Men of Am., 1983; recipient Outstanding Service award 9th Cir. Jud. Conf., 1986. Mem. ABA, Calif. State Bar Ct. (referee 1985-88), Am. Arbitration Assn. (arbitrator 1986-95), Calif. Judges Assn. (mem. criminal law and procedure com. 1997—), Boalt Hall Alumni Assn. (bd. dirs. 1994-97), Claremont McKenna Coll. Alumni Assn. (founding dir. San Diego chpt. 1984—), Rotary (bd. dirs. San Diego club 1995—). Republican. Avocations: music, golf. Office: San Diego Superior Ct PO Box 122724 San Diego CA 92112-2724

**HARVEY, ALBERT C.,** lawyer; m. Nancy Rutherford; children: Anne, Elizabeth. BS, U. Tenn., 1961, J.D., 1967. Asst. pub. defender Tenn. Supreme Ct.; asst. to pub. defender Shelby County, 1969-71; ptnr. Thomason, Hendrix, Harvey, Johnson & Mitchell, Memphis; instr. med. and dental jurisprudence U. Tenn., Memphis. Bd. editors Tennessee Law Review. Pres. Goodwill Boys Club, 1983-85; active YMCA, Arthritis Found., Citizens Assn. Memphis and Shelby County, Shelby County War Memls.; sr. warden of vestry Calvary Episcopal Ch. Maj. gen. USMCR, comdg. gen. 4th Marine div. Recipient Sam A. Myar, Jr. award Tenn. Bd. Law Examiners, 1978. Fellow Am. Bar Found. (life), Tenn. Bar Found. (pres. 1993-94); mem. ABA (bd. govs., ho. dels. charter mem. and coun. sect. litigation, young lawyers sect., fellow young lawyers divsn., com. on ethics and profl. responsibilty, ethics 2000 spl. com.), Am. Judicature Soc. (nat. bd. dirs.), Am. Bd. Trial Advocates (advocate), Tenn. Bar Assn. (bd. govs., pres. young lawyers conf.), Memphis Bar Assn. (v.p. 1989, pres. elect 1990, pres. 1991, pres. young lawyers divsn.), U. Tenn. Nat. Alumni Assn. (pres. Memphis chpt., nat. bd. govs.), Ctrl. Garden Area Assn. (pres.), Memphis Area C. of C. (pres. mil. affairs coun.), Navy League, Phoenix Club (1st v.p.), Kiwanis, University Club of Memphis (v.p.). Construction, Personal injury, Product liability. Office: 1 Commerce Sq 29th Fl Memphis TN 38103

**HARVEY, ALEXANDER, II,** federal judge; b. Balt., May 3, 1923; s. Fred B. and Rose (Hopkins) H.; m. Mary E. Williams, Feb. 24, 1951; children: Elizabeth H., Alexander IV. BA, Yale U., 1947; LLB, Columbia U., 1950. Bar: Md. 1950. Assoc. Ober, William, Grimes & Stinson, Balt., 1950-66, ptnr., 1953-66; asst. atty. gen. Md., 1957-58; judge U.S. Dist. Ct. Md., 1966-86, chief judge, 1986-91; sr. judge U.S. Dist. Ct. Md., Balt., 1991—; mem. Gov.'s Com. To Study Blue Sky Law of Md., 1961; mem. character com. Ct. Appeals Md. for 8th Jud. Cir. Bd. dirs. Balt. Symphony Assn., 1966-68; pres., dir. Balt. Opera Guild, 1960; bd. dirs. Balt. Coun. Social Agys., 1957-63; trustee Ch. Home and Hosp., Balt., 1952-71. 1st lt. AUS, World War II, ETO. Mem. Am., Md., Balt. bar assns., Phi Beta Kappa. Episcopalian (vestry 1967-70). Home: 7300 Brightside Rd Baltimore MD 21212-1011 Office: US Dist Ct 101 W Lombard St Ste 404 Baltimore MD 21201-2626

**HARVEY, ALICE ELEASE,** lawyer; b. Haddonfield, N.J., Apr. 10, 1968; d. Lucious James and Doris Arleen Harvey; m. Joseph Edward Koren, Aug. 17, 1996. BS, Drexel U., 1986; JD, U. Pa., 1994. Bar: Pa. 1995. Law clk. U.S. SEC, Phila., summer 1992; assoc. Morgan, Lewis & Bockius, LLP, Phila., 1994-97, Hangley, Aronchick, Segal & Pudlin, Phila., 1997-99; corp. counsel The Franklin Mint, Franklin Center, Pa., 1999—; tutor Future Investments Tutoring Program, Phila., 1995-98; vol. lawyer Phila. Vol. Lawyers for Arts, 1997—. Editor/mng. editor Housing Law Jour., 1991-94; editor Univ. Pa. Law Rev., 1992-94. Mem. Pa. Bar Assn., Phila. Bar Assn. Avocations: travel, writing, equestrian. General corporate, Mergers and acquisitions, Entertainment. Office: The Franklin Mint Franklin Center PA 19091

**HARVEY, EDMUND LUKENS,** lawyer; b. Chester, Pa., July 21, 1915. BSME, U. Pa., 1937, JD, 1941. Bar: Pa. 1942, U.S. Tax. Ct. 1955, U.S. Dist. Ct. (ea. dist.) Pa. 1961, U.S. Supreme Ct. 1969. Pvt. practice Chester, 1946-70, Media, Pa., 1970-95. Bd. dirs., solicitor J. Lewis Crozer Libr., Chester, 1952-89; bd. dirs. Lindsay Law Libr., Chester, 1967-91. Mem. ABA, Pa. Bar Assn., Del. County Bar Assn. Probate. Home: Whitehorse Village # V-109 Newtown Square PA 19073-2815 Office: 535 Gradyville Rd PO Box 82 Gradyville PA 19039-0082

**HARVEY, ELIZABETH SCHROER,** lawyer; b. Rockford, Ill., June 17, 1960; d. Philip Paul and E. Rebecca (Whisler) Schroer; m. Robert J. Harvey, July 27, 1985 (div. Nov. 1995). BA in History and Polit. Sci., U. Iowa, 1982; JD, So. Ill. U., 1986. Bar: Ill. 1986, U.S. Dist. Ct. (no. dist.) Ill. 1990, U.S. Dist. Ct. (cen. and so. dists.) Ill. 1995. Rsch. atty. Ill. Supreme Ct., Springfield, 1986-87; atty. Ill. Pollution Control Bd., Chgo., 1987-95; environ. atty. McKenna, Storer, Rowe, White & Farrug, Chgo., 1995—. Contbr. articles to profl. publs. Mem. Ill. State Bar Assn., Chgo. Bar Assn. (chmn. practice and procedure com. of environ. law sect. 1989-90), Environ. Law Inst., So. Ill. U. Law Alumni Assn., U. Iowa Alumni Assn. Presbyterian. Avocations: gardening, reading, walking, sports. Environmental. Office: McKenna Storer Rowe White & Farrug 200 N Lasalle St Ste 3000 Chicago IL 60601-1083

**HARVEY, ELTON BARTLETT, III,** lawyer; b. Albany, N.Y., Oct. 26, 1946; s. Elton Bartlett Jr. and Marjorie Irene (Johnson) H.; children: Tamilyn, Jocelyn Janel, Josiah Bartlett, James Mullen, Benjamin Dante. BA, U. Conn., 1969; MA, U. New Haven, 1976; JD, Western New Eng. Coll., 1986. Bar: Conn. 1986, U.S. Dist. Ct. Conn. 1986. Title officer Conn. Atty.'s Title Ins. Co., Rocky Hill, Conn., 1980-83; counsel, mgr. Safeco Title Ins. Co., Hartford, Conn., 1983-87, Am. Title Ins. Co., Hartford, 1987-88; prin. Osborne & Harvey, Farmington, 1988-95; ptnr. Harvey Law Assocs., Farmington, 1995—. Mem. ABA, Conn. Bar Assn. Real property. Office: Harvey Law Assocs 3 Melrose Dr Farmington CT 06032-2249

**HARVEY, JAMES CLEMENT,** lawyer; b. Shattuck, Okla., June 8, 1941; s. T.C. Jr. and Loucille (Miller) H.; m. Sue Simmons White, Aug. 11, 1962 (div. Feb. 1970); 1 child, Shannon Suzanne; m. Sherry L. Grant, Sept. 24, 1979. BBA, So. Meth. U., 1963, JD, 1966. Bar: Tex., 1966; U.S. Dist. Ct. (no. dist.) Tex. 1968. Pvt. practice, Dallas, 1966. Methodist. Real property, Banking, Finance. Home: 4129 Bowser Ave Dallas TX 75219-3719 Office: 3811 Turtle Creek Blvd Ste 350 Dallas TX 75219-4450

**HARVEY, JONATHAN MATTHEW,** lawyer; b. Worcester, Mass., July 6, 1955; s. Irwin and Hannah H.; m. Lyssa Lynn Kligman, Dec. 17, 1977; children: Laurel Eden, Jordane Mills, Kyle Michael. BA cum laude, U. Ga., 1977; JD, U. S.C., 1981. Bar: S.C. 1981, U.S. Dist. Ct. S.C. 1982, U.S. Ct. Appeals (4th cir.) 1992. Asst. solicitor Fifth Judicial Circuit Solicitor's Office, Columbia, S.C., 1982-83; asst. atty. gen. Office of the Atty. Gen., Columbia, S.C., 1983-86; lawyer pvt. practice, Columbia, 1986—. Fin. dir. Richland County Dems., Columbia, S.C., 1987-88, mem. exec. com. 1987-90, 1998—; vice chmn. commr. E. Richland County Pub. Svc. Dist., Richland County, S.C., 1990—. Mem. ATLA, S.C. Bar Assn., S.C. Assn. Criminal Defense Lawyers, Richland County Bar Assn., S.C. Trial Lawyers.. Democrat. Avocations: tennis, outdoor activities. Criminal, Administrative and regulatory, Personal injury. Office: 1804 Bull St Columbia SC 29201-2506

**HARVEY, LEIGH KATHRYN,** lawyer; b. Abilene, Tex.; d. Jasper Elliott and Kathryn E. (McDaniel) H.; m. Bert Gubbels, Oct. 1983 (div. 1993). BA cum laude, U. Tex., 1971, JD, 1974. Bar: Tex. 1975. Asst. atty. City of San Angelo, Tex., 1974-77; asst. dist. atty. County of Fort Bend, Richmond, Tex., 1978; pvt. practice various cities, Tex., 1977—. Bd. dirs. Tom Green County Community Action Council, San Angelo, 1975-77, pres. 1976; vol. judge bd. advs. U. Tex. Law Sch., Austin, 1980; mem. Met. Austin 2000, 1982; mem. vestry St. Mary's Episcopal Ch., Lampasas, Tex., 1989-91; mem. Natural Resources Def. Coun., The Heritage Found., 1994-98; host for Jan Patterson Austin/Temple receptions Ct. Appeals 3rd cir., 1998. Keeton fellow U. Tex., 1997—; recipient Young Careerist award Dist. 7 Bus. and Profl. Women's Club, 1977, Cert. of Achievement Rep. Nat. Conv., 1998; named Guardian of the Wild Nat. Wildlife Fedn., 1998. Mem. ABA, Tex. Bar Assn. (legal forms com. manual for Real Estate Transactions rev. edit. 1986-92), Travis County Bar Assn., Bell Lampasas Mills County Bar Assn. (sr. citizen project 1986). Episcopalian. General practice. Office: PO Box 926 Lampasas TX 76550-0926

**HARVEY, MARC SEAN,** lawyer; b. N.Y.C., May 4, 1960; s. M. Eugene and Coleen (Jones) H. BA with honors, So. Ill. U., 1980; JD, Southwestern U., 1983; postgrad., Loyola Marymount U., L.A., 1984-86. lectr. Loyola Marymount U., 1986; judge pro tem Culver (Calif.) Mcpl. Ct., 1991—. Counsel U.S. SBA, L.A., 1982-83; counsel enforcement div. U.S. SEC, L.A., 1983-84; counsel State Farm Ins. Co., L.A., 1984-85, 20th Century Ins. Co., Woodland Hills, Calif., 1985-86; pvt. practice Encino, Calif., 1986—; lectr. Loyola Marymount U., 1986; judge pro tem Culver (Calif.) Mcpl. Ct., 1991—. Charter mem., trustee Rep. Presdl. Task Force, Washington, 1981—; mem. Nat. Rep. Senatorial Com., Washington, 1983—, Rep. Congl. Leadership Coun., Washington, 1987—, Rep. Senatorial Inner Cir., Washington, 1988—; victory fund sponsor Nat. Rep. Congl. Com., Washington, 1984—; judge pro tem Culver Mcpl. Ct., 1991— (Judge Pro Tem of Yr. award 1991). Recipient 1st Pl. Essay award VFW, 1976, So. Ill. U. scholarship, 1979-81. Mem. ABA, AFTRA, SAG, Am. Trial Lawyers Assn., Calif. Trial Lawyers Assn., L.A. Bar Assn., L.A. Trial Laywers Assn., Themis Soc., Nat. Honor Soc. General civil litigation, Entertainment.

**HARVEY, MARGOT MARIE,** lawyer; b. Lancaster, Pa., Apr. 21, 1941; d. George Claude and Roma (Ember) Spiese; m. Donald Eugene Harvey, Jan. 22, 1962; children: Katherine Marie, Mary Leigh. AA, Santa Ana Coll., 1968; BA, Calif. State U., Fullerton, 1972; JD, Western State U., Fullerton, 1983. Bar: Calif. 1984, U.S. Dist. Ct. (ctrl. dist.) Calif. 1984. With Clk.'s Office, Orange County Juvenile Ct., Orange, Calif., 1970-73; ct. clk. to Judge Robert H. Green, Orange County Superior Ct., Orange, 1973-83; atty. Safco Ins. Co., Fountain Valley, Calif., 1984-87, Gt. Am. Ins. Co., Orange, 1987-89; ptnr. Law Offices Mercer and Zinder, Orange, 1989-96; sr. trial atty. Laskero and Assocs., Santa Ana, Calif., 1996—. With USAF, 1958-62. Mem. ABA, ATLA, Calif. State Bar, Calif. Women Lawyers, Orange County Women Lawyers, Calif. Trial Lawyers Assn., Orange County Trial Lawyers Assn., Orange County Bar Assn. (speaker bridging the gap 1986—), Orange County Ins. Def. Assn. (bd. dirs.), Orange County Barristers (speaker bridging the gap 1986—, bd. dirs.). Lutheran. Avocations: reading, music, gardening, travel. Personal injury, State civil litigation, Construction. Office: Laskero and Assocs 1551 N Tustin Ave Ste 100 Santa Ana CA 92705-8639

**HARVEY, MORRIS LANE,** lawyer; b. Madisonville, Ky., Apr. 22, 1950; s. Morris Lee and Margie Lou (Wallace) H.; divorced; children: Morris Lane Jr., John French, Laura Kathleen. BS, Murray State U., 1972; JD, U. Ky., 1974. Bar: Ill. 1975, U.S. Dist. Ct. (so. dist.) 1979. Assoc. Hanagan & Dousman, Mt. Vernon, Ill., 1975-77; ptnr. Feiger, Quindry, Molt & Harvey and successor firms, Fairfield, Ill., 1977-85; sole practice Fairfield, 1986-97, Mt. Vernon, 1997—; instr. Frontier C.C., Fairfield, 1977-79; spl. asst. atty. gen. State of Ill., Fairfield, 1977-82; Ill. pres. Woodman of World Life Inst. Soc., 1985-87; mem. nat. fraternal com., 1987-89, nat. legis. com., 1989-93, nat. jud. com., 1993-97. Recipient Outstanding Young Man Am. U.S. Jaycees, 1978, 81, 89. Mem. ABA, Ill. Bar Assn., Assn. Trial Lawyers Am., Ill. Trial Lawyers Assn., Am. Judicature Soc. State civil litigation, Family and matrimonial, Personal injury. Home: 5 Webster Hills Estates Mount Vernon IL 62864-6274 Office: 2029 Broadway St Mount Vernon IL 62864-2910

**HARVEY, NICHOLAS D. N., JR.,** lawyer; b. Balt., May 7, 1948; m. Margaret K. (Knox) H.; 2 children. BA, Colgate U., 1970; LLM, U. Puget Sound, 1976. Bar: Wash. 1976, N.H. 1980, Vt. 1980. Atty. Stebbins, Bradley Wood & Harvey, P.A., Hanover, N.H., 1980—. 1st lt. USAF, 1970-72. Estate planning, Corporate taxation, Estate taxation. Office: Stebbins Bradley Wood & Harvey 41 S Park St Hanover NH 03755-2109

**HARVIE, CRAWFORD THOMAS,** lawyer; b. N.Y.C., Mar. 28, 1943; s. William Mead and Barbara Adele (Johnson) H.; m. Iris Ruth Alofsin, June 10, 1972; children: Katherine, Edward. AB, Stanford U., 1965; LLB, Yale U., 1968; cert. advanced mgmt. program, Harvard U., 1992. Bar: N.Y. 1969. Assoc. Debevoise & Plimpton, N.Y.C., 1971-75; counsel TRW, Inc., Cleve., 1976-77, sr. counsel, 1978-79, asst. gen. counsel, v.p., 1980-83; v.p. law TRW Automotive, Cleve., 1983-90; v.p., assoc. gen. counsel TRW Inc., 1990-95; sr. v.p., gen. counsel Goodyear Tire and Rubber Co., Akron, Ohio, 1995—. Trustee Cleve. Inst. of Music, 1989—, Akron Art Mus., Cleve. Opera, Cleve. Coun. on World Affairs; bd. overseers Blossom Music Ctr. Mem. Am. Corp. Counsel Assn., Assn. of Gen. Counsel, Chief Legal Officer Roundtable-U.S., Assn. of Bar of City of N.Y. General corporate. Home: 6537 Thornbrook Cir Hudson OH 44236-3552 Office: Goodyear Tire and Rubber Co 1144 E Market St Akron OH 44316-0002

**HARVIN, L(UCIUS) SCOTT,** lawyer; b. Columbia, S.C., Aug. 3, 1965; m. Rachel Marion Forbes, May 20, 1995. BA, Duke U., 1987; JD, U. S.C., 1991. With Hood Law Firm, Charleston, S.C., 1991-93; hwy. safety prosecutor Ninth Cir. Solicitors Office, Charleston, 1993-94; sole practitioner

Charleston, 1994-97; with Hetrick Law Firm, Walterboro, S.C., 1997—; founding mem. Nat. Coll. for DUT Def., Cambridge, Mass. Mem. Assn. Trial Lawyers of Am., S.C. Trial Lawyers Assn., S.C. Criminal Def. Lawyers Assn., S.C. Bar Assn. Criminal, Personal injury, General civil litigation. Office: Hetrick Law Firm PO Box 139 Walterboro SC 29488-0002

**HARVIN, WESLEY REID,** lawyer; b. Thomasville, Ga., Jan. 4, 1944; s. Henry Ellis and Bertha Mae Harvin; m. Kay Kerce, Aug. 9, 1964; 1 child, Wesley Reid II. BA in Psychology, U. South Fla., 1971; JD, Stetson U., 1976. Bar: Fla. 1976, Fla. Trial Bar 1977, U.S. Dist. Ct. (so. dist.) Fla. 1977, U.S. Ct. Appeals (11th cir.) 1977, U.S. Supreme Ct. 1980. Pvt. practice Stuart, Fla., 1976—; past legal counsel St. Lucie County Code Enforcement Bd.; past gen. counsel Thomas J. White Devel. Corp. Chmn. planned giving bd. dirs. Am. Heart Assn. Martin County; bd. dirs. Treasure Coast Wildlife Hosp.; past bd. dirs. presch. First United Meth. Ch.; past pres. Martin County Band Boosters, Inc.; past asst. scoutmaster Boy Scouts Am., founder ann. fundraiser dinner. Served with Fla. Army N.G. Mem. ABA, ATLA, Fla. Bar Assn., Martin County Bar Assn., Am. Arbitration Assn., Real Property Coun. of Martin Coun. (pres.). Avocations: physical exercise, biking, scuba diving. Federal civil litigation, General civil litigation, State civil litigation. Office: 900 E Ocean Blvd Ste B-210 Stuart FL 34994-2471

**HARVITT, ADRIANNE STANLEY,** lawyer; b. Chgo., May 15, 1954; d. Stanley and Maryln (Loye) H.; m. Donald Martin Heinrich, Aug. 27, 1977; children: Patrick Loye, Christina Marie. AB, U. Chgo., 1975, MBA, 1976; JD with honors, Ill. Inst. Tech., 1980. Bar: Ill. 1980, U.S. Dist. Ct. (no. dist.) Ill. 1980, U.S. Ct. Appeals (7th cir.) 1985, (9th cir.) 1988, U.S. Supreme Ct. 1985, Wis. 1993. Fin. analyst Bell & Howell Co., Chgo., 1976-77; trial atty. U.S. Commodity Futures Trading Commn., Chgo., 1980-83; assoc. Hannafan & Handler, Chgo., 1983-85; ptnr. Harvitt & Gekas, Ltd., Chgo., 1985-97, Harvitt & Assoc., Ltd., Milw., 1997-98; appt. pub. svc. spl. prosecutor Milw. County Dist. Atty.'s Office, 1998; v.p., assoc. gen. counsel Stephens Inc., Little Rock, 1999—; adj. prof. securities regulation U. Ark. Sch. of Law, Little Rock, Ark., 1999. Mem. Law Rev. Chgo.-Kent Coll. Law, 1979-80. Mem. ABA, Ill. Bar Assn. (article hon. mention 1982), Chgo. Bar Assn., Assn. Women Lawyers, U. Chgo. Alumni Assn. (svc. citation 1995, bd. govs. 1996-98), U. Chgo. Women's Bus. Group (v.p. 1988-90), U. Chgo. Women's Bd., Art Inst. Chgo. Avocations: skiing, swimming, scuba diving. Federal civil litigation, Securities, Commodities.

**HARWELL, DAVID WALKER,** retired state supreme court chief justice; b. Florence, S.C., Jan. 8, 1932; s. Baxter Hicks and Lacy (Rankin) H.; divorced; children: Robert Bryan, William Baxter. LL.B., J.D., U. S.C., 1958; HHD (hon.), Frances Marion U., 1987. Bar: S.C. 1958, U.S. Dist. Ct. S.C. 1958, U.S. Ct. Appeals 1964, U.S. Supreme Ct. 1961. Circuit judge 12th Jud. Ct. S.C., 1973-80; justice S.C. Supreme Ct., 1980-91, chief justice, 1991-94; ret., 1994; spl. counsel Nelson, Mullins, Riley and Scarborough. Mem. S.C. Ho. of Reps., 1962-73. Served with USNR, 1952-54. Mem. Am. Bar Assn., Am. Trial Lawyers Assn., S.C. Bar Assn., S.C. Trial Lawyers Assn. (Portrait and Scholarship award 1986). Presbyterian. Office: PO Box 2459 Myrtle Beach SC 29578-2459

**HARWICK, DENNIS PATRICK,** lawyer; b. Nampa, Idaho, May 27, 1949; s. T. Dale and Lois L. (Patrick) H.; m. Rebecca Cowgill, May 10, 1980. BA, U. Idaho, 1971, JD, 1974. Bar: Idaho 1974, U.S. Dist. Ct. Idaho 1974. Legal officer Idaho Bank & Trust, Pocatello, 1974-79, v.p.-legal, Boise, 1979-85, spokesman, 1983-85, editor corp. newsletter, 1983-85; mem. adv. coun. U. Idaho Coll. Letters and Sci., 1986-90; exec. dir. Idaho State Bar and Idaho Law Found., Inc., 1985-90; exec. dir., CEO Washington State Bar Assn., 1990-97; pres. Kans. Lawyers Svc. Corp., 1998—; exec. dir. Kans. Bar Assn./Kans. Bar Found., Topeka, 1998—. Bd. dirs. Boise Philharm., 1984-89, v.p. adminstrn., 1985-87; chmn. Idaho Commn. U.S. Constl. Bicentennial, 1986-88; chmn. Idaho Bus. Week Program, 1984; treas. Idaho State Dem. Conv., 1980. Mem. ABA, Nat. Assn. Bar Execs. (mem. exec. com., pres. 1996-97), Nat. Conf. Bar Founds. (trustee), Idaho State Bar (examiner/grader 1975-90), Idaho Bankers Assn. (spokesman), Am. Inst. Banking (state chmn. 1982-83), Idaho Assn. Commerce and Industry (chmn. coms.), Boise Bar Assn., Bar Assn. Adminstrn., Phi Beta Kappa. Democrat. Clubs: Boise Racquet and Swim (bd. dirs. 1988-90, pres. 1990). Office: Kans Bar Assn PO Box 1037 Topeka KS 66601-1037

**HASBROUCK, CATHERINE O'MALLEY,** lawyer; b. Chgo., June 10, 1964; d. Arthur Stephen and Mary Catherine O'Malley; m. Peter Voss Hasbrouck, Sept. 24, 1994; children: Clare McCuiston, Henry Arthur. BA with honors, U. N.C., Chapel Hill, 1986, JD with honors, 1989. Bar: N.Y. 1990, Ga. 1993. Assoc. Winthrop, Stimson, Putnam & Roberts, N.Y.C., 1989-92, Troutman Sanders LLP, Atlanta, 1992-96; v.p., gen. counsel, corp. sec. Paragon Trade Brands, Inc., Norcross, Ga., 1996—. Mem. Am. Soc. Corp. Secs. Avocations: running, reading, music. General corporate, Securities. Office: Paragon Trade Brands Inc 180 Technology Pkwy Norcross GA 30092-2907

**HASELTON, RICK THOMAS,** lawyer; b. Albany, Oreg., Nov. 5, 1953; s. Shirley (Schantz) H. AB, Stanford U., 1976; JD, Yale U., 1979. Chair Oreg. State Bd. Bar Examiners, 1988-89, bd. dirs., 1986-88; mem. adv. com. on rules of practice 9th Cir. Ct., 1991-93. Law clk. U.S. Ct. Appeals (9th cir.) Oreg., Portland, 1979-80; from assoc. to ptnr. Lindsay, Hart, Neil & Weigler, Portland, 1979-93; sole practice Portland, 1993-94; assoc. judge Oreg. Ct. Appeals, Salem, 1994—. Chair Multnomah County Legal Aid, Portland, 1985-86, bd. dirs., 1982-87. Mem. ABA, Oreg. Bar Assn., ACLU (cooperating atty. 1982-94), Phi Beta Kappa. Jewish. Federal civil litigation, State civil litigation. Office: 300 Justice Blvd Salem OR 97310-0001

**HASENAUER, JUDITH ANNE,** lawyer; b. Rochester, N.Y., Sept. 28, 1946; d. William F. and Arline (Burns) H. AA, Monroe C.C., 1966; AB, U. Rochester, 1969; JD, Golden Gate U., 1973; CLU, Am. Coll., 1974. Bar: Calif. 1974, Conn. 1974, U.S. Dist. Ct. Conn. 1975, N.Y. 1983, D.C. 1983, Fla. 1993. Ptnr. Blazzard, Grodd & Hasenauer, Westport, Conn., 1974—; co-chmn. regulatory affairs com. Nat. Assn. for Variable Annuities, 1997—. Contbr. articles to profl. jours. Bd. dirs. Friends of Norwalk C.C., Conn., 1977-83; sec. Fairfield County CLUs, Conn., 1983-85. Securities, Insurance. Office: Blazzard Grodd & Hasenauer 4401 W Tradewinds Ave Laud By Sea FL 33308-4463

**HASKEL, JULES J.,** lawyer; b. Bklyn., Sept. 9, 1929; s. Manny and Sadie H.; m. Arlene Teitelbaum, Apr. 19, 1957; children: Lynn S. Haskel Lancaster, Barbara I. Haskel Weiner, Carol Haskel Solomon. BS in Journalism, Medill Sch. Journalism, Northwestern U., 1951; JD, NYU, 1954. Bar: N.Y. 1955, U.S. Dist. Ct. (so. and ea. dists.) N.Y. 1957, U.S. Tax Ct. 1958, U.S. Ct. Apls. (2d cir.) 1981, U.S. Supreme Ct. 1962. Assoc. Grossman & Grossman, N.Y.C., 1954-55; exec. dir. membership campaign ABA, N.Y.C., 1955-56; assoc. Otterbourg, Steindler, Houston & Rosen, N.Y.C., 1956-57, Newman & Bisco, N.Y.C., 1957-59; ptnr. Koopersmith & Haskel, Jamaica, N.Y., 1960-77, Durben & Haskel, Garden City, N.Y., 1977-87, Haskel, Hand & Lancaster, 1988-96, Jaspan Schlessinger, Silverman & Hoffman L.L.P., 1996—; mem. surrogate's ct. adv. com. N.Y. State Office of Ct. Adminstrn., 1995—. Mem. law com. UJA-Fedn. Jewish Philanthropies of N.Y., 1978—; bd. dirs. Queens Legal Svcs. Corp., 1970-73. Fellow Am. Coll. Trust and Estates Counsel (mem. fiduciary litigation com. 1994—); mem. ABA, N.Y. State Bar Assn. (mem. ho. of dels. 1975-92, chmn. trusts and estates law sect. 1982, v.p. 1984-86, mem. exec. com. 1986-89, chair action unit 4 judicial selection and ct. merger 1990-93), N.Y. State Bar Found. (bd. dirs. 1986—), Queens County Bar Assn. (pres. 1973-74, chmn. judiciary com. 1978-79, editor bar bull. 1964-66), Jamaica Lawyers Club (pres. 1968-69), Nassau County Bar Assn., NYU Law Alumni Assn. (v.p. 1970-73, 77-81). Jewish. Probate, Estate planning, Estate taxation. Office: Jaspan Schlessinger Silverman & Hoffman LLP 300 Garden City Plz Garden City NY 11530-3302

**HASKELL, DONALD MCMILLAN,** lawyer; b. Toledo, July 2, 1932; s. Irwin Wales and Grace (Lee) H.; m. Carol Jean Ross, June 19, 1954; children: Deborah Lee, Catherine Jean, David Ross. BA, Coll. of Wooster, 1954; JD, U. Mich., 1957. Bar: Ill. 1957, U.S. Dist. Ct. (no. dist.) Ill. 1958, U.S. Ct. Appeals (7th cir.) 1960, U.S. Supreme Ct. 1963, U.S. Ct. Appeals (10th cir.) 1974, Oreg. 1990. Ptnr. McKenna, Storer, Rowe, White & Haskell and predecessors, Chgo., 1957-75; sr. ptnr. Haskell & Perrin, Chgo., 1975-89, of counsel, 1989—; commr. Clatsop County, Oreg., 1991-94; bd. dirs. N.W. Oreg. Econ. Alliance, 1993-98. Trustee Columbia River Maritime Mus., 1991—; chmn. Clatsop County Rep. Com., 1994-95; Astoria planning commr., 1999—. Fellow Am. Bar Found., Ill. Bar Found.; mem. ABA (ho. of dels. 1982-92, bd. govs. 1987-90), Law Club Chgo., Legal Club Chgo., Astoria Country Club. Lutheran. Insurance, Aviation, Admiralty. Home: 600 W Lexington Ave Astoria OR 97103-5726 Office: Wecoma Ptnrs Ltd PO Box 777 100 16th St Astoria OR 97103-3634 also: Haskell & Perrin 200 W Adams St Ste 2600 Chicago IL 60606-5233

**HASKIN, J. MICHAEL,** lawyer; b. Kansas City, Mo., Sept. 25, 1949; s. Harley V. and Geraldine E. (Porterfield) H.; m. Pamela J. Lutz, May 22, 1999. BA, Baker U., 1971; JD, U. Mo., 1976. Bar: Kans. 1976, Mo. 1987, U.S. Fed. Tax Ct., U.S. Supreme Ct. Ptnr., atty. Haskin, Hinkle, Slater & Snowbarger, Olathe, Kans., 1976-83, Dietrich, Davis, Dicus, Rowlands, Schmitt & Gorman, Kansas City, Mo., 1984-88; pres., atty. J. Michael Haskin, PA, Olathe, 1989—; bd. dirs., exec. com., The Assn. K-10 Corridor Devel., Inc., Lawrence, 1993-95. City councilman-at-large City of Olathe, 1989-93, mayor, 1993-95; mem., vice chmn., chmn. Stormwater Mgmt. Adv. Coun., Johnson County, Kans., 1989-95; bd. dirs. Olathe Pub. Libr., 1989-90, 93-95; bd. dirs. Hidden Glen Arts Festival, vice chmn., chmn., 1990—); mem. Mid-Am. Regional Coun. Perimeter Transp. Com., 1995—. Recipient Boss of Yr. award Johnson County Legal Secs. Assn., 1991-92, Cmty. Leadership award Olathe Area C. of C., 1992. Mem. Kans. Bar Assn., Mo. Bar Assn., Olathe Rotary Club (bd. dirs., pres. 1981—, Paul Harris award 1992, Olathe Rotarian of Yr. 1995), Olathe Arts Alliance (pres. 1988), Kaw Valley Philological Soc. Republican. Methodist. Avocations: golfing, sailing. Estate planning, Probate, Real property. Office: PO Box 413 100 E Park St Ste 203 Olathe KS 66061-3463

**HASKINS, CHARLES GREGORY, JR.,** lawyer; b. Chgo., Jan. 27, 1951; s. Charles G. and Ellen Barbara (Essman) H.; m. Gail Beaubien Ferbend, June 14, 1987; 1 child, Charles Robert. BA, U. Ill., 1972; JD, John Marshall Law Sch., 1976. Bar: Ill. 1976, U.S. Dist. Ct. (no. dist.) Ill. 1976. Assoc. George J. Cullen, Ltd., Chgo., 1976-82; shareholder George J. Cullen & Assoc., Ltd., Chgo., 1982-89, Cullen, Haskins, Nicholson & Menchetti, Chgo., 1989—. Mem. ATLA, Workers Compensation Lawyers Assn. (bd. dirs. 1986-96, pres. 1989), Ill. Bar Assn., Ill. Trial Lawyers Assn. (bd. mgrs. 1989—, treas. 1997, co-chmn. Workers Compensation com. 1991—, co-editor Case Notebook 1992—), Chgo. Bar Assn. (cham. indsl. commn. com. 1987-88), Workplace Injury Litigation Group (bd. dirs. 1997—). Democrat. Roman Catholic. Avocations: golf, water skiing, snow skiing. Workers' compensation. Office: Cullen Haskins Nicholson & Menchetti 35 E Wacker Dr Ste 1760 Chicago IL 60601-2271

**HASKO, JUDITH ANN,** lawyer; b. Waterbury, Conn., Feb. 11, 1964. BA, Vassar Coll., 1986; MPhil, U. Sussex, Brighton, Eng., 1988; JD, U. Wis., 1994. Bar: Wis. 1995, Calif. 1995, U.S. Patent and Trademark Office 1998. Rsch. assoc. Genentech Inc., South San Francisco, Calif., 1988-92; assoc. Cooley Godward, Palo Alto, Calif., 1994—; articles editor Wis. Law Rev., 1993-94. Mem. ABA, AAAS. Avocation: long distance running. Contracts commercial, Intellectual property. Office: Cooley Godward 5 Palo Alto Sq Palo Alto CA 94306-2122

**HASL, HANNELORE VERA MARGARETE,** lawyer; b. Hersbruck, Bavaria, Fed. Republic Germany, June 13, 1955; came to U.S., 1956; d. Siegfried C. and Gunda (Aures) H. AB, Duke U., 1976; MBA, Cornell U., 1978; JD, Rutgers U., 1981. Bar: N.J. 1982, D.C. 1982, U.S. Dist. Ct. N.J 1982, U.S. Dist. Ct. D.C. 1982, U.S. Ct. Appeals (5th cir.) 1982, U.S. Ct. Internat. Trade 1984, U.S. Ct. Appeals (fed. cir.) 1984. Assoc. Duncan, Allen & Mitchell, Washington, 1981-83; atty., advisor U.S. Internat. Trade Commn., Washington, 1983-84; v.p., gen. counsel Alloy Tool & Mold Mfg. Corp. and IML Tech. Inc., North Branch, N.J., 1984—. Editor-in-chief JD/MBA Quarterly, 1983. Mem. ABA, Internat. Platform Assn., N.J. Bar Assn., D.C. Bar Assn., Soc. Plastics Engrs., Nat. Assn. JD/MBA Profls. (incorporating dir. 1982, trustee 1982). General corporate, Private international, Public international. Office: IML Tech Inc 80 Liberty Corner Rd Warren NJ 07059-6708

**HASSAN, ALLEN CLARENCE,** lawyer, physician, surgeon, educator; b. Red Oak, Iowa, Mar. 29, 1936; s. Oman Diab Hassan and Dorothea Tuttle. DVM, Iowa State U., 1962; MD, U. Iowa, 1966; JD, Lincoln U., 1978. Bar: Calif. 1981, U.S. Dist. Ct. (ea. dist.) Calif. 1981, U.S. Supreme Ct. 1981; diplomate Am. Bd. Family Practice, Am. Bd. Sports Medicine. Intern Mt. Zion Hosp., San Francisco, 1966-67; residency Mendolino State Hosp. Psychiatry, Talmage, Calif., 1967-70; sole practice Sacramento, Calif., 1981—; clin. instr. family pracitce, U. Calif., Davis, 1976-86. Author: Diagnosis and Treatment of Brain and Spinal Cord Trauma, 1992, Failure to Atone, 1969. Served as sgt. USMC, 1954-57, comdr. USCG. Fellow Coll. of Legal Medicine; mem. AMA, Am. Acad. Family Physicians (program chmn. 1973-76, sec., treas. 1974, 75, pres. 1975-76), Calif. Bar Assn., Calif. Trial Lawyer Assn., Calif. Med. Assn. Avocations: reading, jogging, golf, flying, scuba diving. Personal injury, Workers' compensation, Professional liability. Home: 401 Bret Harte Rd Sacramento CA 95864-5602 Office: 2933 El Camino Ave Sacramento CA 95821-6012

**HASSELL, FRANK BRADLEY, SR.,** lawyer; b. Atlanta, Apr. 14, 1955; s. Emory Frank and Ava Nell (Hooker) H.; m. Lynn Louise Schaller, Oct. 14, 1989; children: Frank Bradley Jr., Nicole Lynn Hassell. BSBA, Fla. Tech. U., 1975; JD, U. Fla., 1978. Bar: Fla. 1978, U.S. Dist. Ct. (mid. dist.) Fla. 1981, U.S. Ct. Appeals (5th cir.) 1981, U.S. Ct. Appeals (11th cir.) 1983; cert. Civil Trial Lawyer, Fla. Bar, 1994, U.S. Dist. Ct. (so. dist.) Fla. 1996. Acting clk., marshal Fla. Ct. Appeal (5th dist.), Daytona Beach, Fla., 1979; judicial rsch. asst. Fla. Ct. Appeal (5th dist.), Daytona Beach, 1979-82; from assoc. to ptnr. Smalbein, Eubank, Johnson, Rosier and Bussey, Daytona Beach, 1981-88; ptnr. Eubank, Hassell & Lewis, Daytona Beach, 1988-95, Eubank, Hassell & Assocs., Daytona Beach, 1995—. Mem. Volusa County Civil Trial Attys. Assn. (sec. 1990), Nat. Inst. Trial Advocacy, Defense Rsch. Inst. (mem. aviation law com. 1990-95). Avocations: flying (FAA lic. comml. pilot), sailing, skiing. Insurance, General civil litigation, Aviation. Office: Eubank Hassell & Assocs PA PO Box 2229 Daytona Beach FL 32115-2229

**HASSELL, LEROY ROUNTREE, SR.,** state supreme court justice; b. Aug. 17, 1955. BA in Govt. and Fgn. Affairs, U. Va., 1977; JD, Harvard U., 1980. Bar: Va. Former ptnr. McGuire, Woods, Battle and Boothe; now justice Supreme Ct. of Va.; former mem. Va. gen. assembly task force to study violence on sch. property. Former mem. adv. bd. Massey Cancer Ctr.; mem. policy com., former chmn. Richmond Sch. Bd., ; former bd. dirs. Richmond Renaissance, Inc., richmond chpt. ARC, Garfield childs Fund, Carpenter Ctr. for Performing Arts, St. John's Hosp., Legal Aid Ctrl. Va.; vol. Richmond Pub. Schs., Hospice vol.; elected sch. bd. chmn. 4 terms. Recipient Liberty Bell award 1985, 86, Black Achievers award, 1985-86, Outstanding Young Citizen award Richmond Jaycees, 1987, Outstanding Young Virginian award Va. Jaycees, 1987; one of youngest persons to both serve on the Richmond Sch. Bd. and to serve as bd. chmn. Mem. Va. Trial Lawyers Assn., Assn. Trial Lawyers Am., Va. Assn. Def. Attys., Old Dominion Bar Assn., Va. Bar Assn. Office: Supreme Ct of Virginia PO Box 1315 Richmond VA 23218-1315

**HASSELL, MORRIS WILLIAM,** judge; b. Jacksonville, Tex., Aug. 9, 1916; s. Alonzo Seldon and Cora Lee (Rainey) H.; m. Mauriete Watson, Sept. 3, 1944; children: Morris William, Charles Robert. AA, Lon Morris Coll., 1936; JD, U. Tex., Austin, 1942. Bar: Tex. 1941, U.S. Dist. Ct. 1948, U.S. Supreme Ct. 1973. County atty. Cherokee County, Tex., 1943-47; mem. Norman Hassell Spiers & Thrall of Rusk and Jacksonville, Tex., 1948-78; sr. judge 2d Jud. Dist. Tex., 1978—; chmn. bd. Swift Oil Co., 1964-77, H & I Oil Co., 1968-77; dir. First State Bank, Rusk, Tex., 1959-78. Mayor, City of Rusk, Tex., 1959-63, 73-78; trustee Rusk Ind. Sch. Dist., 1967-73; chmn. bd. trustees, chmn. exec. com. Lon Morris Coll., Jacksonville; chmn. bd. trustees Tex. conf. United Methodist Ch.; vice-chmn. bd. trustees Lakeview Meth. Assembly; trustee Tex. ann. conf. United Meth. Found. Recipient Disting. Alumnus award Community Svc. U. Tex. Law Sch., 1994. Mem. State Bar Tex., ABA; fellow Tex. Bar Found., Am. Bar Found. Democrat. Lodges: Kiwanis (lt. gov. 1964), Masons, Odd Fellow. Home: 1300 Copeland St Rusk TX 75785 Office: Second Jud Dist Ct PO Box 196 Rusk TX 75785-0196

**HASSELQUIST, MAYNARD BURTON,** lawyer; b. Amador, Minn., July 1, 1919; s. Harry and Anna F. (Froberg) H.; m. Lorraine Swenson, Nov. 20, 1948; children: Mark D., Peter L. BSL, U. Minn., 1941; JDL, U. Minn., 1947. Bar: Minn. 1948. Asst. mgr. taxation Gen. Mills Inc., Mpls., 1947-53; chmn. internat. dept. Dorsey & Whitney, Mpls., 1953-81, of counsel, 1981-91; retired, 1991; bd. dirs. McLaughlin Gormley King Co., Mpls. Bd. dirs. Gustavus Adolphus Coll., St. Peter, Minn., Swedish Council Am.; past chmn. Japan-Am. Soc. Minn.; bd. dirs., counsel James Ford Bell Library. Served with USN, 1941-46. Decorated knight Royal Order of North Star (Sweden). Mem. ABA, Minn. Bar Assn. Lutheran. Club: Mpls. Avocations: swimming, fishing, hiking, travel. Private international, General corporate. Address (winter): 6834 E Russet Sky Dr Scottsdale AZ 85262-7155 Office: Dorsey & Whitney 220 S 6th St Ste 2200 Minneapolis MN 55402-1498

**HASSETT, JOSEPH MARK,** lawyer; b. Buffalo, May 1, 1943; m. Carol A. Melton, June 23, 1984; children: Matthew, Meredith. B.A. summa cum laude, Canisius Coll., 1964; LL.B. cum laude, Harvard U., 1967; M.A. with 1st class honors, Univ. Coll. Dublin, 1981, Ph.D., 1985. Bar: N.Y. 1967, D.C. 1970, U.S. Supreme Ct. 1976. Assoc. Hogan & Hartson, Washington, 1970-74, ptnr., 1974—; bd. trustees Canisius Coll. Author: Yeats and the Poetics of Hate, 1986; contbr. articles to profl. publs. Mem. ABA, D.C. Bar Assn. General civil litigation, Federal civil litigation, State civil litigation. Home: 6035 Crimson Ct Mc Lean VA 22101-1818 Office: 555 13th St NW Washington DC 20004-1109

**HASSETT, ROBERT WILLIAM,** lawyer; b. Franklin, Va., June 17, 1950; s. George Abe and Peggy Rita (Scher) H.; m. Lynn Ellen Shier, June 12, 1983; children: Laura, Elizabeth, Joe. B in Indsl. Engring., Ga. Inst. Tech., 1973; JD, U. Ga., 1976. Bar: Ga. 1976. Assoc. Garland Nuckles & Kadish, Atlanta, 1976-80; ptnr. Gort Hassett & Shannon, Atlanta, 1980-84, Rubin & Hassett, Atlanta, 1984-88, Hassett, Cohen, Beitchman & Goldstein, LLP, Atlanta, 1988—; chair multimedia fair Ind. Media Artists of Ga., 1995, membership chair, 1994-97, also bd. dirs.; bd. dirs., spl. events chmn. Ga. chpt. Internat. Interactive Comm. Soc., Atlanta, 1994-97; spkr. profl. confs. Contbr. articles to profl. jours. Mem. ABA (co-chair subcom. top level domain names 1998-99). Avocations: computers, multimedia, running. Website: www.internetlegal.com. E-mail: rob@internetlegal.com. Computer, Entertainment, Intellectual property. Office: Hassett Cohen Beitchman & Goldstein LLP 990 Hammond Dr NE Ste 990 Atlanta GA 30328-5589

**HASSINGER, TIMOTHY WILLIAM,** lawyer, realtor; b. New Orleans, Dec. 3, 1971; s. Lambert J. Hassinger. BA in Philosophy, Loyola U., New Orleans, 1995, JD, 1997. Bar: U.S. Dist. Ct. (ea. dist.) La. 1997, U.S. Ct. Appeals (5th cir.) 1997. Realtor Gertrude Gardner Realtors, Inc., New Orleans, 1995-98; assoc. Sacks & Raines, New Orleans, 1997—; realtor REMAX, New Orleans, 1998—; jud. extern La. Fifth Cir. Ct. Appeals, Gretna, 1996-97. Mem. editl. bd. New Orleans Inn of Ct., 1998—, La. Bar Jour., 1998—. Mem. ABA, La. State Bar Assn., New Orleans Bar Assn (civil law and litigation com.), Jefferson Bar Assn., New Orleans Met. Assn. Realtors (govtl. affairs and litigation com. 1996). E-mail: gosacks@worldnet.att.net. Office: Sacks & Raines 225 Baronne St Ste 910 New Orleans LA 70112-1704

**HASTINGS, DOUGLAS ALFRED,** lawyer; b. Oak Park, Ill., July 28, 1949; s. Douglas A. and Elaine M. (Schramm) H.; m. Virginia Joslin, June 28, 1982; children: Corey, Douglas. BA, Duke U., 1971; MPA, Memphis State U., 1977; JD, U. Va., 1981. Bar: D.C. 1981. Assoc. dir. Inst. for Govt. Studies, Memphis State U., 1976-77; adminstrv. intern Fed. Exec. Inst., Charlottesville, Va., 1977-78; project coord. Assn. Acad. Health Ctrs., Charlottesville, 1978-80; cons. Shenandoah PSRO, Charlottesville, 1980-81; ptnr. Epstein Becker & Green, Washington, 1981—; vis. lectr. dept. health adminstrn. Duke U., Durham, N.C., 1985-90. Contbr. articles to profl. jours. Mem. ABA, Washington Coun. Lawyers, Am. Health Lawyers Assn. (bd. dirs. 1991—), Order of Coif, Phi Beta Kappa. Democrat. Unitarian. Avocations: karate, tennis, basketball, coaching. Health, Administrative and regulatory, General corporate. Home: 7525 Elba Rd Alexandria VA 22306-2504 Office: Epstein Becker & Green 1227 25th St NW Fl 7 Washington DC 20037-1156

**HASTINGS, EDWIN H(AMILTON),** lawyer; b. Yonkers, N.Y., Jan. 2, 1917; s. Edwin H. Jr. and Emily (Clark) H.; m. Mabel Hurst, July 12, 1941 (div. June 1957); children: Judy H. Hastings Johnson, Jill S. Hastings Cane; m. Suzanne Saul, July 1, 1957; 1 child, Andrew C. AB, Amherst Coll., 1938; LLB, Columbia U., 1941. Bar: N.Y. 1941, R.I. 1946, U.S. Dist. Ct. R.I. 1947, U.S. Ct. Appeals (1st cir.) 1950, Mass. 1951. Assoc. Larkin, Rathbone & Perry, N.Y.C., 1941-42, Tillinghast, Collins & Tanner, Providence, 1946-53; ptnr. Tillinghast Collins & Graham, Providence, 1953-96, Tillinghast Licht & Semonoff, Providence, 1996—; cons. ptnr. estate planning and adminstrn.; bar examiner State of R.I., 1968-74, chmn. of bd., 1972-74; chmn. com. on future of criminal law R.I. Supreme Ct., 1973-75; bar examiner U.S. Dist. Ct. R.I., 1981-84. Served to 1st lt. U.S. Army, 1942-46, 51-52, Korea. Mem. ABA, R.I. Bar Assn., Lawyers Alliance World Security. Baptist. Avocation: bird watching. Estate planning, Probate. Home: 210 Payton Ave Warwick RI 02889-5133 Office: Tillinghast Licht & Semonoff 1 Park Row Ste 1 Providence RI 02903-1288

**HASTINGS, JOYCE R.,** editor. Editor Wis. Lawyer, Madison. Office: State Bar Wis 402 W Wilson St Madison WI 53703-3689

**HASTINGS, THOMAS WARREN,** lawyer, prosecutor; b. North Conway, N.H., Apr. 25, 1956; s. Hugh Warren II and Norene (Mattson) H.; m. Sabina Edith Robiller, June 26, 1982 (div. Nov. 1985); m. Lynn Marie Rushing, Apr. 16, 1994. BA in Econs., U. Maine, 1978; JD, New Eng. Sch. Law, 1982. Bars: Fla. 1982, U.S. Dist. Ct. (mid. dist.) Fla. 1983. Asst. state atty., chief of career criminal divsn. State of Fla., Office of State Atty., Sanford, 1982—; lectr., instr., law enforcement agys. and related groups, 1987—; police chief search com. Casselberry (Fla.) Police Dept., 1990. Chmn. legal mentor program, Lake Brantley H.S., Altamonte Springs, Fla., 1992—. Mem. Seminole County Bar Assn. (chmn. criminal law sect. 1993). Republican. Avocations: boating, SCUBA diving, tennis. Office: Office of State Atty 100 E 1st St Sanford FL 32771-1302

**HASTINGS, WILLIAM CHARLES,** retired state supreme court chief justice; b. Newman Grove, Nebr., Jan. 31, 1921; s. William C. and Margaret (Hansen) H.; m. Julie Ann Simonson, Dec. 29, 1946; children—Pamela, Charles, Steven. B.Sc., U. Nebr., 1942, J.D., 1948; LHD (hon.), Hastings Coll., 1991. Bar: Nebr. 1948. With FBI, 1942-43; mem. firm Chambers, Holland, Dudgeon & Hastings, Lincoln, 1948-65; judge 3d jud. dist. Nebr., Lincoln, 1965-79; judge Supreme Ct. Nebr., Lincoln, 1979-88, chief justice, 1988-95; ret., 1995; bd. dirs. Nat. Conf. Chief Justices, 1989-91. Pres. Child Guidance Ctr., Lincoln, 1962, 63; v.p. Lincoln Community Coun., 1968, 69; vice chmn. Antelope Valley coun. Boy Scouts Am., 1968, 69; pres. 1st Presbyn. Ch. Found., 1968—; mem. Lincoln Parks and Recreation Adv. Bd. Served with AUS, 1943-46. Named to Nebr. Jaycee Hall of Fame, 1998. Mem. ABA, Nebr. Bar Assn. (George H. Turner award 1991, Pioneer award 1992), Am. Jud. Soc., Lincoln Bar Assn., Nebr. Dist. Judges Assn. (past pres.), Nat. Conf. Chief Justices (past bd. dirs.), Am. Judicature Soc. (Herbert Harley award 1997), Phi Delta Phi. Republican. Presbyterian (deacon, elder, trustee). Club: East Hills Country (pres. 1959-60). Home: 1544 S 58th St Lincoln NE 68506-1407

**HASTY, WILLIAM GRADY, JR.,** lawyer; b. Canton, Ga., July 7, 1947; s. William Grady and Hazel Bonnie (Wyatt) H.; m. Linda Lacey Nichols, Aug. 9, 1969; children: William Grady III, Lauren Elise, Jeffrey Nichols. AA, Reinhardt Coll., 1967; BS, U. Ga., 1969; JD, Mercer U., 1974. Bar: Ga. 1974, U.S. Dist. Ct. (no. dist.) Ga. 1975, U.S. Ct. Appeals (11th cir.) 1975. bd. dirs. Bank of Canton, The Presdl. Roundtable. Chmn. Cherokee County Recreation Commn., 1975-85; charter mem. Leadership Cherokee County, 1987, steering com., 1988—; mem. Leadership Ga.; trustee Canton 1st United Meth. Ch., sec., exec. com.; bd. trustees Reinhardt Coll., Cherokee County Hosp. Authority, Northside Hosp., Cherokee; exec. bd. Cherokee

Founder's Club; bd. dirs. Northside Hosp., Cherokee. Named Outstanding Citizen Cherokee County Commr., 1986, 87. Mem. VFW, ATLA, Ga. Bar Assn., Canton Bar Assn., Blue Ridge Bar Assn., Trial Lawyers Assn. Ga., Phoenix Soc. Atlanta, Canton Golf Club, Moose Club, Atlanta Track Club, Cherokee County C. of C., Commerce Club Atlanta. Avocations: tennis, running, fishing, hunting. Personal injury, General civil litigation, Banking. Home: 1746 Cumming Hwy Canton GA 30114-8043 Office: William G Hasty Jr PC PO Box 1818 211 E Main St Canton GA 30114-2710

**HATCH, HAZEN VAN DEN BERG,** lawyer; b. Battle Creek, Mich., Jan. 18, 1932; s. Hazen Jesse and Clare Janet (van den Berg) H.; m. Mary Lou Holmes, Dec. 27, 1955; children: Mary, David. BA, Dartmouth Coll., 1953; JD, U. Mich., 1956. Bar: Mich. 1956, U.S. Supreme Ct. 1959. Ptnr. various firms, Marshall, Mich., 1960-81, Hatch & Smith, Kalamazoo, Mich., 1981-93, Butler Durham & Willoughby, Kalamazoo, Mich., 1993—. Contbr. articles to profl. jours. Del. Mich. Constitutional Conv., Lansing, 1961-62; trustee Marshall Sch. Bd., 1971-72. Lt. USAR, 1957-60. Recipient citation Mich. State Bar Assn., 1962. Fellow Mich. State Bar Found., Am. Coll. Trial Lawyers; mem. ABA, Kalamazoo County Bar Assn. Republican. Episcopalian. Avocation: golf. General civil litigation, Personal injury, Estate planning. Office: Butler Durham & Willoughby 202 N Riverview Dr Kalamazoo MI 49004-1310

**HATCH, HILARY JOY,** lawyer; b. L.A., Nov. 3, 1969; d. Robert Fred and Sandra Thunander H. BA, U. Calif., Berkeley, 1991; JD cum laude, Loyola U., 1994. Bar: Calif. 1994, U.S. Dist. Ct. (cen. dist.) Calif. 1994. Assoc. Gibson, Dunn & Crutcher, L.L.P., L.A., 1994—. Republican. Presbyterian. Avocations: skiing, running, travel, biking, reading. General corporate, Securities, Mergers and acquisitions. Office: Gibson Dunn & Crutcher LLP 333 S Grand Ave Ste 4400 Los Angeles CA 90071-3197

**HATCH, JOHN D.,** lawyer; b. Atlanta, Aug. 26, 1942; s. Ernest Healey and Charlotte Blanchard (Chazal) H.; m. Pamela Faye Carr, June 13, 1964; children: Wendy H. Duncan, A. Candice Hatch, Teresa H. Caraker. AA, Ctrl. Fla. Jr. Coll., Ocala, 1962; BS, Fla. State U., 1964; JD, Georgetown U., 1971. Bar: Fla. 1971, Conn. 1972, Tex. 1992, U.S. Dist. Ct. Conn. 1973, U.S. Dist. Ct. (no. dist.) Tex. 1992, U.S. Tax Ct. 1979, U.S. Supreme Ct. 1979; gen. securities lic., gen. prin. lic. Lt. USNR, 1964-71; atty. AEtna Life & Casualty, Hartford, Conn., 1971-74, counsel, 1974-83; v.p. and gen. counsel Continental Corp., N.Y.C., 1983-85; v.p. spl. ops. Comml. Life Ins. Co., Piscataway, N.J., 1985-87; v.p. and gen. counsel Associated Madison Cos., Inc., N.Y.C., 1987-88; sr. v.p. Resource Deployment, Inc., N.Y.C. and Ft. Worth, 1988-91; pres. Ins. Horizons, Inc., Ocala, Fla., 1992—, John D. Hatch, P.C., Ocala, 1992—; bd. dirs. Pub. Svc. Mut. Ins. Co., N.Y.C., Haubourton Reassurance Inc., Aurora, Colo.; gen. counsel Am. Health & Life Ins. Co., Ft. Worth, 1995—. Mem. ABA (chmn. TIPS employee benefits com. 1983-84, TIPS fin. svcs. com. 1992-93), Assn. Life Ins. Counsel, Fed. Bar Assn., Internat. Assn. Ins. Law. Republican. Catholic. Avocations: reading, boating, tennis. Insurance, General corporate, Consumer commercial. Home and Office: 840 SE 5th St Ocala FL 34471-2306

**HATCH, MICHAEL WARD,** lawyer; b. Pittsfield, Mass., Nov. 19, 1949; s. Ward Sterling and Elizabeth (Hubbard) H.; m. Lisa Schilling, June 8, 1974; children: Stuart, Andrew, Gillian. AB in Econs., St. Lawrence U., 1971; JD, Yale U., 1974. Bar: Wis. 1974, N.Y. 1980. Ptnr., chmn. real estate group Foley & Lardner, Milw., 1974—. Mem. ABA, N.Y. State Bar Assn., Wis. Bar Assn., Milw. Bar Assn., Am. Coll. Real Estate Lawyers, Urban Land Inst., Nat. Multi Housing Coun., Mortgage Bankers Assn. Wis., Bldg. Owners and Mgrs. Assn., Local Initiatives Support Corp., Milw. Athletic Club, Town Club. Avocations: architecture, historic preservation. Real property, Finance, Contracts commercial. Office: Foley & Lardner 777 E Wisconsin Ave Ste 3800 Milwaukee WI 53202-5367

**HATCH, MIKE,** state attorney general; m. Patti Hatch; 3 children. BS in Polit. Sci. with honors, U. Minn., Duluth, 1970; JD, U. Minn., 1973. Commr. of commerce State of. Minn., 1983-89; pvt. practice law; atty. gen. State of Minn., 1999—. Office: Minn Atty Gen's Office 102 State Capitol Saint Paul MN 55155-1622*

**HATCHER, JAMES GREGORY,** lawyer; b. Charleston, S.C., May 30, 1968; m. Quinton Larue and Wilma Pearl H.; m. Julia Kate Harris, Sept. 20, 1997. BA in History, Philosophy, Vanderbilt U., 1990; JD, Wake Forest U., 1993. Bar: N.C. 1993, S.C. 1995, U.S. Dist. Ct. (we. dist.) N.C. Atty. Russell & King, PA, Asheville, N.C., 1993-94, Erdman & Hockfield, LLP, Charlotte, N.C., 1995-98, The McIntosh Law Firm P.C., Charlotte, 1998—. Mem. N.C. Bar Assn., S.C. Bar Assn., N.C. Acad. Trial Lawyers, Mecklenburg County Bar Assn. (family law sect.). Family and matrimonial. Office: The McIntosh Law Firm PC 428 E Fourth St Ste 201 Charlotte NC 28202

**HATCHETT, CYNTHIA M.,** lawyer; b. Santa Ana, Calif., Sept. 16, 1964; m. Michael K. Hatchett, Nov. 26, 1993; 1 child, Madelaine Ann. BA, UCLA, 1987; JD, U. Houston, 1991, MBA, 1991. Bar: U.S. Dist. Ct. (so. dist.) Tex. 1993. Ptnr. Boudreaux, Hatchett, Washington & Sparks, Houston, 1991-96, The Hatchett Law Firm, Houston, 1996—. Mem. African-Am. mktg. com. United Way Tex. Gulf Coast, Houston, 1995—. Mem. State Bar Tex. (opportunites for minorities in legal profession 1996—), Houston Bar Assn. (mem. elder law com. 1996—), Women Attys. in Tax and Probate (v.p. 1996—). State civil litigation, Probate, Estate planning. Office: The Hatchett Law Firm 1001 West Loop S Ste 100 Houston TX 77027-9002

**HATFIELD, JACK KENTON,** lawyer, accountant; b. Medford, Okla., Jan. 26, 1922; s. Loate L. and Cora (Walsh) H.; m. D. Ann Keltner, Dec. 5, 1943 (dec. Sept. 1988); children: Susan Kathryn Hatfield Bechtold, Sally Ann Hatfield Clark; m. K. Dean Walker, Aug. 7, 1997. BS in BA, Phillips U., Enid, Okla., 1947; BA, Phillips U., 1953; LLB, Oklahoma City U., 1954, JD, 1967. Bar: Okla. 1954; CPA 1954. Pvt. practice, Enid, Okla., 1954-58; with Dept. Interior, Tulsa, 1958-77; pvt. practice, Tulsa, 1977—. Mem. ABA, Okla. Bar Assn., Tulsa Co. Bar Assn., Am. Inst. CPA's, Okla. Soc. CPA's. Club: Petroleum. Avocations: photography, tennis. Probate, Personal income taxation, Estate planning. Home: 4013 E 86th St Tulsa OK 74137-2609 Office: 7060 S Yale Ave Ste 601 Tulsa OK 74136-5739

**HATFIELD, PAUL GERHART,** federal judge; b. Great Falls, Mont., Apr. 29, 1928; s. Trueman LeRoy and Grace Lenore (Gerhart) H.; m. Dorothy Ann Allen, Feb. 1, 1958 (dec. Aug. 1992); children: Kathleen Helen, Susan Ann, Paul Allen. Student, Coll. of Great Falls, 1947-50; LL.B., U. Mont., 1955. Bar: Mont. bar 1955. Asso. firm Hoffman & Cure, Gt. Falls, Mont., 1955-56, Jardine, Stephenson, Blewett & Weaver, Gt. Falls, 1956-58, Hatfield & Hatfield, Gt. Falls, 1959-60; chief dep. county atty. Cascade County, Mont., 1959-60; dist. ct. judge 8th Jud. Dist., Mont., 1961-76; chief justice Supreme Ct. Mont., Helena, 1977-78; U.S. Senator from Mont., 1978-79; U.S. dist. judge for Dist. of Mont., Gt. Falls, 1979-96; chief judge, 1990-96, sr. judge, 1996—; Vice chmn. Pres.'s Council Coll. of Great Falls. Author standards for criminal justice, Mont. cts. Served with U.S. Army, 1951-53. Korea. Mem. Am., Mont. bar assns., Am. Judicature Soc. Roman Catholic. Office: US Dist Ct US Post Office & Cthouse PO Box 1529 Great Falls MT 59403-1529

**HATHAWAY, GERALD THOMAS,** lawyer; b. Frankfurt, Fed. Republic of Germany, Aug. 5, 1954; came to U.S., 1955; s. Robert Ernest Hathaway and Jacqueline Anne (Hughes) Gouin; m. Kathleen Ann McCauley, Dec. 27, 1980; children: Michael, Anne, Thomas. BA, LaSalle U., 1976; JD, U. Pitts., 1979. Bar: Pa. 1979, N.J. 1980, N.Y. 1983, U.S. Dist. Ct. (ea. dist.) Pa. 1980, U.S. Dist. Ct. N.J. 1980, U.S. Ct. Appeals (3d cir) 1980, U.S. Dist. Ct. (cen. dist.) Ill. 1981, U.S. Dist. Ct. (so. and ea. dists.) N.Y. 1984, U.S. Supreme Ct., 1988, U.S. Ct. Appeals (2d cir.) 1988. Assoc. Cunniff, Bray & McAleese, Phila., 1979-82; assoc. Holtzmann, Wise & Shepard, N.Y.C., 1982-86, ptnr., 1987-91; ptnr. Marks & Murase, L.L.P., N.Y.C., 1991—. Author: (musical play) Ire, 1984; contbg. editor (3d edit., 2d and 3d supplements) The Developing Labor Law, 1987, 88; contbr. articles to profl. jours. Vol. dir. NYU Grad. Sch. Bus., 1983-87; asst. sec. Riverside Opera Ensemble, N.Y.C., 1984-91. Mem. ABA, N.Y. State Bar Assn., Pa. Bar Assn., Assn. Bar of City of N.Y., Wyoming Club (Millburn, N.J.). Republican. Roman Catholic. Avocations: theatre, photography, sailing. Labor, Federal civil litigation, Entertainment. Home: 53 Chestnut St Millburn NJ 07041-2003 Office: Marks & Murase LLP 399 Park Ave New York NY 10022-4614

**HATLEY, RODNEY JAMES,** lawyer, naval officer; b. Millington, Tenn., May 25, 1961; s. Carmon Warren and Lorraine Elizabeth (Kapustka) H. BA, Rhodes Coll., 1983; JD, Memphis State U., 1986. Bar: Tenn. 1987, Calif. 1992, U.S. Dist. Ct. (we. dist.) Tenn. 1987, U.S. Dist. Ct. (ea. dist.) Calif. 1992, U.S. Ct. Mil. Appeals 1990, U.S. Ct. Appeals (6th cir.) 1992, U.S. Supreme Ct. 1991, U.S. Tax Ct. 1993, U.S. Dist. Ct. (mid. and ea. dists.) Tenn. 1994, U.S. Dist. Ct. (no., cen. and so. dists.) Calif. 1994. Assoc. Byrd, Cobb, et al., Memphis, 1987-88, Gatti, Keltner and Bienvenu, Memphis, 1988-89; judge adv. Naval Legal Svc. Office, San Francisco, 1989-91; staff judge adv. Naval Air Weapons Sta., China Lake, Calif., 1991—; special asst. U.S. atty. Naval Air Weapons Sta., 1993—. Co-author: California Probate Information Booklet, 1990. Legal counsel San Francisco Jaycees, 1990, pres., 1991. Lt. USNR, 1988—. Mem. ABA, Fed. Bar Assn., Assn. Trial Lawyers Am., Calif. State Bar Assn., Calif. Trial Lawyers Assn., Memphis Bar Assn., Tenn. Bar Assn., Phi Alpha Delta Legal Fraternity, China Lake Rotary Club, Commonwealth Club Calif., Ridgecrest-China Lake Optimist Club, Masons (Indian Wells Valley lodge). Republican. Roman Catholic. Avocations: flying, sky diving, sail planing, scuba diving, collecting Beatles' memorabilia. Military, Environmental, Taxation, general. Home: 10027 Rio San Diego Dr Apt 223 San Diego CA 92108-5644 Office: Naval Air Weapons Sta Code C0807 # 00001 China Lake CA 93555

**HATTEN, ROBERT RANDOLPH,** lawyer; b. Charlottesville, Va., Jan. 27, 1948; s. John Quackenbush and Mary Lou (Payne) H.; m. Anne Meredith Sherman, Aug. 14, 1970 (div. Jan. 9181); children: Catharine Cary, Anne Meredith; m. Shirley Kaye Ambrose, Feb. 21, 1981; 1 stepchild, Christopher Hilton. BA, Hampden-Sydney Coll., 1969; JD, Washington & Lee U., 1972. Bar: Va. 1972, U.S. Dist. Ct. (ea. dist.) Va. 1973, U.S. Ct. Appeals (4th cir.) 1973, U.S. Supreme Ct. 1982. Law clk. U.S. Dist. Ct. (ea. dist.) Va., Norfolk, 1972-73; assoc. Patten & Wornom, Newport News, Va., 1973-75; ptnr. Patten, Wornom & Watkins, Newport News, 1976—; bd. dirs. Asbestos Health Claimants Com., Johns Manville Bankruptcy Region, N.Y.C., 1983-89; mem. MDL Steering Com., 1991—. Contbr. articles to profl. jours. Bd. dirs. Peninsula Big Bros. Assn. Hampton Va., 1974-79; chmn. Newport News League of Downtown Churches, 1978; bd. trustees Lexington (Ky.) Theol. Sem., Hampden-Sydney Coll., 1994—. Mem. ATLA (mem. key congl. liaison, spl.), Am. Bd. Trial Advocates, Va. Trial Lawyers Assn. (bd. govs. 1985-91, spl. award for courageous advocacy 1987), Newport News Bar Assn. Democrat. Club: James River Country (Newport News). Avocations: golf, boating. Personal injury, Workers' compensation, Admiralty. Home: 9 Hopemont Dr Newport News VA 23606-2116 Office: Patten Wornom & Watkins 12350 Jefferson Ave Ste 360 Newport News VA 23602-6951

**HATTEN, W. EDWARD, JR.,** lawyer; b. Jackson, Miss., May 8, 1965. BS, U. Southern Miss., 1987; JD, U. Miss., 1990. Bar: Miss. 1991, U.S. Dist. Ct. (no. and so. dists.) Miss. 1991, U.S. Ct. Appeals (5th cir.) 1991. Spl. asst. atty. gen. Office of Atty. Gen., Jackson, Miss., 1990-93; assoc. Waycaster & Warren, Jackson, 1993-95, Dukes, Dukes, Keating & Faneca, P.A., Gulfport, Miss., 1995—. Mem. Miss. Bar Assn., Harrison County Bar Assn. General civil litigation, Real property, Civil rights. Office: Dukes Dukes Keating & Faneca PO Drawer W Gulfport MS 39502

**HATTER, TERRY JULIUS, JR.,** federal judge; b. Chgo., Mar. 11, 1933. A.B., Wesleyan U., 1954; J.D., U. Chgo., 1960. Bar: Ill. 1960, Calif. 1965, U.S. Dist. Ct. 1960, U.S. Ct. Appeals 1960. Adjudicator Chgo., 1960-61; assoc. Harold M. Calhoun, Chgo., 1961-62; asst. pub. defender Cook County Chgo., 1961-62; asst. U.S. atty. No. Dist. Calif., San Francisco, 1962-66; chief counsel San Francisco Neighborhood Legal Assistance Found., 1966-67; regional legal svcs. dir. Exec. Office Pres. OEO, San Francisco, 1967-70; exec. dir. Western Ctr. Law and Poverty, L.A., 1970-73; exec. asst. to mayor, dir. criminal justice planning L.A., 1974-75; spl. asst. to mayor, dir. urban devel., 1975-77; judge Superior Ct. Calif., L.A., 1977-80; judge U.S. Dist. Ct. (cen. dist.) Calif., L.A., 1979-98, chief judge, 1998—; lectr. Police Acad., San Francisco Police Dept., 1963-66, U. Calif., San Diego, 1970-71, Colo. Jud. Conf., 1973; assoc. clin. prof. law U. So. Calif. Law Ctr., L.A., 1970-74, mem. bd. councilors; prof. law Loyola U. Sch. Law, L.A., 1973-75; mem. faculty Nat. Coll. State Judiciary, Reno, 1974. V.p. Northbay Halfway House, 1964-65; vice chmn. Los Angeles Regional Criminal Justice Planning Bd., 1975-76; mem. Los Angeles Mayor's Cabinet Com. Econ. Devel., 1976-77, Mayor's Policy Com., 1973-77, chmn. housing econ. and community devel. com., City Los Angeles, 1975-77, chmn. housing and community devel. tech. com., 1975-77; vice chmn. Young Dems. Cook County, 1961-62; chmn. bd. Real Estate Coop; bd. dirs. Bay Area Social Planning Coun., Contra Costa, Black Law Center L.A., Nat. Fedn. Settlements & Neighborhood Ctrs., Edn. Fin. & Governance Reform Project, Mexican Am. Legal Def. & Ednl. Fund, Nat. Health Law Program, Nat. Sr. Citizens Law Ctr., Calif. Law Ctr., L.A. Regional Criminal Justice Planning Bd.; mem. exec. com. bd. dirs. Constl. Rights Found; trustee Wesleyan Univ. Meth. Ch.; mem. bd. visitors U. Chgo. Law Sch. Mem. NAACP (exec. com., bd. dirs. Richmond chpt.), Nat. Legal Aid & Defender Assn. (dir., vice chmn.), L.A. County Bar Assn. (exec. com.), Am. Judicature Soc., Charles Houston Law Club, Phi Delta Phi, Order Coif. Office: US Dist Ct 312 N Spring St Los Angeles CA 90012-4701

**HATTERVIG, KAREN ANN,** lawyer; b. Mitchell, S.D., Oct. 13, 1948; d. Gordon E. and Emma Sophia (Wiken) Larson; m. Jack A. Hattervig, Dec. 20, 1967 (div. Aug. 1973); children: Kimberly A., Thorpe-Jeffrey M. AA, BS, U. S.D., 1977, JD, 1981. Bar: S.D. 1981, U.S. Dist. Ct. (so. dist.) 1981, U.S. Ct. Appeals (8th cir.) 1981. Assoc. Strange, Strange & Palmer, Sioux Falls, S.D., 1981-82; supervising atty. East River Legal Svcs., Sioux Falls, 1982—. Chair Minnehaha County Family Violence Task Force, Sioux Falls, S.D., 1982—, S.D. Advocacy Network for Women, Sioux Falls, 1995—; mem. Wheels to Work Com., Sioux Falls, 1997—; treas. S.D. Coalition for Children, Sioux Falls, 1992—; chair Cmty. Outreach, Inc., Sioux Falls, 1994—. Named Friend of Social Work Nat. Assn. Social Workers. Democrat. Lutheran. Family and matrimonial, Civil rights, Government contracts and claims. Office: East River Legal Svcs 335 N Main Ave Ste 300 Sioux Falls SD 57104-6038

**HAUBENREICH, JOHN GILMAN,** lawyer; b. Lewisburg, Tenn., Feb. 24, 1953; s. Albert Dyer Haubenreich and Gladys Louise Edwards; m. Carol V. Clark, Nov. 4, 1995. BA, U. Tenn., 1973; JD, Emory U., 1976. Bar: Ga. 1976, U.S. Dist. Ct. (no. dist.) Ga. 1976, U.S. Ct. Appeals (5th cir.) 1976, U.S. Dist. Ct. (mid. dist.) Ga. 1978, U.S. Supreme Ct. 1979, U.S. Dist. Ct. (we. dist.) Tenn. 1980, U.S. Ct. Appeals (11th cir.) 1981, U.S. Tax Ct. 1981, U.S. Ct. Appeals (9th cir.) 1982. Atty. Bovis Kyle & Burch, Atlanta, 1976-80, Somers & Altenbach, Atlanta, 1980-82; sole practice Atlanta, 1982—. Mem. Lawyers Club Atlanta (sec. 1997-98, treas. 1998—). Methodist. Avocations: scuba diving, flying, skiing. General civil litigation, Insurance, Personal injury. Office: 6100 Lake Forrest Dr NW Ste 400 Atlanta GA 30328-3836

**HAUCK, DAVID LEAHIGH,** lawyer; b. Ft. Belvoir, Va., Jan. 8, 1954; s. Raymond Leahigh Hauck and Mary Virginia Carpenter; m. Marsha G. Woolard, Apr. 16, 1988; children: Sarah Hauck Bolton, Somer Pittman, John David, Benjamin L. BA in Psychology, U. Va., 1976; JD, Emory U., 1980. Bar: Va. 1981, U.S. Dist. Ct. (ea. dist.) Va. 1981. Assoc. Nikas, Englisby and Barnes, Richmond, Va., 1981-83; asst. Commonwealth atty. Chesterfield County, Richmond, 1984-86, asst. county atty., 1987; assoc., dir. Duane and Shannon, P.C., Richmond, 1988—; substitute judge for gen. dist., juvenile, and domestic rels., Chesterfield, Va., 1996—. Mem. Chesterfield County Bar Assn. (v.p. 1997-98, pres.-elect 1998-99). Insurance, Product liability, Criminal. Office: Duane and Shannon PC 10 E Franklin St Richmond VA 23219-2131

**HAUER, JAMES ALBERT,** lawyer; b. Fond du Lac, Wis., Apr. 3, 1924; s. Albert A. and Hazel M. (Corcoran) H.; children: Stephen, John, Paul, Christopher, Patrick. BCE, Marquette U., 1948, LLB, 1949; bank mgmt. cert., Columbia U., 1957, U. Wis., 1959. Bar: Wis., U.S. Dist. Ct. (ea. dist.), U.S. Ct. Appeals (9th cir.), U.S. Dist. Ct. (fed. dist.) 1958. Patent counsel Ira Milton Jones, Milw., 1949; chief counsel Wauwatosa Realty, Milw., 1950-57; v.p. Wauwatosa (Wis.) State Bank, 1957-67; pres. Milw. We. Bank, 1967-69, Prem Constrn. Co., Milw., 1969-73; pvt. practice Elm Grove, Wis., 1973-86, Sun City, Ariz., 1986—. Pres., bd. dirs. Sunshine Svc., Sun City, Meals on Wheels, Sun City. With USMCR, 1942-45. Mem. Wis. Bar Assn., Ariz. Patent Law Assn. (charter). Roman Catholic. Land use and zoning (including planning), Patent, Real property. Office: 9915 W Royal Oak Rd # Gh1078 Sun City AZ 85351-3163

**HAUGHT, JACK GREGG,** lawyer; b. Indpls., Dec. 18, 1958; s. Jack Laidley and Marilyn Louise (Richardson) H.; m. Sherry Jean Bush, Dec. 28, 1979 (div. Dec. 1988); m. Sarah Edith Lynn, Sept. 28, 1991; children: Elizabeth, Jack. AB, Ind. U., 1980; JD, U. Mich., 1983. Bar: Ohio 1983, D.C. 1986, U.S. Dist. Ct. (so. dist.) Ohio 1984, U.S. Ct. Appeals (6th cir.) 1983. Assoc. Topper, Alloway, Goodman, DeLeone & Duffey, Columbus, Ohio, 1983-85; assoc. Benesch, Friedlander, Coplan & Aronoff, Columbus, 1986-89, ptnr., 1993—; assoc. Dickstein, Shapiro & Morin, Washington, 1989-90; dep. atty. gen. of Ohio Atty. Gen. of Ohio, Columbus, 1991-93. Contbg. editor The Developing Labor Law, 2d edit., 1987. Sr. advisor to Ohio campaign Clinton/Gore 1992 Campaign, Columbus, 1992; polit. dir. Ohio primary election Dukakis for Pres., Boston, 1988; chair Ohio Elections Commn., Columbus, 1993-94; mem. Presdl. Rank Rev. Bd., Washington, 1993; del. Dem. Nat. Conv., Atlanta, 1988, N.Y. 1980. Democrat. Fax: 614-223-9330. E-mail: jghaught@bfca.com. Legislative, Labor, Government contracts and claims. Home: 140 S Cassingham Rd Bexley OH 43209-1845 Office: Benesch Friedlander Coplan & Aronoff 88 E Broad St Ste 900 Columbus OH 43215-3553

**HAUGHT, SHARON KAY,** lawyer; b. East Chicago, Ind., Jan. 31, 1959; d. Edwin Frank and Shirlee Mae Lebryk; m. Jeffrey Paul Haught, Aug. 17, 1991; children: Don Roger, Stephanie Marie. BS, Ball State U., 1981; JD, U. Dayton, 1984. Bar: Ohio 1984. Assoc. atty. Bank One Dayton (Ohio) NA, 1983-85; assoc. counsel Rubbermaid Inc., Wooster, Ohio, 1985—. Mem., program chair St. Mary of the Immaculate Conception Sch.-Sch. Support Orgn., Wooster, 1998. Mem. ABA, Ohio Bar Assn. Republican. Roman Catholic. Avocations: music, art, photography, computers. Contracts commercial, Environmental, Real property. Home: 1589 Brentwood Dr Wooster OH 44691-2527 Office: Rubbermaid Inc 1147 Akron Rd Wooster OH 44691-2596

**HAUGHT, WILLIAM DIXON,** lawyer; b. Kansas City, Kans., June 12, 1939; s. Walter Dixon and Florence Louise (Rhoads) H.; m. Julia Jane Headstream, July 22, 1967; 1 dau., Stephanie Jane. B.S., U. Kans., 1961; LL.B., U Kans., 1964; LL.M., Georgetown U., 1968. Bar: Kans. 1964, Ark. 1971. Assoc. Stanley, Schroeder, Weeks, Thomas & Lysaught, Kansas City, Kans., 1968-70; ptnr. Wright, Lindsey & Jennings, Little Rock, 1970-91; pvt. practice Little Rock, 1991-95; ptnr. Haught & Wade, 1996—. Author: Arkansas Probate System, 1977, 5th ed. 1992, (with others) Probate and Estate Administration: The Law in Arkansas, 1983. Served to capt. USAR, 1964-68, Korea, Washington. Mem. ABA (coun. chmn. coms.), Am. Coll. Trust and Estate Counsel (regent, editor studies program, chmn. editl. bd., state chair), Internat. Acad. Estate and Trust Law, Am. Law Inst., Am. Counsel Assn., Ark. Bar Assn. (chmn. probate law sect. 1981-82, chmn. econs. of law practice com. 1982-84, chmn. agrl. law com. 1986-88), Ctrl. Ark. Estate Coun., Pulaski County Bar Assn., Ark. Bar Found., Country Club of Little Rock. Presbyterian. Estate planning, Probate, Estate taxation. Office: Haught & Wade 111 Center St Ste 1320 Little Rock AR 72201-4405

**HAUGHTON, BRIAN STEPHENS,** lawyer, educator; b. San Jose, Calif., May 6, 1958; s. Kenneth Elwood and Beverly Mae (Bacon) H.; m. Tracy Ann Stephens, July 28, 1984; children: Katharine Ina, Stephanie Alma, Jacqueline Amy. Student, U. Sussex, Eng., 1978-79; BS in Physics with highest honors, U. Calif., Davis, 1980; JD, U. Calif. Berkeley/Harvard U., 1983. Bar: Calif. 1983, U.S. Dist. Ct. (no. dist.) Calif. 1983, U.S. Dist. Ct. (ea. and ctrl. dists.) Calif. 1986, U.S. Dist. Ct. (so. dist.) Calif. 1987, U.S. Ct. Appeals (9th cir.) 1987, U.S. Supreme Ct. 1987. Assoc. Landels, Ripley & Diamond, San Francisco, 1983-86, Ellman, Burke & Cassidy, San Francisco, 1986-89; assoc. Landels Ripley & Diamond LLP, San Francisco, 1989-91, ptnr., 1992—; adj. prof. Hastings Coll. Law, San Francisco, 1994—, U. San Francisco Sch. Law, 1991-93; lectr. U. Calif. Extension, others. Contbr. articles to profl. jours. Watson scholar, 1976; Kraft scholar, 1976. Mem. ABA (litigation sect., environ. litigation com.), State Bar Calif. (environ. law sect.), Bar Assn. San Francisco, Phi Kappa Phi. Avocation: theater. Environmental, Real property, Land use and zoning (including planning). Office: Landels Ripley & Diamond LLP 350 The Embarcadero San Francisco CA 94105-1204

**HAUPT, FRED JERRY,** lawyer; b. Alliance, Ohio, Nov. 17, 1941; s. Fred F. and Christina Haupt; m. Victoria E. Tzetzu, Apr. 29, 1967; children: Erika L., Jason F., Lindsay B. BA, Mt. Union Coll., 1963; JD, Case Western Res. U., 1967. Lawyer Krugliak, Wilkins, Griffiths and Dougherty Co. LPA, Canton, Ohio, 1967—; H-P Products, Inc., Louisville, Ohio; chair of bd. Alpha Land Title Agy., Inc., 1985—. Bd. dirs. Stark Devel. Bd., Canton, 1989-93, Leadership Stark County, 1995—; chair of bd. Mt. Union Coll., 1992—; mem. exec. coun. Boy Scouts Am. Mem. Canton Regional C. of C. (chair of bd. 1990), Jackson-Belden C. of C. (pres. 1996-98, bd. dirs. 1992—), Congress Lake Club (pres. 1988-90). Republican. Episcopalian. Avocations: golf, exercise. General corporate, Health, Estate planning. Office: Krugliak Wilkins Griffiths Dougherty Co LPA PO Box 36963 Canton OH 44735-6963

**HAUSCH, ADRIENNE LOUISE FLIPSE,** lawyer, minister; b. Bklyn., Oct. 23, 1950; d. William Jay and Mignon (Sorg) Flipse; m. Roger H. Hausch, Apr. 13, 1991. BA in Polit. Sci. with honors, Hofstra U., 1972; postgrad. C.W. Post Coll., L.I. U., 1973; JD, St. John's U., 1976; MDiv New Brunswick Theol. Sem., 1995. Bar: N.Y. 1977, U.S. Dist. Ct. (so., no. and ea. dists.) N.Y. 1983, U.S. Ct. Appeals (2d cir.) 1983, U.S. Tax Ct. 1983, U.S. Supreme Ct. 1986, Ariz. 1995. Law asst. Am. Ins. Assn., N.Y.C., 1975-76; law asst. law dept. N.Y.C. Criminal Ct., 1976; asst. counsel Senate Com. on Ins., Garden City, N.Y., 1977; assoc. counsel transp. com. N.Y. State Senate, Albany, 1977-82; pvt. practice, Williston Park, N.Y., 1977-81; asst. counsel N.Y. State Assembly, Albany, 1982-83; ptnr. Carway, Flipse & Moroney, Williston Park, N.Y., 1981-84, Carway, Flipse & Hannon, 1984-86, Carway & Flipse, Mineola, 1986—; adj. prof. dept. soc. scis. N.Y. Inst. Tech., Old Westbury, N.Y., 1981-91; adj. asst. prof. dept. paralegal studies St. John's U., 1986-93; instr. dept. continuing edn. C.W. Post, 1993—; counsel Westbury NAACP, 1983-90, St. Francis Hosp. Guild, Roslyn, N.Y., 1978-91. Republican candidate for N.Y. State Assembly, 1980; bd. dirs. Nassau County Youth Bd., Mineola, N.Y., 1970-94; v.p. fin. Scouting for the Handicapped divsn. Boy Scouts Am., Nassau County, 1982-85; sec. Nassau council Girl Scouts U.S.A., Inc., 1983-85; mem. Town of North Hempstead Cable TV Commn., Manhasset, N.Y., 1984. Recipient George N. Estabrook Disting. Svc.award Hofstra Alumni Assn., 1974; Dist. X Young Careerist award Bus. and Profl. Women's Clubs, 1980. Mem. Bar Assn. of Nassau County (bd. dirs. 1983-86, editor-in-chief Nassau Lawyer 1989-90, 98—, We Care bd. 1999—, mem. ann. dinner com. 1978—, mem. ins. com. 1978-80, chmn. subcom. on ins. availability 1978-79, mem. continuing legal edn. com. 1979-80, mem. gen. practice com. 1981-93, chmn. cmty. rels. and pub. edn. com. 1981-83, mem. criminal law and procedure com. 1987—, chmn. pro bono com. 1983-85), N.Y. State Bar Assn. (mem. law day com. 1984-93, mem. com. on assn. ins. plans), Assn. Trial Lawyers Am., Phi Delta Phi. Republican. Mem. Dutch Reformed Ch. Criminal, Family and matrimonial, Personal injury. Home: 42 Clinton Rd Garden City NY 11530-6356

**HAUSELT, DENISE ANN,** lawyer; b. Wellsville, N.Y., Oct. 12, 1956. BS, Cornell U., 1979, JD, 1983. Bar: N.Y. 1984, Ill. 1984, U.S. Dist. Ct. (we. dist.) N.Y. 1984, U.S. Bankruptcy Ct. 1984. Summer assoc. Wildman, Harrold, Allen & Dixon, Chgo., 1982; assoc. Nixon Hargrave Devans & Doyle, Rochester, N.Y., 1983-86; asst. counsel Corning (N.Y.) Inc., 1986-93, divsn. counsel, 1993-99, asst. gen. counsel, 1999—; Bd. dirs. So. Tier Legal Svcs., Bath, N.Y., 1986-89, Home Health Svcs., Inc., Corning, 1986-99, 171 Cedar Arts Ctr., 1999—. Mem. Cornell Law Sch. adv. coun. Recipient Am. Jurisprudence Constl. Law prize, Cornell U., 1981, others. Mem. ABA, Am. Corp. Counsel Assn., Cornell Law Assn., Keuka Yacht Club. Republican. Avocations: sailing, skiing. Antitrust, General civil litigation, Contracts commercial. Home: 164 Delevan Ave Corning NY 14830-3224 Office: Corning Inc Riverfront Plz Mp Hq E2 Corning NY 14831-0001

**HAUSER, CHRISTOPHER GEORGE,** lawyer; b. Syracuse, N.Y., May 15, 1954; s. W. Dieter and Nancy (Keating) H. BA, Washington & Jefferson Coll., 1976; JD, Dickinson Sch. Law, 1979. Bar: Pa. 1979, U.S. Dist. Ct. (we. dist.) Pa. 1981, N.Y. 1987, U.S. Supreme Ct. 1992. Legal asst. Pa. Dept. of Justice, Harrisburg, 1978-79; assoc. McDowell, McDowell, Wick & Daly, Bradford, 1979-83; ptnr. McDowell, Wick, Daly, Gallup, Hauser, & Hartle and predecessor firm McDowell, McDowell, Wick & Daly, Bradford, 1983—; broker, owner Re/Max Alpine Sales, Ellicottville, N.Y., 1991-93; pres./owner Alpine Sales and Rental Mgmt., Inc., Ellicottville, N.Y., 1987-94; chmn. adv. bd. Office Econ. Cmty. Devel., Bradford, 1988—. Chmn. campaign Bradford Area United Way, 1984, v.p., 1987-89, pres., 1990-92; chmn. Downtown Bradford Revitalization Corp., 1986—; Bradford Parking Authority, 1986-94; pres. Alleghany Highlands coun. Boy Scouts Am., Falconer, N.Y., 1986-88; dir. Bradford Econ. Devel. Corp., 1987—, Exch. Club, 1989-91; sec., treas. Bradford Redevel. Authority, 1992-96, chmn., 1996—; active Bradford Area Citizens Adv. Com., 1992—; dir. Pa. Economy League, 1997—; dir., sec. Bradford Area Alliance, 1997—; bd. dirs. Rte. 219 Assn., 1996—; dir. Continental One Alliance. Recipient Outstanding Svc. award Bradford Area United Way, 1985, Silver Beaver award Allehany Highlands coun. Boy Scouts Am., 1990, Founder's award Order Arrow Boy Scouts Am., 1991, Cmty. Svc. award City of Bradford Office Econ. and Cmty. Devel., 1995; named Bus. Person of Yr. Bradford C. of C., 1986, One of Outstanding Young Men Am. U.S. Jaycees, 1983. Mem. N.Y. Bar Assn., Pa. Bar Assn., McKean County Bar Assn. (v.p. 1992-93, pres. 1994-96), Bradford Area Jaycees (pres. 1983-85), Pennhills Club (sec. 1985-90, 99—, pres. 1990-92), Bradford Club. Republican. Episcopalian. General corporate, Real property, Finance. Home: 110 Congress St Bradford PA 16701-2228 Office: McDowell Wick Daly Gallup Hauser & Hartle PO Box 361 78 Main St Bradford PA 16701-2026

**HAUSER, HELEN ANN,** lawyer; b. Miami, Fla., July 23, 1948; d. Philip Jay and Ruth (Saltman) Fruitstone; m. Mark Jay Hauser; children: Robert Jeffrey, Cheryl Elaine, Lauren Yvonne. BA in English, Duke U., 1970; MA in English, U. Fla., 1972, PhD, 1975; JD, U. Miami, 1982. Bar: Fla. 1982, U.S. Dist. Ct. (so. dist.) Fla. 1982, U.S. Ct. Appeals (11th cir.) 1986, U.S. Supreme Ct. 1987, U.S. Dist. Ct. (mid. dist.) Fla. 1994. Instr. various colls., 1973-79; clk. to presiding justice Fla. 3d Ct. of Appeals, 1982-84; ptnr. Pines & Hauser, Miami, 1984-89; assoc. Law Offices of David P. Dittmar, Miami, 1989-91; ptnr. Dittmar & Hauser, P.A., Miami, 1991—. Vol. Guardian ad Litem Program, Juvenile Ct., Miami, 1985—. Angier B. Duke scholar Duke U., 1966-70; Harvey T. Reid fellow U. Miami Law Sch., 1979-82. Mem. Dade County Bar Assn., South Miami-Kendall Bar Assn., Fla. Assn. Women Lawyers. Avocations: playing violin, viola. Appellate, Insurance, General civil litigation. Office: Dittmar & Hauser 3250 Mary St Ste 400 Miami FL 33133-5232

**HAUSER, RITA ELEANORE ABRAMS,** lawyer; b. N.Y.C., July 12, 1934; d. Nathan and Frieda (Litt) Abrams; m. Gustave M. Hauser, June 10, 1956; children: Glenvil Aubrey, Ana Patricia. AB magna cum laude, CUNY Hunter Coll., 1954; D in Polit. Economy with highest honors, U. Strasbourg, France, 1955; Licence en Droit, U. Paris, 1958; student law sch., Harvard U., 1955-56; LLB with honors, NYU, 1959; LLD (hon.), Seton Hall U., 1969, Finch Coll., 1969, U. Miami, Fla., 1971, Colgate U., 1995. Bar: D.C. 1959, N.Y. 1961, U.S. Supreme Ct. 1967. Atty. U.S. Dept. Justice, 1959-61; pvt. practice N.Y.C., 1961-67; ptnr. Moldover, Hauser, Strauss & Volin, 1968-72; sr. ptnr. Stroock & Stroock & Lavan, N.Y.C., 1972-92, of counsel, 1992—; pres. The Hauser Found., N.Y.C., 1990—; Handmaker lectr., Louis Brandeis Lecture Series, U. Ky. Law Sch.; lectr. on internat. law Naval War Coll. and Army War Coll.; Mitchell lectr. in law SUNY, Buffalo; USIA lectr. constl. law Egypt, India, Australia, New Zealand; bd. dirs. The Eisenhower World Affairs Inst.; U.S. chmn. Internat. Ctr. for Peace in Middle East, 1984-92; bd. dirs. Internat. Peace Acad., 1990—, chair 1993—; U.S. pub. del. to Vienna follow-up meeting of Conf. on Security and Cooperation in Europe, 1986-88; mem. adv. panel in internat. law U.S. Dept. State, 1986-92, Am. Soc. Internat. Law Award to honor Women in Internat. Law; mem. Pacific Coun. on Internat. Policy, 1998—; bd. dirs. The Rand Corp. Contbr. articles on internat. law to profl. jours. U.S. rep. to UN commn. on Human Rights, 1969-72; mem. U.S. del. to Gen. Assembly UN, 1969; vice chmn. U.S. Adv. Com. on Internat. and Cultural Affairs, 1973-77; mem. N.Y.C. Bd. Higher Edn., 1974-76, Stanton Panel on internat. info., edn., cultural rels. to reorganize USIA and Voice of Am., 1974-75, Mid. East Study Gruop Brookings Inst., 1975, 87-88, U.S. del. World Conf. Internat. Women's Yr., Mexico City, 1975; co-chair Com. for Re-election Pres., 1972, Presdl. Debates project LVW, 1976, Coalition for Regan/Bush; adv. bd. Nat. News Coun., 1977-79; bd. dirs. Bd for Internat. Broadcasting, 1977-80, Catalyst, Internat. Peace Acad., The Aspen Inst., The RAND Corp., U.S. Coun. Germany; trustee, exec com. N.Y. Philharm. Soc.; trustee Lincoln Ctr. Performing Arts; adv. bd. Ctr. For Law and Nat. Security, U. Va. Law Sch., 1978-84; vis. com. Ctr. Internat. Affairs Harvard U., 1975-81, John F. Kennedy Sch. Govt., Harvard U., 1992—; dean's bd. advisor's Harvard Law Sch., 1996—, vice-chair, nat. co-chair univ. fund-raising campaign, 1997—; mem. bd. advisors Middle East Inst., Harvard U.; bd of visitors Georgetown Sch. Fgn. Svc., 1989-94; chmn. adv. panel Internat. Parlimentatry Group for Human Rights in Soviet Union, 1984-86; mem. Lawyers Com. for Human Rights, 1995—; mem. spl. refugee adv. panel Dept. State, 1981; bd. fellows Claremont U. Ctr. & Grad. Sch., 1990-94; former trustee Internat. Legal Ctr., Legal Aid Soc. N.Y., Freedom House; mem. Lawyer's Comm. Human Rights, 1996—. Fulbright grantee U. Strasbourg, 1955; Intellectual Exch. fellow Japan Soc.; recipient Jane Addams Internat. Women's Leadership award, 1996, women in internat. law award Am. Soc. Internat. Law, 1995, Fulbright award for Fulbright Alumni, 1997. Fellow ABA (life, mem. standing coms. on law and nat. security 1979-85, standing com. on world order under law 1969-78, standing com. on jud. selection, tenure, compensation 1977-79, coun. sect. on ind. rights and responsibilities 1970-73, advisor bd. jour. 1973-78); mem. Am. Soc. Internat. Law (v.p. 1988—, mem. exec. com. 1971-76), Am. Fgn. Law Assn. (bd. dirs.), Am. Arbitration Assn. (past bd. dirs.), Ams. Soc. (bd. dirs. 1988—), Coun. Fgn. Rels. (bd. dirs.), Internat. Inst. for Strategic Studies (London, bd. dirs. 1994—), Am. Coun. on Germany, The Atlantic Coun. U.S., Friends of the Hauge Acad. Internat. Law (bd. dirs.), Assn. of Bar of City of N.Y., Catalyst (bd. dirs. 1989-96). Republican. Banking, Private international, Public international. Office: Stroock & Stroock & Lavan 180 Maiden Ln New York NY 10038-4925 also: The Hauser Found Office of Pres 712 5th Ave New York NY 10019-4108

**HAUSHALTER, HARRY,** lawyer; b. Tel Aviv, Israel, July 7, 1945; s. Leo and Ruth H.; m. Theresa Ann Lukowicz. BA magna cum laude, Rutgers U., 1967, JD, 1970. Bar: N.J. 1970, U.S. Dist. Ct. 1970, U.S. Ct. Appeals (3rd cir.) 1972, U.S. Supreme Ct. 1982. Tax atty. Arthur Anderson & Co., Newark, 1970-71; dep. atty. gen. N.J. Atty. Gen.'s Office, Trenton, 1972-90; atty. Conley & Haushalter, Princeton, N.J., 1990-98; pvt. practice Hamilton, N.J., 1998—. Author: Matthew Bender/N.J. Taxes, 1982. Trustee Rutgers Ctr. for Govt. Svcs., 1994—; mem. Supreme Ct. Com. on N.J. Jud. Tax Ct., 1982-96. Mem. Phi Beta Kappa. State and local taxation. Office: Harry Haushalter Atty-at-Law 2119 Route 33 Ste A Hamilton NJ 08690-1740

**HAUSMAN, BRUCE,** retired lawyer; b. N.Y.C., Mar. 4, 1930; s. Samuel and Vera (Kuttler) H.; m. Jeanne Epstein, June 8, 1952 (div. Oct. 1992); children: Robert Lloyd, Arlene; m. Amy Kadin, Dec. 12, 1992. BA, Brown U., 1951; MS, Columbia U., 1952; postgrad., N.Y. Law Sch., 1979. Bar: N.Y. 1980. Dir. Belding Real Estate Corp., Corticelli Real Estate Corp., 1960-63; pres., dir. Va. Dyeing Corp., 1962-64; div. mgr. M. Hausman & Sons, Inc. (named changed to Belding Hausman Fabrics Inc.), 1952-64; ptnr. Kastex Corp., L.A., 1964; regional sales mgr. Belding Heminway Co., Inc., 1965; pres., dir. contract knitting divsn. Mozzil Knits Inc., 1969-73; exec., adminstrv. officer apparel fabric divsn. Belding Heminway Co., Inc., N.Y.C., 1966-73, exec. asst. to chmn. bd., 1973-74, group pres. home furnishings divsn., 1975-79, corp. v.p., 1979; corp. counsel Belding Heminway Co., Inc., 1980-85; sr. vice chmn. Belding Heminway Co., Inc., N.Y.C., 1980-86, chmn. exec. com., 1981-86, cons., 1987-88, sr. v.p., 1988-92; ret., 1993; exec. adminstrv. head Belding Hausman Fabrics Inc., 1975-79; adminstrv. officer Va. Dyeing Corp., Belding Corticelli Fiberglass Fabrics Inc.; pres. M.K. Leasing Corp., 1974; mem. exec. com. Daltex Med. Scis., Inc., 1993, pres., CEO, 1995—. Bd. overseers Parsons Sch. Design, 1975-91; trustee, mem. exec. com. Beth Israel Med. Ctr., N.Y.C., 1976-93, hon. trustee, 1993—; trustee, mem. exec. com. Beth Israel Nursing Home, 1991-93, hon. trustee, 1994—. Named Man of Yr., Fabric Salesmens Guild, Inc., 1972. Mem. Textile Salesmen's Assn. (bd. govs., Man of Yr. award 1987), Textile Distbrs. Assn. (gov. 1979, v.p. 1982, sec. 1983-87), Am. Arbitration Assn., NCCJ (bd. dirs. 1974-88). General corporate, Health, Pension, profit-sharing, and employee benefits. *To maintain a high standard of ethics in dealing with others. To respect my fellow persons and treat them with dignity. To devote part of my life in helping others less fortunate than I.*

**HAUSMAN, C. MICHAEL,** lawyer, judge; b. Chgo., Oct. 4, 1940; s. Charles Martin and Evelyn (Partridge) H.; children: Laura, Sarah, Craig, Karen, Richard, Ronald, Charles, Ashley, Courtney Megan. BS, Marquette U., 1962, JD, 1967. Bar: Wis. 1967, U.S. Dist. Ct. (ea. dist.) Wis. 1967, U.S. Supreme Ct. 1972. Ptnr. Frisch, Dudek & Slattery, Ltd., Milw., 1967-88, Slattery & Hausman, Ltd., Waukesha, 1988—; mcpl. judge City of Delafield, Wis., 1983—; lectr. State Bar of Wis. Family Law Seminars, Am. Acad. Matrimonial Lawyers. Named Outstanding Young Man Brookfield (Wis.) Jaycees, 1975. Fellow Internat. Acad. Matrimonial Lawyers, Am. Acad. Matrimonial Lawyers (pres. Wis. chpt. 1988-89); mem. Assn. Trial Lawyers Am., Am. Arbitration Assn., Wis. Acad. Trial Lawyers, State Bar Wis., Milw. Jr. Bar Assn. (bd. dirs. 1969-71), Brookfield C. of C. (pres. 1977-78), Brookfield Rotary (pres. 1980-81). Avocations: fishing, hiking, stamp and coin collecting. Family and matrimonial, Personal injury, Workers' compensation. Home: South 608 St Johns Dr Delafield WI 53018

**HAUSNER, JOHN HERMAN,** judge; b. Detroit, Oct. 31, 1932; s. John E. and Anna (Mudrak) H.; m. Alice R. Kieltka, Aug. 22, 1959. Ph.B. cum laude, U. Detroit, 1954, M.A., 1957, J.D. summa cum laude, 1966. Bar: Mich. 1967, U.S. Ct. Appeals (6th cir.) 1968, U.S. Supreme Ct. 1971, U.S. Tax Ct. 1976, U.S. Ct. Claims 1976, U.S. Ct. Mil. Appeals 1976. Tchr. Detroit Pub. Schs., 1954, 56-59; tchg. fellow U. Cin., 1959-61; instr. U. Detroit, 1961-74; sole practice U. Detroit, Detroit, 1967-69; asst. U.S. atty. Detroit, 1969-73; chief asst. U.S. atty. ea. dist. Mich., 1973-76; judge 3rd Jud. Cir. Mich., Wayne County, 1976-94; ret. 3d Jud. Cir. Mich., Wayne County, 1994, 1994; lectr. Law Sch.; faculty adviser Nat. Jud. Coll., 1978-79. Author: Sebastian, The Essence of My Soul, 1982; contbr. articles to Detroit Advertiser. Active Civic Searchlight. Served with U.S. Army, 1954-56. Mem. Fed. Bar Assn. (mem. exec. bd. Detroit chpt. 1976-82), State Bar Mich., Mich. Retired Judges Assn., Blue Key, Alpha Sigma Mu. Republican. Home: 22433 Louise St Saint Clair Shores MI 48081-2034 also: 8420 E Desert Palm Tucson AZ 85730-4723

**HAUSRATH, LES A.,** lawyer; b. Cleve., June 8, 1947; m. Linda, June 26, 1971; 1 child, Daniel. BA, U. Calif., Berkeley, 1969, JD, 1973. Bar: Calif. 1973, U.S. Dist. Ct. (no. dist.) Calif. 1973, U.S. Ct. Appeals (9th cir.) 1975. Atty. Legal Aid Soc. Alameda County, Oakland, Calif., 1973-77, Sullivan, Jones & Archer, San Francisco, 1977-79, Armour, St. John, Wilcox & Goudin, San Francisco, 1979-81; ptnr. Wendel, Rosen, Black & Dean, Oakland, 1981—; lectr. Contbr. articles to profl. jours. Commr., vice chair City Planning Commn., Oakland, 1997—; commr., chair Landmarks Adv. Bd., Oakland, 1991-96; mem. Gen. Plan Congress, Oakland, 1993-97. Mem. Internat. Right of Way Assn. (exec. bd. 1998—), Phi Beta Kappa. Land use and zoning (including planning), Condemnation, Real property. Office: Wendel Rosen Black & Dean LLP 1111 Broadway Fl 24 Oakland CA 94607-4036

**HAVEN, MILTON M.,** lawyer; b. Paterson, N.J., July 12, 1909; s. Harry and Minnie (Brown) H.; m. Phyllis Grossman, Dec. 23, 1938; children: Miles J., Constance A. AB, Syracuse U., 1931, LLB, 1933, JD, 1968. Bar: N.Y. Assoc. Hon. John E. Mack, Poughkeepsie, N.Y., 1933-46; rent examiner OPA, Poughkeepsie, 1946-50; acting sitting city judge, clk. of City Ct., Poughkeepsie, 1950-54; assoc. Edward J. Mack, Poughkeepsie, 1954-62, 66-70; judge City Ct., Poughkeepsie, 1962-66, 70-72; counsel to firm McCabe & Mack, Poughkeepsie, 1972-80, Corbally, Gartland & Rappleyea, Poughkeepsie, 1980—; jud. hearing officer 9th Jud. Dist., Poughkeepsie, 1978-81; mem. N.Y. State Mental Hygiene Coun. Pres. Poughkeepsie Jewish Ctr., 1942-43; pres. Temple Beth-El, Poughkeepsie, 1959-60, hon. trustee, 1985—; mem. adv. com. police sci. and correction adminstrn. CC, 1966-71; pres. Dutchess County Mental Health Assn., 1970-71, hon. trustee, 1990—; mem. adv. com. Pub. Welfare, Poughkeepsie, 1966-71; chmn. City Trial Com., Poughkeepsie, 1972-75; budget chair Dutchess County Area Chest and Coun., Poughkeepsie, 1952-54; mem. adv. bd. Marist Coll., Poughkeepsie, 1970-75; chmn. Dem. Com. City of Poughkeepsie, 1954-57; mem. bd. visitors Hudson River Psychiat. Ctr., 1977-88. Served with U.S. Army, 1942-43. Recipient Cert. of Appreciation Dutchess C.C., 1965, Dutchess Interfaith Coun., Poughkeepsie, 1990, Disting. Svc. award Mental Health Assn., Poughkeepsie, 1992, Van Bramer award, 1992. Mem. N.Y. State Bar Assn., Dutchess County Bar Assn. (pres. 1977-78), Masons, Harding Club (pres. 1937-38). Avocation: choir singing. Estate planning, General practice, Estate taxation. Home: 3 Ivy Ter Poughkeepsie NY 12601-4804

**HAVENS, HUNTER SCOTT,** lawyer; b. Cleve., Dec. 6, 1954; s. George Noble and Virginia Councell Havens; m. Gale Ann Havens, Oct. 18, 1996. BA, Case Western Res. U., 1980; JD, Cleve.-Marshall Coll. Law, 1984. Bar: Ohio 1984, U.S. Dist. Ct. (no. dist.) Ohio 1984. Ptrn. Quandt, Giffels & Buck, Cleve., 1984—. Personal injury, Product liability, General civil litigation. Office: Quandt Giffels & Buck Co LPA 800 Leader Bldg Cleveland OH 44114

**HAVERKAMP, JUDSON,** editor. AB in History, Earlham Coll., 1967; MEd, U. Mass., 1976, postgrad. With U.S. Peace Corps/Ministry of Pub. Helath, Bangkok, Thailand, 1967-70; asst. fgn. student advisor U. Mass., Amherst, 1971-75, publs. coord. Ctr. for Internat. Edn., 1975-79; dir. residence, acad. advisor Bradford (Mass.) Coll., 1979-81; freelance writer and editor Mpls., 1981-84; assoc. editor Minn. State Bar Assn., Mpls., 1984-85, dir. publs., editor, 1985—. Office: Minn State Bar Assn 600 Nicollet Ave Ste 380 Minneapolis MN 55402-1641

**HAVERMAN, DANIEL LIPMAN,** lawyer; b. Detroit, May 23, 1956; s. Samuel and Esther Haverman; m. Holly Gayle Gershon, Nov. 22, 1985; children: David, Elsie. Bs, Fla. State U., 1979; JD, Nova Southeastern U., 1984. Bar: Fla. 1984, U.S. Dist. Ct. Fla. 1985, U.S. Supreme Ct. 1990. Assoc. Jay B. Green, P.A., Ft. Lauderdale, Fla., 1985-90; ptnr. Green, Haverman, P.A., Ft. Lauderdale, 1990-96; pvt. practice law Boca Raton, Fla., 1990—. Mem. ATLA, Acad. Fla. Trial Lawyers, Def. Rsch. Inst., Broward Bar Assn. (chmn. legal ethics com.). Avocations: golf, tennis, boating. Personal injury, Insurance, General civil litigation. Office: 150 E Palmetto Park Rd Ste 500 Boca Raton FL 33432-4834

**HAVIGHURST, CLARK CANFIELD,** dean, law educator; b. Evanston, Ill., May 25, 1933; s. Harold Canfield and Marion Clay (Perryman) H.; m. Karen Waldron, Aug. 28, 1965; children: Craig Perryman, Marjorie Clark. BA, Princeton U., 1955; JD, Northwestern U., 1958. Bar: Ill. 1958, N.Y. 1961. Assoc. Debevoise Plimpton Lyons & Gates, N.Y.C., 1958, 61-64; assoc. prof. law Duke U., Durham, N.C., 1964-68, prof., 1968-86; William Neal Reynolds prof. Duke U., 1986—; interim dean Duke U. Sch. of Law, 1999—; dir. Program on Legal Issues in Health Care Duke U., 1969-88; adj. scholar Am Enterprise Inst. Pub. Policy Rsch., 1976—; resident cons. FTC, Washington, 1978, Epstein, Becker & Green, Washington, 1989-90; scholar in residence Inst. Medicine of NAS, Washington, 1972-73, RAND Corp., Santa Monica, 1999. Author: Deferred Compensation for Key Employees, 1964, Regulating Health Facilities Construction, 1974, Deregulating the Health Care Industry, 1982, Health Care Law and Policy, 1988, 2d edit., 1998, Health Care Choices: Private Contracts as Instruments of Health Reform, 1995; editor Law and Contemporary Problems jour., 1965-70. Served with U.S. Army, 1958-60. Mem. Inst. Medicine of Nat. Acad. Sci., Order of Coif. Office: Duke U Sch Law PO Box 90360 Durham NC 27708-0360

**HAVILAND, DONALD EDWARD, JR.,** lawyer; b. Meadowbrook, Pa., June 22, 1965; s. Donald Edward Sr. and Dolores Marion Haviland. BA, Rutgers U., 1987; JD, Villanova U., 1992. Bar: Pa. 1992, U.S. Dist. Ct. (ea. dist.) Pa. 1992, U.S. Ct. Appeals (3d cir.) 1993, N.J. 1994, U.S. Dist. Ct. N.J. 1994. Law clk. Herbert B. Newberg, P.C., Phila., 1991-92; assoc. Kronfeld, Newberg & Duggan, Phila., 1991-93, Harvey Pennington, Phila., 1993-94, Levin Fishbein, Phila., 1994—. Mem. ABA, Pa. Bar Assn., Phila. Bar Assn. Antitrust, Federal civil litigation, State civil litigation. Office: Levin Fishbein Sedran & Berman 510 Walnut St Ste 500 Philadelphia PA 19106-3601

**HAWES, SUE,** lawyer; b. Washington, Mar. 30, 1937; d. Alexander Boyd and Elizabeth (Armstrong) H.; m. James E. Brodhead, June 21, 1963; children: William James Pusey Brodhead, Daniel Alexander Hawes Brodhead. BA, Sarah Lawrence Coll., 1959, MA, 1963; JD, Whittier (Calif.) Sch. of Law, 1983. Bar: Calif. 1988, U.S. Dist. Ct. (cen. dist.) Calif. 1990. Dancer and choreographer N.Y.C., Washington, Latin Am., Europe, 1959-62; instr., dir. dance program dept. theatre and phys. edn. Smith Coll., Northampton, Mass., 1963-65; instr. dept. dance UCLA, 1973-75; freelance script supr. L.A., 1976-80; prin. Law Office of Sue Hawes, L.A., 1988-96; ptnr., mem. RESULTS. Articles editor Whittier Law Rev., 1982-83. Active Santa Barbara Symphony League. Mem. AAUW, Results, State Bar Calif., Actors' Equity Assn. Democrat. Avocations: music, gardening, politics. General practice.

**HAWK, BARRY EDWARD,** lawyer; b. Reading, Pa., 1940. AB magna cum laude, Fordham U., 1962; postgrad., U. Paris; LLB cum laude, U. Va., 1965. Bar: Pa. 1965, N.Y. 1975. Ptnr. Skadden, Arps, Slate, Meagher & Flom LLP, N.Y.C., 1991—. Editor: Ann. Fordham Corp. Law Inst. Vols. on Internat. Antitrust. Office: Skadden Arps Slate Meagher & Flom LLP 919 3rd Ave New York NY 10022-3902

**HAWKEY, G. MICHAEL,** lawyer; b. Apr. 17, 1941; m. Frances Tripp, Feb. 27, 1971; children: Samuel, Eliza, MacKenzie. AB, Princeton U., 1963; postgrad., Columbia Bus. Sch., 1964; LLB, Cornell U., 1967. Bar: Mass. 1967. Ptnr. Sullivan and Worcester, Boston, Mettowee Valley Partnership, Vt.; lectr. Mass. Restaurant Assn. Author: The Union-Management Controversy Over Subcontracting and Plant Relocation, 1963. Bd. dirs. Pacific Internat. Inst., Lewiston, Idaho, 1992-97, St. Lukes Cancer Rsch. Found., Inc., Cork, Ireland, 1994-97; bd. dirs., sec. mem. N.Am. bd. Michael Smurfit Grad. Sch. Bus., Univ. Coll., Dublin, Ireland, 1994-98; trustee Maruzen Hawthorne Coll., Antrim, N.H., 1991-92; gov. Wianno Club, 1982-98; founder Sun Valley Properties, MeHowee Valley Partnership. Mem. Real Estate Fin. Assn. (bd. dirs. 1989-92), Sr. Execs. Club of Mass. Real Estate Fin. Assn., Mass. Conveyance Assn., Abstract Club, The Country Club (Brookline, Mass.). Avocations: golf, tennis, skiing, real estate development. Land use and zoning (including planning), Landlord-tenant, Real property. Home: 26 Arlington Rd Wellesley MA 02481-6129 Office: Sullivan & Worcester 1 Post Office Sq Ste 2300 Boston MA 02109-2129

**HAWKINS, EDWARD JACKSON,** lawyer; b. Fall River, Mass., June 24, 1927; s. Edward Jackson and Harriet (Sherman) H.; children: Daniel, George, Robert, Harriet. Grad., Phillips Acad., Andover, Mass., 1945; AB summa cum laude, Princeton U., 1950; LLB magna cum laude, Harvard U., 1953. Bar: Ohio 1954, D.C. 1990. Assoc., ptnr. Squire, Sanders & Dempsey, Cleve., 1953-78; ptnr. Squire, Sanders & Dempsey, Cleve. and Washington, 1982-96, counsel, 1997—; chief tax counsel U.S. Senate Fin. Com., Washington, 1979-80, minority tax counsel, 1981; gen. chmn. Cleve. Tax Inst., 1969. Contbr. articles to profl. jours. With U.S. Army, 1945-46. Mem. ABA (vice chmn. govt. rels. tax sect. 1987-89), FBA, Ohio Bar Assn., D.C. Bar Assn., Phillips Acad. Alumni Assn. (alumni coun. 1967-70), Quadrangle Club. Democrat. Corporate taxation, Taxation, general, Personal income taxation. Home: 7404 Park Terrace Dr Alexandria VA 22307-2039 Office: Squire Sanders & Dempsey PO Box 407 1201 Pennsylvania Ave NW Washington DC 20044

**HAWKINS, FALCON BLACK, JR.,** federal judge; b. Charleston, S.C., Mar. 16, 1927; s. Falcon Black Sr. and Mae Elizabeth (Infinger) H.; m. Jean Elizabeth Timmerman, May 28, 1949; children: Richard Keith, Daryl Gene, Mary Elizabeth Hawkins Eddy, Steely Odell II. BS, The Citadel, 1958; LLB, U. S.C., 1963, JD, 1970. Bar: S.C. bar 1963. Leadingman electronics Charleston (S.C.) Naval Shipyard, 1948-60; salesman ACH Brokers, Columbia, S.C., 1960-63; from assoc. to sr. ptnr. firm Hollings & Hawkins and successor firms, Charleston, 1963-79; U.S. dist. judge Dist. of S.C., Charleston, 1979—, chief judge, 1990-93, sr. status, 1993—. Served with Mcht. Marines, 1944-45, with AUS, 1945-46. Mem. Jud. Conf. 4th Jud. Circuit, ABA, S.C. Bar Assn., Charleston County Bar Assn., Am. Trial Lawyers Assn., S.C. Trial Lawyers Assn., Carolina Yacht Club, Hibernian Soc. Charleston, Masons. Democrat. Presbyterian. Fax: (843) 579-1499. Office: Hollings Jud Ctr PO Box 835 Charleston SC 29402-0835

**HAWKINS, LISA LYNNE,** lawyer, municipal official; b. Washington, Mar. 15, 1971; d. Joseph Addison Jr. and Barbara Lynne (Brown) H. BA, Frostburg (Md.) State U., 1993; postgrad., Harvard U., 1995-96; JD, U. Calif., Berkeley, 1996. Bar: Md. 1996, D.C. 1998. Assoc. Patton Boggs, L.L.P., Washington, 1998—; polit. columnist Digital City Washington, Am. Online, Washington. Supervising editor Harvard Jour. on Legislation, Cambridge, Mass., 1995-96. Bd. dirs. Women Leadership Found., Washington, 1996-97; dir. fundraising Montgomery County (Md.) Young Dems., 1996-98; mem. city coun. Takoma Park, Md., 1997-98. Mem. ABA, Am. League of Lobbyists, Women in Govt. Rels., Bar Assn. D.C. Avocations: classic art, theater, mentoring. Office: Patton Boggs LLP 2550 M St NW Ste 400 Washington DC 20037-1301

**HAWKINS, MICHAEL DALY,** federal judge; b. Winslow, Ariz., Feb. 12, 1945; s. William Bert and Patricia Agnes (Daly) H.; m. Phyllis A. Lewis, June 4, 1966; children: Aaron, Adam. BA, Ariz. State U., 1967, JD cum laude, 1970; LLM, U. Va., 1998. Bar: Ariz. 1970, U.S. Ct. Mil. Appeals 1971, U.S. Supreme Ct. 1974. Pvt. practice law, 1973-77, 80-94; U.S. atty. Dept. Justice, Phoenix, 1977-80; judge U.S. Ct. Appeals (9th cir.), Phoenix, 1994—; mem. Appellate Cts. Jud. Nominating Commn., 1985-89. Staff editor: Ariz. State U. Law Jour, 1968-70. Mem. Ariz. Lottery Commn., 1980-83, Commn. on Uniform State Laws, 1988-93. Capt. USMC, 1970-73. Recipient Alumni Achievement award Ariz. State U., 1995. Mem. ABA, Maricopa County Bar Assn. (bd. dirs. 1975-77, 81-89, pres. 1987-88), State Bar of Ariz., Ariz. Trial Lawyers Assn. (bd. dirs. 1976-77, state sec. 1976-77), Phoenix Trial Lawyers Assn., Adminstrv. Conf. U.S. (pub. mem. 1985-94), Nat. Assn. Former U.S. Attys. (pres. 1989-90). Lutheran.

**HAWKINS, RICHARD MICHAEL,** lawyer; b. Nevada City, Calif., July 23, 1949; s. Robert Augustus and Virginia June (Hawke) H.; m. Linda Lee Chapman, Sept. 27, 1975; child, Alexandra Michelle. BS in Math., U. Calif., Davis, 1971; JD, U. Calif., San Francisco, 1974; LLM in Taxation, U. Pacific, 1983. Bar: Calif. 1974, U.S. Dist. Ct. (ea. dist.) Calif. 1974, U.S. Dist. Ct. (no. dist.) Calif. 1982, U.S. Ct. Claims 1982, U.S. Tax Ct. 1982, U.S. Ct. Appeals (9th cir.) 1982, U.S. Supreme Ct. 1982. From assoc. to ptnr. Larue & Francis, Nevada City, 1974-76; ptnr. Larue, Roach & Hawkins, Nevada City, 1977-78; of counsel Berliner & Ellers, Nevada City; ptnr. Berliner, Spiller & Hawkins, Nevada City, 1981; sole practice Grass Valley, Calif., 1981—. Bd. dirs. 49ers Fire Dist., Nevada City, 1977-81, 89-98, asst. fire chief, 1981-83, fire chief, 1983-89. Mem. ABA, Calif. State Bar (cert. specialist in estate planning, trust and probate law 1990), Nevada County Bar Assn. (v.p. 1976), Order of Coif, Phi Kappa Phi. Republican. Roman Catholic. Avocations: bicycling, snow and water skiing, running, showing Morgan horses. E-mail: rhawk53@aol.com. Fax: (530) 272-7861. Probate, Estate taxation, Estate planning. Home: 14762 Banner Quaker Hill Rd Nevada City CA 95959-8813 Office: 10563 Brunswick Rd Ste 2 Grass Valley CA 95945-7801

**HAWKINS, SCOTT ALEXIS,** lawyer; b. Des Moines, Nov. 24, 1954; s. Alexis Merrill and Rosemary Kathryn (Carney) H. BS, Drake U., 1977, JD, 1981. Bar: Iowa 1982, U.S. Dist. Ct. (no. dist.) Iowa, Tex. 1983, U.S. Dist. Ct. (no. and we. dists.) Tex., U.S. Ct. Appeals (5th cir.) Tex. 1988. In house counsel Internat. Housing Systems Inc., Dallas, 1982-84; assoc. Durant & Mankoff, Dallas, 1984-85; ptnr. Hawkins & Hawkins, Dallas, 1985—. Gen. counsel Wednesday's Child Benefit Corp., Dallas, 1987-88; pres., gen. counsel Hunger Solutions, Inc., a non-profit orgn., 1989. Mem. ABA, State Bar Tex. General civil litigation, Personal injury, Landlord-tenant. Office: Hawkins & Hawkins 5747 Ridgetown Cir Dallas TX 75230-2657

**HAWKS, TIMOTHY EDWARD,** lawyer; b. San Antonio, May 9, 1952; s. James E. and Charlene (Vorwald) H.; m. Mary Lewis McCormick, Aug. 8,

1980; children: Colleen, Laura, Tyler. BA, Georgetown U., 1974; JD, U. Iowa, 1977. Bar: Iowa 1978, Wis. 1981. Staff atty. Wis. Employment Rels. Commn., Madison, Wis., 1978-81; ptnr. Shneidman, Myers, Dowling & Blumenfield, Milw., 1981--. Mem. ABA, Wis. Bar Assn. (dir. labor law sect. 1983-84, officer 1990-92). Democrat. Roman Catholic. Labor. Office: Shneidman Myers Dowling & Blumenfield 700 W Michigan St Milwaukee WI 53233-2415

**HAWLEY, WILLIAM LEE,** lawyer; b. Cleve., Sept. 15, 1954; s. Donald Wade and Jane Louise (Lee) H.; m. Monica Oberlin, July 5, 1980; children: Rachel, Douglas. BA, Baldwin-Wallace Coll., 1976; JD, Ohio State U., 1979. Bar: Ohio 1979, U.S. Dist. Ct. (no. dist.) Ohio 1979, U.S. Ct. Appeals (5th cir.) 1984, U.S. Ct. Appeals (6th cir.) 1989, U.S. Supreme Ct. 1996. Assoc. Hoppe, Frey, Hewitt & Milligan, Warren, Ohio, 1979-85; ptnr. Harrington, Hoppe & Mitchell, Warren, 1986-98. Mem. ABA, Ohio State Bar Assn., Ohio Assn. Civil Trial Attys., Trumbull County Bar Assn. Republican. Lutheran. Contracts commercial, Insurance, General civil litigation. Office: Harrington Hoppe & Mitchell 500 Second National Tower Warren OH 44481-1084

**HAWORTH, GREGORY ROBERT,** lawyer; b. Tulsa, Dec. 25, 1954; s. William Edward and Elizabeth Techla (Koellner) H.; m. Mary Elizabeth Burgwinkle, Mar. 31, 1984. BA, Franklin (Ind.) Coll., 1977; JD, Rutgers U., 1982. Bar: N.J. 1983, U.S. Dist. Ct. N.J. 1983, U.S. Ct. Appeals (3rd cir.) 1994. Rsch. asst. Inst. Fgn. and Comparative Law U. South Africa, Pretoria, 1981; law clk. Superior Ct. N.J., Somerville, 1982-83; assoc. Cole, Schotz, Meisel, Forman & Leonard, Hackensack, N.J., 1983-90, ptnr., 1990—; advisor, judge Rutgers Law Sch. Moot Ct. Bd., Newark, 1994—; bd. mem., adv. bd. paralegal studies program Fairleigh Dickinson U., Madison, N.J., 1993—. Contbr. articles to profl. jours. Bd. mem. United Way, Plainfield, N.J., 1992—. Mem. N.J. State Bar Assn. (debtor/creditor and banking law sects. 1990—), N.J. Fed. Bar Assn. General civil litigation, Bankruptcy, Insurance. Office: Cole Schotz Meisel Forman & Leonard Ct Plaza N 25 Main St Hackensack NJ 07601

**HAWTHORNE, STAN,** lawyer; b. Cochabamba, Bolivia, June 4, 1950; s. John R. and Sarah (Reese) H.;m. Corinne Ann Hewlitt, Nov. 1, 1974; children: Michelle, Christopher, Kristin, Shana. BA, U. N.H., 1986; JD, Franklin Pierce Law Ctr., 1989. Bar: N.H. 1990, U.S. Dist. Ct. (ea. dist.) N.H. 1990, U.S. Bankruptcy Ct. 1990. Justice of peace, 1987—; pvt. practice law Somersworth, N.H., 1990-91; ptnr. Hawthorne & Brown, Somersworth, 1991-94; sr. atty., owner Hawthorne Law Ctrs., Rochester, Somersworth, Ossipee, Wakefield, N.H., 1994—; nat. drug trafficking def. cons., 1995—; justice of the peace State of N.H.; mem. adj. faculty N.H. Coll. Bus. Law I & II, 1999. Coun. City of Somersworth, 1991-92, mem. sch. bd., 1987-90, conservation commr., 1987-91. Served in USN, 1969-75, S.E. Asia, Mediterranean. Mem. VFW, N.H. Bar Assn. (bd. dirs., publ. com. 1996—), Am. Legion, Eagles. Republican. Protestant. Avocations: mountain climbing, snowmobiling, hunting, fishing, writing. Criminal. Home: 388 Lovell Lake Rd Sanbornville NH 03872-4727 Office: PO Box 946 Wolfeboro Falls NH 03896-0946

**HAY, DENNIS LEE,** lawyer; b. L.A., Feb. 18, 1958; s. Frank Henry, Jr. and Kyoko (Sukuya) H.; m. Kerry Lynne Hatfield, Aug. 11, 1984; children: Michelle, Jason, Katheryne. BS in Fin., San Jose State U., 1984; JD, U. Honolulu, 1988. Bar: Calif. 1989. Law clk. Legal Aid Soc. of Alameda Co., Hayward, Calif., 1985-87, Cohn, Becker & Jacquint, Hayward, Calif., 1987; law clk. Souza, Coats, McInnis, Mehlhaff & Hay, Tracy, Calif., 1987-89, assoc. counsel atty., 1989-92; ptnr. Mehlhaff & Hay, Tracy, Calif., 1992—; judge pro tem San Joaquin Superior Cts.; prof. law U. Honolulu Law Sch., Modesto, Calif., 1990—. Mem. ABA, Calif. Bar Assn., San Joaquin County Bar Assn. (chairperson bus. litig. sect. com. 1997-98). Republican. Presbyterian. Avocations: drag racing, horse back riding, raquetball. General civil litigation, Consumer commercial, Contracts commercial. Office: Mehlhaff Hay & Adrejko PO Box 1129 1011 Parker Ave Tracy CA 95376-3933

**HAY, JOHN LEONARD,** lawyer; b. Lawrence, Mass., Oct. 6, 1940; s. Charles Cable and Henrietta Dudley (Wise) H.; m. Ruth Murphy, Mar. 16, 1997; 1 child, Ian. AB with distinction, Stanford U., 1961; JD, U. Colo., 1964. Bar: Colo. 1964, Ariz. 1965, D.C. 1971. Assoc. Lewis and Roca, Phoenix, 1964-69, ptnr., 1969-82; ptnr. Fannin, Terry & Hay, Phoenix, 1982-87, Allen, Kimerer & LaVelle, Phoenix, 1987-94, Gust Rosenfeld, Phoenix, 1994—; judge pro tem Ariz. Ct. Appeals, 1999—; bd. dirs. Ariz. Life and Disability Ins. Guaranty Fund, 1984-95, chmn., 1993-95. Co-author: Arizona Corporate Practice, 1996, Representing Franchisees, 1996. Mem. Dem. Precinct Com., 1966-78, Ariz. State Dem. Com., 1968-78; chmn. Dem. Legis. Dist., 1971-74; mem. Maricopa County Dem. Cen. Com., 1971-74; bd. dirs. ACLU, 1973-78; bd. dirs. Community Legal Svcs., 1983-89, pres., 1987-88; bd. dirs. Ariz. Club, 1994-96. Mem. ABA, Ariz. Bar Assn., Maricopa County Bar Assn. (bd. dirs. 1972-85), Assn. Life Ins. Counsel, Ariz. Licensors and Franchisors Assn. (bd. dirs. 1985—, pres. 1988-89), Ariz. Civil Liberties Union (bd. dirs. 1967-84, 95—, pres. 1973-77, 97—, Disting. Citizen award 1979), Phoenix C. of C. (chmn. arts and culture task force 1997—). General corporate, Franchising, Insurance. Home: 201 E Hayward Ave Phoenix AZ 85020-4037 Office: Gust Rosenfeld 201 N Central Ave Ste 3300 Phoenix AZ 85073-3300

**HAYASHI, ARTHUR,** prosecutor; b. Spokane, Wash., Aug. 18, 1955; s. Kaoru and Mary I. (Ogata) H.; m. Lynda C. Egger, Mar. 31, 1984. BA in Polit. Sci., Gonzaga U., 1977; JD, U. Wash., 1980. Bar: Wash. 1981, U.S. Dist. Ct. (ea. and we. dists.) Wash. 1981, U.S. Ct. Appeals (9th cir.) 1981. Assoc. McKanna, Herman & Toreson, Spokane, 1980-83, Salter, McKeehen, Gudger & Rabine, Seattle, 1983-84; pvt. practice Spokane, 1984-87; dep. prosecutor Spokane County, 1987—; chmn. bd. dirs. Spokane Fed. Credit Union, 1994—; exec. mem. Wash. State Family Support Coun., Seattle, 1987-94; exec. mem. legal sec.'s adv. com. Spokane C.C., 1992—. Co-contbr.: Best Practices for State Family Law Cases, 1996. Mem. nominating com. Inland Empire coun. Girl Scouts U.S.A., Spokane, 1994—; trustee St. Paul's United Meth. Ch., Spokane, 1994—. Mem. Inns of Ct. (Charles Powell chpt.). Avocations: tennis, basketball, softball. Office: Spokane County Prosecutors Office 1124 W Riverside Ave # LL2 Spokane WA 99201-1132

**HAYCOX, ROLANDA MOORE,** lawyer, nurse; b. Indpls., July 19, 1964; d. Richard Roland and Roberta Joyce Moore; m. James William Haycox, Aug. 7, 1986. BSN with honors, Ind. U., Indpls., 1986, JD magna cum laude, M in Health Adminstrn., 1992. Bar: Ind. 1992, U.S. Dist. Ct. (no. and so. dists.) Ind. 1992; RN, Ind. Nurse Cmty. Hosp. East, Indpls., 1986-91, St. Francis Hosp., Beech Grove, Ind., 1990; rsch. asst. Ind. U. Sch. Law, 1990-92; assoc. Baker & Daniels, 1992-95; region dir. clin. analysis and compliance NovaCare, Inc., Carmel, Ind., 1995-96; counsel Anthem, Inc., Indpls., 1996—; condr. seminars in nursing and legal fields. Editor-in-chief Ind. Law Rev., 1991-92; contbr. articles to profl. jours. Bd. dirs. Alpha Home Assn. Greater Indpls., 1993-96; vol. Meth. Hosp. Hospice of Indpls., 1993-95, Hospice of Ind., 1995-96. Lloyd G. Balfour scholar, 1991, alumni scholar Eli Lilly & Co., 1992. Mem. ABA, Ind. Bar Assn., Indpls. Bar Assn., Hendricks County Bar Assn., Am. Health Lawyers Assn., Med. Group Mgmt. Assn., Am. Soc. Writers on Legal Subjects, Pi Alpha Alpha, Phi Delta Phi. Republican. Episcopalian. Avocations: violinist, gardening, cooking. Health, General corporate, Insurance. Office: Anthem Inc 120 Monument Cir Indianapolis IN 46204-4906

**HAYDEN, JOSEPH A., JR.,** lawyer; b. Newark, Apr. 2, 1944; s. Joseph A. and Mary (Giblin) H.; m. Donna Heinrich, Aug. 26, 1967; children: Kathryn Elizabeth, Patrick Joseph; m. Katharine Jackson Sweeney, July 19, 1987. Student, Boston Coll., 1966; JD magna cum laude, Rutgers U., 1969. Bar: N.J. 1969, U.S. Dist. Ct. N.J. 1969, N.Y. 1981. Law sec. to chief justice N.J. Supreme Ct., Trenton, 1969-70; dep. atty. gen. organized crime and spl. prosecution sect. Div. Criminal Justice, Atty. Gen.'s Office, Trenton, 1970-73; pvt. practice Newark, Hoboken and Weehawken, N.J., 1973—. Mem. editl bd. N.J. Law Jour., 1998—. Counsel to Essex County Dems., 1976-80; mem. adv. com. U.S. Dist. Ct. N.J. Named Top Lawyer N.J. Monthly mag., 1997. Fellow Am. Coll. Trial Lawyers, Am. Bar Found.; mem. FBA (trustee 1996-99), N.J. State Bar Assn. (prosecutorial and jud. appointment com. 1992-97, trustee 1998-99), Assn. Criminal Def. Lawyers N.J. (trustee 1985—, founder, 1st pres.), Ct. of Appeal Lawyers 3rd cir. (adv. com.), Fed. Bar Assn. (program chair 1998-99). Democrat. Avocations: running, recreational basketball, skiing. Criminal, General civil litigation, Environmental. Home: 811 Hudson St Hoboken NJ 07030-5003 Office: Hayden & Silber 1500 Harbor Blvd Weehawken NJ 07087-6732

**HAYDEN, RAYMOND PAUL,** lawyer; b. Rochester, N.Y., Jan. 15, 1939; s. John Joseph and Orpha (Lindsay) H.; m. Suzanne Saloy, Sept. 1, 1962; children—Thomas Gerard, Christopher Matthew. BS in Marine Transit, SUNY Maritime Coll., 1960; LLB, Syracuse U., 1963. Bar: N.Y. 1963, U.S. Ct. Appeals (2d cir.) 1963, U.S. Dist. Ct. (ea. and so. dists.) N.Y. 1964, U.S. Supreme Ct. 1967. Assoc. Haight Gardner Poor & Havens, N.Y.C., 1963-70; asst. gen. counsel Commonwealth Oil Co., N.Y.C., 1970-71; ptnr. Hill Rivkins & Hayden LLP, N.Y.C., 1971—. Mem. Coll. Coun., SUNY Maritime Coll., 1977-98, chmn., 1983-98; mem. adv. coun. Tulane U. Admiralty Law Inst. Served as lt. (j.g.) USNR, 1960-70. Mem. ABA (chmn. standing com. on admiralty and maritime law 1982-86), Maritime Law Assn. U.S. (chmn. com. on admissions 1974-82, exec. com. 1988-91, membership sec. 1996-98, 2nd v.p. 1998—), India House Club, Brookville Country Club (N.Y.). Admiralty, Insurance, Private international. Office: Hill Rivkins & Hayden LLP 90 West St New York NY 10006-1039

**HAYDEN, WILLIAM TAYLOR,** lawyer; b. Cin., Feb. 14, 1954; s. Joseph Page Jr. and Lois Elaine (Taylor) H.; m. Debbie Jane Kraus, Nov. 27, 1976; children: Page Ann, William Taylor, Michael Joseph, Amy Weber. BA in Econs., Denison U., 1976; JD, U. Cin., 1979. Bar: Ohio 1979, U.S. Dist. Ct. (so. dist.) Ohio 1979. Assoc. Cohen, Todd, Kite & Stanford, Cin., 1979-85, ptnr., 1986-96, mng. ptnr., mem. mgmt. com., 1988-96; sec. to bd. dirs. The Midland Co., 1988—, also bd. dirs.; trustee Fernald Litigation Settlement Fund, 1990—. Bd. dirs., mem. exec. com. Cin. Restoration, Inc., 1989-98, chair bd. dirs., 1995-96. Mem. ABA (corp. sect., tort and ins. law sect., tax sect., real estate and trust sect.), Ohio State Bar Assn., Queen City Club, Coldstream Country Club, Met. Club. Republican. Methodist. General corporate, Bankruptcy, Contracts commercial. Home: 7266 Nottinghill Ln Cincinnati OH 45255-3964 Office: PO Box 1104 Cincinnati OH 45254-1104

**HAYEK, CAROLYN JEAN,** retired judge, former church administrator; b. Portland, Oreg., Aug. 17, 1948; d. Robert A. and Marion L. (DeKoning) H.; m. Steven M. Rosen, July 21, 1974; children: Jonathan David, Laura Elizabeth. BA in Psychology, Carleton Coll., 1970; JD, U. Chgo., 1973. Bar: Wash. 1973. Assoc. Jones, Grey & Bayley, Seattle, 1973-77; sole practice law Federal Way, Wash., 1977-82; judge Federal Way Dist. Ct., 1982-95; ret., 1995; task force mem. Alternatives for Wash., 1973-75; mem. Wash. State Ecol. Commn., 1975-77; columnist Tacoma News Tribune Hometown Sect., 1995-96. Bd. dirs. 1st Unitarian Ch., Seattle, 1986-89, vice chair 1987-88, pres. 1988-89; ch. adminstr. Northlake Unitarian Universalist Ch.; den leader Cub Scouts Mt. Rainier coun. Boy Scouts Am., 1987-88, scouting coord., 1988-89; bd. dirs. Twin Lakes Elem. Sch. PTA. Recipient Women Helping Women award Federal Way Soroptimist, 1991, Martin Luther King Day Humanitarian award King County, 1993, Recognition cert. City of Federal Way Diversity Commn., 1995. Mem. AAUW (co-pres. Kirland-Redmond br., br. pres. 1978-80, 90-92, chmn. state level conf. com. 1986-87, mem. diversity com. 1991-98, state bd. mem. 1995-97, dir. ESL project), ABA, Wash. Women Lawyers, Wash. State Bar Assn., King County Dist. Ct. Judges Assn. (treas., exec. com. 1990-91, 92-93, com. chmn., chair and rules com. 1990-91, 92-94), Elected Wash. Women (dir. 1983-87), Nat. Assn. Women Judges (nat. bd. dirs., dist. bd. dirs. 1984-86, chmn. rules com. 1988-89, chmn. bylaws com. 1990-91), Fed. Way Women's Network (bd. dirs. 1984-87, 88-91, 95-97, pres. 1985, program co-chair 1989-91, co-editor newsletter), Greater Fed. Way C. of C. (dir. 1978-82, sec. 1980-81, v.p. 1981-82), Sunrise Rotary (com. svc. chair, bd. dirs., membership com., Federal Way chpt. 1991-96, youth exch. officer 1994-95), Washington Women United (bd. dirs. 1995-97), Unitarian Universalist Women's Assn. (chair bylaws com. 1996), Eliot Inst. (bd. dirs. 1996—, vice chmn. 1998-99, bd. chair 1999—), Plaza on State Owners Assn. (bd. dirs. 1997—, pres. 1997-99).

**HAYEK, JOHN WILLIAM,** lawyer; b. Iowa City, Jan. 25, 1941; s. Will J. and Marjorie B. (Kurtz) H.; m. Patricia M. Hess, Dec. 21, 1968; children: Grace, Matthew, Andrew. BA, Harvard U., 1963, JD, 1966. Bar: Iowa 1966, U.S. Dist. Ct. (so. dist.) Iowa 1967, U.S. Dist. Ct. (no. dist.) Iowa 1968, U.S. Ct. Appeals (8th cir.) 1973. Ptnr. Hayek, Hayek & Brown L.L.P., Iowa City, 1966—; 1st asst. county atty. Johnson County, Iowa City, 1967-70; spl. counsel City of Iowa City, 1970-90, city atty., 1974-81; mem. 6th Jud. Dist. Nominating Commn., 1978-83. Fellow Iowa Acad. Trial Lawyers; mem. Iowa Bar Assn. (sec., title standards com.), Johnson County Bar Assn. (pres. 1982-83), Assn. Trial Lawyers Iowa, Nat. Bd. Trial Advocacy, Iowa Def. Counsel Assn. (chmn. 6th jud. dist. bench bar liaison com.), Mason Ladd Inn of Ct. (emeritus master of the bench). Unitarian. General practice, General civil litigation, Real property. Home: 531 Kimball Rd Iowa City IA 52245-5830 Office: Hayek Hayek & Brown 120 1/2 E Washington St Iowa City IA 52240-3924

**HAYES, AUDREY DAWN,** lawyer; b. Atlanta, Oct. 26, 1959; d. Hilton Ray and Joan Armistead Dean. BS, Auburn U., Montgomery, Ala., 1981; JD, Cumberland Sch. Law, Birmingham, Ala., 1984. Bar: Fla.; bd. cert. in workers' compensation. Atty. Earle & Thompson, St. Petersburg, Fla., 1985-86, Law Offices of John W. Cash, Tampa, 1986-89, Rywant, Alvarez, Jones & Russo, Tampa, 1989-91, Haas, Austin, Ley, Roe & Patsko, P.A., Tampa, 1991-93; mng. shareholder Tampa office The O'Riorden Law Firm, P.A., 1993-96; shareholder, mng. ptnr. Hayes, Eraclides, Johns, Hall, Greene & Gelman, LLP, Tampa, 1996—; cir. ct. mediator Fla. Supreme Ct., Tampa, 1991—; lectr. in field. Bd. dirs. Head Liners, Tampa Performing Arts Ctr., 1998. Mem. ABA, Fla. Bar Assn., Hillsborough County Bar Assn. (chmn. workers compensation sect. 1995-97), Def. Rsch. Inst. Baptist. Avocations: oil painting, golf. Workers' compensation. Office: Hayes Eraclides Johns Hall Greene & Gelman LLP 3805 Henderson Blvd Tampa FL 33629-5013

**HAYES, BYRON JACKSON, JR.,** retired lawyer; b. L.A., July 9, 1934; s. Byron Jackson and Caroline Violet (Scott) H.; m. DeAnne Saliba, June 30, 1962; children: Kenneth Byron, Patricia DeAnne. Student, Pomona Coll., 1952-56; BA magna cum laude, Harvard U., LB cum laude, 1959. Bar: Calif. 1960, U.S. Supreme Ct. 1963. Assoc. McCutchen, Black, Verleger & Shea, L.A., 1960-68, ptnr., 1968-89; ptnr. Baker & Hostetler, 1990-97; ret., 1998. Trustee L.A. Urban Found., 1996—, CFO, 1998—; trustee L.A. Ch. Ext. Soc. United Meth. Ch., 1967-77, pres., 1974-77, chancellor ann. conf. Pacific and S.W., 1979-86, dir. 1010 devel. corp., 1993—, v.p., 1995—; dir., pres. Pacific and S.W. United Meth. Found., 1978-84; dir., v.p. Padua Hills, Inc., 1999—. Named Layperson of yr. Pacific and S.W. Ann. Conf., United Meth. Ch., 1981; recipient Bishop's award, 1992. Mem. ABA, Am. Coll. Mortgage Attys. (regent 1984-93, pres. 1993-94), Calif. Bar Assn., Los Angeles County Bar Assn. (chmn. real property sect. 1982-83), Toluca Lake Property Owners Assn. (sec. 1990-94), Pomona Coll. Alumni Assn. (pres. 1984-85), Lakeside Golf Club. Real property, Contracts commercial, General corporate. Office: Baker & Hostetler 600 Wilshire Blvd Fl 12 Los Angeles CA 90017-3212

**HAYES, DAVID JOHN ARTHUR, JR.,** legal association executive; b. Chgo., July 30, 1929; s. David J.A. and Lucille (Johnson) H.; m. Anne Huston, Feb. 20, 1963; children—David J.A. III, Cary. A.B., Harvard U., 1952; J.D., Ill. Inst. Tech.-Kent Coll. Law, 1961. Bar: Ill. Trust officer, asst. sec. First Nat. Bank of Evanston, Ill., 1961-63; gen. counsel Ill. State Bar Assn., Chgo., 1963-66; asst. dir. ABA, Chgo., 1966-68, div. dir., 1968-69, asst. exec. dir., 1969-87, v.p., 1987-88, assoc. exec. v.p., 1989-90, sr. assoc. exec. v.p., 1990, exec. dir., 1990-94, exec. dir. emeritus, 1994—; exec. dir. Naval Res. Lawyers Assn., 1971-75; asst. sec. gen. Internat. Bar Assn., 1978-80, 90—, Inter-ABA, 1984—. Contbr. articles to profl. jours. Capt. JAGC, USNR. Fellow Am. Bar Found. (life); mem. Ill. State Bar Assn. (ho. of dels. 1972-76), Nat. Orgn. Bar Counsel (pres. 1967), Chgo. Bar Assn., Michigan Shores Club. Home: 908 Pontiac Rd Wilmette IL 60091-1349 Office: ABA 750 N Lake Shore Dr Chicago IL 60611-4403

**HAYES, DAVID MICHAEL,** lawyer; b. Syracuse, N.Y., Dec. 2, 1943; s. James P. and Lillie Anna (Wood) H.; m. Elizabeth S. Tracy, Aug. 26, 1972; children: Timothy T., AnnElizabeth S. AB, Syracuse U., 1965; LLB, U. Va., 1968. Bar: Va. 1968, N.Y. 1969. Assoc. Hiscock & Barclay, Syracuse, 1968-72; asst. gen. counsel Agway Inc., Syracuse, 1972-81, gen. counsel, sec., 1981-87, v.p., gen. counsel, sec., 1987-92, sr. v.p., gen. counsel, sec., 1992—; adj. prof. law Syracuse U. Coll. Law; former chmn. Nat. Coun. of Farmer Coops. Legal Tax and Acctg. Com. Bd. dirs., former pres. Boys and Girls Club of Syracuse. With Army N.G., 1968-74. Fellow N.Y. Bar Found.; mem. ABA, Onondaga County Bar Assn. (pres. 1998), N.Y. State Bar Assn. (ho. of dels.), Va. State Bar, Century Club, Skaneateles Country Club. Democrat. General corporate. Office: Agway Inc PO Box 4933 Syracuse NY 13221-4933

**HAYES, DEWEY,** lawyer; b. Ga., July 27, 1923; s. J.C. and Mary (Walsh) H.; m. Margaret Haley, June 16, 1951; children: Dewey Jr., Franklin, Candy. AB, Mercer U., JD, 1949. Bar: Ga. 1949, U.S. Supreme Ct. 1966. Mem. Ga. Ho. of Reps., 1953-56; dist. atty. Waycross Jud. Cir., Ga., 1957-80; sole practice Douglas, Ga., 1980—; instr. law South Ga. Coll., 1973. Author: You and the Law, 1970, Georgia Warrants, 1972; Miranda, 1973; Search and Seizure, 1973. Mem. Ga. State Crime Commn., 1973-74. Served with U.S. Army, 1942-46, ETO, PTO. Mem. Nat. Dist. Atty.'s Assn., Dist. Attys. Assn. Ga. (pres. 1972), Am. Legion, V.F.W., Douglas Bar Assn. (pres. 1962—), Delta Theta Phi (pres. 1949), Kappa Sigma. Methodist. Lodges: Elk, Lion, Woodman of World. Insurance, Personal injury, Workers' compensation. Office: 107 Madison Ave S Douglas GA 31533-5321

**HAYES, GEORGE NICHOLAS,** lawyer; b. Alliance, Ohio, Sept. 30, 1928; s. Nicholas John and Mary Irene (Fanady) H. BA, U. Akron, 1950; MA, Western Res. U., 1953, LLB, 1955. Bar: Ohio 1955, U.S. Dist. Ct. Alaska 1957, U.S. Ct. Appeals (9th cir.) 1958, Alaska 1959, U.S. Supreme Ct. 1964, Wash. 1972. Mcpl. ct. prosecutor, asst. county prosecutor Portage County, Ravenna, Ohio, 1955-57; asst. U.S. atty. Fairbanks and Anchorage, Alaska, 1957-59; dep. atty gen. State of Alaska, Anchorage, 1959-62; dist. atty. 3d Jud. Dist., Anchorage, 1960-62; atty gen. Juneau, Alaska, 1962-64; spl. counsel to Gov. on earthquake recovery program State of Alaska, Washington, 1964; stockholder Delaney, Wiles, Hayes, Gerety & Ellis, Inc. and predecessor, Anchorage, 1964-92, of counsel, 1992. Mem. ABA, Wash. State Bar Assn., Alaska Bar Assn, Ohio Bar Assn., Anchorage Bar Assn. Democrat. Personal injury, Federal civil litigation, State civil litigation. Office: Delaney Wiles Hayes 1007 W 3rd Ave Anchorage AK 99501-1936

**HAYES, GERALD JOSEPH,** lawyer; b. Bronx, N.Y., July 24, 1950; s. James Joseph and Gladys (Guest) H.; m. Diane Elizabeth Willoughby, July 21, 1984; children: Erin Jane, Thomas Joseph, Cara Elizabeth. BA, U. Mass., 1972; JD, U. Miami, 1978. Bar: N.Y. 1979, U.S. Dist. Ct. (so. dist.) N.Y. 1979. Assoc. Baker & McKenzie, N.Y.C., 1978-85, ptnr., 1985—, mng. ptnr., 1995, 97, mem. policy com., 1997—; mem. Bus. Coun. for UN, 1990-95. Nat. alumni adv. bd. U. Miami Sch. Law, 1992—. Mem. ABA (atomic energy com. publ utility law sect. 1983, vice chair internat. tort & ins. law com., tort & ins. practice sect. 1997—), Assn. Bar City N.Y. (com. on nuclear tech. and law 1979-82, 85-88, com. on ins. law 1983-84), Nat. Assn. Ins. Commrs. (adv. com. on internat. law 1989-90), Nat. Risk Retention Assn. (govt. affairs com.). Insurance, Private international, Nuclear power. Office: Baker & McKenzie 805 3rd Ave New York NY 10022-7513

**HAYES, J. MICHAEL,** lawyer; b. St. Louis, Dec. 10, 1946; s. Frank J. and Louise J. (Lough) H.; m. Vicky J. Verbocy, May 27, 1972; children: Thomas K., James M. BS summa cum laude, SUNY, Brockport, 1973; JD, SUNY, Buffalo, 1976. Bar: N.Y. 1977, U.S. Dist. Ct. (we. dist.) N.Y. 1977. Assoc. Smith, Murphy & Schoepperle, Buffalo, 1977-79, Tenney, Smith & Scott, Buffalo, 1979-82, Terry D. Smith, Buffalo, 1982-86; ptnr. Smith, Keller, Hayes & Miner, Buffalo, 1986-94; pvt. practice Buffalo, 1994—. General civil litigation, Personal injury, Product liability. Office: 69 Delaware Ave Rm 1111 Buffalo NY 14202-3805

**HAYES, JEREMIAH MICHAEL,** lawyer; b. Postdam, N.Y., Nov. 28, 1947; s. W. Bernard and Grace B. (Smith) H.; m. Eileen King, June 10, 1972; children: Megan, Jeremiah, Brigid, Brendan, Michael. BA in History, Lemoyne Coll., 1970; JD, Albany Law Sch., 1973. Bar: N.Y. 1974, U.S. Dist. Ct. (no. dist.) N.Y. 1974. Assoc. Devine & Hayes, Postdam, 1974-77; pvt. practice Tupper Lake, N.Y., 1977--; asst. dist. atty., Franklin County, N.Y., 1978-94; sec. bd. dirs. Mercy Healthcare Ctr. Inc., Tupper Lake, 1978—; mem. com. profl. standards Appellate Div., 3d Dept., Albany, N.Y., 1983-89. Bd. trustees Adirondack Med. Ctr., 1997—. Mem. N.Y. State Bar Assn., ATLA, Tupper Lake C. of C. (pres. 1986-87), KC. Republican. Roman Catholic. Avocations: golf, hockey, skiing. General practice, Personal injury, Criminal. Office: 86 Racquette River Rd Tupper Lake NY 12986-9719

**HAYES, JOHN T.,** lawyer, accountant; b. Chgo., Oct. 9, 1927; s. Frank D. and Mildred G. (McEvoy) H.; m. Dolores J. Donahue, Aug. 21, 1954; 1 child, Virginia M. O'Sullivan. BS in Commerce, Loyola U., 1952; JD, I.I.T.-Chgo. Kent Coll. Law, 1960. Bar: Ill. 1960; CPA, Ill. Ptnr. Arthur Young & Co., Chgo., 1952-85; of counsel Schiff, Hardin & Waite, Chgo., 1985—; bd. dirs. Erikson Inst., Chgo.; adj. prof. Loyola U., Chgo., 1961-71; mem. com. planned giving Art Inst. Chgo., 1985—. mem. editl. bd. Estate Planning Mag., N.Y.C., 1975—; mem. charitable adv. bd. Trusts and Estates Mag., N.Y.C., 1995—; contbr. articles to profl. jours., chpts. to book. Bd. dirs. Kohl Children's Mus., Wilmette, Ill., 1992—, Grover Hermann Found., Chgo., 1992—. Pvt. 1st class USA, 1946-47. Mem. Chgo. Estate Planning Coun. (disting. svc. award 1995), Chgo. Bar Assn., Chgo. Athletic Assn., Ill. State Bar Assn., Ill. CPA Soc. Avocations: reading, chess, opera. Home: 444 Wagner Rd Northfield IL 60093-2922 Office: Schiff Hardin & Waite 233 S Wacker Dr Ste 7200 Chicago IL 60606-6473

**HAYES, KARLA LAVON,** legal assistant, marketing executive, civil rights advocate; b. Phillips, Tex., Aug. 21, 1947; d. Buster LeRoy and Elna Lavon (Ostrom) Caviness; children: Stephen Brent Turner, Lane Randall Rose, Lyndsy Caviness Rose; m. Joseph William Hayes Jr., Sept. 23, 1987. Student, Okla. U., West Tex. A & M, Amarillo Coll.; continuing edn. symposiums, 1992—. Legal asst. Joe W. Hayes, P.C.; pub. rels. Panhandle Youth Football League, 1997—; pub. rels., interview coach Miss Amarillo Area U.S.A., 1997—; adv. to end family violence, 1986—; polit. cons., 1988-91. Bd. dirs. Women's Forum, Tex. Fedn. Rep. Women; co-chmn. Formerly Battered Women's Task Force, 1990-92; lobbyist on child abuse, domestic violence, Tex. oil and gas legislation, batterer's treatment; DHS Domestic Violence Com. State of Tex. appt., 1989-92; vol. United Way Agys., govtl. affairs 1995—; pub. rels./media vol. new non-profit orgns.; introduced designated driver program to State of Tex.; developed and led 12 step program for battered women in 44 countys; media spokesperson, created sponsorship with Tex. Head Injury Found. and Tex. Hotel Motel Assn. Recipient Merit award Amarillo's 7 Who Care Program, 1992-93. Mem. Amarillo Symphony Guild, Downtown Merchants (pres.), Tex. Coun. on Family Violence, Nat. Coalition Against Domestic Violence, Women's Network, Alpha Phi. Republican. Methodist. Avocations: family, reading, aerobics. Fax: 806-352-1554. Home and Office: 3412 Danbury St Amarillo TX 79109-4024

**HAYES, LARRY B.,** lawyer; b. Atlanta, Oct. 4, 1939; s. Luther F. and Ruby (Thomas) H.; m. Rebecca Thomason, Feb. 12, 1959; children: Laura Alison, Lawrence Bruce. BS in Pharmacy, U. Fla., 1962; JD, St. Mary's U., 1977. Bar: Tex. 1978, U.S. Dist. Ct. (no. dist.) Tex. 1979, U.S. Ct. Appeals (5th cir.) 1979; cert. personal injury trial law, Tex. Trial counsel Windle Turley PC, Dallas, 1978-82; ptnr. Ware & Hayes, Dallas, 1982-83; sr. trial atty. Green, Hayes & Ryan, Dallas, 1983-86; ptnr. Cantey & Hanger, Ft. Worth, 1986—. Mem. Tex. Bar Assn., Tex. Assn. Def. Counsel, Def. Rsch. Inst., Tarrant County Bar Assn., Tarrant County Civil Trial Lawyers Assn., Ridglea Country Club, Phi Delta Phi. Health, Personal injury, Product liability. Home: 910 Houston St Apt 802 Fort Worth TX 76102-6228 Office: Cantey & Hanger 2100 Burnett Plaza 801 Cherry St Ste 2100 Fort Worth TX 76102-6898

**HAYES, LEWIS MIFFLIN, JR.,** lawyer; b. Mpls., May 5, 1941; s. Lewis Mifflin and Helen Camille (Vail) H.; m. Patricia Louise Schwab, June 3, 1967; m. Roberta Jane Hobson, Dec. 29, 1977; m. Diana Amorosino, Mar. 31, 1983; m. Debra Hines, Nov. 12, 1993; children: Rhoda Margaret, Lewis Mifflin, III, Robert Nelson. AB cum laude in Polit. Sci., Kenyon Coll., Gambier, Ohio, 1963; LLB with distinction, Duke U., 1966. Bar: N.Y. 1967, N.J. 1974, U.S. Sup. Ct. 1974, U.S. Tax Ct. 1978, U.S. Dist. Ct. (so. and ea.

dist.) N.Y. 1968, U.S. Dist. Ct. N.J. 1974, U.S. Ct. Apls. (2d cir.). Assoc. Mudge Rose Guthrie & Alexander, N.Y.C., 1966-73, Gifford, Woody, Carter & Hays, N.Y.C., 1973-76; ptnr. Hayes and Jenkins, N.Y.C. and Elizabeth, N.J., 1976-80; pvt. practice Elizabeth, 1980-88, N.Y.C., 1980—, Summit, N.J., 1988-92, Scotch Plains, N.J., 1992—. Trustee The Vail-Deare Sch., 1979-83. With U.S. Navy, 1966-68. Mem. N.J. State Bar Assn. Presbyterian. Clubs: Seaside Park (N.J.) Yacht. General civil litigation, General corporate, Contracts commercial. Home: 310 Pearl Pl Scotch Plains NJ 07076-1328 Office: 1810 Front St Scotch Plains NJ 07076-1103

**HAYES, NEIL JOHN,** lawyer; b. N.Y.C., Nov. 16, 1951; s. John T. and Marion G. (Watson) H.; m. Rebecca A. Wisner, Dec. 8, 1985. BA, Villanova U., 1973; JD, Stetson U., 1981. Bar: Fla. 1982, U.S. Dist. Ct. (so. and mid. dists.) Fla. 1982, U.S. Supreme Ct. 1986. Detective Mt. Laurel (N.J.) Police Dept., 1974-79; law clk. to chief judge Fla. 5th Dist. Ct. Appeals, Daytona Beach, 1982-83; assoc. Jones & Foster P.A., West Palm Beach, Fla., 1983-88, Bobo, Spicer & Ciotoli, West Palm Beach, 1988-89; pvt. practice West Palm Beach, 1989—. Assoc. editor Stetson U. Law Rev., 1981. Mem. ABA, Fla. Bar Assn., Palm Beach County Bar Assn., Palm Beach County Claims Assn., Fla. Def. Lawyers Assn., Tuscawilla Club. Roman Catholic. Avocations: motorcycling, aviation, photography. State civil litigation, Insurance, Workers' compensation. Home: 8733 Marlamoor Ln West Palm Beach FL 33412-1614 Office: 4365 Northlake Blvd Palm Beach Gardens FL 33410-6253

**HAYES, NORMAN ROBERT, JR.,** lawyer; b. Schenectady, N.Y., Apr. 12, 1948; s. Norman Robert Sr. and Ethel May (Blair) H.; m. Alice S. Margitan, Oct. 14, 1972; children: Robert, Charles. BS, Clarkson U., 1970; JD, Union U., 1973. Bar: N.Y. 1974, U.S. Dist. Ct. (no. dist.) N.Y. 1974, U.S. Supreme Ct. 1978. Ptnr. Wemple, Daly, Casey, Hayes, Watkins & Harter, Schenectady, 1973-86; pvt. practice Clifton Park, N.Y., 1986-96; ptnr. Gordon, Siegel, Mastro, Mullaney, Gordon & Galvin, Clifton Park, N.Y., 1996—; pres. S.P.B. Industries, Clifton Park, 1979—; chmn. Active Industries Inc.; bd. dirs. Saratoga Econ. Devel. Corp., Saratoga Springs, N.Y., adv. bd. dirs. Chase Manhattan Bank. Pres. County Knolls South Civic Assn., Clifton Park, 1975-76. Served to capt. U.S. Army, 1973-74. Mem. ABA, N.Y. State Bar Assn., Schenectady County Bar Assn. Republican. Banking, Contracts commercial, General corporate. Home: PO Box 4395 Queensbury NY 12804-0395 Office: 20 Solar Dr Clifton Park NY 12065-3401

**HAYES, PHILIP HAROLD,** lawyer; b. Battle Creek, Mich., Sept. 1, 1940; s. Robert Harold and Maurine (Page) H.; m. Robin Hayes, May 20, 1995; 1 child, Rian; children from previous marriage: Elizabeth, Courtney. AB, Ind. U., 1963, JD, 1967. Bar: Ind. 1967, U.S. Dist. Ct. (so. dist.) Ind. 1967, D.C. 1977, U.S. Ct. Appeals (7th cir.) 1992. Dep. prosecutor Vanderburgh County, Evansville, Ind., 1967-68; ptnr. Cox & Hayes, Evansville, 1969-72; senator State of Ind., Evansville, 1971-74; pvt. practice Evansville, 1973-74, 77-79, 1990—; U.S. congressman U.S. Ho. of Reps., Washington, 1975-77; ptnr. Hayes & Young, Evansville, 1980-90, Hayes & Tornatta, Evansville, 1990-92; legal counsel Airport Authority Dist., Evansville, 1980-84, Redevel. Commn., Evansville, 1984-88, Health and Hosp. Corp., Evansville, 1984-88. Editor, moderator pub. affairs TV program, 1977-78. Mem. Evansville Bar Assn., D.C. Bar Assn., Ind. Trial Lawyers Assn. Democrat. Real property, General civil litigation, Administrative and regulatory. Home: 218 Glenview Dr Evansville IN 47710-3737 Office: 100 NW 2d St Ste 08 Evansville IN 47708

**HAYES, RAY, JR.,** lawyer; b. Kansas City, Mo., Feb. 27, 1925; s. Ray and Kathryn L. (O'Hara) H.; m. Millifred Ann Schultz, Jan. 22, 1948; children: Leslie, Rick Lynn, Pat. B.S., U. Denver, 1947, J.D., 1949. Bar: Wash., U.S. Dist. Ct. (we. dist.) Wash., U.S. Supreme Ct., Ariz. 1996, U.S. Dist. Ct. Ariz. 1996. Assoc. Stinson & Hayes, Chehalis, Wash., 1950-53; dep. pros. atty. Lewis County (Wash.), 1953-58, sole practice, Chehalis, 1953-69; of counsel Davies, Pearson, P.C., and predecessor, Tacoma, 1969—. Served to capt. USMC, 1942, 1956. Mem. Wash. State Bar Assn., ABA, Fed. Bar Assn., Assn. Trial Lawyers Am., Wash. State Trial Lawyers Assn., Nat. Transp. Safety Bd. Bar Assn. (founding mem.). State civil litigation, Estate planning, Personal injury. Office: Hayes Jefferson PLC 12425 W Bell Rd Ste 202 Surprise AZ 85374-9002

**HAYES, RICHARD JOHNSON,** association executive, lawyer; b. Chgo., May 25, 1933; s. David John Arthur and Lucille Margaret (Johnson) H.; m. Mary R. Lynch, Dec. 2, 1961; children: Susan, Richard, Jr., John, Edward. B.A., Colo. Coll., 1955; J.D., Georgetown U., 1961. Bar: Ill. 1961. Assoc. firm Barnabas F. Sears, Chgo., 1961-63, Peterson, Lowry, Rall, Barber and Ross, Chgo., 1963-65; staff dir. Am. Bar Assn., Chgo., 1965-70; exec. dir. Internat. Assn. Def. Counsel, Chgo., 1970—; instr. various legal programs, 1966—; pres. Heritage Resource Mgmt. Group, 1997—, Tri Star Corp., 1997—; dir. nat. jury innovations program Internat. Assn. Def. Counsel, Chgo., 1998—; dir. Def. Counsel Trial Acad., 1973—; exec. dir. Nat. Pre-Suit Mediation, 1991—. Editor: Antitrust Law Jour., 1969-71. 1st lt. USAR, 1955-57. Mem. ABA (chmn. various coms. 1977—), Ill. Bar Assn., Chgo. Bar Assn., Jr. Bar (chmn. 1965), Am. Soc. Assn. Execs., Chgo. Soc. Assn. Execs., Nat. Conf. Lawyers and Ins. Cos. (bd. dirs. 1983—), Rotary/One (Chgo.), Tower Club (Chgo.), Monroe Club (Chgo.), Met. Club (Chgo.), Mich. Shores Club (Wilmette, Ill.). Clubs: Rotary/One (Chgo.), Tower (Chgo.); Mich. Shores (Wilmette, Ill.). Home: 1920 Thornwood Ave Wilmette IL 60091-1403 Office: One N Franklin Ste 2400 Chicago IL 60606

**HAYES, TIMOTHY GEORGE,** lawyer, consultant; b. New London, Conn., June 27, 1954; s. George Melen and Lauretta C. (Bresnahan) H.; m. Barbara Joan White, Jan. 27, 1983; children: Laura Katherine, Kevin Michael. BS, Fla. State U., 1976, MS, 1977; JD, Stetson Coll. Law, 1982. Bar: Fla. 1982, U.S. Dist. Ct. (mid. dist.) Fla. 1983. Legis. aide Fla. State Rep. George H. Sheldon, Tallahassee, 1978-79; assoc. Alice K. Nelson, P.A., Tampa, Fla., 1982-83; ptnr. Cotterill, Gonzalez & Hayes, Lutz, Fla., 1983-84, Cotterill, Gonzalez, Hayes & Grantham, Lutz, 1984-88; sr. ptnr. Hayes & McClelland, Lutz, 1988-90, Hayes, Winick & Albrechta, Lutz, 1990-91, Hayes & Albrechta, P.A., Lutz, 1991-93, Hayes & Assocs., Lutz, 1993—. V.p. Hillsborough County Young Dems., Tampa, 1978, pres., 1979; bd. dirs. Tampa Bay Commuter Rail Authority, Tampa, 1990-97, Pasco County Econ. Devel. Coun., New Port Richey, Fla., 1990-92, Ctrl. Pasco Coalition, Land O' Lakes, Fla., 1991-95, Pasco Food Bank, 1996—, Sunshine Youth Soccer Assn., 1997—; bd. dirs., coach Ctrl. Pasco United Soccer Assn., 1995—, pres., 1996-98; mem. Tampa-Orlando High-Speed Transp. Study Task Force, 1992-94; mem. adv. bd. Pasco-Hernando C.C., 1994-95; bd. dirs., v.p. Heritage Park Found., 1997—. Named Outstanding Young Man in Am. by Jaycees, 1980; recipient Sam Walton Bus. Leader award, 1998. Mem. ABA (real property, probate and trust law sect.), Fla. Bar Assn. (environ. and land use law sect., real property, probate and trust law sect.), Hillsborough County Bar Assn. (environ. and land use law sect.), Land O' Lakes C. of C. (v.p. 1988-89, pres. 1991-92, chmn. bd. 1992-93, bd. dirs. 1995—). Roman Catholic. Avocations: soccer, bicycling, camping, gardening. Real property, Probate, Land use and zoning (including planning). Office: Hayes & Assocs 21859 State Road 54 Ste 200 Lutz FL 33549-6986

**HAYGOOD, JOHN WARREN,** retired lawyer; b. Richmond, Tex., Sept. 16, 1924; s. Claude Culberson and Jessie (Scott) H.; m. Mary Forea McGill, Aug. 25, 1946 (div. 1979); children: Scott McGill Haygood, Holly Mary Haygood. BA, Centenary Coll., 1947; JD, Tulane U., 1950. Bar: La. 1950, U.S. Dist. Ct. (we. dist.) La. 1952, U.S. Ct. Mil. Appeals 1956, U.S. Supreme Ct. 1959, U.S. Ct. Appeals (5th cir.) 1960, U.S. Dist. Ct. (ea. dist.) La. 1966, U.S. Dist. Ct. (mid. dist.) La. 1966, U.S. Dist. Ct. (so. dist.) Miss. 1968. Pvt. practice Shreveport, La., 1950; assoc. Brown & Fleniken, Shreveport, 1952-53; atty. Ark. Fuel Oil Corp., Shreveport, 1953-58; ptnr. Stagg, Cady, Haygood & Beard, Shreveport, 1958-65, Jones, Walker, Waechter, Poitevent, Carrere & Denegre, New Orleans, 1965-87; ret., 1987; instr. trial practice Tulane U. Law Sch., 1974;. Named Outstanding Class Agt. Tulane Alumni Fund, 1980. Mem. Kappa Alpha Order. Federal civil litigation, General civil litigation, State civil litigation. Home: 1300 Aris St Metairie LA 70005-1714

**HAYMANS, MICHAEL P.,** lawyer; b. Jacksonville, Fla., Oct. 19, 1954; s. Kenton H. and Margaret E. Haymans; m. Deborah L. Brown, Sept. 5, 1975; children: Dylan H., Donovan M. JD, U. Fla., 1982. Bar: Fla. 1983. Atty. Farr Law Firm, Punta Gorda, Fla., 1983—. Avocations: poetry, song writing, singing, folk music. Land use and zoning (including planning), Real property. Office: Farr Law Firm 115 W Olympia Ave Punta Gorda FL 33950-4430

**HAYNER, HERMAN HENRY,** lawyer; b. Fairfield, Wash., Sept. 25, 1916; s. Charles H. and Lillie (Reifenberger) H.; m. Jeannette Hafner, Oct. 24, 1942; children: Stephen, James K., Judith A. BA, Wash. State U., 1938; JD with honors, U. Oreg., 1946. Bar: Wash. 1946, Oreg. 1946, U.S. Dist. Ct. Wash. 1947, U.S. Ct. Appeals (9th cir.) 1947. Asst. U.S. atty. U.S. Dept. Justice, Portland, Oreg., 1946-47; atty. City of Walla Walla, Wash., 1949-53; ptnr. Minnick-Hayner, Walla Walla, 1949—; mem. Wash. State exec. bd. U.S. West, Seattle, 1988-95. Regent Wash. State U., Pullman, 1965-78; dir. YMCA, Walla Walla, 1956-67. Lt. col. Infantry, 1942-46. Decorated Bronze Star medal and four Battle Stars; recipient Disting. Svc. award Jr. C. of C., 1951, Wash. State U. Alumni award, 1988. Fellow ABA, Am. Coll. Trust & Estate Counsel; mem. Wash. State Bar Assn., Walla Walla County Bar Assn. (pres. 1954-55), Walla Walla C. of C. (merit award 1977, dir. 1973-88), Rotary (pres. 1956-57), Walla Walla Country Club (pres. 1956-57). Republican. Lutheran. Avocations: golf, photography. Probate, General corporate. Home: PO Box 454 Walla Walla WA 99362-0013 Office: Minnick-Hayner PO Box 1757 Walla Walla WA 99362-0348

**HAYNES, JEAN REED,** lawyer; b. Miami, Fla., Apr. 6, 1949; d. Oswald Birnam and Arleen (Wiedman) Dow. AB with honors, Pembroke Coll., 1971; MA, Brown U., 1971; JD, U. Chgo., 1981. Bar: Ill. 1981, U.S. Ct. Appeals (7th cir.) 1982, U.S. Dist. Ct. (no. dist.) Ill. 1983, U.S. Dist. Ct. (cen. dist.) Ill., 1988, N.Y. 1991, U.S. Dist. Ct. (so. dist.) N.Y. 1991, U.S. Dist. Ct. (no. and ea. dists.) N.Y. 1992, U.S. Ct. Appeals (10th cir.) 1993, U.S. Ct. Appeals (11th cir.) 1995. Tchr. grades 1-4 Abbie Tuller Sch., Providence, 1971-72; tchr., facilitator St. Mary's Acad., Riverside, R.I., 1972-74; tchr., head lower sch. St. Francis Sch., Goshen, Ky., 1974-78; law clk. U.S. Ct. Appeals (7th cir.), Chgo., 1981-83; assoc. Kirkland & Ellis, Chgo., 1983-87, ptnr., 1987—; assoc. editor Litigation Mag., 1997-99. Assoc. editor: Litigation Mag. Governing mem. Art Inst. Chgo., 1982-90, mem. aux. bd., 1986-90, membership com. aux. bd., 1987-90, v.p. for devel., 1988-90; vis. com. U. Chgo. Law Sch., 1990-92; pres. comm. Cmty. Literacy Rsch. Project, 1997—; adv. com. Youth Devel. Ctr., 1997—. Mem. ABA (com. on affordable justice litigation sect. 1988—), Ill. Bar Assn. (life), Assn. Bar City N.Y., Internat. Bar Assn., Am. Judicature Soc. (life, chmn. membership com. 1991-97, treas. 1997-99, chmn. fin. com. 1997-99, v.p. 1994-97, exec. com. 1992—, pres. 1999—, bd. dirs. 1991—, mem. adminstrv. com. 1997—), Three Lincoln Ctr. Condominium Assn. (pres. 1995—), Law Club Chgo., Mid-Am. Club. Federal civil litigation, Bankruptcy, State civil litigation. Office: Kirkland & Ellis Citicorp Ctr 153 E 53rd St New York NY 10022-4611

**HAYNES, PAUL R.,** lawyer; b. Danbury, Conn., Dec. 15, 1950; s. Richard Osborn and Doris Louise (Rowe) H.; m. Karen Marie Traboldt, Nov. 3, 1979; children: Matthew, Joshua, Laura. BA, SUNY, Oneonta, 1972; JD, Albany U., 1976. Bar: N.Y. 1977, U.S. Dist. Ct. (so., ea. and no. dists.) N.Y. 1979, U.S. Ct. Appeals (2d cir.) 1979, U.S. Supreme Ct. 1980. Law clk. Hon. Allan Dixon Rensselaer County Family Ct., Troy, N.Y., 1975-76; assoc. Reed & Reed, Esqs., Poughkeepsie, N.Y., 1977-80; pvt. practice Wappingers Falls, N.Y., 1980—. Mem. tel-law com. United Way of Dutchess County, Poughkeepsie, N.Y., 1977; mem. Cmty. Ambulance Svc., Wappingers Falls, N.Y., 1986—; cubmaster Pack 40 Dutchess County Coun., Boy Scouts Am., Wappingers Falls, 1991-94; asst. scoutmaster Troop 40, Hudson Valley Coun., Hopewell Junction, N.Y., 1996—. Mem. ABA, ATLA, N.Y. State Bar Assn., Dutchess County Bar Assn., Rotary (sec. 1985-87, pres. 1987-88, Paul Harris fellow 1987), Greater So. Dutchess C. of C. (county issues com. 1980—), Wappingers Falls Bus. and Profl. Assn. (charter), Pi Gamma Mu. Republican. General practice, Real property, Probate. Office: 161 W Main St Wappingers Falls NY 12590-1524

**HAYNES, RICHARD TERRY,** lawyer; b. Detroit, Dec. 10, 1946; s. Charles Hawley and Elizabeth (Powers) H.; m. Jan Michele Ouillette, Dec. 22, 1980. BBA, U. Mich., 1969; JD, Wayne U., 1972. Bar: Mich. 1973, U.S. Dist. Ct. (ea. dist.) Mich. 1973. Ptnr. Draugelis, Ashton, Scully and Haynes, Plymouth, Mich., 1973--. Capt. USAR, 1965-80. Mem. ABA, Mich. Bar Assn., Detroit Bar Assn., Washtenaw County Bar Assn., Def. Rsch. Inst. General civil litigation, Insurance, Personal injury. Office: Draugelis Ashton Scully & Haynes 843 Penniman Ave Plymouth MI 48170-1690

**HAYNES, WILLIAM ERNEST,** lawyer, financial consultant, educator; b. Peoria, Ill., Aug. 22, 1936; s. Clarence Ernest and Lucille Ann Haynes; m. Willette Lancia Rothschild, Dec. 2, 1972; children: Lancia Ann, Sharon Elizabeth. BA in Fin., Loras Coll., Dubuque, Iowa, 1959; JD, Marquette U., Milw., 1964; MBA in Bus. Econs., Loyola U., Chgo., 1969. Bar: Wis. 1964, Ill. 1965, Calif. 1970; cert. specialist taxation law, Calif. Corp. counsel Gen. Fin. Co., Evanston, Ill., 1964-69; asst. contr. internat. tax Wells Fargo Bank, San Francisco, 1969-76; tax counsel Kaiser Aluminum and Chem. Corp., Oakland, Calif., 1976-79; prin. Law Offices of William E. Haynes and Assocs., San Francisco, 1979—; chief fin. officer Pacific Rim Ptnrs. Ltd., San Francisco, 1989—; pres. Gryphon Group Ltd., econ. cons., 1981-86; prin. The Bus. Mart Bus. Brokers, San Francisco, 1987-94; prof. taxation, adj. faculty, McLaren Coll. of Bus., U. San Francisco; lectr. on law, taxation and fin. Mem. adv. com. on edn. State Bar of Calif.; bd. dirs. Meals on Wheels of San Francisco. With U.S. Army, 1959-61. Mem. ABA, Calif. Bar Assn., Am. Econs. Assn., San Francisco Internat. Tax Group, Internat. Assn. Fin. Planners, Calif. Hist. Soc., San Francisco Mus. Soc., World Affairs Council, Civil Air Patrol (capt.). Republican. Roman Catholic. Lodge: Rotary, Elks. Taxation, general, Estate planning, Private international. Office: 225 Bush St Fl 16 San Francisco CA 94104-4213

**HAYNES, WILLIAM J(AMES), II,** lawyer; b. Waco, Tex., Mar. 30, 1958; s. William James and Caroline (Bynum) H.; m. Margaret Frances Campbell, Aug. 21, 1982; children: William James III, Sarah Insley, Taylor Bynum. BA, Davidson Coll., 1980; JD, Harvard U., 1983; LLD (hon.), Stetson U., 1999. Bar: N.C. 1983, Ga. 1989, D.C. 1990. Law clk. to Hon. James B. McMillan U.S. Dist. Ct. N.C., Charlotte, 1983-84; assoc. Sutherland, Asbill & Brennan, Washington, 1989; spl. asst. to gen. counsel Dept. Def., Washington, 1989-90; gen. counsel Dept. Army, Washington, 1990-93; ptnr. Jenner & Block, Washington, 1993-96; v.p., assoc. gen. counsel Gen. Dynamics Corp., Falls Church, Va., 1996-98; gen. counsel Gen. Dynamics Marine Group, 1997-98; ptnr. Jenner & Block, Washington, 1999—. Capt. U.S. Army, 1984-88. Mem. ABA, N.C. Bar Assn., D.C. Bar Assn., Ga. Bar Assn., Army-Navy Club. Presbyterian. Avocation: tennis. Government contracts and claims, Environmental, Federal civil litigation. Office: Jenner and Block 601 13th St NW Ste 1200S Washington DC 20005-3823

**HAYNIE, TONY WAYNE,** lawyer; b. Houston, Sept. 26, 1955; m. Mary E. Steward, Sept. 1, 1978. BA, U. Okla., 1978; postgrad., Boston U., Heidelberg Br., Fed. Republic Germany, 1980-81; JD, U. Tulsa, 1984; MBA, Okla. State U., 1993. Bar: Okla. 1985, U.S. Dist. Okla. 1985, U.S. Ct. Appeals (10th cir.) 1987, U.S. Ct. Appeals (5th cir.) 1992, U.S. Ct. Appeals (7th and D.C. cirs.) 1998, U.S. Supreme Ct. 1990. Assoc. Conner & Winters, Tulsa, 1984-90, ptnr., 1991-92, shareholder, 1992—; pres., CEO The Colonneh Co., Tulsa, 1991—; arbitrator N.Y. Stock Exch., 1991—; trustee Transvoc, Inc., 1995—, pres. bd. trustees, 1998-99. Adv. bd. mem. Tulsa Area United Way, 1998—. 1st lt. U.S. Army, 1978-82. Mem. ABA (sect. bus. law and litig., chair subcom. on expert witness on trial evidence com. of litig. sect. 1991-94), Am. Inns of Ct. (barrister Hudson-Hall-Wheaton chpt. 1996—), Okla. Bar Assn., Okla. Bar Found., Tulsa County Bar Assn., Tulsa County Bar Found., Phi Delta Phi. Democrat. Methodist. Federal civil litigation, Bankruptcy, General civil litigation. Office: Conner & Winters 3700 1st Place Tower 15 E 5th St Tulsa OK 74103-4391

**HAYS, MELISSA PADGETT,** lawyer; b. West Islip, N.Y., June 18, 1968; d. Olin Wright Jr. and Ellen (Medlin) Padgett; m. Robert Bond Hays, III, Mar. 21, 1998. BA, Emory U., 1990; JD, U. Ga., 1994. Bar: Ga. 1994, U.S. Dist. Ct. (so. dist.) Ga. 1994, Supreme Ct. of Ga., 1994, Tenn. 1998, Supreme Ct. of Tenn. 1998. Atty. Harrison & Shapiro, Augusta, Ga., 1994-95, Garrett & Gilliard, P.C., Augusta, 1995-97; sole practitioner Augusta, 1997-98; atty., asst. counsel Provident Cos., Inc., Chattanooga, 1998—. Alumni mem. Leadership Augusta, 1997-98. Mem. ABA, State Bar of Ga., Tenn. Bar Assn. Insurance. Office: Provident Cos Inc Law Dept 1 Fountain Sq Chattanooga TN 37402-1307

**HAYS, STEELE,** retired state supreme court judge; b. Little Rock, Mar. 25, 1925; s. L. Brooks and Marion (Prather) H.; m. Peggy Wall, July 12, 1980; children from previous marriage: Andrew Steele, Melissa Louise, Sarah Anne. B.A., U. Ark., 1948; J.D., George Washington U., 1951. Bar: Ark. 1951. Adminstrv. asst. to Congressman Brooks Hays, 1951-53; practice in Little Rock, 1953-79; mem. firm Spitzberg, Mitchell & Hays, 1953-79; circuit judge 6th Jud. Circuit Ark., Little Rock, 1969-70; judge Ark. Ct. Appeals, 1979-81; assoc. justice Ark. Supreme Ct., 1981-95; ret., 1995; chmn. Bd. Law Examiners, 1968-70. Mem. Ark. com. U.S. Civil Rights Commn.; del. Presbyn. Ch. Consultation on Ch. Union, 1968-70; trustee Presbyn. Found.; chancellor Episcopal Diocese of Ark. Mem. Ark. Bar Assn. (past sec.-treas.), Sigma Chi, Delta Theta Phi. Home: 12 Deerwood St Conway AR 72032-6113

**HAYTHE, THOMAS MADISON,** lawyer; b. N.Y.C., Aug. 28, 1939; s. Madison H. and Barbara (Belt) H.; m. Sabine Cailliau-de Gaulle, Jan. 28, 1967; children: Pamela F., Jennifer H. BA, Havard U., 1961, LLB, 1964. Bar: N.Y. 1967, Conn. 1975. Ptnr. Casey, Lane & Mittendorf, N.Y.C., 1971-81; sr. ptnr. Haythe & Curley, N.Y.C., 1982—; bd. dirs. Novametrix Med. Systems, Inc., Wallingford, Conn., Guest Supply, Inc., North Brunswick, N.J., Westerbeke Corp, Avon., Mass., Ramsay Youth Svcs. Inc., Coral Gables, Fla. Mem. ABA, Conn. Bar Assn., N.Y. Bar Assn., Assn. of Bar of City of N.Y. Republican. Episcopalian. General practice, General corporate, Mergers and acquisitions. Office: Haythe & Curley 237 Park Ave New York NY 10017-3140

**HAYTHE, WINSTON MCDONALD,** lawyer, educator, consultant, real estate investor; b. Reidsville, N.C., Oct. 10, 1940; s. McDonald Swann and Henrietta Elizabeth (East) H.; m. Glenann Leigh Rogers, Aug. 17, 1963 (div. 1977); children: Sheila Elaine, Kevin McDonald, Rhonda Leigh. BS, S.W. Mo. State U., 1963; JD, Coll. William and Mary, 1967; postgrad., U. Va., 1968-69; grad., Command and Gen. Staff Sch., Ft. Leavenworth, Kans., 1982, U.S. Def. U., 1984. Bar: Va. 1967, D.C. 1969. Assoc. Rhyne & Rhyne, Washington, 1969-72; sr. trial atty. AEC, Washington, 1972-73; asst. gen counsel, sr. atty. Consumer Produce Safety Commn., Washington, 1973-82; staff dir. legal office EPA, Washington, 1982-83, sr. atty. for enforcement policy, 1985-91, sr. atty. Nat. Enforcement Tng. Inst., 1991-94, asst. dir., 1994-96, sr. legal counsel, 1996—; legis. fellow U.S. Senate, Washington, 1983-85; mem. adv. com. paralegal studies U. Md., 1980-95, chmn., 1992-95; adj. prof. law, 1978—; mem. law faculty U.S. Army Judge Adv. Gen.'s Sch., Charlottesville, Va., 1969-94; cons. Barrister Ent., Washington, 1978—; elected mem. undergrad. programs adv. coun. U. Md., 1993-95. Trustee Georgetown Presbyn. Ch., 1995-98, v.p. trustees, 1996, pres. trustees, 1997-98. Col. JAGC, USAR, 1967-94, ret. Mem. Va. State Bar Assn., D.C. Bar Assn., Fed. Bar Assn. (chmn. nat. com. 1981—), Coll. William and Mary Law Sch. Assn. (bd. dirs. 1988-95), Kappa Mu Epsilon. Presbyterian. Avocations: playing organ, piano, theater, concerts, reading. Home: 2141 P St NW Apt 402 Washington DC 20037-1031 Office: EPA 401 M St SW Washington DC 20460-0002

**HAYWARD, DANIEL THOMAS,** lawyer; b. Des Moines, Jan. 25, 1969; s. H. Dean and Aletha May Hayward. BA with distinction, Iowa State U., 1991; JD with high distinction, U. Iowa, 1994. Bar: Mo. 1994, Kans. 1995, Nev. 1996, U.S. Dist. Ct. (we. dist.) Mo. 1994, U.S. Dist. Ct. Kans. 1995, U.S. Dist. Ct. Nev. 1996. Assoc. Morrison & Hecker, LLP, Kansas City, Mo., 1994-96, Laxalt & Nomura, Ltd., Reno, 1996—. Mem. Ptnrs. in Edn., Reno, 1998—; mentor Big Bros./Big Sisters of Greater Kansas City, Mo., 1995-96. Mem. State Bar Nev., State Bar Kans., State Bar Mo., Washoe County Bar Assn. (vol. atty. project 1997—). Avocations: skiing, hiking, weightlifting, martial arts. Insurance, Product liability, General civil litigation. Office: Laxalt & Nomura Ltd 50 W Liberty St Ste 700 Reno NV 89501-1947

**HAYWARD, SAMUEL GEORGE, SR.,** lawyer; b. Hanover, N.H., Feb. 17, 1946; s. Frederick Reynolds and Lucy Eleanor Hayward; m. Barbara Baumann, Dec. 13, 1969; children: Samuel George Jr., Elizabeth Dalton. BA in History, Norwich U., 1968; JD, U. Louisville, 1973. Bar: Ky. 1974, U.S. Ct. Appeals (6th cir.) 1974. Pres., pvt. practice Louisville, 1980-98; ptnr. Nicolas, Welsh & Hayward, Louisville, 1993—. Soccer coach Assumption H.S., Louisville, 1991-98; pres. Ky. Youth Soccer, Lexington, 1992-93. 1st lt. U.S. Army, 1968-71, Korea. Mem. ABA, Ky. Bar Assn., Ky. Trial Lawyers Assn. Home: 5512 Apache Rd Louisville KY 40207 Office: Nicolas Welsh & Hayward 1009 S 4th St Louisville KY 40203-3207

**HAYWARD, THOMAS ZANDER, JR.,** lawyer; b. Evanston, Ill., Apr. 21, 1940; s. Thomas Zander and Wilhelmina (White) H.; m. Sally Ann Madden, June 24, 1964; children: Thomas Z. III, Wallace M., Robert M. BA, Northwestern U., 1962, JD, 1965; MBA, U. Chgo., 1970. Bar: Ill. 1966, Ohio 1966, U.S. Dist. Ct. (no. dist.) Ill. 1966, U.S. Supreme Ct. 1970. Assoc., ptnr. Defrees & Fiske, Chgo., 1965-81; ptnr. Boodell, Sears, Giambalvo, Chgo., 1981-87, Bell, Boyd & Lloyd, Chgo., 1987—. Trustee Northwestern U., Evanston, Chgo. Bar Found., Legal Svcs./Chgo. Cmty. Trust. Recipient Svc. award Northwestern U. Alumni Assn. Mem. ABA (bd. govs. 1998-2001), Chgo. Bar Assn. (pres. 1983-84), Barrington Hills Country Club (pres.). Republican. Presbyterian. Avocations: golf, tennis, fishing. Office: Bell Boyd & Lloyd 70 W Madison St Ste 3300 Chicago IL 60602-4284

**HAZARD, GEOFFREY CORNELL, JR.,** law educator; b. Cleve., Sept. 18, 1929; s. Geoffrey Cornell and Virginia (Perry) H.; m. Elizabeth O'Hara; children: James G., Katherine W., Robin P., Geoffrey Cornell III. BA, Swarthmore Coll., 1953, LLD (hon.), 1988; LLB, Columbia U., 1954; LLD (hon.), Gonzaga U., 1985, U. San Diego, 1985, Ill. Inst. Tech., 1990, Republica Italiana, 1998. Bar: Oreg. 1954, Calif. 1960, Conn. 1982, Pa. 1994. Assoc. Hart, Spencer, McCulloch, Rockwood & Davies, Portland, Oreg., 1954-57; exec. sec. Oreg. Legis. Interim Com. Jud. Adminstrn., 1957-58; assoc. prof. law, then prof. U. Calif., Berkeley, 1958-64; prof. law U. Chgo., 1964-71; prof. law Yale U., 1971-94, prof. mgmt., 1979-83, acting dean Sch. Orgn. and Mgmt., 1980-81, Sterling prof. law, 1986-94; trustee prof. U. Pa., Phila., 1994—; mem. Adminstrv. Conf. U.S., 1971-78; jud. conf. U.S. com. on rules practice and procedure, 1994—. Author: (with D.W. Louisell, C. Tait and W. Fletcher) Pleading and Procedure, 1972, 8th edit., 1999, Research in Civil Procedure, 1963, (with F. James and J. Leubsdorf) Civil Procedure, 4th edit., 1992, Ethics in the Practice of law, 1978, (with W. W. Hodes) Law of Lawyering, 2d edit., 1990), (with S. Koniak and R. Cramton) Law and Ethics of Lawyering, 3rd edit., 1999, (with M. Tanruffu) Am. Civil Procedure, 1994; editor: Law in a Changing America, 1968, (with D. Rhode) Legal Profession: Responsibility and Regulation, 1985, 3d edit., 1994; contbr. articles to profl. jours. Served with USAF, 1948-49. Fellow Am. Bar Found. (exec. dir. 1964-70, rsch. award 1986), Am. Acad. Arts and Scis.; mem. ABA (cons. code jud. conduct 1970-72, reporter stds. jud. adminstrn. 1971-77, reporter model rules of profl. conduct 1978-83), Am. Law Inst. (reporter restatement of judgments 1973-81, dir. 1984-99), Nat. Legal Aid and Defender Assn., Inst. Jud. Adminstrn., Am. Judicature Soc., Selden Soc., Pa. Bar Assn., Calif. State Bar, Conn. Bar Assn., Assn. Bar City N.Y., Phi Beta Kappa. Episcopalian. Avocations: tennis, history, golf.

**HAZELTON, PENNY ANN,** law librarian, educator; b. Yakima, Wash., Sept. 24, 1947; d. Fred Robert and Margaret (McLeod) Pease; m. Norris J. Hazelton, Sept. 12, 1971; 1 dau., Victoria MacLeod. BA cum laude, Linfield Coll., 1969; JD, Lewis and Clark Law Sch., 1975; M in Law Librarianship, U. Wash., 1976. Bar: Wash. 1976; U.S. Supreme Ct. 1982. assoc. law libr., assoc. prof. U. Maine, 1976-78, law libr., assoc. prof., 1978-81; asst. libr. for rsch. svcs. U.S. Supreme Ct., Washington, 1981-85, law libr., 1985; law librarian U. Wash., Seattle, 1985—, prof. law, 1985—; tchr. legal rsch., law librarianship, Indian law; cons. Maine Adv. Com. on County Law Librs., Nat. U. Sch. Law, San Diego, 1985-88, Lawyers Cooperative Pub., 1993-94. Author: Computer Assisted Legal Research: The Basics, 1993; contbr. articles to legal jours. Recipient Disting. Alumni award U. Wash., 1992. Mem. ABA (sect. legal edn. & admissions to bar, chair com. on librs. 1993-94, vice chair 1992-93, 94-95), Am. Assn. Law Schs. (com. law librs. 1991-94), Law Librs. New Eng. (sec. 1977-79, pres. 1979-81), Am. Assn. Law Librs. (cert., program chmn. ann. meeting 1984, exec. bd. 1984-87, v.p., pres.-elect 1989-90, pres. 1990-91, program co-chair Insts. 1983, 95), Law Libr. Soc. Washington (exec. bd. 1983-84, v.p., pres.-elect 1984-85), Law Librs. Puget Sound, Wash. State Bar Assn. (chair editl. adv. bd. 1990-91), Wash. Adv. Coun. on Librs., Westpac. Office: U Wash Marian Gould Gallagher Law Libr 1100 NE Campus Pkwy Seattle WA 98105-6605

**HEAD, BEN THOMAS,** lawyer; b. Oklahoma City, Nov. 1, 1920; s. Ben Thomas Head and Virginia (Broados) Pine; m. Mary C. Johnston, Feb. 28, 1930 (div. June 1983); children: Marcy, Paul, Eric; m. June Leftwich, Mar. 22, 1986. BBA, U. Okla., 1942, LLB, 1948, JD, 1970. Bar: Okla., Tex. Pres., chmn., chief exec. officer RepublicBank, Austin, Tex., 1978-84; sr. lectr. banking U. Tex., Austin, 1984-88; U.S. trustee U.S. Dist. Ct. (so. and we. dists.) Tex., Houston, 1988-93; pres., CEO United Va. Bank (now Crestar), Newport News, Va., 1975-78; chmn. City Savs., San Angelo, Tex., 1986-87. V.p. Oklahoma City C. of C., 1973, chmn. Austin C. of C., 1983; pres. progress com. Newport News., Va., 1978; bd. dirs., chmn. fin. com. Austin Presbyn. Sem., 1982-90; bd. dirs. fin. com. Tex. Presbyn. Found., 1988—; trustee, vice chmn. bd., Hampton U., 1980—. Col. U.S. Army, 1942-46, India. Named Exec. of Yr. Austin C. of C., 1983. Mem. Rotary. Avocations: golf, walking. Home: 3234 Tarryhollow Dr Austin TX 78703-1639 Office: 816 Congress Ave Ste 1200 Austin TX 78701-2443

**HEAD, HAYDEN WILSON, JR.,** judge; b. Sherman, Tex., Nov. 12, 1944; s. Hayden W. Head and Marshall (Elmore) Skinner. Student, Washington and Lee U., 1962-64; B.A., U. Tex., 1967, LL.B., 1968. Bar: Tex. Assoc. Head & Kendrick, Corpus Christi, Tex., 1968-69, 1972-76, ptnr., 1976-81; judge U.S. Dist. Ct. (so. dist.) Tex., Corpus Christi, 1981—. Lt. JAGC, USNR, 1969-72. Fellow Tex. Bar Found.; mem. State Bar Tex. Office: US Dist Ct 521 Starr St Fl 2 Corpus Christi TX 78401-2349

**HEAD, PATRICK JAMES,** lawyer; b. Randolph, Nebr., July 13, 1932; s. Clarence Martin and Ellen Cecelia (Magirl) H.; m. Eleanor Hickey, Nov. 24, 1960; children: Adrienne, Ellen, Damian, Maria, Brendan, Martin, Sarah, Daniel, Brian. A.B. summa cum laude, Georgetown U., 1953, LL.B., 1956, LL.M. in Internat. Law, 1957. Bar: D.C. 1956, Ill. 1966. Assoc. John L. Ingolsby (and predecessor firm), Washington, 1956-64; gen. counsel internat. ops. Sears, Roebuck & Co., Oakbrook, Ill., 1964-70; counsel midwest ter. Sears, Roebuck & Co., Skokie, Ill., 1970-72; v.p. Montgomery Ward & Co., Inc., Washington, 1972-76; v.p., gen. counsel, sec. Montgomery Ward & Co., Inc., Chgo., 1976-81; v.p., gen. counsel FMC Corp., Chgo., 1981-96; ptnr. Altheimer E. Gray, Chgo., 1997—; bd. visitors Northwestern Law, 1988-91. Mem. Chgo. Crime Commn.; bd. regents Georgetown U., Washington, 1981-87; bd. visitors Georgetown Law Sch., 1992—. Mem. ABA, D.C. Bar Assn., Chgo. Bar Assn., Am. Law Inst. Democrat. Roman Catholic. Clubs: Met. (Washington); Chgo, Internat. General corporate, Administrative and regulatory, Federal civil litigation. Office: Altheimer & Gray 10 S Wacker Dr Fl 36 Chicago IL 60606-7407

**HEAD, WILLIAM CARL,** lawyer, author; b. Columbus, Ga., Mar. 4, 1951; s. Louis Bernice and Betty June (Vickery) H.; m. Sandra Earle, Sept. 3, 1972 (div. 1979); m. Kathleen Crenshaw, Aug. 8, 1981 (div. 1988); 1 stepchild, Stephanie A. Hansen; m. Kris L. Foreman, Feb. 14, 1990; children: Lauren Ansley, Shelby Jordan. BA cum laude, U. Ga., 1973, JD, 1976. Bar: Ga. 1976, U.S. Dist. Ct. (mid. dist.) Ga. 1976, U.S. Ct. Appeals (5th and 11th cirs.) 1979, S.C. 1990. Ptnr. Galis, Timmons, Andrews & Head, Athens, Ga., 1977-79, Andrews & Head P.C., Athens, 1979-82; pvt. practice Athens, 1982-85; ptnr. McDonald, Head, Carney & Haggard, Athens, 1985-88; real estate developer Athens, 1979-88; regent, co-founder Nat. Coll. DUI Def., Inc. Author: The Georgia DUI Trial Practice Manual, 1998, Handling License Revocations and Suspensions in Georgia, 1993, Georgia DUI Trial Practice, 1998; co-author: 101 Ways to Avoid A Drunk Driving Conviction, 1991. Pres. Joseph Henry Lumpkin Found., Inc., Athens, 1979; chmn. Bridge the Gap seminar, Atlanta, 1980. Awardee Athens-Clarke Heritage Found. Inc., Athens, 1983. Mem. ABA, Ga. Bar Assn., S.C. Bar Assn., Assn. Trial Lawyers Am., Ga. Trial Lawyers Assn., Def. Drinking Drivers Network (founder), Order of Barristers, U. Ga. Pres.'s Club. Democrat. Presbyterian. Product liability, Personal injury, Criminal. Home: 6115 Spalding Bluff Ct Norcross GA 30092-4540 Office: 750 Hammond Dr NE Ste 12-100 Atlanta GA 30328-6135

**HEADMAN, ARLAN OSMOND, JR.,** lawyer; b. Salt Lake City, Utah, Oct. 22, 1952; s. Arlan O. and Ione (Ficklin) H.; m. Debra Card, Aug. 20, 1973; 1 child, Alexander Oliver. B.S., U. Utah, 1974, J.D., 1977. Bar: Utah 1977, U.S. Dist. Ct. Utah 1977, U.S. Dist. Ct. Ariz. 1992, U.S. Ct. Appeals (10th cir.) 1993, U.S. Supreme Ct. 1993. Cons., Ra-Tek Investment, Denver, 1981-82; sole practice, Salt Lake City, 1982-84; ptnr. Smith & Headman, Salt Lake City, 1984-89; of counsel Wilkins, Oritt & Ronnow, Salt Lake City, 1989-92; ptnr. Wilkins, Oritt & Headman, Salt Lake City, 1992-94, Cohne, Rappaport & Segal, Salt Lake City, 1994; mem. rule change com. Ad Hoc Com., Utah State Securities Div., 1984; mem. Utah Securities Adv. Bd. Del., Utah Dem. Conv., 1972, state and county Dem. Conv., 1986. U. Utah scholar, 1971. Mem. ABA (arbitration subcom. bus. law sect.), Nat. Assn. Security Dealers (bd. arbitrators 1991—, Utah State Bar (continuing legal edn. com. 1990-91, chmn. 1991-92, legis. affairs com. 1991, securities sect., corp. sect., administrv. law sect.), Mormon, Phi Eta Sigma. Securities, General corporate, Real property. Office: Cohnes Rappaport & Segal 525 E 100 S Fl 5 Salt Lake City UT 84102-1956

**HEADY, EUGENE JOSEPH,** lawyer; b. Poughkeepsie, N.Y., Jan. 25, 1958; s. William and Margaret Patricia Heady; m. Susan Leigh Snead, July 31, 1987; children: Anthony Rey, Emily Rene, Katie Shanell. BS in Engring., U. Hartford, 1981; JD cum laude, Tex. Tech. U., 1996. Bar: Tex. 1996, Ga. 1997, Colo. 1997, Fla. 1998, Supreme Ct. Ga. 1997, U.S. Dist. Ct. (no. dist.) Ga. 1997, U.S. Ct. Appeals Ga. 1997. V.p. Heady Electric Co., Inc., Poughkeepsie, 1980-83; project mgr. ANECO, Inc., West Palm Beach, Fla., 1987-93; assoc. Smith, Currie & Hancock LLP, Atlanta, 1996—. Editor-in-chief Tex. Tech Law Rev. vol. 27, 1995-96; editor Tex. Tech Legal Rsch. Bd., 1995-96; co-author: Ga. Suppl. to Fifty State Construction Lien and Bond Law, 1996, 97, 98, Ga. chpt. Fifty State Construction Lien and Bond Law, 1999; author: chpts. in Alternative Clauses to Standard Construction Contracts, 1998. Mem. ABA (forum on the constrn. industry), Scribes-The Am. Soc. Writers on Legal Subjects. Avocations: writing, reading. E-mail: gjheady@smithcurrie.com. Fax: 404-688-0671. Construction, Government contracts and claims. Home: 2412 Waterscape Trl Snellville GA 30078-7700 Office: Smith Currie & Hancock LLP 2600 Harris Tower 233 Peachtree St NE Atlanta GA 30303-1530

**HEALY, GEORGE WILLIAM, III,** lawyer, mediator; b. New Orleans, Mar. 8, 1930; s. George William and Margaret Alford H.; m. Sharon Saunders, Oct. 26, 1974; children: George W. IV, John Carmichael, Floyd Alford, Hyde Dunbar, Mary Margaret. BA, Tulane U., 1950, JD, 1955. Bar: La. 1955, U.S. Supreme Ct. 1969. Assoc. Phelps, Dunbar, Marks, Claverie & Sims, New Orleans, 1955-58; ptnr. Phelps Dunbar, 1958-95, of counsel, 1996—; mem. U.S. del. Comité Maritime Internat., Tokyo, 1969, Lisbon, 1985, Paris, 1990, Sydney, 1994, titulary mem. Mem. planning com. Tulane U. Admiralty Law Inst., dir. World Trade Ctr., 1993—; dir. New Orleans Pro Bono Project, 1995-97. Fellow Am. Bar Found., Am. Coll. Trial Lawyers, Maritime Law Assn. U.S. (mem. exec. com. 1984-87, 2d v.p. 1988-90, 1st v.p. 1990-92, pres. 1992-94), La. Bar Found.; mem. New Orleans Bar Assn. (pres. 1992), Def. Rsch. Inst., La. Assn. Def. Counsel, New Orleans Assn. Def. Counsel, Com. Maritime Internat. Am. Found. (dir. 1990—), New Orleans Bar Assn. Inn of Ct. (master), Boston Club., La. Club, Stratford Club, Plimsoll Club, Recess Club (pres. 1978), Pinfeathers Hunting Club, New Orleans Lawn Tennis Club, Propeller Club, Mariners Club. Republican. Episcopalian. Fax: (504) 568-9130; e-mail: healyg@phelps.com. Admiralty. Home: 6020 Camp St New Orleans LA 70118-5902 Office: 400 Poydras St New Orleans LA 70130-3245

**HEALY, JAMES CASEY,** lawyer; b. Washington, Feb. 19, 1956; s. Joseph Francis Jr. and Patricia Ann (Casey) H.; m. Kelly Anne Quinn, Nov. 4, 1995; 1 child, Caitlin Quinn. BS, Spring Hill Coll., 1978; JD, Emory U., 1982. Bar: Ga. 1983, Conn. 1983, U.S. Dist. Ct. Conn. 1984, U.S. Tax Ct. 1984, U.S. Supreme Ct. 1987. Assoc. Gregory and Adams PC, Wilton, Conn., 1982-87, ptnr., 1988-89, mng. ptnr., 1990-94; v.p. Gregory and Adams PC, Wilton, 1995—; spl. counsel Wilton Police Commn., 1986-98; mem. Parks and Recreation Commn., 1991—, sec., 1991-93, chmn., 1997—; corporator Ridgefield Bank, 1997—. Bd. dirs. Mark Lavin Meml. Offshore Med. and Safety Found., Empire, Mich., 1987-97, Village Market Inc., 1988-90; chmn. leadership giving program United Way, 1991; bd. mgrs. Wilton Childrens. Ctr., 1996-98; mem. athletic fields subcom. of bldg. com. Wilton H.S., 1998-99; active various charity and athletic orgns. Mem. ABA, State Bar Ga., State Bar Conn. (exec. com., planning and zoning sect. 1992-94, 98—), Am. Planning Assn., Stamford/Norwalk Regional Bar Assn. (law office mgmt. com. 1994-96, co-chmn. land use com. 1996—, real estate broker's contract com. 1997-98), Wilton C. of C. (bd. dirs. 1994-96), Silver Spring Country Club. Republican. Roman Catholic. E-mail: jhealy@gregoryandadams.com. Land use and zoning (including planning), Real property. Office: Gregory and Adams 190 Old Ridgefield Rd Wilton CT 06897-4023

**HEALY, JOSEPH FRANCIS, JR.,** lawyer, arbitrator, retired airline executive; b. N.Y.C., Aug. 11, 1930; s. Joseph Francis and Agnes (Kett) H.; m. Patricia A. Casey, Apr. 23, 1955; children: James C., Timothy, Kevin, Cathleen M., Mary, Terence. BS, Fordham U., 1952; JD, Georgetown U., 1959. Bar: D.C. 1959. With gen. traffic dept. Eastman-Kodak Co., Rochester, N.Y., 1954-55; air transp. examiner CAB, Washington, 1955-59; practiced in Washington, 1959-70, 80-81; asst. gen. counsel Air Transport Assn. Am., 1966-70; v.p. legal Eastern Air Lines, Inc., N.Y.C. and Miami, Fla., 1970-80; ptnr. Ford, Farquhar, Kornblut & O'Neill, Washington, 1980-81; v.p. legal affairs Piedmont Aviation, Inc., Winston Salem, N.C., 1981-84, sr. v.p., gen counsel, 1984-89, ret., 1989; sr. v.p. gen. counsel Trans World Airlines Inc., Mt. Kisco, N.Y., 1993-94. Mem. bd. visitors Sch. Law Wake Forest U., 1988-96. 1st lt. USAF, 1952-54. Mem. FBA, Am. Arbitration Assn. (mem. nat. panel arbitrators 1989—), Nat. Aero. Assn., Internat. Aviation Club (Washington), Univ. Club (Washington), Beta Gamma Sigma, Phi Delta Phi. Home: 104 Overlink Ct Lynchburg VA 24503-3200

**HEALY, MICHAEL PATRICK,** lawyer; b. Sioux Falls, S.D., Apr. 27, 1962; s. Patrick Joseph and Carolyn Cathrine (Billion) H.; m. Sarah E. Recker, Dec. 30, 1989 (div. Nov. 19, 1992). Bar: Mo. 1987, Kans. 1989, U.S. Dist. Ct. (we. dist.) Mo. 1987, U.S. Ct. Appeals (8th cir.), U.S. Ct. Appeals (10th cir.), U.S. Dist. Ct. Kans. 1989, U.S. Supreme Ct. 1995. Assoc. Stites McIntosh Knepper & Hopkins, Kansas City, Mo., 1987-94; ptnr. McIntosh Knepper Hobson & Healy, Kansas City, 1994—; v.p., gen. coun. D.M.I., Inc., Sioux Falls, 1994—; v.p., gen. counsel J.L. Healy Constrn. Co., Sioux Falls, 1993—. Mem. Am. Trial Lawyers Assn., Mo. Assn. Trial Lawyers, Mo. Bar Assn. Republican. Roman Catholic. Federal civil litigation, Professional liability, Securities. Office: McIntosh Knepper Hobson & Healy 1125 Grand Blvd Ste 1800 Kansas City MO 64106-2506

**HEALY, NICHOLAS JOSEPH,** lawyer, educator; b. N.Y.C., Jan. 4, 1910; s. Nicholas Joseph and Frances Cecilia (McCarthy) H.; m. Margaret Marie Ferry, Mar. 29, 1937; children: Nicholas, Margaret Healy Parker, Rosemary Healy Bell, Mary Louise Healy White, Donall, Kathleen Healy Hamon. AB, Holy Cross Coll., 1931; JD, Harvard U., 1934. Bar: N.Y. 1935, U.S. Supreme Ct. 1949. Pvt. practice N.Y.C., 1935-42, 48—; mem. Healy & Baillie (and predecessor law firms), 1948—; spl. asst. to atty. gen. U.S., 1945-48; tchr. admiralty law NYU Sch. Law, 1947-86, adj. prof., 1960—; Niels F. Johnsen vis. prof. maritime law Tulane Maritime Law Ctr., 1986; vis. prof. maritime law Shanghai Maritime Law Inst. (now Shanghai Maritime U.), 1981, 86, 88. Contbr. chpts. on admiralty to Ann. Survey Am. Law, 1948-87; author: (with Sprague) Cases on Admiralty, 1950, (with Currie) Cases and Materials on Admiralty, 1965, (with Sharpe) Cases and Materials on Admiralty, 1974, 3rd edit., 1998, (with Sweeney) The Law of Marine Collision, 1998; editor: Jour. Maritime Law and Commerce, 1980-90, mem. bd. editors, 1969-79, 91—; assoc. editor: American Maritime Cases; mem. bd. dirs. Il Dirittimo Marittimo; contbr. to Ency. Brit. Chmn. USCG Adv. Panel on Rules of the Road, 1966-72; mem. permanent adv. bd. Tulane Admiralty Law Inst. Lt. (s.g.) USNR, 1942-45. Fellow Am. Coll. Trial Lawyers; mem. ABA (ho. of dels. 1964-66), N.Y. State Bar Assn., Assn. of Bar of City of N.Y., N.Y. County Lawyers Assn., Maritime Law Assn. U.S. (pres. 1964-66), Assn. Average Adjusters U.S. (chmn. 1959-60), Com. Maritime Internat. (exec. coun. 1972-79, v.p. 1985-91, hon. v.p. 1991—), Ibero-Am. Inst. Maritime Law (hon.). Admiralty. Home: 132 Tullamore Rd Garden City NY 11530-1139 Office: Healy & Baillie 29 Broadway Fl 27 New York NY 10006-3201

**HEALY, WALTER F. X.,** lawyer; b. N.Y.C., Sept. 15, 1941; s. Walter Patrick and Helen Theresa (Fischer) H.; BA, St. Joseph's Coll., Yonkers, N.Y., 1963; LLB, Fordham U., 1966; m. Margaret O'Hanlon, Nov. 26, 1966; 1 child, Katherine Healy Burrows. Bar: N.Y. 1967, Pa. 1980, U.S. Ct. Appeals (9th cir.) 1983; assoc. Dewey, Ballantine, Bushby, Palmer & Wood, N.Y.C., 1966-76; corp. counsel Singer Co., N.Y.C., 1976; corp. sec., dep. gen. counsel Studebaker-Worthington, Inc., N.Y.C., 1976-79; v.p., gen. counsel UGI Corp., Valley Forge, Pa., 1979-84; ptnr. Windels, Marx, Davies & Ives, N.Y.C., 1984—. Mem. ABA, Assn. Bar City of N.Y., N.Y. Athletic Club. Avocations: squash, basketball, theatre. Mergers and acquisitions, Finance, Securities. Office: Windels Marx Davies & Ives 156 W 56th St Fl 23 New York NY 10019-3867

**HEALY, WILLIAM TIMOTHY,** lawyer; b. Babylon, N.Y., Sept. 13, 1932; s. John B. and Mary B. H.; m. Gail H.; children: Virginia Mary, William Timothy Jr., Sean Patrick. Colgate U., 1954; LLB, U. Ariz., 1960. Asst. city atty. City Attys. Office, Tucson, Ariz., 1961-62; deputy atty. Pima County Attys. Office, Tucson, Ariz., 1962-63, chief trial atty., 1963-66; atty. pvt. practice, Tucson, Ariz., 1966—. Treas. Pima County Dem. Ctrl. Com., 1962-64, pres. Young Dems. Greater Tucson, 1964-65; bd. dirs. Downtown YMCA, 1972-74. 1st lt. USAF, 1955-57; capt. Ariz. Air NG, 1958-62. Mem. ABA, Am. Bd. Trial Advocacy, Assn. Trial Lawyers Am., Am. Arbitration Assn., State Bar Assn. Ariz., Colgate U. Alumni Assn. (regional dir. 1968-84), U. Ariz. Wildcat Club. Personal injury. Office: Healy & Studwell 5210 E Williams Cir Ste 720 Tucson AZ 85711-4424

**HEAP, ROBERT A.,** lawyer; b. Lincoln, Nebr., Nov. 25, 1955; s. Duane E. and Pat R. (Buster) H.; m. Jane S. Fawell, June 26, 1981; children: Andrew, Emily, Wesley. BS in Edn., No. Ill. U., 1978, MS in Ednl. Adminstrn., 1980; JD with honors, IIT, 1983. Bar: Ill., U.S. Dist. Ct. (no. dist.) Ill., U.S. Ct. Appeals (7th cir.), U.S. Supreme Ct. Tchr. Naperville (Ill.) Sch. Dist. 203, 1978-81; atty. DuPage County States Attys. Office, Wheaton, Ill., 1983-86, Fawell, James & Brooks, Naperville, 1986-88; pvt. practice pvt. practice, Naperville, 1988-91; ptnr. Kuhn & Heap, Naperville, 1991—. Mem. DuPage County Bd., 1990—; commr. DuPage County Forest Preserve, 1990—; chmn. Citizens Adv. Bd. Solid Waste, Wheaton, 1988-90; mem. DuPage County Affordable Housing Task Force, Wheaton, 1990-91; chmn. Intergovtl. Coop. Com., Naperville, 1996. Mem. Ill. Bar Assn., DuPage County Bar Assn. (chmn. legis. 1986-96). General practice, Constitutional. Office: Kuhn & Heap 552 S Washington St Naperville IL 60540-6658

**HEAREY, ELIZABETH BERLE,** lawyer; b. East Orange, N.J., Mar. 3, 1947; d. Charles Henry and Winifred (McCubbin) Berle; m. Charles DeLisle Hearey Jr., June 13, 1970; children: Raymond DeLisle, Katherine Berle, Sarah Elizabeth. BA with honors, Wellesley Coll., 1969; JD, U. Calif., San Francisco, 1974. Bar: Calif. 1974, U.S. Dist. Ct. (no. dist.) Calif. 1974. Dep. county counsel Contra Costa County, Martinez, Calif., 1975-86; assoc. Williams & Woods, Martinez, 1992-95, Atkinson, Andelson, Loya, Ruud & Romo, Pleasanton, Calif., 1995—. Mem. Contra Costa County Bar Assn., Phi Beta Kappa. Education and schools, Labor. Office: Atkinson Andelson Loya Ruud & Romo 5776 Stoneridge Mall Rd Pleasanton CA 94588-2832

**HEARIN, ROBERT MATLOCK, JR.,** lawyer; b. Tuscaloosa, Ala., Jan. 15, 1946; s. Robert M. Hearin and Annie Laurie Swaim; m. Zetta M. Bryant, Mar. 25, 1972; children: Andrew, Timothy. BA, U. Miss., 1968; JD, Tulane U., 1971. Bar: La. 1971, Calif. 1976, Tex. 1993. Mng. atty. New Orleans Legal Assistance Corp., 1972-75; sole practice law New Orleans, 1976-95; mng. atty. Hearin & Warriner, New Orleans, 1995—. Baseball coach Carrollton Booster Club, Inc., New Orleans, 1991, 92, 95, 97. With U.S. Army, 1971-72. Fellow La. Bar Found. (life). Presbyn. Avocations: travel, sports, cooking. Personal injury, General civil litigation, Admiralty. Office: Hearin & Warriner 338 Baronne St Ste 200 New Orleans LA 70112-1693

**HEARN, HOLLY MICHELLE,** lawyer; b. Atlanta, June 19, 1967; d. Jerald Pershing and Jackie Gamble Hart. BS in Mgmt., Ga. Inst. Tech., 1989; JD magna cum laude, Ga. State U., 1996. Bar: Ga. 1996, Wash. 1997, U.S. Dist. Ct. (we. dist.) Wash. 1997. Assoc. Davis Wright Tremaine, Seattle, 1996—. Bd. dirs. New Beginnings, Seattle, 1997-98. Labor. Office: Davis Wright Tremaine 1501 Fourth Ave 2600 Century Sq Seattle WA 98101

**HEARN-HAYNES, THERESA,** lawyer; b. Chgo., Feb. 27, 1954; d. Gustia L. and Johnnie Hearn; m. Emil P. Haynes, Dec. 20, 1985 (dec. Apr. 1990); children: Dominique, Ashley, Alexis; m. William Ivory Murphy, 1993; 1 child, William Myles Murphy. BS, U. Ill., 1975; MS, U. Iowa, 1980; JD, South Tex. Coll. Law, 1986; postgrad. in mediation tng., A.A. White Dispute Resolution Inst., 1997. Ordained to ministry, Ch. of Yahvah Ala Hay, 1991. Pvt. practice Spring, Tex., 1986—, gubernatorial candidate for Tex., 1989—; specialist pub. interest law, excessive taxation, unconstnl. statutory and case law, pub. corruption, 1989—. Author: 20th Century Slavery in America, How to Stop Homeowner Association Abuse, 1999. Chairperson Senatorial dist. 18, Fort Bend County, Tex., 1988; v.p. Southside Comty. Improvement Assn., Houston, 1985; active African-Am. Legal Def. Fund, 1994; bd. dirs. Harris County Coop. Resources, 1994; dist. supt. for state of Tex., Ch. of Yahvah Ala Hay. Named Hon. Tuskegee alumni, 1994. Mem. Trial Lawyers of Am., Landowners Assn. (bd. dirs. 1984—), Wild Heather Civic Club. Avocations: singing, dancing, teaching, sewing, jogging. Personal injury, Real property, Administrative and regulatory. Office: PO Box 1495 Spring TX 77383-1495

**HEARTFIELD, THAD,** judge; b. 1940. Student, Notre Dame U., 1959-60, Southwest Tex. Jr. Coll., 1960; BA, St. Mary's U., 1962, JD, 1965. Asst. dist. atty. Jefferson County, 1965-66; assoc. Weller, Wheelus & Green, 1966-69; city atty. Beaumont, 1969-73; ptnr. O'Brian, Richards & Heartfield, 1973-77, Crutchfield, DeCordova, Brocato & Heartfield, 1981-85; dir. Lower Neches Valley Authority, 1983-94; dist. judge U.S. Dist. Ct. (ea. dist.)Tex., 1995—. adv. dir. St. Elizabeth Hosp., 1992-94. Office: US Dist Ct PO Box 949 Beaumont TX 77704-0949

**HEATH, CHARLES DICKINSON,** lawyer, telephone company executive; b. Waterloo, Iowa, June 28, 1941; s. George Clinton and Dorothy (Dickinson) H.; m. Carilyn Frances Cain, June 3, 1972. BBA, U. Iowa, 1962, JD, 1966; MBA, U. Ariz., 1963. Bar: Iowa 1966, Pa. 1969, Ind. 1970, U.S. Supreme Ct. 1971, Wis. 1973, Ariz. 1975, Mich. 1979, Fla. 1979, Calif. 1989. Asst. gen. counsel Kohler Co., Wis., 1973-79; securities and tax counsel Kellogg Co., Battle Creek, Mich., 1979-81; assoc. gen. counsel Universal Telephone Inc., Milw., 1981-89, also corp. sec., 1987-89; atty. CenturyTel, Inc., LaCrosse, Wis., 1989—. Securities, Public utilities, Corporate taxation.

**HEATH, CLAUDE ROBERT,** lawyer; b. Commerce, Tex., May 4, 1947; s. H. Harold and Laura (Hammond) H.; m. Jean L. Manning, May 18, 1974; children: John Hammond, William Hunter. BA, U. Tex., 1969, JD, 1972. Bar: Tex. 1972, U.S. Dist. Ct. (we. dist.) Tex. 1977, U.S. Ct. Appeals (5th cir.) 1981, U.S. Dist. Ct. (no. and so. dists.) Tex. 1991. Law clk. U.S. Dist. Ct. (we. dist.) Tex., Austin, 1972-73; asst. atty. gen., chmn. opinion com. Atty. Gen.'s Office, Austin, 1973-80; ptnr. Bickerstaff, Heath, Smiley, Pollan, Kever & McDaniel, Austin, 1980—. Mem. ABA, Tex. Bar Found., State Bar of Tex., Travis County Bar Assn. Democrat. Administrative and regulatory, Civil rights, Appellate. Home: 7605 Rustling Cv Austin TX 78731-1332 Office: Bickerstaff Heath Pollan Kever & McDaniel 816 Congress Ave Ste 1700 Austin TX 78701-2443

**HEATH, THOMAS CLARK,** lawyer; b. Sarasota, Fla., Feb. 6, 1948; s. Roy Fulmer and Ruby (Clark) H.; m. Marsha Robert Hubbard, June 26, 1971 (div. Dec. 1977); m. Anne Frances Wilson, Sept. 6, 1980; 1 child, Benjamin. BSBA, U. Fla., 1970, JD, 1973. Bar: Fla. 1973, U.S. Dist. Ct. (so. dist.) Fla. 1976, U.S. Ct. Appeals (11th cir.) 1976. Assoc. Howell, Kirby, Montgomery et al, Ft. Lauderdale, Fla., 1973-75, Carey, Dwyer, Cole, Selwood & Bernard, Ft. Lauderdale, Fla., 1975-81; ptnr. Hainline, Billing, Cochran & Heath, Ft. Lauderdale, Fla., 1981-85; ptnr. Billing, Cochran, Heath, Lyles & Mauro, Ft. Lauderdale, Fla., 1985—, West Palm Beach, Fla., 1985—. Fellow Am. Bd. Trial Advocacy (charter); mem. Am. Assn. Hosp. Attys., Assn. Trial Lawyers Am., Trial Attys. Am., Fla. Defense Lawyers Assn. Avocations: fishing, hunting. General civil litigation, Personal injury, Product liability. Office: Billing Cochran Heath Lyles & Mauro 888 SE 3rd Ave Ste 301 Fort Lauderdale FL 33316-1159

**HEATON, JON C.,** lawyer; b. Brigham City, Utah, Aug. 31, 1942; s. Harley Lowry and Anne Jane (Lundburg) H.; m. Penny Bourquin, Dec. 30, 1961; children: John Patrick, Timothy A., J. Scott, Jennifer, L., Annelise. BS in Bus. with honors, U. Colo., 1964; JD, Vanderbilt U., 1972. Bar: Utah 1972, U.S. Dist. Ct. Utah 1972. Assoc. Butler, McHugh, Butler, Tune & Watts, Nashville, 1972; assoc. Prince, Yeates & Geldzahler, Salt Lake City, 1972-76, ptnr., 1976-80, sr. ptnr., 1980—; bd. dirs., officer Koflach USA, Salt Lake City, 1988-92, Marker Bindings, Salt Lake City, 1983-96; atty. Park City (Utah) Ski Resort, 1975—, U.S. Ski Team, Park City, 1978-84, Whitmores Inc., Star Resorts, Pentalon Corp.; judge pro tem 3d Cir. Cts., Salt Lake City, 1980—; mem. archtl. bd. State Utah. With USAF, 1964-69; brig. gen. Utah Air N.G. Mem. ABA, Utah State Bar, Salt Lake County Bar Assn., N.G. Assn. U.S., Order of Coif, Pi Kappa Alpha. Republican. Avocations: tennis, boating, wilderness areas, skiing, flying. Real property, General corporate, Administrative and regulatory. Office: 175 E 4th S Salt Lake City UT 84111-2314

**HEBBLE, NANCY L.,** editor. Editor Phila. Bar Reporter. Office: Phila Bar Assn 1101 Market St Ste 11 Philadelphia PA 19107-2935

**HEBENSTREIT, MICHAEL JOSEPH,** lawyer; b. Indpls., Sept. 23, 1952; s. Robert Joseph and Patricia (Hagan) H.; m. Robyn L. Moberly, May 13, 1978; children: Cory M., Megan L., H. Kyle. BA, Xavier U., 1974; JD, Ind. U., Indpls., 1977. Bar: Ind. 1977, U.S. Dist. Ct. (so. dist.) Ind. 1977. Staff atty. Nisenbaum & Brown, Indpls., 1977-79; assoc. William R. Richards, P.C., Indpls., 1979-82; ptnr. Hebenstreit & Moberly, Indpls., 1982-96; of counsel Kroger, Gardis & Reyas, 1996—; spkr. continuing legal edn. seminar, 1993. Mem. 500 Festival Assocs., Indpls., 1989—; adult leader Boy Scouts Am., Indpls., 1990—; bd. mem. Girls Inc., 1996—; pres. Brebery Jesuit Oreparatory Sch. Dad's Club, 1996—; co-chair 500 Festival Parade Band Com., 1997—. Mem. Indpls. Bar Assn. (exec. com. family law 1991—, grievance com. family law 1990—, comml. and bankruptcy com. 1990—), Ind. State Bar Assn. (ho. dels. 1989—), Indpls. Bar Assn. (bd. mgrs. 1998—). Roman Catholic. Avocations: water sports, boating, snow skiing, camping, travel. Consumer commercial, Bankruptcy, Family and matrimonial. Office: Kugin Gardis & Ryan 111 Monument Cir Ste 900 Indianapolis IN 46204-5106

**HEBENTHAL, M(ARGARETA) ELAINE,** law librarian; b. Bartlesville, Okla., May 16, 1960; d. Alan D. II and LaVerne (Duckwall) Cochrane; m. Daniel P. Hebenthal, Oct. 24, 1992; 1 child, Evan Daniel. BA, Huntingdon Coll., 1981; MLS, Fla. State U., 1989. Info. mgr. Barrett and Pelham, Tallahassee, 1990—. Vol. Leon County Pub. Libr., Tallahassee, 1994, Literacy Vols. of Leon County, 1986-91. Mem. Assn. Legal Adminstrs., Tallahassee Assn. Law Librs. (pres. 1996-97), Tallahassee Netware Users Group (pres. 1994-99), Legal Adminstrs. Assn. Tallahassee. Episcopalian. Avocation: writing poetry. Office: Barrett and Pelham 111 S Monroe St Ste 3000 Tallahassee FL 32301-1583

**HECHT, CHARLES JOEL,** lawyer; b. N.Y.C., Mar. 15, 1939; s. Charles Maurice and Jane Ann Hecht; children: Stacey Ann, Eric Simon. BA, Cornell U., 1961, LLB, 1963. Bar: N.Y. 1965, U.S. Dist. Ct. (ea. and so. dists.) N.Y. 1971, U.S. Supreme Ct. 1971, U.S. Ct. Appeals (2d cir.) 1975, U.S. Ct. Appeals (5th and 7th cirs.) 1979, U.S. Ct. Appeals (6th cir.) 1985, U.S. Ct. Appeals (3d cir.) 1988, U.S. Ct. Appeals (9th cir.) 1992. Atty. SEC, Washington, 1966-69; assoc. Mermelstein, Burns & Lesser, N.Y.C., 1969-71; sole practice N.Y.C., 1971-89, Hecht & Steckman, P.C., N.Y.C., 1989—. Contbr. articles to profl. jours. Served to 1st lt. U.S. Army, 1963-65. Mem. ABA (commodities regulation com.), N.Y. State Bar Assn. (gen. securities litigation com.). Club: Lotos (N.Y.C.) (fin. com. 1983-92, membership com. 1985-87, bd. dirs. 1986-97). Avocations: scuba diving, bicycling, stamp collecting, golf. Fax: (212) 490-3263. Securities, General corporate, Federal civil litigation. Office: 60 E 42nd St New York NY 10165-0006

**HECHT, DONALD STUART,** lawyer; b. N.Y.C., Mar. 20, 1941; s. Murray Hecht and Jeanne (Morris) Friedman; m. Laura Ruth Dodes, Sept. 9, 1967; children: Brian, Daniel. BA, Hofstra Coll., 1962; JD, Bklyn. Law Sch., 1969. Bar: N.Y. 1970, U.S. Dist. Ct. (so. and ea. dists.) N.Y. 1975. Assoc. Sitomer, Sitomer & Porges, N.Y.C., 1970-73, Silver, Saperstein, Barnet & Soloman, N.Y.C., 1973-81; ptnr. Weber & Scharf, Massapequa, N.Y., 1981-82; sole practice Port Washington, N.Y., 1982-90; pvt. practice Manhasset, N.Y., 1991-96; small claims arbitrator Dist. Ct. Nassau County, 1988—; pvt. practice Garden City, N.Y., 1996-98; pvt. prac. Jericho, NY, 1998—; cons., lectr. Bd. Cooperative Ednl. Svcs., Nassau County, N.Y. 1985—. Co-author, editor: Guardianship Practice in New York State, 1997; law columnist: Able Newspaper for the Disabled. Bd. dirs. United Cerebral Palsy Assn. Nassau County, 1982-87, Epilepsy Found. of Long Island, 1983-99, v.p. 1987-96; bd. appeals Village of Port Washington North, 1984-85, trustee, 1985-87, dep. mayor, 1986-87; mem. Nassau County Dem. Com., 1984-87. 1st lt. USAF 1962-66. Mem. ABA, New York State Bar Assn., Bar Assn. Nassau County, Nat. Acad. Elder Law Attys., Am. Judges Assn., Lions (bd. dirs. 1982-83, asst. sec. 1983-84, Disting. Svc. award 1983, Lion of Yr. 1984), Iota Theta. Avocations: hiking, cooking, gardening. E-mail: dschecht@ix.netcom.com. Estate planning, Probate, Elder. Home: 37 Seaview Ln Port Washington NY 11050-1737 Office: 350 Jericho Tpke Jericho NY 11753-1317

**HECHT, FRANK THOMAS,** lawyer; b. Ann Arbor, Mich., June 18, 1944; s. Hans H. and Ilse (Wagner) H. AB, Stanford U., 1966; postgrad., Johns Hopkins U., 1966-68, U. Chgo., 1968; JD, U. Chgo., 1975. Bar: Ill. 1975, U.S. Dist. Ct. (no. dist.) 1975, U.S. Ct. Appeals (7th cir.) 1975, U.S. Supreme Ct. 1981, Colo. 1991. Lawyer Migrant Farmworker Litigation Project, Chgo., 1978-81, dir., 1981-82; assoc. Levy & Erens, Chgo., 1982-85, ptnr., 1985-86; ptnr. Hopkins & Sutter, Chgo., 1986—, vice chair trial sect., pro bono coord., 1996—; cooperating atty. ACLU, Ill., 1983—, bd. dirs. 1985—; bd. dirs. Cook County Legal Assistance Found., 1984-85, Nat. Inst. for Trial Advocacy, 1978. Contbr. Civil Rights Law Reporter. Exec. dir. New Univ. Conf., 1970-72, Indochina Peace Campaign, 1973-75; exec. com. ACLU, 1986-87. Reginald Heber Smith fellow, 1975-78. Mem. ATLA, Assn. Trial Lawyers Am., Def. Rsch. Inst. Federal civil litigation, State civil litigation, Civil rights. Home: 240 Maplewood Rd Riverside IL 60546-1846 Office: Hopkins & Sutter 3 First National Plz Chicago IL 60602

**HECHT, NATHAN LINCOLN,** state supreme court justice; b. Clovis, N.Mex., Aug. 15, 1949; s. Harold Lee and Mary Loretta (Byerly) H. BA, Yale U., 1971; JD cum laude, So. Meth. U., 1974. Bar: Tex. 1974, D.C. 1975, U.S. Dist. Ct. D.C. 1975, U.S. Dist. Ct. (no. and we. dists.) Tex. 1976, U.S. Ct. Appeals (D.C. cir.) 1975, U.S. Ct. Appeals (5th cir.) 1976, U.S. Supreme Ct. 1979. Law clk. to judge U.S. Ct. Appeals (D.C. cir.), 1974-75; assoc. Locke, Purnell, Boren, Laney & Neely, Dallas, 1976-80, ptnr., 1981; dist. judge 95th Dist. Ct., Dallas, 1981-86; justice Tex. 5th Dist. Ct. Appeals, 1986-89, Texas Supreme Ct., Austin, 1989—. Contbr. articles to profl. jours. Bd. visitors So. Meth. U., Dallas, 1984-87; trustee Children's Med. Found., Dallas, 1983-89; bd. dirs. Children's Med. Ctr. North, Dallas, 1985-89; elder Valley View Christian Ch., Dallas, 1981—. Lt. USNR, 1971-79. Named Outstanding Young Lawyer of Dallas, Dallas Assn. of Young Lawyers, 1984. Fellow Tex. Bar Found., Am. Bar Found.; mem. ABA, Dallas Bar Assn., D.C. Bar Assn., Am. Law Inst. Republican. Avocations: piano, organ, jogging, bicycling. Office: Tex Supreme Ct PO Box 12248 201 West 14th Room 104 Austin TX 78711

**HECKATHORN, I. JAMES,** lawyer; b. Wolf Creek, Mont., Sept. 4, 1923; s. Lee and Wilhelmina (Sacht) H.; m. Vera Jean Hensrud; children: James (dec.), Martha. LLB, U. Mont., 1950. Bar: Mont. 1950, U.S. Dist. Ct. Mont., 1950, U.S. Ct. Appeals (9th cir.), Tribal Ct. of Confederated Salish and Kootenai Tribes; cert. civil trial specialist, Nat. Bd. Trial Advocacy. Atty. VA, Helena, Mont., 1952-54; ptnr. Haswell & Heckathorn, Whitefish, Mont., 1954-58, Murphy, Robinson, Heckathorn & Phillips, PC, Kalispell, Mont., 1958-97, Murphy, Robinson, Heckathorn & Phillips (merged with Crowley, Haughey, Toole & Dietrich, 1997—; former mem. Com. for Civil Justice Expense and Delay Reduction Plan, U.S. Dist. Cts. for Dist. of Mont.; standing com. for rev. of discovery practices and litigation conduct of U.S. Dist. Cts. for Mont.; civil rules com. Supreme Ct. of Mont., com. on uniform dist. ct. rules; chmn. settlement masters com. 11th Jud. Dist. With AUS, 1943-46, lt. col. USAR. Mem. ABA, ATLA, Am. Bd. Trial Advocacy (charter mem. Mont. chpt.), N.W. Mont. Bar, State Bar of Mont., Mont. Def. Trial Lawyers Assn. (pres.). General civil litigation, Insurance, Personal injury. Home: PO Box 516 Whitefish MT 59937-0516 Office: Crowley Haughey Hansen Toole & Dietrich LLP 431 1st Ave W Kalispell MT 59901-4835

**HECKENKAMP, ROBERT GLENN,** lawyer; b. Quincy, Ill., June 29, 1923; s. Joseph Edward and Ethel E. (Requet) H.; m. Jean E. Duker, June 22, 1946 (dec. 1983); children: Gae Kelly, Joy Heckenkamp-Roate; m. Wilma E. Dobbs, Nov. 15, 1985. BS, Quincy Coll., 1947; JD, DePaul U., 1949. Bar: Ill. 1949, U.S. Dist. Ct. (cen. and so. dists.) Ill. 1949, U.S. Ct. Appeals (7th cir.) 1952, U.S. Supreme Ct. 1965. Sr. ptnr. Heckenkamp, Simhauser, Ward & Zerkle, Springfield, Ill. Fellow Am. Coll. Trial Lawyers (com. chmn. 1983-86), Internat. Acad. Trial Lawyers; mem. ABA, Ill. State Bar Assn. (pres. 1980-81), Sangamon County Bar Assn., Assn. Trial Lawyers Am., Ill. Trial Lawyers Assn. (pres. 1977-78). Soc. Trial Lawyers. Avocations: hunting, fishing. General civil litigation, Personal injury, Insurance. Home: 60 Yacht Club Rd Springfield IL 62707-9525 Office: Heckenkamp Simhauser Ward & Zerkle West Mezzanine Hilton Hotel 7th & Adams Springfield IL 62701

**HECKER, LESLIE FAYE,** lawyer; b. Park Ridge, Ill., Oct. 22, 1960; d. Earl Edward and Joanne H. BA, U. Colo., 1983; JD, U. Miami, 1987. Assoc. Walton, Lantaff, Miami, Fla., 1989-92, Parenti, Falk, Miami, Fla., 1992-96; ptnr. Leslie Heules Law Office, Miami, Fla., 1996—. Mem. Am. Counsel Soc., Dade County Bar Assn. (professionalism com. 1998—), Viscayans. Personal injury, Insurance. Office: 1320 S Dixie Hwy Ste 1100 Miami FL 33146-2942

**HECKER, ROBERT J.,** lawyer; b. White Plains, N.Y.. AB, Brandeis U., 1959; JD, Fordham U., 1962. Bar: N.Y. 1962, U.S. Dist. Ct. (so. and ea. dists.) N.Y., U.S. Supreme Ct. assoc. judge City Ct., White Plains, 1977-81; lectr., bd. dirs. Nat. Home Equity Mortgage Assn. Mem. N.Y. State Bar Assn., Westchester County Bar Assn., White Plains Bar Assn. (pres. 1971), N.Y. State Magistrates Assn. Republican. General corporate, Real property, Finance. Office: Hecker Colasurdo & Assocs PC 707 Westchester Ave White Plains NY 10604-3102

**HECKLER, GERARD VINCENT,** lawyer; b. Utica, N.Y., Feb. 18, 1941; s. Gerard Vincent and Mary Jane (Finocan) H. BA, Union Coll., Schenectady, 1962; JD, Syracuse U., 1970; MA in Clin. Psychology, Antioch U., 1994; postgrad., The Fielding Inst., 1995—. Bar: Ill. 1971, Calif. 1980, Mass. 1986, N.Y. 1986, U.S. Supreme Ct. 1985. Assoc. Martin, Craig, Chester & Sonnenschein, Chgo., 1970-73, Goldstein, Goldberg & Fishman, Chgo., 1973-76; ptnr. Heckler & Enstrom, Chgo., 1976-80; pvt. practice law L.A., Irvine, 1980-85; sr. trial atty. Law Office of Harden Bennion, L.A., 1985-87, Rafferty & Polich, Cambridge, Mass., 1987-8; trial atty. Acret, Gropman & Turner, L.A., 1989-92; instr. trial skills and evidence Calif. State Bar, 1987—; judge pro tem L.A. Mcpl. Ct., 1991—. Lt. USCG, 1964-67, Vietnam. Mem. Calif. State Bar (Bd. Govs. commendation 1986), L.A. County Bar Assn., Acad. Family Mediators, Ill. Bar Assn., Mass. Bar Assn., N.Y. Bar Assn. Avocations: sports, theater, public speaking. General civil litigation, Construction, Bankruptcy. Office: 400 N Tustin Ave Ste 120 Santa Ana CA 92705-3879

**HECKMAN, JEROME HAROLD,** lawyer; b. Washington, June 7, 1927; s. Morris and Pauline (German) H.; m. Margot Resh, June 16, 1948 (div. Oct. 1977); children: Eric Stephen, Carey Eugene; m. Ilona Ely Grenadier, Jan. 2, 1986. BSS, Georgetown U., 1948, LLB, 1953, JD, 1967. Bar: D.C. 1953, U.S. Supreme Ct. 1965. Assoc. Dow, Lohnes & Albertson, Washington, 1954-59, ptnr., 1959-62; sr. ptnr. Keller and Heckman, Washington, 1962—; gen. counsel Soc. of Plastics Industry Inc., N.Y.C., Washington, 1954—, Broadcasting Publs. Inc. Mag., Washington (co. sold to L.A. Times), 1968-87, Disposables Assn. Inc. (now named Internat. Nonwovens and Disposables Assn.), 1958-67. Contbr. articles to profl. jours. Chmn. regional Rep. com., Md., 1966-72; pres. Plastics Acad., 1995-97. Named to Hall of Fame of Plastics Industry, 1987; recipient Spes Hominum award, Nat. Sanitation Found., 1987. Mem. ABA, Bar Assn. D.C., George Town Club, Woodmont Country Club, Phi Delta Phi. Avocations: golf, tennis. Antitrust, Communications, Administrative and regulatory. Office: Keller & Heckman 1001 G St NW Ste 500 Washington DC 20001-4545

**HECTOR, BRUCE JOHN,** lawyer; b. Newark, Feb. 18, 1950; s. Henry Francis and Doris Mary (Campbell) H.; m. Carol Ann Seely, Aug. 10, 1974. BA in English, Coll. of the Holy Cross, 1971; JD, NYU, 1974. Bar: N.J. 1974, U.S. Dist. Ct. N.J. 1974, N.Y. 1976, U.S. Dist. Ct. (ea. and so. dists.) N.Y. 1976, U.S. Ct. Appeals (4th cir.) 1977, U.S. Ct. Appeals (3d cir.) 1981. Assoc. Podvey & Sachs, Newark, 1974-75, Hill, Rivkins et al, N.Y.C., 1975-81; atty. Becton Dickinson & Co., Franklin Lakes, N.J., 1981-87, sr. atty., 1987-91; assoc. gen. counsel Becton Dickinson & Co., Franklin Lakes, 1992—; lectr. in field. Contbr. articles to profl. publs. Leader explorer law post Boy Scouts Am., Glen Rock, N.J., 1985-88; lectr. environ. law Hazardous Waste Expo '87, Chgo., HWAC Ann. Meeting, Washington, 1988, N.J. Environ. Expn., 1988, 90, Inside Superfund Conf., Washington, 1989-90, Calif. Inst. Bus. Law, 1991-92, Am. Soc. Microbiology, 1992, ACCA Nat. Meeting, 1995, NJCCA Diversity Forum, 1996, NJCCA Forum for Outside Counsel, 1997, others. Mem. Maritime Law Assn. U.S. (proctor in admiralty 1981—), Am. Corp. Counsel Assn., N.J. State Bar Assn., N.J. Corp. Counsel Assn. (bd. dirs. 1995-97, v.p., sec. 1997—), Am. Soc. Microbiol. Democrat. Roman Catholic. Avocations: jazz and classical guitar. Fax: (201) 848-9228. Federal civil litigation, General corporate, Environmental. Home: 170 Gramercy Pl Glen Rock NJ 07452-2310 Office: Becton Dickinson & Co 1 Becton Dr Franklin Lakes NJ 07417-1880

**HEDGEPETH, CURTIS GRANT,** lawyer; b. Laurel, Miss., Aug. 13, 1961; s. Walter Curtis and Aline Graves (Anderson) H.; m. Susan Wells Loper, July 9, 1994; children: Derek Loper, Lily. AA in Acctg., Jones County Jr. Coll., Ellisville, Miss., 1981; BS in BA, U. So. Miss., 1984; JD, U. Miss., 1987. Bar: Miss. 1987, U.S. Dist. Ct. (so. dist.) Miss. 1994. Pub. defender City of Ellisville, 1987-88, pros., 1988-91; city atty. Town of Beaumont, Miss., 1992—; pub. defender Town of Soso, Miss., 1997—. Mem. Jones County Bar Assn., Sertoma (bd. dirs. 1997), Kiwanis. Methodist. Avocations: music, farming. Office: PO Box 413 1 Kampers Alley Laurel MS 39441

**HEDGES, DONALD WALTON,** lawyer; b. Kansas City, Mo., May 24, 1921; s. Byron C. and Irma (McCleary) H.; m. Mary Elizabeth Mancill, Jan. 29, 1944 (div.); children: Judith Elizabeth, Donna Louise, Byron C. III, Steven M.; m. Diane Scheid, Jan. 15, 1965; children: Scott Andrew, Hillary Carson. Student, Principia Coll., 1939-40; BS, U. Pa., 1943, LLB, 1947; D. Bus. Sci. (hon.), Webber Coll., 1947. Bar: Pa. 1949, U.S. Ct. Appeals (3d cir.) 1979, U.S. Dist. Ct. (ea. dist.) Pa. 1949. Law clk. to Chief Justice Horace Stern Pa. Supreme Ct., 1948-49; mem. firm Mancill, Cooney, Semans & Hedges, 1949-64; ptnr. Wolf, Block, Schorr & Solis Cohen, Phila., 1965-82, Obermayer, Rebmann, Maxwell & Hippel, Wayne, Pa., 1986-88; pvt. practice law Wayne, Pa., 1989—; dir. Servotronics, Inc. Trustee Atwater Kent Mus. Served as lt. (j.g.) Air Force, USNR, 1943-46. Decorated Distinguished Flying Cross, Air medal. Mem. ABA, Pa. Bar Assn., Phila. Bar Assn., Juristic Soc. Phila., Beta Theta Pi. Episcopalian. Clubs: Union League (Phila.); Sharswood Law (U. Pa.), Merion Cricket. General corporate, Mergers and acquisitions, Securities. Home: 538 Whitford Hills Rd Exton PA 19341-2050

**HEDGES, RICHARD HOUSTON,** lawyer, epidemiologist; b. Louisville, July 16, 1952; s. Houston and Frances Ruth (Zemo) H.; m. Donna Jean Hough. BA, U. Ky., 1974; MA, Ea. Ky. U., 1975, MPA, 1983; PhD, U. Ky., 1986; JD, Capital U. Law, 1994. Bar: Ohio 1995. Rehab. specialist Commonwealth of Ky., Somerset, 1976-81; chief health planner Commonwealth of Ky., Frankfort, 1981-82; asst. prof. U. Ky., Lexington, 1985-87; rsch. assoc. dept. med. behavioral sci. U. Ky. Coll. Medicine, Lexington, 1982-85; program adminstr. Rollman Psychiat. Inst., Cin., 1987-88; asst. prof. Ohio U., 1988-92, assoc. prof., 1992—; assoc. law Garry Hunter, LPA, Athens, Ohio, 1997-98; ptnr. Thomas & Hedges LLC, 1998-99; sole practice, 1999—; asst. city atty. City of Nelsonville, Ohio, 1997—, city pros., 1997—; dir. divsn. on aging Ohio U. Health Promotion and Rsch., 1990-92, MHA Grad Prog. Coord., 1995-96; bd. dirs. Washington County Mental Health and Addiction Recovery, 1998-99; exec. dir. pro tem Health Recovery Svcs., 1998. Contbr. articles to profl. jours. Mem. Athens County Domestic Violence Task Force, Athens County Victim's Assistance Adv.; treas. Athens County Heart Assn.. 1998. Fellow NIMH, 1984-86. Mem. ABA, ATLA, APHA, Ohio Acad. Trial Lawyers, Healthcare Fin. Mgmt. Assn., Am. Coll. Health Care Execs., Nat. Health Lawyers Assn., Ohio State Bar Assn., Pi Sigma Alpha, Phi Delta Phi. Democrat. Episcopalian. Fax: 592-3424. Avocations: backpacking, volleyball, bicycling, sailing. Health, Labor, Family and matrimonial. Home: RR 2 Box 14 Belpre OH 45714-9702 Office: 11 E Washington St Athens OH 45701-2412 also: Ohio U Sch Health Scis 413 Tower Athens OH 45201

**HEDIEN, COLETTE JOHNSTON,** lawyer; b. Chgo., 1939; d. George A. and Catherine (Bugan) Johnston; m. Wayne E. Hedien; 3 children. BS with honors, U. Wis., 1960; JD, DePaul U., 1981. Bar: Ill. 1981. Tchr. Sch. Dist. 39, Wilmette, Ill., 1960-63, Tustin (Calif.) Pub. Schs., 1964-66; extern law clk. to judge Chgo., 1980, U.S. Atty.'s Office, Chgo., 1980; pvt. practice Northbrook, Ill., 1981—; atty. Chgo. Vol. Legal Svcs.; mem. Chgo. Appellate Law Com., 1982-83, chmn., 1987-88; chmn. Northbrook Planning Commn., 1984-89; founder Am. Women of Surrey (Eng.), 1975-77; founding dir. U. Irvine Friends of Libr., 1965-66; guidance vol. Glenbrook High Sch., 1984-89; trustee Village of Northbrook, 1989—; mem. Women's Bd. Field Mus. Bd. dirs. Ill. Project for Spl. Needs Children, 1998—. NSF scholar, 1962. Mem. ABA (com. on real property), Ill. Bar Assn., Chgo. Bar Assn., North Shore Panhellenic Assn. (rep. 1989—), Phi Kappa Phi, Kappa Alpha Theta (bd. dirs.).

**HEDLUND, PAUL JAMES,** lawyer; b. Abington, Pa., June 26, 1946; s. Frank Xavier and Eva Ruth (Hoffman) H.; m. Marta Louise Brewer, Dec. 7, 1985; children: Annemarie Kirsten, Brooke Ashley, Tess Kara. BSME, U. Mich., 1968; JD, UCLA, 1973. Bar: Calif. 1973, D.C. 1994, U.S. Dist. Ct. (ctrl. dist.) Calif. 1977, U.S. Dist. Ct. (ea. dist.) Calif. 1991, U.S. Dist. Ct. (no. dist.) N.Y. 1994, U.S. Patent and Trademark Office 1978, U.S. Ct. Appeals (9th cir.) 1994, U.S. Supreme Ct. 1997. Staff engr. So. Calif. Edison, L.A., 1968-70; ptnr. Hedlund & Samuels, L.A., 1974-88, Kananack, Murgatroyd Baum & Hedlund (and predecessor firms), L.A., 1988-92; shareholder Baum, Hedlund, Aristei, Guilford & Downey (and predecessor firms), L.A., 1993—; lectr. in field. *Paul Hedlund has spent the last 26 years fighting for individual's rights as a plaintiffs' lawyer. With involvement in complex issues of multi-district litigation and choice of law analysis, he aggressively sued huge corporations in protecting victims' rights in general and commercial aviation, tractor-trailer, bus and train accident litigation. His extensive academic and work background in mechanical and nuclear engineering formed the foundation for his licensing as a patent attorney which led to concentrating in mass transportation accident litigation. His most recent achievement is arguing a case of a highspeed police pursuit (Lewis v. Sacramento County) before the U.S. Supreme Court.* Mem. Bar. Assn. D.C., Consumer Attys. Calif., L.A. County Bar Assn. Aviation, Personal injury, Product liability. Office: Baum Hedlund Aristei Guilford & Downey 12100 Wilshire Blvd Ste 950 Los Angeles CA 90025-7107

**HEDMAN, GEORGE WILLIAM,** lawyer; b. Chgo., Sept. 29, 1923; s. George Edward and Susan Welde (Dent) H.; m. Louisa Wetherbee, Apr. 26, 1947 (div. 1973); children: Mark, C. William, Jason; m. Evelyn L. Ramey, Jan. 1, 1987; children: David, Rebecca, Richard. JD, Ill. Tech., 1950; PhD in Psychology, Fla. Inst. Tech., 1981. Bar: Hawaii 1950, Am. Samoa 1953, Fla. 1956. Pvt. practice Honolulu, 1950-53, Melbourne, Fla. and Port Angeles, Wash., 1962—; attorney gen. Govt. Am. Samoa, Pago Pago, 1953-55; exec. Edison Electric Inst., N.Y.C., 1956-62. Author: Florida's New No-Fault Divorce Law, 1973, Divorce Without (Much) Agony, 1978, Jesus Didn't TellUs Everything, 1996, The Secret Life of Jesus Christ, 1999. Mem. Brevard County Sch. Bd., Titusville, Fla., 1968-72. Sgt. U.S. Army, 1943-46. Mem. Fla. Bar Assn., Hawaii State Bar Assn. Home: 877 N Miramar Ave Apt 1106 Indialantic FL 32903-3028

**HEDRICK, MARK,** lawyer; b. Sweetwater, Tex., Nov. 21, 1951; m. Gail Shackelford Hedrick; children: Gabriel, Alexandra. BA, Southwestern U., 1973; postgrad., Harvard U., 1973-74; JD, U. Tex., 1979. Lawyer Hallmark, Villa & Keith, El Paso, Tex., 1979-82, Hardie & Hallmark, El Paso, 1982-90, Hallmark & Hedrick, El Paso, 1990-98, Kemp, Smith, Duncan & Hammond, El Paso, 1999—; spkr. in field. Bd. dirs. Hospice El Paso, 1980-84, Visiting Nurse Assn., El Paso, 1983-85; adv. dir. KTEP-TV Pub. TV, El Paso, 1986-88. General corporate, Estate planning, Probate. Home: 705 River Elms Ct El Paso TX 79922-2118 Office: Kemp Smith Duncan & Hammond 1900 Norwest Plaza El Paso TX 79901

**HEDRICK, PEGGY SHEPHERD,** lawyer; b. Lake City, Iowa, Dec. 30, 1936; d. Clayton Conner and Clyttie Lucinda (Leake) Shepherd; m. Charles Webster Hedrick Sr., Dec. 8, 1955; children: Charles Jr., J. Lucinda Kennaley, Lois Kathryn. BA in Sociology and German, Pitzer Coll., 1972; JD, U. LaVerne Coll. Law, 1980, Yeshiva U., 1981. Bar: Mo. 1981, U.S. Dist. Ct. (so. dist.) Mo. 1981, U.S. Ct. Appeals (8th cir.) 1981. Pvt. practice Springfield, Mo., 1981; staff atty. Legal Aid Southwest Mo., Springfield, Mo.; pvt. practice Springfield, Mo., 1984—. Contbr. articles and photographs to profl. jours; team mem. Archeol. projects in Egypt, 1970-75, 84, sponsored by Smithsonian Inst. bd. dir. Mayor's Commn. Human Rights, Dogwood Coun. Girl Scouts Am., Rape Crisis, Green County League Women Voters; candidate Cir. Ct. Judge, 1988. Nominated Danforth Found. scholar, Pitzer Coll. Democrat. Southern Baptist. E-mail: peggy@peggyhedrick.com. Civil rights, Family and matrimonial, General practice. Office: PO Box 11027 Springfield MO 65808-1027

**HEED, PETER W.,** lawyer; b. West Chester, Pa., Apr. 2, 1950; s. Walter R. and Elizabeth Allen Hed; m. Patricia Longo, Sept. 3, 1983; children: Travis, Ethan. BA, Dartmouth Coll., 1972; JD, Cornell U., 1975. Bar: N.H. 1975, U.S. Dist. Ct. N.H. 1975, U.S. Ct. Appeals (1st cir.) 1976. Asst. atty. gen. State of N.H., Concord, 1975-80; assoc. Cristiano and Krumphold, Keene, N.H., 1980-82; sr. ptnr. Green, McMahon & Heed, Keene, N.H., 1982—; instr., paralegal studies, Keene State Coll., 1980-84; bd. govs. N.H. Health & Welfare Coun., Keene, 1985-90. Co-author: Canoe Racing: The Competitor's Guide, 1992; dir./prodr. (video) The General Clinton Regatta, 1989. Moderator, Town of Westmoreland, N.H., 1998—; mem. zoning bd. adjustment, Town of Roxbury, N.H., 1989-90; bd. govs., v.p. Norris Cotton Cancer Ctr., Dartmouth-Hitchand Hosp., Lebanon, N.H., 1993—; mem. U.S. Marathon Canoe and Kayak Team, 1982-83. Mem. Am. Trial Lawyers Assn. (sustaining mem. 1987—), N.H. Trial Lawyers Assn. (bd. dirs. 1987-93). Avocations: canoe and kayak racing (7 times Nat. Marathon and Downriver Canoe Champion, current World Masters Marathon Canoe Champion, Nike World Masters Games, 1998), nordic ski racing, marathon running, U.S. history. Aviation, Personal injury, Criminal. Office: Green McMahon & Heed 28 Middle St Keene NH 03431-3305

**HEENAN, CYNTHIA,** lawyer; b. Kalamazoo, June 5, 1959; d. John Ambrose and Shirley Jeanne (Blalock) H. BS, U. Mich., 1992; JD, U. Detroit, 1995. Bar: Mich. 1995, U.S. Dist. Ct. (ea. and we. dist.) Mich., U.S. Dist. Ct. (so. and mid. dist.) Fla., U.S. Ct. Appeals (6th and 11th cir.). Paralegal rsch. Dennis Hayes, Esq., Ann Arbor, Mich., 1980-89, Student Legal Svcs., Ann Arbor, Mich., 1986-88; paralegal adminstrv. Hugh M. Davis, P.C., Detroit, 1989-95; mng. ptnr. Constl. Litigation Assocs., Detroit, 1995—. Civil rights, Constitutional. Office: Constitutional Litigation Assocs 719 Griswold St Ste 1630 Detroit MI 48226-3317

**HEERENS, JOSEPH ROBERT,** lawyer; b. Park Ridge, Ill., Aug. 9, 1962; s. Joseph Allen and Priscilla Joan (Pearson) H.; m. Anne Elizabeth Heerens, Sept. 14, 1991. BA, DePauw U., 1984; JD, Ind. U., 1987. Bar: Ind. 1987, U.S. Ct. Appeals (7th cir.) 1990. Assoc. Wooden McLaughlin & Sterner, Indpls., 1987-90; sr. law clk. Ind. Ct. Appeals, Indpls., 1990-92; from staff atty. to assoc. gen. counsel Marsh Supermarkets LLC, Indpls., 1992—, asst. sec., bd. dirs., 1996—; bd. dirs. S.D. Isle Sportswear, Indpls. Vice chmn. bd. dirs. Am. Heart Assn., Indpls., 1994-96, chmn. bd. dirs., 1996—; co-chmn. com. Newman for Prosecutor, Indpls., 1992-94; active United Way Leadership Series, Indpls., 1991-92; bd. dirs. Rep. for Ind., Indpls., 1992. Mem. ABA, Ind. Bar Assn., Indpls. Bar Assn. Presbyterian. Avocations: reading, home renovation, basketball, golf. General corporate, Private international, Real property. Home: 14494 Stephanie St Carmel IN 46033-8641 Office: Marsh Supermarkets LLC 9800 Crosspoint Blvd Indianapolis IN 46256-3350

**HEFFERNAN, JAMES VINCENT,** lawyer; b. Washington, Oct. 6, 1926; s. Vincent Jerome and Hazel Belle (Wiltfong) H.; m. Virginia May Adams, June 26, 1954; children: David V., Douglas J., Alan P., Margaret L., Thomas A. AB, Cornell U., 1949, JD with distinction, 1952. Bar: D.C., 1953, Md., 1959, U.S. Ct. Claims, 1955, U.S. Tax Ct., 1953, U.S. Supreme Ct., 1958. Assoc. Sutherland, Asbill & Brennan, Washington, 1952-59, ptnr., 1959—; adj. prof. Georgetown U., Washington, 1978-79. Contbr. articles on tax subjects to profl. jours. Served with USN, 1945-46. Mem. ABA, Bar Assn. of D.C., Order of Coif, Phi Alpha Delta. Democrat. Roman Catholic. Clubs: Metropolitan (Washington); Kenwood Golf and Country (Bethesda, Md.). Lodge: KC. Corporate taxation, Estate taxation, Personal income taxation. Home: 5216 Falmouth Rd Bethesda MD 20816-2913 Office: Sutherland Asbill & Brennan 1275 Pennsylvania Ave NW Ste 1 Washington DC 20004-2415

**HEFFERNAN, MICHAEL STEWART,** lawyer; b. Sheboygan, Wis., Sept. 24, 1951; s. Nathan Stewart and Dorothy Lucille H.; m. Barbara Jean Zellmer, Apr. 30, 1988; children: Cyrus, Nathan. BA, U. Wis., 1974, JD, 1977. Bar: Wis. 1977, U.S. Dist. Ct. (ea. and we. dists.) Wis. Law clk. to chief justice Supreme Ct. of Wis., Madison, 1977-78; staff atty. Wis. Ct. Appeals, Madison, 1978-84; assoc. Walther & Halling, Milw., 1985-87, Stolper, Koritzinsky, Brewster & Neider, Madison, 1987-94; spl. counsel Foley & Lardner, Madison, 1994—. Author: (book) Appellate Practice and Procedure in Wisconsin, 1995. Fellow Am. Bar Found.; mem. ABA, Seventh Cir. Bar Assn., Dane County Bar Assn., Wis. Bar Assn. Appellate, Family and matrimonial. Office: Foley & Lardner 150 E Gilman St Madison WI 53703-1499

**HEFFERNAN, NATHAN STEWART,** retired state supreme court chief justice; b. Frederic, Wis., Aug. 6, 1920; s. Jesse Eugene and Pearl Eva (Kaump) H.; m. Dorothy Hillemann, Apr. 27, 1946; children: Katie (Mrs. Howard Thomas), Michael, Thomas. BA, U. Wis., 1942, LLB, 1948; postgrad. in bus., Harvard U. Sch. Bus. Adminstrn., 1943-44; LLD (hon.), Lakeland Coll., 1995; LLD, U. Wis., 1999. Bar: Wis. 1948, U.S. Dist. Ct. (we. dist.) Wis. 1948, U.S. Dist. Ct. (ea. dist.) Wis. 1950, U.S. Ct. Appeals (7th cir.) 1960, U.S. Supreme Ct. 1960. Assoc. firm Schubring, Ryan, Peterson & Sutherland, Madison, Wis., 1948-49; practice in Sheboygan, Wis., 1949-59; partner firm Buchen & Heffernan, 1951-59; counsel Wis. League Municipalities, 1949; research asst. to gov. Wis., 1949; asst. dist. atty. Sheboygan County, 1951-53; city atty. City of Sheboygan, 1953-59; dep. atty. gen. State of Wis., 1959-62; U.S. atty. Western Dist. Wis., 1962-64; justice Wis. Supreme Ct., 1964—, chief justice, 1983-95; lectr. mcpl. corps., 1961-64, appellate procedure and practice U. Wis. Law Sch., 1971-83; faculty Appellate Judges Seminar, Inst. Jud. Adminstrn., NYU, 1972-87; former mem. Nat. Council State Ct. Reps., chmn., 1976-77; ex-officio dir. Nat. Ctr. State Cts., 1976-77, mem. adv. bd. appellate justice project; former mem. Wis. Jud. Planning Com.; chmn. Wis. Appellate Practice and Procedure Com., 1975-76; mem. exec. com. Wis. Jud. Conf., 1978—, chmn., 1983; pres. City Attys. Assn., 1958-59; chair Citizens Panel on Election Reform; co-chair Equal Justice Coalition. Wis. chmn. NCCJ, 1966-67; past exec. bd. Four Lakes Coun., Boy Scouts Am.; gen. chmn. Wis. Dem. Conv., 1960, 61; mem. Wis. Found.; bd. dirs. Inst. Jud. Adminstrn.; visitors U. Wis. Law Sch., 1970-83, chmn., 1973-76; past mem. corp. bd. Meth. Hosp.; former curator Wis. Hist. Soc., curator emeritus, 1990; trustee Wis. Meml. Union, Wis. State Libr., William Freeman Vilas Trust Estate; v.p. U. Wis. Meml. Union Bldg. Assn.; former deacon Conglist. Ch. Lt. (s.g.) USNR, 1942-46, ETO, PTO. Recipient Disting. Svc. award NCCJ, 1968, Ann. Disting. Svc. award Wis. Mediation Assn., 1995, Lifetime Achievement award Milw. Bar Assn., 1995, Disting. Svc. award Dem. Party Sheboygan County, 1995; Disting. Jud. fellow Marquette U. Law Sch., 1996. Fellow Am. Bar Found. (life), Inst. for Jud. Adminstrn. (hon., bd. dirs., mem. faculty seminar); mem. ABA (past mem. spl. com. on adminstrn. criminal justice, mem. com. fed.-state delineation of jurisdiction, jud. adminstrn. com. on appellate ct., com. appellate time standards), Am. Law Inst. (life, adv. com. on complex litigation), Wis.

Bar Assn. (chmn. Wis. bar com. study on legal edn. 1995-96, hon. chmn. Equal Justice Coalition 1997—, Goldberg award for disting. svc.), Dane County Bar Assn., Sheboygan County Bar Assn., Am. Judicature Soc. (dir. 1977-80, chmn. program com. 1979-81), Wis. Law Alumni Assn. (bd. dirs., Disting. Alumni Svc. award 1989), Nat. Conf. Chief Justices (bd. dirs.), Nat. Assn. Ct. Mgmt., Order of Coif, Iron Cross, U. Club (Madison, Wis.), Phi Kappa Phi, Phi Delta Phi. Clubs: Madison Lit. (pres. 1979-80); Harvard (Milw.); Harvard Bus. Sch. (Wis.). Home: 17 Thorstein Veblen Pl Madison WI 53705

**HEFFERON, THOMAS MICHAEL,** lawyer; b. Mt. Vernon, N.Y., Sept. 20, 1960; s. George Joseph and Julia Theresa Hefferon; m. Elizabeth Ann Rosnagle, May 27, 1990; children: David, Margaret, Robert. BA, Trinity Coll., 1982; JD, U. Chgo., 1986. Bar: Mass. 1986, U.S. Dist. Ct. Mass. 1987, U.S. Ct. Appeals (1st cir.) 1987, U.S. Dist. Ct. (we. dist.) Mich. 1997, U.S. Dist. Ct. D.C. 1998, U.S. Ct. Appeals (D.C., 6th and 11th cirs.) 1998, U.S. Supreme Ct. 1998, D.C. 1999. Asst. prof. Boston Coll. Law Sch., Newton, Mass., 1989-90; assoc. Goodwin, Procter & Hoar, Boston, 1986-89, 90-95, ptnr., 1995—. Mem. ABA, Boston Bar Assn., Order of Coif. Federal civil litigation, Consumer commercial, Insurance. Office: Goodwin Procter & Hoar 1717 Pennsylvania Ave NW Washington DC 20006-4614

**HEFTER, LAURENCE ROY,** lawyer; b. N.Y.C., Oct. 13, 1935; s. Charles S. and Rose (Postal) H.; m. Jacqulyn Maureen Miller, June 13, 1957; children—Jeffrey Scott, Sue-Anne. B.M.E., Rensselaer Poly. Inst., 1957, M.S. in Mech. Engring., 1960; J.D. with honors, George Washington U., 1964. Bar: Va. 1964, N.Y. 1967, D.C. 1973. Instr. Rensselaer Poly. Inst., Troy, N.Y., 1957-59; patent engr. Gen. Electric Co., Washington, 1959-63; sr. patent atty. Atlantic Research Corp., Alexandria, Va., 1963-66; assoc. firm Davis, Hoxie, Faithfull & Hapgood, N.Y.C., 1966-69; mem. firm Ryder, McAulay & Hefter, N.Y.C., 1970-73, Finnegan, Henderson, Farabow, Garrett & Dunner, LLP, Washington, 1973—; professorial lectr. trademark law George Washington U., 1981-90; mem. adv. com. U.S. Patent and Trademark Office, 1988-92, Trademark Rev. Commn., 1986-89. Named in Best Lawyers in Am., Best Lawyers in Washington. Mem. ABA (chmn. patent office affairs com. patent, trademark and copyright sect. 1976-80, unfair competition com. 1980-81, governing com. franchise forum 1994-97), N.Y. State Bar Assn., D.C. Bar Assn., Va. Bar Assn. (dir. patent, trademark and copyright sect. 1976-78), Internat. Bar Assn. (chmn. trademark com. 1986-90), Am. Patent Law Assn. (chmn. trademark com. 1979-81, dir. 1981-84), U.S. Trademark Assn. (dir. 1982-84, elected Guide to World's Leading Experts in Trademark Law, Guide to World's Leading Experts in Patent Law), Order of Coif, Alpha Epsilon Pi. Trademark and copyright, Patent, Federal civil litigation. Home: 6904 Loch Lomond Dr Bethesda MD 20817-4756 Office: 1300 I St NW Washington DC 20005-3314

**HEGARTY, MARY FRANCES,** lawyer; b. Chgo., Dec. 19, 1950; d. James E. and Frances M. (King) H. BA, DePaul U., 1972, JD, 1975. Bar: Ill. 1975, U.S. Dist. Ct. (no. dist.) Ill. 1976, U.S. Supreme Ct. 1980. Ptnr. Lannon & Hegarty, Park Ridge, Ill., 1975-80; pvt. practice, Park Ridge, 1980—; dir. Legal Assistance Found. Chgo., 1983—. Mem. revenue study com. Chgo. City Coun. Fin. Com., 1983; mem. Sole Source Rev. Panel, City of Chgo., 1984; pres. Hist. Pullman Found., Inc., 1984-85; apptd. Park Ridge Zoning Bd., 1993-94. Mem. Ill. State Bar Assn. (real estate coun. 1980-84), Chgo. Bar Assn., Women's Bar Assn. Ill. (pres. 1983-84), NW Suburban Bar Assn., Park Ridge Women Entrepreneurs, Chgo. Athletic Assn. (pres. 1992-93). Democrat. Roman Catholic. Real property, Probate, General corporate. Office: 301 W Touhy Ave Park Ridge IL 60068-4204

**HEGGEN, IVAR NELSON,** lawyer; b. Tulsa, Sept. 22, 1954; s. Ivar George Lewis and Marley L. (Whitson) H.; m. Caroline Ann Driscoll, Dec. 20, 1976 (div. 1980); children: Kristin Dominique. BS, Charter Oaks Coll., 1979; JD cum laude, U. Houston, 1983. Bar: Tex. 1983, U.S. Ct. Appeals (5th cir.) 1987, U.S. Ct. Appeals (11th cir.) 1994; cert. in personal injury and civil trial law Tex. Bd. Legal Specialization and Nat. Bd. Trial Advocates. Assoc. Dibrell & Greer, Galveston, Tex., 1983-86, Schmidt & Matthews, Houston, 1986-87, Hornbuckle & Windham, Houston, 1987-89; pvt. practice, Houston, 1989—. Mem. ABA, Tex. Bar Assn., Coll. of State Bar Tex., Houston Bar Assn., Tex. Trial Lawyers Assn. (lectr.), Order of the Baron. Avocations: theater, music. General civil litigation, Insurance, Personal injury. Home: 422 W 15th St Houston TX 77008-4122 Office: 2211 Norfolk St Ste 820 Houston TX 77098-4030

**HEIDELBERG, JAMES HINKLE,** lawyer; b. Pasacagoula, Miss., July 15, 1953; s. Samuel Terril and Lillian (Merriweather) H.; m. Jennye W. Heidelberg, Nov. 29, 1981; children: Mary C., Laura Kate. BS, U. Southern Miss., Hattiesburg, 1975; JD, U. Miss., Oxford, 1978. Bar: Miss. 1979, U.S. Supreme Ct. 1984, U.S. Dist. Ct. (so. dist.) 1980 (no. dist.) 1978 (5th cir.) 1984, U.S. Dist. Ct., Ala. 1979. Mem. Internat. Assn. of Def. Counsel, Def. Rsch. Inst., Am. Inns. of Ct. Toxic tort, Personal injury, Appellate. Office: PO Box 1407 Pascagoula MS 39568-1407

**HEIDER, JON VINTON,** retired lawyer, corporate executive; b. Moline, Ill., Mar. 1, 1934; s. Raymond and Doris (Hinch) H.; m. Barbara L. Bond, Dec. 27, 1960 (div.); children: Loren P., John C., Lindsay L.; m. Mary R. Murray, Jan. 27, 1984. AB, U. Wis., 1956; JD, Harvard U., 1961; grad., Advanced Mgmt. Program, 1974. Bar: Pa. 1962, U.S. Dist. Ct. (ea. dist.) Pa. 1962, U.S. Ct. Appeals (3d cir.) 1962, U.S. Supreme Ct. 1991. Assoc. Morgan Lewis & Bockius, Phila., 1961-66; counsel Catalytic, Inc., Phila., 1966-68, Houdry Process & Chem. Co., Phila., 1968-70; counsel chems. group Air Products & Chems., Inc., Valley Forge, Pa., 1970-75, asst. gen. counsel, 1975-76, assoc. gen. counsel, 1976-78; gen. counsel Air Products & Chems., Inc., Allentown, Pa., 1978-80; v.p. corp. affairs, sr. adminstrv. officer-Europe, Air Products Europe, Inc., London, 1980-83; v.p. corp. devel. Air Products & Chems., Inc., 1983-84; v.p., gen. counsel BF Goodrich Co., Akron, Ohio, 1984-88, sr. v.p., gen. counsel, 1988-94, exec. v.p., gen. counsel, 1994-98; ret., 1998. Trustee Bluecoats, Inc.; mem. distbn. m. Charles E. and Mabel M. Ritchie Meml. Found. Lt. USNR, 1956-58. Mem. ABA, Am. Law Inst., Assn. Gen. Counsel, Blossom Music Ctr. Bd. Overseers, Sisler McFawn Found. (distbn. com.), U. Wis. Found., Portage Country Club, Rolling Rock Club, Key Biscayne Yacht Club. General corporate.

**HEIDGERD, FREDERICK CAY,** lawyer; b. Sewickley, Pa., Sept. 27, 1950; s. Diederich W.F. and Margaret (Ozburn) H.; m. Sarah H. Beck, Jan. 16, 1976; children: Rebecca, Rachel, Christian. BA, Wake Forest U., 1972; JD, U. Fla., 1975. Bar: Ga. 1975, Fla. 1976, U.S. Dist. Ct. (mid. dist.) Fla. 1981, U.S. Dist. Ct. (so. dist.) Fla. 1977, U.S. Ct. Appeals (5th and 11th cirs.) 1981, U.S. Supreme Ct. 1980. Assoc. Haynsworth, Baldwin & Miles, Greenville, S.C., 1976, Cabot, Wenkstern & Casteel, Ft. Lauderdale, Fla., 1976-78; from assoc. to ptnr. Lunny, Tucker & Heidgerd, Ft. Lauderdale, Fla., 1978-82; ptnr. Heidgerd, Martin & Bennis, P.A., Ft. Lauderdale, Fla., 1982—; mem. traffic ct. rev. com. Fla. Supreme Ct., Tallahassee, 1980-89. Mem. law rev. U. Fla. Law Sch., 1975. Pres. Broward County Citizens Safety Coun., Inc., Ft. Lauderdale, Fla., 1981-83; mem. planning and zoning bd. City of Deerfield Beach, Fla., 1979-81. Carswell scholar Wake Forest U., 1968-72. Mem. Broward County Bar Assn. (sec., treas., exec. com. young lawyers sect. 1980-84), Kiwanis (pres. Ft. Lauderdale southside club 1994-95). Banking, Probate, General civil litigation. Office: Heidgerd Martin & Bennis PA 319 SE 14th St Fort Lauderdale FL 33316-1929

**HEIFETZ, ALAN WILLIAM,** federal judge; b. Portland, Maine, Jan. 15, 1943; s. Ralph and Bernice (Diamon) H.; m. Nancy Butler Stone, Aug. 11, 1968; children: Andrew Stone, Peter Stone. A.B., Syracuse U., 1965; J.D., Boston U., 1968. Bar: Maine 1968, Mass. 1968, U.S. Dist. Ct. Mass. 1969, U.S. Supreme Ct. 1972. Assoc. Chayet and Flash, Boston, 1968-70; trial atty. ICC, Washington, 1970-72, counsel to chmn., 1972-78, adminstrv. law judge, 1978-80; adminstrv. law judge Fed. Labor Relations Authority, Washington, 1980-82; chief adminstrv. law judge Dept. HUD, Washington, 1982—; mem. forum faculty Am. Arbitration Assn., Washington, 1983; mem. faculty Nat. Jud. Coll., U. Nev., Reno, 1988-94; mem. Adminstrv. Conf. U.S., 1986-95; mem. Forum U.S. Adminstrv. Law Judges, v.p., 1986-87, pres., 1987-89; mem. exec. com. Fed. Adminstrv. Law Judges Conf., 1982-90; jurist-in-residence The John Marshall Law Sch., 1995. Contbr. articles to profl. jours. Mem. Fallsmead Civic Assn. (Md.). Mem. ABA, Potomac Tennis Club. Home: 23 Infield Ct N Potomac MD 20854-5506 Office: Dept of Housing & Urban Devel 409 3rd St SW Ste 320 Washington DC 20024-3212

**HEILIGENSTEIN, CHRISTIAN E.,** lawyer; b. St. Louis, Dec. 7, 1929; s. Christian A. and Louisa M. (Dixon) H.; children: Christie; m. Liselotte Warbanoff, Feb. 6, 1981. BS in Law, U.Ill., 1953, JD, 1955. Bar: Ill. 1956, U.S. Dist. Ct. (so. dist.) Ill. 1956, U.S. Ct. Appeals (7th cir.) 1956, U.S. Dist. Ct. (cen. dist.) Ill. 1960, U.S. Supreme Ct. 1978. Assoc. Listeman & Bandy, East St. Louis, Ill., 1955-61; sole practice Belleville, Ill., 1962-84; ptnr., pres. Heiligenstein & Badgley, Belleville, 1984-98; pres. C.E. Heiligenstein, P.C., Belleville, 1998—; chair audit com. Magna Group, Inc., 1994-98; bd. dirs. Union Planters Corp., Union Planters Bank NA, 1998—, chair audit com. 1999—. Recipient Alumni of Month award U. Ill. Law Sch., 1982. Mem. Ill. State Bar Assn., Internat. Acad. Trial Lawyers (bd. dirs. 1991-97), St. Clair County Bar Assn., St. Louis Bar Assn., Inner Circle Advs., Am. Bd. Trial Advs. (nat. bd. dirs. 1992, pres. St. Louis, So. Ill. region 1993), Am. Acad. Profl. Liabilities Attys. (Nat. bd. dirs., 1990-99), ATLA (bd. govs. 1985-87), Ill. Trial Lawyers Assn. (bd. mgrs. 1975-88, pres. 1989), Mo. Athletic Club, Beach Club (bd. dirs. 1996, v.p. 1998). Democrat. Personal injury, Workers' compensation, Product liability. Home: 5200 Turner Hall Rd Belleville IL 62220-5628 Office: Heiligenstein & Badgley 30 Public Sq Belleville IL 62220-1693

**HEILMAN, CARL EDWIN,** lawyer; b. Elizabethville, Pa., Feb. 3, 1911; s. Edgar James and Mary Alice (Bechtold) H.; m. Grace Emily Greene, Nov. 29, 1934 (div. 1952); children: John Greene, Elizabeth Greene; m. Claire Virginia Phelps, Oct. 10, 1952 (dec. June 1990); m. Marie Wilmot Russ, Nov. 23, 1990. *Carl's son John Heilman, Lafayette College 1964, PhD New York University 1973, professor of Political Science at Auburn University, became dean of Auburn's College of Liberal Arts in 1999. John's wife Ursula for many years taught German at Auburn. Their son David, graduated from Harvard College in 1995, is an analyst with Credit Suisse First Boston Technology Group in Palo Alto, California, working on mergers and acquisitions in the information technology industry. Their daughter Catherine, graduated from Wellesley College in 1998, is an investment banking analyst with Merrill Lynch in New York City, specializing in leveraged buyouts.* BA, Lafayette Coll., Easton, Pa., 1932, MA, 1933; JD magna cum laude, U. Pa., 1939. Bar: N.Y. 1940, Pa. 1940, Mass. 1973, U.S. Supreme Ct. 1960. Tchr. English Easton High Sch., 1934-36; assoc. Dwight, Harris, Koegel & Caskey, N.Y.C., 1939-42; atty. OPA, Washington, 1942-43, N.Y. Gov.'s Commn. to Investigate Workmen's Compensation Law, N.Y.C., 1943-44; assoc. Dewey, Ballantine, Bushby, Palmer & Wood, N.Y.C., 1944-59, ptnr., 1959-73; counsel to firm Csaplar & Bok, Boston and San Francisco, 1973-90; trustee Upsala Coll., East Orange, N.J., 1970-73. Fellow Am. Bar Found., mem. ABA, Nat. Trust for Hist. Preservation, Order of Coif. Republican. Episcopalian. General corporate, Real property, Finance. Home: 5850 Meridian Rd Apt 508A Gibsonia PA 15044-9683

**HEILMANN, DAVID MICHAEL,** lawyer; b. Evergreen Park, Ill., Oct. 10, 1962; s. Joseph Christian Heilmann and Therese Mary Murphy. BS in Broadcast Journalism, U. Ill., 1984; JD, DePaul U., 1987. Bar: Ill. 1987, U.S. Dist. Ct. (no. dist.) Ill. 1987. Ptnr. Clausen Miller, P.C., Chgo., 1987—; advisor, counsel Corp. Event Planners, Oak Lawn, 1997—; pro bono counsel Comedy Sportz Chgo., 1995-96; panel counsel, Ill. Risk Mgmt. Assn., Chgo., 1994. Past pres., v.p. Oak Lake Park Dist. Bd. Commrs., 1989—; hwy. commr. Worth Twp., Ill., 1997—; performer, dir. several south suburban cmty. and charitable orgns., 1977—; mem. Oak Lawn Environ. Task Force, Oak Lawn Adv. Resident Com.; vol. Am. Cancer soc.; founder Oak Lawn Cmty. Theatre; founder scholarship fund Worth Twp.; hon. chmn. Park Lawn Assn. Telethon, 1996. Recipient Gold medal Am. Legion, 1980. Mem. Chgo. Bar Assn. Republican. Roman Catholic. Avocations: theater, golf, politics, writing. General civil litigation, Insurance, Construction. Home: 5225 W 105th Pl Oak Lawn IL 60453-5145 Office: Clausen Miller PC 10 S Lasalle St Ste 1600 Chicago IL 60603-1098

**HEIM, THOMAS GEORGE,** lawyer; b. Phila., Feb. 5, 1945; s. Joseph E. and Lillian H.; m. Anne Mary Fatkin, Aug. 23, 1969; children: Thomas George, Susan, James, Christopher. AB, Seton Hall U., 1967; JD, Rutgers U., 1971. Bar: N.J. 1971, U.S. Dist. Ct. N.J. 1971, U.S. Ct. Mil. Appeals 1971, U.S. Ct. Appeals (3d cir.) 1976, U.S. Supreme Ct. 1992. Ptnr. Granite & Heim, Woodbury Hts., N.J., 1979—; mcpl. prosecutor Borough of Woodbury Heights, 1979-81, solicitor Woodbury Heights Planning Bd., 1983-87; mcpl. ct. judge Borough of Woodbury Hts., 1998—. Pres. St. Margeret Regional Sch .Bd., 1978-87; lector St. Margaret Ch., Woodbury Hts.; chmn. local adv. com. probation dept. Gloucester County, chmn. Human Rels. Commn., 1994-96. Capt. JAGC, U.S. Army, 1971-74. Named Profl. Lawyer of Yr., N.J. Commn. on Professionalism in Law, 1998. Mem. ABA, N.J. State Bar Assn., Gloucester County Bar Assn. Democrat. Roman Catholic. Criminal, General practice, Personal injury. Home: 228 Cherry Ave Woodbury Heights NJ 08097-1111 Office: PO Box 69 Woodbury Heights NJ 08097-0069

**HEINDL, PHARES MATTHEWS,** lawyer; b. Meridian, Miss., Dec. 14, 1949; s. Paul A. and Leila (Matthews) H.; m. Linda Ann Williamson, Sept. 21, 1985; children: Lori Elizabeth, Jesse Phares, Jared Matthews. BS in Chem. Engring., Miss. State U., 1972; JD, U. Fla., 1981. Bar: Fla. 1981, Calif. 1982, U.S. Dist. Ct. (cen. dist.) Calif. 1983, U.S. Dist. Ct. (mid. dist.) Fla. 1983; bd. cert. civil trial lawyer Fla. Bar. Assoc. Lafollette, Johnson et al, L.A., 1982-83, Sam E. Murrell & Sons, Orlando, Fla., 1983-84; pvt. practice Orlando, Fla., 1984-93, Altamonte Springs, Fla., 1993—; bd. cert. civil trial lawyer. Precinct coord. Freedom Coun., Orlando, 1986; pres. Friends of the Wekiva River, 1998. Mem. Fla. Bar Assn., Calif. Bar Assn., Seminole County Bar Assn. (pres. civil trial sect. 1998), ATLA, Christian Legal Soc. (past pres. Ctrl. Fla.), Fla. Acad. Trial Lawyers (Eagle mem.), Workers Compensation Rules Com. Republican. Avocation: kayak racing. Personal injury, State civil litigation, Workers' compensation. Home: 2415 River Tree Cir Sanford FL 32771-8334 Office: 222 S Westmonte Dr Ste 208 Altamonte Springs FL 32714-4269

**HEINEMAN, ANDREW DAVID,** lawyer; b. N.Y.C., Nov. 5, 1928; s. Bernard and Lucy (Morgenthau) H. BA, Williams Coll., 1950; LLB, Yale U., 1953. Bar: N.Y. 1953. Assoc. Proskauer Rose Goetz & Mendelsohn, N.Y.C., 1953-63; ptnr. Proskauer Rose LLP, N.Y.C., 1963—. Pres., chmn. bd. dirs. Ernest and Mary Hayward Weir Found., N.Y.C., 1969-87, trustee Mt. Sinai Hosp. Med. Sch. and Med. Ctr., 1976—, Williams Coll., 1980-95, Abelard Found., 1976-96; Asphalt Green, 1992-96; bd. dirs. Jewish Home and Hosp. for Aged, 1967—, vice chmn. bd. dirs., 1992, chmn. bd. dirs. 1993-97; exec. asst. Citizens for Kennedy and Johnson, N.Y.C., 1960; mem. N.Y. Gov.'s Commn. on Minorities in Med. Schs., 1982. Mem. Yale Law Sch. Assn. N.Y. (pres. 1970-73), Yale Law Sch. Alumni Assn. (v.p. 1973-76, exec. com.). Estate planning. Office: Proskauer Rose LLP 1585 Broadway New York NY 10036-8200

**HEINEMAN, BENJAMIN WALTER, JR.,** lawyer; b. Chgo., Jan. 25, 1944; s. Benjamin Walter and Natalie (Goldstein) H.; m. Jeanne Cristine Russell, June 7, 1975; children: Zachary R., Matthew R. B.A. magna cum laude, Harvard U., 1965; B.Letters, Balliol Coll., Oxford U., Eng., 1967; J.D., Yale U., 1971. Bar: D.C. 1973, U.S. Supreme Ct. 1973. Reporter Chgo. Sun Times, 1968; law clk. Assoc. Justice Potter Stewart U.S. Supreme Ct., 1971-72; staff atty. Center for Law and Social Policy, 1973-75; with Williams Connolly and Califano, Washington, 1975-76; exec. asst. to sec. HEW, Washington, 1977-78, asst. sec. for planning and evaluation, 1978-79; partner Califano, Ross & Heineman, Washington, 1979-82, Sidley & Austin, Washington, 1982-87; sr. v.p., gen. counsel, sec. Gen. Electric Co., Fairfield, Conn., 1987—. Author: The Politics of the Powerless: A Study of the Campaign Against Racial Discrimination, 1972, Memorandum for the President: A Strategic Approach to Domestic Affairs in the 1980's, 1981; editor-in-chief: Yale Law Jour., 1970-71. Rhodes scholar, 1965-67. Mem. Phi Beta Kappa. Office: General Electric Co 3135 Easton Tpke Fairfield CT 06431-0001*

**HEINICHEN, JEFFREY KIRK,** lawyer, business executive; b. Cin., Jan. 13, 1952; s. Albert James and Shirley Beverly (Frisch) H.; m. Noel Susan Keefer, June 6, 1987; children: Laura Marie, Katherine Noel, Kelly Frisch, Brooke Turner. BBA, Tex. Christian U., 1974; JD, No. Ky. U., 1978. Bar: Ohio 1978. Assoc. Keating Muething & Klekamp, Cin., 1978-82; assoc. gen counsel Am. Fin. Corp., Cin., 1982-86; owner, gen. counsel, dir., v.p. Cambridge Gen. Inc., Cin., 1986-88; pres. Gen. Polymers Corp., Cin., 1988—. Bd. dirs. Springer Sch., Cin., 1986—. Mem. ABA, Ohio Bar Assn., Cin. Bar Assn., Constrn. Specification Inst., Cin. Country Club, Queen City Club. Home: 5280 Ivyfarm Rd Cincinnati OH 45243-3745

**HEINLE, RICHARD ALAN,** lawyer; b. New Kensington, Pa., May 13, 1959; s. Robert Alan and Barbara Jane Heinle; m. Sharon Eileen Farrell, Oct. 20, 1990; children: Kelly, Kyra. AB with highest honors, U. Chgo., 1981; JD cum laude, Georgetown U., 1984. Bar: Ill. 1984, Fla. 1994. Assoc. Arnstein & Lehr, Chgo., 1984-89, Foley & Laroner, Chgo., 1989-93; ptnr. Foley & Laroner, Orlando, Fla., 1993—; counsel Better Bus. Bur. Ctrl. Fla., Orlando, 1996—. Mem. Mfrs. Assn. Ctrl. Fla. (bd. dirs. 1995—), Phi Beta Kappa. Roman Catholic. Avocations: golf, running. Mergers and acquisitions, Securities. Home: 8100 Vineland Oaks Blvd Orlando FL 32835-8215 Office: Foley & Lardner 111 N Orange Ave Ste 1800 Orlando FL 32801-2386

**HEINRICH, RANDALL WAYNE,** lawyer, investment banker; b. Houston, Nov. 29, 1958; s. Albert Joseph Sr. and Beverly June Earles; m. Linda Carol Cheek, June 6, 1993; children: Angela Leigh, Conrad Randall. BA, Baylor U., 1980, postgrad., 1981; postgrad., Rice U., 1981-82; JD, U. Tex., 1985. Bar: Tex. 1985. Assoc. Baker & Botts, Houston, 1985-87, Chamberlain, Hrdlicka, White, Williams & Martin, Houston, 1987-91, Norton & Blair, Houston, 1991-92; of counsel Gillis & Slogar, Houston, 1992—; mng. dir. Baytree Investors, Houston, 1993—. Mem. dirs.' circle Houston Grand Opera, 1991, The Arts Symposium, 1991, Center Stage, Alley Theater, Houston, 1992-93, Houston Entrepreneurs' Forum, 1990-91; bd. dirs. The Cadre, 1991-92; pres. Exchange Club of Bayou City, 1992-93. Mem. ABA (YLD securities law com. 1993-95, vice chmn. 1994-95), NASD Pool Securities Arbitrators, Am. Arbitration Assn. (mem. nat. panel neutrals), Houston Bar Assn., Forum Club Houston, Phi Delta Theta. Republican. Baptist. Securities, Mergers and acquisitions, General corporate. Home: 4318 Saint Michaels Ct Sugar Land TX 77479-2986 Office: Gillis & Slogar 1000 Louisiana St Ste 6905 Houston TX 77002-5014

**HEINRICH, STEVEN ALLAN,** lawyer; b. Missoula, Mont., Mar. 1, 1962; s. Albert Carl and Mary Morlan H. BA, U. Calgary, Alberta, Can., 1984; MA, U. Ill., 1989, PhD, 1991; postgrad., U. B.C., Vancouver, Can., 1991-92; JD, U. Wash., 1994. Bar: Oreg. 1994, U.S. Dist. Ct. Oreg. 1995, U.S. Ct. Appeals (9th cir.) 1995. Law clk. Mortimer & Rose, Vancouver, B.C., Can., 1992; jud. intern, clk. Benton County Cir. Ct., Corvallis, Oreg., 1993; assoc. Morley, Thomas & McHill, Lebanon, Oreg., 1994-98; atty. pvt. practice, Corvallis, 1998—. Contbr. articles to profl. jours. Rsch. travel grantee U. Ill., 1989; U. Ill. fellow, 1990; MacArthur Found. scholar, 1989, Panvini scholar, 1992, Philip J. Weiss scholar, U. Wash., 1993. Mem. Oreg. Bar Assn., Oreg. Criminal Defense Lawyers Assn., Benton County Bar Assn., Order of Coif, Phi Kappa Phi. Avocations: flying, scuba diving, canoeing, hiking. Family and matrimonial, General civil litigation, General practice. Office: 27 NW 3d St Corvallis OR 97330

**HEINRICH, TIMOTHY JOHN,** lawyer; b. Houston, Nov. 30, 1961; s. Albert J. and Beverly J. Heinrich; m. Tammy K. Morgan, Aug. 10, 1985; children: John, Allison, Michelle, Philip. BA, Washington U., St. Louis, 1984; JD, U. Tex., 1987. Bar: Tex. 1987. Assoc. Hiller Kornfeld Axelrad & Falik, Houston, 1987-90; assoc., shareholder Boyar Simon & Miller, Houston, 1990—. Lay leader Terrace United Meth. Ch., Houston, 1994-97. Mem. Kiwanis (lt. gov. Houston 1997-98). Real property, Mergers and acquisitions, Contracts commercial. Office: Boyar Simon & Miller 4265 San Felipe St Ste 1200 Houston TX 77027-2917

**HEINS, SAMUEL DAVID,** lawyer; b. Providence, May 31, 1947; s. Maurice Haskell and Hadassah (Wagman) H.; children: Madeleine Sarah, Nora Anne. BA, U. Minn., 1968, JD, 1972. Bar: Minn. 1973, U.S. Dist. Ct. Minn., U.S. Ct. Appeals (8th cir.). Law clk. U.S. Dist. Ct. Minn., Mpls., 1972-73; assoc. Firestone Law Firm, St. Paul, 1973-76; ptnr. Tanick & Heins, Mpls., 1976-89, Opperman & Heins, Mpls., 1989-94, Heins, Mills & Olson, Mpls., 1994—; vis. asst. prof. Sch. Architecture, U. Minn.-Mpls., 1974-89. Mem. Mpls. Charter Commn., 1983-84; pres. Minn. Lawyers Internat. Human Rights Com., Mpls., 1983-85, Minn. Ctr. for Torture Victims, Mpls., 1985-87, chmn., pres. Mem. ABA, Minn. State Bar Assn. (bd. govs. 1978-84). Federal civil litigation, State civil litigation.

**HEINTZ, BARON STRUM,** lawyer; b. Des Moines, Feb. 1, 1966; s. Larry and Janice H. BA, Saint Ambrose U., 1987; MPA, George Washington U., 1991, JD, 1991. Bar: Ill 1992; U.S. Dist. Ct. (cen. dist.) Ill. 1994; U.S. Ct. Appeals (7th cir.) 1994. Asst. state's atty. Mercer County, Aledo, Ill., 1992-96, state's atty., 1996—. Vol./advisor Mercer County DARE, Inc., Aledo, 1992—. Mem. Mercer County Bar Assn. (sec./treas. 1993-95, pres. 1995—), Ill. Bar Assn., ABA, Nat. Dist. Attys. Assn., Ill. State's Attys. Assn. Home: PO Box 243 Aledo IL 61231-0243 Office: States Attys Office Mercer County Courthouse Aledo IL 61231

**HEINTZ, PAUL CAPRON,** lawyer; b. Urbana, Ill., June 4, 1940; s. Leo H. and Allyn Capron H.; m. Jane Develin, June 8, 1963; children: Helen C., Sandra DeH., Robert B.D., Edward S.A. AB, Kenyon Coll., 1962; LLB, U. Pa., 1965. Bar: Pa. 1965, U.S. Dist. Ct. (ea. dist.) Pa. 1965. Assoc. Obermayer, Rebmann, Maxwell & Hippel LLP, Phila., 1965-74, ptnr., 1974—. Author: Remick's Pennsylvania Orphans' Court Practice (7 vols.), 1982—, Dunlap-Hanna Forms (14 vols.), 1984—; author newspaper column Aviation, 1969-82. Bd. dirs. Aviation Coun. Pa., 1980—; chmn. bd. Phila. divsn. Am. Cancer Soc., 1985-87; trustee Franklin Inst., Phila., 1982—; pres. Lower Merion Bd. Sch. Dirs., Montgomery County, Pa., 1983-86; bd. dirs. Nat. Constitution Ctr., 1994—; bd. dirs. Com. of 70, 1997—. Recipient Disting. Svc. award Am. Cancer Soc., 1983, Gov.'s Aviation trophy Aviation Coun. Pa., 1984, Disting. Estates Planners award Phila. Estate Planning Coun., 1996. Mem. ABA, Am. Coll. Trust and Estate Counsel, Pa. Bar Assn. (chmn. aviation law sect. 1975-80, ho. dels. 1980-90), Phila. Bar Assn. (bd. govs. 1979, 89-92, 93-94, chmn. probate law sect. 1979, asst. treas. 1993-94), Phila. Bar Edn. Ctr. (treas. 1992-94), Phila. Estate Planning Coun. (bd. dirs. 1997—), Haverford Civic Assn. (bd. dirs. 1972—), Aircraft Owners and Pilots Assn. (vice-chmn. bd. dirs. 1974—), Merion Cricket Club, Union League (bd. dirs. 1992-96, v.p. 1993-96). Republican. Episcopalian. Avocations: flying, sailing, swimming, tennis. Aviation, Non-profit and tax-exempt organizations, Probate. Home: 269 Booth Ln Haverford PA 19041-1716 Office: Obermayer Rebmann Maxwell & Hippel LLP 1617 JfK Blvd Philadelphia PA 19103-1895

**HEINY, JAMES RAY,** lawyer; b. Albert Lea, Minn., Oct. 7, 1928; s. Albin James and Lola Marguerite (Keig) H.; m. Wava Jeanine Isaacson, Sept. 2, 1951 (dec. 1980); children: Jon Carl, Jane Ellen Heiny Smith, Ann Elizabeth Heiny Hohenshell, Thomas James; m. Norma Lou West, July 24, 1982. BA, Grinnell Coll., 1950; JD, U. Iowa, 1953. Bar: Iowa 1953. Assoc. Westfall, Laird & Burington, Mason City, Iowa, 1955-58; ptnr. Laird, Heiny, McManigal, Winga, Duffy & Stambaugh, Mason City, 1958—. Pres. Good Shepherd Geriatric Ctr., Inc., Mason City, 1960-72; bd. dirs. YMCA, Mason City, 1972-75; pres. Luth. Social Svcs. Iowa FODN, 1987—. With U.S. Army, 1953-55. Mem. ABA, Iowa State Bar Assn. (bd. govs. 1986-91), Cerro Gordo County Bar Assn. (pres. 1976). Republican. Avocations: amateur radio, bird watching, sports. Probate, Real property, Personal income taxation. Home: 2040 Hunters Ridge Dr Mason City IA 50401-7500 Office: Laird Heiny McManigal Winga Duffy & Stambaugh 300 Norwest Bank Bldg Mason City IA 50401

**HEIPLE, JAMES DEE,** state supreme court justice; b. Peoria, Ill., Sept. 13, 1933; s. Rae Crane and Harriet (Birkett) H.; B.S., Bradley U., 1955; J.D., U. Louisville, 1957; Certificate in Internat. Law, City of London Coll., 1967; grad. Nat. Jud. Coll., 1971; LLM U. Va., 1988; m. Virginia Kerswill, July 28, 1956 (dec. Apr. 16, 1995); children: Jeremy Hans, Jonathan James, Rachel Duffield. Bar: Ill. 1957, Ky. 1958, U.S. Supreme Ct. 1962; partner Heiple and Heiple, Pekin, Ill., 1957-70; circuit judge Ill., 10th Circuit 1970-80; justice Ill. Appellate Ct., 1980-90; justice Ill. Supreme Ct., 1990—. V.p., dir. Washington State Bank (Ill.), 1959-66; dir. Gridley State Bank (Ill.), 1958-59; village atty., Tremont, Ill., 1961-66, Mackinaw, Ill., 1961-66; asst. pub. defender Tazewell County, 1967-70., jud. clerk Ill. Appellate Ct., 1968-70. Chmn. Tazewell County Heart Fund, 1960. Pub. Adminstr. Tazewell

County, Ill., 1959-61; sec. Tazewell County Republican Central Com. 1966-70; mem. Pekin Sch. Bd., 1970; mem. Ill. Supreme Ct. Com. on Profl. Responsibility, 1978-86. Recipient certificate Freedoms Found., 1975, George Washington honor medal, 1976, Bradley Centurion award Bradley U., 1995; named Disting. Alumnus, U. Louisville, 1992. Fellow ABA (life), Ill. Bar Found. (life), Ky. Bar Found. (life); mem. Ky., Ill. (chmn. legal edn. com. 1972-74, chmn. jud. sect. 1976-77, chmn. Bench and Bar Council 1984-85), Tazewell County Bar Assn. (pres. 1967-68), Ill. Judges Assn. (pres. 1978-79), Ky., Ill., Pa. hist. socs., S.A.R., War of 1812, Sons of Union Vets., Delta Theta Phi, Sigma Nu, Pi Kappa Delta. Methodist. Clubs: Filson; Union League (Chgo.), Country (Peoria). Lodge: Masons (33 degree). Office: 207 Main St Ste 500 Peoria IL 61602-1362

**HEISE, JOHN IRVIN, JR.,** lawyer; b. Balt., Dec. 13, 1924; s. John Irvin and Ruby Belle (Carpenter) H.; m. Jacqueline Mosey Morley, Sept. 3, 1949; children: John Irvin III, Liane Des Roches, Jeff Howard, Suzanne, Wolfrom. AB, U. Md., 1947; JD, U. Va., 1950. Bar: Md. 1950, D.C. 1953, U.S. Sup. Ct. 1962. Trial atty. civil div. Dept. Justice, Washington, 1950-52; assoc. Shea Greenman Gardner & McConnaughey, Washington, 1952-57; ptnr., pres. Heise Jorgensen & Stefanelli, P.A., Silver Spring, Md., 1957—. Committeeman, merit badge counselor, dist. chmn. sustaining mem. dr. Boy Scouts Am.; chmn. Md. Ednl. Found., Inc., 1972-92. Maj. USAF, 1942-45. Recipient Gottwals award U. Md., 1978. Mem. Am. Bar Assn., Fed Bar Assn., Md. Bar Assn., D.C. Bar Assn., Montgomery County Bar Assn., Md. Alumni Assn. (pres. 1972-73), Omicron Delta Kappa, Phi Kappa Phi. Republican. Episcopalian. Clubs: M (pres. 1966-67), Terrapin (pres. 1961-62). Federal civil litigation, Administrative and regulatory, General corporate.

**HEISINGER, JAMES GORDON, JR.,** lawyer; b. Carmel, Calif., Aug. 17, 1952; s. James Gordon Sr. and Rosemary F. (Walters) H.; m. Pamela Quinn, Mar. 24, 1979; children: Michael, Alexander. BA, U. Calif., Santa Cruz, 1974; JD, Lewis and Clark Coll., Portland, 1979. Bar: Calif. 1979, U.S. Dist. Ct. (no. dist.) Calif. 1979, U.S. Ct. Appeals (9th cir.) 1985, U.S. Supreme Ct. 1985. Pvt. practice Carmel, 1980-87; atty. City of Sand City, Calif., 1985—; ptnr. Heisinger, Buck, Morris & Rose, Carmel, Calif., 1987—; instr. Monterey (Calif.) Coll. of Law, 1983-87. Bd. dirs. Carmel Pub. Libr. Found., 1998—; chmn. Carmel chpt. ARC, 1985-87; bd. dirs. Vols. in Action, Monterey, 1983-85. Mem. ABA, Calif. Bar Assn., Monterey County Bar Assn. Republican. Roman Catholic. Avocation: sailing, skiing. Real property, Administrative and regulatory. Office: Heisinger Buck Morris & Rose Dolores & 6th PO Box 5427 Carmel CA 93921-5427

**HEISKELL, EDGAR FRANK, III,** lawyer; b. Morgantown, W.Va., Oct. 10, 1940; s. Edgar Frank Jr. and Barbara Baker H.; n. Jerri Frances Deegan (div. May 1997); m. Morgan Peyton, Julu 19, 1998; children: Christopher, Edgar F. IV, Ryan, Justin, Gretchen. AB in Polit. Sci., W.Va. U., 1963; JD, U. Va., 1966. Bar: W.Va. 1966, U.S. Supreme Ct. 1985, U.S. Cts. Appeals (4th, 6th, 9th and fed. cirs.). Acting pros. atty. Monongalia County, W.Va., 1970-71; commr. W.Va. Workmen's Comp., Charleston, 1971-73; sec. of state State of W.Va., Charleston, 1973-75; ptnr. Haden & Heiskell, Morgantown, W.Va., 1975-85, Rose, Schmidt & Hasley, Pitts., 1985-88, Spilman, Thomas & Battle, Charleston, 1988-93; atty. pvt. practice, Charleston, 1993—. State rep. chmn. W.Va. GOP, Charleston, 1987-90; exec. Rep. Nat. Com., Washington, 1987-90; chmn. com. election reform Nat. Assn. Secs. of State, Washington, 1973-75. 1st lt. USAF, 1966-70. Mem. W.Va. State Bar Assn., Attys. Info. Exch. Group. Republican. Presbyterian. Avocations: writing, flying, skiing, rollerblading. Product liability, Aviation, Personal injury. Office: PO Box 3761 Charleston WV 25337-3761

**HEISLER, JOHN CHARLES,** lawyer; b. Balt., Aug. 31, 1960; s. Charles David and Gloria Barbara (Knoerlein) H. BS in Acctg., Mt. St. Mary's Coll., Emmitsburg, Md., 1982; JD, U. Balt., 1985. Bar: Md. 1985, U.S. Ct. Appeals (4th cir.) 1987, U.S. Ct. Appeals (D.C. cir.) 1988, D.C. Ct. Appeals 1988; CPA, Md. Assoc. Bregel, Kerr & Heisler, Towson, Md., 1986-88; mem. Heisler, Williams & Lazzaro LLC, Towson, 1988—. Mem. Assn. Trial Lawyers Am., Balt. County Bar Assn., Balt. City Bar Assn. (com. mem.), Md. Assn. CPAs. Republican. Roman Catholic. Avocations: running, hiking. Estate planning, Probate, Estate taxation. Office: Heisler Williams & Lazzaro 102 W Pennsylvania Ave Ste 200 Baltimore MD 21204-4544

**HEISLER, STANLEY DEAN,** lawyer; b. The Dalles, Oreg., Jan. 11, 1946; s. Donald Eugene and Roberta (Van Valkenburgh) H. BA, Willamette U., 1968, JD, 1972. Bar: Oreg. 1972, U.S. Ct. Claims 1972, U.S. Tax Ct. 1972, U.S. Ct. Appeals (9th cir.) 1972, D.C. 1973, U.S. Ct. Appeals (fed. cir.) 1973, U.S. Ct. Mil. Appeals 1973, N.Y. 1985, U.S. Supreme Ct. 1985. Assoc. Heisler & Van Valkenburgh, The Dalles, 1973-74; ptnr. Heisler, Van Valkenburgh & Coats, The Dalles, 1975-81, Heisler & Heisler, The Dalles, 1982-84, Cohen & Shalleck, N.Y.C., 1985-88, Phillips, Nizer, Benjamin, Krim & Ballon, N.Y.C., 1988-91, Squadron, Ellenoff, Plesent, Sheinfeld & Sorkin, N.Y.C., 1991-94; mng. ptnr. Shays & Kemper, LLP, N.Y.C., 1994-98, Shays, Rothman, & Heisler, LLP, N.Y.C., 1999—. Speechwriter Sec. of State Tom McCall, Salem, 1965, Gov. Tom McCall, Salem, 1966-68; speechwriter, legis. asst. U.S. Senator Bob Packwood, Washington, 1969-73; vice chmn. Pres.'s Air Quality Adv. Bd., Washington, 1973-76. Mem. ABA, N.Y. State Bar Assn., Assn. of Bar of City of N.Y., Arlington Club, Univ. Club (N.Y.C. and Portland, Oreg.), Soc. Mayflower Descs., Soc. of the Descs. Washington's Army at Valley Forge, Soc. for the Promotion of Hellenic Studies (London), Edmund Rice (1638) Assn. Republican. Family and matrimonial, State civil litigation. Home: 400 E 77th St Apt 8J New York NY 10021-2342 Office: Shays Rothman & Heisler LLP 276 5th Ave New York NY 10001-4509

**HEITKAMP, HEIDI,** state attorney general; b. Breckenridge, Minn.; m. Darwin Lange; children: Alethea Lange, Nathan Lange. BA, U. N.D., 1977; JD, Lewis and Clark Coll., 1980. Intern asst. Environ. Study Conf., Washington, 1976; legis. intern N.D. Legis. Coun., Bismarck, 1977; exec. dir. Northwestern Environ. Def. Ctr., Portland, 1978-79; rsch. asst. Nat. Resources Law Inst., Portland, 1979; atty. enforcement divsn. EPA, Washington, 1980-81; asst. atty. gen. Office of N.D. State Tax Commr., Bismarck, 1981-85, adminstrv. counsel, 1985-86, tax commr., 1986-92; atty. gen. State of N.D., Bismarck, 1993—; del. Am. Coun. Young Polit. Leaders, UK Internat. Def. Conf., 1988; trustee Fedn. Tax Adminstrs., 1991; presdl. appointee trade and environment policy adv. com. Office of Trade Reps., 1996. N.D. State Crusade chmn. Am. Cancer Soc., 1988—. Recipient Young Achiever award Nat. Coun. Women, 1987; named One of 20 Young Lawyers Making a Difference, ABA Barrister mag., 1990; Toll fellow Coun. State Govts., 1986. Mem. Nat. Assn. Atty. Gens. Office: Attorney General State Capitol 600 E Boulevard Ave Dept 125 Bismarck ND 58505-0040*

**HEITLER, PERRIE NANETTE,** lawyer; b. Flushing, N.Y., June 5, 1953; d. Arthur and Sylvia Barbara Heitler; m. John M. Kasel. BA, Hamline U., 1974, JD, 1978. Bar: Minn. 1978, U.S. Dist. Ct. Minn. 1981. Govt. cons. Edman & Assoc., St. Paul, 1975-78; ptnr. Caldwell & Heitler, Mpls., 1978-80; pvt. practice, Roseville, Minn., 1980—. Mem. Roseville City Ctr. Task Force, 1998-99. Mem. Minn. Bar Assn., Ramsey County Bar Assn. Avocations: tennis, fishing, reading. Fax: 651-484-9189. E-mail: heitler@gateway.net. Probate, Real property, Estate planning. Office: 2345 Rice St Ste 165 Roseville MN 55113-3720

**HEJTMANEK, DANTON CHARLES,** lawyer; b. Topeka, July 22, 1951; s. Robert Keith and Bernice Louise (Krause) H.; m. Julie Hejtmanek; 1 child, Brian J. BBA in Acctg., Washburn U., 1973, JD, 1975. Bar: Kans. 1976, U.S. Dist. Ct. Kans. 1976, U.S. Tax Ct. 1976. Ptnr. Schroer, Rice, Bryan & Lykins, P.A., Topeka, 1975-86, Bryan, Lykins & Hejtmanek, P.A., Topeka, 1986—. Mem. ABA (rep. young lawyers Kans. and Nebr.), ATLA, Kans. Bar Assn. (pres. young lawyers 1985), Kans. Trial Lawyers Assn., Sertoma (pres. 1983, internat. pres. 1998-99). Republican. Presbyterian. Avocations: snow skiing, travel. Personal injury, Probate, Family and matrimonial. Home: 2800 SW Burlingame Rd Topeka KS 66611-1316 Office: Bryan Lykins & Hejtmanek PA 222 SW 7th St Topeka KS 66603-3734

**HEKTNER, CANDICE ELAINE,** lawyer; b. Fargo, N.D., Apr. 22, 1948; d. Alfred G. and Hope E. Hektner; children: Nicole A, Brittany T. BA, Concordia Coll., Moorhead, Minn., 1970; JD, Valparaiso U., 1975. Bar: Minn. 1975, N.D. 1975, U.S. Dist. Ct. Minn. 1975, U.S. Dist. Ct. N.D. 1975. Assoc. Ochs Larsen Law Firm, Mpls., 1975-80; ptnr. Chadwick, Johnson & Condon, P.A., Mpls., 1980-91, Peterson & Hektner Ltd., Mpls., 1991—. Mem. ABA, Minn. Bar Assn., Minn. Def. Lawyers Assn. Lutheran. Workers' compensation, Family and matrimonial, Insurance. Office: Peterson & Hektner Ltd 7831 Glenroy Rd Minneapolis MN 55439-3132

**HELBERT, MICHAEL CLINTON,** lawyer; b. Wichita, Kans., Dec. 30, 1950; s. Robert Lee and Carrollyn Jean (Stull) H.; m. Sandra Sue Ziegler, Aug. 26, 1978; 1 son, Michael Ryan. BA, U. Kans.-Lawrence, 1972, J.D., 1975. Bar: Kans. 1975, U.S. Dist. Ct. Kans. 1975, U.S. Supreme Ct. 1980, U.S. Ct. Appeals (10th cir.) 1984. Intern, Douglas County Legal Aid, Lawrence, 1974-75; assoc. law firm Atherton, Hurt & Sanderson, Emporia, Kans., 1975-77; ptnr. firm Helbert & Bell, and predecessor firms, Emporia, 1978-81, prin., 1981-97; pvt. practice, 1998—; mem. Kans. Justice Iniative Commn., 1997—. Treas. Lyon County Rep. Ctrl. Com., 1986-94; mem. adv. bd. Kans. U. Endowment Assn., 1977-81; chmn. profl. divsn. United Way of Emporia, 1978. Mem. Kans. Trial Lawyers Assn. (bd. govs. 1988—, state parliamentarian 1988-89, sec. 1989-90, v.p., 1997-99, pres.-elect 1999—), Kans. Bar Assn., Assn. Trial Lawyers Am., Lyon-Chase County Bar Assn. (treas. 1982, v.p. 1983, pres. 1984), Emporia C. of C. (past dir., past vice-chmn.), Emporia Jaycees (past dir.), Kans. Jaycees (past dir.). Republican. Presbyterian. State civil litigation, Personal injury, Workers' compensation. Home: 1721 Hammond Dr Emporia KS 66801-5312 Office: 519 Commercial St Emporia KS 66801-4005

**HELBLING, LAUREN A.,** lawyer; b. Niantic, Conn., Feb. 20, 1961; d. Roger Allen and Mary Jo Yeary; m. Kenneth Michael Hebling, July 12, 1986. BS in Fin., Ohio State U., 1984; posrgrad., U. Houston, 1985; JD, Cleve. State U., 1987. Bar: Ohio, U.S. Dist. Ct. (no. dist.) Ohio. Atty. Porter, Wright, Morris & Arthur, Cleve., 1987-90, pvt. practice, Cleve., 1990-92, 97—; law clk. Cuyahoga County Ct., Cleve., 1992-93, U.S. Bankruptcy Ct., Cleve., 1993-97. Mem. Nat. Assn. Bankruptcy Trustees, Cleve. Bar Assn., Verea Animal Rescue Fund. Avocations: power boating, softball, rollerblading. Bankruptcy, Consumer commercial. Office: Seraien M Haygood & Assocs 1422 Euclid Ave Ste 1366 Cleveland OH 44115-2001

**HELD, EDWIN WALTER, JR.,** lawyer; b. Jacksonville, Fla., Feb. 14, 1947; m. Leslie Edwards, Aug. 18, 1974; children: Kimberly M., Eric E. BSBA, U. Fla., 1970; JD, Stetson U., 1973. Bar: Fla. 1973, U.S. Dist. Ct. (mid. dist.) Fla. 1973, U.S. Ct. Appeals (11th cir.) 1973. Assoc. Fischette, Parrish & Owen, Jacksonville, 1973-75; mem. Fischette, Parrish, Owen & Held, Jacksonville, 1975-90, Fischette, Owen & Held, Jacksonville, 1990-97, Fischette, Owen, Held & McBurney, Jacksonville, 1997—. Founding dir., bd. dirs. Jewish Cmty. Alliance, Jacksonville, 1990. Mem. Comml. Law League Am. (exec. con. bankruptcy and insolvency sect. 1990—, chmn. sect. 1997-98). Democrat. Avocations: boating, skiing, tennis, fishing, golf. Bankruptcy, Contracts commercial, General corporate. Office: Fischette Owen Held & McBurney 1301 Riverplace Blvd Ste 1916 Jacksonville FL 32207-9073

**HELD, MARC JASON,** lawyer; b. Bronx, N.Y., Sept. 7, 1972; s. Edward and Barbara Anne Held. BA cum laude, Brandeis U., 1993; JD, NYU, 1996. Bar: N.J. 1996, N.Y. 1997. Intern hon. Joe Levine Bklyn., 1994; legal extern Neil B. Cheekman, N.Y.C., 1995; ptnr. Held, Held & Held, Bklyn., 1996—. Mem. N.Y.C. Trial Lawyers Assn., Civil Term Forum. Personal injury, Real property, General civil litigation. Office: Held Held & Held 6920 Bay Pkwy Brooklyn NY 11204-5508

**HELDER, JAN PLEASANT, JR.,** lawyer; b. Marysville, Calif., Jan. 18, 1963; s. Jan Pleasant Sr. and Roleane Phylis (Harrison) H.; m. Barbara Irene Loring, July 14, 1990; children: Russell Wright, Zachary Allen, David Grant. BA in Econs., Calif. State U., Sacramento, 1986; JD, Georgetown U., 1989. Bar: Mo. 1989, U.S. Dist. Ct. (we. dist.) Mo. 1989, Kans. 1990, U.S. Dist. Ct. Kans. 1990, U.S. Ct. Appeals (10th cir.) 1994, U.S. Tax Ct. 1994. Exec. asst. to pres. Sacramento Trade Exch., 1983-84; legis. asst. Calif. Postsecondary Edn. Commn., Sacramento, 1985-86; assoc. Spencer, Fane, Britt & Browne, Kansas City, Mo., 1989-94; assoc. Sonnenschein Nath & Rosenthal, Kansas City, Mo., 1994-96, ptnr., 1996—; judge pro tem City of Prairie Village (Kans.) Mcpl. Ct.; bd. dirs. Edn., Inc., bd. sec., 1994-95; bd. dirs. Young Audiences, vice pres., 1997-98, vice chmn., 1999—. Bd. editor Bus. Torts Reporter, 1996—. Chair Calif. State Student Assn., Sacramento and Long Beach, 1984-85; mem. Leadership Mo., Jefferson City, 1992; mem. Centurions Leadership Program, 1993-95, mem. steering com., 1994-95. Pursuit of Worthwhile Endeavors scholar Calif. State U., Sacramento, 1982. Mem. ABA (vice-chair bus. torts subcom., bus. and corp. litigation com., bus. sect. 1993-95, task force on Litigation Reform, chair bus. torts subcom. 1995—, co-chair, Task Force on Year 2000 Legislation, 1999—), co-chair, Task Force on Litigation Reform and Rule Revision, 1999—; Nat. Inst. Trial Advocacy (western regional 1993), Mo. Bar Assn., Kans. Bar Assn., Kansas City Met. Bar Assn., Johnson County Bar Assn., Greater Kansas City C. of C. (chair subcom. on labor and jud. 1990-91, fed. affairs com. 1989—), Ross T. Roberts Inn Ct. (barrister 1991-92). Republican. Presbyterian. Avocations: jazz and classical and choral music, golf, tennis, running, politics. Federal civil litigation, General civil litigation, State civil litigation. Home: 2216 W 63rd St Shawnee Mission KS 66208-1903 Office: Sonnenschein Nath & Rosenthal 4520 Main St Ste 1100 Kansas City MO 64111-7700

**HELDMAN, JAMES GARDNER,** lawyer; b. Cin., Mar. 7, 1949; s. James Norvin and Jane Marie (Gardner) H.; m. Wendy Maureen Saunders, Sept. 3, 1978; children: Dustin A., Courtney B. AB cum laude, Harvard U., 1971; JD with honors, George Washington U., 1974. Bar: D.C. 1975, U.S. Dist. Ct. (D.C. dist.) 1975, U.S. Ct. Appeals (D.C. cir.) 1975, U.S. Supreme Ct. 1980, Ohio 1981. Assoc. Perazich & Kolker, Washington, 1974-79, Wyman, Bautzer, Kuchel & Silbert, Washington, 1979-81; assoc. Strauss & Troy, Cin., 1981-83, ptnr., 1984—. Mem. ABA, Ohio State Bar Assn., Cin. Bar Assn. Avocations: tennis, platform tennis, swimming. Real property, Securities, Finance. Office: Strauss & Troy The Fed Res Bldg 150 E Fourth St Cincinnati OH 45202-4018

**HELDMAN, PAUL W.,** lawyer, grocery store company executive. BS, Boston U., 1973; JD, U. Cin., 1977. Bar: Ohio 1977. Assoc. Beckman, Lavercombe & Well, 1977-82; atty. The Kroger Co., Cin., 1982-86; sr. atty. Kroger Co., Cin., 1986-87, sr. counsel, 1987-89, v.p., gen. counsel, 1989-92; v.p., sec., gen. counsel The Kroger Co., 1992-97, sr. v.p., sec., gen. counsel, 1997—. Securities, General corporate. Office: The Kroger Co 1014 Vine St Ste 1000 Cincinnati OH 45202-1100

**HELENIAK, DAVID WILLIAM,** lawyer, educator; b. St. Paul, June 27, 1945; s. George L. and Elizabeth (Child) H.; m. Kathryn Moore, Jan. 14, 1967; children: Claire Elizabeth Moore, Charlotte Margaret Moore. AB, U. Mich., 1967; MSc in Econ., London Sch. of Econ., 1969; JD, Columbia U., 1974. Bar: N.Y. 1975. Assoc. Shearman & Sterling, N.Y.C., 1974-77, 79-81, ptnr., 1981—; exec. asst. to dep. sec. U.S. Dept. of the Treasury, Washington, 1977-78, asst. gen. counsel, 1978-79; instr. in econs. U. Wis., Eau Claire, 1974-77. Pres. The MacDowell Colony Inc., N.Y.C., 1987-93. Mem. Lawrence Beach Club, Century Assn. Mergers and acquisitions, General corporate, Public international. Office: 599 Lexington Ave Fl C2 New York NY 10022-6030

**HELFAND, MARCY CAREN,** lawyer; b. Chgo., Sept. 2, 1954; d. Irwin and Pauline H.; children: Eric and Alexis Weisbrod. BS with high hons., So. Meth. U., 1976, JD cum laude, 1979. Bar: Tex. 1979, U.S. Dist. Ct. (no. dist.) Tex.; cert. comml. real estate law, Tex. Bd. of Legal Specialization. Assoc. Freytag, Marshall, et al, Dallas, 1979-83, Jones, Day, Reavis & Pogue, Dallas, 1983-84; Of Counsel Morgan & Weisbrod, Dallas, 1984-94; pvt. practice Dallas, 1994—. Precinct chair Dallas Dem. Orgn., 1979—. Mem. ABA (chair remedies, miscellaneous clauses real property, probate and trust section 1993-95), Dallas Assn. Young Lawyers (chair continuing legal edn. com. 1983), Dallas Bar Assn., Coll. State Bar of Tex., Order of Coif. Real property, Contracts commercial, Finance. Home: 7191 Kendallwood Dr Dallas TX 75240-5510 Office: 5580 Lbj Fwy Ste 270 Dallas TX 75240-6293

**HELFER, MICHAEL STEVENS,** lawyer; b. N.Y.C., Aug. 2, 1945; s. Robert Stevens and Teresa (Kahan) H.; m. Ricki Rhodarmer Helfer; children: David, Matthew, Lisa. BA summa cum laude, Claremont Men's Coll., 1967; JD magna cum laude, Harvard U., 1970. Bar: D.C. 1971. Law clk. to chief judge U.S. Ct. Appeals D.C., 1970-71; asst. counsel subcom. on constl. amendments Senate Judiciary Com., 1971-73; assoc. Wilmer, Cutler & Pickering, Washington, 1973-78, ptnr., 1978—, mem. mgmt. com., 1990-98, chmn., 1995-98; professorial lectr. George Washington U. Law Sch., 1982; bd. dirs. 1st Cmty. Bankshares, Inc., Houston. Trustee Legal Aid Soc. D.C., 1983-95, pres., 1990-92; v.p., bd. dirs. Lawyers for Children Am., Inc., 1995—. Fellow Am. Bar Found.; mem. Am. Law Inst. Democrat. Banking, Administrative and regulatory, Federal civil litigation. Home: 1336 31st St NW Washington DC 20007-3347 Office: 2445 M St NW Washington DC 20037-1435

**HELLAWELL, ROBERT,** law educator; b. Long Island, N.Y., Jan. 24, 1928; s. Edwin V. and Nora D. (Mahoney) H.; m. Jane Buck, June 16, 1951; 1 child, Kathleen Abbott. AB, Williams Coll., 1950; LLB, Columbia U., 1953. Bar: N.Y. 1954, Ohio 1955. Law clk. U.S. Circuit Ct. judge, 1953-54; with firm Jones, Day, Cockley & Reavis, Cleve., 1954-61; ptnr. Jones, Day, Cockley & Reavis, 1961; atty., adviser formation Peace Corps, 1961; dir. projects in Peace Corps, Tanganyika, 1961-63; dep. assoc. dir. Peace Corps, 1963-64; assoc. prof. law Columbia Law Sch., N.Y.C., 1964-67, prof. law, 1967-89, Wilber Friedman prof. emeritus, 1989—, vice dean, 1973-76, acting dean, 1976-77, dir. African Law Center, 1971-77, co-dir. Investment Negotiation Center, 1973-82, dir. Center for Law and Econs., 1978-79; vis. prof. U. Ghana, 1969; cons. admiralty law UN Commn. Internat. Trade Law, 1971. Co-author: Taxation of Business Enterprises, 1987, Taxation of Transnational Transactions, 1989; editor: United States Taxation and Developing Countries, 1980; co-editor: Competition in International Business, 1981, Negotiating Foreign Investments, 1982; notes editor: Columbia Law Rev, 1952-53. Bd. dirs. Internat. Law Inst., Georgetown U., 1973-85. With AUS, 1946-48, Korea. Mem. Delta Kappa Epsilon, Phi Delta Phi. Home: 410 Heron Pt Chestertown MD 21620-1679 Office: Columbia Law Sch New York NY 10027

**HELLBECK, ECKHARD ROBERT,** lawyer; b. Hong Kong, Hong Kong, May 18, 1961; came to the U.S., 1991; s. Hannspeter and Ursula H.; m. Arminda Buria, July 15, 1988; children: Alexander Peter Buria-Hellbeck, Stephanie Michelle Buria-Hellbeck. 1st and 2d state exams. in law, Freie U. Berlin, 1986; LLM, Am. U., 1987. Bar: N.Y. 1996. Legal asst. Internat. Monetary Fund, Washington, 1987; diplomat/lawyer German Fgn. Office, Bonn, Germany, 1988-91, Permanent Mission to Germany to UN, N.Y.C., 1991-95, German Fgn. Office, Bonn, 1995-96; lawyer Mielicke, Hoffmann & Ptnr., Bonn, 1997, White & Case LLP, Washington, 1998—. Co-author: Kaufrecht in AnwaltFormulare, 1997; editor: Am. U. Jour. Internat. Law and Policy, 1987, German-Am. Law Jour., 1998—. Fulbright fellow, 1986-87; scholar German Acad. Exchange Svc., 1985. Mem. ABA, Internat. Law Assn., German-Am. Law Assn., Am. Soc. Internat. Law. Avocations: photography, literature, music, art. Fax: 202-639-9355. E-mail: hellbec@washde.whitecase.com. Contracts commercial, Private international, Public international. Office: White & Case LLP 601 13th St NW Ste 600S Washington DC 20005-3807

**HELLDORFER, BERNARD GEORGE,** law educator, lawyer; b. Bklyn., Aug. 4, 1955; s. Bernard John and Lillian Elizabeth (Stietz) H.; m. Linda Helen Sturm, June 14, 1980. BS, St. John's U., Jamaica, N.Y., 1977, JD, 1980. Bar: N.Y. 1981, U.S. Dist. Ct. (so. and ea. dists.) N.Y. 1981, Pa. 1989, U.S. Supreme Ct. 1989. Assoc. counsel Mobil Oil Corp., N.Y.C., 1979-81, counsel, 1981-83; instr. St. John's U., 1983-84, asst. prof., 1984-89, assoc. prof., 1989—, dir. paralegal studies program, 1987—, 1983—, assoc. prof., 1989—; arbitrator N.Y. Stock Exchange, 1983—, Am. Stock Exchange, N.Y.C., 1984—, N.Y.C. Civil Ct., 1984—; of counsel Puskuldjian & Frustaci, Bklyn., 1984—. Sect. editor The Bus. Lawyer jour., 1986—; editor: N.Y.C. Consumers' Law Guide. 1988; co-producer (film) Careers in Law, 1986. Pro bono counsel Our Lady of Hope Athletic Assn., Middle Village, N.Y., 1981—, German-Am. Dance Group, Ridgewood, N.Y., 1981—; trustee Christ the King Regional High Sch., Middlevillage, 1990—. Mem. ABA, N.Y. State Bar Assn. (Outstanding Service award 1984), Assn. Bar City of N.Y., Holy Name Soc., Am. Assn. Paralegal Edn., Phi Delta Phi. Republican. Roman Catholic. Lodge: KC. Avocations: music, fishing, boating, photography. Home: 60-67 69th Ln Maspeth NY 11378-2911 Office: St Johns U Grand Cen Utopia Pkwy Jamaica NY 11439-0001

**HELLER, DONALD HERBERT,** lawyer; b. N.Y.C., June 1, 1943; s. Nathan and Sylvia (Wexler) H.; m. Lesley Siskin, July 24, 1976; children: Michael, Joshua, Alexandra. BA in Econs., Queens Coll., 1966; JD, Bklyn. Law Sch., 1969. Bar: N.Y. 1969, Calif. 1973, U.S. Dist. Ct. (cen., no. and ea. dists.) Calif. 1974, U.S. Ct. Appeals (9th cir.) 1974. Asst. dist. atty. N.Y. County, N.Y.C., 1969-73; asst. U.S. atty. Calif. Dist. Ct. (ea. dist.), Sacramento, 1973-77; sole practice Sacramento, 1977—; judge pro tempore Sacramento County Superior Ct., 1986—. Mem. ABA, Sacramento County Bar Assn. Republican. Avocation: golf. Criminal, General civil litigation. Home: 205 Dunbarton Cir Sacramento CA 95825-6808 Office: A Law Corp 455 Capitol Mall Ste 405 Sacramento CA 95814-4496

**HELLER, FRED IRA,** lawyer; b. Bklyn., July 3, 1945; s. Murray Joseph and Pearl (Epstein) H.; m. Lynne Sue Shusterman, June 9, 1968; children: Robert, Jason. BA, Hofstra U., 1968; JD, Bklyn. Law Sch., 1972. Bar: N.Y. 1974, U.S. Dist. Ct. (ea. dist.) N.Y. 1974, U.S. Ct. Appeals (2d cir.) 1975, U.S. Supreme Ct. 1977. From law clk. to ptnr. Speiser & Krause PC, N.Y.C., 1972-80; pres., cons. Heller Assocs. Ltd., Merrick, N.Y., 1980—; lectr. Practicing Law Inst., N.Y.C., 1981-87. Author: Advanced Litigation Skills Using Video, 1987, Video Technology: Its Use and Applications in Law, 1984, Video Techniques in Trial and Pretrial, 1983; planner, producer: (video) Day in the Life, 1989; co-author: How to Use Video in Litigation, 1986; contbr. articles to profl. jours. Mem. ABA, Assn. Trial Lawyers of Am., N.Y. State Bar Assn., Mass. Continuing Legal Edn. Assn., N.Y. State Trial Lawyers Assn., Nat. Spinal Cord Injury Assn., Nat. Forensic Video Assn. Avocations: photography, hiking, video documentary production for use in litigation. Media. Office: Heller Assocs Ltd 33 Fox Blvd Merrick NY 11566-4039

**HELLER, PHILIP,** lawyer; b. N.Y.C., Aug. 12, 1952; s. Irving and Dolores (Soloff) H.; divorced; 1 child, Howard Philip. Attended, Harvard Coll.; BA summa cum laude, Boston U., 1976, JD, 1979. Bar: Mass. 1979, N.Y. 1980, U.S. Ct. Appeals (1st, 2nd and 9th cirs.) 1980, U.S. Supreme Ct. 1983, Calif. 1984, U.S. Dist. Ct. (all dists.) Calif., U.S. Dist. Ct. (ea. and so. dists.) N.Y., U.S. Dist. Ct. Mass. Law clk. to judge Cooper So. Dist. N.Y., N.Y.C., 1979; ptnr. Fagelbaum & Heller LLP, L.A. *Born in New York City. Skipped high school, was admitted to college at age 14. Attended Harvard College and Boston University. Graduated as University Professors' Scholar from Boston University with a BA, summa cum laude, 1976. Received his JD from Boston University School of Law in 1979 and is admitted to practice in New York, Massachusetts and California. Mr. Heller was a partner in one of the largest law firms in California prior to starting his own firm with Jerold Fagelbaum. Mr. Heller's practice is comprised primarily of complex civil litigation matters with an emphasis in securities and antitrust law.* Mem. ABA (litigation sect.), Calif. Bar Assn., L.A. County Bar Assn. E-mail: bestlawyers@worldnet.att.net. Fax: 310-286-7086. Federal civil litigation, State civil litigation, General civil litigation. Office: Fagelbaum & Heller LLP 2049 Century Park E Ste 2050 Los Angeles CA 90067-3168

**HELLER, ROBERT MARTIN,** lawyer; b. N.Y.C., Feb. 12, 1942; s. Philip B. and Mildred S. (Friedman) H.; m. Amy S. Wexler, July 11, 1965; children: David B., Pamela L. BA, Columbia U., 1963, LLB, 1966. Bar: N.Y. 1967, D.C. 1992, U.S. Dist. Ct. (so. and ea. dists.) N.Y. 1970, U.S. Ct. Appeals (2d cir.) 1967, U.S. Supreme Ct. 1976. Law clk. to judge U.S. Ct. Appeals (2d cir.), N.Y.C., 1966-67; atty. adviser to commr. FTC, Washington, 1967-69; asst. to mayor for housing, city planning, transp. and model cities, sec. to cabinet City of N.Y., 1971-73; ptnr. Kramer Levin Naftalis & Frankel LLP, N.Y.C., 1974—, mng. ptnr., 1991-94; adj. prof. architecture Columbia U., 1975-77; bd. visitors Columbia Law Sch., 1992—. Bd. govs. Hebrew Union Coll./Jewish Inst. Religion, 1996—; pres. bd. dirs. 1056 Fifth Ave. Corp., 1994-96; officer Union Am. Hebrew Congregations, 1997—, mem. joint commn. on social action, 1992—; trustee Rabbi Marc H. Tanenbaum Found.

James Kent scholar; Harlan Fiske Stone scholar. Mem. ABA, N.Y. State Bar Assn., Assn. of Bar of City of N.Y. (com. on antitrust and trade regulation 1996—), Phi Beta Kappa. Avocations: aerobic walking, photography. Antitrust, Federal civil litigation, Mergers and acquisitions. Home: 1056 5th Ave New York NY 10028-0112 Office: Kramer Levin Naftalis & Frankel LLP 919 3rd Ave New York NY 10022-3902

**HELLER, RONALD IAN,** lawyer; b. Cleve., Sept. 4, 1956; s. Grant L. and Audrey P. (Lecht) H.; m. Shirley Ann Stringer, Mar. 23, 1986; 1 child, David Grant. AB with high honors, Univ Mich., 1976, MBA, 1979, JD, 1980. Bar: Hawaii 1980, U.S. Ct. Claims 1982, U.S. Tax Ct. 1981, U.S. Ct. Appeals (9th cir.) 1981, U.S. Supreme Ct. 1992; Trust Ter. of Pacific Islands 1982, Republic of Marshall Islands 1982; CPA, Hawaii. Assoc. Hoddick, Reinwald, O'Connor & Marrack, Honolulu, 1980-84; ptnr. Reinwald, O'Connor & Marrack, 1984-87; stockholder, bd. dirs. Torkildson, Katz, Fonseca, Jaffe & Moore, Honolulu, 1988—; adj. prof. U. Hawaii Sch. Law, 1981; arbitrator ct.-annexed arbitration program First Cir. Ct., State of Hawaii; author, instr. Hawaii Taxes. Bd. dirs. Hawaii Women Lawyers Found., Honolulu, 1984-86, Hawaii Performing Arts Co., Honolulu, 1984-93; mem. panel. of arbitrators Am. Arbitration Assn.; named NFIB Hawaii Oustanding Sml. Bus. Vol. of 1998. Actor, stage mgr. Honolulu Community Theatre, 1983-87, Hawaii Performing Arts Co., Honolulu, 1982-87. Fellow Am. Coll. Tax Counsel; mem. AICPA (mem. coun. 1994-96), ABA, Hawaii State Bar Assn. (chair tax sect. 1997-98, chair state and local tax com. 1994-95), Hawaii Soc. CPAs (chmn tax com. 1985-86, legis. com. 1987-88, bd. dirs. 1988-98, pres. 1994-95), Hawaii Women Lawyers. Taxation, general, General civil litigation, State and local taxation. Office: Torkildson Katz 700 Bishop St Fl 15 Honolulu HI 96813-4187

**HELLER, SANDERS D.,** lawyer; b. Montpelier, Vt., Apr. 19, 1923; s. Hymon and Annie Dorothy Heller; m. Helen Heller, Jan. 22, 1948; children: Howard, Jeffrey, David, Stephen. BA, Ohio State U., 1948, JD, 1950. Bar: Ohio 1950, N.Y. 1952. Sole practitioner Columbus, Ohio, 1950-51, Gouverneur, N.Y., 1952—; asst., acting dist. atty. St. Lawrence County, Canton, N.Y., 1961-64, spel. prosecutor, 1983-84, adminstr. assigned counsel plan, 1965-81. N.Y. state chmn. March of Dimes, 1970-73; v.p. Congregation Anshe Zophen, 1985—. Recipient Disting. Vol. Svc. award Nat. Found. March of Dimes. Mem. Fedn. Bar Assns. Fourth Judicial Dist. (past pres.), St. Lawrence County Bar Assn. (past pres.), Gouverneur Lions Club (past dist. gov., Melvin Jones fellow 1993-94), Tau Epsilon Phi (past pres., C.C. Lilienfield award 1981). General practice, Oil, gas, and mineral, Probate. Office: PO Box 128 Gouverneur NY 13642-0128

**HELLER, STEPHEN REID,** lawyer; b. Norfolk, Va., Jan. 25, 1956; s. Selwyn Bernard and Dorothy Leah H.; m. Karen Heller, June 13, 1982; children: Ilana Ruth, Naomi Ann. Degree in psychology, U. South Fla., 1978; JD, So. Meth. U., 1982. Bar: Tex. 1983, U.S. Ct. Appeals (5th cir.) 1983, U.S. Supreme Ct. 1988. Assoc., pvt. firm Dallas, 1982-84; assoc. gen. counsel Safeco Title Co., Dallas, 1984-86; from assoc. to shareholder Stigall and Maxfield, Dallas, 1986-89; shareholder Hutchison, Boyle, Brooks and Fisher, Dallas, 1989-93; pvt. practice Dallas, 1993—; bd. dirs. various internat. cos. Co-founder Dallas Virtual Jewish Cmty. web-page, 1994—, Bridwell Judaica lectr. series, 1994—; dir. Am. Jewish Com., 1990—, Dallas Jewish Hist. Soc., 1992-96; founder Classic Jewish Text Seminars, 1989—; founding dir. Am. Zionist Movement Dallas, 1999—; gen. counsel Solomon Schechter Acad. Dallas, 1997—. Mem. Dallas Bar Assn., Internat. Law Soc. Avocations: weight lifting, hiking. Office: 2651 N Harwood St Ste 200 Dallas TX 75201-1506

**HELLMAN, MICHAEL DAVID,** lawyer; b. L.A., Jan. 31, 1964; s. Herbert Lloyd and Carol Lee Hellman; m. Kara Michele Munro, Sept. 7, 1996. BA in Econs. and Bus., UCLA, 1986; JD, U. Calif., San Francisco, 1991. Bar: Calif. 1991, U.S. Dist. Ct. (ctrl. dist.) Calif. 1992, U.S. Ct. Appeals (9th cir.) 1992. Assoc. Fell, Marking, Abkin et al, Santa Barbara, Calif., 1991-97, ptnr., 1998—. Mem. Santa Barbara Inns of Ct., Barristers Club of Santa Barbara (dir. 1992, v.p. 1993-94). Avocations: travel, all things Canadian. General civil litigation, Consumer commercial. Office: Fell Marking Abkin et al 222 E Carrillo St Ste 400 Santa Barbara CA 93101-7148

**HELLMAN, THEODORE ALBERT, JR.,** lawyer; b. Orange, N.J., June 4, 1946; s. Theodore A. Sr. and Jean Florence (Chrystie) H.; m. Janice Anne Reed, July 12, 1969; children: Theodore A. III, Anne, Karen, Julia. BA, Yale U., 1968; MA in Govt., Georgetown U., 1971; JD, U. Va., 1974. Bar: Calif. 1974. Assoc. Pettit & Martin, San Francisco, 1974-78; ptnr. Hanson, Bridgett, Marcus, Vlahos & Rudy, San Francisco, 1978—; dir. Pacific Presbyn. Med. Found., San Francisco. Author: (supplement) Drafting California Irrev. Intervivos Trusts 1985, 1984; co-author: (chpt.) California Will Drafting, 1982; mem. editorial bd. U. Va. Law Rev. Lt. (j.g.) USNR, 1968-71. Mem. Bar Assn. of San Francisco (chmn. estate planning and probate sect. 1991—). Avocation: running. Estate planning, Probate, Estate taxation. Home: 445 Lovell Ave Mill Valley CA 94941-1053 Office: Hanson Bridgett Marcus Vlahos & Rudy 333 Market St Fl 23D San Francisco CA 94105-2102

**HELLMUTH, THEODORE HENNING,** lawyer; b. Detroit, Mar. 28, 1949; s. George F. and Mildred Lee (Henning) H.; m. Laurie Kincaid, May 29, 1970; children: Elizabeth Ann, Theodore Henning, Sara Marie. BA, U. Pa., 1970; JD cum laude, U. Mo.-Columbia, 1974. Bar: Mo. 1974, U.S. Dist. Ct. (ea. dist.) Mo. 1974, U.S. Ct. Appeals (8th cir.) 1978. Assoc., then ptnr. Armstrong Teasdale LLP, St. Louis, 1974—. Author: Missouri Real Estate, 1985, 2d edit., 1998, Lease Audits: The Essential Guide, 1994; editor Distressed Real Estate Law Alert, 1987-88, Litigated Commercial Real Estate Document Reports, 1987-95. Mem. ABA (vice-chmn., chmn. litigation and dispute resolution com. real property and probate sect. 1991-95, mng. book editor real property and probate sect. 1998—), Am. Coll. Real Estate Lawyers (chmn. alternative dispute resolution com. 1993-96), Order of Coif. Real property, General civil litigation. Office: Armstrong Teasdale LLP 1 Metropolitan Sq Ste 2600 Saint Louis MO 63102-2740

**HELM, HUGH BARNETT,** retired judge; b. Bowling Green, Ky., Dec. 27, 1914; s. Hugh Barnett and Ermine (Cox) H.; BA, Vanderbilt U., 1935, postgrad. law sch., 1936-37, 52-53, Stanford U., 1953-56, Nat. Coll. Judiciary, 1976; m. Vivian Loreen Downing, June 5, 1943; children: Beverly Barron, Hugh B. III, Nathaniel Henry. Bar: Ky. 1938, Tenn. 1938, U.S. Supreme Ct. 1942; atty. Trade Practice Conf., FTC, Washington, 1938-42; asso. counsel U.S. Internat. Prosecution Sect. Gen. Hdqrs., SCAP, Tokyo, 1946; practiced in Nashville, 1946-53; bond specialist Swett & Crawford, San Francisco, 1956-57; resident mgr. Totten & Co., San Francisco, 1958, v.p. gen. mgr., 1959-60; sr. trial atty. Bur. Restraint of Trade, FTC, Washington, 1961-66, chief div. of adv. opinions, 1966-70, acting dir. Bur. Industry Guidance, 1969-70, atty. adviser FTC Bur. Consumer Claims, until 1971; adminstrv. law judge Bur. Hearing and Appeals, Social Security Adminstrn., HEW, Chattanooga, 1971-73, adminstrv. law judge charge Western Ky. and So. Ill., Paducah, Ky., 1973-76, Louisville, 1976-78; adminstrv. law judge in charge Miami (Fla.) Office Hearings and Appeals, 1979-81, adminstrv. law judge, Louisville, 1981-82; mem. regional jud. council Social Security Adminstrn. Pres. Surety Claims Assn. No. Calif., 1957-58. Mem. Tenn. Ho. of Reps., 1949-50. Served with inf. USAAF, 1941-45; served to capt. U.S. Army, 1950-52. Decorated Bronze Star, Combat Infantry Badge; recipient Founders medal for oratory Vanderbilt U., 1935, Disting. Service Commendation FTC, 1969. Mem. Nat. Lawyers Club, Pi Sigma Alpha, Tau Kappa Alpha. Presbyterian (deacon). Home: 6479 Randall Ct Pleasanton CA 94566-7725

**HELM, THOMAS KENNEDY, JR.,** retired lawyer; b. Louisville, Ky., Sept. 16, 1918; s. Thomas Kennedy and Elizabeth Tebbs (Nelson) H.; m. Nell Hoge, Jan. 2, 1943,children: T. Kennedy III, Peyton Randolph, Hunt Chouteau. BA, Washington & Lee U., 1940; JD, U. Louisville, 1942. Assoc. Stites & Harbison Attys., Louisville, Ky., 1941-53; ptnr. Stites & Harbison Attys., Louisville, 1953-88, mng. ptnr., 1975; of counsel Stites & Harbison Attys., 1989—; bd. dirs. Griffin Chem. Co., Louisville, Marwood, Inc., Louisville, Frame House Galleries, Louisville, Whayne Supply Co., Louisville. Author: Kentucky Airport Law and Management, 1989. Chmn. bd. Ky. Country Day Sch., Louisville. Comdr. USCG Aux. Capt. AUS Res., 1942-46. Mem. Gen. Soc. Colonial Wars (gov. gen. 1990-93). Avocations: boating, woodworking, photography. Home: 321 Mockingbird Hill Rd Louisville KY 40207-1852

**HELMAN, STEPHEN JODY,** lawyer; b. Houston, Dec. 14, 1949; m. Gail Stevenson, 1974; children: Kimberley Brooke, Courtney Elizabeth, Caitlin Rebecca. BA in Spanish and Religion, So. Meth. U., 1971; postgrad., Perkins Sch. Theology, 1971-73; JD with honors, U. Tex., 1978. Bar: Tex., 1978; cert. estate planning and probate law, 1987. Assoc. Graves, Dougherty, Hearon & Moody, Austin, Tex., 1978-85, ptnr., shareholder, 1985-93; ptnr. Osborne, Lowe, Helman & Smith, L.L.P., Austin, Tex., 1993—; exam commr. in estate planning and probate law, Tex. Bd. Legal Specialization, 1990-94. Contbr. articles to profl. jours. Fellow Am. Coll. Trust and Estate Counsel (mem. profl. standards com. 1990-93); mem. ABA (mem. real property, probate, and trust law sects.), Coll. of the State Bar of Tex., State Bar Tex. (mem. real property, probate and trust law sects.), Travis County Bar Assn. (mem. probate and estate planning sect., pres. 1991-92, dir. 1989-92, ex-officio dir. 1992-93), Order of Coif. Avocations: nature photography, hiking. Probate, Estate planning, Estate taxation. Office: Osborne Lowe Helman & Smith LLP 301 Congress Ave Ste 1900 Austin TX 78701-4041

**HELMER, DAVID ALAN,** lawyer; b. Colorado Springs, May 19, 1946; s. Horton James and Alice Ruth (Cooley) H.; m. Jean Marie Lamping, May 23, 1987. BA, U. Colo., 1968, JD, 1973. Bar: Colo. 1973, U.S. Dist. Ct. Colo. 1973, U.S. Ct. Appeals (10th cir.) 1993, U.S. Ct. Claims 1990, U.S. Supreme Ct. 1991. Assoc. Neil C. King, Boulder, Colo., 1973-76; mgr. labor rels., mine regulations Climax Molybdenum Co., Inc. divsn. AMAX, Inc., Climax, Colo., 1976-84; prin. Law Offices David A. Helmer, Frisco, Colo., 1983—; sec., bd. dirs. Z Comm. Corp., Frisco, 1983-90; cmty. bd. dirs .Norwest Bank Colo., N.A., Frisco, 1996—. Editor U. Colo. Law Rev., 1972-73; contbr. articles to legal jours. Bd. dirs. Summit County Coun. Arts and Humanities, Dillon, Colo., 1980-85; advisor Advocates for Victims of Assault, Frisco, 1984—; legal counsel Summit County United Way, 1983-95, v.p., bd. dirs., 1983-88; bd. dirs., legal counsel Summit county Alcohol and Drug Task Force, Inc., Summit Prevention Alliance, 1984—, Pumpkin Bowl Inc./Children's Hosp. Burn Ctr., 1989—; chmn. Summit County Reps., 1982-89; chmn. 5th Jud. Dist. (Colo.) Rep. Com., 1982-89; chmn. resolutions com. Colo. Rep. Conv., 1984, del. Rep. Nat. Com., 1984; chmn. reaccreditation com. Colo. Mountain Coll., Breckenridge, 1983, mem. steering com., 1997-99; founder, bd. dirs. Dillon Bus. Assn., 1983-87, Frisco Arts Coun., 1989—; atty. N.W. Colo. Legal Svcs. Project, Summit County, 1983—; mcpl. judge Town of Dillon, 1982—, Town of Silverthorne, Colo., 1982—; dir. Snake River Water Dist., 1998—. Sgt. USAR, 1968-74. Mem. ABA, Colo. Bar Assn., (bd. govs. 1991-93, mem. exec. com. 1995-97), Continental Divide Bar Assn. (prs. 1991-95, v.p. 1995-97), Summit County Bar Assn. (pres. 1990-99), Dillon Corinthian Yacht Club (commodore local club 1987-88, 95-97, vice commodore 1994, club champion 1989-91, 94, 95, 97, winner Colo. Cup, Colo. State Sailing Championships 1991), Phi Gamma Delta. Lutheran. General practice, Real property, State civil litigation. Home: PO Box 300 352 Snake River Dr Dillon CO 80435-0300 Office: PO Box 868 611 Main St Frisco CO 80443-0868

**HELMRICH, JOEL MARC,** lawyer; b. Bklyn., Apr. 15, 1953; s. William and Edna (Steigman) H.; m. Barbara Ellen Richter, Sept. 2, 1984; children: Joshua David, Rachel Marysa. BS, Cornell U., 1975, MBA, 1976; JD, Syracuse U., 1979. Bar: Pa. 1979, U.S. Dist. Ct. (we. dist.) Pa. 1979. Assoc. Tucker Arensberg, P.C., Pitts., 1979-86; shareholder Tucker Arensberg, Pitts., 1986-99; ptnr. Meyer, Unkovic & Scott, LLP, Pitts., 1999—. Mem. Pa. Bar Assn., Allegheny County Bar Assn., Comml. Law League Am., Am. Bankruptcy Inst., Rolling Hills Country Club, Cornell Club. Avocations: golf, tennis. Bankruptcy, Consumer commercial, General corporate. Office: Unkovic & Scott LLP 1300 Oliver Bldg Pittsburgh PA 15222-2304

**HELMS, CATHERINE HARRIS,** lawyer; b. Hampton, Va., Feb. 12, 1961; d. Roy Vincent Jr. and Mary Susan (Hill) Harris; m. Jack Jeffrey Helms Jr., June 10, 1989. BA, U. Va., 1983; JD, U. Ga., 1986. Bar: Ga. 1986. Assoc. Peterson Young Self & Asselin, Atlanta, 1986-89; asst. dist. atty. So. Jud. Cir., Valdosta, 1989-90; ptnr. Helms & Helms, P.C., Homerville, Ga., 1990—; barrister Lumpkin Inn of Ct., Athens, 1989—. Contbr. articles to profl. publs. Coach high sch. mock trial competition, Homerville, 1992—. Mem. ABA, Ga. Bar Assn., Alapaha Bar Assn., Valdosta Bar Assn., Ga. Law Sch. Assn. Coun., Order of Barristers. Avocations: reading, sailing, running, gardening. General civil litigation, Criminal, Personal injury. Home: Esperance Farm PO Box 537 Homerville GA 31634 Office: Helms & Helms PC PO Box 537 100 N College St Homerville GA 31634-1401

**HELMS, ROGER D.,** lawyer; b. Orlando, June 11, 1953; s. V.S. and Eunice H.; divorced. BS magna cum laude, U. Ctrl. Fla., 1980; JD, U. Fla. Sch. Law, 1982. Bar: Fla. From assoc. to ptnr. Troutman, Williams, Irvin & Green, Winter Park, Fla., 1983—. Mem. ABA, Acad. Fla. Trial Lawyers. Avocation: boating, fishing. Home: 2840 Bear Island Pointe Winter Park FL 32792-9426 Office: Troutman Williams Irvin Green & Helms 311 W Fairbanks Ave Winter Park FL 32789-5094

**HELMS, WILLIAM COLLIER, III,** lawyer; b. Atlanta, July 11, 1945; s. William Collier and Helen (Meharg) H.; m. Anne Moultrie Ball, July 1, 1967; children: William C. IV, Moultrie B., R. Carter. BA, Emory U., 1967, JD, 1970. Bar: S.C. 1970, U.S. Dist. Ct. S.C. 1971, U.S. Ct. Appeals (4th cir.) 1979. Atty. Barnwell, Whaley, Patterson & Helms, Charleston, S.C., 1970—. Mem. ABA, S.C. Defense Trial Attys. Assn. (exec. com. 1984-87), Am. Bd. Trial Advocates, Internat. Assn. Defense Coun., Rotary. General civil litigation, Construction, Personal injury. Office: Barnwell Whaley Patterson & Helms 134 Meeting St Ste 300 Charleston SC 29401-2240 also: PO Drawer H Charleston SC 29402

**HELT, CHRISTOPHER WILLIAM,** lawyer; b. Chgo., Apr. 28, 1968; s. William and Mary Ann Helt. BA cum laude, Loyola U., Chgo., 1990; JD, Loyola U., 1993. Bar: Ill. 1994, Ind. 1999, U.S. Supreme Ct. 1998. Ptnr. Helt & Assocs., Chgo.; founder Indo-Pak Law Offices, Chgo., 1998—. Editor-in-chief Chgo. Barrister, 1998—. Mem. ABA, Am. Immigration Lawyers Assn. Democrat. Roman Catholic. Avocations: writing, reading. Civil rights, Immigration, naturalization, and customs, Federal civil litigation. Home: 230 W Huron St Chicago IL 60610-3681 Office: 325 W Huron St Chicago IL 60610-3636 also: 6357 N Maplewood Ave Chicago IL 60659-1905

**HELTON, ARTHUR CLEVELAND,** advocate, lawyer; b. St. Louis, Jan. 24, 1949; s. Arthur Cleveland Sr. and Marjorie Jane (Russell) H.; m. Jacqueline Dean Gilbert, May 14, 1982. AB, Columbia Coll., 1971; JD, NYU, 1976. Bar: N.Y. 1977, U.S. Dist. Ct. (so. and ea. dists.) N.Y. 1977, U.S. Ct. Appeals (2d cir.) 1978, U.S. Ct. Appeals (1st cir.) 1980, U.S. Ct. Appeals (4th and 9th cir.) 1988, U.S. Ct. Appeals (5th, 7th and 11th cir.) 1989, U.S. Ct. Appeals (3d cir.) 1994, U.S. Supreme Ct. 1980. Assoc. appellate counsel Legal Aid Soc., N.Y.C., 1976-79; assoc. Mailman & Rutheizer, N.Y.C., 1979-82; dir. refugee project Lawyers Com. Human Rights, N.Y.C., 1982-94; dir. migration programs, forced migration projects Open Soc. Inst., N.Y.C., 1994-99; vis. prof. internat. rels. Ctrl. European U., 1997—; adj. prof. law NYU, 1986-99. Contbr. articles to profl. jours. Recipient Pub. Svc. award Law Alumni Assn. NYU, 1987; grantee The German Marshall Fund, The Ford Found.; sr. fellow Coun. Fgn. Rels., 1999—. Fellow Am. Bar Found.; mem. Coun. Fgn. Rels., ABA (co-chmn. immigration and nationality law com. sect. internat. law and practice, coord. com. on immigration law 1997—), Internat. Bar Assn., Assn. Bar N.Y.C. (chmn. com. on immigration and nationality law 1982-85, legal assistance com. 1985-88, civil rights com. 1988-91, internat. human rights com. 1991-94, internat. law com. 1995-98, adminstrv. law com. 1999—), Pub. internatl. imm., naturalization, and customs. Home: 245 7th Ave Apt 10B New York NY 10001-7301 Office: Coun Fgn Rels 58 E 68th St New York NY 10021

**HELTON, ROBERT MOORE,** lawyer, geologist; b. Enid, Okla., Jan. 23, 1913; s. Robert Isaac and Stella Ann (Moore) H.; m. Emma Katherine Gibson, June 8, 1935; 1 child: John Robert. AA, Kemper Coll., 1931; BA, Okla. U., 1933; JD, U. Mich., 1936. Bar: Tillman County Okla. 1936, Okla. 1936, Okla. (we. dist.) 1936, U.S. Ct. Appeals (10th cir.) 1936, Wichita County (Tex.) 1967, Tex. 1967, U.S. Dist. Ct. (no. dist.) Tex. 1969, U.S. Ct. Appeals (5th cir.) 1969, Okla. U.S. Dist. Ct. (no. dist.) Okla. 1970. Pvt. practice Wichita Falls, Okla., 1936-69, Wichita Falls, Tex., 1969—; mem. law libr. com. Wichita County Bar Assn., 1967-77; original mem. U.S. Hwy. 70 Assn., 1945. Pres. Grandfield (Okla.) C. of C., 1945-57. Flight officer USAF, 1942-45. Named Gen. Practitioner of Yr. Wichita County Bar Assn., 1974. Republican. Presbyterian. Avocation: hunting for crude oil with a rotary drilling rig. General practice, Constitutional, Administrative and regulatory. Home and Office: 2407 Martin St Wichita Falls TX 76308-1908

**HELTON, THOMAS OSWALD,** lawyer; b. Pulaski, Tenn., June 1, 1940; s. Thomas O. and Alameda (Beeler) H.; m. Barbara Sue Brown, May 29, 1965; 1 child, Joshua M. BS, U. Tenn., Knoxville, 1963; LLB, Vanderbilt U., 1966. Bar: Tenn. 1966, Ga. 1976, U.S. Ct. Appeals (6th and 11th cirs.), U.S. Dist. Ct. (ea. and mid. dists.) Tenn., U.S. Dist. Ct. (no. dist.) Ga., U.S. Supreme Ct. Law clk. to Hon. Frank Gray, Jr. U.S. Dist. Ct. Middle Dist. Tenn., Nashville, 1966-67; law clk. to Hon. Paul C. Weick U.S. Ct. Appeals for 6th Cir., Cin., 1967-68; assoc., mem. Stophel, Caldwell & Heggie, P.C., Chattanooga, 1968-86; mem. firm Caldwell, Heggie & Helton, P.C., Chattanooga, 1986-93; mem. Baker, Donelson, Bearman & Caldwell, Chattanooga, 1993—. Mem. fundraising and allocation United Way, Chattanooga, 1972-88; bd. dirs. Family and Children Services, Inc., Chattanooga, 1980-87; trustee Tenn. River Gorge Trust, 1997—. Fellow Tenn. Bar Found.; mem. Tenn. Bar Assn. (bd. govs. 1985-93), Chattanooga Bar Assn. (bd. govs. 1976-78, sec.-treas. 1978-79, pres.-elect 1979-80, pres. 1980-81), Ga. Bar Assn., Greater Chattanooga Area C. of C. Episcopalian. General civil litigation, Intellectual property, Labor. Home: 200 Fairy Trl Lookout Mountain TN 37350-1604 Office: Baker Donelson Bearman & Caldwell PC 633 Chestnut St Ste 1800 Chattanooga TN 37450-1800

**HELVEY, EDWARD DOUGLAS,** lawyer; b. West Palm Beach, Fla., Apr. 26, 1956; s. Wilfred Douglass (dec.) and Alice Garr (Campbell) H.; m. Mary Patricia McGraw, Oct. 26, 1985; children: Megan Anne, Andrew Douglas. BA, Ohio State U., 1978; JD, Cleve. State U., 1981. Bar: Ohio 1982, U.S. Dist. Ct. (no. and so. dists.) Ohio 1982, U.S. Supreme Ct. 1993. Asst. atty. gen. Office of Ohio Atty. Gen., Columbus, 1981-84, spl. counsel, 1987-94; staff atty. ITT Consumer Fin. Corp., Columbus, 1984-85, reg. adminstr. govtl. affairs, 1985-88; legis. agt. Ohio Edn. Assn., Columbus, 1988-97, labor. rels. cons., 1997—; mem. exec. com. Profl. Staff Union Ohio, 1988—, v.p., 1995-98; del. Nat. Staff Orgn., 1994-98, 99. Bd. dirs. N.W. Civic Assn., Columbus, 1984; exec. v.p. Am. Ionized Pasteurization Coun., 1993-95; alt. del. Nat. Dem. Conv., 1996; mem. Delaware County Dem. Ctr. Com., 1996—, St. Anthony Parish coun., 1997—. Mem. Nat. Assn. Legis. and Polit. Specialists in Edn., Ohio Bar Assn., Columbus Bar Assn., Ohio Consumer Fin. Assn. (bd. dirs. 1985-88), Pa. Fin. Svcs. Assn. (bd. dirs. 1985-88), Va. Consumer Fin. Assn. (bd. dirs. 1985-88), Md. Fin. Svcs. Assn. (bd. dirs. 1985-88), Internat. Found. Employee Benefits, Nat. Staff Orgn., Nat. Assn. Legis. and Polit. Specialists in Edn., Ohio Soc. Assn. Execs., Richland Co. Bar Assn. Democrat. Roman Catholic. Home: 410 Ashford Dr Westerville OH 43082-7446

**HELWEG, M. DIANA,** lawyer; b. Abington, Pa., Aug. 3, 1966; d. Joseph Earley Helweg and Mary Welham (Walbridge) Helweg Campbell. BA in East Asian Studies, Yale Coll., 1988; JD, Boston U., 1992. Bar: Md. 1992, Mass. 1993, D.C. 1993, U.S. Ct. Internat. Trade 1994, Ct. Appeals (fed. cir.) 1995. Coord. internat. rels. Yamaguchi Prefectural Govt., Yamaguchi, Japan, 1988-89; assoc. Morrison & Foerster, Washington, 1992—. Contbr. articles to profl. jours. Mem. Women in Internat. Trade. General corporate, Private international.

**HELWIG, BILL J.,** lawyer; b. San Angelo, Tex., Jan. 21, 1954; s. Billy Joe and June Lois H. m. Debi Elaine Helwig, Sept. 4, 1998; children: Brandon Howard, Chad, Jodee. BS, Tex. A&M, 1976; JD, Tex. Tech. Sch. Law, Lubbock, Tex., 1979. Lawyer Coke County, Robert Lee, Tex., 1980-92; asst. gen counsel Tex. A&M U. System, College Station, Tex., 1992-97; pvt. practice Denver City, Tex., 1997—; coord. High Edn. Law Symposium, 1996; spkr. in field. trustee emeritus Tex. 4-H Found. Recipient Tex. 4-H Alumni award, Tex. Agrl. Ext. Svc., 1990, Dist. 7 Alumni award. Avocations: hunting, fishing. Office: Bill Helwig Atty at Law 317 N Main Ave Denver City TX 79323-3241

**HEMEON-HEYER, SHEILA MARIE,** lawyer; b. Quincy, Mass., Feb. 11, 1959; d. Ronald Eugene and Katherine Joan (Finnerty) Hemeon; m. Mark Christopher Heyer, July 23, 1983; children: Ellis, Travis. BS in Biomed. Engrng., Boston U., 1981; MS in Biomechs., U. Mass., 1987; JD, Western New Eng. Coll., 1997. Instr. computer, electronics SUNY, Farmingdale, 1981-82, Holyoke (Mass.) C.C., 1982-86; sci. reviewer FDA, Washington, 1987-90; cons. regulatory affairs Amherst, Mass., 1990-97; jud. law clk. Mass. Supreme Ct., Boston, 1997-98. Contbr. articles to sci. and profl. jours. Pres. Wildwood Afterschool Parent Bd., Amherst, 1997-98; mem. religious edn. com. Unitarian-Universalist Ch., Amherst, 1995-97. Mem. Regulatory Affairs Profl. Soc., Mass. Bar Assn. Democrat. Avocations: running, volleyball, skiing.

**HEMINGWAY, RICHARD WILLIAM,** law educator; b. Detroit, Nov. 24, 1927; s. William Oswald and Iva Catherine (Wildfang) H.; m. Vera Cecilia Eck, Sept. 12, 1947; children: Margaret Catherine, Carol Elizabeth, Richard Albert. B.S. in Bus, U. Colo., 1950; J.D. magna cum laude (J. Woodall Rogers Sr. Gold medal 1955), So. Meth. U., 1955; LL.M. (William S. Cook fellow 1968), U. Mich., 1969. Bar: Tex. 1955, Okla. 1981. Assoc. Fulbright, Crooker, Freeman, Bates & Jaworski, Houston, 1955-60; lectr. Bates Sch. Law, U. Houston, 1960; assoc. prof. law Baylor U. Law Sch., Waco, Tex., 1960-65; vis. assoc. prof. So. Meth. U. Law Sch., 1965-68; prof. law Tex. Tech U. Law Sch., Lubbock, 1968-71, Paul W. Horn prof., 1972-81, acting dean, 1974-75, dean ad interim, 1980-81; prof. law U. Okla., Norman, 1981-83, Eugene Kuntz prof. oil, gas and natural resources law, 1983-92, Eugne Kuntz prof. emeritus oil, gas & natural resources law, 1992—. Author: The Law of Oil and Gas, 1971, 2d edit., 1983, lawyer's edit., 1983, 3d edit., 1991, West's Texas Forms (Mines and Minerals), 1977, 2d edit., 1991, 85; contbg. editor various law reports, cases and materials. Served with USAAF, 1945-47. Mem. Tex. Bar Assn., Scribes, Order of Coif (faculty), Beta Gamma Sigma. Lutheran. Home: 5000 Old Shepard Pl Apt 518 Plano TX 75093-4402

**HEMINGWAY, WHITLEY MAYNARD,** lawyer; b. Webster City, Iowa, Oct. 21, 1915; s. Max Maynard and Grace B. (Whitley) H.; m. Elsie Mae O'Connor, Feb. 12, 1994; cildren from previouse marriage: John, Susan, Sarah, Frances. BA, U. Iowa, 1936, JD, 1938. Bar: Iowa 1938. Ptnr. Burnstedt & Hemingway, Webster City, 1938-42, Hemingway and predecessor firms, Webster City, 1946—; atty. City of Webster City, 1946-57; jud. commr. 2d Jud. Dist. Iowa, 1965-71. Trustee Morrison Charitable Trust, Webster City, 1953—; trustee, treas. Kendall Young Libr., Webster City, 1958-79. Lt. USN, 1942-46, ETO. Mem. ABA, Iowa Bar Assn., Hamilton County Bar Assn., Rotary, Elks, Webster City Country Club. Republican. Avocations: golf, motorcycles. Probate, Real property, Personal income taxation. Office: Hemingway Law Offices 741 2nd St Webster City IA 50595-1436

**HEMLEBEN, SCOTT P.,** lawyer; b. Floral Park, N.Y., Nov. 18, 1943; s. Sylvester John and Mary Ruth (Bingham) H.; m. Suzanne Whatley, Aug. 4, 1973; children: Sarah Elizabeth, Mark Elliott, John Parker, Joseph Scott. BAE, U. Miss., 1964, JD, 1967. Bar: Miss. 1967, U.S. Dist. Ct. (so. dist.) Miss. 1969, U.S. Ct. Appeals (5th cir.) 1985, U.S. Supreme Ct. 1971. Law clk. to chief justice Miss. Supreme Ct., Jackson, 1967-68; from assoc. to ptnr. Wells, Gerald, Brand, Watters & Cox, Jackson, 1968-77; ptnr. Gerald, Brand, Watters, Cox & Hemleben, 1977-90, Gerald & Brand, 1990—; bd. dirs. Mid-Continent Oil and Gas Assn.; gov.'s rep. to Interstate Oil and Gas Compact Commn., 1992—. Fellow Miss. Bar Found.; mem. Hinds County Bar Assn. (pres. 1987-88), Miss. Bar Assn. (chmn. natural resources sect. 1989-90), Miss. Oil and Gas Lawyers Assn. (pres. 1973-74). Avocation: saltwater fishing. Federal civil litigation, Environmental, Administrative and regulatory. Home: 43 Avery Cir Jackson MS 39211-2403 Office: Gerald & Brand Ste 900 One Jackson Pl Jackson MS 39201

**HEMPSTEAD, GERARD FRANCIS,** lawyer; b. St. Louis, Feb. 20, 1944; s. Edward James and Helen Amelia (Ebeling) H.; m. Kathryn Elizabeth Yoch, Aug. 17, 1967; children: Helen, Gerard, Christopher. BA in Classics, St. Louis U., 1965, JD, 1968. Bar: Mo. 1969, U.S. Dist. Ct. (ea. dist.) Mo.

1970, U.S. Ct. Appeals (8th cir.) 1971, U.S. Ct. Appeals (7th cir.) 1982. Assoc. Evans and Dixon, St. Louis, 1969-75, Susman, Stern, St. Louis, 1975-80, Suelthaus & Kaplan, P.C., St. Louis, 1980—. Bd. dirs. Sacred Heart Program, Inc., 1988—, United Way Allocations Com., 1984-86; mem. devel. bd. Cardinal Glennon Children's Hosp., 1988—. With USAR, 1968-74. Mem. ABA (gen. practice sect., vice-chmn. litigation com. 1987—, chmn. trial sect. 1988-89, Merit award 1976), Bar Assn. St. Louis. Republican. Roman Catholic. Federal civil litigation, Personal injury, Environmental. Office: Suelthaus & Kaplan PC 7733 Forsyth Blvd Fl 12 Saint Louis MO 63105-1817

**HENCK, CHARLES SEYMOUR,** lawyer; b. Knoxville, Apr. 28, 1947; s. F. Seymour and Martha M. Henck; m. Christine Gorenflo Henck, June 16, 1973; children: Stephanie, Alison. BA, Emory Coll., 1969, JD, 1975; LLM, Georgetown U., 1979. Bar: Ga. 1975, U.S. Tax Ct. 1979, D.C. 1979. Atty. Office of Chief Counsel IRS, Washington, 1975-79; assoc. Ballard Spahr Andrews & Ingersoll, Washington, 1980-84, ptnr., 1984—. Fellow Am. Coll. Bond Counsel; mem. ABA, Nat. Assn. Bond Lawyers (bd. dirs. 1992-94). Taxation, general, Municipal (including bonds), Finance. Office: Ballard Spahr Andrews & Ingersoll LLP 601 13th St NW Ste 1000S Washington DC 20005-3882

**HENDERSON, ALBERT JOHN,** federal judge; b. Canton, Ga., Dec. 12, 1920; s. Albert Jefferson and Cliffie Mae (Cook) H.; m. Jenny Lee Medford, Feb. 24, 1951; children—Michael John, Jenny Lee. LL.B., Mercer U., 1947. Bar: Ga. bar 1947. Practiced law Marietta, Ga., 1948-60; judge Juvenile Ct. Cobb County, Ga., 1953-60, Superior Ct. Cobb County, 1961-68, U.S. Dist. Ct. for No. Dist. Ga., Atlanta, 1968-76; chief judge U.S. Dist. Ct. for No. Dist. Ga., 1976-79; judge U.S. Circuit Ct. of Appeals for 5th Circuit, 1979-81; judge U.S. Circuit Ct. Appeals for 11th Circuit, 1981-86, sr. judge, 1986-99; asst. solicitor gen. Blue Ridge Jud. Circuit, 1948-52. Chmn. Cobb dist. Atlanta council Boy Scouts Am., 1964. Served with AUS, 1943-46. Fellow Am. Bar Found.; mem. ABA, FBA, Am. Judicature Soc., State Bar Ga., Atlanta Bar Assn., Cobb Jud. Bar Assn., Lawyers Club Atlanta, Old War Horse Lawyers Club. Office: US Ct Appeals 11th Circuit 56 Forsyth St NW Atlanta GA 30303-2205 *Died May 11, 1999.*

**HENDERSON, CAROL,** lawyer; b. Smithtown, N.Y., Apr. 11, 1956; d. Harold John and Mary A. (Rogers) Henderson; m. Craig Trocino, 1995. BA, U. Fla., 1976; JD, George Washington U., 1980. Bar: Fla. 1981, U.S. Dist. Ct. (so. dist.) Fla. 1986, U.S. Supreme Ct. 1986. Spl. asst. U.S Atty's. Office, Washington, 1981-84, asst. U.S. atty., 1984-85; sr. litigation assoc. Finley, Kumble, Wagner, Heine, Underberg, Manley, Myerson & Casey, Miami, Fla., 1985-86; vis. prof. Nova Southeastern U. Law Sch., Ft. Lauderdale, Fla., 1986-87, asst. prof., 1987-90, assoc. prof., 1990-91, prof., 1991—; rsch. analyst U.S. Bur. Prisons, Miami, Washington, 1976-77; law clk. criminal div. Dept. Justice, 1977-80; adj. prof. The Am. U., Washington, 1981-85; guest lectr. The Nat. Law Ctr. George Washington U., 1983-85; spl. master Broward County Cir. Ct., Ft. Lauderdale, 1988. Co-author: Investigation for Determination of Fact, 1988, Scientific Evidence in Civil and Criminal Cases, 1995; contbr. articles to profl. jours; appeared on CBS 48 Hours, 1999. Named Cyril Wecht Dist. Lectr. in legal medicine Am. Coll. Legal Medicine, 1999. Fellow Am. Acad. Forensic Scis. (bd. dirs. 1995-98, program co-chmn. jurisprudence sect. 1989, sec., 1990, chairperson, 1991, Jurisprudence Sect. Harold A. Feder award 1999); mem. ATLA, NACDL (forensic evidence com.). Episcopalian. Avocation: gardening. Criminal. Office: Nova U Law Sch 3305 College Ave Fort Lauderdale FL 33314-7721

**HENDERSON, DAN FENNO,** lawyer, law educator; b. Chelan, Wash., May 24, 1921; s. Joe and Edna (Fenno) H.; m. Carol Drake Hardin, Sept. 14, 1957; children: Louis, Karen, Gail, Fenno. AB, Whitman Coll., 1944, LLD, 1983; AB, U. Mich., 1945; JD, Harvard U., 1949; PhD in Polit. Sci. U. Calif., Berkeley, 1955. Bar: Wash. 1949, Korea 1954, Japan 1955, Calif. 1956. Movie, radio censor U.S. Dept. Def., Japan, 1946-47; teaching asst. polit. sci. dept. U. Calif., Berkeley, 1949-51; atty. firm Little, LeSourd, Palmer & Scott, Seattle, 1951-52; instr. ext. div. U. Calif., Berkeley, 1952-54; atty. firm Graham James & Rolph, San Francisco, 1955-57; ptnr. Graham James & Rolph, Tokyo, 1957-62; prof. law, dir. Asian Law Program U. Wash. Sch. Law, 1962-91; prof. law Hastings. Coll. U. Calif., San Francisco, 1991—; ptnr. firm Adachi, Henderson, Miyatake and Fujita, Tokyo, 1973-91; of counsel Graham and James/Riddell Williams, Seattle, 1990-97; vis. prof. law Harvard U., 1968-69, Monash U., Melbourne, Australia, 1979, Cambridge (Eng.) U., 1980, U. Melbourne, 1988, Beijing U., 1988, Erasmus U., The Netherlands, 1989, Duke U., 1990, U. Calif., Hastings, 1991, Washington U., St. Louis, 1993, U. Tokyo, 1994, U. Hawaii, 1999; cons. Asia Found., 1967-92, Battelle Inst., 1969-92. Author: Conciliation and Japanese Law, 1965, The Constitution of Japan, Its First Twenty Years, 1969, Foreign Enterprise in Japan, 1973, Village Contracts in Tokugawa, Japan, 1975, Law and Legal Process in Japan, 2d edit., 1988, Civil Procedure in Japan, 1981, 2d edit., 1985; contbr. articles to profl. jours. Trustee Seattle Art Mus., 1975-95, Blakemore Found., 1998—; overseer Whitman Coll., 1985—. Served to lt. AUS, 1943-46. Investment fellow Am. Soc. Internat. Law, 1962-64. Mem. Internat. Acad. Comparative Law, Internat. Acad. Comml. and Consumer Law, Am. C. of C. Japan (past sec., dir.), Japanese-Am. Soc. Legal Studies (pres.), Am. Assn. Comparative Study of Law (dir.), Hastings 65 Club, Bohemian Club (San Francisco), Rainier Club, Univ. Club (Seattle), Tokyo Lawn Tennis Club. Admiralty, General corporate. Home: 530 McGilvra Blvd E Seattle WA 98112-5048 Office: Hastings Law Coll 200 Mcallister St San Francisco CA 94102-4707

**HENDERSON, DAVID ALLEN,** lawyer; b. Japan, Feb. 18, 1948; s. Frank David and Pauline Elizabeth (Patton) H. BA, Miami U., Oxford, Ohio, 1970; LLB, U. Cin., 1974. Bar: Calif. 1974, U.S. Ct. Appeals (9th cir.) 1975, U.S. Dist. Ct. (no. dist.) Calif. 1976, U.S. Dist. Ct. (ea. dist.) Calif. 1978, U.S. Supreme Ct. 1978, D.C. 1980, N.Y. 1981, U.S. Ct. Appeals (D.C. cir.) 1982, Ariz. 1983, U.S. Dist. Ct. Ariz. 1983, U.S. Dist. Ct. (no., cen., and we. dists.) Tex. 1996. Law clk. to presiding justice U.S. Ct. Appeals (9th cir.), San Diego, 1974-75; adj. prof. U. San Diego Coll. Law, 1975; assoc. Pillsbury, Madison & Sutro, San Francisco, 1975-79, Chadbourn, Park, Whiteside & Wolfe, N.Y.C. and Washington, 1981-82; dep. gen. counsel Pres.'s Council on Wage and Price Stability, Washington, 1979-81; ptnr. Brown & Bain, Phoenix and Palo Alto, Calif., 1983-93, Fish & Richardson, Menlo Park, Calif., 1993-95, Jenkens & Gilchrist, Dallas, 1995—; mem. adv. bd. St. Francis Meml. Hosp., 1978—, Ctr. Nat. Policy, Washington, 1981—, Corp. Pub. Broadcasting, Washington, 1969-70; counsel to Alfred Kahn, inflation advisor to Pres., Washington, 1979-81; superior ct. judge pro tem Maricopa County, Ariz. Editor in chief U. Cin. Law Rev., Jour. World Intellectual Property and Trade Forum. Mem. ABA (litigation and anti-trust sects.), Order of Coif, St. Francis Yacht Club (San Francisco). Avocations: sailing, horseback riding, competitive skiing. Federal civil litigation, Intellectual property, Patent. Office: Jenkens & Gilchrist 1445 Ross Ave Ste 3200 Dallas TX 75202-2799

**HENDERSON, EUGENE LEROY,** lawyer; b. Columbus, Ind., July 21, 1925; s. Harry E. and Verna (Guffey) H.; m. Mary Louise Beatty, Sept. 6, 1948; children: Andrew, Joseph, Carrie Henderson Walkup. BA, Franklin Coll., 1950; JD, Harvard U., 1953. Bar: Ind. 1953. Assoc. Baker & Daniels, Indpls., 1953-59, ptnr., 1959-65; sr. ptnr. Henderson, Daily, Withrow & DeVoe, Indpls., 1965—; bd. dirs. Pinnacle Tech., Inc., Maplehurst Farms, PHD Venture Capital Corp., Periculum Capital Co., LLC; bd. advisors BMT Corp. Mem. Ind. State Bd. Edn., 1984-89; gen. counsel Franklin Coll., Igo Family Found., Lacy Found.; pres., bd. dirs. Branigin Found., Indpls. Athletic Club Art Found.; mem. Indpls. Mus. Art. With U.S. Maritime Svc., 1943-44, AUS, 1944-46. Fellow Ind. Bar Found.; mem. ABA, Am. Arbitration Assn., Ind. Bar Assn., Indpls. Bar Assn., Internat. Law Assn., Indpls. Athletic Club, Venture Club, Lawyers Club, Econ. Club, Rotary. Democrat. General corporate, Mergers and acquisitions, Insurance. Home: 6225 Sunset Ln Indianapolis IN 46260-4705 Office: Henderson Daily Withrow & Devoe 2600 One Indiana Sq Indianapolis IN 46204

**HENDERSON, HELENA NAUGHTON,** legal association administrator; b. New Orleans, Mar. 19, 1956; d. John Francis and Helen Naughton; div.; children: William Henry Henderson, Kevin Richard Henderson. BS in Psychology, Harvard U., 1976, Newcomb Coll, 1978; postgrad., Tulane U., 1990—. Exec. dir. New Orleans Bar Assn.; chair Subcom. to Establish La. Women's Commn. on Policy and Rsch., 1998-99, Juvenile Law Conf. for La., 1999. Bd. dirs. La. Ctr. for Law-Related Edn., New Orleans, 1992—, New Orleans Police Found., 1996—, Voices for Children, 1997—, Voice for Children, 1997—. Mem. ABA (assoc.), Am. Soc. Assn. Execs., Nat. Assn. Bar Execs. (chair strategic planning com. 1996-98), Nat. Ctr. for Nonprofit Bds. Office: New Orleans Bar Assn 228 Saint Charles Ave Ste 1223 New Orleans LA 70130-2643

**HENDERSON, JAMES FORNEY,** lawyer; b. Bloomington, Ill., Oct. 10, 1921; s. Ernest James and Helen Darlene (Forney) H.; m. Shirley May Lawson, June 10, 1943 (div. Oct. 1979); children: James Dale, Helen Diane, Lynda Joanne; m. Sonja Ramona Hayward, Nov. 8, 1979. BS, Northwestern U., 1943, JD, 1948. Bar: Ill. 1948, Ariz. 1949, U.S. Dist. Ct. Ariz. 1950, U.S. Ct. Appeals (9th cir.) 1954. Assoc., ptnr. Gust, Rosenfeld & Henderson, Phoenix, 1950-92; ptnr. Scult, French, Zwillinger & Smock, Phoenix, 1992-95, Morrison & Hecker, Phoenix, 1995—; counsel mem. Libel Def. Resource Ctr., N.Y.C., 1989—. Bd. dirs. Samaritan Health Svcs., 1974-92. Lt. USN, 1943-46. Recipient Disting. Svc. award Ariz. Press Club 1986, First Amendment Rights award Sigma Delta Chi 1980-81. Mem. ABA, Def. Rsch. Inst., Fedn. Corp. and Ins. Counsel, Ill. Bar Assn., Ariz. Bar Assn., Ariz. Assn. Def. Counsel. Communications, General civil litigation, Constitutional. Office: Morrison & Hecker 2800 N Central Ste 1600 Phoenix AZ 85004-1047

**HENDERSON, JANICE ELIZABETH,** law librarian; b. N.Y.C., Dec. 22, 1952; d. James and Adeline M. (Fitzgerald) H. BA in Psychology, Hunter Coll., 1974; MS in Spl. Edn., CUNY, 1979; MS in Library Sci., Pratt Inst., 1980; JD, Bklyn. Law Sch., 1986. Law librarian Morgan, Lewis & Bockius, N.Y.C., 1977-83; reference librarian Weil, Gotshal & Manges, N.Y.C., 1983-85; law librarian Tenzer, Greenblatt et. al., N.Y.C., 1985-86, Robinson, Silverman et. al., N.Y.C., 1986-88, Kirkland & Ellis, N.Y.C., 1991-93; assoc. law libr. prof. CUNY Law Sch., N.Y.C., 1989-91; dir. libr. svcs. Epstein, Becker & Green, P.C., 1993-98; dir. profl. devel. and libr. svcs. Baker & McKenzie, 1998—; assoc. adj. prof. Sch. Libr. and Info. Sci., St. John's U., N.Y.C., 1990-93. Book reviewer Legal Info. Alert newsletter, 1984-86. Mem. Am. Assn. Law Librs., Law Libr. Assn. Greater N.Y. (advt. mgr. 1986-89, bd. dirs. 1989-90, mem. MCLE com. 1990-92, co-chair 1992-94, v.p. 1995-96, pres. 1996-97, immediate past pres. 1997-98. Democrat. Roman Catholic. Home: PO Box 020196 Brooklyn NY 11202-0196

**HENDERSON, JOAN BLUST,** lawyer, educator, writer, mediator; b. Paterson, N.J., July 7, 1936; d. Vincent M. and Ellen Kennedy (Adams) Blust; m. J. Eber henderson, June 26, 1959 (div. 1976); children: Ian Scott, Heather Jo. BA, Cedar Crest Coll., 1958; MA, U. Louisville, 1967; JD, 1978. Bar: Ind. 1979, U.S. Dist. Ct. (so. dist.) Ind. 1979, U.S. Supreme Ct. 1988. Tchr. New Providence (N.J.) Sch., 1960-61, Army Sch., Ft. Campbell, Ky., 1961-62; tchr. chronically ill Louisville Pub. Schs., 1962-65; exec. dir. Rauch Ctr. Handicapped, New Albany, Ind., 1965-72; instr. Webster U. Jeffersonville Campus, St. Louis, 1983; dept. chmn. health svcs. mgmt., 1988—; sole practice Jeffersonville, Ind., 1979—; lectr. various orgns. Author: A Good Worker, 1971, A Good Citizen, 1973, A Good Neighbor, 1976. Mem. adv. com. on child abuse Clark County Welfare, Jeffesonville, 1980-84; edn. com. ARC, Louisville, 1982—. Recipient Jeffersonville United to Make Progress Bus. aard, 1985. Mem. Am. Bus. Women's Assn. (Jeffersonville chpt.), Ind. Bar Assn., Clark County Bar Assn., Assn. Trial Lawyers Am., Kappa Delta Pi, Phi Alpha Delta. Personal injury. Home: 400 E Terrace Hts Jeffersonville IN 47130-4720 Office: 521 E 7th St Jeffersonville IN 47130-4031

**HENDERSON, JOE H.,** lawyer, mediator, arbitrator, college dean; b. Pangburn, Ark., Apr. 14, 1936; s. John H. and Nancy L. (Johnston) H.; m. Marian Jones, July 31, 1965 (div. Feb. 1978); 1 child, James H.; m. Linda Gaye Bertucelli, Mar. 21, 1981; stepchildren: Jason, Daniel. BA in Pub. Adminstrn., Calif. State U., Sacramento, 1960; JD, Lincoln U., 1968. Bar: Calif. 1971. Budget and mgmt. analyst Sacramento County, 1960-64; asst. dir. pub. works Marin County, San Rafael, Calif., 1964-66; asst. city mgr. City of Santa Rosa (Calif.), 1966-71; dean sch. of law Empire Coll., Santa Rosa, 1989-97; pvt. practice Santa Rosa, 1971-97; arbitrator, mediator, 1972—. Recipient 1 of 7200 Best Attys. in U.S. award Steven Naifeh & Gregory White Smith, 1987. Mem. Nat. Acad. Arbitrators. Avocation: fishing. Fax: 707-573-1322. E-mail: joehh@sonic.net. Office: PO Box 463 Santa Rosa CA 95402-0463

**HENDERSON, KAREN LECRAFT,** federal judge; b. 1944. BA, Duke U., 1966; JD, U. N.C., 1969. Ptnr. Wright & Henderson, Chapel Hill, N.C., 1969-70, Sinkler, Gibbs & Simons, P.A., Columbia, S.C., 1983-86; asst. atty. gen. Columbia, 1973-78; sr. asst. atty. gen., dir. of spl. litigation sect., 1978-82, deputy atty. gen., dir. of criminal div., 1982; judge U.S. Dist. Ct. S.C., Columbia, 1986-90, U.S. Ct. Appeals (D.C. cir.), Washington, 1990—. Apptd. Dist. Ct. Adv. Com. Mem. ABA (litigation sect. and urban, state and local government law sect.), N.C. Bar Assn., S.C. Bar (government law sect., trial and appellate practice sect., fed. judges assn.). Office: US Ct Appeals DC Cir US Courthouse 333 Constitution Ave NW Washington DC 20001-2802*

**HENDERSON, KELLY JAMES,** lawyer; b. Wausau, Wis.; s. Robert C.B. Henderson; m. Adrienne Rabinowitz, May 27, 1991; children: Logan James, Hayley Rose. BA in Philosophy, U. Wis., 1977; JD, Nova-Southeastern Law Sch., Ft. Lauderdale, Fla., 1993. Bar: Fla. 1993, U.S. Dist. Ct. (so. dist.) Fla. 1994, U.S. Dist. Ct. (mid. dist.) Fla. 1995, U.S. Ct. Appeals (11th cir.) 1995; cert. in money market trading; cert. mediator. Trial atty. U.S. EEOC, Miami, Fla., 1994—. Mem. ABA (labor and employment law sect.), Am. Inns of Ct. Office: US EEOC 2 S Biscayne Blvd Ste 2700 Miami FL 33131-1804

**HENDERSON, MARK GORDY,** lawyer; b. Berkeley, Calif., Feb. 21, 1954; s. John Nelson and Shirley Belle (Queen) H.; m. Elizabeth Andrea Fulmer, June 24, 1978; children: Emily MacCaughey, James Ellis. BA, U. of the Pacific, 1976, JD, 1981, LLM in Bus. and Tax, 1985. Bar: Calif. 1981, U.S. Ct. Appeals (9th cir.) 1985, U.S. Dist. Ct. (ctrl. dist.) Calif. 1988, U.S. Dist. Ct. (ea. dist.) Calif. 1992; cert. specialist in estate planning, trust and probate law. Ptnr. Hiroshima, Jacobs & Roth, Sacramento, 1981-91; pvt. practice law Davis, Calif., 1991—. Exec. dir. Citizens Who Care, Inc., Davis. Mem. Calif. State Bar Assn. (estate planning, trust and probate law sect.), Yolo County Bar Assn., Order of the Coif. Probate, Estate planning, General civil litigation. Office: PO Box 73914 Davis CA 95617-3914

**HENDERSON, STEPHEN PAUL,** lawyer; b. Oakland, Calif., July 14, 1949; s. Carl Edward and Esther Minnie (Miller) H.; m. Josephine Ann Bartlett. BA, Wash. State U., 1971; JD, U. Oreg., 1974; LLM, NYU, 1978. Bar: Oreg. 1974, U.S. Ct. Mil. Appeals 1978, U.S. Tax Ct. 1979, U.S. Ct. Appeals (9th cir.) 1979, U.S. Ct. Appeals (6th cir.) 1990, U.S. Supreme Ct. 1979. Atty. GE Credit Corp., Providence, 1979-81; dept. counsel GE, Schenectady, N.Y., 1981-83; operation counsel GE, Atlanta, 1983-86, divsn. counsel, 1987-89; divsn. counsel GE Aircraft Engines, Cin., 1990-97; gen. counsel GE Engine Svcs., Inc., Cin., 1998—. Editor U. Oreg. Law Rev., 1972-73. Nat. Merit scholar, 1967. Mem. ABA, Oreg. Bar Assn., Ohio Bar Assn., Cin. Bar Assn., Corp. Counsel Assn. of Atlanta Bar Assn., Fed. Bar Assn., Horseshoe Bend Country Club, Phi Beta Kappa, Phi Kappa Phi, Phi Eta Sigma. Republican. Episcopalian. Mergers and acquisitions, General corporate, Private international. Office: GE 1 Neumann Way # F17 Cincinnati OH 45215-1915

**HENDERSON, SUSAN ELLEN FORTUNE,** lawyer, educator; b. Bluefield, W.Va., Dec. 21, 1957; d. William Edward and Gladys Ellen (Scott) Fortune. Student, Randolph-Macon Woman's Coll., 1976-78; BS summa cum laude, Bluefield State Coll., 1986; JD cum laude, Washington & Lee U., 1994. Bar: Va. 1994, W.Va. 1995. Legal sec., paralegal, office mgr. Katz, Kantor & Perkins, Bluefield, 1979-86; paralegal, office mgr. David Burton, Atty. at Law, Princeton, W.Va., 1986-91; assoc. Burton & Kilgore, Princeton, W.Va., 1994-95; sole practice Bluefield, 1995-97; instr. Bluefield State Coll., 1996-98; ptnr. Henderson & Fuda, 1997—; tchr. Legal Learning Inst., Manassas, Va., 1995-96. Nat. Merit scholar, 1976, Disting. scholar Randolph-Macon Woman's Coll., 1976, Law scholar Washington & Lee U., 1991. Mem. ABA, ATLA, W.Va. Trial Lawyers Assn., Va. Trial Lawyers Assn., Main St. Bluefield Bd. of Dirs. Avocations: tennis, skiing, music, reading, landscaping. Criminal, General civil litigation, General practice. Home: 6 Oak Ln Bluefield WV 24701-4741 Office: Henderson & Fuda 3107 E Cumberland Rd Bluefield WV 24701-4960

**HENDERSON, THELTON EUGENE,** federal judge; b. Shreveport, La., Nov. 28, 1933; s. Eugene M. and Wanzie (Roberts) H.; 1 son, Geoffrey A. B.A., U. Calif.-, Berkeley, 1956, J.D., 1962. Bar: Calif. 1962. Atty. U.S. Dept. Justice, 1962-63; assoc. firm FitzSimmons & Petris, 1964, assoc., 1964-66; directing atty. San Mateo County (Calif.) Legal Aid Soc., 1966-69; asst. dean Stanford (Calif.) U. Law Sch., 1968-76; ptnr. firm Rosen, Remcho & Henderson, San Francisco, 1977-80; judge U.S. Dist. Ct. (no. dist.) Calif., San Francisco, 1980-90, 98—, chief judge, 1990-97; asso. prof. Sch. Law, Golden Gate U., San Francisco, 1978-80. Served with U.S. Army, 1956-58. Mem. ABA, Nat. Bar Assn., Charles Houston Law Assn. Office: US Dist Ct US Courthouse PO Box 36060 San Francisco CA 94102

**HENDERSON, THOMAS HENRY, JR.,** lawyer, legal association executive; b. Birmingham, Ala., Feb. 4, 1939; s. Thomas Henry and Edna (Green) H.; m. Elaine Dauphin (div. 1983); children: Ashley, Michelle; m. Paulette Maehara, June 1988. BSBA, Auburn U., 1961; JD, U. Ala., 1966; LLM, Nat. Law Ctr., George Washington U., 1977. Bar: D.C. 1970, Ala. 1966. Trial atty. organized crime and racketeering sect. U.S. Dept. Justice, Washington, 1966-70, dep. sect. chief mgmt. labor sect., 1970-73; dep. chief counsel, subcom. on adminstrn. practice and procedure U.S. Senate, Washington, 1973-74; dep. sect. chief mgmt. and labor sect. Dept. Justice, Washington, 1974-76, chief pub. integrity sect., 1976-80, sr. counsel criminal div., 1980-83; bar counsel D.C. Ct. Appeals, Washington, 1983-87; exec. dir. ATLA, Washington, 1988—. Columnist Bar Counsels Page, Washington Lawyer mag., bi-monthly, 1983-87. Pres. Christmas in April, Washington, 1986-87. Mem. Am. Soc. Assn. Execs. (bd. dirs. 1994-97, vice chair 1997-98), Omicron Delta Kappa. Avocations: golf, skiing, fitness, outdoor adventure. Home: 6698 Glenbrook Rd Chevy Chase MD 20815-6515 Office: ATLA 1050 31st St NW Washington DC 20007-4409

**HENDLER, MICHAEL G.,** lawyer; b. Balt., May 16, 1942; s. Nathan and Mrs. Hendler; m. Royce Hendler; children: Andrea G., Eileen B. Fox. BA, U. Md., College Park, 1963; JD, U. Md., Balt., 1965. Bar: Md. 1965. Staff atty. Legal Aid Bur., Balt., 1965-66; assoc. Adelberg, adelberg & Rudow, Balt., 1967-74; ptnr., mem. Adelberg, Rudow, orf Hendler & Sameth, LLC, Balt., 1974—. Pres. Box 414 Assn., Inc., Balt., 197678; patrol dir. Nat. Ski Patrol, 1983-85. Fellow Am. Acd. Matrimonial Lawyers (v.p. 1997-99, bd. govs. 1998—). Family and matrimonial. Office: Adelberg Rudow et al 2 Hopkins Plz Ste 600 Baltimore MD 21201-2908

**HENDREN, JIMM LARRY,** federal judge; b. 1940. BA, U. Ark., 1964, LLB, 1965. With Little & Enfield, 1968-69; pvt. practice Bentonville, Ark., 1970-77, 79-92; chancellor, probate judge Ark. 16th Chancery Dist., 1977-78; chief judge U.S. Dist. Ct. We. Dist., Ark., 1997—. Served to lt. comdr. JAGC, USN, 1965-70, USNR, 1970-83. Mem. ABA, Ark. Bar Assn. Office: US Dist Ct PO Box 3487 Fayetteville AR 72702-3487

**HENDRICK, BENARD CALVIN, VII,** lawyer; b. Odessa, Tex., Oct. 7, 1964; s. Benard Calvin IV and Marita Hendrick; m. Amy Camille Weatherby, Nov. 17, 1990; children: Benard Calvin VIII, Kaitlin Camille. BBA summa cum laude, Angelo State U., San Angelo, Tex., 1987; JD, U. Tex., 1990. Bar: Tex. 1990, U.S. Dist. Ct. (ea., we. and no. dists.) Tex. 1991, U.S. Ct. Appeals (5th cir.) 1995. Assoc. Shafer, Davis, Ashley, O'Leary & Stoker, Odessa, 1990-92, ptnr., 1992—. Bd. dirs. Permian Basin Rehab. Ctr., Odessa, 1992-97, Crystal Ball Found., Odessa, 1993-96; elder First Christian Ch., Odessa, 1995-98. Fellow Tex. Bar Found.; mem. Tex. Assn. Def. Counsel (bd. dirs. 1998—), State Bar Tex., Ector County Bar Assn. (pres. 1998—), Ector County Young Lawyers Assn. (pres. 1995), Def. Rsch. Inst. Republican. Mem. Christian Ch. (Disciples of Christ). Avocations: hunting, fishing, karate. Personal injury, Insurance, General civil litigation. Home: 6201 Montana Ave Odessa TX 79762-9350 Office: Shafer Davis Ashley O'Leary & Stoker 700 N Grant Ave Ste 201 Odessa TX 79761-4576

**HENDRICKS, JAMES W.,** lawyer, real estate executive; b. Palisades, Park, N.J., Mar. 31, 1924; s. William R. and Grace W. (Womack) H.; m. Frances E. Earls, Feb. 24, 1945; children: Rickey Lynn, Janet Leigh, Barbara Louise, James W. Jr. BS, Ohio State U., 1947; JD, Columbia U., 1949. Bar: Ky. 1949. Assoc. Bullitt, Dawson & Tarrant, Louisville, 1949-54; ptnr. Marshall, Cochran, Heyburn & Wells, Louisville, 1957-67; individual practice law, Louisville, 1968—; owner Holiday Inn, Key Largo, Fla., African Queen; ptnr. Holiday Manor, Inc.; pres. Key Largo Holiday Harbour, Key Largo Marine Tours and related cos. Served with USMC, 1943-46. Fellow Am. Bar Found. (life); mem. ABA, Ky. Bar Assn., Louisville Bar Assn., Am. Judicature Soc. Presbyterian. Clubs: Ocean Reef, Harmony Landing, Cat Cay, Jefferson, Louisville Boat, Key Largo Angler's. Real property. Home: 49 Spadefish Ln Key Largo FL 33037-5226 Office: 6401 Upper River Rd Harrods Creek KY 40027

**HENDRICKS, NATHAN VANMETER, III,** lawyer; b. Decatur, Ga., Dec. 16, 1943; s. Nathan VanMeter and Ella L. (Ward) H.; B.A., Washington and Lee U., 1966, LL.B., 1969; m. Kathryn A. Barnes, Aug. 19, 1972; children—Nathan VanMeter, Seaton Grantland. Bar: Ga. 1970. Practiced in Atlanta, 1969—; assoc. firm Swift, Currie, McGhee and Hiers, 1969-70, Henning, Chambers and Mabry, 1970-71; asso. firm Redfern, Butler and Morgan, 1971-73, partner, 1973-77; partner firm Cobb, Hyre, Hendricks & Ferguson, Atlanta, 1978—. Chmn. Younger Lawyers Com. Campaign for mayor, Atlanta, 1972, re-election campaign for chmn. of Fulton County Bd. Commnrs., 1986; active host com. 1988 Dem. Nat. Conv. Mem. High Mus. of Art, group leader ann. fund-raising campaign, 1973-75, chmn. young careers group, 1972-73, sec. young men's round table, 1974-75; active ann. fund raising campaign Atlanta Symphony Orch. Assn., 1977-78, Atlanta Arts Alliance, 1977-79, Atlanta Botanical Garden, 1986-88; bd. dirs. Atlanta Hunter-Jumper Classic, 1978-79, pres., 1979; bd. dirs. Save America's Vital Environment, sec., 1971-74; bd. dirs. Merrie-Woode Found., v.p., 1978-79, chmn., pres., 1981—, exec. com. Give Wildlife a Chance fund Ga. Dept. Natural Resources, 1988. Mem. Am., Atlanta (mem. real estate sect. 1972—, com. 1978) bar assns., State Bar of Ga. (mem. real estate sect. 1972—), Lawyers Club Atlanta, Washington and Lee U. Alumni Assn. (dir. 1972—, pres. Atlanta chpt. 1973-75), Beta Theta Pi, Phi Delta Phi. Episcopalian. Clubs: Ansley Golf, Piedmont Driving, Wildcat Cliffs Country, The Nine O'Clocks, Pan Tex. Assembly, N.C. Soc. of the Cincinnati. Home: 230 The Prado NE Atlanta GA 30309-3336 Office: 6085 Lake Forrest Dr NW Ste 200 Atlanta GA 30328-3846

**HENDRICKS, RANDAL ARLAN,** lawyer; b. Kansas City, Mo., Nov. 18, 1945; s. Clinton H. and Edith T. (Anderson) H.; m. Suann Rose, June 1, 1965 (div. 1976); children: Kristin Lee, Daehne Lynn; m. Jill Edith Duke, Mar. 22, 1982; 1 child, Bret Larson-Hendricks. Student, U. Mo.-Kansas City, 1963-65; BS with honors, U. Houston, 1968, JD with honors, 1970. Bar: Tex. 1970, U.S. Dist. (so. dist.) Tex. 1970, U.S. Tax Ct. 1985. Assoc. Baker & Botts, Houston, 1970-71; pvt. practice, Houston, 1971—; ptnr. Hendricks Sports Mgmt., Houston, 1977-81; pres. Hendricks Mgmt. Co., Inc., Houston, 1981—. Author: Inside the Strike Zone, 1994. Dir. profl. div. Excellence Campaign, U. Houston, 1971; bd. dirs. Cypress Creek Christian Ch., Spring, Tex., 1979-85; expert witness U.S. Senate Subcom. on Antitrust and Monopoly, 1972; mem. pub. adv. com. Houston/Harris County Sports Facility, 1995-96. Mem. Houston Bar Assn., Assn. Reps. Profl. Athletes (bd. dirs. 1978-88, mem. at large 1978-79, treas. 1979-80, v.p. 1980-81, pres. 1981-82, chmn. ethics com. 1978-80, chmn. baseball com. 1981-88), Sports Lawyers Assn. (bd. dirs. 1992—), Order of Barons (chancellor 1969-70), Phi Kappa Phi, Phi Delta Phi. Sports, Real property, Personal income taxation. Home: 20802 Highet Pl Tomball TX 77375-7042 Office: 400 Randal Way Ste 106 Spring TX 77388-8908

**HENDRICKS, STEPHEN,** lawyer; b. Portland, Oreg., Apr. 6, 1954. BA in History, Cornell U., 1976; JD, U. Oreg., 1979. Bar: Oreg. 1979, U.S. Dist. Ct. Oreg. 1979. Assoc. Martin, Biscloff et al, Portland, Grenley, Rotenburg et al, Portland; pvt. practice Portland. Personal injury, General corporate. Office: 1708 SW Columbia St Portland OR 97201-2539

**HENDRICKSON, GEORGE M.,** prosecutor; b. 1952. BA, U. Calif., Berkeley, 1974; JD, U. of the Pacific, 1977. Bar: Calif. 1977. Dep. dist. atty. Sacramento County Dist. Atty.'s Office, 1978-84; dep. atty. gen. Calif. Atty. Gen.'s Office, Sacramento, 1984—. Author: (manual) People's Remedies, 1986. Office: Attys Gens Office 1300 I St Sacramento CA 95814-2919

**HENDRICKSON, THOMAS ATHERTON,** lawyer; b. Indpls., May 12, 1927; s. Robert Augustus and Eleanor Riggs (Atherton) H.; m. Sandra Bly Shepard, Feb. 6, 1960; children: Thomas Shepard, Heidi Bly, Melanie Parke. BA, Yale U., 1949; LLB, Ind. U., 1952. Bar: Ind. 1952; cert. level II tax assessor-appraiser Ind. Former ptnr. Hendrickson, Travis, Pantzer & Miller. Mem. Indpls. Hist. Preservation Commn., 1982-83; mem. Marion County/Indpls. Hist. Soc., pres., 1984-85; mem. adv. bd. Fund for Landmark Indpls. Properties, 1984-85, Cath. Sem. Found. Indpls., Inc., 1985-94; former Marion County lay rep. planning com. Central Ind. Library Services Authority, recipient Outstanding Service award; former council pres. Indpls. Great Books. Served to lt. (s.g.) USNR, 1945-56. Fellow Ind. Bar Found.; mem. ABA (sect. on taxation, com. on State and local taxation) Ind. State Bar Assn. (taxation sect., ho. of dels. 1971-75, 79-89, asst. editor ABA Property Tax Handbook, author How to Challenge an Indiana Realty Assessment in Interstate Tax Insights, 1992, Indpls. Bar Assn. (taxation sect.), Nat. Tax Assn. (property tax com.), Quality for Ind. Tax Payers, Lawyers' Club, Columbia Club. E-mail address: greycoat@ameritech.net. State and local taxation. Office: 7979 Lantern Rd Indianapolis IN 46256-1827

**HENDRY, ANDREW DELANEY,** lawyer, consumer products company executive; b. N.Y.C., Aug. 9, 1947; s. Andrew Joseph and Virginia (Delaney) H.; 1 child, Robert. AB in Econs., Georgetown U., 1969; JD, NYU, 1972. Bar: N.Y. 1973. Va. 1981, Mich. 1984, Pa. 1987. Assoc. Battle and Fowler, N.Y.C., 1972-79; sr. corp. and fin. atty. Reynolds Metals Co., Richmond, Va., 1979-82; sr. staff counsel Burroughs Corp., Detroit, 1982-83, assoc. gen. coun., 1983-86, dep. gen. counsel, 1986-87; v.p. legal affairs Unisys Corp, Blue Bell, Pa., 1987-88, v.p., gen. counsel, 1988-91; sr. v.p., gen. counsel, sec. Colgate-Palmolive Co., N.Y.C., 1991—. Bd. dirs. Youth Power (formerly Just Say No Internat.), Oakland, Calif., 1994—; dir., chmn., corp. adv. bd. Nat. Legal Aid & Def., Washington, 1992—. With JAGC USAF, 1973. Mem. ABA (corp. gen. counsel, com. chmn. 1996-98, standing com. on substance abuse, com. on corp. laws), Am. Law Inst., Am. Corp. Counsel Assn. (pres. Mich. chpt. 1985, bd. dirs. emeritus N.Y. chpt., chmn. nat. pro bono com. 1985-88), N.Y. Athletic Club. General corporate, Securities, Mergers and acquisitions. Office: Colgate-Palmolive Co 300 Park Ave New York NY 10022-7499

**HENDRY, JOHN,** state supreme court justice; b. Omaha, Aug. 23, 1948. BS, U. Nebr., 1970, JD, 1974. Pvt. practice Licoln, 1974-1995; county ct. judge 3d Jud. Dist., 1995-98; chief justice Nebr. Supreme Ct., 1998—. Office: Rm 2214 State Capitol Lincoln NE 68509*

**HENDRY, NANCY H.,** lawyer; b. Beijing, China, Jan. 28, 1949; m. William Joseph Baer, 1979; two children. BA, Radcliff Coll., Cambridge, MA, 1970; J.D., Stanford U Law Sch., CA, 1975. Vol. Peace Corps, Senegal, 1970-72; Assoc. Wald Harkrader and Ross, 1975-80; special asst. to the general counsel Dept. of Edn., 1980-81; VP, dep. general counsel and asst. corp. secy. Public Broadcasting Service, 1981-96; general counsel Peace Corps, 1996—; adjunct prof. Georgetown U Law Sch., Washington, DC, 1989-90. Office: Peace Corps General Counsel 1990 K St NW Washington DC 20526-0002

**HENDRY, ROBERT RYON,** lawyer; b. Jacksonville, Fla., Apr. 23, 1936; s. Warren Candler and Evalyn Marguerite (Ryon) H.; children by previous marriage: Lorraine Evalyn, Lynette Comstock, Krista Ryon; m. Janet LaCoste. BA in Polit. Sci., U. Fla., 1958, JD, 1963. Bar: Fla. 1963; bd. cert. in internat. law. Assoc. Harrell, Caro, Middlebrooks & Whiltshire, Pensacola, Fla., 1963-66; assoc. Hewlliwell, Melrose & DeWolf, Orlando, Fla., 1966-67, ptnr., 1967-69; ptnr., pres. Hoffman, Hendry, Parker & Smith and predecessor Hoffman, Hendry & Parker, Orlando, 1969-77, Hoffman, Hendry & Stoner and predecessor, Orlando, 1977-82, Hendry, Stoner, Sims & Sawicki, Orlando, 1982-88, Hendry, Stoner, Townsend Sawicki & Brown, 1988-92, Hendry, Stoner, Sawicki & Brown, 1992—. Author: U.S. Real Estate and the Foreign Investor, 1983; contbr. articles to profl. jours. Mem. Dist. Export Coun., 1977-91, vice chmn., 1981, chair, 1995—, mem. nat. steering com., 1997—; bd. dirs. World Trade Ctr. and predecessor, Orlando, 1979-89, pres., 1980-82, 84; chmn. Fla. Gov.'s Conf. on World Trade, 1983; chmn. Fla. coun. on internat. edn., 1993-96; mem. internat. fin. and mktg. adv. bd. U. Miami Sch. Bus., Fla., 1979-90, Commn. on Internat. Edn., 1986-88; mem. Metro Orlando Internat. Bus. Coun., 1994-96, Metro Orlando Internat. Affairs Commn., 1995—, Fla. Econ. Summit, 1996—; mem. internat. trade and econ. devel. bd. and audit com. Enterprise, Fla., 1997—; chmn. Fla. Trade Grant Review Panel, 1998—. Lt. U.S. Army, 1958-60, capt. Army N.G., 1960-70. Mem. Fla. Coun. Internat. Devel. (bd. dirs. 1972-85, chmn. 1977-79, adv. bd. 1985-95, chmn. emeritus, 1991—, vice chair 1995-96, chair 1996-98), Fla. Bar (bd. cert. internat. lawyer 1999—, vice chmn. internat. law com. 1974-75, chmn. com. 1976-77, mem. exec. coun. internat. law sect. 1982—, original internat. law certification com. 1998—), Fla. Assn. Voluntary Agys. for Caribbean Action (bd. dirs. 1987—, pres. 1989-91, past pres. 1991—), Orange County Bar Assn. (treas. 1971-74), Soc. Internat. Bus. Fellows, Brit.-Am. C. of C. (bd. dirs., sec. 1984-85), Swiss Am. C. of C. (sec. Fla. chpt. 1996—), Univ. Club. Private international, General corporate, Real property. Office: Hendry Stoner Sawicki Et Al 200 E Robinson St Ste 500 Orlando FL 32801-1956

**HENEGAN, JOHN C(LARK),** lawyer; b. Mobile, Ala., Oct. 14, 1950; s. Virgil Baker and Marie (Fife) Gunter; m. Morella Lloyd Kuykendall, Aug. 5, 1972; children: Clark, Jim. BA in English and Philosophy, U. Miss., 1972, JD with honors, 1976. Bar: Miss. 1976, U.S. Dist. Ct. (no. dist.) Miss. 1976, N.Y. 1978, U.S. Dist. Ct. (so. dist.) N.Y. 1979, U.S. Ct. Appeals (5th and 11th cirs.) 1982, U.S. Ct. Appeals (2nd cir.) 1984, U.S. Dist. Ct. (so. dist.) Miss. 1984, U.S. Ct. Appeals (fed. cir.) 1995, U.S. Supreme Ct. 1995. Law clk. to judge U.S. Ct. Appeals (5th cir.), N.Y.C., 1976-77; atty. Dewey, Ballantine, Bushby, Palmer & Wood, N.Y.C. and Washington, 1977-81; exec. asst., chief of staff to Gov. William Winter Jackson, Miss., 1981-84; atty. Butler, Snow, O'Mara, Stevens & Cannada, PLLC, Jackson, 1984—; lectr. U. Miss. Ctr. for Continuing Legal Edn., 1985, 87, Miss. Jud. Coll., Oxford, 1982; mem. lawyers adv. com. U.S. Ct. Appeals for 5th Cir. Jud. Conf., 1991-93. Editor-in-chief Miss. Law Jour., 1976; editor Miss. Lawyer, 1985; contbr. articles to legal jours. Bd. dirs. Mississippians for Ednl. Broadcasting, Jackson, 1983-90, North Jackson Youth Baseball, Inc., 1991-97, Ctrl. Miss. Legal Svcs., 1997—; co-pres. Chastain Mid. Sch. Parent Tchrs. Students Assn., 1995-96; mem. Miss. Ethics Commn., Jackson, 1984-87; del. Hinds County Dem. Conv., 1988; mem. Miss. Dem. Fin. Coun., 1988, Hinds County Dem. Exec. Com., 1989-92; Sunday sch. supt. Covenant Presbyn. Ch., 1989-90, elder, 1996—, deacon, 1991-96, moderator of diaconate, 1993-94. Recipient Cmty. Svc. award Hinds County Bar Assn., 1998. Mem. ABA, FBA, Miss. Bar Assn. (chmn. Law Day U.S.A. 1983), Miss. Def. Lawyers Assn., Miss. Law Jour. Alumni Assn. (bd. dirs. 1985—), 5th Cir. Bar Assn., Jackson C. of C., Am. Inns of Ct. (barrister Charles Clark chpt. 1991-93), Phi Kappa Phi, Phi Delta Phi, Omicron Delta Kappa. Avocations: reading, running. Antitrust, Federal civil litigation, Libel. Home: 2441 Eastover Dr Jackson MS 39211-6727 Office: 210 E Capitol St Fl 17 Jackson MS 39201-2307

**HENG, DONALD JAMES, JR.,** lawyer; b. Mpls., July 12, 1944; s. Donald James and Catharine Amelia (Strom) H.; m. Kathleen Ann Bailey, Sept. 2, 1967; 1 child, Francesca Remy. BA cum laude, Yale U., 1967; JD magna cum laude, Minn., 1971. Bar: Calif. 1971, U.S. Dist. Ct. (no. dist.) Calif. 1971, U.S. Ct. Appeals (9th cir.) 1971. Assoc. Brobeck, Phleger & Harrison, San Francisco, 1971-73, ptnr., 1978-90; atty.-adviser Office Internat. Tax Counsel, Dept. Treasury, Washington, 1973-75; pvt. practice law San Francisco, 1990—; lectr., writer on tax-related subjects. Note and comment editor Minn. Law Rev., 1970-71. Co-recipient award for outstanding performance Am. Lawyer Mag., 1981; Fulbright scholar, Italy, 1967-68. Mem. ABA, Calif. Bar Assn., Oakland Mus. Assn. (pres. 1985-87, bd. dirs. 1983-89), Mus. Soc. San Francisco, Fine Arts Mus. (bd. dirs. 1989-90), Order Coif. Republican. Congregationalist. Personal income taxation, Private international. Office: 388 Market St Ste 500 San Francisco CA 94111-5313

**HENG, GERALD C. W.,** lawyer; b. London, Mar. 6, 1941; came to U.S., 1964; s. Chong-Kwai and York-Choo (Eng); m. Eileen B-Y Tang; 1 child, Sharmaine. BS with honors, Harvard U., 1967; LLM in Taxation, Boston U., 1985; LLB, London U., 1973; JD, Suffolk U., 1983. Tchr. Malay and English langs. Ministry of Edn., Malaysia and Singapore, 1959-60; adminstr. hosp. and health Ministry of Health, Malaysia and Singapore, 1960-64; Fulbright fellow, scholar Inst. Internat. Edn., N.Y.C., 1964-69; atty. Heng Assocs., London, 1973-83; ptnr. Heng Assocs., Brookline, Mass., 1983—. Contbr. articles to newspapers including Boston Globe, Singapore Mirror, Boston Mag. and community newspapers. Com. mem. internship program Sch. Theology, Boston U., 1987; founding sponsor Civil Justice Found., 1987—; campaign vol., amb. Elliot L. Richardson for U.S. Senate, Boston, 1984. Mem. ABA, ATLA, Asian-Am. Lawyers Assn., Internat. Assn. Asian Ams. (pres. Boston chpt. 1981—), Boston Bar Assn. (specialist on internat. trade and human rights 1987—, gen. law practice and coms.), Mass. Acad. Trial Attys. Avocations: travel, hiking, horseback riding, sailing, golf. E-mail: gcwebheng@gis.net. Taxation, general, General practice, Communications. Home and Office: 19 Lillian Rd Framingham MA 01701-4820

**HENGBER, GREGORY PAUL,** lawyer; b. Sayreville, N.J., July 5, 1967; s. Stuart Lawrence and Donna Barbra (Toback) H. AA, Broward C.C., Coconut Creek, Fla., 1990; BA, Stetson U., Deland, Fla., 1992; JD cum laude, Stetson U., St. Petersburg, Fla., 1995. Bar: Fla. 1995, U.S. Dist. Ct. (so. dist.) Fla. 1996. Assoc. Davis & Wood, Miami, Fla., 1995-96, Wood & Quintairos, Miami, 1996-98; ptnr. Wood & Hengber, Miami, 1998-99, Hengber & Goldstein, Coral Gables, Fla., 1999—. Mem. ABA, ATLA, Def. Rsch. Inst., Fla. Def. Lawyers Assn., Dade County Def. Bar Assn., Dade County Bar Assn., Med. Claims Def. Network. Avocations: scuba diving, basketball, weight training, softball, golf. State civil litigation, Personal injury, Insurance. Office: Wood & Hengber 95 Merrick Way Coral Gables FL 33134-5323

**HENGSTLER, GARY ARDELL,** publisher, editor, lawyer; b. Wapakoneta, Ohio, Mar. 23, 1947; s. Luther C. and N. Delphine (Sims) H.; m. Linda K. Spreen, Mar. 8, 1969 (div. Aug. 1986); children: Dylan A., Joel S.; m. Laura M. Williams, Dec. 15, 1986. BS, Ball State U., 1969; JD, Cleve. State U., 1983. Bar: Ohio 1984, U.S. Dist. Ct. (no. dist.) Ohio 1984. Assoc. Blaszak, Schilling, Coey & Bennett, Elyria, Ohio, 1984-85; editor The Tex. Lawyer, Austin, 1985-86; news editor ABA Jour., Chgo., 1986-89, editor, pub., 1989—. Home: 834 N Arlington Hts Rd Arlington Heights IL 60004-5666 Office: ABA Jour 750 N Lake Shore Dr Chicago IL 60611-4403

**HENKE, MICHAEL JOHN,** lawyer, educator; b. Evansville, Ind., Aug. 3, 1940; s. Emerson Overbeck and Beatrice (Arney) H.; m. Leni Edith Anderson, Mar. 20, 1966; children: Blake, Paige, Britt. BA summa cum laude, Baylor U., 1962, LLB, 1965; LLM, NYU, 1966. Bar: Tex. 1965, D.C. 1967. Assoc. Covington & Burling, Washington, 1966-73; assoc. Vinson & Elkins, Washington, 1974-76, ptnr., 1976—; adj. prof. U. Va. Law Sch., 1988-94, 96—; chmn. pro bono adv. com. Legal Aid Soc., D.C., 1990-96, trustee, 1992—, chmn. ways & means com., 1997—; mem. Washington adv. coun. Baylor Washington Program, 1989-92; mem. sesquicentennial coun. of 150 Baylor U., 1993-95. Author: (with others) Petroleum Regulation Handbook, 1980, Natural Gas Yearbook, 1995; mem. editl. adv. bd. Nat. Gas Mag., 1992-97, Best Lawyers in America, 1989—, Best Lawyers in Washington, 1997, Worlds Leading Competition and Antitrust Lawyers, 1997—, World's Leading Litigation Lawyers, 1997—; contbr. articles to profl. jours. Founder, chmn. Old Presbyn. Meeting House Day Care Ctr., Alexandria, Va., 1970-74. Mem. ABA (chmn. energy antitrust subcom. litigation sect. 1987-88, vice chmn. energy litigation com. 1988-89, chmn. 1989-92, chmn. ann. fall meeting 1993, divsn. dir. 1993-95, co-chmn. audiotaping & videotaping com. 1995-96, co-chmn. ins. coverage litigation com. 1996-98, coun. mem. 1998—), D.C. Bar Assn., Tex. Bar Assn., Coll. State Bar Tex., Baylor U. Alumni Assn. (bd. dirs. 1994-98), Met. Club, Belle Haven Country Club, Farmington Country Club (Charlottesville). Democrat. Avocations: skiing, flyfishing, tennis, backpacking. Administrative and regulatory, Antitrust, Federal civil litigation. Home: 310 Charles Alexander Ct Alexandria VA 22301-1500 Office: Vinson & Elkins 1455 Pennsylvania Ave NW Fl 7 Washington DC 20004-1013

**HENKE, ROBERT JOHN,** lawyer, mediator, consultant, engineer; b. Chgo., Oct. 13, 1934; s. Raymond Anthony and May Dorothy (Driscoll) H.; m. Mary Gabrielle Handrigan, June 18, 1960; children: Robert Joseph, Ann Marie. BSEE, U. Ill., 1956; MBA, U. Chgo., 1964; JD, No. Ill. U., 1979, postgrad. John Marshall Law Sch. Bar: Ill. 1980, Wis. 1980, U.S. Dist. Ct. (no. dist.) Ill. 1980, U.S. Dist. Ct. (we. and ea. dists.) Wis. 1980, U.S. Supreme Ct. 1984; registered profl. engr., Ill., Wis. Sr. elec. engr. Commonwealth Edison Co., Chgo., 1956-80; elec. engr. Peterson Builders, Sturgeon Bay, Wis., 1982-83; sr. elec., cost estimating engr. Sargent & Lundy Engrs., Chgo., 1985-94; instr. econs. and criminal law NE Wis. Tech. Inst., 1981-82; asst. dist. atty. Door County, Wis., 1981, ct. commr., 1981-82; sole practice, Door County, 1981-84, Lake County, Ill., 1984-94; pvt. practice cons., mediator, Fish Creek, Wis., 1995—; dir. Scand, Door County, 1981-82. Vice chmn. Door County Bd. Adjustment, 1983-84; atty. coach Wis. Bar Found. High Sch. Moot Ct. Competition, Door County, 1984; vol. lawyers program, Lake County, Ill., 1985-95; sec., counsel, bd. dirs. Woodland Hills Condominium Assn., Gurnee, Ill., 1993-94. Served with USAR, 1958-63. Recipient award for pro bono work, 1994. Mem. ABA, Wis. Bar Assn., Door Kewaunee Bar Assn. (pres. 1983-84), Chgo. Bar Assn., IEEE, Am. Assn. Cost Engrs. Roman Catholic. Office: PO Box 827 Fish Creek WI 54212-0827

**HENKE, ROBERT JOHN,** lawyer; b. Hammond, Ind., Mar. 25, 1958; s. Robert L. and Lucille Adeana (Wright) H.; m. Jo Ellen Hurst, Mar. 24, 1979; children: Emily Jo, Robert James. Student, Ind. U., 1982-84; BA cum laude, Trinity Coll., 1986; JD with high distinction, Valparaiso U., 1990. Bar: Ind. 1990, Ill. 1990, U.S. Dist. Ct. (no. and so. dists.) Ind. 1990, U.S. Dist. Ct. (no. dist.) Ill. 1990. Assoc. atty. Schlyer & Assoc., Griffith, Ind., 1990-92; judicial clk. Lake County Ind. Criminal Divsn., Crown Point, Ind., 1992—; atty. Carr & Henke, Portage, Ind., 1993-95; pvt. practice Portage, Ind., 1995—. Contbr. chpts. to books on trial practice and discovery. Sr. pastor Chapel of the Dunes, Gary, Ind., 1986-98; sub-deacon Holy Resurrection Orthodox Ch., Hobart, Ind., 1998—. Hoosier State scholar State of Ind., 1976, Law scholar, Valparaiso U. Sch. Law, 1989-90. Mem. ABA, Ill. Bar Assn., Ind. Bar Assn., Lake County Bar Assn., Federalist Soc., Jus Vitia, Delta Theta Phi. Republican. Orthodox. Avocations: woodworking, church history researcher, hunting, fishing, power lifting. Contracts commercial, Criminal, Personal injury. Office: 5955 Central Ave Portage IN 46368-2945

**HENKELMAN, WILLARD MAX,** lawyer; b. Scranton, Pa., June 7, 1914; s. Max Frederick and Emilie (Neuls) H.; m. Elizabeth Tweedle, Feb. 21, 1943; children—Elizabeth L., Steven W. Grad., Phillips Exeter Acad., Exeter, N.H., 1932; A.B., Princeton U., 1936; LLB, Harvard U., 1939. Bar: Pa. 1940, U.S. Ct. Appeals (3d cir.) 1941. Practiced in Scranton, 1940-41; asso. Henkelman, Kreder, O'Connell & Brooks (and predecessor firms), Scranton, 1946-52; ptnr. Henkelman, Kreder, O'Connell & Brooks (and predecessor firms), 1952-86, of counsel, 1987—; Gen. counsel, advisory dir. Citizens Savs. Assn. Mem. Exeter Grad. Council, Princeton Alumni Council. Served from pvt. to maj. AUS, 1942-46, PTO; col. Res. ret. Decorated Bronze Star. Mem. ABA, Pa. Bar Assn., Lackawanna Bar Assn. (exec. com. 1974-79), Am. Coll. Real Estate Lawyers, Waynewood Assn. (pres. 1969-70), Lackawanna Hist. Soc. (v.p. 1969-72), N.E. Pa. Princeton Alumni Assn. (pres. 1952-55, chmn. alumni schs. com. 1960-70), Northeast Pa. Exeter Assn. (pres. 1953-55). Presbyn. Clubs: Kiwanis (pres. 1961), Scranton, Princeton Tower. Probate, Real property, Banking. Home: 1741 N Washington Ave Scranton PA 18509-1958 Office: 200 Bank Towers PO Box 956 Scranton PA 18501-0956

**HENKIN, LOUIS,** lawyer, law educator; b. Russia, Nov. 11, 1917; came to U.S., 1923, naturalized, 1930; s. Yoseph Elia and Frieda Rebecca (Kreindel) H.; m. Alice Barbara Hartman, June 19, 1960; children: Joshua, David, Daniel. AB, Yeshiva Coll., 1937; DHL, Yeshiva U., 1963; LLB, Harvard U., 1940; LLD, Columbia U., 1995; JD (hon.), Bklyn. Law Sch., 1997. Bar: N.Y. 1941, U.S. Supreme Ct. 1947. Law clk. to Judge Learned Hand, 1940-41, law clk. to Justice Frankfurter, 1946-47; cons. legal dept. UN, 1947-48; with State Dept., 1945-46, 48-57; U.S. rep. UN Com. Refugees and Stateless Persons, 1950; adviser U.S. del. UN Econ. and Social Coun., 1950, UN Gen. Assembly, 1950-53, Geneva Conf. on Korea, 1954; assoc. dir. Legis. Drafting Rsch. Fund, lectr. law Columbia U., 1956-57; prof. law U. Pa., 1958-62; prof. internat. law and diplomacy, prof. law Columbia U., 1962, mem. Inst. War and Peace Studies, 1962—, Hamilton Fish prof. internat. law and diplomacy, 1963-78, Harlan Fiske Stone prof. constl. law, 1978-79, univ. prof., 1979-88, prof. emeritus and spl. svc. prof., 1988—; co-dir. Ctr. for Study of Human Rights, 1978-86, chmn. of directorate, 1986—; U.S. mem. Permanent Ct. Arbitration, 1963-69; adviser U.S. Del. UN Conf. on Law of the Sea, 1972-80; adv. panel on internat. law Dept. State, 1975-80, 93—; human rights com. U.S. Commn. for UNESCO, 1977-80; Carnegie lectr. Hague Acad. Internat. Law, 1965; Frankel lectr. U. Houston, 1969; Gottesman lectr. Yeshiva U., 1975; Lockhart lectr. U. Minn. Law Sch., 1976; Francis Biddle lectr. Harvard Law Sch., 1978; lectr. Columbia U., 1979; Sherrill lectr. Yale U. Law Sch., 1981; Jefferson lectr. U. Pa. Law Sch., 1983; Irvine lectr. Cornell U., 1986; disting. lectr. Coll. Physicians and Surgeons, Columbia U., 1988; Solf lectr. Judge Adv. Gen.'s Sch., 1988; Cooley lectr. U. Mich. Law Sch., 1988; White lectr. La. State U., 1989; prin. lectr. The Hague Acad. Internat. Law, 1989; Blaine Sloane lectr. Pace U. Law Sch., 1991; Gerber lectr. U. Md. Law Sch., 1991; Nathanson lectr. law sch. U. San Diego, 1994; Sibley lectr. U. Ga. Law Sch., 1994; Brandeis lectr. Israel Acad. Scis. and Humanities, 1994; Phi Kappa Phi lectr., James Madison U., 1996, Doris and A. Leo Levin lectr. Bar Ilan U., Israel, 1996; cons. to govt., pres. U.S. Inst. Human Rights, 1970-93, Robert L. Levine lectr. Fordham Law Sch.; chief reporter Am. Law Inst., Restatement of the Law (3d), Fgn. Rels. Law of the U.S., 1979-87; bd. dirs. Lawyers Com. Human Rights, Immigration and Refugee Svcs. Am., v.p., 1994—; pres. Am. Soc. Internat. Law, 1992-94; vis. prof. U. Pa., 1957-58. Author: Arms Control and Inspection in American Law, 1958, The Berlin Crisis and the United Nations, 1959, Disarmament: The Lawyer's Interests, 1964, Law for the Sea's Mineral Resources, 1968, Foreign Affairs and the Constitution, 1972, 2nd edit., 1996, The Rights of Man Today, 1978, How Nations Behave: Law and Foreign Policy, 2nd edit., 1979; (with others) Human Rights in Contemporary China, 1986, Right v. Might: International Law and the Use of Force, 1989, 2nd edit., 1991, The Age of Rights, 1990, Constitutionalism, Democracy and Foreign Affairs, 1990, International Law: Politics and Values, 1995; editor: Arms Control: Issues for the Public, 1961, (with others) Transnational Law in a Changing Society, 1972, World Politics and the Jewish Condition, 1972, The International Bill of Rights: The International Covenant of Civil and Political Rights, 1981; (with others) International Law: Cases and Materials, 3d edit., 1993, Constitutionalism and Rights: The Influence of the United States Constitution Abroad, 1989, Foreign Affairs and the U.S. Constitution, 1990, Human Rights: Cases and Materials, 1999; bd. editors: Am. Jour. Internat. Law, 1967—, co-editor-in-chief, 1978-84; bd editors Ocean Devel. and Internat. Law Jour., 1973—, Jerusalem Jour. Internat. Relations, 1976—; contbr. articles to profl. jours. Served with AUS, 1941-45. Decorated Silver Star; recipient Law Alumni medal of excellence Columbia U. Sch. Law, 1982, Friedmann Meml. award Columbia Soc. Internat. law, 1986, Hudson medal Am. Soc. Internat. Law, 1995, Leadership in Human Rights award Columbia Human Rights Law Rev., 1995, Human Rights award Lawyers Com. for Human Rights, 1995, Outstanding Rsch. in Law and Govt. award Fellows of Am. Bar Found., 1997; Guggenheim fellow, 1979-80; Festschrift (Liber Amicorum): Politics, Values and Functions, Internat. Law in the 21st Century, Essays on Internat. Law in his honor, 1997, Louis Henkin Professorship in Human and Constitutional Rights established in his honor Columbia Law Sch., 1999. Fellow Am. Acad. Arts and Scis.; mem. Coun. Fgn. Rels., Am. Soc. Internat. Law (v.p. 1975-76, 88-90, pres. 1992-94, hon. v.p. 1994—), Internat. Law Assn. (v.p. Am. br., 1973—), Am. Soc. Polit. and Legal Philosophy (pres. 1985-87), Inst. de Droit Internat., Am. Polit. Sci. Assn., Internat. Assn. Constl. Law (v.p. 1982-95, hon. pres. 1995—), U.S. Assn. Constl. Law (hon. pres. 1997—), Am. Philos. Soc. Home: 460 Riverside Dr New York NY 10027-6801

**HENNEBERRY, MICHAEL L.,** defender; b. Decatur, Ill., Aug. 6, 1955; s. Harry Lee and Rita Marie (Walsh) H.; m. Sheri L Smith, May 13, 1989. AA, Black Hawk Coll., 1975; BA, Ill. State U., 1977; JD, DePaul U., 1980. Asst. pub. defender Bureau County, Princeton, Ill., 1992-94; pub. defender Bureau County, Princeton, 1994—; bd. mem. Bureau County & Wynet Mut. Ins., Wynet, Ill., 1985-97. Author: Driver's Legal Handbook, 1981. Mem. Knights of Columbia. Office: Michael L Henneberry PC 408 S Main St Princeton IL 61356-2005

**HENNEKE, EDWARD GEORGE,** lawyer; b. Flint, Mich., Jan. 28, 1940; s. Edward G. and Anna I. (Kielhorn) H.; m. Donna M. Wardosky, Jan. 24, 1970; children: Dawn, Shelley, Charlene; stepchildren: Scott, Tracy, Kurt Fraim. AA, Flint Jr. Coll., 1960; BS, U. Mich., Flint, 1962; JD, U. Mich., Ann Arbor, 1965. Bar: Mich. 1965, U.S. Dist. Ct. (ea. dist.) Mich. 1967, U.S. Ct. Appeals (6th cir.) 1974, U.S. Supreme Ct. 1971. Asst. pros. atty. Genesee County Pros. Atty., Flint, 1965-67; assoc. Ransom, Fazenbaker & Ransom, Flint, 1967-74; prin. ptnr. Keil, Ransom & Henneke, Flint, 1975-88, Henneke, McKone & Fraim, Flint, 1988—. Mem. planning com. Flushing Twp., 1986-92; bd. appeals, 1993—. Named Outstanding Alumnus, Flint U. Mich., 1971. Mem. Genesee County Bar Assn. (dir. 1978-81, pres. 1981-83), ABA. Avocations: hunting, golf, skiing. General civil litigation, Insurance, Probate. Office: Henneke McKone & Fraim 2222 S Linden Rd Ste G Flint MI 48532-5460

**HENNELLY, EDMUND PAUL,** lawyer, oil company executive; b. N.Y.C., Apr. 2, 1923; s. Edmund Patrick and Alice (Laccorn) H.; m. Josephine Kline; children: Patricia A. Anglin, Pamela J. Farley. BCE, Manhattan Coll., 1944; JD, Fordham U., 1950. Bar: N.Y. 1950. Instr. Manhattan Coll., 1947-50; litigation assoc. Cravath, Swaine & Moore, 1950-51, sr. litigation assoc., 1953-54; asst. gen. counsel CIA, Washington, 1951-52; assoc. counsel Time, Inc., N.Y.C., 1954-56; asst. legis. cons. Mobil Oil Corp., N.Y.C., 1956-60, legis. cons., 1960-61, mgr. domestic govt. rels. dept., 1961-67, mgr. govt. rels. dept., 1967-73, gen. mgr. govt. rels. dept., 1974-78, gen. mgr. pub. affairs dept., 1978-86; pres., chief exec. officer Citroil Enterprises, N.Y.C., 1986—; bd. dirs. South Cay Trust, Republic Nat. Bank N.Y., N.Y.C. Contbr. articles on engring. and law to profl. jours. Trustee, vice chmn. Daytop Village Found.; mem. adv. com. N.Y. State Legis. Com. on Higher Edn., Nassau County (N.Y.) Energy Commn., L.I. Citizens' Com. for Mass Transit, N.Y. State Def. Coun.; mem. White House Conf. on Natural Beauty, 1963; bd. dirs. Nat. Coun. on Aging; exec. com. Pub. Affairs Rsch. Coun. of Conf. Bd.; mem. Nassau County Econ. Devel. Planning Coun.; commr. nat. com. Commn. for UNESCO, 1982-85, head U.S. del. with personal rank of amb. 22d Gen. Conf., 1983, mem. internat. adv. panel, 1989—; mem. Pres.' Intelligence Transition Team, 1980-81; cons. Pres.'s Intelligence Oversight Bd.; trustee Austen Riggs Ctr., Pub. Affairs Found. Lt., USNR, 1943-46, PTO, ETO. Decorated Knight of Malta, Knight of Holy Sepulchre. Mem. ABA, Fed. Bar Assn., Assn. Bar City of N.Y., Acad. Polit. and Social Scis., Am. Good Govt. Soc. (trustee), Tax Coun. (bd. dirs.), Pub. Affairs Coun. (bd. dirs.), Freedom House (trustee), Am. Mgmt. Assn., Pi Sigma Epsilon, Delta Theta Phi, Army-Navy Club, Meadows Country Club, Sarasota Yacht Club, Island Hills Country Club, Explorers Club, Knights of Malta, Knights Holy Sepulchre. Clubs: Army-Navy, Explorers. Lodges: K.M., Knights Holy Sepulcher. Oil, gas, and mineral. Home: 84 Sequams Ln E West Islip NY 11795-4508 also: 3941 Hamilton Club Cir Sarasota FL 34242-1109 Office: Citroil Enterprises 21 Argyle Sq Babylon NY 11702-2712

**HENNESSY, DEAN MCDONALD,** lawyer, multinational corporation executive; b. McPherson, Kans., June 13, 1923; s. Ernest Weston and Beulah A. (Dunn) H.; m. Marguerite Sundheim, Sept. 6, 1946 (div. Sept. 1979); children: Joan Hennessy Wright, John D., Robert D. (dec.), Scott D. (dec.); m. Darlene MacLean, Apr. 4, 1981. A.B. cum laude, Harvard U., 1947, LL.B., 1950; M.B.A., U. Chgo., 1959. Bar: Ill. 1951. Assoc. Carney, Crowell & Leibman, Chgo., 1950-53; atty. Borg-Warner Corp., Chgo., 1953-62; with Emhart Corp., Farmington, Conn., 1962-88, asst. sec., 1964-67, sec., gen. counsel, 1967-74, v.p., sec., gen. counsel, 1974-76, v.p., gen. counsel, 1976-86, sr. v.p., gen. counsel, 1986-88, ret., 1988. Incorporator Ill. Citizens for Eisenhower, 1952; chmn. Citizens Activities, Ill. Citizens for Eisenhower, 1952, 56; Justice of the peace, mem. bd. suprs. Proviso Twp., Ill., 1952-56; vice chmn. Jr. Achievement Chgo., 1959; program chmn. trade and industries divsn. United Rep. Fund Ill., 1961; trustee West Hartford Bicentennial Trust, Inc., 1976-77, Friends and Trustees of Bushnell Meml., Hartford, 1978-84; bd. dirs. Royal Homestead Condominium Assn., Juno Beach, Fla., 1990-93. Served to lt. (j.g.) USNR, 1943-46. Sheldon fellow Harvard U., 1943-46. Mem. ABA, Mfrs. Alliance for Productivity and Innovation (vice chmn. law coun. 1984-87, chmn. 1987, 88), John Harvard Soc. Republican. Presbyterian. General corporate. Home: 70 Wagner Rd Westerly RI 02891-4719

**HENNESSY, ELLEN ANNE,** lawyer, benefits compensation analyst, educator; b. Auburn, N.Y., Mar. 3, 1949; d. Charles Francis and Mary Anne (Roan ) H.; m. Frank Daspit, Aug. 27, 1974. BA, Mich. State U., 1971; JD, Cath. U., 1978; LLM in Taxation, Georgetown U., 1984. Bar: D.C. 1978, U.S. Ct. Appeals (D.C. cir.) 1978, U.S. Supreme Ct. 1984. Various positions NEH, Washington, 1971-74; atty. office chief counsel IRS, Washington, 1978-80; atty.-advisor Pension Benefit Guaranty Corp., Washington, 1980-82; assoc. Stroock & Stroock & Lavan, Washington, 1982-85; assoc. Willkie Farr & Gallager, Washington, 1985-86, ptnr., 1987-93; dep. exec. dir. and chief negotiator Pension Benefit Guaranty Corp., Washington, 1993-98; sr. v.p. Actuarial Sci. Assocs., Inc., Washington, 1998—; adj. prof. law Georgetown U., Washington, 1985—; mem. com. on continuing profl. edn. Am. Law Inst./ABA, 1994-97. Mem. ABA (supervising editor taxation sect. newsletter 1984-87, mem. standing com. on continuing edn. 1990-94, chairperson joint com. on employee benefits 1991-92), Women in Employee Benefits (pres. 1987-88), D.C. Bar Assn. (mem. steering com. tax sect. 1988-93, chairperson continuing legal edn. com. 1993-95). Democrat. Avocation: whitewater canoeing. Pension, profit-sharing, and employee benefits, Bankruptcy. Home: 1926 Lawrence St NE Washington DC 20018-2734 Office: 601 Pennsylvania Ave NW Ste 900 Washington DC 20004-2601

**HENNESSY, JOSEPH H.,** lawyer; b. Nov. 16, 1937. BA, LaSalle Coll., 1959; MA, U. Notre Dame, 1962, PhD, 1967; JD, Temple U., 1971. Bar: Pa. 1971, D.C. 1978, U.S. Supreme Ct. 1977. Ptnr. Morgan, Lewis & Bockius, Phila. General corporate, Private international, Mergers and acquisitions. Office: Morgan Lewis & Bockius 1701 Market St Philadelphia PA 19103-2903

**HENNESSY, MICKEE M.,** lawyer; b. New Orleans, Aug. 6, 1968; d. William P. and Marilyn H. Imwalle; m. Michael P. Hennessy, Oct. 21, 1995; 1 child, Devon Marie. BA in Music, SUNY, Pottdam, 1990; JD, Fordham U., 1995. Bar: N.Y. 1996, U.S. Dist. Ct. (so. and ea. dists.) N.Y. 1997. Assoc. Battle Fowler LLP, N.Y.C., 1995—. Mem. ABA, N.Y. State Bar Assn. Federal civil litigation, General civil litigation, State civil litigation. Office: Battle Fowler LLP 75 East 55th St Park Ave Twr New York NY 10022

**HENNIGER, DAVID THOMAS,** lawyer; b. Cuyahoga Falls, Ohio, Dec. 12, 1936; s. Herman Harrison and Wilma (Weeks) H.; m. LaRayne Virginia Kerlin, Apr. 9, 1965; children: Mark, Jill, Matthew, Michael. AA, St. Petersburg Jr. Coll., 1957; BS summa cum laude, Fla. So. Coll., 1959; JD cum laude, Stetson U., 1965. Bar: Fla. 1965, U.S. Dist. Ct. (mid. dist.) Fla. 1965, U.S. Ct. Appeals (5th cir.) 1966, U.S. Supreme Ct. 1971, U.S. Ct. Appeals (11th cir.) 1981. Diplomate Nat. Bd. Trial Advocacy. Assoc. Masterson, Lloyd, Sundberg & Rogers, St. Petersburg, Fla., 1965-75; ptnr. Lloyd and Henniger, P.A., St. Petersburg, 1975-84; assoc. Greene and Mastry, P.A., St. Petersburg, 1984-91; coll. atty. St. Petersburg Jr. Coll.; instr. Stetson Coll. Law, Gulfport, Fla., 1972-73; St. Petersburg Jr. Coll., 1968-73; pres. St. Petersburg Legal Aid Soc., 1976. Pres. Christian Arbitration Ctr., St. Petersburg, 1987—; v.p. Christian Businessmen's Com., 1981-82; chmn. sch. adv. com. Dixie Hollins High Sch., Kenneth City, Fla., 1985-86, pres. Parent Tchrs. Student Assn., 1987-88. Mem. ABA, Fed. Bar Assn., Am. Judicare Soc., Assn. Trial Lawyers Am., Fla. Trial Lawyers Soc., Am. Arbitration Assn. (panel arbitrators 1977-88), Christian Legal Soc. (treas. St. Petersburg 1984—). Avocations: basketball, photography. General civil litigation. Home: 5862 32nd Ave N Saint Petersburg FL 33710-1837 Office: St Petersburg Jr Coll PO Box 13489 Saint Petersburg FL 33733-3489

**HENNING, JOEL FRANK,** lawyer, author, publisher, consultant; b. Chgo., Sept. 15, 1939; s. Alexander M. and Henrietta (Frank) H.; m. Grace Weiner, May 24, 1964 (div. July 1987); children: Justine, Sarah-Anne, Dara; m. Rosemary Nadolsky, June 21, 1992; 1 child, Alexandra. AB, Harvard U., 1961, JD, 1964. Bar: Ill. 1965. Assoc. Sonnenschein, Levinson, Carlin, Nath & Rosenthal, Chgo., 1965-70; fellow, dir. program Adlai Stevenson Inst. Internat. Affairs, Chgo., 1970-73; nat. dir. Youth Edn. for Citizenship, 1972-75; dir. profl. edn. Am. Bar Assn., Chgo., 1975-78; asst. exec. dir. comm. and edn. ABA, 1978-80; ptnr. Joel Henning & Assocs., 1980-87; sr. v.p., gen. counsel, mem. exec. com. Hildebrandt, Inc., 1987—; pres., pub. LawLetters, Inc., 1980-89; pub. Lawyer Hiring and Tng. Report, 1980-89; Chgo. theater critic Wall St. Jour., 1989—; pub. Almanac of Fed. Judiciary, 1984-89; editor Bus. Lawyer Update, 1980-87; mem. faculty Inst. on Law and Ethics, Council Philos. Studies; chmn. Fund for Justice, Chgo., 1979-85. Author: Law-Related Education in America: Guidelines for the Future, 1975, Holistic Running: Beyond the Threshhold of Fitness, 1978, Mandate for Change: The Impact of Law on Educational Innovaiton, 1979, Improving Lawyer Productivity: How to Train, Manage and Supervise Your Lawyers, 1985, Law Practice and Management Desk Book, 1987, Lawyers Guide to Managing and Training Lawyers, 1988, Maximizing Law Firm Profitability: Hiring, Training and Developing Productive Lawyers, 1991-98, also articles. Chmn. Gov.'s Commn. on Financing Arts in Ill., 1970-71; bd. dirs. Ill. Arts Council, 1971-81, Columbia Coll., Chgo.; bd. dirs., v.p., pub. edn. exec. com. ACLU of Ill.; trustee S.E. Chgo. Commn.; mem. Joseph Jefferson Theatrical Awards Com. Fellow Am. Bar Found. (life); mem. Am. Law Inst., ABA (ho. of dels.), Chgo. Bar Assn., Chgo. Council Lawyers (co-founder), Social Sci. Edn. Consortium. General corporate, General practice. Office: 150 N Michigan Ave Ste 3600 Chicago IL 60601-7572 *The hardest question for me to answer is, "What do you do?" I do a lot. Some of it returns money and satisfaction. Some returns more of one than the other. And, I do some things that make me feel fit. The best of what I do helps integrate my various selves and improves my relations with the world. But I have no facile way to say all of this at cocktail parties when, invariably, that question is popped.*

**HENRICK, MICHAEL FRANCIS,** lawyer; b. Chgo., Feb. 29, 1948; s. John L. and A. Madeline (Hafner) H.; m. Cissi F. Henrick, Aug. 9, 1980; children: Michael Francis Jr., Derry Patricia. BA, Loyola U., 1971; JD with honors, John Marshall Law Sch., 1974. Bar: Ill. 1974, U.S. Dist. Ct. (no. dist.) Ill. 1974, U.S. Supreme Ct. 1979, Wis. 1985, U.S. Dist. Ct. (ea. dist.) Wis. 1985. Ptnr. Hinshaw & Culbertson, Chgo., Waukegan, Ill., 1974—. Recipient Corpus Juris Secundum award West Publ. Co., 1974. Mem. ABA, Def. Rsch. Inst., Ill. Bar Assn., Lake County Bar Assn., Ill. Hosp. Attys. Assn., Internat. Assn. of Defense Counsel, Ill. Defense Attys. Assn., Soc. Trial Lawyers Def. Rsch. Inst., Am. Inns of Ct. Personal injury. Office: Hinshaw & Culbertson 110 N West St Waukegan IL 60085-4330

**HENRIKSEN, C. RICHARD, JR.,** lawyer; b. Salt Lake City, May 15, 1953; s. C. Richard and Evelyn (Pay) H.; m. Elaine Morrison, Mar. 27, 1975; children: Emily, C. Richard III, Robert, Holly, Melissa, Daniel. BS in Polit. Sci., U. Utah, 1976, JD, 1979. Bar: Utah 1979, U.S. Dist. Ct. Utah 1979, U.S. Ct. Appeals (10th cir.) 1979, U.S. Supreme Ct. 1993. Legal asst. Henriksen Bradford Forbes, Salt Lake City, 1970-72; missionary Australia West Mission, 1972-74; legal asst. Henriksen Fairbourne & Tate, Salt Lake City, 1974-76; law clk. Henriksen & Tate, Salt Lake City, 1976-79; atty., founder Henriksen & Henriksen, P.C., Salt Lake City, 1979—, sr. ptnr., pres., 1987—. Del., voter dist. chairperson Rep. Party, Salt Lake City, 1975-95; scoutmaster Boy Scouts of Am., 1988-95, cubmaster, 1983-87. Mem. Assn. Trial Lawy of Am. (bd. govs. 1986—), Western Trial Lawyers Assn. (bd. govs. 1983—), Utah Trial Lawyers Assn. (bd. govs. 1980—, pres. 1984-85, Presdl. award 1985). Republican. LDS. Avocations: scouting, camping, cycling, scuba diving. Personal injury, General civil litigation, Contracts commercial. Office: Henriksen & Henriksen PC 320 S 500 E Salt Lake City UT 84102-4022

**HENRY, BRIAN THOMAS,** lawyer; b. Chgo., Dec. 25, 1954; s. Thomas Joseph and Shirley Grace (Pfaff) H.; m. Mary Elizabeth Collins, Sept. 17, 1983; children: Kyle J., Erin Maureen, Colin Thomas. BA Honors in History magna cum laude, Loyola U., Chgo., 1977; JD, U. Ill., 1980. Bar: Ill. 1980, U.S. Dist. Ct. (no. dist.) Ill. 1980. Assoc. Pretzel & Stouffe Chtd., Chgo., 1980—; faculty instr. Ill. Assn. of Def. Trial Counsel Trial Acads., 1990-99; seminar speaker Chgo. Bar Assn. Comparative Negligence Seminar, 1990, '91; cons. health care com. Inst. of Medicine of Chgo.; frequent lectr. med. groups. Editor-in-chief Recent Decisions Sect. of Ill. Bar Jour., 1979-80. Mem. ASTL, ABA, Ill. Assn. Hosp. Attys., Ill. Assn. Defense Trial Counsel, Internat. Assn. Defense Counsel, Chgo. Bar Assn., Ill. Bar Assn., Phi Alpha Theta, Phi Alpha Delta. Personal injury, Professional liability, General civil litigation. Office: Pretzel & Stouffer Chtd 1 S Wacker Dr Ste 2500 Chicago IL 60606-4614

**HENRY, CARL NOLAN,** lawyer; b. Washington, Sept. 30, 1965; s. Robert Benjamin Covington III and Inola Francis Henry. BA in Polit. Sci., U. Calif., Berkeley, 1987, JD, 1993. Bar: Calif. 1993, U.S. Supreme Ct. 1997, U.S. Ct. Appeal (9th cir.) 1993, U.S. Dist. Ct. (no., ctrl. dists.) Calif. 1993. Dep. atty. gen. Calif. Dept. Justice, L.A., 1994-99, 99—; staff atty. to Hon. Janice Rogers Brown Calif. Supreme Ct., San Francisco, 1999. Career Awareness Acad. scholar Home Savings Am., 1983; Liberl Arts award Bank Am., 1983. Mem. L.A. Angel City Links Assn. (O. J. Simpson Acad. scholar 1983), L.A. Ephebian Honor Soc. Democrat. Methodist. Avocations: sports, politics, music, history, education. Office: Calif Dept Justice 300 S Spring St Ste 5000 Los Angeles CA 90013

**HENRY, DAVID PATRICK,** lawyer; b. Terre Haute, Ind., June 2, 1960; s. Joseph C. and Sara F. Henry; children: Hannah Lane, Blake Ryan. BS, U. Mo., 1982; JD, Oklahoma City U., 1985. Bar: Okla., U.S. Dist. Ct. (we., no. and ea. dists.) Okla., U.S. Ct. Appeals (10th cir.). Assoc. Hughes & Nelson, Oklahoma City, Okla., 1985-88; ptnr. Coyle & Henry, P.C., Oklahoma City, 1988-91, Henry Law Office, Oklahoma City, 1991—. Mem. ATLA, Okla. Criminal Def. Bar Assn., Okla. County Bar Assn. Democrat. Baptist. Avocations: golf, poker. Criminal, Family and matrimonial, Personal injury. Office: Henry Davidson & Hill 3315 NW 63rd St Oklahoma City OK 73116-3787

**HENRY, DELYSLE LEON,** lawyer; b. Cumberland, Apr. 17, 1935; s. Clarence Philip and Lillian Pauline (Hartley) H.; m. Kaye Claire Grulke, June 23, 1960; children: Reginald DeLysle, Lisa Kay. BA, Ea. Nazarene Coll., 1956; MA, U. Pa., 1958; JD, U. Balt., 1966; postgrad., Mich. State U. Bar: Mich. 1971, U.S. Dist. Ct. (ea. dist.) Mich. 1978, U.S. Ct. Appeals (6th cir.) 1979. Instr. law and govt. Alpena (Mich.) Community Coll., 1959-61, 66-89; pvt. practice Alpena, 1971—. Commr. County of Alpena, 1974-76. Mem. ABA, Nat. Orgn. Social Security Claimants' Reps., State Bar Mich., Am. Judicature Soc., Am. Bus. Law Assn., Fed. Bar Assn. (Detroit chpt.). Presbyterian. Avocations: hiking, swimming. Pension, profit-sharing, and employee benefits, Federal civil litigation.

**HENRY, EDWIN MAURICE, JR.,** lawyer, electrical engineer, consultant; b. Cambridge, Md., June 26, 1930; s. Edwin Maurice Henry Sr. and Emma Lee (Wilson) Clayton; m. Barbara Ann Brittingham, Feb. 2, 1952; children: Barbara Jo, Kim M. Student, U.S. Naval Acad., 1949-51; BSEE, John Hopkins U., 1957; JD, U. Balt., 1972. Bar: Md. 1974, U.S. Dist. Ct. Md. 1974; registered profl. engr., Md. Assoc. Pairo & Pairo, Balt., 1973-76; ptnr. Pairo & Henry, Ellicott City, Md., 1976-86; sole practice Ellicott City, 1986-95; pvt. practice LLC, 1996—; mem. Md. Atty. Grievance Rev. Bd., 1980-83. Author: Defense of Speeding Vascar, 1974. Served with USN, 1947-51. Mem. Md. Bar Assn., Howard County Bar Assn., Am. Legion, Masons, Shriners, Jesters, Eastern Shore Soc., St. Andrew's Soc., Cambridge Yacht Club. Methodist. Avocations: travel. Estate planning, Family and matrimonial, General practice. Home: 9035 Overhill Dr Ellicott City MD 21042-5246 Office: PO Box 309 8433 Main St Ellicott City MD 21043-4665

**HENRY, JAMES FRED,** lawyer; b. Russell, Kans., Sept. 22, 1957; s. William Robert and Dorothea Katherine H.; m. Kelly Jo Morrison, June 17, 1993; children: Camille Marie, Natalie Suzanne, Karla Marie. BS, U. North Ala., 1978; MBA, Samford U., 1982; JD, Cumberland U., 1997. Bar: Ala. 1997, U.S. Dist. Ct. (no. dist.) Ala. 1997. Sales rep. AT&T, Birmingham, 1979-82; mgr. tech. support AT&T, Mobile, 1983-86; br. mgr. Bell South, Louisville, 1987-88; regional mgr. Bell South, Nashville, 1988-89; dir. mktg. Bell South, Birmingham, 1989-94; atty. Johnston, Barton, Proctor & Powell, LLP, Birmingham, 1997—. Bd. trustees Highlands United Meth. Ch., Birmingham, 1998—, Found. Ileitis and Colitis, Birmingham, 1982-87. Mem. ABA, Am. Mgmt. Assn., Birmingham Bar Assn., Phi Gamma Delta. Methodist. Health, General civil litigation, Administrative and regulatory. Home: 543 Bristol Ln Birmingham AL 35226-1986 Office: Johnston Barton Proctor & Powell LLP 2900 S Harbert Plz Birmingham AL 35203

**HENRY, JAMES RICHARD,** lawyer. BA, SUNY, Potsdam, 1976; JD, Yale U., 1979. Bar: N.Y. 1980. Assoc. White & Case, N.Y.C. and Washington, 1979-81, Luster & Salk, Groton, N.Y., 1982-84; ptnr. Luster, Salk & Henry, Groton, 1984-87, Luster, Salk, Henry & Tischler, Groton, 1987-88; pvt. practice, Groton, 1989—. Mem. ABA, N.Y. State Bar Assn., Tompkins County Bar Assn., Groton Bus. Assn. Real property, Probate, General practice. Office: PO Box 95 Groton NY 13073-0095

**HENRY, KELLY SUE,** lawyer; b. Pikeville, Ky., July 22, 1969; d. Dennis William and Wanda (Murray) Henry; m. Francisco Javier Fajardo-Ocana, Sept. 23, 1995. AB, Smith Coll., 1991; JD, U. Louisville, 1994. Bar: Ky. 1994, U.S. Dist. Ct. (ea. dist.) Ky. 1997, U.S. Ct. Appeals (6th cir.) 1997. Assoc. Coopers & Lybrand, LLP, Louisville, 1994-96, Tilford, Dobbins, Alexander, Buckaway & Black, Louisville, 1997, Ogden Newell & Welch, Louisville, 1997—. Editor U. Lousville Jour. Family Law, 1993-94. Mem. ABA, Ky. Bar Assn., Louisville Bar Assn., Jefferson County Women Lawyers Assn. (sec. 1997-98, v.p. 1998-99), Estate Planning Coun. Louisville, Jr. League of Louisville. Roman Catholic. Estate planning, Probate, Estate taxation. Office: Ogden Newell & Welch 1700 Citizens Plz 500 W Jefferson St Louisville KY 40202-2874

**HENRY, KENNETH ALAN,** lawyer; b. Chgo., Jan. 21, 1951; s. Marvin David and Diane Dina (Kraft) H.; m. Amyra Weissberg, July 1, 1979; children: Oren Meron, Orly Michal. BS with distinction, U. Wis., Madison, 1972; JD, Ill. Inst. Tech., 1976; postgrad., Northwestern U., 1982-87. Bar: Ill. 1976, U.S. Dist. Ct (no. dist.) Ill. 1976, U.S. Ct. Appeals (7th cir.) 1976, U.S. Supreme Ct. 1981, U.S. Ct. Appeals (fed. cir.) 1986. Assoc. Edes & Rosen, Chgo., 1976-78; trial atty. office of solicitor region 5 U.S. Dept Labor, Chgo., 1978-85; ptnr. Weissberg & Henry, Ltd., Chgo., 1985-87; pvt. practice law Chgo., 1987—; arbitrator Am. Arbitration Assn., Chgo., 1982—; hearing officer Ill. State Bd. Edn., Chgo., 1982—; mem. Ill. Pub. Employee Mediation-Arbitration Roster, Chgo., 1986—; adj. asst. prof. health policy and adminstrn. divsn. Sch. Pub. Health, U. Ill., Chgo., 1998—. Author: The Labor Handbook, 1984, 2nd edit., 1986. Mem. Environ. Control Commn., Highland Park, Ill., chmn., 1989-91; mem. North Shore Sch. Dist. 112, Highland Park, 1995—; mem. Highwood-Highland Park Sch. Dist. 111, 1992-93. Mem. ABA, Chgo. Bar Assn., Decalogue Soc. Lawyers. Jewish. Avocations: athletics, theater, dance, symphony, reading. Fax: (312) 857-1157. E-mail: khenry@kahlaw.com. Labor, General civil litigation, Bankruptcy. Home: 2847 Idlewood Ln Highland Park IL 60035-1125 Office: 120 W Madison St Ste 600 Chicago IL 60602-4106

**HENRY, PETER YORK,** lawyer, mediator; b. Washington, Apr. 28, 1951; s. David Howe II and Margaret (Beard) H.; children: Ryan York, Zachary Price, Chance Hagdorn; m. Deidra B. Hagdorn, May 1995; 1 child, Chance Hagdorn Henry; stepchildren: Nathan Hebert, Christopher Hebert. B.B.A., Ohio U., 1973; J.D. St. Mary's U., San Antonio, 1976. Bar: Tex. 1976. Sole practice, San Antonio, 1976—. Mem. ATLA, Tex. Bar Assn., Tex Trial Lawyers Assn., San Antonio Trial Lawyers Assn. (bd. dirs. 1989-90), San Antonio Bar Assn., Phi Delta Phi. Personal injury, Insurance, Workers' compensation. Home: 7642 Bluesage Cv San Antonio TX 78249-2541 Office: 224 Casa Blanca St San Antonio TX 78215-1232

**HENRY, RAGAN AUGUSTUS,** lawyer, communications executive; b. Sadiesville, Ky., Mar. 20, 1980; s. Augustus Wilson and Ruby Helen H.; m. Regina Amanda, Mar. 20, 1980. BA, Harvard U., 1956, LLM, 1961. Assoc. Narin, Garfinkel & Mann, Phila., 1961-64; ptnr. Goodis, Greenfield, Henry, Edelstein, Phila., 1964-77, Wolf, Block, Schorr & Solis-Cohen, Phila., 1977-94; chmn. US Radio, Inc., Phila., 1980-96, MediaComm Nat., Inc., Phila., 1988—; cons. Clear Channel Comm. Inc., San Antonio, 1996-97; tchr. S.I. Newhouse Sch., Syracuse, N.Y., 1979-83; lectr. Law Sch. Temple U., Phila., 1971-73, La Salle U., Phila., 1971-73. Bd. dirs. Phila. Mus. Art, 1986—; bd. dirs., treas. United Way Am., Washington, 1993-95, Elderhostel, Boston, 1984—. Pvt. U.S. Army, 1957-59. Recipient Outstanding Bus. award Urban Bankers Del. Valley, 1978, Human Rels. award Nat. Conf. Christians and Jews, 1981; named Broadcaster of Yr. Nat. Assn. Black Broadcasters, 1981. Methodist. General corporate, Communications. Office: MediaComm Nat Inc 1420 Walnut St Ste 715 Philadelphia PA 19102-4006

**HENRY, ROBERT HARLAN,** federal judge, former attorney general; b. Shawnee, Okla., Apr. 3, 1953. BA, U. Okla., 1974, JD, 1976. Bar: Okla. 1976. Atty. Henry, West, Still & Combs, Shawnee, Okla., 1977-83, Henry, Henry & Henry, Shawnee, 1983-87; mem. Okla. Ho. of Reps., 1976-86; atty. gen. State of Okla., Oklahoma City, 1987-91; dean, prof. law. Law Sch. Okla. City U., 1991-94; judge U.S. Ct. Appeals (10th cir.), Oklahoma City, 1994—; mem. Nat. Conf. Commrs. on Uniform State Law. Fellow Am. Bar Found.; mem. Okla. Bar Assn., Am. Coun. Young Polit. Leaders, Nat. Assn. Attys. Gen. (chmn. state constl. law adv. com., vice-chmn. civil rights com.). Office: US Ct Appeals 10th Cir 200 NW 4th St Oklahoma City OK 73102-3026*

**HENRY, ROBERT JOHN,** lawyer; b. Chgo., Aug. 1, 1950; s. John P. and Margaret P. (Froelich) H.; children: Cherylyn, Deanna, Laurin. BA cum laude, Loyola U., Chgo., 1973, JD cum laude, 1975. Bar: Ill 1975, U.S. Dist. Ct. (no. dist.) Ill. 1975. Atty. Continental Ill. Nat. Bank, Chgo., 1975-77; atty. Allied Van Lines, Inc., Chgo., 1977-81, assoc. gen. counsel, 1981-88, gen. counsel, 1988-90, v.p. adminstrn., gen. counsel, 1990-93; v.p. gen. counsel, 1993—; gen. counsel NFC N.Am., 1996—. Alt. scholar Weymouth Kirkland Found., 1971. Mem. ABA, Chgo. Bar Assn., Am. Corp. Counsel Assn. Contracts commercial, General corporate, Securities. Office: Allied Van Lines Inc PO Box 4403 Chicago IL 60680-4403

**HENRY, SALLY MCDONALD,** lawyer; b. Durham, N.C., Aug. 1, 1948; d. John Frederick and Mary Frances (McDonald) Henry; m. Bradley Lewis Rudin. BA, Duke U., 1970; MA in Anthropology, SUNY, Binghamton, 1973; JD, NYU, 1982. Tchr. Endicott (N.Y.) Pub. Schs., 1971-75, Monticello (N.Y.) Pub. Schs., 1975-79; clk. U.S. Bankruptcy Ct., Bklyn., 1982-83; assoc. Skadden, Arps, Slate, Meagher & Flom, N.Y.C., 1983-91, ptnr., 1991—. Editor articles Rev. Law and Social Change, 1981-83; contbr. numerous articles to profl. jours. Mem. rules com. E.D.N.Y., Bklyn, 1984. Home: 395 Riverside Dr Apt 6A New York NY 10025-1843 Office: Skadden Arps Slate Meagher & Flom 919 3rd Ave New York NY 10022-3902

**HENRY, VIC HOUSTON,** lawyer; b. Big Spring, TX, Apr. 23, 1958; s. Don Vernor and Patricia Jean (Ezell) H.; m. Candace Lee McComb, Dec. 27, 1980; children: Taylor McComb, Lee Houston. BA with highest honors, U. Tex., 1980; JD cum laude, Georgetown U., Washington, 1983. Bar: Tex. 1983, U.S. Ct. Appeals (5th, 8th, 10th and D.C. cirs.) 1985, U.S. Ct. Appeals (fed. cir.) 1987, U.S. Dist. Ct. (no. dist.) Tex. 1983, U.S. Dist. Ct. (ea. and we. dists.) Tex. 1985, U.S. Dist. Ct. (ea. and we. dists.) Okla. 1985, U.S. Dist. Ct. (ea. and we. dists.) Ark. 1985, U.S. Dist. Ct. (no. dist.) Ala. 1985, U.S. Claims Ct., 1986, U.S. Supreme Ct. 1985. Law clk. to presiding justice U.S. Dist. Ct., Dallas, 1983-84; assoc. Storey Armstrong Steger & Martin, Dallas, 1984-88, ptnr., 1989-97; ptnr. Henry Oddo Austin & Fletcher, P.C., Dallas, 1997—; mem. faculty U. Tex. Arlington Asbestos Abatement, 1987; mem. adv. group Civil Justice Reform, U.S. Dist. Ct. (no. dist.) Tex., 1990; speaker seminars including Am. Corp. Counsel Assn., 1987. Adminstrv. asst. Tex. senate, Austin, 1976-78, Tex. Ho. of Reps., Austin, 1979-80, U.S. Ho. of Reps., Washington, 1980-82; chmn. deacons Gaston Ave. Baptist Ch., Dallas, 1988. Mem. ABA (labor-OSHA subcom. 1985-86, 90—, mem. ins. environ. com., chmn. litig. subcom. firms 5-15 lawyers), Tex. State Bar, Dallas Bar Assn., Dallas Assn. Young Lawyers (chmn. fed. casenotes com. 1985-87), Conf. Freight Counsel, Dallas Inn Ct. (barrister 1988-91). Avocations: basketball, travel. General civil litigation, Transportation, Insurance. Home: 4903 Heritage Cir Sachse TX 75048-4560 Office: Henry Oddo Austin & Fletcher PC 1717 Main St Ste 3850 Dallas TX 75201-7353

**HENRY, WENDELL S.,** lawyer; b. Bklyn., Apr. 16, 1963; s. Kermit W. and Eloise (Bell) H.; m. Deborah Arnelle Gilbert, June 8, 1996; 1 child, Chantel Janai. BS in Broadcast & Film, Boston U., 1985; JD, So. U., 1990. Bar: Ga. Assoc. Divida Gude, Atlanta, 1990-91; atty. State of Ga., Fulton County Office of Pub. Defender, Atlanta, 1991-95; prin. Henry & Assocs., Decatur, Ga., 1995—. Mem. adv. bd. DeKalb Youth Detentio Ctr., 1996. Mem. Dekalb Lawyers Assn., Kappa Alpha Psi, Delta Theta Phi. Democrat. Avocations: tennis, basketball, woodwork. Personal injury, Bankruptcy. Office: 315 W Ponce De Leon Ave Decatur GA 30030-2441

**HENRYSON, HERBERT, II,** lawyer; b. N.Y.C., Mar. 9, 1940; s. Herbert and Adeline (Grey) H.; m. Maxine Mosher, Sept. 4, 1965; children: Dylan Melville, Stefan Friend. BSE, Princeton U., 1962; PhD, U. Calif., Berkeley, 1968; JD, U. Chgo., 1984. Bar: N.Y., Pa., Minn. Vis. scientist U.K. Atomic Energy Authority, Winfrith, Eng., 1967; sr. scientist, mgr. LMFBR physics design Argonne (Ill.) Nat. Lab., 1968-84; assoc., vis. prof. Northwestern U., Evanston, Ill., 1982-84; assoc. Skadeen Arps Slate Meagher & Flom, N.Y.C., 1984-92; dep. gen. counsel Honeywell Inc., Mpls., 1992-96; ptnr., co-chair corp. dept. Wolf, Block, Schorr & Solis-Cohen LLP, Phila., 1996—; vis. assoc. prof. U. Pa., Phila., 1998-99. Contbr. articles to profl. jours. Bd. dirs. Hyde Park Neighborhood Club, Chgo., 1980-84, Honeywell Found. Arts Com., Mpls., 1994-96, Theatre de la Jeune Lune, Mpls., 1994-96, Venture Theatre, Phila., 1997-99. U.S. AEC spl. fellow in sci. and engring., 1962-65, U. Calif. sci. fellow, 1965-66, Fulbright Hays fellow, London, 1966-67. Mem. Phi Beta Kappa. Achievements include participation in many of the most significant negotiated and unsolicited merger and acquisitions of 1980s and 90s. Mergers and acquisitions, Securities, General corporate. Home: 478 W Broadway New York NY 10012-3168 Office: Wolf Black et al 250 Park Ave New York NY 10177-0001

**HENSCHEL, JOHN JAMES,** lawyer; b. Mineola, NY, Aug. 11, 1954; s. John Jr. and Lilyan Marie (Dodge) H.; m. Yasmin Islami, May 26, 1980; children: John Christopher, Theodore Martin, Jessamyn Susanna. BA in Psychology, Fairfield U., 1976; JD, Seton Hall U., 1984. Bar: N.J. 1984, U.S. Dist. Ct. N.J. 1984, U.S. Dist. Ct. (so. and ea. dists.) N.Y. 1985, U.S. Ct. Appeals (3d cir.) 1996. Law sec. Hon. Marshall Selikoff, J.S.C., Freehold, N.J., 1984-85; assoc. McElroy, Deutsch & Mulvaney, Morristown, N.J., 1985-88, Bumgardner, Hardin & Ellis, Springfield, N.J., 1988-90; ptnr. Tompkins McGuire & Wachenfeld, Newark, 1990-97; trial counsel Caron McCormick Constants & Wilson, Rutherford, N.J., 1997—; mediator Superior Ct. N.J., 1999—. Trustee Abdol H. Islami M.D. Found. for Med. Edn. Mem. ABA, N.J. Bar Assn., N.J. Bar Found. (trustee 1995—, treas. 1999—), Am. Inns of Ct. (Justice William Brennan Jr. chpt.; master Seton Hall Law Alumni chpt., Marie L. Garibaldi chpt.), Essex County Bar Assn. Avocations: reading, sports. Alternative dispute resolution, General civil litigation, Insurance. Home: 3 Birchmont Ln Warren NJ 07059-5437 Office: 201 Route 17 Rutherford NJ 07070-2574

**HENSEN, STEPHEN JEROME,** lawyer; b. Durango, Colo., Nov. 8, 1961; s. Ronald Jerome and Sandra Lucille (Monroe) H.; m. Janice Lynn Lamunyon; children: Amanda, Stephanie, Cory. BS in Econs., Colo. State U., 1984; JD, Gonzaga U., 1987. Bar: Colo. 1987, U.S. Dist. Ct. Colo. 1987, U.S. Ct. Appeals (10th cir.) 1988, U.S. Supreme Ct. 1994. Atty. Cortez Friedman, P.C., Denver, 1987-93; atty. McKenna & Cuneo, Denver, 1993-95; ptnr. Richman & Hensen, P.C., Denver, 1995—. Mem. Colo. Bar Assn., Denver Bar Assn., Colo. Supreme Ct. Bar Com. Republican. General civil litigation, Insurance, Professional liability. Office: Richman & Hensen PC 1775 Sherman St Ste 1717 Denver CO 80203-4318

**HENSEY, CHARLES MCKINNON,** retired lawyer; b. Ft. Bragg, N.C., Aug. 20, 1934; s. Charles Walter and Sarah McQueen (McKinnon) H.; m. Edna May Railey, July 9, 1966; children: Charles Gordon, Walter Thomas. BA in Bus. Adminstrn., Duke U., 1957; JD, U. N.C., 1962. Bar: N.C. 1962, U.S. Ct. Appeals (4th cir.) 1984, U.S. Supreme Ct. 1972. Assoc. Johnson, Biggs & Britt, Lumberton, N.C., 1962-65; asst. atty. gen. N.C. Dept. Justice, Raleigh, 1965-85, spl. dep. atty. gen., 1985-86, mem. spl. litig. counsel, 1985-91, counsel N.C. State Bd. Elections, 1991-97. Bd. dirs. Montessori Sch., Raleigh, 1978. Lt. (j.g.) USNR, 1957-59; capt. USNR ret. Mem. N.C. Bar Assn., N.C. State Bar. Democrat. Avocations: genealogy, historical research. Home: 2051 White Oak Rd Raleigh NC 27608-1449

**HENSLEIGH, HOWARD EDGAR,** lawyer; b. Blanchard, Iowa, Oct. 29, 1920; s. Albert Dales and Eula Fern (Bair) H.; m. Janice Lee Pedersen, Aug. 15, 1948; children: Susan Lee Hensleigh Harvey, Nancy Ann Hensleigh-Quinn, Jonathan Blair. BA, Iowa U., 1943, JD, 1947; postgrad., Columbia U., 1954-55. Bar: Iowa 1947, N.Y. 1955, Mass. 1968. Commd. U.S. Army, 1943, advanced through grades to col., 1965, ret., 1973; legal adviser U.S. Mission to NATO, Paris, 1958-60; dep. asst. gen. counsel office of Sec. Def. U.S. Govt., Washington, 1960-67, dep. asst. to sec. treas., 1967-68; asst. gen. counsel Raytheon Co., Bedford, Mass., 1968-91, ret., 1991; pvt. practice Carlisle, Mass., 1991—; participated in U.S. Italy Internat. Ct. Justice, The Hague, 1989. Chmn. town com. Carlisle Reps., 1972-80, sch. com. Carlisle, 1973-75, bd. selectmen, 1977-80. Mem. ABA (chmn. region I), Fed. Bar Assn., Am. Soc. Internat. Law. Government contracts and claims, Private international, Public international. Home and Office: 50 School St Carlisle MA 01741-1709

**HENSLEY, WILLIAM MICHAEL,** lawyer; b. Fresno, Calif., Apr. 25, 1954; s. Goldie Reeves and Allene (Watson) H.; m. Mari Bordona Calabrese, May 1981 (div. Jan. 1984); 1 child, Gilliann Mar; m. Anne Fields, Nov. 20, 1988. BA in Speech Comm., U. So. Calif., 1976; JD, Rutgers U., Camden, N.J., 1979. Bar: Calif. 1979, U.S. Dist. Ct. (no., ea., ctrl. and so. dists.) Calif., U.S. Ct. Appeals (9th cir.). Law clk. to Hon. Zenovich Calif. Ct. Appeals, 5th Appellate Dist., Fresno, 1979-81; assoc. Kadison, Pfaelzer, Woodard, Quinn & Rossi, L.A., 1981-87, Irell & Manella, L.A., 1987-92, Menke, Fahrney & Carroll, Costa Mesa, Calif., 1992-95; atty. Jackson, DeMarco & Peckenpaugh, Irvine, Calif., 1995—. Mem. editl. bd. Matthew Bender Calif. Real Estate Reporter, 1993—; contbr. articles to profl. jours. Mem. Orange County Bar Assn. Democrat. Mem. Ch. of Christ. Achievements include arguing some 60 appellate cases in Calif. state and federal courts. Avocations: gardening, walking, hiking, cooking. General civil litigation, Securities, Appellate. Home: 25 Pacific Crst Laguna Niguel CA 92677-5314 Office: Jackson DeMarco & Peckenpaugh 4 Park Plz Fl 16 Irvine CA 92614-8560

**HENVEY, JOHN WILLIAM,** lawyer; b. Washington, Aug. 18, 1945; s. John and Thelma Edna (Swaffar) H.; children: Kate, Scott. BA in Econs., Hardin-Simmons U., 1968; JD, U. Tex., 1973. Bar: Tex. 1973; cert. personal injury and civil trial specialist. Pvt. practice Dallas, 1973-76, 86—; assoc. Timothy E. Kelley, Dallas, 1976-86. 1st lt. U.S. Army, 1969-71, Vietnam. Decorated Bronze star. Mem. Coll. State Bar of Tex. Democrat. Methodist. General civil litigation, Product liability, Personal injury. Office: 5310 Forest Ln Ste 204 Dallas TX 75244-8031

**HENWOOD, WILLIAM SCOTT,** lawyer; b. Toronto, Ont., Can., May 24, 1949; s. William John and Muriel Mae (Scott) H.; m. Carol Elizabeth Nichols, Nov. 17, 1973; children: William Scott Jr., Cameron Nichols. BBA, Ga. State U., 1976; JD, Woodrow Wilson Coll. Law, 1978. Bar: Ga. 1979. Law clk. to reporter of decisions Supreme Ct. Ga., Atlanta, 1974-80, asst. reporter of decisions, 1980-84, reporter of decisions, 1984—. Co-author: Georgia's Appellate Judiciary: Profiles and History, 1987. Pres. Leafmore-Creek Park Civic Assn., Decatur, Ga., 1982-83, Briarcliff Cmty. Sports, Decatur, 1986-87; mem. Sesquicentennial Com., Supreme Ct. of Ga. With Army N.G., 1968-74. Fellow Ga. Bar Found.; mem. Assn. of Reporters of Jud. Decisions (pres. 1988-89), Ga. Legal History Found. (treas. 1984-96), Gridiron Secret Soc., Lawyers Club Atlanta (mem. exec. com. 1998—), Advocates Club (exec. bd. 1996-98), Burns Club (sec. 1992-93), Old War Horse Lawyers Club. Democrat. Presbyterian. Avocations: travel, hunting, sports car racing. Appellate. Home: 2247 Springwood Dr Decatur GA 30033-2722 Office: Supreme Ct Ga Judicial Bldg Atlanta GA 30334

**HERB, ALICE H.,** lawyer; b. Vienna, Austria, Feb. 17, 1933; came to U.S., 1939; d. Joseph and Emma (Teichner) Hoenig; m. Robert I.S. Herb, June 17, 1951 (dec. Dec. 1965); children: Eric L. (dec.), Peter L.; m. Matthe W. Boxer, Nov. 5, 1970 (dec. Jan. 1984). AB, Syracuse U., 1953; JD, NYU, 1955, LLM, 1992. Bar: N.Y. 1956. Atty. various firms N.Y.C., 1955-66; with ABC News, N.Y.C., 1966-81, CBS Cable, N.Y.C., 1981, Newsweek, N.Y.C., 1982; ind. prodr. N.Y.C., 1982-87; intern in ethics Montefiore Med. Ctr., Bronx, 1987, atty./ethicist, 1988-92; atty./ethicist SUNY Health Sci. Ctr., Bklyn., 1992—; cons. in ethics Bklyn. Hosp. Ctr., 1994—; mem. instnl. rev. bd. ERIA, N.Y.C., 1993-97. Writer/prodr. (video): A Choice Among Risks, 1992. Office: SUNY Health Sci Ctr PO Box 116 Brooklyn NY 11203-0116

**HERB, F(RANK) STEVEN,** lawyer; b. Cin., Nov. 9, 1949; s. Frank X. and Jean M. (Zurcher) H.; m. Jean L. Jeffers, June 21, 1971; children: Tracy Lynn, Jacquelyn Anne. BS, Bowling Green U., 1971; JD, U. Cin., 1974. Bar: Ohio 1974, Fla. 1978, U.S. Dist. Ct. (no., mid., and so. dists.) Fla., U.S. Ct. Appeals (11th cir.). Assoc. Connaughton Law Offices, Hamilton, Ohio, 1974; jud. advocate gen., chief of civil law USAF, Tyndall AFB, Fla., 1975-78; mng. ptnr. Nelson Hesse, Sarasota, Fla., 1979—. Author: (with others) Bennedicts on Admiralty, 1996, 97, 98; contbr. chpts. to books. Bd. dirs. Brock Wilson Found., Sarasota, 1983-92; pres. Riegels Landing Assn., Sarasota, 1986-90, 98-2000; dir., vice chmn. Siesta Key Utilities Assn., 1994—; mem. govt. rels. com. Nat. Marine Mfrs. Assn. Capt. JAGC USAF, 1975-78. Decorated USAF Meritorious Svc. medal. Mem. Ohio Bar Assn., Fla. Bar Assn. (chmn. 12th Jud. cir. unauthorized practice of law com. 1986-93, fee arbitration com. 12th jud. cir. 1996—), Sarasota Bar Assn., Def. Rsch. Inst., Maritime Law Assn., Am. Boat and Yacht Counsel, Nat. Marine Mfrs. Assn. (govt. rels. com.), The Field Club (dir. exec. com.). Republican. Roman Catholic. Avocations: boating, woodworking, skiing, tennis. General corporate, Admiralty, Product liability. Office: Nelson Hesse 2070 Ringling Blvd Sarasota FL 34237-7002

**HERBST, ABBE ILENE,** lawyer; b. N.Y.C., June 19, 1955; d. Seymour and Charlotte (Wolper) H. BA summa cum laude, Fordham U., 1976, JD, 1979. Bar: N.Y. 1980, N.J. 1980, U.S. Supreme Ct. 1986. Law clk. Keenan, Powers & Andrews, N.Y.C., 1978-79, assoc., 1980-83; assoc. DeForest & Duer, N.Y.C., 1983-90, ptnr., 1991—. Editor: Fordham Urban Law Journal, 1978-79. Recipient Outstanding Presentation award Cmty. Svc. Soc., N.Y.C., 1986. Mem. ABA, N.Y. State Bar Assn., N.J. State Bar Assn., N.Y. County Lawyers Assn., Fin. Women's Assn. N.Y., Riverdale Mental Health Assn., Soc. for Bus. Ethics, Phi Beta Kappa. Avocations: traveling, collecting miniature cat figurines. Estate planning, Probate, Estate taxation. Office: DeForest & Duer 90 Broad St Fl 18 New York NY 10004-2276

**HERBST, TODD L.,** lawyer; b. N.Y.C., July 15, 1952; s. Seymour and Charlotte (Wolper) H.; m. Robyn Beth Kellman, June 3, 1979; children: Scott Marshall, Carly Nicole. BA, CUNY, 1974; JD, John Marshall Law Sch., 1977. Bar: N.Y. 1978. Assoc. Max E. Greenberg, Cantor & Reiss, N.Y.C., 1977-83, mng. ptnr., 1984-87; sr. ptnr. Max E. Greenberg, Trager, Toplitz & Herbst, N.Y.C., 1988—; bus. cons. Shimizu Corp., U.S., 1983—, NTT Internat. Corp., Japan and U.S., 1996—, Dillingham Constrn. Holdings, Inc., San Francisco, 1987—, Gottlieb Skanska, Inc., N.Y.C., 1980—, Jolly Hotels, Italy, 1993—; lectr. Nat. Assn. Corp. Real Estate Execs. Exec. editor John Marshall Law Rev. Mem. ABA, N.Y. State Bar Assn., Am. Corp. Counsel Assn., N.Y. County Lawyers Assn. Jewish. Avocations: writing poetry, automobiles. Contracts commercial, Construction, Real property. Home: 7 Brookwood Ln New City NY 10956-2203 Office: Max E Greenberg Trager Toplitz & Herbst 100 Church St New York NY 10007-2601

**HERCH, FRANK ALAN,** law librarian, lawyer; b. Chgo., May 5, 1949; s. Robert Gilbert and Shirley (Berman) H.; m. Ruth Blackwell, Dec. 29, 1971; children: Nathaniel, Rachmiel. BA in Sociology and History, U. Calif., Davis, 1971; MLS, U. Calif., Berkeley, 1972; JD, U. Calif., Davis, 1975. Bar: Calif. 1981, U.S. Dist. Ct. (no. dist.) Calif. 1981. Reference libr. Alameda County Law Libr., Oakland, Calif., 1975-78; asst. law libr. Georgetown U. Law Ctr., Washington, 1978-81; atty. Blackwell, Herch & Herch, Oakland, 1981-87; libr. Cityline Info. Svc. Oakland Pub. Libr., 1984-87; dir. Clark County Law Libr., Las Vegas, Nev., 1987—; lectr. John F. Kennedy U. Sch. of Law, 1977-78, St. Mary's Coll. Paralegal Program, Moraga, Calif., 1981-87; law libr. and rsch. cons. Nev. Civil Jury Instructions Com. Monterey Coll. of Law, Alameda County Bar Assn., Oakland, 1981-87. Editor U. Calif. Davis Law Rev., 1974-75, writer, 1973-74; editor Jazz Rag mag., 1975-85, book revs. Legal Pub. Rev., Legal Information Alert, Business Information Alert, 1989—. Steering com. Second Start: Adult Literacy Program, Oakland, 1984-87; mem. exec. bd. East Bay Info. and Referral Network, Berkeley, 1984-87; mem. Clark County Merit Ins. Task Force, 1992. Recipient Cert. of Leadership Nat. U., Oakland, 1987, Leadership award City of Oakland, 1987. Mem. Am. Assn. Law Librs. (cert. 1978, v.p. West Pacific chpt. 1991-92, pres. 1992-93, sec. and treas. state, city and county law librs. spl. interest sect. 1989-92, chmn. regional meeting com., key issues forums, gov.'s conf. on future of librs. 1990, v.p., pres. elect, 1994—, legal info to the pub. special interest sect.), Nev. Libr. Assn. (chmn., bd. rep. so. dist. 1989). Avocations: writing fiction, playing guitar and keyboards, tennis, videotaping jazz performances. Office: Clark County Law Libr 304 Carson Ave Las Vegas NV 89101-5903 *I have been asked repeatedly how I can maintain my optimism and motivation when things appear to have gone wrong. I respond by insisting that even the most adverse events in our economy, the environment and our lives will bring lessons to be embraced and circumstances than can be turned into more positive results, Tolerance, flexibility and adaptability have been my watchwords.*

**HERDZIK, ARTHUR ALAN,** lawyer; b. Buffalo, June 6, 1950; s. Arthur Chester and Lottie Marie (Kowalczyk) H.; m. Jean Marie Rozler, Aug. 3, 1973; children: Julie, Karen, Lisa, Molly. BA magna cum laude, SUNY-Buffalo, 1972, JD, 1975. Bar: N.Y. 1976, U.S. Dist. Ct. (we. dist.) N.Y. 1976. Assoc. Miles, Cochrane, Grosse, Rossetti & Chelus, P.C., Buffalo, 1976-84; mem. Chelus, Herdzik & Speyer, P.C., Buffalo, 1985—; acting judge Village of Lancaster, N.Y., 1980-82, village prosecutor, 1982-92, village atty., 1988—. Sr. editor Buffalo Law Rev., 1975. Committeeman Erie County Dem. Com., 1978-80, 82— (Lancaster chpt. chmn. 1998—, exec. com. 1998—). Mem. ABA, N.Y. State Bar Assn., Erie County Bar Assn. (negligence com. 1990-93), Trial Lawyers Assn. Erie County, Phi Beta Kappa, Lodge: Lions (pres. 1998-99). Democrat. State civil litigation, Federal civil litigation, Insurance. Home: 68 Church St Lancaster NY 14086-2638 Office: Chelus Herdzik & Speyer PC 1560 Statler Towers Buffalo NY 14202-7502

**HEREDIA, F. SAMUEL,** lawyer; b. Santa Monica, Calif., Dec. 13, 1965; s. Franklin and Alicia Heredia; m. Bertha Alicia Cisneros, Aug. 17, 1996. BA in History, UCLA, 1989; JD, U. San Diego, 1992. Bar: Calif. 1992. Atty. Heredia & Assocs., Oxnard, Calif., 1996—. Mem. Consumer Attys. Calif., Consumer Attys. L.A. Democrat. Personal injury, Civil rights, Professional liability. Office: Heredia & Assocs 300 Esplanade Dr Ste 1170 Oxnard CA 93030-0238

**HERGE, J. CURTIS,** lawyer; b. Flushing, N.Y., June 14, 1938; s. Henry Curtis and Josephine E. (Breen) H.; m. Joyce Dorean Humbert, Aug. 20, 1960 (div. 1988); children: Cynthia Lynda, Christopher Curtis; m. Shirley Brooks Labonte, Dec. 22, 1989. Student, Cornell U., 1956-58; BA, Rutgers U., 1961, JD (Sebastian Gaeta scholar), 1963. Bar: N.Y. 1964, U.S. Supreme Ct. 1970, U.S. Ct. Claims 1974, D.C. 1974, Va. 1976. Assoc. firm Mudge Rose Guthrie & Alexander, N.Y.C., 1963-71; spl. asst. to atty. gen. U.S. Dept. Justice, Washington, 1973; assoc. solicitor conservation and wildlife U.S. Dept. Interior, Washington, 1973-74; asst. to sec. and chief staff U.S. Dept. Interior, 1974-76; ptnr. Sedam & Herge, McLean, Va., 1976-85, Herge, Sparks & Christopher LLP, McLean, Va., 1985—; bd. dirs. Diversified Labs., Inc., Ann E.W. Stone & Assocs., Inc., Palmer Tech. Svcs., Inc., Eaton Design Group, Inc., George Washington Banking Corp., Eaton Purchase Mgmt., Inc., George Washington Nat. Bank, Congl. Inst. Inc., Citizens United for Am., Am. Def. Lobby, Coun. Nat. Def., Renascence Found., The Am. Lobby Econ. Recovery Taskforce, Nat. Bank No. Va., Am. Freedom Found., Creative Response Concepts Inc. With Congl. Inst. Inc.; mem. adv. bds. Washington Legal Found., Nat. Taxpayers Legal Fund; Va. Commonwealth escheator Loudoun County and City of Fairfax, 1979-83; co-dir. spokesmen resources Com. for Re-election of Pres., 1971-72; mem. No. Va. Estate Planning Council; mem. natural resources coun. Rep. Nat. Com.; mem. Fairfax County Rep. Com., Conservative Rep. Com.; mem. Office Pres.-Elect Fed. Election Commn. Transition Team, 1980; co-chmn. N.Y. Honor Am. Day, 1970; speaker estate planning and fed. election laws; expert witness, charitable fund-raising, U.S. Tax Ct. Mem. Am., N.Y. State, Va., D.C. bar assns., Phi Kappa Sigma. Club: Capitol Hill. Administrative and regulatory, Non-profit and tax-exempt organizations, Probate. Home: 35 Rutherford Cir Potomac Falls VA 20165-6221 Office: Herge Sparks & Christopher LLP 6862 Elm St Ste 360 Mc Lean VA 22101-3862

**HERGOTT, DANIEL WELDON,** lawyer; b. LeSueur, Minn., June 11, 1950; s. Raymond Henry and Veronica Helen H.; m. Gail Lorraine Hayden, June 24, 1972; children: Nicholas, Kathryn. AB, Dartmouth Coll., 1972; JD, William Mitchell Coll. Law, 1976. Bar: Minn. 1976. Assoc. Rodney M. Hynes and Assocs., Mpls., 1976-78; ptnr. Hanley, Hergott & Hunziker, Mpls., 1979-84; shareholder Dunkley, Bennett & Christensen, P.A., Mpls., 1985—; referee Hennepin County Conciliation Ct., Mpls., 1979—, mem. ethics com., 1981-84. Youth coach Edina Athletic Assn., 1984-95. Mem. Rooster Found. (bd. dirs. 1991—). Avocations: racquetball, golf, tennis. Real property, Family and matrimonial, General corporate. Home: 5804 Garden Ave Edina MN 55436-2268 Office: Dunkley Bennett & Christensen PA 701 4th Ave S Ste 700 Minneapolis MN 55415-1812

**HERIN, DAVID V.,** lawyer; b. Bemidji, Minn., Aug. 17, 1944; s. Robert and Betty (Smithkey) H.; m. Cynthia Ann Duran, Apr. 12, 1969; children: David, Monica Ann. BA, Baylor U., Waco, Tex., 1966; JD, Baylor U., 1969. Bar: Tex. 1969, U.S. Dist. Ct. (so. dist.) Tex. 1973, U.S. Ct. Appeals (5th cir.) 1973, U.S. Tax Ct. 1973, U.S. Supreme Ct. 1973, U.S. Ct. Appeals (11th cir.) 1980. Assoc. Fischer & Fischer, Corpus Christi, Tex., 1973-80, Barnhart & Luther, Corpus Christi, 1980-81; judge 148th Jud. Dist. Tex., Corpus Christi, 1981-83; of counsel Coover & Coover, Corpus Christi, 1983-85; ptnr. Herin & Johnson, Corpus Christi, 1985-87, Herin & Miller, Corpus Christi, 1987-90; pvt. practice law Corpus Christi, 1990—. Capt. USAF, 1969-73. Mem. Tex. Bar Assn. (pres. 1980-81), Nueces County Bar Assn. (pres. 1977-81, Outstanding Young Lawyer 1981). Republican. Bankruptcy, State civil litigation, General practice. Office: 710 Buffalo St Corpus Christi TX 78401-1933

**HERLIHY, THOMAS MORTIMER,** lawyer; b. N.Y.C., Apr. 8, 1953; s. John Wilfred and Mary Frances (O'Sullivan) H.; m. Janice Anne Lazzaro, Aug. 26, 1978; children: Carolyn Jane, John Wilfred II. BA in History, Columbia U., 1975; JD, Fordham U., 1978. Bar: Calif. 1978, U.S. Dist. Ct. (no. dist.) Calif. 1978, U.S. Dist. Ct. (ea. and so. dists.) Calif. 1979, U.S. Dist. Ct. (cen. dist.) Calif. 1984, U.S. Ct. Appeals (9th cir.) 1979. Assoc. Pettit & Martin, San Francisco, 1978-82; ptnr. Kornblum, Kelly & Herlihy, San Francisco, 1982-88, Kelly, Herlihy, Advani & Klein, San Francisco, 1988—; lectr. Rutter Group, trial skills program Calif. Continuing Edn. of Bar, 1983-86, 87, 88; adj. faculty Nat. Inst. Trial Advocacy, 1997-98. Mem. ABA (litigation sect., torts and ins. practice sect.), Calif. Bar Assn., San Francisco Bar Assn., Calif. Def. Counsel, Def. Research Inst. Republican. Roman Catholic. Clubs: Olympic, Columbia U. Alumlni Club. Insurance, Federal civil litigation, State civil litigation. Home: 1424 Cortez Ave Burlingame CA 94010-4711 Office: Kelly Herlihy Advani & Klein 44 Montgomery St Ste 2500 San Francisco CA 94104-4712

**HERLING, MICHAEL JAMES,** lawyer; b. Bayshore, N.Y., Aug. 29, 1957; s. William Robert and Kathleen Joan (Meyer) H.; m. Nancy Ann Campbell, Nov. 28, 1981; children: Douglas Campbell, Scott Campbell, William Campbell. BA, Colgate U., 1979; JD, Stanford U., 1982. Bar: Conn. 1982. Assoc. Cummings & Lockwood, Stamford, Conn., 1982-86; ptnr. Finn Dixon & Herling, LLP, Stamford, 1986—; bd. dirs. Ring's End, Inc., Darien, Conn.; sec., gen. counsel Mormac Marine Group, Inc., Stamford, 1987—, The Interlake Steamship Co., Cleve., 1987—; sec. Meridian Aggregates Co., Denver, 1991—. Trustee Darien Library, 1989-95, Stamford Health System, 1998—, Darien YMCA, 1998—; bd. visitors Stanford Law Sch., 1996-98; chmn. Pres.'s Club Colgate U., 1998—; dir. Darien United Way, 1992-94. Mem. ABA, Conn. Bar Assn. (exec. com. bus. law sect., co-reporter bus. corp. act revision com.), Noroton Yacht Club, Wee Burn Country Club, Phi Beta Kappa. Republican. Episcopalian. Mergers and acquisitions, Securities, Finance. Office: Finn Dixon & Herling LLP One Landmark Sq Stamford CT 06901

**HERLONG, HENRY MICHAEL, JR.,** federal judge; b. Washington, June 1, 1944; s. Henry Michael Sr. and Josie Payne (Blocker) H.; m. Frances Elizabeth Thompson, Dec. 30, 1983; children: Faris Elizabeth, Henry Michael III. BA, Clemson U., 1967; JD, U. S.C., 1970. Bar: S.C. 1970, U.S. Ct. Appeals (4th cir.) 1972, U.S. Dist. Ct. S.C. 1972. Legis. asst. U.S. Senator Strom Thurmond, Washington, 1970-72; asst. U.S. atty. Dept. Justice, Greenville, S.C., 1972-76, Columbia, S.C., 1983-86; U.S. Magistrate judge U.S. Dist. Ct., Columbia, S.C., 1986-91; U.S. Dist. judge U.S. Dist. Ct., Greenville, S.C., 1991—; prin. Coleman & Herlong, Edgefield, S.C., 1976-83. Dir. Edgefield (S.C.) Devel. Bd., 1978-83, S.C. Assn. of Counties, 1980-83; active S.C. Rural Devel. Bd., 1980-83, Edgefield County Coun., 1979-83. Capt. USAR , 1970-75. Mem. S.C. Bar, Edgefield County Bar, Lions Club, Sertoma Club. Republican. United Methodist. Avocations: hunting, fishing, gardening. Office: US Dist Courts PO Box 10469 300 E Washington St Greenville SC 29603-1000

**HERMAN, FRED L.,** lawyer; b. New Orleans, Mar. 25, 1950; s. Harry and Reba (Hoffman) H.; m. Amanda Luria, Mar. 4, 1975. BA, Tulane U., 1972; JD, Loyola U.-New Orleans, 1975. Bar: La. 1975, U.S. Dist Ct. (ea. dist.) La. 1975, U.S. Ct. Appeals (5th cir.) 1978, U.S. Dist. Ct. (we. and mid. dists.) La. 1981, U.S. Ct. Appeals (11th cir.) 1981. Assoc. Herman & Herman, New Orleans, 1975-80; ptnr. Herman, Herman, Katz & Cotlar, New Orleans, 1980-87; sole practice New Orleans, 1987—; of counsel Garner and Munoz, Attys. at Law, 1988—; ltd. ptnr. New Orleans Saints, 1985, legis. counsel, chief negotiator for mng. ptnr., 1987; adj. faculty Tulane U.; lectr. Loyola Sch. Law, New Orleans, La. Trial Lawyers Assn. Commr. New Orleans Pub. Belt R.R. Commn., 1983-93; mem. Jefferson Parish Child Abuse Advocacy Program, 1980-81; spl. counsel litigation, State of La.; spl. counsel City of New Orleans; judge pro tem., First City Ct., New Orleans, 1998; mem. adv. coun. Adult Rehab. Ctr. Salvation Army, 1991—. Mem. ATLA, Am. Arbitration Assn. (mediator, arbitrator), Nat. Health Lawyer Assn. (panel of mediators and arbitrators), Fed. Bar Assn. (bank counsel sect.), La. Bankers' Assn., La. State Bar Assn. General civil litigation, Personal injury, General corporate. Office: 1010 Common St Ste 3000 New Orleans LA 70112-2401

**HERMAN, ROBERT STEPHEN,** lawyer; b. Pitts., Aug. 1, 1954; s. Earl and Lena Herman; m. Joan Optican, July 24, 1982; children: Kelsey, Brian, Kaley. Student, Tulane U., 1972-74; BA, U. Fla., 1976; JD, Loyola U., 1981. Bar: La. 1982, Tex. 1984, Mo. 1987. Assoc. Newman Drolla, New Orleans, 1982-84, Howard Abramson, Dallas, 1984-86, McDowell Rice, Kansas City, Mo., 1987-92; of counsel Kurlbaum Stoll, Kansas City, 1992-98; atty. Norris & Keplinger LLC, Overland Park, Kans., 1998—; approved agt. The Bar Plan Title Ins. Co., Kansas City, 1997—; spkr. Paine Webber Fin. Planning Seminars, Overland Park, Kans., 1998—. Coach Blue Valley Soccer Club, Overland Park, 1993-98; scout leader Boy Scouts Am., Leawood, Kans., 1998. Mem. ABA, Nat. Network Estate Planning Attys., The Midwest Estate Planning Inst., Kansas City Metro. Bar Assn. Avocations: tennis, golf, scuba, travel. Real property, Contracts commercial, Estate planning. Office: Norris & Keplinger LLC 6800 College Blvd Ste 630 Overland Park KS 66211-1556

**HERMAN, ROSS NEIL,** lawyer; b. N.Y.C., Feb. 19, 1956; s. Jack L. and Arlene (Zohn) H.; m. Judith D. Neuss, July 22, 1990. BA summa cum laude, Hobart Coll., 1980; MA, U. Chgo., 1981; JD magna cum laude, Yeshiva U., 1987. Bar: N.Y. 1988, U.S. Dist. Ct. (so. and ea. dists.) N.Y. 1989, U.S. Tax Ct. 1990, Fed. Cir. Ct. Appeals 1990, U.S. Ct. Appeals (2d cir.) 1993, U.S. Ct. Appeals (5th cir.) 1995, U.S. Ct. Appeals (3d cir.) 1997. Assoc. Kramer, Levin, Nessen, Kamin & Frankel, N.Y.C., 1987-89, Kostelanetz Ritholz Tigue & Fink, N.Y.C., 1989-93, Morvillo, Abramowitz, Grand, Iason & Silberberg, P.C., N.Y.C., 1993-97, Sills, Cummis, Radin, Tischman, Epstein & Gross, P.A., Newark, 1997—. Jacob Burns scholar Yeshiva U., 1984. Mem. ABA, Assn. of Bar of City of N.Y., N.Y. State Bar Assn., Nat. Assn. Criminal Def. Lawyers, Amnesty Internat., Phi Beta Kappa. Federal civil litigation, Criminal, State civil litigation. Office: Sills Cummis Radin Tischman Epstein & Gross PA Tigue & Fink 1 Riverfront Plz Newark NJ 07102

**HERMAN, RUSS MICHEL,** lawyer; b. New Orleans, Apr. 26, 1942; s. Harry and Reba Nell (Hoffman) H.; m. Barbara Ann Kline, July 5, 1965; children: Stephen Jay, Penny Lynn, Elizabeth Rose. BA, Tulane U., 1963, LLB, 1966. Bar: La. 1966, U.S. Dist. Ct. (ea. dist.) La. 1966, U.S. Ct. Appeals (5th cir.) 1970, U.S. Supreme Ct., 1972. Law clk. La. Ct. Appeals (4th cir.), New Orleans, 1965-66; ptnr. Herman, Herman, Katz & Cotlar (formerly Herman & Herman), New Orleans, 1966—; sec. Citizens for Justice, Inc., 1980; guest lectr. Loyola U. Law Sch., La. State U. Law Sch., Practising Law Inst.; adj. prof. law Tulane U. Law Sch., 1979—; spl. trial counsel New Orleans Aviation Bd., 1974-76, 88-89; mem. adv. council La. chpt. Am. Arbitration Assn., 1976—; mem. Civil Dist. Ct. Commn. on Local Rules and Forms, 1979, U.S. Dist. Ct. Com. on Disciplinary Rules and Revision Local Rules, 1979-80; mem. disciplinary com. U.S. Dist. Ct. (ea. dist.) La., 1980—. Mem. New Orleans Bd. Zoning Appeals, 1974-80; bd. dirs. Jewish Welfare Fedn., New Orleans; trustee Jewish Family and Children's Services, New Orleans; campaign chmn. for Gov. David C. Treen in Greater Met. area, 1980, 84; pres. Civil Justice Found., 1988-89. With U.S. Air N.G., 1959-65. Named Boss of Yr., New Orleans Legal Secs. Assn., 1981. Fellow Internat. Acad. Trial Lawyers, Roscoe Pound Found. (life, trustee, pres.); mem. ABA, Am. Soc. Profl. Liability Attys (diplomate), Fed. Bar Assn., Assn. Trial Lawyers Am. (bd. govs. 1986—, parlimentarian 1987—, pres.-elect 1988-89, pres. 1989—), La. Bar Assn. (ho. of dels. 1980-81, 85-86, asst. bar examiner 1975-80), La. Bar Found. (trustee 1980—), La. Trial Lawyers Assn. (pres. 1980-81, named Outstanding La. Trial Lawyer 1977, Leadership award 1981-82), Acad. Fla. Trial Lawyers, Boge Doga Soc. of Barristers, Ky. Trial Lawyers Assn., N.Y. State Trial Lawyers Assn., Calif. Trial Lawyers Assn., Pa. Trial Lawyers Assn., Trial Lawyers for Pub. Justice (trustee, bd. dirs. 1987-89), La. Found. for Law and Soc. (trustee), Ariz. Trial Lawyers Assn., Coalition for Consumer Justice. Democrat. Jewish. Federal civil litigation, State civil litigation, Personal injury. Home: 5346 Chestnut St New Orleans LA 70115-3053 Office: Herman Herman Katz & Cotlar 820 Okeefe Ave New Orleans LA 70113-1116

**HERMAN, STEPHEN ALLEN,** lawyer; b. Suffolk, Va., Nov. 27, 1943; m. Sally Jean Mansbach, Sept. 7, 1968; children: Braden, Andrew. BS, U. Pa., 1965; LLB, U. Va., 1968. Bar: Va. 1968, D.C. 1970, U.S. Ct. Appeals (D.C. cir.) 1970. Instr. law U. Chgo., 1968-70; assoc. Kirkland & Ellis, Washington, 1970-75, ptnr., 1975-90; sr. v.p., gen. counsel U.S. Generating Co., Bethesda, Md., 1990—. Author: FERC Practice and Procedure, 1984. Mem. Energy Bar Assn. (past pres.). FERC practice, Contracts commercial, Administrative and regulatory. Office: US Generating Co 7500 Old Georgetown Rd Ste 1300 Bethesda MD 20814-6161

**HERMAN, STEPHEN CHARLES,** lawyer; b. Johnson City, N.Y., Apr. 28, 1951; s. William Herman and Myrtle Stella (Clark) Keithline; m. Jeanne Ellen Nelson, Sept. 9, 1972; children: Neelie Kristine, Stefanie Anne, Christopher William. Student, Cedarville Coll., 1969-72; BA, Wright State U., 1973; JD, Ohio No. U., 1976. Bar: Mo. 1977, Ill. 1977; U.S. Dist. Ct. (ea. dist.) Mo. 1978, U.S. Dist. Ct. (no. dist.) Ill. 1979, U.S. Dist. Ct. (ea. dist) Mich. 1988, U.S. Dist. Ct. (so. dist.) Tex. 1997; U.S. Ct. Appeals (D.C. cir.) 1979, U.S. Ct. Appeals (7th cir.) 1979, U.S. Ct. Appeals (5th cir.) 1980, U.S. Ct. Appeals (10th cir.) 1992; U.S. Supreme Ct. 1986, U.S. Ct. Internat. Trade, 1998. Atty. Mo. Pacific Railraod Co., St. Louis, 1977-78; assoc. Belnap, McCarthy, Spencer, Sweeney & Harkaway, Chgo., 1978-82; ptnr. Belnap, Spencer & McFarland, Chgo., 1982-83, Belnap, Spencer, McFarland & Emrich, Chgo., 1983-84, Belnap, Spencer, McFarland, Emrich & Herman, Chgo., 1984-89, Belnap, Spencer, McFarland, Herman, 1990-96, McFarland & Herman, 1996—. Mem. ABA, Mo. Bar Assn., Met. Bar Assn. St. Louis, Ill. State Bar Assn., Chgo. bar Assn., Met. Bar Assn. St. Louis, Assn. Transp. Law, Logistics and Policy, Tower Club, Univ. Club (Chgo.). Transportation, Administrative and regulatory, General civil litigation. Home: 440 E Wisconsin Ave Lake Forest IL 60045-1452 Office: McFarland & Herman 20 N Wacker Dr Ste 1330 Chicago IL 60606-2902

**HERMAN-GIDDENS, GREGORY,** lawyer; b. Birmingham, Ala., Aug. 8, 1961. BA, U. N.C., 1984; JD, Tulane U., 1988; LLM in Estate Planning, U. Miami, 1993. Bar: N.C. 1988, U.S. Dist. Ct. (mid. dist.) N.C. 1988, Fla. 1992, U.S. Supreme Ct. 1998; cert. specialist in estate planning and probate law, N.C. State Bar Bd. Legal Specialization; grad. leadership triangle program 1996. Assoc. N. Joanne Foil, Atty. at Law, Durham, N.C., 1988-92, Catalano, Fisher, Gregory & Crown, Chartered, Naples, Fla., 1993, Northen, Blue, Rooks, Thibaut, Anderson & Woods, L.L.P., Chapel Hill,

N.C., 1994-96; pvt. practice Chapel Hill, 1996—; profl. adv. com. Triangle Cmty. Found., 1999—. Mem. Chapel Hill Bd. Adjustment, 1989-92; bd. dirs. Friends of Chapel Hill Sr. Ctr., 1994-97; mem. Orange County Adv. Bd. on Aging, 1994-97, vice-chair, 1996-97; treas., bd. dirs. Orange County Literacy coun., Carrboro, N.C., 1994-98; mem. nat. com. on planned giving N.C. Planned Giving Coun. Mem. ABA (coms. on stds. of tax practice and tax practice mgmt. of tax sect., coms. on lifetime and testamentary charitable gift planning and planning for execs. and profls. of real property, probate and trust sect. 1996—), N.C. Bar Assn. (law and aging com. young lawyers divsn. 1994-98, elder law sect. coun. 1998—, career devel. com. young lawyers divsn. 1990-91, dir. young lawyers divsn. 1997-98, endowment com. 1997—, estate adminstrn. manual com. estate planning & fiduciary law sect. 1997—), Nat. Acad. Elder Law Attys., Durham/Orange Estate Planning Coun., Kiwanis Club Orange County (pres. 1998-99), Phi Beta Kappa, Psi Chi. Estate planning, Probate, Estate taxation. Office: 1829 E Franklin St Ste 600 Chapel Hill NC 27514-5863

**HERMANN, DONALD HAROLD JAMES,** lawyer, educator; b. Southgate, Ky., Apr. 6, 1943; s. Albert Joseph and Helen Marie (Snow) H. AB (George E. Gamble Honors scholar), Stanford U., 1965; JD, Columbia U., 1968; LLM, Harvard U., 1974; MA, Northwestern U., 1979, Ph.D., 1981; MA in Art History, Sch. Art Inst. Chgo., 1993; postgrad., U. Chgo. Bar: Ariz. 1968, Wash. 1969, Ky. 1971, Ill. 1972, U.S. Supreme Ct. 1974. Mem. staff, directorate devel. plans U.S. Dept. Def., 1964-65; With Legis. Drafting Research Fund, Columbia U., 1966-68; asst. dean Columbia Coll., 1967-68; mem. faculty U. Wash., Seattle, 1968-71, U. Ky., Lexington, 1971-72; mem. faculty DePaul U., 1972—, prof. law and philosophy, 1978—, dir. acad. programs and interdisciplinary study, 1975-76, assoc. dean, 1975-78, dir. Health Law Inst., 1985—; lectr. dept. philosophy Northwestern U., 1979-81; counsel DeWolfe, Poynton & Stevens, 1984-89; vis. prof. Washington U., St. Louis, 1974, U. Brazilia, 1976, U. P.R. Sch. Law, 1993; lectr. law Am. Soc. Found., 1975-78, Sch. Edn. Northwestern U., 1974-76, Christ Coll. Cambridge (Eng.) U., 1977, U. Athens, 1980; vis. scholar U. N.D., 1983; mem. NEH seminar on property and rights Stanford U., 1981; participant law and econs. program U. Rochester, 1974; mem. faculty summer seminar in law and humanities UCLA, 1978; Bicentennial Fellow of U.S. Constitution Claremont Coll., 1986; Law and Medicine fellow Cleve. Clinic., 1990; bd. dirs. Coun. Legal Edn. Opportunity, Ohio Valley Consortium, 1972, Ill. Bar Automated Rsch. Corp., 1975-81, Criminal Law Consortium Cook County, Ill., 1977-80; cons. Adminstrv. Office Ill. Cts., 1975-90; reporter cons. Ill. Jud. Conf., 1972-90; mem. Ctr. for Law Focused Edn., Chgo., 1977-81; faculty Instituto Superiore Internazionale Di Science Criminali, Siracusa, Italy, 1978-82; cons. Commerce Fedn., State of São Paulo, Brazil, 1975. Editor: Jour. of Health and Hosp. Law, 1986-96, DePaul Jour. Healthcare Law, 1996—, AIDS Monograph Series, 1987—. Bd. dirs. Ctr. for Ch.-State Studies, 1982—, Horizons Cmty. Svcs., 1985-88, Chgo. Area AIDS Task Force, 1987-90, Howard Brown Health Ctr., 1994—; dir., v.p. Inst. for Genetics, Law and Ethics, Ill. Masonic Hosp., 1993—; trustee 860 N. Lakeshore Trust, Chgo., Ill., 1993-95; bd. visitors Oriental Inst., U. Chgo., 1995—, bd. dirs. Renaissance Soc., 1995—; mem. Cook County States Atty. Task Force on Drugs, 1985-90, Cook County States Atty. Task Force on Gay and Lesbian Issues, 1990—; mem. Ill. HIV Prevention Cmty. Planning Group, Ill. Dept. Pub. Health. John Noble fellow Columbia U., 1968, Internat. fellow, NEH fellow, Law and Humanities fellow U. Chgo, 1975-76, Law and Humanities fellow Harvard U., 1973-74, Northwestern U., 1978-82, Criticism and Theory fellow Stanford U. 1981, NEH fellow Cornell U., 1982, Judicial fellow U.S. Supreme Ct., 1983-84; Univ. scholar Northwestern U., 1979. Mem. ABA, Ill. Bar Assn., Chgo. Bar Assn., Am. Acad. Polit. and Social Sci., Am. Law Inst., Am. Soc. Law and Medicine, Am. Soc. Polit. and Legal Philosophy, Nat. Health Lawyers Assn., Am. Judicature Soc., Am. Philos. Assn., Soc. for Bus. Ethics, Soc. for Phenomenology and Existential Philosophy, Internat. Assn. Philosophy of Law and Soc., Soc. Writers on Legal Subjects, Internat. Penal Law Soc., Soc. Am. Law Tchrs., Am. Assn. Law Schs. (del., sect. chmn., chmn. sect. on jurisprudence), Am. Acad. Healthcare Attys., Ill. Assn. Hosp. Attys., Evanston Hist. Soc., Northwestern U. Alumni Assn., Signet Soc. of Harvard, Hasty Pudding Club, University Club, Quadrangle Club, Tavern Club, Cliff Dwellers Club, Arts Club Chgo., Legal Club Chgo., Law Club Chgo. Episcopalian. Home: 1243 Forest Ave Evanston IL 60202-1451 Office: DePaul U Coll Law 25 E Jackson Blvd Chicago IL 60604-2287 also: 880 N Lake Shore Dr Chicago IL 60611-1761

**HERMANN, PHILIP J.,** lawyer; b. Cleve., Sept. 17, 1916; s. Isadore and Gazella (Gross) H.; m. Cecilia Alexander, Dec. 28, 1945; children: Gary, Ann. Student, Hiram Coll., 1935-37; B.A., Ohio State U., 1939; J.D., Western Res. U., 1942. Bar: Ohio 1942. With Hermann Cahn & Schneider and predecessors, Cleve., 1946-86; founder, former chmn. bd. Jury Verdict Rsch., Cleve.; pres. Legal Info. Pubs. Author: 1956, Better Settlements Through Leverage, 1965, Do You Need a Lawyer?, 1980, Better, Earlier Settlements through Economic Leverage, 1989, Injured? How to Get All the Money You Deserve, 1990, The 96 Billion Dollar Game: You are Losing, 1993, How to Select Competent Cost-effective Legal Counsel, 1993, Profit With the Right Lawyer; contbr. articles to profl. jours. Served to lt. comdr. USNR, 1942-46, PTO. Mem. ABA (past vice chmn. casualty law com., past chmn. use of modern tech. com.), Ohio Bar Assn. (past chmn. ins. com., past chmn. fed. ct. com., past mem. ho. of dels.), Cleve. Bar Assn. (past chmn. membership com.), Am. Law Firm Assn. (past chmn. bd.), Fedn. Ins. Counsel. Club: Walden Golf and Tennis. Personal injury, Product liability, Insurance. Home: 615 Acadia St Aurora OH 44202 *Being what some people label "a perfectionist" is not easy and certainly not popular. It takes time and effort to collect information, to analyze it, to apply these to decisions and to insist upon careful work, but in the long run it is rewarding.*

**HERMANN, ROBIN L.,** lawyer; b. Ames, Iowa, May 23, 1943; s. Robert L. and Helen Ann Hermann; m. Peggy J. Hermann, Aug. 31, 1968; 4 children. LLB, U. Iowa, 1968. Bar: Iowa. Ptnr. Patterson Lorentzen Duffield Timmons Irish Becker Ordway LLP, Des Moines, 1968—. With USAR, 1961-68. Mem. ABA, Iowa Bar Assn., Polk County Bar Assn. Personal injury, Professional liability. Office: Patterson Lorentzen Duffield Timmons Irish Becker Ordway 505 5th Ave Ste 729 Des Moines IA 50309-2318

**HERMUNDSTAD, SARA SEXSON,** lawyer; b. Stuttgart, West Germany, Mar. 29, 1955; came to U.S., 1956, naturalized, 1970; d. Julius Calvin and Coyla Jeane (Fields) Sexson; m. Mark Allen Hermundstad, Oct. 18, 1980. BA, Colo. State U., 1977; JD, U. Colo., 1980. Bar: Colo. 1980. Law clk. NW Coun. of Govts., Frisco, Colo., 1979-80; assoc. Gerald B. Feather, P.C., Grand Junction, Colo., 1981-82; sole practice Grand Junction, 1982—; mediator 1991—; mem. selection com. for Fed. Magistrate, Grand Junction, 1981, Mesa County Judges, 1993-96. Mem. adv. bd. Salvation Army, 1987-97; spkr. various orgns., including Women's Resource Center, 1981-83; mem. adv. bd. for day care for sick children Family Health West, 1986-88; pres., treas., dir. Schuman Singers; bd. dirs. Western Colo. Bot. Soc., 1994-97. Mem. ABA, Colo. Bar Assn., Mesa County Bar Assn., Mesa County Bar Assn. Pro Bono Project, Inc. (sec., treas., bd. dirs.), PEO, Attrusa (bd. dirs.). Alternative dispute resolution, Family and matrimonial. Office: PO Box 2539 Grand Junction CO 81502

**HERNANDEZ, CARLOS ENRIQUE, JR.,** lawyer; b. Brownsville, Tex., Dec. 23, 1966; s. Carlos Enrique Sr. and Lorraine Renee Hernandez; m. Sophia Alexa Salinas, Mar. 22, 1996; 1 child, Carlos Enrique III. BA in Polit. Sci., Tex. A&M U., 1989; JD, South Tex. U., 1993. Bar: Tex. Assoc. Willette & James, Brownsville, Tex., 1993-94, Sweetman & Wise LLP, Harlingen, Tex., 1995-96, Hirsch, Sheiness & Garcia PLLC, Harlingen, Tex., 1997—. Mem. Brownsville C. of C. Democrat. Roman Catholic. Avocations: Internet, travel, golf. Office: Hirsch Sheiness & Garcia PLLC 1221 Mckinney St Ste 3700 Houston TX 77010-2010

**HERNANDEZ, DANIEL MARIO,** lawyer; b. Tampa, Fla., Sept. 26, 1951; s. Mario and Margaret (Alvarez) H.; m. Debra Sue Coleman, Dec. 6, 1980. BA, U. South Fla., 1972; JD, U. Fla., 1976. Bar: Fla. 1977, U.S. Dist. Ct. (mid. dist.) Fla. 1977, U.S. Supreme Ct. 1977. Asst. state atty. State Atty.'s Office, Tampa, 1977-82; assoc. Wilson and Sawyer P.A., Tampa, 1983; sole practice Tampa, 1983—. Mem. NCDFL, FBA, Hillsborough County Bar Assn. Democrat. Baptist. Avocations: tennis, jogging. Criminal, Family and matrimonial, Personal injury. Office: 902 N Armenia Ave Tampa FL 33609-1707

**HERNÁNDEZ, FERNANDO VARGAS,** lawyer; b. Irapuato, México Sept. 8, 1939; came to U.S., 1942, naturalized, 1957; s. José Espinosa and Ana María (Vargas) H.; m. Bonnie Corrie, Jan. 8, 1966 (div. Feb. 1991); children: Michael David, Alexandra Rae, Marcel Paul. BS, U. Santa Clara, 1961, MBA, 1962; JD, U. Calif.-Berkeley, 1966. Bar: Calif. 1967, U.S. Dist. Ct. (no. dist.) Calif. 1967. Sole practice law, San Jose, Calif., 1967—; lectr. law Lincoln U.; lectr. bus. U. Santa Clara. Mem. San Jose Housing Bd., 1970-73; arbitrator, judge protem Santa Clara County Superior Cts., 1979-98. Chmn. bd. trustees Calif. Rural Legal Assistance, 1973-75; bd. dirs. San Jose Civic Light Opera, 1981-83. Served with AUS, 1962-63. Mem. Calif. State Bar Assn., Santa Clara County Bar Assn. (chmn. torts sect. 1977-78, features editor In Brief mag. 1990-93), Calif. Trial Lawyers Assn., (bd. govs. 1979-82), Santa Clara County Trial Lawyers Assn. (pres. elect 1981), U. Santa Clara Alumni Assn. (pres. San Jose chpt. 1977-78), La Raza Lawyers Assn. Democrat. Roman Catholic. Club: Democratic Century. Contbg. editor to legal pleadings books. General civil litigation, Personal injury, Real property. Office: 64 W Santa Clara St Fl 2D San Jose CA 95113-1806

**HERNANDEZ, GARY A.,** lawyer; b. Merced, Calif., Feb. 15, 1959; s. Rosendo and Margaret (Salazar) H.; m. Teri L. Bond, Sept. 9, 1989. AB, U. Calif., Berkeley, 1981; JD, U. Calif., Davis, 1984. Bar: Calif. 1985. Dep. city atty. City and County of San Francisco, 1988-90; dep. ins. commr. Calif. Dept. Ins., San Francisco, 1990-95; ptnr. Long & Levit, San Francisco, 1995-97, Sonnenschein Nath & Rosenthal, San Francisco, 1997—; chmn. Claif. Coastal Conservancy, 1999—; dir. U.S. Pub. Technologies, San Diego, 1995—. Editor (newspaper) Perspectiva, 1984-88; editor Calif. Ins. Law Reporter, 1988—. Dir. Hispanic Cmty. Found., San Francisco, 1997—, Am. Cancer Soc., San Francisco, 1997—; bd. dirs. Calif. Coastal Conservancy, Oakland, 1998—. Mem. City Club of San Francisco, Club Mercedes. Democrat. Roman Catholic. Administrative and regulatory, Insurance. Home: 167 Knockash Hl San Francisco CA 94127-1237 Office: Sonnenschein Nath & Rosenthal 685 Market St San Francisco CA 94105-4200

**HERNANDEZ, H(ERMES) MANUEL,** lawyer; b. Bronx, N.Y., Mar. 16, 1955; s. Manuel and Aurora O'Neill H.; m. Hortensia Beatriz Carrasquillo, Aug. 28, 1980; children: Antonio, Victoria, Stephanie. BS in Criminal Justice magna cum laude, Met. State Coll. of Denver, 1976; JD, U. Denver, Denver, 1979. Bar: Colo. 1979, N.Y. 1986, D.C. 1986, Fla. 1988; cert. trial adv Nat. Bd. Trial Advocacy; cert. criminal trial specialist and criminal appellate specialist Fla.. Bar 1993. Trial atty. criminal div. U.S. Dept. Justice, Washington, 1979-80; asst. U.S. atty. criminal and civil div. U.S. Dept. Justice (Colo., Puerto Rico, Fla. mid. dist.), 1980-89; pvt. practice Orlando, Fla., 1989—; chmn. civilian rev. bd. Seminole County Sheriff's Office, Orlando, 1992-93. Mem. Nat. Criminal Def. Lawyers Assn., Fla. Fed. Bar Assn. (Orlando chpt., v.p. 1988-89, pres. 1989-90, 90-91, 99—, nat. del. 1991, 92, 93), Fla. Bar, Fla. Assn. Criminal Def. Lawyers, Hispanic Bar Assn. (charter mem. Orlando chpt.), Ctrl. Fla. Criminal Trial Lawyers Assn.. Republican. Roman Catholic. Avocations: music, history. Criminal, Appellate, Federal civil litigation. Office: 646 E Colonial Dr Orlando FL 32803-4603

**HERNANDEZ, JACQUELINE CHARMAINE,** lawyer; b. Trinidad, W.I., Nov. 1, 1960; came to U.S., 1975; d. Desmond and Jocelyn Virginia (Felix) H. BA, L.I. U., 1982; JD, NYU, 1985. Bar: N.Y. 1986, N.J. 1987, U.S. Dist. Ct. (so. and ea. dists.) N.Y. 1988, U.S. Dist. Ct. N.J. 1996. Assoc. Cooper and Kenny, N.Y.C., 1985-87, Semel, Boeckmann, Diamond, Schepp & Yuhas, N.Y.C., 1987-88, Wood, Williams, Rafalsky & Harris, N.Y.C., 1988-90; from assoc. to ptnr. Cooper, Liebowitz, Royster & Wright, Elmsford, N.Y., 1990-96; assoc. Gordon & Silber, P.C., N.Y.C., 1996—. Mem. ABA, Nat. Bar Assn., Black Bar Assn. Bronx County, Assn. Black Lawyers of Westchester County Inc., Internat. Platform Assn. Roman Catholic. Avocations: theatre, travel. Insurance, Personal injury, Product liability. Home: Paladins Keep 24 Carhart Ave White Plains NY 10605-1448 Office: Gordon & Silber PC 355 Lexington Ave New York NY 10017-6603

**HERNANDEZ, MACK RAY,** lawyer; b. Austin, Tex., Sept. 8, 1944; s. Mack and Mary (Prado) H.; m. Mary Lynn McGuire, May 11, 1979 (div. Sept. 1988); 1 child, John Christopher. BA, U. Tex., 1967, JD, 1970. Bar: Tex. 1970, U.S. Dist. Ct. (we. dist.) Tex. 1972. Staff atty. Travis County Legal Aid Soc, Austin, 1970-71; pvt. practice law Austin, 1971—. Mem. bd. dirs. Austin C. of C., 1983-86, Meals on Wheels, Austin, 1972-76; trustee Austin C.C., 1988—; vice chair, 1990-92, chair, 1992—; chmn. bd. dirs. Am. Cancer Soc., Austin, 1988—. Mem. Tex. Bar Assn., Travis County Bar Assn., Coll. of State Bar, Tex. Bar Found. Avocations: travel, jogging, hiking, backpacking. E-mail: mackrayh@bga.com. State civil litigation, Contracts commercial, Probate. Office: 700 N Lamar Blvd Ste 200 Austin TX 78703-5416

**HERNANDEZ, MICHAEL VINCENT,** law educator; b. Richmond, Va., Apr. 29, 1962; s. Henry Vincent and Betty Jane (Fulwider) H.; m. Laura Ruth Brown, Sept. 16, 1989; children: Justin Michael, Nathan Marc, Alicia Joy. BA in Govt. with high distinction, U. Va., 1984, JD, 1987. Bar: Va. 1987, U.S. Dist. Ct. (ea. and we. dists.) Va., 1987, U.S. Ct. Appeals (4th cir.) 1987, U.S. Supreme Ct. 1990. Assoc. McGuire, Woods, Battle & Boothe, Richmond, 1987-89, McSweeney, Burtch & Crump, Richmond, 1990-92; adj. asst. prof. Regent U. Sch. Law, Virginia Beach, Va., 1992, asst. prof., 1992-98, faculty advisor moot ct., 1994—, assoc. prof., 1998—; mem. Tidewater Va. Tchg. Consortium, spring 1995; counsel for State of N.C. re interstate dispute over Coastal Zone Mgmt. Act, 1994, and challenge to fed. fishing regulations, 1995-98. Contbr. articles to law jours., chpt. to book. Pro bono counsel tenants coalition and lead com. Washington Park, Portsmouth, Va., 1992—; gen. counsel Richmond AIDS Ministry, spring 1992; vol. STEP (Strategies To Elevate People), Richmond, 1987-92; asst. homegroup leader, Sunday sch. tchr. Southside Ch. Richmond, 1990-92; asst. homegroup leader, nursery vol. Episcopal Ch. of Messiah, Chesapeake, Va., 1993-94, 95; nursery vol. Kempsville Presbyn. Ch., Virginia Beach, 1994, 95-96, 97-98; children's Sunday sch. tchr., substitute lector Christ Covenant Ref. Episcopal Ch., Virginia Beach, 1996-97. Mem. ABA, Va. State Bar, Va. Bar Assn. Avocations: golf, tennis, basketball. Office: Regent U Sch Law 1000 Regent University Dr Virginia Beach VA 23464-5037

**HERNANDEZ-DENTON, FEDERICO,** supreme court justice; b. Santurce, P.R., Apr. 12, 1944; s. Federico and Teresa (Denton) Hernandez-Morales; m. Isabel Pico, 1966. BA, Harvard U., 1966, JD, 1969. Bar: P.R. 1971. Dir. Consumer Rsch. Ctr. and Bus. Adminstrn. Rsch. Ctr. U. P.R., 1970-72; dir. P.R. Consumer Svc. Adminstrn., 1973; sec. P.R. Dept. Consumer Affairs, 1973-76; asst. prof. Law Sch. Interam. U., P.R., 1977-84, dean, 1984-85; now justice Supreme Ct. P.R, San Juan; chair Bd. Bar Examiners. Mem. ABA, Am. Law Inst., P.R. Bar Assn. Office: Supreme Ct of PR PO Box 9022392 San Juan PR 00902-2392

**HERNANDEZ-GONZALEZ, GLORIA MARIA,** lawyer, consultant; b. Santo Domingo, Dominican Republic, May 8, 1959; came to U.S., 1990; d. Lupo Hernandez-Rueda and Gloria E. (Contreras) Hernandez; m. Ramon Horacio Gonzalez-Perez, June 27, 1986; children: Ramon Horacio, Maria de Fatima, Patricia Antonia, David Rafael. JD magna cum laude, U. Nat. Pedro Henriquez Urena, Santo Domingo, 1981. Bar: Dominican Republic 1982, N.Y. 1991. Atty., ptnr. Ortiz, Hernandez & Assocs., Santo Domingo, 1976—; internat. legal cons. Ortiz, Hernandez & Assocs., Albertson, N.Y., 1991—; legal advisor Nat. Coun. for Higher Edn., Santo Domingo, 1986—. Author: La Responsabilidad Patrimonial del Estado, 1985, Tratado de Responsabilidad Civil, 1991. Mem. ABA, Dominican Bar Assn., Inter-Am. Bar Assn., N.Y. State Bar Assn., N.Y. State Trial Lawyers Assn., Instituto Derecho del Trabajo, Am. C. of C. of Dominican Republic. Roman Catholic. Avocations: piano, painting, horseback riding, lecturing. Contracts commercial, General civil litigation, Labor. Home and Office: 158-34 90th St Howard Beach NY 11414-3112

**HEROLD, KARL GUENTER,** lawyer; b. Munich, Feb. 3, 1947; came to U.S., 1963; s. Guenter K.B. and Eleonore E.E. H.; children: Deanna, Donna, Nicole, Jessica, Christine, Karl-Matthäus. BS, Bowling Green State U., 1969; JD, Case Western Res. U., 1972. Bar: Ohio 1972, N.Y. 1985, Conseil Juridique, France, 1990, Rechtskundiger, Germany, 1991, Avocat, France, 1992. Ptnr.-in-charge, European bus. practice coord. Jones, Day, Reavis & Pogue, Frankfurt, Germany, 1972—; coord. bus. practice Europe and Ctrl. and Ea. Europe Jones, Day, Reavis & Pogue; trustee Internat. and Comparative Law Ctr. Southwest Legal Found., Dallas, 1983; bd. dirs. Didier Taylor Refractories Corp., Cin., Redland Corp., San Antonio, v.p., Redland Credit Corp., San Antonio, v.p., Redland Fin. Inc., San Antonio, v.p., 1979-86, Zircoa Inc., Solon, Ohio, 1988-92. Contbr. numerous articles to legal jours. Trustee Cleve. Internat. Program, 1982-88; chmn. bd. dirs. Frankfurt Internat. Sch., 1991-93. Mem. ABA, Internat. Bar Assn., Order of Coif, Omicron Delta Kappa. Private international, General corporate. Office: Jones Day Reavis & Pogue 599 Lexington Ave Fl C1A New York NY 10022-6030 also: Jones Day Reavis & Pogue, Hochhaus am Park Grueneburg Weg, 60323 Frankfurt Germany

**HERON, JULIAN BRISCOE, JR.,** lawyer; b. Washington, Dec. 17, 1939; s. Julian B. Sr. and Doris S. (Strange) H.; m. Kathleen Ann Sweeney, Aug. 13, 1983; children: Kimberle, Melissa, Julian III, Kevin, Kathleen. BS, U. Ky., 1962, LLB, 1965. Bar: Ky. 1965, D.C. 1966, U.S. Dist. Ct. D.C. 1966, Md. 1968, U.S. Ct. Appeals (D.C. cir.) 1968, U.S. Supreme Ct. 1968. Ptnr. Pope, Ballard & Loos, Washington, 1968-81, Heron, Burchette, Ruckert & Rothwell, Washington, 1981-90, Tuttle, Taylor & Heron, Washington, 1990—; chmn. U.S. Agrl. Export Devel. Coun., 1983-85. Pres. Washington Internat. Horse Show, 1984, 85, Nat. Horse Show, 1994-96. Capt. USAF, 1965-68. Fellow ABA (chmn. agr. com. of adminstrv. law sect.); mem. D.C. Bar Assn. (chmn. ethics com.), Ky. Bar Assn., Md. Bar Assn., Bar Assn. D.C., Barristers, Faquier Springs Country Club. Republican. Roman Catholic. Administrative and regulatory, Private international, Legislative. Office: Tuttle Taylor & Heron Ste 407 1025 Thomas Jefferson St NW Washington DC 20007-5201

**HERPE, DAVID A.,** lawyer; b. Chgo., May 2, 1953; s. Richard S. and Beverly H.; m. Tina Demsetz, Aug. 21, 1977; children: Lauren E., Stacy P. BA in Econs., U. Ill., 1975; JD, U. Chgo., 1978. Bar: Ill. 1978, U.S. Dist. Ct. (no. dist.) Ill. 1979, U.S. Tax Ct. 1991. Assoc. then ptnr. Schiff, Hardin & Waite, Chgo., 1978-1996; ptnr. McDermott, Will & Emery, Chgo., 1996—. Co-author: Illinois Estate Planning, Will Drafting and Estate Administration Forms-Practice, 2nd edit., 1994; contbr. articles to legal jours. Mem. and dir. Chgo. Estate Planning Coun. (v.p. 1999—). Fellow Am. Coll. of Trust and Estate Counsel; mem. ABA. Estate planning, Probate, Estate taxation. Office: McDermott Will & Emery 227 W Monroe St Ste 3100 Chicago IL 60606-5096

**HERR, BRUCE,** lawyer; b. Chgo., Aug. 12, 1943; s. Ross and Emilie (Robert) H.; m. Ellen Epstein, Feb. 22, 1968; children: Sarah, Rachel. BA cum laude, Harvard U., 1965, JD, 1968. Bar: N. Mex. 1969, Ill. 1970, U.S. Dist. Ct. N. Mex. 1969, U.S. Ct. Appeals (10th cir.) 1969, U.S. Supreme Ct. 1973. Staff atty. DNA Legal Svcs., Shiprock, N. Mex., 1969-70, Appellate Defender Project, Springfield, Ill., 1970-73; legal dir. Office of Ill. Appellate Defender, Springfield, 1973; appellate defender N. Mex. Pub. Defender Dept., Santa Fe, 1973-76; assoc., shareholder Montgomery & Andrews, PA, Santa Fe, 1976—; Mem. N. Mex. Supreme Ct. Com. on Civil Procedure Rules, 1983-98, chair, 1996-98, chair task force on electronic filing, 1994-96; mem. adv. opinions com. N. Mex. State Bar, 1985-88, 96—, chair employment and labor law sect., 1994-95. Pres. Friends of Santa Fe Pub. Libr., 1997; tutor Literacy Vols. Santa Fe, 1996—; bd. dirs. Santa Fe Bus. Incubator, Inc., 1995-96; v.p. Sante Fe Econ. Devel., Inc., 1999—. Lifetime hon. bd. mem. Santa Fe Bus. Incubator, Inc., 1996. Mem. ABA, First Jud. Dist. Bar Assn., Oliver Seth Am. Inn of Ct., Santa Fe County C. of C. (dir. 1992-96, chair 1995-96, Bd. Mem. of Yr. 1993-94), Rotary Club. Avocations: running, hiking, reading, community activities. Labor, General civil litigation, Civil rights. Home: 148 Elena St # A Santa Fe NM 87501-6528 Office: Montgomery & Andrews PA 325 Paseo De Peralta Santa Fe NM 87501-1860

**HERR, STANLEY SHOLOM,** law educator; b. Newark, Aug. 7, 1945; s. Louis J. and Ruth G. (Greenberg) H.; m. Raquel Schuster, June 17, 1979; children: David Louis, Deborah Ann, Ilana Ruth. BA cum laude, Yale U., 1967, JD, 1970; DPhil, Oxford U., 1979. Bar: D.C. 1971, U.S. Dist Ct. D.C. 1971, U.S. Ct. Appeals (5th cir.) 1972, Md. 1984, U.S. Supreme Ct. 1984. Staff atty. Stern Community Law Office, Washington, 1970-71; sr. staff atty. Nat. Law Office of Nat. Legal Aid Defender Assn., Washington, 1971-73; Joseph P. Kennedy Jr. fellow Balliol Coll. Oxford (Eng.) U., 1973-76; vis. scholar, instr. Law Sch. Harvard U., Cambridge, Mass., 1976-80; Rockefeller Found. fellow, vis. scholar Law Sch. Columbia U., N.Y.C., 1980-82; project dir. mental patients' rights guidebook NIMH, Northampton, Mass. and Bethesda, Md., 1982-83; vis. assoc. prof. law U. Md., Balt., 1983-84, assoc. prof. law, 1984-95, prof. law, 1995—; sr. rsch. fellow Schell Ctr. for Internat. Human Rights, Yale Law Sch., 1995—; cons. U.S. Dist. Ct. Mass., Boston, 1979-81; co-founder, v.p. Homeless Persons Representation Project, Balt., 1987—; vis. prof. Tel Aviv U., 1990-91; vis. scholar Law Sch., Hebrew U., Jerusalem, 1990-91; Kennedy Pub. Policy fellow, The White House, 1993-95; cons. NAS; Switzer disting. rsch. fellow Nat. Inst. on Disability and Rehab. Rsch., 1999—; vis. Grossman prof. Haifa U., 1999—. Author: The New Clients: Legal Services for Mentally Retarded Persons, 1979, Rights and Advocacy for Retarded People, 1983, Legal Rights and Mental Health Care, 1983, A Guide to Consent, 1999, Aging, Rights and Quality of Life, 1999; contbr. articles to legal jours., chpts. to books. Bd. dirs. Am. Jewish Soc. for Svc., N.Y.C., 1972—, Am. Assn. Mental Retardation, Internat. Acad. Law & Mental Health; cons. U.S. Pres.'s Com. on Mental Retardation, 1978-80; mem. Md. Gov.'s Commn. to Revise Mental Retardation and Devel. Disability Laws, 1985-86; pres. Greater Balt. Shelter Network, 1987. Recipient Rosemary F. Dybwad Internat. award Nat. Assn. Retarded Citizens, 1973, Leadership award Region IX Am. Assn. Mental Deficiency, 1984, Thomas Ferciot Disting. Profl. Svc. award Balt. Assn. Retarded Citizens, 1987, Swartz medallion for Humanitarian Svc., Swartz found., 1990, Burton Blatt award Young Adult Inst., Rights of the Disadvantage award Md. Bar Found., 1999, Regent's faculty award for excellence in pub. svc., 1999; named Fulbright scholar 1990-91, fellow World Inst. on Disability, 1993; Switzer Disting. Rsch. fellow, 1999—. Fellow Am. Assn. Mental Retardation (pres. legal process divsn. 1978-80, 82-84, bd. dirs. 1993-95, v.p. 1996, pres.-elect 1997, pres. 1998, Humanitarian award 1996, Sandra Jensen Humanitarian award Region II 1997); mem. ABA (commn. on mental and phys. disability law 1997, chair editl. adv. bd., mental and phys. disability law reporter), Assn. Retarded Citizens U.S. (chmn. legal advocacy com. 1984-90). Avocations: long-distance running, foreign travel. Office: U Md Law Sch 515 W Lombard St Baltimore MD 21201-1701

**HERRING, GROVER CLEVELAND,** lawyer; b. Nocatee, Fla., Dec. 9, 1925; s. Joseph I. and Martha (Selph) H.; m. Dorothy L. Blinn, Apr. 17, 1947; children: Stanley T., Kenneth Lee. JD, U. Fla., 1950. Bar: Fla. 1950. Assoc. Haskins & Bryant, 1950-52; sole practice West Palm Beach, Fla., 1952-60, 64—; ptnr. Blakeslee, Herring & Bie and predecessor firm, 1953-60, Warwick, Paul & Herring, 1964-70, Herring & Evans now Arnstein & Lehr, 1970-95, Baldwin & Herring, West Palm Beach, Fla., 1995—; atty. City of Atlantis, Fla., City of West Palm Beach, 1960-63, Town of Ocean Ridge, Fla., 1953-61, 64-66, Village of Royal Palm Beach, Fla., 1964-72, Town of South Palm Beach, Fla., 1966-72; spl. master-in-chancery 15th Jud. Cir. Palm Beach County, 1953-54; judge ad litem Mcpl. Ct., West Palm Beach, 1954-55; bd. dirs. Lawyers Title Services Inc., West Palm Beach. Contbr. legal articles to profl. revs. Active PTA, Family Service Agy., Palm Beach County Mental Health Assn.; chmn. profl. sect. ARC, 1960; mem. Charter Revision Com. West Palm Beach, 1960-65, Palm Beach County Resources Devel. Bd., 1959—, Dem. Exec. Com., 1965-70; apptd. mem. Govtl. Study Commn. by Fla. Legis.; bd. dirs. Community Chest. Served with USNR, 1944-46. Mem. ABA, Palm Beach County Bar Assn. (treas. 1960), John Marshall Bar Assn., Fla. Bar Assn., Am. Judicature Soc., Lawyers Title Guaranty Fund (field rep. 1955-60, 64—), East Coast Estate Planning Council, Nat. Inst. Mcpl. Law Officers, Law-Sci. Acad., Assn. Trial Lawyers Am. (assoc. editor 1960—), Lawyers Lit. Club, Nat. Mcpl. League, U. Fla. Law Ctr. Assn., World Peace Through Law Ctr., Fla. Sheriff's Assn. (hon.), U. Fla. Alumni Assn., VFW, Am. Legion, West Palm Beach C. of C., Civic Music Assn., Palm Beach County Hist. Soc. (pres. 1969-72), New Eng. Hist. Geneal. Soc. Boston. Clubs: West Palm Beach Country (hon.); Airways (N.Y.C.). Lodges: Eight Oaks River, Masons (32 deg.), Elks, Moose. Home: 3507 N Australian Ave West Palm Beach FL 33407 Office: Baldwin & Herring Ste G 1675 P B Lakes Blvd West Palm Beach FL 33401

**HERRING, JERONE CARSON,** lawyer, bank executive; b. Kinston, N.C., Sept. 27, 1938; s. James and Isabel (Knight) H.; m. Patricia Ann Hardy, Aug. 6, 1961; children—Bradley Jerone, Ansley Carole. A.B., Davidson Coll., 1960; LL.B., Duke U., 1963. Bar: N.C. 1963. Assoc. McElwee & Hall, North Wilkesboro, N.C., 1965-69; ptnr. McElwee, Hall & Herring, North Wilkesboro, 1969-71; exec. v.p., sec., gen. counsel Br. Banking & Trust Co., Winston-Salem, N.C., 1971—, BB&T Corp., Winston-Salem, 1995—. Served to capt. U.S. Army, 1963-65. Mem. ABA, N.C. Bar Assn., Am. Soc. Corp. Secs., Am. Corp. Counsel Assn. Presbyterian. Banking, General corporate. Office: 200 W 2d St Winston Salem NC 27101

**HERROLD, DAVID HENRY,** lawyer; b. Corpus Christi, Tex., Sept. 4, 1969; s. Donald Erwin and Mary Louise Herrold; m. Amy Lynn Fisher, Aug. 14, 1993. BA in Liberal Arts, U. Tex., 1992; JD, U. Tulsa, 1996. Bar: Okla. 1996, U.S. Dist. Ct. (no., and ea. dists.) Okla. 1996, U.S. Dist. Ct. (we. dist.) Okla. 1997, U.S. Ct. Appeals (10th cir.) 1997, U.S. Ct. Appeals (11th cir.) 1999. Law clk. Herrold, Herrold & Davis, Tulsa, 1992-94, Huffman Arrington et al, Tulsa, 1994-95; law clk., summer assoc. Conner & Winters, P.C., Tulsa, 1995-96, assoc., 1996—; mem. ct. ops. com. Tulsa Bar, 1997-98; mem. bankruptcy sect. Okla. Bar, 1997-98, mem. civil procedure sect. Okla. Bar, 1999—. Articles editor Tulsa Jour. of Comparative & Internat. Law, 1993-95; staff mem. Tulsa Law Jour., 1993-94. Participant Tulsa Bus. Forum, 1996-97; conflict juvenile atty. Okla. Juvenile Cts., Tulsa, 1996-98; active campaign com. R. Hayden Downie, Tulsa, 1998. Recipient Jurisprudence award Am. Jurisprudence, Tulsa, 1992, First Pl. award St. Francis Corp. Challenge, Tulsa, 1997-98. Mem. ABA, Okla. Bar Assn., Taka County Bar Assn., The Summit, Nicholas Club, Tulsa Tex. Execs. (pres. 1996-98), Am. Inns Ct., Phi Delta Phi. Republican. Methodist. Avocations: swimming, water sports, running, racquetball. Consumer commercial, General civil litigation, Contracts commercial. Office: Conner & Winters PC 15 E 5th St Ste 3700 Tulsa OK 74103-4304

**HERRON, DONALD PATRICK,** lawyer, psychologist; b. Springfield, Ill. Feb. 6, 1954; s. Donald Franklin and Patricia Ann (Flynn) H.; m. Kristine Lydia Gish, Aug. 7, 1976. B.A. in Psychology and Sociology, U. Mo.-Kansas City, 1976, M.A. in Psychology, 1978, J.D., 1981. Bar: Mo. 1981, U.S. Dist. Ct. (we. dist.) Mo. 1981. Counselor, Johnson County Mental Retardation Ctr., Kans., 1976-77; lectr. in psychology, acad. adviser U. Mo.-Kansas City, 1977-80; assoc. Morris and Foust, Kansas City, 1981-85; ptnr. Herron and Lewis, Kansas City, 1985—; cons. psychology, Kansas City, 1978—. Author profl. papers in psychology. Named one of Outstanding Young Men in Am. Mem. ABA (litigation sect.), Mo. Bar Assn., Kansas City Bar Assn., Assn. Trial Lawyers Am., Mo. Trial Lawyers Assn., Nat. Assn. For Behavior Analysis, AAAS, Phi Delta Phi, Phi Kappa Phi, Psi Chi. Roman Catholic. Avocation: sports. Personal injury, Insurance, General civil litigation. Home: 11333 W 121st Ter Shawnee Mission KS 66213-1979 Office: Herron and Lewis Country Club Pla 400 E 95th St Ste E Kansas City MO 64131-3018

**HERRON, ROY BRASFIELD,** lawyer; b. Martin, Tenn., Sept. 30, 1953; s. Clarence Grooms and Mary Cornelia (Brasfield) H.; m. Nancy Carol Miller, Jan. 3, 1987; children: John, Richard, Benjamin. BS with highest honors, U. Tenn., 1975; MDiv, Vanderbilt U., 1980, JD, 1980. Bar: Tenn. 1980, U.S. Dist. Ct. Tenn. 1980, U.S. Ct. Appeals (6th cir.). Ptnr. Herron & Miller-Herron, Dresden, Tenn., 1991-97, Neese, Herron & Miller-Herron, Dresden, 1997—; pres. Grooms Herron Found., Dresden; bd. dirs. Herron Farms Inc., Dresden. Author: Things Held Dear. Mem. Tenn. Ho. of Reps., Nashville, 1986-96, Tenn. State Senate, Nashville, 1996—. Rotary scholar U. St. Andrews, Scotland, 1975-76. Democrat. United Methodist. Avocations: hunting, fishing, triathlons, marathons, writing. General civil litigation, General practice, Consumer commercial. Home: 545 Meadowlawn Dresden TN 38225-1394 Office: Neese Herron & Miller-Herron PO Box 5 Dresden TN 38225-0005

**HERRON, VINCENT H.,** lawyer; b. Santa Monica, Calif., June 1, 1967; s. Thomas Litchfield and Bonnie (Quinn) H. BA in Econs., UCLA, 1990; JD, U. So. Calif., 1994. Bar: Calif., U.S. Tax Ct. Assoc. Latham and Watkins, L.A., 1994-98. General civil litigation. Office: Latham and Watkins 633 W 5th St Ste 4000 Los Angeles CA 90071-2005

**HERSH, ROBERT MICHAEL,** lawyer, insurance company executive; b. N.Y.C., Feb. 12, 1940; s. Esaac and Esther (Cohen) H.; m. Louise Jersh, ept. 23, 1984; 1 child, Lauren. BA, Columbia U., 1960; JD, Harvard U. Bar: N.Y. 1964. Assoc. Malcolm & Hoffmann, N.Y.C., 1964-66, Valicenti, Leighton, Reid & Pine, N.Y.C., 1966-68; atty. Lraftco Corp., N.Y.C., 1968-74; assoc. counsel Equitable Life Assurance Soc. U.S., N.Y.C., 1974-76, asst. gen. counse., 1976-78, v.p., counsel, 1978-83, v.p., assoc. gen. counsel, 1983-88; v.p., gen. counsel Integrity Life Ins. Co., N.Y.C., 1988-93; assoc. gen. counsel Met. Life ins. Co., N.Y.C., 1994—; dir. Ideal Mut. Ins. Co., 1972-74; chief announcer Madison Sq. Garden Track Meets, 1974—; chief Eng. lang. athletics announcer Olympic Games, 1984, 88, 92, 96 World Championships, 1991, 93, 95, 97, 99 World Indoor Championships, 1987, 99, World Jr. Championships, 1994-98. Columnidst: Track & Field News, 1973-84, sr. editor, 1974—; contbg. editor Runner Mag., 1980-87; contbr. articles to profl. jours. With USAR, 1963-69. Mem. Assn. of Bar of City of N.Y. (com. profl. and jud. ethics 1978-81, consumer affairs com. 1984-85, ins. com. 1985-88), USA Track & Field (dir. 1979—, chmn. records com. 1979-88, chmn. rules com. 1989-98, gen. counsel 1989-98, chmn. grand prix 1982-96, Robert Giegengack award for outstanding svc. 1997), Internat. Amateur Athletic Fedn. (tech. com. 1984—), Assn. Track & Field Statisticians, Fedn. Am. Statisticians of Track. General corporate, Insurance, Securities. Home: 92 Club Dr Roslyn Heights NY 11577-2732 Office: MetLife 1 Madison Ave New York NY 10010-3603

**HERSHATTER, RICHARD LAWRENCE,** lawyer, author; b. New Haven, Sept. 20, 1923; s. Alexander Charles and Belle (Blenner) H.; m. Mary Jane McNulty, Aug. 16, 1980; children by previous marriage; Gail Brook, Nancy Jill, Bruce Warren; 1 stepdau., Kimberly Ann Matlock Kleiman. BA, Yale U., 1948; JD, U. Mich., 1951. Bar: Conn. 1951, Mich. 1951, U.S. Supreme Ct. 1959. Pvt. practice New Haven, 1951-85, Clinton, Conn., 1985—; state trial referee, 1984—. Author: The Spy Who Hated Licorice, 1966, Fallout For a Spy, 1968; The Spy Who Hated Fudge, 1970, Hu'g Jury, 1999. Mem. Clinton Rep. Town Com., Conn., 1982—, chmn., 1984-88; mem. Branford (Conn.) Bd. Edn., 1963-71. With Air Corps, U.S. Army, 1942-44, AUS, 1944-46. Mem. Conn. Sch. Attys. Coun. (pres. 1977), Middlesex County Bar Assn., Mystery Writers Am., Masons. Alternative dispute resolution, Landlord-tenant, Probate. Office: 41 West Rd Clinton CT 06413-2316 also: 166 Route 81 Killingworth CT 06419-1469

**HERSHMAN, SCOTT EDWARD,** lawyer; b. N.Y.C., Mar. 31, 1958; s. Harold Martin and Barbara (Goldberg) H. BA, Am. U., 1980; JD, Yeshiva U., 1983. Bar: N.Y. 1984, U.S. Dist. Ct. (so. and ea. dists.) N.Y. 1986, U.S. Supreme Ct. 1994. Asst. dist. atty. N.Y. County Dist. Atty.'s Office, N.Y.C., 1983-86; ptnr. Graubard, Mollen & Miller, N.Y.C., 1986—. Mem. ABA, N.Y. State Bar Assn., Assn. Bar City of N.Y. Securities, General civil litigation, Criminal. Office: Graubard Mollen & Miller 600 3rd Ave New York NY 10016-1901

**HERSHNER, ROBERT FRANKLIN, JR.,** judge; b. Sumter, S.C., Jan. 21, 1944; s. Robert Franklin and Druie (Goodman) H.; m. Sally Sinclair, May 19, 1990; children: Bryan, Andrew. AB, Mercer U., 1966, JD, 1969. Bar: Ga. 1971, U.S. Dist. Ct. (mid. dist.) Ga. 1971, U.S. Dist. Ct. (so. dist.) Ga. 1979, U.S. Ct. Appeals (11th cir.) 1981, U.S. Supreme Ct. 1978. Atty. Ga. Legal Svcs. Corp., Macon, 1972; assoc. Adams, O'Neal, Hemingway & Kampal, Macon, 1972-76; ptnr. Kaplam & Hershner, P.A., Macon, 1976-80; judge U.S. Bankruptcy Ct. for Mid. Dist. Ga., Macon, 1986—, chief bankruptcy judge, 1986—; chair Fed. Jud. Ctr. Com. on Bankruptcy Edn., 1994—, active, 1990—; active Fed. Jud. Ctr. Com. on Bankruptcy Edn., 1990-99, chair, 194-99. Contbr. Georgia Lawyers Basic Practice Handbook, 2d edit., Post-Judgment Procedures, 1979; cons. Norton Bankruptcy Law and Practice. V.p. Macon Heritage Found., 1977-78; pres. student body Mercer U., 1965-66, interfraternity coun., 1964-65. Capt. U.S. Army, 1970-75. Mem. Ga. Bar Assn., Macon Bar Assn., Nat. Conf. Bankruptcy Judges (gov., v.p. 1996-97, pres. 1997-98), Blue Key Honor Soc., Phi EWta Sigma. Methodist. Office: US Bankruptcy Ct PO Box 86 Macon GA 31202-0086

**HERSKOVITZ, S(AM) MARC,** lawyer; b. Munich, Jan. 1, 1949; came to U.S., 1949; s. Max and Bella Herskovitz; 1 child from previous marriage, David Michael; m. Barbara Hobbs, Nov. 28, 1990; 1 child, Daniel Max. BA, Pa. State U., 1970; MS in Edn. with high honors, So. Ill. U., 1974; JD with honors, Fla. State U., 1987. Bar: Fla. 1987, U.S. Dist. Ct. (mid. dist.) Fla. 1988, U.S. Ct. Appeals (11th cir) 1988. Agy. mgr. Sun Personnel Svcs., Inc., Sarasota, Fla., 1978-80; claims adjuster Allstate Inc. Co., Lake Worth, Fla., 1980-84; sr. litigation atty. Fla. Dept. Ins., Tallahassee, 1987—. Mem. ABA, Assn. Trial Lawyers Am., Phi Kappa Phi. Democrat. Jewish. Avocations: volleyball, softball, reading, photography. Home: 707 Lothian Dr Tallahassee FL 32312-2858 Office: Fla Dept Ins 612 Larson Bldg Tallahassee FL 32399-0333

**HERTZ, NATALIE ZUCKER,** lawyer; b. Cleve., Sept. 23, 1934. AB, Cornell U., SUNY, 1956; JD, N.Y.U., 1976. Bar: N.Y. 1976, U.S. Dist. Ct. (so. dist.) N.Y. Pvt. practice Harrison, N.Y.; mem. Order of Coif; asst. in legal writing N.Y.U. Sch. Law, 1975-76. Assoc. editor: Annual Survey of American Law, N.Y.U., 1974-75; Author: The National Environmental Policy Act, 1974. Recipient Pomeroy prize, 1974, 75. Mem. Westchester County and N.Y. State Bar Assns., Westchester Women's Bar Assn. (v.p. 1987-89, dir. 1989-91, chairperson Trusts and Estates com., 1989-91, chairperson Real Property com. 1984-86), Women's Bar Assn. of State N.Y. (dir. 1991-94), Westchester County Bar Assn. (ethics com. 1991-99), Nat. Acad. Elder Law Attys. General practice, Estate planning, Probate. Office: 451 Harrison Ave Harrison NY 10528-2119

**HERZ, ANDREW LEE,** lawyer; b. N.Y.C., Nov. 12, 1946; s. John W. and Elise J. H.; m. Jill K. Herz; children: Adam, Matthew, Daniel, Michael. BA, Columbia U., 1968, JD, 1971. Bar: N.Y. 1972. Assoc. Milbank, Tweed, Hadley & McCloy, N.Y.C., 1971-75, Nickerson, Kramer, Lowenstein, Nessen, Kamin & Soll, N.Y.C., 1975-76, Marshall, Bratter, Greene, Allison & Tucker, N.Y.C., 1977-80; gen. counsel N.Y. State Mortgage Loan Enforcement and Adminstrn. Corp., N.Y.C., 1980-81; ptnr. Richards & O'Neil, LLP, N.Y.C., 1981—; lectr. Real Estate Inst., NYU, 1988-93; cons. N.Y. Real Property Svcs., 1987; pres., dir. Hotel Carlyle Owners Corp. Author: Office Lease Operating Expense Clauses-Definitional Problems, 1986, Renegotiating Commercial Leases, 1993, Liability Risks for Ducting Loan Commitments, 1995; co-author: Japanese Yen Financing of U.S. Real Estate, 1989, Real Estate Management Agreements, 1990. Chmn. zoning bd. appeals Village of Ossining, N.Y., 1980-88; bd. dirs. Planned Parenthood N.Y.C., 1987-94, AIDS Resource Ctr., 1991-94. Harlan Fiske Stone Scholar, 1971. Mem. ABA (real property divsn., comml. office leasing com. 1999—, chair real estate mgmt. com. 1990-91, vice chmn. 1988-90, cochair real estate asset mgmt. com. 1992-94, chair real estate asset mgmt. com. 1994-95, lending and financing subcom. 1997-99, co-chair comml. leasing com. 1999—), Am. Coll. Real Estate Lawyers (vice chair office leasing com. 1997-98, chair office leasing com. 1999—), N.Y. State Bar Assn. (co-chmn. comml. leasing com. 1991-96, exec. com. 1991-96, real property sect., editor N.Y. Real Property Jour. 1996-97), Assn. of Bar of City of N.Y., Real Estate Bd. N.Y., Urban Land Inst. Democrat. Real property, Contracts commercial. Home: 31 Flint Ave Larchmont NY 10538-3807 Office: Richards & O'Neil LLP 885 3rd Ave New York NY 10022-4834

**HERZECA, LOIS FRIEDMAN,** lawyer; b. N.Y.C., July 7, 1954; d. Martin and Elaine Shirley (Rapoport) Friedman; m. Christian S. Herzeca, Aug. 15, 1980; children: Jane Leslie, Nicholas Cameron. BA, SUNY-Binghamton, 1976; JD, Boston U., 1979. Bar: N.Y. 1980, U.S. Dist. Ct. (so. and ea. dist.) N.Y. 1980. Atty. antitrust div. U.S. Dept. Justice, Washington, 1979-80; assoc. Fried, Frank, Harris, Shriver & Jacobson, N.Y.C., 1980-86, ptnr., 1986—. Editor Am. Jour. Law and Medicine, 1978-79. Mem. ABA, N.Y.C. Bar Assn. Securities, General corporate. Office: Fried Frank Harris Shriver Jacobson 1 New York Plz Fl 22 New York NY 10004-1980

**HERZOG, BRIGITTE,** lawyer; b. St. Sauveur, France, Jan. 11, 1943; came to U.S., 1970, naturalized, 1976; d. Roger and Berthe (Niobey) Ecolivet; m. Peter E. Herzog, June 29, 1970; children: Paul Roger, Elizabeth Ann. Licence en Droit, Law Sch. Pantheon, Paris, 1967, diploma in internat. and criminal law d'Etudes Superieures, 1968; diploma Acad. Internat. Law, The Hague, Netherlands, 1969; JD Syracuse Coll. Law, 1975. Bar: Paris, 1968, N.Y. 1976. Assoc. Chardenon Law Firm, Paris, 1968-70, Cleary, Gottlieb et al, Paris, 1976-77; staff atty. Carrier Corp., Syracuse, N.Y., 1977-83, sr. atty., 1983-84, asst. gen. counsel, 1984-86, counsel European and Transcontinental Ops., Surrey, Eng., 1986-89, assoc. gen. counsel Carrier Corp., Syracuse, 1990; dir. legal affairs Otis, Paris, 1990-92; v.p. legal affairs European and Transcontinental Ops. Otis Internat., Inc., 1992-97; dep. gen. counsel Otis Elevator Co., Europe and vice pres. legal affairs Otis Elevator North European Area, 1998—. Contbr. to Harmonization of Laws in the EEC Fifth Sokol Colloquium, 1983; contbr. articles on French and internat. law to profl. jours. Bd. Dirs. Syracuse Stage Guild, 1974-77; chair legal com. European Elevator Assn. Mem. ABA, Am. Fgn. Law Assn. Roman Catholic. General corporate, Private international. Home: 112 Erregger Rd Syracuse NY 13224-2220 Office: Otis, 4 Place Victor Hugo, Courbevoie France

**HERZOG, CAROLYN BETH,** lawyer; b. Madison, Wis., Oct. 2, 1966; d. Paul Arthur and Janet Marion Herzog. BA, Washington U., St. Louis, 1988; JD, U. Wis., 1996. Bar: Wis. 1996, U.S. Ct. Appeals (7th cir.) 1996. Staff asst. The World Bank, Washington, 1990-93; legal intern Jalenques, Boxer, Chammard & Assocs., Paris, summer 1994, Washington Area Lawyers for the Arts, summer 1995; staff atty. Internat. Law Inst., Washington, 1996-98; corp. counsel Axent Techs., Inc., Rockville, Md., 1998—. Vol., mem. Washington Area Lawyers for the Arts, 1997—; jr. bd. dirs. The Source Theater, Washington, 1997—. Mem. ABA (regional coord. sect. internat. law 1996—, vice chair sect. internat. law 1998—, com. mem. intellectual property law 1998—), Assn. Women in Internat. Trade (organizer, meetings promoter 1997—). Avocations: musician, sailing, literature, tennis. Contracts commercial, Intellectual property, General corporate. Home: 1811 Wyoming Ave NW Apt 24 Washington DC 20009-1848 Office: Axent Techs Inc 2400 Research Blvd Rockville MD 20850-3243

**HERZOG, FRED F.,** law educator; b. Prague, Czech Republic, Sept. 21, 1907; s. David and Anna (Reich) H.; m. Betty Ruth Cohen, Mar. 27, 1947 (dec. Sept. 1984); children: Stephen E., David R. Dr. Juris, U. Graz (Austria), 1931; JD with high distinction U. Iowa, 1942; LL.D. (hon.), John Marshall Law Sch., 1983. Bar: Iowa 1942, Ill. 1946, U.S. Supreme Ct. 1965. Judge, Vienna, Austria, 1937-38; prof. and dean Chgo.-Kent Coll. Law, 1947-73; spl. atty. Met. San. Dist. Greater Chgo., 1962-70; 1st asst. atty. gen. Ill., 1973-76; dean John Marshall Law Sch., Chgo., 1976-83, prof., 1976—. Recipient Americanism award DAR, 1978; Golden Doctor diploma U. Graz, 1981; award of Excellence, John Marshall Law Sch. Alumni Assn., 1981; cert. of Appreciation, Ill. Dept. Registration and Edn., 1978; Ill. Atty. Gen.'s award for Outstanding Pub. Service, 1976; Torch of Learning award Am. Friends of the Hebrew U., 1986; named to Sr. Citizens Hall of Fame, City of Chgo., 1983. Mem. ABA, Ill. Bar Assn., Chgo. Bar Assn., Ill. Appellate Lawyers Assn., Decalogue Soc. Lawyers, Mid-Am. Club, Internat. Club (Chgo.), Union League Club (Chgo.). Contbr. articles to legal jours. Office: John Marshall Law Sch 315 S Plymouth Ct Chicago IL 60604-3969

**HERZOG, LESTER BARRY,** lawyer, educator; b. Presov, Czechoslovakia, July 3, 1953; came to U.S., 1965; s. Alexander and Flora (Braun) H.; m. Terry Lynn Hochhauser, Feb. 6, 1979; children: Simcha, Sarah, Chaim, Judah, Leah. BA, Rabbinical Sem. Belz, Bklyn., 1974; MBA with distinction, L.I. U., 1977; JD cum laude, Bklyn. Law Sch., 1983. Bar: N.Y. 1984, U.S. Dist. Ct. (ea. and so. dists.) N.Y. 1984; CPA, N.Y. Sr. auditor Seidman & Seidman, N.Y.C., 1977-83; sr. trial atty. Office Corp. Counsel N.Y.C. Law Dept., Bklyn., 1983-89; pvt. practice N.Y.C., 1989—; adj. assoc. prof. law and acctg. L.I. U., Bklyn., 1985—. Contbr. articles to profl. jours. Mem. ABA, AICPA (exam grader 1981-83), N.Y. State Bar Assn. Democrat. Jewish. Avocations: chess, fishing, gardening. Home and Office: 1729 E 15th St Brooklyn NY 11229-2084

**HESKETH, THOMAS A.E.,** lawyer, arbitrator, educator; b. Toronto, July 22, 1951; s. Thomas William Hesketh and Mary Patricia Bell Kindermann. BA, Claremont Men's Coll., 1975; JD, U. Calif., San Franciso, 1979. Bar: Calif. 1980, U.S. Supreme Ct. 1989. Tchr. Peace Corps, Morocco, 1973-76; atty. Law Offices of Daryl R. Hawkins, San Francisco, 1980-87, Dinkelspiel & Dinkelspiel, San Francisco, 1987-90; instr. legal rsch. and writing Hastings Coll. of the Law, U. Calif., San Francisco, 1985-88; atty., arbitrator Chickering & Gregory, San Francisco, 1990-94, Law Offices of Thomas A.E. Hesketh, San Francisco, 1995—; judge pro tem, arbitrator San Francisco Mcpl. Ct., 1988—; settlement judge pro tem, arbitrator San Francisco Superior Ct., 1992—; tchr. San Francisco Unified Sch. Dist., 1996-98; arbitrator Nat. Assn. Securities Dealers, 1988—, Pacific Stock Exch., 1992—. Sr. articles editor Hastings Constnl. Law Quar., 1978-79. Mem. Civil Grand Jury, San Francisco, 1991-92. Calif. State scholar, 1969-73. Mem. Bar Assn. San Francisco (vol. legal svcs. program). Democrat. Avocations: chess, baseball, international affairs. Office: Law Offices of Thomas AE Hesketh 303 31st Ave San Francisco CA 94121-1706

**HESKIN, KEERSTEN LEE,** lawyer; b. Fargo, N.D., Aug. 28, 1967; d. Robert Allen and JoAnn Molta Heskin. BS in Aviation Mgmt. and Flight Tech., Fla. Inst. Tech., 1990; JD, U. Fla., 1995. Bar: Fla. 1996, U.S. Dist. Ct. (mid. dist.) Fla. 1996, U.S. Dist. Ct. (no. and so. dists.) Fla. 1997. Assoc. Fisher, Rushmer, Werrenrath, Dickson, Talley & Dunlap P.A., Orlando, Fla., 1996—. Mem. Ctrl. Fla. Assn. Women Lawyers, Orange County Bar Assn. Family and matrimonial, Pension, profit-sharing, and employee benefits, Insurance. Office: Fisher Rushmer Werrenrath Dickson Talley & Dunlap PA 20 N Orange Ave Ste 1500 Orlando FL 32801-4623

**HESLIN, GARY PHILLIP,** lawyer; b. Phila., Oct. 16, 1951; s. James Phillip and Margaret Mary (McConnell) H.; m. Maureen Ann Burnley, Feb. 13, 1982; 1 child, Lindsay. BA in Polit. Sci., La Salle U., Phila., 1973; JD, Loyola U., New Orleans, 1977. Bar: Pa., U.S. Dist. Ct. (ea. dist.) Pa. Law clk. Phila. Ct. Common Pleas, 1979-80; assoc. Woluv & Rosenberg, Phila., 1981-86; ptnr. Krain & Heslin, Phila., 1986-97. Mem. Pa. Bar Assn., Phila. Bar Assn., Pa. Trial Lawyers Assn., Phila. Trial Lawyers Assn. Personal injury, Workers' compensation. Office: Krain & Heslin The Bourse Bldg 21 S 5th St Ste 1002 Philadelphia PA 19106-2515

**HESS, EMERSON GARFIELD,** lawyer; b. Pitts., Nov. 13, 1914. A.B., Bethany Coll., 1936; J.D., U. Pitts., 1939. Bar: Pa. 1940. Sr. ptnr. Hess, Reich, Georgiades, Wile & Homyak and predecessor firm Emerson G. Hess & Assocs., Pitts., 1940-92; of counsel DeMarco & Assocs., Pitts., 1992—; solicitor Scott Twp. Sch. Bd., 1958-65; legal counsel Judiciary com. Pa. Ho. of Reps., 1967-69; solicitor Scott Twp., 1968-69, Crafton Borough, 1974-78, Authority for Improvements in Municipalities of Allegheny County, 1977-80. Bd. dirs. Golden Triangle YMCA, Pitts., 1945—, WQED Ednl. TV, Pitts., 1952-68; pres., dir. Civic Light Opera Assn., Pitts., 1967-68; mem. internat. com. YMCA World Svc., N.Y.C., 1968-78; trustee, chmn. Cen. Christian Ch., Pitts., 1962-63; pres. Anesthesia and Resuscitation Found., Pitts., 1964-88, Pa. Med. Rsch. Found., 1960-88. Mem. ABA, Pa. Bar Assn., Allegheny County Bar Assn. General corporate, Probate, Real property. Home: 43 Robin Hill Dr Mc Kees Rocks PA 15136-1238 Office: DeMarco & Assocs 946 Gulf Tower 707 Grant St Pittsburgh PA 15219-1908

**HESS, GEORGE FRANKLIN, II,** lawyer; b. Oak Park, Ill., May 13, 1939; s. Franklin Edward and Carol (Hackman) H.; m. Diane Ricci, Aug. 9, 1974; 1 child, Franklin Edward. BS in Bus., Colo. State U., 1962; JD, Suffolk U., 1970; LLM, Boston U., 1973. Bar: Pa. 1971, Fla. 1973, U.S. Tax Ct. 1974, U.S. Dist. Ct. (so. dist.) Fla. 1975. Assoc. Hart, Childs, Hepburn, Ross & Putnam, Phila., 1970-72; instr. Suffolk U. Law Sch., Boston, 1973-74; ptnr. Henry, Hess & Hoines, Ft. Lauderdale, Fla., 1974-79; with Mousaw, Vigdor, Reeves & Hess, Ft. Lauderdale, Fla., 1979-94; pvt. practice Ft. Lauderdale, Fla., 1995—. Bd. dirs. Childrens Home Soc., Ft. Lauderdale, 1985-89, Nadeau Charitable Found., 198—. Lt. USNR, 1963-66. Mem. ABA, SAR, Fla. Bar Assn., Broward County Bar Assn., Lauderdale Yacht Club, USN League, Phi Alpha Delta. Episcopalian. Estate planning, Probate, Personal income taxation. Home: 2524 Castilla Is Fort Lauderdale FL 33301-1505 Office: 333 N New River Dr E Fort Lauderdale FL 33301-2241

**HESS, JEFFERY L.,** lawyer; b. Ft. Bragg, Calif., Feb. 24, 1949; s. Robert A. and Audrey J. Hess; m. Linda M. Hess, Dec. 6, 1951; children: Jason, Jaymi, Jenna, Jared. AA, Santa Rosa Jr. Coll., 1970; BS, Wash. State U., 1989; JD, U. Idaho, 1991. Bar: Idaho. Br. mgr. Household Fin. Corp., San Bruno, Calif., 1970-74; carpenter, millwright Ga. Pacific, Ft. Bragg, 1975-78, head constrn. dept., 1981-88; gen. contractor Hess' Homes, Ft. Bragg, 1978-88; tchr. Mendocino County Schs., Ft. Bragg, 1983-88; law clk./intern U.S. Ct. Appeals (9th cir.), Boise, Idaho, 1992; law clk. Idaho Supreme Ct., Boise, 1992-93; gen. counsel Hawkins-Smith, Boise, 1993—. Contbr. articles to profl. jours. Planning commr. City of Ft. Bragg, 1976-78; pres. Internat. Woodworkers Am., Ft. Bragg, 1984-88; pres., founder Am. Futbol Soccer Club, Boise, 1992-98. Recipient State Vol. of Yr. award Idaho Youth Soccer Assn., 1998. Mem. Internat. Coun. Shopping Ctrs., Idaho Bar (real estate sect.). Democrat. Avocations: soccer coaching, fly fishing, gardening, camping, hunting. Real property, General corporate, Construction. Home: 3309 Chuckwagon Ave Boise ID 83713-3710 Office: Hawkins-Smith 8645 Franklin Rd Boise ID 83709-0632

**HESS, LAWRENCE EUGENE, JR.,** lawyer; b. Phila., Aug. 18, 1923; s. Lawrence Eugene and Charlotte (Engel) H.; m. Jane Strayer, June 11, 1949; children: Lawrence Edward, Charlotte Jane. Student, Princeton U., 1942-43; BS, U.S. Naval Acad., 1946; JD with honors, George Washington U., 1954. Bar: Pa. 1954, D.C. 1954, U.S. Supreme Ct. 1963. Commd. ensign USN, 1946, advanced through grades to lt. comdr., assigned to various ships and stas.; ret., 1966; house counsel Nat. Liberty Life Ins. Co., Valley Forge, Pa., 1966-67, Standard Computers, Inc., 1967-68; atty. Def. Pers. Support Ctr., Phila., 1968-69; counsel Am. Acceptance Corp., Phila., 1969-74; pvt. practice law Fort Washington, 1974—. Mem. editorial bd. George Washington U. Law Rev., 1952-53. Mem. Sch. Bd. Upper Dublin Sch. Dist., Montgomery County, Pa., 1981-85; chmn. bd. trustees Glenside (Pa.) United Meth. Ch., 1973-76, 89-91, vice chmn. bd. trustees, 1988-89, 92-93. Mem. ABA, Fed. Bar Assn., Pa. Bar Assn., Phila. Bar Assn., Montgomery Bar Assn.,Comml. Law League Am., Judge Advs. Assn., Montgomery Trial Lawyers Assn., Fleet Res. Assn., Navy League U.S., U.S. Naval Acad. Alumni Assn. Phila. (past pres., bd. dirs), The Ret. Officers Assn. (life, bd. dirs., pres. WG chpt. 1990-91., pres. Pa. Coun. of chpts., 1995-97, v.p. Pa. coun. of chpts. 1993-95), Am. Legion, Mil. Order World Wars, Army-Navy Country Club, Mfrs. Golf and Country Club, Masons. Republican. General practice, Probate, Family and matrimonial. Home and Office: 515 Dreshertown Rd Fort Washington PA 19034-3022

**HESS, MICHAEL DAVID,** lawyer; b. N.Y.C., Nov. 8, 1940; s. Jacques J. and Lee B. (Berman) H.; m. Lynn Carol Levine, June 16, 1963; children: Laurie R., Geoffrey N. AB, Yale Coll., 1962; JD, Harvard U., 1965. Bar: N.Y. Chief civil divsn. Office of U.S. Atty., N.Y.C., 1966-73; ptnr. Weil Gotshal, N.Y.C., 1973-83; sr. ptnr. Gelberg & Abrams, N.Y.C., 1983-86, White & Case, N.Y.C., 1986-93, Chadbourne & Parke, N.Y.C., 1993-98; corp. counsel, law dept. head City of N.Y., 1998—. Chmn., trustee Horace Mann Sch., Bronx, N.Y., 1994—. Mem. ABA, N.Y. State Bar Assn., N.Y.C. Bar Assn., Phi Beta Kappa. Office: NYC Law Dept 100 Church St New York NY 10007-2601

**HESSE, MARGARET ANN,** lawyer; b. St. Louis, Oct. 10, 1966; d. Richard Paul and Frances Mary H. BA, Fontbonne Coll., 1989; JD, Washington U., St. Louis, 1994. Bar: Mo. 1994, Ill. 1995, U.S. Dist. Ct. (ea. dist.) Mo. 1995, U.S. Dist. Ct. (so. dist.) Ill. 1995. Assoc. Hinshaw & Culbertson, St. Louis, 1994-97, Peper, Martin, et. al., St. Louis, 1998, Blackwell, Sanders, Peper & Martin, St. Louis, 1998—. Bd. dirs. Literacy Coun. of Greater St. Louis, 1996-97. Mem. Women's Lawyer Assn., Bar Assn. Met. St. Louis, Internat. Acad. Trial Lawyers. Democrat. Roman Catholic. Avocations: golf, weight lifting, reading, Karate. Labor, Professional liability, Product liability. Office: Blackwell Sanders Peper Martin 720 Olive St Fl 24 Saint Louis MO 63101-2338

**HESSER, RANDALL GARY,** lawyer; b. Nuremburg, Germany, Sept. 17, 1958; came to U.S., 1959; s. Gary Leslie and Mary Jean Hesser; m. Mary Deters, Aug. 14, 1982; children: Anna, Frederick, John. BA, Ind. U., 1980; JD, Boston Coll., 1983. Bar: Ind. 1983, Mich. 1984. Atty., ptnr. Warrick & Boyn, Elkhart, Ind., 1983—. Bd. dirs., pres. Loveway, Inc., Middlebury, Ind., 1992-96; bd. dirs. Youth Svcs. Bur., Inc., Elkhart, 1984—, also past pres. Mem. Exch. Club (past pres., bd. dirs.). Labor, General corporate,

Estate planning. Home: 56277 County Road 31 Goshen IN 46528-6707 Office: Warrick & Boyn 121 W Franklin St Ste 400 Elkhart IN 46516-3201

**HESTER, FRANCIS (FRANK) BARTOW, III,** lawyer; b. Interlachen, Fla., Oct. 13, 1920; s. Francis Bartow Jr. and Flora McRae H.; m. Joyce Slate, Dec. 12, 1946; children: Susan Hester Elmore, Blanche Hester Wolfson, F. Bartow Hester Jr. Student, Ga. Inst. Tech., 1938-42, U. Ga., 1946; LLB, Emory U., 1948. Bar: Ga. 1952, U.S. Dist. Ct. (no. dist.) Ga. 1952, U.S. Ct. Appeals (4th cir.) 1990, U.S. Ct. Appeals (5th cir.) 1955, U.S. Ct. Appeals (6th cir.) 1967, U.S. Ct. Appeals (7th cir.) 1994, U.S. Ct. Appeals (11th cir.) 1981, U.S. Bd. Immigration Appeals 1985, U.S. Supreme Ct. 1960. Spl. agt. FBI, Cleve., Phila., Atlanta, 1948-51; criminal case trial lawyer Hester & Hester, 1952-99; spl. investigator of fraud in Ga. State Govt., 1958-59. With Air Corp., U.S. Army, 1942-45. Commendation Ga. Ho. of Reps., 1997. Mem. Ga. Bar Assn., Ga. Assn. Criminal Lawyers, Former Spl. Agts. of FBI Assn., Inc., Atlanta Bar Assn., Mason (32d degree), 6th Bomb Group Assn. (Tinian 1945), Cherokee Town & Country Club, Shriner (Yaarab temple), Sigma Alpha Epsilon. Democrat. Avocation: boating. Criminal. Home and Office: 5350 Larch Ln Gainesville GA 30506-6282

**HESTER, JULIA A.,** lawyer; b. L.A., Nov. 14, 1953; d. Robert William and Bertie Ella (Gilbert) H.; m. Fred M. Haddad, Aug. 2, 1980; children: Allison Hester-Haddad, Nancy Hester-Haddad. BA, Fla. Atlantic U., 1984; JD, Nova U., 1990. Bar: Fla. 1990, U.S. Dist. Ct. (mid. dist.) Fla. 1993. Asst. pub. defender Broward Pub. Defender, Ft. Lauderdale, Fla., 1990-93; atty., ptnr. Haddad & Hester, Ft. Lauderdale, 1993-95, 97—. Bd. dirs. St. Anthony Found., Ft. Lauderdale, 1995—, Ft. Lauderdale Billfish Tournament, 1992-96, BACDL, St. Thomas Aquinas Found., 1999—; mem. Sunrise Intracoastal Bd., Ft. Lauderdale, 1995; bd. dirs., officer Kids Inn Distress Aux., Ft. Lauderdale, 1984-87; bd. dirs. St. Thomas Found., 1999—, mem. exec. bd., 1999. Avocations: skiing, fishing, swimming. Criminal, Appellate, Juvenile. Office: 1 Financial Plz Ste 2612 Fort Lauderdale FL 33394-0061

**HESTER, PATRICK JOSEPH,** lawyer; b. Worcester, Mass., Aug. 14, 1951; s. Joseph P. and Anne T. (O'Brien) H.; m. Ann E. Riley, July 11, 1987; children: Maureen M., Colleen A., Margaret R., Molly E. BS in Civil Engr., W.P.I., Worcester, Mass., 1973; MS in Civil Engr., Northeastern U., Boston, 1979; JD, Suffolk Law Sch., Boston, 1983. Bar: Mass. 1983, U.S. Dist. Ct. Mass. 1984, 1st Cir. Ct. Appeals, 1999. Civil engr. Stone & Webster, Boston, 1973; dist. engr. Algonquin Gas Transmission Co., Boston, 1973-75, engr., 1975-78, sr. engr., 1978-79, supr.,engr., 1979-82, project mgr., 1982-83, asst. mgr. gas supply, 1983-84, corp. atty., 1984-92, v.p., gen. counsel, 1992-97; asst. gen. counsel Duke Energy Corp., Boston, 1998—; gen. counsel M & N Mgmt. Co., 1998-99, jr. v.p. and gen. counsel, 1999—; profl. engr., Mass. Mem. Am. Bar Assn., Mass. Bar Assn., Fed. Energy Bar Assn., Boston Bar Assn., New England Corp. Counsel Assn., Guild Gas Mgrs., Chi Epsilon, Phi Delta Phi. Democrat. Roman Catholic. Avocation: sports. FERC practice, Contracts commercial, General corporate. Office: Duke Energy Corp 1284 Soldiers Field Rd Boston MA 02135-1003

**HESTER, THOMAS PATRICK,** lawyer, business executive; b. Tulsa, Okla., Nov. 20, 1937; s. E.P. and Mary J. (Layton) H; m. Nancy B. Scofield, Aug. 20, 1960; children: Thomas P. Jr., Ann S., John L. BA, Okla. U., 1961, LLB, 1963. Bar: Okla. 1963, Mo. 1967, N.Y. 1970, D.C. 1973, Ill. 1975. Atty. McAfee & Taft, Okla. City, 1963-66, Southwestern Bell Telephone Co., Okla. City, St. Louis, 1966-72, AT&T, N.Y.C., Washington, 1972-75; gen. atty. Ill. Bell Telephone Co., Springfield, 1975-77; gen. solicitor Ill. Bell Telephone Co., Chgo., 1977-83, v.p., gen. counsel, 1983-87; sr. v.p., gen. counsel Ameritech, Chgo., 1987-91, exec. v.p., gen. counsel, 1991-97; ptnr. Mayer, Brown & Platt, Chgo., 1997—; sr. v.p., gen. counsel, sec. Sears, Roebuck and Co., 1998-99; corp. counsel ctr. adv. bd. Northwestern U., 1987-97. Mem. Taxpayers' Fed. of Ill., Springfield, 1987-97, chmn. bd. trustees 1987-88; mem. adv. bd. Ill. Dept. Natural Resources, 1991—, chmn., 1993-98; mem. Am. arts com. Art Inst. Chgo., 1994—, trustee, 1995—. Fellow Am. Bar Found.; mem. Am. Law Inst. General corporate, Public utilities, Administrative and regulatory. Office: Mayer Brown & Platt 190 S LaSalle St Chicago IL 60603-3441

**HETHERINGTON, JOHN JOSEPH,** lawyer; b. Phila., Jan. 22, 1947; s. Jack Joseph and Josephine J. (Krawiec) H.; m. Janet Louise Erven; children: Wendy Lynn, John Joseph, Patrick John. BA, U. Pa., 1974; JD, Gonzaga U., 1977. Bar: Pa. 1977, U.S. Dist. Ct. (ea. dist.) Pa. 1979, U.S. Ct. Appeals (3d cir.) 1983. Staff atty. Legal Services Northeast Pa., Wilkes-Barre, 1977-79; sole practice Chalfont, Pa., 1979-82, Hilltown, Pa., 1986—; assoc. Toll, Hetherington & Ghen, Doylestown, Pa., 1982-86; cons., lectr. pre-retirement workshops, Devon, Pa., 1984—; solicitor Hilltown (Pa.) Twp. Townwatch Assn., 1982—; lectr. programs on elder law and social security claims CLE, 1981—. Bd. dirs. Bucks County Legal Aid Soc. With USAF, 1966-69. Mem. Pa. Bar Assn. (chmn. com. legal affairs elderly and social security law 1987), Bucks County Bar Assn. (bd. dirs. 1987-90, com. legal problems of elderly, panelist), Nat. Acad. Elder Law Attys. Republican. Roman Catholic. Avocations: horticulture, collecting contemporary music, golf. Elder, General practice, General civil litigation. Office: PO Box 229 Hilltown PA 18927-0229

**HETHERWICK, GILBERT LEWIS,** lawyer; b. Winnsboro, La., Oct. 30, 1920; s. Septimus and Addie Louise (Gilbert) H.; m. Joan Friend Gibbons, May 31, 1946 (dec. Aug. 1964); children: Janet Hetherick Pumphrey, Ann Hetherwick Lyons Winegeart, Gilbert, Carol Hetherwick Sutton, Katherine Hetherwick Hummel; remarried Mertis Elizabeth Cook, June 7, 1967. BA summa cum laude, Centenary Coll., 1942; JD, Tulane U., 1949. Bar: La. 1949. With legal dept. NorAm Energy Corp., Shreveport, La., 1949-53; dir. Blanchard, Walker, O'Quin & Roberts, PLC, Shreveport, 1953—. Mem. Shreveport City Charter Revision Com., 1955; Shreveport Mcpl. Fire and Police Civil Svc. Bd., 1956-92, vice chmn., 1957-78, chmn., 1978-88. Served with AUS, 1942-46. Recipient Tulane U. Law Faculty medal, 1949. Mem. ABA, La. Bar Assn., Shreveport Bar Assn. (pres. 1987), Fed. Energy Bar Assn., Order of Coif, Phi Delta Phi, Omicron Delta Kappa. Episcopalian. General practice, FERC practice. Home: 4604 Fairfield Ave Shreveport LA 71106-1432 Office: Bank One Tower Shreveport LA 71101

**HETLAGE, ROBERT OWEN,** lawyer; b. St. Louis, Jan. 9, 1931; s. George C. and Doris M. (Talbot) H.; m. Anne R. Willis, Sept. 24, 1960; children: Mary T., James C., Thomas K. AB, Washington U., St. Louis, 1952, LLB, 1954; LLM, George Washington U., 1957. Bar: Mo. 1954, U.S. Dist. Ct. (ea. dist.) Mo. 1954, U.S. Supreme Ct. 1957. Ptnr., Hetlage & Hetlage, 1958-65, Peper, Martin, Jensen, Maichel & Hetlage, St. Louis, 1966-97, chmn., 1994-97; of counsel Blackwell Sanders Peper Martin LLP, 1998—. Served to 1st lt. U.S. Army, 1954-58. Fellow Am. Bar Found. (life); mem. Bar Assn. Met. St. Louis (pres. 1967-68), Mo. Bar (pres. 1976-77), ABA (chmn. real property, probate and trust law sect. 1981-82), Am. Coll. Real Estate Lawyers (pres. 1985-86), Am. Bar Found. (bd. trustees 1996—), Am. Judicature Soc., Anglo-Am. Real Property Inst. (chmn. 1991). Real property, Construction, Contracts commercial. Office: Blackwell Sanders Peper Martin LLP 720 Olive St Saint Louis MO 63101-2338

**HETLAND, JOHN ROBERT,** lawyer, educator; b. Mpls., Mar. 12, 1930; s. James L. and Evelyn (Lundgren) H.; m. Mildred Woodruff, Dec. 1951 (div.); children: Lynda Lee Catlin, Robert John, Debra Ann Allen; m. Anne Kneeland, Dec. 1972; children: Robin T. Willcox, Elizabeth J. Pickett. B.S.L., U. Minn., 1952, J.D., 1956. Bar: Minn. 1956, Calif. 1962, U.S. Supreme Ct. 1981. Practice law Mpls., 1956-59; prof. law U. Calif., Berkeley, 1959-91; prof. emeritus, 1991—; prin. Hetland & Kneeland, PC, Berkeley, 1959—; vis. prof. law Stanford U., 1971, 80, U. Singapore, 1972, U. Cologne, Fed. Republic Germany, 1988. Author: California Real Property Secured Transactions, 1970, Commercial Real Estate Transactions, 1972, Secured Real Estate Transactions, 1974, 1977; co-author: California Cases on Security Transactions in Land, 2d edit., 1975, 3d edit., 1984, 4th edit., 1992; contbr. articles to legal, real estate and fin. jours. Served to lt. comdr. USNR, 1953-55. Fellow Am. Coll. Real Estate Lawyers, Am. Coll. Mortgage Attys., Am. Bar Found.; mem. ABA, State Bar Calif., State Bar Minn., Order of Coif, Phi Delta Phi. Home: 20 Red Coach Ln Orinda CA 94563-1112 Office: 2600 Warring St Berkeley CA 94704-3415

**HETRICK, BRENDA DRENDEL,** lawyer; b. Rota, Spain, May 21, 1968; d. Richard L. and Maria Diaz Drendel; m. Randall Scott Hetrick, June 28, 1997. BS in Fin., U. Ala., 1990; JD, U. Birmingham, 1995. Data info. coord. UAB Health Svcs. Found., Birmingham, Ala., 1991-94; runner, law clk. London, Yancey, Elliott & Burgess, Birmingham, Ala., 1994-95; atty. William L. Howell, Mobile, Ala., 1995—. Bd. dirs. Salvation Army Womens Shelter, Mobile, 1998—; mem. Mobile Opera Guild, 1998—. Mem. ABA, Am. Trial Lawyers Assn., Ala. Bar Assn., Ala. Trial Lawyers Assn., South Ala. Trial Lawyers Assn., Mobile Bar Assn., Alice Meadows Coun., Women Lawyers. Roman Catholic. General civil litigation, Alternative dispute resolution, General practice.

**HETSKO, JEFFREY FRANCIS,** lawyer; b. Glen Ridge, N.J., Apr. 25, 1950; s. Cyril Francis and Josephine (Stein) H. BA, Williams Coll., 1972; JD, U. Fla., 1978. Bar: Fla. 1978, Ga. 1978. Assoc. Troutman, Sanders, Lockerman & Ashmore, Atlanta, 1978-86, ptnr., 1987; v.p., gen. counsel Grove Properties, Inc., Atlanta, 1987-89; ptnr. Troutman Sanders LLP, Atlanta, 1989—. Mem. ABA, State Bar Assn. Ga., Fla. State Bar Assn., Atlanta Bar Assn. Real property, Trademark and copyright. Office: Troutman Sanders LLP 600 Peachtree St NE Ste 5200 Atlanta GA 30308-2231

**HETTINGER, SUSAN,** lawyer; b. Riverton, Wyo., Jan. 28, 1956; d. James Lewis and Sheila Marie (Bleösch) H. BA, U. Utah, 1978; JD, U. Wash., 1981. Jud. law clk. Superior Ct., Everett, Wash., 1983-84; contracting officer Dept. Social and Health Svcs., Olympia, Wash., 1984-86; analyst Data Processing Authority, Olympia, 1986; mgmt. cons. Arthur Young & Co., Seattle, 1987-89; sr. cons. State of Wash., Olympia, 1989-92; asst. dir. Dept. of Info. Svcs., Olympia, 1992-98; sr. mgr. dept. real estate Eddie Bauer, Redmond, Wash., 1998—; mem. steering com. Women & Leadership, Tacoma, Wash., 1997-98, exec. com. Tech. and Human Resources, Olympia, 1996-98. Author: (short story) Departure, 1997 (Best Short Story award Seattle mag. 1997), (essay) If I Were Governor . . ., 1992 (1st place award The Olympian newspaper 1992). Vol. lawyer Thurston County Legal Svcs., Olympia, 1997—; mediation trainer Lawyers and Students Engaged in Resolution, Olympia, 1996—. Mem. Nat. Minority Supplier Devel. Coun., Wash. State Bar Assn., Wash. Women Lawyers, Soc. for Info. Mgmt., Asst. Dirs. of Adminstrv. Svcs. (exec. steering com. 1995-97), Odd Lots Investment Club (pres. 1997-98), Phi Beta Kappa, Phi Kappa Phi. Home: 5847 Swayne Dr NE Olympia WA 98516-9547 Office: Eddie Bauer PO Box 97000 Redmond WA 98073-9700

**HETZNER, MARC ANDREW,** lawyer; b. Logansort, Ind., Apr. 24, 1953; s. John R. and Nelma L. (Byrt) H.; m. Rosalie M.; children: Collette N., Christopher R., Kimberly A. BA, Ind. U., 1975, MBA, 1983, JD, 1983. Bar: Ind. 1983, U.S. Dist. Ct. (so. dist.) Ind. 1983, U.S. Tax Ct. 1983, U.S. Ct. Appeals (7th cir.) 1988. Ptnr. Krieg Devault Alexander & Capehart, Indpls., 1989—. Contbr. articles to profl. jours. Mem. St. Vincent Hosp. Found., Planned Giving Com., 1995—. 1st lt. U.S. Army, 1975-79. Fellow Am. Coll. Trust & Estate Counsel; mem. Ind. Estate Bar Found., Indpls. Estate Planning Coun. Estate planning, Taxation, general, Estate taxation. Office: Krieg DeVault Alexander & Capehart 1 Indiana Sq Ste 2800 Indianapolis IN 46204-2079

**HEUBAUM, WILLIAM LINCOLN,** retired lawyer; b. Chgo., Jan., 1938; s. Lincoln William and Hazel Lillian (Kvilvang) H.; m. Mary Lynn Gilbert, June 19, 1965; children: Karl Franz, Joy Ann. B.S. (Forrestel scholar), Northwestern U., 1959, J.D. (Kosmerl scholar), 1965. Bar: Ill. 1965, Iowa 1973, Nebr. 1982. Atty. Hopkins & Sutter, Chgo., 1965-72; v.p., sec., gen. counsel IBP (formerly Iowa Beef Processors, Inc.), Dakota City, Nebr., 1972-82; ptnr. Bikakis, Heubaum, Vohs & Storm, Sioux City, Iowa, 1983-85; founder, mem. Crime Stoppers, 1982-98; lectr. Chgo. Bar Assn. Continuing Legal Edn. Com. Mem. Local Bd. 12; asso. govt. appeal agt. Local Bd. 30, Ill. Selective Service System, 1967-72. Served to lt. Supply Corps USNR, 1959-62. Mem. Ill. Bar Assn., Nebr. Bar Assn., Acacia, Masons, Moose, Rotary, Phi Alpha Delta. Republican. Methodist. Home: 204 Calumet Dr Yankton SD 57078-6751

**HEUER, SAM TATE,** lawyer; b. Batesville, Ark., July 11, 1952; s. Albert A. and Mary (Baker) H.; children: Noal Tate, Polly Anna, Charles Albert; m. Max Parker. BBA in Banking and Fin., U. Miss., 1974; JD, U. Ark., 1978. Bar: Ark. Dep. pros. atty. 4th Jud. Dist., Fayetteville, Ark., 1979-80; assoc. Davis Bracey & Heuer, Springdale, Ark., 1980-81; pvt. practice, Batesville, 1981-86; pros. atty. 16th Jud. Dist., Batesville, 1983-86; assoc., salesman Crews & Assocs., Little Rock, 1987-88; assoc. John Wesley Hall P.C., Little Rock, 1988-93; ptnr. Thurman, Lawrence & Heuer, PLC, Little Rock, 1994—. Mem. ATLA, Ark. Prosecutor's Assn. (bd. dirs. 1984-86, v.p. 1985-86), Ark. Trial Lawyers Assn., Am. Trial Lawyers Assn., Pulaski County Attys. Assn. Democrat. Episcopalian. Criminal, General civil litigation, Family and matrimonial. Office: Thurman Lawrence & Heuer 124 W Capitol Ave Ste 1650 Little Rock AR 72201-3758

**HEUISLER, CHARLES WILLIAM,** lawyer; b. Phila., May 24, 1941; s. Isaac Kilner and Mary Gertrude (Smith) H.; m. Judith Ann Hargadon, June 26, 1965; children: Karen L. Heuisler Murphy, Susan M. Heuisler McCabe, Charles W. Jr. BA in Modern Lang., Coll. of Holy Cross, 1963; JD, Villanova U., 1966. Bar: N.J. 1966, U.S. Dist. Ct. N.J. 1966, U.S. Ct. Appeals (3d cir.) 1970, U.S. Supreme Ct. 1972; cert. civil trial atty. Am. Bd. Trial Advs. Law clk. to Hon. John B. Wick, Superior Ct. of N.J., Chancery Divsn., Camden, 1966-67; shareholder Archer & Greiner, Haddonfield, N.J., 1972—. Counsel, mem. adv. bd. Haddonfield Symphony Soc., 1980—; chmn. South Jersey Performing Arts Ctr., 1992-98. Mem. FBA, N.J. Bar Assn. (trustee from Camden County 1989-93), Camden County Bar Assn. (pres. 1985-86, trustee, Peter J. Devine award 1991), Rotary (pres. Camden 1987-88). Avocations: tennis, sailing. General civil litigation, Intellectual property, Professional liability. Home: 1236 Folkestone Way Cherry Hill NJ 08034-3021 Office: Archer & Greiner PC One Centennial Sq Haddonfield NJ 08033

**HEUMAN, DONNA RENA,** lawyer; b. Seattle, May 27, 1949; d. Russell George and Edna Inez (Armstrong) H. BA in Psychology, UCLA, 1972; JD, U. Calif., San Francisco, 1985. Cert. shorthand reporter, Calif. Owner Heuman & Assocs., San Francisco, 1978-86; real estate broker Calif., 1990—; co-founder, chair, CFO Atherton Park Foods, Inc., 1996—; mem. Hastings Internat. and Comparative Law Rev., 1984-85; bd. dirs. Saddleback, 1987-89. Jessup Internat. Moot Ct. Competition, 1985, bBd. dirs. N. Fair Oaks Adv. Coun., vice chair, sec. 1993-95. Mem. ABA, NAFE, ATLA, AOPA, Nat. Shorthand Reporters Assn., Women Entrepreneurs, Mensa, Calif. State Bar Assn., Nat. Mus. of Women in the Arts, Calif. Lawyers for the Arts, San Francisco Bar Assn., Commonwealth Club, World Affairs Coun., Zonta (bd. dirs.). Home: 750 18th Ave Menlo Park CA 94025-2018 Office: Superior Ct Calif Hall Of Justice Redwood City CA 94063

**HEWES, GEORGE POINDEXTER, III,** lawyer; b. Jackson, Miss., Oct. 25, 1928; s. George P. Jr. and Gertrude (Turner) H.; m. Helen Elizabeth Morrison, Nov. 19, 1954 (dec. July 1997); children: George P. IV, Laura L., Robert Russelll m. Joan Dean, Dec. 27, 1998. BBA, U. Miss., 1950, JD, 1954. Bar: Miss. 1954, U.S. Dist. Ct. (so. and no. dists.) Miss. 1954, U.S. Ct. Appeals (5th cir.) 1954, U.S. Supreme Ct. 1970. Enlisted U.S. Marine Corps., 1950, advanced through grades to lt. col., ret., 1975; sr. ptnr. Brunini, Grantham, Grower & Hewes, Jackson, 1955—; bd. dirs. Trustmark Nat. Bank, Jackson. Chmn. United Way Campaign, 1985; chmn. bd. dirs. Magnolia Speech Sch. Deaf, 1986-87; chancellor Episc. Diocese Miss., 1984—. Fellow Am. Coll. Trial Lawyers (regent 1984-88); mem. ABA, Miss. State Bar Assn. (pres. young lawyers sect. 1963-64), Hinds County Bar Assn., Nat. Conf. Commrs. Uniform State Laws, Jackson Symphony Orch. Assn. (past pres.), Met. YMCA (past pres.), Jackson Jr. C. of C. (Young Man Yr. local and state 1962), Jackson Country Club, One Hundred Club Jackson (sec. 1984—, past pres.). Democrat. Product liability, Federal civil litigation, State civil litigation. Home: 40 Eastbrooke Jackson MS 39216-4714 Office: Brunini Grantham Grower & Hewes PO Box 119 Jackson MS 39205-0119

**HEWETT, ARTHUR EDWARD,** real estate developer, lawyer; b. Dallas, Oct. 16, 1935; s. Arthur Elton and Clara Mae (Wagoner) H.; m. Helen Yvonne Barry, May 20, 1959; children: Julie, Matthew, Clara. B.B.A., So. Methodist U., 1957, LL.B., 1965. Bar: Tex. 1965. Asst. to exec. v.p. Diversa, Inc., Dallas, 1960-61; asst. to pres. RichPlan Corp., Dallas, 1961-62; ptnr. Vial, Hamilton and Koch, 1965-69; founder, mng. ptnr. firm Hewett Johnson Swanson & Barbee, 1970-80; pres., chief executive officer Thompson Realty Corp., Dallas, 1980-83; pres., chief exec. officer Republic Property Group, Inc., 1983-97; vice-chmn. RCS Investments, Dallas, 1997—. Served to lt. USNR, 1957-60. Mem. Tex. Bar Assn., Bohemian Club (San Francisco), Park City Club. Presbyterian. Home: PO Box F2 Snowmass Village CO 81615-5026 Office: RCS Investments 8th Fl Lockbox 4 8440 Walnut Hill Ln Dallas TX 75231-3833

**HEWITT, JAMES WATT,** lawyer; b. Hastings, Nebr., Dec. 25, 1932; s. Roscoe Stanley and Willa Manners (Watt) H.; m. Marjorie Ruth Barrett, Aug. 8, 1954; children: Mary Janet, William Edward, John Charles, Martha Ann. Student, Hastings Coll., 1950-52; BS, U. Nebr., 1954, JD, 1956, MA, 1994. Bar: Nebr. 1956. Practice Hastings, 1956-57, Lincoln, Nebr., 1960—; v.p., gen. counsel Nebco, Inc., Lincoln, 1961—; vis. lectr. U. Nebr. Coll. Law, 1970-71. Mem. state exec. com. Rep. Party, 1967-70, mem. state ctrl. com., 1967-70, legis chmn., 1968-70; bd. dirs. Lincoln Child Guidance Ctr., 1969-72, pres., 1972; bd. dirs. Lincoln Cmty. Playhouse, 1967-73, pres., 1972-73; trustee Bryan Meml. Hosp., Lincoln, 1968-74, 76-82, chmn., 1972-74; bd. dirs. Lincoln Libr., 1990-97; trustee U. Nebr. Found., 1979—; dir. Bryan Meml. Hosp. Found., Lincoln, 1994—; exec. v.p., dir. Nebr. State Hist. Soc. Found., Lincoln, 1994—; dir. Nebr. state chpt. The Nature Conservancy, 1993-97. Capt. USAF, 1957-60. Fellow Am. Bar Found. (Nebr. state chmn. 1988-92, 99—, chmn. 1994-95); mem. ABA (Nebr. state del. 1972-80, bd. govs. 1981-83), Nebr. State Bar (chmn. ins. com. 1972-76, chmn. pub. rels. com. 1982-84, pres. 1985-86), Fed. Bar Assn., Lincoln Bar Assn., Newcomen Soc. (Nebr. chair 1995—), Am. Rose Soc., Nebr. Rose Soc., Lincoln Rose Soc., Nebr. Club, Country of Lincoln Club, Round Table, Beta Theta Pi, Phi Delta Phi. Congregationalist. General corporate, Administrative and regulatory, Construction. Home: 2990 Sheridan Blvd Lincoln NE 68502-4241 Office: PO Box 80268 1815 Y St Lincoln NE 68508-1233

**HEWITT, OTTO D., III,** lawyer; b. Hillsboro, Tex., Oct. 21, 1946; s. Otto D. Jr. and Marguerite (Porter) H.; m. Sunny N. Martin, Aug. 1970; children: Heather Eleanor, Heidi Elizabeth. BA, Baylor U., 1969, JD, 1980. Bar: Tex. 1980, U.S. Dist. Ct. (so., ea. and we. dists.) Tex. 1981, U.S. Ct. Appeals (5th cir.) 1983, U.S. Ct. Appeals (10th cir.) 1988, U.S. Supreme Ct. 1984. Staff atty. Ct. Appeals, Eastland, Tex., 1980-81; assoc., firm officer McLeod, Alexander, p.c., Galveston, Tex., 1981-91; participating atty. Davenport Law Firm, Alvin, Tex., 1991-94; owner, lawyer Hewitt Law Firm, Alvin, Tex., 1994—; adj. prof. civil rights and constitutional law Baylor Law Sch., Waco, Tex., 1990—. Contbr. articles to profl. jours. law enforcement officer State of Calif., 1970-78; law grad. asst. Gov's. War Against Crime Commn., 1980; pres. AFSCME, AFL-CIO, 1975-78, sec. 1972-75; vice-chmn. Merced County Dem. Cen. Com., Calif., 1972-78; commnr. Mcpl. Airport Commn., Atwater, Calif., 1977-78. Sgt. USAF, 1969-72. named one of Outstanding Young Men of Am., 1978, Boss of Yr. Galveston Legal Secretaries Assn., 1985, 90. Mem. Tex. Bar Assn., Tex. Bar Found., Tex. Indian Bar Assn., Galveston Bar Assn., Brazoria County Bar Assn., 5th Cir. Bar Assn. (founding mem.), Assn. Civil Trial and Appellate Specialists, Coll. State Bar Tex., Southeastern Cherokee Confederation (cert. mediator state and fed. cts.). Personal injury, General civil litigation, Civil rights. Office: Hewitt Law Firm 1600 E Highway 6 Ste 302 Alvin TX 77511-2560

**HEWITT, RICHARD GILBERT,** lawyer; b. Boston, Jan. 1, 1927; s. Ely Shepard and Frieda (Pike) H.; m. Shirley Adele Keddy, Mar. 18, 1950 (dec. Dec. 1986); children: Carolyn Spiegel, William; m. Genevieve Madeleine Fisch, Aug. 3, 1989. BA, Williams Coll., 1948; LLB, Columbia U., 1951. Bar: N.Y. 1951, U.S. Dist. Ct. (so., ea. and we. dists.) N.Y. 1954. Atty. Port of N.Y. Authority, N.Y.C., 1950-53; assoc. Myles, Wormser & Koch, N.Y.C., 1953-56; ptnr. Wormser, Kiely, Galef & Jacobs and predecessor firms, N.Y.C., 1957—. Trustee Hale Matthews Found., N.Y.C., 1980—, Am. Contract Bridge League Charity Found., Memphis, 1983-91, Nat. Com. for Prevention of Child Abuse, Chgo., 1988-92; trustee Rsch. to Prevent Blindness, N.Y.C., 1993—, Scoville Found., N.Y.C., 1992—. Mem. Westchester Country Club. Avocations: duplicate bridge, golf. Estate planning, Probate, Estate taxation. Office: Wormser Kiely Galef & Jacobs 711 3rd Ave New York NY 10017-4014

**HEYBURN, JOHN GILPIN, II,** federal judge; b. 1948; m. Martha Keeney, 1976. BA, Harvard U., 1970; JD, U. Ky., 1976. Ptnr. Brown, Todd & Heyburn, Louisville, 1976-92; fed. judge U.S. Dist. Ct. (we. dist.) Louisville, 1992—. Bd. dirs. Kentuckians for Jud. Improvement, 1975-76; mem. Budget Com. Jud. Conf.of U.S., 1994—, chmn. 1997—; chair Jefferson County Crime Commn.; mem. vis. com. U. Ky., 1980; active Leadership Louisville Found. With USAR, 1970-76. Mem. ABA, Ky. Bar Assn., Louisville Bar Assn., U. Ky. Coll. Law Alumni Assn., Louisville Com. Fgn. Rels. Office: US Dist Ct 601 W Broadway Ste 450 Louisville KY 40202-2227

**HEYCK, JOSEPH GIRAUD, JR.,** lawyer; b. Lake Charles, La., Sept. 25, 1935; s. Joseph G. Sr. and Frances (Hunter) H.; m. Marilyn C. Grace, Dec. 26, 1964; children: Laura Frances, Thomas Michael. B in Indsl. Engring., U. Fla., 1958, JD, 1963. Bar: Fla. 1964, U.S. Dist. Ct. (mid. dist.) Fla. 1965, U.S. Ct. Appeals (5th and 11th cirs.) 1968. Law clk. to presiding judge U.S. Dist. (mid. dist.) Fla., Tampa, 1963-64; ptnr. Allen, Dell, Frank & Trinkle, Tampa, 1964—. Active parish council Our Lady of the Rosary Cath. Ch., Land O'Lakes, Fla., 1975; bd. dirs. Am. Cancer Soc., Hillsborough County, Fla., 1972. Capt. USNR, 1958-81. Mem. ABA, Fla. Bar Assn., Hillsborough County Bar Assn., Am. Judicature Soc., Tampa Yacht and Country Club (bd. dirs. 1978). Avocations: tennis, fishing, golf. Real property, Contracts commercial, Probate. Home: 3624 Crenshaw Lake Rd Lutz FL 33549-4755 Office: Allen Dell Frank & Trinkle PO Box 2111 Tampa FL 33601-2111

**HEYCK, THEODORE DALY,** lawyer; b. Houston, Apr. 17, 1941; s. Theodore Richard and Gertrude Paine (Daly) H. *Theodore Daly Heyck, son of Gertrude Paine Daly and Theodore Richard Heyck. Gertrude Daly, daughter of David Daly and Gertrude Paine and granddaughter of Robert Paine, all instrumental in the formation of early Houston social and business life. The Paine lineage includes Thomas Paine, colonial revolutionary and David Daly, Harvard graduate, descended from a line of Boston Irish. Theodore Richard Heyck, son of Theodore Frantz Valentin Heyck and Frances Catherine Girand, whose ancestries trace back respectively through Friedrich Heinrich Theodore Heyck who emmigrated to Galveston, Texas from Holstein in 1852 and through Sophia Caroline Hanauer whose ancestors emmigrated from Wiltenheim, Alsace in 1843.* BA, Brown U., 1963; postgrad. Georgetown. U., 1963-65, 71-72; JD, N.Y. Law Sch., 1979. Bar: N.Y. 1980, Calif. 1984, U.S. Ct. Appeals (2nd cir.) 1984, U.S. Supreme Ct. 1984, U.S. Dist. Ct. (so. and ea. dists.) N.Y. 1980, U.S. Dist. Ct. (we. and no. dists.) N.Y. 1984, U.S. Dist. Ct. (cen. and so. dists.) Calif. 1984, U.S. Ct. Appeals (9th cir.) 1986. Paralegal dist. atty. Bklyn., 1975-79; asst. dist. atty. Bklyn. dist., Kings County, N.Y., 1979-85; dep. city atty., L.A., 1985—; bd. dirs. Screen Actors Guild, N.Y.C., 1977-78. Mem. ABA, AFTRA, NATAS, SAG, Bklyn. Bar Assn., Assn. Trial Lawyers Am., N.Y. Trial Lawyers Assn., N.Y. State Bar Assn., Calif. Bar Assn., Fed. Bar Council, L.A. County Bar Assn., Actors Equity Assn. Home: 2106 E Live Oak Dr Los Angeles CA 90068-3639 Office: Office City Atty City Hall E 200 N Main St Los Angeles CA 90012-4110

**HEYDEN, MICHAEL C.,** lawyer; b. L.I., Nov. 7, 1955; s. Edward and Lois Heyden. BS, U. Del., 1977; JD, Widener U., 1980. Bar: Del., Pa., U.S. Dist. Ct., U.S. Supreme Ct. Pvt. practice Wilmington, Del. Mem. Trial Lawyers Assn. Personal injury. Office: 1201 N King St Wilmington DE 19801-3217

**HEYER, JOHN HENRY, II,** lawyer; b. Rochester, N.Y., May 4, 1946; s. Joseph Lester and Margaret Mary (Darcy) H.; m. Charla Ann Prewitt (dec.); children: Thomas, William, John III, Richard, Mary. BA, U. Colo., 1969; JD, U. Denver, 1972. Bar: Colo. 1973, U.S. Dist. Ct. Colo. 1973, N.Y. 1976, Pa. 1979, U.S. Dist. Ct. (we. dist.) N.Y. 1980, U.S. Supreme Ct. 1982. Atty. Texaco, Inc., Denver, 1973-75; sole practice Olean, N.Y., 1975—; pres. Northeastern Land Svcs., Inc., Olean, N.Y., 1982—; v.p. Vector Capital Corp., Rochester, N.Y., 1985-87; chpt. 7 trustee U.S. Bankruptcy Ct., we. dist. N.Y., 1986—. Editor: New York Oil and Gas Statutes, 1985. Asst. dist. atty. Cattaraugus County, Olean, 1978-81; bd. dirs. Olean YMCA,

1989—, v.p. 1993-94, pres., 1994-99; bd. dirs. Buffalo Philharm. Symphony Cir., v.p., 1993, pres., 1994-95; bd. dirs. Friends of Good Music, pres. 1994-95. Mem. N.Y. State Bar Assn. (real property sect., real property devel. com.), Erie County Bar Assn., Cattaraugus County Bar Assn. (sec.-treas. 1997, v.p. 1998, pres. 1999), Eastern Mineral Law Found. (trustee 1984—, exec. com. 1994-95), Ind. Oil and Gas Assn. N.Y. (bd. dirs. 1986—, sec. 1986-87, v.p. 1988—), SAR, Selden Soc. Roman Catholic. Oil, gas, and mineral, Real property, Bankruptcy. Office: PO Box 588 201 N Union St Olean NY 14760-2738

**HEYL, ERICA LYNN,** mediator, lawyer; b. St. Louis, Jan. 7, 1965; d. Bruce Anthony and Carol Arlene (Johnson) H.; m. Richard Bancroft Dowd, June 29, 1985 (div. Sept. 1992); children: William Heyl Dowd, Sarah Ann Dowd. BA in Russian, U. Wis., 1988, JD, 1992. Bar: Ill. 1992, U.S. Dist. Ct. (no. dist.) Ill. 1993; lic. notary public, title agt. Lawyer, sole practitioner Antioch, Ill., 1993—; JD with honors. Advocate for mediation of family law issues; family law mediator. Title VI FLAS fellow in Russian Area Studies, U. Wis., 1988-89; recipient Joseph Bercovici award for Jurisprudence and Legal Philosophy, U. Wis., 1992. Mem. Ill. State Bar Assn., Lake County Bar Assn. (vol. lawyers program 1994—). Avocations: classical piano, yoga, Russian literature, volunteer soccer referee. Office: 392 Lake St Antioch IL 60002-1404

**HEYMAN, SIDNEY,** lawyer, educator; b. Riga, Latvia, Feb. 1, 1925; came to U.S., 1927; s. Seymour and Paula H.; m. Doris A. Groudine, Sept. 9, 1-51; children: Susan Cohn, Sharon McDermott. BS, L.I. U., 1949; LLB, Bklyn. Law Sch., 1953, JD, 1967. Trial atty. Great Am. Ins., N.Y.C., 1953-59, Julius Diamond, N.Y.C., 1959-68, Chikovsky, Snyder & Heyman, Rochester, N.Y., 1969-82; ptnr. Cory & Heyman, Staten Island, 1969; pvt. practice Rochester, 1983—; tchr. polit. sci. SUNY, Geneseo, 1989, 95. Staff sgt. U.S. Army, 1943-46, PTO. Avocation: competitive swimming. Personal injury, Insurance. Office: 36 W Main St Ste 604 Rochester NY 14614-1701

**HEYMANN, PHILIP BENJAMIN,** law educator, academic director; b. Pitts., Oct. 30, 1932. B.A., Yale U., 1954; LL.B., Harvard U., 1960. Bar: D.C. 1960, Mass. 1969. Trial atty. gen. Dept. Justice, Washington, 1961-65, asst. atty. gen. criminal div., 1978-81, dep. atty. gen., 1993-94; dep. adminstr. Bur. Security and Consular Affairs, Dept. State, Washington, 1965; acting adminstr. Bur. Security and Consular Affairs, Dept. State, to 1967; dep. asst. sec. of state for Bur. Internat. Orgns., 1967, exec. asst. to under sec. of state, 1967-69; with Legal Aid Agy. of D.C., 1969; faculty law Harvard U., 1969—, James Barr Ames prof. law, dir. Harvard Law Sch. Ctr. for Criminal Justice; assoc. prosecutor and cons. to Watergate Spl. Prosecution Force, summers 1973-75. Served with USAF, 1955-57.

**HEYWOOD, ROBERT GILMOUR,** lawyer; b. Berkeley, Calif., May 18, 1949; m. Carolyn Cox, June 10, 1972. AB with distinction, Stanford U., 1971; MA, U. Calif., Berkeley, 1972; JD cum laude, Santa Clara U., 1975. Bar: Calif. 1975, U.S. Dist. Ct. (no. and ea. dists.) Calif. 1975, U.S. Ct. Appeals (9th cir.) 1976, U.S. Supreme Ct. 1979; cert. specialist workers' compensation law Calif. Bd. Legal Specialization, State Bar Calif. Ptnr. Hanna, Brophy, MacLean, McAleer & Jensen, Oakland, Calif., 1976—; instr. Santa Clara U., 1975-77, advocacy skills workshop Stanford U. Law Sch., 1994—; faculty ctr. for trial and appellate adv. Hasting Coll. of Law, San Francisco; mem. faculty Calif. Ctr. for Jud. Edn. and Rsch., 1998; mem. intensive advocacy program faculty U. San Francisco Sch. Law, 1995—; adj. prof. law U. Calif., Hastings, 1982-86; arbitrator Alameda County Superior Ct. Mem. bd. editl. cons. Calif. Compensation Cases. Bd. dirs. Alameda County Legal Aid Soc., Oakland, 1978-87, Cazadero Performing Arts Camp, 1994—; bd. govs. Oakland East Bay Symphony, pres., 1991-93. Mem. ABA, Calif. Bar Assn., Calif. Continuing Edn. of Bar (editor, lect., author), Alameda County Bar Assn., Calif. Compensaton Def. Attys. Assn. Personal injury, Workers' compensation, Insurance. Office: Hanna Brophy MacLean Et Al 155 Grand Ave Ste 600 Oakland CA 94612-3747

**HIBBERT, DAVID WILSON,** lawyer; b. Atlanta, Nov. 21, 1950; s. George Wilfred and Dorothy Marie H.; m. Mary Frances Disco, June 21, 1975; children: Jaxon, Taj. BA, Mercer U., 1972; JD, Emory U., 1972. Bar: Ga. 1975, U.S. Dist. Ct. (no. dist.) Ga. 1975. Sole practice Atlanta, Tucker, Ga., 1975-89. Mem. ATLA, Ga. Bar Assn., Atlanta Bar Assn. (chmn. referral com. 1981-89). Democrat. Baptist. Club: Lawyers of Atlanta, Atlanta Radio, Atlanta Bonsai (treas. 1982). Avocations: bonsai, amateur radio. Family and matrimonial, Personal injury, Workers' compensation.

**HIBBERT, ROBERT GEORGE,** lawyer, food company executive; b. Marlboro, Mass., July 3, 1950; s. Charles Harris and Mary Barbara (Sauage) H.; m. Cynthia Joan Miller, June 12, 1971; children: Lauren, Meg, Robert J. BA, Columbia U., 1972; JD, Am. U., 1975. Bar: Mass. 1975, Md. 1975, D.C. 1985. Trial atty. office of gen. counsel USDA, Washington, 1975-79, dir. standards and labeling divsn. food safety inspection service, 1980-85; v.p., gen. counsel Am. Meat Inst., Arlington, Va., 1985-88; with McDermott, Will & Emery, Washington. Mem. ABA, Mass. Bar Assn., Md. Bar Assn., D.C. Bar Assn., Am. Agrl. Law Assn. Home: 621 Whittingham Dr Silver Spring MD 20904-6332 Office: McDermott Will & Emery 600 13th St NW Fl 12-8 Washington DC 20005-3005

**HIBBS, JOHN STANLEY,** lawyer; b. Des Moines, Sept. 19, 1934; s. Ray E. Hibbs and Jean Waller (Lackey) Gravender; m. John S. II, Kari S. Hibbs Carroll, Jennifer R. Hibbs-Kraus. BBA, U. Minn., 1956, JD cum laude, 1960. Bar: Minn. 1960, U.S. Dist. Ct. Minn. 1960, U.S. Ct. Appeals (8th cir.) 1963, U.S. Tax Ct. 1965, U.S. Supreme Ct. 1970. Ptnr. Dorsey and Whitney, Mpls., 1960—, Health Practice Group; chmn. Adv. Task Force on Minn. Corp. Law, Mpls., 1979-82, tax policy study group of Minn. Bus. Climate Task Force, Mpls., 1978-80; coun. Med. Group Practice Attys. Author: Minnesota Nonprofit Corporations-A Corporate and Tax Guide, 1979; contbr. over 150 profl. papers to publs. Served to capt. USAR, 1956-66. Fellow Am. Coll. Tax Counsel; mem. ABA (cons. com. on corp. laws 1981-82), Nat. Health Lawyers Assn., Am. Acad. Healthcare Attys., Coun. Med. Group Practice Attys., Minn. Bar Assn., Hennepin County Bar Assn. Republican. Lutheran. Avocations: sports, reading, travel, gardening. General corporate, Health, Taxation, general. Home: 25 Cooper Cir Minneapolis MN 55436-1316 Office: Dorsey & Whitney 220 S 6th St Ste 2200 Minneapolis MN 55402-1498

**HIBBS, LOYAL ROBERT,** lawyer; b. Des Moines, Dec. 24, 1925; s. Loyal B. and Catharine (McClymond) H.; children: Timothy, Theodore, Howard, Dean. BA, U. Iowa, 1950, LLB, JD, 1952. Bar: Iowa 1952, Nev. 1958, U.S. Supreme Ct. 1971. Ptnr. Hibbs Law Offices, Reno, 1972—. Moderator radio, TV Town Hall Coffee Breaks, 1970-72; mem. Nev. State Bicycle Adv. Bd., 1996—, Reno Bicycle Coun., 1995—, Reno Park Recreation Commn., 1999—. Fellow Am. Bar Found. (Nev. chmn. 1989-94); mem. ABA (standing com. Lawyer Referral Svc. 1978-79, steering com. state dels. 1979-82, consortium on legal svcs. and the pub. 1979-82, Nev. State Bar del. to Ho. of Dels. 1978-82, 89-90, bd. govs. 1982-85, mem. legal tech. adv. coun. 1985-86, standing com. on nat. conf. groups 1985-91, chmn. sr. lawyers divsn. Nev. 1988—), Nat. Conf. Bar Pres.'s Iowa Bar Assn., Nev. Bar Assn. (bd. govs. 1968-78, pres. 1977-78), Washoe County Bar Assn. (pres. 1966-67), Nat. Jud. Coll. (bd. dirs. 1986-92, sec. 1988-92), Assn. Def. Counsel No. Calif., Assn. Def. Counsel Nev., Assn. Ski Def. Attys., Aircraft Owners and Pilots Assn. (legal svcs. plan 1991—), Washoe County Legal Aid Soc. (co-founder), Lawyer-Pilots Bar Assn. (chmn. Nev.), Greater Reno C. of C. (bd. dirs. 1968-72), Phi Alpha Delta. General civil litigation, Aviation, Probate. Home: 1489 Foster Dr Reno NV 89509-1209 Office: 290 S Arlington Ave Ste 250 Reno NV 89501-1793

**HICKEN, JEFFREY PRICE,** lawyer; b. Macomb, Ill., Oct. 25, 1947; s. Victor and Mary Patricia (O'Connell) H.; m. Mary Sarah Schmidt, Aug. 23, 1969; children: Andrew, Molly, Elizabeth. BA, Cornell Coll., 1969; JD, U. Ill., 1972. Bar: Minn. 1972, U.S. Dist. Ct. Minn. 1980, U.S. Ct. Appeals (8th cir.). Assoc. Weaver, Talle & Herrick, Anoka, Minn., 1972-77; sr. ptnr. Hicken, Scott & Howard, P.A., Anoka, 1977-97, 1998—. Bd. dirs. Anoka Lyric Arts; precinct chair Dem. Farmer-Labor Party, Anoka, 1976—. Capt. U.S. Army, 1969-77. Recipient J. Franklin Littel scholarship Cornell Coll., Mt. Vernon, Iowa, 1969. Fellow Am. Acad. Matrimonial Lawyers (cert. arbitrator, bd. mgrs.); mem. Minn. State Bar Assn., Anoka County Bar Assn. (pres. 1990-91), City of Anoka Charter Commn. (chmn. 1978-84). Democrat. Avocations: running, violin. Family and matrimonial. Home: 1700 West Ln Anoka MN 55303-1923 Office: Hicken Scott & Howard PA 2150 3rd Ave Ste 300 Anoka MN 55303-2200

**HICKEY, JOHN HEYWARD,** lawyer; b. Miami, Fla., Dec. 18, 1954; s. Weyman Park Hickey and Alice Joan (Heyward) Brown. BA magna cum laude, Fla. State U., 1976; JD, Duke U., 1980. Bars: Fla. 1980, U.S. Dist. Ct. (so. dist.) Fla. 1980, U.S. Dist. Ct. (mid. dist.) Fla. 1982, U.S. Ct. Appeals (5th cir.) 1982, U.S. Ct. Appeals (11th cir.) 1983, U.S. Supreme Ct. 1985. Trial lawyer Smathers & Thompson, Miami, 1980-85; trial lawyer Hornsby & Whisenand P.A., Miami, 1985—, ptnr., 1988; ptnr. Hickey & Jones, Miami, 1988—; lectr. securities litigation Internat. Assn. Fin. Planners, 1989, 90, Fla. Inst. CPAs, 1990, Flood Ins. Conf., Columbus, Ohio, 1991, Scottsdale, Ariz., 1992, Orlando, Fla., 1993; lectr. admiralty law, Fla. Bar, 1994. Contbg. author: Fla. Bar Jour., 1990. Interviewer of prospective undergrads. Duke U. Alumni Adv. Com., 1984—; arbitrator Miami Marine Arbitration Coun. Mem. ABA (litigation mgmt./econs. com. 1986—, comml. transactions and banking com. 1986—), Fla. Bar (chmn. grievance com. 1986-89, vice chmn. 1999—, lectr. Bridge the Gap seminars 1984-85, jud. evaluation com. 1985, chmn. 11th cir. fee arbitration com. 1991—, cert. civil trial lawyer 1990, lectr. admiralty law 1994, vice chair admiralty law com. 1997—), Dade County Bar Assn. (bd. dirs. 1998—, media rels. com. 1982-83, membership com. 1982-83, legal edn. com. 1983-84, cir. ct. com. 1983-84, dir. 1984-86, chmn. young lawyers sect. meetings and programs com. 1985-86, chmn. young lawyers sect. sports com. 1984-85, exec. com. 1985—, chmn. profl. arbitration subcom. 1986—, cert. of merit 1985, 88, 89, 91, 921, 93, bd. dirs. 1990-93, 97—, chmn. banking and corp. litigation com. 1990, 91, 92, chmn. civil litigation com. 1992-93, exec. com. 1992-93, treas. 1999—), Greater Miami C. of C., Coral Gables C. of C., Propellor Club of U.S. (Miami divsn.), Marine Coun. So. Fla. (bd. dirs.), Southeastern Admiralty Law Inst. (proctor), Maritime Law Assn., Miami Marine Arbitration Coun., Phi Beta Kappa. Admiralty, General civil litigation, Personal injury. Office: Hickey & Jones PA 1401 Brickell Ave Ste 510 Miami FL 33131-3501

**HICKEY, JOHN KING,** lawyer, career officer; b. Mt. Sterling, Ky.; s. John Andrew and Anna Christine H.; m. Elizabeth Jane Pattavina, Nov. 23, 1944; children: Roger Dennis, John King, Patricia Elizabeth Corsini. JD, U. Ky., 1948; M in Internat. Affairs, George Washington U., 1974. Bar: Ky. 1949, Colo. 1958, U.S. Ct. Military Appeals 1959, U.S. Supreme Ct. 1959. Commd. 2d. lt. U.S. Army Air Forces, 1942; advanced through grades to col. USAF, 1974, ret., 1970; dir. legal judicial adminstrn. Council State Govts., Lexington, Ky., 1971-73; dir. continuing legal edn. U. Ky. Coll. Law, Lexington, Ky., 1973-86; pvt. practice Lexington, Ky., 1986—. Mem. Nat. Assn. Attorneys Gen. (outstanding contributions award 1973, sec.), U. Ky. Law Alumni Assn. (sec., treas. 1973-76, appreciation award 1976), Ctrl. Ky. Knife Club (plaque 1997). Democrat. Roman Catholic. Avocations: machairologist, reading, walking, swimming. Military, Public international, General practice. Office: 3340 Nantucket Rd Lexington KY 40502-3205

**HICKEY, JOHN MILLER,** lawyer; b. Cleve., June 4, 1955; s. Lawrence Thomas and Margaret (Miller) H.; m. Sharon Salazar, Aug. 4, 1984; children: Theodore James, John Salazar, Margaret Maureen. Student, U. Wales, U.K., 1975-76; BA, Tulane U., 1977; JD cum laude, Calif. We. Sch. Law, 1981; LLM in tax, NYU, 1982. Bar: Calif. 1981, N.Mex. 1983, U.S. Dist. Ct. N.Mex. 1983, U.S. Tax Ct. 1983, U.S. Ct. Appeals (10th cir.) 1983. Prodn. control mgr. Randall-Textron, Inc., Wilmington, Ohio, 1977-78; assoc. Montgomery & Andrews, Santa Fe, 1983-88; shareholder, dir. Compton, Coryell, Hickey & Ives, Santa Fe, 1988-93, Hickey & Ives, Santa Fe, 1993-97, Hickey & Johnson PA, Santa Fe, 1998-99, White, Koch, Kelly & McCarthy, P.A., Santa Fe, 1999—. Bd. dirs. Los Alamos (N.Mex.) Econ. Devel., Hospice Ctr., Inc., Santa Fe; sec. Inst. Water Policy Studies, Santa Fe. Republican. Roman Catholic. Avocations: bicycling, squash, reading. Estate planning, Taxation, general, Probate. Home: 806 Camino Zozobra Santa Fe NM 87505-6101 Office: White Koch Kelly & McCarthy PA 433 Paseo De Peralta Santa Fe NM 87501-1958

**HICKEY, PAUL JOSEPH,** lawyer; b. Cheyenne, Wyo., May 20, 1950; s. John Joseph and Winifred (Espy) H.; m. Jeanne M. Mrak, Dec. 29, 1973; children: Mary Bridget, Patrick, Joseph. BA, U. Wyo., 1972, JD, 1975. Bar: Wyo. 1975, U.S. Ct. Appeals (10th cir.) 1976, U.S. Supreme Ct. 1988, Colo. 1990. Law clk. to judge U.S. Ct. Appeals for 10th Cir., Cheyenne, 1975-76; ptnr. Rooney, Horiskey, Bagley, Hickey, Cheyenne, 1976-78, Horiskey, Bagley & Hickey, Cheyenne, 1978-82, Bagley, Hickey, Evans & Statkus, Cheyenne, 1982-88, Hickey & Evans, Cheyenne, 1988-94; Hickey, Mackey, Evans, Walker & Stewart, 1995—; atty. Laramie County Sch. Dist. 1, Cheyenne, 1979—; atty., mem. Wyo. Natural Gas Pipeline Authority, Cheyenne, 1989-94. Mem. Wyo. Water Devel. Com., Cheyenne, 1987-95; bd. dirs. Goodwill Industries, Cheyenne, 1988, United Way, Cheyenne, 1990; pres. Old West Mus., Cheyenne, 1987. Mem. ABA, Nat. Sch. Bds. Assn., Coun. Sch. Attys., Internat. Soc. Barristers, Wyo. State Bar (pres. 1997), Wyo. State Bar Found. (pres. 1993), Laramie County Bar Assn. (pres. 1985), Rotary (bd. dirs. Cheyenne 1988, pres. 1993). Democrat. Roman Catholic. Administrative and regulatory, General civil litigation, Public utilities. Home: 4000 Bent Ave Cheyenne WY 82001-1133 Office: 1712 Carey Ave Cheyenne WY 82001-4420

**HICKEY, TIMOTHY ANDREW,** lawyer; b. Cin., Feb. 24, 1945; s. Clifford Michael and Ellen Margaret (Hart) H.; m. Debra Dessart, June 30, 1973; children: Erin, Meghan, T. Andrew Jr., Kristin. BA, Georgetown U., 1967; JD, Chase Coll. Law, 1971. Bar: Ohio 1971, U.S. Ct. Appeals (6th cir.) 1971. Coord. Hamilton County Juvenile Ct., Cin., 1967-71, chief pub. defender, 1971-72; pvt. practice Cin., 1971—; lectr. U. Cin., 1983—. Capt. USAR, 1967-75. Mem. ABA, Ohio State Bar Assn., Cin. Bar Assn. (chmn. various coms.), Georgetown Club, Kenwood Country Club. Republican. Roman Catholic. Avocations: tennis, golf, coaching youth baseball. Juvenile, Family and matrimonial, Criminal.

**HICKLE, WILLIAM EARL,** lawyer, judge; b. Ft. Worth, Aug. 23, 1957; s. John Edward Sr. and Jean Gore Hickle; m. Debra Kruse, Jan. 27, 1982; children: David John, Mark Daniel, Nathan William, Sarah Elaine, Rachel Diane. BA in Chemistry, Baylor U., 1979; JD, U. Mo., 1982. Bar: Mo. 1983. Ptnr. Carnahan, Hickle & Calvert, L.L.C., Rolla, Mo., 1983—; part-time mcpl. judge City of Rolla, 1996—; chmn. Mo. Head Injury Adv. Coun. to Gov., Jefferson City, 1996-98. Mem. Phelps County Bar Assn. (pres. 1988), Rolla Rotary Club (pres. 1992-93). Avocations: basketball, hunting, piano. Personal injury, Product liability, Estate planning. Home: 904 Southview Dr Rolla MO 65401-4719 Office: Carnahan Hickle & Calvert LLC PO Box 698 406 N Main St Rolla MO 65401-3016

**HICKLIN, EDWIN ANDERSON,** lawyer; b. Wapello, Iowa, June 13, 1922; s. Edwin Reichley and Leona Irene (Anderson) H.; m. Carolyn Woods, June 21, 1947; children—Kathryn Hicklin Gerst, Martha Hicklin Remley, Elizabeth Hicklin Barber. B.A., U. Iowa, 1946, J.D., 1948. Bar: Iowa 1948, U.S. Dist. Ct. (so. dist.) Iowa 1953, U.S. Ct. Appeals (8th cir.) 1964. Ptnr. Hicklin & Hicklin, Wapello, 1948-57, Hicklin & Matthews, Wapello, 1962—; county atty. Louisa County, Wapello, 1952-56. Mem. Iowa Ho. of Reps., Des Moines, 1967-68; mem. Iowa State Bd. Tax Rev., Des Moines, 1969-74, chmn., 1969-70. Served to 1st lt. USAF, 1943-45; PTO. Mem. Iowa State Bar Assn. (com. on jud. adminstrn. 1969-73, chmn. 1972-73), ABA, Phi Delta Phi. Republican. Episcopalian. Lodge: Masons. General practice. Office: Hicklin & Matthews 326 Van Buren St Wapello IA 52653-1223

**HICKMAN, FRANK ROBERT,** lawyer; b. Tulsa, July 5, 1923; s. Frank N. and Ruth L. H.; m. June M. Hickman, Apr. 15, 1952; children: William, Steven, Scott. Grad., U.S. Merchant Marine Acad., 1945; LLB, Tulsa U., 1949. Bar: Okla. 1949, U.S. Dist. Ct. (no. dist.) Okla. With Hickman & Hickman, Tulsa, 1949-59, ptnr., 1983—; pub. defender Tulsa County, 1950-52; past pres. Tulsa County Jr. Bar. Lt.j.g. USNR. General corporate, Criminal. Office: Hickman & Hickman 1601 S Main St Ste 104 Tulsa OK 74119-4430

**HICKMAN, JAMES K.,** lawyer; b. Pitts., July 27, 1966; s. James Harry and Shirley Marlene H.; m. Susan Marie Stoeffler, Aug. 4, 1990; children: James David, Jason William. BA, U. Fla., 1988; JD, Stetson Coll. Law, 1991. Bar: Fla. 1991, U.S. Dist. Ct. (ctrl. dist.) Fla. 1992, U.S. Ct. Appeals (11th cir.) 1997. Atty. Blasingame, Forizs & Smiljanich PA, St. Petersburg, Fla., 1991-97, James, Hoyer, Newcomer, Forizs & Smiljanich PA, St. Petersburg, 1997—. Chairperson Christmas in Jan., St. Petersburg Bar Assn., 1994-97. Mem. ABA, Fla. Def. Lawyer Assn. General civil litigation, Consumer commercial. Office: James Hoyer Newcomer Forizs & Smiljanich 300 1st Ave S Saint Petersburg FL 33701-4236

**HICKMAN, LORI A. DEMOND,** lawyer; b. Otis AFB, Mass., Aug. 11, 1965; d. Loren G. and Judith A. (Hawkins) DeMond. BS in Bus. Mgmt., Brigham Young U., 1988, JD, 1991. Bar: N.Y. 1992, U.S. Dist. Ct. (so. dist.) N.Y. 1992, U.S. Dist. Ct. (ea. dist.) N.Y. 1993, Utah 1995, U.S. Dist. Ct. Utah 1995. Assoc. Latham & Watkins, N.Y.C., 1992-95, Holme Roberts & Owen, Salt Lake City, 1995-96; assoc. gen. counsel Micron Tech., Inc., Boise, Idaho, 1996—; mentor Mentor Law Program, N.Y.C., 1992-95, Salt Lake City, 1995-96. Mem. ABA, Utah Bar Assn., N.Y. State Bar Assn. Avocations: scuba, skiing, triathlons. General corporate, Intellectual property, Contracts commercial. Office: Micron Technology Inc MS 507 8000 Federal Way Boise ID 83716-9632

**HICKS, BETHANY GRIBBEN,** judge, commissioner, lawyer; b. N.Y., Sept. 8, 1951; d. Robert and DeSales Gribben; m. William A. Hicks III, May 21, 1982; children: Alexandra Elizabeth, Samantha Katherine. AB, Vassar Coll., 1973; MEd, Boston U., 1975; JD, Ariz. State U., 1984. Bar: Ariz. 1984. Pvt. practice Scottsdale and Paradise Valley, Ariz., 1984-91; law clk. to Hon. Kenneth L. Fields Maricopa County Superior Ct. S.E. dist., Mesa, 1991-93; commr., judge pro tem Maricopa County Superior Ct. Ctrl. and S.E. Dists., Phoenix and Mesa, with domestic rels. and juvenile divsns., 1993-99; magistrate Town of Paradise Valley, Ariz., 1993-94; judge ctrl. dist. domestic rels. Maricopa County Superior Ct., Phoenix, 1999—. Mem. Jr. League of Phoenix, 1984-91; bd. dirs. Phoenix Children's Theatre, 1988-90; parliamentarian Girls Club of Scottsdale, Ariz., 1985-87, 89-90, bd. dirs., 1988-91; exec. bd., sec. All Saints' Episcopal Day Sch. Parents Assn., 1991-92, pres., 1993-94; active Nat. Charity League, 1995-99, Valley Leadership Class XIX, 1997-98; vol., Teach for Am., 1997—. Mem. ABA, State Bar Ariz., Maricopa County Bar Assn., Ariz. Women Lawyers' Assn. (steering com. 1998—). Republican. Episcopalian. Club: Paradise Valley Country. Office: 201 W Jefferson Phoenix AZ 85003

**HICKS, C. FLIPPO,** lawyer; b. Fredericksburg, Va., Feb. 24, 1929; s. Robert A. and Nell (Jones) H.; m. Patricia DeHardit (dec. 1983); children: Robert, Patricia Shull, J. Flippo (dec. 1995), Paula Mooradian. BS in Commerce, U. Va., 1950, LLB, 1952. Bar: Va. 1952, U.S. Supreme Ct. 1955. Asst. atty. gen. Commonwealth of Va., Richmond, 1953-59; ptnr. Martin, Hicks, Ingles, Ltd., Gloucester, Va., 1959-91; gen. counsel Va. Assn. Counties, Richmond, 1991—; bd. dirs., v.p. Williamsburg (Va.) Nat. Bank, 1965-75; bd. dirs. 1st Va. Bank, Commonwealth Williamsburg. Presdl. elector 1968, 76, 80; pres. exec. coun. Episcopal Diocese of Va., 1970-71, mem. standing com., 1971-74. Fellow Am. Bar Found.; mem. ABA (Leader of Yr. award Gen. Practice Sect., Constbar Leader of Yr. 1992), Va. State Bar (pres. 1990-91), Nat. Assn. of Counties Civil Attys. (pres. 1999—). Democrat. Episcopalian. Avocations: gardening, college sports. General civil litigation. Office: Va Assn Counties Old City Hall 10th and Broad Sts Richmond VA 23234

**HICKS, C. THOMAS, III,** lawyer; b. N.Y.C., Sept. 14, 1945; s. Charles Thomas and Jeane (Merritt) H.; m. Susan Massie, Dec. 30, 1967 (div. Dec. 1997); children: Melissa, Merritt. BSCE, Va. Tech. U., 1967; JD, U. Ga., 1970; LLM in Tax, Georgetown U., 1975. Bar: Ga. 1970, Va. 1972, D.C. 1981. Assoc. Boothe, Prichard & Dudley, Fairfax, Va., 1975-78; ptnr. Wickwire, Gavin & Gibbs, P.C., Vienna, Va., 1978-83, Shaw, Pittman, Potts & Trowbridge, McLean, Va., 1983-98, Greenberg Traurig, McLean, 1998—; gen. counsel Wolf Trap Found. Performing Arts, 1998—. Judge advocate USMC, Washington, 1971-75; co-founder, dir. No. Va. Transp. Alliance, McLean, Va., 1987, gen. counsel, 1987—. Mem. Va. Bar Assn. (mem. bus. law coun.), Va. State Bar (bus. law sec. bd. governors, chmn.), Fairfax Bar Assn., Nat. Assn. Bond Lawyers, Va. Assn. Comml. Real Estate (pres., co-founder, dir.), NAIOP (pres., dir. Va. chpt. 1990), No. Va. Tech. Coun. (dir., gen. counsel 1996—), Greater Washington Bd. Trade, Fairfax County C. of C. (dir. 1998—). Avocations: sailing, tennis, golf. Home: 6443 Madison McLean Dr Mc Lean VA 22101 Office: Greenberg Traurig 1750 Tysons Blvd Ste 12 Mc Lean VA 22102-4220

**HICKS, DERON RAY,** lawyer; b. Athens, Ga., June 5, 1968; s. Jesse Ray and Joanna Parker (Flynn) H.; m. Angela Medders Hicks, Aug. 21, 1995; 1 child, Margaret Anna. BFA, U. Ga., Athens, 1990; JD, Mercer U., Macon, Ga., 1993. Law clk. to Judge Owens U.S. Dist. Judge Middle Dist. Ga., Macon, 1993-95; assoc. Hicks, Mullins, Robinson, Marchetti & Kamensky PC, Columbus, Ga., 1995-97, ptnr., 1998; ptnr. Page, Scranton, Sprouse, Tucker & Ford PC, Columbus, Ga., 1998—. Co-author: Georgia Law of Torts: Preparasentor Trial, 1996; contbr. articles to profl. jours. Counsel person City Coun. Warm Springs, Ga., 1998—. Mem. State Bar Ga., Columbus Bar Assn., ABA. Presbyterian. Avocation: painting. Insurance, Appellate, Civil rights. Office: Page Scranton Sprouse Tucker & Ford 1043 3rd Ave Columbus GA 31901-2501

**HICKS, DONALD CADE, III,** lawyer; b. Raleigh, N.C., Jan. 19, 1948; s. Donald Cade and Charlotte Pollock H.; m. Grethen E. Kemmer, May 26, 1978 (div. 1986); 1 child, Kathryn; m. Susan Ellen Everett, Jan. 1, 1995. AB in Econs., U. N.C., 1970, JD, 1974. Asst. dist. atty. 3d Jud. Dist., Greenville, N.C., 1975-79; assoc. Taft & Taft, Greenville, N.C., 1979-81; pub. def. 3d Jud. Dist., Greenville, 1981-85, asst. dist. atty., 1985-89; asst. dist. atty. 3d Jud. Dist., New Bern, 1989—. With USMC, 1970-76. Mem. Phi Beta Kappa. Methodist. Avocations: boating, antique automobiles. Office: Dist Attys Office Broad St New Bern NC 28563

**HICKS, ELLIOT GENE,** lawyer; b. Charleston, W.Va., Dec. 3, 1955; m. Nancy A. Abt, May 10, 1997; 1 child, Lauren Camilla. BA in Polit. Sci., W.Va. U., 1978, JD, 1981. Bar: Va., U.S. Dist. Ct. (no. and so. dists.) W.Va. Pvt. practice Charleston, W.Va., 1981-82; ptnr. Dues, Tyree & Hicks, Charleston, W.Va., 1982-83; pvt. practice Charleston, W.Va., 1983-84; assoc. Kay, Casto, Chaney, Love & Wise, Charleston, W.Va., 1984-89, ptnr., 1989—. Chmn. Kanawha County Housing & Redevel., Charleston, 1991-98; chmn. bd. trustees 1st Bapt. Ch., Charleston, 1991—. Mem. W.Va. State Bar Assn. (pres. 1998—, bd. govs. 1993-96), Kanawha County Bar Assn. (pres. 1988-89), Sigma Pi Phi. General civil litigation, Product liability. Home: 8 Druid Pl Charleston WV 25314-1127 Office: Kay Casto Chaney Love & Wise 1600 Bank One Ctr 707 Virginia St E Fl 16 Charleston WV 25301-2702

**HICKS, J. PORTIS,** lawyer; b. Detroit, May 16, 1938; s. Livingstone Porter and Mildred (Portis) H.; m. Julie A. Gildersleeve, June 1, 1963 (div. Apr. 1977); children: Darcy A., Tyler P; m. Laura J. Corwin, Oct. 25, 1995. BA in History, U. Mich., 1962, JD, 1964; cert., London Sch. Econs.-Polit. Sci., 1965. Bar: N.Y. 1966, U.S. Dist. Ct. (so. and ea. dists.) N.Y. 1971, U.S. Ct. Appeals (2d cir.) 1972, U.S. Supreme Ct. 1981. Assoc. Kelley Drye & Warren, N.Y.C., 1965-69, Pinheiro Neto, Barros & Freire, Sao Paulo, Brazil, 1969-71; assoc., then ptnr. Marks, Murase & White, N.Y.C., 1971-82; ptnr. Boulanger, Finley & Hicks, N.Y.C., 1982-84, 89-91; ptnr. Drinker, Biddle, & Reath, N.Y.C., 1984-89, of counsel, 1989-91; ptnr. Boulanger, Hicks, & Churchill, N.Y.C., 1991-96, Winthrop Stimson Putnam & Roberts, N.Y.C., 1996—. Mem. ABA, N.Y. State Bar Assn., Assn. Bar City N.Y. Private international, General civil litigation. Office: Winthrop Stimson Putnam & Roberts 1 Battery Park Plz Fl 31 New York NY 10004-1490

**HICKS, JAMES HERMANN,** lawyer; b. Wassertruding, Germany, Jan. 29, 1955; came to U.S., 1956.; s. W.B. Hicks and Marlena (Hahnlein) Reimer; m. Sarah Murphy, June 12, 1988; children: Jordan Schlam, Addison Blade, Alexandra Starr. BA, Coll. William & Mary, Williamsburg, Va., 1977; JD, Nova U., Ft. Lauderdale, Fla., 1980. Bar: Fla. 1980, U.S. Dist. Ct. (so. dist. and so. dist. trial bar) Fla. 1981. Assoc. Law Office of Ronald Sales, West Palm Beach, Fla., 1980-81, McKeown & Gamot, P.A., Palm Beach, Fla., 1981-87; sr. ptnr. Hicks and Brams, P.A., West Palm Beach, 1987—; legal counsel Palm Beach County Sheriff Dept., West Palm Beach, 1981—, Fla. Hwy. Patrol, West Palm Beach, 1987—; mem. Palm Beach Jud. Rels. Com. Contbr. article to U.S. and internat. pubs. Mem. Palm Beach County Sports Authority, 1991—. Mem. ABA, Assn. Trial Lawyers Am., Acad. Fla. Trial

Lawyers, Florida Bar, Palm Beach County Bar Assn., Palm Beach County Police Assn. Republican. Lutheran. Avocations: white water rafting, skiing, karate, racquetball, running. General civil litigation, Personal injury, Family and matrimonial. Office: Hicks and Brams PA 1645 Palm Beach Lakes Blvd # 0 West Palm Beach FL 33401-2204

**HICKS, RENEA,** lawyer; b. Denison, Tex., May 12, 1947; s. Crayton and Eleanor H.; m. Susan Godsey, May 16, 1970; 1 child, Michael. BA, U. Tex., 1969, JD, 1976. Bar: Tex. 1977, U.S. Ct. Appeals (5th cir.) 1978, U.S. Dist. Ct. (we. and no. dist.) Tex. 1980, U.S. Dist. Ct. (ea. and so. dists.) Tex. 1981, U.S. Supreme Ct. 1981, U.S. Ct. Appeals (9th cir.) 1985, U.S. Ct. Appeals (D.C. and 1st cirs.) 1986, U.S. Ct. Appeals (10th cir.) 1988. Law clk. U.S. Dist. Judge Sarah Hughes, Dallas, 1976-77; dir. litigation Advocacy, Inc., Austin, 1980-84; state solicitor, spl. asst., asst. atty. gen. Tex. Atty. Gen.'s Office, Austin, 1977-80, 84-95; with George, Donaldson & Ford, L.L.P., Austin, 1995-96, ptnr., 1996-99; ptnr. George & Donaldson, L.L.P., Austin, 1999—; mem. adv. bd. Women's Advocacy Project, Austin, 1990—. With U.S. Army, 1970-71. Recipient Pres.'s Disting. Svc. award Nat. Assn. Attys. Gen., 1989. Fellow Tex. Bar Found.; mem. ABA, Bar Assn. 5th Fed. Cir., Travis County Bar Assn. Democrat. Methodist. Appellate, General civil litigation, Environmental. Home: 4112 Ramsey Ave Austin TX 78756-3511 Office: George & Donaldson LLP 1100 Norwood Tower 114 W 7th St Austin TX 78701-3000

**HICKTON, DAVID JOHN,** lawyer; b. Columbus, Ohio, Aug. 14, 1955; s. John Joseph and Gloria Catherine (McDermott) H.; m. Dawne Eileen Sepanski, June 16, 1984; children: Conor David, Audrey Rose, Daniel McDermott, Keenan Richard, Declan John. Student, Exeter U., U.K., 1977; BA, Pa. State U., 1978; JD, U. Pitts., 1981. Bar: Pa. 1981, U.S. Dist. Ct. (we. dist. 1981) Pa., U.S. Ct. Appeals (3d cir.) 1985, U.S. Supreme Ct. 1993. Law clk. to Hon. Gustave Diamond U.S. Dist. Ct. (we. dist.) Pa., Pitts., 1981-83; assoc. Dickie, McCamey & Chillote, Pitts., 1983-87; ptnr. Burns, White & Hickton, Pitts., 1987—; adj. prof. law Duquesne U. Bd. dirs. Family House, 1985—; mem. Big Bros.-Big Sisters Greater Pitts., 1987. Mem. ABA, Pa. Bar Assn., Allegheny County Bar Assn., Acad. Trial Lawyers, Nat. Assn. R.R. Trial Counsel, Am. Arbitration Assn. Democrat. Roman Catholic. Avocations: tennis, golf. General civil litigation, Construction, Antitrust. Office: Burns White & Hickton 2400 5th Ave Pl 120 5th Ave Ste 2400 Pittsburgh PA 15222-3011

**HIDEN, ROBERT BATTAILE, JR.,** lawyer; b. Boston, May 8, 1933; s. Robert Battaile Sr. and Clotilda (Waddell) H.; m. Ann Eliza McCracken, Mar. 27, 1956; children: Robert B. III, Elizabeth Patterson, John Hughes. BA, Princeton U., 1955; LLB, U. Va., 1960. Bar: N.Y. 1961, U.S. Ct. Appeals (2d cir.) 1974, U.S. Dist. Ct. (so. dist.) N.Y. 1975. Assoc. Sullivan & Cromwell, N.Y.C., 1960-67, ptnr., 1968-98, of counsel, 1999—. Articles editor and contbr. U. Va. Law Rev., 1959-60; contbr., mem. bd. editors Futures Internat. Law Letter, 1987-92. Trustee Hampton (Va.) U. and Hampton Inst., 1984—; commr. Larchmont Little League, N.Y., 1964-68; chmn. Larchmont Jr. Sailing Program, 1977-78; vestry, jr. warden St. John's Episc. Ch., Larchmont, 1982-86, 99—. Served to lt. (j.g.) USNR, 1955-57. Mem. ABA, N.Y. State Bar Assn., Assn. of Bar of City of N.Y., N.Y. County Bar Assn., Am. Judicature Soc., Raven Soc., Order of Coif, Omicron Delta Kappa. Democrat. Clubs: Larchmont U. (pres. 1976-77), Larchmont Yacht (trustee 1979-85, sec. 1990—); N.Y. Yacht (N.Y.C.); Scarsdale Golf (N.Y.). Avocations: skiing, golf, sailing, tennis. General corporate, Securities, Mergers and acquisitions. Home: 2 Walnut Ave Larchmont NY 10538-4232 Office: Sullivan & Cromwell 125 Broad St Fl 28 New York NY 10004-2489

**HIEKEN, CHARLES,** lawyer; b. Granite City, Ill., Aug. 15, 1928; s. Samuel and Margaret (Isaacs) H.; m. Donna Jane Clanin, Jan. 6, 1961; children: Tina Jane, Seth Paul. SBEE, MIT, 1952, SMEE, 1952; LLB, Harvard U., 1957. Bar: Ill. 1957, Mass. 1958, U.S. Supreme Ct. 1960, U.S. Ct. Customs and Patent Appeals 1961, U.S. Ct. Claims 1963, U.S. Ct. Appeals (fed. cir.) 1982. Patent asst. Lab. Electronics, Boston, 1954-56, Fish, Richardson & Neave, Boston, 1956-57; assoc. Hill, Sherman, Meroni & Simpson, Chgo., 1957, Joseph Weingarten, Boston, 1957-58; assoc. Wolf, Greenfield & Hieken, Boston, 1958-61, ptnr., 1961-70; prin. Charles Hieken Law Offices, Waltham, Mass., 1970-87; ptnr. Fish & Richardson, Boston, 1987-94, prin., 1995—. Mem. pres.'s adv. coun. Bentley Coll., 1993—; mem. coun. Harvard Law Sch. Assn., 1998—. Served with U.S. Merchant Marine, 1944-47, U.S. Army, 1952-54. Mem. Boston Bar Assn. (mem. civil procedure com. 1959—), Mass. Bar Assn. (chmn. intellectual property com. 1977-80), Ill. State Bar Assn., Boston Patent Law Assn. (chmn. pub. rels. com. 1965-66, chmn. antitrust law com. 1966-70, 78-80, treas. 1970-71, v.p. 1971-72, pres.-elect 1972-73, pres. 1973-74), IEEE (sr., life), Down Town Club (bd. govs.), Tau Beta Pi, Eta Kappa Nu. Patent, Federal civil litigation, Trademark and copyright. Home: 193 Wilshire Dr Sharon MA 02067-1561 Office: Fish & Richardson PC 225 Franklin St 31st Fl Boston MA 02110-2804

**HIER, MARSHALL DAVID,** lawyer; b. Bay City, Mich., Aug. 24, 1945; s. Marshall George and Helen May (Copeland) H.; m. Nancy Speed Brown, June 26, 1970; children: John, Susan, Ann. BA, Mich. State U., 1966; JD, U. Mich., 1969. Bar: Mo. 1969. Assoc. Peper, Martin, Jensen, Maichel and Hetlage, St. Louis, 1969-76, ptnr., 1976-95; prin. Bertram, Peper and Hier, P.C., St. Louis, 1996—; bd. dirs. Gateway Ctr. Met. St. Louis, Mercantile Libr. Assn., St. Louis Soc. Blind and Visually Impaired. Contbr. articles to profl. jours. Mem. St. Louis Bar Assn. (editor jour. 1988—), St. Louis Civil Round Table (former pres.). Baptist. General corporate, Securities, Private international. Home: 17141 Chaise Ridge Rd Chesterfield MO 63005-4457

**HIESTAND, SHEILA PATRICIA,** lawyer; b. Levittown, Pa., July 10, 1969; d. John Douglas Lloyd and Eileen Ann Cassidy; m. David Michael Hiestand, July 25, 1992; 1 child, Michael David. BA in Spanish and English, Centre Coll., Danville, Ky., 1990; JD, U. Ky., 1993. Bar: Ky. 1993, U.S. Dist. Ct. (ea. and we. dists.) Ky. 1994, U.S. Ct. Appeals (6th cir.) 1997. Assoc. Landrum & Shouse, Lexington, Ky., 1993-98; ptnr. Landrum & Shouse, Lexington, 1999—. Bd. dirs., officer Vol. Ctr. of the Bluegrass, 1995-98; girls basketball coach Christ the King Sch., 1993-98. Mem. Fayette County Bar Assn. (Outstanding Young Lawyer 1998, pres. young lawyers sect. 1996-98, bd. dirs. 1996-99), Ky. Bar Assn. (bd. dirs. young lawyers sect., convention CLE com. 1997-98). Roman Catholic. General civil litigation, Civil rights, Workers' compensation. Office: Landrum & Shouse 106 W Vine St Ste 800 Lexington KY 40507-1688

**HIGDON, FREDERICK ALONZO,** lawyer, accountant; b. Lebanon, Ky., Aug. 30, 1950; s. William Joseph and Mary Rita Higdon; m. Nancy Lawrence Brents, Aug. 4, 1972; children: Ashley, Matthew, Scott. BS cum laude, Western Ky. U., 1972; JD, U. Louisville, 1975. Bar: Ky. 1975. Staff acct. Coopers & Lybrand, Louisville, 1972-74; tax acct. Peat, Marwick & Mitchell, Louisville, 1974-76; lawyer Spragens, Smith & Higdon, P.S.C., Lebanon, Ky., 1976—; bd. dirs., vice chair Peoples Bank, Lebanon; asst. county atty. Marion County, Ky., 1992-96. Past pres. Lebanon/Marion County C. of C., Lebanon/Marion County Leadership Alumni Assn., Marion County Jr. Miss, Inc.; pres., dir. Marion County Pub. Libr., Lebanon, 1993—, Marion County Indsl. Found., Lebanon, 1997—. Mem. Ky. Bar Assn., Ky. Soc. CPAs, Marion County Bar Assn. (treas. 1978—). Avocations: snow skiing, hunting, fishing. General practice, Probate, Taxation, general. Office: Spragens Smith and Higdon PSC 15 Court Sq Lebanon KY 40033-1257

**HIGDON, JAMES NOEL,** lawyer; b. McAlester, Okla., Oct. 20, 1944; s. Wilford Dain and Ida Jean (Douglass) H.; m. Barbara Ann Downing, Feb. 8, 1969; children: Travis Noel, Charles Andrew. BA, U. Tex., 1967; MBA, U. West Fla., 1973; JD, St. Mary's U., 1975. Bar: Tex. 1976; U.S. Dist. Ct. (we. dist.) Tex. 1978, U.S. Dist. Ct. (no. dist.) Tex. 1979, U.S. Dist. Ct. (ea. dist.) Tex. 1980; U.S. Ct. Appeals (5th cir.) 1979, U.S. Supreme Ct. 1979; bd. cert. family law, civil appellate law; trained mediator, arbitrator. Briefing atty. 4th Ct. Civil Appeals, San Antonio, 1976-77; assoc. Wiley, Plunkett, Gibson and Allen, San Antonio, 1977-79; ptnr. Wiley, Garwood, Hornbuckle and Higdon, San Antonio, 1979-81; ptnr., sec., treas. Hornbuckle, Higdon and Young, P.C., San Antonio, 1981-83; ptnr., v.p. Bass, Higdon and Hardy, Inc., San Antonio, 1983-97; ptnr. Higdon, Hardy & Zuflacht, L.L.P., San Antonio, 1997—; bd. dirs. Alamo Masonic Cemetery Corp., San Antonio. Troop com. chmn. Boy Scouts Am., 1989-91, cubmaster, treas., dean leader, 1982-87; commr. City San Antonio AIDS/HIV Commn., 1990-93; chmn. San Antonio Navy Recruiting Dist. Assistance Coun., 1989-91; mem. Alamo Coun., Navy League of U.S.; bd. dirs. Bexar County Dispute Resolution Ctr., 1997—, San Antonio Pub. Libr. Found., 1997—. Capt. USNR, ret. Fellow Am. Acad. Matrimonial Lawyers, Tex. Bar Found., San Antonio Bar Found.; mem. State Bar Tex. (mem. Tex. Bar Jour. Commn., 1980-95, family law, ADR, mil. law, litigation, appellate advocacy secs.), San Antonio Bar Assn. (chmn. continuing legal edn. com. 1990-92, bd. dirs. 1992-94, founder, charter chmn. family law sec. 1992-94), San Antonio Family Lawyers Assn. (sec. 1987-88, v.p. 1988-89, pres. 1989-90, bd. dirs. 1986-91, 98-99), Tex. Acad. Family Law Specialists, Rotary (San Antonio Oak Hills, v.p. program chmn. 1989-90, pres. 1991-92, bd. dirs. 1986-93, sec. dist. 5840 1992-93), Masons (pres. lodge 1980-81, chpt. 1983-84, coun. 1984-85, commandery 1992, york rite coll. 1994-95, s.a. coun. # 261 1997-98), Masonic Grand Lodge Tex. (dist. deputy grand master-39A 1989-90, dist. Masonic rels. officer-39A 1990-93), Knights Templar of Tex. (grand commandery, grand line officer 1996—), Sigma Phi Epsilon. Southern Baptist. Family and matrimonial, General civil litigation, Appellate. Home: 10122 N Manton Ln San Antonio TX 78213-1948 Office: Higdon Hardy & Zuflacht LLP 1848 Lockhill Selma Ste 102 San Antonio TX 78213-1566

**HIGDON, POLLY SUSANNE,** federal judge; b. Goodland, Kans., May 1, 1942; d. William and Pauline Higdon; m. John P. Wilhardt (div. May 1988); 1 child, Liesl. BA, Vassar Coll., 1964; postgrad., Cornell U., 1967; JD, Washburn U., 1975; LLM, NYU, 1980. Bar: Kans. 1975, Oreg. 1980. Assoc. Corley & Assocs., Garden City, Kans., 1975-79, Kendrick M. Mercer Law Offices, Eugene, Oreg., 1980-82; pvt. practice law Eugene, 1983; judge U.S. Bankruptcy Ct., Eugene, 1983-95; judge U.S. Bankruptcy Ct., Portland, Oreg., 1995-97, chief judge, 1997—. Active U.S. Peace Corps, Tanzania, East Africa, 1965-66. Mem. Am. Bankruptcy Inst., Nat. Conf. Bankruptcy Judges, Oreg. Women Lawyers. Office: US Bankruptcy Ct 1001 SW 5th Ave Fl 7 Portland OR 97204-1147

**HIGGINBOTHAM, JOHN TAYLOR,** lawyer; b. St. Louis, Feb. 10, 1947; s. Richard Cann and Jocelyn (Taylor) H.; m. Lauren Flint Totty, Aug. 9, 1975 (div. 1979). BA, UCLA, 1969; JD, Columbia U., 1972. Bar: N.Y. 1975, Calif. 1976. Assoc., Kirlin, Campbell & Keating, N.Y.C., 1972-74; atty. Nat. Bank of N.Am., N.Y.C., 1974-76, Bank of Am., 1977; assoc. Barger & Wolen, L.A., 1977-78, Halperin, Shivitz, Scholer, Schneider & Eisenberg, 1978-79; atty., dir. real estate Korvettes Inc., N.Y.C., 1979-82; assoc. Leon Katz, Bklyn., 1983-84; assoc. Finley, Kumble, Wagner, Heine, Underberg, Manley & Casey, N.Y.C., 1984-86; assoc. regional counsel HUD, N.Y.C., 1986-88, assoc. Fink, Weinberger, Fridman, Berman, Lowell & Fensterhein, 1988-89, Sterling Securities, Inc., Manhasset, N.Y., 1989-93, Willkie, Farr & Gallagher, N.Y.C., 1993. Editor: Safe Deposit Decisions and Practice, 1977—. Mem. NARAS, NATAS, Acad. Motion Picture Arts and Scis., League Am. Theatres and Producers, Inc. Real property, General civil litigation, Entertainment.

**HIGGINBOTHAM, PATRICK ERROL,** federal judge; b. Ala., Dec. 16, 1938. Student, U. Ala., 1956, Arlington State Coll., 1957, North Tex. State U., 1958, U. Tex., 1958; B.A., U. Ala., 1960, LL.B., 1961; LLD (hon.), So. Meth. U., 1989. Bar: Ala. 1961, Tex. 1962, U.S. Supreme Ct. 1962. Assoc. to ptnr. Coke & Coke, Dallas, 1964-75; judge U.S. Dist. Ct. (no. dist.) Tex., Dallas, 1976-82, U.S. Ct. Appeals (5th cir.), Dallas, 1982—; adj. prof. So. Meth. U. Law Sch., 1971—, adj. prof. constl. law, 1981—; conferee Am. Assembly, 1975, Pound Conf., 1976; bd. suprs. Inst. Civil Justice Rand. Contbr. articles, revs. to profl. publs.; note editor: Ala. Law Rev., 1960-61. With USAF, 1961-64, JAG. Recipient Dan Meador award U. Ala., Samuel E. Gates Litigation award Am. Coll. Trial Lawyers, 1997; named Outstanding Alumnus U. Tex., Arlington, 1978, One of Nation's 100 Most Powerful Persons for the 80's Next Mag. Fellow Am. Bar Found.; mem. ABA (chmn. com. to compile fed. jury charges antitrust sect., mem. coun. antitrust sect., bd. editors Jour. chair appellate judges conf. 1989—), Dallas Bar Assn. (dir., chmn. cons. legal aid civic affairs), Dallas Bar Found. (bd. dirs.), Am. Law Inst., S.W. Legal Found. (chmn. bd. of trustees), Am. Judicature Soc. (bd. dirs., trustee), Nat. Jud. Coun. State and Fed. Cts., Dallas Inn of Ct. (pres. 1996—, chair adv. com. on civil rules jud. conf. U.S. 1993-96), Farrah Law Soc., Order of Coif (hon.), Bench and Bar, Am. Inns. of Ct. Found. (pres. 1996—), Omicron Delta Kappa. Office: US Ct Appeals 13E1 US Courthouse 1100 Commerce St Dallas TX 75242-1027

**HIGGINS, JOHN STUART, JR.,** lawyer; b. Providence, Nov. 9, 1939; s. John Stuart and Frances Hanna (Bell) H.; m. Karon Ellen Brigman, May 30, 1975; children: Jennifer Reyes, Nathan, Christopher, John, Nicholas. AB cum laude, Harvard U., 1961, JD, 1964. Bar: Calif. 1966, U.S. Dist. Ct. (no. dist.) Calif. 1966, U.S. Ct. Appeals (9th cir.) 1966, U.S. Dist. Ct. (ea. dist.) Calif. 1975, U.S. Supreme Ct. 1986, U.S. Dist. Ct. (ctrl. dist.) Calif. 1989. Assoc. Chickering & Gregory, San Francisco, 1965-66; staff atty. San Francisco Neighborhood Legal Assistance Found., 1966-67, Tulare County Legal Svcs. Assn., Tulare, Calif., 1972-75; staff atty., then sr. staff atty. Contra Costa Legal Svcs. Found., Richmond, Calif., 1967-71; pvt. practice, Pleasant Hill, Calif., 1971-72; dep. dist. atty. Tulare County, Visalia, 1975—; chmn. appellate com. Calif. Family Support Coun., Sacramento, 1986—. Contbr. articles to law publs. Trustee, chmn. bd. St. Paul's Sch., Visalia, 1978-81, 84-92; vestryman St. Paul's Episcopal Ch., 1975-77, 92-94, 97-99, treas. 1976-77, sr. warden, 1994. Mem. State Bar Calif., Calif. Dist. Attys. Assn., Tulare County Bar Assn., Marines Meml. Assn. Avocations: Hiking, bicycling, skiing. Office: Office Dist Atty Family Support Divsn 8040 W Doe Ave Visalia CA 93291-9721

**HIGGINS, JOHN WAYNE,** lawyer; b. Nashville, Dec. 24, 1943; s. Frank Higgins and Madeline Wolfe; m. Nancy Farrington, Jan. 21, 1964 (div. Dec. 1994); children: Madeline Kim Higgins Scates, Susan Rebecca Higgins Goldway, John Frank. BA, U. N.Mex., 1968; JD, Oklahoma City U., 1973. Secondary sch. tchr. Okla. Pub. Schs., Oklahoma City, 1968-72; legal intern Freeman, Heffron and Pittman Law Firm, Oklahoma City, 1972-73; legal advisor Albuquerque Police Dept., 1973; pvt. practice, ptnr. Higgins, Mescall & Lee, Albuquerque, 1973—; temporary mcpl. ct. judge City of Albuquerque, 1977-80, temporary met. ct. judge, 1980-82; legal counsel Office Sheriff Bernalillo County, 1991-95; former panel mem. bd. trustees U.S. Bankruptcy Ct., Albuquerque; former mem. rules com. of the cts. of limited jurisdiction State of N.Mex.; former mem. jud. selection com. Bernalillo County Met. Ct.; lectr. in field. Scholar Oklahoma City U., 1970, 71, 72. Mem. Okla. Fed. Bar Assn., Okla. Bar Assn., N.Mex. Bar Assn., N.Mex. Trial Lawyers Assn., U.S. Dist. Ct. Dist. N.Mex., Albuquerque Bar Assn., Comml. Law League Am., Phi Alpha Delta. Office: Higgins Mescall & Lee 515 Roma Ave NW Albuquerque NM 87102-2124

**HIGGINS, MARY CELESTE,** lawyer, researcher; b. Chgo., Feb. 9, 1943; d. Maurice James and Helen Marie (Egan) H. AB, St. Mary-of-the-Woods Coll., Ind., 1965; JD, DePaul U., 1970; LLM, John Marshall Law Sch., Chgo., 1976; postgrad., Harvard U., 1981, 82, MPA, 1982; MPhil, U. Cambridge (Eng.), 1983. Bar: Ill., 1970, U.S. Dist. Ct. (no. dist.) Ill. 1970. Sole practice Chgo., 1970-72, 79-80; atty. corp. counsel dept. Continental Bank, Chgo., 1972-76; asst. sec., asst. counsel Marshall Field & Co., Chgo., 1976-79; sr. atty. Mattel, Inc., Hawthorne, Calif., 1980-81; rch. in revitalization and adjustment of U.S. Industries in U.S. and world markets, 1981-83; legal cons., 1983-85; Midwest regional officer Legal Svcs. Corp., 1985-87, assoc. dir., 1986, acting dir. office of field svcs., 1986-87, dir., 1987-89; dir. Meridian One Corp., Alexandria, Va., 1990—. Recipient Am. Jurisprudence awards for acad. excellence, 1966-70. Mem. Ill. Bar Assn. General corporate, Private international, Public international. Home: 203 Yoakum Pkwy Apt 508 Alexandria VA 22304-3711

**HIGGINS, ROBERT FREDERICK,** lawyer; b. Olney, Ill., July 8, 1944; s. Robert Kenneth and Betty (Travers) H.; m. Barbara Bowman, Aug. 27, 1966 (dec.); children: Jennifer M., Matthew B., Kathryn C. BA, Marietta Coll., 1966; JD, Wash. U., St. Louis, 1969. Bar: Fla. 1972, Mo. 1969, Ohio 1969. Asst. county counselor legal dept. St. Louis County, St. Louis, 1969; judge advocate USAF, Keesler AFB, Biloxi, Miss., 1969-71; trial counsel USAF, Southeast U.S., 1971-72; mil. judge USAF, Calif. and Nev., 1972-73; assoc. Van Den Berg, Gay & Burke, PA, Orlando, Fla., 1974-76, Lowndes, Piersol, Drosdick & Doster, Orlando, 1977-79; ptnr. Lowndes, Drosdick, Doster, Kantor & Reed, PA, Orlando, 1979—. Pres. Christian Svc. Ctr., Orlando, 1983-85; chmn. Ctrl. Fla. chpt. ARC, Orlando, 1992-94; bd. dirs. ARC in Ctrl. Fla., 1990—; mem. cmty. redevelopment adv. bd. City Winter Park, 1995-97. Mem. Fla. Bar Assn. (UCC/bankruptcy com. 1990—), Orange County Bar Assn. (exec. coun. 1983-89), Comml. Law League, Orlando Area Dolfins (pres. 1983-84), Interlachen Country Club. Lutheran. Bankruptcy, Banking, General civil litigation. Office: Lowndes Drosdick Doster Kantor & Reed PO Box 2809 215 N Eola Dr Orlando FL 32802

**HIGGINS, THOMAS A.,** federal judge; b. 1932. AA, Christian Bros. Coll., 1952; BA, U. Tenn., 1954; LLB, Vanderbilt U., 1957. Bar: U.S. Dist. Ct. (mid. dist.) Tenn., U.S. Ct. Mil. Appeals, U.S. Ct. Appeals (6th cir.), U.S. Supreme Ct. Ptnr. Willis & Higgins, 1960-61; assoc., then. ptnr. Cornelius, Collins, Higgins & White, 1961-84; judge U.S. Dist. Ct. (mid. dist.) Tenn., Nashville, 1984—. Served with AUS, 1957-60. Fellow Am. Coll. Trial Lawyers; mem. ABA, Tenn. Bar Assn., Nashville Bar Assn. Office: US District Court A-845 US Courthouse Nashville TN 37203-3816

**HIGGINS, VALERIE JAN,** lawyer. BA in History with honors, UCLA, 1978; JD, Glendale U., 1981; diploma, Inst. Internat. & Comparative Law, Paris, 1981; cert., Hague Acad. Internat. Law, The Netherlands, 1985; diploma, Inst. Internat. Law, Dublin, Ireland, 1993. Bar: Calif. 1982, U.S. Dist. Ct. (ctrl. and no. dists.) Calif. 1982, U.S. Ct. Appeals (9th cir.) 1982. Legal rsch. asst. civil default and law and motion depts. L.A. Mcpl. Ct., 1980-82; ptnr., atty. Law Offices of Higgins and Higgins, San Francisco, 1982—; settlement conf. judge pro tem San Francisco Superior Ct., 1985—, arbitrator, 1985—; arbitrator San Francisco Mcpl. Ct., 1995—; mediator in field. Mem. State Bar Calif., PEO Sisterhood. Avocations: equestrienne, music, writing. State civil litigation, Private international, Probate. Office: Higgins and Higgins 1255 Post St Ste 1037 San Francisco CA 94109-6705

**HIGGINSON, CARLA JEAN,** lawyer; b. Snoqualmie, Wash., Jan. 27, 1955; d. William Hollis and Jean Marie (Landahl) H.; m. Jack (A. John) Wuebker, Feb. 14, 1987; 1 stepchild, Cody Wuebker. BA cum laude, Western Wash. U., 1976; JD, U. Wash., 1979. Bar: Wash. 1980, U.S. Dist. Ct. (we. dist.) Wash. 1980, U.S. Supreme Ct. 1987. Assoc. Gaddis & Fox, Seattle, 1979, Francis, Lopez & Ackerman, Seattle, 1980-81; pvt. practice Friday Harbor, Wash., 1980—; judge Town of Friday Harbor, 1981-89. Mem. San Juan County Bd. Realtors, ABA, San Juan County Bar Assn., Wash. State Bar Assn. Land use and zoning (including planning), Probate, General civil litigation.

**HIGGS, DAVID LAWRENCE,** lawyer; b. Canton, Ill., Aug. 14, 1951; s. Louis Wilson and Lois (Gentle) H.; m. Carolyn Jean Perardi, June 24, 1973; children: Craig, Scott. BS with high honors, Western Ill. U., 1972; JD summa cum laude, So. Ill. U., 1981. Bar: Ill. 1981, U.S. Dist. Ct. (no. dist.) Ill. 1981, U.S. Ct. Appeals (7th cir.) 1982, U.S. Tax Ct. 1982. Ptnr. Sutkowski & Washkuhn Assocs., Peoria, Ill., 1981-91, Husch & Eppenberger, Peoria, 1991—. Contbr. articles to profl. jours. Mem. ABA, Ill. State Bar Assn. (employee benefits sect. coun. 1990-91, Chmn. award 1991), Peoria County Bar Assn., Estate Planning Coun. of Peoria, Peoria-North Rotary. Presbyterian. Avocation: golf. Pension, profit-sharing, and employee benefits, Estate taxation, Estate planning. Office: Husch & Eppenberger LLC 401 Main St Ste 1400 Peoria IL 61602-1258

**HIGGS, JOHN H.,** lawyer; b. Balt., Mar. 10, 1934; s. E. Homer and Josephine (Doughty) H.; m. Helen Platt, Aug. 25, 1956; children: Sarah, Anne, Julia, Susan. AB, Dartmouth Coll., 1956; LLB, U. Pa., 1960. Bar: N.Y. 1961. Founder Higgs Pavements Co., Milford, Conn., 1953-56; assoc. Sullivan & Cromwell, N.Y.C., 1960-61, 62-68; assoc. Wickes, Riddell, Bloomer, Jacobi & McGuire, N.Y.C., 1968, ptnr., 1969-79; ptnr. Morgan, Lewis & Bockius, LLP, N.Y.C., 1979-97, counsel, 1997—; ptnr. Skyport Indsl. Park, Newark, N.J.; sec. Ea. States Bankcard Assn., Lake Success, N.Y., 1970-88; bd. dirs. Indsl. Bank Japan Trust Co., N.Y., 1974—, IBJ Found. Inc., N.Y., 1989—; mem. staff adv. com. on comml. bank supervision State N.Y., 1965-66. Contbr. articles to profl. jours. Mayor Village of Pelham Manor, N.Y., 1979-81. Banking, Private international, Finance. Home: 20 Beechtree Ln Pelham NY 10803-3502 Office: Morgan Lewis & Bockius 101 Park Ave Fl 44 New York NY 10178-0060

**HIGH, DAVID ROYCE,** lawyer; b. Oklahoma City, Aug. 28, 1950; s. Jack Eugene and Harriett Ann High; m. Charlotte Anne Bonsteel, Dec. 28, 1975; 1 child, Katie McKenzie. BA, U. Okla., 1973; JD, Oklahoma City U., 1978. Bar: Okla. 1978, U.S. Dist. Ct. (we. dist.) Okla. 1978, U.S. Ct. Appeals (10th cir.) 1990. Assoc. Tomerlin & High, Oklahoma City, 1978-80; ptnr. Tomerlin, High & High, Oklahoma City, 1980-92, pvt. practice law, 1992—. Legal counsel The Children's Ctr., Bethany, Okla., 1978—, Oklahoma City Beautiful Inc., 1982-89. Mem. ABA, Okla. Bar Assn. (gov. 1988-91), Oklahoma County Bar Assn. (bd. dirs. 1981-91, v.p. 1984-85, Outstanding Oklahoma County Young Lawyer award 1981). Avocation: tennis. General corporate, Probate, General civil litigation. Office: Tomerlin High & High 3601 N Classen Blvd Ste 203 Oklahoma City OK 73118-3269

**HIGHBERGER, WILLIAM FOSTER,** lawyer; b. Suffern, N.Y., May 15, 1950; s. John Kistler and Helen Stewart (Foster) H.; m. Carolyn Barbara Kuhl, July 12, 1980; children: Helen Barbara, Anna Mary. AB, Princeton U.; JD, Columbia U. Bar: Calif. 1976, U.S. Dist. Ct. (cen. dist.) Calif. 1976, U.S. Ct. Appeals (2d cir.) 1976, U.S. Ct. Appeals (9th cir.) 1977, U.S. Dist. Ct. (so. and ea. dists.) Calif. 1979, U.S. Supreme Ct. 1980, D.C. 1981, U.S. Dist. Ct. (no. dist.) Calif. 1981, U.S. Dist. Ct. D.C. 1982, U.S. Ct. Appeals (D.C. cir.) 1982, U.S. Ct. Appeals (3d cir.) 1983, N.Y. 1984, U.S. Dist. Ct. (so. dist.) N.Y. 1984, U.S. Dist. Ct. (ea. dist.) N.Y. 1985. Law clk. to judge U.S. Ct. Appeals (2d cir.), Bridgeport, Conn., 1975-76; assoc. Gibson, Dunn & Crutcher, Washington and L.A., 1976-82, ptnr., 1983—. Notes and comments editor Columbia U. Law Rev., 1974. Mem. Nature Conservatory, Calif., 1981—; active Pacific Palisades (Calif.) Presbtn. Ch., 1987—. James Kent scholar Columbia U., 1973. Mem. ABA (com. on individual rights and responsibilities in workplace, labor sect.), L.A. County Bar Assn., Indsl. Rels. Rsch. Assn., Am. Employment Law Coun., Univ. Cottage Club. Republican. Labor, Pension, profit-sharing, and employee benefits, Federal civil litigation. Office: Gibson Dunn & Crutcher 333 S Grand Ave Ste 4400 Los Angeles CA 90071-3197

**HIGHSMITH, SHELBY,** federal judge; b. Jacksonville, Fla., Jan. 31, 1929; s. Isaac Shelby and Edna Mae (Phillips) H.; m. Mary Jane Zimmerman, Nov. 25, 1972; children—Holly Law, Shelby. A.A., Ga. Mil. Coll., 1948; B.A., J.D., U. Kansas City, 1958. Bar: Fla. 1958. Trial atty. Kansas City, Mo., 1958-59, Miami, Fla., 1959-70; circuit judge Dade County, Fla., 1970-75; sr. ptnr. Highsmith, Strauss, Glatzer & Deutsch, P.A., Miami, 1975-91; judge U.S. Dist. Ct. (so. dist.) Fla., Miami, 1991—. Chief legal adviser Gov.'s War on Crime Program, 1967-68; spl. counsel Fla. Racing Commn., 1969-70; mem. Inter-Agy. Law Enforcement Planning Counsel of Fla., 1969-70. Served to capt. AUS, 1949-55. Decorated Bronze Star; recipient Outstanding Alumni Achievement Law award, U. Mo., 1998. Fellow Internat. Soc. Barristers; mem. ABA, Dade County Bar Assn., Bench and Robe, Torch and Scroll, Miami Nat. Golf Club, Wildcat Cliffs Country Club, (Highlands, N.C.), Omicron Delta, Phi Alpha Delta. Republican. Roman Catholic. Office: Fed Justice Bldg 99 NE 4th St Rm 1027 Miami FL 33132-2138

**HIGHTOWER, JACK ENGLISH,** former state supreme court justice, congressman; b. Memphis, Tex., Sept. 6, 1926; s. Walter Thomas and Floy Edna (English) H.; m. Colleen Ward, Aug. 26, 1950; children—Ann, Amy, Alison. B.A., Baylor U., 1949; JD, 1951; LLM, Univ. Va., 1992. Bar: Tex. 1951. Since practiced in Vernon; mem. Tex. Ho. of Reps., 1953-54; dist. atty. 46th Jud. Dist. Tex., 1955-61; mem. Tex. Senate, 1965-75, pro tempore, 1971; mem. 94th-98th Congresses from 13th Tex. Dist., 1975-85; 1st asst. atty. gen. State of Tex., 1985-87; justice Texas Supreme Ct., Austin, 1988-95; ret., 1996. Mem. Tex. Law Enforcement Study Commn., 1957; del. White House Conf. Children and Youth, 1970; alt. del. Democratic Nat. Conv., 1968; bd. regents Midwestern U., Wichita Falls, Tex., 1962-65; trustee Baylor U., 1972-81, acting gov., 1971; trustee Wayland Bapt. Univ., Plainview, Tex., 1991—, Tex. Bapt. Children's Home, 1959-62, Tex. Scottish Rite Hosp. Children, 1991—, Human Welfare Commn.; bd. dirs. Bapt. Standard, 1959-68. With USNR, 1944-46. Named Outstanding Dist. Atty, Tex., Tex. Law Enforcement Found., 1959, Disting. Alumnus, Baylor U., 1978; recipient Knapp-Porter award Tex. A&M Univ., 1980. Mem. Tex.

Dist. and County Attys. Assn. (pres. 1958-59), Scottish Rite Ednl. Assn. Tex. (exec. com. 1990—), Tex. Supreme Ct. Historical Soc. (pres. 1991-98), Tex. Bar. Found. (fellow 1992), SAR, U.S. Supreme Ct. Historical Soc., Tex. State Historical Assn. (exec. coun. 1998—), Masons (grand master Tex. 1972), Lions (pres. Vernon 1961).

**HIGINBOTHAM, JACQUELYN JOAN,** lawyer; b. Dec. 15, 1951; d. Ivan Lyle and Ruth Harriet (La Point) H.; m. Robert Redditt; children: Altara Roxana, Rigel Rowena. AA, Northeastern Jr. Coll., Sterling, Colo., 1972; BA, U. No. Colo., 1974; JD, U. Colo., 1978. Bar: Colo. 1978, U.S. Dist. Ct. Colo. 1978, U.S. Ct. Appeals (10th cir.) 1983. Staff, mng. atty. Colo. Rural Legal Svcs., Ft. Morgan, 1979—. Precinct committeewoman Ft. Morgan Dem. Com., 1984—; mem. adv. bd. Caring Ministries Morgan County, 1986-87; mem. Ft. Morgan Parent-Tchr. League, 1987—. Mem. Colo. Bar Assn., Nat. Lawyers Guild, Christian Legal Soc., Order of Coif. Democrat. Episcopalian. Avocations: astronomy, music, skating. Family and matrimonial, Health, Pension, profit-sharing, and employee benefits. Home: 702 Sherman St # 1123 Fort Morgan CO 80701-3540 Office: Colo Rural Legal Svcs 209 State St Fort Morgan CO 80701-2115

**HIIGEL, F. EUGENE,** lawyer; b. Lamar, Colo., 1943. BA, U. Colo., 1967; MA, U. Denver, 1977; JD, NYU, 1979. Bar: N.Y. 1980. Ptnr. Skadden, Arps, Slate, Meagher & Flom LLP, N.Y.C. Securities. Office: Skadden Arps Slate Meagher & Flom LLP 919 3rd Ave New York NY 10022-3902

**HILBERG, LANCE MICHAEL,** lawyer, historian; b. Michigan City, Ind., Sept. 24, 1939; s. Karl and Evelyn (Gropp) H.; m. Norma Jean Cochran, Dec. 24, 1960; children: Jennifer, Nathan, Jane. LLB, LaSalle Extension U., Chgo., 1969; PhD, Columbia State U., 1998. Bar: Ind. Capt. Police Dept., Michigan City, 1961-78; corp. state tax lawyer Sullair Corp., Michigan City, 1978—; v.p., bd. dirs., chair edn. com. Gt. Lakes Mus. Mil. History, Michigan City. Mil. history educator local TV program Another Voice--For Freedom We Served. Task force mem. Urban Enterprise Zone Bd., Michigan City, 1992-93; chmn. coun. Grace Ch., Michigan City, 1994-96. Served with U.S. Army, 1958-61, Korea. Mem. NRA (life, endowment mem., instr. emeritus), Nat. Lawyers Assn., Co. Mil. Historians, U.S. Cavalry Assn., VFW. Avocation: army military history. Office: Sullair Corp 3700 E Michigan Blvd Michigan City IN 46360-6500

**HILBERT, OTTO KARL, II,** lawyer; b. Colorado Springs, Colo., Feb. 9, 1962; s. Otto Karl and Mary Rachel (Shine) H.; m. Lucille Megan O'Shaughnessy, Apr. 21, 1995. BA, U. Notre Dame, 1984, postgrad., 1985; JD, U. Colo., 1988. Bar: Colo. 1989, Ariz. 1989, Wis. 1998, U.S. Dist. Ct. (no. dist.) Calif, U.S. Ct. Appeals (9th cir.) 1991, U.S. Tax Ct. 1992, U.S. Ct. Appeals (10th cir.) 1993, U.S. Supreme Ct. 1995. Assoc. Kelly, Stansfield & O'Donnell, Denver, 1988-89, 92-93, Russell Piccoli, Ltd., Phoenix, 1989-92, LeBoeuf, Lamb, Greene & MacRae LLP, Denver, 1993-96; shareholder Reinhart, Boerner, Van Deuren, Norris & Rieselbach PC, Denver, 1996—; arbitrator Nat. Assn. Securities Dealers, Inc., 1993—, Nat. Futures Assn., 1993—. Mem. law sch. adv. coun. U. Notre Dame, 1989-92; cons. Ariz. Spl. Olympics, Phoenix, 1989-92; mem. Edward Frederick Sorin Soc., Notre Dame, Ind., 1989—. Mem. ABA, Colo. Bar Assn., Denver Bar Assn., Ariz. Bar Assn., Wis. Bar Assn., Notre Dame Club of Phoenix (1st v.p. 1991-92, bd. dirs. 1989-92, Award of the Yr. 1992), Notre Dame Club of Denver (bd. dirs. 1995-97), Lakewood Country Club (bd. dirs. 1998—). Republican. Roman Catholic. Avocations: piano, guitar, golf. Securities, Sports, Federal civil litigation. Office: Reinhart Boerner Van Deuren Norris Rieselbach PC 1 Norwest Ctr 1700 Lincoln St Ste 3725 Denver CO 80203-4537

**HILBORNE, THOMAS GEORGE, JR.,** lawyer; b. Oklahoma City, Sept. 8, 1946; s. Thomas George and Bula LaFern (Buercklin) H. BBA, U. Okla., 1968, JD, 1971. Bar: Okla. 1971, U.S. Dist. Ct. (we. dist.) Okla. 1974, U.S. Dist. Ct. (no. dist.) Okla. 1977, U.S. Ct. Mil. Appeals 1972, U.S. Supreme Ct. 1975. Ptnr. Hirsh, Johanning & Hudson, Oklahoma City, 1971-74; assoc. Crowe & Dunlevy, Oklahoma City, 1974-77; mem. firm, officer, dir. Jones, Givens, Gotcher, Bogan & Hilborne, P.C., Tulsa, 1977-90; pres. Hilborne & Weidman, P.C., Tulsa, 1990—; mem. select com. to advise Okla. Securities Commn., Oklahoma City, 1988; assoc. mem. Nat. Assn. Mpl. Law Officers, Oklahoma City, 1986-89, expert assoc. mem. com. mpl. bonds, 1986-89. Bd. dirs. Tulsa Zoo Devel., Inc., 1985—. Lt. comdr. JAGC, USNR, 1972-82. Mem. Okla. Bar Assn. (commr. profl. responsibility com. 1983-85), Nat. Assn. Bond Lawyers (charter mem.), Econ. Club Okla., So. Hills Country Club, Com. of One Hundred of Tulsa, Golf Club Okla. Methodist. Avocation: golf, tennis. Municipal (including bonds), Finance, Transportation. Home: 2712 E 31st St Tulsa OK 74105-2302 Office: Hilborne & Weidman PC 2405 E 57th St Tulsa OK 74105-7548

**HILBRECHT, NORMAN TY,** lawyer; b. San Diego, Feb. 11, 1933; s. Norman Titus and Elizabeth (Lair) H.; m. Mercedes L. Sharratt, Oct. 24, 1980. B.A., Northwestern U., 1956; J.D., Yale U., 1959. Bar: Nev. 1959, U.S. Supreme Ct. 1963. Assoc. counsel Union Pacific R.R., Las Vegas, 1962; ptnr. Hilbrecht & Jones, Las Vegas, 1962-69; pres. Hilbrecht, Jones, Schreck & Bernhard, 1969-83, Hilbrecht & Assocs, 1983—, Mobil Transport Corp., 1970-72; gen. counsel Bell United Ins. Co., 1986-94; mem. Nev. Assembly, 1966-72, minority leader, 1971-72; mem. Nev. Senate, 1974-78; legis. commn., 1977-78; asst. lectr. bus. law U. Nev., Las Vegas.; oper. mem. Corp. Svcs. Group, 1998—; pres. Corp. Svcs. Co., 1998—, Nev. Incorporating Co., 1998—. Author: Nevada Motor Carrier Compendium, 1990. Mem. labor mgmt. com. NCCJ, 1963; mem. Clark County (Nev.) Dem. Ctrl. Com., 1959-80, 1st vice chmn., 1965-66; del. Western Regional Assembly on Ombudsman; chmn. Clark County Dem. Conv., 1966, Nev. Dem. Conv., 1966; pres. Clark County Legal Aid Soc., 1964, Nev. Legal Aid and Defender Assn., 1965-83; assoc. for justice Nat. Jud. Coll., 1993, 94, 95, 96. Capt. AUS, 1952-67. Named Outstanding State Legislator Eagleton Inst. Politics, Rutgers U., 1969, Best Lawyers in Am., Bar of Nev., 1993. Mem. ABA, ATLA, Am. Judicature Soc., Am. Acad. Polit. and Social Sci., State Bar Nev. (chmn. adminstrv. law 1991-94, chmn. sect. on adminstrv. law 1996), Nev. Trial Lawyers (state v.p. 1966), Am. Assn. Ret. Persons (state legis. com. 1991-94), Rotary, Elks, Phi Beta Kappa, Delta Phi Epsilon, Theta Chi, Phi Delta Phi. Lutheran. Office: 723 S Casino Center Blvd Las Vegas NV 89101-6716

**HILDEBRAND, CHRISTA,** lawyer; b. Warstein, Germany, Dec. 27, 1945; came to U.S., 1970; d. Fritz and Hilde (Pothoff) H.; m. Jeffrey Abrams; 1 child. Grad., Acad. Sci. and Tech., Isny, Germany, 1970; BA, BS, U. Wis., 1972, MA, 1973, PhD, 1980, JD, 1983. Bar: Wis. 1983, N.Y. 1985, Patent Bar 1986. Assoc. David Hoxie Faithful & Hapgood, N.Y.C., 1983-85, Fish & Neave, N.Y.C., 1985-90, Egli Internat., N.Y.C., 1990-94; assoc., resident atty. Cohen Pontani Lieberman & Pavane, N.Y.C., 1994-96; of counsel Darby & Darby, N.Y.C, 1997—. Mem. ABA, Am. Intellectual Property Law Assn., N.Y. Patent Law Assn. Office: Darby & Darby PC 805 3rd Ave Fl 27 New York NY 10022-7557

**HILDEBRAND, DANIEL WALTER,** lawyer; b. Oshkosh, Wis., May 1, 1940; s. Dan M. and Rose Marie (Baranowski) H.; m. Dawn E. Erickson; children: Daniel G., Douglas P., Elizabeth A., Rachel E., Jacob E. BS, U. Wis., 1962, LLB, 1964. Bar: Wis. 1964, U.S. Dist. Ct. (we. dist.) Wis. 1964, N.Y. 1965, U.S. Dist. Ct. (so. and ea. dists.) N.Y. 1967, U.S. Ct. Appeals (2d cir.) 1968, U.S. Dist. Ct. (ea. dist.) Wis. 1970, U.S. Ct. Appeals (7th cir.) 1970, U.S. Supreme Ct. 1970, U.S. Tax Ct. 1986, U.S. Ct. Appeals (8th cir.) 1988, U.S. Ct. Appeals (D.C. cir.) 1991. Assoc. Willkie, Farr & Gallagher, N.Y.C., 1964-68; from assoc. to ptnr. DeWitt Ross & Stevens S.C., Madison, Wis., 1968—; lectr. U. Wis. Law Sch., Madison, 1972—; mem. Joint Survey Com. on Tax Ememptions Wis. Editor: U. Wis. Law Rev., 1963-64. Pres. Wis. Law Foun., 1993-95, Wis. Jud. Commn., 1992-98, chairperson, 1997-98. Fellow Am. Bar Found.; mem. ABA (mem. fed. cts. com. litigation sect., ho. of dels. 1992—, standing com. on ethics 1997—, Wis. state delegate 1995—), Wis. Bar Assn. (bd. govs. 1981-85, 86-93, mem. exec. com. 1987-93, chmn. 1988-89, pres. 1991-92), N.Y. State Bar Assn., Dane County Bar Assn. (pres. 1980-81), 7th Cir. Bar Assn., Am. Law Inst., Am. Acad. Appellate Lawyers, James E. Doyle Inn of Ct. Roman Catholic. Federal civil litigation, State civil litigation. Office: 2 E Mifflin St Ste 600 Madison WI 53703-2890

**HILDEBRAND, DONALD DEAN,** lawyer; b. Emden, Ill., Aug. 9, 1928; s. Henry John and Ethel Paulena (Weimer) H.; m. Jewell Howell, Jan. 4, 1959. BA, Ill. Wesleyan U., 1950; JD, Vanderbilt U., 1955; postgrad., U. Ill., U. Nev.; nat. advocacy cert., U. Nev. Nat. Coll. Advocacy, 1984. Bar: Tenn. 1957, U.S. Dist. Ct. (mid. dist.) Tenn. 1957, U.S. Supreme Ct. 1980. Claims rep. State Farm Mut. Ins., Nashville, 1957-62; pvt. practice, Nashville, 1962—; advocate Tenn. chpt. Am. Bd. Trial Advocates, sec., 1990—. Prodr., host (local TV show) Law: Cases & Comment, 1989-95. Rep. candidate for Tenn. Supreme Ct., 1973. With U.S. Army, 1952-54, Korea; col. Tenn. Def. Force, 1984—. Mem. Tenn. Bar Assn., Tenn. C. of C. (chmn. mil. affairs com. 1978-82), Am. Legion (state comdr. 1970-73, post comdr. 1978, Shriners (life, Legion of Honor 1982). Methodist. Avocations: walking, weightlifting, gardening, world-wide travel. Personal injury, Workers' compensation, Federal civil litigation. Home: 132 Hardingwoods Pl Nashville TN 37205-3612 Office: 214 3d Ave Nashville TN 37201

**HILDNER, PHILLIPS BROOKS, II,** lawyer; b. Battle Creek, Mich., June 26, 1944; s. Phillips Brooks and Eva Marie (Burek) H.; divorced; 1 child, Phillips Brooks III. BS, Western Mich. U., 1967; JD, Detroit Coll. Law, 1971. Bar: Mich. 1971. Asst. prosecuting atty. Genesee County, Flint, Mich., 1971-73; ptnr. Conover, Hildner & Zielinski, Fenton, Mich., 1973-79; sole practice Fenton, 1980—; sponsoring atty. Law Day, Fenton High Sch., 1973—. Mem. State Bar Mich., Genesee County Bar Assn., Fenton C. of C., 2d Century Club Detroit Coll. Law, Delta Theta Phi. Episcopalian. Avocations: fly fishing, hunting, running, exercise. General practice, Probate. Office: PO Box 87 111 W Shiawassee Ave Fenton MI 48430-2005

**HILDRETH, GARY R.,** lawyer; b. Valparaiso, Ind., May 18, 1938; s. Harry S. and Gladys V.; m. June A Martin, Dec. 20, 1958; children: Teri A. Hildreth Hawkins, Kellee L. Hildreth McEntee, Matthew H. BS, Ind. U., 1960, JD, 1963. Bar: Ind. 1963, Calif. 1970, Tex. 1980, Ohio 1982, Pa. 1994. Atty. U.S. Atomic Energy Commn., 1963-67; contracts counsel Honeywell, Inc., 1967-68; divsn. counsel Lockheed Missiles & Space Co., 1968-71; gen. counsel Hitco, 1971-78; gen. atty. Armco, Pitts., 1978-80; corp. counsel Armco, 1980-86; asst. gen. counsel Armco, Pitts., 1986-90, assoc. gen. coun., 1990-92, asst. v.p. law, 1992-93, gen. counsel, 1993—; v.p., gen. counsel sec. Armco, Inc. Pitts., 1993. Mem. Bd. of Adjustments Chester Twp. N.J., 1992-93. Mem. ABA, Am. Corp. Counsel Assoc., Am. Soc. Corp. Sec., Duquesne club. Avocation: gardening, hiking, reading. General corporate, Mergers and acquisitions. Office: ARMCO Inc One Oxford Ctr 1 Oxford Ct Pittsburgh PA 15219-1407

**HILES, BRADLEY STEPHEN,** lawyer; b. Granite City, Ill., Nov. 11, 1955; s. Joseph J. and Betty Lou (Goodman) H.; m. Toni Jonine Failoni, Aug. 12, 1977; children: Eric Stephen, Nina Catherine, Emily Christine. BA cum laude, Furman U., 1977; JD cum laude, St. Louis U., 1980. Bar: Mo. 1980, U.S. Dist. Ct. (ea. dist.) Mo., 1980, Ill. 1981. From assoc. to ptnr. Blackwell Sanders Peper Martin, St. Louis, 1980—; v.p., sec., gen. counsel Miss. Lime Co., 1992. Editor-in-chief St. Louis Univ. Law Jour., 1979-80; contbr. articles to profl. jours. Pres. Second Baptist Ch. of St. Louis, 1988. Mem. Bar Assn. of Met. St. Louis (chmn. environ. and conservation law com. 1993-94). Republican. Baptist. Avocations: gospel singing, cycling. Environmental, Labor. Home: 34 Meditation Way Ct Florissant MO 63031-6535 Office: Blackwell Sanders Peper Martin 720 Olive St Fl 24 Saint Louis MO 63101-2338

**HILF, MICHAEL GARY,** law administrator, prosecutor; b. Hollis, N.Y., June 11, 1955; s. Victor and Dorothy (Goldwasser) H. AB, Cornell U., 1976; JD, Harvard U., 1979. Bar: N.Y. 1980, U.S. Dist. Ct. (no., ea., and so. dists.) N.Y. 1980. Asst. dist. atty. N.Y. County, N.Y.C., 1979-86; sr. staff atty. N.Y. State Edn. Dept., Office Profl. Discipline, N.Y.C., 1987-89, dep. dir. prosecutions, 1989—; vis. asst. prof. law Coll. Law, U. Toledo, 1986-87. Mem. Alumni Assn. of Bronx H.S. of Sci. (trustee 1981—, chmn. bd. trustees 1981-86, 87-91, 92-95), Phi Beta Kappa. Office: NY State Edn Dept 6th Fl One Park Ave New York NY 10016-5802

**HILKER, WALTER ROBERT, JR.,** lawyer; b. L.A., Apr. 18, 1921; s. Walter Robert and Alice (Cox) H.; children: Anne Katherine, Walter Robert III. BS, U. So. Calif., 1942, LLB, 1948. Bar: Calif. 1949. Sole practice Los Angeles, 1949-55; ptnr. Parker, Milliken, Kohlmeier, Clark & O'Hara, 1955-75; of counsel Pacht, Ross, Warne, Bernhard & Sears, Newport Beach, Calif., 1980-84. Trustee Bella Mabury Trust; bd. dirs. Houchin Found. Served to lt. USNR, 1942-45. Decorated Bronze Star. Mem. ABA, Calif. Bar Assn., Orange County Bar Assn. Republican. Clubs: Spring Valley Lake Country (Apple Valley, Calif.); Balboa Bay (Newport Beach, Calif.). Estate planning, Probate, Estate taxation. Home and Office: 154 Stonecliffe Aisle Irvine CA 92612-5700

**HILL, ALFRED,** lawyer, educator; b. N.Y.C., Nov. 7, 1917; m. Dorothy Turck, Aug. 12, 1960; 1 dau., Amelia. B.S., Coll. City N.Y., 1937; LL.B., Bklyn. Law Sch., 1941, LL.D., 1986; S.J. D., Harvard U., 1957. Bar: N.Y. State bar 1943, Ill 1958. With SEC, 1943-52; prof. law So. Meth. U., 1953-56, Northwestern U., 1956-62; prof. law Columbia U., 1962-75, Simon H. Rifkind prof. law, 1975-87, Simon H. Rifkind prof. law emeritus, 1988—. Contbr. articles on torts, conflict of laws, fed. cts. constl. law to legal jours. Mem. Am. Law Inst. Home: 79 Sherwood Rd Tenafly NJ 07670-2734 Office: Columbia Law Sch New York NY 10027

**HILL, BARRY MORTON,** lawyer; b. Wheeling, W.Va., Sept. 13, 1946; m. Jacqueline Sue Jackson, Aug. 12, 1967 (div. Mar. 1988); children: Jackson Duff, Brandy; m. Lisa C. Wien, Jan. 7, 1989; 1 child, Gabriel Hunter. BS in Journalism, W.Va. U., 1968, JD, 1977. Bar: W.Va. 1977, U.S Dist. Ct. (no. and so. dists.) W.Va. 1977, Ohio 1978, U.S. Dist. Ct. (no. dist.) Ohio 1978, U.S. Ct. Appeals (3d, 4th, 6th and D.C. cirs.) 1984, U.S. Supreme Ct. 1984, U.S. Ct. Appeals (2d and 11th cirs.) 1986, Pa. 1986, U.S. Ct. Appeals (5th, 7th and 10th cirs.) 1988; cert. civil trial specialist Nat. Bd. Trial Adv. Ptnr. Parsons Thompson & Hill, Wheeling, W.Va.; mem. W.Va. Pattern Jury Instrn. Panel, 1986; mem. exec. com. for rev. jury selection U.S. Dist. Ct. (no. dist.) W.Va.; mem. W.Va. Bar Civil Procedure Rules Rev. com., 1987; draftsman Interprofl. Code for Attys. and Physicians W.Va., 1987-88; adj. prof. Saba U. Sch. of Medicine, 1994—. Founding sponsor Civil Justice Found. Served to 1st lt. U.S. Army, 1969-71. Mem. ABA (regional editor torts and ins. practices sect. of newsletter 1987-88), Assn. Trial Lawyers Am. (sec. Pres.' coun. 1987-88, key person com., 1987-88, Pres.' coun. study com. 1988—, ins. practices com. 1988—), Am. Bd. Profl. Liability Attys. (diplomate), Ohio Acad. Trial Lawyers, Pa. Trial Lawyers Assn., W.Va. Trial Lawyers Assn. (pres. 1987-88, Outstanding mem. 1984), So. Trial Lawyers Assn. (bd. govs. 1988—). Democrat. Avocations: SCUBA, tennis, travel, writing, golf. Federal civil litigation, State civil litigation, Personal injury. Office: Parsons Thomson & Hill 1325 National Rd Wheeling WV 26003-5705

**HILL, CINDY ELLEN,** lawyer; b. Atlantic City, N.J., Nov. 29, 1963; d. William Gilbert and Dorothy Evelyn Hill; m. Jon Christopher Frappier, Aug. 1, 1998; 1 child, Evelyn Mae. BA in Polit. Sci., SUNY, Stony Brook, 1984; M in Environ. Legal Studies, U. Vt., 1987, JD, 1987. Mng. ptnr. Couture and Hill, Northampton, Mass., 1987-92; mng. atty. Law Office of Cindy Hill, Middlebury, Vt., 1992—. Selectman Bd. of Selectmen, Middlebury, 1997—. Avocations: black and white photography, handspinning and knitting, writing. Criminal, Environmental, Land use and zoning (including planning). Office: 10 Merchants Row Middlebury VT 05753-1436

**HILL, CLYDE VERNON, JR.,** prosecutor; b. Oxford, Miss., May 30, 1952; s. Clyde Vernon and Doris Elizabeth Hill; m. Lisa K. Proctor, Aug. 18, 1984; children: Tara C., Ami E. (dec.), Christina K., Amanda G., Lisa Michelle. BS, Miss. State U., 1978; JD, U. Miss., 1983. Bar: Miss. 1983, U.S. Dist. Ct. (no. dist.) Miss. 1983. Asst. dist. atty. 11th Cir. Miss., Clarksdale, 1983-94, 5th Cir. Miss., Grenada, 1994—. Sunday sch. tchr. adult bible study. Mem. Miss. Prosecutors Assn. (bd. dirs. 1995—). Baptist. Avocation: farming. Home: 14 Northwoods Dr Grenada MS 38901-9274 Office: Dist Attys office 234 1st St Grenada MS 38901-2602

**HILL, DOUGLAS JENNINGS,** lawyer; b. Detroit, Jan. 8, 1933; s. Wade Flowers and Bernice (Champion) H.; m. Sylvia Kay Seelye, July 20, 1957; children: Cynthia Kay, Elizabeth Ann, Stephen Wade. BA in Bus. Adminsrn., U. Mich., 1955, LLB, 1960. Atty. Cadick, Burns, Duck & Neighbors, Indpls., 1960-81, Hill, Fulwider, McDowell, Funk & Matthews, Indpls., 1981—; mem. Ind. Jud. Nominating Commn., Indpls., 1996-98. With U.S. Army, 1955-57. General civil litigation, Alternative dispute resolution, Professional liability. Office: Hill Fulwider McDowell Funk & Matthews 1 Indiana Sq Ste 2000 Indianapolis IN 46204-2031

**HILL, EARL MCCOLL,** lawyer; b. Bisbee, Ariz., June 12, 1926; s. Earl George and Jeanette (McColl) H.; m. Bea Dolan, Nov. 22, 1968 (dec. Aug. 1998); children: Arthur Charles, John Earl, Darlene Stern, Tamara Fegert. BA, U. Wash., 1960, JD, 1961. Bar: Nev. 1962, U.S. Ct. Clms. 1978, U.S. Ct. Apls. (9th cir.) 1971, U.S. Sup. Ct. 1978. Law clk. Nev. sup. ct., Carson City, 1962; assoc. Gray, Horton & Hill, Reno, 1962-65, ptnr. 1965-73; ptnr. Marshall Hill Cassas & de Lipkau (and predecessors), Reno, 1974—, Sherman & Howard, Denver, 1982-91; judge pro tem Reno mcpl. ct., 1964-70; lectr. continuing legal edn.; mem. Nev. Commn. on Jud. Selection 1977-84; trustee Rocky Mountain Mineral Law Found. 1976-95, sec. 1987-88. Contbr. articles to profl. jours. Mem. ABA, ATLA, State Bar Nev. (chmn. com. on jud. adminstrn. 1971-77), Washoe County Bar Assn., Am. Judicature Soc., Lawyer Pilots Bar Assn., Soc. Mining Antiquarians (sec.-treas. 1975—), Prospectors Club. General civil litigation, Environmental, Real property. Office: Holcomb Profl Ctr 333 Holcomb Ave Ste 300 Reno NV 89502-1648

**HILL, GARY D.,** lawyer; b. Eugene, Oreg., Apr. 7, 1952; s. Virgil R. and Doris H.; m. Patricia L. Hill, July 10, 1976. BA, Linfield Coll., McMinnville, Oreg., 1974; JD, Northwestern Sch. of Law, Portland, 1981. Bar: Oreg. 1982. News anchor KPTV, Portland, Oreg., 1976-92; pvt. practice Portland, Oreg., 1981-84, 88-92; atty. Hergert & Assocs., Oregon City, Oreg., 1992—. Vol. Oreg. Rep. Party, Portland, 1996, Oregon Dole-Kemp presdl. campaign, 1996. Recipient Am. Juris Prudence award, Lawyers Coop. Pub. Co., 1981; recognized for participation in CLE Oreg. State Bar, 1985, 91. Mem. Oreg. State Bar Assn. (law related edn. com. 1996—, chair-elect small firm and sole practitioner sect. 1997-98, Juvenile and Family Law Sect. 1992—, chair 1998-99), Oreg. Assn. of Family Law Practitioners. Avocations: golf, sailing, fishing. Family and matrimonial, Estate planning. Office: Hergert & Assocs 1001 Molalla Ave Ste 201 Oregon City OR 97045-3768

**HILL, JAMES CLINKSCALES,** federal judge; b. Darlington, S.C., Jan. 8, 1924; s. Albert Michael and Alberta (Clinkscales) H.; m. Mary Cornelia Black, June 7, 1946; children: James Clinkscales, Albert Michael. BS in Commerce, U. S.C., 1948; JD, Emory U., 1948. Bar: Ga. 1948, U.S. Supreme Ct. 1969. Assoc. Gambrell, Russell, Killorin & Forbes, Atlanta, 1948-55, ptnr., 1955-63; ptnr. Hurt, Hill & Richardson, Atlanta, 1963-74; judge U.S. Dist. Ct. (no. dist.) Ga., 1974-76, U.S. Cir. Ct. (5th cir.), Atlanta, 1976-81, U.S. Cir. Ct. (11th cir.), Atlanta, 1981-89; sr. U.S. cir. judge U.S. Ct. Appeals, Atlanta, 1989—; past chmn. com. on appellate ednl. programs Fed. Jud. Ctr.; former mem. com. on intercir. assignments Jud. Conf. U.S. With USAAF, 1943-45. Fellow ACTL, Am. Bar Found. (life); m. ABA, Am. Law Inst., World Assn. Judges, State Bar Ga., Atlanta Bar Assn., Am. Judicature Soc., Lawyers Club Atlanta (life), Old War Horse Lawyers. Republican. Baptist. Office: US Ct Appeals PO Box 52598 Jacksonville FL 32201-2598

**HILL, JEFFREY LEE,** lawyer; b. Oak Ridge, Tenn., Sept. 14, 1967; s. Thomas A. H. and Joan O'Steen; m. Michele Johnson, Apr. 20, 1996. BA in Polit. Sci., East Tenn. State U., 1989; JD, U. Tenn., 1994. Bar: Tenn. 1994, U.S. Dist. Ct. (ea., mid. and we. dists.) Tenn. 1995, U.S. Ct. Appeals (6th cir.) 1995. Asst. atty. gen. Tenn. Atty. Gen., Nashville, 1994—. Democrat. Methodist. Home: 1715 Linden Ave Nashville TN 37212-5111 Office: Tenn Atty Gen 425 5th Ave N Nashville TN 37243

**HILL, JOHN BRIAN,** lawyer; b. Independence, Mo., Apr. 9, 1957; s. John Howard and Jennie (Smith) H.; m. Tona Lynn Bevier, Oct. 27, 1984; children: John Benjamin, Abigail Lynn. BA, U. Mo., 1979, JD, 1982. Bar: Mo. 1982, U.S. Dist. Ct. (we. dist.) Mo. 1982, U.S. Ct. Appeals (10th cir.) 1983. Ptnr. Schulz, Bender, Maher, Lee, Sexton & Hill, Kansas City, Mo., 1983—. Chmn. planning and zoning commn., tax increment financing commn., City of Gladstone, Mo. Mem. Mo. Bar Assn., Kansas City Bar Assn. Contracts commercial, Real property, Estate planning. Office: Schulz Bender Maher Lee Sexton & Hill Woodlands Office Bldg 2900 NE Brooktree Ln Kansas City MO 64119-1873

**HILL, JOHN HOWARD,** lawyer; b. Pitts., Aug. 12, 1940; s. David Garrett and Eleanor Campbell (Musser) H. B.A., Yale U., 1962, J.D., 1965. Bar: Pa. 1965, U.S. Dist. Ct. (we dist.) Pa. 1965, U.S. Ct. Appeals (3d cir.) 1965, U.S. Supreme Ct. 1982. Assoc. Reed, Smith, Shaw & McClay, Pitts., 1965-75, ptnr., 1975-90; of counsel Jackson, Lewis, Schnitzler & Krupman, Pitts., 1991—. Bd. dirs. Travelers Aid Soc., Pitts., 1972—, treas., 1982-87, pres., 1987-90; bd. dirs. Pitts. Opera, Pitts. Symphony Soc. Mem. ABA, Pa. Bar Assn., Allegheny County Bar Assn., Hosp. Assn. Pa., Pa. Soc., Duquesne Club, Fox Chapel Golf Club, Rolling Rock Club, Phi Gemma Delta. Republican. Presbyterian. E-mail: hillj@jacksonlewis.com. Labor. Home: 4722 Bayard St Pittsburgh PA 15213-1708 Office: Jackson Lewis Schnitzler & Krupman One PPG Pl 28th Fl Pittsburgh PA 15222-5414

**HILL, JOSEPH C.,** lawyer; b. Kingston, N.Y., Sept. 23, 1964. BA, Fordham U., 1986; JD, Columbia U., 1989. Bar: N.Y., Spain. With Uria & Menendez, Madrid, Spain, Mayer, Brown & Platt, N.Y.C.; v.p., asst. gen. counsel The Chase Manhattan Bank, N.Y.C., 1994—. Mem. Assn. Bar City N.Y. (chair inter-Am. affairs com.), Coun. on Fgn. Rels., Phi Beta Kappa. Private international, Banking, Mergers and acquisitions. Office: The Chase Manhattan Bank 270 Park Ave Fl 40 New York NY 10017-2014

**HILL, MARCUS EDISON,** lawyer; b. Asheville, N.C., June 5, 1955; s. G. Edison and Helen Hill. BA in Psychology, U. N.C., 1978, JD, 1983. Bar: N.C. 1984. Atty. Clayton, Myrick, McClanahan & Coulter, Durham, N.C., 1985-92, Bryant, Patterson, Covington & Idol, Durham, 1992-95; pvt. practice Durham, 1995—. Criminal. Office: PO Box 1411 Durham NC 27702-1411

**HILL, MELISSA CLUTE (LISA HILL),** lawyer; b. Madisonville, Tex., Apr. 15, 1965; d. Donald Ray and Peggy Ann (Waller) Clute. BBA in Fin., Sam Houston State U., 1987; student, Cambridge U., 1991; JD, South Tex. Coll., 1992. Bar: Tex. 1993, U.S. Dist. Ct. (we. dist.) Tex. 1996. Asst. atty. gen. Tex. Atty. Gen.'s Office, Austin, 1993-94; lawyer Lea & Chamberlain, Austin, 1994—. Mem. Tex. Assn. Def. Coun., Def. Rsch. Inst., Travis Co. Bar Assn. Pension, profit-sharing, and employee benefits, Labor, General civil litigation. Office: Lea & Chamberlain 301 Congress Ave Ste 1800 Austin TX 78701-4041 Office: PO Box 684158 Austin TX 78768-4158

**HILL, MILTON KING, JR.,** lawyer; b. Balt., Nov. 29, 1926; s. Milton King and Mary Fusselbaugh (Hall) H.; m. Agnes Ciotti, June 11, 1949; children: Thomas Michael, Milton King, III, Susan Hill. BS in Bus. and Pub. Adminstrn., U. Md., 1950, JD, 1952. Bar: Md. 1952, U.S. Dist. Ct. Md. 1952, U.S. Ct. Appeals (4th cir.) 1952. Assoc. Smith, Somerville & Case, Balt., 1952-55, ptnr., 1955-90; ret.; mem. faculty Md. Hosp. Ednl. Inst. Served with USAF, 1944-46. Fellow Am. Coll. Trial Lawyers, Internat. Soc. Barristers; mem. Md. State Bar Assn., Md. Bar Assn., Nat. Conf. Commrs. Uniform State Laws (pres. 1981-83, chmn. model punitive damages act drafting com.), Assn. Def. Trial Counsel (pres. 1964-65), Internat. Assn. Ins. Counsel, ABA (ho. of dels. 1981-83), Md. Bar Found., Am. Acad. Hosp. Attys. Clubs: Potapskut Sailing Assn., Wednesday Law. State civil litigation, Federal civil litigation, Insurance. Home: 8810 Walther Blvd Apt 2329 Parkville MD 21234-0025

**HILL, MORRIS GERARD,** lawyer; b. New Orleans, Sept. 2, 1948; s. Morris Richard and Eunice (Pecot) H.; children: Emily Grayson, Morgan Spencer. JD, Tulane U., 1976. Bar: La. 1976, Calif. 1981. Assoc. Knutson, Tobin et al, La Mesa, Calif., 1981-82, Minyard & Minyard, Orange, Calif., 1982-87; dep. county counsel County of San Diego, 1987—. Office: County of San Diego 1600 Pacific Hwy Ste 355 San Diego CA 92101-2437

**HILL, OLIVER WHITE, SR.,** lawyer, consultant; b. Richmond, Va., May 1, 1907; s. William Henry White Jr. and Olivia (Lewis) White-Hill; m. Beresenia Ann Walker, Sept. 5, 1934; children: Oliver White Hill, Jr. AB,

Howard U., 1931, JD, 1933; LLD (hon.), St. Paul's Coll., 1978, Va. State U., 1982, Va. Union U., 1988, U. Richmond, Coll. William & Mary, 1996; LHD (hon.) Va. Commonwealth U., 1991. Bar: Va. 1934, U.S. Dist. Ct. (ea. dist.) Va. 1939, U.S. Ct. Appeals (4th cir.) 1940, U.S. Dist. Ct. (we. dist.) Va. 1947, U.S. Supreme Ct. 1950. Sole practice, Roanoke, Va., 1934-36, Richmond, Va., 1939-43, 59-61; ptnr. Hill, Martin & Robinson, Richmond, 1943-55, Hill Martin & Olphin, Richmond, 1955-59; asst. to commr. FHA, Washington, 1961-66; asst. to asst. sec. Mortgage Credit and Fed. Housing Commn., Washington, 1966; ptnr. Hill, Tucker, & Marsh, Richmond, 1966—; dir. HTM, Inc., Richmond; mem. President's Commn. on Govt. Contract Compliance, Washington, 1951-53, Commn. on Constl. Revision for Commonwealth of Va., U. Va., 1968-69, Va. State Bar Disciplinary Bd., 1976-82. Bd. dirs. Richmond br. NAACP, 1940-61 ( Outstanding Svc. award 1992), Richmond Urban League, 1950-61; mem. City Council, Richmond, 1948-50, Richmond Citizens Assn., 1950-54, Richmond City Dem. Com., 1956-61, 67-72, Va. Regional Med. Program, 1969-76; chmn. legal com. Va. State Conf. of NAACP, 1940-61. Staff sgt. U.S. Army, 1943-45, ETO. Recipient Chgo. Defender Merit award, 1949, Howard U. Alumni award, 1950, Nat. Publ. Assn. Russwurm award, 1952, Disting. Service award Delver Women's Club, 1954, Va. State Conf. of NAACP award, 1957, Ann. Conv. award NAACP, 1964, Disting. Service award Va. Tchrs. Assn., 1964, Francis Ellis Rivers award NAACP Legal Def. and Edn. Fund, 1976, Charles Hamilton Houston Medallion of Merit award Washington Bar Assn., 1976, Outstanding Pub. Service award The Moles, 1977, Disting. Service award Va. Union U. Am. Black Soc. Workers, 1978, John Mercer Langston Outstanding Alumnus award Howard U. Student Bar Assn., 1980, William Robert Ming Advocacy award NAACP, 1980, Appreciation award Va. State U., 1981, William P. Robinson Meml. award Democratic Party Va., 1981, Alumnus of Yr. award Howard U. Alumni Assn., 1981, Disting. Service award Va. State U., 1981, Distinguished Scholar award Oliver W. Hill Pre-Law Assn. of U. Va., 1983, award Commn. on Women and Minorities in Legal System Va. State Bar, 1987, Citizen of the Yr. award Alpha Kappa Alpha, 1992, Pro Bono Publico award ABA standing com. on lawyer's pub. svc. responsibility, 1993, Justice Thurgood Marshall award commn. for opportunities in the profession, 1993; citation for Disting. Legal Service, Richmond chpt. Frontiers of Am., 1954, Cert. of Appreciation, Assn. for Study of Afro-Am. Life and History, 1974, Brotherhood citation NCCJ, 1982, Thomas Jefferson Pub. Svc. award Richmond chpt. Pub. Rels. Soc. Am., 1995; Oliver Hill Cts. Bldg named in his honor, 1996. Fellow Am. Coll. Trial Lawyers, Old Dominion Bar Assn. Found. (pres. 1985—), Va. Bar Found.; mem. Old Dominion Bar Assn. (pres. 1941-43, 46-56, recipient numerous awards), Va. Bar Found., Richmond Bar Assn. (Hill-Tucker Pub. Svc. award 1989), Nat. Bar Assn. (C. Francis Stradford award 1959, Wiley A. Branton Symposium award), NAACP (legal def. fund The Simple Justice award 1986), George C. Marshall Found. (bd. dirs. 1989-94), Evolutionary Change Inc. (bd. dirs. 1990—), Strong Men and Women Excellence in Leadership award Va. and N.C. Power Co. 1992, Lewis F. Powell Jr. Pro Bono award Va. State Bar 1992, Harry L. Carrico Professionalism award; Friend of Edn. award Va. Edn. Assn. 1992; Apex Museum tribute Atlanta Ga. 1992, Va. Senate commendation 1992, NAACP Branches hall of fame Va. State Conference 1992. Sigma Pi Phi (grand sire archon 1964-66), Omega Psi Phi (Omega Man of Yr. 1957), Omicron Delta Kappa. Baptist. Civil rights, General practice, Probate. Home: 3108 Noble Ave Richmond VA 23222-2528 Office: Hill Tucker & Marsh 600 E Broad St Ste 402 Richmond VA 23219-1800

**HILL, PETER WAVERLY,** lawyer; b. White River Junction, Vt., June 24, 1953; s. Richard Bert and Elaine Etta (Kimball) H.; m. Eileen Winderman, Aug. 27, 1994; 1 stepchild, Marshall Jackson Miller. BA in Philosophy and Govt., U. Ariz., 1975, JD, 1978. Bar: Ariz. 1978, U.S. Dist. Ct. (no. dist.) N.Y. 1979, N.Y. 1980, U.S. Ct. Appeals (2d cir.) 1982. Staff atty. Legal Aid Soc. Mid N.Y., Utica, 1978-79, Oneonta, 1979-83; assoc. Law Offices of Paternoster & O'Leary, Walton, N.Y., 1983-84; pvt. practice, Oneonta, 1985—. Contbr. articles to profl. jours. Mem. N.Y. State com. Socialist Party, Syracuse. Mem. Nat. Lawyers Guild, Nat. Orgn. Social Security Claimants Reps., N.Y. State Bar Assn., Otsego County Bar Assn., Delaware County Bar Assn., Injured Workers' Bar Assn., Inc. Unitarian Universalist. Probate, Pension, profit-sharing, and employee benefits, Workers' compensation. Office: 384 Main St Oneonta NY 13820-1930

**HILL, PHILIP,** retired lawyer; b. East Saint Louis, Ill., Mar. 13, 1917; s. Nehemiah William and Lulu Myrtle (Johnson) H.; m. Betty Jean Stone, July 4, 1942; children: William Stone, Thomas Chapman, Nancy Layton, Mary Anne. AB in Chemistry, U. Ill., 1937; PhD in Chemistry, Ohio State U., 1941; JD, John Marshall Law Sch., Chgo., 1968. Bar: Ill. 1968, U.S. Patent Office 1969, U.S. Ct. Appeals (fed. cir.) 1982. With Standard Oil Co. Ind., 1941-78, patent atty., 1969-73, dir. petroleum and corp. patents and licensing, 1973-78; ptnr. Hill & Hill, Lansing, Ill., 1978-86, pvt. practice law Philip Hill, P.C., 1987-96; ret., 1996; cons. Univ. Patents, Inc., Norwalk, Conn., 1980-89; treas. Am. Waste Reduction Corp., 1992-96. Mem. ABA, AAAS, Ill. State Bar Assn., Am. Intellectual Property Law Assn., Chgo. Patent Law Assn., Am. Chem. Soc., Phi Beta Kappa, Sigma Xi, Phi Kappa Phi. Methodist. Clubs: Kiwanis (Lansing, pres. 1959, 84). Contbr. articles to profl. jours.; patentee in field. Patent, General corporate, Trademark and copyright. Home: 3241 N Schultz Dr Lansing IL 60438-3205 Office: PO Box 187 Lansing IL 60438-0187

**HILL, PHILIP BONNER,** lawyer; b. Charleston, W.Va., May 1, 1931. AB, Princeton U., 1952; LLB, W.Va. U., 1957. Bar: W.Va. 1957, Iowa 1965. Assoc. Dayton, Campbell & Love, Charleston, W.Va., 1957-61; ptnr. Porter, Hill, Thomas, Williams & Hubbard, Charleston, 1961-65; v.p. Thomas & Hill, Charleston, 1961-65; assoc. counsel Equitable Life Ins. Co. of Iowa, Des Moines, 1965-68, counsel, 1968-75; ptnr. Reimenschneider, Hanes & Hill, Des Moines, 1975-79, Austin & Gaudineer, Des Moines, 1979-82; ptnr. Snyder & Hassig, Des Moines, 1982-96, of counsel, 1997—. Mem. staff W.Va. Law Rev., 1955-57; contbr. articles to profl. jours. Lt. USNR, 1952-54. Mem. ABA (exec. coun. young lawyers sect. 1966-67), W.Va. State Bar (chmn. jr. bar sect. 1961-62, bd. govs. 1989-92), W.Va. Bar Assn. (pres. 1998-99), Iowa State Bar Assn., Assn. Life Ins. Counsel, Am. Land Title Assn., Am. Judicature Soc., Phi Delta Phi. Real property, Banking, Estate planning. Office: Snyder & Hassig PO Box 189 233 Main St New Martinsville WV 26155-1213*

**HILL, RICHARD PAUL,** lawyer; b. San Francisco, Oct. 1, 1946; s. Leo L. and Evelyn H. Hannon Hill; m. Diane M. Molyneux, May 17, 1975; children: Miranda, Nathaniel. AB in Rhetoric, U. Calif., Berkeley, 1968, JD, 1971. Bar: Calif. 1972, U.S. Dist. Ct. (no. and ea. dist.) Calif., U.S. Dist. Ct. (no. dist.) Tex. Atty. Law Offices of John Wynne Herron, San Francisco, 1972-76, Memorex Corp., Santa Clara, Calif., 1976-78; atty., ptnr. Neisar, Moody Hill & Massey, San Francisco, 1978-84; ptnr. Moody & Hill, San Francisco, 1984—; lectr. Calif. Continuing Edn., Berkeley, 1984-96, Hastings Coll. Law Continuing Edn., San Francisco, 1994-97. Editor: California Forms of Pleading and Practice, 1997. Founding mem., sch. bd. Immaculate Heart of Mary Parish Sch., Belmont, Calif., 1988-90; mem. Olympic Club, 1988—, Million Dollar Advocates Forum, 1999. Roman Catholic. Avocations: youth sports coaching (baseball, basketball). General civil litigation, Constitutional, Labor. Office: Moody & Hill 214 Grant Ave Ste 301 San Francisco CA 94108-4692

**HILL, ROBERT F.,** lawyer; b. Clarinda, Iowa, Mar. 5, 1945; s. Gordon and Irma M. Hill; m. Laura L. Hill; children: Kristine, Lisa, Catherine. BA, U. Nebr., 1967; JD, U. Colo., 1970. Bar: Calif., D.C. 1971, Colo. 1975, U.S. Supreme Ct. 1975. Law clk. Hon. Warren J. Ferguson, U.S. Dist. Ct., L.A., 1970-71; assoc. Covington & Burling, Washington, 1971-74; staff atty. Neighborhood Legal Svcs. Prog., Washington, 1973; vis. assoc. prof. law U. Colo., Boulder, 1974-75; 1st asst. atty. gen. Antitrust Sect., State of Colo., Denver, 1975-78; ptnr. Hill & Robbins, P.C., Denver, 1978—. Co-editor-in-chief U. Colo. Law Rev., 1969-70. Founding mem. bd. dirs. Project Safeguard, 1985-87; pres. bd. dirs. Tech. Assistance Ctr., 1984-85; mem. bd. dirs. Colo.: Ocean Journey, 1997—, Colo. Common Cause, 1994—, L.Am. Rsch. and Svc. Agy., 1994—. Storke scholar, Dunklee awardee. Mem. ABA, Colo. Bar Assn. (Hoagland award Pro Bono Svc. 1997), Denver Bar Assn., Boulder County Bar Assn., Colo. Lawyers Com. (chmn. bd. dirs. 1985-87), Order of the Coif. Antitrust, Securities, Federal civil litigation. Home: 700 High St Denver CO 80218-3698 Office: Hill & Robbins PC 1441 18th St Ste 100 Denver CO 80202-5932

**HILL, ROBYN MARCELLA,** lawyer; b. Schenectady, Aug. 18, 1951; d. Fred Warren Hill Jr. and Prudence Alberta (Lamper) Shackford; m. Charles A. Boenecke, Jr., Sept. 16, 1977; children: Blake Elizabeth Hill Boenecke, Hayley Alexandra Hill Boenecke. BA with distinction, Simmons Coll., 1973; JD, Rutgers U., Camden, 1976. Bar: N.J. 1977, Pa. 1977, U.S. Dist. Ct. N.J. 1977, U.S. Supreme Ct. 1985. Staff atty. for hearings and regulations N.J. Dept. Pers., Trenton, 1977-79; atty. div. ethics and profl. svcs. Adminstrv. Office Cts., Trenton, 1979-83; dep. ethics counsel Office Atty. Ethics, Supreme Ct. N.J., Trenton, 1983-89, chief counsel disciplinary rev. bd., 1989—, mem. staff N.J. Ethics Commn., 1991-94. Mem. ABA, Nat. Orgn. Bar Counsel, N.J. Bar Assn. (profl. responsibility com., lawyers in pub. employment com.), Burlington County Bar Assn. Unitarian. Office: Disciplinary Rev Bd RJ Hughes Justice Complex CN962 Trenton NJ 08625

**HILL, SONIA ELIZABETH,** lawyer, educator; b. Fairmont, N.C., May 12, 1965; d. James Franklin and Edythe Brenda Hill. BS in Math., Howard U., 1987; JD, Duke U., 1990. Bar: Ga. 1992, U.S. Dist. Ct. (no. dist.) Ga., U.S. Ct. Appeals (4th and 11th cirs.). Ptnr. Mack & McLean, P.A., Atlanta, 1990—. Anna Pierce scholar. Mem. ABA, DeKalb Lawyers Assn., Alpha Kappa Alpha, Phi Beta Kappa. Avocations: creative writing, racquetball. Civil rights, Labor. Office: Mack & McLean PA 100 Peachtree St NW Ste 600 Atlanta GA 30303-1909 also: 2255 Glades Rd Ste 234W Boca Raton FL 33431-7391

**HILL, STEPHEN L., JR.,** prosecutor; m. Marianne Matteson; 2 children. BS in Polit. Sci., Southwest Mo. State U., 1981; JD, U. Mo., 1986; postgrad., London U. Trial atty. Smith, Gill, Fisher & Butts, Kansas City, 1986-94; U.S. atty. Western Dist. Mo., Kansas City, 1994—. Office: Office US Atty We Dist Mo 400 E 9th St Ste 5510 Kansas City MO 64106-2637*

**HILL, THOMAS ALLEN,** lawyer; b. Salem, Ohio, Mar. 29, 1958; s. Charles Spencer and Dorothy Jane (Allen) H. *During WWII father Charles served in the 586th B-26 Bomb Squadron of the 397th Bomb Group, U.S. Army Air Force, and was in France in 1945 with the 1259th Combat Engineer Battalion. Mother Dorothy worked for Lockheed Aircraft Corp., 1943-1945. Father descends from Sir Moyses Hill, who accompanied the Earl of Essex to Ireland in 1573 and was dubbed a Knight Bachelor in 1616. Mother descends from the immigrant Ralph Allen of Sandwich, Mass. and his son, Jedediah Allen, the latter having been a minister among the Quakers as early as 1685 and a member of the first New Jersey Colonial Assembly in 1703.* BA magna cum laude, Hiram Coll., 1980; JD, George Washington U., 1984. Bar: Ohio 1984, Pa. 1987, D.C. 1988, U.S. Supreme Ct. 1989, Tex. 1990, Okla. 1991; registered rep. series 6 and 63 Nat. Assn. Securities Dealers. Legis. intern Office of Hon. John Conyers, Jr., Washington, 1979; asst. to dean campus Life for Housing, conf. dir. Hiram (Ohio) Coll., 1980-81; corp. counsel Capital Oil & Gas Inc., Austintown, Ohio, 1984-93; gen. counsel, sec. North Coast Energy, Inc., Bedford Heights, Ohio, 1987—, Trinity Oil & Gas, Inc. subs. North Coast Energy Inc., Warren, Ohio, 1990-93; mem. mini-task force on notices of violation Ohio Div. Oil and Gas, Columbus, 1988-90; part-time fin. analyst Primerica Fin. Svcs., Inc., 1997—. *Tom Hill has been the General Counsel of North Coast Energy, Inc. (NCE) since its acquisition of Capital Oil & Gas, Inc. in 1987. NCE is publicly traded on NASDAQ under the symbol NCEB and is a major Appalachian Basin exploration and production company which in 1998 acquired the assets of BTI Energy, Inc. and Kelt-Ohio, Inc. Since 1997 NCE has been an affiliate of NUON International, whose parent, Nuon-ENW, is the largest public utility company in the Netherlands and a leader in the development of co-generation facilities. NCE's second largest shareholder is Fort Worth-based Range Resources Corporation.* Mem. ABA, Ohio Bar Assn., Mahoning County Bar Assn., Pa. Bar Assn., Okla. Bar Assn., D.C. Bar Assn., State Bar Tex., Trumbull County Bar Assn., Ohio Oil and Gas Assn., Christian Legal Soc., Ea. Mineral Law Found., Fed. Energy Bar Assn., Ohio Land Title Assn., Ohio Geneal. Soc., Mahoning Valley Hist. Soc., Austintown Hist. Soc., Gen. Soc., War of 1812, SAR, Order of Arrow, Kappa Delta Pi, Pi Gamma Mu. Republican. Avocations: local history, study of Amaranth. Oil, gas, and mineral, Real property, General corporate. Home: 4841 Westchester Dr Apt 102 Youngstown OH 44515-2548 Office: North Coast Energy Inc 1993 Case Pkwy Twinsburg OH 44087-2343 *Motto: I Peter 1: 23-25.*

**HILL, THOMAS CLARK,** lawyer; b. Prestonsburg, Ky., July 17, 1946; s. Lon Clay and Corinne (Allen) H.; m. J. Barbarie Friedly, June 13, 1968; children: Jason L., Duncan L. BA, Case Western Reserve U., 1968; JD, U. Chgo., 1973. Bar: Ohio 1973, U.S. Supreme Ct. 1976. Assoc. atty. Taft, Stettinius & Hollister LLP, Cin., 1973-81, ptnr., 1981—. Author: Monthly Meetings in North America: A Quaker Index, 4th edit., 1998. Trustee, treas. Wilmington (Ohio) Coll., 1982-94, 99—; treas. Friends World Commn. for Consultation, Sect. of the Ams., 1990-95, presiding clk., 1995-99; trustee Wilmington Yearly Meeting of Friends (Quakers), 1986-98, Friends United Meeting, 1999—. Mem. ABA, Ohio State Bar Assn., Cin. Bar Assn., Friends Hist. Assn. (bd. dirs. 1994-95). Republican. Mem. Soc. of Friends. Avocation: Quaker history. Antitrust, Insurance, Environmental. Office: 1800 Firstar Tower 425 Walnut St Cincinnati OH 45202-3923

**HILL, THOMAS WILLIAM, JR.,** lawyer, educator; b. N.Y.C., Dec. 25, 1924; s. Thomas William Sr. and Marion (Bond) H.; m. Elizabeth Rowe, June 18, 1949; children: Gretchen P., Catharine B., Thomas William III. BS, U. Pa., 1948; MBA, NYU, 1950; JD, Columbia U., 1953. Bar: N.Y. 1953, D.C. 1954, U.S. Supreme Ct. 1958, Fla. 1989; CPA, N.Y. Sr. tax acct. Hurdman & Cranstoun, 1949-50; asst. U.S. atty. So. Dist. N.Y., 1953-54; assoc. Cahill, Gordon, Reindel & Ohl, 1954-58; sr. ptnr. Spear & Hill, 1958-75; ptnr. Sidley & Austin, 1981-86; pres. Belco Petroleum Co., N.Y.C., 1962-63; legal adviser Sultanate of Oman, 1972-76; adj. prof. law U. Miami, 1986-97. Contbr. articles to profl. jours. Vice chmn., pres., trustee Internat. Coll., Beirut, Lebanon, 1978-91. 1st lt. AUS, 1943-46. Decorated Bronze Star, Purple Heart, Medal of Oman (Sultanate of Oman), Order of Homayun (Iran). Mem. ABA, Assn. of Bar of City of N.Y., IBA, Racquet and Tennis Club (N.Y.C.), Mayacoo Golf Club, Taconic Golf Club, Phi Delta Phi, Kappa Sigma. Private international, Public international. Home: 2627 Muirfield Ct West Palm Beach FL 33414-7019

**HILL, WILLIAM U.,** state supreme court justice. Atty. gen. Cheyenne, Wyo., 1995-98; justice Wyo. Supreme Ct., Cheyenne, 1998—. Office: Wyoming Supreme Court 2301 Capitol Ave Cheyenne WY 82001-3644

**HILLBERG, MARYLOU ELIN,** lawyer; b. Chgo., Nov. 6, 1950; d. Harold Andrew Hillberg and Eunice Elin (Anderson) Peterson; m. Andrew Charles Lennox, Aug. 6, 1983; children: Elin Elizabeth Lennox, David Andrew Lennox. BFA, San Francisco Art Inst., 1973; JD, U. Calif., San Francisco, 1979. Bar: Calif. 1979, U.S. Dist. Ct. (no. dist.) Calif. 1979. Dep. dist. atty. Sonoma County, Santa Rosa, Calif., 1980; sole practice Santa Rosa, 1981—; asst. prof. Sonoma State U., Rohnert Park, Calif., 1982—; mem. United Christian Ch., mem. cmty. adv. coun., 1992—, chair, 1994-95. Chmn. bd. dirs. Sonoma County Drug Abuse Alternatives Ctr., Santa Rosa, 1983-84; bd. dirs. ACLU, Santa Rosa, 1982-84; mem. adv. coun. Sonoma County Cmty., 1992—. Mem. Sonoma County Women in Law (chairperson 1983-84), Calif. Pub. Defenders Assn., Criminal Appellate Def. Counsel, Calif. Atty. Criminal Justice. Democrat. Criminal, Juvenile, Appellate. Office: 2500 Vallejo St Ste 200 Santa Rosa CA 95405-6959

**HILLE, ROBERT JOHN,** lawyer, trust officer; b. St. Louis, July 20, 1953; s. Robert E. and Virginia (Curry) H.; m. Carol A. Fukuchi, May 30, 1982; children: Jessica, Stephanie. BS, U. Tulsa, 1976; JD, Washington U., St. Louis, 1983. Bar: Mo. 1983. Assoc. Mathis and Long, P.C., St. Louis, 1983-84; ptnr. Anderson, Preuss and Bachman, St. Louis, 1984-86; pvt. practice St. Louis, 1986-88; ptnr. Brackman, Hille and Freed, P.C., St. Louis, 1988-94; trust officer Bank Am. and Pvt. Bank, St. Louis, 1994—. Mem. ABA, Mo. Bar Assn., Bar Assn. Met. St. Louis. General corporate, Estate planning, Probate. Office: Boatmen's Trust Co 100 N Broadway Saint Louis MO 63102-2728

**HILLER, NEIL HOWARD,** lawyer; b. Detroit, Jan. 21, 1950; s. Leo and Rita Dorothy Hiller; m. Peggy Lee Abrams, Aug. 27, 1972; children: Evan, Kimberly. BA, U. Mich., 1971; JD cum laude, Wayne State U., 1974. Bar: Ariz. 1974, U.S. Dist. Ct. Ariz. 1975, U.S. Tax Ct. 1984. Atty. Burch & Cracchiolo, Phoenix, 1975-78, Lane & Smith, Ltd., Phoenix, 1978-79; shareholder Ehmann & Hiller, P.C., Phoenix, 1979—. Pres., v.p., treas. Jewish Fedn. Phoenix, 1994-98. Pension, profit-sharing, and employee benefits, Estate planning, Taxation, general. Office: Ehmann & Hiller PC 2525 E Camelback Rd Ste 720 Phoenix AZ 85016-4229

**HILLESTAD, CHARLES ANDREW,** lawyer; b. McCurtain, Okla., Aug. 30, 1945; s. Carl Oliver and Aileen Hanna (Sweeney) H.; m. Ann Ramsey Robertson, Oct. 13, 1973. BS, U. Oreg., 1967; JD, U. Mich., 1972. Bar: Colo. 1972, U.S. Dist. Ct. Colo. 1972, U.S. Ct. Appeals (10th cir.) 1972, Oreg. 1993; lic. real estate broker, Colo. Law clk. to presiding justice Colo. Supreme Ct., Denver, 1972-73; ptnr. DeMuth & Kemp, Denver, 1973-83, Cornwell & Blakey, Denver, 1983-90, Scheid & Horlbeck, Denver, 1990-93, Gablehouse & Epel, Denver, 1993-94; pvt. practice Cannon Beach, Oreg., 1994—; co-developer award winning Queen Anne Inn, Capitol Hill Mansion and Cheyenne Canyon Inn Hotels (4-diamond award AAA); mem. ad hoc com. Denver Real Estate Atty. Specialists. Author: Preventive Law for Innkeepers, co-author: Annual Surveys of Real Estate Law for Colorado Bar Association; contbr. articles to profl. jours.; assoc. editor Inn Times. Past coun. mem. Denver Art Mus.; past chmn. Rocky Mountain chpt. Sierra Club; past v.p., bd. dirs. Seaside C. of C.; past bd. dirs. Hist. Denver, Inc. Staff sgt. U.S. Army, 1968-70. Recipient Colo. Co. of Yr. award Colo. Bus. Mag., Award of Honor Denver Ptnrship., Newsmaker of Yr. and Outstanding Achievement awards Am. Assn. Hist. Inns, Tourism Person of Yr. award Denver Conv. and Visitor's Bur., Rocky Mountain Spectacular Inn award B&B Rocky Mountains Assn., Best Inns of Yr. awards County Inns Mag. and Adventure Rd. Mag., Best of Denver award Westward newspaper. Mem. ABA, Colo. Bar Assn., Oreg. Bar Assn., Denver Bar Assn., Colo. Lawyers for the Arts, POETS, Astoria C. of C., Seaside C. of C., Cannon Beach C. of C. Avocations: photography, art collecting, historic and environmental preservation, history and architecture reading, rafting. Real property, Landlord-tenant, Contracts commercial. Office: PO Box 1065 1347 S Hemlock Cannon Beach OR 97110

**HILLIARD, DAVID CRAIG,** lawyer, educator; b. Framingham, Mass., May 22, 1937; s. Walter David and Dorothy (Shortiss) H.; m. Celia Schmid, Feb. 16, 1974. BS, Tufts U., 1959; JD, U. Chgo., 1962. Bar: Ill. 1962, U.S. Supreme Ct. 1966. Mng. ptnr. Pattishall, McAuliffe, Newbury, Hilliard & Geraldson, Chgo., 1984—; adj. prof. law Northwestern U., 1971—, chmn. Symposium Intellectual Property Law and the Corp. Client, 1987—; lectr. in advanced trademark law U. Chgo. Law Sch., 1999—. Author: Unfair Competition and Unfair Trade Practices, 1985, Trademarks, 1987, Trademarks and Unfair Competition, 1994, 3d edit., 1998, Trademarks and Unfair Competition Deskbook, 1996, 3d edit., 1998; editor-in-chief Chgo. Bar Record, 1978-81. Trustee Art Inst. Chgo., 1980—, chmn. sustaining fellows, 1981-85, chmn. adv. com. dept. architecture, 1981—, pres. aux. bd., 1977-79, chmn. exhbns. com., 1993—, exec. com., 1995—, chmn. bd. govs. of the sch., 1997—; trustee Newberry Libr., 1983—, exec. com., 1987—; pres. Lawyers Trust Fund Ill., 1985-88; mem. vis. com. DePaul U. Law Sch., U. Chgo. Sch. of Law, chmn., 1987-88, Northwestern U. Assocs., 1985—; mem. profl. adv. bd. Atty. Gen. Ill., 1982-84; mem. Ill. Commn. on Rights of Women, 1983-85; bd. dirs. Ill. Inst. Continuing Legal Edn., 1980-82; pres. Planned Parenthood Assn. Chgo., 1975-77. Lt. JAGC, USN, 1962-66. Recipient Maurice Weigle award, 1974, Chgo. Coun. Lawyers award for jud. reform, 1983. Fellow Am. Coll. Trial Lawyers (chmn. courageous adv. com. 1995-97); mem. ABA (chmn. trademark divsn. 1986-87, mem. coun. 1991-95, intellectual property law sect.), Ill. Bar Assn., Chgo. Bar Assn. (pres. 1982-83, founding chmn. young lawyers sect. 1971-72), Internat. Trademark Assn. (bd. dirs. 1989-91, ADR panel of neutrals 1994—), Arts Club, Chgo. Club, Econ. Club, Grolier Club, Law Club, Legal Club (pres. 1989-90), Univ. Club, Casino, Wayfarers Club (pres. 1994-95). Trademark and copyright, Federal civil litigation, Intellectual property. Home: 1320 N State Pky Chicago IL 60610-2118 Office: Pattishall McAuliffe Newbury Hilliard & Geraldson 311 S Wacker Dr Ste 5000 Chicago IL 60606-6622

**HILLJE, BARBARA BROWN,** lawyer; b. Carlisle, Pa., Dec. 18, 1942; d. R. Morrison and Gladys M. (Lauver) Brown; m. John W. Hillje, Mar. 23, 1968. AB, Vassar Coll., 1964; BS in Edn., Ind. U. Pa., 1965; MA, Temple U., 1971, ABD, 1977; JD, Villanova U., 1984. Bar: Pa. 1984, U.S. Dist. Ct. (ea. dist.) Pa. 1984, N.J. 1985, U.S. Dist. Ct. N.J. 1985, U.S. Supreme Ct. 1990. English tchr. Council Rock Sr. High Sch., Newtown, Pa., 1965-68; assoc. Harry J. Agzigian and Assocs., Levittown, Pa., 1985-87; pvt. practice Langhorne, Pa., 1987—. Contbr. articles to profl. journals. Bd. dirs., pres. bd. Children of Aging Parents, Levittown, 1985-93; mem. facility ethics com. Statesman Health & Rehab. Ctr., Levittown, Pa., 1996—. Recipient Women Helping Women award Soroptimists of Indian Rock, Inc., 1995; named Woman of Yr., Lower Bucks AAUW, 1985, Neshaminy BPW, 1987, Legal Humanitarian of Yr., Bucks County United Way, 1994, Consumer Connection award, 1996. Mem. ABA, AAUW (bd. dirs. 1978—, legis. cons. Pa. division 1990-92), Middletown-Newtown LWV (bd. dirs. 1983-89, citizen campaign watch adv. panel 1992, 94, 96), Pa. Bar Assn., Bucks County Bar Assn. (bd. dirs. 1991-93), Nat. Acad. Elder Law Attys., Older Women's League (legis. chair 1984-94, Women of Worth award 1993). Family and matrimonial, Probate, Elder. Office: 506 Corporate Dr W Langhorne PA 19047-8011

**HILLMAN, DOUGLAS WOODRUFF,** federal judge; b. Grand Rapids, Mich., Feb. 15, 1922; s. Lemuel Serrell and Dorothy (Woodruff) H.; m. Sally Jones, Sept. 13, 1944; children: Drusilla W., Clayton D. Student, Phillips Exeter Acad., 1941; A.B., U. Mich., 1946, LL.B., 1948. Bar: Mich. 1948, U.S. Supreme Ct. 1967. Assoc. Lilly, Luyendyk & Snyder, Grand Rapids, 1948-53; partner Luyendyk, Hainer, Hillman, Karr & Dutcher, Grand Rapids, 1953-65, Hillman, Baxter & Hammond, 1965-79; U.S. dist. judge Western Dist. Mich., Grand Rapids, 1979—; chief judge Western Dist. Mich., 1986-91, sr. judge, 1991—; instr. Nat. Inst. Trial Adv., Boulder, Colo; dir. Fed. Judges Assn.; mem. jud. conf. com. on Adminstrn. of Magistrate Judges Sys., 1993—; chair 6th Circuit Standing Com. on Jud. Conf. Planning; mem. exec. com. ABA jud. adminstrn. divsn. Nat. Conf. Fed. Trial Judges, 1995-98. Co-author articles in legal publs. Chmn. Grand Rapids Human Relations Commn., 1963-66; chmn. bd. trustees Fountain St. Ch., 1970-72; pres. Family Service Assn., 1967. Served as pilot USAAF, 1943-45. Decorated DFC, Air medal; recipient Annual Civil Liberties award ACLU, 1970, Disting. Alumni award Ctrl. High Sch., 1986, Raymond Fox Advocacy award, 1989, Champion of Justice award State Bar Mich., 1990, Profl. & Cmty. Svc. award Young Lawyers Sect., 1996, Svc. to Profession award Fed. Bar Assn., 1991; named one of 25 Most Respected Judges Mich. Lawyers Weekly. Fellow Am. Bar Found.; mem. ABA, Mich. Bar Assn. (chmn. client security fund), Grand Rapids Bar Assn. (pres. 1963), Am. Coll. Trial Lawyers (Mich. chmn. 1979, com. on teaching trial and appellate adv.), 6th Circuit Jud. Conf. (life), Internat. Acad. Trial Lawyers, Fedn. Ins. Counsel, Internat. Assn. Ins. Counsel, Internat. Soc. Barristers (pres 1977-78, chair annual Hillman Trial Adv. Seminar 1982—), M Club of U. Mich. (com. visitors U. Mich. Law Sch.), Univ. Club (Grand Rapids), Torch Club. Office: US Dist Ct 682 Fed Bldg 110 Michigan St NW Grand Rapids MI 49503-2363

**HILLMAN, JORDAN JAY,** law educator; b. 1924. M.A. in Polit Sci., U. Chgo., 1947, JD, 1950; SJD, Northwestern U., 1965. Bar: Ill. 1950. Mem. legal staff Ill. Commerce Commn., 1950-53; with Chgo. and Northwestern Ry., 1954-67, gen. counsel, 1963-67, v.p. law, 1966-67; prof. emeritus law Northwestern U., 1967-89, prof., rsch. counsel, prof. transp. ctr., 1989-91; sr. legal cons., gen. counsel U.S. Ry. Assn., 1974-76, spl. counsel, 1976-79; legal cons. Amtrak, 1978. Mem. Constn. Study Commn., State of Ill., 1963-67; mem. Zoning Amendment Com., Evanston, Ill., 1963-68; mem. Bd. Edn., Dist. 202, Evanston Twp. H.S., 1968-71; mem. Chgo. Transit Authority Bd., 1981-87. Mem. Phi Beta Kappa. Author: Competition and Railroad Price Discrimination, 1968; The Parliamentary Structuring of British Road-Rail Freight Coordination, 1973; The Export-Import Bank at Work; Promotional Financing in the Public Sector, 1982; Price Level Regulation for Diversified Public Utilities, 1989. Office: Northwestern U Sch Law 317 E Chicago Ave Chicago IL 60611-3008

**HILLMAN, ROGER LEWIS,** lawyer; b. Newark, May 10, 1944; s. Fred and Pauline (Kantrowitz) H.; m. Joanne Leslie Kaufman, Aug. 3, 1969; children: Matt, Meredith. BA, Tufts U., 1966; JD, U. Mich., 1969. Bar: N.J. 1969, Wash. 1989. Dep. atty. gen. State of N.J., Trenton, 1970-73; assoc. Stark and Stark, Trenton, 1974-77; litigation mgr. Chubb Group of

Ins. Cos., Warren, N.J., 1977-81; v.p. Aetna Ins. Co., Hartford, Conn., 1981-82; sr. v.p. U.S. Ins. Group, Basking Ridge, N.J., 1982-85, Reliance/United Pacific Ins. Co., Federal Way, Wash., 1985-88; owner Garvey, Schubert & Barer, Seattle, 1995—. Mem. ABA, Fedn. Ins. & Corp. Counsel, N.J. Bar Assn., Wash. Bar Assn., Seattle/King County Bar Assn., Wash. Def. Trial Lawyers, Def. Rsch. Inst. General civil litigation, Insurance, Professional liability. Home: 8284 SE 82nd St Mercer Island WA 98040-5652 Office: Garvey Schubert & Barer 1191 2d Ave Ste 1800 Seattle WA 98101-2939

**HILLMAN, SHELTON B., JR.,** lawyer; b. Walnut Ridge, Ark., Mar. 18, 1944; s. Shelton R. Hillman Sr. and Anne (Brown) Worley; m. Gay K. Hillman, Feb. 6, 1971; children: Kate, Seth. BS, U. Tenn., 1966, JD, 1971. Law clk. 4th cir. U.S. Ct. Appeals, Richmond, Va., 1973-74; atty. Gore and Hillman, Bristol, Tenn., 1974—. Mcpl. judge City of Bristol, 1982—. Lt. col. USAF, 1966-71. General practice, Personal injury, Real property. Office: Gore and Hillman 917 Anderson St Bristol TN 37620-2105

**HILLS, CARLA ANDERSON,** lawyer, former federal official; b. Los Angeles, Jan. 3, 1934; d. Carl H. and Edith (Hume) Anderson; m. Roderick Maltman Hills, Sept. 27, 1958; children: Laura Hume, Roderick Maltman, Megan Elizabeth, Alison Macbeth. AB cum laude, Stanford U., 1955; student, St. Hilda's Coll., Oxford (Eng.) U., 1954; LLB, Yale U., 1958; hon. degrees, Pepperdine U., 1975, Washington U., 1977, Mills Coll., 1977, Lake Forest Coll., 1978, Williams Coll., 1981, Notre Dame U., 1993, Wabash Coll., 1997. Bar: Calif. 1959, DC 1974, U.S. Supreme Ct. 1965. Asst. U.S. atty. civil divsn. L.A., 1958-61; ptnr. Munger, Tolles, Hills & Rickershauser, L.A., 1962-74; asst. atty. gen. civil divsn. Justice Dept., Washington, 1974-75; sec. HUD, 1975-77; ptnr. Latham, Watkins & Hills, Washington, 1978-86, Weil, Gotshal & Manges, Washington, 1986-88; U.S. trade rep. Exec. Office of the Pres., 1989-93; chmn., CEO Hills & Co., 1993—; bd. dirs. Inter-Am. Dialogue, Am. Internat. Group, Time-Warner, Lucent Techs., Inc., Bechtel Enterprises Holdings, Chevron Corp., TCW Group, Inc.; adj. prof. Sch. Law, UCLA, 1972; mem. Trilateral Commn., 1977-82, 93—, Am. Com. on East-West Accord, 1977-79, Internat. Found. for Cultural Cooperation and Devel., 1977-89, Fed. Acctg. Standards Adv. Council, 1978-80; mem. corrections task force L.A. County Sub-Regional; adv. bd. Calif. Council on Criminal Justice, 1969-71; standing com. discipline U.S. Dist. Ct. for Central Calif., 1970-73; mem. Adminstrv. Conf. U.S., 1972-74; exec. com. law and free soc. State Bar Calif., 1973; bd. councillors U. So. Calif. Law Center, 1972-74; trustee Pomona Coll., 1974-79; trustee Brookings Instn., 1985; mem. at large exec. com. Yale Law Sch., 1973-78; mem. com. on Law Sch. Yale U. Council; Gordon Grand fellow Yale U., 1978; mem. Sloan Commn. on Govt. and Higher Edn., 1977-79; advisory com. Princeton U., Woodrow Wilson Sch. of Pub. and Internat. Affairs, 1977-80; trustee Am. Productivity and Quality Ctr., 1988; council mem. Calif. Gov. Coun. Econ. Policy Adv., 1993-98, Coun. on Fgn. Rels., 1993—; vice-chair Nat. Com. on U.S.-China Rels., 1993—; bd. dirs., U.S.-China Bus. Coun., vice-chair, 1995—. Co-author: Federal Civil Practice, 1961; co-author, editor: Antitrust Adviser, 1971, 3d edit., 1985; contbg. editor: Legal Times, 1978-88; mem. editorial bd. Nat. Law Jour., 1978-88. Trustee U. So. Calif., 1977-79, Norton Simon Mus. Art, Pasadena, Calif., 1976-80; trustee Urban Inst., 1978-89, chmn., 1983-89; co-chmn. Alliance to Save Energy, 1977-89; vice chmn. adv. coun. on legal policy Am. Enterprise Inst., 1977-84; bd. visitors, exec. com. Stanford U. Law Sch., 1978-81; bd. dirs. Am. Coun. for Capital Formation, 1978-82, Interam. Dialogue, 1997—; mem. exec. com. Inst. for Internat. Econs., 1993—; mem. adv. com. MIT-Harvard U. Joint Ctr. for Urban Studies, 1978-82. Fellow Am. Bar Found.; mem. L.A. Women Lawyers Assn. (pres. 1964), ABA (chair publs. com. antitrust sect. 1972-74, council 1974, 77-84, chair 1982-83), Fed. Bar Assn. (pres. L.A. chpt. 1963), L.A. County Bar Assn. (fed. rules and practice com. 1963-72, chair issues and survey 1963-72, chair sub-com. revision local rules for fed. cts. 1966-72, jud. qualifications com. 1971-72), Am. Law Inst., Am. China Soc. (bd. dirs. 1995—), Yale of So. Calif. Club (bd. dirs. 1972-74), Yale Club. Clubs: Yale of So. Calif. (dir. 1972-74); Yale (Washington). Antitrust. Office: Hills & Co 1200 19th St NW Ste 201 Washington DC 20036-2429

**HILPERT, EDWARD THEODORE, JR.,** lawyer; b. Frazee, Minn., Apr. 29, 1928; s. Edward Theodore Sr. and Hulda Gertrude (Wilder) H.; m. Susan Hazelton, May 5, 1973. AB, U. Wash., 1954, JD, 1956. Bar: Wash. 1956, U.S. Dist. Ct. (we. dist.) Wash. 1956, U.S. Tax Ct. 1959, U.S. Ct. Appeals (9th cir.) 1959, U.S. Supreme Ct. 1970. Law clk. to Hon. George H. Boldt U.S. Dist. Ct. (we. dist.) Wash., Tacoma, 1956-58; assoc. Ferguson & Burdell, Seattle, 1958-63, ptnr., 1963-91; sr. ptnr. Schwabe, Williamson, Ferguson & Burdell, Seattle, 1992—; mem. exec. com. 9th cir. Jud. Conf., San Francisco, 1987-90. Judge pro tem Seattle Mcpl. Ct., 1971-80. Capt. USAR, 1946-49, 50-52, Korea. Mem. ABA, Mensa, Rainer Club, Seattle Tennis Club, Broadmoor Golf Club. Republican. Lutheran. General corporate, Estate planning, State and local taxation. Home: 1434 Broadmoor Dr E Seattle WA 98112-3744 Office: Schwabe Williamson Ferguson & Burdell US Bank Ctr 1420 5th Ave Ste 3400 Seattle WA 98101-2339

**HILSABECK, MICHAEL D.,** lawyer, judge; b. Oklahoma City, Mar. 26, 1952; s. Don Arthur Jr. and Dorene Hubbs Hilsabeck; m. Linda Dickey, June 11, 1977; children: Seth, Natalie, Alex. BA in History, Comm., Oral Roberts U., 1975; JD, U. Tulsa, 1980. Bar: Okla. 1980, U.S. Dist. Ct. (no. dist.) Okla. 1981, U.S. Ct. Appeals (10th cir.) 1985, U.S. Supreme Ct. 1985. Assoc. Chapel, Wikinson, Riggs & Abney, Tulsa, Okla., 1979-82; pvt. practice Tulsa, Okla., 1982, 84-85; ptnr. Barnard, Lee & Hilsabeck, Tulsa, Okla., 1983-84; assoc. Allis & Vandivort, Tulsa, Okla., 1986-87; ptnr. Edgar, Perigo & Hilsabeck, Tulsa, Okla., 1987—; instr. Tulsa Jr. Coll., 1982-84; mcpl. judge City of Owasso, Okla., 1987—. Scoutmaster Troop 1, Boy Scouts of Am., Tulsa, 1993—. Recipient Scoutmaster Award of Merit, Boy Scouts of Am., Tulsa, 1997. Mem. Okla. Bar Assn., Tulsa County Bar Assn., Rotary (Southside Tulsa officer). Presbyterian. Avocations: scouting, outdoors, coaching kids sports. Contracts commercial, General corporate, Real property. Office: Edgar Perigo and Hilsabeck 2615 E Fifteenth Tulsa OK 74104

**HILTON, CLAUDE MEREDITH,** federal judge; b. Scott County, Va., Dec. 8, 1940; s. Claude Swanson and Edna (Fletcher) H.; m. Joretta Cabaniss, June 16, 1963; children: John, Rachel. BS, Ohio State U., 1963; JD, Am. Univ., 1966. Bar: Va. 1966, U.S. Ct. Appeals ( 4th cir.) 1967, U.S. Supreme Ct. 1981. Dep. clk. of cts. Arlington County, Va., 1964-66, asst. commonwealth atty., 1967-68, commonwealth atty., 1974; sole practice Arlington, 1967-85; judge U.S. Dist. Ct. (ea. dist.) Va., Alexandria, 1985—, now chief judge; asst. commonwealth atty., Arlington, 1967-68, commonwealth atty., 1974; dep. clk. ct., Arlington, 1964-66; commr. in chancery U.S. Ct. Appeals (4th cir.), 1976-85; bd. govs. criminal law sect. Va. State Bar, 1979-84, chmn., 1982-83, mem. ins. com., 1981-85. Mem. ABA, Va. Bar Assn., Arlington County Bar Assn. Republican. Methodist. Lodges: Masons, Alexandria Lodge of Perfection, Kena Temple. Home: 3912 N Upland St Arlington VA 22207-4642 Office: US Courthouse 401 Courthouse Sq Alexandria VA 22314-5704

**HILTON, STANLEY GOUMAS,** lawyer, educator, writer; b. San Francisco, June 16, 1949; s. Loucas Stylianos and Effie (Glafkides) Goumas; m. Raquel Estrella Villalba, Feb. 25, 1996. BA with honors, U. Chgo., 1971; JD, Duke U., 1975; MBA, Harvard U., 1979. Bar: Calif. 1975, U.S. Dist. Ct. Calif. 1975, U.S. Ct. Appeals (9th cir.) 1983, U.S. Supreme Ct. 1985. Libr. asst. Duke U. Libr., Durham, N.C., 1972-75, Harvard U. Libr., Cambridge, Mass., 1977-79; minority counsel U.S. Senator Bob Dole, Washington, 1979-80; adminstrv. asst. Calif. State Senate, Sacramento, 1980-81; pvt. practice San Francisco, 1981—; adj. assoc. prof. Golden Gate U., San Francisco, 1991—. Author: Bob Dole: American Political Phoenix, 1988, Senator for Sale, 1995, Glass Houses, 1998 (best writer 1998). Pres. Com. to Stick With Candlestick Park, San Francisco, 1992-96, Value Added Tax Now, San Francisco, 1994—, Save the 4th Amendment, San Francisco, 1995—. Mem. Calif. State Bar, Hellenic Law Soc., Bechtel Toastmasters Club (pres.). Democrat. Avocations: philately, photography, classical music, ancient Greek and Roman history. Constitutional, Labor. Office: 580 California St Ste 500 San Francisco CA 94104-1000

**HILTS, EARL T.,** lawyer, government official; educator; b. Ilion, N.Y., Mar. 31, 1946; stepson Leon Thomas and Gertrude Annette (Daly) Butler; m. Mae Hwa Kim, Apr. 13, 1973; children: Troy Alan, Kimberly Michelle. BS, St. Lawrence U., 1967; JD, Albany Law Sch., 1970. Bar: N.Y. 1972. Gen. atty.-advisor Dept. Army, Watervliet Arsenal, N.Y., 1978-80, supervisory atty.-advisor, Watervliet 1980—; adj. prof. Schnectady C.C., 1985—. Catechism instr. St. Mary's Ch., 1990-92; pee wee football coach, wrestling coach Shenendehowa Sch., 1983-87; little league coach West Crescent Halfmoon Baseball League, 1980-90. Capt. JAGC, U.S. Army, 1972-76. Scholar St. Lawrence U., 1963-67, Albany Law Sch., 1967-70. Mem. N.Y. State Bar Assn., Am. Legion, Pi Mu Epsilon. Republican. Roman Catholic. Home: 28 Oakwood Blvd Clifton Park NY 12065-7413 Office: Legal Office Watervliet Arsenal Watervliet NY 12189

**HIMELEIN, LARRY M.,** judge; b. Buffalo, June 27, 1949; s. Levant Maurice and Barbara McKenzie (Neilson) H.; m. Julie Ann Peglowski, Mar. 20, 1982; children: Ryan Charles, Brendan Levant, Meghan Lee. BA, Ithaca Coll., 1971; JD, Suffolk U., 1975. Bar: N.Y. 1976. Pvt. practice, Gowanda, N.Y., 1977-79; assoc. Levant Himelein, Jr., Gowanda, 1979-82; dist. atty. Cattaraugus County, Little Valley, N.Y., 1982-92; judge Cattaraugus County, Little Valley, 1993—; mem. Arson Task Force, Little Valley, 1982-92, Traffic Safety Bd., 1982-92, Cattaraugus County Police Chiefs, Little Valley, 1982-92. Bd. dirs. Tri-County Meml. Hosp., Gowanda, N.Y., 1987-96. Mem. N.Y. State Bar Assn., N.Y. State County Judges Assn., N.Y. State Family Judges Assn., N.Y. State Surrogate Ct. Assn., Cattaraugus County Bar Assn., Erie County Bar Assn., Am. Legion, Slovenian Club, Gowanda Country Club (bd. dirs. 1997—). Democrat. Episcopalian. Home: 40 W Hill St Gowanda NY 14070-1428 Office: 303 Court St Little Valley NY 14755-1028

**HIMELES, MARTIN STANLEY, JR.,** lawyer; b. Balt., Mar. 13, 1956; s. Martin Stanley and Betty Jean (Applebaum) H.; m. Paula Kilimnik, Aug. 26, 1984. BA summa cum laude, Yale U., 1978; JD magna cum laude, Harvard U., 1981. Bar: N.Y. 1982, U.S. Dist. Ct. (so. and ea. dists.) N.Y. 1982, U.S. Ct. Appeals (4th cir.) 1982, U.S. Dist. Ct. Md. 1986, Md. 1989, U.S. Ct. Appeals (8th cir.) 1999. Law clk. to judge U.S. Ct. Appeals (4th cir.), Balt., 1981-82; assoc. Parker, Auspitz, Neesemann & Delehanty P.C., N.Y.C., 1982-86; asst. U.S. atty. U.S. Atty's. Office, Balt., 1986-90; ptnr. Zuckerman, Spaeder, Goldstein, Taylor & Better, Balt., 1990—. Mem. Fed. Bar Assn. (v.p. Md. chpt.), Am. Jewish Com. (v.p. Md. chpt.), Phi Beta Kappa. Democrat. Federal civil litigation, General civil litigation, Criminal. Office: 100 E Pratt St Ste 2440 Baltimore MD 21202-1031

**HIMELFARB, STEPHEN ROY,** lawyer; b. Washington, Feb. 19, 1954; s. Jordan Sheldon and Marion (Soloman) H.; m. Anne Patricia Spille, June 26, 1983; children: Kara Michelle, Bradley Richard. BSBA, Am. U., 1976; JD, George Mason U., 1980. Bar: D.C. 1982, Md. 1982, Va. 1988, U.S. Dist. Ct. D.C. 1982, U.S. Dist. Ct. Md. 1982, U.S. Ct. Appeals (D.C. and 4th cirs.) 1982, U.S. Dist. Ct. (ea. dist.) Va. 1988, U.S. Tax Ct. 1990, U.S. Bankruptcy Ct. (ea. div.) Va. 1988, U.S. Supreme Ct. 1985. From v.p. to pres. ECA Bus. Comm. Network, Washington, 1982-85; ptnr. Himelfarb & Podryhula, Washington, 1984-93, Speights & Micheel, Washington, 1986-88, Sheeskin, Hillman & Lazar, PC, Rockville, Md., 1989-90, Ahmad & Himelfarb, PC, Rockville, Md., 1993-95; pvt. practice Bethesda, Md., 1995—; v.p. Video Shack Inc., Woodbridge, Va., 1984-95. Mem. ABA, Md. State Bar Assn., Va. Bar Assn., Assn. Trial Lawyers Am., Phi Delta Phi. Democrat. Jewish. Avocations: electronics, coin-op/americana collecting, model trains, radio control models. Contracts commercial, General corporate, Personal injury. Home: 1214 Winter Hunt Rd Mc Lean VA 22102-2434 Office: 4701 Sangamore Rd Ste S-225 Bethesda MD 20816-2508

**HIMES, A. LYNN,** lawyer; b. Raleigh, N.C., Oct. 25, 1947; s. Winfred Phillip and Alice Ruth (Jones) H.; m. Bodil Feleciann Anderson, Nov. 28, 1980; 1 child, Parker Russell. AB in Econs., Davidson Coll., 1970; JD, U. N.C., 1973; LLM in Labor, Georgetown U., 1978. Bar: N.C. 1973, U.S. Dist. Ct. (ea. dist.) N.C. 1973, U.S. Claims Ct. 1974, U.S. Ct. Mil. Appeals 1974, U.S. Supreme Ct. 1977, Ill. 1979, U.S. Dist. Ct. (no. dist.) Ill. 1979, U.S. Ct. Appeals (7th and D.C. cirs.) 19799, U.S. Ct. Appeals (fed. cir.) 1983. Assoc. Braude, Margulies, Sacks & Repalan, Washington, 1978-79, Brydges, Riseborough & Morris, Chgo., 1979-81; ptnr. Brydges, Riseborough, Morris, Franke & Miller, Chgo., 1981-86, Scariano, Kula, Ellch & Himes, Chgo., 1986—. Capt. U.S. Army, 1973-78. Mem. ABA, Fed. Bar Assn., N.C. Bar Assn. (labor law sect.), Ill. State Bar Assn. (labor law sect., sch. law sect.), N.C. State Bar, D.C. Bar Assn., Lake County Bar Assn. (sch. law sect., labor law sect.), Nat. Coun. Sch. Attys., Ill. Coun. Sch. Attys., Phi Delta Phi. Avocation: tennis. Labor, Education and schools, Construction. Office: Scariano Kula Ellch & Himes Two Prudential Plaza 180 N Stetson Ave Ste 3100 Chicago IL 60601-6702

**HIMMELREICH, DAVID BAKER,** lawyer; b. Reading, Pa., Feb. 11, 1954; s. Lester Leon and Jane (Baker) H. AB in Econs., Lafayette U., 1976; JD, U. Pitts., 1979. Bar: Pa. 1980, U.S. Tax Ct. 1980. Sr. atty. Ayco Corp., Albany (N.Y) and Stamford (Conn.), 1979-84; sr. cons. Peat Marwick Main & co., N.Y.C., 1984-86; ptnr. Hynes, Himmelreich, Glennon & Co., Stamford, 1986—. Bd. dirs. Project Return, Westport, Conn., 1986—; dir. Alcohol and Drug Dependency Coun. of Conn., Westport. Republican. Lutheran. Estate planning, Personal income taxation, Estate taxation. Home: 190 Gregory Blvd Norwalk CT 06855-2620 Office: Hynes Himmelreich Glennon & Co One Dock St Stamford CT 06902

**HIMMELREICH, DAVID MERRILL,** attorney general; b. Smyrna, Tenn., June 29, 1954; married; 3 children. BA in History, Wash. U., St. Louis, 1976; JD, Vanderbilt U., 1979. Bar: Tenn. 1979, U.S. Dist. Ct. (mid. dist.) Tenn. 1979, U.S. Ct. of Appeals (6th cir.) 1980, U.S. Ct. Appeals (8th cir.) 1984. Atty. Bruce, Weathers, Dughman & Himmelreich, Nashville, 1979-80; asst. atty. gen. criminal justice divsn. State of Tenn., Nashville, 1980-85, dep. atty. gen., 1986, dep. atty. gen. spl. litigation, 1986-91, dept. atty. gen. enforcement divsn., 1991—. Office: Office of the Atty Gen 425 5th Ave N Nashville TN 37243

**HINCHEY, JOHN WILLIAM,** lawyer; b. Knoxville, Tenn., June 18, 1941; s. Roy William and Ruth (Owenby) H.; m. Sherie Paulette Archer, May 12, 1968; children: Paul William, Meredith Marie, John Oliver. A.B., Emory U., 1964, LL.B., 1965; LL.M., Harvard U., 1966; M.Litt., Oxford U., 1980. Bar: Ga. 1965, U.S. Dist. Ct. (no., mid. and so. dists.) Ga. 1968, U.S. Ct. Appeals (11th cir.) 1968, U.S. Supreme Ct. 1969. Asst. atty. gen. State of Ga., Atlanta, 1968-72; ptnr. McConaughey & Hinchey, Decatur, Ga., 1972-76, Phillips & Mozley, Atlanta, 1976-84, Phillips, Hinchey & Reid, Atlanta, 1984-92, King and Spalding, Atlanta, 1992—. Contbr. to profl. jours. and treatises. Mem. ABA (chair Forum on Constrn. Industry), Am. Coll. Constitution Lawyers, Am. Arbitration Assn., Ga. Bar Assn., Atlanta Bar Assn. (chair constrn. law sect. 1999—), London Ct. of Internat. Arbitration, Druid Hills Golf Club. Republican. Methodist. Construction, Contracts commercial, Alternative dispute resolution. Office: King & Spalding 191 Peachtree St SW Atlanta GA 30303-3637

**HINDELANG, ROBERT LOUIS,** lawyer; b. Detroit, Nov. 21, 1946; s. John Louis and Louise M. (Vantiem) H.; m. Paula Marie Hirzel, July 13, 1973; children: Marianne, Maureen, Michael, Matthew, Mark. BS, Wayne State U., 1968, MBA, 1970; JD, U. Detroit, 1975. Bar: Mich. 1975, U.S. Dist. Ct. Mich. 1975, U.S. Ct. Internat. Trade 1976, U.S. Supreme Ct. 1980, U.S. Tax Ct. 1987; CPA, Mich. Sec., treas. Barry Steel Corp., Detroit, 1973-80, chief exec. officer, 1980-82; sole practice E. Detroit, Mich., 1982-87, Grosse Pointe Farms, Mich., 1987—. Mem. ABA, Mich. Bar Assn., Mich. Assn. CPA's. Roman Catholic. Private international, General corporate, Corporate taxation. Office: 18430 Mack Ave Grosse Pointe MI 48236-3221

**HINDEN, BARRY HARRIS,** lawyer; b. Bklyn., Sept. 21, 1943; s. Richard A. and Freda (Zucker) H.; m. Marilyn Hausner, July 19, 1970; children: Stephen M., Traci M. BA, Calif. State U., 1970; JD, Southwestern U., L.A., 1974. Bar: Calif. 1974, U.S. Ct. Appeals 1974. Pvt. practice law L.A., 1974-78; sr. ptnr. Sobo & Hinden, Beverly Hills, Calif., 1978-88, Hinden, Rodich & Grueskin, L.A., 1988-90, Hinden & Grueskin, L.A., 1989-96, Hinden, Glauber, Grueskin & Aguirre, L.A., 1996-97, Hinden, Grueskin & Aguirre, L.A., 1997—; lectr. CompPro Seminars, L.A., 1992-95, Westwood Seminars, Encino, Calif., 1992, Coalition of Medicare Providers, L.A., 1992, Calif. Soc. Indsl. Medicine; adj. prof. Calif. Poly. U., 1996—. Author: Surviving the Storm of Reform, 1993, How to Prepare Your Client for Trial, Medical Control: Advanced Worker's Compensation in California, 1997, Workers Compensation in California, 1998, How to Litigate the Post Termination Claim: Indentifying the Collateral Issues to Workers Compensation. Judge pro tem Workers Compensation Appeals Bd., Santa Monica, Calif., L.A., 1989-95; adminstrv. asst. Calif. Polit. Forum, 1968; vol. Beverly Hills Edn. Found., 1988-95; coach Beverly Hills Little League, Am. Youth Soccer Orgn.; scoutmaster Boy Scouts Am., 1962-65, 73-76, cubmaster, 1982-85; baseball & football coach U.S. Army Dependents, 1962-65; bd. dirs., v.p. Nat. Kidney Assn., Westside Jewish Cmty. Ctr., 1980-88, Temple Emanuel, Beverly Hills, 1989-92, also pres. brotherhood, 1990-92; vol. L.A. Mission, 1993-95, Lokrantz Sch. for Retarded, 1969-70; mem. L.A. Mid City Redevel. P.A.C. Served in U.S. Army, 1962-65, Germany. Mem. Calif. Applications Atty. Assn. (edn. chair 1992-93), L.A. County Bar Assn. (lectr.), L.A. Trial Lawyers Assn., Consumer Attys. of Calif., L.A. Lawyers Club, Mid City C. of C. Democrat. Avocations: cross-country skiing, golf, travel, jogging, baseball card collecting. Workers' compensation. Office: Hinden Grueskin & Aguirre 4661 W Pico Blvd Los Angeles CA 90019-4237

**HINDERAKER, JOHN HADLEY,** lawyer; b. Watertown, S.D., Sept. 19, 1950; s. Irving Alden and Eula Mae (Jertson) H.; m. Shannon Faye Smith, Jan. 3, 1981 (div. 1993); children: Eric, Laura, Alison, Kathryn; m. Loree Kay Miner, June 4, 1994. AB magna cum laude, Dartmouth Coll., 1971; JD cum laude, Harvard U., 1974. Bar: Minn. 1974. Assoc. Faegre & Benson, Mpls., 1974-81, ptnr., 1981—; chmn. practice standards com., Faegre & Benson, 1986—; lectr. in field. Contbr. articles to profl. jours. Bd. dirs. Ctr. of the Am. Experiment, 1996—. Mem. ABA, Minn. State Bar Assn. (mem. ethics com. 1979-85), Hennepin County Bar Assn. Republican. Lutheran. Avocations: authoring commentaries on polit. and econ. issues, weightlifting. General civil litigation, Construction, Product liability. Office: Faegre & Benson 2200 Norwest Ctr 90 S 7th St Ste 2200 Minneapolis MN 55402-3901

**HINDMAN, LARRIE C.,** lawyer; b. Meservey, Iowa, Mar. 30, 1937; s. Marvin C. and Fredona E. (Lemke) H.; m. Jeannie Carol Richey, June 18, 1961; children: Bryant C., Derek Cory. BS, Iowa State U., 1959; JD, U. Iowa, 1962. Bar: Mo. 1963, Kans. 1975. Ptnr. Morrison & Hecker LLP, Kansas City, Mo., 1962—. Contbr. legal articles to profl. jours. Mem. ABA, Am. Coll. Real Estate Lawyers, Am. Coll. Mortgage Attys., Am. Land Title Assn. (lender counsel), Lawyers Assn. Kansas City, Indian Hills County Club. Real property, Finance. Home: 6432 W 101st St Overland Park KS 66212-1603 Office: Morrison & Hecker LLP 2600 Grand Blvd Ste 1200 Kansas City MO 64108-4606

**HINDS, ROBERT TAYLOR, JR.,** lawyer; b. Jamaica, N.Y., May 8, 1940; s. Robert Taylor Sr. and Evelyn (Kipp) H.; m. Donna Kearney Castrigano, Jan. 6, 1968; children: Robert, Christopher, Timothy, Michael. AS, Cobleskill (N.Y.) Coll., 1960; BA, Drew U., 1964; JD, U. Denver, 1967. Bar: Colo. 1968, U.S. Dist. Ct. Colo. 1968. Pvt. practice Littleton, Colo., 1968-80; pres. Robert T. Hinds Jr. & Assocs. P.C., Littleton, 1980—; judge City of Morrison, Colo., 1970-72; lectr. to bar assns., 1975—. Co-author: Colorado Domestic Relations Forms, 1988—; contbr. articles to profl. jours. Mem. Gov.'s Commn. on Child Support, 1985-86, Gov.'s Commn. on Child Support and Family Law Matters, 1985—. Fellow Am. Acad. Matrimonial Lawyers (legis. chmn. Colo. chpt., v.p. Colo. chpt. 1991, pres., 1992-93); mem. Colo. Bar Assn. (family law sect., bd. govs. 1981); Colo. Trial Lawyers Assn. (chmn. 1977—, family law editor), Arapahoe County Bar Assn. (pres. 1979, Outstanding Young Lawyer 1975). Family and matrimonial.

**HINE, JOHN C.,** lawyer; b. Winston-Salem, N.C., Dec. 30, 1948; s. George H. and Laura L. H.; m. Ann Moore, Aug. 14, 1971; childre: Neil, Laura. BS, U. N.C., 1971; JD, U. Tenn., 1974; LLM in Taxation, NYU, 1977. Bar: N.C., U.S. Surpeme Ct., U.S. Tax Ct., Ct. Mil. Appeals. Atty. IRS, Raleigh, N.C., 1974-76, Baddour, Parker & Hine, Goldsboro, N.C., 1977—. Treas. Goldsboro-Wayne Airport Authority, 1982-87, N.C.; dir. Econ. Deve. Comm., Goldsboro, 1992-96. Lt. col. USAF, 1975-98. Mem. Rotary. Republican. Episcopalian. Avocations: hunting, camping, sports, flying. Estate planning, Probate, Corporate taxation. Home: 2507 Peachtree St Goldsboro NC 27534-4311 Office: PO Box 916 Goldsboro NC 27533-0916

**HINES, BARBARA C.,** lawyer. Student, Universidad Nacional Autonoma, Mexico City, 1965, U. Ams., 1965, Universidad de Madrid, 1967-68; BA in Latin American Studies with honors, U. Tex., 1969, postgrad., 1970, 72, 74-75; JD, Northeastern U., 1975. Bar: Tex. 1975, U.S. Supreme Ct., U.S. Dist. Ct. (we., so., and no. dists.) Tex., U.S. Ct. Appeals (1st, 4th, and 5th cirs.). Teaching asst. dept. Spanish & Portuguese U. Tex., Austin, 1970; staff atty., mng. atty. Legal Aid Soc. Ctrl. Tex., Austin, 1975-82; of counsel lawyers com. Civil Rights Under Law Tex., Immigrant & Refugee Rights Project, 1994—, co-dir., 1991-94; pvt. practice, 1982—; pres. bd. dirs. Human Rights Documentation Exch., Austin, 1988-90, sec. bd. dirs., 1990-98; mem. adv. bd. Tex. Immigrant & Refugee Coalition, 1993-96, Tibetal Resettlement Project Austin, 1995—; bd. dirs. Lawyers Com. Civil Rights Under Law Tex., Polit. asylum Project Austin; mem. Working Group Battered Immigrant Women, 1994—, United Network Immigrants' Rights, Austin, 1993—; lectr. Univ. Tex. Sch. Law, 1999—. Mem. City of Austin Commn. on Immigrant Affairs, 1998—. Recipient Best Immigration Lawyer award Austin Chronicle, 1993, Pro Bono award Immigration, 1989; Fulbright scholar, 1996. Mem. Nat. Lawyers Guild (steering com. nat. immigration project 1997—), Am. Immigration Lawyers Assn. (nat. exec. office immigration review liaison com. 1992-93, nat. asylum & refugee liaison com. 1988-89, mem. ctrl. office liaison com. 1997-98, treas. Tex. chpt. 1986-87, enforcement liaison com. 1997—, mentor program 1990—, Jack Wasserman Meml. award 1992, Litigation award Tex. chpt. 1993), Am. Immigration Law Found. (adv. bd. 1991-95), Travis County Bar Assn. (internat. law sect.). E-mail: barbarahines@austintx.com. Office: 1005 E 40th St Austin TX 78751-4805

**HINES, EDWARD FRANCIS, JR.,** lawyer; b. Norfolk, Va., Sept. 5, 1945; s. Edward Francis and Jeanne Miriam (Caulfield) H.; m. Elaine Geneva Carroll, Aug. 21, 1971; children: Jonathan Edward, Carolyn Adele. AB, Boston Coll., 1966; JD, Harvard U., 1969. Bar: Mass. 1969. Assoc. Choate Hall & Stewart, Boston, 1969-77, ptnr., 1977—; bd. dirs. Univ. Hosp., Boston, 1990-96, vice-chmn., 1994-96. With USAR, 1969-75. Mem. Boston Bar Assn. (pres. 1988-89), Boston Bar Found. (pres. 1995-97), Mass. CLE (pres. 1985-87), Carroll Ctr. for Blind (bd. dirs. 1983-89, 90-96, chmn. 1994-96), Mass. Taxpayers Found. (bd. dirs. 1987—), Am. Heart Assn. (bd. dirs. Dallas 1984-86, 91—, chmn. 1998-99, award of merit 1983), Assoc. Industries Mass. (bd. dirs. 1990—, chmn. 1996-98), Am. Coll. Greece (Athens, bd. dirs., vice chmn. 1988-97), Fed. Tax Inst. New Eng. (treas. 1994—), Social Law Libr. (trustee 1993-98), Supreme Jud. Ct. Hist. Soc. (trustee 1989-96), Accion Internat. (bd. dirs. 1999—), North Andover Country Club, Boston Coll. Club, Bay Club. General corporate, Taxation, general, State and local taxation. Office: Choate Hall & Stewart Exchange Pl 53 State St Boston MA 02109-2804

**HINES, N. WILLIAM,** dean, law educator, administrator; b. 1936. AB, Baker U., 1958; LLD, U. Kans., 1999, LLB, 1961; LLD, Baker U., 1999. Bar: Kans. 1961, Iowa 1965. Law clk. U.S. Ct. Appeals 10th cir., 1961-62; tchg. fellow Harvard U., 1961-62; asst. prof. law U. Iowa, 1962-65, assoc. prof., 1965-67, prof., 1967-73, disting. prof., 1973—, dean, 1976—; vis. prof. Stanford U., 1974-75. Notes and comments editor Kans. Law Rev. Grad. fellow Harvard U., 1961-62. Fellow ABA Found., Iowa State Bar Found.; mem. Environ. Law Inst. (assoc.), Jo. Co. Her. Trust (founder, pres.), Order of Coif. Office: U Iowa Coll Law Iowa City IA 52242-0001

**HINES, PRESTON HARRIS,** state supreme court justice; b. Atlanta, Sept. 6, 1943. AB in Polit. Sci., Emory U., 1965, JD, 1968. Bar: Ga. 1968, U.S. Dist. Ct. Ga. 1973. Law clk. Civil Ct. Fulton County, 1968-69; pvt. practice Marietta, Ga., 1969-74; judge State Ct. of Cobb County, 1974-82, Superior Ct. of Ga., 1982—. Chmn. attys. divsn. Cobb County United Appeal, 1972; participant Leadership Ga., 1975, Leadership Atlanta, 1978-79; pres. YMCA Cobb County, 1976; co-treas. Cobb Landmarks Soc., 1976-77; former bd. dirs. Cobb County Emergency Aid Assn., Cobb-Marietta Girls Club, Ga. chpt. Leukemia Soc. Am., Cobb County Children's Ctr., Met. Atlanta Red Cross, First Presbyn. Day Kindergarten; mem. cmty. adv. com. Marietta-Cobb County LWV; bd. dirs. Kennesaw Coll. Found.; trustee Cobb Cmty. Symphony. Named Outstanding Young Man of Yr., Ga. Jaycees, 1975, Boss of Yr., Cobb County Legal Secs. Assn., 1975-76, 83-84. Mem. ABA, State Bar Ga. (chmn. Law Day com. 1975, mem. exec. com. younger lawyers sec.

1974-76), Cobb Jud. Cir. (sec. 1972-73, chmn. Law Day com. 1972), Joseph Henry Lumpkin Inn of Ct. Ga., Atlanta Lawyers Club, Kiwanis (bd. dirs. Marietta chpt., chmn. Key Club com., past chmn. spiritual aims com., past pres.), Cobb County C. of C., Sigma Alpha Epsilon (Atlanta and Marietta chpts.). Office: Supreme Court 504 State Judicial Bldg Atlanta GA 30334

**HINES, SUZANNE,** lawyer; b. Moline, Ill., Feb. 24, 1947; d. William Joseph and Janice E. (Sersig) H.; m. Stuart N. Emanuel, July 10, 1965 (div. June 1980); children: William, Margaret, Robert; m. E. Vaughn Gordy III, Jan. 27, 1990. BA, Loyola U., Chgo., 1978, JD, 1981. Bar: Ill. 1981, U.S. Dist. Ct. (no. dist.) Ill. 1981, U.S. Ct. Appeals (fed. cir.) 1990. Jud. clk. to Hon. Helen McGillicuddy and Hon. Maurice Perlin Ill. Appellate Ct. (1st dist.), Chgo., 1982-85; assoc. Welsh & Katz, Ltd., Chgo., 1985-90, prin., 1990-95; gen. counsel Precious Moments, Inc., St. Charles, Ill., 1995—; instr. legal writing Sch. Law Loyola U., 1984-90. Mem. ABA, Internat. Trademark Assn. Intellectual property, General corporate, Federal civil litigation. Office: Precious Moments Inc 2210 Dean St Ste G Saint Charles IL 60175-1059

**HINGSON, JOHN HENRY, III,** lawyer; b. Phoenix, Mar. 2, 1946; s. John Henry Jr. and Virginia Seagrave (Marxsen) H.; m. Susan Kay DeWitz, Feb. 25, 1989; children: John Henry IV, Sarah Ainsley. BA, So. Meth. U., 1968; JD, U. Tex., 1971. Bar: Oreg. 1971, U.S. Dist. Ct. Oreg. 1971, U.S. Supreme Ct. 1975, U.S. Ct. Appeals (9th cir.) 1977. Pvt. practice Oregon City, Oreg., 1971—. Author: How to Defend a Drunk Driving Case, 5th edit., 1990. Pres. Oreg. Criminal Def. Lawyers Assn., Eugene, 1982-84, Clackamas County (Oreg.) Bar Assn., Oregon City, 1982-83. Mem. Nat. Assn. Criminal Def. Lawyers (pres. 1993-94). Democrat. Methodist. Criminal, Constitutional. Office: 421 High St Oregon City OR 97045-2214

**HINKLE, CHARLES FREDERICK,** lawyer, clergyman, educator; b. Oregon City, Oreg., July 6, 1942; s. William Ralph and Ruth Barbara (Holcomb) H. BA, Stanford U., 1964; MDiv, Union Theol. Sem., N.Y.C., 1968; JD, Yale U., 1971. Bar: Oreg. 1971; ordained to ministry United Ch. of Christ, 1974. Instr. English, Morehouse Coll., Atlanta, 1966-67; assoc. Stoel Rives LLP (formerly Stoel, Rives, Boley, Jones & Grey), Portland, Oreg., 1971-77, ptnr., 1977—; adj. prof. Lewis and Clark Law Sch., Portland, 1978—; bd. govs. Oreg. State Bar, 1992-95. Oreg. pres. ACLU, Portland, 1976-80, nat. bd. dirs., 1979-85; bd. dirs. Kendall Cmty. Ctr., 1987-93, Youth Progress Assn., 1994-98, Portland Baroque Orch., 1999—; mem. pub. affairs com. Am. Cancer Soc., 1994-99; mem. Oreg. Gov.'s Task Force on Youth Suicide, 1996. Recipient Elliott Human Rights award Oreg. Edn. Assn., 1984, E.B. MacNaughton award ACLU Oreg., 1987, Wayne Morse award Dem. Com. Oreg., 1994, Tom McCall Freedom of Info. award Women in Comm., 1996, Civil Rights award Met. Human Rights Commn., 1996, Pub. Svc. award Oreg. State Bar, 1997. Fellow Am. Bar Found.; mem. ABA (ho. of dels. 1998—), FBA, Multnomah County Bar Assn., City Club Portland (pres. 1987-88). Democrat. Libel, Constitutional, Communications. Home: 14079 SE Fairoaks Way Milwaukie OR 97267-1017 Office: Stoel Rives 900 SW 5th Ave Ste 2600 Portland OR 97204-1268

**HINMAN, HARVEY DEFOREST,** lawyer; b. Binghamton, N.Y., May 7, 1940; s. George Lyon and Barbara (Davidge) H.; m. Margaret Snyder, June 23, 1962; children: George, Sarah, Marguerite. BA, Brown U., 1962; JD, Cornell U., 1965. Bar: Calif. 1966. Assoc. Pillsbury, Madison & Sutro, San Francisco, 1965-72, ptnr., 1973-93, v.p., gen. counsel Chevron Corp., 1993—; bd. dirs. Legal Aid Soc., San Francisco. Bd. dirs., sec. Holbrook Palmer Park Found., 1977-86; bd. dirs. Phillips Brooks Sch., 1978-84, pres. 1983-84; trustee Castillija Sch., 1988-89; bd. govs. Filoli Ctr., 1988—, pres. 1994-95. Fellow Am. Bar Found.; mem. ABA, San Francisco Bar Assn. Private international, Contracts commercial, Oil, gas, and mineral. Office: Chevron Corporation 575 Market St San Francisco CA 94105-2856

**HINMAN, JAMES STUART,** lawyer; b. Phila., Apr. 30, 1955; s. Herbert Stuart Hinman and Marion Dorothy (Bolton) Northrup; m. Joan Brenda Karas, Aug. 16, 1980; children: Joseph Stuart, Robert James. BA, Gettysburg Coll., 1976; JD, Syracuse U., 1980. Bar: N.Y. 1981, U.S. Dist. Ct. (we. dist.) N.Y. 1981. Assoc. Antell & Harris, Rochester, N.Y., 1980-82, ptnr., 1983-84; ptnr. Antell, Harris & Hinman, Rochester, N.Y., 1985-86, Antell & Hinman, Rochester, 1987-88; pvt. practice Rochester, N.Y., 1988—. Asst. scoutmaster Boy Scout Am., Irondequoit, N.Y., 1982-91, com. chair, 1991-98, scoutmaster, 1998—. Recipient Am. Jurisprudence awards Bancroft Whittney Lawyers Co-op, Rochester, N.Y., 1980. Mem. ABA, N.Y. Bar Assn., Assn. Trial Lawyers Am. Congregationalist. General practice, Criminal, Family and matrimonial. Home: 103 Minocqua Dr Rochester NY 14617-4427 Office: 19 Main St W Ste 600 Rochester NY 14614-1586

**HINMAN, MICHAEL J.,** lawyer; b. Drayton, N.D., July 4, 1943; s. Ivan James and Edna Ray (Johnson) H.; m. Joyce Gayle Becker, June 11, 1973; children: Joy, Daniel. BA in Polit. Sci., U. N.D., 1970, JD, 1973. Law clk. N.D. Supreme Ct., Bismarck, 1973-74; staff atty. Basin Electric Power Coop., Bismarck, 1974-77, asst. gen. counsel, 1977-79, gen. counsel, 1979—. City commr. City of Bismarck, 1992-96. Served with USN, 1964-68. Recipient Pro Bono Publico award N.D. State Bar Assn., 1988. Administrative and regulatory, General corporate, Public utilities. Office: Basin Electric Power Coop 1717 E Interstate Ave Bismarck ND 58501-0564

**HINOJOSA, FEDERICO GUSTAVO, JR.,** judge; b. Edinburg, Tex., Apr. 16, 1947; s. Federico Gustavo and Zulema (Trevino) H.; m. Yolanda Silva, 1970 (div. 1977); 1 child, Cynthia; m. Magdalena Garza, Oct. 30, 1992. BA, Pan Am. U., 1969; JD, U. Houston, 1977. Bar: Tex. 1977, U.S. Dist. Ct. (so. dist.) Tex. 1977, U.S. Ct. Appeals (5th cir.) 1980, U.S. Supreme Ct. 1980. Assoc. Clark, Lowes & Carrithers, Houston, 1977-79; ptnr. Clark & Hinojosa, Houston, 1979-81; child support atty. Tex. Dept. Human Resources, McAllen, 1981-83; asst. dist. atty. Hidalgo County, Edinburg, 1983-84; assoc. Atlas & Hall, McAllen, 1984-87; ptnr. Lewis, Pettitt & Hinojosa, McAllen, 1987-91; justice Tex. Ct. Appeals for 13th Dist., Corpus Christi, 1991—. Sgt. USAF, 1970-74. Mem. State Bar Tex., Mexican-Am. Bar Tex., Mexican-Am. Bar Assn. Coastal Bend (dir. 1993-94), Hidalgo County Bar Assn. (dir. 1986-90). Democrat. Office: 13th Ct Appeals 100 E Cano St Edinburg TX 78539-4548

**HINOJOSA, RICARDO H.,** federal judge; b. 1950. BA, U. Tex., 1972; JD, Harvard U., 1975. Judge U.S. Dist. Ct. (so. dist.) Tex.; law clk. Tex. Supreme Ct., 1975-76; assoc. Ewers & Toothaker, McAllen, Tex., 1976-79, ptnr., 1979-83; judge U.S. Dist. Ct. (so. dist.) Tex., McAllen, 1983—. Office: US Dist Ct So Dist Tex 1701 W Bus Hwy 83 Ste 1028 Mcallen TX 78501

**HINSDALE, BETH A.,** lawyer; b. Montclair, N.J., June 25, 1965; d. Robert Joseph and Sandra Elvira Drew. BA, Pa. State U., 1987; JD, Villanova U., 1990. Bar: N.J. 1990, U.S. Dist. Ct. N.J. 1990, U.S. Ct. Appeals (3d cir.) 1996. Assoc. Grotta, Glassman & Hoffman, Roseland, N.J., 1990—. Mem. ABA, N.J. Bar Assn. Labor. Office: Grotta Glassman & Hoffman 75 Livingston Ave Roseland NJ 07068-3701

**HINSON, REID GARRETT,** lawyer; b. Rockingham, N.C., Nov. 11, 1956; s. Robin Ledbetter and Frances (Garrett) H.; m. Melinda Mills, May 16, 1992; children: Reid Garrett Jr., Mills Gray. BA, Davidson Coll., 1978; JD, U. N.C., Chapel Hill, 1986. Bar: N.C. 1986, U.S. Dist. Ct. (ea. dist.) N.C. 1986, U.S. Ct. Appeals (4th cir.) 1988, U.S. Dist. Ct. (mid. dist.) N.C. 1988. Ptnr. Murchison, Taylor, Kenddrick, Gibson & Davenport, Wilmington, N.C., 1986-91, Clark, Newton, Hinson & McLean, L.L.P., Wilmington, N.C., 1991—; mem. Southeastern Admiralty Law Inst., 1992-94, dir., 1996-98. Lt., USN, 1978-83, U.S. Pacific Fleet. Avocations: bluegrass guitar, fly fishing, sailing, piloting. Admiralty, Federal civil litigation, State civil litigation. Office: Clark Newton Hinson & McLean LLP 509 Princess St Wilmington NC 28401-4130

**HINTON, CHARLES FRANKLIN,** prosecutor; b. Des Moines, June 30, 1932; s. Charles Franklin and Wilma Pearl (Nuzum) H. BA, U. Iowa, 1957, JD, 1959. Bar: Iowa 1959. Owner, Hinton Law Firm, Waterloo, Iowa, 1959-62; asst. county atty. Black Hawk County, Iowa, 1960-64; asst. city solicitor City of Waterloo, 1966-68; spl. prosecutor Black Hawk County, 1972—; atty. Heart Fund, 1966-70. Mem. Black Hawk County Rep. Com., 1962-64. Mem. ABA, N.Y. State Trial Lawyers Assn., Iowa Bar Assn., Black Hawk County (v.p. 1997) Bar Assn., ATLA, Sertoma (dist. pres. 1968). Home and Office: 3908 Midway Dr Waterloo IA 50701-3152

**HINTON, FLOYD,** lawyer; b. Olympia, Wash., Sept. 11, 1923; s. Irma (Yost) Ness; m. Feb. 1, 1946; children—Denise C. Hinton Maaranen, Stefan J., Bradford R. B.S., U. Oreg., 1948; LL.B., Northwestern Sch. Law, Portland, Oreg., 1958. Bar: Oreg. 1958, U.S. Dist. Ct. Oreg. 1959, U.S. Ct. Appeals (9th cir.) 1980. Sole practice, Portland, 1958-61; ptnr. Deich Hinton & Meece and predecessors Deich & Hinton and Deich, Deich & Hinton, Portland, 1961-88; in house counsel Oreg. Ctrl. Credit Union, 1988—. chmn. supervisory com. Oreg. Cen. Credit Union. Active in fin. devel. Oreg. Lung Assn., Portland, 1982-85; bd. dirs. Northwest Native Am. Arts Council, 1985—. Served with U.S. Army, 1943. Mem. Oreg. State Bar (author ins. and creditor rights for continuing legal edn. com.), Multnomah County Bar, Oreg. Trial lawyers Assn., Am. Arbitration Assn., Portland Art Assn. Democrat. Clubs: Portland City (mem. study groups), Viking Athletic Assn. (bd. dirs. 1985). Lodge: Elks (trustee). State civil litigation, Consumer commercial, Family and matrimonial. Home: 1303 Moore St Unit 303 Brookings OR 97415-9049

**HINTON, JAMES FORREST, JR.,** lawyer; b. Gadsden, Ala., Nov. 19, 1951; s. James Forrest Sr. and Juanita Grey (Weems) H.; m. Rosalind Flynn, Nov. 10, 1979. BA, Vanderbilt U., 1974; JD, U. Ala., 1977. Bar: Ala. 1977, D.C. 1979, U.S. Dist. Ct. (so. dist.) Ala. 1979, U.S. Ct. Appeals (5th cir.) 1980, U.S. Ct. Appeals (11th cir.) 1981, La. 1982, U.S. Dist. Ct. (ea. and mid. dists.) La. 1982, U.S. Dist. Ct. (no. dist.) Ala 1982, U.S. Supreme Ct. 1982, U.S. Dist. Ct. (we. dist.) La. 1983, U.S. Dist. Ct. (no. dist.) Ohio 1983, U.S. Ct. Appeals (D.C. cir.) 1984, U.S. Ct. Appeals (fed. cir.) 1985, U.S. Dist. Ct. (so. dist.) Tex. 1987, U.S. Dist. Ct. (no. dist.) Tex. 1991, Tex. 1992, Tenn. 1992, U.S. Dist. Ct. (ea. and we. dists.) Ark. 1992, U.S. Ct. Appeals (6th and 8th cirs.) 1992, U.S. Dist. Ct. (ea. and we. dists.) Tex. 1993, U.S. Dist. Ct. (mid. dist.) Ala. 1993, U.S. Dist. Ct. (ea. and mid. dist.) Tenn. 1994. Law clk. to chief judge U.S. Dist. Ct. (so. dist.) Ala., Mobile, 1977-79; ptnr. Darby, Myrick & Hinton, Mobile, 1979-82; dir. McGlinchey Stafford Lang, New Orleans, 1982-93; ptnr. Adams & Reese, New Orleans, 1993-97; shareholder Berkowitz, Lefkovits, Isom & Kushner, Birmingham, 1997—. Contbr. articles to profl. jours. Mem. ABA (antitrust, intellectual property, litigation sects.), FBA, La. Assn. Def. Counsel, Order of Coif, Phi Beta Kappa. General civil litigation, Antitrust, Intellectual property. Office: Berkowitz Lefkovits Isom & Kushner 1600 South Trust Twr 420 20th St N Birmingham AL 35203-5200

**HINTON, RHETTA ANN,** legal assistant, educator; b. Tulare, Calif., June 2, 1941; d. M. E. and Helen (Ehrich) Willeford; m. George E. Hinton; children: Dwight, Kent, Kevin. BA, U. Calif., Berkeley, 1962; Cert. atty. asst. program, Sonoma State U., 1985. Cert. legal asst., Nat. Assn. Legal Assts., 1997. Substitute tchr. pub. schs. Santa Rosa, Calif., 1964-74; pvt. practice paralegal Santa Rosa, 1985-86; legal asst./paralegal Shapiro, Glavin, Shapiro, Piasta & Moran, Santa Rosa, 1986—; instr. atty. asst. program Sonoma State U., Rohnert Park, Calif. 1987-95. Active Symphony League, Santa Rosa, 1982-86; mem. Citizens Com. Bd. Edn., Santa Rosa, 1973, 1983-84; bd. dirs. We Care, Santa Rosa, 1983-84; bd. dirs., sec. Santa Rosa Inst. Mental Health, Santa Rosa, 1991-95. Mem. ATLA (paralegal subsect.), Redwood Empire Legal Assts. Assn. (v.p. 1987-88, pres. 1998-99), Am. Assn. Paralegal Educators, Sonoma County Bar Assn. (Paragon award 1997), Nat. Assn. Legal Assts. Avocations: reading, swimming, running, T'ai Chi. Office: Shapiro Galvin Shapiro Piasta & Moran 640 3rd St Fl 2 Santa Rosa CA 95404-4418

**HINTZEN, ERICH HEINZ,** lawyer; b. Grosse Pointe, Mich., June 9, 1960; s. Heinz and Hanna Hintzen; m. Valerie L. Parker; children: Andrew P., Emma L. AB, U. Mich., 1983; JD, U. Minn., 1989. Bar: Tex. 1989, Mich. 1990, U.S. Dist. Ct. (we. dist.) Mich. 1991, U.S. Ct. Appeals (6th cir.) 1991, U.S. Dist. Ct. (ea. dist.) Mich. 1992, U.S. Dist. Ct. (ea. dist.) Tex. 1995, U.S. Dist. Ct. (we. dist.) Tex. 1995, U.S. Ct. Appeals (5th cir.) 1995, U.S. Supreme Ct. 1996, U.S. Dist. Ct. (no. dist.) Tex. 1997, U.S. Dist. Ct. (so. dist.) Tex. 1998. Briefing atty. to Justice C.L. Ray Tex. Supreme Ct., Austin, 1989-90; assoc. Miller, Canfield, Paddock & Stone, PLC, Detroit, 1990-95, Parkers Parks & Rosenthal, LLP, Austin, 1995-96; assoc. Miller Canfield Paddock & Stone, PLC, Austin, 1996-98, prin., 1998—; prin. Miller Canfield Paddock & Stone, PLC, Bloomfield Hills. Product liability, Appellate. Office: Miller Canfield Paddock & Stone PLC 1400 N Woodward Ave Ste 100 Bloomfield Hills MI 48304-2855

**HIPP, KENNETH BYRON,** lawyer; b. Charlotte, N.C., Aug. 4, 1945; s. Junius B. and Jeanne Carol (Gwaltney) H.; m. Ann Winfield Birmingham, Sept. 23, 1966; children: Kenneth Byron Jr., Andrew Clay. AB, Duke U., 1967; JD with high honors, U. N.C., Chapel Hill, 1971. Bar: N.C. 1971, Hawaii 1987, U.S. Dist. Ct. (no. dist.) Tex. 1978, U.S. Dist. Ct. Hawaii 1987, U.S. Ct. Appeals (2d, 4th and 5th cirs.) 1972, U.S. Ct. Appeals (9th cir.) 1976, U.S. Ct. Appeals (10th cir.) 1977, U.S. Supreme Ct. 1993. Assoc. Micronesian Claims Com., Saipan, Northern Mariana Islands, 1973-74; regional dir. Micronesian Claims Co., Palau, Western Caroline Islands, 1974-76; atty. enforcement litigation NLRB, Washington, 1971-73, 76-77, supr. atty. enforcement litigation, 1977, dep. asst. gen. counsel spl. litigation, 1977-78, dep. asst. gen. counsel appellate litigation, 1978-86, dep. asst. gen. counsel contempt litigation, 1986-87; ptnr. Goodsill Anderson Quinn & Stifel, Honolulu, 1987-95; mem. Nat. Mediation Bd., Washington, 1995-98, chmn., 1996-98; ptnr. Marr Hipp Jones & Pepper, Honolulu, 1998—; bar examiner State of Hawaii, 1988-92; vis. assoc. prof. Law Sch., Boston Coll., 1983-84; adj. prof. Law Sch., Cath. U. Am., 1978-79, Law Ctr., Georgetown U., Washington, 1984-87; adj. prof. Grad. Sch. Bus. U. Hawaii, 1989-94. Mem. Hawaii State Bar Assn. (chair labor and employment law sect. 1990-91), Order of Coif. Presbyterian. Labor. Home: 314 Poipu Dr Honolulu HI 96825-2125 Office: Marr Hipp Jones and Pepper Ste 1550 1001 Bishop St Pauahi Tower Honolulu HI 96813

**HIRES, JACK MERLE,** law educator; b. Kansas City, Kans., Jan. 28, 1932; s. William Lewis Hires and Roberta Carmen (Farris) Herod; m. Dorie Denessen, Aug. 3, 1973. JD, Valparaiso U., 1983; BS magna cum laude, Ind. U., 1980; student, U. Denver, 1951-53. Bar: Mich. 1983, U.S. Dist. Ct. (we. dist.) Mich. 1983, U.S. Tax Ct. 1983. Engr., surveyor Abrams Aerial Survey Corp., Lansing, Mich., 1954-59; sales engr. CEWA, Inc., South Bend, Ind., 1959-70; v.p. mktg. Laird Co., Appleton, Wis., 1970-74; pres. Jack M. Hires, Assocs., Inc., Wheaton, Ill., 1974-79; prof. Valparaiso (Ind.) U., 1983—; bd. dirs. Am. Redecorating, Kalamazoo, Mich., 1982—; mem. ednl. policy com. Valparaiso U., 1987-88, chmn. curriculum com. 1985-86, admissions, advisement and scholarship com. 1983-86, chmn. 1985-86, prelaw adv. com. 1984—, prelaw advisor to students in the Coll. of Bus. Adminstrn., 1983—, student fair practices com. 1983-85, mem. univ. senate 1984-86, ednl. policy com. 1987-88, com. on acad. and profl. standards 1988—, chmn. 1990-92, faculty tenure promotion and retention rev. com. 1989—, sec. 1991. Author: (with others) Partnership Formation, 1987; reviewer (book) Legal Environment, 1984; contbr. articles to profl. jours. Pres. Northside Little League, South Bend, 1969-70; advisor Spl. Olympics, Green Bay, Wis., 1976, Alpha Xi Epsilon sorority, Valparaiso, 1985—, Kemper Scholar Program, Valparaiso, 1989—. Rsch. grantee Kemper Found., Valparaiso, 1987, 89, 90, 91, 92, 93. Mem. ABA, Mich. Bar Assn., Am. Bus. Law Assn., Berrien County Bar Assn., Midwest Bus. Law Assn., Phi Alpha Delta. Republican. Roman Catholic. Avocations: model shipbuilding, fishing, history of Pacific War. Home: 1806 Clover Ln Valparaiso IN 46385-2858 Office: Valparaiso U 211 Urschel Hall Valparaiso IN 46383

**HIROZAWA, KENT Y.,** lawyer; b. Wyandotte, Mich., Jan. 31, 1955. BA, Yale U., 1977; JD, N.Y. U. Sch. Law, 1982. Bar: N.Y. 1983, so. and ea. dists. N.Y. 1983. Law clerk U.S. Ct. Appeals, 2d Cir., N.Y.C., 1982-84; atty. NLRB, N.Y.C., 1984-86; assoc. Gladstein, Reif & Meginniss, N.Y.C., 1986-89, ptnr., 1990—. Labor, Pension, profit-sharing, and employee benefits, Civil rights. Office: Gladstein Reif & Meginniss LLP 361 Broadway New York NY 10013-3903

**HIRREL, MICHAEL JOHN,** lawyer; b. Buckroe Beach, Va., Oct. 13, 1951; s. Michael Ambrose and Evelyn Louise (Nuissl) H.; m. Mary Helen Ratchford, Apr. 16, 1984; 1 child, Shannon Maureen. BA magna cum laude, Boston Coll., Chestnut Hill, Mass., 1973; JD, George Washington U., 1977. Bar: D.C. 1977, U.S. Ct. Appeals (D.C. cir.) 1978, Fla. 1991, U.S. Supreme Ct. 1993. Atty. Hamel Park McCabe & Saunders, Washington, 1977-80, Arent, Fox, Kintner, Plotkin & Kahn, Washington, 1980-87, Davis, Graham & Stubbs, Washington, 1987-90; pvt. practice Washington, 1990—; speaker numerous convs. and seminars concerning Washington events. Contbr.: Cablespeech, The Case for First Amendment Protaection, 1983, articles to profl. jours. mem. ABA, Fed. Comm. Bar Assn. (co-chmn. jud. practice com. 1993—), D.C. Bar Assn., Fla. Bar Assn. (pub. utilites law com. 1992—). Democrat. Roman Catholic. Avocation: Shakespeare. Communications, Administrative and regulatory, Federal civil litigation. Address: 1300 New York Ave NE Ste 200E Washington DC 20002-1621

**HIRSBERG, DAVID M.,** lawyer; b. Clarksdale, Miss., Nov. 4, 1962; s. George M. and Goldie S. Hirsberg. Student, Harvard U.; BS in Acctg., U. Ala., Tuscaloosa, 1984; JD, Washington and Lee U., 1987; LLM in Taxation, NYU, 1988. Bar: Ohio 1988, Ga. 1992, U.S. Ct. Appeals (6th cir.) 1988. Assoc. Dinsmore & Shohl, Cin., 1988-89, Katz, Teller, brant & Hild, Cin., 1989-92; ptnr., head tax group Hunter, MacLean, Exley & Dunn, Savannah, Ga., 1992—; spkr. on estate planning. Mem. fin. counseling svcs. com. Meml. Found., 1995—. Mem. ABA (tax sect.), Savannah Bar Assn., Savannah Estate Planning Coun., Am. Acad. Estate Planning Attys. Avocations: tennis, skiing. Estate planning, General corporate. Office: Hunter MacLean et al PO box 9848 200 E Saint Julian St Savannah GA 31412-2700

**HIRSCH, ALAN SETH,** lawyer; b. Miami Beach, Fla., May 22, 1950; s. Morse Sable and Belle (Falk) H.; m. Marsha Fay Yellin, June 9, 1974; children: Melanie, Sara. BA, U. N.C., 1971; JD, Columbia U., 1974; program for sr. mgrs. in govt. John F. Kennedy Sch. Govt. Harvard U., 1984. Bar: N.C. 1974, U.S. Dist. Ct. (ea., we. and mid. dists.) N.C. 1975, U.S. Ct. Appeals (4th cir.) 1975. Assoc. atty. gen. N.C. Dept. Justice, Raleigh, 1974-75, asst. atty. gen., 1976—, chief counsel consumer protection div., 1976-85, environ. protection div., 1985-89, counsel to Sec. of State, N.C., 1989—; adj. prof. polit. sci. N.C. State U., Raleigh, 1977-80, U. N.C., 1989—. Mem. N.C. Bar Assn., Nat. Assn. Attys. Gen. (chmn. coop. enforcement com. 1982-84). Democrat. Jewish. Home: 6 Lacrosse Pl Chapel Hill NC 27514-8664 Office: NC Dept Justice PO Box 629 Raleigh NC 27602-0629

**HIRSCH, BARRY,** lawyer; b. N.Y.C., Mar. 19, 1933; s. Emanuel M. and Minnie (Levenson) H.; m. Myra Seiden, June 13, 1963; children—Victor Terry II, Neil Charles Seiden, Nancy Elizabeth. BSBA, U. Mo., 1954; J.D., U. Mich., 1959; LL.M., N.Y. U., 1964. Bar: N.Y. bar 1960. Assoc., then partner firm Seligson & Morris, N.Y.C., 1960-69; v.p., sec., gen. counsel dir. B.T.B. Corp., 1969-71; v.p., sec., gen. counsel Loews Corp. (and subsidiaries), 1971-86, sr. v.p., sec., gen. counsel, 1986—; bds. dirs. Neuberger and Berman Fixed Income Funds. Served to 1st lt. AUS, 1954-56. Mem. ABA, Assn. of Bar of City of N.Y., N.Y. State Bar Assn., Zeta Beta Tau, Phi Delta Phi. Securities, Finance, General corporate. Home: 1010 5th Ave New York NY 10028-0130 Office: Loews Corp 667 Madison Ave Fl 7 New York NY 10021-8087

**HIRSCH, DANIEL,** lawyer; b. Bklyn., Feb. 26, 1940; s. Burton and Lee (Roller) H.; m. Trina Lutter, July 15, 1965 (div.); children: Jessica Elyse, Jeremy Bram. BS, U. Pa., 1960; JD, Columbia U., 1963. Bar: N.Y. 1964. Assoc. Carter Ledyard & Milburn, N.Y.C., 1964-68; pvt. practice N.Y.C., 1968-74; prin. Jones, Hirsch, Connors & Bull, P.C., N.Y.C., 1974—; dir. Loral Orion. Lt. USNR, 1965-75. Mem. N.Y. State Bar Assn., Assn. of Bar of City of N.Y., Fedn. Ins. and Corp. Counsel, Univ. Club. General corporate, Insurance, Private international. Office: Jones Hirsch Connors & Bull 101 E 52nd St Fl 22 New York NY 10022-6061

**HIRSCH, DAVID L.,** lawyer, corporate executive. BA, Pomona Coll., 1959; JD, U. Calif., Berkeley, 1962. Bar: Calif. 1963. V.p. Masco Tech./NI Industries, Inc., Taylor, Mich., 1966—; v.p. mem. commn. on Govt. Procurement for U.S. Congress, 1971. Mem. editorial bd. Bur. Nat. Affairs' Fed. Contracts Report. Fellow Am. Bar Found.; mem. ABA (life fellow of fellows, chair emerging issues com. sect. pub. contract law, sec. pub. contract law sect. 1977-78, mem. council 1978-80, chmn. 1981-82), Calif. Bar (bd. advisors pub. law sect.), Los Angeles County Bar Assn., Fed. Bar Assn., Nat. Contract Mgmt. Assn. (nat. bd. advisors), Fin. Exec. Inst. (legal advisor com. on govt. bus.). Contracts commercial, Government contracts and claims. Office: Masco Tech Corp/NI Industries Inc 21001 Van Born Rd Taylor MI 48180-1340

**HIRSCH, JEROME S.,** lawyer; b. N.Y.C., 1948. BA in Econs., SUNY, Binghamton, 1970; JD, Fordham U., 1974. Bar: N.Y. Assoc. Skadden, Arps, Slate, Meagher & Flom, N.Y.C., 1974-81, ptnr., 1982—. Mem. ABA (class action and derivative lawsuits subcom. 1982-85, corp. counsel com., co-chmn. subcom. on settlement techniques), N.Y. State Bar Assn., Assn. of Bar of City of N.Y. Securities, Federal civil litigation, State civil litigation. Office: Skadden Arps Slate Meagher & Flom 919 3rd Ave New York NY 10022-3902

**HIRSCH, MELISSA,** lawyer; b. Midland, Tex., Mar. 10, 1952; d. Nolan and Lila Sue (Caruthers) H. BA, Austin Coll., Sherman Tex., 1975; JD, St. Mary's U., San Antonio, 1978. Bar: Tex. 1980, U.S. Dist. Ct. (we. and no. dists.) Tex. 1980, U.S. Ct. Claims 1994, U.S. Ct. Appeals (5th cir.) 1994, U.S. Supreme Ct. 1994. Assoc. Hirsch & Bartley, Odessa, Tex., 1979-80; pvt. practice, Odessa, 1980—; chmn. Tex. Bd. Pvt. Investigators, 1993-97; spkr. U. Houston Law Sch., 1995, U. Tex. Law Sch., 1996-98. Mem. Odessa City Coun., 1983-87. Mem. State Bar Tex. (spkr. 1990-98, labor and employment law seminar 1990-98). Office: 201 E 4th St Odessa TX 79761-5178

**HIRSCH, MICHAEL,** lawyer; b. Hamilton, Ohio, Aug. 27, 1949. BA, Duke U., 1971; JD, George Washington U., 1974. Atty. advisor U.S. Gen. Acctg. Office, Washington, 1974-76, Dept. Housing and Urban Devel., Washington, 1976-79; atty. advisor Fed. Emergency Mgmt. Agy., Washington, 1979-90, assoc. gen. counsel, 1991-96, dep. gen. counsel, 1997—. Office: Fed Emergency Mgmt Agy 500 C St SW Ste 840 Washington DC 20472-0001

**HIRSCH, MILTON CHARLES,** lawyer; b. Chgo., Sept. 10, 1952; s. Charles Ira and Beverly Ruth (Kelner) H.; m. Ilene Lonnie Schreer, Feb. 16, 1986. BA, U. Calif., San Diego, 1974; MS, DePaul U., 1979; JD, Georgetown U., 1982. Bar: Fla. 1982, U.S. Dist. Ct. (so., mid. dists.) Fla. 1983, U.S. Dist. Ct. (no. dist.) Fla. 1985, U.S. Ct. Appeals (5th and 11th cirs.) 1983, U.S. Tax Ct. 1983, U.S. Ct. Claims 1983, U.S. Supreme Ct. 1988. Acct. Arthur Young & Co., CPAs, Chgo., 1977-79; asst. state atty. Office State Atty., Miami, Fla., 1982-84; assoc. Finley, Kumble, Wagner, Heine, Underberg, Manley et al, Miami, 1985-87; pvt. practice Miami, 1987—; adj. prof. Nova U. Law Sch., Ft. Lauderdale, Fla., 1988, 94, 95. Author: Florida Criminal Trial Procedure; contbg. editor Jour. Nat. Assn. Criminal Def. Attys., 1987—; contbr. articles to profl. jours. Mem. ABA (litigation sect.), Nat. Assn. Criminal Def. Lawyers, Fla. Bar Assn.), Fla. Criminal Def. Attys. Assn. (former pres., Presdl. award for Disting. Svc. 1987-88). Criminal, General practice. Office: 9130 S Dadeland Blvd Ste 1504 Miami FL 33156-7850

**HIRSCH, RICHARD GARY,** lawyer; b. L.A., June 15, 1940; s. Charles and Sylvia (Leopold) H.; m. Claire Renee Recsei, Mar. 25, 1967; 1 child, Nicole Denise. BA, UCLA, 1961; JD, U. Calif., Berkeley, 1965. Bar: Calif. 1967, U.S. Dist. Ct. (ctrl. dist.) Calif. 1967, U.S. Supreme Ct. 1972, U.S. Ct. Appeals (9th cir.) 1989, U.S. Dist. Ct. (ea. dist.) Calif. 1991. Dep. dist. atty. L.A. Dist. Atty.'s Office, 1967-71; ptnr. Nasatir, Hirsch & Podberesky, Santa Monica, Calif., 1971—; commr. Calif. Coun. Criminal Justice, 1977-81; mem. Spl. Com. on Cts. in the Media/Judicial Coun. Calif., 1979. Co-author: California Criminal Law Procedings/Practice, 1986, 2d edit. 1994. Pres. bd. trustees Santa Monica Mus. Art, 1984-91; chmn. Greek Theatre Adv. Com., L.A., 1976-79; mem. L.A. Olympic Organizing Com., 1981-84; bd. dirs. Ocean Park Cmty. Ctr., 1995—, bd. chair, 1997—. Recipient Spl. Merit Resolution, L.A. City Coun., 1984, Criminal Def. Atty. of Yr. award Century City Bar Assn., 1996. Fellow Am. Bd. Criminal Lawyers (bd. dirs., v.p. 1998—); mem. Calif. Attys. Criminal Justice (pres. 1987, bd. trustees), Criminal Cts. Bar Assn. (pres. 1981, Spl. Merit award 1988), L.A. County Bar Assn. (Criminal Def. Atty. of Yr. 1999), Santa Monica C. of C. (bd. dirs.

1995-97). Avocations: cooking, reading, community service. Criminal. Office: Nasatir Hirsch Podberesky 2115 Main St Santa Monica CA 90405-2215

**HIRSCHEL, REBECCA L.,** lawyer; b. Spokane, Wash.; d. Delbert Ray and Carol Ann H.; m. Erich Alan Prahl, Jan. 12, 1991. BA, Gonzaga U., 1986, JD, 1990. Bar: Wash. 1990, U.S. Dist. Ct. (ea. dist.) Wash. 1992. Assoc. Miller Law Office, Cheney, Wash., 1990; asst. city prosecutor City of Cheney, Wash., 1990; asst. pub. defender City of Spokane, Wash., 1991—. Mem. Wash. Defender Assn., Spokane Ski Club, Mt. Spokane Zoo. Democrat. Roman Catholic. Avocations: art, music, golf. Office: City of Spokane Public Defender Office 824 N Monroe St Spokane WA 99201-2110

**HIRSCHFELD, MICHAEL,** lawyer; b. Bronx, N.Y., July 4, 1950; s. Lawrence John and Ida (Miller) H.; m. Heidi P. Greenspan, June 17, 1973; children: Adam Lawrence, Philip Richard. BEE summa cum laude, CCNY, 1972; JD cum laude, U. Pa., 1975; LLM in Taxation, NYU, 1980. Bar: N.Y. 1976, U.S. Dist. Ct. (so. and ea. dists.) N.Y. 1976, U.S. Tax Ct. 1978. Assoc. Shearman and Sterling, N.Y.C., 1975-80, Roberts and Holland, N.Y.C., 1980-83; assoc. Carro, Spanbock, Kaster and Cuiffo, N.Y.C., 1983-85, ptnr., 1985-88; ptnr. Winstown & Strawn, N.Y.C., 1988-98, Dechert, Price & Rhoads, N.Y.C., 1998—; lectr. NYU, Assn. of Bar of City of New York, ABA, ALI-ABA, PLI, Syracuse U., U. Tex., Tulane U., Georgetown U.; chmn. NYU Inst. Real Estate Taxation; co-chmn. 49th, 50th, 52d, 53d and 54th ann. Fed. Income Taxation Confs.; 11th-21st ann. NYU Confs. on Fed. Taxation of Real Estate Taxations: mem. nat. edn. bd., Business Entities (RIA publ.) Real Estate Tax Digest, Jour. of Internat. Tax, Tax. Mgmt. Real Estate Jour.; mem. adv. bd. Tax Mgmt. Real Estate, Inst. Fed. Tax. Co-author: Real Estate Limited Partnerships, 3rd edit., 1991; bd. editors Real Estate Tax Digest, BNA Tax Mgmt.; editl. adv. bd. NYU Real Estate Adv. Bd. Mem. ABA (lectr. taxation sect., mem. coun. 1997—, co-chmn. govt. subcom. 1992-94, chmn. govt. subcom. 1994-97, chmn. real estate tax problems com. 1989-91, chmn. syndications subcom. 1985-87, vice chmn. ACRS depreciation recapture subcom. 1983-85, task force pres.'s tax reform proposals minimum tax subcom. 1985-86, vice chmn. gov. submission com. 1992-95), Am. Law Inst. (lectr.), N.Y. State Bar Assn. (lectr., co-chmn. coms. on income from real property tax sect. 1988-91, co-chmn. com. on preferences and minimum tax 1991-92, co-chmn. com. in individuals 1992-93, co-chmn. com. U.S. activities of fgn. taxpayers 1993-96, co-chmn. com. on real property, 1996-98, co-chmn. tax accts. 1998—, exec. com. 1987—, com. on internat. members), Assn. of Bar of City of N.Y. (mem. com. on internat. transactions), Internat. Tax Assn., Am. Coll. Tax Counsel. Avocation: music (drum). Fax: (212) 698-3599. E-mail: Mhirschf@Dechert.com. Corporate taxation, Personal income taxation, Taxation, general. Office: Dechert Price & Rhoads 30 Rockefeller Plz Fl 22 New York NY 10112-2200

**HIRSCHHORN, HERBERT HERMAN,** lawyer; b. Bklyn., Apr. 13, 1909; s. Bernard and Rae (Greenberg) H.; m. Rose Kopal, July 10, 1968. BA, NYU, 1930, JD, 1932, Dr. Jud. Sci., 1934, MA, 1937. Bar: N.Y. 1934, U.S. Supreme Ct. 1959, U.S. Dist. Ct. (so. and ea. dists.) N.Y. 1962, U.S. Dist. Ct. (we. dist.) N.Y. 1964, U.S. Ct. Appeals (2d cir.) 1966. Assoc. Gair Gair Conason Steigman & Mackauf and predecessor firms, N.Y.C., 1932—; dir. emeritus NYU Alumni Fedn. Recipient Alumni Meritorious Svc. award NYU, 1982, Disting. Svc. award NYU and Washington Sq. Coll., 1992, Judge Edward Weinfeld award NYU Law Ctr., 1993; inscribed on the Wall of Honor, NYU Sch. of Law 1996. Mem. ABA, N.Y. State Bar Assn., N.Y. County Lawyers Assn., Am. Judicature Soc., Assn. Trial Lawyers Am., Soc. Med. Jurisprudence, Met. Women's Bar Assn., Internat. Assn. Jewish Lawyers and Jurists, N.Y. State Trial Lawyers Assn. (dir. 1954-80, dir. emeritus 1982—). Personal injury. Home: 40 Central Park S New York NY 10019-1633 Office: Gair Gair Conason Steigman & Mackauf 80 Pine St Fl 34 New York NY 10005-1768

**HIRSCHKLAU, MORTON,** lawyer; b. N.Y.C., Mar. 9, 1932; s. Joseph I. and Sylvia (Kleiner) H.; m. Martha R. Silverstein, June 21, 1953; children: Mitchell L., Deborah E. Hirschklau Loeber, Susan I. AB, Syracuse U., 1953, JD, 1959. Bar: N.Y. 1959, N.J. 1960, U.S. Supreme Ct. 1963, U.S. Ct. Appeals (3d cir.) 1982. Law sec. Superior Ct. N.J., Paterson, 1959-60; assoc. Theodore D. Rosenberg, Esquire, Paterson, 1960-63; ptnr. Hirschklau, Wasserman & Welch, Oakland, N.J., 1963-73; pvt. practice Fair Lawn, N.J., 1973-76; ptnr. Hirschklau, Feitlin & Trawinski, Fair Lawn, 1976-84, Muscarella, Hirschklau, Bochet, Feitlin, Trawinski & Edwards, Fair Lawn, 1984-90, Karas, Kilstein, Hirschklau, Feitlin & Youngman, Fair Lawn, 1990-99, Morton Hirschklau, Esq. and Assocs., 1999—; planning bd. atty. Borough of Fair Lawn, 1961-65, Borough atty., 1965, 81-83; planning bd. atty., Borough of Emerson, 1967-71, zoning bd. atty., 1971-83; zoning bd. atty. Village of Ridgewood, 1977—, Borough of Saddle River, 1996—; spl. counsel Bergen County Park Commn., Paramus, N.J., 1987-88; chmn. N.J. Supreme Ct. Com. on Ethics, 1987-88. Bd. dirs., atty. Fair Lawn Mental Health Ctr., 1965—; bd. dirs., past pres. Opportunity Ctr., Inc., Fair Lawn; pres. Fair Lawn Clean Govt. Assn., 1968-70. Lt. USNR, 1953-56. Mem. N.J. Bar Assn., Bergen County Bar Assn. (chmn. real estate com.), Fair Lawn Rotary Club (past pres.). Avocations: golf, tennis, collecting porcelains. Land use and zoning (including planning), Real property, State and local taxation. Office: 9-10 Saddle River Rd Fair Lawn NJ 07410-5721

**HIRSCHKOP, PHILIP JAY,** lawyer, educator; b. Bklyn., May 14, 1936; s. Abraham and Frances (Krumholz) H.; children: Jacqueline, Jon David, Adam Abraham. AB, Columbia Coll., 1960; BS in Engring., Columbia U., 1961; JD, Georgetown U., 1964. Bar: Va. 1964, U.S. Dist. Ct. (ea. and we. dists.) Va. 1964, U.S. Dist. Ct. D.C. 1964, U.S. Ct. Mil. Appeals 1964, U.S. Ct. Appeals (4th and D.C. cirs.) 1965, U.S. Supreme 1967, U.S. Ct. Claims 1969, U.S. Dist. Ct. (no. dist.) Tex. 1973, U.S. Ct. Appeals (5th cir.) 1973, U.S. Tax Ct. 1974, U.S Ct. Appeals (11th cir.), 1981, N.Y., 1982, U.S. Dist. Ct. (ea. dist.) N.C., U.S. Dist. Ct. D.C. Patent examiner U.S. Patent Office, Washington, 1961-63; legis. asst. congressman Richard Ichord, Washington, 1964; pvt. practice Alexandria, Va., 1964—; adj. prof. law Georgetown U., Washington, 1969-75; chair steering com. Nat. Prison Project, Washington, 1975—; spkr. in field. Contbr. articles to profl. jours. Nat. bd. dirs. ACLU, N.Y.C., 1966-86. With Spl. Forces, U.S. Army, 1954-56. Fellow Va. Law Found.; mem. ATLA (state committeeman), PETA (gen. counsel), NCIA (dir., counsel), Va. Bar Assn. (coun. 1979-85), Alexandria Bar Assn., Trial Lawyers for Pub. Justice (bd dirs., founder 1986—), Va. State Bar Coun., Law Students Civil Rights Rsch. Coun. General civil litigation, Constitutional, Personal injury. Office: Hirschkop & Assocs PC 108 N Columbus St Alexandria VA 22314-3013

**HIRSCHMAN, SHERMAN JOSEPH,** lawyer, educator; b. Detroit, May 11, 1935; s. Samuel and Anna (Maxmen) H.; m. Audrey Hecker, 1959; children: Samuel, Shari. BS, Wayne State U., 1956, JD, 1959, LLM, 1968, D in Bus. Adminstrn., Nova Southeastern U., 1996. Bar: Mich. 1959, Fla. 1983; CPA, Mich., Fla.; cert. tax lawyer, Fla. Pvt. practice, Mich., 1959—; instr. comml. law Detroit Coll. Bus., 1971—; adj. instr. Nova Southeastern U., 1997—. With USAR, 1959-62. Mem. Mich. Bar Assn., Fla. Bar Assn., Am. Arbitration Assn., Am. Assn. CPA Attys. Corporate taxation, Personal income taxation, Pension, profit-sharing, and employee benefits. Office: 340 Woodlake Wynde Oldsmar FL 34677-2190

**HIRSCHSON, LINDA BENJAMIN,** lawyer; b. N.Y.C., Jan. 21, 1941; d. Philip David and Ruth (Levy) Benjamin; m. Albert M. Hirschson, Dec. 22, 1963; children: Jay Philip, Pamela Ellen. AB, Barnard Coll., 1962; JD, Columbia U., 1965; LLM in Taxation, NYU, 1973. Bar: N.Y. 1965, U.S. Tax Ct. 1975, U.S. Dist. Ct. (so. and ea. dists. N.Y. 1976. Assoc. Kaye, Scholer, et. al., N.Y.C., 1965-70; teaching fellow NYU Law Sch., N.Y.C., 1970-73; assoc. prof. Hofstra Law Sch., Hempstead, N.Y., 1974-77; assoc. Gilbert Segall and Young, N.Y.C., 1977-79, ptnr., 1979-93; ptnr. Katten, Muchin & Zavis, N.Y.C., 1994-96, Parson & Brown, N.Y.C., 1996-98; shareholder Greenberg Traurig, N.Y.C., 1998—. Contbg. editor Rev. of Taxation/Individual jour., 1982-89, editor-in-chief, 1976-79, (book chpt.) Estate and Gift Tax After ERTA, 1982; chmn. CLE Satellite Network, Current Estate Planning, 1990. Treas. Friends of Joffrey Ballet, N.Y. chpt., 1988-91; treas., bd. dirs. Barnard Bus. and Profl. Women, N.Y.C., 1982-86; trustee The Calhoun Sch., N.Y.C., 1986-92; mem. EPTL Adv. Com. to N.Y. State Legislature, 1990-94, 97—, advisor, 1997. Named Outstanding Alumna The Calhoun Sch., 1985. Fellow Am. Coll. Trust and Estate Counsel (chmn. transfer tax com. 1998—); mem. ABA (chmn. marital deduction com. real property, probate and trust sect. 1996—, co-chmn. estate and gift tax com. of tax sect., 1981-89), N.Y. State Bar Assn. (chmn. taxation com. of tax sect. 1986-89, chair trusts and estates law sect. 1996), Assn. Bar City N.Y. (chmn. Mortimer Hess lectr. com. 1992-94, estate and gift tax com. 1989-92, trustee, bd. dirs. Assn. Bar City N.Y. Fund). Avocations: skiing, tennis, jogging. Estate planning, Estate taxation, Probate. Home: 501 E 79th St New York NY 10021-0735 Office: Greenberg Traurig 200 Park Ave Fl 14 New York NY 10166-1400

**HIRSH, ROBERT JOEL,** lawyer; b. Shamokin, Pa., May 18, 1935; s. David and Rose (Koplansky) H.; children: Christine, Jonathan, Thomas. BS, U. Ariz., 1960, LLB, 1964. Bar: Ariz. 1964, U.S. Dist. Ct. Ariz. 1964, U.S. Ct. Appeals (9th cir.) 1968, U.S. Supreme Ct. 1971; cert. criminal specialist, State Bar of Ariz. Ptnr. firm Messing Hirsh & Franklin, Tucson, 1969-72, Hirsh & Hooker, Tucson, 1972-73, Hirsh, Shiner & Walker, Tucson, 1973-77, Hirsh & Bayles, Tucson, 1977-82, Hirsh & Fines, P.C., Tucson, 1982-84, Hirsh, Sherick & Murphy, P.C., 1985-90, Hirsh & Sherick, P.C., 1990-91, Hirsh, Davis, Walker & Piccarreta, P.C., 1991-95, Hirsh, Davis & Piccarreta, D.C., 1995-97, Hirsh, Byorgaard & Rogers, P.L.C., 1998—. Mem. ABA, State Bar Ariz., Ariz. Attys. for Criminal Justice (founder, pres. 1990), 9th Cir. Jud. Conf. (del. 1986-88), Ariz. Supreme Ct. Commn. on Courts (task force mem.), Pima County Bar Assn. Ariz. State Bar Assn., Nat. Assn. Criminal Def. Lawyers, Calif. Attys. for Criminal Justice, Am. Bd. Criminal Lawyers, Am. Coll. Trial Lawyers. Criminal. Office: 177 N Church Ave Ste 700 Tucson AZ 85701-1119

**HIRSHFIELD, STUART,** lawyer; b. N.Y.C., Dec. 31, 1941; s. William Louis and Anne (Frank) H.; m. Susanne Drucker, Jan. 22, 1967; children: Matthew S., Edward R. BA, Syracuse U., 1963, JD, 1966. Bar: N.Y. 1966, U.S. Dist. Ct. (so. and ea. dists.) N.Y. 1968, U.S. Ct. Appeals (2nd cir.) 1968. Assoc. Krauss & Krauss, N.Y.C., 1966-67; atty. N.Y. Cen. RR, N.Y.C., 1967-69; assoc. Blum, Haimoff, Gersen, Lipson & Szabad, N.Y.C., 1969; atty. CIT Fin., N.Y.C., 1970-72; assoc. Shea & Gould, N.Y.C., 1972-77, ptnr., 1977-88; ptnr., chmn. bankruptcy practice group Dewey Ballantine, N.Y.C., 1988—; Bd. dirs. 565 Tenants Corp. Contbr. Asset Based Financing--A Transactional Guide, 1985. Assn. atty. Allenwood Civic Assn., Great Neck, N.Y., 1984; bd. visitors Syracuse U. Coll. Law, 1990—, exec. com., 1991-96. With USAR, 1966-72. Fellow Am. Coll. Bankruptcy (2d cir. admissions coun. 1994—, chair 1998—, bd. regents 1998—), Am. Bar Found.; mem. ABA (com. on bankruptcy 1983—), N.Y. Bar Assn., Assn. Bar City N.Y. (corp. reogn. com. 1975-78, 82-85), Assn. Comml. Fin. Attys. (dir. 1980-93), Rockefeller Ctr. Club. Bankruptcy, Contracts commercial. Office: Dewey Ballantine 1301 Avenue Of The Americas New York NY 10019-6022

**HIRSHON, JACK THOMAS,** lawyer; b. L.A., July 25, 1931; s. Jack W. Hirshon and Dorothy Sanborn; m. Patricia Lee Boldt, Mar. 30, 1957; children: David, Susan, Lori, Thomas. BBA, UCLA, 1955; JD, Golden Gate Coll., 1962. Bar: Calif. 1963. Ins. adjuster, claim mgr. United Pacific Ins. Co., San Francisco, 1962-63; pvt. practice law Santa Clara County, 1963—. Planning commr. City of Cupertino, Calif., 1964-72. 1st lt. U.S. Army, 1955-57. Mem. Assn. Trial Lawyers Am., Calif. Trial Lawyers Assn., Santa Clara County Bar Assn., Santa Clara County Trial Lawyers Assn., Sunnyvale Bar Assn. (pres.), Kiwanis. Democrat. Roman Catholic. Avocations: golf, skiing, running, football, genealogy. Personal injury, Insurance. Office: 111 N Market St Ste 1040 San Jose CA 95113-1118

**HIRSHON, ROBERT EDWARD,** lawyer; b. Portland, Maine, Apr. 2, 1948; s. Selvin and Gladys (Wein) H.; m. Roberta Lynn Miller, Aug. 16, 1969; children: Todd, Sara, Jason, Miriam. BA, U. Mich., 1970, JD, 1973. Bar: Maine 1973, U.S. Dist. Ct. Maine 1973, U.S. Ct. Appeals (1st cir.) 1977. Shareholder Drummond, Woodsum & MacMahon P.A., Portland, 1973—; adj. prof. law U. Maine Law Sch. Contbr. articles to profl. jours. Chairperson Breakwater Sch Bd., Portland, 1978-85; mem. Zoning Bd. Appeals, Cape Elizabeth, Maine, 1983-90. Mem. ABA (mem. Ho. of Dels. 1992—, chair standing com. lawyers pub. svc. responsibility 1990-93, chair steering com. pro bono ctr. 1991-96, chair torts and ins. practice sect. 1996-97, chair standing com. on membership 1997—), Maine Bar Assn. (pres. 1986, chair continuing legal edn. com. 1975-83), Cumberland County Bar Assn., Maine Bar Found. (pres. 1990). Avocations: reading, tennis, skiing. General civil litigation, Banking, Insurance. Home: 2 Oakhurst Rd Cape Elizabeth ME 04107-1406 Office: Drummond Woodsum & MacMahon PO Box 9781 Portland ME 04104-5081

**HIRSHOWITZ, MELVIN STEPHEN,** lawyer; b. N.Y.C., Dec. 11, 1938; s. Samuel Albert and Lillian Rose (Minkow) H.; m. Susan Bonnie Brezel, June 19, 1983; children: Lauren Allison, Emily Sara. BA with hons., Cornell U., 1960; LLB cum laude, Harvard U., 1963; MA in Biology, CUNY, 1977. Bar: N.Y. 1963, N.J. 1987, U.S. Dist. Ct. (so. dist.) N.Y. 1969, (ea. dist.) N.Y. 1977, N.J. 1993, U.S. Ct. Appeals (2d cir.) 1978, U.S. Supreme Ct. 1994. Assoc. atty. SEC, N.Y.C., 1963-65; sole practitioner Melvin Hirshowitz Law Office, N.Y.C., 1966-76, 87--; of counsel Hyman Bravin Law Offices, N.Y.C., 1976-87. Author: (manual) Proof of an Over the Counter Manipulation, 1964. Vice chmn. N.Y. Libertarian Party, 1970-72, candidate for surrogate ct. judge and ct. of appeals judge. Mem. N.Y. County Lawyers Assn. (com. on profl. ethics 1986-92, com. fed. legislation 1986-88, com. on profl. discipline 1993—), Assn. of Bar of City of N.Y. (com. on the civil ct. 1986-89), N.Y. State Bar Assn., Harvard Club of N.Y.C., Phi Beta Kappa, Pi Delta Epsilon. Republican. Jewish. Avocations: bird watching, art, tennis. State civil litigation, General civil litigation, Probate. Office: 630 3rd Ave New York NY 10017-6705

**HIRST, RICHARD B.,** lawyer. Sr. v.p., gen. counsel Northwest Airlines, 1990-94, sr. v.p. corp. affairs, 1994—. Office: Northwest Airlines Inc 5101 Northwest Dr Saint Paul MN 55111-3027*

**HITCHCOCK, BION EARL,** lawyer; b. Muscatine, Iowa, Oct. 9, 1942; s. Stewart Edward and Arlene Ruth (Eichelberger) H. BSEE, Iowa State U., 1965; JD, U. Iowa, 1968. Bar: Iowa 1968, Okla. 1968, U.S. Ct. Customs and Patent Appeals 1973, U.S. Ct. Appeals (fed. cir.) 1982. Attyl Phillips Petroleum Co., Bartlesville, Okla., 1968-69, 73-76; mgr. licensing Phillips Petroleum Co. Europe-Africa, Brussels, 1977-80; sr. patent counsel Phillips Petroleum Co., Bartlesville, 1980-84, assoc. gen. patent counsel, 1984—. Bd. dirs. Bartlesville Symphony Orch., 1973-77, 80-91, pres., 1975-77, 82-84; bd. dirs. Bartlesville Allied Arts and Humanities Coun., 1976-77, 80-86, 1st v.p., 1982-83; mem. Govt. and Fin. Goals for Bartlesville Com., 1974-75; bd. dirs. Bartlesville Cmty. Concert Assn., 1982-90, Okla. Assn. Symphony Orchs., 1983-88. Lt. JAGC, USN, 1969-73. Mem. ABA, Okla. Bar Assn. (dir. patent trademark and copyright sect. 1980-86, sec. 1982-83, vice chmn. 1983-84, chmn. 1984-85), Iowa Bar Assn., Washington County Bar Assn. (pres. 1981-82), Am. Intellectual Property Law Assn., Am. Judicature Soc., Am. Corp. Counsel Assn., Fed. Cir. Bar Assn., Licensing Execs. Soc., Eta Kappa Nu. Patent, Private international, Trademark and copyright. Home: 1227 Misty Lake Ct Sugar Land TX 77478-5613 Office: Phillips Petroleum Co 236 Plb Bartlesville OK 74004-0001

**HITE, DAVID L.,** lawyer; b. Thornville, Ohio, Apr. 30, 1916; s. Frank C. Hite and Mary Pannabaker; m. Maxine Witherbee, July 15, 1943; 1 child, Diane. BS, Kent Sate U., 1938; JD, Capital U., 1946. Neuropsychiat. fellow Psychology Ct. Neuropsychiat. Inst., Hartford, Conn., 1939; pvt. practice Utica and Newark, Ohio, 1946—. Capt. OSS, 1942-46. Mem. ABA (pub. utilities sect., small trusts and estate com., adminstrn. and distbrn. of estates com.), Ohio Bar Ass., Cleve. Bar Assn., Licking Bar Assn. Public utilities, Probate. Office: Hite & Hite 964 N 21st St Ste D Newark OH 43055-7230

**HITE, RICHARD C.,** lawyer; b. Iola, Kans., Sept. 13, 1928; s. Cecil Clifford and E. Marie (Harlan) H.; m. Edith Olson Davies, Dec. 28, 1994; children: Elizabeth, Richard, Robert. BS, Kans. U., 1950; LLB, Washburn U., 1953. Bar: Kans. 1953, U.S. Dist. Ct. Kans. 1953, U.S. Ct. Appeals (10th cir.) 1960. Claims atty. USF&G Co., Wichita, Kans., 1956-59; ptnr. Kahrs, Nelson, Fanning, Hite & Kellogg, Wichita, 1960—. Bd. dirs. Via Christi Regional Med. Ctr., Wichita, 1995—, chmn., 1995-98; bd. dirs. St. Francis Regional Med. Ctr., Wichita, 1982-93, chmn. 1994—, United Way of the Plains, Wichita, 1968-86, pres 1980; bd. dirs. Preferred Health Sys., 1998—. Fellow Am. Coll. Trial Lawyers (state chmn. 1987-88), Am. Bar Found.; mem. ABA (state del. 1986-95), Kans. Bar Assn. (gov. 1986-95, Outstanding Svc. award 1972, 86, Phil Lewis medal of Disting., 1995), Nat. Conf. Commrs. on Uniform State Laws (commr., exec. com. 1985-97, pres. 1993-95), Crestview Country Club (pres. 1977). Republican. Congregationalist. Avocation: golf. General civil litigation. Home: 1440 N Gatewood St Apt 26 Wichita KS 67206-1253 Office: Kahrs Nelson Fanning Hite & Kellogg 200 W Douglas Ave Ste 630 Wichita KS 67202-3089

**HITES, EARLE FLOYD,** lawyer; b. Indpls., Oct. 18, 1947; s. Earle F. and Era L. Hites; m. Katherine Sanders, Aug. 23, 1969; children: Kevin, Sarah. BS, Ind. U., 1969; JD, Valparaiso U., 1972. Bar: Ind. 1972, U.S. Dist. Ct. (no. and so. dists.) Ind. 1972, U.S. Ct. Appeals 1975. Assoc. Hodges & Davis, P.C., Merrillville, Ind., 1972—. Mem. editl. bd. Valparaiso U. Law Rev., 1971-72. Past pres., bd. dirs. Vis. Nurse Assn. Porter County, Ind., Valparaiso, 1985-88, Home Health Svcs. Porter County, Ind., Valparaiso, 1985-88. Capt. USAR, 1969-79. Fellow Ind. Bar Found., 1989. Mem. ABA, Ind. State Bar Assn., Am. Acad. Hosp. Attys., Nat. Health Lawyers Assocs., Lake County Bar Assn., Rotary (past pres., bd. dirs. Merrillville chpt. 1980-81). Avocations: golfing, skiing. Health, General corporate, Real property. Office: Hodges & Davis PC 8700 Broadway Merrillville IN 46410-7036

**HITESMAN, DARCY L.,** lawyer; b. St. Paul, Sept. 11, 1962; d. Donald Joel and Kathryn Corrine (White) H.; m. Mark Valdmar Steffenson, Sept. 5, 1987. BA summa cum laude, Coe Coll., 1984; JD cum laude, U. Minn., 1987. Bar: Minn., U.S. Dist. Ct. Minn. Atty. Lefevere, Lefler, Kennedy, O'Briwn & Drawz, Mpls., 1987-88, Felhaber, Larson, Fenlon & Vogt, Mpls., 1989-90, Doherty, Rumble & Butler, P.A., Mpls., 1990-95, 96—, Briggs and Morgan, Mpls., 1995-96; presenter in field, various orgns. including Minn. Inst. Legal Edn., Minn. Counties Ins. Trust, Workers' Compensation Inst., others. Contbg. editor: 401(k) Plans: A Comprehensive Guide, 1993; author Minn. Rules Part 7190.0100-7190.0108, Household Labor Compensation; contbr. articles to various jours. and newsletters. Mem. Met. Airports Commn., chair affirmative action com.; adv. bd. Hennepin County Sheriff; vol. atty. Project Offstreets, 1998—, Maple Grove (Minn.) D.A.R.E. Ho., 1996; coord. Habitat for Humanity, 1997, 98; campaign mgr. Hennepin County Sheriff Patrick McGowan, 1994—; treas., exec. com. mem., North Hennepin C.C. Found., 1995-98; chair cmty. svc., Rotary Internat. Maple Grove, 1995-96; mem. Maple Grove Planning Comm., 1989-95; chair Mpls. Crisis Nursey, Once Upon a Saturday Night fundraiser, 1994-96; mem. Gov. Arne Carlson fundraising com., 1988-94; mem. regional rev. com., West-Metro area, 1988-90. Recipient Rising Star designation, Jour. Law & Politics, Mpls., 1998; recipient pres. award for Exceptional Svc. Above Self, Rotary, 1995-96, Dist. Gov.'s award for Cmty., Internat. Rotary, 1996. Mem. ABA (labor and employment law sect. 1995), Minn. State Bar Assn. (employee benefits sect. 1987, mock trial coach), Hennepin County Bar Assn. (tax law sect. 1987, former chair young lawyers sect., past mem. professionalism com.), TwinWest C. of C. (chair Karen Gibb's career change scholarship com. 1998, chair pres.'s task force regarding awards programs 1998, chair women's network com. 1997,chair Women of Achievement 1996, award 1995), Phi Beta Kappa, Delta Theta Phi. Fax: 612-677-4814. E-mail: hitesd@drblaw.com. Pension, profit-sharing, and employee benefits. Home: 12628 88th Ave N Maple Grove MN 55369-3044 Office: Doherty Rumble & Butler PA 3500 5th St Towers 30 7th St E Ste 2800 Saint Paul MN 55101-4999

**HITT, LEO N.,** lawyer, educator; b. Pitts., Oct. 20, 1955; s. Joe Stephen and Laurene (Lally) H.; m. Mary Elizabeth Wolf, Jan. 26, 1985; children: Nancy Anne, Elizabeth Lea. BA summa cum laude, U. Pitts., 1977, JD cum laude, 1980; LLM in Taxation, N.Y.U., 1983. Bar: Pa. 1980, U.S. Dist. Ct. (we. dist.) Pa. 1983, U.S. Tax Ct. 1981, U.S. Ct. Fed. Claims, 1997. Atty., tax sr. Kenneth Leventhal & Co., N.Y.C., 1980-81; atty., tax counsel Touche Ross & Co., Pitts., N.Y.C., 1981-83; assoc. Reed Smith Shaw & McClay, Pitts., 1983-88, ptnr., 1989—; adj. prof. tax. grad. sch. Robert Morris Coll., Pitts., 1983—, tax grad. sch., law sch. Duquesne U., Pitts., 1987—, sch. law U. Pitts., 1988—; seminar speaker various profl. orgns., Pitts., 1983—. Comments editor: U. Pitts. Law Review, 1979-80. Mem. ABA, Allegheny County Bar Assn., Pitts. Internat. Tax Soc., Allegheny Tax Soc., Pitts. Tax Club. Democrat. Roman Catholic. Avocations: alpine skiing, opera, gourmet cooking. Corporate taxation, Taxation, general. Home: 4209 Summervale Dr Murrysville PA 15668-3515 Office: Reed Smith Shaw & McClay 435 6th Ave Ste 2 Pittsburgh PA 15219-1886

**HITTER, JOSEPH IRA,** lawyer; b. Bklyn., Nov. 1, 1944; s. Harry H. and Annette (Fidler) H.; m. Ann Lois Jaffe, May 28, 1966; children: Jonathan C., Evan R. BS in Acctg., L.I. U., 1966; JD, St. John's U., 1969; LLM in Taxation, NYU, 1973. Bar: N.Y. 1970, U.S. Tax Ct. 1971, U.S. Supreme Ct. 1974. Tax specialist Arthur Young & Co., N.Y.C., 1969-72; tax atty. Pfizer, Inc., N.Y.C., 1972-73, supr. tax planning, 1973-74; sr. tax. specialist Mead Corp., Dayton, Ohio, 1974-76, mgr. fed. and internat. taxes, 1976-77, mgr. tax affairs, 1977-82, dir. taxation, 1982-98; v.p. Mead Corp., Dayton, 1999—; chmn. tax policy com. Am. Paper Inst., 1987—. Advisor YWCA, Dayton, 1985-87; dir. Hillel Acad., Dayton, 1981-83. Mem. ABA Tax Execs. Inst. (chpt. pres. 1984-85), N.Y. State Bar Assn., Dayton Bar Assn. Republican. Clubs: Meadowbrook Country, Dayton Racquet. Avocations: golf, tennis. Corporate taxation, Taxation, general, State and local taxation. Office: The Mead Corp Courthouse Plz NE Dayton OH 45402

**HITTLE, DAVID WILLIAM,** lawyer; b. Medford, Oreg., Apr. 28, 1947; s. Merritt Lyle and Mary Jane (Williams) H. BS, Oreg. State U., 1969; JD, Lewis & Clark Coll., 1974. Bar: Oregon 1974, U.S. Dist. Ct. Oreg. 1974, U.S. Ct. Appeals (9th cir.) 1976, U.S. Supreme Ct. 1977. Assoc. William Claussen PC, Salem, Oreg., 1974-75, Dye & Olson, Salem, 1975-79; ptnr. Olson, Hittle & Gardner, Salem, 1979-82, Callahan, Hittle & Gardner, Salem, 1982-89; now with Burt, Swanson, Lathen, Alexander & McCann, Salem, 1989—; instr. Linfield Coll., McMinnville, Oreg., 1982—, Coll. of Law Willamette U., Salem, 1987; mcpl. judge pro tem City of Salem, 1978-85; dist. judge pro tem Oreg., 1982—, cir. judge pro tem, 1990—; mem. Oreg. Supreme Ct. Disciplinary Bd., 1984-85. Mem. Oreg. Trial Lawyers Assn. (legis. chmn. workers compensation 1985, bd. dirs. 1988-92), Oreg. Bar Assn. (worker's compensation sect. sec. 1982, chmn. 1984, bd. govs. 1985-88, v.p. 1987-88, bd. dirs. civil rights sect. 1993—, contbr. author Bar Book on Worker's Compensation 1980, 84, Real Property 1985, Legislation 1985), Oreg. Law Found. (bd. dirs. 1988-92, pres. 1991), Marion County Bar (bd. dirs. 1984-86, v.p. 1987, pres. 1988), Oreg. Law Inst. (bd. dirs. 1988—), Oreg. Worker's Compensation Attys. (exec. com. 1978-88). Avocations: snow skiing, flying, mountain climbing, fly fishing. Workers' compensation, Personal injury. Home: 1580 Fairmount Ave S Salem OR 97302-5103 Office: Burt Swanson Lathen Alexander & McCann 388 State St Ste 1000 Salem OR 97301-3538

**HITTLE, KATHLEEN J.,** lawyer; b. New Orleans, Nov. 1, 1949; d. Ray L. and Vivian J. Tiemeier; m. Richard M. Hittle, Sept. 9, 1972; children: Timothy, Valerie, David, Mark. BA, U. Ill., 1971; JD, U. Chgo., 1974. Bar: Ill. 1974, U.S. Dist. Ct. (no. dist.) Ill. 1974. Lawyer Liberty Mutual Ins., Chgo., 1974-76, Pretzel & Stouffer Chartered, Chgo., 1976-80; pvt. practice law Naperville, Ill., 1980-96; ptnr. Glaser & Hittle, Naperville, 1996—. Leader, organizer Girl Scouts Am., Naperville, 1985-96; pack and troop com. mem. Boy Scouts Am., Naperville, 1986—. Mem. Ill. State Bar Assn., DuPage County Bar Assn. Lutheran. Family and matrimonial, General practice, Alternative dispute resolution. Office: Glaser & Hittle 15 W Jefferson Ave Naperville IL 60540-5375

**HITTLE, LARRY GLENN,** lawyer, electrical engineer; b. Seattle, Apr. 5, 1933; s. Oliver Glenn and Ruth Pauline (Stryker) H.; m. Betty Ann Davis, Jan. 30, 1954; children: Vanessa Ann Hittle Jordan, Gretchen Lynn. BSEE, Wash. State U., 1954; JD, Lewis & Clark Coll., 1968. Bar; Oreg. 1968, U.S. Dist. Ct. Oreg. 1968, U.S. Ct. Appeals (9th cir.) 1990; registered profl. engr., Wash. Flight test instrument engr. Douglas Aircraft Co., Santa Monica, Calif., 1954; elec. engr. Boeing Airplane Co., Seattle, 1956-57; engr. Lewis County Pub. Utility Dist. #1, Chehalis, Wash., 1957-64; contract engr. Bonneville Power Adminstrn., Portland, Oreg., 1964-67; head power contracts Bonneville Power Adminstrn., Portland, 1967-72; spl. asst. regional solicitor U.S. Dept. of Interior, Portland, 1972-78; asst. gen. counsel Bonneville Power Adminstrn., Portland, 1978-81; ptnr. Lindsay, Hort, Neil & Weigler, Portland, 1981-90, Ater Wynne Hewitt, Dodson & Skeritt, Portland, 1990-93, 96—; pvt. practice Portland, 1993-95; of counsel Ater Wynne LLP, Portland, 1996—. Served with U.S. Army, 1954-56. Mem. ABA,

Oreg. Bar Assn., Multnomah County Bar Assn., Mulnomah Club. Democrat. Public utilities.

**HITTNER, DAVID,** federal judge; b. Schenectady, N.Y., July 10, 1939; s. George and Sophie (Moskowitz) H.; children: Miriam, Susan, George. BS, NYU, 1961, JD, 1964. Bar: N.Y. 1964, Tex. 1967. Pvt. practice, Houston, 1967-78; judge Tex. 133d Dist. Ct., Houston, 1978-86, U.S. Dist. Ct. (so. dist.) Tex., Houston, 1986—. Author 2 books; contbr. articles to profl. jours. Mem. Nat. coun. Boy Scouts Am. Capt. inf., paratrooper U.S. Army, 1965-66. Recipient Silver Beaver award Boy Scouts Am., 1974, Silver Antelope award Boy Scouts Am., 1988, Samuel E. Gates award Am. Coll. Trial Lawyers. Mem. ABA (merit award), State Bar Tex. (Outstanding Lawyer in Tex. award), Houston Bar Assn. (president's and Dirs.' award), Am. Law Inst., Masons (33d degree). Office: US Courthouse 515 Rusk St Ste 8509 Houston TX 77002-2603

**HIX, ANDREA NOEL,** lawyer; b. Guantanamo Bay, Cuba, Dec. 11, 1969; d. James O'Fallon III and Ann Marie Hix. BS in Mktg., Okla. State U., 1991; JD, Oklahoma City U., 1995. Bar: Colo. 1996, U.S. Dist. Ct. Colo. 1997, U.S. Ct. Appeals (10 cir.) 1998. Assoc. Featherstone & Shea LLP, Denver, 1996-97, Berryhill Cage & North P.C., Denver, 1997—. Mem. ABA, Colo. Bar Assn., Denver Bar Assn. Avocations: running, hiking, skiing, reading, traveling. General civil litigation. Office: Berryhill Cage & North PC 1433 17th St Ste 300 Denver CO 80202-1273

**HIXSON, WENDELL MARK,** lawyer, judge; b. Oklahoma City, Dec. 6, 1966; s. Wendell Dee and Mary Theresa (Landgraf) H.; m. Shaa Marie Green, June 22, 1996. BA, Conception Sem. Coll., 1989; JD, U. Okla., 1992. Bar: Okla. 1992, U.S. Dist. Ct. (we. dist.) Okla. 1992, U.S. Dist. Ct. (ea. and no. dists.) 1993, U.S. Ct. Appeals (10th cir.) 1993, U.S. Supreme Ct. 1995. Assoc. Stan Chatman, P.C., Yukon, Okla., 1992-94, Bill James, Yukon and Oklahoma City, 1994-96; pvt. practice Yukon, 1996—; spl. mcpl. judge, Oklahoma City, 1997—; juvenile defender, City of Yukon, 1994—; indigent defender Okla. Indigent Def. Sys., Norman, 1994—. Mem. troop com. Boy Scouts Am., Oklahoma, 1992-97. Fellow Okla. Bar Found.; mem. U.S. Supreme Ct. Hist. Soc., Okla. Criminal Def. Lawyers Assn., Cath. Lawyers Guild of Archdiocese of Oklahoma City, Okla. Bar Assn. (litigation sect., sec. 1998-99, family law sect., mem. criminal law com., mem. rules of profl. conduct com., del. ho. of dels. 1996, 97, 98, Outstanding Young Lawyer 1998), Canadian County Bar Assn. (pres. 1997-98). Republican. Roman Catholic. Criminal, Family and matrimonial, General practice. Office: 800 W Main St Yukon OK 73099-1040

**HJELMFELT, DAVID CHARLES,** lawyer; b. Chgo., Nov. 25, 1940; s. Allen T. and Doris (Hauber) H.; m. Kendall L. Lawrence, Aug. 17, 1969; children: Trevor Christian, Rebecca Kirstan. AB cum laude, Kans. State U., Manhattan, 1962; LLB, Duke U., 1965. Bar: Kans. 1965, Colo. 1965, D.C. 1973, U.S. Supreme Ct. 1978, U.S. Ct. Appeals (D.C. cir.) 1973, U.S. Ct. Appeals (5th and 11th cirs.) 1981, U.S. Ct. Appeals (10th cir.) 1982. Vis. prof. Sch. Law U. Okla., Norman, 1970-71; staff atty. U.S. AEC, Albuquerque, 1971-73; ptnr. Goldberg, Fieldman & Hjelmfelt, Washington, Colo., 1973-78; sole practice Fort Collins, Colo., 1978-81; ptnr. Hjelmfelt & Larson, Fort Collins, Colo., 1981-90; sole practice Fort Collins, Denver, Colo., 1990—. Author: Antitrust and Regulated Industries, 1985; contbr. articles to profl. jours. Mem. coun. liberal edn. Kans. State U.; bd. dirs. Heritage Christian Sch., 1988; bd. dirs. Christian Conciliation Svc., Fort Collins. Lt. JAGC USNR, 1965-68. Mem. ABA (essential facilities monograph com. antitrust sect.), Colo. Bar Assn., Rep. Sen. Inside Circle Club. Antitrust, Public utilities, Federal civil litigation. Office: 417 17th St Ste 1200 Denver CO 80202-4005

**HJELMSTAD, WILLIAM DAVID,** lawyer; b. Apr. 4, 1954; s. Alvin Gordon and a. thecla (Walz) H.; m. Jenny M. Dube, Nov. 27, 1993; children: Jennifer Ashley, Allison Caitlin. AA in Social Sci., Casper Coll., 1974; BS in Psychology, U. Wyo., 1976, JD, 1979. Bar: Wyo. 1979, U.S. Dist. Ct. Wyo. 1979. Dept. county pros. atty. Hot Springs County, Thermopolis, Wyo., 1979-80; asst. pub. defender Natrona County, Casper, Wyo., 1980-82; sole practice Casper, Wyo., 1981—. Mem. ATLA, ABA (mem. family law com. 1983-84, adoption com. 1983-84), Wyo. State Bar Assn. (mem. alcohol and substance abuse com., lawyers assistance com. 1988-95, computer and technical com. 1997-99), Natrona County Bar Assn., Wyo. Trial Lawyers Assn., Am. Judicature Soc., Acad. Family Mediators, U. Wyo. Alumni Assn., Casper Coll. Alumni Assn., Wyo. Cowboy Shootout Com., Elks, Kiwanis. General civil litigation, Family and matrimonial, Probate. Home: PO Box 90001 Casper WY 82609-1001

**HJORTH, ROLAND L.,** dean, educator; b. 1935; m. Mary Byrne; 1 child, Heather Byrne. AB, U. Nebr., 1957; JD, NYU, 1961. Bar: Wash., N.Y., U.S. Tax Ct. Assoc. atty. Paul, Weiss, Rifkind, Wharton & Garrison, N.Y.C., 1961-64; of counsel Preston, Thorgrimson, Starin, Ellis & Holman, 1971-72, Perkins Coie, Seattle, 1980-95; asst. prof. U. Wash., Seattle, 1964-67, assoc. prof., 1967-69, prof., 1969—, assoc. dean for acad. affairs, 1994-95, dean Sch. Law, 1995—; vis. prof. NYU, 1969-70, U. Tex., 1976, U. Mich., 1980, U. Fla., 1982, U. Melbourne, Australia, 1989. Author: Taxation of Business Enterprises, 1981, also monographs; note and comment editor NYU Law Rev., 1960-61; contbr. numerous articles to profl. jours. Fulbright scholar, 1957-58; Root-tilden scholar, 1958-61. Fellow Am. Bar Found. (life); mem. ABA, Wash. State Bar Assn., Order of Coif, Phi Beta Kappa. Address: 5636 NE Keswick Dr Seattle WA 98105-2856

**HOAGLAND, KARL KING, JR.,** lawyer; b. St. Louis, Aug. 21, 1933; s. Karl King and Mary Edna (Parsons) H.; m. Sylvia Anne Naranick, July 13, 1957; children: Elizabeth Parsons, Sarah Stewart, Karl King III, Alison T. BS in Econs., U. Pa., 1955; LLB, U. Ill., 1958. Bar: Ill. 1958, U.S. Dist. Ct. (so. dist.) Ill. 1958. V.p., gen. counsel, sec. Jefferson Smurfit Corp., St. Louis, 1960-92, Container Corp. Am., St. Louis, 1986-92; of counsel Hoagland, Fitzgerald, Smith & Pranaitis, Alton, Ill., 1987—; chmn. bd. dirs. Millers' Mut. Ins. Assn. Ill., 1989-92. Asst. editor: U. Ill. Law Forum, 1957-58. Trustee, treas. Monticello Coll. Found., 1965—. 1st lt. USAF, 1958-60. Mem. Ill. Bar Assn., Madison County Bar Assn., Alton-Wood River Bar Assn., Lockhaven Country Club, Mo. Athletic Club, Crystal Lake Club, Order of the Coif, Beta Gamma Sigma. Episcopalian. Avocations: tennis, skiing, hunting, fishing, golf. General corporate. Home: Fairmount Addition 91 Hawthorne Dr Alton IL 62002-3209

**HOAGLAND, SAMUEL ALBERT,** lawyer, pharmacist; b. Mt. Home, Idaho, Aug. 19, 1953; s. Charles Leroy and Glenna Lorraine (Gridley) H.; m. Karen Ann Mengel, Nov. 20, 1976; children: Hiliary Anne, Heidi Lynne, Holly Kaye. BS in Pharmacy, Idaho State U., 1976; JD, U. Idaho, 1982. Bar: Idaho 1982, U.S. Dist. Ct. Idaho 1982, U.S. CT. Appeals (9th cir.) 1984. Lectr. clin. pharmacy Idaho State U., Pocatello, 1976-78, lectr. pharmacy law, 1985-86, dean's adv. council Coll. Pharmacy, 1987-92; hosp. pharmacist Mercy Med. Ctr., Nampa, Idaho, 1978-79; retail pharmacist Thrifty Corp., Moscow, Idaho, 1980-82; assoc. Dial, Looze & May, Pocatello, 1982-89, Prescott & Foster, Boise, Idaho, 1989-90; pvt. practice, 1990—; gen. counsel Design Innovations and Rsch. Corp., 1991-95; chmn. malpractice panel Idaho Bd. Medicine, Boise, 1983-92, adminstrv. hearing officer, 1989-92. Contbr. to law publs. Bd. dirs. Cathedral Pines Camp, Ketchum, Idaho. Mem. Idaho State Bar Assn., Idaho Pharm. Assn., Idaho Trial Lawyers Assn., Boise Bar Assn., Capital Pharm. Assn., Am. Pharm. Assn., Idaho Soc. Hosp. Pharmacists (bd. dirs.), Am. Soc. Pharmacy Law, Flying Doctors Am. (Atlanta) (bd. dirs.). Administrative and regulatory, General civil litigation, General practice. Home: 11901 W Mesquite Dr Boise ID 83713-0813 Office: 1471 Shoreline Dr Ste 100 Boise ID 83702-9104

**HOAR, SEAN BENNETT,** lawyer; b. Massena, N.Y., Mar. 6, 1958; s. Thomas James and Marcia Mae (Miller) H.; m. Judith Ellen Abel, June 1, 1986; children: Rachel Louise, Keenan Alexander. BA, Linfield Coll., McMinnville, Oreg., 1980; MS, Fla. State U., 1981; JD, U. Oreg., 1987. Bar: Oreg. 1987, U.S. Dist. Ct. Ore. 1991, U.S. Ct. Appeals (9th cir.) 1991, U.S. Supreme Ct. 1997. Asst. dir. residential and jud. affairs Vanderbilt U., Nashville, 1981-84; asst. dist. atty. Lane County Dist. Atty.'s Office, Eugene, 1987-91; asst. U.S. atty. U.S. Atty.'s Office, Eugene, 1991—. Mem. Gov.'s Coun. on Domestic Violence, 1998—; coach baseball and soccer Kidsports, Eugene, 1998—. Recipient Centurian award U. Oreg., 1987. Mem. Oreg. State Bar Assn. (criminal jury instrn. com. 1989-92), Lane County Bar Assn. (fed. cts. com. 1993-94). Avocations: athletics, coaching. Office: US Attys Office 701 High St Eugene OR 97401-2713

**HOBBS, GREGORY JAMES, JR.,** state supreme court justice; b. Gainesville, Fla., Dec. 15, 1944; s. Gregory J. Hobbs and Mary Ann (Rhodes) Frakes; m. Barbara Louise Hay, June 17, 1967; children: Daniel Gregory, Emily Mary Hobbs Wright. BA, U. Notre Dame, 1966; JD, U. Calif., Berkeley, 1971. Bar: Colo. 1971, Calif. 1972. Law clk. to Judge William E. Doyle 10th U.S. Cir. Ct. Appeals, Denver, 1971-72; assoc. Cooper, White & Cooper, San Francisco, 1972-73; enforcement atty. U.S. EPA, Denver, 1973-75; asst. atty. gen. State of Colo. Atty. Gen.'s Office, Denver, 1975-79; ptnr. Davis, Graham & Stubbs, Denver, 1979-92; shareholder Hobbs, Trout & Raley, P.C., Denver, 1992-96; justice Colo. Supreme Ct., Denver, 1996—; counsel No. Colo. Water Conservancy, Loveland, Colo., 1979-96. Contbr. articles to profl. jours. vol. Peace Corps-S.Am., Colombia, 1967-68; vice chair Colo. Air Quality Control Com., Denver, 1982-87; mem. ranch com. Philmont Scout Ranch, Boy Scouts Am., Cimarron, N.Mex., 1988-98; co-chair Eating Disorder Family Support Group, Denver, 1992—. Recipient award of merit Denver Area Coun. Boy Scouts, 1993, Pres. award Nat. Water Resources Assn., Washington, 1995. Fellow Am. Bar Found.; mem. ABA, Colo. Bar Assn., Denver Bar Assn. Avocations: backpacking, fishing, writing poetry. Office: Colo Supreme Ct 2 E 14th Ave Denver CO 80203-2115

**HOBBS, J. TIMOTHY, SR.,** lawyer; b. Yakima, Wash., Sept. 23, 1941; s. Leonard M. and Virginia (Snider) H.; m. Barbara J. Hatfield, June 14, 1964; children: Amy Elizabeth, J. Timothy Jr. BA in Polit. Sci., U. Wash., 1964; JD, Am. U., 1968. Bar: D.C. 1969, U.S. Ct. Supreme Ct. 1973, U.S. Ct. Appeals Fed. Crct. 1982, U.S. Ct. Appeals (11th cir.) 1986, U.S. Ct. Appeals (5th cir.) 1989, U.S. Ct. Appeals (6th cir.) 1996. Assoc. Mason Fenwick & Lawrence, Washington, 1969-76, ptnr., 1977-82, sr. ptnr., 1982-91; ptnr., head intellectual property dept. Dykema Gossett, 1991—. Author chpt. on copyright law, West's Federal Practice Manual, 1983. Pres. Arlington Outdoor Edn. Assn., 1990-92. Mem. D.C. Bar (chmn. trademark com. 1982-84), U.S. Trademark Assn. Forums (speaker 1988), Washington Golf and Country Club. Trademark and copyright. Home: 6135 Lee Hwy Arlington VA 22205-2134 Office: Dykema Gossett Franklin Square Ste 300 West 1300 I St NW Washington DC 20005

**HOBBS, TRUMAN MCGILL,** federal judge; b. Selma, Ala., Feb. 8, 1921; s. Sam F. and Sarah Ellen (Greene) H.; m. Joyce Cummings, July 9, 1949; children—Emilie C. Reid, Frances John Rose, Dexter Cummings, Truman McGill. A.B., U. N.C., 1942; LL.B., Yale U., 1948. Bar: Ala. 1948. Practiced in Montgomery, 1951-80; law clk. U.S. Supreme Ct., 1948-49; ptnr. Hobbs, Copeland, Franco & Screws, 1951-80; U.S. dist. judge Montgomery, 1980—; now sr. judge; Chmn. Ala. Unemployment Appeal Bd., 1952-58. Pres. United Appeal Montgomery; pres. Montgomery County Tb Assn.; v.p. Ala. Com. for Better Schs.; Chmn. Montgomery County Exec. Democratic Com., 1970. Served to lt. USNR, 1942-46, ETO, PTO. Decorated Bronze Star medal. Fellow Am. Coll. Trial Lawyers; mem. Internat. Acad. Trial Lawyers, Ala. Plaintiffs Lawyers Assn. (past pres.), Ala. Bar Assn. (pres. 1970-71), Montgomery County Bar Assn. (past pres.). Home: 2301 Fernway Dr Montgomery AL 36111-1603

**HOBELMAN, CARL DONALD,** lawyer; b. Hackensack, N.J., Dec. 26, 1931; s. Alfred Charles and Marion (Gerrish) H.; m. Grace Palumbo, Apr. 25, 1964. BCE, Cornell U., 1954; JD, Harvard U., 1959. Bar: N.Y. 1960, U.S. Supreme Ct. 1975, D.C. 1980, Calif. 1993. Assoc. LeBoeuf, Lamb, Greene & MacRae, N.Y.C., 1959-64; ptnr. LeBoeuf, Lamb, Greene & MacRae, L.A., N.Y.C., Washington, 1965-94; of counsel LeBoeuf, Lamb, Greene & MacRae, Washington, 1995—. Contbr. articles on energy-related topics to profl. jours. Served to 1st lt. U.S. Army, 1954-56. Mem. ABA, Fed. Energy Bar Assn. (pres. 1980-81), D.C. Bar Assn., Met. Club (Washington), Univ. Club (N.Y.C.). Avocations: travel, philately. Administrative and regulatory, General corporate, FERC practice. Office: LeBoeuf Lamb Greene & MacRae 1875 Connecticut Ave NW Washington DC 20009-5728

**HOBERMAN, STUART A.,** lawyer; b. N.Y.C., Nov. 21, 1946. BBA, Baruch Coll., N.Y.C., 1969; JD, Bklyn. Law Sch., 1972; LLM, NYU, 1973. Bar: N.Y. 1973, N.J. 1977, Pa. 1979, U.S. Supreme Ct. 1976. Assoc. Windels & Marx, N.Y.C., 1973-77, Wilentz, Goldman & Spitzer, Woodbridge, N.J., 1977-80; ptnr. Wilentz, Goldman & Spitzer, 1980—. Trustee, Emmanuel Cancer Found., Kenilworth, N.J., 1983-90. Mem. N.J. State Bar Assn. (trustee 1990-94, 97—, corp. and bus. law sect. chmn. 1988-90, bank law sect. chmn. 1986-87, chmn. exec. com. of gen. coun. 1990-92, trustee N.J. State Bar Found. 1992—, treas. 1995, 96, 1st v.p. 1997—). General corporate, Banking, Finance. Office: Wilentz Goldman & Spitzer PO Box 10 90 Woodbridge Ctr Dr Ste 900 Woodbridge NJ 07095-1142

**HOBSON, JAMES RICHMOND,** lawyer; b. Atlanta, Sept. 13, 1937; s. Richmond Pearson and Alice Chambers (Carey) H.; m. Nancy Hulbert Saussy, Nov. 29, 1963; children: Kathleen Hunter, Caroline Richmond, Susan Saussy. BA in English, Cornell U., 1959; MA in Govt., Georgetown U., 1963; JD, U. San Francisco, 1971. Bar: Calif. 1972, U.S. Ct. Appeals (9th cir.) 1972, U.S. Dist. Ct. (no. dist.) Calif. 1972, D.C., 1973, U.S. Ct. Appeals (D.C. cir.) 1973, U.S. Dist. Ct. D.C. 1973. Staff writer Charlotte (N.C.) Observer, 1963; rschr., writer Rep. Nat. Com., Washington, 1964-65; Washington editor Med. Econs. Mag., 1965; info. officer Hoover Instn., Stanford, Calif., 1966-72; atty., mgr. FCC, Washington, 1972-78; asst. v.p. GTE Svc. Corp., Washington, 1978-81; Washington counsel GTE Corp., Washington, 1982-91; v.p. Donelan, Cleary, Wood & Maser, PC, Washington, 1991-95, prin., 1995—, pres., 1997—. Bd. dirs. Mid-Peninsula Citizens for Fair Housing, Palo Alto, Calif., 1971-72; sr. warden Immanuel Ch. on the Hill, Alexandria, Va., 1977, 90, jr. warden, 1976, 88; traffic and parking bd. City Alexandria, 1980-82; mem. Alexandria Libr. Co., 1991—, pres., 1995-96; mem. panel arbitrators Am. Arbitration Assn., 1994-97; adv. bd. Inst. for Conflict Analysis and Resolution, George Mason U., 1989—, chmn., 1995-98; bd. trustees Goodwin House, Inc., 1996—, exec. com., 1998—. Mem. ABA, Fed. Comm. Bar Assn. (exec. com. 1984-87, 94-96), Met. Club Washington, Sigma Alpha Epsilon. Episcopalian. Administrative and regulatory, Communications, Public utilities. Home: 3613 Trinity Dr Alexandria VA 22304-1840 Office: Donelan Cleary Wood & Maser 1100 New York Ave NW Ste 750W Washington DC 20005-3934

**HOCH, RAND,** lawyer, mediator; b. Everett, Wash., Apr. 2, 1955; s. Harold S. and Thelma (Frisch) H. AB in Am. Govt., Georgetown U., 1977; JD, Stetson U., 1985. Bar: Fla. 1985, U.S. Dist. Ct. (mid., so. dists.) Fla. 1986, U.S. Ct. Appeals (11th cir.) 1986, D.C. 1989. Adminstrv. aide Henry M. Jackson for Pres. Com., Washington, 1974-76; research dir. Council Active Ind. Oil and Gas Producers, Washington, 1977; polit. cons. New South Communications, Washington and Fla., 1977-82; asst. to regional coordinator North Shore Council on Alcoholism, Mass., 1978; exec. dir. Fund for A New Direction, Washington and West Palm Beach, Fla., 1979-91; real estate salesman Adams Cameron/Realty World, Ormond Beach, Fla., 1980-81; real estate broker South 1st Realty Inc., Ormond Beach, 1981-82; research asst. Stetson U., St. Petersburg, Fla., 1983-85; law clk. real estate and constrn. De Santis, Cook, Gaskill & Silverman, North Palm Beach, Fla., 1984; labor, election and ERISA atty. Kaplan, Sicking & Bloom P.A., West Palm Beach, 1985-88; workers' compensation atty. Law Offices of Gerald Rosenthal P.A., West Palm Beach, 1989-91; gen. master div. worker's compensation Fla. Dept. Labor & Employment Security, 1991-92; judge compensation claims State of Fla., Daytona Beach, 1992-96; pvt. practice The Law & Mediation Office of Rand Hoch, West Palm Beach, Fla., 1996—; cons. in field. Contbr. articles to profl. jours. Mem. Dem. Exec. Com., Volusia County Fla., 1980-82, Pinellas County, Fla., 1983, Palm Beach County, 1989-92, 96—, chair, 1990, vice-chair, 1989-90; del. Fla. Dem. Conv., 1981, 83, 85, 87, 89, 91; alt. del. Dem. Nat. Conv., 1988; bd. dirs. ACLU, Palm Beach and Martin Counties, 1985-87, Fla. Consumer Fedn., 1987-89, Fla. Task Force, 1987-89, Nat. Gay & Lesbian Task Force, 1989-92, Palm Beach County Human Rights Coun., Inc., 1990-92, Cen. Fla. Friends of 440, 1995-96; mem. exec. com. Lesbian and Gay Dems. of Am., 1988-92; regional coord. Dukakis for Pres., Fla., 1987-88; pres. Palm Beach County Human Rights Coun., 1987-92; chmn. pro tem employment practices rev. com. City West Palm Beach, 1990-91; mem. ethics ordinance adv. com. Palm Beach County, 1991-92; mem. Young Friends of Bob Graham, 1989-92, 96—, Leadership 2000, 1990-92, Young Friends of the Kravis Ctr., 1996—; mem. adv. bd. Volusia County Elections, 1993-94. Recipient Am. Jurisprudence Book awards, 1983, 84, Fred C. Fantz award, 1985, Hank Godley Meml. award Met. Bus. Orgn. of South Fla., 1992, Spectrum Lifetime Achievement award Greater Orlando Gay & Lesbian Cmty. Ctr., 1994; named Charles A. Dana scholar, 1983-85. Mem. ABA (young lawyers divsn. 1985-91, labor and employment law sect. 1986-92, mem. sect. on individual rights and responsibilities 1990-92, campaign ethics com. 1987-92), Fla. Bar Assn. (labor and employment law sect. 1989—, mem. editl. bd. Fla. Bar News and Fla. Bar Jour. 1995—), D.C. Bar Assn., Acad. Trial Lawyers Am., Assn. Bipartisan Cons., Fla. Acad. Trial Lawyers, Am. Mediation Assn. (nat. bd. accredited mediators 1993—), Internat. Assn. Lesbian and Gay Judges (bd. dirs. 1993-95, v.p. 1995-97), Nat. Gay and Lesbian Lawyers Assn., Fla. Conf. Judges of Compensation Claims (pres. 1994-95, mem. exec. com. 1995-96), Volusia County Bar Assn. (mem. jud. evaluation rev. com. 1994), Palm Beach County Bar Assn. (alt. dispute resolution com. 1997—, workers compensation com. 1997—), Phi Alpha Delta, Lambda Legal Def. and Edn. Fund. Jewish. Avocation: political button collecting. E-mail: rand-hoch@usa.net. Labor, Workers' compensation, Civil rights. Office: 400 N Flagler Dr Apt 1402 West Palm Beach FL 33401-4315

**HOCHBERG, FAITH S.,** prosecutor. BA summa cum laude, Tufts U., 1972; JD magna cum laude, Harvard U., 1975. Law clk. to Hon. Spottswood W. Robinson III U.S. Ct. Appeals (D.C. cir.), 1975-76; pvt. practice Washington, Boston, Roseland, N.J., 1977-83; asst. U.S. atty. Dist. N.J., Newark, 1983-87, U.S. atty., 1994—; ptnr. Cole, Schotz, Bernstein, Meisel & Forman, Hackensack, N.J., 1987-90; past sr. dep. chief counsel Office Thrift Supervision, Jersey City; former dep. asst. sec. law enforcement U.S. Treasury Dept., Washington; U.S. Atty. Dist. of N.J., 1994—. Office: US Attorney for District of NJ Federal Bldg 970 Broad St Newark NJ 07102-2506

**HOCHBERG, RONALD MARK,** lawyer; b. Bklyn., Apr. 3, 1955; s. Fred S. and Adele (Gunsberg) H.; m. Sharon A. Berg, Aug. 11, 1985; children: Rachel, Sarah. BA, Rutgers U., 1977; JD, Bklyn. Law Sch., 1980; LLM, U. Miami, 1982. Assoc. Klatsky & Klatsky, Red Bank, N.J., 1980-81, Fuerst, Singer & Yusem, Somerville, N.J., 1982-83, Law Offices of Steven Schanker, Melville, N.Y., 1983-86; ptnr. Schanker & Hochberg, Attys., Huntington, N.Y., 1986—; frequent lectr. on estate planning; instr. Adelphi U., 1984-93. Columnist Financial World Mag., 1993-97; contbr. articles to profl. publs. Mem. ABA, N.Y. State Bar Assn., Estate and Tax Planning Coun. Avocations: skiing, sailing. Estate taxation, Estate planning, Pension, profit-sharing, and employee benefits. Office: Schanker & Hochberg 27 W Neck Rd Huntington NY 11743-2618

**HOCHMAN, ALAN ROBERT,** lawyer; b. Maplewood, N.J., Aug. 19, 1950; s. Ralph and Pearl (Gelb) H.; m. Barbara Ann Bitman, Aug. 10, 1975; children: Jennifer Susan, Michael Robert. BA, George Washington U., 1972; JD, U. Miami (Fla.), 1975. Bar: Fla. 1975, U.S. Dist. Ct. (so. dist.) Fla. 1975, U.S. Ct. Appeals (5th cir.) 1975. Assoc. Donald M. Coon, P.A., Miami, 1975-77; founder Alan R. Hochman P.A., Miami, 1977—; co-founder Teardrop Golf. Bd. dirs., state rep. Khoury League Continental Kendall Boys and Girls Club, Miami, 1990—; active Dade County Dem. party. Recipient Recognition award nat. Assn. Legal Investigators, 1994. Mem. ABA, Fla. Bar Assn. State civil litigation, Personal injury, Insurance. Office: 13015 SW 89th Pl Ste 206 Miami FL 33176-5812

**HOCHMAN, KENNETH GEORGE,** lawyer; b. Mt. Vernon, N.Y., Nov. 12, 1947; s. Benjamin S. and Lillian (Gilbert) H.; m. Carol K. Hochman, Apr. 8, 1979; children: Brian Paul, Lisa Erin. BA, SUNY, Buffalo, 1969; JD, Columbia U., 1972. Bar: Ohio 1973, Fla. 1977, N.Y. 1979. Assoc. Jones, Day, Reavis & Pogue, Cleve., 1972-79, ptnr., 1980—; trustee Katharine Kenyon Lippitt Found., Cleve., 1988, Kenridge Fund, Cleve., 1989, Bolton Found., Cleve., 1990, Elisha-Bolton Found., Cleve., 1993. Harlan Fiske Stone scholar Columbia U., 1971, 72. Fellow Am. Coll. Trusts and Estate Counsel; mem. Phi Beta Kappa, Oakwood Club (Cleve.) (trustee 1997). Estate planning, Probate, Estate taxation. Office: Jones Day Reavis & Pogue 901 Lakeside Ave E Cleveland OH 44114-1116

**HOCHMAN, STEPHEN ALLEN,** lawyer; b. N.Y.C., June 25, 1935; s. Henry and Ida Hochman; m. Judith Cole, June 16, 1957; children: Glen, Susan, Lisa. BA, Cornell U., 1957, JD with distinction, 1959. Bar: N.Y. 1960, U.S. Supreme Ct. 1963, U.S. Dist. Ct. (so. dist.) N.Y. 1963. Assoc. Proskauer Rose Goetz & Mendelsohn, N.Y.C., 1960-64; ptnr. Feldman, Kramer, Bam & Nessen, N.Y.C., 1964-66, Kramer, Nessen & Hochman, 1966-68, Kramer, Levin, Nessen, Kamin & Frankel, N.Y.C., 1968-86, Friedman, Wittenstein & Hochman, N.Y.C., 1986—; chmn. ALI/ABA Ann. Program on Corp. Acquisitions, 1985—, Program on Arbitration, Mediation and ADR, 1993—; mediator U.S. Dist. Ct. (so. and eas. dists.) N.Y., U.S. Bankryptcy Ct. (so. dist.) N.Y., N.Y. State Supreme Ct., NASD mediator, arbitrator. Contbr. articles to profl. jours. Trustee, sec. Beth Israel Med. Ctr., N.Y.C., 1982—, Jewish Communal Fund N.Y., N.Y.C., 1982—; mem. N.Y. State Adv. Commn. on Substance Abuse, 1977-83; trustee State Communities Aid Assn., N.Y. State, 1976—. 1st lt. USAR, 1959-60. Mem. ABA (former chair arbitration com. sect. dispute resolution, co-chair large/complex case sub-com.), Assn. of Bar of City of N.Y., Am. Arbitration Assn., Am. Law Inst., Order of Coif, Phi Kappa Phi. General corporate, Mergers and acquisitions, Alternative dispute resolution. Home: 303 West St White Plains NY 10605-5304 Office: Friedman Wittenstein & Hochman 101 E 52nd St New York NY 10022-6018

**HOCK, FREDERICK WYETH,** lawyer; b. Newark, July 10, 1924; s. Herbert Hummel and Carol (Wyeth) H.; m. Alfeld Catherine Larsen, Mar. 4, 1945; children: Carolyn, Sandra, Rhonda; m. 2d, Ellen Barbara Weidner, June 28, 1975. AA, Princeton U., 1944; BA, Rutgers U., 1948, LLB, 1950, JD, 1968. Bar: N.J. 1949. Assoc. Stevenson, Willette & McDermott, 1949-51; sole practice, 1951-65; ptnr. Hock & Sharkey, East Orange, N.J., 1965-79; sr. ptnr. Hock Silverlieb & Kramer, Livingston, N.J., 1979-93, Gulkin, Hock & Lehr, 1994—; acting judge East Orange Mcpl. Ct., 1954-57; mem. adv. bd. Maplewood Bank and Trust Co., Livingston, 1987-91, Summit Trust Co., 1991-98. Chmn. Juvenile Conf. Com. 1958-62; trustee Community Day Nursery of the Oranges & Maplewood, 1962-75, pres., 1973-75; trustee Founders Endowment Fund, 1954-87, House of Good Shepherd 1970-90, Nu Beta Found., 1970-91; bd. dirs. Essex County chpt. ARC, 1987-91; post adv. VFW post 5445, 1955-90. Served with USMC 1942-46. Mem. ABA, N.J. Bar Assn., Northwestern N.J. Estate Planning Council (dir. 1981-90), No. N.J. Estate Planning Coun. Estate planning, Probate. Office: 354 Eisenhower Pkwy Livingston NJ 07039-1022

**HOCKENBERRY, JOHN FEDDEN,** counselor; b. Bronxville, N.Y., Sept. 2, 1945; m. Nina Gail Levitt; 1 child, Mark S. AB in Econ. summa cum laude, Princeton U., 1969; JD, Yale Law Sch., 1972. Bar: N.Y., D.C. Atty. Cravath, Swaine & Moore, N.Y.C., 1973-80; assoc. gen. counsel The Washington Post Co., 1980—. General corporate, Mergers and acquisitions, Intellectual property. Office: The Washington Post Co 1150 15th St NW Washington DC 20071-0002

**HOCKETT, CHRISTOPHER BURCH,** lawyer; b. Hutchinson, Kans., Sept. 6, 1959; s. George Rundell and Shirley (Corker) H. BA, William & Mary, 1981; JD, U. Va., 1985. Bar: Calif. 1985, U.S. Dist. Ct. (no. dist.) Calif. 1985, U.S. Dist. Ct. (cen.dist.) Calif. 1988, U.S. Ct. Appeals (9th cir.) 1988. Assoc. McCutchen, Doyle, Brown, & Enersen, San Francisco, 1985-92, ptnr., 1992—. Author: (chpt.) State Antitrust Law Handbook, 1990, 2nd edit., 1999; assoc. editor Antitrust Mag., 1990-91. Bd. dirs. San Francisco Neighborhood Legal Assistance Found., 1992—. Mem. ABA (council sect. of antitrust law, 1998—, vice chairperson antitrust law civil practice and procedure com. 1991-95, chairperson 1995-98, mem. task force on civil justice reform 1992-93), No. Calif. Assn. Bus. Trial Lawyers, Bar ASsn. San Francisco, Barristers Club. Avocations: mountaineering, golf. Antitrust, General civil litigation, Securities. Office: McCutchen Doyle Brown & Enersen 3 Embarcadero Ctr Fl 18 San Francisco CA 94111-4021

**HODAN, PATRICK JOHN,** lawyer; b. San Francisco, Aug. 8, 1962; s. Theodore and Mary Francis (Vidas) H.; m. Kerry Hickey, Aug. 25, 1990; children: Patrick Jr., Bridget, Colleen. B of Bus. Adminstrn. summa cum laude, Georgetown U., 1985; JD cum laude, Marquette U., 1990. Bar: Wis. 1990, U.S. Dist. Ct. (ea. and we. dists.) Wis. 1990. Ptnr. Reinhart Boerner

Van Deuren Norris & Rieselbach, Milw., 1990—; pub. spl. prosecutor Milw. County Dist. Atty.'s Office, 1995. Mem. Wis. Acad. Trial Lawyers, Milw. Bar Assn. General civil litigation, Product liability, Legislative. Office: Reinhart Boerner Van Deuren Norris & Rieselbach 1000 N Water St Ste 2100 Milwaukee WI 53202-3197

**HODES, PAUL WILLIAM,** record company executive, lawyer; b. N.Y.C., Mar. 21, 1951; s. Robert Bernard and Florence (Rosenberg) H.; m. Margaret Ann Horstmann; children: Maxwell, Ariana. BA, Dartmouth Coll., 1972; JD, Boston Coll., 1978. Bar: N.H. 1978, Mass. 1980. Asst. atty. gen. Office of N.H. Atty. Gen., Concord, 1978-82; pres. Big Round Records, Inc., Concord, N.H., 1986—; co-owner Peggosus Music, 1986—. Bd. dirs. Capital Ctr. for Arts, 1990-97, chair 1990-96; bd. dirs. Children's Entertainment Assn., 1995-99, Concord Cmty. Music Sch., 1997—, N.H. Children's Alliance, 1997—. Recipient hon. award Parents Choice Found., 1987, 96. Mem. Am. Bd. Trial Advocates, NARAS, ASCAP, ATLA, Nat. Assn. Criminal Def. Lawyers, N.H. Assn. Criminal Def. Lawyers, N.H. Trial Lawyers. Federal civil litigation, Entertainment, Criminal. Office: Shaheen & Gordon PA PO Box 2703 Concord NH 03302-2703 also: Big Round Records Inc PO Box 610 Concord NH 03302-0610

**HODGE, JAMES EDWARD,** lawyer; b. Alexander City, Ala., Sept. 24, 1936; s. William H. and Nellie (Greene) H.; m. Nancy Bates, Aug. 24, 1963; children: Stephanie, Christopher, Timothy, Michael. BA, Stetson U., 1958; JD, U. Fla., 1963. Bar: Fla. 1963, U.S. Dist. Ct. (mid. dist.) Fla. 1963, U.S. Ct. Appeals (5th cir.) 1963, U.S. Supreme Ct. 1972, U.S. Ct. Appeals (11th cir.) 1981. Ptnr. Jones, Foerster & Hodge, Jacksonville, Fla., 1966-74, Foerster & Hodge, Jacksonville, 1974-82, Milne, Hodge & Milne, Jacksonville, 1982-85; pvt. practice Jacksonville, 1985-86; ptnr. Blackwell, Walker, Fascell & Hoehl, Jacksonville, 1986-87; chmn. Bus. Acquisitions, Inc., Jacksonville, 1988-91; pvt. practice Jacksonville, Fla., 1991—; Spl. counsel Gov. Fla. 1981-82. Pres. Cerebral Palsy Jacksonville, 1972; bd. dirs. Little League Baseball, Jacksonville, 1976-81, Bolles Sch. Dads Assn., Jacksonville, 1978-82; bd. dirs. Jacksonville Port Authority, 1980-86, chmn., 1986-88. Named one of Outstanding Young Men Am., 1968. Mem. ABA, Fla. Bar Assn., Jacksonville Bar Assn. (bd. govs. 1972-73), Stetson U. Alumni Assn. (pres. 1968), Rotary (pres. West Jacksonville club 1979-80, The Robert T. Shircliff Svc. award 1988), Phi Delta Phi. Episcopalian. Avocations: tennis, reading biographies, spectator sports, walking. Banking, Contracts commercial, Real property. Office: PO Box 27055 Jacksonville FL 32205-0055

**HODGE, VICTOR A(NTHONY),** lawyer; b. Louisville, Apr. 4, 1947; s. Lester D. and Bridget T. (DeGeorge) H.; m. Barbara A. Downs, June 24, 1967; children—James Eric, Jill Marie. B.A. in Chemistry, Bellarmine Coll.; J.D. cum laude, U. Dayton. Bar: Ohio 1981, Fla. 1982. Forensic chemist Sanford Crime Lab., Fla., 1974-75, Miami Valley Regional Crime Lab., Dayton, Ohio, 1973-74, 75-80; assoc. Brannon & Cox Law Offices, Dayton, 1981-83; sole practice, Dayton, 1983—. Youth sports coach Merlin Heights Baseball Assn., Dayton. Served to sgt. U.S. Army, 1969-71. Mem. Ohio State Bar Assn., Dayton Bar Assn., Fla. Bar Assn., Assn. Trial Lawyers Am., Am Legion. Democrat. Roman Catholic. Office: 130 W 2nd St Ste 810 Dayton OH 45402-1501

**HODGES, CHARLES ROBERT,** lawyer; b. Dallas, June 11, 1946; s. Robert L. and Geraldine (Pearson) H. BA, U. Tex., 1968, JD, 1974. Bar: Tex. 1974, U.S. Dist. Ct. (no., ea. and we. dists.) Tex. 1976, U.S. Ct. Appeals (5th cir.) 1976, U.S. Dist. Ct. (so. dist.) Tex. 1977, U.S. Supreme Ct. 1978; bd. cert. family law Tex. Bd. Legal Specialization. Spl. asst. U.S. Senator Lloyd Bentsen, Washington, 1971-72; asst. atty. gen. Tex. Atty. Gen.'s Office, Austin, 1974-75; spl. counsel Tex. Sec. of State, Austin, 1975; atty. Law Offices of James K. Presnal, Austin, 1976-77; v.p. mktg. Nat. Data Commn., Dallas, 1977-83; ptnr. Hooks & Hodges, Attys., Dallas, 1983-92, Massingill, Bennett, Hodges & Leslie, LLP, Dallas, 1992-94; sr. ptnr. Law Offices of Charles R. Hodges, PC, Dallas, 1994—. Bd. dirs. Dallas (Tex.) Summer Musicals, 1988-93; v.p. Tom Hughes Found., Dallas, 1988-94. Mem. Tex. Acad. Family Law Specialists, Coll. State Bar Tex., Dallas Bar Assn. (bd. dirs. family law sect.). Family and matrimonial, Alternative dispute resolution. Office: 3838 Oak Lawn Ave Ste 1800 Dallas TX 75219-4519

**HODGES, JOSEPH GILLULY, JR.,** lawyer; b. Denver, Dec. 7, 1942; s. Joseph Gilluly Sr. and Elaine (Chanute) H.; m. Jean Todd Creamer, Aug. 7, 1971; children: Ashley E., Wendy C., Elaine V. BA, Lake Forest Coll., 1965; JD, U. Colo., 1968. Bar: Colo. 1968, U.S. Dist. Ct. Colo. 1969, U.S. Ct. Mil. Appeals 1969. Assoc. Hodges, Kerwin, Otten & Weeks, Denver, 1969-73; assoc. Davis, Graham & Stubbs, Denver, 1973-76, ptnr., 1976-86; pvt. practice, Denver, 1986—. Bd. dirs. Arapahoe Colo. Nat. Bank, Littleton, Colo., 1971-90, Cherry Creek Improvement Assn., Denver, 1979-91; bd. trustees Lake Forest (Ill.) Coll., 1977-87; pres. Colo. Arlberg Club, Winter Park, Colo., 1984-85; treas. St. Johns Episcopal Cathedral, Denver, 1981-96; chmn. bd. Spalding Cmty. Found., 1995—. Capt. USAR, 1969-74. Named Best Lawyers in Am., Woodward/White, N.Y.C., 1994-95. Fellow Am. Coll. Trust and Estate Counsel (state chmn. 1991-96); mem. ABA (chmn. probate divsn. G-2 Tech. 1990-95, coun. mem. real property, probate and trust law sect. 1996—), Am. Judicature Soc., Colo. Bar Assn. (chair probate coun. 1981-82), Denver Bar Assn., Denver Estate Planning Coun., Colo. Planned Giving Roundtable (bd. 1991-94), Rotary Club Denver, Kappa Sigma, Phi Alpha Delta. Republican. Avocations: skiing, hiking, fishing, photography, computers. Estate planning, Probate, Non-profit and tax-exempt organizations. Office: 3300 E 1st Ave Ste 600 Denver CO 80206-5809

**HODGES, JOT HOLIVER, JR.,** lawyer, business executive; b. Archer City, Tex., Nov. 16, 1932; s. Jot Holiver and Lola Mae (Hurd) H.; m. Virginia Cordray Pardue, June 11, 1955; children: Deborah, Jot, Darlene. BS, BBA, Sam Houston State U., 1954; JD, U. Tex., 1957. Bar: Tex., U.S. Dist. Ct. (so. dist.) Tex., U.S. Ct. Appeals (5th cir.). Asst. atty. gen. State of Tex., Austin, 1958-60; chmn. bd. Presidio Devel. Corp., Missouri City, Tex.; organizer, founder 3 banks, several corps. and ltd. partnerships; residential and comml. real estate developer. Contbr. articles to legal, med., pharm., and hosp. jours. Capt. U.S. Army. Mem. Houston Club. General practice, Real property, General corporate. Home: 3527 Thunderbird St Missouri City TX 77459-2445 Office: 3660 Hampton Dr Ste 200 Missouri City TX 77459-3044

**HODGES, RALPH B.,** state supreme court justice; b. Anadarko, Okla., Aug. 4, 1930; s. Dewey E. and Pearl R. (Hodges) H.; m. Janelle H.; children: Shari, Mark, Randy. B.A., Okla. Baptist U.; LL.B., U. Okla. Atty. Bryan County, Okla., 1956-58; judge Okla. Dist. Ct., 1959-65; justice Okla. Supreme Ct., Oklahoma City, 1965—. Office: Okla Supreme Ct State Capital Bldg Oklahoma City OK 73105

**HODGES, WILLIAM TERRELL,** federal judge; b. Lake Wales, Fla., Apr. 28, 1934; s. Haywood and Clara Lucy (Murphy) H.; m. Peggy Jean Woods, June 8, 1958; children: Judson, Daniel, Clay. B.S.B.A., U. Fla., 1956, J.D., 1958. Bar: Fla. 1959. Mem. firm Macfarlane, Ferguson, Allison & Kelly, Tampa, 1958-71; instr. bus. law U. South Fla., Tampa, 1961-66; judge U.S. Dist. Ct. (mid. dist.) Fla., Tampa, 1971-82, 89—; mem. com. on ops. jury system Jud. Conf., 1982-87, cir. coun., 11th cir., 1981-86; adv. com. on rules criminal procedure and evidence Jud. Conf., 1987—, ad hoc com. on habeas corpus reform; mem. bench book com. Fed. Jud. Ctr., 1984—, chmn., 1987—. Exec. editor, U. Fla. Law Rev., 1957-58. Mem. Am., Tampa-Hillsborough County bar assns., Fla. Bar (chmn. grievance com. 1967-70, chmn. uniform comml. code com. 1970-71), Dist. Judges Assn. 5th Circuit (co-chmn. com. on pattern jury instrn. 1977-81), Dist. Judges Assn. 11th Circuit (chmn. jury instrns. com. 1982—, pres. 1981-82) Am. Judicature Soc. Office: US Dist Ct 512 US Courthouse 311 W Monroe St Jacksonville FL 32202-4242

**HODGSON, ARTHUR CLAY,** lawyer; b. Little River, Kans., Aug. 22, 1907; s. Edward Howard and Flora Cleveland (Perry) H.; m. Annie Letitia Green, Jan. 5, 1939; children: Richard, David, Edward, Alice Anne, James. AB, U. Kans., 1929; JD, George Washington U., 1937. Bar: Kans. 1936, D.C. 1936, U.S. Supreme Ct. 1950. Sole practice law, Washington, 1936-38; practice, Lyons, Kans., 1938—, ptnr. Hodgson & Kahler, 1969—. Pres. Lyons Jaycees; bd. dirs. Lyons C. of C. With USN, 1943-45. Recipient Disting. Svc. award Lyons C. of C. Mem. ABA (ho. of dels. 1976-82), Kans. Trial Lawyers Assn. (bd. govs. 1957-89, pres. 1972-73), ATLA (bd. govs. 1973-76), Rice County Bar, S.W. Kans. Bar, Kans. Bar Assn. (del., disting. service award 1985), City Attys. Assn. Kans. (pres. 1960-61), Kans. State Hist. Soc. (pres. 1996-97), Rotary, Masons. Democrat. Congregationalist. General practice, State civil litigation, Probate. Home: 1240 28th Rd Little River KS 67457-9004 Office: Hodgson & Kahler 119 1/2 W Main St Lyons KS 67554-1927

**HODINAR, MICHAEL,** lawyer, publishing company executive; b. Prague, Czechoslovakia, Dec. 25, 1954; came to U.S., 1969; s. Adolf and Dagmar (Dosoudilova) H.; m. Bernadette Callerame, Nov. 10, 1979. BA, Columbia U., 1977, MIA, 1981; JD, N.Y. Law Sch., 1983. Bar: N.J. 1984, N.Y. 1985, Conn. 1985, U.S. Dist. Ct. N.J. 1984, U.S. Dist. Ct. (ea. dist.) N.Y. 1985, U.S. Dist. Ct. (so. dist.) N.Y. 1986. Pvt. practice Paramus, N.J., 1984-92, Pelham Bay, N.Y., 1985—, Conn., 1985—; pres., pub. VonPalisaden Publs., Inc., Paramus, 1986-92; pvt. practice Hillsdale, N.J., 1992—; fin. cons., N.Y., N.J., Conn. Bus. editor Jour. Internat. Affairs, 1979-80. John Jay Nat. scholar, 1973, Solomon scholar, 1981. Mem. ABA, N.J. Bar Assn., N.Y. State Bar Assn., Columbia U. Sailing Club, Blue Key Soc., Phi Gamma Delta. Democrat. Roman Catholic. Avocations: tennis, sailing, skiing, traveling. General practice, Personal injury, Probate. Home and Office: 60 Saddlewood Dr Hillsdale NJ 07642-1336

**HODOUS, ROBERT POWER,** lawyer; b. Zanesville, Ohio, July 29, 1945; s. Robert Frank and Nancy Aurelia (Power) H.; m. Susan Cottrell Birkhead, Feb. 1, 1969; children: Robert Everett, Shannon Alycia. BA, Miami U., Oxford, Ohio, 1967; JD, U. Va., Charlottesville, 1970. Bar: Va. 1970. Assoc. firm McGuire, Woods & Battle, Charlottesville, 1970-71; asst. trust officer Nat. Bank & Trust Co., Charlottesville, 1971-72, trust officer, 1972-75, sec., 1975-79; sec. Jefferson Bankshares, Inc. (formerly NB Corp.), Charlottesville, 1979-91, v.p., sec., 1985-91, sr. v.p., sec., 1987-91; asst. to pres. Jefferson Nat. Bank, Charlottesville, 1987-91; pvt. practice law Charlottesville, 1991-92; mem. firm Payne & Hodous, Charlottesville, 1992—. Chmn. profl. div. Thomas Jefferson Area United Way, 1973, vice-chmn., 1978-79, campaign chmn., 1979-80, v.p. planning, 1981, pres., 1983; bd. dirs. Central Va. chpt. ARC, 1972-78, treas., 1972-75, chmn., 1975-77; commr. Charlottesville Redevel. and Housing Authority, 1974-78; mem. Region X Community Mental Health and Retardation Services Bd., 1973-79, chmn., 1974-76, mem. exec. com., 1976-78; v.p. Soccer Orgn. of Charlottesville-Albemarle, 1985-86, pres., 1986-88; co-pres. Greenbier Sch. PTA, 1985-86; chmn. recreation precinct Charlottesville City Dem. Com., 1971, Rep. com., 1992—; bd. dirs. Charlottesville-Albemarle Community Found., 1987—, chmn. devel. com., 1991-93, mem. exec. and fin. coms., 1991—, chmn. fin. com., 1997—. Mem. Va. Bar Assn., Charlottesville-Albemarle Bar Assn., Va. State Bar, Va. Bankers Assn. (com. drafted Va. Trust Subs. Act 1973, trust com. 1974-77, legal affairs com. 1986-91, large bank legis. coord. 1987-91), Computer Law Assn., Albemarle C. of C. (legis. action com. 1996—), Fairview Club (Charlottesville, pres. 1974-75). Roman Catholic. Banking, General corporate, Pension, profit-sharing, and employee benefits. Home: 1309 Lester Dr Charlottesville VA 22901-3143 Office: 412 E Jefferson St Charlottesville VA 22902-5109 *To me success is indicated by feelings of personal peace and satisfaction, not by external possessions. My goals are to do my best in contributing to the success of endeavors in which I become involved and to remember that the people involved in activities are the most important part of the activities. I feel my family is my most important endeavor. I hope never to become so involved in activities that I cannot enjoy my family, my surroundings and people I meet, or that I cannot spend the time necessary to do well those activities in which I am involved.*

**HOEFLE, PAUL RYAN,** lawyer; b. Aurora, Ill., July 25, 1956; s. Ronald Anthony and Shirley Anne Hoefle; m. Mary Beth Wredling, June 25, 1983; children: Mary Elyse, Mitchell, Matthew. BS in Fin. summa cum laude, U. Ill., 1978; JD, U. Mich., 1981. Bar: Wis., U.S. Dist. Ct. (ea. and we. dists.) Wis. Assoc. Frisch, Dudek & Slattery, Milw., 1981-86, shareholder, 1986-88; shareholder Slattery, Hausman & Hoefle, Waukesha, Wis., 1988-98; shareholder, mng. ptnr. Bode, Carroll, McCoy & Hoefle, Waukesha, 1998—. Bd. dirs. Wildlife in Need, Oconomowoc, Wis., 1998—. Mem. State Bar Wis., Milw. Bar Assn., Waukesha Bar Assn., Wis. Acad. Trial Lawyers (bd. dirs. 1988—, exec. com. 1997—), Waukesha Rotary Club. Avocations: outdoor activities, children's activities. Personal injury, Professional liability, Product liability. Office: Bode Carroll McCoy & Hoefle SC 20700 Swenson Dr Ste 250 Waukesha WI 53186-0905

**HOEFLICH, MICHAEL HARLAN,** law school dean; b. N.Y.C., Jan. 11, 1952; s. Sterling Martin and Barbara Su (Junger) H.; m. Karen Nordheden, Sept. 13, 1986. BA, MA in Canon Law, Haverford (Pa.) Coll., 1973; MA, Cambridge (Eng.) U., 1976; JD, Yale U., 1979. Bar: N.Y. 1980. Rsch. fellow Cambridge U., 1975-77; tax assoc. Cravath, Swaine & Moore, N.Y.C., 1978-79, 79-81; asst. prof. law U. Ill., Champaign, 1981-84, assoc. prof., 1984-86, prof., univ. scholar, dir. rsch. on legal history, 1986-88; prof. law and history Syracuse (N.Y.) U., 1988-94, dean coll. law, 1988-94; dean sch. law U. Kans., Lawrence, 1994—, John M. and John H. Kane Disting. prof., 1997—. Author: Roman and Civil Law, and the Development of Anglo-American Jurisprudence, 1997; co-author: Cases and Materials on Federal Taxation of Deferred Compensation, 1989; co-editor Property Law and Legal Education, 1988; editor The Gladsome Light of Jurisprudence, Learning the Law in England and the United States in the 18th and 19th Centuries, 1988; legal columnist Lawrence Jour.-World, 1994—; contbr. numerous articles to profl. publs. Housing commr. Champaign County Housing Authority, 1987-88; host weekly radio show on sta. WILL-AM, Champaign, 1986-88; bd. dirs. U. Ill. Libr. Friends, Champaign, 1988-90. Recipient Surrency Prize Am. Soc. Legal History, 1985. Fellow Am. Bar Found., Am. Philos. Soc. (Phillips); mem. Onondaga County Bar Assn. (bd. dirs. 1991-93), N.Y. State Bar Assn. (com. on professionalism 1988-94), Am. Law Inst. (advisor restatement, property, security and mortgages coms. 1989-93), Fund for Modern Cts. (bd. dirs. 1988-90), Kans. Bar Assn. Contracts commercial. Office: U Kansas Sch Law Green Hall Lawrence KS 66044-7577

**HOELSCHER, MICHAEL RAY,** lawyer; b. Rosebud, Tex., Dec. 15, 1947; s. Clarence Raymond and Helen (Buster) H.; m. Anita R. Clark, June 6, 1975; children: Jennie, Matt. BA, Baylor U., 1970, JD, 1972. Bar: Tex. 1972, U.S. Dist. Ct. (so. dist.) Tex. 1976. Assoc. Law Office of Phillip Goode, College Station, Tex., 1974-78; shareholder Hoelscher, Lipsey & Elmore, College Station, 1978—, 1995—; lectr. Tex. A&M U., 1975-76; shareholder, officer Univ. Title Co., College Station, 1982—. Pres. Brazos Valley Rehab. Ctr., Bryan, Tex., 1980-82, Am. Heart Assn., 1992. Mem. Coll. State Bar Tex., Brazos County Bar Assn. (pres. 1988-89), The Dispute Resolution Ctr. (pres. 1997-99), Tex. Bar Found. (1999—), Lions (pres. College Station club 1982-83), Tiger Club (pres. 1995-96). State civil litigation, Personal injury, Family and matrimonial. Office: Hoelscher Lipsey Elmore PC 1021 University Dr E College Station TX 77840-2120

**HOELZEL, SALLY ANN,** lawyer; b. Knoxville, Iowa, Apr. 5, 1962; d. Clement C. and Helen J. (Falck) H.; m. Peter M. Eckblad, Oct. 11, 1986. BS, U. Wis., 1984, JD, 1987. Bar: Wis. 1987, U.S. Dist. Ct. (we. dist.) Wis. 1987. Assoc. McBurney, Perina, Wyngaard, Wilson & Raymond, Madison, Wis., 1987-88; staff atty. Office of State Pub. Defender, Racine, Wis., 1988-96; pvt. practice Racine, 1996—. Mem. ACLU, NOW, State Bar Wis., Racine County Bar Assn., People for the Ethical Treatment of Animals, ASPCA, Planned Parenthood, Ctr. for Reproductive Law and Policy. Criminal, Family and matrimonial, Juvenile. Office: 201 6th St Ste 300 Racine WI 53403-1264

**HOENIG, GERALD JAY,** lawyer, insurance company executive; b. N.Y.C., Sept. 25, 1944; s. Sidney Benjamin and Florence (Greenberg) H.; m. Susan Leslie Hoenig; children: Anne, Lesley, Deborah, Spencer. BA, CCNY, 1966; JD, Boston Coll., 1969. Atty. Met. Life Ins. Co., N.Y.C., 1969-75; atty. Met. Life Ins. Co., Oak Brook, Ill., 1975-80, asst. gen. counsel, 1980-86; assoc. gen. counsel Met. Life Ins. Co., Itasca, Ill., 1986-92, Atlanta, 1992—; bd. dirs., sec. Metmor Fin., Inc., Overland Park, Kans., 1987-94, Farmers Nat. co., Omaha, 1987-97, Met. Farm & Ranch, Inc., Overland Park, 1986-96; mem. faculty Practicing Law Inst., N.Y.C., 1988-91. Expert, originator Expert System, CLINT, 1989. Youth soccer coach Naperville (Ill.) Park Dist., 1979-91. Mem. ABA (co-chmn. com. on design and constrn. 1989-92, chair com. agribus. 1992-97, chair com. on tech. and comml. mortgage financing). Avocations: computer programming and applications, tennis, soccer, sports. Real property, General corporate, Construction. Home: 8495 Caney Creek Lndg Alpharetta GA 30005-7847 Office: Met Life Ins Co 2400 Lakeview Pkwy Alpharetta GA 30004-1976

**HOERNER, ROBERT JACK,** lawyer; b. Fairfield, Iowa, Oct. 12, 1931; s. John Andrew and Margaret Louise (Simmons) H.; m. Judith Chandler, Apr. 21, 1954 (div. Feb. 1975); children: John Andrew II, Timothy Chandler, Blayne Marie, Michelle Margaret Hoerner Smith; m. Mary Paolano, June 3, 1989. BA, Cornell Coll., 1953; JD, U. Mich., 1958. Bar: Ohio 1960, U.S. Supreme Ct. 1964, U.S. Ct. Appeals (6th cir.) 1972, U.S. Ct. Appeals (Fed. cir.) 1990. Law clk. to hon. Chief Justice Earl Warren U.S. Supreme Ct., Washington, 1958-59; assoc. Jones, Day, Reavis & Pogue, Cleve., 1959-63, 65-66; chief evaluation sect. antitrust divsn. Dept. Justice, Washington, 1963-65; ptnr. Jones, Day, Reavis & Pogue, Cleve., 1967-93. Contbr. articles to prof. jours. Trustee New Orgn. of the Visual Arts, Cleve., 1976-80, 87-90. With Counter Intelligence Corps, U.S. Army, 1953-55. Mem. ABA (antitrust sect., patent sect.), Ohio Bar Assn., Greater Cleve. Bar Assn., Cleve. Intellectual Property Law Assn., Leland (Mich.) Country Club, Order of Coif, Phi Beta Kappa. Democrat. Antitrust, Patent, Federal civil litigation. Home: 360 Darbys Run Bay Village OH 44140-2968 Office: Jones Day Reavis & Pogue 901 Lakeside Ave E Cleveland OH 44114-1116

**HOEVELER, WILLIAM M.,** federal judge; b. Aug. 23, 1922; m. Mary Griffin Smith, 1950; 4 children. Student, Temple U., 1941-42; B.A., Bucknell U., 1947; LL.B., Harvard U., 1950. Bar: Fla. 1951. Practice law Miami, Fla., 1951-77; firm individual practice law; judge U.S. Dist. Ct. for Fla. So. Dist., 1977—; federal judge U.S. Dist., Miami, Fla., now sr. judge; lectr. in field. Incorporator, bd. dirs. Youth Industries, Inc.; mem. vestry St. Stephens Episcopal Ch., 1973-75, chancellor, 1973. Served to lt. USMC, 1942-46. Mem. Am. Judicature Soc., Fla. Bar (personal injury and wrongful death adv. com. 1976), Phila. Bar Assn., Dade County (Fla.) Bar Assn. (chmn. charity drives com. 1966), Am. Bar Assn. (chmn. com. on products, profl. and gen. liability law 1972-73, program chmn. sec. ins., negligence and compensation law 1975, mem. sect. governing council 1975-78, mem. governing com. of forum com. on constrn. industry), Omicron Delta Kappa. Office: US Dist Ct 301 N Miami Ave Fl 9 Miami FL 33128-7702

**HOEY, WILLIAM EDWARD,** lawyer; b. Mckeesport, Pa., Sept. 22, 1930; s. Edward Duane and Helen (Damm) H.; m. Shirley Morgan, Dec. 27, 1954; children—Gregory, Jonathan, Jessica, Christopher, Erica. A.B., Dickinson Coll., 1952, LL.B., 1954. Bar: Pa. 1957, U.S. Dist. Ct. (we. dist.) Pa. 1957, U.S. Supreme Ct. 1970, Fla. 1972, U.S. Dist. Ct. (so. dist.) Fla. 1975. Sole practice, Pitts., 1957-75, Miami, Fla., 1975—; Served with M.C., U.S. Army, 1954-56. Mem. ABA, Pa. Bar Assn., Allegheny County Bar Assn., Pa. Def. Inst., Am. Arbitration Assn., Fla. Bar, Dade County Bar Assn., Fla. Def. Lawyers Assn., Def. Research Inst., Internat. Assn. Def. Counsel, Phi Kappa Psi, Pi Delta Epsilon. State civil litigation, Federal civil litigation, Insurance. Home: 7400 Laurels Pl Port Saint Lucie FL 34986-3268

**HOFELICH, JAMES ALBERT,** lawyer; b. Cleve., June 1, 1943; s. Charles G. and Jean L. (Zander) H.; m. Susan LaPorte, Jan. 31, 1970; children: James, Amy, Clay, Emily, Mark. BS in Chemistry, Wittenberg U., Springfield, Ohio, 1966; JD, Case Western Res. U., Cleve., 1969. Bar: Ohio 1969, U.S. Dist. Ct. (no. dist.) Ohio 1969, U.S. Ct. Appeals (6th cir.) 1969, (2d cir.) 1979, (5th cir.) 1982, U.S. Patent and Trademark Office 1970. Assoc. McCoy, Greene & Howell, Cleve., 1969-70; ptnr. Spangenberg, Shibley, Traci, Lancione, Cleve., 1971-85, Jones, Day, Reavis & Pogue, Cleve., 1985-91, Hofelich & King, Cleve., 1992—; spkr. various seminars; host/moderator TV 54 Ohio Supreme Ct. Candidate. Columnist, Cleve. Bar Jour., 1972-75. Bd. dirs. The Covenant, Cleve., 1984—; legal advisor Ohio Disaster Relief, 1980-84. Mem. ABA (litigation sect.), Ohio State Bar Assn., Cuyahoga County Bar Assn., Cleve. Bar Assn., Ohio Acad. Trial Lawyers, Assn. Trial Lawyers Am., Lakewood Country Club (caddie chmn. 1985—). General civil litigation, Personal injury, Intellectual property. Home: 30880 Clinton Dr Bay Village OH 44140-1526 Office: Hofelich & King One Cleveland Ctr 200 Public Sq Ste 2920 Cleveland OH 44114-2301

**HOFER, STEPHEN ROBERT,** lawyer; b. Anderson, Ind., July 25, 1950; s. Robert E. and Maxine (Hert) H.; m. Cheryl A. Stiles, Aug. 27, 1994; 1 child, Victoria Sloane. AB, Ind. U., 1976; JD, Northwestern U., 1980. Bar: Calif. 1980, U.S. Dist. Ct. (ctrl. dist.) Calif. 1980, U.S. Ct. Appeals (9th cir.) 1980, U.S. Dist. Ct. (ea., no., and so. dists.) Calif. 1982, U.S. Supreme Ct. 1995. Mng. editor Daily Herald-Tel., Bloomington, Ind., 1972-74; asst. city editor Miami Herald, Ft. Lauderdale, Fla., 1976-77; atty. Gibson Dunn & Crutcher, L.A., 1980-84; venue press chief L.A. Olympic Organizing Com., 1983-84; v.p., gen. counsel Am. Golf Corp., Santa Monica, Calif., 1984-92; atty., ptnr. Bailey & Marzano, Santa Monica, 1992—; instr. law U. So. Calif., L.A., 1983-84. Sec., bd. dirs. Mus. of Flying, Santa Monica, 1986-89; bd. dirs. L.A. Philharmonic Assn., 1992-95, Santa Monica Symphony Assn., 1999—; pres. L.A. Philharmonic Bus. and Profl. Assn., 1992-95. Democrat. Avocations: symphonic music, mountain climbing, travel, wine, photography. Aviation, General corporate, Real property. Office: Bailey & Marzano 2d Fl 2828 Don Douglas Loop N Santa Monica CA 90405-2959

**HOFF, JONATHAN M(ORIND),** lawyer; b. Chgo., July 4, 1955; s. Irwin S. and Ida (Indritz) H. AB, U. Calif., Berkeley, 1978; JD, UCLA, 1981. Bar: Calif. 1981, U.S. Dist. Ct. (no. and cen. dists.) Calif. 1981, N.Y. 1982, U.S. Dist. Ct. (so. dist.) N.Y. 1982, U.S. Ct. Appeals (4th, 5th, 7th, 8th, 9th, 10th cirs.) 1982. Ptnr. Weil, Gotshal & Manges, N.Y.C., 1981-98, Cadwalader, Wickersham & Taft, N.Y.C., 1998—. Comment editor UCLA Law Rev., 1980-81; contbr. articles to law jours. Mem. ABA, Calif. Bar Assn. General civil litigation, Mergers and acquisitions, Securities. Office: Cadwalader Wickersham & Taft 100 Maiden Ln New York NY 10038-4818

**HOFFA, ROBERT ALAN,** lawyer; b. West Reading, Pa., Mar. 4, 1957; s. Edwin Jacob and Maggie E. Hofa; married, Sept. 1984 (dec. Aug. 1994); 1 child, Taylor. BA, Washington & Jefferson Coll., 1979; JD, Del. Law Sch., 1982. Bar: Pa. 1982, U.S. Dist. Ct. (ea. dist.) Pa. 1984, U.S. Ct. Appeals (3d cir.) 1986, U.S. Supreme Ct. 1991. Assoc. Nino V. Tinari P.C., Phila., 1982-87; ptnr. Hoffa and Freemas, Bensalem, Pa., 1987-92; pvt. practice, Bensalem, 1992—; cons. Nat. Reining Horse Assn., Oklahoma City, 1987—; instr. Salem Teikyo U., 1996—; panel mem. Gryphon Equine Ins., Woodland Hills, Calif., 1998. Mem. Am. Trial Lawyers Assn., Pa. Bar Assn. (agrl. law com. 1997—). Insurance, State civil litigation, Equine. Office: The Ctr Schoolhouse 3360 Knights Rd Bensalem PA 19020-2819

**HOFFA, THOMAS EDWARD,** lawyer; b. Marshalltown, Iowa, Sept. 20, 1935; s. Harvey Edward and Janette (Nason) H. BS, Iowa State U., 1958; JD, John Marshall Law Sch., 1972. Bar: Ill. 1972, U.S. Dist. Ct. (no. dist.) Ill. 1972 (Gen. Bar), U.S. Tax Ct. 1976, U.S. Dist. Ct. (no. dist.) Ill. 1983, U.S. Ct. Appeals (7th cir.) 1987. Sole practice Chgo., 1972—. With USAF, 1958-60. Mem. ABA, Assn. Trial Lawyers Am., Ill. State Bar Assn., Chgo. Bar Assn. Republican. Presbyterian. Appellate, General civil litigation, Criminal. Office: 30 W Chicago Ave Ste 1320 Chicago IL 60610-4339

**HOFFHEIMER, DANIEL JOSEPH,** lawyer; b. Cin., Dec. 28, 1950; s. Harry Max and Charlotte (O'Brien) H.; children: Rebecca, Rachel, Leah. Grad., Phillips Exeter Acad., 1969; AB cum laude, Harvard Coll., 1973; JD, U. Va., 1976. Bar: Ohio 1976, U.S. Dist. Ct. (so. dist.) Ohio 1976, U.S. Ct. Appeals (6th crct.) 1977, U.S. Ct. Appeals (D.C. and fed. crcts.) 1986, U.S. Ct. Internat. Trade 1986, U.S. Tax Ct. 1992, U.S. Supreme Ct. 1980, U.S. Tax Ct. 1992. Assoc. Taft, Stettinius & Hollister, Cin., 1976-84, ptnr., 1984—; lectr. law Coll. Law, U. Cin., 1981-83; trustee Judges Hogan & Porter Meml. Trust; mem. adv. bd. Ohio Dist. Ct. Rev. Editor-in-chief U. Va. Jour. Internat. Law, 1975-76; co-author: Practitioners' Handbook Ohio First District Court Appeals, 1984, 2d edit., 1991, Federal Practice Manual, U.S. 6th Circuit Court of Appeals, 1993, Manual on Labor Law, 1988; contbr. articles to profl. jours. Mem. Cin. Symphony Bus. Rels. Com., 1977-86, Cin. Composers Guild, 1988-93, Ohio Supreme Ct. Com. Racial Fairness, 1993—; trustee Underground R.R. Freedom Mus., 1995—; mem. adv. bd. for Consumer Protection, Cin., 1978-80, Hoxworth Blood Ctr. Univ. Cin. Hosp., 1994—; mem. bd. Hebrew Union Coll. Jewish Inst. Religion, 1994—, WGUC-FM Pub. Radio, 1988—, vice chmn., 1993-96, chmn., 1996-98; trustee Cin. Chamber Orch., 1977-80, Seven Hills Sch., Cin., 1980-86, Internat. Visitors Ctr., Cin., 1980-84, Friends Coll. Conservatory of Music, Cin., 1985-86, Cin. Symphony Orch., 1988-94, 96—, sec., 1996-99, vice chair

1999—, Children's Psychiat. Ctr., Cin., 1986-89, treas., 1987-89; vice chmn. Jewish Hosp., Cin., 1989-92; Leadership Cin., 1989-90; sec., trustee Cin. Symphony Musicians Pension Fund, 1989-99, Jewish Cmty. Rels. Coun., 1990-98, v.p., 1996-98; sec. Nat. Conf. Commn. Justice, 1992-99, treas. 1999—; counsel Cin. AIDS Commn., 1991—, Cin. Inst. Fine Arts Govt. Affairs Com., 1993-94, B'nai B'rith Nat. Coun. Legacy Devel., 1996-97. Named Outstanding Young Man, U.S. Jaycees, 1984, 98. Life fellow Am. Bar Found., Ohio Bar Found.; fellow Am. Coll. of Trust & Estate Counsel; mem. ABA, Internat. Bar Assn., Internat. Trade Bar Assn., Internat. Arbitration Assn. (comml. arbitrator 1991-95), Fed. Bar Assn. (treas. 1984, sec. 1985, v.p. 1986-87, pres. 1987-88), Ohio State Bar Assn., Cin. Bar Assn. (trustee 1988-93, v.p. 1990-91, pres. 1992-93, dean Cin. Acad. Leadership for Lawyers 1998—), Harvard Club of Cin. (bd. dirs. 1980-88, v.p. 1983-86, pres. 1986-87). Democrat. Avocations: music, tennis, Chinese and Japanese art. General practice, Estate planning, Probate. Home: 3672 Willowlea Ct # A Cincinnati OH 45208-1816 Office: 1800 Firstar Tower 425 Walnut St Cincinnati OH 45202-3923 *The elusive meaning of life is really at our fingertips: to create and execute the purpose of making life better for others today and after. Felicitously, that is our joy.*

**HOFFLUND, PAUL,** lawyer; b. San Diego, Mar. 27, 1928; s. John Leslie and Ethel Frances (Cline) H.; m. Anne Marie Thalman, Feb. 15, 1958; children: Mark, Sylvia. BA, Princeton (N.J.) U., 1950; JD, George Washington U., 1956. Bar: D.C. 1956, U.S. Dist. Ct. D.C. 1956, U.S. Ct. Appeals (D.C. cir.) 1956, Calif. 1957, U.S. Dist. Ct. (so. dist.) Calif. 1957, U.S. Ct. Mil. Appeals 1957, U.S. Ct. Claims 1958, U.S. Ct. Appeals (9th cir.) 1960, U.S. Supreme Ct. 1964, U.S. Tax Ct. 1989. Assoc. Wencke, Carlson & Kuykendall, San Diego, 1961-62; ptnr. Carlson, Kuykendall & Hofflund, San Diego, 1963-65, Carlson & Hofflund, San Diego, 1965-72; Christian Sci. practitioner San Diego, 1972-84; arbitrator Mcpl. Cts. and Superior Ct. of Calif., San Diego, 1984—; pvt. practice San Diego, 1985—; adj. prof. law Nat. U. Sch. Law, San Diego, 1985-94; judge pro tem Mcpl. Ct. South Bay Jud. Dist., 1990—; disciplinary counsel to U.S. Tax Ct., 1989—; asst. U.S. atty. U.S. Dept. of Justice, L.A., 1959-60, asst. U.S. atty. in charge, San Diego, 1960-61, spl. hearing officer, San Diego, 1962-68; asst. corp. counsel Govt. of D.C., 1957-59. Author: (chpt. in book) Handbook on Criminal Procedure in the U.S. District Court, 1967; contbr. articles to profl. jours. Treas. Princeton Club of San Diego; v.p. Community Concert Assn., San Diego; pres. Sunland Home Found., San Diego, Trust for Christian Sci. Orgn., San Diego; chmn. bd. 8th Ch. of Christ, Scientist, San Diego. With USN, 1950-53, comdr. JAGC, USNR, 1953-72, ret. Mem. ABA, San Diego County Bar Assn., Inst. Global Ethics, World Affairs Coun., Phi Delta Phi. Democrat. Avocations: theater, classical music, bridge, fine art, biblical study. General practice, Estate planning, Probate. Home and Office: 6146 Syracuse Ln San Diego CA 92122-3301 *Decisions should be based on divine direction rather than human determination. Pray first; then act. A life devoid of sprirituality lacks dimension. The steps of a good man are ordered by the lord: And he delighteth in his way.*

**HOFFMAN, ALAN CRAIG,** lawyer, consultant; b. Chgo., Oct. 1, 1944; s. Morris Joseph and Marie E. H.; m. Pamela Hoffman. BA, Carthage Coll., 1968; JD, John Marshall Law Sch., 1973. Bar: Fla. 1973, Ill. 1973, U.S. Dist. Ct. (no dist.) Ill. 1974, U.S. Dist. Ct. (mid. dist.) Fla. 1981, U.S. Ct. Appeals (7th cir.) 1974, U.S. Ct. Appeals (5th and 11th cirs.) 1981, U.S. Supreme Ct. 1977. Staff atty. Cook County Legal Assistance Found., Brookfield, 1973-74, Patient Legal Svcs., Chgo., 1974; pvt. practice law, Chgo., 1973—, River Grove, Ill., 1973-86, Oak Brook, Ill., 1980-87—, Hinsdale, Ill., 1987-93; with assocs., 1980—; spl. asst. atty. gen. Ill. Criminal Justice Div., Chgo., 1977-79, Ill. Condemnation Div., Chgo., 1980-87; pres. Almar, Ltd., 1986-91; v.p. Marach, Ltd., 1986-89, Hoffman Realty, 1978—; pres., dir. North Shore Greenview Bldg. Corp., 1978—; asst. prof. law Lewis U., 1974-79, vis. prof. Coll. Law Paraprofl. Center, 1974-76, adj. prof., 1979-80; assoc. prof. No. Ill. U., 1979-80; v.p. Adv. Adv. Service, Inc.; cons. med.-legal cases, 1982—. Mem. Oak Park Twp. (Ill.) Mental Health Bd., 1975-80, v.p. 1975, chmn. program com. 1975-77, pres. 1978; governing bd. Women In Need Growing Stronger, 1993-96; bd. govs. Jewish Fedn. of Chgo., coun. for elderly, 1995—; co-chair Rainbow House Bread and Roses Ann. Fundraiser, 1997-98. Fellow Am. Coll. Legal Medicine (assoc. in law 1975, profl. devel. com. 1990—, student awards com. 1993—, moot court competition com. 1992—, co-chair com. violence and abuse in the family 1993, textbook update com. 1988, program com. 1988—, legal com. 1988—, editl. bd. med. and legal textbook com. 1987—); mem. ABA (civil procedure and evidence com. 1993—, commercial tort com. 1993—), Ill. State Bar Assn. (vice-chmn. standing com. on mentally disabled 1975-77, chmn. 77-78), Chgo. Bar Assn., DuPage Bar Assn., West Suburban Bar Assn., Chgo. Acad. Law and Medicine, Am. Soc. Law and Medicine, Mensa, Ill. Trial Lawyers Assn. (profl. negligence com. 1982), Fla. Bar Assn. (health law com. 1983-84, out-of-state practitioner com. 1988-91), Assn. Trial Lawyers Am., Phi Alpha Delta, Mensa. Author: (with F. Lane and D. Birnbaum) Lane's Medical Litigation Guide, 1981; contbr. articles to Med. Trial Technique Quar., numerous articles in field; speaker, lectr., presenter in field U.S., Europe, Israel, Africa; editorial bd. Jour. Legal Medicine, 1980—, Medical Malpractice Prevention, 1986-96, Medical Malpractice Prevention Ob-Gyn, 1987-96; contbg. author Legal Medicine: Legal Dynamics of Med. Encounters, 1988, 2d edit., 1991, supplement, 1990, 91, 92, 93, 94, 3rd. edit. 1995. Personal injury, State civil litigation, Workers' compensation.

**HOFFMAN, ALAN JAY,** lawyer; b. Phila., Aug. 31, 1948; s. Heinz Julius and Sylvia (Wise) H.; children: Jennifer, Lauren, Allison. BBA, Temple U., 1970; JD, Villanova U., 1973. Bar: Pa. 1973, U.S. Dist. Ct. (ea. dist.) Pa. 1973, U.S. Dist. Ct. Del. 1973, U.S. Ct. Appeals (3rd cir.) 1973, Del. 1977, U.S. Supreme Ct. 1984, D.C. 1990. Asst. U.S. atty. U.S. Dept. Justice, Wilimington, Del., 1973-78; ptnr. Dilworth, Paxson, Kalish & Kauffman, Phila., 1979-92, mem. exec. mgmt. com., 1989-90, chmn. new bus. com., 1990-91; ptnr. Blank, Rome, Comisky and McCauley, Phila., 1992—, mem. exec. mgmt. com., 1998—, co-chmn. atty. recruiting com.; adminstrv. ptnr. in charge Blank, Rome, Comisky and McCauley, Wilmington, Del., chmn. litigation and dispute resolution dept., 1996—; lectr. Widener Del. Law Sch., Wilmington, 1974. Contbg. co-editor Villanova Law Rev., 1972-73; contbr. articles to profl. jours. Bd. dirs. Men's Club Temple Adath Israel, Merion, Pa., 1993—. Recipient Atty. Gen.'s Spl. Commendation U.S. Dept. Justice, Washington, 1977. Mem. ABA, Pa. Bar Assn., Fed. Bar Assn., Phila. Bar Assn., Del. Bar Assn., Assn. Trial Lawyers Am., Del. Trial Lawyers Assn., Pa. Trial Lawyers Assn., White Manor Country Club (pres. 1993—, 1st v.p. 1990-93, bd. dirs. 1988-90, admissions chmn. 1989—). Avocation: golf. General civil litigation, Criminal, General practice. Office: Blank Rome Comisky & McCauley One Logan Sq Philadelphia PA 19103-6998

**HOFFMAN, ALAN S.,** lawyer; b. Bronx, N.Y., July 9, 1962; s. Robert and Doris Lenore Hoffman; m. Marla Sue Hoffman, Apr. 30, 1989; children: Danielle Kayli, Nicole Remi. Student, SUNY, Albany, 1980-84; JD, Georgetown U., 1987. Bar: N.Y. 1987. Assoc. Reid & Priest, N.Y.C., 1987-95, Dewey Ballantine, N.Y.C., 1995-96; ptnr. Whitman Breed Abbott & Morgan LLP, N.Y.C., 1997—. General corporate, Securities, Finance. Office: Whitman Breed Abbott & Morgan 200 Park Ave New York NY 10166-0005

**HOFFMAN, BARRY PAUL,** lawyer; b. Phila., May 29, 1941; s. Samuel and Hilda (Cohn) H.; m. Mary Ann Schrock, May 18, 1978; children: Elizabeth Barron, Hayley Rebecca. BA, Pa. State U., 1963; JD, George Washington U., 1968. Bar: Pa. 1972, Mich. 1983. Asst. U.S. Senator Wayne Morse, Oreg., Washington; spl. agt. FBI, Washington; asst. dist. atty. Phila. Dist. Atty.'s Office; exec. v.p., gen. counsel Valassis Communications, Inc., Livonia, Mich. 1st lt. U.S. Army, 1963-65, Korea. General corporate. Home: 49933 Standish Ct Plymouth MI 48170-2882 Office: Valassis Communications Inc 19975 Victor Pkwy Livonia MI 48152-7001

**HOFFMAN, CARL H(ENRY),** lawyer; b. St. Louis, May 28, 1936; s. Carl Henry and Anna Marie (Remlinger) H.; m. Pamela L. Polk, May 8, 1971 (div. Novl 1982); children: Kurt M., Jennifer K. BS, St. Louis U., 1958; postgrad., U. Mex., Mexico City, 1958, U. Nev., 1960-61, Tex. Technol. Coll., 1961-62; JD, Washington U., St. Louis, 1966. Bar: Mo. 1966, Fla. 1969, U.S. Supreme Ct. 1970; cert. civil trial adv. Nat. Bd. Trial Advocacy. Pilot Eastern. Airlines, Inc., Miami, Fla.; assoc. Spencer & Taylor, Miami, Fla., 1969-70; pvt. practice, Miami, 1970-80; ptnr. Hoffman & Hertzig, P.A., Coral Gables, Fla., 1980—. Capt. USAF, 1958-63. Mem. ABA, ATLA, Fla. Bar (cert. civil trial lawyer, cert. bus. litigation lawyer, civil procedure rules com., chmn. aviation law com. 1997-98), Fla. Acad. Trial Lawyers, Am. Jurisprudence Soc., Greater Miami C. of C. (trustee). Aviation, General civil litigation, Personal injury. Office: Hoffman & Hertzig PA 241 Sevilla Ave Ste 900 Coral Gables FL 33134-6600

**HOFFMAN, CARL K.,** lawyer; b. Plant City, Fla., Mar. 10, 1929; s. Virginia Bautier (Randolph) H.; m. Patricia Ray Shepard Hoffman, Mar. 18, 1961; children: Debra, Sandra, David, William. BS, Northwestern U., Evanston, Ill., 1951; JD, Yale U., New Haven, Conn., 1957. Bar: Fla., Va., D.C. Ptnr. Kinbrell & Hamann PA, Miami, 1960-93. Lt. USN, 1951-54, Korea. Mem. Nat. Soc. Sons of the Am. Revolution. Avocations: stamp collecting, historical research, travel. Home: 1291 Beach Ave Atlantic Beach FL 32233

**HOFFMAN, DANIEL STEVEN,** lawyer, legal educator; b. N.Y.C., May 4, 1931; s. Lawrence Hoffman and Juliette (Marbes) Ostrov; m. Beverly Mae Swenson, Dec. 4, 1954; children: Lisa Hoffman Ciancio, Tracy Hoffman Cockriel, Robin Hoffman Black. BA, U. Colo., 1951; LLB, U. Denver, 1958. Bar: Colo. 1958. Assoc., then ptnr. Fugate, Mitchem, Hoffman, Denver, 1951-55; mgr. of safety City and County of Denver, 1963-65; ptnr. Kripke, Hoffman, Carrigan, Denver, 1965-70, Hoffman, McDermott, Hoffman, Denver, 1970-78; of counsel Hoffman & McDermott, Denver, 1978-84; mem. Holme Roberts & Owen, LLC, Denver, 1984-94; dean Coll. Law, U. Denver, 1978-84, dean emeritus, prof. emeritus, 1984—; ptnr. McKenna & Cuneo LLP, Denver, 1994—; bd. dirs. CLE in Colo., 1971-74; chmn., mem. Merit Screening Com. for Bankruptcy Judges, Denver, 1979-84; chmn. subcom. Dist. Atty.'s Crime Adv. Commn., Denver, 1984—; chmn. Senator Wirth's jud. nomination rev. com.; mem. Senator Campbell's jud. nomination rev. com. Contbr. chpts. to books. Mem. Rocky Mountain region Anti-Defamation League, Denver, 1985; bd. dirs. Colo. chpt. Am. Jewish Com., 1985, Legal Ctr., Denver, 1985—; mem. adv. com. Samaritan Shelter, Denver, 1985; chmn. Rocky Flats Blue Ribbon Citizens Com., Denver, 1980-83; mem. bd. visitors J. Reuben Clark Law Sch. Brigham Young U., 1986-88. With USAF, 1951-55. Recipient Am. Jewish Com. Nat. Judge Learned Hand award, 1993, Humanitarian award Rocky Mountain chpt. Anti-Defamation League, 1984, Alumni of Yr. award U. Denver Coll. Law, 1997. Fellow Am. Coll. Trial Lawyers (state chmn. 1975-76), Internat. Soc. Barristers, Colo. Bar. Found., Am. Bar Found.; mem. Colo. Bar. Assn. (pres. 1976-77, Young Lawyer of Yr. award 1965), Colo. Trial Lawyers Assn. (pres. 1961-62), Assn. Trial Lawyers Am. (nat. com. mem. 1962-63), Am. Judicature Soc. (bd. dirs. 1977-81), Order of Coif (hon.). Democrat. Jewish. Avocation: platform tennis. Federal civil litigation, State civil litigation, Personal injury. Office: McKenna & Cuneo LLP 370 17th St Ste 4800 Denver CO 80202-5648

**HOFFMAN, DARNAY ROBERT,** management consultant; b. N.Y.C., Nov. 25, 1947; s. Bill and Toni (Darnay) H.; B.A., SUNY, 1977; M.B.A., Baruch Coll., City U. N.Y., 1980; J.D., Yeshiva U., 1982; m. Jennifer Lea Sheppard, Aug. 20, 1984; children by previous marriage—Brandon, Brett. Pres., Darnay Hoffman Assos., Inc., mgmt. cons., N.Y.C., 1969—, Hoffman Research Group, Inc., mgmt. cons., N.Y.C., 1977—; research asso. Baruch Coll., 1977-79; bd. dirs. Hobton Realty Corp.; dir. Nat. Conf. Law Historians Am., 1987—. Mem. ABA, Am. Mgmt. Assn., Am. Mktg. Assn., Acad. Mgmt. Scis., Beta Gamma Sigma, Alpha Delta Sigma. Club: Player's. Author: Murder in the Wilderness, Alien Contact, 1980; (pamphlet) Products in Decline, 1980.

**HOFFMAN, DAVID NATHANIEL,** lawyer; b. N.Y.C., Aug. 10, 1960; s. Martin J. and Edith D. Hoffman; m. Joan Lynne Fiden, Feb. 18, 1990; children: Benjamin, Emily. JD, SUNY, Buffalo, 1986; cert. in bio-ethics, Columbia U., 1996. Bar: N.Y. 1997, U.S. Dist. Ct. (ea. dist.) N.Y. 1997, U.S. Dist. Ct. (so. dist.) N.Y. 1997. Litigation assoc. Martin, Clearwater & Bell, N.Y.C., 1986-88; assoc., then ptnr. Kanterman, Taub & Breitner, N.Y.C., 1988-94; founding ptnr. Breitner & Hoffman, N.Y.C., 1994-99, Law Offices of David N. Hoffman, P.C., N.Y.C., 1999—. Mem. Am. Soc. Law Medicine and Ethics, Nature Conservancy, Amnesty Internat., Habitat for Humanity, Assn. of Bar of City of N.Y. (legis. liaison com. on med. malpractice 1988-96, chmn. subcom. on organ donation 1996—, com. on bioethics). Avocations: sailing, SCUBA diving, woodworking, bicycling, philosophy. Professional liability, Health, Alternative dispute resolution. Office: 233 E 69th St New York NY 10021-5414

**HOFFMAN, DONALD ALFRED,** lawyer; b. Milw., May 4, 1936; s. Harry Gustav and Emily Frances (Schwartz) H.; m. Louise Hardie Chapman, June 8, 1963; children: Donald Hardie, Richard Rainey. BBA, U. Wis., 1958, JD, 1968. Bar: La. 1969, U.S. Supreme Ct. 1972, U.S. Ct. Appeals (5th cir.) 1973, U.S. Dist. Ct. (ea., mid. and we. dists.) La. Assoc. Lemle & Kelleher, New Orleans, 1968-73; ptnr. Lemle, Kelleher, Kohlmeyer, Matthews & Schumacher, New Orleans, 1973-75, McGlinchey, Stafford, Mintz & Hoffman, New Orleans, 1975-78; city atty. City of New Orleans, 1978-79; dir. Carmouche, Gray & Hoffman, New Orleans, 1979-82, sr. dir., 1982-88; sr. dir. Hoffman, Siegel, Seydel, Bienvenu & Centola, New Orleans, 1989—. Fellow Am. Bar Found., La. Bar Found.; mem. Am. Bd. Trial Advocates, French-Am. C. of C. (pres. La. chpt.). Democrat. Presbyterian. General civil litigation, Personal injury. Home: 1524 4th St New Orleans LA 70130-5918 Office: Hoffman Sutterfield 650 Poydras St New Orleans LA 70130-6101

**HOFFMAN, DOUGLAS RAYMOND,** lawyer; b. Kankakee, Ill., June 29, 1957; s. Daniel P. and Madonna J. (Emling) H. BS, Ill. Benedictine Coll., Lisle, 1979; JD, IIT/Chgo.-Kent Coll. Law, 1982. Bar: Ill. 1982, U.S. Dist. Ct. (no. dist.) Ill. 1982, U.S. Ct. Appeals (fed. cir.) 1983, U.S. Ct. Appeals (7th cir.) 1984. Assoc. Supena & Nyman, Chgo. and Oak Brook, Ill., 1982-87; assoc. Wilson & McIlvaine, Chgo., 1987-90, ptnr., 1990-99; ptnr. Quarles & Brady, 1999—; cons. Ill. Sec. of State, Chgo. and Springfield, 1992—. Contbr. chpt. to book, articles to profl. jours. Chair pastoral coun. Holy Name Cathedral, Chgo., 1989-91; regent Mercy Home for Boys and Girls, Chgo., 1990—; mem. planned giving com. Boy Scouts Am., Chgo., 1988—. Mem. ABA, Internat. Bar Assn., Union League Club. General corporate, Private international, Contracts commercial. Office: Wilson & McIlvaine 500 W Madison St Ste 3700 Chicago IL 60661-2592

**HOFFMAN, HARVEY JOHN,** judge; b. Hastings, Mich., Aug. 3, 1950; s. Kenneth Harvey and G. Elizabeth Hoffman; m. Susan Mary Kelsch, June 17, 1978; children: Elizabeth, John, Tammara, Julie, Ashleigh. BA, Western Mich. U., 1972; JD, Thomas M. Cooley Law Sch., 1981. Bar: Mich. 1982, U.S. Dist. Ct. (we. dist.) Mich. 1982. Assoc. Law Offices of Albert J. Thunburr, Lansing, Mich., 1982-85; pvt. practice Lansing, 1986-96; judge 56-A Dist. Ct., Charlotte, Mich., 1997—. Exetor County (Mich.) Rep. chair Exetor County Reps., 1986-88; chmn. Mich. Rural Devel. Coun., 1996-97. Mem. KC (Grand Lodge), Charlotte Rotary. Office: 115 W Allegan St Ste 10B Lansing MI 48933-1712

**HOFFMAN, IRA ELIOT,** lawyer; b. Highland Park, Mich., Jan. 3, 1952; s. Maxwell Mordecai and Leah (Silverman) H.; m. Ruth Felsen, Aug. 19, 1975 (div. 1981); 1 child, Daniel Gideon; m. Meredith Lippman, Dec. 17, 1988; 1 child, Lauren Samantha. BA, U. Mich., 1973; MSc in Econs., London Sch. Econs., 1975; JD cum laude, U. Miami, 1983. Bar: Fla. 1983, U.S. Ct. Appeals (D.C. cir.) 1984, D.C. 1985, Md. 1991, U.S. Ct. Appeals (10th cir., 4th cir) 1992, U.S. Dist. Ct. (D.C. dist.) 1992, U.S. Dist. Ct. Md., 1992, U.S. Ct. Appeals (fed. cir.) 1994, U.S. Ct. Fed. Claims, 1998. Tchr. London Sch. Econs., 1975-77; rsch. assoc. Shiloah Ctr. Mid. East Studies, Tel Aviv U., 1978-80; staff atty. FTC, Washington, 1983; law clk. U.S. Ct. Appeals (D.C. cir.), Washington, 1983-84; assoc. Fried, Frank, Harris, Shriver & Jacobson, Washington, 1984-86, 87-88; counsel Ministry of Def. Mission to the U.S., Govt. of Israel, N.Y.C., 1986-87; counsel to vice chmn. U.S. Internat. Trade Commn., Washington, 1988-89; assoc. Howrey & Simon, Washington, 1989-91; pres. Israel Housing Investors, Inc., Rockville, Md., 1990-92; v.p. H.P.F. Prefab Constrn., Ltd., Givatayim, Israel, 1991-92; of counsel Savage & Schwartzman, Balt., 1992-94, McAleese & Assocs., P.C., McLean, Va., 1995-98, Grayson and Assocs. P.C., McLean, 1998—; pres. Smart Planet, LLC, Rockville, Md., 1998—. Translator: The Emergence of Pan-Arabism in Egypt, 1980; contbr. articles to profl. jours. Spl. counsel Nat. Sudden Infant Death Syndrome Found., Landover, Md., 1984-86; hon. counsel to chmn. Nat. Holocaust Meml. Coun., Washington, 1985. Mem. ABA. Jewish. Avocations: travel, sports, history. E-mail: hoffmani@erols.com. Government contracts and claims, Private international, Public international.

**HOFFMAN, JAMES PAUL,** lawyer, hypnotist; b. Waterloo, Iowa, Sept. 7, 1943; s. James A. and Luella M. (Prokosch) H.; 1 child, Tiffany K. B.A., U. No. Iowa, 1965, J.D. U. Iowa, 1967. Bar: Iowa 1967, U.S. Dist. Ct. (no. dist.) Iowa 1981, U.S. Dist. Ct. (so. dist.) Iowa 1968, U.S. Dist. Ct. (so. dist.) Ill, U.S. Tax Ct. 1971, U.S. Ct. Appeals (8th cir.) 1970, U.S. Supreme Ct. 1974. Sr. mem. James P. Hoffman, Law Offices, Keokuk, Iowa, 1967—; chmn. bd. Iowa Inst. Hypnosis. Fellow Am. Inst. Hypnosis; mem. ABA, Iowa Bar Assn., Lee County Bar Assn., Assn. Trial Lawyers Am., Ill. Trial Lawyers Assn., Iowa Trial Lawyers Assn. Democrat. Roman Catholic. Author: The Iowa Trial Lawyers and the Use of Hypnosis, 1980. Personal injury, Workers' compensation, State civil litigation. Home and Office: PO Box 1087 Middle Rd Keokuk IA 52632-1087

**HOFFMAN, JOHN FLETCHER,** lawyer; b. N.Y.C., May 22, 1946; s. George Fletcher and Helen (Gilbert) H.; m. Coralie Tallman, June 29, 1969; children: Julie Gilbert, William Delano. BS, St. Lawrence U., 1969; JD, Washington and Lee U., 1975. Bar: N.Y. 1976, U.S. Dist. Ct. (so. dist.) N.Y. 1976, U.S. Dist. Ct. (ea. dist.) N.Y. 1978, U.S. Supreme Ct. 1980, U.S. Ct. Appeals (2d cir.) 1982, U.S. Dist. Ct. (no. dist.) Tex. 1988, U.S. Ct. Appeals (11th cir.) 1991. Assoc. Cadwalader, Wickersham & Taft, N.Y.C., 1975-83, ptnr., 1983-94; v.p., assoc. gen. counsel Schering-Plough Corp., Kenilworth, N.J., 1995—. Trustee First Unitarian Congl. Soc. Bklyn., 1980-83; trustee, treas. Bklyn. Children's Mus., 1985-95. Mem. ABA, Fed. Bar Coun., Order of Coif, Omicron Delta Kappa. Antitrust, Federal civil litigation, State civil litigation. Office: Schering Plough Corp 2000 Galloping Hill Rd Kenilworth NJ 07033-1328

**HOFFMAN, JOHN RICHARD,** mediator, arbitrator; b. Rochester, Minn., Nov. 23, 1940; s. John Ralph and Helen Gertrude (Romens) H.; m. Carol Jean Hoffmann, May 9, 1964; children: Stephen John Raymond, Melinda Carol. BA in History, U. Minn., 1964; JD, William Mitchell Coll. of Law, 1968. Bar: Minn. 1968, Wis. 1984. Assoc. Mordaunt Walstad Cousineau & McGuire, Mpls., 1968-70, Murnane, Murnane Battis De Lambert & Conlin, St. Paul, 1970-76; ptnr. Murnane Conlin, White Brandt & Hoffman, St. Paul, 1976-92; pvt. practice mediation and arbitration John R. Hoffman & Assocs., Mpls., 1992—. Office: 1300 Nicollet Mall Ste 5002 Minneapolis MN 55403-2606

**HOFFMAN, LARRY J.,** lawyer; b. N.Y.C., Aug. 20, 1930; s. Max and Pauline (Epstein) H.; m. Deborh E. Alexander, Oct. 2, 1954; children: Lisa, Ken, Heidi, Mark. AA, U. Fla.; JD, U. Miami. Bar: Fla. 1954. Chmn. Greenberg, Traurig, PA, Miami, 1968—; also bd. dirs. Greenberg, Traurig, Hoffman, Lipoff, Rosen & Quentel, PA, Miami. Mem. ABA, Fla. Bar Assn., Dade County Bar Assn. Avocations: music, art, tennis. Securities, General corporate, Contracts commercial. Office: Greenberg Traurig 1221 Brickell Ave Miami FL 33131-3224

**HOFFMAN, MARK FREDERICK,** lawyer; b. Bellevue, Wash., Mar. 30, 1971; s. Frederick Joseph and Molly K. Hoffman; m. Elizabeth Briggs, Aug. 17, 1996. AB summa cum laude, Princeton U., 1993; JD cum laude, U. Mich., 1996. Bar: Wash. 1996. Assoc. Graham & James LLP, Seattle, 1996—. Mem. ABA, Order of the Coif. Avocations: running, skiing, hiking, biking, reading. Securities, General corporate, Finance. Office: Graham & James LLP 1001 4th Ave Ste 4500 Seattle WA 98154-1192

**HOFFMAN, MICHAEL WILLIAM,** lawyer, accountant; b. Bowling Green, Ohio, Feb. 5, 1955; s. Oscar William and Marie Louise (Carlson) H.; m. Lynne Ellen Steele, Aug. 31, 1975; children: Megan, Jessica, Kristine, Robert. BA in Acctg. summa cum laude, Bowling Green State U., 1976; JD, U. Toledo, 1981. Bar: Ohio 1981, Ga. 1983; CPA, Ga., Ohio. Acct. Ernst & Whinney, Toledo, 1976-81; acct., ptnr. Touche Ross & Co., Atlanta, 1981-86; v.p. Profl. Svcs. Network Inc., Atlanta, 1986; assoc. Chamberlain, Hrdlicka, White, Johnson & Williams, Atlanta, 1986-89; ptnr. Somers & Altenbach, Atlanta, 1989-91; atty. Hoffman & Assocs., Atlanta, 1991—; organizing dir. Paces Bank & Trust Co., Atlanta; spkr. in field. Author: RIA's U.S.A. News for the Inbound Investor, 1983. Treas. Friendship Force Internat., 1984; mem. troop com. Boy Scouts Am. Recipient Leadership award Boy Scouts Am., 1986. Mem. ABA, AICPA, State Bar Ga. (fiduciary law and tax sects.), State Bar Ohio, Ga. Soc. CPAs (chmn. estate, gift and trust sect.; Atlanta chpt. estate, gift and trust sect., Disting. Com. Chair award 1998-99), Bowling Green State U.-Atlanta Alumni Assn. (pres. 1988-90), Atlanta Country Club (bd. dirs. 1998—), Serra. Republican. Roman Catholic. Avocations: golf, tennis, coaching Little League basketball. Email: mhoffman@avana.net. Estate planning, Taxation, general, State and local taxation. Home: 535 Willow Knolls Dr Marietta GA 30067-4647 Office: 6075 Lake Forrest Dr NW Ste 200 Atlanta GA 30328-3845

**HOFFMAN, NANCY E.,** lawyer; b. N.Y.C., Mar. 19, 1944; d. Jack and Catherine (Wertheim) H.; m. Thomas G. Spagnoletti. BS in Indsl. and Labor Rels., Cornell U., 1966; MA in Am. History, N.Y.U., 1968; JD, St. John's U., 1973. Bar: N.Y. 1974, U.S. Dist. Ct. (so. and ea. dists.) N.Y. 1975, U.S. Dist. Ct. (we. and no. dists.) N.Y. 1984, U.S. Supreme Ct. 1975, U.S. Ct. Appeals (2d cir.) 1975. Asst. corp. counsel N.Y. Dept. Law, 1973-75; assoc. Plunkett & Jaffee, 1978-79; assoc. counsel Office Gen. Counsel N.Y. State United Tchrs., 1975-78, 79-84; asst. atty. gen. State of N.Y., Albany, 1984-85; dep. counsel div. legal affairs N.Y. State Dept. Social Svcs., 1985-86, first asst. counsel for fair hearings, 1986-89; gen. counsel Civil Svc. Employees Assn., Inc., 1989—. Recipient Disting. Svc. award Am. Arbitration Assn., 1997. Mem. ABA (labor/employment law sect., coun. mem., com. on state and local govt. bargaining, commn. on women in the profession), N.Y. State Bar Assn. (labor/employment law sect., future directions com., govt. bargaining com.), Women's Bar Assn. State of N.Y. Office: Civil Svc Employees Assn 143 Washington Ave Albany NY 12210-2303

**HOFFMAN, PAUL SHAFER,** lawyer; b. Harrisburg, Pa., Dec. 12, 1933; s. Paul and Lucy Rose (Shafer) H.; m. Patricia Ann Rudisill, 1958; children: Eric, Kathryn, Julia, Margot. AB in Physics, Gettysburg Coll., 1957; JD, Harvard U., 1962. Bar: N.Y. 1963, U.S. Patent Office 1963, U.S. Dist. Ct. (so. dist.) N.Y. 1977, U.S. Ct. Appeals (2d cir.) 1977, U.S. Supreme Ct. 1977. Assoc. Kenyon & Kenyon, N.Y.C., 1962-63; application analyst IBM-ASDD, Yorktown, N.Y., 1963-66; dir. tech. research Matthew Bender Co., N.Y.C., 1966-68; v.p. Bowne and Co., Inc., N.Y.C., 1968-77; sole practice Croton-on-Hudson, N.Y., 1977—. Mem. Croton Sch. Bd., 1972-75, pres., 1974-75; trustee Village Croton-on-Hudson, 1977-81, acting village justice, 1991—; bd. dirs. Croton Caring Com., Inc., 1982—. Served to cpl. U.S. Army, 1952-54. Mem. N.Y. State Bar Assn. (assoc. editor-in-chief N.Y. State Bar jour. 1991-98), Westchester County Bar Assn., Computer Law Assn. (bd. dirs. 1984-94, 96—). Republican. Lutheran. Club: Harvard (N.Y.C.). Lodge: Masons. Computer, Trademark and copyright, Contracts commercial. Office: 139 Grand St Croton On Hudson NY 10520-2306

**HOFFMAN, ROBERT DEAN, JR.,** lawyer; b. New Orleans, Dec. 15, 1954; s. Robert Dean Sr. and Ruth Ann (Wheelahan) H.; m. Katherine Bel Thielen, 1987; children: Taylor Ann, R. Dean III. BS, Auburn U., 1975; JD, Loyola U., New Orleans, 1978; LLM in Taxation, Emory U., 1980. Bar: La. 1978, U.S. Dist. Ct. (ea. dist.) La. 1978, U.S. Ct. Appeals (5th cir.) 1979, U.S. Tax. Ct. 1981, U.S. Ct. Appeals (11th cir.) 1981, U.S. Dist. Ct. (mid. dist.) La. 1982, U.S. Dist. Ct. (we. dist.) La. 1995. Ptnr. Ballin & Hoffman, New Orleans, 1978-90; shareholder Burke & Mayer, 1994—; hearing com. mem. La. Atty. Disciplinary Bd., 1999—. Lanaza-Greco Meml scholar Loyola U., 1978. Fellow La. Bar Found.; mem. ABA, La. Bar Assn. Club: Over the Mountain Athletic (commr. 1985—, sportsmanship award 1986), Krewe of Olympia. Personal income taxation, Real property, Contracts commercial. Home: 12 Oaklawn Dr Covington LA 70433-4510 Office: 1100 Poydras St Ste 2000 New Orleans LA 70163-1121

**HOFFMAN, VALERIE JANE,** lawyer; b. Lowville, N.Y., Oct. 27, 1953; d. Russell Francis and Jane Marie (Fowler) H.; m. Michael J. Grillo, Apr. 4, 1996. Student, U. Edinburgh, Scotland, 1973-74; BA summa cum laude, Union Coll., 1975; JD, Boston Coll., 1978. Bar: Ill. 1978, U.S. Dist. Ct. (no. dist.) Ill. 1978, U.S. Ct. Appeals (3rd cir.) 1981, U.S. Ct. Appeals (7th cir.) 1983. Assoc. Seyfarth, Shaw, Fairweather & Geraldson, Chgo., 1978-87, ptnr., 1987—; adj. prof. Columbia Coll., 1985. Contbr. articles to legal publs. Dir. Remains Theatre, Chgo., 1981-95, pres., 1991-93, v.p., 1991-95; dir. The Nat. Conf. for Cmty. and Justice, Chgo. Region, 1993—, nat. trustee, 1995—; trustee bd. advisors Union Coll., 1996—; dir. AIDS Found. of Chgo., 1997—, sec., 1999—; trustee Union Coll., 1999—. Mem. ABA, Chgo. Bar Assn., Law Club Chgo., Univ. Club Chgo. (bd. dirs. 1984-87), Phi Beta Kappa. Labor, Entertainment, Administrative and regulatory. Office: Seyfarth Shaw Fairweather & Geraldson 55 E Monroe St Ste 4400 Chicago IL 60603-5713

**HOFFMANN, CHRISTOPH LUDWIG,** lawyer; b. Elsterwerda, Germany, Oct. 9, 1944; came to U.S., 1965; s. Gunther and Ruth (Hornschuh) H.; m. Susan Magnuson, June 18, 1983. Student, Freie U. Berlin, 1964-65; BA, U. Wis., 1966; JD, Harvard U., 1969. Bar: Mass. 1969, R.I. 1977. Assoc. Bingham, Dana & Gould, Boston, 1969-76; asst. gen. counsel Textron Inc., Providence, 1976-83; v.p., gen. counsel, sec. Pneumo Corp., Boston, 1983-85; sr. v.p., gen. counsel, sec. Pneumo Abex Corp., Boston, 1985-91; v.p., sec., gen. counsel Raytheon Co., Lexington, Mass., 1991-94, sr. v.p. law, human resources and corp. adminstrn., sec., 1994-95, exec. v.p. law and corp. adminstrn., sec., 1995-98; ltd. ptnr. Carlisle 1999, L.P., 1998—; bd. dirs. Assoc. Industries Mass., 1994-98; trustee Deaconess Glover Hosp., 1994-98. Mem. ABA, New Eng. Legal Found. (bd. dirs. 1991—), Mass. Bar Assn., R.I. Bar Assn., Assn. Gen. Counsel.

**HOFFMANN, MARTIN RICHARD,** lawyer; b. Stockbridge, Mass., Apr. 20, 1932; m. Margaret Ann McCabe; children: Heidi H. Slye, William, Bern. AB, Princeton U., 1954; LLB, U. Va., 1961. Bar: D.C. 1961. Law clk. U.S. Ct. Appeals (4th cir.), 1961-62; asst. U.S. atty. Washington, 1962-65; minority counsel com. on judiciary Ho. of Reps., Washington, 1965-67; legal counsel to U.S. senator C. Percy Washington, 1967-69; asst. gen. counsel Univ. Computing Co., Dallas, 1969-71; gen. counsel Atomic Energy Commn., Washington, 1971-73; spl. asst. to sec. and dep. sec. def. Washington, 1973-74; gen. counsel Dept. Def., Washington, 1974-75; sec. Dept. Army, Washington, 1975-77; mng. ptnr. Gardner, Carton & Douglas, Washington, 1977-89; v.p., gen. counsel, sec. Digital Equipment Corp., Maynard, Mass., 1989-93; of counsel Skadden, Arps, Slate, Meagher & Flom, Washington, 1996—; sr. vis. fellow Ctr. for Policy, Tech. and Indsl. Devel., MIT, Cambridge, 1993-95; trustee Assn. U.S. Army, Washington; bd. dirs. Castle Energy, Phila., Sea Change Corp., Maynard, Mass., Mitretek Systems, Inc. Maj. USAR, 1954-73. Mem. Met. Club. General corporate, Computer, Government contracts and claims. Home: 1546 Hampton Hill Cir Mc Lean VA 22101-6021 Office: 1440 New York Ave NW Washington DC 20005-2111

**HOFFMANN, MICHAEL RICHARD,** lawyer; b. Des Moines, Apr. 26, 1947; s. Robert Wyman and Margaret Inez Wagner (stepmother) H. and Patricia Hilliard; m. Amy Marie Gales; children: Kurt Michael, Kristen Elaine, Kevin Richard. BS in Chemistry and Zoology, U. Iowa, 1969; JD, Drake U., 1972; LLM in Patent and Trade Regulation, George Washington U., 1973. Bar: Iowa 1972, U.S. Ct. Customs and Patent Appeals 1972, U.S. Patent and Trademark Office 1973, U.S. Dist. Ct. (so. and no. dists.) Iowa 1974, U.S. Ct. Appeals (8th cir.) 1976, U.S. Supreme Ct. 1977. Clerk Jones, Hoffmann & Davison, Des Moines, 1970-73; assoc. Bacon and Thomas, Arlington, Va., 1973-74; assoc. Jones, Hoffmann & Davison, Des Moines, 1974-79, ptnr., 1979-83; pres. Michael R. Hoffmann, P.C., Des Moines, 1983-95; pvt. practice, 1995—; del. U.S./Japan Bilateral Session: A New Era in Legal and Econ. Relations, Tokyo, 1988; mem. Iowa Def. Counsel, Def. Research Inst., Inc. Recipient Am. Jurisprudence award Bancroft-Whitney Co. and Lawyers Coop. Pub. Co., 1970-72. Mem. Iowa State Bar Assn., ABA (sci. and tech. sect.), Iowa Patent Bar Assn. (charter mem.), Am. Patent Law Assn., Am. Judicature Soc., Polk County Bar Assn., Iowa Assn. Workers' Compensation Lawyers, Internat. Assn. Indsl. Accident Bds. and Commns., Prairie Club (pres. Des Moines chpt. 1993-94), Nat. Rifle Club (Washington). Office: 3708 75th St Des Moines IA 50322-3002

**HOFFMEYER, WILLIAM FREDERICK,** lawyer, educator; b. York, Pa., Dec. 20, 1936; s. Frederick W. and Mary B. (Stremmel) H.; m. Betty J. Hoffmeyer, Feb. 6, 1960 (divorced); 1 child, Louise C.; m. Karen L. Semmelman, 1985. AB, Franklin and Marshall Coll., 1958; JD, Dickinson Sch. Law, 1961. Bar: Pa. 1962, U.S. Dist. Ct. (mid. dist.) Pa. 1981, U.S. Supreme Ct. 1983. Pvt. practice law, 1962-81; sr. ptnr. Hoffmeyer & Semmelman, 1982—; adj. prof. real estate law York Coll. Pa., 1980-92, real estate law, paral legal program Pa. State U., 1978—. Author: The Abstractor's Bible, 1981, Pennsylvania Real Estate Installment Sales Contract Manual, 1981, Real Estate Settlement Procedures, 1982, Contracts of Sale, 1985, How to Plot a Deed Description, 1986; author, lectr., moderator and course planner numerous Pa. Bar Inst. CLE Programs. Recipient Disting. Svc. award Gen. Alumni Assn. of Dickinson Sch. Law, 1993, Pa. Bar medal, 1997. Mem. ABA, Pa. Bar Assn. (chmn., unauthorized practice of law com.), York County Bar Assn. (chmn. continuing legal edn. com., 1992-96), Am. Coll. Real Estate Lawyers, Lions (past pres. East York club), Masons (past pres. York County Shrine club), York Area C. of C. (chair small bus. support network 1997—). Real property, Probate, General practice. Address: 30 N George St York PA 17401-1214

**HOGAN, CHARLES MARSHALL,** lawyer; b. Columbus, Ohio, June 3, 1911; s. Timothy Sylvester and Mary Adele (Deasy) H.; m. Joan Elizabeth Ziegler, June 22, 1940; children: Timothy, John, Diane, Dennis. AB, Xavier U., Cin., 1930, MA, 1972; BSEE, Purdue U., West Lafayette, Ind., 1932; JD, Capital U., Columbus, Ohio, 1939, U. Cin., 1954, DePaul U., Chgo., 1953; PhD in History, U. Cin., 1986. Assoc. H.B. Reese, Wellston, Ohio, 1940-42; patent examiner U.S. Patent Office, Richmond, Va.; patent atty. L.B. Dodds, N.Y.C., 1943-44, C. Loftus, Chgo., 1946-47, Crosley & Avco, Cin., 1947-66; gen. patent counsel Avco Corp., Cin., 1966-76; cons. Textron, Inc. (successor of Avco), Cin., 1976-89; sec. Hogan Fin., Cin.; witness Sen. Hart Patent Subcom., 1973; mem. numerous patent law reform coms. Author: Timothy S. Hogan, 1972, Wayne B. Wheeler, 1986; contbr. articles to profl. jours. V.p. Ohio Hist. Soc., Columbus, 1976-82, Ohioana Libr., Columbus, 1982-92. Lt. USN, 1944-46. Named Outstanding Alumnus Law Sch. Capital U., Columbus, 1993. Mem. Am. IPL Assn. (jud. selection com. 1970), Cin. IPL Assn. (pres. 1961), 6th Cir. Jud. Conf., Assn. Corp. Patent Counsel. Republican. Roman Catholic. Patent.

**HOGAN, DANIEL JAMES,** lawyer; b. Hammond, Ind., Jan. 3, 1961; s. Daniel Vincent and Mary Rita (Murray) H.; m. Cathy Marie Lynch, Aug. 3, 1985; 1 child, Daniel Curtis. BA in History, St. Bonaventure U., 1983; JD, Touro Coll., 1989. Bar: N.Y. 1990, U.S. Dist. Ct. (so. and ea. dists.) N.Y. 1990, (no. dist.) 1994. Paralegal, law clk. Cahn, Wishod & Lamb, Melville, N.Y., 1985-89; assoc. Weil, Gotshal & Manges, N.Y.C., 1989-93, McPhillips, Fitzgerald & Meyer, Glens Falls, N.Y., 1993—. Pres. Glens Falls Family YMCA, 1997-99. Republican. Office: McPhillips Fitzgerald & Cullum LLP PO Box 299 Glens Falls NY 12801-0299

**HOGAN, ELWOOD,** lawyer; b. Augusta, Ga., Mar. 4, 1929; s. William Elwood and Geneva Isabell H.; m. Myrtle Elizabeth McCall, June 15, 1957; children: Martha Elizabeth Ondrejcal, Darrell William Hogan. BBA, U. Ga., 1954; JD, Stetson U., 1958. Bar: Fla. Supreme Ct. 1958, U.S. Dist. Ct. Fla. 1959, U.S. Ct. Appeals (11th cir.) 1959, U.S. Tax Ct. 1965, U.S. Supreme Ct. 1973; cert. cir. ct. mediator. Assoc. Wolfe & Bonner Attys., Clearwater, Fla., 1958-63; ptnr. Wolfe, Bonner & Hogan, Clearwater, 1964-75; pres. Bonner & Hogan P.A., Clearwater, 1975-98, Hogan & Breakstone, P.A., Clearwater, 1998—; prosecutor Mcpl. Ct., Clearwater, 1966-68, judge, 1968-74; bd. trustees Morton Plant Hosp., Clearwater, 1981-86, chmn., 1984-86; pres. Fla. Mcpl. Judges Assn., 1972; Fla. Cir. Ct. mediator. Mem. ABA, Clearwater Bar Assn. (pres. 1972-73), Fla. Acad. Profl. Mediators, Kiwanis Club, Phi Alpha Delta. Avocations: swimming, tennis, fishing. Probate, Estate planning, Real property. Office: Hogan & Breakstone PA 613 S Myrtle Ave Clearwater FL 33756-5615

**HOGAN, MICHAEL R(OBERT),** judge; b. Oregon City, Oreg., Sept. 24, 1946; married; 3 children. A.B., U. Oreg. Honors Coll., 1968; J.D., Georgetown U., 1971. Bar: Oreg. 1971, U.S. Ct. Appeals (9th cir.) 1971. Law clk. to chief judge U.S. Dist. Ct. Oreg., Portland, 1971-72; assoc. Miller, Anderson, Nash, Yerke and Wiener, Portland, 1972-73; magistrate judge U.S. Dist. Ct. Oreg., Eugene, 1973-91, dist. judge, 1991—, chief judge, 1995—; bankruptcy judge U.S. Dist. Oreg., Eugene, 1973-80. Mem. ABA, Oreg. State Bar Assn. Office: US Courthouse 211 E 7th Ave Eugene OR 97401-2722

**HOGAN, RICHARD PHILLIPS,** lawyer; b. Troy, Ohio, June 21, 1931; s. George Thomas and Florence Anna (Phillips) H.; m. Jane Conti, June 21, 1958; children: Richard P. Jr., Mary Sean Hogan Harvin, Kathleen Keally Hogan Hoeffner. BS, Xavier U., 1953; attended, Georgetown U. Law Ctr.; LLB, South Tex. Coll., 1961. Bar: Tex. 1962, U.S. Supreme Ct., U.S. Dist Ct. (so. dist.) Tex., U.S. Ct. Appeals (5th cir.). Sales staff 3M Co., St. Paul, Albuquerque, Houston, 1958-62; asst. dist. atty. Harris County, Houston, 1962-63; ptnr. Helm, Pletcher, Hogan, Bowen & Saunders, Houston, 1963-93; atty. of counsel Holman, Hogan, Dubose & Townsend, Houston, 1993-95, Hoeffner, Bilek & Edman, 1995—. Bd. dirs. Nottingham Civic Assn., Houston, 1965-69, Young Life, Houston, 1976-79, Irish Am. Partnership, Boston, 1993—, Guadalupe Area Social Svcs., Houston, 1987-92. 1st lt. U.S. Army, 1953-56. Mem. ABA (ho. of del.), Am. Soc. Legal Mecine & Ethics, Am. Coll. Legal Medicine, Am. Bd. Trial Advocates (pres. Houston chpt.), Am. Bar Found., Tex. Bar Found. (sec.), Tex. Bar Assn. (bd. dirs.), Tex. Trial Lawyers Assn. (bd. dirs.), Houston Jr. Bar Assn. (bd. dirs.), Houston Bar Assn. (bd. dirs., 1st v.p.), Houston Trial Lawyers Assn. (pres.), Houston Bar Found. (chmn. bd. dirs.), Internat. Soc. Barristers, Lakeside Country Club, Ocean Forest Golf Club. Roman Catholic. Avocations: travel, gardening, reading, golf. Federal civil litigation, State civil litigation, Personal injury.

**HOGAN, THOMAS FRANCIS,** federal judge; b. Washington, May 31, 1938; s. Bartholomew W. and Grace (Gloninger) H.; m. Martha Lou Wyrick, July 16, 1966; 1 son, Thomas Garth. A.B., Georgetown U., 1960, J.D., 1966; postgrad., George Washington U., 1960-62. Bar: Md. 1966, U.S. Dist. Ct. D.C. 1967, D.C. 1967, U.S. Ct. Appeals (D.C. cir.) 1972, U.S. Dist. Ct. Md. 1973, U.S. Supreme Ct. 1973. Law clk. to presiding judge U.S. Dist. Ct. D.C., 1966-67; counsel Nat. Commn. on Reform of Fed. Criminal Laws, Washington, 1967-68; ptnr. McCarthy & Wharton, Rockville, Md., 1968-75, Kenary, Tietz & Hogan, Rockville, 1975-81, Furey, Doolan, Abell & Hogan, Chevy Chase, Md., 1981-82; judge U.S. Dist. Ct. D.C., Washington, 1982—; asst. prof. Potomac Sch. Law, Washington, 1977-79; adj. prof. law Georgetown Law Ctr., 1985—. Pub. mem. Officer Evaluation Bd. U.S. Fgn. Service, 1973; chmn. Christ Child Inst. for Disturbed Children, 1975; bd. dirs. Providence Hosp., Washington, 1984-86. Recipient cert. recognition and appreciation for vol. services Montgomery County Govt., 1976; recipient cert. appreciation Christ Child Soc., 1976; St. Thomas More fellow Georgetown U. Law Ctr., 1965-66. Mem. ABA (Md. chmn. Drug Abuse Edn. Program, Young Lawyers sect. 1970-73, mem. Litigation sect.), Bar Assn. D.C. (mem. com. on D.C. cts.), Md. State Bar Assn. (Litigatin sect.), Montgomery County Bar Assn. (chmn. legal ethics com. 1973-74, lawyer referral service com. 1974-75, adminstrn. justice com. 1979-82, bd. govs. 1977-78), Nat. Inst. for Trial Advocacy Assocs., Def. Research Inst., Md. Assn. Def. Trial Counsel, Md. Trial Lawyers Assn., Georgetown U. Alumni Assn., Smithsonian Assocs., John Carroll Soc., Knights of Malta. Clubs: Barristers, Chevy Chase, Lawyers.

**HOGAN, THOMAS PATRICK,** lawyer; b. Binghamton, N.Y., Mar. 30, 1948; s. Edward P. and Elizabeth Hogan; m. Linda S. Scheffler, Aug. 18, 1973; children: Edward, Michael, Kathleen. BBA, U. Notre Dame, 1970, JD, 1974. Atty. Rhoades, McKee, Boer, Goodrich & Titta, Grand Rapids, Mich., 1974—; adj. faculty Grand Rapids C.C., 1980-97; chmn. exec. com. Rhoades, McKee, Boer, Goodrich and Titta, 1998. Dir. Kent County Am. Cancer Soc., Grand Rapids, 1995-98, Grand Rapids Dental Found., 1996-98. Mem. State Bar Mich., Grand Rapids Bar Assn. General corporate, Real property, Estate planning. Office: Rhoades McKee Boer Goodrich and Titta 600 Waters Bldg 161 Ottawa Ave NW Grand Rapids MI 49503-2701

**HOGE, CHRIS,** lawyer; b. Katonah, N.Y., June 12, 1948. BA, U. N.C., 1970; JD, Am. U., 1974. Bar: D.C. 1975, U.S. Ct. Appeals (D.C.) 1977, U.S. Supreme Ct. 1987. Law clk. Hon. George Revercomb Superior Ct. D.C., Washington, 1974-75; ptnr. Crowley, Hoge & Fein, PC, Washington. Mem. ABA, D.C. Bar Assn. (pres.), Md. State Bar Assn., George Washington Am. Inn Ct. (pres. 1996-97). General civil litigation, Family and matrimonial, Estate planning. Office: Crowley Hoge & Fein PC Ste 100 1717 Massachusetts Ave NW Washington DC 20036-2013

**HOGEBOOM, ROBERT WOOD,** lawyer; b. Joplin, Mo., Dec. 28, 1947; s. Robert William and Betty (Wood) H.; m. Anne Fitz; children: Robert Fitz, Jeffrey Marshall. BA, Stanford U., 1970; JD, Calif. Western Sch. Law, San Diego, 1974. Bar: Calif. 1974, U.S. Dist. Ct. (cen. dist.) 1974. Assoc. DeMarco, Barger & Beral, L.A., 1975-76; assoc. Barger & Wolen, L.A., 1976-80, ptnr., 1980—. Contbr. articles to profl. jours. Bd. dirs. San Marino (Calif.) City Club, 1988-90, San Marino Schs. Found., 1983-86, St. Edwards Nursery Sch., San Marino, 1984-87; pres. San Marino Little League, 1990-91. Mem. Conf. of Ins. Counsel (pres. 1990—, dir.), ABA, Fedn. of Ins. Counsel, dir. conf. of Ins. Couns., L.A. County Bar Assn., State Bar Calif. (ins. law com., dept. ins. task force on rates). Republican. Episcopalian. Administrative and regulatory, Insurance, General corporate. Office: Barger & Wolen 515 S Flower St Fl 34 Los Angeles CA 90071-2201

**HOGEN-KIND, VANYA S.,** lawyer; b. Vermillion, S.D., Feb. 14, 1968; d. Philip N. and Marilyn J. Hogen; m. Brian C. Kind, July 27, 1991. BA, U. Minn., 1990, JD cum laude, 1993. Law clk. Hennepin County Atty.'s Office, Mpls., 1992, Blue Dog Law Office, Mpls., 1992-93; atty. Blue Dog, Olson & Small, Mpls., 1993—. Mem. Minn.-Am. Indian Bar Assn. (v.p. 1997—, bd. dirs. 1995—), ABA, Fed. Bar Assn., S.D. Bar Assn. Avocations: reading, playing piano, golf. Native American, General civil litigation, Environmental. Office: Blue Dog Olson & Small 5001 W 80th St Ste 500 Minneapolis MN 55437-1116

**HOGG, DAVID KENNETH,** lawyer; b. Dothan, Ala., Feb. 6, 1961; s. Kenneth Talmage Hogg and Cora Juanita Sasnett; m. Lisa Jane Lathem, June 12, 1981; children: Daniel Anderson, Amelia Leanna. BA, U. Ala., 1984; JD, Jones Sch. Law, 1996. Bar: Ala. 1996, U.S. Dist. Ct. (mid. dist.) Ala. 1996. Assoc. Merrill, Harrison and Adams, Dothan, 1996-98; pvt. practice Dothan, 1998—. Deacon 1st Presbyn. Ch., Dothan, 1996—; bd. dirs. S.E. Ala. Youth Svcs., Dothan, 1997—. Mem. Houston County Bar Assn. Avocation: genealogy. General civil litigation, Consumer commercial, Criminal. Home: 509 Baywood Rd Dothan AL 36305-6321 Office: Ste 106 188 N Foster St Dothan AL 36303-4568

**HOGG, JAMES STUART,** lawyer; b. N.Y.C., Aug. 5, 1952; s. John S. and Rosalie (Smith) H.; m. Kathleen Anne Rhoades, May 20, 1978; children: John S., Robert W., Elizabeth A. BA, Kalamazoo Coll., 1974; JD, U. Mich., 1977. Bar: N.Y. 1978, Ohio 1985. Assoc. Brown, Wood, Ivey, Mitchell & Petty, N.Y.C., 1977-80, Carter, Ledyard & Milburn, N.Y.C., 1980-83; sr. counsel The Standard Oil Co., Cleve., 1983-87; asst. gen. counsel GenCorp Inc., Fairlawn, Ohio, 1987-88; v.p. law GenCorp Automotive, Akron, Ohio, 1989-93; of counsel Ulmer & Berne, LLP, Cleve., 1994-96; prin. Cowden, Humphrey & Sarlson Co., L.P.A., Cleve., 1996—. Mem. ABA, Cleve. Bar Assn., Ohio Bar Assn. Republican. Episcopalian. Avocations: golf, tennis. Finance, Securities, Mergers and acquisitions. Office: Cowden Humphrey & Sarlson 1414 Terminal Tower Cleveland OH 44113

**HOGLE, SEAN SHERWOOD,** lawyer; b. Del Rio, Tex., Oct. 7, 1967; s. Walter S. Jr. and Janet L. (Stow) H.; m. Cynthia R. Abesa, Aug. 7, 1993. BBA, James Madison U., 1990; JD, Coll. William and Mary, 1993. Bar: Va. 1993, Colo. 1995, U.S. Dist. Ct. Colo. 1995. Jud. clk. to Hon. Juan G. Burciaga U.S. Dist. Ct. Dist. of N.Mex., Albuquerque, 1993-95; assoc. atty. Moye, Giles, O'Keefe, Vermeire & Gorrell LLP, Denver, 1995-98; counsel Sun Microsystems, Inc., Broomfield, Colo., 1998—. Mem. ABA (intellectual property sect.), Am. Intellectual Property Law Assn., Computer Law Assn., Colo. Bar Assn. (patent, trademark and copyright sect.), Order of Coif. Avocations: skiing, hiking, computers. Computer, Intellectual property, Trademark and copyright. Office: Sun Microsystems Inc MS 01-205 500 Eldorado Blvd Broomfield CO 80021-3400

**HOGLUND, JOHN ANDREW,** lawyer; b. Cleve., July 19, 1945; s. Paul Franklin and Louise (Anderson) H.; m. Patricia Olwell, May 27, 1972; children: Britt Hannah, Maeve Olwell, Marc Paul-Joseph. BA, Augustana Coll., 1967; JD, George Washington U., 1972. Bar: Wash. 1973, U.S. Dist. Ct. (we. dist.) Wash. 1973, U.S. Ct. Appeals (9th cir.) 1973. Law clk. Wash. State Supreme Ct., 1973-74; assoc. Mooney, Cullen & Holm, Olympia, 1973-75; ptnr. Cullen, Holm, Hoglund & Foster, Olympia, 1975-81; pvt. practice Olympia, 1981—; pres. Hoglund Enterprises, 1987—; adj. prof. law sch. U. Puget Sound, Tacoma, Wash., 1989-90, trustee, 1984-92. Co-author: SKYCYL Practicing Law Manual, 1986-95, WSBA Book Automobile Negligence Law, 1988. Vice chmn. Group Health Coop., Olympia, 1978, Thurston County Dem. Cen. Com., Olympia, 1980; chmn. bd. dirs. S.W. Wash. Health Sys. Agy., 1979; alumni bd. dirs. George Washington U. Nat. Law Ctr., 1994-97, emeritus mem., 1997—. With U.S. Army, 1967-69. Named Boss of Yr. Thurston County Legal Secs. Assn., 1985. Mem. ABA, Thurston County Bar Assn. (trustee 1988-90, Svc. awards 1987, 90), ATLA, Wash. State Trial Lawyers Assn. (pres. 1983-84, Brandeis award 1980), Wash. State Trial Lawyers Found. (pres. 1985-87), Wash. State Bar Assn. (chmn. UPL com. 1979, CPR com., pub. rels. com., chmn. Lawyer Protection Fund com. 1991), Nat. Law Ctr. George Washington U. (alumni bd. 1994-97), Kiwanis (Disting. Pres. award 1980). Personal injury, Insurance. Address: Hoglund Counselors PO Box 11189 Olympia WA 98508-1189

**HOGSHIRE, EDWARD LEIGH,** lawyer; b. Norfolk, Va., Apr. 14, 1943; s. Russell Blake and Margaret Maria (Johnston) H.; m. Diane Hoyle Austin, June 12, 1992; children by previous marriage: Edward Carlisle, Charles Kent; stepchildren: Jason Austin, Jennie Austin, Benjamin Austin. B.A. in English, J.D., U. Va. Bar: Va. 1970, D.C. 1972. Staff atty. Council of Better Bus. Burs., Washington, 1971-72; dir. Student Legal Services, Charlottesville, Va., 1972-73; assoc. Lowe & Gordon, Ltd., 1973-76; ptnr. Paxson, Smith, Boyd, Gilliam & Gouldman, 1976-82, Buck, Hogshire & Teresherz, Ltd., Charlottesville, 1982-98 ; lectr. in law U. Va. Sch. Law, 1980-98 ; dir. criminal practice clinic, 1987-98; judge Charlottesville Cir. Ct., 1998—. Chmn. Criminal Justice Adv. Council, Charlottesville, 1975-76; pres. Charlottesville/Albemarle Mental Health Assn., 1981-83. Served as 1st lt. U.S. Army, 1965-67. Recipient Scribner-Garnett award Charlottesville/Albemarle Mental Health Assn., 1981; Cert. of Merit, Criminal Justice Adv. Council, Thomas Jefferson Planning Dist. Com., 1978. Mem. Va. Coll. Criminal Def. Attys., NACDL, Va. Bar Assn., (statewide coordinator inmate assistance project 1977-79, Citation for Significant Svc.). Democrat. Episcopalian. Office: Buck Hogshire & Teresker 315 E High St Charlottesville VA 22902-5118

**HOGUE, DALE CURTIS, SR.,** lawyer; b. St. Louis, Feb. 11, 1942; s. William Curtis Hogue and Juanita Estel Bean; m. Alice Jeam Smith, 1963 (div. 1964); m. Carolyn Frances Jones, Oct. 24, 1965; children: Dale Curtis Jr., Sean Cyril Raymond, Stuart Ridgely. Student, U.S. Naval Acad., 1961; BS in Engring. Sci., Washington U., St. Louis, 1964; JD, Georgetown U., 1972. Bar: Va. 1972, D.C. 1973, N.C. 1990. Ptnr. Hogue, Rhodes & Boss, Washington, 1972-74, Cross, Murphy & Smith, Washington, 1974-77, Hogue, Crothers & Bernard, Washington, 1977-79; corp. sec., gen. counsel ADI, Las Vegas, Nev., 1979-81; pvt. practice Washington, 1981-88, Charlotte, N.C., 1988-89; atty. IBM, Charlotte, 1989-90; assoc. Pennie & Edmonds, Washington, 1990-92; ptnr. Mason, Fenwick & Lawrence (merged with Popham Haik Schnobrich & Kaufman 1994), Washington, 1992-95, Marks & Murase LLP, Washington, 1995-98, Kilpatrick & Cody, Washington, 1996-98, Coudert Bros., Washington, 1998-99, Antonelli, Terry, Stout & Kraus, LLP, Arlington, Va., 1999—; sec. Nat. Motor Vehicle Safety Adv. Coun., Dept. Transp., Washington, 1971-77. Author: (with others) Association of University Technology Managers Manual, 1992, 94. Minority opinion reporter Alexandria Va. Charter Rev. Commn. Capt. USAF, 1964-68, Vietnam. Mem. Am. Intellectual Property Law Assn., Internat. Fedn. of Intellectual Property Attys., Licensing Execs. Soc., Assn. of Univ. Tech. Mgrs., Internat. Fedn. of Indsl. Property Attys., Assn. of Univ. Tech. Mgrs. Republican. Episcopalian. Avocations: flying, golfing, sailing. Fax: 703-312-6666. E-mail: dhogue@antonelli.com. Intellectual property, Trademark and copyright, Patent. Office: Antonelli Terry Stout & Kraus LLP 1300 17th St N Ste 1800 Arlington VA 22209-3873

**HOGUE, TERRY GLYNN,** lawyer; b. Merced, Calif., Sept. 23, 1944; s. Glynn Dale and Lillian LaVonne (Carter) H.; m. Joanne Laura Sharples, Oct. 3, 1969; children: Morgan Taylor, Whitney Shannon. BA, U. Calif., Fresno, 1966, postgrad., 1967; JD, U. Calif., San Francisco, 1972. Bar: Calif. 1972, Idaho 1975, U.S. Dist. Ct. (cen. dist.) Calif. 1973, U.S. Dist. Ct. Idaho 1975, U.S. Supreme Ct. 1976. Assoc. Reid, Babbage & Coil, Riverside, Calif., 1972-75; pvt. practice, Hailey, Idaho, 1975-77; ptnr. Campion & Hogue, Hailey, 1977-80, Hogue & Speck, Hailey and Ketchum, Idaho, 1980-82, Hogue, Speck & Aanestad, Hailey and Ketchum, 1982-97, Hogue & Dunlap, L.L.P., Hailey and Ketchum, 1998—. Bd. dirs. Blaine County Med. Ctr., Hailey, 1975-91. Sgt. U.S. Army, 1969-71. Mem. ABA, Calif. Bar Assn., Idaho Bar Assn. (hearing panel of profl. conduct bd. 1991-97, chmn. profl. conduct bd. 1994-95), 5th Jud. Dist. Bar Assn. (magistrate com. 1991-93, ethics com. 1991-93), Idaho Trial Lawyers Assn. (bd. dirs. 1982-93, treas. 1985-86, sec. 1986-87, v.p. 1988-89, pres. 1989-90), Assn. Trial Lawyers Am. (sec. coun. of pres. 1989-90, Atla Weideman Wisocki award 1990), Am. Inns. of Ct. (charter Master Bench chpt.), Hailey C. of C. (bd. dirs. 1975-83), Rotary. General practice, Family and matrimonial, General civil litigation. Home: PO Box 1259 500 Onyx Dr Ketchum ID 83340-1259 Office: Hogue & Dunlap LLP PO Box 460 Hailey ID 83333-0460 also: PO Box 538 Ketchum ID 83340-0538

**HOHMAN, DAVID MICHAEL,** lawyer; b. Omaha, Dec. 11, 1964; s. John Roger and Susan Mary (Stahl) H.; m. Eleanor Ann Skrupa, Feb. 5, 1994; 1 child, Harrison John. Student, Oxford (Eng.) U., 1985; BA, Stanford U., 1987; JD, U. Nebr., 1992. Bar: Calif. 1992, Nebr. 1993. Assoc. Gray, Cary, Ware & Friedenrich, Palo Alto, Calif., 1992-93, Dixon & Jessup LLP, Omaha, 1993-95, Blackwell, Sanders, Peper & Martin, Omaha, 1995—. Bd. dirs. Mt. Michael Benedictine H.S. Alumni, Elkhorn, Nebr., 1997—. Mem. Nebr. Young Lawyers, Nebr. State Bar (corp. counsel sect.), Future Omaha Young Profls. Group, Stanford Alumni Assn. (pres. Nebr.-Western Iowa chpt. 1996—). Republican. Roman Catholic. Avocations: family, fly fishing, golf, gardening. E-mail: dhohman@bspmlaw.com. General corporate, Securities. Office: Blackwell Sanders Peper Martin 13710 Fnb Pkwy Ste 200 Omaha NE 68154-5298

**HOHNHORST, JOHN CHARLES,** lawyer; b. Jerome, Idaho, Dec. 25, 1952; m. Raelene Casper; children: Jennifer, Rachel, John. BS in Polit. Sci./Pub. Adminstrn., U. Idaho, 1975, JD cum laude, 1978. Bar: Idaho 1978, U.S. Dist. Ct. Idaho 1978, U.S. Ct. Appeals (9th cir.) 1980, U.S. Ct. Claims 1983, U.S. Supreme Ct. 1987. Adminstrv. asst. to Sen. John M. Barker Idaho State Senate, 1975; ptnr. Hepworth, Lezamiz & Hohnhorst, Twin Falls, Idaho, 1978—. Contbr. articles to profl. jours. Mem. planning & zoning commn. City of Twin Falls, 1987-90. Mem. ABA, ATLA, Idaho State Bar (commr. 1990-93, pres. 1993), Idaho Trial Lawyers Assn. (regional dir. 1985-86), 5th Dist. Bar Assn. (treas. 1987-88, v.p. 1988-89, pres. 1989-90), Am. Acad. Appellate Lawyers, Greater Twin Falls C. of C. (chmn. magic valley leadership program 1988-89, bd. dirs. 1989-92), Phi Kappa Tau (Beta Gamma chpt., Phi award 1988). General civil litigation, Contracts commercial, Real property. Office: Hepworth Lezamiz & Hohnhorst PO Box 389 133 Shoshone St N Twin Falls ID 83301-6150

**HOINES, DAVID ALAN,** lawyer; b. St. Paul, Oct. 18, 1946; s. Arnold H. and Patricia (Olson) H.; m. Bonnie K. Smith, June 4, 1983. BA, Calif. State U., San Jose, 1969; JD, Santa Clara U., 1972; LLM in Taxation, Boston U., 1973. Bar: Fla. 1975, Calif. 1975, N.Y. 1999, U.S. Dist. Ct. (so. dist.) Fla. 1975, U.S. Dist. Ct. (no. dist.) Calif. 1980, U.S. Dist. Ct. (mid. dist.) Fla. 1984, U.S. Dist. Ct. (ctrl. dist.) Calif. 1990, U.S. Ct. Claims 1980, U.S. Tax Ct. 1975, U.S. Ct. Appeals (fed. cir.) 1990, U.S. Ct. Appeals (4th cir.) 1985, U.S. Ct. Appeals (5th cir.) 1978, U.S. Ct. Appeals (9th cir.) 1980, U.S. Ct. Appeals (11th cir.) 1981, U.S. Supreme Ct. 1980, N.Y. 1999; cert. civil trial lawyer. Pvt. practice Ft. Lauderdale, Fla., 1975—; adj. instr. Nova U. Ctr. for Study of Law, 1977. Author: Taxman and the Textbook, The Ripon Forum, 1972. Mem. ABA, Assn. Trial Lawyers Am., Broward County Bar Assn., Fla. Bar Assn., Calif. Bar Assn., State Bar of N.Y., Hundred Club of Broward County, Tau Delta Phi. Avocations: ocean diving (free and scuba), snowskiing, running, boating, reading. General civil litigation, Taxation, general, Probate. Office: 1290 E Oakland Park Blvd Fort Lauderdale FL 33334-4443

**HOLBROOK, DONALD BENSON,** lawyer; b. Salt Lake City, Jan. 4, 1925; s. Robert Sweeten and Kinnie Benson H.; m. Bety J. Gilchrist, Apr. 23, 1947; children: Mark, Thomas, Gregory, Mary.; Student, Colo. Coll., U. Utah; JD, U. Utah, 1952, PhD (hon.), 1990; PhD (hon.), HHD (hon.), Utah Valley C.C., 1990; DFA (hon.), 1990; DHL (hon.), Salt Lake City C.C. Bar: Utah 1953. Pres. Jones Waldo, Holbrook and McDonough, Salt Lake City, 1973-89; of counsel, 1995—; exec. v.p., legal officer Am. Stores Co., 1990-95; bd. dirs. Blue Cross/Blue Shield Utah, The Regence Group; commr. Utah Bar, 1983-87; bd. advs. Mountain Bell, 1974-84. Editor in chief: Utah Law Rev., 1951-52. Bd. dirs. Utah Ass. UN, 1963-64; bd. dirs., exec. com. Utah Coop. Assn., 1962-83, vice chmn., 1970-73, chmn., 1974-82, 83-85; chmn. Utah Partnership for Ednl. and Econ. devel., 1987-95; pres. and chmn. bd. Ballet West, 1982-84; bd. dirs. Utah Dem. Party, exec. sec., 1955-65, exec. com., 1956-65; chmn. antitrust and monopoly subcom. Western States Dem. Conf., 1962-66; campaign mgr. Gov. Calvin L. Rampton, 1964-68; candidate for U.S. Senate, 1964; commr. Western Interstate Commn. on Higher Edn., 1978-83, chmn., 1982. Recipient Disting. Alumni award U. Utah, 1985, Resolution of Appreciation Utah Ste Bd. Regents, 1990, Light of Learning award Utah State Bd. Edn., 1994; named Lawyer of Yr. Utah State Bar, 1990. Fellow Internat. Acad. Trial Lawyers, Am. Bar Found.; mem. U. Utah Coll. Law Alumni Assn. (pres. 1957), ABA (gen. chmn. Rocky Mountain region 1962, Utha chmn., mem. com. sect. corp., banking, bus. law 1962-95), Utah Bar Assn. (bd. commrs. 1982-87, chmn. com. World Peace Through Law 1964, pres. 1964-65), Order of the Coif (award for contbns. to law, scholarship and cmty. svc. 1968), Salt Lake City Country Club, Beta Theta Phi, Phi Kappa Phi, Delta Theta Phi (disting. alumni award 1967). Antitrust, Administrative and regulatory, Federal civil litigation. Home: 1752 Laurelhurst Dr Salt Lake City UT 84108-3310

**HOLBROOK, FRANK MALVIN,** lawyer; b. Atlanta, Mar. 26, 1952; s. James David and Mary Linda (Fambrough) H.; m. Julie Melissa Holley, Aug. 30, 1975; children: Holley Marie, James Clinton. AA with honors, Brevard Community Coll., Cocoa, Fla., 1972; BS cum laude, Fla. State U., 1974; JD cum laude, U. Ga., 1979. Bar: Ga. 1979, Miss. 1979, U.S. Dist. Ct. (no. and so. dists.) Miss. 1979, U.S. Ct. Appeals (5th cir.) 1979, U.S. Ct. Appeals (11th cir.) 1982. Assoc. Fuselier, Ott & McKee, Jackson, Miss., 1979-83; assoc. Thompson, Alexander & Crews, Jackson, 1983-85, ptnr., 1985-95; v.p., shareholder Edmonson, Biggs, Mozingo & Holbrook P.A., Jackson, Miss., 1995-97; ptnr. Butler, Snow, O'Mara, Stevens & Cannada, PLLC, Jackson, 1997—. Mem. ABA, Fed. Bar Assn. (pres. Miss. chpt. 1991-92), Miss. State Bar Assn., State Bar Ga., Hinds County Bar Assn. Republican. Methodist. Avocations: music, skiing, backpacking. General civil litigation, Contracts commercial, Insurance. Office: PO Box 22567 Jackson MS 39225-2567

**HOLBROOK, REID FRANKLIN,** lawyer; b. Kansas City, Jan. 19, 1942; s. Henry Edmiston and Margaret Dorothy H.; m. Mary Lynn Rogers, Feb. 16, 1968; children: Ann Holbrook Johnson, Katherine Reid. AB in Econs., U. Kans., 1964, JD, 1966. Bar: Kans. 1967, U.S. Dist. Ct. Kans. 1967, U.S. Dist. Ct. D.C. 1970, U.S. Ct. Appeals (D.C. cir.) 1970, U.S. Mil. Ct. Appeals 1970, U.S. Supreme Ct. 1970, Mo. 1990, U.S. Dist. Ct. (we. dist.) Mo. 1981, U.S. Ct. Appeals (8th and 10th cirs.) 1977. Judge 29th Jud. Dist. Kans., Kansas City, 1967-71, spl. counsel to dist. atty., 1971-75; spl. asst. atty. gen. State of Kans., Kansas City, 1971-74; ptnr. Holbrook, Heaven & Osborn, Kansas City, 1975—. Co-author: Child Abuse and Neglect: A Medical Reference, 1982. Maj. U.S. Army, 1966-80. Fellow Am. Acad. Hosp. Attys.; mem. Kans. Assn. Hosp. Attys., Kansas City Soc. Hosp. Attys. Avocations: flying, golf, travel. Health, Personal injury, General civil litigation. Home: 11101 W 119th Ter Overland Park KS 66213-2051 Office: Holbrook Heaven & Osborn 757 Armstrong Ave Kansas City KS 66101-2701

**HOLCOMB, LYLE DONALD, JR.,** retired lawyer; b. Miami, Fla., Feb. 3, 1929; s. Lyle Donald and Hazel Irene (Watson) H.; m. Barbara Jean Roth, July 12, 1952; children: Susan Holcomb Davis, Douglas J., Mark E. BA, U. Mich., 1951; JD, U. Fla., 1954. Bar: U.S. Supreme Ct. 1966, U.S. Ct. Appeals (5th and 11th cirs.) 1981. Ptnr. Holcomb & Holcomb, Miami, 1955-72; assoc. Copeland, Therrel, Baisden & Peterson, Miami Beach, Fla., 1972-75; ptnr. Therrel, Baisden, Stanton, Wood & Setlin, Miami Beach, 1976-85; ptnr. Therrel Baisden & Meyer Weiss, Miami Beach, 1985-93; pvt. practice, Tallahassee, Fla., 1993-95; mem. organizing bd. Econ. Opportunities Legal Svcs. Program (now Legal Svcs. of Greater Miami, Inc.), 1965-75; organizing pres. So. Fla. Migrant Legal Svcs. Program (now Fla. Rural Legal Svcs.), 1966-68. Mem. exec. coun. So. Fla. coun. Boy Scouts Am., 1958-93; past pres. Miami chpt., past counselor state soc. Huguenot Soc. Fla. Served with USNR, 1947-53. Recipient Silver Beaver award So. Fla. coun. Boy Scouts Am., 1966. Fellow Am. Coll. Trust and Estate Counsel, 1980-94, Acad. Fla. Probate and Trust Litigation Attys., 1980-95; mem. Dade County Bar Assn. (dir. 1960-71, sec. 1963-71), Miami Beach Bar Assn. (pres. 1980), Estate Planning Council Greater Miami., Soc. Mayflower Descs. (past pres. Miami club, past counselor state soc.), SAR (past pres. Miami chpt.), Univ. Yacht Club. Republican. Mem. United Ch. of Christ. Home: 3538 Killarney Plaza Dr Tallahassee FL 32308-3491

**HOLCOMB, MARK ELLIOTT,** lawyer; b. Miami, June 23, 1960; s. Lyle D. and Barbara Jean (Roth) H.; m. Lori Sue Leifer Holcomb, July 11, 1987; children: Steven Andrew, Michael Ross. BA, U. Fla., Gainesville, 1982; JD, Fla. State U., Tallahassee, 1985. Bar: Fla. 1985, U.S. Ct. Appeals (11th cir.) 1986, U.S. Dist. Cts. (no. and middle dists.) Fla. 1986. Assoc. atty. Akerman, Senterfitt & Eidson, Tallahassee, 1985-86; assoc. atty. Huey, Guilday, Kuersteiner & Tucker, Tallahassee, 1986-92, ptnr., 1992-94; ptnr. Holland & Knight LLP, Tallahassee, 1995—. Treas., pres.-elect, counsel Capital Area Healthy Start, Tallahassee, Fla., 1991—; mem. Human Svcs. Adv. Com. 21st Century Coun., Tallahassee, 1997—. Mem. Fla. Bar Tax Sect., Order of Coif, Phi Beta Kappa. Republican. Office: Holland & Knight LLP 315 S Calhoun St Ste 600 Tallahassee FL 32301-1872

**HOLDAWAY, RONALD M.,** federal judge; b. Afton, Wyo.; m. Judy Janowski, Dec. 1958; children: Denise, Georgia. BA, U. Wyo., 1957, JD, 1959. Bar: Wyo. 1959, U.S. Dist. Ct. (Wyo.), U.S. Ct. Mil. Appeals, 1960, U.S. Army Ct. Mil. Rev., U.S. Supreme Ct., 1967. Commd. 2nd lt. U.S. Army., 1960, advanced through grades to brig. gen., 1989; legal staff officer U.S. Army, Ft. Lewis, Washington, 1960-63; legal staff instr. U.S. Army, Hawaii, 1963-66; instr. criminal law, Judge Advocate Gen.'s Sch. U.S. Army, Charlottesville, Va., 1966-69; staff judge advocate 1st cav. divsn. U.S. Army, Vietnam, 1969-70; chief govt. appellate divsn. U.S. Army, Washington, 1971-75, chief of pers., 1975-77; staff judge advocate U.S. Army, Stuttgart, Germany, 1978-80; exec. to judge advocate gen. U.S. Army, Washington, 1980-81, asst. judge advocate gen., 1981-83; judge advocate U.S. Army Europe, Heidelberg, Germany, 1983-87; chief judge Ct. Mil. Review U.S. Army, Washington, 1987-89; judge U.S. Ct. of Vets. Appeals, Washington DC, 1990—. Decorated Bronze Star, Legion of Merit, Disting. Svc. medal with Oak Leaf Cluster, Meritorious Svc. medal with Oak Leaf Cluster, Air medal, Nat. Def. Svc. medal, Vietnam Campaign medal with 4 campaign stars, Vietnam Svc. medal, Overseas medal (3). Mem. Wyo. State Bar Assn., Assn. U.S. Army, Ft. Myer Officers Club, Army Navy Club. Office: US Ct of Appeals for Vets Claims 625 Indiana Ave NW Ste 900 Washington DC 20004-2917

**HOLDEN, C. BYRON,** lawyer; b. Southport, N.C., July 14, 1950; s. Ernest D. and Marjorie P. H.; m. Christine M. Holden, June 20, 1972; children: Heather Elizabeth, C. Byron Jr., Katherine Mary. BA, Yale U., 1972; JD, Wake Forest U., 1975. Bar: N.C. 1975, U.S. Dist. Ct. N.C. Atty. Golding, Meekins, Holden, Cosper & Stiles, Charlotte, N.C., 1975—. Mem. Def. Rsch. Inst., N.C. Assn. Arson Investigators, N.C. I.C.I.E. Insurance, Personal injury. Office: Golding Meekins Holden Cosper & Stiles 301 S Mcdowell St Ste 1200 Charlotte NC 28204-2681

**HOLDEN, MARY GAYLE REYNOLDS,** lawyer; b. Charlottesville, Va., Oct. 21, 1948; d. Bruce Dodson and Jane Rust (Monroe) R.; m. William L. Ashley III, June 7, 1970 (div. Dec. 1980); children: William Lloyd Ashley IV, David Monroe Ashley; m. Peter Randolph Holden, June 15, 1985; children: Peter Reynolds Holden, Benjamin Willson Holden. BA, Roanoke Coll., 1970; JD, U. Va., 1980. Bar: Va. 1980, U.S. Dist. Ct. (fed. dist.) 1980, U.S. Ct. Appeals (4th cir.) 1994. Assoc. McGuire, Woods, Battle & Boothe, Fairfax, Va., 1980-83; pvt. practice Sterling, Va., 1983-84; assoc. Frank, Bernstein, Conway & Goldman, McLean, Va., 1985; corp. counsel Crippen Cos., Gt. Falls, Va., 1986-88; assoc. Caligaro & Mutryn, Washington, 1988-89; ptnr. Leonard, Ralston & Stanton, Washington, 1990-97, Hopkins & Sutter, Washington, 1997—; Bd. dirs. Am. Cancer Soc., Loudoun County, Va., 1997—, Com. for Dulles, 1987-89, 98—, Jackson-Field Home for Girls, Jarrett, Va., 1988-89, Fairfax Choral Soc., 1983-89; mem. Loudoun Vol. Fin. Coun., 1994—, Loudoun County Leadership Ext. Coun., 1995—, Zonta Internat., 1997—. Mem. Loudoun County Affirmative Action Com., 1995—, chmn. 1995. Mem. Va. Bar. Assn., D.C. Bar Assn., Women in Tehc. (bd. dirs. 1999—), Reston C. of C., Dulles Area Transp. Assn., Loudoun County Transp. Assn. (bd. dirs. 1999—). Episcopalian. Avocations: skiing, Am. history. Contracts commercial, General corporate, Intellectual property.

**HOLDER, ERIC H.,** prosecutor; b. N.Y.C., Jan. 21, 1951; s. Eric H. and Miriam R. (Yearwood) H. BA, Columbia Coll., 1973, JD, 1976. Bar: N.Y. 1977, D.C. 1980. Trial atty. pub. integrity sect. U.S. Dept. Justice, 1976-88; assoc. judge Superior Ct., Washington, 1988-93; U.S. atty. Dept. Justice, Washington, 1993-97, U.S. dep. atty. gen., 1997—. Mem. Concerned Black Men. Democrat. Office: Dep Atty Gen Dept Justice 950 Pennsylvania Ave NW Washington DC 20530-0001*

**HOLDER, JANICE MARIE,** state supreme court justice; b. Canonsburg, Pa., Aug. 29, 1949; d. Louis V. and Sylvia (Abraham) H.; m. George W. Loveland II, June 5, 1976 (div. Mar. 1987). Student, Allegheny Coll., 1967-68, Sorbonne, 1970; BS summa cum laude, U. Pitts., 1971; JD, Duquesne U., 1975. Bar: Pa. 1975, Tenn. 1979, D.C. 1988. Sr. law clk. to chief judge U.S. Dist. Ct. for Western Dist. Pa., Pitts., 1975-77; assoc. Catalano & Catalano, P.C., Pitts., 1977-79, Holt, Batchelor, Spicer & Ryan, Memphis, 1980-82; pvt. practice Memphis, 1983-87; assoc. James S. Cox & Assocs., Memphis, 1987-89; pvt. practice law Memphis, 1989-90; judge 30th Jud. Dist., Memphis, 1990-96; justice Tenn. Supreme Ct., 1996—; solicitor Borough of McDonald (Pa.), 1978-79. Bd. dirs. Alliance for Blind and Visually Impaired, Memphis, 1985-94, Midtown Mental Health Ctr., 1995-97; trustee Memphis Botanical Garden Found., 1996—. Fellow Tenn. Bar Found. (trustee 1995—); mem. ABA, Am. Bar Found., Tenn. Bar Assn., Memphis Bar Assn. (bd. dirs. 1986-87, 93-94, editor Memphis Bar Forum 1987-91, 93-94, sec. 1993, treas. 1994, Sam A. Myar award 1990, Judge of Yr. divorce and family law sect. 1992, Chancellor Charles A. Rond award Outstanding Jurist 1992), Assn. for Women Attys. (treas. 1989, v.p. 1991), Tenn. Jud. Conf., Am. Inns Ct., Memphis Trial Lawyers Assn. (bd. dirs. 1988-90), Tenn. Task Force Against Domestic Violence (mem. state coordinating coun. 1994-96), Tenn. Lawyers' Assn. for Women, Tenn. Trial Judges Assn. (exec. com. 1994-96), Tenn. Judicial Conf. (treas. 1993-94, exec. com. 1993-96). Office: Tenn Supreme Ct 5050 Poplar Ave Ste 820 Memphis TN 38157-0820

**HOLDER, THOMAS LEE,** lawyer; b. Bklyn., Feb. 15, 1956; s. Howard Martin and Joan Roslyn (Geffner) H.; m. Laura Mary Mantrone, Sept. 13, 1987. Student, U. Lancaster, Eng., 1975-76; BA, Case Western Res. U., 1977; JD, Emory U., 1981. Bar: Ga. 1981; U.S. Dist. Ct. (no. dist.) Ga. 1981; U.S. Ct. Appeals (11th cir.) 1981. Assoc. Appel, Strickland & Robins, Atlanta, 1981-84, Siler & Jonap, Atlanta, 1984-86; ptnr. Long & Holder, Atlanta, 1986—. Vice-chmn. Young Careers Group High Mus. of Art, Atlanta, 1986-87. Named to Outstanding Young Men of Am., 1986. Mem. Atlanta Bar Assn. (chmn. workers compensation sect. 1987-89), State Bar of Ga., Ga. Trial Lawyers Assn., Assn. of Trial Lawyers of Am. Avocations: basketball, running, reading. Workers' compensation, Personal injury. Home: 1124 Alta Ave NE Atlanta GA 30307-2515 Office: Long & Holder 127 Peachtree St NE Ste 1515 Atlanta GA 30303-1809

**HOLDERMAN, JAMES F., JR.,** federal judge; b. 1946. BS, U. Ill., 1968, JD, 1971. Judge U.S. Dist. Ct. (no. dist.) Ill., Chgo., 1985—; asst. U.S. atty. City of Chgo., 1972-78; ptnr. Sonnenschein, Carlin et al, Chgo., 1978-85; lectr. law U. Chgo., 1983—. Office: US Dist Ct US Courthouse 219 S Dearborn St Ste 2146 Chicago IL 60604-1801

**HOLEWINSKI, PAUL PATRICK,** lawyer; b. Green Bay, Wis., Sept. 16, 1968; s. Gene Anthony and Margaret Ann Holewinski; m. Amy Dickinson, Sept. 6, 1998. BS in Fin., St. Louis U., 1991, MBA, 1994, JD, 1994. Bar: Mo. 1994, Kans. 1995, D.C. 1996. Assoc. Watson & Marshall LLC, Kansas City, Mo., 1994-96, Bryan Cave LLP, Kansas City, Mo., 1996—; bd. dirs. Ozanam, Kansas City. Mem. Kansas City Met. Bar Assn. Republican. Roman Catholic. Avocations: reading, running, golf, travel. General corporate, Securities, Finance. Office: Dickinson Fin Corp 1100 Main St Ste 350 Kansas City MO 64105

**HOLL, JEFFREY P.,** lawyer; b. San Francisco, June 19, 1954. BA, U. Calif., Davis, 1976; JD, Santa Clara U., 1981, MBA, 1981. Ptnr. Walkup, Melodia, Kelley & Echeverria, San Francisco. Chmn. bd. dirs. Archbishop Riordan H.S., San Francisco, 1993—. Office: Walkup Melodia et al 650 California St Fl 26 San Francisco CA 94108-2702

**HOLLADAY, ROBERT LAWSON,** lawyer; b. Greenwood, Miss., Jan. 28, 1948; s. Robert William and Jo (Coleman) H.; children: Rob, Jennifer. BS, Delta State U., 1970; JD, U. Miss., 1973. Bar: Miss. 1973, U.S. Dist. Ct. (no. dist.) Miss. 1973, U.S. Ct. Appeals, (5th cir.) 1975. Ptnr. Towsend, McWilliams & Holladay, Drew and Indianola, Miss., 1973—; Miss. Bar Found. fellow, 1983. Mem. Miss. Trial Lawyers Assn. (bd. dirs. 1975—). Avocations: hunting, fishing. Personal injury, General civil litigation, Criminal. Office: Townsend McWilliams & Holladay PO Box 288 Drew MS 38737-0288

**HOLLAND, FRED ANTHONY,** lawyer; b. Wilmington, Del., Aug. 29, 1955; s. Bernard Allen and Rosalie May (Wellman) H.; m. Martha Jean Barry, July 29, 1978; 1 child, Maureen Patricia. BA, U. Del., 1977; JD, Coll. William and Mary, 1980. Bar: Pa. 1981, U.S. Dist. Ct. (mid. dist.) Pa. 1985. Law clk. to presiding judge Ct. Common Pleas, Williamsport, Pa., 1981-82; asst. dist. atty. Lycoming County, Williamsport, 1983; assoc. Kieser & Gahr, Williamsport, 1983-84, Liebert, Short, Fitzpatrick & Hirshland, Williamsport, 1985-88; ptnr. Murphy, Butterfield & Holland PC, 1988—; adj. instr. Pa. State U., State College, 1986-89. Banking, Contracts commercial, Real property. Home: 508 Highland Ter Williamsport PA 17701-1707 Office: Murphy Butterfield & Holland PC 442 William St Williamsport PA 17701-6116

**HOLLAND, H. RUSSEL,** federal judge; b. 1936; m. Diane Holland; 3 children. BBA, U. Mich., 1958, LLB, 1961. With Alaska Ct. System, Anchorage, 1961, U.S. Atty.'s Office, Dept. Justice, Anchorage, 1963-65; assoc. Stevens & Savage, Anchorage, 1965-66; ptnr. Stevens, Savage, Holland, Erwin & Edwards, Anchorage, 1967-68; sole practice Anchorage, 1968-70; ptnr. Holland & Thornton, Anchorage, 1970-78, Holland, Thornton & Trefry, Anchorage, 1978, Holland & Trefry, Anchorage, 1978-84, Trefry & Brecht, Anchorage, 1984; judge U.S. Dist. Ct. Alaska, Anchorage, 1984—. Mem. ABA, Alaska Bar Assn., Anchorage Bar Assn. Office: US Dist Ct 222 W 7th Ave Unit 54 Anchorage AK 99513-7504

**HOLLAND, LYMAN FAITH, JR.,** lawyer; b. Mobile, Ala., June 17, 1931; s. Lyman Faith and Louise (Wisdom) H.; m. Leannah Louise Platt, Mar. 6, 1954; children: Lyman Faith III, Laura. BS in Bus. Adminstrn, U. Ala., 1953; LLB, 1957. Bar: Ala. 1957. Assoc. Hand, Arendall & Bedsole, Mobile, 1957-62; ptnr. Hand, Arendall, Bedsole, Greaves & Johnston, 1963-94, mem., 1995; mem. Hand Arendall LLC, 1996—. Mem. Mobile Hist. Devel. Com., 1965-69, v.p., 1967-68; bd. dirs. Mobile Azalea Trail, Inc., 1963-68, chmn. bd., 1963-65; bd. dirs. Mobile Mental Health Ctr., 1969-76, v.p., 1972, pres., chmn. bd., 1973; bd. dirs. Mobile chpt. ARC, 1969-89, 91-97, vice chmn., 1975-77, exec. vice chmn., 1978-80, chmn., 1980-82, life bd. dirs. emeritus, 1997—; bd. dirs. Deep South coun. Girl Scouts U.S., 1965-77, Gordan Smith Ctr. Inc., 1973, Bay Area Coun. on Alcoholism, 1973-76, Comty. Chest, Coun. of Mobile County, Inc., 1976-81; bd. dirs. Greater Mobile Mental Health-Mental Retardation, 1975-81, pres., 1975-77; mem. exec. com. Mobile Estate Planning Coun., 1988-97, pres., 1994-95. 1st lt. USAF, 1953-55; lt. col. USAF ret. Mem. ABA, Mobile County Bar Assn., Ala. State Bar (chmn. sect. corp., banking and bus. law 1978-80), Am. Counsel Assn., Am. Coll. Trust and Estate Counsel, Am. Coll. Trust and Estate Counsel Found. (bd. dirs. 1990-96), Ala. Law Inst. (coun. 1978—), Athleston Club (Mobile), Country Club of Mobile, Bienville Club, Lions, Pi Kappa Alpha, Phi Delta Phi. Baptist (deacon, ch. trustee 1968-73, chmn. trustees 1971-73). Estate planning, Probate, Real property. Home: 3606 Provident Ct Mobile AL 36608-1534 Office: Hand Arendall LLC PO Box 123 Mobile AL 36601-0123

**HOLLAND, RANDY JAMES,** state supreme court justice; b. Elizabeth, N.J., Jan. 27, 1947; s. James Charles and Virginia (Wilson) H.; m. Ilona E. Holland, June 24, 1972. B.A. in Econs., Swarthmore Coll., 1969; J.D. cum laude, U. Pa., 1972; LLM, Univ. Va., 1998. Bar: Del. 1972. Ptnr. Dunlap, Holland & Rich and predecessors, Georgetown, Del., 1972-80, Morris, Nichols, Arsht & Tunnell, Georgetown, Del., 1980-86; justice Supreme Ct. Del., Georgetown, 1986—; mem. Del. Bar Examiners, 1978-86; mem. Gov.'s Jud. Nominating Commn., 1978-86, sec., 1982-85, chmn., 1985-86; mem. Del. Supreme Ct. Consol. Com., 1985-86; pres. Terry-Carey Inn of Ct., 1991-94; v.p. Am. Inns of Ct., 1996—; co-chair Racial and Ethnic Task Force, 1995—; adj. prof. Widener U. Sch. Law, 1991—, U. Pa. Sch. Law, 1993-94; co-chair Del. Cts. Planning Com., 1996; chair nat. jud. adv. com. fed. Office of Child Support Enforcement; Jud. Ethics Adv. Commn., 1994—; del. Code Jud. Conduct Rev. Commn., 1991-94; del. Bar Bench Media Conf., 1990—. Mem. editorial bd. Del. Lawyer Mag., 1981-85; contbr. chpt. Del. Appellate Handbook, 1985—. Pres. adminstrv. bd. Ave. United Meth. Ch., Milford, Del. Bar Found.; hon. chmn. History of the Del. Bar in 20th Century, 1992—. Recipient Henry C. Loughlin prize for legal ethics U. Pa. 1972, St. Thomas More award, 1999; named Judge of the Yr. Nat. Child Support Enforcement Assn., 1992. Mem. ABA (standing com. on lawyer competence, nat. jud. coll. adv. commn. model rules jud. disclosure enforcement 1996), Am. Judicature Soc. (nat. trustee 1992—), Am. Inns of Ct. Found. (trustee 1992—, nat. trustee 1996—, v.p. 1996—), Am. Law Inst., Del. Bar Found., Am. Law Inst. Republican. Office: Del Supreme Ct Family Court Bldg 22 The Cir Georgetown DE 19947-1500

**HOLLAND, ROBERT DALE,** retired magistrate, consultant; b. Sayre, Okla., June 10, 1928; s. Claude Henry and Alva Mae (Joyce) H.; children: Arlene, Burton Dale, Rhonda Jo. Student, Tex. A&M, 1946, Internat. Corr. Schs., 1963, 65, 67-68; PhD of Sociology (hon.), Scholars U., 1975. Safety, security, loss prevention officer Copper Queen Br. Phelps Dodge Corp., Bisbee, Ariz., 1946-85; probation officer State of Ariz., Bisbee, 1986-87; safety dir., loss prevention dir. Spray Sys. Environ., Phoenix, 1987-93; city magistrate City of Bisbee, 1989-93; pres., owner Copper City Cons., Bisbee, 1989—; referee & hearing officer Cochise County Juvenile Ct., 1969-78; juvenile ct. judge pro tem, 1990-93; justice ct. judge pro tem, 1991-93; bd. dirs. Southern Ariz. Safety Coun., Tucson, 1986-91. Councilman City of Bisbee, 1973-82; chmn. relief com. Salvation Army, 1980—. With USMC, 1947-52. Mem. ADHS (water quality com. 1974), Am. Mining Congress (ad-hoc com. 1980), Perfect Ashlar Lodge F&AM (master 1964), Scottish Yorkrite Bodies Ariz. Democrat. Avocations: gun collecting, reading, church work. Home and Office: PO Box 5427 206 Black Knob Vw Bisbee AZ 85603-1906

**HOLLAND, SUZANNE KARAPASHEV,** lawyer; b. Akron, Oct. 31, 1965; d. Naum N. and Ljubka N. Karapashev; m. Andrew Paul Holland, Sept. 28, 1991; 1 child, Nathaniel. BA, Coll. of Wooster, 1988; JD, Ohio State U., 1991. Bar: Wis. 1991, Ohio 1992. Jud. atty. Summit County, Akron, 1992-94; atty., litigation specialist Progressive Cos., Mayfield Heights, Ohio, 1994-96; atty. Roetzel & Andress, Akron, 1996—. Mem. fundraising com. Western Res. Girl Scout Coun., Akron, 1996—. Avocations: white water rafting, mountain biking, creative writing, ceramics. Environmental. Office: Roetzel & Andress 222 S Main St Akron OH 44308-1533

**HOLLAND, TROY WHITZHURST,** lawyer; b. St. Petersburg, Fla., Mar. 11, 1961; s. William Langsdon and Carol Whitehurst H.; m. Judith Stanton, Sept. 23, 1989; children: Rosslyn, Frances. BA, Duke U., 1983; JD, U. Fla., 1986. Bar: Fla., U.S. Dist. Ct. (mid. dist.) Fla. Asst. states atty. Office of States Atty., Clearwater, Fla., 1986-89; assoc. Harris, Barrett, Mann & Dew, St. Petersburg, Fla., 1989-95, ptnr., 1995—. Mem. Fla. Bar Assn. (bd. govs. young lawyers divsn. 1994-98), St. Petersburg Bar Assn. (chair young lawyers sect. 1993-94). Republican. Methodist. Avocations: golf, reading, kids. State civil litigation, Condemnation, Insurance. Office: Harris Barrett Mann & Dew 150 2d Ave N Ste 1500 Saint Petersburg FL 33701

**HOLLAND, WILLIAM MEREDITH,** lawyer; b. Live Oak, Fla., Feb. 6, 1922; s. Isaac and Annie Elizaa (Williams) H.; m. Mamie Smith, June 3, 1947; children—William Meredith, Maurice, Gian, Gaelim, Shakira; m. 2d, Margaret Elizabeth Erving, Apr. 9, 1976. B.A., Fla. A. & M. U., 1947; J.D., Boston U., 1951. Bar: Fla. 1951, U.S. Dist. Ct. (so. dist.) Fla. 1952, U.S. Ct. Appeals (5th cir.) 1953, U.S. Supreme Ct. 1956, Ptnr., Holland & Smith, Lake Park, Fla., 1954—; mcpl. judge City of Riviera Beach, Fla., 1973-77. Served with AUS, 1943-46. Mem. Fla. Bar Assn., ABA, Nat. Bar Assn., Am. Judicature Soc., ACLU, NAACP, Council Human Relations, Urban League. Civil rights, Federal civil litigation, State civil litigation. Home and Office: 611 W Kalmia Dr West Palm Beach FL 33403-2109

**HOLLEN, THEODORE THOMAS,** lawyer; b. El Paso, Tex., July 19, 1942; s. Theodore T. Jr. and K.W. Cheta (Weatherford) H.; m. Judy Ann Couser, Aug. 29, 1968; children: Theodore IV, Lin Anne, Jason Tiller. BS in Econs., Sul Ross U., 1966; JD, U. Tex., 1969. Bar: Tex. 1969, U.S. Dist. Ct. (we. dist.) Tex. 1970, U.S. Dist. Ct. (no. dist.) Tex. 1980, U.S. Dist. Ct. (so. dist.) Tex. 1980. Assoc. Pearson & Speer, El Paso, 1969-72; mem. election staff Hon. John G. Tower, Austin, Tex., 1972; staff-adminstrv. asst. Hon. Kay Bailey, Austin, 1973; pvt. practice Austin, 1973—. Vol. Austin Lawyers Care, 1977-90. Republican. Baptist. Avocations: golf, roping, race horses. Real property, Finance, Probate. Office: 8705 Shoal Creek Blvd Ste 209 Austin TX 78757-6848

**HOLLENBAUGH, H(ENRY) RITCHEY,** lawyer; b. Shelby, Ohio, Nov. 12, 1947; m. Diane Robinson Nov. 21, 1973 (div. 1989); children: Chad Ritchey, Katie Paige; m. Rebecca U., Aug. 8, 1995. BA, Kent State U., 1969; JD, Capital U., 1973. Bar: Ohio 1973, U.S. Dist. Ct. (so. dist.) Ohio 1974, U.S. Ct. Appeals (6th cir.) 1976, U.S. Supreme Ct. 1978. Investigator Ohio Civil Rights Com., Columbus, Ohio, 1969-72; legal intern City Atty.'s Office, Columbus, Ohio, 1972-73, asst. city prosecutor, 1973-75, sr. asst. city atty., 1975-76; ptnr. Hunter, Hollenbaugh & Theodotou, Columbus, Ohio, 1976-85, Delligatti, Hollenbaugh, Briscoe & Milless, Columbus, Ohio, 1985-91, Climaco Seminatore Delligatti & Hollenbaugh, Columbus, 1991-93, Delligatti, Hollenbaugh & Briscoe, Columbus, 1993-95, Draper, Hollenbaugh, Briscoe, Yashko & Carmany, 1996-; mem. Ohio Pub. Defender Commn., 1988-94; chmn. Franklin County Pub. Defender Commn., 1986-92. Treas. The Gov's. Com., 1987-96, Friends With Celeste, Friends of Gov's. Residence, 1987-92, Participation 2000, 1987-91. Fellow ABA Found. (chair commn. on advt. 1993-97, ho. of dels. 1993—); mem. Ohio State Bar Assn. (bd. govs. 1989-94, pres. 1992-93), Columbus Bar Assn. (pres. 1987-88), Nat. Conf. Bar Pres., Nat. Assn. Criminal Def. Lawyers, Capital Club. Democrat. Methodist. Avocations: golf, politics. Criminal, Federal civil litigation, State civil litigation. Home: 8549 Glenalmond Ct Dublin OH 43017-9737 Office: Draper Hollenbaugh Briscoe Yashko & Carmany 175 S 3rd St Columbus OH 43215-5134

**HOLLENBECK, FRED DRURY,** lawyer; b. Neenah, Wis., Mar. 22, 1942; s. Fred Drury and Margaret Louise (Knight) H.; m. Susan Virginia Rhyner Bishop, Dec. 29, 1984; children: Fred D. IV, Martha E. BS in History, U. Wis., 1964, JD, 1967. Bar: Wis. 1967, U.S. Dist. Ct. (we. dist.) Wis. 1969, U.S. Dist. Ct. (ea. dist.) Wis. 1984, U.S. Ct. Appeals (7th cir.) 1984, U.S. Supreme Ct. 1995. Atty. Curran, Hollenbeck & Orton, S.C., Mauston, Wis., 1967—. Past chmn., mem. Juneau County Rep. Party, Mauston, 1967—, Housing Authority City of Mauston, 1970—. Avocation: tennis. Family and matrimonial, Personal injury, General practice. Home: 108 W Monroe St Mauston WI 53948-1130 Office: Curran Hollenbeck & Orton SC 111 Oak St Mauston WI 53948-1332

**HOLLENBERG, HARVARD,** lawyer; b. N.Y.C., Dec. 14, 1938; s. William Gustave and Harriet Grace (Renault) Von Höllenberg. BA, NYU, 1960; MA in Polit. Sci., Victoria U., Wellington, New Zealand, 1962; JD, Harvard U., 1965. Bar: N.Y. 1967, U.S. Dist. Ct. (so. and ea. dists.) N.Y. 1993. Sr. atty. Supreme Ct. Mental Hygiene Legal Svc., N.Y.C., 1965-70; chief counsel, staff dir. N.Y. State Commn. to Evaluate the Drug Laws, N.Y.C.,

Albany, N.Y., 1970-76; asst. state atty. gen. litigation N.Y. State Dept. Law, N.Y.C., 1976-78; spl. counsel to speaker N.Y. State Assembly, N.Y.C., Albany, 1978-83; dep. pub. advocate N.J. Dept. Pub. Advocate, 1983-85; gen. counsel N.Y.C. Dept. Mental Hygiene, 1985-88; pvt. practice specializing in govt. rels., healthcare, and state and fed. constnl. law, pvt. internat. law N.Y.C., 1988—. Author: Employing the Rehabilitated Addict, 1972, Drug Abuse Prevention, 1973, How People Overseas Deal with Drugs, 1974, A Law of Vengeance, 1993, The Vinyard Diamonds, 1994; contbr. frequent articles to N.Y. Law Jour., Nat. Law Jour.; contbr. articles to newspapers including N.Y. Times, Atlanta Constn., St. Louis Post-Dispatch; regular monthly food and travel columnist World's Fare in Newsday. Vol., Met. Opera Guild, N.Y.C. Fulbright scholar Inst. for Internat. Edn., New Zealand, 1960-62, Felix Frankfurter scholar Harvard Law Sch., 1962-65. Mem. N.Y. State Bar Assn., Assn. of Bar of City of N.Y., N.Y. County Bar Assn., Phi Beta Kappa. Democrat. Jewish.

**HOLLERAN, JOHN W.,** lawyer; b. Poughkeepsie, N.Y., June 17, 1954. BA, Gonzaga U., 1976, JD, 1979. Bar: Wash. 1979, Idaho, 1980, Calif. 1987. Counsel Boise (Idaho) Cascade Corp., 1979-83, assoc. gen. counsel, 1983-91, v.p., gen. counsel, 1991-96, sr. v.p., gen. counsel, 1996—; chmn. Fibre Box Assn. Legal adv. com., 1989-91; bd. advisors Gonzaga U. Sch. Law, 1991—; mem. Idaho Vol. Lawyers Program Policy Coun., 1991—. Mem. ABA, Wash. State Bar Assn., Boise Bar Assn., Idaho State Bar, State Bar Calif., Am. Corp. Counsel Assn. General corporate, Antitrust. Office: Boise Cascade Corp PO Box 50 1111 W Jefferson St Boise ID 83728-2800

**HOLLEY, STEVEN LYON,** lawyer; b. Ft. Wayne, Ind., Apr. 5, 1958; s. Wesley Lewis and Cornelia Alice (Reeder) H. BA in History/Polit. Sci., Ind. U., 1980; JD, NYU, 1983. Bar: N.Y. 1984, U.S. Dist. Ct. (so. and ea. dist.) N.Y. 1985, U.S. Dist. Ct. (no. dist.) N.Y. 1988. Law clk. Hon. Jose' A. Cabranes, Hartford, Conn., 1983-84; assoc. Sullivan & Cromwell, N.Y.C., 1984-90; ptnr. Sullivan & Cromwell, 1991—. Mem. Assn. Bar City of N.Y. (sec. com. on profl. and jud. ethics 1988-90). Democrat. Antitrust, Mergers and acquisitions, Securities. Home: 832 Broadway New York NY 10003-4813 Office: Sullivan & Cromwell 125 Broad St Fl 28 New York NY 10004-2489

**HOLLIDAY, JAMES SIDNEY, JR.,** lawyer; b. Baton Rouge, Mar. 6, 1941; s. James S. and Ione (McKay) H.; m. Bonnie Walker, June 19, 1965; children: Stephen J., Laurie F., Amy E., Jennie. BS in Fin. and Econs., La. State U., 1962, JD, 1965. Bar: La. 1965, U.S. Dist. Ct. (ea., mid., we. dists.) La. 1965, D.C. 1977, U.S. Supreme Ct. 1977. Ptnr. McCollister, McCleary, Fazio & Holliday, Baton Rouge, 1965-86; sr. ptnr. Anderson, Holliday & Jones, Baton Rouge, 1986-88; sole practice Baton Rouge, 1988—; pres. Baton Rouge Bank Counsel Group, 1986; seminar speaker, 1975—. Co-author: Construction Law in Louisiana, 1982, Louisiana Corporation Law, 1988; contbr. articles to profl. publs. Mem. exec. bd. Baton Rouge area Boy Scouts Am., 1976. Mem. ABA, La. State Bar Assn., La. Trial Lawyers Assn., Assn. Trial Lawyers Am., Maritime Law Assn. U.S., Baton Rouge Marine Inst. (pres., bd. dirs. 1986-90), Baton Rouge Country Club, City Club Baton Rouge, Delta Sigma Pi, Lambda Chi Alpha. Democrat. Roman Catholic. Avocations: running, scuba diving, skiing. General corporate, Construction, General civil litigation. Office: PO Box 65203 Baton Rouge LA 70896-5203

**HOLLINGSWORTH, JONATHAN,** lawyer; b. Marion, Ark., Dec. 22, 1957; s. Robert Lee Hollingsworth and Claretha (Robinson) Cole; m. Linda K. Payne, Nov. 7, 1987; children: Christopher, Kimberly, Demetrius, Bradford, Natasha. BA, Harvard U., 1980; JD, U. Mich., 1983. Bar: Ohio 1983, U.S. Dist. Ct. (so. dist.) Ohio 1983, U.S. Ct. Appeals (6th cir.) 1984. Assoc. Porter, Wright, Morris & Arthur, Dayton, Ohio, 1983-92, ptnr., 1992—. Legal advisor Ohio mock trial program Miamisburg (Ohio) H.S., 1991-94; trustee Big Bros.-Big Sisters, Dayton, 1994, Family Svcs. Assn., Dayton, 1994—; legal advisor Dayton Urbal League, 1996—, 2nd v.p., 1998-99. Recipient appreciation award for leadership and guidance Miamisburg H.S., 1992. Mem. Dayton Bar Assn. (counsel 1991—). Baptist. Avocation: sports enthusiast. Federal civil litigation, General civil litigation, Civil rights. Office: Porter Wright Morris Arthur One South Main St Dayton OH 45402

**HOLLINS, C(ORDELIA) RENITA,** lawyer, researcher; b. Cleveland, Miss., Jan. 14, 1967; d. Mavis Jean Hollins. BA, Alcorn State U., Lorman, Miss., 1989; MS in Pub. Mgmt. and Policy, Carnegie Mellon U., 1991; JD, U. Fla., 1995. Bar: Fla. 1995, Tenn. 1996. Rsch. analyst Comptr. of Treasury, Nashville, 1996-97; atty. Three Rivers Legal Svcs., Lake City, Fla., 1997—. Vol. Hands on Nashville, 1996-97, Ct. Appointed Spl. Advocate, Nashville, 1996-97. Mem. Nat. Bar Assn., Napier Looby Bar Assn., J.T. Walls Bar Assn. Democrat. Baptist. Avocations: travel, reading, aerobic and anaerobic activity, weight training. Home: RR 10 Box 805B Lake City FL 32025-9142 Office: Three Rivers Legal Svcs 2111 Sisters Welcome Rd PO Box 3067 Lake City FL 32056-3067

**HOLLINS, MITCHELL LESLIE,** lawyer; b. N.Y.C., Mar. 11, 1947; s. Milton and Alma (Bell) H.; m. Nancy Kirchheimer, Mar. 27, 1977 (div. 1999); children: Herbert K. II, Dorothy Ann. BA, Case Western Res. U., 1967; JD, NYU, 1971. Bar: Ill. 1971, U.S. Dist. Ct. (no. dist.) Ill. 1971. Assoc. Sonnenschein Nath & Rosenthal, Chgo., 1971-78, ptnr., 1978—; asst. sec., dir. Jr. Achievement Chgo., 1980—; bd. dirs. Young Men's Jewish Coun., 1973-75; bd. dirs. young people's div. Jewish United Fund Met. Chgo., 1972-76; bd. dirs. Med. Rsch. Inst. Coun. Mem. exec. com., 1979-92, sec., 1981-82, gen. counsel, 1983-86, vice chmn., 1987-92, chmn. jr. bd., 1978-79. Editor NYU Jour. Internat. Law and Politics, 1970-71. Asst. sec., dir. Jr. Achievement Chgo., 1980—; bd. dirs. Young Men's Jewish Coun., 1973-75; bd. dirs. young people's divsn. Jewish United Fund Met. Chgo., 1972-76; bd. dirs. Med. Rsch. Inst. Coun., mem. exec. com., 1979-92, sec., 1981-82, gen. counsel, 1983-86, vice chmn., 1987-92, chmn. jr. bd., 1978-79. Mem. ABA, Am. Coll. Investment Counsel, Chgo. Bar Assn., Standard Club, Lake Shore Country Club (mem. bd. govs. 1984-92, sec. 1985-92), Legal Club, Law Club. Republican. General corporate, Securities. Office: Sonnenschein Nath & Rosenthal 8000 Sears Tower Chicago IL 60606

**HOLLINSHEAD, EARL DARNELL, JR.,** lawyer; b. Pitts., Aug. 1, 1927; s. Earl Darnell and Gertrude (Cahill) H.; m. Sylvia Antion, June 29, 1957; children: Barbara, Kim, Earl III, Susan. AB, Ohio U., 1948; LLB, U. Pitts., 1951. Bar: Pa. 1952, U.S. Ct. Mil. Appeals 1954, U.S. Dist. Ct. (we. dist.) Pa. 1955, U.S. Supreme Ct. 1956, U.S. Ct. Appeals (3d cir.) 1959, U.S. Dist. Ct. (ea. dist.) Ohio 1978. Sole practice Pitts., 1955-70; ptnr. Hollinshead and Mendelson, Pitts., 1970-89, Hollinshead, Mendelson, Bresnahan & Nixon, P.C., Pitts., 1990-97; sole practitioner Pitts., 1997—; mem. Pitts. Estate Planning Council. Contbr. articles to profl. jours. Served to lt. USNR, 1951-55. Fellow Pa. Bar Found. (life); mem. Pa. Bar Assn. (chmn. real property divsn. 1983-85, real property, probate and trust secs. 1985-86), Allegheny County Bar Assn. (chmn. real property sect. 1975-76), Pa. Bar Inst. (lectr., planner, bd. dirs. 1988-94), Am. Coll. Real Estate Lawyers. Real property, Bankruptcy, Probate. Home: 2535 Windgate Rd Bethel Park PA 15102-2730 Office: 630 Grant Bldg Pittsburgh PA 15219-2105

**HOLLIS, ANDRE DALE,** lawyer; b. Washington, Jan. 8, 1966; s. Andrew Dale and Phyllis Joyce (Duvall) H. AB, Princeton U., 1988; JD, U. Va., 1991. Bar: Va. 1992, D.C. 1993, U.S. Ct. Appeals (4th cir.) 1992, U.S. Ct. Appeals (8th, 11th, D.C. and Fed. cirs.) 1993. Assoc. Burt, Maner & Miller, Washington, 1991-93, Slover & Loftus, Washington, 1993-95, Alexander, Aponte & Marks, Silver Spring, Md., 1995, Mays & Valentine, Tysons Corner, Va., 1995-98; counsel for oversight and investigations com. on commerce U.S. Ho. of Reps., Washington, 1998—; gen. counsel Alpha of Va., Inc. Active Big Bros. Nat. Capital Area, Washington, 1992—, sec., 1993, chmn. ann. giving campaign, 1993, v.p. recruitment, 1997—; mem. adv. coun. Woodberry Forest Sch. 1st lt. USAR, 1988-96. Mem. Concerned Black Men, Pigskin Club of D.C., Nassau Club. Republican. African Meth. Episcopal. Avocations: basketball, skydiving, rugby. Fax: 202-226-4303. Home: 4902 S 28th St Arlington VA 22206-1409 Office: Ho of Reps Com on Commerce 2125 Rayburn Office Bldg Washington DC 20515-0001

**HOLLIS, CHARLES HATFIELD,** lawyer; b. Washington, Feb. 27, 1956; s. Charles Bernard and Mary Rebecca (Hatfield) H.; m. Catherine Anne Gleason, Sept. 1, 1979; children: Mary Catherine, Charles Joseph. BSBA, U. Md., 1978; JD, U. Ga., 1981. Bar: Ga. 1981, La. 1981, U.S. Dist. Ct. (ea. dist.) La. 1981, U.S. Supreme Ct. 1981, U.S. Ct. Appeals (5th cir.) 1982, U.S. Ct. Appeals (11th cir.) 1984, U.S. Dist. Ct. (mid. dist.) La. 1985, U.S. Dist. Ct. (we. dist.) La. 1988. Assoc. The Kullman Firm, New Orleans, 1981-86, ptnr., 1986—. Mem. ABA, New Orleans Bar Assn., Beta Gamma Sigma. Republican. Avocations: hunting, golf. Labor. Home: 3756 Lake Charles Dr Gretna LA 70056-8350 Office: The Kullman Firm 1600 Energy Ctr 1100 Poydras St New Orleans LA 70163

**HOLLIS, DARYL JOSEPH,** judge; b. Pitts., Oct. 22, 1946; s. Joseph and Margaret Clara (Meszar) H.; m. Linda Eardley, July 18, 1970. BS in Edn., Pa. State U., 1968, MEd in Remedial Reading, 1971; JD, Cath. U. Am., 1984. Bar: Pa. 1987, D.C. 1989. Law clk. D.C. Office of Employee Appeals, Washington, 1984-85, adminstrv. law judge, 1985-97, sr. adminstrv. law judge, 1997—; lectr. D.C. Bar Assn. Pro Bono Svcs., Washington, 1985—; mem. Transplant Recipients Internat. Orgn., Nat. Capital Area Chpt., 1993—. Mem. Columbia Pines Citizens Assn., 1993—. Mem. Transplant Recipients Internat. Orgn. Democrat. Roman Catholic. Avocations: woodworking, hiking, Civil War, baseball history, sports. Home: 4002 Rose Ln Annandale VA 22003-1943

**HOLLIS, JOHN LEE,** lawyer; b. Seattle, Dec. 29, 1943; s. Gerald John and Ruth Alene Hollis; m. May 27, 1984 (div. Mar. 1987). BA, U. N.Mex., Albuquerque, 1966, JD, 1968. Bar: N.Mex. 1968, U.S. Dist. Ct. N.Mex. 1968, U.S. Ct. Appeals (10th cir.) 1968, U.S. Ct. Appeals (5th cir.) 1972. Field atty. NLRB, Albuquerque, 1968-75; ptnr. Kool, Kool & Hollis, P.A., Albuquerque, 1975-91; pvt. practice Albuquerque, 1991—. Mem. Albuquerque Bar Assn., N.Mex. Trial Lawyers Assn. Democrat. Avocations: horseback riding, skiing, fishing, hunting. Labor, General civil litigation, Construction. Address: 4221 Silver Ave SE Albuquerque NM 87108-2720

**HOLLIS, LOUIE ANDREW,** lawyer; b. Enteprise, Ala., Nov. 10, 1942; s. Louie Andrew and Bonnie Ruth (Jones) H. m. Carol Duke, Dec. 20, 1979; m. Jean Virginia Grimes, Sept. 27 (div. 1976); children—Kelly, Allison. B.S., U. Ala., 1965, J.D., 1968. Bar: Ala. 1968, U.S. Dist. Ct. (so., mid. and no. dists.) Ala. Sole practice, Enterprise, Ala., 1970-76; assoc. Emond & Vines, Birmingham, Ala., 1976-81, Hardin & Hollis, 1981—. Contbr. articles to profl. jours. Served to capt. U.S. Army, 1968-78. Vietnam. Decorated Bronze Star; Vietnamese Commendation medal. Mem. Ala. Trial Lawyers Assn. (pres.-elect, treas., sec., 2d v.p. bd. govs., exec. com.), Assn. Trial Lawyers Am. ABA. Democrat. Methodist. Personal injury, Federal civil litigation, State civil litigation. Home: 1120 Beacon Pky E Apt 607 Birmingham AL 35209-1024 Office: PO Box 11328 Birmingham AL 35202-1328

**HOLLIS, SHEILA SLOCUM,** lawyer; b. Denver, July 15, 1948; d. Theodore Doremus and Emily M. (Caplis) Slocum; m. John Hollis; 1 child, Windsong Emily Lanford. BS in Journalism with honors, U. Colo., 1971, BS in Gen. Studies cum laude, 1971; JD, U. Denver, 1973. Bar: Colo. 1974, D.C. 1975, U.S. Supreme Ct. 1980. Trial atty. Fed. Power Commn., Washington, 1974-75; assoc. firm Wilner & Scheiner, Washington, 1975-77; dir. office enforcement Fed. Energy Regulatory Commn., Washington, 1977-80; pvt. practice, 1980-87; ptnr. Vinson & Elkins, Washington, 1987-92; sr. ptnr. Metzger, Hollis, Gordon & Alprin, Washington, 1992-97; ptnr. in charge, chair energy practice Duane, Morris & Heckscher, LLP, Washington, 1997—; professorial lectr. in energy law George Washington U., 1980—. Co-author: Energy Decision Making, 1983, Energy Law and Policy, 1989; mem. editl. bd. Oil and Gas Reporter, Pub. Utility Fortnightly; contbr. articles to profl. publs. Established and developed enforcement program Fed. Energy Regulatory Commn.; mem. adv. bd. Pub. Utility Ctr., N.Mex. State U., 1986-94, Gas Industry Stds. Bd., 1998—; pres. Women's Coun. Energy and Environ., 1997—; mem. bd. dirs. Nat. Assn. Vets. Health Care. U. Denver scholar, 1972-73. Fellow ABA (mem. ho. of dels., vice chair sect. environ., energy and resources, chair coord. group energy law 1989-92, 95-97, chair standing com. environ. law 1997—); mem. Internat. Bar Assn., Am. Law Inst., Nat. Gas Inst. (chmn. 1983-90), Fed. Energy Bar Assn. (pres. 1991-92), Oil and Gas Ednl. Inst. (v.p.), Southwestern Legal Found. (trustee), Colo. Bar Assn., D.C. Bar Assn., Women's Bar Assn. D.C., Nat. Press Club, Cosmos Club, George Washington U. Club. Roman Catholic. FERC practice, Environmental, Administrative and regulatory. Office: Duane Morris & Heckscher LLP 1667 K St NW Ste 700 Washington DC 20006-1608

**HOLLO, LESLIE STEPHEN,** lawyer; b. N.Y.C., Sept. 14, 1963; s. Leslie and Rita B. (Nagy) H.; m. Alison P. Ball, Sept. 28, 1991; children: Barrett, Stephen. BA in Psychology summa cum laude, Columbia U., 1986, JD, 1987. Bar: N.Y. 1988, Conn. 1992, U.S. Dist. Ct. (so. and ea. dists.) N.Y. 1988, Conn. 1992, U.S. Ct. Fed. Claims 1994. Law clk., assoc. Reavis & McGrath, N.Y.C., 1986-88; assoc. Dow, Lohnes & Albertson, N.Y.C., 1988-92, Wiggin & Dana, New Haven, Conn., 1992-94; counsel Marlowe, Snow & Atticks, Madison, Conn., 1995-96, ptnr., 1996-97; ptnr. Snow, Atticks & Hollo, LLC, Madison, 1997—; lectr. Sch. Vols. New Haven, Inc., 1995—; bd. dirs. SARAH Tuxis Residential Svcs., Inc.; mem. devel. com. SARAH Orgn., 1995—; counsel Law Works for People Pro Bono Lawyer referral Svc., 1996—. Mem. ABA, Conn. Bar Assn., New Haven County Bar Assn., N.Y.C. Bar Assn., Phi Beta Kappa. Democrat. Roman Catholic. General civil litigation, Contracts commercial, Personal injury. Office: Snow Atticks & Hollo LLC 69 Wall St Madison CT 06443-3121

**HOLLON, GREGORY J.,** lawyer; b. St. Louis, Sept. 5, 1969; s. C. Frederick Hollon and Carole Lynn Rolando. BA with distinction and honors, Stanford U., 1991; JD magna cum laude, Harvard U., 1996. Bar: Wash., U.S. Dist. Ct. (ea. and we. dists.) Wash. Law clk. to hon. William Fremming Nielsen U.S. Dist. Ct., Spokane, Wash., 1996-97; lawyer McNaul Ebel Nawrot Helgren & Vance, Seattle, 1997—. Mem. FBA (western dist. Wash.), Phi Beta Kappa. Avocations: skiing, rock and Alpine climbing. General civil litigation, Criminal. Office: McNaul Ebel Nawrot Helgren & Vance 600 University St Ste 2700 Seattle WA 98101-3143

**HOLLON, JOHN OAKS,** lawyer; b. Taunton, Mass., Sept. 8, 1968; s. Alva Adams Jr. and Laura Barnes Hollon; m. Julia Long Kincaid, Aug. 15, 1992; 1 child, Elizabeth Darden. BA, Vanderbilt U., 1991; JD, U. Ky., 1994. Bar: Ky. 1994, U.S. Dist. Ct. (we. and ea. dists.) Ky. 1995, Fla. 1997, U.S. Ct. Appeals (6th cir.) 1997, U.S. Dist. Ct. (mid. dist.) Fla. 1998, U.S. Ct. Appeals (11th cir.) 1999. Lawyer Hollon, Hollon & Collins, Hazard, Ky., 1994-95, Clark, Ward & Cave, Lexington, Ky., 1995-97, Sams & Hollon, Jacksonville, Fla., 1997—. Class agt. Woodberry Forest (Va.) Sch., 1987-93. Mem. ABA, Ky. Bar Assn., Fla. Bar. Avocations: golf, jogging, reading. General civil litigation, Insurance, Personal injury. Office: Sams & Hollon 7835 Bayberry Rd Jacksonville FL 32256-6845

**HOLLOWAY, DONALD PHILLIP,** lawyer; b. Akron, Ohio, Feb. 18, 1928; s. Harold Shane and Dorothy Gayle (Ryder) H.; BS in Commerce, Ohio U., Athens, 1950; JD, U. Akron, 1955; MA, Kent State U., 1962. Bar: Ohio 1955. Title examiner Bankers Guarantee Title & Trust Co., Akron, 1950-54; acct. Robinson Clay Product Co., Akron, 1955-60; librarian Akron-Summit Pub. Library, 1962-69, head fine arts and music div., 1969-71, sr. librarian, 1972-82; pvt. practice law, Akron, 1982—. Payroll treas. Akron Symphony Orch., 1957-61; treas. Friends Library Akron and Summit County, 1970-72. Mem. Music Library Assn., ABA, Ohio Bar Assn., Akron Bar Assn., Ohio Library Assn., ALA, Nat. Trust for Hist. Preservation, Internat. Platform Assn., Soc. Archtl. Historians, Coll. Art Assn., Art Libraries North Am., Akron City Club, North Coast Soc. Republican. Episcopalian. Avocations: art and architecture, music, travel. Probate. Home: 601 Nome Ave Akron OH 44320-1682

**HOLLOWAY, GORDON ARTHUR,** lawyer; b. Wichita, Kans., July 27, 1938; s. George Arthur and Margurite (Bondurant) H.; m. Carol H. Criss, Sept. 1, 1960; children: Gregory Arthur, Suzanne Criss, Garrett Austin. BBA, U. Tex., 1960, JD, 1963. Bar: Tex. 1963, Colo. 1993. Assoc. McGregor, Sewell, Junell & Riggs, Houston, 1963-71; ptnr. Sewell and Riggs, Houston, 1971-93, Holloway & Rowley, 1994—. Staff sgt. Air N.G., 1964-71. Mem. Am. Bd. Trial Advocates (diplomate), Nat. Assn. Railroad Trial Counsel, Internat. Assn. Defense Counsel, Tex. Bd. Legal Specialization (cert. personal injury, civil trial law), Houston Club, Intertel. General civil litigation, Personal injury, Product liability. Office: Holloway & Rowley P C 1415 Louisiana St Ste 2550 Houston TX 77002-7360

**HOLLOWAY, HILIARY HAMILTON,** retired lawyer, banker; b. Durham, N.C., Mar. 7, 1928; s. Joseph Sim and Zelma (Slade) H.; m. Beatrice Gwen Larkin, Dec. 22, 1951; children: Hiliary H., Janis L. BBA, N.C. Central U., 1949; EdM, Temple U., 1956, JD, 1964. Bar: Pa. 1965, U.S. Dist. Ct. (ea. dist.) Pa. 1967, U.S. Supreme Ct. 1977. Bus. mgr. St. Augustine's Coll., Raleigh, N.C., 1950-53; nat. exec. dir. Kappa Alpha Psi, Phila., 1953-65; assoc. Hazell & Bowser, Phila., 1965-68; asst. counsel Fed. Res. Bank, Phila., 1968-72, v.p., gen. counsel, 1973-82, sr. v.p., gen. counsel, 1982-89; ptnr. Marshall, Dennehey, Warner, Coleman & Goggin, Phila., 1990-99; ret.; arbitrator Am. Arbitration Assn.; cons. U. Pa., Phila., 1976; chmn. Urban Edn. Found., Phila., 1986-89; bd. dirs. Mellon PSFS Bank, Berean Fed. Savings Bank; mem. adv. coun. NIH, 1989-93; CEO, chmn. New Atlantic Bank, Norfolk, Va., 1989-93. Chmn. oversight commn. overseeing fin. for City of Phila., Pa. Inter-govtl. Coop. Authority, 1993-95. Recipient Disting. Cmty. Svc. award Chapel of Four Chaplains, Phila., 1975, Martin Luther King award Educator's Roundtable, Phila., 1977, Laurel Wreath award Kappa Alpha Psi, Detroit, 1982, Disting. Alumni award N.C. Ctrl. U., 1986. Mem. ABA, Nat. Interfrat. Conf. (pres. 1996). General corporate, Banking.

**HOLLOWAY, PAUL WILLSEY,** lawyer; b. July 28, 1962; m. Eileen Louise Holloway, May 20, 1989; children: Jennifer, Emma. BA cum laude, Georgetown U., 1984; JD, Vanderbilt U., 1988; MA, U. Va., 1992. Bar: N.Y. 1988. Assoc. Harter, Secrest & Emery, Rochester, N.Y., 1988-90, 92-98; ptnr. Harter, Secrest & Emery, Rochester, 1999—. Co-author: Employers' Handbook for 401(k) Plan Administration, 1992; editor: NYS Jurisprudence 2d, Taxation, 1992; mem. law rev. Vanderbilt U. Pres. Nat. Kidney Found. Upstate N.Y., Rochester, 1997-98; treas. Kids Adjusting Through Support, Rochester, 1997-98. Mem. ABA, Internat. Found. Employee Benefit Plans. Home: 130 Newcastle Rd Rochester NY 14610-1449 Office: Harter Secrest & Emery 700 Midtown Tower Rochester NY 14604-2006

**HOLLOWAY, WILLIAM JUDSON, JR.,** federal judge; b. 1923. AB, U. Okla., 1947; LLB, Harvard U., 1950; LLD (hon.), Oklahoma City U., 1991. Ptnr. Holloway & Holloway, Oklahoma City, 1950-51; atty. Dept. Justice, Washington, 1951-52; assoc., ptnr. Crowe and Dunlevy, Oklahoma City, 1952-68; judge U.S. Ct. Appeals (10th cir.), Oklahoma City, 1968-84, chief judge, 1984-91, sr. judge, 1992—. Mem. ABA, Fed. Bar Assn., Okla. Bar Assn., Oklahoma County Bar Assn. Office: US Ct Appeals 10th Cir PO Box 1767 Oklahoma City OK 73101-1767

**HOLLYER, A(RTHUR) RENE,** lawyer; b. Wycoff, N.J., July 28, 1938; s. Richard W. and Florence (Vervaet) H.; m. Lauraine Dennis, Apr. 8, 1978; children: James Richard, Jennifer Ashley. BA, Williams Coll., 1961; MPA, Woodrow Wilson Sch., Princeton, 1963; LLB, Columbia U., 1966. Bar: N.J. 1966, U.S. Dist. Ct. N.J. 1966, N.Y. 1968, U.S. Dist. Ct. (so. and ea. dists.) N.Y. 1969, U.S. Ct. Appeals (3rd cir.) 1970, U.S. Ct. Appeals (2d cir.) 1971, D.C. 1972, U.S. Supreme Ct. 1974. Law sec. to judge chancery divsn. N.J. Superior Ct., Newark, 1966-67; assoc. Olwine, Connelly, Chase, O'Donnell & Weyher, N.Y.C., 1968-70, 72-74; asst. U.S. atty. Dist. N.J., 1970-71; ptnr. Hollyer, Brady, Smith, Troxell, Barret, Rockett, Hines & Mone, L.L.P. and predecessor firms, N.Y.C., 1974—. Mem. N.Y. State Bar Assn., Assn. of Bar of City of N.Y. (profl. discipline com. 1990-92, 95-98, chmn. complaint mediation panel 1991-92, ethics com. 1992-95, profl. responsibility com. 1998—). Federal civil litigation, State civil litigation, General practice. Home: 50 Hamilton Rd Glen Ridge NJ 07028-1109 Office: Hollyer Brady Smith Troxell Barrett Rockett Hines & Mone LLP 551 5th Ave New York NY 10176-0001

**HOLMAN, BUD GEORGE,** lawyer; b. N.Y.C., June 30, 1929; s. Harry and Fannie Abrams (Bass) H.; m. Kathleen Barbara McLean, Sept. 1, 1961; children: Jennifer Jean, Wayne George. BBA, CCNY, 1950; LLB, Yale U., 1956. Bar: N.Y. 1956, Conn. 1979, D.C. 1982. Law sec. to judge N.Y. Ct. Appeals, 1956-58; practice in N.Y.C., 1958—; ptnr. Kelley Drye & Warren (and predecessor firms), 1965—; pres., chmn. bd. dirs. Sixty Sutton Corp., 1969-97; lectr. Practising Law Inst., Wage Price Inst., Young Pres. Orgn. Editor: The Bar, 1949-50, Yale Law Jour., 1955-56. Trustee U.S. Naval Acad. Found., 1978-85; bd. dirs. USO Met. N.Y. Mem. Naval Res. Assn. (pres. 3d naval dist. chpts. 1973-75, mem. nat. adv. coun. 1975-94), Am. Arbitration Assn. (bd. dirs., mem. exec. com.), Navy League (bd. dirs. coun. N.Y. chpt. 1979-99), Yale U. Law Sch. Assn. (mem. exec. com. 1987-90, 93-96, bd. dirs.), Yale Law Sch. Assn. N.Y.C. (bd. dirs.), Met. Club, Yale Club, Beta Gamma Sigma. Democrat. Presbyterian. Antitrust, General civil litigation, Product liability. Home: 60 Sutton Pl S New York NY 10022-4168 Office: Kelley Drye & Warren LLP 101 Park Ave New York NY 10178-0002

**HOLMAN, JOSEPH FREDERICK,** lawyer; b. Farmington, Maine, Aug. 15, 1925; s. Currier Carleton and Rosa (Skillings) H.; m. Brenda Hart, June 24, 1977. AB, Bowdoin Coll., 1947; LLB, Boston U., 1950. Bar: Maine 1951, U.S. Dist. Ct. Maine 1963, U.S. Supreme Ct. 1963. Pvt. practice Farmington, 1951—; atty. Franklin County, Farmington, 1953-58. Sen. State of Maine, 1970; mem. Maine State Claims Comm., 1990—. Mem. ABA, Maine Bar Assn. (exec. com. 1963-71, pres. 1971-72), Franklin County Bar Assn. (pres. 1993), Assn. Trial Lawyers Am., Maine Trial Lawyers Assn. Republican. Avocations: hunting, fly fishing. General practice, Probate, Real property. Home: Cutler Ln Farmington ME 04938 Office: 41 Main St Farmington ME 04938-1924

**HOLME, HOWARD KELLEY,** lawyer; b. Denver, May 5, 1945; s. Peter Hagner Jr. and Lena (Phillips) H.; m. Barbara Lynn Shaw, June 16, 1968; children: Timothy Peter, Lisa. AB in History with distinction and honors in humanities, Stanford U., 1967; JD, Yale U., 1972. Bar: Colo. 1972, U.S. Dist. Ct. Colo. 1972, U.S. Ct. Appeals (10th cir.) 1972, U.S. Supreme Ct. 1984. Staff Denver U. Law Sch., 1969-71; assoc. Fairfield and Woods, Denver, 1972-77; ptnr., dir., pres., mng. dir., Fairfield & Woods, P.C., Denver; cons. Fryingpan-Ark. Project, Southeastern Colo. Water Conservation Dist., 1976—. Editor: National Water Resources Regulation: Where is the Environmental Pendulum Now?, 1994; contbr. articles to profl. jours. Bd. dirs. nat. legal adv. com. Planned Parenthood Fedn. Am., N.Y.C.; active Colo. Supreme Ct. law com., Denver. Mem. Colo. Bar Assn., Denver Bar Assn., Denver Law Club, Cactus Club. Environmental, Federal civil litigation. Home: 5833 Montview Blvd Denver CO 80207-3923 Office: Fairfield & Woods PC 1700 Lincoln St Ste 2400 Denver CO 80203-4524

**HOLMES, CHARLES EVERETT,** lawyer; b. Wellington, Kans., Dec. 21, 1931; s. Charles Everett and Elizabeth Francis (Bergin) H.; m. Lynn Lacy, Jan. 2, 1954; children: Anne Lacy, Charles Everett, Rebecca. BA, Wichita U., 1953; LLB, U. Okla., 1961. Bar: Okla. 1961. Practice, Tulsa, after 1961; sec. Sinclair Oil & Gas Co., Sinclair Can. Oil Co., Mesa Pipeline Co., Border Pipe Line Co., Sinclair Transp. Co., Ltd.; ptnr. Rogers, Bell & Robinson, Tulsa, 1969-71; v.p. Nat. Bank of Tulsa, 1971-78; atty. Petro-Lewis Corp., Denver, 1978-87; v.p. Freeport-McMoRan Oil & Gas Co., 1987-92; v.p. FM Properties, Inc., 1992-95; ret., 1995; pvt. practice, Denver, 1996—. Served with USAF, 1954-56, 61-62. Mem. ABA, Okla. Bar Assn., Colo. Bar Assn., Denver County Bar Assn. Roman Catholic. (del. Okla. Council Cath. Diocese 1966—, chmn. Cath. Parish Governing Body 1968—, bd. dirs. Youth Services, Travelers Aid, Com. Fgn. Relations). Oil, gas, and mineral, General corporate, Administrative and regulatory.

**HOLMES, CLIFTON LEE (SCRAPPY HOLMES),** lawyer; b. Kilgore, Tex., Feb. 17, 1939; s. Clyde Frank and Ima Edith (Osborne) H.; m. Edwina McKellar, Jan. 19, 1960 (dec. 1979); children: Niki, Bryan, Lacy, Shelly. BA, U. Tex.-Austin, 1961; JD with honors, George Washington U., 1966. Bar: Tex. 1967, U.S. Dist. Ct. (ea. dist.) Tex. 1973, U.S. Supreme Ct. 1974, U.S. Dist. Ct. (we. dist.) Tex. 1974, U.S. Ct. Appeals (5th cir.) 1974, U.S. Dist. Ct. (no. dist.) Tex. 1979, U.S. Ct. Appeals (11th cir.) 1981, U.S. Dist. Ct. (so. dist.) Tex. 1984. Regional rep. U.S. Dept. Labor, Austin, Tex., 1966-67; sole practice, Gilmer, Tex., 1967-68; asst. dir. Job Corps, Washington, 1968-70; editor State Bar Tex., Austin, 1970-71; sole practice, Austin, 1971-74, Kilgore/Longview, Tex., 1974—. Editor: Federal Criminal Practice Manual, 1975, Voice for the Defense, 1977-81, Capital Murder Defense, 1978. State del. Democratic Party, 1976, 80, 90. Mem. State Bar Tex. (bd. dirs. 1986-89, criminal justice coun. 1993-99, chair 1997-98), Tex. Criminal Def. Lawyers Assn. (bd. dirs. 1974-81, v.p., 1982-83, pres.-elect 1983-84, pres. 1984-85;

commendation award 1974, 77, 79, 82), Tex. Trial Lawyers Assn., Nat. Criminal Def. Lawyers Assn. Democrat. Criminal, Personal injury, Workers' compensation. Home: PO Box 8 Diana TX 75640-0008 Office: 431 N Center St Longview TX 75601-6404

**HOLMES, HENRY W.,** lawyer; b. Malden, Mass., Apr. 1, 1943; s. Henry W. Holmes. BA, U. Calif., 1966, JD, 1969. Bar: Calif. 1970, U.S. Dist. Ct. (cen. dist.) Calif. 1970, U.S. Ct. Appeals (9th cir.) 1970. Lawyer Pacht, Ross, Warne, Bernhard & Sears, L.A., 1972-78; prin. Schiff, Hirsch & Schreiber, Beverly Hills, Calif., 1978-79; ptnr. Butler, Davidson & Holmes, Beverly Hills, Calif., 1979-84; counsel Cooper, Epstein & Hurewitz, Beverly Hills, Calif., 1984-94; counsel, sports and entertainment law Weissman, Wolff, Bergman, Coleman & Silverman, Beverly Hills, Calif., 1994—; spkr. in field; adj. prof. sports UCLA; adj. prof. sports law Pepperdine U. Law Sch. Contbr. articles to profl. jours. Trustee U.S. Womens Sports Found., N.Y., 1984-97. Named one of Top 20 Sports Lawyers Daily Jour., 1993; Ford Found. fellowship, New Delhi, India, 1969-70. Mem. SAG, Beverly Hills Bar Assn., L.A. Bar Assn., Calif. Bar Assn., Am. Somoa Bar Assn., Explorer's Club. Roman Catholic. Avocations: surfing, acting, art appreciation, scuba diving. Entertainment. Home: 21096 Pacific Coast Hwy Malibu CA 90265-5242 Office: Weissman Wolff Bergman Coleman & Silverman 9665 Wilshire Blvd Fl 9 Beverly Hills CA 90212-2316

**HOLMES, JAMES HILL, III,** lawyer; b. Birmingham, Ala., Sept. 10, 1935; s. Houston Eccleston and Celia Lindsey (Wearn) H.; m. Julia (Judy) Ryman, Aug. 17, 1963; children: James H. IV, Randell Ryman, Tucker Malone. BBA, So. Meth. U., 1957, LLB, 1959. Bar: Tex. 1959, U.S. Dist. Ct. (no. dist.) Tex. 1963, U.S. Dist. Ct. (ea. dist.) Tex. 1966, U.S. Dist. Ct. (we. dist.) Tex. 1979, U.S. Ct. Appeals (5th and 11th cirs.) 1981, U.S. Ct. Mil. Appeals 1960, U.S. Supreme Ct. 1974. Ptnr. Burford & Ryburn, Dallas, 1962—; spkr. State Bar Tex. Profl. Devel. Program, 1987-93; mock trial participant Tex. Nurses Assn., 1978-86; co-chair Supreme Ct. Adv. Com. on Professionalism for Supreme Ct. Tex., 1989-90. Contbr. articles to profl. jours. Past mem. University Park (Tex.) Bd. Adjustment; chmn. University Park Planning and Zoning Commn., 1988-94; city councilman City of University Park, 1994—, mayor pro tem, 1998-99; past. dir. Child Guidance Clinic; past dir., pres. All Sports Assn., Dallas, 1977; pres. University Park Cmty. League, 1987-88; past bd. dirs. Park Cities Town North YMCA; numerous other offices in civic orgns. With USAF, 1959-62. Recipient Presdl. Citation State Bar of Tex., 1995. Fellow Am. Coll. Trial Lawyers, Tex. Bar Found.; mem. ABA, Dallas Assn. Def. Counsel (chmn. 1984-85), Tex. Assn. Def. Counsel (pres. 1992-93, Founder's award 1997), Assn. Def. Trial Attys., Internat. Assn. Def. Counsel, Def. Rsch. Inst., Dallas Bar Assn. (numerous offices and coms.), Tex. Bar Assn., Am. Bd. Trial Advocates (sec.-treas., pres.-elect Dallas chpt. 1999), Patrick E. Higginbotham Am. Inn of Ct. (master 1989-95), State Bar Coll. (Tex.), Blue Key, Phi Alpha Delta, Phi Delta Theta. Episcopalian. Avocations: jogging, spectator sports, outdoors. Personal injury, Product liability, General civil litigation. Home: 3804 Lovers Ln Dallas TX 75225-7101 Office: Burford & Ryburn LLP 3100 Lincoln Pla 500 N Akard St Ste 3100 Dallas TX 75201-6697

**HOLMES, JEANNE L.,** lawyer; b. Brockton, Mass., Apr. 5, 1955; d. John Jadis and Gloria Katherine H.; m. Paul Arthur Kireilis, May 8, 1982; children: Alexander Holmes Kireilis, Courtney Amber Kireilis. AB in English, Polit. Sci., Boston Coll., 1977; JD, Ohio Northern U., 1981. Bar: Mass., U.S. Dist. Ct. Mass. Supr. attorney Plymouth County Dist. Attorney, Brockton, Mass., 1982—. Treas. Whitman Elem. Sch., Brockton, 1992—; sch. choice bd. Brockton (Mass.) Pub. Schs., 1996—, sch. improvement bd., 1996—. Mem. Nat. Dist. Attorney Assn. (Mass. chpt. child abuse subgroup 1987—), Mass. Bar Assn., Plymouth County Bar Assn. Episcopalian. Avocations: advocating for children, dancing, sports, sewing, antique collecting. Home: 65 Belcher Ave Brockton MA 02301-4103 Office: Plymouth County District Attorneys Office 231 Main St Brockton MA 02301-4342

**HOLMES, KAREN ANDERSON,** lawyer; b. Arcadia, Calif., Nov. 7, 1957; d. Harold F. and Maureen L. Anderson; m. Richard N. Holmes, June 25, 1988; 1 child, Haley E. BA in Polit. Sci., San Diego State U., 1979; JD, Calif. Western Sch. of Law, 1983. Bar: Calif. 1983, U.S. Dist. Ct. (so. dist.) Calif. 1983, U.S. Ct. Appeals (9th cir.) 1984. Assoc. Alford & MacLeod, San Diego, 1983-86; from assoc. to ptnr. Edwards, Sooy & Byron (formerly Edwards, White & Sooy), San Diego, 1986—. Bd. dirs., pres. San Diego State Alumni, 19889-91. Mem. So. Calif. Def. Lawyers, Def. Rsch. Inst. (vice-chair 1995—), San Diego Def. Lawyers (bd. dirs., pres. 1991-95), San Diego County Bar Assn. (chair constrn. sect. 1997—). General civil litigation, Construction, Insurance. Office: Edwards Sooy & Byron 101 W Broadway Fl 9 San Diego CA 92101-8201

**HOLMES, KURT STUART,** legal administrator; b. Freeport, N.Y., Oct. 16, 1960; s. Chester Edward and Rose (Kaplan) H. BA, Hofstra U., 1982, JD, 1985. Bar: N.Y. 1986, U.S. Dist. Ct. (ea. dist.) N.Y. 1989. Intern Coffey, McHale, McBride, Olsen & Shoolz, Melville, N.Y., 1983-84, Solerwitz, Solerwitz & Leeds, Garden City, N.Y., 1985; sr. law asst. 1st Dist. Ct., Hempstead, N.Y., 1985-90; law sec. to Hon. Zelda Jonas County Ct., Mineola, N.Y., 1990—. Contbr. articles to profl. jours. Committeeman Bellmore (N.Y.) Rep., 1992—. Mem. N.Y. State Bar Assn., Nassau County Bar Assn. (student mentor 1996-97, criminal procedure com.), Nassau County Courthouse Kiwanis (coord. Island Harvest 1993—, Disting. Kiwanian 1994-95). Avocations: ballroom competitive dancing, politics, chess. Office: Nassau County Courthouse 262 Old Country Rd Mineola NY 11501-4255 Home: 2692 Boundary Rd Bellmore NY 11710-4736

**HOLMES, MICHAEL GENE,** lawyer; b. Longview, Wash., Jan. 14, 1937; s. Robert A. and Esther S. Holmes; children: Helen, Peyton Robert. AB in Econs., Stanford U., 1958, JD, 1960. Bar: Oreg. 1961, U.S. Dist. Ct. Oreg. 1961, U.S. Ct. Appeals (9th cir.) 1961, Temp. Emergency Ct. Appeals 1976, U.S. Supreme Ct. 1976. Assoc. Spears, Lubersky, Bledsoe, Anderson, Young & Hilliard, Portland, 1961-67, ptnr., 1967-90; ptnr. Lane Powell Spears Lubersky, Portland, 1990-95, of counsel, 1995; mem. Oreg. Joint Com. of Bar, Press & Broadcasters, 1982-85, sec., 1983-84, chmn. 1985. Author Survey of Oregon Defamation and Privacy Law, ann., 1982-95. Trustee Med. Rsch. Found. Oreg., Portland, 1985-94, exec. com., 1986-94; hon. trustee Oreg. Health Scis. Found., 1995—; trustee Portland Civic Theatre, 1962-66. Mem. Oreg. Bar Assn., Phi Beta Kappa. Labor, General civil litigation, Administrative and regulatory.

**HOLMES, PAUL KINLOCH, III,** prosecutor; b. Newport, Ark., Nov. 10, 1951; s. Paul K. Jr. and Virginia (Harrison) H.; m. Katherine Hewitt, July 28, 1978; children: Christopher, Stephen. BA, Westminster Coll., 1973; JD, U. Ark., Fayetteville, 1978. Bar: Ark. 1978. Ptnr. Warner & Smith Attys. at Law, Ft. Smith, Ark., 1978-93; U.S. atty. Western Dist. Ark., Ft. Smith, Ark., 1993—. Office: US Courthouse 6th and Rogers Fort Smith AR 72901

**HOLMES, RICHARD WINN,** lawyer, retired state supreme court justice; b. Wichita, Kans., Feb. 23, 1923; s. Winn Earl and Sidney (Clapp) H.; m. Gwen Sand, Aug. 19, 1950; children—Robert W., David K. B.S., Kans. State U., 1950; J.D., Washburn U., 1953, LLD (hon.), 1991. Bar: Kans. 1953, U.S. Dist. Ct. 1953. Practice law Wichita, Kans., 1953-77; judge Wichita Mcpl. Ct., 1959-61; instr. bus. law Wichita State U., 1959-60; justice Kans. Supreme Ct., 1977-90, chief justice, 1990-95; ret., 1995; of counsel Goodell, Stratton, Edmonds & Palmer, Topeka, 1995—. Served with USNR, 1943-46. Mem. ABA, Kans., Topeka, Wichita bar assns., Am. Judges Assn. (founder, bd. govs. 1980-88). Home: 2535 SW Granthurst Ave Topeka KS 66611-1271 Address: 515 S Kansas Ave Topeka KS 66603-3415

**HOLMES, ROBERT ALLEN,** lawyer, educator, consultant, lecturer; b. Sewickley, Pa., Dec. 12, 1947; s. Lee Roy John and Nellie Ann (Kupits) H.; divorced; children: Wesley Paige, Ashley Reagan. BA in Bus. Adminstrn., Coll. William and Mary, 1969, JD, 1972. Bar: Md. 1972, U.S. Dist. Ct. Md. 1972, Va. 1973, U.S. Dist. Ct. (ea. dist.) Va. 1973, U.S. Dist. Ct. (no. dist.) Ohio 1988, U.S. Ct. Appeals (6th cir.) 1988. Assoc. Ober, Grimes & Shriver, Balt., 1972-73, Kellam, Pickrell & Lawler, Norfolk, Va., 1973-75; ptnr. Holliday, Holmes & Inman, Norfolk, 1975-77; asst. prof. law Bowling Green State U., Ohio, 1977-82, assoc. prof., 1982—; dir. Purchasing Law Inst., 1979—, EEO-Affirmative Action Rsch. Group, 1978—; lectr. in field. Author: (books) (with others) Computers, Data Processing and the Law, 1984; numerous manuals on discrimination and affirmative action law, corp. purchasing law and internat. bus. law. Contbg. editor, monthly columnist Midwest Purchasing, 1983-84. Recipient Outstanding Young Man award William and Mary Soc. Alumni, 1973. Mem. Md. Bar Assn., Va. Bar Assn., Am. Bus. Law Assn., Am. Soc. Pers. Adminstrs., Nat. Assn. Purchasing Mgmt., Mensa. Republican. Home: 1030 Conneaut Ave Bowling Green OH 43402-2118 Office: Bowling Green State U Legal Studies and Internat Bus Dept Bowling Green OH 43403-0001

**HOLMES, WILLIAM JAMES,** lawyer; b. Hamilton, Ohio, June 2, 1955; s. William J. and Barbara A. (Huff) H.; m. Traci L. Gossett, Sept. 30, 1995; 1 child, Sarah Ashley. BA, Ohio No. U., 1977; JD, Capital U., Columbus, Ohio, 1980. Bar: Ohio 1980, Va. 1988, U.S. Ct. Claims 1992, U.S. Ct. Mil. Appeals 1981, U.S. Ct. Appeals (Fed. cir.) 1993, U.S. Supreme Ct. 1986. Pvt. practice, Virginia Beach, Va., 1984—. Note editor Capital U. Law Rev., 1979, symposium editor, 1980. Capt. USMC, 1981-84. Military, Criminal, Family and matrimonial. Home: 5121 Stonington Ln Virginia Beach VA 23464

**HOLMQUIST, MICHAEL G.,** lawyer; b. Summit, N.J., Apr. 12, 1964; m. Elizabeth A. Holmquist, Aug. 13, 1988; children: Quinn A., Peyton H. BS in Acctg., Miami U., Oxford, Ohio, 1986; JD, Case Western Res. U., 1994. Audit mgr. KPMG Peat Marwick, Short Hills, N.J., 1986-91; assoc. Buchanan Ingersoll P.C., Pitts., 1994-98; counsel Bank of Am., Charlotte, N.C., 1998—. Securities. Office: Bank of America NCI-007-20-01 100 N Tryon St Charlotte NC 28255-0001

**HOLMSTEAD, JEFFREY RALPH,** lawyer; b. American Fork, Utah, June 20, 1960; s. R. Kay and Mary L. (Gillison) H.; m. Elizabeth Tisdel, Aug. 17, 1985; children: Emily Kay, Eric Noble, Elizabeth Anne, Eli Jeffrey. BA, Brigham Young U., 1984; JD, Yale U., 1987. Bar: Pa. 1988, D.C. 1998. Jud. clk. to Hon. Douglas H. Ginsburg D.C. Cir. Ct. Appeals, Washington, 1987-88; assoc. Davis Polk & Wardwell, Washington, 1988-89; asst. counsel to Pres. of U.S. The White House, Washington, 1989-90, assoc. counsel, 1990-93; assoc. Latham & Watkins, Washington, 1993-95, ptnr., 1996—. Republican. Mem. LDS Ch. Administrative and regulatory, Environmental. Office: Latham & Watkins Ste 1300 1001 Pennsylvania Ave NW Washington DC 20004-2585

**HOLSCHUH, JOHN DAVID,** federal judge; b. Ironton, Ohio, Oct. 12, 1926; s. Edward A. and Helen (Ebert) H.; m. Carol Eloise Stouder, May 25, 1952; 1 child, John David Jr. BA, Miami U., 1948; JD, U. Cin., 1951. Bar: Ohio 1951, U.S. Dist. Ct. (so. dist.) Ohio 1952, U.S. Ct. Appeals (6th cir.) 1953, U.S. Supreme Ct. 1956. Atty. McNamara & McNamara, Columbus, Ohio, 1951-52, 54; law clk. to Hon. Mell. G. Underwood U.S. Dist. Ct., Columbus, 1952-54; ptnr. Alexander, Ebinger, Holschuh, Fisher & McAlister, Columbus, Ohio, 1954-80; judge U.S. Dist. Ct. (so. dist.) Ohio, 1980—, chief judge, 1990-96; adj. prof. law Ohio State U. Coll. Law, 1970; mem. com. on codes of conduct Jud. Conf. U.S., 1985-90. Pres. bd. dirs. Neighborhood House, Columbus, 1969-70; active United Way of Franklin County, Columbus. Fellow Am. Coll. Trial Lawyers; mem. Order of Coif, Phi Beta Kappa, Omicron Delta Kappa. Home: 2630 Charing Rd Columbus OH 43221-3628 Office: US Dist Ct 109 US Courthouse 85 Marconi Blvd Rm 109 Columbus OH 43215-2823

**HOLSCHUH, JOHN DAVID, JR.,** lawyer; b. Columbus, Ohio, Dec. 21, 1955; s. John D. and Carol Elouise (Stouder) H.; m. Wendy G. Ellis, Sept. 22, 1984; children: Heather Elyse, John David III, Jacob Alexander. BS, Miami U., Oxford, Ohio, 1977; JD, U. Cin., 1980. Bar: Ohio 1980, U.S. Dist. Ct. (so. dist.) Ohio 1980, U.S. Ct. Appeals (6th cir.) 1986, U.S. Supreme Ct. 1986, U.S. Dist. Ct. (ea. dist.) Ky. 1987, Ky. 1991. Assoc. Santen, Shaffer & Hughes, Cin., 1980-87, ptnr., 1987-89; ptnr. Santen & Hughes, Cin., 1989—; pros. atty. City of Loveland, Ohio, 1987-92, magistrate, 1992—; magistrate Village of Fairfax, Ohio, 1999—; mem. faculty Nat. Inst. Trial Advocacy, 1990, 91, 96; participant Pretrial Civil Litigation Skills Workshop, 1991. Author: Medical Malpractice, 1986, Tort Reform Pleading, 1987, Civil Procedure, 1986, rev. edit., 1989, Damages for Plaintiff and Defense Attorneys in Ohio, 1990, 2d edit., 1991, Tort Reform Update, 1990. Recipient Merit award Ohio Legal Ctr. Inst., 1986; named with Best Lawyers of Am., 1996-97, 97-98. Mem. ATLA, Am. Bd. Trial Advs., Ohio Acad. Trial Lawyers (trustee 1991-95, 1998—), Ohio State Bar Assn., Hamilton County Trial Lawyers (pres. 1990-92), Cin. Bar Assn. (chmn. common pleas ct. 1991-93, trustee 1995—, sec. 1999—, co-chmn. bench-bar conf. 1997-98, sec. 1999—), 6th Cir. Jud. Conf. (del. 1983-88, life mem.), Potter Stewart Inns of Ct. (emeritus mem.), Order of Barristers. Avocations: sports, travel. General civil litigation, Personal injury, Federal civil litigation. Office: Santen & Hughes 312 Walnut St Ste 3100 Cincinnati OH 45202-4044

**HOLSENBACK, J. DANIEL,** lawyer, actor; b. Augusta, Ga., Apr. 29, 1964; s. John Alfred H. and Kathleen Elaine Hanley. BA in Politics and Govt., U. Puget Sound, 1986; JD, U. Calif., Davis, 1989. Bar: Calif., 1989. Assoc. Gray, Cary, Ames & Frye, San Diego, 1989-92; ptnr. Tremblay & Holsenback, La Jolla, Calif., 1992—. Contbr. article to U. Calif. Davis Law Rev.; performances include 15 plays, 1992—, 5 films and tv shows, 1992—. Mem. Calif. State Bar Assn., Screen Actors Guild, San Diego County Bar Assn. Democrat. Avocation: surfing. Office: Tremblay & Holsenback 9404 Genesee Ave Ste 300 La Jolla CA 92037-1355

**HOLSINGER, JOHN PAUL,** lawyer; b. New Kensington, Pa., June 22, 1963; s. Perry Lanson and Jayne (Devine) H.; m. Amy O'Leary, May 20, 1989; children: Sarah Jayne, Thomas O'Leary, Julia Margaret. BBA, George Washington U., 1985, MBA, 1987; JD, U. Va., 1990. Bar: Pa., U.S. Dist. Ct. (we. dist.) Pa. Counsel Alcoa Inc., Pitts., 1990—. General corporate, Real property, FERC practice. Office: Alcoa Inc 201 Isabella St Pittsburgh PA 15212-5858

**HOLSTEIN, JOHN CHARLES,** state supreme court judge; b. Springfield, Mo., Jan. 10, 1945; s. Clyde E. Jr. and Wanda R. (Polson) H.; m. Mary Frances Brummell, Mar. 26, 1967; children: Robin Diane Camacho, Mary Katherine Link, Erin Elizabeth. BA, S.W. Mo. State Coll., 1967; JD, U. Mo., 1970; LLM, U. Va., 1995. Bar: Mo. 1970. Atty. Moore & Brill, West Plains, Mo., 1970-75; probate judge Howell County, West Plains, 1975-78, assoc. cir. judge, 1978-82; cir. judge 37th Jud. Cir., West Plains, 1982-87; judge so. dist. Mo. Ct. Appeals, Springfield, 1987-88, chief judge so. dist., 1988-89; judge Supreme Ct. Mo., Jefferson City, 1989—, chief justice, 1995-97; instr. bus. law S.W. Mo. State Coll., 1976-77. Lt. col. USAR, 1969-87. Office: Supreme Ct Mo PO Box 150 Jefferson City MO 65102-0150

**HOLT, CHARLES WILLIAM, JR.,** lawyer, mediator; b. Dallas, Aug. 8, 1951; s. Charles William Sr. and Oletha Ruth (Leonard) H.; m. Claudia Capeau, Dec. 2, 1978; 1 child, Auston Charles. BS, East Tex. State U., 1973; JD, So. Meth. U., 1977. Bar: Tex. 1977, U.S. Dist. Ct. (fed. dist.) 1978. Assoc. Ralph M. Hall Law Office, Rockwall, Tex., 1977-89; pvt. practice Rockwall, 1990—. Chmn. Rockwall Firefighter Support Com., 1996—. Mem. State Bar Tex., Rockwall Bar Assn. (pres. 1986-87), Rockwall Area C. of C. (bd. dirs. 1982-84, 97—). Methodist. Avocations: video production, camping, outdoors, arts. Contracts commercial, Personal injury, Real property. Office: 500 Turtle Cove Blvd Ste 140 Rockwall TX 75087-5300

**HOLT, MARJORIE SEWELL,** lawyer, retired congresswoman; b. Birmingham, Ala., Sept. 17, 1920; d. Edward Rol and Juanita (Felts) Sewell; m. Duncan McKay Holt, Dec. 26, 1946; children: Rachel Holt Tschantre, Edward Sewell, Victoria. Grad., Jacksonville Jr. Coll., 1945; JD, U. Fla., 1949. Bar: Fla. 1949, Md. 1962. Pvt. practice Annapolis, Md., 1962; clk. Anne Arundel County Circuit Ct., 1966-72; mem. 93d-99th Congresses from 4th Dist. of Md., 1973-86; armed services com.; vice-chmn. Office Tech. Assessment, 1977; chmn. Republican Study com., 1975-76; of counsel Smith, Somerville & Case, Balt., 1986-90; supr. elections Anne Arundel County, 1963-65; del. Rep. Nat. Conv., 1968, 76, 80, 84, 88; mem. Pres.'s Commn. on Arms Control and Disarmament; mem. ind. commn. USAR; bd. dirs. Annapolis Fed. Savs. Bank; mem. adv. bd. Crestar. Co-author: Case Against The Reckless Congress, 1976, Can You Afford This House, 1978. Bd. dirs. Md. Sch. for the Blind, Hist. Annapolis Found. Recipient Disting. Alumna award U. Fla., 1975, Trustees award U. Fla. Coll. Law, 1984, Alumnae Outstanding Achievement award, 1997. Mem. ABA, Md. Bar Assn., Anne Arundel Bar Assn., Phi Kappa Phi, Phi Delta Delta. Presbyterian (elder 1959).

**HOLT, MICHAEL BARTHOLOMEW,** lawyer; b. Jersey City, July 10, 1956; s. William A. and Grace (Donohue) H.; m. Mary Patricia Butler, Aug. 14, 1982; children: Melissa Aislynn, Scott Michael, Eric Michael. BA magna cum laude, Providence Coll., 1978; JD, Seton Hall U., 1982. Bar: N.J. 1982, U.S. Dist. Ct. N.J. 1982, U.S. Dist. Ct. (ea. and so. dists.) N.Y. 1985, U.S. Ct. Appeals (3d cir.) 1985, U.S. Supreme Ct. 1986, N.Y. 1990. Assoc. Keane, Brady & Hanlon, Jersey City, 1982-84, Waters, McPherson, McNeill P.A., Secaucus, N.J., 1984-87; ptnr. O'Halloran, Holt and Assocs., Bayonne, N.J., 1987-89, Carroll & Holt, Secaucus, 1989-91; pvt. practice Secaucus, 1991-95; corp. counsel NYK Lines (N.Am.) Inc., Secaucus, 1995—. Mem. ABA, N.J. State Bar Assn., N.Y. State Bar Assn. (corp. counsel com.). Transportation, General corporate, General practice. Home: 9 Melrose Ave North Arlington NJ 07031-5917 Office: NYK Line Inc 300 Lighting Way Secaucus NJ 07094-3679

**HOLT, RICHARD DUANE,** lawyer; b. Champaign, Ill., Aug. 1, 1942. BS, Eastern Ill. U., 1964; JD, U. Fla., 1969. Bar: Fla. 1970. Ptnr. Gunster, Yoakley, Valde-Fauli & Stewart, PA, West Palm Beach, Fla. Mem. ABA, Fla. Bar, Palm Beach County Bar Assn., Phi Delta Phi. Real property, Finance. Office: Phillips Point Ste 500 E 777 S Flagler Dr West Palm Beach FL 33401-6161

**HOLT, RONALD LEE,** lawyer; b. Reading, Pa., Dec. 23, 1952; s. Carl John and Mary Catherine (Rossi) H.; m. Sharon Louella Nelsen, June 2, 1973; children: Angela, Valerie, Jeremy. BS in Speech summa cum laude, Evang. Coll., Springfield, Mo., 1975; JD with highest honors, Rutgers U., 1979. Bar: Mo. 1980, U.S. Dist. Ct. (we. dist.) Mo. 1980, U.S. Ct. Appeals (5th and 10th cirs.) 1988, U.S. Ct. Appeals (8th cir.) 1992. Law clk. to presiding judge U.S. Dist. Ct. (we. dist.) Mo., Kansas City, 1979-81; assoc. Stinson, Mag & Fizzell, Kansas City, 1981-86, ptnr., 1986-88; ptnr. Bryan Cave and predecessor firm Bryan, Cave, McPheeters & McRoberts, Kansas City, 1988—. Mng. editor Rutgers U. Law Rev., 1978-79. Bd. dirs. Christian Conciliation Svc. of Kansas City, 1986-95, pres., 1989-91); bd. dirs. Christian Legal Soc. (bd. dirs. 1991-95, pres. Kansas City chpt. 1990, Mo. state membership dir., 1991-93). Mem. Kansas City Met. Bar Assn., Christian Legal Soc. Federal civil litigation, General civil litigation, Antitrust. Office: Bryan Cave 1200 Main St 3500 One Kansas City Pl Kansas City MO 64105-2100

**HOLTMAN, DONALD RICHARD,** lawyer; b. Glens Falls, N.Y., Mar. 6, 1936; s. George John and Marguerite Rosa (Resta) H.; m. Verena Eva Elisabeth Gaitsch, Dec. 6, 1963; children: Peter Richard, Stephenie Eva Elisabeth. BA, Valparaiso U., 1956, LLB, 1958; LLM, NYU, 1963. Bar: Conn. 1958, U.S. Dist. Ct. Conn. 1967, U.S. Ct. Appeals (3d cir.) 1980, U.S. Ct. Appeals (2d cir.) 1988, U.S. Supreme Ct. 1961. Assoc. Law Offices of Herbert Watstein, Bristol, Conn., 1958-59; ptnr. Kiefer & Holtman, Simsbury, Conn., 1965-70, Pelgrift, Byrne, Buck & Connolly (successor firm Connolly, Holtman & Losee), West Hartford, Conn., 1970-78, Kleinman, Lapuk & Holtman (successor firm Stoner, Gross, Chorches, Lapuk & Kleinman), Hartford, Conn., 1978-87, Katz & Seligman, Hartford, Conn., 1988—; town counsel Litchfield, Conn., 1978-88, Hebron, Conn., 1988—, Granby, Conn., 1990—, East Granby, Conn., 1992—. Mem. planning and zoning com. Town of East Granby, 1974, mem. bd. of selectmen, 1976, mem. bd. fin., 1992. Capt. U.S. Army, 1959-65. Mem. Hartford County Bar Assn. (bench bar com. 1990—), Conn. Bar Assn. (exec. com. litigation sect. 1987—), Oliver Elsworth Inn of Ct. (bencher 1990—). Democrat. Lutheran. Avocations: sailing, gardening, reading, music. General civil litigation, Family and matrimonial. Home: 12 Sage Ln East Granby CT 06026-9766 Office: Katz & Seligman 130 Washington St Hartford CT 06106-4405

**HOLTON, WALTER CLINTON, JR.,** lawyer; b. Winston-Salem, N.C.; s. Walter Clinton and Mabel (Hartsfield) H.; m. Lynne Rowley. BA in Polit. Sci., U. N.C., 1977; JD, Wake Forest U., 1984. Bar: N.C. 1984, U.S. Dist. Ct. (mid. dist.) N.C. 1986, U.S. Ct. Appeals (4th cir.) 1990, U.S. Supreme Ct., 1996. Asst. dist. atty. Office 21st Jud. Dist. Atty., Winston-Salem, 1985-87; assoc. White & Crumpler, Winston-Salem, 1987-88; pvt. practice Winston-Salem, 1989; ptnr. Holton & Menefee, Winston-Salem, 1989-92, Tisdale, Holton & Menefee, PA, Winston-Salem, 1992-94; U.S. atty. Office U.S. Atty. Mid. Dist. N.C., Greensboro, N.C., 1994—. Democrat. Office: Office US Atty PO Box 1858 Greensboro NC 27402-1858

**HOLTZ, EDGAR WOLFE,** lawyer; b. Clarksburg, W.Va., Jan. 18, 1922; s. Dennis Drummond and Oleta (Wolfe) H.; m. Alberta Lee Brinkley, May 6, 1944; children: Diana Hilary, Heidi Johanna. BA, Denison U., 1943; JD, U. Cin., 1949. Bar: Ohio 1949, U.S. Supreme Ct. 1957, D.C. 1961. Assoc. firm Matthews & Matthews, Cin., 1949-53; asst. dean Chase Law Sch., Cin., 1952-55; asst. solicitor City of Cin., 1950-55; asst. chief office of opinions and rev. FCC, Washington, 1955-56; dep. gen. counsel FCC, 1956-60; mem. firm Hogan & Hartson, Washington, 1960—. Trustee Denison U., Granville, Ohio, 1974—: chmn. bd. Ctr. for the Arts, Vero Beach, Fla., 1995-97; bd. dirs. Cultural Coun. Indian River County, 1998—. Served to 1st lt. USAAF, 1943-45. Decorated D.F.C., Air medal with 2 clusters, 8 Battle Stars; recipient Alumni citation Denison U., 1993. Fellow Am. Bar Found.; mem. ABA (standing com. on gavel awards), Ohio Bar Assn., D.C. Bar Assn., Fed. Comms. Bar (pres. 1977-78), Am. Juicature Soc., Newcomen Soc. N.Am., Moorings Club (Vero Beach, Fla.), Met. Club (Washington, George Town Club (Washington). Republican. Methodist. Communications, Administrative and regulatory, General corporate. Office: Hogan & Hartson 555 13th St NW Ste 800E Washington DC 20004-1161

**HOLTZLANDER, STEPHANIE FRANCO,** lawyer; b. Indpls., Aug. 14, 1968; d. James Michael and Mary Josephine (Spahn) F.; m. Mark Adam Holtzlander, Dec. 30, 1995. BA, Ind. U., 1990; JD, Drake U., 1993, M, 1993. Bar: Ind. 1993, U.S. Dist. Ct. (no. and so. dist.) Ind. 1993. Litig. assco. Price & Barker, Indpls., 1993-96, Bose, McKinney & Evans, Indpls., 1996—. Contbr. articles to profl. jours. Vol. Jr. League Indpls., 1995-96. Recipient AmJur award Am. Jurisprudence, Inc., 1991-92. Mem. ABA, Ind. Bar Assn., Indpls. Bar Assn., Def. Rsch. Inst. Roman Catholic. Avocations: gourmet cooking, entertaining, reading. Product liability, Personal injury, General civil litigation. Office: Bose McKinney & Evans 2700 First Indiana Plaza 135 N Pennsylvania St Indianapolis IN 46024

**HOLTZMANN, HOWARD MARSHALL,** lawyer, judge; b. N.Y.C., Dec. 10, 1921; s. Jacob L. And Lillian (Plotz) H.; m. Anne Fisher, Jan. 14, 1945 (dec. Aug. 1967); children: Susan Holtzmann Richardson, Betsey; m. Carol Ebenstein Van Berg, Dec. 23, 1972. AB, Yale Coll., 1942, JD, 1947; LittD (hon.), St. Bonaventure U., 1952; LLD (hon.), Jewish Theol. Sem., N.Y.C., 1990. Bar: N.Y. 1947. Atty. Colorado Fuel & Iron Corp., Buffalo, N.Y., 1947-49; ptnr. Holtzmann, Wise & Shepard, N.Y.C., 1949-95; judge Iran-U.S. Claims Tribunal, The Hague, Netherlands, 1981-94; arbitrator and dispute resolution cons., 1994—; arbitrator Claims Resolution Tribunal for Dormant Accounts, Zurich, Switzerland, 1998—; U.S. del. UN Commn. on Internat. Trade Law, 1975—, Hague Conf. on Pvt. Internat. Law, 1985; advisor U.S.A. Arbitration agreements with USSR, Russian Fedn., China, Hungary, Bulgaria, Czechoslovakia, Poland and German Dem. Republic. Author, editor: A New Look at Legal Aspects of Doing Business with China, 1979; co-author: A Guide to the Unicitral Model Law on International Commercial Arbitration—Legislative History and Commentary, 1988 (cert. of merit Am. Soc. Internat. Law 1991); contbr. chpts. to books and articles to law jours. Mem. governing coun. Downstate Med. Sch. SUNY, Bklyn., 1961-78; trustee St. Bonaventure U., Olean, N.Y., 1968-90, trustee emeritus, 1990—; chmn. bd. Jewish Theol. Sem., N.Y.C., 1983-85, hon. chmn., 1985—; trustee Inst. Internat. Law, Pace U. Sch. Law, 1992—. Mem. ABA (chmn. com. code ethics comml. arbitrators 1973-77), Internat. Council for Comml. Arbitration (hon. vice chmn.), Am. Arbitration Assn. (hon. chmn., adv. bd. Bahrain arbitration ctr., adv. bd. Stockholm arbitration inst., Gotshal Internat. Arbitration award 1980), Internat. Arbitration Commn. (chmn.), Internat. C. of C. (vice chmn. arbitration commn. 1979—), Am. Bar Found., N.Y. County Lawyers Assn., Internat. Law Assn., Am. Fgn. Law Assn. (v.p. 1995, dir. 1995—), Internat. Bar Assn., N.Y. State Bar Assn., Assn. of Bar of City of N.Y., Am. Soc. Internat. Law (cert. merit 1991), Soc. Profls. in Dispute Resolution, Indsl. Relations Research Assn.,

N.Y. Law Inst., Am. Judicature Soc., Am. Assn. for Internat. Commn. of Jurists. Private international, General corporate.

**HOLTZSCHUE, KARL BRESSEM,** lawyer, author, educator; b. Wichita, Kans., Mar. 3, 1938; s. Bressem C. and Josephine E. (Landsittel) H.; m. Linda J. Gross, Oct. 24, 1959; children: Alison, Adam, Sara. AB, Dartmouth Coll., 1959; LLB, Columbia U., 1966. Bar: N.Y. 1967, U.S. Dist. Ct. (so. and ea. dists.) N.Y. 1968. Assoc. Webster & Sheffield, N.Y.C., 1966-73, ptnr., 1974-88; ptnr., head real estate dept. O'Melveny and Myers, N.Y.C., 1988-90; pvt. practice N.Y.C., 1990—; adj. prof. Fordham U. Law Sch., 1990—; adj. prof. Bus. Sch., Columbia U., 1990-96, Law Sch., 1991; mem. coun. advisors Ticor Title Guarantee Co., 1988-98; mem. nat. panel arbitrators Am. Arbitration Assn., 1995—. Author: Holtzschue on Real Estate Contracts, 1997, New York Practice Guide: Real Estate, Vol. 1 on Purchase and Sale, 1997, Real Estate Transactions: Purchase and Sale of Real Property, 1997; author: (with others) American Law of Real Property, 1991, Real Estate Development, 1991. Trustee Soc. of St. Johnland, 1980-86, Ensemble Studio Theatre, 1986-88; bd. dirs. The Bridge, 1990—, pres., 1992-95; mem. alumni bd. Dartmouth Ptnrs. in Cmty. Svc., 1994—, chmn., 1994-99. Lt. (j.g.) USN, 1959-62. Mem. ABA (com. on internat. investment in real estate 1987—, com. on legal opinions in real estate trans. 1990—), Am. Arbitration Assn. (nat. panel of arbitrators 1995—), N.Y. State Bar Assn. (exec. com. real property sect. 1998—, com. on attys. opinions 1992—, com. on title and transfer 1998—, co-chmn. 1998—), Assn. Bar City N.Y. (com. on real property law 1977-80, chmn. 1987-90, 95-98, com. ctrl. and east Europe 1998—), Am. Coll. Real Estate Lawyers (opinions com. 1989—, vice chmn. 1992-95), Tri Bar (opinions com. 1990—). Episcopalian. Real property.

**HOLZ, MICHAEL HAROLD,** lawyer; b. Dayton, Ohio, Apr. 10, 1942; s. Harold L. and Norma (Montgomery) H.; m. Tanya Noffsinger, July 22, 1972 (div. Jan. 1983). BA, Wittenberg U., 1964; JD, U. Cin., 1967; MBA, U. Dayton, 1979. Bar: Ohio 1968, U.S. Dist. Ct. 1971, U.S. Tax Ct. 1975. With office of legal assistance Butler County OEO, Hamilton Ohio, 1968; legal dep. probate Montgomery County, Dayton, Ohio, 1971-73; asst. pros. atty. Greene County, Xenia, Ohio, 1973; sole practice, Dayton, 1974—. Mem. Montgomery County Democratic Central Com., 1972-84. Served with U.S. Army, 1968-70, Vietnam. Mem. ACLU (dir.), Dayton Bar Assn. (unauthorized practice of law com. 1990-95, ethics com. 1985-89, bar exam and qualifications com. 1996—), Ohio Bar Assn., Vietnam Vets. Am., Greater Dayton Real Estate Investors Assn., Mensa, Phi Alpha Delta. Episcopalian. General practice, Criminal, Real property. Home: 507 Wilmington Ave Apt 1 Dayton OH 45420-1876

**HOLZMAN, JAMES L(OUIS),** lawyer; b. Bklyn., Jan. 7, 1949; s. Robert Conrad and Muriel Claire (Smith) H.; m. Jonnie Irene Frisbie; children: James Casey, Meredith Claire, Jon Carroll. BA, John B. Stetson U., 1970; JD, U. Fla., 1972. Bar: Fla. 1973, Del. 1973, U.S. Dist. Ct. Del. 1974, U.S. Dist. Ct. (so. dist.) Fla. 1973, U.S. Tax Ct. 1973, U.S. Ct. Appeals (3d cir.) 1976, U.S. Ct. Appeals (fed. cir.) 1983. Assoc., Prickett, Ward, Burt & Sanders, Wilmington, Del., 1973-77, ptnr., 1977-79; ptnr. Prickett, Jones, Elliott, Kristol & Schnee, Wilmington, 1979—, mng. ptnr., 1986-90. Trustee Tower Hill Sch., v.p., 1996—. Author Rev. Devel. Corp. Law. Mem. ABA (sect. bus. law, chair bus. and corp. litigation com., mem. task force litigation reform and rules revision, mem. corp. counsel com., mem. com. on law firms), Del. State Bar Assn. (mem. corp. law sect., mem. corp. law sect. coun. 1998—), Assn. of Bar of City of N.Y., Fla. Bar, Fed. Bar Assn., Wilmington Club. General corporate, Federal civil litigation. Home: 3213 Fordham Rd Wilmington DE 19807-3117 Office: Prickett Jones Elliott Kristol & Schnee 1310 N King St Wilmington DE 19801-3220

**HOMEIER, MICHAEL GEORGE,** lawyer, educator; b. Santa Monica, Calif., Dec. 31, 1958; s. George Vincent Homeier and Nancy Van Noorden Field. BA cum laude, UCLA, 1979; JD, U. So. Calif., 1983. Bar: Calif. 1984, U.S. Dist. Ct. (ctrl. dist.) Calif. 1984. Corp. assoc. Zobrist, Vienna & McCullough, L.A., 1982-84, Ball Hunt Hart Brown and Baerwitz, L.A., 1984-86; staff counsel Hebalife Internat., Inc., L.A., 1986-87; assoc. prof. bus. law Calif. State U., Northridge, 1989-92; atty. Law Offices of Lewis W. Boies, Jr., Santa Monica, Calif., 1992-98; pvt. practice Santa Monica, 1999—; adj. lectr. in bus. law Calif. State U., L.A., 1995, Northridge, 1997—. Dir. Young Adults Conquering Cancer Aux. to the Children's Cancer, L.A., 1992-95; peer counselor Teen Impact Program L.A. Children's Hosp., 1990-95; co-dir. The Vagabond Players Theatre Co., 1997—. Legion lex scholar U. So. Calif., 1982-84. Republican. Avocations: acting, theatre producing, art, writing. E-mail: mhomeier@linkonline.net. Entertainment, Contracts commercial, General corporate. Office: PO Box 3514 Santa Monica CA 90408-3514

**HOMER, THOMAS J.,** judge, former state legislator; b. Canton, Ill., Jan. 12, 1947; s. Clarence E. and Lena (Riccioni) H.; m. Sandra J. Homer; children: Katelyn L., Natalie, Samuel. BA, U. Ill., 1970; JD, Chgo.-Kent Coll. Law, 1974. Bar: Ill. 1974, U.S. Dist. Ct. (no. dist.) Ill. 1974. Asst. states atty. (cen. dist.) Lake County, Waukegan, Ill., 1974-75; state's atty. Fulton County, Lewistown, Ill., 1976-82; mem. Ill. Ho. of Reps., 1982-94; state judge Ill. Appellate Ct., 3d Dist., Naperville, 1996—. Lt. USAR, 1968-78. Mem. Ill. State Bar Assn., Ill. Judges Assn. Home: 95 Salt River Ct Naperville IL 60565-6367 Office: 300 E 5th Ave Ste 300 Naperville IL 60563-3177

**HOMICK, DANIEL JOHN,** lawyer, financial executive; b. Cleve., Nov. 10, 1947; s. John and Frances (Ziherl) H.; m. Victoria Frances Majoros, Sept. 1, 1974; children: Alexandra Victoria, Christopher Daniel, Andrew William, Elizabeth Irene. AB, John Carroll U., 1969, MA, 1971; diploma, U. Vienna, Strobl, Austria, 1972; JD, Capital U., 1978. Bar: Ohio, 1978. Asst. mgr. Shaker Heights (Ohio) Theatre, 1968-71; teaching assoc. John Carroll U., Univ. Heights, Ohio, 1969-71; dept. chmn. Magnificat High Sch., Rocky River, Ohio, 1972-73; asst. to dir. Dept. Human Resources and Econ. Devel. City of Cleve., 1973-75; acting state dir., program officer U.S. Govt. ACTION, Columbus, Ohio, 1975-79; assoc. gen. counsel Am. Invsco, Atlanta and Chgo., 1980-82; program mgr. Mortgage Guaranty Ins. Corp., Milw., 1982-86, v.p. mortgage securities, 1986-87; sr. v.p. capital markets and mktg. CenTrust Savs. Bank, Miami, 1987-89; v.p. negotiated transactions, capital markets Gen. Electric Mortgage Securities Corp., Raleigh, N.C., 1989-93; registered rep. GECC Capital Mkts., Inc., 1990-96; v.p. structured transactions GE Capital Mortgage Svcs., Inc., Raleigh, N.C., 1993-94; v.p. direct placements GE Capital Mortgage Corp., 1994-96; v.p. structured finance, registered rep. Berean Capital Inc., Raleigh, N.C., 1996—; prin., v.p. Berean Capital Ptnrs., Inc., 1998—; pvt. practice law, Columbus, 1978-79; instr., tng. cons. Columbus Tech. Inst., 1978-79. Mem. fin. devel. com. Raleigh Boychoir, 1998—; mem. Ctrl. YMCA Long Bow Coun., 1996—; bd. dirs. Mental Health Assn. Dade County, Miami, 1987-89, Cherrywood Viillage Condominium Assn., Brown Deer, Wis., 1983-84, Summit Chase Condominium Assn., Columbus, Ohio, 1979-80; campaign coord. Andrew Young for Mayor, Atlanta, 1982. Mem. ABA (chmn. mortgage guaranty ins. subcom. 1985-87, chmn. securitization mortgages subcom. 1987-93, chmn. securitization com. 1987-94, ad hoc com. on ctrl. and ea. European law initiative 1991-93, financing affordable housing com. 1991—, internat. investment in real estate com. 1991-95, ad hoc com. on tech. asst. to emerging econs. 1993—, co-chair conf. The Evolving Worldwide Legal and Regulatory Climate for Securitization, Brussels 1993, standing com. on CLE 1993-97, group chair real estate and mortgage investment coms. 1994-95, coun. real property, probate and trust law sect. 1995-98, standing com. on membership 1995—, co-chair 1998—, standing com. on publs. 1995-97, standing com. on goal IX/Diversity 1997—, task force on securitization of assets 1996-98, com. fed. regulation of securities 1996—, task force on fin. svcs. and European Cmty. 1996—, com. internat. bus. law 1996—, subcom. fgn. investments in U.S. 1996—, com. internat. real property fin. and secured transactions 1998—, com. newly ind. states of the former Soviet Union 1998—, subcom. securitization of assets 1998—, subcom. multinat. merger and acquisitions 1998—), Mortgage Banker's Assn. (comml. real estate fin. com. 1990-92, secondary market and securitization subcom. 1990-92), Am. Assn. Advancement Slavic Studies, Delta Sigma Rho, Phi Alpha Theta. Avocations: Russian history, travel. Finance, Real property, Securities. Home and Office: 8608 Cold Springs Rd Raleigh NC 27615-3107

**HOMISAK, THERESA,** lawyer; b. Pitts., Jan. 13, 1950; d. John and Mary (Mordovancy) H. BA, U. Pitts., 1971, MA, 1974; JD, Duquesne U., 1980. Bar: Pa. 1980, U.S. Dist. Ct. (we. dist.) Pa. 1980, U.S. Ct. Appeals (3d cir.) 1984, U.S. Supreme Ct. 1985, U.S. Dist. Ct. (mid. dist.) Pa. 1990, N.J. 1994, U.S. Dist. Ct. N.J. 1994. Assoc. Sharlock, Repcheck and Mahler, Pitts., 1980-87, 90-94; asst. chief counsel Pitts. regional office Pa. Human Relations Commn., 1987-88; ptnr. J.B. Clark Fine Art Co., Pitts., 1989-91; sole practice, 1994-96; devel. assoc. Am. Sch. Classical Studies, 1996-97; of counsel Law Offices of Katherine Benesch, Lawrenceville, N.J., 1997-98; sr. assoc. Wong Fleming, Edison, N.J., 1999—. Contbg. author: Medical Malpractice, 1987-88, State by State Guide to Managed Care Law, 1998; editor: Desktop Guide to Good Juvenile Probation Practice, 1990, Design Guidelines for Juvenile Ct. Facilities, 1993; contbg. editor: Policy Alternatives and Family Court Jurisdiction, 1993. Republican. Presbyterian. General civil litigation, Personal injury. Home: 323 Franklin Ave Princeton NJ 08540-3959 Office: Wong Fleming 2035 Lincoln Hwy Ste 1050 PO Box 985 Edison NJ 08818-0985

**HON, DONALD ALLEN,** retired lawyer; b. Pleasant Hill, Mo., Apr. 5, 1942; s. William Harris and Ella Frances (Raffurty) H.; m. Rita Ann Renner, Aug. 27, 1967 (div. 1976); children: Michael Thomas, Michelle Ann. AA, Palomar Coll., 1966; BS, San Diego State U., 1969; JD, Western State U., 1973. Bar: Calif. 1973, U.S. Dist. Ct. (so. dist.) Calif. 1973, U.S. Ct. Appeals (9th cir.) 1983. Assoc. Greer, Popko, Miller & Forester, San Diego, 1974—; pvt. practice, San Diego, from 1974; del. Calif. State Bar, 1984. With USMC, 1961-64. Mem. San Diego County Bar Assn., United Comml. Travelers Club (San Diego, sr. counselor 1974-75), Optimists. Labor. Home: 6911 Dylan St San Diego CA 92139-2110

**HONAKER, JIMMIE JOE,** lawyer, ecologist; b. Oklahoma City, Jan. 21, 1939; s. Joe Jack and Ruby Lee (Bowen) H.; children: Jay Jimmie, Kerri Ruth. BA, Colo. Coll., 1963; MA, U. No. Colo., 1991; JD, U. Wyo., 1966, MS, 1995; postgrad., Utah State U., 1995—. Bar: Colo. 1966, U.S. Dist. Ct. Colo., U.S. Ct. Appeals (10th cir.), Ute Indian Tribal Ct. Pvt. practice Longmont, Colo., 1966-91. Incorporator Longmont Boys Baseball, 1969; chmn. Longmont City Charter Commn., 1973; chmn. ch. bd. 1st Christian Ch., Longmont, 1975, 76; chmn. North Boulder County unit Am. Cancer Soc., 1978, 79. Recipient Disting. Svc. award Longmont Centennial Yr., 1971; named Outstanding Young Man, Longmont Jaycees, 1973. Mem. ABA, Colo. Bar Assn. (interprofl. com. 1972-91, environ. law sect. 1999—), Denver Bar Assn., Christian Legal Soc., Internat. Assn. Approved Basketball Ofcls. (cert.), Nat. Eagle Scout Assn., Ecol. Soc. Am., Colo. Mountain Club, Uintah Mtn. Club, Phi Alpha Delta, Alpha Kappa Psi, Xi Sigma Pi. Avocations: private pilot, mountain climbing. Real property, Environmental, Contracts commercial. Address: Utah State U PO Box 1320 Logan UT 84322-0001

**HONEA, FLOYD FRANKLIN,** lawyer; b. Dallas, May 20, 1950; s. Floyd Franklin and Gloria Anne H. BS, North Tex. State U., 1973; JD, U. Tex., 1976. Bar: Tex. 1976, U.S. Supreme Ct., U.S. Ct. Appeals (5th and 10th cirs.), U.S. Ct. Claims, U.S. Dist. Ct. (no., ea. and we. dists.) Tex. Ptnr. Payne & Vendig, Dallas, 1976-97; shareholder Winstead Sechrist & Minick, P.C., Dallas, 1997—. Mem. Dallas Hist. Soc., 1978—; mem. Rep. Nat. Com. Rep. party Tex., 1979—; Keeton fellow, mem. dean's coun. U. Tex. Sch. Law; active Dallas Zool. Soc., 1986—, Dallas Symphony Assn.; sponsor Kimbell Art Mus., Smithsonian Inst., WMS Civic Trust, Dallas Mus. Art. Mem. ABA, State Bar Tex., Dallas Bar Assn., The 500, Inc., Crescent Club Dallas. Baptist. General civil litigation, Appellate, Oil, gas, and mineral. Home: 8865 Flint Falls Dr Dallas TX 75243-7542 Office: 5400 Republic Nat Bank Towe Dallas TX 75201

**HONEGGER, ANDREW ALAN,** lawyer; b. Sept. 30, 1968. BA, U. Ill., 1991; JD, Boston U., 1994. Bar: Mass. 1994, Ill. 1995, U.S. Dist. Ct. Mass. 1998, U.S. Ct. Appeals (1st cir.) 1999. Assoc. Bellotti & Barretto, P.C., Cambridge, Mass., 1994-97, Gadsby & Hannah LLP, Boston, 1997—; instr. legal rsch. and writing Boston U. Sch. Law, 1996-98. Recipient Homer Albers Moot Ct. prize 1993. Avocation: golf. General civil litigation, Appellate. Home: 432 Marlborough St Apt G Boston MA 02115-1221 Office: Gadsby & Hannah LLP 225 Franklin St Boston MA 02110-2804

**HONEYCHURCH, DENIS ARTHUR,** lawyer; b. Berkeley, Calif., Sept. 17, 1946; s. Winston and Mary Martha (Chandler) H.; m. Judith Ann Poliquin, Oct. 5, 1969; children: Sean, James, Thomas. BA, UCLA, 1968; JD, U. Calif., San Francisco, 1972. Bar: Calif. 1972, U.S. Dist. Ct. (no. dist.) Calif. 1972, U.S. Ct. Appeals (9th cir.) 1972. Dep. pub. defender Sacramento County Calif., Sacramento, 1973-75; supervising asst. pub. defender Solano County, Fairfield, Calif., 1975-78; ptnr. Honeychurch & Finkas and predecessor firm, Fairfield, 1978—. Bd. dirs. Fairfield-Suisun Unified Sch. Dist., Fairfield, 1979-83, Solano Coll., Fairfield, 1985—; chmn. bd. dirs. Downtown Improvement Dist., Fairfield, 1980-82; mem. Dem. Ctr. Com. Solano County, 1994-98. Mem. ABA, Nat. Assn. Criminal Def. Lawyers, Calif. Attys. Criminal Justice, Calif. Pub. Defenders Assn., Solano County Bar Assn. (pres. 1991), Calif. Bd. Legal Specialization (cert.), Nat. Bd. Trial Advocacy (cert.). Democrat. Criminal. Office: Honeychurch & Finkas 823 Jefferson St Fairfield CA 94533-5591

**HONI, RAGHUBEER S.,** lawyer, arbitrator, consultant; b. Delhi, India, Nov. 2, 1922; came to U.S., 1970; s. Jagan Nath Singh and Kala Wati. Intermediate in commerce honors in Hindi, Panjab U., Allahabad, India, 1951; BA, U. Panjab, Solan, 1953; LLB, Delhi U., 1959; proficiency in law, —, 1960; LLM, Utkal U., India, 1962. Bar: Infia 1962, N.Y. Pvt. practice, Delhi, 1962-70, N.Y.C., 1974—; case commr. Delhi cts.; commr. of oaths; standing counsel to Provident Fund commr., Delhi State To Conduct Govt. Cases; arbitrator Civil Ct. County New York, 1991—. Mem. Am. Judges Assn. (ct. adminstrn. com. 1997-98), New York County Lawyers Assn. (appellate ct. com., internat. and fgn. affairs com.), Assn. Arbitration City N.Y. Office: 160 Broadway Rm 704 New York NY 10038-4201

**HONIG, STEPHEN MICHAEL,** lawyer; b. Albany, N.Y., Nov. 10, 1942; s. Morris and Betty (Tash) H.; m. Laura M. Unflat, June 25, 1989; children: Jennifer, Peter, Charles. AB, Columbia U., 1963; LLB, Harvard U., 1966. Bar: Mass. 1966, U.S. Dist. Ct. Mass. 1968, U.S. Ct. Appeals (1st cir.) 1967. Atty. Widett & Widett, Boston, 1966-75, Goldstein & Manello PC, Boston, 1976—. Computer, General corporate, Securities. Home: 519 Lewis Wharf Boston MA 02110-3914 Office: Goldstein & Manello PC 265 Franklin St Ste 2000 Boston MA 02110-3192

**HONIGMAN, STEVEN,** lawyer; b. Bklyn., May 14, 1948. BA, NYU, 1969; JD, Yale U., 1972. Bar: N.Y. 1973, D.C. 1976, U.S. Supreme Ct., U.S. Ct. Appeals (2d and D.C. cirs.), U.S. Ct. Mil. Appeals, U.S. Dist. Ct. D.C., U.S. Dist. Ct. (so. and ea. dists.) N.Y. Gen. counsel Dept. Navy, Washington, 1992-98; ptnr. Thelen, Reid & Priest, 1998—. Recipient Disting. Pub. Svc. award Dept. of Navy, 1998, Aegis Excellence award, 1995. Fellow Am. Bar Found.; mem. ABA (chmn. standing com. on mil. law 1986-89), N.Y. State Bar Assn., D.C. Bar Assn., Assn. of Bar of City of N.Y., Yale Law Sch. Assn. (mem. exec. com.), U.S. Naval Inst. *

**HONSAKER, MARK LLEWELLYN,** lawyer; b. Warren, Ohio, Feb. 24, 1966; s. Paul R. and Frances Jean (Stewart) H.; m. Darlene Regina Nagel, Aug. 31, 1991; children: Nathaniel David, Amber Marie. BA in Polit. Sci., Ohio State U., Columbus, 1988; paralegal cert., Tex. Sch. Bus., Houston, 1990; JD, South Tex. Coll. Law, Houston, 1995. Bar: Tex. 1996, U.S. Dist. Ct. (so. dist.). Paralegal Fisher & Cain PC, Houston, 1990-94; law clk. Horan & Devlin PC, Houston, 1994-95; atty. LeJune & Singer, Houston, 1995-97, Sheri Y. Dean & Assocs., Houston, 1997, pvt. practice, 1997—. Chmn, Bd. of Adjustment, Seabrook, Tex., 1997-98. Mem. ABA, State Bar of Tex. (bus. sect.), Houston Bar Assn. Personal injury. Office: 18333 Egret Bay Blvd Ste 101 Houston TX 77058-3200

**HOOD, JOSEPH M.,** federal judge; b. 1942. BS, U. Ky., 1965, JD, 1972. Law clk. U.S. Dist. Ct. (ea. dist.) Ky., 1972-76, magistrate, 1976-90, judge, 1990—. Active United Cerebral Palsy Ea. Ky.; bd. trustees Alice LLoyd Coll. Decorated Bronze Star with V device and 4 oak leaf clusters. Mem. YMCA, Rotary, Bellefonte Country Club. Office: US Dist Ct 354 Federal Bldg 330 W Broadway St Frankfort KY 40601-1922

**HOOD, ROBERT HOLMES,** lawyer; b. Charleston, S.C., Oct. 5, 1944; s. James Albert and Ruth (Henderson) H.; m. Mary Agnes Burnham, Aug. 5, 1967; children: Mary Agnes, Elizabeth, Robert Holmes Jr., James Bernard. BA, U. of the South, 1966; JD, U. S.C., 1969. Bar: U.S. Supreme Ct. 1969, S.C. 1969, U.S. Dist. Ct. S.C. 1969, U.S. Ct. Appeals (4th cir.) 1969. Asst. atty. gen. State of S.C., Columbia, 1969-70; ptnr. Sinkler, Gibbs & Simons, Charleston, 1970-85; prin. Hood Law Firm, Charleston, 1985--. Mem. Assn. Def. Trial Attys. (pres. 1985-86), Am. Bd. Trial Advs. (diplomate, pres. Charleston chpt. 1997), Internat. Assn. Def. Counsel, Def. Rsch. and Trial Inst. (bd. dirs. 1987-90), Fedn. Ins. and Corp. Counsel (state chmn. 1997—), S.C. Def. Trial Attys. Assn. (pres. 1980-81), Network of Trial Law Firms. Episcopalian. General civil litigation, Personal injury, Consumer commercial. Office: 172 Meeting St Charleston SC 29401-3126

**HOOD, WILLIAM WAYNE, JR.,** lawyer; b. Tulsa, July 22, 1941; s. William Wayne and Alys (Charles) H.; m. Nancy Raynolds; children—W. Wayne III, Kristina L. B.A., U. Okla., 1963; LL.B., U. Tulsa, 1966. Bar: Okla. 1966, U.S. Dist. Ct. (no. dist.) Okla. 1966. Diplomate Am. Coll. Matrimonial Trial Lawyers. Pvt. practice, Tulsa, 1966-70; pub. defender Tulsa County, 1966-68; ptnr. Hood & Lindsey, Tulsa, 1970-87, Hood & Raynolds, 1989—. Served to maj. JAGC, USAR, 1966-84. Fellow Am. Acad. Matrimonial Lawyers (v.p. 1985-88, pres. Okla. chpt. 1991-93), Internat. Acad. Matrimonial Lawyers (bd. govs. Am. chpt. 1987-91); mem. Okla. Bar Assn. (dir. continuing legal edn.-family law 1980-84, chmn. family law sect. 1975-77, 80-82), Tulsa County Bar Assn. (exec. com. 1979). Republican. Roman Catholic. Family and matrimonial. Office: Hood & Raynolds 1914 S Boston Ave Tulsa OK 74119-5222

**HOOGLAND, ROBERT FREDERICS,** lawyer; b. Paterson, N.J., Apr. 3, 1955; s. Robert J. and Lucretia H.; m. Diane Wood, Sept. 21, 1983 (div. Mar. 1985). BA, U. Fla., 1976; MBA, Rollins Coll., 1977; JD, U. Fla., 1982. Bar: Fla. 1983, U.S. Dist. Ct. (mid. dist.) Fla. 1989. Assoc. Giles, Hedrick & Robinson, Orlando, Fla., 1983-89; ptnr. Hoogland & Durket, P.A., Longwood, Fla., 1989-92, Robert F. Hoogland, P.A., Altamonte Springs, Fla., 1992—. Mem. ABA, Fla. Bar Assn., Orange County Bar Assn., Seminole County Bar Assn., Winter Park C. of C., Phi Delta Phi. Republican. Roman Catholic. Avocations: tennis, golf, fishing. Real property, Consumer commercial, Banking. Home: 139 Olive Tree Cir Altamonte Springs FL 32714-3240 Office: PO Box 160021 Altamonte Springs FL 32716-0021

**HOOGSTRA, SHIRLEY VOGELZANG,** lawyer; b. Holland, Mich., July 30, 1956; d. William and Betty Jane (Bergsma) Vogelzang; m. Jeffrey Hoogstra, Aug. 19, 1978; children: David Jacob, Mary Elizabeth. BS in Regular and Spl. Edn., Calvin Coll., 1978; postgrad., Inst. Internat. & Comp. Law, Paris, 1984; JD with honors, U. Conn., 1986. Bar: Conn. 1986, U.S. Dist. Ct. Conn. 1986, U.S. Tax Ct. 1986. Tchr. English Covenant Christian Sch., Cranford, N.J., 1979-82; legal asst. Office of Gen. Counsel Yale U., New Haven, 1982-83, law clk. Office of Gen. Counsel, summer 1984; atty. Jacobs, Grudberg & Belt, New Haven, 1986-99; v.p. student life Calvin Coll., Grand Rapids, Mich., 1999—; tchg. asst. legal writing U. Conn. Sch. Law, Hartford, 1984-85, 85-86. Assoc. editor: Soviet Law and Economy, 1985. Bd. trustees Calvin Coll., 1995—, exec. com., chmn. devel. com., mem. steering com. Campaign for Calvin Coll., 1991-94; bd. dirs. Bridgeport (Conn.) Rescue Mission, 1997—, v.p.; chair 40th anniversary com. St. Thomas's Day Sch. Mem. ABA (mem. litigation and family law sects.), Am. Inns of Ct., Conn. Bar Assn. (mem. family law sect., Conn. coun. of bar pres.), Conn. Bar Examining Com., Conn. Trial Lawyers Assn., New Haven County Bar Assn. (pres. exec. com. 1988-99), New Haven County Bar Found. (pres., mem. exec. com. 1997-99). Office: Jacobs Grudberg Belt & Dow PC 350 Orange St New Haven CT 06511-6415

**HOOKER, WADE STUART, JR.,** lawyer; b. Brockton, Mass., Sept. 23, 1941; s. Wade S. and Eleanor M. (Tolan) H.; m. Susan M. Levine, May 20, 1984; children: Thomas A., Richard P. BA, Harvard Coll., 1963; LLB, U. Va., 1966. Bar: N.Y. 1969. Assoc. Casey, Lane & Mittendorf, N.Y.C., 1968-77; ptnr. Burlingham Underwood LLP, N.Y.C., 1979—; spkr. in field. Contbr. articles to profl. jours. Maxwell fellow Syracuse U., Resident scholar Indian Law Inst., New Delhi, 1966-67. Mem. ABA, Assn. Bar City of N.Y., Computer Law Assn., Inc., Internat. Bar Assn., Maritime Law Assn. U.S. (chair com. maritime regulation and promotion 1990-94), Mensa. Admiralty, Computer, Finance. Office: Burlingham Underwood LLP One Battery Pk Plaza New York NY 10004

**HOOKS, WILLIAM HENRY,** lawyer; b. Memphis, July 30, 1953; s. H.A. Jr. and Eleanor Patricia (Cummings) H.; m. Debra S. Parrish, Jan. 5, 1975; children: Mariah S., Ashley S. BA in Sociology/Criminal Justice, DePaul U., Chgo., 1975; JD, Ill. Inst. Tech., Chgo., 1981. Bar: Ill. 1981, U.S. Ct. Appeals (7th cir.) 1981, U.S. Tax Ct. 1982, U.S. Ct. Mil. Appeals 1982, U.S. Dist. Ct. 1981, Trial Bar U.S. Dist. Ct. (no. dist.) Ill. 1985. Watch officer Naval Security Group, 1978-81; assoc. Hinshaw & Culbertson, Chgo., 1986-89; prin. Hooks Law Offices P.C., Chgo., 1989—; adj. prof. Advanced Trial Adv. DePaul Coll. of Law, 1995—, Trial Adv. IIT Chgo.-Kent Coll. of Law; res. judge advocate USMCR, Chgo., 1985—; mem. rules com. U. S. Dist. Ct., Chgo., 1990—; commn. Ill. Supreme Ct., Chgo., 1992—; chair hearing panel Atty. Disciplinary Commn. Lt. col. USMCR, 1974-92. Mem. ABA, NBA, Assn. Trial Lawyers Am., Fed. Bar Assn. (v.p. Chgo. chpt.), Nat. Eagle Scout Assn., Cook County Bar Assn. (v.p., past chmn. atty. disciplinary liaison com., com. on jud. investigations), Chgo. Bar Assn. (com. on jud. hearings, com. on jud. investigations, past chmn.). Criminal, Insurance, Professional liability. Office: Hooks Law Offices PC 3 1st Nat Plz Ste 5200 Chicago IL 60602

**HOOPER, PERRY OLLIE,** state supreme court judge; b. Birmingham, Ala., Apr. 8, 1925; s. Ernest J. and Mary Lou (Perry) H.; m. Marilyn Yost, May 16, 1953; children: Perry O. Jr., Walter, Conwell, John. BS, U. Ala., 1950, LLB, 1953. Bar: Ala. 1953, U.S. Dist. Ct. (so. dist.) Ala. 1953. Pvt. practice Montgomery, Ala., 1953-64, 83—; probate judge Montgomery County, Montgomery, 1964-76; cir. ct. judge State of Ala., Montgomery, 1975-83, presiding cir. judge, 1978-83, chief justice Supreme Ct., 1995—. Mem. Nat. Republican Com., 1972-96. Methodist. Avocations: golf, gardening. Home: 3191 Thomas Ave Montgomery AL 36106-2425 Office: 300 Dexter Ave Montgomery AL 36104-3741

**HOOPES, ROBERT PATRICK,** lawyer; b. Phila., Feb. 2, 1947; s. Edward Wakefield and Marie Alma (Hoover) H.; m. Theresa Marie Moran; children: Dawn Marie, Amy Lynn, Lynne Marie, Samantha Marie, Christian Marie Hamilton. BA, Trenton (N.J.) State Coll., 1979; Jd, Widener U., 1988. Real estate developer Doylestown, 1986-89, pvt. practice, 1990—; Bar: N.J. 1989, Pa. 1990, U.S. Dist. Ct. N.J. 1989, U.S. Dist. Ct. (ea. dist.) Pa. 1991, U.S. Tax Ct., U.S. Ct. Appeals (3d cir.) 1991, U.S. Supreme Ct. 1994. Decorated Bronze star, Purple Heart. Mem. ABA, Bucks County Bar Assn., Am. Trial Lawyers Assn. Republican. Roman Catholic. Avocations: golf, hunting, fishing. Personal injury, Family and matrimonial, Criminal. Home: 1 Mercer Gate Dr Doylestown PA 18901-3147 Office: 573 N Main St Ste 203 Doylestown PA 18901-3929

**HOOVER, DAVID CARLSON,** lawyer; b. Waterville, Maine, Apr. 22, 1950; s. Jack Cauldwell and Mary Elizabeth (Donavan) H.; m. Kathleen Delia Powell, June 28, 1981; children: Maegan Elizabeth, Peter Daniel, Christian Shaw. BA, U. N.H., 1972; JD cum laude, Suffolk U., 1976. Bar: Mass. 1977, U.S. Dist. Ct. Mass. 1982, U.S. Supreme Ct. 1982, U.S. Ct. Appeals (1st cir.) 1983. Atty. advisor NOAA, Washington, 1976-79; gen. counsel Mass. Div. Marine Fisheries, Boston, 1979-83; spl. asst. atty. gen. Mass. Dept. Atty. Gen., Boston, 1980—; gen. counsel Mass. Dept. of Fisheries, Wildlife and Environ. Law Enforcement, Boston, 1983—; adminstrv. law judge Commonwealth of Mass., 1979; lectr. Franklin Pierce Law Ctr., Concord, N.H., 1984. Mem. editorial bd. Territorial Sea Jour., U. of Maine Sch. of Law; contbr. articles to profl. jours. Ch. lector; tchr. Cath. Youth Orgn.; vol. New England Shelter for Homeless Vets.; exec. dir. Mass. Wildcats AAU Basketball Club. Recipient Am. Jurisprudence award Lawyers Cooperative Pub. Co. Mem. Mass. Bar Assn., Com. on Chemical Dependency, Atty. advisor to Mock-Trial Tournament, Law Related Edn. Com., Lawyers Concerned for Lawyers, Internat. Assn. of Approved Basketball Offcls. Avocations: miniaturist, woodworking, civil war history, coaching youth basketball. Home: 808 Watertown St Newton MA 02465-

2116 Office: Dept Fisheries Wildlife and Environ Law Enforcement 100 Cambridge St Rm 1901 Boston MA 02202-0044

**HOOVER, R. SAM,** lawyer; b. Alameda, Calif., Oct. 16, 1931; s. Ralph Miller and Vera Marie H.; m. Sheila, July 2, 1955; children: Sue, Sarah, Sharon, Mary, Robert. BA, Notre Dame U., 1953; MA, Iowa U., 1957; MPH, Harvard U., 1962; JD, Loyola U., 1994. Bar: Ill., U.S. Supreme Ct. Ptnr. R.S. Hoover & Assocs., Chgo., 1994—. Capt. USAR, 1958-62. Mem. Ill. State Bar Assn., Alpha Omega Alpha. Avocations: golf, squash. Health, General civil litigation, Administrative and regulatory. Home: 444 Thorne Ln Lake Forest IL 60045-2343 Office: 20 N Clark St Ste 3600 Chicago IL 60602-5088

**HOPCROFT, ANN VICTORIA,** lawyer; b. Tawas City, Mich., July 13, 1950; d. Robert J. and Marion V. (Haglund) H.; 1 child, Natalie Jordan. BA in Psychology, Mich. State U., 1972; JD, U. Detroit, 1978. Bar: Colo. 1978. Assoc. Lawrence Litvak, P.C., Denver, 1978-79; asst. county atty. Adams County, Brighton, Colo., 1980-81; litigation cons., Holland, Mich., 1981-84, Boulder, Colo., 1984-85; litigation counsel Aldefer & Herm, Denver, 1985-87; corp. counsel IDHHB, Inc., Nevada City, Calif., 1987—. Chmn., bd. dirs. Mus. Ancient and Modern Art, Penn Valley, Calif., 1990-97; election judge Dem. Orgn., Boulder, 1980-87. Designer (mag.) Galaxy Sci. Fiction, 1994-95. Mem. ABA, NOW (media task chair state bd. dirs. 1978-80), Labyrinth Readers Soc., Grass Valley Graphics Group (artist), Order of Barristers. Home and Office: PO Box 878 Penn Valley CA 95946-0878

**HOPE, JOHN CHARLES, JR.,** lawyer; b. Cleve., Nov. 12, 1948; s. John Charles and Ruth Marie (Carens) H. B.A., U. Nev.-Reno, 1974; J.D., Western State U., 1977. Bar: Nev. 1978, Calif. 1977, U.S. Dist. Ct. Nev. 1979, U.S. Ct. Appeals (9th cir.) 1981, U.S. Dist. Ct. (so. dist.) Calif. 1982, U.S. Dist. Ct. (ea. dist.) Calif. 1983. Atty., Corn and Hardesty, Reno, Nev., 1979-82; sole practice, Reno, 1982—. Republican. Roman Catholic. Home: 3820 Piccadilly Dr Reno NV 89509-5625 Office: PO Box 13043 Reno NV 89507-3043

**HOPE, RONALD ARTHUR,** lawyer; b. Mineral Wells, Tex., Jan. 8, 1956; s. Arthur Virgil and Barbara Louise (Wester) H.; m. Mary Katharyn Howell, Oct. 3, 1987; children: Katharyn Rachel, Laura Anderson, John Arthur. BSBA in Acctg., U. Ark., 1978, JD, 1981. Bar: Ark. 1981, U.S.Dist. Ct. (ea. and we. dists.) Ark. 1982, U.S. Ct. Appeals (8th cir.) 1991, U.S. Supreme Ct. 1987. Atty. Howell, Price & Trice, P.A., Little Rock, 1981-85; ptnr. Howell, Price, Trice, Basham & Hope, P.A., Little Rock, 1985-93; shareholder Howell, Trice & Hope, P.A., Little Rock, 1993—; city atty. City of Wrightsville, Ark., 1988—; atty. Ark. Property and Casualty Guaranty Fund. Mem. legal com. NCIGF, 1996—. Century mem. Boy Scouts Am. Mem. ATLA, Ark. Bar Assn., Ark. Trial Lawyers Assn., Pulaski County Bar Assn., Rotary, Masons, Shriners, Phi Alpha Delta, Sigma Chi. Methodist. Avocations: duck hunting, deer hunting, golf. General civil litigation, Insurance, Family and matrimonial. Office: Howell Trice & Hope PA 211 S Spring St Little Rock AR 72201-2405

**HOPEN, ANTON JOHN,** lawyer; b. Phila., Aug. 31, 1969; s. John Hopen and Joan Girard; m. Lisa Michelle Nicholson, May 27, 1995; 1 child, Anna Noel. BA in Biology, U. South Fla., 1991; JD, U. Fla., 1995. Bar: Fla. 1995, U.S. Dist. Ct. (mid. dist.) Fla. 1997, (no. dist.) Fla. 1999, U.S. Patent and Trademark Office 1998, U.S. Dist. Ct. (so. dist.) Fla. 1999, U.S. Ct. Appeals (fed. cir.) 1999, (11th cir.) 1999. Asst. state atty. 6th Jud. Cir., Clearwater, Fla., 1995-98; registered patent atty. Lott & Friedland, Coral Gables, Fla., 1998-99; ptnr. Smith & Hopen, Clearwater, 1999—; lectr. forensic DNA, Fla. Dept. Law Enforcement, Tallahassee, 1998—; trial judge U. Miami Coll. Law, 1998-99. Mem. Am. Intellectual Property Law Assn., Patent Law Assn. South Fla. (officer 1998-99). Republican. Avocations: golf, saltwater fishing. Fax: 727-507-8668. E-mail: ajhopen@baypatents.com. Patent, Trademark and copyright, Intellectual property. Office: Smith & Hopen PA 15950 Bay Vista Dr Ste 220 Clearwater FL 33760-3131

**HOPEN, RICHARD MARTIN,** lawyer, marketing consultant; b. Phila., Jan. 30, 1958; s. Bernard Charles and Bertie H.; m. Joanne Wolf, Nov. 26, 1988; children: Sydney, Bernadette. BA, Clark U., 1980; M in Pub. Adminstrn., San Diego State U., 1984; JD, Calif. Western Sch. Law, 1985. Bar: Fla., Pa., D.C. Sole practice Ft. Lauderdale, Fla., 1992-99; pres. R. Hopen Mktg. Svcs., Inc., Ft. Lauderdale, Fla., 1999—. Author: (audio tape program) Marketing Secrets for Lawyers, 1999; columnist Daily Bus. Rev. newspapers, 1999. Chmn. Braund County Brownfields Redevel. Task Force, Braund City, Fla., 1998-99. Environmental. Office: 1776 N Pine Island Rd Fort Lauderdale FL 33322-5233

**HOPF, JAMES FREDRIK,** lawyer; b. Taipei, Taiwan, Dec. 21, 1961; s. William H.; m. Julie Carole Bunch, May 22, 1982; children: Christopher James, Benjamin Thomas, Maggie Elizabeth. BA, Campbell U., N.C., 1983; JD, U. N.C., 1986. Bar: N.C. 1986, U.S. Dist. Ct. (mid. and ea. dists.) N.C. 1986, U.S. Ct. Appeals (4th cir.) 1988. Assoc. Smith, Anderson, Blount, Dorsett, Mitchell & Jernigan, Raleigh, 1986-90, Law Offices of Marvin Blount, Jr., Greenville, N.C., 1990-95; pvt. practice Law Offices of James F. Hopf, Greenville, 1995-96; ptnr. Barefoot & Hopf, L.L.P., Greenville and Raleigh, 1996-98; pvt. practice, 1998—; assoc. Smith, Anderson, Blount, Dorsett, Mitchell & Jernigan, Raleigh, 1986-90. Mem. ABA, ATLA, N.C. Bar Assn., N.C. Acad. Trial Lawyers, Order of Barristers, Omicron Delta Kappa, Phi Kappa Phi. Baptist. Personal injury, Environmental, General civil litigation. Office: 1694 E Arlington Blvd Ste E Greenville NC 27858-5331

**HOPKINS, CHARLES PETER, II,** lawyer; b. Elizabeth, N.J., June 16, 1953; s. Charles Peter Sr. and Josephine Ann (Battaglia) H.; m. Elizabeth Anna Altinger, Jan. 21, 1984; children: Courtney Alexandra, Ashley Elizabeth, Brooke Anne, Brittany Emilia. AB summa cum laude, Boston Coll., 1975, JD, 1979; MBA, Rutgers U., 1987. Bar: N.J. 1979, U.S. Dist. Ct. N.J. 1979, U.S. Ct. Appeals (3d cir.) 1982, U.S. Supreme Ct. 1985, U.S. Tax Ct. 1988. Assoc. Gagliano, Tucci & Kennedy, West Long Branch, N.J., 1980; pvt. practice West Long Branch, 1980-81; assoc. Richard J. Sauerwein (formerly Sparks & Sauerwein), Shrewsbury, N.J., 1981-83, trial atty., 1983-87, sr. trial atty., 1987-90; mng. trial atty. Law Offices Charles Peter Hopkins II, Shrewsbury, N.J., 1990—; arbitrator U.S. Dist. Ct. N.J., 1985—, N.J. Civil arbitrator program, 1987—, Am. Arbitration Assn., 1991—. Mem. Def. Rsch. Inst., West Long Br. Sch. Bd., 1980-82. Mem. Monmouth Bar Assn., N.J. Def. Assn. (regional v.p. ctrl. region 1994-95, chmn. leadership com. 1994-98, chmn. pub. rel. com. 1994-98, chmn. tech. com. dir. 1995-98, sec.-treas. 1996-97, pres.-elect 1997-98, pres. 1998—, bd. dirs.), Def. Rsch. Inst. (So. N.J. chair 1995-97, state rep. 1997—, chmn. tech. com. 1997—, chmn. tech. com.), Phi Beta Kappa. Republican. Roman Catholic. Avocations: fitness, politics, mil. history. General civil litigation, Personal injury, Insurance. Office: Shrewsbury Sq Office Ctr 655 Shrewsbury Ave Shrewsbury NJ 07702-4151

**HOPKINS, GEORGE MATHEWS MARKS,** lawyer, business executive; b. Houston, June 9, 1923; s. C. Allen and Agnes Cary (Marks) H.; m. Betty Miller McLean, Aug. 21, 1954; children: Laura Hopkins Corrigan, Edith Hopkins Collins. Student, Ga. Tech., 1943-44; BSChemE, Ala. Poly. Inst., 1944; LLB, JD, U. Ala., 1949; postgrad., George Washington U., 1949-50. Bar: Ala. 1949, Ga. 1954; registered patent lawyer, U.S.; registered profl. engr., Ga.; Can. qualified deep-sea diver. Instr. math. U. Ala., 1947-49; assoc. A. Yates Dowell, Washington, 1949-50, Edward T. Newton, Atlanta, 1950-62; ptnr. Newton, Hopkins and Ormsby (and predecessor), Atlanta, 1962-87; sr. ptnr. Hunt, Richardson, Garner, Todd & Cadenhead, Atlanta, 1987-91; ptnr. Hopkins & Thomas, 1991-95; ret., 1996; spl. asst. atty. gen. State of Ga., 1978; chmn. bd. Southeastern Carpet Mills, Inc., Chatsworth, Ga., 1962-77, Thomas-Daniel & Assocs., Inc., 1981-85, Ea. Carpet Mills, Inc., 1983-87; CEO, Airamar Chem. Engring., Inc., Doraville, Ga., 1997—; asst. dir. rsch., legal counsel Auburn (Ala.) Rsch. Found., 1954-55; spl. asst. atty. gen. State of Ga., 1978; chmn. bd. S.E. Carpet Mills, Inc., Chatsworth, Ga., 1962-77, Thomas-Daniel & Assocs., Inc., 1981-85, Ea. Carpet Mills, Inc.; dir. Xepol Inc. Served as lt., navigator, Submarine Service USNR, 1944-46, 50-51. Mem. ABA, Ga. Bar Assn. (chmn. sect. patents 1970-71), Atlanta Bar Assn., Am. Intellectual Property Law Assn., Am. Soc. Profl. Engrs., Submarine Vets. World War II (pres. Ga. chpt. 1977-78), Phi Delta Phi, Sigma Alpha Epsilon, Atlanta Lawyers Club, Phoenix Soc., Cherokee Town and Country Club, AtlantaSoc. Episcopalian. Patent, Federal civil litigation, Trademark and copyright. Home: 795 Old Post Rd NW Atlanta GA 30328-4758

**HOPKINS, HARRY L.,** lawyer; b. Piggott, Ark., Aug. 11, 1935; s. Marcus Vann and Nellie Mae (Branson) H.; m. Martha Markline, Feb. 4, 1940; children: Peter Ashley, Heather Caroline. BA, U. So. Miss., 1960; LLB, Tulane U., 1964. Bar: Miss. 1964, Ala. 1973. Pvt. practice Meridian, Miss., 1964-65; trial atty. NLRB, New Orleans, 1965-69, gen. atty., 1969-73; ptnr. Lange, Simpson, Robinson & Somerville, Birmingham, Ala., 1973-97, Ogletree, Deakins, Nash, Smoke and Stewart, Birmingham, 1997—; adj. prof. econs. U. So. Miss., Hattiesberg, 1968-72; adj. prof. labor law U. Ala. Sch. Law, Tuscaloosa, 1979—; pres. Klondike Cattle Co. Maj. U.S. Army, 1953-56. Fellow Coll. of Labor and Employment Lawyers; mem. Briarwood Country Club, Klondike Hunting Club. Labor, Constitutional. Home: 1800 Woodcrest Rd Birmingham AL 35209-1364 Office: 1900 Southtrust Tower Birmingham AL 35203-3212

**HOPKINS, JOHN DAVID,** lawyer; b. Memphis, Feb. 8, 1938; s. John and Helen (Sweeney) H.; m. Evelyn Harry, June 8, 1963 (div. Feb. 1985); children: John David III, Katharine Jane, Matthew Joseph; m. Laurie Eileen House, June 3, 1987. BA, Vanderbilt U., 1959; LLB, U. Va., 1965. Bar: Ga. 1966, D.C. 1979. From assoc. to ptnr. King & Spalding, Atlanta, 1965-93; exec. v.p., gen. counsel Jefferson-Pilot Corp., Greensboro, N.C., 1993—; bd. dirs., mem. exec. com. Rock-Tenn Co., Atlanta; mem. Guilford Coll. Bd. of Visitors, 1994—; bd. dirs. Univ. N.C. at Greensboro Excellence Found. Bd. dirs. Atlanta Ballet, 1991-93, Greensboro United Arts Coun., 1994-97; trustee Children's Sch., Inc., Atlanta, 1971-79, 88-89, Nat. Assn. Children's Hosps. and Related Instns., Alexandria, Va., 1973-79. Lt. USN, 1959-62. Mem. ABA, Ga. Bar Assn. (chmn. corp. code revision com., corp. and banking sect. 1970-79), D.C. Bar Assn., Atlanta Lawyers Club, Greensboro Country Club, Cherokee Town and Country Club (Atlanta), Order of Coif, Omicron Delta Kappa. Democrat. Episcopalian. General corporate, Mergers and acquisitions, Finance. Office: 100 N Greene St Greensboro NC 27401-2507

**HOPKINS, KEVIN L.,** law educator, consultant; b. Milford, Del., Sept. 3, 1959; s. Kendall B. Hopkins and Dorothy M. Cirwithian. BA, U. Del., 1981; AM, Duke U., 1983; JD, Coll. William & Mary, 1989. Bar: Ky. 1990, U.S. Dist Ct. (we. dist.) Ky. 1990, U.S. Ct. Appeals (6th cir.) 1990. Rsch. asst. Nat. Ctr. State Cts., Williamsburg, Va., 1986-87; law clerk Del. Family Ct., Georgetown, 1987, Office Atty. Gen., Richmond, Va., 1989; assoc. Woodward, Hobson & Fulton, Louisville, 1989-91; mem. faculty Widener U. Sch. Law, Wilmington, Del., 1991-96, John Marshall Law Sch., Chgo., 1996—; faculty staff mem. Inst. Commitment Workshop, 1987; summer assoc. Woodward, Hobson & Fulton, 1987; legal counsel Del. Community Reinvestment Action Com., Wilminton, 1992-96. Mem. ABA, Ky. Bar Assn., Am. Assn. Law Schs., Legal Writing Inst. Democrat. Methodist. Avocations: jogging, music, sports, literature, art. Home: 800 S Wells St Chicago IL 60607-4529 Office: John Marshall Law Sch 315 S Plymouth Ct Chicago IL 60604-3968

**HOPKINS, WILLIAM CARLISLE, II,** lawyer; b. Mason City, Iowa, Apr. 11, 1945; s. William C. and Dorothy (Purcey) H.; m. Sandra Janssen, Apr. 22, 1978; children: William C. III, Ryan Lee, Leigh Alexandra. BA, S.W. Mo. State U., 1967; JD, U. Mo., Columbia, 1970. Bar: Mo. 1970, U.S. Dist. Ct. (we. and ea. dists.) 1970, U.S. Ct. Appeals (8th cir.) 1970, U.S. Supreme Ct. 1973, Calif. 1983. Assoc. Lathrop Koontz et al., Kansas City, Mo., 1970-75; freelance TV writer Universal, Fox, MTM, L.A., 1975-82; assoc. atty. Mix & Assocs., Redondo Beach, Calif., 1982-83; ptnr. Hubbell Sawyer Peak & O'Neal, Kansas City, 1983-94, Stites McIntosh & Hopkins, Kansas City, 1993-94, Stites Hopkins Fair & Riederer, Kansas City, 1994—; v.p. Spl. Event Entertainment, L.A., 1975-77. Writer various TV shows including Paper Chase, Lou Grant, Quincy; feature writer The K.C. Counsellor, 1993—. Vol. Head Injury Assn. Greater Kansas City, 1993-94. Mem. ATLA, Mo. Assn. Trial Attys. (com. chair 1983—, chair pub. awareness com. 1994-95, mem. bd. 1994—), Mo. Bar Assn. (Tort Com. coun. 1993), Kansas City Met. Bar Assn., Brain Injury Assn. of Mo. (contributing writer to newsletter The Focus 1993—). Avocations: golf, coaching little league. Personal injury, State civil litigation, Federal civil litigation. Office: Stites Hopkins Fair & Riederer 1101 Walnut St Ste 1400 Kansas City MO 64106-2182

**HOPKINS, WILLIAM HAYES,** lawyer, writer; b. Moscow, Idaho, Aug. 5, 1943; s. Bert Earl and Marie Hayes H.; m. Rachel Pomeroy, Aug. 28, 1965; children: Alaa Christina, Elizabeth Anne, Amelia Jeanne, William, Rachel G. BA, Yale U., 1965; JD, Vanderbilt U., 1986. Bar: Conn. 1968, N.H. 1969, U.S. Dist. Ct. N.H. 1969, U.S. Ct. Appeals (1st cir.) 1983. Assoc. atty. Wakefield & Ray, Plymouth, N.H., 1969-75; ptnr. Ray & Hopkins, Plymouth, 1975-88; sr. ptnr. Hopkins & Blaine, Plymouth, 1989-94; pvt. practice Plymouth, 1995—; vice chmn. N.H. Adult Parole Bd., Concord, 1988—; chmn. N.H. Wine Law Revision Commn., Concord, 1979-81. Mem. N.H. Bridge Assn. (pres. 1996-98), Plymouth Wine Patrol (guru 1984-93), James Hogan Bridge Club (pres. 1996-98), Yale Club N.H. (pres. 1997—). Avocations: oenology, skiing, hiking. General civil litigation, Workers' compensation, Family and matrimonial. Home: PO Box 126 Plymouth NH 03264-0126 Office: PO Box 270 Plymouth NH 03264-0270

**HOPP, DANIEL FREDERICK,** manufacturing company executive, lawyer; b. Ann Arbor, Mich., Apr. 14, 1947; s. Clayton A. and Monica E. (Williams) H.; m. Maria G. Lopez, Dec. 20, 1968; children: Emily, Daniel, Melissa. BA in English, U. Mich., 1969; JD, Wayne State U., 1973. Bar: Ill. 1974, Mich. 1980. Atty. Mayer, Brown and Platt, Chgo., 1973-79; atty. Whirlpool Corp., Benton Harbor, Mich., 1979-84, asst. sec., 1984-85, sec., asst. gen. counsel, 1985-89, v.p., gen. counsel, sec., 1989-98, sr. v.p., corp. affairs and gen. counsel, 1998—; past co-chmn. Conf. Bd. Legal Quality Coun. Mem. City of St. Joseph (Mich.) Planning Comm.; bd. dirs. Lakeland Regional Health Sys., Joseph, Mich. With U.S. Army, 1969-71. Mem. Am. Soc. Corp. Secs. (past pres., bd. dirs. Chgo. chpt.), Mich. Bar Assn. (mem. Open Justice Commn.), Ill. Bar Assn., Berrien County Bar Assn. Republican. Mem. Ch. of Christ. Avocation: golf. Office: Whirlpool Corp Adminstrv Ctr 2000 N M 63 Benton Harbor MI 49022-2692

**HOPPEL, ROBERT GERALD, JR.,** lawyer; b. Scranton, Pa., Dec. 26, 1921; s. Robert Gerald and Ellen Amelia (Casey) H. B.S., U. Scranton, 1950; J.D., Georgetown U., 1954. Bar: D.C. 1955, U.S. Ct. Appeals (D.C. cir.) 1955, U.S. Supreme Ct. 1974. Supervising auditor GAO, Washington, 1950-57; ptnr. Coles & Goertner, Washington, 1957-82; ptnr. Hoppel, Mayer & Coleman, Washington, 1982-84; sole practice, 1984—. Served to cpl. USAAF, 1943-45. Mem. ABA, Maritime Adminstrv. Bar Assn., D.C. Bar, Bar Assn. D.C., Internat. Platform Assn., Am. Legion, Nat. Lawyers Club. Republican. Roman Catholic. Clubs: Propellor (Washington). Administrative and regulatory, Admiralty, Government contracts and claims. Office: 3600 Massachusetts Ave NW Washington DC 20007-1449

**HOPPER, WALTER EVERETT,** lawyer; b. Houghton, Mich., Oct. 29, 1915; s. Walter E. and Maude (Crum) H.; m. Jeannette Ross, Aug. 23, 1941 (dec. 1947); 1 dau., Nancy Cameron Hopper Marcovici; m. Diana Kerensky, Sept. 24, 1958; 1 stepdau., Nicole Sudrow Hopper Neilan. A.B., Cornell U., 1937, J.D., 1939; grad., Command and Gen. Staff Sch., Indsl. Coll. Armed Forces. Bar: N.Y. 1939, U.S. Supreme Ct. 1946, D.C. 1959. Practice in Ithaca, 1939-42, N.Y.C., 1946—; mobilization designee, office dep. chief of staff mil. ops. Dept. of Army, 1952-67; chmn., chief exec. officer Fort Amsterdam Corp., 1973-81; dir. Davis Brake Beam Co. Chmn. trustees Loyal Legion Found.; trustee Inst. on Man and Sci., 1969-71, Signal Hill Ednl. Ctr.; bd. dirs. U.S. Flag Found. Lt. col., inf. ETO, col. AUS (ret.). Decorated Army Commendation medal with oak leaf cluster; N.Y. State Conspicious Service Cross with Maltese Cross; Order Ruben Dario Nicaragua; comdr. Order Orange-Nassau, Netherlands; Order St. John of Jerusalem. Mem. Internat. Assn. Protection Indsl. Property (exec. com. Am. group 1958-71), Internat. Fiscal Assn., British Fifth Army Old Comrades Assn., Nat. Fgn. Trade Council (mem. coms.), Internat. C. of C. (rep. internat. conf. revision internat. conv. protection indsl. property 1958, U.S. council 1949-71, mem. coms.), Am. Arbitration Assn. (panelist), U.S. Trademark Assn. (past v.p., dir., chmn. internat. com.), UN Assn. (dir. N.Y. chpt. 1964-66), Holland Soc. (pres. 1966-71), Loyal Legion (comdr.-in-chief 1964-67), Assn. Bar City N.Y., N.Y. State Criminal Bar Assn., Res. Officers Assn. (pres. N.Y. State 1949), Confrerie des Chevaliers du Tastevin, Pilgrims, Soc. War 1812, Founders and Patriots of Am., Mayflower Descs., Soc. Colonial Wars, St. Nicholas Soc. (pres. 1982-84), S.R., Huguenot Soc. Am. (pres. 1972-75), Mil. Order Fgn. Wars, Soc. of Cin., St. Andrews Soc., Explorers Club (N.Y.C.), Univ. Club (N.Y.C.), Met. Club (Washington), Army-Navy Club (Washington). General civil litigation, Criminal, Probate. Home: 715 Park Ave New York NY 10021-5047 *The key to success in human endeavor is determination.*

**HOPPS, RAYMOND, JR.,** lawyer, film producer; b. Balt., July 26, 1949; s. Raymond Hopps Sr. and Ella Louise Dixon. BA cum laude, Howard U., 1971; JD, Loyola U., Chgo., 1974. Bar: Ill. 1975. CEO, art atty. Cmty. Legal Counsel, Chgo., 1972; staff and adminstr. Chgo. Vol. Legal Svcs., 1972-74; assoc. Archie B. Weston Sr. Ltd., Chgo., 1975-77; pvt. practice Chgo., 1977-78, film prodr., 1978; prodr. N.Y. Film Colony, 1979; with svc. work Internat. Econs.; owner, prodr., artist Am. Oriental Internat. Ltd., Balt., 1980—; staff rschr. Task Force for Cmty. Broadcasting, Chgo., 1973-78; atty. cons. Assn. of AudioVisual Prodrs., Chgo., 1978; coord. N.Y. Film Colony, 1979; staff atty. Ebony Talent Assocs., Chgo. Composer: Concerto Impossible, 1987, For Your Eyes Only, 1981, Victory for the Free Planet, 1991; author: (prose) Master E, 1986; composer, author: Free Planet, 1991; writer, film prodr. for screen. Staff artist Eubie Blake Cultural Ctr., Balt., 1990—; assoc. Nat. Football League and Balt. Ravens. With USAF, 1968-91, brig. gen. Res. Mem. NAACP, Internat. Mid. East Assn., Am. Mgmt. Assn., Equal Opportunity Found., Jim Straw Heritage Exch., WFI Corp. Democrat. Avocations: music, dancing, films, walking. Trademark and copyright, Intellectual property, Entertainment. Office: AMI Ltd Motion Pictures PO Box 67585 Baltimore MD 21215-0016 also: 2806 Garrison Blvd Apt 1 Baltimore MD 21216-1846

**HOPSON, EDWIN SHARP,** lawyer; b. Louisville, Apr. 23, 1945; s. Henry Dockins and Martha (Linton) H.; m. Jane Mayo Fitzpatrick, July 20, 1968; children: Edwin Hopson Jr., Martha. BSL, U. Louisville, 1967, JD, 1969; LLM, George Washington U., 1971. Bar: Ky. 1969, Fla. 1969, U.S. Supreme Ct. 1972, U.S. Dist. Ct. (we. dist.) Ky. 1974, U.S. Ct. Appeals (6th cir.) 1977. Atty. Solicitor's Office, U.S. Dept. Labor, Washington, 1969-72; field atty. NLRB, Balt., 1972-74; assoc. Tarrant, Combs, Blackwell & Bullitt, Louisville, 1974-77; ptnr. Tarrant, Combs & Bullitt, Louisville, 1977-80, Wyatt, Tarrant & Combs, Louisville, 1980—. Editor Ky. Bench & Bar, 1989-91; chpt. editor: How Arbitration Works, 1989, 2d edit., 1991; contbr. articles to profl. jours. Bd. dirs. Bellewood Presbyn. Children's Home, Louisville, 1988-96, pres., 1991-93; bd. dirs. Louisville Ballet, 1991—, v.p., 1992-93, pres., 1993-94; bd. dirs. Bellewood Children's Found., 1995—, pres., 1995-96. Fellow Coll. Labor & Employment Lawyers, Inc.; mem. ABA (co-chmn. future directions of arbitration subcom. 1989-94), FBA (chpt. pres. 1991-92), Louisville Bar Assn. (co-chmn. labor and employment law sect. 1982-83), Ky. Bar Assn. (co-chmn. labor and employment law sect. 1987-89, mem. ho. of dels. 1996—). Republican. Presbyterian. Avocations: flying, various sports, reading. Labor. Home: 3003 Lightheart Rd Louisville KY 40222-6138 Office: Wyatt Tarrant & Combs Citizens Plz Louisville KY 40202

**HOPSON, EVERETT GEORGE,** retired lawyer; b. Stillwell, Ill., Sept. 4, 1922; s. Carman Roy and Adella (George) H.; m. Doris May Hutchins, Aug. 15, 1953; children: Christine E., Eugene G. AA, Springfield Jr. Coll., 1942; BS, U. Ill., 1947, JD, 1949; MS in Internat. Affairs, George Washington U., 1967. Bar: Ill. 1949, U.S. Ct. Mil. Appeals 1957, U.S. Supreme Ct. 1957. Dep. collector U.S. Treasury, IRS, Carlinville, Ill., 1949-51; commd. officer USAF, 1951, advanced to col., judge advocate, 1951-71; spl. asst. to asst. sec. def. Dept. Def., Washington, 1971; sr. atty. U.S. Postal Svc., Washington, 1972-73; dep. chief gen. law divsn. USAF, Washington, 1973-75, chief gen. law divsn., 1975-94, ret., 1994. Trustee USAF JAG Sch. Found. Served with U.S. Army, 1943-46. Decorated Legion of Merit; recipient Presdl. Rank of Meritorious Exec., USAF, 1981, 87, 92, Freedoms Found. award, 1961, 62, 66. Mem. ABA, Ill. Bar Assn., Fed. Bar Assn., Judge Advocates Assn., Am. Inns of Ct., Phi Alpha Delta. Democrat. Methodist. Avocations: coin collecting, gardening. Home: 9719 Limoges Dr Fairfax VA 22032-1115 *Helpful advice and good counsel need to make sense and be reasonable to be effective. In my professional career and in life, I have attempted, with some degree of success, to let common sense prevail and reason rule the land.*

**HORACE, DONALD,** lawyer; b. Dermott, Ark., Dec. 31, 1968; s. Robert Lee Jr. and Hester Griffin; m. Karen Samuels, Aug. 30, 1997. BA, Vanderbilt U., 1991; JD, U. Cin., 1994. Bar: Ga. 1994. Staff atty. Atlanta Legal Aid, 1994-97; assoc. Duvall, McChamber & Doverspike, P.C., Decatur, Ga., 1997, Arnall, Golden & Gregory, LLP, Atlanta, 1997—; mem. charter revision com. Avondale Estates, Ga., 1998—. United Methodist. Health. Office: Arnall Golden & Gregory LLP 1201 W Peachtree St Atlanta GA 30002

**HORBACZEWSKI, HENRY ZYGMUNT,** lawyer, publishing executive; b. Bristol, Eng., June 11, 1950; Came to U.S., 1951; s. Henry S. and Zofia (Rozmyslowicz) H.; m. Ann M. Baker, Aug. 19, 1972; children: Stephanie A., Nicholas H. AB, Harvard Coll., 1972, JD, 1975. Bar: N.Y. 1976, Mass. 1989. Assoc. Hale, Russell & Gray, N.Y.C., 1975-76; assoc. Coudert Bros., N.Y.C., 1976-84, ptnr., 1984-86; sr. v.p. and gen. counsel Reed Elsevier Inc., Newton, Mass., 1986—. Mem. ABA, Bar Assn. of City of New York. General corporate, Mergers and acquisitions, Intellectual property. Home: 48 Thackeray Rd Wellesley MA 02481-3414 Office: Reed Elsevier Inc 275 Washington St Newton MA 02458-1646

**HORN, ANDREW WARREN,** lawyer; b. Cin., Apr. 19, 1946; s. George H. and Belle (Collin) H.; m. Melinda Fink; children: Lee Shawn, Ruth Belle. B.B.A. in Acctg., U. Miami, 1968, J.D., 1971. Bar: Fla. 1971, Colo. 1990, U.S. Dist. Ct. (so. dist.) Fla. 1972, U.S. Tax Ct. 1974. Ptnr. Gillman & Horn P.A., Miami, Fla., 1973-74; pvt. practice Miami, 1974—. Active civic coun. Children's Hosp., Miami. Recipient Am. Jurisprudence award Lawyers Coop. Pub. Co., 1970. Mem. ABA, Fla. Bar, Assn. Trial Lawyers Am., Acad. Fla. Trial Lawyers. State civil litigation, Personal injury, Consumer commercial.

**HORN, BRENDA SUE,** lawyer; b. Beech Grove, Ind., Apr. 22, 1949; d. Donald Eugene Horn and Barbara Joyce (Waggoner) Christie. AB with distinction, Ind. U., 1971; MS, Purdue U., 1975; JD summa cum laude, Ind. U., 1981. Bar: Ind. 1981, U.S. Dist. Ct. (so. dist.) Ind. 1981. Assoc. Ice Miller Donadio & Ryan, Indpls., 1981-87, ptnr., 1988—. Assoc. editor Ind. Law Rev., 1980-81. Bd. dirs. Ballet Internationale, 1995—, treas., 1996—; pres. Greenleaf Cmty. Ctr., 1992-93, 95-98, v.p., 1991, sec., 1990; bd. dirs., v.p. Cmty. Alliance for the Far East Side, 1997-99, hon. dir. 1999—; bd. dirs. Big Sisters of Ctrl. Ind., 1995-98, hon. dir., 1998—. Named among Influential Women in Indpls., Ind. Lawyer and Indpls. Bus. Jour., 1998. Mem. ABA, Am. Coll. Bond Counsel (bd. dirs., v.p. 1995-98, pres. 1998—), Ind. Bar Assn., Indpls. Bar Assn. (bd. mgrs. 1992), Ind. Mcpl. Lawyers Assn., Nat. Assn. Bond Lawyers, Phi Beta Kappa. Municipal (including bonds), Health. Office: Ice Miller Donadio & Ryan Box 82001 One American Sq Indianapolis IN 46282

**HORN, CHARLES M.,** lawyer; b. Boston, Sept. 28, 1951; s. Garfield Henry and Alexandra (Matz) H.; m. Jane Charlotte Luxton, May 29, 1976; children: Andrew L., Caroline C. AB magna cum laude, Harvard Coll., 1973; JD, Cornell Law Sch., 1976. Bar: D.C. 1976, U.S. Dist. Ct. D.C. 1977, U.S. Ct. Appeals (D.C. cir.) 1977, U.S. Supreme Ct. 1980. Atty. U.S. Securities and Exchange Commn., Washington, 1976-82, br. chief divsn. enforcement, 1982-83; asst. dir. securities and corp. practices Office Comptroller of Currency, Washington, 1983-86, dir. securities and corp. practices, 1986-89; ptnr. Stroock & Stroock & Lavan, Washington, 1989-92, Mayer, Brown & Platt, Washington, 1992—; mem. faculty Am. Bankers Assn. Nat. Grad. Compliance Sch., 1991-92, 94, Fed. Fin. Instns. Exam. Coun. (programs off-balance-sheet risk, Trust Exams. Sch.); lectr. in field. Edit. adv. bd. Bank Acctg. and Fin., 1993—; contbr. articles to profl. jours. Mem. ABA (banking law com., subcom. securities, com. fed. regulation securities ), D.C. Bar Assn., Harvard Club Washington, Washington Golf and Country Club.

Banking, Securities, Administrative and regulatory. Home: 1918 Massachusetts Ave Mc Lean VA 22101-4907 Office: Mayer Brown & Platt 2000 Pennsylvania Ave NW Washington DC 20006-1812

**HORN, DOUGLAS MICHAEL,** lawyer; b. Lake Success, N.Y., July 2, 1966; s. Sidney and Doris Horn; m. Jenny Eileen Benson, Mar. 9, 1997. BS, U. Fla., 1988; JD, Nova Southeastern U., Davie, Fla., 1991. Bar: Fla. 1991, U.S. Dist. Ct. (so. dist.) Fla. 1992, U.S. Ct. Appeals (11th cir.) 1993. Assoc. atty. Kusnick & Rothstein, P.A., Ft. Lauderdale, Fla., 1991-95; ptnr. Fronstin & Horn, P.A., Ft. Lauderdale, 1995-96; sr. atty. Andrew Hall & Assocs., P.A., Miami, Fla., 1996-97; sole practitioner Boca Raton, Fla., 1997—. Bd. dirs. Am. Heart Assn., Ft. Lauderdale, 1996; mem. Leukemia Soc. Am., 1997-98. Mem. Fla. Bar (chair vol. bar liaison com. 1997-98), Greater Ft. Lauderdale Road Runners Cub (bd. dirs. 1992-96). Avocations: marathon running, football, reading. General civil litigation, Intellectual property, General corporate. Office: 20423 State Road 7 Ste 170 Boca Raton FL 33498-6797

**HORN, GEORGE EDWARD, JR.,** lawyer; b. Woodbury, N.J., July 4, 1961; s. George E. and Virginia B. (Taylor) H.; m. Dixie Horn; children: Ryan, Adam, Frankie, Kenny. AS, Glen Oaks C.C., 1981; BA, U. Notre Dame, 1984, JD, 1987. Bar: Ind. 1987, Mich. 1987, U.S. Dist. Ct. (no. dist.) Ind. 1987, U.S. Dist. Ct. (so. dist.) Ind. 1996, U.S. Dist. Ct. (we. dist.) Mich. 1996, U.S. Dist. Ct. (no. dist.) Tex. Law clk. U.S. Atty.'s Office, South Bend, Ind., 1985-87; spl. asst. U.S. atty. U.S. Atty.'s Office, Indpls., 1994-95; chief asst. prosecutor Cass County Pros. Office, Cassopolis, Mich., 1987-91; dep. prosecutor Marion County Pros. Office, Indpls., 1991-95; assoc. Barnes & Thornburg, South Bend, 1995—; lectr. Nat. Coll. Dist. Attys., Huston, 1993-95; guest lectr. Pros. Atty.'s Assn., Mich., Lansing, 1995, Marion County Law Enforcement Agys., Indpls., 1991-95. Coach Franklin (Ind.) Rocket Football, 1993, Niles (Mich.) YMCA Basketball, 1995—; mem. Cassopolis Athletic Boosters, 1996—. Mem. Ind. Bar Assn., Mich. Bar Assn. Avocations: sports, working with children. Criminal, Personal injury, Product liability. Office: Barnes & Thornburg 100 N Michigan St Ste 600 South Bend IN 46601-1632

**HORN, JOHN HAROLD,** lawyer; b. Eugene, Oreg., Mar. 4, 1927; s. Harold William and Mildred A. (Truesdale) H.; m. Deloris Eileen Davis, Aug. 22, 1948; children: Lorraine, Deborah, Lisa, Darren. BS, U. Oreg., 1949, JD, 1951. Bar: Oreg. 1951, U.S. Dist. Ct. Oreg. 1957. Ptnr. Horn & Slocum, Roseburg, Oreg., 1951-65, Riddlesbarger, Pederson, Young & Horn, Eugene, 1970-74, Young, Horn, Cass & Scott, Eugene, 1974-82; pvt. practice Roseburg, 1965-70; pvt. practice, Eugene, 1982—. Chmn. fund raising Douglas County unit ARC, 1966, county chmn., 1968; exec. bd., legal advisor Eugene Mission, 1979—; pres. bd. dirs. Jubilee Ministries, Eugene, 1980—; v.p., bd. dirs. His Word Broadcasting, 1989-91, pres. bd. dirs., 1991—. Recipient Outstanding Svc. award ARC, 1968. Mem. ABA, Oreg. Bar Assn., Douglas County Bar Assn. (pres. 1960, chmn. grievance com. 1961-62), Lake County Bar Assn., Lions. Republican. Avocations: aviation, golf, skiing. Probate, Real property, General civil litigation. Home: 640 Elwood Ct Eugene OR 97401-2235 Office: 875 Country Club Rd Eugene OR 97401-2255

**HORN, JOSEPH PETER,** lawyer, mediator; b. Houston, Sept. 26, 1960; s. Jack Herbert and Patricia Martha (Hyder) H.; m. Anna Sergeivna Shuklina, June 5, 1993. BA, U. Tex., 1983, JD, 1986; LLM, London Sch. Econs./Polit. Sci., 1987. Bar: D.C. Report examiner Office of Clk., U.S. Ho. of Reps., Washington, 1989-91; legal counsel and mediator Office Fair Employment, U.S. Ho. of Reps., Washington, 1991-96; 1st ADA coord. for House Chief Adminstrv. Office, U.S. Ho. of Reps., Washington, 1997-99, mgr. pilot workplace conflict resolution program, 1999—; mediator D.C. Superior Ct. Multi-door, Washington, 1992—, D.C. Fed. Dist. Ct., 1998—, D.C. Pilot Employee Mediation Program; spkr. in field. Trustee Hamrah Charitable Trust, Houston, 1993—; mem. nat. scholarship com. Am. Friends of the London Sch. Econs. and Polit. Sci. Mem. ABA (dispute resolution sect., labor and employment law sect., internat. law and practice sect.), Soc. for Profls. in Dispute Resolution, Washington Area Lawyers for the Arts. Methodist. Avocations: reading, travel, learning about other cultures, fencing. Home: PO Box 1769 Washington DC 20013-1769 Office: US Ho of Reps Chief Adminstrv Office O Neill House Ofc Bldg 722 Washington DC 20515-0001

**HORN, MARIAN BLANK,** federal judge; b. N.Y.C., June 24, 1943; d. Werner P. and Mady R. Blank; m. Robert Jack Horn; children: Juli Marie, Carrie Charlotte, Rebecca Blank. AB, Barnard Coll., 1962; student, Cornell U., Columbia U., 1965, NYU, 1965-66; JD, Fordham U., 1969. Bar: N.Y. 1970, D.C. 1973, U.S. Supreme Ct. 1973. Asst. dist. atty. Bronx County, N.Y., 1969-72; assoc. Arent, Fox, Kintner, Plotkin & Kahn, 1972-73; project mgr. Am. U. Law Sch. study on alts. to conventional criminal adjudication U.S. Dept. Justice, 1973-75; litigation atty. Fed. Energy Adminstrn., 1975-76; sr. atty. office gen. counsel strategic petroleum res. br. Dept. Energy, 1976-79, dep. asst. gen. counsel for procurement and fin. incentives, 1979-81; dep. assoc. solicitor div. surface mining Dept. Interior, 1981-83, assoc. solicitor div. gen. law, 1983-85, prin. dep. solicitor, acting solicitor, 1985; judge U.S. Ct. of Federal Claims, 1986—; adj. prof. law Washington Coll. Law, Am. U., 1973-76, George Washington U. Sch. Law, 1992—. Office: US Ct Fed Claims 717 Madison Pl NW Washington DC 20005-1011

**HORN, MARK,** lawyer; b. Bronx; s. Harry and Sala H.; m. Yael T. Frydman, July 30, 1996; 1 child, Chava. BA, Fla. Internat. U., 1989; JD, Touro Coll., 1990. Bar: Fla. 1990, N.Y. 1991, D.C. 1991, U.S. Dist. Ct. (so. dist.) Fla. 1991, U.S.Ct. Appeals (11th cir.) 1992, U.S. Supreme Ct. 1993. Dir. gen. counsel ALEPH Inst., Surfside, Fla., 1991-96. Contbr. articles to profl. jours. Mem. Nat. Assn. Criminal Def. Lawyers, Dade County Bar Assn., Jewish Lawyers Network (vice-chmn. 1998). Jewish. Criminal, Constitutional, Administrative and regulatory. Office: 18800 NW 2nd Ave Ste 211 Miami FL 33169-4044

**HORN, RICHARD LESLIE,** lawyer; b. Rochester, N.Y., Sept. 30, 1940; s. Norman and Alice Horn; m. Sharon Lee Shapiro, June 2, 1962 (div. Mar. 1977); children: Bevin G., Michael A.; m. Robin Lee Smith, Apr. 24, 1977; 1 child, Leslie. BA magna cum laude, U. Miami, 1962; JD with high honors, U. Fla., 1965. Bar: Fla. 1965, Ill. 1967. With Rutledge & Milledge, Miami, Fla., 1965-67, Milledge & Horn, Miami, 1967-76, Karon, Savikas & Horn, Chgo., 1976-88, Keck, Mahin & Cate, Chgo., 1988-94, Wilson & McIlvaine, Chgo., 1994-98, Quarles & Brady, LLC, Chgo., 1999—; dir. Bascomb Meml. Broadcasting Co., Miami, 1974-76. Alt. conv. del. Dems., Chgo., 1968. Mem. ABA, Am. Intellectual Property Law Assn., Fla. Bar Assn., Miami-Dade County Bar Assn. Jewish. Avocations: reading, music, sports. Intellectual property, Antitrust, Federal civil litigation. Office: Quarles & Brady LLC 500 W Madison St Ste 3700 Chicago IL 60661-2592

**HORN, ROBERT ALLEN,** lawyer; b. St. Joseph, Mo., Feb. 10, 1954; s. James Harold Horn and Emma L. Bailey; m. Tammy L. Womack, July 19, 1999; children: Zachary A., Scott E., Rachel E., James K. BA, U. Mo., 1976, JD, 1979. Bar: Mo., U.S. Dist. Ct. (we. dist.) Md. 1979, U.S. Dist. Ct. Kans. 1998. Assoc. Blackwell Sanders, Kansas City, Mo., 1979-84; ptnr. Blackwell Sanders, Kansas City, 1984-99, Horn Aylward & Gardy, Kansas City, 1999—. Mem. Kans. City Bar Assn., Trucking Industry Def. Assn. (bd. dirs.). General civil litigation, Product liability, Insurance. Home: 8029 Manor Rd Leawood KS 66206-1220 Office: Horn Aylward & Bardy 2600 Grand Blvd Ste 500 Kansas City MO 64108-4623

**HORN, ROBERT F.,** lawyer; b. Phila., Jan. 9, 1959; s. Albert B. and Helen K. (Earley) H. BS in Edn., West Chester (Pa.) U., 1982; JD, Widener U., 1996. Bar: Pa., N.J.; assoc. in claims Chartered Property Casualty Underwriters. Realtor Carr Real Estate Co., Drexel Hill, Pa., 1986-89; classroom tchr. Gloucester Twp. Sch. Dist., Blackwood, N.J., 1982-88; sr. claim rep. Allstate Claim Office, Exton, Pa., 1988-90, claim support mgr., 1990-91; paralegal Allstate Staff Counsel, Phila., 1991-93, legal unit mgr., 1994-96, trial atty., 1996—; pres. Wynnwood Condominium Assn., Wilmington, Del., 1998. Mem. Pa. Bar Assn., N.J. Bar Assn., Phila. Bar Assn., Brehon Law Soc., Men of Malvern. Democrat. Insurance, Personal injury. Office: Allstate Staff Counsel Two Logan Sq Ste 300 Philadelphia PA 19103

**HORNAK, MARK RAYMOND,** lawyer; b. Homestead, Pa., Mar. 31, 1956; s. Raymond John and Margaret W. (Somiak) H.; m. Elizabeth Ann Meyer, Jan. 30, 1982; children: Samuel A., Rachel A., Rebecca A., Mary R. BA (cum laude), U. Pitts., 1978, JD (summa cum laude), 1981. Bar: Pa. 1981, W.Va. 1982, U.S. Dist. Ct. (we. dist.) Pa. 1981, U.S. Dist. Ct. (so. dist.) W.Va. 1983, U.S. Dist. Ct. (no. dist.) W.Va. 1991, U.S. Ct. Appeals (3rd and 4th cirs.) 1982, U.S. Supreme Ct. 1996. Law clk. to James M. Sprouse U.S. Ct. Appeals (4th cir.), Charleston, W.Va., 1981-82; assoc. Buchanan Ingersoll, P.C., Pitts., 1982-88, shareholder, 1989—; adj. prof. law U. Pitts., 1988-92; solicitor, gen. counsel Pub. Auditorium Authority of Pitts., Allegheny County, 1994—; editor-in-chief U. Pitts. Law Rev., 1981; mem. Leadership Pitts., 1989. Pres. Bd. Sch. Dirs., Steel Valley Sch. Dist., 1987-89, mem. Allegheny Intermediate Unit, 1987-90; mem. Mon-Valley Commn., Pitts., 1988-90; chief Munhall Vol. Fire Co. #4, 1982. Univ. scholar U. Pitts., 1981, James Fulton Congl. intern, 1977. Mem. ABA, Allegheny County Bar Assn., Am. Law Inst., Am. Bar Found., Acad. of Trial Lawyers, Order of Coif. Labor, Libel, General civil litigation. Home: 2368 Mill Grove Rd Uppr Saint Clair PA 15241-2731 Office: Buchanan Ingersoll PC 301 Grant St Fl 20 Pittsburgh PA 15219-1410

**HORNBECK, DAVID ARTHUR,** lawyer; b. Reno, Nev., May 9, 1943; s. William Hornbeck and Sarah (Dixon) Ercolini. BS in Physics and Math., U. Nev., Reno, 1968; JD, U. of Pacific, Sacramento, 1979. Bar: Nev. 1979, Calif. 1980, U.S. Dist. Ct. Nev. 1980, U. S. Ct. Appeals (9th cir.) 1987. Law clk. 2d Jud. Dist. Ct. Nev., Reno, 1979-80; dep. pub. defender Washoe County Pub. Defender, Reno, 1980-84; pvt. practice Reno, 1984—; dep. atty. gen. Environ. Protection divsn. State of Nev., 1993-95; bd. dirs. Washoe Legal Svcs., Reno, 1985-88. Bd. dirs. No. Nev. Mental Health Adv. Bd., Reno, 1988-91; founding bd. dirs. Friends of Pyramid Lake, Reno, 1982—; bd. dirs., past treas., past pres. Reno Chamber Orch., Inc., 1987-95. Lt. USNR, 1968-73. Mem. ABA, Assn. Trial Lawyers Am., Nat. Assn. Criminal Def. Lawyers, Nev. Trial Lawyers Assn., Washoe County Bar Assn. Avocations: skiing, soaring, tennis, racquetball, hiking, camping, photography. Fax: 775-322-0223. E-mail: davidühornbeck@email.msn.com. General civil litigation, Environmental, Family and matrimonial. Office: 1675 Lakeside Dr Reno NV 89509-3408

**HORNBERGER, LEE,** lawyer; b. Elizabethtown, Pa., Oct. 31, 1946; s. Lee and Peggy (Mann) H. AB, U. Mich., 1966, JD cum laude, 1968; LLM in Labor Law, Wayne State U., 1982. Bar: Mich. 1969, Ohio 1982, U.S. Dist. Ct. (no. dist.) Ohio 1971, U.S. Dist. Ct. (so. dist.) Ohio 1982, U.S. Dist. Ct. (we. and ea. dists.) Mich. 1973, U.S. Dist. Ct. (ea. dist.) Ky., U.S. Ct. Mil. Appeals 1970, U.S. Ct. Appeals (6th cir.) 1972, U.S. Supreme Ct. 1998. Atty. Office of Solicitor, U.S. Dept. Labor, Washington, 1971-75; adj. prof. U. Cin., 1985-87; adj. prof. law U. Cin., 1985-87, Chase Coll., 1992—; presenter Employment Lawyers Assn., Lake Tahoe, 1990, Cin., 1991, Cin. Bar Assn., 1990, 91, 92, 93, 95, 97, Ohio State Bar Assn., Cin., 1991, Nat. Employment Lawyers Assn., Cape Code, 1991, Advanced Ednl. Seminars, Cin., 1991, Ohio Employment Lawyers Assn., Columbus, 1991, Ohio Edn. Assn., Cin., 1992, Nat. Edn. Network, Cin., 1993, 94, Ky. Employment Lawyers Assn., 1996, U. Ky., 1996, among others. Contbr. articles to profl. jours. Dem. candidate spl. election, 2d dist. Ohio for U.S. Congress. Capt. U.S. Army, 1969-71, Vietnam. Mem. ABA (labor and employment law sect.), Ohio State Bar Assn., Cin. Bar Assn. (chair, civil rights com. 1990-92), Ohio Employment Lawyers Assn. (exec. bd. 1990—), Cin. Employment Lawyers Assn. (CLE chair), Nat. Employment Lawyers Assn. (chmn. Cin. chpt. 1987-90). Avocations: camping, sailing, employment law seminars. Civil rights, Education and schools, Labor. Office: 910 Mercantile Libr Bldg 414 Walnut St Cincinnati OH 45202-3908

**HORNBLASS, JEROME,** lawyer, mediator, arbitrator, former judge; b. N.Y.C., June 20, 1941; s. Maurice and Betty (Krieger) H.; m. Ann Herman; children: Jonathan, Elliott, Jessica. BA, Yeshiva U., 1962; JD, Bklyn. Law Sch., 1965. Bar: N.Y. 1965. Commr. N.Y.C. Addiction Svcs. Agy., 1974-77; judge N.Y.C. Criminal Ct., 1977-81; justice N.Y. State Supreme Ct., 1982-97; atty., mediator, arbitrator U.S. Post Office, Bankruptcy Ct. & Family Dispute, N.Y.C., 1997—; assoc. prof. law and sociology CCNY; lectr. New Sch. for Social Rsch., throughout U.S. Past pres. Civic Ctr. synagogue, N.Y.C., 1979; pres. Yeshiva Etz Chaim Found., Bklyn., 1980—; bd. dirs. Union Orthodox Jewish Congregations. Mem. ABA, Internat. Assn. Jewish Lawyers and Jurists (v.p. 1982-86, pres. Am. sect. 1986—). Criminal.

**HORNBY, DAVID BROCK,** federal judge; b. Brandon, Manitoba, Can., Apr. 21, 1944; s. William Ralph Hornby and Retha Patricia (Fox) Sword; m. Helaine Cora Mandel, Oct. 9, 1946; children: Kirstin, Zachary. BA, U. Western Ont., 1965; JD, Harvard U., 1969. Bar: Va. 1973, Maine 1974, U.S. Supreme Ct. 1980. Law clk. U.S. Ct. Appeals, New Orleans, 1969-70; assoc. prof. U. Va. Sch. Law, Charlottesville, 1970-74; ptnr. Perkins, Thompson, Hinckley & Keddy, Portland, Maine, 1974-82; U.S. magistrate Dist. Maine, Portland, 1982-88; assoc. justice Maine Supreme Jud. Ct., Portland, 1988-90; judge U.S. Dist. Ct. Maine, 1990—; chief judge, 1996—; mem. Fed. Jud. Ctr.'s Com. on Dist. Judge Edn., 1994-98, chair 1995-98; com. on ct. adminstrn. and case mgmt. Jud. Conf. of the U.S., 1990—, chair 1997—. Contbr. articles to profl. jours.; editor, officer Harvard Law Rev., 1967-69. Fellow Am. Bar Found.; mem. ABA, Am. Law Inst., Maine State Bar Assn., Maine Bar Found. (bd. trustees 1990-94), Cumberland County Bar Assn. Office: US Dist Ct Edward T Gignoux Courthouse 156 Federal St Portland ME 04101-4152

**HORNE, MICHAEL STEWART,** lawyer; b. Mpls., May 10, 1938; s. Owen Edward and Adeline (DiGeorgio) H.; m. Martha Brean, Sept. 11, 1965; children: Jennifer, Katherine, Sarah, Owen. BA, U. Minn., 1959; LLB, Harvard U., 1962. Bar: D.C. 1963, U.S. Ct. Appeals (D.C. cir.) 1964, U.S. Supreme Ct. 1968, U.S. Ct. Appeals (6th cir.), 1966, U.S. Ct. Appeals (9th cir.) 1978, U.S. Ct. Appeals (4th cir.) 1979, U.S. Ct. Appeals (5th cir.), 1979, U.S. Ct. Appeals (2d cir.) 1980, U.S. Ct. Appeals (11th cir.) 1983, U.S. Ct. Appeals (8th cir.) 1984, U.S. Ct. Appeals (10th cir.), 1997. Assoc. Covington & Burling, Washington, 1964-71, ptnr., 1971—. Mem. D.C. Bar Assn., ABA, FCC Bar Assn., Am. Judicature Soc. Democrat. Administrative and regulatory, Labor, Libel. Home: 9008 Levelle Dr Bethesda MD 20815-5608 Office: Covington & Burling 1201 Pennsylvania Ave NW PO Box 7566 Washington DC 20044-7566

**HORNE, THOMAS CHARLES,** lawyer; b. Montreal, Que., Can., Mar. 28, 1945; s. George Marcus and Ludwika (Tom) H.; m. Martha Louise Presbry, June 25, 1972; children: Susan Christine, Mary Alice, David Charles, Mark Walter. BA magna cum laude, Harvard U., 1967, JD with honors, 1970. Bar: Mass. 1970, Ariz. 1972, U.S. Supreme Ct. 1974. Assoc. Donovan, Leisure, Newton & Irvine, N.Y.C.; sr. ptnr. Lewis & Roca, Phoenix; mng. ptnr. Horne, Bistrow & Dulberg P.C., Phoenix. Author: Arizona Construction Law, 1978. Chmn. Ariz. Air Pollution Control Hearing Bd., Phoenix, 1976-78; mem. Paradise Valley (Ariz.) Sch. Bd., 1978—, pres., 1981-83, 85-88, 90-91, 94; mem. Ariz. Ho. of Reps., 1997—. Mem. Ariz. Bar Assn. (former chmn. constrn. law com. litigation sect.). Republican. Jewish. Office: Horne Bistrow & Dulberg 40 N Central Ave Ste 2800 Phoenix AZ 85004-4497

**HORNER, CLIFFORD R.,** lawyer; b. June 21, 1963. BS in Bus., Calif. Poly., 1985; JD, U. Calif., San Francisco, 1991. Atty. Zankel & McGrane, San Francisco, 1991-95, Morgan, Miller & Blair, Walnut Creek, Calif., 1995—. Contbg. author: (book) California Eviction Defense Manual, 1998; cons.: (book) California Landlord-Tenant Practice, 1998; guest editor: Contra Costa Lawyer, 1998. Co-chair Contra Costa (Calif.) Legis. Coun., 1998—. Mem. Hastings Alumni Assn. (C.C. chpt. pres. 1998—), Walnut Creek C. of C. (dir. 1998—, chair civic affairs com. 1997—). General civil litigation, Landlord-tenant, Real property. Office: Morgan Miller & Blair 1676 N California Blvd Ste 200 Walnut Creek CA 94596-4137

**HORNER, RUSSELL GRANT, JR.,** energy and chemical company executive. BA, U. Okla., 1961, LLB, 1963. Bar: Okla. 1963. Ptnr. Kerr-Davis, 1963-69; div. counsel Kerr-McGee Corp., Oklahoma City, 1969-75, sr. v.p., gen. counsel, corp. sec., 1997—; v.p. land Transworld Drilling Co., 1975-82, exec. v.p., 1982-86, v.p. gen. counsel, 1986-87. Office: Kerr McGee Corp PO Box 25861 Oklahoma City OK 73125-0861

**HORNSCHEMEIER, PATRICK,** lawyer; b. Hamilton County, Ohio, June 20, 1945; m. Margaret A. Clark. AB cum laude, Athenaeum of Ohio, 1967, MA, 1968; student Xavier U., summers, 1965-68; Grad. Sch. Theology postgrad. Mt. St. Mary's Sem. 1968-71; JD, U. Cin., 1977. Bar: Ohio, U.S. Dist. Ct. (so. dist.) Ohio 1977. Exec. dir. Housing Opportunities Made Equal, Cin., 1971-74; staff atty. Legal Aid Soc. Cin., 1977-81; asst. pros. atty. Clermont County, Ohio, 1981-84; ptnr. Clark and Hornschemeier, Georgetown, Ohio. Family and matrimonial, Probate, Real property. Address: 104 1/2 S Main St Georgetown OH 45121-1221

**HORNTHAL, LOUIS PHILIP, JR.,** lawyer; b. Tarboro, N.C., Oct. 16, 1936; s. Louis Phillip and Mildred (Lane) H.; m. Harriett Phillips Lang, Aug. 17, 1963; children: Louis Phillip III, William Lang. AB in History, U. N.C., 1958, LLB, 1963. Bar: N.C. 1963, U.S. Supreme Ct. 1979. Law clk. Justice W.B. Rodman, Jr., N.C. Supreme Ct., Raleigh, 1963-64; staff atty. N.C. Atty. Gen., Raleigh, 1964-65; assoc. LeRoy, Wells & Shaw, Elizabeth City, N.C., 1965-66; ptnr. Hornthal, Riley, Ellis & Maland and predecessor cos., Elizabeth City, 1966—; bd. dirs. N.C. Lawyers Mutual Ins. Corp., Raleigh, 1988—; mem. N.C. State Bar Disciplinary Hearing Commn., Raleigh, 1985-92. Vestry, sr. warden Christ Episcopal Ch., Elizabeth City, 1966—; active in past various charitable orgns.; bd. visitors U. N.C., Chapel Hill, 1994—. Fellow Am. Coll. Trial Lawyers; mem. N.C. Bar Assn. (pres. 1996-97, bd. govs. 1986-89), N.C. Assn. Def. Attys. (pres.), Internat. Assn. Ins. Counsel, Assn. Ins. Attys., Am. Bd. Trial Attys. (advocate), U. N.C. Chapel Hill Law Alumni Assn. (pres. 1991-92). Democrat. Episcopalian. Avocations: tennis, reading, travel, sports spectator. Alternative dispute resolution, General civil litigation, Education and schools.

**HOROWITZ, DONALD,** lawyer; b. N.Y.C., Nov. 18, 1936; s. Louis and Ethel (Kaplan) H.; m. Rosalind Jean Odrezin Horowitz, Dec. 17, 1967; children: Louis A., Jill, Gary N. BA, Rutgers U., 1958; LLB, Columbia U., 1961. Bar: N.J. 1962, N.Y. 1983, U.S. Dist. Ct. N.J. 1962, U.S. Dist. Ct. (so. dist.) N.Y. 1986, U.S. Dist. Ct. (ea. dist.) N.Y., 1986, U.S. Ct. Appeals (3rd cir.) 1965, U.S. Tax Ct. 1972, U.S. Supreme Ct. 1966; cert. civil & criminal trial atty. Supreme Ct. N.J. 1983. Asst. U.S. Atty.'s Office, Newark, 1963-66, asst.-chief criminal divsn., 1966-68, first asst., 1968-69, U.S. atty. dist. of N.J., 1969; spl. dep. atty. gen. State of N.J., 1969-70; ptnr. Cummins, Dunn, Horowitz & Pashman, Hackensack, N.J., 1969-82; sole practice Hackensack, N.J., 1982-85, 89—; ptnr. Horowitz & Jacobs, Hackensack, N.J., 1985-89; mem. Criminal Justice Adv. Com. Bergen C.C., Paramus, N.J., 1992—. Dem. County Committeeman, Ridgewood, N.J., 1993—. Staff Sgt. U.S. Army, 1962-68. Mem. ABA, Fed. Bar Assn. (pres. N.J. chpt. 1977-78, 79-80), Nat. Assn. Criminal Def. Lawyers, Assn. Criminal Def. Lawyers of N.J. Jewish. Criminal, General civil litigation. Home: 563 Eastbrook Rd Ridgewood NJ 07450-2114 Office: 24 Bergen St Hackensack NJ 07601-5461

**HOROWITZ, EDWARD JAY,** lawyer; b. Milw., Feb. 13, 1942; s. Aaron and Sue Horowitz; m. Marcia Gold, Apr. 29,1990; children: Amy, Aaron. BA, UCLA, 1963; JD, Harvard U., 1966. Dep. atty. gen. Calif. Dept. Justice, L.A., 1960-69; ptnr. Goldhammer & Horowitz, L.A., 1969-72; sr. atty. Calif. Ct. Appeals, L.A., 1972-76; ptnr. Horvitz, Greines & Horowitz, Encino, Calif., 1976-78; pvt. practice L.A., 1978—. Author: (book) Appellate Practice Handbook, 1982. Fellow Am. Acad. Appellate Lawyers; mem. Calif. Acad. Appellate Lawyers (pres. 1985). Avocations: swimming, backpacking, skiing. Appellate. Office: 11661 San Vicente Blvd Ste 1015 Los Angeles CA 90049-5118

**HOROWITZ, ROBERT M.,** lawyer; b. N.Y.C., Feb. 14, 1963; s. Harold M. and Charlotte R. (Rosenblatt) H. BA, Coll. of William and Mary, 1985; JD, U. Colo., 1988. Bar: Colo. 1988, U.S. Dist. Ct. Colo. 1988, U.S. Ct. Appeals (10th cir.). Instr. People's Law Sch., 1991-93, Nat. Inst. Trial Advocacy, 1993; shareholder Pearson, Milligan & Horowitz, P.C., Denver, 1991—; mem. faculty 3rd Ann. Rocky Mountain Child Advocacy Tng. Inst., Million Dollar Advs. Forum. Mem. ABA (litigation sect.), Denver Bar Assn., Colo. Bar Assn. (litigation sect.), Colo. Trial Lawyers Assn. Avocations: backpacking, rock climbing, music. General civil litigation, Contracts commercial, Entertainment. Office: Pearson Milligan & Horowitz PC 1999 Broadway Ste 2300 Denver CO 80202-5750

**HORRIGAN, JOSEPH STEWART,** lawyer; b. Houston, Nov. 22, 1938; s. Joseph Raymond and Ruth (Mize) H.; (div. Nov. 1986); children: Elizabeth, Katherine, Erin; m. Katherine K. Horrigan, Aug. 20, 1988. BA, Duke U., 1961; LLB, U. Tex., 1964. Bar: Tex. 1964, U.S. Dist. Ct. (we. and so. dists.) Tex., 1966, U.S. Ct. Appeals (5th cir.), 1981, U.S. Supreme Ct. 1995; cert. in estate planning and probate law Tex. Bd. Legal Specialization. Law clk. U.S. Dist. Ct., 1964-65, U.S. Ct. Appeals (5th cir.), 1965-66; assoc. Bryan, Suhr, Bering, & Bailey, Houston, 1966-71; ptnr. Dyche & Wright, Houston, 1973-81, Armogida & Coats, Houston, 1981-84, Coats, Yale, Holm, Horrigan & Lee, Houston, 1984-85, Horrigan & Goehrs, Houston, 1986—. Fellow Am. Coll. Trust and Estate Counsel, Tex. Bar Found., Houston Bar Assn. (charter sustaining); mem. ABA, State Bar Tex., Houston Bus. and Estate Planning Coun. Club: Houston Center. Probate, State civil litigation. Home: 2310 Mimosa Dr Houston TX 77019-6024 Office: 1000 Two Houston Ctr Houston TX 77010

**HORSLEY, JACK EVERETT,** lawyer, author; b. Sioux City, Iowa, Dec. 12, 1915; s. Charles E. and Edith V. (Timms) H.; m. Sallie Kelley, June 12, 1939 (dec.); children: Pamela, Charles Edward; m. Bertha J. Newland, Feb. 24, 1950 (dec.); m. Mary Jane Moran, Jan. 20, 1973; 1 child, Sharon. AB, U. Ill., 1937, JD, 1939. Bar: Ill. 1939. Ptnr. Craig & Craig, Mattoon, Ill., 1939—, sr. atty.-of counsel, 1983—; vice-chmn. bd. dirs. Ctrl. Nat. Bank, 1976-91, chmn. trustee com., mem. exec. com., 1986-91, dir. emeritus; mem. Harlan Moore Heart Rsch. Found., 1968—, asst. treas., 1996—; mem. lawyers adv. coun. U. Ill. Law Forum, 1960-63; lectr. Practicing Law Inst., N.Y.C., 1967-73, U. Ill., Champaign, 1974, Ct. Practice Inst., Chgo., 1974—, Coll. Law Inst. Continuing Legal Edn. U. Mich., 1967, Bankers' Seminar, 1992; vis. lectr. Orange County (Fla.) Med. Soc., 1985, San Diego Med. Soc., 1970, U. S.C., 1976, Duquesne Coll., 1970, U. Ill. Law Forum, 1972, alumni adv. com., 1991—; vis lectr. trial practice NYU Coll. Law, 1972; faculty banker seminar Wis. Med. Assn., Lake Geneva, 1997; lectr. med./legal seminars on tour Chgo., Cleve., Pa., Orlando, 1995; chmn. rev. bd. Ill. Supreme Ct. Disciplinary Commn., 1973-76, adv. cons., 1976—; lectr. Cleve. Hosp., Shelby, N.C., 1976; legal cons. Cenbank Trust Co., 1992-95; vis. prof. trial practice Fordham Law Sch., N.Y.C., 1998. Narrator Poetry Interludes, Sta. WLBH-FM, 1977-91; author: Trial Lawyer's Manual, 1967, Voir Dire Examinations and Opening Statements, 1968, Current Development in Products Liability Law, 1969, Illinois Civil Practice and Procedure, 1970, The Medical Expert Witness, 1973, Testifying in Court, 1973, 5th edit., 1997, supplement 4th edit., 1993, The Doctor and the Law, 1975, The Doctor and Family Law, 1975, The Doctor and Business Law, 1976, The Doctor and Medical Law, 1977, Anatomy of a Medical Malpractice Case, 1984, 3rd edit., 1993, History of Craig & Craig, Attorneys, 1968-89, 1990, supplement, 1993, 2nd edit., 1994, Municipals: G.O. of Revenue, 1992, World War II, D-Day, 1st edit., 1994, 2nd edit., 1998, Trial Techniques, 1995, Legal Liability Exposure of Trust Co. Officers, 1996, On Trust Dept. Guide-lines and Risks, 1996, On Federal Evidence and Examination, 1995, 96, 97, Memories of World War II In the European Theater, Purple Heart, 1997, History of the Bar in East Central Illinois, 1997, Remembrances: An Autobiography, 1998; co-author: RN Legally Speaking, 1998, Matthew Bender Forensic Sciences, 1999; editor Med. Econs., 1969—, Fifty Eight Years as Attorney, 1997, 2nd edit., 1998; legal cons. Mast-Head, 1972; contbr. A.L.L. Life, Stafford, Va., 1988—, Fed. Evidence Rules, 1996, Cross-Exam. Techniques and Potential Traps, 1996, Forensic Scis. on Texts and Treatises, 1981, 2d edit. 1999, Christianity: The Origin of Man Creationism vs. Darwinism, 1999; cons., reviewer Civil Practice State and Fed. Cts., 1998-99; contbr., cons. editor Eagle Forum; contbr. articles to profl. jours. Alt. del. to Rep. Platform Com., 1992; active Senatorial Reelection Com., 1993; mem. exec. com. Ill. Rep. Election Campaign, 1997; founding mem. U.S. Air Mus., Am. Air Mus.; pres. bd. edn. sch. dist. 100, 1946-48; bd. dirs. Harlan Moore Heart Rsch. Found., 1968-91, hon. dir., 1991—; vol. reader in rec. texts Am. Assn. for Blind, 1970-72; chmn. exec. com. U. Ill. Law Forum, 1990-91; pres. Res. Officers Assn. East Cen. Ill., 1988-89; founder Bertha Newland Horsley award St. John's Coll. Nursing, Springfield, Mary Jane Horsley award trophy Mattoon (Ill.) H.S.; mem. exec. com. Ill. Rep. Election Campaign, 1997. Col. U.S. Army, 1942-46, ETO, USA JAGD (hon., ret., promoted hon. full col., 1997). Recipient Disting. Svc. award U. Ill., 1995. Fellow Am. Coll. Trial Lawyers (co-chair membership commn. 1998); mem. ABA, Ill. Bar Assn. (exec. coun. ins. law 1961-63, com. chmn. banking law 1972, lectr. law course for attys. 1962, 64-65, sr. counsellor 1989—, Disting. Svc. award 1982-83), Assn. of Bar of City of N.Y. (non-resident), Coles-Cumberland Bar Assn. (v.p. 1968-69, pres. 1969-70, chmn. com. jud. inquiry 1976-80, chair meml. com. 1989-99, mem. exec. com. 1998, sr. counsellor 1989, co-author Forensic Scis. Jour. 1991, 2d edit. 1999), Am. Arbitration Assn. (nat. panel arbitrators, counsel advisor hearing officers in Ill. 1996-97), U. Ill. Law Alumni Assn. (life mem., pres. 1966-67, Alumni of Month Sept. 1974, exec. com. 1990-91), Ill. Appellate Lawyers Assn., Soc. Legal Scribes, Ill. Def. Counsel Assn. (pres. 1967-88), Soc. Trial Lawyers (chmn. profl. activities 1960-61, bd. dirs. 1966-67), U.S. Supreme Ct. Hist. Soc. (co-chmn.), Adelphic Debating Soc., Assn. Ins. Attys., Internat. Assn. Ins. Counsel, Am. Judicature Soc., Res. Officers Assn. (pres. 1997-98, chair exec. com., pres. emeritus 1999), U. Ill. Alumni Assn. (exec. com. 1990-91), Soc. Legal Scribes, Masons (Sr. Master award 1992), Delta Phi (exec. com. alumni assn. 1960-61, 67-68), Sigma Delta Kappa. Lutheran. Health, State civil litigation, Personal injury. Home: 913 N 31st St Mattoon IL 61938-2271 Office: Craig & Craig 1807 Broadway PO Box 689 Mattoon IL 61938-0689 also: 227 1/2 S 9th St PO Box 1545 Mount Vernon IL 62864-0030 *Time is a controlling asset. Using it effectively and discharging duties promptly are essential to leaving a creditable legacy and producing accomplishments.*

**HORSLEY, WALLER HOLLADAY,** lawyer; b. Richmond, Va., July 2, 1931; s. John Shelton Jr. and Lilian (Holladay) H.; m. Margaret Stuart Cooke, Dec. 3, 1955; children: Margaret Terrell, Stuart W., John Garrett. BA with distinction, U. Va., 1953, LLB, 1959. Bar: Va. 1959, U.S. Dist. Ct. (ea. dist.) Va. 1959, U.S. Tax Ct. 1959, U.S. Ct. Appeals (4th cir.) 1959, U.S. Supreme Ct. 1969. Ptnr. Hunton & Williams, Richmond, 1965-92, Horsley & Horsley, Richmond, 1992—; lectr. taxation U. Va. Law Sch., 1961-65, 69. Mem. editorial bd. Taxation for Lawyers, 1975-86, Probate Lawyer, 1976-87, Probate Notes, 1976-87, editor, 1986-87; bd. advisors Va. Tax Rev., 1981—; contbr. articles to legal jours. Mem. adv. coun. Sch. Bus., Va. Commonwealth U., 1983-91; sr. warden St. Stephen's Episcopal Ch., 1977-79; gen. conv. dep. Diocese of Va., 1979, 85; pres. Richmond Tennis Patrons Assn., 1969, Va. Silver Star Found., 1985-86; mem. bd. visitors U. Va., 1988-92. With USN, 1953-56; to lt. comdr. USNR, 1956-62. Recipient Algernon Sydney Sullivan award, 1953; named Outstanding Young Man of Yr., Richmond Jr. C. of C., 1965. Fellow Am. Bar Found., Va. Bar Found.; mem. ABA, Va. State Bar (pres. 1982-83), Va. Bar Assn., Am. Coll. Trust and Estate Counsel (pres. 1990), Country Club of Va., Bull and Bear Club, Westwood Club, Omicron Delta Kappa, Phi Beta Kappa, Order of Coif. Democrat. Episcopalian. Estate planning, Probate, Estate taxation. Office: Horsley & Horsley 5020 Monument Ave Fl 2 Richmond VA 23230-3620

**HORTON, LAURA M.,** lawyer; b. Miami, Fla., May 7, 1965; d. Charles Oxford Jr. and Marabel (Hawk) Morgan; m. Mallory McCall Horton, Aug. 5, 1989. BA, Wheaton Coll., 1987; JD, U. Fla., 1990. Bar: Fla. 1990. Ptnr. Charles O. Morgan, Jr. P.A., Miami, Fla., 1990—; corp. sec. Don Shula Found., Inc., Miami, 1991—. Mem. alumni bd. Miami Country Day Sch., 1990-98. Mem. Christian Legal Soc. (bd. dirs. 1995-98). Office: Charles O Morgan Jr PA 1300 NW 167th St Miami FL 33169-5738

**HORTON, ODELL,** federal judge; b. Bolivar, Tenn., May 13, 1929; s. Odell and Rosa H.; m. Evie L. Randolph, Sept. 13, 1953; children: Odell, Christopher. AB, Morehouse Coll., 1951; cert., U.S. Navy Sch. Journalism, 1952; JD, Howard U., 1956; HHD (hon.), Miss. Indsl. Coll., 1969; LLD (hon.), Morehouse Coll., 1983. Bar: Tenn. 1956. Pvt. practice law Memphis, 1957-62; asst. U.S. atty. Western Dist. Tenn., Memphis, 1962-67; dir. div. hosp. and health services City of Memphis, 1968; judge Criminal Ct. Shelby County, Memphis, 1969-70; pres. LeMoyne-Owen Coll., Memphis, 1970-74; commentator Sta. WREC-TV (CBS), Memphis, 1972-74; judge U.S. Dist. Ct. (we. dist.) Tenn., 1980—, chief judge, 1987; mem. Jud. Conf. of U.S. Com. on Defender Svcs.; chair com. to establish a Death Penalty Resource Ctr., Nashville. Bd. mgrs. Meth. Hosp., Memphis, 1969-79; bd. dirs. Family Svc. Memphis, United Negro Coll. Fund, N.Y.C., 1970-74. With USMC, 1951-53. Recipient Disting. Alumni award Howard U., 1969, L. M. Graves Meml. Health award Mid-South Med. Ctr. Coun., Memphis, 1969, Bill of Rights award West Tenn. chpt. ACLU, 1970, Disting. Service award Mallory Knights Charitable Orgn., 1970, Disting. Service award Smothers Chapel C.M.E. Ch., 1971, Outstanding Citizen award Frontiers Internat., 1969, Ralph E. Bunche Humanitarian award Boy Scouts Am., 1972, Outstanding Educator and Judge award Salem-Gilfield Bapt. Ch., 1973, Spl. Tribute award A.M.E. Ch., 1974, United Negro Coll. Fund award, 1974, Humanities award Citizens Com. Coun. of Memphis, 1969, Shelby County Penal Farm award, 1974, Disting. Service award LeMoyne-Owen Coll., 1974, Disting. Service award Lane Coll., 1977, Dedicated Community Service award Christian Meth. Episc. Ch., 1979. Mem. NAACP, ABA (sr., chair conf. fed. trial judges, jud. adminstrn. divsn., chair exec. com. nat. conf. fed. trial judges 1994-95).

**HORTON, PAUL BRADFIELD,** lawyer; b. Dallas, Oct. 19, 1920; s. Frank Barrett and Hazel Lillian (Bradfield) H.; m. Susan Jeanne Diggle, May 19, 1949; children: Bradfield Ragland, Bruce Ragsdale. B.A., U. Tex., Austin, 1943, student Law Sch., 1941-43; LL.B., So. Methodist U., 1947. Bar: Tex. 1946. Ptnr. McCall, Parkhurst & Horton, Dallas, 1951—; lectr. mcpl. bond law and pub. finance S.W. Legal Found.; drafter Tex. mcpl. bonds legislation, 1963—. Mem. Gov.'s Com. Tex. Edn. Code, 1967-69. Served to lt. USNR, 1943-46. Mem. ABA, Dallas Bar Assn., Southwestern Legal Found., Nat. Water Resources Assn., Tex. Water Conservation Assn., Govt. Fin. Officers Assn., The Barristers, Dallas Country Club, Crescent Club, Tower Club, Delta Theta Phi, Beta Theta Pi. Municipal (including bonds). Home: 5039 Seneca Dr Dallas TX 75209-2219 Office: McCall Parkhurst & Horton 717 N Harwood St Ste 900 Dallas TX 75201-6586

**HORTON, SHERMAN D., JR.,** state supreme court justice; b. 1931. AB, Dartmouth Coll.; LLB, Harvard U. Assoc justice. N.H. Supreme Ct., Concord, NH, 1990—. Office: NH Supreme Court One Noble Dr Concord NH 03301-6160*

**HORTY, JOHN FRANCIS,** lawyer; b. Johnstown, Pa., Oct. 21, 1928; s. John Frank and Nancy Bolsinger (Dibert) H.; m. Christine Kennamer, June 1979; children: John Francis, Jon Michael, Kathryn Camille, Roger Lawrence, Jason Lawrence. BA cum laude, Amherst Coll., 1950; JD, Harvard U., 1953. Bar: Pa. 1956, D.C., 1981. Prof. U. Pitts., 1956-68; pres. Aspen Systems Corp., Pitts., 1966-71; mng. ptnr. Horty, Springer & Mattern, P.C., Pitts., 1971—; pres. Action Kit for Hosp. Law, Pitts., 1971—; chmn. bd. St. Francis Ctrl. Hosp., Pitts., 1973—; chmn. Estes Park Inst., Denver, 1984—; chmn. Indigo Inst., Washington, 1988—; pres. Nat. Coun. Cmty. Hosps., Washington, 1974—; bd. dirs. Hosp. Coun. Western Pa., St. Francis Health Sys., Pitts., Health Alliance of Pa. Editor and pub. (manuals, newsletters, chpts.) Hospital Law Manual, 1956, Action Kit for Hospital Law, 1973, Action Kit for Hospital Trustees, 1977, Patient Care Law, 1981, Treatise on Hospital Law, 1977, Medical Staff Law, 1984. Named Hon. Fellow Am. Coll. Hosp. Execs., 1965; recipient award of honor Am. Hosp. Assn., 1970. Mem. ABA, Am. Hosp. Assn. (life, hon.), Pa. Bar Assn., D.C. Bar Assn., Allegheny County Bar Assn., Ponte Vedra Country Club, Tournament Players Club. Democrat. Avocation: golf. Health. Home: 4614 5th Ave Pittsburgh PA 15213-3663 also: 637 Ponte Vedra Blvd Apt D Ponte Vedra FL 32082-2723 Office: Horty Springer & Mattern 4614 5th Ave Pittsburgh PA 15213-3663

**HORVATH, JANE CHURCH,** lawyer; b. Pitts., May 15, 1964; d. Charles Henry and Julia (Davis) Church; m. Laszlo Horvath, Mar. 1, 1997. BS, Coll. William and Mary, 1986; JD, U. Va., 1991. Bar: Va. 1991. Assoc. Gibson, Dunn & Crutcher, Washington, 1991-93, Hogan & Hartson, Washington, 1993-95; counsel Am. Online, Inc., Vienna, Va., 1995-97; sr. counsel Digital City, Inc., a subs. of Am. Online, Inc., Vienna 1996—; asst. gen. counsel, gen. counsel Digital City, Inc. Am. Online, Inc., 1997—. Mem. Women in Technology (founder, v.p. 1994-95). Office: America Online Inc 8615 Westwood Center Dr Vienna VA 22182-2218

**HORWIN, LEONARD,** lawyer; b. Chgo., Jan. 2, 1913; s. Joseph and Jennie (Fuhrmann) H.; m. Ursula Helene Donig, Oct. 15, 1939; children—Noel Samuel, Leonora Marie. LLD cum laude, Yale U., 1936. Bar: Calif. 1936, U.S. Dist. Ct. (cen. dist.) Calif. 1937, U.S. Ct. Appeals (9th cir.) 1939, U.S. Supreme Ct. 1940. Assoc., Lawler, Felix & Hall, 1936-39; ptnr. Hardy & Horwin, Los Angeles, 1939-42; counsel Bd. Econ. Warfare, Washington, 1942-43; mem. program adjustment com. U.S. War Prodn. Bd., 1942-43; attache, legal advisor U.S. Embassy, Madrid, Spain, 1943-47; sole practice, Beverly Hills, Calif., 1948—; dir., lectr. Witkin-Horwin Rev. Course on Calif. Law, 1939-42; judge pro tempore Los Angeles Superior Ct., 1940-42; instr. labor law U. So. Calif., 1939-42. U.S. rep. Allied Control Council for Ger., 1945-47; councilman City of Beverly Hills, 1962-66, mayor, 1964-65; chmn. transp. Los Angeles Goals Council, 1968; bd. dirs. So. Calif. Rapid Transit Dist., 1964-66; chmn. Rent Stabilization Com., Beverly Hills, 1980. Fellow Am. Acad. Matrimonial Lawyers; mem. ABA, State Bar Calif., Order Coif, Balboa Bay Club, Aspen Inst., La Costa Country Club. Author: Insight and Foresight, 1990, Plain Talk, 1931—; contbr. articles to profl. jours. E-Mail address: lhorwin@mindspring.com. Family and matrimonial, General practice, Real property. Office: 121 S Beverly Dr Beverly Hills CA 90212-3002

**HORWITZ, MELVIN,** lawyer, physician; b. N.Y.C., Nov. 20, 1926; m. Dorothy G. Horwitz. BA, Columbia U., 1945; MD, Harvard U., 1949; JD, Yale U., 1986. Bar: Conn. 1986. Resident in surgery Yale-New Haven Hosp., New Haven, 1959-52; resident Columbia-Presbyterian Med. Ctr., 1954-55; surgeon Manchester (Conn.) Meml. Hosp., 1956-86, chief of surgery, 1976-81, sr. surgeon emeritus, 1981—; rsch. cons., vis. lectr. dept. animal pathology and virology U. Conn., Storrs, 1962-73; adj. prof. Western New Eng. Law Sch., Springfield, Mass., 1986-87; pres. Helapol Assocs., Manchester, 1987—; chmn. Nutmeg Inst. Rev. Bd., 1991—; cons. Inst. Medicine, Washington, 1985. Health, Personal injury. Office: Helapol Assoc 223 Ludlow Rd Manchester CT 06040-4546

**HOSEMAN, DANIEL,** lawyer; b. Chgo., Aug. 18, 1935; s. Irving and Anne (Pruzansky) H.; m. Susan H. Myles, Aug. 7, 1960; children: Lawrence N., Joan E., Jonathan W. B.A., U. Ill., 1956, J.D., 1959. Bar: Ill. 1959, U.S. Dist. Ct. (no. dist.) Ill. 1960, U.S. Ct. Appeals (7th cir.) 1967, U.S. Supreme Ct. 1976. Sole practice, Chgo., 1959—; mem. panel pvt. atty. trustees U.S. Bankruptcy Ct. No. Dist. Ill., 1979—; arbitrator Cir. Ct. Cook County. Trustee Ill. Legal Svcs. Fund, 1978—; v.p. Allied Jewish Sch. Bd. Met. Chgo., 1977—; v.p. United Synagogue Am., 1978—. Served with USAFR, 1959-65. Mem. Am. Bankruptcy Inst., Advs. Soc., Decalogue Soc. Lawyers (pres. 1981-82, award of merit 1979-80), Ill. Bar Assn. (gen. assembly, long-range planning com.), Lake County Bar Assn. (com. on bankruptcy 1980—), Chgo. Coun. Lawyers, Comml. Law League Am., Am. Bankruptcy Inst., Nat. Assn. of Bankruptcy Trustees. Bankruptcy, Consumer commercial, Contracts commercial. Home: 2151 Tanglewood Ct Highland Park IL 60035-4231 Office: 77 W Washington St Ste 1220 Chicago IL 60602-2901

**HOSKINS, SONYA DENISE,** lawyer; b. Bryan, Tex., Feb. 16, 1966; d. Lillian Delois (Lucas) H. BS, U. Tex., Arlington, 1987; JD cum laude, So. U. La., 1992. Bar: La. 1992, Tex. 1993, U.S. Dist. Ct. (no. dist.) Tex., 1995. Law clk. Law Office Julius Whittier, Dallas, 1989-90, Law Office Johnnie Matthew, Baton Rouge, 1991-92; student asst. dist. atty. East Baton Rouge (La.) Dist. Attys. Office, 1992; assoc. Robinson West & Gooden, P.C., Dallas, 1993—. Legal advisor Antioch Missionary Bapt. Ch., Dallas, 1994—. Mem. ABA, FBA, Nat. Bar Assn. (regional dir. 1996—, Outstanding Region award 1997), Tex. State Bar Assn. (dir. minority African-Am. sect. 1996—), La. State Bar Assn., The Coll. State Bar of Tex., J.L. Turner Legal Assn. (mentor 1994—, rec. sec. 1993-95, v.p. 1996, pres.-elect 1998, Jurist African Am. award 1991-92, Pres.'s award 1997), Dallas Bar Assn. (bd. dirs.). Avocations: jogging, reading. General civil litigation, State civil litigation, Real property. Office: Robinson West & Gooden PC 400 S Zang Blvd Ste 600 Dallas TX 75208-6641

**HOSSLER, DAVID JOSEPH,** lawyer, law educator; b. Mesa, Ariz., Oct. 18, 1940; s. Carl Joseph and Elizabeth Ruth (Bills) H.; m. Gretchen Anne, Mar. 2, 1945; 1 child, Devon Annagret. BA, U. Ariz., 1969, JD, 1972. Bar: Ariz. 1972, U.S. Dist. Ct. Ariz. 1972, U.S. Supreme Ct. 1977. Legal intern to chmn. FCC, summer 1971; law clk. to chief justice Ariz. Supreme Ct., 1972-73; chief dep. county atty. Yuma County (Ariz.), 1973-74; ptnr. Hunt, Kenworthy and Hossler, Yuma, Ariz., 1974—; instr. in law and banking, law and real estate Ariz. Western Coll.; instr. in bus. law, mktg., ethics Webster U; co-chmn. fee arbitration com. Ariz. State Bar, 1990—; instr. agrl. law U. Ariz. Editor-in-chief Ariz. adv., 1971-72. Mem. precinct com. Yuma County Rep. Ctrl. Com., 1974-98, vice chmn., 1982; chmn. region II Acad. Decathalon competition, 1989; bd. dirs. Yuma County Ednl. Found., Yuma County Assn. Behavior Health Svcs., also pres., 1981; coach Yuma H.S. mock ct. team, 1987-94; bd. dirs. friends of U. Med. Ctr. With USN. Recipient Man and Boy award Boys Clubs Am., 1979, Freedoms Found. award Yuma chpt., 1988, Demolay Legion of Honor, 1991; named Vol. of Yr., Yuma County, 1981-82. Mem. ATLA, Am. Judicature Soc., Yuma County Bar Assn. (pres. 1975-76), Navy League, VFW, Am. Legion, U. Ariz. Alumni Assn. (nat. bd. dirs., past pres., hon. bobcat 1996, Disting. Citizen award 1997), Rotary (pres. Yuma club 1987-88, dist. gov. rep. 1989, dist. gov. 1992-93, findings com. 1996, dist. found. chair 1996—, Van Houton Look Beyond Yourself award 1995, Roy Slayton Share Rotary Share People award 1996, Al Face You Are the Key award 1997, Ted Day Let Svc. Light the Way award 1998, Rotary Found. citation for meritorious svc.). Episcopalian (vestry 1978-82). State civil litigation, Personal injury, Family and matrimonial. Home: 2802 S Fern Dr Yuma AZ 85364-7909 Office: Hunt and Hossler 330 W 24th St Yuma AZ 85364-6455 also: PO Box 2919 Yuma AZ 85366-2919

**HOSTERMAN, J. MICHAEL,** lawyer; b. Kansas City, Mo.; s. John Richard and Shirley Mae Hosterman; m. Jennifer Ann Judge, July 6, 1980; children: Heather Rose, Sarah Lynn, Megan Ann. Student, UCLA, 1969-71; BA, U. Calif., Berkeley, 1973; JD cum laude, Santa Clara U., 1977. Bar: Calif. 1977, U.S. Dist. Ct. (no. dist.) Calif. 1977. Assoc. Popelka, Allard, et. al., San Jose, Calif., 1977-80; ptnr. Hosterman & Oushalem, San Jose, 1980-85, Hosterman, Oushalem, et. al., San Jose, 1985-95; prin. Law Office J. Michael Hosterman, Pleasanton, Calif., 1990—; mem. adv. bd. Pleasanton Downtown Assn., 1994-97, bd. dirs.; bd. dirs. Ea. Alameda City Bar, Pleasanton. Bd. dirs. Pleasanton Girls Soccer Assn., 1998—. Mem. Pleasanton Downtown Rotary. Avocations: golf, tennis, traveling. Office: 555 Peters Ave Ste 115 Pleasanton CA 94566-6595

**HOSTNIK, CHARLES RIVOIRE,** lawyer; b. Glen Ridge, N.J., Apr. 8, 1954; s. William John and Susan (Rivoire) H. AB, Dartmouth Coll., 1976; JD, U. Puget Sound, 1979. Bar: Wash. 1980, U.S. Dist. Ct. (we. dist.) Wash. 1980, U.S. Dist. Ct. (ea. dist.) Wash. 1982, U.S. Ct. Appeals (9th cir.) 1983, Hoh Tribal Ct. 1984, Nisqually Tribal Ct. 1984, Puyallup Tribal Ct. 1984, Shoalwater Bay Tribal Ct. 1984, Skokomish Tribal Ct. 1984. Asst. atty. gen. Atty. Gen.'s Office State of Wash., Olympia, 1980-84; assoc. Kane, Vandeberg, Hartinger & Walker, Tacoma, 1984-87; ptnr. Anderson, Burns & Hostnik, Tacoma, 1988—; trial and appellate judge N.W. Intertribal Ct. Sys., Edmonds, Wash., 1986—. Author: (chpt.) Washington Practice, 1989. Com. mem. to re-elect Justice R. Guy, Olympia and Tacoma, 1990. Mem. N.W. Tribal Ct. Judges Assn. General practice, Personal injury, Native American. Office: Anderson Burns & Hostnik 6915 Lakewood Dr W Ste A1 Tacoma WA 98467-3299

**HOTH, STEVEN SERGEY,** lawyer; b. Jan. 30, 1941; s. Donald Leroy and Ina Dorothy (Barr) H.; m. JoEllen Maly, July 29, 1967; children: Andrew Steven, Peter Lindsey. AB, Grinnell Coll., 1962; JD, U. Iowa, 1966; postgrad., U. Pa., 1968, Oxford (Eng.) U., 1973. Bar: U.S. Ct. Appeals (8th cir.) 1966, U.S. Tax Ct. 1967, U.S. Ct. Claims 1967, U.S. Dist. Ct. Iowa 1968, U.S. Dist. Ct. N.D. 1968, U.S. Dist. Ct. S.D. 1968, U.S. Supreme Ct. 1973, U.S. Ct. Appeals (7th cir.) 1982. Law clk. to chief justice U.S. Ct. Appeals (8th cir.), Fargo, N.D., 1967-68; assoc. Hirsch, Adams, Hoth & Krekel, Burlington, Iowa, 1968-72, ptnr., 1972-91; pvt. practice Burlington, 1992—; asst. atty. Des Moines County, Burlington, 1968-72, atty., 1972-83; alt. mcpl. judge, Burlington, 1968-69; lectr. criminal law Southeastern C.C., West Burlington, 1972-82; assoc. prof. polit. sci. Iowa Wesleyan Coll., Mt. Pleasant, 1981-82, Iowa Truck Rail; pres. Burlington Truck Rail, Burlington Short Line RR. Inc., Iowa Internat. Investments; sec. Burlington Loading Co. Contbr. numerous articles to profl. jours. Chmn. Des Moines County Civil Svc. Commn.; trustee Charles H. Rand Lecture Trust; mem. Des Moines County Conf. Com., Des Moines County Conf. Bd.; dir. Burlington Med. Ctr. Staff Found.; moderator 1st Congl. Ch., Burlington; bd. dirs. UN Assn., Burlington Med. Ctr. Staff Found.; clk. Burlington North Bottoms Levy and Drainage Dist.; bd. mem., pres. Burlington Cmty. Sch. Dist. Bd. Edn., chmn. commn. on ministry, mem. exec. com. Nat. Assn. Congl. Christian Chs., moderator; treas. 1st dist. Dem. Com.; bd. dirs. Legal Aid Soc. Planned Parenthood Des Moines County. Recipient Chmn.'s award ARC, 1980; Reginald Heber Smith fellow in legal aid Cheyenne River Indian Reservation, Eagle Butte, S.D., 1967-68. Mem. ABA (internat. sect., tax sect.), Iowa State Bar Assn., Des Moines County Bar Assn., Am. Judicature Soc., Agrl. Law Com., Iowa Def. Coun., Grinnell Coll. Alumni Assn. (bd. dirs.), Burlington-West Burlington C. of C. (bd. dirs.), Nat. Assn. Congrl. Christian Chs., Burlington Golf Club, New Crystal Lake Club (pres.), Elks, Eagles, Masons, Rotary. General practice, General corporate, Private international. Office: PO Box 982 Hoth Bldg 200 Jefferson St Burlington IA 52601

**HOUCK, CHARLES WESTON,** federal judge; b. Florence, S.C., Apr. 16, 1933; s. William Stokes and Charlotte Barnwell (Weston) H.; children from previous marriage: Charles Weston, Charlotte Elizabeth. Grad., U. N.C., 1954; LLB, U. S.C., 1956. Bar: S.C. Mem. firm Willcox, Hardee, Houck, Palmer & O'Farrell, 1956, 58-70;; ptnr. Houck, Clarke & Johnson, 1971-79; judge U.S. Dist. Ct. S.C., Florence, 1979—, now chief justice. Mem. S.C. Ho. of Reps., 1963-66; chmn. Florence City-County Bldg. Commn., 1968-76. Served with AUS, 1957-58. Mem. ABA, S.C. Bar Assn. Episcopalian. Office: US Dist Ct PO Box 2317 Florence SC 29503-2317

**HOUGH, MARK MASON,** lawyer; b. Uniontown, Pa., Jan. 21, 1945; s. Carl H. and Ruth Ann (Mason) H.; children: Benjamin, Daniel; m. Sharon Fay Jesperson, Oct. 26, 1985. BA in Econs., U. Wash., 1966, JD, 1971. Bar: Wash. 1971, U.S. Dist. Ct. (we. dist.) Wash. 1973, U.S. Dist. Ct. (ea. dist.) Wash. 1976, U.S. Ct. Appeals (9th cir.) 1979. Staff atty. Bur. of Competition FTC, Washington, 1971-73; from assoc. to ptnr. Schweppe Krug & Tausend, P.S., Seattle, 1973-89; ptnr. Reed & McClure, Seattle, 1989—. Mem. ABA (sect. on antitrust, litigation and bus.), Wash. State Bar Assn. (sect. on antitrust, litigation and bus.). Antitrust, General civil litigation, General corporate. Office: Reed McClure 3600 Columbia Ctr 701 5th Ave Seattle WA 98104-7097

**HOUGH, STEVEN HEDGES,** lawyer; b. Cleve., May 24, 1938; s. William Rockwell and Virginia Hull (Olds) H.; m. Carolyn Millicent Day, July 29, 1968 (dec. July 1981); children: Glenn, Holly, Heather. BSBA, Chico State Coll., 1961; JD, U. Calif., San Francisco, 1964. Bar: Calif. 1966, U.S. Dist. Ct. (no. dist.) Calif. 1966, U.S. Ct. Appeals (9th cir.) 1966, U.S. Supreme Ct. 1975. Trial atty. L.A. County Pub. Defender, L.A., 1966-76, head dep., 1976—; pres. Criminal Cts. Bar Assn., L.A., 1984; asst. presiding referee state bar ct. State Bar Calif., L.A., San Francisco, 1985-91, chair standing com. on delivery of legal svcs. to criminal defendants, 1978-79; bd. govs. Long Beach (Calif.) Bar Assn., 1990, 91; instr., lectr., panelist trial advocacy clinic, day in ct. program; mtgs. L.A. County Pub. Defenders, marshal program Calif. Youth Authority, Long Beach Police Dept., other orgns. Mem. First Congregational Ch., Santa Ana, Calif., deacon, 1985-87, 91-93, 96—; mem. PTA several schs.; referee, coach, bd. dirs. region 5 Am. Youth Soccer Orgn.; referee, coach North Huntington Beach Soccer Club, Coast Soccer League; treas. Orange County Soccer Referees Assn., 1986; sustaining mem. Boy Scouts Am., Girl Scouts U.S.; mem. Westhaven Homeowners Assn., Gifted Children's Assn. Orange County; life mem. So. Calif. Acro Team; fund raising solicitor United Way Crusade, Brotherhood Crusade. Recipient Charitable Giving Hon. award Brotherhood Crusade, 1982. Mem. ABA (criminal law sect.), Criminal Cts. Bar Assn., Calif. Pub. Defenders Assn., Calif. Attys. for Criminal Justice, S.E. Bar Assn., Calif. State Bar Assn., Long Beach Bar Assn. (bd. govs. 1990, 91), South Bar Bar Assn., U.S. Supreme Ct. Bar Assn., Nat. Coll. Criminal Def. Lawyers and Pub. Defenders, Nat. Assn. Criminal Def. Lawyers, Am. Judicature Soc., Am. Contract Bridge League (Bronze life master), Mission Viejo Country Club, Hastings Alumni Assn., Univ. Sch. Alumni Assn., Lambda Chi Alph. Republican. Avocations: golf, bridge, soccer, travel. Office: LA County Pub Defenders Office 210 W Temple St Fl 19 Los Angeles CA 90012-3210

**HOUGH, THOMAS HENRY MICHAEL,** lawyer; b. Midland, Pa., Aug. 4, 1933; s. Bert Patrick and Marguerite (Mullen) H.; m. Jocelyn Peltz, Aug. 20, 1956 (div. 1996); children: Jocelyn, Thomas Henry Michael. AB, Dickinson Coll., 1955; JD, Dickinson Sch. Law, 1958. Bar: Pa. 1959, U.S. Ct. Appeals (3d cir.) 1975, U.S. Supreme Ct. 1970. Field atty. NLRB, Pitts., 1959-60; atty. United Steelworkers Am., 1960-68; ptnr. Lucchino, Gaitens & Hough, Pitts., 1968-79, Hough & Gleason, P.C., Pitts., 1980-84, Barry Fasulo & Hough, P.C., Pitts., 1994—; adj. assoc. prof. pub. sector arbitration and pub. sector collective bargaining Grad. Sch. Pub. and Internat. Affairs, U. Pitts., 1970-97. Labor, Health. Office: Barry Fasulo & Hough 3700 Gulf Tower 707 Grant St Pittsburgh PA 15219-1908

**HOUGHTALING, CHRIS ALLEN,** lawyer; b. Muskegon, Mich., Sept. 12, 1964; s. Larain Donald and Suzan Kay H.; m. Christine Ann Rose, June 18, 1988; m. Klintworth W. Erkes, Kohl A. Houghtaling, Kollin P. Houghtaling. AA, Muskegon C.C., 1990; BS, Grand Valley State U., 1991; JD, Valparaiso U., 1995. Bar: Mich. 1995, Fla. 1996. Asst. pros. atty. Muskegon (Mich.) County Prosecutors Office, 1994-97; atty. Vander Ploeg & Wells, LLP, Whitehall, 1997-99, Cook & Houghtaling, PLC, Muskegon, 1999—. Active Boy Scouts Am.; regional AYSO referee; chief referee Tri-Cities Am. Youth Soccer Orgn.; referee U.S. Soccer Fedn. Mem. Muskegon County Bar Assn. (dir. bd. dirs.), Ct. Appointed Spl. Advs. (dir. exec. bd.), Child Abuse Coun. (bd. dirs.). Avocations: soccer, bicycling. Fax: 231-722-8312. General practice, Probate, Juvenile. Home: 18463 Iroquois Dr Spring Lake MI 49456-9128 Office: Cook & Houghtaling PLC 40 Concord Ave Ste 2 Muskegon MI 49442-3437

**HOULE, JEFFREY ROBERT,** lawyer; b. Biddeford, Maine, July 27, 1965; s. Marcel Paul and Lois Marie (Jackson) H.; m. Lorren Johnston Houle, Oct. 11, 1997; 1 child, Grace Morgan. AB, Boston Coll., Chestnut Hill, Mass., 1987; JD, Western New Eng. Coll., Springfield, Mass., 1991; LLM in Taxation, Cert. in Employee Benefits Law, Georgetown U., Washington, 1992, LLM in Securities Regulation, 1995. Bar: D.C., N.Y., Conn., Mass., Maine. Pres. A.F.I. Investments, Springfield, Mass., 1988-91, Washington Capital Ventures, LP, Washington, 1995-98; law clk. Stones Solicitors, Exeter, Devon, Eng., 1989; jud. intern to the Hon. Joan Glazer Margolis U.S. Magistrate Judge, New Haven, Conn., 1990; legal intern Office of Atty. Gen. Robert Abrams, N.Y.C., 1990; analyst The Bur. of Nat. Affairs, Inc., Washington, 1992; assoc. Andros, Floyd & Miller PC, Hartford, Conn., 1992-94, Elias, Matz, Tiernan & Herrick LLP, Washington, 1994-98; ptnr. Greenberg Traurig, McLean, Va., 1998—. Contbr. articles to profl. jours. With U.S. Army, 1984-86. Mem. ABA, The Army and Navy Club, The Federalist Soc.,The Tower Club, Phi Alpha Delta. Republican. Roman Catholic. Avocations: hiking, swimming, horseback riding, internat. travel. Securities, General corporate, Taxation, general. Home: 444 New Jersey Ave SE Washington DC 20003-4008 Office: Greenberg Traurig Ste 1200 1750 Tysons Blvd McLean VA 22102

**HOULIHAN, CHARLES DANIEL, JR.,** lawyer; b. Boston, June 15, 1953; s. Charles Daniel and Barbara Ann (Keohane) H.; m. Shelley Savran, May 28, 1978; children: Meghan, Brenna. BA, U. Mass., 1975; JD, Syracuse U., 1978. Bar: Tex. 1979, U.S. Ct. Appeals (5th cir.) 1983, U.S. Dist. Ct. (we. dist.) Tex. 1984, Conn. 1993, U.S. Dist. Ct. Conn. 1993; cert. mediator. Law clk. to chief judge U.S. Dist. Ct. Va., Roanoke, 1978-79; shareholder Matthews & Branscomb, San Antonio, 1979-92; of counsel Hebb & Gitlin, Hartford, Conn., 1992-94; pvt. practice Simsbury, Conn., 1995—; speaker in field. Chair Simsbury Econ. Devel. Commn., 1995-98; bd. dirs. Hartford Symphony Orch., 1997—; pres. Simsbury Main St. Partnership, 1997-98, dir. 1996—; vice chair Talcott Mountain Music Festival, 1996-98, chair, 1999. Mem. ABA (vice chmn. torts and non-profit, charitable and religious orgns. 1990—), Conn. Bar Assn. (exec. com. constrn. law sect.), San Antonio Bar Assn. (chmn. fed. pre-trial study group fed. cts. com. 1986-92), Am. Inns of Ct. (San Antonio and Hartford chpts., sec. William Sessions chpt. 1985—, pres. 1997-98), Order of Coif, Phi Beta Kappa. Roman Catholic. General civil litigation, Construction, Bankruptcy. Home: 235 Stratton Brook Rd PO Box 56 West Simsbury CT 06092-0056 Office: 930 Hopmeadow St PO Box 582 Simsbury CT 06070-0582

**HOULIHAN, CHRISTOPHER MICHAEL,** lawyer; b. N.Y.C., Nov. 4, 1949; s. Walter M. and Rose Anne (King) H.; m. Nancy Ellen Grealy, Aug. 12, 1978; 1 child, Andrew Justin. BA, Marquette U., 1971; JD, N.Y. Law Sch., 1975. Bar: N.Y. 1976, D.C. 1979, U.S. Dist. Ct. (so. and ea. dists.) N.Y. 1976, U.S. Dist. Ct. (no. dist.) N.Y. 1981, U.S. Dist. Ct. D.C. 1991, U.S. Dist. Ct. Conn. 1991, U.S. Dist. Ct. Vt. 1995, U.S. Ct. Claims 1982, U.S. Ct. Appeals (2d cir.) 1978, U.S. Ct. Appeals (fed. cir.) 1987, U.S. Ct. Appeals (3rd cir.) 1996, U.S. Supreme Ct. 1979. Asst. corp. counsel City of N.Y.C., 1976-77; assoc. Judge Livoti & Bernstein, N.Y.C., 1977-78; assoc. Galef & Jacobs, N.Y.C., 1979-83, ptnr., 1984-87; mng. ptnr. Roemer & Featherstonhaugh, P.C., N.Y.C., 1988-94; ptnr. Putney, Twombly, Hall & Hirson, LLP, N.Y.C., 1995—. Mem. ABA, N.Y. State Bar Assn. (com on civil practice law and rules, com. on cert. and specialization trial lawyers), Assn. Bar City N.Y., D.C. Bar, New York County Lawyers Assn. (com. on fed. cts., chmn. fed. civil practice continuing edn. program 1985, lectr. fed. practice 1985), Am. Arbitration Assn. (nat. panel arbitrators), N.Y. Athletic Club, Watch Hill Yacht Club. General civil litigation, General corporate. Office: Putney Twombly Hall Hirson LLP 521 5th Ave Fl 10 New York NY 10175-0010

**HOULIHAN, F(RANCIS) ROBERT, JR.,** lawyer; b. Boston, May 27, 1944; s. F. Robert Sr. and Elizabeth A. (Mullen) H.; m. Susan M. Forti, June 11, 1977. AB, Bates Coll., 1966; MA, Northwestern U., 1967; JD, Boston U., 1972. Bar: Mass. 1972, U.S. Dist. Ct. Mass. 1983. Atty. Boston Legal Services, 1972-74; assoc. Kunen & Hart, Marlboro, Mass., 1974-77; asst. dist. atty. Middlesex County, Cambridge, Mass., 1977-81; ptnr. Heavey, Houlihan, Kraft & Cardinal, Brookline, Mass., 1981—. Mem. ABA, Mass. Bar Assn., Longwood Indoor Tennis Country Club (Chestnut Hill, Mass.). Democrat. Roman Catholic. Avocations: amateur ice hockey, adult soccer. General practice, State civil litigation, Federal civil litigation. Office: Heavey Houlihan Kraft & Cardinal 229 Harvard St Brookline MA 02446-5004

**HOULIHAN, GERALD JOHN,** lawyer; b. Cortland, N.Y., Aug. 26, 1943; s. Robert Emmett and Helen (Corsi) H.; m. Claudia C. Kitchens; children: Andrea, Gerald Jr., Maureen, Katherine, Colleen. BS, U. Notre Dame, 1965; JD, Syracuse U., 1968. Bar: N.Y. 1968, U.S. Dist. Ct. (we. dist.) N.Y. 1968, U.S. Ct. Appeals (2nd cir.) 1972, U.S. Supreme Ct. 1980, U.S. Ct. Appeals (5th cir.) 1981, U.S. Ct. Appeals (11th cir.) 1981, Fla. 1985, U.S. Dist. Ct. (so. dist.) Fla. 1985, U.S. Dist. Ct. (so. dist.) N.Y. 1986, U.S. Dist. Ct. (no. dist.) Fla. 1986, U.S. Ct. Appeals (4th and D.C. cirs.) 1987, U.S. Dist. Ct. (middle dist.) Fla., 1987. Assoc. Harris, Beach, Keating et al., Rochester, N.Y., 1968-72; asst. U.S. atty. U.S. Atty.'s Office, Rochester, 1972-81; sr. litigation counsel U.S. Dept. Justice, Rochester, 1981-82; chief asst. U.S. atty. U.S. Atty.'s Office, Miami, Fla., 1982-85; ptnr. Steel Hector & Davis, Miami, 1985-91; mem. Greenberg, Traurig, Hoffman, Lipoff, Rosen & Quentel, P.A., Miami, 1991-95; ptnr. Houlihan & Ptnrs., P.A., 1995—. Advocate Am. Bd. Trial Advocates. Belle L. Landry scholar Syracuse Soc. Mem. Fed. Bar Assn. (pres. 1993-94, bd. dirs. Miami chpt. 1988—), Order of Coif. Democrat. Roman Catholic. Federal civil litigation, Antitrust, Criminal. Home: 5191 SW 76th St Miami FL 33143-6015 Office: Houlihan & Ptnrs PA 2600 S Douglas Rd Ste 600 Miami FL 33134-6100

**HOUPT, JAMES EDWARD,** lawyer; b. Calif., 1951; m. Leslie Ann Jones Houpt. BA with distinction, Calif. State U., Chico, 1976; JD cum laude, Harvard U., 1992. Bar: Va. 1992, D.C. 1992, Md. 1993, U.S. Ct. Appeals (4th cir.) 1992, Calif. 1997, U.S. Ct. Appeals (9th cir.) 1997. News dir. Sta. KNVR-FM, Paradise, Calif., 1978-80; anchor, reporter Sta. KHSL-AM-TV, Chico, 1980-85; sr. reporter Sta. KOLO-TV, Reno, 1985-89; assoc. Baker & Hostetler, Washington, D.C., 1992-97, Orrick, Herrington & Sutcliffe LLP, Sacramento, Calif., 1997—; lectr. journalism Calif. State U., 1981, 85; adj. prof. law sch. U. Calif., Davis, vis. prof., 1999. Author: (booklet) Access to Electronic Records, 1990, The Libel Curtain: A Comparison of Canadian & American Libel Law, 1994, Going On-Line: Is the World Wide Web a Web for the Unwary?, 1996, Boarding a Moving Bus: Developing an Internet Risk Management Strategy, 1997; contbr. articles to legal and gen. interest publs. With USN, 1970-74. Recipient Cert. of Merit, Calif.-Nev. AP TV-Radio Assn., 1983, 84, 86. Mem. ABA, Va. State Bar Assn., D.C. Bar, Calif. Bar Assn., VFW. Avocations: photography, hiking. General civil litigation, Libel. Office: Orrick, Herrington & Sutcliffe LLP 400 Capitol Mall Ste 3000 Sacramento CA 95814-4421

**HOUSER, BARBARA J.,** lawyer; b. Scottsbluff, Nebr., Jan. 29, 1954. BS with honors, U. Nebr., 1975; JD, So. Meth. U., 1978. Bar: Tex. 1978, U.S. Dist. Ct. (no., so., ea., and we. dists.) Tex., U.S. Dist. Ct. (ea. dist.) Mich., U.S. Ct. Appeals (5th, 6th, and 11th cirs.), U.S. Supreme Ct. Shareholder Sheinfeld Maley & Kay, Houston; lectr. nationally on insolvency, bankruptcy, and debtor/creditor relationships. Author: The Fifth Circuit in Review: A Retrospective of the First Decade Under the Bankruptcy Code, 1989; casenote and comment editor Southwestern Law Jour., 1977-78; contbg. author: Collier on Bankruptcy, 15th edit., Collier Bankruptcy Manual, 3d edit. Named One of Fifty Top Women Lawyers Nat. Law Jour., 1998. Fellow Am. Coll. Bankruptcy, Am. Bar Found., Tex. Bar Found.; mem. ABA, Nat. Bankruptcy Conf., Alpha Lambda Delta, Phi Delta Phi. Bankruptcy. Office: Sheinfeld Maley & Kay 1700 Pacific Ave Ste 4400 Dallas TX 75201-4678*

**HOUSER, RONALD EDWARD,** lawyer, mediator; b. Fairbury, Nebr., Aug. 11, 1949; s. Edward Erle and Lois Charlotte (Dux) H.; m. Linda Marie Webber, June 13, 1971 (div. 1985); children: Angela Marie, Brian Edward, Darren James; m. Beatrice Virginia McMullen Bupp, July 24, 1993. DVM, U. Mo., 1974; MS, Ohio State U., 1979; JD, U. Ga., 1990. Bar: Ga. 1990, U.S. Dist. Ct. (mid., no. and so. dist.) Ga. 1990, U.S. Ct. Appeals (11th cir.) 1990, U.S. Ct. Mil. Appeals 1993, U.S. Supreme Ct. 1993. Asst. instr. Univ. Nebr., Lincoln, 1979-83; owner, mgr. Lincoln Animal Health Clinic, 1983-85; atty. Cook, Noell, Tolley, Bates & Michael, Athens, Ga., 1990—. Contbr. articles to profl. jours. Mem. Nebr. State Bd. Health, 1980-84. Mem. Nat. Lawyers Assn., Nebr. Vet. Med. Assn. (dist. pres. 1979-81), Christian Legal Soc., Res. Officers Assn., Am. Legion, Phi Alpha Delta, Sigma Xi. Avocations: sports, reading, gardening. Alternative dispute resolution, Appellate, Criminal. Home: PO Box 502 Athens GA 30603-0502 Office: Cook Noell Tolley Bates & Michael LLP 304 E Washington St Athens GA 30601-2751

**HOUSER, STEPHEN DOUGLAS BARLOW, III,** lawyer; b. Hartford, Conn., Feb. 19, 1952; s. Stephen Douglas Barlow Jr. and Lynn (Cunningham) H.; m. Barbara Ann Houser, Mar. 24, 1989. BSMetE, Purdue U., 1974; JD, U. Fla., 1984. Bar: Fla. 1985, U.S. Dist. Ct. (so. dist.) Fla. 1992. Jr. engr. Pratt & Whitney Aircraft, East Hartford, Conn., 1975-76; engr. Pratt & Whitney Aircraft, West Palm Beach, Fla., 1976-78, sr. engr., 1978-81; assoc. Wicker, Smith, Tutan et al, West Palm Beach, Fla., 1985-89, ptnr., 1990-95; sole practitioner Palm Beach Gardens, Fla., 1995-98, Jupiter, Fla., 1998—. Campaign treas.. Thomas Bermingham, Candidate for County Commr., Palm Beach County, 1988. Mem. ABA, Palm Beach County Bar Assn. Republican. Avocations: sailing, tennis, rugby, football, motorcycling, camping. General civil litigation, Personal injury, Construction. Office: 50 S Us Highway 1 Ste 210 Jupiter FL 33477-5114

**HOUSER, TIMOTHY CURTIS,** lawyer; b. Knoxville, Tenn., May 15, 1953; s. Raymond Curtis and Wanda (Cowan) H.; 1 child, Adrienne Celeste Rose. BA, U. Tenn., 1984, JD, 1988. Bar: Tenn. 1989, U.S. Dist. Ct. (ea. dist.) Tenn. 1989, U.S. Ct. Appeals (6th cir.) 1990. Assoc. Arnett Draper & Hagood, Knoxville, 1989-91, Leibowitz & Cohen, Knoxville, 1991-95; pvt. practice Knoxville, 1995-97; founding ptnr. Houser & Hodge P.C., Knoxville, 1997—; spl. judge City of Knoxville, 1994—. Adv. bd. Pellissippi State Coll., Knoxville, 1994—; vol. Habitat for Humanity, 1996. Mem. ABA, Tenn. Bar Assn., Knoxville Bar Assn. (Golden Gavel award 1996), Phi Kappa Phi. Republican. Avocations: hiking, backpacking, camping. General civil litigation, Personal injury, Workers' compensation. Office: Houser & Hodge PC 11826 Kingston Pike Ste 210 Knoxville TN 37922-3842

**HOUSH, TEDRICK ADDISON, JR.,** lawyer; b. Kansas City, Mo., Jan. 11, 1936; s. Tedrick Addison and Margaret Eleanor Housh; m. Barbara Jane Pearl, Sept. 5, 1959; children: Tedrick Addison III, Frank Thomas. BA in Psychology, U. Mo., 1959, JD, 1961. Bar: Mo. 1962, U.S. Dist. Ct. (we. dist.) Mo. 1962. Law clk. U.S. Dist. Ct. We. Dist. Mo., Kansas City, 1961-63; counsel for litigation Office of the Solicitor, U.S. Dept. Labor, Washington, 1972-73; trial atty. Office of the Solicitor, U.S. Dept. Labor, Kansas City, Mo., 1963-72, regional solicitor, 1973-98, retired, 1998—. Avocations: reading, writing.

**HOUSH, TEDRICK ADDISON, III,** lawyer; b. Kansas City, Mo., Apr. 21, 1962; s. Tedrick Addison Jr. and Barbara Jane (Pearl) H.; m. Shelly Lynne Peterson, June 23, 1990; children: Adidja Mampuya, Abdul Mampuya, Saida Mampuya, Tedrick Addison IV, Madeleine Jane. BA, U. Oreg., 1984; JD, U. Kans., 1991. Bar: Mo. 1991, U.S. Dist. Ct. (we. dist.) Mo. 1991, Kans. 1992, U.S. Dist. Ct. Kans. 1992, U.S. Ct. Appeals (8th cir.) 1995. Vol. Peace Corps, Congo, Africa, 1985-87; ESL tchr. Blue Valley Sch. Dist., Overland Park, Kans., 1987-88; atty. Swanson, Midgley, Gangwere, Kitchin & McLarney LLC, Kansas City, 1991-99; of counsel Lathrop & Gage L.C., Kansas City, 1999—. Bd. pres. Kansas City Acad. Preparatory Sch., 1996—, bd. dirs., 1994-96. Mem. ABA (chair young lawyers divsn. children and the law com. 1997-98, vice-chair 1995-97), Lawyers Assn. Kansas City (bd. dirs. 1993-97, chair pub. svc., Pub. Svc. award 1995), Kansas City Metro Bar Assn. (Pro Bono award 1992). Labor, Federal civil litigation, State civil litigation. Office: Lathrop & Gage LC Ste 2800 2345 Grand Blvd Kansas City MO 64108-2612

**HOUSTON, JAMES GORMAN, JR.,** state supreme court justice; b. Eufaula, Ala., Mar. 11, 1933; s. James Gorman and Mildred (Vance) H.; m. Martha Martin, Dec. 3, 1955; children: Mildred Vance, J. Gorman III. BS, Auburn U., 1955; LLB, U. Ala., 1956, JD, 1969. Bar: Ala. 1956. Law clk. to chief justice Ala. Supreme Ct., Montgomery, 1956-57; ptnr. Houston & Martin, P.C., Eufaula, 1960-85; assoc. justice Ala. Supreme Ct., Montgomery, 1985—; county atty. Barbour County, Clayton, Ala., 1961-79. Contbr. numerous opinions to So. Reporter; contbr. articles to profl. jours. Mayor pro tem, alderman City of Eufaula, 1964-70; pres. Heritage Assn., Eufaula, Ala., 1979-82; mem. Ala. Commn. on Uniform State Laws. 1st lt. JAGC, USAF, 1957-60. Named Citizen of Yr., City of Eufaula, 1979; recipient Alumni Achievement in Humanities award Auburn Univ., 1993. Fellow Am. Bar Found.; mem. ABA, Ala. Bar Assn., Ala. State Bar (examiner 1979-82, disciplinary commn. 1984-85, state bar commr. 1982-85), Barbour County Bar Assn. (pres. 1975), Eufaula C. of C. (pres. 1974). Republican. Methodist. Office: Ala Supreme Ct 300 Dexter Ave Montgomery AL 36104-3741

**HOUSTON, JOHN R.,** lawyer; b. Midland, Tex., Aug. 3, 1952; s. William Robert and Mary Elizabeth Houston; m. Patricia K. Houston, Mar. 19, 1978; children: Katherine, Michael. BA, Mich. State U., 1978; JD, St. Louis U., 1981. Bar: Minn. 1981, U.S. Dist. Ct. Minn., U.S. Ct. Appeals (8th cir.). Ptnr. Lindquist & Vennum, Mpls., 1981—; lectr. continuing legal edn., Minn. Mem. Corp. Counsel Assn. (pres. 1995, 98). Securities, Mergers and acquisitions, General corporate. Office: Lindquist & Vennum 4200 IDS Ctr Minneapolis MN 55402

**HOUSTON, WILLIAM MCCLELLAND,** lawyer; b. Pitts., Jan. 19, 1923; s. Fred C. and Fame (Whiteside) H.; m. Josephine Simpson, Feb. 4, 1950 (div. 1989); children: William McClelland Jr., Ann A. Houston Kelley, Barbara S. Houston Kinek; m. Carolyn B. Rehmus, July 7, 1990. BS, Haverford Coll., 1943; JD with distinction, U. Mich., 1945. Bar: Pa. 1946. Ptnr. Houston Donnelly & Meck, Pitts., 1946-98; of counsel Kabala & Geeseman, Pitts., 1998—; chmn. decedents' estates adv. com. Pa. Joint State Govt. Commn.; past mem. Pa. Supreme Ct. Orphans' Ct. Rules Com. Past pres. Western Pa. Heart Assn. Served with AUS, 1945-46. Mem. ABA, Pa. Bar Assn. (past chmn. real property, probate and trust sect.), Allegheny County Bar Assn. (past. chmn. ethics com., probate and trust sect.), Am. Coll. Trust and Estate Counsel, Pitts. Estate Planning Council (past pres.). Republican. Presbyterian. Clubs: Duquesne (Pitts.); Edgeworth (Sewickley, Pa.). Estate planning, Probate, Estate taxation. Office: Kabala & Geeseman 200 1st Ave Ste 4 Pittsburgh PA 15222-1575

**HOVDE, F. BOYD,** lawyer; b. Mpls., Aug. 7, 1934; s. Frederick L. and Priscilla L. (Boyd) H.; m. Alice Austell, Feb. 21, 1981; children by previous marriage: Frederick R., Debra L., Kristine L., Sarah L. AB, Princeton U., 1956; JD, U. Mich. 1959. Bar: Ind. 1959, U.S. Dist. Ct. (no. and so. dists.) Ind. 1959, U.S. Ct. Appeals (7th cir.) 1960, U.S. Supreme Ct. 1977. Assoc. Ice, Miller, Donadio & Ryan, Indpls., 1959-67, ptnr., 1967-69; ptnr. Townsend, Hovde & Townsend, Indpls., 1969-77; mem. Townsend, Hovde, Townsend & Montross, P.C., 1977-84; mem. Townsend, Hovde & Montross, P.C., 1984-85; mem. F. Boyd Hovde, P.C., 1985—, Hovde Law Firm, 1997—; mem. com. on character and fitness Ind. Supreme Ct., 1976—, rules of practice and procedure, 1980-92. Mem. Indpls. Bar Assn. (treas. 1969, v.p. 1974, pres. 1979), ABA (del. 1980-83), Ind. Trial Lawyers Assn. (bd. dirs. 1970—, pres. 1976-77), Assn. Trial Lawyers Am., Am. Coll. Trial Lawyers, Internat. Acad. Trial Lawyers, Ind. Coll. Trial Lawyers, Indpls. Jaycees (pres. 1963-64), Ind. Golf Assn. (pres. 1974-75), Western Golf Assn. (dir. 1969-81, v.p. 1972-81). Clubs: Crooked Stick Golf (Carmel, Ind.); Pine Valley Golf (Clementon, N.J.); Old Marsh Golf (Palm Beach Gardens, Fla.). Personal injury, Product liability, Professional liability. Office: Hovde Law Firm One Meridian Plaza 10585 N Meridian St Ste 345 Indianapolis IN 46290-1068

**HOVDE, FREDERICK RUSSELL,** lawyer; b. Lafayette, Ind., Oct. 1, 1955; s. F. Boyd and Karen (Sorenson) H. BBA, So. Meth. U., 1977; JD, Ind. U., 1980. Bar: Ind. 1980, U.S. Dist. Ct. (no. and so. dists.) Ind. 1980, U.S. Ct. Appeals (7th cir.) 1980. Ptnr. Hovde Law Firm, Indpls., 1980—; bd. visitors Ind. U. Sch. of Law, Indpls., 1993—. Bd. dirs. Ind. Golf Found., 1998—. Fellow Ind. Coll. Trial Lawyers, Indpls. Bar Found.; mem. ABA, Ind. Bar Assn. (bd. dirs. young lawyers sect. 1983-86), Indpls. Bar Assn. (bd. dirs. young lawyers sect. 1986-89), Assn. Trial Lawyers Am. (sustaining), Ind. Trial Lawyers Assn. (bd. dirs. 1990—, exec. com. 1995—, treas. 1997-99, sec. 1999), Am. Bd. Trial Advs., Tex. Trial Lawyers Assn., Ind. Golf Assn. (pres. 1995-97), Sagamore Inn of Ct., Indpls. Athletic Club, Crooked Stick Golf Club (pres. 1992-93). Personal injury, Product liability. Office: Hovde Law Firm 10585 N Meridian St Indianapolis IN 46290-1069

**HOVER, JOHN CHARLES,** lawyer; b. Wichita, Kans., Jan. 18, 1935; s. John Charles and Mabel Alice (Kirk) H.; m. Mary E. Hover, 1955 (div. 1966); children: John Charles, Kirk Ellis, Holley Anne. BS in Bus., LLB, U. Colo., 1959. Bar: Colo. 1959, Ariz. 1961, Idaho 1982. Assoc. Gordon & Gordon, Lamar, Colo., 1959-60; ptnr. Lewis & Roca, Phoenix, 1960-70, Moeller, Hover, Jensen & Henry, Phoenix, 1970-72; pvt. practice, Phoenix, 1972-78, McCall, Idaho, 1982-85; atty. Mountain Bell, Phoenix, 1978-80; of counsel Allen, Kimerer & La Velle, Phoenix, 1985-86, Harrison & Lerch, Phoenix, 1986-88; ptnr. Hover & Slomski, Phoenix, 1988-93, John C. Hover, P.C., Phoenix, 1994-95, 99—; sabbatical, 1980-82, 96-99. Fellow Ariz. Bar Assn.; mem. ABA, Ariz. Bar Assn. (Outstanding Svcs. award 1977), Colo. Bar Assn., Idaho Bar Assn., Order of Coif. Republican. Avocations: golf, fishing. General civil litigation, Contracts commercial, Bankruptcy. Home: 4816 E Fernwood Ct Cave Creek AZ 85331-6391 Office: Hover & Slomski 11811 N Tatum Blvd Ste 3031 Phoenix AZ 85028-1621

**HOVIS, ROBERT HOUSTON, III,** lawyer; b. Washington, Apr. 19, 1942; s. Robert Houston and Lera Frances (Robbins) H.; m. Mary Ann Jennings, Dec. 27, 1965. BS, U. Tenn., 1964, JD, 1966. Bar: Tenn. 1967, Va. 1967, U.S. Dist. Ct. (ea. dist.) Va. 1973. Asst. commonwealth atty. Fairfax County, Va., 1969-71; pvt. practice law Fairfax County, Fairfax County, 1971—; prin. Robert H. Hovis III PC, Annandale, Va.; commr. in chancery Circuit Ct. Fairfax County, 1969—; commr. in chancery Cir. Ct. Fairfax County, 1969—. Mem. adv. coun. Salvation Army, Annandale, 1984—; bd. dirs. Annandale C. of C., 1984. With U.S. Army, 1967-69, Germany. Mem. ATLA (cert. Nat. Coll. Advocacy 1981, cert. Med. Malprctice Advanced Coll. 1983), Va. Trial Lawyers Assn. (profl. negligence sect.), Va. State Bar, Fairfax County Bar Assn., Trial Lawyers for Pub. Justice (Va. state coord. 1993—), Fairfax County Cir. Ct. (ind. case evaluator), Ethridge Soc., Rotary (pres. 1983-84). Mem. ATLA (cert. Nat. Coll. Advocacy 1981, cert. Med. Malpractice Advanced Coll. 1983), Va. Trial Lawyers Assn. (profl. negligence sect.), Fairfax County Bar Assn., Va. State Bar, Trial Lawyers for Pub. Justice (Va. state coord. 1993—), Fairfax County Cir. Ct. (ind. case evaluator), Ethridge Soc., Million Dollar Advocates Forum. Democrat. Methodist. Lodge: Rotary (pres. 1983-84). Personal injury, Professional liability. Home: 2700 Green Holly Springs Ct Oakton VA 22124-1457 Office: 4544 John Marr Dr Annandale VA 22003-3308

**HOWALD, JOHN WILLIAM,** lawyer; b. St. Louis, Dec. 21, 1935; s. Herbert John and Irene Dorothy (Weber) H.; m. Nina M. Zierenderg, June 15, 1957 (div. 1970); children: Deborah A., Catherine A., Laura A., John William; m. Betty L. Curtis, Feb. 14, 1971; 1 stepchild, Tracy L. BS, U. Mo., 1957; JD, St. Louis U., 1962. Bar: Mo. 1962, U.S. Dist. Ct. (ea. dist.) Mo. 1962, U.S. Ct. Appeals (8th cir.) 1965, U.S. Supreme Ct. 1985. V.p. sales Eureka Svc. and Equip. Co., Eureka, Mo., 1959-62; ptnr. Sheehan, Furtaw & Howald, Hillsboro, Mo., 1963-64, Thurman, Nixon, Smith & Howald, Hillsboro, 1964-70, Thurman, Nixon, Smith, Howald, Weber & Bowles, Hillsboro, 1970-80, Thurman, Smith, Howald, Weber & Bowles, Hillsboro, 1989-91, Thurman, Howald, Weber, Bowles & Senkel, Hillsboro, 1991-95, Thurman, Howald, Weber, Senkel & Norrick, L.L.C., Hillsboro, 1995—; bd. dirs. LaBarque Ent. of Jefferson County, Hillsboro, 1965—, Rustic Hills Resort Ltd., Hillsboro, 1968—. Mem. Mo. Ethics Commn., 1994-98, vice-chmn., 1995-96, chmn., 1996-98. Lt. (j.g.) USN, 1957-59. Recipient Spl. award, Meramec Basin Assn., 1967, 69. Fellow Am. Bar Found., Am. Coll. Trust and Estate Counsel (Mo. chmn. 1987-92); mem. ABA, Estate Planning Coun. St. Louis (pres. 1990-91), Mo. Bar Assn. (bd. govs. 1975-87, Pres. Spl. award 1979), Jefferson County Bar Assn. (pres. 1963-64). Avocations: travel, golf. Estate planning, Real property, General corporate. Home: 3360 Franks Ct House Springs MO 63051-1005 Office: Thurman Howald Weber Senkel & Norrick LLC PO Box 800 One Thurman Ct Hillsboro MO 63050

**HOWARD, ALEX T., JR.,** federal judge; b. 1924. Student, U. Ala., 1942, U. Ala., 1946, Auburn U., 1942-44; JD, Vanderbilt U., 1950. U.S. probation officer Mobile, Ala., 1950-51; ptnr. Johnstone, Adams, Howard, Bailey & Gordon, Mobile, 1951-86; U.S. commr. U.S. Dist. Ct. (so. dist.) Ala., 1956-70; judge U.S. Dist. Ct. (so. dist.) Ala., Mobile, 1986—, chief judge, 1989-94; assoc. editor Am. Maritime Cases for Port of Mobile. Served to 2d lt. U.S. Army, 1943-46. Mem. ABA, Internat. Soc. Barristers, Internat. Assn. of Ins. Counsel, Maritime Law Assn. of U.S., Southeastern Admiralty Law Inst. (dir. 1978-80), Ala. Bar Assn., Ala. Def. Lawyers Assn. (dir. late 1950's), Mobile Bar Assn. (pres. 1973). Office: US Courthouse 113 Saint Joseph St Mobile AL 36602-3606

**HOWARD, ANDREW BAKER,** lawyer; b. Watertown, N.Y., July 26, 1969; s. Courtland Rogers and Maryanne H.; m. Elizabeth Edge, June 8, 1996; 1 child, Christopher Baker. BA cum laude, St. Lawrence U., 1991; JD cum laude, Union U., 1994. Bar: N.Y. 1995. Atty. Connor, Curran & Schram, Hudson, N.Y., 1994—; asst. dist. atty. Columbia County Dist. Atty., Hudson, 1995; instr. Am. Inst. Banking, Albany, 1997—. Mem. N.Y. State Bar Assn., Columbia County Bar Assn., Justinian Soc. Republican. Roman Catholic. Avocations: mountain biking, skiing, shooting. General civil litigation, Banking, Personal injury. Home: 216 Long Pond Rd Hewitt NJ 07421-3118 Office: Connor Curran & Schram PC 441 E Allen St Hudson NY 12534-2422

**HOWARD, BLAIR DUNCAN,** lawyer; b. Alexandria, Va.; s. T. Brooke and Elizabeth Duncan H.; m. Catherine Cremins; children: Thomas Brooke II, Caitlin Margaret. BA, U. Va., 1960; LLB, American U., 1963. Ptnr. Howard, Leino & Howard, Alexandria, Va., 1966—. Capt. USA, 1963-65. Named One in Best Lawyers of America (book), 1989—, Superstar Ohio Assn. Criminal Defense Lawyers, Columbus, 1994, One of Top Lawyers in Met. Washington, Washingtonian Mag. article, 1997. Fellow Am. Coll. Trial Lawyers; mem. ABA, ATLA, Alexandria Bar Assn., Va. State Bar Assn. (faculty professionalism course 1990-93). Office: Howard Leino & Howard 19 Culpeper St Warrenton VA 20186-3319

**HOWARD, CHARLES,** lawyer. Gen. counsel Appalachian Regional Commn., Washington. Office: Appalachian Regional Commn 1666 Connecticut Ave NW Washington DC 20009-1039*

**HOWARD, CHRISTOPHER HOLM,** lawyer; b. Cleve., Sept. 28, 1956; s. George Thomas and Karen Miriam (Holm) H.; m. Jaime Vaughn Austen, Dec. 18, 1988; 1 child, Alexandria Vaughan Austen Howard. AB in Polit. Sci., Johns Hopkins U., 1977; JD, Stanford U., 1980. Bar: Wash. 1980, U.S. Dist. Ct. (we. dist.) Wash. 1980, U.S. Ct. Appeals (9th cir.) 1981, U.S. Ct. Claims 1994, U.S. Dist. Ct. (ea. dist.) Wash. 1996. Assoc. Reed and McClure, Seattle, 1980-85, dir., 1986-88; shareholder, dir. Weiss Jensen Ellis & Howard, Seattle and Portland, Oreg., 1988—; dir. Weiss, Jensen, Ellis & Howard, Seattle and Portland, Oreg., 1989—. Mem. Wash. State Bar Assn. (interprofl. com. 1990-93, mem. rules profl. conduct com. 1999—), Wash. Soc. Hosp. Attys., Wash. Soc. Def. Trial Lawyers, Def. Rsch. Inst. Professional liability, Federal civil litigation, Health.

**HOWARD, DAVIS JONATHAN,** lawyer, educator; b. S.I., N.Y., Dec. 8, 1954; s. Royal Marwin and Muriel Lu (Russell) H. BA summa cum laude, Wagner Coll., 1976; JD, Yale U., 1982. Bar: N.Y. 1983, N.J. 1986, U.S. Dist. Ct. (so. and ea. dists.) N.Y. 1983, U.S. Dist. Ct. N.J. 1986, U.S. Ct. Appeals (3d cir.) 1987, U.S. Ct. Appeals (4th cir.) 1988, U.S. Ct. Appeals (2d cir.) 1994. Assoc. Robson & Miller, N.Y.C., 1983-85, Sills Cummis Zuckerman Radin Tischman Epstein & Gross, P.A., Newark, 1985-92; ptnr. Parry & Howard, P.A., Elizabeth, N.J., 1993-98; lectr. law Rutgers U. Sch. Law, Newark, 1987-89; faculty legal seminars, symposiums; adjunct Coll. of Staten Island, CUNY, 1999. Contbr. articles to legal jours.; editor-in-chief, co-founder Shepard's N.J. Ins. Law and Regulation Reporter, 1991. Dir. alumni sch. com. Yale U., 1989-96. Mem. ABA (tort and ins. practice sect., bus. law sect., sect. of litigation, com. on ins. coverage litigation, com. on ins. insolvency), N.Y. State Bar Assn. (com. on fed. cts. 1985-86, com. ins. coverage), N.J. Bar Assn., N.Y. County Lawyers Assn. (mem. com. on ins.), Def. Rsch. Inst., Assn. of Trial Lwayers of Am., Am. Soc. of Writers on Legal Subjects, Scribes. Fax number: 718-816-4961. Insurance, Federal civil litigation, General civil litigation. Home and Office: 46 Longfellow Ave Staten Island NY 10301-4616

**HOWARD, GEORGE, JR.,** federal judge; b. Pine Bluff, Ark., May 13, 1924. Student, Lincoln U., 1951; B.S., U. Ark., J.D., 1954; LL.D., 1976. Bar: Ark. bar 1953, U.S. Supreme Ct. bar 1959. Pvt. practice law Pine Bluff, 1953-77; spl. assoc. justice Ark. Supreme Ct., 1976, assoc. justice, 1977; justice U.S. Ct. Appeals, Ark., 1979-80; U.S. dist. judge, Eastern dist. Little Rock, 1980—; Mem. Ark. Claims Commn., 1969-77; chmn. Ark. adv. com. Civil Rights Commn.. Recipient citation in recognition of faithful and disting. svc. as mem. Supreme Ct. Com. of Profl. Conduct, 1980, disting. jurist award Jud. Coun. Nat. Bar Assn., 1980, Wiley A. Branton Issues Symposium award, 1990; voted outstanding trial judge 1984-85 Ark. Trial Lawyers Assn.; inducted Ark.'s Black Hall of Fame, 1994; recipient keepers of the spirit award Univ. Ark., Pine Bluff, 1995, quality svc. award Ark. Dem. Black Caucus, 1995. Mem. ABA, Ark. Bar Assn., Jefferson County Bar Assn. (pres.). Baptist.

**HOWARD, JEFFREY HJALMAR,** lawyer; b. N.Y.C., Aug. 23, 1944; s. Virgil Edward and Margaretta E. H.; m. Brenda H. Howard, June 19, 1966; children: Taggart Harrison, Brooke Kennedy. BA in Philosophy, Randolph-Macon Coll., 1966; postgrad. (English Speaking Union scholar) U. Edinburgh (Scotland), 1965; LLB, U. Va., 1969. Bar: D.C. 1970, U.S. Sup. Ct. 1978, Va. 1987. Law clk. Circuit Ct., Montgomery County, Md., 1969-70; assoc. Covington & Burling, Washington, 1970-74; assoc. gen. counsel for toxics, pesticides and solid waste U.S. EPA, Washington, 1974-76; ptnr. Crowell & Moring, 1989—; lectr. antitrust and environ. law U. Va. 1976-89; lectr. environ. law Peking U., Peoples Republic of China, 1986. Mem. ABA, D.C. Bar Assn., Va. Soc. Fellows, Order Coif, Alpha Psi Omega, Alpha Epsilon Pi, Delta Sigma Rho-Tau Kappa Alpha, Omicron Delta Kappa. Editorial bd. Va. Law Rev., 1967-69; contbr. chpts. to books and articles to profl. jours. Administrative and regulatory, Antitrust, Environmental. Home: 1021 Duchess Dr Mc Lean VA 22102-2007 Office: 1001 Pennsylvania Ave NW Washington DC 20004-2505

**HOWARD, JEFFREY R.,** lawyer, former state attorney general; b. Claremont, N.H.. BA, Plymouth St Coll-Univ N.H., 1978; JD, Law Ctr-Georgetown U, 1981. Assoc. atty. gen. Div. Legal Counsel; atty. Antitrust Div-Atty. Gen. Ofc., 1981; U.S. atty. Dist. of N.H., Concord, 1989-92; atty. gen. State of N.H., 1993-97; ptnr. Choate Hall & Stewart. Mem. Atty. Gen. Adv. Committee for Attys. Gen. Thornburg & Barr. *

**HOWARD, JOHN WAYNE,** lawyer; b. Newport, R.I., Dec. 17, 1948; s. Joseph Leon and Irene Elizabeth (Silver) H.; m. Kathleen Amanda Busby, Oct. 7. 1978. B.A., U. Calif.-San Diego, 1971; J.D. Calif. Western Sch. Law, 1976; postgrad. San Diego Inn of Ct., 1979, Hastings Coll. Advocacy, 1981. Harvard Law Sch., Program of Instructions for Lawyers, 1992, Bar: Calif. 1978, U.S. Dist. Ct. (so. dist.) Calif. 1978, U.S. Supreme Ct. 1989, Colo. 1989, U.S. Dist. Ct. (cen. dist.) Calif. 1991, U.S. Dist Ct. (no. dist.) Calif., U.S. Dist. Ct. (ea. dist.) Calif., U.S. Ct. of Appeals (9th cir.) 1995, U.S Ct. Appeals (D.C. cir.) 1996, U.S. Ct. of Claims, 1996. Assoc. Robert T. Dierdorff, San Diego, 1978-79; sole practice, San Diego, 1979-82; ptnr. Howard & Neeb, San Diego, 1982-84; prin. John W. Howard and Assocs., San Diego, 1984-86; gen. counsel Ace Parking, Inc., 1986-89, CCCA Inc., 1989-93; pres. Individual Rights Found. Inc., 1993-95, pres. Inst. for Constitutional Rights, Inc., 1995—, John W. Howard and Assoc., 1995—; jud. arbitrator Superior Ct. Calif., 1983—. Chmn., San Diego County Indigent Def. Adv. Bd., 1981-84, mem. subcom. on def. monitoring and budget for Office Defender Services of San Diego County; mem. select com. on small bus. Calif. State Assembly, 1983-90; chmn. San Diego Pub. Arts Adv. Bd.; mem. San Diego County Council of Com. Chairs; chmn. precinct orgn. Roger Hedgecock for Supt. Campaign Com., 1976, mem. steering com., 1976; chmn. steering com. Hedgecock for Mayor, 1982, Cleator for Mayor, 1986; chmn. Muscular Dystrophy Telethon, San Diego, 1983; vice chmn. San Diego Festival of Arts, 1983-84; pres. Bowery Theatre, San Diego, 1984-89; pres., bd. dirs. La Jolla Stage Co.; founder, bd. dirs. San Diego Theatre League; 1st v.p., bd. dirs. Muscular Dystrophy Assn.; bd. dirs. Patrick Henry Meml. Found., Brookneal, Va., The Poe Mus., Richmond, Va., San Diego Med. Oncology Research Found., Ilan-Lael Found., Multiple Sclerosis Soc., Am. Ballet Found., Wellness Community, Teatro Mascara Magica; bd. dirs., chmn. legal affairs subcom. Calif. Motion Picture Council; mem. adv. bd. dirs. San Diego Motion Picture Bur.; mem. pub. edn. com. Am. Cancer Soc.; founder, bd. dirs. San Diego Theatre Found., 1984—; mem. 44th Congl. Dist. Adv. Com.; mem. Com. to Re-Elect Congressman Bill Lowery; mem. San Diego County 4th Dist. Adv. Com. Mem. ABA, Calif. State Bar, Assn. Trial Lawyers Am., Am. Corp. Counsel Assn., U. Calif.-San Diego Alumni Assn. (past v.p., bd. dirs.), Calif. Western Sch. Law Alumni Assn., Friendly Sons of St. Patrick, Delta Kappa Epsilon, Phi Alpha Delta. Republican. Lodge: Rotary, Enright Inn of Ct., Am. Inns of Ct. State civil litigation, Federal civil litigation, Constitutional.

**HOWARD, LEWIS SPILMAN,** lawyer; b. Knoxville, Tenn., Oct. 10, 1930; s. Frank Catlett and Lillian (Spilman) H.; m. Anne Robinson, Dec. 26, 1953 (div. 1976); children: Catherine C., Martha S., Lewis S. Jr., Laura A. BSBA, U. Tenn., 1953, JD, 1953. Bar: Tenn. 1953, U.S. Ct. Mil. Appeals 1954, U.S. Dist. Ct. Ga. 1954, U.S. Dist. Ct. Tenn. 1956, U.S. Ct. Appeals (6th cir.) 1959. Ptnr. Kennerly, Montgomery, Howard & Finley, Knoxville, 1957-84, Howard & Ridge, Knoxville, 1984—; gen. counsel Coal Creek Mining and Mfg. Co., Knoxville, 1969—, pres., 1971—. Vice chmn. Knoxville Bd. Edn., 1968-71. Capt. JAGC, USAR, 1953-56. Mem. ABA, Tenn. Bar Assn., Knoxville Bar Assn., Cherokee Country Club, Club LeConte. Republican. Presbyterian. Avocation: boating. General corporate, Mergers and acquisitions, Natural resources. Home: 1604 Kenesaw Ave Knoxville TN 37919-7863 Office: Howard & Ridge First Tennessee Tower #1304 Knoxville TN 37929

**HOWARD, LOWELL BENNETT, JR.,** lawyer; b. Nelsonville, Ohio, Oct. 19, 1959; s. Lowell Bennett and Jeanetta (Turner) H.; m. Christine Ellen Briggs, Sept. 1, 1984; children: Lowell Bennett III, Geoffrey Hamilton Briggs. AB, Miami U., Oxford, Ohio, 1982; MBA, U. Mich., 1985; JD, Ohio State U., 1987. Bar: Ohio 1987, U.S. Dist. Ct. (so. dist.) Ohio 1988. Law clk. Supreme Ct. of Ohio, Columbus, 1987-88, 92; assoc. Vorys, Sater, Seymour and Pease, Columbus, 1988-91; asst. counsel Honda of Am. Mfg., Inc., Marysville, Ohio, 1992-96, sr. asst. counsel, 1996—. Mng. editor Ohio State Law Jour., 1986-87. Mem. ABA, Ohio Bar Assn., Columbus Bar Assn., Union County Bar Assn. Democrat. Christian. Avocations: reading, cycling, skiing, trivia. Private international, Pension, profit-sharing, and employee benefits, Administrative and regulatory. Home: 207 W Dominion Blvd Columbus OH 43214-2502 Office: Honda of Am Mfg Inc 24000 Honda Pkwy Marysville OH 43040-9251

**HOWARD, MALCOLM JONES,** federal judge; b. Kinston, N.C., June 24, 1939; s. Clayton and Thelma (Jones) H.; m. Eloise McGinty, Nov. 24, 1964; children: Shannon Lea, Joshua Brian. BS, U.S. Mil. Acad., 1962; JD, Wake Forest U., Winston Salem, N.C., 1970. Bar: N.C. 1970, U.S. Ct. Appeals (4th cir.) 1973. Sec. Judge Adv. Gen. Sch., Charlottesville, Va., 1970-71; legis. counsel to sec. U.S. Army, Washington, 1971-72; asst. U.S. atty. Ea. Dist. N.C., Raleigh, 1972-73; dep. spl. counsel to Pres. U.S. Washington, 1974; sr. ptnr. Howard Browning Sams & Poole, Greenville, S.C., 1974-88; U.S. dist. judge Ea. Dist. N.C., Greenville, 1988—. With U.S. Army, 1962-82. Office: US Dist Ct PO Box 5006 Greenville NC 27835-5006

**HOWARD, MARILYN HOEY,** lawyer; b. Keene, N.H., Aug. 17, 1952; d. Thomas John and Arleen Carol (Grimmelman) Hoey; m. Charles Taylor Howard, Apr. 14, 1984; children: Joseph Dale, John Thomas. BA, Univ. Fla., 1975; JD, Duke Univ. Sch. Law, 1978. Bar: Fla. 1979, U.S. Cir. Ct. (5th and 11th cirs.) Fla. 1980. Sr. coun. Harris Corp., Melbourne, Fla., 1978-98; mem. adv. bd. Indian River Nat. Bank, 1998—. Mem. Fla. Bar (chair corp. counsel com. Bus. Law Sect. 1996-98, chair quality of life, stress mgmt. com. 1995-97),. Republican. Avocations: writing, poetry, Italian. Contracts commercial, Intellectual property, Communications. Home: 2552 King St NE Palm Bay FL 32905-4704

**HOWARD, STEVEN GRAY,** lawyer; b. Lafayette, Ind., Aug. 9, 1951; s. C. Warren and Joan Elizabeth (Gray) H.; m. Deborah F. Mooring, July 24, 1982; children: Jeremy, Jessica, Judd, Christopher, Adrienne. BA, Purdue U., 1973; JD with honors, U. Ark., 1977. Bar: Ark. 1977, U.S. Dist. Ct. (ea. and we. dists.) Ark. 1978. Assoc. Thaxton & Hout, Newport, Ark., 1977-86; ptnr. Thaxton, Hout & Howard, Newport, Ark., 1986—; mcpl. judge City of Tuckerman, Ark., 1979—; city atty. Campbell Sta., Ark., 1977—. Assoc. editor U. Ark. Law Rev., 1976-77. Bd. dirs. Northeast Ark. Legal Services, Inc., Newport, 1978-82, Legal Services of Ark., Little Rock, 1980-82. Mem. ABA, Ark. Bar Assn., Jackson County Bar Assn. (pres. 1979-80), Ark. Trial Lawyers Assn., Delta Theta Phi, Order of Barristers. Democrat. Methodist. Lodge: Rotary. Avocations: hunting, fishing. Real property, State civil litigation, General practice. Office: Thaxton Hout & Howard 600 3rd St Newport AR 72112-3218

**HOWARD, SUSANNE C.,** lawyer; b. White Plains, N.Y., July 14, 1951; d. Leonard F. and Trudy Howard. AB in History, Washington U., St. Louis, 1973; JD, Cath. U., Washington, 1977. Bar: Mass. 1978, U.S. Dist. Ct. Mass. 1978, U.S. Ct. Appeals (1st cir.) 1979. Researcher Environ. Law Inst., Washington, 1976-77; mng. ptnr. Thomas & Howard, Cambridge, Mass., 1977-80; sr. assoc. Choate, Hall & Stewart, Boston, 1981-86; v.p., asst. gen. counsel Aldrich, Eastman & Waltch, Inc., Boston, 1986-87; sr. assoc. Csaplar & Bok, Boston, 1987-88; counsel Warner & Stackpole, Boston, 1988-92; New England regional counsel Trust for Public Land, Boston, 1992-94; pres. Consensus Capital, Inc., Cambridge, Mass., 1995-99; pres. L.F. Howard Assocs., Inc., N.Y.C., 1998—, also bd. dirs.; mem. faculty Mass. Continuing Legal Edn. Programs, Boston, 1988-92. Contrb. articles to profl. jours. Mem. Environ. Adv. Com. to Atty. Gen., Mass., 1990-95; bd. dirs. Cambridge YWCA, 1987-93, pres., 1991-92. Mem. Boston Bar Assn. (mem. steering com. environ. sect. 1987-91, chair wetlands and waterways com. 1989-91), Women's Bar Assn. Mass. (bd. dirs. 1981-83, co-chair legis. policy com. 1979-81, Pub. Svc. to Bar and Cmty. award 1991). Finance, Real property, Environmental. Office: LF Howard Assocs Inc 60 E 42nd St Rm 1644 New York NY 10165-0044

**HOWE, DRAYTON FORD, JR.,** lawyer; b. Seattle, Nov. 17, 1931; s. Drayton Ford and Virginia (Wester) H.; m. Joyce Arnold, June 21, 1952; 1 son, James Drayton. AB, U. Calif., Berkeley, 1953; LLB, U. Calif., San Francisco, 1957. Bar: Calif. 1958. CPA Calif. Atty. IRS, 1958-61; tax dept. supr. Ernst & Ernst, San Francisco, 1962-67; ptnr. Bishop, Barry, Howe, Haney & Ryder, San Francisco, 1968—; lectr. on tax matters U. Calif. extension, 1966-76. Mem. Calif. Bar Assn., San Francisco Bar Assn. (chmn. client relations com. 1977), Calif. Soc. CPA's. State civil litigation, Corporate taxation, Estate planning. Office: Bishop Barry Howe Haney & Ryder 44 Montgomery St Ste 1300 San Francisco CA 94104-4615

**HOWE, EDWIN A(LBERTS), JR.,** lawyer; b. Cleve., Jan. 21, 1939; s. Edwin Alberts and Helen Dorothy (Beck) H.; m. Margaret Joan Webber, Sept. 12, 1964; children: Christopher, Melissa, Katie. BA, Yale U., 1961; JD with honors, U. Mich., 1964. Bar: N.Y. 1965, U.S. Supreme Ct. 1976. Assoc. Devevoise and Plimpton, N.Y.C., 1964-70; ptnr. Howe & Addington LLP, N.Y.C., 1970—. Trustee Garden City (N.Y.) Pub. Libr., 1982-86, chmn., 1986-88; trustee Village of Garden City, 1988-89; mem. Garden City Environ. Adv. Bd., 1994-98; mem. Westport Land Acquisitions Com., 1999—. Fellow Inst. Dirs.; mem. ABA, Internat. Fiscal Assn., Counselors of Real Estate, Urban Land Inst., Nat. Real Estate Forum (chmn. 1996—), Assn. of Bar of City of N.Y., N.Y. State Bar Assn., Internat. Bar Assn., Internat. Law Assn. (Am. Br.), Am. Soc. Internat. Law, Am. Fgn. Law Assn., Sky Club, Yale Club, Netherland Club, No. Lake George Yacht Club, Lake George Assn., Rogers Rock Club. Republican. Episcopalian. Avocation: fishing, golf, reading, theatre, languages. Private international, General corporate, Real property. Home: 164 Roseville Rd Westport CT 06880-2617 Office: Howe & Addington LLP 450 Lexington Ave New York NY 10017-3911

**HOWE, JONATHAN THOMAS,** lawyer; b. Evanston, Ill., Dec. 16, 1940; s. Frederick King and Rosalie Charlotte (Volz) H.; m. Lois Helene Braun, July 12, 1963; children: Heather C., Jonathan Thomas Jr., Sara E. BA with honors, Northwestern U., 1963; JD with distinction, Duke U., 1966. Bar: Ill. 1966, U.S. Dist. Ct. (no. dist.) Ill. 1966, U.S. Ct. Appeals (7th cir.) 1967, U.S. Tax Ct. 1968, U.S. Supreme Ct. 1970, U.S. Ct. Appeals (D.C. cir.) 1976, U.S. Ct. Appeals (9th cir.) 1980, U.S. Ct. Appeals (4th, 5th, 11th dirs.) 1983, U.S. Claims Ct. 1990. Ptnr. Jenner & Block, Chgo., 1966-85, sr. ptnr. in charge assn. and adminstrv. law dept., 1978-85; founding and sr. ptnr., pres. Howe & Hutton, Chgo., Washington, 1985—; exec. and adv. coms. to Ill. Sec. of State to revise the Ill. Not for Profit Act, 1983-86; dir. Pacific Mut. Realty Investors, Inc., 1985-86; dir. cable TV options for public Chgo. Access Corp., 1995-97. Contbg. editor Ill. Inst. for Continuing Legal Edn., 1973—, Sporting Goods Bus., 1977-91, Meeting News, 1978-88, Meetings Mgr., 1988—, Meetings and Convs., 1991—; contbr. articles to profl. jours.; legal editor Meetings and Convs., 1990—. Mem. Dist. 27 Bd. Edn., Northbrook, Ill., 1969-89, sec., 1969-72, pres., 1973-84; chmn. bd. trustees Sch. Employee Benefit Trust, 1979-85; founding bd. dirs., pres. Sch. Mgmt. Found. Ill., 1976-84; mem. exec. com. Northfield Twp. Rep. Orgn., 1967-71; bd. deacons Village Presbyn. Ch. Northbrook, 1975-78, trustee, 1981-83; mem. Arts and Music Forum, 4th Presbyn. Ch., Chgo., 1990-93; spl. advisor Pres.'s Coun. Phys. Fitness and Sports, 1983-87, Duke Univ. Sch. of Law Bd. of Visitors (life mem.). Named Industry Leader of Yr., Meeting Industry, 1987, Sch. Bd. Mem. Yr. (twice) , Ill. State Bd. Edn.; recipient Internat. Found. PaceSetters award Hospitality Sales Mktg. Assn., 1996. Fellow Internat. Forum of Travel and Tourism Advs., Am. Soc. Assn. Execs. (vice-chmn. legal com. 1983-86); mem. Internat. Assn. Conv. and Hosp. Indsl. Attys. (founder), ABA (antitrust sect. Nat. Inst. com., trade assn. law com. corp. banking and bus. law sect., sect. on litigation, adminstrv. law sect.; mem. internat. law com., continuing edn. com., tort and ins. practice, vice-chmn. com. sports law 1986—, standing com. meetings and travel 1988-93, spl. advisor 1993—), Task Force on Membership Benefits for Disabled Lawyers, Ill. Bar Assn. (antitrust sect., civil practice sect., sch. law sect., adminstrv. law sect.; co-editor Antitrust Newsletter 1986-70), Chgo. Bar Assn. (def. of prisoners com. 1966-83, antitrust law com. 1971—, continuing edn. com. 1977—, chmn. assn. and non-profit soc. law com. 1984-86), Am. Soc. Assn. Execs. (vice-chmn. legal com., founding mem. legal sect.), Assn. Hospitality Industry Attys. (founder, bd. dirs. 1994—), Nat. Sch. Bds. Assn. (nat. bd. dirs. 1979-89, exec. com. 1981-89, sec.-treas. 1983-85, 2d v.p. 1985-86, pres.-elect 1986-87, chmn. devel. com. 1982-87, pres. 1987-88), D.C. Bar Assn., Am. Judicature Soc., Ill. Assn. Sch. Bds. (pres. 1977-79, bd. dirs. 1971-88), Chi Bar Found. (life), Assn. Forum Chicagoland (assoc., formerly Chgo. Soc. Assn. Execs.), Nat. Sch. Bds. Assn. Found. (pres./trustee 1995—), Greater Washington Soc. Assn. Execs., Legal Club, Law Club, Mid-Am. Club, Tower Club, Univ. Club Chgo., Psi Upsilon. Non-profit and tax-exempt organizations, General practice, General civil litigation. Home: 126 W Delaware Pl Chicago IL 60610-3252 Office: 20 N Wacker Dr Ste 4200 Chicago IL 60606-3191 also: 1899 L St NW Washington DC 20036-3804

**HOWE, KAREN LOUISE,** lawyer; b. Corning, N.Y., Jan. 2, 1964; d. George R. Cleveland and Alberta B. Rhoda; m. William Earl Howe, May 1, 1993. BS, Keuka Coll., 1986; JD, Syracuse Coll., 1989. Bar: N.Y. 1990. Pub. defender Cortland (N.Y.) County Pub. Defender's Office, 1990—. Mem. N.Y. State Bar Assn., Cortland County Bar Assn. Office: Cortland County Pub Defender 60 Central Ave Cortland NY 13045-2746

**HOWE, RICHARD CUDDY,** state supreme court chief justice; b. South Cottonwood, Utah, Jan. 20, 1924; s. Edward E. and Mildred (Cuddy) H.; m. Juanita Lyon, Aug. 30, 1949; children: Christine Howe Schultz, Andrea Howe Reynolds, Bryant, Valerie Howe Winegar, Jeffrey, Craig. B.S., U. Utah, 1945, J.D., 1948. Bar: Utah. Law clk. to Justice James H. Wolfe, Utah Supreme Ct., 1949-50; judge city ct. Murray, Utah, 1951; individual practice law Murray, 1952-80; assoc. justice Utah Supreme Ct., Salt Lake City, 1980—, justice, chief justice; mem. Utah Constnl. Revision Commn., 1976-85. Chmn., original mem. Salt Lake County Merit Coun.; mem. Utah Ho. of Reps., 1951-58, 69-72, Utah Senate, 1973-78. Named Outstanding Legislator Citizens' Conf. State Legislatures, 1972. Mem. ABA, Utah Bar Assn., Sons of Utah Pioneers. Mem. LDS Ch. Office: Utah Supreme Ct 450 S State St PO Box 140210 Salt Lake City UT 84114-0210

**HOWE, RICHARD RIVES,** lawyer; b. Portland, Oreg., Dec. 21, 1942; s. Hubert Shattuck Jr. and Anna Gertrude (Moody) H.; m. Elizabeth Anne Crowell, Aug. 29, 1964; 1 child, Richard Rives Jr. BA, Yale U., 1964; JD, Harvard U., 1967. Bar: N.Y. 1968, U.S. Ct. Appeals (2d cir.) 1973, U.S. Dist. Ct. (so. and ea. dists.) N.Y. 1973, U.S. Supreme Ct. 1973. Assoc. Sullivan & Cromwell, N.Y.C., 1967-74, ptnr., 1974—. Bd. dirs. Peoples' Symphony Concerts, N.Y.C., 1983—, Bar Assurance and Reinsurance Ltd., Bermuda, 1994—, Nat. Com. Am. Fgn. Policy, Inc., 1999—. Mem. ABA (mem. com. on corp. practice, bus. law sect.), N.Y. State Bar Assn. (mem. exec. com. 1982-99, chmn. 1992-93, bus. law sect., chmn. securities regulation com. 1982-86), Assn. Bar City of N.Y., Phi Beta Kappa, Pi Sigma Alpha. Democrat. Securities, General corporate, Mergers and acquisitions. Home: 86 Woodfield Dr Short Hills NJ 07078-1654 Office: Sullivan & Cromwell 125 Broad St Fl 28 New York NY 10004-2489

**HOWELL, ALLEN WINDSOR,** lawyer; b. Montgomery, Ala., Mar. 10, 1949; s. Elvin and Bennie Merle (Windsor) H.; m. Donna K. Graffander, Sept. 2, 1989; children: Christopher Darby, Joshua Darby, Jeremiah Graffander. BA, Huntington Coll., 1971; JD, Jones Sch. Law, 1974. Bar: Ala. 1974, U.S. Supreme Ct. 1977, U.S. Ct. Appeals (fed. cir.) 1983, U.S. Ct. Appeals (11th cir.) 1981, U.S. Tax Ct. 1979, U.S. Claims Ct. 1982, U.S. Dist. Ct. (mid. dist.) Ala. 1975, U. Dist. Ct. (so. dist.) Ala. 1978. Archivist Hist. Rsch. Ctr. Air U., Maxwell AFB, Ala., 1972-75; pvt. practice Montgomery, 1975-82, 83—; adj. prof. Faulkner U., Montgomery, 1975—, law sch. 1983-85; asst. atty. gen., chief legal sect. Ala. Medicaid Agy., Montgomery, 1982-83. Author: Alabama Civic Practice Forms, 1986, 3d edit., 1992, Alabama Torts Case Finder, 1988, Alabama Personal Injury and Torts, 1996, Trial Handbook for Alabama Lawyers, 2d edit., 1998. Hon. lt. col., aide de camp Gov. Ala., 1974. Mem. ABA (contbr. editor profl. liability newsletter, litigation sect. 1990-92), Assn. Trial Lawyers Am., Montgomery County Bar Assn. (newsletter editorial com. 1984-85), Nat. Bd. Trial Adv. (cert. civil litigation 1981, 86, 91, examiner ethics, evidence and civil procedure). Mem. Ch. of Christ. Insurance, Personal injury, Probate. Office: PO Box 70367 Montgomery AL 36107-0367

**HOWELL, ARTHUR,** lawyer; b. Atlanta, Aug. 24, 1918; s. Arthur and Katharine (Mitchell) H.; m. Caroline Sherman, June 14, 1941; children: Arthur, Caroline, Eleanor, Richard, Peter, James; m. Janet Kerr Franchot, Dec. 16, 1972. AB, Princeton U., 1939; JD, Harvard U., 1942; LLD (hon.), Oglethorpe U., 1972. Bar: Ga. 1942. Assoc. F.M., 1942-45; ptnr. Alston & Bird (and predecessor firms), 1945-89, of counsel, 1989—; bd. dirs., gen. counsel Atlantic Steel Co., 1960-93; pres., bd. dirs. Summit Industries, Inc.; bd. dirs. Enterprise Funds; chmn. bd. dirs. Crescent Banking Co.; past pres. Atlanta Legal Aid Soc.; emeritus mem. bd. dirs. Crescent Bank and Trust Co. Pres. Met. Atlanta Cmty. Svcs., 1956, dir., 1953—; pres. Cmty. Planning Coun., 1961-63; gen. chmn. United Appeal, 1955; spl. atty. gen. State Ga., 1948-55; spl. counsel Univ. Sys. Ga., State Sch. Bldg. Authorities, 1951-70; adv. com. Ga. Corp. Code, 1967—; chmn. Atlanta Adv. Com. Pks.; trustee, past chmn. Oglethorpe U.; trustee Princeton, 1964-68, Atlanta Speech Sch., Westminister Schs., Atlanta, Episcopal H.S., Alexandria, Va.; emeritus trustee Morehouse Coll., past trustee Inst. Internat. Edn., mem. exec. com. 1969-72; elder, trustee, chmn. bd. trustees Presbyn. Ch., 1985-89. Named hon. alumnus Ga. Inst. Tech. Mem. ABA, Ga. Bar Assn., Atlanta Bar Assn., Am. Law Inst. (life), Lawyers Club of Atlanta (past pres.), Am. Judicature Soc., Soc. Colonial Wars, Capital City Club, Piedmont Driving Club, Commerce Club, Homosassa Fishing Club, Nassau Club, Princeton Club, Phi Beta Kappa. Probate, General corporate. Home: 200 Larkspur Ln Highlands NC 28741-8388 Office: Alston & Bird One Atlantic Ctr 1201 W Peachtree St NW Ste 4200 Atlanta GA 30309-3424

**HOWELL, DENNIS LEE,** lawyer; b. Marion, N.C., Oct. 2, 1951; s. Clayton Lee and Herma (Thomas) H.; m. Marilyn Howell, Apr. 27, 1980; children: Christopher Lee, Andrew Jackson. BS in Bus. Adminstrn. summa cum laude, Western Carolina U., 1969-73; JD, U.N.C., 1973-76. Bar: N.C. 1976, U.S. Dist. Ct. 1976, U.S. Ct. Appeals (4th cir.) 1976. Partner Howell & Howell, Marshall, N.C., 1976; assoc. partner Pritchard & Hise, Spruce Pine, N.C., 1976-77; partner Pritchard, Hise & Howell, Spruce Pine, N.C., 1977-78, Hise, Howell & Harrison, Spruce Pine, N.C., 1978-79; pvt. practice Burnsville, N.C., 1979-85; partner Howell & Peterson, Burnsville, N.C., 1985-87; pvt. practive Burnsville, N.C., 1987—; atty. Yancey County Bd. Edn., Burnsville, N.C.; bd. dirs. Southeastern Savings & Loan, Burnsville, N.C. Vice-chmn. Yancey County (N.C.) Bd. Edn., Burnsville, 1986-90; pres. Yancey County Youth Football League, 1985-87; coach Yancey County Youth Basketball, 1993—. Mem. N.C. Acad. Trial Lawyers, Alpha Phi Sigma, Phi Kappa Phi. Dem. Presbyn. Avocations: biking, hiking, basketball, fishing, golf. General practice, Criminal, Personal injury. Office: 9 E Main St Ste 100 Burnsville NC 28714-2916

**HOWELL, DONALD LEE,** lawyer; b. Waco, Tex., Jan. 31, 1935; s. Hilton Emory and Louise (Hatchett) H.; m. Gwendolyn Avera, June 13, 1957; children: Daniel Liege, Alison Avera, Anne Turner. BA cum laude, Baylor U., 1956; JD with honors, U. Tex., 1963. Bar: Tex. 1963. Assoc. Vinson & Elkins, Houston, 1963-70, ptnr., 1970—, mem. mgmt. com., 1980—. Capt. USAFR, 1956-59. Fellow Am. Bar Found., Tex. Bar Found., Houston Bar Found., Am. Law Inst.; mem. ABA, Am. Coll. Bond Counsel, Houston Bar Assn., Nat. Assn. Bond Lawyers (pres. 1981-82, bd. dirs. 1979-83), Attys. Liability Assurance Soc. (Bermuda bd. dirs. 1992—, U.S. bd. dirs, 1992—), Houston Club, Houston Ctr. Club, Order of Coif, Phi Delta Phi. Democrat. Episcopalian. Finance, Municipal (including bonds), Public utilities.

**HOWELL, GEORGE COOK, III,** lawyer; b. New Orleans, June 27, 1956; s. George C. Jr. and Billie Grace (Webb) H.; children: Margaret Sloan, George C. IV. AB magna cum laude, Princeton U., 1978; JD, U.Va., 1981. Bar: Va. 1981, U.S. Dist. Ct. (ea. dist.) Va. 1982, U.S. Ct. Appeals (4th cir.) 1982. Law clk. U.S. Dist. Ct. (ea. dist.) Va., Alexandria, 1981-82; assoc. Hunton & Williams, Richmond, Va., 1982-89, ptnr., 1989—. Contbr. Va. Law Rev., 1980; editor-in-chief Va. Tax Rev., 1980-81; articles editor The Tax Lawyer, 1983-86, mng. editor, 1987-89. Mem. usher's guild 1st Presbyn. Ch., Richmond, 1986-90; participant Leadership Metro Richmond, 1987-88. Mem. ABA (taxation sect. chmn. remic task force 1987-88, chmn. mini-program on mortgage-backed securities 1988, chmn. subcom. on asset securitization 1988-90, vice chmn. com. on fin. trans. 1990-92, chmn. com. on fin. trans. 1992-94, sec. taxation 1995-97, mem. sect. taxation coun., 1997—), Princeton Assn. Va. (treas. 1987-89, pres. 1989-91), Order of Coif, Phi Beta Kappa. Republican. Avocations: golf, tennis, basketball, running, the stock market. Corporate taxation. Office: Hunton & Williams 951 E Byrd St Ste 200 Richmond VA 23219-4074

**HOWELL, HARLEY THOMAS,** lawyer; b. Chgo., June 5, 1937; s. Harley W. and Geneva (Engelmann) H.; m. Aliceann A. McLaughlin, Apr. 23, 1983; children by previous marriage: Shelley A. Young, Rebecca L., Emily S. AB, Princeton U., 1959; JD, Yale U., 1962. Bar: Md. 1962, U.S. Supreme Ct. 1966, D.C. 1972. Law clk. to chief judge U.S. Ct. Appeals (4th cir.), 1962-63; assoc. Semmes, Bowen & Semmes, Balt., 1966-72, ptnr., 1972-92; ptnr. Howell, Gately, Whitney & Carter LLP, Towson, Md., 1992-98; counsel Howell, Gately, Whitney & Carter LLP, Towson, 1998-99; ptnr. Howell & Gately, Towson, 1999—; mem. Gov.'s Commn. to Revise Annotated Code Md., 1975-85; mem. standing com. on rules of practice and procedure Ct. Appeals of Md., 1985—. Bd. dirs. Balt. Symphony Orch., 1975—, sec., 1986—; trustee Sheppard & Enoch Pratt Hosp., Towson, 1991—. Capt. JAG Corps, U.S. Army, 1963-66. Decorated Army Commendation medal. Fellow Am. Coll. Trial Lawyers, Am. Acad. Appellate Lawyers, Md. Bar Found.; mem. ABA, Md. State Bar Assn., Bar Assn. Balt. City, Balt. County Bar Assn., D.C. Bar Assn., Fed. Bar Assn., Wine and Food Soc., Wranglers Law Club (Balt.). State civil litigation, Federal civil litigation, Appellate. Home: 1012 Chestnut Ridge Dr Lutherville Timonium MD 21093-1716 Office: Howell & Gately Court Towers 210 W Pennsylvania Ave Ste 240 Baltimore MD 21204-5325

**HOWELL, JAMES F.,** lawyer; b. Wewoka, Okla., July 14, 1934; s. F.F. and Lena Howell; m. Diann Harris; children: Cheryl, David F., Mark. Student, Ea. Okla. A&M Jr. Coll., 1954; BS, Okla. Bapt. U., 1956; JD, Okla. U., 1963. Bar: Okla. 1963, U.S. Dist. Ct. (we. dist.) Okla., U.S. Dist. Ct. (ea. dist.) Okla, U.S. Ct. Appeals (10th cir.), U.S. Supreme Ct. Sr. ptnr. James F. Howell and Assocs., Parklawn, Reno, Okla., Midwest City, Okla.; mcpl. judge, Midwest City, 1963-70; mem. Okla. State Senate, 1970-86. Chmn. grantors com. Midwest City Hosp., 1998; bd. dirs. Bapt. Hosp., 1971-97; trustee Okla. Bapt. U., 1973; chmn. of deacons, First Bapt. Ch. of Midwest City, trustee, supt. and tchr. Sunday Sch., 1957—. Mem. ATLA, Okla. Bar Assn., Oklahoma County Bar Assn. (past bd. dirs.), Okla. trial Lawyers Assn., Alumni Assn. of Okla. Bapt. U. (pres. bd. dirs.), Midwest City C. of C. (past pres.), Delta Theta Phi, Rotary *pres. 1970-71). Personal injury. Office: PO Box 10798 Midwest City OK 73140-1798

**HOWELL, JAY CHARLTON,** lawyer; b. Findlay, Ohio, June 28, 1949; s. Carl K. and Loucille (Mullen) H. BA, U. Fla., 1972; JD, So. Meth. U., 1976. Bar: Tex. 1976, U.S. Dist. Ct. (no. dist.) Tex. 1977, U.S. Supreme Ct. 1983. Pvt. practice Dallas, 1976-77; asst. state atty. Office of State Atty., Jacksonville, Fla., 1977-81; chief counsel U.S. Senate Subcom. in Investigations, Washington, 1981-84; exec. dir. Nat. Ctr. for Missing/Exploited Children, Washington, 1984-87; ptnr. Anderson and Howell, Jacksonville, 1987—; mem. adv. bd. Nat. Ctr. Prosecution Child Abuse, Alexandria, Va., 1987—; mem. Mayors Com. on Children, Jacksonville, 1988; chmn. Victims Con Amend Com., Fla., 1987—. Author: Laws to Protect Children, 1985. Bd. dirs. Youth Crisis Ctr., Jacksonville, 1987. Mem. Assn. Trial Lawyers Am., Nat. Assn. Counsael Children, Nat. Assn. Victim Assistance, Sigma Chi. Personal injury. Office: Anderson and Howell 2029 3rd St N Jaxville Bch FL 32250-7429

**HOWELL, MARK FRANKLIN,** lawyer; b. El Paso, Tex., Nov. 19, 1934; s. Benjamin Randolph and Romaine (Safford) H.; m. Linda O'Reilly (div.); m. Jayne Upton (div.); m. Linda Way; children: Madeline, Celia, Cara. BA in History, Stanford U., 1956; LLB, U. Tex., 1961. Bar: Tex. 1961, U.S. Ct. Customs and Patent Appeals 1967, U.S. Supreme Ct. 1971. Ptnr. Howell & Fields, El Paso, 1961-86; sole practice El Paso, 1986—; founder El Paso Legal Svcs., 1970; bd. dirs. Tex. Property and Casualty Guaranty Fund Assn., 1992-97; mem. State Bar Pattern Jury Change Com., 1994-98. Contbr. articles to profl. jours. Chmn. Mayor's Com. on Housing, El Paso, 1970; vice chmn., commr. El Paso Housing Authority, 1970-72. Served to capt. U.S. Army, 1956-58. Diplomate Am. Bd. Trial Advs. (nat. bd. dirs. 1994—, pres. El Paso chpt. 1993-94); mem. ATLA (sustaining; state del. 1981-83), Tex. Bar Assn. (chmn. state bar tort and compensation sect. 1988-89), El Paso County Bar Assn. (bd. dirs. 1984-85), Tex. Trial Lawyers Assn. (bd. dirs. 1973-81, 86-87), El Paso Trial Lawyers Assn. (pres. 1975). Democrat. Episcopalian. Federal civil litigation, State civil litigation. Home: 310 N Mesa St El Paso TX 79901-1364

**HOWELL, R(OBERT) THOMAS, JR.,** lawyer, former food company executive; b. Racine, Wis., July 18, 1942; s. Robert T. and Margaret Paris (Billings) H.; m. Karen Wallace Corbett, May 11, 1968; children: Clarinda, Margaret, Robert. AB, Williams Coll., 1964; JD, U. Wis., 1967; postgrad., Harvard U., 1981. Bar: Wis. 1968, Ill. 1968, U.S. Dist. Ct. (no. dist.) Ill.

1968, U.S. Tax Ct. Assoc. Hopkins & Sutter, Chgo., 1967-71; atty. The Quaker Oats Co., Chgo., 1971-77, counsel, 1977-80, v.p., assoc. gen. corp. counsel, 1980-84, v.p., gen. corp. counsel, 1984-96, corp. sec., 1994-96; of counsel Seyfarth, Shaw, Fairweather & Geraldson, Chgo., 1997—; bd. dirs. Ill. Inst. of Continuing Legal Edn. Editor: (mags.) Barrister, 1975-77, Compleat Lawyer, 1983-87. Bd. dirs. Metro. Family Svcs.; bd. dirs. Chgo. Bar Found., 1987—, pres., 1991-93; trustee 4th Presbyn. Ch., Chgo., 1989-92, pres., 1994-96; bd. dirs. Chgo. Equity Fund, 1992-96. Capt. USAR, 1966-72. Mem. ABA, Ill. Bar Assn., Wis. Bar Assn., Chgo. Bar Assn. (bd. mgrs. 1977-79, chmn. young lawyers sect. 1974-75), Food and Drug Law Inst. (bd. dirs. 1986—), LawClub Chgo., Econ. Club Chgo., Univ. Club Chgo. (bd. dirs. 1982-85, 87-88, v.p.). Presbyterian. General corporate, Antitrust, Mergers and acquisitions. Home: 853 W Chalmers Pl Chicago IL 60614-3233 Office: Seyfarth Shaw Fairweather & Geraldson 55 E Monroe St Ste 4200 Chicago IL 60603-5863

**HOWELL, WILLIAM ASHLEY, III,** lawyer; b. Raleigh, N.C., Jan. 2, 1949; s. William Ashley II and Caroline Erskine Greenleaf; m. Esther Holland, Dec. 22, 1973. BS, Troy State U., 1972; postgrad. U. Alabama, Birmingham, 1974-75; JD, Birmingham Sch. Law, 1977. Bar: Ala. 1977, U.S. Dist. Ct. (no. dist.) Ala. 1977, U.S. Ct. Appeals (5th cir.) 1977, U.S. Supreme Ct. 1982, U.S. Ct. Appeals (11th cir.) 1983, U.S. Dist. Ct. (mid. dist.) Ala. 1987. Atty. pub. defender div. Legal Aid. Soc. of Birmingham, 1977-78, civil divsn. Legal Aid Soc. Birmingham, 1978-81; dist. office atty. SBA, Birmingham, 1980-82, supervising atty. Ala. Dist., 1982—; spl. asst. U.S. Atty. (Middle Dist.), Ala., 1988—; part-time instr. legal and social environ. and human resources mgmt. Jefferson State C.C., Birmingham, 1993. Contbr. articles to profl. jours. Bd. dirs. Hoover Homeowners Assn., 1977-81, Southside Ministries, Inc., 1990-91, v.p. bd. dirs., 1990-91; bd. dirs. SafeHouse of Shelby County, Inc., 1990-93, vice chmn., 1991-93; mem. outreach comm., Episc. Ch. of St. Francis of Assisi, Pelham, Ala., 1992, 95, 97; del. State Conv., alternate del., 1993, 94; vol. reader Radio Reading Svc. Network for Blind, 1991-93; active Shelby County Econ. Devel. Coun., 1993-94. Recipient Am. Jurisprudence Criminal Procedure Book award. Mem. ABA (sect. corporation, banking and bus. law), Nat. Parks and Conservation Soc. (life), Fed. Bar Assn. (sec. Birmingham chpt. 1980-81, del. nat. conv. 1993, 94, del. mid year meeting, 1994-95), Ala. Bar Assn. (com. on future of the profession 1978-81, 83-84, com. on quality of life 1992-93, sect. bankruptcy and corp. law, sect. bankruptcy and comml. law, sect. corp. counsel, sect. banking and bus. law), Nature Conservancy (life), Birmingham Bar Assn., Birmingham Venture Club, Sierra Club (life), Sigma Delta Kappa (v.p., Outstanding Sr. award 1977). Episcopalian. Office: US SBA 2121 8th Ave N Ste 200 Birmingham AL 35203-2326

**HOWES, BRIAN THOMAS,** lawyer; b. Sioux Falls, S.D., July 23, 1957; s. Thomas A. and Joyce L. (McFarland) H.; m. Robin Kay Schoonover, June 2, 1979; children: Phillip, Adam, Jason. BSBA in Acctg., BA in Polit. Sci., Kans. State U., 1979; JD, U. Kans., 1982. Bar: Mo. 1982, U.S. Dist. Ct. (we. dist.) Mo. 1982, U.S. Supreme Ct. 1989. Assoc. Shughart, Thomson & Kilroy, Kansas City, Mo., 1982-85; exec. v.p., COO, gen. counsel Tenenbaum & Assocs., Inc., Kansas City, 1985-95; ptnr., nat. dir. property tax svcs. Ernst & Young LLP, Kansas City, Mo., 1995—; pres. Nat. Coun. Property Taxation, 1999—. Contr. articles to profl. jours; writer, speaker in field. Contbg. mem. Dem. Nat. Com.; bd. dirs. Kansas City Wheelchair Athletic Commn., 1987-89, Vol. Atty. Project, 1984—, Nat. Youth Sprots Coaches Assn., 1994—. Mem. ABA, Assn. Trial Lawyers Am., Kansas City Met. Bar Assn., Lawyers Assn. Kansas City, Am. Corp. Counsel Assn., Inst. Property Taxation, Internat. Assn. of Assessing Officers, Urban Land Inst. Episcopalian. State and local taxation, Real property, General corporate. Home: 4901 W 130th St Shawnee Mission KS 66209-1864 Office: Ernst & Young LLP One Kansas City Pl 1200 Main St Ste 2000 Kansas City MO 64105-2143

**HOWETT, JOHN CHARLES, JR.,** lawyer; b. Tampa, Fla., Feb. 11, 1946; s. John Charles and Martha Carlton (Durrance) H.; m. Mary K. Sheehan, Oct. 12, 1974; children: Timothy S., Julia K. BA, U. Pa., 1968; JD, Dickinson Sch. of Law, 1974. Bar: Pa. 1974, U.S. Supreme Ct. 1979. Law clk. Hon. Roy Wilkinson Commonwealth Ct. Pa., Harrisburg, 1974-75; sr. ptnr. Howett, Kissinger & Miles, P.C., Harrisburg, 1975—. Contbr. articles to profl. jours. 1st lt. U.S. Army, 1968-71, Vietnam. Mem. Pa. Bar Assn. (chmn. family law sect. 1995-96, bd. govs. 1978-81, 88-91, pres. young lawyers divsn. 1979-80), Am. Acad. Matrimonial Lawyers (pres. Pa. chpt. 1999—), Dauphin County Bar Assn. (pres. 1994-95, chmn. family law sect. 1990-91), Internat. Acad. Matrimonial Lawyers. Family and matrimonial. Office: Howett Kissinger & Miles PC PO Box 810 130 Walnut St Harrisburg PA 17101-1612

**HOWIE, JOHN ROBERT,** lawyer; b. Paris, Tex., June 29, 1946; s. Robert H. and Sarah Francis (Caldwell) H.; m. Evelyn Eileen Yates, May 3, 1969; children: John Robert, Ashley Elizabeth, Lindsey Leigh. BBA, North Tex. State U., 1968; JD, So. Meth. U., 1976. Bar: Tex. 1976, U.S. Dist. Ct. (no. dist.) Tex. 1977, U.S. Ct. Appeals (5th, 9th, 10th and 11th cirs.), U.S. Supreme Ct. 1985, U.S. Dist. Ct. (so., ea., and we. dists.) Tex. 1987; cert. in personal injury trial law Tex. Bd. Legal Specialization, 1982. Law Offices of Windle Turley, Dallas, 1976-88, Misko & Howie, 1988-95, ptnr. Howie & Sweeney, LLP, 1995—; adj. prof. trial advocacy So. Meth. U. Sch. Law, 1988-89, 92—, So. Meth. Sch. Law exec. brd. mem., mem. exec. com. Editor The Verdict, 1981-87. Lt. comdr. USN, 1968-73. Fellow So. Trial Lawyers Assn., Roscoe Pound Found. Civil Trial Adv.-Nat. Bd. Trial Adv. (cert. civil trial law), Internat. Acad. Trial Lawyers; mem. Tex. Trial Lawyers Assn. (bd. dirs. 1983—, chmn. product liability com. 1988-89), Dallas Trial Lawyers Assn. (sec.-treas. 1984, v.p. 1985, pres. 1986), Assn. Trial Lawyers Am. (vice chmn. aviation sect. 1984-85, chmn. 1986, Wiedemann Wysocki award 1990), Am. Bd. Trial Advocates (sec. Dallas chpt. 1988, pres. 1989), ABA (vice chmn. aviation law sect. 1986-91, chair 1992), State Bar Tex. (aviation law sect. coun. 1994—, personal injury trial specialist), Lawyer/Pilots Bar Assn., Flight Safety Found, Million Dollar Advs. Forum, Trial Lawyers for Pub. Justice Found., Ark. Trial Lawyers Assn., Ga. Trial Lawyers Assn., Com. for a Qualified Judiciary, Safe Communities Exec. Adv. Com., So. Meth. U. Jour. Air Law and Commerce (bd. advs.), fellow Tex. Bar Found., rsch. fellow Southwestern Legal Found., fellow Dallas Bar Found., Internat. Soc. Air Safety Investigators (contbr. Million Dollar Argument series 1989), Pres.'s Coun. U. North Tex. Democrat. Presbyterian. Personal injury, Aviation, Product liability. Home: 6508 Turtle Creek Blvd Dallas TX 75205-1244 Office: Howie & Sweeney LLP 2911 Turtle Creek Blvd Ste 1400 Dallas TX 75219-6258

**HOWLAND, JOAN SIDNEY,** law librarian, law educator; b. Eureka, Calif., Apr. 9, 1951; d. Robert Sidney and Ruth Mary Howland. BA, U. Calif., Davis, 1971; MA, U. Tex., 1973; MLS, Calif. State U., San Jose, 1975; JD, Santa Clara (Calif.) U., 1983; MBA, U. Minn., 1997. Assoc. librarian for pub. svcs. Stanford (Calif.) U. Law Library, 1975-83, Harvard U. Law Library, Cambridge, Mass., 1983-86; dep. dir. U. Calif. Law Library, Berkeley, 1986-92; dir. law libr., Roger F. Noreen prof. law, dir. info. tech. U. Minn. Sch. of Law, 1992—. Questions and answers column editor Law Libr. Jour., 1986-91; memt. column editor Trends in Law Libr. Mgmt. & Tech., 1987-94. Mem. ALA (chmn. cultural diversity com. 1995-97), Am. Assn. Law Librs. (chmn. edn. com. 1987-90, 95-97), Am. Assn. Law Schs. (libr. tech. com. 1998—), Am. Indian Libr. Assn. (treas. 1992—), Am. Law Inst. Office: U Minn Law Sch 229 19th Ave S Minneapolis MN 55455-0400

**HOWLAND, RICHARD MOULTON,** lawyer; b. Glen Cove, L.I., N.Y., Jan. 2, 1940; s. Richard Moulton and Natalie (Fuller) H.; m. Julie Rose Keschl, Sept. 28, 1974 (div.); children: Kimberly Merrill, Gillian Fuller. BA, Amherst Coll., 1961; JD, Columbia U., 1968. Bar: Mass. 1968. Assoc. firm Nutter, McLennen & Fish, Boston, 1968-69, DiMento & Sullivan, Boston, 1969-70; atty. for students U. Mass., Amherst, 1970-74; practice law Amherst, 1974—; Legal Infirmary Amherst, 1997—; adj. prof. U. Mass., 1972-76, Western New Eng. Coll. Sch. Law, 1993-94; vis. lectr. Amherst Coll., 1983, mock trial team coach, 1989-98; mock trial team coach Tufts Coll., 1998, Deerfield Acad., 1999—. Co-editor Mass. Lawyers Weekly, 1979-94, emeritus, 1994; statistician New England Blizzard, 1996-98, Springfield Sirens Pro Soccer, 1999—. Asst. moderator Town of Leverett, 1988-93, moderator, 1993-96; mem. Leverett Sch. Bldg. Com., 1988-89; trustee Art Inst. Boston, 1990-92, Greenfield C. C. Found., 1991-97, Amherst Regional High Sch. Coun., 1993-95; trustee Amherst Hist. Soc., 1990-95; pres. Leverett PTO, 1981-85; mem. devel. com. Pioneer Valley High Sch. of the Performing Arts, 1996-97; pres. Interfaith Housing Corp., Amherst, 1984-93; bd. dirs. Leverett Craftsmen and Artists, Inc., 1986—, treas., 1988-89, v.p., 1988-89, pres., 1989—; bd. dirs. Community Multisvc. Inc., Northampton, Mass., 1987-93; trustee Wildwood Cemetery Assn., 1987—; bd. dirs., sec. Responsible Hospitality Inst., 1990-95; mem. host com. Russia-Amherst Exchange City of Petrozavadsk, 1988—; del. rep. Town of Amherst to Sister City, Kanegasaki, Japan, 1992-95; chair Amherst-Kanegasaki Sister Com., 1994-95; mem. bd. career com., Hampshire-Franklin Sch., 1995—; cert. ofcl. U.S. Assn. Track and Field, 1996—; Western Mass. track and field ofcl., 1995—; We. Mass. football ofcl., 1995—; referee FIFA Soccer, 1997—; collegiate water polo ofcl., 1997—; asst. coach varsity girls soccer Amherst Regional H.S., 1995—. Lt. (j.g.) USNR, 1961-65. Mem. ABA (chmn. profl. liability com. Gen. Practice Sect. 1987-90, chmn. certification and specialization com. Gen. Practice Sect. 1992-95, chmn. family law com. 1995-96, chmn. certification, specialization and law sch. curriculum com. 1996-98, mem. coun. 1997—), Mass. Bar Assn. (chmn. com. on chem. dependency, Mass. Community Svc. award 1984), Franklin Bar Assn., Hampshire Bar Assn. (del. to Mass. Bar Assn., sec., v.p. 1986), Mass. Acad. Trial Lawyers, Amherst C. of C. (pres. 1985-93, Dakin medallion 1995), Nat. High Sch. Slavic Honor Soc. (hon.), Amherst Alumni Athletic Assn. (bd. dirs. 1995—), Skating Club (past v.p., treas. 1987-96, Amherst). Democrat. E-mail: howland@crocker.com. General civil litigation, Family and matrimonial, General practice. Home: 326 N Pleasant St Amherst MA 01002-1706

**HOWLEY, JAMES MCANDREW,** lawyer; b. Dunmore, Pa., Oct. 3, 1928; s. Joseph Austin and Mary Helene (Ruddy) H.; m. Mary McDade; 1 child, Maura. BS, U. Scranton, 1952; LLB, U. Pa., 1955. Bar: Pa. 1956, U.S. Dist. Ct. (mid. dist.) Pa. 1956, U.S. Ct. Appeals (3d cir.) 1960. Pvt. practice Scranton, Northeastern Pa., 1956—; panel mem. and speaker at various legal symposiums; chmn. and commr. Pa. State Ethics Commn.; chmn. Gov.'s Spl. Trial Ct. nomination commn., Lackawanna County, Pa., 1987; disciplinary bd. Supreme Ct. Pa. hearing com., 1987; lawyer's adv. com. U.S. Ct. Appeals (3d cir.), 1983-86, U.S. Dist. Ct. (mid. dist.) Pa., 1981-86. Chmn. and trustee Marywood Coll., trustee St. Mary's Villa. Fellow Am. Coll. Trial Lawyers; mem. ABA, Pa. Bar Assn., Pa. Def. Inst., Pa. Trial Lawyers Assn., Am. Bd. Trial Advs. (cert.), Lackawanna County Bar Assn., Scranton C. of C. (bd. dirs.), Country Club of Scranton (pres. 1974-79), Friendly Sons of St. Patrick (pres. 1986). Roman Catholic. Avocations: golf, tennis. General civil litigation, Federal civil litigation, State civil litigation. Home: 115 Maple Ave Clarks Summit PA 18411-2513 Office: 1000 Bank Towers 321 Spruce St Scranton PA 18503-1400

**HOWORTH, ANDREW KINCANNON,** lawyer; b. Memphis, Nov. 12, 1955; s. Marion Beckett and Mary (Hartwell) H.; m. Laura Stewart Cantral, Dec. 28, 1985; children: Marian, Stewart; m. Susan S. Barksdale, Oct. 10, 1998. BBA, U. Miss., 1984, JD, 1987. Bar: Miss. 1987, U.S. Dist. Ct. (no. and so. dists.) Miss. 1987, U.S. Dist. Ct. (5th cir.) Miss. 1987. Atty., ptnr. Hickman, Goza & Gore, Oxford, Miss., 1987-98, Howorth Law Firm, P.A., Oxford, Miss., 1998—. Pres. Oxford Lafayette County United Way, Oxford, 1989. Paul Harris fellow; mem. Miss. Bar Assn. (commr. 1992-94), 3rd Cir. Bar Assn. (pres. 1992), Tri-county Bar Assn. (pres. 1990), Lafayette County Bar Assn. (pres. 1989), Rotary. Personal injury, Probate, Real property. Office: Howorth Law Firm PA 409 N 9th St Oxford MS 38655-3101

**HOWSER, RICHARD GLEN,** lawyer; b. Tulsa, Apr. 5, 1951; s. Richard Glen and Mary Ann Howser; m. Judith Anne Howser, Sept. 1, 1986; children: Crystal, Benton, Elizabeth, Richard. BA, U. Ill., 1973; JD, Loyola U., 1977. Assoc. Clausen Miller P.C., Chgo., 1977-83, ptnr., 1983—, dir., 1992—, corp. sec., 1996—. Treas. Wilmette (Ill.) Luth. Ch., 1991-95, pres., 1995-96; area chmn. New Trier Republican Orgn., Kenilworth, Ill., 1992—. Mem. ABA, Soc. Trial Lawyers, Ill. State Bar Assn., Chgo. Bar Assn. Avocations: soccer coach, Sunday school teacher, gardener, history buff, politics. General civil litigation, Product liability, Personal injury. Office: Clausen Miller PC 10 S Lasalle St Ste 1600 Chicago IL 60603-1098

**HOYLE, LAWRENCE TRUMAN, JR.,** lawyer; b. Greensboro, N.C., Oct. 6, 1938; s. Lawrence Truman and Martha Parks (Lane) H.; m. Molly Hoyle, Oct.1993; children: Eric L., Alison D. AB in History, Duke U., 1960; JD, U. Chgo., 1965. Bar: Pa. 1965, U.S. Dist. Ct. (ea. dist.) Pa. 1966, U.S. Ct. Appeals (3d cir.) 1966, U.S. Dist. Ct. (no. dist.) Miss. 1968, U.S. Supreme Ct. 1970, U.S. Ct. Appeals (4th, 5th, 6th and 11th cirs.) 1984, U.S. Ct. Appeals (D.C. cir.) 1988. Assoc. Schnader, Harrison, Segal & Lewis, Phila., 1965-71; dep. atty. gen., chief civil litigation divsn. Pa. Dept. Justice, Harrisburg, Pa., 1971-72; exec. dir. Pa. Crime Commn., Harrisburg, Pa., 1972-74; ptnr. Schnader, Harrison, Segal & Lewis, Phila., 1974-85, Hoyle, Morris & Kerr, Phila., 1985—; lectr. Sch. Law, Temple U., 1969-71; mem. vis. com. Law Sch., U. Chgo., 1975-77, 88-90, 96—; mem. nominating com. Pa. Appellate Ct., 1979-86; mem. Pa. Jud. Inquiry Rev. Bd., 1988-90. Bd. vis. Duke U. Trinity, 1992-99; bd. dirs. The Lighthouse, Phila., 1968-77, United Communities of S.E. Phila., 1983-86, Pub. Interest Law Ctr., Phila., 1976—, Fox Chase Cancer Ctr., 1992—; vol. atty. Lawyers' Com. for Civil Rights Under the Law, 1968; trustee Acad. Natural Scis. Fellow Am. Bar Found., Am. Coll. Trial Lawyers; mem. ABA, Pa. Bar Assn., Phila. Bar Assn., Racquet Club Phila., Blooming Grove Hunting and Fishing Club. Democrat. General civil litigation, Securities, Toxic tort. Home: 404 Spruce St Philadelphia PA 19106-4216 Office: Hoyle Morris & Kerr One Liberty Pl 1650 Market St Ste 1 Philadelphia PA 19103-7397

**HOYNES, LOUIS LENOIR, JR.,** lawyer; b. Indpls., Sept. 23, 1935; s. Louis L. and Catharine (Parker) H.; m. Judith E. Kass, Oct. 12, 1958 (div. 1979); children: Thomas M., William D., Ellen B.; m. Virginia Devin, Dec. 9, 1979. AB, Columbia U., 1957; JD cum laude, Harvard U., 1962. Bar: N.Y. 1963, U.S. Supreme Ct. 1967, U.S. Dist. Ct. (so. dist.) N.Y., U.S. Ct. Appeals (2d, 7th and 9th cirs.). Assoc. Willkie, Farr & Gallagher, N.Y.C., 1962-68, ptnr., 1969-90; counsel Nat. League Profl. Baseball Clubs, 1970-90; sr. v.p., gen. counsel Am. Home Products Corp., 1990—; lectr. law Columbia U., N.Y.C., 1982-91; bd. dirs. Cytec Industries Inc.; trustee Food and Drug Law Inst. Served to lt. USNR, 1957-59, PTO. Mem. ABA, N.Y. State Bar Assn., Assn. of City of Bar of N.Y., The Assn. Gen. Counsel. Federal civil litigation, General corporate, Labor. Home: 47 Cornwells Beach Rd Sands Point NY 11050-1305

**HOYT, BROOKS PETTINGILL,** lawyer; b. Tampa, Fla., Oct. 31, 1929; s. Robert Denny and Mary Elizabeth (Macfarlane) H.; m. Patricia Amelia Young, June 13, 1953; children: Kathryn Ann Hoyt Hindman, Nancy Hoyt O'Connell. AB with honors, U. Fla., 1952, LLB with high honors, 1954; LLM, Columbia U., 1962. Bar: Fla. 1955, U.S. Dist. Ct. (so. and mid. dist.) Fla. 1956, 64, U.S. Ct. Appeals (5th and 11th cirs.) 1964, 92. Assoc. Macfarlane, Ferguson, Allison & Kelly, Tampa, 1954-57, 62-63, ptnr., 1964-76; asst. prof. law U. Fla., Gainesville, 1957-62; ptnr. Stichter, Stagg, Hoyt, Riedel & Fogarty, Tampa, 1977-79, Holland & Knight, Tampa, 1980-92, Hoyt, Colgan & Andreu, P.A., Tampa, 1992-97; of counsel Macfarlane Ferguson & McMullen, Tampa, 1998—; mem. Jud. Nominating Commn. 2d Dist. Ct. Appeals, 1987-91, vice chmn., 1989-90, chmn., 1990. Bd. dirs. Southeastern Admiralty Law Inst., 1979-81. Served as cpl. USAF, 1948. Mem. Maritime Law Assn. Am., Fla. Bar, Tampa and Hillsborough County Bar Assn., Ye Mystic Krewe of Gasparilla, Tampa Yacht and Country Club, Order of Coif, Phi Beta Kappa. Democrat. Methodist. Avocations: tennis, reading, swimming. Admiralty, State and local taxation, General civil litigation. Home: 3435 Bayshore Blvd Apt 1401 Tampa FL 33629-8880 Office: Macfarlane Ferguson & McMullen 400 N Tampa St Ste 2300 Tampa FL 33602-4708

**HOYT, KENNETH M.,** federal judge; b. 1948. AB, Tex. So. U., 1969, JD, 1972. Mem. firm Wickliff, King, Hoyt & Jones, 1972-75, Anderson, Hodge, Jones & Hoyt, 1975-79, Webster & Andrews, 1979-81; presiding judge 125th Civil Dist. Ct., 1981-82; pvt. practice law Kenneth M. Hoyt & Assocs., 1983-85; justice U.S. Ct. Appeals (1st cir.), 1985-88; judge U.S. Dist. Ct. (so. dist.)Tex., Houston, 1988—; faculty trial advocacy program South Tex. Coll., 1981-82; adj. prof. Thurgood Marshall Sch. Law, 1983-84. Contbr. articles to profl. jours. Former bd. dirs. Bus. and Profl. Men's Club; judge trial advocacy program U. Houston, 1982-84, 87-88; former mem. Juvenile Justice & Delinquency Prevention Adv. Bd., Blue Ribbon Commn., Rev. Criminal Justice Corrections System, Referendum Force, Selection of Judges; former mem. adv. bd. Parents of Murdered Children and Coalition of Victims Rights; formerly active Salvation Army; former chmn. Capital Devel. Com., Wheeler Ave. Bapt. Ch.; past dir. Houston Lawyer's Referral Svc. With USNG, 1972-78. Decorated Am. Spirit medal; recipient Outstanding Community Svc. award Kendleton, Tex., Ethel Ranson Art & Literary Club award, Outstanding Acheivement award Thurgood Marshall Sch. Law Alumni Assn., 1986; named one of Most Outstanding Black Rep. South Tex. Mem. Nat. Bar Assn., State Bar Tex. (task force, minimum continuing legal edn.). Office: US District Courthouse 9513 US Courthouse Houston TX 77002 Office: US District Courthouse Suite 11144 515 Rusk St Houston TX 77002-2605

**HRANITZKY, RACHEL ROBYN,** lawyer; b. Irving, Tex., Mar. 16, 1968; d. Dennis Rogers and Jeanne Beverly (Crooks) H. BA, Tex. Christian U., 1987, U. Tex., 1988; JD, So. Meth. U., 1995. Bar: Tex. 1995, U.S. Dist. Ct. (no. dist.) Tex. 1997, U.S. Dist. Ct. (ea. dist.) Tex. 1999. Tchr. Grapevine (Tex.) H.S., 1988-92; clk. to Hon. Candace Tyson, 44th Dist. Ct., Dallas, 1993; assoc. coun. Mesa, Inc., Dallas, 1995; assoc. Hiersche, Martens, Hayward, Drakeley & Urbach, Dallas, 1996—; rsch. asst. William V. Dorsaneo, III, 1993-95; clinic atty. So. Meth. U. Legal Clinics, Dallas, 1995. Mem. ATLA, Dallas Bar Assn., Delta Theta Phi. Avocations: art, music, sports, cooking, dancing. General civil litigation, Insurance, Consumer commercial. Home: 5400 Preston Oaks Rd Apt 2021 Dallas TX 75240-8444 Office: 15303 Dallas Pkwy Ste 700 LB-17 Dallas TX 75248

**HRIBERNICK, PAUL R.,** lawyer; b. LaGrande, Oreg., Oct. 28, 1954. BS, U. Oreg., 1977, JD, 1980. Bar: Oreg. 1980, U.S. Dist. Ct. Oreg. 1980, U.S. Ct. Appeals (9th cir.) 1985, U.S. Supreme Ct. 1988. Dep. dist. atty. Klamath County, Klamath Falls, Oreg., 1980; rsch. lawyer La. Sea Grant Program, Baton Rouge, 1981-82; jud. clk. U.S. Dist. Ct. (ea. dist.) La., New Orleans, 1983-84; lawyer Black Helterline LLP, Portland, Oreg., 1984—. Contbg. author: Immigration and Nationality Law Handbook, 1990, 93, 94, 96, 99; assoc. editor: H-1B Toolbox, 1994-98; editor: AILA Western Regional Directory, 1998. Adminstrv. coun. All Saints Parish, Portland; mem. polit. action com. Oreg. Concrete and Aggregate Prodrs. Assn., Salem. Fulbright scholar USIA/Commn. Fulbright, Lima, Peru, 1982-83. Mem. Am. Immigration Lawyers Assn. (bd. govs. 1992-94, chair nat. membership com.). Avocations: hunting, kayaking, fishing. Immigration, naturalization, and customs, Land use and zoning (including planning). Office: Black Helterline LLP 1200 Union Bank Calif Tower 707 SW Washington St Portland OR 97205-3536

**HRITZ, GEORGE F.,** lawyer; b. Hyde Park, N.Y., Aug. 28, 1948; s. George F. and Margaret M. (Callahan) H.; m. Mary Elizabeth Noonan; 1 child, Amelia C. Hritz. AB, Princeton U., 1969; JD, Columbia U., 1973. Bar: N.Y. 1974, D.C. 1978, U.S. Supreme Ct. 1979. Law clk. U.S. Dist. Ct. (ea. dist.) N.Y., N.Y.C., 1973; assoc. Cravath, Swaine & Moore, N.Y.C., 1974-77; counsel U.S. Senate Select Com. Ethics Korean Inquiry, Washington, 1977-78; ptnr. Moore & Foster, Washington, 1978-80, Davis, Weber & Edwards, N.Y.C., 1980—; assoc. ind. counsel Washington, 1986-89; mem. adv. com. U.S. Dist. Ct. (ea. dist.) N.Y., 1990—. Trustee Fed. Bar Found., 1998—; bd. dirs. gen. counsel exec. com. Internat. Rescue Com., 1982—; chmn. planning bd. Village of Sleepy Hollow, N.Y., 1993-97. Mem. Fed. Bar Coun., D.C. Bar Assn. Federal civil litigation, State civil litigation, Private international. Home: 505 Cognewaugh Rd Greenwich CT 06807-1110 Office: Davis Weber & Edwards 100 Park Ave Ste 3200 New York NY 10017-5516

**HRONES, STEPHEN BAYLIS,** lawyer, educator; b. Boston, Jan. 20, 1942; s. John Anthony and Margaret (Baylis) H.; m. Anneliese Zion, Sept. 11, 1970; children: Christopher, Katja. BA cum laude, Harvard U., 1964; postgrad., U. Sorbonne, Paris, 1964-65; JD, U. Mich., 1968. Bar: Iowa 1969, Mass. 1972, U.S. Dist. Ct. Mass. 1973, U.S. Ct. Appeals (1st cir.) 1979, U.S. Tax Ct. 1985, U.S. Supreme Ct. 1991. Pvt. practice Heidelberg, Germany, 1970-72, Boston, 1973-86; ptnr. Hrones and Harwood, Boston, 1986-90, Hrones and Garrity, Boston, 1990—; clin. assoc. Suffolk U. Law Sch., Boston, 1979-82; faculty advisor Harvard Law Sch., 1988—; instr. Northeastern Law Sch., 1998; advisor Mass. CLE Trial Practice Programs, 1990—, Mass. Continuing Legal Edn. Programs, 1988—. Author: How To Try a Criminal Case, 1982, Criminal Practice Handbook, 1995, Massachusetts Jury (Criminal) Instructions, 1999; contbr. articles to profl. jours. Trustee Orgn. for Assabet River; mem. schs. and scholarship com. Harvard U.; fundraiser Harvard Coll. Fund, 1985—; candidate for bd. overseers Harvard U., 1999. Fulbright scholar, 1968-69. Mem. ACLU, Nat. Assn. Criminal Def. Lawyers, Mass. Assn. Criminal Def. Lawyers, Mass. Bar Assn., Boston Bar Assn., Nat. Lawyers Guild. Democrat. Avocations: squash, skiing, wind-surfing, vegetable gardening. E-mail: Azhro@aol.com. Criminal, Civil rights, Personal injury. Home: 39 Winslow St Concord MA 01742-3817 Office: Hrones and Garrity Lewis Wharf Bay 232 Boston MA 02110

**HRYCAK, MICHAEL PAUL,** lawyer; b. Mpls., May 12, 1959; s. Peter and Rea Meta (Limberg) H. BA, Rutgers U., 1981, JD, 1989; MS, N.J. Inst. Tech., 1983. Bar: N.J. 1990, N.Y. 1990, Conn. 1990, D.C. 1992, U.S. Dist. Ct. N.J. 1990. Systems analyst RCA Astro-Electronics Divsn., Princeton, N.J., 1983-86; prin. atty. Law Office of Michael P. Hrycak, Westfield, N.J., 1990—. Lt. USNG, 1981-87, capt., 1987-96, maj., 1996—. Mem. ABA, N.J. Bar Assn., Ukrainian Am. Bar Assn., Ukrainian Engrs. Soc. Am. (treas. 1984—). Republican. Ukrainian Catholic. Avocations: skiing, backpacking, marksmanship, traveling, current events. Computer, Family and matrimonial, Criminal. Home: 199 Bexley Ln Piscataway NJ 08854-2180 Office: 316 Lenox Ave Westfield NJ 07090-2138

**HSIAO, MONICA LO-CHING,** lawyer; b. L.A., Mar. 3, 1970; d. Joseph Lan-Nan and Kathleen Hsiao; m. Jean-Marie Barreau, Sept. 2, 1995. BA in Econs., Stanford U., 1991, MA in Internat. Policy Studies, 1993; JD, UCLA, 1995. Bar: N.Y. 1995. Intern U.S. State Dept., Tokyo, summer 1992, U.S. Trade Rep. Office, Washington, summer 1993; assoc. Fried, Frank, Harris, Shriver & Jacobson, N.Y.C., summer 1994, 1995—. Scholarship advisor No. Calif. Scholarship Found. Mem. Phi Beta Kappa, Omicron Delta Epsilon. Avocations: drawing, painting. General corporate, Mergers and acquisitions. Office: Fried Frank Harris Shriver & Jacobson One New York Plaza New York NY 10004

**HSU, JULIE L.,** lawyer; b. Chayi, Taiwan, Jan. 4, 1971; came to U.S., 1973; d. Winston Kuo Wen and Grace Kun Mahn Hsu. BA in English and Econs., UCLA, 1993; JD, U. So. Calif., 1996. Bar: Calif. 1996. Atty. Greenfield & Assocs., L.A., 1996-97; assoc. Kaye, Scholer, Fierman, Hays & Handler, LLP, L.A., 1997—. Mem. Women's Law Assn., Los Angeles County Bar Assn. Democrat. General corporate, Mergers and acquisitions, Securities. Office: Kaye Scholer et al Ste 1500 1999 Avenue Of The Stars Los Angeles CA 90067-6112

**HU, DANIEL DAVID,** lawyer; b. N.Y.C., 1960. BA, Rice U., 1982, MA, 1984; Jd, U. Tex., 1986. Bar: Tex. 1986. Jud. clk. Hon. Norman W Black, Houston, 1986-88; assoc. Royston Rayzor, Houston, 1988-91; asst. U.S. atty. U.S. Attys. Offie, Houston, 1992—. Mem. State Bar Tex. (bd. mem.), Guld Coast Legal Found. (bd. mem.), Houston Asian Bar. Avocation: running. Office: US Attys Office PO Box 61129 Houston TX 77208-1129

**HU, PATRICK HAIPING,** lawyer; b. Shanghai, China, June 27, 1956; s. Enze Hu and Yunyu Wu; m. Susan Shen, June 30, 1989. BA, Shanghai Conservatory Music, 1981; MA, UCLA, 1986, PhD, 1991; JD, U. Minn., 1995. Bar: D.C., Minn. Atty. Popham Haik, Mpls., 1995-97, Chadbourne & Parke, Washington, 1997-98, Coudert Bros., Washington, 1998—. Mem. ABA. Finance, Private international, Securities. Office: Coudert Bros 1627 I St NW Washington DC 20006-4007

**HUANG, THOMAS WEISHING,** lawyer; b. Taipei, Taiwan, Feb. 1, 1941; came to U.S., 1967; s. Lienden and Helen (Yen) H. BA, Taiwan U., 1964; JD magna cum laude, Ind. U., Indpls., 1970; LLM, Harvard U., 1971, SJD, 1975. Bar: D.C. 1975, Mass. 1976, U.S. Dist. Ct. Mass. 1976, U.S. Ct. Appeals (1st cir.) 1978, N.Y. 1980. Judge adv. Chinese Army, Taiwan, 1964-65; legal officer Treaty and Legal Dept., Ministry of Fgn. Affairs, Taiwan, 1966-67; assoc. Chemung County Legal Svcs., Elmira, N.Y., 1975-76; assoc.

law firm Taylor Johnson & Wieschhoff, Marblehead, Mass., 1980; prin. Reiser & Rosenberg, Boston, 1982-86, Huang & Assocs., Boston, 1987-88, Hale, Sanderson, Byrnes & Morton, Boston, 1988-96; of counsel Chin, Wright & Branson P.C., Boston, 1996-97; shareholder Sherburne, Powers & Needham, P.C., Boston, 1997-98, ptnr. Holland & Knight, LLP, Boston, 1998—; exec. v.p. Excel Tech. Internat. Co., Brunswick, N.J., 1982-88; bd. dirs. Asian Am. Bank & Trust Co., Boston, exec. com., clk., 1993—; legal counsel Nat. Assn. Chinese Ams., Washington, 1979-80. Mem. editl. staff Ind. Law Rev., 1969-70; contbr. articles to legal jours. Bd. dirs. Chinese Econ. Devel. Coun., Boston, 1978-80; mem. Gov.'s Adv. Coun. on Guangdong, 1984-87; mem. minority bus. task force Senator Kerry's Office, 1988—. Mem. Boston Bar Assn. (mem. internat. law sect. steering com. 1979-90, mem. ad hoc com. on code of profl. conducts), Nat. Assn. Chinese Ams. (v.p. Boston chpt. 1984-86, pres. 1986-88, 1st. v.p. nat. assn. 1994-97), Taiwan C. of C. in New Eng. (clk., bd. dirs. 1996—). Democrat. Contracts commercial, Immigration, naturalization, and customs, Private international. Home: 30 Farrwood Dr Andover MA 01810-5233 Office: Holland & Knight LLP One Beacon St Boston MA 02108

**HUBAND, FRANK LOUIS,** educational association executive; b. Washington, July 12, 1938; m. Carol Singer. BS, Cornell U., 1961, PhD, 1967; JD, Yale U., 1975. Bar: D.C. 1975, U.S. Patent Office, 1977; registered prof. engr., Tex. Asst. prof. elec. engring. and math. scis. Rice U., Houston, 1966-72; owner, pres. Engring. Systems, Houston, 1972-73; atty., advisor FEA, Washington, 1975-76; div. dir. NSF, Washington, 1976-90; exec. dir. Am. Soc. for Engring. Edn., Washington, 1990—; cons. Tex. Instrument, 1968-75; lectr. George Mason U., Fairfax, Va., George Washington U. Author: Protection of Computer Systems and Software, 1986. Mem. ABA, IEEE. Office: Am Soc for Engring Edn 1818 N St NW Ste 600 Washington DC 20036-2476

**HUBBARD, CAROLYN MARIE,** lawyer; b. Vancouver, Wash., Aug. 27, 1956; d. Kenneth D. Hubbard and Beverly J. Richards. AA, Richland Coll., 1977; BS, East Tex. State U., 1979; JD, Rutgers U., 1988. Bar: Tex., N.J., U.S. Dist. Ct. (no. dist.) Tex., U.S. Dist. Ct. (no. dist.) N.J., U.S. Tax Ct. Pvt. practice Camden, N.J., 1988-90; partner Byrne, Downing, Hubbard, Jackson & Ratliff, Dallas, Tex., 1990-94; assoc. Michael Wigton, Dallas, Tex., 1994-95, Baker, Brown & Dixon, Arlington, Tex., 1995-97, Wald and Assocs., Richardson, Tex., 1997-98. Vol. Dallas Tenant's Assn., Hillcrest Ch., Dallas, Alcoholics Anonymous, Dallas. Mem. Dallas Women's Lawyers Assn., Christian Legal Soc. Avocations: walking, knitting, writing, theology. Family and matrimonial, Alternative dispute resolution, Nonprofit and tax-exempt organizations. Office: Wald & Associates 1600 Promenade Ctr # 1616 Richardson TX 75080-5400

**HUBBARD, ELIZABETH LOUISE,** lawyer; b. Springfield, Ill., Mar. 10, 1949; d. Glenn Wellington and Elizabeth (Frederick) H.; m. A. Jeffrey Seidman, Oct. 27, 1974 (div. May 1982). B.A., U. Ky., 1971; JD with honors, Ill. Inst. Tech.-Chgo. Kent Coll. Law, 1974. Bar: Ill. 1974, U.S. Dist. Ct. (no. dist.) Ill. 1974, U.S. Ct. Appeals (7th cir.) 1976, U.S. Supreme Ct. 1984. Atty. Wyatt Co., Chgo., 1974-75, Gertz & Giampietro, Chgo., 1975-76, Baum, Sigman, Gold, Chgo., 1976-81, Elizabeth Hubbard, Ltd., 1981-98, Hubbard & O'Connor, Ltd., 1998—; legal counsel NOW, Chgo., 1978-94, sec., 1977. Editor Chgo. Kent Law Rev., 1970; supplement editor Litigating Sexual Harassment and Sex discrimination Cases, 1997, 98, 99. Bd. dirs., mem. The Remains Theatre, 1985-94. Mem. Chgo. Bar Assn. (fed. civil procedure com.), Ill. State Bar Assn., Nat. Employment Lawyers Assn. (chair Ill. chpt. 1992-95, sec.-treas. 1997—). Civil rights, General corporate, Family and matrimonial. Home: 420 W Grand Ave Apt 4A Chicago IL 60610-4087 Office: 55 E Monroe St Chicago IL 60603-5713

**HUBBARD, MICHAEL JAMES,** lawyer; b. N.Y.C., Dec. 8, 1950; s. William Neil and Elizabeth (Terleski) H. AB, U. Mich., 1976; JD, Marquette U., 1979. Bar: Wis. 1980, Mich. 1980. Assoc. Kidston, Peterson P.C., Kalamazoo, 1980, Barbier, Goulet & Petersmarck, Mt. Clemens, Mich., 1981; pvt. practice Detroit, 1982-86, Belleville, Mich., 1990-98; assoc. Lawrence J. Stockler, P.C., Southfield, Mich., 1987; staff atty. Hyatt Legal Svcs., Southgate, Mich., 1988; assoc. Dunchock, Linden & Wells, Coruna, Mich., 1989. Mem. Mich. Trial Lawyers Assn., State Bar Mich. Republican. Avocations: reading, racquetball. General civil litigation, General corporate, Finance.

**HUBBARD, PETER LAWRENCE,** lawyer; b. Syracuse, N.Y., Apr. 4, 1946; s. Bardwell B. and Barbara (Bowen) H.; m. Hannah R., June 21, 1967; 1 child, Brian C. BA, Syracuse U., 1968, JD, 1971; postgrad., Judge Advocate Gen.'s Sch., Charlottesville, Va., 1976. Bar: N.Y. 1972, U.S. Dist. Ct. (no. and we. dists.) N.Y. 1972, U.S. Ct. Appeals (2d cir.) 1983. Assoc. Smith & Sovik, Syracuse, N.Y., 1971-72; asst. dist. counsel U.S. SBA, Syracuse, 1972-80; ptnr. Menter, Rudin & Trivelpiece, Syracuse, 1980—; lectr. in field. Contbr. articles to profl. jours. Pres. Reachout Inc., County Drug Rehab. Agy., Syracuse, 1979. Bankruptcy, Banking, Contracts commercial. Office: Menter Rudin & Trivelpiece 500 S Salina St Ste 500 Syracuse NY 13202-3300

**HUBBARD, THOMAS EDWIN (TIM HUBBARD),** lawyer; b. Roseboro, N.C., July 10, 1944; s. Charles Spence and Mary Mercer (Reeves) H.; children: Marvin Gannon, Caitlin Kable York. BS in Biomed. Engring., Duke U., 1970, postgrad., 1970-71; JD, U. N.C., 1973. Bar: N.C. 1973. Regulation writer, med. devices FDA, Washington, 1974-75; asst. dir. clin. affairs Zimmer USA, Warsaw, Ind., 1975, dir. regulatory affairs, 1975-76; house counsel Gen. Med. Cor., Richmond, Va., 1976-79; pvt. practice Pittsboro, N.C., 1979—; pres. Chathamborough Rsch. Group, Inc., Pittsboro, 1979—, Chathamborough Farms Inc., 1982—; sec.-treas. Hubbard-Corry, Inc., Pittsboro, 1981—; chmn. Hubbard Bros., Inc., Chapel Hill, N.C., 1982-87; bd. dirs. No. State Legal Svc., Hillsborough, N.C., 1980—, pres., 1986-89, MDR Svcs., Inc., 1991—; adj. instr. U. N.C. Law Sch., 1983. V.p. N.C. Young Dems. 4th Congl. Dist., 1970-71; mem. State Dem. Exec. Com., 1972-73; mem. paralegal adv. com. Ctrl. Carolina C.C., Sanford, N.C., 1987-93, legal svcs. N.C. Long Range Planning Com., 1987-93; bd. dirs. Chatham Soccer League, 1993—, sec.-treas., coach coord., 1994-98, v.p., 1998-99, pres., 1999—; mem. Chatham Coalition to Improve Quality of Life, 1992-93, chmn. single parent com.; pres. Pittsboro Elem. PTAA 1996-98. Sgt. USMC, 1963-68. Named Top N.C. Young Dem., 1971. Mem. ABA (vice chmn. health law com. gen. practice sect. 1991-93), N.C. Bar Assn. (legal svcs. planning com. 1988-94), Chatham County Bar Assn., Assn. for Advancement Med. Instrumentation (govt. affairs com. 1976). Democrat. Methodist. Administrative and regulatory, Personal injury, Product liability. Office: PO Box 939 Pittsboro NC 27312-0939 also: Chathamborough Rsch Group Inc 105 West St Pittsboro NC 27312-9470

**HUBBELL, BILLY JAMES,** lawyer; b. Pine Bluff, Ark., May 21, 1949; s. Arley E. and Mary M. (Duke) H.; m. Judy C. Webb, Feb. 21, 1981; children: Jennifer Leigh, William Griffin. BE, U. Cen. Ark., 1971; JD, U. Ark, Little Rock, 1978. Bar: Ark. 1978, U.S. Dist. Ct. (ea. dist.) Ark. 1978, U.S. Ct. Appeals (8th cir.) 1987. Tchr. Grady (Ark.) High Sch., 1971-78; assoc. Smith and Smith, McGehee, Ark., 1978-79; ptnr. Smith, Hubbell and Drake, McGehee, 1979-86, Griffin, Rainwater & Draper, P.A., Crossett, Ark., 1987-90; dep. prosecuting atty. Ashley County, Ark., 1989-90; mcpl. judge Crossett, 1991—, pvt. practice, 1991—. Candidate Ark. Ho. of Reps., Lincoln County, 1984, 10th Jud. Dist. Cir./Chancery Judge, 1998. Sgt. USAR, 1970-76. Mem. Ark. Bar Assn., S.E. Ark. Legal Inst. (chmn. 1984-85, Ashley County Bar Assn. (past pres.), Ark. Trial Lawyers Assn. Democrat. Seventh Day Adventist. Avocations: jogging, computers. General civil litigation, Personal injury, Contracts commercial. Office: PO Box 574 Crossett AR 71635-0574

**HUBBELL, ERNEST,** lawyer; b. Trenton, Mo., Aug. 28, 1914; s. Platt and Maud Irene (Ray) H.; m. Nevah Smith, Apr. 25, 1943; 1 child, Platt Thorpe. AA, North Cen. Mo. Coll. (formerly Trenton Jr. Coll.), 1934; JD, Georgetown U., 1938. Bar: D.C. 1937, Mo. 1938, U.S. Supreme Ct. 1946. Practiced in Trenton, 1938-39, Jefferson City, Mo., 1939-42; pvt. practice, Kansas City, Mo., 1947-52; ptnr. Hubbell, Sawyer, Peak, O'Neal & Napier (formerly Hubbell, Lane & Sawyer), Kansas City, 1952—; asst. atty. gen. Mo., 1939-42; first chmn. bench, bar com. 16th Jud. Cir. Ct., Kansas City, 1964-69, mem 16th Cir. Jud. Nominating Commn., 1970-75; mem. U.S. Cir. Judge Nominating Commn., 1977-80. Trustee Legal Aid and Defender Soc. Greater Kansas City, 1964-73; mem. Law Found. U. Mo. Kansas City, 1966-71; chmn. Nat. Council on Crime and Delinquency, 1966-76; pres. Hubbell Family Hist. Soc., 1981-85; mem. Soc. Fellows Nelson Art Gallery. With USAAF, 1942-44, capt. JAGC, 1944-46. Mem. ABA, Kansas City Met. Bar Assn. (pres. 1963-64, ann. Achievement award 1974, 1st ann. Litigator Emeritus award), Mo. Bar Assn., Assn. Trial Lawyers Am. (assoc. editor R.R. law sect. of jour. 1951—), Mo. Assn. Trial Attys. (pres. 1954, editor bull. 1955), Lawyers Assn. Kansas City, Lawyers Assn. St. Louis, Archeol. Inst. Am., Sierra Club (life). Episcopalian. Democrat. Club: Kansas City. Personal injury, Federal civil litigation, State civil litigation. Home: 1210 W 63d St Kansas City MO 64113-1513 Office: Hubbell Sawyer Peak O'Neal & Napier Power and Light Bldg 106 W 14th St Fl 12 Kansas City MO 64105-1914

**HUBBELL, LINDA,** publishing executive. Pub. Calif. Lawyer, San Francisco. Office: Daily Jour Corp 1390 Market St Ste 1210 San Francisco CA 94102-5306

**HUBBY, BERT GORMAN,** lawyer; b. Waco, Tex., July 15, 1951; s. Albert G. and Pattye Jane (Cayton) H.; m. Loye Dell Noah, Oct. 4, 1980. BA in Psychology and Polit. Sci., North Tex. State U., Denton, 1974; JD, South Tex. Coll. Law, Houston, 1978. Bar: Tex. 1978, U.S. Dist. Ct. (no. dist.) Tex. 1980; bd. cert. personal injury, Tex. Assoc. Foster & Garrett, Arlington, Tex., 1978-80, John B. Foster, P.C., Arlington, 1980-86; pvt. practice Arlington, 1986—. Mem. Am. Trial Lawyers Assn., Tex. Trial Lawyers Assn., Arlington Bar Assn. (past pres.), Tarrant County Bar Assn., Kiwanis Arlington S.W. (past pres.), Tarrant County Trial Lawyers, State Bar Tex. Methodist. Avocations: scuba diving, hunting, fishing. Toxic tort, Personal injury. Office: 4200 S Cooper St Ste 210 Arlington TX 76015-4139

**HUBEL, DENNIS JAMES,** judge; b. N.Y.C., Nov. 3, 1947. BS in Electrical Engring., Cornell U., 1969; postgrad., U. Wash., 1972-73; JD cum laude, Lewis & Clark Coll., 1976. Bar: Oreg. 1976, Wash. 1985, U.S. Dist. Ct. Oreg., U.S. Dist. Ct. (ea. and we. dists.) Wash., U.S. Ct. Appeals (9th cir.), U.S. Supreme Ct. Judge U.S. Magistrate, Portland, 1998—; adj. prof. Lewis & Clark Coll., Portland, Oreg., 1980-82. Mem. Am. Bd. Trial Advs., Oreg. State Bar Assn. (chmn. jury instrn. com. 1988-91, chmn. procedure & practice com. 1991-93). Office: 927 US Courthouse 1000 SW 3rd Ave Portland OR 97204-2930

**HUBEN, BRIAN DAVID,** lawyer; b. Inglewood, Calif., May 14, 1962; s. Michael Gerald and Dorothy (Withers) H.; m. Kathy Henson Johnson, Apr. 6, 1991; children: Kaitlin Johnson, Mariana Johnson. BA, Loyola Marymount U., 1984; JD, Loyola Law Sch., 1987. Bar: Calif. 1988, U.S. Dist. Ct. (no., ce., ea. and so. dists.) Calif. 1988, Ariz., 1994, U.S. Ct. Appeals (9th cir.) 1988, D.C. 1989, U.S. Supreme Ct. 1996. Assoc. Steinberg, Nutter & Brent, Santa Monica, Calif., 1988-89, Smith & Hilbig, Torrance, Calif., 1989-95, Robie & Matthai, L.A., 1995—; spl. master State Bar of Calif., 1995-99; del. L.A. County Bar Assn. State Conv., 1990—. Mem. instl. rev. bd. Torrance Meml. Med. Ctr., 1990-95. Mem. Calif. Bar Assn., D.C. Bar Assn., L.A. County Bar Assn., Loyola Marymount Univ. Alumni Assn. (dir., bd. dirs. 1995—). Democrat. Roman Catholic. Avocations: travel, sports, current events. General civil litigation, Bankruptcy, Contracts commercial. Office: Robie & Matthai 500 S Grand Ave 15th Fl Los Angeles CA 90071-2609

**HUBER, RICHARD GREGORY,** lawyer, educator; b. Indpls., June 29, 1919; s. Hugh Joseph and Laura Marie (Becker) H.; m. Katherine Elizabeth McDonald, June 21, 1950; children: Katherine, Richard, Mary, Elizabeth, Stephen, Mark. BS, U.S. Naval Acad, 1942; JD, U. Iowa, 1950; LLM, Harvard U., 1951; LLD (hon.), New England Sch. Law, 1985, Northeastern U., 1987, Roger Williams U., 1996. Instr. law U. Iowa, 1950; assoc. prof. law U. S.C., 1952-54; assoc. prof. Tulane U., 1954-57; assoc. prof. Boston Coll., 1957-59, prof., 1959-90, dean, 1970-85; disting. prof. Roger Williams U., Bristol, R.I., 1993-95; prof. New England Sch. Law, Newton, Mass., 1995-99; adj. faculty Boston Coll., 1999—. Contbr. articles and book revs. to profl. jours. Past chairperson pers. and fin. coms. Mass. chpt. Multiple Sclerosis Soc.; past pres. bd. trustees Beaver Country Day Sch. With USN, 1941-47, 51-52. Mem. ABA (del., mem. coun. legal edn. 1981-85, trustee law sch. admissions coun 1983-85), Soc. Am. Law Tchrs., Assn. Am. Law Schs. (pres. 1988-89), Coun. Legal Edn. Opportunity (pres. 1975-79), Am. Judicature Soc., Mass. Bar Assn., Mass. Bar Found. Democrat. Roman Catholic. Home: 406 Woodward St Waban MA 02468-1523 Office: 885 Centre St Newton MA 02459-1154

**HUBER, WILLIAM EVAN,** lawyer; b. Celina, Ohio, Mar. 10, 1943; s. W. Evan and Genevieve Rose Huber; m. E. Marie Schwaberow, June 24, 1966 (div. Aug. 1994); children: Michael D., Mark William. BSEd, Ohio No. U., 1965, JD, 1968. Bar: Ohio 1968, U.S. Dist. Ct. (no. dist.) Ohio 1972, U.S. Supreme Ct. 1972, U.S. Ct. Appeals (6th cir.) 1990, U.S. Tax Ct. Ohio. Asst. pros. atty. Auglaize County, Ohio, 1969-76; pvt. practice St. Marys, Ohio, 1976—; asst. law dir. City of St. Marys, Ohio, 1972-79. Past pres., past state dir. St. Marys Jaycees; past state v.p. Ohio Jaycees, 1969; mem. Jr. Chamber Internat. Senate; past trustee Auglaize County Mental Health Assn.; past gen. chmn. St. Mary's Area United Way; past chmn. St. Marys City Recreational Adv. Bd.; past pres. St. Marys Nat. Little League; past chmn. St. Marys Medic-Search Com.; mem., past trustee St. Marys Cmty. Improvement Corp.; past mem. Mayor's Downtown Re-vitalization Com.; past mem., chmn. St. Marys Civil Svc. Commn., 1993-97; mem. Auglaize County Bd. Elections, 1994-97; past mem. Auglaize County Dem. Exec. Com., chmn., 1992-97. Named Outstanding Jaycee, St. Marys Jaycees, 1971; recipient Ohio Jaycees Presdl. award of Honor, 1972, Disting. Svc. award Ohio Dem. Party, 1997. Mem. Ohio State Bar Assn., Auglaize County Bar Assn. (past pres.), St. Marys C. of C. (past trustee, past pres.). Family and matrimonial, General practice, General civil litigation. Office: PO Box 298 Saint Marys OH 45885-0298

**HUCHTEMAN, RALPH DOUGLAS,** lawyer; b. Garland, Tex., Oct. 8, 1946; s. Ray Edwin and Hazel Laverne (Clark) H.; m. Sherry Lynn Horner, Mar. 12, 1994; children: Lara Victoria, Brett Norman, Bryan Randolff. AA, Okla. Mil. Acad., 1966; BA in Polit. Sci., Okla. State U., 1969; JD, Okla. U., 1972. Bar: Okla. 1972, U.S. Dist. Ct. (we. dist.) Okla. 1972. Ptnr. Doak & Huchteman, Oklahoma City, 1972-73, Wolf & Wolf P.C. (formerly Wolf, Wold, Huchteman & Graven), Norman, Okla., 1982-88; prin. Huchteman Law Offices, Norman, 1989-98; staff atty. Legal Svcs. of Eastern Okla., Inc., Bartlesville, 1998-99, mng. atty., 1999—; assoc. mcpl. judge, Noble, Okla., 1990-98, Blanchard, Okla., 1992-98; vis. asst. prof. Coll. Bus., Okla. U., 1972-73; temporary justice Okla. Ct. Appeals, Oklahoma City, 1982-83. State exec. sec. Student Lobby for Higher Edn., Stillwater, Okla., 1968-69. 1st lt. U.s. Army, 1973. T.A. Shadid scholar Okla. U., 1969; recipient A.C. Hunt Practice award Okla. U., 1972. Mem. ATLA, Okla. Bar Assn., Okla. Trial Lawyers Assn. Democrat. Family and matrimonial, Pension, profit-sharing, and employee benefits, State civil litigation. Office: Legal Svcs Eastern Okla 217 S Choctaw Ave Bartlesville OK 74003-2837

**HUCK, RICHARD FELIX, III,** lawyer; b. St. Louis, Mar. 4, 1957; s. Richard Felix Jr. and Agnes Stewart (Kinsella) H.; m. Kathryn Ewing Otto, Apr. 7, 1984; children: Richard Dalton, Emily Stewart. BA, Washington & Lee U., 1979; JD, St. Louis U., 1982. Bar: Mo. 1982, U.S. Dist. Ct. (we. dist.) Mo. 1982, Ill. 1983, U.S. Dist. Ct. (ea. dist.) Mo. 1983, U.S. Ct. Appeals (8th cir.) 1983, U.S. Ct. Fed. Claims 1996. From assoc. to ptnr. Evans & Dixon, St. Louis, 1982-96; ptnr. Blumenfeld Kaplan & Sandweiss PC, St. Louis, 1996—. Mem. John Marshall Rep. Club., St. Louis, 1989. Mem. ABA, Bar Assn. Met. St. Louis, Forum on Constrn. Industry, Racquet Club, Noonday Club, St. Louis Country Club. Roman Catholic. Avocations: golf, squash. General civil litigation, Construction, Insurance. Home: 5 Glenmary Rd Saint Louis MO 63132-3608 Office: Blumenfeld Kaplan & Sandweiss PC 168 N Meramec Ave Ste 400 Saint Louis MO 63105-3758

**HUCKABEE, HARLOW MAXWELL,** lawyer, writer; b. Wichita Falls, Tex., Jan. 22, 1918; s. Edwin Cleveland and Gladys Idella (Bonney) H.; m. Gloria Charlotte Comstock, Jan. 10, 1942; children: Bonney M., David C., Stephen M. BA, Harvard U., 1948; JD, Georgetown U., 1951. Bar: U.S. Dist. Ct. D.C. 1952, U.S. Ct. Appeals (D.C. cir.) 1952. Cashier br. office Columbian Nat. Life Ins. Co., Boston, 1935-40; lawyer Fed. Housing Adminstrn., Washington, 1955-56; trial lawyer, criminal sect., tax divsn. U.S. Justice Dept., Washington, 1956-63; lawyer IRS, Washington, 1963-67; trial lawyer organized crime and racketeering sect. U.S. Justice Dept., Washington, 1967-68, trial lawyer criminal sect., tax divsn., 1968-80. Author: Lawyers, Psychiatrists and Criminal Law, 1980; contbr. articles to profl. jours. and legal publs. including Diminished Capacity Dilemma in the Federal System, 1991. Maj. U.S. Army, 1940-45, 48-55, ETO, Korea; lt. col. USAR, 1961. Methodist. Home: 5100 Fillmore Ave Apt 913 Alexandria VA 22311-5048

**HUCKIN, WILLIAM PRICE, JR.,** prosecutor; b. Okmulgee, Okla., Aug. 20, 1920; s. William Price and Mary Louise H.; m. Freda Croom, Nov. 15, 1947; children: William Price III, David, Elizabeth, Barbara. BA, U. Okla., 1942, LLB, 1947. Bar: Okla. 1947; U.S. Dist. Ct. (no. dist.) 1953, U.S. Dist. Ct. (we. dist.) 1950, U.S. Ct. Appeals, 1994. Asst. county atty. Tulsa, Okla., 1951-52, prosecutor, 1954-55, pvt. practice, 1956—; apttd. city prosecutor, Tulsa. Active First Presbyn. Ch., clk. of session, permanent jud. commn. 1st lt., pilot, U.S. Army Air Corps, 1943-45. Decorated EAME (Rome Arno and Air Offensive Europe) Theatre ribbon with 2 bronze stars, air medal, 1944, 2nd oak leaf cluster, 1944, unit citation, 1944. Mem. ATLA, Okla. Bar Assn., Tulsa County Bar Assn. (Disting. Svc. award 1986), Beta Theta Pi (pres. 1947). Republican. Avocations: genealogy, chess. Home: 6706 S Florence Ave Tulsa OK 74136-4556 Office: 1206 Philtower Bldg 427 S Boston Ave Tulsa OK 74103-4141

**HUDACEK, DANIEL ANDREW,** lawyer, financial planner; b. Memphis, Oct. 29, 1951; s. Andrew Gabriel and Ann Elizabeth (Thrower) H.; m. Sharon Ann Moran, May 21, 1982; children: Shannon, Ashley, William. AB, Princeton U., 1973; JD, Dickinson Sch. Law, 1979. Bar: Pa. Supreme Ct. 1979, N.J. Supreme Ct. 1980, U.S. Dist. Ct. N.J. 1980, U.S. Tax. Ct. 1980; CFP. Staff atty. AYCO Corp., Albany, N.Y., 1979-83; dir. fin. planning Fin. Blueprints, Inc., Florham Park, N.J., 1983-85; asst. v.p. N.Y. Life Ins. Co., N.Y.C., 1985-98; v.p. Eagle Strategies Corp., N.Y.C., 1989-98; pvt. practice, 1998—. Mem. Internat. Assn. for Fin. Planning. Avocation: international travel. Estate planning, Probate, Estate taxation. Office: 486 Schooleys Mountain Rd Hackettstown NJ 07840-4000

**HUDDLESTON, JOSEPH RUSSELL,** judge; b. Glasgow, Ky., Feb. 5, 1937; s. Paul Russell and Laura Frances (Martin) H.; m. Heidi Wood, Sept. 12, 1959; children: Johanna, Lisa, Kristina. AB, Princeton U., 1959; JD, U. Va., 1962, LLM, 1997. Bar: Ky. 1962, U.S. Ct. Appeals (6th cir.) 1963, U.S. Supreme Ct. 1970. Ptnr. Huddleston Bros., Bowling Green, Ky., 1962-87; judge Warren Cir. Ct. Divsn. I, Bowling Green, Ky., 1987-91, Ky. Ct. appeals, Bowling Green, Ky., 1991—; mem. Adv. Com. for Criminal Law Revision, 1969-71; mem. exec. com. Ky. Crime Commn., 1972-77. Named Ky. Outstanding Trial Judge, 1990. Mem. ABA, Ky. Bar Assn. (ho. of dels. 1971-80), Assn. Trial Lawyers Am. (state del. 1981-82), Ky. Acad. Trial Attys. (bd. govs. 1975-87, pres. 1978), Bowling Green Bar Assn. (pres. 1972), So. Ky. Estate Planning Coun. (pres. 1983), Bowling Green-Warren County C. of C. (bd. dirs. 1987-91), Port Oliver Yacht Club (Comodore). Democrat. Episcopalian. Home: 644 Minnie Way Bowling Green KY 42101-9210 Office: 1945 Scottsville Rd Ste 101 Bowling Green KY 42104-5824

**HUDIAK, DAVID MICHAEL,** academic administrator, lawyer; b. Darby, Pa., June 27, 1953; s. Michael Paul and Sophie Marie (Glowaski) H.; m. Veronica Ann Barbone, Aug. 28, 1982; children: David Michael, Christopher Andrew, Jonathan Joseph. BA, Haverford Coll., 1975; JD, U. Pa., 1978. Bar: Pa. 1979, U.S. Dist. Ct. (ea. dist.) Pa. 1979, N.J. 1981, U.S. Dist. Ct. N.J. 1981. Assoc. Jerome H. Ellis, Phila., 1978-79, Berson, Fineman & Bernstein, Phila., 1979-80; pvt. practice Aldan, Pa., 1980-81; dir. tng. paralegal program PJA Sch., Upper Darby, Pa., 1982—, acting dir., 1983-89, dir., 1989—; v.p. The PJA Sch., Inc., 1989—, bd. dirs.; v.p., sec.-treas., bd. dirs. 7900 West Chester Pike Corp., 1994—; mem. staff Nat. Ctr. Ednl. Testing, Phila., 1982-87; instr. Villanova (Pa.) U., 1985. Mem. Havertown Choristers; active U. Pa. Light Opera Co., 1977-84. Mem. ABA, Pa. Bar Assn., Founders Club Haverford Coll. Office: PJA Sch 7900 W Chester Pike Upper Darby PA 19082-1917

**HUDKINS, JOHN W.,** lawyer; b. Inglewood, Calif., Jan. 12, 1946; s. Ralph Emerson and Genevieve Delores H.; m. Diana Byler, Feb. 16, 1969. BA, Calif. State U., Hayward, 1968; MBA, U. Nev., Las Vegas, 1971; JD, U. of Pacific, 1976; LLM, George Washington U., 1983. Bar: Fla. 1976, Iowa 1976, Calif. 1977, U.S. Ct. Mil. Appeals 1976. Commd. 2d lt. USAF, 1968, advanced through grades to lt. col., 1983, ret., 1988; sr. counsel Aerojet-Gen. Corp., Sacramento, 1988-94; dir. bus. mgmt. Olin Irdnance, Downey, Calif., 1994-95; sr. counsel Olin Ordnance, St. Petersburg, Fla., 1995-96; v.p., chief counsel Olin Irdnance, St. Petersburg, Fla., 1996-97; v.p., dep. gen. counsel Primex Tech., Inc., St. Petersburg, Fla., 1997—. Bd. dirs. Vandenberg Fed. Credit Union, Lompoc, Calif., 1983-85, Prince William (Va.) County Soccer Assn., 1985-88. Mem. ABA (pub. contract law sect.), Nat. Security Indsl. Assn. (chair legal com.). Government contracts and claims, General corporate, Administrative and regulatory. Home: 1339 Forestedge Blvd Oldsmar FL 34677-5119 Office: Primex Tech Inc 10101 9th St N St Petersburg FL 33716-3807

**HUDNUT, STEWART SKINNER,** manufacturing company executive, lawyer; b. Cin., Apr. 29, 1939; s. William Herbert and Elizabeth Allen (Kilborne) H.; children: Alexander Putnam, Andrew Gerard, Nathaniel Parker. AB (summa cum laude), Princeton U., 1961; postgrad., Oxford U., Eng., 1962; JD, Harvard Law Sch., 1965; Environ. Law Cert., Pace U., 1991. Bar: N.Y. 1965, U.S. Dist. Ct. (so. and ea. dists.) N.Y., U.S. Ct. Appeals (2d cir.), U.S. Supreme Ct. Assoc. Davis Polk & Wardwell, N.Y.C., 1965-67, 71-73, Paris, 1968-70; v.p., counsel Bankers Trust Co., 1973-77; v.p., gen. counsel, sec. Scovill Mfg. Co., Waterbury, Conn., 1977-87; sr. v.p., gen. counsel, sec. Mcpl. Bond Investors Assurance Corp., White Plains, N.Y., 1987-89, Ill. Tool Works Inc., Glenview, Ill., 1992—. Bd. dirs., exec. com. Lyric Opera Guild of Chgo.; instr. Voyageur Outward Bound Sch., 1989-90. Woodrow Wilson fellow, Keasbey fellow Christ Ch. Oxford U., Eng., 1962. Mem. ABA, Ill. Bar Assn., Phi Beta Kappa. Republican. Presbyterian. Home: 56 Indian Hill Rd Winnetka IL 60093-3938 Office: Ill Tool Works Inc 3600 W Lake Ave Glenview IL 60025-5811

**HUDSON, ANN,** circuit clerk; b. Cash, Ark., Nov. 28, 1946; d. Brisco Floyd and Jennie Ruth (McQuay) Coots; children: Kristi, Jamie. Cert. of election, Ark. Credit bur. worker Jonesboro, 1966-68; libr. worker Ark. State U., Jonesboro, 1969-71; deputy cir. clk. Jonesboro, 1971-80, apptd. cir. ct. clk., 1980; mcpl. ct. deputy Jonesboro, Ark., 1983-96; cir. ct. clk. Jonesboro, 1997—. Office: 511 S Main St Jonesboro AR 72401-2859

**HUDSON, DENNIS LEE,** lawyer, retired government official, arbitrator, educator; b. St. Louis, Jan. 5, 1936; s. Lewis Jefferson and Helen Mabel (Buchanan) H.; children: Karen Marie, Karla Sue, Mary Ashley. BA, U. Ill., 1958; JD, John Marshall Law Sch., 1972. Bar: Ill. 1972, U.S Dist. Ct. (so. dist.) Ill. 1972, U.S. Dist. Ct. (no. dist.) Ill. 1972. Insp., IRS, Chgo., 1962-72; spl. agt. GSA, Chgo., 1972-78, spl. agt.-in-charge, 1978-83, regional insp. gen., 1983-87; supervisory spl. agt., Dept Justice-GSA Task Force, Washington, 1978; arbitrator Cir. Ct. Cook County, Ill.; prof. of criminal justice Coll. Dupage. Bd. govs. Theatre Western Springs, Ill., 1978-81, 91-92; deacon Grace Lutheran Ch., LaGrange, Ill., 1977-81. Served with U.S. Army, 1959-61. John N. Jewett scholar, 1972. Mem. ABA, Ill. Bar Assn. Home: 109 51st Pl Western Springs IL 60558-2002 Office: Coll Dupage Bus & Svcs Div 22D Saint Lambert Rd Glen Ellyn IL 60137

**HUDSON, LEIGH CARLETON,** lawyer; b. Fort Scott, Kans., Apr. 18, 1948; s. Howard Carleton and Dorothy Delano H.; m. Marsha Ann Corn, July 30, 1971; children: Tyler William, Ryan Carleton. BS in Bus., Emporia State U., 1971; JD, Washburn U., 1975. Bar: Kans. 1975, U.S. Dist. Ct. Kans. 1975, Kansas Supreme Ct. 1975, U.S. Ct. Appeals (10th cir.) 1997. Mem. White & Hudson, Pittsburg, Kans., 1975-82, Hudson & Mullies, Fort Scott, 1982—. Contbr. articles to profl. jours. Fellow Am. Coll. Trial Lawyers (mem. state com. 1993); mem. Kans. Bar Assn. (bd. govs. 1981-87), Kans. Def. Assn. (pres. 1993), Am Bd. Trial Advs., Rotary. Personal injury, Workers' compensation, Professional liability. Home: 601 Fairway Dr Fort Scott KS 66701-3130 Office: Hudson & Mullies LLC 102 S Main St Fort Scott KS 66701-1415

**HUDSON, LISE LYN,** lawyer; b. Miami, Fla., Mar. 18, 1962; d. Richard Hudson and Bette Anne (Graham) H. BA in Internat. Affairs, George Washington U., 1984; JD, Mercer Law Sch., 1988. Bar: Fla. 1988, U.S. Dist. Ct. (so. dist.) Fla. 1989. Assoc. Montgomery and Larmoyeux, West Palm Beach, Fla., 1988-94; pvt. practice Law Office of Lise Hudson, Palm Beach, Fla., 1994—. Dir. Palette, Mask and Lyre Children's Theatre, West Palm Beach, 1994—; mem. Acad. Fla. Trial Lawyers, 1988—, vice-chmn. family law divsn., 1997—. Recipient Pro Bono award Palm Beach County Bar Assn., 1989. Mem. Acad. Fla. Trial Lawyers (vice chmn. family law divsn. 1996—). State civil litigation, Family and matrimonial, Professional liability. Office: Hudson & Assocs 224 Datura St Ste 1300 West Palm Beach FL 33401-5641

**HUDSON, ROBERT FRANKLIN, JR.,** lawyer; b. Miami, Fla., Sept. 20, 1946; s. Robert Franklin and Jane Ann (Reed) H.; m. Edith Mueller, June 19, 1971; children: Daniel Warren, Patrick Alexander. BSBA in Econs., U. Fla., 1968, JD, 1971; summer cert., U. London, 1970; LLM in Taxation, NYU, 1972. Bar: Fla. 1971, N.Y. 1975. Law clk. to judge Don N. Laramore U.S. Ct. Claims, Washington, 1972-73; assoc. Wender, Murase & White, N.Y.C., 1973-77; ptnr. Arky, Freed, Stearns et al, Miami, 1977-86; ptnr. Baker & McKenzie, Miami, 1986—, mem. policy com., 1990-93, mem. client credit com., 1992—, mng. ptnr. Miami office, 1996-98; mem. adv. bd. Tax Mgmt., Inc., Washington, 1986—, Fgn. Investment N.Am., London, 1990-96; legal counsel to her majesty's Britanic Counsel, Miami. Author: Federal Taxation of Foreign Investment in U.S. Real Estate, 1986; contbr. articles to legal publs. Bd. dirs. Fla. Philharmonic, 1996-97, Performing Arts Ctr. Found., 1994—, Concert Assn. Fla., 1992—, exec. com., 1993-98, vice chmn., 1994-98. Mem. ABA, Fla. Bar Assn. (chmn. tax sect. 1989-90, Outstanding Spkr. 1995), Internat. Fiscal Assn. (v.p. S.E. region U.S. br. 1985-92, exec. coun. 1987—), Inter-Am. Bar Assn., Internat. Bar Assn., Internat. Tax Planning Assn., Coll. Tax Lawyers, World Trade Ctr. (bd. dirs. 1992-94), S.E./U.S. Japan Assn., Japan Soc. South Fla. (chmn. pub. affairs com. 1991-93, bd. dirs. 1993—, treas. 1995-96, pres. 1996-99. Democrat. Methodist. Avocations: skiing, boating, photography, travel, hiking. Corporate taxation, Private international. Office: Baker & McKenzie 1200 Brickell Ave Ste 1900 Miami FL 33131-3257

**HUDSPETH, HARRY LEE,** federal judge; b. Dallas, Dec. 28, 1935; s. Harry Ellis and Hattilee (Dudney) H.; m. Vicki Kathryn Round, Nov. 27, 1971; children: Melinda, Mary Kathryn. BA, U. Tex., Austin, 1955, JD, 1958. Bar: Tex. 1958. Trial atty. Dept. Justice, Washington, 1959-62; asst. U.S. atty. Western Dist. Tex., El Paso, 1962-69; assoc. Peticolas, Luscombe & Stephens, El Paso, 1969-77; U.S. magistrate El Paso, 1977-79; judge U.S. Dist. Ct. (we. dist.) Tex., El Paso, 1979—; chief judge U.S. Dist. Ct. (we. dist) Tex., El Paso, 1992—. Bd. dirs. Sun Carnival Assn., 1976, Met. YMCA El Paso, 1980-88. Mem. ABA, El Paso Bar Assn., U. Tex. Ex-students Assn. (exec. coun. 1980-86), Chancellors, Order of Coif, Phi Beta Kappa. Democrat. Mem. Christian Ch. (Disciples of Christ). Office: US Dist Ct We Dist Tex 433 US Courthouse 511 E San Antonio St El Paso TX 79901-2401

**HUDSPETH, HARVEY GRESHAM,** history educator; b. Clarksdale, Miss., Oct. 17, 1955; s. Joseph MacDonald Hudspeth and Martha Lou Shelton; m. Mary Ruth Chambley, May 25, 1999. BA in History and Polit. Sci., U. Miss., 1978, JD, 1981, PhD in History, 1994. Bar: Miss. 1981, U.S. Dist. Ct. (no. dist.) M iss. 1981, U.S. Dist. Ct. (so. dist.) Miss. 1984, U.S. Ct. Appeals (5th cir.) 1985, Ill. 1989. Staff atty. Miss. Sec. of State, Jackson, 1981-83; pvt. practice Gulfport, Miss., 1983-85; land analyst Shell Oil Co., Houston, 1985-87; title examiner 1st Am. Title, Chgo., 1987-89; credit adminstr. Citicorp, Chgo., 1989-90; tchg. asst. U. Miss., University, 1991-94; history program coord., asst. prof. history Mississippi Valley State U., Itta Bena, Miss., 1994—; presenter in field. Contbr. to books: Tennessee Encyclopedia of History, 1998, Booker T. Washington: Essays, 1998; contbr. articles to profl. jours. Chmn. Com. to Elect Joe Hudspeth Pub. Svc. Commr., Miss., 1983. Mem. Am. Hist. Assn., Orgn. Am. Historians, Miss. Hist. Assn., Gulf South Hist. Assn., So. Conf. on Afro-Am. Studies, Inc., Econ. and Bus. Hist. Soc., Miss. Bar Assn., Ill. Bar Assn. Republican. Presbyterian. Avocations: travel, politics, reading. Home: PO Box 5045 Itta Bena MS 38941 Office: Mississippi Valley State U 14000 Highway 82 W Itta Bena MS 38941-1400

**HUENERGARDT, DARREL J.,** lawyer; b. Kearney, Nebr., June 20, 1943; s. LaVern O. and Dorothy J. (Rouse) H.; m. Carol A. Barker, Jan. 3, 1970; children: Benjamin, Samuel, Joshua. BS, Union Coll., Lincoln, Nebr., 1965; JD, U. Nebr., 1968. Bar: Nebr. 1968, Colo. 1992, U.S. Ct. Appeals (8th cir.) 1968, U.S. Supreme Ct. 1975, U.S. Tax Ct. 1985. Dep. county atty. Gage County, Nebr., 1968-70; ptnr. O'Brien, Huenergardt & Cook, Kimball, Nebr., 1970-98, Huenergardt & Neilan, Kimball, Nebr., 1998—. Dir. pub. affairs Mid Am. Conf. of SDA, Lincoln, 1976—. General practice, Probate, Oil, gas, and mineral.

**HUETTNER, RICHARD ALFRED,** lawyer; b. N.Y.C., Mar. 25, 1927; s. Alfred F. and Mary (Reilly) H.; children—Jennifer Mary, Barbara Bryan; m. 2d, Eunice Bizzell Dowd, Aug. 22, 1971. Marine Engrs. License, N.Y. State Maritime Acad., 1947; B.S., Yale U. Sch. Engring., 1949; J.D., U. Pa., 1952. Bar: D.C. 1952, N.Y. 1954, U.S. Ct. Mil. Appeals 1953, U.S. Ct. Claims 1961, U.S. Supreme Ct. 1969, U.S. Ct. Appeals (fed. cir.) 1982, also other fed. cts, registered to practice U.S. Patent and Trademark Office 1957, Canadian Patent Office 1968. Engr. Jones & Laughlin Steel Corp., 1954-55; assoc. atty. firm Kenyon & Kenyon, N.Y.C, 1955-61; mem. firm Kenyon & Kenyon, 1961-96, of counsel, 1996-98; specialist patent, trademark and copyright law. Trustee N.J. Shakespeare Festival, 1972-79, sec., 1977-79; trustee Overlook Hosp., Summit, N.J., 1978-84, 86-89, vice chmn. bd. trustees, 1980-82, chmn. bd. trustees, 1982-84; trustee Overlook Found., 1981-89, chmn. bd. trustees, 1986-89, emeritus trustee, 1991; trustee Colonial Symphony Orch., Madison, N.J., 1972-82, v.p. bd. trustees 1974-76. pres. 1976-79; chmn. bd. overseers N.J. Consortium for Performing Arts, 1972-74; mem. Yale U. Council, 1978-81; bd. dirs. Yale Communications Bd., 1978-80; chmn. bd. trustees Center for Addictive Illnesses, Morristown, N.J., 1979-82; rep. Assn. Yale Alumni, 1975-80, chmn. com. undergrad. admissions, 1976-78, bd. govs., 1976-80, chmn. bd. govs., 1978-80; chmn. Yale Alumni Schs. Com. N.Y., 1972-78; assoc. fellow Silliman Coll., Yale U., 1976—; bd. dirs., exec. com. Yale U. Alumni Fund, 1978-81; mem. Yale Class of 1949 Council, 1980—; bd. dirs. Overlook Health Systems, 1984—. Served from midshipman to lt. USNR, 1945-47, 52-54; cert. JAGC 1953; Res. ret. Recipient Yale medal, 1983, Disting. Svc. to Yale Class of 1949 award, 1989, Yale Sci. and Engring. Meritorious Svc. award, 1992. Fellow N.Y. Bar Found.; mem. ABA, N.Y. State Bar Assn., Assn. Bar City N.Y., N.Y. Patent Trademark Copyright Law Assn. (chmn. com. mtgs. 1961-64, chmn. com. econ. matters 1966-69, 72-74), AAAS, N.Y. Acad. Scis., N.Y. County Lawyers Assn., Am. Intellectual Property Law Assn., Internat. Patent and Trademark Assn., Am. Judicature Soc., Yale Sci. and Engring. Assn. (v.p. 1973-75, pres. 1975-78, exec. bd. 1972-79), Fed. Bar Coun. Clubs: Yale (N.Y.C.); Yale of Central N.J. (Summit) (trustee 1973-88, pres. 1975-77), Morris County Golf (Convent, N.J.); The Graduates (New Haven). Patent, Trademark and copyright, Federal civil litigation. Home: 150 Green Ave Madison NJ 07940-2513

**HUEY, DAVID W.,** lawyer; b. Fargo, N.D., Aug. 5, 1947; s. Robert N. and Muriel Ekness H.; m. Marcia Miller, Aug. 18, 1967; children: Sara Marie, James Andrew, Jonathan Lund. BA with honors, U. N.D., 1976; JD cum laude, U.Minn., 1979. Assoc. Muir Law Firm, Jackson, Minn., 1979-81, ptnr., 1981-87; asst. atty. gen. N.D. Office Atty. Gen., Bismarck, 1988—. Com. mem. Boy Scouts Am., 1990—. With USN, 1965-68. Recipient Someone Spl. Vol. award Legal Assistance N.D., 1993. Mem. State Bar Assn. N.D. (com. law related edn. 1995—). Presbyterian. Avocations: backpacking, skiing, camping, basketball. Office: ND Atty Gen 600 E Boulevard Ave Bismarck ND 58505-0660

**HUEY, FRANCES COLLEEN,** lawyer; b. Sacramento, Sept. 15, 1954; d. Francis Edward Huey and Gladys Colleen (Stone) Huey. AA, Am. River Coll.; BA, Calif. State U., Sacramento, 1977; JD, Hamline U., St. Paul, 1980. Bar: Minn. 1980, Calif., 1982, U.S. Dist. Ct. (ea. dist.) Calif. Rsch. asst. to assoc. dean Hamline U., 1978-80; assoc. editor Law Rev. Digest, Mpls., 1979-80; legal intern Freeman, Rishwain, Hall & Shore, Stockton Calif., 1982; sole practice, Sacramento, 1983—; mem. Indigent Criminal Def. Panel, Sacramento, 1983—. Author short stories. Rep. Sacramento County Council Folkdance Clubs, 1982—, v.p., 1985, 86. Mem. Asian ABA, ABA, Calif. State Bar Assn., Assn. Trial Lawyers Am., Calif. Trial Lawyers Assn., Fed. Bar Assn., Minn. State Bar Assn., Sacramento County Bar Assn. Democrat. Mem. Universal Freedom Ch. Home: 2017 Maryal Dr Sacramento CA 95864-0638 Office: 2240 Tamarack Way Sacramento CA 95821-4609

**HUFF, MARILYN L.,** federal judge; b. 1951. BA, Calvin Coll., Grand Rapids, Mich., 1972; JD, U. Mich., 1976. Assoc. Gray, Cary, Ames & Frye, 1976-83, ptnr., 1983-91; judge U.S. Dist. Ct. (so. dist.) Calif., San Diego, 1991-98, chief judge, 1998—. Contbr. articles to profl. jours. Mem. adv. coun. Calif. LWV, 1987—, Am. Lung Assn.; bd. dirs. San Diego and Imperial Counties, 1989—; mem. LaJolla Presbyn. Ch. Named Legal Profl. of Yr. San Diego City Club and Jr. C. of C., 1990; recipient Superior Ct. Valuable Svc. award, 1982. Mem. ABA, San Diego Bar Found., San Diego Bar Assn. (bd. dirs. 1986-88, v.p. 1988, chmn. profl. edn. com. 1990, Svc. award to legal profession, 1989, Lawyer of Yr. 1990), Calif. State Bar Assn., Calif. Women Lawyers, Am. Bd. Trial Advs., Libel Def. Resource Ctr., Am. Inns of Ct. (master 1987—, exec. com. 1989—), Lawyers' Club San Diego (adv. bd. 1989-90, Belva Lockwood Svc. award 1987), Univ. Club, Aardvarks Lt. Office: US Dist Ct Courtroom 1 940 Front St San Diego CA 92101-8994

**HUFF, THOMAS E.,** judge; b. Augusta, Ga., June 5, 1949; s. Ernest Roscoe and Trilby Collen Huff; m. Patricia Dale Tucker, May 5, 1974; 1 child, Tiffany Dale. Student, U. S.C., Aiken, 1969, Augusta State U., 1971; JD, U. S.C., 1975. Judge S.C. Ct. Appeals, Aiken. Address: PO Box 3247 Aiken SC 29802-3247

**HUFFAKER, JOHN BOSTON,** lawyer; b. Nashville, Nov. 1, 1925; s. William Bruce and Pauline (Watson) H.; m. Grace Murray Logan, Jan. 14, 1954 (dec. June 15, 1989); children: Margaret, Christiana H. Logansmith; m. Judith Hudson Webster, Oct. 24, 1992. B.S., Yale U., 1946; LL.B., U. Va., 1948. Bar: Va., Pa., D.C., U.S. Supreme Ct. Assoc. Cummings, Stanley, Truitt & Cross, Washington, 1949-51; legis. atty. Joint Com. on Taxation, Washington, 1953-56; assoc. Duane, Morris & Heckscher, Phila., 1956-61; ptnr. Rawle & Henderson, Phila., 1961-66, Pepper Hamilton LLP, Berwyn, Pa., Phila. and Washington, 1966—; spl. advisor Tax Mgmt., 1960—; pres. Consular Corps of Phila., 1990-91. Departmental editor Jour. Taxation, 1976—; contbr. articles to profl. jours. Named hon. consul Republic of Madagascar, 1982—; bd. dirs. Welcome House, Doylestown, Pa., 1970—, v.p., 1976-80, pres., 1980—, chmn. overseas ops. com., 1984—, chmn., 1988—, bd. dirs. Pearl S. Buck Found., 1984—, vice chmn. internat. ops., 1994-96, chmn. 1990-94, chmn. fin. com., 1998—; chmn. Wharton Sch. Tax Conf., 1981-83, Phila. Tax Conf., 1996-97, planned giving coun. U. Va. Lt. USN, 1951-53. Bldg. in The Philippines named in recognition of work (with wife) in behalf of neglected and abandoned children in The Philippines. Fellow Am. Coll. Tax Counsel; mem. ABA (chmn. com. income of estates and trusts, sect. taxation 1981-83, spl. adviser 1983-85, chmn. QSST subcom. 1984—), Phila. Bar Assn. (tax sect. coun. 1976-81), Consular Corps Phila. (pres. 1989-91), Merion Cricket Club, Phila. Skating Club & Humane Soc., Univ. Club Washington, Sons of Confederate Vets. Republican. Presbyterian. Estate planning, Personal income taxation, Taxation, general. Home: 229 Pennswood Rd Bryn Mawr PA 19010-3615 Office: Pepper Hamilton & Scheetz 1235 Westlakes Dr Ste 400 Berwyn PA 19312-2416 also: 3000 N 2nd St Philadelphia PA 19133-3610

**HUFFMAN, DIANE RAUSCH,** lawyer; b. Napoleon, Ohio, Nov. 25, 1952; d. James D. and Emily (Baughman) Rausch; m. Rex Hartley, June 28, 1975; children: Benjamin, Anna. BS, Miami U., Oxford, Ohio, 1975; JD, U. Toledo, 1981. Bar: Ohio 1982, U.S. Dist. Ct. (no. and we. dists.) Ohio 1982. Tchr. Dixie High Sch., New Lebanon, Ohio, 1975-76; employment interviewer Jobst Inst., Toledo, 1976-78; staff atty. Spitler Vogtsberger & Huffman, Bowling Green, Ohio, 1982-87; ptnr. Spitler Vogtsberger & Huffman, Bowling Green, 1987—. Pres. bd. trustees La Libr., Wood County, Ohio, 1987-88; bd. dirs. United Way, Child Support Enforcement Agy.; mem. bus. adv. coun. to Bowling Green City Schs. Mem. ABA, Ohio Bar Assn. (com. on alternative dispute resolution), Ohio Land Title Assn., Wood County Bd. Realtors, Bowling Green C. of C. (Athena award 1992), Miami U. Alumni Assn. (bd. dirs., nat. pres. 1992-93). Democrat. Methodist. Avocations: sports, golf, family. Juvenile, Real property, Probate. Office: Spitler Vogtsberger & Huffman 131 E Court St Bowling Green OH 43402-2402

**HUFFMAN, JARED WILLIAM,** lawyer; b. Independence, Mo., Feb. 18, 1964; s. William Ward and Phyllis Jean Huffman; m. Susan E. Musgrove, May 13, 1995. BA in Polit. Sci. magna cum laude, U. Calif., Santa Barbara, 1986; JD cum laude, Boston Coll., 1990. Bar: Calif. 1990, U.S. Dist. Ct. (no. dist.) Calif. 1990. Assoc. McCatchen Doyle Brown & Enersen, San Francisco, 1990-92; ptnr. Boyd Huffman Williams & Urla, San Francisco, 1992-96, The Legal Solutions Group LLP, San Rafael, Calif., 1996—; commr. Marin County Adult Criminal Justice Commn., San Rafael, 1996—; bd. dirs. Marin Mcpl. Water Dist., Corte Madera, Calif. Contbg. editor Legal Practice Guide, 1995-96. Mem. Rotary Club San Rafael. Democrat. Avocations: volleyball, golf, basketball. Labor, General civil litigation, Civil rights. Office: The Legal Solutions Group LLP 1629 5th Ave San Rafael CA 94901-1828

**HUFFMAN, ROBERT ALLEN, JR.,** lawyer; b. Tucson, Dec. 30, 1950; s. Robert Allen and Ruth Jane (Hicks) H.; m. Marjorie Kavanagh Rooney, Dec. 30, 1976; children: Katharine Kavanagh, Elizabeth Rooney, Robert Allen III, Simeon Ross. BBA, U. Okla., 1973, JD, 1976. Bar: Okla. 1977, U.S. Dist. Ct. (no. dist.) Okla. 1977, U.S. Ct. Appeals (10th cir.) 1978, U.S. Supreme Ct. 1982. Assoc. Huffman, Arrington, Kihle, Gaberino & Dunn, Tulsa, 1977-81, ptnr. 1981-97, ptnr. Edwards & Huffmann LLP, 1997—. Mem. ABA, Tulsa County Bar Assn., Fed. Energy Bar Assn. Republican. Roman Catholic. Clubs: Southern Hills Country (Tulsa), Summit Club. General corporate, Public utilities, Real property. Home: 4136 S Wheeling Ave Tulsa OK 74105-4232 Office: Edwards & Huffman LLP South Yale Ste 1470 Two Warren Pl 6120 Tulsa OK 74136

**HUFFSTETLER, PALMER EUGENE,** lawyer; b. Shelby, N.C., Dec. 21, 1937; s. Daniel S. and Ethel (Turner) H.; m. Mary Ann Beam, Aug. 9, 1958; children: Palmer Eugene, Ben Beam, Brian Tad. BA, Wake Forest U., 1959, JD, 1961. Bar: N.C. 1961. Practiced in Kings Mountain, N.C., 1961-62, Raleigh, N.C., 1962-64; with State Farm Ins. Co., Orlando, Fla., 1962; gen. legal counsel Carolina Freight Corp., Cherryville, N.C., 1964-93, sec., 1969-90, sr. v.p., 1969-89, also dir., 1971-94, exec. v.p., 1985-93, pres., 1993-95; ret., 1995; pres., CEO Blue Chip Inc., 1997—. Author, composer: Senior Man on Carolina Line, Fifty Years Ago. Chmn. Cherryville Zoning Bd. Adjustment, 1967-70; mem. N.C. Gasoline and Oil Insp. Bd., 1974-76; class chmn. Wake Forest Coll. Fund, 1971-79, decade chmn., 1981-82; mem. governing body, chmn. adminstrv. com. So. Piedmont Health Systems Agy., 1975-77; mem. Cherryville Econ. Devel. Commn., 1982-87, Cherryville Econ. Devel. Com., 1995-97; pres. Cherryville Devel. Corp., 1986—; bd. dirs. C. Grier Beam Truck Mus., 1982—, pres. 1982-96; bd. dirs. Schiele Mus., Gastonia, N.C., 1985-88, Gaston Meml. Hosp., 1990-93, vice-chmn. bd.; mem. N.C. Gov.'s Hwy. Safety Commn., 1985-88; mem. v.p. Ctrl. and So. Rate Bur., 1984-89; trustee Brevard Coll., 1987-93. Mem. N.C. State Bar, N.C. Bar Assn. Methodist (mem. adminstrv. bd. 1965-69, 71-72, chmn. adminstrv. bd., trustee 1970-73, fin. com. 1994—, fin. com. 1994—). General corporate, Labor, Transportation. Home: 2141 Fairways Dr Cherryville NC 28021-2115

**HUFSTEDLER, SHIRLEY MOUNT (MRS. SETH M. HUFSTEDLER),** lawyer, former federal judge; b. Denver, Aug. 24, 1925; d. Earl Stanley and Eva (Von Behren) Mount; m. Seth Martin Hufstedler, Aug. 16, 1949; 1 son, Steven Mark. BBA, U. N.Mex., 1945, LLD (hon.), 1972; LLB, Stanford U., 1949; LLD (hon.), U. Wyo., 1970, Gonzaga U., 1970, Occidental Coll., 1971, Tufts U., 1974, U. So. Calif., 1976, Georgetown U., 1976, U. Pa., 1976, Columbia U., 1977, U. Mich., 1979, Yale U., 1981, Rutgers U., 1981, Claremont U. Ctr., 1981, Smith Coll., 1982, Syracuse U., 1983, Mt. Holyoke Coll., 1985; PHH (hon.), Hood Coll., 1981, Hebrew Union Coll., 1986, Tulane U., 1988. Bar: Calif. 1950. Mem. firm Beardsley, Hufstedler & Kemble, L.A., 1951-61; practiced in L.A., 1961; judge Superior Ct., County L.A., 1961-66; justice Ct. Appeals 2d dist., 1966-68; circuit judge U.S. Ct. Appeals 9th cir., 1968-79; sec. U.S. Dept. Edn., 1979-81; ptnr. Hufstedler & Kaus, L.A., 1981-95; sr. of counsel Morrison & Foerster LLP, L.A., 1995—; emeritus dir. Hewlett Packard Co., US West, Inc.; bd. dirs. Harman Internat. Industries. Mem. staff Stanford Law Rev, 1947-49; articles and book rev. editor, 1948-49. Trustee Calif. Inst. Tech., Occidental Coll., 1972-89, Aspen Inst., Colonial Williamsburg Found., 1976-93, Constl. Rights Found., 1978-80, Nat. Resources Def. Coun., 1983-85, Carnegie Endowment for International Peace, 1983-94; bd. dirs. John T. and Catherine MacArthur Found., 1983—; chair U.S. Commn. on Immigration Reform, 1996-97. Named Woman of Yr. Ladies Home Jour., 1976; recipient UCLA medal, 1981. Fellow Am. Acad. Arts and Scis.; mem. ABA (medal 1995), L.A. Bar Assn., Town Hall, Am. Law Inst. (coun. 1974-84), Am. Bar Found., Women Lawyers Assn. (pres. 1957-58), Am. Judicature Soc., Assn. of the Bar of City of N.Y., Coun. on Fgn. Rels., Order of Coif. Antitrust, Federal civil litigation, State civil litigation. Office: Morrison & Foerster LLP 555 W 5th St Ste 3500 Los Angeles CA 90013-1024

**HUG, PROCTER RALPH, JR.,** federal judge; b. Reno, Mar. 11, 1931; s. Procter Ralph and Margaret (Beverly) H.; m. Barbara Van Meter, Apr. 4, 1954; children: Cheryl Ann English, Procter James, Elyse Marie Pasha. BS, U. Nev., 1953; LLB, JD, Stanford U., 1958. Bar: Nev. 1958. With firm Springer, McKissick & Hug, 1958-63, Woodburn, Wedge, Blakey, Folsom & Hug, Reno, 1963-77; U.S. judge 9th Circuit Ct. Appeals, Reno, 1977—; U.S. chief judge 9th Circuit Ct. Appeals, 1996—; dep. atty. gen. State of Nev.; v.p. dir. Nev. Tel. & Tel. Co., 1958-77. Mem. bd. regents U. Nev., 1962-71, chmn., 1969-71; bd. visitors Stanford Law Sch.; mem. Nev. Humanities Commn., 1988-94; vol. civilian aid sect. U.S. Army, 1977. Lt. USNR, 1953-55. Recipient Outstanding Alumnus award U. Nev., 1967, Disting. Nevadan citation, 1982; named Alumnus of Yr. U. Nev., 1988. Mem. ABA (bd. govs. 1976-78), Am. Judicare Soc. (bd. dirs. 1975-77), Nat. Judicial Coll. (bd. dirs. 1977-78), Nat. Assn. Coll. and Univ. Attys. (past mem. exec. bd.), U. Nev. Alumni Assn. (past pres.), Stanford Law Soc. Nev. (pres.). Office: US Ct Appeals 9th Cir US Courthouse Fed Bldg 400 S Virginia St Ste 708 Reno NV 89501-2181

**HUGGARD, JOHN PARKER,** lawyer; b. Midland, Tex., Dec. 7, 1945; s. Peter John and Dorothy (Sampson) H. BA, U. N.C., 1971, JD, 1975; MA, Duke U., 1989. Bar: N.C. 1975, U.S. Dist. Ct. (ea. dist.) N.C. 1975, U.S. Ct. Appeals (4th cir.) 1975, U.S. Tax Ct. 1976, U.S. Ct. Claims 1976, U.S. Ct. Customs 1977, U.S. Ct. Mil. Appeals 1977, U.S. Dist. Ct. D.C. 1979, U.S. Supreme Ct. 1979, U.S. Ct. Internat. Trade 1981, U.S. Ct. Customs and Patent Appeals 1982; cert. fin. planner. Sr. ptnr. Hensley & Overby, Raleigh, N.C., 1975-88, Huggard, Obiol & Blake, PLLC, Raleigh, 1988—; alumni disting. prof. Law and Econs. N.C. State U., Raleigh, 1975—. Author: The Adminstration of Decedents' Estates in North Carolina, 1985, North Carolina Estate Settlement Guidebook, 1995, Living Trust/Living Hell-Why You Should Avoid Living Trusts, 1998; contbr. articles to profl. publs. With USMC, 1964-68, capt. USNR. Mem. ABA, Am. Bus. Law Assn., Assn. Trial Lawyers Am., N.C. Bar Assn., N.C. Acad. Trial Lawyers, N.C. Coll. Advocacy, Acad. Outstanding Tchrs., Wake County Bar Assn., Phi Beta Kappa. Democrat. Roman Catholic. Avocation: flying. Finance, Probate, Military. Home: 8621 Kings Arms Way Raleigh NC 27615-2029 Office: Huggard Obiol & Blake PLLC 124 Saint Marys St Raleigh NC 27605-1809

**HUGGLER, DAVID H.,** lawyer; b. Bryn Mawr, Pa., July 30, 1944; s. George W. and Salley L. (Horton) H.; m. Ann Blattner, May 10, 1969; children: Matthew, Catherine. BSBA, U. N.C., 1966; JD, Villanova U., 1969. Bar: Pa., N.J. From assoc. to ptnr. Pepper, Hamilton & Scheetz, Phila., 1970-84; ptnr. Huggler & Silverang, Phila., 1984-95, Miller, Dunham & Doering, Phila., 1995-96, Pepper Hamilton LLP, Berwyn, Pa., 1996—. Mem. Easttown Twp. Zoning Hearing Bd., Berwyn, 1986-88, 90—, Easttown Twp. Planning Commn., Berwyn, 1989. Real property, Contracts commercial, Finance. Office: Pepper Hamiltn LLP 1235 Westlakes Dr Ste 200 Berwyn PA 19312-2412

**HUGHES, BYRON WILLIAM,** lawyer, oil exploration company executive; b. Clarksdale, Miss., Nov. 8, 1945; s. Byron B. and Francis C. (Turner) H.; m. Sarah Eileen Goodwin, June 23, 1973 (div.); children: Jennife Eileen, Stephanie Ann. BA, U. Miss., 1968; JD, Jackson Sch. Law (now Miss. Coll. Law), 1971. Bar: Miss. 1971, U.S. Supreme Ct. 1975; cert. real estate appraiser. Atty., abstractor Miss. Hwy. Dept., 1971-76; atty., ind. landman Byron Hughes Oil Exploration Co., Jackson, Miss., 1976-92; prosecutor, child support enforcement atty. Miss. Dept. Human Svcs., 1992—; tchr. high sch.; real estate broker. Mem. ABA, Miss. Bar Assn., Hinds County Bar Assn., Bolivar County Bar Assn., Am. Judicature Soc., Nat. Assn. Real Estate Appraisers, Miss. Child Support Assn., Miss. Assn. Petroleum Landmen, Ala. Landmen Assn., Black Warrior Basin Petroleum Landmen Assn., Am. Assn. Petroleum Landmen (cert. profl. landman 1991), Ole Miss. Alumni Assn., Miss. Coll. Alumni Assn., Miss. Art Assn., Sigma Delta Kappa. Methodist. Oil, gas, and mineral, Real property, Family and matrimonial. Home: PO Box 1485 Jackson MS 39215-1485 Office: PO Box 1485 Jackson MS 39215-1485

**HUGHES, CARL DOUGLAS,** lawyer; b. Sapulpa, Okla., Aug. 29, 1946; s. Kenneth Gordon and Louise (Coffield) H.; m. Alice M. Hughes, May 12, 1978; children—Sarah Elizabeth, Kenneth James. B.B.A., U. Okla., 1968, J.D., 1971. Bar: Okla. 1971, U.S. Sup. Ct. 1974. Assoc. Stipe, Gossett, Stipe & Harper, Oklahoma City, 1971-76; ptnr. Hughes, White, Adams & Grant and predecessors, Oklahoma City, 1976—. Legal counsel Okla. Democratic Party, 1978-83; gen. counsel Spl. Olympics, 1976—, chmn., 1981, 84, 85, 86, 87; legal counsel Okla. Horseman's Assn., Okla. Alliance, 1990—. Served to capt. U.S. Army Res., 1968-73. Mem. Okla. Trial Lawyers Assn. (dir. 1971-78, chmn. judiciary com. 1977-78, chmn. criminal law com. 1981), Okla. Bar Assn., Oklahoma County Bar Assn. Episcopalian. Mem. editorial bd., torts editor Advocate mag., 1975-78. Personal injury, Criminal, Federal civil litigation. Office: 5801 Broadway Ext Ste 302 Oklahoma City OK 73118-7483

**HUGHES, (TERRY) CHRIS(TOPHER),** lawyer; b. Fitzgerald, Ga., Nov. 11, 1959; s. Paul Daniel and Virginia (Puckett) H.; m. Sara Jane Wilson, July 13, 1985. AB, U. Ga., 1981, JD, 1984. Bar: Ga. Ptnr. Ellis & Hughes, Fitzgerald, 1984-86; sole practice Fitzgerald, 1987-93; ptnr. Hughes & Hobby, P.C., Fitzgerald, 1993—. Clk. 1st Bapt. Ch., Fitzgerald, 1986—, trustee, 1992—, Sunday sch. dir., 1994—, vice chmn. deacons, 1995; active Fitzgerald-Ben Hill County Devel. Authority, 1994; pres. Burch-Hudson Funeral Home, Inc.; bd. dirs. Ben Hill Edn. Found. and Comtys. in Schs., Inc. Named one of Outstanding Young Man of Am., 1985. Mem. Ga. Trial Lawyers Assn., Cordele Cir. Bar Assn., Fitzgerald-Ben Hill C. of C. (chmn. 1994), Kiwanis (treas. 1985-88, v.p. 1989, pres. 1990). Republican. Avocations: Civil War history, walking. General practice, General civil litigation, Criminal. Office: 413 S Grant St PO Box 5149 Fitzgerald GA 31750-5149

**HUGHES, DEBORAH ANN,** lawyer; b. Wilkes-Barre, Pa., Jan. 8, 1954; d. Marvin M. and Sonia K. Hughes; m. John C. Kern. BA, Dickinson Coll., 1975, JD, 1979. Bar: Pa. 1979, U.S. Dist. Ct. (mid. dist.) Pa. 1979. Sole practice Harrisburg, Pa., 1979—. Contbr. articles to profl. jours. Mem. ABA (bankruptcy com.). Avocations: golf, gardening, interior design, antiques, travel. Bankruptcy.

**HUGHES, DEBORAH ENOCH,** circuit court clerk; b. Lynchburg, Va., Mar. 24, 1953; d. George Alexander Enoch and Inez (Hailey) Enoch Green; m. Frank Plunkett Hughes, Apr. 24, 1971; children: Frank P. II, Neal Thomas. Grad. in Data Processing, Ctrl. Va. C.C., 1974. Cert. circuit ct. clk., Va. Dep. real estate office Divsn. Commr. of Revenue, Rustburg, Va., 1971-75; data processing chief entry clk. Campbell County Sch. Bd., Rustburg, Va., 1975-79; dep. clk. Circuit Ct. Clk.'s Office, Campbell County, 1979-91, clk., 1992—. Mem. Va. Circuit Ct. Clk.'s Assn., Va. Assn. Elected Constnl. Officers (sec.). Office: Campbell County Circuit Ct Clks Office PO Box 7 Rustburg VA 24588-0007

**HUGHES, JAMES DONALD,** lawyer; b. Houston, June 5, 1951; s. D. E. and Ruby Christine (Wagstaff) H. BS, Stanford U., 1973; JD, U. Tex., 1976; LLM in Taxation, NYU, 1978. Bar: Tex. 1976, Ala. 1979, U.S. Dist. Ct. (so. dist.) Ala., 1979, U.S. Tax Ct. 1987. Assoc. O.N. Baker Inc., Houston, 1977; ptnr. Armbrecht, Jackson, Demovy, Crowe, Holmes & Reeves, Mobile, Ala., 1978-99, Bradley, Arant, Rose & White, LLP, Birmingham, Ala., 1999—.

Mem. ABA (taxation and real property probate and trust sects.), Small Bus. Coun. Am. (bd. legal advisers). Avocations: photography, stained glass, sports. Pension, profit-sharing, and employee benefits, Estate planning, Taxation, general. Office: Bradley Arant Rose & White LLP 2001 Park Pl Ste 1400 Birmingham AL 35203-2736

**HUGHES, KEVIN JOHN,** lawyer; b. St. Cloud, Minn., July 27, 1936; s. Fred James and Valeria Mary (Spaniol) H.; m. Joanne Margaret Robertson, July 27, 1936; children: Anne, Thomas, Jennifer, James, Emily. BA in Philosophy and Polit. Sci., St. John's U., Collegeville, Minn., 1958; JD, U. Minn., 1962. Bar: Minn. 1962, U.S. Dist. Ct. Minn. 1963, U.S. Ct. Appeals (8th cir.) 1973, U.S. Supreme Ct. 1973. Law clerk Minn. Supreme Ct., 1962-63; assoc. Fred J. Hughes Atty., St. Cloud, 1963; ptnr. Hughes Thoreen & Sullivan, Hughes Thoreen Mathews & Knapp, St. Cloud, 1964-94, Hughes Mathews & Didier PA, St. Cloud, 1994—. Bd. dirs. Ctrl. Minn. Cmty. Found., United Way, YMCA. 1st lt. U.S. Army, 1959. Mem. Minn. State Bar, Am. Health Lawyers Assn., St. Cloud C. of C. General civil litigation, Contracts commercial, Labor. Home: 295 Waite Ave S Saint Cloud MN 56301-7335 Office: Hughes Mathews & Didier PO Box 548 Saint Cloud MN 56302-0548

**HUGHES, LYNN NETTLETON,** federal judge; b. Houston, Sept. 9, 1941; m. Olive Allen. BA, U. Ala., 1963; JD, U. Tex., 1968; LLM, U. Va., 1992. Bar: Tex., 1966. Pvt. practice, Houston, 1966-79; judge Dist. Ct. Tex., Houston, 1979-85; U.S. dist. judge So. Dist. Tex., Houston, 1985—; adj. prof. South Tex. Coll. Law, 1973—, U. Tex., 1990-91; Tex. del. Nat. Conf. State Trial Judges, 1983-85; cons. Tex. Jud. Budget Bd., 1984; lectr. Tex. Coll. Judiciary, 1983; mem. task force on revision rules of civil procedure Supreme Ct. Tex., 1993-94; cons. on constn. Republic of Moldova, 1993, European Community, 1989, Ukraine, 1995, Romania, 1996, Albania, 1997. Mem. adv. bd. Houston Jour. Internat. Law, 1981—, chmn., 1989-99; mem. adv. dirs. Internat. Law Inst., U. Houston, 1995—. Trustee Rift Valley Rsch. Mission, 1978—; mem. St. Martin's Episcopal Ch.; dir. Houston World Affairs Coun., 1997—, co-chair 1999-00. Fellow Tex. Bar Found.; mem. ABA, Fed. Bar Assn. (bd. dirs. Houston chpt. 1986-89), Am. Law Inst., Maritime Law Assn., Houston Bar Assn., Tex. Bar Assn. (nominations com. jud. sect. 1983, court cost, delay and efficiency com. 1981-90, vice chmn. 1984-86, selection, compensation and tenure state judges com. 1981-85, vice chmn. 1982-83, liaison with law schs. com. 1987-92, plain lang. com. 1989-96), Am. Judicature Soc., Am. Soc. Legal History, Am. Anthrop Assn., Houston Philos. Soc., Am. Inns of Ct. XV (pres. 1986-92), Phi Delta Phi. Office: US Court House 11122 515 Rusk St Houston TX 77002-2600

**HUGHES, MARCIA MARIE,** lawyer, mediator, trainer; b. Montrose, Colo., Oct. 12, 1949; d. John Atkinson and Catherine Marie (Buskirk) H.; m. James Terrell, Dec. 26, 1990; 1 child, Julia. BA, U. Colo., 1972; JD with honors, George Washington U., 1976; MA in Psychology, U. Colo. Bar: Colo. 1976, U.S. Dist. Ct. Colo. 1976, U.S. Ct. Appeals (10th cir.) 1976. Adminstrv. aide Bur. Accounts Treasury Dept., Washington, 1972-73; legis. aide to Congresswoman Patricia Schroeder Washington, 1973-74; legal intern Consumer Product Info. Ctr., Washington, 1974-75, Media Access Project, Washington, 1975-76; law clk. to Hon. William E. Doyle U.S. Ct. Appeals (10th cir.), Denver, 1976-77; asst. atty. gen. Colo. Atty. Gen.'s Office, Denver, 1977-79; spl. asst. to dir. Colo. Dept. Health, Denver, 1979-81; assoc. Rothgerber, Appel, Powers & Johnson, Denver, 1982-85; ptnr. Cockrel, Quinn & Creighton, Denver, 1985-87; pres. Hughes, Duncan & Dingess, Denver, 1987-90, Marcia M. Hughes, P.C., Denver, 1990-99, Collaborative Growth, L.L.C., 1993—; exec. dir. Salt Creek Sch., 1998—; exec. dir. Salt Creek Sch. Youth Edn. Corp., 1999—; pub. speaker on conflict resolution, mediation, environ. issues and child abuse awareness and prevention. Bd. dirs. Jefferson County chpt. ARC, 1999—, Influence Denver X, Capitol Hill United Neighborhoods, 1977-86; v.p. Nat. Assn. Neighborhoods, 1980-81; bd. dirs. Ecumenical Housing Corp., 1982-85; participant Leadership Denver, 1984-85; active Big Sisters Colo., Denver, 1987-93; vice chmn. Kempe Children's Found., bd. dirs., 1991-95, chair pub. affairs Com.; bd. dirs. Colo. Found. Children and Families, 1993-96, pres., 1995-96; apptd. mem. family issues task force Colo. Legislature, Influence X Denver. Named one of Outstanding Young Women in Colo., 1980, Big Sister of Yr., 1991. Mem. Colo. Profl. Soc. on Abuse of Children (bd. dirs.), Colo. Bar Assn. (chmn. environ. sect., officer 1982-86), Colo. Hazardous Waste Com. (chmn. 1982-85). Avocations: writing, hiking, gardening, reading. Environmental, Family and matrimonial, Alternative dispute resolution. Home: PO Box 10758 Golden CO 80401-0610

**HUGHES, SARAH JANE,** law educator, writer, consultant; b. Chgo., June 26, 1949; m. A. James Barnes, June 19, 1976; children: Morey Elizabeth, Laura L., Catherine Farrell. AB cum laude, Mt. Holyoke Coll., 1971; JD, U. Wash., 1974. Bar: Wash. 1974, D.C. 1975. With consumer protection divsn. FTC, Seattle and Washington, 1974-88; mem. faculty Cath. U. Am. Columbus Sch. Law, Washington, 1991, Ind. U. Sch. Law, Bloomington, 1988-90, 91—; reporter ABA Bus. Sect. Cyberspace Law Subcom., 1998—; mem. faculty at nat. confs. Am. Bankers Assn., 1989-93; expert advisor Office Tech. Assessment, U.S. Congress, 1994-95; cons. law firms on payments sys. problems and malpractice; cons. econ. cos. on payment sys. and privacy; participant nat. and internat. confs. on payments and ecommerce. Mem. editl. bd. Money Laundering Alert, 1992-94; contbr. articles to legal jours. Vol., bd. dirs. The Yard, modern dance, Chilmark, Mass., 1993—. Mem. ABA, D.C. Bar, Wash. State Bar, Edgartown Yacht Club, Vineyard Haven Yacht Club, Skyline Club (Ind.). Republican. Office: Ind U Sch Law 3d St and Indiana Ave Bloomington IN 47405

**HUGHES, STEVEN JAY,** lawyer; b. Fayetteville, Ark., Nov. 7, 1948; s. Howard and Jimmie Louise (Williams) H.; m. Leora Donna Halfhill, July 22, 1972; children: Christopher Blake, Clayton Brent. BS in Edn., U. Ark., Fayetteville, 1970; JD, U. Ark., Little Rock, 1978; LLM, DePaul U., 1993. Bar: Ark. 1978, U.S. Dist. Ct. (ea. dist.) Ark. 1978, U.S. Ct. Appeals (8th cir.) 1978, U.S. Supreme Ct. 1981, Mo. 1993. Sole practice Jacksonville, Ark., 1978-92; owner Hughes Legal Rsch., 1994-96; assoc. Mickel Law Firm, PA, Little Rock, 1998—; bd. dirs. Tiara Condominium Property Owners Assn., chmn., 1994-96. Alderman Jacksonville City Coun., 1979-81; commr. Jacksonville Planning Commn., 1982-85; mem. U. Ark. Razorback Letterman's Club, Little Rock, 1985, Ark. Sports Hall of Fame, 1985; bd. dirs. Jacksonville Boys Club, 1979-92, pres., 1982-83. Mem. Assn. Trial Lawyers Am., Ark. Bar Assn., Delta Theta Phi (life, dist. chancellor 1983-93). Baptist. Lodge: Kiwanis (pres. Jacksonville club 1983-84, Kiwanian of Yr. award 1979-80, Disting. Club Pres. award 1984). Avocation: sports. Real property, General practice, Bankruptcy. Home: 7502 W Markham St Little Rock AR 72205-2608 Office: 1501 N University Ave Ste 966 Little Rock AR 72207-5238

**HUGHES, STEVEN LEE,** lawyer; b. Big Spring, Tex., May 31, 1953; s. Oscar Gordon and Mary Alice Hughes; m. Cynthia A. Oldham, June 12, 1982. BM with highest honors, Tex. Tech. U., 1975, MM, 1976; JD with honors, U. Tex., 1985. Bar: Tex. 1985, U.S. Ct. Appeals (5th cir.) 1987, U.S. Dist. Ct. (we. dist.) Tex. 1987, U.S. Supreme Ct. 1993. Briefing atty. Dallas Ct. Appeals, 1985-86; assoc. Mounce Green Myers Safi & Galatzan, El Paso, Tex., 1986-91, shareholder, 1992—. Appellate, Education and schools, Labor. Office: Mounce Green Myers Safi & Galatzan 100 N Stanton St Ste 1700 El Paso TX 79901-1448

**HUGHES, TERESA LEE,** lawyer, educator; b. Little Rock, Mar. 6, 1953; d. William Lindsay and Lillian Phyllis Cloud; m. Thomas Morgan Hughes III, Aug. 10, 1974; 1 child, Gwyneth Leigh. BA in Humanities, Hendrix Coll., 1975; JD, U. Ark., Little Rock, 1978. Bar: Ark. 1978, U.S. Dist. Ct. Ark. 1978. Ptnr. Hughes & Hughes PA, Searcy, Ark., 1978—; former adj. prof. Ark. State U., Beebe. Pres. White County Dem. Women, 1993; chmn. com. White County Dems., 1994—, White County Election Com., 1994—; trustee White County Libr. Sys., 1987-97, chmn. bd. trustee, 1995-97; sec. Gov.'s Commn. Librs., 1997. Mem. Ark. Bar Assn., Ctrl. Ark. Debtor-Creditor Bar Assn., Bus. & Profl. Women Beebe (sec. 1998-99, pres. 1995, Woman of the Yr. 1989), White County Bar Assn. (pres. 1993), Ark. Assn. Women Lawyers. Bankruptcy, Family and matrimonial, Pension, profit-sharing, and employee benefits. Office: Hughes & Hughes 407 W Arch Ave Searcy AR 72143-5202

**HUGHES, VESTER THOMAS, JR.,** lawyer; b. San Angelo, Tex., May 24, 1928; s. Vester Thomas and Mary Ellen (Tisdale) H. Student, Baylor U., 1945-46; B.A. with distinction, Rice U., 1949; LLB cum laude, Harvard U., 1952. Bar: Tex. 1955. Law clk. U.S. Supreme Ct., 1952; assoc. Robertson, Jackson, Payne, Lancaster & Walker, Dallas, 1955-58; ptnr. Jackson, Walker, Winstead, Cantwell & Miller, Dallas, 1958-76, Hughes, Luce, Hennessy, Smith & Castle, Dallas, 1976—, Hughes & Hill, Dallas, 1979-85, Hughes & Luce, Dallas, 1985—; bd. dirs. Exell Cattle Co., Amarillo, Tex., LX Cattle Co., Amarillo, Murphy Oil Corp., El Dorado, Ark., Austin Industries, Dallas ; adv. dir. First Nat. Bank Mertzon; tax counsel Communities Found. of Tex., Inc.; mem. adv. com. Tex. Supreme Ct., 1985-93. Contbr. articles on fed. taxation to profl. jours. Bd. dirs. Juvenile Diabetes Found. Inc., Dallas, 1982—; trustee Dallas Bapt. Coll., 1967-77; v.p., trustee, exec. com. Tex. Scottish Rite Hosp. for Children, 1967—; bd. overseers vis. com. Harvard Law Sch., 1969-75. 1st lt. JAGC U.S. Army, 1952-55. Mem. ABA (coun. sect. taxation 1969-73), Tex. Bar Assn., Dallas Bar Assn., Am. Law Inst. (coun. 1958—), Am. Coll. Tax Counsel, Southwestern Legal Found., Am. Coll. of Trust and Estate Counsel, Met. Club (Washington), Harvard Club (N.Y.C.), Masons, Order Ea. Star, Phi Beta Kappa, Sigma Xi. Democrat. Baptist. Avocations: traveling, community and church activities, reading. Corporate taxation, Estate taxation, Personal income taxation. Office: Hughes & Luce 1717 Main St Ste 2800 Dallas TX 75201-4685

**HUGHEY, RICHARD KOHLMAN,** author, lawyer; b. Chgo., July 6, 1934. BA cum laude, Santa Clara U., 1958, JD cum laude, 1963. Bar: Calif. 1964, U.S. Ct. Appeals (9th cir.) 1964, U.S. Supreme Ct. 1972. Atty. Pacific Gas & Elec. Co., San Francisco, 1963-69, Berry, Davis & McInerny, Oakland, Calif., 1969-71; ptnr. Caputo, Liccardo, Rossi & Kohlman, San Jose, 1971-75; lectr. law, dir. CLE Santa Clara (Calif.) U., 1975-80; mng. editor Bancroft-Whitney Co., San Francisco, 1980-91, Lawyers Coop. Pub. Co., Rochester, N.Y., 1992-94; history and lit. biography writer, 1995—; columnist Mountain Democrat, Placerville, Calif., 1997—. Bd. editors Calif. State Bar Jour., 1972-75; editor-in-chief Santa Clara Law Rev., 1961-63; author: Jeffers Country Revisited: Beauty Without Price, 1996, Computer Technology in Civil Litigation, 1990, Trial Lawyers Manual, 1978, Abalone Lite, 1997; co-author: Petroglyphs: Poetry and Fiction, 1994, Hey Lew: Homage to Lew Welch, 1997; editor: Am Jur Trials, 1980-90, Proof of Facts, 1982-90. Mem. citizen's adv. commn. U.S. Postal Svc., San Francisco, 1989-92; mem. adv. bd. Commn. on Future of the Cts., Jud. Coun. of Calif., 1992; dir. Cmty. Legal Svcs., San Jose, 1973-78. Recipient Merit award Calif. Psychol. Assn., 1985, Santa Clara County Bar Assn., 1973-75. Mem. ABA, Am. Acad. Forensic Scis., Assn. Trial Lawyers Am., Practicing Law Inst., Def. Rsch. Inst., Internat. Platform Assn., Writers and Books Club, Acad. Am. Poets, Modern Poetry Assn., San Jose Ctr. for Poetry and Lit. Avocations: creative writing, photography.

**HULIN, FRANCES C.,** prosecutor. AB, Northwestern U., 1957; JD, U. Ill., Urbana, 1971. Bar: Ill. 1973. Asst. states atty. Champaign County, IL, 1973-76, Macon County, Ill., 1977-78; prosecutor U.S. Attys. Office, Ctrl. Dist. Ill., 1978-93; U.S. atty. Dept. Justice, Springfield, Ill., 1993—. Office: US Attys Office 600 E Monroe St Ste 312 Springfield IL 62701-1626

**HULL, E. PATRICK,** lawyer; b. Jefferson City, Tenn., Mar. 17, 1949; s. Erwin and Elizabeth Sue (Shipley) H.; m. Sarah Jane Quarles H., Dec. 14, 1974; children: Daniel Patrick, Christopher Douglas, Michael Erwin. BSIE, U. Tenn., 1971, JD, 1975. Bar: Tenn. 1976, U.S. Dist. Ct. (ea. dist.) Tenn. 1977, U.S. Ct. Appeals (6th cir.) 1988, U.S. Supreme Ct. 1995. Assoc. Wilson, Worley, Gamble & Ward, Kingsport, Tenn., 1976-79, ptnr., 1980-82; ptnr. Hull & Hansen, Kingsport, 1982-84; min. Columbia, S.C., 1984-86; pvt. practice Kingsport, 1986—; adj. faculty East Tenn. State U., Johnson City, 1993—. Editor: Spl. Edn. Newsletter, 1988-92; contbr. articles to profl. jours. Com. mem. ARC, Kingsport, 1994-95; bd. dirs., sec. Youth Athletic Adv. Bd., Kingsport, 1994-95; bd. assocs. Emmanuel Sch. Religion, 1996—. Mem. Tenn. Bar Assn., Tenn. Coun. Sch. Bd. Attys. (pres. 1990-92), Nat. Coun. Sch. Bd. Attys. Avocations: coaching youth athletics, fly fishing, writing. Education and schools, Insurance, General civil litigation. Home: 2109 Heatherly Rd Kingsport TN 37660-3446 Office: 229 E New St Kingsport TN 37660-4326

**HULL, FRANK MAYS,** federal judge; b. Augusta, Ga., Dec. 9, 1948; d. James M. Hull Jr. and Frank (Mays) Pride; m. Antonin Aeck, Apr. 16, 1977; children: Richard Hull Aeck, Molly Hull Aeck. AB, Randolph-Macon Women's Coll., 1970; JD cum laude, Emory U., 1973. Bar: Ga. 1973, U.S. Ct. Appeals (5th cir.) 1973, U.S. Dist. Ct. (no. dist.) Ga. 1974, U.S. Ct. Appeals (11th cir.) 1982. Law clk. to Hon. Elbert P. Tuttle U.S. Ct. Appeals (5th cir.), Atlanta, 1973-74; assoc. Powell, Goldstein, Frazer & Murphy, Atlanta, 1974-80, ptnr., 1980-84; judge State Ct. Fulton County, Atlanta, 1984-90, Superior Ct. Fulton County, Atlanta, 1990-94, U.S. Dist. Ct. (no. dist.) Ga., 1994-97, U.S. Ct. Appeals (11th cir.), 1997—; mem. commn. on family violence State of Ga., 1992-94, commn. on gender bias in jud. sys., 1988-90. Bd. dirs. Met. Atlanta Mediation Ctr., Inc., 1976-79, Atlanta Vol. Lawyers Assn., 1988-91; mem. Leadership Atlanta, 1986—, program co-chair criminal justice com., 1988-89; Sunday sch. tchr. Cathedral St. Philip, Atlanta, 1983-88, childrens com., 1981-82, outreach com., 1989-91. Fellow AAUW, 1973—. Mem. ABA (fin. sec. long range planning com. tort and ins. practice sect. 1979-82, chmn. contract documents divsn., forum com. on constrn. industry 1983-85, editl. staff jour. 1981-85, vice chmn. fidelity and surety law com. 1978-85), Ga. Bar Assn., Am. Judicature Soc. (bd. dirs. 1990-96), Atlanta Bar Assn., Ga. Assn. Women Lawyers, Nat. Assn. Women Judges, Order of Coif. Office: US Ct of Appeals 56 Forsyth St NW Atlanta GA 30303-2289

**HULL, J(AMES) RICHARD,** retired lawyer, business executive; b. Keokuk, Iowa, Dec. 5, 1933; s. James Robert and Alberta Margaret (Bouseman) H.; m. Patricia M. Kiesner, June 14, 1958; children—Elizabeth Ann Hull Whims, James Robert, David Glen. B.A., Ill. Wesleyan U., 1955; J.D., Northwestern U., 1958. Bar: Ill. 1958, Fla. 1978. V.p., sec., gen. counsel Honeggers & Co., Inc., Fairbury, Ill., 1959-65, also bd. dirs.; staff atty. Am. Hosp. Supply Corp., Evanston, Ill., 1965-68, chief atty., asst. sec., 1968-70, corp. sec., 1970-71, corp. sec., corp. gen. counsel, 1971-79, gen. counsel, 1979-84; sr. v.p., sec., gen. counsel Household Internat. Inc., Northbrook, Ill., 1984-93, sr. v.p., of counsel, 1993-94; ret.; ret.; mem. planning com. Northwestern U. Corp. Counsel Inst., 1992-93, chmn. Northwestern Corp. Counsel Ctr., 1993. Bd. trustees, bd. visitors Ill. Wesleyan U.; pres. Prestancia Cmty. Assn. Fellow Am. Bar Found., Am. Law Inst.; mem. ABA, Ill. Bar Assn., Fla. Bar Assn., Chgo. Bar Assn. (chmn. corp. law dept.), North Shore Gen. Counsels, Northwestern U. Sch. Law Alumni Assn. (pres.), Sigma Chi, Legal Club (Chgo.), Law Club (Chgo.), Skokie Country Club (Glencoe, Ill.), Gator Creek Golf Club (Sarasota, Fla.), T.P.C. Club (Prestancia, Fla.), Prestancia Cmty. Assn. (pres. 1995-96), Champion Hills Golf Club (Hendersonville, N.C.). General corporate, Antitrust, Contracts commercial. Home: 21 La Coste Dr Hendersonville NC 28739 Summer Home: 4634 Mirada Way Unit 24 Sarasota FL 34238-4547 *Success will come to those who plan and rehearse. Set your goals, define your strategies and implement your tactics. Your goals must always determine and never justify the means toward achievement.*

**HULL, JOHN DANIEL, IV,** lawyer; b. Washington, Feb. 27, 1953; s. John Daniel III and Arlene (Reemer) H. BA cum laude, Duke U., 1975; JD, U. Cin., 1978. Bar: D.C. 1978, U.S. Dist. Ct. D.C. 1983, U.S. Ct. Appeals (D.C. cir.) 1984, Md. 1989, Pa. 1989, U.S. Dist. Ct. (we. dist.) Pa. 1989, U.S. Ct. Appeals (3d cir.) 1989, U.S. Supreme Ct. 1989. Legis. asst. 93d & 96th U.S. Congresses, Washington, 1974, 78-81; assoc. Rose, Schmidt & Dixon, Washington, 1981-87, ptnr., 1988-92; with Hull McGuire PC, Pitts., Washington, and San Diego, 1992—. Mem. U. Cin. Law Rev., 1976-77, editor student articles, 1977-78. Mem. ABA (sect. natural resources, energy and environ. law and litigation, intellectual property), Bar Assn. D.C., Md. Bar Assn., Pa. Bar Assn., Calif. Bar Assn., Duke Club, Tara Club. Federal civil litigation, Environmental, Legislative. Office: Hull McGuire PC 32d Fl USX Tower 600 Grant St Pittsburgh PA 15219-2702 also: Hull McGuire PC 1155 Connecticut Ave NW Ste 300 Washington DC 20036-4327 also: Hull McGuire PC 15644 Via Calanova San Diego CA 92128-4462

**HULL, PHILIP GLASGOW,** lawyer; b. St. Albans, Vt., Feb. 17, 1925; s. Charles Herman and Gladys Gertrude (Glasgow) H.; AB, Middlebury Coll., 1949; LLB (Ellis fellow, Kent scholar, Stone scholar), Columbia U., 1952; m. Gretchen Elizabeth Gaebelein, Oct. 24, 1952; children: Jeffrey R., Sanford D., Meredyth Hull Smith. Bar: N.Y. 1952, Fla. 1977. Staff mem. sub-com. on adminstrn. internal revenue laws, com. on ways and means U.S. Ho. of Reps., Washington, 1951; assoc. Winthrop, Stimson, Putnam & Roberts, N.Y.C., 1952-63, ptnr., 1964-97, sr. counsel, 1998—. Mem. Sch. Revenue Com., Cold Spring Harbor, N.Y., 1963-65; bd. dirs. Eagle Dock Found., Cold Spring Harbor, 1971-74, People's Symphony Concerts, N.Y.C., 1977—. L.I. Philharm, 1979-81; trustee Latin Am. Mission, Miami, Fl., 1969-79; elder Ctrl. Presbyn. Ch., Huntington, N.Y., 1958-78; mem. nat. missions bd. United Presbyn. Ch. U.S.A., 1967-73; trustee Madison Ave. Presbyn. Ch., N.Y.C., 1989-94, pres., 1993-94; mem. Lloyd Harbor Conservation Adv. Coun., 1973-77. With U.S. Army, 1943-46. Mem. N.Y. State Bar Assn., Fla. Bar Assn., Am. Coll. Trust and Estate Counsel, Christian Legal Soc. (dir. 1984-97), Fellowship Christians in Univs. and Schs. (trustee 1983-90), Univ. Club N.Y.C. (bd. dirs. 1986-90), Cold Spring Harbor Beach, Blue Key, Phi Beta Kappa. Estate planning, Probate, Estate taxation. Office: Winthrop Stimson Putnam & Roberts One Battery Park Pla New York NY 10004-1490

**HULL, ROBERT JOE,** lawyer; b. Ft. Monmouth, N.J., Dec. 16, 1944; s. Thurman Beuford and Helen Louise (Bracey) H.; m. Susan Diane Hull, Mar. 12, 1966; 1 child, Robert Steven. BA, U. Tex., 1966, JD, 1969. Bar: Tex. 1969, Calif. 1970, U.S. Dist. Ct. (ctrl. dist.) Calif. 1970, U.S. Ct. Appeals (9th cir.) 1970, U.S. Tax. Ct. 1971, U.S. Supreme Ct. 1992. Assoc. Sheppard, Mullin, Richter & Hampton, L.A., 1969-76, ptnr., 1976-98; ptnr. Bracewell & Patterson LLP, Houston, 1998—. Co-author: Representing Start-Up Companies, 1992, (annual) ABA Sales & Use Tax Handbook, ABA Property Tax Deskbook; mem. editorial bd., contbr. Jour. Multistate Taxation, 1991—. Mem. Tex. Bar Found., Brae Burn Country Club, Annandale Golf Club, PGA West Golf Club. Avocation: golf. Taxation, general, State and local taxation. Home: 2607 Sutton Ct Houston TX 77027-5246 Office: Bracewell & Patterson LLP S Twr Penzoil Pl 711 Louisiana St Ste 2900 Houston TX 77002-2781

**HULL, THOMAS GRAY,** federal judge; b. 1926; m. Joan Brandon; children: Leslie, Brandon, Amy. Student, Tusculum Coll.; JD, U. Tenn., 1951. Atty. Easterly and Hull, Greeneville, Tenn., 1951-63; mem. Tenn. Ho. of Reps., 1955-65; atty., prin. Thomas G. Hull, 1951-72; chief clk. Tenn. Ho. of Reps., 1969-70; judge 20th Jud. Cir., Greeneville, Morristown and Rogersville, Tenn., 1972-79; legal counsel to Tenn. Gov. Lamar Alexander, 1979-81; judge U.S. Dist. Ct. (ea. dist.) Tenn., 1983—. Served as cpl. U.S. Army, 1944-46. Mem. Tenn. Bar Assn. (chmn. East dist. com. 1969), Greeneville Bar Assn. (pres. 1969-71), Tenn. Jud. Conf. (del. 1972-79, vice chmn. 1974-75, com. to draft uniform charges for trial judges). Republican. Office: Office of US Dist Judge 211 US Courthouse 101 W Summer St Greeneville TN 37743-4944

**HULSTRAND, GEORGE EUGENE,** lawyer; b. Cannon Falls, Minn., Aug. 3, 1918; s. John George and Alice Elizabeth (Holm) H.; m. Mabel Elizabeth Ericson, Sept. 7, 1946; children: George E. Jr., Brian Douglas, Darlene Lucette, Jeanne Louise. BA, Gustavus Adolphus Coll., 1943; JD, Yale U., 1946. Bar: Minn. 1947, U.S. Dist. Ct. Minn. 1951, U.S. Supreme Ct. 1977, U.S. Ct. Claims 1990. Assoc. Roy A. Hendrickson, Willmar, Minn., 1947-53; ptnr. Hulstrand, Anderson, Larson, Hanson & Saunders, Willmar, 1953-97; pvt. practice Willmar, 1997—; asst. county atty. Kandiyohi County, Willmar, 1947-50. Contbr. articles to mags. Mem. Willmar City Coun., 1953-56; chmn. Willmar Planning Commn., 1956-67, 74-80, Kandiyohi County Dem.-Farmer-Labor Party, Willmar, 1957-72; bd. dirs. Willmar Cmty. Coll. Found., 1965-94. Mem. ABA, Minn. Bar Assn. (bd. govs. 1977-83, cert. sr. counselor 1997), 12th Dist. Bar Assn., Am. Judicature Soc., Willmar Jaycees (Disting. Service award 1952, Outstanding Citizen award 1979). Lutheran. Lodges: Lions, Elks. Avocations: music, writing, golf, travel. General practice, Probate, Real property. Home: 325 N 7th St Willmar MN 56201 Office: PO Box 1860 Wilmar Bldg 201 4th St SW Willmar MN 56201-1860

**HULT, STEPHANIE SMITH,** lawyer, education consultant; b. Berkeley, Calif., Jan. 31, 1950; d. Daniel Malloy and Caroline Aladeen Smith; m. James Hult, Aug. 9, 1975; 1 child: Caroline. BA, U. Colo., 1973; JD, U. Denver, 1988. Bar: Colo. 1989. Mem. Murray, Thompson & Hult, Boulder, 1989-91, Hult, Garlin, Driscoll & Murray LLC, Boulder, 1991—; co-chmn. Boulder Bar Assn. Young Lawyers, 1990-92. Mem. sch. bd. Boulder Valley Schs., 1993-97, pres. 1995-97. Mem. Colo. Bar Assn., Colo. Trial Lawyers Assn., Boulder County Bar Assn. Republican. Roman Catholic. Avocations: skiing, gardening, travel. Personal injury. Home: 405 Oneida St Boulder CO 80303-4113 Office: Hult Garlin Driscoll & Murray LLC 2338 Broadway St Boulder CO 80304-4107

**HULTQUIST, STEVEN JOHN,** lawyer; b. Sioux City, Iowa, Jan. 29, 1949; s. Robert Edward and Betty (Van Dyck) H.; m. Judith Ann Raymond, July 10, 1972 (div. May 1981); m. Donna Marie DeMichele, Nov. 18, 1981 (div. Feb. 1995); 1 child, Liana Rose. BSChemE, Wash. U., 1970, MSChemE, 1972; JD, Fordham U., 1979. Bar: U.S. Patent and Trademark Office 1976, N.Y. 1980, Calif. 1981, U.S. Dist. Ct. (cen. dist.) Calif. 1982, U.S. Ct. Appeals (9th cir.) 1982, Conn. 1984, U.S. Ct. Appeals (fed. cir.) 1985, N.C. 1987. Lab. researcher Carboline Co., St. Louis, 1969-72; patent engr. Union Carbide Co., Tonawanda, N.Y., 1972-74; patent trainee Union Carbide Co., N.Y.C., 1974-76, patent agt., 1976-80, patent atty., 1980-81; patent atty. Tosco Corp., L.A., 1981-82; patent counsel Am. Cyanamid Corp., Stamford, Conn., 1982-85; pvt. practice Weston, Conn., 1985-86; assoc. Olive & Olive P.A., Durham, N.C., 1986-87; ptnr. Olive & Olive P.A., Durham, 1988-89; of counsel Harlow, Derr & Stark, Research Triangle Park, N.C., 1990; ptnr. Harlow, Stark, Hultquist, Evans & London, Research Triangle Park, 1990-92; prin. Intellectual Property/Tech. Law, Research Triangle Park, 1992; adj. prof. engring. N.C. State U., 1994-97; chmn. Incutech Com., 1987, Tech. Exch. Com., 1989; pres. Tri-Letix Corp., 1995-97; v.p. CaroTech LLC, 1995-96, pres., 1996-99; bd. dirs. Coun. Entrepreneurial Devel. Author: North Carolina General Practice Deskbook, 1995—; editor Tech. Exch. Newsletter; patentee in semiconductor mfg., material scis. fields; contbr. articles to profl. jours. Fundraiser YMCA of Wake County, Raleigh N.C., 1988. Mem. ABA (Intellectual Property Law Chpt. Deskbook award 1998), N.C. Bar Assn. (intellectual property sect., counsel mem. 1992-95), Copyright Law Assn., Durham C. of C., Coun. for Entrepreneurial Devel., N.C. Acad. Trial Lawyers, Licensing Exec. Soc., Raleigh Athletic Club, Sigma Xi. Republican. Presbyterian. Avocations: civic affairs, bus. devel. and networking, pro bono law, psychology of learning. Patent, Trademark and copyright, Contracts commercial. Home: 6728 Queen Annes Dr Raleigh NC 27613-3326 Office: Intellectual Property/Tech Law 6320 Quadrangle Dr Ste 110 Chapel Hill NC 27514-7890

**HUMICK, THOMAS CHARLES CAMPBELL,** lawyer; b. N.Y.C., Aug. 7, 1947; s. Anthony and Elizabeth Campbell (Meredith) H.; m. Nancy June Young, June 7, 1969; 1 child, Nicole Elizabeth Campbell. BA, Rutgers U., 1969; JD, Suffolk U., 1972; postgrad. London Sch. Econs. and Polit. Sci., 1977-78. Bar: N.J. 1972, U.S. Ct. Appeals (3d cir.) 1976, U.S. Supreme Ct. 1977, N.Y. 1981. Law clk. Superior Ct. N.J., 1972-73; assoc. Riker, Danzig, Scherer & Debevoise, Newark and Morristown, N.J., 1973-77; ptnr. Francis & Berry, Morristown, 1978-84, Dillon, Bitar & Luther, Morristown, 1985-92, Schenck, Price, Smith & King, Morristown, 1992—; arbitrator U.S. Dist. Ct. N.J., 1985—; del. to Jud. Conf. for Third Jud. Cir. U.S., 1975-79; mem. dist. X ethics com. N.J. Supreme Ct., 1983-87; judicial selection com. Morris County, 1995-99. Contbr. author: Valuation for Eminent Domain, 1973; mem. editl. bd. Suffolk U. Law Rev., 1970-71, New Jersey Lawyer, 1993-94. Trustee The Peck Sch., 1993-98, Richmond Fellowship of N.J., 1982-89, pres., 1984. Mem. ABA, N.J. Bar Assn., Fed. Bar Assn., Morris County Bar Assn. (trustee 1995—), Bay Head Yacht Club. Republican. Presbyterian. General corporate, State civil litigation, Federal civil litigation. Home: PO Box 191 Oldwick NJ 08858-0191 Office: Schenck Price Smith & King 10 Washington St Morristown NJ 07960-7117

**HUMMEL, GREGORY WILLIAM,** lawyer; b. Sterling, Ill., Feb. 25, 1949; s. Osborne William and Vivian LaVera (Guess) H.; m. Teresa Lynn Beveroth, June 20, 1970; children: Andrea Lynn, Brandon Gregory. BA, MacMurray Coll., 1971; JD, Northwestern U., 1974. Bar: Ill. 1974, U.S. Dist. Ct. (no. dist.) Ill. 1974. Assoc. Rusnak, Deutsch & Gilbert, Chgo., 1974-78; ptnr. Rudnick & Wolfe, Chgo., 1978-97, Bell, Boyd & Lloyd,

Chgo., 1997—. Editor Jour. Criminal Law & Criminology Northwestern U., 1973-74; co-author: Illinois Real Estate Forms, 1989; contbr. articles to law jours. Mem. gov. coun. Luth. Gen. Hosp. Advocate Health Care Sys.; trustee Mac Murray Coll., Jacksonville, Ill., 1986—. Homes for Children Found; bd. dirs. Chgo. area coun. Boy Scouts Am., ChildServ. Mem. Nat. Inst. Constrn. Law and Practice, Internat. Bar Assn. (co-chmn. com. internat. constrn. projects), Am. Coll. Constrn. Lawyers (past pres.), Urban Land Inst. (chmn. pub.-pvt. partnership coun.), Chgo. Dist. Coun. (chmn.), Lambda Alpha Internat. (Ely chpt. past pres.). Real property, Construction, Municipal (including bonds). Office: Bell Boyd & Lloyd Three First Nat Plaza 70 W Madison St Ste 3300 Chicago IL 60602-4284

**HUMMEL, HOLLY JANE,** lawyer; b. Woodbury, N.J., July 13, 1957; d. John Richard and Mary Lou (Dodson) H. BA with highest honors, Rochard Stockton Coll., 1979; JD, U. Oreg., 1982. Bar: Oreg., U.S. Ct. Appeals (9th cir.), U.S. Dist. Ct. Oreg. Law clerk Idaho Supreme Ct., Boise, 1982-84; assoc. Heller, Ehrman et al, Portland, Oreg., 1984-87, Rudnick & Assocs., Portland, 1987-89; pvt. practice Portland, 1990-97; ptnr. Hummel & Assocs., Portland, 1997-99; mem. Uniform Civil Jury Instrn. Com., Lake Oswego, Oreg., 1995-98, chair, 1997-98; bd. dirs. Goodwin Family Ltd. Partnership, Portland; spkr. in field. Rsch. asst.: The Law of Environment Protection, 1982; contbr. articles to profl. jours. Mem. Kiwanis Club. Avocations: rafting, bridge, property renovation. Real property, Personal injury, General civil litigation. Office: Hummel & Assocs 522 SW 5th Ave Ste 812 Portland OR 97204-2125

**HUMPHERYS, LEGRANDE RICH,** lawyer; b. Provo, Utah, May 16, 1949; m. Susan J. Olson, May 28, 1971; children: Daniel, Benjamin, Christa, Alissa, Joseph, Sara. BA, Brigham Young U., 1973, JD, 1976. Bar: Utah 1976, U.S. Dist. Ct. Utah 1976, U.S. Ct. Appeals (10th cir.) 1984, U.S. Claims Ct. 1991. Shareholder Christensen & Jensen, Salt Lake City, 1980-98, pres., 1998—; v.p. Christensen, Jensen & Powell, Salt Lake City, 1986—, also bd. dirs.; adj. assoc. prof. U. Utah., Salt Lake City, 1981—; v.p. Lo-Vo Tech. Inc., Salt Lake City, 1984-90, also dir. Bd. dirs. Davis County Mental Health Assn., Farmington, Utah, 1985-89; vice chmn. Indian Springs coun. Boy Scouts Am., 1985-86; state and county del. Rep. party, Davis County, 1982. Mem. ATLA, Am. Bd. Trial Advocates, Utah State Bar, Def. Rsch. Inst., Barrister Inns of Ct., Utah Trial Lawyers Assn. Mormon. Avocations: racquetball, fly fishing. Personal injury, Insurance, General civil litigation. Office: Christensen & Jensen Ste 510 50 S Main St # 1500 Salt Lake City UT 84144-0103

**HUMPHREVILLE, JOHN DAVID,** lawyer; b. Harrisburg, Pa., Feb. 4, 1953; s. Robert E. and Winifred (MacNulty) H.; m. Laurie Wettstone, Mar. 6, 1976; children: Caroline Elizabeth, John Evin. BS, Pa. State U., 1977; MA in Govt. Adminstrn., U. Pa., 1984; JD, Cath. U. Am., 1986. Bar: Fla. 1986, U.S. Dist. Ct. (mid. dist.) Fla. 1987, D.C. 1988. Dir. bur. real estate Pa. Dept. Gen. Svcs., Harrisburg, 1979-80; dep. adminstrv. asst. to gov. State of Pa., Harrisburg, 1980-83; assoc. Shackleford, Farrior, Stallings & Evans, P.A., Tampa, Fla., 1986-90; ptnr. Icard, Merrill, Cullis, Timm, Furren & Ginsburg, P.A., Tampa, 1990; asst. to atty. gen. U.S. Dept. Justice, Washington, 1990-91, spl. counsel Asst. Atty. Gen. environ. divsn., 1991; ptnr. Quarles & Brady, Naples, Fla., 1991—; mem. Fed. Jud. Adv. Commn., 1989-91. Avocations: surfing, swimming, triathlons. Real property, Environmental, Land use and zoning (including planning). Office: Quarles & Brady 4501 Tamiami Trl N Ste 300 Naples FL 34103-3023

**HUMPHREY, CARLOS M.,** lawyer; b. Mexico City, Mar. 8, 1966; s. Carlos Andres and Cecilia (Sanchez-Gavito) H.; m. Cecilia Bonilla Humphrey, Mar. 6, 1992; 1 child, Ainsley Isabel. JD, U. Nac. Autonoma de Mex., Mexico City, 1990; LLM in Corp. and Fin. Law, Widener U., 1996. Bar: Mex., 1991. Paralegal/jr. assoc. Ritch, Heather & Mueller, Mexico City, 1987-91; asst. gen. counsel InterDigital, King of Prussia, Pa., 1991-95; asst. v.p. Hyde & Assocs., Media, Pa., 1995-97; v.p., gen. counsel InterConsult, Inc., Media, 1997—. Contracts commercial, General corporate, Private international. Office: InterConsult Inc 202 Northbrook Dr Media PA 19063-5124

**HUMPHREY, THEODORE JAMES,** screenwriter, producer; b. Youngstown, Ohio, Aug. 6, 1969; s. Theodore Sr. and Marian H. BA in History & Govt., Georgetown U., 1991; JD, U. Va., 1994, MA in History, 1994. Bar: Va. 1994, D.C. 1995, Md. 1995, U.S. Dist. Ct. Md. 1995, U.S. Ct. Appeals (4th cir.) 1995, U.S. Dist. Ct. (ea. dist.) Va. 1995. Assoc. David & Hagner, Washington, 1994-96; prin. Pinetree Entertainment, L.A., 1996—. Mem. Writers Guild Am., West. Avocations: travel, rugby. Office: c/o The Shuman Co 225 Santa Monica Blvd Fl 7 Santa Monica CA 90401-2207

**HUMPHREYS, GENE LYNN,** lawyer; b. Lexington, Ky., Aug. 9, 1962; s. Eugene Paschal and Evelyn (Osborn) H.; m. Tracey Renee Scarlott, May 15, 1993; children: Molly Elizabeth, Emily Catherine. BA, Emory & Henry Coll., Emory, Va., 1984; MA, Bowling Green (Ohio) State U., 1986; JD, U. Ky., 1989. Bar: Ky. 1989, U.S. Dist. Ct. (ea. dist.) Ky. 1989, U.S. Dist. Ct. (we. dist.) Ky. 1990, U.S. Ct. Appeals (6th cir.) 1991. Grad. teaching asst. Bowling Green State U., 1984-86; summer assoc. Sturgill, Turner & Truitt, Lexington, 1987, Sulloway, Hollis & Soden, Concord, N.H., 1988; assoc. Sturgill, Turner & Truitt, Lexington, 1989-95, Ogden, Newell & Welch, Louisville, 1995—; legal writing instr. U. Ky., Lexington, 1990-92, 94—. Contbr. articles to profl. jours.; editor-in-chief Ky. Law Jour., 1988-89. Mem. Ky. Bar Assn., Louisville Bar Assn. Bankruptcy, General civil litigation, Contracts commercial. Home: 13502 Broken Branch Way Louisville KY 40245-2084 Office: Ogden Newell & Welch 1700 Citizens Plz 500 W Jefferson St Ste 1700 Louisville KY 40202-2874

**HUMPHREYS, KEVIN LEE,** lawyer; b. Kentwood, La., Aug. 7, 1963; s. Franklin Adrian and Ola Mae (Kyle) H.; m. Julie Elizabeth Hartness, Aug. 21, 1993; 1 child, Kyle Richmond. BS, Miss. Coll., 1985; JD, Vanderbilt U., 1988. Bar: Miss. 1989, U.S. Dist. Ct. (no. and so. dists.) Miss. 1989, U.S. Ct. Appeals (5th cir.) 1989. Law clk. Supreme Ct. of Miss., Jackson, 1988-90; pvt. practice Jackson, 1990-92; atty., sr. analyst PEER Com., Jackson, 1992-97; lawyer So. Farm Bur. Casualty Ins. Co., Ridgeland, Miss., 1997—. Author: (literary compilation) Arrowhead, 1985. Vol. Cmty. Stewpot, Jackson, 1993—; trustee Madison County Libr. Sys., 1999—. Recipient First Pl. Winner and Spl. citation Am. Scholastic Press Assn., 1984, Nat. Excellence in Program Evaluation Group award Nat. Legis. Program Evaluation Soc., 1994; named one of Outstanding Young Men of Am., 1989. Mem. ABA (contbg. book reviewer sect. of law practice mgmt. 1993-96), Miss. Bar Assn., Hinds County Bar Assn. Methodist. Avocations: golf, reading, music. General corporate, General civil litigation, Insurance. Home: 313 Autumn Crest Dr Ridgeland MS 39157-2604 Office: So Farm Bur Casualty Ins Co Ste 400 1800 E County Line Rd Ridgeland MS 39157-1916 also: PO Box 1800 Ridgeland MS 39158-1800

**HUMPHRIES, J. BOB,** lawyer; b. Birmingham, Ala., Nov. 18, 1946. BS, Fla. State U., 1968, MBA, 1972, JD cum laude, 1971. Bar: Fla. 1972, Ga. 1974. Atty. Fowler, White, Gillen, Boggs, Villareal and Banker P.A., Tampa, Fla. Bus. editor Fla. State U. Law Rev., 1971. Chmn. bd. Tampa-Hillsborough County Pub. Libr., 1986-87; bd. trustees Cmty. Found. Tampa Bay; bd. dirs., exec. mem. Tampa Bay Performing Arts Ctr.; trustee Cmty. Found. Tampa Bay; bd. dirs. Tampa Bay Downtown Partnership. Mem. ABA, State Bar Ga., Fla. Bar (chmn. tax sect., mem. environ. and land use law sect., corp., banking and bus. law sect., and real property, probate and trust law sect.), Phi Delta Phi. E-mail: bhtaxlaw@fowlerwhite.com. Real property, Taxation, general. Office: Fowler White Gillen Boggs Villareal and Banker 501 E Kennedy Blvd Ste 1700 Tampa FL 33602-5239

**HUNDLEY, LAURA S.,** lawyer; b. Boston, July 31, 1967; d. Franklin M. and Priscilla C. Hundley. AB, Harvard Coll., 1989; JD, Cornell U., 1994. Bar: Mass. 1994, Colo. 1996. Atty. Ropes & Gray, Boston, 1994-96, Holland & Hart LLP, Boulder, Colo., 1996—. Trustee, legal com. mem. The Cmty. Found., Boulder, Colo., 1997—. Mem. ABA, Colo. Bar Assn., Denver Bar Assn., Boulder County Bar Assn. Estate planning, Estate taxation, Probate. Office: Holland & Hart LLP 1050 Walnut St Ste 500 Boulder CO 80302-5144

**HUNEYCUTT, ALICE RUTH,** lawyer; b. New Haven, Jan. 10, 1951; d. C. Jerome and Alberta (Piner) H.; m. Howard Mark Bernstein, Nov. 28, 1981; children: Ashley Laughton, Laura Whitney. BA in History, Duke U., 1972; JD, U. Miami (Fla.), 1979. Bar: Fla. 1980, U.S. Dist. Ct. (so. dist.) Fla. 1980, U.S. Ct. Appeals (5th cir.) 1980, U.S. Dist. Ct. (mid. dist.) Fla. 1982, U.S. Ct. Appeals (11th cir.) 1982. Corp. counsel Burger King Corp., Miami, 1980-82; assoc. Stearns Weaver Miller Weissler Alhadeff & Sitterson, P.A., Tampa, Fla., 1982-84; ptnr. Stearns Weaver Miller Weissler Alhadeff & Sitterson, P.A., Tampa, 1984—. Bd. dirs. Am. Heart Assn., Tampa, 1986-91, chmn. elect, 1988-89, chmn. 1990-91. Mem. ABA (subcom. franchising, small bus. com., corp., banking and bus law sect.), Fla. Bar Assn. (pres.'s Pro Bono Svc. award 1987), Fla. Assn. Women Lawyers. Democrat. Methodist. General civil litigation. Home: 1400 72nd Ave NE Saint Petersburg FL 33702-4610 Office: 401 E Jackson St Ste 2200 Tampa FL 33602-5236

**HUNKINS, RAYMOND BREEDLOVE,** lawyer, rancher; b. Culver City, Calif., Mar. 19, 1939; s. Charles F. and Louise (Breedlove) H.; m. Mary Deborah McBride, Dec. 12, 1968; children: Amanda, Blake, Ashley. BA, U. Wyo., 1966, JD, 1968. Ptnr. Jones, Jones, Vines & Hunkins, Wheatland, Wyo., 1968—; mem. local rules com. U.S. Dist. Ct., 1990—; spl. counsel U. Wyo., Laramie, State of Wyo., Cheyenne; mem. faculty Western Trial Adv. Inst., 1993—, Wyo. Supreme Ct. Commn. Jud. Salary and Benefits, 1996—; owner Thunderhead Ranches, Albany and Platte Counties, Wyo.; gen. ptnr. Split Rock Land & Cattle Co.; spl. asst. atty. gen., Wyo. Chmn. Platte County Reps., Wheatland, 1972-74, chmn. adv. coun. Coll. of Commerce and Industry, U. Wyo., 1978-79; bd. dirs. U. Wyo. Found., 1996—, Am. Heritage Ctr., 1995—; mem. Gov.'s Crime Commn., 1970-78; pres. Wyo. U. Alumni Assn., 1973-74, commr. Wyo. Aeronautics Commn., 1987-98; moderator United Ch. Christ, 1997-98. With USMC, 1955-57. Fellow Am. Coll. Trial Lawyers (Wyo. state chmn.), Internat. Soc. Barristers, Am. Bd. Trial Advs.; mem. ABA (aviation com. 1980-86, forum com. on constrn. industry litigation sect.), Wyo. Bar Assn. (chmn. grievance com. 1980-86, mem. com. on civil pattern jury instrns.), Wyo. Trial Lawyers Assn. (past pres.), Lions, Elks. Federal civil litigation, Personal injury, Construction. Office: Jones Jones Vines & Hunkins PO Drawer 189 9th and Maple Wheatland WY 82201

**HUNSAKER, RICHARD KENDALL,** lawyer; b. L.A., June 2, 1960; s. Richard Allan and Patricia Kendall (Cook) H.; m. Laura Constance Haile, Oct. 8, 1988; children, Charles Nicholas, Laura Caroline. BA, U. Ill., 1982, MA, 1983; JD, Washington U., St. Louis, 1986. Bar: Ill. 1986, U.S. Dist. Ct. (cen. and no. dists.) Ill. 1987, U.S. Ct. Appeals (7th cir.) 1990, Wis. 1992. Speech coach Champaign (Ill.) Central High Sch., 1979-81; instr. speech communications, asst. debate coach U. Ill., Urbana, 1982-83; assoc. Heyl, Royster, Voelker & Allen, Springfield, Ill., 1986-87; assoc. Heyl, Royster, Voelker & Allen, Rockford, Ill., 1987-93, ptnr., 1994—. Author: Advanced Real Estate Law in Illinois - Environmental Liabilities, 1992, (with others) Advanced Real Estate Law in Illinois: Environmental Liability, 1992. Mem. ABA (tort and ins. practice, litigation and natural resources, energy and environ. law sects.), Ill. Bar Assn. (assoc., ins. law sect. 1990-92, civil practice and procedure, workers compensation, tort law and environ. control law sects.), Ill. Assn. Def. Trial Counsel, Winnebago County Bar Assn. (editl. bd. lawyer, legal-med., trial practice and continuing legal edn. coms.), Seventh Cir. Bar Assn., Def. Rsch. Inst. Methodist. Avocations: golf, biking, backpacking. General civil litigation, Insurance, Workers' compensation. Home: 1418 National Ave Rockford IL 61103-7144 Office: Heyl Royster Voelker & Allen 321 W State St Rockford IL 61101-1137

**HUNSTEIN, CAROL,** state supreme court justice; b. Miami, Fla., Aug. 16, 1944. AA, Miami-Dade Jr. Coll., 1970; BS, Fla. Atlantic U., 1972; JD, Stetson U., 1976, LLD (hon.), 1993. Bar: Ga. 1976; U.S. Dist. Ct. 1978; U.S. Ct. Appeals 1978; U.S. Supreme Ct. 1989. Legal practice Atlanta, 1976-84; judge Superior Ct. of Ga. (Stone Mt. cir.), 1984-92; justice Supreme Ct. of Ga., Atlanta, 1992—; chair Ga. Commn. on Gender Bias in the Judicial System 1989—; pres. Coun. of Superior Ct. Judges of Ga., 1990-91; adj. prof. Sch. Law Emory U., 1991—. Bd. dirs. Ga. Campaign Adolescent Pregnancy Prevention, 1992—. Recipient Clint Green Trial Advocacy award 1976, Women Who Made A Difference award Dekalb Women's Network 1986, Outstanding Svc. commendation Ga. Legislature, 1993, Cmty. Svc. award Emory U. Legal Assn. for Women Students., 1993. Mem. Ga. Assn. of Women Lawyers, Nat. Assn. of Women Judges (dir. 1988-90), Bleckley Inn of Ct., State Bar Ga. Office: Supreme Ct Ga 523 State Judicial Bldg Atlanta GA 30334-9007*

**HUNT, AMY KATHERINE,** lawyer; b. Corvallis, Oreg., Mar. 7, 1967; d. Michael Dennis and Judith Ann Campbell; m. Carter Joe Hunt, Apr. 20, 1991; 1 child, Natalie Anne. BBA, BA, U. Tex., 1989; JD, So. Meth. U., 1994. Bar: Tex. 1994, U.S. Dist. Ct. (no. and ea. dists.) Tex., U.S. Ct. Appeals (5th cir.). Cons. Price Waterhouse, Dallas, 1990-91; law clk. to Hon. Patrick E. Higginbotham U.S. Ct. Appeals (5th cir.), Dallas, 1994-95; assoc. Carrington, Coleman, Sloman & Blumenthal, LLP, Dallas, 1995—; legal writing instr. So. Meth. U. Sch. of Law, Dallas, 1997-98. Mem. ABA, State Bar Tex., Dallas Assn. Young Lawyers. Antitrust, General civil litigation, Professional liability. Office: Carrington Coleman Sloman & Blumenthal LLP 200 Crescent Ct Ste 1500 Dallas TX 75201-1848

**HUNT, CYNTHIA ANN,** paralegal; b. Kittery, Maine, Jan. 31, 1956; d. Thomas L. and Barbara C. (Cullinane) Hunt; 1 child, Amanda. BA in Bus. Mgmt., Simmons Coll., 1979; Cert. in Paralegal Studies, Bentley Coll., 1982. Legal asst. Wedgestone, Newton, Mass., 1982-85; corp. paralegal Rackemann, Sawyer & Brewster, Boston, 1985-87; sr. paralegal Berkshire Group, Boston, 1987-89; legal asst. Choate Hall & Stewart, Boston, 1989-92; sr. paralegal Millipore Corp., Bedford, Mass., 1992-95; corp. paralegal U.S. Filter, Lowell, Mass., 1995-96; sr. paralegal Ropes & Gray, Boston, 1996-98; legal asst. coord. Palmer & Dodge LLP, Boston, 1998—; notary pub. Commonwealth of Mass., 1982—. Mem. ABA, Mass. Bar Assn., Legal Asst. Mgmt. Assn., Mass. Paralegal Assn. Home: 78 Middlesex Ave Reading MA 01867-2425 Office: Palmer & Dodge LLP One Beacon St Boston MA 02108

**HUNT, DAVID EVANS,** lawyer; b. Wilkes-Barre, Pa., May 10, 1953; s. James Dixon and Twyla (Burkert) H.; m. Denise M. Barbera, Aug. 21, 1976 (div. 1984); 1 child Christopher Evans; m. Elizabeth S. Pearce, Sept. 5, 1987; children: Alexandra Stacy, Thomas Dixon. AB, Dartmouth Coll., 1975; JD, U. Chgo., 1978. Bar: N.Y. 1979, U.S. Dist. Ct. (so. and ea. dists.) N.Y. 1979, Maine 1982, U.S. Dist. Ct. Maine 1982, U.S. Tax Ct. 1982. Assoc. Debevoise & Plimpton, N.Y.C., 1978-81; ptnr. Pierce, Atwood, Scribner, Allen, Smith & Lancaster, Portland, Maine, 1981-92, McCandless & Hunt, Portland, Maine, 1992-97; sole practitioner Portland, 1997—; adjunct prof. Univ. Maine Law Sch. Portland, Maine, 1991-92. Co-author: Maine Will and Trust Forms, 1994, Maine Estate Administration, 1996. Officer, dir. Maine Estate Planning Coun., Portland, 1986-94. Fellow Am. Coll. Trust & Estate Counsel; mem. Maine State Bar Assn., N.Y. State Bar Assn., Cumberland County Bar Assn., Woodlands Club. Episcopalian. Avocations: classical Latin, skiing. Estate planning, Probate, Taxation, general. Home: 6 Highland St Portland ME 04103-3005 Office: 75 Market St Portland ME 04101-5031

**HUNT, GEORGE ANDREW,** lawyer; b. Salina, Utah, Mar. 5, 1949; s. Loyd G. and Inez Hunt; m. Elizabeth Jean Brandise, July 28, 1973 (div.); children: Rachael, Rinaldo, Andrew, Geoffrey. BS in Internat. Relations cum laude, U. Utah, 1971, JD, 1974. Bar: Utah 1974, U.S. Dist. Ct. Utah 1974, U.S. Ct. Appeals (10th cir.) 1976, U.S. Supreme Ct. 1978, U.S. Ct. Appeals (9th cir.) 1984. Assoc. Snow, Christensen & Martineau, Salt Lake City, 1974-78, ptnr., 1978-90; founding ptnr. Williams & Hunt, Salt Lake City, 1991—. Pres. U. Utah Coll. of Law, Salt Lake City, 1974. Mem. Utah Bar Assn. (bar examiner 1976-80, chmn. constrn. law sect. 1985-88), Salt Lake County Bar Assn. (mem. exec. com. 1979-90, treas. 1984, sec. 1985, v.p. 1986-87, pres. 1987-88), U. Coll. of Law (bd. trustees 1993-96), Alta Club. Republican. Roman Catholic. Avocations: flying, reading, music, gardening. Construction, Real property, Contracts commercial. Office: Williams & Hunt PO Box 45678 Salt Lake City UT 84145-0678

**HUNT, GERALD WALLACE,** lawyer; b. Portland, Oreg., Oct. 31, 1939. BSBA in Econs., U. Denver, 1961, JD, 1964; LLM in Taxation, Washington U., 1981. Bar: Colo. 1964, Ariz. 1968, Tex. 1996; cert. tax splst. Ariz. Bd. Legal Specialization. Asst. trust officer The Ariz. Bank, Phoenix, 1967-69; atty. Westover, Keddie, et al, Yuma, Ariz., 1969-73; pvt. practice law Yuma, 1973-74; atty. Hunt & Clark, Yuma, 1974-75, Hunt, Staney & Hossler, Yuma, 1975-96, Hunt, Tallan & Hossler, Yuma, 1996-97, Hunt and Hossler, Yuma, 1998—; fin. com. chair Excel Group, Yuma, 1998. Fellow Am. Coll. Trust and Estate Counsel; mem. ABA, Internat. Mcpl. Lawyers Assn., Ariz. State Bar, Colo. State Bar. Probate, Taxation, general, Estate planning. Office: Hunt and Hossler 330 W 24th St Yuma AZ 85364-6455

**HUNT, HEATHER M.,** lawyer; b. Madison, Wis., June 21, 1971; d. Charles Leonard Wnukowski and Nancy M. Marek; m. Rick J. Hunt, July 11, 1992. BS, U. Wis., Eau Claire, 1993; JD, U. Wis., Madison, 1997. Bar: Wis. 1997, U.S. Dist. Ct. (we. dist.) Wis. 1997. Intern Legal Assistance to Institutionalized Persons Program, Madison, 1995-96, LaCrosse County Dist. Atty.'s Office, LaCrosse, 1996, Wis. Supreme Ct., Madison, 1996; assoc. Wiley Colbert Norseng Cray & Herrell, S.C., Chippewa Falls, Wis., 1997—. Note and comment editor U. Wis. Law Rev., 1995-97. Dir. Chippewa Valley Cultural Assn., Inc., 1997—. Mem. Chippewa County Bar Assn., State Bar of Wis., Rotary (cmty. svc. chair 1997—). Estate planning, Real property, Contracts commercial. Home: 921 W Willow St Chippewa Falls WI 54729-2149 Office: Wiley Colbert Norseng Cray & Herrell 119 1/2 N Bridge St Chippewa Falls WI 54729-2404

**HUNT, JAMES L.,** lawyer; b. Tuscumbia, Ala., Dec. 18, 1936; s. James H. and Myrtle J. Hunt. BA, U. North Ala., 1959; JD, U. Ala., 1962. Bar: Ala., U.S. Dist. Ct. (no. dist.) Ala. Mcpl. judge City of Tuscumbia, Ala., 1967-72; sole practice Tuscumbia. Sgt. U.S. Army, 1962-68. Democrat. General practice, State civil litigation, Criminal. Office: 304 N Water St PO Box 8 Tuscumbia AL 35674-0008

**HUNT, JEFFREY BRIAN,** lawyer; b. Huntington, W.Va., Sept. 23, 1958; s. Bernard Ray and Nadine Dora (Meadows) H.; m. Krista Moorman, May 14, 1983. BA magna cum laude, Marshall U., 1980; JD summa cum laude, U. Ky., 1983. Bar: Mo. 1983, Ill. 1984, U.S. Ct. Appeals (8th cir.) 1984. Assoc. Lewis & Rice, 1983-93; mem. Lewis, Rice & Fingersh, L.C., St. Louis, 1993—; adj. instr. Washington U., St. Louis, 1983-89, 96—. Mem. ABA (vice chair TIPS sect. civil procedure and evidence 1996—), Bar Assn. M et. St. Louis, Order of Coif, Omicron Delta Kappa. Democrat. Methodist. Avocations: tennis, softball, baseball, basketball, golf. Admiralty, Federal civil litigation, Personal injury. Home: 2220 Stonegate Manor Ct Chesterfield MO 63017-7126 Office: Lewis Rice and Fingersh LC 500 N Broadway Ste 2000 Saint Louis MO 63102-2147

**HUNT, JOHN ROBERT,** lawyer; b. Kingston, N.Y., Feb. 17, 1957; s. Robert Wright and Joan Sickler H.; m. Diane Marie DiPaola, Aug. 15, 1980; 1 child, Sarah M. BA magna cum laude, Boston U., 1979, BS magna cum laude, 1979; JD, William & Mary Coll., 1982. Bar: Va. 1982, U.S. Ct. Appeals (4th cir.) 1983, U.S. Dist. Ct. (ea. dist.) Va. 1983, Ga. 1984, U.S. Dist. Ct. (no. dist.) Ga. 1984, U.S. Dist. Ct. (mid. dist.) Ga. 1990, U.S. Ct. Appeals (2d cir.) 1990, U.S. Ct. Appeals (11th cir.) 1992, U.S. Supreme Ct. 1993, U.S. Dist. Ct. (we. dist.) Va. 1994, U.S. Ct. Appeals (7th and 8th cirs.) 1994, U.S. Ct. Appeals Fed. Cir. 1995, U.S. Dist. Ct. (ea. dist.) Mich. 1997. Law clk. to Hon. Albert V. Bryan U.S. Ct. Appeals (4th cir.), Richmond and Alexandria, Va., 1982-83; atty. Kilpatrick & Cody, Atlanta, 1983-86, Stokes, Lazarus & Carmichael, Atlanta, 1986-92, Stokes & Murphy, Atlanta, 1992—. Exec. editor William & Mary Law Rev., 1981-82. Mem. Assn. Trial Lawyers Am., Ga. Trial Lawyers Assn., Atlanta Bar Assn., Confrerie de la Chaine des Rotisseurs. Avocations: running, skiing, reading, golfing. Labor, Federal civil litigation, General civil litigation. Office: Stokes & Murphy PO Box 87468 Atlanta GA 30337-0468

**HUNT, KAY NORD,** lawyer; b. Carver, Minn., June 26, 1955; d. Edward John and Carol Valentine (Lunde) Nord; m. Gary C. Hunt, June 25, 1977 (div. Dec. 1987). BA, Gustavus Adolphus, 1977; JD, Marquette U., 1981. Law clk. Wis. Ct. Appeals, Milw., 1981-82; atty. Lommen Nelson Cole & Stageberg, Mpls., 1982—. Bd. mem. Ramsy County Humane Soc., St. Paul, 1997—. Mem. Am. Acad. Appellate Lawyers, Minn. Def. Lawyers (amicus curia com.), Amdahl Inn of Ct. Office: Lommen Nelson Cole & Stageberg 80 S 8th St Minneapolis MN 55402-2100

**HUNT, LAWRENCE HALLEY, JR.,** lawyer; b. July 15, 1943; s. Lawrence Halley Sr. and Mary Hamilton (Johnson) H.; children: Caroline Smith, Laura Hamilton, Darwin Halley. AB, Dartmouth Coll., 1965; cert., l'Inst. de'Etudes Politiques, Paris, 1966; JD, U. Chgo., 1969. Bar: N.Y. 1970, Ill. 1971, U.S. Ct. Appeals (9th cir.) 1980, U.S. Ct. Appeals (2d cir.) 1981, U.S. Supreme Ct. 1981. Assoc. Davis Polk & Wardwell, N.Y.C., 1969-70; assoc. Sidley & Austin, Chgo., 1970-75, ptnr., 1975—; advisor securities adv. com. Ill. Sec. of State, Springfield, 1977-87; prof. grad. program fin. svcs. law Ill. Inst. Tech.-Chgo.-Kent Coll. Law, 1987—. James D. Reynolds scholar Dartmouth Coll., 1965-66. Mem. ABA (com. on commodity regulation, past chmn. subcom. on futures commn. merchants, mem. exec. coun.), Mid-Day Club, Chgo. Club, Indian Hill Club. Private international, Administrative and regulatory. Office: Sidley & Austin One First Nat Plz Chicago IL 60603

**HUNT, MERRILL ROBERTS,** retired lawyer; b. Portland, Maine, Jan. 23, 1939; s. Merrill Dewey and Lillian Katherine (McIntosh) H.; m. Janet McLean, July 21, 1962; 1 dau., Virginia Elizabeth. BA, Trinity Coll., 1962; JD, U. Maine, 1969. Bar: Maine 1969. Assoc., Mahoney, Robinson, Mahoney & Norman (and predecessors), Portland, 1969-70, ptnr., 1971-75; ptnr. Robinson, Hunt & Kriger, Portland, 1976-78; founding ptnr. Hunt, Thompson & Bowie, Portland, 1979-90; retired 1990. Chmn., Falmouth (Maine) Sewer Bd. Appeals, 1972-73; mem. Falmouth Bd. Zoning Appeals, 1974-78, chmn., 1976-78. Mem. ABA, Maine Bar Assn., Cumberland County Bar Assn., Am. Judicature Soc., Def. Research Inst. Federal civil litigation, State civil litigation, Personal injury.

**HUNT, RONALD FORREST,** lawyer; b. Shelby, N.C., Apr. 18, 1943; s. Forrest Elmer and Bruna Magnolia (Brackett) H.; m. Judy Elaine Shultz, May 19, 1965; 1 child, Mary. A.B., U. N.C., 1966, J.D., 1968. Bar: N.C. 1968, D.C. 1973. Mem. staff SEC, Washington, 1968-69, legal asst. to chmn., 1970-71, sec. of commn., 1972-73; dep. gen. counsel, sec. Student Loan Mktg. Assn., Washington, 1973-78, sr. v.p., gen. counsel, sec., 1979-83, exec. v.p., gen. counsel, 1983-90; pvt. practice New Bern, N.C., 1991—; vice chmn. First Capital Corp., Southern Pines, N.C., 1984-90; bd. dirs. Student Loan Mktg. Assn., Washington., SLM Holding Corp., Reston, Va.; chmn. bd. dirs. Nat. Student Loan Clearinghouse, Reston, 1993-95, 97—. Mem. Montgomery County Commn. Landlord and Tenant Affairs, Md., 1976-81, chmn., 1979-81; bd. dirs. D.C. chpt. ARC, 1976-83; trustee Arena Stage, Washington, 1984-89, Washington Theatre Awards Soc., 1988-90. Republican. Presbyterian. Avocations: sailing; gardening. General corporate, Securities.

**HUNT, SEAN ANTONE,** lawyer, civil engineer; b. Warrenton, Va., Sept. 6, 1965; s. John Booker, Jr. and Isabelle H. H.; m. Clarice Turner, Dec. 2, 1995. BS in Civil Engring., Tenn. State U., 1988; JD, Vanderbilt U. Sch. Law, 1993. Bar: Tenn. 1993, U.S. Dist. Ct. (ea., mid. and we. dists.) Tenn. 1993, Ga. 1994, U.S. Dist. Ct. (no. dist.) Ga. 1994. Assoc. hwy. engr. N.C. Dept. Transportation, Raleigh, 1988-90, bridge design engr., 1990; intern Tenn. Atty. Gen's. Office, Nashville, 1993, U.S. Dist. Ct. Judge Robert L. Echols, Nashville, 1993; law clerk Law Offices Raymond G. Prince, Nashville, 1993; atty. Leitner, Warner, Moffitt, Williams, Dooley, Carpenter, & Napolitan, PLLC, Chattanooga, 1993-96, Spicer, Flynn & Rudstrom, P.L.L.C., Nashville, 1996—. Com. mem. Martina O'Bryan Ctr., Nashville, 1996-97; com. co-chair Bethlehem Ctrs. Nashville, 1998; treas., Friends in Gen. (Gen. Hosp.), Nashville, 1998—. With USAFR, 1983-87. General civil litigation, Construction, Personal injury. Office: Spicer Flynn & Rudstrom 424 Church St Ste 1350 Nashville TN 37219-2326

**HUNT, THOMAS REED, JR.,** lawyer; b. Elkton, Md., Feb. 22, 1948; s. Thomas R. and Marian D. (Decker) H.; children: Reed Thomas, Clifton Bowie, Molly Dustin, Travis John. Ptnr. Morris, Nichols, Arsht & Tunnell, Wilmington, Del., 1972—.

**HUNT, WILLIAM E., SR.,** state supreme court justice; b. 1923. BA, LLB, U. Mont., JD, 1955. Bar: 1955. Judge State Workers' Compensation Ct.,

1975-81; justice Mont. Supreme Ct., Helena, 1984—. Office: Mont Supreme Ct Justice Bldg Rm 315 215 N Sanders St Helena MT 59601-4522*

**HUNT, WILLIS B., JR.,** federal judge. Former judge Houston, Superior Ct. Ga.; justice Ga. Supreme Ct., Atlanta, 1986-95, chief justice, 1994-95; justice U.S. Dist. Ct. (no. dist.) Ga., Atlanta, 1995—. Office: US Dist Ct no dist Ga 75 Spring St SW Atlanta GA 30306

**HUNTER, DONALD FORREST,** lawyer; b. Mpls., Jan. 30, 1934; s. Earl Harvey and Ruby Cecilia (Lagerson) H.; m. Marlys Ann Zilge; Jeffrey, Cheri, Kathryn. BA, U. Minn., 1961, JD, 1963. Bar: Minn. 1963, U.S. Dist. Ct. Minn. 1965, U.S. Ct. Appeals (8th cir.) 1965, Ill. 1977, U.S. Dist. Ct. (no. dist.) Ill. 1991, U.S. Supreme Ct. 1986. Assoc., then ptnr. Gislason, Dosland, Hunter & Malecki, New Ulm, Minn., 1963-76; exec. v.p., sec., gen. counsel Wirtz Prodn. Ltd. Ice Follies/Holiday on Ice, Chgo., 1976-79; ptnr. Gislason, Dosland, Hunter & Malecki, Mpls., 1979-99; of counsel Gislason & Hunter, 1999—; chmn. bd. dirs. Chgo. Milw. Corp., 1977-81; pres. Chgo. Milw. R.R., 1977-81; bd. dirs. First Security Bank, Chgo.; bd. dirs., officer First Security Bancorp, Inc., Chgo., 1993—; bd. dirs., sec. Wirtz Corp., Chgo. Blackhawk Hockey Team and related cos. Fellow Am. Coll. Trial Lawyers; mem. ABA, Am. Judicature Soc., Minn. Bar Assn. (bd. of govs. 1973-76), 5th Dist. Bar Assn. (pres. 1971-72), Hennepin County Bar Assn., Minn. Def. Lawyers Assn. (bd. dirs. 1976), Internat. Assn. Ins. Counsel, U.S. Supreme Ct. Hist. Assn. General civil litigation, Contracts commercial, General corporate. Office: Gislason & Hunter PO Box 5297 9900 Bren Rd E Ste 215E Hopkins MN 55343-9666

**HUNTER, EDWIN FORD, JR.,** federal judge; b. Alexandria, La., Feb. 18, 1911; s. Edwin Ford and Amelia (French) H.; m. Shirley Kidd, Nov. 9, 1941; children—Edwin Kidd, Janin, Kelley. Student, La. State U., 1930-33; LL.B., George Washington U., 1938. Bar: La. bar 1938. Mem. firm Smith, Hunter, Risinger & Shuey, Shreveport, 1940-53; mem. La. Legislature, 1948-52; exec. counsel Gov. La., 1952-53; mem. La. State Mineral Bd., 1952; judge, now sr. judge U.S. Dist. Ct., Western Dist. La., 1953—, also mem. adv. com. on civil rules., 1971-76. Served as lt. USNR, 1942-45. Mem. Am. Bar Assn. (La. state chmn. jr. bar sect. 1945), Am. Legion (post comdr. 1945, judge adv. Dept. La. 1948), Sigma Chi. Roman Catholic. Home: 1000 Bayou Oak Ln Lake Charles LA 70605-2634 Office: US Dist Ct 611 Broad St Ste 243 Lake Charles LA 70601-4380

**HUNTER, ELMO BOLTON,** federal judge; b. St. Louis, Oct. 23, 1915; s. David Riley and Della (Bolton) H.; m. Shirley Arnold, Apr. 5, 1952; 1 child, Nancy Ann (Mrs. Ray Lee Hunt). AB, U. Mo., 1936, LLB, 1938; Cook Grad. fellow, U. Mich., 1941; PhD (hon.), Coll. of Ozarks, 1988. Bar: Mo. 1938. Pvt. practice Kansas City, 1938-45; sr. asst. city counselor, 1939-40; ptnr. Sebree, Shook, Hardy and Hunter, 1945-51; state circuit judge Mo., 1951-57; Mo. appellate judge, 1957-65; judge U.S. Dist. Ct., Kansas City, Mo., 1965—, now sr. judge; instr. law U. Mo., 1952-62; mem. jud. selection Elmo B. Hunter Citizens Ctr., Am. Judicature Soc. Contbr. articles to profl. jours. Mem. Bd. Police Commrs., 1949-51; Trustee Kansas City U., Coll. of Ozarks; fellow William Rockhill Nelson Gallery Art. 1st lt. M.I., AUS, 1943-46. Recipient 1st Ann. Law Day award U. Mo., 1964, Charles E. Whittaker award, 1994, SAR Law Enforcement Commendation medal, 1994, citation of Merit Mo. Law Sch., 1996. Fellow ABA; mem. Fed., Mo. bar assns., Jud. Conf. U.S. (mem. long range planning com., chmn. ct. adminstrn. com.), Am. Judicature Soc. (bd. govs., mem. exec. com., pres., chmn. bd., Devitt Disting. Svc. to Justice award 1987), Acad. Mo. Squires, Order of Coif, Phi Beta Kappa, Phi Delta Phi. Presbyterian (elder). Office: US Dist Ct 659 US Courthouse 811 Grand Blvd Ste 201 Kansas City MO 64106-1904

**HUNTER, HOWARD OWEN,** dean, law educator; b. Brunswick, Ga., Oct. 14, 1946; m. Susan Frankel, Nov. 27, 1971; 1 child, Emily Atwood. BA in Russian Studies, Yale U., 1968, JD, 1971. Bar: Ga. 1971. Assoc. atty. Hogan & Hartson, Washington, 1971-72, Hansell, Post, Brandon & Dorsey, Atlanta, 1972-76; asst. prof. Emory U. Sch. Law, Atlanta, 1976-79, assoc. prof., 1979-82, assoc. dean, 1979-80, prof., 1982—, prof. law, dean, 1989—; dir. Ga. Vol. Lawyers for the Arts, Inc., 1975-89, sec., 1975-77, treas., 1978-80, v.p., 1980-82, pres., 1984-87; vis. prof. law U. Va. Sch. Law, Charlottesville, 1982-83; hon. prof. law U. Hong Kong, 1986; vis. Mills E. Godwin prof. law Coll. William & Mary, Williamsburg, Va., 1989; mem. Chief Justice Commn. on Professionalism, 1990—; bd. trustees Fed. Def. Program, 1991—; lectr. in field. Author: Freedom of Information Handbook: Georgia, 1979, Modern Law of Contracts: Breach and Remedies, 1986, supplements, 1987, 88, 89, 90, 91, 92, 93, Modern Law of Contracts: Formation, Performance, Relationships, 1987, supplements, 1988, 89, 90, 91, 92, 93, Modern Law of Contracts, revised edit., 1993, supplements, 1994, 95, 96, 97, (with Mogens Pedersen) Recent Reforms in Swedish Higher Education, 1980; contbr. articles to profl. jours.; mem. editl. bd. Jour. of Contract Law, 1988—. Fulbright Sr. scholar U. Sydney, 1988. Mem. ABA, Assn. Am. Law Schs., Am. Law Inst. (mem. consultative com. on revisions to article 2 of UCC), State Bar Ga. (mem. editl. bd. Ga. State Bar Jour. 1977-82), Decatur-DeKalb Bar Assn., Atlanta Bar Assn. (vol. lawyer project on illegal Cuban immigrants 1985-87, vol. lawyer in representation of Cuban inmates at fed. prison in Talladega, Ala. 1988, bd. dirs. internat. transaction sect. 1995—), Inst. Continuing Legal Edn. (vice-chmn. bd. trustees 1993—), Inst. Continuing Judicial Edn. (bd. trustees 1989—). Avocations: riding and training show hunters, jogging, fishing, travel. Office: Emory U Sch Law Gambrell Hall 1301 Clifton Rd NE Atlanta GA 30322-1013

**HUNTER, JACK DUVAL,** lawyer; b. Elkhart, Ind., Jan. 14, 1937; s. William Stanley and Marjorie Irene (Upson) H.; m. Marsha Ann Goodsell, Nov. 14, 1958; children: Jack, Jon, Justin. BBA, U. Mich., 1959, LLB, 1961. Bar: Mich. 1961, Ind. 1962. Atty. Lincoln Nat. Life Ins. Co., Ft. Wayne, Ind., 1961-64, asst. counsel, 1964-68, v.p., gen. counsel, 1975-79, sr. v.p., gen. counsel, 1979-86, exec. v.p., gen. counsel, 1986—; asst. gen. counsel, asst. sec. Lincoln Nat. Corp., Ft. Wayne and Phila., 1968-71, gen. counsel, 1971—, v.p., 1972-79, sr. v.p., 1979-86, exec. v.p., 1986—. Life trustee Ind. Nature Conservancy, chmn. bd. trustees, 1993-95. Recipient Oak Leaf award Nature Conservancy, 1997. Mem. ABA, Ind. State Bar Assn., Allen County Bar Assn., Assn. Life Ins. Counsel (pres. 1995-96), Am. Coun. Life Ins. (chmn. legal sect. 1991). General corporate. Office: Lincoln Nat Corp 1500 Market St Ste 3900 Philadelphia PA 19102-2100

**HUNTER, JACK DUVAL, II,** lawyer; b. Ann Arbor, Mich., July 15, 1959; s. Jack Duval and Marsha Ann (Goodsell) H.; m. Denise Marie Hodge, June 27, 1981; children: Adam Duval, Benjamin Robert. BSCE, Purdue U., 1982, MSCE, 1984; JD, St. Mary's U., 1986. Bar: Tex. 1986, U.S. Dist. Ct. (so. dist.) Tex. 1987, U.S. Ct. Appeals (5th cir.) 1987, U.S. Supreme Ct. 1990; engr. in tng., Ind., Tex. Assoc. Johnson & Davis, Harlingen, Tex., 1986-88; asst. dist. atty. Hidalgo County Courthouse, Edinburg, Tex., 1989-91; gen. atty. Immigration and Naturalization Svc., 1991-93; pvt. practice lawyer Harlingen, Tex., 1993—, Edinburg, 1996—; adj. prof. Reynaldo G. Garza Sch. of Law, 1989-91. Assoc. editor St. Mary's Law Jour., 1984-86. Bd. dirs. Harlingen Boys' and Girls' Club, 1987-88. Mem. NRA (life), Coll. State Bar Tex., State Bar Tex. (adminstrn. of rules and evidence com.), Cameron County Bar Assn., Hidalgo County Bar Assn., Juvenile Ct. Conf. Com. (lectr. 1990), Tex. State Rifle Assn. (life), Buckmasters (life), Valley Sportsmen Club of the Lower Rio Grande Valley (life), Order of Barristers, Whittington Ctr. (life), Phi Delta Phi. Democrat. Baptist. Fax: 956-383-3736. Criminal. Office: 204 E Cano St Edinburg TX 78539-4510

**HUNTER, JAMES AUSTEN, JR.,** lawyer; b. Phoenix, June 19, 1941; s. James Austen and Elizabeth Aileen (Holt) H.; m. Donna Gabriele, Aug. 24, 1973; 1 child, James A. A.B., Cath. U. Am., 1963, LL.B., 1966. Bar: N.Y. 1967, Pa. 1975, U.S. Supreme Ct. 1974. Assoc. firm Sullivan & Cromwell, N.Y.C., 1967-74; assoc. firm Morgan, Lewis & Bockius, Phila., 1974-77; ptnr. Morgan, Lewis & Bockius, 1977—. Banking, General corporate, Real property. Home: 1001 Red Rose Ln Villanova PA 19085-2118 Office: Morgan Lewis & Bockius 1701 Market St Philadelphia PA 19103-2903

**HUNTER, JAMES GALBRAITH, JR.,** lawyer; b. Phila., Jan. 6, 1942; s. James Galbraith and Emma Margaret (Jehl) H.; m. Pamela Ann Trott, July 18, 1969 (div.); children: James Nicholas, Catherine Selene; m. Nancy Grace Scheurwater, June 21, 1992. B.S. in Engring. Sci., Case Inst. Tech., 1965; J.D., U. Chgo., 1967. Bar: Ill. 1967, U.S. Dist. Ct. (no. dist.) Ill. 1967, U.S. Ct. Appeals (7th cir.) 1967, U.S. Ct. Claims, 1976, U.S. Ct. Appeals (4th and 9th cirs.) 1978, U.S. Supreme Ct. 1979, U.S. Dist. Ct. (cen. dist.) Ill. 1980, Calif. 1980, U.S. Dist. Ct. (cen. and so. dists.) Calif. 1980, U.S. Ct. Appeals (5th cir.) 1982, U.S. Ct. Appeals (fed. cir.) 1982. Assoc. Kirkland & Ellis, Chgo., 1967-68, 70-73, ptnr., 1973-76; ptnr. Hedlund, Hunter & Lynch, Chgo., 1976-82, Los Angeles, 1979-82; ptnr. Latham & Watkins, Hedlund, Hunter & Lynch, Chgo. and Los Angeles, 1982—. Served to lt. JAGC, USN, 1968-70. Mem. ABA, State Bar Calif., Los Angeles County Bar Assn., Chgo. Bar Assn. Clubs: Metropolitan (Chgo.), Chgo. Athletic Assn., Los Angeles Athletic. Exec. editor U. Chgo. Law Rev., 1966-67. Federal civil litigation, State civil litigation, Antitrust. Office: Latham & Watkins Sears Tower Ste 5800 Chicago IL 60606-6306 also: 633 W 5th St Los Angeles CA 90071-2005

**HUNTER, JOHN LESLIE,** lawyer; b. Miss., Aug. 15, 1946; s. Leslie Hunter; m. Judy G. Hunter; children: John Leslie II, Lee Joseph, Kristy Lynn. BS, Miss. State U., 1969; JD, U. Miss., 1972. Bar: U.S. Dist. Ct. (no. dist.) Miss. 1972, U.S. Dist. Ct. (so. dist.) Miss. 1973, U.S. Ct. Appeals (5th cir.) 1974, U.S. Supreme Ct. 1978, U.S. Dist. Ct. (so. dist.) Ala. 1980, U.S. Ct. Appeals (11th cir.) 1981. Ptnr. Cumbest Cumbest Hunter & McCormick, Pascagoula, Miss., 1975—; atty. Jackson county Port Authority. Mem. ABA, Assn. Trial Lawyers of Am. (sustaining mem.), Am. Bd. Trail Advocates, Miss. Bar Assn. (exec. com. bd. commrs.), Miss. Trial Lawyers Assn. (sustaining), Jackson County Bar Assn. Methodist. Admiralty, Insurance, Personal injury. Office: Cumbest Cumbest Hunter McCormick 707 Watts Ave PO Box 1287 Pascagoula MS 39568-1287

**HUNTER, LARRY DEAN,** lawyer; b. Leon, Iowa, Apr. 10, 1950; s. Doyle J. and Dorothy B. (Grey) H.; m. Rita K. Barker, Jan. 24, 1971; children: Nathan (dec.), Allison. BS with high distinction, U. Iowa, 1971; AM, U. Mich., 1974, JD magna cum laude, 1974, CPhil in Econs., 1975. Bar: Va. 1975, Mich. 1978, Calif. 1992. Assoc. McGuire Woods & Battle, Richmond, Va., 1975-77; asst. counsel, internat. counsel Clark Equipment Co., Buchanan, Mich., 1977-80; ptnr. Honigman, Miller, Schwartz and Cohn, Detroit, 1980-93; asst. gen. counsel Hughes Electronics Corp., L.A., 1993-98, corp. v.p., 1998—; sr. v.p., gen. counsel DIRECTV, Inc., El Segundo, Calif., 1996—; chmn. pres. DIRECTV Japan Mgmt., Inc., Tokyo, 1998—; mem. faculty Wayne State U. Law Sch., Detroit, 1987-89. Mem. Order of Coif. General corporate, Securities, Contracts commercial. Home: 306014 Shiroganedai, Minato-ku, Tokyo 108-0071, Japan Office: DIRECTV Japan Mgmt Inc, 4-20-3 Ebisu, Shibuya-ku, Tokyo 150-6023, Japan

**HUNTER, RICHARD SAMFORD, JR.,** lawyer; b. Montgomery, Ala., May 8, 1954; s. Richard Samford and Anne (Arendell) H.; m. Jane Messer, June 28, 1981; children: Richard Samford III, Benjamin Arendell. Student, Berklee Coll. of Music, 1974-75; BA, U. N.C., 1977; JD, Cumberland Sch Law of Samford U., 1980. Bar: N.C. 1980, U.S. Dist. Ct. (ea. and mid. dists.) N.C. 1981; cert. Am. Bd. Trial Advs. Assoc. Green & Mann, Raleigh, N.C., 1980-82, Smith, Debnam, Hibbert & Pahl, Raleigh, 1982-85; ptnr. Futrell, Hunter & Bingham, Raleigh, 1985-97; Pres., North Carolina Acad. of Trial Lawyers, 1993-94; pres. elect, 1992-93; exec. comm., 1987-94; bd., 1984-87; chair, Auto Torts Sect., 1998—, program chmn. media law U. N.C., Chapel Hill, 1983-84; mem. faculty NCATL Nat. Inst. Trial Advocacy, 1987; lectr. in field. Author: Insurance Law for the General Practitioner, 1992, North Carolina Bar Assn. Desk Book, 1992, Traumatic Medicine, 1995; composer, performer (TV musical) The Tomorrow Show, 1975; contbr. articles to profl. jours. Corp. fund raiser United Way, Wake County, N.C., 1984-85; mem. clergy's sermon evaluation com. Christ Episc. Ch., Raleigh; bd. dirs. Raleigh Chamber Music Guild, 1986-88; bd. dirs. Food Bank of N.C., 1990—. Fellow So. Trial Lawyers Assn., Roscoe Pound Found.; mem. ABA (mem. litigation sect.), ATLA, Am. Bd. Trial Advocates (cert.), N.C. Bar Assn., Wake County Bar Assn. (bd. dirs. 1987-88, chmn. 1988), Assn. Trial Lawyers Am. (Stalwart fellow Roscoe Pound Found.), N.C. Acad. Trial Lawyers (speaker various seminars, chmn. speakers bur. 1984-85, bd. govs. 1986—, v.p. pub. svc. and info. com. 1988-90, v.p. membership 1990-91, v.p. legis. 1991—, pres. 1993-94, exec. com. 1987-94, chmn. auto torts sect. 1998—, mem. edn. com. 1985-88), Kiwanis, Sphinx, Phi Alpha Delta. Democrat. Avocations: sports, music, hunting, fishing. Fax: 919-831-8734. E-mail: hunteratty@aol.com. State civil litigation, Personal injury, Insurance. Home: 813 Graham St Raleigh NC 27605-1124 Office: Futrell Hunter & Bingham 1st Union Capitol Ctr 1700 150 Fayetteville Street Mall Raleigh NC 27601-1395

**HUNTER, ROBERT FREDERICK,** lawyer; b. Ft. Worth, June 7, 1937; s. Homer Alexander and Pauline (Steely) H.; m. Elisabeth Loader, July 1, 1961 (div. Sept. 1982); children: Homer Alexander II, Robert Frederick Jr.; m. Barbara Bailey, June 7, 1984. BBA, BS in Civil Engring., Tex. A&M U., 1960; MS, M.I.T., 1964; JD, So. Meth. U., 1974. Bar: Tex. 1975, Mo. 1976. Pres., chief exec. officer Hydro-Air Engring., St. Louis, 1974-84; sole practice Dallas, 1985-86; ptnr. Ashley and Welch, Dallas, 1987-90; pvt. practice Dallas, 1990—. Mem. ABA, ASCE, Tex. Bar Assn., Mo. Bar Assn., Phi Delta Phi. Republican. Lodge: Rotary (pres. 1970). Avocations: cameras, woodworking. General corporate, Contracts commercial, Private international. Home: 3517 Villanova St Dallas TX 75225-5008

**HUNTER, THEODORE PAUL,** lawyer, energy consultant; b. St. Clair, Mich., Dec. 14, 1951; s. James Peter and Esther (Breuehner) H.; m. Ramona Holmes, Sept 5, 1977; children: Justin, Brandon. BS with honors, Portland (Oreg.) State U., 1973; JD, U. Wash., 1978. Bar: Wash. 1978, U.S. Dist. Ct. (we. dist.) Wash. 1978, U.S. Ct. Appeals (9th cir.) 1979, U.S. Supreme Ct. 1993. Ptnr. Lippek, Hunter, Caryl & Raan, Seattle, 1978-83; chief counsel Wash. State Legis. Energy Com., Olympia, 1983-88; dir. Pacific Energy Inst., Seattle, 1988—; ptnr. Driscoll & Hunter, 1988—; arbitrator King County Superior Cts., Seattle, 1985—; prof., instr. Evergreen Coll., Olympia, 1986—. Contbr. articles to profl. jours. Fellow Environ. Law Inst., Washington, 1979. Mem. Washington State Bar Assn. (chair dispute resolution sect.), Environ. Lawyers of Wash., Soc. Profls. in Dispute Resolution, Klapa Sokoli. Democrat. Lutheran. Avocations: squash, running, pvt. pilot, playing trumpet. Office: 101 Yesler Way Ste 607 Seattle WA 98104-2580

**HUNTLEY, DONALD WAYNE,** lawyer; b. Chgo., Sept. 22, 1942; s. Joseph Edward and Emily Rose (Beran) H.; m. Margaret Helen Kopacek, Aug. 27, 1966 (div. 1994); children: Richard A. II, Scott J., Mark B., C. Frederick M. BS, U. Ill., 1963, JD, 1966. Bar: D.C. 1967, Del. 1981, U.S. Supreme Ct. 1973. Patent counsel E. I. du Pont de Nemours & Co., Wilmington, Del., 1966-92, Remington Arms Co., 1985-89; founder present firm, 1993; asst. pub. defender State of Del., Wilmington, 1972-78; pntr. Huntley & Assocs., Wilmington. Bd. dirs. Del. Symphony Assn., 1972-86, 98—, pres., 1976-79, chmn. music com., 1979-86, trustee, 1988-98, chmn. past pres. coun., 1990—; bd. dirs. Kalmar Nyckel Commemorative Com., 1983-91, chmn. cultural com., 1983-86, mem. exec. com., 350th anniversary com., 1986-88; counsel Ctr. for Creative Arts, Yorklyn, Del., 1983-84. Mem. Rotary Club Wilmington, ABA, Del. Bar Assn., Phila. Intellectual Property Law Assn., Phi Delta Phi. Republican. Episcopalian. Patent, Trademark and copyright, Intellectual property. Home: 838 Summerset Dr Hockessin DE 19707-9338 Office: Huntley & Assocs PO Box 948 1105 N Market St Wilmington DE 19899-0948

**HUNTSBERGER, THOMAS ALLEN,** lawyer; b. Palo Alto, Calif., Apr. 22, 1949; s. Ralph Francis and Margaret Ruth (Kroener) H.; m. Barbara Doyle, May 12, 1973; children: Briana, Jenna, Alex. AB, Harvard U., 1972; JD, U. Oreg. Law Sch., 1976. Assoc. Ackerman & Dewenter, Springfield, Oreg., 1977-80; ptnr. Ackerman, Dewenter & Huntsberger, Springfield, 1981—, Thomas A. Huntsberger, PC, Springfield, 1996—; trustee U.S. Trustees Office, Eugene, Oreg., 1980. Mem. Oreg. State Bar, Lane County Bar (bankruptcy com. 1986). Democrat. Episcopalian. Fax: 541-746-3201. Home: 2212 Agate St Eugene OR 97403-1761 Office: Thomas A Huntsberger PC 870 W Centennial Blvd Springfield OR 97477-2835

**HUNTSMAN, PETER R.,** lawyer; b. Boston, Aug. 11, 1952; s. Robert Fletcher Huntsman and Eleanor Dorothy Burckel; m. D'Innocenzo Huntsman, Jan. 30, 1981; children: Julia, Andrew. AB, Harvard U., 1974; JD, Boston U., 1979. Bar: Mass. 1979, Conn. 1983, U.S. Dist. Ct. Mass. 1979, U.S. Dist. Ct. Conn. 1983, U.S. Ct. Appeals (1st cir.) 1980. Assoc. Updike Kelly & Spellacy, P.C., Falls Church, Va., 1983-90; prin. Updike Kelly & Spellacy, P.C., Hartford, Conn., 1991-93; asst. atty. gen. State of Conn., Hartford, 1993—. Mem. U.S. Olympic Women's Rowing Com., Phila., 19976-80, U.S. Lightweight Women's Rowing Com., Indpls., 1980-82, 85-90; mem. allocations com. United Way of the Capital Region, Hartford, 1992-94, 96—. Capt., U.S. Army JAGC, 1980-83. Home: 155 Terry Rd Hartford CT 06105-1121 Office: Office of Atty Gen 55 Elm St Hartford CT 06106

**HUPP, HARRY L.,** federal judge; b. L.A., Apr. 5, 1929; s. Earl L. and Dorothy (Goodspeed) H.; m. Patricia Hupp, Sept. 13, 1953; children: Virginia, Karen, Keith, Brian. AB, Stanford U., 1953, LLB, 1955. Bar: Calif. 1956, U.S. Dist. Ct. (cen. dist.) Calif. 1956, U.S. Supreme Ct. Pvt. practice law Beardsley, Hufstedler and Kemble, L.A., 1955-72; judge Superior Ct. of Los Angeles, 1972-84; appointed fed. dist. judge U.S. Dist. Ct. (cen. dist.) Calif., L.A., 1984-97, sr. judge, 1997—. Served with U.S. Army, 1950-52. Mem. Calif. Bar Assn., Los Angeles County Bar Assn. (Trial Judge of Yr. 1983), Order of Coif, Phi Alpha Delta. Office: US Dist Ct 312 N Spring St Ste 218P Los Angeles CA 90012-4704

**HUPPE, MICHAEL J.,** lawyer; b. Wilmington, Del., Feb. 2, 1968. BA with honors, U. Va., 1990; JD, Harvard U., 1995. Bar: Va., D.C., U.S. Dist. Ct. (ea. dist.) Va., U.S. Ct. Appeals (4th cir.). With Akin, Gump, Strauss, Hauer & Feld, LLP, Washington. Office: Akin Gump Strauss Hauer & Feld LLP Ste 400 1333 New Hampshire Ave NW Washington DC 20036-1564

**HURD, DOUGLAS HEROLD,** lawyer; b. Summit, N.J., Sept. 15, 1969; s. Richard Hanford and Janet (Binder) H.; m. Mindy Kain. BA, U. Del., 1991; JD (cum laude), Widener U., 1994. Bar: Pa. 1994, N.J. 1994, U.S. Dist. Ct. N.J. 1994. Law clk. Judge John F. Kingfield, Belvidere, N.J., 1994-95; assoc. Mason, Griffin & Pierson, PC, Princeton, N.J., 1995-98; asst. counsel Office of Counsel to the Gov., Trenton, N.J., 1998—. Chair Hunterdon County Young Reps., Flemington, N.J., 1997—; vice-chair Red Cross Leadership Coun., Princeton, 1998—. Mem. ABA (exec. coun. mem., dist. rep. young lawyers divsn. 1997—). Avocations: running marathons, basketball. Home: 15 Rock Creek Woods Dr Lambertville NJ 08530-1111 Office: Govs Office State House Trenton NJ 08625-0001

**HURD, JAMES A., JR.,** prosecutor. BA, Howard U., 1968; JD, U. Md., 1975. Dep. dist. atty. Dept. Justice, Denver, chief counsel for Met. Consumer Fraud Office, chief dep. dist. atty., until 1980; asst. U.S. atty. for V.I. Dept. Justice, St. Croix, 1980-81; with dist. atty. office Dept. Justice, St. Thomas, 1984-92, 1st asst. U.S. atty., 1992-94; dir. Office Legal Edn. Dept. Justice, Washington, 1994-95; U.S. atty. for dist. V.I. Dept. Justice, St. Thomas, 1995—. Office: Fed Bldg & US Courthouse 5500 Veterans Dr Rm 260 Charlotte Amalie VI 00802-6214*

**HURD, PAUL GEMMILL,** lawyer; b. Salt Lake City, Nov. 23, 1946; s. Melvin and Marjorie Hurd. BS, Portland State U., 1968; JD, Lewis and Clark Coll., 1976. Bar: Oreg. 1976, Wash. 1984, U.S. Dist. Ct. Oreg. 1980, U.S. Ct. Appeals (9th cir.) 1981, U.S. Supreme Ct. 1988. Sr. dep. dist. atty. Multnomah County Dist. Atty., Portland, Oreg., 1976-80; trial counsel Burlington No. R.R., Portland, 1980-84; asst. gen. counsel Freightliner Corp., Portland, 1984-89, assoc. gen. counsel, 1989—. Trustee Leukemia Assn. of Oreg., Portland, 1984-90. Mem. ABA, Oreg. Bar Assn., Wash. Bar Assn., Multnomah Bar Assn., Am. Corp. Counsel Assn. (bd. dirs. N.W. chpt.), Nat. Inst. for Trial Adv. (diplomate 1982). Republican. Presbyterian. Avocations: cross country skiing, reading history, bicycling. Antitrust, Federal civil litigation, General corporate. Office: Freightliner Corp Legal Dept PO Box 3849 Portland OR 97208-3849

**HUREWITZ, PHALEN GILBERT,** lawyer; b. Fall River, Mass., Nov. 25, 1936; s. Samuel and Lillian Hurewitz; m. Renee Rosengarten, June 18, 1961; children: Deborah, Matthew, Daniel. AB magna cum laude, Dartmouth Coll., 1958; LLB, Stanford U., 1961. Bar: Calif. 1962. Clk. to justice Calif. Dist. Ct. Appeal for 1st Dist., awd, 1961-62; assoc. McCarthy & Johnson, San Francisco, 1962-64, Arnold & Gold, Beverly Hills, Calif., 1964-66; ptnr. Cooper, Epstein & Hurewitz, Beverly Hills, Calif., 1966-93, Manatt, Phelps & Phillips, L.A., 1993-97, Isaacman, Kaufman & Painter P.C., Beverly Hills, 1997—; prof. Calif. Coll. Law, 1967-70. Co-founder Widow's Ctr., Temple Isaiah, 1975, Am. Chamber Symphony, 1982; past pres. Temple Isaiah, 1975-76; mem. legal adv. com. Beverly Hills Bd. Edn., 1980-83; bd. dirs., past pres. Alternative Living for Aging; pres. Met. region United Jewish Fund Campaign, 1986-88; bd. dirs. Jewish Fedn. Coun.; pres. Jewish Family Svc., 1991-94, Bur. Jewish Edn., 1994-97; vice chair L.A. County Commn. Children and Families; also bd. mem. numerous other orgns. Mem. ABA, State Bar Calif., Los Angeles County Bar Assn., Beverly Hills Bar Assn., Calif. Copyright Conf., L.A. Copyright Soc. Home: 522 N Alpine Dr Beverly Hills CA 90210-3316 Office: Isaacman Kaufman & Painter 8484 Wilshire Blvd Ste 850 Beverly Hills CA 90211

**HURLEY, DANIEL T. K.,** judge; b. Fitchburg, Mass., Feb. 24, 1943; A.B. cum laude, St. Anselm's Coll., 1964; J.D., George Washington U., 1968. Bar: Fla. 1969, Calif. 1979, D.C. 1969. Asst. county solicitor Palm Beach County (Fla.), 1970-73; exec. asst. state atty. 15th Jud. Circuit Fla., West Palm Beach, 1973-75, judge, 1977-79, 86-94, chief judge, 1988-93; judge Palm Beach County Ct., 1975-77, 4th Dist. Ct. Appeals, Fla., West Palm Beach, 1979-86; U.S. Dist. judge So. Dist. Fla., West Palm Beach, 1994—. Office: US Courthouse 701 Clematis St Rm 352 West Palm Beach FL 33401-5111

**HURLEY, DENIS R.,** federal judge; b. 1937. BS, U. Pa., 1959; MBA, Columbia U., 1962; LLB, Fordham U., 1966. Assoc. Bond, Schoenck and King, Syracuse, N.Y., 1966-68; prin. asst. dist. atty. Dist. Attys. Office, Suffolk County, N.Y., 1968-70; assoc., then ptnr. Pike, Behringer & Hurley (and successor firms), Riverhead, N.Y., 1970-82; judge N.Y. State Family Ct., 1983-87; acting justice N.Y. Supreme Ct., Suffolk County, 1987-88; judge N.Y. State County Ct., Suffolk County, 1988-91; fed. judge U.S. Dist. Ct. (ea. dist.) N.Y., Bklyn., 1991—. Office: US Dist Ct 225 Cadman Plz E Brooklyn NY 11201-1818

**HURLEY, LAWRENCE JOSEPH,** lawyer; b. Plainfield, N.J., Nov. 17, 1946; s. Luke Michael and Gertrude Marie (Bremer) H.; m. Allyson J. Kingsley, May 28, 1977; children: Michael William, Kathryn Elizabeth. BS, U. Dayton, 1969; JD, Cath. U. Am., 1974. Bar: N.J. 1974, U.S. Dist. Ct. N.J., 1974, D.C. 1976, N.Y. 1980, U.S. Ct. Appeals (3rd cir.) 1980, U.S. Dist. Ct. (ea. and so. dists.) N.Y. 1981, U.S. Ct. Appeals (2nd cir.) 1981, U.S. Ct. Appeals (D.C. cir.) 1982. Law clk. Superior Ct. N.J., New Brunswick, 1974-75; assoc. Lynch, Mannion, Lutz & Lewandowski, New Brunswick, 1975-76, Stryker, Tams & Dill, Newark, 1976-79; atty. AT&T Comm., Basking Ridge, N.J., 1979-85; asst. prosecutor in charge of econ. crimes and ofcl. corruption Morris County Prosecutor's Office, Morristown, N.J., 1985-89; ptnr. Voorhees & Acciavatti, Morristown, 1989-91; sr. atty. AT&T, 1991-96; mng. corp. labor and employment counsel Lucent Techs., 1996—. With U.S. Army, 1969-71. Decorated Bronze Star. Mem. ABA (litigation sect. 1976—, labor law sect. 1981-86, criminal law sect. 1985-91, labor law sect. 1991—), N.J. State Bar Assn. (labor law sect. 1981—). Criminal, Labor. Office: Lucent Techs Rm B2D10 283 King George Rd Warren NJ 07059-5134

**HURLOCK, JAMES BICKFORD,** lawyer; b. Chgo., Aug. 7, 1933; s. James Bickford and Elizabeth (Charls) H.; m. Margaret Lyn Holding, July 1, 1961; children: James Bickford III, Burton Charls, Matthew Hunter. AB, Princeton U., 1955; BA, Oxford U., 1957, MA, 1960; JD, Harvard U., 1959. Bar: N.Y. 1960, U.S. Supreme Ct. 1967. Assoc. White & Case, N.Y.C., 1959-66, ptnr., 1967—. Trustee N.Y. Presbyn. Hosp., Parker Sch. Fgn. and Comparative Law, Internat. Devel. Law Inst., Mystic Seaport Mus., Woods Hole Oceanog. Inst. Rhodes scholar, 1955. Mem. ABA, N.Y. State Bar Inst., Am. Law Inst., Am. Assn. Internat. Law. Republican. Episcopalian. Clubs: Links, River, N.Y. Yacht. Antitrust, General corporate, Private international. Home: 46 Byram Dr Greenwich CT 06830-7008 Office: White & Case Bldg Ll 1155 Avenue Of The Americas New York NY 10036-2787

**HURNYAK, CHRISTINA KAISER,** lawyer; b. Noblesville, Ind., Dec. 22, 1949; d. Albert Michar=el and Lois Angie (Gatton) Kaiser; m. Cyril Hurnyak, June 24, 1972. BA cum laude, Wittenberg U., 1972; JD, SUNY-Buffalo, 1979. Bar: N.Y. 1980, Pa. 1996, U.S. Dist. Ct. (we. dist.) Pa. 1998. Mem. support staff McKinsey & Co., Inc., mgmt. cons., Chgo., 1972-75; law clk. Justice Norman J. Wolf, N.Y. Supreme Ct., Buffalo, 1980-81; assoc.

Dempsey & Dempsey, Buffalo, 1979-80, 81-90, Grossman, Levine & Civiletto, Niagara Falls, N.Y., 1990-95, The Tarasi Law Firm, Pitts., 1998—. Mem. ABA, N.Y. State Bar Assn., Allegheny County Bar Assn., Pa. State Bar Assn., Pa. Trial Lawyers Assn. Democrat. Lutheran. Personal injury, Federal civil litigation, State civil litigation. Office: Tarasi Law Firm 510 3rd Ave Pittsburgh PA 15219-2107

**HURSH, JOHN R.,** lawyer; b. Scottsbluff, Nebr., Feb. 16, 1943; s. R. Max and Virginia Hursh; m. Judy Ann Lopez, Mar. 10, 1978; 1 child, Bryan W. BA, U. Wyo., 1965, JD, 1968. BAr: Wyo. 1968, U.S. Dist. Ct. Wyo. 1968, U.S. Ct. Appeals (10th cir.), U.S. Claims Ct., U.S. Supreme Ct. Assoc. atty. Paul Godfrey Law Offices, Cheyenne, Wyo., 1972-73; atty. Ctrl. Wyo. Law Assocs., Riverton, 1973—. Mem. Wyo. State Legislature, Cheyenne, 1974-80. Capt. USMCR, 1968-72. Mem. Wyo Trial Lawyers (pres. 1991-92). Republican. Episcopalian. General civil litigation. Home: 1497 S Hwy 20 Thermopolis WY 82443 Office: Ctrl Wyo Law Assocs 105 S 6th St E Riverton WY 82501-4456

**HURSH, LYNN WILSON,** lawyer; b. Kansas City, Kans., Apr. 24, 1953; s. Frank Whitaker and Mary Alice (Walker) H.; m. Michelle Winter, June 27, 1987. BA, U. Kans., 1975, JD, 1979. Bar: Kans. 1979, Mo. 1989, U.S. Ct. Appeals (10th cir.) 1979, U.S. Dist. Ct. Mo. 1989, U.S. Dist. Ct. Kans. 1979. Assoc. Turner & Boisseau, Great Bend, Kans., 1979-87; ptnr. Armstrong, Teasdale Schlafly, Kansas City, Mo., 1987—. Co-author: Insurance Litigation in Missouri, 1992, Compensation Law in Kansas, 1987. Mem. Mo. Bar Assn., Kans. Bar Assn., Mo. Orgn. Def. Lawyers, Kansas City Claims Assn., Johnson County Bar Assn., Internat. Assn. Defense Counsel. Product liability, Personal injury, Insurance. Office: Armstrong Teasdale Schiafly 2345 Grand Blvd Ste 2000 Kansas City MO 64108-2617

**HURST, CHARLES WILSON,** lawyer; b. Salt Lake City, July 4, 1957; s. John Vann and Myra (Kasik) Piscane; m. Karen Buck, Jan. 5, 1985; children: Jeanette Q., Daniel C., Brian K., Matthew C., Robert W. Student, U. Chgo., 1975-77; BA cum laude, Wesleyan U., Conn., 1979; JD, Duke U., 1983. Bar: Pa. 1983, U.S. Dist. Ct. (ea. dist.) Pa. 1985, Calif. 1986, U.S. Dist. Ct. (cen. dist.) Calif. 1990. Assoc. Saul, Ewing, Remick & Saul, Phila., 1983-85; assoc. Wyman Bautzer Kuchel & Silbert, Orange County, Calif., 1985-89, ptnr., 1990; ptnr. Snell & Wilmer LLP, Orange County, 1990—. Dir. Pacific Art Found., 1994—; trustee Pegasus Sch., 1996—. Mem. ABA (comml. leasing com. of real property, probate and trust law sect.), Orange County Bar Assn. Real property, Contracts commercial, Land use and zoning (including planning). Office: Snell & Wilmer 1920 Main St Ste 1200 Irvine CA 92614-7230

**HURST, MARGARET ANNE,** lawyer; b. Raleigh, N.Y., Dec. 30, 1957; m. William W. and Elizabeth Hurst. BMus, Greensboro Coll., 1979; JD, Wake Forest U., 1982. Bar: Fla., N.Y. Asst. dist. atty. Nassau County Dist. Atty., Mineola, N.Y., 1984-90; pvt. practice Garden City, N.Y., 1990-97; atty. Brady & Hurst, LLP, Westbury, N.Y., 1997—. Republican. United Methodist. Bankruptcy, Non-profit and tax-exempt organizations. Office: Brady & Hurst LLP 900 Merchants Concourse Ste 405 Westbury NY 11590-5114

**HURT, JENNINGS LAVERNE, III,** lawyer; b. Sanford, Fla., Oct. 25, 1952; s. Jennings Laverne Jr. and Virginia (Ludwig) H.; m. Maribeth O'Connor, June 24, 1978; children: Jennings Laverne IV, Matthew Alexander, Natalie Elizabeth, Joseph Connor. AA, Seminole Jr. Coll., 1972; BSBA, U. Fla., 1974; JD with honors, Cumberland Sch. Law, 1977. Bar: Fla. 1977, U.S. Dist. Ct. (mid. dist.) 1978, U.S. Dist. Ct. (no. and so. dists.) Fla. 1982, U.S. Ct. Appeals (11th cir.) 1988; cert. trial lawyer Nat. Bd. Trial Advocacy. Assoc. D'Aiuto, Walker & Buckmaster, P.A., Orlando, Fla., 1977-79; ptnr. Anderson & Hurt, P.A., Orlando, 1979-87; mng. ptnr. Rissman, Weisberg, Barrett & Hurt, P.A., Orlando, 1987—. Contbr. articles to profl. jours. Recipient Am. Jurisprudence award, 1974. Mem. ABA, Orange County Bar Assn., Fla. Bar Assn. (bd. cert. trial lawyer), Assn. Trial lawyers Am., Fla. Def. Lawyers Assn., Def. Rsch. Inst., Cen. Fla. Med. Malpractice Claims Assn. (treas. 1992-95). Republican. Roman Catholic. Avocations: golf, tennis. Personal injury, Insurance, General civil litigation. Home: 1655 Barcelona Way Winter Park FL 32789-5614 Office: Rissman Weisberg Barrett & Hurt PA 201 E Pine St Fl 15 Orlando FL 32801-2738

**HURWITZ, BARRETT ALAN,** lawyer; b. New Bedford, Mass., Dec. 9, 1948; s. Harold and Claire (Wollison) H. BA, Colby Coll., 1970; JD, Suffolk U., 1973. Bar: Mass. 1973, U.S. Dist. Ct. Mass. 1974. Intern U.S. Atty.'s Office, Boston, 1972-73; ptnr. Hurwitz and Hurwitz, New Bedford, 1973-97, owner, 1997—. Author weekly newspaper column: The Legal Forum, 1982-84. Bd. dirs. New Bedford Legal Aid Soc., 1976—. Recipient Achievement award in oral advocacy Suffolk U. Law Sch., 1971, Achievement award in brief writing, 1971, Excellence award in corps. Am. Jurisprudence, 1973. Mem. New Bedford Bar Assn. (bar coun. 1975-82, pres. 1982-84), Bristol County Bar Assn. (bd. dirs. 1982-84), Mass. Bar Assn. General practice, General corporate, Probate. Home: 74 William St South Dartmouth MA 02748-3703 Office: Hurwitz and Hurwitz 888 Purchase St New Bedford MA 02740-6217

**HURWITZ, IRVING LEONARD,** lawyer; b. Boston, Feb. 25, 1941; s. Saul and Pauline Josephine (Goldin) H.; m. Barbara Ruth Sidel, Aug. 14, 1966; children: Cheryl, Jeffrey. BA, U. Mass., 1963; LLB cum laude, Boston U., 1966; LLM, N.Y.U., 1967. Bar: Mass. 1966, N.J. 1973, U.S. Dist. Ct. (no. dist.) N.J. 1973, U.S. Ct. Appeals (3d cir.) 1989, U.S. Ct. Appeals (D.C. cir.) 1993, U.S. Supreme Ct. 1991. Atty. Nat. Labor Relations Bd., Buffalo, 1967-72; ptnr. Carpenter, Bennet and Morrissey, Newark, 1973—. Author, editor: Boston U. Law Review, 1965-66. V.p. Matawan-Aberdeen Regional Bd. Edn., 1984-85, pres. 1985-87. Mem. ABA, N.J. Bar Assn., Essex County Bar Assn. (dist. ethics com. 1987-91), Assn. Fed. Bar of the State N.J. Labor. Home: 39 Poet Dr Matawan NJ 07747-3414 Office: Carpenter Bennett & Morrissey Gateway 3 100 Mulberry St Newark NJ 07102

**HURWITZ, JOEL MICHAEL,** lawyer; b. Lancaster, Pa., May 25, 1951; s. Leon Arnold and Helen (Lubit) H.; m. Jill Rosenheim, July 10, 1983; children: Jacqueline, Michael. BA, U. Pitts., 1973; MBA in Corp. Fin., U. Chgo., 1975, JD, 1976. Bar: Ill., 1976. Lawyer law divsn. The First Nat. Bank of Chgo., 1976-77; shareholder Lurie, Sklar & Simon, Ltd., Chgo., 1977-87; ptnr. Neal, Gerber & Eisenberg, Chgo., 1987—; instr. real estate law Chgo.-Kent Law Sch., 1980-81; dir. Capitol Analysts Network, Inc., Bethesda, Md., 1997—. Dir. Jewish Vocat. Svcs., Chgo., 1987-94; bd. dirs. Lawyers Com. for Better Housing, Chgo., 1978-81, Anti-Defamation League, 1992—, civil rights com., 1995; co-chair Chgo./Wis. region Assoc. Nat. Commrs., 1998—; co-chair, bd. dirs. Midwest civil rights com., 1995—; head coach Am. Youth Soccer Orgn., Highland Park, Ill., 1995-97. Mem. U. Pitts.-Pitt. Club of Chgo. (exec. com., chmn. Midwest scholarship 1994-98), Std. Club. Avocations: golf, art collecting, coin collecting, investment. Banking, General corporate, Real property. Office: Neal Gerber & Eisenberg Two N La Salle St Chicago IL 60602

**HURWITZ, MICHAEL A.,** lawyer; married. JD, Hastings Coll. of Law, 1980. Prin. Law Office of Michael A. Hurwitz, San Jose, Calif., 1980—. Mem. ABA, Calif. Bar, Santa Clara Bar Assn. Personal injury, Health, Alternative dispute resolution. Office: 2 N Market St Ste 444 San Jose CA 95113-1211 also: PO Box 90036 San Jose CA 95109-3036

**HURYN, CHRISTOPHER MICHAEL,** lawyer; b. Akron, Ohio, June 1, 1967; s. Michael Alexander and Eileen Ruth (McFadden) H.; m. Leslie Marie Vitale, Oct. 9, 1993; 1 child, Samuel. BS in Bus., Miami U., Oxford, Ohio, 1989; JD, U. Akron, 1993. Bar: Ohio 1993, U.S. Dist. Ct. (no. dist.) Ohio 1994, U.S. Ct. Appeals (6th cir.) 1994. Jud. law clk. to Hon. Frank J. Bayer, Summit County Ct. Common Pleans, Akron, 1990-93; assoc. Tzangas, Plakas, Mannos & Recupero, Canton, Ohio, 1993—. Dean's Club scholar, Sch. Law scholar and Judge and Mrs. Charles Sacks scholar U. Akron Sch. Law, 1992-93. Mem. Ohio Bar Assn., Ohio Acad. Trial Lawyers, Stark County Acad. Trial Lawyes (trustee 1997). Personal injury. Office: Tzangas Plakas Mannos Et Al 454 Citizens Bldg Canton OH 44702

**HUSIC, YVONNE M.,** lawyer; b. Harrisburg, Pa.; d. Anthony J. and Catherine M. Husic. BA, Temple U., 1977; MS, Shippensburg (Pa.) U., 1980; JD, Widener U., 1994. Bar: Pa. 1994, U.S. Dist. Ct. (mid. dist.) Pa. 1997, U.S. Ct. Appeals (3d cir.) 1998. Case mgmt. supr. Cumberland/Perry, Carlisle, Pa., 1980-83; dir. advocacy The Arc of Pa., Harrisburg, 1983-97; atty. Law Offices of Nicholas & Foreman, P.C., Harrisburg, 1995—. Mem. ATLA, Pa. Bar Assn., Dauphin County Bar Assn., Nat. Bar Assn. Avocations: rollerblading, cycling, skiing, boating. Education and schools, General civil litigation, Civil rights. Office: 4409 N Front St Harrisburg PA 17110-1709

**HUSICK, LAWRENCE ALAN,** lawyer; b. Bklyn., Feb. 15, 1958; s. Charles Bernard and Babette Ann (Kraus) H.; m. Margaret Levy, Aug. 23, 1987; children: Andrew Jacob, Carly Elizabeth. BSc cum laude, Muhlenberg Coll., 1980; JD, Washington Coll. of Law, 1983. Bar: Pa. 1983, U.S. Dist. Ct. (ea. dist.) Pa. 1983, U.S. Ct. Appeals (3d cir.) 1989, U.S. Ct. Appeals (fed. cir.) 1990. Chemist Air Products and Chem. Inc., Allentown, Pa., 1979-80; cons. Hilton-Alan Assoc., Chevy Chase, Md., 1980-83; assoc. Ratner & Prestia, Valley Forge, Pa., 1983-88; head intellectual property dept. Dilworth, Paxson, Kalish & Kauffman, Phila., 1988-91; sole practitioner Southeastern, Pa., 1991-95; ptnr. Lipton, Weinberger & Husick, Malvern, Pa., 1995—; co-founder, prin. Informatics, Inc., Wayne, Pa., 1992—; mem. adv. com. for patents, Washington, 1987-91. Pres. Helen Beebe Speech and Hearning Ctr., Easton, Pa., 1989-92. Recipient Advocacy award Assn. Trial Lawyers Am., 1983. Avocations: computing, sailing. E-mail: Lawrence@LawHusick.com. Patent, Trademark and copyright, Federal civil litigation. Office: PO Box 587 Southeastern PA 19399-0587

**HUSKINS, MICHAEL LOUIS,** lawyer; b. Lincoln, Nebr., Feb. 27, 1970; s. Louis Anthony and Gail Hartmann Huskins; m. Priya S. Cherian, Aug. 8, 1998. AB cum laude, Princeton U., 1992; JD cum laude, U. Chgo., 1996. Bar: Calif. 1998. Jud. clk. judge Frank Magill U.S. Ct. Appeals (8th cir.), Fargo, N.D., 1996-97; assoc. Wilson, Sonsini, Goodrich & Rosati, Palo Alto, Calif., 1997—. Avocations: music, hiking, fitness. General corporate, Securities. Office: Wilson Sonsini Goodrich & Rosati 650 Page Mill Rd Palo Alto CA 94304-1050

**HUST, BRUCE KEVIN,** lawyer; b. Cin., Aug. 16, 1957; s. George Julius and Shirley Mae (Glaser) H. BA, U. Cin., 1979; JD, No. Ky. U., 1985. Bar: Ohio 1986, U.S. Dist. Ct. (so. dist.) Ohio 1987. Pvt. practice Cin., 1986-99; trial counsel Hamilton County Pub. Defender's Office, Cin., 1988—; assoc. Wm. Eric Minamyer Esq. Co., LPA, Cin., 1999—. Vol. Lawyers for Poor, Cin., 1986-87, 90—; precinct exec. mem. Hamilton County Rep. Ctrl. Com., 1988—. With Ohio Naval Militia, 1988-94; journalist USNR, 1994—. Mem. Ohio State Bar Assn., Cin. Bar Assn., Ohio Assn. Criminal Def. Lawyers, Masons, Odd Fellows. Mem. United Ch. of Christ. Avocations: reading, current events, politics, writing and performing comedy. Criminal, Appellate, General practice. Home: 4247 Delridge Dr Cincinnati OH 45205-2025 Office: Pub Defender's Office Wm Howard Taft Law Ctr 230 E 9th St Fl 2D Cincinnati OH 45202-2174

**HUSTON, BARRY SCOTT,** lawyer; b. Bronx, N.Y., July 17, 1946; s. Irving and Estelle Huston; m. Audrey Jill Kimmel, Mar. 29, 1970; children: Jared, Brett. BA, CUNY, 1969; JD, Bklyn. Law Sch., 1972. Bar: N.Y. 1973, U.S. Dist. Ct. (ea. and so. dists.) N.Y. 1975, U.S. Ct. Appeals (2d cir.) 1975, U.S. Tax Ct. 1978, U.S. Supreme Ct. 1978. Assoc. Dreyer & Traub, N.Y.C., 1972-75, Reich & Reich, N.Y.C., 1975-77; pvt. practice N.Y.C., 1977-80, Gt. Neck, N.Y., 1985-87; sr. ptnr. Arenstein & Huston, PC, N.Y.C., 1980-85; ptnr. Edelman & Edelman, PC, N.Y.C., 1987-94, Baron & Kesel, PC, Kew Gardens, N.Y., 1994; sr. trial atty. Schneider Kleinick Weitz Damashek & Shoot, N.Y.C., 1994-97; sr. ptnr. Huston & Schuller, PC, N.Y.C., 1997—. Pres. Roslyn (N.Y.) Pines Civic Assn., 1983-85; bd. dirs. Sid Jacobson Jewish Cmty. Ctr., East Hills, N.Y., 1989—. Mem. Penn Club N.Y.C. Avocations: golf, travel, reading. Personal injury, Health, Entertainment. Home: 20 Melby Ln Roslyn NY 11576-2519 Office: Huston & Schuller PC 470 Park Ave S New York NY 10016-6819

**HUSTON, GARY WILLIAM,** lawyer; b. Velasco, Tex., Aug. 25, 1953; s. Robert Frank and Gloria Esther Marie Huston; m. Mary Ellen Meyer, May 28, 1977; children: Kyle Patrick, Megan Emily. BA, La. State U., 1974; JD, U. Va., 1978; LLM, U. Fla., 1994. Bar: Mo. 1978, U.S. Dist. Ct. (we. dist.) Mo. 1978, Fla. 1995; cert. tax lawyer and wills, trusts and estates, Fla. Bd. Legal Specialization and Edn. Assoc. Smith Gill Fisher Butts, Kansas City, Mo., 1978-79; ptnr. Grier & Swartzman, Kansas City, 1979-89; of counsel Armstrong, Teasdale, Kansas City, 1989-93; atty. Beggs & Lane, Pensacola, Fla., 1994-99, Clark, Partington, Hart, Larry, Bond, Stackhouse & Stone, Pensacola, 1999—. Atty. Greater Escambia Cmty. Found., Pensacola, 1995-97. Top 100 scholar La State U. Alumni Fedn., 1971-74, scholar Sigma Nu Ednl. Found., 1975-76. Mem. Pensacola Estate Planning Coun. (bd. dirs. 1997—). Lutheran. Avocations: golf, running, fishing. Taxation, general, Estate planning, General corporate. Office: Clark Partington Hart Larry Bond Stackhouse & Stone 125 W Romana St Ste 800 Pensacola FL 32501-5856

**HUSTON, KENNETH DALE,** lawyer; b. Watsonville, Calif., Aug. 2, 1936; s. Charles Edward Huston and Chauncey Elfie (Bivens) Stephen; m. Janet Joyce Markarian, Dec. 31, 1971; children: Jennifer, Brian. Student, U. Okla., 1954-56, U. Utah, 1958-60; BA in Engring. and Math., San Diego State U., 1972; JD, U. San Diego, 1979. Bar: Calif. 1979, U.S. Dist. Ct. (so. dist.) Calif. 1979. Assoc. Higgs, Fletcher & Mack, San Diego, 1980-88; dir. Grace, Neumeyer & Otto, L.A. and San Diego, 1988-89; dir., shareholder Grace, Scocypek, Cosgrove & Schirm, L.A. and San Diego, 1989-94; ptnr. Lewis, D'Amato, Brisbois & Bisgaard, San Diego, 1994—; judge pro-tem San Diego Mcpl. Ct. South Bay, Chula Vista, Calif., 1988—. Author: Defending Claimed Mild Brain Injury Cases. With USN, 1956-78. Mem. Def. Rsch. Inst., Soc. Automotive Engrs., Calif. State Bar, San Diego Def. Lawyers. Republican. Product liability, Personal injury, Insurance. Office: Lewis D'Amato Brisbois & Bisgaard 550 W C St Ste 800 San Diego CA 92101-3573

**HUSTON, STEVEN CRAIG,** lawyer; b. Morris, Ill., June 3, 1954; s. Raymond P. and Evelyn M. (Bass) H. BA, Ill. Coll., 1977; JD, John Marshall Law Sch., 1980; MBA, Northwestern U., 1989. Bar: Ill. 1980, U.S. Dist. Ct. (no. dist.) Ill. 1980, U.S. Ct. Appeals (7th cir.) 1980. Assoc. Siegel, Denberg et al, Chgo., 1980-83; staff atty. Wm. Wrigley Jr. Co., Chgo., 1983-84; asst. sec. legal William Wrigley Jr. Co., Chgo., 1984-94, asst. v.p. legal, 1994-96, counsel North Am., 1996—. Mem. ABA, Chgo. Bar Assn. General corporate, Trademark and copyright, Securities. Office: Wm Wrigley Jr Co 410 N Michigan Ave Chicago IL 60611-4213

**HUSZAGH, FREDRICK WICKETT,** lawyer, educator, information management company executive; b. Evanston, Ill., July 20, 1937; s. Rudolph LeRoy and Dorothea (Wickett) H.; m. Sandra McRae, Apr. 4, 1959; children: Floyd McRae, Fredrick Wickett II, Theodore Wickett II. B.A., Northwestern U., 1958; J.D., U. Chgo., 1962, LL.M., 1963, J.S.D., 1964. Bar: Ill. 1962, U.S. Dist. Ct. D.C. 1965, U.S. Supreme Ct. 1966. Market researcher Leo Burnett Co. Chgo., 1958-59; internat. atty. COMSAT, Washington, 1964-67; assoc. Debevoise & Liberman, Washington, 1967-68; asst. prof. law Am. U., Washington, 1968-71; program dir. NSF, Washington, 1971-73; assoc. prof. U. Mont., Missoula, 1973-76, U. Wis.-Madison, 1976-77; exec. dir. Dean Rusk Ctr., U. Ga., Athens, 1977-82; prof. U. Ga., 1982—; chmn. TWH Corp., Athens, 1982—; chmn. Profession Mgmt. Techs., Inc., Athens, 1993-96; cons. TWH Scv. Corp.; cons. Pres. Johnson's Telecommunications Task Force, Washington, 1967-68; co-chmn. Nat. Gov.'s Internat. Trade Staff Commn., Washington, 1979- 81. Author: International Decision-Making Process, 1964; Comparative Facts on Canada, Mexico and U.S., 1979; also articles. Editor Rusk Ctr. Briefings, 1981-82. Mem. Econ. Policy Council, N.Y.C., 1981-89. NSF grantee, 1974-78. Republican. Presbyterian. Home: 151 E Clayton St Athens GA 30601-2702 Office: U Ga Law Sch Athens GA 30602

**HUSZAR, ARLENE CELIA,** lawyer, mediator; b. N.Y.C., May 1, 1952; d. Charles and Dora (Toffoli) H.; m. Victor M. Yellen, May 6, 1978; 1 child: Mariette Huszar Yellen. BA, Fla. Atlantic U., 1973; JD, U. Fla., 1976. Bar: Fla. 1977, U.S. Dist. Ct. (mid. and no. dists.) Fla. 1978, U.S. Ct. Appeals (5th and 11th cirs.) 1978, D.C. 1979, U.S. Supreme Ct. 1982; cert. fed. and cir. ct. mediator, arbitrator. Pvt. practice Gainesville, Fla., 1977-80; mng. atty. Fla. Instl. Legal Svcs., Gainesville, 1980—. Author: (with others) Adoption, 1992, Termination of Parental Rights, 1997. Mem. City of Gainesville Citizens Adv. Com. for Cmty. Devel., 1976-79, Fla. Bar Com. on the Legal Needs of Children, 1984-85; mem. steering com. juvenile law sect. Nat. Legal Aid and Defender Assn., 1986-87; vice chmn. Alachua County Citizens Adv. Com., Dept. Criminal Justice Svcs., 1986-95; precinct committeewoman Alachua County Dem. Exec. Com., 1986-96; Queen of Peach parish coun. (sec. 1995-97, pres. 1998). Named one of Outstanding Young Women of Am., 1975. Mem. ATLA, Nat. Assn. Counsel for Children, Eighth Jud. Cir. Bar Assn. (bd. dirs. 1994—), Fla. Acad. Profl. Mediators, North Ctrl. Fla. Mediation Coun. Roman Catholic. Office: Fla Instl Legal Svcs 1110 NW 8th Ave Ste C Gainesville FL 32601-4969

**HUTCHENS, CHARLES KENNETH,** lawyer, environmental consultant; b. Oil Dale, Calif., Oct. 9, 1947; s. Charley H. and Marjorie E. (Speares) H.; m. Yolanda M. Vercher, Aug. 9, 1991; 1 child, Casey Harrington. BA, U. Southern Colo., Pueblo, 1969; JD, U. Colo., Boulder, 1972. Bar: Colo. 1973, U.S. Dist. Ct. Colo. 1973, La. 1980, U.S. Dist. Ct. (we. & ea. dists.) La. 1980, U.S. Supreme Ct. 1985, U.S. Ct. Appeals (5th cir.) 1986. Intern U.S. Senate, Washington, 1968; sole practitioner Boulder, 1973-75; exec. dir. Counsel on Environment, Lafayette, La., 1975-78; sole practitioner Lafayette, 1980—; cons. U.S. EPA, 1978; speaker in field. Mem. Gov.'s Adv. Task Force on Environment, Baton Rouge, 1992, La. Dept. Environ. Quality Citizens Adv. Com., 1984-88; mem. steering com. Southwestern U.S. Environ. Leaders Conf., Atlanta, 1977; tech. advisor Vermilion Devel. Dist., 1985-87; chmn. State Conf. on Water Quality & Citizen Action, Baton Rouge, 1977; task force mem., subcom. chmn. La.: Priorities for the Future, 1977; bd. dirs. Downtown Lafayette Unltd., 1985-87, Environ. & Occupational Med. Rsch. Inst., Lafayette, 1990-92, affiliate, 1990-92; incident comdr. Hazardous Waste Ops. and Emergency Response, 1991. Named Outstanding Young Man Am. U.S. Jaycees, 1979. Mem. ABA, Assn. Trial Lawyers Am., La. Trial Lawyers Assn., Lafayette Parish Trial Lawyers Assn., Lafayette Trial Lawyers Assn. Avocations: fishing, reading, cooking. Environmental, Personal injury. Office: 802 Johnston St Lafayette LA 70501-7902

**HUTCHESON, J(AMES) STERLING,** lawyer; b. Nanking, China, Oct. 17, 1919; s. Allen Carrington and Strausie (McCaslin) H.; m. Marilyn Brown, Dec. 26, 1944; children—James Sterling, Holly Hutcheson Jasperson, Joanne Hutcheson Denton, Scott Brown, Allen McCaslin. B.A., Princeton U., 1941; LL.B., Stanford U., 1949. Bar: Calif. 1949, U.S. Dist. Ct. (no. dist.) Calif. 1949, U.S. Ct. Apls. (9th cir.) 1949, U.S. Dist. Ct. (so. dist.) Calif. 1950, U.S. Ct. Mil. Appeals 1955, Clk. jud. com. Calif. State Assembly, 1949; assoc., then ptnr. Gray, Cary, Ames & Frye, San Diego, 1950-93; ptnr. emeritus Gray, Cary Ware & Freidenrich, 1994—. Mem. San Diego City Traffic Commn.; bd. dirs. San Diego County Hosp. and Health Facility Planning Commn.; trustee Francis Parker Sch., San Diego, 1956-59, pres. bd., 1957-58; trustee La Jolla (Calif.) Country Day Sch., 1956-59. Served to comdr. USNR, 1941-45. Mem. Internat. Assn. Def. Counsel (state editor 1958, 61-63, 66-67, chmn. legal malpractice subcom. 1962, exec. com. 1976-79), State Bar Calif. (lectr. continuing edn. bar 1960, 63, mem. disciplinary bd. 1973-77, referee rev. bd. 1979-83, client security fund 1977-78), San Diego County Barristers, San Diego County Bar Assn. (sec. 1963-64, v.p. 1964-65, chmn. med. legal com. 1961-62), Am. Bd. Trial Advs., Assn. So. Calif. Def. Counsel (dir. 1974-76), Southwestern Legal Found. (lectr. 1963), Am. Coll. Trial Lawyers, Def. Research Inst. (regional v.p. Pacific 1971-74), Navy League, Phi Alpha Delta. Republican. Presbyterian. Club: Princeton of San Diego (pres. 1955-71). General civil litigation, Insurance, Professional liability. Home: 7784 Hillside Dr La Jolla CA 92037-3944 Office: Gray Cary Ware & Freidenrich 401 B St Ste 1700 San Diego CA 92101-4240

**HUTCHESON, MARK ANDREW,** lawyer; b. Phila., Mar. 29, 1942; s. John R. and Mary Helen (Willis) H.; m. Julie A. Olander, June 13, 1964; children: Kirsten Elizabeth, Mark Andrew II, Megan Ann. BA, U. Puget Sound, 1964; LLB, U. Wash., 1967. Bar: Wash. 1967, U.S. Dist. Ct. (we. and ea. dists.) Wash., U.S. Ct. Appeals (9th cir.), U.S. Supreme Ct. Staff counsel Com. on Commerce U.S. Senate, Washington, 1967-68; assoc. Davis Wright Tremaine, Seattle, 1968-72; ptnr. Davis, Wright Tremaine, Seattle, 1973—; mng. ptnr., chief exec. officer Davis Wright Tremaine, Seattle, 1989-94; chmn. Davis, Wright Tremaine, Seattle, 1994—; mem., co-founder labor law com. Nat. Banking Industry, 1984—. Co-author: Employer's Guide to Strike Planning and Prevention, 1986; contbr. articles to profl. jours. Pres., trustee Virginia Mason Hosp., Seattle, 1980—, Overlake Sch., Redmond, Wash., 1984-89, Epiphany Sch., Seattle, 1982-84, Legal Aid for Wash. Fund, 1991—; bd. dirs. Vis. Nurse Svcs., Seattle-King County, 1985-88; trustee Pacific N.W. Ballet, 1991—, Pacific N.W. Assn. Ind. Schs., 1996-98. Nelson T. Hartson scholar U. Wash., 1966; Deerfield fellow Heritage Found., Deerfield, Mass., 1963. Mem. ABA (health care forum, employment law sect.), Seattle-King County Bar Assn. (employment law sect.), Am. Acad. Hosp. Attys., Am. Hosp. Assn. (labor rels. adv. com. 1978—), Coll. Labor and Employment Lawyers, Greater Seattle C. of C. (bd. dirs. 1991-94), Rainier Club, Seattle Tennis Club, Univ. Club, Order of Coif. Episcopalian. Avocations: sailing, tennis, skiing, reading, travel. Labor, Health. Office: Davis Wright Tremaine 2600 Century Sq 1501 4th Ave Ste 2600 Seattle WA 98101-1688

**HUTCHINS, ROBERT BRUCE,** lawyer; b. Audubon, Iowa, Nov. 22, 1953; s. Leslie D. and Carma I. (Hogueisson) H.; m. Marla A. Nelson, Aug. 20, 1988; 1 child, Grant N. BA, Yale U., 1975; JD, UCLA, 1988. Bar: Calif. 1988, U.S. Dist. Ct. (ctrl. dist.) Calif. 1989, U.S. Dist. Ct. (so. dist.) Calif. 1992, U.S. Tax Ct. 1990, U.S. Ct. Appeal (9th cir.) 1992. Asst. editor Anchor Press/Doubleday, N.Y.C., 1976-79; editor Facts on File, N.Y.C., 1979-82; atty. Jeffer, Mangels, Butler & Marmaro, L.A., 1988—. Mem. ABA, State Bar Calif., Los Angeles County Bar Assn., Assn. Bus. Trial Lawyers. Democrat. General civil litigation, State civil litigation, Federal civil litigation. Office: Jeffer Mangels Butler & Marmaro 2121 Avenue Of The Stars Los Angeles CA 90067-5010

**HUTCHINSON, STEPHEN ALOYSIUS,** lawyer; b. Indpls., Nov. 12, 1940; s. Thomas Eugene and Rose Elizabeth (Adams) H.; m. Kathryn Lucille Martin, Sept. 10, 1966; children: Mark Stephen, Scott Martin, Sarah Kathryn. BS, BA, Oreg. State U., 1963; postgrad., U. Pavia, Italy; JD, U. Oreg., 1967. Bar: Oreg. 1967, U.S. Dist. Ct. Oreg. 1968, U.S. Ct. Appeals (9th cir.) 1988. Dep. dist. atty. Lane County Dist. Atty. Office, Eugene, Oreg., 1967-70; ptnr. Hutchinson, Harrell, Cox & Teising and predecessor firms, Eugene, 1970-81, Hutchinson, Anderson, Cox, Coons & DuPriest P.C., Eugene, 1981—; adj. prof. law U. Oreg., Eugene, 1985-88; judge pro tem Lane County Dist. Ct., Eugene, Marion County Dist. Ct., Salem; city atty. pro tem, Eugene and Springfield (Oreg.) Mcpl. Cts. Contbr. articles to Advising Oreg. Bus., rev., 1980, Labor Law--Law Rev., 1966. Pres. O'Hara Sch. Found., Eugene, 1980-82; gen. counsel Western Rivers council Girl Scouts Am., 1983—; chmn. Econ. Lane Coun. Govts., Eugene, 1986; pres. Marist High Sch. Bd., 1992-93. Named Outstanding Citizen Yr., Lane County Coun. Govts., 1986, Outstanding Svc. award Western Rivers coun. Girl Scouts Am., 1994. Mem. Assn. Trial Lawyers Am., Oreg. Bar Assn. (trial counsel 1971-75, editor Practice Mgmt. newsletter 1996—), Oreg. Trial Lawyers Assn., Active 20-30 Club, Rotary (pres. 1995). Democrat. Roman Catholic. Avocations: skiing, golf, jogging. Fax: 541-343-8693. E-mail: stevehutch@haccd.com. Personal injury, General civil litigation, General practice. Office: Hutchinson Anderson Cox Coons & DuPriest PC 200 Forum Bldg 777 High St Eugene OR 97401-2782

**HUTH, LESTER CHARLES,** lawyer; b. Tiffin, Ohio, Nov. 21, 1924. JD, U. Notre Dame, 1951. Bar: Ohio 1954. Pvt. practice, Fostoria, Ohio, 1954-97. Tiffin, Ohio, 1997—; acting mcpl. judge, Fostoria, 1970, city solicitor, 1954-56, 60-64, police prosecutor, 1964-68; magistrate Common Pleas Ct., Seneca County, Ohio, 1995—; legal counsel to St. Wendelin Parish, Fostoria, 1972—, Cmty. Hospice, 1992—; atty. Selective Svc. Bd. Appeals, 1956-75. Clk. city council, Fostoria, 1957-58; sec.-treas. Karrick Sch. Handicapped Children, 1956-77; Cub scoutmaster Boy Scouts Am., 1967-68; adviser to Fostoria Family and Child Service, 1977-83. Recipient Certs. of Appreciation Pres. Lyndon Johnson, 1966, SSS, 1975. Mem. Ohio Bar Assn., Senece County Bar Assn., C. of C. (dir. 1970-71), Fostoria Jaycees (founding pres. 1954), Fostoria A.M. Exchange Club. General practice. Home and Office: 80 Northwood Dr Tiffin OH 44883-1997

**HUTH, WILLIAM EDWARD,** lawyer; b. South Bend, Ind., July 26, 1931; s. Edward Andrew and Margaret Mary (Emonds) H.; m. Mary Pamela Hall, Aug. 11, 1962; children: Katharine Louise, Stephen Edward (dec.), Alan Edward. BS, U. Dayton, 1952; JD, Yale, 1957. Bar: N.Y. 1958, U.S. Dist. Ct. (so. dist.) N.Y. 1959, Mich. 1962, U.S. Dist. Ct. (ea. dist.) Mich. 1962, U.S. Supreme Ct. 1969, Pa. 1975, Conn. 1978. Assoc. Kelley, Drye, Newhall & Maginnes, N.Y.C., 1958-61; group counsel Chrysler Corp., Detroit, 1962-72; ptnr. Ziegler, Dykhouse, Wise & Huth, Detroit, 1973-74; assoc. gen. counsel Westinghouse Electric Corp., Pitts., 1974-76; asst. sec., asst. gen. counsel Combustion Engring., Inc., Stamford, Conn., 1976-90; ptnr. Huth, Grinnell & Flaherty, Stamford, 1991—; adj. prof. law Wayne State U., Detroit, 1969-74. Contbr. articles to profl. publs. 1st lt. AUS, 1952-54. Mem. ABA (antitrust sect., internat. law sect., bus. law sect., intellectual property sect.), Am. Soc. Internat. Law, Am. Arbitration Assn. (Blue Ribbon Panel Arbitrators & Mediators, mem. copr. coun. com.), Inter-Am. Bar Assn., Inter-Pacific Bar Assn., Internat. Bar Assn., Conn. Bar Assn. (chmn. corp. coun. sec. 1991-94), Assn. of Bar of City of N.Y., Westchester-Fairfield Corp. Counsel Assn. (pres. 1987, bd. dirs. 1984-88), U.S. C. of C. (mem. antitrust adv. coun.), Yale Club N.Y.C., N.Y. Yacht Club, The Army and Navy Club (Washington), Indian Harbor Yacht Club (Greenwich), Order of Coif. Roman Catholic. Antitrust, Private international, Contracts commercial. Home: 39 Balmaha Ct Fairfield CT 06432-1173 Office: Huth Grinnell & Flaherty 1055 Washington Blvd Stamford CT 06901-2216

**HUTSON, BENNE COLE,** lawyer; b. Southgate, Mich., Aug. 21, 1957; s. Andrew Woodrow Hutson and Hedzeebenn Bova; m. Martha Dobie Hennessy, Apr. 30, 1983; children: Michael, Kathleen, Patrick, Colleen. BA summa cum laude, Hillsdale Coll., 1979; JD cum laude, Harvard Law Sch., 1982. Assoc. Bricker & Eckler, Columbus, Ohio, 1982-85; ptnr. Smith Helms Mulliss & Moore, Charlotte, 1985—. Mem. ABA, N.C. Bar Assn., Mecklenburg County Bar Assn., Myers Park Country Club.j. Republican. Roman Catholic. Avocations: golf, travel, reading. Environmental. Office: Smith Helms et al PO Box 31247 Charlotte NC 28231-1247

**HUTSON, JEFFREY WOODWARD,** lawyer; b. New London, Conn., July 19, 1941; s. John Jenkins and Kathryn Barbara (Himberg) H.; m. Susan Office, Nov. 25, 1967; children: Elizabeth Kathryn, Anne Louise. AB, U. Mich., 1963, LLB, 1966. Bar: Ohio 1966, Hawaii 1970. Assoc. Lane, Alton & Horst, Columbus, Ohio, 1966-74, ptnr., 1974—. Trustee, vice-chmn. Six Pence Sch., 1983-88; mem. com. creeds and professionalism Ohio Supreme Ct., 1989-90; chair, bd. dirs. Northwest Counseling Svcs., 1990-92; regional v.p. Def. Rsch. Inst, 1991-93. Lt. comdr. USNR, 1967-71. Fellow Am. Coll. Trial Lawyers; mem. ABA, Ohio Bar Assn. (past chmn. litigation sect.), Ohio Assn. Civil Trial Attys. (past pres.), Columbus Bar Assn., Internat. Assn. Def. Counsel, Faculty Def. Coun. Trial Acad., Scioto Country Club, Athletic Club. Avocations: cycling, reading, music. Federal civil litigation, State civil litigation, Construction. Office: Lane Alton & Horst 175 S 3rd St Ste 700 Columbus OH 43215-5100

**HUTT, LAURENCE JEFFREY,** lawyer; b. N.Y.C., Dec. 15, 1950; s. George Joseph and Miriam Martha (Cohen) H.; children: Marcie Arin, Ethan Lance, Amanda Rachel, Denver Allison. BA in History, U. Pa., 1972; JD, Stanford U., 1975. Bar: Calif. 1975, Colo., 1995. Assoc. Kadison, Pfaelzer, Woodard, Quinn & Rossi, L.A., 1976-82, ptnr., 1982-87; shareholder Quinn, Kully and Morrow, L.A., 1987-96; ptnr. Arnold & Porter, L.A., 1996—; judge pro tem L.A. Mcpl. Ctr.; judge pro tem settlement officer L.A. Superior Ct. Mem. State Bar Calif. (mem. exec. com. conf. del. 1992-95, legis. chair and vice chair 1994-95), L.A. County Bar (del. to Calif. State Bar Conv. 1980-92, 97-98, mem. del. exec. com. 1986-92, del. chair 1991-92, state cts. com. 1989-93, vice chair 1989-90, chair superior cts. subcom. 1988-89, Calif. jud. sys. com. 1988-90, liaison bench and bar com. 1988-90), Assn. Bus. Trial Lawyers (L.A. chpt.), Constnl. Rights Found. (high sch. moot ct. scoring att. of coach 1985-90), Order of Coif, Phi Beta Kappa. Avocations: wine tasting, theater, film. General civil litigation, Sports, Real property. Office: Arnold & Porter 777 S Figueroa St Fl 44 Los Angeles CA 90017-5800

**HUTTO, RICHARD JAY,** lawyer; b. Fitzgerald, Ga., Oct. 7, 1952; s. O.J. and Reba Ivalow (Gossett) H.; m. Katherine Anne Johnston, Aug. 3, 1991; children: Katherine Tod, Bradley Martin. BA, U. Ga., 1974; JD, Mercer U., 1984. Bar: Ga., 1984, D.C., 1985. Polit. coord. Jimmy Carter Presdl. Campaign, Atlanta, 1975-76; Carter family appointments sec. The White Ho., Washington, 1977-78; asst. to Lt. Gov. Zell Miller Lt. Gov. Zell Miller, Atlanta, 1978; program coord. White Ho. Conf. on Small Bus., Washington, 1979-80; dir. spl. projects White Ho. Conf. for Children and Youth, Washington, 1980-81; atty. Barrett, Montgomery and Murphy, Washington, 1984-87; v.p. Challenger Ctr. Space Sci. Edn., Alexandria, Va., 1987-89; pvt. practice Alexandria, Va., 1989-93; asst. v.p. devel. Mercer Univ., Macon, Ga., 1995-96. Commr. for Arts, City of Alexandria, 1989-93; mng. dir. The Grand Opera House, Macon, Ga.; Gov.'s appointee Ga. Coun. for Arts, 1995—; chmn., 1997—; bd. dirs. So. Arts Found., 1997—; pres. Macon-Bibb County Convention and Visitors Bur. Mem. Nat. Assembly State Arts Agys. (bd. dirs.), Nat. Dem. Club, Macon C. of C. (bd. dirs.). Episcopalian. Avocations: book collecting, travel. Home: 1269 Jackson Springs Rd Macon GA 31211-1731

**HUTTON, G. THOMPSON,** lawyer; b. Greensboro, N.C., Oct. 1, 1946; s. Charles Coble and Annie (Lee) H.; children: Jason, Jennifer, Logan. BA with honors, U. N.C., 1968; JD, Columbia U., 1971. Bar: N.Y. 1972, U.S. Dist. Ct. (so. dist.) N.Y. 1976, U.S. Ct. Appeals (2nd cir.) 1976. Assoc. Shea & Gould, N.Y.C., 1971-79, ptnr., 1979-89; founding ptnr. Hutton Ingram, Yuzek Gainen Carroll & Bertolotti, N.Y.C., 1989-99, Law Offices of G. Thompson Hutton, 1999—. Mem. ABA, N.Y. State Bar, Assn. of Bar of City of N.Y., Phi Beta Kappa. General corporate, Securities, Mergers and acquisitions. Office: 250 Park Ave New York NY 10177-0001

**HUTTON, HERBERT J.,** federal judge; b. 1937. AB, Lincoln U., 1959; JD, Temple U., 1962. With Housing and Home Fin. Agy., 1962-64; mem. firm Norris Brown & Hall, 1964-69, Norris, Wells & Neal, 1969-72, Norris & Wells, 1972-76, Simpkins & Tucker, 1977-88; hearing officer Bd. Revision Taxes, Phila., 1982-88; judge U.S. Dist. Ct. (ea. dist.) Pa., Phila., 1988—. Recipient Bd. Dirs. City Trusts' award, 1988. Mem. Phila Bar Assn. (Medal of Svc. 1982), Phila. Bar Found. (trustee), Fed. Judges Assn. Office: US Dist Ct 9614 US Courthouse 601 Market St Philadelphia PA 19106-1713 *Notable cases include: Antinoph, et al. vs. Laverall Reynolds Securities, Inc., et al., U.S. Dist.Ct., ea. dist. Pa., C.A. No. 88-3664, 703 F.Supp. 1185, which involved securities, fraud and breach of contract; Johnson vs. Phila. Electric Co., U.S. Dist.Ct., ea. dist. Pa., C.A. No. 88-0085, which involved civil rights, Title VII Civil Rights Act of 1964 and 42 U.S.C. 1981.*

**HUUSKO, GARY LAWRENCE,** lawyer; b. Ashland, Wis., Mar. 19, 1957; m. Laurie Ann Paulsen, may 30, 1981. BA, U. Minn., Duluth, 1979; JD, William Mitchell Coll. Law, 1983. Bar: Minn. 1983, U.S. Dist. Ct. Minn. 1984, U.S. Tax Ct. 1984, U.S. Ct. Appeals (8th cir.) 1984. Registered patent atty. Atty. London, Anderson, Antolak & Hoeft, Ltd., Apple Valley, Minn. Mem. Capital Facilities Devel. and Fin. Commn. of the Minn. Conf. of the United Meth. Ch.; trustee Minn. United Meth. Found. Mem. Minn. Bar Assn., Dakota County Bar Assn., Dakota County Econ. Devel. Partnership, Minn. Intellectual Property Law Assn., Apple Valley C. of C., Rotary. Republican. Avocations: fly fishing, hockey, tennis, golf, reading. Intellectual property, Patent, Trademark and copyright. Office: 130 Anchor Bank Bldg 14665 Galaxie Ave W Apple Valley MN 55124-4507

**HWANG, MARIAN C.,** lawyer; b. Mineola, N.Y., Sept. 14, 1950; d. John Y. and Betty Hwang; m. Arcangelo M. Tuminelli; 1 child, Catherine. BA, Hofstra U., 1972; postgrad., Brandeis U., 1973; JD, Georgetown U., 1984. Bar: Md. 1984, U.S. Dist. Ct. Md., U.S. Ct. Appeals (4th cir.). Investigator Mass. Commn. Against Discrimination, Boston, 1974-75; equal opportunity specialist EPA, HEW, HHS, Boston and Washington, 1975-82; law clk. to chief judge Robert C. Murphy, Md. Ct. Appeals, Annapolis, 1984-85; assoc. Tydings & Rosenberg, Balt., 1985-87; prin., ptnr. Miles & Stockbridge P.C., Balt., 1987—; mem. inquiry panel Md. Atty. Grievance Commn., Balt., 1997—; lectr. tng. seminars on environ. matters, 1990—. Pres.-elect Network 2000, Inc., Balt., 1997—, also past sec.; bd. girls. Ctrl. Md. coun. Girl Scouts U.S.A., Balt., 1997—. Named One of Top 100 Women, The Daily Record, Balt., 1997, One of Md.'s Top Bus. Women, Balt. mag., 1997. Mem. ABA, Def. Rsch. Inst., Nat. Bar Assn., Md. Bar Assn., Monumental City Bar Assn., ELI, SONREEL (vice chmn.). Avocations: cooking, politics, travel. Environmental. Office: Miles & Stockbridge PC 10 Light St Ste 1100 Baltimore MD 21202-1487

**HWANG, VICTOR W.,** lawyer; b. Baton Rouge, La., May 27, 1971; s. C.J. and Betty W. Hwang. AB with honors, Harvard U., 1993; JD, U. Chgo., 1996. Staff Clinton Presdl. Campaign and Inauguration, Washington, 1995-97; law clk. U.S. AID, Washington, 1997; atty. Mayer, Brown & Platt, L.A., 1997—. Bd. dirs. San Gabriel Valley Habitat for Humanity, San Gabriel, Calif., 1998. Office: Mayer Brown & Platt 3 Embarcadero Ctr San Francisco CA 94111-4003

**HYAMS, HAROLD,** lawyer; b. Bklyn., May 19, 1943; s. Frank Charles and Celia (Silverstein) H.; m. Simone Elkeharrat, Nov. 18, 1973; children: Gabriel, Galite, Emilie, Jonathan. BA, U. Vt., 1965; MA in Latin Am. Studies, Georgetown U., 1966; JD, Syracuse U., 1970. Bar: N.Y. 1971, Ariz. 1974, U.S. Dist. Ct. Ariz. 1974, U.S. Ct. Appeals (9th cir.) 1974. Asst. to the gen. counsel Am. Express Co., N.Y.C., 1970-72; atty. Legal Aid Soc., Bklyn., 1973; ptnr. Harold Hyams and Assocs., Tucson, 1974—; mem. panel of arbitrators Am. Arbitration Assn., N.Y.C., 1971-73. Mem. Commn. on Ariz. Environ., 1988. Mem. Am. Bd. Trial Advs., Ariz. Trial Lawyers Assn., Pima County Bar Assn., Assn. Trial Lawyers Am. (adv. bd. trial advocates 1990, cert. specialist in personal injury and wrongful death 1991). Avocation: travel. Federal civil litigation, Personal injury. Home: 3175 N Elena Maria Tucson AZ 85750-2915 Office: 680 S Craycroft Rd Tucson AZ 85711-7197

**HYATT, DAN RICHARD,** judge; b. Seattle, Nov. 23, 1949; m. Robin L. Hinkle, Dec. 20, 1973 (div. 1988); m. Kathleen Lyons; children: Casey, Dorianne. BA in English, U. Oreg., 1975; JD, Lewis & Clark Coll., Eugene, Oreg., 1978. Bar: Oreg. 1978, U.S. Dist. Ct. Oreg. 1978, U.S. Ct. Mil. Appeals 1984, U.S. Ct. Appeals (9th cir.) 1985, U.S. Ct. Fed. Claims 1986, U.S. Supreme Ct. 1993. Ptnr. Hyatt, Jackson & Vause, Portland, Oreg., 1978-82; sr. def. counsel USN, Guam, 1983-84; spl. asst. U.S. atty. Dept. Justice, Seattle, 1984-85; pvt. practice, Portland, 1985—; lawyer's chair MOMS, Frederick, Md., 1991—; nat. counsel Am. Fighter Aces Assn., Mesa, Ariz., 1994—, Nat. Spiritualist Assn., Lilydale, N.Y., 1990-94. Elder Westminster Presbyn. Ch., Portland, 1986-89. Comdr. USNR, 1984—. Mem. Oreg. State Bar Assn. (counsel to bar-ethics 1993—, chair mil. and vets. sect. 1995—, bd. govs. (ex-officio 1995—), Judge Advocates Assn., Am. Legion, Am. Fighter Aces Mus. Found. (counsel 1994—), False Memory Syndrome Found. Avocations: forensic psychology, carpentry. Office: 522 SW 5th Ave Ste 200 Portland OR 97204-2119

**HYBL, WILLIAM JOSEPH,** lawyer, foundation executive; b. Des Moines, July 16, 1942; s. Joseph A. and Geraldine (Evans) H.; m. Kathleen Horrigan, June 6, 1967; children: William J. Jr., Kyle Horrigan. BA, Colo. Coll., 1964; JD, U. Colo., 1967. Bar: Colo. 1967. Asst. dist. atty. 4th Jud. Dist. El Paso and Teller Counties, 1970-72; pres., dir. Garden City Co., 1973—; dir. Broadmoor Hotel, Inc., 1973—, also vice-chmn., 1987—; chmn., CEO, trustee El Pomar Found., Colorado Springs, Colo., 1973—; pres. U.S. Olympic Com., 1991-92, 96—; vice chair USAA, San Antonio; dir. KN Energy Inc., Lakewood, Colo., FirstBank Holding Co. of Colo., Lakewood; mem. Colo. Ho. Reps., 1972-73; spl. counsel The White House, Washington, 1981. Pres. Air Force Acad. Found.; sec., dir. Nat. Jr. Achievement; vice chmn. bd. U.S. Adv. Commn. on Pub. Diplomacy, 1990-97; civilian aide to sec. of army, 1986—. Capt. U.S. Army, 1967-69. Republican. Real property.

**HYDE, CAROL ANN,** lawyer; b. Detroit, May 20, 1959; m. Sanjay Marc Correa, May 10, 1980; children: Sarah, Kiran. B of Gen. Studies, U. Mich., 1981; JD, Albany Law Sch., 1984. Bar: N.Y. 1985, U.S. Dist. Ct. (no. dist.) N.Y. 1986, U.S. Tax Ct. 1985. Atty. adv. U.S. Tax Ct., Washington, 1984-86; assoc. De Graff, Foy, Conway, Holt-Harris & Mealey, Albany, N.Y., 1986-91; ptnr. Iseman, Cunningham, Riester & Hyde, L.L.P., Albany, N.Y., 1991—. Mem. Nat. Health Lawyers Assn., N.Y. State Bar Assn., Albany County Bar Assn. Health, General corporate, Taxation, general. Office: Iseman Cunningham Riester Hyde LLP 9 Thurlow Ter Albany NY 12203-1005

**HYDE, HOWARD LAURENCE,** lawyer; b. Boston, Sept. 4, 1957; s. Morris Morton and Evelyn Lee (Weinstein) H.; m. Nancy J. Paulu, May 18, 1985; children: Emma Catherine, Benjamin Tuttle. AB, Dartmouth Coll., 1979; JD, Harvard U., 1982. Bar: Mass. 1983, D.C. 1987, U.S. Dist. Ct. Mass. 1984, U.S. Ct. Appeals (1st cir.) 1984. Jud. clk. Minn. Supreme Ct., St. Paul, 1982-83; assoc. Gaston Snow & Ely Bartlett, Boston, 1983-86; assoc. Arnold & Porter, Washington, 1986-91, spl. counsel, 1992—. Mem. ABA (Bus. law sect.). Avocations: fly fishing, canoeing. Banking, Securities, General corporate. Office: Arnold & Porter 555 12th St NW Washington DC 20004-1206

**HYDE, THOMAS D.,** lawyer. Sr. v.p., sec., gen. counsel Raytheon Co., Lexington, Mass. Office: Raytheon Co 141 Spring St Lexington MA 02421-7899

**HYLAND, STEPHEN JAMES,** lawyer; b. Phila., Dec. 12, 1953; s. William F. and Joan E. Hyland. BS, Pa. State U., 1978; JD, South Tex. Coll., 1996. Bar: Tex. 1996, U.S. Dist. Ct. (so. dist.) Tex. 1997, U.S. Dist. Ct. (no. dist.) Tex. 1998. Computer scientist SAIC, McLean, Va., 1983-84, 85-86, San Diego, 1987-88; computer scientist Adasoft, Washington, 1984-85, Alsys, Inc., Irvine, Calif., 1986-87; pres. AdaPWS, Houston, 1988-96; ptnr. Hyland Law Firm, P.C., Houston, 1996—. Mem. ABA, Houston Bar Assn. (chair sect. on computer law 1998—). Democrat. Jewish. Avocations: reading, drawing. Computer, Intellectual property. Office: Hyland Law Firm PC 440 Louisiana St Ste 1515 Houston TX 77002-1691

**HYLTON, MYLES TALBERT,** lawyer; b. Pearisburg, Va., Apr. 22, 1954; s. Joseph Gordon and Ruby Viola (Clarkson) H.; 1 child, Jessica Kathleen. BSME, U. Mich., 1976, MSME, 1978; JD, U. Va., 1983. Bar: Va. 1983, U.S. Ct. Appeals (4th cir.) 1983, U.S. Patent Office 1985. Mech. engr. White Motor Co., New River, Va., 1979-80; atty. Gentry, Locke, Rakes & Moore, Roanoke, Va., 1983-86, Stone & Hamrick, Radford, Va., 1986-89; Haga & Hylton, 1989-90; atty. Pavin, Wilson, Barnett & Hopper, Roanoke, 1990—. Mem. Va. Trial Lawyers, Assn. Trial Lawyers Am., Nat. Assn. Criminal Def. Lawyers, Soc. Automotive Engrs. Republican. Avocations: racquetball, weight lifting, boxing, scuba diving. General civil litigation, Criminal, Personal injury. Home: 1812 Sheffield Rd SW Roanoke VA 24015-3022 Office: Parvin Wilson Barnett & Hopper 23 Franklin Rd SW Roanoke VA 24011

**HYMAN, MICHAEL BRUCE,** lawyer; b. Elgin, Ill., July 26, 1952; s. Robert I. and Ruth (Cohen) H.; m. Leslie Bland, Aug. 14, 1977; children: Rachel Joy, David Adam. BSJ with honors, Northwestern U., 1974, JD, 1977. Bar: Ill. 1977, U.S. Supreme Ct. 1989. Asst. atty. gen. Antitrust div. State of Ill., Chgo., 1977-79; atty. Much Shelist Freed Denenberg Ament & Rubenstein, Chgo., 1979-85, ptnr., 1985—; chmn. panelist various continuing legal edn. seminars. Columnist Editor's Briefcase, CBA Record, 1988-90, 93—, The Red Pencil, 1986-89; contbr. chpt. to book, articles to profl. jours. Trustee North Shore Congregation Israel, Glencoe, 1980-89, 95—, v.p., 1987-89. Mem. ABA (mem. sect. litigation, chmn. antitrust litigation com. 1987-90, editor-in-chief Litigation News 1990-92, mng. editor 1989-90, assoc. editor 1985-89, chmn. monographs and unpub. papers com. 1992-95, task force on civil justice reform 1991-93, editor-in-chief Litigation Docket, 1995—, mem. jud. divsn., lawyers conf., membership com. chair 1999—), Chgo. Bar Assn. (editor-in-chief CBA Record 1988-90, 93—, CBA News 1994-98, bd. mgrs. 1992-94, vice chair class action com. 1999—), Ill. Bar Assn. (rep. on assembly 1986-92, 94-99, antitrust coun. 1981-87, chmn. coun. 1985-86, vice chair, sec., co-editor newsletter 1982-85, chmn. bench and bar sect. coun. 1990-91, professionalism com. 1992-95, chair 1993-94, vice chair ARDC com. 1995-96, chair ARDC com. 1996-97, mem. cable tv com. 1995—, chair 1997-99), Am. Soc. Writers on Legal Subjects (mem., chair book award com. 1997—), others. Jewish. Avocations: books, writing, Abraham Lincoln. Antitrust, Securities, General civil litigation. Office: Much Shelist Freed Denenberg Ament & Rubenstein 200 N La Salle St Ste 2100 Chicago IL 60601-1026

**HYMAN, MONTAGUE ALLAN,** lawyer; b. N.Y.C., Apr. 19, 1941; s. Allan Richard and Lilyan P. (Pollock) H.; m. Susann Podell, Jan. 25, 1965; children—Jeffrie-Anne, Erik. B.A., Syracuse U., 1962; J.D., St. Johns U., 1965. Bar: N.Y. 1965, U.S. Dist. Ct. (so. and ea. dists.) N.Y. 1967, U.S. Supreme Ct. 1973, U.S. Ct. Appeals (2d cir.) 1982. Assoc. Warburton, Hyman, Deeley & Connelly, Mineola, N.Y., 1965-67; ptnr. Hyman & Deeley, Mineola, 1967-69, Koeppel, Hyman, Sommer, Lesnick & Ross, Mineola, 1969-72, Hyman & Hyman, P.C., Garden City, N.Y., 1972-80, Costigan, Hyman, Hyman & Herman, P.C., Mineola, 1980-87, Certilman Haft Balin Buckley Kremer & Hyman, 1987-88, Certilman Balin Adler & Hyman, 1988—; lectr. Hofstra U., Adelphi U., Columbia Appraisal Soc., Practicing Law Inst. Trustee L.I. Jewish Med. Ctr.; chmn. The Rehabilitation Inst.; bd. trustees North Shore L.I. Jewish Health System. Mem. Nassau County Bar Assn., N.Y. State Bar Assn., Inst. Property Taxation. Contbr. articles to profl. jours. Real property, State and local taxation, Federal civil litigation. Office: Certilman Balin Adler & Hyman LLP 90 Merrick Ave East Meadow NY 11554-1571

**HYMAN, ROGER DAVID,** lawyer; b. Oak Ridge, Tenn., Apr. 23, 1957; s. Marshall Leonard and Vera Lorraine (McKinney) H.; m. Elsa Laurencio; 1 child, Cristina Alicia. BA, Vanderbilt U., 1979; JD, U. Tenn., 1984. Clk. Oak Ridge Nat. Lab., 1977-78, 81; air personality, news reporter Stas. WKDA, WKDF, Nashville, 1979; program dir. Sta. WBIR-FM, Knoxville, Tenn., 1979-80; assoc. atty. Hindman & Holt, Attys., Knoxville, Tenn., 1984-85; asst. atty. gen. State of Tenn., Knoxville, 1986-95; with Law Offices of Roger D. Hyman Powell, Tenn., 1995-97; ptnr. Hyman & Carter, Attys., Powell, Tenn., 1997—. Bd. dirs. Knoxville Christian Sch., 1991-93. Democrat. Mem. Ch. of Christ. Home: 2713 Windemere Ln Powell TN 37849-3782 Office: Hyman & Carter PO Box 1304 Powell TN 37849-1304

**HYMEL, L(EZIN) J(OSEPH),** prosecutor; b. Baton Rouge, July 2, 1944; s. Lezin Joseph Sr. and Alma K. Hymel; m. Linda N., Oct. 6, 1973; children: Traci Lyn, Shea Roach Bonaventure, Kimberly Kaye. BS in Geology, La. State U., 1966, JD, 1969. Bar: La., U.S. Dist. Ct. (ea. dist.) La., U.S. Dist. Ct. (mid. dist.) La., U.S. Dist. Ct. (we. dist.) La., U.S. Ct. Appeals (5th cir.). Pvt. practice Baton Rouge, 1969-70; staff atty. Office State Atty. Gen., Baton Rouge, 1970-71, asst. atty. gen., 1972-78, dir. criminal divsn., 1992-93; asst. dist. atty. Office 19 Jud. Dist. Atty., Baton Rouge, 1978-79; city judge Baton Rouge City Ct., 1980-83; state dist. ct. judge criminal divsn. 19th Jud. Dist. Ct, Baton Rouge, 1983-90, state dist. ct. judge civil divsn., 1991-92; U.S. atty. Office U.S. Atty., Dept. Justice, Baton Rouge, 1994—. Office: US Atty Mid Dist La Russell B Long Fed Bldg 777 Florida St Baton Rouge LA 70801-1717*

**HYNES, PATRICIA,** lawyer; b. N.Y.C., Jan. 26, 1942. BA, CUNY, 1963; LLB, Fordham U., 1966. Bar: N.Y. 1966, U.S. Dist. Ct. (so. and ea. dists.) N.Y. 1969, U.S. Ct. Appeals (2d cir.) 1982. Law clk. Hon. Joseph C. Zavatt U.S. Dist. Ct. (ea. dist.) N.Y., 1966-67; asst. U.S. atty. U.S. Dist. Ct. (so. dist.) N.Y., 1967-82, exec. asst. U.S. atty., 1980-82, chief ofcl. corruption and spl. pros. unit, 1978-80, mem. consumer fraud unit, 1971-78, mem. civil divsn., 1967-71; ptnr. Milberg Weiss Bershad Hynes & Lerach LLP, N.Y.C.; adj. prof. law Fordham U., 1978-83; law lectr. Sch. Trial Advocacy Harvard U., 1983; lectr. Practising Law Inst.; mem. criminal justice act peer rev. panel U.S. Dist. Ct. (so. dist.) N.Y., 1982-83, mem. discovery com., 1982-84, mem. civil litig. com., 1983-84, mem. merit selection panel, for N.Y. magistrate judges, 1994—. Mem. Fordham Law Rev., 1964-66; mem. editl. bd. N.Y. Law Jour., 1994—. Mem. Gov.'s Exec. Adv. Com. on Adminstrn. Criminal Justice, 1981-82, N.Y. Gov.'s Commn. on Govt. Integrity, 1987-90; mem. Mayor's Adv. Com. on Jud., 1994—; chairperson N.Y. Regional Consumer Protection Coun., 1971-72. Named one of 50 Top Women Lawyers Nat. Law Jour., 1998. Fellow Am. Coll. Trial Lawyers; mem. ABA (standing com. on fed. jud. 1995—, coun. litig. sect. 1989-92, chair pre-trial practice and discovery com. 1992-94, chair govt. litig. com. litig. sect. 1984-87, chair securities litig. com. 1987-89, criminal justice sect.), Am. Law Inst. (spl. adviser 1995—), Fordham Law Alumni Assn., Assn. of the Bar of the City of N.Y. (del. to ABA, ho. dels. 1990-94, chair fed. cts. com. 1992-95, sec. 1982-84, exec. com. 1984-88, second century com. 1988-92, criminal law com. 1980-84, police law and policy com. 1981-83, consumer affairs com. 1974-78), N.Y. State Bar Assn. (del., ho. dels. 1983-84), Fed. Bar Coun. (v.p. 1990, 96—, treas. 1987-90, trustee 1983-91), N.Y. Coun. Def. Lawyers. Criminal, Securities, General civil litigation. Office: Milberg Weiss Bershad Hynes & Lerach LLP One Pennsylvania Plz New York NY 10119*

**HYNES, TERENCE MICHAEL,** lawyer; b. Jersey City, Mar. 26, 1954; s. Robert Francis and Eleanor (McGuirk) H.; m. Kathryn Wilson, Jan. 25, 1986; children: Shaylyn Michelle, Meaghan Elizabeth, Patrick Francis. BA in Polit. Sci. with highest distinction, Rutgers Coll., 1976; JD, Duke U., 1979. Bar: D.C. 1979, Interstate Commerce Commn. 1979, U.S. Dist. Ct. (D.C. dist.) 1979, U.S. Ct. Appeals (D.C. cir.) 1979, U.S. Ct. Appeals (7th cir.) 1981, U.S. Ct. Appeals (1st and 2d cirs.) 1997. Assoc. Sidley & Austin, Washington, 1979-86, ptnr., 1986—. With comml. practice clinic Duke U. Law Sch., 1983-89; mem. nat. coun. law sch. fund Duke U., 1986-91; mem. Duke Law Sch. Alumni Coun., 1997—. Mem. ABA (pub. utility law sect. 1979—, antitrust law sect. 1979—), Assn. Transp. Law, Logistics and Policy, Duke U. Gen. Alumni Assn. (bd. dirs. 1984-86). Roman Catholic. E-mail: thynes@sidley.com. Administrative and regulatory, Antitrust, Transportation. Office: Sidley & Austin 1722 I St NW Ste 600 Washington DC 20006-3705

**HYTKEN, LOUISE PARKS,** lawyer; b. Toronto, Ont., Can., Feb. 22, 1951; d. Edwin Ketchum and Lucille Mabel (Hansen) Parks; m. Franklin Harris Hytken, Aug. 11, 1979; 1 child, Rachel Lee. BS, U. Ariz., 1972; JD, Ariz. State U., 1976. Bar: Ariz. 1976, Tex. 1979. Atty. tax divsn. U.S. Dept. Justice, Washington, 1976-83; atty. tax divsn. U.S. Dept. Justice, Dallas, 1976-83, atty. in charge, 1984-95, chief tax divsn., 1995—; prin. Hytken & Hytken, Dallas, 1983-84. Fellow Tex. Bar Assn., ABA, Dallas Bar Assn., Dallas Women Lawyers Assn. (pres. 1986-87). Avocations: tennis, golf. Office: Dept Justice Tax Divsn 717 N Harwood St Ste 400 Dallas TX 75201-6598

**IAMELE, RICHARD THOMAS,** law librarian; b. Newark, Jan. 29, 1942; s. Armando Anthony and Evelyn Iamele; m. Marilyn Ann Berutto, Aug. 21, 1965; children: Thomas, Ann Marie. BA, Loyola U., L.A., 1963; MSLS, U. So. Calif., 1967; JD, Southwestern U., L.A., 1976. Bar: Calif. 1977. Cataloger U. So. Calif., L.A., 1967-71; asst. cataloger L.A. County Law Libr., 1971-77, asst. ref. libr., 1977-78, asst. libr., 1978-80, libr. dir., 1980—. Mem. ABA, Am. Assn. Law Librs., Calif. Libr. Assn., So. Calif. Assn. Law Librs., Coun. Calif. County Law Librs. (pres. 1981-82, 88-90). Office: LA County Law Libr 301 W 1st St Los Angeles CA 90012-3140

**IANNACONE, RANDOLPH FRANK,** lawyer; b. Paterson, N.J., Nov. 19, 1953; s. Anthony and Dorothy Mae (Russo) I. BSc in Pharmacy, St. John's U., N.Y.C., 1979; JD, N.Y. Law Sch., 1990. Bar: N.Y. 1990, U.S. Dist. Ct. (no., so. and ea. dists.) N.Y. 1990, U.S. Ct. Appeals (2d cir.) 1990, N.J. 1991, U.S. Dist. Ct. N.J. 1991, U.S. Ct. Appeals (11th cir.) 1993, U.S. Fed. Ct. of Claims, 1995, U.S. Tax Ct. 1995, U.S. Dist. Ct. (we. dist.) N.Y. 1999. Community pharmacist Dan Drug Co., Englewood, N.J., 1979-85; v.p., tech. dir. Reliance Packaging Corp., Paterson, 1985-87; assoc. Bower & Gardner, N.Y.C., 1990-91; with Med. Malpractice Ins. Assn., N.Y.C., 1991-93; pres. Middle Village (N.Y.) Law Assocs., 1993—. Mem. West Paterson (N.J.) Jaycees, 1979-81; mem. Allendale (N.J.) Rep. Party, 1985—. Mem. ABA, N.Y. State Bar Assn., N.Y. County Lawyers (med. malpractice com. 1990—), N.J. Bar Assn., Assn. Trial Lawyers Am., Am. Pharm. Assn. (coord. continuing edn. com. Trenton com. 1979-82). Avocations: computers, golf, photography, music. Personal injury, Insurance, Product liability.

**IANNAZZONE, JOSEPH CHARLES,** judge; b. Camp Kilmer, N.J., Oct. 15, 1954; s. Ralph Louis and Constance Margaret Iannazzone; m. Shirley Angela Williams, July 7, 1990; children: Joseph Adam, Matthew Streicher, Christie Streicher. BS, Ga. Inst. Tech., 1975; JD, Emory U., 1979. Bar: Ga. 1979. Asst. gen. counsel Internat. Ladies' Garment Workers' Union, AFL-CIO, Atlanta, 1979-86; lawyer Lawrenceville, Ga., 1987-95; part-time judge

Magistrate Ct. of Gwinnett County, Lawrenceville, 1988-96, judge, 1997—; officer Ga. Coun. Magistrate Ct. Judges, pres.-elect, 1999, pres. 1999—; dir. Gwinnett County Pro Bono Project, 1990—; mem. Jud. Coun. Ga., 1998—; mem. Ga. Cts. Automation Commn., 1997—. Editor Ga. Magistrate Ct. Newsletter, 1996—; contg. author: Georgia Magistrate Benchbook, 1991—; contbr. aticles to profl. jours. Pres., Flowers Crossing Neighborhood Assn., Lawrenceville, 1998; den leader Boy Scouts Am., Lawrenceville, 1997—. Avocations: fly fishing, backpacking, woodworking, photography. Home: 4015 Vicksburg Dr Lawrenceville GA 30044-5986 Office: Magistrate Ct Gwinnett County 75 Langley Dr Lawrenceville GA 30045-6935

**IANNUZZI, JOHN NICHOLAS,** lawyer, author, educator; b. N.Y.C., May 31, 1935; s. Nicholas Peter and Grace Margaret (Russo) I.; m. Carmen Marina Barrios, Aug. 1979; children: Dana Alejandra, Christina Maria, Nicholas Peter II, Alessandro Luke; children from previous marriage: Andrea Marguerite, Maria Teresa. BS, Fordham U., 1956; JD, N.Y. Law Sch., 1962. Bar: N.Y., U.S. Dist. Ct. (so. and ea. dists.) N.Y. 1964, U.S. Dist. Ct. (no. and we. dists.) N.Y. 1965, U.S. Ct. Appeals (2d cir.) 1965, U.S. Supreme Ct. 1971, U.S. Dist. Ct. Conn. 1978, U.S. Tax Ct. 1978, U.S. Ct. Appeals (5th and 11th cirs.) 1982, U.S. Ct. Appeals (4th cir.) 1988, Wyo. 1994. Assoc. Law Offices of H.H. Lipsig, N.Y.C., 1962, Law Offices of Aaron J. Broder, N.Y.C., 1963; ptnr. Iannuzzi & Iannuzzi, N.Y.C., 1963—; adj. prof. trial advocacy Fordham U. Law Sch. Author: (fiction) What's Happening, 1963, Part 35, 1970, Sicilian Defense, 1974, Courthouse, 1977, J.T., 1984, (non-fiction) Cross-Examination: The Mosaic Art, 1984, Trial Strategy and Psychology, 1992. Mem. ABA, N.Y. County Bar Assn., N.Y. Criminal Bar Assn., Columbian Lawyers Assn., Lipizzan Internat. Fedn. (v.p.). Roman Catholic. Criminal, Federal civil litigation, State civil litigation. Home: 118 Via Settembre, 9 Rome Italy Office: Iannuzzi & Iannuzzi 233 Broadway New York NY 10279-0001 also: 775 Park Ave Huntington NY 11743-3976 also: Front St Millbrook NY 12545 also: 345 Franklin St San Francisco CA 94102-4427 also: Advokatunburo Schumacher, Bunishoferstrasse 51, 8706 Zurich Switzerland also: 1592 Pine Ave W, Montreal, PQ Canada also: 120 Adelaide St W, Toronto, ON Canada H3B 3G3

**IAPOCE, MICHAEL ANTHONY,** lawyer; b. N.Y.C., Sept. 23, 1963; s. John Alfred and Elizabeth (Kaufman) I.; m. Judith Katherine Vizvary, Nov. 19, 1988; children: John Anthony, Samuel Murcer, Maggie Beth. BA, St. Michael's Coll., 1985; JD, Northeastern U., 1990. Bar: Vt. 1991, N.Y. 1993. Customs inspector U.S. Customs Svc., Burlington, Vt., 1992; legal advisor U.S. Customs Svc., St. Albans, Vt., 1992-93; staff atty. Ulster County Dept. Social Svcs., Kingston, N.Y., 1993—; pvt. practice Kingston, N.Y., 1995—. Office: PO Box 3741 Kingston NY 12402-3741

**IATESTA, JOHN MICHAEL,** lawyer; b. Orange, N.J., Dec. 29, 1944; s. Thomas Anthony and Marie Monica I.; m. Paulina Clare Pascuzzi, July 11, 1971. BS magna cum laude, Seton Hall U., 1967, JD cum laude, 1976; MS, Fordham U., 1968; LLM in Corp. Law, NYU, 1986. Bar: N.J. 1976, U.S. Dist. Ct. N.J. 1976, U.S. Ct. Appeals (3d cir.) 1981, N.Y. 1982, U.S. Supreme Ct. 1985. Law sec. to presiding judge appellate div. Superior Ct. N.J., Trenton, 1976-77; assoc. Wilentz, Goldman & Spitzer, Woodbridge, N.J., 1977-81, D'Alessandro, Sussman & Jacovino, Florham Park, N.J., 1981-83; corp. counsel, 1983—, Rhodia Inc., Cranbury, N.J. Recipient Book prize Tchrs. Coll. Columbia U., 1967. Mem. ABA, N.J. Bar Assn., Am. Corp. Counsel Assn., Order of the Cross & Crescent, Delta Epsilon Sigma, Kappa Delta Pi. General corporate, Finance, Real property. Office: Rhodia Inc 259 Prospect Plains Rd Cranbury NJ 08512-3712

**IBANEZ, SILVIA SAFILLE,** lawyer; b. Havana, Cuba, Nov. 3, 1952; d. Eduardo and Alicia (Martin) Safille; m. Juan Antonio Ibáñez, July 5, 1974; children: Juan-Carlos and Cristina (twins); came to U.S., 1961. BBA, U. Miami, Fla., 1973, MS in Acctg., 1974; JD, U. P.R., 1981. Bar: Fla. 1983; CPA, Fla. Auditor, Coopers & Lybrand, Miami, Fla., 1974-75, tax specialist, 1977-81; prof. U. Católica Mad. & Meastra, Santiago, Dominican Republic, 1975-76; tax mgr. Main Hurdman CPAs, St. Petersburg, Fla., 1981-84; fin. planner Interstate Securities Co., Fort Myers, Fla., 1985; fin. cons., Fort Myers, Fla., 1985-87; pvt. practice law, Winter Haven, 1988-93, Orlando, Fla., 1994—. inst. U. Ctrlo. Fla., 1993-97. Vol. guardian ad-litem representing abused/neglected children 20th and 10th Jud. Cir. Ct. Lee, Polk and Orange Counties, 1986—; active Orange County League of Women Voters; former mem. coun. bd. Polk County Children's Svcs. Mem. ABA, AICPA, Fla. Inst. CPAs (Outstanding Grad. 1974), Fla. Bar Assn., Am. Assn. Attys.-CPAs, Orlando Opera Chorus. Democrat. Presbyterian. Avocations: reading, singing, piano, family. Estate planning, Probate, Taxation, general. Office: 7380 Sand Lake Rd Ste 500 Orlando FL 32819-5257

**IBEKWE, EDEBEATU,** lawyer; b. Onitsha, Nigeria, Mar. 25, 1954; came to U.S., 1972; s. Michael Aniemeka and Victoria Ezidilim (Egwuatu) I.; m. Magdalene Nmame Osakwe, 1981 (dec. May 4, 1984); children: Aniemeka, Edebeatu II; m. Ada Esieje Ejikeme, 1989; children: Afamefuna, Odinakaolisa. AB, Miami U., 1976; MBA, U. Santa Clara, 1979; BL, Nigerian Law Sch., 1984; JD, UCLA, 1983. Bar: Calif. 1984, Nigeria 1984. Assoc. Irell & Manella, L.A., 1985-90, ptnr., 1990—; mem. Fin. Lawyers Conf., L.A., 1988—, Calif. State Bar UCC subcom. Dir. Legal Aid L.A., 1993—. Avocations: tennis, golf, soccer, jogging. Banking, Contracts commercial, Real property. Office: Irell and Manella 333 S Hope St Ste 7500 Los Angeles CA 90071-1406

**ICHIKAWA, ROBERT K.,** lawyer; b. Honolulu, Mar. 7, 1962; s. George K. and Judy Ichikawa; m. Grace S. Ichikawa, Mar. 23, 1991; 1 child, Drew K. BS in Acctg./Fin., U. Colo., 1984; JD, U. Santa Clara, 1987. Bar: Hawaii. Assoc. Kobayashi, Watanabe, et al, Honolulu, 1987-90; assoc. Kobayashi, Sugita & Goda, Honolulu, 1990-94, ptnr., 1994—; past pres. Hawaii chpt. Am. Immigration Lawyers Assn., Honolulu, 1996-98. Bd. mem. Na'Ohana Bd., Honolulu, 1998-99. Avocations: golf, school charities. General corporate, Immigration, naturalization, and customs. Office: Kobayashi Sugita & Goda 999 Bishop St Ste 2600 Honolulu HI 96813-4430

**ICHINOSE, SUSAN M.,** lawyer; b. Honolulu, Mar. 5, 1944; d. Eugene T. and Harriet C. (Toi) I.; m. Martin D. Plotnick, Aug. 3, 1983; 1 child, Andrei I. AB, George Washington U., 1968; JD, Richardson Sch. of Law, Honolulu, 1977. Bar: Hawaii 1977, U.S. Dist. Ct. Hawaii 1977, U.S. Ct. Appeals (9th cir.) 1978, U.S. Supreme Ct. 1985. Assoc. Mukai Ichiki Raffetto & MacMillan, Honolulu, 1977-80, ptnr., 1981-84; mng. ptnr. Miller & Ichinose, Honolulu, 1985-91; ptnr. Foley Maehara Judge Nip & Chang, 1991-95; dir. Simons & Ichinose, 1995-99; pres. Hawaii Women Lawyers, 1997-98; pvt. practice, 1999—; mem. State Supreme Ct. Com. on Pattern Civil Jury Instrns., 1990—; mem. nat. panel of arbitrators Am. Arbitration Assn., 1990—; adj. prof. Richardson Sch. of Law, 1985, 87, 91, 93. Commr. Gov.'s Adv. Commn. on Librs., Honolulu, 1982-84; trustee Friends of Libr. of Hawaii, Honolulu, 1984-87. Mem. ABA (labor and employment law com., law office mgmt. com.), Assn. Trial Lawyers Am., Hawaii Bar Assn. Democrat. General civil litigation, Labor, Contracts commercial. Office: 701 Bishop St Honolulu HI 96813-4814

**IDEMAN, JAMES M.,** federal judge; b. Rockford, Ill., Apr. 2, 1931; s. Joseph and Natalie Ideman; m. Gertraud Erika Ideman, June 1, 1971. BA, The Citadel, 1953; JD, U. So. Calif., 1963. Bar: Calif. 1964, U.S. Dist. Ct. (cen. dist.) Calif. 1964, U.S. Ct. Mil. Appeals 1967, U.S. Supreme Ct. 1967. Dep. dist. atty. Los Angeles County, 1964-79; judge Los Angeles County Superior Ct., 1979-84; appointed judge U.S. Dist. Ct. (cen. dist.) Calif., L.A., 1984-98, sr. judge, 1998. Served to 1st lt. U.S. Army, 1953-56, col. AUS Ret. Republican. Office: US Dist Ct 312 N Spring St Los Angeles CA 90012-4701

**IDING, ALLAN EARL,** lawyer; b. Milw., Apr. 29, 1939; s. Earl Herman and Erna Adeline (Albrecht) I.; m. Anne Louise Chaconas, July 9, 1961; children: Kent Earl, Krista Anne Templeman, Bradford A., Andrea Beth Brozynski. BS, Marquette U., 1961, LLB, 1963; DHL (hon.), Nashotah (Wis.) House, 1990. Bar: Wis. 1963, U.S. Dist. Ct. (ea. dist.) Wis. 1963, U.S. Ct. Appeals (7th cir.) 1963. Law clk. U.S. Ct. Appeals (7th cir.), Chgo., 1963-64; assoc. Whyte Hirschboeck Dudek, S.C., Milw., 1964-71, mem., 1971—; bd. dirs. Elicar Corp. Trustee Nashotah House, 1976—; pres., bd. dirs. Wis. DeMolay Found., Milw., 1985—, Wis. Health and Ednl. Facilities Authority, 1978-85, Todd Wehr Found., Inc., Wis. Masonic Home, Inc.; mem. Wauwatosa (Wis.) Police and Fire Commn., 1978-83. Mem. Blue Mound Golf and Country Club (bd. dirs.), Milw. Athletic Club, Masons (grand master Wis. 1981-82). Republican. Episcopalian. Avocation: golf. Estate planning, Probate, General corporate. Home: 9212 Wilson Blvd Milwaukee WI 53226-1729 Office: Whyte & Hirschboeck Dudek SC Ste 2100 111 W Wisconsin Ave Milwaukee WI 53203-2501

**IEYOUB, RICHARD PHILLIP,** state attorney general; b. Lake Charles, La., Aug. 11, 1944; s. Phillip Assad and Virginia Khoury I.; m. Caprice Brown, Feb. 3, 1995; children: Amy Claire, Nicole Anne, Brnnan Jude, Richard Phillip Jr., Khoury Myhand. BA in history, McNeese State U., 1968; JD, La. State U., 1972. Bar: La. 1972, U.S. Supreme Ct. Spl. prosecutor to atty. gen. State of La., Baton Rouge, 1972-74; assoc. Camp, Carmouche, Lake Charles, 1974-76; mem. Stockwell, Sievert, Lake Charles, 1976-78, Baggett, McCall, Singleton, Ranier, Ieyoub, Lake Charles, from 1978; sole practice Lake Charles; dist. atty. Calcasieu Parish, 1985-92; atty. gen. State of La., 1992—; instr. criminal law McNeese State U.; chmn. La. Drug Policy Bd., New Orleans Met. Crime Task Force; mem. La. Commn. on Law Enforcement, President's Commn. on Model State Drug Laws, 1992—; mem. bd. dirs. La. State U. Alumni Assn. Bd. dirs. S.W. La. Health Counseling Svcs., Crime Stoppers of Lake Charles, St. Jude Children's Rsch. Hosp., 1998-99; mem. Parish coun. Immaculate Conception Cathedral Parish, Lake Charles; vice chmn. La. coord. coun. on the prevention of drug abuse and treatment of drug use; mem. La. commn. on law enforcement; apptd. by gov. to adv. bd. La. D.A.R.E.; chmn. New Orleans Metropolitan Crime Task Force, Gov's. Military Adv. Commn. Named Outstanding Pub. Ofcl. for Diocese Lake Charles, 1990; recipient Disting. Alumnus award McNeese State U., 1994, Legis. Leadership award, Nat. Coun. Against Drinking and Driving, 1996, Ochsner Humanitarian award, 1998. Mem. ABA (vice chmn. prosecution function com.), Assn. Trial Lawyers Am., Nat. Assn. Criminal Def. Lawyers, La. Bar Assn. (lectr. criminal law), Nat. Dist. Attys. Assn. (pres., bd. dirs. 1990-91), Nat. Assn. Attys. Gen. (exec. working group on prosecutorial rels.), La. Dist. Attys. Assn. (pres., bd. dirs. 1989-90), Nat. Coll. Dist. Attys. (bd. regents 1991), S.W. La. Bar Assn. (exec. com. 1979), So. Attys. Gen. Assn. (elected chmn.), Sierra Club. Democrat. Roman Catholic. Office: Justice Dept PO Box 94005 Baton Rouge LA 70804-9005

**IGLEHEART, TED LEWIS,** lawyer; b. Shelbyville, Ky., Feb. 17, 1930; s. James Hayden and Mary Gladys Igleheart; m. Elizabeth Ann Craig, Feb. 5, 1956; children: Gladys Woods, Ted L. II, Margaret Sparks. BA, Centre Coll., 1951; LLB, U. Ky., 1957, JD, 1970. Bar: Ky. 1957, U.S. Dist. Ct. (we. dist.) Ky. 1989. Pvt. practice law Shelbyville, 1957—; adminstrv. asst. Gov.'s Office, Frankfort, Ky., 1957-59; atty. Shelby County Suburban Fire Dist., Shelbyville, 1967-87, Shelbyville Water and Sewer Commn., Shelbyville, 1969—; judge City of Shelbyville, 1961-63; county atty. Shelby County, Shelbyville, 1970-78; commonwealth atty. Commonwealth Ky., Shelbyville, 1982-94. Contbr. articles to profl. jours. Pres. Shelby County Hist. Soc., Shelbyville, 1958—; past chmn. bd. Am. Cancer Soc., Ky., 1960—. Cpl. U.S. Army, 1953-55, Korea. Named Outstanding Young Man, Shelbyville Jaycees, 1958. Mem. Ky. Bar Assn., 53rd Jud. Dist. Bar Assn. (sec.), Rotary Club (past pres.), Phi Delta Theta. Democrat. Methodist. Avocations: tennis, golf, fishing, photography, model railroads. General practice. Office: 543 Main St Shelbyville KY 40065-1119

**IHM, STEPHEN LAWRENCE,** lawyer; b. Galena, Ill., Apr. 28, 1962; s. Lawrence Charles Ihm and Elvera Ann Schardt; m. Terry Lee Swenson, May 31, 1986; children: Dietrich John, Nathan Paul. BA, Carthage Coll., 1984; JD magna cum laude, No. Ill. U., 1988. Bar: Ill. 1988, Ill. 1989, N.Y. 1997; U.S. Dist. Ct. (no. dist.) Ill. Asst. counsel Allstate Ins. Co., Northbrook, Ill., 1991-93; gen. counsel Allstate Enterprises, Inc., Arlington Heights, Ill., 1994-95; counsel Allstate Ins. Co., Northbrook, Ill., 1995—; zone rep. Nat. Autp Travel Orgn., 1994; faculty Exec. Enterprises N.Y.C., 1996, 97. Editor: Centrique, 1984, No. Ill. U. Law Rev., 1988; author: Criminal Justice, 1988. Lobbyist Allstate Ins. Co., N.Y., Conn., 1995-97, N.C., S.C., 1989-93; mem. Chgo. Sister Cities Internat., 1998—. Recipient writing award Lexis, 1988, award Am. Juriprudence, 1988. Mem. ABA, N.Y. State Bar Assn., Ill. Bar Assn. Avocations: golf, bicycling. Insurance, Private international, Legislative. Office: Allstate Ins Co 2775 Sanders Rd Northbrook IL 60062-6127

**IIJIMA, CHRIS K.,** law educator; b. N.Y.C., Dec. 19, 1948; s. Takeru and Kazuko (Ikeda) I.; m. Karen Asakawa (div. Aug. 1991); m. Jane Ann Dickson, Feb. 17, 1993; children: Alan Kando, Christopher Takeru. BA, Columbia U., 1969; JD, N.Y. Law Sch., 1988. Bar: N.Y. 1989, U.S. Dist. Ct. (so. and ea. dists.) N.Y. 1989. Jud. clk. U.S. Dist. Ct. (so. dist.) N.Y., N.Y.C., 1988-90; litigation assoc. Friedman & Kaplan, N.Y.C., 1990-93; lawyering instr. NYU Sch. Law, N.Y.C., 1993-95; asst. prof., dir. lawyering process program Western New Eng. Coll. Sch. Law, Springfield, Mass., 1995-98; asst. prof., dir. pre-admission program William S. Richardson Sch. Law, Honolulu, 1998—; bd. dirs. Na Loio Pub. Interest Legal Ctr., Honolulu, 1998—; mem. Manoa Network for Minority Students, Honolulu, 1998—. Mem. bd. advisors Rosenberg Fund for Children, Springfield, Mass., 1997—; mem. Asian Pacific Ams. in Philanthropy, N.Y.C., 1997-98. Office: William S Richardson Sch Law 2515 Dole St Honolulu HI 96822-2328

**ILLNER, MICHAEL DOUGLAS,** lawyer; b. Hamilton, Ohio, Nov. 17, 1948; s. Arthur George and Grace Louise Illner; m. Andrea Taylor. BS in Edn., Bowling Green State U., 1972; MA in Edn., Baldwin-Wallace Coll., 1978; JD, U. Akron, 1985. Bar: Ohio 1985. Tchr. Midria Local Schs., Grafton, Ohio, 1972-85; asst. prosecutor Lorain County, Elyria, Ohio, 1985-97; atty. Spike & Meckler, Elyria, 1997—. Roman Catholic. Family and matrimonial, Criminal. Office: Spike & Meckler 1551 W River Rd N Elyria OH 44035-2729

**ILLSTON, SUSAN Y.,** judge; b. 1948. BA, Duke U., 1970; JD, Stanford U., 1973. Ptnr. Cotchett, Illston & Pitre, San Francisco, 1973-95; judge U.S. Dist. Ct. (no. dist.) Calif., San Francisco, 1995—. Author: Insurance Coverage in a Toxic Tort Case, A Guide to Toxic Torts, 1987, California Complex Litigation Manual, 1990. Active Legal Aid Soc. San Mateo County, Svc. League San Mateo County. Recipient Appreciation for Vol. Svcs. cert. No. Dist. Calif. Fed. Practice Program, 1989, Svc. and Appreciation cert. 1992. Mem. ABA, ATLA, Assn. Bus. Trial Lawyers, San Mateo County Bar Assn. (Eleanor Falvey award 1994), State Bar Calif. (mem. jud. coun., mem. ethics com. 1975-79, mem. com. on women in law 1985-87, mem. jud. nominees evaluation commn. 1988, mem. exec. com. on litigation 1990-93), Calif. Women Lawyers, Calif. Trial Lawyers Assn., Trial Lawyers for Pub. Justice. Office: US Dist Ct No Dist Calif PO Box 36060 450 Golden Gate Ave San Francisco CA 94102-3661

**IMBER, ANNABELLE CLINTON,** state supreme court justice; b. Heber Springs, Ark., July 15, 1950; m. Ariel Barak Imber; 1 child, William Pierce Clinton. BA magna cum laude, Smith Coll., 1971; postgrad., Inst. for Paralegal Tng., 1971, U. of Houston, 1973-75; JD, U. Ark., 1977. Atty. Wright, Lindsey & Jennings Law Firm, Little Rock, Ark., 1977-88; apptd. cir. judge (5th divsn.) Pulaski and Perry Counties, Ark., 1984, elected chancery and probate judge (6th divsn.), 1989-96; elected assoc. justice Ark. Supreme Ct., 1997—. Bd. dirs. Ark. Advs. for Children and Families, 1985-90, pres. 1986-88; bd. dirs Pulaski County Hist. Soc., 1992-95, Congregation B'Nai Israel, 1988-92, Kiwanis Club 1995-98, YMCA of Greater Little Rock and Pulaski County, Our House-A Shelter for Homeless, 1992—, St. Vincent Fevel. Found., 1989-93. Mem. ABA, AAUW, Nat. Assn. Women Judges, Ark. Bar Assn., Ark. Women Exec., Assn. of Ark. Women Lawyers (pres. 1980-81, Judge of the Year award 1994), Pulaski County Bar Assn. (bd. dirs. 1982-84). Office: Ark Supreme Ct Justice Bldg 625 Marshall St Little Rock AR 72201-1054

**IMBIEROWICZ, ANGELA,** lawyer; b. Holmstak, Sweden, Aug. 11, 1946; came to U.S., 1949; d. Walerian and Elizabeth Teresa (Tylman) I. EdB, No. Ill. U., 1967, MEd, 1971; JD highest distinction, John Marshall Law Sch., 1985. Bar: Ill. 1985, U.S. Dist. Ct. (no. dist.) Ill. 1985, U.S. Ct. Appeals (7th cir.) 1993, U.S. Supreme Ct. 1994. Assoc. O'Brien & Assocs., P.C., Oakbrook Terrace, Ill., 1985-94; pvt. practice Hinsdale, Ill., 1994—; arbitrator 18th Jud. Cir. Recipient Disting. Svc. award John Marshall Law Sch., 1998. Fellow Ill. Bar Found.; mem. Ill. State Bar Assn. (civil practice sect. coun., gen. practice sect. coun., task force on the future of the profession), DuPage Bar Assn. (civil law and litigation com., ad hoc rules com., real estate law and practice com., bar brief publs. bd., chair law day com.), DuPage Assn. Women Lawyers (past pres.), DuPage Am. Inn of Ct., Child Friendly Cts. Found. (pres.), Advs. Soc., Willowbrook Racquet Club. Labor, Real property, General civil litigation. Office: 15 N Lincoln St Hinsdale IL 60521-3436

**IMBLUM, GARY JOSEPH,** lawyer, educator; b. Monogehela, Pa., May 24, 1959; s. Raymond J. and Kathleen I.; m. Lois Breon, July 2, 1988; children: Courtney, Brittney. BA in Sci. and Computer Sci., U. Pitts., 1981, JD, 1984. Bar: Pa. 1984, U.S. Dist. Ct. (mid. dist.) Pa. 1989. Law clk. Judge J.W. Myers, Bloomsburg, Pa., 1984-85; atty. Houck & Gingrich, Lewiston, Pa., 1985-87, Knupp & Kodak, P.C., Harrisburg, Pa., 1987—; adj. prof. Harrisburg Area C.C., 1992—. Mem. Sertoma (pres. Capital area chpt. 1990-91, Cmty. Achievement award 1991). Avocations: jogging, tennis, raquetball. Bankruptcy, Family and matrimonial, Estate planning. Office: Knupp & Kodak PC PO Box 11848 407 N Front St Harrisburg PA 17108-1848

**IMMERMAN, WILLIAM JOSEPH,** lawyer, motion picture producer; b. N.Y.C., Dec. 29, 1937; s. Nathan and Sadye (Naumoff) I.; children: Scott, Eric, Lara. BS, U. Wis., 1959; JD, Stanford U., 1963. Bar: Calif., 1964. Dep. dist. atty. L.A. County, L.A., 1963-65; v.p. bus. affairs Am. Internat. Pictures, L.A., 1965-72; sr. v.p. 20th Century Fox Film Corp., L.A., 1972-77; producer Warner Bros. Pictures, L.A., 1977-79; pres. Scoric Prodns., Inc., L.A., 1977—, Salem Prodns., Inc., L.A., 1978—, Distbn. Expense Co., L.A., 1986-95; of counsel Barash and Hill, L.A., 1983-93, Kenoff and Machingter, L.A., 1993—; pres. Immkirk Fin. Corp., 1987—; chmn. Cinema Group, Inc., L.A., 1979-82; vice-chmn. Cannon Pictures, Inc., L.A., 1989-90; cons. to pres. Pathe Comm. Corp., L.A., 1988-89; dir. Heritage Entertainment Corp., L.A., 1987-91. Dir. The Thalians, L.A., 1978-99. Capt. USAR, 1959-68. Mem. Assn. Motion Picture and TV Producers (bd. dirs. 1972-77), Ind. Film and Distbr. Assn. (bd. dirs. 1966-70), Acad. Motion Picture Arts and Sci., State Bar Calif, Los Angeles County Bar Assn. Avocations: tennis, theater, sporting events, travel. Intellectual property, Trademark and copyright. Office: Kenoff and Machingter Ste 1250 1999 Avenue Of The Stars Los Angeles CA 90067-4609

**IMMKE, KEITH HENRY,** lawyer; b. Peoria, Ill., Jan. 18, 1953; s. Francis William and Pearl Lenora (Kime) I. BA, U. Ill., 1975; JD, So. Ill. U., 1978. Bar: Ill. 1978, U.S. Dist. Ct. (so. and ea. dist.) Ill. 1978. Assoc. Lawrence E. Johnson & Assocs., P.C., Champaign, Ill., 1979-87; staff atty. Dept. Ins. State Ill., Springfield, 1987-88; legal counsel Underground Storage Tank program (now Divsn. Petroleum and Chem. Safety), 1988-98; asst. legal counsel Office Fire Marshal State Ill., 1988—; legal counsel Underground Storage Tank Program (now Div. Petroleum and Chem. Safety 1988-98), asst. legal counsel; Office Fire Marshal State Ill., 1998—. Mem. ABA, Ill. State Bar Assn., U. Ill. Alumni Assn., Phi Kappa Phi, Pi Sigma Alpha, Phi Alpha Delta. Environmental. Office: State Ill Office Fire Marshal Div Petroleum and Chem Safety 1035 Stevenson Dr Springfield IL 62703-4259

**IMPERATO, GABRIEL LOUIS,** lawyer; b. Teaneck, N.J., June 22, 1950; s. Gabriel and Edelweiss I.; m. Cynthia Gelmine, May 4, 1991; children; Alexander, Ashley. BA magna cum laude, U. Mass., 1973; JD, DePaul U., 1977. Bar: Ill. 1977, U.S. Dist. Ct. (no. dist.) Ill. 1977, U.S. Ct. Appeals (6th, 7th and 8th cirs.) 1981, U.S. Dist. Ct. Md., 1987, U.S. Ct. of Appeals (4th, 5th, 10th and 11th cirs.) 1987, Fla. 1989, U.S. Dist. Ct. (so. and mid. dists.) Fla. 1989, D.C. 1989. Counsel Office of the Gen. Counsel Health and Human Svcs., Chgo, Washington, Dallas, 1976-87; assoc. Becker & Poliakoff, Ft. Lauderdale, Fla., 1987-88; ptnr. Dykema, Gossett, Ft. Lauderdale, 1988-93, Broad & Cassal, Ft. Lauderdale, 1993—. Mem. ABA (antitrust, health care, white collar crime, health care fraud sects.), Am. Acad. Hosp. Attys. (chair com. on reimbursement and payment 1991-92)), Fla. Bar (health law sect.), D.C. Bar Assn. (health law administrn., antitrust sects.), Am. Health Lawyers Assn. (chair health care reform task force). Criminal, Health. Office: Broad and Cassel 500 E Broward Blvd Ste 1130 Fort Lauderdale FL 33394-3077

**IMRE, CHRISTINA JOANNE,** lawyer; b. Gary, Ind., Oct. 25, 1950; d. Joseph and Ruth Leone I.; m. Richard Long, Dec. 31, 1991. BA, Mt. St. Mary's Coll., L.A., 1972; MA, U. Notre Dame, 1974; JD, Loyola Law Sch., L.A., 1980. Bar: Calif. 1980, U.S. Ct. Appeals (ninth cir.) 1982, U.S. Dist. Ct. (ctrl. dist.) Calif. 1983, U.S. Dist. Ct. (no. dist.) Calif. 1988,U.S. Dist. Ct. (so. dist.) Calif. 1995. Assoc. Lascher & Lascher, Ventura, Calif., 1980-83, Law Office of Errol Berk, Ventura, Calif., 1983-84, Pachter, Gold & Schaffer, L.A., 1984-87; sr. atty. Kornblum & McBride, L.A., 1987-89; atty. Horvitz & Levy LLP, Encino, Calif., 1989—; bd. govs. Calif. Continuing Edn. of Bar, Berkeley, Calif., 1996—; chair Calif. Continuing Edn. of Bar Joint Adv. Com., Berkeley, 1995; editorial bd. L.A. Lawyer Mag., L.A., 1996-99; cons. Handling Civil Appeals, Berkeley, 1996, Calif. Trial Practice, Berkeley, 1995; lectr. in field. Editor-in-chief: Loyola of Los Angeles International & Comparative Law Journal, 1979-80; contbr. articles to profl. jours. and chpts. to books. Named one of 50 Most Powerful Women in L.A. Law, L.A. Business Journal, 1998; Loyola Law Sch. fellow, 1979-80, U. Notre Dame fellow, 1972-74. Mem. L.A. County Bar Assn., Defense Rsch. Inst., So. Calif. Defense Counsel Assn. Avocations: music, Shakespeare, history, philosophy. E-mail: CImre@horvitzlevy.com. Appellate, Insurance, State civil litigation. Office: Horvitz & Levy LLP 15760 Ventura Blvd Fl 18 Van Nuys CA 91436-3000

**INAMA, CHRISTOPHER ROY,** lawyer, educator; b. Burbank, Calif., Apr. 4, 1952; s. Leo H. Inama and Jeanne (Bauer) Truax; m. Colleen J. Deal, Dec. 30, 1986. BA, U. Calif., Santa Barbara, 1974; JD, U. Calif., San Francisco, 1977; MA in Econs., Calif. State U., Hayward, 1996. Bar: Calif. 1977, U.S. Dist. Ct. (no. dist.) Calif. 1977. Pvt. practice Law Office of Christopher R. Inama, Redwood City, Calif., 1978—; chief of security San Francisco Giants, 1974-89; adj. prof. econs. U. Phoenix, 1996—, Golden Gate U., 1996—. County chair Calif. Libertarian Party, San Mateo County, 1990-92; candidate Calif. State Assembly, Dist. 21, 1990, 96, Calif. State Senate, Dist. 11, 1992. Chief warrant officer USCGR, 1987—. Mem. Mensa, Hastings Old Boys Rugby Club, St. Thomas More Soc., Native Sons of Golden West #66. Libertarian. Roman Catholic. Criminal, General civil litigation, Appellate. Office: 399 Bradford St Ste 102 Redwood City CA 94063-1584

**INCLIMA, CHARLES P.,** lawyer; b. Rochester, N.Y., Dec. 12, 1946; s. Charles Jr. and Mary (Nicoletti) I.; m. Marjorie Inclima, June 8, 1968 (div. 1980); m. Deborah J. Inclima, Sept. 11, 1982; 1 child, Brian M. Standish. BA, St. John Fisher Coll., 1968; JD, U. Toledo, 1973. Bar: N.Y. 1974, U.S. Dist. Ct. (we. dist.) N.Y. 1974. Assoc. Biernbaum & Vorrasi, Rochester, 1973-76; ptnr. Biernbaum & Inclima, Rochester, 1976-86, Biernbaum, Inclima & Nowak, Rochester, 1986-88, Biernbaum, Inclima & Meyer, Rochester, 1988—; adj. prof. Rochester Inst. Tech., 1976—; lectr., panelist N.Y. State Bar Assn., 1983—. Fellow Am. Acad. Matrimonial Lawyers; mem. Monroe County Bar Assn. (chair family law sect., trustee 1987-89, dean acad. of law, chair continuing legal edn. com. 1984—). Democrat. Roman Catholic. Avocations: golf, photography, teaching. Family and matrimonial, State civil litigation. Home: 36 Woodcliff Ter Fairport NY 14450-4209 Office: Biernbaum Inclima & Meyer 19 Main St W Ste 900 Rochester NY 14614-1586

**INCORVAIA, SANTO THOMAS,** lawyer; b. Cleve., Dec. 31, 1957; s. Santo Francis and Frances Mary (Liotta) I. BA, Cleve. State U., 1985; JD, Case Western Res. U., 1988. Bar: Ohio 1988, U.S. Dist. Ct. (no. dist.) Ohio 1988. Prin. Santo T. Incorvaia, Atty. at Law, Cleve., 1988—. Mayor City of Maple Heights, Ohio, 1991—; mem. exec. com. Cuyahoga County Dem. Com., Cleve., 1992. Named Outstanding Young Men of Am., 1987; Norgar Academic scholar, 1988. Mem. Ohio Bar Assn., Cuyahoga County Mayors and Mgrs. Assn. Democrat. Criminal, Personal injury, Municipal (including bonds). Home: 5736 South Blvd Maple Heights OH 44137-3433 Office: Santo T Incorvaia Atty At Law 5005 Rockside Rd Ste 600 Cleveland OH 44131-6827

**INDURSKY, ARTHUR,** lawyer; b. Bklyn., Jan. 1, 1943; s. David and Anne (Levine) I.; m. Deanne Fiedler, Mar. 26, 1967; 1 child, Blake. BBA, CCNY, 1964; JD, Bklyn. Law Sch., 1967. Bar: N.Y., 1968. Entertainment counsel Columbia Pictures, N.Y.C., 1969-72; mng. ptnr. Grubman Indursky Schindler & Goldstein P.C., N.Y.C., 1973—; bd. dirs. Alliance Artists and Rec. Cos.; guest spkr. Can. Rec. Industry Seminar, 1986, Entertainment Law Soc., Bklyn. Law Sch., 1987, 92, Copyright Soc., 1988, Disting. Alumni Lecture Series Bklyn. Law Sch., 1989, Hofstra Law Sch., 1995. Bd. dirs. T.J. Martell Found. for Leukemia, Cancer and AIDS Rsch., 1993—. Recipient 1st Ann. Alumni Achievement award Bklyn. Law Sch., 1992, Outstanding Leadership award Meml. Sloan Kettering Cancer Ctr., 1994, City of Hope award, 1995, Jule Styne Humanitarian award Childrens Hearing Inst., 1998. Entertainment. Office: Grubman Indursky Schindler & Goldstein PC 152 W 57th St New York NY 10019-3310

**INFANTI, ANTHONY C.,** lawyer; b. Point Pleasant, N.J., Aug. 29, 1968; s. Anthony and Margarete (Matern) I. BA, Drew U., 1990; JD, U. Calif., Berkeley, 1993; LLM, NYU, 1996. Bar: Calif. 1993, U.S. Dist. Ct. (so. dist.) Calif. 1993, N.Y. 1995, U.S. Dist. Ct. N.J. 1995. Law clk. to Hon. E.J. Schwartz U.S. Dist. Ct., San Diego, 1993-94; assoc. Curtis, Mallet-Prevost, Colt and Mosle, N.Y.C., 1994-95, 97—, Rosenman & Colin, N.Y.C., 1996-97. Articles editor Internat. Tax and Bus. Lawyer, 1992-93. Mem. State Bar Calif., N.Y. State Bar Assn., Assn. of the Bar of the City of N.Y., Phi Beta Kappa, Sigma Delta Pi. Democrat. Roman Catholic. Taxation, general. Office: Roberts & Holland LLP 825 8th Ave New York NY 10019-7416

**INFELISE, ROBERT DONALD,** lawyer, educator; b. Long Beach, Calif., Nov. 23, 1955; s. Phil and Mary Infelise; m. Linda Burrell, Mar. 1, 1986; children: Tyler, Whitney. AB, U. Calif., Berkeley, 1977, JD, 1980. Bar: Calif. 1980, U.S. Dist. Ct. (so. dist.) Calif. 1980, U.S. Dist. Ct. (no. dist.) Calif. 1987. Ptnr. Cox Castle and Nicholson LLP, L.A., San Francisco, 1980—; prof. Bolt Sch. of Law U. Calif., Berkeley, 1994—. Environmental. Office: Cox Castle & Nicholson LLP 505 Montgomery St San Francisco CA 94111-2552

**INGALLS, EVERETT PALMER, III,** lawyer; b. Portland, Maine, Nov. 21, 1947; s. Everett Palmer and Joyce (Iveney) I.; m. Susan Wilson, Feb. 15, 1992; 1 child, Abigail Valentine. AB, Brown U., 1969; JD, Harvard U., 1972. Bar: Maine 1972, U.S. Dist. Ct. Maine 1972. Assoc. Pierce & Atwood, Portland, 1972-77, mem., 1977—. Area chmn. Harvard Law Sch. Fund, Cambridge, Mass., 1978-82; pres. Portland Widows' Wood Soc., 1982-86; bd. dirs. Portland Stage Co., 1979-82; pres. Portland Performing Arts, 1992—. Fellow Am. Coll. Trust & Estate Counsel; mem. ABA (real property, probate & trust law and taxation), Harvard Law Sch. Assn. in Maine (pres. 1982-85), Phi Beta Kappa. Administrative and regulatory, Estate planning, General corporate. Home: 125 Neal St Portland ME 04102-3209 Office: Pierce & Atwood One Monument Sq Portland ME 04101

**INGALSBE, WILLIAM JAMES,** lawyer; b. Guam, June 5, 1947; came to U.S., 1953; s. Wilbur and Erma I.; m. Heidi Marie Freed, June 21, 1969; 1 child, James. BA, Calif. State U., San Diego, 1969; JD, Southwestern U., 1975. Bar: Calif., 1975, U.S. Ct. Appeals (9th cir.) 1984, U.S. Dist. Ct. (cen. and so. dist.) Calif. 1976, U.S. Dist. Ct. (no. dist.) Calif. 1984, U.S. Claims Ct. 1979. Assoc. Spray, Gould & Bowers, L.A., 1975-76; ptnr. Monteleone & McCrory, L.A., Calif., 1976—. Editor-in-chief: Southwestern U. Law Rev., 1974. Vol. investigative atty. State Bar Calif., L.A., 1986. Mem. Assoc. Gen. Contractors Calif., L.A. County Bar Assn. (judge pro tem mcpl. ts. com. 1984-86, vol. atty. client rels. com. 1984-90). Avocations: fishing, golf, photography. Federal civil litigation, State civil litigation, Construction. Office: Monteleone & McCrory 1551 N Tustin Ave Ste 750 Santa Ana CA 92705-8663

**INGBER, MARVIN C.,** lawyer; b. St. Paul, Feb. 28, 1941; s. Sam and Leah Ingber; m. Diane C. Ingber, Aug. 30, 1965; children: Matthew C., Jessica S. BA, U. Minn., 1963, JD, 1966; LLM, NYU, 1970. Ptnr. Mackall, Crowse & Moore, PLC, Mpls., 1970-93; shareholder Winthrop & Weinstine, Mpls., 1993—. Capt. U.S. Army, 1967-69. Estate planning, Estate taxation, General corporate. Office: Winthrop & Weinstine PA 60 S 6th St #3000 Minneapolis MN 55402-4430

**INGERSOLL, MARC W.,** lawyer; b. Columbus, Ohio, Oct. 4, 1964; s. ralph Walter and Reta Irene Ingersoll; m. Julia L. Ingersoll, July 11, 1987; children: Jessica L., Meagan E. BS in Acctg., Bob Jones U., Greenville, S.C., 1986; JD, Wake Forest U., 1990. Bar: N.C. 1990, U.S. Dist. Ct. (mid. dist.) N.C. 1994. Atty. Hollowell & Assocs., Raleigh, 1990-94, House Law Firm, Winston-Salem, 1994-97; ptnr. House & Ingersoll, PLLC, Winston-Salem, 1997—; spkr. N.W. Piedmont of CPAs, Winston-Salem, 1997; lectr. St. Mary's Coll., Raleigh, 1993-94. Recipient Am. Jurisprudence award Bur. Nat. Affairs, 1990, Award of Distinction, Wake Forest Sch. Law, 1990; named Best Class Lectr. of S.E., Am. Inst., Winston-Salem, 1994. Mem. N.C. Bar Assn. (bus. sect., tax sect.), Estate Planning Coun. Avocations: writing, golf, softball. Estate planning, General corporate, Taxation, general. Office: House & Ingersoll PLLC 3325 Healy Dr Winston Salem NC 27103-1479

**INGERSOLL, RICHARD KING,** lawyer; b. Algoma, Wis., Aug. 13, 1944; s. Robert Clive and Bernice Eleanore (Koehn) I.; m. Caroline Soi-Keu Yee, Aug. 31, 1968; children: Kristin Paula Juk-Yee, Karin Eleanor Juk-Ling. BBA, U. Mich., 1966; JD, U. Calif.-Berkeley, Berkeley, 1969. Bar: Ill. 1969, Hawaii 1973. Asst. prof. U. Ill.-Champaign, Champaign, 1969-70; assoc. Sidley & Austin, Chgo., 1970-73; ptnr. Rush, Moore, Craven, Kim & Stricklin, Honolulu, 1973-88, Gelber, Gelber, Ingersoll Klevansky & Faris, Honolulu, 1989—; speaker tax law seminars. Author various law materials. Bd. dirs. MacFarms of Hawaii, Inc., Honolulu. Mem. ABA (taxation, bus. and internat. law coms.), Waialae Country Club (chmn. by-laws com.). Corporate taxation, General corporate, Private international. Home: 944 Waiholo St Honolulu HI 96821-1226

**INGERSOLL, WILLIAM BOLEY,** lawyer, real estate developer; b. Washington, Sept. 21, 1938; s. William Brown and Loraine (Boley) I.; m. Carolyn Grace Potter, Sept. 8, 1963; children: William Brett, Courtney Lynn, Wayne Brandon, Dana Lee. BS, Brigham Young U., 1964; JD, Cath. U. Am., 1968. Bar: Va. 1968, D.C. 1969. Atty. Office of Corp. Counsel D.C., 1967-69; atty. Office Gen. Counsel, HUD, 1969-70; ptnr. Fried, Klewans, Ingersoll & Bloch, Washington, 1970-72; pres. Ingersoll and Bloch Chartered, Washington, 1972—; of counsel Holland & Knight, Washington, 1998—; mng. ptnr. JC Assocs. Real Estate Devel., Washington, 1973—; gen. counsel Am. Resort Devel. Assn.; lectr. in field. Bd. dirs. Nat. Timesharing Coun., 1981—; mem. Garrison Presdl. Commn., 1984; mem. bd. adv. J. Ruben Clark Law Sch., 1987-93, chmn. 1991-93; bishop McLean (Va.) Ward, LDS Ch. Mem. ABA, Fed. Bar Assn., D.C. Bar Assn., Va. Bar Assn., Va. Assn. Trial Lawyers, Land Devel. Inst. (vice chmn.), Brigham Young U. Alumni Assn. (bd. dir. 1984-92), Order of Coif, Univ. Club Washington. Coeditor-in-chief of Land Devel. Law Reporter, Land Trends, 1973—. Co-editor-in-chief Law Reporter and Land Trends, 1973—, Time Sharing Law Reporter, 1980—, The Digest of State Land Sales, 1976—, D.C. Real Estate Reporter, 1982—, Real Estate Opportunity Report, 1986. Contbr. in field. Mem. nat. adv. com. Inside Real Estate, 1985—. Real property, Administrative and regulatory, Legislative. Home: 713 Potomac Knolls Dr Mc Lean VA 22102-1421 also: Holland & Knight 2100 Pennsylvania Ave NW Washington DC 20037-3202

**INGLE, JOHN DAVID,** lawyer; b. Indpls., Sept. 15, 1940; s. G. Clyde and Harriet (Neideffer) I.; m. Margaret Messer, Oct. 5, 1976. BS, Ind. U., 1963; JD, Mercer U., 1970; cert., Campbell Coll., 1971. Bar: U.S. Ct. Appeals (4th cir.) 1986; cert. mediator and arbitrator. Corr. banking rep. Mchts. Nat. Bank, Indpls., 1965-67; trust officer 1st Nat. Bank, Hickory, N.C., 1970-73; judge N.C. Dist. Ct., 1973-75; sole practice Hickory, N.C., 1975-80; ptnr., pres. Lovekin & Ingle, Hickory, 1980-97; prin. officer John Ingle Assocs., PLLC, Hickory, 1997—; fin. officer USA, BadKreuznach, Fed. Rep. of Germany, 1963-65; park ranger U.S. Park Service, Macon, Ga., 1968-70. Pres. Western Piedmont Humane Soc., Hickory, 1975. Served to capt. Fin. Corps., 1963-65. Mem. N.C. State Bar Assn., Acad. Trial Lawyers, Def. Research Inst. Republican. Lutheran. Lodges: Masons, Shriners. Personal injury, Workers' compensation, Pension, profit-sharing, and employee benefits. Home: Hwy 16 North Conover NC 28613 Office: John Ingle Assocs PLLC PO Box 1728 Hickory NC 28603-1728

**INGRAM, DENNY OUZTS, JR.,** lawyer, educator; b. Kirbyville, Tex., Mar. 23, 1929; s. Denny Ouzts and Grace Bertha (Smith) I.; m. Ann Elizabeth Rees, July 11, 1952; children: Scott Rees, Stuart Tillman. B.A., U. Tex., 1955, J.D. with honors, 1957. Bar: Tex. 1956, N.Mex. 1967, Utah 1968. Editor Kirbyville Banner, 1949-50; mem. Tex. Ho. of Reps., 1951-52; assoc. Graves, Dougherty, Gee and Hearon (and predecessors), Austin, Tex., 1957, 59-60; partner Graves, Dougherty, Gee and Hearon (and predecessors), 1961-66; asst. prof. law U. Tex., 1957-59, U. N.Mex., 1966-67; prof. U. Utah, 1968-77; ptnr. McGinnis, Lochridge, and Kilgore, Austin, 1977-90, of counsel, 1991—; prof. law Tex. Wesleyan U. Sch. Law, 1991—; vis. prof. U. Calif., Davis, 1973-74, U. Tex., summers 1968, 75, U. San Diego, 1993; research fellow Southwestern Legal Found., lectr. in field. Contbr. numerous articles to law revs., chpts. to books; assoc. note editor: Tex. Law Rev., 1956-57. Research dir. Utah Constn. Revision Com., 1969-71, 73-74. Served with U.S. Army, 1951-54. Fellow Am. Coll. Trust and Estate Counsel, Am. Coll. Tax Counsel, Tex. Bar Found.; mem. ABA, Am. Law Inst. (life), Tex. Bar Assn., Utah Bar Assn., N.Mex. Bar Assn., Chancellors, Order of Coif, Phi Delta Phi. Democrat. Episcopalian. Home: 4055 Hildring Dr E Fort Worth TX 76109-4712 Office: Tex Wesleyan U Sch Law 1515 Commerce St Fort Worth TX 76102-6509

**INGRAM, GEORGE CONLEY,** lawyer, judge; b. Dublin, Ga., Sept. 27, 1930; s. George Conley and Nancy Averett (Whitehurst) I.; m. Sylvia Williams, July 26, 1952; children: Sylvia Lark, Nancy Randolph, George Conley. A.B., Emory U., 1949, LL.B., 1951. Bar: Ga. 1952. City atty. City of Smyrna, Ga., 1958-64, City of Kennesaw, Ga., 1964; judge Cobb County Juvenile Ct., 1960-64, Superior Ct., Cobb Jud. Cir., 1964-68; justice Supreme Ct. Ga., 1973-77; spl. asst. atty. gen. State of Ga., 1979-86; ptnr. Alston & Bird, Atlanta, 1977-98; sr. judge State of Ga., 1998—; staff, faculty Judge Advocate Gen. Sch. U.S. Army U. Va., 1952-54. Former trustee Scott Coll., U. Ark., Kennesaw Coll. Found.; trustee Cobb Cmty. Found., The Eleventh Cirs. Hist. Soc. Inc., Tommy Nobbis Ctr. Found., Inc.; emeritus mem. Emory Law Sch. Coun.; past pres. Cobb County YMCA, Cobb Landmarks Soc.; chmn. ofcl. bd. 1st Meth. Ch. of Marietta. 1st lt. JAGC, USAR, 1952-54. Recipient Emory U. medal and Disting. Svc. award Kennesaw Mountain Jaycees, 1961, Ga. Jaycees, 1961, Emory Law Sch. Alumni Assn., 1985; Disting. Citizen award City of Marietta, Ga., 1973; Len Gilbert Leadership award Cobb County C. of C., 1985; Cobb County Citizen of Yr. award, 1990; hon. life mem. Ga. PTA. Fellow Am. Bar Assn. Found., Am. Coll. Trial Lawyers, Internat. Soc. Barristers, Am. Acad. Appellate Lawyers, Marietta-Cobb Mus. Art; mem. ABA, Am. Law Inst., State Bar Ga. (Tradition of Excellence award 1987), Cobb and Atlanta Bar Assn., Lawyers Club of Atlanta, Old War Horse Lawyers Club, Cobb County C. of C. (Pub. Svc. award, 1970) Georgian Club (bd. mem., founding chmn.), Rotary (award for vocat. excellence 1999), Order of Coif (hon.), Phi Delta Phi, Omicron Delta Kappa. Methodist. Federal civil litigation, State civil litigation, General practice. Home: 540 Hickory Dr Marietta GA 30064-3602

**INGRAM, KENNETH FRANK,** retired state supreme court justice; b. Ashland, Ala., July 7, 1929; s. Earnest Frank and Alta Mary (Allen) I.; m. Judith Louise Brown, Sept. 3, 1954; children: Jennifer Lynn Ingram Malone, Kenneth Frank Jr. BS, Auburn U., 1951; LLB, Jones Law Sch., 1963. Bar: Ala. 1963, U.S. Dist. Ct. (no. dist.) Ala. 1965, U.S. Dist. Ct. (mid. dist.) Ala. 1966. City councilman City of Ashland, Ala., 1956-58; mem. Ho. of Reps., Ala., 1958-66; presiding judge 18th Jud. Cir. Ct., Ala., 1968-87; judge Ala. Ct. Civil Appeals, Montgomery, 1987-89, presiding judge, 1989-91; assoc. justice Ala. Supreme Ct., Montgomery, 1991-97; mem., chmn. Ala. Jud. Inquiry Commn., 1979-87. Contbr. articles on jud. ethics to profl. pubs. With USMC, 1952-54. Mem. Ala. Bar Assn., Masons. Democrat. Methodist. Avocations: woodworking, metalcrafting, tennis, swimming. Home: 264 1st St N PO Box 729 Ashland AL 36251-0729

**INGRAM, SAMUEL WILLIAM, JR.,** lawyer; b. Utica, N.Y., Mar. 20, 1933; s. Samuel William and Mary Elizabeth (Rosen) I.; m. Jane Austin Stokes, Sept. 30, 1961; children: Victoria, William. BS, Vanderbilt U., 1954; LLB, Columbia U., 1960. Bar: N.Y. 1960. Assoc. Sullivan & Cromwell, N.Y.C., 1960-67; assoc. Shea Gallop Climenko & Gould, N.Y.C., 1967-68; ptnr. Shea & Gould and predecessors, N.Y.C., 1968-89, Hutton, Ingram, Yuzek, Gainen, Carroll & Bertolotti LLP, N.Y.C., 1989—. Bd. dirs. Legal Aid Soc., N.Y.C., 1974-86, sec., 1978-86; trustee Green Mountain Valley Sch., Waitsfield, Vt., 1984-87. Served to 1st lt. USMC, 1954-57. Mem. ABA, N.Y. State Bar Assn., Assn. of Bar of City of N.Y. Avocations: athletic and outdoor activities. Real property. Home: 332 Long Ridge Rd Pound Ridge NY 10576-2005 Office: Hutton Ingram Yuzek Gainen Carroll & Bertolotti LLP 250 Park Ave Ste 600 New York NY 10177-0600

**INGRAM, TEMPLE BYRN, JR.,** lawyer; b. Gilmer, Tex., Mar. 12, 1949; s. Temple Byrn and Janet (Wofford) I.; m. Janet Marie Bandy, Mar. 11, 1979; children: Lon Cartwright, James Ross, Katherine Anne. BA, Harvard U., 1971; JD, So. Meth. U., 1979. Bar: Tex. 1979, N.M. 1982, U.S. Ct. Appeals (10th cir.) 1984, U.S. Ct. Appeals (5th cir.) 1987, U.S. Supreme Ct. 1984. Consumer safety officer EPA, Boston, 1972-76; law clk. to presiding justice U.S. Dist. Ct. (we. dist.) Tex., San Antonio, 1979-81; assoc. Studdard, Melby, Schwartz, Crowson & Parrish, El Paso, Tex., 1981-83, ptnr., 1983-86; ptnr. Crowson & Ingram, El Paso, 1986—. Mem. ABA, Tex. Bar Assn., N.Mex. Bar Assn. Methodist. Avocations: flying, backpacking, canoeing. General civil litigation, Consumer commercial, Contracts commercial. Home: 810 Fairway Cir El Paso TX 79922-2135 Office: Crowson & Ingram 310 N Mesa St Ste 706 El Paso TX 79901-1301

**INGRAM, WILLIAM AUSTIN,** federal judge; b. Jeffersonville, Ind., July 6, 1924; s. William Austin and Marion (Lane) I.; m. Barbara Brown Lender, Sept. 18, 1947; children: Mary Ingram Mac Calla, Claudia, Betsy Ingram Friebel. Student, Stanford U., 1947; LL.B., U. Louisville, 1950; LLD honoris causas, Santa Clara U., 1994. Assoc., Littler, Coakley, Lauritzen & Ferdon, San Francisco, 1951-55; dep. dist. atty. Santa Clara (Calif.) County, 1955-57; mem. firm Rankin, O'Neal, Luckhardt & Center, San Jose, Calif., 1955-69; judge Mcpl. Ct., Palo Alto-Mountain View, Calif., 1969-71, Calif. Superior Ct., 1971-76; judge U.S. Dist. Ct. (no. dist.) Calif., San Jose, 1976-88, chief judge, 1988-90; sr. judge, 1990—. Served with USMCR, 1943-46. Fellow Am. Coll. Trial Lawyers. Republican. Episcopalian. Office: US Dist Ct 280 S 1st St Rm 5198 San Jose CA 95113-3002

**INKLEY, JOHN JAMES, JR.,** lawyer; b. St. Louis, Nov. 7, 1945; s. John James Sr. and Morjorie Jane (Kenna) I.; m. Catherine Ann Mattingly, Apr. 13, 1971; children: Caroline Marie, John James III. BSIE, St. Louis U., 1967, JD, 1970; LLM in Taxation, Washington U., St. Louis, 1976. Bar: Mo. 1970, U.S. Dist. Ct. (we. dist.) Mo. 1970, U.S. Dist. Ct. (ea. dist.) Mo. 1975, U.S. Tax Ct. 1975, U.S. Supreme Ct. 1975. Assoc. Padberg, Raack, McSweeney & Slater, St. Louis, 1970-73; ptnr. Summer, Hanlon, Summer, MacDonald & Nouss, St. Louis, 1973-81; city atty. City of Town and Country, Mo., 1979-84, spl. counsel, 1984-88; ptnr. Hanlon, Nouss, Inkley & Coughlin, St. Louis, 1981-83; ptnr., chmn. banking and real estate dept. Suelthaus & Kaplan, St. Louis, 1983-91; ptnr. Armstrong Teasdale LLP (and predecessor firm), St. Louis, 1991—; co-chmn. bus. svcs. group, 1993—; exec. com. St. Louis, 1994—. Mem. ABA, Mo. Bar Assn., Bar Assn. Met. St. Louis. Roman Catholic. Banking, General corporate, Real property. Home: 35 Muirfield Ln Saint Louis MO 63141-7382 Office: Armstrong Teasdale LLP 1 Metropolitan Sq Ste 2600 Saint Louis MO 63102-2740

**INMAN-CAMPBELL, GAIL,** lawyer; b. Harrison, Ark., Nov. 12, 1956; d. John Blaine and Frances Helen (Kennedy) Inman; m. Ronald Dale Campbell, July 17, 1976; children: Heather Ryan, Lee Inman C. BA, U. Ark., Little Rock, 1979, JD, 1982. Bar: Ark. 1983, U.S. Dist. Ct. (ea. and we. dist.) Ark. 1983. Ptnr. Walker, Campbell & Campbell PLC, Harrison, 1983—. Bd. dirs. Ozark Rape Crisis, Inc., 1992-96, AM/PM Care, Inc. 1988-93. Mem. Bus. and Profl. Women (pres. harrison 1986-87, Woman of Yr. 1991), Boone-Newton Bar Assn. (pres. 1987), 20th Century Club of Harrison. Mem. Ch. of Christ. Consumer commercial, Bankruptcy, General practice. Office: Walker Campbell & Campbell PLC Security Pla 303 N Main St Ste 201 Harrison AR 72601-3526

**INNAMORATO, DON ANTHONY,** lawyer; b. Perth Amboy, N.J., Sept. 10, 1961; s. Anthony John Innamorato and Caroline Elizabeth Rusin; m. Laura Ann Russo, Nov. 9, 1996; 1 child, Anthony. BA in Psychology, Columbia U., 1983; JD, Villanova U., 1986. Bar: Pa. 1986, N.J. 1987, U.S. Dist. Ct. (ea. dist.) Pa. 1987, U.S. Dist. Ct. N.J. 1987, U.S. Ct. Appeals (3rd cir.) 1987. Assoc. Reed Smith Shaw & McClay, Phila., 1986-95; ptnr. Reed Smith Shaw & McClay, Princeton, N.J., 1995—. Labor. Office: Reed Smith Shaw & McClay Princeton Forrestal Village 136 Main St Princeton NJ 08540-5735

**INNES, KENNETH FREDERICK, III,** lawyer; b. San Francisco, May 15, 1950; s. Kenneth F. Jr. and Jean I.; m. Patricia Ann Graboyes, May 12, 1973; children: Kenneth F. IV, Julia Christine. BA, San Francisco State U., 1972, JD, 1984. Bar: Calif. 1984, U.S. Dist. Ct. (no. dist.) Calif. 1987, U.S. Dist. Ct. (ea. dist.) Calif. 1988. Tchr. secondary schs. Red Bluff, Calif., 1973-74; postal clk. U.S. Postal Svc., Vallejo, Calif., 1977-84; postal insp. U.S. Postal Svc., Denver, 1984-87; regional atty. U.S. Postal Inspection Svc., Memphis, 1987-90, fin. auditor, 1990-92; regional atty. U.S. Postal Inspection Svc., San Francisco, 1992—. Capt. USMCR, 1974-77. Mem. ABA, Calif. Bar Assn., Mensa, Elks. Democrat. Roman Catholic. Home: 157 Heartwood Ct Vallejo CA 94591-5638 Office: US Postal Insp Svc PO Box 882528 San Francisco CA 94188-2528

**INSEL, MICHAEL S.,** lawyer; b. N.Y.C., Apr. 19, 1947; s. Ralph David and Lillian Ruth (Solomon) I.; married; 1 child, Louis Leo. BA, Duke U., 1969; JD, NYU, 1973. Bar: N.Y. 1974, Fla. 1984. Assoc. Kelley Drye & Warren, N.Y.C., 1973-82, ptnr., 1982—; pres. French Am. Vintners LLC; bd. dirs. Kobrand Corp., N.Y.C., Maison Louis Jadot, S.A., Beaune, France, L & L, S.A., Boe, France, Western Wine Svcs., Inc., North Bergen, N.J., Kobrand Found., N.Y.C., E.C. Kopf Found., N.Y.C., Goodwill Industries, Astoria, N.Y.; trustee Elsie del Fierro Charitable Trust, N.Y.C., 1985—, Barbara Bell Cumming Found., N.Y.C., 1991—. Bd. dirs. St. Francis Vineyards, Sonoma, Calif.; bd. dirs. Domaine Carneros, Napa, Calif. Mem. ABA, N.Y. State Bar Assn., Fla. Bar, Assn. Bar of City of N.Y. Avocations: sailing, golf, opera. Office: Kelley Drye & Warren 101 Park Ave Fl 30 New York NY 10178-0062

**INTRILIGATOR, MARC STEVEN,** lawyer; b. Oceanside, N.Y., July 14, 1952; s. Alan and Sally (Jacobs) I.; m. Roxann Kathleen Hoff, Aug. 28, 1977; children: Seth Adam, Joshua Ross, Daniel Benjamin. BA, SUNY, Binghamton, 1974; JD, Boston U., 1977. Bar: N.Y. 1978. Assoc. Dreyer and Traub, N.Y.C., 1977-83, assoc. ptnr., 1984-85, sr. ptnr., 1985-96; of counsel Fischbein Badillo Wagner Harding, N.Y.C., 1996—. Projects editor: Boston U. law rev., 1976-77. Trustee, past pres. Croton Jewish Ctr. Mem. ABA, Assn. of Bar of City of N.Y., Highlands Country Club (pres., trustee), Tau Epsilon Phi. Real property, Landlord-tenant. Office: Fischbein Badillo Wagner Harding 909 3rd Ave New York NY 10022-4731

**INZETTA, MARK STEPHEN,** lawyer; b. N.Y.C., Apr. 14, 1956; s. James William and Rose Delores (Cirnigliaro) I.; children: Michelle, Margot, Mallory. BBA summa cum laude, U. Cin., 1977; JD, U. Akron, 1980. Bar: Ohio 1980, U.S. Dist. Ct. (no. dist.) Ohio 1980. Legal intern City of Canton, Ohio, 1979-80; assoc. W.J. Ross Co., LPA, Canton, 1980-84; asst. gen. counsel Wendy's Internat. Inc., Columbus, Ohio, 1984—; instr. real estate law Stark Tech. Coll., Canton, 1983. Case and comment editor: Akron Law Rev., 1979-80. Instr. religious edn. St. Peter's Cath. Ch.; bd. dirs. Brookside Village Civic Assn., 1985-87, treas., 1986-87; chmn. campaign Earle Wise Appellate Judge, North Canton, Ohio, 1982; legis. dir. Children's and Parents' Rights assn., 1996-97, chmn., 1997—, State of Ohio Child Support Guidelines Commn., 1995-97, 99—; State of Ohio Task Force on Family Law and Children, 1998-99, treas. Recipient Am. Jurisprudence award Lawyers Coop. Pub. Co., 1978, Dir. of Yr. award North Canton Jaycees, 1982, Presdl. award of honor, 1984, Dist. Dir. award of honor Ohio Jaycees, 1984. Mem. ABA, Ohio Bar Assn., North Canton Jaycees (bd. dirs. 1981-82, v.p. 1982-83, pres. 1983-84), North Canton C. of C. (bd. dirs. 1983-84). Democrat. Roman Catholic. Real property, General corporate, Private international. Home: 775 Suntree Dr Westerville OH 43081-5086 Office: Wendy's Internat Inc 4288 W Dublin Granville Rd Dublin OH 43017-1442

**IOANES, JOYCE,** lawyer, social worker; b. Washington, Feb. 23, 1944; d. Raymond Andrew and Irma Elizabeth (Blazo) I.; BA in French Lit., Dunbarton Coll., Washington, 1965; MS in Psychiat. Social Work, Simmons Coll., 1971; JD cum laude, Suffolk U., 1983. Bar: R.I. 1983, U.S. Cts. 1984, Mass. 1985; cert. Acad. Cert. Social Workers, 1978; lic. real estate broker. Social caseworker R.I. Dept. Social and Rehab. Services, Cranston and Providence, 1968-74, casework supr., Cranston and Johnston, R.I., 1974-77; therapist Northwestern Mental Health Clinic, Greenville, R.I., 1974-75, Washington County Mental Health Clinic, Charlestown, R.I., 1977-79; mental health profl. R.I. Mental Health Advs. Office, Cranston, 1977—, atty., 1983—; sole practice, Jamestown, 1983—; field instr. R.I. Coll., Roger Williams Coll., 1975-77, Providence Coll., 1975-81; mem. Gov.'s Task Force Community Placement of Geriatric Patients, 1977-81. Recipient Am. Jurisprudence award, 1980-81, R.I. Community Person of Yr. award, 1993. Mem. ABA, Nat. Assn. Social Workers, Mass. Bar Assn., R.I. Bar Assn. Avocations: jogging, gardening. Home: 78 Columbia Ave Jamestown RI 02835-1345 Office: RI Mental Health Cottage 405 Cranston RI 02920

**IONETZ, RONALD GEORGE,** lawyer, real estate broker; b. Detroit, May 27, 1953; s. George and Dorothy I.; div. 1984; children: Adam, Kendra; m. Kay Seals, Aug. 20, 1997; children: Austin, Jonathan, Mason. BS, Wayne State U., 1976; JD, Detroit Coll. Law, 1981. Bar: Mich., U.S. Dist. Ct. Mich., U.S. Ct. Appeals (6th cir.). Lic. builder Macomb, Mich., 1978-83; real estate broker Action Real Estate, Macomb, 1978—; pvt. practice atty. Macomb, 1981—; title examiner Genesis Title Co., 1998. Bd. dirs. Police Athletic League, Warren, Mich., 1995-97; assoc. mem. Fraternal Order of Polic, 1986-97. Democrat. Criminal, Family and matrimonial, General civil litigation. Office: 23750 Gratiot Ave Eastpointe MI 48021-1659

**IOPPOLO, FRANK S., JR.,** lawyer; b. Rockville Centre, N.Y., Nov. 13, 1966; s. Frank S. and Carmella L. (Marrone) I. BA, Wake Forest U., 1988; JD, Fordham U., 1991. Bar: Fla. 1991, U.S. Dist. Ct. (mid. dist.) Fla. 1991, D.C. 1992, N.Y. 1992, U.S. Dist. Ct. (so. dist.) Fla. 1992, U.S. Supreme Ct. 1995. Assoc. Baker & Hostetler, Orlando, Fla., 1991-96, Greenberg Traurig, Orlando, 1996—. Bd. regents Leadership Fla., 1995-96, 97-98; chmn. bd. Orlando Marine Insts., Inc., 1995-97; bd. dirs. Assoc. Marine Insts., Inc., 1995-97; pres., chmn. bd. Bay Point of Bay Hill Property Owners Assn., Inc., Orlando, 1994-96; bd. dirs. Communities in Schs., Orange County, Fla., 1997-99. Mem. ABA, Fla. Bar Assn., Orange County Bar Assn., N.Y. State Bar Assn., D.C. Bar Assn., Wake Forest U. Alumni Assn. Ctrl. Fla. (pres. 1995-98). Avocations: sailing, snow and water skiing, reading, fishing, target shooting. General corporate, Private international, Securities. Office: Greenberg Traurig 111 N Orange Ave Fl 20 Orlando FL 32801-2316

**IORIO, THEODORE,** lawyer; b. Waterbury, Conn.; s. Donato and Josephine Iorio; m. Gretchen Jean Sawyer, Dec. 12, 1969; children: Fillipe, Toby, Rachael. BA, U. Toledo, 1966, JD, 1969. Bar: Ohio 1969, Mich. 1989. Ptnr. Kalniz Iorio & Feldstein, Toledo, 1969—; instr. Defiance (Ohio) Coll., Ohio State Labor Extension Svc., Mich. State Labor Studies Program; guest speaker NLRB, Nat. Assn. Police Officers, Ohio Jud. Coun. Mem. U. Toledo Law Rev., 1968-69. Bd. dirs. Community Concern; atty. Farm Labor Organizing Com., 1969—. Recipient Pub. Employee Labor Rels. plaque U. Toledo, 1985, UniServ plaque Ohio Edn. Assn. 1986. Mem. Ohio Bar Assn., Mich. Bar Assn., Toledo Bar Assn. Avocations: walking, reading, family. Labor, Constitutional, Workers' compensation. Home: 1941 Lake Dr SE Grand Rapids MI 49506-3020 Office: PO Box 352170 Toledo OH 43635-2170

**IRAK, JOSEPH S.,** lawyer; b. Gary, Ind., May 7, 1955; s. John Jr. and Evelyn (Scott) I.; m. Kristi M. Irak, May 21, 1988; children: Christopher Joseph, Nicholas Arthur. BA, Valparaiso U., 1978, JD, 1981. Bar: Ind. 1982, U.S. Dist. Ct. (no. dist.) Ind. 1982, U.S. Supreme Ct. Pvt. practice Merrillville, Ind., 1982—; asst. county atty., atty. plan commn. Lake County Ind., Crown Point, 1985—. Mem. precinct com. Lake County Dem. Party, 1983—. Mem. Lake County Bar Assn., Gary Sportsman Club. Avocations: fishing, handball, hunting, skiing, boating. Personal injury, Real property, General practice. Office: 9219 Broadway Merrillville IN 46410-7046

**IRBY, HOLT,** lawyer; b. Dodge City, Kans., July 4, 1937; s. Jerry M. and Virgie (Lorean) I.; m. LaVerne Smith, May 27, 1956; children: Joseph,

Kathy, Kay, Karon, James. BA, Tex. Tech. U., 1959; JD, U. Tex., 1962. Bar: Tex. 1962, U.S. Dist. Ct. (no. dist.) Tex. 1963. Asst. city atty. City of Lubbock, Tex., 1962-63; assoc. Hugh Anderson, Lubbock, 1963-66; gen. counsel, sec. Mercantile Fin. Corp., Dallas, 1966-69; gen. counsel, v.p. Ward Food Restaurants, inc., Dallas, 1969-71; pvt. practice Garland, Tex., 1971—; mem. lawyer referal com. State Bar Tex., 1977, 78. Mem. bd. deacons First Bapt. Ch., Garland, 1979-84, chmn., 1976-77; bd. dirs. Garland Assistance Program, 1980, Habitat for Humanity of Greater Garland, Inc., 1997—, Dallas Life Found., 1980-90, Toler Children's Cmty., 1983-85; bd. dirs. Garland Civic Theatre, 1986—, pres., 1990-91, 92-93, v.p., 1991-92; mem. Garland Drug Task Force, 1990; deacon South Garland Bapt. Ch., 1992—, chmn., 1993-94, 98-99. Mem. Tex. Trial Lawyers Assn., Tex. Assn. Bank Counsel, Tex. Bar Assn., Garland Bar Assn. (bd. dirs. 1986-96, sec. 1992-93, v.p. 1993-94, pres. 1995-96), Dallas Bar Assn., Praetor Legal Frat. (named outstanding mem. 1962), Lubbock Jaycees (dir. 1963-65), Kiwanis (dir. 1973-74). General practice, State civil litigation, Contracts commercial. Office: Bank of Am Tower 705 W Avenue B Ste 404 Garland TX 75040-6241

**IREDALE, EUGENE GERALD,** lawyer; b. Louisville, Nov. 16, 1951; children: Danielle, Jake; m. Leah Singer, Jul. 14, 1996. BA in History and Sociology, Columbia U., N.Y.C., 1973; JD, Harvard U., 1976. Bar: Mass. 1977, Calif. 1977. Atty. Fed. Defenders of San Diego, 1977-82; chief trial atty. Fed. Defenders of San Diego, San Diego, 1982-83; prin. Law Offices of E. G. Iredale, San Diego, 1983—. Editor: Defending a Federal Criminal Case, 1980-83. Instr. Nat. Coll. for Criminal Def., Houston and Macon, Ga., 1979—. Mem. Nat. Assn. Criminal Def. Lawyers, Calif. Attys. for Criminal Justice, Criminal Def. Lawyers Club. Democrat. Criminal, General civil litigation. Office: 105 W F St Fl 4 San Diego CA 92101-6036

**IRELAND, D. JEFFREY,** lawyer; b. Dayton, Ohio, Feb. 28, 1954; s. Don R. and Beth P. Ireland; m. Ellen S. Ireland, Aug. 25, 1979; children: Elizabeth Jean, Olivia Kathryn. BA, Denison U., 1976; JD, U. Dayton, 1980. Bar: Ohio, U.S. Dist. Ct. (so. dist.) Ohio, U.S. Ct. Appeals (6th, 7th 8th and 9th cirs.), U.S. Supreme Ct. Assoc., ptnr. Smith & Schnacke, Dayton, 1980-89; founding ptnr. Faruki Gilliam & Ireland, Dayton, 1989—. Councilman, City of Oakwood, Ohio, 1983-85, mayor, 1985-95; trustee Miami Valley Regional Transit Authority, Dayton, 1998—; bd. dirs., chair Affordable Housing Fund, Dayton, 1989—; mem. adv. bd. Salvation Army, 1993—. Recipient Up and Comers award Price Waterhouse, 1989. Mem. ABA, Fed. Bar Assn., Ohio State Bar Assn., Dayton Bar Assn., Dayton Rotary Club. Avocations: running, reading, golf. Antitrust, Federal civil litigation, Environmental. Office: Faruki Gilliam & Ireland 600 Courthouse Plz SW 10 N Ludlow St Dayton OH 45402-1826

**IRELAND, FAITH,** judge; b. Seattle, 1942; d. Carl and Janice Enyeart; m. Chuck Norem. BA, U. Wash.; JD, Willamette U., 1969; M in Taxation with honors, Golden Gate U. Past assoc. McCune, Godfrey and Emerick, Seattle; pvt. practice Pioneer Square, Wash., 1974; judge King County Superior Ct., 1984-98; justice Wash. Supreme Ct., 1998; past dean Washington Jud. Coll., past mem. Bd. Ct. Edn. Served on numerous civic and charitable bds.; past pro-bono atty. Georgetown Dental Clin.; past bd. dirs. Puget Sound Big Sisters, Inc.; founding mem. Wing Luke Asian Mus., 1967—, past pres., past bd. dirs.; bd. dirs. Youth and Fitness Found., 1998. Recipient Disting. Svc. award Nat. Leadership Inst. Jud. Edn., 1998; named Judge of Yr. Washington State Trial Lawyer's Assn., Man of Yr. for efforts in founding Wing Luke Asian Mus. Mem. Washington Women Lawyer's (founding mem., Pres.'s award, Vanguard award), Wash. State Trial Lawyer's Assn. (past chair bd. dirs), Superior Ct. Judges Assn. (past bd. dirs., pres. 1996-97, vice chair bd. dirs. jud. adminstrn. 1996-98), Rainer Valley Hist. Soc. (founding mem., life), Rotary (bd. dirs. Seattle No. 4 1998). Office: Washington Supreme Ct Temple Justice PO Box 40929 Olympia WA 98504-0929*

**IRELAND, RODERICK L.,** state supreme court justice; m. Alice Ireland; 1 stepchild, Melanee Alexandra. Bachelor's degree, Lincoln U., 1966; Master's degree, Harvard U.; JD, Columbia U., 1969; postgrad., Northeastern U. Assoc. justice Mass. Supreme Jud. Ct., 1997—; former judge Boston Juvenile Ct., 1977. Mem. Eliot Congregational Ch. Office: Mass Supreme Jud Ct Pemberton Square 1300 New Courthouse Boston MA 02108*

**IRENAS, JOSEPH ERON,** judge; b. Newark, July 13, 1940; s. Zachary and Bessie (Shain) I.; m. Nancy Harriet Jacknow, 1962; children: Amy Ruth, Edward Eron. A.B., Princeton U., 1962; J.D. cum laude, Harvard U., 1965; postgrad. NYU Sch. Law, 1967-70. Bar: N.J. 1965, N.Y. 1982. Law sec. to justice N.J. Supreme Ct., 1965-66; assoc. McCarter & English, Newark, 1966-71, ptnr., 1972-92, judge U.S. Dist. Ct. N.J., 1992—; trustee Hamilton Investment Trust, Elizabeth, N.J., 1980-83; mem. N.J. Supreme Ct. Dist. Ethics Com., 1984-86, vice chmn., 1986; adj. prof. law Rutgers Sch. Law, Camden, 1985-86, 88-97, N.J. Bd. Bar Examiners, 1986-88. Contbr. articles to legal jours. Chmn. bd. trustees United Hosps. of Newark, 1982-83; trustee United Hosps. Found., 1985-92, United Way Essex County, 1988-92, treas., 1990-92. Fellow Royal Chartered Inst. Arbitrators (London), Am. Bar Found.; mem. ABA, Am. Law Inst., N.J. Bar Assn., Camden County Bar Assn., Nassau Club, Harbor League Club. Republican. Jewish. Office: Mitchell H Cohen US Courthouse One John F Gerry Plaza PO Box 2097 Camden NJ 08101-2097

**IRISH, LEON EUGENE,** lawyer, educator, non-profit executive; b. Superior, Wis., June 19, 1938; s. Edward Eugene and Phyllis Ione (Johnson) I.; m. Karla W. Simon; children: Stephen T., Jessica L., Thomas A., Emily A. B.A. in History, Stanford U., 1960; J.D., U. Mich., 1964; D.Phil in Law, Oxford (Eng.) U., 1973. Law clk. to Asso. Justice U.S. Supreme Ct. Byron R. White, 1967; cons. Office Fgn. Direct Investments, Dept. Commerce, 1967-68; spl. rep. sec. def. 7th session 3d UN Conf. Law of Sea; mem. Caplin & Drysdale, chartered, Washington, 1968-85; prof. law U. Mich. Law Sch., Ann Arbor, 1985-88; ptnr. Jones, Day, Reavis & Pogue, Washington, 1988-93; v.p., sr. counsel Aetna Life and Casualty Co., Hartford, Conn., 1993-95; pres. Internat. Ctr. Not-for-Profit Law, Washington, 1994—; pres., CEO United Way Internat., Alexandria, Va., 1996; sr. legal cons. World Bank NGO Law, 1997—; adj. prof. Georgetown U. Law Ctr., 1975-85; regent Am. Coll. Tax Counsel, 1986-89; mem. IRS Commr.'s Adv. Group, 1987; bd. dirs. Vols. Tech. Assistance, Found. for Devel. of Polish Agr.; vis. fellow World Bank, 1995-96. Contbr. articles to legal jours. Bd. dirs., sec. Ctr. Comm., Health and Environ. Mem. ABA, D.C. Bar Assn., Am. Law Inst., Am. Coll. Tax Counsel, Coun. on Fgn. Rels. Democrat. Episcopalian. Home: 1410 Hopkins St NW Washington DC 20036-5904

**IRONS, PAULETTE RILEY,** lawyer, state senator; b. New Orleans, May 19, 1953; d. Florida Wilson; m. Alvin L. Irons; children: Marseah Irons Delatte, Paul-Alvin. BBA, Loyola U., New Orleans, 1975; JD, Tulane U., 1991. Bar: La. 1991. Sr. cons. Small Bus. Devel. and Mgmt. Inst., New Orleans, 1992-93; mem. La. Ho. of Reps., Baton Rouge, 1992-94, La. Senate, Baton Rouge, 1994—; vice chmn. transp., hwys. and pub. works com., mem. health and welfare com., formr mem. fin. com., pres. women's caucus,1998, sgt.-at-arms legis. black caucus, 1993-95; sr. cons. Small Bus. Devel. and Mgmt. Inst., New Orleans, 1992-93; adj. prof. Tulane U. Law Clinic, New Orleans, fall 1995; atty. Office of Constable, 1at City Ct., New Orleans, 1996-98; atty. Recorder of Mortgages Office, New Orleans, 1997—; mem. adv. bd. women's network Nat. Conf. State Legislators, Denver, 1996—. Pres. bd. dirs. La. Initiative on Teen Pregnancy Prevention, 1995—; bd. dirs. New Orleans Area Literacy Coalition. Recipient Woman of Excellence award 2d Bapt. Ch., 1994, Outstanding African Am. Woman, Tulane Black Law Students, 1996; named Legislator of Yr., New Orleans Alliance for Good Govt., 1995. Mem. LWV, AAUW, Nat. Order Women Legislators, Nat. Order Black Elected Legislators, Women for a Better La., Ind. Women's Orgn., La. League Good Govt. Democrat. Avocations: reading, travel. Office: La Senate 3308 Tulane Ave Ste 300 New Orleans LA 70119-7160

**IRONS, SPENCER ERNEST,** lawyer; b. Chgo., Sept. 15, 1917; s. Ernest Edward and Gertrude Bertwhistle (Thompson) I.; m. Betty M. Chesnut, Jan. 16, 1954; children: Janet L., Nancy G., Edward S. AB, U. Chgo., 1938; JD, U. Mich., 1941. Bar: Ill. 1941, U.S. Dist. Ct. (no. dist.) Ill. 1953, U.S. Supreme Ct. 1962. Assoc. Holmes, Dixon, Knouff & Potter, Chgo., 1946-50; assoc. McKinney, Carlson, Leaton & Smalley, Chgo., 1950-54, ptnr., 1955-58; sr. atty. Brunswick Corp., Skokie, Ill., 1959-82; pvt. practice Flossmoor, Ill., 1983-92; ret., 1992. Mem. bd. editors U. Mich. Law Rev., 1939-41. Mem. bd. trustees Flossmoor Pub. Library, 1959-61; mem. Chgo. Crime Commn., 1954-82. Lt. col. U.S. Army, 1941-46, 61-62. Mem. ABA, Ill. Bar Assn., Chgo. Bar Assn. (bd. of mgrs. 1954-56), Law Club, Legal Club. Republican. Unitarian. Real property, General corporate, General practice. Home: 2020 Plymouth Ln Northbrook IL 60062-6064

**IRONS, SUE E. FRAYLE,** judge; b. Ogdensburg, N.Y., Aug. 21, 1941; d. Edward Victor and Martha (Martin) Frayle; m. John T. Irons (div. 1972). BS, So. Meth. U., 1963; JD, U. Calif., San Francisco, 1974. Bar: Calif. 1974. Sole practice law San Francisco, 1975-77; atty. Law Office of John Thorpe, Hayward, Calif., 1977-79; counsel Stanford Applied Engring., Santa Clara, Calif., 1980-90; adminstrv. law judge Calif. Unemployment Ins. Appeals Bd., Rancho Cucamonga, Calif., 1990—. Cmty. rels. bd. Prototypes Women's Ctr., Pomona, Calif.; mem. Beyond War, Palo Alto, Calif., 1984-90. Mem. Nat. Audubon Soc. Democrat. Avocations: quilting, travel. Home: 10962 Menlo Ct Alta Loma CA 91701-7730 Office: Calif Unemployment Ins Appeals Bd 9655 Arrow Rte Rancho Cucamonga CA 91730-4514

**IRVINE, LYNDA MYSKA,** lawyer; b. Richmond, Tex., Aug. 24, 1952; d. Clifford E. and Evelyn Blair (Walzel) M.; m. John A. Irvine, May 24, 981; children: James Woolrich, William Myska. BA, Rice U., 1973; postgrad., U. Tex., Austin, 1993-94; JD, U. Houston, 1976. Bar: Tex. 1976, U.S. Dist. Ct. (so. dist.) Tex. 1977, U.S. Ct. Appeals (5th cir.) 1979, Ohio 1981, U.S. Dist. Ct. (so. dist.) Ohio 1981, U.S. Dist. Ct. (no. dist.) Tex. 1992. Assoc. Hutchson & Grundy, Houston, 1976-81; assoc., shareholder Smith & Schnache, Dayton, Ohio, 1981-84; ptnr. Hutchson & Grundy, Houston, 1984-95; counsel Hutcheson & Grundy, Houston, 1996-98; sr. antitrust counsel Equira Svcs. LLC, Houston, 1998—. Mem. Tex. Bar Assn. Antitrust. Home: 3428 Meadow Lake Ln Houston TX 77027-4107 Office: 910 Lousiana OSP 1138 Houston TX 77082

**IRVING, JEANNE ELLEN,** lawyer; b. Brighton, Mass., Aug. 26, 1953. JD, Harvard U., 1978. Assoc. Hennigan, Mercer & Bennett, Los Angeles. State civil litigation, Professional liability. Office: Hennigan Mercer & Bennett 601 S Figueroa St Los Angeles CA 90017-5704

**IRWIN, IVAN, JR.,** lawyer; b. Dallas, Dec. 10, 1933; s. Ivan and Charlotte (Shoupe) I.; m. Carol Eklund; children: Catherine Ann, Ivan III, Margaret Lynn, Kevin. BA, So. Meth. U., 1954, LLB, 1957. Bar: Tex. 1957. Assoc. Fulbright & Jaworski, Houston, 1957-60; ptnr. Shank, Irwin, Conant, Lipshy & Casterline, Dallas, 1960-90, Vinson & Elkins, Dallas, 1990—. Contbr. articles to profl. pubs. Mem. Dallas Citizens Coun., 1988—; bd. dirs., trustee trust fund Dallas Lighthouse for Blind; bd. dirs. Anita N. Martinez Ballet Folklorico, Dallas, 1991-92; mem. photography com. Dallas Mus. Art, 1988—. Mem. Dallas Bar Assn. (corp. coun. and internat. bar sects.). Avocations: photography, golf, tennis. General corporate, Securities, Oil, gas, and mineral. Office: Vinson & Elkins 2001 Ross Ave Ste 3700 Dallas TX 75201-2975

**IRWIN, JAMES BURKE, V,** lawyer; b. St. Louis, June 11, 1947; s. James Burke and June (Cullen) I.; m. Stephanie Lottinger, June 22, 1996; children: James VI, Christopher, Burke. AB, Kenyon Coll., 1969; JD, Case Western Res. U., 1973. Bar: Ohio 1973, La. 1974, U.S. Dist. Ct. (we. dist.) La. 1974, U.S. Dist. Ct. (ea. and mid. dists.) La. 1975, U.S. Ct. Appeals (5th and 11th cirs.) 1975, U.S. Ct. Appeals (3d cir.) 1996, U.S. Supreme Ct. 1983. Law clk. to judge U.S. Dist. Ct., Alexandria, La., 1973-75; ptnr. Montgomery, Barnett, Brown, Read, Hammond & Mintz, New Orleans, 1975—, mng. ptnr., 1998—. Mem. Met. Area Com., New Orleans, 1973. Fellow Am. Coll. Trial Lawyers; mem. ABA, FBA, La. Bar Assn., New Orleans Bar Assn., Internat. Assn. Def. Counsel, La. Assn. Def. Counsel (pres.-elect 1998-99), Def. Rsch. Inst. (state chmn. 1991—). Republican. Episcopalian. Avocations: skiing, golf. General civil litigation, Insurance, Personal injury. Home: 461 Browning Loop Mandeville LA 70448-1914 Office: Montgomery Barnett Brown Read Hammond & Mintz 3200 Energy Ctr New Orleans LA 70163

**IRWIN, LAUREN SIMON,** lawyer, associate; b. St. Louis, Dec. 13, 1968; d. James F. and Marcia Simon; m. Thomas F. Irwin, May 29, 1994. BA, Wesleyan U., 1991; JD cum laude, Boston U., 1994. Bar: N.H. 1994, U.S. Dist. Ct. N.H. 1994. Law clk. N.H. Superior Ct. (rotation), 1994-96; assoc. Upton, Sanders & Smith, Concord, N.H., 1996—. Bd. dirs. Dress for Success N.H., Concord, 1998—; mem. N.H. Coun. Sch. Attys., 1997—. Mem. William Batchelder Inn of Ct. General civil litigation, Civil rights, Education and schools. Office: Upton Sanders & Smith PO Box 1090 Concord NH 03302-1090

**IRWIN, PAT,** federal judge; b. Leedey, Okla., June 12, 1921; s. Marvin J. and Ollie D. (Newton) I.; m. Margaret Boggs, Aug. 18, 1950; children: William, Margaret. Student, Southwestern State Coll., 1939-41, U. Okla., 1941-42, 46-49; LLB, U. Okla., 1949, JD, 1961. Bar: Okla. 1949. County atty. Dewey County, 1949-50; sec. to commrs. land office Okla. Sch. Land Commn., 1955-58; justice Okla. Supreme Ct., 1959-83, chief justice, 1969-70, 81-82; U.S. magistrate judge western dist. Okla., 1983-99; presiding judge appellate div. Okla. Ct. on Judiciary, 1971-74; mem. exec. council Conf. Chief Justices, 1971-72. Mem. Okla. Senate, 1951-54. U.S. Naval aviation cadet, 1942-43, capt. USMCR, 1943-46, PTO. Decorated DFC (2), Air medal (8). Mem. Am. Legion, Masons, Delta Theta Phi. Office: US Courthouse 200 NW 4th St Oklahoma City OK 73102-3026

**IRWIN, R. ROBERT,** lawyer; b. Denver, July 27, 1933; s. Royal Robert and Mildred Mary (Wilson) I.; m. Sue Ann Scott, Dec. 16, 1956; children—Lori, Stacy, Kristi, Amy. Student U. Colo., 1951-54, B.S.L., U. Denver, 1955, LL.B., 1957. Bar: Colo. 1957, Wyo. 1967. Asst. atty. gen. State of Colo., 1958-66; asst. div. atty. Mobil Oil Corp., Casper, Wyo. 1966-70; prin. atty. No. Natural Gas Co., Omaha 1970-72; sr. atty. Coastal Oil & Gas Corp., Denver 1972-83, asst. sec. 1972-83; ptnr. Baker & Hostetler, 1983-87; pvt. practice 1987—. Mem. Colo. Bar Assn., Arapahoe County Bar Assn., Rocky Mountain Oil and Gas Assn. Republican. Clubs: Los Verdes Golf, Petroleum, Denver Law (Denver). General corporate, Oil, gas, and mineral, Real property. Office: 650 S Alton Way Apt 4D Denver CO 80231-1669

**ISAACS, DOROTHY ANN,** lawyer, community activist; b. St. Thomas, V.I., Nov. 20, 1948; d. Walter John and Thelma Ruth (Watson) Maguire; m. Mark Aldes Isaacs, Apr. 8, 1972; children: Julie, Elisabeth. BA, BS, Castleton State Coll., 1970, JD, George Mason U. Sch. of Law, 1988. Lic. atty., Va., D.C. Assoc. Surovell, Jackson, Colten and Dugan P.C., Fairfax, Va., 1988-91; prin. The Law Offices Dorothy M. Isaacs, Alexandria, Va., 1991—. Rep., Mt. Vernon Citizens Assn. Edn. Com., Fairfax County, Va., 1983-85, Task Force on Declining Enrollment, Fairfax County, Va., 1984, Mt. Vernon Ednl. Adv. Com., Fairfax County, 1985. Bd. dirs. Belle View PTA, Fairfax County, 1980-91, pres., 1981-82, West Potomac High Sch. PTA, 1993—; unit co-chair League Women Voters, Fairfax County, 1984-85; bd. dirs. Tauxemont Pre-Sch., Alexandria, 1977-84; bd. dirs. The Women's Ctr. Mem. ABA (law student div., 4th cir. gov. chmn.-publs. com. 1987-88), Am. Assn. Trial Lawyers, Va. Trial Lawyers Assn., Va. Women Lawyers Assn., Fairfax Bar Assn., Alexandria Bar Assn., Phi Delta Phi. General civil litigation, Family and matrimonial, Personal injury. Home: 7204 Marlan Dr Alexandria VA 22307-1912 Office: 100 N Pitt St Ste 201 Alexandria VA 22314-3134

**ISAACS, LEONARD BERNARD,** lawyer; b. Bklyn., Feb. 1, 1951; s. Louis Jack and Sadie (Groman) I.; m. Allison Meryl Grushack, Aug. 23, 1986 (dec.); children: Samantha Nicole, Justin Lance, Adam Tyler. BA, Queens Coll., CUNY, 1973; JD, Hofstra U., 1976. Bar: N.Y. 1977, U.S. Dist. Ct. (ea. and so. dists.) N.Y. 1977, U.S. Ct. Appeals (2d cir.) 1978, U.S. Ct. Claims 1978, U.S. Tax Ct. 1978, U.S. Ct. Mil. Appeals 1978, U.S. Customs Ct. 1978, U.S. Ct. Customs and Patent Appeals 1980, U.S. Ct. Internat. Trade 1980, U.S. Supreme Ct. 1980, U.S. Ct. Appeals (fed. cir.) 1982, U.S. Dist. Ct. (no. dist.) N.Y. 1983. Assoc. in law office Mineola, N.Y., 1977-80; sole practice Valley Stream, N.Y., 1980—. Mem. N.Y. State Bar Assn., Nassau County Bar Assn. Republican. Jewish. Criminal, Personal injury, Family and matrimonial. Office: 108 S Franklin Ave Ste 16 Valley Stream NY 11580-6105

**ISAACS, ROBERT CHARLES,** retired lawyer; b. N.Y.C., July 16, 1919; s. David and Elsie (Weiss) I.; m. Doris Frances Shapiro, Nov. 20, 1943 (dec. 1982); 1 child, Leigh Richard; m. Mary Lou Anderson, Dec. 12, 1986. BA cum laude, NYU, 1941, JD (Maurice Goodman Meml. prize), 1943. Bar: N.Y. 1943. Asst. dep. atty. gen. N.Y. State Dept. Law, Albany, 1943, spl. asst. atty. gen., 1946; ptnr. Nordlinger Riegelman Benetar, N.Y.C., 1946-71, Aranow Brodsky Bohlinger Benetar & Einhorn, N.Y.C., 1972-79; ptnr. Benetar Isaacs Bernstein & Schair, N.Y.C., 1979-88; vice chmn. Lebanon (N.H.) Zoning Bd. Adjustment, 1988—; adj. prof. law St. John's U. Sch. Law, N.Y.C., 1961-72. Served to capt. U.S. Army, 1943-45, 51. Mem. ABA, N.Y.C. Bar Assn., N.Y.U. Alumni Club. Contbr. articles to profl. publs. Labor, Federal civil litigation. Home: 5 Village Grn West Lebanon NH 03784-1506

**ISAACS, SABRINA,** lawyer; b. N.Y.C., July 24, 1966; d. Abby and Jacqueline Setaveh; m. Jeffrey S. Isaacs, Oct. 12, 1991; children: Corey, Jason. BA, Colgate U., 1988; JD, Cardozo Law Sch., 1991. Assoc. Kucker, Kraus & Bruh, N.Y.C., 1992-98, ptnr., 1998—; arbitrator Civil Ct. N.Y.C., 1997—. Mem. N.Y.C. Bar Assn. (housing ct. com. 1997—). Home: 652 Oak Tree Rd Palisades NY 10964-1531 Office: Kucker Kraus and Bruh 36 W 44th St New York NY 10036-8102

**ISABELLA, MARY MARGARET,** lawyer; b. Pitts., Oct. 16, 1947; d. Sebastian C. and Joanna C. (dec.) (Ferris) I. BS in Biology, Duquesne U., 1969; cert. med. technologist, Mercy Hosp., Pitts., 1970; JD, Duquesne U., 1975. Bar: Pa. 1976, U.S. Dist Ct. (we. dist.) Pa. 1976, U.S. Supreme Ct., 1982. Sole practice Pitts., 1977—; instr. Wheeling (W.Va.) Coll., 1978-80. mem. coun. Brentwood Whitehall Assn., Pitts., 1984-90; bd. dirs. Dukes Ct., Duquesne U.; bd. govs. Law Alumni Assn., treas., 1993, sec., 1994-95. Mem. ABA ( vice chair sole practice sect., 1994—), Pa. Bar Assn., Allegheny County Bar Assn., Delta Theta Phi (past asst. dist. chancellor). Republican. Roman Catholic. Lodge: Italian Sons and Daughters of Am. (trustee local chpt.). Family and matrimonial, Probate. Office: 4101 Brownsville Rd Bldg 200 Pittsburgh PA 15227-3336

**ISAF, FRED THOMAS,** lawyer; b. Jacksonville, N.C., Nov. 18, 1950; s. Thomas Fred and Rowanda (Maloof) I.; m. June J. Jeffcoat, Aug. 18, 1973; children: Julie, Thomas, Christa. BA, Duke U., 1972; JD, Emory U., 1975, LLM in Taxation, 1978. Bar: Ga. 1975. Ptnr. Peterson, Young, Self & Asselin, Atlanta, 1980-86; shareholder Roberts and Isaf, PC, Atlanta, 1986-94, Roberts, Isaf & Summers, PC, Atlanta, 1994—. Contbr. article to profl. jour. Dir. Pinecrest Acad., 1995—. Mem. State Bar Ga., Cherokee Town and Country Club (dir. 1994-96, 99, sec. 1993, v.p. 1997, pres. 1998), Order of the Coif, Order of Barristers. General corporate, Securities, Real property. Office: Roberts Isaf & Summers PC 1100 Abernathy Rd NE Ste 1100 Atlanta GA 30328-5629

**ISBELL, DAVID BRADFORD,** lawyer, legal educator; b. New Haven, Feb. 18, 1929; s. Percy Ernest and Dorothy Mae (Crabb) I.; m. Florence Bachrach, July 21, 1971; children: Christopher Pascal, Virginia Anne, Nicholas Bradford. BA, Yale U., 1949, LLB, 1956. Bar: Conn., 1956, D.C. 1957. Assoc. Covington & Burling, Washington, 1957-59, 61-65, ptnr., 1965-98, sr. counsel, 1998—; asst. staff dir. U.S. Commn. on Civil Rights, Washington, 1959-61; lectr. Sch. Law U. Va., 1962—, Georgetown U. Law Ctr., 1996—. Bd. dirs. ACLU, 1965-92. 2nd lt. U.S. Army, 1951-53. Mem. ABA (mem. ho. dels. 1986-96, chairperson com. on ethics and profl. responsibility 1991-94), D.C. Bar (gov. 1978-82, pres. 1983-84), Cosmos Club. Federal civil litigation, Libel, General corporate. Home: 3709 Bradley Ln Bethesda MD 20815-4256 Office: Covington & Burling 1201 Pennsylvania Ave NW PO Box 7566 Washington DC 20044-7566

**ISCOE, CRAIG STEVEN,** lawyer; b. Austin, Tex., May 10, 1953; s. Ira and Louise N. (Kosches) I.; m. Rosemary Anne Hart, Apr. 16, 1983; children: David Hart, Mark Samuel. BA, U. Tex., 1974; JD, Stanford U., 1978; LLM, Georgetown U., 1979. Bar: D.C. 1978, U.S. Dist. Ct. D.C. 1978, U.S. Dist. Ct. Tenn., 1992, U.S. Supreme Ct. 1982, Tenn. 1992. Grad. fellow/staff atty. Inst. for Pub. Representation, Washington, 1978-79; asst. to dir. FTC, Washington, 1980-82; assoc. Arent, Fox, Washington, 1982-85; vis. prof. Georgetown U., Washington, 1986; asst. U.S. atty. U.S. Atty. for D.C., 1986-91, 92-97; asst. prof. Vanderbilt U., Nashville, 1991-92; counsel to the Dep. Atty. Gen., 1997—; adj. prof. Georgetown U. Law Sch., 1990, 92—; instr. Nat. Inst. Trial Advocacy, Washington, 1993-95, N.Mex., 1995. Contbr. articles to profl. jours., chpts. to books. Bd. dirs. Wash. Coun. Lawyers, 1989-91, 93-95, cons. Am. Bar Assn. Ctrl. & East European Law Initiative, (CEELI). Recipient Spl. Achievement award Dept. Justice, 1994, 95. Democrat. Jewish. Avocations: running, woodworking. Office: Office of US Atty 555 4th St NW Washington DC 20001-2733

**ISENBERG, ANDREW BRIAN,** lawyer; b. Buffalo, N.Y., Sept. 10, 1967. BA in Econs., Northwestern U., 1989; JD cum laude, SUNY, Buffalo, 1992. Bar: N.Y. 1993, Fla. 1995, D.C. 1994, U.S. Dist. Ct. (we. dist.) N.Y. 1994. Law clk. N.Y. State Supreme Ct. Appellate Divsn., Rochester, 1992-94; assoc. Offermann, Cassano, Greco & Slisz LLP, Buffalo, N.Y., 1994-98, Gresens & Gillen LLP, Buffalo, N.Y., 1998—. Articles editor Buffalo Law Rev., 1991-92. V.p. Am. Jewish Com., Buffalo, 1997—. Mem. N.Y. State Bar Assn. (com. atty. professionalism 1994-97), Erie County Bar Assn. (chair appellate practice com. 1998—), Sertoma Club, Northwestern Alumni Assn., Nichols Sch. Alumni Assn. (class agt.), Rep. Lawyers Club (treas. 1997—), Phi Beta Kappa. Avocation: tennis. Consumer commercial, Appellate, General civil litigation. Office: Gresens & Gillen LLP 12 Fountain Plz Rm 510 Buffalo NY 14202-2222

**ISERN, KEVIN ANTHONY,** lawyer; b. San Juan, P.R., Oct. 5, 1966; s. Janet Rae Isern; m. Karem Amelia Upchurch, Dec. 19, 1992. BS, Ariz. State U., 1988; JD, So. Meth. U., 1991. Bar: Tex. 1991. Briefing atty. Tex. Ct. Appeals (5th cir.), Dallas, 1991-92; assoc. Tom Upchurch Jr. & Assocs., Amarillo, Tex., 1992—. Vol. Big Bros., Phoenix, 1986, Juvenile Diabetes Assn., Dallas, 1990—. Mem. ABA, Tex. Bar Assn., Dallas Bar Assn., Amarillo Bar Assn., Tex. Trial Lawyers Assn. Republican. Methodist. Avocations: all sports, reading. General civil litigation, Criminal, Personal injury. Office: Tom Upchurch Jr & Assocs 3310 W Interstate 40 Amarillo TX 79102-2109

**ISLA, EXU REIDEMER Q.,** corrections professional, lawyer; b. Villasis, Pangasinan, The Philippines, May 30, 1941; camd to U.S., 1990; s. Francisco Lopez and Rosenda (Quero) I.; m. Carmen Rosales Isla, June 7, 1970; children: Mary, Christian, John, Imelda, Theresa, Francis. AA, U. Pangasinan, 1960, edn. degree, 1965, postgrad., 1970-72, 80-81, JD, 1985; BA, U. of East, Manila, 1963; bus. adminstrn. degree, Arellano U., The Philippines, 1969; legal asst. diploma, Internat. Corr. Schs., 1969. Instr. social studies U. Pangasinan, 1964-68, 69-72; cmty. devel. worker Presdl. Arms Cmty. Devel., The Philippines, 1968-69; tchr. social studies Manila Pub. Schs., 1968-69; tng. officer Capital Planning Corp., The Philippines, 1971-74; regional tng. officer Bur. Lands, The Philippines, 1974-79; manpower devel. officer Nat. Manpower, The Philippines, 1979-87; election registrar Commn. on Elections, The Philippines, 1987-89; legal asst. Nat. Bur. Investigation, The Philippines, 1989-90; probation officer Gary (Ind.) City Ct., 1991—; rural devel. cons. Presdl. Office for Devel., The Philippines, 1978-81; youth devel. cons. Youth Movement in Barrios, The Philippines, 1978-86. Columnist North Tribune and Ilocos Times, The Philippines, 1974-87, Weekly Express, The Philippines, 1987-89. Presdl. asst. for Province of Abra, Presdl. Regional Office for Devel. Regional Mgmt. Staff, 1978-81; regional sec. Rural Adv. Bd., The Philippines, 1978-81. Recipient provincial award Pangasinan-Dagupan City YMCA, nat. award Nat. YMCA, The Philippines, 1965, Found. for Youth Devel. in The Philippines, award of recognition Ministry Pub. Info., Ilocos Region, 1980, Pangasinan State U., 1981, Provincial Agr. Office Pangasinan, 1984, Mcpl. Coun. Urdaneta, Pangasinan, 1989, Outstanding Adminstr. award KC, The Philippines, 1982, Outstanding Parent award U. Pangasinan H.S., Dagupan City, 1989, Lew Wallace H.S., Gary, 1994. Mem. Am. Correctional Assn., Ind. Correctional Assn., Philippine Profl. Assn. (officer 1991—), Internat. Inst. N.W. Ind. (officer 1991—). Home: 5066 Pennsylvania St Gary IN 46409-2738 Office: Gary City Ct 1301 Broadway Gary IN 46407-1326

**ISQUITH, FRED TAYLOR,** lawyer; b. N.Y.C., June 6, 1947; s. Stanley and Rita (Hoskwith) I.; m. Susan Nora Goldberg, May 23, 1976; children:

Fred, Rebecca. BA, Brooklyn Coll. of CUNY, 1968; JD, Columbia U., 1971. Bar: N.Y. 1972, D.C. 1976, U.S. Dist. Ct. (so. and ea. dists.) N.Y. 1975, U.S. Dist. Ct. (no. dist.) N.Y. 1988, U.S. Dist. Ct. (we. dist.) Mich. 1992, U.S. Dist. Ct. Ariz. 1994, U.S. Dist. Ct. (ctrl. dist.) Ill. 1996, U.S. Ct. Appeals (2d cir.) 1975, U.S. Ct. Appeals (8th cir.) 1985, U.S. Ct. Appeals (3d cir.) 1986, U.S. Ct. Appeals (4th cir.) 1990, U.S. Supreme Ct. 1983. Assoc. Fulbright & Jaworski, N.Y.C., 1971-75, Kaye Scholer et al, N.Y.C., 1975-80; ptnr. Wolf Haldenstein Adler Freeman & Herz, N.Y.C., 1980—; bd. trustees St. Chad's Coll. Found.; bd. dirs. 103 East 84th St. Corp., N.Y.C., Sheinkopf Communications, Ltd.; lectr. Am. Conf. Inst., N.Y. State Bar Assn.; mediator Supreme Ct. State N.Y. County N.Y. Comml. Divsn.; arbitrator Am. Arbitration Assn. Author: An Introduction to Securities Arbitration, 1994, Real Estate Exit Strategies, 1994; editor, weekly columnist The Class Act. Mem. ABA, N.Y. State Bar Assn. (coms. on securities and legis.), N.Y. County Lawyers Assn. (chair bus. torts), D.C. Bar Assn., Assn. of Bar of City of N.Y., Bklyn. Bar Assn. (civil practice law and rules com., legis. com. and fed. ct. coms.), Columbia Club. Federal civil litigation, Securities, State civil litigation. Office: Wolf Haldenstein Adler Freeman & Herz 270 Madison Ave New York NY 10016-0601

**ISRAEL, BARRY JOHN,** lawyer; b. Rockford, Ill., Mar. 14, 1946; s. Robert John and Bettie Jane (Erickson) I.; m. Lynne Charlene Thomsen; children: Alison, Ashley, Brenna. BA, U. So. Calif., L.A., 1968; JD, George Washington U., 1974. Bar: Calif. 1975, D.C. 1976, U.S. Supreme Ct. 1978, U.S. Dist. Ct. Mariana Islands 1985. Assoc. Clifford & Warnke, Washington, 1975-83; ptnr. Stovall, Spradlin, Armstrong & Israel, Washington, 1983-86, Dorsey & Whitney, Washington, 1988-92, Stroock, Stroock & Lavan, Washington, 1992-95; spl. counsel, pres. Federated States of Micronesia, 1982-84; spl. asst. atty. gen. Territory Guam, 1990-95; bd. dirs. Bank of the Federated States of Micronesia. Author: (guides) Investment Guides to the Federated States of Micronesia and the Republic of the Marshall Islands, 1989. 1st lt. U.S. Army, 1969-72. Democrat. Avocations: travel, tennis. Private international, Public international, Administrative and regulatory. Home: 1310 Shoreline Dr Santa Barbara CA 93109-2124

**ISRAEL, DEBORAH JEAN,** lawyer; b. Atlantic City, N.J., Nov. 10, 1964; d. Gary Philip and Alice Louise Israel. BA, Rutgers U., 1986, JD, 1990. Assoc. Melrod, Redman & Gartlan, Washington, 1990-93, Colton & Boykin, Washington, 1992-95; mem. Silverstein & Mullens, P.L.L.C., Washington, 1995—. Bd. dirs. Metro Teen AIDS, Washington, 1996—; co-chair WBA Cmty. Project Com., 1992-95. Mem. D.C. Women's Bar Assn. Found. (pres. 1996-98, v.p. 1995-96). Federal civil litigation, Trademark and copyright, Contracts commercial. Home: 1713 Preston Rd Alexandria VA 22302-2126 Office: Silverstein & Mullens PLLC 1776 K St NW Washington DC 20006-2304

**ISRAELS, MICHAEL JOZEF,** lawyer; b. N.Y.C., Sept. 27, 1949; s. Carlos Lindner and Ruth Lucille (Goldstein) I.; m. Maija-Sarmite Jansons, Aug. 31, 1980; children: Aleksandrs Lehman, Peter Carlos. A.B. magna cum laude, Amherst Coll., 1972; J.D., Harvard U., 1975. Bar: N.Y. 1976, U.S. Dist. Ct. (so. and ea. dists.) N.Y. 1976, D.C. 1977, N.J. 1980, U.S. Dist. Ct. N.J. 1980. Assoc. Shearman & Sterling, N.Y.C., 1975-79; sole practice, N.Y.C., 1979-81; ptnr. Courter, Kobert, Laufer & Pease, P.A., Hackettstown, N.J., 1981-83, Fitzpatrick & Israels, Bayonne and Secaucus, N.J., 1983-87, 89-94; sr. ptnr. Waters, McPherson, McNeill, Fitzpatrick, P.A., Secaucus, N.J., 1987-89; ptnr. Broscious, Israels, Glynn & Gentile, Washington, N.J., 1994-96; counsel Fitzpatrick & Waterman, 1996—; gen. counsel Kearny (N.J.) Mcpl. Port Authority, 1985-90, Jersey City Mcpl. Port Authority, 1986-96; Kearny Mcpl. Utilities Authority, 1988-95; mem. N.J. Debt. Mgmt. Adv. Com., 1986—; cons. U.S./USSR Trade Council, N.Y.C., 1979, Council on Religion and Internat. Affairs, N.Y.C., 1980. Author: (with Moore, Thomson and Linsky) Report of the New England Conference on Conflicts Between Media and Law, 1977. Contbr. articles to legal jours. Bd. dirs. Community Tax Aid, Inc., N.Y.C., 1976-82, Am. Jewish Com., N.Y.C., 1980-88 , Anti-Defamation League N.J., Livingston, 1981—, U.S. Assn. Internat. Migration, 1988-94; mem. religious sch. com. Temple Emanu-El, N.Y.C., 1972-84. Mem. ABA (gov. Law Student div. 1974-75), Assn. Bar City N.Y., N.J. Bar Assn. Clubs: Met. Opera, Harvard (N.Y.C.). General corporate, Estate taxation, Municipal (including bonds). Home: 160 W 66th St Apt 51E New York NY 10023-6567 Office: Fitzpatrick & Waterman 227 Main St Hackettstown NJ 07840-2001

**ISRAELS, VALLI KATRINA,** prosecutor; b. Modesto, Calif.; m. Andrew Mendlin, Oct. 9, 1994. BA, U. Calif., Berkeley, 1989; JD, U. of the Pacific, 1989. Bar: Calif. 1994. Dep. dist. atty. Sacramento County, Sacramento, Calif., 1994-95, San Joaquin County, Stockton, Calif., 1995—. Mem. Stanslaus Bar. Office: San Joaquin County Dist Atty 222 E Weber Ave Ste 202 Stockton CA 95202-2709

**ISRAELSTAM, ALFRED WILLIAM,** lawyer; b. Chgo., Nov. 8, 1908; s. Adolph and Tillie Block Israelstam; m. Beatrice Ruden, Oct. 29, 1934; children: David M., Frances. JD, U. Chgo., 1933. Bar: U.S. Dist. Ct. (no. dist.) Ill. 1934. Sole practice Chgo., 1934-98, Buffalo Grove, Ill., 1998—; bd. dirs. Erect-A-Tube Inc., Harvard, Ill. Author: Verses for 21st Century, 1997. Jewish. Avocation: poetry—sonnet writing. General practice, Real property, General corporate. Home: 360 Lincolnwood Rd Highland Park IL 60035-5214 Office: 1111 W Lake Cook Rd Buffalo Grove IL 60089-1926

**ISSELBACHER, RHODA SOLIN,** lawyer; b. Springfield, Mass., June 12, 1932; d. Jay Zachary and Theo L. (Michelman) S.; m. Kurt J. Isselbacher, June 22, 1955; children: Lisa Isselbacher-Ramirez, Karen Isselbacher-Epstein, Jody Isselbacher-Coukos, Eric M. BA, Cornell U., 1954; JD, Harvard U., 1959. Bar: Mass. 1960, U.S. Dist. Ct. Mass. 1984. Assoc. firm Melvin Dangel, Boston, 1960-67, Sherin & Lodgen, Boston, 1965-67, Pollock & Katz, Boston, 1967-70; ptnr. firm Epstein, King & Isselbacher, Boston, 1971-91; gen. counsel Dana-Farber Cancer Inst., Boston, 1979-89; pvt. practice law, Newton Centre, Mass., 1989-91; of counsel Edwards and Angell, Boston, 1991-92; legal counsel Mass. Gen. Hosp. Svc. League, 1969-85; legal cons. Children's Sch. of Sci., Woods Hole, Mass., 1969—; cons. med. programming WGBH-TV, 1972-73. Alderman, Woods Hole, Mass., 1968; chmn. Newton United Fund, Mass., 1961; trustee, Beaver Country Day Sch., 1975-77. Mem. Mass. Bar Assn., Boston Bar Assn., Mass. Health Lawyers Assn. Health, Probate, Real property. Home and Office: 20 Nobscot Rd Newton MA 02459-1323

**ISSLER, HARRY,** lawyer; b. Cologne, Germany, Nov. 14, 1935; came to U.S., 1937; s. Max and Fanny (Grunbaum) I.; m. Doris Helen Lukow, June 1, 1958; children: Adriane P. Schorr, M. Valerie Priestley, Stephanie L. Beck. BS, U. Wis., 1955; JD, Cornell U., 1958. Bar: N.Y. 1958, U.S. Supreme Ct. 1962, U.S. Ct. Mil. Appeals 1967, U.S. Dist. Ct. (so. and ea. dists.) N.Y. 1960, U.S. Customs Ct. 1964, U.S. Tax Ct. 1964; cert. specialist in civil trial advocacy Nat. Bo. Trial Advocacy. Assoc. Wing & Wing, N.Y.C., 1958-60, Fuchsberg & Fuchsberg, N.Y.C., 1960-62; ptnr. Issler & Fein, N.Y.C., 1963-68, Shaw, Issler & Rosenberg, N.Y.C., 1968-70; pvt. practice N.Y.C., 1970-79; sr. ptnr. The Law Firm of Harry Issler PLC, N.Y.C., 1979—; arbitrator Civil Ct., N.Y. County, 1979-91; hearing officer N.Y. State Tax Appeals, 1975-77, Supreme Ct. of N.Y., N.Y. County Med. Malpractice Panel, 1980-91; judge advocate N.Y. State; mem. neutral evaluator mediation panel Supreme Ct., N.Y. County, 1997—. Trustee N.Y. State Mil. Ednl. Found., 1997—. With U.S. Army, 1958-59, N.Y. Army N.G., 1963-88, ret. brig. gen., 1988. Ford Found. scholar, 1951-55. Mem. N.Y. State Bar Assn., Assn. of Bar of City N.Y., Am. Trial Lawyers Assn., N.Y. State Trial Lawyers Assn., 42d Infantry Div. Officers Club (N.Y.C., pres. 1979-80), Officers Club (U.S. Mcht. Marine Acad.), 42d Infantry Rainbow Div. Assn. (pres. 1989), Phi Alpha Delta, Pi Lambda Phi (Omega chpt. pres. 1953-54). Family and matrimonial, Personal injury, Military. Home: 50 Sutton Pl S New York NY 10022-4167 Office: The Law Firm of Harry Issler PLC 65 E 55th St New York NY 10022-3219

**ITKOFF, DAVID F.,** lawyer; b. Cin., Dec. 30, 1953. BA magna cum laude, Boston U., 1976; JD, Villanova U., 1979. Bar: Pa. 1979, U.S. Dist. Ct. (ea. dist.) Pa. 1979, U.S. Supreme Ct. 1983, U.S. Ct. Appeals (3d cir.) 1986. Pvt. practice, Phila., 1979—. Mem. ABA, Assn. Trial Lawyers Am., Pa. Bar Assn., Phila. Trial Lawyers Assn. State civil litigation, Insurance, Personal injury. Home: Zenas Buckman House 1300 Wrightstown Rd Newtown PA 18940-9602 Office: Penns Park Place PO Box 528 2325 2d Street Pike Penns Park PA 18943

**ITO, LANCE ALLAN,** judge; b. L.A., Aug. 2, 1950; s. Jim and Toshi I.; m. Margaret York. BA cum laude, UCLA, 1972; JD, U. Calif., Berkeley, 1975. Bar: Calif. 1976. Civil atty., 1975-77; dep. dist. atty. gang unit, complaints divsn., organized crime unit L.A. County Dist. Attys. Office, 1977-87; judge L.A. County Mcpl. Ct., 1987-89, Superior Ct. Calif., L.A. County, 1989—; vice chair Calif. Task Force on Youth Gang Violence, 1986, 89, Calif. Task Force on Victims Rights, 1988. Named Trial Judge of Yr. L.A. County Bar Assn., 1992. Mem. Calif. Judges Assn. (bd. dirs., mem. calif. coun. on criminal justice), L.A. County Bar Assn., Japanese-Am. Bar Assn. Democrat. Office: Criminal Cts Bldg 210 W Temple St Los Angeles CA 90012-3210*

**IVANCIC, GREGORY THOMAS,** lawyer, accountant, educator; b. Buffalo, July 18, 1955; s. John G. and Gladys J. Ivancic; m. Diane M. Hess, Aug. 25, 1984; children: Thomas, William, Alexander. BBA, U. Notre Dame, 1977; JD, SUNY, Buffalo, 1982. Bar: N.Y. 1983, U.S. Dist. Ct. (we. dis.) N.Y. 1983; CPA, N.Y. Acct. Price Waterhouse Coopers, Buffalo, 1977-79; atty., ptnr. Cohen Swados Wright Hanifin Bradford & Brett, Buffalo, 1983—; adj. prof. acctg. Canisius Coll., Buffalo, 1988—. Chmn. bd. dirs. Gateway Longview Inc., Buffalo, 1998. Mem. Notre Dame Club Western N.Y. (pres.), Buffalo Sabres Alumni Assn. (bd. dirs., sec. 1990—). Avocations: golf, skiing. General corporate, Taxation, general, Sports. Office: Cohen Swados Wright Hanifin Bradford & Brett 70 Niagara St Ste 1 Buffalo NY 14202-3467

**IVARY, ERIC HENRY,** lawyer; b. Oakland, Calif., Sept. 15, 1946; s. Toivo Henry and Margaret Aldrich (Ames) I.; children: Amy, Andrew; m. Rebecca Jo Brittain, Jan. 30, 1984; children: Debra, James. BA, St. Mary's Coll., 1968; JD, U. Santa Clara, 1971. Bar: Calif. 1972, U.S. Dist. Ct. (no. dist.) Calif. 1972, U.S. Ct. Appeals (9th cir.) 1972. From assoc. to ptnr. Alfred Naphan Law Office, Oakland, Calif., 1971-78; v.p., mng. ptnr. Gwilliam, Ivary, Chiosso, Cavalli & Brewer, Oakland, Calif., 1978—. Co-author: Winning at Arbitration, 1992. Mem. ATLA, Alameda Countra-Costa County Trial Lawyers Assn. (past pres., chpt. bd. dirs. 1975-90), Am. Bd. Trial Advs., Alameda County Lawyers' Club (Lawyer of Yr. 1995). Avocations: running, golfing. Professional liability, Insurance, Product liability. Office: Gwilliam Ivary et al 1999 Harrison St Ste 1600 Oakland CA 94612-3577

**IVERS, DONALD LOUIS,** judge; b. San Diego, May 6, 1941; s. Grant Perrin and Margaret (Ware) I. BA, U. N.Mex., 1963; JD, Am. U., 1971. Bar: U.S. Dist. Ct. (D.C. 1972, U.S. Ct. Appeals (D.C. cir.) 1972, U.S. Ct. Mil. Appeals 1972, U.S. Supreme Ct. 1975. Assoc., Brault, Graham, Scott, Brault, Washington, 1972-78; chief counsel Republican Nat Com., Washington, 1978-81, gen. counsel 1980 Rep. Nat. Conv. Site Selection Com., 1979-80; chief counsel Fed. Hwy. Adminstrn., U.S. Dept. Transp., Washington, 1981-85; counselor to sec., chmn. sec.'s safety rev. task force U.S. Dept. Transp., Washington, 1984-85; gen. counsel VA, 1985-89; acting gen. counsel U.S. Dept. Vet. Affairs, 1989-90, asst. to the sec., 1990; assoc. judge U.S. Ct. Appeals Vet. Claims, 1990—. Capt. U.S. Army, 1963-68, Vietnam, lt. col. Res., ret. Decorated Bronze Star, Air medal, Parachute badge. Mem. D.C. Bar Assn., Delta Theta Phi. Office: US Ct Appeals Vet Claims 625 Indiana Ave NW Washington DC 20004-2923

**IVERSON, DALE ANN,** lawyer; b. Ann Arbor, Mich., Feb. 3, 1956; d. Arthur T. Jr. and Ann Lois (Geary) I. BA, Oberlin Coll., 1979; JD, U. Wis., 1983. Bar: Wis. 1983, Mich. 1983, U.S. Dist. Ct. (we. dist.) Mich. 1983, U.S. Dist. Ct. (ea. dist.) Mich. 1984. Ptnr. Smith, Haughey, Rice & Roegge, Grand Rapids, Mich., 1983—. Contbr. articles to profl. publs. Bd. Dirs. Urban League for Contemporary Art; mem. Leadership Grand Rapids. Mem. ABA, State Bar of Mich. (exec. coun. ADR sect., Supreme Ct. dispute resolution task force, cert. mediator Western dist., coun. alt. dispute resolution sect., character and fitness com. 1986-92), Grand Rapids Bar Assn. (trustee 1992-95, v.p. 1999—). Avocations: sailing, horseback riding, gardening. General civil litigation, Alternative dispute resolution, Non-profit and tax-exempt organizations. Office: Smith Haughey Rice & Roegge 250 Monroe Ave NW Ste 200 Grand Rapids MI 49503-2251

**IVES, ANSON BRADLEY,** lawyer; b. Jacksonville, Fla., Sept. 8, 1964; s. William Maner and Sue (Howe) I. BA, U. N.C., 1986, JD, 1989. Bar: Va., N.Y. Assoc. Hunton and Williams, Richmond, Va., 1989-91, N.Y.C., 1991-92; assoc. Orrick, Herrington & Sutcliffe, N.Y.C., 1993—. Bd. dirs. William Byrd Community House, Richmond, 1990. Morehead scholar U. N.C., 1986. Mem. ABA, Va. Bar Assn, Round Table Internat. Republican. Episcopalian. Office: Orrick Herrington & Sutcliffe 666 5th Ave Fl 18 New York NY 10103-0001

**IVES, DANIEL DELBERT,** lawyer; b. Tulsa, Nov. 27, 1951; s. Delbert Ennis and Mary (Bunch) I.; m. Rebecca Mulligan, Mar. 17, 1984; children: Mary Nell, David Daniel. BBA, Ark. U., 1975, MBA, 1976, JD, 1978. Bar: Ark. 1979, U.S. Dist. Ct. (we. dist.) Ark. 1979. Ptnr. Rollins & Ives, Camden, Ark., 1981—; dep. pros. atty. 13th Jud. Dist., Camden, Ark., 1987-98; city atty. Chidester, Ark., 1991—, East Camden, Ark., 1992-98; mcpl. judge East Camden, 1999—. Pres. Rotary Club, Camden, 1988-89; v.p. United Way, Camden, 1992-93, C. of C., Camden, 1990. Mem. ABA, Ark. Bar Assn., Ouachita County Bar Assn. Baptist. Avocations: golf, tennis, swimming. General practice, Bankruptcy, Personal injury. Office: Rollins & Ives PA 143 Jackson Camden AR 71701

**IVES, STEPHEN BRADSHAW, JR.,** retired lawyer; b. N.Y.C., Oct. 6, 1924. AB, Harvard U., 1948; LLB, Yale U., 1951. Bar: R.I. 1952, D.C. 1970, U.S. Supreme Ct. 1960. Assoc. Hinckley, Allen, Salisbury & Parsons, Providence, 1952-57, ptnr., 1957-61; exec. asst. to adminstr. AID, Washington, 1961-62, dir. Office Korea Affairs, 1962-64, dir. Office East Asian Affairs, 1964-66, assoc. asst. adminstr. Far East, 1966-67, dept. asst. adminstr. East Asia, 1967-68, gen. counsel, 1968-70; ptnr. Wald, Harkrader and Ross, Washington, 1970-87; of counsel Pepper, Hamilton & Scheetz, 1987-95; mem. R.I. Mechanics Lien Law Commn., R.I. Commn. Interstate Coop. Bd. dirs. Providence Community Fund, Children's Friend and Svc. R.I.; mem. U.S. del. U.S.-USSR Comml. Commn., 1975; dir. Bus. Coun. S.E. Europe, 1977-95, vice. chmn. 1991-95. Mem. ABA, D.C. Bar Assn. (chmn. div. internat. law and transactions 1976-77), R.I. Bar Assn. (past mem. exec. com.), Fed. Bar Assn., Washington Fgn. Law Soc. (past pres.), Am. Soc. Internat. Law, Am. Arbitration Assn. (panel), Order of Coif, Phi Beta Kappa. Private international, Public international. Home: 3508 Macomb St NW Washington DC 20016-3162

**IVEY, JACK TODD,** lawyer; b. Galveston, Tex., Apr. 26, 1967; s. Jack Lyndon Ivey and Catherine Ann (Kemmerer) Harward; m. Jane Marie Gurley, May 7, 1994. BA, U. Tex., 1989; JD, So. Tex. U., 1992. Bar: Tex. 1993, U.S. Dist. Ct. (so., no., and ea. dists.) Tex. 1994, U.S. Ct. Appeals (5th cir.), U.S. Supreme Ct. Assoc. Holland & Stephens, Houston, 1993-95, Holland & Assocs., Houston, 1995-97; ptnr. Ivey & Kadlec, Houston, 1997—. Vol. HTLF Adopt-a-Sch., Houston, 1993-99. Mem. Tex. Trial Lawyers Assn., Houston Trial Lawyers Assn., Houston Bar Assn. (com. mem. 1995-97), Houston Trial Lawyers Found. (bd. dirs. 1996-99), Coll. of the State Bar. Personal injury, Consumer commercial, General civil litigation. Home: 11306 Del Monte Dr Houston TX 77077-6408 Office: 440 Louisiana St Ste 715 Houston TX 77002-1634

**IVEY, JOHN KEMMERER,** lawyer; b. Ft. Worth, Aug. 31, 1961; s. Jack Lyndon Ivey and Catherine (Kemmerer) Harward. BBA in Fin., U. Tex., 1983, JD, 1985; grad., Nat. Inst. Trial Advocacy, 1989. Bar: Tex. 1986, U.S. Dist. Ct. (no. dist.) Tex. 1986, U.S. Dist. Ct. (ea. dist.) Tex. 1988, U.S. Dist. Ct. (so. and we. dists.) Tex. 1989, U.S. Dist. Ct. (ea. dist.) Ark. 1987, U.S. Dist. Ct. Minn. 1990, U.S. Ct. Appeals (5th and 11th cirs.) 1987, Bd. Cert. Personal Inj. Trial Law Tex. Bd. Legal Specialization (1994), Coll. of The State Bar of Tex., 1995—. Assoc. Cowles & Thompson, Dallas, 1985-86, Hopkins & Sutter, Dallas, 1987-89, Meshbesher & Spence Ltd., Mpls., 1990-92, Jim S. Adler P.C., Houston, 1992-94; pvt. practice Houston, 1994-96; James W. Shoecraft P.C. Dallas, 1996-99; with Kraft & Assocs. PC, 1999—; dir. and lectr. seminars Video Software Dealer's Assn., 1990, 91. Contbr. articles to profl. jours. Mem. State Bar Tex., ATLA, Tex. Trial Lawyers Assn., Dallas Trial Lawyers Assn., Houston Trial Lawyers Assn., Houston Trial Lawyers Found. (vol., team capt. JFK Elem. Sch. project 1994-96, bd. dirs. 1996), ABA (Inns of Ct. com. 1990-92, Pro Bono com. 1991-92), Houston Bar Assn., Citizens for Qualified Judiciary. Native American, Product liability, Insurance. Home: 3209 Chippenham Dr Plano TX 75093-3117 Office: 2777 N Stemmons Fwy Dallas TX 75207-2277

**IVEY, RUTH PROUDMAN,** lawyer; b. Jersey City, N.J., Nov. 10, 1921; d. Chester Frederick and Ruth Merriam (Walters) Proudman; m. William Hamilton Ivey, 1946 (div. 1972); 1 child, Marilyn Carlyle. BA, Barnard Coll., 1948; MLS, Columbia Sch. Libr. Svcs., 1951; JD, NYU, 1961. Bar: N.Y. 1962. Sec. to chief counsel Shearman & Sterling, N.Y.C., 1941-42; adminstrv. asst. David E. Lilienthal, N.Y.C., 1951-62; libr. Dade County Sch. System, Miami, Fla., 1967-90. Lt. (j.g.) WAVES, 1942-46. Avocations: playing piano, gardening.

**IVEY, STEPHEN DAVID,** lawyer; b. Glen Ridge, N.J., Jan. 15, 1953; s. Henry Franklin and Sylvia (Berg) I. BA in History, Polit. Sci., Pa. State U., 1975; JD, Georgetown U., 1978. Bar: Pa. 1978, U.S. Dist. Ct. (ea. dist.) Pa. 1979, U.S. Ct. Appeals (3d cir.) 1979, U.S. Supreme Ct. 1982, U.S. Ct. Appeals (fed. cir.) 1984. Law clk. to judge Supreme Ct. Pa., Phila., 1978-81; pvt. practice Phila., 1981—. General civil litigation, Criminal. Office: 325 S 16th St Philadelphia PA 19102-4936

**IWAI, WILFRED KIYOSHI,** lawyer; b. Honolulu, Aug. 21, 1941; s. Charles Kazuo and Michiko (Sakimoto) I.; m. Judy Tomiko Yoshimoto, Mar. 1, 1963; children: Kyle K., Tiffany Seiko. BS in Bus., U. Colo., 1963, JD, 1966. Bar: Hawaii 1966, Colo. 1966, U.S. Dist. Ct. Hawaii 1966, U.S. Ct. Appeals (9th cir.) 1966. Dep. corp. counsel State of Hawaii, Honolulu, 1966-71; assoc. Kashiwa & Kanazawa, Honolulu, 1971-75; ptnr. Kashiwa, Iwai, Motooka & Goto, Honolulu, 1975-82, also bd. dirs.; ptnr. Iwai & Morris, Honolulu, 1982—, also bd. dirs. Mem. ABA, Hawaii Bar Assn., Assn. Trial Lawyers Am., Bldg. Industry Assn., Bldg. Owners & Mgrs. Assn. Hawaii. Club: Draftsmen's (Honolulu) (pres.). State civil litigation, Construction, General practice. Office: Iwai & Morris 820 Mililani St Ste 502 Honolulu HI 96813-2935

**IWAN, LORI E.,** lawyer; b. Chgo., Jan. 17, 1958. BA in Fin. with distinction. U. Ill., 1980, JD, 1983. Bar: Ill. 1983. Ptnr. Iwan, Cray, Huber, Horstman & VanAusdal LLC, Chgo. Author internet column Lori's Links, 1997—; editor (newsletter) Year 2000 Update, 1998. Mem. Fedn. Ins. and Corp. Counsel (Y2K sect. vice-chair task force 1998, product liability chair), Def. Rsch. Inst. (trial tactics and techniques steering com. 1996-97, co-editor newsletter 1996-97, Internet rsch. subcom. chair 1998, CLE co-chair annual meeting 1999—). Fax: 312-332-8451. E-mail: lei@iwancray.com. General civil litigation, Personal injury, Product liability. Office: Iwan Cray Huber Horstman & VanAusdal LLC 29 N Wacker Dr Chicago IL 60606-3203

**IYEKI, MARC HIDEO,** lawyer; b. Bklyn., May 3, 1957; s. Donald Shozo and Fusaye (Hayashida) I.; m. Aoi Soya, May 18, 1991. BA cum laude, Washington U., St. Louis, 1979; postgrad., U. Pa., 1980-81; JD, NYU, 1984. Bar: N.J. 1985, N.Y. 1985, U.S. Dist. Ct. N.J. 1985. Asst. dep. pub. advocate N.J. Dept. Pub. Advocate, Newark, 1985-87; sr. enforcement atty. N.Y. Stock Exch., Inc., N.Y.C., 1987—, spl. coun., 1988-89, sr. spl. counsel, 1989-92, trial counsel, 1992—. Contbr. articles to profl. publs.; mem. staff Rev. Law and Social Change NYU, 1983-84. Arbitrator, vol. Small Claims sect. Civil Ct. of City of N.Y., 1997—; bd. dirs., vol. Asian Am. Legal Def. and Edn. Fund., Inc., N.Y.C., 1986-87, pro bono atty., 1985-86. Samuel Fels fellow, 1980-81. Mem. Am. Assn. Individual Investors, N.Y. County Lawyers' Assn., Omicron Delta Ep—ilon. Avocations: Japanese language, jogging, tennis, basketball. Administrative and regulatory, Securities. Office: NY Stock Exch Inc 2 World Trade Ctr Fl 30 New York NY 10048-0203

**IZZO, JOHN A.,** lawyer; b. Chgo., Apr. 14, 1968; s. Richard John and Janice Elaine (Potocki) I. BA in Polit. Sci., U. Ill., 1986; JD, U. Akron, 1990. Bar: Ohio 1993, U.S. Dist. Ct. (so. dist.) Ohio 1994, Ill. 1995. Staff atty. Champaign County Child Support Enforcement Agy., Urbana, Ohio, 1994-98; enforcement coord. State Med. Bd. of Ohio, Columbus, 1998—. Mem. ABA, Ohio State Bar Assn., Ill. State Bar Assn., Champaign County Bar Assn. (v.p. 1996, pres. 1997).

**JAASMA, KEITH DUANE,** lawyer, educator; b. Long Branch, N.J., Oct. 15, 1969; s. Edward George and Dorothy Ruth (Koopman) J. BA, Rice U., 1992; JD, UCLA, 1995. Bar: Tex., U.S. Dist. Ct. (so. dist.) Tex., U.S. Ct. Appeals (9th cir.). Law clk. Chambers of Charles E. Wiggins, U.S. Ct. Appeals (9th cir.), Reno, 1995-96; with Baker & Botts, L.L.P., Houston, 1996—; adj. prof. legal rsch. and writing U. Houston Law Ctr., 1998—. Avocations: running, basketball. Labor, Antitrust, Intellectual property. Office: Baker & Botts LLP 910 Louisiana St Ste 3000 Houston TX 77002-4991

**JABLONSKI, RAYMOND LEO,** lawyer; b. Southampton, N.Y., July 8, 1952; s. Raymond Leo and Isabel J.; m. Maureen Ruth, Oct. 23, 1982; children: Valerie, Christine. BA, Syracuse U., 1973; JD, Marquette U., 1977. Bar: Wis. 1977, U.S. Dist. Ct. (ea. and we. dists.) Wis. 1977. Asst. dist. atty. Dodge County Dist. Atty., Juneau, Wis., 1977-79, Rock County Dist. Atty., Janesville, Wis., 1979-93; dep. dist. atty. Rock County Dist. Atty., Janesville, 1993-95; asst. dist. atty. Rock County Dist. Atty., Beloit, Wis., 1995—; Mem. Profl. Responsibility Com., Madison, Wis., 1997—. Pres. Janesville Libr. Bd., 1990. Mem. Janesville Evening Lions Club, Janesville Noon Lions Club. Office: Rock County Dist Atty Office 51 S Main St Janesville WI 53545-3951

**JABRO, JOHN A.,** lawyer; b. Detroit, May 22, 1947; s. John P. and May E. Jabro; m. Brenda A. Jabro, Sept. 30, 1984; 1 child, John Paul. BA, Sacred Heart Sem., Detroit, 1969; JD cum laude, Detroit Coll. Law, 1982. Bar: Fla. 1983, U.S. Dist. Ct. (mid. dist.) Fla. 1983; cert. instr. high liability subjects Fla. Ops. mgr. CETA program Sarasota Bd. County Commrs., Sarasota, Fla., 1978-79; intern to Hon. Ralph B. Guy, U.S. Dist. Ct. for Ea. Dist. Mich., Detroit, 1981-82; asst. pub. defender Office Pub. Defender for 12th Jud. Cir., Sarasota, 1982-86; asst. pub. defender, chief Upper Keys Office, Office Pub. Defender for 16th Jud. Cir., Key West, Fla., 1986-89, chief asst. pub. defender, 1989-90; assoc. Russell H. Cullen, P.A., Key Largo, Fla., 1990-91; ptnr. Cullen & Jabro, P.A., Key Largo, 1992-94; pvt. practice, Tavernier, Fla., 1994—; adj. prof. dept. criminal justice, instr. high liability subjects Fla. Keys C.C., Key West, 1987-90. Mng. editor Detroit Coll. Law Law Rev., 1982. Mem. Fla. Bar (chmn. grievance com. 1996-97, Pro Bono Svc. award 1996), Upper Keys Bar Assn. (pres. 1995—), Kiwanis (pres. Upper Keys 1993-96). Avocations: fly fishing, chess, amateur radio. General civil litigation, Criminal, Personal injury. Office: 90311 Overseas Hwy Tavernier FL 33070

**JACK, JANIS GRAHAM,** judge; b. 1946. RN, St. Thomas Sch. Nursing, 1969; BA, U. Balt., 1974; JD summa cum laude, South Tex. Coll., 1981. Pvt. practice Corpus Christi, Tex., 1981-94; judge U.S. Dist. Ct. (so. dist.) Tex., Corpus Christi, 1994—; jud. mem. The Maritime Law Assn. U.S.; bd. dirs. South Tex. Coll. Law. Mem. ABA, Fed. Judges Assn., Fifth Cir. Dist. Judges Assn., Nat. Assn. Women Judges, Tex. Bar Found., State Bar Tex., The Philos. Soc. Tex., Order of Lytac, Phi Alpha Delta. Office: US Dist Ct 521 Starr St Corpus Christi TX 78401-2349

**JACK, WILLIAM WILSON, JR.,** lawyer; b. Grand Rapids, Mich., June 23, 1947; s. William Wilson and Mary Bennett Jack; m. Kathy J. Anderson, June 20, 1986; 1 child, Katherine Bennett. BA, Denison U., 1969; secondary edn. cert., U. Denver, 1970; JD, George Washington U., 1973. Bar: U.S. Dist. Ct. (we. dist.) Mich. 1977. With Smith Haughey Rice & Roegge, Grand Rapids; pres. Mich. Def. Trial Counsel, 1987-88; mem. faculty NITA, 1985—, ICLE, Ann Arbor, 1985—, Hillman Advocacy Program, Grand Rapids, 1980—; team leader advocacy course U. Mich. Law Sch., Ann Arbor, 1980—. Pres. Planned Parenthood, Grand Rapids, 1992; v.p. Kent Med. Found., Grand Rapids, 1998. Master Am. Inns of Ct. (pres. Grand Rapids chpt. 1997-98); fellow Am. Bar Found., Mich. Bar Found.; Grand Rapids Bar Assn. (pres. 1988-99). Avocations: tennis, skiing, bicycling, birding. General civil litigation, Health, Personal injury. Office: Smith Haughey Rice & Roegge 200 Calder Plz Grand Rapids MI 49503

**JACKLEY, MICHAEL DANO,** lawyer; b. Balt., Oct. 1, 1942; s. Francis Dano and Jean Diantha (Dietz) J.; m. Mary Margaret Mixer, July 5, 1977 (div.); children: Megan, Dano Mixer, Jackley; m. Karen Klare Blocher, Oct. 5, 1987. BA, U. Md., 1965, JD, 1970; LLM in Corp. Law with highest honors, George Washington U., 1977. Bar: D.C., Md. 1971, U.S. Tax Ct. 1973. Assoc. Williams, Brown, Eklund & Baldwin, Washington, 1971-74; assoc. Smith, Joseph, Greenwald & Laake and predecessor firms, Hyattsville, Md., 1974-77; prin. Joseph, Greenwald & Laake, P.A., 1977—; mem. Select Com. to Redraft D.C. Corp. Statute, 1977-86; tchr. Paralegal Inst., 1977-80. Adv. bd. Prince George's County Mental Health Assn., 1978—. Key Delta Theta Phi scholar, 1970. Mem. ABA, Md. State Bar Assn., Prince George's County Bar Assn. Democrat. Unitarian. General corporate, Corporate taxation. Address: 6404 Ivy Ln Ste 400 Greenbelt MD 20770

**JACKMAN, J. WARREN,** lawyer; b. Overton, Tex., Aug. 16, 1934; s. James A. and Nettie S. Jackman; m. Barbara Johnston Lawrence, Nov. 23, 1957 (div. June 1971); children: Jay, Jera, Jeff, Jana; m. Lavonne M. Marrs, July 13, 1973. AB, Washburn U., 1957, MD, 1959. Bar: Okla., U.S. Ct. Appeals (10th cir.). Asst. dist. atty. Office of Dist. Atty., Tulsa, 1962-63; assoc. Wheeler & Wheeler, Tulsa, 1963-65; ptnr. Northcut, Northcutt & Jackman, Ponca City, Okla., 1965-69, Iverson & Jackman, Tulsa, 1969-71, Jackman McQueen & Tanner, Tulsa, 1971-73. Walker, Jackman and Assocs., Tulsa, 1973-79, Pray, Walker Jackman et al, Tulsa, 1979—. Capt. USAF, 1959-62. Fellow Am. Coll. Trial Lawyers, Am. Bar Found. Republican. Presbyn. Avocations: golf, sailing. Federal civil litigation, General civil litigation, State civil litigation. Office: Pray Walker Jackman et al 900 Oneok Plaza Tulsa OK 74103

**JACKMAN, JAMES DAVID,** lawyer; b. Stubenville, Ohio, Aug. 13, 1960; s. Merle M. and Sarah L. Jackman; m. Lorraine P. Jackman, Apr. 30, 1988; children: Joshua A., Jeremy S. BS in Acctg., U. Akron, 1982; JD, Nova Southeastern U., 1985. Bar: Fla. 1985, Ohio 1990; cert. Am. Bd. Certification Consumer Bankruptcy. Pvt. practice law, pres. Bradenton, Fla., 1986—. Coach YMCA Youth Sports, Bradenton, 1994—. Mem. Kiwanis (com. chmn. 1990—), Masonic Lodge, Shriners. Avocations: football, basketball, youth sports coaching, movies, family activities. Bankruptcy.

**JACKOWIAK, PATRICIA,** lawyer; b. Chgo., Feb. 3, 1959; d. Leonard John and Margaret Mary (Iozzi) J. BA, Loyola U., Chgo., 1981; JD, John Marshall Law Sch., 1984. Bar: Ill. 1985. Asst. state's atty. Cook County, Chgo., 1987-89, supr. trial atty. bur. child support enforcement, legal advisor law student's spl. and perjury projects, chmn. employee rels. com., 1988-89, com. mem. domestic rels. div. Pro-se task force, 1989; dep. commr. Consumer Protection div. Dept. Consumer Svcs. City of Chgo., 1989-96; dep. dir. Dept. Adminstrv. Hearings City of Chgo., 1996—; summer atty. Ct. Claims and Antitrust divsn. Office of Ill. Atty. Gen., 1985, 86; com. mem. domestic rels. divsn. Cook County The Pro-Se Task Force Com.; mem. Chgo. divsn. Ford Consumer Appeals Bd., 1989-92, chair, 1991-92. Pres. Santa Lucia Sch. Bd., Chgo., 1987—; chairperson Santa Lucia Parish Carnival Com., 1987—; chairperson employee rels. com. Child Support divsn., 1988-89; dir. religious edn. Santa Lucia Parish, 1985—; mem. freshman recruiting and fundraising coms. Parents Assocs. Loyola U., Chgo., 1987-90; mem. elder care task force Dept. Health, Aging and Disability, Dept. Consumer Svcs. City of Chgo., 1989-96; commencement speaker St. Barbara High Sch., Chgo., 1993, 97, adv. bd., 1994—, co-chair 1998—. Recipient Local Parish award Cath. Youth Orgn./Archdiocese of Chgo., 1991; disting. elem. grad. award Nat. Cath. Ednl. Assn., Santa Lucia Sch., 1994, Superior Pub. Svc. award, 1998. Mem. ABA, Nat. Assn. Adminstrv. Law Judges, Nat. Indsl. Scale Assn., Nat. Conf. Weights and Measures, Blue Key, Pi Sigma Alpha. Democratic. Roman Catholic. Office: Dept Adminstrv Hearings 740 N Sedgwick St Fl 6 Chicago IL 60610-3478

**JACKSON, CAROL E.,** federal judge. BA, Wellesley Coll., 1973; JD, U. Mich., 1976. With Thompson & Mitchell, St. Louis, 1976-83; counsel Mallinckrodt, Inc., St. Louis, 1983-85; magistrate U.S. Dist. Ct., Ea. Dist. Mo., 1986-92, dist. judge, 1992—; adj. prof. law Washington U., St. Louis, 1989-92. Trustee St. Louis Art Mus., 1987-91; dir. bi-state chpt. ARC, 1989-91, Mo. Bot. Garden. Mem. Nat. Assn. Women Judges, Fed. Magistrate Judges Assn., Mo. Bar, St. Louis County Bar Assn., Bar Assn. Metro. St. Louis, Mound City Bar Assn., Lawyers Assn. St. Louis. Office: US Courthouse 1114 Market St Rm 812 Saint Louis MO 63101-2034

**JACKSON, DILLON EDWARD,** lawyer; b. Washington, Apr. 18, 1945; s. Paul David and Virginia (Dillon) J.; children: David I., Anne E.; m. Misha Halvarsson, Aug. 19, 1989. BA, Middlebury (Vt.) Coll., 1967; JD, U. Wash., 1970. Bar: Wash. 1970, U.S. Dist. Ct. (we. and ea. dists.) Wash. 1970, U.S. Ct. Appeals (9th cir.) 1970, U.S. Dist. Ct. Ariz. 1991. Assoc. Kleist & Helmick, Seattle, 1971-73, Powell Livengood & Silvernale, Kirkland, Wash., 1973-75; ptnr. Keller Jacobsen Jackson & Snodgrass, Bellevue, Wash., 1975-85, Hatch & Leslie, Seattle, 1985-91, Foster Pepper & Shefelman, Seattle, 1991—; chairperson creditor rights and bankruptcy dept. Am. Bankruptcy Bd. Cert.; bd. mem. Consumer Credit Counseling, Seattle, 1975-79; chmn. publs. com. Am. Bankruptcy Inst., bd. mem., 1999—. Co-author: Commercial Law Desk Book, 1995; contbg. author: Advance Chapter 11 Bankruptcy Practice, 1989-95. Pres. Dox Coop., Seattle, 1989-91. Fellow Am. Coll. Bankruptcy (co-founder, mem. copyright com.); mem. ABA, Wash. State Trial Lawyers Assn., Wash. State Bar Assn. (creditor-debtor sect., chairperson 1984-88), Continuing Legal Edn. Bd. (chairperson 1991-92). Bankruptcy, General corporate. Office: Foster Pepper & Shefelman PLLC 1111 3rd Ave Ste 3400 Seattle WA 98101-3299

**JACKSON, GARY DEAN,** lawyer; b. Dallas, Sept. 13, 1935; s. Troy Byrl and Leslie Evelyn (Sitton) J.; m. Gloria Ann Galouye, Dec. 22, 1957; children—David MacArthur, Daniel Marshall. B.A. in Govt., So. Meth. U., 1957; J.D., Baylor U., 1961; grad. U.S. Army War Coll., 1979. Bar: Tex. 1961, U.S. Ct. Mil. Appeals 1968, U.S. Supreme Ct. 1968, U.S. Dist. Ct. (no., so., ea., we. dists.) Tex., U.S. Dist. Ct. (no. dist.) Ala., U.S. Dist. Ct. (ea. and we. dists.) Ark., 1988, U.S. Dist. Ct. (no. dist.) Iowa, 1999, U.S. Army Ct. Review, 1975, U.S. Ct. Claims, U.S. Ct. Appeals (1st, 3d, 4th, 5th, 7th, 8th, 9th, 10th ctrs.). Budget examiner Tex. Legis. Budget Bd., 1957-59; ptnr. Pace, Jarvis & Jackson, Tyler, Tex., 1961-66; mcpl. judge Arlington, Tex., 1966-69; spl. asst. Dept. Justice, Washington, 1969-74; ptnr. Colvin & Jackson, Dallas, 1974-78; ptnr. Jackson Jenkins & Rowton, Dallas, 1978-81, Jackson, Jackson & Loving, 1982-83, Jackson, Jackson, Loving & Gutman, 1984-86, Jackson, Loving & Kindred, 1986-92; pvt. practice, Lindale, Tex., 1992—; instr. in bus. law Tyler Jr. Coll., 1962-65, fraud seminars, 1972—. Contbr. articles to legal jours. Pres. Smith County Republican Men's Club, 1965; counselor Baylor U. Law Sch., 1974; chmn. Lindale Area Water Devel. Com.; vice chmn. exec. com. Upper Sabine Water Alliance; voting mem. Region Water Planning Group "D" (NE Tex ). Recipient commendations Dir. FBI, 1971, 72, Atty. Gen. U.S., 1971, also others. Mem. ABA, So. Meth. U. Alumni Assn., Baylor U. Law Sch. Alumni Assn., Mil. Order World Wars, Civil Affairs Assn., Army Res. Assn., Baylor Law Rev. Former Editors (pres. 1979), Masons, Scottish Rite, Delta Theta Phi. Republican. Baptist. Home: PO Box 2229 Lindale TX 75771-2229 Office: 1500 CR 472 PO Box 1210 Lindale TX 75771-1210

**JACKSON, JAMES B.,** lawyer; b. Kansas City, Mo., Oct. 22, 1951; s. Claude James and Evalyn Nadine (Smith) J.; m. Merrily Teresa Thomson, Oct. 23, 1982. BA, U. Ariz., 1973; JD, U. Mo., Kansas City, 1977. Bar: Mo. 1977, U.S. Dist. Ct. (we. dist.) Mo. 1977, Ariz. 1985, Kans. 1990, U.S. Dist. Ct. Kans. 1990, U.S. Ct. Appeals (8th cir.) 1991. Assoc. counsel Mo. State Hwy. Dept., Kansas City, 1977-85; pvt. practice law Kansas City, 1985—; adj. prof. Avila Coll. Paralegal Program, Kansas City, 1989-93. Officer Sierra Club Sect., Kansas City, 1985-90. Mem. Ariz. Bar Assn., Mo. Bar Assn., Kans. Bar Assn., Greater Kansas City Bar Assn., Wyandotte County Bar Assn., Alliance Francaise (sec.), Univ. Club (chair Cincinnatus com. 1996—), Phi Delta Theta. Republican. Methodist. Avocations: scuba, private pilot, amateur radio technician. Condemnation, Real property, State civil litigation. Home: 4417 Harrison St Kansas City MO 64110-1627 Office: 1102 Grand Blvd # 1604 Kansas City MO 64106-2316

**JACKSON, JAMES RALPH,** lawyer; b. Oakland, Calif., Mar. 20, 1967; s. Thomas Edwin and Lillian Nan (Robinson) J.; m. Lisa Carolyn Ferrell, Feb. 14, 1998. BA in History, Hendrix Coll., 1989; JD, U. Ark., 1993. Bar: Ark. 1993. Office asst. Sen. Dale Bumpers U.S. Senate, Washington, 1990; dep. campaign mgr. Jay Bradford for Congress, Pine Bluff, Ark., 1993-95; assoc. Law Offices of Gary Green, Little Rock, 1995-98, Boswell Law Firm, Bryant, Ark., 1998—. Counsel Dem. Party of Ark., Little Rock, 1998; mentor Big Bros./Big Sisters, Little Rock, 1997-98. Mem. Ark. Bar Assn., Ark. Trial Lawyers Assn., Saline County Bar Assn. Methodist. Avocations: reading, basketball. Personal injury, Product liability, General civil litigation. Home: 7 Berkshire Dr Little Rock AR 72204-4805 Office: Boswell Law Firm PO Box 798 Bryant AR 72089-0798

**JACKSON, JOHN HOLLIS, JR.,** lawyer; b. Mongomery, Ala., Aug. 21, 1941; s. John Hollis and Erma (Edgeworth) J.; m. Rebecca Mullins, May 27, 1967; 1 child, John Hollis III. AB, U. Ala., 1963, JD, 1966. Bar: Ala. 1966, U.S. Dist. Ct. (no. dist.) Ala. 1969, U.S. Ct. Appeals (11th cir.) 1993. Pvt. practice Clanton, Ala., 1967—; county atty. Chilton County Commn., Clanton, 1969—; mcpl. judge Clanton, 1971—, Jemison, Ala., 1984—; dir. First Nat. Bank, Clanton, 1974-83; mem. adv. bd. Colonial Bank, Clanton, 1983—. Bd. dirs. Chilton-Shelby Mental Health Bd., Calera, Ala., 1974-83, pres., 1974-79; active State Dem. Exec. Com., Birmingham, Ala., 1974-98, County Dem. Exec. Com., Chilton County, 1982-94; del. Dem. Nat. Conv., N.Y.C., 1976. 1st lt. U.S. Army, 1966-67. Mem. Ala. Young Lawyers Sect. (exec. com. 1969-70), Chilton County Bar Assn. (pres. 1969, 74), Ala. State Bar Assn. (bd. bar commrs. 1984-87, 93-99, chmn. adv. com. to b. bar examiners 1986-87, 93—, 19th cir. indigent def. commn. 1983—), Kiwanis, Phi Alpha Delta. Democrat. Methodist. General practice. Home: Samaria Rd Clanton AL 35045 Office: PO Box 1818 500 2nd Ave S Clanton AL 35046-1818

**JACKSON, KENNETH MONROE,** lawyer, mediator, actor; b. Kenedy, Tex., Sept. 9, 1936; s. Harry Monroe and Harriette Gould (Hughes) J.; m. Judith Ann Foster J.; 1 child, Kenneth Davis J. BA, So. Meth. U., 1960, JD, 1962. Bar: Tex. 1962, Tenn. 1991, U.S. Supreme Ct. 1996, U.S. Dist. Ct. (mid. dist.) Tenn. 1996; cert. civil and family law mediator, Tenn. V.p. contracts, gen. counsel Recon/Optical Inc., Barrington, Ill., 1985-90; v.p., gen. counsel Textron Aerostructures, Nashville, 1990-95; of counsel Neal & Harwell, Nashville, 1995—; artibrator, mediator NASD; mem. Fed. Ct. ADR panel. Contbr. articles to profl. publs. Bd. dirs. Nashville Shakespeare Festival, 1996. Recipient Disting. Svc. award Soc. Am. Value Engrs., 1971. Fellow Nat. Contract Mgmt. Assn. (hon. life, cert profl. contract mgr., nat. pres. 1983-84, Charles J. Delaney Meml. writing award 1984); mem. Am. Corp. Counsel Assn. (pres. Tenn. chpt. 1992-93), Nashville Bar Assn. (chairperson ethics and professionalism com. 1994, ADR com. 1998, Pres.'s award 1994), Coll. of the State Bar Tex., Soc. Profls. in Dispute Resolution, Acad. Family Mediators, Mediation Assn. Tenn.,. Avocations: tennis. Alternative dispute resolution, Government contracts and claims, General corporate. Office: Neal & Harwell 2000 First Union Tower 150 4th Ave N Ste 2000 Nashville TN 37219-2498

**JACKSON, LEAH WITCHER,** lawyer, law educator; b. Waco, Tex., July 15, 1961; d. Thomas Albert and Bessie Virginia (Cooper) Witcher; m. Phillip Edwin Jackson, June 11, 1982; children: Nicole Lea, Ashley Virginia. BBA, Baylor U., 1983, JD, 1985. Bar: Tex. 1985. Assoc. Naman, Howell, Smith & Lee, Waco, 1986-89; asst. prof. law Baylor U. Law Sch., Waco, 1989-92, assoc. prof. law, assoc. dean, 1992-96, prof. law, assoc. dean, 1996—. Bd. mem. The Art Ctr., Waco, 1995—; chair Leadership Waco adv. bd., 1997-98. Recipient Woman of Distinction award, Blue Bonnett Coun. Girl Scouts, Ctrl. Tex., 1997, Outstanding Alumni award Leadership Waco, 1996. Fellow Tex. Bar Found.; mem. Waco-McLennan County Bar Assn. (bd. dirs. 1992—, v.p. 1997, pres. elect 1998, pres. 1999), Leadership Am., Leadership Tex. Baptist. Avocations: oil painting, coaching softball. Personal income taxation, Taxation, general, Corporate taxation. Office: Baylor U Law Sch PO Box 97288 Waco TX 76798-7288

**JACKSON, LYNN ROBERTSON,** lawyer; b. Montgomery, Ala., Nov. 20, 1947; d. Arthur Borders Jr. and Mozelle (Martin) Robertson; m. George Thomas Jackson, Aug. 16, 1969; children: Katherine, William Borders. BS, U. Ala., 1970; JD, Faulkner U., 1979. Bar: Ala. 1981, U.S. Dist. Ct. Ala. 1984. Ptnr. Jackson and Faulk, Clayton, 1981-83, Andrews and Jackson, Clayton, 1983-84; pvt. practice Clayton, 1984-92; ptnr. Jinks, Smithart & Jackson, Clayton, 1992-99, Jinks, Smithart, Jackson & Jackson, Clayton, 1999—; chair mandatory legal edn. Ala. State Bar, 1990—; mem. permanent code com., bench and bar rels. com. Ala. State Bar. City atty. City of Clayton, 1984—; bd. trustees Town and County Libr., Clayton, 1990—; trustee Ala. Law Found., 1989—. Mem. ABA, Ala. State Bar Assn. (bar commr. 1985—), Assn. Trial Lawyers Am. Episcopalian. Avocation: raising Arabian show horses and Doberman Pinschers. General civil litigation, Real property, Probate. Home: Licklog Farm Clayton AL 36016 Office: Jinks Smithart and Jackson Court Sq Clayton AL 36016

**JACKSON, MARK BRYAN,** lawyer; b. San Jose, Calif., Aug. 20, 1963; s. Clyde Andrew and Diane May (Wilcox) J. BS, Colo. State U., 1985; JD, Calif. Western Sch. Law, San Diego, 1989. Bar: Nev. 1991, U.S. Dist. Ct. Nev. 1991, U.S. Ct. Appeals (9th cir.) 1991. Assoc. Terzich, Cauley, Herbig & Krom, Ltd., Gardnerville, Nev., 1991-92; ptnr. Terzich, Herbig & Jackson, Ltd., Gardnerville, 1992-95, Terzich & Jackson, Ltd., Gardnerville, 1995—. Coach Pop Warner Football League. Mem. ABA, ATLA, Nev. Trial Lawyers Assn., Nat. Assn. Criminal Def. Lawyers, Douglas County Bar Assn. (pres. 1994-95), Masons. Republican. Avocations: community youth activities, rugby. Criminal, Personal injury. Home: PO Box 1576 Minden NV 89423-1576 Office: Terzich & Jackson 1470 Us Highway 395 N Gardnerville NV 89410-5256

**JACKSON, NICHOLAS MILLER,** lawyer, researcher; b. Colon, Panama, Sept. 23, 1950; came to U.S., 1966; s. William Merrill J. and Barbara Margaret Malo; m. Jennifer Jewel Watson, Feb. 9, 1971 (div. June 1990); children: Nathaniel Todd, Robert Sean. BA, Mich. State U., 1976; JD, Detroit Coll. Law, 1990. Bar: Mich. 1991, U.S. Supreme Ct. 1997, La. 1998, Fla. 1999. Law clk. 16th Cir. Ct., Mt. Clemens, Mich., 1990-91, rsch. atty., 1991—; cons. in field. Asst. scoutmaster Great Sauk Trail Coun. Boy Scouts Am., Ypsilant, Mich., 1995—; vol. libr. LDS Family History Ctr., Ann Arbor, Mich., 1990-93. With U.S. Army Res., 1978-81. Mem. State Bar Mich., La. State Bar Assn., Macomb County Bar Assn., Panama Canal Soc. Fla. Independent. Mem. LDS Ch. Avocations: genealogy, jogging, amateur radio, photography. Home: 135 N Edgemont St Belleville MI 48111-2849 Office: Macomb County Cir Ct 40 N Main St Mount Clemens MI 48043-8607

**JACKSON, RAYMOND A.,** federal judge; b. 1949. BA, Norfolk State U., 1970; JD, U. Va., 1973. Capt. U.S. Army JAGC, 1973-77; asst. U.S. atty. Ea. Dist. Va., Norfolk, 1977-93; judge U.S. Dist. Ct. (ea. dist.) Va., Norfolk, 1993—; mem. judicial conf. U.S. Ct. Appeals (4th cir.). Active Day Care and Child Devel. Ctr., Tidewater, 1980-86; bd. dirs. Peninsula Legal Aid Ctr., 1977. Col. USAR, ret. Mem. U.S. Dist. Judges Assn., Va. State Bar, Old Dominion Bar Assn. (pres. 1984-86), Norfolk-Portsmouth Bar Assn., South Hampton Rds. Bar Assn., Am. Inn Ct. (Hoffman-l'Anson chpt.), Va. Law Found., U.S. Judicial Conf. Com. Adminstrn. Magistrate Judge System. Office: 600 Granby St Norfolk VA 23510-1915

**JACKSON, RAYMOND SIDNEY, JR.,** lawyer; b. Bklyn., Sept. 17, 1938; s. Raymond Sidney and Mary Frost (McInerney) Van Vranken. BA, William Coll., 1960; JD, Harvard U., 1966. Bar: N.Y. 1967, U.S. Dist. Ct. (so. and ea. dists.) N.Y. 1969, U.S. Ct. Appeals (2d cir.) 1969. Assoc. Thacher, Proffitt & Wood, N.Y.C., 1966-76, ptnr., 1976-94, of counsel, 1994—. Mem. South St. Seaport Mus., N.Y.C., 1974—, Gramercy Neighborhood Assocs., N.Y.C., 1974—, Nat. Assn. Coll. and Univ. Attys., 1972. Mem. ABA (vice chmn. admiralty and maritime law com. sect. of tort and ins. practice 1990-92), N.Y. State Bar Assn. (admiralty and maritime com. internat. law and practice sect. 1989-94), Assn. Bar City N.Y. (admiralty com. 1984-85, 88-91), Maritime Law Assn. U.S. (com. on practice and procedure 1976-91). E-mail: RSJacksonJ@aol.com. Admiralty, General civil litigation. Office: Thacher Proffitt & Wood 2 World Trade Ctr New York NY 10048-0203

**JACKSON, RENEE LEONE,** lawyer; b. Winter Park, Fla., Sept. 26, 1966; d. Richard Lee and Jean Karen (Bergmann) Wiechmann; m. J. David Jackson, Dec. 10, 1994; stepchildren: Ian, Kelsey. AA, Bethany Lutheran Coll., 1986; BS with high honors, U. Fla., 1988; JD magna cum laude, U. Minn. Law Sch., 1991. Lawyer Dorsey & Whitney, Mpls., 1991-93, Larkin, Hoffman, Daly & Lindgren, Bloomington, Minn., 1993—. Bd. dirs. Bloomington Cmty. Found., 1996—. Mem. ABA. Lutheran. General civil litigation, Intellectual property. Office: Larkin et al 7900 Xerxes Ave S Bloomington MN 55431-1106

**JACKSON, RICHARD BROOKE,** judge; b. Bozeman, Mont., Mar. 5, 1947; s. William T. and Myra (McHugh) J.; m. Elizabeth Ciner, Sept. 19, 1971; children: Jeffrey, Brett, Jennifer. AB magna cum laude, Dartmouth Coll., 1969; JD cum laude, Harvard U., 1972. Bar: Colo. 1972, U.S. Dist. Ct. Colo. 1972, D.C. 1980, U.S. Dist. Ct. D.C. 1980,U.S. Ct. Appeals (10th cir.) 1972, U.S. Ct. Appeals (D.C. cir.) 1980, U.S. Supreme Ct. 1980. Assoc. Holland & Hart, Denver, 1972-78; ptnr. Holland & Hart, Denver and Washington, 1978-98; dist. ct. judge Jefferson County, Golden, Colo., 1998—; instr. in trial practice U. Colo. Law Sch., Boulder, 1984-85, 87, 88, 89, 91, 98, Nat. Inst. Trial Advocacy, 1986, 87, 90, 91. Co-author: Manual for Complex Insurance Coverage Litigation, 1993; editor: A Better New Hampshire, 1968; contbr. articles to profl. jours. Fellow Am. Coll. Trial Lawyers; mem. ABA (former co-chair ins. coverage com. sect. of litigation), Colo. Bar Assn., Denver Bar Assn. Democrat. Avocations: running, golf, reading, travel, Spanish. Home: 5355 Yellowstone St Bow Mar CO 80123-1423 Office: Dist Ct Jefferson Cty 100 Jefferson County Pkwy Golden CO 80401-6000

**JACKSON, ROBBI JO,** non-hazardous agricultural products company executive, lawyer; b. Nampa, Idaho, Apr. 12, 1959; d. William R. Jackson and Marilyn K. Samp Jackson Nunez. BS in Fin., U. Colo., Boulder and Denver, 1981; JD, U. Denver, 1987, LLM in Taxation, 1990. Bar: Colo. Asst. office mgr. Jerome Karsh & Co., Denver, 1982; office mgr. Almirall & Assocs., Englewood, Colo., 1983-84; assoc. Moye, Giles, O'Keefe, Vermeire & Gorrell, Denver, 1989-90, Holme Roberts & Owen, Denver, 1990-92; in-house gen. counsel Cmty. Corrections Svcs., Denver, 1992-96; CEO Enviro Cons. Svc., LLC, Evergreen and Lakewood, Colo., 1996—. Mem. staff Adminstrv. Law Rev., Denver, 1985, editor, 1985, mng. editor, 1986-87; co-author course of study materials; presenter in field. Mem. fin. com. Mile-High chpt. ARC, Denver, 1990-92; food delivery person Vols. of Am., Meals-on-Wheels, Denver, 1990-92. Recipient scholarships. Mem. ABA, Colo. Bar Assn. (ethics com.). Republican. Avocations: running marathons and other races, biking, hiking, swimming, piano and organ playing.

**JACKSON, ROBERT TOUSSAINT, JR.,** lawyer, retired army officer; b. Detroit, Feb. 24, 1948; s. Robert Toussaint and Katrine (Hazely) J.; m. Peggy Hanna, Dec. 30, 1978; 1 child, Christopher Jason. BS, Mich. State U., 1969; JD, U. Detroit, 1972. Bar: Mich. 1973, U.S. Dist. Ct. (ea. dist.) Mich. 1973, U.S. Ct. Mil. Appeals 1973, U.S. Supreme Ct. 1978, U.S. Tax Ct. 1993, Ga. 1994, U.S. Dist. Ct. (no. dist.) Ga. 1994, U.S. Ct. Appeals Ga. 1994. Commd. 2d lt. U.S. Army, 1973, advanced through grades to lt. col., 1986; def. counsel, adminstrv. law atty U.S. Army, Ft. Bragg, N.C., 1977-82; dep. staff judge advocate U.S. Army, Ft. Devens, Mass., 1982-85; mil. judge U.S. Army Trial Judiciary, Legal Svcs. Agy. U.S. Army, Falls Church, Va., 1985-88; staff judge advocate U.S. Army, Ft. McPherson, Ga., 1988-91, dep. staff judge advocate Res. command, 1991-93; asst. clinic dir. Ga. State U. Coll. Law Tax Clinic, 1993—; mem. svc. acad. screening com. U.S. Senate, 1991. Contbr. articles to profl. jours. Decorated Legion of Merit. Mem. Nat. Bar Assn. Avocations: tennis, reading. Home: 100 Senoya Trce Fayetteville GA 30214-7332

**JACKSON, RONI D.,** lawyer, consultant. BS, U. Pa., 1984, JD, 1987. Atty. Rutan & Tucker, Costa Mesa, Calif., 1987-89, Pactel Corp./Air Touch Comms., Irvine, Calif., 1989-94; dir. legal affairs DIRECTV, Inc., El Segundo, Calif., 1994-96; asst. gen. counsel Cox Comms. PCS, L.P., Irvine, 1996-98; ptnr. Jackson Downes, LLP, San Diego, 1998—; mem. PCIA Broadband PCS Alliance Coun., Alexandria, Va., 1996-98; bd. dirs. PCIA Microwave Clearinghouse, Alexandria, 1996-98. Mem. ABA, Orange County Bar Assn. General corporate, Communications. Office: Jackson Downes LLP 12707 High Bluff Dr Ste 200 San Diego CA 92130-2037

**JACKSON, TERRY D.,** lawyer; b. Oak Ridge, Tenn., Apr. 3, 1963; s. Randall Harness and Daisy Nell Jackson; m. Bridget Ann Casey, Dec. 11, 1964; children: Maria Elizabeth, Lilian Katherine. BSBA, U. Tenn., 1985, M in Acctg. Tax., 1986; JD, U. Ga., 1993. Bar: Ga. 1993; CPA, Ga. Acct. Peat, Marwick KPMG, Atlanta, 1986-90; tax cons. BellSouth, Atlanta, 1993-94; assoc. Ford Law Firm, Atlanta, 1994-96; pvt. practice Atlanta, 1996—. Capt. USAR, 1960-93. Mem. ABA, State Bar Assn. Ga., ATLA, Ga. Trial Lawyers Assn. General civil litigation, Estate taxation, Taxation, general. Office: 1776 Peachtree St NW Ste 306S Atlanta GA 30309-2344

**JACKSON, THOMAS FRANCIS, III,** lawyer; b. Memphis, Oct. 21, 1940; s. Thomas Francis and Sarah Elizabeth (Farris) J.; children: Thomas Francis, Wythe Macrae Bogy; grad. The Taft Sch.; B.A., Rhodes Coll., 1962; LL.B., George Washington U., 1967. Bar: Tenn. 1967, U.S. Supreme Ct. 1974. Law clk. to chief judge U.S. Dist. Ct., Western Dist. Tenn., 1967-68; assoc. Armstrong, Allen, Braden, Goodman, McBride & Prewitt, Memphis, 1968-72; assoc. Lawler, Humphrey, Dunlap & Wellford, P.C., Memphis, 1972-76, ptnr./owner, 1976-83; sole practice, Memphis, 1983—. Served to lt. USNR, 1962-67. Mem. ABA, Tenn. Bar Assn., Memphis Bar Assn. Episcopalian. Fax: 901-324-6997. E-mail: tfj@lawtenn.com. General practice, General corporate, Probate. Home: 532 S Highland St # 1202 Memphis TN 38111-4304 Office: PO Box 111221 Memphis TN 38111-1221

**JACKSON, THOMAS GENE,** lawyer; b. N.Y.C., Mar. 9, 1949; s. Alan Clark and Clare Seena (Werther) J.; m. Beatrice Lafrance Korab, June 11, 1972; children: Sarah Ann, Alan Edward. AB magna cum laude in English, Dartmouth Coll., 1971; JD, U. Va., 1974. Bar: N.Y. 1975, U.S. Dist. Ct. (so. and ea. dists.) N.Y. 1975, U.S. Ct. Appeals (2d cir.) 1975, U.S. Ct. Appeals (5th cir.) 1978, U.S. Supreme Ct. 1978, U.S. Ct. Appeals (D.C. cir.) 1986. Editor The Rsch. Group, Charlottesville, Va., 1973-74; assoc. Phillips Nizer Benjamin Krim & Ballon LLP, N.Y.C., 1974-82, ptnr., 1982—; fed. bar coun. com. 2d Cir. Cts., 1997—, chmn. subcom. on tech. in the cts., 1997—. Mem. Village of Irvington Cable TV Adv. Com., N.Y., 1979-91, 95—, chmn. franchise renewal com., 1991-95; sec. Village of Irvington Environ. Conservation Bd., 1983-87, chmn., 1987—; mem. Dartmouth Coll. Alumni Coun., 1986-89. Mem. ABA (sect. antitrust law, Clayton Act com., premerger notification subcom. 1982—), Fed. Bar Coun. (com. 2d cir. cts. 1997—, chmn. subcom. tech. in cts. 1997—), Am. Arbitration Assn. (panel of arbitrators, comml. tribunal 1986—), Assn. of Bar of City of N.Y. (antitrust and trade regulation com. 1988-92, mergers acquisitions and joint ventures subcom. 1991-92), Dartmouth Coll. Club Officers Assn. (exec. com. 1988-91), Dartmouth Coll. Class Secs. Assn. (v.p. 1984-85, pres. 1985-86), Dartmouth Club Westchester (sec. 1984-87, 90—, pres. 1987-90). Federal civil litigation, Antitrust. Home: 32 Hamilton Rd Irvington NY 10533-2311 Office: Phillips Nizer Benjamin Krim & Ballon LLP 666 5th Ave New York NY 10103-0001

**JACKSON, THOMAS PENFIELD,** federal judge; b. Washington, Jan. 10, 1937; s. Thomas Searing and May Elizabeth (Jacobs) J. A.B. in Govt., Dartmouth Coll., 1958; LL.B., Harvard U., 1964. Bar: D.C., Md., U.S. Supreme Ct. 1970. Assoc., ptnr. Jackson & Campbell, P.C., Washington, 1964-82; U.S. dist. judge U.S. Dist. Ct. D.C., Washington, 1982—. Vestryman All Saints' Episcopal Ch., Washington, 1969-75; trustee Gallaudet Univ., Washington. Served to lt. (j.g.) USN, 1958-61. Fellow Am. Coll. Trial Lawyers; mem. ABA, Bar Assn. D.C. (pres. 1982-83), Rotary. Republican. Clubs: Chevy Chase, Metropolitan, Lawyers', Barristers. Office: US Dist Ct US Courthouse 3rd & Constitution Ave NW Washington DC 20001

**JACKSON, VELMA LOUISE,** lawyer; b. Sewickley, Pa., Aug. 2, 1945; d. Matthew Edward and Sarah Frances (Carter) J. BS, Duquesne U., 1968; MEd, U. Pitts., 1977; JD, U. Cin., 1982. Bar: W.Va. 1985, Pa. 1986. Chemist Calgon Corp., Pitts., 1969-70; mgr. lab. svcs. Polytech Inc., Cleve., 1970-76; engr. Procter & Gamble Co., Cin., 1976-79; v.p. F.U.T.U.R.E. Assocs., Sewickley, 1982—; law clk., jud. asst. Orphans Ct. div. Ct. Common Pleas, Pitts., 1985-89; pvt. practice Pitts., 1989—; environ. cons.

Creative Mgmt. Systems, Detroit, 1979-81; tech. writer O.H. Materials Inc., Findlay, Ohio, 1980-81; instr. bus. law Carlow Coll., Pitts., 1986-91; bd. dirs. Sentinel Fin. Svcs. Inc. Writer poetry; contbr. articles to profl. jours.; developed cut plant preservative, 1975. Bd. dirs. Sewickley Community Ctr., 1983-89, 91—, Group Against Smog and Pollution, Pitts., 1987—; treas. Quaker Valley Dist. Dems., 1984-92, commr. Police Civil Svcs. Commn., Sewickley, 1986—; invitee Citizen Amb. Project to India, Republic of China and USSR Internat. Amb. Programs Inc., Spokane, Wash., 1987-88. Mem. ABA, AAUW, Nat. Assn. Colored Women's Club (local pres. 1985-87, state 1st v.p. 1988-92), Nat. Assn. Negro Bus. and Profl. Women, Pa. Bar Assn., W.Va. Bar Assn., African Ams. for Self-Determination (co-founder), Am. Biographical Inst. Rsch. Assn. (mem. adv. coun.), Internat. Biographical Ctr., Delta Sigma Theta. Baptist. Avocation: fiction and poetry writing. Probate, Labor. Home: 339 Little St Sewickley PA 15143-1468

**JACKSON, WILLIAM ELDRED,** lawyer; b. Jamestown, N.Y., July 19, 1919; s. Robert Houghwout and Irene Alice (Gerhart) J.; m. Nancy Dabney Roosevelt, Sept. 24, 1944; children—Miranda, Melissa, Melanie, Melinda, Marina. BA, Yale U., 1941; LLB, Harvard U., 1944. Bar: N.Y. 1944, U.S. Supreme Ct. 1952, D.C. 1960. Assoc. Milbank, Tweed, Hadley & McCloy, N.Y.C., 1947-54; ptnr. Milbank, Tweed, Hadley & McCloy, 1954—; chmn. appellate div. 1st Dept. Disciplinary Com., 1985-90; vice chmn. Internat. Ct. Arbitration, 1988-94. Mem. staff Nuremburg trial; trustee Supreme Ct. Hist. Soc., 1987—. Lt. (j.g.) USNR, 1944-46. Mem. Am. Coll. Trial Lawyers, Am. Soc. Internat. Law, Assn. Bar City N.Y. (sec. 1953-54), N.Y. State Bar Assn., ABA, Fed. Bar Coun., Am. Judicature Soc., Coun. Fgn. Rels., Century Club, Downtown Club, Pilgrims Club, River Club. Democrat. Episcopalian. Antitrust, General civil litigation, Private international. Home: 530 E 72nd St New York NY 10021-4855 Office: Milbank Tweed Hadley & McCloy 1 Chase Manhattan Plz Fl 47 New York NY 10005-1413

**JACKSON-HOLMES, FLORA MARIE,** lawyer, educator; b. Miami, Fla., June 1, 1957; d. Andrew and Elizabeth (Oliver) Jackson; m. Myron William Holmes, Apr. 16, 1988. BS, Fla. Meml. Coll., 1978; JD, Howard U., 1982. Bar: Fla. 1984, U.S. Dist. Ct. (so. dist. Fla.). Staff atty. James E. Scott Cmty. Assn., Miami, 1985-87, sr. atty., 1987-89; pvt. practice Miami, 1990—; code enforcement hearing officer Dade County; adj. prof. law, Fla. Meml. Coll., Miami, 1989—; legal advisor Delta Sigma Theta Alumnae of Dade County, 1997. Recipient Pro Bono award Domestic Violence Legal Aid of Greater Miami, 1996, Cert. Appreciation Charles R. Drew Elem. Sch., 1997, Miami Golden Glades Optimists, 1996. Mem. Nat. Black Lawyers (treas. 1986-87), Fla. Bar Assn. (women lawyer's divsn.), NBAWLD (sec. 1996), Delta Sigma Theta. Democrat. Baptist. Avocations: reading, working with youth, travel. Home: 15728 NW 7th Ave Miami FL 33169-6255 Office: 10735 NW 7th Ave Miami FL 33168-2103

**JACOB, BRUCE ROBERT,** law educator; b. Chgo., Mar. 26, 1935; s. Edward Carl and Elsie Berthe (Hartmann) J.; m. Ann Wear, Sept. 8, 1962; children: Bruce Ledley, Lee Ann, Brian Edward. BA, Fla. State U., 1957; JD, Stetson U., 1959; LLM, Northwestern U., 1965; SJD, Harvard U., 1980; LLM in Taxation, U. Fla., 1995. Bar: Fla. 1959, Ill. 1965, Mass. 1970, Ohio 1972. Asst. atty. gen. State of Fla., 1960-62; assoc. Holland, Bevis & Smith, Bartow, Fla., 1962-64; asst. to assoc. prof. Emory U. Sch. Law, 1965-69; rsch. assoc. Ctr. for Criminal Justice, Harvard Law Sch., 1969-70; staff atty. Cmty. Legal Assistance Office, Cambridge, Mass., 1970-71; assoc. prof. Coll. Law, Ohio State U., 1971-73, prof., dir. clin. programs, 1973-78; dean, prof. Mercer U. Law Sch., Macon, Ga., 1978-81; v.p., dean, prof. Stetson U. Coll. Law, St. Petersburg, Fla., 1981-94, dean emeritus and prof., 1994—. Contbr. articles to profl. jours. Mem. Fla. Bar, Sigma Chi. Democrat. Home: 1946 Coffee Pot Blvd NE Saint Petersburg FL 33704-4632 Office: Stetson U Coll Law 1401 61st St S Saint Petersburg FL 33707-3246

**JACOB, EDWIN J.,** lawyer; b. Detroit, Aug. 25, 1927; s. A. Aubrey and Estelle R. (Vesell) J.; m. Constance Dorfman, June 15, 1948; children—Louise B., Beth D., Ellen P. AB cum laude, Harvard U., 1948, JD cum laude, 1951. Bar: N.Y. 1951, U.S. Dist. Ct. (so. dist.) N.Y. 1953, U.S. Dist. Ct. (ea. dist.) N.Y. 1953, U.S. Ct. Appeals (2d cir.) 1954, U.S. Supreme Ct. 1963, U.S. Ct. Appeals (8th cir.) 1981, U.S. Ct. Appeals (10th cir.) 1987. Assoc. Davis Polk Wardwell Sunderland & Kiendl, N.Y.C., 1951-62; ptnr. Cabell, Medinger, Forsyth & Decker, N.Y.C., 1962-69, Lauterstein & Lauterstein, N.Y.C., 1969-72, Jacob, Medinger & Finnegan, LLP, N.Y.C., 1973—; bd. advisors Inst. for Health Policy Analysis, Georgetown U., 1987-90. Contbr. articles to profl. jours. Mem. nat. bd. Assn. Ref. Zionists Am., 1991-97; trustee Stephen Wise Free Synagogue, 1991—, pres., 1994-96. With USN, 1945-46. Mem. Am. Law Inst., Am. Judicature Soc., Assn. Bar City N.Y. Club: Harvard of N.Y.C. Federal civil litigation, State civil litigation, Product liability. Office: Jacob Medinger Finnegan LLP 1270 Ave of Americas New York NY 10020

**JACOB, SHALOM,** lawyer; b. N.Y.C., Mar. 10, 1962; s. Marvin and Atara (Bin-Nun) J.; m. Sarah Hubner, Aug. 31, 1989; children: Rivka R., Avraham M., Moshe S. BS, Bklyn. Coll., 1983; JD, Columbia U., 1986; Grad., Yeshiva Rabbi Chaim Berlin, Theol. Seminary. Bar: N.Y. 1988, U.S. Dist. Ct. (so. and ea. dists.) N.Y. 1988. Assoc. Rosenman & Colin, N.Y.C., 1986-93, Shereff, Friedman, Hoffman & Goodman LLP, N.Y.C., 1994—. Republican. Jewish. Bankruptcy, Probate. Office: Shereff Friedman Hoffman & Goodman LLP 919 3rd Ave New York NY 10022-3902

**JACOBOWITZ, HAROLD SAUL,** lawyer; b. N.Y.C., Aug. 26, 1950; s. William and Miriam (Spector) J.; m. Estrella B. Rivera, Oct. 26, 1972. BA, CUNY, 1972; JD, Rutgers U., 1977. Bar: N.Y. 1977, U.S. Dist. Ct. (so. dist.) N.Y. 1978, U.S. Dist. Ct. (ea. dist.) N.Y. 1978. Assoc. Goldman & Heffernan, N.Y.C., 1977-78, Zola & Zola, N.Y.C., 1978-79, Goldberg & Lysaght, N.Y.C., 1979-82; atty. of record Am. Internat. Group (Jacobowitz, Spessard, Garfinkel & Lesman), N.Y.C., 1982-88, regional mng. atty., 1988-89, chief counsel, 1989-90, v.p., 1990—, chief tech. officer property/casualty claims, 1998—; arbitration panel U.S. Dist. Ct. (ea. dist.) N.Y. Mem. ABA, N.Y. State Bar Assn., Assn. Bar City N.Y., N.Y. County Lawyers Assn., Assn. Trial Lawyers N.Y.C. (bd. dirs.). Personal injury, Insurance, State civil litigation. Office: Am Internat Group 70 Pine St New York NY 10270-0002

**JACOBS, ALAN,** lawyer; b. Balt., Jan. 7, 1947; s. Jerome and Mildred (Carlin) J.; m. Paula Ference Kaiser, May 16, 1979; children: Mark, Michelle, Jeremy, Katherine. BS, U. Md., 1969; JD, U. Balt., 1975. Bar: Calif. 1977, D.C. 1978, Tex. 1993; CPA, Md., Calif. Staff SEC, Washington, 1972-76; mem. Zipser, Snyderman, et al., L.A., 1976-79; gen. counsel House of Fabrics, Inc., Van Nuys, Calif., 1979-80; v.p., sec., gen. counsel ICN Pharms., Inc., Costa Mesa, Calif., 1980-81; mem. Jones, Day, Reavis & Pogue, L.A., 1981-86, Dallas, 1986-91; exec. v.p., sec., gen. counsel D.R. Horton, Inc., Arlington, Tex., 1991-92, also bd. dirs.; mem. McGlinchey Stafford A Profl. LLC, Dallas, 1993—, pres.; adj. prof. Southwestern U. Sch. of Law, 1985-86. With USAR, 1969-75. General corporate, Securities, Banking.

**JACOBS, ALAN J.,** lawyer, editor; b. Englewood, N.J., July 23, 1951; s. David and Rose (Friedman) J. BA, Montclair State Coll., 1974; JD, N.Y. Law Sch., 1990. Editl. asst. Clark Boardman Co., N.Y.C., 1976-77, copy editor, 1977-85, assoc. editor, 1985-89, legal editor, 1989-91; mng. editor Clark Boardman Callaghan, N.Y.C., 1991-92, sr. mng. editor, 1992-93, editor-in-chief, 1993-96, sr. project editor, 1996-97; editor-in-chief Practising Law Inst., N.Y.C., 1997—. Pres., founder 9th St A-1 Block Assn., N.Y.C., 1980-85; v.p., founder W. 13th St. 100 Block Assn., 1997—; mem. Dem. County Com., 1997—. Recipient New Yorkers for N.Y. award, Citizens Com. N.Y.C., 1984. Mem. ABA, City of N.Y. Bar Assn., Lesbian & Gay Lawyers-N.Y. Avocations: history, bicycling. Office: Practising Law Inst 810 7th Ave Fl 26 New York NY 10019-5818

**JACOBS, ANDREW ROBERT,** lawyer; b. Newark, Sept. 18, 1946; s. Seymour B. and Pearle (Flaschen) J.; m. Yardana Steinberg, July 10, 1976; 1 child, Suzanne Michal. BA with high honors, Rutgers U., 1968; JD, Columbia U., 1971. Bar: N.J. 1971, U.S. Dist. Ct. N.J. 1971, U.S. Ct. of Appeals (3rd cir.) 1974, U.S. Ct. Appeals (D.C. cir.) 1976, U.S. Supreme Ct. 1979, U.S. Dist. Ct. (ea. and so. Dists.) N.Y. 1980, N.Y. 1980, Pa. 1981, U.S. Ct. Appeals (2nd cir.) 1984, U.S. Claims Ct. 1986. Law clk. to chief judge U.S. Dist. Ct., Newark, 1971-72; asst. U.S. atty. U.S. Atty.'s Office, Newark, 1972-76; assoc. Cole Berman & Belsky, Rochelle Park, N.J., 1976; assoc. Lanigan O'Connell Jacobs & Chazin, Basking Ridge, N.J. and N.Y.C., 1977-78, ptnr., 1979-82; asst. U.S. atty., chief spl. pros., dep. chief criminal div. U.S. Atty.'s Office (ea. dist.), N.Y., 1983-85; ptnr. Horowitz & Jacobs, Hackensack, N.J. and N.Y.C., 1985-89, Gern, Dunetz, Davison & Weinstein, Roseland, N.J. and N.Y.C., 1990-93, Fitzsimmons Ringle & Jacobs, Newark, N.J., Hackensack, N.J. and N.Y.C., 1993—; faculty Practicing Law Inst., N.Y.C., 1980-82; legal writing instr. N.Y. Law Sch., 1981-82; master Justice William J. Brennan, Jr. Inns of Ct., 1995—. Bd. trustees N.J. YM-YWHA Camps, Fairfield, N.J. and Milford, Pa., 1985—, v.p. 1998—; trustee Congregation Shomrei Emunah, Montclair, N.J., 1985-96; pres. Rutgers Coll. Alumni Class 1968. Capt. U.S. Army, 1977. Harlan Fiske Stone scholar; recipient U.S. Dept. Justice Spl. commendation award, 1973, 75, U.S. Dept. Treasury ATF cert. of Appreciation, 1976, Jerome Michal prize for Excellence in Trial Advocacy Columbia U. Mem. ABA, ATLA, N.J. State Bar Assn., N.Y. County Lawyers Assn. (fed. cts. com.), N.Y. State Trial Lawyers Assn., Assn. Criminal Def. Lawyers N.J., Bergen County Bar Assn., Essex County Bar Assn., Assn. Fed. Bar N.J., Soc. of Loyal Sons of Rutgers (elected), Phi Beta Kappa. Criminal, Federal civil litigation, State civil litigation. Home: 153 Lloyd Rd Montclair NJ 07042-1732 Office: Fitzsimmons Ringle & Jacobs PC 50 Park Pl 4th Fl Newark NJ 07102-4305 also: 2 Park Ave New York NY 10016 also: 2 University Plaza Hackensack NJ 07601-6202

**JACOBS, ANN ELIZABETH,** lawyer; b. Lima, Ohio, July 28, 1950; d. Warren Charles and Virginia Elizabeth (Lewis) J.; m. Mark S. Bush, Nov. 26, 1988; 1 child, Whitney Elizabeth. BA, George Washington U., 1972; JD, Cath. U., 1976. Bar: Ohio 1977, Calif. 1977, U.S. Ct. Appeals (D.C. cir.) 1980, U.S. Dist. Ct. (no. dist.) Ohio 1982. Asst. atty. gen. State of Ohio, Columbus, 1977-78; trial atty. EEOC of Ohio, Miami, Fla., 1978-80; sole practice Lima, 1980—; bd. dirs. Allen County Blackhoof Area Legal Svcs. Assn., Marimor Industries, Inc., Lima. Fundraiser Lima Symphony Orch., 1985; trustee Lima Art Assn., YWCA; bd. dirs. Sr. Citizens; mem. bd. elders Market St. Presbyn. Ch. Recipient Recognition award US Naval Air Sta., Jacksonville, Fla., 1979. Mem. LWV, Ohio Bar Assn., Calif. Bar Assn., D.C. Bar Assn., Allen County Bar Assn. (chmn. juvenile ct. com. 1993). Avocations: sailing, golf, reading. General practice, General civil litigation, Personal injury. Home: 1529 Shawnee Rd Lima OH 45805-3801 Office: Jacobs & Von der Embse 558 W Spring St Lima OH 45801-4728

**JACOBS, CHRISTOPHER B.,** patent lawyer; b. Columbus, Ohio, Jan. 18, 1969; m. Carolyn Marie Broering, May 21, 1994. BSME, Ohio State U., 1992, JD, 1995. Bar: Ohio 1995, U.S. Dist. Ct. (no. dist.) Ohio 1996, U.S. Ct. Appeals (fed. cir.) 1997, U.S. Patent and Trademark Office 1994. Patent atty. Renner, Otto, Boisselle & Sklar, Cleve., 1995—. Mem. Am. Intellectual Property Law Assn., Cleve. Intellectual Property Law Assn. Intellectual property, Patent, Trademark and copyright. Office: Renner Otto Boisselle & Sklar 1621 Euclid Ave Fl 19 Cleveland OH 44115-2107

**JACOBS, CURTIS MARSHALL,** lawyer; b. Louisville, Oct. 4, 1942; s. William Willard and Ruth Adell (Marshall) J.; m. Susan Delong; children: Curtis Jr., Sarah, William. BA, Hanover Coll., 1964; JD, Ind. U., 1967. Bar: Ind. 1967, U.S. Dist. Ct. (so. dist.) Ind. 1967, U.S. Ct. Appeals (6th cir.) 1990, Ky. 1993. Ptnr. Cooper, Cox, Jacobs & Kemper, Madison, Ind., 1967-88; dir. litigation Merchant's Nat. Bank, Indpls., 1988-93; chief counsel and sr. v.p. Nat. City Bank of Ky., Louisville, 1993—, Nat. City Bank of Ind., Indpls., 1997—. Office: Nat City Bank of Ky 101 S 5th St # T-37 Louisville KY 40202-3103 also: Nat City Bank Ind One Nat City Ctr Indianapolis IN 46255

**JACOBS, DARLEEN M.,** lawyer; b. New Orleans, June 18, 1945; d. Arthur Paul and Ann (Imbornone) J.; widowed. BA, U. New Orleans, 1966; JD, Tulane U. Law Sch., 1970. Pvt. practice law New Orleans, 1970—. Fellow Am. Coll. Trial Advocacy; mem. La. State Bar Assn., N.Y. State Bar Assn. Democrat. Jewish. Office: 823 Saint Louis St New Orleans LA 70112-3415

**JACOBS, DENNIS,** federal judge; b. N.Y.C., Feb. 28, 1944; s. Harry N. and Rose J.; m. Judith Weissman. BA, Queens Coll., 1964; MA, NYU, 1965, JD, 1973. Atty. Simpson Thacher & Bartlett, N.Y.C., 1973-92; judge U.S. Ct. Appeals (2d cir.), N.Y.C., 1992—. Office: US Ct Appeals US Courthouse 40 Foley Sq New York NY 10007-1502*

**JACOBS, H. VINCENT,** lawyer; b. Saskatoon, Sask., Can., Feb. 3, 1943; came to U.S., 1956; m. Suzanne R. Jacobs; 2 children. BS, Calif. Poly. State U., 1965, MA, 1967; JD, U. of the Pacific, 1971. Bar: Calif. 1972, U.S. Dist. Ct. (ea. dist.) Calif.; cert. family law specialist. Atty., shareholder Hiroshima, Jacobs, Roth & Lewis, Sacramento, 1972—; mem. Calif. Bd. Legal Specialization, State Bar Calif., 1997—; arbitrator Better Bus. Bur., 1980—, Am. Arbitration Assn., 1985—; lectr. in field. Trustee Sacramento Country Day Sch., 1992-98, treas., 1996-98. Mem. Calif. Poly. Alumni Assn. (Alumni of Yr. 1981). Avocation: fly fishing. Family and matrimonial. Office: Hiroshima Jacobs et al 1420 River Park Dr Fl 2D Sacramento CA 95815-4506

**JACOBS, HARA KAY,** lawyer; b. Phila., Dec. 22, 1969; d. Ellis R. Jacobs and Sandy K. Sacks; m. Clifford I. Ward, Oct. 10, 1998. BA, U. Mich., 1991; JD, Duke U., 1994. Bar: Pa. 1994, U.S. Dist. Ct. (ea. dist.) Pa. 1995, N.J. 1995, U.S. Dist. Ct. N.J. 1995, U.S. Dist. Ct. (ea. and so. dists.) N.Y. 1997, N.Y. 1998. Assoc. Ballard Spahr Andrews & Ingersoll, Phila., 1994-97, Hall Dickler, N.Y.C., 1997-98, Pryor Cashman Sherman & Flynn, N.Y.C., 1998—. Mem. ABA (intellectual property sect.), Internat. Trademark Assn. (project editl. bd.), N.Y. Bar Assn., Phi Beta Kappa. Avocations: basketball, skiing, running. General civil litigation, Trademark and copyright. Office: Pryor Cashman Sherman & Flynn 410 Park Ave Fl 10 New York NY 10022-4441

**JACOBS, HARVEY S.,** lawyer; b. Bradley Beach, N.J., Dec. 15, 1958; s. Joseph and Leatrice J.; m. Marcia E. Clarke; children: Jeffrey, Leah. BBA in Acctg., George Washington U., 1980; JD, Bklyn. Law Sch., 1983. Bar: N.Y. 1984, D.C. 1985, Md. 1995. Assoc. Graham & James (merger Austrian, Lance & Stewart and Graham & James), N.Y.C., 1984-87, Mudge Rose Guthrie Alexander & Ferdon, N.Y.C., 1987-88, Ginsburg Feldman & Bress, Washington, 1988-89; ptnr. Joyce & Jacobs, Washington, 1989—. Editor: D.C. Bar Practice Manual; contbr. articles on Internet and real estate to Unique Homes, Dist. Lawyer mags., Internet: Legal and Business Aspects, Small Bus. News, Georgetowner. Precinct coord. U.S. Rep. Connie Morella, 8th dist., Md. Mem. ABA (sect. on bus. law), D.C. Bar Assn. (various sects., real estate legis. coalition, chair real property transactions subcom.), Assn. of Bar of City of N.Y., Fin. Info. Protection Assn. (charter mem.), D.C. Tech. Coun., George Washington U. Sch. Govt. and Bus. Alumni Assn. (pres. 1986-88), Balt.-Washington Venture Group, Kiwanis (dir.). E-mail: jacobs@jandjlaw.com. Computer, Real property, General corporate. Office: Joyce & Jacobs Attys 1019 19th St NW Ph Two Washington DC 20036-5105

**JACOBS, JACK BERNARD,** judge; b. July 23, 1942; s. Louis K. and Phoebe J.; m. Marion Antiles, Apr. 2, 1967; 1 child, Andrew Seth. AB, U. Chgo., 1964; LLB, Harvard U., 1967. Bar: Del. 1968, U.S. Dist. Ct. Del. 1968, U.S. Ct. Appeals (3d cir.) 1968, U.S. Supreme Ct. 1975. Law clk. Del. Chancery and Superior Cts., 1967-68; assoc. Young, Conaway, Stargatt & Taylor, Wilmington, Del., 1968-71; ptnr. Young, Conaway, Stargatt & Taylor, Wilmington, 1971-85; vice chancellor Ct. of Chancery State of Del., 1985—; adj. prof. Widener U. Sch. Law, 1986—; chmn. Bar-Bench-Media Conf. Del., 1992-93; mem. various faculty continuing legal edn. programs. Contbr. articles to profl. jours. Vice chmn. Nat. Jewish Cmty. Rels. Adv. Coun., 1985-89; bd. dirs. Jewish Fedn. Del., 1981-87, Del. Symphony Assn., 1991-95, Del. Cmty. Found., 1994—, chair grants com., 1998—; pres. Milton & Hattie Kutz Home, 1990-92. Mem. ABA (litigation sect., bus. law sect.), Am. Law Inst., Del. Bar Assn., Harvard Law Sch. Del. (pres. 1986-87), Phi Beta Kappa. Democrat. Jewish. Home: 28 Beethoven Dr Wilmington DE 19807-1923 Office: Ct of Chancery 1000 N King St Wilmington DE 19801-3334

**JACOBS, JEFFREY LEE,** lawyer, education network company executive; b. Boston, Jan. 20, 1951; s. Philip and Millicent T. (Katz) J.; m. Deborah R. Rath, June 7, 1981; children: Alison, Hannah. BA, U. Pa., 1973; MPA, U. So. Calif., 1979; JD, Pace U., 1985. Bar: Conn. 1985, N.Y. 1988. Asst. to comptroller gen. U.S. Gen. Acctg. Office, Washington, 1976-80; sr. rsch. assoc. Nat. Acad. Pub. Adminstrn., Washington, 1980-83; dir. of seminars Prentice Hall, Clifton, N.J., 1985-87; pres. Profl. Edn. Network, Inc., Westport, Conn., 1987—; lectr. Ga. Tax Inst., Ohio Fed. Tax Inst.; adj. prof. Quinnipiac Coll., U. New Haven; cons. Primedia Workplace Learning. Co-author: GAO: Government Accountability, 1979; producer, writer TV series The CPA Report, 1988-91; producer, writer radio series Legal Practice Alert, 1990—. Trustee Westport Pub. Libr. Mem. ABA (taxation sect.), Acad. Legal Studies in Bus. General corporate, Taxation, general. Home: 16 Janson Dr Westport CT 06880-2568 Office: Profl Edn Network 181 Post Rd W Westport CT 06880-4626

**JACOBS, JOHN E.,** lawyer; b. Detroit, Feb. 13, 1947; s. Morton and Gilberta (Jewell) J.; m. Gilda Gail Zalenko, June 6, 1971; children: Rachel H., Jessica E. BA, Mich. State U., 1968; JD, U. Mich., 1971. Bar: Mich. 1971, U.S. Dist. Ct. (ea. dist.) Mich. 1971, U.S. Ct. Appeals (6th cir.) 1984, U.S. Dist. Ct. (we. dist.) Mich. 1997. Assoc. Butzel, Levin, Winston & Quint, Detroit, 1971-76, ptnr., 1976-81; shareholder Mason, Steinhardt, Jacobs, Perlman & Pesick, P.C., Southfield, Mich., 1981—. Contbr. articles to profl. jours. Pres. Jewish Family Svc., Southfield, 1991-93, Temple Emanu-El, Oak Park, Mich., 1995-97. Mem. ABA (mem. consumer fin. svcs. com. 1978—), Jewish Fedn. Met. Detroit (bd. govs. 1997—, mem. exec. com. 1998—). Democrat. Avocations: golfing, bicycling. General corporate, Real property, Contracts commercial. Home: 8353 Hendrie Blvd Huntington Woods MI 48070-1613 Office: Mason Steinhardt Jacobs Perlman & Pesick 4000 Town Ctr Ste 1500 Southfield MI 48075-1588

**JACOBS, JOHN PATRICK,** lawyer; b. Chgo., Oct. 27, 1945; s. Anthony N. and Bessie (Montgomery) J.; m. Linda I. Grams, Oct. 6, 1973; 1 child, Christine Margaret. BA cum laude, U. Detroit, 1967, JD magna cum laude, 1970. Bar: Mich. 1970, U.S. Dist. Ct. Mich. (ea. dist.) 1970, U.S. Ct. Appeals (6th cir.) 1974, U.S. Ct. Appeals (D.C. cir.) 1988, U.S. Supreme Ct. 1978. Law clk. to chief judge Mich. Ct. Appeals, Detroit, 1970-71; assoc., then ptnr. Plunkett & Cooney P.C., Detroit, 1972-92, also bd. dirs.; founding ptnr., prin. mem. O'Leary, O'Leary, Jacobs, Mattson, Perry & Mason P.C., Southfield, Mich., 1992—; investigator Atty. Grievance Com., Detroit, 1975-84; mem. hearing panel Atty. Discipline Bd., Detroit, 1984-87, 94—; adj. prof. law Sch. Law, U. Detroit, 1983-84, faculty advisor, 1984-89, Pres.'s Cabinet, 1982—; elected rep. State Bar Rep. Assembly, Lansing, Mich., 1980-82, 91-92, 93-96; fellow Mich. State Bar Found., 1990-98; treas., mem. steering com. Mich. Bench-Bar Appellate Conf. Com., 1994—; apptd. mem. Mich. Supreme Ct. Com. on Appellate Fees, 1990; spl. mediator appellate negotiation program Mich. Ct. Appeals, 1995—; mem. exec. com. Mich. Appellate Bench-Bar Conf. Found., 1996—. mem. profl. ethics com. State Bar Mich., 1998, mem. multi-disciplinary practice com., 1999. Bd. dirs. Boysville of Mich., Clinton, 1988-95, 99—, chmn. pub. policy com., 1993-95, pub. policy liaison, 1999—; apptd. mem. State Bar Mich. Blue Ribbon Com. Improving Def. Counsel-Insurer Rels., 1998-99, spl. amicus curiae counsel to Mich. Supreme Ct., 1999. Recipient Robert E. Dice Med. Malpractice Def. Atty. award Mich. Physicians, 1986; Reginald Heber Smith fellow, 1971-72. Fellow Am. Acad. Appellate Lawyers, Mich. Std. Jury Instn. (subcom. employment law 1984-87); mem. ABA (litigation sect., appellate subcom., torts and ins. practice), Internat. Assn. Def. Counsel (v.p., amicus curiae com., med. and legal malpractice coms., product liability com.), Fedn. Ins. and Corp. Counsel, Mich. Def. Trial Counsel (chmn. amicus curiae com. 1986-88, chmn. future planning com., bd. dirs. 1989—, treas. 1993-94, sec. 1994-95, v.p. 1995-96, program chair 1990, 94, 95, pres., 1996-97), Def. Rsch. Inst. (state rep. 1997-98, Outstanding Performance Citation 1997, appellate com. steering com. 1997—), Cath. Lawyers Soc. (bd. dirs. 1988-98, emeritus dir. 1998—, pres. 1994-95). Democrat. Roman Catholic. Avocations: collecting antique law books, film. Appellate, Federal civil litigation, State civil litigation. Office: O'Leary O'Leary Jacobs Mattson Perry and Mason PC 26777 Central Park Blvd Ste 275 Southfield MI 48076-4137

**JACOBS, JULIAN I.,** federal judge; b. Balt., Aug. 13, 1937; s. Sidney and Bernice (Kellman) J.; m. Donna Buffenstein; children: Richard S., Jennifer K. B.A., U. Md., 1958, J.D., 1960; LL.M., Georgetown U., 1965. Bar: Md., 1960. Atty. chief counsel's office IRS, Washington, 1961-65; trial atty. regional counsel's office IRS, Buffalo, 1965-67; assoc. Weinberg & Green, Balt., 1967-69, Hoffberger & Hollander, Balt., 1969-72; assoc. Gordon Feinblatt Rothman Hoffberger & Hollander, Balt., 1972-74, ptnr., 1974-84; judge U.S. Tax Ct., Washington, 1984—; chmn. study commn. Md. Tax Ct., 1978-79, mem. rules com., 1980; mem. spl. study group Md. Gen. Assembly, 1980; adj. prof. grad. tax program U. Balt., 1991-93. Mem. U. Md. Law Rev. Bd. dirs. Md. Med. Research Inst., Inc. Mem. Md. State Bar Assn. (past chmn. taxation sect.), Balt. City Bar Assn. (past chmn. tax legis. subcom.). Office: US Tax Ct 400 2nd St NW Washington DC 20217-0002

**JACOBS, LAWRENCE H.,** lawyer; b. Paterson, N.J., Feb. 8, 1955; s. Bernard Jacobs and Hortense (Grossman) Roemer; m. Sue Ann Luckman, May 27, 1990; 1 child, Alanna Brooke. BA summa cum laude, Fairleigh Dickinson U., 1977; JD cum laude, Seton Hall U., 1980. Bar: N.J. 1980, U.S. Ct. Appeals (3rd cir.) 1980, Fla. 1982. Assoc. Pitney, Hardin, Kipp & Szuch, Morristown, N.J., 1980-83; assoc. Francis & Berry, Morristown, 1983-87, ptnr., 1987-88; assoc. Hein, Smith, Berezin, Maloof & Spinella, Hackensack, N.J., 1988-91; ptnr. Hein, Smith, Berezin, Maloof, Spinella & Rogers, Hackensack, 1991-96, Hein, Smith, Berezin, Maloof, Davidson & Jacobs, Hackensack, 1996-98, Hein Smith Berezin Maloof & Jacobs, Hackensack, 1999—. Mem. ABA, N.J. State Bar Assn., Fla. Bar Assn., Bergen County Bar Assn. Avocations: tennis, racquetball, golf. Personal injury, Health, General civil litigation. Office: Hein Smith Berezin Maloof & Jacobs 19 Main St Hackensack NJ 07601-7043

**JACOBS, MARK RANDOLPH,** lawyer; b. Columbus, Ohio, June 7, 1953; s. Lee Randolph and Sally Ann (Cummins) J.; m. Linda Beth Rogozinski, Oct. 29, 1983; children: Philip Randolph, Gregory Cummins. BA cum laude with distinction, Yale U., 1979, JD, 1982. Bar: N.Y. 1983, U.S. Dist. Ct. (so. dist.) N.Y. 1983, Conn. 1993. Law clerk Hon. S.W. Kram U.S. Dist. Judge, N.Y., 1983-84; ptnr. Pryor, Cashman, Sherman & Flynn, N.Y., 1988-90, Cadwalader, Wickersham & Taft, N.Y., 1990-92; of counsel Gregory & Adams, Wilton, Conn., 1992-96; ptnr. Jacobs Goldman LLC, Norwalk, Conn., 1997—. Bankruptcy, Federal civil litigation. Office: Jacobs Goldman LLC Merritt View 383 Main Ave Norwalk CT 06851-1543

**JACOBS, MARY LEE,** lawyer; b. Pitts., June 29, 1950; d. George and Mary Jane (Swinderman) Jacobs. BA in History, Wellesley Coll., 1972; JD, Boston U., 1974. BAr: Mass. 1975, U.S. Dist. Ct. Mass. 1976, U.S. Ct. Appeals (1st cir.) 1978, U.S. Supreme Ct. 1981. Gen. counsel Tufts U., Medford, Mass., 1984—. Mem. ABA, Boston Bar Assn., Nat. Assn. Coll. and Univ. Attys. Education and schools. Office: Tufts Univ Ballou Hall 3d Fl Medford MA 02155

**JACOBS, RICHARD LOUIS,** lawyer, writer; b. Merced, Calif., Sept. 3, 1953; s. George Paul and Emma Frances (Schrettner) J.; m. Marjorie Ann Kosatka, Aug. 22, 1986. BA in Journalism, Pa. State U., 1975; JD, Duquesne U., 1978. Bar: Pa. 1978, U.S. Dist. Ct. (we. dist.) Pa. 1978, U.S. Supreme Ct. 1991. Reporter Pa. Daily Mirror, State College, 1975; trial atty. Legal Svcs. Corp., Beaver Falls, Pa., 1978-81; assoc. Miller & Templin, Pitts., 1981-86; adminstrv. trial atty. Nationwide Ins. Co., Warrendale, Pa., 1986—. Contbr. articles to Strategy Plus mag. Bd. dirs. Family Svcs., Inc., Beaver, Pa., 1980; press liaison Fred Kotrozo Campaign for Pa. Legislature, 1980, John Foley Campaign for Pa. Legislature, 1980. Mem. Am. Corp. Counsel Assn., Pa. Bar Assn. (mem. in-house counsel com.), Allegheny County Bar Assn., Butler County Bar Assn., Pa. Def. Inst., Am. Youth Hostels, Kappa Tau Alpha. Roman Catholic. Avocations: computer science, World War II studies, freelance writing. Insurance, Personal injury, General civil litigation. Office: Nationwide Ins Co One Williamsburg Pl Ste 200 Warrendale PA 15086-7568

**JACOBS, ROLLY WARREN,** lawyer; b. Nashville, Aug. 26, 1946; s. William Clinton Jr. and Eleanor Olive (Warren) J.; m. Karen Lee Ponist, Sept. 16, 1972; children: Collin Wayne, Tyler Warren. BA in Econs., Washington & Lee U., 1968; JD, U. S.C., 1974. Bar: S.C. 1975, U.S. Dist. Ct. for S.C. 1975. Assoc. Carl R. Reasonover, Camden, S.C., 1975-77; ptnr. Reasonover

& Jacobs, Camden, S.C., 1977-80; pvt. practice law Camden, S.C., 1988-99; family ct. judge Fifth Jud. Cir. Ct., 1999—; asst. city judge Mcpl. Ct., Camden, 1976-77; master in equity S.C. Jud. Sys., Camden, 1978-99; mem. Jud. Coun. for S.C., Columbia, 1989—, Fee Dispute Panel, 1986-93; family ct. judge U.S. Cir. Ct. (5th cir.) S.C., 1999—. d. dirs. ARC, Camden, 1976-78, Am. Cancer Soc., Camden, 1976-78, United Way, Camden, 1978-82; active Boy Scouts Am., Camden, 1984-96. Capt. U.S. Army, 1968-72. Recipient Dist. Award of Merit Indian Waters Coun. Boy Scouts Am., 1991. Mem. ABA, VFW, S.C. Bar Assn., Am. Legon, Res. Officers Assn., Elks. Methodist. Avocations: yard work, swimming. Family and matrimonial, General practice, Real property. Home: 418 Lafayette Way Camden SC 29020-1642 Office: 612 Lafayette St Camden SC 29020-3520

**JACOBS, RONALD HEDSTROM,** lawyer; b. York, Pa., Oct. 23, 1945; s. Jerry S. and Ann E. (Hedstrom) J.; 1 dau., Heidi. AB, Dickinson Coll., 1967; JD, U. Denver, 1970. Bar: Colo. 1971. Regional counsel Transam Title Ins. Co., Denver, 1971-75; v.p., resident counsel Midland Fed. Savs. and Loan Assn., Denver, 1975-81; ptnr. Brownstein, Hyatt, Farber & Madden, Denver, 1981-84, Sherman & Howard, 1984-91; prin. Ronald H. Jacobs, A Profl. Corp., 1992—; mem. adv. bd. Arapahoe Community Coll., 1974-76; instr. in real estate law Emily Griffith Opportunity Sch., 1971-73, Inst. Fin. Edn., 1975-78; lectr. continuing legal edn., title ins. and real estate seminars. Mem. ABA (past mem. exec. coun. law, young lawyers sect.), Colo. Bar Assn. (forms com., chmn. legal asst. com. 1976-78, ad hoc com. Uniform Condominium Act 1977-80, chmn. young lawyers sect. 1981-82, chmn. by laws com. 1983-85, mem. long range planning com. 1983-85, conv. com. 1985— ), Denver Bar Assn. (past chmn. topical luncheon com., professionalism com. 1991—), Am. Arbitration Assn., U.S. Savs. and Loan League (attys. com.). Banking, Real property. Home and Office: 730 17th St Ste 900 Denver CO 80202-3520

**JACOBS, STEPHEN LOUIS,** lawyer; b. Staples, Minn., June 22, 1953; s. James P. and Gertrude G. (Willis) J.; m. Sue E. Bell, June 14, 1975; 2 children. BA, St. John's U., 1975; JD, William Mitchell Coll. of Law, St. Paul, 1979. Bar: Minn. 1979, U.S. Dist. Ct. Minn. 1979. Assoc. Bertie, Bettenburg & Strong, St. Paul, 1979-84; ptnr. Bertie, Bettenberg, Jacobs & Bettenburg, St. Paul, 1984-89; pvt. practice law St. Paul, 1989—. Mem. Minn. Bar Assn., Kiwanis (pres. St. Paul-Midway chpt. 1987-88, 97-98, bd. dirs. 1984—). Roman Catholic. Probate, Real property, General practice. Office: 190 Midtown Commons 2334 University Ave W Saint Paul MN 55114-1802

**JACOBS, THOMAS E.,** lawyer; b. Tacoma, Wash., May 17, 1949; s. Edmund F. and Barbara J. J.; m. Gayle L. McFarland, Mar. 4, 1972; children: Joshua, Rebecca, Andrew. BA, Whitworth Coll., 1971; JD, Gonzaga Law Sch., 1976. Bar: U.S. Dist. Ct. (we. dist.) Wash. 1979. Intern Lukins, Amis, Spokane, Wash., 1975-76; ptnr. Jacobs & Jacobs, Puyallup, Wash., 1977—; prosecuting atty. City of Puyallup, 1977-82; pres. Puyallup Yacht Charter, Inc., 1992-97. Bd. dirs. Puyallup YMCA, 1982-84, Puyallup Ch. of Nazarene, 1977—; gen. coun. Wstn. Pacific Dist. Ch. of Nazarene, Seattle, 1982—; bd. dirs. Crisis Pregnancy Ctr., Tacoma, Wash., 1998—. Mem. Wash. State Bar Assn. (investigation coun. 1990-96, bar examiner 1998—), Pierce County Bar Assn. (trustee 1991-92), Inn of Ct. Republican. Avocations: boating, snow skiing, hunting, fishing, flying. Office: Jacobs & Jacobs 114 E Meeker Puyallup WA 98372-3243

**JACOBS, WENDELL EARLY, JR.,** lawyer; b. Detroit, Nov. 15, 1945; s. Wendell E. and Mildred P. (Horton) J.; m. Elaine M. Lott (div.); children: Wendell Early III, Damon R. BFA, Denison U., 1969; JD, Wayne State U., 1972. Bar: Mich. 1972, U.S. Dist. Ct. (ea. dist.) Mich. 1973, Fla. 1974. Asst. prosecutor Jackson County, Mich., 1973-76; ptnr. Jacobs & Engle, Jackson, 1977—. Mem. Mich. Coun. on Crime and Delinquency. Mem. Nat. Assn. Criminal Def. Lawyers, Criminal Def. Attys. Mich., Jackson County Bar Assn., Eagles Club, Grotto Club, Elks. Avocations: paddleball, motorcycling. Criminal, Family and matrimonial, General practice. Home: 9281 Greenwood Rd Grass Lake MI 49240-9590 Office: Jacobs & Engle 1104 W Michigan Ave Jackson MI 49202-4123

**JACOBS, WILLIAM RUSSELL, II,** lawyer; b. Chgo., Oct. 26, 1927; s. William Russell and Doris B. (Desmond) J.; m. Shirley M. Spiegler, Mar. 21, 1950; children: William R. III, Richard W., Bruce Allen. BS, Northwestern U., 1950, JD, 1953. Bar: Ill. 1953, U.S. Dist. Ct. (no. dist.) Ill. 1958, U.S. Ct. Appeals (7th cir.) 1958, U.S. Supreme Ct., 1962. Atty. Continental Casualty Co., Chgo., 1955-58; assoc. Horwitz and Anesi, Chgo., 1958-62; prin. William R. Jacobs and Assocs., Chgo., 1962—; adj. prof. Lewis Coll. Law, Glen Ellyn, Ill., 1975-76; dir., tchr. Ct. Practice Inst., Chgo., 1974—; lectr. Ill. Inst. Continuing Legal Edn., Chgo., 1967—. Elected alderman Des Plaines (Ill.) City Coun., 1953-54; mem. Ill. Bar Assembly, 1973—. 1st lt. inf. U.S. Army, 1946-48. Mem. Ill. State Bar Assn., Am. Acad. Matrimonial Lawyers. Congregationalist. General civil litigation, Family and matrimonial, Personal injury. Office: William R Jacobs & Assocs 601 Lee St Des Plaines IL 60016-4616

**JACOBSEN, RAYMOND ALFRED, JR.,** lawyer; b. Wilmington, Del., Dec. 14, 1949; s. Raymond Alfred and Margaret (Walters) J.; m. Marilyn Perry, Aug. 4, 1973. BA, U. Del., 1971; JD, Georgetown U., 1975. Bar: D.C. 1975, U.S. Supreme Ct. 1982. From assoc. to ptnr. Howrey & Simon, Washington, 1975-97; dir. Antitrust/Trade Reg. Grp. McDermott, Will & Emery, Washington, 1997-, ptnr., 1997—; adj. prof. internat. anti-trust law Am. U. Law Sch. Spl. projects editor Law & Policy in International Business, 1974-75. Served to capt. U.S. Army, 1975. Mem. ABA (antitrust law sect., adminstrv. law sect., corp. banking and bus. law sect., litigation sect., internat. law sect., pub. contract law sect.), D.C. Bar Assn., U.S. Supreme Ct. Bar Assn. Republican. Club: Army & Navy, City (Washington). Antitrust, Federal civil litigation, Mergers and acquisitions. Home: 4205 Maple Tree Ct Alexandria VA 22304-1035 Office: McDermott Will & Emery 600 13th St NW Fl 12 Washington DC 20005-3096

**JACOBSEN, VAN PAUL,** lawyer; b. Olivia, Minn., Nov. 26, 1954; s. Ivan Robert and Nola Ruth Jacobsen; children: Natalie, Evan. BS, U. Minn., 1977, JD, 1982. Bar: Minn. 1982, U.S. Dist. Ct. Minn. 1986, U.S. Supreme Ct. 1997. Law clk. Dakota County Atty.'s Office, Hastings, Minn., 1980-82; asst. county atty. Renville County, Olivia, Minn., 1982-84; assoc. Simmons, Hunt & Jacobsen, Olivia, Minn., 1985-87, Steward, Perry, Mahler & Bird, Rochester, Minn., 1985-87; ptnr. Bird and Jacobsen, Rochester, Minn., 1987—. Vol. Legal Assistance of Olmsted County, Rochester, 1985—; mem. social concerns com. 1st Presbyn. Ch., Rochester, 1997—; bd. dirs. Vol. Connection, Rochester, 1990-92. Mem. Minn. Trial Lawyers Assn., Minn. State Bar Assn., Nat. Orgn. Social Security Claimant's Reps., Minn. Arabian Horse Assn., Internat. Arabian Horse Assn. Workers' compensation, Pension, profit-sharing, and employee benefits. Home: 628 73rd St NW Rochester MN 55901-5509 Office: Bird and Jacobsen 305 Ironwood Sq 300 3rd Ave SE Rochester MN 55904-4619

**JACOBSON, BARRY STEPHEN,** lawyer, judge; b. Bklyn., Mar. 30, 1955; s. Morris and Sally (Ballaban) J.; m. Andrea Jacobson; children: Faith Blair, Matthew Aaron Jacobson. Cert. in drama, Sch. of Performing Arts, N.Y.C., 1973; BA, CUNY, 1977, MA, 1980; JD, Bklyn. Sch. Law, 1980. Bar: N.Y., 1981, U.S. Dist. Ct. (ea. and so. dists.) N.Y. 1981, U.S. Dist. Ct. (we. and no. dists.) N.Y., 1988, U.S. Dist. Ct. D.C., 1988, U.S. Ct. Appeals (2d cir.) 1981, U.S. Ct. Appeals (fed. and D.C. cirs.) 1988, U.S. Supreme Ct. 1984, U.S. Ct. Claims, 1985, U.S. Tax Ct. 1988 and others. Sole practice Bklyn., 1981; asst. corp. counsel N.Y.C. Law Dept., Bklyn., 1981-84; asst. dist. atty. Borough of Queens, Kew Gardens, N.Y., 1984-85; judge adminstrv. law N.Y. Dept. Motor Vehicles, Bklyn., 1985-86, 87-92; assoc. counsel N.Y. State Dept. Health, N.Y.C., 1986; arbitrator N.Y.C. Small Claims Ct., 1986-91; pvt. practice Bklyn., 1992—; gen. counsel Amersfort Flatlands Devel. Corp., Bklyn., 1981-82; arbitrator N.Y.C. Civil Ct. 1987-92; adminstrv. law judge N.Y.C. Parking Violators Bur., 1987-93; mem. Indigent Defenders Appeal Panel, 1988-96; sr. adminstrv. law judge N.Y.C. Parking Violation Bur., 1989-93; leader Nat. Jud. Coll., N.Y. Mem. Roosevelt Dem. Party, Bklyn., 1984-95, mem. adv. bd., 1989-92, treas., 1990-92; active Kings Hwy. Dem. Party, Bklyn., 1982-95, Dem. com. 1986-95; active King's County Young Dems., 1985-86; gen. counsel Bklyn. Coll. Hillel, Bklyn. Coll. Student Govts., 1980-90, also advisor; treas. local div. dept. mtr. vehicles pub. employees fedn. AFL-CIO; coun. ldr. div. #255 Pub. Employee's Fedn., 1989-92, conv. del. 1989, 90, 91; chmn. Bklyn. Traffic Employee Assistance Prog., 1989-92. Named one of Outstanding Young Men Am., 1983, 85, 86, 87, 88. Mem. ABA (judicial sect., spl. const. judges traffic cts. com.), Am. Judges Assn. (hwy. safety com.), Bklyn. Bar Found. (trustee, bd. dirs.), Am. Arbitration Assn. (forums 1988—), Am. Judicature Soc., Assn. Adminstrv. Law Judges (pres.), N.Y. State Dept. Motor Vehicles (v.p.), N.Y. State Adminstrv. Law Judges Assn. (pres. bd. dirs. parking violation com., v.p.), N.Y. State Bar Assn. (pres. for DMV, spl. com. juvenile justice, adminstrv. law jud. coms., jud. adminstrn. com.), Bklyn. Bar Assn. (family ct. com., chmn. young lawyers sect., trustee 1991, chmn. adminstrn. law com.), N.Y. County Lawyers Assn. (family Ct. Com.), Bklyn. Coll. Alumni Assn. (gen. counsel student govt. affiliate 1983-92, bd. dirs. 1985-92), Jaycees, B'nai B'rith, Hillel (bd. dirs. 1983-91, gen. counsel 1987-91), many others. Jewish. Avocations: motorcycling, drama, theatre, target shooting, flying. Criminal, Administrative and regulatory, Family and matrimonial. Home: 342 Coleridge Ln Jericho NY 11753-2605 Office: 26 Court St Ste 810 Brooklyn NY 11242-1108

**JACOBSON, BERNARD,** lawyer; b. Hartford, Conn., Feb. 27, 1930; s. Samuel Barnard and Lillian Jacobson; m. Florence Ellen Greenberg, Oct. 7, 1956; children: Daniel John, Alice Lash, Nancy. AB, Amherst Coll., 1951; LLB, Columbia U., 1954. Bar: Conn. 1955, Fla. 1957, U.S. Dist. Ct. (so. dist.) Fla. 1957, U.S. Ct. Appeals (11th cir.) 1961. Pvt. practice Miami, Fla., 1957-68; ptnr. Fine, Jacobson, Miami, Fla., 1968-94, Holland & Knight LLP, Miami, Fla., 1994—; pres., CEO Rep. Mortgage Investors, Miami, 1973-81; presenter in field. Contbr. articles to profl. jours. Chmn. Fla. Congl. Partnership, Miami, 1987; vice chmn. Greater Miami C. of C., 1988-92. With U.S. Army Counter Intelligence Corps, 1955-57. Mem. ABA, Fla. Bar Assn. Avocations: tennis, boating, skiing. General corporate, Private international, Securities. Office: Holland & Knight LLP 701 Brickell Ave Ste 3000 Miami FL 33131-2898

**JACOBSON, DENNIS JOHN,** lawyer; b. Racine, Wis., June 1, 1953; s. Donald Lee and Donna Marie (Andress) J.; m. Debra Jean Tully, Dec. 21, 1981; 1 child, Rebecca Michelle. BA, Western State Coll., Gunnison, Colo., 1975; JD, U. Denver, 1978. Bar: Colo. 1978, U.S. Dist. Ct. Colo. 1978, U.S. Ct. Appeals (10th cir.) 1987. Dep. dist. atty. 1st Jud. Dist. Colo., Golden, 1978-81; assoc. Polidori, Rasmussen & Gerome, Lakewood, Colo., 1981-83; ptnr. Polidori, Gerome, Franklin & Jacobson, Lakewood, 1983—; lectr. Colo. Law enforcement Tng. Acad., Golden, 1979—. Co-author: DUI Manual State of Colorado, 1981. Mem. cen. com. Jefferson County Rep. Com., Colo., 1986-88; lay leader St. James United Meth. Ch., Central City, Colo., 1986-90. Mem. ABA, Colo. Bar Assn. (bd. govs. 1988-90, v.p. 1990-91), 1st Jud. Dist. Bar Assn. Colo. (pres. 1987-88, contbr. to newsletter 1985—, Outstanding Young Lawyer award 1983, Merit award 1998). Avocations: instrumental and vocal music, sports, scuba diving. General civil litigation, Criminal, Family and matrimonial. Office: Polidori Gerome Franklin & Jacobson 550 S Wadsworth Blvd Ste 300 Lakewood CO 80226-3117

**JACOBSON, EARL JAMES,** lawyer, tax leasing executive; b. Chgo., May 10, 1940; s. Benjamin L. and Mary (Urman) J.; children: Joan, John. BA, U. Ill., 1961; MBA, U. Chgo., 1963; JD, Loyola U., Chgo., 1980. Bar: Ill. 1980, U.S. Dist. Ct. (no. dist.) Ill. 1980, U.S. Ct. Internat. Trade 1980, U.S. Ct. Customs and Patent Appeals 1980, U.S. Tax Ct. 1985, U.S. Supreme Ct. 1985. Indsl. salesman Honeywell, Xerox, Chgo., 1964-67; dir. mktg. Mastech Computer, Chgo., 1967-71, Datronic Rental Co., Chgo., 1971-81; v.p. Dearborn Computer Co., Park Ridge, Ill., 1981-82; sr. syndication officer Seattle 1st Nat. Bank, Schaumburg, Ill., 1982-83; v.p. fin. and syndication Hartford Fin. Svcs., Inverness, Ill., 1983-85; v.p. corp. fin. and corp. counsel Lease Investment Corp., Chgo., 1985-86; dir. equity placement CIS Corp., Syracuse, N.Y., 1986-87; pres. Mid Tech Funding, 1987-89, Smith Wilson Acceptance Corp., 1989-99; regional mgr. Deloitte & Touche, Chgo., 1999; funding mgr. Internat. Profit Assocs., Buffalo, N.Y., 1999—; dir., gen. counsel Info. Systems, Arlington Heights, Ill., 1st Securities, Inc., Chgo., Citifirst, Inc., Chgo. Served with USAF, 1963-69. Mem. ABA, Nat. Assn. Securities Dealers, Equipment Syndication Assn., Ill. State Bar Assn., Chgo. Bar Assn. Club: 20 Plus (Chgo.) (pres. 1980-82). Home: 4200 W Lake Ave Apt A102 Glenview IL 60025-7402

**JACOBSON, JEFFREY ELI,** lawyer, consultant; b. N.Y.C., Aug. 19, 1956; s. Murray and Adele (Ebert) J.; m. Linda Moel, Aug. 11, 1984; children: Justin Myles, Sari Amanda. BA, Fordham U., 1976; JD, N.Y. Law Sch., 1980. Bar: N.Y. 1982, D.C. 1982, U.S. Tax Ct. 1982, U.S. Ct. Internat. Trade 1982, U.S. Dist. Ct. (so. and ea. dists.) N.Y. 1982, U.S. Ct. Appeals (2d cir.) 1988, U.S. Supreme Ct. 1988. Assoc. SESAC, Inc., N.Y.C., 1980-82; sole practice N.Y.C., 1982-85; sr. ptnr. Jacobson & Colfin, P.C., N.Y.C. and L.I., 1985-90; mng. mem. Jacobson & Colfin, P.C., N.Y.C. and Washington, 1991—; v.p., sec. Fifth Ave. Media, Ltd., N.Y.C., 1995—; asst. mgr. Embassy Theatre, N.Y.C., 1975, Victoria Theatre, N.Y.C., 1975; asst. Theatre Confections, Inc., N.Y.C., 1975; mgr. Criterion Theatre, N.Y.C., 1976; mgr., sec. Squirrels Prodns. Ltd., N.Y.C., 1976-88; pres. Aldous Demian Prodns., Ltd., N.Y.C., 1980-82; counsel Box Office Media, N.Y.C., 1982-88, Eggink, N.Y.C., 1982-89, Performance Records, 1988-97, J&J Mus. Enterprises, Ltd., 1982-95,, Anamaze Records, 1982-95, Cynthia Entertainment Group, Ltd., 1989-91, Roir Records, 1992—, Super Bubble Music Corp., 1992—, Sergei Artemiev Benefit, 1993, New Riders of the Purple Sage, 1985—, Mick Taylor Music, 1985—, Best Film and Video Corp., 1988-91, Marty Balin, 1988—, Andrew Tosh, 1990—; spkr. CMJ Music Marathon & Musicfest, 1995, Phila. Music Confs., 1993, 94, 95, 96, 97. Mem. editl. bd. Mealey's Intellectual Property Litigation Law Report, 1992-93; contbr. articles to profl. jours.; music and internat. promotion mgmt., 1984-85; columnist IMPS Jour., 1990-95, Replication News, 1998—. Mem. Rep. candidate assembly; v.p. Pelham Pkwy., 1983-88; speaker Songwriter's Guild, N.Y.C., 1983-88, NARAS, 1991; entertainment arbitrator Am. Arbitration Assn., N.Y.C., 1984-95; guest speaker Ctr. for Media Arts, N.Y.C., 1985, Fordham U., N.Y.C., 1986, N.Y. Law Sch., 1987, Detroit Sch. Law, 1991, 93; counsel Pelham Pkwy. Block Assn., Inc., 1991; panelist Mid-Am. Music Conf., Detroit, 1993, Black Radio Exclusive, Econs. of Music, 1993; league lawyer Hewlett-Woodmere Little League, 1994—. Recipient Eagle Scout Silver Palm award Boy Scouts Am., 1972, Cert. of Merit Bronx House, Nathan Burkan award ASCAP, 1980, Plaque of Appreciation, Am. Arbitration Assn., 1985; named Most Admired Men and Women of Yr., 1993, Two Thousand Notable Am. Men, 1993, Man of Yr., 1996. Mem. ABA (chmn. subcom. on satellites, chmn. subcom. on copyright compliance, chmn. subcom. on copyright renewal, mem. patent trademark, copyright law sect., forum com. on entertainment and sports law sects., mem. spl. com. on corp. practice 1992-97, mem. spl. com. on atty. opinions 1994—, mem. spl. com. on internet 1997—), forum com. on comm. law, young lawyer's divsn., vice chmn. 1992-94, patent, trademark, intellectual property sect. exec. com., 1992-93, media law com., young lawyers divsn., founder Urban Intellectual Property Law seminars 1993-95, dir., 1993-95, mem. com. on atty./client opinions, mem. spl. com. Internet usage), Assn. of Bar of City of N.Y. (entertainment law com. 1992-95, trademark law com. 1997—), Copyright Soc. USA (com. on Bicentennial of copyright, mem. editl. bd. Jour. of Copyright Soc. 1991-93, 97—), Nat. Acad. Rec. Arts and Scis. (edn. com., columnist N.Y. chpt. newsletter 1997—), Rock and Roll Hall of Fame and Museum, Internat. Assn. Entertainment Lawyers, B'nai B'rith (v.p. 1988-91), Order of the Arrow Brotherhood, Sephardic Jewish Brotherhood Am., Audubon Soc. Inc., Phi Delta Phi. Jewish. Avocations: music, photography, swimming, stereo equipment, traveling. Entertainment, Trademark and copyright, Federal civil litigation. Office: Jacobson & Colfin PC 156 5th Ave Ste 434 New York NY 10010-7002

**JACOBSON, JEROLD DENNIS,** lawyer; b. N.Y.C., Oct. 12, 1940; s. Sidney and Lillian D. (Fink) J.; m. Gertraude M.J. Holle-Suppa, May 4, 1998; children—Diana, Lisa, Pamela. A.B., U. Vt., 1962; J.D., Cornell U., 1965; LL.M. in Labor Law, NYU, 1966. Bar: N.Y. 1966, U.S. Dist. Ct. (so. and ea. dists.) N.Y. 1968, U.S. Dist. Ct. (no. dist.) N.Y. 1981, U.S. Ct. Appeals (2d cir.) 1979, U.S. Ct. Appeals (5th cir.) 1980, U.S. Ct. Appeals (11th cir.) 1981, U.S. Supreme Ct. 1982. Assoc. to gen. counsel ILGWU, AFL-CIO, N.Y.C., 1966-69; assoc. Rains, Pogrebin and Scher, N.Y.C. and Mineola, N.Y., 1969-70; assoc. Guggenheimer & Untermyer, N.Y.C., 1970-74, ptnr., 1975-85; ptnr. Summit, Rovins & Feldesman, N.Y.C., 1986-89, Patterson, Belknap, Webb & Tyler, N.Y.C., 1989-91, Proskauer Rose LLP, N.Y.C., 1991—; lectr. in labor and employment relations law Practising Law Inst., Am. Soc. Law and Medicine, Profl. Edn. Systems, Inc. Bd. dirs. Nassau County chpt. N.Y. State Civil Liberties Union; mem. adv. bd. U. Vt. Holocaust Study Ctr., U. Vt. Coll. Arts and Scis. Mem. ABA, Legal Aid Soc., Am. Arbitration Assn., Am. Acad. Hosp. Attys., Nat. Health Lawyers Assn., N.Y. State Bar Assn. (lectr.) Contbr. articles to profl. jours. Active, Inst. for Internat. Rsch., Coun. on Edn. in Mgmt.; bd. dirs. Nassau County chpt. N.Y. State Civil Liberties Union. Labor, Administrative and regulatory, Health. Office: Proskauer Rose LLP 1585 Broadway New York NY 10036-8200

**JACOBSON, LEON IRWIN,** lawyer; b. Boston, Apr. 9, 1943; s. Max and Dora Katz; m. Judith Seidel, Aug. 30, 1970; children: Alexander, Matthew. AB magna cum laude, Harvard Coll., 1963; JD cum laude, Harvard U., 1967; postgrad., London Sch. Econs., 1964. Bar: N.Y., Fla. Assoc. Paul Weiss Rifkind Wharton & Garrison, N.Y.C., 1967-74, Freeman, Meade, N.Y.C., 1974-76; pres. Jacobson, Mermelstein & Squire LLP and predecessor firms, N.Y.C., 1976—. Contbr. chpt. to book. Mem. Phi Beta Kappa. Fax: 212-697-1427. Corporate taxation, Insurance, General corporate. Home: 277 W End Ave Apt 7D New York NY 10023-2611 Office: Jacobson Mermelstein & Squire 52 Vanderbilt Ave New York NY 10017-3808

**JACOBSON, MARY CAROL,** lawyer; b. Jersey City, N.J., Oct. 8, 1953; d. William Walter and Katherine Cawley J.; m. James Howard Laskey, Oct. 1, 1983; children: Michael, Kevin, Katherine. BA, Smith Coll., 1975; JD, NYU, 1978. Bar: N.J. 1978, U.S. Dist. Ct. N.J. 1978, U.S. Ct. Appeals (3d and D.C. cirs.) 1980, U.S. Supreme Ct. 1983. Law clk. to Hon. Samuel Larner, Newark, 1978-79; dep. atty. gen. N.J. Dept. Law, Trenton, 1979-93, asst. atty. gen., 1993—. Office: Office Atty Gen NJ PO Box 112 25 Market St Trenton NJ 08625-0112

**JACOBSON, PETER A.,** lawyer; b. Stamford, Conn., Apr. 2, 1944; s. Arthur V. and Teresa (Cesare) J. BA, Union Coll., 1966; JD, Albany Law Sch., 1969. Bar: N.Y. 1971, U.S. Dist. Ct. (we. dist.) N.Y. 1971. Spl. agt. FBI, Rochester, N.Y., 1969-76; asst. dist. atty. Monroe County Dist. Atty.'s Office, Rochester, 1976-85; ptnr. Trevett, Lenweaver & Salzer, P.C., Rochester, 1985—. Mem. N.Y. State Bar Assn. Personal injury, Criminal. Home: 222 Fairhaven Rd Rochester NY 14610-2203 Office: Trevett Lenweaver & Salzer PC 700 Reynolds Arcade 16 Main St E Ste 700 Rochester NY 14614-1813

**JACOBSON, RICHARD LEE,** lawyer, educator; b. Los Angeles, Nov. 2, 1942; s. Joseph and Betty (Koenig) J.; children: David, Peter, Michael. S.B., U. Chgo., 1964; J.D., U. So. Calif., 1970. Bar: Calif. 1971, U.S. Ct. Appeals (9th cir.) 1971, D.C. 1980, U.S. Ct. Appeals (4th cir.) 1980, U.S. Ct. Appeals (D.C. cir.) 1980, U.S. Supreme Ct. 1980, U.S. Ct. Appeals (6th cir.) 1983. Law clk. U.S. Ct. Appeals (9th cir.), 1970-71; law clk. to Assoc. Justice William O. Douglas U.S. Supreme Ct., Washington, 1971-72; assoc. Irell & Manella, Los Angeles, 1973-76; mem. trial unit SEC, Washington, 1977-78, spl. counsel to chmn., 1978-79; ptnr. Mayer, Brown & Platt, Washington, 1980-85; spl. counsel Heller, Ehrman, White & McAuliffe, Palo Alto, 1986-88; of counsel Fulbright & Jaworski, Washington, 1988-89, ptnr., 1990—; adj. prof. law Georgetown U. Law Ctr., Washington, 1979-86; mem. bd. advisors, sec. Reform Act Litig. Reporter, 1998—. Exec. editor So. Calif. Law Rev., 1969-70; contbr. articles to profl. jours. Bd. dirs. Washington Lawyers Com. for Civil Rights and Urban Affairs, 1983—. Mem. ABA (chmn. subcom. uniformity of local discovery rules 1983-85, chmn. subcom. securities class actions 1995—, fed. regulation securities com., securities litigation com.), Am. Law Inst., Washington Coun. Lawyers (bd. dirs. 1982-86, 88-99, pres. 1985-86), D.C. Bar Assn. (nominations com. 1984-85, steering com. computer law divsn. 1985-86), Assn. SEC Alumni (pres. 1995-97, dir. 1998—), Order of Coif. Federal civil litigation, Securities. Office: Fulbright & Jaworski LLP 801 Pennsylvania Ave NW Washington DC 20004

**JACOBSON, RONALD H.,** lawyer; b. Chgo., July 23, 1963. BA, U. Ill., 1985; JD, Loyola U., Chgo., 1988; M Mgmt., Northwestern U., 1990. Bar: Ill. 1988. Assoc. Winston & Strawn, Chgo., 1990-96, ptnr., 1997—. Mem. ABA (bus. law sect.), Comml. Fin. Assn. (governing bd. 1998—), Loan Syndications and Trading Assn. Finance, Banking, Contracts commercial. Office: Winston & Strawn 35 W Wacker Dr Ste 4200 Chicago IL 60601-1695

**JACOBSON, SANDRA W.,** lawyer; b. Bklyn., Feb. 1, 1930; d. Elias and Anna (Goldstein) Weinstein; m. Irving Jacobson, July 31, 1955; 1 child, Bonnie Nancy. BA, Vassar Coll., 1951; LLB, Yale U., 1954. Bar: N.Y. 1955, U.S. Supreme Ct. 1960, U.S. Dist. Ct. (so., ea. dists.) N.Y. 1972, U.S. Ct. Appeals (2nd cir.) 1975. Ptnr. Mulligan, Jacobson & Langenus, N.Y.C., 1964-88, Hall, McNicol, Hamilton & Clark, N.Y.C., 1988-92; sole practitioner N.Y.C., 1992—; lectr. in family law. Contbr. articles to profl. jours. and chpts. to books. Mem. ABA (family law sect.), N.Y. State Bar Assn. (family law sect., legis. and exec. com., co-chair lawyer specialization 1999—), N.Y. Women's Bar Assn. (pres. 1989-90, matrimonial and family law com. 1984—, chmn. 1986-88, jud. screening com. 1987-88), Women's Bar Assn. of State of N.Y. (matrimonial com. 1986—, co-chair 1987-89, chair cts. com. 1987-88, amicus com. 1994-96, CLE com. 1998-99, by-laws 1999—), Assn. of Bar of City of N.Y. (com. matrimonial law 1984-87, chair 1990-93, com. women in the cts. 1986-96, sec. 1987-90, state cts. of superior juridiction 1987-90, women in the profession 1989-92, judiciary 1995-99, family law 1999—), Westchester County Bar Assn., Am. Acad. Matrimonial Lawyers (chair lawyer specialization com., bd. mgrs. N.Y. chpt. 1987-89, 91-93, 95-98, v.p. 1998—, interdisciplinary com.), Com. to Improve Availability of Legal Svcs., Ind. Jud. Screening Panel, Westchester Women's Bar Assn., Internat. Acad. of Matrimonial Lawyers (bd. govs. U.S. chpt. 1994-97, chair pub. rels. and mktg. com.), Phi Betta Kappa. Family and matrimonial, State civil litigation. Office: 295 Madison Ave New York NY 10017-6304

**JACOBSON, STEPHEN WAYNE,** lawyer; b. Girard, Kans., June 26, 1947; s. Victor and Wilda Dean (Miller) J.; m. Laurel Francine Arbogast, Aug. 9, 1968; children—Wendy, Nicole, Stephen. B.A., Northwestern U., 1969; J.D. with honors, U. Md., 1973. Bar: Mo. 1973, U.S. Dist Ct. (we. dist.) Mo. 1975, U.S. Ct. Appeals (8th cir.) 1976. Computer programmer Social Security Adminstrn., Balt., 1971-73; law clk. to judge U.S. Ct. Appeals (8th cir.), Kansas City, Mo., 1973-75; assoc. Lathrop, Koontz, Righter, Clagett & Norquist, Kansas City, Mo., 1975-81, ptnr., 1981—. Mem. ABA, Lawyers Assn. of Kansas City, Kansas City Bar Assn., Order of Coif. Club: Homestead (Mission, Kans.). Environmental, Federal civil litigation. Home: 370 Red Bay Rd Kiawah Island SC 29455-5603

**JACOBUS, CHARLES JOSEPH,** lawyer, title company executive, author; b. Ponca City, Okla., Aug. 21, 1947; s. David William and Louise Graham (Johnson) J.; m. Heather Jeanne Jones, June 6, 1970; children: Mary Helen, Charles J. Jr. BS, U. Houston, 1970, JD, 1973. Bar: Tex. 1973; cert. specialist residential and commerical real estate law Tex. Bd. Legal Specialization. Pvt. practice Houston, 1973-75; staff counsel Tenneco Realty, Inc., Houston, 1975-78; gen. counsel Tenneco Realty, Inc., Deerfield, Ill., 1979-83; chief legal counsel Speedy Muffler King, Deerfield, 1978-79; v.p. Commerce Title Co., Houston, 1983-85; sr. v.p. Charter Title Co., Houston, 1986—; ptnr. Jacobus & Melamed PC, Houston; 1998 Jenkens & Gilchrist, Houston, 1998-99; pvt. practice Bellaire, Tex., 1999—; adv. dir. Heritage Bank, Houston; adj. faculty Tex. A&M U., 1986-90; adj. prof. U. Houston Law Ctr., Houston C.C., Champions Sch. Real Estate; instr. advanced real estate law State Bar Tex., course dir., 1990, Tex. Land Title Assn. Sch. Author: Real Estate Law, 1996, Texas Real Estate, 8th edit., 1998; co-author: Mastering Real Estate Titles and Title Insurance in Texas, 1996, Georgia Real Estate, 1995, Ohio Real Estate, 2d edit., 1990, Calif. Real Estate, 1989, Keeping Current with Texas Real Estate, updated annually, Real Estate Principles, 8th edit., 1999, Real Estate, An Introduction to the Profession, 8th edit., 1999, Texas Title Insurance, updated annually, Texas Real Estate Brokerage and the Law of Agency, 1999; co-author: Real Estate Brokerage Law and Practice; editor: Building Blocks of a Commercial Transaction, 1992, Building Blocks of a Residential Real Estate Transaction, 1994, Texas Real Estate Law Deskbook, 1995; editor-in-chief Tex. Forms Manual. Chmn. Planning and Zoning Commn., Bellaire, Tex., 1976-77; bd. dirs. Tax Increment Fin. Dist., Bellaire, 1984-91; chmn. profl. adv. com. dept. urban and regional planning Tex. A&M U., 1988-89; 1st asst. scoutmaster Boy Scout World Jamboree, Holland, 1995, scoutmaster, Chile, 1998; scoutmaster Nat. Boy Scout Jamboree, 1997; mayor City of Bellaire, 1998—; sec.-treas. Harris County Mayors and Coun. Assn. Recipient Peggy Hayes Tchg. Excellence award TLTA, 1993. Mem. ABA (acquisitions editor books and pubs. com., chmn. brokers and brokerage com. 1986-93), Internat. Wine Food Soc. (host Houston chpt. 1993-94), Am. Coll. Real Estate Lawyers, Nat. Assn. Corp. Real Estate Execs. (chpt. v.p.), Am. Land Devel. Assn. (bd. dirs.), Tex. Land Title Assn. (chmn. forms manual com., TREC earnest money contract task force), Houston Real Estate Lawyers Coun., Real Estate Educator's Assn. (pres. 1987-88), Houston Bar Assn. (chmn. real estate sect. 1987-88), Bellaire/S.W. Houston C. of C. (Real Estate Educator of Yr. 1986, Outstanding Real Estate Educator in Tex. 1986, Outstanding Businessman of Yr. 1990), U. Tex. Mortgage Lending Inst. (faculty), U. Houston Law Alumni Assn. (bd. dirs.). Universal Order Knights of Vine (master barrister Houston chpt.), Les Amis Escoffler, Amici della Vite. Republican. Roman Catholic. Real property, Probate. Home: 5223 Pine St Bellaire TX 77401-4820 Office: 6800 West Loop S Ste 460 Bellaire TX 77401-4523

**JACONETTY, THOMAS ANTHONY,** lawyer; b. Chgo., May 21, 1953; s. George Bernard and Mary Jane (Sgarioto) J.; m. Judith Hamill; 1 child, Nicole Alicia. AB in History and Polit. Sci. summa cum laude with honors, Loyola U., Chgo., 1975; JD, Northwestern U., 1978. Bar: Ill. 1978, U.S. Dist. Ct. (no. dist.) Ill. 1978, U.S. Ct. Appeals (7th cir.) 1979; cert. rev. appraiser. Adminstrv. asst. Chgo. Dept. Aviation, 1979; asst. corp. counsel Chgo. Dept. Law, 1980; asst. to commr. Cook County Bd. Tax Appeals, Chgo., 1981-83, dep. commr., 1983-87, commr., 1988-89, chief dep. commr., 1989—; sole practice Chgo.; lectr. Ill. Inst. for Continuing Legal Edn.; lectr. and presenter Lorman Edn. Svcs., Lincoln Inst. Land Policy. Asst. editor, indexer: Corwin on the Constitution, 1981; author book chpts., articles and papers on real estate taxation, assessment adminstrn. and election law. Mem. Cook County Dem. Orgn.; pres., bd. dirs. Polish and Am. Citizens Club, 1981—; pres. Italian Am. Cath. Assn., Chgo., 1981—; mem. Old Timers' Baseball Assn., Art Inst. Chgo., Channel 11-PBS, Mus. Sci. and Industry, Ill. Spl. Olympics, Nat. Trust Hist. Preservation, Libr. of Congress, Ill. Alzheimer's Assn., Civic Fedn. Tax Com.; mem. planning com. Nat. Conf. State Tax Judges, 1999—. Mem. ABA, Ill. Bar Assn. (mem. assembly 1988-91, 92-94, state and local taxation sect. coun., chmn. 1994-95, vice chmn. 1993-94, ad hoc and civic fedn. com. on property tax reform, 1994-96), Chgo. Bar Assn. (chmn. election law com.), Internat. Assn. Assessing Officers (arbitrator cir. ct. Cook County, 1990-97, various sects., legal coms., chmn. legal com. 1995-96, 97-98, 98-99, recipient Donohoo Essay award, 1996), Justinian Soc. Italian Lawyers, Northwestern Law Sch. Alumni Assn., Loyola U. Alumni Assn., Pi Sigma Alpha, Alpha Sigma Nu. Avocations: travel, reading. Office: Cook County Bd of Review 118 N Clark St Ste 601 Chicago IL 60602-1311

**JACOVER, JEROLD ALAN,** lawyer; b. Chgo., Mar. 20, 1945; s. David Louis and Beverly (Funk) J.; m. Judith Lee Greenwald, June 28, 1970; children: Aric Seth, Evan Michael, Brian Ethan. BSEE, U. Wis., 1967; JD, Georgetown U., 1972. Bar: Ohio 1972, Ill. 1973, U.S. Ct. Appeals (7th cir.) 1974, U.S. Ct. Appeals (fed. cir.) 1983. Atty. Ralph Nader, Columbus, Ohio, 1972-73, Brinks Hofer, Gilson and Lione, Chgo., 1973—. Mem. ABA, Am. Intellectual Property Law Assn. (com. chmn. 1980-86, bd. dirs. 1994-98), Decalogue Soc. Lawyers, Intellectual Property Law Assn. Chgo. (treas. 1983-84, bd. dirs. 1993-94, 98-99), Intellectual Property Law Assn. Chgo. Ednl. Found. (pres. 1990-93), Am. Techion Soc. (v.p. 1985-91, treas. 1988-91, bd. dirs. 1985—, pres. 1994-97). Patent, Trademark and copyright, Federal civil litigation. Home: 1409 Lincoln St Evanston IL 60201-2336 Office: Brinks Hofer Gilson & Lione Ste 3600 455 N Cityfront Plaza Dr Chicago IL 60611-5599

**JACQUENEY, STEPHANIE A(LICE),** lawyer; b. Freeport, N.Y.; d. Theodore and Mona (Graubart) J. BS, Cornell U., 1979; MPA, JD, Syracuse U., 1982. Bar: N.Y. 1983, U.S. Dist. Ct. (so. and ea. dists.) N.Y. 1983. Law clk. to U.S. atty. U.S. Dist. Ct. (No. Dist.) N.Y., Syracuse, 1981-82; assoc. Olwine, Connelly, Chase, O'Donnell & Weyer, N.Y.C., 1982-84, Cadwalader, Wickersham & Taft, N.Y.C., 1984-87; asst. counsel Manhattan Cable TV, Inc., N.Y.C., 1987-89, gen. counsel, 1989-90, v.p., gen. counsel, 1990-92; v.p. legal dept. Time Warner Cable of N.Y.C., 1992-94; dir. bus. affairs Radio City Prodns., N.Y.C., 1994-97, sr. dir. bus. affairs, 1997-99; v.p. legal and bus. affairs Madison Square Garden, N.Y.C., 1999—. Mem. ABA, N.Y. State Bar Assn., Assn. of Bar of City of N.Y. (com. on arbitration 1984-88, com. on copyright and intellectual property 1996-99), N.Y. County Lawyers Assn. Communications, Entertainment, General civil litigation. Office: Radio City Entertainment Madison Square Garden 2 Penn Plz 14th Flr New York NY 10121

**JACQUES, NIGEL EDWARD,** lawyer; b. Leicester, Eng., Aug. 14, 1968. LLB with honors, U. Exeter, Eng., 1989. Bar: England & Wales 1990, Calif. 1994, U.S. Dist. Ct. (ctrl. dist.) Calif. 1998, U.S. Dist. Ct. (ea. dist.) Calif. 1998. Solicitor Norton Rose, London, 1990-97; assoc. Baker & Hostetler, L.A., 1997—. Mem. L.A. World Affairs Coun. Mem. ABA, State Bar Assn. of Calif., Law Soc. of Eng. and Wales. Avocations: skiing, photography, travel, cinema, tennis. Federal civil litigation, General civil litigation, State civil litigation. Home: 390 S Sepulveda Blvd Apt 202 Los Angeles CA 90049-3140 Office: Baker & Hostetler 600 Wilshire Blvd Los Angeles CA 90017-3212

**JAFFA, JONATHAN MARK,** lawyer; b. Pitts., Sept. 13, 1948; s Harold Seymour and Ellen Chersky Jaffa; m. Sandra Pelton, June 20, 1971; children: Miriam Nicole, Randi Sarah. BA, Wayne State U., 1970; JD, Detroit Coll. Law, 1974. Bar: Mich. 1974, U.S. Dist. Ct. (ea. dist.) Mich. 1976, U.S. Ct. Appeals (6th cir.) 1977, U.S. Supreme Ct. 1985. Assoc. Law Office of Sol E. Goldberg, Southfield, Mich., 1974-76; ptnr. Natinsky and Jaffa, Southfield, 1976-94, Sullivan, Ward, Bone, Tyler & Asher, Southfield, 1994—; Mich. def. trial counsel; lectr. Nat. Bus. Inst., 1997-98. Pres. Detroit Friends of Alyn Hosp., 1998-99—; past pres. Hillel of Met. Detroit. Mem. ACLU, Handgun Control Fedn. Met. Detroit (past pres. young adult divsn.). Avocations: tennis, physical fitness, reading, travel, philately. Personal injury, Product liability, Professional liability. Office: Sullivan Ward Bone Et Al 25900 Northwestern Hwy Southfield MI 48075-1067

**JAFFE, ALAN STEVEN,** lawyer; b. Portland, Maine, Nov. 11, 1939; s. Herman and Rose (Simon) J.; m. Elizabeth L. Reiss, Nov. 3, 1943; children: David, Robert, Richard. BS cum laude, Cornell U., 1961; LLB cum laude, Columbia U., 1964. Bar: N.Y. 1964. Assoc. Poletti, Freiden, Prashker and Gartner, N.Y.C., 1964-65; asst. chief counsel N.Y.C. Anti-Poverty Program, 1965-66; ptnr. Proskauer Rose LLP, N.Y.C., 1966—, chmn., 1999—; bd. dirs. Lincoln Savs. Bank, N.Y.C., 1984-92. Editor Columbia Law Rev., 1962-64. Bd. dirs., v.p. Coun. Jewish Fedns. N.Am., N.Y.C., 1992-99, Jewish Cmty. Rels. Coun., N.Y., 1987-91; bd. dirs., mem. exec. com. Beth Israel Med. Ctr., 1995—, Am. Jewish Joint Distbn. Com., 1991—; bd. govs. Jewish Agy. for Israel, 1999—; pres. Altro Health and Rehab. Svcs., Inc., N.Y.C., 1983-86, pres. UJA Fedn. of N.Y., 1992-95, bd. dirs. 1980—, chmn. bd. domestic affairs, 1988-91; bd. dirs. N.Y.C. Coalition for Homeless, 1995-98; mem. N.Y.C. Sports Devel. Corp., 1995-98. Office: Proskauer Rose LLP 1585 Broadway New York NY 10036-8200

**JAFFE, F. FILMORE,** lawyer, retired judge; b. Chgo., May 4, 1918; s. Jacob Isadore and Goldie (Rabinowitz) J.; m. Mary Main, Nov. 7, 1942; children: Jo Anne, Jay. Student, Southwestern U., 1936-39; J.D., Pacific Coast U., 1940. Bar: Calif. 1945, U.S. Supreme Ct. 1964. Practiced law Los Angeles, 1945-91; ptnr. Bernard & Jaffe, Los Angeles, 1947-74, Jaffe & Jaffe, Los Angeles, 1975-91; apptd. referee Superior Ct. of Los Angeles County, 1991-97, apptd. judge pro tem, 1991-97; ret., 1997; atty. in pvt. practice L.A., 1997—; mem. L.A. Traffic Commn., 1947-48; arbitrator Am. Arbitration Assn., 1968-91; chmn. pro bono com. Superior Ct. Calif., County of Los Angeles, 1980-86; lectr. on paternity. Served to capt. inf. AUS, 1942-45. Decorated Purple Heart, Croix de Guerre with Silver Star, Bronze Star with oak leaf cluster; honored Human Rights Commn. Los Angeles, Los Angeles County Bd. Suprs.; recipient Pro Bono award State Bar Calif., commendation State Bar Calif., 1983. Mem. ABA, Los Angeles County Bar Assn. (honored by family law sect. 1983), Los Angeles Criminal Ct. Bar Assn. (charter mem.), U.S. Supreme Ct. Bar Assn., Masons, Shriners. State civil litigation, Family and matrimonial, General practice. Office: 433 N Camden Dr Ste 400 Beverly Hills CA 90210-4408

**JAFFE, MARK M.,** lawyer; b. Paterson, N.J., Sept. 18, 1941; s. Irving and Bertha (Margolis) J.; m. June A. Fisher, June 19, 1977. BS in Econs., U. Pa., 1962; JD, Columbia U., 1985. Bar: N.J. 1965, La. 1968, N.Y. 1970, U.S. Dist. Ct. (ea. dist.) N.Y., U.S. Ct. Mil. Appeals, U.S. Ct. Appeals (2d and 5th cirs.), U.S. Dist. Ct. N.J., U.S. Supreme Ct. Assoc. Hill, Betts & Nash, LLP, N.Y.C., 1969-72; ptnr. Hill, Betts & Nash, N.Y.C., 1972—. Lt. USCGR, 1965-68. Mem. ABA, N.J. Bar Assn., La. Bar Assn., Assn. of Bar of City of N.Y., Am. Judicature Soc., Maritime Law Soc. General corporate, General civil litigation, Admiralty. Home: 377 Rector Pl New York NY 10280-1432 Office: Hill Betts & Nash 1 World Trade Ctr Ste 5215 New York NY 10048-5299

**JAFFE, MATTHEW ELY,** lawyer; b. N.Y.C., Mar. 22, 1941; s. Irving and Alice B. (Bein) J.; m. Els Litjens, Dec. 25, 1971 (dec. Apr. 1987); children: Paul, Mark; m. Karen Diane Weiss, Feb. 19, 1989; children: Ilona, Aaron. BA, Bucknell U., 1963; LLB, Georgetown U., 1966. Bar: Md. 1966, D.C. 1967. Atty. advisor SEC, Washington, 1967-72; trial atty. U.S. Dept. of Justice, Washington, 1972-85; pvt. practice Rockville, Md., 1985—. Criminal, Family and matrimonial, General practice. Office: 10215 Nolan Dr Rockville MD 20850-3507

**JAFFE, PAUL LAWRENCE,** judge, lawyer; b. Phila., June 24, 1928; s. Albert L. and Elsie (Peiser) J.; m. Susan Oppenheim, Apr. 16, 1993; children from previous marriage: Marc David, Richard Alan, Peter Edward. B.A., Dickinson Coll., 1947; J.D., U. Pa., 1950. Bar: Pa. Assoc. Wolf, Block, Schorr and Solis-Cohen, Phila., 1950-57; sole practice Phila., 1957-59; mng. ptnr. Mesirov, Gelman, Jaffe, Cramer and Jamieson and predecessor firms, 1959-98; judge Common Pleas Ct. of Phila., 1996-98; of counsel Mesirov, Gelman, Jaffe, Cramer and Jamieson, 1998—; of counsel Mesirov, Gelman, Jaffe, Cramer and Jamieson, 1998—. Pres. Reform Congregation Keneseth Israel, 1974-77; trustee Jewish Fedn. Phila.; trustee Moss Rehab. Hosp., pres., 1977-80, chmn. bd., 1980-84, hon. chmn. bd., 1984—; emeritus dir. Albert Einstein Healthcare Network, 1997—; chmn. United Law Network, 1987-89; vice chmn. Phila. Parking Authority, 1992-96. Mem. ABA, Pa. Bar Assn., Phila. Bar Assn., Am. Coll. Real Estate Lawyers, Lawyers Club Phila., Pyramid Club (chmn. bd. govs. 1999—), Penn Club N.Y., Banyan Country Club (Palm Beach, Fla.), Union League of Phila. Home: 1820 Rittenhouse Sq Philadelphia PA 19103-5832 Office: 1735 Market St Fl 38 Philadelphia PA 19103-7501

**JAFFE, SARI BLONDER,** lawyer; b. N.Y.C., Oct. 22, 1948; d. Edward and Selma (Riesel) Blonder; m. Alan H. Jaffe, May 31, 1970; children: David, Devra. BS, U. Conn., 1970; JD, Pace U., 1984. Bar: Conn. 1984, U.S. Dist. Ct. Conn. 1984. Atty. Kelley Drye & Warren, Stamford, Conn., 1984-87, Silverberg Marvin & Swaim, New Canaan, Conn., 1987-90; ptnr. Jaffe & Jaffe, New Canaan, 1990—. Chair ARI of Conn., Stamford, 1994—. Mem. ABA, Conn. Bar Assn. (family law sect.), New Canaan Bar Assn. (treas., v.p., pres.). Family and matrimonial. Office: Jaffe & Jaffe 140 Elm St New Canaan CT 06840-5406

**JAGIELLA, DIANA MARY,** lawyer; b. Chgo., Sept. 16, 1959; d. John James and Mildred Helen (Lapinskas) J.; m. Charles John Thorbjornsen, June 9, 1984; children: Kenneth James, Rachael Frances, Lauren Kellie. BA, Purdue U., 1983; JD, DePaul U., 1987; postgrad., U. Chgo., 1989—. Bar: Ill. 1987, U.S. Dist. Ct. (cen. dist.) Ill. 1987, U.S. Ct. Appeals (7th cir.) 1989. Assoc. Hinshaw & Culbertson, Chgo., 1987-88, Howard & Howard, Attys., P.C., Peoria, Ill., 1991—; atty. CilCorp, Inc., Peoria, 1988-91. Contbr. articles to legal jours. Chmn. Police and Fire Commn., Peoria, 1990—; mem. allocation panel United Way, Peoria, 1991—; mem. spl. com. Peoria C. of C., 1989-90; pres., bd. dirs. Abuse Shelter, Peoria, 1991-92; mem. Rotary North Peoria Sch. Bd., 1989—. Sheridan scholar, 1986; recipient Recognition award Women's Law Caucus, 1986. Mem. ABA (environ. sect.), Ill. Bar Assn. (environ. sect.), Peoria Bar Assn. (chmn. law day 1990-91, pres. women lawyers sect. 1988-90). Republican. Roman Catholic. Avocations: coaching youth soccer, gardening, horses, politics. Environmental. Office: Howard & Howard Attys PC 321 Liberty St Peoria IL 61602-1403

**JAGLOM, ANDRE RICHARD,** lawyer; b. N.Y.C., Dec. 23, 1953; s. Jacob and Irene (Moore) J.; m. Janet R. Stampfl, Apr. 12, 1980; children: Peter Stampfl Jaglom, Wendy Stampfl Jaglom. BS in Mgmt., BS in Physics, MIT, 1974; JD, Harvard U., 1977. Bar: N.Y. 1978, U.S. Dist. Ct. (so. and ea. dists.) N.Y. 1978, U.S. Supreme Ct. 1982, U.S. Ct. Appeals (2d cir.) 1987. Assoc. Paul, Weiss, Rifkind, Wharton & Garrison, N.Y.C., 1977-84; mng. ptnr. Stecher Jaglom & Prutzman LLP, N.Y.C., 1984—; bd. dirs. Cmty. Fund of Bronxville, Eastchester and Tuckahoe, Inc., 1988-94. Computer mktg. and distbn. editor Computer Law Reporter, 1984-90; Am. Law Inst. ABA course of study on product distbn. and mktg., mem. faculty 1983—, chmn., 1989—; contbr. article to law jours.; contbr chpt. to Legal Checklists, 1988—. Trustee bd. edn. Bronxville Union Free Sch. Dist., 1997—. Mem. ABA, Bar Assn. City N.Y. (computer law com. 1986-89, sec. 1990-94, com. on tech. and practice of law 1993-96), Am. Inst. Wine and Food (bd. dirs. N.Y. chpt. 1991—, treas. 1992—. Intellectual property, Contracts commercial, General corporate. Office: 900 3d Ave New York NY 10022-4728

**JAIN, LALIT K.,** lawyer; b. Bhagalpur, Bihar, India, Aug. 10, 1944; came to U.S. 1971; s. Baij Nath and Janki Devi (Agrawal) J.; m. Abha Gupta, May 28, 1973; children; Monika, Konika. B in Commerce, Patna U., India, 1964, LLB with distinction, 1967. Bar: India 1975, N.Y. 1978, U.S. Tax Ct. 1979, U.S. Supreme Ct. 1982, U.S. Dist. Ct. (so. and ea. dists.) N.Y. 1983. Pvt. practice tax and acctg. Patna, Bihar, India, 1967-71; sr. tax acct. Gen. Adjustment Bur., Inc., N.Y.C., 1972; sr. tax acct. St. Regis Corp., N.Y.C., 1973-76, legal asst., 1976-78, atty., 1978-80, gen. atty., 1981-83; mgr. tax research and plannig St. Regis Corp., 1983-85; sr. atty. corp. law dept. Merrill Lynch and Co., Inc., N.Y.C., 1985-86, v.p. corp. staff, counsel, 1986-87, sr. counsel, 1987-92, v.p., sr. counsel, office of gen. counsel, 1992-94; prin. C'mmonSense Counsel, Inc., N.Y.C., 1995-97, KuttingEdge KommonSense, Inc., N.Y.C., 1997—; bd. dirs. Forest Industries Tele-Communications, Eugene, Oreg. Nat. Merit scholar Govt. of India, 1960, 64, 67. Fellow Inst. Chartered Accts. (S. Vaidyanath Aiyar Meml. scholar 1966); mem. Chartered Inst. Secs. and Adminstrs., Inst. Co. Secs. India, Inst. Cost and Works Accts. India. Hindu. Avocations: tennis, swimming, bowling, billiards, table tennis. Constitutional, Pension, profit-sharing, and employee benefits, Taxation, general. Home: 61-22 Booth St Rego Park NY 11374-1034 Office: KuttingEdge KommonSense Inc 61-22 Booth St Rego Park NY 11374-1034

**JAIRAM, KHELANAND VISHVAYKANAND,** lawyer; b. Queenstown, Essequibo, Guyana, Nov. 29, 1946; came to U.S., 1988; s. Kaiser and Narainee Jairam; m. Joyce B. Gafur, Dec. 2, 1967; children: Shashi, Nishall, Ashwini. Barrister at Law, Inns Ct. Sch., London, 1974; LLB with honors, U. London, 1988; LLM, U. N.Y., N.Y.C., 1990. Bar: Eng. 1974, Wales 1974, Guyana 1974, N.Y. 1991, U.S. Dist. Ct. (so. and ea. dists.) 1991, Trinidad and Tobago, 1997. Pvt. practice Georgetown, Guyana, 1974-88; tax counsel N.Y.C. Dept. Fin., 1991-94; pvt. practice Law Office K.V. Jairam, N.Y.C., 1994—; mem. parliament, Govt. of Guyana, 1980-85. Mem. ABA, Am. Trial Lawyers Assn., N.Y. State Bar Assn., Queens County Bar Assn. Democrat. Hindu. Avocations: tennis, cricket. General civil litigation, Family and matrimonial, Real property. Home: 11620 237th St Elmont NY 11003-3902 Office: 18836 Jamaica Ave Hollis NY 11423-2512

**JALBERT, MICHAEL JOSEPH,** lawyer; b. Coventry, R.I., July 31, 1951; s. Charles Edward and Josephine Elizabeth (Stoy) J.; m. Patricia Heather Gibson, Nov. 19, 1983; children: Brett Allen Conley, Thomas Michael. BS, U. R.I., 1973; MS, U. Mass., 1975; JD, U. Akron, Ohio, 1983. Bar: R.I. 1983, Ohio 1984, U.S. Dist. Ct. (no. dist.) Ohio 1984, U.S. Ct. Appeals (6th cir.) 1984. Rsch. coord. office collective bargaining State of R.I., Providence, 1974-75; rsch. assoc. Cobleigh & Fleury, Warwick, R.I., 1975-79; assoc. Nicely & Wagner, Akron, 1984—; vis. lectr. Providence Coll., R.I., 1975-79; vis. prof. Bryant Coll., R.I., 1979; prof. U. Akron, 1979—; labor edn. cons. Ohio State U., 1981—. Counsel Brimfield (Ohio) Lake, Inc., 1985—. Mem. Ohio Bar Assn., R.I. Bar Assn., Akron Bar Assn., IRRA, Am. Arbitration Assn., K.C. Democrat. Roman Catholic. Avocations: golf, tennis, traveling. Labor, General practice, Workers' compensation. Office: U Akron 131 The Polsky Bldg Akron OH 44325-0001

**JALBUENA, ARNEL BABIERA,** lawyer; b. Lucena, Quezon, The Philippines, Oct. 19, 1961; came to U.S., 1988; s. Pedro Ravina and Clotilde (Babiera) J.; m. Mildred Bravo Allas, Nov.10, 1990; children: Amica Alexa, Arnel II, Alexander. BS in Biology, De La Salle U., Manila, 1982; LLB, San Beda Coll., Manila, 1987. Bar: The Philippines 1988, Calif. 1991, D.C. 1997, U.S. Dist. Ct. (cen. dist.) Calif. 1991, U.S. Ct. Appeals (9th cir.) 1995. Profl. svc. rep. Boehringer-Ingelheim, Manila, 1983-87; law clk. Tucker & Kodani, Santa Monica, Calif., 1988-91; pvt. practice Law Office of Arnel Jalbuena, L.A., 1991—; of counsel Law Offices of Salvador Tuy, L.A., 1991—, Richard Chiu & Assocs., L.A., 1992—. Pres. Lucena Assn. So. Calif., L.A., 1989. Mem. ABA, Am. Trial Lawyers Assn., Calif. Trial Lawyers Assn., Lions. Roman Catholic. Avocations: scuba diving, fishing, shooting, golf. Personal injury, Immigration, naturalization, and customs, State civil litigation. Home: 11743 Doral Ave Northridge CA 91326-1218 Office: Law Offices Arnel Jalbuena 3250 Wilshire Blvd Los Angeles CA 90010-1577

**JALENAK, JAMES BAILEY,** lawyer; b. New Orleans, Sept. 5, 1939; s. Leo R. and Reha (Lichterman) J.; m. Natalie Block, Dec. 27, 1965; children: Margaret Amie Jalenak Wexler, Catherine Ann Jalenak Levit. BA in Politics & Econs. magna cum laude, Yale U., 1961, JD, 1964. Assoc. Paul, Weiss, Rifkind, Wharton & Garrison, N.Y.C., 1964-65; ptnr. Hanover, Walsh, Jalenak & Blair, Memphis, 1965—; lectr. in law U. Memphis, 1971-76. Sec., gen. counsel Memphis Zool. Soc., also past bd. dirs.; v.p. S.W. coun. Union Am. Hebrew Congregations; mem. adv. com. Memphis Urban League; chmn. legal com. Henry S. Jacobs Camp; pres. Temple Israel, Memphis, 1992-94; past pres. Memphis Pub. Edn. Fund, Memphis Yale Club; past bd. dirs. Jewish Children's Regional Svc., New Orleans, Memphis Jewish Cmty. Ctr.; past officer, bd. dirs. Plough Towers, Jewish Family Svc.; past chmn. ctrl. area adv. com., supt.'s adv. com., commn. on excellence Memphis City Schs.; v.p. Memphis Jewish Fedn. Recipient Golden Rule award Vol. Ctr. of Memphis, 1994. Fellow Tenn. Bar Found.; mem. Memphis Bar Assn. (bd. dirs.), Memphis Rotary (past pres.), Order of Coif, Phi Delta Phi. Jewish. Avocation: photography. Real property, General corporate, Estate planning. Home: 5260 Sycamore Grove Ln Memphis TN 38120-2242 Office: Hanover Walsh Jalenak Blair 22 N Front St Memphis TN 38103-2162

**JALLINS, RICHARD DAVID,** lawyer; b. L.A., Mar. 21, 1957; s. Walter Joshua and Elaine Beatrice (Youngerman) J.; m. Katherine Sue Pfeiffer, June 12, 1982; children: Stephen David, Rachel Marie. BA, U. Calif., Santa Barbara, 1978; JD, Calif. Western Sch. Law, 1981. Bar: Calif. 1988, U.S. Dist. Ct. (so. dist.) Calif. 1988. Panel atty. Bd. Prison Terms, Sacramento, 1989-96, Appellate Defenders, Inc., San Diego, 1989-91, Calif. Dept. Corrections, Parole Hearings Divsn., Sacramento, 1992-94; dep. commr. Bd. Prison Terms, 1996—. Mem. ABA, San Diego County Bar Assn., Phi Alpha Delta.

**JAMAR, STEVEN DWIGHT,** law educator; b. Ishpeming, Mich., May 11, 1953; s. Dwight W. and Lorraine (Persgard) J.; m. Shelley June Von Hagen-Jamar, May 19, 1979; children: Alexander S., Eric D. BA, Carleton Coll., 1975; JD cum laude, Hamline U., 1979; LLM with distinction, Georgetown U., 1994. Bar: Minn. 1979, D.C. 1993, U.S. Supreme Ct. 1985. Jud. clk. Minn. Supreme Ct., St. Paul, 1979-80; assoc. Meagher & Geer, Mpls., 1980-86; clin. instr. William Mitchell Coll. of Law, St. Paul, 1987-89; pvt. practice Mpls., 1987-89; vis. asst. prof. law U. Balt., 1989-90; asst. prof. law Sch. Law Howard U., Washington, 1991-94, assoc. prof. law, 1994-96, prof. law, 1996—, dir. legal rsch. and writing program, 1990—; cons. on environ. legal info. sys. project NASA, 1998—. Co-author: Essential Lawyering Skills: Interviewing, Counseling, Negotiation, and Persuasive Fact Analysis, 1999; contbr. articles to profl. jours. Bd. dirs. Legal Advice Clinics, Hennepin County, Mpls., 1980-89, mem. exec. com., 1986-89, sec.-treas., 1988-89; coach Soccer Assn. Columbia, 1991-96. Mem. Legal Writing Inst., 1990— (exec com., 1994-98, pres., 1997-98), ABA, ACLU, Am. Soc. Internat. Law, Amnesty Internat., Computer Law Assn., Assn. Legal Writing Dirs. (bd. dirs., exec. com. 1996-97), Sierra Club, Howard County Go Club. Avocations: canoe camping, soccer, go. Office: Howard U Sch Law 2900 Van Ness St NW Washington DC 20008-1106

**JAMES, CHARLES E., JR.,** lawyer; b. Pontiac, Mich., Sept. 19, 1948. BA, Occidental Coll., 1970; JD with highest distinction, U. Ariz. Bar: Ariz. 1973. Ptnr. Snell & Wilmer, Phoenix, 1990. Mem. ABA, Nat. Assn. Bond Lawyers. Finance, Municipal (including bonds), Securities. Office: Snell & Wilmer 1 Arizona Ctr 400 E Van Buren St Phoenix AZ 85004-2223

**JAMES, CHRISTOPHER,** lawyer; b. Portland, Oreg., Nov. 26, 1948; s. Arthur Montague and Martha Rose (Lehman) J.; m. Christine Ruth Ehrsam, Jan. 28, 1972; children: Aaron Thomas, David Christopher, Daniel Jonathan. BA, U. Oreg., 1970, JD, 1974. Bar: Oreg. 1974. Assoc. James C. Maletis, P.C. Portland, 1974-81; ptnr. Maletis and James, 1981-83, Mitchell, Lang & Smith, 1983-86; prin. Christopher James P.C., Portland, 1987-90, James & Denecke, Portland, 1991-95, James, Denecke, Urrutia, Marmaduke & Lawson, 1995—. Mem. ABA, Oreg. State Bar, Multnomah Athletic Club. Avocation: running. General civil litigation, Real property, Mergers and acquisitions. Home: 4140 SW Greenleaf Ct Portland OR 97221-3215

**JAMES, GORDON, III,** lawyer; b. Montclair, N.J., Feb. 24, 1947; s. Ernest Gordon Jr. and Betty (Wackerman) J.; m. Adelia Louise Medlin (div. Sept. 1989); children: Deidre Leigh, Diana Catherine, Gordon Daniel; m. Gwen Aline Campanile, Jan. 5, 1991 (div. June 1993). BS, U. Tenn., 1969; JD, Vanderbilt U., 1972. Bar: Fla. 1972, U.S. Dist. Ct. (so. dist.) Fla. 1972, D.C. 1973, U.S. Ct. Appeals (11th cir.) 1980, U.S. Dist. Ct. (mid. dist.) Fla. 1985, U.S. Dist. Ct. (no. dist.) Fla. 1986, U.S. Supreme Ct. 1988. Assoc. Bradford, Williams, Kimbrell, et al, Miami, Fla., 1972-76; ptnr. Druck, Grimmett, Norman, Weaver, Scherer, Ft. Lauderdale, Fla., 1976-77, Druck, Grimmett, Scherer, James, Ft. Lauderdale, 1977-78, Grimmett, Scherer, James, Ft. Lauderdale, 1978-79, Conrad, Scherer, James & Jenne, Ft. Lauderdale, 1979-95, Heinrich Gordon Hargrove Weihe & James, Ft. Lauderdale, 1995—. Eucharistic lay minister, All Saints Episcopal Ch., 1991—. Capt. USAR, 1969-77. Mem. ABA, Fla. Bar Assn. (vice chmn. civil rule of procedure com. 1990-91), Nat. Assn. R.R. Counsel, Am. Acad. Hosp. Attys., Am. Bd. Trial Advs. (cert., Ft. Lauderdale chpt. pres. 1998), Def. Rsch. Inst., Fla. Def. Lawyers (pres. 1991-92). Republican. Avocations: fishing, snow skiing, scuba diving, physical and aerobics exercise. Product liability, Personal injury, General civil litigation. Office: Heinrich Gordon Hargrove Weihe & James 500 E Broward Blvd Fort Lauderdale FL 33394-3000

**JAMES, KEITH ALAN,** lawyer; b. Wichita, Kans., Sept. 29, 1957; s. Anthony Ray James and Patricia Ann Jones; Elaine Penelope Johnson, Aug. 14, 1982. BA, Harvard U., 1979, JD, 1982. Bar: Pa. 1982, U.S. Dist. Ct. (ea. dist.) Pa. 1982, Fla. 1988. Atty. Girard Bank, Phila., 1982-84; assoc. Wolf, Block, Schorr & Solis-Cohen, Phila., 1984-87, West Palm Beach, Fla., 1987-88; assoc. Shapiro & Bregman, West Palm Beach, 1988-90, ptnr., 1990-91; ptnr. Greenberg, Traurig, Hoffman, Lipoff, Rosen & Quentel, P.A., West Palm Beach, 1991-96; founder, pvt. practice Keith A. James, P.A., West Palm Beach, 1996—. Bd. dirs. A Better Chance in Lower Merion, Ardmore, Pa., 1984-87; mem. Leadership Fla., 1988-90, bd. regents, 1989-90, 91-93, chmn., 1995-96; mem. Fla. Commn. Human Rels., 1992-97, chmn., 1993-95; bd. dirs. Edn. Partnership Palm Beach County, Inc., 1988-91; bd. dirs. Cmty. Found. Martin and Palm Beach Counties, 1994—, vice chair, 1996-97; trustee JFK Med. Ctr., 1994-95, Quantum Found., 1995—, Norton Art Mus., 1996—. Mem. Associated Marine Insts. (trustee 1989-96), Palm Beach Marine Inst. (bd. dirs. 1989-96, chmn. 1994-95), Harvard Club of the Palm Beaches (pres. 1990), Fox Club. Democrat. Banking, General corporate, Contracts commercial. Office: 5725 Corporate Way Ste A106 West Palm Beach FL 33407-2007

**JAMES, RONALD EUGENE,** lawyer; b. Frankfort, Ind., Aug. 17, 1954; s. Earl Alvin and Peggy Zoe (Amy) J.; m. Mary Ann Freygang, Aug. 7, 1982; children: Nathaniel Earl, Zachary Luke. Student, St. Joseph's Coll., Rensselaer, Ind., 1972-74; BA, Ind. U., 1976, JD, 1979. Bar: Ind. 1979, U.S. Dist. Ct. (no. dist.) Ind. 1979, U.S. Ct. Appeals (7th cir.) 1988, U.S. Ct. Appeals (5th cir.) 1988, U.S. Supreme Ct. 1982, U.S. Dist. Ct. (so. dist.) Ind. 1997. Law clk. Superior Ct., Ft. Wayne, Ind., 1979-80; assoc. Sowers & Benson, Ft. Wayne, 1980-83; ptnr. Benson, Pantello, Morris, James & Logan, Ft. Wayne, 1983—; atty. Vol. Lawyers Program, Ft. Wayne, 1987—; sub-chair Allen County Law Library, Ft. Wayne, 1994-96. Author column K's Pouch Zoo News, 1987-92. Pres. Rudisill-Plaza Neighborhood Assn., Ft. Wayne, 1985-86; docent Ft. Wayne Children's Zoo, 1985-95; dir., pres.

Little River Wetlands Project, Inc., 1997-98; dir. Cedar Creek Wildlife Project, Inc., 1990—. Recipient Am. Jurisprudence award Lawyer's Coop. Pub., 1977. Mem. Assn. Trial Lawyers Am., Izaak Walton League Am. (dir., pres. Ft. Wayne chpt. 1997—), Ind. Bar Assn., Ind. Trial Lawyers Assn., Allen County Bar Assn., Sierra Club. Methodist. Avocations: gardening, hiking/camping, flying, photography. General civil litigation, Workers' compensation, Probate. Home: 17525 Griffin Rd Huntertown IN 46748-9730 Office: Benson Pantello Morris James & Logan 3505 Lake Ave Fort Wayne IN 46805-5549

**JAMES, STUART FAWCETT,** lawyer; b. Daytona Beach, Fla., May 17, 1957; s. George M. and Gertrude (Fawcett) J.; m. Vicki Lawrence, Aug. 4, 1990. B in Polit. Sci., U. Cen. Fla., 1981; JD, Samford U., 1989. Bar: Tenn. 1990, Ga. 1991, U.S. Dist. Ct. (ea. dist.) Tenn. 1990, U.S. Dist. Ct. (no. dist.) Ga. 1992, U.S. Ct. Appeals (6th and 11th cir.) 1992, Ala. 1993. Atty, mng. mem. Manuel & James PLLC, Chattanooga, 1996—. Assoc. editor Cumberland Sch. Law Law Rev., 1989. Mem. LAS adv. coun. U. Tenn., Chattanooga. Mem. ABA, Fed. Bar Assn., Tenn. Bar Assn. (chair law office tech./mgmt. sect. 1996, co-chair AIDS awareness com., chmn. computer and tech. com. young lawyers divsn., mem. mock trial com., chair disciplinary diversion project, mem. young lawyers divsn. fellow, Pres.'s Disting. Svc. award 1994), Chattanooga Bar Assn. (pres. 1997, sec.-treas., bd. govs., legis. chair young lawyers sect., chmn., past pres.'s com. 1999, Robert Horton Campbell award), Dem. Leadership Counsel. Episcopalian. Avocations: photography, hiking. General civil litigation, Personal injury, Product liability. Office: Manuel & James James Bldg Ste 702 Chattanooga TN 37402-1804

**JAMES, WALTER D., III,** lawyer; b. Omaha, Apr. 16, 1957; s. Walter D. Jr. and Josephine M. James; m. Carole A. James, June 21, 1980; children: W. Taylor, Delaney E. BS in Polit. Sci., U. Nebr., Omaha, 1984; JD, U. Nebr., 1987. Assoc. Winstead Sechrest & Minick, Dallas, 1987-95, Hutcheson & Grundy LLP, Dallas, 1995-98; sr. counsel Strasburger & Price LLP, Dallas, 1998—. Environmental, General civil litigation, Toxic tort. Office: Strasburger & Price LLP 901 Main St Ste 4300 Dallas TX 75202-3714

**JAMES, WILLIAM RICHARD,** lawyer; b. Union, S.C., July 9, 1937; s. John Byrd and Louise Aline (Kirby) J.; m. Carolyn Cash Holder, Mar. 2, 1968 (div.); children: Allison Louise, Richard Foster; m. Sandra Gail Burgin, mar. 13, 1984. BA, U. S.C., 1961, LLB, 1964, JD, 1970. Bar: S.C. 1964, U.S. Dist. Ct. S.C. 1964, U.S. Ct. Appeals (4th cir.) 1974. Assoc. Edens & Hamer, Columbia, S.C., 1964-65, Richard Foster, Greenville, S.C., 1965-66; pvt. practice law Greenville, 1966—; cons. Southeastern Products, Greenville, 1985—. Contbg. atty. ACLU, Greenville, 1970. Recipient Am. Jurisprudence award, 1964, Disting. Svc. award S.C. Assn. Deaf, 1973. Mem. S.C. Trial Lawyers Assn. (treas. 1967), Assn. Trial Lawyers Am., Nat. Assn. Criminal Def. Lawyers, Am. Legion, Moose, Sigma Alpha Epsilon. Democrat. Episcopalian. General civil litigation, Criminal. Office: 611 N Main St Greenville SC 29601-1611

**JAMIESON, LINDA SUSAN,** judge; b. Rockville Centre, N.Y., June 22, 1954; d. Joseph C. and Harriet L. (Schlegel) J.; m. Laurence Keiser, Sept. 9, 1984; children: Heather, Jamieson, Ross. BA in Psychology, Hofstra U., 1976; JD, Pace U. Sch. of Law, 1979. Bar: N.Y. 1980, U.S. Dist. Ct. (so. and ea. dists.) N.Y. 1980, N.J. 1981, U.S. Dist. Ct. N.J. 1981, Fla. 1982, Conn. 1989. Law intern Westchester Legal Svcs., Inc., White Plains, N.Y., 1978-79; rsch. asst. Pace U. Sch. of Law, 1978-79; assoc. Addesso & Merovitch, Mount Vernon, N.Y., 1979-80, Eugene L. Scancarelli, Mount Vernon, N.Y., 1980-82; sole practitioner White Plains, 1982—; family ct. judge County of Westchester, N.Y., 1996-97; adj. prof. Iona Coll., 1984-86, Westchester C.C., 1989-94. Bd. mem. Westchester Children's Assn. rsch. and advocacy, campaign for kids and family ct. children's ctr. com.; mem. adv. bd. Yonkers Family Ct. Children's Ctr.; bd. mem., past v.p. Juvenile Law Edn. Project, Inc.; adv. bd. mem. Hudson Valley Bank Found., Inc.; past v.p. White Plains Rep. Club; judge Pace U. Sch. of Law Moot Ct.; small claims arbitrator White Plains City Ct., Mt. Vernon City Ct.; mem. White Plains Exch. Club, Lions Club. Mem. N.Y. State Women Judges Assn., Nat. Assn. Women Judges, Nat. Coun. of Juvenile and Family Ct. Judges, Assn. Judges of Family Ct. of State of N.Y., N.Y. State Bar Assn. (mem. family law sect.), Westchester County Bar Assn. (mem. family law sect., past chair new lawyers sect. 1984, 86, past com. mem. county ct., family ct., nominating and grievances com., law guardian panel Appellate Divsn. Supreme Ct., supervising atty. for panel applicants), White Plains Bar Assn. (bd. dirs.), N.Y. Women's Bar Assn. (Westchester chpt. co-chair judiciary, past chairperson legal referral, family ct. and legal rights of children coms.), Estate Planning Coun. of Westchester County, Inc. Office: State of NY Family Ct 420 North Ave New Rochelle NY 10801-4105

**JAMIESON, MICHAEL LAWRENCE,** lawyer; b. Coral Gables, Fla., Mar. 2, 1940; s. Warren Thomas and Ruth Amelia (Gallman) J.; children: Ann Layton, Thomas Howard; m. Elizabeth Marie Peeples, Dec. 31, 1992. BA in English, U. Fla., 1961, JD with honors, 1964. Bar: Fla. 1964, U.S. Dist. Ct. (mid. dist.) Fla. 1964, D.C. 1998. Teaching asst. U. Fla., 1964; law clk. U.S. Ct. Appeals (5th cir.), 1964-65; assoc. Holland & Knight LLP and predecessor firms, Tampa, Fla., 1965-69; ptnr. Holland & Knight and predecessor firms, Tampa, Fla., 1969—, chmn. bus. law dept., 1992—. Editor-in-chief U. Fla. Law Rev., 1963. Trustee Law Ctr. U. Fla., chmn. bd. dirs., 1986-88; bd. dirs., chmn. Bus. Com. for the Arts Inc., 1989-90; trustee Tampa Bay Performing Arts Ctr. Inc., 1989—, chmn. devel. coun., 1990-91; trustee Cmty. Found. Greater Tampa, 1990-97, chmn. devel. com. Fla. C. of C. Found., 1992-95; mem. Tampa Leadership Conf., Golden Triangle Civic Assn. Recipient Gertrude Brick Law Rev. award, 1963. Fellow Am. Bar Found.; mem. ABA (mem. com on corp. laws, mem. com. on fed. regulation of securities), Am. Law Inst., Hillsborough County Bar Assn., Greater Tampa C. of C. (mem. bd. govs. 1988-91), Com. 100 (mem. policy bd. 1989-92, trustee 1998—), Univ. Club, Tampa Club (bd. dirs. 1985-89, pres. 1987-88), The Down Town Assn., Order of Coif, Phi Kappa Phi. General corporate, Securities, Contracts commercial.

**JAMIN, MATTHEW DANIEL,** lawyer, magistrate judge; b. New Brunswick, N.J., Nov. 29, 1947; s. Matthew Bernard and Frances Marie (Newburg) J.; m. Christine Frances Bjorkman, June 28, 1969; children: Rebecca, Erica. BA, Colgate U., 1969; JD, Harvard U., 1974. Bar: Alaska 1974, U.S. Dist. Ct. Alaska 1974, U.S. Ct. Appeals (9th cir.) 1980. Staff atty. Alaska Legal Svcs., Anchorage, 1974-75; supervising atty. Alaska Legal Svcs., Kodiak, Alaska, 1975-81; contract atty. Pub. Defender's Office State of Alaska, Kodiak, 1976-82; prin. Matthew D. Jamin, Atty., Kodiak, 1982; ptnr. Jamin & Bolger, Kodiak, 1982-85, Jamin, Ebell, Bolger & Gentry, Kodiak, 1985-97; part-time magistrate judge U.S. Cts., Kodiak, 1984—; shareholder Jamin, Ebell, Schmitt & Mason, Kodiak, 1998—. Part-time instr. U. Alaska Kodiak Coll., 1975—; active Theshold Svcs., Inc., Kodiak, 1985—, pres., 1985-92, 95-96. Mem. Alaska Bar Assn. (Professionalism award 1988), Kodiak Bar Assn. General civil litigation, Family and matrimonial, Probate. Office: US Dist Ct 323 Carolyn Ave Kodiak AK 99615-6348

**JAMISON, DANIEL OLIVER,** lawyer; b. Fresno, Calif., Nov. 28, 1952; s. Oliver Morton and Margaret (Ratcliffe) J.; m. Debra Suzanne Parent, May 23, 1981; l child, Holly Elizabeth. Student, Claremont Men's Coll., 1970-72; BA in Philosophy, U. Calif., Berkeley, 1974; JD, U. Calif., Davis, 1977. Bar: Calif. 1977, U.S. Dist. Ct. (ea. dist.) Calif. 1977, U.S. Dist. Ct. (no. dist.) Calif. 1982, U.S. Ct. Appeals (9th cir.) 1987. Law clk. to judge M.D. Crocker U.S. Dist. Ct. (ea. dist.) Calif., Fresno, 1977-78; from assoc. to ptnr. Stammer, McKnight, Barnum & Bailey, Fresno, 1978-95; ptnr. Sagaser, Franson Jamison & Jones PC, Fresno, 1995-99; pvt. practice Fresno, 1999—. Vol. atty. Calif. H.S., Fresno, 1983-87, 89-94; mem. Assocs. of Valley Children's Hosp., Fresno, 1980-81; co-chmn. Fresno County Law Day, 1995-96; panelist Selected Issues in Handling Discrimination and Wrongful Termination Cases. Mem. ABA, Fed. Bar Assn., Def. Rsch. Inst., No. Calif. Assn. Def. Counsel, Fresno County Bar Assn. Republican. Avocations: golf, jogging, aerobics. General civil litigation, Health, Personal injury. Office: 2444 Main St Ste 170 Fresno CA 93721-2736

**JAMISON, JUDITH JAFFE,** retired judge, lawyer, arbitrator, consultant; b. Phila., Aug. 19, 1924; d. Selig and Mary J.; m. I.I. Jamison, June 23, 1957; 1 child, Sara. BA, Antioch Coll., 1946; student, U. Chgo. Law Sch., 1945-46; JD, Temple U., 1948. Bar: Pa. 1949, U.S. Dist. Ct. (ea. dist.) Pa. 1949, U.S. Ct. Appeals (3d cir.) 1949. Gen. practice Phila., 1949-51, 91-96; spl. dep., asst. atty. gen. Pa. Dept. Justice, Phila., 1956-73; judge Ct. Common Pleas, Phila., 1974-90; of counsel Cozen and O'Connor, Phila., 1997—; mem. Supreme Ct. Orphan's Ct. Procedural Rules Commn., Pa., 1985-91, 96—; advisor Mayor's Commn. on Women, 1976-86; lectr. Pa. Coll. Judiciary, 1978-90. Contbr. articles to law jours. Bd. dirs. Fox Chase Cancer Ctr., Phila., 1980—; dir. Bd. Dirs. City Trusts, Phila., 1990—, Wills Eye Hosp., 1991—; trustee Ctr. for Literacy, Phila., 1990—; dir. Jenkins Law Libr. Recipient Spl. Achievement award Temple Law Alumni-Alumnae Assn., 1984, Legion of Honor, Chapel of the Four Chaplains. Mem. ABA, Nat. Coll. Probate Judges, Nat. Assn. Women Judges, Pa. Bar Assn., Phila. Bar Assn. Democrat. Jewish. Probate, Estate planning, Alternative dispute resolution. Home: 2119 Delancey St Philadelphia PA 19103-6511 Office: Cozen and O'Connor 1900 Market St Philadelphia PA 19103-3527

**JANECEK, JEANETTE MARY,** lawyer; b. Morris, Minn., Aug. 28, 1934; m. James Janacek, Oct. 13, 1956; children: Sarah, Karen Hoyt, James E. BS, Hamline U., 1956; JD, William Mitchell Coll., 1977. Bar: Minn. 1977. Ptrn. Janecek & Wright, New Brighton, Minn., 1978-91; pvt. practice New Brighton, 1991-99; retired, 1999. Coun. mem. City of New Brighton, 1978-85. Mem. Minn. Bar Assn., Ramsey County Bar Assn., Collaborative Law Inst. (bd. dirs. 1991-93). Family and matrimonial, Probate.

**JANECKY, JOHN FRANKLIN,** lawyer; b. Crookston, Minn., Nov. 26, 1944; s. Franklin Alfred and Betty (Bohlig) J.; m. Barbara Kearley, Sept. 26, 1970; children: Caryn Montgomery, Susan, John Jr. BS, USAF Acad., 1966; JD, U. Ala., 1975. Bar: Ala. 1975, Fla. 1976, U.S. Dist. Ct. (so. dist.) Ala., U.S. Dist. Ct. (no. dist.) Fla., U.S. Ct. Appeals (5th and 11th cirs.). Assoc. Nettles & Cox, Mobile, Ala., 1974-78; ptnr. Nettles, Barker & Janecky, Mobile, Ala., 1979-94; sr. ptnr. Janecky, Newell, Potts, Wilson, Smith & Masterson, Mobile, Ala., 1994—. Bd. dirs. Vols. Am., Mobile, 1980—; chmn. bd. deacons First Bapt. Ch., Mobile, 1991-93, deacon, 1977—; pres. Leadership Mobile, 1995. Capt. USAF, 1967-71. Mem. Ala. State Bar Assn. (vice chair ethics edn. com. 1993—), Mobile Bar Assn. (chmn. ethic com. 1998—), Ala. Def. Lawyers Assn. (v.p. 1997-98, bd. dirs., exec. com. 1994-95), Mobile Inns of Ct. (master bencher 1993—). Avocations: hunting, fishing, computers. Workers' compensation, General civil litigation, Insurance. Home: 112 Lanier Ave Mobile AL 36607-3214 Office: Janecky Newell Potts Wilson Smith & Masterson 3300 AmSouth Bank Bldg Mobile AL 36602

**JANGER, RICHARD K.,** lawyer; b. Chgo., Oct. 31, 1936; s. Max and Myrtle (Levy) J.; m. Lois Lieberman, Dec. 20, 1959; children: Seth, Joanna, Lee. BS, Northwestern U., 1958, JD, 1961. Assoc. McDermott Will & Emery, Chgo., 1962-64; ptnr. Levenfeld, Eisenberg, Janger & Glassberg, Chgo., 1964-98, Eisenberg & Janger, Chgo., 1999—. Served in U.S. Army, 1961. Mem. ABA, Chgo. Bar Assn., Ill. Bar Assn. Home: 250 Cedar Ave Highland Park IL 60035-4138 Office: Eisenberg & Janger 77 W Wacker Dr Fl 46 Chicago IL 60601-1635

**JANIGIAN, BRUCE JASPER,** lawyer, educator; b. San Francisco, Oct. 21, 1950; s. Michael D. Janigian and Stella (Minasian) Amerian; m. Susan Elizabeth Frye, Oct. 4, 1986; children: Alan Michael, Alison Elizabeth. AB, U. Calif., Berkeley, 1972; JD, U. Calif., San Francisco, 1975; LLM, George Washington U., 1982. Bar: Calif. 1975, U.S. Supreme Ct. 1979, D.C. 1981. Dir. Hastings Rsch. Svcs., Inc., San Francisco, 1973-75; judge adv. in Spain, 1976-78; commr. U.S. Navy and Marine Corps Ct. Mil. Rev., 1978-79; atty. advisor AID U.S. State Dept., Washington, 1979-84; dep. dir., gen. counsel Calif. Employment Devel. Dept., Sacramento, 1984-89; Fulbright scholar, vis. prof. law U. Salzburg, Austria, 1989-90; chmn. Calif. Agrl. Labor Rels. Bd., 1990-95; v.p. Europe, resident dir. Salzburg (Austria) Seminar, 1995-96; U.S. legate European Acad. Scis. and Art, 1996—; Rapporteur World Economic Forum, 1996; of counsel Weintraub Genshlea & Sproul Law Corp., Sacramento, 1998—; prof. law McGeorge Sch. Law, U. Pacific, Sacramento, 1986—, Inst. on Internat. Legal Studies, Salzburg, summer 1987, London Inst. on Comml. Law, summers 1989, 92, 93; vis. scholar Hoover Inst. War, Revolution and Peace, Stanford U., 1991-92; dir. Vienna-Budapest East/West Trade Inst., 1993; vis. prof. law U. Salzburg, 1995-96. Editor: Financing International Trade and Development, 1986, 87, 89, International Business Transactions, 1989, 92, International Trade Law, 1993, 94. Coord. fund raiser March of Dimes, Sacramento, 1987. Capt. USNR, JAGC, 1976-79, mem. Res. Fulbright scholar, 1989-90; decorated Meritorious Achievement medal; recipeint USAID Meritorious Honor award. Mem. Calif. Bar Assn., D.C. Bar Assn., Sacamento Bar Assn. (exec. com. taxation sect. 1988-89), Anthony M. Kennedy Am. Inn of Ct. (barrister 1998—), Carnegie Endowment for Internat. Peace, Sacramento Met. C. of C. (award for program contbns. and cmty. enrichment 1989), European Acad. Scis. and Art, World Art Forum, Austro-Am. Soc. (v.p. 1996), Navy League (gen. counsel 1997—), Naval Res. Officers Assn. (life), Marine Meml. Assn., Fulbright Assoc. (life), Knights of Vartan, Phi Beta Kappa. Avocations: cross-country skiing, tennis, bicycling. Home: 1631 12th Ave Sacramento CA 95818-4146 Office: 400 Capitol Mall Fl 11 Sacramento CA 95814-4407

**JANIS, N. RICHARD,** lawyer; b. Washington, Nov. 23, 1946; s. Mortimer Lewis and Mildred (Sacks) J.; m. Jan C. Campbell, July 23, 1972 (div. 1980); 1 child, Taylor Lael. BA, U. Wis., 1968; JD, Harvard U., 1972. Bar: D.C. 1973, U.S. Dist. Ct. D.C. 1973, U.S. Ct. Appeals (D.C. cir.) 1973, U.S. Supreme Ct. 1978, U.S. Dist. Ct. Md. 1985. Asst. U.S. atty. U.S. Dept. Justice, Washington, 1972-76; ptnr. Sharp, Randolph & Janis, Washington, 1976-79; sole practice Washington, 1979; ptnr. Janis, Schuelke & Wechsler, Washington, 1979—; lectr. George Washington U. Grad. Sch. Forensic Sciences, Washington, 1977-83. Mem. D.C. Bar Assn. (hearing com. chmn. bd. on profl. responsibility 1985-91), Edward Bennett Williams Inn of Ct. Avocations: golf, oriental rugs, antiques. Federal civil litigation, Criminal, Personal injury. Home: 5063 Overlook Rd NW Washington DC 20016-1911 Office: Janis Schuelke & Wechsler 1728 Massachusetts Ave NW Washington DC 20036-1933

**JANNEY, DONALD WAYNE,** lawyer; b. Clinton, N.C., Jan. 9, 1952; s. Wayne Columbus and Bernice (Talley) J.; m. Sydney Louise Rhame, May 28, 1977; children: Taylor Columbus, Camden St. Clair. BA, Furman U., 1974; JD, U. Va., 1978. Bar: Ga. 1978, U.S. Dist. Ct. (no. dist.) Ga. 1978, U.S. Ct. Appeals (11th cir.) 1982. Assoc. Troutman Sanders, Atlanta, 1978-85; ptnr. Troutman Sanders and predecessor firm, Atlanta, 1985—. Bd. dirs. State YMCA Ga., Atlanta, 1980-91. Mem. ABA, Ga. Bar Assn., Atlanta Bar Assn., Lawyers Club Atlanta, Phi Beta Kappa. Baptist. Condemnation, General civil litigation. Home: 705 E Morningside Dr Atlanta GA 30324-5220 Office: Troutman Sanders 5200 NationsBank Plz 600 Peachtree St NE Ste 5200 Atlanta GA 30308-2231

**JANNEY, OLIVER JAMES,** lawyer, plastics and chemical company executive; b. N.Y.C., Feb. 11, 1946; s. Walter Coggeshall and Helen Jennings (James) J.; m. Suzanne Elizabeth Lenz, June 21, 1969; children: Oliver Burr, Elizabeth Flower. BA cum laude, Yale Coll., 1967; JD, Harvard U., 1970. Bar: Mass. 1970, N.Y. 1971, Fla. 1991. With Walston & Co., Inc., N.Y.C., 1970-73, asst. v.p., 1971-73; assoc. Cleary, Gottlieb, Steen & Hamilton, N.Y.C., 1973-76; with RKO Gen., Inc., N.Y.C., 1976-90, asst. sec., 1977-85, asst. gen. atty., 1978-82, asst. gen. counsel, 1982-85, sec., gen. counsel, 1985-89; v.p., gen. counsel, sec. Uniroyal Tech. Corp., Sarasota, Fla., 1990—. Former pres. River Rd. Assn., Scarborough, N.Y.; vestryman, treas. All Angels by the Sea, Longboat Key, Fla., 1999—. Served to 1st lt. USAR, 1969-77. Mem. ABA, N.Y. State Bar Assn., Assn. of Bar of City of N.Y., Sleepy Hollow Country Club (Scarborough), Longboat Key (Fla.) Club. Republican. General corporate, Administrative and regulatory, Environmental. Home: 3651 Bayou Cir Longboat Key FL 34228-3005 Office: Uniroyal Tech Corp 2 N Tamiami Trl Ste 900 Sarasota FL 34236-5568

**JANNUZZO, JEFFREY ANTHONY,** lawyer; b. N.Y., Feb. 26, 1949; s. Anthony C. and Marjorie R. (Falk) J.; m. Anne Marie Thompson, Nov. 2, 1991. BS, Skidmore Coll., 1971; JD, Yale U., 1976. Bar: N.Y. 1977. With Debevoise & Plimpton, N.Y.C., 1976-85, Jones, Day, Surrey & Morse, Saudi Arabia, 1985-88, Coudert Bros., N.Y.C., 1989-93, Layton, Brooks & Hecht, N.Y.C., 1993-99. Author: (video) Preparing For a Deposition in a Business Case, 1984 (Hugo award 1984). Mem. ABA (internat. sect.), Assn. of Bar of City of N.Y. Private international, Federal civil litigation. Home: 375 Riverside Dr Apt 4A New York NY 10025-2120

**JANOWITZ, JAMES ARNOLD,** lawyer; b. N.Y.C., Sept. 2, 1946; s. Arnold and Erna (Frankel) J.; m. Katherine Eva Sborovy, Aug. 6, 1967; children: Jessie Elizabeth, William Aaron. BA, Haverford Coll., 1967; JD, NYU, 1971. Bar: N.Y. 1972, U.S. Dist Ct. (so. dist.) N.Y. 1972. Tchr. St. David's Sch., N.Y.C., 1968-72; assoc. Guzik & Boukstein, N.Y.C., 1972-73, Reavis & McGrath, N.Y.C., 1973-74, Pryor, Cashman & Sherman, N.Y.C., 1974-76; ptnr. Pryor, Cashman, Sherman & Flynn, N.Y.C., 1977—; adj. prof. Cardozo Law Sch., Yeshiva U., N.Y.C., 1992; bd. dirs. Avenue Entertainment, 1986—. Editor NYU Jour. Internat. Law and Politics, 1970-71. Mem. N.Y. State Bar Assn., Assn. of Bar of City of N.Y. General civil litigation, Entertainment, Finance. Office: Pryor Cashman Sherman & Flynn 410 Park Ave Fl 10 New York NY 10022-4441

**JANSEN, DONALD WILLIAM,** lawyer, legislative administrator; b. Luverne, Minn., Aug. 21, 1948; s. William John and Florence Catherine (Tisdell) J.; m. Jacqueline Skeens, Sept. 30, 1978; children: Christopher Donald, Morgan Whitney, Madison Maarten. BA in Polit. Sci., Ariz. State U., 1970; JD, Gonzaga U., 1975. Bar: Ariz. 1975, U.S. Dist. Ct. Ariz. 1977, U.S. Supreme Ct. 1987, U.S. Ct. Appeals (9th cir.) 1998. Asst. rules atty., counsel to ethics com. Ariz. Ho. of Reps., Phoenix, 1976-83, counsel to majority leader, 1983-87, gen. counsel, 1987; dir. Ariz. Legis. Coun., Phoenix, 1987-92; policy advisor and counsel Ariz. Ho. of Reps., Phoenix, 1992-98, gen. counsel, 1998—. Contbr. to Ariz. State Law Jour., 1988. 1st lt. U.S. Army, 1970-72. Mem. State Bar Ariz., Nat. Conf. State Legislatures, Western Legis. Conf. Roman Catholic. Home: 4389 E Olney Dr Phoenix AZ 85044-1018 Office: Ariz House of Reps 1700 W Washington St Phoenix AZ 85007-2812

**JANSEN, LAMBERTUS,** judge; b. Salt Lake City, Oct. 27, 1934; s. Lambertus Christianus and Cobi Maria (van Ekelenburg) J.; m. Rosemary Van Dyke, Aug. 22, 1958 (div. 1969); children: Jackie Lyn, David Scott; m. LaNita Joyce Lindley, Sept. 10, 1982. AA, Westminster Coll., Salt Lake City, 1954, BS, 1959; JD, U. Utah, 1968. Bar: Utah 1968, N.Y. 1983. Tchr. English Jordan Sch. Dist., Sandy, Utah, 1959-62; fraud investigator Utah Job Svc., Salt Lake City, 1962-65; instr. U. Utah, Salt Lake City, 1965-68; lawyer Jansen Law Office, Salt Lake City, 1968-83, Hyatt Legal Svcs., Syracuse, N.Y., 1983-87, Shanley Law Office, Oswego, N.Y., 1987-92; city ct. judge Oswego, 1992—. Dir. Utah Housing Devel. Agy., Salt Lake City, 1969-71; mem. steering com. Oswego County Anti-Drug Program, 1996-97; mem. Oswego County Drug Ct. Program, 1996-97. Mem. Am. Judges Assn., N.Y. State City Ct. Judges Assn., Am. Trial Lawyers Assn., Oswego County Bar Assn., Onondaga County Bar Assn. Roman Catholic. Avocations: skiing, hiking, golf, camping. Home: 30 Talisman Ter Oswego NY 13126-6142 Office: Oswego City Ct 20 W Oneida St Oswego NY 13126-2574

**JARPE, GEOFFREY PELLAS,** lawyer; b. Milw., Aug. 2, 1945; s. Gunnar E. and Laura Johnson (Camp) J.; m. Lezlie J. Myhra, Aug. 10, 1968; children: Nathan M., Rachel K., Joseph S. BA, U. Mich., 1967, JD, 1969. Bar: Minn. 1970, U.S. Dist. Ct. Minn. 1973, U.S. Ct. Appeals (8th cir.), 1973, U.S. Dist. Ct. (ea. dist.) Mich. 1982, U.S. Dist. Ct. (ea. dist.) Wis. 1987, U.S. Claims Ct. 1990, Wis. 1989, U.S. Dist. Ct. (we. dist.) Wis., 1995, U.S. Supreme Ct. 1990; cert. Nat. Bd. Trial Advocacy. Spl. asst atty. gen. State of Minn., St. Paul, 1970-72; assoc. Maun & Simon, St. Paul, 1972-78, ptnr., 1978—. Mem. ABA, Minn. State Bar Assn. (cert. civil trial specialist, civil litigation sect.), Ramsey County Bar Assn., U. Mich. Club (pres. Twin Cities chpt. 1985-87). Lutheran. Federal civil litigation, General civil litigation, State civil litigation. Office: Maun & Simon 801 Nicollet Mall 200 Midwest Plz Bldg W Minneapolis MN 55402-2534

**JARVIS, BARBARA ANNE,** lawyer; b. Kansas City, Mo., Apr. 14, 1934; d. Herman Edward and Marjorie Maude (Graber) Spitzenfeil; A.A., Kansas City Jr. Coll., 1953; B.S. in Polit. Sci. magna cum laude, Ariz. State U., 1976, J.D., 1979; m. Thomas B. Jarvis, Sept. 9, 1965; 1 son, Kenneth Mark. Technologist Menorah Med. Center, Kansas City, Mo., 1955-56, Ariz. State U. Student Health Service, 1960-62, Scottsdale (Ariz.) Bapt. Hosp., 1962-65; chief technologist Skyline Lab., Globe, Ariz., 1967-72; practice law, Phoenix, 1979—; pro tem judge Ashland (Oreg.) Municipal Ct., 1990—. Sec. Globe Planning and Zoning Commn., 1970-75; assoc. coordinator Women's Polit. Caucus Ariz.; 1st vice chmn. Ariz. Democratic Com.; mem. Dem. Nat. Com. from Ariz.; chmn. neighborhood rehab. com. Phoenix Urban Form, 1976-77, mem. steering com., 1976-79; mem. Phoenix Bd. Adjustment, 1977-82, chmn., 1980-81; chmn. Village 4 Planning Com., City of Phoenix; chmn. citizens adv. com. Ariz. Dept. Corrections, 1983-85, Paradise Corridor, 1986-88; chmn. planning commn. City of Ashland, Oreg., 1992—; bd. dirs. Salvation Army, Globe, Gila Pueblo campus Eastern Ariz. Coll., Gila County Guidance Clinic, On Track, Medford, Oreg., 1990—; mem. gov's. com. on alcohol and drug abuse, 1994—. Mem. State Bar Ariz., State Bar Orge., Maricopa County Bar Assn. (co-chmn. alternatives to sentencing com. 1980-81), Ariz. Assn. Criminal Justice, Nat. Orgn. Criminal Def. Lawyers, Oreg. Criminal Def. Lawyers Assn., Ariz. Women Lawyers, Women in Law (chmn.), Jackson County Bar Assn., Ariz. State U. Law Sch. Alumni Assn., Charter 100, Pi Sigma Alpha, Phi Kappa Phi. Family and matrimonial, Criminal. Office: 1159 Emma St Ashland OR 97520-3470

**JARVIS, DONALD BERTRAM,** judge; b. Newark, N.J., Dec. 14, 1928; s. Benjamin and Esther (Golden) J.; BA, Rutgers U., 1949; JD, Stanford U., 1952; m. Rosalind C. Chodorcove, June 13, 1954; children: Nancie, Brian, Joanne. Bar: Calif. 1953. Law clk. Justice John W. Shenk, Calif. Supreme Ct., 1953-54; assoc. Erskine, Erskine & Tulley, 1955; assoc. Aaron N. Cohen, 1955-56; law clk. Dist. Ct. Appeal, 1956; assoc. Carl Hoppe, 1956-57; adminstrv. law judge Calif. Pub. Utilities Commn., San Francisco, 1957-91, U.S. Dept. of Labor, 1992—; mem. exec. com. Nat. Conf. Adminstrv. Law Judges, 1986-88, sec. 1988-89, vice-chair, 1990-91, chair-elect, 1991-92, chair 1992-93; pres. Calif. Adminstrv. Law Judges Coun., 1978-84; mem. faculty Nat. Jud. Coll., U. Nev., 1977, 78, 80. Chmn. pack Boy Scouts Am., 1967-69, chmn. troop, 1972; class chmn. Stanford Law Sch. Fund, 1959, mem. nat. com., 1963-65; dir. Forest Hill Assn., 1970-71. Served to col. USAF Res., 1949-79. Decorated Legion of Merit. Mem. ABA (mem. ho. of dels. 1993—, vice chair jud. divsn. 1997-98, chair elect 1998-99), State Bar Calif., Bar Assn. San Francisco, Calif. Conf. Pub. Utility Counsel (pres. 1980-81), Air Force Assn., Res. Officers Assn., Ret. Officers Assn., De Young Museum Soc. and Patrons Art and Music, San Francisco Gem and Mineral Soc., Stanford Alumni Assn., Rutgers Alumni Assn., Phi Beta Kappa (pres. No. Calif. 1973-74), Tau Kappa Alpha, Phi Alpha Theta, Phi Alpha Delta. Home: 530 Dewey Blvd San Francisco CA 94116-1427 Office: 50 Fremont St San Francisco CA 94105-2230

**JARVIS, JAMES HOWARD, II,** judge; b. Knoxville, Tenn., Feb 28, 1937; s. Howard F. and Eleanor B. J.; m. Martha Stapleton, June 1957 (div. Feb. 1962); children—James Howard III, Leslie; m. Pamela K. Duncan, Aug. 23, 1964 (div. Apr. 1991); children: Ann, Kathryn, Louise; m. Gail Stone, Sept. 4, 1992. BA, U. Tenn., 1958, JD, 1960. Bar: Tenn. 1961, U.S. Dist. Ct. (ea. dist.) Tenn. 1961, U.S. Ct. Appeals (6th cir.) 1965. Assoc. O'Neil, Jarvis, Parker & Williamson, Knoxville, Tenn., 1960-68, mem., 1968-70; mem. Meares, Dungan, Jarvis, Maryville, Tenn., 1970-72; judge Law and Equity Ct., Blount County, Tenn., 1972-77, 30th Jud. Cir. Ct., Blount County, 1977-84, U.S. Dist. Ct. (ea. dist.) Tenn., Knoxville, 1984-91, chief judge, 1991—. Past bd. dirs. Maryville (Tenn.) Coll.; mem. and past chmn. fin. com. St. Andrews Episc. Ch.; past bd. dirs. Detoxification Rehab. Inst. of Knoxville; mem. com. on codes of conduct Jud. Conf. U.S. Mem. ABA (com. ethics and profl. responsibility), Tenn. Bar Assn. (bd. govs. 1983-84), Am. Judicature Soc., Tenn. Trial Judges Assn. (past mem. exec. com.), Tenn. Jud. Conf. (pres. 1983-84), Blount County Bar Assn., Knoxville Bar Assn., Great Smoky Mountains Conservation Assn., Phi Delta Phi, Sigma Chi (significant Sigma Chi). Republican. Home: 6916 Stone Mill Rd Knoxville TN 37919-7431 Office: Howard H Baker Jr US Courthouse 800 Market St Knoxville TN 37902-2303

**JARVIS, PERCY ALTON, JR.,** lawyer, entertainment consultant; b. Orange, N.J., July 3, 1941; s. Percy Alton and Madeline (Hanna) J. BA, Bloomfield Coll., N.J., 1964; JD, Seton Hall U., 1971. Bar: N.J. 1974. Legal rschr. Firemen's Fund Ins. Co., Newark, 1964-70; asst. dir. alcoholic beverage control State of N.J., Trenton, 1970-74; counsel Nat. Wine &

Liquor, Capitol Wine & Spirits, 1974-75; sr. ptnr. Jarvis Lorentz & Wood, Esquires, 1975—. Vice chmn. Republican County Com., Millburn, N.J., 1977-79; atty. bd. adj. City of Summit. Mem. Union County Bar Assn., Summit Bar Assn., Am. Legion (judge adv. 1976—), Phi Alpha Delta (justice N.J. alumni chpt. 1980-84), Elks (Summit). Consumer commercial, Probate, Real property. Office: Jarvis Lorentz & Wood PO Box 357 45 River Rd Summit NJ 07902

**JARVIS, ROBERT GLENN,** lawyer; b. San Benito, Tex., Jan. 20, 1938; s. Robert Harral and Helen Aline (Cruse) J.; m. Patricia Joyce Morgan, June ll, 1960; children: Jeffrey, Todd, Tate. BA, Rice U., 1960; JD, U. Tex., 1963. Bar: Tex. 1963, U.S. Dist. Ct. (so. dist.) Tex. 1963, U.S. Ct. Appeals (5th cir.) 1968, U.S. Ct. Appeals (D.C. cir.) 1970, U.S. Supreme Ct. 1975. Assoc. Ewers & Toothaker, McAllen, Tex., 1963-65, ptnr., 1965-85; ptnr. Jarvis, Schwarz & Kittleman, McAllen, 1985-90; pres. Jarvis & Kittleman, PC, McAllen, 1991-98; pvt. practice McAllen, 1998—; adv. coun. Tex. Commerce Bank, McAllen, 1981-84; mem., bd. dirs. Internat. Bank McAllen, 1984—. Mem. Watermaster planning adv. com. Tex. Water Commn., Austin, 1987-91; pres. McAllen Ind. Sch. Dist. Bd. Edn., 1979; bd. dirs. McAllen Econ. Devel. Corp., 1987-98; chmn. McAllen Infrastructure Planning Coun., 1989-94; bd. dirs. Tex. Turnpike Authority, 1997—. Fellow Tex. Bar Found.; mem. ABA, State Bar Tex. (labor law adv. com. bd. legal specialization 1978—), Coll. State Bar Tex., Hidalgo County Bar Assn., McAllen C. of C. (bd. dirs. 1987-97), Rio Grande Valley C. of C. (bd. dirs. 1992-95, pres. 1995-96). Labor, Environmental, Administrative and regulatory. Office: PO Box 4828 McAllen TX 78502-4828

**JARVIS, ROBERT MARK,** law educator; b. N.Y.C., Oct. 17, 1959; s. Rubin and Ute (Hacklander) J.; m. Judith Anne Mellman, Mar. 3, 1989. BA, Northwestern U., 1980; JD, U. Pa., 1983; LLM, NYU, 1986. Bar: N.Y. 1984, D.C. 1985, U.S. Dist. Ct. (ea. and so. dists.) N.Y. 1984, U.S. Ct. Mil. Appeals 1985, U.S. Ct. Internat. Trade 1987, U.S. Ct. Appeals (2d cir.) 1987, U.S. Supreme Ct. 1987, U.S. Ct. Appeals (11th cir.) 1989, U.S. Ct. Appeals (D.C. cir.) 1990, U.S. Claims Ct. 1990, Fla. 1990. Assoc. Haight Gardner Poor & Havens, N.Y.C., 1983-85, Baker & McKenzie, N.Y.C., 1985-87; asst. prof. law ctr. Nova Southeastern U., Ft. Lauderdale, Fla., 1987-90, assoc. prof., 1990-92, prof., 1992—; adj. instr. law Yeshiva U., N.Y.C., 1986-87; vis. asst. prof. Tulane U., New Orleans, 1988; adj. prof. law St. Thomas U., Miami, 1991-95; lectr. BAR/BRI bar rev. courses, 1990-95; chmn. bd. dirs. Miami Maritime Arbitration Bd., 1993-94; vice chmn. bd. dirs. Miami Internat. Arbitration and Mediation Inst., 1993-94; mem. adv. bd. Carolina Acad. Press, 1996—. Co-author: AIDS: Cases and Materials, 1989, 2d edit., 1995, AIDS Law in a Nutshell, 1991, 2d edit., 1996, Notary Law and Practice: Cases and Materials, 1997, Travel Law: Cases and Materials, 1998, Sports Law: Cases and Materials, 1999; author: Careers in Admiralty and Maritime Law, 1993, An Admiralty Law Anthology, 1995; co-editor: Prime Time Law: Fictional Television as Legal Narrative, 1998; mem. editl. bd. Washington Lawyer, 1988-94, Jour. Maritime Law and Commerce, 1990-92, assoc. editor, 1993-95, editor, 1996—, Hospitality Law, 1999—, Maritime Law Reporter, 1991—; mem. editl. adv. bd. Transnat. Lawyer, 1991—; mem. adv. bd. World Arbitration and Mediation Report, 1990—, U. San Francisco Maritime Law Jour., 1992-95; contbg. editor Preview U.S. Supreme Ct. Cases, 1990-95; mem. editl. bd. Hospitality Law, 1999—. Mem. ABA (vice chmn. admiralty law com. young lawyers divsn. 1992-93, chair 1993-94), Fla. Bar Assn. (admiralty law com. 1988-95, vice chmn. 1991-92, chmn. 1992-93, exec. coun. internat. law sect. 1992-96), Maritime Law Assn. U.S., Southeastern Admiralty Law Inst., Assn. Am. Law Schs. (chmn.-elect maritime law sect. 1991-93, chmn. 1993-94), Northwestern U. Club South Fla. (v.p. 1992-93, pres. 1993-95), Phi Beta Kappa, Phi Delta Phi (province pres. 1989-91, coun. 1991-93), Acacia. Democrat. Jewish. Avocations: theatre, running. Office: Nova Southeastern U Law Ctr 3305 College Ave Fort Lauderdale FL 33314-7721

**JASCOURT, HUGH D.,** lawyer, arbitrator, mediator; b. Phila., Mar. 25, 1935; s. Jacquard A. and Gladys Mae (Bregen) J.; m. Resa B. Zall, Nov. 28, 1963; children: Stephen, Leigh. AB, U. Pa., 1956; JD, Wayne State U., 1960. Bar: Mich. 1961, U.S. Supreme Ct. 1965, D.C. 1967. Atty. advisor U.S. Dept. Labor, Washington, 1960-64; asst. dir. employee-mgmt. rels. Am. Fedn. Govt. Employees, Washington, 1964-65; atty. advisor Nat. Labor Rels. Bd., Washington, 1965-66; exec. dir. Fed. Bar Assn., Washington, 1966-67; house counsel Am. Fedn. of State, County, & Mcpl. Employees, Washington, 1967-69; sr. labor-law counsel Bd. of Gov. Fed. Reserve Bd., Washington, 1969-72; dir. Pub. Employment Rels. Rsch. Inst., Washington, 1972-74; asst. solicitor U.S. Dept. of Interior, Washington, 1974-82; sr. labor-law counsel U.S. Dept. Commerce, Washington, 1982-90; pres. Agency for Dispute Resolutions and Synergistic Rels., Greenbelt, Md., 1991—; lectr. George Washington U. Law Sch., Washington, 1970-75; chmn. unfair labor practice panel Prince George County Employee Rels. Bd., Upper Marlboro, Md., 1972-83, mem. Greenbelt (Md.) Employee Rels. Bd., 1984—; arbitrator/mediator, 1973—. Author, editor: Trends in Public Sector Labor Relations, 1973, Government Labor Relations, 1979; author: (with others) Labor Relations, 1978-82; Collective Bargaining, 1980; labor rels. editor Jour. Law and Edn., 1972—. Pres. Road Runners Club Am., 1962-66, Prince George County (Md.) Fedn. of Recreational Couns., 1969, Prince George County Coun. of PTAs, 1989-90; coach U.S. track and field team AAU So. Games, Trinidad, 1964, Internat. Cross Country Championship, Morocco, 1966; v.p. Am. Running and Fitness Assn., 1968-84. Inductee Road Runners Club Am. Hall of Fame, 1986; initial inductee D.C. Road Runners Club Hall of Fame, 1994. Fellow Coll. of Labor and Employment Lawyers; mem. ABA (com. on state and local labor employment and law, chmn. subcom. 1982—, co-chmn. com. on fed. svc. labor and employment law 1985-97, mem. mediation com., sect. on dispute resolution), ASPA, Soc. Fed. Labor Rels. Profls. (bd. dirs. 1992-93), Soc. Profls. in Dispute Resolution (charter mem.), Indsl. Rels. Rsch. Assn., Internat. Pers. Mgmt. Assn., Am. Arbitration Assn., Md. Coun. on Dispute Resolution. Office: Agency Dispute Resolution & Synergistic Rels 18 Maplewood Ct Greenbelt MD 20770-1907

**JASEN, MATTHEW JOSEPH,** lawyer, state justice; b. Buffalo, Dec. 13, 1915; s. Joseph John and Celina (Perlinski) Jasinski; m. Anastasia Gawinski, Oct. 4, 1943 (dec. Aug. 1970); children: Peter M., Mark M., Christine (Mrs. David K. Mac Leod), Carol Ann, (Mrs. J. David Sampson); m. Gertrude O'Connor Travers, Mar. 25, 1972 (dec. Nov. 1972); m. Grace Yungbluth Frauenheim, Aug. 31, 1973. Student, Canisius Coll., 1936; LLB, U. Buffalo, 1939; postgrad., Harvard U., 1944; LLD (hon.), Union U., 1980; LL.D. (hon.), N.Y. Law Sch., 1981. Bar: N.Y. 1940. Ptnr. firm Beyer, Jasen & Boland, Buffalo, 1940-43; pres. U.S. Security Rev. Bd., Wurttemberg-Baden, Germany, 1945-46; judge U.S. Mil. Govt. Ct., Heidelberg, Germany, 1946-49; sr. ptnr. firm Jasen, Manz, Johnson & Bayger, Buffalo, 1949-57; justice N.Y. Supreme Ct. (8th jud. dist.), 1957-67; judge N.Y. Ct. Appeals, 1968-85; U.S. Supreme Ct. spl. master S.C. v. U.S., 1987-88; spl. master Ill. vs. Ky. U.S. Supreme Ct., 1989-95; of counsel Moot & Sprague, Buffalo, 1986-90; counsel Jasen, Jasen & Sampson, P.C., Buffalo, 1990-99, Jasen & Jasen, P.C., Buffalo, 1999—; mem. N.Y. State Jud. Screening Com., 1996—. Contbr. articles to profl. jours. Mem. council U. Buffalo, 1963-66; trustee Canisius Coll. Chair of Polish Culture, also, Nottingham Acad. Served to capt. AUS, 1943-46, ETO. Fellow Hilbert Coll.; recipient Disting. Alumnus award SUNY-Buffalo Sch. Law, 1969, Disting. Alumnus award Alumni Assn., 1976, Disting. Alumnus award Canisius Coll., 1978, Edwin F. Jaeckle award SUNY-Buffalo Sch. Law, 1982. Mem. Nat. Conf. Appellate Judges, State U. N.Y. at Buffalo Law Sch. Alumni Assn. (pres. 1964-65), Am., N.Y. State, Erie County bar assns., Am. Law Inst., Am. Judicature Soc., Lawyers Club Buffalo (pres. 1961-62), Nat. Advocates Club, Profl. Businessmen's Assn. Western N.Y. (pres. 1952), Phi Alpha Delta, DiGamma Soc. Roman Catholic (mem. Bishop's Bd. Govs., Buffalo diocese 1951—). Clubs: K.C. (4 deg.). General civil litigation, Personal injury, General corporate. Home: 26 Pine Ter Orchard Park NY 14127-3928 Office: 69 Delaware Ave Rm 700 Buffalo NY 14202-3805

**JASINSKI, GEORGE JOHN,** lawyer; b. Chgo., Dec. 12, 1954; s. George Ambrose and Geraldine Marie (Orowick) J.; m. Kathy Mary Procenti, Nov. 8, 1980; children: George Ambrose, David Francis, Gabrielle Kathryn. BS, Bradley U., 1976; JD, John Marshall Law Sch., 1979. Bar: Ill. 1979, U.S. Dist. Ct. (no. dist.) Ill. 1979, U.S. Ct. Appeals (7th cir.) 1979. Assoc. Law Offices of Phillip F. Maher, Chgo., 1979-80; ptnr. Barrett, Sramek & Jasinski, Palos Heights, Ill., 1980-98; owner Law Offices George J. Jasinski, Palos Heights, Ill., 1998—. Mem. ABA, Assn. Trial Lawyers Am., Ill. Bar Assn. (torts sect. 1980—, civil practice and procedure sect. 1980—, workers compensation sec. 1980—), Ill. Trial Lawyers Assn., Chgo. Bar Assn. (young lawyers sect. 1979—), Am. Arbitration Assn., S.W. Suburban Bar Assn., Palos Heights C. of C. Roman Catholic. Avocations: golf, all sports, travel. Fax: (708) 4483200. General civil litigation, Personal injury, Product liability. Home: 12311 S Pine Pl Palos Heights IL 60463-1885 Office: Law Offices George J Jasinski 7330 W College Dr Ste 101 Palos Heights IL 60463-1160 also: 77 W Washington St Ste 600 Chicago IL 60602-2803

**JASPER, SEYMOUR,** lawyer; b. N.Y.C., May 15, 1919; s. Louis and Gussie (Levitch) J.; m. Geulah Eidelsberg, Nov. 24, 1940 (dec.); children: Michael, Ronald, Jeffrey, Idylia; m. Barbara Gray, Feb. 11, 1975. BS, NYU, 1939; JD, Columbia U., 1956. Bar: N.Y. 1956. Assoc. Young, Kaplan & Edelstein, N.Y.C., 1956-59; ptnr. Jasper, Sandler & Lipsay, N.Y.C., 1959-62; pvt. practice N.Y.C., 1962—. With USN. Probate, Estate planning. Office: 115 E 87th St New York NY 10128-1136

**JASSY, EVERETT LEWIS,** lawyer; b. N.Y.C., Feb. 4, 1937; s. David H. and Florence A. (Pollak) J.; m. Margery Ellen Rose; children: Katherine Savitt Lennon, Andrew Ralph, Jonathan Scott. AB, Harvard U., 1957, JD, 1960. Bar: N.Y. 1960, D.C. 1975. Assoc. Dewey Ballantine, N.Y.C., 1960-68, ptnr., 1968—, chmn. mgmt. com., 1996—. Mem. ABA, N.Y. State Bar Assn., Assn. of Bar of City of N.Y., The Tax Club, Harmonie Club (bd. govs. 1999—), Fairview Country Club, Washington Athletic Club. Avocations: golf, travel. Corporate taxation, Personal income taxation. Home: 20 Tompkins Rd Scarsdale NY 10583-2838 Office: Dewey Ballantine LLP 1301 Avenue Of The Americas New York NY 10019-6022

**JAUDES, RICHARD EDWARD,** lawyer; b. St. Louis, Feb. 22, 1943; s. Leo August Jr. and Dorothy Catherine (Schmidt) J.; m. Mary Kay Tansey, Sept. 22, 1967; children: Michele, Pamela. BS, St. Louis U., 1965, JD, 1968. Bar: Mo. Supreme Ct. 1968, Ky. 1984, Ill. 1990, U.S. Dist. Ct. (ea. dist.) Mo. 1973, U.S. Dist. Ct. (ea. dist.) Ky. 1985, U.S. Dist. Ct. (we. dist.) 1986, U.S. Dist. Ct. (so. dist.) Ill. 1991, U.S. Ct. Appeals (8th cir.) 1973, U.S. Supreme Ct. 1990. With Peper, Martin, Jensen, Maichel & Hetlage, St. Louis, 1973-97, mng. ptnr., 1990-93; lawyer, co-chair labor and employment practice group Thompson Coburn, St. Louis, 1997—, mem. mgmt. com.; bd. dirs. Baldor Electric Co. Vol. Civic Entrepreneurs Orgn., St. Louis, 1990; vol. counsel St. Louis chpt. MS Soc., 1990, exec. com. Lt. USN, 1968-73; comdr. USNR, ret. Labor. Office: Thompson Coburn One Mercantile Ctr Saint Louis MO 63101-1693

**JAVIER, RAMON EMILIO,** lawyer; b. Elmhurst, N.Y., Oct. 24, 1969; s. Ramon Emilio Sr. and Carmen Margarita Javier; m. Debra Castro de Javier, June 14, 1998. AA, NYU, 1989, BA, 1991; JD, Touro Coll., 1995. Bar: N.Y. 1996, U.S. Dist. Ct. (ea. and so. dists.) N.Y. 1997, D.C. 1997, U.S. Ct. Appeals (fed. cir.) 1999, U.S. Ct. Appeals for the Armed Forces 1999, U.S. Ct. Fed. Claims 1999, U.S. Supreme Ct. 1999. Rsch. asst. Prof. Peter Zablotsky, Hempstead, N.Y., 1994; clk. Hon. Steven W. Fisher, Jamaica, N.Y., fall 1994; staff atty. Legal Aid Soc., Hempstead, N.Y., 1996-97; founder, prin. Law Office of Ramon E. Javier, N.Y.C., 1997—. Bd. dirs. LEAP Alumni Assn.-Touro Law Sch., Huntington, N.Y., 1998—. Mem. N.Y. State Assn. Criminal Def. Lawyers, Assn. of the Bar of the City of N.Y. Democrat. Roman Catholic. Avocations: skiing, mountain biking, writing. Criminal, General practice. Office: Law Offices of Ramon E Javier 40 Exchange Pl Ste 1800 New York NY 10005-2701

**JAVORE, GARY WILLIAM,** lawyer; b. San Antonio, Apr. 3, 1952; s. Fred Walter and Glennice Jean (Gilbert) J. BA, Kent (Ohio) State U., 1975; JD, Cleve. State U., 1978. Bar: Tex. 1978, U.S. Dist. Ct. (we. dist.) Tex. 1981, U.S. Ct. Appeals (5th cir.) 1981, U.S. Supreme Ct. 1981. Atty. Bexar County Legal Aid, San Antonio, 1979-81; prin. Johnson, Christopher, Javore & Cochran, San Antonio, 1981—; bd. dirs. Bexar County Legal Aid, San Antonio, 1986—. Author, speaker legal seminars. Mem. Leadership San Antonio Class XXIV. Fellow Tex. Bar Found., San Antonio Bar Found.; mem. San Antonio Trial Lawyers Assn. (bd. dirs. 1986—, treas. 1991, pres. 1993, Outstanding Young Lawyer award 1986), Greater San Antonio Builders Assn. (cons., exec. bd. 1990—, v.p. assoc. coun. 1993), Tex. Trial Lawyers Assn., Order of Barristers. Avocations: wood carving, tennis, scuba diving. Alternative dispute resolution, Consumer commercial, Construction. Office: Johnson Christopher Javore & Cochran 5802 Northwest Expy San Antonio TX 78201-2851

**JEANSONNE, MARK ANTHONY,** lawyer, mayor; b. Hessmer, La., Oct. 5, 1962; s. Milburn Joseph and Wava (Normand) J.; m. Shannon Descant, Dec. 12, 1992. BA in Polit. Sci., La. State U., 1988; JD, Loyola U., 1991. Bar: La., U.S. Dist. Ct. (we. dist.) La., U.S. Dist. Ct. (mid. dist.) La. Mayor Village of Hessmer, La., 1993—, magistrate, 1993—; magistrate Town of Cottonport, La., 1996—, Town of Mansura, La., 1997—; pvt. practice Hessmer, 1998—. Recipient Small Town Leadership award Wal-Mart, 1997. Mem. La. State Bar, Avoyelles Parish Bar (pres. 1995-96). Avocations: collecting gold and silver coinage, antiques. General civil litigation, Personal injury, General practice. Home: PO Box 301 2540 Main St Hessmer LA 71341-4058 Office: 2472 Main St Hessmer LA 71341-4034

**JEFFERIES, JACK P.,** lawyer; b. Radford, Va., Dec. 5, 1928; s. Raymond L. and Artelia P. Jefferies; m. Patricia Ann Carl, Sept. 8, 1962; m. 2d, Karen S. Sommarstrom, Oct. 14, 1972; 1 child, Elizabeth Karling. BS in Commerce, U. Va., 1949, JD, 1951, LLM, 1952; JSD, Yale U., 1954. Bar: Va. 1953, N.Y. 1959, U.S. Dist. Ct. (so. dist.) N.Y., U.S. Ct. Appeals (D.C. cir.), U.S. Supreme Ct. Ptnr. Lord, Day, Lord, Barrett & Smith, N.Y.C., 1958-88, of counsel, 1988-94; spl. cons. McDermott, Will & Emery, N.Y.C., 1994—; legal cons. Office Gen. Counsel, U.S. Dept. Def., 1957; mem. White House Conf. on Equality to Fulfill These Rights, 1966; mem. U.S. Pres.'s Com. on Employment of Handicapped, 1981. Author: Understanding Hotel/Motel Law, 1983, 3d edit., 1995, Important New York State Laws for Hotels/Motels; primary editor for Dept. Army publs. on internat. law, 1956; editl. bd. Va. Law Rev., 1950-51; contbr. articles to legal jours. UN rep. Internat. Hotel Assn., 1993—; pres. Policy Scis. Ctr.; exec. com., bd. dirs. Downtown Lower Manhattan Assn.; trustee Am. Waterways Wind Orch.; mem. adv. bd. NYU Hospitality Mgmt. Sch.; treas., trustee Historic House Trust for N.Y.C.; elder Presbyn. Ch., Palisades, N.Y.; bd. dirs. Newport Hist. Soc. Served with JACG, U.S. Army, 1954-57. Mem. Assn. of Bar City of N.Y., ABA, U. Va. Alumni Assn. of N.Y. (exec. com.), Les Amis d'Escoffier Soc. (bd. dirs.). Democrat. Club: Down Town Assn. (N.Y.C.). Lodge: Masons. General corporate, Private international, Non-profit and tax-exempt organizations. Home: 111 Harrison Ave Apt B-6 Newport RI 02840-3712 Office: McDermott Will & Emery Ste 4300 50 Rockefeller Plaza New York NY 10020-1605

**JEFFERIS, PAUL BRUCE,** lawyer; b. Barnesville, Ohio, Jan. 11, 1952; s. Maurice D. and Ruth C. (Rinehart) J.; m. Shirley R. Zervos, Sept. 13, 1997; children: Paul M., Elaini Noel Zervos. BA, Ohio State U., 1977; JD, U. Akron, 1980. Bar: Ohio 1980. Asst. prosecutor Belmont County, St. Clairsville, Ohio, 1981-83; pvt. practice, Barnesville, 1983—. Bd. dirs. St. Clairsville Drug and Alcohol Coun., 1982—. With USN, 1975-77. Mem. ABA, Belmont County Bar Assn., Am. Legion, Moose. Roman Catholic. Avocations: reading, hunting. Criminal, Family and matrimonial, General practice. Office: 58884 Wright Rd Barnesville OH 43713-9799

**JEFFERS, JOHN WILLIAM,** lawyer; b. N.Y.C., May 11, 1936; s. William Hicks and Thelma Leone (Seeger) J.; children: Michael D., Thomas W., James B., John P. AB cum laude, Harvard U., 1958; JD, U. Pa., 1964. Bar: Ohio, 1964, U.S. Dist. Ct. (no. dist.) Ohio 1965. Assoc. Rosenthal,Roesch, Buckman & McLandrich, Cleve., 1964-67; assoc. Weston, Hurd, Fallon, Paisley & Howley, Cleve., 1967-71, ptnr., 1971—. Mem. Ohio Assn. Civil Trial Attys. (chmn. med. malpractice com. 1987-94, exec. com. 1990-97), Cleve. Bar Assn. (past chmn. Cuyahoga County Common Pleas and Ct. Appeals com.). Avocations: travel, tennis, basketball, volleyball, biking. State civil litigation, Personal injury, Product liability. Office: Weston Hurd Fallon Paisley & Howley 2500 Terminal Tower Cleveland OH 44113

**JEFFORDS, EDWARD ALAN,** former assistant state attorney general; b. Rector, Ark., Nov. 28, 1945; s. Roy Ezra and Sylvia Belle (Dickinson) J.; AA, Victor Valley Coll., 1967; student U. Wis. Mgmt. Inst., 1977; BS, USNY-Albany, 1983; JD, Baylor U. Sch. Law, 1985; postgrad. Harvard U., 1991; DHL (hon.) Harington Coll., 1976. Bar: Tex. 1985, U.S. Dist Ct. (we. dist.) Tex. 1985, U.S. Ct. Appeals (5th cir.) 1985, U.S. Dist. Ct. (so. dist.) Tex. 1986, U.S. Dist. Ct. (no. dist.) Tex. 1988, U.S. Supreme Ct. 1989; bd. cert. civil trial law, personal injury law, Tex. bd. legal specialization, 1990; cert. civil trial adv., Nat. Bd. Trial Advocacy, 1995. Editor, Auburn (Wash.) Globe-News, 1967-70; fine arts editor Tacoma News-Tribune, 1970-75; exec. dir. Ozark Inst., Eureka Springs, 1976-82; asst. atty. gen. State of Tex., Austin, 1985-92; exec. editor Baylor Law Rev., 1984-85; adj. prof. Nat. U. of Costa Rica, 1989-90; exec. dir. Pan Am. Ednl. Found., 1989—; trustee Regents Coll. Alumni Assn., USNY, 1990-99; advocate Nat. Coll. Advocacy. With USAF, 1963-67. Mem. ABA, Travis County Bar Assn., Tex. Trial Lawyers Assn., Assn. Trial Lawyers Am., Am. Judicature Assn., Order of Barrister, State Bar Coll., State Pro Bono Coll., Univ. Club, Million Dollar Adv. Forum, Delta Theta Phi. Office: PO Box 2521 Austin TX 78768-2521

**JEFFREYS, ALBERT LEONIDAS,** lawyer; b. Chase City, Va.; m. Lee H. Hickson. AB in History and Govt., Fla. So. Coll.; JD, So. Meth. U., 1969. Bar: Tex. 1971. Contract negotiator LTV Electro Systems, Dallas, 1960-71; corp. atty., asst. sec. Earth Resources Co., Dallas, 1971-73; gen. counsel, asst. sec. Liquid Paper Corp., Dallas, 1973-80; gen. counsel, dir. of contracts Electrospace Systems, Inc., Richardson, Tex., 1980-81; pvt. practice Richardson and Dallas, 1981—; gen. counsel Ratheal Cos., Garland, Tex., 1991-92; spl. counsel to office of econ. devel. City of Dallas, 1999—. Sgt. U.S. Army. Mem. ABA, Tex. Bar Assn., Dallas Bar Assn. General corporate, General practice, Probate. Home: 328 Huffhines St Richardson TX 75081-4113

**JEFFS, M. DAYLE,** lawyer; b. Provo, Utah, Mar. 7, 1930; s. Alvin Woolley and Melvina (Payne) J.; m. Janice Parker, Dec. 18, 1950; children: David D., James H., Robert L., William M. JD, U. Utah, 1957. Bar: Utah, U.S. Dist. Ct. (10th dist.), U.S. Supreme Ct. Ptnr. Jeffs & Jeffs, Provo, 1957—; county atty. Utah County, Provo, Utah, 1966-70; mem. ad hoc com. Am. Inns of Ct. of Judicial Conf., U.S., 1983-85; mem. adv. com. rules of evidence Utah Supreme Ct., 1986—, mem. task force on regulation of practice of law, 1990-91; mem. Utah State Bar Commn., 1979-85; mem. fed. rules com. U.S. Dist. Ct., Salt Lake City, 1990—; master of bench Am. Inn of Ct., Provo, 1983—. Rep. state del. Provo, 1990-96. With U.S. Army 1952-54. Mem. Defense Attys. Assn., Utah County Bar Assn. (pres. 1959). Mem. LDS Ch. Avocations: hunting, fishing, snowmobiling, boating, hiking. Fax: (801) 373-8878. Insurance, General civil litigation, Real property. Office: Jeffs & Jeffs PO Box 888 Provo UT 84603-0888

**JEHANI, AHMED,** lawyer; b. Beghazi, Libya, Oct. 15, 1946; came to U.S., 1972; s. Mohamed and Massauda (Kadiki) J.; m. Mariem Ghrairi, Nov. 12, 1994; 1 child, Lyn. LLM, Harvard U., 1973; MA, Tufts U., 1976, MALD, 1977, PhD, 1978. Legal cons. Boston, 1975-79; gen. counsel Ageco, B.P., Benshazi, Libya, 1967-75; sr. counsel World Bank, Washington, 1979—. Office: World Bank 1818 H St NW Washington DC 20433-0002

**JEHU, JOHN PAUL,** lawyer; b. N.Y.C., Oct. 17, 1908; s. John Milton and Pauline (Burger) J.; m. Dorothy Elvira Kellog Ferris (dec.); children: Lynn Jehu Amadon, Susan Jehu Kessler; m. Virginia Linder Corones, 1974; 1 stepson, James P. Student U. Munich, U. Leipzig, U. Erlangen, Germany, 1927-32; D in Roman and Canon Law, U. Erlangen, 1932; LLB, Cornell U., 1937. Bar: N.Y. 1939; U.S. Dist. Ct. (no. dist.) N.Y. 1954, U.S. Dist. Ct. (so., ea. dists.) N.Y. 1963, U.S. Ct. Appeals (2d cir.) 1965, U.S. Supreme Ct. 1968, U.S. Dist. Ct. (we. dist.) N.Y. 1971. Assoc. firm Sherry and Picarello, 1937-39; with contract div. Mergenthaler Linotype Co., 1937-42; research counsel Temp. N.Y. State Commn. for Revision and Codification of Laws relating to Mcpl. Fin., Albany, 1942-43, asst., then assoc. counsel to Joint Legis. Com. on State Edn. System, 1945-47, sr. atty. law div. State Edn. Dept., 1947-50, dir. law div., 1950-67, assoc. counsel to Bd. Regents, 1967-76, assoc. counsel State Dept. Edn., 1967-76; sole practice, Albany, 1976—; legal cons. to state comptroller, comptroller's com. on Constl. Tax and Debt Limitations and City-Sch. Fiscal Relations, Temp. State Commn. on Ednl. Fin.; assoc. prof. ednl. adminstrn. SUNY-Albany, 1956-76; spl. counsel V.I. Bd. Edn., 1967-68, assoc. counsel, 1968-76; lectr. univs., colls. including NYU, Rochester, SUNY-Buffalo. Bd. dirs. Albany Symphony Orch., 1973—, mem. exec. com., chmn. nominating com.; elder Presbyn. Ch. Author: (poetry) Autumn Leaves, 1989, Onomatology, 1993, Autobiography, 1995. Served with M.P., JAGC, AUS, 1943-45, ETO. Decorated 3 Battle Stars. Mem. N.Y. State Bar Assn., Albany County Bar Assn., Cornell Law Assn., St. David's Soc. (pres. Capital dist. 1976-84, counsellor state orgn. 1977—, hon. sec. 1980-87, v.p. 1988—), Am. Legion (Blanchard Post), Albany Inst. of History and Art, Nat. Welsh-Am. Found. (adv. coun. 1979—, counsel 1986—), Assn. Counsel Welsh-Am. Legal Def., Edn. & Devel. Fund (Twm Sion Cati), bd. dirs. English-Speaking Union, Torch Club, Capital Dist. Mineral Club, Evergreen Country, University, Cornell, Powysland (Welshpool, Wales), State Mus. Assocs. Episcopalian. Education and schools, Federal civil litigation, Constitutional. Address: 30 S Pearl St Ste 1100 Albany NY 12207-3425

**JELINCH, FRANK ANTHONY,** lawyer; b. San Jose, Calif., July 22, 1943; s. Frank Anthony and Minnie Leona J.; m. Roberta Katherine Magi, Dec. 27, 1975; 1 child, Michelle. BA cum laude, San Jose State U., 1965; JD, U. Calif., Berkeley, 1968. Bar: Calif. 1969, U.S. Dist. Ct. (no. dist.) Calif. 1969, U.S. Supreme Ct. 1972. Ptnr. Jelinch & Rendler, Cupertino, Calif., 1980—; instr. Lincoln U. Sch. Law, San Jose, 1980; founder Cupertino Nat. Bank. Chmn. San Francisco Shakespeare Festival, 1997-98, Terra Found., San Jose, 1980—; commr. Los Gatos Parks Commn., 1980-88, Cupertino Parks & Recreation, 1996—, Cupertino Fine Arts Commn., 1990-94. Capt. U.S. Army, 1969-73. Recipient Bronze Star, Oak Leaf Cluster, Vietnam. Mem. ABA, Sunnyvale-Cupertino Bar Assn. (pres. 1990), Cupertino C. of C. (pres. 1998-99), Santa Clara County Bar Assn., Calif. State Bar Assn., Santa Clara County Trial Lawyers Assn. Personal injury, General civil litigation, Insurance. Office: Jelinch & Rendler 20863 Stevens Creek Blvd Cupertino CA 95014-2125

**JELKIN, JOHN LAMOINE,** lawyer; b. Hildreth, Nebr., Dec. 24, 1952; s. Lamoine George and Verna Mae (DeJonge) J.; m. Diane Louise Davis, June 10, 1978; children: Jessica Jean, Jaclyn Jade. BA, Univ. Nebr., 1975; JD, U. Nebr., 1978. Bar: Nebr. 1978, U.S. Dist. Ct. Nebr. 1978. Assoc. Duncan & Duncan, Franklin, Nebr., 1978-81; ptnr. Duncan, Duncan & Jelkin, Franklin, 1981-87, Duncan, Duncan, Jelkin & Walker, Franklin, 1987—; bd. dirs. Nebr. Continuing Legal Edn., Inc., 1995—; sec.-treas. Hildreth Area Bus. Devel. Corp., 1983-88; dep. atty. Buffalo County, Kearney, Nebr., 1986. Vol. fireman; chmn. Franklin County Dems., 1984—; dep. atty. Franklin County, Nebr.; seminar presenter, speaker NCLE, Inc., 1991, 92, 93 94, 98; mem. ch. council St. Peters Luth. Ch., Hildreth, Nebr., 1988, pres., 1989-90; pres. Hildreth Alumni Assn., 1990-95, Hildreth Cmty. Improvement Project, 1992-93; active Hildreth Industrial Devel. Com., 1995, chmn., 1997; bd. dirs. Franklin County Cmty. Found., 1995—, Nebr. Child Abuse Prevention Fund, 1996—. Mem. ABA (mem. real estate probate & trust sect.), Nebr. Bar Assn. (exec. com. real estate, proate & trust sect. 1992-94, chmn. 1994-95, real estate practice guidelines com. 1991—), Buffalo County Bar Assn., Nebr. Assn. Trial Attys., 10th Jud. Bar Assn. (pres. 1983-84, 2nd pres. 1998—), Lions (bd. dirs. 1993—). Democrat. Lutheran. Lodge: Lions (pres. Hildreth 1985-86, v.p. 1982-85, sec. 1981-82). Probate, Real property, Personal income taxation. Office: Duncan Duncan Jelkin & Walker PO Box 340 Hildreth NE 68947-0340

**JENKINS, BRIAN RENNERT,** lawyer; b. Puunene, Hawaii, June 18, 1953; s. John Denison and Margaret (Rennert) J. BA in English, U. Hawaii, 1982; JD, Lewis and Clark Coll., 1986. Bar: Hawaii 1986, U.S. Dist. Ct. Hawaii 1986, U.S. Ct. Appeals (9th cir.) 1988. Assoc. Brown & Johnson, Honolulu, 1986-88, Boyce R. Brown, Jr., A.L.C., Honolulu, 1988, Rush, Moore et al, Honolulu and Wailuku, Hawaii, 1989-93; ptnr. Rush, Moore et al, Wailuku, Hawaii, 1993-95; ptnr. Brumbaugh & Jenkins, Wailuku, 1995—, Wailuku, Hawaii, 1986—. Mem. ABA, Hawaii Bar Assn. Avocations: history, natural sciences. Fax: 808-243-8293. E-mail: lawmaui@maui.net. Real property, Land use and zoning (including planning), General civil litigation. Office: Brumbaugh & Jenkins Wailuku Bus Plz 2065 Main St Ste 101 Wailuku HI 96793-1693

**JENKINS, BRUCE STERLING,** federal judge; b. Salt Lake City, Utah, May 27, 1927; s. Joseph and Bessie Pearl (Iverson) J.; m. Margaret Watkins, Sept. 19, 1952; children—Judith Margaret, David Bruce, Michael Glen, Carol Alice. BA with high honors, U. Utah, 1949, LLB, 1952, JD, 1952. Bar: Utah 1952, U.S. Dist. Ct. 1952, U.S. Supreme Ct. 1962, U.S. Circuit Ct. Appeals 1962. Pvt. practice Salt Lake City, 1952-59; assoc. firm George McMillan, 1959-65; asst. atty. gen. State of Utah, 1952; dep. county atty. Salt Lake County, 1954-58; bankruptcy judge U.S. Dist. Ct., Utah, 1965-78, judge, 1978—, chief judge, 1984-93; adj. prof. U. Utah, 1987-88, 96—. Research, publs. in field; contbr. essays to Law jours.; bd. editors: Utah Law Rev, 1951-52. Mem. Utah Senate, 1959-65, minority leader, 1963, pres. senate, 1965, vice chmn. commn. on orgn. exec. br. of Utah Govt., 1965-66; Mem. adv. com. Utah Tech. Coll., 1967-72; mem. instl. council Utah State U., 1976. Served with USN, 1945-46. Named Alumnus of Yr. award Coll. Law Univ. Utah, 1985; recipient Admiration and Appreciation award Utah State Bar, 1995, Emeritus Merit of Honor award U. Utah Alumni Assn., 1997. Fellow Am. Bar Found.; mem. ABA, Am. Inn Ct., Utah State Bar Assn. (Judge of Yr. 1993), Salt Lake County Bar Assn., Fed. Bar Assn. (Disting. Jud. Svc. awrd Utah chpt. 1993), Order of Coif, Phi Beta Kappa, Phi Kappa Phi, Phi Eta Sigma, Phi Sigma Alpha, Tau Kappa Alpha. Democrat. Mormon. Office: US Dist Ct 462 US Courthouse 350 S Main St Ste 150 Salt Lake City UT 84101-2180

**JENKINS, DAVID LYNN,** lawyer; b. Madison, Wis., Feb. 9, 1943; s. Roger Dewey and Dorothy Joanna (Cuff) J.; m. Kristine Jane Kettunen, July 13, 1974; children—Siiri Lynn, Alison Jane, Jonathon Pryce, Philip Kettunen. J.D., U. Wis., 1972. Bar: Wis. 1972, U.S. Dist. Ct. (we. dist.) Wis. 1972. Assoc. R.D. Endicott & Assoc., Hillsboro, Wis., 1972-77; ptnr. Jenkins and Stittleburg, Viroqua, Wis., 1977—; city atty. Viroqua, 1978—. Treas. Vernon County Republican Party, Viroqua, 1983. Served to sgt. U.S. Army, 1966-69; W. Ger. Mem. Vernon County Bar Assn. Real property, Personal income taxation, Contracts commercial. Home: 428 S Main St Viroqua WI 54665-2056 Office: Jenkins and Stittleburg 428 S Main St Viroqua WI 54665-2056

**JENKINS, JAMES C.,** lawyer; b. Logan, Utah, July 16, 1948. BA in Fin., U. Utah, 1972; JD, Gonzaga U., 1976. Bar: Utah 1976, U.S. Dist. Ct. Utah 1976, U.S. Ct. Appeals (10th cir.) 1992, U.S. Tax Ct. 1985, U.S. Supreme Ct. 1981. Ptnr. Olson & Hoggan, P.C., Logan, Utah; Rich county atty., 1978-81, Cache county dep. atty., 1981-95; gen. counsel Bear Lake Spl. Svcs. Dist., Rich County, Utah, 1978—; instr. Utah State U., 1976; trustee Utah Bankruptcy Ct., 1977-80. Chair jud. conduct commn. Utah Jud. Coun., 1996-97, mem. jud. performance and evaluation com., mem. adv. bd. Utah State Crime Lab. Mem. ABA (trial practice com., litig. sect. 1986-95), Utah State Bar Assn. (pres.-elect 1997-98, pres. 1998-99, law benefit com. 1978-80, law day com. 1989-90, ethics and discipline com. 1992-93, exec. com., litig. com. 1993-95, bd. commrs. 1993-96), Utah Statewide Assn. Pros., Cache County Bar Assn. (sec.-treas. 1978-81). General civil litigation, Real property, Personal injury. Office: Olson & Hoggan PC PO Box 525 88 W Center St Logan UT 84323-0525*

**JENKINS, JOHN RICHARD, III,** lawyer; b. Phila., Apr. 14, 1946; s. John Richard Jr. and Barbara (Ladd) J.; m. Judy Long, June 19, 1971; children: Leigh, John IV, Matthew. BA, UCLA, 1968; JD, U. Tex., 1971; LLM, So. Meth. U., 1977. Bar: Tex. 1971, U.S. Dist. Ct. (no. dist.) Tex. 1972, U.S. Tax Ct. 1972. Cert. Tax Law Tex. Bd. Legal Splization. Assoc. Law, Snakard, Brown & Gambill, Ft. Worth, 1971-72; chief counsel Nu-Way Oil, Ft. Worth, 1972-73; assoc. Ashley & Welch, Dallas, 1973-78; ptnr. Tanner & Jenkins, Dallas, 1978-80, McMullen, Porter, Jenkins, Smith, Dallas, 1980-87, Graham Bright & Smith, Dallas, 1987-91; pvt. practice Dallas, 1991—. spkr. estate planning, 1980—. Past pres. YMCA, 1988. Mem. ABA, Dallas Bar Assn., Rotary, Masons (past master). Republican. Methodist. Avocation: golf. Corporate taxation, Estate taxation, Taxation, general. Office: 14651 Dallas Pkwy Ste 102 Dallas TX 75240-8887

**JENKINS, OLNEY DALE,** lawyer; b. Ludowici, Ga., Oct. 9, 1952; s. Olney Alexander and Olive Modesta (Howard) J.; children: Jessica Dawn, Shelsea Brooke. BA, Auburn U., 1974; JD, Oglethorpe U., 1984. Bar: Ga., U.S. Dist. Ct. (so. and no. dists.) Ga., U.S. Ct. Appeals (llth cir.). Pvt. practice, Darien, Ga., 1985—. Mem. ABA, State Bar Ga., Assn. Trial Lawyers Am., Nat. Assn. Criminal Def. Lawyers, Ga. Assn. Criminal Def. Lawyers, Ga. Trial Lawyers Assn. Criminal, Personal injury. Office: PO Box 1168 Darien GA 31305-1168

**JENKINS, RICHARD ERIK,** patent lawyer; b. Newport News, Va., Jan. 12, 1946; s. Willard Erette and Ina Beatrice (Porter) J.; m. Susan Rankin Thurston, Aug. 24, 1968 (div. Nov. 1991); 1 child, Anna. BS, N.C. State U., 1968, M in Stats. and Econs., 1971; JD, U. N.C., 1975. Engr. Celanese Corp., Charlotte, N.C., 1971-72; assoc. atty. Stevens, Davis, Miller & Mosher, Washington, D.C., 1975-76, Bell, Seltzer, Park & Gibson, Charlotte, N.C., 1976-78; ptnr. Adams &Jenkins, Charlotte, 1978-80; asst. patent counsel Burlington Industries, Inc., Greensboro, N.C., 1980-84; sr. ptnr. Jenkins & Wilson, Durham, N.C., 1984—; adj. assoc. prof. Duke U., Durham, 1989—, N.C. State U., Raleigh, N.C., 1992—. Trustee N.C. Ctrl. U., Durham, 1992-95; bd. govs. Univ. Club, Durham, 1994-98; bd. dirs. Coun. Entrepreneurial Devel., 1988-90. Mem. AMA, N.C. Bar Assn., Rotary, Hope Valley Country Club, Univ. Club, Carolina Club. Republican. Presbyn. Avocations: golf, yard, reading, sports cars. Patent, Intellectual property. Office: Jenkins & Wilson PA 3100 Tower Blvd Ste 1400 Durham NC 27707-2575

**JENKINS, ROBERT ROWE,** lawyer; b. Norwalk, Ohio, Aug. 8, 1933; s. Robert Leslie and Millie Leona (Rowe) J.; m. Francis Jean Cline, June 12, 1955 (div. July 1972); children: Diane Elaine, Katherine Eileen; m. Jean Dingus, July 9, 1972. Student, Lebanon Valley Coll., 1951-55; BS in Chemistry, Eastern Coll. (now U. Balt.), 1967; JD, U. Balt., 1975. Bar: Md. 1976, U.S. Dist. Ct. Md. 1976, U.S. Ct. Appeals (4th cir.) 1979, U.S. Supreme Ct. 1979. Atty. Social Security Adminstrn., Balt., 1975-76; trial atty. Nelson R. Kandel, Balt., 1976-77; sole practice Balt., 1977-81; ptnr. Jenkins Block & Mering, Balt., 1981—; faculty continuing profl. edn. of lawyers Md. Inst., Balt., 1986—. Ruling elder Faith Christian Fellowship Presbyterian Ch. Am., Balt., 1982—. Served with U.S. Coast Guard, 1955-59. Mem. ABA, Md. Bar Assn., Balt. City Bar Assn., Assn. Trial Lawyers Am., Md. Trial Lawyers Assn., Christian Legal Soc., Nat. Orgn. Social Security Claimant's Rep. (exec. com.). Republican. Avocations: fishing, boating. Administrative and regulatory, Pension, profit-sharing, and employee benefits, Personal injury. Home: 1003 Travers St Cambridge MD 21613-1543 Office: Jenkins Block and Assocs 711 W 40th St Ste 235 Baltimore MD 21211-2186 also: 1011 E Main St Ste 212 Richmond VA 23219-3537 also: 516 Poplar St Cambridge MD 21613-1834 also: 33 W Franklin St Ste 102 Hagerstown MD 21740-4826

**JENKINS, RONALD WAYNE,** lawyer; b. Johnson City, Tenn., Aug. 14, 1950; s. James Herman and Peggy Sue (Hutchison) J.; children: April Chalice, Kimberly Michelle, Robert Herman, Ronald Wayne II. BSEE, U. Tenn., 1972, JD, 1980. Bar: Tenn. 1980, U.S. Supreme Ct. 1986, U.S. Ct. Appeals (6th cir.) 1986, U.S. Dist. Ct. (ea. dist.) Tenn. 1986. Assoc. M. Lacy West, P.C., Kingsport, Tenn., 1980-83, Herndon, Coleman, Brading & McKee, Johnson City, 1984-86; ptnr. Herndon, Coleman, Brading & McKee, 1986—. Editor-in-chief Tenn. Law Rev., 1979. Mem. ABA, Tenn. Bar Assn., Washington County Bar Assn., Nat. Aeronautic Assn., Aircraft Owners and Pilots Assn., Tau Beta Pi (Tenn. col.), Eta Kappa Nu. Avocations: agriculture, aviation. General civil litigation, Insurance, Professional liability. Office: Herndon Coleman PO Box 1160 104 E Main St Johnson City TN 37604-5735

**JENKINSON, WILLIAM ELDRIDGE, III,** lawyer; b. Kingstree, S.C., June 27, 1946; s. William Eldridge Jr. and Gordon (Brockington) J.; m. Salley K. Jenkinson, July 20, 1974; children: William E. IV, Anne Gordon, Louisa K. BA, The Citadel, 1968; JD, U. S.C., 1971. Bar: S.C., U.S. Dist. Ct. S.C., U.S. Ct. Appeals (4th cir.), U.S. Supreme Ct. Sr. ptnr. Jenkinson & Jenkinson, P.A., Kingstree, S.C., 1971—. Vice chmn., bd. vis. The Citadel, Charleston, S.C., 1992—; trustee The Meth. Oaks, Orangeburg, S.C., 1997—; sec. Williamsburgh Hist. Soc., Kingstree, 1990—. 1st lt. U.S. Army, 1971. Mem. Lions. General civil litigation, Contracts commercial, Criminal. Office: Jenkinson & Jenkinson PA 120 W Main St Kingstree SC 29556-3344

**JENKS, GEORGE MILAN,** retired lawyer; b. Dickinson, N.D., Feb. 26, 1933; s. John Leo and Mary Magdalene (Bleth) J.; m. Elaine Marjorie Ketterling, May 12, 1956; children: Gregory Martell, Jeffrey Michael. AS in Civil Engring., Multnomah Jr. Coll., 1958; BS, U. Oreg., 1960, MEd, 1961; JD, Lewis & Clark Coll., 1971. Bar: Oreg. 1972, U.S. Ct. Appeals, 1977, U.S. Supreme Ct. 1977. Assoc. Law Firm David Weinstein, Portland, Oreg., 1972-75; sr. ptnr. Jenks & Weinstein, P.C., Portland, 1975-98; retired, 1998, ret., 1998; lectr., instr. Bus. Law Inst., Portland, 1975-82; sec. Levesque & Assocs., Portland, 1985—; advisor ct. rules Multnomah County Dist. Ct. Contbr. articles to profl. jours. Pres. Milwaukie (Oreg.) Luth. Ch., 1973-75; bd. dirs. Luth. Family Svcs. Oreg. and S.W. Wash., 1975-82; chmn. bd. dirs. Milwaukie Luth. Found., 1975—. With U.S. Army, 1953-56. Mem. ABA, Oreg. State Bar Assn., Multnomah County Bar Assn., Clackamas County Bar Assn., Kiwanis. Republican. Avocations: fishing, clamming, crabbing, boating, gardening. Landlord-tenant, Probate, General practice. Office: Jenks and Weinstein 1112 NE 21st Ave Portland OR 97232-2114

**JENNER, EVA CATHERINE,** lawyer; b. Taipei, Taiwan, Feb. 2, 1968; d. William John and Kitty J. BA, U. Calif., 1990; JD magna cum laude, Syracuse U., 1995. Bar: N.Y. 1996. Paralegal Hawaii Lawyers Care, Honolulu, 1992; legal intern Bklyn. Legal Svcs., N.Y.C., 1993; assoc. Rogers & Wells, N.Y.C., 1995-97; staff atty., Cleary fellow Lawyers Alliance N.Y., N.Y.C., 1998; assoc. Cleary, Gottlieb, Steen & Hamilton, N.Y.C., 1997—. Andrews scholar Syracuse U., 1992-95. Democrat. Buddhist. Avocations: painting, photography, basketball. Mergers and acquisitions, Securities, General corporate. Office: 1 Liberty Plz Fl 38 New York NY 10006-1470

**JENNETTE, NOBLE STEVENSON, III,** lawyer; b. Brunswick, Ga., May 20, 1953; s. Noble Stevenson Jr. and Geraldine Elanor (Emmanuel) J.; m. Linda Lee King, May 13, 1978; children: N. Stevenson IV, Emily King, Nicholas Andrew. BS, Ind. U., 1980; JD cum laude, Harvard U., 1984. Bar: Ind. 1984, U.S. Dist. Ct. Ind. 1984, Mich. 1986, U.S. Dist. Ct. Mich. 1987, U.S. Ct. Appeals (6th and 7th cirs.) 1989, U.S. Supreme Ct. 1990. Assoc. Baker & Daniels, Indpls., 1984-86; assoc. Varnum, Riddering, Schmidt & Howlett, Grand Rapids, Mich., 1987-90, ptnr., 1991—; vice chairperson zoning and land use com. State Bar Mich., Lansing, 1989-92. Author: Real Estate Development: Business, Commercial, Industrial and Major Residential Properties, 4 vols., 1988, A Practical Guide to Obtaining Land Use Approvals and Permits, 1989; contbr. articles to profl. publs. With USN, 1971-74. Mem. ABA (child custody com. family law sect. 1993—), Grand Rapids Hockey Assn. (commr.), Harvard Club Western Mich. Avocations: ice hockey, writing. Family and matrimonial, General civil litigation, Land use and zoning (including planning). Home: 1094 Idema Dr SE Grand Rapids MI 49506-3149 Office: Varnum Riddering Schmidt & Howlett PO Box 352 Grand Rapids MI 49501-0352

**JENNINGS, JAMES WILSON, JR.,** lawyer; b. Temple, Tex., Aug. 10, 1943; s. James W. and Mary Lee (Patton) J.; m. Anne Rita Moran, Aug. 9, 1969; children: Helene, Anne Conway, Mary. BA in English, Washington and Lee U., 1965, JD, 1972. Bar: Va. 1972, U.S. Dist. Ct. (we. dist.) Va. 1972, U.S. Ct. Appeals (4th cir.) 1980, U.S. Supreme Ct. 1991. Law clk. Supreme Ct. of Va., Richmond, 1972-73; ptnr. Woods, Rogers & Hazlegrove, Roanoke, Va., 1973—; adj. prof. Washington and Lee Sch. of Law, 1999—. Chmn. bd. editors Jour. Civil Litig., 1990-94, Mcpl. Liability Reporter, 1990-93; bd. editors Def. Coun. Jour.; contbr. articles to profl. jours. Co-chmn. drive for attys. United Way, 1975; chmn. fund drive for attys. Am. Cancer Soc., 1976; bd. dirs. Art Mus. of Western Va., v.p., 1995; bd. dirs. Opera Roanoke, 1988-96, pres., 1996; trustee Funds of Diocese of Southwestern Va.; v.p. Art Mus. of Western Va., 1995-96. Lt. (j.g.) USN, 1965-69. Fellow Va. Law Found., 1997. Fellow Va. Law Found.; mem. ABA, Nat. Assn. Ry. Trial Counsel, Am. Bd. Trial Advocates (pres. Va. chpt. 1995-96), Va. Bar Assn., Va. Assn. Def. Attys. (pres. 1988-89), Roanoke City Bar Assn., Internat. Assn. Def. Counsel, Assn. Def. Trial Attys. (exec. coun. 1997—, v.p. 1999), Def. Rsch. Inst. (Exceptional Performance citation 1989), Assn. Internat. de Droit des Assurances, Downtown Roanoke Inc. (bd. dirs. 1981-89), Washington and Lee Alumni Assn. (bd. dirs. 1984-88), Roanoke Regional C. of C. (bd. dirs. 1989-93), Order of Coif, Roanoke Country Club (bd. govs.), Shenandoah Club. Episcopalian. Federal civil litigation, General civil litigation, Product liability. Home: 2710 Rosalind Ave SW Roanoke VA 24014-2330 Office: Woods Rogers & Hazlegrove 10 S Jefferson St Ste 1400 Roanoke VA 24011-1314

**JENNINGS, KATHLEEN M.,** laweyr; b. Wilmington, Del., Apr. 4, 1953; d. George and Margaret (Rafal) Bosch; m. William Jennings, May 4, 1983 (div.); children: William E., Rebecca; m. Carl E. Hostetter, June 13, 1998. BA, U. Del., 1975; JD, Villanova U., 1978. Bar: Del. 1978, U.S. Dist. Ct. Del. 1978. Dep. atty. gen. State of Del., Wilmington, 1978-83, 84-93, chief dep. atty. gen., 1993-95; assoc. Bayard, Brill & Handelman, Wilmington, 1983-84; ptnr. Oberly & Jennings, Wilmington, 1995—. Active Big Bros./Big Sisters program of United Way; dive rescue vol. Mem. Nat. Assn. Criminal Def. Lawyers, Del Trial Lawyers Assn., Del. Assn. Criminal Def. Lawyers, Del. Bar Assn. (exec. com., past sec.). Office: Oberly Jennings & Drexler 800 Delaware Ave Wilmington DE 19801-1322

**JENNINGS, THOMAS PARKS,** lawyer; b. Alexandria, Va., Nov. 16, 1947; s. George Christian and Ellen (Thompson) J.; m. Shelley Corrine Abernathy, Oct. 30, 1971; 1 child, Kathleen Eaye. BA in History, Wake Forest U., 1970; JD, U. Va., 1975. Bar: Va. 1975. Assoc. Lewis, Wilson, Lewis & Jones, Arlington, Va., 1975-78; atty. First Va. Banks, Inc., Falls Church, 1978-80, gen. counsel, 1980—, sec., 1993—, sr. v.p., 1995—; adj. prof. George Mason U. Sch. Law, Arlington, 1987-88. Trustee Arlington Cmty. Found., 1998—; dir. Rixey St. Found., Inc., 1997—; deacon Georgetown Presbyn. Ch., Washington, 1979-82, elder, 1982-85, 95-97, trustee, 1988-90. With U.S. Army, 1970-71. Mem. ABA, Am. Soc. Corp. Secs., Va. State Bar Assn., Va. Bankers Assn. (legal affairs com.), Fairfax County Bar Assn., Am. Corp. Counsel Assn., Washington Met. Area Corp. Counsel Assn. (bd. dirs. 1984-87). Avocations: bridge, kayaking. Banking, Contracts commercial, General corporate. Office: First Va Banks Inc 6400 Arlington Blvd Ste 420 Falls Church VA 22042-2336

**JENSCH, CHARLES CAMPBELL,** lawyer; b. St. Paul, Apr. 15, 1929; s. Charles C. Jensch and Dorothy Blanche (Tilden) Stoms; m. Helen Joan Alan, Jan. 26, 1957; children: Jeanne, Clifton, Diana, Charles, Marianne, Chistine. AB, Williams Coll., 1950; JD, U. Mich., 1953. Bar: Ill. 1953, Minn. 1978; cert. real property law specialist. Assoc. Wilson & McIlvaine, Chgo., 1953-58; sec. Story & Clark Piano Co., Chgo., 1958-60; v.p. A.E. Staley Mfg. Co., Decatur, Ill., 1960-69; pres., sec. Sunstar Foods, Inc., Mpls., 1969-80; v.p., dir. Petersen, Tews & Squires, St. Paul, 1980-96; of counsel Krass Monroe, P.A., Mpls., 1997—. Mem. Minn. State Bar Assn. Landlord-tenant, Real property. Home: 197 Avon St S Saint Paul MN 55105-3319 Office: Krass Monroe PA Southpoint Office Ctr 1650 West 82nd St Ste 1100 Minneapolis MN 55431-1447

**JENSEN, D. LOWELL,** federal judge, lawyer, government official; b. Brigham, Utah, June 3, 1928; s. Wendell and Elnora (Hatch) J.; m. Barbara Cowin, Apr. 20, 1951; children: Peter, Marcia, Thomas. A.B. in Econs, U. Calif.-Berkeley, 1949, LL.B., 1952. Bar: Calif. 1952. Dep. dist. atty. Alameda County, 1955-66, asst. dist. atty., 1966-69, dist. atty., 1969-81; asst. atty. gen. criminal div. Dept. Justice, Washington, 1981-83, assoc. atty. gen., 1983-85, dep. atty. gen., 1985-86; judge U.S. Dist. Ct. (no. dist.) Calif., Oakland, 1986—; mem. Calif. Council on Criminal Justice, 1974-81; past pres. Calif. Dist. Atty.'s Assn. Served with U.S. Army, 1952-54. Fellow Am. Coll. Trial Lawyers; mem. Nat. Dist. Atty.'s Assn. (victim/witness commn. 1974-81), Boalt Hall Alumni Assn. (past pres.). Office: US Dist Ct 1301 Clay St Rm 490C Oakland CA 94612-5217

**JENSEN, DALLIN W.,** lawyer; b. Afton, Wyo., June 2, 1932; s. Louis J. and Nellie B. Jensen; m. Barbara J. Bassett, Mar. 22, 1958; children: Brad L., Julie N. BS, Brigham Young U., 1954; JD, U. Utah, 1960. Bar: Utah 1960, U.S. Dist. Ct. Utah 1962, U.S. Ct. Appeals (10th cir.) 1974, U.S. Ct. Appeals D.C. 1980, U.S. Supreme Ct. 1971. Asst. atty. gen. Utah Atty. Gen., Salt Lake City, 1960-83, solicitor gen., 1983-88; shareholder Parsons, Behle & Latimer, Salt Lake City, 1988—; alt. commr. Upper Colo. River Commn., 1983—; mem. Colo. River Basin Salinity Adv. Council, 1975—; spl. legal cons. Nat. Water Commn., Washington, 1971-73; mem. energy law center adv. council U. Utah Coll. Law, 1976—. Mem. editl. bd. Rocky Mountain Mineral Law Found., 1983-85. Author: (with Wells A. Hutchins) The Utah Law of Water Rights, 1965. Contbr. articles on water law and water resource mgmt. to profl. jours. Served with U.S. Army, 1955-57. Mem. LDS Ch. Natural resources, Real property, Administrative and regulatory. Home: 3565 S 2175 E Salt Lake City UT 84109-2902 Office: PO Box 45898 Salt Lake City UT 84145-0898

**JENSEN, DARRELL ALF,** lawyer; b. Columbus, Ga., Feb. 13, 1942; s. Alf Henry Jensen and Charlotte E. Olson; m. Barbara A. Yuzer, June 8, 1968; children: Andrea, Christine. BA, U. Minn., 1967; JD, William Mitchell Coll. Law, 1973. Bar: Minn. 1973. Ptnr. Barna, Guzy & Steffen, Ltd., Mpls. With USN, Vietnam. Mem. ABA, Minn. Bar Assn., Hennepin County Bar Assn., Anoka County Bar Assn. Fax: 612-780-1777. E-mail: djensen1@ix.netcom.com and djensen@bgslaw.com. General civil litigation, Land use and zoning (including planning), Alternative dispute resolution. Office: 200 Coon Rapids Blvd NW Ste 400 Minneapolis MN 55433-5894

**JENSEN, DOUGLAS BLAINE,** lawyer; b. Fresno, Calif., Feb. 10, 1943; s. Rodger Blaine and Margaret Mae J.; m. Lesley S. Smith, Sept. 4, 1967 (div.); children—Clayton B., Kelly E.; m. Patty Stocking Telles, Aug. 5, 1988. AB, Stanford U., 1964, JD, 1967. Bar: Calif. 1967, U.S. Dist. Ct. (ea. dist.) Calif., U.S. Dist. Ct. (no. dist.) Calif., U.S. Ct. Appeals (9th cir.). Clk. to judge U.S. Ct. Appeals 9th Cir., Fresno and San Francisco, 1967-68; Internat. Legal Ctr. fellow, Santiago, Chile, 1968-70; assoc. Miller, Groezinger, Pettit, Evers & Martin, San Francisco, 1970-72, Baker, Manock & Wanger, Fresno, Calif., 1972-74; ptnr. Baker, Manock & Jensen, Fresno, 1974—; adj. prof. water law San Joaquin Coll. Law, 1980-83. Chmn. Valley Children's Hosp., 1976-93 . Mem. ABA, State Bar Calif., Fresno County Bar Assn. (pres. 1982-83). Club: Rotary (pres. 1992-93). Contbr. article to legal publ. Real property, General corporate, Municipal (including bonds). Office: 5260 N Palm Ave Ste 421 Fresno CA 93704-2217

**JENSEN, HOWARD FERNANDO,** lawyer; b. Olympia, Wash., Feb. 8, 1969; s. Robert Victor and Maria Inez Jensen. BA in History, Whitman Coll., Walla Walla, Wash., 1991; JD, U. Wash., 1995. Bar: Wash. 1995, U.S. Dist. Ct. (we. dist.) Wash. 1997. Assoc. Ogden Murphy Wallace PLLC, Seattle, 1995—. Mem. Wash. State Bar Assn., King County Bar Assn., Wash. State Assn. Mcpl. Attys. Environmental, Land use and zoning (including planning), Real property. Office: Ogden Murphy Wallace PLLC 1601 5th Ave Ste 2100 Seattle WA 98101-1686

**JENSEN, JILL ELLEN,** lawyer; b. Modesto, Calif., Oct. 30, 1967; d. Jack Lowell and June Ellen Jensen. BA, NYU, 1990; JD, Lewis & Clark U., 1995. Bar: Alaska 1996, U.S. Dist. Ct. Alaska 1996. Assoc. Leutwyler, Brion & Assocs., Anchorage, Alaska, 1996-98, Fortier & Mikko, P.C., Anchorage, Alaska, 1998—. Mem. ABA (Alaska pro bono panel 1996—), Alaska Bar Assn. (young lawyers rep. historian's com. 1998—, mem. law-related edn. com. 1999—). Democrat. Avocations: reading, computers, animals, travel. Criminal, Appellate, General civil litigation. Office: Fortier & Mikko PC 2550 Denali St Ste 1500 Anchorage AK 99503-2753

**JENSEN, JOHN ROBERT,** lawyer; b. Rapid City, S.D., Aug. 9, 1946; s. Edwin Robert and Roxina Althier (Hollinger) J.; m. Susan McClelland, Aug. 27, 1977; children: Margaret Marie, Jennifer Jo, Edwin Robert II, James Peder. BA, Calif. State U.-Northridge, 1971; JD, Baylor U., 1976. Bar: Tex. 1977, U.S. Dist. Ct. (no. dist.) Tex. 1977, U.S. Ct. Appeals (5th cir.) 1982. Asst. ins. dir. Groesbeck Fin., Los Angeles, 1971-73; v.p. Capital Cons., Dallas, 1973-74; assoc. McConnell & Assocs., Arlington, Tex., 1977; sole practice, Arlington, 1978-84; ptnr. Jensen & Jensen, Arlington, 1984—. Author: Checklist for Texas Lawyers, 1979, 81. Served with U.S. Army, 1966-68, Vietnam. Decorated Army Commendation medal. Mem. Arlington Bar Assn., Baylor Order Barristers, Tex. Bd. Legal Specialization (cert. personal injury trial law), Nat. Bd. Trial Adv. (cert. civil trial adv.), Delta Theta Phi (treas. Baylor chpt. 1976). Lutheran. State civil litigation, Personal injury, Federal civil litigation. Office: Jensen & Jensen 6025 Interstate 20 W Arlington TX 76017-1077

**JENSEN, LANCE PRIEST,** prosecutor; b. Palo Alto, Calif., May 18, 1960; s. Pierce Andrew Jensen Jr. and Pat Priest Hansing; m. Ann Elizabeth Moore, Feb. 5, 1994; 1 child, Elizabeth. BS, U. So. Calif., L.A., 1982; JD, Western State Law Sch., 1989. Dept. dist. atty. Orange County Dist. Atty., Santa Ana, Calif., 1990—. Bd. mem. North Tustin Adv. Com., Santa Ana, 1997—. Mem. Calif. Dist. Attys. Assn., Calif. Hazardous Materials Investigators Assn., Orange County Bar Assn. (bd. dirs. 1996—), Assn. Orange County Dep. Dist. Attys. (bd. dirs. 1992—, named Outstanding Prosecutor 1994), Orange County Lincoln Club. Republican. Avocations: skiing, woodworking. Home: 13681 Newport Ave # 8610 Tustin CA 92780-4689 Office: Orange County Dist Atty Office 700 Civic Center Dr W Santa Ana CA 92701-4045

**JENSEN, RICHARD CURRIE,** lawyer; b. Flushing, N.Y., June 5, 1939; s. David T. and Isabel (Currie) J.; m. Leslie Dodge, Jan. 9, 1965; children: Tracy, Richard, David, Meredith, Lauren, Christopher. BS in Social Studies, Villanova U., 1961; JD, Fordham U., 1964. Bar: N.Y. 1965. Staff atty. Comml. Union Ins. Co., N.Y.C., 1965-67; ptnr. Morris, Duffy, Ivone & Jensen, N.Y.C., 1967-85, Ivone, Devine & Jensen, Lake Success, N.Y., 1985—. Mem. ABA, N.Y. State Bar Assn., Nassau County Bar Assn., Am. Soc. Law & Medicine. Republican. Roman Catholic. Personal injury, Product liability, State civil litigation. Office: Ivone Devine & Jensen 2001 Marcus Ave Ste 100N New Hyde Park NY 11042-1024

**JENSEN, WALTER EDWARD,** lawyer, educator; b. Chgo., Oct. 20, 1937. A.B., U. Colo., 1959; J.D., Ind. U., 1962, M.B.A., 1964; Ph.D. (Univ. fellow), Duke U., 1972. Bar: Ind. 1962, Ill. 1962, D.C. 1963, U.S. Tax Ct. 1982, U.S. Supreme Ct. 1967. Assoc. prof. Colo. State U., 1964-66; assoc. prof. Ill. State U., 1970-72; prof. bus. adminstrn. Va. Poly. Inst. and State U., beginning 1972, now prof. fin., ins. and law; with Inst. Advanced Legal Studies, U. London, 1983-84; prof. U.S. Air Force Grad. Mgmt. Program, Europe, 1977-78, 83-85; Duke U. legal research awardee, researcher, Guyana, Trinidad and Tobago, 1967; vis. lectr. pub. internat. law U. Istanbul, 1988, Roberts Coll. U. of Bosporous, Istanbul, Uludag Univ., Turkey, 1988; researcher U. London Inst. Advanced Legal Studies, London Sch. Econs. and Inst. Commonwealth Studies, summers, 1969, 71, 74, 76, winter 1972-73; Ford Found. research fellow Ind. U., 1963-64; faculty research fellow in econs. U. Tex., 1968; Bell Telephone fellow in econs. regulated pub. utilities U. Chgo., 1965. Recipient Dissertation Travel award Duke U. Grad. sch., 1968; Ind. U. fellow, 1963, 74, scholar, 1963-64. Mem. D.C. Bar Assn., Ill. Bar Assn., Ind. bar Assn., ABA, Am. Polit. sci. Assn., Am. Soc. Internat. Law, Am. Judicature Soc., Am. Bus. Law Assn., Alpha Kappa Psi, Phi Alpha Delta, Pi Gamma Mu, Pi Kappa Alpha, Beta Gamma Sigma. Contbr. articles to profl. publs.; staff editor Am. Bus Law Jour., 1973—; vice chmn. assoc. editor for adminstrv. law sect. young lawyers Barrister (Law Notes), 1975-83; book rev. and manuscript editor Justice System Jour: A Mgmt. Rev., 1975—; staff editor Bus. Law Rev., 1975—. Home: PO Box 250 Blacksburg VA 24063-0250 Office: Va Poly Inst and State U Blacksburg VA 24060

**JENSEN, WILLIAM POWELL,** lawyer; b. Newport, R.I., Apr. 4, 1963; s. William Marvin and Jean (Powell) J.; m. Robin R. Jensen. BS in Indsl. Engring., Tex. A&M U., 1985; JD, St. Mary's U., 1989. Bar: Tex. 1989. Law clk. Matthews and Assoc. LLP, Houston, 1987, 88; rsch. asst. St. Mary's Law Sch., 1988; law clk. Gunn, Lee and Miller, San Antonio, 1988; equity participating assoc. Matthews and Assoc. LLP, Houston, 1989-96, Browing Bushman, Houston, 1997—; cons. Houston Vol. Lawyers, 1989; designated expert in litig., Houston, 1994-95; bd. dirs. K.K.G. Enterprises, Inc., San Antonio; spkr. Tex. A&M U., College Station, 1993—. Author: (with others) Punitive Damages, Modern Dictionary for the Legal Profession, 1993; contbr. articles to profl. jours. Youth counselor Chapelwood Meth. Ch., Houston, 1990-92; pres. Korean Martial Arts Acad., Houston, 1993-94. Mem. State Bar Tex., Am. Intellectual Property Law Assn., Houston Intellectual Property Law Assn. Avocations: martial arts, running. Trademark and copyright, Intellectual property, Patent. Office: Browning Bushman 5718 Westheimer Rd Ste 1800 Houston TX 77057-5771

**JENTZ, GAYLORD ADAIR,** law educator; b. Beloit, Wis., Aug. 7, 1931; s. Merlyn Adair and Delva (Mullen) J.; m. JoAnn Mary Hornung, Aug. 6, 1955; children: Katherine Ann, Gary Adair, Loretta Ann, Rory Adair. BA, U. Wis., 1953, JD, 1957, MBA, 1958. Bar: Wis. 1957. Pvt. practice law Madison, 1957-58; from instr. to assoc. prof. bus. law U. Okla., 1958-65; vis. instr. to vis. prof. U. Wis. Law Sch., summers 1957-65; asso. prof. to prof. U. Tex., Austin, 1965-68, prof., 1968-98, prof. emeritus, 1998—, Herbert D. Kelleher prof. bus. law, 1982-98, chmn. gen. bus. dept., 1968-74, 80-86. Author: (with others) Business Law Text and Cases, 1968, Business Law Text, 1978, Texas Uniform Commercial Code, 1967, rev. edit., 1975, West's Business Law: Alternate Edition, 7th edit., 1999, Legal Environment of Business, 1989, Texas Family Law, 7th edit., 1992, West's Business Law: Text and Cases, 7th edit., 1998, Fundamentals of Business Law, 5th edit., 2000, Business Law Today, 5th edit., 2000, Business Law Today-Comprehensive Edition, 5th Edit., 2000, Business Law Today-The Essentials, 5th edit., 2000, Business Law Today-Alternate Essentials Edition, 4th edit., 1997; dep. editor Social Sci. Quar., 1966-82, editl. bd., 1982-94; editor-in-chief Am. Bus. Law Jour., 1969-74, adv. editor, 1974—. Served with AUS, 1953-55. Recipient Outstanding Tchr. award U. Tex. Coll. Bus., 1967, Jack G. Taylor Tchg. Excellence award, 1971, 89, Joe D. Beasley Grad. Tchg. Excellence award, 1978, CBA Found. Adv. Coun. award, 1979, Grad. Bus. Coun. Outstanding Grad. Bus. Prof. award, 1980, James C. Scorboro Meml. award for outstanding leadership in banking edn. Colo. Grad. Sch. Banking, 1983, Utmost Outstanding Prof. award, 1989, CBA award for excellence in edn., 1994, Banking Leadership award Western States Sch. Banking, 1995, U. Tex. Civitatis award, 1997; inducted to CBA Hall of Fame, 1999. Mem. Southwestern Fedn. Adminstrv. Disciples (v.p. 1979-80, pres. 1980-81), Am. Arbitration Assn. (nat. panel 1966-96), Acad. Legal Studies in Bus. (pres. 1971-72, exec. com. 1989-94, Faculty award of excellence 1981), So. Bus. Law Assn. (pres. 1967), Tex. Assn. Coll. Tchrs. (pres. Austin chpt. 1967-68, exec. com. 1979-80, state pres. 1971-72), Wis. Bar Assn., Omicron Delta Kappa, Phi Kappa Phi (pres. 1983-84). Home: 4106 N Hills Dr Austin TX 78731-2826 Office: U Tex CBA 5.202 MSIS Dept Austin TX 78712

**JEPPESEN, ALAN KARL,** prosecutor; b. Nampa, Idaho, Dec. 19, 1941; s. Karl and Kleo B. Jeppesen; m. Jeanne Nelson Jeppesen, Aug. 20, 1965; children: Rebeca Rae Jeppesen Christensen, Amelia Anne, Kevin Karl, Erik Alan, Kristen Kaye. BA in English, U. Idaho, 1967; JD in Law, U. Utah, 1970. Bar: Utah, U.S. Dist. Ct. Utah. Assoc. Clyde & Pratt, Salt Lake City, 1970-75; atty. Tooele (Utah) City Corp., 1975-80; pvt. practice law Tooele, 1980-92; prosecutor Tooele County Atty., 1992—. Avocations: stained glass, photography. Home: 468 S 300 W Tooele UT 84074-2944 Office: Tooele County Atty 47 S Main St Tooele UT 84074-2194

**JEPPSON, ROGER WAYNE,** lawyer; b. San Francisco, June 26, 1936; s. Wayne O. and Maude (Josephson) J.; m. Janet Strong, Nov. 27, 1957; children: Jennifer, Jill. B.S. in Polit. Sci., Brigham Young U., 1958; J.D., Duke U., 1961. Bar: Oreg. 1961, Nev. 1961. Law clk. Justice Kenneth J. O'Connell of Oreg. Sup. Ct., 1961-62; assoc. Woodburn, Wedge and Jeppson and predecessors, Reno, 1962-65, ptnr., 1965-91; shareholder Jeppson & Lee, Reno, 1991-98; ptnr. Van Cott, Bagley, Cornwall & McCarthy, 1991-98; shareholder Hale Lane Peek Dennison Howard and Anderson, 1998—. Mem. Nev. State Bar Assn. (chmn. ethics com. 1979-82, del. 9th cir. judicial conf. 1979-82), Oreg. State Bar Assn., Washoe County Bar Assn. (pres. 1974-75), Rocky Mountain Mineral Law Found. (trustee). Democrat. Oil, gas, and mineral, General corporate. Office: 100 W Liberty St Ste 990 Reno NV 89501-1990

**JEPSEN, PETER LEE,** court reporter; b. Virginia, Minn., Dec. 23, 1952; s. Peter Frederick and Delores Audrey (Sorenson) J.; m. Valerie Lynn Tow, Mar. 20, 1976; children: Sarah Jo, Jennifer Lynn, Elizabeth Ann. Student, St. Cloud State U., 1971, Mankato State U., 1972, Southwestern AVTI, Jackson, Minn., 1978. Registered profl. reporter; chartered shorthand reporter. Freelance ct. reporter Carney & Assocs., Rochester, Minn., 1978-79; ofcl. ct. reporter State of S.D., Sioux Falls, 1979-80; part owner, reporter Carney & Assocs., Rochester, 1980-83; realtime captioner Can. Captioning Devel. Agy., Toronto, Ont., 1984-85, mgr. live captioning services, 1985-87; captioning trainer and cons. XScribe Corp., San Diego, 1987-88, mgr. captioning products and services, 1988-91; dir. U.S. Senate Office of Captioning Svcs., Washington, 1991-92; v.p. U.S. Captioning, Inc., San Diego, 1992-93; dir. U.S. Senate Office Captioning Svcs., Washington, 1994—. Lutheran. Avocations: reading, music, writing. Office: St 54 The Capitol Washington DC 20510-0001

**JEPSEN, WILLIAM E.,** lawyer; b. Omaha, July 1, 1947; s. Herschel Lewis and Ellen (Viola) J.; m. Cynthia Cadden, Aug. 22, 1969 (div. Aug. 1989); children: David, John. BS, U. Nebr., 1969; JD, U. Minn., 1972. Bar: Minn. 1972, U.S. Dist. Ct. Minn. 1973, U.S. Ct. Appeals (8th cir.) 1973. Atty., ptnr. Karon, Jepsen & Daly, Stillwater, minn., 1972-85; atty., pres. Hebert, Cass, Jepsen & Doyscher, St. Paul, 1985-96; atty. Schwebel, Goetz & Stieben, Mpls., 1996—; mem., chair Minn. Bd. Continuing Legal Edn., St. Paul, 1993—; bd. dirs. Creative Dispute Resolution, Mpls., 1997—. Mem. city coun. Mainre On St. Croix, Minn., 1978-80. Mem. Minn. State Bar Assn. (bd. govs. 1997—), Minn. Trial Lawyers Assn. (pres. 1990-91, Mem. of Yr. 1986). Personal injury, State civil litigation. Home: 321 Boutwell Pl Stillwater MN 55082-4518 Office: Schwebel Goetz & Sieben 5120 IDS Center Minneapolis MN 55402

**JEREN, JOHN ANTHONY, JR.,** lawyer; b. Youngstown, Ohio, Feb. 23, 1946; s. John and Irene E. (Struharik) J.; m. Marjorie C. Barbarie, July 11, 1973; children: Lisa Ann, Christine Alicia, Suzanne Beth, John A. III. BS in Bus., Ohio State U., 1968; JD, Ohio No. U., 1973. Bar: Ohio 1973, U.S. Dist. Ct. (no. dist.) Ohio 1974. Ptnr. Wellman & Jeren Co., L.P.A., Youngstown, 1973-93, Talback, Wellman, Jeren, Hackett & Skoufatos Co., L.P.A., Youngstown, 1993—. Recipient Willis Soc. award Ohio No. U., 1974. Mem. ATLA, Ohio Trial Lawyers Assn., Ohio State Bar Assn. (chmn. workers compensation sect. 1994-95). Personal injury, Workers' compensation, General practice. Home: 8199 Burgess Lake Dr Youngstown OH 44514-2745 Office: Tablack Wellman Jeren Hackett & Skoufatos Co LPA 67 Westchester Dr Youngstown OH 44515-3902

**JERNIGAN, JAY LAWRENCE,** lawyer; b. El Dorado, Ark., July 31, 1954; s. Alfred Benjamin and Betty Jean (Weatherford) J.; m. Kelly Ruth Faris (div.); 1 child, Jacqueline Sophia. BBA, U. Miss., 1976, JD, 1979. Bar: Miss. 1979. Asst. dist. atty. 12th Jud. Dist., Hattiesburg, Miss., 1978-79; assoc. Holmes & Dukes, Hattiesburg, 1979-82; ptnr. Dukes & Jernigan, Hattiesburg, 1983; prin. Hattiesburg, 1983—; tchr. Miss. Prosecutors Conf., 1987, Miss. Jud. Coll., 1988. Mem. Am. Trial Lawyers Assn., 5th Cir. Bar Assn., Miss. Trial Lawyers Assn., Miss. State Bar, South Miss. Bar Assn., Mason. Baptist. Avocation: golf. General civil litigation, Personal injury, Product liability. Office: PO Box 427 Hattiesburg MS 39403-0427

**JERNIGAN, JOHN LEE,** lawyer; b. Atlanta, May 29, 1942; s. Alton Lee and Marian (Heidt) J.; m. Virginia McKinney; children: Lee Ashley, Frank McKinney. AB, Davidson Coll., 1964; JD, U. N.C., 1967. Bar: N.C. 1967. Assoc. Smith, Anderson, Blount, Dorsett, Mitchell & Jernigan, Raleigh, N.C., 1969-72; ptnr. Smith, Anderson, Blount, Dorsett, Mitchell & Jernigan, Raleigh, 1972—; bd. adv. U. N.C. Banking Law Inst. Contbr. articles to profl. jours. Mem. bd. visitors Davidson (N.C.) Coll., 1986—; mem., trustee Choate-Rosemary Hall, Wallingford, Conn., 1989-92. Capt. U.S. Army, 1967-69. Fellow N.C. Bar Found.; mem. N.C. Bar Assn. (chmn. bus. law sect. 1985-87, bd. govs. 1989-92, chmn. bar ctr. cabinet 1994-98, pres.-elect 1998-99), Wake County Bar Assn., Cardinal Club (bd. dirs.), So. Conf. Bar Pres., Nat. Conf. Bar Pres., Supreme Ct. Hist. Soc. Episcopalian. Contracts commercial, Banking, General corporate. Office: PO Box 2611 Raleigh NC 27602-2611

**JERNSTEDT, KENNETH ELLIOTT,** lawyer; b. Rockeville Center, N.Y., Feb. 27, 1944; s. Kenneth Allen and Laura Jean (Elliott) J.; m. Sandra Reece, Aug. 20, 1967; children: Erik, Matt, Kaitlin. BA in History, Stanford U., 1966; JD, U. Calif., Berkeley, 1969. Bar: Calif. 1970, Oreg. 1970, U.S. Dist. Ct. Oreg., U.S. Ct. Appeals (9th cir.), U.S. Supreme Ct. 1977. Assoc. Spears, Lubersky, Campbell, Bledsoe & Young, Portland, Oreg., 1970-75; ptnr. Spears, Lubersky, Campbell, Bledsoe & Young, Portland, 1975-80; ptnr., exec. com. Bullard, Korshoj, Smith & Jernstedt, Portland, 1980—. Bd. dirs. Vis. Nurses Assn., Portland, 1973-82; mem. Oreg. Fish and Wildlife Commn., 1987-92, chmn., 1988-90; basketball coach Sellwood Boys Club, Portland, 1981-87, West Sylvan Sch., Portland, 1987-90; coach S.E. Soccer Assn., Portland, 1981-90; coach Lake Oswego Soccer Assn. 1992; coach youth basketball YMCA, 1992-93; pres., coach Lake Oswego Youth Traveling Basketball Assn., 1995-97. Mem. ABA (labor sect.), Calif. Bar Assn., Oreg. State Bar Assn. (exec. bd. labor sect. 1975), Multnomah Athletic Club, Stanford Club (pres. 1974-75). Republican. Avocations: skiing, fishing, hunting, biking, running. Labor. Office: Bullard Korshoj Smith & Jernstedt 1000 SW Broadway Ste 1900 Portland OR 97205-3071

**JEROME, JOSEPH BEN,** lawyer; b. Cleve., Sept. 8, 1950; s. Rudolph J. and Mary R. (Consiglio) J.; m. Sharon A. Tersigni, Sept. 10, 1988. BSBA, Bowling Green State U., 1972; JD cum laude, Cleve. Marshall Sch. Law, 1975. Bar: Ohio 1975, U.S. Dist. Ct. (no. dist.) Ohio 1976, U.S. Tax Ct. 1977. With safety dept. City of Cleve., 1973-75; ptnr. Boylan and Jerome, Cleve., 1976-80, Jerome and Smith, Cleve., 1980-88, Jerome, Smith & Condeni, Cleve., 1989-92; with Jerome & Zoller, 1992-95, Joseph B. Jerome and Assocs., 1995—; arbitrator, chmn. Cuyahoga County Arbitration Commn., Cleve., 1978-84; arbitrator Am. Arbitration Commn., 1980—. Referee Cleve. Civil Svc. Commn., 1978—; pres., mem. The Playhouse Sq. Bus. Coun., 1989—. Mem. ABA, Edgewater Yacht Club (assoc.), Pi Kappa Alpha (trustee 1982—), Beta Gamma Sigma. Republican. Roman Catholic. Avocations: sailing, golf, personal computer, home remodelling. Construction.

**JESKE, CHARLES MATTHEW,** lawyer; b. Bartlesville, Okla., July 16, 1964; s. Arnold Carl and Maudie Marie (Matthews) J.; m. Pamela Kay Paholek, May 20, 1989. BBA in Fin./Acctg., Tex. A&M U., 1986; JD, South Tex. Coll. Law, Houston, 1989. Bar: Tex. 1989, U.S. Dist. Ct. (so. dist.) Tex. 1990, U.S. Ct. Appeals (5th cir.) 1990. Briefing atty. 14th Dist. Ct. of Appeals Tex., Houston, 1989-90, 90-91; sr. assoc. atty. Renneker & Assocs., Houston, 1991-96; pvt. practice Houston, 1996—; Contractor, investment analyst Jeske Homes, Bryan, Tex., 1986—. Trustee, officer Meml. Hollow Citizens, Inc., Houston, 1994-96. Mem. Houston Bar Assn., Houston Young Lawyers Assn., Tex. A&M U. Former Students Assn., Phi Alpha Delta Alumni Assn. Republican. Lutheran. Avocations: photography, travel. Estate planning, Probate, Estate taxation. Home and Office: 12407 Barryknoll Ln Houston TX 77024-4113

**JESPERSEN, ROBERT RANDOLPH,** legal consultant; b. N.Y.C., June 17, 1936; s. Randolph Foyen and Marie (Larsen) J.; m. Shirley Dubber, Dec. 20, 1958; children: Robert Randolph Jr., Craig Christopher. AB, Columbia U., 1958, AM, 1964; JD, U. Houston, 1975; LLM, U. Tex., 1987. Bar: Tex. 1975, Ark. 1981, U.S. Supreme Ct., U.S. Ct. Appeals (5th and 8th cirs.), U.S. Dist. Ct. (so. dist.) Tex., U.S. Dist. Ct. (ea. dist.) Ark., U.S. Ct. Mil. Appeals. Pvt. practice law, 1975—; moderator Am. Arbitration Assn. conf., Little Rock, 1987; asst. atty. gen. Tex., 1975-76; apprentice banker The Bank of N.Y., N.Y.C., 1964-66; mgmt. analyst U.S. Govt., Washington, 1961-62; hon. consul Kingdom of Lesotho, Jurisdiction of Tex., 1972-75; legal cons., 1995—; adj. prof. law U. Ark.-Little rock, 1987-91, prof. bus. law, 1980-95, prof. emeritus, 1995—; vis. prof. law, 1993; vis. sr. lectr. bus. law Massey U., N.Z., 1991; vis. disting. lectr. internat. bus. Calif. State U., Long Beach, 1987; vis. prof. bus. law U. Tex., Austin, 1987; part-time instr. Houston C.C., 1975-76; part-time tchg. fellow U. Houston, 1974-75; sr. advisor Assn. African Univs., Accra, Ghana, 1971-72; headmaster Kurisini Internat. Edn. Ctr., Dar-es-Salaam, Tanzania, 1969-71; dir. devel. African-Am. Inst., N.Y.C., 1967-69; assoc. dir. career svcs. Princeton U., 1966-67; asst. dir. univ. placement Columbia U., 1962-64. Co-author: Business Law: Comprehensive Edit., 1987, Business Law: Text and Cases, 1984, 5th edit., 1996, American Legal System, 1986; editor, contbr.: Industrial Laws, 1980; editl. bd. Jour. Legal Studies Edn., 1983-85, The Houston Lawyer, 1978-80; editor: Proc. of Internat. Legal Studies Assn. Ann. Mtg., 1988; contbr. numerous articles to profl. jours. 1st lt. USMC, 1958-61, col. USMCR, 1961-88. Recipient Tchg. Excellence award Nat. Conf. of Acad. Bus. Adminstrn., 1993, Faculty Excellence award Coll. Bus. Adminstrn., U. Ark.-Little Rock, 1992; Sam M. Walton Free Enterprise fellow, 1995, Peace Rsch. fellow U. Auckland Ctr. for Peace Studies, 1992. Mem. Nat. Assn. Scholars, The Federalist Soc. for Law and Pub. Policy Studies (lawyers divsn. Ark. chpt. dir. 1992-93, 94-95, pres. 1991-92), Am. Bus. Law Assn. (pres. 1988-89), So. Reg. Bus. Law Assn. (pres. 1983-84), Ark. Bar Assn. (mem. alternative dispute resolution com. 1987-88, 92-93, internat. law com. 1983-84), State Bar of Tex. (exec. com. mil. law sect. 1978-80), Southwestern Fedn. Adminstrv. Disciplines (bd. dirs. 1982-84), Internat. Consular Acad., Am. Arbitration Assn., Assn. Law Tchrs. G.B., Assn. of Attenders and Alumni of the Hague Acad. Internat. Law, Order of Barristers, Order of Advocates, Golden Key, Beta Gamma Sigma (chpt. pres. 1985-86), Phi Kappa Phi (chpt. pres. 1984-85), Phi Alpha Delta, Alpha Kappa Psi, Alpha Phi Omega. Office: PO Box 410471 Melbourne FL 32941-0471

**JESSEE, ROY MARK,** lawyer; b. Kingsport, Tenn., Feb. 8, 1966; s. Roy Claude and Myrtle Delight (Robinette) J.; m. Cortney Wynn Williams, June 30, 1990. BA, King Coll., 1988; JD, U. Va., 1991. Bar: Va. 1991, U.S. Dist. Ct. (we. dist.) Va. 1992. Law clk. Ct. of Appeals of Va., Bristol, 1991-92; assoc. atty. Mullins, Thomason & Harris, Norton, Va., 1992-94; shareholder, prin., atty. Mullins, Thomason, Harris & Jessee, Norton, Va., 1995-98; shareholder, prin. Mullins, Harris & Jessee, Norton, Va., 1998—. Contbr. articles to legal jours. Chmn. Scott County Dem. Party, 1993-95, 95-97. Named one of Outstanding Young Men in Am., 1989. Mem. ABA, Wise County Bar Assn. (pres.-elect 1998, pres. 1999), Am. Judicature Soc., Va. Assn. Def. Attys. Democrat. Baptist. Avocations: running, weight lifting, reading, writing poetry. General civil litigation, Personal injury, Product liability. Home: PO Box 353 112 B Elm St Gate City VA 24251 Office: Mullins Thomason Harris & Jessee PO Box 1200 30 Seventh St Norton VA 24273

**JESSOP, JEANETTE WANLESS,** lawyer; b. Portage, Wis., Mar. 10, 1948; d. Gale L. and Marie Joyce Wanless; m. Gerald E. Jessop, Feb. 6, 1971. BA in Psychology, U. Wis., 1970, JD, 1976. Assoc. Quale, Hartmann, Bohl & Evenson, Baraboo, Wis., 1976-77; ptnr. Quale, Hartmann, Bohl & Evenson, Baraboo, 1978-85; sr. atty. law dept. Firstar Corp., Milw., 1985-98. Mem. ABA, State Bar Wis., Sauk County Bar Assn. Real property, Contracts commercial, Taxation, general.

**JESSUP, JAMES R.,** lawyer; b. Grosse Pointe, Mich., Aug. 31, 1949; s. James Robert and Joan (Coffman) J.; m. Elizabeth Ann Cooper, Aug. 9, 1975 (div. Mar. 1996); children: William, Rebecca, Steven; m. Lee Anne Wysocki, May 11, 1997. BA, Mich. State U., 1976; JD, Detroit Coll. Law, 1976. Atty. Levinson, Disney et al, Detroit, 1979-82, Makower & Jessup, Detroit, 1983-84, Raoul Robar, Ishpeming, Mich., 1984-85, Kendricks, Bordeau et al, Marquette, Mich., 1985-92, pvt. practice, Marquette, Mich., 1992—; treas. Upper Peninsula Children's Mus., Marquette, 1991—; pres. Red Earth Loppet, Inc., Marquette, 1994—; commr. Commn Aging, Marquette, 1994-96; trustee U.S. Bankruptcy, Marquette, 1993-95. Mem. Mich. State Bar Assn., County Bar Assn., Kiwanis. Avocations: cross-country skiing, hunting, outdoor activities. Bankruptcy, General corporate. Office: 315 S Front St Marquette MI 49855-4644

**JESTER, CARROLL GLADSTONE,** lawyer; b. Macon, Ga., May 5, 1957; s. Carroll Gladstone and Annie Jean (Bazemore) J.; m. Laura Ann Spencer, Aug. 17, 1985; children: Annie Catherine, Carroll Elizabeth. BA, U. Ga., 1979, JD, 1982. Bar: Ga. 1982, U.S. Dist. Ct. (no. dist.) Ga. 1982, U.S. Ct. Appeals (11th cir.) 1983, U.S. Dist. Ct. (mid. dist.) Ga. 1989, U.S. Dist. Ct. (so. dist.) Ga. 1991. Assoc. Rogers, Magruder, Hoyt, Sumner & Brinson, Rome, Ga., 1982-85, Swift, Currie, McGhee & Hiers, Atlanta, 1985-89; assoc. Goldner, Sommers, Scrudder & Bass, Atlanta, 1989-91, ptnr., 1991-98; ptnr. Mozley, Finlayson & Loggins, Atlanta, 1998—. Contbg. friend Friends of Zoo Atlanta; angel The Alliance Theatre, Atlanta; mem. The Ga. Conservancy, Ga. Trust for Hist. Preservation, St. Luke's Presbyn. Ch. Mem. ABA (torts and ins. sect.), Atlanta Bar Assn., Ga. Def. Lawyers Assn., U. Ga. Bulldog Club, SAR, Honorable Order Ky. Cols. (col.), Sigma Chi (undergrad. treas. 1978, Best Pledge 1976), Phi Delta Phi, Phi Alpha Theta. Avocations: golf, raquetball, chess, finishing furniture, gardening. General civil litigation, Insurance, Contracts commercial. Office: Mozley Finlayson & Loggins 5605 Glenridge Dr NE Atlanta GA 30342-1365

**JESTER, JACK D.,** lawyer; b. Columbus, Ohio, Jan. 31, 1946. BS, Ohio State U., 1968, JD, 1971; LLM, U. Mo., 1972. Bar: Ohio 1971, Ill. 1978. Gen. counsel, atty. inspector Ohio Divsn. Securities, 1973-74; mem. Coffield, Ungaretti & Harris (now named Ungaretti & Harris), Chgo.; spl. counsel City Counselors Office, Kansas City, Mo., 1971-72; counsel Mayor's Environ. Control Task Force, Kansas City, 1971-72. Contbr. articles to profl. jours. Mem. ABA, Urban Land Inst., Mortgage Bankers Assn., Nat. Assn. Bond Lawyers, Ill. State Bar Assn., Ohio State Bar Assn., Internat. Coun. Shopping Ctrs. Real property, Municipal (including bonds). Office: Ungaretti & Harris 3500 Three 1st Nat Plz Chicago IL 60602

**JESTER, MICHAEL HENRY,** patent lawyer; b. Trinidad, British W.I., June 9, 1951; s. Malvern Hill Lash and Frances (Henry) J.; m. Dorothy Kay Rottschafer, Oct. 6, 1979; children: John, James, Julia. BS, U. Calif., Davis, 1973; JD, U. Calif., San Francisco, 1976. Bar: Calif. 1976, U.S. Patent and Trademark Office 1976, U.S. Ct. Appeals (9th cir.) 1976, U.S. Ct. Appeals (fed. cir.) 1988. Assoc. Townsend & Townsend, San Francisco, 1976-78, Klarquist, Sparkman, Portland, Oreg., 1978-79, Brown and Martin, San Diego, 1979-84; prin. Baker, Maxham, Jester and Meador, San Diego, 1984-98; pvt. practice San Diego, 1998—; instr. U. Calif., San Diego, 1997—. Mem. Am. Intellectual Property Law Assn., San Diego Intellectual Property Law Assn. Patent, Trademark and copyright.

**JESTER, WILLIAM DAVID,** lawyer; b. Jacksonville, Fla., May 18, 1954; s. Harold Leon Jester and Betty Lee (Babb) Notestine; children: Joanna Megan, Zachary Kegan. BS, Troy (Ala.) State U., 1988; JD, U. Fla., 1991. Bar: Fla. 1991, Ala., 1998, Md., U.S. Dist. Ct. (mid. dist.) Fla. 1991, U.S. Dist. Ct. (no. dist.) Fla. 1993, U.S. Dist. Ct. (so. dist.) Fla. 1996, U.S. Dist. Ct. (ctrl. dist.) Ala. 1998, U.S. Dist. Ct. (so. dist.) Ala. 1999, U.S. Ct. Appeals (11th cir.) 1998. Assoc. Coker, Myers, Schickel, Cooper & Sorenson, PA, Jacksonville, Fla., 1991-93; ptnr. Boyes & Jester P.A., Gainesville, Fla., 1993-96; sr. assoc. Galloway Johnson Tompkins and Burr, PLC, Gulf Breeze, Fla., 1996—. Bd. dirs. N.W. Fla. Rape Crisis Ctr., Pensacola, 1985. Mem. ABA, Inns. of Ct. Avocations: flying, golf, reading, snow skiing. General civil litigation, Admiralty, Insurance. Office: 55 Baybridge Dr Gulf Breeze FL 32561

**JETER, KATHERINE LESLIE BRASH,** lawyer; b. Gulfport, Miss., July 24, 1921; d. Ralph Edward and Rosa Meta (Jacobs) Brash; m. Robert McLean Jeter, Jr., May 11, 1946. BA, Newcomb Coll. of Tulane U., 1943; JD, Tulane U., 1945. Bar: La. 1945, U.S. Dist. Ct. (we. dist.) La. 1948, U.S. Tax Ct. 1965, U.S. Supreme Ct. 1971, U.S. Dist. Ct. (ea. dist.) La. 1975, U.S. Ct. Appeals (5th cir.) 1981, U.S. Dist. Ct. (mid. dist.) La. 1982. Assoc. Montgomery, Fenner & Brown, New Orleans, 1945-46, Tucker, Martin, Holder, Jeter & Jackson, Shreveport, 1947-79; ptnr. Tucker, Jeter, Jackson and Hickman and predecessors, Shreveport, 1980—; judge pro tem 1st Jud. Dist. Ct., Caddo Parish, La., 1982-83; mem. adv. com. to joint legis. subcom. on mgmt. of the community; pres. YWCA of Shreveport, 1963; hon. consul of France; Shreveport, 1982-91; pres. Little Theatre of Shreveport, 1966-67; pres. Shreveport Art Guild, 1974-75; mem. task force crim justice La. Priorities for the Future, 1978; pres. LWV of Shreveport, 1950-51. Recipient Disting. Grad. award Tulane U., 1983. Mem. Am. Law Inst., La. State Law Inst. (mem. coun. 1980—, adv. com. La. Civil Code 1973-77, temp. ad hoc. com. 1976-77, sr. officer 1993—), Am. Law Inst., Pub. Affairs Rsch. Coun. (bd. trustees 1976-81, 91—, exec. com. 1981-84, area exec. committeeman Shreveport area 1982), ABA, La. Bar Assn., Shreveport Bar Assn. (pres. 1986), Nat. Assn. Women Lawyers, Shreveport Assn. for Women Attys., C. of C. Shreveport (bd. dirs. 1975-77), Order of Coif, Phi Beta Kappa. Author: (with Fredricka Doll Gute) Historical Profile, Shreveport 1850, 1982; author: A Man and His Boat, The Civil War Career and Correspondence of Lieutenant Jonathan H. Carter, 1996; contbr. articles on law to profl. jours. General corporate. Home: 3959 Maryland Ave Shreveport LA 71106-1021 Office: 401 Edwards St Ste 905 Shreveport LA 71101-5509

**JETTE, ERNEST ARTHUR,** lawyer; b. Nashua, N.H., Apr. 19, 1945; s. Fernand Ernest and Jeannette M. (Thibodeau) J.; m. Bridget Belton, Sept. 4, 1977; 1 child, Alexandra. BA, Boston Coll., 1967, JD, 1970. Bar: N.H. 1970, U.S. Dist. Ct. N.H. 1971, U.S. Tax Ct. 1972; diplomate Trial Practice Inst. Mng. atty. N.H. Legal Assistance, Nashua, 1970-72; ptnr. Janelle, Nadeau & Jette, Nashua, 1972-81; dir. Hamblett & Kerrigan, P.A., Nashua, 1981-93; pvt. practice Nashua, 1993—; lectr. paralegal studies Rivier Coll., Nashua, 1977-78. Chmn. Nashua Regional Planning Commn., 1981-82; mem. Town of Merrimack (N.H.) Master Plan Com., 1981, dir. Nashua Youth Coun., Inc., 1975-80, pres., 1978-79; dir. NEEDS, Inc., 1972-75; chmn. Heart Sunday, N.H. Heart Assn., 1973; mem. pub. affairs com. N.H. Assn. Commerce and Industry, 1983-93; mem. sch. bd. Bishop Guertin H.S., 1994-96. Capt. U.S. Army, 1970. Mem. ABA (state com. disaster legal assistance 1973-75, litigation, tort and ins. practice sects.), N.H. Bar Assn. (past mem. law related edn., coop. with the cts., profl. responsibility coms.), N.H. Bar Found., N.H. Trial Lawyers Assn., Nashua Bar Assn. (pres. 1990-91), Greater Nashua C. of C. (dir. 1985-96), Four Seasons Property Owners' Assn. (pres. 1977-78), Rotary Club Nashua (dir. 1978-79, pres. 1992-93). General practice, General civil litigation, Personal injury. Home: 9 Westbrook Dr Nashua NH 03060-5314 Office: 7 Concord St Nashua NH 03064-2328

**JETTON, C. LORING, JR.,** lawyer; b. Pitts., Feb. 10, 1943; s. Clyde Loring and Barbara (Lewis) J.; m. Marion Luyken, Feb. 19, 1966; children: Ada Elizabeth, Christopher Loring. AB, Harvard U., 1964; JD, Columbia U., 1969. Bar: N.Y. 1969, D.C. 1970. Law clk. to Hon. W. Feinberg U.S. Ct. Appeals (2d. cir.), 1969-70; assoc. Wilmer, Cutler & Pickering, Washington, 1970-76, ptnr., 1977—. Lt. U.S. Army, 1964-66. Mem. ABA, D.C. Bar. Antitrust, Private international, General civil litigation. Office: Wilmer Cutler & Pickering 2445 M St NW Ste 500 Washington DC 20037-1487

**JEWELER, ROBIN,** lawyer; b. Washington, Sept. 11, 1951; d. David Baer and Jeanne Carolyn (Weiss) J.; m. Laurence Donald Wiseman, May 29, 1978; children: Justin Jeweler, David Baer. BA with honors, U. Md., 1973; JD, George Washington U., 1976. Bar: Md., Washington. Jud. clk. Supreme Ct. Appeals, Charleston, W.Va., 1977-78; atty. Matthew Bender, Inc., N.Y.C., 1978-79; legis. atty. Congrl. Rsch. Svc., Libr. Congress, Washington, 1980—. Contbr. articles to profl. jours. Bd. dirs. Jewish Hist. Soc., Washington, 1996-98, sec., 1999; pres. Bells Mill PTA, 1993. Mem. Internat. Women's Insolvency and Restructuring Confedn., Fed. Bar Assn., Am. Bankruptcy Inst. Fax: 202-707-8595. E-mail: rjeweler@crs.loc.gov. Home: 10621 Democracy Ln Potomac MD 20854-4016 Office: Libr Congress 101 Independence Ave SE Washington DC 20540-0002

**JEWELL, GEORGE BENSON,** lawyer, educator, minister; b. Evanston, Ill., Mar. 26, 1944; s. Benson Murray and Ellen Louise (Mahle) J.; m. Pamela Elaine Peterson, Aug. 12, 1967; children: Jeffrey Benson, Brian Edward. BA, Beloit (Wis.) Coll., 1966; MDiv, Gordon-Conwell Theol. Sem., 1978; JD, Washington U., St. Louis, 1971. Bar: Ill. 1971, Mo. 1972, Mass. 1990, U.S. Dist. Ct. (ea. dist.) Mo. 1973, U.S. Dist. Ct. Mass. 1991. Trust adminstr. Ill. Nat. Bank, Springfield, 1971; corp. atty. Ralston Purina Co., St. Louis, 1971-75; assoc. pastor Westminster Presbyn. Ch., Bluefield, W.Va., 1978-81; sr. pastor Westminster Presbyn. Ch., Cape Girardeau, Mo., 1981-86, Evang. Free Ch., Cape Girardeau, 1986-88; pvt. practice Cape Girardeau, 1988-89; counsel, dir. gift planning, adj. assoc. prof. bus. law Gordon Coll., Wenham, Mass., 1989-97; dir. legal support svcs. Renaissance Inc., Carmel, Ind., 1997-98, v.p. client svcs., sr. counsel, 1998—; instr. in bus. law S.E. Mo. State U., Cape Girardeau, 1986; cons. Stone, McGhee, Feuchtenberger & Barringer, Bluefield, 1980-81; mng. editor Washington U. Law Quar. Deacon Ctrl. Presbyn. Ch., St. Louis, 1974-75; scoutmaster Appalachian coun. Boy Scouts Am., Bluefield, 1979; bd. advisors Sta. KUGT, Cape Girardeau, 1988, Boston Rescue Mission, 1994-97; baccalaureate spkr. Ctrl. H.S., Cape Girardeau, 1988; workshop presenter Congress '93 and Congress '94, Boston; bd. dirs. Young Life of Cape Girardeau. Mem. Nat. Assn. Coll. and Univ. Attys. (ad hoc com. on income devel. 1990-91, ad hoc com. svcs. small colls. 1991-93, com. profl. devel., 1993-97), Mass. Soc. Sons Am. Revolution, Boston Bar Assn. (coll. and univ. com., estate planning com.), Planned Giving Group of New Eng., Christian Fin. Advisors Network (founder), Mo. Bar Assn. (franchise tax subcom. corp. law and bus. orgn. coms.), Evang. Free Ch. Ministerial Assn., Sigma Alpha Epsilon. Avocations: swimming, tennis, biking, sailing. Estate taxation, Estate planning,

Personal income taxation. Home: 553 Melark Dr Carmel IN 46032-2312 Office: Renaissance Inc 11595 N Meridian St Ste 250 Carmel IN 46032-6922

**JEWELL, JOHN J.,** lawyer; b. Kokomo, Ind., Aug. 31, 1954; s. G.M. and Kathryn (Knepper) J. AB, Ind. U., 1975, JD, 1979, MBA, 1979. Bar: Ind. 1979, U.S. Dist. Ct. (so. dist.) Ind. 1979. Assoc. Trimble & Jewell, Evansville, Ind., 1979—. Mem. ABA, Ind. Bar Assn., Evansville Bar Assn., Ind. Jaycees (legal counsel 1983-84, Internat. Senator), Evansville Jaycees (pres. 1982-83). Episcopalian. Real property, Landlord-tenant, Consumer commercial. Home: PO Box 291 Evansville IN 47702-0291 Office: Trimble & Jewell PO Box 1107 Evansville IN 47706-1107

**JEWETT, JAMES MICHAEL,** lawyer; b. Columbus, Ohio, Jan. 4, 1948; s. James Howard and Edna Ruth Jewett. BS, Ohio State U., 1970; JD, Capital U., 1974. Bar: Ohio 1974, U.S. Dist. Ct. (so. dist.) Ohio 1975, U.S. Supreme Ct. 1978. Pvt. practice Columbus, 1974—. Mem. ABA, Ohio State Bar Assn., Columbus Bar Assn., Franklin County Trial Lawyers Assn. Probate, Real property, Family and matrimonial. Office: 2577 N High St Columbus OH 43202-2555

**JILES, GARY D.,** lawyer; b. Newport, Ark., Jan. 27, 1963; s. Randolph and Frances N. Jiles; m. Elisa A. Litchfield, Oct. 26, 1985; children: Katherine E., Trevor G. BSBA in Acctg., U. Ark., Fayetteville, 1985; JD with honors, U. Ark., Little Rock, 1988. Bar: Ark. 1988. Atty., ptnr. Jack, Lyon & Jones, P.A., Little Rock, 1988—. Author: Employment Law Deskbook for Arkansas Employers, 1996—; editor/author newsletter Ark. Employment Law Letter, 1995—. Mem. ABA, Ark. Bar Assn. (treas., sec., chmn. labor and employment law sect., Best of CLE Speaker 1998, 99). E-mail: gdj@jlj.com. Labor, Banking, General civil litigation. Office: Jack Lyon & Jones PA 3400 TCBY Tower 425 W Capitol Ave Little Rock AR 72201-3405 also: Park Pl Office Complex 400 Salem Rd Ste 3 Conway AR 72032-7534

**JIMÉNEZ, EMILIO,** corporate lawyer; b. San Juan, Puerto Rico, Feb. 27, 1967; s. Emilio and Ana Lidia (Colón) Jiménez; m. Alicia María Alvarez, Mar. 30, 1996. BA cum laude, Harvard Coll., 1989; JD, NYU, 1992. Bar: N.Y. 1993, Mass. 1992. Assoc. Jones, Day, Reavis & Pogue, N.Y.C., 1992-93, Brown & Wood, N.Y.C., 1993-95; asst. v.p., legal and compliance dept. CSFP Capital, Inc., N.Y.C., 1995-97; v.p., asst. gen. counsel J.P. Morgan & Co. Inc., N.Y.C., 1997—. Staff editor NYU Law Review, 1990-92. Mem. Am. Bar Assn., N.Y. State Bar Assn., Fly Club, Harvard Club of N.Y.C. Republican. Roman Catholic. Avocations: golf, marksmanship. Finance, Contracts commercial, Securities. Home: 422 E 72nd St Apt 6F New York NY 10021-4618 Office: JP Morgan & Co Inc 60 Wall St New York NY 10005-2888

**JINNETT, ROBERT JEFFERSON,** lawyer; b. Birmingham, Ala., May 9, 1949; s. Bryan Floyd Jr. and Elizabeth Coleman (Borders) J.; m. Doreen S. Ziff, Aug. 2, 1975; children: Brynn Leigh, Maren Alexandra. BA, Harvard U., 1971; JD, Cornell U., 1975. Bar: N.Y. 1976, U.S. Dist. Ct. (no. dist.) N.Y. 1976, U.S. Dist. Ct. (so. dist.) N.Y. 1978, U.S. Dist. Ct. (ea. dist.) N.Y. 1979, U.S. Supreme Ct. 1988. Law clk. N.Y. State Ct. Appeals, Albany, 1975-77; assoc. Rogers & Wells, N.Y.C., 1977-82, LeBoeuf, Lamb, Greene & MacRae, N.Y.C., 1983-85; ptnr. LeBoeuf, Lamb, Leiby & MacRae, N.Y.C., 1986-94; ptnr. LeBoeuf, Lamb, Greene & MacRae, L.L.P., N.Y.C., 1994, of counsel, 1995—; pres. LeBoeuf Computing Techs., LLC., N.Y.C., 1996—; sr. cons. Cutter Consortium Year 2000 Adv. Svc. Co-editor: Year 2000 Law Deskbook, 1999; contbr. articles to profl. jours. Recipient 3d nat. prize Nathan Burkan Meml. Competition, ASCAP, 1974; German Acad. Exch. Svc. fellow U. Heidelberg, Germany, 1971-72. Mem. S.R., Jamestowne Soc. Republican. Episcopalian. Avocation: poetry. General corporate, Computer. Office: LeBoeuf Lamb Greene MacRae 125 W 55th St New York NY 10019-5369

**JIROTKA, GEORGE M.,** lawyer; b. Berwyn, Ill., May 8, 1957; s. Zdenek F. and Jaromira (Kralovec) J. BA, Columbia U., 1979; MBA, U. Chgo., 1980; JD, U. Tex., 1983. Assoc. Annis, Mitchell, Cockey, Edward & Roehn, P.A., Tampa, Fla., 1984-86; assoc. Fowler, White, Gillen, Boggs, Villareal & Banker, P.A., Tampa/Clearwater, Fla., 1986-91, ptnr./shareholder, 1991—. Commr./mayor Belleair Shore, Fla., 1986-98; chmn. Pinellas County (Fla.) Planning Coun., 1988-98; pres. Suncoast League of Municipalities, Fla. west coast, 1994—; dir. Fla. League of Cities, 1997-98, Pinellas Suncoast Transit Authority, 1996-98; mem. Pinellas County Pub. Employee Rels. Commn., 1996—. Mem. Gulf Beaches on Sand Key C. of C. (Outstand Cmty. Svc. award 1994). Rep. Roman Cath. Avocations: politics, fin. Real property, Probate. Office: Fowler White Gillen Boggs Villareal & Banker PA 601 Cleveland St Ste 800 Clearwater FL 33755-4169

**JOBE, TONY BRYSON,** airline executive, lawyer; b. Washington, Aug. 29, 1943; s. William Theodore and Marguerite (Hendrickson) J.; m. Beverly June Bryant, Aug. 15, 1987. BA in English, Southwestern U., Memphis, 1966; JD, Tulane U., 1974. Bar: La. 1975. Prin. Jobe & Assocs., New Orleans, 1975—; pres., chief exec. officer Air New Orleans, 1981—; with Olsen, Gilman & Pangia, Washington, 1988—, of Counsel Ryon and Willeford. Bd. dirs. New Orleans Ballet, 1981-83. Capt. (pilot) USMC, 1967-71. Decorated D.F.C. Mem. Internat. Soc. Air Safety Investigators, ABA, NTCB Bar Assn., Assn. Bar City N.Y., Assn. Trial Lawyers Am., Attys. Info. Exchange Group (exec. bd. 1979—). Republican. Presbyterian. also: Ryon and Willeford 201 Saint Charles Ave Ste 3701 New Orleans LA 70170-3703 also: 14465 Settlers Landing Way Gaithersburg MD 20878-4304

**JOCHNER, MICHELE MELINA,** lawyer; b. Naperville, Ill., May 19, 1966. BA summa cum laude, Mundelein Coll., Chgo., 1987; JD with honors, DePaul U., 1990, LLM in Taxation Law, 1992. Bar: Ill. 1990, U.S. Dist. Ct. (no. dist.) Ill. 1990, U.S. Ct. Appeals (7th cir.) 1996, U.S. Supreme Ct. 1996. Law clk. U.S. Securities & Exch. Commn., Chgo., 1989; legal rsch. asst. to prof. Marlene Nicholson DePaul U. Sch. Law, Chgo., 1989-91; legal rsch. asst. to assoc. dean Vincent Vitullo DePaul U. Sch. Law, 1989-91; law clk. extern U.S. Dist. Ct. (no. dist.) Ill., Chgo., 1989-90; judicial law clk. Cir. Ct. of Cook County, Chgo., 1991-92; staff atty. Cir. Ct. of Cook County, 1992-93, sr. staff atty., 1993-95, acting supr. legal rsch. divsn., 1995-96; staff atty. permanency project child protection divsn. Cir. Ct. Cook County, Chgo., 1996-97; jud. law clk. to Hon. Mary Ann G. McMorrow Ill. Supreme Ct., Chgo., 1997—; mem. subcom. money transfers and adminstrv. regulations Ill. Supreme Ct., 1995-96; adj. prof. law John Marshall Law Sch., Chgo., 1994—, judge Herzog moot ct.competition, 1997—; adj. prof. law DePaul U. Coll. Law, 1998—; spkr. in field. Contbr. articles to profl. jours. Recipient Harold A. Shertz award Film, Air & Package Carriers Conf., Alexandria, Va., 1990. Mem. ABA, Ill. Bar Assn. (Lincoln award 2d pl. 1994, 97, 1st pl. 1996, 99, mem. gen. practice sect. coun.), Fed. Bar Assn., Chgo. Bar Assn., U.S. Supreme Ct. Hist. Soc., Order of Coif, Kappa Gamma Pi, Phi Sigma Tau. Avocations: writing fiction, non-fiction.

**JOCK, PAUL F., II,** lawyer; b. Indpls., Jan. 25, 1943; s. Paul F. and Alice (Sheehan) J.; m. Gail A. Webre, Sept. 16, 1967; children: Craig W., Nicole L. BBA, U. Notre Dame, 1965; JD, U. Chgo., 1970. Bar: Ill. 1970, N.Y. 1990. Ptnr. Kirkland & Ellis, Chgo. and N.Y.C., 1970—; v.p. legal affairs Tribune Co., Chgo., 1981. Assoc. editor U. Chgo. Law Rev., 1969-70. Served to lt. USN, 1965-67. Mem. ABA, Chgo. Bar Assn., Assn. of the Bar of City of N.Y. Securities, Banking, General corporate. Office: Kirkland & Ellis 200 E Randolph St Fl 54 Chicago IL 60601-6636 also: Citicorp Ctr 153 E 53rd St New York NY 10022-4611

**JOERLING, DALE RAYMOND,** lawyer; b. St. Louis, Apr. 11, 1949; s. Raymond H. and Opal M. (Hoffman) J.; m. Cozette Joyce Turner, Apr. 7, 1979; children: Jeffrey Dale, Jill Lorraine. BA in Econ. cum laude, Southeast Mo. State U., 1971; JD, U. Mo., 1976. Bar: Mo. 1976, D.C. 1980, U.S. Dist. Ct. (ea. dist.) Mo. 1982, Ill. 1990. Atty. FTC, Washington, 1976-81; assoc. Guilfoil, Petzall & Shoemake, St. Louis, 1981-85; ptnr. Thompson & Coburn, St. Louis, 1985—. Served as sgt. U.S. Army, 1971-73. Mem. ABA, Mo. Bar Assn., Bar Assn. of St. Louis, Ill. Bar Assn. Club: Mo. Athletic (St. Louis). Avocation: juggling. General civil litigation, Antitrust, Environmental. Home: 23 S Elm Ave Saint Louis MO 63119-3015 Office: Thompson & Coburn One Mercantile Ctr Saint Louis MO 63101

**JOFFE, DAVID JONATHON,** lawyer; b. Manhatten, N.Y., Mar. 8, 1962; s. Seymour Joffe and Saretta Hoyt (Hill) Prescott; m. Hillary Ray Joffe, June 25, 1994; 1 child, Alexander Seymour. BA, Fla. State U., 1984; JD, U. Miami, Coral Gables, Fla., 1988. Bar: Fla. 1989, U.S. Dist. Ct. (so. dist.) Fla. 1989, U.S. Dist. Ct. (mid. dist.) Fla. 1989, U.S. Ct. Appeals (11th cir.) 1989. Legal intern Dade County Pub. Defenders, Miami, 1988-89; assoc. Randy S. Maultasch, Esquire, Miami, 1989-90; owner, ptnr. Ticket Attys., P.A., Coconut Grove, Fla., 1992—; pvt. practice Coconut Grove, 1990—; mem. C.J.A. Panel Atty. for So. Dist. of Fla. Dir., chmn. com. Dade County Young Dems., Miami, 1990. Mem. ABA, ATLA, Nat. Assn. Criminal Def. Lawyers, Assn. Fla. Trial Lawyers, Fla. Assn. Criminal Def. Attys. Democrat. Jewish. Avocations: working out (exercise), reading, pistol and skeet shooting. Criminal, Juvenile, Personal injury. Office: 2900 Bridgeport Ave Ste 401 Coconut Grove FL 33133-3606

**JOFFE, ROBERT DAVID,** lawyer; b. N.Y.C., May 26, 1943; s. Joseph and Bertha (Pashkovsky) J.; children by prior marriage: Katherine, David; m. Virginia Ryan, June 20, 1981; stepchildren: Elizabeth DeHaas, Ryan DeHaas. A.B., Harvard U., 1964, J.D., 1967. Bar: N.Y. 1970, U.S. Dist. Ct. (so. and ea. dists.) N.Y. 1971, U.S. Ct. Appeals (2d cir.) 1972, U.S. Supreme Ct. 1973. Maxwell Sch. Africa Pub. Svc. fellow (funded by Ford Found.) Republic of Malawi, 1967-69, state counsel, 1968-69; assoc. Cravath, Swaine & Moore, N.Y.C., 1969-75, ptnr., 1975—, dep. presiding ptnr., 1997-98, presiding ptnr., 1999—; apptd. to bd. dirs. by Pres. Clinton, Romanian Am. Enterprise Fund, 1994—. Bd. dirs. Lawyers Com. for Human Rights; bd. dirs. The Jericho Project, 1985-97; chair Harvard Law Sch. Nat. Fund, 1995-97, Dean's Adv. Bd., 1997—. Mem. ABA, N.Y. Bar Assn., Assn. of the Bar of the City of N.Y. (chmn. trade regulation com. 1980-83, exec. com. 1995-99), Coun. on Fgn. Rels., Human Rights Watch/Africa (adv. com.), Harvard Club. Antitrust, Federal civil litigation, Communications. Home: 300 W End Ave Apt 13A New York NY 10023-8156 Office: Cravath Swaine & Moore 825 8th Ave Fl 46 New York NY 10019-7416

**JOHANNSEN, MARC ALAN,** lawyer; b. Victorville, Calif., Feb. 14, 1964; s. Gerald W. and Sharon K. J.; m. Kimberly Kriss, Sept. 29, 1990. BSBA magna cum laude, Carroll Coll., 1986; JD cum laude, U. Minn., 1989. Bar: Minn. 1989, U.S. Dist. Ct. Minn. 1990, Wis. 1997. Jud. clk. Hennepin County Dist. Ct., Mpls., 1989-90, Minn. Ct. Appeals, St. Paul, 1990-91; atty., shareholder Lommen, Nelson, Cole & Stageberg, Mpls., 1991—. Vol. pro bono atty. Vol. Lawyers Network, Mpls., 1991—; mem. city coun. City of Vadnais Heights, Minn., 1995—. Mem. ABA, Minn. Bar Assn., Hennepin County Bar Assn. Avocations: hiking, gardening, computers, politics. Family and matrimonial, General civil litigation. Office: Lommen Nelson Cole & Stageberg 80 S 80th St 1800 IDS Minneapolis MN 55127

**JOHANSON, DAVID RICHARD,** lawyer; b. St. Paul, Sept. 27, 1957; s. Carol Lyle and Mabel Ruth (Person) J.; children: David Richard II, Britta Mae. AA in Liberal Arts, Columbia Coll., 1980; B in Individualized Studies summa cum laude, U. Minn., 1983, JD cum laude, 1986. Bar: Minn. 1986, D.C. 1989, Md. 1990, Calif. 1993, U.S. Dist. Ct. Minn. 1987, U.S. Dist. Ct. (no. dist.) Calif. 1994, U.S. Tax Ct. 1987, U.S. Ct. Appeals (8th cir.) 1987. Assoc., law clk. Bowman & London, St. Paul, 1984-85, 86-87; tax cons. Ernst & Whinney, Mpls., 1986-87; assoc. Ober, Kaler, Grimes & Shriver, Balt., 1988-93; mem. Ludwig & Jeans, San Francisco, 1993; income ptnr. Keck, Mahin & Cate, San Francisco, 1993-95; equity ptnr. Graham & James LLP, San Francisco, 1995-97; of counsel Case Bigelow & Lombardi, Honolulu, 1997—. Author: (introduction) Selling to an ESOP, 1998, Employee Stock Ownership Plans 1996 Yearbook, and subsequent edits.; editor (periodical) ESOP Calif., 1993—; bd. editors Jour. Employee Ownership Law and Fin., 1994—, ESOP Report, Legal Update, 1992—, The Stock Options Book, Employee Stock Options and Related Equity Incentives, 1997. Pro bono work Bar Assn. San Francisco, 1993-97, Napa County (Calif.) Pub. Defender's Office, 1994. Sgt. USAF, 1976-80. Mem. The Employee Stock Ownership Plan, Assn. (bd. dirs. 1994-96, chair legis. and regulatory adv. com. 1993-95, chair adv. com. chairs coun. 1994-96, Calif./western states chpt. steering com. 1993—, v.p. profl. mems. 1996-98, Outstanding Adv. Com. Chair 1993-94, monthly columnist 1992—), Nat. Ctr. for Employee Ownership (bd. dirs. 1996—, stock options adv. bd. 1997—), Found. for Enterprise Devel. Avocations: running, cycling, hiking, traveling. E-mail: drj@esop-law.com. Pension, profit-sharing, and employee benefits, Mergers and acquisitions, Finance.

**JOHN, ROBERT MCCLINTOCK,** lawyer; b. Phila., May 21, 1947; s. Lewis Timothy and Marie (McClintock) J.; m. Barbara Ann Weand, May 10, 1975; children: Jennifer, Ryan. BA, Villanova U., 1969, JD, 1972. Bar: Pa. 1972, U.S. Dist. Ct. (ea. dist.) Pa. 1973, U.S. Ct. of Appeals (3d cir.) 1998. Atty. Schneider, Nixon & John, Hatboro, Pa., 1972-74, ptnr., 1975-93, sole proprietor, 1993—. Scoutmaster Boy Scouts Am., Hatboro, 1972—, long range planning com., 1979; lectr. and student loan com. Hatboro-Horsham High Sch., 1972-95, co-chmn. Tip of the Hat Cavalcade of Bands, 1994, 95, 96; co-prs. Hatters for Music, 1997-99; prodr. multi media banquet show Marching Hatters, 1994-98; mgr. Little League, Horsham, Pa., 1985-96, girls' sr. tournament coach, 1993; referee Hatboro-Horsham Youth Basketball Assn., 1990-91, mgr., 1991-94. Recipient award Hatboro-Horsham Sch. Bd., 1979, medal Hatboro YMCA Triathlon, 1983, Silver Beaver award Boy Scouts Am., 1981, Scoutmaster's award of Merit, 1989, Nat. God and Svc. award, 1991, Hatboro-Horsham H.S. Prin.'s Golden Apple award, 1997, Martin Luther King Humanitarian award Upper Moreland Mid. Sch., 1997, others. Mem. Pa. Bar Assn., Montgomery County Bar Assn., Greater Hatboro C. of C. (pres. 1983, Honored Citizen Svc. to Youth award 1984, judge advocate 1984—, chmn. awards com. and prod. multimedia awards ceremony biannual borough ball, 86, 89, 97, 99), Navy League (sec. southeastern Pa. coun. 1975-88, pres. 1989, S.E. Pa. Coun. Svc. to Youth and Community award 1990, Willow Grove naval Air Sta. svc. award 1986), Rotary (pres. 1984, Dist. Gov.'s Outstanding Pres.'s award 1984, host family foreign exch. students). Republican. Roman Catholic. Avocations: scouting, swimming, cycling, backpacking. Family and matrimonial, General practice, Probate. Home: 83 Home Rd Hatboro PA 19040-1830 Office: Schneider Nixon & John 76 Byberry Ave # 698 Hatboro PA 19040-3419

**JOHNS, DEBORAH ANN HENRY,** lawyer; b. Cin., Aug. 14, 1954; d. Don P. and Dorine N. Henry; m. Robert John, Dec. 29, 1998; children: Jennifer, Ane, Jessica, Judith. BSE in Edn., Ark. State U.; JD, U. Ark. Staff atty. West Tex. Legal Svcs., Ft. Worth, 1991-94, Ark. Ct. of Appeals, Little Rock, Ark., 1985-90; pvt. practice Fort Worth, 1994—. Vol. Batter Womens Shelter, Fort Worth, 1995, 96, Open Arms, Fort Worth, 1994—. Avocations: reading, needlework, swimming. Family and matrimonial, Alternative dispute resolution, Landlord-tenant. Office: 610 E Weatherford St Fort Worth TX 76102-3264

**JOHNS, LARRY CHARLES,** lawyer; b. Las Vegas, Dec. 23, 1944; s. Raymond Mark and Helen Marie (Holmes) J.; m. Mary Louise Pratt, June 4, 1966; children: Charles, Laura, Julianna, Jason. BA, U. Ariz., 1966, JD, 1968. Assoc. E.M. Gunderson, Las Vegas, 1968-69; dep. dist. atty. Clark County Dist. Atty., Las Vegas, 1969-71; ptnr., shareholder Johns & Johns Ltd., Las Vegas, 1971-96; pres., shareholder Larry C. Johns, P.C., Las Vegas, 1996—. mem. ATLA, Nev. Trial Lawyers Assn., Nev. Am. Inns of Ct. Republican. Methodist. Office: 517 S 3rd St Las Vegas NV 89101-6501

**JOHNS, MICHAEL A.,** prosecutor. 1st asst. U.S. atty. State of Ariz., Phoenix. Office: US Courthouse and Fed Bldg 230 N 1st Ave Phoenix AZ 85025-0230

**JOHNS, RICHARD SETH ELLIS,** lawyer; b. Eugene, Oreg., Apr. 23, 1946; s. Frank Errol Jr. and Emily Elizabeth (Ellis) J.; m. Eleanor Lee Kuntz, Mar. 8, 1981. BA in English, U. Calif., Santa Barbara, 1968; JD, U. Calif., San Francisco, 1971. Bar: Calif. 1971, Ill. 1972. Instr. law U. Chgo., 1972-73; assoc. Atchison, Topeka & Santa Fe RR, Chgo., 1973-75, Furth, Fahrner, Bluemle & Mason, San Francisco, 1975-84; of counsel Maier, Dimitriou & Ross, San Francisco, 1984; ptnr. Rubenstein, Bohachek & Johns, San Francisco, 1985-88, Kipperman & Johns, San Francisco, 1988—. Contbr. articles to Calif. Law Rev. Bd. dirs. Congregation Beth Shalom, San Francisco, 1982-92, Bay Area sect. Am. Jewish Com., 1984—; leader Family Policy Task Force, 1987-88; guest of Christian Dem. Union, Konrad Adenhauer Stiftung-German-Am. Jewish Exchange Program, Fed. Republic Germany, 1985; dir. Mus. of the City of San Francisco, 1996-97, v.p., 1997—. 1st lt. U.S. Army, 1972-75. Mem. ABA, Calif. Bar Assn., Concordia-Argonaut Club, Ill. State Bar. Federal civil litigation, General civil litigation, Real property. Office: Kipperman & Johns 3 Embarcadero Ctr Ste 28 San Francisco CA 94111-4074

**JOHNS, WARREN LEROI,** lawyer; b. Nevada, Iowa, June 9, 1929; s. Varner Jay and Ruby Charlene (Morrison) J.; m. Elaine C. Magnuson, July 24, 1955 (div. June 1983); children: Richard Warren, Lynn Cherie Johns-Pence; m. Ruth Page Scott, Sept. 29, 1985. BA, La Sierra U., 1950; MA, Andrews U., 1951; JD, U. So. Calif., 1958. Bar: Calif. 1959, U.S. Dist. Ct. (cen. dist.) Calif. 1959,U.S. Supreme Ct. 1963, Md. 1976, D.C. 1976, U.S. Dist. Ct. Md. 1976, U.S. Dist. Ct. D.C. 1976, U.S. Tax Ct. 1976, U.S. Ct. Appeals (4th cir.) 1976, U.S. Ct. Appeals (10th cir.) 1977, U.S. Ct. Customs and Patent Appeals 1979. Gen. counsel So. Calif. Conf. Seventh-day Adventists, Glendale, 1959-63, Pacific Union Conf. Seventh-day Adventists, Glendale and Sacramento, 1964-69; pvt. practice Sacramento, 1969-75; gen. counsel Gen. Conf. Seventh-day Adventists, Washington, 1975-92, trustee; pvt. practice Brookeville, Md., 1992-98; mem. adv. bd. Ctr. for Ch./State Studies, De Paul U. Coll. Chgo., 1987-93, spl. counsel to gen. conf., 1992-95; spl. counsel Adventist HealthCare Corp., Columbia Union HealthCare Corp., 1992-97. Author: Dateline Sunday USA, 1967, Ride to Glory, 1999; founding editor JD, 1978-92. Chmn. bd. dirs., pres. Sacramento Area Econ. Opportunity Coun., 1974. Recipient Frank Yost award Ch. State Coun., Glendale, Alumnus of Achievement award Andrews U., 1981, Alumnus of Yr. award La Sierra U., 1994. Mem. AAAS, ABA (vice-chmn. com. on torts, non-profit, charitable and religious orgns., sect. of tort and ins. practice 1990-91). Democrat. Avocations: sports, photography, book collecting. General corporate, General practice, Alternative dispute resolution. Office: 21320 Georgia Ave Brookeville MD 20833-1132

**JOHNSON, ALAN BOND,** federal judge; b. 1939. BA, Vanderbilt U., 1961; JD, U. Wyo., 1964. Pvt. practice law Cheyenne, Wyo., 1968-71; assoc. Hanes, Carmichael, Johnson, Gage & Speight P.C., Cheyenne, 1971-74; judge Wyo. Dist. Ct., 1974-85; judge U.S. Dist. Ct. Wyo., 1986-92, chief judge, 1992—; part-time fed. magistrate U.S. Dist. Ct. Wyo., 1971-74; substitute judge Mcpl. Ct., Cheyenne, 1973-74. Served to capt. USAF, 1964-67, to col. Wyo. Air N.G., 1973-90. Mem. ABA, Wyo. State Bar, Laramie County Bar Assn. (sec.-treas. 1968-70), Wyo. Jud. Conf. (sec. 1977-78, chmn. 1979), Wyo. Jud. Council. Office: US Dist Ct O'Mahoney Fed Ctr 2120 Capitol Ave Ste 2242 Cheyenne WY 82001-3666

**JOHNSON, ALEXANDER CHARLES,** lawyer, electrical engineer; b. Richmond, Va., Aug. 1, 1948. BSEE, The Citadel, 1970; MSEE, Purdue U., 1974; JD cum laude, Brigham Young U., 1978. Bar: Oreg. 1978, U.S. Patent and Trademark Office 1979, U.S. Ct. Appeals (8th, 9th and Fed. cirs.) 1984. From assoc. to ptnr. Klarquist, Sparkman, Campbell, Leigh & Whinston, Portland, Oreg., 1978-86; prin. Marger, Johnson, & McCollom, P.C., Portland, 1986—. Author: IP Protection in Semiconductor Industry, 1989. Capt. USAF, 1975, USAFR, 1975-83. Mem. ABA (intellectual property sect.), Am. Intellectual Property Law Assn., Oreg. Bar Assn., Order of Barristers, Tau Beta Pi. Patent, Trademark and copyright. Office: Marger Johnson & McCollom PC 1030 SW Morrison St Portland OR 97205-2626

**JOHNSON, ALISE M.,** lawyer; b. Gainesville, Fla., Dec. 17, 1968; d. Gregory William and Jean (Long) J. BA, Vanderbilt U., 1989; JD, U. Fla., 1993. Bar: Fla. 1994, U.S. Dist. Ct. (so., mid. and no. dists.) Fla. Law clk. U.S. Magistrate Chief William Turnoff, Miami, Fla., 1994-97; assoc. Akerman Senterfitt, Miami, 1997—. Articles editor U. Fla. Law Rev., 1993. Mem. Jr. League of Miami, 1995—; participant Leadership Miami, 1998. Municipal (including bonds), General civil litigation, Insurance. Office: Akerman Senterfitt One SE 3d Ave 28th Fl Miami FL 33131

**JOHNSON, ANNE STUCKLY,** lawyer; b. Axtell, Tex., Jan. 8, 1921; d. Arnold Joseph and Angeline (Morris) Stuckly; m. Edward James Johnson, Oct. 9, 1943 (dec. 1967); children: edward M., Ronald J., Dennis L., Shawn T., Rozlynn Jan, Anne J'lynn, Kevin J, Karal Ian, Donna Lynn. BA, Baylor U., 1940; MA in Econs., St. Mary's U., 1974, JD, 1980. Bar: Tex. 1980. Claims clk. Social Security Adminstrn., Amarillo, Tex., 1940-42; asst. chief divsn. pers. Pantex Ordnance Plant, Amarillo, Tex., 1942-43; chief divsn. pers. Cactus Ordnance Works, Dumas, Tex., 1943-44; citations unit supr. Gen. Hdqrs. Far East Command, Tokyo, 1950-51; v.p., treas. Drive-Safe Corp., San Antonio, 1967-69; counseling psychologist ARC, San Antonio, 1968-69; counseling psychologist Divsn. Pers. Office, Ft. Sam Houston, 1969, pers. mgmt. specialist, 1969-77; pvt. practice Oliver B. Chamberlin Offices, San Antonio, 1981-86; pvt. practice San Antonio, 1987-93, ret., 1994. Active Am. Heart Assn., 1983—. Mem. ABA, San Antonio Bar Assn., Tex. Bar Assn., Am. Trial Lawyers Assn., Assn. Social Econs., Tex. Trial Lawyers Assn., Phi Alpha Delta, Pi Gamma Mu, Omicron Delta Epsilon. Home: 115 Meadowood Ln San Antonio TX 78216-7323

**JOHNSON, BARBARA JEAN,** retired judge, lawyer; b. Detroit, Apr. 9, 1932; d. Clifford Clarence and Orma Cecile (Boring) Barnhouse; m. Ronald Mayo Johnson, June 24, 1965; 1 dau., Belinda Etezad. B.S., U. So. Calif., 1953, J.D., 1970. Bar: Calif. 1971. Ptnr. Anglea, Burford, Johnson & Tookay, Pasadena, Calif., 1970-77; judge L.A. Mcpl. Ct., 1977-81; judge L.A. Superior Ct., 1981-97; ret., 1997; lectr. U. So. Calif. Law Sch. profl. program; adj. prof. Southwestern U. Law Sch. Recipient Ernestine Stahlhut award, 1981. Mem. Calif. Judges Assn., Nat. Assn. Women Judges, Calif. Women Lawyers Assn. (pres. 1976-77), Women Lawyers Assn. L.A. (pres. 1975-76), Internat. Assn. Women Judges, World Jurist Assn. Home: 1000 Prospect Blvd Pasadena CA 91103-2810

**JOHNSON, BENJAMIN F(RANKLIN), III,** lawyer; b. Atlanta, Aug. 20, 1943; s. Benjamin Franklin Jr. and Stella Byrd (Darnell) J.; m. Ann Armistead, Aug., 6, 1966; children: Benjamin Franklin IV, James Leslie Armistead. BA, Emory U., 1965; JD, Harvard U., 1968. Bar: Ga. 1968, U.S. Ct. Appeals (5th cir.) 1973, U.S. Ct. Appeals (11th cir.) 1982, U.S. Dist. Ct. (no. dist.) Ga. 1969, U.S. Dist. Ct. (so. dist.) Ga. 1978, U.S. Dist. Ct. (mid. dist.) Ga. 1981. Law clk. to judge Griffin B. Bell U.S. Ct. Appeals (5th cir.), Atlanta, 1968-69; assoc. Alston, Miller & Gaines, Atlanta, 1971-76; ptnr. Alston & Bird and predecessor firm Alston, Miller & Gaines, Atlanta, 1976—; mem. faculty Stonier Grad. Sch. Banking, Newark, Del., 1982-91. Co-author: Problem Loan Strategies, 1985. chmn. governing bd. Woodward Acad., College Park, Ga., 1982-95; chmn. bd. trustees Atlanta Leadership Devel. Found., 1994-95; trustee Emory U., 1995, Charles Loridans Found., 1991-95; pres. Rsch. Atlanta, 1988. 1st lt. U.S. Army, 1969-71, Vietnam. Recipient Disting. Alumnus award Woodward Acad., 1981. Mem. Ga. Bar Assn., Atlanta Bar Assn. (chmn. litigation sect. 1980), Atlanta Lawyer's Club, Commerce Club, Ansley Golf Club. Democrat. Avocations: reading, music, politics, exercise. Banking, General civil litigation, Construction. Home: 288 The Prado NE Atlanta GA 30309-3336 Office: Alston & Bird One Atlantic Ctr 1201 W Peachtree St NW Ste 4200 Atlanta GA 30309-3424

**JOHNSON, BERNETTE J.,** state supreme court justice; b. Ascension Parish, La.; d. Frank Joshua Jr. and Olivia W. Johnson. BA, Spelman Coll., Atlanta, 1964; JD, La. State U., 1969. Bar: La. Law intern Civil Rights divsn. U.S. Dept. Justice; judge La. Civil Dist. Ct., 1984-94, chief judge, 1994; assoc. justice La. Supreme Ct., New Orleans, 1994—; legal svc. atty. New Orleans Legal Asst. Corp. Bd. dirs. YMCA, New Orleans; chmn. bd. Learning Ctr., Great St. Stephen Full Gospel Bapt. Ch. Named Woman of Yr., LaBelle chpt. Am. Bus. Women's Assn., 1994. Office: Supreme Ct Bldg 301 Loyola Ave New Orleans LA 70112-1814*

**JOHNSON, BETH EXUM,** lawyer; b. Beaumont, Tex., July 4, 1952; d. James Powers Jr. and Betty Jean (Clement) Exum; m. Walter William Johnson, Apr. 25, 1981; children: Stratton William, Jacqueline Clement, Jacob Claiborne. BA in Psychology, Tulane U., 1974; JD, Loyola U., New Orleans, 1985; LLM in Energy and Environ., Tulane U., 1989. Bar: La. 1985, Tex. 1993, U.S. Dist. Ct. (ea. dist.) La. 1985, U.S. Dist. Ct. (we. and mid. dists.) 1989. Paralegal McCloskey, Dennery, Page & Hennesy, New Orleans, 1975-80; oil and gas abstractor of title Frawley, Wogan, Miller & Co., New Orleans, 1980-82; assoc. trust counsel, asst. v.p. and trust officer Hibernia Nat. Bank, New Orleans, 1985-95; legal cons. New Orleans, 1995-96; assoc. Gelpi and Assocs., PLC, New Orleans, 1996—; mem. faculty succession practice Tulane U., New Orleans, 1990-94, 97, environ. law practice, 1991-94; mem. fundraising com. and atty. honor roll New Orleans Pro

Bono Project. Mem. New Orleans Estate Planning Coun. Mem. ABA, La. Bar Assn., New Orleans Bar Assn., Jr. League New Orleans, Friends City Park, La. Children's Mus., Audubon Zoo, Aquarium and La. Nature Ctr., Phi Alpha Delta, Kappa Alpha Theta. Avocations: tennis, Thoroughbred horse racing, interior decorating, travel. Probate, Oil, gas, and mineral. Home: 959 Harrison Ave New Orleans LA 70124-3837 Office: 203 Carondelet St Ste 907 New Orleans LA 70130-3087

**JOHNSON, BRENT ALLEN,** lawyer; b. Anchorage, Alaska, May 1, 1959; s. Emil Charles and Irene Mary Petersen; m. Debra Lynn Appleton Johnson, June 24, 1982; children: Staci Wood, Robert Collier, Marcus. BSBA, Chapman U., 1988; JD, Gonzaga U., 1991. Bar: Alaska, U.S. Dist. Ct., U.S. Ct. Appeals (9th cir.). Assoc. Fortier & Mikko, P.C., Anchorage, Alaska, 1992-93, Royce & Brain, Anchorage, 1993-95; ptnr. Johnson & Kim, LLC, Anchorage, 1995-98; rates and tariffs analyst Anchorage Mcpl. Light and Power, 1998—; adj. prof. U. Alaska, 1996—. Coach, mgr. Simonian Little League, Anchorage, 1996—. Mem. Phi Delta Phi. Republican. Roman Catholic. E-mail: JohnsonBA@ci.anchorage.ak.us and bjlaw@gci.net. Bankruptcy, Family and matrimonial, Estate planning. Home: PO Box 111797 Anchorage AK 99511-1797 Office: Anchorage Mcpl Light and Power 1200 E 1st Ave Anchorage AK 99501-1658

**JOHNSON, BRUCE CARLTON,** lawyer; b. Moline, Ill., Mar. 17, 1949; s. Kenneth Mauritz and Phyllis Jean (Armstrong) J. BS in Comm., U. Ill., 1970, MS in Comm., 1972; JD, U. Mich., 1977. Bar: N.Y. 1978, U.S. Dist. Ct. (so. and ea. dists.) N.Y. 1978. Assoc. Chadbourne, Parke, Whiteside & Wolff, N.Y.C., 1977-84, Wofsey, Certilman, Haft et al, N.Y.C., 1984-87, Parker Chapin Flattau & Klimpl, N.Y.C., 1987-93, Rosen & Reade, N.Y.C., 1993-94, Graubard Mollen & Miller, N.Y.C., 1994-98, Hall Dickler Kent Friedman & Wood, N.Y.C., 1998—. Mem. parish coun. St. Peter's Ch., N.Y.C.; chmn. bd. Canterbury Choral Soc., N.Y.C.; trustee Phi Sigma Kappa Found., Indpls. Mem. ABA, N.Y. State Bar Assn., Assn. Bar City N.Y. Lutheran. Avocations: singing, college alumni affairs, theater, canoeing. Probate, Estate taxation, Estate planning. Home: 300 E 40th St Apt 19-t New York NY 10016-2152 Office: Hall Dickler Kent Friedman & Wood 909 3d Ave New York NY 10022

**JOHNSON, BRUCE EDWARD HUMBLE,** lawyer; b. Columbus, Jan. 22, 1950; s. Hugo Edward and M. Alice (Humble) J.; m. Paige Robinson Miller, June 28, 1980; children: Marta Noble, Winslow Collins, Russell Scott. AB, Harvard U., 1972; JD, Yale U., 1977; MA, U. Cambridge, Eng., 1978. Bar: Wash. 1977, Calif. 1992. Atty. Davis Wright Tremaine LLP, Seattle, 1977—; King County Gov. Access Channel Oversight com., 1996—. Bd. dirs. Seattle Repertory Theatre, 1993—, pres., 1999—. Mem. ABA (tort and ins. practice sect., media law and defamation torts com. chair 1999—). Constitutional, General civil litigation, Libel. Home: 711 W Kinnear Pl Seattle WA 98119-3621 Office: Davis Wright Tremaine LLP 2600 Century Sq 1501 4th Ave Seattle WA 98101-1688

**JOHNSON, BYRON JERALD,** retired state supreme court judge; b. Boise, Idaho, Aug. 2, 1937; s. Arlie Johnson and V. Bronell (Dunten) J.; children: Matthew, Ethan, Elaine, Laura; m. Paticia G. Young, 1984. AB, Harvard U., 1959, LLB, 1962. Bar: Idaho, 1962. Justice Idaho Supreme Ct., Boise, 1988-98; ret., 1998.

**JOHNSON, BYRON JOHN,** lawyer, real estate developer, educator; b. Bessemer, Mich., June 15, 1944; s. Roy John and Betty Jeanette (Hagelin) J.; m. Karen Lee Borre, Aug. 21, 1971; children: Eric, Travis. BS, No. Mich. U., 1968; MA, Ea. Mich. U., 1968; JD, Thomas M. Colley Law Sch., 1977. Bar: Mich. 1977, U.S. Dist. Ct. (we. dist.) Mich. 1979. Assoc. Foley, Rasmusson & Emerson, Lansing, Mich., 1977; Assoc. Smith & Johnson, Traverse City, Mich., 1977-80; gen. counsel J.D. Hitchens, Traverse City, Mich., 1980-83; sr. corp. counsel Amway Corp., Ada, Mich., 1983—; v.p., gen. counsel Nutrilite Products Divsn.; gen. ptnr. Cmty. Housing, Traverse City, 1982—; adj. prof., former adv. bd. mem. paralegal program Davenport Bus. Coll. Grand Rapids, Mich.; former adj. prof. Grand Valley State U., Allendale, Mich.; bd. dirs. Coun. for Responsible Nutrition. Former chmn. bd. trustees Ada Congl. Ch. With U.S. Army, 1969-71, Vietnam. Decorated Bronze Star with two oak leaf clusters. Mem. ABA, State Bar Mich., Grand Rapids Bar Assn., Am. Corp. Counsel Assn., No. Mich. U. Alumni Assn. (ex officio past pres., nat. bd. dirs. 1987—). General practice, Mergers and acquisitions, Real property. Home: 7777 Kirkwall Dr SE Ada MI 49301-9389 Office: Amway Corp 7575 E Fulton St Ada MI 49301 also: Nutrilite Divsn 5600 Beach Blvd Buena Park CA 90621-2007

**JOHNSON, C. TERRY,** lawyer; b. Bridgeport, Conn., Sept. 24, 1937; s. Clifford Gustave and Evelyn Florence (Terry) J.; m. Suzanne Frances Chichy, Aug. 24, 1985; children: Laura Elizabeth, Melissa Lynne, Clifford Terry. AB, Trinity Coll., 1960; LLD, Columbia U., 1963. Bar: Ohio 1964, U.S. Ct. Appeals (6th cir.) 1966, U.S. Dist. Ct. (so. dist.) Ohio 1970. Legal dep. probate ct. Montgomery County, Dayton, Ohio, 1964-67; head probate dept. Coolidge Wall & Wood, Dayton, 1967-79, Smith & Schnacke, Dayton, 1979-89, Thompson, Hine and Flory, Dayton, 1989-92; head estate planning and probate group Porter, Wright, Morris & Arthur, Dayton, 1992—; frequent lectr. on estate planning to various profl. orgns. Contbr. articles to profl. jours. Fellow Am. Coll. Trust and Estate Counsel; mem. Ohio Bar Assn. (bd. govs. probate and trust law sect., chmn. 1993-95), Dayton Bar Assn. (chmn. probate com. 1992-94), Ohio State Bar Found. (trustee 1995-99), Ohio CLE Inst. (trustee 1995-99, chair 1998-99), Dayton Legal Secs. Assn. (hon.), Dayton Racquet Club, Dayton Bicycle Club. Estate planning, Probate, Estate taxation. Home: 8307 Rhine Way Centerville OH 45458-3017 Office: Porter Wright Morris & Arthur 1 S Main St Ste 1600 Dayton OH 45402-2028

**JOHNSON, CAROLYN JEAN,** law librarian; b. Beaver Dam, Wis., Nov. 7, 1938; d. Henry William and Bernice Mae (Haas) Krueger; m. Robert Edward Johnson, June 19, 1960; children: Eric Steven, Kristin Elizabeth. BS in Edn., Wartburg Coll., 1960. Tchr. various locations, 1960-64, Hennepin County Library, 1972-81; libr. 3M Tech. Libr., St. Paul, 1981-86; law libr. 3M Ctr. Law Libr., St. Paul, 1986—. Mem. Am. Assn. Law Libraries, Minn. Assn. Law Libraries. Lutheran. Avocations: reading, walking, cooking. Office: 3M Co Ctr Law Library PO Box 33355 Saint Paul MN 55133-3355

**JOHNSON, CHARLES WILLIAM,** state supreme court justice; b. Tacoma, Wash., Mar. 16, 1951. BA in Econs., U. Wash., 1973; JD, U. Puget Sound, 1976. Bar: Wash. 1977. Justice Wash. Supreme Ct., 1991—; mem. Wash. State Minority and Justice Commn. Bd. dirs. Wash. Assn. Children and Parents; mem. vis. com. U. Wash. Sch. Social Work; bd. visitors Seattle U. Sch. Law, mem. Washington State Courthouse Sec. Task Force. Mem. Wash. State Bar Assn., Tacoma-Pierce County Bar Assn. (Liberty Bell award young lawyers sect. 1994). Avocations: sailing, downhill skiing, cycling. Office: Wash State Supreme Ct Temple of Justice PO Box 40929 Olympia WA 98504-0929*

**JOHNSON, CHERYL ANN,** judge; b. Aurora, Ill., Sept. 30, 1946; d. Ellsworth Tower and Vava Vieda (Munson) J.; m. Gregory William Lasley, May 27, 1989. BS, Ohio State U., 1968; MS, U. Ill., Urbana, 1970; JD, John Marshall Law Sch., Chgo., 1984. Bar: Tex. 1983, Ill. 1984, U.S. Ct. Appeals (7th cir.) 1986, U.S. Dist. Ct. (we. dist.) Tex. 1991; cert. in criminal law Tex. Bd. Legal Specialization. Jud. clk. U.S. Ct. Appeals for 5th Circuit, 1983-84; pvt. practice Austin, 1984-98; judge Tex. Ct. Criminal Appeals, Austin, 1999—. Tutor Literacy Austin, 1997—. Mem. State Bar Coll., Tex. Criminal Def. Lawyers Assn., Austin Criminal Def. Lawyers Assn. Office: Tex Ct Criminal Appeals Capitol Sta PO Box 12308 Austin TX 78711-2308

**JOHNSON, CHRISTIAN KENT,** lawyer; b. Hays, Kans., Dec. 11, 1935; s. Joseph Claude and Arleen (Wilson) J.; m. Jeanne Aldridge, June 16, 1957 (div. 1982); children: Kimberly Ann, Christian Kent Jr.; m. Judith Ann Tucker, Sept. 10, 1982. BS in Acctg., U. Colo., 1957, JD, 1961. Bar: Colo. 1961. Ptnr. Gordon, Gordon & Johnson, Lamar, Colo., 1961-64; trust officer 1st Interstate Bank, Denver, 1964-67, sr. v.p., 1967-76, exec. v.p., 1976-79; owner, mgr. Equity Mgmt. Group, Inc., Denver, 1979-80; ptnr. Buchanan, Thomas & Johnson, P.C., Lakewood, Colo., 1980-88; pvt. practice Ouray, Colo., 1988-95; ptnr. Johnson & Link, P.C., Ouray, 1995—. Bd. dirs. Craig Hosp., Englewood, Colo., 1978-86, pres., 1983-85. Mem. ABA, Colo. Bar Assn., Denver Bar Assn., Denver Estate Planning Coun. (bd.d irs. 1965), Lions (bd. dirs. Denver 1966-78), Montrose County Rotary. Presbyterian. Avocations: reading, outdoor activities. Estate planning, Probate, Estate taxation. Home: PO Box 662 Ouray CO 81427-0662 Office: PO Box 663 Ouray CO 81427-0663

**JOHNSON, CHRISTOPHER GEORGE,** lawyer; b. Aug. 22, 1963; s. Alexander Chester and Virginia Ann J.; m. Diane Marie Dorkey, June 30, 1990; children: Stephanie, Samantha. BA (hons.) in History, Canisius Coll., 1985; JD, U. Detroit, 1988. Bar: N.Y. 1989, U.S. Dist. Ct. (we. dist.) N.Y. 1993. Pvt. practice Rochester, N.Y., 1989; assoc. attorney Darweesh, Callen & Lewis, Rochester, N.Y., 1989; asst. dist. attorney Monroe County Dist. Attorney's Office, Rochester, N.Y., 1989—. Rschr. Mich. Criminal Law Update, 1988. Mem. CURE Childhood Cancer, Mock Trial Law Explorers (winning coach 1992), Neighborhood Enforcement team, Rochester, 1997—; active Leadership Rochester, 1998—; steering com. Minority Achiever's Program, YMCA Metro Rochester, 1996—. Mem. N.Y. Welfare Fraud Investigation Assn., United Counsel on Welfare Fraud. Roman Catholic. Avocations: my children, reading, home brewing, physical fitness. Office: Monroe County District Attorneys Office 832 Ebenezer Watts Bldg Rochester NY 14617

**JOHNSON, CHRISTOPHER PAUL,** lawyer; b. Bklyn., Apr. 25, 1960; s. Edward William and Margaret Sheridan (Lynch) J.; m. Maureen Elizabeth Piga, Jan. 30, 1983; children: Caitlin Marie, Christopher Paul Jr., Megan Cecilia. BA, Fordham U., N.Y.C., 1982; JD, U. Va., 1986. Bar: N.Y. 1987, U.S. Dist. Ct. (so. and ea. dists.) N.Y. 1987, U.S. Dist. Ct. (we. dist.) Mich. 1996, U.S. Ct. Appeals(3d cir.) 1994, U.S. Ct. Appeals (2d and 6th cirs.) 1996, Ct. Internat. Trade 1989, U.S. Tax Ct. 1994. Assoc. Donovan Leisure Newton & Irvine, N.Y.C., 1986-95, ptnr., 1995-97; ptnr. Brobeck Phleger & Harrison, LLP, N.Y.C., 1997—. Mem. ABA, N.Y. State Bar Assn., Bar Assn. City of N.Y. Product liability, General civil litigation, Criminal. Office: Brobeck Phleger & Harrison LLP 1633 Broadway Fl 47 New York NY 10019-6708

**JOHNSON, CLARENCE TRAYLOR, JR.,** federal judge; b. Trenton, Fla., Aug. 16, 1929; s. Clarence Traylor and Jessie Granade (Wilson) J.; m. Shirley Ann Traxler, Aug. 30, 1957; children: James Waring, Robert Dale, Douglas Earl, Jan Elizabeth. BSBA, U. Fla., 1955, JD, 1958. Ptnr. Cone, Wagner, Nugent, Johnson, McKeown & Dell, West Palm Beach, Fla., 1958-71; cir. ct. judge 18th Jud. Cir. of Fla., Brevard and Seminole Counties, 1971-92; chmn. Fla. Conf. of Cir. Judges, 1990-91; mem. Fla. Bench Bar Commn., State of Fla., 1990-92; faculty Fla. Jud. Coll., 1988-90; mem. Fla. Fed.-State Jud. Coun., 1989-91, Jud. Coun. Fla., 1989-91. Pres. Jr. C. of C., Cocoa, Fla., 1963-64; chmn. bd. Cen. Brevard YMCA, Cocoa, 1965-66; pres. YMCA, Brevard County, 1968-71, Rotary, Cocoa, 1965-66; charter pres. Vassar B. Carlton Am. Inn of Ct., 1992-93. With USAF, 1950-54. Recipient Disting. Svc. award Cocoa Jaycees, 1965, Jud. Achievement award Acad. Fla. Trial Lawyers, 1987. Mem. ABA, Brevard County Bar Assn. (pres. 1969-70), The Fla. Bar (bd. govs. 1970-71). Lutheran. Avocation: fishing. Home: 600 Heron Dr Merritt Island FL 32952-4022

**JOHNSON, CRAIG EDWARD,** lawyer; b. Orange, N.J., Oct. 30, 1953; s. Charles Armond Johnson and Ruth Evans Sweeny; m. Kimberly Ellen Young, Oct. 8, 1983; children: Alec Daniel, Evan McFarland, Conor Thomas. BS, Cornell U., 1976; JD, Syracuse U., 1981. Bar: D.C. 1983, N.J. 1991, U.S. Dist. Ct. D.C., U.S. Dist. Ct. N.J. 1993. Law clk. U.S. Dist. Ct., Norfolk, Va., 1981-82; atty. U.S. Dept. Energy, Washington, 1982-86; sr. atty. U.S. Dept. Justice, Washington, 1986-91; of counsel Gibbons Del Deo Dolan Griffinger Vechione, Newark, 1991-94; asst. gen. counsel, dir. litig. ITT Industries, N.Y.C., 1994—. Mem. ABA (chair real estate sect. 1994-96, chair corp. environ. enforcement coun. 1999). Environmental, General civil litigation. Office: ITT Industries 4 W Red Oak Ln Fl 2 West Harrison NY 10604-3617

**JOHNSON, CYNTHIA L(E) M(AE),** lawyer; b. Detroit, Mar. 1, 1952; d. Robert Alexander and Frances Esedell (Peeples) J.; children: Alexandra, Lauren Gayle. BA, U. Mich., 1973, MPH, 1975, JD cum laude, 1984. Bar: Mich. 1984, U.S. Dist. Ct. (ea. dist.) 1984, U.S. Supreme Ct. 1989. Health planning asst. Charles R. Drew Postgrad. Sch. Medicine, L.A., 1974; dep. project dir. Mich. Health Maintenance Orgn. Plans, Detroit, 1975; sr. health program analyst N.Y. Health and Hosps. Corp., N.Y.C., 1975-77; health care cons. UAW, Detroit, 1977-84; jud. law clk. Mich. Ct. Appeals, 1984-86, Mich. Supreme Ct., 1986-87; ptnr. Clark, Klein & Beaumont (now Clark Hill, PLC), Detroit, 1987—. Mem. ABA, Mich. Bar Assn., Detroit Bar Assn., Wolverine Bar Assn., Delta Sigma Theta. General practice, Health. Office: Clark Hill PLC 500 Woodward Ave Ste 3500 Detroit MI 48226-3435

**JOHNSON, DARRELL THOMAS, JR.,** lawyer; b. Columbia, S.C., Oct. 10, 1949; Darrell Thomas and Lorena Beckett (McDonald) J.; m. Wanda Jones, June 2, 1972; children: Darrell Thomas III, Warren Paul. BS, U. S.C., 1971; JD, 1974. Bar: S.C. 1975, U.S. Dist. Ct. S.C. 1976, U.S. Ct. Appeals (4th cir.) 1981. Criminal defense S.C., 1973; town atty. Hardeeville, S.C., 1975-81, Bluffton, S.C., 1982-83; county atty. Jasper, S.C., 1984-85. Author: (with others) Crime Law and Justice, 1974, Criminal Defense in S.C., 197. Bd. dirs. Jasper Dept. Social Svcs., S.C., 1978-82; adv. mem. Coastal Coun., Jasper, 1978-79; treas. Dem. Party, 1978-87; mem. election commn., Jasper, 1978-87, Beaufort-Jasper Bd. Higher Edn., 1999—. Mem. ABA, AIEG, Def. Trial Lawyer Assn., Assn. Trial Lawyers Am., S.C. Trial Laywrs Assn. Office: 7 Hwy 17 S Hardeeville SC 29927

**JOHNSON, DARRYL TODD,** lawyer; b. Suttons Bay, Mich., Sept. 7, 1962; s. Roderic M. and Laura J. (Steffens) J.; m. Susan E. Peckham, Sept. 6, 1986; children: Laura A., Austin T., Kelsey A. BS, Ferris State U., 1984; JD, Mich. State U., 1991. Bar: Mich. 1991, U.S. Dist. Ct. (we. dist.) Mich. 1992. Pvt. practice Darryl T. Johnson, PLC, Suttons Bay, 1991—. Candidate County Bd. Commrs., Leland, Mich., 1995; v.p. coun. Immanuel Luth. Ch., Suttons Bay, 1994-98. Mem. Rotary of Suttons Bay. Republican. Lutheran. Avocations: running, camping, home computing, home repair. General practice, Family and matrimonial, Municipal (including bonds). Home: 172 S Shore Dr Suttons Bay MI 49682-9629 Office: PO Box 811 406 St Joseph Suttons Bay MI 49682

**JOHNSON, DAVID REYNOLD,** lawyer; b. Binghamton, N.Y., Aug. 8, 1945; s. Reynold Benjamin and Beatrice (Rashleigh) J.; m. Judith Harvey, Dec. 22, 1968; children: Bryan, Kathryn. BA, Yale U., 1967, JD, 1972; student, Univ. Coll., Oxford, England, 1967-68. Bar: D.C. 1973, U.S. Ct. Appeals (5th and 11th cirs.) 1973. Law clk. to Hon. Malcolm R. Wilkey U.S. Ct. of Appeals, Washington, 1972-73; ptnr. Wilmer, Cutler & Pickering, Washington, 1973-92, 1998—, counsel, 1993-98; pres., CEO Counsel Connect; founding pres., CEO and chmn. Counsel Connect; co-dir. Cyberspace Law Inst.; speaker, writer on computerization of law and hypertext. Contbr. articles to profl. jours. Computer. Office: Wilmer Cutler & Pickering 2445 M St NW Ste 500 Washington DC 20037-1487

**JOHNSON, DAVID WESLEY,** lawyer; b. Rochester, N.Y., Mar. 13, 1933. BA, U. Rochester, 1954; LLB, Columbia U., 1959. Bar: N.Y. 1961, U.S. Dist. Ct. (so. dist.) N.Y. 1961, U.S. Dist. Ct. (no. dist.) N.Y. 1971. Counsel, sec., v.p. Textile Banking Co., N.Y.C., 1959-68; legis. counsel CIT Fin. Corp., N.Y.C., 1968-70; ptnr. Otterbourg, Steindler, Houston & Rosen, N.Y.C., 1970-71, Palmer & Johnson, Tupper Lake, N.Y., 1971-74; pvt. practice Tupper Lake, 1974—; bd. dirs. Adirondack Cmty. Trust;. Trustee, chmn. bd. North Country C.C., Saranac Lake, N.Y., 1973-82; bd. dirs., pres. High Peaks Hospice, Inc., Saranac Lake, 1988-92; bd. dirs., v.p. Lake Placid (N.Y.) Ctr. for Arts, 1989-97, Franklin County Children's Legal Svcs., Inc., pres., 1991—. Mem. Franklin County Bar Assn. (pres. 1979-81), N.Y. State Bar Assn., Lawyers Assn. Textile Industry (bd. dirs., sec.-treas. 1962-71), Assn. Comml. Fin. Attys. (bd. dirs., v.p. 1962-71). General practice. Office: 51 Lake St Tupper Lake NY 12986-1624

**JOHNSON, DEANNA K.,** educator, court reporter; b. Aug. 12, 1942, Paragould, Ark.; d. Howard and Agnes (Christian) Nichols; divorced; 1 child, Terri-Anne. Student Oakland City Coll., 1961-62, Acad. Steno Arts, 1973-76, Bay Area Inst. Ct. Reporting, 1976-78, Gadsden State Community Coll., 1983-84. Registered profl. reporter; cert. shorthand reporter, Calif. Exec. sec. various, Calif., 1960-75; ct. reporter Hendersheid & Assocs, San Francisco, 1976-78, DeSouza & Assocs., San Mateo, Calif., 1978-79; agy. owner, ct. reporter Johnson & Assocs., San Leandro, Calif., 1979-80; part-time ct. reporter freelance, Gadsden, Ala., 1980—; dir. Sch. Ct. Reporting, Gadsden State Community Coll., 1982—; hon. mem. faculty Ala. Supreme Ct./Jud. Coll., 1984. Honors com. Gadsden State Community Coll., 1983-85, Pres.' Cup selection com., 1983. Author: Deposition Manual, 1985, rev., 1989; editor Under the Bench, 1983-85; reviewer occupational brief Ct. Reporters, No. 202, 1982, 86. Ct. Reporter Pres.'s Council on Mental Health, San Francisco, 1978; guest speaker in field. Mem. NAFE, Ala. Ct. Reporters Assn. (sec., chmn. pub. relations, various coms. 1983—, pres.-elect 1987-88, pres. 1988-89, Ala. del. to nat. conv. 1984-88), Nat. Ct. Reporters Assn. (conv. planning com., 1985-86, 86-87, 87-88, chmn. Midyear Seminar 1988, Ala. chief examiner, 1983—, sch. evaluator for Bd. Approved Student Edn., various coms. 1983—, bd. dirs. 1990—), Nat. Notary Assn., Calif. Ct. Reporters Assn., Ala. Edn. Assn., NEA. Republican. Lodge: Internat. Order Job's Daus. (honored queen 1959, sec. 1973-77), Order of Eastern Star. Avocations: antiques, boating, reading, knitting, travel. Office: Gadsden State Community Coll PO Box 227 Gadsden AL 35902-0227

**JOHNSON, DENISE REINKA,** state supreme court justice; b. Wyandotte, Mich., July 13, 1947. Student, Mich. State U., 1965-67; BA, Wayne State U., 1969; postgrad., Cath. U. of Am., 1971-72; JD with honors, U. Conn., 1974. Bar: Conn. 1974, U.S. Dist. Ct. Conn. 1974, Vt. 1980, U.S. Ct. Appeals (2d cir.) 1983, U.S. Dist. Ct. Vt. 1986. Atty. New Haven (Conn.) Legal Assistance Assn., 1974-78; instr. legal writing Vt. Law Sch., South Royalton, 1978-79; clerk Blodgett & McCarren, Burlington, Vt., 1979-80; chief civil rights divsn. Atty. Gen.'s Office, State of Vt., 1980-82; chief pub. protection divsn. Atty. Gen.'s Office, Montpelier, Vt., 1982-88; pvt. practice Shrewsbury, Vt., 1988-90; assoc. justice Vt. Supreme Ct., Montpelier, 1990—. Chair Vt. Human Rights Commn., 1988-90. Mem. Am. Law Inst. Office: Vt Supreme Ct 109 State St Montpelier VT 05609-0001*

**JOHNSON, DON EDWIN,** lawyer; b. Decatur, Ill., Jan. 29, 1939; s. B. Edwin and Mary Louise (Pitzer) J.; m. Suzanne Curtis, Aug. 23, 1959; children: Jennifer, Marc Wade. BA cum laude, Millikin U., 1959; LLB, U. Ill., 1961, JD, 1968. Bar: Ill. 1961, U.S. Dist. Ct. (so. dist.) Ill. 1961, U.S. Tax Ct. 1986. Law clk. Ill. Supreme Ct., Springfield, 1961-63; assoc. Hohlt, House & DeMoss, Pinckneyville, Ill., 1961-66; ptnr. Johnson Seibert & Bigham, Pinckneyville, 1966—; state's atty. Perry County, Ill., Pinckneyville, 1968-72; bd. dirs. 1st Nat. Bank, Pinckneyville, First Perry Bancorp, Pinckneyville. Contbr. articles to profl. jours. City atty. DuQuoin, Ill., 1965-68, Pinckneyville, 1983—; bd. dirs. Rend Lake Coll. Found., Ina, Ill., 1981-90; bd. visitors U. Ill. Coll. Law, 1984-88. Fellow Am. Coll. Trust and Estate Counsel, Am. Bar Found., Ill. Bar Found. (chmn. 1986-87); mem. Ill. State Bar Assn. (chmn. fed. tax sect. 1983-84, chmn. mineral law sect. 1984-86, 94-95, 96-97), Energy and Mineral Law Found. (trustee 1985—), Nat. Acad. Elder Law Attys., Pinckneyville C. of C. (pres. 1968), So. Ill. Golf Assn. (pres. 1997—), USGA (sectional affairs com. 1994—), Rotary (pres. 1966, 76), Elks, Scottish Rite, Shriners, Chaine des Rotisseurs, Red Hawk Country Club, Crab Orchard Golf Club, Kelly Greens Golf and Country Club, Delta Sigma Phi. Republican. Presbyterian. Avocations: golf, travel, stamp and coin collecting. Fax: 618-357-3314. E-mail: JSBAttorneys@Midamer.net. Probate, Real property, Oil, gas, and mineral. Home: 605 W South St Pinckneyville IL 62274-1236 Office: Johnson Seibert & Bigham One N Main St Pinckneyville IL 62274

**JOHNSON, DONALD WAYNE,** lawyer; b. Memphis, Feb. 2, 1950; s. Hugh Don and Oline (Rowland) J.; m. Jan Marie Mullinax, May 12, 1972 (div. 1980); 1 child, Scott Fitzgerald; m. Cindy L. Walker, Dec. 10, 1988; children: Trevor Christian, Mallory Faith. Student, Memphis State U., 1968, Lee Coll., 1968-72; JD, Woodrow Wilson Coll. Law, 1975. Bar: Ga. 1975, U.S. Dist. Ct. (no. dist.) Ga. 1975, U.S. Ct. appeals (5th cir.) 1976, U.S. Ct. Appeals (11th, 9th, DC cirs.) 1984, U.S. Ct. Claims 1978, U.S. Tax Ct. 1978, U.S. Supreme Ct. 1979. Ptnr. Barnes & Johnson, Dalton, Ga., 1975-77, Johnson & Fain, Dalton, 1977-80; pvt. practice Dalton, 1975-85, Atlanta, 1985—; city atty. City of Forest Park, Ga., 1996-97. Bd. dirs. Pathway Christian Sch., Dalton, 1978-85, Jr. Achievement of Dalton, 1978-84, Dalton-Whitfield County Day Care Ctrs., Inc.; legal counsel Robertson for Pres. Com., Ga., 1988; bd. chmn. Ga. Family Coun., 1990-97; Rep. chmn. Clayton County, 1993-95; Rep. gen. counsel 3rd Congl. Dist., 1993-95, Clayton County Rep. Com., 1995-96; Rep. candidate for Ga. Senate, 1998. Recipient Power of One award Ga. Family Coun., 1997. Mem. Ga. Assn., Christian Legal Soc. Mem. Ch. of God. Workers' compensation, Personal injury, State civil litigation. Office: PO Box 187 Fayetteville GA 30214-0187

**JOHNSON, DOUGLAS WELLS,** lawyer; b. Denver, May 31, 1949; s. Robert Douglas and Mildred Irene (Fehr) J.; m. Kathryn Ann Hoberg, Oct. 18, 1980. BA, U. Denver, 1971, JD, 1974. Bar: Colo. 1974, U.S. Dist. Ct. Colo. 1974, U.S. Ct. Appeals (10th cir.) 1974; U.S. Supreme Ct. 1977, Ill. 1980, U.S. Dist. Ct. (no. dist.) Ill. 1980, U.S. Ct. Appeals (7th cir.) 1981, D.C. 1981, U.S. Ct. Internat. Trade 1981, U.S. Dist. Ct. (ea. dist.) Mich. 1983, U.S. Ct. Appeals (6th cir.) 1984, U.S. Ct. Appeals Fed. Cir. 1984, U.S. Dist. Ct. (no. dist.) Ind. 1986, U.S. Ct. Appeals (4th and 8th cirs.) 1986. Ptnr. Mellman, Mellman & Thorn, Denver, 1974-80; sr. atty. Amoco Corp., Chgo., 1980-91, mgr. real estate Amoco Oil Co., Chgo., 1991-4; sr. atty. Amoco Corp., Chgo., 1994-98; prin. legal counsel Amoco Pipeline Co., 1998—. U. Denver Alumni scholar, 1967-71. Mem. ABA, Ill. Bar Assn., D.C. Bar Assn., Chgo. Bar Assn., Kappa Delta Pi. Antitrust, Contracts commercial, Franchising. Office: BP Amoco Corp 200 E Randolph St Ste 1907B Chicago IL 60601-6436

**JOHNSON, EARL M., JR.,** lawyer; b. Jacksonville, Fla., Aug. 19, 1965; s. Earl M. and Janet R. Johnson; m. Margo D. Campbell, Aug. 18, 1989; 1 child, Earl M. III. BS, Fla. State U., 1987; JD, Stetson U., 1993. Bar: Fla. 1993. Litigation atty. Holland & Knight, Tampa, 1993-95; law clk. to Hon. Henry Lee Adams, Jr. U.S. Dist. Ct., Tampa, Fla., 1996-98; trial atty. Law Offices of Earl M. Johnson, Jr., Jacksonville, 1998—. Democrat. Roman Catholic. Avocations: discus throwing. Office: Blackstone Bldg 233 E Bay St Ste 901 Jacksonville FL 32202-3456

**JOHNSON, EDWARD CARL,** lawyer; b. Jackson, Mich., Nov. 9, 1938; s. Erling C. and Helen Mills (Frost) J.; m. Elizabeth R. Rooney, May 1, 1965; children: Julia, Bridget, Kristin, Edward Jr. AB, Princeton U., 1960; JD, U. Mich., 1963. Bar: Mich. 1963. Assoc. Marentay, Rouse, Selby, Webber & Dickinson, Detroit, 1963-65; ptnr. Cozadd, Shangle & Smith, Detroit, 1965-70; pvt. practice Detroit, 1970-72; ptnr. Berry, Hopson, Francis, Mack, Johnson & Seifman, Detroit, 1972-80, Johnson & Valentine, Detroit, 1980-96, Johnson & McPherson, PLC, Detroit, 1996—. Mem. ABA, Detroit Racquet Club (pres. 1980-84), Princeton Club Mich. (pres. 1973-74). Republican. General practice, Real property, Securities. Home: 41 Lakecrest Ln Grosse Pointe MI 48236-3714 Office: Johnson & McPherson PLC 81 Kercheval Ave Grosse Pointe MI 48236-3603

**JOHNSON, EDWARD MICHAEL,** lawyer; b. Waco, Tex., July 12, 1944; s. Edward James and Anne Margaret (Stuchly) J.; m. Yvonne Margaret Hill, May 7, 1977; children: Hilary Yvonne, Megan Joy, Michael David. BA in Polit. Sci., S.W. Tex. State U., 1967; JD, St. Mary's U., 1970. Bar: Tex. 1971, U.S. Dist. Ct. (we. and so. dist.) Tex. 1972, U.S. Ct. Claims, 1972, U.S. Supreme Ct. 1976. Asst. law libr. Bexar County Law Libr., 1968-69; briefing clk. Judge Preston H. Dial, Jr., 1969-70; briefing atty. U.S. Dist. Judge John H. Wood Jr., San Antonio, Tex., 1971-72; asst. U.S. atty. Dept. Justice, San Antonio, 1972-76; sole practice San Antonio, 1976-81; sr. atty. Wiley, Garwood, Hornbuckle, Higdon & Johnson, San Antonio, 1980-81; pres. McCabe Petroleum Corp., San Antonio, 1981; chmn. bd., CEO, gen. counsel Blue Chip Petroleum Corp., San Antonio, 1981-83; pres., gen. counsel Harvest Investments Corp., San Antonio, 1983-87, also dir.; gen. ptrn. Med. Mobility Ltd. IV, San Antonio, 1984-87; mgr. Med. Mobility Joint Venture, San Antonio, 1984-87; exec. cons. Advance Tax Representation, Inc., 1987-88; gen. ptrn. Harvest Venture Capital Ltd. I, San Antonio, 1986-87; pres., gen. counsel Blue Chip Securities Corp., San Antonio, 1984-87; rep. First Investors Corp., 1988-89; pres., CEO Johnson, Curney, Garcia, Wise & Farmer P.C., 1990—; pres. E.Y.J. Internat. L.L.C., 1996—; host (radio program) The Christian Lawyers, 1990-91, (TV program) God's Army, 1990-

98; mem. adv. bd. Red McCombs Galleria Imports, 1996-98, Hovey Motorcars, 1999—; internat. spkr. GlobalNet, LLC, 1997—; bd. dirs. 1997—, Diamond Direct Distributor, Amway Corp., 1997—. Co-chmn. fund raising Am. Heart Assn., San Antonio, 1982-84; bd. dirs. Am. Cancer Soc., San Antonio, 1982-84; chmn. San Fernando Cathedral Endowment Fund, San Antonio, 1986; mem. Gideons Internat., San Antonio, 1982-86, mem. exec. bd. San Antonio Christian Schs., 1983-84, San Antonio Christian Legal Soc., 1991—, Fed. Bar Licensing Bd., 1976-78; bd. dirs. Tex. Bible Coll., 1984-87, Christian Businessmen's Com., San Antonio, 1981-88, Cornerstone Christian Schs., San Antonio, 1991-92, mem., spkr., pres. Med. Ctr. chpt. 1988-91, mem. Full Gospel Businessmen's Fellowship, 1981-92, pres. 1985-88, field rep., 1988-92; bd. dirs. Assn. Spirit Filled Fellowships, 1991-93; pres. God's Army Internat. Found., Inc., 1990-92; gen. counsel, bd. dirs. Four Winds Ministries, Inc., 1992-93; scoutmaster Alamo area coun. Boy Scouts Am., San Antonio, 1973-74; founder, chmn. Christian Businessmen's Focus on the Family, San Antonio, 1984-85. Recipient spl. commendation Dept. Transp. 1973, Dept. Air Force HQ, ATC, 1974, Dept. Treasury, 1974; named Outstanding Asst. U.S. Atty. Dept. Justice, 1974-75, one of Outstanding Young Men Am., 1975, one of Outstanding Young Texans, 1976. Mem. Fed. Bar Assn. (pres. San Antonio chpt. 1975-76, v.p. 1973-74, sec. 1972-73, treas. 1971-72, named outstanding chpt. pres. 1976), Tex. Bar Assn., San Antonio Bar Assn. Republican. Insurance, Securities, Federal civil litigation. Office: 800 Spectrum Bldg 613 NW Loop 410 San Antonio TX 78216-5507

**JOHNSON, EINAR WILLIAM,** lawyer; b. Fontana, Calif., Apr. 6, 1955; s. Carl Wilbur and Judith Priscilla (Orcutt) J.; m. Cynthia Jeanne Bailey, Oct. 9, 1976; children: Brian Mark (dec.), Carl Einar, Gregory Daniel, Christopher James, Shaun Curtis, Bradford Keith. BA in Speech Communications, Brigham Young U., 1980; JD, J. Reuben Clark Law Sch., Provo, Utah, 1983. Bar: Calif. 1983, U.S. Dist. Ct. (cen. dist.) Calif. 1984, U.S. Ct. Appeals (9th cir.) 1986, U.S. Supreme Ct. 1987. Asst. debate coach Brigham Young U., Provo, Utah, 1979-80; fin. committeeman Jed Richardson for Congress, Provo, 1980; sales mgr./salesman Ortho Mattress, Orem, Utah, 1979, 81; law clk. Acret & Perrochet, L.A., 1982; jud. clk. U.S. Cts., Salt Lake City, 1983-84; litigation atty. Smith & Hilbig, Torrance, Calif., 1984-90; litigation ptnr. Smith & Hilbig, 1990-93; owner, founder Johnson and Assocs., 1993—; editor Moot Ct. program J. Reuben Clark Law Sch., 1982-83. Contbr. articles to profl. jours. Missionary, leader Ch. of Jesus Christ of Latter Day Saints, Denver, 197476, Sunday sch. tchr., L.A., 1986-89, stake high counselor, 1989-92, 1st counselor ward bishopric, 1992-93, pres. elders quorum, 1993-94, high counselor, 1994—. Recipient A.H. Christensen award, Am. Jurisprudence awards Bancroft-Whitney, 1981. Mem. ABA, Calif. Bar Assn., L.A. County Bar Assn., Assn. Trial Lawyers Am., Internat. Platofrm Assn., Order Barristers, Kappa Tau Alpha. Republican. Mormon. Avocations: photography, guitar, fishing, house remodeling, automobile restoration. General civil litigation, Labor, Landlord-tenant. Office: Johnson & Assocs 3655 Torrance Blvd Ste 470 Torrance CA 90503-4848

**JOHNSON, ELIZABETH DIANE LONG,** lawyer; b. Pasadena, Calif., Nov. 16, 1945; d. Volney Earl and Sylvia Irene (Drury) Long; m. Lynn Douglas Johnson, Oct. 22, 1966; 1 child, Barbara Annette. BA, U. of Houston, 1967; JD, Rutgers U., 1980. Bar: N.J. 1980, U.S. Dist. Ct. N.J. 1980, Pa. 1984, U.S. Supreme Ct. 1986. Pvt. practice Riverside, N.J., 1980-96; pub. defender Riverside Twp., 1988-91; speaker Comprehensive Justice Ctr. Burlington County, 1987-89. Del. Women in Law to Peoples Republic of China Citizen Amb. Program of People to People Internat., 1989; mem. Orchid Found., 1989-97, rec. sec., 1991-97; mem. Tenby Chase Civic Assn., Delran, N.J., 1972-87, treas., 1976, v.p., 1974; trustee Drenk Mental Health Ctr., 1988-95, pres., 1991-94, chair bd. trustees, 1993-94, vice chair bd. trustees, 1995. Mem. N.J. Women Lawyers Assn., Burlington County Bar Assn. (chmn. bench and bar com. 1989-91), Burlington County Bar Found. (trustee 1988-91, treas. 1988-90, v.p. 1990-91, pres. 1991-92), Soc. for Right to Die, Nat. Trust for Hist. Preservation, Mensa, Rotary (sec. Riverside 1991-92, v.p. 1992-93, pres.-elect 1993-94, pres. 1994-95, dir. 1995-96, area rep. 1995-96), Delta Gamma. Methodist. General practice.

**JOHNSON, ERIC GATES,** lawyer; b. Utica, N.Y., Apr. 12, 1961; s. Grant E. and Barbara G. Johnson; m. Catherine Keib. BA, Colgate U., 1983; JD, Coll. William and Mary, 1986. Bar: N.Y., U.S. Dist. Ct. (no. and we. dists.) N.Y. Atty. Mackenzie Smith Lewis Michell & Hughes, LLP, Syracuse, N.Y., 1986—. Bd. dirs., pres. Am. Diabetes Assn., Syracuse, 1994-98. Mem. Def. Rsch. Inst. Avocations: downhill skiing, running. General civil litigation, Personal injury, Professional liability. Office: McKenzie Smith et al 101 S Salina St Syracuse NY 13202-1301

**JOHNSON, ERIK REID,** lawyer; b. L.A., Jan. 13, 1950. BA in Psychology magna cum laude, UCLA, 1973; JD, Loyola U., 1978. Bar: Calif. 1978, Nev. 1984. Dep. dist. atty. L.A. County, 1979-86; dep. state pub. defender State of Nev., Carson City, 1986-89; pvt. practice Carson City, 1989—. 1st lt. USAR, 1973-79. Criminal, Juvenile, Appellate. Office: 711 E Washington St Carson City NV 89701-4063

**JOHNSON, FRED MACK,** lawyer; b. Panama City, Fla., Nov. 5, 1948; s. Ted Johnson and Mary Pogue; m. Gwen Marie Parrot, Aug. 8, 1970; children: MacKenzie Lane, Bonnie Katherine, Frederick Carter. BS, U. Fla., 1970, JD, 1972. Bar: Fla. 1973, U.S. Dist. Ct. (mid. dist.) Fla. 1974), U.S. Dist. Ct. (no. dist.) Fla. 1980, U.S. Ct. Appeals (11th cir.) 1981. Atty. Fla. Atty. Gen., Tallahassee, 1973-74, Howell, Kirby, Montgomery, et al, Jacksonville, Fla., 1974-78, Fuller, Johnson & Farrell, P.A., Tallahassee, 1978—. Author: (booklet) Understanding Extra Contractual Liability, 1994. Mem. Nat. Bd. Trial Advocacy (cert. civil trial advocacy 1984), Tallahassee Inns of Ct. (charter mem. 1995). Republican. Methodist. Avocations: golfing, fishing. Insurance, General civil litigation. Home: 3234 W Lakeshore Dr Tallahassee FL 32312-1809 Office: Fuller Johnson & Farrell PA 111 N Calhoun St Tallahassee FL 32301-1505

**JOHNSON, G. ROBERT,** lawyer; b. Mpls., July 2, 1940. BA, U. Minn., 1965, JD, 1968. Bar: Minn. 1968. Spl. asst. atty. gen. Minn. Pollution Control Agy., 1968-71; past ptnr. Popham, Haik, Schnobrich & Kaufman Ltd., Mpls.; ptnr. Oppenheimer, Wolff & Donnelly LLP, Mpls., 1997—. Mem. ABA, Minn. Bar Assn. chmn. continuing legal edn. 1986-87), Nat. Coun. State Legislatures (liaison 1987—). Administrative and regulatory, Environmental, Natural resources. Office: Oppenheimer Wolff & Donnelly LLP 3400 Plaza VII 45 S 7th St Ste 3400 Minneapolis MN 55402-1609

**JOHNSON, GARY THOMAS,** lawyer; b. Chgo., July 26, 1950; s. Thomas G. Jr. and Marcia (Lunde) J.; m. Susan Elizabeth Moore, May 28, 1978; children: Christopher Thomas, Timothy Henry, Anna Louisa. AB, Yale U., 1972; Hons. BA, Oxford U., 1974, MA, 1983; JD, Harvard U., 1977. Ba: Ill. 1977, U.S. Dist. Ct. (no. dist.), Ill. 1977, U.S. Ct. Appeals (7th cir.) 1985, U.S. Supreme Ct. 1986, N.Y. 1993. Assoc. Mayer, Brown & Platt, Chgo., 1977-84, ptnr., 1985-94; ptnr. Jones, Day, Reavis & Pogue, Chgo., 1994—; mem. Spl. Commn. on Adminstrn. of Justice Cook County, Chgo., 1984-88; v.p. Criminal Justice Project of Cook County, 1987-91; bd. dirs. Lawyers' Com. for Civil Rights Under Law, 1992—, trustee, 1994—, regional vice chair, 1996—; mem. Ill. Supreme Ct. Spl. Commn. on the Adminstrn. of Justice, 1992-94. Bd. dirs. Chgo. Lawyers' Com. for Civil Rights Under Law, 1981-90, Legal Assistance Found., Chgo., 1987-96, pres., 1994-96. Rhodes scholar Oxford U., 1972-74. Fellow Am. Bar Found. (life), Ill. Bar Found.; mem. ABA (Ho. of Dels. 1991-97), Internat. Bar Assn., Chgo. Bar Assn., Chgo. Coun. Lawyers (pres. 1981-83), Am. Judicature Soc. (bd. dirs. 1987-91). Democrat. Securities, General corporate, Finance. Office: Jones Day Reavis & Pogue 77 W Wacker Dr Chicago IL 60601-1692

**JOHNSON, GOODYEAR See O'CONNOR, KARL WILLIAM**

**JOHNSON, GRANT LESTER,** lawyer, retired manufacturing company executive; b. Virginia, Minn., Aug. 16, 1929; s. Ernest and Anna Elizabeth (Nordstrom) J.; m. Esther Linnea Nystrom, June 16, 1956 (dec. July 1985); children: Karen Elisabeth, Elise Ann; m. Amy Rowe Fetzer, July 18, 1992. AB, Cornell U., 1951; LLB, Harvard U., 1957. Bar: Ohio 1958, Ill. 1972. Assoc. Squire, Sanders & Dempsey, Cleve., 1957-58; atty. Pickands Mather & Co., Cleve., 1958-71, assoc. gen. counsel, 1967, gen. counsel, 1968-71, sec., 1969-71; corporate counsel Interlake, Inc., Chgo., 1971-73, v.p. law, 1974-78, v.p. law and adminstrn., 1978-84, sr. v.p., gen. counsel, 1984-86; sr. v.p., gen. counsel The InterLake Corp., 1986-91, ret., 1991. Lt. (j.g.) USN, 1951-54. General corporate. Home: 4 Oakbrook Club Dr Apt G-205 Oak Brook IL 60523-1328

**JOHNSON, GREGORY L.,** lawyer. BA, Fordham U.; MBA, Columbia U.; JD. Bar: N.Y. 1973. V.p., gen. counsel Warner Lambert Co., Morris Plains, N.J.; lawyer. BA Fordham U.; MBA Columbia U., JD. Bar: N.Y. 1973. Vice pres., gen. counsel Warner Lambert Co., Morris Plains, N.J. General corporate. Office: Warner-Lambert Co 201 Tabor Rd Morris Plains NJ 07950-2693

**JOHNSON, HAROLD GENE,** lawyer; b. St. Louis, July 20, 1934; s. Edward Henry Johnson and Betty (Burton) Pallister; m. Susan Ann Giesecke, Oct. 10, 1953; children: H. Mark, Deborah S. Johnson Schnitzer, Michael R., Laura A. Johnson Schwent, Mitchell D. BSBA, Washington U., St. Louis, 1961, LLB, 1962. Bar: Mo. 1962, U.S. Dist. Ct. (ea. dist.) Mo. 1964, U.S. Ct. Appeals (8th cir.) 1981. Assoc. Schomburg, Marshall & Craig, St. Louis, 1962-63, Green & Raymond, St. Louis, 1963-64; ptnr. Johnson & Hayes, St. Louis, 1978-85, Law Offices Mitchell D. Johnson, St. Louis, 1988-93, Johnson & Johnson, 1993—. Judge mcpl. ct. City of Bridgeton, Mo., 1973-85. Served with U.S. Army 1954-56. Recipient Spl. Service award City of Bridgeton, 1985; Honored with ann. presentation of The Judge Harold Johnson award Pro-Life Direct Action League, 1985. Bar: Mo. Bar Assn., Met. Bar St. Louis, St. Louis County Bar Assn. Avocation: woodworking. State civil litigation, General practice, Personal injury. Office: 500 Northwest Plz Ste 715 Saint Ann MO 63074-2222

**JOHNSON, HELEN SCOTT,** lawyer; b. Shreveport, La., Nov. 26, 1950; d. Robert Beard and Adeline (LeComte) S.; div. BA, U. Southwestern La., 1973; JD, Paul M. Hebert Law Ctr., 1981. Bar: La. 1982, U.S. Dist. Ct. (we. and mid. dists.) La. 1985. Law clk. Hon John Parker U.S. Dist. Ct., Baton Rouge, La., 1982-83; law clk. Hon Tom Stagg U.S. Dist. Ct., Shreveport, La., 1983-85; law clk. Hon John M. Duhe U.S. Dist. Ct., Lafayette, La., 1985; assoc. Jeansonne & Brinney, Lafayette, 1985-86; pvt. practice Lafayette, La., 1986—. Author La. Law Rev., 1980. Fellow Am. Acad. Matrimonial Lawyers; mem. Acadiana chpt. Am. Inns of Court, Lafayette's Vol. Lawyers. Avocations: judo (instr., referee), dancing, reading. Family and matrimonial. Office: Helen Scott Johnson 321 W Main St Ste 2-6 Lafayette LA 70501-6858

**JOHNSON, HJALMA EUGENE,** lawyer, rancher, banker; b. Bradenton, Fla., Aug. 16, 1934; s. Bethel Curtis and Florence Elizabeth Johnson; m. Laura McLeod; 1 child, Leonard Hjalma. B in Indsl. Engring. with honors, U. Fla., 1958; JD, U. Ala., 1965. Bar: Ala. 1965, U.S. Dist. Ct. (no. dist.) Ala. 1968, U.S. Ct. Appeals (11th cir.) 1981, U.S. Tax Ct. 1982, U.S. Ct. Appeals D.C. 1983, U.S. Supreme Ct. 1974. Sales engr. Buckeye Cellulose Corp., Memphis, 1958-62; data processing account rep. IBM, Birmingham, Ala., 1962-65; v.p. mgr. mktg. dept. Regions Fin. Corp., Birmingham, Ala., 1965-70; chmn. bd., CEO North Fla. Bank Corp. and Bank of Madison County, 1971-88; pres., CEO, bd. dirs. Ctrl. Fla. Bank Corp. and Bank of Pasco County, Dade City, Fla., 1971-85; cons., First Union Nat. Bank of Fla., Dade City, Fla., 1987-89; chmn. bd., CEO., vice chmn. bd. Cypress Banks, Inc., First Nat. Bank of the South, Dade City, Fla., 1990-95; cons. SouthTrust Corp. Fla., Jacksonville, 1989-97; founding ptnr., mng. dir. Synagen Capital Ptnrs., Inc., Orlando, Fla., 1989-97; pres. Investment Advisors, Inc., Dade City, Fla., 1987—; chmn. bd., CEO East Coast Bank Corp., Bank at Ormond By-The-Sea, Ormond Beach, Fla., 1973—; pres., treas. real estate Four Score Corp.; pres. Triple J. Ranch, Inc., 1975—. Bd. dirs. Com. of 100 of Pasco County, 1987-88, Enterprise Fla. Capital Partnership, 1992-94, Fla. Coun. Econ. Edn., 1996—, Fannie Mae Nat. Adv. Coun., 1996-98, Fla. Interchange Group Inc., 1983; mem. Tampa Bay Forum, 1984-89; deacon, past mem. stewardship com. First Bapt. Ch., Dade City, Fla. 2d lt. U.S. Army, 1956-59, USAR, 1959-62. Mem. Ala. Bar Assn., ABA, Am. Bankers Assn. (cmty. banking leaders coun. adv. bd. 1981-83, state v.p. 1985-87, govt. rels. coun. 1987-91, BankPac com. 1992-94, chmn. fed. home loan bank task force 1994-95, bd. dirs. 1993—, treas. 1995-97, 1st v.p. 1997-98, pres. elect 1998—), Fla. Bankers Assn. (vice chmn. group IV 1978-79, bd. dirs. 1980-83, chmn. state legia. com. 1981-82, coun. 1981-83, chmn. govt. rels. divsn. 1982-83, pres.-elect 1983-84, pres. 1984-85, chmn. coun. 1985-86, chmn. govt. rels. divsn. 1986-89, dir. Fla. BankPac 1990-94, fed. legis. com. 1990—), Am. Inst. Indsl. Engrs., Phi Kappa Phi, Beta Gamma Sigma, Pi Kappa Alpha, Sigma Tau, Tau Beta Pi. Home: 14435 Hale Rd Dade City FL 33523-7524 Office: East Coast Bank Corp PO Box 1075 Dade City FL 33526-1075

**JOHNSON, HOWARD PRICE,** lawyer; b. Clarksburg, W.Va., July 12, 1954; s. Oscar Price and Frances Ann (Coleman) J. BS, U. Utah, 1975, JD, 1978. Bar: Utah 1978, U.S. Dist. Ct. Utah 1978, U.S. Ct. Appeals (10th cir.) 1979. Assoc. Utah Legal Svcs., Salt Lake City, 1978-80, 83-85, Woodger Mortgage, Salt Lake City, 1985-88, Richard Calder, Salt Lake City, 1990-91; pvt. practice Salt Lake City, 1980—. Mem. ctrl. com. Utah State Dem. Orgn., Salt Lake City, 1994—, Salt Lake County Dem. Orgn., 1990—; treas. Gay and Lesbian Polit. Action Com., Salt Lake City, 1997; sec. Utah Lawyers for Human Rights, Salt Lake City, 1998—. Mem. Utah Bar Assn. (presiding judge moot ct. competition 1992—). Avocations: politics, computers, reading, travel. Bankruptcy, Personal injury, Family and matrimonial. Office: Schiess & Emmett PC 7050 Union Park Ctr Ste 520 Midvale UT 84047-6005

**JOHNSON, JAMES HAROLD,** lawyer; b. Galesburg, Ill., May 3, 1944; s. Harold Frank and Marjorie Isabel J.; m. Judith Eileen Moore, June 5, 1966; children: Todd James, Tiffany Nicole. BA, Colo. Coll., 1966; JD, U. Tex., 1969. Bar: N.Y. 1970, Colo. 1971, Tex. 1975. Assoc. Winthrop, Stimson, Putnam & Roberts, N.Y.C., 1969-70, Sherman & Howard, Denver, 1970-72; corp. counsel Tex. Instruments, Inc., Dallas, 1972-85; v.p., gen. counsel, sec. Am. Healthcare Mgmt., Dallas, 1985-86, Ornda Healthcorp, Dallas, 1986-94; shareholder Jenkens & Gilchrist, PC, Dallas, 1994-97; ast. gen. counsel Sulzer Medica Inc., Houston, 1997—. Mem. ABA, Tenn. Bar Assn., Tex. Bar Assn., Am. Health Lawyers Assn. Republican. Methodist. Avocations: skiing, horseback riding. Health, Securities, Mergers and acquisitions. Home: 3907 N Kimball Ct Missouri City TX 77459-6230 Office: Sulzer Medica 3 E Greenway Plz Ste 1600 Houston TX 77046-0303

**JOHNSON, JAMES J.,** lawyer. BA, U. Mich.; JD, Ohio State U. Bar: Ohio 1972. V.p., gen. counsel Proctor & Gamble Co., Cin., 1991—, now sr. v.p., gen. counsel, 1991—. Office: Procter & Gamble Co 1 Procter And Gamble Plz Cincinnati OH 45202-3393*

**JOHNSON, JAMES JOSEPH SCOFIELD,** lawyer, judge, educator, author; b. Washington, Apr. 28, 1956; s. Richard Carl and Harriette (Benson) J.; m. Sherry Bekki Hall; children: Andrew Joel Schaeffer Johnson. AA with high honors, Montgomery Coll., Germantown, Md., 1980; BA with honors, Wake Forest U., 1982; JD, U. N.C., 1984; ThD with highest honors, Emmanuel Coll. Christian, 1996; PhD with highest honors, Cambridge Grad. Sch., Springdale, Ark., 1996, MSc, M of Liberal Arts, 1999. Bar: Tex. 1985, U.S. Dist. Ct. (no. dist.) Tex. 1986, U.S. Dist. Ct. (ea. dist.) Tex. 1987, U.S. Ct. Appeals (5th cir.) 1989, U.S. Dist. Ct. (we. and so. dists.) Tex. 1990; bd. cert. bus. bankruptcy law Tex. Bd. Legal Specialization, 1990, 95, Am. Bankruptcy Bd. Cert., 1992; cert. water quality monitor Tex. Natural Resource Conservation Commn., 1994. Assoc. various orgns., Dallas, 1985—; pvt. practice law Dallas, 1993—; adj. prof. LeTourneau U., Dallas, 1991—, Dallas Christian Coll., 1995—; lectr. History, Ecology, Culture, Norwegian Cruise Lines, 1998—. Author: Introduction to Environmental Studies, 1995, 98, Doxological Zoology and Zoogeography, 1998; sr. editl. staff N.C. Jour. Internat. Law and Comml. Regulation, 1983-84; conf. issue editor Harvard Jour. Law & Pub. Policy, 1984; contbr. articles to profl. jours. Protestant chaplain Boy Scouts Am., Goshen, Va., 1976; libr. vol. N.W. Bible Ch., Dallas, 1991-98; cmty. program dir. Southwestern Legal Founds. Conf. on Internat. and Am. Law, 1991-92; active mem. Pro Bono Coll. State Bar Tex., Dallas, 1992—98; scripture chmn. Gideons Internat., North Dallas, Tex., 1993-94. Recipient award for excellence in biblical studies and biblical langs. Am. Bible Soc., 1982. Mem. Coun. Cert. Bankruptcy Specialists (cert.), Tex. River & Reservoir Mgmt. Soc., Soc. Christian Philosophers, Sangre de Cristo Mountain Coun., Creation Rsch. Soc., Evangel. Theol. Soc. Republican. Avocations: reading, writing, birding, traveling, hiking. General civil litigation, Bankruptcy, Environmental. Office: PO Box 2952 Dallas TX 75221-2952

**JOHNSON, JAMES RANDALL,** lawyer; b. Flint, Mich., Sept. 12, 1951; s. James Bryant and Dorothy Mae (Perkins) J.; m. Darlene J. Scott, Jan. 25, 1975 (div. 1982); m. Gail Leslie Hoffman, Mar. 5, 1984; children: Christopher Randall, Adam Powell, Alexandra Leslie. BS, Ea. Mich. U., 1977; JD, T.M. Cooley Law Sch., 1981; postgrad, Harvard U., 1988, 90, Dartmouth Coll., 1993. Bar: N.D. 1982, Mich. 1985, U.S. Ct. Mil. Appeals 1982. Assoc. Stertz and Weaver, P.C., Saginaw, Mich., 1984-87; chief oper. officer, exec. v.p., gen. counsel Meml. Hosp., Owosso, Mich., 1987-90; pres. The Health Support Corp.; of counsel Cox & Hodgman, Troy, Mich.; COO Meml. Healthcare Ctr., 1991-92, pres., CEO, 1992-94; pres., CEO, corporate gen. counsel Zero Parallax Inc., Owosso, Mich., 1994—; adj. prof. Spring Arbor (Mich.) Coll., 1979-81, Coll. Lake County, Chgo., 1982-84, Lansing (Mich.) Community Coll., 1984—, Saginaw Valley State U., 1985; pres. Medico-Legal Consultation Svc., Ltd., Mich., 1987—; bd. dirs. Key State Bank, Owosso, Ackco Industries, Owosso, Health Support Corp., Support Svcs. Corp. Candidate Mich. State Senate, 1974, Mich. Ho. of Reps., 1976; chmn. bd. United Way of Shiawassee County. With JAGC, USN, 1978-84. Recipient Alfred award USN League, 1982. Mem. ABA, Am. Coll. Healthcare Execs., Mich. Bar Assn., Am. Assn. Hosp. Attys., Mich. Def. Trial Counsel. Republican. Episcopalian. Health, State civil litigation, General corporate. Office: Meml Hosp 826 W King St Owosso MI 48867-2198

**JOHNSON, JEH CHARLES,** lawyer; b. N.Y.C., Sept. 11, 1957; s. Jeh Vincent and Norma (Edelin) J.; m. Susan M. DiMarco, Mar. 18, 1994. BA in Polit. Sci. cum laude, Morehouse Coll., Atlanta, 1979; JD, Columbia U., 1982. Bar: N.Y., 1983, U.S. Dist. Ct. (so. and ea. dists.) N.Y., U.S. Dist. Ct. (ea. dist.) Mich., U.S. Ct. Appeals (2d, 4th, 6th, and D.C. cirs.). Litigation assoc. Sullivan & Cromwell, N.Y.C., 1982-84; assoc. Paul, Weiss, Rifkind, Wharton & Garrison, N.Y.C., 1984-88, 92-93; asst. U.S. atty. So. Dist. N.Y., 1989-91; ptnr. Paul, Weiss, Rifkind, Wharton & Garrison, N.Y.C., 1994-98; gen. counsel USAF, Washington, 1998—; adj. lectr. law Columbia U. Sch. Law, N.Y.C., 1995-97; dir. Com. for Modern Cts., 1993—. Mem. bd. visitors Columbia U. Sch. of Law, 1993—; mem. N.Y. County Dem. Com., 1993—; dir. Legal Aid Soc., Lawyers Com. for Civil Rights, Vera Inst. for Justice, Film Soc. Lincoln Ctr. Mem. N.Y. State Bar. Assn. (mem. jud., profl. and jud. ethics coms.). Office: Dept of Air Force General Counsel 1740 Air Force Pentagon Washington DC 20330-1740*

**JOHNSON, JENIFER L.,** defender; b. Springfield, Ill., Oct. 9, 1968; d. Robert A. and LuAnn Johnson; m. Rudolph M. Brand, Jr., Nov. 15, 1996. BS, U. Ill., 1990; JD, No. Ill. U., 1994. Bar: Ill. 1994, U.S. Dist. Ct. (no. dist.) Ill. 1996, U.S. Dist. Ct. (ctrl. dist.) 1998. Assoc. Law Offices of Dennis Schumacher, Mt. Morris, Ill., 1994-97; asst. defender Office of the State Appelate Defender, Springfield, 1997—; alumni coun. bd. mem. No. Ill. U. Coll. Law, DeKalb, 1998—. Scoring chmn. LPGA State Farm Rail Classic, Springfield, 1990—. Mem. ABA, Ill. State Bar Assn. Office: Office State Appellate Defender PO Box 5750 Springfield IL 62705-5750

**JOHNSON, JENNIFER JERIT,** lawyer; b. Courtland, N.Y., Apr. 23, 1960. BA magna cum laude with distinction, U. Ill., 1982; JD, Loyola U., Chgo., 1985. Bar: Ill. Atty. McKenna, Storer, Rowe, White & Farrug, Chgo., 1985-86; assoc. Tressler, Soderstrom, Maloney & Priess, Chgo., 1986-93, ptnr., 1993—. Bd. dirs. Youth Care divsn. Gateway Found., Chgo., 1997—. Mem. Ill. Assn. Def. Counsel (bd. dirs. 1996—), Def. Rsch. Inst. (chair trial, tactics and techniques com. 1998—, steering com. drug and med. device divsn. 1997—). Toxic tort, Product liability, Personal injury. Office: Tressler Soderstrom et al 233 S Wacker Dr Ste 22D Chicago IL 60606-6427

**JOHNSON, JIM D.,** lawyer, judge; b. Andrews, Tex., Jan. 30, 1953; s. J.E. and Eddie Bea Johnson; m. April K. Hayes, Feb. 14, 1986; children: Derrek Collins, Stacey Collins, Kim Johnson, Dyland Johnson. AA, Western Tex. Coll., 1973; BA, U. Ark., 1981, JD, 1983. Bar: Ark. 1984, U.S. Dist. Ct. Ark. 1984, U.S. Ct. Appeals 1985. Dep. pub. defender Benton County, Ark., 1984-87; pvt. practice Bentonville, Ark., 1984—; city atty. Cave Springs, Ark., 1987—, city judge, 1989—. Avocations: music, painting, walking, hiking, tennis. Office: 913 SE J St Bentonville AR 72712-6522

**JOHNSON, JOHN LYNN,** lawyer; b. Amarillo, Tex., Apr. 10, 1938; s. Alton Amos Johnson and Amelia (Tunnell) Kitchens; m. Brenda Kay Leathers, June 9, 1962 (div. Feb. 1978); children: John Lynn II, Jennifer; m. Janet Ellen Janes, Dec. 22, 1978. AS, Tarleton State Coll., 1958; BA, U. Tex., 1960, LLB, 1963. Bar: Tex. 1963, U.S. Dist. Ct. (no., so., ea., and we. dists.) Tex. 1971, U.S. Supreme Ct. 1971. Asst. county atty. Wichita County, Wichota Falls, Tex., 1963-64; assoc. Short & Smith, Wichota Falls, 1965, Law Office Philip S. Kouri, Wichota Falls, 1965-67, Law Office William R. Edwards/ Edwards & DeAnda, Corpus Christi, Tex., 1967-72; pvt. practice Corpus Christi, 1972-86; ptnr. Johnson & Tower, Corpus Christi, 1987-98, mediation, arbitrator, 1998—. 2d lt. U.S. Army, 1960-61. Mem. State Bar Tex., Assn. Trial Lawyers Am., Tex. Trial Lawyers Assn., Elks. Democrat. Methodist. Avocations: golf, old cars. Alternative dispute resolution, Workers' compensation, Family and matrimonial. Home: 6030 Ennis Joslin Rd Corpus Christi TX 78412-2806 Office: 611 S Tancahua St Corpus Christi TX 78401-3425

**JOHNSON, JOHN WALTER, III,** lawyer; b. Nashville, Mar. 3, 1947; s. John Walter and Nancy Thornton (Pierce) J.; m. Margaret Hamilton Mebane, Oct. 5, 1973 (div. June 1980); m. Susan T. Johnson, May 18, 1985; children: Virginia Hamilton, Margaret Peyton, John Walter IV. BS, U. Tenn., Knoxville, 1969, JD, 1973. Bar: Tenn. 1973, Ga. 1976, U.S. Dist. Ct. (no. dist.) Ga. 1976, U.S. Dist. Ct. Tenn. 1974, U.S. Tax Ct. 1974. Assoc. Grant, Clements & Bower, Chattanooga, 1973-74; ptnr. Anderson & Johnson, Chattanooga, 1975-83, Hatcher & Johnson, Chattanooga, 1983-85, Hatcher, Johnson & Meaney, Chattanooga, 1985—; Bd. dirs. Multiple Sclerosis, Chattanooga, 1978; pres. Luth. Ch. of the Good Shepherd, Chattanooga, 1983, Chattanooga Cerebral Palsy, 1978-81; housing trustee Kappa Sigma Fraternity, Chattanooga, 1992; mem. Univ. Alumnae Coun., Chattanooga, 1990—. Bd. dirs. Walter E. Boehm Birth Defects Ctr. Mem. Tenn. Trial Lawyers Assn., Chattanooga Trial Lawyers (treas., v.p., pres. 1977-81). Republican. Avocations: golf, skiing, water skiing, football. Workers' compensation, Personal injury, State civil litigation. Home: 416 N Hermitage Ave Lookout Mountain TN 37350-1234 Office: Hatcher Johnson & Meaney 2901 E 48th St Chattanooga TN 37407-3303

**JOHNSON, JOSEPH CLAYTON, JR.,** lawyer; b. Vicksburg, Miss., Nov. 15, 1943; s. Joseph Clayton and Rose Butler (Levy) J.; m. Cherrian Frances Turpin, Oct. 24, 1970; children: Mary Clayton, Erik Cole. BS, La. State U., 1965, JD, 1969. Bar: La. 1969, U.S. Dist. Ct. (ea. dist.) La. 1969, U.S. Dist. Ct. (mid. dist.) La. 1969, U.S. Dist. Ct. (we. dist.) La. 1979, U.S. Ct. Appeals (5th cir.) 1982. Ptnr. Taylor, Porter, Brooks & Phillips, Baton Rouge, 1969—; mem. civil justice reform act com. U.S. Dist. Ct. (mid. dist.) La., 1995-97, chmn. 1996-97; mem. La. Atty. Disciplinary Bd., 1997—. Bd. Editors Oil and Gas Reporter. Pres. Baton Rouge area Am. Cancer Soc., 1987-88. With U.S. Army, 1969-75. Mem. ABA, La. Bar Assn. (mem. ho. of dels. 1979-92, council rep. mineral law sect. 1986-94, chmn. mineral law sect. 1992-93), La. State Law Inst. (mineral code com.), Baton Rouge Bar Assn., Dean Henry George McMahon Am. Inn of Ct. Republican. Methodist. Oil, gas, and mineral. Office: PO Box 2471 Baton Rouge LA 70821-2471

**JOHNSON, JOSEPH H., JR.,** lawyer; b. Dothan, Ala., July 14, 1925. Student, La. Poly. Inst.; LLB, U. Va., 1949. Bar: Ala. 1949. Of counsel Lange, Simpson, Robinson & Somerville, Birmingham, Ala. Recipient Bernard P. Friel medal for disting. svc. in pub. fin., 1997. Mem. ABA (mem. coun. 1962-66, 68-72, 73-77, chmn. 1981-82, sec. of urban, state and local govt. law), Assn. of Bar of City of N.Y., Birmingham Bar Assn. (chmn. com. on profl. ethics 1978-79), Ala. State Bar, Nat. Assn. bond Lawyers (pres. 1988-89), Am. Coll. Bond Counsel (bd. dirs. 1998—). Municipal (including bonds), Securities. Office: Lange Simpson Robinson & Somerville 1700 Regions Bank Bldg # A Birmingham AL 35203-3217

**JOHNSON, JULIE ASHLEY,** lawyer; b. Louisville, Ky., Oct. 7, 1968; d. Robert Reiner and Mildred Wallace Johnson; m. Christopher Thomas Fulks, Aug. 1, 1992. BA, Centre Coll., 1990; JD, U. Louisville, 1994. Bar: Ky. 1994, U.S. Dist. Ct. (ea. dist.) Ky. 1998, U.S. Dist. Ct. (we. dist.) Ky. 1998. Assoc. Sparks & Assocs., Louisville, 1994-96; jr. ptnr. Sparks Johnson Malone PLLC, Louisville, 1997-98; assoc. Dinsmore and Shohl LLP, Louisville, 1998, Thompson and Miller PLC, Louisville, 1998—; moot ct. team, moot ct. bd. Nat. Environ. Law. Alumni editor Brandeis Brief mag., 1993-94; mem. Jour. Family Law, Jour. Law and Edn. Dir. Old Brownsboro Rd. Arts and Crafts Festival, Louisville, 1994-96; mem. Mayor's Coun. on Outside Activities, Louisville, 1994-96. Mem. ABA, Am. Inns. of Ct., Louisville Bar Assn., Ky. Bar Assn., Phi Beta Kappa. Avocations: Taoist Tai Chi, gardening, exercise, reading. Office: Thompson and Miller PLC 220 W Main St Ste 1700 Louisville KY 40202-1390

**JOHNSON, KATHERINE ANNE,** health research administrator, lawyer; b. Medford, Mass., Apr. 20, 1947; d. Lester and Eileen Anne (Henaghan) J. BS, La. State U., 1969; MSA, George Washington U., 1972; JD, Cath. U., 1985. Bar: Md. 1985. Pub. health adviser HHS, Washington, 1970-76; dir. plan implementation SE Colo. Health Sys. Agy., Colorado Springs, 1976-78; sr. mng. assoc. CDP Assocs., Inc., Atlanta, 1978-87, dir. legal affairs, 1986-87; v.p. Cancer CarePoint Inc., Atlanta, 1987; sr. mgr. Salick Health Care, Inc., Bethesda, Md., 1987-89; pvt. practice atty. cons., Potomac, Md., 1989-90; assoc. dir. for adminstrn. San Antonio Cancer Inst., 1990-96; assoc. dir. planning and adminstrn. CTRC Rsch. Found., San Antonio, 1996-97, v.p., 1997-98; COO Inst. Drug Devel., San Antonio, 1997-98; prin. biomed. program devel. consulting Inst. Drug Devel., 1998—; spkr. in field. Contbr. articles to profl. jours. Vol. Ct.-Apptd. Spl. Adv. for Abused Children. Mem. Md. Bar Assn., Am. Health Lawyers Assn., Leadership Tex. Class of 1996, Soc. Rsch. Adminstrs. Avocations: skiing, reading, antique collecting. Office: 15228 Antler Creek Dr San Antonio TX 78248-2009

**JOHNSON, KEVIN RAYMOND,** lawyer, educator; b. Culver City, Calif., June 29, 1958; s. Kenneth R. Johnson and Angela J. (Gallardo) McEachron; m. Virginia Salazar, Oct. 17, 1987; children: Teresa, Tomás, Elena. AB in Econs. with great distinction, U. Calif., 1980; JD magna cum laude, Harvard U., 1983. Bar: Calif. 1985, U.S. Dist. Ct. (no., ea. and so. dists.) Calif. 1985, U.S. Ct. Appeals (9th cir.) 1985, U.S. Supreme Ct. 1991. Rsch asst. to Charles Haar prof. Harvard U., Cambridge, Mass., 1982-83, instr. legal writing, 1982; law clk. to Hon. Stephen Reinhardt U.S. Ct. Appeals (9th cir.), L.A., 1983-84; atty. Heller Ehrman White & McAuliffe, San Francisco, 1984-89; acting prof. law U. Calif., Davis, 1989-92, prof. law, 1992—, assoc. dean for acad. affairs, 1998—; instr. civil procedure, complex litigation, immigration law, refugee law, acting dir. clin. legal edn., spring 1992; mem. legal del. to El Salvador, 1987. Author: How Did You Get To Be Mexican? A White/Brown Man's Search for Identity, 1999; editor: Harvard Law Review, 1981-83; contbr. articles to profl. jours. Bd. dirs. Legal Svcs. No. Calif., 1996—, exec. com., 1997—; bd. dirs. Yolo County ACLU, 1990-93, chmn. legal com., 1991-93; magistrate merit selection panel U.S. Dist. Ct. for Ea. Dist. Calif.; vol. Legal Svcs. Program, San Francisco, Sacramento, Calif.; mem. Lawyers Com. for Civil Rights of the San Francisco Bay Area, 1991—; various pro bono activies. Recipient Commendation, Calif. State Bar, 1985-90, Disting. Tchr. award U. Calif. Davis Sch. of Law, 1993. Mem. ABA (coordinators com. immigration 1998—), Calif. Bar Assn. (standing com. legal svcs. for poor 1992-94, gov. com. continuing edn. bar 1993-98), U. Calif. Alumni Assn. (class sec. Class of 1980), Harvard Club San Francisco, Phi Beta Kappa. Democrat. Roman Catholic. Office: U Calif Sch Law King Hall Davis CA 95617

**JOHNSON, KRAIG NELSON,** lawyer, mediator; b. Landstuhl, Germany, July 8, 1959; came to U.S., 1966; s. Howard Arthur and Joy Anne (Nelson) J.; m. AmberJade F. Leca, Nov. 13, 1993. BA with honors, Eckerd Coll., 1981; M in Internat. Mgmt., Am. Grad. Sch. Internat. Mgmt., Glendale, Ariz., 1982; JD, Baylor U., 1992. Bar: Fla. 1993; cert. mediator and arbitrator Supreme Ct. of Fla. Mktg. mgr. Jack Eckerd Corp., Clearwater, Fla., 1982-85; mktg. systems mgr. NCS, Inc., Houston, 1985-87; dir. ops. Petro, Inc., El Paso, 1987-90; atty. and shareholder Zimmerman, Shuffield, Kiser & Sutcliffe, P.A., Orlando, Fla., 1992—. Editor: Florida Workers' Compensation Practice, 1994; contbr. articles to profl. jours. Mem. internat. trade and investment adv. bd. Econ. Devel. Commn. of Mid-Fla., Orlando, 1997—; mem. Task Force on Title IX, Baylor U. Bd. of Regents, Waco, 1992-93; bd. dirs. Asian-Am. C. of C., Orlando, 1994-95. Fellow Soc. of Antiquaries of Scotland; mem. Am. Immigration Lawyers Assn., St. Andrew's Soc. of Ctrl. Fla. (bd. dirs., v.p. 1996-98, pres. 1998—), Fla. Bar Assn. (sect. on internat. law and litig.), Order of Barristers. Avocations: sailing, flying, shooting sports, Mandarin Chinese and German languages. Private international, Immigration, naturalization, and customs, General civil litigation. Home: 509 N Hampton Ave Orlando FL 32803-5516 Office: Zimmerman Shuffield Kiser & Sutcliffe PA 315 E Robinson St Ste 600 Orlando FL 32801-4308

**JOHNSON, LAEL FREDERIC,** lawyer; b. Yakima, Wash., Jan. 22, 1938; s. Andrew Cabot and Gudney M. (Fredrickson) J.; m. Eugenie Rae Call, June 9, 1960; children: Eva Marie, Inga Margaret. AB, Wheaton (Ill.) Coll., 1960; JD, Northwestern U., 1963. Bar: Ill. 1963, U.S. Dist. Ct. (no. dist.) Ill. 1964, U.S. Ct. Appeals (7th cir.) 1966. V.p., gen. counsel Abbott Labs., Abbott Park, Ill., 1981-89, sr. v.p., sec., gen. counsel, 1989-94; of counsel Schiff Hardin & Waite, Chgo., 1995—. Mem. Chgo. panel CPR Inst. for Dispute Resolution; chair Northwestern U. Law Sch. Bd. Mem. ABA, Chgo. Bar Assn., Assn. Gen. Counsel. Antitrust, General corporate, Securities. Office: Schiff Hardin & Waite 6600 Sears Tower Chicago IL 60606

**JOHNSON, LAURENCE FLEMING,** lawyer; b. Dallas, Oct. 14, 1948; s. Milton G. and Miriam (Fleming) J.; m. Mary Louise Nichols, May 10, 1980; children: Andrew William, Margaret Elizabeth, Paul Nichols. BA, U. Md., 1970, JD, 1973. Bar: Md. 1974, D.C. 1978, U.S. Dist. Ct. Md. 1977, U.S. Dist. Ct. D.C. 1978, U.S. Ct. Appeals (4th cir.) 1977, U.S. Ct. Appeals (D.C. cir.) 1980, U.S. Supreme Ct. 1977. Staff atty. Md. Pub. Interest Research Group, College Park, 1974-76; sole practice, Silver Spring, Md., 1976-77; spl. asst. to commr. Pub. Service Commn. Md., Balt., 1977-78; asst. to U.S. Congressman, Silver Spring, 1979-80; sole practice, Wheaton, Md., 1980-82; pres. Laurence F. Johnson, P.C., Wheaton, 1982-87; mng. ptnr. Johnson & Freedman, 1987—; legis. agt. Greenbelt Consumer Services, Inc., Savage, Md., 1977-81; research asst. various state legislators, Annapolis, Md., 1976-77. Pres. Ayrlawn Citizens Assn., Bethesda, Md., 1984-87. Recipient Outstanding Performance award Montgomery County Dem. Com., Kensington, Md., 1976, Citation of Appreciation, Greenbelt Consumer Services, 1978; named one of Outstanding Young Men Am., 1977. Mem. Am. Immigration Lawyers Assn. (softball chmn. 1983, 84, 86, chmn. office tech. and econs. com. 1989), ABA (chmn. subcom. nonimmigrant visas, gen. practice sect. 1984), Fed. Bar Assn., Md. State Bar Assn., Bar Assn. Montgomery County (co-chmn. immigration 1984, chmn. 1986), Nat. Eagle Scout Assn., Alpha Phi Omega. Democrat. Roman Catholic. Immigration, naturalization, and customs. Home: 6004 Henning St Bethesda MD 20817-3464 Office: 11141 Georgia Ave Ste 418 Silver Spring MD 20902-4659

**JOHNSON, LAURENCE MICHAEL,** lawyer; b. N.Y.C., Feb. 8, 1940; s. Edgar and Eleanor (Kraus) J.; m. Benita Kalnins, Feb. 15, 1975; children: Mark Steven, Lisa Arienne, Laura Elizabeth, Daniel Milton. A.B. cum laude, Harvard U., 1961; LL.B. cum laude, Columbia U., 1964. Bar: Mass. 1964. Research asst. Columbia U., 1962-64; law clk. Supreme Jud. Ct. Mass., 1964-65; from assoc. to ptnr. firm Nutter, McClennen & Fish, Boston, 1965-77; ptnr. firm Newman & Meserve, Boston, 1977-78, Palmer & Dodge, Boston, 1978-83; sole practice law Boston, 1983-85; ptnr. firm Johnson & Polubinski, Boston, 1985-86, Johnson & Schwartzman, Boston, 1986—; teaching team Harvard Trial Adv. Workshop, 1976—; mem. trial adv. faculty Mass. Continuing Legal Edn. of New Eng. Law Inst., 1979—; arbitrator Am. Arbitration Assn., 1976—. Group chmn. larger law firms United Way of Mass. Bay, 1976; mem. Sudbury Human Rights Council, 1964-68, pres., 1965-66; mem. steering com. Lawyers Com. for Civil Rights under Law, Boston Bar Assn., 1976—. Patriot award, 1976. Fellow Am. Coll. Trial Lawyers; mem. Boston Bar Assn. (steering com. lawyers com. for civil rights under law), ABA (jud. adminstrn. div., litigation and anti-trust sects.), Am. Law Inst. Democrat. Club: Union (Boston). Home: 11 Northway Rd Randolph MA 02368-2913 *The trial lawyer's art requires a combination of knowledge, both specialized and general, experience (and the judgment that comes with it), energy, determination, uncompromising self-appraisal and receptivity to the ideas of others. Its object is effective communication and to achieve it, it draws upon not only the law, but every area of human interest. It provides boundless opportunities for creative achievement, but they are realized only in proportion to the effort actually expended.*

**JOHNSON, LAWRENCE WILBUR, JR.,** lawyer; b. Columbia, S.C., Apr. 17, 1955; s. Lawrence Wilbur and Ruth (Cooper) J.; m. Cindy Ann Small, May 26, 1979. BS in Acctg., U. S.C., 1976, JD, 1979. Bar: S.C. 1979, U.S. Dist. Ct. S.C. 1979, U.S. Ct. Appeals (4th cir.) 1980. Jud. clk. 3d Jud. Cir. Ct., Bishopville, S.C., 1979-80; ptnr. Robinson, McFadden, Moore, Pope, Williams, Taylor & Brailsford, P.A., Columbia, 1980-87; shareholder Adams, Quackenbush, Herring & Stuart, P.A., Columbia, 1987-94; ptnr. Young, Clement, Rivers & Tisdale, LLP, Columbia, 1994-96, Johnson Law Firm, Columbia, 1996—. Mem. S.C. Bar Assn., Richland County Bar Assn. (pres. bankruptcy law sect. 1982-85), S.C. Bankruptcy Law Assn. (bd. dirs.), S.C. Bar Ho. of Dels., Greater Columbia C. of C. (bd. dirs.), Com. of 100 (chmn.), Forest Lake Club , U. S.C. Alumni Assn. (bd. dirs. 1980-82), Chi Psi, Omicron Delta Kappa. Republican. Baptist. Avocation: golf. Banking, Bankruptcy, Consumer commercial. Home: 713 Harborview Ct Chapin SC 29036-7716 Office: Johnson Law Firm PA 1728 Main St Ste 221 Columbia SC 29201-2844 also: PO Box 883 Columbia SC 29202-0883

**JOHNSON, LEANNE,** lawyer; b. Bossier City, La., Oct. 18, 1961. BS magna cum laude, So. Ark. U., 1983; JD with high honors, U. Ark., 1986. Bar: Ark. 1986, Tex. 1987, U.S. Dist. Ct. (so. and ea. dists.) Tex. 1987; bd. cert. in personal injury trial law Tex. Bd. Legal Cert. Clk. to Hon. Nauman Scott U.S. Dist. Ct. (we. dist.) La., Alexandria, 1986-87; from assoc. to ptnr. Orgain, Bell & Tucker, LLP, Beaumont, Tex., 1987—. Dir., sec., officer Beaumont YMCA. Mem. Jefferson County Young Lawyers Assn. (former officer, dir.), Jefferson County Bar Assn. (bd. dirs.). Contracts commercial, Personal injury, Toxic tort. Office: Orgain Bell & Tucker LLP 470 Orleans St Ste 400 Beaumont TX 77701-3076

**JOHNSON, LEONARD HJALMA,** lawyer; b. Thomasville, Ga., May 22, 1957; s. Hjalma Eugene and Laura Nell (McLeod) J.; m. Nancy Louise Brock, Dec. 13, 1981; children: Brock Hjalma, Paige McLeod. BSBA, U. Fla., 1978, JD, 1980. Assoc. Dayton, Sumner, Luckie and McKnight, Dade City, 1981-83, Greenfelder and Mander, Dade City, 1983-84; pres. East Coast Bank Corp., Ormond Beach, Fla., 1982—; pvt. practice Dade City, 1984-89; ptnr. Schrader, Johnson, Auvil & Brock, P.A., Dade City, 1990—; vice chmn. Bank of Madison (Fla.) County, 1985-88, N. Fla. Bank Corp., Madison, 1985-88, Bank at Ormond By-the-Sea, 1983—; vice chmn. Lake State Bank, 1989-96. Bd. dirs. Downtown Dade City Main St. Inc., 1987-96, East Pasco Habitat for Humanity, 1998—; trustee Dade City Hosp., 1994-96, chmn., 1996; mem. Leadership Fla. Mem. ABA, Fla. Bar Assn., Pasco County Bar Assn. (sec. 1982-83), Young Pres. Orgn. (edn. chmn. Fla. chpt. 1997-98, chpt. chmn. 1998-99), Dade City C. of C., Fla. Blue Key. Republican. Methodist. Banking, General corporate, Real property.

**JOHNSON, LON M., JR.,** lawyer; b. Pikeville, Ky., May 21, 1950; s. Lon M. Sr. and Edith Bentley Johnson. BS, Pikeville Coll., 1972; JD, U. Ky., 1977. Bar: Ky. 1977, U.S. Dist. Ct. (ea. dist.) Ky. 1981. Assoc. Baird & Baird, Pikeville, 1977-78; pvt. practice Pikeville, 1978—. Republican. Southern Baptist. Fax: 606-432-1482. Consumer commercial, Bankruptcy, General practice. Home: 5105 Collins Hwy Pikeville KY 41501-6843 Office: 317 2nd St Pikeville KY 41501-1128

**JOHNSON, LYNNE A.,** lawyer; b. Oct. 25, 1951; d. Gaylar Winton and Donna Lucille (Tolford) J. AB in Econs. with departmental honors and distinction, Vassar Coll., 1973; JD, Yale U., 1976. Bar: Ga. 1977, N.Y. 1981. Asst. to gen. counsel Sys. and Technics, S.A., Gland, Switzerland, 1976-77; assoc. Powell, Goldstein, Frazer & Murphy, Atlanta, 1977-79; assoc. Fried, Frank, Harris, Shriver & Jacobson, N.Y.C., 1979-97, spl. counsel, 1997—, dir. corp. adminstrn., 1998—. Contgb. author: Exit Age: Reconsidering Compulsory Education for Adolescents: Studies in Law, Education and Social Science, 1981. Hon. grad. fellow for legal studies, 1973-74. Mem. ABA, Am. Soc. Internat. Law, Internat. Bar Assn., Inter-Am. Bar Assn., Assn. Immigration and Nationality Lawyers, N.Y. County Lawyers' Assn., State Bar Ga., N.Y. State Bar Assn., Soc. Univ. Patent Adminstrs., Lotus Club. General corporate, Private international, Mergers and acquisitions. Office: One New York Plz New York NY 10004

**JOHNSON, MARK ANDREW,** lawyer; b. Plainville, Kans., Feb. 27, 1959; s. Delton Lee and Margaret Ellen (McCracken) J. BA in Chemistry, Reed Coll., 1982; JD, U. Calif., Berkeley, 1987. Bar: Oreg. 1987, U.S. Supreme Ct. 1991. Jud. clk. U.S. Dist. Ct. Oreg., Portland, 1987-88, Oreg. Ct. of Appeals, Salem, 1988-89; assoc. Gevurtz, Menashe, Larson, Kurshner & Yates, PC, Portland, 1989-93; ptnr. Findling & Johnson LLP, Portland, 1993-99; of counsel Bennett, Hartman & Reynolds, Portland, 1999—. Mem. ABA, Nat. Gay and Lesbian Law Assn. (co-chmn. 1994-95), Oreg. Gay and Lesbian Law Assn. (co-chair 1990-92), Oreg. State Bar (pres.). Family and matrimonial, Appellate. Office: Bennett Hartman & Reynolds 300 Jefferson Sta 851 SW 6th Ave Ste 1600 Portland OR 97204-1307

**JOHNSON, MARK EUGENE,** lawyer; b. Independence, Mo., Jan. 8, 1951; s. Russell Eugene and Reatha (Nixon) J.; m. Vicki Ja Lane, June 11, 1983. AB with honors, U. Mo., 1973, JD, 1976. Bar: Mo. 1976, U.S. Dist. Ct. (we. dist.) Mo. 1976, U.S. Ct. Appeals (8th cir.) 1984, U.S. Supreme Ct. 1993. Ptnr. Morrison & Hecker, LLP, Kansas City, Mo., 1976—. Editor: Mo. Law Rev., 1974-76. Pres. Lido Villas Assn., Inc., Mission, Kans., 1979-81. Mem. ABA, Mo. Bar Assn., Kansas City Bar Assn., Lawyers Assn. Kansas City, Def. Research Inst., Internat. Assn. Defense Counsel, Mo. Orgn. Def. Lawyers, Carriage Club, Order of Coif, Phi Beta Kappa, Phi Eta Sigma, Phi Kappa Phi, Omicron Delta Kappa. Republican. Presbyterian. Federal civil litigation, State civil litigation. Home: 4905 Somerset Dr Shawnee Mission KS 66207-2230 Office: Morrison & Hecker LLP 2600 Grand Blvd Ste 1200 Kansas City MO 64108-4606

**JOHNSON, MARK HAROLD,** lawyer; b. Grants Pass, Oreg., June 12, 1956; s. Harold R. and Dorothy A. Johnson; m. Susan M. Johnson, June 16, 1979; children: Eric M., Sarah S. BA, Harvard U., 1978; JD, U. Calif. Hastings Coll. Law, San Francisco, 1981. Bar: Calif. 1981. Ptnr. Fenton & Keller (formerly Hoge, Fenton, Jones & Appel, Inc.), Monterey, Calif., 1981-97, Johnson, Gaver & Leach, LLP, Monterey, 1997—. Estate planning, Probate. Office: Johnson Gaver & Leach LLP 2801 Monterey Salinas Hwy Ste B Monterey CA 93940-6401

**JOHNSON, MARK WAYNE,** lawyer; b. Dallas, June 6, 1959; s. W.A. and Wanda Louise (Follis) J.; m. Helene Denise Metz, June 7, 1987; children: Benjamin Gates, Andrew Noah. BS, Belhaven Coll., Jackson, Miss., 1980; JD, U. Miss., Oxford, 1983. Bar: Miss. 1983, U.S. Dist. Ct. (no. and so. dists.) Miss. 1983, U.S. Ct. Appeals (5th cir.) 1990; cert. govt. fin. mgr. Sole practice Jackson, Miss., 1983-86; investigative auditor Miss. Dept. Audit, Jackson, 1986-92; budget analyst Office Budget and Fund Mgmt., Jackson, 1992—; owner Possum Press, 1998—. Contbr. articles to profl. jours. Dir. Miss. Coun. Compulsive Gamblin, 1996-98, adv. bd., 1998—; bd. dirs. Miss. Pub. Employees Credit Union, 1994—. Recipient Spl. Merit award for traffic safety and edn. Nat. Assn. Chiefs of Police, 1987; named one of Outstanding Young Men of Am., 1988. Mem. Miss. Bar. Republican. Avocations: writing, computers. Legislative, State and local taxation, Finance. Office: DFA-Office of Budget and Fund Mgmt 303 Walter Sillers Bldg Jackson MS 39201-1113

**JOHNSON, MARTIN WOLFE,** lawyer; b. Benton, Ky., July 25, 1941; s. Jack William and Mary Irene (Wolfe) J.; m. Sandra Landon, Dec. 28, 1972; children: Kem Renee', Kurt, Kelly. BS in History/Sociology, Lambuth U., Jackson, Tenn., 1967; JD, U. Memphis, 1970. Bar: Ky. 1970, U.S. Dist. Ct. (we. dist.) Ky. 1972, U.S. Ct. Appeals (6th cir.) 1989. Assoc. Lovett & Lewis, Benton, 1970-72; ptnr. Lovett, Lewis & Johnson, Benton, 1972-74, Lovett, Johnson & Shapiro, Benton, 1974-86; ptnr. Lovett & Johnson, Benton, 1986-87, sole ptnr., 1987—; dir. Bank of Benton, Calvert Bank, Calvert City, Ky., Benton Bancorp, Inc., also gen. counsel; city atty. City of Benton, 1972-80, 84—; atty. Marshall County, Ky., 1980-84. Atty., Marshall County Bd. Edn., Benton, 1972—. Named Citizen of the Yr., Marshall County C. of C., 1994, Am. Jurisprudence award, 1969. Mem. Ky. Bar Assn. (mem. CLE com., CLE award 1994). Ch. of Christ. Avocations: biking, hiking, outdoor related activities. Banking, Education and schools, Municipal (including bonds). Office: Lovett and Johnson 1114 Main St Benton KY 42025-1450

**JOHNSON, MATTHEW KINARD,** lawyer; b. Columbia, S.C., Feb. 26, 1969; s. R. Kinard Jr. and Carol McKinney Johnson. BA, Rhodes Coll., 1991; JD, U. Memphis, 1996. Bar: S.C. 1996, U.S. Dist. Ct. S.C. 1997, U.S. Ct. Appeals (4th cir.) 1998. Atty. Mitchell, Bouton, Duggan, Yokel & Childs, Greenville, S.C., 1996-97, Gibbes, Gallivan, White & Boyd, P.A., Greenville, 1997—. Mem. ABA, Def. Rsch. Inst., S.C. Def. Trial Attys. Assn., S.C. Bar Assn., Greenville County Bar Assn. General civil litigation, Insurance, Personal injury. Office: Gibbes Gallivan White & Boyd PA PO Box 10589 Greenville SC 29603-0589

**JOHNSON, MICHAEL A.,** lawyer; b. Hornell, N.Y., Mar. 5, 1955; s. Richard C. and Patricia A. J.; m. Katherine A. Sheridan, Aug. 9, 1980; children: Michael Patrick, Kaitlyn Meghan. BA, St. Vincent Coll., 1977; JD, Ohio No. U., 1980. Bar: Pa. 1980, U.S. Dist. Ct. (we. dist.) Pa. 1980, U.S. Ct. Appeals (3rd cir.) 1991, U.S. Supreme Ct. 1988. Assoc. Hammer & Pollins, Greensburg, Pa., 1981-84; pvt. practice Mt. Pleasant, Pa., 1984—. Active Boy Scouts Am., 1969. Mem. Pa. Bar Assn. (zone 6 bd. dels. 1996—), Mental Health Assn. (pres. 1996-97, Fred Funari award 1998), Westmoreland Bar Assn. (chair planning com. 1990-92, mock trial advisor Mt. Pleasant Sch. 1993-95), Lawyers Abstract Westmoreland County (bd. dirs./ officer 1997—), Westmoreland Inn of Ct. (barrister, sec. 1997-99). Avocations: automotive restoration, reading, coaching soccer. Workers' compensation, General corporate, Real property. Office: 749 N Church St Mount Pleasant PA 15666-9147

**JOHNSON, MICHAEL DENNIS,** lawyer; b. Upper Darby, Pa., Sept. 2, 1948; s. Peter Joseph and Gloria Veronica (Magro) Caruso; 1 child, Monica Ann. BA in political sci., Washington State Univ., 1970; JD, Univ. Washington, 1973. Bar: Wash., Ct. of Appeals Bar (5th cir.), Ct. of Appeals Bar (8th cir.). Trial lawyer Civil Rights Divsn., Washington, 1973-76; sr. trial lawyer Criming Sect. Civil Rights Divsn., Washington, 1976-84; sr. litigation counsel U.S. Dept. Justice, Little Rock, Ark., 1984-93, first asst. U.S. atty., 1993—; adj. prof. Univ. Ark., Little Rock, 1985—; instr. Nat. Inst. of Trial Advocacy, So. Bend, Ind., 1988—, U.S. Dept. Justice Advocacy Inst., Washington, 1980—, Criminal Justice Inst., Little Rock, 1993-97. Author: Management of Civil Rights Allegation, 1994. Recipient Cert. of Appreciation ATF, 1986, 88, 97, Spl. Recognition award, 1988, LECC, 1993, Outstanding Svc. award IRS, 1992, Exceptional Svc. award FBI, 1989, Cert. of Achievement award Ark. Trial Lawyers Assn., 1991, Ark. Investigation, 1990, DOJ Trial Advocacy, 1987, Outstanding Achievement award Secret Svc., 1998. Mem. William R. Overton Inn of Ct. Avocations: photography, travel, athletics. Criminal, Civil rights. Office: US Atty Office 425 W Capitol Ave Ste 500 Little Rock AR 72201-3405

**JOHNSON, NORMA HOLLOWAY,** federal judge; b. Lake Charles, La.; d. H. Lee and Beatrice (Williams) Holloway; m. Julius A. Johnson, June 18, 1964. B.S., D.C. Tchrs. Coll., 1955; J.D., Georgetown U., 1962. Bar: D.C. 1962, U.S. Supreme Ct. 1967. Pvt. practice law Washington, 1963; atty. civil divsn. Dept. Justice, Washington, 1963-67; asst. corp. counsel Office of Corp. Counsel, Washington, 1967-70; judge D.C. Superior Ct., 1970-80; judge U.S. Dist. Ct. (D.C. dist.), Washington, 1980-97, chief judge, 1997—. Bd. dirs. Judiciary Leadership Devel. Coun. Fellow Am. Bar Found.; mem. Nat. Bar Assn., Fed. Judges Assn., Am. Judicature Soc., Supreme Ct. Hist. Soc., Am. Inns of Ct. (William Bryant inn). Office: US Dist Ct US Courthouse 333 Constitution Ave NW Washington DC 20001-2802

**JOHNSON, PAUL OWEN,** lawyer; b. Ft. Wayne, Ind., Jan. 26, 1919; s. Paul Ephriam and Pauline May (Ebersole) J.; m. Arlyn Marie Munson, Aug. 3, 1945; m. Louise Marie Skoglund, Feb. 11, 1972; children: Roxanne Marie, Dianne Marie. BSL, U. Minn., 1941, LLB, 1943, JD, 1967. Bar: Minn. 1943, U.S. Dist. Ct. Minn. 1948. V.p., counsel United Capital Life Ins., Mpls., 1965-70; assoc. editor Am. Trial Lawyers Jour., 1970-75; ptnr. Johnson & Ildstad, Edina, Minn., 1975—; bd. dirs. Interchange Investors, Mpls.; corp. counsel Thunderbird Hotel and Conv. Ctr. Corp.; mem. alt. dispute resolution com. Minn. Supreme Ct. Contbr. articles to Minn. Trial Lawyer Jour. Mem. Mayo Found. Lt. comdr. USN, 1941-46, PTO. Mem. ABA, Am. Arbitration Assn. (lectr.), Am. Judicature Soc., Minn. Bar Assn., Am. Trial Lawyers Assn., Minn. Trial Lawyers Assn. (pres. 1957, bd. dirs.), U.S. Naval Inst., Am. Legion (comdr., judge adv. 1980—), Minn. Alumni Assn. (life), U.S. Navy League (nat. dir. 1995), Submarine Vets. U.S. (life, submarine chaser), VFW, Fireside Investors Club, Masons, Shriners, Gamma Eta Gamma. Episcopalian. Avocations: tennis, boating, travel. Personal injury, Insurance, Alternative dispute resolution. Home: 109 Meadow Ln S Minneapolis MN 55416-3404

**JOHNSON, PHILIP LESLIE,** lawyer; b. Beloit, Wis., Jan. 24, 1939; s. James Philip and Christabel (Williams) J.; m. Kathleen Rose Westover, May 12, 1979; children: Celeste Marie, Nicole Michelle. AB, Princeton U., 1961; JD, U. South Calif., 1973. Bar: Calif. 1973, U.S. Ct. Appeals (9th cir.) 1975, U.S. Ct. of Military Appeals, 1978, U.S. Supreme Ct. 1980. Pilot U.S. Marine Corps., 1961-70; assoc. Law Office Wm. G. Tucker, L.A., 1973-78; ptnr. Engstrom, Lipscomb & Lack, L.A., 1978-92; judge pro tem Calif. State Bar Ct., 1990-95; ptnr. Lillick & Charles, Long Beach, Calif., 1993-99, Cogswell Woolley Nakazawa & Russell, Long Beach, 1999—; chmn. aerospace law com. Def. Rsch. Inst. Contbr. articles to profl. jours. Pres., bd. dirs. U. So. Calif. Legion Lex, 1992-93; chmn. com. to nom. alumni trustees Princeton U., 1996-97, mem. exec. com. of alumni coun., 1996-97; chmn. Marine Corps Scholarship Found. L.A. Ball, 1997-99. Mem. ABA, (aviation & space law com., torts & ins. practice section), Princeton Club (So. Calif., bd. dirs.). Avocations: flying, snow skiing, jazz. Aviation, Product liability, Insurance. Home: 5340 Valley View Rd Rancho Palos Verdes CA 90275-5089 Office: Cogswell Woolley Nakazawa & Russell 111 W OceanBlvd #2000 Long Beach CA 90802

**JOHNSON, PHILIP MARTIN,** lawyer; b. Boston, Feb. 22, 1940; s. Philip E. and Catherine (Martin) J.; children: Charles T., Jennifer M., Melissa C.; m. Carolyn Moxley, Feb. 14, 1981. BA, Colgate U., 1963; LLB, Union U., 1966, JD, 1968; grad., Nat. Coll. Trial Advocacy, 1975. Bar: N.Y. 1967, U.S. Dist. Ct. (we. dist.) N.Y. 1967, Vt. 1970, U.S. Dist Ct. Vt. 1970, U.S. Dist. Ct. N.H. 1975. Asst. dist. atty. County of Livingston, N.Y., 1968-70; ptnr. Niles, Johnson & Brush, Woodstock, Vt., 1970-80; sr. ptnr. Johnson & Dunne, Norwich, Vt., 1980-84; sole practice Taftsville, Vt., 1985—; bd. dirs. Vt. Assn. Blind and Visually Impaired. Justice Village of Dansville, 1967-68, moderator, 1971-73, Village of Woodstock, 1971-73, Town of Woodstock, 1972-80; chmn. Woodstock Zoning Bd. Adjustment, 1972-74, chmn. fin. com., 1986-87; bd. dirs. Woodstock Recreation Assn., 1972-79, chmn., 1973-76, 78-79; bd. dirs. Woodstock Union High Sch., 1974-79, chmn., 1975-79; trustee Ottaquechee Health Ctr., 1979-83, chmn., 1980-83; judge moot ct. competition Vt. Law Sch. Mem. N.Y. Bar Assn., Vt. Bar Assn. (coms. bus. cop. law, unauthorized practice). Avocations: golf, sailing, hunting. General corporate, Estate planning, Real property. Home and Office: 1 River Rd PO Box 67 Taftsville VT 05073-0067

**JOHNSON, PHILIP MCBRIDE,** lawyer; b. Springfield, Ohio, June 18, 1938. AB with honors, Ind. U., 1959; LLB, Yale U., 1962. Bar: Ill. 1962, D.C. 1983, N.Y. 1984. Ptnr. Kirkland & Ellis, Chgo., 1962-81; chmn. Commodity Futures Trading Commn., Washington, 1981-83; ptnr. Wiley, Johnson & Rein, Washington, 1983-84, Skadden, Arps, Slate, Meagher & Flom, Washington, 1984—; lectr. on commodities regulation U. Va. Law Sch., 1993—; spkr. panelist on Commodity Exch. Act Fed. Bar Assn., others; mem. adv. com. definition and regulation Commodity Futures Trading Commn., adv. com. state jurisdiction and responsibility; adv. com. regulatory coordination, adv. com. fin. products Commodity Futures Trading Commn. Author: Commodities Regulation, 2 vols., 1997, Derivatives: A Manager's Guide to the World's Most Powerful Financial Instruments, 1999; mng. editor Yale U. Law Jour, 1962, Agrl. Law Jour; contbr. articles to legal jours. Mem. ABA (founder, chmn. com. on futures regulation 1975-81, mem. governing coun. sect. on bus. law 1981-83), Futures Industry Assn. (bd. dirs. 1980-81, 86-87), Internat. Bar Assn. (founder, chmn. subcom. on commodities, futures and options law 1986-90), N.Y. Stock Exch. (mem. regulatory adv. com. 1988—). Commodities, Administrative and regulatory, Securities. Office: Skadden Arps Slate Meagher & Flom 1440 New York Ave NW Ste 700 Washington DC 20005-2111

**JOHNSON, PHILIP WAYNE,** judge; b. Greenwood, Ark., Oct. 24, 1944; s. John Luther and Flora (Joyce) J.; m. Carla Jean Newsom, Nov. 6, 1970;

children: Betsy, Carl, Jeff, Laura, Philip. B.A., Tex. Tech. U., 1965, J.D., 1975. Bar: Tex. 1975, U.S. Dist. Ct. (no. and we. dists.) Tex. 1976, U.S. Ct. Appeals (5th cir.) 1984, U.S. Supreme Ct. 1984; cert. in civil trial and personal injury trial law, Tex. Bd. Legal Specialization. Assoc. Crenshaw Dupree & Milam, Lubbock, Tex., 1975-80; ptnr. Crenshaw Dupree & Milam, 1980-98; justice Tex. State Ct. of Appeals (7th dist), Amarillo, 1999—; mem. pattern jury charge and state judiciary rels com. State Bar Tex. Bd. dirs., pres. Lubbock County Legal Aid Soc., Tex., 1977-79; bd. dirs., chmn. Trinity Christian Schs., Lubbock, 1978-83, 85-89; bd. dirs., pres. S.W. Lighthouse for Blind, Lubbock, 1978-85. Served to capt. USAF, 1965-72. Decorated Silver Star, D.F.C.; Cross of Gallantry (Vietnam). Fellow Am. Bar Found., Tex. Bar Found. (life); mem. ABA, Tex. Bar Assn., Amarillo Bar Assn., Lubbock County Bar Assn. (pres. 1984-85), Phi Delta Phi. Home: 2301 60th St Lubbock TX 79412-3304 Office: Seventh Ct of Appeals 501 S Fillmore St Rm 2A Amarillo TX 79101-2449

**JOHNSON, RICHARD ARLO,** lawyer; b. Vermillion, S.D., July 8, 1952; s. Arlo Goodwin and Edna Marie (Styles) J.; m. Diane Marie Zephier, Aug. 18, 1972 (div. Jan. 1979); m. Sheryl Lavonne Mader, June 5, 1981; 1 stepchild, Chadwick O. Wagner; 1 child, Sarah N. BA, U. S.D., 1974, JD, 1976. Bar: S.D. 1977, U.S. Dist. Ct. S.D. 1977. Ptnr. Pruitt, Matthews, Muilenberg & Strange, Sioux Falls, S.D., 1977-92, Strange, Farrell & Johnson, P.C., Sioux Falls, 1992—. Mem. Pub. Defender Adv. Bd., Sioux Falls, 1983-98; mem. S.D. Dental Peer Rev. Com. S.E. Dist. Fellow Am. Acad. Matrimonial Lawyers; mem. ATLA, ABA, S.D. Trial Lawyers Assn., State Bar S.D. (chmn. family law com. 1989-92), Phi Delta Phi (pres. 1976-77), Masons, Shriners. Democrat. Lutheran. Family and matrimonial, Criminal, Consumer commercial. Home: 409 E Lotta St Sioux Falls SD 57105-7109 Office: Strange Farrell & Johnson PC 141 N Main Ave Ste 200 Sioux Falls SD 57104-6429

**JOHNSON, RICHARD BRUCE,** lawyer; b. Leavenworth, Wash., Nov. 10, 1928; s. William E. and Frances (Cameron) J.; m. Ann Lohrman Heaps, Feb. 4, 1984. BA, Washington State U., 1950; JD, U. Wash., Seattle, 1959. Bar: Wash. 1960, U.S. Dist. Ct. (we. dist.) Wash. 1960. Sole practice Everett, Wash., 1959—. Mem. Wash. Bar Assn., Def. Research Inst., Wash. Assn. Def. Counsel (pres. 1983), Fedn. Ins. And Corp. Counsel. Republican. Avocations: boating, golfing. State civil litigation, Personal injury, General practice. Office: 1604 Hewitt Ave Ste 301 Everett WA 98201-3536

**JOHNSON, RICHARD FRED,** lawyer; b. Chgo., July 12, 1944; s. Sylvester Hiram and Naomi Ruth (Jackson) J.; m. Sheila Conley, June 26, 1970; children: Brendon, Bridget, Timothy, Laura. BS, Miami U., Oxford, Ohio, 1966; JD cum laude, Northwestern U., 1969. Bar: Ill. 1969, U.S. Dist. Ct. (no. dist.) Ill. 1969, U.S. Ct. Appeals (7th cir.) 1977, U.S. Supreme Ct. 1978, U.S. Ct. Appeals (2d cir.) 1980, U.S. Ct. Appeals (9th cir.) 1991, U.S. Ct. Appeals (5th cir.) 1993. Law clk. U.S. Dist. Ct. (no. dist.) Ill., Chgo., 1969-70; assoc. firm Lord, Bissell & Brook, Chgo., 1970-77, ptnr., 1977—; lectr. legal edn. Contbr. articles to profl. jours. Recipient Am. Jurisprudence award, 1968. Mem. Chgo. Bar Assn., Union League. Insurance, Personal injury, Admiralty. Home: 521 W Roscoe St Chicago IL 60657-3518 Office: Lord Bissell & Brook 115 S La Salle St Ste 3200 Chicago IL 60603-3972

**JOHNSON, RICHARD TENNEY,** lawyer; b. Evanston, Ill., Mar. 24, 1930; s. Ernest Levin and Margaret Abbott (Higgins) J.; m. Marilyn Bliss Meuth, May 1, 1954; children: Ross Tenney, Lenore, Jocelyn. AB with high honors, U. Rochester, 1951; postgrad., Trinity Coll., Dublin, Ireland, 1954-55; LLB, Harvard, 1958. Bar: D.C. 1959. Trainee Office Sec. Def., 1957-59; atty. Office Gen. Counsel. Dept. Def., 1959-63; dep. gen. counsel Dept. Army, 1963-67, Dept. Transp., 1967-70; gen. counsel CAB, 1970-73, mem., 1976-77; gen. counsel NASA, 1973-75, ERDA, 1975-76; chmn. organizational integration Dept. Energy Activation, Exec. Office of Pres., 1977; ptnr. firm Sullivan & Beauregard, 1978-81; gen. counsel Dept. Energy, 1981-83; ptnr. Zuckert, Scoutt, Rasenberger & Johnson, 1983-87; prin. Law Offices of R. Tenney Johnson, Esq., Washington, 1987—; gen. counsel Assn. of Univs. for Rsch. in Astronomy, 1987—. Lt. USNR, 1951-54. Mem. ABA, Fed. Bar Assn., Cosmos Club, Phi Beta Kappa, Theta Delta Chi. Government contracts and claims, Administrative and regulatory, Aviation. Office: 2121 K St NW Ste 800 Washington DC 20037-1829

**JOHNSON, RICHARD WESLEY,** lawyer; b. Stockton, Calif., Aug. 15, 1933; s. Ralph Wesley and Elizabeth Louise (Pucci) J.; m. Suzanne Marie Waldron, Feb. 18, 1962 (div. 1979); children: Scott Wesley, Elizabeth Nancye, Alexis Marie. BA, U. Calif., San Francisco, 1957, JD, 1961. Bar: Calif. 1961, U.S Dist. Ct. Utah., U.S. Dist. Ct. (no. dist.) Calif., U.S. Ct. Appeals (9th cir.). Assoc. Pillsbury, Madison & Sutro, San Francisco, 1961-65; sole practice A&J Publs., Walnut Creek, 1963—, ptnr., 1985—. Author: Express Your Love, 1986; editor-in-chief: Hastings Law Rev. Founding trustee J.F.K. Univ., Orinda, Calif., 1963-66, sec., dean of law, 1964-66. Served as pvt. U.S. Army, 1953-55. Mem. Calif. Bar Assn. (com. mem. 1972), Calif. Bar Assn., Mt. Diablo Bar Assn. (bd. dirs. 1974), Nat. Ski Patrol (patrol leader), Contra Costa Bar Assn. Republican. Roman Catholic. Avocations: photography, sailing, poetry, songwriting. Criminal, Personal injury, State civil litigation.

**JOHNSON, ROBERT ALAN,** lawyer; b. Harrisburg, Pa., June 18, 1944; s. Harry Andrew and Minna Melissa (Ebert) J.; m. Selina Braham Pedersen, Aug. 25, 1979; children: Isabella P., Robert A. Jr. BA, Washington and Jefferson Coll., 1966; JD, Harvard U., 1969. Bar: Pa. 1969. Assoc. Buchanan Ingersoll, Pitts., 1969-76, ptnr., 1977—. Contbr. legal articles to profl. jours. Pres. Bach Choir Pitts., 1979-81; bd. dirs. Pitts. Opera, 1985-94, River City Brass Band, Pitts., 1986-95, Renaissance and Baroque Soc., Pitts., 1994—, Friends of the Music Libr., Carnegie Libr. of Pitts., 1995—. Fellow Am. Coll. Tax Counsel; mem. ABA, Am. Arbitration Assn. (panel arbitrators), Allegheny County Bar Assn., Allegheny Tax Soc. (chmn. 1982-83), Pitts. Tax Club, Duquesne Club. Presbyterian. Avocation: avid collector classical music recs. Pension, profit-sharing, and employee benefits, Nonprofit and tax-exempt organizations. Home: 601 St James St Pittsburgh PA 15232-1434 Office: Buchanan Ingersoll 301 Grant St Ste 20 Pittsburgh PA 15219-1410

**JOHNSON, ROBERT MAX,** lawyer; b. Thomas, Okla., Aug. 20, 1942; s. Claude L. and Jesse C. (Stimmel) J.; m. Virginia A. LeForce, May 31, 1964; children: Kelli Brook, Brent Matthew. BS, Okla. State U., 1964; JD, U. Okla., 1967. Bar: Okla. 1967. Shareholder Crowe & Dunlevy, Oklahoma City, 1967—, pres., 1985-87, exec. com., 1992—; spl. lectr. in land fin. and real estate contracts U. Okla. Coll. of Law, Norman, 1973, 84. Mng. editor: Oklahoma Environmental Law Handbook, 1992-96; contbr. to book: The Law of Distressed Real Estate, 1987; case editor Okla. Law Rev., 1966. Bd. dirs. Redbud Found., Oklahoma City, 1987-96, Myriad Gardens Conservatory, Oklahoma City, 1987-89, Myriad Gardens Found., 1993-96, ARC, 1994-96, Arts Coun. Oklahoma City, 1994—, Am. Heart Assn., 1999—; chmn. Oklahoma City Festival of Arts, 1993-94, Murrah Fed. Bldg. Meml. Task Force, 1995-96, Oklahoma City Nat. Meml. Found., 1996-98, Oklahoma City Nat. Meml. Trust, 1998—. Capt. U.S. Army, 1968-70. Recipient Outstanding Svc. to the Pub. award Okla. Bar Assn., 1998. Fellow Am. Coll. Mortgage Attys. (bd. regents, pres. 1994-95, chmn. exec. com. 1995-96); mem. Am. Coll. Real Estate Lawyers, Oklahoma City Golf and Country Club (bd. dirs. 1981-82, sec. 1982), Order of Coif, Phi Delta Phi (magister 1966-67), Lambda Alpha. Avocations: golf, quail hunting, fly fishing, skiing. Finance, Landlord-tenant, Real property. Home: 1701 Dorchester Dr Oklahoma City OK 73120-1005 Office: Crowe & Dunlevy 1800 Mid Am Tower Oklahoma City OK 73102

**JOHNSON, ROBERT VEILING, II,** lawyer; b. Laconia, N.H., Apr. 29, 1939; s. Robert Veiling and Pauline Leora (Roberts) J.; children: Celia Annah, Jared Veiling. BA, Boston U., 1961; diploma, Internat. Grad. Sch., Sweden, 1963; MS, U. Stockholm, 1964; JD, Boston U., 1967. Bar: N.H. 1967, U.S. Dist. Ct. N.H. 1968, U.S. Ct. Appeals (1st cir.) 1971, U.S. Supreme Ct. 1974. Instr. Wilbraham-Monson Acad., Wilbraham, Mass., 1961-62; assoc. Upton, Sanders & Smith, Concord, N.H., 1967-71; asst. atty. gen. Chief of Criminal Div., State of N.H., Concord, 1971-77; chmn. Bd. of Tax and Land Appeals, State of N.H., Concord, 1977-82; sr. ptnr. Law Offices of Robert V. Johnson II, Concord, 1977—; bd. dirs. Warren Electrical, Inc., Concord, N.H. Electric Cooperative, Inc., Plymouth; vice chmn. bd. dirs. exec. com., fin., engring. and ops. coms. N.H. Electric Cooperative, 1995—. Author: European Economic Community Law, 1964. Instr. Am. Inst. Banking, 1971; chmn. Concord Conservation Commn., 1971-84; bd. dirs. N.H. Assn. Conservation Commns., Concord, 1977-78, Concord Heritage Commn., 1998—; legal counsel Exec. Council, State of N.H., Concord, 1974; bd. trustees First Congl. Ch., Concord, 1998—. Am.-Scandinavian Found. fellow, Sweden, 1962; recipient leadership award Rotary Internat., Laconia, N.H., 1955. Mem. ABA, N.H. Trial Lawyers Assn., Assn. Trial Lawyers Am., Internat. Assn. Assessing Ofcls., Boston U. Alumni Assn. Republican. General practice, State civil litigation, Federal civil litigation. Home: 130 Oak Hill Rd Concord NH 03301-8632 also: PO Box 1425 Center Harbor NH 03226-1425 Office: 64 N State St Concord NH 03301-4330

**JOHNSON, RODNEY MARCUM,** lawyer; b. Dayton, Ohio, Feb. 6, 1947; s. Marvin Clarence and Frances (Marcum) J.; m. Martha Elizabeth Mapp, Sept. 3, 1967 (div. 1974); m. Madolyn Gorman, May 5, 1979; children: Kristine Janeen, Jarrod Marcum, Jason Oliver. AS in Bus. Mgmt., Sinclair C.C., 1968; BS in Bus. Econs., Wright State U., 1975; JD, Cleve. State U., 1978. Bar: Ohio 1979, U.S. Dist. Ct. (so. dist.) Ohio 1980, U.S. Tax Ct. 1980, U.S. Ct. Mil. Appeals 1983, U.S. Supreme Ct. 1983, Fla. 1985, U.S. Dist. Ct. (no. dist.) Fla. 1986. Methods engr. Delco Moraine Divsn. GMC, Dayton, 1965-71; sys. analyst D.W. Mikesell, Inc., Dayton, 1971-74; prin. Johnson Tool Co., Savannah, Ga., 1974-75; pvt. practice Dayton, 1979-81; dist. chief legal counsel Fla. Dept. Health, Pensacola, 1986—. Lt. comdr. JAGC, USN, 1981-86. Mem. Escambia-Santa Rosa Bar Assn. Avocations: boating, fishing, scuba diving. Office: Fla Dept Health 1295 W Fairfield Dr Pensacola FL 32501-1107

**JOHNSON, RUFUS WINFIELD,** lawyer; b. Montgomery County, Md., May 1, 1911; s. Charles L. and Margaret (Smith) J.; m. Rosena L. Allen, June 21, 1939 (div. May 1971); m. Vaunda Louise Griffith, May 29, 1971; step-children: Yvonne, Jackie, Karen, Rodney, Michelle. AB, Howard U., 1934, postgrad., 1934-36, LLB, 1939. Bar: Calif., Ark., Supreme Ct. Ark., Supreme Ct. Calif., D.C. Dist. Ct., U.S. Ct. Appeals, D.C., U.S. Supreme Ct., Supreme Ct. Korea; cert. counsel Judge Advocate Gen. Sch., Washington. Pvt. practice D.C., Calif., Ark., 1945—; originator Lawyer's Pro Bono Svc. Ret. lt. col. USAR. Recipient Combat Infantry badge, U.S. Army, 1944, Purple Heart, 1944, Bronze Star, 1944, Spl. Citation Bravery, 1944. Mem. VFW (life), Am. Judicature Soc., Am. Acad. Polit. and Social Sci., Mil. Order Purple Heart, Internat. Soc. Poets, Am. Kempo Karate Assn., Sr. Citizens Coalition, Ret. Officers Assn., Am. Legion, Masons, Am. Karate Assn. (5th degree Shorin-Ryu Black Belt), Lions. Baptist. Criminal, Appellate, Military. Home: PO Box 776 Mason TX 76856-0776

**JOHNSON, RUSSELL A.,** lawyer; b. Vincennes, Ind., Dec. 9, 1954; s. Pascal Hicox and Leona Irene Johnson; m. Carol Yarbrough, Aug. 16, 1981; children: Heath Y., Kyle A. Assocs., Vincennes U., 1978; BS, JD, Ind. U., 1981. Bar: Ind., U.S. Dist. Ct. (so. dist.) Ind. Assoc. Jones & Loveall, Franklin, Ind., 1981-85; ptnr. Jones Loveall & Johnson, Franklin, 1986-92, Johnson Gray & MacAbee, Franklin, 1992—. exam. author Nat. Bd. Trial Advocacy, 1985-86; regional editor DUI Jour. Nat. Publ., 1985-86. Criminal, General civil litigation. Home: 433 Macy Way Greenwood IN 46142-7482 Office: Johnson Gray & MacAbee PO Box 160 Franklin IN 46131-0160

**JOHNSON, SHIRLEY Z.,** lawyer; b. Burlington, Iowa, Mar. 6, 1940; d. Arthur Frank and Helen Martha (Nelson) Zaiss; m. Charles Rumph, Jan. 19, 1979. BA summa cum laude, U. Iowa, 1962; JD with honors, U. Mich., 1965. Bar: Calif. 1966, D.C. 1976, U.S. Supreme Ct. 1979. Trial atty. antitrust divsn. U.S. Dept. Justice, San Francisco, 1965-72; counsel antitrust subcom. U.S. Senate Jud. Com., Washington, 1973-75; ptnr. Baker & Hostetler, Washington, 1976-85; pvt. practice Washington, 1985-98; ptnr., chair antitrust and trade regulations dept. Greenberg Traurig, Washington, 1998—; mediator U.S. Dist. Ct., Washington, 1990—. Contbr. articles to profl. jours. Trustee The Textile Mus., Washington, 1991—, v.p. bd. trustees, 1994—. Mem. ABA, Women's Bar Assn. (bd. dirs. 1989-91), Am. Law Inst., Order of Coif, Phi Beta Kappa. Democrat. Avocation: collecting Asian art. Antitrust, Administrative and regulatory, Legislative. Office: Greenburg Traurig 1300 Connecticut Ave NW Washington DC 20036-1703

**JOHNSON, STEPHEN PATRICK HOWARD,** lawyer; b. Holmfirth, England, Feb. 23, 1957; came to U.S., 1982; s. Herbert Edward and Margaret Patricia Johnson; 1 child, Graham Johnson. BA in Genetics, Cambridge (Eng.) U., 1978, MA (hon.), 1993; solicitors final exam. with honors, Coll. of Law, London, 1980; JD with high honors, Ill. Inst. Tech., 1984. Bar: Ill. 1984, N.Y. 1991; solicitor Supreme Ct. Eng. 1982. Solicitor, trainee Bird & Bird, London, 1980-82; assoc. Kirkland & Ellis, Chgo., 1982-88, ptnr., 1988-90; ptnr. Kirkland & Ellis, N.Y.C., 1990—. Contbr. chpt. to book. Intellectual property, Private international. Office: Kirkland & Ellis 153 E 53rd St New York NY 10022-4611

**JOHNSON, STEPHEN W.,** lawyer; b. Pitts., Jan. 29, 1959; s. John F. and Audrey F. Johnson; m. Tracey A. Johnson, June 5, 1982; children: Samuel Peter, Adam D. BA, U. Va., 1981; JD, U. Pitts., 1984. Bar: Pa. 1984. Shareholder Buchanan Ingersoll P.C., Pitts., 1984—. General corporate, Securities. Home: 229 Hickory Heights Dr Bridgeville PA 15017-1084 Office: Buchanan Ingersoll PC One Oxford Ctr, Grant Pittsburgh PA 15219

**JOHNSON, STERLING, JR.,** federal judge; b. 1934. BA, Bklyn. Coll., 1963; LLB, Bklyn. Sch. Law, 1966. With N.Y.C. Police Dept., 1957-67; asst. U.S. atty. U.S. Atty. Office (ea. dist.) N.Y., 1967-70; atty. civilian complaint rev. bd. U.S. Atty. Office (so. dist.) N.Y., 1970-74, atty. drug enforcement adminstrn., 1974-75, spl. narcotics prosecutor, 1975-91; fed. judge U.S. Dist. Ct. (ea. dist.) N.Y., Bklyn., 1991—; active Second Cir. Task Force on Gender, Racial, and Ethnic Fairness in Cts.; mem. Nat. Conf. Fed. Trial Judges Exec. Com. Bd. dirs. Bedford Stuyvesant Restoration Corp., Cardinal Cook Com. on Substance Abuse; active Police Athletic League, Pres. Drug Adv. Coun. With USMC, 1952-55, USNR, 1975—. Mem. ABA, N.Y. State Bar Assn., Nat. Black Prosecutors Assn., Nat. Orgn. Black Law Enforcement Execs., N.Y. State Dist. Attys. Assn. Office: US Dist Ct 225 Cadman Plz E Rm 432 Brooklyn NY 11201-1818

**JOHNSON, STEVEN BOYD,** lawyer; b. Springfield, Tenn., July 19, 1953; s. Ammon and Dorothy Jean (Anderson) J.; m. Martha Jane Yoakum, 1981 (div. Mar. 1987) 1 child, Eleanor Danielle; m. Betsy Lou Brown, Jan. 4, 1989. BA, Vanderbilt U., 1975; MA, Webster Coll., 1977; JD, U. Memphis, 1979. Bar: Tenn. 1979, U.S. Dsit. Ct. (we., mid. and ea. dists.) Tenn., U.S. Ct. Appeals (6th cir.). Law clk. to Judge Robert M. McRae U.S. Dist. Ct. (we. dist.) Tenn., Memphis, 1980-81; assoc. Apperson, Crump, Duzane & Maxwell, Memphis, 1981-83; ptnr. Horne & Peppel, Memphis, 1983-84; mem., ptnr. Butler Vines & Babb, P.L.L.C., Knoxville, 1985—; assoc. prof. entertainment law U. Memphis, 1980. Co-author: Tennessee Workers Compensation Practice, 1995. Served with USN, 1975-77. Mem. Tenn. Bar Assn., Knoxville Bar Assn., Def. Rsch. Inst., Delta Theta Phi, Omicron Delta Kappa. Republican. Avocations: skiing, water skiing, boating, reading. Personal injury, Workers' compensation, Insurance. Home: 3434 Harbour Front Way Knoxville TN 37922-9422 Office: Butler Vines & Babb PLLC First Am Bank Ctr Ste 810 Knoxville TN 37902

**JOHNSON, TERRI SUE,** lawyer; b. Saginaw, Mich., Sept. 18, 1961. BA, Mich. State U., 1983; JD, U. Fla., 1988. Bar: Fla. 1989. Assoc. Roy J. Morgan & Assocs., P.A., Orlando, Fla., 1980-92; ptnr. Morgan & Johnson, P.A., Orlando, Fla., 1992—. Assoc. editor Acad. Fal. Trial Lawyers Jour., 1994—. Mem. Fla. Bar Assn., Nat. Orgn. Social Security Reps., Acad. Fla. Trial Lawyers, Orange County Bar Assn. (guardian ad litem). Personal injury, Insurance, Pension, profit-sharing, and employee benefits. Office: Morgan & Johnson PA 221 N Joanna Ave Tavares FL 32778-3217

**JOHNSON, THOMAS STUART,** lawyer; b. Rockford, Ill., May 21, 1942; s. Frederick C. and Pauline (Ross) J. BA, Rockford Coll. 1964, LLD, 1989; JD, Harvard U., 1967. Bar: Ill. 1967. Pres.Williams & McCarthy, Rockford, 1967—; lectr. in field. Contbr. numerous articles to profl. jours. Chmn. bd. trustees Rockford Coll., 1986-89; trustee Eastern Ill. U., 1996—; chmn. bd. dirs. Ill. Inst. Continuing Legal Edn., Chgo., 1984-86; trustee Emanuel Med. Ctr., Turlock, Cal., 1984-86, trustee Swedish Covenant Hosp., Chgo., 1984-86; treas. Lawyers Trust Fund of Ill., Chgo., 1984-86; trustee, Lincoln Acad. of Ill., 1999—, mem. bd. govs., 1985-90, Regent's Coll., London, 1985-89; bd. dir. benevolence bd. Covenant Ch. Am., Chgo., 1984-86; chmn. Regent's Found. for Internat. Edn., London. With U.S. Army, 1965-67. Fellow Am. Bar Found., Am. Coll. Trust and Estate Counsel; mem. ABA (ho. dels. 1982-89, chmn. comm. on advt. 1984-88), Ill. Bar Assn. (bd. govs. 1976-82, sec. 1981-82, medal of honor 1997), Winnebago County Bar Assn. (pres. 1990), Am. Judicature Soc. (bd. dirs. 1986-90), Rockford Country Club, Rotary (pres. Rockford 1992-93). Republican. Estate planning, General corporate, General practice. Home: 913 N Main St Rockford IL 61103-7068

**JOHNSON, THOMAS WEBBER, JR.,** lawyer; b. Indpls., Oct. 18, 1941; s. Thomas W. and Mary Lucinda (Webber) J.; m. Sandra Kay McMahon, Aug. 15, 1964 (div. 1986); m. Deborah Joan Collins, May 17, 1987 (div. 1990); m. Barbara Joyce Walter, Mar. 13, 1992. BS in Edn., Ind. U., 1963, JD summa cum laude, 1969. Bar: Ind. 1969, Calif. 1970. Law clk. Ind. Supreme Ct., Indpls., 1968-69; assoc. Irell & Manella, L.A., 1969-76; ptnr. Irell & Manella law firm, L.A., 1976-84, Newport Beach, Calif., 1984—; chair Com. on Group Ins. Programs for State Bar of Calif., San Francisco, 1978-79; adj. prof. law UCLA, 1996—; lectr. for Practicing Law Inst., Calif. Continuing Edn. of the Bar, Calif. Judges Assn., seminars on ins. and bus. litigation. Editor-in-chief: Ind. Law Review, 1968-69; contbr. articles to profl. jours. With USNR, 1959-65. Named Outstanding Grad. Province XII, Phi Delta Phi legal fraternity, 1969. Mem. ABA (lectr. chair ins. coverage litigation com., tort and ins. practice sec. 1995-96), Calif. Bar Assn., Orange County Bar Assn., Masons, Newport Beach Country Club. Republican. Mem. Christian Ch. Insurance, General civil litigation. Office: Irell & Manella 840 Newport Center Dr Ste 400 Newport Beach CA 92660-6323

**JOHNSON, TIGE CHRISTOPHER,** lawyer; b. Morris, Ill., Oct. 20, 1970; s. H. Craig and Sandra K. J.; m. Yvonne C. Rubio, May 22, 1993. BA with distinction, U. N.Mex., 1992; JD, Vanderbilt U., 1996; LLM with merit, London Sch. Econ. and Polit. Sci., 1997. Bar: Mich. 1998, D.C. 1999. Assoc. Varnum, Riddering, Schmidt & Howlett LLP, Grand Rapids, Mich., 1997-99, Altheimer & Gray, Chgo., 1999—; adj. prof. depts. legal studies and criminal justice Grand Valley State U., 1999; cons. Jr. Achievement, Grand Rapids, 1998. Mem. Mich. Bar Assn., Grand Rapids Bar Assn., D.C. Bar Assn., Phi Alpha Delta (pres. 1995—, law-related instr. 1995-96), Alpha Tau Omega (various coms. 1988—). Republican. Lutheran. Avocations: snowboarding, traveling, reading, in-line skating. Fax: 312-715-4800. E-mail: johnsontc@altheimer.com. Mergers and acquisitions, General corporate, Private international. Home: 225 W Huron St Apt 207 Chicago IL 60610 Office: Altheimer & Gray 10 S Wacker Dr Chicago IL 60606-7482

**JOHNSON, TODD ALAN,** lawyer; b. Lansing, Mich., Oct. 23, 1965; s. Austin Lawrence and Mary Roxanne Johnson; m. Tracy Larned, May 13, 1989; children: Amy Larned, Mary Larned, Samuel Grant. BA, Western Mich. U., 1987; JD, U. Iowa, 1989. Bar: Tex. 1990, Mich. 1994. Summer clk. Varnum, Riddering et al, Grand Rapids, Mich., 1989; assoc. Fulbright & Jaworski, Dallas, 1989-94, Van Eenenaam White et al, Grand Haven, Mich., 1994-97, Johnson McNally, Grand Haven, 1997—; CFO Millenium Land Devel., Spring Lake, Mich., 1997—. Mem. Spring Lake Country Club, Kiwanis (pres.-elect 1998—). General corporate, Estate planning, General practice. Office: Johnson McNally 222 Franklin St Grand Haven MI 49417-1336

**JOHNSON, WALTER FRANK, JR.,** lawyer; b. Georgiana, Ala., Apr. 14, 1945; s. Walter F. and Marjorie Ellen (Carnathan) J.; m. Emily Waldrep, Nov. 23, 1969; children—Brian W., Stacey E. BS in Bus. Adminstrn., Auburn U., 1968; JD, Samford U., 1973. Bar: Ala. 1973, Ga. 1974. Assoc. Hatcher, Meyerson, Oxford and Irvin, Atlanta, 1973-74, Thompson and Redmond, Columbus, Ga., 1974-78; sole practice, Columbus, Ga., 1978—; asst. pub. defender, Columbus, 1978; acct. Union Camp Corp., 1968-70. Mem. ABA, Ala. State Bar, State Bar of Ga., Columbus Lawyers Club. Methodist. Real property, Bankruptcy, Probate. Home: 3235 Flint Dr Columbus GA 31907-2029 Office: PO Box 6507 3006 University Ave Columbus GA 31907-2106

**JOHNSON, WATTS CAREY,** lawyer; b. Chgo., June 21, 1925; s. Carey R. and Leone (VanMechelen) J.; m. Claire Hayes Johnson, June 4, 1950; children: Gregory, Philip, Carolyn, Brian, Barbara. BA, Western Mich. U., 1947; JD, Northwestern U., 1950. Bar: Ill. 1950, U.S. Supreme Ct. 1967. Justice of the peace Princeton Twp., Bureau County, Ill., 1952-56; asst. state's atty. State's Atty. Office, Bureau County, 1957-64; ptnr. Peterson, Johnson & Martin, 1960-69, Johnson, Martin & Russell, Princeton, Ill., 1969-88; ptnr. Johnson, Martin, Russell, English, Scoma & Beneke, Princeton, Ill., 1988-95, ret., 1995; of counsel Johnson, Martin, Russell, English, Scoma & Beneke, Princeton, 1995-97, Russell, English, Scoma & Beneke, P.C., Princeton, 1997—; mem. rules commn. Ill. Supreme Ct., 1977-95; commr. State of Ill. Ct. of Claims, 1989-95; ret. 1996; mem. Atty. Registration and Disciplinary Commn. State of Ill., 1973-92, inquiry divsn., 1973-76, hearing divsn., 1976-78, rev. bd., 1979-90, commr., 1991-95. Pres. Bureau County chpt. ARC, 1959-62; pres. Princeton Jaycees, 1954; chmn. Bureau County Merit Commn., 1985-88. Fellow Am. Coll. Trust and Probate Counsel; mem. Ill. Cts. Commn., Ill. Appellate Lawyers Assn., Ill. Def. Counsel, Internat. Assn. Def. Counsel. Republican. Baptist. Avocation: computers. State civil litigation, Family and matrimonial, General practice. Office: Russell English Scoma & Beneke PC 10 Park Ave W Princeton IL 61356-2019

**JOHNSON, WELDON NEAL,** lawyer; b. Lovington, N.Mex., Apr. 3, 1961; s. Ben and O. Annette Johnson; m. Kellie Marie Nolfo, June 22, 1962; children: Kaitlyn Elizabeth, Shannon Christine. BS in Bus. Adminstrn., Columbia Coll., 1992; JD, St. Louis U., 1996. Bar: Mo. 1996, Ill. 1997, U.S. Dist. Ct. (ea. dist.) Mo. 1997. With Anheuser-Busch, Inc., St. Louis, 1980-93; assoc. The O'Malley Law Firm, St. Louis, 1996—. Mem. ABA, Mo. Bar Assn., Ill. State Bar Assn., Bar Assn. Met. St. Louis, Alpha Chi. Avocations: golf, baseball, snow skiing. Personal injury, Insurance, Labor. Office: The O'Malley Law Firm 10 S Brentwood Blvd Ste 102 Saint Louis MO 63105-1694

**JOHNSON, WILLIAM H.,** lawyer; b. Orangeburg, S.C., July 10, 1945; s. Wayman and Lila (McKiever) J.; m. Annette Bell; children: William, Lionel, Immanuel. BA, Claflin Coll., 1972; JD, Duke U., 1975; LLM in Trial Advocacy, Temple U., 1997. Bar: N.C. 1975, D.C. 1979, Pa. 1981, U.S. Ct. Appeals (3d and fed. cirs.), U.S. Supreme Ct. Atty. ICC, Washington, 1975-78; chief counsel transp. subcom. of commerce com. U.S. Senate, Washington, 1978-81; William Henry Johnson gen. atty. Norfolk Southern Corp., Norfolk, 1981—; arbitrator Common Pleas Ct., Phila., 1985—, U.S. Dist. Ct. for Ea. Dist. Pa., Phila., 1987—; mem. bd. advisors paralegal studies Phila. C.C., 1996—. Bd. dirs. Met. Career Ctr., Phila., 1993—. With USN, 1968-72. Mem. ABA, Nat. Bar Assn. (regional bd. dirs. 1991-93), Am. Corp. Counsel Assn., Phila. Bar Assn. (bd. dirs. Edn. Ctr. 1995—), Barristers Assn. Phila. (pres. 1993-94). Avocations: golf, gardening. Bankruptcy, Administrative and regulatory, General civil litigation. Home: 2804 Ocean Mist Ct Virginia Beach VA 23454-1230 Office: Norfolk Southern Corp 3 Commercial Pl Norfolk VA 23510-2108

**JOHNSON, WILLIAM R.,** state supreme court justice; b. Oct. 21, 1930; married; 2 children. Student, Dartmouth Coll., Harvard U. Pvt. practice law Hanover; state senator N.H. Gen. Assembly, Concord, state rep.; judge N.H. Superior Ct., Concord, 1969-85; assoc. judge N.H. Supreme Ct., Concord, 1985—; instr. law Dartmouth Coll., Hanover. Office: NH Supreme Ct One Noble Dr Concord NH 03301*

**JOHNSON, WILLIE DAN,** lawyer; b. Senatobia, Miss., Mar. 26, 1948; s. Beauregard and Geraldine J.; m. Marilyn Ann Stamps, Jan. 4, 1967; children: Renita Annette, Jamaal Curtis, Courtnay Erin. BA, UCLA, 1973, JD, 1977. Bar: Calif. 1978, U.S. Dist. Ct. (cen.) Dist. Calif. 1978. Lawyer, sole practice L.A. Sgt. USAF, 1966-70. Mem. ABA, ATLA, Consumer Atty. Assn. Calif., Consumer Atty. Assn. L.A. General civil litigation, Personal injury, Workers' compensation. Office: Law Offices of Willie Dan Johnson 3500 S Figueroa St Ste 217 Los Angeles CA 90007-4363

**JOHNSTON, COYT RANDAL,** lawyer, poet; b. Wheeler, Tex., Nov. 17, 1946; s. Coyt Edward Johnston and Valrea Joyce (Hirons) Chase; m. Sandra

Susan Ramos, Sept. 4, 1970 (div. Aug. 1993). BA, Brigham Young U., 1971; JD with honors, U. Tex., 1974. Bar: Tex. 1974. Assoc. Baker & Botts, Houston, 1974-78, Hewett, Johnson, Swanson & Barbee, Dallas, 1979-81; owner Coyt Randal Johnston, Dallas, 1981-82; atty. Davenport & Brown, Dallas, 1982-84; shareholder Johnston & Budner, Dallas, 1984-97; founder, shareholder Johnston & Tobey, Dallas, 1997—; mem. Tex. Bd. Legal Specialization, Austin, 1980-83, mem. personal injury adv. commn., 1990—. Author poems. Avocations: water skiing, poetry and song writing, guitar playing. Professional liability, Personal injury, General civil litigation. Office: Johnston & Tobey PC 900 Jackson St Ste 710 Dallas TX 75202-4427

**JOHNSTON, JOANNE SPITZNAGEL,** lawyer, writing consultant; b. Peoria, Ill., Mar. 11, 1930; d. Elmer Florian and Anna E. (Kolb) Spitznagel; m. Charles Helm Bennett, June 12, 1951 (div. 1978); children—Mary Jaquelin Bennett Graub, Ariana Holliday, Caroline Helm Bennett Ammerman, Joanne Mary Jeffers; m. Donald Robert Johnston, Nov. 25, 1981. A.B., Vassar Coll., 1951; M.A., Ind. U., 1970, Ph.D., 1974; J.D., Ind. U.-Indpls., 1980. Bar: Ind. 1980, Minn. 1985. Lectr., Ind. U., Indpls., 1968-81, U.-Indpls., 1970-76; writing cons. U. Minn., Mpls., 1982-91; sole practice, Indpls., 1980-86, Mpls., 1986-91. Mem. Jr. League Sarasota, Dramatic Club; Indpls. Womans Club, Garden Club Am. (Indpls.). Methodist. Home: 9845 S Harbour Pointe Dr Bloomington IN 47401-8423

**JOHNSTON, JOCELYN STANWELL,** paralegal; b. Evanston, Ill., Feb. 16, 1954; d. Gerald and Dorothy Jeanne (Schoenfield) Stanwell; m. Thomas Patrick Johnston, Nov. 28, 1986. BA, U. Minn., 1981; cert., Phila. Inst. Paralegal Tng., Phila., 1986. Paralegal Fredrikson & Byron P.A., Mpls., 1981-84, Reed, Smith, Shaw and McClay, Phila., 1984-85, McCausland, Keen & Buckman, P.C., Radnor, Pa., 1985-86, Harris, Guenzel, Meier & Nichols, P.C., Ann Arbor, Mich., 1986-87, Conner & Bentley, P.C., Ann Arbor, 1987-88, Cichocki & Armstrong, Ltd., Oak Park, Ill., 1988-90, Bishop and Bishop, Oak Brook, Ill., 1994-95, Martin, Breen & Merrick, Oak Park, 1994-95, Saitlin, Patzik, Frank & Samotny, Ltd., Chgo., 1995, Bryson R. Cloon, Esquire, Leawood, Kans., 1996—. Mem. Kans. Bar Assn. Democrat. Home: 14501 Marty St Overland Park KS 66223-2300 Office: Bryson R Cloon Esquire 11350 Tomahawk Creek Pkwy Leawood KS 66211-2670

**JOHNSTON, JOHN JOSEPH,** lawyer; b. East St. Louis, Ill., Jan. 19, 1954; s. Joseph J. and Marilyn A. (McAteer) J.; m. Becky Boulware, Aug. 14, 1976; children: Hilary, Laura, Ellen Scott, David. BS in Journalism, U. Kans., 1976; JD, U. Ill., 1979. Bar: Ill. 1979, Nebr. 1986, U.S. Dist. Ct. (so. dist.) Ill. 1982, U.S. Ct. Appeals (7th cir.) 1983. Assoc. Meyer, Capel, Hirschfeld et al, Champaign, Ill., 1979-81, Richard Reed Law Offices, Belleville, Ill., 1981-83; ptnr. Johnston & Kavanaugh, Belleville, 1983-90, Ripplinger, Dixon & Johnston, Belleville, 1990-94; Dixon & Johnston, Belleville, 1994—. Bd. dirs. Children First Found., 1997—. Mem. ABA (ho. of dels. 1988-90), Ill. State Bar Assn. (bd. govs. 1990-92), Attys. Title Guaranty Fund, Sierra Club (chair 1986), KC (pres. # 592 1988-91). Personal injury, Family and matrimonial. Office: Dixon & Johnston 103 W Main St Belleville IL 62220-1501

**JOHNSTON, LOGAN TRUAX, III,** lawyer; b. New Haven, Dec. 9, 1947; s. Logan Truax Jr. and Elizabeth (Josey) J.; m. Celeste Linguere; children: Charlotte Hathaway, Logan Truax IV, Owen Conrad, Oritse J., Gboyega P. BA, Yale U., 1969; JD, Harvard U., 1973. Bar: Ill. 1973, Ariz. 1984, U.S. Ct. Appeals (2d cir.) 1982, U.S. Ct. Appeals (7th cir.) 1973, U.S. Ct. Appeals (9th cir.) 1986, U.S. Ct. Appeals (fed. cir.) 1990, U.S. Supreme Ct. 1991. Assoc. Winston & Strawn, Chgo., 1973-79, ptnr., 1979-83; ptnr. Winston & Strawn, Phoenix, 1983-89; mng. ptnr. Johnston Maynard Grant & Parker, Phoenix, 1989-97, Johnston & Dodd, Phoenix, 1997—; spl. asst. state's atty. Du Page County, Ill., Wheaton, 1976-77; cons. Community Legal Svcs., Phoenix, 1984—. Contbg author: Arizona Appellate Handvook, Vol. III. Served with U.S. Army N.G., 1970-76. Mem. ABA, Maricopa County Bar Found., Maricopa County Bar Assn., Ariz. Bar Found., Ariz. State Bar Assn., Phoenix Heroes Endowment Fund. Presbyterian. Avocations: books, movies, golf, hiking, travel. General civil litigation, Administrative and regulatory, Health. Office: Johnston & Dodd PLC 1 N 1st St Phoenix AZ 85004-2357

**JOHNSTON, MICHAEL WAYNE,** lawyer; b. Houston, TX, Mar. 23, 1955; m. M. Katherine Johnston, June 2, 1979; children: K. Elizabeth, M. Phillip. BA, Trinity U., San Antonio, 1977; JD, Baylor U., 1980. Bar: Tex. 1980, U.S. Dist. Ct. (no. dist.) Tex. 1980, U.S. Ct. Claims 1981, U.S. Supreme Ct. 1988, U.S. Dist. Ct. (so. dist.) Tex. 1988, U.S. Dist. Ct. (we. dist.) Tex. 1989; bd. cert. civil trial law; bd. cert. consumer law. Shareholder Simon, Anisman, Doley & Wilson, Fort Worth, 1980-86; ptnr. Thompson, Coe, Cousins & Irons, Dallas, 1986-89, Knox, Beadles & Johnston, Dallas, 1989-94, Broude, Nelson & Harrington, Ft. Worth, 1994-97, Johnston & Minton, Ft. Worth, 1997—. Contbr articles to profl. jours. Pres. Univ. West Neighborhod Assn., Ft. Worth. Mem. Def. Rsch. Inst., Tarrant Bar Assn., Dallas Bar Assn., Legal Network for Deaf, Coll. State Bar of Tex. General civil litigation, Consumer commercial, Insurance. Office: Johnston & Minton 307 W 7th St Ste 825 Fort Worth TX 76102-5108

**JOHNSTON, NEIL CHUNN,** lawyer; b. Mobile, Ala., Feb. 23, 1953; s. Vivian Gaines and Sara Niel (Chunn) J.; m. Ashley Monroe Hocklander, Dec. 20, 1980; children: Katie, Neil Jr. BA, Southwestern at Memphis (name changed to Rhodes Coll.), 1975; JD, U. Ala., 1978. Atty. Hand, Arendall L.L.C., Mobile, Ala., 1978—; Com. mem. Ala. Law Inst. Com., Tuscaloosa, Ala., 1990; mem. Gov.'s Wetland Mitigation Task Force, 1994. Contbr. articles to profl. jours. Pres. Project CATE Found, Inc., Mobile, 1987—; trustee Nature Conservancy, Ala., 1990-96; mem. Wetland Mitigation Banking Task Force, 1994-96; bd. dirs. Am. Jr. Miss Program. Recipient Ala. Gov.'s award-Water Conservationist, Ala. Wildlife Fedn., 1987. Mem. ABA, Ala. State Bar Assn. (chmn. environ. law sect. 1984-91, corp. banking, bus. law sect. 1993, Mobile Bar Assn., Ala. Forestry Assn., Ala. Law Inst. (mem. com. 1990), Rotary (pres. Mobile 1996-97). Environmental, Real property, Contracts commercial. Office: Hand Arendall LLC 3000 FNB Bldg Royal St Mobile AL 36602

**JOHNSTON, OSCAR BLACK, III,** lawyer; b. Tulsa, Oct. 1, 1941; s. Oscar Black Jr. and Carol (VanDerwiele) J.; m. Ruth Archdeacon Darrough; children: Eric Oscar, David Darrough. BBA, Baylor U., 1963; JD, U. Tulsa, 1966. Bar: Okla. 1966, U.S. Dist. Ct. (no., ea., we. dists.) Okla., U.S. Ct. Claims, U.S. Ct. Appeals (10th cir.), U.S. Supreme Ct. Asst. U.S. attorney U.S. Dist. Ct. (we. dist.) Okla., 1970-76; ptnr. Logan & Lowry, L.L.P., Vinita, Okla., 1979—. Assoc. editor Tulsa Law Review, 1964-66. Presiding judge divsn. 54 Okla. Temp. Ct. Appeals, 1980-81, judge divsn. XIV, 1991-93; presiding judge panel VI Lawyer-Staffed Ct. Appeals, 1992. Capt. JAGC, U.S. Army, 1966-70. Fellow Am. Bar Found., Okla. Bar Found. (trustee 1988-96, pres. 1995); mem. ABA (sects. litigation, family law and criminal), Fed. Bar Assn. (pres. Oklahoma City chpt. 1975), Craig County Bar Assn. (pres. 1986-88), Okla. Bar Assn. (adminstrn. of justice, bench and bar coms.), Okla. Trial Lawyers Assn., Rotary (pres. Vinita 1983-84), Phi Alpha Delta. Republican. Methodist. General civil litigation, Family and matrimonial, Criminal. Office: Logan & Lowry PO Box 558 Vinita OK 74301-0558 Home: 116 Westwood Ave Vinita OK 74301-2703

**JOHNSTON, SHARON A.,** lawyer; b. Jefferson Parish, La., Mar. 25, 1963; d. Thomas D. and Dorothy Genevieve Marie (Arceneaux) J. BA in Polit. Sci., U. N.C., 1985; JD, Campbell U., Buies Creek, N.C., 1989. Bar: N.C. 1989. Assoc. Crossley, McIntosh, Prior & Collier, Wilmington, N.C., 1989—. Tutor Cape Fear Literacy Coun., Wilmington, N.C., 1991; bldg. fundraiser Habitat for Humanity, Wilmington, 1994. Mem. 5th Judicial Dist. Bar Assn. (rep. young lawyer's divsn.), New Hanover County Bar Assn. Insurance, Consumer commercial, General civil litigation. Office: Crossley McIntosh et al 616 Market St Wilmington NC 28401-4637 Address: PO Box 2366 Surf City NC 28445-9821

**JOHNSTONE, DEBORAH BLACKMON,** lawyer; b. Birmingham, Ala., Jan. 26, 1953; d. T.C. Blackmon and Joan (Thompson) Ryals; m. David Johnstone, July 26, 1968 (div. 1976); children: Pamela, Robin. A.S., Jefferson Sch. Nursing, Birmingham, 1976; BA, Birmingham-So. Coll., 1982; JD, Birmingham Law Sch., 1986. Bar: Ala. 1986. Nurse Carraway Med. Ctr., Birmingham, 1976-86; assoc. Emond & Vines, Attys., Birmingham, 1986-88; atty., med.-legal cons. Am. Internat. Group, Bedford, Dallas, Ft. Worth, 1988—. Founder, v.p. Burleson Animal Soc., 1998—. Mem. ABA, ATLA, ACLU, AAAS, Ala. Trial Lawyers, Ala. State Bar, Tex. Bd. Nurse Examiners, Ala. Bd. Nursing, Consumers Union. Democrat. Roman Catholic. Avocations: history, golf, writing non-fiction, jewelry design. Personal injury, Product liability, Health. Office: 849 E Renfro St Burleson TX 76028-5019

**JOHNSTONE, DOUGLAS INGE,** judge; b. Mobile, Ala., Nov. 15, 1941; s. Harry Inge and Kathleen (Yerger) J.; m. Mary Jayne Baynes (div.); 1 child, Francis Inge. BA, Rice U., 1963; JD, Tulane U., 1966. Bar: Ala. 1966, U.S. Dist. Ct. Ala. 1966, U.S. Ct. Appeals (5th cir.) 1968, U.S. Supreme Ct. 1969. Pvt. practice Mobile, 1966-84; dist. judge Ala. Cir. Ct., Mobile, 1984-85, presiding dist. judge, 1985, cir. judge, 1985-99; justice Supreme Ct. Ala., Montgomery, 1999—; rep. State of Ala., 1974-78. MKem. Jaycees, Mobile, Mobile County Wildlife; bd. advisors Salvation Army, Mobile, 1989—; bd. dirs. Mental Health Assn., Mobile, 1990-92. Capt. U.S. Army, 1963-72. Elected Outstanding Freshman Rep., Capital Prses Corps., 1975; recipient Meritorious Svc. award Mobile County Bd. of Health, 1968, Humanitarian Svc. award Mobile Cerebral Palsy Assn., 1973. Mem. ABA, Am. Judges Assn., Ala. Bar Assn., Mobile Bar Assn., Internat. Acad. Trial Judges. Democrat. Episcopalian. Office: Supreme Ct of Ala 300 Dexter Ave Montgomery AL 36104-3741

**JOHNSTONE, EDWARD HUGGINS,** federal judge; b. 1922. J.D., U. Ky., 1949. Bar: Ky. 1949. Ptnr. firm Johnstone, Eldred & Paxton, Princeton, Ky., 1949-76; judge 56th Cir. Ct. Ky, 1976-77; judge U.S. Dist. Ct. (we. dist.) Ky., 1977—, chief judge, 1985-90; sr. judge, 1993—. Mem. ABA, Ky. Bar Assn. Office: US Dist Ct 219 Fed Bldg 501 Broadway St Paducah KY 42001-6856 Also: 262 US Courthouse 601 E Broadway Louisville KY 40202-1709

**JOHNSTONE, IRVINE BLAKELEY, III,** lawyer; b. Newark, Dec. 21, 1948; s. Irvine Blakeley Jr. and Ruth (Morton) J.; m. Phyllis Nevins, Oct. 16, 1983. BA with honors, Lehigh U., 1972; JD, Duke U., 1975. Bar: N.J. 1975, U.S. Dist. Ct. N.J. 1975, U.S. Ct. Appeals (3d cir.) 1979, N.Y. 1981. Assoc. Riker, Danzig, Scherer & DeBevoise, Newark, 1975-76, Shanley & Fisher, Newark, 1976-80; ptnr. Johnstone, Skok, Loughlin & Lane, Westfield, N.J., 1980—. Mem. bd. of govs. Blair Acad., 1978-84; atty. Rahway Lifers Group (N.J.) State Prison, 1980-85, Planning Bd., Clark, N.J., 1981-82, Bd. of Adjustment, Clark, 1982-84. Mem. ABA, N.J. Bar Assn., Union County Bar Assn., Def. Rsch. Inst., Union County Arbitration Bd. (cert. civil trial atty. N.J. Supreme Ct.), N.J. Trial Lawyers Assn., Am. Trial Lawyers Assn., R.J. Hughes Am. Inns of Ct. (master 1995—). Republican. Presbyterian. Club: Baltusrol (Springfield, N.J.). Avocations: flying, golf, sports. Personal injury, General civil litigation, General corporate. Home: 5 Bartles Rd Lebanon NJ 08833-4606

**JOHNSTONE, MARTIN E.,** state supreme court justice. BA, Western Ky. U.; JD, U. Louisville. Bar: Ky. Judge 3d Magisterial Dist., Ky., 1976-78; dist. judge Jefferson County, Ky., 1978-83, chief judge, 1987-93, circuit judge, 1985-87; justice Ky. Ct. Appeals, 1993-96, chief judge pro tem, 1996; justice Ky. Supreme Ct., 1996—, dep. chief justice, 1998—. Recipient Outstanding Trial Judge award Ky. Acad. Trial Attys., 1991. Mem. Louisville Bar Assn. (Judge of Yr. 1981). Office: State Capitol Capitol Bldg Rm 235 700 Capitol Ave Frankfort KY 40601-3410*

**JOHNSTONE, PHILIP MACLAREN,** lawyer; b. Sharon, Conn., Mar. 24, 1961; s. Rodney Stuart and Frances Louise (Davis) J.; m. Elizabeth Laird McGovern, Sept. 10, 1988. BA in Econs. magna cum laude, Duke U., 1983; JD, U. Pa., 1986. Bar: Mass. 1986, Conn. 1987, U.S. Dist. Ct. Conn. 1988, R.I. 1998. Ptnr. Waller, Smith & Palmer, P.C., New London, Conn., 1997—; bd. dirs. J Boats, Inc., Newport, R.I., 1987—. Mem. ABA, Mass. Bar Assn., Conn. Bar Assn., R.I. Bar Assn. Republican. Episcopalian. Avocations: tennis, golf. General corporate, Real property, Estate planning. Home: 17 Cliff St Stonington CT 06378-1249 Office: Waller Smith and Palmer PC 52 Eugene Oneill Dr New London CT 06320-6324

**JOHNTING, WENDELL,** law librarian; b. Winchester, Ind., Aug. 30, 1952; s. Ernest K. and Jewell G. (Browning) J. AB, Taylor U., 1974; MLS, Ind. U., 1975. Asst. dir. tech. svcs. Ind. U. Sch. Law Libr., Indpls., 1975—; project dir. Indpls. Law Cataloging Consortium, 1980-92; vis. libr. Cambridge U., Squire Law Libr., Cambridge, Eng., 1985; founding mem. Info. Online Project Leaders, 1987-90; spkr. in field. Libr. vol. Beech Grove (Ind.) Pub. Libr., 1993-95; reader, vol. Marion County Health Care Home, Indpls., 1989. Mem. Ohio Region Assn. Law Librs. (exec. bd. 1982-85, sec. 1982), Ind. U. Librs. Assn. (v.p. 1986-87, exec. bd. 1982-85), Dramatic Order Knights Khorassen, Knights of Pythias (chancellor comdr. 1997), Beta Phi Mu, Chi Alpha Omega, Alpha Phi Gamma. Republican. Baptist. Avocations: gardening, astronomy, cooking. Home: 420 N 23rd Ave Beech Grove IN 46107-1032 Office: Ind U Sch Law Libr 735 W New York St Indianapolis IN 46202-5222

**JOINER, CHARLES WYCLIFFE,** judge; b. Maquoketa, Iowa, Feb. 14, 1916; s. Melvin William and Mary (von Schrader) J.; m. Ann Martin, Sept. 29, 1939; children: Charles Wycliffe, Nancy Caroline, Richard Martin. BA, U. Iowa, 1937, JD, 1939. Bar: Iowa 1939, Mich. 1947. With firm Miller, Huebner & Miller, Des Moines, 1939-47; part-time lectr. Des Moines Coll. Law, 1940-41; faculty U. Mich. Law, 1947-68, assoc. dean, 1960-65, acting dean, 1964-65; dean Wayne State U. Law Sch., Detroit, 1968-72; U.S. dist. judge, sr. judge, 1972-99, ret., 1999; assoc. dir. Preparatory Commn. Mich. Constl. Conv., 1961, co-dir. research and drafting com., 1961-62; civil rules adv. com. U.S. Jud. Conf. Com. Rules Practice and Procedure, 1959-70, evidence rules adv. com., 1965-70; rep. Mich. Atty. Gens. Com. Ct. Congestion, 1959-60. Author: Trials and Appeals, 1957, Civil Justice and the Jury, 1962, Trial and Appellate Practice, 1968; Co-author: Introduction to Civil Procedures, 1949, Jurisdiction and Judgments, 1953, (with Delmar Karten) Trials and Appeals, 1971. Mem. charter rev. com. Ann Arbor Citizens Council, 1959-61; mem. Mich. Commn. on Uniform State Laws, 1963—; Mem. Ann Arbor City Council, 1955-59. Served to 1st lt. USAAF, 1942-45. Fellow Am. Bar Found. (chmn. 1977-78); mem. ABA (chmn. com. specialization 1952-56, spl. com. uniform evidence rules fed. cts. 1959-64, adv. bd. jour. 1961-67, spl. com. on specialization 1966-69, ethics com. 1961-70, council mem. sect. individual rights and responsibilities 1967-77, chairperson 1976-77), State Bar Mich. (pres. 1970-71, chmn. joint com. Mich. procedural revision 1956-62, commr. 1964—), Am. Judicature Soc. (chmn. publs. com. 1959-62), Am. Law Student Assn. (bd. govs.), Am. Law Inst., Scribes (pres. 1963-64).

**JOITY, DONNA MARIE,** law librarian; b. Detroit, June 1, 1947; d. Alex and Helen Marie (Illin) Iukov; m. John Frank Joity, Nov. 23, 1969. BA in pre-legal studies, U. Mich., 1969, MA in Libr. Sci., 1972. Cataloger Tulane U. Law Libr., New Orleans, 1973-78; reference libr. Okla. State Capital Law Libr., Oklahoma City, 1979; reference/acquisitions libr. Baker & Botts, LLP, Houston, 1981-82, asst. mgr., supr. tech. svcs., 1986—. Mem. ABA, Am. Assn. Law Librs., S.W. Assn. Law Librs., Houston Area Law Librs. (sec. 1981-82, v.p., program chair 1990-91, pres. 1991-92). Eastern Orthodox. Avocations: hiking, travel. Office: Baker & Botts LLP 1 Shell Plz 910 Louisiana St Ste 3000 Houston TX 77002-4991

**JOLLES, JANET KAVANAUGH PILLING,** lawyer; b. Akron, Ohio, Sept. 5, 1951; d. Paul and Marjorie (Logue) Kavanaugh; m. Martin Jolles, Mar. 6, 1987; children: Madeleine Sloan Langdon Jolles, Jameson Samuel Rhys Jolles. BA, Ohio Wesleyan U., 1973; JD, U. Mo., 1976; LLM, Villanova U., 1985. Bar: Pa. 1976, U.S. Tax Ct. 1976, U.S. Dist. Ct. (ea. dist.) Pa. 1976, Ohio 1996. Atty. Schnader, Harrison, Segal & Lewis, Phila., 1976-83; gen. counsel Kistler-Tiffany Cos., Wayne, Pa., 1983-95; lawyer Janet Kavanaugh Pilling Jolles & Assocs., Berea, Ohio, 1996—. Mem. Phila. Estate Planning Coun., Estate Planning Coun. Cleve. Mem. ABA, Ohio State Bar Assn., Cleve. Bar Assn., Cuyahoga County Bar Assn., Phila. Bar Assn. (probate sect., tax sect.), Pa. Bar Assn., Berea Women's League, Phi Beta Kappa, Phi Delta Phi. Estate taxation, Probate, Estate planning. Office: 43 E Bridge St Ste 101 Berea OH 44017-1909

**JOLLEY, R. GARDNER,** lawyer; b. Salt Lake City, May 12, 1944; s. Reuben G. and Varno J.; m. Sharon Lea Thomas, Aug. 21, 1965; children—Christopher Gardner and Jennifer Lea. B.S. in Econs., U. Utah, 1966; J.D., U. Calif.-Berkeley, 1969. Bar: Calif. 1970, Nev. 1970, U.S. Dist. Ct. Nev. 1970. Law clk. to presiding justice Nev. Supreme Ct., 1969-70; assoc. Wiener, Goldwater and Galatz, Las Vegas, 1970-73; ptnr. Jolley, Urga, Wirth & Woodbury, Las Vegas, Nev., 1974—; lectr. new law clks. for Nev. judges, 1973-74; instr. Clark County Community Coll., 1975-77; instr. Nev. Continuing Legal Edn., 1983. Bd. dirs. Catholic Community Services, 1973-80; bd. govs. Easter Seal Soc., 1977-78. Mem. Nev. State Bar Assn. (bd. govs. 1976-86, pres. 1985-86), ABA (Nev. rep. to Ho. Dels. 1986-88), Assn. Trial Lawyers Am., Nev. Trial Lawyers Assn. Banking, State civil litigation, Contracts commercial.

**JOLLY, E. GRADY,** federal judge; b. 1937. BA, U. Miss., 1959, LLB, 1962. Trial atty. NLRB, Winston-Salem, N.C., 1962-64; asst. U.S. atty. No. Dist. Miss., 1964-67; trial atty. Dept. Justice Tax Div., Washington, 1967-69; pvt. practice Jolly, Miller & Milam, Jackson, Miss., 1969-82; judge U.S. Ct. Appeals (5th cir.), Jackson, 1982—. Office: US Ct Appeals James O Eastland Courthouse 245 E Capitol St Ste 202 Jackson MS 39201-2414

**JOLLY, JOHN RUSSELL, JR.,** lawyer; b. Charlotte, N.C., Sept. 7, 1942; s. John Russell and Mildred Inez (Hovis) J.; m. Mary Angela Blanton, Dec. 28, 1963 (div. 1987); children: John R. III, Christopher E. BA, U. N.C., 1964, JD with honors, 1967. Bar: N.C. 1967, U.S. Ct. Appeals (4th cir.) 1970, U.S. Dist. Ct. (ea., mid. & we. dists.) N.C. 1970, U.S. Supreme Ct. 1972. Ptnr. Poyner & Spruill, Raleigh, Charlotte, N.C., Rocky Mount, N.C., 1967-79, 82—; superior ct. judge N.C. Gen. Ct. of Justice, 1979-82. Mem. Nat. Assn. Railroad Trial Counsel, N.C. Bar Assn., N.C. Assn. Def. Attys. (pres., bd. dirs. 1988-91). Democrat. Episcopalian. Avocations: boating, golf, exercise. Federal civil litigation, General civil litigation, State civil litigation. Office: Poyner & Spruill PO Box 10096 Raleigh NC 27605-0096

**JONAS, GAIL E.,** lawyer; b. Tacoma, Wash., Apr. 20, 1940; d. Paul E. and Bernadine G. (Cronin) Temple; m. Ron Jonas, Sept. 2, 1960 (div. 1974). BS, U. Md., Riverside, 1962; JD, U. Calif., Hastings, 1976. Bar: Calif., U.S. Dist. Ct. (no. dist.) Calif., U.S. Ct. Appeals. Tchr. Balt. Schs., Balt., 1960-64; sole practice, 1977—; mem. bd. dirs. Tile Heritage Found., 1990—; mem. Am. Acad. Family Mediators, Wis., 1993—; officer alt. dispute reolution ctr. Sonoma County Bar Assn., 1994—. mem. adv. coun. Conservation Action, Santa Rosa, Calif., 1990—; wilderness guardian Sierra Club, San Francisco, 1994—. Named Environmentalist of the Yr. COAAST Environ. Group, 1974. Democrat. Avocations: marathons, triathlons, whitewater kayaking. FAX: (707) 433-8314. E-mail: gjonas@pon.net. Alternative dispute resolution, Family and matrimonial, Estate planning. Office: 521 Brown St Healdsburg CA 95448-3965

**JONASSON, WILLIAM BRADFORD,** lawyer; b. Portland, Oreg., Jan. 29, 1946; m. Karen Young Longanecker, Dec. 29, 1984; children: Carrie, Lindsay, Samantha. BA in Psychology, Yale U., 1968; JD, U. Oreg., 1976. Bar: Oreg. 1976, U.S. Dist. Ct. (fed. dist.) 1977. Assoc., ptnr. Santos & Schneider, Oregon City, Oreg., 1976-80; pvt. practice Oregon City, Oreg., 1980—; mem. bd. govs. Oreg. State Bar, Lake Oswego, 1991-94; pres. Clackamas County Bar, Oregon City, 1991; bd. pres. Clackamas Indigent Def. Corp., Oregon City, 1988—; mem. adv. bd. Family Ct. Svc., Oregon City, 1980—. Lt. comdr. USNR, 1968-77. Criminal, State civil litigation, Family and matrimonial. Office: 1317 7th St Oregon City OR 97045-2003

**JONDLE, ROBERT JOHN,** patent lawyer; b. Iowa City, Aug. 8, 1946; s. Clarence A. and Modesta (Duwa) J.; m. Sharon Walsh, Aug. 16, 1969; children: Julie, Dan. BS in Botany, Iowa State U., 1968, PhD in Plant Breeding and Genetics, 1974; JD, Georgetown U., 1991. Bar: Md., D.C., Nebr. Coord. Pioneeer Hi-Bred, Johnston, Iowa, 1975-80, dir., 1980-85; v.p. rsch. Stauffer Seeds, Iowa City, 1985-87; patent agt. Venable Baetjer et al, Washington, 1987-90, patent atty., 1991-92; patent atty. Henderson & Sturm, Omaha, 1992-95, Rothwell Figg et al, Omaha, 1995—. Contbr. articles to sci. publs. Capt. U.S. Army, 1968-73. Mem. Phi Kappa Phi, Gamma Sigma Delta, Phi Eta Sigma. E-mail: rjondle@rfek.com. Patent, Trademark and copyright, Intellectual property. Office: Rothwell Figg et al 13906 Gold Cir Ste 204 Omaha NE 68144-2336

**JONES, ALLEN, JR.,** lawyer; b. Washington, May 24, 1930; s. Allen Sr. and Gladys May (Bunch) J.; m. Gloria Jean Clyma, Nov. 29, 1952 (div. June 1989); children: Victoria, Jennifer, Matthew; m. Cheryl B. Crook, Aug. 11, 1991. BA, Mich. State U., 1952; JD, Georgetown U., 1957. Bar: D.C. 1957, U.S. Supreme Ct. 1961, Md. 1962. Sales rep. Ethyl Corp., Salt Lake City, 1952; sr. atty. Wilkes, Artis, Hedrick & Lane, Washington, 1957—; mem. exec. com., treas. Coun. for Ct. Excellence, Washington, 1988-98. Mem. Civil Delay Reduction Task Force, Washington, 1988-92; co-founder Washington Lawyers Against Drugs, 1986-87; mediator Superior Ct. of D.C., 1986—; vice chmn. Children's Hosp. Found., Washington, 1988-92; chmn. Children's Hosp. Telethon, Washington, 1988-89. Mem. ABA (Ho. of Dels. D.C. chpt. 1986-87), D.C. Bar Assn. (pres. 1986-87, pres. rsch. found. 1984-85), The Barristers (pres. 1982-83), Lawyers Club, Jud. Conf. of D.C., Rotary Club Washington (pres.-elect 1997, pres. 1998-99). Republican. Lutheran. Avocations: golf, biking, hiking. General civil litigation, General corporate, General practice. Home: 703 Penny Ln Stevensville MD 21666-3731 Office: Wilkes Artis Hedrick & Lane 1666 K St NW Ste 1100 Washington DC 20006-2897

**JONES, B. TODD,** prosecutor; s. Paul and Sylvia Jones. Grad., Macalester Coll., 1979; JD, U. Minn., 1983. Former mng. ptnr. Greene Espel, Mpls.; asst. U.S. atty. for Minn.; U.S. atty. Minn. dist. U.S. Dept. Justice. With USMC. Office: Ste 600 300 S 4th St Minneapolis MN 55415*

**JONES, BRUCE ALAN,** lawyer; b. Newton, N.J., Aug. 22, 1950; s. George William and Elda J.; m. Melinda M. Frank, June 22, 1972; children: Alison E., Michael B. BS, Widenor U., 1971; JD, U. Balt., 1975. Bar: N.J., U.S. Dist. Ct. Law clk. N.J. Superior Court Warren County, Belvidere, N.J., 1975-76; staff atty. Warren County Legal Svcs., Belvidere, 1976-77, exec. dir., 1977-81; ptnr. Curry & Jones, Phillipsburg, N.J., 1981-99; mcpl. prosecutor, planning bd. atty. Lopatcong and Harmony Twps., Phillipsburg, 1993—; sole practitioner Phillipsburg, 1999—; mem. adv. bd. Warren County Office on Aging, Belvidere, N.J., 1978—, Warren County Mental Health, Belvidere, 1978—. Mem. Phillipsburg Riverview Orgn. Avocations: skiing, gardening. E-mail: bjlaw@nac.net. General civil litigation, Family and matrimonial, Land use and zoning (including planning). Home: 11 Camp Rd Blairstown NJ 07825-9655 Office: Curry & Jones 8 Market St Phillipsburg NJ 08865

**JONES, C. PAUL,** lawyer, educator; b. Grand Forks, N.D., Jan. 7, 1927; s. Walter M. and Sophie J. (Thorton) J.; m. Helen M. Fredel, Sept. 7, 1957; children—Katherine, Sara H. B.B.A., U. Minn., 1950, J.D., 1950; LL.M., William Mitchell Coll. of Law, 1955. Assoc. Lewis, Hammer, Heaney, Weyl & Halverson, Duluth, Minn., 1950-51; asst., chief dep. Hennepin County Atty., Mpls., 1952-58; asst. U.S. atty. U.S. Atty.'s Office, St. Paul, 1959-60; assoc. Maun & Hazel, St. Paul, 1960-61; ptnr. Dorfman, Rudquist, Jones, & Ramstead, Mpls., 1961-65; state pub. defender Minn. State Pub. Defender's Office, Mpls., 1966-90; adj. prof. law William Mitchell Coll. of Law, St. Paul, 1953-70, prof. law, 1970—, assoc. dean for acad. affairs, 1991-95; adj. prof. U. Minn., Mpls., 1970-90; mem. adv. com. on rules of criminal procedure Minn. Supreme Ct., 1970—. Author: Criminal Procedure from Police Detention to Final Disposition, 1981; Jones on Minnesota Criminal Procedure, 1955, 64, 70, 75; Minnesota Police Law Manual, 1955, 67, 70, 76. Mem. Minn. Gov.'s Crime Commn., St. Paul, 1970s, Minn. Fair Trial-Free Press Assn., Mpls., 1970s, Citizens League, Mpls., 1955—, Mpls. Aquatennial Assn., Mpls., 1955-60, Minn. Citizens Coun. on Crime and Justice, 1991—. Recipient Reginald Heber Smith award Nat. Legal Aid and Defender Assn., 1969. Fellow Am. Coll. Trial Lawyers; mem. Am. Bd. Trial Advs., ABA, Minn. State Bar Assn., Hennepin County Bar Assn., Ramsey County Bar Assn., Nat. Legal Aid & Defender Assn. Democrat. Lutheran. Clubs: Suburban Gyro of Mpls., Mpls. Athletic. Lodge: Rotary. Avocations: fishing; hunting; golfing; desert watching. Home: 5501 Dewey Hill Rd Edina MN 55439-1906 Office: William Mitchell Coll Law 875 Summit Ave Saint Paul MN 55105-3030

**JONES, CHARLES E.,** state supreme court justice. BA, Brigham Young U., 1959; JD, Stanford U., 1962. Bar: Calif. 1962, U.S. Dist. Ct. Ariz. 1963, U.S. Ct. Appeals (9th cir.) 1963, Ariz. 1964, U.S. Ct. Appeals (10th cir.) 1974, U.S. Supreme Ct. 1979. Law clk. to Hon. Richard H. Chambers U.S. Ct. Appeals (9th cir.), 1962-63; assoc., ptnr. Jennings, Strouss & Salmon, Phoenix, Ariz., 1963-96; apptd. justice Ariz. Supreme Ct., Phoenix, 1996, vice chief justice, 1997—. Bd. visitors Brigham Young U. Law Sch., 1973-81, chmn., 1978-81. Named Avocat du Consulat-Gen. de France, 1981—; Alumni Dist. Svc. award Brigham Young U., 1982; recipient Aaron Feuerstein award U. Ariz., 1998. Mem. ABA, State Bar Ariz., Fed. Bar Assn. (pres. Ariz. chpt. 1971-73), J. Reuben Clark Law Soc. (nat. chmn. 1994-97), Maricopa County Bar Assn., Pi Sigma Alpha. Office: Ariz Supreme Court 1501 W Washington St Phoenix AZ 85007-3231

**JONES, CHARLES ERIC, JR.,** lawyer; b. Phila., Dec. 21, 1957; s. Charles Eric and Janith (Van Orden) J.; m. Ronda Nolen, May 16, 1981; children: Charles Eric III, Courtney Elaine, Camille Elizabeth. BBA, U. Tex., 1980; JD, St. Mary's U., 1983. Bar: Tex. 1983, U.S. Dist. Ct. (no. dist.) Tex. 1985, U.S. Dist. Ct. (we. dist.) Okla. 1986, U.S. Dist. Ct. (we. and ea. dists.) Ark. 1987, U.S. Supreme Ct. 1988, U.S. Ct. Appeals (5th cir.) 1988, U.S. Dist. Ct. (ea. dist.) Tex. 1992. Briefing atty. Tex. Ct. Criminal Appeals, Austin, 1983-84; assoc. Nunn Griggs & Wetsel, Sweetwater, Tex., 1984; ptnr. Nunn, Griggs, Wetsel & Jones, Sweetwater, 1985-88, 1985-89; ptnr. Nunn, Griggs, Jones & Sheridan, Sweetwater, 1989-91, Jones & Edwards, L.L.P., Sweetwater, 1992-94, Jones, Edwards & Young, L.L.P., Sweetwater, 1995, Jones & Young, LLP, Sweetwater, Tex., 1995-97, Charles E. Jones, Jr. & Assocs., 1997—; chmn. St. Mary's Legal Rsch. Bd., San Antonio, 1982-83; student instr. St. Mary's U., San Antonio, 1982-83, The Order of Barristers, 1983. Bd. dirs. Nolan County Hospice, Inc., Sweetwater, 1984-92, Nolan County Crimestoppers, Inc., Sweetwater, 1985-90, chmn., 1987-89; dir. adminstrv. bd. United Meth. Ch., Sweetwater, 1985-88; chmn. Nolan County United Way, 1985-87; co-chmn. City Coun. Libr. Bd., 1987—. Mem. ABA, Assn. Trial Lawyers Am., Tex. Bar Assn., Tex. Trial Lawyers Assn., Tex. State Bar Coll., Order of Barristers, Tex. Assn. Banking Counsel, Indp. Bankers Assn. Tex., Tex. Bd. of Legal Specialization (bd. cert. civil trial law). Avocations: flying, scuba diving, skiing, golf. Federal civil litigation, State civil litigation, Consumer commercial. Home: 804 Josephine St Sweetwater TX 79556-3312 Office: Charles E Jones Jr & Assocs PO Box 188 Sweetwater TX 79556-0188

**JONES, CHRISTOPHER DON,** lawyer; b. Longview, Tex., Jan. 23, 1964; s. Donald and Audrey Gale Jones; m. Michelle McCullough, Feb. 16, 1991; children: Catherine Abigail, Christopher Andrew. BBA, Baylor U., 1987, JD, 1989. Bar: Tex. 1989. Assoc. Worsham, Forsythe, Sampels & Wooldrige, Dallas, 1989-92, Misko, Howie & Sweeney, LLP, Dallas, 1992-95, Howie & Sweeney, LLP, Dallas, 1995-96, Erskine, McMahon & Stroup, LLP, Longview, 1996-97; ptnr. Stroup & Jones, LLP, Longview, 1997—. Asst. mng. editor Baylor Law Rev., 1989. Mem. Leadership Longview, 1998-99. Named Kiwanian of Yr., Kiwais Club Dallas, 1993. Mem. ABA, Tex. Bar Assn., Tex. Trial Lawyers Assn. (sustaining). Democrat. Avocations: golf, hunting, running. Product liability, Personal injury, Labor. Office: Stroup & Jones LLP 420 N Green St Ste C Longview TX 75601-6409

**JONES, CLIFFORD AARON, SR.,** lawyer, international businessman; b. Long Lane, Mo., Feb. 19, 1912; s. Burley Monroe and Arlie (Benton) J.; children: Clifford A. Jones II, Joni Lee Jones Ryan; m. Marilyn T. Hayes, May 1, 1995. LL.B., U. Mo., 1938, J.D., 1969. Bar: Nev. 1938, U.S. Dist. Ct. Nev. 1939, D.C. 1982, U.S. Ct. Appeals (9th and D.C. cirs.) 1983, U.S. Supreme Ct. 1983. Founder, sr. ptnr. Jones Vargas (formerly Jones, Jones, Close & Brown), Las Vegas, Nev., 1938-93, retired, 1993; majority leader Nev. Legislature, 1941-42; judge 8th Jud. Dist., Nev., 1945-46; lt. gov. State of Nev., 1946-54; owner, builder, chmn. bd. Thunderbird Hotel, Inc., Las Vegas, 1948-64; founder Valley Bank of Nev., 1953; founder, sec., bd. dirs. First Western Savs. and Loan Assn., 1964-66; pres., chmn. bd. Caribbean-Am. Investment Co., Inc., 1960-78; pres., bd. dirs. Income Investments, Inc., 1963-65; sr. v.p., bd. dirs. Barrington Industries, Inc., 1966-70; chmn. bd., pres. Cen. African Land Co. Mem. Clark County (Nev.) Democratic Central Com., 1940-80, chmn., 1948; nat. committeeman from Nev. Dem. Party, 1954; mem. Nev. Dem. State Central Com., 1945-60; 4 time del. Dem. Nat. Conv. Served as lt. col. F.A. U.S. Army, 1942-46, ETO. Mem. ABA (past mem. tax sect.), Am. Coll. Trust and Estate Counsel, Nev. Bar Assn., D.C. Bar Assn., Am. Legion, VFW, Phi Delta Phi, Kappa Sigma. Clubs: United Nations Lions (N.Y.C.); Elks (Las Vegas), Lions (Las Vegas) (past pres.). General corporate, Private international, Probate.

**JONES, CRAIG WARD,** lawyer; b. Pitts., June 14, 1947; s. Curtis Edison and Margaret (McFarland) J.; m. Sarah Dowding; children: Laura McFarland, Rebecca Long, Nancy Harper. BA, Carleton Coll., 1969; JD, U. Pitts., 1976. Bar: Pa. 1976, U.S. Dist. Ct. (we. dist.) Pa. 1976, U.S. Ct. Appeals (3d cir.) 1981. Ptnr. Reed, Smith, Shaw & McClay, Pitts., 1976—. Served to lt. USNR, 1969-73. Mem. Allegheny County Bar Assn. Presbyterian. Federal civil litigation, State civil litigation. Home: 208 Cornwall Dr Pittsburgh PA 15238-2639 Office: Reed Smith Shaw & McClay Mellon Sq 435 6th Ave Pittsburgh PA 15219-1886

**JONES, DALE EDWIN,** public defender; b. Rahway, N.J., Oct. 22, 1948; s. Horatio Gates and Audrey Irma (Morgan) J.; m. Karen Anne Woodhall, June 19, 1971; children: Sharon, Michael, Stephan; m. Maria D. Noto, Aug. 2, 1987 (div. 1989); m. Joan E. DiTullio, Oct. 18, 1991; 1 child, Trevor. BA, Rutgers U., 1970, JD, 1973. Bar: N.J. 1973, U.S. Dist. Ct. N.J. 1973, U.S. Supreme Ct. 1977, N.Y. 1983. 1st asst. pub. defender Office Pub. Defender, Newark, 1974-84; dep. pub. defender in charge of capital litigation Office Pub. Defender, 1984-87; asst. pub. defender Office of Pub. Defender, Trenton, N.J., 1987—; mem. model jury charge com., N.J. Supreme Ct., 1983-88, criminal practice com., Trenton, 1983—, com. media rels., 1987-89, strategic planning com., 1996-98, rules of evidence com., 1998—. Mem. editorial bd. N.J. Lawyer. Mem. ACDL-N.J., Nat. Assn. Criminal Def. Lawyers (cert. criminal atty.), Amnesty Internat. Democrat. Office: Pub Defender Office PO Box 850 Trenton NJ 08625-0850

**JONES, DANIEL W.,** lawyer; b. Washington, Jan. 1, 1945. BA, Yale Coll., 1967; JD, Boston U., 1972. Pvt. practice Exeter, N.H., 1976—. Rep. N.H. House, Concord, N.H., 1978. With U.S. Army, 1968-70. Estate planning, Probate, Real property. Office: 129 Water St Exeter NH 03833-2456

**JONES, DAVID EDWIN,** lawyer; b. Gainesville, Fla., May 18, 1963; s. C. Jerome and Dorothy (Roberts) J.; m. Holly Dickey, Dec. 17, 1983; children: Sydney Unell, Madeleine Dorothy. BSBA, Creighton U., 1985, JD, 1987. Bar: Nebr. 1987, D.C. 1993, Wis. 1996. Law clk. to Judge David B. Sentelle U.S. Ct. Appeals (D.C. cir.), Washington, 1991-92; assoc. Shea & Gardner, Washington, 1992-95; asst. U.S. Atty. Madison, Wis., 1995—; lectr. on judiciary CloseUp Found., Washington, 1988-95; lectr. legal rsch. and writing U. Wis. Law Sch., 1998—; instr. Bill of Rights program D.C. Bar, Washington, 1988-95. Contbr. articles to legal jours. Capt. U.S. Army, Gen. Counsel's Office, 1987-91. Recipient Dir.'s award for Superior Performance, U.S. Dept. Justice, 1998. Mem. ABA, Nebr. Bar Assn., D.C. Bar Assn., Wis. Bar Assn. Presbyterian. Administrative and regulatory, Environmental.

**JONES, DEANNE FORTNA,** lawyer; b. Sidney, Ill., Sept. 15, 1963; d. Paul Ernest and Janet Elizabeth (Haas) F.; m. Steven Gary Jones, Dec. 11, 1993. AA, Parkland Jr. Coll., Champaign, Ill., 1982; student, U. Stirling, Scotland, 1986-88; BS, U. Ill., 1988; JD, So. Ill. U., Carbondale, 1991. Bar: Ill. 1991, U.S. Dist. Ct. (ctrl. dist.) Ill., U.S. Ct. Appeals (7th cir.). Law clk. U.S. Dist. Ct. Jr. Richard H. Mills, Springfield, Ill., 1991-93; assoc. Kehart, Shafter, Hughes & Webber, Decatur, Ill., 1993-97, Hughes & Hill, L.L.C., Decatur, 1997—; adj. assoc. prof. Millikin U., Decatur, 1998—. Contbr. articles to profl. jours. Mem. Theatre 7, Decatur, 1996; treas. Altrusa Internat., Decatur, 1996; bd. mem. Decatur Arts Coun., 1997; mem. adv. bd. Vis. Nuses Assn., Decatur, 1997. Recipient Cert. of Appreciation, U.S. Dept. Justice, 1993. Mem. Ill. State Bar Assn. (Cert. of Recognition for Pub. Svc. 1991), Decatur Bar Assn. (treas. 1996—), Ill. Assn. Def. Trial Counsel, Adjusters Assn. Ctrl. Ill. Avocations: travel, cooking, painting. Personal injury, Workers' compensation, Product liability. Office: Hughes & Hill LLC 160 E Main St Ste 200 Decatur IL 62523-1283

**JONES, DOUGLAS W.,** lawyer; b. Fort Lauderdale, Fla., 1948. AB, Princeton U., 1970; JD, Harvard U., 1973. Bar: N.Y. 1974. Mem. Milbank, Tweed, Hadley & McCloy LLP, N.Y.C. Mem. ABA, Assn. of the Bar of the City of N.Y. Private international, Securities, General corporate. Office: Milbank Tweed Hadley & McCloy LLP 1 Chase Manhattan Plz Fl 47 New York NY 10005-1413

**JONES, E. STEWART, JR.,** lawyer; b. Troy, N.Y., Dec. 4, 1941; s. E. Stewart and Louise (Farley) J.; m. Constance M., Dec. 28, 1968; children: Christopher, Brady, Erin. BA, Williams Coll., 1963; JD, Albany Law Sch., 1966. Bar: N.Y. 1966, U.S. Dist. Ct. (no. dist.) N.Y. 1966, U.S. Dist. Ct. (so. and ea. dist.) N.Y. 1994, U.S. Dist. Ct. (we. dist.) N.Y. 1987, U.S. Claims Ct. 1991, U.S. Ct. Appeals (2d cir.) 1976, U.S. Supreme Ct. 1976. Asst. dist. atty. Rensselaer County (N.Y.), 1968-70, spl. prosecutor, 1974; ptnr. E. Stewart Jones, Troy, 1974—; lectr. in field; mem. com. on profl. standards of 3d jud. dept. State of N.Y., 1977-80, mem. 3d jud. screening com., Albany County; mem. merit selection panel for selection and appointment of U.S. magistrate for No. Dist. N.Y., 1981, 91; bd. dirs. Univ. Found. at Albany, trustee Troy Savs. Bank. Contbr. numerous articles to profl. jours. Trustee The Albany Acad., Albany Law Sch.; active Nat. Alumni Coun. Albany Law Sch. With USNG. Fellow Am. Bar Found., Am. Inns Ct., Internat. Acad. Trial Lawyers, Am. Bd. Criminal Trial Lawyers (Upstate N.Y. chmn. 1998—), Am. Coll. Trial Lawyers, Inner Circle of Advs., Am. Bd. Profl. Liability Attys. (diplomate), Internat. Soc. Barristers (chmn. upstate N.Y. 1998—); mem. N.Y. State Bar Assn. (Outstanding Practitioner award 1980, mem. exec. com. of criminal justice sect. 1977-90, mem. exec. com. trial lawyers sect. 1981-94, mem. spl. com. med. malpractice, other coms.), N.Y. State Trial Lawyers Assn. (bd. dirs. 1982-91, dir. emeritus 1991), Capital Dist. Trial Lawyers Assn. (bd. dir. 1973-76), ABA (numerous coms.) Calif. Attys. for Criminal Justice, Practising Law Inst., Am. Judicature Soc. (sustaining), Renssealer County Bar Assn., Am. Soc. Law and Medicine, Albany County Bar Assn., N.Y. State Defenders Assn., Am. Arbitration Assn. (nat. panel of arbitrators), Dispute Resolutions, Inc. (nat. panel of arbitrators), Fed. Bar Coun., Upstate Trial Attys. Assn., Inc., Nat. Bd. Trial Advocacy (diplomate), Nat. Assn. Criminal Def. Lawyers, N.Y. State Assn. Criminal Def. Lawyers, Am. Bd. Trial Advocates (advocate), Inst. for Injury Reduction (founder), Trial Lawyers for Pub. Justice (founder), Civil Justice Found. (founding sponsor), Schuyler Meadows Club, Troy Country Club, Troy Club, Steuben Athletic Club, Ft. Orange Club, Stone Horse Yacht Club (Harwich Port, Mass.), Equinox Country Club (Manchester, Vt.), Williams Club (N.Y.C.). Personal injury, Federal civil litigation, Criminal. Home: 46 Schuyler Rd Loudonville NY 12211-1447 Office: 28 2nd St Troy NY 12180-3986

**JONES, E. THOMAS,** lawyer; b. Buffalo, July 19, 1950; s. Thomas Kenneth and Marian Arlene (Turk) J.; m. Jennifer Dee Lowery, Oct. 19, 1974; children: Evan Thomas III, Courtney Bree. BA, SUNY, Buffalo, 1972; JD, Cleve. State U., 1981. Bar: N.Y. 1982, U.S. Dist. Ct. (we. dist.) N.Y. 1982, U.S. Ct. Appeals (2d cir.) 1987. Mem. mgmt. staff Marine Midland Bank, Buffalo, 1971-76, M&T Bank, Buffalo, 1976-78, 81-82, Nat. City Bank, Cleve., 1978-81; sole practice Buffalo, 1982—. Committeeman Amherst Rep. Party, N.Y., 1984—; fire fighter Getzville Fire Co., Inc., Amherst, 1988-91; town councilman, Amherst, 1990-91; coach, bd. dirs. Amherst Youth Hockey Assn.; dep. town atty. Town Amherst, N.Y., 1996—. Mem. ABA, Erie County Bar Assn. General practice, General civil litigation, Probate. Home: 1375 N French Rd Amherst NY 14228-1908

**JONES, EDITH HOLLAN,** judge; b. Phila., Apr. 7, 1949; BA, Cornell U., 1971; JD with honors, U. Tex., 1974. Bar: Tex. 1974, U.S. Supreme Ct. 1979, U.S. Ct. Appeals (5th and 11th cirs.), U.S. Dist. Ct. (so. and no. dists.) Tex. Assoc. Andrews & Kurth, Houston, 1974-82, ptnr., 1982-85; judge U.S. Ct. Appeals (5th cir.), Houston, 1985—. Gen. counsel Rep. Party of Tex., 1981-83. Mem. ABA, State Bar Tex. Presbyterian. Office: US Ct Appeals Bob Casey US Courthouse 515 Rusk St Ste 12505 Houston TX 77002-2605*

**JONES, ERIC S.,** lawyer; b. Lansing, Mich., Sept. 28, 1967; s. Stephen Albert and Judith H. J. BA, U. Richmond, 1989; JD, Emory U., 1992. Bar: Ga. 1992, U.S. Dist. Ct. (no. dist.) Ga. 1992. Assoc. Zirkle & Smith, Atlanta, 1992-93; assoc. Zirkle & Hoffman, Atlanta, 1993-97, ptnr., 1997—. Mem. ABA, Ga. Bar Assn., Atlanta Bar Assn., Def. Rsch. Inst., Atlanta Claims Assn., Ga. Self Insurers Assn. Avocation: coaching soccer. Insurance, Personal injury, Workers' compensation. Office: Zirkle & Hoffman Ste 2900 Five Concourse Pkwy Atlanta GA 30328

**JONES, EVAN WIER,** lawyer; b. Warwick, R.I., Sept. 25, 1966; s. Richard Morris and Suzanne Wier J.; m. Andrea Squire, Aug. 15, 1992; children: Connor Evan, Sarah Kathryn. BA with honors, U. Ga., 1988, JD, 1991. Bar: Ga. 1991, U.S. Dist. Ct. (no. dist.) Ga. 1996, U.S. Ct. Appeals (11th cir.) 1996, U.S. Army Ct. Appeals 1996, Ga. Supreme Ct. 1996. Legal assistance atty. 7th inf. div. U.S. Army, Monterey, Calif., 1991-92, spl. asst. U.S. atty. 7th inf. div., 1992-93; trial counsel U.S. SETAF U.S. Army, Vicenza, Italy, 1994-95; assoc. Sistrunk & Assocs., Atlanta, 1995-99; ptnr. Insley & Race, LLP, 1999—; lectr. on basic med. malpractice ICLE, 1999; faculty mem. Ga. Trial Skills Clinic, 1999. Mem. Aspiring Youth Program, 1998—, Ga. Pro Bono Honor Roll, 1997—. Capt. U.S. Army, 1991-95. Mem. Atlanta Bar Assn., Ga. State Bar Assn. (Pro Bono Honor Roll), Gridiron Secret Soc., Christian Bus. Mens Coun., Def. Rsch. Inst. Avocations: running, weightlifting, reading, fishing, history. General civil litigation, Personal injury, Product liability. Office: Sistrunk & Assocs 127 Peachtree St NE Ste 800 Atlanta GA 30303-1809

**JONES, G. DOUGLAS,** prosecutor. U.S. atty. no. dist. State of Ala., Birmingham, 1997—. Office: Robert S Vance Fed Bldg Courthouse 1800 5th Ave N Birmingham AL 35203-2111

**JONES, GARTH LEWIS,** lawyer; b. Seattle, Wash., Aug. 24, 1954; s. Myles C. and Rosetta (Holmes) J.; m. Nyree Rose Cropp, Nov. 19, 1977 (div. 1993); children: Meredyth Elise, Graham Lewis; m. Patricia Dewey, Nov. 11, 1993; 1 child, Randall Dewey. BS in pysch. and sociology, Brigham Young U., 1979, JD, 1984. Legal analyst Washington Supreme Ct. Ofc. of the Admistr. for the Cts., Olympia, Wash., 1984-93; atty. Stritmatter Kessler, Hoquiam, Wash., 1993—. Reporter Supreme Ct. com. on Pattern Jury instructions, Olympia, 1986-93, Supreme Ct. Com. on Pattern Forms, Olympia, 1984-93, Washington Pattern Jury Instructions - Criminal Practice (vol. 11 & 11A), Washington, 1993, Washington Pattern Jury Instructions - Civil Practice (vol. 6 west), Washington, 1989; staff & rep. Superior Ct. Judges' Benchbook Com., Olympia, 1984-93; reporter, author Washington Judges' Benchbook - Civil, 1985. Eagle mem. Washington State Trial Lawyers Assn. Personal injury. Home: 712 Hill Ave Hoquiam WA 98550-1435 Office: Stritmatter Kessler 407 8th St Hoquiam WA 98550-3607

**JONES, GARY KENNETH,** lawyer; b. Wiesbaden, Germany, Sept. 7, 1952; came to U.S., 1953; s. Grafton K. and Ethel L. Jones; m. Joan E. Bergkamp, May 22, 1982; children: Geoffrey, Thomas, Christopher, Alice. AA, Longview C.C., 1972; BS, U. Mo., 1975; MA, U. Kans., 1979; JD, U. Ark., 1985. Bar: Kans. 1985, U.S. Dist. Ct. Kans. 1985, U.S. Ct. Appeals (10th cir.) 1986. Lawyer Turner & Boisseau, Chartered, Wichita, Kans., 1985-88, Smith, Shay, Farmer & Wetta, LLC, Wichita, 1988—. Mem. Kans. Bar Assn., Kans. Trial Lawyers Assn. General civil litigation, Personal injury, Workers' compensation. Office: Smith Shay Farmer & Wetta LLC 200 W Douglas Ave Ste 830 Wichita KS 67202-3094

**JONES, GLOWER WHITEHEAD,** lawyer; b. Atlanta, May 4, 1936; s. Samuel L. and Alma (Powell) J.; m. Joanna Dayvault, Apr. 5, 1980; children: Mark, Jeff, Tom, Frank, Michael. Grad. Dartmouth Coll. 1958; JD, Emory U., 1963. Bar: Ga. 1962, U.S. Dist. Ct. Ga. 1963, U.S. Ct. Appeals (5th and 11th cirs.), U.S. Ct. Claims, U.S. Supreme Ct. Assoc. Smith, Swift, Currie, McGhee & Hancock, Atlanta, 1963-65; ptnr. Smith Currie & Hancock, Atlanta, 1967—. Author: Legal Aspects of Doing Business in North America and Canada, 1987, Alternative Clauses to Standard Construction Contracts, 1990, editor 2d edit., Construction Subcontracting: A Legal Guide for Industry Professionals, 1991, Wiley Construction Law Update, 1992, 93, 94, Construction Contractors: The Right To Stop Work, 1992, Remedies for International Sellers of Goods, 1993; mem. editorial bd. Ga. State Bar Jour.; contbr. articles to profl. jours. Mem. exec. bd. Met. Atlanta Boys' & Girls' Clubs, Inc., asst. sec., 1973-80, sec., 1980-83; bd. dirs. Samuel L. Jones Boys & Girls' Club, Inc., So. Region Boys Clubs Am.; trustee, past pres. Atlanta Florence Crittendon Services, Inc.; bd. dirs. Carrie Steele Pitts Home; bd. dirs. Gate City Day Nursery Assn. Recipient Golden Boy award Met. Atlanta Boys' Club, 1971. Fellow Chartered Inst. Arbitrators; mem. ABA, Fed. Bar Assn., Internat. Bar Assn. (chmn. internat. sales com., chmn. UNCITRAL subcom., chmn. membership com., mem. governing coun. sect. bus. law), Ga. Bar Assn., State Bar Ga., Atlanta Bar Assn. (former chmn. prepaid legal svcs. com., engr. lawyers rels. com.), Lawyers Club Atlanta, Am. Judicature Soc., Assn. Trial Attys. Am., Ga. Assn. Trial Lawyers, Dartmouth Coll. Alumni Club, Baylor Alumni Club, Emory U. Alumni Club, Atlanta Athletic Club, Ansley Park Golf Club, Dartmouth Club, World Trade Club, Phi Delta Theta. Construction, Public international, Contracts commercial. Home: 78 Peachtree Cir NE Atlanta GA 30309-3519 Office: Smith Currie & Hancock 2600 Harris Tower 233 Peachtree St NE Ste 2600 Atlanta GA 30303-1530

**JONES, GREGORY G.,** lawyer; b. Milw., Nov. 3, 1955; s. George Dean and Barbara Lucile (Aamodt) J.; m. Lori C. Jones, May 30, 1981; children: Whitney Schafer, Kendall Court. BA, So. Meth. U., Dallas, 1978; JD, So. Meth. U., 1982. Bar: Tex. 1982, U.S. Dist. Ct. (no. dist.) Tex. 1982; bd. cert. personal injury trial law. Ptnr. Russell, Turner, Laird & Jones, Ft. Worth, 1983—, Russell, Turner, Laired & Jones; adj. prof. bus. law Tex. Christian U.. Bd. dirs. Enchanted Lake Estates Homeowners Assn., 1989-91, Tex. Citizen Action, 1991—; mem. adminstrv. bd. Trinity Meth. Ch.; chair adv. bd. Tex. Citizen Action, Ft. Worth, 1991—. Fellow Roscoe Pound Found.; mem. AMA, Tarrant County Young Lawyers Assn. (bd. dirs.), Tarrant County Bar Assn., Tex. Bar Assn. (com. for adminstr. of rules of evidence), Tex. Trial Lawyers Assn. (bd. dirs.), Tarrant County Trial Lawyers Assn. (bd. dirs. 1989-91, pres.-elect 1991—), Assn. Trial Lawyers Am. (sustaining, co-chair nat. student trial adv. com.), Acad. Polit. Sci., Tarrant County So. Meth. U. Alumni Assn. (pres. 1982-84), MClub, Phi Alpha Delta. Methodist. Personal injury, Product liability, Insurance. Office: Russell Turner Laird Jones 2400 Scott Ave Fort Worth TX 76103-2245 also: Los Colinas Urban Ctr 1159 Cottonwood Ln Ste 150 Irving TX 75038-6110

**JONES, GREGORY ROBERT,** lawyer; b. San Marcos, Tex, Apr. 12, 1952; s. Robert Calvin and Dorothy Jeanne J.; m. Julia Ann Paris, Mar. 23, 1985; children: Richard, Andrew, Michael. BS cum laude, W.Va. U., 1974; MBA, Ala. A&M U., 1977; JD, Samford U., 1981. Bar: Ala., Ga. Atty. Humphrey & Smith, P.C., Huntsville, Ala., 1981, Thrasher & Whitley, P.C., Atlanta, 1982-85; atty., mgr. contracts Sci. Atlanta, Inc., Atlanta, 1986-88, Thiokol Corp., Huntsville, 1988-91; v.p., gen. counsel QMS, Inc., Mobile, Ala., 1991-96; atty. Hand Arendall, L.L.C., Mobile, 1996—. Bd. dirs., sec. German Ala. Partnership, Birmingham, 1998; bd. dirs., treas. Goodwill Industries of Gulf Coast, Inc., Mobile, 1995—. 1st lt. U.S. Army, 1974-78. Mem. Japan Am. Soc. Ala. (bd. dirs. 1997—), Ala. Export Coun., Fairhope Yacht Club (youth sailing advisor 1996-97). Republican. Episcopalian. Avocations: sailing, writing. Fax: 334-694-6375. E-mail: gregj@handarendall.com. Office: Hand Arendall LLC PO Box 123 Mobile AL 36601-0123

**JONES, GRIER PATTERSON,** lawyer; b. Ft. Worth, June 26, 1942; s. Kenneth Hugh and Nancy (Culver) J.; m. Mary Ransford, Mar. 17, 1979; children: Allison Culver, Megan Elizabeth. BA, U. of South, 1964; JD, U. Tex., 1967. Bar: Tex. 1967, Ill. 1978. Asst. sec. and counsel Southland Fin. Corp., Dallas, 1969-74; atty. Mobil Oil Corp., Dallas, 1974-77; litigation mgr. Mobil Oil Corp., Chgo., 1977-79; corp. counsel Hunt Energy Corp., Dallas, 1979-83; pvt. practice Dallas, 1983-95; asst. dist. atty. Dallas County, 1995—; mem. Tex. Unauthorized Practice of Law Com., 1987-95. Speaker to various groups. Lay reader, vestryman Good Shepherd Episcopal Ch. Fellow Coll. State Bar Tex.; mem. Dallas Bar Assn. (bd. dirs. 1998-99, chmn. house com. 1996-98), Tex. Steeplechase Club, Phi Gamma Delta. Republican. Probate, General civil litigation. Home: 9048 Stone Creek Pl Dallas TX 75243-6213 Office: Dallas County Juvenile Justice Ctr 2600 Lone Star Dr # Lb22 Dallas TX 75212-6307

**JONES, HARTWELL KELLEY, JR.,** lawyer; b. Columbia, S.C., Mar. 4, 1941; s. Hartwell Kelley and Lora (Bussey) J. B.A. in Journalism, U. S.C., 1963, M.A. in Internat. Studies, 1966, J.D., 1970. Bar: S.C. 1970, U.S. Ct. Appeals (4th cir.) 1974, U.S. Dist. Ct. 1975, U.S. Supreme 1976. Reporter Columbia Record, 1961-64; press sec. to U.S. Rep. A. W. Watson, 1964-67; reporter govt. affairs The State newspaper, Columbia, 1967-68, night city editor, 1968-70; legal asst., press sec. to Gov. of S.C., 1970-74; gen. counsel S.C. Ins. Dept., Columbia, 1974-78; sole practice Cayce, S.C., 1978-83, West Columbia, S.C., 1983-92, Columbia, S.C., 1992—; exec. v.p., counsel Profl. Ins. Agents S.C.; gen. counsel S.C. Optometric Assn.; legis. counsel S.C. Assn. Veterinarians; counsel, monitor S.C. Child Care Assn. V.p., dir. This Magic Moment Original R&B Festival; bd. dirs. Riverland Park Neighborhood Assn. Served with U.S. Army, 1964. Decorated Order of Palmetto, S.C., State of S.C. Highest Civilian award. Mem. S.C. Bar, S.C. Law Enforcement Officers Assn. Baptist. Insurance, Personal injury. Office: PO Box 2561 West 1286 Picken St Ste 203 Columbia SC 29201

**JONES, JAMES ALTON,** lawyer; b. Palestine, Tex., Feb. 26, 1956; s. Ralph A. and Jo Nell (Broadway) J. JD magna cum laude, Tulane U., 1983. Bar: Tex. 1985, U.S. Dist. Ct. (so. dist.) Tex. 1985, U.S. Dist. Ct. (no. and eas. dists.) Tex. 1986, U.S. Dist. Ct. (we. dist.) Tex. 1988, U.S. Ct. Appeals (5th cir.) 1985, Minn. 1993, U.S. Dist. Ct. Minn. 1993, U.S. Ct. Appeals (8th cir.) 1993. Law clk. U.S. Ct. Appeals (5th cir.), Houston, 1983-84; assoc. Holtzman & Urquhart, Houston, 1984-86, Johnson & Swanson, Dallas, 1986, Figari & Davenport, Dallas, 1986-89; ptnr. Doke & Riley, Dallas, 1989-92, Sprenger & Lang, Mpls., 1992-95; shareholder Jones & Assocs. P.C., Dallas, 1995—; instr. legal rsch. and writing Tulane U., 1983. Mem. ABA, State Bar Tex., Dallas Bar Assn., Dallas Assn. Young Lawyers, Order of Coif. Baptist. Avocations: tennis, skiing. E-mail: titlvii@anet-dfw.com. Fax: 214-219-9309. Labor, Civil rights, Federal civil litigation. Office: Jones & Associates PC 5015 Tracy St Ste 100 Dallas TX 75205-3400

**JONES, JEFFREY FOSTER,** lawyer; b. Phila., Apr. 24, 1944; s. Richard L. and Dorothy A. (Shaw) J.; m. Susan Craft, Aug. 22, 1970; children: Amanda, Michael. BA, Williams Coll., 1966; JD, Harvard U., 1973. Bar: Mass. 1973, U.S. Dist. Ct. Mass. 1974, U.S. Dist. Ct. Appeals (1st cir.) 1974. Law clk. Supreme Jud. Ct., Boston, 1973-74; assoc. Palmer & Dodge, Boston, 1974-80, ptnr., 1980-88, mng. ptnr., 1998—; chmn. bd. Law Firm Resources Project., 1981—. Overseer Boys and Girls Clubs of Boston, 1974-93, sec., bd. dirs., 1993—; trustee Radcliffe Coll., 1995—, Sterling and Francine Clark Art Inst., 1995-98. Lt. USN, 1966-70. Mem. ABA, Nat. Assn. Coll. and Univ. Attys., Boston Bar Assn., Mass. Bar Assn. Democrat. Avocations: racquetball, golfing, reading. General civil litigation, Public utilities, Education and schools. Office: Palmer & Dodge 1 Beacon St Ste 22 Boston MA 02108-3190

**JONES, JENIVER JAMES,** lawyer; b. Sutton, W.Va., Sept. 24, 1915; s. Lee Jackson J. and Mary Ida (Lewis) J.; m. Maxine Hickman, Oct. 3, 1939 (dec. Dec. 1993); children: Gary Keith, Glendon Kent, Ronnie Dale; m. Mary Frame, July 30, 1994; stepchildren: Debra Frame Brady, Joseph Brady. Student, Glenville (W. Va.) Coll., 1938; JD, W. Va. U., 1947. Bar: W. Va. 1947. Tchr. Braxton County Bd. Edn., Sutton, W. Va., 1936-43; attendance dir. Braxton County Bd. Edn., Sutton, 1947-48; aircraft inspector Glen L. Martin, Middle River, Md., 1943-45; pvt. practice Sutton, 1948-91, Gassaway, 1991-99. W. Va. Rep. Supreme Ct. nominee, 1988. Mem. Lions Club Internat. (dist. gov. 1963-64, Sutton, W.Va.). Methodist. Avocations: reading, tennis, baseball, golfing. General practice, Family and matrimonial, Real property. Office: Law Offices of Jeniver J Jones HC 62 Box 75 Gassaway WV 26624-9405

**JONES, JOHN BAILEY,** federal judge; b. Mitchell, S.D., Mar. 30, 1927; s. John B. and Grace M. (Bailey) J.; m. Rosemary Wermers; children: John, William, Mary Louise, David, Judith, Robert. BSBA, U. S.D., 1951, LLB, 1953. Bar: S.D. 1953. Sole practice Presho, S.D., 1953-67; judge Lyman County, Kennebec, S.D., 1953-56; mem. S.D. Ho. of Reps., Pierre, 1957-61; judge S.D. Cir. Ct., 1967-81, U.S. Dist. Ct. S.D., Sioux Falls, 1981—; now sr. judge. Mem. Am. Judicature Soc., S.D. Bar Assn., Fed. Judges Assn., VFW, Am. Legion. Methodist. Lodges: Elks, Lions. Avocation: golf. Office: US Dist Ct 400 S Phillips Ave Rm 302 Sioux Falls SD 57104-6851

**JONES, JOHN FRANK,** retired lawyer; b. Carrington, N.D., Feb. 24, 1922; s. Dwight Frank and Veronica Esther (Sheehy) J.; m. Sally Oppegard; children: Janna Jones Bellwin, John M., Jeramy Ridder, Jill Jones Nester, Julie, Jeffrey, J. David. BS, U. N.D., 1946; MS in Organic Chemistry, U. Wis., 1953; JD, U. Akron, 1956. Bar: Ohio 1956, U.S. Patent Office, U.S. Ct. Appeals. Patent atty. B. F. Goodrich Co., Akron, Ohio, 1956-62; sr. patent atty. Standard Oil Co., Cleve., 1962-70, patent counsel, 1970-81, food and drug atty. Vistron Corp. subs. Standard Oil Co., Cleve., 1968-81, ret., 1981; cons. to Standard Oil Co., Cleve. and Ashland Chem. Co. (div. Ashland Oil Co.), Columbus, Ohio, 1981-95, B.F. Goodrich Co. Served with USAAF, 1943-46. Decorated D.F.C., Air medal. Mem. Am. Chem. Soc., Ohio Bar Assn., ABA, Cleve. Intellectual Property Law Assn., CBI Hump Pilots Assn. Republican. Patentee in chem. and polymer fields; contbr. articles on polymer sci. to profl. jours. Patent, Trademark and copyright. Home and Office: 2724 Cedar Hill Rd Cuyahoga Falls OH 44223-1226

**JONES, JOHN PAUL,** probation officer, psychologist; b. Blanchard, Mich., July 23, 1944; s. Lawrence John and Thelma Blanche (Eldred) J.; m. Joan Margaret Bruder, Aug. 18, 1972; children: Jason John, Justin John, Jessica Joan-Margaret. BS, Cen. Mich. U., 1970, MA, 1974; PhD, Wayne State U., Detroit, 1980. Diplomate Am. Bd. Forensic Medicine, Am. Bd. Cert. Forensic Examiners, Am. Bd. Psychol. Specialties, Am. Acad. of Experts in Traumatic Stree; cert. addictions counselor. Mgr. F. W. Woolworth Co., Bay City, Mich., 1970; probation officer Oakland County Cir. Ct., Pontiac, Mich., 1970-74, probation officer supr., 1974-78, dir. spl. probation program, 1978-80; chief probation officer County of Oakland, Pontiac, 1980-93; outpatient clin. dir. Auro Med. Ctr., Bloomfield Hills, 1993—; lectr. Oakland U., Rochester, Mich., 1978-82; lic. psychologist Psychol. Svcs. of Bloomfield Hills, Mich., 1980-82, Family Treatment Ctr., Pontiac, Mich., 1983-84, Associated Profls., Bloomfield Hills, 1984-85, Auro Med. Ctr., Bloomfield Hills, 1985—. Pres. Pontiac Lions Club, 1986-87; study subcom. Oakland County Jail, 1982-84; mem. Oakland County Child Sexual Abuse Task Force, 1982-83. With U.S. Army, 1966-68. Mem. APA (bd. govs.), Internat. Neuropsychol. Assn., Am. Correctional Psychologist Assn., Am. Acad. Experts in Traumatic Stress, Am. Coll. Forensic Examiners (BCFE, BCFM), Mich. Corrections Assn., Mich. Assn. Probation Officers Svcs., Mich. Psychol. Assn., Fraternal Order of Police, Cen. Mich. U. Alumni Assn. (bd. dirs. Mt. Pleasant chpt. 1989-93), Mich. Neuropsychol. Soc., Am. Psychol. Assn. Republican. Avocations: travel, horseback riding, reading, fencing. Home: 2915 Masefield Dr Bloomfield Hills MI 48304-1951 Office: Auro Med Ctr Ste 102 1711 S Woodwood Ave Bloomfield Hills MI 48302

**JONES, JOSEPH HAYWARD,** lawyer; b. Shamokin, Pa., July 9, 1924; s. Joseph H. and Anna Elizabeth (Lippiatt) J.; m. Grace Loretta Hicks, Mar. 17, 1951; children: Elizabeth Christie, Joseph H. Jr., Gregory H. BA, Ursinus Coll., 1947, LLD (hon.), 1987; JD, Dickinson Sch. Law, Carlisle, Pa., 1950; LLM, NYU, 1954. Bar: Pa. 1950, U.S. Supreme Ct. 1959. Ptnr. Williamson, Friedberg & Jones, Pottsville, Pa., 1950—; mem. Pa. Judicial Reform Commn., 1987. Past pres. Appalachian Trail coun. Boy Scouts Am., Hawk Mountain coun. Boy Scouts Am.; sec., past pres. Schuylkill Econ. Devel. Corp.; pres. Pottsville Area Devel. Corp., 1986; bd. dirs. Salvation Army, Pa. Lawyers Trust Account Bd., 1989-96. Lt. (j.g.) USN, 1942-45, PTO. Recipient Silver Beaver award Boy Scouts Am., Disting. Citizen award Pa. State U., Schuylkill, 1987, Citizen of Yr. award St. David's Soc. Schuylkill and Carbon Counties; named Young Man of Yr., Pottsville Area Jaycees, Vol. of Yr., So. Schuylkill United Fund, 1972. Mem. Pa. Bar Assn. (pres. 1987-88, recipient Pa. Bar medal, chmn. task force legal svcs. to poor 1989-90, recipient ADL torch of Liberty 1997), Pa. Bar Found. (pres.), Masons (33 deg.), Lions (past pres.). General practice, Taxation, general, Probate. Home: 2100 Mahantongo St Pottsville PA 17901-3112 Office: Williamson Friedberg & Jones Ten Westwood Rd Pottsville PA 17901

**JONES, KEITH DUNN,** lawyer; b. Monroe, La., July 17, 1951; s. Arnott Lewis and Edwina Lorraine (Dunn) J.; m. Eilleen Kean, July 5, 1974; children—Christopher Keith, Kathleen Conley, Gordon Lewis. B.A., La. Tech. U., 1973; J.D., La. State U., 1976. Bar: La. 1976, U.S. Dist. Ct. (mid. dist.) La. 1977, U.S. Ct. Appeals (5th cir.) 1982, U.S. supreme Ct. 1982. Ptnr. firm McKernan & Jones, Baton Rouge, La., 1976-80, firm Gill, Bankston & Morgan, Baton Rouge, 1980-81; sole practice, Baton Rouge, 1981-85, 1992-98; ptnr. Jones & Counce; 1985-92, ptnr. Jones & Aaron Law Firm, 1998—; counsel La. Ins. Rating Commn., Baton Rouge, 1977-80. Pres. Oak Hills Civic Assn., Baton Rouge, 1981. Mem. La. State Bar Assn., ABA, Assn. Trial Lawyers Am., La. Trial Lawyers Assn. (bd. govs. 1980—), Kappa Sigma Alumni Assn. (pres. 1982). Club: Baton Rouge Country. Lodge: Cortana Kiwanis (Baton Rouge). Personal injury, Insurance, State civil litigation. Home: 1033 Woodstone Dr Baton Rouge LA 70808-5171

**JONES, KEN PAUL,** lawyer; b. DeRidder, La., Jan. 5, 1959; s. Benjamin Paul and Frances (Causey) J.; m. Kari Stuart, 1990. BS in Fin., U. Utah, Salt Lake City, 1980; BS in Mgmt., U. Utah, 1980, JD, 1983. Bar: Tex. 1983, Utah 1984, U.S. Dist. Ct. Utah 1984. Assoc. McGinnis, Lochridge & Kilgore, Austin, Tex., 1983-84; mem. firm Watkiss & Saperstein, Salt Lake City, 1984-92, Parsons, Davies, Kinghorn & Peters, Salt Lake City, 1992—. Mem. Order of the Coif. Avocations: running, reading, biking. Real property, Contracts commercial, Landlord-tenant. Office: Parsons Davies Kinghorn & Peters 185 S State St Ste 700 Salt Lake City UT 84111-1550

**JONES, LAUREN EVANS,** lawyer; b. Lawrence, Kans., Jan. 10, 1952; s. Kevin Rice and Marcia Jo Ann (Peterson) J.; m. Vivien Craig Long, Mar. 26, 1978; children: Dylan Tyler, Hayden Blake, Carson Reed. BA in History, U. Mich., 1973; JD, Duke U., 1977. Bar: R.I. 1978, U.S. Dist. Ct. R.I. 1978, U.S. Ct. Appeals (1st cir.) 1985, U.S. Ct. Appeals (9th cir.) 1994, U.S. Supreme Ct. 1991. Assoc. Lovett, Morgera, Schefrin & Gallogly, Providence, R.I., 1979-83; ptnr. Jones & Aisenberg, Providence, 1983-89; owner Jones Assocs., Providence, 1990—; mem. Jud. Performance Eval. Commn., 1993—; mem. R.I. Supreme Ct. Com. on Profl. and Civility, 1995-96. Editor R.I. Bar Jour., 1989-95; contbr. articles to profl. jours. Nominee R.I. Supreme Ct., 1993, 95, 96, 97. Mem. R.I. Bar Assn. (exec. com. 1989—, sec. 1995, v.p. 1996, pres. elect 1997, pres. 1998-99). General civil litigation, Appellate, Personal injury. Office: Jones Assocs 72 S Main St Providence RI 02903-2907

**JONES, LAWRENCE TUNNICLIFFE,** lawyer; b. Mineola, N.Y., Jan. 20, 1950; s. Carroll Hudson Tunnicliffe and Florence Virginia (Greene) J. BA, U. Va., 1972; JD, U. Richmond, 1975. Bar: Va. 1975, D.C. 1976, N.Y. 1976, U.S. Dist. Ct. (ea. and so. dist.) N.Y. 1976, U.S. Supreme Ct. 1986. Bus. mgr. law review U. Richmond, Va., 1974-75; ptnr. Carroll Hudson Tunnicliffe Jones and Lawrence Tunnicliffe Jones Attys. at law, Mineola, 1976-91. Trustee Nassau County Hist. Soc., 1976—, pres., 1983-89; bd. dirs. Friends of Hist. St. George's Ch., Hempstead, N.Y., 1982—, v.p., 1990-92, pres., 1992-94; bd. dirs. St. Mary's Devel. Fund, Garden City, N.Y., 1983-89, pres., 1987-89; pres. coun. Cathedral Sch. St. Paul Alumni Fund, Inc., Garden City, 1984—; bd. govs. Cathedral Sch. St. Mary, Garden City, 1983-86. Mem. ABA, Va. State Bar Assn., N.Y. State Bar Assn., Nassau County Bar Assn., Nassau County Tax and Estate Planning Coun., Univ. Club (N.Y.C.), Univ. Club (L.I., pres. 1986-87, 93-94, bd. dirs. 1983-86, 89—), Mineola C. of C. (dir. 1993—), Garden City Golf Club, Mineola-Garden City Rotary (dir. 1991-94), Garden City Fellowship (pres. 1993-94, dir. 1994—), Cathedral Club (Garden City) (pres. 1993-95), Garden City C. of C. Episcopalian. Avocation: historic building preservation. Probate, Real property, General practice. Home: 158 Cathedral Ave Hempstead NY 11550-1140 Office: Jones & Jones 286 Old Country Rd Ste 22 Mineola NY 11501-4106

**JONES, LINDA SCHORSCH,** lawyer; b. Balt., Mar. 21, 1964; d. Daniel and Ellen (Goldstein) Schorsch; m. Stephen Randolph Jones, July 25, 1992; children; Zachary Stephen, Seth Randolph. BA, U. Va., 1986; JD, U. Richmond, 1989. Clk. Va. Supreme Ct., Richmond, 1989-90; asst. atty. State of Va., Harrisonburg, 1990-91; ptnr. Poindexter & Schorsch, Waynesboro, Va., 1991—. Mem. Va. State Bar., Waynesboro/Staunton/Augusta County Bar Assn. Fax: 540-949-6476. E-mail: poindex@cfw.com. Family and matrimonial, Criminal, Juvenile. Office: Poindexter & Schorsch 404 S Wayne Ave Waynesboro VA 22980-4740

**JONES, LOUIS, JR. (BUCKY JONES),** academic administrator. Dir. Fayetteville (Ark.) regional campus Webster U. Mem. Ark. Bar Assn. (pres. 1999—). Office: Webster U 3448 N College Ave Fayetteville AR 72703*

**JONES, LUCIAN COX,** lawyer; b. Kew Gardens, N.Y., Dec. 22, 1942; s. Richard Jeter and Ruth Virginia (Cox) J.; m. Ann Waters, Aug. 22, 1964; children—L. Rustin, Norman W., Warren R. A.B., Davidson Coll., 1964; J.D., Columbia U., 1967. Bar: N.Y. 1967. Assoc. Shearman & Sterling, N.Y.C., 1967-68, 70-76, ptnr., 1976-98; lectr.Cameron Sch. Bus. U. N.C., Wilmington, 1998—; bd. dirs. The Nash Engrng. Co., Trumbull, Conn. 1994—. Served to capt. U.S. Army, 1968-70. Mem. ABA, N.Y. State Bar Assn., Assn. Bar City N.Y. Banking, Antitrust, Contracts commercial. Office: U NC Cameron Sch Bus 601 S College Rd Wilmington NC 28403-3297

**JONES, MICHAEL FRANK,** lawyer; b. Chgo., May 5, 1948; s. Martin F. and Joan M. (Harvey) J.; m. Susan D. Drozda. AB in Econs., Middlebury Coll., 1970, JD, 1973. Bar: Ill. 1973, Utah 1981. Assoc. Coles & Wise Ltd., Chgo., 1973-78; assoc. Rosenberg, Savner & Unikel, Chgo., 1978-80, ptnr., 1980-81; assoc. Fabian & Clendenin, Salt Lake City, 1981-82, mem., 1982-83; assoc. Hansen, Jones, Maycock & Leta, Salt Lake City, 1983-84; ptnr. Tibbals, Howell, Jones & Moxley, Salt Lake City, 1984-88, Hones & Farr, Salt Lake City, 1988-90, Pruitt, Gushee & Bachtell, Salt Lake City, 1990-95, Michael F. Jones P.C., Salt Lake City, 1995-96; mem. Moxley Jones & Campbell, L.C., Salt Lake City, 1996-98, Baird & Jones, L.C., Salt Lake City, 1998—. Contbr. articles to profl. jours. Trustee Utah Heritage Found., Salt Lake City, 1984-93. Mem. ABA, Ill. Bar Assn., Am. Coll. Real Estate Lawyers, Utah State Bar (chmn. real property sect. 1985-86). Real property, Contracts commercial, General corporate. Home: 1703 Yalecrest Ave Salt Lake City UT 84108-1839 Office: Baird & Jones LC One Utah Ctr Ste 900 Salt Lake City UT 84111

**JONES, NAPOLEON A., JR.,** judge; b. 1940. BA, San Diego State U., 1962, MSW, 1967; JD, U. San Diego, 1971. Legal intern, staff atty. Calif. Rural Legal Assistance, Modesto, Calif., 1971-73; staff atty. Defenders, Inc., San Diego, 1973-75; ptnr. Jones, Cazares, Adler & Lopez, San Diego, 1975-77; judge San Diego Mcpl. Ct., 1977-82, San Diego Superior Ct., 1982-94, U.S. Dist. Ct. (so. dist.) Calif., San Diego, 1994—; mem. San Diego County Indigent Def. Policy Bd. Bd. visitors Sch. Social Work San Diego State U.; active Valencia Park Elem. Sch. Mem. San Diego County Bar Assn., Earl B. Gilliam Bar Assn., San Diego Bar Found., Nat. Bar Assn., Calif. Bar Assn., Calif. Black Attys. Assn., Nat. Assn. Women Judges, Masons, Sigma Pi Phi, Kappa Alpha Psi. Office: US Dist Ct So Dist Calif US Courthouse 940 Front St Ste 2125 San Diego CA 92101-8912

**JONES, NATHANIEL RAPHAEL,** federal judge; b. Youngstown, Ohio, May 13, 1926; s. Nathaniel B. and Lillian J. (Rafe) J.; m. Lillian Graham, Mar. 22, 1974; 1 dau., Stephanie Joyce; stepchildren: William Hawthorne, Rickey Hawthorne, Marc Hawthorne, Pamela Haley. A.B., Youngstown State U., 1951, LL.B., 1955, LL.D. (hon.), 1969; LL.D. (hon.), Syracuse U., 1972. Editor Buckeye Rev. newspaper, 1956; exec. dir. FEPC, Youngstown, 1956-59; practiced law, 1959-61; mem. firm Goldberg & Jones, 1968-69; asst. U.S. atty., 1961-67; asst. gen. counsel Nat. Adv. Commn. on Civil Disorders, 1967-68; gen. counsel NAACP, 1969-79; judge U.S. Ct. of Appeals, 6th Circuit, 1979-95, sr. judge, 1995—; adj/ prof. U. Cin. Coll. Law, 1983—; trial observer South Africa, 1985; dir. Buckeye Rev. Pub. Co.; chmn. Con. on Adequate Def. and Incentives in Mil.; mem. Task Force-Vets. Benefits; lectr. South African Judges seminar, Johannesburg. Co-chmn. Cin. Roundtable, Black-Jewish Coalition Cin.; observer Soviet Union Behalf com. on Soviet Jewry; bd. dirs. Interights, USA. Served with USAAF, 1945-47. Mem. Ohio State Bar Assn., Mahoning County Bar Assn., Fed. Bar Assn., Nat. Bar Assn., Am. Arbitration Assn., Youngstown Area Devel. Corp., Urban League, Nat. Conf. Black Lawyers, ABA (co-chmn. com. constl. rights criminal sect. 1971-73), Kappa Alpha Psi. Baptist. Clubs: Houston Law (Youngstown); Elks. Office: US Ct Appeals US Courthouse 100 E 5th St Rm 610 Cincinnati OH 45202-3905*

**JONES, OWAIIAN MAURICE,** lawyer; b. Roanoke, Va., July 24, 1961; s. Owaiian W. and Mary D. Jones; m. Joy A. Ingram; children: Shadei E., Owaiian W. Cert. Human Rels., Dale Carnegie Inst., 1978; BS in Bus. Adminstrn. summa cum laude, Va. State U., 1982; JD, U. Tenn., 1986. Dist. mgr. Char Anne Corp., Altavista, Va., 1979; intern fin. unit corp. audit dept. Aetna Life Casualty, Hartford, Conn., 1981, asst. staff auditor employee benefits unit, 1982-83; chief fin. collegian Office Student Affairs Va. State U., 1980-81; ctr. mgr. Jr. Achievement Richmond (Va.) Inc., 1981-82; coord. black alumni activities and affairs U. Tenn., Knoxville, 1984-86, counselor, privatdocent Office Minority Affairs, 1985-86, asst. dir. alumni affairs dept. alumni affairs, 1986; chief intern law internship program Knoxville Area Urban League, 1985-86; pvt. practice Fredericksburg, Va., 1986—; pastor Ministry of Everlasting Life. Author: Draughtsman, The UTK Black Alumni Associates Constitution and Bylaws, 1984; contbg. author: The Tenn. Jud. Newsletter, 1985-86; editor, pub. U. Tenn.-Knoxville Black Alumni Report, 1984-86. Mem. NAACP, ABA (law student div. 1983-86), Va. State Bar, Fredericksburg Area Bar Assn., Am. Christian Assn. (pres.). Republican. Baptist. Avocations: tennis, golf, debating, history, chess. Family and matrimonial, Criminal, General civil litigation. Office: 406 Chatham Square Office Park Fredericksburg VA 22405-2544

**JONES, PHILIP KIRKPATRICK, JR.,** lawyer; b. Baton Rouge, June 26, 1949; s. Philip Kirkpatrick and Mary Jane (Kincade) J.; m. Serena Catherine Cockayne, Apr. 5, 1980; children: Veronica Cockayne, Nicola Kincade, Clare Kirkpatrick, Philip Carruth Elliot. BA in Govt., Dartmouth Coll., 1971; JD, La. State U., 1974; LLB, diploma in legal studies, Cambridge (U.K.) U., 1976. Bar: La. 1974, U.S. Dist. Ct. (ea. and we. dist.) La. 1980, U.S. Ct. Appeals (5th and 11th cirs.) 1981, U.S. Dist. Ct. (mid. dist.) La. 1987, U.S. Supreme Ct. 1992. Law clk. to John A. Dixon Jr. Supreme Ct. La., New Orleans, 1974-75; staff atty. Presdl. Clemency Bd., Washington, 1975; lectr. U. Singapore, 1977-79; from assoc. to ptnr. Liskow & Lewis, New Orleans, 1980—. 1st lt. USAF, 1975. Republican. Presbyterian. Bankruptcy, Federal civil litigation, Private international. Office: Liskow & Lewis PC 50th Fl One Shell Square New Orleans LA 70139

**JONES, PHILLIP JEFFREY,** lawyer; b. Elkins, W.Va., Mar. 24, 1953; s. Harry Richard and Mary Jones; m. Melissa First, Feb. 2, 1980. AB, Coll. William & Mary, 1974; JD, Stetson U., 1977. Bar: Fla. 1977, U.S. Dist. Ct. (mid. dist.) Fla. 1978, U.S. Ct. Appeals (11th cir.) 1981, Colo. 1991. Assoc. Devito & Colen, St. Petersburg, Fla., 1977-79; asst. state atty. 20th Jud Ct., Punta Gorda, Fla., 1979-80; assoc., ptnr. Wotitzky & Wititzky, Punta Gorda, Fla., 1980-88; shareholder Wilkins, Frohlich, Jones, Hevia, Russell & Sutter, Port Charlotte, Fla., 1988—. Dist. chmn. Boy Scouts Am., Charlotte County, Fla., 1998-99; co-chmn. Charlotte Homeless Coalition, 1998—. Mem. Rotary (dir. 1998—). Bankruptcy, General civil litigation, Criminal. Office: Wilkins Frohlich Jones Hevia Russell & Sutter 18501 Murdock Cir Fl 6 Pt Charlotte FL 33948-1039

**JONES, R. BRANDON,** lawyer; b. Deming, N.Mex., Oct. 21, 1944; s. Ralph B. and Lillian Mae Jones; m. Lois P. Jones, June 17, 1966; children: Kelly-Snow, Tiffany, Rourke. BA, U. Del., 1966; JD, U. Va., 1969. Bar: Del. Ptnr. Hudson, Jones, Jayvort, Fisher & Ligouri, Dover and Rehoboth Beach, Del., 1970—; pres. Kent County Bar Assn., Dover. Parlimentarian Kent County Rep. Com., Dover, 1972-82; trustee, mem. Frederica Meth. Ch., 1980s; mem. Felton Meth. Ch., Del., 1990—. Republican. Personal injury, Probate, Real property. Office: Hudson Jones Jayvort Fisher & Ligouri 225 S State St Dover DE 19901-6756

**JONES, RANDY KANE,** lawyer; b. Jacksonville, N.C., Oct. 25, 1957; s. Henry and Julia Mae (Saunders) J.; m. Traci Eileen Williams, Feb. 21, 1998; 1 child, Randy Kane Baker. BA in Polit. Sci., U. N.C., 1979, JD, 1982; LLD (hon.), Claflin Coll., 1998. Judge adv. Dept. Navy, San Diego, 1982-86; asst. U.S. atty. Dept. Justice, San Diego, 1987—. counselor Nu-Way Youth Gang Diversion, San Diego, 1990-96; dir. Voices for Children, San Diego, 1992-97; moderator Christian Fellowship Ch., San Diego, 1997—; bd. dirs. San Diego Crime Victims Fund, 1993—. With USNR, 1988-98. Recipient San Diego County Pub. Lawyer of Yr. award, 1994, Disting. Alumni award U. N.C. Chapel Hill, 1998; named one of 100 Most Influential Leaders, Ebony Mag., 1998. Mem. ABA, Nat. Bar Assn. (pres. 1997-98), Earl B. Gillian Bar Assn. (pres. 1990-91). Avocations: singing, mentoring, sports, travel. Office: US Attys Office 880 Front St Fl 6 San Diego CA 92101-8897

**JONES, REGINALD NASH,** lawyer; b. Jarratt, Va., Feb. 11, 1943; s. Jesse Everett and Ruby Lee (Parson) J.; m. Anne Johnson Askew, Aug. 28, 1965; children: Charles Everett, Emily Reed. BA in Econs., U. Richmond, 1965, JD, 1968. Bar: Va. 1968. Assoc., ptnr. Willey, Jones & Waechter, Richmond, Va., 1970-79; prin. Press, Jones & Waechter, P.C., Richmond, 1979-93; pres. Press, Jones & Waechter, P.C., Richmond, 1986-93; ptnr. Williams, Mullen, Christian & Dobbins, Richmond, 1993—; mem. adv. bd. BB&T Bank, 1987—; asst. staff judge adv. for So. Thailand, 1970; mem. Va. State Bar Coun., 1985-91. State youth coord., asst. campaign coord. Com. to Re-elect U.S. Sen. A. Willis Robertson, Richmond, 1966; citizen mem. Va. Bd. Medicine, 1986-91; trustee U. Richmond, 1982-86, mem. bd. assocs., mem. exec. com., 1986—; active River Rd. Bapt. Ch., Richmond, 1972—; v.p. bd. dirs. Jamestown-Yorktown Ednl. Trust, 1993—, Robins Found., 1996—; mem. Pres.'s Coun. Va. Hist. Soc., 1996—. Recipient Disting. Svc. award U. Richmond Alumni, 1986. Fellow Va. Law Found. (bd. dirs. 1986-92, pres. 1989); mem. ABA (com. on credit union law 1981—), Richmond Bar Assn. (chmn. real estate sect. 1976-77, exec. com. 1976-78), Va. Bar Assn (bar coun. 1985-91, chmn. legis. com. 1989-92), Henrico County Bar Assn. (founding pres. 1974-75), Hermitage Country Club, Foundry Golf Club, Scabbard and Blade, Omicron Delta Kappa, Theta Chi, Phi Delta Phi. Avocations: golf, travel. Banking, General corporate, Legislative. Home: 321 Clovelly Rd Richmond VA 23221-3701 Office: Williams Mullen Clark & Dobbins PO Box 1320 1021 E Cary St Richmond VA 23219-4000

**JONES, RICHARD MICHAEL,** lawyer; b. Chgo., Jan. 16, 1952; s. Richard Anthony and Shirley Mae (Wilhelm) J.; m. Catherine Leona Ford, May 25, 1974. BS, U. Ill., 1974; JD, Harvard U., 1977. Bar: Colo. 1977, U.S. Dist. Ct. Colo. 1977. Assoc. Davis, Graham & Stubbs, Denver, 1977-81; corp. counsel Tosco Corp., Denver, 1981-82; asst. gen. counsel Anschutz Corp., Denver, 1982-88, gen. counsel, v.p., 1989—. Mem. ABA, Colo. Bar Assn., Denver Bar Assn. Oil, gas, and mineral, General corporate, Private international. Office: Anschutz Corp 555 17th St Ste 2400 Denver CO 80202-3987

**JONES, ROBERT EDWARD,** federal judge; b. Portland, Oreg., July 5, 1927; s. Howard C. and Leita (Hendricks) J.; m. Pearl F. Jensen, May 29, 1948; children—Jeffrey Scott, Julie Lynn. BA, U. Hawaii, 1949; JD, Lewis and Clark Coll., 1953, LHD (hon.), 1995; LLD (hon.), City U., Seattle, 1984, Lewis and Clark Coll., 1995. Bar: Oreg. Trial atty. Portland, Oreg., 1953-63; judge Oreg. Circuit Ct., Portland, 1963-83; justice Oreg. Supreme Ct., Salem, 1983-90; judge U.S. Dist. Ct. Oreg., Portland, 1990—; mem. faculty Nat. Jud. Coll., Am. Acad. Jud. Edn., ABA Appellate Judges Seminars; former mem. Oreg. Evidence Revision Commn., Oreg. Ho. of Reps.; former chmn. Oreg. Commn. Prison Terms and Parole Stds.; adj. prof. Northwestern Sch. Law, Lewis and Clark Coll., 1963—, Willamette Law Sch., 1988—. Author: Rutter Group Practice Guide Federal Civil Trials and Evidence, 1999. Bd. overseers Lewis and Clark Coll. Served to capt. JAGC, USNR. Recipient merit award Multnomah Bar Assn., 1979; Citizen award NCCJ, Legal Citizen of the Yr. award Law Related Edn. Project, 1988; Service to Mankind award Sertoma Club Oreg.; James Madison award Sigma Delta Chi; named Disting. Grad., Northwestern Sch. Law. Mem. Am. Judicature Soc. (bd. dirs. 1997—), State Bar Oreg. (past chmn. Continuing Legal Edn.), Oregon Circuit Judges Assn. (pres. 1967—), Oreg. Trial Lawyers Assn. (pres. 1959, chair 9th cir. edn. com. 1996-97). Office: US Dist Ct House 1000 SW 3rd Ave Ste 1407 Portland OR 97204-2944

**JONES, ROBERT GRIFFITH,** lawyer, mayor; b. State Coll., Pa., Mar. 25, 1936; s. Edward H. and Dorothy (Griffiths) J.; m. Carolyn E. Hazard, Aug. 29, 1959; Robert Griffith Jr., Chester H. AB, Davidson (N.C.) Coll., 1958; MDiv, Yale U., 1961; PhD, Duke U., 1966; JD, U. Va., 1974. Bar: Va. 1974, U.S. Supreme Ct. 1977. Asst. prof. Davidson (N.C.) Coll., 1964-65; assoc. prof. Lehigh U., Bethlehem, Pa., 1965-71; prof. U. Va., Charlottesville, 1971-74; mayor City of Virginia Beach, Va., 1986-88; chmn. Jones, Russotto & Walker P.C., Virginia Beach, 1991—; adv. bd. mem. Princess Anns Bank, 1997—. Vice-chmn. Tidewater Transp. Dist. Commn., 1987-88, chmn., 1988; councilman City Council of Virginia Beach, 1982-88. Mem. ABA, Va. Bar Assn., Virginia Beach Bar Assn. Democrat. Presbyterian. Home: 2716 Robin Dr Virginia Beach VA 23454-1814 Office: 128 S Lynnhaven Rd Virginia Beach VA 23452-7417

**JONES, ROBERT JEFFRIES,** lawyer; b. Atlantic City, N.J., Sept. 7, 1939; s. Robert Lewis and Mildred Laura (Jeffries) J.; m. Joan Mary Feichtner, Aug. 17, 1963; children: Christopher, Kendall, Stephen. BA, Colgate U., 1961; LLB with honors, U. Pa., 1964. Bar: Pa. 1965, U.S. Dist. Ct. (ea. dist.) Pa. 1965, U.S. Ct. Appeals (3d cir.) 1965. Assoc. Saul, Ewing, Remick & Saul, Phila., 1964-71, ptnr., 1971—; mem. steering com. Bond Atty.'s Workshop, Chgo., 1980. Mem. Montgomery County Rep. Com., Norristown, Pa., 1967-71; chmn. Whitpain Twp. Park and Recreation Bd., Blue Bell, Pa., 1980-84; bd. dirs. Phila. YMCA Camps, 1970-76; trustee Colgate U., 1999—; mem. gen. counsel alumni corp., 1993-99, pres. Phila. chpt., 1980-84. Fellow Am. Coll. Bond Counsel (founder); mem. ABA, Phila. Bar Assn. (chmn. tax exempt fin. com. 1985-86), Pa. Bond Lawyers Assn. (founder Harrisburg, Pa. 1987), Pa. Economy League (bd. dirs. 1994—). Avocations: skiing, golf, history. Municipal (including bonds), Securities, Finance. Office: Saul Ewing Remick & Saul 3800 Centre Sq W Philadelphia PA 19102

**JONES, SANDRA YVONNE,** lawyer; b. Chgo., July 13, 1952; d. Fred Alexander and Luenettie (Joiner) J. B.S., U. Ill., 1975; J.D., Valparaiso U., 1977; diploma Nat. Jud. Coll., 1981. Bar: Ill. 1978, U.S. Dist. Ct. (no. dist.) Ill., U.S. Supreme Ct. 1983. Legal asst. Porter County Prosecutor's Office, Valparaiso, Ind., 1977; legal counsel Cook County Legal Asst.'s Office, Maywood, Ill., 1978-81; adminstrv. law judge Human Rights Commn., Chgo., 1981-85; asst. regional civil rights counsel Office Civil Rights, U.S. Dept. Edn., Chgo., 1985—, supervising atty. Office Pub. Guardian, Chgo., 1987-94, adminstrv. hearing officer expedited child support divsn. Cir. Ct. Cook County, Chgo., 1994—. Author: Tenant's Guide to Self-Help, 1981. Mem. ABA, Ill. Assn. Adminstrv. Law Judges (v.p. 1984—), Ill. Assn. Trial Lawyers, Chgo. Bar Assn., Ill. Bar Assn. Home: 3316 S Calumet Ave Chicago IL 60616-3992 Office: Human Rights Commn 32 W Randolph St Chicago IL 60601-3405

**JONES, SHELDON ATWELL,** lawyer; b. Melrose, Mass., Apr. 20, 1938; s. Sheldon Atwell and Hannah Margaret (Andrews) J.; m. Priscilla Ann Hatch, Sept. 10, 1966; children: Sarah Percy, Abigail Atwell. BA, Yale U., 1959; LLB, Harvard U., 1965. Bar: Mass. 1965, U.S. Dist. Ct. Mass. 1967. Assoc. Gaston, Snow, Motley & Holt, Boston, 1965-72; ptnr. Gaston Snow & Ely Bartlett, Boston, 1972-87, Dechert Price & Rhoads, Boston, 1987—; past sec. H&Q Healthcare Investors, Boston. Contbr. articles to profl. jours. Lt. (j.g.) USN, 1959-62. Mem. ABA (past chmn. subcom. on investment cos., state regulation of securities com.), Mass. Bar Assn., Boston Bar Assn. (past co-chmn. subcom. on investment cos. and investment advisers), Yale Club, Harvard Club. Congregationalist. Avocations: skiing, sailing. Securities, General corporate, Investment. Home: 70 Indian Spring Rd Concord MA 01742-5512 Office: Dechert Price & Rhoads 12th Fl Ten Post Office Sq Boston MA 02109

**JONES, STEPHEN,** lawyer; b. Lafayette, La., July 1, 1940; s. Leslie William and Gladys A. (Williams) J.; m. Virginia Hadden (dec.); 1 child, John Chapman; m. Sherrel Alice Stephens, Dec. 27, 1973; children: Stephen Mark, Leslie Rachael, Edward St. Andrew. Student, U. Tex., 1960-63; LLB, U. Okla., 1966. Sec. Rep. Minority Conf., Tex. Ho. of Reps., 1963; personal asst. to Richard M. Nixon N.Y.C., 1964; adminstrv. asst. to Congressman Paul Findley, 1966-69, legal counsel to gov. of Okla., 1967; spl. asst. U.S. Senator Charles H. Percy and U.S. Rep. Donald Rumsfeld, 1968; mem. U.S. del. to North Atlantic Assembly NATO, 1968; staff counsel censure task force Ho. of Reps. Impeachment Inquiry, 1974; spl. U.S. atty. No. Dist. Okla., 1979; spl. prosecutor, spl. asst. dist. atty. State of Okla., 1977; judge Okla. Ct. Appeals, 1982; civil jury instrn. com. Okla. Supreme Ct., 1979-81; adv. com. ct. rules Okla. Ct. Criminal Appeals, 1980; now mng. ptnr. Jones and Wyatt, Enid, Okla.; adj. prof. U. Okla., 1973-76; instr. Phillips U., 1982-

90; bd. dirs. Coun. on the Nat. Interest Found. Author: Oklahoma and Politics in State and Nation, 1907-62, Others Unknown: The Oklahoma City Bombing Case and Conspiracy (Public Affairs, 1998); co-author: France and China, The First Ten Years, 1964-74, 1991; contbr. articles to various jours. Bd. dirs., coun. mem. Nat. Interest Found.; acting chmn. Rep. State Com., Okla., 1982; Rep. nominee Okla. atty. gen., 1974, U.S. Senate, 1990; spl. counsel to Gov. Okla., 1995; apptd. chief def. counsel by U.S. Dist. Ct., Oklahoma City, U.S. vs. Tim McVeigh, Oklahoma City Bombing Case, 1995-97; mem. vestry St. Matthews Episc. Ch., 1974, sr. warden, 1983-84, 89-90. Mem. ABA, Okla. Bar Assn., Garfield County Bar Assn., Beacon Club, Petroleum Club (Oklahoma City), Oakwood Country Club (Enid). Criminal, Taxation, general, General civil litigation. Office: PO Box 472 Enid OK 73702-0472

**JONES, STEPHEN M.,** lawyer, accountant; b. Decatur, Ala., Nov. 9, 1954; s. William E. and Elease M. Jones; m. Joann G. Jones, Apr. 19. 1980; children: Mitchell, Brandon, Wesley. BS, U. of Ala., 1977; JD, Birmingham Sch. of Law, 1983. Contr. Bessemer (Ala.) Carraway Med. Ctr., 1983—, gen. counsel, 1983—. Mem. Am. Assn. of Health Lawyers. Health, Nonprofit and tax-exempt organizations. Office: Bessemer Carraway Med Ctr PO Box 847 Bessemer AL 35021-0847

**JONES, STEPHEN WITSELL,** lawyer; b. Honolulu, Aug. 12, 1947; s. Allen Newton Jr. and Maude Estelle (Witsell) J.; m. Judy Kaye Mason, Aug. 13, 1977; children: MaryAnn, Adam, Kathleen. Student, Hendrix Coll., 1965-66; AB with high honors, U. Ill., 1969; JD with highest honors, U. Ark., Little Rock, 1978. Bar: Ark. 1978, U.S. Dist. Ct. (ea. and we. dists.) Ark. 1978, U.S. Ct. Appeals (7th and 8th cirs.) 1978, U.S. Supreme Ct. 1984. Rsch. statistician Ark. Dept. Parks and Tourism, Little Rock, 1971-72, dir. tourist info. ctr., 1972-74; affirmative action specialist Office of the Gov., Little Rock, 1974-75; dir. pers. Ark. Social Svcs. Div., Little Rock, 1975-77; mgmt. info. specialist Ark. Health Dept., Little Rock, 1977-78; assoc. House, Holmes & Jewell, Little Rock, 1978-84; ptnr. House, Wallace, Nelson & Jewell, Little Rock, 1984-86; mng. ptnr. Jack, Lyon & Jones, P.A., Little Rock, 1986—; adj. instr. div. lifelong edn. U. Ark., Little Rock, 1992-95. Co-author: Employment Law Deskbook for Arkansas Employers, 1997; editor-in-chief U. Ark. Little Rock Law Rev., 1977; editor Ark. Employment Law Letter, 1996—; contbg. author: Employment Discrimination Law, 2d edit., 1983; editor. Bd. dirs. United Cerebral Palsy of Ctrl. Ark., Little Rock, 1978—; bd. dirs. Ark. Ice Hockey Assn., 1992—. With U.S. Army, 1969-71. Recipient Svc. Recognition award United Cerebral Palsy of Ctrl. Ark., 1986, 95. Fellow Greater Little Rock C. of C.; mem. ABA (labor/litigation law practice mgmt. sect.), Ark. Bar Assn., Def. Rsch. Inst. Episcopalian. Avocations: photography, golf. Federal civil litigation, Civil rights, Labor. Home: 1724 S Arch St Little Rock AR 72206-1215 Office: Jack Lyon & Jones PA 3400 TCBY Tower 425 W Capitol Ave Little Rock AR 72201-3405

**JONES, STEVEN EMRYS,** judge; b. Tokyo, Nov. 17, 1957; came to U.S., 1958; s. Stanley Emrys and Nellie Rae (Hunt) J.; m. Jill Dana Witbeck, Apr. 10, 1981 (div. Feb. 1984); m. Deborah Jo Gefken, June 20, 1985; children: Ashley Danielle, Spencer Emrys, Isaac. BS, Brigham Young U., 1981; JD magna cum laude, Calif. Western U., San Diego, 1984. Bar: Nev. 1985, U.S. Dist. Ct. Nev. 1985, U.S. Ct. Appeals (9th cir.) 1985. Jud. law clk. to presiding justice Nev. Supreme Ct., Carson City, 1984-85; assoc. Stewart L. Bell, Charted, Las Vegas, Nev., 1985-89; ptnr. Bell, Davidson & Jones, Las Vegas, 1990-92; chief/presiding judge family divsn. 8th Jud. Dist. Ct., 1992—; atty. Clark County Pro Bono Project, Las Vegas, 1985-90; elected judge 8th Jud. Dist. Ct. Clark County; domestic rels. referee State of Nev., 1991-92; lectr. in field. Participant Am. Cancer Soc., Las Vegas, 1988, 89—; bd. dirs. Clark County Health Dist. Air Pollution Bd., Las Vegas, 1987—; mem. Clark County Clean Air Task Force, 1991—. Mem. ABA, Am. Judges' Assn., Nev. Dist. Judges' Assn., Nev. Bar Assn. (bd. govs. 1994—), Clark County Bar Assn., Assn. Trial Lawyers Am. Republican. LDS. Avocations: reading, sports, hunting, music. Office: 601 N Pecos Rd Las Vegas NV 89101-2408

**JONES, STEVEN GARY,** lawyer; b. Flora, Ill., Dec. 29, 1966; s. Robert Gary and Erma Kay Jones; m. Deanne Fortna, Dec. 11, 1993. BA, Ea. Ill. U., 1989; JD, So. Ill. U., 1992. Bar: U.S. Dist. Ct. (so. dist.) Ill. 1992, U.S. Dist. Ct. (cen. dist.) Ill. 1993. Assoc. Brian P. McGarry, Marion, Ill., 1992-93, Bickes & Bickes, Decatur, Ill., 1993-94, Shay & Perbix, Decatur, 1994-98; ptnr. Willoughby, Hopkins & Jones P.C., Decatur, 1998—. Precinct committeeman Dem. Party, Louisville, Ill., 1986-89; bd. dirs. CHELP, Decatur, 1998—. Gen. Assembly scholar Ill. Gen. Assembly, 1986-87. Mem. Ill. State Bar Assn., Decatur Bar Assn. (comty. involvement com. 1997-98). Democrat. Avocation: cooking. General civil litigation. Office: Willoughby Hopkins & Jones PC 502 W Prairie Ave Decatur IL 62522-2422

**JONES, SYLVANUS BENSON,** adjudicator, consultant; b. Southport, N.C., Nov. 21, 1928; s. Thomas Henry and Katie Mable J.; m. Karen Ann Charbonneau, Aug. 10, 1970 (div. May 1975); 1 child, Donovan. Student, Howard U., 1945-48; AD in Fin., Peter's Bus. Coll., Washington, 1955; postgrad., Fgn. Svc. Inst., Arlington, Va., 1956, George Washington U., 1959-60, Bibliothèque de la Sorbonne U. de Paris, Paris, 1962, Georgetown U., Washington, 1962, Am. U., Washington, 1966-68. Lic. real estate agt.; lic. gen. contractor, Md.; lic. ins. agt., Md., D.C. Enumerator, IBM computer operator U.S. Census Bur., Suitland, Md., 1950-51; clk. typist, claims div. VA, Washington, 1951-52; rsch. clk. Bur. Security and Consular Affairs, U.S. Dept. State, Washington, 1952-53, supr. passport processing sect., 1953-56, from jr. to sr. adjudicator domestic adjudication div., 1956-61, consular affairs officer adv. opinions div., 1961-63, chief pvt. bill staff, office of dep. dir. for ops., 1963-68, chief fraud and investigation unit, 1968-72; adjudicator, gen. cons., 1972—; editor-in-chief The Washington Press, 1957-63; founder, dir. Mut. Fund Investment Program for Govt. Employees, Washingotn, 1969-73; instr. Tennis U. Puebla (Mex.), 1973-75; editor-in-chief The Annapolis (Md.) Press, 1989—; chmn. ad hoc com. to repeal the utilities tax, Annapolis, 1992—. Contbr. articles to profl. jours; grantee hub cap locking device. Treas. Annapolis City Dem. Ctrl. Com., 1992, 97; Dem. candidate for mayor, Annapolis, 1993, 97; chmn. trans. adv. bd., Annapolis, 1992-98. Recipient Cert. of Disting. Citizenship, City of Annapolis, 1987, 97, Gov.'s Citation for Outstanding Svc. to Citizens, State of Md., 1997, Red Cross Citizenship award, Trailblazer award U.S. Dept. State, 1998; numerous meritorious svc. awards; Howard U. scholar. Home: 16 Bausum Dr Annapolis MD 21401-4309

**JONES, THEODORE LAWRENCE,** lawyer; b. Dallas, Nov. 29, 1920; s. Theodore Evan and Ernestine Lucy (Douthit) J.; m. Marion Elizabeth Thomas, Feb. 29, 1944; children: Suzanne Maas, Scott Evan, Stephen Lawrence, Shannon Ritter. BBA, U. Tex., 1944, JD, 1948; postgrad., So. Meth. U., 1950-52, Am. U., 1965-66. Bar: Tex. 1948, D.C. 1988, U.S. Supreme Ct. 1962; cert. panelist for arbitration and mediation Internat. Ctrs. for Arbitration, 1994—. Assoc. Carrington, Gowan, Johnson & Walker, Dallas, 1948-51; gen. counsel W. H. Cothrum & Co., Dallas, 1951-54; pvt. practice law Dallas, 1955-56; asst. atty. gen., chief ins., banking and corp. div. Atty. Gen. Office, Tex., 1957-60; ptnr. Herring & Jones, Austin, Tex., 1960-61; gen. counsel maritime adminstrn. U.S. Dept. Commerce, 1961-63; dep. gen. counsel Dept. Commerce, 1963-64, dep. fed. hwy. adminstr., 1964-66; pres. Am. Ins. Assn., N.Y.C., 1967-86; counsel Hunton & Williams, Washington, 1986—; chmn. interdeptl. com. for bilateral agreements for acceptance of nuclear ship, Savannah, 1962-63; lectr. Fgn. Service Inst., 1962-64; alt. U.S. rep. 11th session Diplomatic Conf. on Maritime Law, Brussels, 1962; advisor U.S. del. 6th session Coun., Intergovtl. Maritime Consultative Orgn., London, 1962; mem. maritime subsidy bd. U.S. Dept. Commerce, 1962-63; acting hwy. beautification coord., 1965-66; del. White House Conf. on Internat. Cooperation; mem. Property-Casualty Ins. Coun., 1976-86, Internat. Ins. Adv. Coun., 1980-87; mem. adv. com. Pension Benefit Guaranty Corp., 1977; mem. Time Newstour, Ea. Europe and Persian Gulf, 1981, Mexico and Panama, 1983, Pacific Rim, 1985; bd. dirs. Nat. Safety Coun., 1967, Ins. Inst. for Hwy. Safety, 1967-86. Contbr. articles to profl. jours. Lt. (j.g.) USNR, 1944-46; lt. commdr. 1962-66. Mem. ABA, D.C. Bar Assn., Bar Assn. of D.C., Fed. Bar Assn. (chmn. nat. spkrs. bur. 1964), Tex. Bar Assn., Am. Judicature Soc., Friars, Phi Delta Phi, Beta Gamma Sigma, Phi Eta Sigma. Democrat. Presbyterian. Insurance, Environmental, Legislative. Home: 648 S Carolina Ave SE Washington DC 20003-2701 Office: Hunton & Williams 1900 K St NW Ste 1100 Washington DC 20006-1110

**JONES, THOMAS BROOKS,** lawyer; b. Atmore, Ala.; s. John Maxwell and Marjorie Lee (Brooks) J. BA, U. Ala., 1949, JD, 1951; LLM, Columbia U., 1958; postgrad. legal studies, U. Stockholm, Sweden, 1973. Bar: Ala. 1951. Sole practice Escambia County, Ala., 1951-52; judge Escambia County, 1953-57; interim asst. prof. U. Fla. Law Sch., Gainesville, 1958-60; atty. Dept. of the Army, various cities, 1961-83; instr. Anchorage Community Coll., Chapman Coll., Anchorage, 1982—. Author: Munich, 1977; contbr. articles to profl. jours. Served with AUS, 1946-47. Mem. ABA, Fla. Bar Assn. Democrat. Baptist. Avocations: foreign travel, sports. Home and Office: 836 M St Apt 208 Anchorage AK 99501-3355

**JONES, TOM GEORGE,** lawyer; b. Defiance, Ohio, Oct. 21, 1934; s. Russell George and Edith (Guinn) J.; m. Annette Huttmacher, June 14, 1959 (div. Mar. 1979); children: Amy Jones Rogers, Mary Margaret, Russell Nicholas, Jennifer Jones Auger; m. Susan Lee Crawford Whitacre, Sept. 17, 1981; stepchildren: Robert Parker Whitacre, James Alan Whitacre, Elizabeth Lee Whitacre. BS in Mktg., Ind. U., 1956; JD, Ind. U., Indpls., 1961. Bar: Ind. 1961, U.S. Dist. Ct. (so. dist.) Ind. 1961, U.S. Ct. Appeals (7th cir.) 1961. Ptnr. Jones, Hoffman, Franklin, Ind., 1961—; dep. pros. atty. Johnson County, 1960-61; lectr. Ind. Continuing Legal Edn. Forum, Indpls., 1982—; mem. faculty Nat. Inst. Trial Adv., Washington, 1985—. Contbr. articles to profl. jours. Atty. Johnson County Planning Commn. and Zoning Bd., Ind., 1961-66. Fellow Ind. Trial Lawyers Assn. (chmn. criminal law sect. 1981-83, bd. dirs., 1982-95), Roscoe Pound Found.; mem. ABA, Indpls. Bar Assn., Johnson County Bar Assn.(sec. 1962, pres. 1974), Am. Bd. Trial Advocates (pres. Ind. chpt. 1990-95, nat. bd. dirs. 1990-96), Internat. Soc. Barristers, Nat. Assn. Criminal Def. Lawyers, Assn. Trial Lawyers Am. (sustaining), Tex. Trial Lawyers Assn., Melvin N. Bellie Soc., Phi Kappa Psi. Presbyterian. Lodges: Elks, Shriners, Masons, Scottish Rite. Fax: 317-736-4440. E-mail: tommygjones@hotmail.com. Personal injury, Criminal, State civil litigation. Home: 200 N Water St Franklin IN 46131-1725 Office: Jones Hoffman & Ullrich 150 N Main St Franklin IN 46131-1721

**JONES, TRACY WEBB,** lawyer; b. Lexington, Jan. 14, 1965; s. John Morland and Carol Tracy Webb; m. Robert Bondurant Jones, June 3, 1995. BA in Polit. Sci., U. Ky., 1987, JD, 1990. Bar: Ky. 1990, U.S. Dist. Ct. (we. dist.) Ky. 1991, U.S. Dist. Ct. (ea. dist.) Ky. 1992, U.S. Ct. Appeals (6th cir.) 1996. Staff atty. Fruit of the Loom, Bowling Green, Ky., 1990-91; assoc. Gallion, Baker & Bray, Lexington, 1991-98; atty. pvt. practice, Versailles, Ky., 1998—. Bd. dirs. Visually Impaired Presch. Svcs., Lexington, 1994—. Construction, Government contracts and claims, General civil litigation. Office: 808 Royal Ridge Ct Versailles KY 40383-1922

**JONES, WILLIAM ALLEN,** lawyer, entertainment company executive; b. Phila., Dec. 13, 1941; s. Roland Emmett and Gloria (Miller) J.; m. Margaret Smith, Sept. 24, 1965 (div. 1972); m. Dorothea S. Whitson, June 15, 1973; children—Darlene, Rebecca, Gloria, David. BA, Temple U., 1967; MBA, JD, Harvard U., 1972. Bar: Calif. 1974. Atty. Walt Disney Prodns., Burbank, Calif., 1973-77, treas., 1977-81; atty. Wyman Bautzer et al, L.A., 1981-83; atty. MGM/UA Entertainment Co., Culver City, 1983, v.p., gen. counsel, 1983-86; sr. v.p., corp. gen. counsel, sec. MGM/UA Communications Co., Culver City, Calif., 1986-91; exec. v.p., gen. counsel, sec. Metro-Goldwyn-Mayer Inc., Santa Monica, Calif., 1991-95, exec. v.p. corp. affairs, 1995-97, sr. exec. v.p., 1997—; bus. mgr. L.A. Bar Jour., 1974-75; bd. dirs. The Nostalgia Network Inc.; mem. bd. of govs. Inst. for Corp. Counsel, 1990-93. Charter mem. L.A. Philharm. Men's Com., 1974-80; trustee Marlborough Sch., 1988-93, Flintridge Preparatory Sch., 1993-96. With USAF, 1960-64. President's scholar Temple U., 1972. Mem. Harvard Bus. Sch. Assn. So. Calif. (bd. dirs. 1985-88). Home: 1557 Colina Dr Glendale CA 91208-2412 Office: Metro-Goldwyn-Mayer Inc 2500 Broadway Santa Monica CA 90404-3065

**JONES, WILLIAM REX,** law educator; b. Murphysboro, Ill., Oct. 20, 1922; s. Cluade E. and Ivy P. (McCormick) J.; m. Miriam R. Lamy, Mar. 27, 1944; m. Gerri L. Haun, June 30, 1972; children: Michael Kimber, Jeanne Keats, Patricia Combs, Sally Instone, Kevin. B.S., U. Louisville, 1950; J.D., U. Ky., 1968; LL.M., U. Mich., 1970. Bar: Ky. 1969, Fla. 1969, Ind. 1971, U.S. Supreme Ct. 1976. Exec. v.p. Paul Miller Ford, Inc., Lexington, Ky., 1951-64; pres. Bill's Seat Cover Ctr., Inc., Lexington, Ky., 1952-65, Bill Jones Real Estate, Inc., Lexington, Ky., 1965-70; asst. prof. law Ind. U., Indpls., 1970-73, assoc. prof., 1973-75, prof., 1975-80; dean Salmon P. Chase Coll. Law, No. Ky. U., Highland Heights, 1980-85, prof., 1980-93, prof. emeritus, 1993—; vis. prof. Shepard Broad Law Ctr., Nova Southeastern U., Ft. Lauderdale, Fla., 1994-95; mem. Ky. Pub. Advocacy Commn., 1982-93, 97—, chmn., 1986-93. Author: Kentucky Criminal Trial Practice, 2d edit., 1991, Kentucky Criminal Trial Practice Forms, 2d edit., 1993. Served as 1st sgt. U.S. Army, 1940-44. Cook fellow U. Mich., 1969-70; W.G. Hart fellow Queen Mary Coll. U. London, 1985. Mem. ABA, Nat. Legal Aid and Defenders Assn., Nat. Dist. Attys. Assn., Order of Coif. Office: No Ky U Nunn Hall Highland Heights KY 41099-1400

**JONESCO, JANE RIGGS,** lawyer, development officer; b. Delaware, Ohio, Feb. 7, 1949; d. Edgar Gray and Bettie Pauline (Lowther) Riggs; m. John Michael Jonesco, Aug. 8, 1970; children: Amy Jane, John Michael III, Michael Andrew, Katherine Elizabeth. BA, Ohio Wesleyan U., 1971; JD, DePaul U., 1980. Bar: Ohio 1980. Atty. in pvt. practice Oberlin, Ohio, 1981-91; dir. planned giving Oberlin Coll., 1991—; mem. adminstrn. and profl. coun. Oberlin Coll., 1992-93; chair, mem. Oberlin City Income Tax Bd. of Rev., 1995. Mem. Oberlin Bd. Edn., 1987-93, v.p., 1988-89, pres., 1990-93; founder, mem. Oberlin Interagy. Coun., 1990-93; mem. Oberlin Community Svcs. Coun., 1986-90; mem. Oberlin Bicentennial Commn., 1985-86; pres., mem. Oberlin Baseball Softball Fedn., 1981-86; mem. Nat. Planned Giving Coun., No. Ohio Planned Giving Coun.; mem. Jr. League of Columbus, 1979-80, Oberlin Schs. Endowment Bd., 1996—. Episcopalian. Avocations: family activities, tennis. Home: 440 E College St Oberlin OH 44074-1305 Office: Oberlin Coll 208 Bosworth Hall Oberlin OH 44074

**JONG, JAMES C. (CHUANPING ZHANG),** lawyer, educator; b. Wuhan, China. LLB, South Ctrl. U., Wuhan, 1977; LLM, Peking U., Beijing, China, 1982; JD, Columbia U., 1986. Bar: N.Y. 1992, U.S. Dist. Ct. (so. dist.) N.Y. 1993, China 1983. Dir. China Higher Edn. Assn., Beijing, 1981-88, China Civil Law Soc., Beijing, 1983-86; sec.-gen. Grad. Assn. of Peking U., Beijing, 1983-86; legal counsel Longyi Co., Ltd., Beijing, 1985-86; assoc. Menaker & Herrmann, N.Y.C., 1989-95; vis. prof. South Ctrl. U., Wuhan, 1993—; sole practitioner N.Y.C., 1995—; legal counsel U.S. China Trade Ctr. in Oakland City, Calif., 1997—; cons. Metro Internat., Stockholm, 1998—. Author: Handbook of Chinese Law, 1986; editor Jour. China Law, Columbia U., 1987-89; contbr. articles to profl. jours. Banking, Private international, Immigration, naturalization, and customs. Office: 40-41 81st St New York NY 10000

**JONSEN, ERIC R.,** lawyer; b. San Francisco, June 5, 1958; s. Richard William and Ann Margaret (Parsons) J.; m. Ida-Marie, May 8, 1982; children: Kaitlyn, Jeremy, Michelle. BA, Hartwick Coll., 1980; JD, U. Colo., 1985. Bar: Colo., N.Y., U.S. Dist. Ct. Colo., U.S. Ct. Appeals (10th cir., Fed. cir.), U.S. Ct. Appeals (fed. cir.). Assoc. William P. DeMoulin, Denver, 1986-88, Fairfield & Woods, Denver, 1988-90; ptnr. Ciancio & Jonsen PC, Denver, 1990—. Mem. ABA, Colo. Bar Assn. E-mail: jonsen@csn.net. General civil litigation, Federal civil litigation, Intellectual property. Office: Ciancio & Jonsen PC 12000 Pecos St Ste 200 Denver CO 80234-2079

**JONSSON, JON MARVIN,** lawyer; b. Seattle, Mar. 22, 1928; s. Thorbjorn and Brynhildur S. Jonsson; m. Marlene Pederson, Oct. 23, 1948 (div. Oct. 1953); 1 child, Dwight; m. Ellen Joanne Sivertsen, Dec. 27, 1960; children: Bryndis, Geir Thorbjorn. BA in Econs. and Bus., U. Wash., 1952, JD, 1954. Bar: Wash. 1954. Pvt. practice, Seattle, 1955—; apptd. hon. consul for Iceland, 1968, consul gen., 1990. Mem. Wash. State Ho. of Reps., 1959-60. With USMC, 1946-47. Named to Order of Falcon Gov. of Iceland, 1977. Probate, Personal injury, Native American. Office: 5610 20th Ave NW Seattle WA 98107-5290

**JONTZ, JEFFRY ROBERT,** lawyer; b. Stuart, Iowa, May 28, 1944; s. John Leo Jontz and Leora Burnette (Pittman) Myers; m. Sharyn Sue Kopriva, June 8, 1968; 1 son, Eric Barrett. BA, Drake U., 1966; JD with distinction, U. Iowa, 1969. Bar: Iowa 1969, Fla. 1971, Ohio 1972, U.S. Dist. Ct. (mid. dist.) Fla. 1971, U.S. Ct. Appeals (5th cir.) 1971, fla. 1972, U.S. Ct. Appeals (11th cir.) 1981, U.S. Tax Ct. 1983. Law clk. to Hon. Charles R. Scott U.S. Dist. Ct. (mid. dist.) Fla., Jacksonville, 1969-70; to Hon. Bryan Simpson U.S. Ct. Appeals (5th cir.), Jacksonville, 1970-71; assoc. Jones, Day, Cockley & Reavis, Cleve., 1971-72; asst. U.S. atty. U.S. Dist. Ct. (mid. dist.) Fla., Orlando, 1972-74; pvt. practice Orlando, 1974—; ptnr. Young, Turnbull & Linscott, Orlando, 1974-79, Baker & Hostetler, Orlando, 1979, DeWolf, ward & Morris, Orlando, 1979-84, Jontz, russell & Hull, Orlando, 1985-86, Holland & Knight, 1986-96, Carldon Fields, Orlando, 1996—. Contbr. articles to legal jours.; bd. editors Iowa Law Rev., 1968. past bd. dirs. The Door Drug Rehab. Ctr. of Ctrl. Fla.; past chmn. bd. trustees First Congregational Ch. of Winter Park, Fla., mem. com., long range planning com.; former county committeeman Rep. Party of Orange County, Fla.; bd. dirs. Fla. Symphony Orch., 1985-93, Jr. Achievement Ctrl. Fla., Inc.; mem. Rollins Coll. Tar Boosters; chmn. bankruptcy com. Orange County Bar Assn., 1986-87, chmn. jud. rels. com., 1998—; chmn. bankruptcy com. Code Enforcement Bd. City of Maitland, Fla., 1990-92; chmn. bd. adjustment City of Winter Park, 1995—; mem. parents com. Dartmouth Coll., 1995-99. Recipient Outstanding Individual Cmty. Leadership award Vol. Ctr. Ctrl. Fla., 1991. Mem. Am. Bankruptcy Inst., Ctrl. Fla. Bankruptcy Lawyers Assn., Fla. Bar (ith cir. grievance com. 1979-82, chmn. comml. litigation com. 1981-82, bankruptcy and creditor's rights com. corp. bus. and banking law sect., com. on jud. adminstrn., selection and tenure 1985-86, mem. jud. nominating procedures com. 1995-96, lectr. seminars), Orange County Bar Assn. (chmn. jud. rels. com. 1995—, bankruptcy com.), ABA (mem. comml. transactions litigation com., numerous other coms.), Drake U. Nat. Alumni Assn. (past chmn. ctrl. Fla. chpt., sec., bd. dirs. 1981-93, pres.'s circle coun.), Iowa State Bar Assn., Order of Coif, Winter Park Racquet Club (mem. bd. govs., sec., v.p., pres. 1989-94, 96—), Tiger Bay Club Orlando, Citrus Club, Omicron Delta Kappa, Tau Kappa Epsilon, Phi Delta Phi. General civil litigation, Bankruptcy, Banking. Office: Carlton Fields Ward Emmanuel Smith Cutler PA Ste 1600 PO Box 1171 255 South Orange Ave Orlando FL 32802

**JORDAN, ALEXANDER JOSEPH, JR.,** lawyer; b. New London, Conn., Oct. 11, 1938; s. Alexander Joseph and Alice Elizabeth (Mugovero) J.; m. Mary Carolyn Miller, Aug. 8, 1964; children: Jennifer, Michael, Stephanie. BS, U.S. Naval Acad., 1960; LLB, Harvard U., 1968. Ptnr. Gaston & Snow, Boston, 1968-91, Bingham, Dana & Gould, Boston, 1991-93, Nixon Peabody LLP, Boston, 1994—. Mem., past chmn. adv. com. Town of Hingham, Mass., 1989-95. With USN, 1960-65, capt. USNR, 1965-94, ret. Mem. ABA, Mass. Bar Assn., Boston Bar Assn., U.S. Naval Inst., Naval Res. Assn., Harvard Alumni Assn. (regional dir.), Harvard Club Hingham (trustee, chmn. com. schs. and scholarships, past pres.), Harvard Club of Boston. General corporate, Finance, Securities. Office: Nixon Peabody LLP 101 Federal St Fl 13 Boston MA 02110-1800

**JORDAN, CHARLES MILTON,** lawyer; b. Houston, Apr. 3, 1949; s. Milton Reginald and Jean (Burris) J.; m. Jeanette Lutz; children: Nicole Catherine, John Milton, Rebecca Louise Darnell. BBA, U. Tex., 1971, JD, 1975. Bar: Tex. 1975, U.S. Dist. Ct. (so. dist.) Tex. 1976, U.S. Supreme Ct. 1978, U.S. Ct. Appeals (5th cir.) 1979, U.S. Dist. Ct. (no. dist.) Tex. 1982, U.S. Dist. Ct. (we. and ea. dists.) Tex. 1983. Assoc. Troutman, Earle & Hill, Austin, 1975-76, Simpson & Burwell, Texas City, 1976-78, Smith & Herz, Galveston, Tex., 1978-80; ptnr. Dibrell & Greer, Galveston, 1980-85, Barlow, Todd, Crews & Jordan PC, Houston, 1986-88, Barlow, Todd, Jordan & Oliver, LLP, Houston, 1988-99, Barlow, Todd, Jordan & Jones, LLP, Houston, 1999—. Commr. Commn. Texas City/Galveston Ports, 1984. 1st lt. USAF, 1971-77. Recipient Outstanding Young Man Am. award, U.S. Jaycees, 1980. Mem. Tex. Bar Assn., Galveston County Bar Assn. (pres. 1981-82, bd. dirs. 1985-88), Tex. Young Lawyers Assn (bd. dirs. 1982-85, Outstanding Dir. award 1983-84), Galveston County Young Lawyers Assn. (pres. 1979-80, Outstanding Young Lawyer award 1981). Federal civil litigation, State civil litigation. Office: Barlow Todd Jordan LLP 17225 El Camino Real Ste 400 Houston TX 77058-2768

**JORDAN, DAVID FRANCIS, JR.,** retired judge; b. N.Y.C., Apr. 18, 1928; s. David Francis Jordan and Frances Marion (J.) Edebohls; m. Bess Vukas, Aug. 4, 1956; children: Melissa Marie, David Francis III, Dennis Paul. AB, Princeton U., 1950; JD, NYU, 1953, LLM in Taxation, 1970. Law clk. U.S. Ct. Appeals (2d cir.), 1957-58, chief dep., clk., 1958-59; sole practice, Smithtown, N.Y., 1959-63; ptnr. O'Rourke & Jordan, Central Islip, N.Y., 1963-67; asst. dist. atty. Suffolk County, Riverhead, N.Y., 1969-74; law clk. Supreme Ct., Suffolk County, 1975; investigator N.Y. Supreme Ct. Appellate Div. 2d dept., Bklyn., 1976; corp. counsel City of Newburgh, N.Y., 1976-78; acting city mgr., 1978; U.S. magistrate judge Ea. Dist. N.Y., Bklyn., Uniondale and Hauppauge, N.Y., 1978-94, So. Dist. Calif., San Diego, 1994, So. Dist. Ohio, 1996; mil. judge U.S. Army Judiciary, Washington, 1969-80; legislative analyst Cen. and Ea. European Law Initiative. Served with JAGC, U.S. Army, 1954-57, to col. USAR. Decorated Meritorious Service medal. Mem. ABA (vice chair sr. lawyers divsn. jud. com. 1994-97). Home: 15732 Vista Vicente Dr Ramona CA 92065-4323

**JORDAN, EDDIE J.,** prosecutor; b. Ft. Campbell, Ky., Oct. 6, 1952. BA with honors, Wesleyan U., 1974; JD, Rutgers U., 1977. Bar: Pa. 1977, La. 1982. Law clk. for Hon. Clifford Scott Green U.S. Dist. Ct. (ea. dist.) Pa., Phila.; assoc. Pepper, Hamilton & Scheetz, Phila.; asst. prof. law So. U., Baton Rouge, 1981-83; asst. U.S. atty. U.S. Dept. Justice, New Orleans, 1984-87; assoc. Sessions & Fishman, New Orleans, 1987-91, ptnr., 1991-92; of counsel Bryan Jupiter, New Orleans, 1992-94; U.S. atty. for ea. dist. La. U.S. Dept. Justice, New Orleans, 1994—. Mem. adv. com. on humam rels. City of New Orleans, 1993; mem. various bds. of dirs. Recipient A.P. Tureaud award Louis A. Martinet Legal Soc., 1992. Office: US Atty Ea Dist La Hale Boggs Bldg 501 Magazine St New Orleans LA 70130-3319*

**JORDAN, JOHN JOSEPH,** lawyer; b. Scranton, Pa., Jan. 30, 1965; s. John Joseph and Anne Marie Jordan; m. Lorena M. Alvarez, Dec. 26, 1993; 1 child, Maximiliano José. BS in Agr., U. Ariz., 1989; JD, St. Mary's U., 1996. Bar: Tex. 1996, U.S. Dist. Ct. (so. dist.) Tex. 1997, U.S. Ct. Appeals (5th cir.) 1997. Briefing atty. U.S. Dist. Ct. (so. dist.) Tex., Brownsville, 1996-97; atty. Roerig Oliveira & Fisher, Brownsville, 1997—. Federal civil litigation, State civil litigation, Insurance. Home: 1244 Cedar Ridge Dr Brownsville TX 78520-9208 Office: Roerig Oliveira & Fisher 855 W Price Rd Brownsville TX 78520-8718

**JORDAN, PAUL RODGERS, III,** lawyer; b. Marion, Ohio, July 6, 1948; s. Paul Rodgers and Joyce Leora (Cox) J.; m. Virginia Lee Morris, Mar. 1966 (div. Jan. 1976); children: Kristina Lee, Timothy Owen; m. Pamela Jane Wright, Jan. 27, 1979; children: Samuel Zachary, Laura Wright. BA cum laude, Millsaps Coll., 1970; JD, Emory U. Sch. Law, 1973. Bar: Ga. 1973. Atty. Rich, Bass, Kidd & Broome, Decatur, Ga., 1973, Westmoreland, Hall & McGee, Atlanta, 1974-79, Fine & Block, Atlanta, 1979-96; atty., ptnr. Lawson, Davis, Pickren & Seydel, Atlanta, 1996—. Mem. Am. Trial Lawyers Assn., Ga. Trial Lawyers Assn., Atlanta Bar Assn., Lawyers Club of Atlanta, Rotary Club Atlanta, West End (sgt. at arms 1998—). Presbyterian. General civil litigation, General practice. Office: Lawson Davis Pickren & Seydel LLP 2500 Marquis Two Tower 285 Peachtree Center Ave NE Atlanta GA 30303-1229

**JORDAN, ROBERT LEON,** lawyer, educator; b. Reading, Pa., Feb. 27, 1928; s. Anthony and Carmela (Votto) J.; m. Evelyn Allen Willard, Feb. 15, 1958 (dec. Nov. 1996); children: John Willard, David Anthony. BA, Pa. State U., 1948; LLB, Harvard U., 1951. Bar: N.Y. 1952. Assoc. White & Case, N.Y.C., 1953-59; prof. law UCLA, 1959-70, 75-91, prof. law emeritus, 1991—, assoc. dean Sch. Law, 1968-69; vis. prof. law Cornell U., Ithaca, N.Y., 1962-63; co-reporter Uniform Consumer Credit Code, 1964-70, Uniform Comml. Code Articles 3, 4, 4A, 1985-90; Fulbright lectr. U. Pisa, Italy, 1967-68. Co-author: (with W.D. Warren) Commercial Law, 1983, 4th edit., 1997, Bankruptcy, 1985, 5th edit., 1999. Lt. USAF, 1951-53. Office: UCLA Sch Law 405 Hilgard Ave Los Angeles CA 90095-9000

**JORDAN, ROBERT LEON,** federal judge; b. Woodlawn, Tenn., June 28, 1934; s. James Richard and Josephine (Broadbent) J.; m. Dorothy Rueter, Sept. 8, 1956; children: Robert, Margaret, Daniel. BS in Fin., U. Tenn., 1958, JD, 1960. Atty. Goodpasture, Carpenter, Dale & Woods, Nashville, 1960-61; mgr. Frontier Refining Co., Denver, 1961-64; atty. Green and Green, Johnson City, Tenn., 1964-66; trust officer 1st Peoples Bank, Johnson City, 1966-69; v.p., trust officer Comml. Nat. Bank, Pensacola, Fla., 1969-71; atty. Bryant, Price, Brandt & Jordan, Johnson City, 1971-80; chancellor 1st Jud. Dist., Johnson City, 1980-88; dist. judge U.S. Dist. Ct. (ea. dist.) Tenn., Knoxville, 1988—; mem. adv. com. U. Tenn. Law Alumni, 1978-80; sec. Tenn. Jud. Conf., 1987-88, mem. exec. com., 1988; del. Tenn. State-Fed. Judicial Coun., 1993—. Bd. dirs., v.p. Tri-Cities estate Planning Coun., Johnson City, 1969; bd. dirs. Washington County Tb Assn., Rocky Mount Hist. Assn., High Rock Camp, Johnson City, Jr. Achievement of Pensacola Inc.; bd. dirs., treas. N.W. Fla. Crippled Children's Assn., Pensacola; chancellor's assoc. U. Tenn. With U.S. Army, 1954-56. Named Boss of Yr. Legal Secs. Assn., Washington, Carter County, Tenn., 1982. Mem. Tenn. Bar Assn., Knoxville Bar Assn. (bd. govs.), Washington County Bar Assn. (pres.-elect 1980), Johnson City C. of C., Hamilton Burnett Am. Inn of Ct. (pres. 1993-94), Kiwanis (pres. Met. Johnson City Club 1969, Kiwanian of Yr. award 1986-87). Republican. Mem. Ch. of Christ. Office: Howard H Baker US Courthouse 800 Market St Ste 141 Knoxville TN 37902-2303

**JORDAN, SANDRA DICKERSON,** law educator; b. Phila., Dec. 3, 1951; m. Byron Neal Jordan, July 21, 1973; children: Nedra Catherine, Byron Neal II. BS in Edn., Wilberforce U., 1973; JD, U. Pitts., 1979. Bar: Pa. 1979, U.S. Dist. Ct. (we. dist.) Pa. 1979, U.S. Ct. Appeals (3d cir.) 1979. Asst. U.S. atty. U.S. Dept. Justice, Pitts., 1979-88; assoc. ind. counsel Ind. Counsel-Iran/Contra, Washington, 1988-91; prof. U. Pitts. Sch. Law, 1988—, assoc. dean, 1993—; jud. ct. bd. Commonwealth of Pa., 1995—; hearing com. disciplinary bd. Pa. Supreme Ct., PItts., 1989-95; lectr. U.S. Dept. Justice, Pa. Trial Judges Assn., Acad. Trial Lawyers, Pa. Bar Inst. Author tng. video in field, 1982; contbr. articles to profl. jours. Vice pres. Health and Welfare Planning Commn., Pitts., 1986-89; mem. Program to Aid Citizen Enterprise, Pitts., 1983—. Mem. ABA (mem. white collar crimes com. 1988—), Homer S. Brown Law Assn., Allegheny County Bar Assn., Nat. Bar Assn., Urban League (v.p. Pitts. chpt. 1988-90), Alpha Kappa Mu, Alpha Kappa Alpha. Avocation: scuba diving. Office: U Pitts Law Sch 3900 Forbes Ave Pittsburgh PA 15213

**JORDAN, SUSAN PATRICIA,** lawyer; b. Oak Park, Ill., Dec. 10, 1952; d. Forbes Edward and Bette (Kleinow) J.; 1 child, Sarah Rose. BA, Northwestern U., 1973, MAT, 1974; CAS, Harvard U., 1978; JD, Georgetown U., 1984. Bar: N.Y. 1985, Ill. 1987, U.S. Dist. Ct. (so. dist.) N.Y. 1985, U.S. Dist. Ct. (no. dist.) Ill. 1987. Assoc. Cravath, Swaine & Moore, N.Y.C., 1984-87, Kirkland & Ellis, Chgo., 1987-92, Lord, Bissell & Brook, Chgo., 1992—. Presbyterian. General civil litigation, Insurance. Home: 1440 N Lake Shore Dr Apt 27D Chicago IL 60610-1686 Office: Lord Bissell & Brook 115 S La Salle St Ste 3200 Chicago IL 60603-3972

**JORDAN, VERNON MURRAY,** judge; b. Floresville, Tex., Feb. 9, 1935; s. Vernon Elton and Gertrude Bailey (Murray) J.; m. Sherron L. Smith (div. 1979); children: Vernon Murray Jr., Jennifer J. Jordan Orrell; m. Jeanette H. Jordan, 1991. BBA, U. Tex., 1957, JD, 1959. Trial counselor U.S. Navy, 1959-62; asst. atty. gen. State of Tex., 1963-64; county atty. McCulloch County, Brady, Tex., 1965-70; dist. atty. 198th Jud. Dist., Tex., 1970-77, dist. judge, 1977-91; sr. dist. judge State of Tex., 1991—. Home: 1501 S Pine St Brady TX 76825-6537

**JORDEN, DOUGLAS ALLEN,** lawyer, zoning hearing officer; b. Ft. Smith, Ark., July 17, 1950; s. James Roy and Gordon P. J.; m. Mary Zoe Arendt, Apr. 23, 1983; children: Michael, Willie, Julia. BA, U. Ark., 1972, JD, 1976. Bar: Ark. 1976, Ariz. 1976, U.S. Dist. Ct. Ariz. 1976, U.S. Ct. Appeals (9th cir.) 1977, Calif. 1992, Colo. 1992, U.S. Supreme Ct. 1996. Assoc. Harold Mott Esq., Phoenix, 1976-78; town atty. Town of Paradise Valley, Ariz., 1978-82; assoc. Fennemore Craig, Phoenix, 1982-84; ptnr. Slavin, Kane & Paterson, Phoenix, 1984-88, Lancy, Scult, McVey, Phoenix, 1988-90, Jorden Law Firm, Phoenix, 1990-92, Kane, Jorden, von Oppenfeld, Phoenix, 1992-98, Jorden & Bischoff, Phoenix, 1998—. Co-author: Arizona Land Use Law, 1988, 2d rev. edit. 1998. Mem. Paradise Valley Village Planning Com. 1988-90; chmn. Phoenix Environ. Quality Commn., 1988-95. Mem. State Bar Ariz. (continuing legal edn. com. 1990-94), Rocky Mt. Land Use Inst. (regional adv. bd. 1992—). Democrat. Methodist. Avocation: hiking. Land use and zoning (including planning), Real property, Environmental. Office: Jorden & Bischoff 4201 N 24th St Ste 300 Phoenix AZ 85016-6268

**JORGENSEN, DONALD LEROY,** judge; b. Kenmare, N.D., Sept. 23, 1944; s. Karl Alfred and Elsie Tina (Erickson) J.; m. Aug. 5, 1967; children: Damon, Heather, Heidi. PhB, U. N.D., 1967, JD, 1970; diploma jud. skills, Am. Acad. Jud. Edn., Tuscaloosa, Ala., 1992. Bar; N.D. 1970, U.S. Federal 1973. Asst. states atty. Stark County, Dickinson, N.D., 1973-82, county judge, 1982-84; dist. judge S.W. Jud. Dist. N.D., Hettinger, 1984-95, South Ctrl. Jud. Dist. N.D., Linton and Bismarck, 1995—. Pres. Dickinson C. of C., 1983. With JAGC, U.S. Army, 1971-73. Mem. Nat. Juvenile and Family Ct. Judges (chmn. rural cts. com. 1993-95), N.D. Bar Assn. (various offices), KC (grand knight). Office: South Ctrl Jud Dist Ct PO Box 1019 Bismarck ND 58502-1019

**JORGENSEN, ERIK HOLGER,** lawyer; b. Copenhagen, July 19, 1916; s. Holger and Karla (Andersen) J.; children: Jette Friis, Lone Olesen, John, Jean Ann. JD, San Francisco Law Sch., 1960. Bar: Calif. 1961. Pvt. practice law, 1961-70; ptnr. Hersh, Hadfield, Jorgensen & Fried, San Francisco, 1970-76, Hadfield & Jorgensen, San Francisco, 1976-88 . Pres. Aldersly, Danish Retirement Home, San Rafael, Calif., 1974-77, Rebild Park Soc. Bay Area chpt., 1974-77. Fellow Scandinavian Am. Found. (hon.); mem. ABA, San Francisco Lawyers Club, Bar Assn. of San Francisco, Calif. Assn. Realtors (hon. life bd. dirs.). Author: Master Forms Guide for Successful Real Estate Agreements, Successful Real Estate Sales Agreements, 1991; contbr. articles on law and real estate law to profl. jours. General practice, Real property, Probate.

**JORGENSEN, LAUREN,** lawyer; b. Miami, Fla., Aug. 14, 1962; d. Otto J. Jorgensen and Sandra Thompson. BS, U. Ala., 1983; JD, Cornell U., 1986. Bar: N.Y. 1987, Fla. 1987. Assoc. Shea & Gould, N.Y.C., 1986-88, Stillman, Friedman & Shaw, N.Y.C., 1988-90; asst. U.S. atty. So. Dist. Fla., Miami, 1990—. Chmn. Beautification Com. City of Coral Gables. Mem. Internat. Palm Soc., Tropical Audubon Soc., Friends of the Everglades, Fairchild Tropical Garden. Democrat. Roman Catholic. Avocations: tennis, running, literature, historic preservation, tropical gardening. Criminal, Environmental, Municipal (including bonds). Office: US Attys Office 99 NE 4th St Ste 411 Miami FL 33132-2131

**JORGENSEN, NORMAN ERIC,** lawyer; b. Oakland, Calif., July 13, 1938; s. Peter Wesley and Janet Marie Jorgensen; m. Concetta Finocchio, Aug. 3, 1963 (div.); children: Eric Vincent, Joseph Peter, Catherine Ann Jorgensen Martinsen, Lara Lynn; m. Connie Enkelking, Feb. 4, 1979. BS in Physics, MIT, 1960; postgrad., Princeton U., 1960-61, U. Calif., Berkeley, 1961-65; JD, U. Calif., Berkeley, 1968. Bar: Calif. 1969, U.S. Dist. Ct. (no. dist.) Calif. 1969, U.S. Ct. Appeals (9th cir.) 1969, Oreg. 1973, U.S. Ct. Claims 1973, U.S.Dist. Ct. (ctrl. dist.) Calif. 1974, U.S. Dist. Ct. Oreg. 1976, U.S. Supreme Ct. 1976, U.S. Ct. Appeals (fed. cir.) 1982, U.S. Patent and Trademark Office 1993. Pvt. practice, Oakland, 1969-71; ptnr. Grose Rose & Jorgensen, Oakland, 1971-73; assoc. gen. counsel Tektronix Inc., Beaverton, Oreg., 1973-90; group counsel Intel Corp., Santa Clara, Calif., 1990-91; pvt. practice, San Jose, Calif., 1991—. Mem. Calif. State Bar, Oreg. State Bar, Santa Clara County Bar Assn. Intellectual property, General corporate, Patent. Office: 3465 Sierra Rd Ste 1000 San Jose CA 95132-3000

**JORGENSEN, RALPH GUBLER,** lawyer, accountant; b. N.Y.C., Mar. 12, 1937; s. Thorvald W. and Florence (Gubler) J.; m. Patricia June Spivey, June 21, 1971 (dec. Oct. 1997); 1 child, Misty. AB, George Washington U., 1960, LLB, 1962. CPA, Md., Nev., N.C. Bar: D.C. 1963, Md. 1963, U.S. Dist. Ct. D.C. 1963, U.S. Ct. Appeals (D.C. cir.) 1963, U.S. Dist. Ct. Md. 1964, U.S. Supreme Ct. 1971, N.C. 1972, U.S. Dist. Ct. (ea. dist.) N.C. 1972, U.S. Ct. Appeals (4th cir.) 1974, U.S. Tax Ct. 1976, U.S. Dist. Ct. (mid. dist.) N.C. 1977, U.S. Ct. Clms. 1979. Sole practice, Washington and Silver Spring, Md., 1963-71, Tabor City, N.C., 1971—. Bd. dirs. Columbus County ARC, N.C., 1974. Mem. ATLA, Am. Assn. Atty.-CPAs, N.C. Bar Assn., N.C. Acad. Trial Lawyers, Alpha Kappa Psi. Democrat. Baptist. Federal civil litigation, State civil litigation, Taxation, general. Home: 101 Pireway Rd Tabor City NC 28463-2021 Office: 116 W 4th St PO Box 248 Tabor City NC 28463-0248

**JOSCELYN, KENT BUCKLEY,** lawyer; b. Binghamton, N.Y., Dec. 18, 1936; s. Raymond Miles and Gwen Buckley (Smith) J.; children: Kathryn Anne, Jennifer Sheldon. BS, Union Coll., 1957; JD, Albany (N.Y.) Law Sch., 1960. Bar: N.Y. 1961, U.S. Ct. Mil. Appeals 1962, D.C., 1967, Mich. 1979. Atty. adviser hdqts. USAF, Washington, 1965-67; assoc. prof. forensic studies U. Ind., Bloomington, 1967-76; dir. Inst. Rsch. in Pub. Safety, 1970-75; head policy analysis divsn. Highway Safety Rsch. Inst. U. Mich., Ann Arbor, 1976-81; dir. transp. planning and policy Urban Tech. Environ. Planning Program, Ann Arbor, 1981-84; prin. Joscelyn and Treat P.C., Ann Arbor, 1981-83, Joscelyn, McNair & Jeffrey P.C., Ann Arbor, 1993—; cons. Law Enforcement Assistance Adminstrn., U.S. Dept. Justice, 1969-72; Gov.'s appointee as regional dir. Ind. Criminal Justice Planning Agy., 1969-72; vice chmn. Ind. Organized Crime Prevention Coun., 1969-72; commr. pub. safety City of Bloomington, Ind., 1974-76. Editor Internat. Jour. Criminal Justice. Capt. USAF, 1961-64. Mem. NAS, ABA, NRC, D.C. Bar Assn., N.Y. State Bar Assn., Internat. Bar Assn., Transp. Rsch. Bd. (chmn. motor vehicle and traffic law com. 1979-82), Am. Soc. Criminology (life), Assn. for Advancement Automotive Medicine (life), Soc. Automotive Engrs., Acad. Criminal Justice Scis. (life), Assn. Chiefs Police (assoc.), Nat. Safety Coun., Assn. Former Intelligence Officers (life), Product Liability Adv. Coun., Sigma Xi, Theta Delta Chi. E-mail: jmjpc@msn.com. General civil litigation, Product liability, Estate planning. Office: Joscelyn McNair & Jeffrey PC PO Box 130589 Ann Arbor MI 48113-0589

**JOSEPH, ALAN LLOYD,** lawyer; b. Monticello, N.Y., Dec. 28, 1953. BS in Criminal Justice magna cum laude, Wilmington Coll., 1974; JD, Cardozo Sch. Law, N.Y.C., 1979. Bar: N.Y. 1979, U.S. Dist. Ct. (so. dist.) N.Y. Atty. Baum & Shawn, Monticello, 1980; paralegal, investigator Sullivan County Legal Aid, Monticello, 1974-76; staff atty. Sullivan County legal Aid, Monticello, 1980-83; asst. dist. atty. Orange County Dist. Atty., Goshen, N.Y., 1983-85, chief asst. dist. atty., 1985-91; sole practitioner Goshen, 1991—. Mem. N.Y. State Bar Assn. Criminal, General corporate, Real property. Office: 261 Greenwich Ave Goshen NY 10924-2028

**JOSEPH, CHARLES IAN,** lawyer; b. Boston, Dec. 24, 1968; s. Larry Michael and Phoebe Geyer J. BA, Conn. Coll., 1991; JD, U. Balt., 1995. Bar: Md. 1995, U.S. Dist. Ct. (no. dist.) Md. 1996. Law clk. to Hon. Robert F. Fischer Annapolis, Md., 1995-96; lawyer Anderson, Coe & King LLP, Balt., 1996—. Mem. Md. Bar Assn., Md. Def. Counsel, Balt. City Lead Paint Commn. Avocations: weightlifting, running, playing guitar. General civil litigation, Product liability, Personal injury. Home: 107 Cross Keys Rd Apt A Baltimore MD 21210-1531 Office: Anderson Coe & King LLP 201 N Charles St Ste 2000 Baltimore MD 21201-4124

**JOSEPH, DANIEL,** lawyer; b. New Kensington, Pa., Apr. 7, 1946; s. Daniel William and Mary Ellen (Anis) J.; m. Judith A. Joseph, Dec. 20, 1969 (div. June 1982); 1 child, Robert Daniel. BS in Math., Mt. Union Coll., 1968; JD, Duquesne U., 1972. Bar: Pa. 1972, U.S. Dist. Ct. (ea. and we dists.) Pa. 1974, U.S. Ct. Appeals (3d. cir.) 1974, U.S. Surpeme Ct. 1977. Law clk. Justice Louis L. Mandarino Pa. Supreme Ct., Monessen, Pa., 1972-74; asst. dist. atty. Dist. Attys. Office Westmoreland County, Greensburg, Pa., 1974-79, asst. pub. defender, 1981-83; atty. pvt. practice, New Kensington, Pa., 1974-94; ptnr. George & Joseph, New Kensington, Pa., 1994—. With U.S. Army, 1968-74. Rev. Cornelius McCardie scholar Duquesne U. Sch. Law, 1970. Mem. Pa. Trial Lawyers Assn., Westmoreland Bar Assn. (bd. dirs. 1993—, pres. 1998), Westmoreland County Bar Assn. (chmn. criminal law com.), We. Pa. Trial Lawyers Assn., Westmoreland County Acad. Trial Lawyers. Avocations: skiing, boating, scuba diving. Criminal, Personal injury, Workers' compensation. Home: 230 White Oak Dr New Kensingtn PA 15068-6724 Office: George & Joseph 2300 Freeport Rd 10 Felderelli Sq New Kensington PA 15068

**JOSEPH, GREGORY PAUL,** lawyer; b. Mpls., Jan. 18, 1951; s. George Phillip and Josephine Sheha (Nofel) J.; m. Barbara, Jan. 19, 1979. BA summa cum laude, U. Minn., 1972, JD cum laude, 1975. Bar: Minn. 1975, N.Y. 1979, U.S. Dist. Ct. Minn. 1975, U.S. Dist. Ct. (so. and ea. dist.) N.Y. 1979, U.S. Ct. Appeals (8th cir.) 1976, U.S. Ct. Appeals (2d cir.) 1979, U.S. Ct. Appeals (D.C. cir.) 1980, U.S. Supreme Ct. 1983, U.S. Tax Ct. 1987, U.S. Ct. Appeals (7th cir.) 1989, (5th cir.) 1992, (6th cir.) 1999. Pvt. practice Mpls., 1975-79; assoc. Fried, Frank, Harris, Shriver & Jacobson, N.Y.C., 1979-82, ptnr., 1982—; asst. U.S. spl. prosecutor N.Y.C., Washington, 1981-82; mem. U.S. Judicial Conf. adv. com. on fed. rules of evidence, 1993-99; chair Com. of Lawyers to Enhance the Jury Process, N.Y. State Cts., 1998-99, mem. Adv. Com. on Civil Practice, 1999—. Author: Modern Visual Evidence, 1984, Sanctions: The Federal Law of Litigation Abuse, 1989 2d edit., 1994, Civil RICO: A Definitive Guide, 1992; co-author: Evidence in America, 1987; editor: Emerging Problems Under the Federal Rules of Evidence, 1983, reporter 2d edit., 1991; co-editor: Sanctions: Rule 11 and Other Powers, 1986, 2d rev. edit., 1988; editorial bd. Moore's Fed. Practice, 1995—; contbr. articles to profl. jours. Fellow Am. Bar Found., Am. Coll. Trial Lawyers (chair downstate N.Y. com. 1996-98); mem. ABA (chmn. litig. sect. 1997-98), Am. Law Inst., N.Y. Bar Assn. (chair trial evidence com. 1988-94), Minn. Bar Assn., N.Y. County Lawyers Assn., Assn. of Bar of City of N.Y. (chmn. profl. responsibility com. 1993-96, mem. exec. com. 1999—). Federal civil litigation, State civil litigation. Home: 188 E 70th St Apt 25A New York NY 10021-5170 Office: Fried Frank Harris Shriver & Jacobson 1 New York Plz Fl 24 New York NY 10004-1901

**JOSEPH, IRWIN H.,** lawyer; b. L.A., Nov. 6, 1947; s. Peter and Gertrude J.; m. Gail Schwartz, Apr. 15, 1981; childre: Noona, Bae-Jin. BA, UCLA, 1969; JD, LaVerne U., 1982. Bar: Calif. 1982, U.S. Dist. Ct. (all dists.) Calif. 1982, U.S. Ct. Claims 1996. Atty. Britton, Jackson, Santa Cruz, Calif., 1982-88; ptnr. Baskin Grant & Joseph, Santa Cruz, 1988-95; atty. pvt. practice, Santa Cruz, 1996—. Sgt. U.S. Army Res., 1969-95. Mem. Santa Cruz Trial Lawyers Assn. (pres. 1996, bd. dirs.). Consumer commercial, Contracts commercial, Alternative dispute resolution. Office: 125 Jewell St Santa Cruz CA 95060-1717

**JOSEPH, JEFFREY ALAN,** lawyer; b. Chgo., Aug. 3, 1947; s. Bryan Kenneth Joseph and Carol Maxine Cummings; m. Valerie Ann Pearson, Sept. 12, 1981; children: Adriana, Bryan. BA, U. Calif., Berkeley, 1969; JD, U. Calif., Davis, 1972. Bar: Calif. 1972, U.S. Dist. Ct. (ea. dist.) Calif. 1972, U.S. Dist. Ct. (so. dist.) Calif. 1973. Dep. atty. Calif. Atty. Gen.'s Office, Sacramento and San Diego, 1972-79; prin. atty. spl. prosecuting unit Calif. Atty. Gen.'s Office, San Diego, 1979-80; dep. chief counsel Calif. Dept. Transp., San Diego, 1980—; arbitrator, mediator San Diego Superior Ct., 1983—, superior judge pro tem, 1992—; adj. prof. law Thomas Jefferson Sch. of Law, San Diego, 1990—; bd. dirs. Assn. Calif. State Attys., 1982-83. Pres. Stella Maris Sch. Bd., La Jolla, Calif., 1996-97. Mem. San Diego County Bar Assn. Roman Catholic. Avocations: music, flute, guitar, basketball, history. Office: Calif Dept Transp Legal Divsn 610 W Ash St Ste 805 San Diego CA 92101-3346

**JOSEPH, JOHN JAMES,** lawyer; b. Owen Sound, Ont., Can., July 10, 1953; came to U.S., 1961; s. Thomas Anthony and Freda (Salome) J.; children: Jamie, Jennifer, Justin; m. Jennifer Jones, Oct. 11, 1991. BE summa cum laude, Ohio State U., 1978, JD with honors, 1981. Bar: Ohio 1981, U.S. Dist. Ct. (so. dist.) Ohio 1982. V.p., asst. to pres. T.A. Joseph Ltd., Owen Sound, 1971-86; assoc. Carlile, Patchen, Murphy & Allison, Columbus, Ohio, 1981-86, ptnr., 1987-88; ptnr. Benesch, Friedlander, Coplan & Aranoff, Columbus, 1988-92, Joseph & Joseph, Columbus, 1992—; lectr. in field. Fellow Columbus Bar Assn. (real property and fin. inst. coms., co-chmn. Real Property Law Inst. 1989-90, chmn. real property com. 1991); mem. ABA (corp. bus. and banking, real property probate and tax law sects.), Ohio Bar Assn., Cen. Ohio Soccer Assn. (pres., trustee 1984-91), Phi Kappa Phi. Democrat. Avocations: jogging, soccer, tennis, photography, music. Real property, Contracts commercial, Landlord-tenant. Home: 8854 Gailes Ct Dublin OH 43017-9408 Office: Joseph & Joseph 931 S Front St Columbus OH 43206-2520

**JOSEPH, MARC WARD,** lawyer, human resources professional; b. Harlan, Ky., Apr. 2, 1953; s. Julius C. and Mildred (Daniel) J.; m. Margaret Ann Lilly, Feb. 6, 1988; children: Christopher Marc, Samuel Morgan. BS, U.S. Naval Acad., 1975; JD, Vanderbilt U., 1983. Bar: Tex. 1983, U.S. Dist. Ct. N.D., Tex. 1983, U.S. Claims Ct. 1984, U.S. Ct. Appeals (5th cir.) 1985. Assoc. Rain Harrell Emery Young & Doke, Dallas, 1983-85, Carrington, Coleman, Sloman & Blumenthal, Dallas, 1985-90; litigation counsel Electronic Data Sys. Corp., Plano, Tex., 1990-94; gen. counsel Haggar Clothing Co., Dallas, 1994-95, v.p., gen. counsel, 1995-98, sr. v.p. human resources, gen. counsel, 1998—. Contbr. articles to law revs. Bd. dirs. Equest, Dallas, 1990-92. Lt. USN, 1975-80. Mem. ABA. Methodist. General civil litigation, Contracts commercial, General corporate. Office: Haggar Clothing Co 6113 Lemmon Ave Dallas TX 75209-5715

**JOSEPH, MICHAEL BRANDES,** lawyer; b. Phila., Oct. 12, 1950; s. Arthur W. and Judith (Brandes) J.; m. Dayle Press, Mar. 25, 1973; children: Adam, Daniel. AB, Rutgers U., 1972; JD, Widener U., 1975. Bar: Del. 1976, N.J. 1977, Pa. 1976, U.S. Dist. Ct. Del. 1976, U.S. Dist. Ct. N.J. 1977, U.S. Dist. Ct. Pa. 1976, U.S. Ct. Appeals (3rd cir.) 1990. Lawyer UAW Legal Svcs. Plan, Wilmington, Del., 1979-81; pvt. practice Wilmington, 1981-90; ptnr. Ferry Joseph & Fink, Wilmington, 1990—. Contbr. articles to profl. jours. Pres., bd. trustees Congr. Beth Emeth, Wilmington, 1993—; chmn., bd. mgrs. YMCA-Resource Ctr., Wilmington, 1984-86. Recipient Outstanding Vol. YMCA-Resource Ctr., 1986. Mem. Nat. Assn. of Chpt. 13 Trustee (com. legis. 1990—), Nat. Assn. of Bankruptcy Trustee, Assn. Bankruptcy Profls. (treas.). Bankruptcy, Consumer commercial. Office: Ferry Joseph & Fink 824 Market St PO Box 1351 Wilmington DE 19899-1351

**JOSEPH, MICHAEL P.,** lawyer; b. Bklyn., Dec. 18, 1945; s. Harry and Stephanie Joseph; m. Anne L. Walker, Dec. 30, 1979; children: Adam, Brett. BA, Franklin and Marshall, 1968; JD, NYU, 1971. Bar: N.Y. 1972, U.S. Dist. Ct. (so. and ea. dists.) N.Y. 1976, U.S. Ct. Appeals (2nd and 11th cirs.) 1976. Lawyer Legal Aid Soc., N.Y.C., 1971-75; ptnr. Joseph and Stalonas, N.Y.C., 1976—. Mem. Criminal Bar State N.Y., Criminal Bar Assn. City N.Y., N.Y. Coun. Lawyers. Family and matrimonial, Criminal. Office: Joseph and Stalonas 233 Broadway New York NY 10279-0001

**JOSEPH, PAUL R,** law educator; b. Los Angeles, Apr. 30, 1951; s. Lawrence H. Joseph and Barbara A. (Acoff) Brittin; m. Lynn Wolf, 1990. BA, Goddard Coll., 1973; JD, U. Calif., Davis, 1977; LLM, Temple U., 1979. Bar: Calif. 1977, U.S. Supreme Ct. 1981, U.S. Ct. Appeals (9th cir.) 1982, U.S. Ct. Appeals (11th cir.) 1987. Lectr. law, teaching fellow Temple U., Phila., 1977-79; asst. prof. Salmon Chase Coll. Law No. Ky. U., Highland Heights, 1979-82, assoc. prof., 1982-84; assoc. prof. Nova Southeastern U., Ft. Lauderdale, Fla., 1984-88, prof., 1988—, dir. internat. programs, 1996-98, Goodwin prof., 1999, assoc. dean internat. and external programs, 1999—; mem. interview team Benjamin Franklin Fellowship Program, 1992; frequent spkr. on law topics, including search and seizure and civil liberties, and the use of computers in legal edn., law and popular culture; lectr. in field, Eng., Russia. Author: Warrantless Search Law, 1991 (updated yearly); co-editor: Prime Time Law: Fictional Television as Legal Narrative, 1998; mem. editl. bd. Human Rights mag., 1986-95, Legal Studies Forum, 1998-99; columnist Visions mag., 1995; contbr. MSNBC Website, 1996-97 and articles to profl. jours.; editor Picturing Justice Website, 1998—. Mem. Broward County Human Rights Bd., 1986-92, vice chmn., 1987-88, chmn., 1991-92; trustee Goddard Coll., 1981-90, 95-96, vice chmn. bd. dirs., 1985-86, chmn. fin. com., 1986-89, chmn. presdl. search com., 1989-90, chmn. acad. and student affairs com., 1995-96; mem. Broward County Dem. Exec. Com., 1988-92; bd. dirs. Inter-Am. Ctr. for Human Rights, 1997—. Mem. ABA (chair, liaison to state and local individual rights sects. 1991-95, individual rights and responsibilities sect. liaison to spl. com. on the drug crisis 1991-95, standing com. on Gavel awards 1996—), ACLU (nat. bd. 1995-97, chmn. Broward County chpt. 1985-86, 90-91, chmn. legal panel 1984-85, 86-87, Fla. state bd. dirs. 1985-97, chmn. legal programs com. 1986-87, pres. 1990-93, del. to nat. conv. 1987, 89, 91, 95, chair nat. affiliate leadership network 1991-93), Fla. Bar Assn. (faculty affiliate, exec. coun. pub. interest sect. 1990-92). Democrat. Avocations: computers, Irish music, travel. Office: Nova Southeastern U Shepard Broad Law Ctr 3305 College Ave Fort Lauderdale FL 33314-7721

**JOSEPH, RAYMOND,** lawyer; b. Lansing, Mich., Jan. 21, 1924; s. John Gamel and Lena (Tobia) J.; divorced; children: Gina Marie, Mark Raymond. Student, Mich. State U., 1948; JD, Wayne State U., 1951. Law clk. to presiding justice Mich. Supreme Ct., 1953-54; with Raymond Joseph & Assocs., Lansing, 1952—. Pres. Lansing Symphony Assn. 1967-69; officer, dir. Opera Co. Mid-Mich., Kresge Art Mus., Lansing Art Gallery, Lansing Ballet Assn., Mich. Orchestral Assn. Lt. USAAF, 1943-45, ETO. Decorated 7 Air medals for combat flying; recipient presdl. citation for 35 combat missions, 1944. Mem. ABA, Mich. Bar Assn., Ingham County Bar Assn. (sec. 1954-56), Assn. Trial Lawyers Am., Mich. Trial Lawyers Assn., Am. Judicature Soc. (fed. ct. mediator), Def. Rsch. Inst. Democrat. Mem. Christian Ch. Avocations: art and art history, classical music, reading, tennis. Insurance, Aviation, Federal civil litigation. Home and Office: 713 Applegate Ln East Lansing MI 48823-2109

**JOSEPH, ROBERT GEORGE,** lawyer, consultant; b. Cleve., Dec. 1, 1948; s. Shaffie Charles and Mary Alice (Joseph) J.; m. Diane Selinger, June 8, 1974; children: Daniel Selinger, Edward Michael. Student, U. Md., 1967-69; BA, U. Tenn., 1972; JD, Ohio State U., 1975. Bar: Ohio 1975, D.C. 1976, U.S. Ct. Appeals (D.C. cir.) 1976. Law clk. to judge U.S. Ct. Appeals (D.C. cir.), Washington, 1975-76; assoc. Howrey & Simon, Washington, 1976-84; officer, dir. Law Resources Inc., Washington, 1984—. Editor-in-Chief Ohio State U. Law Jour., 1974-75. Served with USAF, 1966-70. Mem. ABA, D.C. Bar Assn., Phi Beta Kappa. Republican. Roman Catholic. Home: 6515 Deidre Ter Mc Lean VA 22101-1605 Office: Law Resources Inc 1140 Connecticut Ave NW Washington DC 20036-4001

**JOSEPH, STEVEN JAY,** lawyer; b. Baker, Oreg., Sept. 7, 1950; s. Jay Hyrum and Patricia Jean (Cahill) J.; m. Melissa Davis Joseph, Jan. 1, 1978; children: Lindsey Joseph, Logan Joseph. BS, Ea. Oreg. State Coll., 1972; JD, U. Oreg., 1975. Bar: Oreg. 1975, U.S. Dist. Ct. Oreg. 1975. Assoc. Willard K. Carey P.C., LaGrande, Oreg., 1975-76; ptnr. Carey & Joseph P.C., LaGrande, Oreg., 1976-88, Carey, Joseph & Mendiguren, LaGrande, Oreg., 1988-95, Joseph & Mendiguren P.C., LaGrande, 1995-96; atty. pvt. practice, LaGrande, 1997—. Councilor City of LaGrande, Oreg. 1990-94, 97-98; adv. bd. Salvation Army, 1995—; trustee E.O.S.C. Found., 1980-95, pres. 1988-90. Mem. LaGrande-Union County C. of C. (dir. 1982-84), Rotary, Elks. Republican. Avocations: polo, racquetball, skiing, hunting, golf. General civil litigation, Estate planning, Real property. Home: 806 Highland Pl La Grande OR 97850-3216 Office: 901 Washington Ave La Grande OR 97850-2224

**JOSEPH, SUSAN B.,** lawyer; b. N.Y.C., 1958; d. Alfred A. and Bella J. BS in Econ. and Bus. Mgmt., Ramapo Coll. of N.J., 1981; JD cum laude, Seton Hall U., 1985. Bar: N.J. 1985, U.S. Dist. Ct. N.J. 1985, N.Y. 1988, U.S. Dist. Ct. (so. and ea. dist.) N.Y. 1991. Legal asst. Prudential Ins. Co. Am., Newark, 1982-85; assoc. Fox & Fox, Newark, 1985-86, Elkes, Maybruch & Weiss, P.A., Freehold, N.J., 1986-87; asst. counsel N.Am. Reins. Corp., N.Y.C., 1987-90; assoc. Mark D. Lefkowitz, Esq., 1991; mgr. GRE Ins. Group, Princeton, N.J., 1991; atty. GRE Ins. Group, N.Y.C., 1992-95; cons. Fin. Guaranty Ins. Co., N.Y.C., 1996-97, counsel, 1997—. Vol. campaign Bill Bradley for Senate, 1984, 90; vol. Starlight Found., N.Y.C., 1988—, mem. exec. com. Friends of the Maplewood (N.J.) Lib., 1995; mem Transp. Com., Twp. of Maplewood, 1999—. Mem. N.J. State Bar Assn. (sect. on entertainment and arts law, newsletter editor 1992-93, bd. dirs. 1992—; founding sec. ins. law sect. 1996-98, vice chair 1998-99, chair 1999—). Democrat. Jewish. Avocations: writing, theater, photography. Entertainment, Real property, Insurance. Address: Apt 3K 747 Valley St Maplewood NJ 07040-2664

**JOSEPHSON, WILLIAM HOWARD,** lawyer; b. Newark, Mar. 22, 1934; s. Maurice and Gertrude (Brooks) J.; m. Barbara Beth Haws, June 18, 1995. A.B., U. Chgo., 1952; J.D., Columbia, 1955; commoner, St. Antony's Coll., Oxford (Eng.) U., 1958-59. Bar: N.Y. 1956, D.C. 1966, U.S. Supreme Ct. 1959. Assoc. Paul, Weiss, Rifkind, Wharton & Garrison, N.Y.C., 1955-

58, Joseph L. Rauh, Jr., Washington, 1959; Far East regional counsel ICA, 1959-61; spl. asst. to dir. Peace Corps, 1961-62, dep. gen. counsel, 1961-63, gen. counsel, 1963-66; asso. Fried, Frank, Harris, Shriver & Jacobson, N.Y.C., 1966-67; ptnr. Fried, Frank, Harris, Shriver & Jacobson, 1968-94, counsel, 1994-99; asst. atty. gen. in charge charities bur. N.Y. State Law Dept., 1999—; spl. counsel N.Y.C. Human Resources Adminstrn., 1966-67, City Univ. Constrn. Fund, 1967-96, N.Y.C. Bd. Edn., 1968-71, N.Y.C. Employees' Retirement Sys., 1975-86; Nat. Dem. vice presdl. campaign coord., 1972; pres. Peace Corps Inst., 1980—; mem. N.Y. State Gov. Task Force Pension and Investment, 1987-89, N.Y. State His. Records Adv. Bd., 1990-96, N.Y. State Archives Preservation Trust, 1994-96. Bd. editors: Columbia Law Rev, 1953-55. Trustee and treas. St. Antony's Coll. trust, 1994-99. Recipient William A. Jump award exemplary achievement pub. adminstrn., 1965, Disting. Svc. award, Valerie Kantor award, Corp. Social Responsibility award Mex. Am. Legal Def. and Edn. Fund, 1980, 81, 93. Mem. Assn. Bar City N.Y. (spl. com. on Congl. ethics 1968-70), Council on Fgn. Relations. Jewish. Municipal (including bonds), Education and schools. Home: 58 S Oxford St Brooklyn NY 11217-1305 Office: Charities Bur NY State Law Dept 120 Broadway Fl 3 New York NY 10271

**JOSEY, JON RENE,** prosecutor; b. Jackson, Miss., Nov. 28, 1960; m. Martha Willis, May 28, 1985; 2 children. BA, Clemson U., 1982; JD, U. S.C., 1985. Bar: S.C. 1985, U.S. Dist. Ct. S.C. 1987, U.S. Ct. Appeals (4th cir.) 1987, U.S. Ct. Appeals (fed. cir.) 1992, U.S. Supreme Ct. 1994. Law clk. to Chief Judge C. Weston Houck U.S. Dist. S.C., 1985-87; assoc. Rogers, McBratney and Josey, Florence, S.C., 1987-91, ptnr., 1991-93; lectr. polit. sci. Francis Marion U., Florence, 1992-93; sole practitioner Florence, 1994-96; interim U.S. atty. U.S. Atty. Dist. S.C., 1996, U.S. atty., 1996—. Contbr. articles to profl. jours. Mem. Florence Area Arts Coun., 1992-96, chair, 1996; mem. choir Ctrl. United Meth. Ch., 1992—, mem. adminstrv. bd., 1995—; 1st v.p. Florence County Dem. Party, 1995—, chair Florence City Dem. party, 1995-96; mem. S.C. Coun. for Mediation and Alternative Dispute Resolution, 1995-96. Fellow S.C. Bar Found.; mem. ABA, ATLA, S.C. Trial Lawyers Assn. Office: US Atty for SC 1441 Main St Ste 500 Columbia SC 29201-2862*

**JOSHI, MICHAEL,** lawyer; b. Washington, Sept. 1, 1951; s. Jaimini and Milena Joshi; m. Patricia D. Misencik; children: Mia, Nicole. BA, U. Va., 1975; JD, George Mason U., 1985. Bar: Va. 1985, U.S. Dist. Ct. (ea. dist.) Va., U.S. Ct. Appeals (4th cir.). Atty., ptnr. Miller, Miller, Kearney and Geschickter, Fairfax, Va., 1987—. Mem. Fairfax County Bar assn., Va. Trial Lawyers Assn., Va. Assn. Def. Attys., No. Va. Def. Lawyers Assn. (v.p. 1987—). Roman Catholic. Avocations: golf, sports. Personal injury, General civil litigation, Criminal. Office: Miller Miller Kearney & Geschickter 10400 Eaton Pl Ste 312 Fairfax VA 22030-2208

**JOSLIN, GARY JAMES,** dean, lawyer; b. Glendale, Calif., Nov. 14, 1943; s. James C. and Elsie Victoria (White) J.; m. Connie Ruth Hanson, Sept. 5, 1970; children: Christine E., Julie A., James Scott. AA, Glendale Coll., 1963; grad., Calif. Mil. Acad., 1964; BA, UCLA, 1965; JD, U. So. Calif., 1969; MA in Pub. Affairs, U. Oreg., 1971; LLM in Tax, Washington Inst., 1989; BS, SUNY, 1991; PhD, S.W. U., 1993. Bar: Utah 1972, U.S. Dist. Ct. Utah 1972, U.S. Ct. Appeals (10th cir.) 1975, U.S. Supreme Ct. 1975, U.S. Ct. Claims 1977, U.S. Tax Ct. 1977, U.S. Ct. Appeals (9th cir.) 1977, U.S. Dist. Ct. (so. dist.) Ind. 1978, U.S. Ct. Appeals (7th cir.) 1979, U.S. Ct. Internat. Trade 1982, U.S. Ct. Appeals (D.C. cir.) 1984, U.S. Dist. Ct. Okla. 1986, Mass. 1994; cert. EMT, Utah, emergency response grid leader. Criminal justice planner, region VII Utah Law Enforcement Agy., 1971; sole practice Sandy, Utah; instr. criminal procedure Weber State Coll. Extension; instr. polit. sci. Utah State U. Extension; prof. paralegal studies Am. Legal Svcs. Inst.; prof. taxation, dir. grad. program, dean Washington Sch. of Law; dep. county atty. Duchesne County, Utah; city atty. City of Salem, Utah, City of Santaguin, Utah. Author: The Living Trust, 1978, Family Relations, 1993, Saint Masons, 1993. Scoutmaster Boy Scouts Am., Roosevelt, Utah, 1972; dist. commr. Varsity Scouting, Sandy, 1986, dist. vice chair, 1995. Founder Citizens for Good Govt., Roosevelt, 1972. 2d lt. Calif. N.G. Recipient Commemorative medal of Honor, Am. Biographical Inst., 1991. Republican. Mem. LDS Church. Avocation: good govt., social reform, mental health. Office: 2268 Newcastle Dr Sandy UT 84093-1743

**JOSLIN, LANA ELLEN,** lawyer; b. Manhasset, N.Y., Dec. 8, 1968; d. Richard Ira and Linda Kay Levine; m. Christopher S. Joslin, June 15, 1997. BA, U. Vt., 1990; JD, St. John's U., 1993. Bar: N.Y. 1994, U.S. Dist. Ct. (so and ea. dists.) N.Y. 1994. Atty. Piken & Piken, Lake Success, N.Y., 1993-97, Rivkin, Radler & Kremer, Uniondale, N.Y., 1997—. Mem. N.Y. State Bar Assn., N.Y. State Movers & Warehouseman Assn., NAssau County Bar Assn., L.I. Moving & Storage Assn. Transportation, Administrative and regulatory, General civil litigation. Office: Rivkin Radler & Kremer Eab Plz Uniondale NY 11556-0001

**JOSLYN, ROBERT BRUCE,** lawyer; b. Detroit, Jan. 9, 1945; s. Lee Everett, Jr. and Juanita Constance (McGonegal) J.; m. Karen Sue Glenny, July 8, 1967; children: Gwendolyn Constance, Robert Bruce. B.A., Fla. State U., 1967; J.D., Emory U., 1970. Bar: Mich. 1970. Law clk. Gurney, Gurney & Handley, Orlando, Fla., summer 1969; asso. Joslyn & Keydel, Detroit, 1970-74; ptnr. Joslyn, Keydel & Wallace, 1975-95; pvt. practice Robert B. Joslyn, PC, 1996—; vis. instr. Oakland U., Rochester, Mich., 1974-75; faculty Inst. Continuing Legal Edn., Ann Arbor, Michl, 1975—; guest instr. U. Mich. Law Sch. Co-author: Manual for Lawyers and Legal Assistants: Probate and Trust Administration, 1977, Manual for Lawyers and Legal Assistants: Taxation of Trusts and Estates, 1977, 3d edit., 1980. Mem. U.S. All Am. Prep. Sch. Swim Team, 1963. Mem. ABA, Detroit Bar Assn. (chmn. taxation com. 1985-87), State Bar Mich. (chairperson probate and estate planning sect. 1992-93), Am. Coll. of Trust and Estate Counsel (state chmn. 1987-92, bd. regents 1994—), Internat. Acad. Estate and Trust Law, Fin. and Estate Planning Coun. Detroit (bd. dirs. 1988-92, pres. 1992), Grosse Pointe Club (Commodore 1989-91), Phi Delta Phi, Phi Kappa Psi. Estate planning, Estate taxation, Personal income taxation. Home: 286 Hillcrest Ave Grosse Pointe MI 48236-3123 Office: 200 Maple Park Blvd Ste 201 Saint Clair Shores MI 48081-2211

**JOST, RICHARD FREDERIC, III,** lawyer; b. N.Y.C., Sept. 25, 1947; s. Richard Frederic Jr. and Gertrude (Holoch) J.; m. Sally Ann Galvin, July 29, 1972; children: Jennifer, Richard IV. BA, Dickinson Coll., 1969; JD, Syracuse U., 1975. Bar: N.Y. 1976, Nev. 1978, U.S. Dist. Ct. Nev. 1979, U.S. Supreme Ct. 1984. Dep. dist. atty. Elko (Nev.) County Dist. Atty.'s Office, 1976-80; dep. atty. gen. Nev. Atty. Gen.'s Office, Carson City, 1980-83; ptnr. Jones & Vargas, Las Vegas, Nev., 1983—. Trustee United Meth. Ch., Carson City, Nev., 1982-83; bd. dirs. Ormsby Assn. Retarded Citizens, Carson City, 1982-83. Served to lt. USNR, 1970-74. Mem. ABA (urban, state and local govt. law sect.), Clark County Bar Assn., Nat. Assn. Bond Lawyers. Democrat. Municipal (including bonds), Administrative and regulatory. Home: 2840 S Monte Cristo Way Las Vegas NV 89117-2951 Office: Jones & Vargas 3773 Howard Hughes Pkwy Las Vegas NV 89109-0949

**JOST, TIMOTHY STOLTZFUS,** law educator; b. Reedley, Calif., Nov. 25, 1948; s. Arthur P. and Esther Ruth (Goosen) J.; m. Ruth Stoltzfus, Jan. 2, 1982; children: Jacob, Micah, David. BA, U. Calif., Santa Cruz, 1970; JD, U. Chgo., 1975. Bar: Ill. 1975, Ohio 1982. Atty. Legal Assistance Found. of Chgo., 1975-81; asst./assoc. prof. law Ohio State U., Columbus, 1981-87, prof. law, 1987-92, acting dir. Health Policy Ctr., 1994-96, Newton, Baker, Baker & Hostetler prof., 1992—; cons. Inst. of Medicine, 1984-85; guest prof. U. Gottingen (Germany), 1996-97. Author: (casebook) Health Law, 1987, 2d edit. 1991, 3rd edit., 1997, Property Law, 1989, Regulation of the Health Care Professions, 1997, The Law of Medicare and Medicaid Fraud and Abuse, 1998. Mem., supervising mem. State Mental Bd. of Ohio, Columbus, 1967-92. Deutsche Academische Austausch Dienst grantee, 1995, Fulbright grantee, 1989, 1996-97. Mem. Am. Soc. Law and Med. Ethics, Nat. Health Laywers Assn., AALS (aging and law sect. chair 1990). Democrat. Mennonite. Home: 3445 Live Oak Pl Columbus OH 43221-4725 Office: Ohio State Univ 55 W 12th Ave Columbus OH 43210-1338

**JOURNEY, DREXEL DAHLKE,** lawyer; b. Westfield, Wis., Feb. 23, 1926; s. Clarence Earl and Verna L. Gilmore (Dahlke) Journey Gilmore; m. Vergene Harriet Sandsmark, Oct. 24, 1952; 1 child, Ann Marie. *Wife Vergene Journey, Registered Nurse St Mary's School of Nursing, 1947 and a member of the National Capitol Harp Ensemble, Holds various concert harp performance credits, including ensemble appearances at the White House and the John F. Kennedy Center for the Performing Arts.* BBA, U. Wis., 1950, LLB, 1952; LLM, George Washington U., 1957. Bar: Wis. 1952, U.S. Dist. Ct. (we. dist.) Wis. 1953, U.S. Supreme Ct. 1955, U.S. Ct. Appeals (4th cir.) 1960, U.S. Ct. Appeals (5th cir.) 1961, U.S. Ct. Appeals (D.C. cir.) 1965, U.S. Ct. Appeals (7th and 9th cirs.) 1967, U.S. Ct. Appeals (1st cir.) 1969, D.C. 1970, U.S. Dist. Ct. D.C. 1970, U.S. Ct. Appeals (2d, 3d, 6th, 8th and 10th cirs. ) 1976, U.S. Ct. Appeals (11th cir.) 1981. Counsel FPC, Washington, 1952-66, asst. gen. counsel, 1966-70, dep. gen. counsel, 1970-74, gen. counsel, 1974-77; ptnr. Schiff, Hardin & Waite, Washington, 1977—; mem. mediation program U.S. Dist. Ct. (D.C. cir.), 1989—, early neutral evaluation program, 1989-95; mem. case evaluation program D.C. Superior Ct., 1991—. Author: Corporate Law and Practice, 1975; contbr. articles to profl. jours. Pres. Am. U. Park Citizens Assn., Washington, 1970-72; trustee Lincoln-Wesmoreland Housing Project, Washington, 1978-79. With Mcht. Marine Res., USNR, 1944-46, USNG, 1948-50. Knapp scholar U. Wis., 1952. Mem. ABA, FBA, Fed. Energy Bar Assn., Masons, Army and Navy Club, Phi Kappa Phi, Phi Eta Sigma, Theta Delta Chi. Republican. Congregationalist. Administrative and regulatory, FERC practice, Municipal (including bonds). Home: 4540 Windom Pl NW Washington DC 20016-2452 Office: Schiff Hardin & Waite 1101 Connecticut Ave NW Ste 600 Washington DC 20036-4390

**JOVICK, ROBERT L.,** lawyer; b. Butte, Mont., Oct. 2, 1950; m. Stacy Towle, June 23, 1976; children: Janelle, Torey, Jay. BS in Indsl. Engring., Mont. State U., 1972; JD, U. Mont., 1975. Bar: Mont. 1975, U.S. Dist. Ct. Mont. 1975, U.S. Supreme Ct. Pvt. practice Livingston, Mont., 1975—; city atty. City of Livingston, 1975-95. Sec. Livingston Community Trust, 1987—. Mem. Livingston Golf Club (pres. 1990). Methodist. Avocations: fly fishing, hiking, history of Montana. General civil litigation, Real property, Personal injury. Office: PO 1245 227 S 2nd St Livingston MT 59047-3001

**JOYCE, DONNA MARIE,** lawyer, advertising coordinator; b. New Haven, Oct. 16, 1965; d. Wallace Landon and Rose Marie Joyce. BA in Polit. Sci. with honors in gen. scholarship, Trinity Coll., Hartford, Conn., 1987; JD, Georgetown U., 1991. Bar: Pa., D.C. Legal intern Conn. Conf. Municipalities, New Haven, 1989, Energy and Commerce Com., U.S. Congress, Washington, 1989; law clk. Arch. of the U.S. Capitol, U.S. Congress, Washington, 1990; legal paraprofl. Brown & Welsh, P.C., Meriden, Conn., 1993-95; legal advt. specialist, cons. and trainer Shore Line Newspapers, New Haven, 1995-97; advt. coordinator Wall Street Journal, 1998—. Legis. intern State Rep. Michael Rybak, Hartford, 1985; press intern Senate Caucus Media Office, Hartford, 1986; campaign aide Conn. Senate, Hartford, 1986. Recipient Conn. Gen. Assembly citation for contbn. to legis. process, Conn. House of Reps., 1985, President's Fellow in Polit. Sci., Trinity Coll., 1986, Ferguson Prize in Govt., Trinity Coll., 1987. Mem. Fed. Am. Inn Ct., Amnesty Internat., Georgetown Club at the Chemists' Club N.Y., Pi Gamma Mu, Phi Beta Kappa. Roman Catholic. Avocations: antiques, visual art in several mediums, studying Native American Indian culture, shamanism and theopneusty. Home: 506 Quinnipiac Ave North Haven CT 06473-3760

**JOYCE, JAMES JOSEPH, JR.,** lawyer; b. Worcester, Mass., Apr. 10, 1947; s. James Joseph and Phyllis Mary (Crowley) J.; m. Susan Plummer, Apr. 22, 1972. A.B. summa cum laude, Coll. Holy Cross, 1969; J.D., Harvard U., 1976. Bar: Mass. 1977, U.S. Dist. Ct. Mass. 1978, U.S. Ct. Appeals (1st cir.) 1978, U.S. Supreme Ct. 1980. Assoc. Burns & Levinson, Boston, 1976-82; counsel Norton Co., Worcester, Mass., 1982-92; divisional counsel Norton Co., Saint-Gobain Corp., Worcester, 1992—. Lt. Supply Corps, USN, 1969-73. Mem. ABA, Omicron Delta Epsilon, Alpha Sigma Nu. General corporate, Contracts commercial, Mergers and acquisitions. Office: Norton Co 1 New Bond St Worcester MA 01606-2698

**JOYCE, JOSEPH JAMES,** lawyer, food products executive; b. Chgo., Sept. 28, 1943; s. Edward R. and Mary E. (Jordan) J.; m. Suzanne M. Sheridan, Aug. 26, 1967; children: Joseph, Michael, Peter, Kevin, Edward. BS, Xavier U., 1965; JD, Loyola U., 1968. Bar: Ill. 1968. Mem. Hill, Sherman, Meroni, Gross & Simpson, Chgo., 1968-72; atty. Pepsico, Inc., Purchase, N.Y., 1972-74, trademark counsel, 1974-77, asst. gen. counsel, 1977—, v.p., asst. gen. counsel, 1986—. Contbr. articles to profl. jours. Bd. mgrs. Lincoln Hall Found., Inc., 1989—. Mem. ABA, Ill. Bar Assn., U.S. Trade Assn., Assn. Internationale pour la Protection de la Propiete Industrielle (bd. dirs.), Licensing Execs. Soc., Westchester-Fairfield Corp. Counsel Assn., Inc., Assn. Inter-Am. de la Propriedad Industrial, IIPA (exec. com. 1989—, bd. dirs.). Roman Catholic. Private international, Trademark and copyright, Franchising. Office: Pepsico Inc Anderson Hill Rd Purchase NY 10577

**JOYCE, JOSEPH M.,** lawyer. BSBA, U. Minn., 1973; JD, William Mitchell Coll. Law, 1977. Bar: Minn. 1977. Legal counsel Tonka Corp., Minnetonka, Minn., 1977-81, sec., gen. counsel, 1981-87, v.p., sec., gen. counsel, 1987—. Office: Best Buy Co Inc PO Box 9312 7075 Flying Cloud Dr Eden Prairie MN 55344-3538

**JOYCE, MICHAEL PATRICK,** lawyer; b. Omaha, Oct. 3, 1960; s. Thomas Hunt and Joan Clare (Berigan) J. Student, Miami U., Oxford, Ohio, 1978-79; BSBA, Creighton U., 1982; JD, U. Houston, 1988. Bar: Mo., Kans., U.S. Dist. Ct. (we. dist.) Mo. 1988, U.S. Dist. Ct. Kans. 1989, U.S. Ct. Appeals (8th and 10th cirs.) 1988, U.S. Supreme Ct. 1994. Assoc. mgr. Avco Fin. Svcs. Internat., Inc., Omaha, 1983-85; assoc. Wyrsch, Atwell, Mirakian, Lee & Hobbs, P.C. (formerly Koenigsdorf & Wyrsch, P.C.), Kansas City, Mo., 1988-94; shareholder Wyrsch, Hobbs, Mirakian, & Lee, PC, Kansas City, Mo., 1995-97; pvt. practice, 1997-98; pres. The Joyce Law Firm, LLC, Kansas City, Mo., 1998—; adj. prof. U. Mo. Kansas City Sch. Law, 1997—. Asst. editor (newsletter State Bar Tex.) Caveat Vendor, 1987-88. Grad. NITA, 1992; bd. dirs. Creighton U., 1997-99. Mem. ABA, Nat. Assn. Criminal Def. Lawyers, Am. Health Lawyers Assn., Mo. Bar Assn., Mo. Assn. Criminal Def. Lawyers, Kans. Bar Assn., Kansas City Metro Bar Assn., Johnson County Bar Assn., Creighton U. Alumni Assn. (dir. region IV nat. alumni bd. dirs. 1994-96, pres. 1997-99), Creighton U. Alumni Club (pres. Kansas City area 1992-94). Roman Catholic. Avocations: golf, basketball, community service. E-mail: mpjoyce@worldnet.att.net. General civil litigation, Consumer commercial, Criminal. Office: 104 W 9th St Ste 303 Kansas City MO 64105-1718

**JOYCE, SARAH ELIZABETH,** lawyer; b. St. Paul, Oct. 9, 1969; d. John Paul and Robin Alexandra Joyce; m. Matthew Harrison Koritz, July 20, 1996. BA in Rhetoric, U. Ill., 1991; JD, DePaul U., Chgo., 1994. Bar: Ill. 1994, U.S. Dist. Ct. (no. dist.) Ill. 1994. Atty. Scariano, Kula, Ellch & Himes, Chartered, Chgo., 1994-99, Scariano, Ellch, Himes, Sraja & Petrarca, Chartered, Chgo., 1999—; spkr. in field. Contbr. articles to profl. jours. Vol., Dreams Come True, Chgo., 1997. Mem. Ill. State Bar Assn., Chgo. Bar Assn., Ill. Assn. Sch. Attys., Nat. Sch. Bds. Assn./Coun. Sch. Attys. Education and schools, Labor, Civil rights. Office: Scariano Ellch et al 180 N Stetson Ave Ste 3100 Chicago IL 60601-6702

**JOYCE, STEPHEN MICHAEL,** lawyer; b. Los Angeles, Mar. 19, 1945; s. John Rowland and Elizabeth Rose (Rahe) J.; m. Bernadette Anne Novey, Aug. 18, 1973; children: Natalie Elizabeth, Vanessa Anne. BS, Calif. State U., Los Angeles, 1970; JD, U. LaVerne, 1976. Bar: Calif. 1976, U.S. Dist. Ct. (cen. dist.) Calif. 1977, U.S. Ct. Claims 1981. Pvt. practice Beverly Hills, Calif., 1976-93; ptnr. Gold & Joyce, Beverly Hills, 1982-84; personal atty. to Stevie Wonder and various other celebrities, 1977—. Contbr. articles to profl. jours. Served to pvt. USAR, 1963-69. Mem. ABA, Calif. Bar Assn., Los Angeles County Bar Assn., Beverly Hills Bar Assn., Los Angeles Trial Lawyers Assn., San Fernando Valley Bar Assn., Calabasas Athletic Club. Democrat. Roman Catholic. Avocation: long distance running. State civil litigation, General practice, Entertainment. Home: 4724 Barcelona Ct Calabasas CA 91302-1403 Office: 15260 Ventura Blvd Ste 640 Sherman Oaks CA 91403-5340

**JOYCE, STEPHEN P.,** lawyer; b. San Diego, Nov. 13, 1952; s. Patrick J. Joyce and Barbara Favaloro; 1 child, Stephanie. JD, We. New England Coll., 1980. Bar: N.Y. 1981, Pa. 1987. Pvt. practice Sherburne, N.Y., 1981—. Editor: The So. Tier Jury Verdict and Settlement Reporter, 1989-95. Mem. N.Y. State Trial Lawyers Assn. (bd. trustees 1981—). Democrat. Avocations: boating, skiing, biking. General civil litigation. Office: The Joyce Law Firm 26 N Main St Sherburne NY 13460-9514

**JOYE, MARK CHRISTOPHER,** lawyer; b. Columbia, S.C., Apr. 28, 1963; s. Reese Irby and Jacquelyn (Day) J.; m. Melissa Beaty, Apr. 7, 1990; children: Mason, Eliza. BA in Polit. Sci., U. N.C., 1985; JD, U. S.C., 1989. Bar: S.C. 1989, U.S. Dist. Ct. S.C. 1991; cert. civil trial advocate Nat. Bd. Trial Advocacy. Atty. Clawson & Staubes, LLC, Charleston, S.C., 1989-92, Joye Law Firm, LLP, North Charleston, S.C., 1992—. Mem. Coastal Carolina coun. Boy Scouts Am., 1994—. Mem. ABA, ATLA, S.C. Trial Lawyers Assn., S.C. Bar Assn. (pres. 1998-99, pres.-elect young lawyers divsn. 1997-98, sec.-treas. 1996-97, exec. coun. 1994—, bd. govs. 1999—), Charleston County Bar (exec. coun. 1996-97), Million Dollar Advocates Forum, Charleston Lawyers Club (sec. 1994, treas. 1995, pres.-elect 1996, pres. 1997), Atty. Info. Exchange Group, Rotary. Democrat. Presbyterian. Avocations: Hunting, boating, golf, skiing. Personal injury, Product liability, General civil litigation. Office: Joye Law Firm 5861 Rivers Ave Ste 101 N Charleston SC 29406-6044

**JOYNER, IRVING L.,** law educator, consultant; b. Bklyn., Dec. 11, 1944; s. McLean Spaulding and Dorothy Joyner; children: Lauren, Kwame, Tuere. BS in Acctg., L.I. U., 1972; JD, Rutgers U., 1977. Bar: N.C., U.S. Dist. Ct. (ea. dist.) N.C., U.S. Dist. Ct. (mid. dist.) N.C., 1977, U.S. Ct. Appeals (4th cir.), 1979, U.S. Supreme Ct., 1995. Dir. criminal justice program United Ch. Christ Commn. Racial Justice, N.Y.C., 1968-78; atty. Currie & Joyner, Raleigh, N.C., 1978-80, Currie, Pugh, Simmons & Joyner, Raleigh, 1981-84; staff atty. Nat. Prison Project Am. Civil Liberties Union, Washington, 1980-81; prof. Sch. Law N.C. Ctrl. U., Durham, 1983—. Author: Criminal Procedure in North Carolina, 1989, 2nd edit., 1999; contbr. articles to profl. jours. Mem. ABA, Nat. Bar Assn., N.C. Acad. Trial Lawyers , N.C. Assn. Black Lawyers (pres. 1977-81, Lawyer of Yr. award 1995), Susie Sharp Inn Ct. (exec. bd. 1995—). Office: NC Ctrl U Sch Law 1512 S Alston Ave Durham NC 27707-3252

**JOYNER, J(AMES) CURTIS,** federal judge; b. Newberry, S.C., Apr. 18, 1948; s. George C. and Joan C. (Glenn) J.; m. Mildred Ann Carter, Apr. 5, 1975; children: Jennifer Christine, Nicole Marie, Jacqlyn Ann. Student, Peirce Jr. Coll., Phila., 1967; BS in Acctg., Ctrl. State U., Wilberforce, Ohio, 1971; JD, Howard U., 1974. Bar: Pa. 1975, U.S. Dist. Ct. (ea. dist.) Pa. 1981. Contr. D.C. Project, Washington, 1972-73; legal publ. specialist Fed. Register, Washington, 1974-75; asst. dist. atty. Dist. Atty. Office Chester County, West Chester, Pa., 1975-80, chief dep. dist. atty., 1980-84, 1st asst. dist. atty., 1984-87; judge Ct. of Common Pleas, 15th Jud. Dist., West Chester, 1987-92, U.S. Dist. Ct. (ea. dist.) Pa., Phila., 1992—. Mem. coun. trustees West Chester U., 1983—. Named Trailblazer in Law Enforcement Gov. Thornburgh, 1986; recipient Outstanding Svc. award to law enforcement Pa. Criminal Investigators, 1987, Disting. Law and Justice award County and State Detectives Assn., 1988, Donald K. Anthony Alumni Achievement Hall of Fame Ctrl. State U., 1994. Mem. Fed. Bar Assn. (hon.), Chester County Bar Assn. Avocations: sports, jazz, golf. Office: US Dist Ct 601 Market St Rm 5613 Philadelphia PA 19106-1714

**JUAN, WILLIAM L.,** lawyer; b. Bronxville, N.Y., Oct. 3, 1968. Student, Boston Coll., 1990, grad., 1995; student, U. Pitts., 1991. Assoc. Buchanan Ingersoll, P.C., Pitts., 1995-98; asst. atty. Corning (N.Y.) Inc., 1998—. Home: 12 Churchill St Big Flats NY 14814-9767 Office: Corning Inc One Riverfront Plaza Corning NY 14831

**JUÁREZ, JOSÉ ROBERTO, JR.,** law educator; b. Laredo, Tex., May 25, 1955; s. José Roberto Sr. and María Antonia (Martínez) J.; m. Lorene Martínez Juárez, Aug. 8, 1981; children: Marisa Celia, José Roberto III, Marco Andrés. AB, Stanford U., 1977; JD, U. Tex., Austin, 1981. Bar: Tex. 1981, U.S. Ct. Appeals (5th cir.) 1983, U.S. Ct. Appeals (9th cir.) 1989, U.S. Dist. Ct. (so. and we. dists.) Tex. 1984. Staff atty. Gulf Coast Legal Found., Galveston, Tex., 1982, Mex. Am. Legal Def. & Ednl. Fund (MALDEF), San Antonio, 1983-87; regional counsel, dir. employment program MALDEF, L.A., 1987-90; assoc. prof. law St. Mary's U. Sch. Law, San Antonio, 1990-95, prof. law, 1995—, assoc. dean, 1997—; cons. Ford Found., N.Y.C., 1990—, Intercultural R & D Assn., San Antonio, 1991. Contbr. articles to profl. jours., including Jour. Law & Inequality, St. Mary's Law Jour. Mem. ABA, Assn. Am. Law Schs. (chair sect. on employment discrimination 1994), State Bar Tex. Roman Catholic. Home: 108 Cas Hills Dr Castle Hills TX 78213-3322 Office: St Mary's U Sch Law One Camino Santa Maria San Antonio TX 78228

**JUCHATZ, WAYNE WARREN,** lawyer; b. N.Y.C., June 25, 1946; s. Warren Carl and Margaret E. (Trafford) J.; m. Linda K. Wilson, June 21, 1969; children: Bradley T., Scott W. BA, Franklin & Marshall Coll., 1968; JD, U. Va., 1974. Bar: N.Y. 1975, N.C. 1985. Assoc. Cadwalader, Wickersham & Taft, N.Y.C., 1974-77; asst. counsel R.J. Reynolds Industries Inc., Winston-Salem, N.C., 1977-79, assoc. counsel, 1979-80, sr. assoc. counsel, 1980-81; asst. gen. counsel R.J. Reynolds Tobacco Co., Winston-Salem, 1981-84, dep. gen. counsel, 1984-85, v.p., sec., gen. counsel, 1986-87, sr. v.p., sec., gen. counsel, 1987-93, exec. v.p., gen. counsel, 1993-95; exec. v.p., gen. counsel Textron Inc., Providence, 1995—. Served with U.S. Army, 1969-71. Office: Textron Inc 40 Westminster St Providence RI 02903-2525

**JUDAS, SUZANNE MEYER,** lawyer; b. Eldora, Iowa, Mar. 27, 1946; d. Alan Wallace and Willie Bea (Goodson) M. BA, Jacksonville U., 1969; JD with honors, U. Fla., 1990. Bar: Fla. 1990, U.S. Dist. Ct. (mid. dist.) Fla. 1990, U.S. Supreme Ct. 1990, U.S. Ct. Appeals (11th cir.) 1991. Mktg. rep. IBM Corp., Baton Rouge, La., 1969-70; mgr. account svcs., film & TV prodr. Fla. Prodn. Ctr., Jacksonville, 1980-87; ptnr. Gabel & Hair, Jacksonville, 1990-98, Holland & Knight LLP, Jacksonville, 1998—; barrister Chester Bedell Inn of Ct., Jacksonville, 1993—; trustee Am. Inns Ct. Found., 1994—, chmn. Pegasus scholars subcom. Contbr., editor Maritime Law and Practice of Fla. Bar., 1994. Bd. dirs., sec./treas. Leadership Jacksonville, 1983-85, pres. alumni, 1983-85, chair local govt. symposiums; pres. League of Women Voters, Jacksonville, 1976-78, Fla. bd. dirs., 1978-79, bd. dirs., Baton Rouge, Columbia, S.C., Jacksonville, 1969-76; bd. dirs. Jacksonville Cmty. Coun., Inc., 1978-82, mgmt. team Ind. Authorities Study, 1978, chair civil svc. implementation task force, 1979-85, long range planning com., 1987; bd. dirs. Jacksonville Women's Network, 1987, Jacksonville Urban League, 1994—, Child Guidance Clinic, 1987, Fla. Ballet, Jacksonville, 1986-87; vice chmn. sch. bd., fin. chmn. sch. bd. St. Paul's By the Sea Episc. Day Sch., 1976-82; v.p. Jacksonville chpt. Internat. Assn. Bus. Communicators, 1986-87; bd. dirs. Nat. Conf. Christians and Jews, 1978-87, exec. prodr. ann. brotherhood awards, 1980-87; adv. bd. dirs., co-chair mission implementation com. Jacksonville Hosps. Edn. Program, 1979-85; bd. dirs. Mental Health Resource Ctr., 1983-87, chmn. com. children's delivery svcs., bd. dirs. ctr. corp. & family health; CIS adv bd. dirs. Fla. Jr. Coll, 1983-84; chair United Way Agy. Rev. Com., 1980; mem. adv. com. Northeast Fla. Citizens on 208 Water Quality Planning, 1979; mem. statewide adv. com. Offender Rsch. project, 1978; v.p. Lexington County (S.C.) Young Democrats, 1972, Episcopal Children's Svcs., 1998—; del. S.C. State Democratic Conv.; campaign mgr. Northeast Fla. "Yes on 2", 1978, Lex Hester for Mayor, 1979; pres.-elect The Propeller Club of U.S., Port of Jacksonville, Fla. Named Person of Yr., Propeller Club Port of Jacksonville; Pegasus Trust of Inner Temple scholar, 1992. Mem. Maritime Law Assn. U.S. (maritime pers. com.), Southeast Admiralty Law Inst., Fla. Bar Admiralty Law Com., Propeller Club (pres.-elect 1999—). Democrat. Episcopalian. Admiralty, General civil litigation, Libel. Office: Holland & Knight LLP 50 N Laura St Ste 3900 Jacksonville FL 32202-3622

**JUDD, DENNIS L.,** lawyer; b. Provo, Utah, June 27, 1954; s. Derrel Wesley and Leila (Lundquist) J.; m. Carol Lynne Chilberg, May 6, 1977; children: Lynne Marie, Amy Jo, Tiffany Ann, Andrew, Jacquelyn Nicole. BA in Polit. Sci. summa cum laude, Brigham Young U., 1978, JD, 1981. Bar: Utah 1981, U.S. Dist. Ct. Utah 1981. Assoc. Nielson & Senior, Salt Lake City and Vernal, Utah, 1981-83; dep. county atty. Uintah County, Vernal, 1982-84; ptnr. Bennett & Judd, Vernal, 1983-88; county atty. Daggett County, Utah, 1985-89, 91-99; pvt. practice Vernal, 1988—; county atty. Daggett County, 1991-99; prosecutor City of Naples, Naples, 1996-99; city atty. City of Naples, 1999—, CIty of Naples, 1999—; legal counsel Uintah County Sch. Dist., 1996—; mem. governing bd. Uintah Basin applied Tech. Ctr., 1991-95, v.p., 1993-94, pres., 1994-95. Chmn. bd. adjustment Zoning and Planning Bd., Naples, 1982-91, 94—; mem. Naples City Coun., 1982-91; mayor pro tem City of Naples, 1983-91; legis. v.p. Naples PTA, 1988-90; v.p. Uintah Dist. PTA Coun., 1990-92; mem. resolution com. Utah League Cities and Towns, 1985-86, small cities com., 1985-86; trustee Uintah Sch. Dist. Found., 1988-97, vice chmn., 1991-93; mem. Uintah County Sch. Dist. Bd. Edn., 1991-95, v.p., 1991-92, pres., 1992-95; chmn. Uintah County Rep. Conv., 1998. Hinkley scholar Brigham Young U., 1977. Mem. Utah Bar Assn., Uintah Basin Bar Assn., Statewide Assn. Prosecutors, Vernal C. of C. Republican. Mormon. Avocations: hunting, photography, lapidary. Home: 460 E 1555 S Naples UT 84078 Office: 461 W 200 S Vernal UT 84078-3049

**JUDELL, HAROLD BENN,** lawyer; b. Milw., Mar. 9, 1915; s. Philip Fox and Lena Florence (Krause) J.; m. Maria Violeta van Ronzelen, May 5, 1951 (div.); m. Celeste Seymour Grulich, June 24, 1986. BA, U. Wis., 1936, JD, 1938; LLB, Tulane U., 1950. Bar: Wis. 1938, La. 1950. Mem. Scheinfeld Collins Durant & Winter, Milw., 1938; spl. agt., adminstrv. asst. to dir. FBI, 1939-44; legal attache U.S. Embassy Peru Dauphine Orleans Hotel Corp., 1939-44; ptnr. Foley & Judell, LLP, New Orleans, 1950—; v.p., dir. Dauphine Orleans Hotel Corp., 1970—; mem. Tulane U. Bus. Sch. Coun.; trustee Greater New Orleans YMCA, 1981—. Fellow Am. Coll. Bond Counsel (founding); mem. ABA, La. Bar Assn., Nat. Assn. Bond Lawyers (bd. dirs., pres. 1984-85), New Orleans Country Club, Lawn Tennis Club, Met. Club (N.Y.C.). Municipal (including bonds). Office: Foley & Judell 365 Canal St New Orleans LA 70130-1112

**JUDGE, BERNARD MARTIN,** editor, publisher; b. Chgo., Jan. 6, 1940; s. Bernard A. and Catherine Elizabeth (Halloran) J.; m. Kimbeth A. Wehrli, July 9, 1966; children: Kelly, Bernard R., Jessica. Reporter City News Bur., Chgo., 1965-66; reporter Chgo. Tribune, 1966-72, city editor, 1974-79, asst. mng. editor met. news, 1979-83; editor, gen. mgr. City News Bur. Chgo., 1983-84; assoc. editor Chgo. Sun-Times, 1984-88; editor Chgo. Daily Law Bull., 1988—; pub. Chgo. Lawyer, 1989—; v.p. Law Bull. Pub. Co., Chgo., 1988—. Bd. dirs. Constnl. Rights Found., Chgo., 1992—, chmn. bd. dirs., 1995-97; trustee Fenwick Cath. Prep. H.S., Oak Park, Ill., 1989—. Mem. Sigma Delta Chi. Home: 360 E Randolph St Apt 1905 Chicago IL 60601-7335 Office: Law Bull Pub Co 415 N State St Chicago IL 60610-4631

**JUDGE, BRIAN,** coast guard officer, lawyer; b. N.Y.C., Nov. 16, 1962. BS in Govt., U.S. Coast Guard Acad., 1984; JD, U. Balt., 1992, MBA, 1992. Bar: Md. 1992, U.S. Ct. Appeals (9th cir.) 1997, U.S. Ct. Appeals for Armed Forces, 1992. Commd. ensign USCG, 1984, advanced through grades to lt. comdr., 1986; deck watch officer USCGC Reliance, Port Canaveral, Fla., 1984-86; intelligence officer USCG Intelligence Coordination Ctr., Washington, 1986-89; trial counsel, contracts atty. USCG Maintenance Logistics, N.Y.C., 1992-96; trial atty. civil divsn., torts br. Dept. Justice, San Francisco, 1996-99; dep. dir. Def. Inst. of Internat. Legal Studies, 1999—. Avocation: rowing. Home: 51 Washington St Newport RI 02840 Office: 360 Elliot St Newport RI 02841

**JUDGE, JAMES ROBERT,** lawyer, judge; b. Milw., Mar. 19, 1948; s. Robert James and Margaret D. (Wesli) J.; children: Robert Kanoa, Corrie Malia. BBA, U. Hawaii, 1970; JD, U. Calif., San Francisco, 1973. Bar: Hawaii 1973, U.S. Dist. Ct. Hawaii 1973. Assoc. Okano Noguchi & Wong, Honolulu, 1973-75; from assoc. to ptnr. Woodell Mukai & Ichiki, Honolulu, 1976-81; ptnr. Foley, Maehara, Judge, Choi, Nip & Okamura, Maui, Hawaii, 1982-85, Foley, Maehara, Judge & Nip, Maui, 1986-93; per diem judge 2d Jud. Ct. State of Hawaii, 1981-91. Legal advisor Friends of the Maui Symphony, 1981-84, Maui Hist. Soc., 1985-88; bd. dirs. Maui Community Arts and Cultural Ctr., 1983—. Real property, General corporate. Office: 2233 W Vineyard St Wailuku HI 96793-1621

**JUDGE, JANET PATRICIA,** lawyer; b. Rockville Centre, N.Y., Jan. 6, 1962; d. James Joseph Judge and Barbara Crowley Weber; m. Eric Farnham Saunders, Sept. 3, 1994; children: Kelsey Meaghan Saunders, Emily Lauren Saunders. AB, Harvard Coll., 1985; JD cum laude, Boston U., 1993. Bar: Mass. 1993, Maine 1993, U.S. Dist. Ct. Maine 1994, U.S. Dist. Ct. Mass. 1994, U.S. Ct. Appeals (1st cir.) 1994. Asst. dir. athletic ops. Harvard Coll., Cambridge, Mass., 1985-86, asst. athletic dir., 1986-90; law clk. to Hon. Norman Stahl U.S. Ct. Appeals (1st cir.), Concord, N.H., 1993-94; atty. Moon, Moss, McGill & Batchelder, Portland, Maine, 1994-96, Verrill & Dana LLP, Portland, 1996—; mem. Harvard U. Vis. Com., Portland, 1997—. Allocations vol. United Way, Portland, 1998-99. Labor, Sports. Office: Verrill & Dana LLP PO Box 586 1 Portland Sq Portland ME 04112-0586

**JUDGE, WALTER E.,** lawyer; b. Lowell, Mass., Dec. 20, 1960; s. Walter E. and Jeannie (Sargent) J.; m. Jean C. O'Neill, July 27, 1991; children: Phoebe A., Sophie I. BA, Colby Coll., 1982; MA, Columbia U., 1985; JD, Boston Coll., 1990. Bar: Mass. 1990, Maine 1990, Vt. 1992, U.S. Dist. Ct. Vt. 1992. Assoc. Nutter, McClennen & Fish, Boston, 1990-92, Downs Rachlin & Martin, Burlington, Vt., 1992—. Contbr. articles to Vt. Bar Jour. and Vt. Bus. Mag., 1993—. Mem. Conservation Commn., Charlotte, Vt., 1993, 95, Leadership Champlain, Burlington, 1996—. Avocations: hiking, cooking. Intellectual property, Contracts commercial, Product liability. Office: Downs Rachlin & Martin 199 Main St Burlington VT 05401-8339

**JUDICE, GREGORY VAN,** lawyer, educator; b. Lake Charles, La., June 14, 1966; s. Richard Edward and Anne Lynne J.; m. Caroline Kaye Zama, May 9, 1992. BS in Polit. Sci., McNeese State U., 1989; JD, Notre Dame Law Sch., London, 1994, Wesleyan U., 1995. Bar: La. 1996; cert. mediator. Staff atty. West Pub., Inc., Dallas, 1994-96; atty. Woodley, Williams, Fenet et al, Lake Charles, 1996-97; atty., cert. mediator Hunt Law Firm, Lake Charles, 1997—. Bd. dirs. vol. ctr. United Way, Lake Charles, 1995—. Named to Order of Barristers, 1994; recipient Am. Jurisprudence award Lawyers Coop. Pub. Co., 1994, 95. Mem. ABA (house dels. 1995), La. Bar Assn., Southwest La. Bar Assn. Episcopalian. Avocations: travelling, writing, reading, teaching, outdoor activities. Fax: 318-436-8466. General civil litigation, General corporate, Insurance. Office: Hunt Law Firm 1709 W Prien Lake Rd Ste B Lake Charles LA 70601-8360 also: 132 West Broad St PO Drawer 281 Lake Charles LA 70601

**JUDICE, KENNETH R.,** lawyer; b. Houston, Aug. 19, 1945; s. Morris Joseph and Media (Smith) J.; m. Paula Berron, June 25, 1966; children: Jill, Grant. BA, U. Houston, 1967; JD, South Tex. Coll., 1970. Bar: U.S. Dist. Ct. (so. dist.) Tex. 1974, U.S. Supreme Ct. 1975, U.S. Ct. Appeals (5th cir.) 1995, U.S. Ct. Mil. Appeals 1972. Atty. pvt. practice, Houston. With U.S. Army, 1967. Mem. Katy Bar Assn. (charter). Banking, Consumer commercial, Real property. Office: 15915 Katy Fwy Ste 630 Houston TX 77094-1712

**JUDICE, MARC WAYNE,** lawyer; b. Lafayette, La., Oct. 22, 1946; s. Marc and Gladys B. Judice; m. Anne Keaty; children: Scott, Renee. BS, U. Southwestern La., 1969; MBA, U. Utah, 1974; JD, La. State U., 1977. Bar: La. 1977; CPA, La.; bd. cert. civil trial law, civil trial advocacy Nat. Bd. Trial Advocacy. Ptnr. Voorhies & Labbe, Lafayette, 1977-85, Juneau, Judice, Hill & Adley, Lafayette, 1985-93, Judice & Adley, Lafayette, 1993-94. Bd. dirs. Univ. Med. Ctr., Lafayette, 1991, Home Savs. Bank, Lafayette, 1996—, Women's & Childrens Hosp., Lafayette, 1992-94; bd. trustees Med. Ctr. Southwest La., 1998—, chmn. bd. dirs., 1999—. Republican. Roman Catholic. Insurance, Personal injury. Office: Judice & Adley 926 Coolidge Blvd Lafayette LA 70503-2434

**JUDSON, CHARLES B.,** lawyer; b. Big Rapids, Mich., June 17, 1951; s. Thomas G. and Marilyn R. Judson; m. Susan C. Chapelle, Aug. 6, 1977; children: Alexandria L., Bailey A. BA, Albion Coll., 1973; JD cum laude, U. Detroit, 1980. Bar: U.S. Dist. Ct. (we. dist.) Mich. 1981. Atty. Watson and Alanson, Traverse City, Mich., 1980-82; ptnr. Watson Alanson Gray and Judson, Traverse City, 1982-96; atty., shareholder Smith Haughey Rice & Roegge, Traverse City, 1996—; gen. counsel Traverse Area Dist. Libr., Traverse City, 1981—, Northwestern Regional Airport Commn., Traverse City, 1986—, Grand Traverse Commons Redevel. Corp., 1992—. Bd. dirs. Northwestern Mich. Coll. Found. Bd., 1996—. Fellow Mich. Bar Found.; mem. Order of Barristers, Traverse City Area C of C (bd. dirs. 1996—). Republican. United Methodist. Avocations: golf, downhill skiing. Real property, Municipal (including bonds), Family and matrimonial. Office: Smith Haughey Rice Roegge 202 E State St Traverse City MI 49684-2515

**JUDSON, C(HARLES) JAMES (JIM JUDSON),** lawyer; b. Oregon City, Oreg., Oct. 24, 1944; s. Charles James and Barbara (Busch) J.; m. Diana L. Gerlach, Sept. 7, 1965; children: Kevin, Nicole. BA cum laude, Stanford U., 1966, LLB with honors, 1969. Bar: Wash. 1969, U.S. Tax Ct. 1970, D.C. 1981. Ptnr. Davis Wright Tremaine, Seattle, 1969—; v.p. Eagle River, Inc.; speaker various convs. and seminars. Author: State Taxation of Fin. Instns., 1981; contbr. articles to profl. jours. Chmn. Bus. Tax Coalition, Seattle, 1987; chmn. lawyers div. United Way, Seattle, 1986, 87, commerce and industry div., 1989-91; trustee Wash. State Internat. Trade Fair, Seattle, 1981-86; bd. dirs. Seattle Prep. Sch., 1986-88; bd. dirs. Olympic Park Inst., 1988—, Yosemite Nat. Insts., 1993—; mem. Assn. Wash. Bus. Tax Com., 1978—; tax advisor Wash. State House Reps. Dem. Caucus; advisor Wash. State Dept. Revenue on Tax and Legis. Matters; mem. Seattle Tax Group, 1983—. Fellow Am. Coll Tax Counsel; mem. ABA (chmn. com. on fin. orgns. tax sect. 1978-82, subcom chmn. state and local tax com. tax sect. 1979—, chmn. excise tax com. 1983-90, interorgn. coordination com. 1985—, chmn. environ. tax com. 1991—), Wash. State Bar Assn. (chmn. tax sect. 1984-86, chmn. western region IRS/bar liaison com. 1987-88, mem. rules com. 1991—), Seattle-King County Bar Assn. (mem. tax sect. 1973-86), Seattle C. of C. (tax com. 1982—), Wash. Athletic Club (Seattle), Bear Creek Golf Club (Redmond). Avocation: skiing, basketball, wood working, hiking. State and local taxation, Taxation, general, General corporate. Office: Davis Wright Tremaine 2600 Century Sq 1501 4th Ave Ste 2600 Seattle WA 98101-1688

**JUDSON, PHILIP LIVINGSTON,** lawyer; b. Palo Alto, Calif., Oct. 25, 1941; s. Philip MacGregor and Elizabeth Stuart (Peck) J.; m. Dorothy Louisa Lebohner, Sept. 6, 1963 (div. Jan., 1996); children: Wendy Patricia, Philip Lebohner, Michael Lee; m. Danielle DuPuis Kane, May 18, 1996. BA, Stanford U., 1963; JD, U. Calif., Hastings, 1969. Bar: Calif. 1970, U.S. Dist. Ct. (no. dist.) Calif. 1970, U.S. Ct. Appeals (9th cir.) 1970, U.S. Dist. Ct. (ctrl. dist.) Calif. 1984, U.S. Dist. Ct. (ea. dist.) Calif. 1985, U.S. Supreme Ct. 1987, D.C. 1988, U.S. Dist. Ct. (so. dist.) Calif. 1989. Assoc. Pillsbury, Madison & Sutro, San Francisco, 1969-76, ptnr., 1977-99; ptnr. Skjeren, Morrill, MacPherson, Franklin & Friel, LLP, San Jose, Calif., 1999—; lectr. Practising Law Inst. Pres. St. Mark's Sch., San Rafael, 1983-85, founding mem. trustee 1980-86; trustee Marin Acad., San Rafael, 1985-91. 1st lt. U.S. Army, 1963-65. Mem. ABA (antitrust and litigation sects.), San Francisco Bar Assn., Am. Judicature Soc., Order of Coif, Phi Delta Theta. Republican. Episcopalian. Antitrust, Federal civil litigation, State civil litigation. Home and Office: 19 Byron Cir Mill Valley CA 94941-4627

**JUETTNER, DIANA D'AMICO,** lawyer, educator; b. N.Y.C., Jan. 21, 1940; d. Paris T.R. and Dina Adele (Antonucci) D'Amico; m. Paul J. Juettner, June 29, 1963; children: John, Laura. BA, Hunter Coll., 1961; postgrad., Am. U., 1963; JD cum laude, Touro Coll., 1983. Bar: N.Y. 1984, U.S. Dist. Ct. (so. dist.) N.Y. 1984, U.S. Supreme Ct. 1987. Office mgr. Westchester County Dem. Com., White Plains, N.Y., 1976-79; dist. mgr. for Westchester County U.S. Bur. Census, N.Y.C., 1979-80; pvt. practice, Ardsley, N.Y., 1984—; prof. law, program dir. for legal studies Mercy Coll., Dobbs Ferry, N.Y., 1985—, asst. chair dept. law, criminal justice-safety adminstrn., 1994-98, pres. faculty senate, 1996-98; arbitrator small claims matters White Plains City Ct., 1985-89. Co-author booklet: Your Day in Court, How to File a Small Claims Suit in Westchester County, 1976; assoc. editor N.Y. State Probation Officers Assn. Jour., 1990-92; editor-in-chief Jour. Northeast Acad. Legal Studies in Bus., 1996-98; contbr. articles to profl. jours. Councilwoman Town of Greenburgh, N.Y., 1992—; vice chair law com. Westchester County Dem. Com., White Plains, 1987-91; corr. sec. Greenburgh Dem. Town Com., Hartsdale, N.Y., 1986-91; mem. Westchester County Citizens Consumer Adv. Coun., White Plains, 1975-91, chair, 1991; chair Ardsley (N.Y.) Consumer Adv. Commn., 1974-79. Mem. Am. Assn. for Paralegal Edn. (model syllabus task force 1992-95, chair legis. com. 1995-97), N.Y. State Bar Assn. (elder law sect. com. on pub. agy. liaison and legis. 1992-95), Westchester County Bar Assn. (chair paralegal subcom. 1990—, chair bicentennial U.S. Constitution com. 1987-91), Westchester Women's Bar Assn. (v.p. 1989-91, dir. 1994-96, co-chair tech. com. 1996—), Women's Bar Assn. State N.Y. (chair profl. ethics com. 1997-98). Avocation: sailing, walking. Real property, Probate. Office: Mercy Coll 555 Broadway Dobbs Ferry NY 10522-1134

**JUHOLA, MICHAEL DUANE,** lawyer; b. Ashtabula, Ohio, May 11, 1955; s. Kenneth Duane and Lois Rosemary (England) J.; m. Denise H. Juhola, May 2, 1987. BA, Hiram Coll., 1977; JD, Ohio State U., 1980. Bar: Ohio 1980, U.S. Dist. Ct. (so. dist.) Ohio 1987, U.S. Ct. Appeals (6th cir.) 1992. Asst. dir. Ohio Legal Ctr. Inst., Columbus, 1980-88; staff atty. Smith, Clark & Holzapfel, Columbus, 1988-89; exec. dir. Ohio div. Profl. Edn. System, Inc., Columbus, 1989-91; pvt. practice law Columbus, 1991—. Coun. mem. North Community Luth. Ch., Columbus, 1989-93. Mem. Ohio Bar Assn., Columbus Bar Assn., Worthington Estate Planning Coun., Phi Beta Kappa. Avocation: boating. Probate, Personal injury, Family and matrimonial. Office: 4889 Sinclair Rd Ste 204 Columbus OH 43229-5434

**JULIAN, J. R.,** lawyer; b. Wilmington, Del., Apr. 6, 1943. BA, Am U., 1966; JD, Cath. U. Am., 1970. Bar: Del. 1971, U.S. Dist. Ct. Del., U.S. Ct. Appeals (3d cir.), U.S. Supreme Ct. Pvt. practice Wilmington, Del.; mem. bd. bar examiners Supreme Ct. State Del., 1985-89; mem. rules com. Del. Indsl. Accident Bd. Bd. dirs. Hist. Soc. Ct. Chancery. Mem. ABA (litig. sect., bus. law sect.), ATLA, Del. Bar Assn. (v.p. New Castle County chpt., former vice chair jud. appointments com., exec. com., litig. com., alt. dispute resolution com., ins. com., workers' compensation com., pres.), Am. Bd. Trial Advocates, Def. Rsch. Inst., Am. Judicature Soc., Del. Trial Lawyers Assn., Federalist Soc. for Law and Pub. Policy Studies (bd. adv. Del. chpt. lawyers divsn.), St. Thomas More Soc. Del. (pres.), Pi Sigma Alpha, Delta Theta Pi. General civil litigation, Insurance, Product liability. Office: Ste 1001 Market St Mall PO Box 2171 Wilmington DE 19899-2171*

**JULIAN, JIM LEE,** lawyer; b. Osceola, Ark., Dec. 14, 1954; s. John Roland and Lucille Angela (Potts) J.; m. Patricia Lynn Roberts, Jan. 26, 1980; 1 child, Kathryn Elizabeth. BA, Ark. State U., 1976; JD, U. Ark., 1979. Bar: Ark. 1979, U.S. Dist. Ct. (ea. and we. dists.) Ark. 1979, U.S. Ct. Appeals (8th cir.). Assoc. Skillman & Durrett, West Memphis, Ark., 1979-82; staff atty. Ark. Power and Light Co., Little Rock, 1982-84; assoc. House, Wallace & Jewell, Little Rock, 1984-85, ptnr., 1986-89; ptnr. Chisenhall, Nestrud & Julian, Little Rock, 1989—. Pres. Crittenden County (Ark.) Young Dems., 1980-82; chmn. bd. dirs. Northside YMCA, 1992-96. Mem. ABA, Ark. Bar Assn., Pulaski County Bar Assn., Ark. Assn. Def. Counsel, Major Sports Assn., North Hills Country Club. Avocation: golf. General civil litigation, Environmental, Insurance. Home: 3711 Lochridge Rd North Little Rock AR 72116-8328 Office: Chisenhall Nestrud & Julian 2840 First Commercial Bldg Little Rock AR 72201

**JULIANO, JOHN LOUIS,** lawyer; b. Jamaica, N.Y., Oct. 21, 1944; s. John Carmine and Jeannette Helen (Ciotti) J.; m. Maryjane Theresa Groccia, July 4, 1966; children—Jennifer, Jonathan. BBA, St. John's U., 1966; JD, Bklyn. Law Sch., 1969. Bar: N.Y. 1970, U.S. Dist. Ct. (ea. and so. dists.) N.Y., U.S. Ct. Appeals (2d cir.), U.S. Supreme Ct. Ptnr., Juliano, Karlson, Weisberg, 1970-72; sole practice, East Northport, N.Y., 1972—; pres., dir. Hillside Van Lines, Inc.; mem. N.Y. State 10th Jud. Grievance Com., 1998—; lectr. Suffolk Acad. Law. Mem. Am. Trial Lawyers Assn., N.Y. State Bar Assn., Suffolk County Bar Assn. (pres. 1996-97, v.p. 1995-96, treas. 1994-95, sec. 1993-94, bd. dirs. 1998—), N.Y. State Trial Lawyers Assn., ICC Practitioners, Criminal Bar Assn., Columbian Lawyers Assn. (sec. 1972, treas. 1973, pres. 1974-75), Am. Inns of Ct. Personal injury, Criminal, Family and matrimonial. Address: 39 Doyle Ct East Northport NY 11731-6404

**JUN, MEEKA,** lawyer; b. Taegu, South Korea, Aug. 31, 1968; d. Moo Young and Young Hae (Sang) J.; m. Joseph Aaron Bondy, Sept. 6, 1997. BA, U. Pa., 1990; JD, Bklyn. Law Sch., 1994. Bar: N.Y., U.S. Dist. Ct. (so. and ea. dists.) N.Y. Asst. to nat. advt. dir. PC Mag., N.Y.C., 1990-91; assoc. Brown Raysman Millstein Felder & Steiner, N.Y.C., 1994-98; assoc. counsel Time Inc., N.Y.C., 1998—. Mem. ABA, N.Y. State Bar Assn., N.Y. Women's Bar Assn., N.Y. City Bar Assn., Assn. Women in Computing, Asian-Am. Bar Assn. N.Y. Jewish. Avocations: tennis, skiing, swimming, opera. Intellectual property, Computer, Libel. Home: 1365 York Ave Apt 32J New York NY 10021-4048 Office: Time Inc 1271 Avenue Of The Americas New York NY 10020-1300

**JUNELL, WILLIAM EDWARD, JR.,** lawyer; b. Houston, Jan. 2, 1946; s. William Edward and Lily Layne Junell; m. Carol Harrison, Sept. 13, 1969; children: Mark Alan, William Harrison, Ann Elizabeth. Degree in bus., U. Tex., Austin, 1968, JD, 1971. Bar: U.S. Dist. Ct. (so., no., we. and ea. dists.) Tex., U.S. Ct. Appeals (5th cir.), U.S. Supreme Ct. Atty. Reynolds White Allen & Cook, Houston, 1971-88, Andrews & Kurth, Houston, 1988-97, Schwartz Junell Campbell & Oathout, Houston, 1997—. Active St. Luke's United Meth. Ch. Mem. Houston Bar Assn. (bd. dirs.; v.p. 1998—). Avocations: golf, water sports, fishing, skiing. General civil litigation. Home: 410 Thamer Ln Houston TX 77024-6919 Office: Schwartz Junell Campbell & Oathout 909 Fannin Ste 2000 Houston TX 77010

**JUNGEBERG, THOMAS DONALD,** lawyer; b. Berea, Ohio, June 12, 1950; s. Wilbert Donald and Carolyn Francis (Gaube) J.; m. Kathleen Ann Killmer, Oct. 5, 1973; children: Kimberlee Ann, Allison Lynn, Zebulun Thomas, Nathan Aaron. BA, Kent State U., 1972; JD, Cleve. State U., 1976. Bar: Ohio 1976, U.S. Dist. Ct. (no. dist.) Ohio 1977, U.S. Tax Ct. 1980, U.S. Supreme Ct. 1980. Tchr., Berea City Schs., Ohio, 1972-75; staff atty. Palmquist & Palmquist, Medina, Ohio, 1977-80, Gibbs & Craze, Parma Heights, Ohio, 1980-81; sole practice, Medina, 1981-87; v.p., gen. counsel, corp. sec. Shelby (Ohio) Ins. Co., 1987-95; prin. Lexington (Ohio) Ins. Cons., 1995-96; sole practice, Lexington, 1995-96; v.p. legal Reliance Nat., Cleve., 1996-98. Tchr., First Baptist Christian Sch., Medina, 1981-84; elder, sec. First Bapt. Ch. of Medina, 1979-86, chmn. First Bapt. Christian Sch., Medina, 1984; bd. govs. Ohio Med. Profl. Liability Underwriting Assn., 1993-95; dir. Ins. Inst. Ind., 1994-95. Mem. Ohio State Bar Assn., Am. Corp. Counsel Assn., Gideons Internat. (v.p. S.W. Camp). Republican. Avocations: piano; golf; archery. General corporate, Insurance, Labor. Home: 10236 Foxwood Dr N Royalton OH 44133-3365

**JUNIUS, ANDREAS GRETUS,** lawyer, educator; b. Dortmund, Federal Republic of Germany, Sept. 15, 1954; s. Kurt Paul and Beatrix M. (Braunert) J. Diploma, Bonn U., 1981; ML, Columbia U., 1982; Dr. jur., Bonn U., 1988. Bar: N.Y. 1983, Germany 1986. Fgn. assoc. Walter Conston et al, N.Y.C., 1982-83; assessor Circuit Ct., Frankfurt, Germany, 1983-86; ptnr. Puender, Volhard, Weber & Axster, Frankfurt, 1986—; adj. prof. Boston U. Sch. Law, 1990—; mem. adv. bd. European Law Program Tulane Law Sch., 1992-94, Am. Coun. on Germany, N.Y.C., 1991—; bd. dirs. Am. Fgn. Law Assn., N.Y.C., 1990—. Author: UN Council for Namibia, 1988; contbr. articles to profl. jours. Bd. dirs. Deutscher Verein, N.Y.C., 1995-96, 97—. Mem. ABA, Internat. Bar Assn., N.Y. State Bar Assn., Bar Assn. of the City of N.Y., Columbia Law Sch. Assn., Deutscher Anwaltsverein. Lutheran. Avocations: golf, jogging, playing violin. Banking, Mergers and acquisitions, Finance. Home: 55 E 86th St New York NY 10028-1059 Office: Puender Volhard Weber & Axster 152 W 57th St Fl 53 New York NY 10019-3310

**JUNO, CYNTHIA,** lawyer; b. Lubbock, Tex., Feb. 19, 1958. B in Music Edn., Tex. Tech. U., 1980; JD, Georgetown U., 1989. Assoc. atty. Hufstedler, Kaus & Ettinger, L.A., 1989-91, Jeffer, Mangels, Butler & Marmaro, L.A., 1991-93; pres., owner Juno Law Offices, L.A., 1993—. General practice, State civil litigation, Civil rights. Office: Juno Law Offices 8306 Wilshire Blvd Ste 7000 Beverly Hills CA 90211-2382

**JURCYK, JOHN JOSEPH, JR.,** lawyer; b. Kansas City, Kans., Apr. 15, 1930; s. John Joseph Sr. and Ann (Kordash) J.; m. Rita Menghini, July 13, 1957; children: Jeff, John David, Amy L., Alison C., Ann. E. AB in History, Rockhurst Coll., 1952; JD, U. Kans., 1957. Bar: Kans. 1957, U.S. Dist. Ct. Kans. 1957, U.S. Ct. Appeals (10th cir.) 1957, U.S. Ct. Appeals (8th cir.) 1984, U.S. Supreme Ct. 1970. Law clk. to chief judge U.S. Dist. Ct. Kans., Kansas City, 1957; assoc. McAnany, Van Cleave & Phillips, Kansas City, Kans., 1958-63, ptnr., 1963—, sr. trial lawyer, pres. corp., 1978-89; mem. nominating commn. 29th Jud. Dist., 1978-79; mem. merit selection panel for magistrate U.S. Dist. Ct. Kans., 1986-89, mem. adv. group Civil Justice Reform Act, 1991-94, mem. 10th Cir. Adv. Com., 1998—. Editor-in-chief Kans. Law Rev., 1957. Chmn. Civic Arts Council Kansas City (Kans.), 1965-69, Citizens Commn. on Local Govt. Wyandotte County (Kans.), 1969-70, United Way of Wyandotte County, 1995, 96; chmn. bd. edn. Bishop Ward High Sch., 1968-71; pres. St. Patrick Sch. Bd., Kansas City, Kans., 1979-80; bd. dirs. Kansas City region NCCJ, 1964-72, Kansas City, Kans., YMCA, 1971-76, Cath. Housing Svcs., 1978—, pres., 1985—; hon. dir. Rockhurst Coll., Kansas City, Mo.; mem. Kans. Citizen Justice Commn., 1997-99. Recipient Exceptional Performance citation Def. Rsch. and Trial Lawyers Assn., 1985. Fellow Am. Coll. Trial Lawyers, Am. Bar Found., Kans. Bar Found. (pres. 1995-96); mem. ABA, Kans. Bar Assn. (numerous coms., Outstanding Svc. award 1986), Johnson County Bar Assn., Wyandotte County Bar Assn. (pres. 1970-71, editor Advocate 1968-74), Internat. Assn. Def. Counsel, Kans. Assn. Def. Counsel (pres. 1984-85), U. Kans. Law Soc. (bd. govs. 1985-88), U. Kans. Law Alumni Assn. Greater Kansas City (pres. 1966), Kansas City Area C. of C. (sec. 1971-72, bd. dirs., chmn. 1991-92), Cursillo Movement Kansas City (lay dir. 1980-83), Serra Club, Rotary (bd. dirs. Kansas City 1979). Democrat. Roman Catholic. General civil litigation, Labor, Personal injury. Office: McAnany Van Cleave & Phillips PO Box 1300 707 Minnesota Ave Fl 4 Kansas City KS 66101-2703

**JUREWICZ, RICHARD MICHAEL,** lawyer; b. Phila., Jan. 4, 1958; s. Leo Peter and Margaret Carol Jurewicz; m. Susan Mary McElwee, May 18, 1991; children: Kelsey Ann, Kaitlyn Nicole, Karly Renee. BS in Adminstrn. Justice, Pa. State U., 1980; JD, Temple U., 1983. Bar: Pa. 1983, U.S. Dist. Ct. (ea. dist.) Pa. 1984, U.S. Ct. Appeals (3d cir.) 1985. Judicial law clk. Pa. Supreme Ct., Phila., 1983-84; assoc. Galfand Berger Lurie Senesky & March, Phila., 1984-88; ptnr. Galfand Berger Lurie Brigham Jacobs Swan Jurewicz Jensen Ltd, Phila., 1989—. Pres., bd. dirs. Kids Chance Penn. Inc., Phila., 1997—. Mem. Nat. Bd. Trial Advocacy (cert. in civil trial law and advocacy), Million Dollar Advocates Forum. Democrat. Avocations: racketball, camping, biking. Product liability, Construction, General civil litigation. Office: Galfand Berber LLP 1818 Market St Ste 2300 Philadelphia PA 19103-3629

**JURKOWITZ, DANIEL S.,** lawyer, prosecutor; b. Tucson; s. Harvey and Chaya Jurkowitz; m. Lisa A. Klein. BA, U. Ariz., 1994, JD, 1997. Bar: Ariz. 1997, U.S. Dist. Ct. Ariz. 1998, U.S. Ct. Appeals (9th cir.) 1998. Intern Ariz. Atty. Gens. Office, Dept. Econ. Security, Tucson, 1994; appeals clk. criminal divsn. Pima County Attys. Office, Tucson, 1995-96, student prosecutor criminal divsn., 1996; Westlaw student rep. West Pub. Corp., Tucson, 1996-97; law clk. civil divsn. Pima County Attys. Office, Tucson, 1997, dep. county atty. criminal divsn., 1997-98, dep. county atty. civil divsn., 1998—. State and precinct committeeman Ariz. Rep. Party, Tucson, 1994—; sec. exec. com. Pima County Rep. Party, 1999—; sch. coord., tutor Lawyers for Literacy-Pima County Bar Assn.-Young Lawyers Divsn., Tucson, 1997—; pres., v.p., Sienna Homeowners Assn., Tucson, 1998—. Nat. merit scholar Ariz. Rep. Party, Tucson, 1994—. Mem. ABA, ATLA, FBA, Phi Beta Kappa. Jewish. Avocations: guitar, tennis, reading. Office: Pima County Attys Office Civil Divsn 32 N Stone Ave # 1500 Tucson AZ 85701-1403

**JUROW, GEORGE,** judge; b. N.Y.C., Feb. 3, 1943; m. Barbara Hertzberg, Jan. 25, 1995; 1 child, John Ross. BS, U. Pa., 1963; JD, Yale U., 1966; PhD, Adelphi U., 1971. Dep. commr. N.Y.C. Dept. Mental Health, 1972-79; judge N.Y. State Family Ct., N.Y.C., 1982—. Contbr. numerous articles to profl. jours. Office: NY State Family Ct 60 Laayette St New York NY 10013

**JUSTICE, WILLIAM WAYNE,** federal judge; b. Athens, Tex., Feb. 25, 1920; s. William Davis and Jackie May (Hanson) J.; m. Sue Tom Ellen Rowan, Mar. 16, 1947; 1 dau., Ellen Rowan. LL.B., U. Tex., 1942. Bar: Tex. 1942. Ptnr. firm Justice & Justice, Athens, 1946-61; part-time city atty. Athens, 1948-50, 52-58; U.S. atty. U.S. Dist. Ct. (ea. dist.) Tex., Tyler, 1961-68, U.S. dist. judge, 1968—, chief judge, 1980-90, sr. judge, 1998—. Subject of book William Wayne Justice, A Judicial Biography (Frank R. Kemerer), 1991. Vice pres. Young Democrats Tex., 1948; adv. council Dem. Nat.

Com., 1954; alternate del. Dem. Nat. Conv., 1956, presdl. elector, 1960. Served to 1st lt. F.A. AUS, 1942-46, CBI. Recipient Nat. Outstanding Fed. Judge award ATLA, 1982, Outstanding Civil Libertarian award Tex. Civil Liberties Union, 1986, Lifetime Achievement award NACDL, 1996. Episcopalian. Office: 903 San Jacinto Blvd Ste 310 Austin TX 78701-2450

**JUSTUS, JO LYNNE,** lawyer; b. Manhattan, Kans., Jan. 26, 1950; d. William Wade and Gertrude Eunice (Wheeler) J.; 1 child, William Lee Whitson. BA, U. Kans., 1972, JD, 1975; grad., Nat. Inst. Trial Advocacy, 1983. Bar: Kans. 1975, U.S. Dist. Ct. Kans. 1975, U.S. Ct. Claims 1985, U.S. Ct. Appeals (10th cir.) 1985. Legal rschr. Chambers & Mallon, Kansas City, Kans., 1974-75; pvt. practice law Kansas City, 1975-78, Lawrence, Kans., 1978-82; mng. atty. Kans. Legal Svcs., Topeka, 1982-83, regional dir., 1983-84; ptnr. Metcalf and Justus, Topeka, 1984—. Active Douglas County chpt. ARC, Lawrence, 1980-82; coach Sunflower Soccer Assn., 1990—; membership chair Stout Elem. PTA, 1991-92, pres., 1992-93; mem. Stout Elem. Site Coun., 1993-96. Recipient Cert. of Appreciation award Unified Sch. Dist. 501, 1992-96. Mem. Kans. Bar Assn. (family law com. 1977-79, 83-84, legal issues affecting the elderly com. 1984-86), Topeka Area Bankruptcy Coun., U. Kans. Alumni Assn. (life), Lawrence Bus. and Profl. Women's Club (v.p. 1981, pres.-elect 1982, Outstanding Young Woman 1980). Republican. Presbyterian. Bankruptcy, Federal civil litigation, State civil litigation. Office: 3601 SW 29th PO Box 2184 Topeka KS 66601-2184

**KABAK, DOUGLAS THOMAS,** lawyer; b. Elizabeth, N.J., Nov. 19, 1957; s. Aaron and Marilyn Virginia (Johnson) K.; m. Elisabeth Wiggin McDuffie, Oct. 21, 1989; 1 child, Matthew Thomas McDuffie Kabak. BA, Rutgers U., 1979, MBA, 1990; JD, Seton Hall U., 1982; postgrad., U. Exeter, Eng., 1980. Bar. N.J. 1982, U.S. Dist. Ct. N.J. 1982. Law clk. Superior Ct. N.J., Elizabeth, 1982-83; assoc. Z. Lance Samay, Morristown, N.J., 1983-86; asst. dep. pub. defender Office Pub. Defender, Elizabeth, 1986—; legal rep. St. Joseph's the Carpenter Bd. Edn., Roselle, N.J., 1985-87. Dir. St. Joseph the Carpenter Cath. Youth Orgn., Roselle, 1986-88, coach, 1981-86. Mem. ABA, N.J. Bar Assn., Union County Bar Assn., KC. Roman Catholic. Home: 16 Indian Spring Rd Cranford NJ 07016-1616 Office: Pub Defender Office 65 Jefferson Ave Ste 3 Elizabeth NJ 07201-2441

**KABALA, EDWARD JOHN,** lawyer, corporate executive; b. Phila., Mar. 21, 1942; s. Stan and Margaret (Toner) K.; m. Gail L., Dec. 28, 1963; children: Courtenay, Paxson. BS, Pa. State U., 1964; JD, Duquesne U., 1970. Bar: Pa. 1970, U.S. Dist. Ct. (we. dist.) Pa., 3d cir. 1970, U.S. Tax Ct. 1970. Indsl. engr. Allegheny Ludlum Steel Co., 1964-67; sr. indsl. engr. Titanium Metals Corp. Am., 1967-68; patent engr. U.S. Steel Corp., 1969, atty., 1970; atty. Houston, Cooper, Speer and German, Pitts., 1970-73; pres. Kabala & Geeseman and predecessor firm, Pitts., 1973—; counsel Allegheny Med. Soc.; author, lectr. pensions, estate planning, taxation, fin. planning health care law various univs. and profl. orgns. of physicians, attys., accts., dentists, 1976—; editl. bd. Today's Health Care Mag; bd. dirs., chmn. Cancer Support Network, 1994-96. Author: Defending Your Practice in a Blue Sheild Audit, 1992. Recipient Crystal award Cancer Support Network, 1993-95. Mem. ABA (sect. of taxation com. on closely held corps. and com. on profl. service corps., sect. of bus. banking and corp. law com. on employee benefits), Pa. Bar Assn., Allegheny County Bar Assn., Am. Acad. Hosp. Attys. Pension, profit-sharing, and employee benefits, Estate planning, Health. Home: 18 Forest Glen Dr Pittsburgh PA 15228-1513 Office: The Waterfront 200 Forest Ave Pittsburgh PA 15202-1938

**KACIR, BARBARA BRATTIN,** lawyer; b. Buffalo, Ohio, July 19, 1941; d. William James and Jean (Harrington) Brattin; m. Charles Stephen Kacir, June 3, 1973 (div. Aug. 1977). BA, Wellesley Coll., 1963; JD, U. Mich., 1967. Bar: Ohio 1967, D.C. 1980. Assoc. Arter & Hadden, Cleve., 1967-74, ptnr., 1974-79; ptnr. Jones, Day, Reavis & Pogue, Washington, 1980-83, Cleve., 1983-95; dep. gen. counsel-litigation Textron Inc., Providence, 1995—; instr. trial tactics Case-Western Res. U., Cleve., 1976-79. Mem. nat. com. visitors, nat. fund raising com. U. Mich. Mem. ABA, Ohio Bar Assn., D.C. Bar Assn., Cleve. Bar Assn. (trustee 1973-76, treas. 1978-79), Am. Law Inst., Def. Rsch. Inst. Republican. Federal civil litigation, General corporate, Personal injury. Office: Textron Inc 40 Westminster St Ste 2 Providence RI 02903

**KACOYANIS, DENNIS CHARLES,** lawyer; b. Arlington, Mass., Sept. 3, 1953; s. Paul and Faye (Vaghida) K.; m. Anna Makrys, Sept. 16, 1990; children: Paul Dennis, Leah Faye. BA in Polit. Sci. with honors, Northeastern U., 1976; JD, DePaul U., 1979. Bar: Mass. 1979, U.S. Dist. Ct. Mass. 1980, U.S. Ct. Appeals (D.C. cir.) 1980, Va. 1981, U.S. Ct. Appeals (4th cir.) 1981, U.S. Dist. Ct. (ea. dist.) Va. 1991. Trial atty. EEOC, Washington, 1979-87; atty. U.S. Consumer Product Safety Commn., Washington, 1987—. atty. EEOC, Washington. Named one of Outstanding Young Men Am., 1986. Mem. Va. Bar Assn., Mass. Bar Assn., Am. Hellenic Lawyers Assn., Am. Hellenic Edn. Progressive Assn. Greek Orthodox. Avocations: athletics, music. Fax: 301-504-0359. E-mail: dkacoyanis@cpsl.gov. Home: 4301 Hollowstone Ct Chantilly VA 20151-2535 Office: US Consumer Product Safety Commn Washington DC 20207-0001

**KACZANOWSKA, LAURIE HYSON SMITH,** lawyer; b. Palmerton, Pa., July 7, 1953; d. James Donaldson and Mary Ann (Hyson) Smith; m. Donald James Gerber, Aug. 1976 (div. May 1981); m. Witold-K, Dec. 11, 1993; 1 child, Wit Thomas Kaczanowski. BS, Pa. State U., 1975; MSW, U. Denver, 1981; JD, Northeastern U., 1989. Adminstrv. staff, resource coord., vol. coord., counselor Women in Crisis, Lakewood, Colo., 1977-79; program adminstr. Big Sis. of Colo., Life Choices Program, Denver, 1979-80; legis. coord., lobbyist Common Cause, Denver, 1980-81; social work advocate Denver Legal Aid Soc., 1982-86; legis. analyst Nat. Conf. State Legis., Denver, 1987; mediator, intake coord. Harvard Law Sch., Cambridge, Mass., 1988; law clk. Supreme Jud. Ct. State Mass., Boston, 1988-89; legis. staff Rep. Patricia Schroeder, U.S. Congress, Washington, 1989; dir., ptnr. Pfaff & Smith Family Law Clinic, Denver, 1990-91; asst. city atty., sr. atty. unit leader, dir. alternative resolution program Denver City Attys. Office, Denver, 1991—; Co-owner, Arte Gallery, Inc.; pres., Apollon, Inc. Mem. Colo. Women's Bar Assn., Colo. Bar Assn., Colo. Lawyers for the Arts, Denver Bar Assn. Presbyterian. Avocations: daydreaming. Home: 3216 E 6th Ave Denver CO 80206-4407 Office: Denver City Attys Office 303 W Colfax Ave Ste 500 Denver CO 80204-2623

**KADEN, ELLEN ORAN,** lawyer, consumer products company executive; b. N.Y.C., Oct. 1, 1951. AB, Cornell U., 1972; MA, U. Chgo., 1973; JD, Columbia U., 1977. Bar: N.Y., 1978. Law clerk U.S. Dist. Ct. (so. dist.) N.Y., 1977-78; asst. prof. Columbia U. Sch. Law, 1978-82, assoc. prof., 1982-84; exec. v.p., gen. counsel, sec. CBS Inc., N.Y.C., 1991-98; sr. v.p. law and govt. affairs Campbell Soup Co., Camden, N.J., 1998—; reporter jud. coun. 2nd Cir. Adv. Comm. on Planning for Dist. Cts., 1979-81; assoc. Cravath, Swaine & Moore, 1981-86. Trustee Columbia U. Mem. Nat. Legal Aid and Defender Assn. (corp. adv. com.), Inst. Jud. Adminstrn. (trustee), Lawyers' Com. for Civil Rights (internat. rule of law coun.). Office: Campbell Soup Co One Campbell Pl Camden NJ 08103

**KADEN, LEWIS B.,** law educator, lawyer; b. 1942. AB, Harvard U., 1963, LLB, 1967. Bar: N.Y. 1970, N.J. 1974. Harvard scholar Emmanuel Coll. Cambridge U., 1963-64; law clk. U.S. Ct. Appeals, 1967; legis. asst. Senator Robert F. Kennedy, 1968; ptnr. Battle, Fowler, Stokes & Kheel, 1969-73; chief counsel to gov. State of N.J., 1974-76; assoc. prof. Columbia U., 1976-79, prof., 1979-84, adj. prof., 1984—, dir. Ctr. for Law and Econ. Studies, 1979-83; ptnr. Davis, Polk & Wardwell, N.Y.C., 1984—; bd. dirs. Bethlehem Steel Corp. Chmn. N.Y. State Indsl. Coop. Council, 1986-92. Office: Davis Polk & Wardwell 450 Lexington Ave New York NY 10017-3911

**KADISH, SANFORD HAROLD,** law educator; b. N.Y.C., Sept. 7, 1921; s. Samuel J. and Frances R. (Klein) K.; m. June Kurtin, Sept. 29, 1942; children: Joshua, Peter. B Social Scis, CCNY, 1942; LLB, Columbia U., 1948; JD (hon.), U. Cologne, 1983; LLD (hon.), CUNY, 1985, Southwestern U., 1993. Bar: N.Y. 1948, Utah 1954. Pvt. practice law N.Y.C., 1948-51; prof. law U. Utah, 1951-60, U. Mich., 1961-64; prof. law U. Calif., Berkeley, 1964-91, dean Law Sch., 1975-82, Morrison prof., 1973-91, prof. emeritus, 1991—; Fulbright lectr. Melbourne (Australia) U., 1956; vis. prof. Harvard U., 1960-61, Freiburg U., 1967, Stanford U., 1970; lectr. Salzburg Seminar Am. Studies, 1965; Fulbright vis. lectr. Kyoto (Japan) U., 1975; vis. fellow Inst. Criminology, Cambridge (Eng.) U., 1968. Author: (with M.R. Kadish) Discretion to Disobey—A Study of Lawful Departures from Legal Rules, 1973, (with Schulhofer) Criminal Law and Its Processes, 6th edit., 1995, Blame and Punishment—Essays in the Criminal Law, 1987; editor-in-chief Ency. Crime and Justice, 1983; contbr. articles to profl. jours. Reporter Calif. Legis. Penal Code Project, 1964-68; pub. mem. Wage Stblzn. Bd., region XII, 1951-53; cons. Pres.'s Commn. Adminstrn. of Justice, 1966; mem. Calif. Coun. Criminal Justice, 1968-69. Lt. USNR, 1943-46. Fellow Ctr. Advanced Study Behavioral Scis., 1967-68; Guggenheim fellow Oxford U., 1974-75; vis. fellow All Souls Coll. Oxford U. Fellow AAAS (v.p. 1984-86), Brit. Acad. (corr.); mem. AAUP (nat. pres. 1970-72), Am. Assn. Law Schs. (exec. com. 1960, pres. 1982), Order of Coif (exec. com. 1966-67, 74-75), Phi Beta Kappa. Home: 774 Hilldale Ave Berkeley CA 94708-1318

**KADUSHIN, KAREN D.,** dean; b. L.A., Sept. 3, 1943. BA, UCLA, 1964; JD, Golden Gate U., 1977. Bar: Calif. 1977, U.S. Dist. Ct. (no. dist.) Calif. 1977. Mem. adj. faculty law Golden Gate U. and U. San Francisco, 1977-84; assoc. Law Offices Diana Richmond, San Francisco, 1978-80; ptnr. Richmond & Kadushin, San Francisco, 1981-83; prin. Kadushin Law Offices, San Francisco, 1983-88; ptnr. Kadushin-Fancher-Wickland, San Francisco, 1989-94; dean Monterey (Calif.) Coll. Law, Monterey, Calif., 1995—; judge pro tem settlement confs. dept. domestic rels. San Francisco Superior Ct., 1985-95; bd. dirs. Lawyers Mut. Ins. Co. Author: California Practice Guide: Law Practice Management, 1992—. Bd. dirs. Legal Assistance for Elderly, San Francisco, 1983, San Francisco Neighborhood Legal Assistance Found., 1984. Mem. Calif. Women Lawyers, Bar Assn. San Francisco (bd. dirs. 1985-86, pres. 1993, Merit award 1980, 90), Barristers Club (pres. 1982). Office: Monterey Coll Law 404 W Franklin St Monterey CA 93940-2303

**KAESTNER, RICHARD DARWIN,** lawyer; b. Milw., Feb. 10, 1934; s. Henry B. and Sophia (Schley) K.; m. Shirley Sue Higgins, Sept. 16, 1961; children: Richard, Kurtis. BS, Marquette U., 1956, JD, 1961. Bar: Wis. 1961, U.S. Dist. Ct. (ea. dist.) Wis. 1961, U.S. Supreme Ct. 1971. Assoc. Wiernick & Zurlo, Milw., 1961-63, Beaudry & Kershek, Milw., 1963-67; sole practice Milw., 1976-77; ptnr. Harris & Kaestner, Wauwatosa, Wis., 1977-80; sole practice Elm Grove, Wis., 1980—; ct. commr. Circuit Ct. Wis., 1981—, Waukesha County, Wis., 1987—. Examiner, Milwaukee County Civil Svc. Commn., 1983—; officer, bd. dirs. Willaura West Homeowners Assn., 1976-84. Served with AUS, 1956-58. Mem. State Bar of Wis. (bd. attys. profl. responsibility com. 1976-85), Wis. Bar Assn., Milw. Bar Assn., Waukesha Bar Assn., Am. Coll. Trust and Estate Counsel, Delta Theta Phi. Lutheran. Probate, Family and matrimonial. Home: N30 W28935 W Lakeside Dr Pewaukee WI 53072 Office: PO Box 619 Elm Grove WI 53122-0619

**KAFANTARIS, GEORGE NICHOLAS,** lawyer; b. Kardamyla, Chios, Greece, May 11, 1953; came to U.S., 1966; s. Nicholas George and Evangelia M. (Frangias) K.; m. Maria G. Gampieris, June 3, 1977; children: Nicholas, Theologos, Mark, Constantine-Evangelos. BS, Youngstown State U., 1976; JD, U. Toledo, 1979. Bar: Ohio, 1981, U.S. Dist. Ct. (no. dist.) Ohio 1982. Pvt. practice Warren, Ohio, 1981—. Sec. United Chios Soc., Agia Markela, Warren, 1984-85; bd. dirs. St. Demetrios Orthodox Ch., Warren, 1984-85; Trumbull County Rep. Precinct Committeeman, Warren, 1984-85. Mem. ABA, Assn. Trial Lawyers Am., Ohio State Bar Assn. (mem. computer com. 1989—), Ohio Acad. Trial Lawyers, Mahoning County Bar Assn., Trumbull County Bar Assn., Mahoning-Trumbull Acad. Trial Lawyers. Avocations: photography, computers, swimming. State civil litigation, Personal injury, Labor. Home: 734 N Park Ave Warren OH 44483-4821 Office: 720 N Park Ave Warren OH 44483-4821

**KAFIN, ROBERT JOSEPH,** lawyer; b. Phila., Jan. 1, 1942; s. Jacob A. and Anna C. (Cohen) K.; m. Carol A. Friedman, June 20, 1965; children: Tammy Ellen, Peter Douglas. AB, Franklin & Marshall Coll., 1963; JD, Harvard U., 1966. Bar: N.Y. 1967, U.S. Dist. Ct. (so. dist.) N.Y. 1968, U.S. Dist. Ct. (no. dist.) N.Y. 1971, U.S. Dist. Ct. (we. dist.) N.Y. 1974, U.S. Ct. Appeals (2d cir.) 1971, U.S. Supreme Ct. 1972, D.C. 1997. Ptnr. Kafin and Needleman, Glens Falls, N.Y., 1971-78; prin. Miller, Mannix, Lemery & Kafin, Glens Falls, N.Y., 1978-87; assoc. Proskauer Rose LLP, N.Y.C., 1967-71, ptnr., 1987-91, chief operating officer, ptnr., 1991—; trustee Adirondack Conservancy Com., Elizabethtown, N.Y., 1980-87; judge Glens Falls City Ct., 1976; counsel N.Y. State Senate, Albany, N.Y., 1973-87. Editor: N.Y. Environmental Law Handbook, 1988, 92. Bd. dirs. Environ. Planning Lobby, Albany, 1977-88; active Manhattan Solid Waste Adv. Bd., N.Y.C., 1987—; dir. N.Y. Parks and Conservation Assn., 1995—, chmn., 1999; trustee Preservation League N.Y. State, 1997—. Mem. N.Y. Bar Assn. (sec. environ. law sect. 1988, treas. 1989, 1st vice chmn. 1991, chair 1992-93), Assn. Bar City N.Y. (environ. law com. 1987-89). Democrat. Jewish. Environmental, Land use and zoning (including planning). Home: 300 E 75th St Apt 24J New York NY 10021-3379 Office: Proskauer Rose LLP 1585 Broadway New York NY 10036-8200

**KAGAN, ANDREW BESDIN,** lawyer; b. Pittsfield, Mass., Apr. 26, 1949; s. David Bernard and Irene Sylvia (Besdin) K. B.A. in Psychology, Syracuse U., 1971; M.A. in Psychiat. Social Work, U. Chgo., 1975; J.D. with honors, Rutgers U., 1980. Bar: Ill. 1980, U.S. Dist. Ct. (no. dist.) Ill. 1980, U.S. Ct. Appeals (7th cir.) 1980, U.S. Tax Ct. 1994. Psychiat. social worker Austen Riggs Ctr., Stockbridge, Mass., 1971-73, Michael Reese Hosp., Chgo., 1975-77; assoc. Mandel, Lipton & Stevenson, Ltd., Chgo., 1980-82; sole practice, Chgo., 1982-85; of counsel Lawrence Y. Schwartz, Ltd., Lincolnwood, 1985—; arbitrator, comml. panel Am. Arbitration Assn., Chgo., 1984, Better Bus. Bur., Chgo., 1984; instr. Northeastern Ill. U., Chgo., 1984. Mem. Community Devel. Citizens' Adv. Council, Village of Oak Park, Ill., 1986. Recipient Am. Jurisprudence award Lawyer's Coop. Pub. Co., Rochester, N.Y., 1980. Mem. Ill. Bar Assn., Chgo. Bar Assn. (mem. lawyer referral service 1984). Contracts commercial, Health, Real property. Office: Ste 404 7366 N Lincoln Ave Chicago IL 60646-1708

**KAHAN, ROCHELLE LIEBLING,** lawyer, concert pianist; b. Chgo., Sept. 5, 1939; d. Arnold Leo and Helly (Ichilson) Liebling; m. Barry D. Kahan, Sept. 22, 1962; 1 child, Kara. BA, Northwestern U., 1960, JD, 1963. Bar: Ill. 1963, Tex. 1977. Atty. Treasury Dept., Chgo., 1964-65, Boston, 1965-66, 68-72, Washington, 1966-67; atty. pvt. practice, Chgo. and Houston, 1972—. Mem. ABA, Tex. Bar Assn. Houston Bar Assn., Tuesday Musical Club (1st v.p.), Treble Clef Club (pres.), Kappa Beta Pi (past pres.), Mu Phi Epsilon. Avocation: early music. Estate taxation.

**KAHARICK, JEROME JOHN,** lawyer; b. Johnstown, Pa., Apr. 15, 1955; s. Stanley Joseph and Emily (Solic) K.; m. Carolyn Marie Safko, Aug. 7, 1977; children: Natalie, Allison. BA summa cum laude, U. Pitts., 1977; JD, Duquesne U., 1991. Bar: Pa. 1991, U.S. Dist. Ct. (we. dist.) Pa. 1991, U.S. Dist. Ct. (we. dist.) Mich. 1998, U.S. Dist. Ct. (no. dist.) N.Y. 1998, U.S. Ct. Appeals (3d cir.) 1992, U.S. Supreme Ct., 1997. Sales rep. Met. Life, Johnstown, Pa., 1977-84; owner, stockholder Planned Fin. Svcs., Johnstown, Pa., 1984-88; law clk. Wayman, Irvin & McAuley, Pitts., 1988-89; legal analyst Elliott Co., Jeannette, Pa., 1989-92; pvt. practice Johnstown, 1992-95, 97—; asst. pub. defender Cambria County, Pa., 1993-99; ptnr. Weaver and Kaharick, 1995-97; atty. in pvt. practice Johnstown, Pa., 1997—. Exec. production editor Duquesne Law Rev., 1990-91. Mem. ABA, Assn. Trial Lawyers Am., Nat. Assn. Criminal Def. Lawyers, Pa. Bar Assn., Order of Barristers. Republican. Roman Catholic. General civil litigation, Criminal, Civil rights. Office: Lincoln Center 1st Flr 419 Lincoln St Ste 103 Johnstown PA 15901-1906

**KAHLER, RAY WILLIAM,** lawyer; b. Longview, Wash., Oct. 29, 1970; s. Ray E. and Karen G. Kahler. BA in English, U. Puget Sound, 1993; JD, Harvard U., 1996. Bar: Wash. 1996, U.S. Dist. Ct. (we. dist.) Wash. 1997. Lawyer Stritmatter Kessler Whelan Withey, Hoquiam, Wash., 1996—. Personal injury, Product liability, Toxic tort. Office: Stritmatter Kessler Whelan Withey 413 8th St Hoquiam WA 98550-3607

**KAHN, ALAN EDWIN,** lawyer; b. N.Y.C., Aug. 9, 1929; s. Joseph and Harriet Rose (Rubel) K.; m. Regina Wolf, Aug. 7, 1960 (div. Jan. 1978); 1 child, Jolie Galen; m. Patricia Ann Dugan, June 4, 1978. BBA, CCNY, 1950; JD, Bklyn. Law Sch., 1956. Bar: N.Y. 1956, U.S. Dist. Ct. (so. and ea. dists.) N.Y. 1978, U.S. Tax Ct. 1978; CPA, N.Y. Staff asst.-acct. Feinberg, Jacobs & Furman, N.Y.C., 1956-57; pvt. practice N.Y.C., 1957-96, 98—; prin. Law Office of Alan E. Kahn, N.Y.C., 1957-99; sr. ptnr. Kahn, Boyd, Levychin CPAs, N.Y.C., 1993; pvt. practice, 1998—; tax cons. to various nonprofit orgns., N.Y.C., 1977—. Cons. Vol. Lawyers for the Arts, N.Y.C., 1978—. Sgt. U.S. Army, 1951-52. Mem. ATLA (mem. com. 1990—), N.Y. State Bar Assn. (elder law com.), N.Y. State Trial Lawyers Assn. (chmn. subcom. on legis. estate and trusts 1979, spkr. bd. 1990—, mem. com. 1991—), N.Y. County Lawyers Assn. (taxation com. 1988—, sec. com. on taxation 1996—), Spkr.'s Bur., Assn. Trial Lawyers City N.Y., Jewish Lawyers Guild, N.Y. State Soc. CPAs, Nat. Sculpture Soc. (patron mem.), Odd Fellows (grand adv. bd. N.Y. chpt. 1979-80, gen. counsel grand lodge 1989—), Mchts. Club (bd. govs., asst. treas., treas. and gov. 1992—, award chmn. legal com. 1995—). Democrat. Avocation: collecting prints, paintings and oriental ceramics. State civil litigation, Probate, Personal income taxation. Home: 370 1st Ave New York NY 10010-4923 Office: 67 Wall St New York NY 10005-3101

**KAHN, BENJAMIN ALEXANDER,** lawyer; b. Boston, July 8, 1970; s. Michael David and Ruth Jacobson Kahn. BA, Tufts U., 1992; postgrad., U. Colo., 1994; JD, U. Mich., 1995. Bar: Colo. 1997, U.S. Dist. Ct. Colo. 1998. Clk. to Hon. Justice George E. Lohr Denver, 1995-96; assoc. Kennedy & Christopher, P.C., Denver, 1998—. Contbr. articles to profl. jours. such as Stanford Journal of Internat. Laws, Tort and Insurance Law Journal. Clara Belfield-Henry Bates Law Travel fellow, 1997. Mem. Colo. Bar Assn. (environ., natural resources, water, litigation, appellate and judiciary coms.), Adminstrn. Law Forum Com., Denver Bar, Def. Rsch. Inst., Colo. Def. Lawyers Assn., Colo. Indian Bar Assn. Avocations: art, music, outdoor activities, antiques, travel. General civil litigation, Appellate, Administrative and regulatory. Home: 2590 Cherry St Denver CO 80207-3145 Office: 1660 Wynkoop St Ste 900 Denver CO 80202-1115

**KAHN, BERT L.,** lawyer; b. Milw., July 5, 1938; s. David and Rose (Glusman) K.; m. Erika Apt, Sept. 1, 1963; children: Rita, Mitchell, Abigail. BBA, U. Wis., 1960, JD, 1963. Bar: Wis. 1964, Ill. 1971, U.S. Tax Ct. 1966. Atty. Estate & Gift Tax div., IRS, Chgo., 1963-65; trial atty. Reg. Counsels Office-U.S. Treasury Office, St. Paul and Chgo., 1965-72; ptnr. Hirschtritt, Hirschtritt, Gold, P.C., Chgo., 1972-77, Mardell & Kahn, Ltd., Chgo., 1977-81; pvt. practice Bert L. Kahn, Ltd., Skokie, Ill., 1981—; lectr. in field. Pres. Religious Zionists of Chgo., 1979-80, co-nat. pres. 1996-98; bd. dirs. Airie Crown Hebrew Day Sch., Chgo., 1981; chmn. subcom. lawyers div. Jewish United Fund, 1989-90. Mem. ABA (tax com.), Chgo. Bar Assn. (tax com.). Estate planning, Probate, Personal income taxation. Office: 4711 Golf Rd Ste 800 Skokie IL 60076-1246

**KAHN, CHARLES JULES, JR.,** judge; b. San Antonio; s. Charles J. and Bettie Berman Kahn; m. Janet Sorensen, Aug. 7, 1977; children: Julia Aren, Sally Joana. BA, Vanderbilt U., 1973; JD, U. Fla., 1977. Bar: Fla. 1977, U.S. Dist. Ct. (n. dist.) Fla. 1980, U.S. Ct. Appeals (5th and 11th cirs.) 1981, U.S. Army Ct. of Mil. Rev. 1983, U.S. Ct. Appeals (6th cir.) 1988. Asst. state atty. 12th Jud. Cir., Bradenton, Fla., 1977-78; litigation atty. Fla. Dept. Transp., Tallahassee, 1978-79; shareholder Levin, Middlebrook, Mabie, Mitchell, Thomas and Mayes, P.A., Pensacola, Fla., 1979-91; appellate judge Fla. Dist. Ct. Appeal, Tallahassee, 1991—; chair Fla. Jud. Ethics Com., 1996-97. Pres. N.E. Sertoma, Pensacola, 1988-89, Temple Beth El, Pensacola, 1989-91. Jewish. Office: 1st Dist Ct Appeal 301 S ML King Jr Blvd Tallahassee FL 32399-1850

**KAHN, DAVID MILLER,** lawyer; b. Port Chester, N.Y., Apr. 21, 1925; m. Barbara Heller, May 9, 1952; children: William, James, Caroline. BA, U. Ky., 1947; LLB cum laude, N.Y. Law Sch., 1950. Bar: N.Y. 1951, U.S. Dist. Ct. (ea. and so. dists.) N.Y. 1953, U.S. Supreme Ct. 1950. Sole practice White Plains, N.Y., 1951-60; ptnr. Kahn & Rubin, White Plains, 1960-66, Kahn & Goldman, White Plains, 1967-80; sr. ptnr. Kahn & Landau, White Plains, Palm Beach, Fla., 1980-88, Kahn and Kahn, Fla. and N.Y., 1988-95, Kahn, Kahn & Scutieri Esq., Palm Beach Gardens, 1995—; lectr. N.Y. Law Sch., 1982—; spl. counsel Village Port Chester, N.Y., 1960-63; commr. of appraisal Westchester County Supreme Ct., 1973-77; counsel Chemplex Industries, Inc., BIS Communications Corp., Bilbar Realty Co. Chmn. Westchester County Citizens for Eisenhower, 1950-52; pres. Westchester County Young Reps. Clubs, 1958-60; founder, chmn. bd. dirs. Port Chester-Rye Town Vol. Ambulance Corps, 1968-77; pres. Driftwood Corp., Amagansette, L.I., N.Y., 1984-91. Served with Counter Intelligence Corps USAF, 1942-46. Recipient John Marshall Harlan fellow N.Y. Law Sch., 1990-93. Fellow Am. Acad. Matrimonial Lawyers (bd. govs. N.Y. chpt. 1976-79); mem. ABA, N.Y. State Bar Assn., Westchester County Bar Assn., White Plains Bar Assn., N.Y. Law Sch. Alumni Assn. (bd. dirs. 1970-80), Elmwood C.C. (legal counsel), Eastpointe Country Club. Family and matrimonial, Probate, Real property. Home and Office: 6419 Eastpointe Pines St Palm Beach Gardens FL 33418 also: 175 Main St White Plains NY 10601-3105

**KAHN, EDWARD STANTON,** lawyer; b. Trenton, N.J., Aug. 22, 1947; s. Albert B. and Catherine A. (Loll) K.; m. Hana Mary Muzika, Aug. 4, 1974; children: Alicia C., Rachel, Samuel. BA, Amherst Coll., 1969; MEd, Rutgers U., 1974, EdD, JD, 1980. Bar: N.J. 1980, U.S. Dist. Ct. N.J. 1980, Pa. 1983, U.S. Tax Ct. 1984. Ptnr. Kahn, Schildkraut & Levy, Trenton, 1980-86; pvt. practice law Lawrenceville, N.J., 1986—; bd. dirs. H. Gross & Co., Outfitters, Inc., Princeton, N.J. Trustee Mercer County Coll. Found., West Windsor, N.J., 1984—, Har Sinai Hebrew Congregation, Trenton, 1980—. Democrat. Jewish. Estate planning, Personal injury, Real property. Home: 41 Westcott Rd Princeton NJ 08540-3038 Office: 140 Franklin Corner Rd Trenton NJ 08648-2502

**KAHN, EDWIN LEONARD,** lawyer; b. N.Y.C., Aug. 1, 1918; s. Max L. and Julia (Rich) K.; m. Myra J. Green, Oct. 20, 1946 (dec. 1994); children: Martha L., Deborah K. Spiliotopoulos. AB, U. N.C., 1937; LLB cum laude, Harvard U., 1940. Bar: N.C. 1940, D.C. 1949. Atty., asst. head legislation and regulations div. Office Chief Counsel IRS, 1940-52, dir. tech. planning div., 1952-55; ptnr. Arent, Fox, Kintner, Plotkin & Kahn, Washington, 1955-86, of counsel, ret., 1986—; lectr. NYU Tax Inst., mem. adv. bd., 1959-70; lectr. tax insts. Coll. William and Mary, U. Chgo., U. Tex. Editor: Harvard Law Rev, 1939-40; editorial adv. bd. Tax Advisor of Am. Inst. CPA's, 1974-86. Bd. dirs. Jewish Community Ctr. Greater Washington, 1972-78; trustee Cosmos Club Found., 1989-93, chmn., 1989-91. With U.S. Army, 1943-46, ETO. Decorated Bronze Star. Fellow Am. Bar Found. (life); mem. ABA (coun. 1963-66, vice chmn. sect. taxation 1965-66), Fed. Bar Assn. (chmn. taxation com. 1967-68), D.C. Bar Assn., Nat. Tax Assn.-Tax Inst. Am. (adv. coun. 1967-69, bd. dirs. 1969-73), Am. Law Inst. (life), Am. Coll. Tax Counsel, J. Edgar Murdock Am. Inn Ct. (master bencher 1988-91), Phi Beta Kappa (life mem. assocs.). Jewish. Corporate taxation, Personal income taxation, Estate taxation. Home: 4104 40th St N Arlington VA 22207-4805 Office: 1050 Connecticut Ave NW Washington DC 20036-5314

**KAHN, ELLIS IRVIN,** lawyer; b. Charleston, S.C., Jan. 18, 1936; s. Robert and Estelle Harriet (Kaminski) K.; m. Janice Weinstein, Aug. 11, 1963; children: Justin Simon, David Israel, Cynthia Kahn Nirenblatt. AB in Polit. Sci., The Citadel, 1958; JD, U. S.C., 1961. Bar: S.C. 1961, U.S. Ct. Appeals (5th cir.) 1963, U.S. Ct. Appeals (4th cir.) 1964, U.S. Supreme Ct. 1970, D.C. 1978, U.S. Claims Ct. 1988; diplomate Nat. Bd. Trial Advocacy, Am. Bd. Profl. Liability Attys. (trustee 1989—). Law clk. U.S. Dist. Ct. S.C., 1964-66; prin. Kahn Law Firm, Charleston; adj. prof. med.-legal jurisprudence Med. U. S.C., 1978-87; mem. rules com. U.S. Dist. Ct., 1984-96. Chmn. campaign Charleston Jewish Fedn., 1986-87, pres., 1988-90, S.C. Organ Procurment Agy., 1987-94, chmn. bd. 1989-94, mem. nat. coun. Am. Israel Pub. Affairs Com., 1982-88, Hebrew Benevolent Soc., pres., 1994-96; mem. Hebrew Orphan Soc. Capt. USAF, 1961-64. Fellow Internat. Soc. Barristers; mem. S.C. Bar, ABA, ATLA (state committeeman 1970-74), S.C. Trial Lawyers Assn. (pres. 1976-77), 4th Cir. Jud. Conf. (permanent mem.). Federal civil litigation, State civil litigation, Personal injury. Home: 316 Confederate Cir Charleston SC 29407-7431 Office: PO Box 898 Charleston SC 29402-0898

**KAHN, ERIC G.,** lawyer; b. Summit, N.J., Dec. 23, 1967; m. Lynn M. Kahn, Oct. 4, 1997. BA, Haverford Coll., 1990; JD, Rutgers U. Newark, 1993. Bar: Pa. 1993, N.J. 1993, U.S. Dist. Ct. N.J. 1993. Assoc. Javerbaum, Wurgaft, Hicks & Zarin, Springfield, N.J., 1993—. Mem. ATLA, ATLA

N.J., ABA, N.J. State Bar Assn. Avocations: golf, basketball, fin. planning. State civil litigation, Personal injury, Professional liability. Office: Javerbaum Wurgaft Hicks & Zarin 959 S Springfield Ave Springfield NJ 07081-3555

**KAHN, LAURENCE MICHAEL,** lawyer; b. Chgo., May 15, 1947; s. Ernest Newman and Louise (Schoenberg) K.; m. Geraldine Marie Hirsch, July 31, 1971 (div. Oct. 1985); children: Eric M., Melissa M.; m. Candace L. Ross, Sept. 7, 1991. BA magna cum laude, U. Pa., 1969, MS in Edn., 1971; JD cum laude, U. Mich., 1977. Bar: Mich. 1977, D.C. 1980, Md. 1981, U.S. Dist. Ct. Md. 1981, U.S. Dist. Ct. D.C. 1981, U.S. Ct. Claims 1989, U.S. Ct. Appeals (D.C. cir) 1992, Calif. 1994. Tchr. Northbrook (Ill.) Sch. Dist. 27, 1969-70, Abington (Pa.) Sch. Dist., 1971-73, Phila. Sch. Dist., 1973-74; staff atty. FTC, Washington, 1977-81; from assoc. to ptnr. Sherman Meehan & Curtin, PC, Washington, 1981-91; adj. prof. U. Md., College Park, 1981, Nat. U., San Diego, 1997, San Diego State U., 1999. Mem. Assn. Trial Lawyers Am., Md. Bar Assn., D.C. Bar Assn., Montgomery County Bar Assn., Phi Beta Kappa. Avocations: jogging, participating in team sports, canoeing, hiking, ornithology. Alternative dispute resolution, Contracts commercial.

**KAHN, MARK LEO,** arbitrator, educator; b. N.Y.C., Dec. 16, 1921; s. Augustus and Manya (Fertig) K.; m. Ruth Elizabeth Wecker, Dec. 21, 1947 (div. Jan. 1972); children: Ann Mariam, Peter David, James Allan, Jean Sarah; m. Elaine Johnson Morris, Feb. 12, 1988. BA, Columbia U., 1942; MA, Harvard U., 1948, PhD in Econs., 1950. Asst. economist U.S. OSS, Washington, 1942-43; tchg. fellow Harvard U., 1947-49; dir. case analysis U.S. WSB, Region 6-B Mich., 1952-53; mem. faculty Wayne State U., Detroit, 1949-85, prof. econs., 1960-85, prof. emeritus, 1985—, dept. chmn., 1961-68, dir. indsl. rels. M.A. program, 1978-85; arbitrator union-mgmt. disputes. Co-author: Collective Bargaining and Technological Change in American Transportation, 1971; mem. editl. bd. Employee Responsibilities and Rights Jour., 1988-96; contbr. articles to profl. jours. Bd. govs. Jewish Welfare Fedn. Detroit, 1976-82; bd. dirs. Jewish Home for Aged, Detroit, 1978-93, Lyric Chamber Ensemble, Southfield, Mich., 1995-97, Detroit Empowerment Zone Devel. Corp., 1996-99. Capt. AUS, 1943-46. Decorated Bronze Star; recipient Disting. Svc. award U.S. Nat. Mediation Bd., 1987, Am. Arbitration Assn., 1992. Mem. AAUP (past chpt. pres.), Nat. Acad. Arbitrators (bd. govs. 1960-62, v.p. 1976-78, chmn. membership com. 1979-82, pres. 1983-84, chmn. nominating com. 1995-96), Indsl. Rels. Rsch. Assn. (pres. Detroit chpt. 1956, exec. sec. 1979-89, nat. exec. bd. 1985-88), Soc. Profls. in Dispute Resolution (v.p. 1982-83, pres. 1986-87). Home and Office: 15151 Ford Rd Apt 321 Dearborn MI 48126-5027

**KAHN, SCOTT H.,** lawyer; b. Chgo., Dec. 28, 1955; s. Lee K. and Jeannett Kahn; m. Janice M. Aveni, July 28, 1979; children: Justin R., Adam Kadan, Jamie Victoria. BS/BA, John Carroll U., 1979; JD, Cleve. U., 1982. With Moore Bus. Forms, Cleve., 1979-81, Magna Form, Inc., Cleve., 1981-83; assoc. McIntyre, Kahn, Kruse & Gillamabardo, Cleve., 1982—. Karate tchr. Kwanmuzendikia, Cleve., 1988; youth soccer coach Mayfield (Ohio) Soccer Club, 1992. Construction, Real property, Contracts commercial. Office: McIntyre Kahn Kruse et al The Galleria & Towers 1301 E 9th St Ste 1200 Cleveland OH 44114-1823

**KAIER, EDWARD JOHN,** lawyer; b. Sewickley, Pa., Sept. 23, 1945; s. Edward Anthony and Mary Patricia (Crimmins) K.; m. Annette Thomas, July 31, 1976; children: Elizabeth Anne, Charles Crimmins, Thomas Edward. AB, Harvard U., 1967; JD, U. Pa., 1970. Bar: D.C. 1970, Pa. 1970, U.S. Dist. Ct. (ea. dist.) Pa. 1971, U.S. Ct. Appeals (3rd and D.C. cirs.) 1971, U.S. Dist. Ct. D.C., 1971. Law clk. to presiding justice U.S. Dist. Ct. for D.C., Washington, 1970-71; assoc. Dechert Price & Rhoads, Phila., 1971-74; ptnr. Kaier and Kaier, Phila., 1974-77, Hepburn Willcox Hamilton & Putnam, Phila., 1977—; pres. Savoy Co., Phila., 1978-80; bd. dirs. Mgrs. Funds, Norwalk, Conn. Vice chmn. Rosemont (Pa.) Sch. of Holy Child, 1981-90. Mem. ABA, Phila. Bar Assn. (chmn. office practice com. probate sect. 1987-90, exec. com. 1990-92), Merion Cricket Club, Phila. Club, Phila. Country Club, Avalon Yacht Club (trustee 1987-90, 92-93, treas. 1990-92), Harvard-Radcliffe Club (Phila., sec. 1989—). Republican. Roman Catholic. Avocations: sailing, golf. Probate, Estate taxation, Estate planning. Home: 111 N Lowrys Ln Rosemont PA 19010-1408 Office: Hepburn Willcox Hamilton & Putnam 1100 One Penn Ctr Philadelphia PA 19103

**KAILAS, LEO GEORGE,** lawyer; b. N.Y.C., May 28, 1949; s. George and Evanthia (Skoulikas) K.; AB, Columbia U., 1970, JD, 1973; m. Merle S. Duskin; children: Arianne, George, Shirley. Bar: N.Y. 1974. Assoc. firm Olwine, Connelly, Chase, O'Donnell and Weyher, N.Y.C., 1973-77; partner specializing in internat., comml. and admiralty litigation, firm Milgrim Thomajan Jacobs & Lee, P.C., (now Piper & Marbury L.L.P.) N.Y.C., 1977—, mem. internat. trade and litigation group. Mem. ABA, Assn. of Bar of City of N.Y. (chmn. admiralty com. 1985-88). Public international, Commodities. Office: Piper & Marbury LLP 1251 Avenue Of The Americas New York NY 10020-1104

**KAIMOWITZ, GABE HILLEL,** civil rights lawyer; b. N.Y.C., May 5, 1935; s. Abraham and Esther (Bialogursky) K.; children: David, Beth. BS, U. Wis., 1955; MA, U. Cen. Fla., 1988; LLB, NYU, 1967. Bar: N.Y. 1969, Mich. 1971, Fla., 1987, U.S. Dist. Ct. (mid. dist.) Fla., 1987, U.S. Ct. Appeals (6th cir.) 1971, U.S. Ct. Appeals (3d cir.) 1982, U.S. Ct. Appeals (2d cir.) 1983, U.S. Ct. Appeals (11th cir.), 1989 U.S. Ct. Appeals (7th cir.) 1990, U.S. Ct. Appeals (D.C. cir.) 1998. Atty. Ctr. Social Welfare, Politics and Law, N.Y.C., 1967-70; sr. atty. Mich. Legal Services, Detroit, 1971-79; assoc. P.R. Legal Def., N.Y.C., 1980-84; exec. dir. Greater Orlando (Fla.) A. Legal Services, 1985-86; atty. Attys. Against Am. Apartheid, Fla. and various other civil rights orgns., 1969—; lectr., adj. prof. numerous univs. Contbr. articles to profl. jours.; author poems. Served with U.S. Army, 1956-57, with Res. 1958-60. Smith fellow, 1970-71, Legal Services Corp. fellow, 1979-80. Mem. N.Y. State Bar Assn., Fla. Bar Assn. Jewish. Avocations: writing and editing. Civil rights, Federal civil litigation, Constitutional. Home: 4411 SW 34th St Gainesville FL 32608-2562 Office: PO Box 140119 Gainesville FL 32614-0119

**KAINEC, LISA ANNE,** lawyer; b. Cleve., Nov. 10, 1967. BBA cum laude, Cleve. State U., 1990; JD magna cum laude, Case Western Res. U., 1993. Bar: Ohio 1993, U.S. Dist. Ct. (no. dist.) Ohio 1993, U.S. Dist. Ct. Ariz. 1995, U.S. Ct. Appeals (6th cir.) 1995, U.S. Ct. Appeals (4th and 8th cirs.) 1996. Assoc. Millisor & Nobil Co. LPA, Cleve., 1993-98, ptnr., 1999—. Vice chair, assoc. bd. trustees Recovery Resources, Cleve., 1996-98, chair, assoc. bd. trustees, 1999. Mem. ABA, Ohio Bar Assn., Cleve. Bar Assn. Labor. Office: Millisor & Nobil Co LPA 9150 S Hills Blvd Ste 300 Cleveland OH 44147-3506

**KAINEN, BURTON,** lawyer; b. Huntington, N.Y., Dec. 8, 1942; s. Roland and Sylvia J. (Kotler) K.; m. Ann Marston Ehleider, June 12, 1965; children: Michael, Steven. BA, St. Lawrence U., 1964; MBA, Columbia U., 1966; JD, U. Conn., 1971. Bar: Conn. 1971, D.C. 1980, U.S. Dist. Ct. Conn. 1971, U.S. Ct. Appeals (2d cir.) 1975. Assoc. Siegel & O'Connor, Hartford, Conn., 1971-74; ptnr. Siegel, O'Connor & Kainen, Hartford, Conn., 1974-81, mng. ptnr., 1981-85; mng. ptnr. Siegel, O'Connor, Schiff, Zangari & Kainen, Hartford, Conn., 1985-93; ptnr. Kainen, Starr, Garfield, Wright & Escalera, P.C., Hartford, 1993-98, Shipman & Goodwin LLP, Hartford, 1998—. Author: (with others) Labor Arbitrator Development, 1983, A Handbook for Connecticut Elected Officials, 1985, Labor Arbitration, A Practice Guide for Advocates, 1990; contbr. articles to profl. jours. Fellow Coll. Labor and Employment Lawyers; mem. ABA (com. chmn. 1983—), Conn. Bar Assn., Hartford County Bar Assn., Hopmeadow Country Club (dir. 1980-82), Stratton Country Club. Labor, Federal civil litigation. Office: Shipman & Goodwin LLP One American Row Hartford CT 06103-2819

**KAITZ, HASKELL A.,** lawyer, accountant, retired; b. Chelsea, Mass., Nov. 25, 1922; s. Isidor and Anna G. (Cohen) K.; m. Bettie Kahan, Nov. 19, 1944; children: Merrill A., Gary M. BSBA, Boston U., 1943; JD, Suffolk U., 1969. Bar: Mass. 1970, U.S. Tax Ct. 1970, U.S. Supreme Ct. 1979; CPA, Mass., Fed. Dist. Ct. 1982. Ptnr. Kaitz, Levine and Ilacqua and predecessors, CPA's, Boston, 1943—. Contbr. articles to profl. jours. Mem. AICPA (40-yr. hon.), Mass. Soc. CPA's, Mass. Bar Assn. Avocation: computer programming. Estate planning, Probate, Estate taxation.

**KALAT, PETER ANTHONY,** lawyer; b. Worcester, Mass., Nov. 16, 1939; s. Norman William and Priscilla (Rose) K.; m. Lois Campbell, Mar. 24, 1962 (div. 1988); children: Lindsey, Jennifer, Caroline, Peter S.; m. Nie Lih Cheng, Jan. 22, 1994. BA, Middlebury Coll., 1962; LLB, U. Va., 1965. Bar: Va. 1965, N.Y. 1966, D.C. 1979, U.S. Dist. Ct. (so. and ea. dists.) N.Y. 1968, U.S. Supreme Ct. 1976. Assoc. Curtis, Mallet-Prevost, Colt, & Mosle, N.Y.C., 1965-72, ptnr., 1973—; bd. dirs. privately held cos. Mem. Westchester Contract Bridge Assn. (bd. dirs., pres.). General corporate, Private international. Home: 36 Mianus Dr Bedford NY 10506-1909 Office: Curtis Mallet-Prevost Colt & Mosle 101 Park Ave Fl 34 New York NY 10178-0061

**KALER, ROBERT JOSEPH,** lawyer; b. Boston, July 20, 1956; s. Robert Joseph and Joanne (Bowen) K. BA, Dartmouth Coll., 1978; JD, Am. U., 1981. Bar: D.C. 1981, Mass. 1983, U.S. Dist. Ct. D.C. 1982, U.S. Dist. Ct. Mass. 1984, U.S. Ct. Appeals (D.C. cir.) 1983, U.S. Dist. Ct. Appeals (1st cir.) 1984, U.S. Supreme Ct. 1986. Law clk. Sullivan & Cromwell, Washington, 1979-80, U.S. Dept. Justice, Washington, 1980-81; assoc. McKenna, Connor & Cuneo, Washington, 1981-83; ptnr. Gadsby & Hannah, Boston, 1983—. Contbr. articles to profl. jours. Mem. ABA, Internat. Bar Assn., Mass Bar Assn. General civil litigation, Private international, Trademark and copyright. Office: Gadsby & Hannah 225 Franklin St Boston MA 02110-2804

**KALIL, DAVID THOMAS,** lawyer; b. Detroit, Sept. 22, 1926; s. David A. and Rose Kalil; m. Helga A. Kalil, Nov. 1, 1958; children: David E., John T. BSE in Chem. Engring., U. Mich., 1948; LLB, Mich. State U., Detroit, 1951. Bar: Mich. 1952, Pa. 1989, U.S. Dist. Ct. (we. dist.) Pa. Examiner U.S. Patent Office, Washington, 1951-52; pvt. practice, Detroit, 1952-58; patent lawyer Internat. Nickel Co., Inc., N.Y.C., 1959-63; gen. and patent lawyer Kaynar Mfg. Co., Inc., Fullerton, Calif., 1963-64; asst. dir. law dept. Amax, Inc., N.Y.C., 1964-77; v.p., gen. counsel Jones & Laughlin Steel, Pitts., 1977-83; pvt. practice, Pitts., 1989—; cons. D.E. Cummings, Inc., Bethlehem, Pa., 1985—; gen. mgr. Mindlin Co., Pitts., 1983-85. Cpl. USAAF, 1945-46, ETO. Roman Catholic. Avocations: golf, reading, lecturing, mentoring. General corporate, Contracts commercial, Natural resources. Home: 111 Shannon Dr Pittsburgh PA 15238-1713 Office: 260 Alpha Dr Pittsburgh PA 15238-2906

**KALISH, ARTHUR,** lawyer; b. Bklyn., Mar. 6, 1930; s. Jack and Rebecca (Biniamofsky) K.; m. Janet J. Wiener, Mar. 7, 1953; children: Philip, Pamela. BA, Cornell U., 1951; JD, Columbia U., 1956. Bar: N.Y. 1956, D.C. 1970. Assoc. Paul, Weiss, Rifkind, Wharton & Garrison, N.Y.C., 1956-64, ptnr., 1965-95, of counsel, 1996—; lectr. NYU Inst. Fed. Taxation, Hawaii Tax Inst., Law Jour. Seminars. Contbr. articles to legal jours. Assoc. trustee L.I. Jewish Med. Ctr., New Hyde Park, N.Y., 1978-82, trustee, 1982-95, hon. trustee, 1995-97; trustee emeritus North Shore - L.I. Jewish Health Sys., 1997-98, life trustee, 1998—; bd. dirs. Cmty. Health Program of Queens Nassau Inc., New Hyde Park, 1978-94, pres., 1981-89, chmn. emeritus, 1994-97; bd. dirs. Managed Health, Inc., New Hyde Park, 1990-98, chmn., 1994-95. Fellow Am. Coll. Tax Counsel; mem. ABA, N.Y. State Bar Assn., Assn. Bar City N.Y., Columbia Law Sch. Assn. (bd. dirs. 1990-94). Corporate taxation, Personal income taxation. Home: 2 Bass Pond Dr Old Westbury NY 11568-1307 Office: Paul Weiss Rifkind Wharton & Garrison Ste 4200 1285 Avenue Of The Americas Fl 21 New York NY 10019-6064

**KALISH, DANIEL A.,** lawyer; b. N.Y.C., Aug. 22, 1958; m. Hilde, Oct. 28, 1988; children: Jordan, Ryan. BA, Duke U., 1980; JD, Washington U., St. Louis, 1985. Assoc. Kelner & Kelner, N.Y.C., 1985-86, Rheingold & Golomb, N.Y.C., 1987, pvt. practice, White Plains, N.Y., 1988—. Bd. govs. Ardsley (N.Y.) - Secor Vol. Ambulence Corps, 1995—. Mem. Am. Trial Laywers Assn., N.Y. State Trial Lawyers Assn., Westchester County Bar Assn., Trial Lawyers for Pub. Justice. Avocations: family, jogging, reading. Personal injury, State civil litigation. Office: 175 Main St Ste 207 White Plains NY 10601-3128

**KALKSTEIN, JOSHUA ADAM,** lawyer; b. Phila., Oct. 1, 1943; s. Abraham and Helen (Ponemone) K.; children: Aleta K., Trevor W., Maxim J. AB, Brown U., 1965; JD, U. Pa., 1968. Bar: N.Y. 1968, N.J. 1971, Mass. 1978, U.S. Dist. Ct. N.Y. 1968, U.S. Dist. Ct., N.J. 1971, U.S. Dist. Ct., Mass. 1978, U.S. Ct. of Appeals (3d cir.) 1973, U.S. Ct. Mil. Appeals 1969. Sr. corp. counsel rsch. Pfizer Inc., Groton, Conn., 1978—; assoc. Hellring, Lindeman & Landau, Newark, 1972-75; corp. counsel Hooper Holmes Inc., Basking Ridge, N.J., 1975-78; vis. counsel Harvard U., MIT Ctr. for Exptl. Pharmacology and Therapeutics, Cambridge, 1995—. Bd. dirs. Howland Art Ctr., Beacon, N.Y., 1987-91, Congregation Beth El, New London, Conn., 1995-96; commr. Waterfront Redevel. Commn., Beacon, 1990-91. Lt. USNR, 1969-72. Mem. N.Y. State Bar Assn., N.J. Bar Assn., Mass. Bar Assn. Jewish. Avocations: art collecting, book collecting, golf. Home: 76 Library St Mystic CT 06355-2420 Office: Pfizer Inc Eastern Point Rd Groton CT 06340

**KALLGREN, EDWARD EUGENE,** lawyer; b. San Francisco, May 22, 1928; s. Edward H. and Florence E. (Campbell) K.; m. Joyce Elaine Kislitzin, Feb. 8, 1953; children: Virginia K. Pegley, Charles Edward. AB, U. Calif., Berkeley, 1951, JD, 1954. Bar: Calif. Assoc., ptnr. Brobeck, Phleger & Harrison, San Francisco, 1954-93, of counsel, 1993—. Bd. dirs. Olivet Meml. Park, Colma, Calif., 1970-98, pres., 1991-98; chair, pres. Five Bridges Found., 1998—; mem. Berkeley City Council, 1971-75; bd. dirs., v.p./treas. Planned Parenthood Alameda/San Francisco, 1984-89. Served to sgt. USMC, 1945-48. Mem. ABA (ho. of dels. 1985—, state del. 1997-98, coun. sr. law divsn. 1996—, chair 1999—), State Bar of Calif. (bd. govs. 1989-92, v.p. 1991-92), Found. of State Bar Calif. (bd. dirs. 1993-98, v.p., 1994-96, chair fellows soc. 1996-98), Bar Assn. San Francisco (pres. 1988, bd. dirs.), San Francisco Lawyers Com. Urban Affairs (co-chair 1983-85), Lawyers Com. Civil Rights Under Law (trustee 1985—), The TenBroek Soc. (chair bd. dirs. 1992-95). Democrat. General corporate, Contracts commercial. Office: Brobeck Phleger & Harrison Spear St Tower 1 Market Plz Ste 341 San Francisco CA 94105-1420

**KALLIANIS, JAMES H., JR.,** lawyer; b. Chgo., July 4, 1965. BA, U. Ill., 1987; JD, DePaul U., 1990. Bar: Calif. 1990, Ill. 1992, U.S. Ct. Appeals (9th cir.) 1990, U.S. Dist. Ct. (no., ctrl. dists.) Calif. 1990, U.S. Dist. Ct. (ea. dist.) Calif. 1992. Assoc. Crosby, Heafey, Roach & May, Oakland, Calif., 1990-91, Buchalter, Nemer, Fields & Younger, San Francisco, 1991-93, Sedgwick, Detert, Moran & Arnold, Chgo., 1993-95; ptnr. Bates Meckler Bulger & Tilson, Chgo., 1995—. Contbr. articles to profl. jours. Mem. ABA, Am. Health Lawyers Assn., Profl. Liability Underwriting Soc. General civil litigation, Securities, Insurance. Office: Bates Meckler Bulger & Tilson 8300 Sears Tower 233 S Wacker Dr Chicago IL 60606-6306

**KALLINA, EMANUEL JOHN, II,** lawyer; b. Balt., Dec. 18, 1948; s. Robert Wooding and Elanor Lee (Stinson) K.; m. Anne M. Vik, Jan. 16, 1982; children: James E. (dec.), Deborah A., Kristine L., Abigail M. BA in English, Bowdoin Coll., Brunswick, Maine, 1970; JD, U. Md., 1973; LLM in Taxation, NYU, 1974. Bar: Md. 1974, D.C. 1977. Law clk. Hon. R. Dorsey Watkins, U.S. Dist. Judge, Balt., 1974-75; assoc. McKenney, Thomsen & Burke, Balt., 1975-77; pvt. practice Balt., 1977-78; ptnr. Niles, Barton & Wilmer, Balt., 1978-82; pres., atty. Kallina, Levinson & Burns, Balt., 1982-85, Kallina & Assocs., Balt., 1985-92; pres., mng. ptnr. Kallina & Ackerman, Balt., 1993—; real estate broker Kallina Realty Assocs., Balt., 1985—; life ins. agt., Balt., 1990—. Contbr. articles to profl. jours.; frequent speaker in field. Bd. dirs. Nat. Com. on Planned Giving, 1993-95, chmn. govt. rel. com., 1994-98; co-founder Chesapeake Planned Giving Coun.; mem. The Working Group; chmn. bd., pres. The James Found., 1995—. Mem. ABA, Md. Bar Assn., Balt. Assn. Tax Counsel (pres. 1981-82), D.C. Bar Assn. Republican. State civil litigation, Estate taxation. Office: Kallina & Ackerman LLP 6507 York Rd Baltimore MD 21212-2115

**KALLMAN, KRISTOFER,** lawyer; b. Santa Barbara, Calif., Dec. 29, 1948; s. Robert Edward Kallman and Ruth Davis; m. Gwen G. Kallman, Dec. 13, 1981; children: Aimee, Matthew. BA in History, Calif. Poly., 1971; JD, Pepperdine U., 1975. Bar: Calif. 1975, U.S. Dist. Ct. (ctrl. dist.) Calif. 1976. Assoc. Halde, Thomas, Kallman & Hulse, Santa Barbara, 1976-84; ptnr. Law Offices of Kristofer Kallman, Santa Barbara, 1985—; pres. Am. Bd. Trial Advocates, Santa Barbara, 1997-98. Bd. dirs. 19th Dist. Agrl. Assn., 1985-89; pres. Santa Barbara br. Arthritis Found., 1988-89. Mem. Univ. Club of Santa Barbara. Republican. Avocations: music, golf, horseback riding. Personal injury, Product liability. Office: Law Offices of Kristofer Kallman 2019B State St Santa Barbara CA 93105-3553

**KALLMANN, STANLEY WALTER,** lawyer; b. Bklyn., June 6, 1943; s. Silve and Erna (Clesius) K.; m. Carolee A. McDonald, Aug. 23, 1969; children: Alexander, Andrew. BA, Rutgers U., New Brunswick, 1964; LLB, Rutgers U., Newark, 1967. Bar: N.J. 1967, U.S. Dist. Ct. N.J. 1967, N.Y. 1984. Law clk. to judge U.S. Dist. Ct. N.J., Newark, 1967-69; assoc. Stryker, Tams & Dill, Newark, 1969-71; asst. U.S. atty. U.S. Atty.'s Office, Newark, 1971-75; ptnr. Gennet, Kallmann, Antin & Robinson, Parsippany, N.J., 1975—. Mem. ABA, N.J. Bar Assn. State civil litigation, Federal civil litigation, Insurance. Office: Gennet Kallmann Antin & Robinson 6 Campus Dr Parsippany NJ 07054-4401

**KALLSTROM, JAMES DAVID,** lawyer; b. Akron, Ohio, Sept. 20, 1950; s. David H. and Mary (Joshua) K.; m. Phebe Gay Zimmerman, Jan. 2, 1982; 1 child, Adam J. AB, Kenyon Coll., 1973; JD, Case Western Res. U., 1976. Bar: Ohio 1976, Okla. 1982. Gen. counsel Kallstrom Real Estate, Akron, Ohio, 1976-81; ptnr. Kallstrom & Ming, Edmond, Okla., 1982-84, Reed, Kallstrom, Shadid & Pipes, Oklahoma City, 1984-86; of counsel Speck, Philbin, Fleig, Trudgeon & Lutz, Oklahoma City, 1987-99, Lynn & Neville, Oklahoma City, 1999—; instr. real estate law Akron U., 1979-81, Cen. State U., Edmond, 1982-84; instr. bus. law Okla. Christian Coll., Edmond, 1984. Mem. ABA, Okla. Bar Assn., Okla. City Land Title Atty.'s Assn. Real property, Oil, gas, and mineral. Office: Linn & Neville 1200 Bank of Okla Plz 201 Robert S Kerr Ave Oklahoma City OK 73102-4289

**KALOGREDIS, VASILIOS J.,** lawyer, health care management consultant; b. New Bedford, Mass., Mar. 3, 1949; s. John V. and Rose (Simeonidis) K.; m. Stephanie Pahides, May 26, 1974; children: Maria, John. BS in Acctg., Providence Coll., 1971; JD, Villanova U., 1974. Bar: Pa. 1974. Assoc. Beck & Kalogredis, Bala Cynwyd, Pa., 1974-81; ptnr. Kalogredis Law Assocs., Wayne, Pa., 1981-95; founder, pres. Kalogredis Tsoules and Sweeney Ltd., Wayne, 1996—; speaker in field. Contbg. author: The Physician's Practice, 1980. Contbr. articles to profl. jours. Pres. St. George Greek Orthodox Ch., Media, Pa., 1980, 86, chmn. bldg. com., 1984-87. Dougherty fellow Villanova U., 1971-74. Mem. ABA, Pa. Bar Assn., Soc. Med.-Dental Cons., Soc. Profl. Bus. Cons., Nat. Health Lawyers Assn. Republican. Pension, profit-sharing, and employee benefits, General corporate, Health. Office: 995 Old Eagle School Rd Ste 315 Wayne PA 19087-1709

**KALOMIRIS, ERRIKA,** lawyer; b. Valley Stream, N.Y.. BA, Barnard Coll., 1986; MPA, Columbia U., 1987; JD, Vanderbilt U., 1994. Bar: N.J. 1994, N.Y. 1995. Assoc. dir. Barnard Coll., N.Y.C., 1986; grants mgr. N.Y.C. Dept. Transp., N.Y.C., 1987-88; analyst Mayor's Office Ops., N.Y.C., 1988-91; contract mgr. N.Y.C. Transit Authority, 1994-96; dir. mgmt. and tech. assistance United Neighborhood Houses, N.Y.C., 1996—. Mem. bd. campus ministry Episcopal Diocese N.Y., N.Y.C., 1998. Mem. Assn. of the Bar of the City of N.Y. (mem. social welfare law com. 1996—). Episcopalian. Avocation: photography. Labor, Real property. Office: United Neighborhood Houses NY 70 W 36th St Fl 5 New York NY 10018-8007

**KAMAIKO, LAURIE ANN,** lawyer; b. N.Y.C., June 23, 1954. BA, Vassar Coll., 1976; JD, Boston U., 1980. Bar: Mass. 1980, N.Y. 1981, U.S. Dist. Ct. (so. and ea. dist.) N.Y. 1982. Assoc. Bower & Gardner, N.Y.C., 1980-87, ptnr., 1988-91; atty. Newman & Co., P.C., N.Y.C., 1991—. Mem. ABA (tips and health law sects.), Bar Assn. of City of N.Y. (com. on ins. 1990-93, com. on profl. responsibility 1993-96, com. med. malpractice 1996-99, chair com. mediation). Insurance, General civil litigation, Personal injury. Address: Newman & Harrington 830 3rd Ave # 6 New York NY 10022-7521

**KAMBORIAN, LISBETH N.,** lawyer; b. Boston, July 1, 1940; d. Jacob Simon and Elizabeth (Kelloyan) K.; children: Amanda, Meredith. BA, U. Chgo., 1962, MBA, 1964; JD, Georgetown U., 1971. Bar: D.C. 1971, Mass. 1986, Md. 1994. Fin. analyst U.S. SEC, Washington, 1966-68; pvt. practice Washington, 1971-76, 79-99; advance person Carter-Mondale Presdl. Campaign, Washington, 1976; assoc. dir. presdl. pers. The White House, Washington, 1977-78; dep. asst. sec. internat. trade U.S. Dept. Commerce, Washington, 1978-79; legal counsel to commr. U.S. Internat. Trade Commn., 1988-91. Pres., trustee Nat. Child Rsch. Ctr., Washington, 1973-77; trustee The Dana Hall Sch., Wellesley, Mass., 1983-91, corporator, 1991—; vol. Dem. Nat. Com., 1972, 76, 80, 88. Recipient Outstanding Achievement award Women's Equity Action League, Washington, 1977. Mem. ABA, Mass. Bar Assn., D.C. Bar Assn., Washington Fgn. Law Soc., Washington Internat. Trade Assn., New England Beetle Cat Boat Assn. (treas. 1998—), South Yarmouth Tennis (pres. 1985-86), Bass River Yacht, Nat. Press Club, Cosmos Club. Avocations: skiing, sailing, opera, tennis, music. Finance, Public international. Office: Judge Baker Children's Ctr 3 Blackfan Cir Boston MA 02115-5794

**KAMEN, MICHAEL ANDREW,** lawyer; b. N.Y.C., May 13, 1952; s. Milton and Renée (Weiss) K. AB, Columbia Coll., 1974; JD, U. Miami, Fla., 1978. Bar: Fla. 1978, U.S. Dist. Ct. (so. dist.) Fla. 1979, U.S. Ct. Appeals (11th cir.) 1987, U.S. Supreme Ct. 1988. Assoc. Fine & Burton, P.A., Ft. Lauderdale, Fla., 1979-84; of counsel Tworoger & Sader, P.A., Ft. Lauderdale, 1984-88; founding ptnr. Kamen & Orlovsky, P.A., West Palm Beach, Fla., 1988—. Author: (with others) Civil Trial Practice, 1994. Recipient Probate Law award Palm Beach County Bar Assn., 1993. Mem. ABA, Assn. Trial Lawyers Am., Acad. Fla. Trial Lawyers. General civil litigation, Native American, Probate. Office: Kamen & Orlovsky PA 1601 Belvedere Rd West Palm Beach FL 33406-1541

**KAMENS, HAROLD,** lawyer; b. Passaic, N.J., Apr. 28, 1917; s. Isadore and Esther (Reingold) K.; m. Bernice F., Jan. 11, 1949; children—Roberta Kamens Rabin, Edward A., Elizabeth. J.D., Rutgers U., 1940, B.S. in Acctg., 1945. Bar: N.J. 1941, N.Y. 1981, U.S. dist. ct. 1941, U.S. Ct. Appeals (3d cir.), U.S. Supreme Ct. 1970. Sole practice, Newark, 1946—; lectr. Seton Hall U., Fairleigh Dickinson U., Instn. Continuing Legal Edn. and numerous other profl., bus. groups; chmn. estate planning com. probate sect. N.J. State Bar. Mem. Fed. Bar Assn. (chmn. com. taxation 1976-77), N.J. Bar Assn. (chmn. com. fed. taxation 1967), Essex County Bar Assn. (chmn. 1974-65), Passaic County Bar Assn. (chmn. fed. taxation 1965-75), Assn. Fed. Bar N.J. (v.p. taxation 1977—). Contbr. articles to legal jours.; editor, chief 8 vols. on estate planning techniques; editor Fed. Tax Notes of N.J. Law Jour., 1947—; Probate, Corporate taxation, Personal income taxation. Office: 333 Radel Ter South Orange NJ 07079-2101

**KAMERICK, EILEEN ANN,** financial executive, lawyer; b. Ravenna, Ohio, July 22, 1958; d. John Joseph and Elaine Elizabeth (Lenney) K.; m. Victor J. Heckler, Sept. 1, 1990; 1 child, Connor Joseph Heckler. AB in English summa cum laude, Boston Coll., 1980; postgrad., Exeter Coll., Oxford, Eng., 1980; JD, U. Chgo., 1984, MBA in Finance and Internat. Bus. with honors, 1993. Bar: Ill. 1984, U.S. Dist. Ct. (no. dist.) Ill. 1985, Mass. 1986, U.S. Ct. Appeals (7th cir.) 1988, U.S. Supreme Ct. 1993. Assoc. Reuben & Proctor, Chgo., 1984-86, Skadden, Arps et al, Chgo., 1986-89; atty. internat. Amoco Corp., Chgo., 1989-93, sr. fin. mgr. corp. fin., 1993-95, sr. fin. cons., 1995-96, dir. banking and fin. svcs., 1996-97; v.p., treas. IMC Global Inc., Northbrook, Ill., 1997—, Whirlpool Corp., Benton Harbor, Mich., 1997; v.p., gen. counsel GE Capital Auto Fin. Svcs., Barrington, Ill., 1997-98; v.p., treas. Amoco Corp., Chgo., 1998-99; v.p. fin. BP Amoco plc, Chgo., 1999—; CFO BP Am., 1999—; advisor fin. com. Am. Petroleum Inst., 1992; bd. dirs. Century Place Devel. Corp. Vol. adv. 7th Cir. Bar Assn., Chgo., 1987—. Mem. ABA, Phi Beta Kappa. Roman Catholic. Private international, General corporate, General civil litigation. Home: 2658D N Southport Ave Chicago IL 60614-1290 Office: BP Amoco PLC 200 E Randolph St # Mc3206A Chicago IL 60601-6436

**KAMIEN, KALVIN,** lawyer; b. Lakewood, N.J., Dec. 11, 1950; s. Joseph and Frieda (Estreich) K.; m. Rhonda Sherry Greenberg, Feb. 7, 1982; children: Joseph Tyler, Joanna Lynn. BA, NYU, 1973; JD cum laude, Bklyn. Law Sch., 1976. Bar: N.Y. 1977, U.S. Dist. Ct. (ea., so. and no. dists.) N.Y. 1977, U.S. Ct. Appeals (2d cir.) 1994. Law asst. appellate div. 2d Dept. Supreme Ct., Bklyn., 1976-79; assoc. Max E Greenberg, Trager, Toplitz &

Herbst, N.Y.C., 1979-86; ptnr. Max E. Greenberg, Trager, Toplitz & Herbst, N.Y.C., 1987—. Bd. dirs. Fieldpoint Community Assn., Irvington, N.Y., 1991—. Recipient Am. Jurisprudence award, 1975. Avocations: tennis, skiing. Construction, General civil litigation, Contracts commercial. Home: 84 Green Way Dr Irvington NY 10533-1844 Office: Max E Greenberg Trager Toplitz & Herbst 100 Church St New York NY 10007-2601

**KAMIN, SCOTT ALLAN,** lawyer; b. Portland, July 1, 1948; s. Lloyd F. and Edith G. (Goldstein) K.; m. Susan Jo Whitlock, Mar. 12, 1978; children: Sarah R., Leah R. BS, U. Oreg., 1971; JD, Lewis & Clark Coll., 1976. Bar: Oreg. 1976, U.S. Dist. Ct. Oreg. 1976, U.S. Tax Ct. 1976. Assoc. atty. Douglas H. Stearns, P.C., Portland, Oreg., 1976-79; attys., ptnr. Weatherhead & Kamin, Portland, 1979-81; atty., shareholder Scott A. Kamin, P.C., Portland, 1981—; IRS liaison Oreg. State Bar, Lake Oswego, 1989—, tax sect. seminar, 1992, mem. computer subcom. elder law sect., 1998—. Mem. Mensa. Avocations: golfing, fishing, biking, computers. Probate, Real property, Taxation, general. Office: 1020 SW Taylor St Ste 550 Portland OR 97205-2527

**KAMINE, BERNARD SAMUEL,** lawyer; b. Dec. 5, 1943; m. Marcia Phyllis Haber; children: Jorge H., Benjamin H., Tovy H. BA, U. Denver, 1965; JD, Harvard U., 1968. Bar: Calif. 1969, Colo. 1969. Dep. atty. gen. Calif. Dept. Justice, L.A., 1969-72; asst. atty. gen. Colo. Dept. Law, Denver, 1972-74; assoc. Shapiro & Maguire, Beverly Hills, Calif., 1974-76; ptnr. Kamine, Steiner & Ungerer (and predecessor firms), L.A., 1976—; judge pro tem Mcpl. Ct., 1974—, Superior Ct., 1989—; bd. dirs., sec. Pub. Works Stds., Inc., 1996—; arbitrator Calif. Pub. Works Contract Arbitration Com., 1990—, Am. Arbitration Assn., 1976—; mem. adv. com. legal forms Calif. Jud. Coun., 1978-82. Author: Public Works Construction Manual: A Legal Guide for California, 1996; contbr. chpts. to legal texts and articles to profl. jours. Mem. L.A. County Dem. Ctrl. Com., 1982-85; mem. Pacific S.W. regional bd. Anti-Defamation League, 1982—, pres. bd., 1998—, nat. commr., 1998—. Col. USAR, 1969—. Mem. ABA, Calif. State Bar Assn. (chair conf. dels. calendar coordinating com. 1991-92), L.A. County Bar Assn. (chair Superior Cts. com. 1977-79, chair constrn. law subsect. of real property sect. 1981-83), Engring. Contractors' Assn. (bd. dirs. 1985—, affiliate chair 1992-93, affiliate DIG award 1996), Assoc. Gen. Contractors Calif. (L.A. dist. bd. dirs. 1995—), Am. Constrn. Insps. Assn. (bd. registered constrn. inspectors 1990-97), Beavers, Res. Officers Assn. (pres. chpt. 1977-78), Omicron Delta Kappa. Construction, Government contracts and claims, Alternative dispute resolution. Office: 350 S Figueroa St Ste 250 Los Angeles CA 90071-1201

**KAMIN-MEYER, TAMI,** lawyer, writer; b. Cin., Jan. 31, 1964; d. Jeff Israel and Ruth (Flek) K.; m. Andrew Meyer, Mar. 13, 1993; children: Justin Wesley Meyer. BA in Comms., Cert. in Arts, U. Cin., 1985; JD, Capital U., 1990. Bar: Ohio 1991, U.S. Dist. Ct. (so. dist.) Ohio 1992. Educator Jewish, Hebrew, other Judaic topics Kol Ami Hebrew Sch., others, Columbus, 1981-98; staff atty. Hyatt Legal Svcs., Cin., 1991-92, Maxwell Law, Columbus, 1992; pvt. practice Columbus, 1993-94, 95—. Editor: (newsletter) Bexley (Ohio) C. of C., 1998; contbr. articles to profl. jours. Named Jewish Educator of Yr. Columbus Commn. on Jewish Edn., 1994. Mem. Ohio State Bar Assn. (mem. editl. bd. 1998—), Columbus Bar Assn. (mem. editl. bd. 1995—), Winding Hollow Country Club (mem. young social com. 1994). Avocations: softball, arts and crafts. Bankruptcy, Consumer commercial. Home: 98 N Ardmore Rd Bexley OH 43209-1445 Office: 2599 E Main St Ste 207 Bexley OH 43209-2445

**KAMINS, BARRY MICHAEL,** lawyer; b. Oct. 3, 1943; s. Abe and Evelyn Bertha (Goffen) K.; m. Fern Louise Kamins, Mar. 30, 1968; 1 child, Allyson. BA, Columbia U., 1965; JD, Rutgers U., 1968. Bar: N.Y. 1969, U.S. Dist. Ct. (ea. and so. dists.) N.Y. 1973, U.S. Supreme Ct. 1974. Asst. dist. atty., 1969-73; dep. chief Criminal Ct. Bur., 1971-73; ptnr. Flamhaft, Levy, Kamins & Hirsch, 1973—; chmn. grievance com. 2d and 11th Jud. Dist., 1994-98; adj. assoc. prof. Fordham Law Sch.; adj. asst. prof. in criminal law N.Y. Tech. Coll.; apptd. spl. prosecutor, Kings County, 1990-92; adj. assoc. prof. N.Y. criminal procedure, law sch. Fordham U., 1994—. Author: The Social Studies Student Investigates the Criminal Justice System, 1978, New York Search and Seizure, 1991; contbr. numerous articles on criminal law to profl. jours. Mem. ABA, N.Y. State Bar Assn. (mem. ho. dels., co-chair com. on justice and the cmty. 1994—), Bklyn. Bar Assn. (past pres., chair jud. com. 1994—), Kings County Criminal Bar Assn. (past pres.), Nat. Dist. Attys. Assn., Assn. of Bar of City of N.Y. (chair jud. com. 1998—, chairperson oversight com. for criminal def. orgns., 2d appellate divsn. 1997—). Criminal. Office: 16 Court St Brooklyn NY 11241-0102

**KAMINS, JOHN MARK,** lawyer; b. Chgo., Feb. 7, 1947; s. David and Beulah (Block) K.; m. Judith Joan Sperling, May 5, 1968; children—Robert, Heather. AB with high honors and distinction, U. Mich., 1968, JD, 1970. Bar: Mich. 1971, Fla. 1991. Assoc., Honigman Miller Schwartz and Cohn, Detroit, 1971-75, ptnr., 1976—; lectr. Inst. on Continuing Legal Edn. Pres. Mich. chpt. Leukemia Soc. Am., 1991-92, 93-96, nat. trustee, 1996—, nat. exec. com., 1997—; bd. dirs. Goodwill Industries of Greater Detroit Found., 1996—; pres. Temple Beth El, Bloomfield Hills, Mich., 1994-96. Mem. Nat. Assn. Bond Lawyers (vice chmn. com. on opinions 1985-86), Mich. Bar Assn. (chairperson, pub. corp. law sect. 1992-93). Jewish. Municipal (including bonds), Securities, General corporate. Home: 1315 Stuyvessant Rd Bloomfield Hills MI 48301-2144 Office: Honigman Miller Schwartz & Cohn 2290 First National Bldg Detroit MI 48226

**KAMINSKI, GERALD FRANCIS,** prosecutor; b. Cleve., Oct. 15, 1946; s. John and Jessie Kaminski; m. Geraldine Margaret Feigel, Jan. 25, 1969; children: Brian, Becky. BA, U. Dayton, 1967; JD, U. Cin., 1970. Atty. Civil Rights divsn. U.S. Dept. of Justice, Washington, 1970-75; asst. U.S. atty. U.S. Atty's Office So. Dist. Ohio, Cin., 1975-79, dep. chief civil divsn., 1982—; atty. Law Office of John A. Lluto Sr., Cin., 1979-82. Office: US Attys Office Potter Stewart Fed Cthouse 5th & Walnut Sts Rm 200 Cincinnati OH 45202

**KAMINSKY, JUDITH A.,** lawyer; b. New Hyde Park, N.Y., Aug. 17, 1968; d. Sheldon S. and Laura J. K. BA, SUNY, Binghamton, 1990; JD, Fordham Law Sch., N.Y.C., 1993. Bar: N.Y. 1994; U.S. Dist. Ct. (so. and ea. dists.) N.Y., 1995. Assoc. Shukat, Arrow, Hafer & Weber, N.Y.C., 1993-97; counsel and assoc. dir. Internat. Apparel Mktg. Co., N.Y.C., 1997-98; counsel, lic. and bus. affairs Halston, N.Y.C., 1998—. Intellectual property, Contracts commercial. Office: Halston 530 7th Ave Fl 17 New York NY 10018-4804

**KAMINSKY, LARRY MICHAEL,** lawyer, insurance company executive; b. San Diego, Feb. 1, 1952; s. Abram and Shirley Edith (Lederman) K.; m. Barbara Sue Kassenick, July 5, 1981; children: Andrew Joshua, Jason David. BA, UCLA, 1974; JD, U. San Fernando Valley, 1977. Bar: Calif. 1977, U.S. Dist. Ct. (cen. dist.) Calif. 1978, (ea., no. and so. dists.) Calif. 1982, U.S. Ct. Appeals (9th cir.) 1979, U.S. Supreme Ct. 1983. Assoc. Law Office Abeles & Markowitz, Beverly Hills, Calif., 1977-78; ptnr. Go, Kaminsky & Misrahi, Canoga Park, Calif., 1978-81; assoc. counsel Safeco Title Ins. Co., Panorama City, Calif., 1981-84; v.p., asst. gen. counsel Fidelity Nat. Title Ins. Co., Irvine, Calif., 1984—; sr. v.p. Fidelity Nat. Title Ins. Co. Tenn., 1987—; staff grader Harcourt, Brace Jovanovich Legal Publs., L.A., 1978-82. Mem. leadership devel. program of community svc. com. Jewish Fedn. Greater Los Angeles, 1979-80. Mem. Am. Land Title Assn., Calif. Land Title Assn. (title ins. forms com., reinsurance com., forms and practices com.). Republican. Jewish. Real property, Insurance. Office: Fidelity Nat Title Ins Co 17911 Von Karman Ave Ste 300 Irvine CA 92614-6262

**KAMINSKY, RICHARD ALAN,** lawyer; b. Toledo, Nov. 15, 1951; s. Jack and Sally (Kale) K. BA, Johns Hopkins U., 1973; JD, U. Mich., 1975. Bar: Ill. 1976, U.S. Dist. Ct. (no. dist.) Ill. 1976. Assoc. Vedder, Price, Kaufman & Kammholz, Chgo., 1976-83; atty. Borg-Warner Corp., Chgo., 1983-89; v.p., assoc. gen. counsel CNA Ins. Cos., Chgo., 1989—. Contbr. chpt. to book. Mem. ABA, Chgo. Bar Assn., Ill. State C. of C. Labor, General civil litigation. Home: 47 Williamsburg Rd Evanston IL 60203-1813 Office: CNA Ins Cos Cna Pla Chicago IL 60685-0001

**KAMISAR, YALE,** lawyer, educator; b. N.Y.C., Aug. 29, 1929; s. Samuel and Mollie (Levine) K.; m. Esther Englander, Sept. 7, 1953 (div. Oct. 1973); children: David Graham, Gordon, Jonathan; m. Christine Keller, May 10, 1974 (dec. 1997); m. Joan Russell, Feb. 28, 1999. AB, NYU, 1950; LLB, Columbia U., 1954; LLD, CUNY, 1978. Bar: D.C. 1955. Rsch. assoc. Am. Law Inst., N.Y.C., 1953; assoc. Covington & Burling, Washington, 1955-57; assoc. prof., then prof. law U. Minn., Mpls., 1957-64; prof. law U. Mich., Ann Arbor, 1965-92, Clarence Darrow disting. univ. prof., 1992—; vis. prof. law Harvard U., 1964-65; disting. vis. prof. law Coll. William and Mary, 1988; cons. Nat. Adv. Commn. Civil Disorders, 1967-68, Nat. Commn. Causes and Prevention Violence, 1968-69; mem. adv. com. model code prearraignment procedure Am. Law Inst., 1965-75. Reporter-draftsman: Uniform Rules of Criminal Procedure, 1971-73; author: (with W.B. Lockhart, J.H. Choper, S. Shiffrin and R.H. Fallon), Constitutional Law: Cases, Comments and Questions, 9th edit., 1999; (with W. LaFave, J. Israel and N. King) Modern Criminal Procedure: Cases and Commentaries, 8th edit., 1994, Criminal Proedure and the Constitution: Leading Cases and Introductory Text, 1988; (with F. Inbau and T. Arnold) Criminal Justice in Our Time, 1965; (with J. Grano and J. Haddad) Sum and Substance of Criminal Procedure, 1977, Police Interrogation and Confessions: Essays in Law and Policy, 1980; contbr. articles to profl. jours. Served to 1st lt. AUS, 1951-52. Recipient Am. Bar Found. Rsch. award, 1996. Home: 2910 Daleview Dr Ann Arbor MI 48105-9684 Office: U Mich Law Sch 625 S State St Ann Arbor MI 48109-1215

**KAMMERER, MATTHEW PAUL,** lawyer; b. Cin., Jan. 30, 1965; s. Leo Joseph and Suzanne Mathews Kammerer; m. Lisa Elizabeth Donisi, Nov. 15, 1996; children: Lauren Elizabeth, Margaret Suzanne. BS in Bus., Miami U., 1987; JD, U. Toledo, 1991. Bar: Ohio 1991, Ky. 1992, U.S. Dist. Ct. (so. dist.) Ohio 1992, U.S. Ct. Appeals (6th cir.) 1992. Assoc. Kohnen, Patton & Hunt, Cin., 1991-92, Strauss & Troy, Cin., 1993-98; ptnr. Murdock & Goldenberg, Cin., 1998—. Field coord. Kearney for coun. campaign, Cin., 1993. Mem. ABA, Ohio State Bar Assn., Ky. Bar Assn., Cin. Bar Assn., Phhi Alpha Delta. Avocations: swimming, golf, skiing. Federal civil litigation, State civil litigation, Product liability. Office: Murdock & Goldenberg 700 Walnut St Ste 400 Cincinnati OH 45202-2011

**KAMP, ARTHUR JOSEPH, JR.,** lawyer; b. Rochester, N.Y., July 22, 1945; s. Arthur Joseph and Irene Catherine (Ehrstein) K.; m. Barbara Hays, Aug. 24, 1968; children: Sara, Nathaniel. BA, SUNY, 1968, JD, 1970. Bar: N.Y. 1971, U.S. Dist. Ct. (we. dist.) N.Y. 1971, Va. 1973, U.S. Dist. Ct. (ea. dist.) Va. 1973. Atty. Neighborhood Legal Svcs., Buffalo, 1971; assoc. Diamonstein & Drucker, Newport News, Va., 1972-77; ptnr. Diamonstein, Drucker & Kamp, Newport News, 1977-84, Kamp & Kamp, Newport News, 1984-87, Kaufman & Canoles, 1987-96, David, Kamp & Frank L.L.C., 1996—; v.p., Peninsula Legal Aid Ctr., Inc., 1978-92. Chmn. Newport News Planning Commn., 1994-95, commr., 1990-97; bd. vis. Med. Coll. Hampton Rds. Lt. USAF, 1971-72. Mem. ABA, Va. State Bar Assn., Newport News Bar Assn. (past bd. dirs., chmn. legal aid com.), Va. Bar Assn., Va. Peninsula C. of C. (bd. dirs., exec. com., chmn. 1997). Democrat. Real property, General corporate, Finance. Office: David & Kamp LLC 301 Hiden Blvd Ste 200 Newport News VA 23606-2939

**KAMP, DAVID PAUL,** lawyer; b. Cin., Aug. 10, 1952; s. Robert P. and Dolores O. (Koop) K.; m. Eileen J. McDermott, Oct. 24, 1981; children: Jennifer Kathleen, Jeffrey Michael. BA, Thomas More Coll., 1978; JD, U. Cin., 1981. Bar: Ohio 1981, U.S. Dist. Ct. (we. and no. dists.) Ohio, U.S. Dist. Ct. Tenn., U.S. Dist. Ct. Kans., U.S. Dist. Ct. Nev., U.S. Ct. Appeals (6th cir.). Assoc. Dinsmore & Shohl, Cin., 1981-87; mng. ptnr. White, Getgey & Meyer, Cin., 1987—; arbitrator N.Y. Stock Exch., Am. Stock Exch. Assoc. mem. U. Cin. Law Sch. Alumni Bd. Trustees, 1994; trustee Ohio Supreme Ct. Client Security Fund, Columbus, 1992—. Mem. ABA, ATLA, Ohio State Bar Assn., Cin. Bar Assn. (com. on ins. and tort practice, joint com. with Acad. of Medicine, com. on ins. law), Ohio State Trial Lawyers Assn., Hamilton County Trial Lawyers Assn. (pres.), Am. Arbitration Assn. (arbitrator), Nat. Assn. Securities Dealers (arbitrator). General civil litigation, Personal injury, Product liability. Home: 9942 Indian Springs Dr Cincinnati OH 45241-3629 Office: White Getgey & Meyer Co LPA 1 W 4th St Ste 1700 Cincinnati OH 45202-3603

**KAMP, RANDALL WILLIAM,** lawyer, accountant; b. Charlotte, N.C., July 5, 1960; s. John F. and Gayla S. (Roberts) K.; m. Linda A.K. Koster, June 8, 1985; children: Lauren, Jessica, Rebecca. BS, Okla. State U., 1982; JD, U. Okla., 1987. CPA, Okla.; bar: Okla. 1987, U.S. Ct. Appeals (10th cir.) 1992. Acct. Arthur Andersen & Co., Oklahoma City, Okla., 1982-83, Englebach Roberts & Co,., Oklahoma City, Okla., 1983-84; assoc. Lytle Soule & Curlee, Oklahoma City, Okla., 1985-89, McKinney Stringer & Webster, Oklahoma City, Okla., 1989-91, Lee M. Holmes & Assocs., Oklahoma City, Okla., 1991-97; pvt. practice Oklahoma City, 1997—. Mem. ABA, Nat. Acad. Elder Law Attys., Okla. Bar Assn. Republican. Avocation: bicycling. Estate planning, Probate, Taxation, general. Office: 1600 E 19th St Ste 302 Edmond OK 73013-6623

**KANDEL, ALAN HAROLD,** lawyer; b. St. Louis, Mar. 8, 1955. AB universali cum honore, Washington U., St. Louis, 1983; JD cum laude, St. Louis U., 1986. Bar: Mo. 1986. Assoc. Popkin & Stern, St. Louis, 1986-91, Lewis, Rice & Fingersh, St. Louis, 1991-95; of counsel Farnam Law Firm, St. Louis, 1995-96; sr. atty. Peper, Martin, Jensen, Maichel & Hetlage, St. Louis, 1996-97; ptnr. Blackwell, Sanders, Peper, Martin LLP, St. Louis, 1998—. Sr. v.p. H.F. Epstein Hebrew Acad., St. Louis, 1999—; pres. Tpheris Israel Chevra Kadisha Congregation, Chesterfield, Mo., 1997-98, Vaad Hoeir of St. Louis, 1998—. Mem. Mo. Bar Assn. (chmn. employee benefits com. 1991-93), Bar Assn. Met. St. Louis (chmn. employee benefits com. 1995-96). Pension, profit-sharing, and employee benefits. Office: Blackwell Sanders Peper Martin LLP 720 Olive St Fl 24 Saint Louis MO 63101-2338

**KANDEL, NELSON ROBERT,** lawyer; b. Balt., Sept. 15, 1929; m. Brigitte Kleemaier, Feb. 28, 1957; children: Katrin, Christopher, Peter. BA, U. Md., 1951, LLB, 1954. Bar: Md. 1954, U.S. Supreme Ct. 1964, D.C. 1980. Prin. law firm, Kandel & Assocs. P.A., Balt., 1957—. With U.S. Army. Mem. Md. Bar Assn., Balt. Bar Assn. Democrat. Lutheran. General practice, General civil litigation, Contracts commercial. Office: Kandel & Assocs PA Legg Mason Tower 100 Light St Ste 1010 Baltimore MD 21202-1184

**KANDEL, PETER THOMAS,** lawyer; b. Balt.; s. Nelson Robert and Brigitte (Kleemaier) K.; m. Marion Hoogstraten, Nov. 18, 1989; children: Andrew, Margaret, James. Student, Johns Hopkins U., 1980-81; BA magna cum laude, Williams Coll., 1984; JD, Yale U., 1987. Bar: N.Y. 1988, Md. 1989, D.C., 1989. Assoc. Jones Day Reavis & Pogue, N.Y.C., 1987-89, Piper & Marbury, Balt., 1990-93; stockholder Kandel & Assocs. P.A., Balt., 1993—. Vol. New Haven Legal Assistance, 1985-87. Horace F. Clark prize Williams Coll., 1984. Mem. ABA, Md. Bar Assn., Williams Coll. Alumni Assn. Md. (pres., mem. exec. com.), Phi Beta Kappa, Phi Delta Phi, Delta Phi. Democrat. Lutheran. General practice, General civil litigation, General corporate. Office: Kandel & Assocs PA Legg Mason Tower 100 Light St Ste 1010 Baltimore MD 21202-1184

**KANDEL, WILLIAM LLOYD,** lawyer, lecturer, author; b. N.Y.C., Apr. 25, 1939; s. Morton H. and Lottie S. (Smith) K.; m. Joyce Roland, Jan. 27, 1974; 1 child, Aron Daniel (Ari). AB cum laude, Dartmouth Coll., 1961; JD, Yale U., 1964; LLM in Labor Law, NYU, 1967. Bar: N.Y. 1965, U.S. Dist. Ct. (ea., so. and no. dists.) N.Y., U.S. Ct. Appeals (2d cir.), U.S. Dist. Ct. (no. dist.) Calif. 1988, U.S. Ct. Appeals (3rd cir.) 1983. Assoc. Lorenz, Finn & Giardino, N.Y.C., 1964-66; labor atty. NAM, N.Y.C., 1966-68; with Singer Co., N.Y.C., 1968-79, asst. v.p. pers. dept., 1973-76, mng. counsel pers. office of gen. counsel, 1976-79; assoc. Skadden, Arps, Slate, Meagher & Flom, N.Y.C., 1979-85; ptnr. Finley, Kumble, Wagner, Heine, Underberg, Manley, Myerson & Casey, N.Y.C., 1985-87, Myerson & Kuhn, N.Y.C., 1987-89, McDermott Will & Emery, 1989-97, Orrick, Herrington & Sutcliffe, 1997—; lectr. to Law and bus. groups, 1974—; adj. prof. employment law Fordham U., 1983-86; lectr. Practising Law Inst.'s Ann. Inst. on Employment Law, 1980—, co-chair, 1995, chair, 1996—; mem. adv. panel Am. Arbitration Assn., 1996—; mem. adv. com. employment law City Coun. N.Y., 1996—. *William L. Kandel, a litigator and counselor in employment law, brings more than 30 years' experience to his specialty of representing employers. His nation-widetrial practice is before courts, administrative agencies, and arbitration/mediation bodies at the federal, state, and city levels. He defends local and multi-national employers in individual and class actions involving discrimination, wrongful discharge, benefits, unions, and contract or tort claims. He is also active in alternate dispute resolution and non-competition/trade secret and employment-related government contract and defamation cases. His counseling role includes advising employers, adoption and application of policies, work force reductions, affirmative action programs, cost-effective compliance with statutes and regulations, internal investigations and low-risk resolution of employment disputes.* Contbg. editor Employee Rels. Law Jour., 1975—; contbr. articles to profl. jours. V.p., bd. dirs. Assn. for Integration Mgmt., 1979-85; bd. dirs. N.Y. chpt. Am. Jewish Com., 1980-82; mem. human resources com. N.Y. YMCA, 1994—. Recipient award of Merit, Nat. Urban Coalition, 1979. Democrat. Jewish. Labor, Federal civil litigation, Administrative and regulatory. Office: Orrick Herrington & Sutcliffe 666 5th Ave Rm 203 New York NY 10103-1798

**KANDRAVY, JOHN,** lawyer; b. Passaic, N.J., May 9, 1935; s. Frank and Anna (Chan) K.; m. Alice E. Sullivan, Feb. 17, 1962; children: Elizabeth Ann, Katherine Ann. BA, Wesleyan U., Middletown, Conn., 1957; JD, Columbia U., 1960. Bar: N.J. 1960, D.C. 1969, U.S. Supreme Ct. 1973, N.Y. 1982. From assoc. to ptnr. Shanley & Fisher, Newark, 1961-80; ptnr. Shanley & Fisher, Morristown, N.J., 1980—, mng. ptnr., 1983-85, 89—; bd. dirs. Tingue, Brown & Co., G.A.R. Internat. Corp., Ridgewood Savs. Bank of N.J., Ridgewood Fin., Inc. Mem. Gov.'s Mgmt. Commn., State of N.J., 1970; chmn. Planning Bd., Ridgewood, N.J., 1981-85, Zoning Bd. Adjustment, 1979-81; mem. bd. advisors Coll. Bus. Adminstrn., Fairleigh Dickinson U., 1983-87, chmn. bd. advisors, 1985-86; mem. Soc. of Valley Hosp., Ridgewood, 1971—, chmn. bd. trustees Cen. Bergen Cmty. Mental Health Ctr., N.J., 1970-73; trustee Palisades Counseling Ctr., Rutherford, 1968-81, The Forum Sch., Waldwick, N.J., 1987—, The Forum Sch. Found., Waldwick, 1978—, The Valley Hosp., Ridgewood, 1992—, Peer Found. for Plastic Surgery and Rehab., Florham Park, 1996—, Valley Health Sys., Inc., Ridgewood, 1997—, Children's Aid and Family Svcs., Inc., Paramus, N.J., 1998—; mem. lawyers' adv. coun. Rutgers Law Sch., Newark, 1994-98, mem. vis. com., 1994-98. Edward John Noble Found.grantee, 1957-60. Mem. ABA, N.J. Bar Assn., Essex County Bar Assn., D.C. Bar Assn., Morris County Bar Assn., Essex Club (gov. 1976-85), Wesleyan U. Alumni Assn. (chmn. 1981-83), Indian Trail Club (Franklin Lakes, N.J.), Ridgewood Country Club, Park Ave. Club (gov. 1992—). Republican. Presbyterian. General corporate, Mergers and acquisitions, Banking. Home: 56 Monte Vista Ave Ridgewood NJ 07450-2428 Office: Shanley & Fisher 131 Madison Ave Morristown NJ 07960-6097

**KANE, ALICE THERESA,** lawyer; b. N.Y.C., Jan. 16, 1948. AB, Manhattanville Coll., 1969; JD, NYU, 1972; grad., Harvard U. Sch. Bus. Program Mgmt. Devel., 1985. Bar: N.Y. 1973, U.S. Dist. Ct. (so. dist.) N.Y. 1974. Atty. N.Y. Life Ins. Co., N.Y.C., 1972-83, v.p., assoc. gen. counsel, 1983-85, v.p. dept. personnel, 1985, sr. v.p., gen. counsel, 1986-89, corp. sec., 1989-92, exec. v.p., gen. counsel, sec., 1992-95, exec. v.p. corp. mktg., 1995-98; exec. v.p. Am. Gen. Investment Mgmt. Corp., N.Y.C., 1998—. Mem. ABA (chmn. employee benefits com., tort and ins. practice sect. 1984-85, mem. corp., banking and bus. law sects., tort and ins. practice sects.), Assn. of Life Ins. Counsel (deps. solvency com.). General corporate. Office: Am Gen Investment Mgmt Corp 125 Maiden Ln Fl 7 New York NY 10038-4912

**KANE, ARTHUR O.,** lawyer; b. Chgo., Jan. 16, 1918; s. Henry L. and Bertha Y. Kane; m. Bernice Estelle Levine, June 14, 1942 (dec. Aug. 1984); m. Esther Steinback, Apr. 21, 1985. AB, U. Chgo., 1937, JD, 1939. Bar: Ill. 1939, U.S. Dist. Ct. (no. dist.) Ill. 1940, U.S. Ct. Appeals 1961. Ptnr. Henry L. Kane & Arthur Kane, Chgo., 1939-63; sole practitioner Kane, Doy & Harrington, Chgo., 1965-81; pres., CEO Kane, Doy & Harrington, Chgo., 1981-98; chmn. bd. Kane, Doy & Harrington, Chgo., 1998—; instr. Ill. Inst. Continuing Legal Edn., Springfield, Ill., 1990. Capt. J.A.G., U.S. Army, 1947-52. Mem. ABA, Ill. Bar Assn. (chair workers compensation com. 1967-68), Chgo. Bar Assn. (chmn. workers compensation com. 1957-61). Avocations: reading, teaching. Workers' compensation. Office: Kane Doy & Harrington Ltd One N LaSalle St Chicago IL 60602

**KANE, DONALD VINCENT,** lawyer; b. N.Y.C., July 4, 1925; s. Thomas Joseph and Nora O'Kane; m. Margaret Mary Kane, Nov. 25, 1950; children: Mary, Thomas, Donald Jr., Mark, Stephen. JD, St. John's U., 1950. Bar: N.Y. 1950, U.S. Dist. Ct. (so. dist.), U.S. Ct. Appeals (2d cir.) 1953, U.S. V.I. 1981, U.S. Ct. Appeals (3d cir.) 1983. With N.Y.C. Police Dept., 1950-51; with anti-crime com. N.Y.C., 1951-53; with RKO Radio & Picures, N.Y.C., 1953-58; pvt. practice N.Y.C., 1958-69, 83—; asst. atty. gen. U.S. Virgin Islands, St. Thomas, 1979-83. Sgt. USN submarine svc., 1943-46, WWII. Mem. N.Y. State Defenders Assn. (v.p. 1978-79), Nassau County Criminal Courts Bar Assn. (v.p. 1978), Nassau County Bar Assn. (chmn. criminal courts com. 1977-79). Fax: 516-481-0851. Criminal, Personal injury, General civil litigation. Office: 21 W Columbia St Hempstead NY 11550-2410

**KANE, EDWARD K.,** lawyer. LLB, Fordham U., 1959; BBA, Manhattan Coll., 1951. Bar: N.Y. 1959. With Gardian Life Ins. Co. Am., N.Y.C., 1951—; exec. v.p. Guardian Life Ins. Co. Am., N.Y.C., 1971—. Office: Guardian Life Ins Co Am 7 Hanover Sq Fl 14 New York NY 10004-2699

**KANE, JOHN LAWRENCE, JR.,** federal judge; b. Tucumcari, N.Mex., Feb. 14, 1937; s. John Lawrence and Dorothy Helen (Bottler) K.; m. Stephanie Jane Shafer, Oct. 5, 1993; children: Molly Francis, Meghan, Sally, John Pattison. B.A., U. Colo., 1958; J.D., U. Denver, 1961, LL.D. (hon), 1997. Bar: Colo. 1961. Dep. dist. atty. Adams County, Colo., 1961-62; assoc. firm Gaunt, Byrne & Dirrim, 1961-63; ptnr. firm Andrews and Kane, Denver, 1964; pub. defender Adams County, 1965-67; dep. dir. eastern region of India Peace Corps, 1967-69; with firm Holme Roberts & Owen, 1970-77, ptnr., 1972-77; judge U.S. Dist. Ct. Colo., Denver, 1977-88, U.S. sr. dist. judge, 1988—; adj. prof. law U. Denver, U. Colo., 1996—; vis. lectr. Trinity Coll., Dublin, Ireland, winter 1989; adj. prof. U. Colo., 1996. Contbr. articles to profl. jours. Recipient St. Thomas More award Cath. Lawyers Guild, 1983, U.S. Info. Agy. Outstanding Svc. award, 1985, Outstanding Alumnus award U. Denver, 1987, Lifetime Jud. Achievement award Nat. Assn. Criminal Def. Lawyers, 1987, Civil Rights award B'nai B'rith, 1988. Fellow Internat. Acad. Trial Lawyers, Am. Bd. Trial Advs. (hon.). Roman Catholic. Office: US Dist Ct C-428 US Courthouse 1929 Stout St Denver CO 80294-1929 *There is a tendency to gild the past with uncritical generosity but an even more pronounced one to forget Santayana's dictum that one who forgets history is bound to repeat it. Law is that indispensable mechanism by which we may survive as a free people if we use it to apply a critical understanding of history to a confusing and dynamic present.*

**KANE, JOSEPH PATRICK,** lawyer, financial planner; b. Phila., Dec. 5, 1957; s. James Thomas Jr. and Rita Margaret (Pergolese) K.; m. Lynn Marie Danesi, May 6, 1989. BS in Econs. cum laude, U. Pa., 1979; JD, U. Va., 1982; CFP, Coll. for Fin. Planning, Denver, 1988. Bar: Pa. 1982, U.S. Dist. Ct. (ea. dist.) Pa. 1983, U.S. Ct. Appeals (3d cir.) 1983, U.S. Dist. Ct. (mid. dist.) Pa. 1993, U.S. Supreme Ct. 1993. Assoc. Obermayer, Rebmann, Maxwell & Hippel, Phila., 1982-85, Kleinbard, Bell & Brecker, Phila., 1985-86, O'Donnell, Weiss & Mattei PC, Pottstown, Pa., 1989-92, Liebert, Short & Hirshland, Williamsport, Pa., 1992-93; fin. and pension cons. PACS, Inc., Phila., 1986-89; pvt. practice, Williamsport, 1993—; asst. prof. mgmt. and bus. law Pa. Coll. Tech., Williamsport, 1998-99; asst. prof. mgmt. and bus. law Pa. Coll. Tech., Williamsport, 1998-99. Bd. dirs., com. mem. Lycoming United Way, Williamsport, 1994—; bd. dirs. Pa. Coll. Tech. Found., Williamsport, 1995-97, Lycoming County Health Improvement Coalition, Inc., Williamsport, 1995-97, Cmty. Theatre League, Inc., Williamsport, 1996—, Lycoming Mediation Project, Inc., Williamsport, 1997—. Mem. ABA, PBA, Lycoming Law Assn., Williamsport-Lycoming C. of C. (com. mem., chmn. subcom. 1992—), Eagles Mere Country Club, Ross Club (bd. dirs. 1997—). Avocations: choral and barbershop singing, community theatre, golf, tennis, hiking. General corporate, Estate planning, Real property. Office: Penn Tower 25 W 3d St Ste 604 Williamsport PA 17701-6530

**KANE, MARY KAY,** dean, law educator; b. Detroit, Nov. 14, 1946; d. John Francis and Frances (Roberts) K.; m. Ronan Eugene Degnan, Feb. 3, 1987 (dec. Oct. 1987). BA cum laude, U. Mich., 1968, JD cum laude, 1971. Bar: Mich., N.Y., Calif. Rsch. assoc., co-dir. NSF project on privacy, confidentiality and social sci. rsch. data sch. law U. Mich., 1971-72, Harvard U., 1972-74; asst. prof. law SUNY, Buffalo, 1974-77; mem. faculty Hastings Coll. Law U. Calif., San Francisco, 1977—, prof. law, 1979—, assoc. acad. dean Hastings Coll. Law, 1981-83, acting acad. dean Hastings Coll. Law, 1987-88, acad. dean. Hastings Coll. Law, 1990-93, dean Hastings Coll. Law, 1993—; vis. prof. law U. Mich., 1981, U. Utah, 1983, U. Calif., Berkeley, 1983-84, sch. law U. Tex., 1989; cons. Mead Data Control, Inc., 1971, 74, Inst. on Consumer Justice, U. Mich. Sch. Law, 1972, U.S. Privacy Protection Study Commn., 1975-76; lectr. pretrial mgmt. devices U.S. magistrates for 6th and 11th cirs. Fed. Jud. Ctr., 1983; Siebenthaler lectr. Samuel P. Chase Coll. Law, U. North Ky., 1987; reporter ad hoc com. on asbestos litigation U.S. Jud. Conf., 1990-91; mem. 9th Cir. Adv. Com. on Rules Practice and Internal Oper. Procedures, 1993-96; spkr. in field. Author: Civil Procedure in a Nutshell, 1979, 4th edit., 1996, Sum and Substance on Remedies, 1981; co-author: (with C. Wright and A. Miller) Pocket Supplements to Federal Practice and Procedure, 1975—, Federal Practice and Procedure, vols. 10, 10A and 10B, 3d edit., 1998, vols. 7-7C, 2d edit., 1986, vols. 6-6A, 2d edit., 1990, vols. 11-11A, 2d edit., 1995, (with J. Friedenthal and A. Miller) Hornbook on Civil Procedure, 3d edit., 1999, (with D. Levine) Civil Procedure in California, 6th edit., 1998; mem. law sch. divsn. West. Adv. Editl. Bd., 1986—; contbr. articles to profl. jours. Mem. ABA (mem. bar admissions com. 1995—), Assn. Am. Law Schs. (com. on prelegal edn. statement 1982, chair sect. remedies 1982, panelist sect. on prelegal edn. 1983, exec. com. sect. on civil procedure 1983, 86, panelist sect. on tchg. methods 1984, spkr. new tchrs. conf. 1986, 89, 90, chair sect. on civil procedure 1987, spkr. sects. civil procedure and conflicts 1987, 91, chair planning com. for 1988 Tchg. Conf. in Civil Procedure 1987-88, nominating com. 1988, profl. devel. com. 1988-91, planning com. for workshop in conflicts 1988, planning com. for 1990 Conf. on Clin. Legal Edn. 1989, chair profl. devel. com. 1989-91, exec. com. 1991-93), Am. Law Inst. (assoc. reporter complex litigation project 1988-93, coun. 1998—), ABA/Assn. Am. Law Schs. Commn. on Financing Legal Edn., State Bar Mich. Home: 8 Admiral Dr Ste 421 Emeryville CA 94608-1567 Office: U Calif Hastings Coll Law 200 Mcallister St San Francisco CA 94102-4707

**KANE, PAULA,** lawyer; b. Burbank, Calif., Aug. 2, 1949; d. Thomas E. and Annabel Lee K.; m. Michael A. Gold, July 16, 1982. BS, U. So. Calif., 1971, M, 1993, JD, 1980. Bar: Calif. 1980. Atty. Law Offices Stuart Walzer, L.A., 1980-82, Greenberg, Glusker, Clamm, Nachtinger & Fields, L.A., 1982-84, pvt. practice, L.A., 1984—. Mem. L.A. County Bar Assn. (exec. com. 1990-92), Beverly Hills Bar Assn. Avocations: water skiing, architecture, art. Family and matrimonial. Office: 1801 Century Park E Los Angeles CA 90067-2302

**KANE, ROBERT F.,** lawyer; b. San Francisco, Aug. 4, 1951; s. Harold B. and Elayne (Lichtman) K. BA in History, U. Calif., 1973, BS in Conservation, 1973; JD, U. Calif., Davis, 1986. Bar: Calif. 1976, U.S. Dist. Ct. (no. dist.) Calif. 1976, U.S. Dist. Ct. (ea. dist.) Calif. 1977, U.S. Supreme Ct. 1983, U.S. Ct. Appeals (9th cir.) 1984 , Hawaii 1990. Assoc. Rockwell, Keenan & Mathewson, San Francisco, 1977-79, Law Offices of Robert C. Maddox, Tahoe City, Calif., 1979-89; prin. Rockwell & Kane, San Francisco, 1989—; pro tem judge San Francisco Superior Ct., 1990—; arbitrator San Francisco Superior and Mcpl. Ct., Marin County Superior Ct., Alameda County Superior Ct., Solono County Superior Ct. Contbr. numerous articles to profl. jours. Bd. dirs. Legal Svcs. No. Calif., 1984-90, Tahoe Womens Svc., Tahoe City, 1985-89; bd. dirs. Am. Jewish Congress, 1989—, pres. 1995-99; pres. Jewish Family and Children Svcs. of East Bay, 1994-98. Recipient Community Svc. award Legal Svcs. No. Calif., Auburn, 1986. Mem. ATLA, Def. Rsch. Inst., State Bar Calif. (pro bono svc. award 1986), Order of Coif, Phi Beta Kappa. General civil litigation, General practice. Office: Rockwell & Kane 870 Market St Ste 1128 San Francisco CA 94102-2906

**KANE, SIEGRUN DINKLAGE,** lawyer; b. N.Y.C., Sept. 21, 1938; d. Ralph Dieter and Lisbeth (Adam) Dinklage; m. David H.T. Kane, Jan. 24, 1964; children: David D., Brendon T. BA cum laude, Mt. Holyoke Coll., 1960; LLB, Harvard U., 1963. Bar: N.Y. 1963, U.S. Ct. Appeals (2d cir.) 1964, U.S. Ct Appeals (5th cir.) 1978, U.S. Ct. Appeals (7th cir.) 1984. Ptnr. Kane, Dalsimer, Sullivan, Kurucz, Levy, Eisele & Richard, N.Y.C., 1963—; bd. mem. Bur. Nat. Affairs Adv. Com., Washington, 1988—; mem. U.S. Patent and Trademark Office Pub. Adv. Com., Washington, 1989-95; lectr. trademarks Practicing Law Inst., N.Y.C., 1980—. Author: Trademark Law: A Practitioner's Guide, 1987, 3d edit., 1997; contbr. articles on trademark law to profl. jours. Mem. Briarcliff Zoning Bd. Appeals, Briarcliff Manor, N.Y., 1978-90, Briarcliff Hist. Soc. Bd., Briarcliff Manor, 1986-90. Mem. ABA, Internat. Trademark Assn., N.Y. Patent Law Assn. Avocations: aerobics, tennis, travel. Trademark and copyright. Office: Kane Dalsimer Sullivan Kurucz Levy Eisele & Richard 711 3rd Ave Fl 20 New York NY 10017-4014

**KANE, STEPHEN MICHAEL,** lawyer; b. Boston; s. John V. and Mary Thea (Prendergast) K.; m. Cynthia Lynne Boyer, Sept. 29, 1984; children: Matthew A., John L., Victoria J. BA, Columbia Coll., 1980; JD, Columbia U., 1983. Bar: Mass., 1983, Mass. (no. dist.), 1984, Mass. (1st cir.), 1984. Staff Leg. Drafting Rsch. Fund, N.Y.C., 1981-83; ptnr. Rich, May, Bilodeau & Flaherty, Boston, 1983—; asst. clk. CORE Inc., Irvine, Calif., 1985—; asst. sec. HealthGate Data Corp., 1994—. Co-pres. Newton (Mass.) North Little League, 1998, bd. dirs., 1996—. Mem. ABA, Mass. Bar Assn., Boston Bar Assn., MIT Enterprise Forum, Assn. for Corp. Growth. Avocations: coaching youth sports, alumni orgn. activities. E-mail: skane@richmaylaw.com. General corporate, Mergers and acquisitions, Securities. Office: Rich May Bilodeau & Flaherty PC 294 Washington St Ste 1100 Boston MA 02108-4675

**KANER, CEM,** lawyer, computer software consultant; b. Detroit, July 8, 1953; s. Harry and Wilma Kaner; 1 child, Virginia Rose. Student, U. Windsor (Ont., Can.), 1971-72; BA, Brock U., St. Catharines, Ont., 1974; postgrad., York U., Toronto, Ont., 1975-76; PhD, McMaster U., Hamilton, Ont., 1984; JD, Golden Gate U., 1993. Cert. quality engr.; Bar: Calif., 1993. Asst. mgr. Gallenkamp Shoes, Toronto, 1975; systems analyst Kaners and 1 plus 1, Windsor, 1981-83; lectr. McMaster U., 1981-83; software testing supr. MicroPro (WordStar), San Rafael, Calif., 1983-84; human factors analyst, software engr. Telenova, Los Gatos, Calif., 1984-88; software testing mgr. creativity div. Electronic Arts, San Mateo, Calif., 1988; software devel. mgr., documentation group mgr., dir. of documentation and software testing Power Up Software, San Mateo, 1989-94; pvt. practice Calif., 1994—; sr. assoc. Psylomar Orgn. Devel., San Francisco, 1983-85; lectr. U. Calif., Berkeley Ext., 1995—, U. Calif., Santa Cruz Ext., 1998—; spkr. in field. Author: Testing Computer Software, 1988, (with Jack Falk and Hung Q Nguyen) Testing Computer Software, 2d edit., 1993 (award for excellence No. Calif. Tech. Publ. Competition 1993), (with David Pels) Bad Software: What to do when Software Fails, 1998; (video course) Testing Computer Software, 1995; columnist Software QA; contbr. articles to profl. publs. Cons. Dundas (Ont.) Pub. Library, 1982-83; vol. Santa Clara County Dept. Consumer Affairs, San Jose, 1987-88; alt. mem. San Mateo County Dem. Central Com., 1988-89; chmn. Foster City Dem Club, 1989; vol. dep. dist. atty. County of Santa Clara, Calif., 1994; grievance handler, intellectual property, book contract advisor Nat. Writers Union, San Francisco, Calif., 1994—; bd. dir. No. Calif. Hemophilia Found., Oakland, Calif., 1995-97; participating observer NCCUSL drafting com. for UCC article 2B, NCCUSL com. for uniform electronic transaction act. Scholar, Can. Nat. Rsch. Coun., 1977-78, Can. Natural Scis. and Engring. Rsch. Coun., 1979, Golden Gate U. Tuition scholar, 1989-93. Mem. IEEE (Computer Soc.), ABA, ATLA, APA, Assn. for Computing Machinery, Assn. Support Profls., Am. Soc. Quality (sr.), Am. Law Inst. (elected), Human Factors and Ergonomics Soc., Soc. for Tech. Comm. (sr.), Software Support Profls. Assn., Software Pubs. Assn. Jewish. Avocation: development of the law of software products liability. E-mail: kaner@kaner.com. Computer, Contracts commercial, Intellectual property. Office: PO Box 580 Santa Clara CA 95052-0580

**KANE-VANNI, PATRICIA RUTH,** lawyer, production consultant, paleo-educator; b. Phila., Jan. 12, 1954; d. Joseph James and Ruth Marina (Ramirez) Kane; m. Francis William Vanni, Feb. 14, 1980; 1 child, Christian Michael. AB, Chestnut Hill Coll., 1975; JD, Temple U., 1985. Bar: Pa. 1985, U.S. Ct. Appeals (3d cir.) 1988. Freelance art illustrator Phila., 1972-80; secondary edn. instr. Archdiocese of Phila., 1980-83; contract analyst CIGNA Corp., Phila., 1983-84; jud. aide Phila. Ct. of Common Pleas, 1984; assoc. atty. Anderson and Dougherty, Wayne, Pa., 1985-86; atty. cons. Bell Telephone Co. of Pa., 1986-87; sr. assoc. corp. counsel Independence Blue Cross, Phila., 1987-96; pvt. practice law, 1996-97; dinosaur educator Acad. Natural Scis., Phila., 1997—; atty. cons., 1996-99; counsel Reliance Ins. Co., Phila., 1998—; cons. Coll. Consortium on Drug and Alcohol Abuse, Chester, Pa., 1986-89; speaker in field; paleo-sci. educator Pa. Acad. Natural Scis., 1997—. Contbr. articles and illustrations to profl. mags. Judge Del. Valley Sci. Fairs, Phila., 1986, 87, 98, 99; Dem. committeewomen, Lower Merion, Pa., 1983-87; ch. cantor, soloist, mem. choir Roman Cath. Ch.; mem. Phila. Assn. Ch. Musicians, also bd. dirs. Recipient Legion of Honor award Chapel of the Four Chaplins, 1983. Mem. ABA, Pa. Bar Assn., Phila. Bar Assn. (Theatre Wing), Phila. Assn. Def. Counsel, Phila. Vol. Lawyers for Arts (bd. dirs.), Nat. Health Lawyers Assn. (spkr. 1994 ann. conv.), Hispanic Bar Assn., vice pres. Delaware Valley Paleontological Soc., Pa. Acad. Nat. Scis. (vol.), Delaware Valley Paleontological Soc. (v.p. 1998—). Democrat. Avocations: choral and solo vocal music, portrait painting and illustrating, paleontology. E-mail: pkv1@erols.com. General corporate, Health, Insurance. Home: 119 Bryn Mawr Ave Bala Cynwyd PA 19004-3012

**KANG, HELEN HAEKYONG,** lawyer; b. Seoul, Korea, Feb. 15, 1960; came to U.S., 1972; m. Greg Alan Martin; children: Isabel Martin, Elena. BA, Yale U., 1982; JD, U. Calif., Berkeley, 1986. Bar: Calif. 1986, U.S. Dist. Ct. (no. dist.) Calif. 1986, U.S. Dist. Ct. (so. dist.) Calif. 1987, U.S. Dist. Ct. (ea. dist.) Calif. 1988, U.S. Ct. Appeals (9th cir.) 1986, U.S. Dist. Ct. (ctrl. dist.) Calif. 1999. Assoc. Feldman, Waldman & Kline, San Francisco, 1986-90; trial atty. U.S. Dept. Justice, San Francisco, 1990-97; ptnr. Goodman Kang LLP, San Francisco, 1997—; early neutral evaluator U.S. Dist. Ct. (no. dist.) Calif., 1997—. Articles editor Berkeley Women's Law Jour., 1982-83. Bd. dirs. Korean Cmty. Ctr. of the East Bay, Oakland, Calif., 1983-88, Asian Women's Shelter, San Francisco, 1988-89. Recipient Spl. Achievement award U.S. Dept. Justice, 1993. Mem. ABA, State Bar Calif. (environ. law sect.), Bar Assn. San Francisco, Asian Am. Bar Assn., Asian Am. Bar Assn. of the Greater Bay Area (bd. dirs. 1998—). General civil litigation, Environmental. Office: Goodman Kang LLP 177 Post St Ste 600 San Francisco CA 94108-4712

**KANNE, MICHAEL STEPHEN,** federal judge; b. Rensselaer, Ind., Dec. 21, 1938; s. Allen Raymond and Jane (Robinson) K.; m. Judith Ann Stevens, June 22, 1963; children: Anne, Katherine. Student, St. Joseph's Coll., Rensselaer, 1957-58; BS, Ind. U., 1962, JD, 1968; postgrad., Boston U., 1963, U. Birmingham, Eng., 1975. Bar: Ind. 1968. Assoc. Nesbitt and Fisher, Rensselaer, 1968-71; sole practice Rensselaer, 1971-72; atty. City of Rensselaer, 1972; judge 30th Jud. Cir. of Ind., 1972-82, U.S. Dist. Ct. (no. dist.) Ind., Hammond, 1982-87, U.S. Ct. Appeals, Chgo., 1987—; chmn. U.S. Cts. Design Guide, 1988-95; lectr. law St. Joseph's Coll., 1975-89, St. Frances Coll., 1990-91; faculty Nat. Inst. for Trial Advocacy, South Bend, Ind., 1978-88. Bd. visitors Ind. U. Sch. Law, 1987—, Ind. U. Sch. Pub. and Environ. Affairs, 1991—; trustee St. Joseph's Coll., 1984—. Served to 1st lt. USAF, 1962-65. Recipient Disting. Service award St. Joseph's Coll., 1973, Disting. Grad. award Nat Cath. Ednl. Assn.; named Outstanding Alumnus Today's Catholic Teacher, 1991. Mem. Fed. Bar Assn., Ind. State Bar Assn. (bd. dirs. 1977-79, Presdl. citation 1979), Jasper County Bar Assn. (pres. 1972-76), Tippecanoe County Bar Assn., Law Alumni Assn. Ind. U. (pres. 1980). Roman Catholic. Avocations, horseback riding, weightlifting. Home: PO Box 1340 Lafayette IN 47902-1340 Office: US Ct Appeals 219 S Dearborn St Chicago IL 60604-1702

**KANNER, FREDERICK W.,** lawyer; b. N.Y.C., Apr. 25, 1943. BA, U. Va., 1965; JD, Georgetown U., 1968. Bar: N.Y. 1969. Ptnr. Dewey Ballantine LLP, N.Y.C., 1976—. Editor: Georgetown Law Jour., 1967-68. Mem. ABA, N.Y. State Bar Assn., Assn. Bar City N.Y. (former mem. securities regulation com.). Office: Dewey Ballantine LLP 1301 Avenue Of The Americas New York NY 10019-6022

**KANNER, GIDEON,** lawyer; b. Lwów, Poland, Apr. 15, 1930; came to U.S., 1947; s. Stanley and Claire Kanner; children: Jonathan, Jesse. B of Mech. Engring., The Cooper Union, 1954; JD, U. So. Calif., 1961. Bar: Calif. 1962, U.S. Supreme Ct. 1967. Rocket engr. USN, N.J., 1954-55, Rocketdyne, Calif., 1955-64; assoc. Fadem & Kanner, L.S., 1964-74; prof. law Loyola U., L.A., 1974-90; assoc. Crosby, Heafey, Roach & May, L.A., 1990-95; lawyer Berger & Norton, Santa Monica, Calif., 1995—; cons. Calif. Law Revision Comm., 1968-77, 97—. Co-editor: Nichols on Eminent Domain, Compensation for Expropriation-A Comparative Study, Vol. II, 1990, After Lucas: Land Use Regulation and the Taking of Property Without Compensation, 1993; editor, pub. Just Compensation, 1974—; contbr. articles and revs. to profl. law jours. Recipient Shattuck prize Am. Inst. Real Estate Appraisers, Harrison Tweed Spl. Merit award for continuing legal edn. Am. Law Inst.-ABA. Condemnation, State civil litigation. Home: PO Box 1741 Burbank CA 91507-1741 Office: Berger & Norton 1620 26th St Ste 200 Santa Monica CA 90404-4059

**KANNRY, JACK STEPHEN,** lawyer; b. N.Y.C., Oct. 21, 1935. B.C.E., CCNY, 1956; M.I.E., NYU, 1959, M.C.E., 1962; J.D., Fordham U., 1968. Bar: N.Y. 1968, U.S. Ct. Appeals (2d cir.) 1970, U.S. Dist. Ct. (so. and ea. dists.) N.Y. 1970, U.S. Supreme Ct. 1972, U.S. Ct. Claims 1974; lic. profl. engr., N.Y., 1961. Asst. resident engr. Andrews & Clark, N.Y.C., 1957-60; chief contracts engr. Leonard S. Wegman Co., N.Y.C., 1961-68; asst. corp. counsel Law Dept. City of N.Y., 1968-70; spl. counsel to City of N.Y., 1970-71, city of Milford, Conn., 1988-91, govt. of Barbados, West Indies, 1985-88; assoc. Corner, Finn, Cuomo & Charles, Bklyn., 1970-73; ptnr. Berman Paley Goldstein & Kannry, LLP, N.Y.C., 1973—; comml./constrn. arbitrator Am. Arbitration Assn., N.Y.C., 1975—. Contbg. author: Construction Law and the Environment, Hazardous Waste Liability for construction contractors and design profls. in the U.S., 1994; contbr. papers to profl. seminars, contractors, bus. and ednl. orgns. 1st lt. C.E., U.S. Army, 1956-57, 60-61. Mem. Assn. of Bar City of N.Y., N.Y. State Bar Assn., ABA, ASCE, Nat. Soc. Profl. Engrs., Mcpl. Engrs. City of N.Y. Construction, Government contracts and claims, Environmental. Office: Berman Paley Goldstein & Kannry LLP 500 5th Ave Fl 43 New York NY 10110-0375

**KANTER, BURTON WALLACE,** lawyer; b. Jersey City, Aug. 12, 1930; s. Morris and Beatrice (Wilsker) K.; m. Naomi R. Krakow, June 17, 1927; children: Joel, Janis, Joshua. BA, U. Chgo., 1951, JD, 1952. Bar: Ill. 1952. Cons. U.S. Treasury Dept., 1959-61; atty.-advisor Tax Ct. U.S., 1954-56; mem. Law Offices of David Altman, Chgo., 1956-60; ptnr. Altman, Levenfeld & Kanter, Chgo., 1961-64, Levenfeld & Kanter, Chgo. and San Francisco, 1964-80, Kanter & Eisenberg, Chgo., 1980-87, of counsel Neal, Gerber, Eisenberg, 1987—; bd. dirs. Sci. Measurement Systems, Inc., Logic Devices, Inc., First Health Group, Inc.; chmn. Walnut Fin. Svcs. Inc.; faculty U. Chgo. Law Sch. Mem. adv. bd. Wharton Real Estate Ctr. U. Pa.; bd. dirs. Chgo. Internat. Film Festival, Midwest Film Ctr. of Sch. Art Inst.; mem. U. Chgo. Tax Policy Council; trustee Mus. Contemporary Art. Mem. ABA, Ill. Bar Assn., Chgo. Bar Assn., Urban Land Inst. Editor Jour. Taxation; contbr. articles to profl. jours. Corporate taxation, Estate taxation, Taxation, general. Office: 2 N La Salle St Fl 22 Chicago IL 60602-3702

**KANTER, STACY J.,** lawyer; b. N.Y.C., 1958. BS magna cum laude, SUNY, Albany, 1979; JD, Bklyn. Law Sch., 1984. Bar: N.Y. 1985. Ptnr. Skadden, Arps, Slate, Meagher & Flom LLP, N.Y.C. Mng. editor Bklyn. Law Rev., 1983-84. Named among N.Y.'s rising stars in bus. Crain's mag., 1997. Securities, General corporate. Office: Skadden Arps Slate Meagher & Flom LLP 919 3rd Ave New York NY 10022-3902

**KANTER, STEPHEN,** law educator, dean; b. Cin., June 30, 1946; s. Aaron J. and Edythe (Kasfir) K.; m. Dory Jean Poduska, June 24, 1972; children: Jordan Alexander, Laura Elizabeth. BS in Math., MIT, 1968; JD, Yale U., 1971. Spl. asst. Portland (Oreg.) City Commr., 1971-72; from staff atty. to asst. dir. Met. Pub. Defender, Portland, 1972-77; prof. law Lewis and Clark Coll., Portland, 1977—, assoc. dean, 1980-81, acting dean, 1981-82, dean, 1986-94; Fulbright prof. law Nanjing (China) U., 1984-85, U. Athens (Greece) Faculty of Law, 1993; bd. dirs. Northwest Regional China Coun., 1996—, pres.- elect, 1997-98, pres., 1998-99; exec. com. Owen M. Panner Am. Inns of Ct., pres., 1994-95; mem. judicial selection com. U.S. Dist. Ct. Oreg., 1993; cons. on drafting and implementation of Kazakhstan Constn., 1992, 94. Contbr. articles to profl. jours. Mem. bd. overseers World Affairs Coun. Oreg., Portland, 1986-89; mem. Oreg. Criminal Justice Coun., Salem, 1987-92, Oreg. Bicentennial Commn., Portland, 1986-89. Named One of 10 Gt. Portlanders, Willamette Week newspaper, 1980; recipient E.B. MacNaughton Civil Liberties award, 1991. Fellow Am. Bar Found.; mem. ACLU (bd. dirs. Oreg. chpt. 1976-82, pres. 1979-81, lawyers com. 1976—), Oreg. State Bar Assn., Am. Law Inst. (ex-officio 1986-94), Fulbright Assn. (bd. dirs. 1987-93, exec. com. 1989-93). Home: 3142 SW Fairview Blvd Portland OR 97201-1831 Office: Lewis & Clark Coll Northwestern Sch Law 10015 SW Terwilliger Blvd Portland OR 97219-7768

**KANTOR, ISAAC NORRIS,** lawyer; b. Charleston, W.Va., Aug. 29, 1929; s. Israel and Rachel (Cohen) K.; m. Doris Sue Katz, June 17, 1956; children: Mark B., Cynthia Kantor Anderson, Beth Kantor Zachwieja. BA, Va. Mil. Inst., 1953; JD, W.Va. U., 1956. Bar: W.Va. 1956, U.S. Dist. Ct. (so. dist.) W.Va. 1956, U.S. Ct. Mil. Appeals 1957, U.S. Ct. Appeals (4th cir.) 1978, U.S. Dist. Ct. (no. dist.) W.Va. 1991, U.S. Ct. Fed. Claims 1996. Ptnr Katz Katz and Kantor, Bluefield, W.Va., 1958-70, Katz Kantor Katz Perkins and Cameron, Bluefield, W.Va., 1970-82, Katz Kantor and Perkins, Bluefield, 1982—; town atty. Town of Bramwell, W.Va., 1970-75, Town of Petestown, W.Va., 1981-85; bd. dirs. First Cmty. Bank of Mercer County, First Cmty. Bankshares Inc., Princeton, W.Va.; mem. vis. com. W.Va. U. Coll. Law, Morgantown, 1986-89; mem. dean's adv. coun. Appalachian Sch. of Law, Grundy, Va., 1998—. Parliamentarian W.Va. Dem. Exec. Com., 1964-68; co-chmn. W.Va. Gov.'s Jud. Selection Com., 1988-97; chmn. W.Va. Ethics Commn., 1998—; chmn. W.Va. divsn. Am. Cancer Soc., 1990-92, pres. New River Pkwy. Authority, 1996—; mem. adv. bd. Bluefield State Coll., 1997—. Capt. JAGC, USAF, 1956-58; mem. USAFR, 1953-61. Paul Harris fellow Rotary Internat., 1999; recipient Citizen of Yr. award Greater Bluefield Jaycees, 1980, Boss of Yr. award, 1992, St. George medal, Nat. Divsnl. award Am. Cancer Soc., 1993. Mem. W.Va. Trial Lawyers Assn. (pres. 1980-81), B'nai B'rith (pres. W.Va. coun. 1975-76), Rotary Internat. (Paul Harris fellow 1999). Jewish. Avocations: golf, reading, travel, civic activities. Personal injury, Family and matrimonial, Administrative and regulatory. Home: 231 Oakdell Ave Bluefield WV 24701-4840 Office: PO Box 727 Bluefield WV 24701-0727

**KANTOR, THEODORE S.,** lawyer; b. N.Y.C., Feb. 26, 1947; s. Irving Kantor and Ruth (Kaminsky) Weinstein; m. Eleanor Vivian Budner, June 16, 1968; 1 child, Ian Michael. BA, Queens Coll., 1967; JD, SUNY, 1970. Bar: N.Y. 1971, U.S. Dist. Ct. (we. dist.) N.Y. 1972, U.S. Dist. Ct. (no. dist.) N.Y. 1992, U.S. Ct. Appeals (2d cir.) 1987, U.S. Supreme Ct. 1990. Chief confidential law asst. Appellate Divsn. 4th Dept., Rochester, N.Y., 1970-75; exec. dir. Am. Arbitration Assn., Rochester, 1975-78; assoc. Goldstein, Goldman, Kessler & Underberg, Rochester, 1979-81, Weiner, Lawrence & Salzman, Rochester, 1981-84; sole practice Rochester, 1984-93; ptnr. Marianetti & Kantor, Rochester, 1993-94, Bilgore, Reich, Levine, Kroll & Kantor, Rochester, 1995—; bd. dirs. Ctr. for Dispute Settlement, Rochester, 1979-80. Mem. Am. Arbitration Assn., Monroe County Bar Assn., N.Y. State Bar Assn., Ctr. Dispute Settlement, Inc. Avocations: golf, travel. Office: Bilgore Reich Levine Kroll & Kantor 16 E Main St Rochester NY 14614-1808

**KANTOWITZ, JEFFREY LEON,** lawyer; b. Paterson, N.J., Feb. 16, 1959; s. Sam and Hilda (Graubart) K. BA, Yeshiva U., 1979; JD, Harvard U., 1982. Bar: N.J. 1982, N.Y. 1983. Law clk. to justice Alan B. Handler U.S. Supreme Ct., Trenton, N.J., 1982-83; assoc. Clapp & Eisenberg PC, Newark, 1984-88; adj. prof. Seton Hall U. Law Sch., 1995—. Pres. Fair Lawn (N.J.) Jewish Cmty. Coun., 1989-90; mem. Fair Lawn Planning Bd., 1989-95, atty., 1996—; spl. counsel Glen Ridge Planning Bd., 1997. Walter D. Head Found. fellow, Hebrew U. Jerusalem, 1983-84. Mem. ABA, N.J. State Bar Assn. (land use and local govt. law sects.). Land use and zoning (including planning), State civil litigation, Environmental. Home: 15-28 Chandler Dr Fair Lawn NJ 07410-2714 Office: Goldberg Mufson & Spar 200 Executive Dr West Orange NJ 07052-3388

**KANTROWITZ, SUSAN LEE,** lawyer; b. Queens, N.Y., Jan. 15, 1955; d. Theodore and Dinah (Kotick) Kantrowitz; m. Mark R. Halperin; 1 child, Jacob Joseph Kantrowitz-Sirotkin. BS summa cum laude, Boston U., 1977; JD, Boston Coll., 1980. Bar: Mass. 1982. Assoc. producer Sta. KOCE-TV, Huntington Beach, Calif., 1980-81; acct. exec. Bozell & Jacobs, Newport Beach, Calif., 1981; atty. WGBH Ednl. Found., Boston, 1981-84, dir. legal affairs, 1984-86, gen. counsel, dir. legal affairs, 1986—, v.p., gen. counsel, 1993. Co-author: Legal and Business Aspects of the Entertainment, Publishing and Sports Industries, 1984. Mem. ABA, Mass. Bar Assn., Boston Bar Assn. Entertainment.

**KAPLAN, CARL ELIOT,** lawyer; b. N.Y.C., Apr. 17, 1939; s. Lawrence S. and Pearl (Eisenberg) K.; m. Diane L. Garvin, Dec. 16, 1965; children: Lynn, Jonathan. BA, Columbia Coll., 1959; LLB, 1962. Bar: U.S. Dist. Ct. (so. and ea. dists.) N.Y. 1964, U.S. Ct. Appeals (2d cir.) 1966, U.S. Supreme Ct. 1970. Assoc. Fulbright & Jaworski L.L.P., N.Y.C., 1963-69; ptnr., 1969—; sec. Data Gen. Corp., Westboro, Mass. Bd. dirs. Columbia Law Rev., 1961-62. Mem. ABA, N.Y. Bar Assn., Assn. of Bar City of N.Y., Am. Soc. Corp. Secs., Columbia Club (N.Y.C.), Univ. Club (N.Y.C.), Phi Beta Kappa. Avocations: skiing, jogging, tennis. Securities, General corporate, Finance. Office: Fulbright & Jaworski LLP 666 5th Ave Fl 31 New York NY 10103-3198

**KAPLAN, DANIEL,** lawyer; b. Memphis, Sept. 2, 1967; s. Steven Robert and Nancy Bonnie Kaplan. BA, U. Md., 1989; JD, Memphis State U., 1992. Assoc. Rosenthal, Rosenthal and Rasco, Miami, 1992-97, Lawrence A. France, P.A., Miami, 1997-98; ptnr. Daniel Kaplan, P.A., Miami, 1998—. Mem. ABA, Dade County Bar Assn. (dir. 1995-98, Pro Bono Svc. award 1995, 96, 97, 98), Fla. Bar Assn., North Dade Bar Assn. (bd. dirs. 1993—, chmn. family cts. com. 1998—). Office: 28 W Flagler St Fl 12 Miami FL 33130-1806

**KAPLAN, DAVID LOUIS,** lawyer, investment banker; b. Lakeland, Fla., Jan. 10, 1961; s. Donald David and Jane Zelda Kaplan; m. Katherine Ann Gibbons, Jan. 4, 1992. BA, Emory U., 1983, MA, 1983; JD, U. Fla., 1986. Bar: Fla. 1987, U.S. Supreme Ct. 1992; registered rep. Dir. Cegmark Internat., N.Y.C., 1986-87; sr. assoc. Kubicki Draper, Miami, Fla., 1987-94; shareholder, ptnr. Adorno & Zeder, P.A., Miami, 1994-97; mng. dir. Prudential Securities, Coral Gables, Fla., 1997—. Chair devel. com. Girl Scouts U.S., 1997, bd. dirs. Am. Red Cross, exec. bd. dirs. Swithbound of Miami. Republican. Jewish. Avocations: riding, sailing, travel, reading. Finance, Municipal (including bonds). Office: Prudential Securities Inc 2800 Ponce De Leon Blvd Coral Gables FL 33134-6913

**KAPLAN, DAVID S.,** lawyer, educator; b. Newark, Feb. 1, 1954; s. Leonard Kaplan and Gerda Bella; m. Beth Krulewitch, Feb. 27, 1988; children: Carolin, Noah. BA, U. Colo., 1977; JD, U. Denver, 1982. Bar: Colo. 1982, U.S. Dist. Ct. Colo. 1982. Dep. state pub. defender Colo. State Pub. Defender's Office, Denver, 1983-87; ptnr. Pozner & Kaplan, Denver, 1987-97, Holland Kaplan & Pagliuca, Denver, 1997—; mem. adj. faculty U. Denver Coll. Law, 1994—. Contbr. Denver Law Rev., 1997. Mem. NACDL, Colo. Criminal Def. Bar (pres. 1993-94). Criminal, Family and matrimonial, General civil litigation. Office: Holland Kaplan & Pagliuca 730 17th St Ste 730 Denver CO 80202-3544

**KAPLAN, ELI,** lawyer; b. Havana, Cuba, Dec. 1, 1957; s. Samuel and Berta (Kozulchyk) K.; m. Mindy Jill Friedman, June 28, 1980; children: Howard, Jeffrey, Adam. BS cum laude, Am. U., 1980; JD, U. Miami, 1984. Bar: Fla. Lawyer/assoc. Law Offices Harvey Friedman, Miami, Fla., 1984-86; ptnr. Friedman & Kaplan, PA, Miami, Fla., 1986-91, Kaplan & Miller, PA, Miami, Fla., 1991—. Chair Aides for Classroom Tchrs., Miami, 1989; v.p. fund raising Temple Samuel or Olom, Miami, 1990; pres. Temple B'Nai Aviv, Weston, Fla., 1996—; mem. Dem. Exec. Com. Broward County, Fla., 1996. Mem. Dade County Bar Assn., Broward County Bar Assn., Dade County Trial Lawyers Assn. General civil litigation, Personal injury. Office: Kaplan & Miller PA 999 Ponce De Leon Blvd Ste 20 Coral Gables FL 33134-3037

**KAPLAN, ELIOT LAWRENCE,** lawyer; b. Syracuse, N.Y., Sept. 18, 1963; s. Marvin Ruben and Marjorie Ann Kaplan; m. Tiffany Dee Munson, July 14, 1990; 1 child, Mikaela. BS, U. Ariz., 1986; JD, Ariz. State U., 1989; M in Legal Letters, Georgetown U., 1992. Bar: Ariz. 1989, D.C. 1992, Mo. 1994, Kans. 1995. Atty., advisor IRS, Washington, 1989-94; assoc. Lathrop & Gage, L.C., Kansas City, Mo., 1994-97; mem. Lathrop & Gage, L.C., Kansas City, 1998—; advisor Ctr. for Mgmt. Assistance, Kansas City, 1995-97. Mem. Kansas City Tommorrow, Civic Coun. Kansas City, 1995; mem. centurions Greater Kans. City Chamber, Kansas City, 1997—; bd. mem. Am. Diabetes Assn., Kansas City, 1997—. Mem. ABA (sect. on taxation), Kansas City Met. Bar (tax sect.), D.C. Bar Assn. (tax sect.), C. of G. Greater Kansas City (mem. fed. affairs com. 1996—, chair tax com. 1996—). Corporate taxation, Taxation, general, General corporate. Home: 10400 Alhandra Dr Overland Park KS 66207 Office: Lathrop & Gage LC 2345 Grand Blvd Ste 2800 Kansas City MO 64108-2684

**KAPLAN, HOWARD M(ARK),** lawyer; b. Bklyn., Apr. 4, 1938; s. Isaac M. and Dorothy M. (Penn) K.; m. Carol Rose Silber, Aug. 11, 1963; children: Rachel Dale, Deborah Michelle, Sarah Beth. BA cum laude, U. Pa., 1960; JD, Yale U., 1963. Bar: N.J. 1963, U.S. Dist. Ct. N.J. 1963, U.S. Supreme Ct. 1980. Dep. atty. gen. State of N.J., 1966-70; pvt. practice Teaneck, N.J., 1967—; ptnr. Kaplan, Radol, Shapiro & Kaplan, LLC, Teaneck. Chmn. ann. Cmty. Blood Dr., Teaneck, 1980—, Cmty. Scholarship Fund, Teaneck, 1976—. Named Teaneck Man of Yr., 1979. Mem. ABA, N.J. Bar Assn., Bergen County Bar Assn., Assn. Trial Lawyers Am., Yale Sch. Assn. N.J. (pres. 1988-90). Democrat. Jewish. Lodge: B'nai B'rith (pres. Palisades council 1979, pres. Teaneck 1973-76). Contracts commercial, Family and matrimonial, Personal injury. Home: 370 Churchill Rd Teaneck NJ 07666-3008 Office: 1086 Teaneck Rd PO Box 78 Teaneck NJ 07666-0078

**KAPLAN, JARED,** lawyer; b. Chgo., Dec. 28, 1938; s. Jerome and Phyllis Enid (Rieber) K.; m. Rosellen Engstrom, Dec. 28, 1964 (div. 1978); children: Brian F., Philip B.; m. Maridee Quanbeck, June 2, 1990. AB, UCLA, 1960; LLB, Harvard, 1963. Bar: Ill. 1963, U.S. Dist. Ct. (no. dist.) Ill. 1969, U.S. Tax Ct. 1978. Assoc. Ross & Hardies, Chgo., 1963-69, ptnr., 1970; ptnr. Roan & Grossman, Chgo., 1970-83, Keck, Mahin & Cate, Chgo., 1983-94, McDermott, Will & Emery, Chgo., 1994—; bd. dirs. ESOP (Employee Stock Ownership Plan) Assn., Washington, 1987-90, Family Firm Inst., Boston, 1996—; adv. coun. Ill. Employee-Owned Enterprise, Chgo., 1984—; chmn. Ill. Adv. Task Force on Ownership Succession and Employee Ownership, 1994-95. Editor in chief: Callaghan's Fed. Tax Guide, 1988; author: Employee Stock Ownership Plans, 1999. Nat. pres. Ripon Soc., Washington, 1975-76; adv. council mem. Rep. Nat. Com., Washington, 1978-80; alt. delegate Rep. Nat. Conv., Detroit, 1980; bd. dirs. Family Firm Inst., 1996—. Fellow Ill. Bar Found.; mem. ABA (chmn. section of taxation, administrv. practice com. 1978-80), City Club, Chgo. (bd. govs. 1982-92), Univ. Club, Met. Club. Republican. Jewish. Corporate taxation, Mergers and acquisitions, Pension, profit-sharing, and employee benefits. Home: 105 W Delaware Pl Chicago IL 60610-3200 Office: McDermott Will & Emery 227 W Monroe St Fl 44 Chicago IL 60606-5018

**KAPLAN, JOEL STUART,** lawyer; b. Bklyn., Feb. 1, 1937; s. Abraham Larry and Phayne (Moses) K.; m. Joan Ruth Katz, June 19, 1960; children: Andrea Beth, Pamela Jill. BA, Bklyn. Coll., 1958; LLB, NYU, 1961. Bar: N.Y. 1962, U.S. Dist. Cts. (ea. and so. dists.) N.Y. 1964, U.S. Ct. Appeals (2d cir.) 1966, U.S. Supreme Ct. 1979, Fla. 1982, D.C. 1987. Asst. town atty. Town of Hempstead, Nassau County, N.Y., 1962-67; ptnr. Jaspan, Kaplan, Levin & Daniels and predecessors, Garden City, N.Y., 1970-83; sole practice Garden City, 1983-95; counsel Levin Belsky Ross and Daniels, Garden City, 1995—. Chmn. Hempstead Town Pub. Employment Rels. Bd., 1973-81; pres. dist. #1 B'nai B'rith, 1986-87, internat. bd. govs., 1987—; chmn. Nat. Ctr. Cmty. Action, 1996—, B'nai B'rith Found. U.S., 1989-90; rep. candidate N.Y. State Senate, 1974. Mem. ABA, N.Y. State Bar Assn., Nassau County Bar Assn. State civil litigation, Federal civil litigation. Home: 973 E End Woodmere NY 11598-1005 Office: 585 Stewart Ave Ste 700 Garden City NY 11530-4785

**KAPLAN, KEITH EUGENE,** insurance company executive, lawyer; b. Rahway, N.J., Apr. 6, 1960; s. Eugene Aloysius and Barbara Ann (Dempski) K.; m. Rita Maria Baker, Aug. 8, 1987; children: Matthew Joseph Kaplan, William Alexander Kaplan (dec.). BS, U. Pa., 1982; JD, Temple U., 1992. Bar: Pa. 1992. Underwriter Home Ins. Co., Phila., 1982-85, underwriting supr., 1985-86; product line mgr. Home Ins. Co., N.Y.C., 1987; underwriting dir. Reliance Ins. Co., Phila., 1987-88; asst. v.p. Reliance Nat., Phila., 1988-90; asst. v.p. Reliance Nat., N.Y.C., 1990-92, v.p., 1992-96, mng. v.p., 1996—. Mem. ABA, Phila. Bar Assn., Soc. CPCU, Wharton Club. Home: 1240 Pickering Ln Chester Springs PA 19425-1423 Office: Reliance National 77 Water St New York NY 10005-4499 also: Reliance Ins Co Three Parkway Philadelphia PA 19102

**KAPLAN, KENNETH J.,** lawyer; b. N.Y.C., Mar. 29, 1967; s. Samuel Simon and Brenda Joan Kaplan; m. Gloria Kaplan, Sept. 3, 1995. BA, Pomona Coll., 1989; JD, U. of the Pacific, 1992. Bar: Calif. 1992, Ariz. 1993. Atty. Law Office of M. Lucia, Donahue, Pasadena, Calif., 1993-95; sr. trial atty. Santochi, Fitzer & Gable, Glendale, Calif., 1995—. Elected mem. for L.A., Cmty. Redevel. Agy., North Hollywood, 1995-96. Workers' compensation. Office: Santochi Fitzer Gable 700 N Brand Blvd Ste 1100 Glendale CA 91203-1208

**KAPLAN, LAWRENCE I.,** lawyer; b. Bklyn., Mar. 15, 1948; s. M. Milton and Pearl (Mandel) K.; m. Gale Jane Gutman, Jan. 31, 1971; children: Sara Rebecca, Aaron Howard. BA, CUNY, 1969; JD, U. Wis., 1973. Bar: Wis. 1974, N.Y. 1975, U.S. Ct. Appeals (2d cir.). Legis. asst. Assembly Judiciary Com., Madison, Wis., 1973-74; assoc. spl. counsel Rec. Industry Assn. Am., N.Y.C., 1974-80; sole practice N.Y.C., 1980—. Pres. Uplands Civic Assn., Great Neck, N.Y., 1985-86. Mem. ABA, Wis. Bar Assn. Democrat. Jewish. Federal civil litigation, State civil litigation, General practice. Home: 47 Upland Rd Great Neck NY 11020-1133 Office: 321 Broadway New York NY 10007-1111

**KAPLAN, LEWIS A.,** judge; b. S.I., N.Y., Dec. 23, 1944; s. Alfred H. and Dorothy A. K.; m. Nancy Gelberg, Aug. 29, 1968; 1 child, Merrill. AB, U. Rochester, 1966; JD, Harvard U., 1969. Bar: N.Y. 1970, U.S. Ct. Appeals (1st and 2d cirs.) 1970, U.S. Dist. Ct. (so. and ea. dists.) N.Y. 1971, U.S. Ct. Appeals (3d cir.) 1973, U.S. Supreme Ct. 1973, U.S. Dist. Ct. (we. dist.) N.Y. 1975, U.S. Ct. Appeals (D.C. cir.) 1976, U.S. Ct. Appeals (4th and 5th cirs.) 1979, U.S. Dist. Ct. (no. dist.) Calif. 1980, U.S. Ct. Appeals (9th cir.) 1980, U.S. Dist. Ct. (ea. dist.) Mich. 1983, U.S. Ct. Appeals (6th cir.) 1983, D.C. 1985, U.S. Ct. Appeals (Fed. and 11th cirs.) 1987, U.S. Dist. Ct. D.C. 1988. Law clk. to judge U.S. Ct. Appeals (1st cir.), 1969-70; assoc. Paul, Weiss, Rifkind, Wharton & Garrison, N.Y.C., 1970-77, ptnr., 1977-94; judge U.S. Dist. Ct. (so. dist.) N.Y., N.Y.C., 1994—; spl. master Westway litigation U.S. Dist. Ct. (so. dist.) N.Y., 1982; trustee Lawyers Com. for Civil Rights Under Law, 1992-94; mem. Comm. on Automation and Tech., Jud. Conf. U.S., 1997—. Mem. trustees' coun. U. Rochester, 1982-88; mem. trustees' vis. com. William E. Simon Grad. Sch. Bus. Adminstrn., 1986-88; village trustee N.Y., 1988-91. Fellow Am. Coll. Trial Lawyers (jud.); mem. ABA, N.Y. State Bar Assn., Fed. Bar Coun., Am. Law Inst., Fed. Judges' Assn. (dir. 1997—). Office: US Courthouse 500 Pearl St New York NY 10007-1316

**KAPLAN, MADELINE,** legal administrator; b. N.Y.C., June 20, 1944; d. Leo and Ethel (Finkelstein) Kahn; m. Theodore Norman Kaplan, Nov. 14, 1982. AS, Fashion Inst. Tech., N.Y.C., 1964; BA in English Lit. summa cum laude, CUNY, 1982; MBA, Baruch Coll., 1990. Free-lance fashion illustrator N.Y.C., 1965-73; legal asst. Krause Hirsch & Gross, Esquires, N.Y.C., 1973-80; mgr. communications Stroock & Stroock & Lavan Esquires, N.Y.C., 1980-86; dir. adminstrn. Cooper Cohen Singer & Ecker Esquires, N.Y.C., 1986-87, Donovan Leisure Newton & Irvine Esquires, N.Y.C., 1987-93, Proskauer Rose Goetz & Mendelsohn, N.Y.C., 1993-95, Kaye, Scholer, Fierman, Hays & Handler, LLP, N.Y.C., 1995, 1995—; mem. adv. bd. Grad. Sch. Human Resources Mgmt. Mercy Coll., 1997—. Contbr. articles to profl. jours. Founder, pres. Knolls chpt. of Women's Am. Orgn. Rehab. Through Tng., Riverdale, N.Y., 1979-82, v.p. edn., Manhattan region, 1982-83; mentor Suited for Success; vol. Starlight Found. Mem. ASTD, Assn. Legal Adminstrs. (program com.), Career Planning Com., Soc. Human Resources Mgmt., Exec. MBA Alumni Assn. (bd. dirs.), Sigma Iota Epsilon (life). Office: 425 Park Ave New York NY 10022-3506

**KAPLAN, MARC J.,** lawyer; b. Phila., Mar. 12, 1957; s. Ronald L. Kaplan and Sylvia B. (Meyers) Price; m. Mary J. Dulacki, Sept. 16, 1984; children: Alexandra Zoe, Rini Isadora. BA, Duke U., 1979; JD, U. Denver, 1983. Bar: Colo. 1984, Mont. 1999, U.S. Dist. Ct. Colo. 1984, U.S. Ct. Appeals (10th cir.) 1984, Mont. 1999. Asst. for polit. ops. Dem. Nat. Com., Washington, 1979-80; asst. to spl. asst. to pres. White House, Washington, 1980-81; atty. Aisenberg & Kaplan, Denver, 1984-94, Rossi, Cox, Kiker & Inderwish, P.C., Denver, 1994-98; special counsel Gutterman, Carlton & Heckenbach LLP, 1998—; polit. cons. Washington, 1981, lawyering process adj. prof. U. Denver Coll. of Law, 1990-92, faculty basic civil litig. skills continuing legal edn. of Denver, 1990-92, Colo. Supreme Ct. Greivance Com. Hearing Bd., Denver, 1993-98; mem. Supreme Ct. Colo., com. county and dist. ct. cir. and jud. access issues, 1998-99. Contbr. Colo. Auto Litigator's Handbook. Pres. Duke Club of Denver, 1990-92, chmn. Children of Violence Com., Denver, 1993-94; bd. dirs. United Citizens of Arapahoe Neighborhoods, 1997-99. Named Young Polit. Leader U.S. State Dept., Washington, 1979. Mem. ATLA (state del. 1997-99), Colo. Bar Assn. (gov. 1990-93, Pro Bono award 1993), Colo. Trial Lawyers Assn. (pres. 1998-99), Denver and Arapahoe Bar Assn., Thompson G. Marsh Inn of Ct., Faculty of Fed. Advocates. E-mail: Marckaplan@uswest.net. Personal injury, Family and matrimonial, General civil litigation. Office: Gutterman Carlton & Hekenbach LLP 8375 S Willow St Ste 300 Lone Tree CO 80124-2846

**KAPLAN, MARK NORMAN,** lawyer; b. N.Y.C., Mar. 7, 1930; s. Louis and Ruth (Hertzberg) K.; m. Helene L. Finkelstein, Sept. 7, 1952; children: Marjorie Ellen, Sue Anne. A.B., Columbia, 1951; J.D., 1953. Bar: N.Y. 1953. Assoc. firm Garey & Garey, N.Y.C., 1953; law clk. Judge William Bondy, U.S. Dist. Ct. for So. Dist. N.Y., 1953-54; assoc. Columbia Law Sch., 1954-55, Wickes, Riddell, Bloomer, Jacobi & McGuire, N.Y.C., 1955-59; assoc., ptnr., sr. ptnr. Marshall, Bratter, Greene, Allison & Tucker, N.Y.C., 1959-70; sr. ptnr. Burnham & Co., N.Y.C., 1970-71; pres. Drexel Burnham Lambert Inc., N.Y.C., 1972-77; also chief exec. officer Drexel Burnham Lambert Inc., 1976-77; pres. Engelhard Minerals & Chem. Corp., N.Y.C., 1977-79; mem. firm Skadden, Arps, Slate, Meager & Flom, N.Y.C., 1979—; bd. dirs. Am. Biltrite, Grey Advt., Inc., REFAC Tech. Devel. Corp., DRS Techs. Inc., Volt Info. Sci., Inc., Jim Pattison, Ltd., Internat. Creative Mgmt., Inc., MovieFone, Inc., Monte Carlo Grand Hotel, Congoleum Corp., Worldwide Securities Ltd., Smith Barney World Wide Spl. Fund N.V.; vice chmn. Am. Stock Exch., N.Y.C., 1974, bd. govs., 1975, vice chmn. bd. govs., 1975-76; trustee Bard Coll.; chmn. audit com. City of N.Y.; Co-chmn. audit adv. com. Bd. Edn. of City of N.Y.; chmn. Early Edn. Leadership Group; bd. dirs. New Alternatives for Children. Mem. Coun. Fgn. Rels., Econ. Club N.Y., Harmonie Club, City Athletic Club. General corporate, Securities. Home: 146 Central Park W New York NY 10023-2005 Office: Skaden Arps 919 3rd Ave New York NY 10022-3902

**KAPLAN, SHELDON,** lawyer; b. Mpls., Feb. 16, 1915; s. Max Julius and Harriet (Wolfson) K.; m. Helene Bamberger, Dec. 7, 1941; children—Jay Michael, Mary Jo, Jean Burton, Jeffrey Lee. BA summa cum laude, U. Minn., 1935; LLB, Columbia U., 1939. Bar: N.Y. 1940, Minn. 1946. Pvt. practice N.Y.C., 1940-42, Mpls., 1946—; mem. firm Lauterstein, Spiller, Bergerman & Dannett, N.Y.C., 1939-42; ptnr. Maslon, Kaplan, Edelman, Borman, Brand & McNulty, Mpls., 1946-80; chmn. Kaplan, Strangis and Kaplan, Mpls., 1980—; bd. dirs. Stewart Enterprises Inc., Creative Ventures Inc. Decisions editor Columbia Law Review, 1939. Served to capt. AUS, 1942-46. Mem. Minn. Bar Assn., Hazeltime Nat. Golf Club, Mpls. Club, Phi Beta Kappa. General corporate, Mergers and acquisitions, Corporate taxation. Home: 2950 Dean Pkwy Minneapolis MN 55416-4446 Office: Kaplan Strangis & Kaplan 5500 Norwest Ctr Minneapolis MN 55402

**KAPLAN, STEVEN MARK,** lawyer; b. Bklyn., Aug. 12, 1967; s. Edwin and Esther Kaplan. BBA, George Washington U., 1989; JD, Benjamin N. Cardozo Law Sch., 1992. Bar: N.J. 1992, N.Y. 1993. Founder, mng. mem. Kaplan Gottbetter and Levenson LLP, N.Y.C., 1992—. General civil litigation, Intellectual property, Contracts commercial. Office: Kaplan Gottbetter & Levenson LLP 630 3rd Ave New York NY 10017-6705

**KAPLOW, LOUIS,** law educator; b. Chgo., June 17, 1956; s. Mortimer and Irene (Horwich) K.; m. Jody Ellen Forchheimer, July 11, 1982; children: Irene Miriam, Leah Rayna. BA, Northwestern U., 1977; AM, Harvard U., 1981, JD, 1981, PhD, 1987. Bar: Mass. 1983. Prof. law Harvard U., Cambridge, Mass., 1982—, assoc. dean for rsch. and spl. programs, 1989-91. Contbr. articles to profl. jours.; co-author: Antitrust Analysis, 1997; editorial bd. Jour. of Law, Econs. and Orgn., 1989—, Internat. Rev. of Law and Econs., 1988—, Nat. Tax Jour., 1995—, Legal Theory, 1995—. Faculty rsch. assoc. Nat. Bur. Economic Rsch., Cambridge, Mass., 1985—. Mem. Am. Econ. Assn., Nat. Tax Assn. Jewish. Office: Harvard U Law Sch Cambridge MA 02138

**KAPLOW, ROBERT DAVID,** lawyer; b. Bklyn., Feb. 6, 1947; s. Herbert and Geraldine Rhoda K.; m. Lois Susan Silverman, May 22, 1971; children: Julie, Jeffrey. BS, Cornell U., 1968; JD, U. Mich., 1971; LLM, Wayne State U., 1978. Bar: Mich. 1972, U.S. Dist. Ct. (ea. dist. ) Mich. 1972, U.S. Tax Ct. 1976, U.S. Ct. Appeals (6th cir.) 1991. Assoc. Milton Y. Zussman, Birmingham, Mich., 1972-75, Rubenstein, Isaacs, Lax & Bordman, Southfield, Mich., 1975-89; ptnr. Maddin, Hauser, Wartell, Roth, Heller & Pesses P.C., Southfield, 1989—. Bd. dirs. Jewish Assn. Retarded Citizens; mem. Fin. and Estate Planning Coun. of Detroit, Inc., Oakland County Fin. and Estate Planning Coun., Inc. Mem. ABA, Mich. Bar Assn., Oakland County Bar Assn., Cornell Club of Mich. Personal income taxation, General corporate, Estate planning. Office: Maddin Hauser Wartell Roth Heller & Pesses PC 28400 Northwestern Hwy Fl 3 Southfield MI 48034-1839 also: PO Box 215 Southfield MI 48037-0215

**KAPNICK, RICHARD BRADSHAW,** lawyer; b. Chgo., Aug. 21, 1955; s. Harvey E. and Jean (Bradshaw) K.; m. Claudia Norris, Dec. 30, 1978; children: Sarah Bancroft, John Norris. BA with distinction, Stanford U., 1977; MPhil in Internat. Rels., U. Oxford, 1980; JD with honors, U. Chgo., 1982. Bar: Ill. 1982, N.Y. 1993. Law clk. to justice Ill. Supreme Ct., Chgo., 1982-84; law clk. to Justice John Paul Stevens U.S. Supreme Ct., Washington, 1984-85; assoc. Sidley & Austin, Chgo., 1985-89, ptnr., 1989—. Mng. editor U. Chgo. Law Rev., 1981-82. Trustee Chgo. Symphony Orch., 1995—, governing mem., 1988-95; bd. dirs. Cabrini Green Legal Aid Clinic, 1990-94, chmn. bd., 1991-93. Marshall scholar, 1978-80; fellow Leadership Greater Chgo., 1989-90. Mem. Order of Coif, Chgo. Club, Econ. Club Chgo., Law Club Chgo., Phi Beta Kappa. Republican. Episcopalian. General civil litigation, Libel.

**KAPP, C. TERRENCE,** lawyer; b. Pine Bluff, Ark., Oct. 1, 1944; s. Robert Amos and Guenevere Patricia (DeVinne) K.; m. Betsy Langer, May 2, 1987. BA, Colgate U., 1966; JD, Cleve. State U., 1971; MA summa cum laude, Holy Apostles Coll., 1984. Bar: Ohio 1971, U.S. Dist. Ct. (no. dist.) Ohio 1973, U.S. Supreme Ct. 1980, U.S. Tax Ct. 1996. Ptnr. Kapp & Kapp, East Liverpool, Ohio, 1971-84; pvt. practice Cleve., 1984—; ptnr. Marshman, Snyder & Kapp, Cleve., 1991-93, Kapp Law Offices, Cleve., 1994—. Contbr. articles to profl. jours. Pres., bd. dirs. Lake Erie Nature & Sci. Ctr., Bay Village, Ohio, 1991-92; chair St. John's Cathedral Endowment Trust, Cleve., 1992-94. Mem. ABA (commr. presdl. commn. on non-lawyer practice 1992-96; judge finals nat. appellate adv. competition 1987, nat. chmn. divorce laws and procedures com. Family law sect. 1989-93, vice-chmn. step families com. 1991-93, chmn. alternative funding com. 1992—, taxation com. exec. 1988—, task force on client edn. 1991—, chair nat. symposium on Image of Family law Atty.-Fact or Myth 1993, cert. Outstanding Svc. 1988, 89, 93, 95, domestic rels. taxation problems com. exec. Tax sect., Litigation sect.), Ohio State Bar Assn. (family law com. exec. 1987—, family law curriculum com. Ohio CLE Inst. 1992—), Cuyahoga County Bar Assn. (chair family law sect. 1991-92, bar admissions com. exec. 1986—, cert. grievance com. 1990—, jud. selection com. 1991—, unauthorized practice of law com. 1992—, cert. Outstanding Leadership 1992), Cleve. Athletic Club (pres., bd. dirs.), Bay Men's Club. Roman Catholic. Avocations: sailing, handball, racquet sports. Family and matrimonial. Office: Kapp Law Offices 1370 Ontario St Cleveland OH 44113-1701

**KAPP, JOHN PAUL,** lawyer, physician, educator; b. Galax, Va., Feb. 22, 1938; s. Paul Homer and Jesse Kathrine (Vass) K.; m. Emily Lureese Evans, June 23, 1961; children: Paul Hardin, Emily Camille. MD, Duke U., 1963, BS, 1966, PhD in Anatomy, 1967; JD, Wake Forest U., 1990. Bar: N.C. 1990, Va. 1991, Fla. 1991. Intern Med. Coll. Va., Richmond, 1963; resident in surgery Duke U., Durham, N.C., 1964, resident in neurosurgery, 1964-69; asst. prof. neurosurgery U. Tenn., Memphis, 1971-72; attending neurosurgeon Bay Meml. Med. Ctr., Panama City, Fla., 1972-80, Gulf Coast Cmty. Hosp., 1977-80; assoc. prof. neurosurgery U. Miss., Jackson, 1980-83, prof., 1983-85; prof., chmn. dept. neurosurgery SUNY, Buffalo, 1985-87; pvt. practice as lawyer Galax, 1990—. Editor: The Cerebral Venous System and Its Disorders, 1984; contbr. articles to profl. jours. and chpts. to books; patentee arterial pressure control system, prosthetic vertebral body, cranial sensor attaching device. Major U.S. Army, 1969-71. USPHS Neurosurgy fellow, 1965-67; recipient Rsch. award Am. Acad. Neurol. Surgery, 1967. Mem. N.C. Acad. Trial Lawyers, N.C. Bar Assn., Va. State Bar Assn. Democrat. Methodist. Avocations: hunting, dog training. Personal injury. Office: 2433 Thomas Dr # 104 Panama City Beach FL 32408-5808

**KAPP, MARSHALL BARRY,** legal educator, consultant; b. Pitts., July 22, 1949; s. Harold Robert and Beatrice Betty (Shapiro) K.; m. Susan Lee Chamovitz, Aug. 22, 1971; children: Melissa, Andrew. BA, Johns Hopkins U., 1971; JD with honors, George Washington U., 1974; MPH, Harvard U., 1978. Bar: Fla. 1974, U.S. Dist. Ct. (mid. dist.) Fla. 1975, U.S. Ct. Appeals (5th cir.) 1975, U.S. Supreme Ct. 1977; lic. nursing home adminstr., D.C. Law clk. to assoc. judge Superior Ct. D.C., Washington, 1974-75; assoc. Law Offices of James M. Russ, P.A., Orlando, Fla., 1975-77; program analyst HEW, 1978-79; instr. health law Balt. Free U., Chaplain's Office, Johns Hopkins U., 1979; legis. counsel for health affairs N.Y. State Office Fed. Affairs, Washington, 1980; adj. prof. law U. Dayton Sch. Law, Ohio, 1982—; asst. prof. legal medicine dept. cmty. health Sch. Medicine Wright State U., 1980-83, assoc. prof., course dir., 1983-87, prof., 1987—, dir. office geriat. medicine and gerontology, 1989—; mem. Hastings Ctr. Inst. Soc., Ethics and Life Scis., 1979—; mem. adv. bd. Montgomery County Nursing Home Ombudsman Program, 1981-87; mem. sr. law adv. bd. Dayton Legal Aid Soc., 1982-87 ; mem. Ohio Developmental Disabilities Planning Council, 1983-84. Articles reviewer Hosp. and Community Psychiatry, 1981—; assoc. editor Law, Medicine and Health Care, 1983-87; bd. editors Jour. Law, Medicine and Ethics, Generations, 1987—; editor Journ Ethics, Law and Aging; manuscript reviewer Annals Internal Medicine, 1983—, The Gerontologist, 1983—; editor: numerous books; author: Geriatrics and the Law: Patient Rights and Professional Responsibilities, 1985, Legal Guide for Medical Office Managers, 1985, Preventing Malpractice in Long-Term Care: Strategies for Risk Management, 1987, also articles in profl. jours.; co-editor: Legal and Ethical Aspects of Health Care for the Elderly, 1986. Trustee Camp Emanuel for Hearing Impaired Children, 1981-84, pres. bd., 1982-83; chair bd. trustees South Community Inc., 1983-85, sec., 1982-83, bd. dirs., 1981-87; mem. Johns Hopkins U. Alumni Schs. Com., 1980—; trustee Ohio Tourette Syndrome Assn., 1982-84. Served with USPHS, 1978-79. MRobert Wood Johnson faculty fellow, 1987-89. Mem. Am. Soc. Law, Medicine and Ethics, Am. Soc. Law and Medicine (mem. task force on health law teaching programs 1983-85, co-chmn. com. on legal and ethical aspects health care for elderly 1983—), Am. Acad. Hosp. Attys., Gerontol. Soc. Am. (abstracts reviewer ann. meeting 1982—), Am. Soc. on Aging (chmn. edn. com. 1984-86), Fla. Bar Assn. (jour. editorial bd. 1983-85, health law com. 1982-88). Republican. Jewish. Home: 7945 Southbury Dr Dayton OH 45458-2924 Office: Wright State U Med Sch PO Box 927 Dayton OH 45401-0927

**KAPP, MICHAEL KEITH,** lawyer; b. Winston-Salem, N.C., Nov. 28, 1953; s. William Henry and Betty Jean (Minton) K.; m. Mary Jo Chancy McLean, Aug. 13, 1977; 1 child, Mary Katherine. AB with honors, U. N.C., 1976, JD with honors, 1979. Bar: N.C. 1979, U.S. Dist. Ct. (ea. dist.) N.C. 1980, U.S. Ct. Appeals (4th cir.) 1982, U.S. Dist. Ct. (mid. dist.) N.C. 1986, U.S. Supreme Ct. 1988. Law clk. to presiding justice N.C. Ct. Appeals, Raleigh, 1979-80, N.C. Supreme Ct., Raleigh, 1980-81; assoc. Maupin, Taylor & Ellis, Raleigh, 1981-85; ptnr. Maupin, Taylor & Ellis, P.A., Raleigh, 1985—. Research editor U. N.C. Jour. Internat. Law and Comml. Regulation, 1978-79; editor Survey of Significant Decisions of North Carolina Court of Appeals and North Carolina Supreme Court, 1979-81, 2d vol., 1981-82. N.C. teen Dem. advisor, 1983-85; mem. exec. council N.C. Dem. Party, 1983-85; founding dir. N.C. Vol. Lawyers for Arts, Raleigh, 1982-85; counsel Moravian Music Found., Winston-Salem, 1982-85, trustee, 1985-90, pres., 1990-92; counsel Raleigh Little Theatre, 1996—; bd. dirs. Moravian Ch. Archives, Wiston-Salem, 1984-89, Soc. for Preservation of Historic Oakwood, Raleigh, 1981-83, Carolina Charter Corp., 1990—, dir. 1995—. Morehead scholar U. N.C., 1972. Mem. ABA, N.C. Bar Assn. (chmn. young lawyer div. continuing legal edn. 1980-82, membership 1984-86, bd. govs. 1983-86), N.C. State Bar (ethics com. 1981-91, com. on professionalism 1986-87), Wake County Bar Assn. (bd. dirs. 1988-90, pres.-elect 1995, pres. 1996), Kiwanis (Raleigh Kiwanis Found. dir., 1996-98), Raleigh Execs. Club (pres. 1998-99), Phi Beta Kappa, Phi Delta Phi, Pi Lambda Phi. Avocation: historic preservation, hiking, gardening. Administrative and regulatory, Franchising, General civil litigation. Home: 1615 Craig St Raleigh NC 27608-2201 Office: Maupin Taylor & Ellis Highwoods Tower One 3200 Beech Leaf Ct Ste 500 Raleigh NC 27604-1063

**KAPPES, PHILIP SPANGLER,** lawyer; b. Detroit, Dec. 24, 1925; s. Philip Alexander and Wilma Fern (Spangler) K.; m. Glendora Galena Miles, Nov. 27, 1948; children: Susan Lea, Philip Miles, Mark William. Bar: Ind. 1948. Assoc. Armstrong and Gause, 1948-49, C.B. Dutton, 1950-51; ptnr. Dutton, Kappes & Overman, 1952-85, of counsel, 1983-85; ptnr. Lewis Kappes Fuller & Eads, Indpls., 1985-89, Lewis & Kappes, Indpls., 1989-92, Lewis & Kappes PC, Indpls., 1993—, Labeco Properties, Creston Group, Indpls.; pres., dir. K&K Realty, Inc., Indpls.; sec., dir., mem. exec. com. Lab. Equipment Corp., Mooresville, Ind.; instr. bus. law Butler U., 1948-49, chmn. bd. govs., 1965-66, bd. trustees, 1987-90; chmn. Ovid Butler Soc., 1982-83. Life bd. dirs. Crossroads Am. coun. Boy Scouts Am., 1965—, v.p. fin., mem. exec. com., pres., 1977-79, chmn. trustees endowment fund, 1987-92, trustee, 1987—; bd. dirs. Fairbanks Hosp., Indpls., 1986-94, chmn. bd., 1988-91, exec. com., 1987-94, mem. audit and fin. com., 1992-94, life dir. emeritus, 1994—, chmn. nominating com., 1991; trustee Butler U., 1987-90, Children's Mus., Indpls., 1969-88, pres. bd. trustees, 1984-85, bd. disting. advisors, 1990—; mem. First Meridian Heights Presbyn. Ch., 1933—, chmn. bd. trustees, 1958-61, 69-72, 1996— ruling elder 1982-85, 94-99, deacon, 1950-58; mem. planning com. and dir. 32-Degree Scottish rite Children's Learning ctr., 1997—. Recipient Paul H. Buchanan award of excellence Indpls. Bar Found. Mem. ABA (ho. of dels. 1970-71), Ind. State Bar Assn. (ho. dels. 1959—, chmn. pub. rels. exec. com. 1966-69, sec. 1973-74, bd. mgrs. 1975-77, chmn. law practice mgmt. com. 1991-92), Indpls. Bar Assn. (treas., 1st v.p. 1965, pres. 1970, bd. mgrs. 1968-71, 75-77, chmn. law day com. 1991-92, settlement week com. 1989-95, co-chair Family Law Study Commn., co-chair ct. liaison com. 1992-93, family law implementation com. 1993-97, mem. exec. com. bd. mgrs. 1994-96, counsel bd. mgrs. 1994, chmn. sr. lawyers divsn. 1999—), Am. Judicature Soc., Indpls. Legal Aid Soc., Indpls. Jr. C. of C. (past 1st v.p., dir. ct. unification implementation com., chmn. 1995-98), Butler U. Alumni Assn. (past pres.), Mich. Alumni Assn., Meridian Hills Country Club, Lawyers Club, Gyro Club (pres. 1966), Masons (worshipful master 1975), Valley Scottish Rite Found. (33d degree, most wise master 1982-84, trustee 1996—, chmn. bd. trustees 1998-99, pres. Indpls. Scottish Rite Cathedral Found., dir. 1997—, chmn. 1998-99), Shriners, Phi Delta Theta (chpt. advisor 1950-82), Tau Kappa Alpha. Republican. Presbyterian. General corporate, Real property, Taxation, general. Home: 624 Somerset Dr W Indianapolis IN 46260-2924 Office: 1 American Square PO Box 82053 Indianapolis IN 46282-0003

**KAPSNER, CAROL RONNING,** state supreme court justice; b. Bismarck, N.D.; m. John Kapsner; children: Mical, Caithlin. BA in English lit., Coll. of St. Catherine; postgrad., Oxford U.; MA in English lit., Ind. U.; JD, U. Colo., 1977. Pvt. practice Bismarck, 1977-98; justice N.D. Supreme Ct., 1998—. Mem. N.D. Bar Assn. (bd. govs.), N.D. Trial Lawyers Assn. (bd. govs.), Burleigh County Bar Assn. (past pres.). Fax: 701-328-4480. E-mail: kapsner@court.state.nd.us. Office: Supreme Ct State Capitol Bismarck ND 58505-0530*

**KARA, PAUL MARK,** lawyer; b. Valparaiso, Ind., Mar. 7, 1954; s. Charles J. and June F. (Williams) K.; m. Elizabeth Louise Smith, Aug. 18, 1979; children: Adeline M., Emily L., Charles J., Phillip H. BA, Ind. U., 1977,

JD, 1980. Bar: Mich. 1980, U.S. Dist. Ct. (we. dist.) Mich. 1980, U.S. Ct. Appeals (6th cir.) 1985. Assoc. Landman, Luyendyk, Latimer Clink & Robb, Muskegon, Mich., 1980-84, ptnr., 1984-86; ptnr. Varnum, Riddering, Schmidt & Howlett, Grand Rapids, Mich., 1986—. Pres., bd. dirs. Sr. Services of Muskegon, Inc., 1985-86, Cath. Social Services of Muskegon, 1985-86. Glenn Peters fellow, Ind. U., 1977-79, Louden Meml. fellow Ind. U., 1977-79. Mem. ABA (labor law sect., litig. sect., com. on devels. under NLRA), Mich. Bar Assn. (labor rels. law sect. coun. 1985-96, chairperson 1995-96), Muskegon County Bar Assn. (pres. 1985-86), Grand Rapids Bar Assn., Univ. Club Chgo. Republican. Labor, Civil rights, Federal civil litigation. Home: 3905 Norton Hills Rd Muskegon MI 49441-4456 Office: Varnum Riddering Schmidt & Howlett Bridgewater Place PO Box 352 Grand Rapids MI 49501-0352

**KARAFFA, MICHAEL ALAN, SR.,** lawyer; b. Sewickley, Pa., Feb. 9, 1956; s. Mickey W. and Mary L. (Gaydos) K.; m. Susan J. Taylor, Aug. 29, 1981; children: Michael A. Jr., Jennifer A., Stephen T. BS in Math. and Econs., U. Pitts., 1978; JD, Duquesne U., 1981. Pvt. practice Pitts., 1981-90; assoc. Plunkett & Cooney PC, Pitts., 1990—. Chmn. awards and fundraising coms. Cub Scout Pack 310, Moon Township, 1993-96; coach floor hockey, YMCA, Moon Township, 1996—. Mem. ABA, Am. Trial Lawyers Assn., Pa. Trial Lawyers Assn., Pa. Bar Assn. Avocation: sports. General civil litigation, Criminal, Environmental. Home: 120 Olde Manor Ln Moon Township PA 15108-9793 Office: Plunkett & Cooney PC 600 Grant St Ste 3000 Pittsburgh PA 15219-2709

**KARAGEORGE, THOMAS GEORGE,** lawyer; b. Louisville, Sept. 26, 1950; s. George D. Karageorge and Betty Delay. JD, U. Louisville, 1977. Bar: Ky. 1977. Assoc. Stalling & Stalling, Louisville, 1976-80; pvt. practice, Louisville, 1980-93; assoc. Borowitz & Goldsmith, Louisville, 1993—. Mem. Ky. Bar Assn., Louisville Bar Assn., Am. Hellenic Ednl. Progressive Assn. (treas.). State civil litigation, Family and matrimonial. Office: Borowitz & Goldsmith 1825 Meidinger Tower Louisville KY 40202-3455

**KARAM, ERNEST,** magistrate; b. Cleve., Apr. 3, 1909; s. Henry Harvey and Frieda K.; m. Lucille Himebaugh, Nov. 23, 1934 (dec. 1985). BS in Bus. Adminstrn., Ohio State U., 1933; LLB, Chase Coll. Law, Cin., 1947; JD, Chase Coll. Law, 1968. Bar: Ohio, U.S. Ct. Mil. Appeals, 1955, U.S. Tax Ct., 1976, U.S. Supreme Ct., 1955. Circulation exec. Cin. Post, 1933-74; referee Hamilton County Domestic Rels. Ct., Cin., 1976-77, chief referee, 1977-97, dir., 1978-97, chief magistrate, 1997—; lectr. Am. Press Inst., 1961-73; spl. counsel Atty. Gen. Ohio, 1983. Lt. cmdr. U.S. Navy, 1943-46, USNR, 1947-74. Named Citizen of Day and Citizen of Decade, Radio WLW-700, Cin., 1968, Ky. Col., 1969—, Hon. Col., Office of Gov. Okla.,1 969—; Ernest Karam Day named in his honor, Apr. 2, 1999, City of Cin. Mem. ABA, Assn. Trial Lawyers Am., Ohio State Bar Assn., Ohio Circulation Mgrs. Assn., Cin. Bar Assn. Home: 5105 Graves Rd Cincinnati OH 45243-3807

**KARAN, PAUL RICHARD,** lawyer; b. Providence, June 12, 1936; s. Aaron Arnold and Sadye (Persky) K.; m. Susan Clare Brody, Jan. 3, 1964 (dec. Apr. 1986); children: Jennifer Hilary, Steven Lee; m. Linda Doris Adler, July 2, 1987. BA, Brown U., 1957; JD, Columbia U., 1960. Bar: NY 1961, U.S. Dist. Ct. (so. dist.) N.Y. 1962, U.S. Supreme Ct. 1967, U.S. Tax Ct. 1975, U.S. Claims Ct. 1976. Assoc. Demov & Morris, N.Y.C., 1960-65, ptnr., 1966-85; ptnr. Gordon Altman Weitzen Shalov & Wein, N.Y.C., 1985—. Contbr. articles to profl. jours. Chmn. Bd. Assessment Rev., Greenburgh, N.Y., 1978-86; mem. Planning Bd., Greenburgh, 1975-78, Bd. Edn., Greenburgh, 1980-83. Fellow Am. Bar Found., Am. Coll. Trust and Estate Counsel (chmn. downstate N.Y. 1996—), N.Y. Bar Found.; mem. ABA, N.Y. State Bar Assn. (chmn. trusts and estates law sect. 1990-91), Assn. of Bar of City of N.Y. Avocation: golf. Probate, Estate planning, Estate taxation. Office: Gordon Altman Weitzen Shalov & Wein 114 W 47th St New York NY 10036-1510

**KARAYANNIS, MARIOS NICHOLAS,** lawyer; b. Athens, Greece, Mar. 11, 1961; came to U.S., 1965; s. Nicholas Marios and Alexandra N. Karayannis; m. Kathryn Mary Diamond, Oct. 1, 1988; children: Kathleen A., Nicholas M. BS in Psychology, U. Ill., 1983; JD, John Marshall Law Sch., Chgo., 1986. Bar: Ill. 1986, U.S. Dist. Ct. (no. dist.) Ill. 1986, U.S. Supreme Ct. 1996, U.S. Tax Ct. 1997, U.S. Ct. Appeals (7th cir.) 1997. Asst. state's atty. Kane County State's Atty.'s Office, Geneva, Ill., 1986-90; assoc. Brady & Jensen, Elgin, Ill., 1991-95, ptnr., 1996—. Mem. Law Rev. John Marshall Law Sch., 1984-86. Coach Youth Soccer League, Elgin, 1998. Mem. ATLA, Ill. Bar Assn., Ill. Trial Lawyers Assn., Kane County Bar Assn., Kiwanis. Greek Orthodox. Avocations: golf, travel, fishing. Personal injury, Toxic tort, General civil litigation. Office: Brady & Jensen 2425 Royal Blvd Elgin IL 60123-2579

**KARCHER, STEVEN MICHAEL,** lawyer; b. San Diego, Oct. 25, 1956; s. Carl Michael and Margaret Ruby (Hayden) K.; m. Dana C. Karcher, June 8, 1985. BS summa cum laude, Calif. State U., Hayward, 1984; JD, Emory U., 1988. Bar: Calif. 1989, U.S. Dist. Ct. (ea. and no. dist.) Calif. 1990, U.S. Dist. Ct. (ctrl. dist.) Calif. 1992. Legal rschr. S.M. Karcher Co., Decatur, Ga., 1985-88; atty. Ericksen Arbuthnot et al, Sacramento, 1988-92; ptnr. Borton Petrini & Conron, Bakersfield, Calif., 1992—. Contbr. articles to profl. jours. Chmn. site coun. Franklin Elem. Sch., Bakersfield, 1998; bd. dirs. Bakersfield City Sch. Edn. Found., 1993—, Bakersfield Boys & Girls Club; cand. City Schs. Bd. Trustees, Bakersfield, 1996. Mem. Kern County Bar Assn. (co-chmn. Spkrs. Bur.), Greater Bakersfield C. of C., Downtown Bus. Assn., East Bakersfield Rotary. Republican. Episcopalian. Avocations: history, 4-wheel driving, reading, domestic travel. General civil litigation, Consumer commercial, Real property. Office: Borton Petrini & Conron 1600 Truxtun Ave Bakersfield CA 93301-5111

**KARDOS, MEL D.,** lawyer; b. Phila., Feb. 6, 1947; s. Julius S. and Rose (Klein) K.; m. Ellen D. Kleinman, Mar. 1, 1984; children: Lindsay Dara, Matthew Daniel. BS, Temple U., 1970; MEd, Trenton State Coll., 1972; JD, U. Balt., 1975. Bar: Pa. 1975, N.J. 1975, U.S. Dist. Ct. (ea. dist.) Pa. 1975, U.S. Dist. Ct. N.J. 1975, U.S. Supreme Ct. 1984. Asst. pub. defender Bucks County, Doylestown, Pa., 1975-80; ptnr. Kardos & Lynch, Newtown, Pa., 1980, Kardos & Heley, Newtown, 1980-87, Kardos, Rickles & Sellers, Newtown, 1988-; adj. prof. Temple U., Phila., 1987, Bucks County C.C., 1995. Mem. ABA, Bucks County Bar Assn., Assn. Trial Lawyers Am., Soc. for Am. Baseball Research. Democrat. Avocations: sports broadcasting, sports, history, politics. General civil litigation, Criminal, Personal injury. Office: Kardos Rickles & Sellers 626 S State St Newtown PA 18940-1509 also: 194 S Broad St Trenton NJ 08608-2405

**KARKANEN, ALEXANDER MICHAEL,** lawyer; b. L.A., June 28, 1965; s. daniel Virgil and Miriam Cecelia (Sasturain) K.; m. Janet Louise Avery, Nov. 5, 1994. BA in Spanish and Polit. Sci., U. Colo., 1988; JD, U. San Francisco, 1992. Bar: Calif. 1992. Dep. dist. atty. L.A. Dist. Atty., 1992—; judge pro tem L.A. Mcpl. Ct., 1998. Office: LA Dist Atty 18000 Criminal Cts Bldg 210 W Temple St Los Angeles CA 90012-3210

**KARLAN, SANDY ELLEN,** judge; b. N.Y.C.; d. Bernard and Muriel (Richter) K. BA, U. Miami, 1971; JD cum laude, Nova Southeastern U., 1978. Bar: Fla. 1978, U.S. Ct. Appeals (5th and 11th cirs.) 1981, U.S. Bankruptcy Ct. 1985, U.S. Dist. Ct. (so. dist.) Fla. 1988; cert. in matrimonial law, Fla. Law clk. to Hon. Alan R. Schwartz Third Dist. Ct. Appeals, Miami, Fla., 1978-80; assoc. Gars, Dixon & Shapiro, Miami, 1980-82; ptnr. Chaykin, Karlan & Jacobs, Coral Gables, Fla., 1982-85; sr. ptnr. Sandy Karlan, P.A., Miami, 1985-95; judge 11th Jud. Cir. Ct., Miami, 1995—; chair steering com. gender bias commn. Fla. Supreme Ct., 1987, mem. family ct. steering com., 1994, Conf. Cir. Ct. Judges, 1995—; chair on legal needs of children Fla. Bar Commn., 1999—. Author: (with others) Florida Family Law, 1986; contbr. articles to profl. jours. Bd. govs. Shepard Broad Sch. Law Nova Southeastern U., Ft. Lauderdale, Fla.; trustee Dade Marine Inst., Miami, 1993—. Recipient Sojourner Truth award NOW, 1989. Fellow ABA; mem. Nat. Assn. Women Judges, Fla. Bar (mem. legislation com. 184-88, grievance com. 11J 1985-87, vice chair disciplinary rev. com. 1987-89, vice chair access com. 1988-89, bd. govs. 1988-92, chair pub. rels. com. 1989-92, mem. gender equality com. 1994, mem. rules of civil procedure com. 1998—), Fla. Assn. Women Lawyers (pres. Dade County chpt. 1984-85), Dade County Bar Assn. (bd. dirs. 1986-89), Bankruptcy Bar Assn. (bd. dirs. 1991-94), Leadership Miami Alumni Assn. Address: 175 NW 1st Ave Ste 2327 Miami FL 33128-1846

**KARLEN, PETER HURD,** lawyer, writer; b. N.Y.C., Feb. 22, 1949; s. S. H. and Jean Karlen; m. Lynette Ann Thwaites, Dec. 22, 1978. BA in History, U. Calif., Berkeley, 1971; JD, U. Calif., Hastings, 1974; MS in Law and Soc., U. Denver, 1976. Bar: Calif. 1974, Hawaii 1989, Colo. 1991, U.S. Dist. Ct. (so. dist.) Calif. 1976, U.S. Dist. Ct. (no. dist.) Calif. 1983, U.S. Dist. Ct. (Hawaii) 1989, U.S. Supreme Ct. 1990. Assoc. Sankary & Sankary, San Diego, 1976; teaching fellow Coll. of Law U. Denver, 1974-75; lectr. Sch. of Law U. Warwick, United Kingdom, 1976-78; pvt. practice La Jolla, Calif., 1979-86; prin. Peter H. Karlen, P.C., La Jolla, 1986—; adj. prof. U. San Diego Sch. of Law, 1979-84; mem. adj. faculty Western State U. Coll. of Law, San Diego, 1976, 79-80, 88, 92. Contbg. editor Artweek, 1979-95, Art Calendar, 1989-96, Art Cellar Exch. mag., 1989-92; mem. editl. bd. Copyright World, 1988—, IP World, 1997—; contbr. numerous articles to profl. jours. Mem. Am. Soc. for Aesthetics, Brit. Soc. Aesthetics. Trademark and copyright, Intellectual property. Office: 1205 Prospect St Ste 400 La Jolla CA 92037-3613

**KARLIN, CALVIN JOSEPH,** lawyer; b. Hutchinson, Kans., Oct. 31, 1952; s. Norman Joseph and Edith Lucille (Biggs) K.; m. Janice Miller, May 25, 1975. BA, U. Kans., 1974, JD, 1977. Bar: Kans. 1977, U.S. Dist. Ct. Kans. 1977. Mem. Barber, Emerson, Springer, Zinn & Murray, L.C., Lawrence, Kans., 1977—; adj. faculty Sch. Law U. Kans. Note and comments editor U. Kans. Law Rev.; contbr. articles to profl. jours. Bd. dirs. United Way, Lawrence, 1983-85, drive chair, 1993, pres., 1995-96; bd. dirs. Kaw Valley Dance Theatre, Lawrence, 1982-85, Vis. Nurses Assn., 1987—, Lawrence Pub. Libr., 1989—. Mem. Kans. Bar Assn. (exec. com. corp. bus. and banking law sect. 1985-88, exec. com. real estate, probate and trust law sect. 1998—), Douglas County Bar Assn. (sec. 1982-83, v.p. 1986-87, pres. 1987-88), Lawrence C. of C. (bd. dirs. 1997—), Swarthout Soc. (corp. and bus. com. 1983-91), Order of Coif, Phi Beta Kappa. Democrat. Avocation: coaching baseball. Bankruptcy, Consumer commercial, Estate planning. Office: Barber Emerson Springer Zinn & Murray LC PO Box 667 Lawrence KS 66044-0667

**KARLTON, LAWRENCE K.,** federal judge; b. Bklyn., May 28, 1935; s. Aaron Katz and Sylvia (Meltzer) K.; m. Mychelle Stiebel, Sept. 7, 1958 (dec.). Student, Washington Sq. Coll., 1952-54; LL.B., Columbia U., 1958. Bar: Fla. 1958, Calif. 1962. Acting legal officer Sacramento Army Depot, Dept. Army, Sacramento, 1958-60; civilian legal officer Sacramento Army Depot, Dept. Army, 1960-62; individual practice law Sacramento, 1962-64; mem. firm Abbott, Karlton & White, 1964, Karlton & Blease, 1964-71, Karlton, Blease & Vanderlaan, 1971-76; judge Calif. Superior Ct. for Sacramento County, 1976-79, U.S. Dist. Ct. (ea. dist.) Calif., Sacramento, 1979-83; formerly chief judge U.S. Dist. Ct., Sacramento, 1983-90, chief judge emeritus, 1990—. Co-chmn. Central Calif. council B'nai B'rith Anit-Defamation League Commn., 1964-65; treas. Sacramento Jewish Community Relations Council, chmn., 1967-68; chmn. Vol. Lawyers Commn. Sun Valley ACLU, 1964-76. Mem. Am. Bar Assn., Sacramento County Bar Assn., Calif. Bar Assn., Fed. Bar Assn., Fed. Judges Assn., 9th Cir. Judges Assn. Club: B'nai B'rith (past pres.). Office: US Dist Ct 501 I St Sacramento CA 95814-2322

**KARMALI, RASHIDA ALIMAHOMED,** lawyer; b. Uganda, May 12, 1948; came to U.S., 1978; d. Alimahomed and Sakina (Govani) K. BSc, MakerereU., 1971; MSc, Aberdeen U., 1973; PhD, U. Newcastle Upon Tyne, 1976; JD, Rutgers U., 1993. Bar: N.Y. 1994; registered to practice U.S. Patent Office. Fellow Clin. Rsch. Inst., Montreal, 1976-78; rsch. assoc. E. Carolina U., Greenville, N.C., 1978-80, Meml. Sloan-Kettering Inst., N.Y.C., 1980-84; adj. assoc. prof. Cook Coll., New Brunswick, N.J., 1984-90; law clk., assoc. Hopgood, Calimafde, Kalil, N.Y.C., 1992-94; assoc. Pennie & Edmonds, N.Y.C., 1994-95, Bryan Cave LLP, N.Y.C., 1995-97; sr. assoc. Stroock & Stroock & Lavan LLP, N.Y.C., 1997—; bd. dirs. Skin Rsch. Found., N.Y.C. Grantee NIH, Am. Cancer Soc. Mem. ABA, Assn. Bar City N.Y. (com. on patents), Am. Intellectual Property Law Assn. (internat. and fgn. law com.). Intellectual property, Antitrust, Federal civil litigation. Office: 180 Maiden Ln New York NY 10038-4925

**KARMEL, PHILIP ELIAS,** lawyer; b. N.Y.C., Dec. 6, 1963; s. Paul R. and Roberta S. (Segal) K.; m. Barbara A. Landress, June 12, 1994. BA in Econs., U. Pa., 1984; MPhil in Econs., U. Cambridge, Eng., 1985; JD, U. Chgo., 1988. Bar: N.Y. 1989. Law clk. to Hon. Edward R. Becker U.S. Ct. Appeals (3rd cir.), 1988-89; trial atty. U.S. Dept. of Justice, Environtl. Enforcement Sect., Washington, 1989-94; assoc. Robinson Silverman Pearce Aronsohn & Berman LLP, N.Y.C., 1996—. Recipient Spl. Achievement award for Superior Performance of Duty U.S. Dept. of Justice, 1992. E-mail: Karmel@rspab.com. Environmental, General civil litigation, Real property. Office: Robinson Silverman Pearce Aronsohn & Berman LLP 1290 Avenue Of The Americas New York NY 10104-0101

**KARMEL, ROBERTA SEGAL,** lawyer, educator; b. Chgo., May 4, 1937; d. J. Herzl and Eva E. (Elin) Segal; m. Paul R. Karmel, June 9, 1957 (dec. Aug. 1994); children: Philip, Solomon, Jonathan, Miriam; m. S. David Harrison, Oct. 29, 1995. BA, Radcliffe Coll.; LLB, NYU, 1962. Bar: N.Y. 1962, U.S. Dist. Ct. (so. and ea. dists.) N.Y. 1964, U.S. Ct. Appeals (2d cir.) 1968, U.S. Supreme Ct. 1968, U.S. Ct. Appeals (3d cir.) 1987. With SEC, 1962-69, 77-80, asst. regional adminstr., until 1969; commr. SEC, Washington, 1977-80; assoc. Willkie Farr & Gallagher, N.Y.C., 1969-72; ptnr. Rogers & Wells, N.Y.C., 1972-77, of counsel, 1980-85; ptnr. Kelley Drye & Warren, N.Y.C., 1987-94, of counsel, 1995—; adj. prof. law Bklyn. Law Sch., 1973-77, 82-85, prof., 1985—, co-dir. Ctr. for Study of Internat. Bus. Law; bd. dirs. Mallinckrodt, Inc., Kemper Ins Cos.; trustee Practicing Law Inst.; mem. nat. adjudicatory coun. NASDR, 1998—. Author: Regulation by Prosecution, 1982; contbr. articles to legal publs. Fellow Am. Bar Found.; mem. ABA, Assn. Bar City N.Y., Am. Law Inst., Fin. Women's Assn. Securities, General corporate. Home: 66 Summit Dr Hastings On Hudson NY 10706 Office: Bklyn Law Sch 250 Joralemon St Brooklyn NY 11201-3700

**KARMELIN, IRA D.,** prosecutor, educator; b. Suffern, N.Y., Apr. 24, 1964; s. Leonard J. and Sheila Karmelin. BAA, Fla. Atlantic U., 1985; JD, Nova U., 1992. Bd. cert. criminal trial law and criminal appellate law, Fla. Dep. sheriff Palm Beach County Sheriff's Office, West Palm Beach, Fla., 1984-89; adj. instr. Inst. Police Tech. and Mgmt., Jacksonville, Fla., 1990—, Criminal Justice Inst./Palm Beach C.C., Lake Worth, Fla., 1993—; asst. state atty. State Atty.'s Office, West Palm Beach, 1993—. Exec. officer Naval Sea Cadet Corps, Palm Beach Divsn., 1996—. Recipient Disting. Svc. award Traffic Safety Com., Palm Beach County, Fla., 1995, Outstanding DUI Prosecution award MADD, Palm Beach County, 1996, Outstanding Victim Svc. award MADD, Palm Beach County, 1997. E-mail: ikarmelin@sa15.state.fl.us. Office: Office of the State Atty 401 N Dixie Hwy West Palm Beach FL 33401-4209

**KARN, DAVID B.,** lawyer; b. Louisville, Sept. 6, 1959; s. H.T. Jr. and Deborah (Hughes) K.; m. Loulee Williams, Apr. 12, 1986; children: Gilchrist, Grantland, Linlee. BA, Samford U., Birmingham, Ala., 1981, JD, 1984. Bar: Ala. 1984, U.S. Ct. Appeals (11th cir.) 1986. Asst. atty. gen. Ala. Atty. Gen.'s Office, Montgomery, 1985-94; pvt. practice Clanton, Ala., 1994—. Editor: Alabama Peace Officers Handbook, 1986. Bd. dirs. Chilton County YMCA, Clanton, 1994-97, Chilton Edn. Found., 1996-99. Mem. Ala. Bar Assn., Chilton County Bar Assn. (v.p. 1997, pres. 1998-99), Lions (sec., bd. dirs. 1996-97). Baptist. Avocations: golf, basketball, softball, baseball. General practice. Home: 100 Windover Dr Clanton AL 35045-9389 Address: PO Box 108 Clanton AL 35046-0108

**KARNES, EVAN BURTON, II,** lawyer; b. Chgo.; s. Evan Burton and Mary Alice (Brosnahan) K.; m. Bridget Anne Clerkin, Oct. 9, 1976 (dec. June 1994); children: Kathleen Anne, Evan Burton III, Molly Aileen, Lauren Jean; m. Janet Ann Pioli, Nov. 2, 1996. AB, Loyola U., Chgo., 1975; JD, DePaul U., 1978; grad. civil trial advocacy program, U. Calif., 1979. Bar: Ill. 1978, U.S. Dist. Ct. (no. dist.) Ill. 1978, U.S. Ct. Appeals (7th cir.) 1978, U.s. Dist. Ct. (no. dist.) Ind. 1995, U.S. Supreme Ct. 1983. Trial atty. Chgo. Milw. St. Paul & Pacific R.R., Chgo., 1978-81; litigation dept. Baker & McKenzie, Chgo., 1981-87; sr. litigation counsel Levin & Ginsburg Ltd., Chgo., 1987-89; of counsel Oppenheimer, Wolff & Donnelly, 1989-91; prin. Law Offices of Evan B. Karnes (( & Assocs.; bd. dirs. Triad Communications Inc, Albuquerque, chmn. bd., 1988. Trustee Village of Northfield, Ill., 1999—, mem. fin. com., mem. planning and zoning commn., 1990-99, vice chmn., 1994-99. Mem. ABA, ATLA, Ill. Bar Assn., Fed. Bar Assn. (bd. dirs. Chgo. chpt. 1995—), Chgo. Bar Assn., Def. Rsch. Inst., Nat. Assn. R.R. Counsel (chmn. sci. evidence com. 1995—, nat. exec. com. 1995—), Ill. Trial Lawyers Assn., Blue Key (sec. Loyola U. chpg. 1974-75), Phi Sigma Alpha, Phi Alpha Delta. General civil litigation, Contracts commercial. Office: Xerox Centre 55 W Monroe St Fl 32 Chicago IL 60603-5001

**KARON, SHELDON,** laweyr; b. Superior, Wis., Mar. 1, 1930; s. Bert and Betty Karon; m. Lee Goldwasser, Aug. 6, 1950; children: Maureen Byron, Laurie Gilbert, Peggy Pattis. BS, Northwestern U., 1952; JD, Harvard U., 1955. Bar: Ill. 1955. Assoc. Jenner & Block, Chgo., 1955-61; ptnr. Friedman & Koven, Chgo., 1962-75; ptnr., chmn. Karon, Morrison & Savikas, Chgo., 1975-88, Keck, Mahin & Cate, Chgo., 1988-97; of counsel Foley & Lardner, Chgo., 1997—; arbitrator CFR Ctr. for Dispute Resolution, N.Y.C.; mem. Ill. Supreme Ct. Commn. for Jud. Reform, 1993-95. Bd. dirs. Kohl CHildren's Mus., Wilmette, Ill., 1988—, Highland Park (Ill.) Cmty. Edn., 1995—. Fellow Am. Coll. Trial Lawyers; mem. ABA, Ill. State Bar Assn., Chgo. Bar Assn., Fed. Cir. Bar Assn., Am. Arbitration Assn. (chair large complex case panel), Law Club, Legal Club. Federal civil litigation, Intellectual property, Alternative dispute resolution. Office: Foley & Lardner 330 N Wabash Ave Chicago IL 60611-3603

**KARP, DAVID BARRY,** lawyer; b. Milw., Dec. 12, 1955; s. Joseph and Sally P. (Nashinsky) K.; m. Donna L. Boorse, Apr. 8, 1984. BA, U. Wis., Milw., 1977; postgrad., Am. U., 1978; JD, Marquette U., 1982. Bar: Wis. 1982, U.S. Dist. Ct. (we. and ea. dist.) Wis. 1982, U.S. Cir. Ct. (7th cir.) 1982. Assoc. Karp Law Offices, S.C., Milw., 1990—. Mem. ABA, WATL, Wis. State Bar. Avocations: golf, running, music. Family and matrimonial, Personal injury.

**KARP, RONALD ALVIN,** lawyer; b. Bklyn., Feb. 12, 1945. BA, U. Md., 1967; JD, Washington Coll. Law, 1971. Bar: D.C. 1972, Md. 1972, U.S. Dist. Ct. Md. 1972, U.S. Dist. Ct. D.C. 1972, U.S. Ct. Appeals (D.C. cir.) 1972, U.S. Supreme Ct. 1975. Ptnr. Karp, Frosh, Lapidus & Wigodsky, P.A., Washington, 1971-99; mng. ptnr. Karp, Frosh, Lapidus, Wigodsky & Norwind, P.A., Washington, 1999—; faculty Nat. Coll. Advocacy, Georgetown U., Washington, 1983. Producer, moderator legal programs for NBC Radio, 1974-79, pub. TV programs, 1986—. Trustee McLean Sch. Md., 1985-88; bd. govs. Washington Regional Bd., ADL, 1988—, co-chair, 1996—. Mem. ABA (litigation sect.), ATLA (del. D.C. 1986-88), D.C. Bar Assn., Md. Bar Assn., Montgomery County Bar Assn. (chair personal injury sect. 1997-99), Trial Lawyers Assn. Met. Washington D.C. (bd. govs. 1980-82, pres. 1985, Trial Lawyer of Yr. 1988), Am. Bd. Trial Advocates, George Washington Am. Inn of Ct. (pres. 1994-95). Federal civil litigation, State civil litigation, Personal injury. Office: Karp Frosh et al 7475 Wisconsin Ave Ste 800 Bethesda MD 20814-3497 also: 1150 Connecticut Ave NW Washington DC 20036-4104

**KARP, SANDER NEIL,** lawyer; b. Milw., July 4, 1943; s. Harry and Rosalind (Schewitz) K.; m. Lana Faye Thering, June 16, 1968; children: Grady Thomas, Milu Su. BS, U. Wis., Madison, 1965, JD, 1968. Bar: Wis. 1968, Colo. 1973, U.S. Supreme Ct., U.S. Ct. Appeals (7th and 10th cirs.), U.S. Dist. Ct. Ohio, U.S. Dist. Ct. Nebr., U.S. Dist. Ct. (ea. and we. dists.) Wis., U.S. Dist. Ct. (no. and ea. dists.) Ill. Ptnr. Greenberg & Karp, Milw. and Madison, 1968-71, Law Office of Rudolph Schware, Denver, 1973-78, Karp, Goldstein & Stern, Denver, 1978-84, Karp & Dodge, Denver, 1984-89; atty. mil. law office Nat. Lawyers Guild, Angeles City, Olongapo, Philippines, 1971-73; pvt. practice Denver, 1989—; vis. prof. Denver U. Sch. Law, 1989-90; lectr. profl. and ednl. seminars. Pres. Community Resources, Inc., Denver, 1988-90. Mem. Assn. Trial Lawyers Am., Colo. Trial Lawyers Assn., Denver Bar Assn., Colo. Bar Assn., Plaintiff's Employment Lawyers Assn., Nat. Lawyers Guild (exec. bd. Colo. chpt. 1987-90, reg. v.p. 1992—). Avocations: fly-fishing, hiking, reading, climbing. Civil rights, Personal injury, General civil litigation. Office: 1100 Stout St Ste 470 Denver CO 80204-2065

**KARPE, BRIAN STANLEY,** lawyer; b. Hartford, Conn., Aug. 21, 1960; s. Donald Eugene and Patricia Jane (Van Wormer) K.; m. Patricia Lynn Smith, Oct. 10, 1992. BS, U. Maine, Orono, 1982; JD, Drake U., 1985. Bar: Colo. 1985, Conn. 1987. Assoc. Ozer, Kiel, Trueax & Pribila, Denver, 1986, Hunt & Leibert, Hartford, 1987-90, Berman & Russo, South Windsor, Conn., 1990-93; pvt. practice Hartford, 1993—. Mem. Assn. Am. Trial Lawyers, Conn. Trial Lawyers Assn., Hartford County Bar Assn. Republican. Lutheran. Avocations: aviation, music, scuba diving. Personal injury, Criminal, Aviation. Office: 81 Wethersfield Ave Hartford CT 06114-1156

**KARPE, MARK ARK,** lawyer; b. Niles, Ill., Nov. 22, 1968; s. Henry and Ann Karpe. BA, Binghamton (N.Y.) U., 1990; JD, Hofstra U., 1996. Examiner NASD, Washington, 1992-93; legal counsel Funds Distbn., N.Y.C., 1996-97; assoc. Solomon Pearl Blum & Quinn, N.Y.C., 1997—. Securities, General corporate. Home: 1641 3d Ave New York NY 10128 Office: Solomon Pearl et al 233 Broadway Fl 37 New York NY 10279-3799

**KARPINSKI, IRENA IZABELLA,** lawyer; b. Phila., July 6, 1950; d. Zygmunt Karpinski and Izabella Styczek; m. Walter Charles Johnston, Sept. 17, 1988; 1 child, Aleksander Styczek. BA, Manhattanville Coll., 1968-72; JD, Temple U., 1972-75; student, Leningrad (USSR) State U., 1970, U. Fribourg, Switzerland, 1970-71. Bar: Pa., 1975, D.C., 1976, N.Y., 1982, Md., 1982; U.S. Dist. Ct. D.C., 1977, U.S. Dist. Ct. (ea. dist.) Pa., 1978, U.S. Dist. Ct. Md., 1986. Spl. asst. to E.G. Biester U.S. Congress, Washington, 1975-76; assoc. atty. Samuel J. Levine, Esq., Washington, 1976-77; pvt. practice Washington, 1977—; chairperson D.C. Bd. Appeals Rev., Washington, 1984-91; cons. bd. govs. Fed. Res., Washington, 1992-94. Mem. Women's Bar Assn. (chair standing com. 1993—). Avocations: languages, traveling, bridge, chess, tennis. Immigration, naturalization, and customs, Family and matrimonial, Private international. Office: # 111 1330 New Hampshire Ave NW Washington DC 20036

**KARR, DAVID DEAN,** lawyer; b. Denver, Sept. 3, 1953; s. Dean Speece and Jean (Ransbottom) K.; m. Laura A. Foster, Apr. 10, 1982; children: Emily Ann, Bradley Foster. BA, U. Puget Sound, 1975; JD, Loyola U., 1979. Bar: Colo. 1979, U.S. Dist. Ct. 1979, U.S. Ct. Appeals (10th cir.) 1981, U.S. Supreme Ct. 1983. Assoc. Pryor Carney & Johnson, P.C., Englewood, Colo., 1979-84, ptnr., 1984-95; ptnr. Pryor, Johnson, Montoya, Carney and Karr, P.C., Englewood, Colo., 1995—. Mem. ABA (lead atty. pro bono team death penalty project Tex. chpt. 1988—), Colo. Bar Assn. (interprofl. com. 1990—), Arapahoe County Bar Assn., Denver Bar Assn. Personal injury, Insurance, Federal civil litigation. Home: 5474 E Hinsdale Cir Littleton CO 80122-2538 Office: Pryor Johnson Montoya Carney and Karr PC Ste 1313 6400 S Fiddlers Green Cir Englewood CO 80111-4939

**KARR, RICHARD LLOYD,** lawyer; b. Webster City, Iowa, Dec. 7, 1947; s. Lloyd and Margaret P. (Phalen) K.; children: Austen, Brenna. BA, Coll. of Great Falls, 1973; JD, Creighton U., 1972. Bar: Iowa 1973, Nebr. 1973, U.S. Dist. Ct. (no. dist.) Iowa 1973, U.S. Dist. Ct. Nebr. 1973, U.S. Dist. Ct. (so. dist.) Iowa 1978, U.S. Ct. Appeals (8th cir.) 1979. Ptnr. Karr, Karr & Karr, Webster City, 1973—. Mem. Iowa State Bar Assn. (bd. govs. 1988—), Elks, Moose, Lions (pres. 1985-86). Republican. Roman Catholic. General civil litigation, Insurance, Workers' compensation. Office: Karr Karr & Karr PC 711 2nd St Webster City IA 50595-1436

**KARRE, NELSON THOMAS,** lawyer; b. Omaha, Aug. 15, 1952; m. Nancy H. Wade. BA, U. Wyo., 1973; JD, U. Nebr., 1977. Bar: Mich. 1977, U.S. Dist.Ct. (we. dist.) Mich. 1977. Atty. Vandervoort, Christ & Fisher, P.C. and predecessor firm, Battle Creek, Mich., 1977—. Chmn. bd. dirs. United Way, Battle Creek, 1992. Mem. Calhoun County Bar Assn., Battle Creek Area C. of C. (legal counsel, bd. dirs. 1991—). Real property, Estate planning, Contracts commercial. Home: 187 Beckwith Dr Battle Creek MI 49015-4068 Office: Vandervoort Cooke McFee Christ Carpenter & Fisher 312 Old Kent Bank Battle Creek MI 49017

**KARRENBERG, THOMAS RICHARD,** lawyer; b. N.Y.C., Nov. 13, 1948; s. Charles Karrenberg and Mary Elizabeth Shalvey; m. Betty Lea Surdez (div. 1976); children: Jacquelyne, Matthew; m. Diana Baker Karrenberg, Nov. 16, 1985; children: Douglas, Derick, Darin. BA, Columbia Coll., 1970; JD, U. Utah, 1980. Bar: Utah 1982, U.S. Dist. Ct. Utah 1982, U.S. Ct. Appeals (10th cir.) 1986. Assoc. O'Melveny & Myers, L.A., 1980-82, Greene, Callister & Nebeker, Salt Lake City, 1982-84; ptnr. Berman & Anderson, Salt Lake City, 1984-86, Hansen & Anderson, Salt Lake City, 1986-89, Anderson & Karrenberg, Salt Lake City, 1989—; mem. Utah Supreme Ct. Adv. Com. for the Rules of Civil Procedure, 1994—. Capt. USAF, 1970-75. Mem. Alta Club. General civil litigation, Antitrust, Securities. Home: 67 N Fairway Dr North Salt Lake UT 84054-3308 Office: Anderson & Karrenberg 50 W Broadway Ste 700 Salt Lake City UT 84101-2035

**KARSCH, JAY HARRIS,** lawyer; b. Phila., May 11, 1942; s. Eli and Pearl (Parris) K.; m. Mary Lynn Dean, June 30, 1962; 1 child, Tamara Lynn. BA, Temple U., 1964, JD, 1974. Bar: Pa. 1974, U.S. Dist. Ct. (ea. dist.) Pa. 1974, U.S. Dist. Ct. (mid. dist.) Pa. 1986, U.S. Ct. Appeals (3rd cir.) 1982. Assoc. Eastburn & Gray, Doylestown, Pa., 1974-80; ptnr. Eastburn & Gray, Doylestown, 1980—. Bd. dirs. ARC, Doylestown, 1979-81. Fellow Am. Bar Found.; mem. ABA, Pa. Bar Assn., Bucks County Bar Assn. (bd. dirs. 1988-90, v.p., pres.-elect 1991-92, pres. 1992-93). Avocations: running, golf, reading. General civil litigation, Environmental, Personal injury. Home: 2745 Stover Trl Doylestown PA 18901-1887 Office: Eastburn & Gray 60 E Court St Doylestown PA 18901-4350

**KARSHBAUM, BONNIE L.,** lawyer, mediator; b. Boston, Nov. 8, 1967. BA, Brandeis U., 1989; JD, New Eng. Sch. Law, 1992. Bar: Mass. 1992, U.S. Dist. Ct. Mass. 1993, U.S. Ct. Appeals (1st cir.) 1993, U.S. Supreme Ct. 1998. Pvt. practice law Waltham, Mass., 1992—, Woburn, Mass., 1993—; pvt. practice mediator Woburn, 1997—. Mem. ABA, Mass. Bar Assn., Boston Bar Assn., Fourth Middlesex Bar Assn., Mass. Acad. Trial Attys. Family and matrimonial, Personal injury, Civil rights. Office: 44 Pleasant St Woburn MA 01801-4127

**KARSON, BARRY M.,** lawyer; b. Bklyn., July 20, 1942; s. Sydney E. and Etta G. Karson; m. Kathryn Cossman Hegleman, June 6, 1993; children: David Harris, Steven Ryan. BA, SUNY, Binghamton, 1963; JD, St. John's U., 1966. Bar: N.Y. 1967, U.S. Dist. Ct. (so. and ea. dists.) N.Y. 1968, U.S. Ct. Appeals (2d cir.) 1973, Fla. 1982, U.S. Supreme Ct. 1988. Atty. Fed. Poverty Program, Bklyn. and Hempstead, N.Y., 1967-70; assoc. Rothenberg & Kalman, N.Y.C., 1970-71; ptnr. Licht Karson & Margolis, N.Y.C., 1972-73; assoc. Rubin & Eisenberg, Mt. Vernon, N.Y., 1973-78; ptnr. Rubin, Eisenberg & Karson, Mt. Vernon, 1978-82, Katz, Kleinbaum, Farber & Karson, White Plains, N.Y., 1982-92, Ballon, Stoll, Bader & Nadler, N.Y.C., 1992—. Treas. Exch. Club of Downtown White Plains, 1984-87; pres. Woodlands Homeowners Assn., New Rochelle, N.Y., 1980-93. With USAR, 1966-72. Mem. Fla. Bar, N.Y. State Bar Assn., Westchester County Bar Assn. (family law sect. 1986—, vice chmn. 1992-96, chmn. 1996-98), City of Mt. Vernon Bar Assn. (v.p. 1980-82), Phi Delta Phi. Contracts commercial, Family and matrimonial, General civil litigation. Office: Ballon Stoll Bader & Nadler 1450 Broadway New York NY 10018-2201

**KARTIGANER, JOSEPH,** retired lawyer; b. Berlin, June 5, 1935; came to U.S., 1939; s. Harold and Lilly (Wolkowitz) K.; children: Deborah Lynn, Alison Beth. A.B., CCNY, 1955; LL.B., Columbia U., 1958. Bar: N.Y. 1960, Fla. 1978, D.C. 1979. Assoc. White & Case, N.Y.C., 1960-69, ptnr., 1969-88; ptnr. Simpson Thacher & Bartlett, N.Y.C., 1988-99; ret., 1999; lectr. law Columbia Law Sch., N.Y.C., 1973-80; vis. lectr. Sch. Law Yale U., 1997—; mem adv. com. N.Y. EPTL-SCPA, 1997—. Fellow Am. Bar Found., Am. Coll. Trust and Estate Counsel (regent 1978-84), Am. Coll. Tax Counsel, N.Y. State Bar Found.; mem. ABA (chmn. real property, probate and trust law sect. 1986-87), N.Y. State Bar Assn., Assn. of Bar of City of N.Y. (chmn. com. on trusts, estates and surrogate's cts. 1990-92), Nat. Conf. Lawyers and Corp. Fiduciaries (co-chair 1991-93), Am. Law Inst., Internat. Acad. Estate and Trust Law (academician), Scarsdale Golf Club (Hartsdale, N.Y.). E-mail: joekart@yahoo.com. Estate planning, Probate, Estate taxation. Home: 179 E 79th St New York NY 10021-0421 Office: Simpson Thacher & Bartlett 425 Lexington Ave Fl 15 New York NY 10017-3954

**KARU, GILDA M(ALL),** lawyer, government official; b. Oceanport, N.J., Dec. 1, 1951; d. Harold and Ilvy (Meriloo) K.; m. Frederick F. Foy, May 23, 1981. AB, Vassar Coll., 1974; JD, Ill. Inst. Tech., 1987. Bar: Ill. 1987, U.S. Dist. Ct. (no. dist.) Ill. 1987. Quality control reviewer Food and Nutrition Svc. USDA, Robbinsville, N.J., 1974-77, team leader, 1977-78, supr., 1978-81; sect. chief Food and Nutrition Svc. USDA, Chgo., 1991—, acting dir. field ops., 1998; employer adviser Ctr. for Rehab. and Tng. Disabled Persons, Chgo., 1986-93; chief mgmt. negotiator for collective bargaining agreement Nat. Treasury Employees Union, 1990. Bd. dirs., legal counsel, regional dir. North Ctrl. Estonian Am. Nat. Coun., N.Y.C.; v.p. 1st Estonian Evang. Luth. Ch., Chgo., treas., 1994—; mem. Chgo. Vol. Legal Svcs., Friends of Arlington Heights Meml. Libr.; vol. dep. voter registration officer Cook County, Ill.; exec. bd. Arlington Heights-Mt. Prospect-Buffalo Grove area LWV. Recipient cert. of recognition William A. Jump Meml. Found., 1987, Arthur S. Flemming award Washington Downtown Jaycees, 1987, Ill. Dem. Ethnic Heritage award, 1989, cert. of appreciation Assn. for Persons with Disabilities in Agr., 1992, Group Honor award for work on 1993 Miss. River Flood Disaster Relief, Sec. of USDA, 1994. Mem. ABA, AAUW, NAFE, LWV (bd. dirs. 1992—), Ill. Bar Assn., Chgo. Bar Assn., Baltic Bar Assn., United Coun. on Welfare Fraud, Internat. Platform Assn., Nat. Audubon Soc., Chgo. Area Seven Sisters Coll. Consortium (sec. 1995—), Mensa, Vassar Club (chpt. treas. 1988-90, v.p. 1990-91, coord. pub. rels. 1991—). Avocations: photography, reading, travel, crafts. Office: USDA Food and Nutrition Svc 77 W Jackson Blvd Fl 20 Chicago IL 60604-3591

**KARWACKI, ROBERT LEE,** judge; b. Balt., Aug. 2, 1933; s. Lee Daniel and Marie Ann (Budzynski) K.; m. Patricia Ann Deal, Nov. 3, 1956 (dec. May 1972); children: Ann Elizabeth, Lee Daniel, John Robert; m. Marion Elizabeth Harper, June 16, 1973. AB, U. Md., 1954; LLB, U. Md., Balt., 1956. Bar: Md. 1956, U.S. Supreme Ct. 1963, U.S. Dist. Ct. Md. 1957, U.S. Ct. Appeals (4th cir.) 1960. Law clk. to Hon. Stephen R. Collins Ct. Appeals Md., Annapolis, 1956-57; assoc. Miles & Stockbridge, Balt., 1957-63, ptnr., 1965-73; asst. atty. gen. State of Md., Balt., 1963-65; assoc. judge Cir. Ct. Balt. City, 1973-84, Ct. Spl. Appeals Md., Annapolis, 1984-90, Ct. Appeals Md., Annapolis, 1990-97. Pres. Balt. City Sch. Bd., 1970-72. Sgt. USAR, 1956-62. Recipient Man for All Seasons award St. Thomas More Soc., 1977. Fellow Md. Bar Found.; mem. Lawyer's Roundtable, Wednesday Law Club (pres. 1984). Democrat. Roman Catholic. Avocations: golfing, boating, fishing, hunting.

**KARWATH, BART ANDREW,** lawyer; b. Davenport, Iowa, July 6, 1966; s. Robert D. and Linda (Bart) K.; m. Karen Elizabeth Lovich, Aug. 20, 1994. BS in pub. affairs, Ind. U., 1988, JD magna cum laude, 1991. Bar: Ind. 1991, U.S. Dist. Ct. (so., no. dist.) Ind. 1991, U.S. Ct. Appeals (7th cir.) 1993, U.S. Supreme Ct. 1998. Law clerk Ct. Appeals of Ind., Indpls., 1991-92, U.S. Dist. Ct. Southern Dist. Ind., Indpls., 1992-94; lawyer Barnes & Thornburg, Indpls., 1994—. Contbr. articles to profl. jours. Mem. Lawyers for Lugar, Indpls., 1995. Order of Coif Ind. U., 1991; recipient Am. Jurisprudence award Ind. U., 1990, Am. Jurisprudence award Drake U., 1989. Mem. Alpha Sigma Phi. Federal civil litigation, State civil litigation, Pension, profit-sharing, and employee benefits. Office: Barnes & Thornburg 11 S Meridian St Indianapolis IN 46204-3506

**KASHANI, HAMID REZA,** lawyer, computer consultant; b. Tehran, Iran, May 1, 1955; came to U.S., 1976; s. Javad K. BSEE with highest distinction, Purdue U., 1978, MSEE, 1979; JD, Ind. U., 1986. Bar: Ind. 1986, U.S. Dist. Ct. (so. and no. dists.) 1986, U.S. Ct. Appeals (7th cir.) 1986, U.S. Supreme Ct. 1994, U.S. Ct. Appeals (9th cir.) 1996. Rsch. asst. Purdue U., West Lafayette, Ind., 1978-79, 80-81; engr. Cummins Engine Co., Columbus, Ind., 1981-82; assoc. faculty Ind. U.-Purdue U., Indpls., 1983-84; sr. software engr. Engineered System Devel., Indpls., 1985-87; computer cons. Hamid R. Kashani, Indpls., 1986—; pvt. practice law Indpls., 1986—; cons. Good Techs., Indpls., 1987-90; cons. Prism Imaging, Denver, 1990-93, Ind. Bar Assn., 1989-95. Editor: Computer Law Desktop Guide, 1995. Mem., bd. dirs. ACLU, 1997—, Ind. Civil Liberties Union, Indpls., 1987—, mem. legis. com., 1987—, mem. screening com., 1985—, del., 1989, 91, 93, 95, acting v.p. fundraising, 1995-96, v.p. edn., 1996—, chair long-range planning com., 1991-92, 96—, chmn. nominating com., 1997—, pres., 1999—; bd. dirs. ACLU, 1997—. Fellow Ind. U. Sch. Law, 1984; recipient Cert. of Appreciation Ind. Correctional Assn., 1988; named Cooperating Atty. of Yr. Ind. Civil Liberties Union, 1990, 95, 98. Mem. ABA (vice chmn. YLD computer law com. 1990-91, chmn. computer law exec. com. 1991-93, litigation exec. com. 1987-89, 90-93, YLD liaison standing com. on jud. selection, tenure and compensation 1992-94, 95-96, co-chair first amendment rights in the digital age com., vice chair com. on opportunities for minorities and women, YLD liaison to ABA tech. coun. 1992-93, co-chmn. first amendment rights in the digital age com. 1997—, vice chmn. com. on opportunities for minorities women 1997—, vice chmn. nat. info. infrastructure com. sect. sci. and tech. 1993-97, chair privacy info. and civil liberties ABA sect. of individual rights and responsibilities 1998—, mem. standing com. on jud. selection, tenure and compensation 1995-96, chair privacy info. and civil liberties sect. of individual rights and responsibilities 1998—), IEEE (Outstanding Contbns. award 1983), Indpls. Bar Assn. (chmn. articles and bylaws coms. 1994-95), Ind. State Bar Assn. (vice chair computer comms. com. 1995-98, chair computer comms. com. 1998—, chair computer comm. com. 1998—), Eta Kappa Nu, Tau Beta Pi, Phi Kappa Phi, Phi Eta Sigma. Federal civil litigation, Computer, Civil rights. Office: 445 N Pennsylvania St Ste 600 Indianapolis IN 46204-1818

**KASHANIAN, SHAHRIAR,** lawyer; b. Tehran, Iran, Apr. 10, 1960; came to U.S., 1977; s. Haghnazar and Shahin (Missaghian) K. BA in Polit. Sci. and Econs., Hofstra U., 1981, JD, 1984; Baccalaureate degree in Biology and Chemistry, Guadalajara (Mex.) Sch. of Law, 1982. Bar: N.Y. 1985, U.S. Dist. Ct. (so. dist.) N.Y. 1988. Assoc. Morris, Graham, Stephens & McMorrow, Westbury, N.Y., 1984-85, Sebastian Randazzo, Great Neck, N.Y., 1985-86, Morris J. Eisen, P.C., N.Y.C., 1986-88, Richard Furman, P.C., Great Neck, 1989-90; prin. Shahriar Kashanian, Great Neck, 1990—; cons. atty. Monavar Enterprises, Inc., Great Neck, 1987—. Internship Sch. of Law Exeter (Eng.) U., 1983. Mem. ABA, N.Y. State Bar Assn., N.Y. Trial Lawyers Assn. Jewish. Avocations: soccer, volleyball, racquetball, antique cars, racing. General civil litigation, Personal injury, Insurance. Office: 69 Stonehenge Rd Manhasset NY 11030-2522

**KASHKASHIAN, ARSEN,** lawyer; b. Bristol, Pa., July 23, 1938; s. Arsen and Katherine (Mangiaracina) K.; children: Arsen III, Valerie T. Tomaro, Juliet Kashkashian; m. Elizabeth Ann Greaves, Apr. 29, 1995 (dec. Dec. 24, 1997). BS in Econs., Temple U., 1960, JD, 1963. Bar: Pa. 1964, U.S. Dist. Ct. (ea. dist.) Pa. 1964, U.S. Ct. Appeals (3d cir.) 1964, U.S. Tax Ct. 1970. Assoc. Egnal & Simons, Phila., 1964-66; lawyer ea. divsn. Sears, Roebuck Co., Phila., 1966-68; ptnr. Simons, Kashkashian & Kellis, Phila., 1968-75, Kashkashian & Kellis, Phila., 1975-85, Kashkashian & Horn, Phila., 1985; owner Kaskashian & Assocs., Bristol, Pa., 1985—; spl. counsel Redevel. Authority, Phila., 1968-69, Sch. Tchrs. Retirement Fund Pa., 1972-80, Bensalem (Pa.) Twp. Water and Sewer Authority, 1972-78. Inventor, patentee Multiple Credit Card, 1976. Chmn. N.E. Citzens' Planning Coun., Phila., 1972-80. Sgt. First Class, U.S. Army, 1964-65. Named Man of Yr. E. Torresdale Civil Assn., Phila., 1968, Powelton Civil Homeowners Assn., Phila., 1970. Mem. ATLA, Fed. Bar Assn., Phila. Bar Assn., Amigo Club Bucks County, Pa. (chmn. 1996-98). Democrat. Armenian Orthodox. Achievements include representing homeowners association in leading case on urban renewal in U.S. Real property, Contracts commercial, Immigration, naturalization, and customs. Home: 959 Fillmore St Philadelphia PA 19124-2402 Office: Kashkashian & Assocs 1240 Rt 413 Bristol PA 19007

**KASISCHKE, LOUIS WALTER,** lawyer; b. Bay City, Mich., July 18, 1942; s. Emil Ernst and Gladys Ann (Stuady) K.; m. Sandra Ann Colosimo, Sept. 30, 1967; children: Douglas, Gregg. BA, Mich. State U., 1964; JD, Detroit Coll. Law, 1967; LLM, Wayne State U., 1971. Bar: Mich. 1968, U.S. Dist. Ct. (southeastern dist.) Mich. 1968; CPA. Acct. Touche Ross & Co., Detroit, 1967-71; atty. Dykema Gossett, Detroit, 1971—; pres. Pella Window and Door Co., West Bloomfield, Mich., 1990—; bd. dirs. Barton Malow Co., Southfield. Author: Michigan Closely Held Corporations, 1986; contbr. articles to profl. jours. Mem. ABA, AICPA, State Bar Mich. (editor column Mich. Bar Jour. 1971-83), Mich. Assn. CPAs, Am. Coll. Tax Counsel. Republican. Lutheran. Avocations: mountaineering, skiing, running, squash, golf. General corporate, Corporate taxation, Taxation, general. Home: 810 Hidden Pine Rd Bloomfield Hills MI 48304-2409 Office: Dykema Gossett 1577 N Woodward Ave Ste 300 Bloomfield Hills MI 48304-2840

**KASOUF, JOSEPH CHICKERY,** lawyer; b. Syracuse, N.Y., July 3, 1954; s. Herbert Chickery and Helen (Hawa) K.; m. Nancy A. Middleton, Sept. 10, 1977; children: Jennifer C., Lauren E., Joseph P. A, Onondaga C.C., 1976; BA, Syracuse U., 1987, MS, 1990, JD, 1990. Police officer, detective Syracuse Polic Dept., 1977-87; asst. gen. counsel The Pyramid Co., 1988-91; mgr. claims counsel Nationwide Mutual Ins. Co., 1991—; adj. prof. Syracuse Univ., 1991—. Contbr. articles to profl. jour. Mem. Civic Action Program, Syracuse, 1991—. Mem. N.Y. State Bar Assn. sect. torts, ins. and compensation law), Def. Assn. N.Y., Onondaga County Bar Assn., Def. Rsch. Inst. Avocations: golf, skiing. Personal injury, Insurance, General corporate. Office: Nationwide Mutual Ins Co 110 Elwood Davis Rd N Syracuse NY 13212-4304

**KASOWITZ, MARC ELLIOT,** lawyer; b. New Haven, June 28, 1952; s. Robert and Felice Beverly (Molaver) K. BA, Yale U., 1974; JD, Cornell U., 1977. Bar: N.Y. 1978, U.S. Dist. Ct. (so. and ea. dists.) N.Y. 1978. Assoc. Rosenman & Colin, N.Y.C., 1977-86, ptnr., 1986-88; ptnr. Mayer, Brown & Platt, N.Y.C., 1988-93, Kasowitz, Benson, Torres & Friedman LLP, N.Y.C., 1993—. Contracts commercial, Product liability, General civil litigation. Home: 1160 Park Ave Apt 4B New York NY 10128-1212 Office: Kasowitz Benson Torres & Friedman LLP 1301 Ave of Ams New York NY 10019-6022

**KASPER, HORST MANFRED,** lawyer; b. Dusseldorf, Germany, June 3, 1939; s. Rudolf Ferdinand and Lilli Helene (Krieger) K.; 1 child, Olaf Jan. Diploma in chemistry, U. Bonn, 1963, D. in Natural Scis., 1965; JD, Seton Hall U., 1978. Bar: N.J. 1978, U.S. Patent Office 1977. Mem. staff Lincoln Lab., MIT, Lexington, 1967-69; mem. tech. staff Bell Tel. Labs., Murray Hill, N.J., 1970-76; assoc. Kirschstein, Kirschstein, Ottinger & Frank, N.Y.C., 1976-77; patent atty. Allied Chem. Corp., Morristown, N.J., 1977-79; pvt. practice Warren, N.J., 1980-83; with Kasper and Weick, Warren, 1983-85, Kasper and Laughlin, 1985—. Contbr. numerous articles to profl. jours.; patentee semicondr. field. Mem. ABA, AAAS, N.J. Bar Assn., Internat. Patent and Trademark Assn., Am. Patent Law Assn., N.J. Patent Law Assn., Am. Chem. Soc., Electrochem. Soc., Am. Phys. Soc., N.Y. Acad. Scis. Patent, Trademark and copyright, Private international. Home and Office: 13 Forest Dr Warren NJ 07059-5832 Office: ul Na Grzgdkach 9, 30421 Cracow Poland

**KASS, DAVID NORMAN,** accountant, lawyer; b. N.Y.C., Mar. 8, 1951; s. Joseph Zane and Rosalind (Sperber) K.; m. Esta Gail Millman, Nov. 26, 1977; children: Sean N., Joshua A. BS in Acctg., SUNY, Albany, 1973; JD, St. John's U., Jamaica, N.Y., 1982. Bar: N.Y. 1983. Staff acct. Touche Ross & Co., N.Y.C., 1972-74; sr. acct. Reich Weiner & Co., N.Y.C., 1974-76; ptnr. Brandt, Pollack, Kass & Wilkins, N.Y.C., 1976-79, Kass & Kass CPAs PC, Roslyn, N.Y., 1979—; pvt. practice Roslyn, 1983—; seminar leader Nassau Acad. Law, Mineola, N.Y., 1993, seminar leader/lectr., 1995. Contbr. articles to newspapers. Baseball coach Roslyn Little League, 1990-95; active in alumni fund campaign SUNY, Albany, 1994. Mem. Am. Arbitration Assn. (comml. law arbitrator), N.Y. State Bar Assn., Nassau County Bar Assn., Nat. Assn. CPA Practitioners, N.Y. State Soc. CPAs.

**KASS, STEPHEN B.,** lawyer, accountant; b. Hempstead, N.Y., Apr. 22, 1963; s. Mortimer and Marily Wermul. BBA, Hofstra U., 1986, JD, 1992; LLM, NYU, 1996. Bar: N.Y., N.J.; CPA. Intern hon. Dorothy Eisenberg Westbury, N.Y., 1991; sr. cons. Deloitte & Touche, N.Y.C., 1992-94; ptnr. Law Office of Stephen B. Kass, Westbury, N.Y., 1995—; Mem. com. N.Y. County Consumer Bankruptcy, 1998—, Nassau County Bankruptcy. Contbr. articles to profl. jours. Provost scholar Hofstra U., 1985. Mem. Ocean Club Condominium (pres. 1992-98). Avocations: reading, movies, biking. Fax: (516) 222-1929. E-mail: sbesq1@aol.com. Office: 900 Ellison Ave Ste 405 Westbury NY 11590-5114

**KASSEBAUM, JOHN PHILIP,** lawyer; b. Kansas City, Mo., Oct. 24, 1932; s. Leonard Charles and Helen Nancy (Horn) K.; m. Nancy Josephine Landon, June 8, 1955; children: John Philip, Richard L., William A., Linda J. Johnson m. Llewellyn Hood Sinkler, Aug. 4, 1979; stepchildren: G. Dana, J. Marshall, Huger II., Llewellyn H. Sinkler. AB, U. Kans.,1953, Phi Delta Theta, Omicron Delta Kappa; JD, U. Mich., 1956, Phi Delta Phi Barristers. Bar: Kans. 1956, N.Y. 1979, U.S. Ct. Appeals (2d, 4th, 10th, D.C. cirs.), U.S. Tax Ct., 1976, U.S. Supreme Ct., 1971. Sr. ptnr. Kassebaum & Johnson, N.Y.C. and Wichita; spl. asst. atty. gen. Kans., 1970. Chmn. Gov.'s Adv. Commn. Kans. Instl. Mgmt., 1961-69; bd. dirs., pres. Wichita Art Mus. Members, chmn. Kans. Assn. for Mental Health; trustee Price R. and Flora A. Reid Charitable Trust; dir. Wichita Eagle-Beacon Pub. Co.; chmn. bd. dirs. Skowhegan (Maine) Sch. Painting and Sculpture; bd. dirs., pres. Carolina Art Assn. and Gibbes Art Gallery, Charleston, S.C.; pres. Spoleto Festival U.S.A., Charleston; treas. Am. Arts Alliance, Washington; hon. curator of ceramics Spencer Mus. Art, U. Kans.; bd. dirs. Nat. Inst. for Music Theater; mem. endowment art com. Ulrich Mus. Art, Wichita; chmn. adv. com. Spencer Mus. Art U. Kans., pres. Wyoming Paris, Ltd. Mem. ABA (sect. dispute resolution), Am. Arbitration Assn., Nat. Inst. Dispute Resolution, Conflict Resolution Edn. Network, Assn. of Bar of City of N.Y., Assn. Trial Lawyers Am., Kans. Trial Lawyers Assn., Kans. Assn. Def. Counsel, Fedn. Ins. Counsel, Union Club (N.Y.C.), Met. Club (Washington), Phi Delta Theta, Omicron Delta Kappa, Phi Delta Phi. Republican. Episcopalian. Author: Kassebaum Collection, Vol. I, 1981. Art. Home: 2065 Pettigrew St Sullivans Island SC 29482-8760 Office: 652 Hudson St Fl 5 New York NY 10014-1619 also: Ste 585 River Park Pl 727 N Waco St Wichita KS 67203-3951

**KASSINGER, THEODORE WILLIAM,** lawyer; b. Atlanta, Jan. 26, 1953; s. Edward Theodore and Sarah Mell (Laurent) K.; m. Ruth Lynn Good, Oct. 13, 1984; children: Anna Laurent, Austen Elizabeth, Alice Caroline. BLA, U. Ga., 1975, JD, 1978. Bar: Ga. 1978, D.C. 1986. Atty.-advisor U.S. Internat. Trade Commn., Washington, 1978-80; atty., advisor U.S. Dept. State, Washington, 1980-81; internat. trade counsel com. on fin. U.S. Senate, Washington, 1981-85, assoc., 1985-89; ptnr. Vinson & Elkins L.L.P., Washington, 1990—. Co-author: U.S. Regulation of International Trade, 1987, Basic Documents in International Economic Law, 1989. Mem. ABA. Republican. Roman Catholic. Private international, Public international. Office: Vinson & Elkins LLP 1455 Pennsylvania Ave NW Washington DC 20004-1008

**KASSLER, HASKELL A.,** lawyer; b. Boston, Feb. 8, 1936; s. Harry and Natalie (Steinberg) K.; m. Mary Elizabeth Kelligrew, May 30, 1965; children: Marion Adelaide, Sarah Elizabeth. BA, Tufts U., 1957; JD, Boston U., 1960. Bar: Mass. 1960, U.S. Dist Ct. Mass. 1961, U.S. Dist. Ct. (no. dist.) Miss. 1964, U.S. Dist. Ct. (so. dist.) La. 1965, U.S. Ct. Appeals (5th cir.) 1965, U.S. Ct. Appeals (1st cir.) 1969, U.S. Supreme Ct. 1967. Assoc. Poster, Wilinsky & Goldstein, Boston, 1960-64; pvt. practice law, 1964-66, 69-71; asst. dir. Vol. Defenders Com., Inc., Boston, 1967-68; ptnr. Kassler & Feuer (formerly Richmond, Kassler, Feinberg & Feuer), 1971-99, Casner & Edwards, LLP, Boston, 1999—; regional counsel New Eng. Region, Am. Jewish Congress, 1965-67; counsel Civil Liberties Union Mass., 1968-70; asst. prof. criminal justice Northeastern U., Boston, 1969-76; chmn. Mass. Jud. Nominating Coun., 1987-90; mem. Lawyers Constl. Def. Commn., 1964-65. Trustee U. Mass., 1977-81, U. Mass. Bldg. Authority, 1980-81, Mus. Transp., 1991—; selectman Town of Brookline, 1971-74, elected town meeting mem., 1959-84; mem. Local Redistricting Rev. Commn., 1976—. Fellow Am. Acad. Matrimonial Lawyers (chpt. bd. mgrs. 1980-90, v.p. 1981-82, pres. 1984-86, Judge Haskell Freedman award Mass. chpt. 1984); mem. ABA, Mass. Bar Assn., Norfolk County Bar Assn., Tufts U. Alumni Coun. Family and matrimonial, Entertainment, Election. Office: Casner & Edwards LLP 1 Federal St Boston MA 02110

**KASSNER, HERBERT SEYMORE,** lawyer; b. N.Y.C., Dec. 3, 1931; s. Abraham and Rose (Rosenblatt) K.; m. Sheilah Goodwin, 1957 (div. 1965); children: Andrew, Kenneth; m. Marjorie Fern Golding, 1974 (div. 1992); children: Robin, Jeffrey; m. Linda Rubinstein Finder, 1993. BA (hon.), Franklin and Marshall U., 1952; cert., Hague (Netherlands) Acad. of Internat. Law, 1953; MA, NYU, 1955; LLB (hon.), Harvard U., 1955. Bar: N.Y. 1955, Conn. 1986. Atty. Gallap, Climenko & Gould, N.Y.C., 1955, Otterbourg, Steindler, Huston & Rosen, N.Y.C., 1956; pvt. practice law N.Y.C., 1957-65, 1969; atty. Dryer & Traub, N.Y.C., 1966-68, Kassner & Detsky, N.Y.C., 1970-80, Kassner & Haigney, N.Y.C., 1981-90; instr. Ohio State U., Columbus, 1956-57; asst. prof. Ark. State U., Pine Bluff, 1965. Contbr. articles to profl. jours. on 1st amendment law. Mem. Phi Beta Kappa. Real property, Constitutional, Antitrust. Home: 7221 Montrico Dr Boca Raton FL 33433-6931

**KASSOFF, MITCHELL JAY,** lawyer, educator; b. N.Y.C., June 11, 1953; s. Justice Edwin and Phyllis (Brafman) K.; m. Gwendolyn Jones, Mar. 3, 1979; children: Sarah, Jonathan. BS in Pub. Acctg. magna cum laude, SUNY-Albany, 1975; JD, U. Va., 1978. Bar: N.Y. 1979, N.J. 1983, U.S. Supreme Ct. 1982, U.S. Ct. Appeals (2d dir.) 1996, U.S. Ct. Appeals (D.C. cir.) 1979, U.S. Tax Ct. 1979, U.S. Ct. Internat. Trade 1981, U.S. Ct. Customs and Patent Appeals 1979, U.S. Dist. Ct. (so., ea., no. and we. dists.) N.Y. 1979, U.S. Dist. Ct. N.J. 1983. Assoc. Herzfeld & Rubin, P.C., N.Y.C., 1978-82; pvt. practice, N.Y.C. and N.J., 1982—; prof. law and taxation Pace U., N.Y.C., 1979—. Contbr. articles to profl. jours. Mem. ABA, N.Y. State Bar Assn., Essex County (N.J.) Bar Assn. General corporate, Franchising, Real property. Home: 2 Foster Ct South Orange NJ 07079-1002

**KASTENBERG, STEPHEN JOEL,** lawyer; b. Dover, N.J., Feb. 10, 1966. AB, Princeton U., 1988; JD, Harvard Law Sch., 1992. Bar: Pa., N.J., U.S. Dist. Ct. (ea. dist.) Pa., U.S. Ct. Appeals (3d cir.). Clk. U.S. Ct. Appeals (1st cir.), Boston, 1992-93; assoc. Ballard Spahr Andrews & Ingersoll, Phila., 1993—. Mem. U. Pa. Am. Inns Ct. Avocations: reading, cooking, skiing, tennis. Antitrust, General civil litigation, Pension, profit-sharing, and employee benefits. Office: Ballard Spahr et al 1735 Market St Philadelphia PA 19103-7501

**KASTL, DIAN EVANS,** lawyer; b. Oklahoma City, Jan. 5, 1958; d. Jim and Hazel Corrine (Hill) Evans; m. David G. Kastl, Feb. 6, 1987; children: Shea P., R. Patricia. BS in Nursing, U. Okla., 1975, MA in Journalism, 1979; BS in Journalism, U. Md., 1976; JD, Loyola U., 1984; LLM in Trade Regulation, NYU, 1985. Bar: N.J. 1985, N.Y. 1985, Fla. 1985, U.S. Dist. Ct. N.J. 1985, La. 1987, D.C. 1987, U.S. Dist. Ct. (ea., mid. and we. dists.) La. 1987, U.S. Ct. Appeals (5th cir.) 1987. Rsch. asst. NYU Sch. Law, N.Y.C., 1984-85; assoc. Trenam, Simmons, Kemker, Scharf, Barkin, Frye O'Neil, Tampa, Fla., 1985-87, Chaffe, McCall, Phillips, Toler & Sarpy, New Orleans, 1987-91; of counsel Godfrey & Wheeler, New Orleans, 1991-92; pvt. practice New Orleans, 1992—. Author: The Ice Key, 1997, Legal Incubus, 1997; mem. editl. bd., comments editor Loyola Law Rev., 1983-84. Bernard and Pauline Lasker scholar, 1984-85. Mem. ABA (chmn. computer programs subcom. patent trademark and copyright sect. 1988-89, info. distbn. techs. subcom. patent trademark and copyright sect. 1990-91), N.Y. Bar Assn., La. Bar Assn., New Orleans Bar Assn., Sigma Delta Chi, Kappa Tau Alpha. Democrat. Trademark and copyright, Federal civil litigation, Computer. Home: 104 Homestead Ave Metairie LA 70005-3766

**KASTLE, DAVID ANTHONY,** lawyer; b. L.A., Apr. 22, 1957; s. Howard Jean and Sandra Nancy Kastle; 1 child, Jackson James. BA, U. Calif., Santa Cruz, 1979; JD, Gonzaga U., 1983. Bar: Wash. 1983. Sole propr. Lynnwood, Wash., 1983—. Family and matrimonial, Juvenile, State civil litigation. Office: 18720 33d Ave Ste 100 Lynnwood WA 98037

**KASTNER, MENACHEM J.,** lawyer; b. Bronx, N.Y., Oct. 13, 1951; s. Danny and Renee K.; m. Arlene Grunwald, Jan. 24, 1971 (div. Aug. 1987); children: Ernest Joseph, Isaac, Grace. BA, Bklyn. Coll., 1973; JD, NYU, 1976. Bar: N.Y., U.S. Dist. Ct. (so. and ea. dists.) N.Y., U.S. Supreme Ct. Assoc. Parker, Chapin, Flattau & Klimpl, N.Y.C., 1976-85; ptnr. Dreyer & Traub, N.Y.C., 1986-96, Fischbein, Badillo, Wagner, Harding, N.Y.C., 1996—. Contbr. articles to profl. jours. Republican. Jewish. Avocation: skiing. Appellate, Landlord-tenant, Real property. Home: 1329 E 7th St Brooklyn NY 11230-5103 Office: Fischbein Badillo Wagner Harding 909 3rd Ave New York NY 10022-4731

**KASUNIC, ROBERT JOYCE,** lawyer, educator; b. N.Y.C., Feb. 5, 1959; s. R. J. Sr. and Mary Ann Kasunic; m. Carol Schultze, Sept. 7, 1991; children: Katherine Lang, Elizabeth Joyce. BA, Columbia U., 1985; JD, U. Balt., 1992. Bar: Md. 1992, U.S. Dist. Ct. Md. 1993, D.C. 1995, U.S. Supreme Ct. 1998, U.S. Ct. Appeals (4th cir.) 1999. Pvt. practice Darnestown, Md., 1992—; adj. faculty U. Balt. Law Sch., 1995—; speaker Hoffberger Ctr. for Profl. Ethics, 1994. Mem. ABA, FBA, Am. Intellectual Property Law Assn., Md. State Bar, Montgomery County Bar Assn., D.C. Bar Assn., Copyright Soc. U.S.A. Intellectual property, Bankruptcy, Criminal. Office: 14409 Brookmead Dr Darnestown MD 20874-3130

**KATSH, M. ETHAN,** law educator; b. N.Y.C., Sept. 3, 1945; s. Abraham Isaac and Estelle (Wachtell) K.; m. Beverly Schwartz; children: Rebecca, Gabriel, Gideon. BA, NYU, 1967; JD, Yale U., 1970. Bar: N.Y. 1970. Asst. prof. legal studies U. Mass., Amherst, 1970-76, assoc. prof., 1977-88, prof., 1988—, chair legal studies dept., 1993-94; dir. Ctr. Info. Tech. and Dispute Resolution, 1997—. Author: The Electronic Media and the Transformation of Law, 1989, Law in a Digital World, 1995; co-author: Before the Law, 6th edit., 1998; editor: Taking Sides: Clashing Views on Controversial Legal Issues, 1982, 8th edit., 1998; bd. of editors: Cyberspace Law Abstracts; contbr. articles on law, media and computers to profl. jours. and mags. Co-founder U. Mass. Mediation Project, 1980; founder, dir. Online Ombuds Office, 1996—. Mem. Am. Legal Studies Assn. (pres. 1978-80). E-mail: katsh@legal.umass.edu. Office: U Mass Dept Legal Studies Amherst MA 01003

**KATSORIS, CONSTANTINE NICHOLAS,** lawyer, consultant; b. Bklyn., Dec. 5, 1932; s. Nicholas C. and Nafsika (Klonis) K.; m. Ann Kanganis, Feb. 19; children: Nancy, Nicholas, Louis. BS in Acctg., Fordham U., 1953; JD cum laude, 1957; LLM, NYU, 1963. Bar: N.Y. 1957, U.S. Dist. Ct. (so. and ea. dist.) N.Y. 1959, U.S. Tax. Ct. 1959, U.S. Ct. Appeals (2nd cir.) 1959, U.S. Supreme Ct. 1961. Assoc. Cahill, Gordon, Reindel & Ohl, N.Y.C., 1958-64; asst. prof. Law Sch. Fordham U., N.Y.C., 1964-66; assoc. prof. Fordham U., 1966-69; prof., 1969—, apptd. Wilkinson prof. law, 1991; cons. N.Y. State Temporary Commn. on Estates, 1964-67; arbitration panelist N.Y. Stock Exchange, 1971—, Nat. Assn. Securities Dealers, 1968—, 1st Jud. Dept., 1972—; pub. mem. Securities Industry Conf. on Arbitration, 1977-97, emeritus pub. mem., 1997—; pvt. judge adjudication ctr. Duke U. Law Sch., 1989—. Contbr. articles to profl. jours. Mem. sch. bd. Greek Orthodox Parochial Sch. St. Spyridon, 1975-89, chmn. sch. bd., 1983-89. With U.S. Army, 1963. Recipient Cert. Appreciation Nat. Assn. Securities Dealers, 1982, Ellis Is. Medal of Honor award, 1999. Mem. ABA (fed. estate and gift tax com. 1966-68), N.Y. State Bar Assn. (sect. on trust and estates 1969—), Assn. Bar City of N.Y. (trusts, estates and surrogates' cts. com. 1968-70, legal assistance com. 1965-67), Fordham U. Law Alumni Assn. (bd. dirs. 1972—), Fordham U. Law Ref. Alumni Assn. (pres. 1968-64). Republican. Greek Orthodox. Estate taxation, Probate, Personal income taxation. Office: 140 W 62nd St New York NY 10023-7407

**KATSOS, BARBARA HELENE,** lawyer; b. N.Y.C.. MA, NYU; JD, U. of City of N.Y.; PhD, NYU. Bar: N.Y., U.S. Dist. Ct. (so. dist.) N.Y., U.S. Dist. Ct. (ea. dist.) N.Y. Pvt. practice N.Y.C. Contracts commercial, General practice, Private international. Office: Ste 3200 777 3d Ave New York NY 10017

**KATSURINIS, STEPHEN AVERY,** lawyer; b. Houston, Aug. 4, 1966; s. Ted and JoAnn Katsurinis. BA, Southwestern U., 1988; JD, Franklin Pierce Law Ctr., 1991. Bar: Va. 1992, D.C. 1999, U.S. Ct. Appeals (4th cir.) 1992, U.S. Dist. Ct. (ea. dist.) Va. 1995. Legis. counsel to Rep. Dana Rohrabacher Washington, 1991-94; policy analyst Dept. of Planning and Budget, Richmond, Va., 1994-95; of counsel Magenheim, Bateman, Houston, 1995-97; staff atty. McGuire, Woods, Battle & Boothe, LLP, Washington, 1997—. Alt. del. Rep. Nat. Conv., San Diego, 1996; election judge State of Tex., Georgetown, 1986. Recipient Am. Citizenship award DAR, 1980. Mem. Am. Hellenic Progressive Assn. (chpt. sec. 1990-91), Federalist Soc. for Law and Pub. Policy, Charles Fahy Am. Inn of Cts. (barrister). Republican. Greek Orthodox. Legislative, Civil rights. Office: McGuire Woods Battle & Boothe LLP # 1200 1050 Connecticut Ave NW Washington DC 20036-5317

**KATZ, CHEROL BOBBY,** law educator, lawyer; b. Inglewood, Calif., June 12, 1957; d. Milton and Piri (Gross) K.; m. Gary Kleinman, June 26, 1983 (div. May 1985). AS in Biology, Cypress (Calif.) Coll., 1981; BA in Eng. Lit., UCLA, 1983; JD, Western State U., Fullerton, Calif., 1987. Bar: Calif. 1989, U.S. Dist. Ct. (cent. dist.) Calif. 1990, U.S. Ct. Appeals (9th cir.) 1990. Atty. Mitchell, Silberberg & Knupp, L.A., 1990-91, 93; dep. city atty. City of Garden Grove, Calif., 1991-92; asst. v.p. bus. and legal affairs Concorde-New Horizon Corp., L.A., 1993-94; v.p. bus. and legal affairs Tele-Seminars, Inc., Huntington Beach, Calif., 1994; pvt. practice Cypress, Calif., 1989—; adj. prof. law Cerritos Coll., Norwalk, Calif., 1990-92, mem. paralegal adv. bd., 1990-97; prof. law So. Calif. Coll. Bus., Brea, 1996—, Platt Coll., Cerritos, Calif., 1997—; prof. law, instr. Troy H.S., Fullerton, 1996—; prof. paralegal and legal sec. program UCI, 1997—; prof. law South Coast Coll., 1998—, U. Phoenix, 1999—; instr. Cypress High Sch., 1999—; mem. careers in law adv. bd. N. Orange Co. Regl. Occupl. Programs, Anaheim, 1997—; polit. cons., Cypress, 1988-89. Assoc. dir. Anti-defamation League of B'nai B'rith, Santa Ana, Calif., 1990. Mem. ABA (mem. forum com. entertainment and sports law 1989—), Calif. Women Lawyers, Intellectual Property Law sect. of State Bar of Calif., Calif. Elected Women's Assn. Edn. and Rsch. Democrat. Jewish. Avocations: swimming, treadmill walking. Office: 6122 Lincoln Ave Ste 107 Cypress CA 90630-5809

**KATZ, GARY M.,** lawyer; b. N.Y.C., May 10, 1941; s. Leon W. and Helen (Dier) K.; m. Marylyn Dintenfass, Aug. 26, 1963 (div. 1991); children: Robert A., Marc A.; m. Lenore Evans, Apr. 5, 1992. BBA, CUNY, 1963; JD, N.Y. Law Sch., 1965. Bar: N.Y. 1967, U.S. Dist. Ct. (ea. and so. dists.) N.Y. Office mgr. Haft & Haft C.P.A., Jerusalem, 1965-66; assoc. product mgr. General Foods, White Plains, N.Y., 1966-69; v.p. fin. dept. Informa-tion, Inc., N.Y.C., 1969-72; v.p. Fabrics Round the World, N.Y.C., 1972-74; ptnr. Katz, Kleinbaum, Farber & Karson (and predecessor firms), White Plains, 1974-92; pvt. practice N.Y.C., 1993—; dir. IAMGOLD Internat. African Mining Gold Corp., 1993-94; dir. Internat. FIA Holdings Ltd., Agem Ltd. Trustee Young Israel of Scarsdale, N.Y., 1981-85. Mem. ABA, N.Y. State Bar Assn. (del. 9th jud. dist. real property law sect., chmn. com. legis. of landlord and tenant, moderator real estate transactions practical skills course), Internat. Law Practice. Jewish. Private international, General corporate. Office: 780 3rd Ave # 24th-fl New York NY 10017-2024

**KATZ, HAROLD AMBROSE,** lawyer, former state legislator; b. Shelbyville, Tenn., Nov. 2, 1921; s. Maurice W. and Gertrude Evelyn (Cohen) K.; m. Ethel Mae Lewison, July 21, 1945; children: Alan, Barbara, Julia, Joel. A.B., Vanderbilt U., 1943; J.D., U. Chgo., 1948, M.A., 1958. Bar: Ill. 1948. Ptnr. Katz, Friedman, Schur & Eagle, Chgo., 1948—; spl. legal cons. to Gov. of Ill., 1961-63; master-in-chancery, circuit ct. Cook County, Ill., 1963-67; mem. Ill. Ho. of Reps., 1965-83, chmn. judiciary com., co-chmn. rules com.; lectr. U. Coll., U. Chgo., 1959-64; Chmn. Ill. Commn. on Orgn. of Gen. Assembly, 1966-82; del. nat. Democratic conv., 1972. Author: Liability of Auto Manufacturers for Unsafe Design of Passenger Cars, 1956; (with Charles O. Gregory) Labor Law: Cases, Materials and Comments, 1948, Labor and the Law, 1979, Harold A. Katz Memoirs, 1988; editor: Improving the State Legislature, 1967; contbr. articles to mags. Fellow Coll. Labor and Employment Lawyers; mem. ABA, Ill. Bar Assn. (chmn. labor law sect. 1979-80), Internat. Soc. for Labor Law and Social Legislation (U.S. chmn. 1961-67), Am. Trial Lawyers Assn. (chmn. workmen's compensation sect. 1963-64). Jewish. Labor, Federal civil litigation, State civil litigation. Home: 1180 Terrace Ct Glencoe IL 60022-1241 Office: Katz Friedman Schur & Eagle 77 W Washington St Fl 20 Chicago IL 60602-2801

**KATZ, JAMES,** lawyer; b. Brookline, Mass., Aug. 11, 1951; s. Louis Ely and Ruth Katz; m. Donna Laverdiere, Nov. 7, 1976; children: Julia, Joshua, Sarah. BA summa cum laude, Brandeis U., 1973; JD cum laude, U. Pa., 1981. Bar: N.J. 1981, Pa. 1981, U.s. Dist. Ct. N.J. 1981, U.S. Dist. Ct. (ea. dist.) Pa. 1981, U.S. Ct. Appeals (3d and D.C. cirs.) 1982, U.S. Supreme Ct. 1982. Assoc. Tomar, Simonoff, Adourian, O'Brien, Kaplan, Jacoby, Graziano, Cherry Hill, N.J., 1981—. Vol. atty. ACLU, Newark, 1985—; mem. Haddonfield (N.J.) Bd. Edn., 1997—. Mem. Phi Beta Kappa. Home: 50 Lafayette Ave Haddonfield NJ 08033-3308 Office: Tomar Simonoff Dourian O'Brien Kaplan Jacoby & Graziano 20 Brace Rd Ste 100 Cherry Hill NJ 08034-2639

**KATZ, JEFFREY HARVEY,** lawyer, mayor; b. Newark, Apr. 16, 1947; s. Jack and Beatrice (Weinstock) K.; m. Sharon R. Davis, Nov. 7, 1971; children: Stacey, Justin. B of Engring, Stevens Inst. Tech., 1970; JD, Seton Hall U., 1981. Bar: N.J. 1981, U.S. Dist. Ct. N.J. 1981, U.S. Ct. Appeals (3d cir.) 1984, U.S. Supreme Ct. 1985. Engr. RKO Gen., Sta. WOR-AM-FM-TV, N.Y.C., 1967-70; mgr., engr. Pub. Svc. Electric & Gas Co., Newark, 1970—, mgr. telecomm. sys., 1977-90; mgr. telecomm. advanced tech. Pub. Svc. Electric & Gas Co., 1990-93, sr. info. technologies cons., 1993-98; prosecutor Twp. of Springfield, N.J., 1982-85, governing body, 1985-95; cons. Enterprise IT, 1998—; mem. Downtown Redevel. Com., Springfield, 1990-94, Springfield Bicentennial Com., logistics chmn., 1993-94; chmn. adv. com. Mcpl. Cable TV, Springfield, 1974-76; mem. Union County Rep. Com., Springfield Rep. Mcpl. Com., 1986-98; Enterprise IT Cons., 1998—. Mem. bd. health Twp. of Springfield, 1986-87, 1990-93, mayor, 1988-89, planning bd., local assistance bd., commr. pub. safety, 1988-93, dep. mayor, 1992; trustee Stevens Inst. Tech., Hoboken, N.J., 1971-74, mem. pres. sch. and sel. com., fin. com., lower campus lounge project; trustee Union County Coll., Cranford, N.J., 1995—, mem. ednl. planning and policy com., bldgs. and grounds com., vice-chair audit com.; lt. Aux. Police, Springfield, 1968—; mem. Gov.'s Mgmt. Improvement Program, Trenton, N.J., 1982-83; local govt. affairs adv. com. N.J. Assembly, 1989-91, mem. recreation com., 1990-92, 94; logistics chief People for Whitman campaign, 1993. Named One of Outstanding Young Men of Am., U.S. Jaycees, 1971-73, Citizen of Yr. Springfield B'nai B'rith, 1976, Citizen of Yr. Policeman's Benevolent Assn. Local, 1976, Springfield, 1985; recipient award for 25 continuous yrs. of pub. svc. N.J. Bldrs. Assn., 1989, Silver Life Card award Policemen's Benevolent Assn. Local 76, 1991. Mem. ABA, IEEE, Soc. Cable TV Engrs., N.J. State Bar Assn., Union County Bar Assn., Internat. Platform Assn., Jewish War Vets. of U.S., Fed. Comms. Bar Assn. Republican. Jewish. Avocations: amateur radio, running, photography. General practice, Computer, Criminal. Office: 182 Meisel Ave Springfield NJ 07081-1830

**KATZ, JERI BETH,** lawyer; b. Washington, Nov. 6, 1964; d. Stanley J. and Paula (Goldberg) K.; m. Daniel Alan Ezra, June 19, 1988 (div. Dec. 1990). BA, U. Md., 1987; JD, Cath. U., Washington, 1990. Bar: Md. 1990, D.C. 1991, U.S. Ct. Appeals (6th cir.) 1991, U.S. Ct. Internat. Trade 1992, Colo. 1994. Assoc. Winston & Strawn, Washington, 1990; ptnr. Law Offices Royal Daniel, Washington, 1990-94, Daniel & Katz, L.L.C., Breckenridge, Colo., 1994-98; pvt. practice, Breckenridge, 1998—; mem. jud. performance commn. 5th Jud. Dist., 1998—. Bd. dirs. Snowmass Ski Acad., 1995-98, Breckenridge Resort Chamber, 1998—; mem. Breckenridge Town Coun., 1998—; chairperson Summit County Transfer of Devel. Rights Commn., 1998—. Mem. Continental Divide Bar Assn. (v.p. 1997-98), Colo. Criminal Def. Bar (rap sheet com. 1998). State civil litigation, Administrative and regulatory, Criminal. Home: PO Box 6602 Breckenridge CO 80424-6602 Office: PO Box 6602 130 Ski Hill Rd Ste 210 Breckenridge CO 80424-6602

**KATZ, JEROME CHARLES,** lawyer; b. Boston, Sept. 25, 1950; s. Ralph and Thelma M. (Clark) K.; m. Nancy M. Green, Aug. 29, 1976; children: Jonathan Green, Elizabeth Rachel. AB, Duke U., 1972; JD, Columbia U., 1975. Bar: N.Y. 1976, U.S. Dist. Ct. (so. and ea. dists.) N.Y. 1976, U.S. Supreme Ct. 1979, U.S. Ct. Appeals (2d cir.) 1981, U.S. Dist. Ct. (we. dist.) N.Y. 1990. Assoc. Chadbourne & Parke, N.Y.C., 1975-83, ptnr., 1983—. Assoc. editor Columbia Jour. Transnat. Law, 1974-75. Harlan Fiske Stone scholar Columbia U., 1974. Mem. ABA, Assn. of the Bar of the City of N.Y., Phi Beta Kappa. General civil litigation, Federal civil litigation, State civil litigation. Home: 77 E 12th St New York NY 10003-5002 Office: Chadbourne & Parke 30 Rockefeller Plz New York NY 10112-0002

**KATZ, JOETTE,** state supreme court justice; b. Bklyn., Feb. 3, 1953. BA, Brandeis U., 1974; JD, U. Conn., 1977. Bar: Conn. 1977. Pvt. practice, 1977-78; asst. pub. defender Office Chief Pub. Defender, 1978-83; chief legal svcs. Pub. Defender Svcs., 1983-89; judge Superior Ct., 1989-92; assoc. judge Conn. Supreme Ct., Hartford, 1992—; instr. U. Conn. Sch. law, 1981-84; tchr. ethics and criminal law Quinnipiac Coll. Mem. Am. Law Inst. (chairperson evidence code drafting com.), Am. Inns Ct. (past pres. Fairfield County br.). Office: Conn Supreme Ct Drawer N Sta A Hartford CT 06106-1548

**KATZ, JOHN W.,** lawyer, state official; b. Balt., June 3, 1943; s. Leonard Wallach and Jean W. (Kane) K.; m. Joan Katz, June 11, 1969 (div. 1982); 1 child, Kimberly Erin. BA, Johns Hopkins U., 1965; JD, U. Calif., Berkeley, 1969; DDL (hon.) U. Alaska, 1994. Bar: Alaska, Pa., U.S. Dist. Ct. D.C. 1971, U.S. Ct. Appeals (D.C. cir.), U.S. Tax Ct., U.S. Ct. Claims, U.S. Ct. Mil. Justice, U.S. Supreme Ct. Legis. and adminstrv. asst. to Congressman Howard W. Pollock of Alaska, Washington, 1969-70; legis. asst. to U.S. Senator Ted Stevens of Alaska, Washington, 1971; assoc. McGrath and Flint, Anchorage, 1972; gen. counsel Joint Fed. State Land Use Planning Commn. for Alaska, Anchorage, 1972-79; spl. counsel to Gov. Jay S. Hammond of Alaska, Anchorage and Washington, 1979-81; commr. Alaska Dept. Natural Resources, Juneau, 1981-83; dir. state fed. relations and spl. counsel to Gov. Bill Sheffield of Alaska, Washington and Juneau, 1983-86; dir. state-fed. relations, spl. counsel to Gov. Steve Cowper of Alaska, Washington, 1986-90, Gov. Walter J. Hickel of Alaska, Washington, 1990-94, Gov. Tony Knowles, 1994—; mem. Alaska Power Survey Exec. Adv. Com. of FPC, Anchorage, 1972-74; mem. spl. com. hard rock minerals Govs. Council of Sci. and Tech., Anchorage, 1979-80; guest lectr. on natural resources U. Alaska, U. Denver. Contbr. articles to profl. jours.; columnist Anchorage Times until 1991. Acad. supr. Alaska Externship Program, U. Denver Coll. Law, 1976-79; mem. Reagan-Bush transition team for U.S. Dept. Justice, 1980. Recipient Superior Sustained Performance award Joint Fed. State Land Use Planning Commn. for Alaska, 1978, Resolution of Commendation award Alaska Legis., 1988. Republican. Office: State of Alaska Office of Gov 444 N Capitol St NW Ste 336 Washington DC 20001-1529

**KATZ, KENNETH ARTHUR,** lawyer, accountant; b. N.Y.C., Apr. 4, 1955; s. Bernard and Shirley Anne (Schachter) K.; m. Gillian Lynn Bagg, Nov. 29, 1986; children: Melissa Lee, Ashley Dawn. AB in Econs. cum laude, Harvard U., 1976; JD, Yeshiva U., 1980; MBA in Pub. Acctg., Pace U., 1987. Bar: N.Y. 1994, U.S. Tax Ct. 1994, D.C. 1995; CPA, N.Y. Legal asst. Law Offices of Jerome A. Wisselman, Manhasset, N.Y., 1980-81, Law Offices of S. Mac Gutman, Forest Hills, N.Y., 1981-82; asst. contr. Tauck Tours, Inc., Westport, Conn., 1982-84; pvt. practice acct. Eastchester, N.Y., 1984-87; tax specialist KPMG Peat Marwick, White Plains, N.Y., 1987-88; atty., acct., ptnr. Bernard Katz & Co, P.C., Eastchester, 1988—. Mem. ABA (taxation and internat. law sects.), N.Y. State Bar Assn. (tax sect.), D.C. Bar Assn. (taxation and sect. on corps., fin. and securities law), Westchester County Bar Assn. (tax and trusts and estates coms.), N.Y. State Soc. CPAs, Nat. Tax Assn.-Tax Inst. Am. (com. on internat. pub. fin.), Harvard-Radcliffe Club of Westchester. Avocations: sports, music, personal investing. Corporate taxation, Estate taxation, Personal income taxation. Office: Bernard Katz & Co PC 1 Mayfair Rd Eastchester NY 10709-2701

**KATZ, LAWRENCE EDWARD,** lawyer; b. Norfolk, Va., Sept. 15, 1947; s. Hyman and Beatrice (Kellert) K. BA, U. Richmond, Va., 1969; JD, U. Balt., 1973. Contract specialist U.S. Dept. Energy, Washington, 1979-80; law clk. various attys., Fla., 1980-86; atty. Richard M. Labovitz, Balt., 1986-87; pvt. practice law Balt., 1987—; movie critic Sta. WTTR, Westminster, Md., 1987—, Prestige Cablevision, Westminster, 1988—, Montgomery County Cable TV, 1991—, Crix Pix Variety, 1991, Labor Herald Weekly mag., 1991, Norfolk City News, L.A., Navy Voice, North Orange County News; entertainment critic Landmark News, Reisterstown, Md., 1987—; host Pro Wrestling Talk, WCAD AM, Balt., 1989-92. Fundraiser Jewish Nat. Fund, Balt., 1988; vol. Assoc. Jewish Charities, Balt., 1985—, Zionist Orgn. Am., Balt., 1987—. With U.S. Army Res., 1969-75. Mem. B'nai B'rith. Personal injury, Bankruptcy, Entertainment. Home and Office: PO Box 32060 Baltimore MD 21282-2060

**KATZ, MARVIN,** federal judge; b. 1930. B.A., U. Pa., 1951; LL.B., Yale U., 1954. Pvt. practice law, 1954-77; asst. commnr. IRS, 1977-81; assoc. Mesirov, Gelman, Jaffe, Cramer & Jamieson, Phila., 1981-83; judge U.S. Dist. Ct. (ea. dist.) Pa., Phila., 1983-97, sr. judge, 1997—. Office: US Courthouse 13613 US Courthouse Ind Mall W 601 Market St Philadelphia PA 19106-1713

**KATZ, MICHAEL JEFFERY,** lawyer; b. Detroit, May 11, 1950; s. Wilfred Lester and Bernice (Ackerman) K. BE with honors, U. Mich., 1972; JD, U. Colo., 1976; cert. mgmt., U. Denver, 1985, cert. fin. mgmt., 1990. Bar: Colo. 1978. Rsch. atty., immigration specialist Colo. Rural Legal Svcs., Denver, 1976-77, supervising atty. migrant farm lab., 1977-78; ind. contractor Colo. Sch. Fin., Denver, 1978-79; sole practice Denver, 1978-86; assoc. Levine and Pitler, P.C., Denver, 1986-88; gen. counsel, sec. Grease Monkey Internat., Inc., Denver, 1988-92; prin. Katz & Co., Denver, 1992—; exec. v.p. Nat. Network Exchange, Inc., Denver, 1992—; lectr. on incorporating small bus. and real estate purchase agreements Front Range Coll., 1986—, condr. various seminars on real estate and landlord/tenant law, 1980—; of counsel Levine and Pitler, P.C., Englewood, Colo., 1985—. Contbr. Action Line column Rocky Mountain News; contbr. articles to profl. jours. Mem. Assn. Trial Lawyers Am., Am. Arbitration Assn. (mem. panel of arbitrators 1989), Denver Bar Assn. (mem. law day com. 1985—, mem. real estate com. 1980—, mem. pro bono svcs. com. 1984—), U.S. Yacht Racing Assn., Dillon Yacht Club. Avocations: sailing, bicycling, swimming, art collecting, reading. Fax: 303-790-0927. Real property, General corporate, Contracts commercial. Office: Tower One 12835 E Arapahoe Rd Ste 400 Englewood CO 80112-3940

**KATZ, MORTON HOWARD,** lawyer; b. New Orleans, Feb. 5, 1945; s. David and Belle (Estes) K.; m. Carole Rae Deutch, Dec. 22, 1966; children: Brian David, Andrew Blair, Jonathan Ryan. BA, U. So. Miss., 1966; JD, Loyola U., New Orleans, 1969. Bar: La. 1969, U.S. Dist. Ct. (ea. dist.) La., U.S. Ct. Appeals (5th and 11th cirs.) 1970. Assoc. Law Offices of Ivor Trapolin, New Orleans, 1969-71, Herman & Herman, New Orleans, 1971-72; ptnr. Herman, Herman, Katz & Cotlar, New Orleans, 1972—; former owner New Orleans Saints Football Club; lectr. various univs. Prof. Jr. Achievement bd. dirs. Assembly Ctr., U. New Orleans, 1982—; bd. dirs., pres. Jewish Cmty. Ctr., New Orleans, 1993-95, New Orleans Alcohol Beverage & Control Bd., 1986-87; adv. bd. Ponchartrain Bank; mem. exec. bd. La. Mental Health Assn.; bd. trustees Met. Pk. Country Day Sch. Lt. USNG, 1969-74. Recipient first place award Local and Regional World LAw Fund Writing Contest, 1966. Mem. ATLA, Am. Arbitration Assn. (bd. dirs.), La. Trial Lawyers Assn. (bd. govs.), So. Trial Lawyers Assn. (bd. govs.), Loyola Law Sch. Alumni Assn. (bd. dirs.). Democrat. Club: Endymion (New Orleans). Avocations: jogging, woodworking, wine. General corporate, Personal injury, Construction. Home: 6034 Hurst St New Orleans LA 70118 Office: Herman Herman Katz & Cotlar 820 Okeefe Ave New Orleans LA 70113-1125

**KATZ, RICHARD LEONARD,** lawyer; b. N.Y.C., Nov. 4, 1938; s. George Katz and Sylvia Paul; m. Gabrielle Zeeh, Sept. 1973 (div. Jan. 1975); m. Susan Keel, Dec. 26, 1979; children: Natasha, Ariana. BS, BA, U. Fla., 1960; JD, Golden Gate U., 1968. Bar: Calif. 1969. Atty. Hoberg, Finger, Brown & Abramson, 1968-69; atty., ptnr. Miller & Keady (now Richard L. Katz, Inc.), 1969—; lectr. Golden Gate U. Sch. Law, San Francisco, 1970-71, 71-74. Pvt. U.S. Army, 1957. Mem. ABA, ATLA, Am. Arbitration Assn. (panel arbitrators), Bar Assn. Calif., Calif. Trial Lawyers Assn., San Francisco Trial Lawyers Assn. (bd. dirs. 1971-77, parliamentarian 1978). State civil litigation, Insurance, Personal injury. Home: 230 Edgewood Ave Mill Valley CA 94941-2638 Office: 100 Larkspur Landing Cir Larkspur CA 94939-1703

**KATZ, ROBERTA R.,** lawyer; b. Denver, Dec. 12, 1947; m. Charles J. Katz Jr.; children: Sarah, Sydney. BA, Stanford U., 1969; PhD, Columbia U., 1977; JD, U. Wash., 1980. Bar: Wash. 1980, U.S. Dist. Ct. (we. dist.) Wash. 1980. Assoc. Preston, Thorgrimson, Ellis & Holman, Seattle, 1981-83, Sirianni & Youtz, Seattle, 1983-85; assoc. then ptnr. Heller Ehrman White & McAuliffe, Seattle, 1986-92; gen. counsel, sr. v.p. LIN Broadcasting Corp., Kirkland, Wash., 1992-95, McCaw Cellular Comm., Inc., Kirkland, Wash., 1993-95; gen. counsel, sr. v.p., sec. Netscape Comms. Corp., Mountain View, Calif., 1995—. Mem. vis. com. sociology dept. U. Wash., Seattle, 1991—; co-founder, chair Seattle Art Fair, 1992-93; bd. dirs. Seattle Children's Theatre, 1990-93, Lakeside Sch., 1994-97. Fellow Discovery Inst., 1992—. General corporate, Communications.

**KATZ, RONALD SCOTT,** lawyer; b. Norwich, Conn., Dec. 14, 1946; s. Irving David and Joan (Lebovitz) K.; m. Ann Lisa Mark, Dec. 27, 1969; children: Benjamin, Cynthia. BA, Johns Hopkins U., 1968; JD, Columbia U., 1972. Bar: N.Y. 1972, U.S. Ct. Appeals (2d cir.) 1974, U.S. Ct. Appeals (4th cir.) 1993. Assoc. Golenbock & Barell, N.Y.C., 1972-80, ptnr., 1981-89; ptnr. Whitman & Ransom, N.Y.C., 1990-93; shareholder, dir. Shack & Siegel, PC, N.Y.C., 1993—. Mem. ABA, N.Y. State Bar Assn. Avocation: tennis. General corporate, Securities, Mergers and acquisitions. Home: 16 Paxford Ln Scarsdale NY 10583-3318 Office: Shack & Siegel PC 530 5th Ave New York NY 10036-5101

**KATZ, SETH ALAN,** lawyer; b. N.Y.C., Sept. 11, 1968; s. Michael Jacob and Gail Salpeter Katz; m. Erin R. Apfel, Nov. 4, 1995; 1 child, Jessica Sydney. BA, U. Mich., 1990; JD, Boston U., 1993. Bar: N.Y. 1994, U.S. Dist. Ct. (ea. and so. dists.) N.Y. 1997. Asst. dist. atty. Bronx (N.Y.) Dist. Attys. Office, 1993-96; assoc. Melito & Adolfsen, PC, N.Y.C., 1996-97, Loeb & Loeb LLP, N.Y.C., 1997—. General civil litigation, Criminal, Real property. Office: Loeb & Loeb LLP 345 Park Ave Fl 18 New York NY 10154-1895

**KATZ, STEVEN MARTIN,** lawyer, accountant; b. Washington, Feb. 8, 1941; s. Joseph and Pauline (Weinberg) K.; m. Lauri Gail Berman, Aug. 23, 1964; children: Benjamin, Aaron, Rebecca, Joshua. BS, U. Md., College Park, 1962; JD, George Washington U., 1965. Bar: D.C. 1966, Md. 1971; CPA, Md. Ptnr. Euzent, Katz & Katz, Washington, 1969-72; sr. ptnr. Katz, Frome & Bleecker, P.A., and predecessors, Rockville, Md., 1972-95; pvt. practice Rockville, 1995—; mem. Md. State Grievance Commn., 1991—. Mem. Am. Soc. Atty.-CPAs, Md. Bar Assn., Md. Assn. CPAs, D.C. Bar, Montgomery County Bar Assn., Md. Soc. Accts., Md. State Bar Found. Jewish. Fax: 301-294-9484. General corporate, Estate planning, Probate. Office: 401 E Jefferson St Ste 208 Rockville MD 20850-2613

**KATZ, THOMAS OWEN,** lawyer; b. Killeen, Tex., Jan. 15, 1958; s. Herbert D. and Eleanor (Meyerhoff) K.; m. Elissa Ellant, Nov. 6, 1983; children: Joseph, Peyton, Jacob. BS in Econs., U. Pa., 1979; JD, Georgetown U., 1982. Bar: Fla. 1982, U.S. Tax Ct. 1983. Shareholder, chair income tax dept. Ruden, McClosky, Smith, Schuster & Russell, P.A., Ft. Lauderdale, Fla., 1982—. Bd. dirs. Ctr. for Jewish Learning and Leadership, N.Y., 1993—, assoc. chmn., 1997—; bd. dirs. Israel Bonds of South Palm Beach County, 1996—, Donors Forum S.Fla., 1998—. Taxation, general, Estate planning, Probate. Office: Ruden McClosky Smith Sch PO Box 1900 Fort Lauderdale FL 33302-1900

**KATZ-CRANK, SHERRY L.,** lawyer; b. Marshall, Mich., July 20, 1962; 1 child, Connor Alexis Crank. BS, U. Mich., 1984; JD, U. Notre Dame Law Sch., 1987. Bar: Mich., U.S. Dist. Ct. (ea. and we. dists.) Mich., U.S. Ct. Appeals (6th cir.). Assoc. Dickinson, Wright, Lansing, Mich., 1987-92; ptnr. Miller, Ceinfield, Paddock & Stone, Lansing, 1992—; presenter seminar Coun. Edn. Mgmt., Mich., Ill., 1996-98, Mich. Mcpl. Fin. Assn., 1998. Mam. ATLA, Women Lawyers Assn. Labor, Administrative and regulatory. Home: 5875 Printemp Dr East Lansing MI 48823-9778 Office: Miller Canfield et al One Michigan Ave Ste 900 Lansing MI 48933

**KATZEN, SALLY,** lawyer, government official; b. Pitts., Nov. 22, 1942; d. Nathan and Hilda (Schwartz) K.; m. Timothy B. Dyk, Oct. 31, 1981; 1 child, Abraham Benjamin. BA magna cum laude, Smith Coll., 1964; JD magna cum laude, U. Mich., 1967. Bar: D.C. 1968, U.S. Supreme Ct. 1971. Congl. intern Sente Subcom. on Constl. Rights, Washington, 1963; legal rsch. asst. civil rights div. Dept. Justice, Washington, 1965; law clk. to Judge J. Skelly Wright U.S. Ct. Appeals (D.C. cir.), 1967-68; assoc. Wilmer, Cutler & Pickering, Washington, 1968-75, ptnr., 1975-79, 81-93; gen. counsel Coun. on Wage and Price Stability, 1979-80; dep. dir. for policy, 1980-81; adminstr. Office of Info. and Regulatory Affairs, Office of Mgmt. and Budget, Washington, 1993-98; dep. dir. Nat. Econ. Coun., The White House, Washington, 1998-99; counsellor to the dir. Office Mgmt. and Budget, Washington, 1999—; pub. mem. Adminstrv. Conf. U.S., 1988-93, govt. mem. and vice chair, 1993-95; mem. exec. com. Prettyman-Leventhal Inn of Ct., 1988-90, counselor, 1990-91; mem. Jud. Conf. for D.C. Cir., 1972-91; adj. prof. Georgetown U. Law Ctr., 1988, 90-92. Editor-in-chief U. Mich. Law Rev., 1966-67. Mem. com. visitors U. Mich. Law Sch., 1972—. Fellow ABA (ho. of dels. 1978-80, 89-91, coun. adminstrv. law sect. 1979-82, chmn. adminstrv. law and regulatory practice sect. 1988-89, governing com. forum com. communications law 1979-82, chmn. standing com. Nat. Conf. Groups 1989-92); mem. D.C. Bar Assn., Women's Bar Assn., FCC Bar Assn. (exec. com. 1984-87, pres. 1990-91), Women's Legal Def. Fund (pres. 1977, v.p. 1978), Order of Coif. Home: 4638 30th St NW Washington DC 20008-2127 Office: Office Mgmt and Budget Old Exec Office Bldg Rm 260 Washington DC 20503-0001

**KATZENSTEIN, ROBERT JOHN,** lawyer; b. Phila., May 2, 1951; s. Lawrence and Joan I. (Hassall) K.; m. Christine M. Waisanen, Apr. 21, 1979; children: Jeffrey Hunt, Erick Hill. BA, Yale U., 1973; JD, U. Pa., 1976. Bar: Del. 1976, D.C. 1979. Trial atty. antitrust div. U.S. Dept. of Justice, Washington, 1976-78; assoc. Richards, Layton & Finger, Wilmington, Del., 1978-84; ptnr. Katzenstein & Furlow, Wilmington, 1984-85, Lassen, Smith, Katzenstein & Furlow, Wilmington, 1985-91, Smith, Katzenstein & Furlow LLP, Wilmington, 1992—; asst. disciplinary counsel to Del. Bd. Profl. Responsibility, 1986-92; mem. Superior Ct. Civil Adv. Com., 1991—, Richard S. Rodney Inn of Court, 1993—, Product Liability Adv. Coun. Mem. ABA (litig. sect., tort and ins. practice sect.), Del. State Bar Assn. (judicial appts. com. 1991—, co-chair 1999—, corp. law, litigation sect.), Internat. Assn. Def. Coun., Def. Counsel of Del. (pres. 1997-99), Def. Rsch. Inst., Yale Club of Del., ARC (bd. dirs. Del., sec. 1998-99, vice chair 1999—), Mass for the Homeless Inc. (pres. 1998—). Democrat. Insurance, General civil litigation. Home: 1609 Mt Salem Ln Wilmington DE 19806-1134 Office: Smith Katzenstein & Furlow LLP PO Box 410 800 Delaware Ave The Corp Plz Wilmington DE 19899-0410

**KATZMAN, HARVEY LAWRENCE,** lawyer, educator; b. Youngstown, Ohio, Sept. 2, 1948; s. Abraham and Elsie Katzman; m. Elizabeth Viola Ball, Dec. 27, 1980. BA, Ohio No. U., 1971; JD, Glendale U., 1976. Bar: Calif. 1978, U.S. Dist. Ct. (cen. dist.) 1978, U.S. Ct. Appeals (9th cir.) 1979. Pvt. practice L.A., 1978-97; prof. law Glendale (Calif.) U., 1979—; lawyer La Casella & Katzman, Pasadena, Calif., 1997—; cons. to newly admitted attys., so. Calif., 1990—; legal advisor Calif. Inst. Baseball Acad., Riverside, 1995—. Mem. L.A. County Bar Assn. (family law com. 1997-99), Delta Theta Phi. Avocations: gardening, baseball, traveling, writing. Bankruptcy, General corporate, Probate. Office: La Casella & Katzman LLP 234 E Colorado Blvd Ste 800 Pasadena CA 91101-2208

**KATZMAN, IRWIN,** lawyer; b. Windsor, Ont., Can., June 29, 1931; s. Aaron and Rose (Tarnow) K.; m. Helen Frances Blecher, Dec. 20, 1952; children: Barry, Harriet, Kenneth, Rhonda, Aaron. BS, Wayne State U., 1953, MBA, 1963; JD cum laude, Loyola U., L.A., 1974. Bar: Calif. 1974, U.S. Dist. Ct. (cen. dist.) Calif. 1974, U.S. Ct. Appeals (9th cir.) 1980, U.S. Supreme Ct. 1980, U.S. Tax Ct. 1988. Chemist E.I. Dupont de Nemours, Phila., 1953-54; asst. quality mgr. Chrysler Corp., Detroit, 1956-63; mfg. plans mgr. Ford Motor Co., Newport Beach, Calif., 1963-70; prodn. control mgr. Dresser Industries, Huntington Park, Calif., 1970-73; purchasing mgr. Hughes Aircraft Co., Inglewood, Calif., 1973-74; v.p. First Alliance Mortgage Co., Santa Ana, Calif., 1976-77; pvt. practice Anaheim, Calif., 1975-94, San Jose, Calif., 1995—. Pres. Temple Beth Emet, Anaheim, 1988-90. With U.S. Army, 1953-56. Mem. State Bar of Calif., Orange County Bar Assn., Santa Clara County Bar Assn., Alpha Epsilon Pi (life). Avocations: sailing, golf, amateur radio. Family and matrimonial, Personal injury, Bankruptcy. Office: 8346 Riesling Way San Jose CA 95135-1435

**KATZMAN, RICHARD ALAN,** lawyer, arbitrator; b. N.Y.C., N.Y., Sept. 3, 1953; s. George and Ellen Delyse (Shure) K.; 1 child, Braden Michael Harris Katzman. AA, Miami-Dade Jr. Coll., 1972; BA, Fla. Internat. U., 1973; JD, U. Miami, 1976; MA, U. So. Calif., 1981. Bar: Fla. 1976, N.J. 1977, Calif. 1980, U.S. Dist. Ct. (so. dist.) Fla. 1976, U.S. Dist. Ct. N.J. 1977, U.S. Dist. Ct. (cent. dist.) Calif. 1980, U.S. Ct. Appeals (9th cir.) 1980, U.S. Ct. Appeals (5th and 11th cirs.) 1981, U.S. Supreme Ct. 1979. Of counsel Black and Denaro, Miami, 1976-78; rsch. atty. 3d Dist. Ct. Appeal, Miami, 1978; labor atty. Pomona (Calif.) divsn. Gen. Dynamics, 1980-82; assoc. atty. Balowitz & Wolf, Santa Ana, Calif., 1982-84; sr. assoc. Petersen & Ferguson, Santa Ana, Calif., 1984-86; sr. litig. L.A. County Met. Transp. Authority, L.A., 1986-94; prin. dep. county counsel County of L.A., L.A., 1994-96; asst. gen. counsel Santa Clara Valley Transp. Authority, 1996—; jud. arbitrator L.A. County Superior Ct., 1986-96, Orange County Superior Ct., Santa Ana, Calif., 1988-96. Judge Pro Tempore West Orange County Mun. Ct., Westminster, Calif., 1985-96. Mem. Amer. Coll. of Legal Medicine (assoc.-in-law). Avocations: boating, skiing, rv. Home: 310 N 1st St Apt 2 Campbell CA 95008-1341 Office: 3331 N 1st St Fl 2 San Jose CA 95134-1906

**KATZMANN, GARY STEPHEN,** lawyer; b. N.Y.C., Apr. 22, 1953; s. John and Sylvia (Butner) K. AB summa cum laude, Columbia U., 1973; MLitt, Oxford U., 1976; MPPM, JD, Yale U., 1979. Bar: Mass. 1982, U.S. Dist. Ct. Mass. 1983, U.S. Ct. Appeals (1st cir.) 1983, D.C. 1984, U.S. Ct. Appeals (2d cir.) 1987, N.Y. 1990, U.S. Ct. Appeals (fed. cir.) 1991. Law clk. to judge U.S. Dist. Ct. (so. dist.) N.Y., N.Y.C., 1979-80; law clk. to Hon. Stephen Breyer U.S. Ct. Appeals (1st cir.), Boston, 1980-81; rsch. assoc. ctr. criminal justice Law Sch. Harvard U., Cambridge, Mass., 1981-83; asst. U.S. atty., chief appellate atty., dep. chief criminal div., chief legal counsel U.S. Atty.'s Office, Mass., 1983—; assoc. dep. atty. gen. U.S. Dept. Justice, Washington, 1993-94; lectr. Harvard U. Law Sch., 1989—; rsch. fellow J.F. Kennedy Sch. Govt., Harvard U., 1997—; participant Yale Law Sch. Sentencing Seminar, 1999—. Author: Inside the Criminal Process, 1991; editor Yale U. Law Jour. Recipient Dir's. Superior Performance award U.S. Dept. Justice, 1993. Mem. ABA, Phi Beta Kappa. Office: US Attys Offci US Courthouse 1 Courthouse Way Ste 9200 Boston MA 02210-3011

**KATZMANN, ROBERT ALLEN,** law educator, non-profit association executive, political scientist; b. N.Y.C., Apr. 22, 1953; s. John and Sylvia Edith (Butner) K. AB summa cum laude, Columbia U., 1973; MA in Govt., Harvard U., 1975, PhD in Govt., 1978; JD, Yale U., 1980. Bar: Mass. 1982, U.S. Ct. Appeals (1st cir.) 1983, D.C. 1984, U.S. Dist. Ct. Mass. 1984. Law clk. to judge U.S. Ct. Appeals (1st cir.), Concord, N.H., 1980-81; rsch. assoc. Brookings Instn., Washington, 1981-85, fellow, 1985—; adj. prof. law, pub. policy Georgetown U., Washington, 1984-92; William J. Walsh prof. govt., prof. law Georgetown U., 1992—; pres. Governance Inst., Washington, 1986—; acting dir. govt. studies Brookings Instn., Washington, 1998; vis. prof. polit. sci. UCLA, Washington program, 1990-92; vis. chair, Wayne Morse prof. law and politics U. Oreg., 1992; cons. Fed. Cts. Study Com., 1990. Author: Regulatory Bureaucracy: The Federal Trade Commission and Antitrust Policy, 1980, Institutional Disability, 1986, Courts and Congress, 1997; co-editor: Managing Appeals in Federal Courts, 1988; editor: Judges and Legislators, 1988, The Law Firm and the Public Good, 1995; article and book editor Yale U. Law Jour., 1979-80. Mem. ABA (adminstrv. law sect. vice chair com. on govt. ops. and separation of powers 1991-94, pub. mem. adminstrn. conf., 1992-95), Am. Judicature Soc. (bd. dirs. 1992-98), Am. Polit. Sci. Assn., Assn. Pub. Policy Analysis and Mgmt., Phi Beta Kappa. Office: Brookings Instn Govtl Studies Program 1775 Massachusetts Ave NW Washington DC 20036-2188

**KAUCHER, JAMES WILLIAM,** lawyer; b. Belleville, Ill., Oct. 20, 1958; s. Robert Frederick and Mary Ellen (Shepard) K.; m. Janine Kaucher, Oct. 24, 1993. BA, U. Colo., 1980; JD, U. Ill., 1983. Bar: Ariz. 1983, U.S. Dist. Ct. Ariz. 1983. Assoc. Evans, Kitchel & Jenckes, Phoenix, 1983-85, Teilborg, Sanders & Parks, Phoenix, 1985-92; ptnr. Cavett and Kaucher, Tucson, 1992-98; of counsel Goodwin Raup PC, Tucson, 1998—; chmn. human rsch. rev. bd. Humana Hosp., Phoenix, 1989-94. Mem. Maricopa Bar Assn., Def. Rsch. Inst., Forum on Health Law, Ariz. Soc. Health Care Risk Mgrs. (bd. dirs. 1989-91), Ariz. Assn. Def. Counsel, Ariz. Mountaineering Club, Am. Alpine Club. Avocations: mountaineering, flying, bicycle racing. Personal injury, Health, Labor. Office: Goodwin Raup PC Ste 2130 One S Church Ave Tucson AZ 85701

**KAUFFELT, JAMES DAVID,** lawyer; b. Glendale, W.Va., May 5, 1952; s. Thaddeus David and Lois Zeigler (McQuade) K. BA, W.Va. U., 1974, JD, 1977. Ptnr. Kauffelt & Kauffelt, Charleston, W.Va. Public utilities, Transportation, Condemnation. Office: Kauffelt & Kauffelt 803 Kanawha Valley Bldg Charleston WV 25301

**KAUFFMAN, ALAN CHARLES,** lawyer; b. Atlantic City, Aug. 12, 1939; s. Joseph Bernard and Lilyan (Abraham) K.; children: Julie Beth, Debra Amy, Paige Tyler. AB, Rutgers U., 1961; JD, Villanova U., 1964. Bar: Pa. 1964, U.S. Ct. Appeals (3d cir.) 1965, U.S. Dist. Ct. (ea. dist.) Pa. 1965, U.S. Supreme Ct. 1968, Fla. 1985. Pres. Alan C. Kauffamn & Assocs., P.A., Boca Raton, Fla.; Mem., bd. dirs. Am. Diabetic Assn., Fla. Philharmonic Orch., Caldwell Theater; vice chmn. Fla. Victory Com.; founding chmn. Gold Coast Forum; bd. mem. Fla. Elections Commn. Cmty. Rels. bd. City of Boca Raton; mem. Greater Boca Raton Senate, Palm Beach County Film & TV Bd.; mem. Jewish Adv. Coun. U.S. Senator Connie Mack; Mem. Internat Bd. Weizmann Inst., Rep. Senatorial Inner Circle. Mem. ABA, ATLA, Pa. Bar Assn. (fromer mem. bd. govs., former trustee), Palm Beach County Bar Assn., Acad. Fla. Trial Lawyers, Phila. Trial Lawyers Assn., Palm Beach County Film Bd., Boca Roundtable. Antitrust, Federal civil litigation, State civil litigation. Office: PH1102 5355 Town Center Rd Boca Raton FL 33486-1005

**KAUFFMAN, RONALD P.,** lawyer, real estate executive; b. Columbus, Ohio, Mar. 30, 1938; s. Albert Paul K. and Marie Lilus Boston; m. June 8, 1968 (div. Dec. 1994); children: Keith, Kevin, Kurt, Lindsey. BSBA, Ohio State U., 1958, LLB, 1961, JD, 1964. Mem. Singing Buckeyes Barber Shop HarmonyChrous, 1998—. 1st lt. USAF, 1960-62. Mem. Columbus (Ohio) Bar Assn. (chmn., arbitrator 1995). Republican. Roman Catholic. Bankruptcy, State civil litigation, Estate planning. Home: 10233 Southfork Ln Powell OH 43065-9449 Office: 824 S High St Columbus OH 43206-1928

**KAUFFMAN, THOMAS ANDREW,** lawyer; b. Indiana, Pa., Apr. 27, 1966; s. Chester T. and Carol Dickerson Kauffman. BA, Pa. State U., 1989; JD, Widener U., 1992. Clk. Commonwealth Ct. of Pa., Harrisburg, 1991-92, Ct. of Common Pleas, Indiana, 1992-93; ptnr. Tomb, Mack & Kauffman, Indiana, 1993—. Active vol. Big Bros./Big Sisters, Indiana, 1994—; vol., pres. Comty. Living and Learning, Indiana, 1995—. State civil litigation, Criminal, Personal injury. Office: Tomb Mack & Kauffman 52 S 9th St Indiana PA 15701-2664

**KAUFFMAN, THOMAS RICHARD,** lawyer; b. Columbus, Ohio, June 3, 1959; s. James Runyan and Sarah Dillon (Dodd) K.; m. Victoria Doherty Heiden, Nov. 13, 1993. BA in Internat. Rels., Ohio State U., 1983; JD, U. Va., 1991. Bar: Va. 1991, U.S. Ct. Appeals (4th cir.) 1991, D.C. 1992, U.S. Dist. Ct. (ea. dist.) Va. 1996. Imagery analyst CIA, Washington, 1985-88, summer assoc., 1989; lawyer Dyer, Ellis, Joseph & Mills, Washington, 1990, 1991-94; cons. atty. Heiden Assocs., Inc., Washington, 1994-96; pvt. practice law, 1995—; dir., sec. Potomac Riverside Farms, Inc., Martinsburg, W.Va., 1989—. Mem. editl. bd. Va. Jour. Internat. Law, 1989-90, sr. editl. bd., 1990-91; mng. editor (newspaper) Va. Law Weekly, 1988-91. Maj./squadron comdr. USAF Aux.-Civil Air Patrol, Ohio, Va., 1972—. Mem. ABA (sects. on internat. law and practice and law practice mgmt.), Va. Bar Assn. (sect. on law practice mgmt.), D.C. Bar Assn. (sects. on corp., fin. and securities law and internat. law), Arlington County Bar Assn., Fairfax County Bar Assn., Am. Mensa, Phi Delta Phi. Republican. Avocations: politics, reading, sailing. Private international, Legislative, Contracts commercial. Home: 5827 11th St N Arlington VA 22205-2339 Office: PO Box 17655 Arlington VA 22216-7655

**KAUFFMAN, WILLIAM RAY,** lawyer; b. Chambersburg, Pa., Nov. 11, 1947; s. Harold William and Margaret Lenna (McCann) K.; children: Michael Harold, Scott William. BA, Gettsburg (Pa.) Coll., 1969; JD, U. Pitts., 1972. Bar: Pa. 1972, Kans. 1977, U.S. Dist. Ct. Kans. 1977, U.S. Supreme Ct. 1980, Alaska 1986, Mo. 1996. Dir. employee rels. Shippensburg (Pa.) State Coll., 1972-74; asst. atty. gen., regional legal counsel Pa. State Colls. and Univ. System, Millerville, 1974-76; gen. counsel Kans. Bd. of Regents, Topeka, 1976-86; gen. counsel U. Alaska, Fairbanks, 1986-88, v.p., gen. counsel, 1988-95; v.p., gen. counsel, corp. sec. St. Louis U., 1995—; mem. adj. faculty U. Alaska Fairbanks, 1990-91. Incorporator, bd. dirs. Pioneer Village, Inc., Topeka, 1979-84; bd. dirs. Presbyn. Hospitality House, Fairbanks, 1988-92, State of Alaska Phys. Therapy and Occupational Therapy Bd., Juneau, Alaska, 1989-92. Mem. Alaska Bar Assn., Mo. Bar Assn., Nat. Assn. Coll. and Univ. Attys. (bd. dirs. 1989-92, 2nd v.p. 1996-97, 1st v.p. 1997-98), Am. Corp. Counsel Assn. Avocations: sailing, golf, registered American quarter horses. Education and schools, General corporate, Labor. Office: St Louis U 221 N Grand Blvd Saint Louis MO 63103-2006

**KAUFMAN, ADAM D.,** judge; b. N.Y.C., May 8, 1942; s. Solomon and Ray (Egrin) K.; 1 child, Jessica. AB, Drew U., 1963; JD, Northwestern U., 1967. Bar: N.Y. 1970, U.S. Dist. Ct. Appeals (2d cir.) 1977. Judge, mediator NYS PERB, Buffalo, N.Y. Office: NYS PERB 125 Main St Buffalo NY 14203-3026

**KAUFMAN, ALBERT I.,** lawyer; b. N.Y.C., Oct. 2, 1936; s. Israel and Pauline (Pardes) K.; m. Ruth Feldman, Jan. 25, 1959; 1 son, Michael Paul. AA, L.A. City Coll., 1957; BA, U. San Fernando Valley, 1964, JD, 1966. Bar: Calif. 1967, U.S. Ct. Appeals (9th cir.) 1968, U.S. Supreme Ct. 1971, U.S. Dist. Ct. (cen. dist.) Calif. 1967, U.S. Tax Ct. 1971, U.S. Ct. Internat. Trade 1981. Sole practice, Encino, Calif., 1967—; judge pro tem L.A. Mcpl. Ct., 1980—, L.A. Superior Ct., 1991—; family law mediator L.A. Superior Ct., 1980—. Mem. Pacific S.W. regional bd. Anti-Defamation league of B'nai B'rith, 1970-91. Served with USAF, 1959-65, to col. CAP, 1956—. Recipient Disting. Svc. award B'nai B'rith, 1969; Exceptional Svc. award CAP, 1977, 95. Mem. ABA, L.A. County Bar Assn., San Fernando Valley Bar Assn., Consumer Atty. of Calif., Consumer Atty. Assn. L.A. Republican. Clubs: Toastmasters, Westerners 1117 (pres. 1969), B'nai B'rith (pres. 1971-72), Santa Monica Yacht (judge adv.) Personal injury, Family and matrimonial, Civil rights. Office: 17609 Ventura Blvd Ste 201 Encino CA 91316-3825

**KAUFMAN, ANDREW LEE,** law educator; b. Newark, Feb. 1, 1931; s. Samuel and Sylvia (Meltzer) K.; m. Linda P. Sonnenschein, June 14, 1959; children: Anne, David, Elizabeth, Daniel. A.B., Harvard U., 1951, LL.B., 1954. Bar: D.C. 1954, Mass. 1979, U.S. Supreme Ct. 1961. Assoc. Bilder, Bilder & Kaufman, Newark, 1954-55; law clk. to Justice Felix Frankfurter U S Supreme Ct., 1955-57; ptnr. Kaufman, Kaufman & Kaufman, Newark, 1957-65; lectr. in law Harvard U., Cambridge, Mass., 1965-66, prof., 1966-81, Charles Stebbins Fairchild prof. law, 1981—, assoc. dean, 1986-89. Author: (with others) Commercial Law, 1971, 82, Problems in Professional Responsibility, 1976, 84, 89, Cardozo, 1998. Treas. Shady Hill Sch., 1969-76; treas. Hillel Found. Cambridge, Inc., 1977-86. Mem. Mass. Bar Assn. (chmn. com. profl. ethics 1982—). Office: Harvard U Law Sch Cambridge MA 02138

**KAUFMAN, ANDREW MICHAEL,** lawyer; b. Boston, Feb. 19, 1949; s. Earle Bertram and Miriam (Halpern) K.; m. Michele Moselle, Aug. 24, 1975; children: Peter Moselle, Melissa Lanes, Caroline Raney. BA cum laude, Yale U., 1971; JD, Vanderbilt U., 1974. Bar: Tex. 1974, Ga. 1976, Ill. 1993, U.S. Ct. Appeals (5th and 11th cirs.) 1981. Assoc. Vinson & Elkins, Houston, 1974-76, ptnr., 1982-83; ptnr. Vinson & Elkins, Austin, 1983-92, Dallas, 1992; assoc. Sutherland, Asbill & Brennan, Atlanta, 1976-80, ptnr., 1980-81; ptnr. Kirkland & Ellis, Chgo., 1993—. Editor in chief Vanderbilt U. Law Rev., 1973-74. Fund raiser alumni fund Yale U., 1971—, mem. alumni schs. com., 1986—; mem. med. ethics coun. Seton Hosp., 1988-92; participant Leadership Austin, 1987-88; bd. dirs. United Way, Austin, 1988-92, Sta. KLRU-TV, 1989-93, pub. TV, Ballet Austin, 1986-92; mem. adv. bd. Austin Tech. Incubator, 1989-93, Austin-U. Tex. Entrepreneurs Coun., 1991-92; Dallas bus. com. Arts Leadership Inst, 1992-93; mem. nat. alumni bd. Vanderbilt U. Law Sch., 1994—; governing mem. Chgo. Symphony Orch. Mem. ABA (bus. law sect. 1978—, chmn. lease financing and secured transactions subcom. of com. devels. in bus. financing 1993-99, UCC com., legal opinions com.), Tex. Bar Assn., Yale U. Alumni Assn., Order of Coif, Headliners Club, Yale Club, N.Y.C. Club, Chgo. Club, Knights of the Symphony Austin. Avocation: sailing. Finance, Banking, General corporate. Office: Kirkland & Ellis 200 E Randolph St Fl 54 Chicago IL 60601-6636

**KAUFMAN, BRUCE ERIC,** judge; b. Anderson, Ind., Nov. 28, 1929; s. Arthur Dale and Ann M. (Hermansen) K.; m. Hazel Gordon; children: Robert, Jaclyn. AB, DePauw U., 1951; JD, U. Chgo., 1956. Bar: Ill. 1957, N.M. 1972, U.S. Supreme Ct. 1973, U.S. Ct. Internat. Trade 1993. Asst. atty. gen. State of Ill., Springfield, 1956-57; assoc. Dixon & Seidenfield, Waukegan, Ill., 1957-60; ptnr. Kaufman, Strouse, Wasneski & Yastrow, 1961-68; chief dep. dist. atty. State of N.M., Santa Fe, 1973-75, asst. atty. gen., 1975-77, dist. ct. judge, 1977-94; ret., 1994; arbitrator, pro-tem tribal judge Jicarilla Apache Tribe; past. chief legal advisor N.Mex. State Police; past instr. N.Mex. Law Enforcement Acad.; umpire U.S. Dist. Ct. Capt. USMCR, 1948-62. Mem. ABA (past vice chmn. com. on implementation of justice standards and goals, past regional rep. criminal justice ethics com.), N.M. Bar Assn., 1st Dist. Bar Assn. Democrat. Methodist. Home: PO Box 1555 Santa Fe NM 87504-1555

**KAUFMAN, DAVID JOSEPH,** lawyer; b. Harrisburg, Pa., Apr. 7, 1931; s. S. Herbert and Bessie (Claster) K.; m. Virginia Stern, Aug. 30, 1959; children: David J. Jr., James H. BS in Econs. cum laude, Franklin and Marshall Coll., 1952; JD cum laude, U. Pa., 1955. Bar: Pa. 1955. First assoc., to ptnr., then of counsel Wolf, Block, Schorr & Solis-Cohen, Phila., 1957—; chmn., exec. com., 1979, 83. Trustee Abington (Pa.) Meml. Hosp., 1981—, chmn. bd. trustees, 1992-94; pres. Congregation Rodeph Shalom, Phila., 1983-86. Fellow Am. Coll. Trust and Estate Counsel; mem. ABA, Pa. Bar Assn. (chmn. real property, probate and trust sect. 1986-87), Phila. Bar Assn. (chmn. probate sect. 1977). Republican. Estate planning, Probate, Estate taxation. Home: 2191 Paper Mill Rd Huntingdon Valley PA 19006-5817 Office: Wolf Block Schorr & Solis-Cohen LLP 1650 Arch St Philadelphia PA 19103-2029

**KAUFMAN, HELENE,** legal secretary; b. Bklyn., June 16, 1939; d. Jack and Faye Kaufman. Student, San Diego Jr. City Coll., 1959-60, San Diego State Coll., 1960-62; BA, U. Calif., Berkeley, 1963. Legal sec. San Diego, 1965-77; legal sec. City of San Diego, 1980-87, sr. legal sec., 1987—. Avocations: gardening, decorating, investing.

**KAUFMAN, IRA GLADSTONE,** judge; b. N.Y.C., Dec. 13, 1909; s. Joseph and Esther K.; m. Margaret Kaufman, Sept., 1988; children: Harvey David, Sylvia Kaufman Delin. BS, NYU, 1933, JD, 1936; DSc in Bus. Adminstrn. (hon.), Cleary Coll., Ypsilanti, Mich., 1976. Bar: Mich. 1939. Pvt. practice law, Detroit, 1939-59; judge of brobate Wayne County Probate Ct., Detroit, 1958-84, presiding judge, 1962-63, 66-67, 72-73, 77-85; chief judge pro tem Wayne County Probate and Juvenile Ct., 1981-85; Moot Ct. judge U. Detroit, 1966-72; lectr. Trustee Children's Hosp. of Detroit, chmn. devel., 1980-83, hon. chmn. ann. concert 1983, chmn. ad hoc com. alcoholism Detroit United Cmtys. Svcs., 1967-68; chmn. Detroit Com. Fgn. Rels., 1974-76; trustee Mich. Cancer Found., 1973, hon. life trustee emeritus, 1985; trustee Detroit Inst. Tech., 1962-72, Park Cmty. Hosp., 1962-73; pres. Inter-Agy. Council on Alcoholism, 1967; pres., chmn. bd. Met. Soc. for Blind, 1966-70, bd. dirs., 1960—; mem. Gov.'s Com. Mental Health Statute Rev. Commn., 1970-72, Mich. Soc. Mental Health, 1960—; hon. life mem. Children's Charter Mich., 1965-75; exec. bd. League Handicapped-Goodwill 1949-60; bd. overseers Dropsie Coll., 1973-75; bd. dirs. Hebrew Free Loan Soc., Detroit, 1979-84, Jewish Nat. Fund Bd.; v.p. United Hebrew Schs. Detroit, 1947-58; founding sec. Midrasha Coll. Hebrew Studies, 1948-58; pres. Adat Shalom Synagogue, 1945-51, founder cemetary, 1948, hon. life pres. 1953; founding chmn. Einstein Luncheon Forum, 1986—. Fellow Mich. State Bar Found. (life mem.); mem. ABA, Mich. Probate and Juvenile Ct. Assn. (exec. bd. 1969-72, pres. 1970-71), Mich. Bar Assn., Detroit Bar Assn., Supreme Ct. Hist. Soc., Mental Health Assn. Mich. (Advocacy award 1989), U.S. Air Force Assn. (ann. installing officer 1983-84), B'nai B'rith (hon. pres. Tikvah Lodge 1974), Valley of Detroit, Masons (33 degree, sovereign prince), Shriners, Jesters. Contbr. biog. sketches of Mich. judges to Jewish Hist. Soc. publ., 1983-84. Home: 4224 Wabeek Lake Dr S Bloomfield Hills MI 48302-1663

**KAUFMAN, JAMES JAY,** lawyer; b. Newark, N.Y., Jan. 23, 1939; s. Joseph Julius and Ann Gertrude (Quick) K.; m. Patricia Ann Patterson, Sept. 3, 1966; children: Kristine, Jeffrey. BA, Bucknell U., 1960; LLB, JD, Union Coll., Albany, 1964. Bar: N.Y. 1965, U.S. Ct. Appeals (2nd cir.) 1966, U.S. Dist. Ct. (we. and no. dists.) N.Y. 1968, N.C. 1985, Pa. 1985, U.S. Supreme Ct. 1985, U.S. Dist. Ct. (ea. dist.) N.C. 1991, U.S. Ct. Appeals (4th cir.) 1991, U.S. Ct. Appeals (7th cir.) 1992, U.S. Dist. Ct. (mid. dist.) N.C. 1993. Legal counsel, legis. and adminstrv. asst. Rep. Theodore R. Kupferman, U.S. Congress, Washington, 1965-67; assoc. Houghton, Pappas & Fink, Rochester, N.Y., 1967-70; ptnr. Culley, Marks, Rochester, 1970-75; sr. ptnr. James J. Kaufman, P.C., Newark, 1975-84, Kaufman & Forsyth, Rochester, 1984-91, Barefoot & Kaufman, Wilmington, N.C., 1991-93, Kaufman, Barefoot & Green, Wilmington, 1993-94; of counsel Hancock & Estabrook, Syracuse, N.Y., 1994-96; sr. ptnr. Kaufman & Green, L.L.P., Wilmington, 1994—; V.p. Fed. Bar Coun., 1968; mem. 7th Jud. Dist. Grievance Com., 1983-89; del. U.S./China Joint Session on Trade, Investment and Econ. Law, Beijing, 1987; strategic planning cons., Rochester, 1994-95; panel mem. Commerce Tech. Adv. Bd. on Noise Abatement, Washington, 1968; chmn. noise task force Genesee Region Health Planning, Rochester, 1970-71, mem./counsel noise task force, mem./counsel environ. health planning com., 1972-73. Author: What to Do Before the Money Runs Out—A Road Map for America's Automobile Dealers, 1993; contbr. articles to profl. publs. Justice Town of Arcadia, Newark, 1976-89. Mem. N.Y. State Bar Assn. (mem. spl. com. on environ. law 1974-77, mem. com. on profl. discipline, mem. com. on ct. in cmty. banking com. 1986—), Wayne County Bar Assn. (pres. 1986-87, v.p. 1985-86, chmn. family law sect. 1975-80, chmn. com. on profl. discipline 1975-89), N.C. Bar Assn., Pa. Bar Assn., New Hanover County Bar Assn., Monroe County Bar Assn., Wilmington Inns of Ct. (pres. 1994-97). Republican. Presbyterian. Avocations: boating, scuba diving, fishing. Health, Banking, Contracts commercial. Office: Kaufman & Green LLP 1985 Eastwood Rd Ste 200 Wilmington NC 28403-7208

**KAUFMAN, JEFFREY HUGH,** lawyer; b. Washington, June 26, 1952; s. E. Alfred and Florence M. (Nevitsky) K.; m. Sheri Fran Posner, Aug. 20, 1977; children: Jessica, Joshua, Rebecca. BA, U. Md., 1974; JD, George Mason U., 1977. Bar: Va. 1977, U.S. Dist. Ct. (ea. dist.) Va. 1977, U.S. Ct. Appeals (4th cir.) 1977, D.C. 1978, U.S. Dist. Ct. D.C. 1978, U.S. Ct. Appeals (Fed., D.C. cirs.) 1978, Md. 1978, U.S. Dist. Ct. Md. 1979, U.S. Supreme Ct. 1981, U.S. Ct. Appeals (5th cir.) 1988. Atty. U.S. Patent and Trademark Office, Washington, 1977-81; assoc. Fleit, Jacobson, Cohn & Price, Washington, 1981-87, ptnr., 1988-89; mng. trademark ptnr. Oblon, Spivak, McClelland, Maier & Neustadt, P.C., Arlington, Va., 1989—. Exec. bd. Jewish Community Council Greater Washington, 1987-90. Mem. ABA (chmn. subcom. patent, trademark and copyright 1987-90), U.S. Trademark Assn. (chmn. subcom. legislation implementation 1988-89, mem. editorial bd. The Trademark Reporter, 1989-91, internet trademark issues subcom., chair gov. affairs 1995—). Democrat. Avocations: technology, telecommunications. Fax: 703-413-2220. E-mail: jkaufan@oblon.com. Trademark and copyright, Intellectual property, Federal civil litigation. Office: Oblon Spivak McClelland Maier & Neustadt PC 1755 Jefferson Davis Hwy Fl 4 Arlington VA 22202-3509

**KAUFMAN, LEONARD LEE,** lawyer; b. Butte, Mont., May 8, 1939; s. Leonard Carl and Madeline (Marx) K.; m. Mary F. Culleton; children: Jennifer Lee, Julie Lee, Jody Lee. BA, Middlebury Coll., 1961; JD, U. Mont., 1964; LLM in Taxation, Denver U., 1976. Bar: Mont. 1961, U.S. Tax Ct. 1978. Trial atty. Mont. Dept. Hwys., Helena, 1967-69; asst. county atty. County of Lincoln, Mont., 1969-72; ptnr. Murray & Kaufman, P.C. (now Kaufman, Vidal & Hileman, P.C.), Kalispell, Mont., 1972—. Contbr. articles to agrl. and comml. code publs. Pres., bd. dirs. Flathead Valley Ski Found., Kalispell, 1978-88. Capt. U.S. Army, 1964-66. Mem. Mont. Bar Assn. (bd. trustees), Northwest Mont. Bar Assn. (pres. 1978), U.S. Ski Assn. (cert. ofcl.), No. Div. Ski Assn. (v.p. 1988-89). Republican. Avocations: Alpine skiing, hunting, fishing. Alternative dispute resolution, Real property, Taxation, general. Office: Kaufman Vidal & Hilman PC 22 2nd Ave E Kalispell MT 59901-4567

**KAUFMAN, MARK ALAN,** lawyer, educator; b. Grand Forks, N.D., Jan. 21, 1951; s. Victor and Vena Lucille (Lovett) K.; m. Jean Berry Hollingsworth, Sept. 6, 1969; children: Gretchen, Damien. BA with honors, U. Md., 1972, JD with honors, 1975. Bar: Md. 1975, Pa. 1979. Staff atty. Del. County Legal Assistance, Chester, Pa., 1976-93; sr. lectr. Widener U., Chester, Pa., 1995—; adj. prof. Villanova (Pa.) U. Sch. Law, 1984-93; instr. Pa. Bar Inst. Profl. Edn. Sys., Inc.; cons. HUD, 1979-80. Author: (tng. manuals) Mortgage Foreclosure Defense, 1983, Representing Abused Women, 1990. Recipient Domestic Abuse Victims Rights award, 1987, Edward Sparer award for Outstanding Advocacy, 1990. Mem. Soc. of Friends. Avocation: watercolors. Home: 203 Brandywine Blvd Wilmington DE 19809-3239 Office: Widener Univ 522 W 14th St Chester PA 19013

**KAUFMAN, MICHELLE STARK,** lawyer; b. N.Y.C., June 11, 1954; d. Maurice E. and Mary (Murray) Stark; m. Daniel M. Kaufman, Oct. 6, 1984; children: Jane Stark, David Stark, Carolyn Stark. BA, Iowa State U., Ames, 1976; JD, U. Mo., Kansas City, 1983. Bar: Mo. 1983, U.S. Dist. Ct. (we. dist.) Mo. 1983. Graphic artist Douglas Stone & Assocs., Newport Beach, Calif., 1976-78; chief news bur. Midwest Records, Kansas City, Mo., 1978-80; ptnr. Stinson, Mag and Fizzell, P.C., Kansas City, 1983-95, Sonnenschein Nath & Rosenthal, Kansas City, 1995—; lectr. in law U. Mo. Sch. Law, Kansas City, 1984-85; trustee U. Mo.-Kansas City Law Sch. Found., 1992—, exec. com., 1996—, sec., 1998—. Bd. dirs. Heart of Am. Family Svcs., Kansas City, 1989-98, vice-chmn., 1991-93, chmn., 1994-95, bd. mem. of the year award, 1995; bd. dirs., sec. Countryside Homes Assn., Kansas City, 1985. Mem. ABA (forum on franchising), Am. Health Lawyers Assn., Mo. Bar Assn., Greater Kansas City C. of C. (chmn. club 1990-96, vice chmn. 1991-92, chmn. 1992-93, Mo. state affairs com. 1995—, Chmn.'s Club Hall of Fame, 1996), U. Mo. Kansas City Law Alumni Assn. (bd. dirs. 1992-96, pres. 1994-95), Kansas City Tomorrow Alumni Assn. (bd. dirs., pres.-elect 1997-98, pres. 1998-99), Delta Delta Delta (exec.bd. 1979). General corporate, Franchising, Health. Office: Sonnenschein Nath & Rosenthal 4520 Main St Ste 1100 Kansas City MO 64111-7700

**KAUFMAN, ROBERT MAX,** lawyer; b. Vienna, Austria, Nov. 17, 1929; came to U.S., 1939, naturalized, 1945; s. Paul M. and Bertha (Hirsch) K.; m. Sheila Seymour Kelley. BA with honors, Bklyn. Coll., 1951; MA, NYU, 1954; JD magna cum laude, Bklyn. Law Sch., 1957. Bar: N.Y. 1957, U.S. Supreme Ct. 1961. Successively jr. economist, economist, sr. economist N.Y. State Div. Housing, 1953-57; atty. antitrust div. U.S. Dept. Justice, 1957-58; legis. asst. to U.S. Senator Jacob K. Javits, 1958-61; assoc. Proskauer Rose LLP, N.Y.C., 1961-69, ptnr., 1969—; chmn. bd. Pirelli Cables & Systems, LLC, Pirelli Tires LLC, Old Westbury Funds, Inc.; bd. dirs. Roytex Inc., Meadowbrook Equity Fund, L.L.C.; mem. N.Y. State Legis. Adv. Com. on Election Law, 1973-74; chmn. adv. com. N.Y. State Bd. Elections, 1974-78; chmn. N.Y. State Bd. Pub. Disclosure, 1981-82, U.S. Army Chief of Staff's Spl. Commn. on Honor System, 1988-89, N.Y. Chief Judge's Com. on Availability of Legal Svcs., 1988-90; referee Commn. on Jud. Conduct; spl. master N.Y. Supreme Ct. Appellate Divsn., 1999—; mem. Adminstrv. Conf. U.S. (chair com. regulations), 1988-95; chmn. Fund for Modern Cts., 1990-95; mem. Def. Adv. Com. on Women in the Svcs., 1997-99, vice chair com. on equality mgmt., mem. exec. com. 1998—. Co-author: Congress and the Public Trust, 1970, Disorder in the Court, 1973; co-gen. editor: Matthew Bender Treatise on Health Care Law, 4 vols., 1992—. Bd. dirs., mem. exec. com. Lawrence M. Gelb Found., Inc., Lawyers in the Public Interest, 1986-95, Am. Judicature Soc., pres. 1995-97, Citizens Union of N.Y.C., vice chair, 1997—, Citizen's Union Found., 1993—; bd. dirs., chmn. exec. com. Cmty. Action for Legal Svcs., Inc., 1976-78; dir., mem. exec. com. Legal Aid Soc., 1985-90, mem. exec. com. Vols. of Legal Svc., 1986-94; mem. platform com. N.Y. Rep. State Com., 1974; mem. jud. selection adv. coms. Senator Javits, 1972-80, and Senator Moynahan, 1977—; compensation elected ofcl. N.Y.C. Quadrennial Comm., 1995, 99; mem. distbn. com. N.Y. Cmty. Trust; bd. dirs. N.Y. Cmty. Funds, James Found.; bd. vis. U.S. Mil. Acad., 1976-79; dir., mem. exec. com., chmn. bd. Times Square Bus. Improvement Dist.; trustee Bklyn. Law Sch. With U.S. Army, 1957-58. Fellow Am. Bar Found., N.Y. State Bar Found.; mem. ABA, Assn. of Bar of City N.Y. (pres. 1986-88, chmn. com. on bldg. cons., co-chmn. com. on campaign fin. reform 1997—, past chmn. com. on 2d Century; past chmn. exec. com., past chmn. com. profl. responsibility, past chmn. spl. com. on campaign expenditures, past chmn. com. civil rights, com. on past vice chmn. com. grievances, chmn. delegation to state bar ho. dels.), N.Y. State Bar Assn. (ho. of dels. 1978, 86-90), N.Y. County Lawyers Assn. (past chmn. com. on civil rights), Am. Law Inst. Health, General corporate, Non-profit and tax-exempt organizations. Office: Proskauer Rose LLP 1585 Broadway New York NY 10036-8200

**KAUFMAN, SARAH HALL,** legal assistant; b. Danville, Va., Mar. 5, 1964; d. Wallace Vann and Mary Lou (Cooke) Hall; m. Robert Gene Kaufman II, Oct. 25, 1997. BA in Polit. Sci., East Carolina U., 1985; Legal Asst. Cert., Meredith Coll., Raleigh, N.C., 1985. Cert. legal asst., 1987. Legal rschr. N.C. Housing Fin. Agy., Raleigh, 1984-85; legal asst. Moore & Van Allen PLLC, Raleigh, 1985—; adj. prof. legal assts. program Meredith Coll., 1988—; instr. CLA rev. course N.C. Paralegal Assn., Inc., Raleigh, 1996—; instr. notary pub. instr. cert. and re-cert. courses N.C. Sec. of State, 1997. Mem., social chair Chapel Hill (N.C.) Village Band, 1997—. Mem. ABA (assoc.), Raleigh Wake Paralegal Assn. (past v.p., past sec.), N.C. Paralegal Assn., Nat. Assn. Legal Assts. Democrat. Methodist. Home: 3 Kandes Ct Durham NC 27713-9722 Office: Moore & Van Allen PLLC PO Box 26507 Raleigh NC 27611-6507

**KAUFMAN, STEPHEN HERSCU,** lawyer, engineer; b. Bucharest, Romania, Aug. 14, 1945; s. Herscu and Roza Kaufman; m. Aurelia Kaufman, Feb. 14, 1992. BS, Columbia U., 1969, MS, 1974; JD, Fordham U., 1982. Bar: N.Y. 1983, U.S. Dist. Ct. (ea. and so. dists.) N.Y. 1983, U.S. Supreme Ct.; registered profl. engr., N.Y. Civil engr. Dept. Transp., N.Y.C., 1976-84; pvt. practice N.Y.C., 1984—. Mem. Assn. of Bar of City of N.Y. (constrn. law com. 1996-98), N.Y. State Bar Assn. (alt. dispute resolution com. 1998), Columbia Club (assoc.). Jewish. Avocations: investments, table tennis. Construction, Real property, Government contracts and claims. Office: 39 Broadway Rm 2301 New York NY 10006-3003

**KAUFMAN, STEVEN MICHAEL,** lawyer; b. Spokane, Wash., July 2, 1951; s. Gordon Leonard and Terri (Thal) K.; m. Connie Hoopes, June 7, 1973; children: Kristopher, Shana. BS magna cum laude, U. Utah, 1973; JD cum laude, Gonzaga U., 1977. Bar: Utah 1977, U.S. Dist. Ct. Utah, 1977, U.S. Ct. Appeals (10th cir.) 1977, U.S. Supreme Ct. 1985. Founding ptnr. Farr, Kaufman, and Hamilton, 1979-89; mng. ptnr. Farr, Kaufman, Sullivan, Gorman, Jensen, Medsker, Nichols & Perkins, 1989—; judge pro tem, 1981-98, bar commr., 1991-98. Chmn. Commn. on Pub. Defenders, Ogden, 1984. Mem. ATLA, ABA, Utah Bar Assn. (pres.-elect, 1995-96, pres., 1996-97, bar commr. 1992-98, rep. Utah Jud. Coun. 1998-99), Weber County Bar Assn. (pres. 1981-82), Rex E. Lee Inn of Ct. (master). Jewish. Personal injury, Family and matrimonial, Criminal. Home: 5878 S 1050 E Ogden UT 84405-4959 Office: Farr Kaufman Sullivan Gorman Jensen Medsker Nichols & Perkins 205 26th St Ste 34 Ogden UT 84401-3119

**KAUFMAN, THOMAS FREDERICK,** lawyer, legal educator; b. Buffalo, Sept. 10, 1949; s. Frederick J. and Edna M. (Kilian) K.; children: Alycia, Thomas, Jonathan. BSEE, SUNY, Buffalo, 1971; JD, Georgetown U., 1976. Bar: Va. 1976, U.S. Ct. Appeals (6th cir.) 1976, D.C. 1977, U.S. Dist. Ct. D.C. 1981. Law clk. to chief judge U.S. Ct. Appeals (6th cir.), 1976-77; assoc. Melrod, Redman & Gartlan, Washington, 1977-81; assoc. Willkie Farr & Gallagher, Washington, 1981-84, ptnr., 1985-95; ptnr. Hunton & Williams, Washington, 1995—; adj. prof. law Georgetown U., Washington, 1986—. Mem. Am. Coll. Real Estate Lawyers. Real property, Banking. Office: Hunton and Williams 1900 K St NW Washington DC 20006-1110

**KAUFMAN, WILLIAM GEORGE,** lawyer; b. Nappanee, Ind., June 4, 1949; s. Joseph Edwin and Phyllis (Reeder) K. BS in History, Ind. State U., 1972; JD, Emory U., 1976. Bar: Colo., U.S. Dist. Ct. Colo. 1976. Assoc. Law Offices F. Ray DeGood, Loveland, Colo., 1976-82; prin. Law Office William G. Kaufman, Loveland, 1982-87, William G. Kaufman, P.C., Loveland, 1987--. County mgr. Rep. Bill Armstrong for U.S. Senate, 1978; county chmn. Larimer County Colo. Rep. Com., 1979, 81, 92; chmn. Econ. Devel. Com., 1987; campaign mgr. Hank Brown for Congress, 1988; exec. bd. Long Peak coun. Boy Scouts Am., 1980-86, bd. trustees, 1986—; bd. dirs. Ft. Collins-Loveland Airport Authority, 1985-91; mem. Colo. Ho. of Reps., 1992—. Recipient Eagle Scout Silver Beaver award Boy Scouts Am. Memn. ABA, Colo. Bar Assn., Larimer County Bar Assn., Rotary. Methodist. Avocations: snow skiing, golf, reading. Health, Real property, Probate. Office: 200 E 7th St Ste 318 Loveland CO 80537-4870

**KAUGER, YVONNE,** state supreme court chief justice; b. Cordell, Okla., Aug. 3, 1937; d. John and Alice (Bottom) K.; m. Ned Bastow, May 8, 1982; 1 child, Jonna Kauger Kirschner. BS magna cum laude, Southwestern State U., Weatherford, Okla., 1958; cert. med. technologist, St. Anthony's Hosp., 1959; J.D., Oklahoma City U., 1969, LLD (hon.), 1992. Med. technologist Med. Arts Lab., 1959-68; assoc. Rogers, Travis & Jordan, 1970-72; jud. asst. Okla. Supreme Ct., Oklahoma City, 1972-84, justice, 1984-94; vice chief justice Okla. Supreme Ct., 1994-96, Chief Justice, 1997—; mem. appellate div. Ct. on Judiciary; mem. State Capitol Preservation Commn., 1983-84; mem. dean's adv. com. Oklahoma City U. Sch. Law; lectr. William O. Douglas Lecture Series Gonzaga U., 1990. Founder Gallery of Plains Indian, Colony, Okla., Red Earth (Down Towner award 1990), 1987; active Jud. Day, Girl's State, 1976-80; keynote speaker Girl's State Hall of Fame Banquet, 1984; bd. dirs. Lyric Theatre, Inc., 1966—, pres. bd. dirs., 1981; past mem. bd. dirs. Civic Music Soc., Okla. Theatre Ctr., Canterbury Choral Soc.; mem. First Lady of Okla.'s Artisans' Alliance Com. Named Panhellenic Woman of Yr., 1990, Woman of Yr. Red Lands Coun. Girl Scouts, 1990, Washita County Hall of Fame, 1992. Mem. ABA (law sch. accreditation com.), Okla. Bar Assn. (law schs. com. 1977—), Washita County Bar Assn., Washita County Hist. Soc. (life), St. Paul's Music Soc., Iota Tau Tau, Delta Zeta (Disting. Alumna award 1988, State Delta Zeta of Yr. 1987, Nat. Woman of Yr. 1988). Episcopalian.

**KAUTTER, DAVID JOHN,** lawyer; b. Wilkes-Barre, Pa., Mar. 20, 1948; s. William George and Mary (Flanagan) K.; m. Kathy Jane Price, May 22, 1976; children: Hilary, David Jr. BBA, Notre Dame U., 1971; JD, Georgetown U., 1974. Bar: D.C. 1975, U.S. Dist. Ct. D.C. 1981, U.S. Tax Ct. 1981, U.S. Supreme Ct. 1981. Staff acct. Coopers & Lybrand, Washington, 1971-74; mgr. Arthur Young and Co., Washington, 1974-78; legis. asst. Senator John Danforth, Washington, 1979-82; ptnr. Arthur Young and Co., Washington, 1982-89, dir. Wash. Nat. Tax Group, 1986-89; nat. dir. compensation and benefits tax svcs. Ernst & Young, Washington, 1989-98, mem. ptnrs. adv. coun., 1993-96, nat. dir. human resource svcs., 1998—. Contbr. articles to profl. jours. Mem. ABA, Fed. Bar Assn., AICPA's. Republican. Roman Catholic. Avocation: cabinet making. Pension, profit-sharing, and employee benefits, Personal income taxation, Legislative. Home: 8312 Summerwood Dr Mc Lean VA 22102-2212 Office: Ernst & Young 1225 Connecticut Ave NW Ste 700 Washington DC 20036-2621

**KAUTZMAN, JOHN FREDRICK,** lawyer; b. Indpls., Aug. 23, 1959; s. Fred L. and Barbara J. (Seeger) K. BA, Ind. U., 1981; JD, Ind. U., Indpls., 1984. Bar: Ind. 1985, U.S. Dist. Ct. (no. and so. dists.) Ind. 1985, U.S. Ct. Appeals (7th cir.) 1992. Law clk. Marion County Pros. Office, Indpls., 1981; bailiff Marion County Cir. Ct., Indpls., 1981-84, commr., judge pro tempore, 1985-89; assoc. Ruckelshaus, Roland, Hasbrook & O'Conner, Indpls., 1985-89, ptnr., 1990-98; ptnr. Ruckelshaus, Roland, Kautzman & Hasbrook, Indpls., 1998—; mem. faculty Ind. Trial Advocacy Coll., 1998—. Contbg. author The Indiana Lawyer newspaper, 1991—. Mem. bd. assocs. Ind. U. Found., Bloomington, 1993—, v.p. 1997—; precinct committeeman Marion County Rep. Party, Indpls., 1994-96. Mem. ABA, Indpls. Bar Assn. (v.p. 1998, bd. mgrs. 1994-96, young lawyers divsn. chmn. 1988-89, Disting. fellow 1993), Ind. State Bar Assn., Phi Delta Phi. Methodist. Avocations: professional piano, golf. General civil litigation, Criminal, General practice. Office: Ruckelshaus Roland Kautzman & Hasbrook Ste 900 107 N Pennsylvania St Indianapolis IN 46204-2424

**KAVANAUGH, JAMES FRANCIS, JR.,** lawyer; b. New Bedford, Mass., Feb. 20, 1949; s. James Francis and Catherine Mary (Loughlin) K.; m. Cynthia Louise Ward, July 4, 1968; 1 child, James F. III. BA, Coll. of the Holy Cross, 1970; JD magna cum laude, Boston Coll., 1977. Bar: Mass. 1977, U.S. Dist. Ct. Mass., 1978, U.S. Ct. Appeals (1st cir.) 1978, U.S. Supreme Ct. 1990. Law clk. to assoc. justice Mass. Supreme Jud. Ct., Boston, 1977-78; assoc. Burns & Levinson, Boston, 1978-82, ptnr., 1983-88; ptnr. Conn, Kavanaugh, Rosenthal, Peisch & Ford, Boston, 1988—. Editor, contbr. Boston Coll. Law Rev., 1975-77. Mem. ABA, Mass. Bar Assn., Boston Bar Assn. Democrat. Roman Catholic. Clubs: Winchester Country, New Bedford Country. Avocations: golf, skiing, reading fiction and history. Federal civil litigation, State civil litigation, General civil litigation. Office: Conn Kavanaugh Rosenthal Peisch & Ford Ten Post Office Sq Boston MA 02109

**KAVOUKJIAN, MICHAEL EDWARD,** lawyer; b. Mpls., Apr. 19, 1958; s. Antranik M. and Leikny Dorthea (Oines) K.;. AB with distinction, Stanford U., 1980; JD cum laude, Harvard U., 1984. Bar: Minn. 1984, N.Y. 1986, U.S. Dist. Ct. Minn. 1985, U.S. Dist. Ct. (so. dist.) N.Y. 1988, Fla. 1999. From assoc. to ptnr. White & Case, N.Y.C. and Miami, Fla., 1985—. Mem. ABA (chmn. com. estate planning and drafting 1992-94), Minn. State Bar Assn., The Fla. Bar, Assn. of the Bar City of N.Y., Soc. Trust and Estate Practitioners, Harvard Club (N.Y.C., Washington), Nat. Press Club (Washington), Lincoln's Inn Soc. Harvard Law Sch. (bd. gov. 1982-84). Republican. Presbyterian. Estate planning, Probate, Estate taxation. Office: White & Case 1155 Avenue Of The Americas New York NY 10036-2787

**KAVOWRAS, MONA,** lawyer; b. N.Y.C., Apr. 29, 1940; d. Hyman and Mollie Shames; m. Theodore Kavowras, Jan. 25, 1960; children: Kenneth, Theodore Jr. BA, CCNY, 1984; JD, Yeshiva U., 1987. Bar: N.J. 1990, N.Y. 1991, D.C. 1993, U.S. Dist. Ct. N.J. 1990, U.S. Dist. Ct. (all dists.) N.Y. 1991. Asst. dist. atty. Bklyn. Dist. Attys. Office, 1987; atty. pvt. practice, Bklyn., 1991—. Mem. N.Y. State Assn. Criminal Def. Attys., Kings County Criminal Bar Assn., Bklyn. Bar Assn., Phi Beta Kappa. Criminal. Office: 16 Court St Brooklyn NY 11241-0102

**KAWACHIKA, JAMES AKIO,** lawyer; b. Honolulu, Dec. 5, 1947; s. Shinichi and Tsuyuko (Murashige) K.; m. Karen Keiko Takahashi, Sept. 1, 1973; 1 child, Robyn Mari. BA, U. Hawaii, Honolulu, 1969; JD, U. Calif., Berkeley, 1973. Bar: Hawaii 1973, U.S. Dist. Ct. Hawaii 1973, U.S. Ct. Appeals (9th cir.) 1974, U.S. Supreme Ct. 1992. Dep. atty. gen. Office of Atty. Gen. State of Hawaii, Honolulu, 1973-74; assoc. Padgett, Greeley & Marumoto, Honolulu, 1974-75, Law Office of Frank D. Padgett, Honolulu, 1975-77, Kobayashi, Watanabe, Sugita & Kawashima, Honolulu, 1977-82; ptnr. Carlsmith, Wichman, Case, Mukai & Ichiki, Honolulu, 1982-86, Bays, Deaver, Hiatt, Kawachika & Lezak, Honolulu, 1986-95; propr. Law Offices of James A. Kawachika, Honolulu, 1996-98; ptnr. Kawachika & Ozaki, Honolulu, 1999—; mem. Hawaii Bd. of Bar Examiners, Honolulu; arbitrator Cir. Ct. Arbitration Program State of Hawaii, Honolulu, 1986—. Chmn. Disciplinary Bd. Hawaii Supreme Ct., 1991-97; mem. U.S. dist. Ct. Adv. Com. on the Civil Justice Reform Act of 1990, 1991—. Mem. ABA, ATLA, Hawaii Bar Assn. (bd. dirs. Honolulu chpt. 1975-76, young lawyers sect. 1983-84, 92-93, treas. 1987-88, v.p./pres.-elect 1997-98, pres. 1998-99), 9th Cir. Jud. Conf. (lawyer rep. Honolulu chpt. 1988-90). Avocations: running, tennis, skiing. General civil litigation, Personal injury, Insurance. Office: Grosvenor Ctr Mauka Tower 737 Bishop St Ste 2750 Honolulu HI 96813-3216

**KAWITT, ALAN,** lawyer; b. Chgo., 1937. J.D., Chgo.-Kent Coll. Law, 1965; postgrad. Lawyers Inst. John Marshall Law Sch., 1966-68. Bar: Ill. 1966, U.S. Dist. Ct. (no. dist.) Ill. 1967, U.S. Ct. Appeals (7th cir.) 1971, U.S. Supreme Ct., 1971. Sole practice, 1970—. Mem. Am. Arbitration Assn. (arbitrator). Fax: (773) 472-3556. Consumer commercial, Landlord-tenant, Insurance. Office: 226 S Wabash Ave Ste 905 Chicago IL 60604-2319

**KAY, ALAN COOKE,** federal judge; b. 1932; s. Harold Thomas and Ann (Cooke) K. BA, Princeton U., 1957; LLB, U. Calif., Berkeley, 1960. Assoc. Case, Kay & Lynch, Honolulu, 1960-64, ptnr., 1965-86; judge U.S. Dist. Ct. Hawaii, Honolulu, 1986-92, chief judge, 1992—; bd. regents Internat. Coll. and Grad. Sch., 1994—. Mem. steering com. Fuller Theol. Sem. Hawaii, 1985-86; pres., trustee Hawaii Mission Children's Soc., Honolulu, 1980-86; bd. dirs. Good News Mission, 1980-86, Econ. Devel. Corp. Honolulu, 1985-86, Legal Aid Soc., Honolulu, 1968-71. Mem. ABA, Hawaii Bar Assn. (exec. com. 1972-73, bd. dirs. real estate sect. 1983-86), Fed. Judges Assn. (9th cir. jud. coun. 1994—, 9th cir. Pacific Islands com. 1994—), Am. Inns of Ct. (counselor Aloha Inn 1987—). Republican. Office: US Dist Ct C-415 Kuhio Federal Bldg 300 Ala Moana Blvd Rm C304 Honolulu HI 96850-4971

**KAY, HERMA HILL,** dean; b. Orangeburg, S.C., Aug. 18, 1934; d. Charles Esdorn and Herma Lee (Crawford) Hill. BA, So. Meth. U., 1956; JD, U. Chgo., 1959. Bar: Calif. 1960, U.S. Supreme Ct. 1978. Law clk. Justice Roger Traynor, Calif. Supreme Ct., 1959-60; asst. prof. law U. Calif., Berkeley, 1960-62; assoc. prof. U. Calif., 1962, prof., 1963, dir. family law project, 1964-67, Jennings prof., 1987-96, dean, 1992—, Armstrong prof., 1996—; co-reporter uniform marriage and div. act Nat. Conf. Commrs. on Uniform State Laws, 1968-70; vis. prof. U. Manchester, Eng., 1972, Harvard U., 1976; mem. Gov.'s Commn. on Family, 1966. Author: (with Martha S. West) Text Cases and Materials on Sex-based Discrimination, 4th edit., 1996, (with R. Cramton, D. Currie and L. Kramer) Conflict of Laws: Cases, Comments, Questions, 5th edit., 1993; contbr. articles to profl. jours. Trustee Russell Sage Found., N.Y., 1972-87, chmn. bd., 1980-84; trustee, bd. dirs. Equal Rights Advs. Calif., 1976—, chmn., 1976-83; pres. bd. dirs. Rosenberg Found., Calif., 1987-88, bd. dirs. 1978—. Recipient rsch. award Am. Bar Found., 1990, Margaret Brent award ABA Commn. Women in Profession, 1992, Marshall-Wythe medal, 1995; fellow Ctr. Advanced Study in Behavioral Sci., Palo Alto, Calif., 1963. Mem. Calif. Bar Assn., Bar U.S. Supreme Ct., Calif. Women Lawyers (bd. govs. 1975-77), Am. Law Inst. (mem. coun. 1985-), Assn. Am. Law Schs. (exec. com. 1986-87, pres.-elect 1988, pres. 1989, past pres. 1990), Am. Acad. Arts and Scis., Order of Coif (nat. pres. 1983-85). Democrat. Office: U Calif Law Sch Boalt Hall Berkeley CA 94720-7200

**KAY, RICHARD BROUGHTON,** lawyer; b. Cleve., Apr. 7, 1918; s. Joseph Stanley and Frances Anna (Broughton) K.; m. Ellen Fletcher, June 6, 1992. BBA, Miami U. of Ohio, 1939; LLB, Case Western Res. U., 1948. Bar: Ohio, Fla., U.S. Supreme Ct. Pvt. practice Tequesta, Fla. Field organizer Eisenhower for Pres., N.Y.C., 1952; exec. sec. Stassen for Pres., Cleve., 1948; nat. v.p. Wilkie Young Voters, N.Y.C., 1940. Lt. USNR, 1941-61. Mem. Ohio Bar Assn., Fla. Bar Assn., Palm Beach County Bar Assn., North Palm Beach County Bar Assn. (pres. 1988), Attys. Bar of Palm Beach County (pres. 1997-98), Elks, VFW, Am. Legion. Avocation: travel. Home: 19800 Us Highway 1 Apt 506 Tequesta FL 33469-2357 Office: 222 US Hwy # 208 Tequesta FL 33469

**KAYA, RANDALL Y.,** lawyer; b. Honolulu, June 3, 1958; s. Frederick K. and Jane H. Kaya; m. Sara Dawn Smith, Feb. 5, 1994; children: Zachary K., Jourdan M. BA in Polit. Sci., U. Hawaii, 1982; JD, William Richardson Sch. Law, 1985. Bar: Hawaii 1985, U.S. Dist. Ct. Hawaii 1985. Assoc. Ing & Lebb, Honolulu, 1986-90, Perkin & Shimizu, Honolulu, 1990-91, Yempuku & Kugisaki, Honolulu, 1992-95, Craig L. Kugisaki, Honolulu, 1995—. Mem. Am. Inn of Ct. Episcopalian. Avocations: golf, basketball, softball. Insurance, Personal injury, Product liability. Office: Law Office Craig T Kugisaki 1001 Bishop St Honolulu HI 96813-3429

**KAYE, BRUCE JEFFREY,** lawyer; b. Tucson, Ariz., June 11, 1949; s. Edward Arthur and Charllotte K.; children from previous marriage: Tracy Lee, Ellen Courtney; m. Lisa Kutner, May 18, 1996. BA, U. Denver, 1971, JD, 1974. Bar: Colo. 1974, U.S. Dist. Ct. Colo. 1974, U.S. Ct. Appeals (10th cir.) 1990, U.S. Dist. Ct. Ariz. 1997, U.S. Dist. Ct. Nebr. 1997. Dep. dist. atty. Boulder County Dist. Atty., Boulder, Colo., 1974-76; ptnr. Reams & Kaye, Grand Junction, Colo., 1977-85, Kaye & Alvillar, Grand Junction, 1985-86, Leventhal & Bogue PC, Denver, 1986-97, The Leventhal Law Firm PC, Denver, 1998; sole practice law Denver, 1998—. Bd. dirs. Amigos de las Americas, Denver, 1996-98; pres. bd. dirs. Mesa County Ptnrs., 1984-85. Mem. ATLA, Colo. Trial Lawyers Assn., Colo. Bar Assn., Denver Bar Assn., Mesa County Bar Assn. Avocations: fly fishing, reading, hiking. Personal injury, Insurance, Product liability. Office: 1775 Sherman St Ste 2000 Denver CO 80203-4319

**KAYE, JUDITH SMITH,** state supreme court chief justice; b. Monticello, N.Y., Aug. 4, 1938; d. Benjamin and Lena (Cohen) Smith; m. Stephen Rackow Kaye, Feb. 11, 1964; children: Luisa Marian, Jonathan Mackey, Gordon Bernard. BA, Barnard Coll., 1958; LLB cum laude, NYU, 1962; LLD (hon.), St. Lawrence U., 1985, Union U., 1985, Pace U., 1985, Syracuse U., 1988, L.I. U., 1989. Assoc. Sullivan & Cromwell, N.Y.C., 1962-64; staff atty. IBM, Armonk, N.Y., 1964-65; asst. to dean Sch. Law NYU, 1965-68; ptnr. Connelly Chase O'Donnell & Weyher, N.Y.C., 1969-83; judge N.Y. State Ct. Appeals, N.Y.C., 1983-93, chief judge, 1993—; bd. dir. Sterling Nat. Bank. Contbr. articles to profl. jours. Former bd. dirs. Legal Aid Soc. Recipient Vanderbilt medal NYU Sch. of Law, 1983, Medal of Distinction, Barnard Coll, 1987. Fellow Am. Bar Found.; mem. Am. Law Inst., Am. Coll. Trial Lawyers, Am. Judicature Soc. (bd. dirs. 1980-83). Democrat. Office: NY Court of Appeals Court of Appeals Hall 20 Eagle St Albany NY 12207-1009 Office: NY Court of Appeals 230 Park Ave Rm 826 New York NY 10169-0899*

**KAYE, MARC MENDELL,** lawyer; b. Irvington, N.J., Nov. 25, 1959; s. Aaron Morton and Sandra (Hoch) K. AA, BA, Rutgers U., 1980; JD, U. Toledo, 1983. Bar: N.J. 1984, Fla. 1987, D.C. 1991, N.Y. 1998, U.S. Dist. Ct. N.J. 1984, U.S. Supreme Ct. 1992; cert. civil trial atty. 1991. Trial atty. Shevick, Ravich, Koster et al, Rahway, N.J., 1984-85, Greenberg, Margolis et al, Roseland, N.J., 1985-86, Brian Granstrand, Fairfield, N.J., 1986-90; pvt. practice Livingston, N.J., 1986-94, Short Hills, 1994—; counsel CNA Ins. Co., Fairfield, 1986-90; apptd. arbitrator Union County Arbitrator Program, 1993, Essex County Arbitrator and Mediator Programs, 1995, Millburn Citizen Budget Com., 1998—; adv. coun. mem. Chmn.'s Club Summit Bank, 1989-91. Mem. exec. com. Young Leadership div. United Jewish Appeal, Metrowest, N.J, 1988-91; bd. dirs. Jewish Cmty. Ctr. of MetroWest, 1998—, Opera Music Theatre Internat., 1999—. Mem. N.J. Bar Assn., Essex County Bar Assn. (subcom. chmn. legal med. com. 1992-94), Union County Bar Assn., Fla. Bar Assn., D.C. Bar Assn., Assn. Trial Lawyers Am., N.J. Trial Lawyers Assn., Lions Club (v.p. 1993-95), Prime Ministers Club, Israel Bonds. Avocations: golf, swimming, scuba diving, travel. Personal injury, Insurance, General civil litigation. Office: One N Brook Dr at S Orange Ave Short Hills NJ 07078-3126

**KAYE, STUART MARTIN,** lawyer; b. Bronx, N.Y., Dec. 2, 1946; s. Jules Krupnikoff and Gussie (Lipchinsky) Kaye; m. Christine Marie Heitkam, Sept. 25, 1970 (div. 1983); m. Eve C. Farkas, Apr. 2, 1988 (div. 1991); children: Joshua Brandon, Jeremy Jason, Kimberly I. Morlan. AA, Glendale Community Coll., 1971; BS in Polit. Sci., Ariz. State U., 1974; JD, Western State U., 1978. Bar: Calif. 1980, U.S. Dist. Ct. (no. dist.) Calif. 1980, (so. dist.) Calif. 1985, (cen. dist.) Calif. 1987. Assoc. mgmt. analyst State of Calif., Sacramento, 1978-84, legal counsel, 1984-85; indsl. relations counsel State of Calif., San Diego, 1985-92; legal asst. Ariz. Atty. Gen., Phoenix, 1992-93; indsl. rels. coun. State of Calif., Santa Ana, 1993—; pvt. practice, Shigle Springs, 1981-84. With U.S. Army, 1964-68. Democrat. Jewish. Avocation: camping. Office: State Calif Div Labor Standards 28 Civic Center Plz Ste 641 Santa Ana CA 92701-4035

**KAYLOR, CYNTHIA ANNE,** lawyer; b. Hershey, Pa., Dec. 22, 1950; d. James Nelson and Clementine (Beam) Bibber. AA, Harrisburg (Pa.) Community Coll., 1980; BS, Elizabethtown (Pa.) Coll., 1983; JD, Dickinson U., Carlisle, Pa., 1989. Bar: Pa. 1989. Hwy. maintenance specialist Pa. Dept. Transp., Harrisburg, 1971-86; assoc. Hepford, Swartz & Morgan, Harrisburg, 1989-91; sole practitioner Harrisburg, 1991; assoc., ptnr. Archie V. Diveglia, P.C., Harrisburg, 1991—. Mem. Pa. Trial Lawyers Assn. Family and matrimonial, Personal injury, General civil litigation. Home: 104 James Ln Mechanicsburg PA 17055-6033 Office: Archie V Diveglia PC 119 Locust St Harrisburg PA 17101-1411

**KAYLOR, GAY L.,** paralegal, food company administrator; b. Cin., Sept. 6, 1961; d. Kenneth E. and Esther M. Umberger; m. Keith E. Kaylor, Oct. 27, 1984; children: Megan, Mark. Paralegal, Harrisburg (Pa.) Area C.C., 1995. Stockholder rels. adminstr. Hershey Foods Corp., Hershey, Pa., 1992-95, assoc. stockholder rels. rep., 1995-97, stockholder rels. rep., 1998—; mem. client adv. bd. ChaseMellon Shareholder Svcs., N.Y.C., 1998—. Mem. Pa. Assn. Notaries, Ctrl. Pa. Corp. Rels. Soc. Republican. Office: Hershey Foods Corp 100 Crystal A Dr Hershey PA 17033-9702

**KAYSER, KENNETH WAYNE,** lawyer; b. N.Y.C., Apr. 28, 1947; s. William Gilbert and Joan Phyliss (Bach) K.; m. Linda Calcote, Apr. 13, 1968; 1 child, Christopher R. BA, Syracuse U., 1969; JD, Seton Hall, 1977. Bar: N.J. 1977, U.S. Dist. Ct. N.J. 1977, U.S. Cir. Ct. (3d cir.) 1988, U.S. Ct. Internat. Trade 1990. Asst. prosecutor Essex County Prosecutor's Office, Newark, 1978-82; assoc. Brach, Eichler, Rosenberg, Silver, Bernstein & Hammer, Roseland, N.J., 1982-83; sole practice West Orange, N.J., 1983-84, Roseland, 1984—. Mem. ABA, N.J. State Bar Assn., Essex County Bar Assn., Assn. Criminal Def. Lawyers N.J. Democrat. Criminal, General civil litigation, Real property. Office: 120 Eagle Rock Ave East Hanover NJ 07936-3105

**KAZANJIAN, JOHN HAROLD,** lawyer; b. Newport, R.I., Jan. 25, 1949; s. Powel Harold and Louise T. (Alexander) K.; m. Jane Mitchell Kohlmeyer, Sept. 26, 1981; 1 child, Sara Jane. BA, Providence Coll., 1971; JD, Notre Dame U., 1975. Bar: N.Y. 1976, U.S. Dist. Ct. (so. dist.) N.Y. 1976, U.S. Dist. Ct. (ea. dist.) N.Y. 1977, U.S. Supreme Ct. 1980, U.S. Ct. Appeals (2d crct.) 1986, U.S. Ct. Appeals (fed. crct.) 1991. Assoc. Cadwalader, Wickersham & Taft, N.Y.C., 1975-86; ptnr. Anderson, Kill & Olick, N.Y.C., 1986-98, Beveridge & Diamond, N.Y.C., 1999—. Mem. U.S. Naval War Coll. Found., Newport, 1985—. Mem. ABA (sects. on litigation, tort and ins. practice and internat. law), Assn. Bar City N.Y. (chair com. on product liability), N.Y. County Lawyers Assn. (chair com. on ins. law, tort law sect.), Metro. Club. Episcopalian. Avocations: caricatures, cartoons, long distance running. Federal civil litigation, Product liability, Insurance. Office: Beveridge & Diamond 15th Fl 477 Madison Ave New York NY 10022-5802

**KAZANJIAN, PHILLIP CARL,** lawyer, business executive; b. Visalia, Calif., May 15, 1945; s. John Casey and Sat-ten Arlene K.; m. Wendy Coffelt, Feb. 5, 1972; 1 child, John. B.A. with honors, U. So. Calif., 1967; J.D. with honors, Lincoln U., San Francisco, 1973. Bar: Calif. 1979, U.S. Dist. Ct. (cen. dist.) Calif. 1980, U.S. Tax Ct. 1980, U.S. Ct. Appeals (9th cir.) 1980, U.S. Mil. Ct. Appeals 1980, U.S. Supreme Ct. 1983. Ptnr. Brakefield & Kazanjian, Glendale, Calif., 1981-87; sr. ptnr., Kazanjian & Martinetti, 1987—; judge pro tem L.A. County Superior Ct., 1993—; instr. U.S. Naval Acad., Annapolis, Md., 1981; adj. prof. Glendale Cmty. Coll., 1997—. Mem. Calif. Atty. Gen.'s Adv. Commn. on Community-Police Relations, 1973; bd. dirs. L.A. County Naval Meml. Found., Inc., 1981-85; pres. bd. trustees Glendale Community Coll. Dist., 1981-97, L.A. World Affairs Council, Town Hall Calif., Republican Assocs. (dir.), Rep. Lincoln Club; bd. govs. Calif. Maritime Acad., 1986-94. Served to capt. USNR, 1969—. Decorated Navy Commendation medal, Navy Achievement medal, knight Order of Knights Templar, 1990; recipient Patrick Henry medal Am. Legion, 1963, Congressional Record tribute U.S. Ho. of Reps., 1974, Centurion award Chief of Naval Ops., 1978, award Res. Officers Assn. U.S., 1981, commendatory resolutions Mayor of L.A., L.A. City Council, L.A. County Bd. Suprs., Calif. State Assembly and Senate, and Govt. of Calif., 1982, Justice award Calif. Law Student Assn., 1973. Mem. ABA (Gold Key 1972), Calif. Bar Assn., Los Angeles County Bar Assn., Am. Judicature Soc., Assn. Trial Lawyers Am., Glendale C. of C. (bd. dirs., Patriot Yr. 1986), Res. Officers Assn. (nat. judg adv.), Naval Res. Assn. (nat. adv. com.), U.S. Naval Inst., Interallied Confedn. Res. Officers (internat. chmn. 1987-94), Explorers Club. Republican. Episcopalian. Club: Commonwealth of Calif. Author: The Circuit Governor, 1972; editor in chief Lincoln Law Rev., 1973. State civil litigation, Personal injury. Office: Kazanjian & Martinetti 520 E Wilson Ave Ste 250 Glendale CA 91206-4346

**KAZEN, GEORGE PHILIP,** federal judge; b. Laredo, Tex., Feb. 29, 1940; s. Emil James and Drusilla M. (Perkins) K.; m. Barbara Ann Sanders, Oct. 27, 1962; children: George Douglas, John Andrew, Elizabeth Ann, Gregory Stephen. BBA, U. Tex., 1960, JD with honors, 1961. Bar: Tex. 1961, U.S. Supreme Ct., U.S. Ct. Claims, U.S. Ct. Appeals (5th cir.), U.S. Dist. Ct. (so. dist.) Tex. Briefing atty. Tex. Sup. Ct., 1961-62; founder, first pres. Laredo Legal Aid Soc., 1966-69; assoc. Mann, Freed, Kazen & Hansen, 1965-79; judge U.S. Dist. Ct. (so. dist.) Tex., Laredo, 1979-96; founder, first pres. Laredo Legal Aid Soc., 1966-69; chief judge U.S. Dist. Ct. (so. dist.) Tex., Laredo, 1996—; mem. Jud. Conf. Com. Criminal Law, 1990-96, chair com., 1996-99; mem. 5th Cir. Jud. Coun., 1991-94, 96—; adj. prof. law St. Mary's U. Sch. Law, 1990—. Pres. Laredo Civic Music Assn.; chmn. St. Augustine-Ursuline Consol. Sch. Bd.; bd. dirs. Boys' Clubs Laredo; trustee Laredo Jr. Coll., 1972-79; bd. dirs., v.p., pres. Econ. Opportunities Devel. Corp., 1968-70; past bd. dirs. D.D. Hachar Found. With USAF, 1962-65. Decorated Air Force Commendation medal; named Outstanding Young Lawyer, Larado Jaycees, 1970. Mem. ABA, Tex. Bar Found., Tex. Bar Assn., Tex. Criminal Def. Lawyers Assn., Tex. Assn. Bank Counsel, Tex. Assn. Def. Counsel, Laredo C. of C. (bd. dirs. 1975-76), 5th Cir. Dist. Judges Assn. (v.p. 1984-85, pres. 1986-88), U. Tex. Law Sch. Alumni Assn. (bd. dirs. 1976-77). Roman Catholic. Office: US Dist Ct PO Box 1060 Laredo TX 78042-1060

**KEADY, GEORGE CREGAN, JR.,** judge; b. Bklyn., June 16, 1924; s. George Cregan and Marie (Lussier) K.; m. Patricia Drake, Sept. 2, 1950; children: Margaret Keady Goldberg, Marie E., George Cregan, Catherine A. Keady Dunn, Kathleen V. Student, U. Kans., 1943-44; B.S., Fordham U., 1949; J.D., Columbia U., 1950; LL.D., Western New Eng. Coll., 1973. Bar: Mass. 1950. Since practiced in Springfield, Mass.; asso. firm Ganley & Crook, 1950-53; assoc. firm Peter D. Wilson, 1953-57; partner firm Wilson, Keady & Ratner, 1958-79; justice Dist. Ct., Springfield, 1979-82; assoc. justice Superior Ct., Springfield, 1982-93; ret., 1993, freelance mediator and arbitrator, 1993—; dean Western New Eng. Coll. Law Sch., 1970-73; dir. Western Mass. Bar Rev., 1956-63, Western New Eng. Coll. Bar Rev., 1965-72; chmn. Mass. Continuing Legal Edn., Inc., 1977-80; mem. Mass. Commn. on Jud. Conduct, 1988, chmn., 1990-93. Active United Fund, Springfield, 1950-72, Joint Civic Agys.; chmn. fund drive Am. Cancer Soc., 1962, selectman, Longmeadow, Mass., 1958-68, chmn. selectmen, 1960-61, 63-64, 66-68, moderator, 1968-73; vice chmn. Rep. Town Com., Longmeadow, 1956-60; alt. del. Rep. Nat. Conv., 1960, del., 1964; pres. Hampden Dist. Mental Health Clinic, Inc., 1968-71, Child Guidance Clinic, Springfield, 1962-64; corporator, trustee, chmn. bd. Baystate Med. Center, 1985-87, trustee, 1984-92, 94—; chmn. bd. Baystate Health System, 1987-90; trustee Western New Eng. Coll., 1978-84, Baypath Jr. Coll., 1972-87, Baystate Health Systems, 1993-98; dir. BHIC, 1993—. Served with AUS, 1943-46. Decorated Bronze star. Mem. Am. Law Inst., Mass. Bar Assn., Hampden County Bar Assn. (exec. com. 1960-79, pres. 1965-67), Supreme Ct. Hist. Soc., Longmeadow Country Club, Phi Delta Phi. Roman Catholic. Home: 16 Meadowbrook Rd Longmeadow MA 01106-1341

**KEAN, JAMES CAMPBELL,** lawyer; b. Colorado Spring, Colo., July 7, 1956; s. James Edward and Maxine Edna (Wolfe) K.; m. Suzanne Lee Bereswill; children: Kathryn Ashley, Jennifer Campbell. BS, U. Tex., Austin, 1978; JD, U. Houston, 1981, LLM in Environ., Energy & Natural Resources Law, 1996. Bar: Tex. 1981, U.S. Ct. Appeals (5th cir.) 1981, U.S. Dist. Ct. (so. dist.) Tex. 1982, U.S. Dist. Ct. (we. dist.) Tex. 1984, U.S. Dist. Ct. (no. dist.) Tex. 1986, U.S. Supreme Ct. 1987; cert. civil trial law. Assoc. Hoover, Cox & Shearer, Houston, 1981-83; ptnr. Dotson, Babcock & Scofield, Houston, 1983-89; litigation counsel Browning-Ferris Industries, Inc., Houston, 1989-93; sr. litigation counsel Browning-Ferris Industries, Inc., 1993-94, asstn. gen. counsel mgr., litigation sect., 1994-95; sr. environ. counsel Browning-Ferris Industries, Inc., Houston, 1995—; mem. faculty Trial Advocacy Inst., Houston, 1986—. Mem. ABA, Tex. Bar Assn., Fed. Bar Assn., Houston Bar Assn. (chmn. litigation sect. 1990-91). Roman Catholic. Avocations: bicycling, running, guitar. Federal civil litigation, State civil litigation, Environmental. Home: 4811 Fern St Bellaire TX 77401-5031 Office: Browning-Ferris Industries 757 N Eldridge Pky Houston TX 77079-4435

**KEAN, JOHN VAUGHAN,** retired lawyer; b. Providence, Mar. 12, 1917; s. Otho Vaughan and Mary (Duell) K. AB cum laude, Harvard U., 1938, JD, 1941. Bar: R.I. 1942. With Edwards & Angell, Providence, 1941—, ptnr., 1954-87, of counsel, 1987—. Bd. dirs., sec. The Robbins Co., Attleboro, Mass.; chmn. Downtown Providence YMCA, 1964-67; bd. dirs. Greater Providence YMCA, 1964-76. Capt. AUS, 1943-46, 50-52, brig. gen. Decorated Legion of Merit. Mem. ABA, R.I. Bar Assn., N.G. Assn., Res. Officers Assn., Assn. U.S. Army, R.I. Army N.G. (brig. gen. 1964-72), Harvard R.I. Club (pres. 1964-66), Agawam Hunt Club, Hope Club, Providence Art Club, Army and Navy Club (Washington), Sakonnet Golf Club (Little Compton, R.I.). General corporate, Probate, Taxation, general. Home: 518 W Main Rd Little Compton RI 02837-1121 Office: Edwards & Angell 2800 Bank Boston Plz Providence RI 02903-2499

**KEANE, AUSTIN WILLIAM,** lawyer; b. Worcester, Mass., Feb. 7, 1925; s. Austin J. and Catherine (O'Brien) K.; m. Marie Flynn, Oct. 6, 1951; children: Virginia, Marian, John, Catherine. BS, Holy Cross Coll., Worcester, Mass., 1947; JD, Suffolk U., Boston, 1954. Bar: Mass. 1955. Assoc. Bowditch & Dewey, Worcester, 1955—. Chmn. adv. com. Salvation Army, Worcester, 1992—; mem. Airport Commn., Worcester, 1990-96; mem. Mohegan coun. Boy Scouts Am. With USN, 1943-46. Recipient In Hoc Signo award Holy Cross Coll., 1966, St. Thomas More award Diocese of Worcester, 1970, Crusader award Holy Cross Club of Worcester, 1975. Mem. Mass. Conveyancers Assn. (chmn. practice stds. 1970-73, Richard B. Johnson award 1991). Real property. Office: Bowditch & Dewey 311 Main St Worcester MA 01608-1552

**KEANE, MICHAEL J.,** lawyer; b. Boston, Aug. 27, 1953. BA, U. Md., 1974; JD magna cum laude, Stetson U., 1978. Bar: Fla. 1978, U.S. Dist. Ct. (no. and mid. dists.) Fla. 1979, U.S. Dist. Ct. (so. dist.) Fla. 1981; bd. cert. bus. litig and civil trial lawyer, Nat. Bd. Trial Advocacy; cert. mediator, Fla. Law clk. to Hon. Ben F. Overton Fla. Supreme Ct., 1978-79; atty. Baynard, Harrell, Mascara, Ostow & Ulrich, P.A., St. Petersburg, Fla., Keane, Reese & Vesely, P.A., St. Petersburg; adj. prof. Stetson U. Editor-in-chief Stetson Law Rev., 1977-78; contbr. articles to profl. jours. Mem. ABA, The Fla. Bar (cert.), Phi Delta Phi. General civil litigation. Office: Northtrust Bank Building 100 2nd Ave S Ste 1201 Saint Petersburg FL 33701-4360

**KEANE, THOMAS J.,** lawyer; b. N.Y.C., Mar. 12, 1953; s. Raymond T. and Catherine (Mcloughlin) K.; m. Alyson M. Krohne, July 24, 1976; children: Raymond G., Kristen M., Danielle M. BA, St. Anselm Coll., Manchester, N.H., 1975; JD magna cum laude, Western New Eng. Coll., Springfield, Mass., 1980. Bar: Mass. 1980, N.Y. 1981, U.S. Dist. Ct. (so. and ea. dists.) N.Y. 1983. Claims Royal Globe Ins. Cos., White Plains, N.Y., 1975-76; staff atty. Ins. Co. N.Am., Springfield, Mass., 1980-82; assoc. Law Offices of Joseph Conklin, N.Y.C., 1982-84; in house assoc. Cigna Corp., N.Y.C., 1982-84; asst. gen. counsel Liberty Lines Cos., Yonkers, N.Y., 1984-93; atty., ptnr. Nesci, Keane, Piekarski, Keogh & Corrigan, White Plains, 1993—; v.p. Specialized Risk Mgmt. Inc., White Plains, 1993—. Mem. Mass. Jud. Internship Program, Boston, 1980; mem. Rep. Congl. Task Force, Washington, 1995-96. Mem. N.Y. State Bar Assn., Westchester County Bar Assn., Soc. Friendly Sons of St. Patrick on the County of Westchester. Avocations: history, golf. Personal injury, Insurance, General civil litigation. Home: 348 Fort Washington Ave Hawthorne NY 10532-1452 Office: Nesci Keane et al 305 Old Tarrytown Rd White Plains NY 10603-2825

**KEANE, WILLIAM TIMOTHY,** lawyer; b. Norwood, Ohio, Dec. 28, 1939; s. William Timothy and Mina I. (Dischner) K.; m. Carol A. Keane, Oct. 28, 1989. BS in Chemistry, U. Cin., 1961, completed basic med. scis., 1963, MS, 1965, DSc, 1967; JD, U. Ariz., 1972. Toxicologist Shell Oil Co., N.Y.C., 1967-69; assoc. Langerman, Begam, Phoenix, 1972-75; atty. sole practitioner Phoenix, 1975—. Contbr. articles to profl. jours. including Bull. Environ. Contamination and Toxicology, Archives of Environ. Health, Brit. Jour. Indsl. Medicine, Ins. Law Jour., Food, Drug and Cosmetic Law Jour., Am. Indsl. Hygiene Assn. Jour., The Sci. of the Total Environ., Occupational Health and Safety, Argl. Consultant, Ariz. Medicine, Proceedings of Seed Crops, Pollinators and Pesticides Seminar U. Ariz., 1983; presenter at numerous profl. confs. and meetings of indsl. hygienists, toxicologists, environmentalists, lawyers. Recipient M. Brayton Graff award, 1960, Am. Inst. Chemists award, 1961, Nat. Agrl. Aviation Assn. Outstanding svc. award, Acapulco, Mex., 1986. Mem. ABA, ATLA, N.Y. Acad. Scis., Ariz. Trial Lawyers Assn. (bd. dirs. 1976, sec. 1977, treas. 1978, v.p. 1979, pres. 1981, legis. chmn. 1982, 83, 84, 85, 86, 87, 88), Maricopa County Bar Assn., State Bar of Ariz., Am. Indsl. Hygiene Assn. (co-chmn. analytical chemistry and biochem. assay session of ann. conf. in St. Louis 1968, co-chmn. Denver, 1969, v.p. Ariz sect., 1973, 75, pres. 1976), Soc. of Toxicology, Nat. Hon. Chem. Soc., Phi Lambda Upsilon. Personal injury, Product liability, Insurance. Office: 803 N 3rd St Phoenix AZ 85004-2021

**KEAR, MARIA MARTHA RUSCITELLA,** lawyer; b. Phila., May 9, 1954; d. Ulysses Thomas and Joan Marie (Hagner) Ruscitella; m. Daniel John Kear, May 31, 1988; children: Catilin Joan, Daniel John II. BA, Elmira Coll., 1975; JD, Del. Law Sch., 1978. Bar: Pa. 1979, Md. 1985, Va. 1991. Atty. pvt. practice, Wayne, Pa., 1979-80, Paoli, Pa., 1982-83; gen. counsel Theriault's, Inc., Annapolis, Md., 1983-85; corp. counsel Devel. Resources, Inc., Alexandria, Va., 1985-87; st. atty., asst. corp. sec. People's Drug Stores, Inc., Alexandria, Va., 1987-91; gen. counsel Jenco Group, Alexandria, Va., 1991-92; ptnr. Fullerton & Kear, Alexandria, Va., 1992-93; mng. ptnr. Kear & Gilbert, Fairfax, Va., 1993-97; atty. The Kear Law Firm, Fairfax, Va., 1997—. Contbr. monthly newsletter The Dollmasters, 1983; contbr. The Law Forum, 1976—. Mem. Annapolis Law Ctr., 1983—; treas. Women's Law Ctr., Anne Arundel County. Mem. ABA, Pa. Bar Assn., Md. Bar Assn., Va. Bar Assn., Women's Bar Assn. Md., Internat. Conf. Shopping Ctrs., Nat. Retail Tenants Assn., Delta Theta Phi. Republican. Roman Catholic. General corporate, Real property, Landlord-tenant. Home: 6801 Tepper Dr Clifton VA 20124-1639 Office: 10605 Judicial Dr Ste A-2 Fairfax VA 22030-5167

**KEARNEY, DOUGLAS CHARLES,** lawyer, journalist; b. Gloucester, Mass., June 24, 1945; s. Charles Matthew Kearney and Jean (Tarr) Thomas. Student, Brown U., 1963-64; BA, Fla. State U., 1971, JD with high honors, 1973. Bar: Fla. 1974, Calif. 1976, U.S. Ct. Appeals (5th cir.) 1977, U.S. Dist. Ct. (mid. and so. dists.) Fla. 1978, U.S. Ct. Appeals (11th cir.) 1981, U.S. Supreme Ct. 1982, U.S. Dist. Ct. (no. dist.) Tex. 1985, Tex. 1986. Asst. pub. defender Office of Pub. Defender 2d Jud. Cir., Tallahassee, 1973-76; asst. atty. gen. Atty. Gen.'s Office State of Fla., Tallahassee, 1977-78, chief antitrust enforcement unit Atty. Gen.'s Office, 1978-79; prin. Law Offices of Douglas C. Kearney, Tallahassee, 1979-85; assoc. Brice & Mankoff, P.C., Dallas, 1985-87, mem., 1987-89; mem. Choate & Lilly, P.C., Dallas, 1989-92; prin. Kearney & Assocs., Dallas, 1992—. Pres. Legal Aid Found. of Tallahassee, Inc., 1984. With U.S. Army, 1965-68, Vietnam. Mem. Fla. Bar Assn., Tex. Bar Assn., Calif. Bar Assn. Episcopalian. Avocations: sailing, tennis, swimming, gardening. Antitrust, Banking, Federal civil litigation. Office: Kearney & Assocs 15105 Cypress Hills Dr Dallas TX 75248-4914

**KEARNEY, JOHN FRANCIS, III,** lawyer; b. Phila., July 27, 1947; s. John Francis and Adria B. (Linder) K.; m. Roseanne M. McAnally, Feb. 25, 1967 (dec. 1983); children: Jennifer F. Kearney Johnstone, Aileen M. Kearney Jones, John F. IV, Anne L. BBA, Temple U., 1970; JD cum laude, Rutgers U., 1973. Bar: N.J. 1973, U.S. Dist. Ct. N.J. 1973, U.S. Supreme Ct. 1977; cert. criminal trial atty. N.J. Supreme Ct. 1984. Assoc. Tomar, Parks, Seliger, Simonoff & Adourian, Camden, N.J., 1973-74; sr. trial atty. Office of Pub. Defender, Mt. Holly, N.J., 1974-83; pvt. practice Moorestown, N.J., 1983—; judge mcpl. ct. City of Bordentown, Twp. of Delran and Borough of Palmyra, N.J., 1993-97; counsel Burlington County Bd. Social Svcs., Mt. Holly, 1984—; prosecutor Borough of Palmyra, 1992-93; pub. defender Woodland Twp., Chatsworth, N.J., 1990-93, Borough of Riverton, N.J., 1984-93; adj. faculty Burlington County Coll., Pemberton, N.J., 1981; pub. defender Twp. of Mt. Holly and Westampton, 1986-90. Editorial bd. Rutgers Law Jour., 1972-73. Bd. dirs. Camden Regional Legal Svcs., Inc., 1972-74; bd. trustees Burlington County Community Action Program, 1971-74; arbitrator Personal Injury and Comml. Arbitration Programs, Superior Ct. of N.J., Burlington County, 1990—. 1 Lt. U.S. Army, 1973. Recipient Am. Jurisprudence award LCP Pub. Co., 1971. Mem. N.J. Assn. County Welfare Attys., Burlington County Mcpl. Judges Assn., Burlington County Bar Assn. (sec. 1998-99, treas. 1999—), Trial Attys. of N.J., Assn. Trial Lawyers of Am. Republican. Roman Catholic. Avocations: wildlife and underwater photography, boating, travel, hiking and climbing, collecting Inuit and Native American art. General civil litigation, Personal injury, Product liability. Office: 720 E Main St Ste 2S Moorestown NJ 08057-3058

**KEARNEY, PATRICIA ANN,** lawyer; b. Warren, Ohio, Nov. 23, 1951; d. Peter Saurick and Orpha Maxine Slick; m. F. Thomas Kearney Jr., May 21, 1982. BA, Youngstown State U., 1973; JD, Akron State U., 1991. Bar: Ohio 1991, U.S. Dist. Ct. (no. dist.) Ohio 1993. Escrow officer Trumbull Co. Abstract, Warren, 1976-85; mgr. Valley Title, Warren, 1985-88, Youngstown, Ohio, 1988-91; mgr. Title Co. Warren, 1991-94; owner Title Profls., Warren, 1994—. Real property, Estate planning, Probate. Office: Title Profls Inc 295 Harmon Ave NW Warren OH 44483-4804

**KEARNS, JAMES CANNON,** lawyer; b. Urbana, Ill., Nov. 8, 1944; s. John T. and Ruth (Cannon) K.; m. Anne Shapland, Feb. 12, 1983; children: Rose, John. BA, U. Notre Dame, 1966; JD, U. Ill., 1975. Bar: Ill. 1975, U.S. Dist. Ct. (cen. dist.) Ill. 1975, U.S. Ct. Appeals (7th cir.) 1976, U.S. Supreme Ct. 1992. Ptnr. Heyl, Royster, Voelker & Allen, Peoria, Ill., 1975-81, Urbana, 1981—. Mem. ABA, Nat. Assn. RR Trial Coun., Ill. Bar Assn., Champaign County Bar Assn., Def. Rsch. Inst., Ill. Assn. Def. Trial Counsel, Am. Bar Found., Nat. Assn. Coll. and Univ. Attys., Internat. Assn. Defense Coun. Roman Catholic. Avocations: reading, jogging. E-mail: jkearns@hrva.com. General civil litigation, Professional liability, Insurance. Office: Heyl Royster Voelker & Allen PO Box 129 102 E Main St Ste 300 Urbana IL 61801-2733

**KEARNS, JOHN W.,** lawyer; b. Chgo., Sept. 9, 1933; s. John W. and Frances R. (Forch) K.; m. Karen E. Swanson, May 3, 1960 (div. 1979); children: Jennifer F., John W., Charles S. BA, Yale U., 1955; JD, Harvard U., 1958. Bar: Ill. 1958, Fla. 1970, U.S. Dist. Ct. (no. dist.) Ill. 1958, U.S. Dist. Ct. (so. dist.) Fla. 1970, U.S. Ct. Appeals (7th, 5th, 3d and 11th cirs.), U.S. Supreme Ct. 1971. With Peterson, Ross, Rall, Barber & Seidel, Chgo., 1958-61, Kirkland & Ellis, Chgo., 1961-69, Paul & Thompson, Miami, Fla., 1969-73; pvt. practice, Miami, 1973—. Bd. dirs. Fla. Zool. Soc., 1974-79. Mem. ABA, Fla. Bar Assn., Dade County Bar Assn., Chgo. Bar Assn. Clubs: Chgo. Yacht; Coral Reef Yacht (Miami). General practice, State civil litigation, Antitrust. Office: 431 Gerona Ave Miami FL 33146-2807

**KEARNS, ROBERT WILLIAM,** manufacturing inventor; b. Gary, Ind., Mar. 10, 1927; s. Martin William and Mary Ellen (O'Hara) K.; m. Phyllis Joan McElwee, Aug. 1, 1953 (annulled Oct. 1980); children: Dennis M., Timothy B., Patrick S., Kathleen A., Maureen M., Robert M. Student, U.S. Army Fin. Sch., Ft. Aiterbury, Ind., 1945-46; BME, U. Detroit, 1952; MS in Engring. Mechanics, Wayne State U., 1957; cert. Internat. Sch. Nuclear Sci., Argonne Nat. Labs., Chgo., 1958; PhD, Case Inst. Tech., 1964. Registered profl. mech. and elec. engr., Mich.. Rsch. engr. Bendix Rsch. Labs., Detroit, 1952-57; assoc. prof. engring., faculty advisor SPE student br. Wayne State U., Detroit, 1957-67; commr. Dept. Bldgs. & Safety Engring., Detroit, 1967-71; prin. investigator for fed. hwy. Nat. Inst. Sci. & Tech., Gaithersburg, Md., 1971-76; trial litigator U.S. Cts.- Auto U.S. Detroit Dist. Ct., 1978—. Inventor intermittent windshield wiper systems; holder numerous patents. Bd. dirs. Vets. of Office of Strategic Svcs. and William J. Donovan Meml. Found., Inc., 1994—, Queen Anne's County (Md.) Hist. Soc., 1995—; cand. Comptroller for State of Md., 1998—. With U.S. Army, 1945-47. Roman Catholic. Avocation: violinist. Office: Kearns Trust 301 Houghton Lab Ln Queenstown MD 21658-2500

**KEARSE, AMALYA LYLE,** federal judge; b. Vauxhall, N.J., June 11, 1937; d. Robert Freeman and Myra Lyle (Smith) K. B.A., Wellesley Coll., 1959; J.D. cum laude, U. Mich., 1962. Bar: N.Y. 1963, U.S. Supreme Ct. 1967. Assoc. Hughes, Hubbard & Reed, N.Y.C., 1962-69; ptnr. Hughes, Hubbard & Reed, 1969-79; judge U.S. Ct. Appeals (2d cir.), 1979—; lectr. evidence N.Y. U. Law Sch., 1968-69. Author: Bridge Conventions Complete, 1975, 3d edit., 1990, Bridge at Your Fingertips, 1980; translator, editor: Bridge Analysis, 1979; editor: Ofcl. Ency. of Bridge, 3d edit, 1976; mem. editorial bd. Charles Goren, 1974—. Bd. dirs. NAACP Legal Def. and Endl. Fund, 1977-79; bd. dirs. Nat. Urban League, 1978-79; trustee N.Y.C. YWCA, 1976-79, Am. Contract Bridge League Nat. Laws Commn., 1975—; mem. Pres.'s Com. on Selection of Fed. Jud. Officers, 1977-78. Named Women's Pairs Bridge Champion Nat. div., 1971, 72, World div., 1986, Nat. Women's Teams Bridge Champion, 1987, 90, 91. Mem. ABA, Assn. of Bar of City of N.Y., Am. Law Inst., Lawyers Com. for Civil Rights Under Law (mem. exec. com. 1970-79). Office: US Ct Appeals US Courthouse 40 Foley Sq New York NY 10007-1502

**KEATING, DANIEL GERARD,** lawyer; b. Warren, Ohio, Dec. 23, 1956; s. Walter Leo and Moyra Louise (Heltzel) K. BA, Concordia U., Montreal, 1979; JD, U. Toledo, 1982. Bar: Ohio 1982, U.S. Dist. Ct. (no. dist.) Ohio 1983. Ptnr. Keating & Keating, Warren, Ohio, 1982—. Mem. Ohio Bar Assn., Trumbull County Bar Assn., Lawyer-Pilots Bar Assn., Nat. Health Lawyers Assn. Democrat. Roman Catholic. Criminal, Aviation, General practice. Office: 170 Monroe St NW Warren OH 44483-4809

**KEATING, DANIEL LOUIS,** law educator; b. Chgo., Oct. 14, 1961; s. Thomas Joseph and Joanne Clara (Shaughnessy) K.; m. Jane Marie Stevens, Aug. 2, 1986. BA, Monmouth Coll., 1983; JD, U. Chgo., 1986. Bar: Ill. 1986, U.S. Dist. Ct. (no. dist.) Ill. 1986. Lawyer 1st Nat. Bank Chgo., 1986-88; prof. law Washington U., St. Louis, 1988—, assoc. dean. Olin Found. John Olin Fellow, 1985. Mem. Order of Coif. Office: Washington U Sch Law Campus Box 1120 Saint Louis MO 63130*

**KEATING, FRANCIS ANTHONY, II,** governor, lawyer; b. St. Louis, Feb. 10, 1944; s. Anthony Francis and Anne (Martin) K.; m. Catherine Dunn Heller, 1972; children: Carissa Herndon, Kelly Martin, Anthony Francis III. A.B., Georgetown U., 1966; J.D., U. Okla., 1969. Bar: Okla. 1969. Spl. agt. FBI, 1969-71; asst. dist. atty. Tulsa County, 1971-72; mem. Okla. Ho. of Reps., 1972-74, Okla. Senate, 1974-81; U.S. atty. No. Dist. Okla., 1981-84; asst. sec. U.S. Treasury Dept., Washington, 1985-88; assoc. atty. gen. Dept. Justice, 1988-89; gen. counsel, acting dep. sec. Dept. Housing and Urban Devel., Washington, 1989-93; gov. State of Okla., 1995—. Mem. Okla. Bar Assn. Office: Office Gov 212 State Capitol Bldg Oklahoma City OK 73105

**KEATING, STEPHEN JOHN,** lawyer; b. Liverpool, Eng., Nov. 14, 1941; came to U.S., 1964; s. Joseph and Veronica M. K.; m. Natalie Tracy, Nov. 21, 1981. BA with honors, Oxford U., 1964, MA, 1970; JD, Boston Coll. Law, 1970. Atty. Blackwell, Walker & Gray, Miami, Fla., 1970-74; atty. Stephens, Magill, Thornton & Sevier, Miami, 1974-75, Stanley M. Rosenblatt, P.A., Miami, 1975-77, L.J. Spiegel, P.A., Miami, 1977-78; asst. county atty. Met. Dade County Atty., Miami, 1978—. Mem. Fla. Bar Assn., Mass. Bar Assn., Soc for the Preservation and Encouragement of Barbershop Quartet Singing Am. Roman Catholic. Avocations: barbershop harmony, golf, chess. Home: 1037 Valencia Ave Coral Gables FL 33134-5536 Office: Miami Dade County Atty 111 NW 1st St Ste 2810 Miami FL 33128-1930

**KEATINGE, CORNELIA WYMA,** architectural preservationist consultant, lawyer; b. Poughkeepsie, N.Y., July 22, 1952; d. Edwin R. and Josephine B. (Brazis) Wyma; m. Robert Reed Keatinge, Aug. 21, 1982; 1 child, Courtney Elizabeth. BArch, U. Ky., 1974; MA in History and Theory of Architecture, U. Essex, Colchester, Eng., 1976; JD, U. Denver, 1982. Bar: Colo. 1982. Archtl. historian Kans. State Hist. Soc., Topeka, 1975-77; hist. architect Nat. Park Service, Denver, 1977-79; assoc. Richard E. Young, Denver, 1982-84; hist. architect Colo. Hist.Soc., Denver, 1984-86; sole practice, cons. architecture Denver, 1986; hist. preservation specialist Adv. Council Hist. Preservation, Golden, Colo., 1986—. Vol. Denver Art Mus., 1980—, Jr. League Denver, 1983—. Rotary fellow, 1974-75; recipient Spl. Achievement award, Nat. Park Service, 1980. Mem. ABA. Home: 460 S Marion Pky # 1904 Denver CO 80209-2544 Office: 12136 W Bayaud Ave Ste 330 Lakewood CO 80228-2115

**KEATINGE, ROBERT REED,** lawyer; b. Berkeley, Calif., Apr. 22, 1948; s. Gerald Robert and Elizabeth Jean (Benedict) K.; m. Katherine Lou Carr, Feb. 1, 1969 (div. Dec. 1981); 1 child, Michael Towne; m. Cornelia Elizabeth Wyma, Aug. 21, 1982; 1 child, Courtney Elizabeth. BA, U. Colo., 1970; JD, U. Denver, 1973, LLM, 1982. Bar: Colo. 1974, U.S. Dist. Ct. Colo. 1974, U.S. Ct. Appeals (10th cir.) 1977, U.S. Tax Ct. 1980. Ptnr. Kubie & Keatinge, Denver, 1974-76; pvt. practice Denver, 1976; assoc. Richard Young, Denver, 1977-86; counsel Durham & Assoc. P.C., Denver, 1986-89, Durham & Baron, Denver, 1989-90; project editor taxation Shepard's/McGraw-Hill, Colorado Springs, Colo., 1990-96; of counsel Holland & Hart, LLP, Denver, 1992—; lectr. law U. Denver, 1982-92, adj. prof. grad. tax program, 1983-94. Author, cons. (CD-ROM) Entity Expert, 1996; co-author: Ribstein and Keatinge on Limited Liability Companies, 1992; contbr. articles to profl. jours. and treatises. Spkr. to profl. socs. and univs. including AICPA, ALI-ABA, U. TEx., 1984—. Recipient Law Week award U. Denver Bur. Nat. Affairs, 1974. Mem. ABA (chmn. subcom. ltd. liability cos. of com. on partnerships 1990-95, chmn. com. on taxation 1995—, mem. ho. of dels. 1996—, editl. bd. ABA/BNA Lawyer's Manual on Professional Conduct 1998—, joint editl. bd. ABA/NCCUSL on unincorporated orgns. 1996—), Colo. Bar Assn. (corp. code revision com., co-chmn. ltd. liability co. revision com., taxation sect. exec. coun. 1988-94, sec.-treas. 1991-92, chmn. 1993-94), Denver Bar Assn. Corporate taxation, Contracts commercial, General corporate. Home: 460 S Marion Pky # 1904 Denver CO 80209-2544

**KEATON, CHRISTOPHER KEVIN,** lawyer; b. Welch, W.Va., Feb. 20, 1965; s. Kyle and Theodosia K. BA, Marshall U., 1991, MA, 1992; JD, John Marshall Sch. Law, 1995. Law clk. Robinson & Rice, Huntington, W.Va., 1992-95; lawyer Robinson, Rice & Levy, Huntington, 1995—; safety cons., Huntington, 1997—; pres. bd. dirs. Devel. Therapy Ctr., Huntington, 1997—. Vol. Spl. Olympics, Huntington, 1997. Mem. ATLA, Am. Soc. Safety Engrs., W.Va. Trial Lawyers Assn., Nat. Inst. Dispute Resolution. Avocations: golf, fishing, outdoor activities. Home: 215 12th Ave Huntington WV 25701-3126 Office: Robinson Rice & Levy 1032 6th Ave Huntington WV 25701-2308

**KEATY, ROBERT BURKE,** lawyer; b. Baton Rouge, July 7, 1949; s. Thomas St. Paul and Alicia (Armshaw) K.; m. Erin Kenny, July 6, 1973; children: Kellen Elizabeth, Kathryn Ellen, Robert Burke, Kaneil Erin, Rory Bridgette-Anne. BS, U. Southwestern La., 1971; JD, Tulane U., 1974. Bar: La. 1973, Tex. 1986. Law clk. to judge U.S. Dist. Ct. for Ea. Dist. La., New Orleans, 1974-76; ptnr. Keaty & Keaty, Lafayette, La., 1976—; mem. pres.'s com. Offshore Tng. and Survival Ctr., U. Southwestern La. Lafayette, 1988-89; co-chmn. United Giver Fund Jud. Legal, 1994, Bishops Charity Ball Legal Com., 1995. Member dean's adv. com. Tulane U. Law Sch., New Orleans, 1987; mem. dean's exec. adv. com. Coll. Bus. Adminstrn., U. Southwestern La., 1991. Sears scholar, 1971, Teagle scholar, 1973; recipient Most Outstanding Alumnus award U. S.W. La. Coll. Bus. Adminstrs., 1991. Fellow La. Bar Found. (lifetime charter mem.); mem. La. Bankers Assn., La. Trial Lawyers (gov. 1988, 92), Lafayette C. of C. (aviation com.), Mardi Gras Krewes, Gabriel, Townhouse, Kappa Sigma. Avocations: alpine skiing, boating, tennis, hunting, fishing. Personal injury, Admiralty, Aviation. Office: Keaty & Keaty PO Box 51989 Lafayette LA 70505-1989

**KEATY, THOMAS ST. PAUL, II,** lawyer; b. Baton Rouge, Jan. 3, 1943; s. Thomas St. Paul and Alicia Armshaw (Burk) K.; m. Sherrie Kerr, Feb. 4, 1966; children: Thomas St. Paul III, Emily Elizabeth Keaty. B.S., U. Southwestern La., 1966; JD, Tulane U., 1972. Bar: La. 1972, Tex. 1986, U.S. Dist. Ct. (ea. dist.) La. 1972, U.S. Dist. Ct. (we. dist.) La. 1975, U.S. Ct. Appeals (5th cir.) 1975, U.S. Ct. Customs and Patent Appeals 1975, U.S. Dist. Ct. (so. dist.) Tex. 1980, U.S. Dist. Ct. (we. dist.) Tex. 1983, U.S. Dist. Ct. (mid. dist.) La. 1984, U.S. Ct. Appeals (Fed. cir.) 1984. Ptnr. Keaty & Keaty, New Orleans; instr. Tulane U.. Mem. ABA, La. State Bar Assn. (rec. sec. New Orleans chpt. 1986), Fed. Bar Assn. New Orleans (bd. dirs. 1983—), La. Trial Lawyers Assn., Am. Patent Law Soc., San Francisco Patent Law Soc., La. Engring. Soc., Am. Soc. Chem. Engrs., State Trademarks and Unfair Bus. Practices (La. sect.). Roman Catholic. Author: What the U.S. Businessman Should Know About Patents, U.S. and Foreign, 1979, Fed. practice seminar Injunctions, 1985-86. Patent, Trademark and copyright. Office: Keaty & Keaty 2140 World Trade Center New Orleans LA 70130

**KECK, RICHARD PAUL,** lawyer; b. London, Eng., Jan. 19, 1960; s. Wilbur Howard and Susie (McNair) K.; m. Margaret Rene Walker, Apr. 3, 1982; children: Elizabeth Ellen, William Joseph, Katherine Margaret. BS, Emory U., 1982; JD, Harvard U., 1985. Bar: Ga. 1985, U.S. Dist. Ct. (no. dist.) Ga. 1985, Ga. Ct. Appeals 1985, Ga. Supreme Ct. 1985. Tchr. math DeKalb County Schs., Decatur, Ga., 1981-82; assoc. Kilpatrick & Cody, Atlanta, 1985-90; assoc. Kilpatrick & Cody, London, 1991-92, ptnr., 1992—. Mem. ABA (ann. meeting, com. internat. sect. 1990-91), Atlanta Bar Assn. (sec.-treas. internat. transactions sect. 1988-89, vice-chairperson, chairperson elect 1989-90, chairperson 1990-91), State Bar Ga., Harvard Club (U.K.), Harvard Law Sch. Assn. U.K., Phi Beta Kappa. Republican. Baptist. Avocations: running, camping, canoeing, house restoration, antique refinishing. Private international, Finance, Communications. Office: Troutman Sanders LLP 600 Peachtree St Atlanta GA 30308-2265

**KEDIA, SARITA,** lawyer; b. Bombay, India, Jan. 1, 1971; d. Prahlad R. and Sushila P. Kedia; m. Geoffrey R. Goldberg, May 24, 1998. JD, Tulane U., 1994; BS in Econs., U. Pa., 1991. Bar: N.Y. 1995, U.S. Dist. Ct. (so. and ea. dists.) N.Y. 1995, U.S. Ct. Appeals (2d cir.) 1995. Assoc. Law Offices of Mel A. Sachs, N.Y.C., 1994-96, Law Offices of Gerald C. Shargel, N.Y.C., 1996—. Mem. NACDL, N.Y. State Bar Assn. Criminal Def. Lawyers, N.Y. State Bar Assn. Avocations: running, hiking, martial arts, reading, travel. Criminal. Office: Law Offfices of Gerald L Shargel 1585 Broadway Fl 19 New York NY 10036-8200

**KEEDY, CHRISTIAN DAVID,** lawyer; b. Worcester, Mass., Jan. 9, 1945. BBA, Tulane U. La., 1967, JD, 1972. Bar: Fla. 1972; bd. cert. in admiralty and maritime law, Fla. Pvt. practice Christian D. Keedy, P.A., Coral Gables, Fla., 1981—. Mem. ABA, Maritime Law Assn. U.S., Southeastern Admiralty Law Inst. (dir. 1982-83), The Fla. Bar (chmn. 1981-82, admiralty law com.), Miami Maritime Arbitration Coun. (dir.). Admiralty, Federal civil litigation, State civil litigation. Office: Christian D Keedy PA 710 S Dixie Hwy Coral Gables FL 33146-2602

**KEEFE, DEBORAH ELLEN,** lawyer, investor; b. Mpls., Sept. 4, 1953; d. John Elmer and Lillian Mary Keefe. BA with honors, U. Minn., 1978, JD, 1984. Bar: Minn. 1985, Wis. 1985, Ga. 1987. Women's advocate Harriet Tubman Shelter for Battered Women, Mpls., 1977-82; coop. owner People's Co. Bakery, Mpls., 1979-83; student paraprofl. Minn. Dept. Transp., St. Paul, 1982-83; law office assoc. Phila. Assn. for Coop. Enterprise, 1982; assoc., ptnr. Keefe Law Office, Hutchinson, Minn., 1985-87; assoc. Paul C. Parker & Assoc., Atlanta, 1988-89; with Norton & D'Agostino, Atlanta, 1990-95; pvt. practice Atlanta, 1995-96; sr. ptnr. Keefe & Sicay-Perrow, Attys. at Law, Atlanta, 1996—; chairperson Consumer Bankruptcy Group, Atlanta, 1998-99. Chair cultural affairs com. U. Minn. Student Govt., Mpls., 1974-75, vice chair student svc. fees com., 1974-75; bd. dirs. Chrysalis Women's Ctr., Mpls., 1979-80. McGill scholar U. Minn., 1973. Mem. NOW, Nat. Mus. Women in the Arts, Ga. Bar Assn. (bd. dirs. bankruptcy sect. 1995-96), Sierra Club, Nature Conservancy. Democrat. Avocations: rock climbing, mountaineering, backpacking, skiing, boating. Home: 2587 Churchwell Ln Tucker GA 30084-2410 Office: Keefe & Sicay-Perrow 84 Peachtree St NW Ste 700 Atlanta GA 30303-2318

**KEEFFE, JOHN ARTHUR,** lawyer, director; b. Bklyn., Apr. 5, 1930; s. Arthur John and Mary Catherine (Daly) K.; m. Frances Elizabeth Rippetoe, July 24, 1952; children: Virginia Frances, Cynthia Louise, Amy Marie. AB, Cornell U., 1950; JD, U. Va., 1953. Bar: Va. 1953, N.Y. 1956. Asst. U.S. atty. so. dist. State of N.Y., 1955-57; assoc. Rogers, Hoge & Hills, N.Y., 1957-63; of counsel Havens, Wandless, Stitt & Tighe, N.Y., 1963-65; ptnr. Keeffe & Costikyan, N.Y.C. and Washington, 1965-74, Keeffe Bros., N.Y.C. and Washington, 1974-77; sec., mng. dir. Saud Al-Farhan Inc., N.Y.C., 1979-80; pres., dir. J.A. Keeffe, P.C., Eastchester, N.Y., 1981—. Bd. dirs., sec. The Street Theater, White Plains, N.Y., 1973—. 1st lt. USAF, 1953-55. Mem. ABA, ATLA, N.Y. State Bar Assn., Va. Bar Assn., Westchester County Bar Assn. (dir. 1989-90, chmn. com. on fed. courthouse plans and procedures 1994—), N.Y. State Trial Lawyers Assn., Eastchester Bar Assn. (v.p. 1988-89, pres. 1989-90, dir. 1990—), Rotary (bd. dirs. 1991—, sec. 1991-92, pres.-elect 1992-93, pres. 1993-94, co-chair Eastchester Rotary Gift of Life 1993-94, co-chair dist. 7230 Gift of Life 1995-97). Republican. Congregationalist. Avocations: golf, reading. Estate planning, General civil litigation, General corporate. Home: 2 Longview Dr Eastchester NY 10709-1425 Office: 700 White Plains Rd Ste 246 Scarsdale NY 10583-5013

**KEEGAN, JOHN E.,** lawyer; b. Spokane, Wash., Apr. 29, 1943. BA, Gonzaga U., 1965; LLB, Harvard U., 1968. Bar: Wash. 1968, U.S. Ct. Appeals (9th cir.) 1976, U.S. Supreme Ct. Gen. counsel Dept. Housing and Urban Devel., Washington, 1968-70; instr. in bus. sch. and inst. environ. studies U. Wash., 1973-76, instr. land use and environ. law, 1976-78; now ptnr. Davis, Wright & Tremaine, Seattle. Office: Davis Wright Tremaine 2600 Century Sq 1501 4th Ave Ste 2600 Seattle WA 98101-1688

**KEEGAN, KAREN ANN,** lawyer; b. Kewanee, Ill., Apr. 5, 1960; d. Donald Eugene and Marlene Joyce Vyneman; m. Ronald Dale Keegan, May 25, 1992; children: Tyler James, Allison Driessens. BS, U. Ill., 1982; JD, Ga. State U., 1992. Bar: Tex. Adjuster Progressive Ins. Co., Dallas, 1983-86; litigation supr. Transp. Ins. Co., Dallas, 1986-96; atty. Smith Defeo, Dallas, 1996—; vice chair client seminars Def. Rsch. Inst., 1997—. Mem. ABA. Republican. Roman Catholic. General civil litigation, Transportation, Insurance. Home: 4210 Widgeon Ct Mc Kinney TX 75070-4170 Office: Smith Defeo 5910 N Central Expy Ste 1100 Dallas TX 75206-5182

**KEEGIN, STAFFORD WARWICK,** lawyer; b. Washington, Aug. 11, 1942; s. Stafford Warwick and Helen A. (Tilson) K.; m. Susan E. Landor, Sept. 1, 1973; children: Hillary Ellen, Emily Elsie, Mary Katherine. BA in Polit. Sci., Dartmouth Coll., 1964; LLB cum laude, Washington and Lee U., 1968. Bar: Calif. 1969. Assoc. Pillsbury, Madison & Sutro, San Francisco, 1968-70; ptnr. Cotton, Seligman & Ray, San Francisco, 1970-75, Martin, Munter & Keegin, San Francisco, 1975-78; sr. atty. Nat. Econ. Devel. and Law Ctr., Berkeley, Calif., 1978-81; ptnr. Bianchi, Keegin & Talkington, Schoppert, & Harrison, Calif., 1981—. Bd. dirs. Marin Symphony Assn., 1979-85, pres., 1982-85; bd. dirs. St. Francis 12 Found. (1987 America's Cup effort), 1984-87, exec. com.; bd. dirs. Mt. Tamalpais Sch., Mill Valley, Calif., 1985-88, pres., 1987-88; bd. dirs., Marin Gen. Hosp., 1984—. Mem. ABA (taxation sect. com. on small bus. fin.), State Bar Calif. (partnership com. bus. law sect.), Bar Assn. San Francisco, Marin County Bar Assn., Order of Coif. Democrat. Co-author: Organizing Production Cooperatives, 1978; Consumer Food Cooperatives, 1982. General corporate, Corporate taxation, Securities. Office: Bianchi Keegin Talkington Schoppert & Harrison 1000 4th St Ste 600 San Rafael CA 94901-3182

**KEELEY, IRENE PATRICIA MURPHY,** federal judge; b. 1944. BA, Coll. Notre Dame, 1965; MA, W.Va. U., 1977, JD, 1980. Bar: W. Va., 1980. Atty. Steptoe & Johnson, Clarksburg, W.Va., 1980-92; dist. judge U.S. Dist. Ct. (no. dist.), W. Va., 1992—; adj. prof. law W.Va. U., 1990-91; bd. dirs. W.Va. U. Alumni Assn., 1995—, 1st v.p., 1997-98; mem. bd. advisors W.Va. U. Vis. com. W.Va. U. Coll. Law, 1987-91, 94-98; chmn. adv. bd. W.Va. U., 1997-98. Mem. ABA, Nat. Conf. Fed. Trial Judges (exec. com. 1996—,), W.Va. State Bar, W.Va. Bar Assn., Harrison County Bar Assn., Clarksburg Country Club, Oral Lake Fishing Club, Immaculate Conception Roman Cath. Ch. Office: US Courthouse PO Box 2808 500 W Pike St Rm 202 Clarksburg WV 26302-2808

**KEELEY, MICHAEL GLENN,** arbitrator, mediator, consultant; b. Memphis, Jan. 8, 1953; s. Lerman and Benneta (Thompson) K.; m. Sandra Virginia Hughes, Oct. 6, 1978 (div. Aug. 1992); m. Karen Bonner, Dec. 31, 1993; 1 child, Kim. BA, UCLA, 1975; JD, U. Calif., Hastings, 1978. Negotiator for NFL players Profl. Sports Mgmt. Inc., 1979-81; sr. rep. Employers Benefits Ins., 1981-85; claims supr. Claims Mgmt. Svcs., 1985-86; sr. litigation specialist Reliance/United Pacific Ins Co, Rancho Cordova, Calif., 1986-96; ptnr. JKP Mgmt. Svcs. Inc., Sacramento, 1996-97; broker, risk mgmt. cons. J&K Risk and Ins. Svcs., Inc., 1997—; cons. to 3rd party adminstr. in workers' compensation, casualty and auto claims. Mem. Black Ins. Profls. Assn. (pres. 1991-92, student mentor program 1991-93, LINK program 1991), Charles Houston Bar Assn. Avocations: golf, baseball, football, racquetball.

**KEELEY, PATRICK CHRISTOPHER,** lawyer; b. Chgo., July 15, 1952; s. Elaine Antoinette K.; m. Kimberly Miller, Aug. 25, 1979; 1 child, Michael. BS, U. Ill., 1974, MBA, 1976; JD, Loyola U., Chgo., 1979. Ptnr., prin. Piccione Keeley & Assoc. Ltd., Wheaton, Ill., 1979—. Trustee David Kinley Found., Champaign, Ill.; mng. dir. Jacksons Sports, Phoenix. Mem. ABA, ALTA, ILTA, Ill. Bar Assn., Dupage County Bar Assn. Office: Piccione Keeley & Assocs 122 S County Farm Rd Ste C Wheaton IL 60187-4594

**KEELY, GEORGE CLAYTON,** lawyer; b. Denver, Feb. 28, 1926; s. Thomas and Margaret (Clayton) K.; m. Jane Elisabeth Coffey, Nov. 18, 1950; children: Margaret Clayton, George C. (dec.), Mary Anne, Jane Elisabeth, Edward Francis, Kendall Anne. *Wife, Jane Keely, investor, BA Wellesley, MA Columbia University. Daughter, Margaret Stannard, BA, MA, EdD, CCC-SLP, business/education consultant. Husband, Daniel. Residence, Denver, Colorado. Daughter, Mary Keely, BA, MA, CPA. Children: Elisa, Angelo and Lia Marie. Residence, Austin, Texas. Daughter, Elisabeth Wilson, BA, artist and sculptor. Husband, Gregory. Children: Gregory Jr. and Bradley. Residence, Danville, California. Son, Edward Keely, BA, CFA, vice president and portfolio manager of Janus Funds. Wife, Diane. Daughter, Makenzie. Son, Charles Edward. Residence, Castle Pines, Colorado. Daughter, Kendall Picardi, BA, paralegal/office manager. Husband, Steve. Son, Chris. Residence, Arvada, Colorado.* BS in Bus, U. Colo., 1948; LLB, Columbia U., 1951. Bar: Colo. 1951. Assoc. Fairfield & Woods, Denver, 1951-58, ptnr., 1958-86, sr. dir., 1986-90, of counsel, 1990-91, ret., 1991; v.p. Silver Corp., 1966-86; mem. exec. com. Timpte Industries, Inc., 1970-78, dir., 1980-89. Mem. Colo. Commn. Promotion Uniform State Laws, 1967—; regional planning adv. com. Denver Regional Coun. Govts., 1972-74; bd. dirs. Bow Mar Water and Sanitation Dist., 1970-74; trustee Town of Bow Mar, 1972-74; trustee, v.p. Silver Found., 1970-90, mem. bd., 1983-90; trustee, v.p. Denver Area coun. Boy Scouts Am., 1985-90; bd. dirs. Pub. Broadcasting of Colo., Inc., 1986-90, Sta. KCFR. With USAF, 1944-47. Fellow Am. Bar Found., Colo. Bar Found.; mem. ABA (ho. of dels. 1977-79), Denver Bar Assn. (award of merit 1980), Colo. Bar Assn., Nat. Conf. Commrs. Uniform State Laws (sec. 1971-75, exec. com. 1971-79 , chmn. exec. com. 1975-77, pres. 1977-79, co-chmn. com. U.S.-Can. Transboundary Pollution Reciprocal Access Act 1979-82, chmn. com. Determination of Death Act 1979-80), Am. Law Inst., Cath. Lawyers Guild of Denver (dir. 1965-67), Denver Estate Planning Coun., U. Club of Denver, (dir. 1966-75, pres. 1973-74), Law Club of Denver (pres. 1966-67, Lifetime Achievement award, 1994), Pinehurst Country Club, Hundred Club, Cactus Club, Rotary, Phi Delta Phi, Beta Theta Pi, Beta Gamma Sigma. General corporate, Mergers and acquisitions, Banking. Home: 5220 W Longhorn St Littleton CO 80123-1408

**KEENAN, BARBARA MILANO,** state supreme court justice. Judge Gen. Dist. Ct., Fairfax County, Va., 1980-82, Circuit Ct., Fairfax County, Va., 1982-85, Court of Appeals of Va., 1985-91; justice Supreme Court Va., Richmond, 1991—. Office: Va Supreme Ct 101 N 9th St Fl 4 Richmond VA 23219-2307

**KEENAN, C. ROBERT, III,** lawyer; b. Pitts., July 21, 1954; s. C. Robert Jr. and Catherine (Conley) K.; m. Joann R. Fogle, June 9, 1979; children: Rachel, Rosemary. BA, Bucknell U., 1976; JD, U. Pitts., 1979. Bar: Pa. 1979, U.S. Dist. Ct. (we. dist.) Pa. 1979, U.S. Ct. Appeals (3d cir.) 1981, U.S. Supreme Ct. 1983. Assoc. Shire & Bergstein, Monessen, Pa., 1979-80; ptnr. Jones, Gregg, Creehan & Gerace, Pitts., 1980-89; prin. Keenan and Krug, P.C., Pitts., 1989-92, Grigsby, Gaca & Davies (now Davies, McFarland and Carroll, P.C.), Pitts., 1992—. Editor Real News Jour., 1984-92. Trustee Castle Shannon (Pa.) Cmty. Libr., 1982-84; mem. claims adjudication bd. SSS, Pitts., 1984—, chmn., 1987-90; mem. Def. Rsch. Inst., Pa. Def. Inst.; mem. Allegheny County Rep. Com.; chmn. Mt. Lebanon Rep. Com., 1991-93; mem. bd. sch. dirs. Mt. Lebanon Sch. Dist., 1998—. Mem. ABA (govtl. liaibility com.), Pa. Bar Assn. (chmn. specialization com. 1990-93), Federalist Soc. Law and Pub. Studies, Allegheny County Bar Assn. (chmn. bd. dirs. real property sect. 1992, jud. com. 1992-95, workers' compensation sect. coun. 1996-98), Christian Bus. Men's Com. (chmn. outreach 1985-88), Dormont-Mt. Lebanon Sportsmen's Club, Rotary (past pres., Disting. Svc. award 1985), Pi Sigma Alpha, Omicron Delta Kappa. Republican. Avocations: marksmanship, music, swimming. Insurance, Labor, Workers' compensation. Office: Davies McFarland & Carroll 10th Fl One Gateway Ctr Pittsburgh PA 15222

**KEENAN, JEFFREY ALAN,** lawyer; b. Pensacola, Fla., Mar. 25, 1960; s. Henry Donald and Isabel (Bolin) K.; m. Allyn Eileen Schram, Feb. 10, 1996. BA, U. Ctrl. Fla., 1982; JD, La. State U., 1985. Var: La. 1985, S.C. 1991. Law clk. 14th Jud. Dist. Ct., Lake Charles, La., 1985-86; atty. John L. Van Norman, III, Lake Charles, 1986-90, Harry Paviliak & Assocs., P.A., Myrtle Beach, S.C., 1993—. Office: Harry Pavilak & Assocs PA 603 N Kings Hwy Myrtle Beach SC 29577-3744

**KEENAN, JOHN FONTAINE,** federal judge; b. N.Y.C., Nov. 23, 1929; s. John Joseph and Veronica (Fontaine) K.; m. Diane R. Nicholson, Oct. 6, 1956; 1 child, Marie Patricia. BBA, Manhattan Coll., N.Y., 1951; LLD (hon.), Manhattan Coll., 1989; LLB, Fordham U., 1954; LLD (hon.), Mt. St. Vincent Coll., 1989. Bar: N.Y. 1954, U.S. Dist. Ct. (so. dist.) N.Y. 1983. From asst. dist. atty. to chief asst. dist. atty. N.Y. County Dist. Atty.'s Office, 1956-76; spl. prosecutor, dep. atty. gen. City of N.Y., 1976-79; chmn. bd., pres. N.Y.C. Off-Track Betting Corp., 1979-82; criminal justice coord. City of N.Y., 1982-83; judge U.S. Dist. Ct. So. Dist. N.Y., N.Y.C., 1983—; chief asst. dist. atty. Queens County Dist. Atty.'s Office, N.Y., 1973; adj. prof. John Jay Coll. Criminal Justice, N.Y.C., 1979-83, Fordham U. Sch. Sch. Law, N.Y.C., 1992, 93; mem. Fgn. Intelligence Svc. Ct., 1994—, Judicial Panel on Multi-Dist. Litigation, 1998—. Contbr. articles to law jours. Chmn. Daytop Village, Inc., N.Y.C., 1981-83. Served with U.S. Army, 1954-56. Recipient Frank S. Hogan award Citizens Com. Control of Crime in N.Y., 1975, Emory R. Buckner award Federal Bar Coun., 1993; cert. of recognition Patrolmen's Benevolent Assn., 1976; 1st Ann. Hogan-Morgenthau Assocs. award N.Y. County Dist. Atty.'s Office, 1976, Medal of Achievement, 1992; Excellence award N.Y. State Bar Assn., 1978, award N.Y. Criminal Bar Assn., 1979, Disting. Faculty award Nat. Coll. Dist. Attys., 1978, Louis J. Lefkowitz award Fordham Urban Law Jour., 1983, Charles Carroll award Guild Cath. Lawyers, 1994, Ellis Island medal of honor, Nat. Ethnic Coalition of Orgns. Found., Inc., 1998. Mem. Amackassin Club, Skytop Club. Republican. Roman Catholic. Office: US Dist Ct US Courthouse 500 Pearl St Rm 1930 New York NY 10007-1316

**KEENAN, JOHN RAYMOND,** lawyer; b. Ridgewood, N.J., Aug. 18, 1963; s. Raymond P. and Carol Keenan; m. Rebecca K. Keenan, June 8, 1991; children: Taylor, Andrew. BA in Econs., Rutgers U., 1985; JD, U. Memphis, 1988. Bar: Tenn. 1988, U.S. Tax Ct. 1988, U.S. Dist. Ct. (mid. dist.) Tenn. 1989. Staff atty. Office of Chief Counsel IRS, Nashville, 1988-93, sr. atty., 1993—, spl. asst. U.S. atty., 1989—. Notes editor Memphis State U. Law Rev., 1987-88. Mem. McCrory Trace Estates Homeowners Assn., Nashville, 1997—. Recipient awards Am. Jurisprudence. Office: Office of Chief Counsel IRS 810 Broadway Nashville TN 37203-3810

**KEENAN, LINDA LEE,** paralegal; b. Lackawanna, N.Y., Mar. 12, 1951; d. David Lee and Beverly Ingaborg (Palmberg) Conway; m. Robert Joseph Keenan Jr., Sept. 10, 1983; children: Kristyn Marie, Beau, Bear, Tammy Ann. AS in Legal Studies, Teikyo Post U., 1995, BS in Liberal Arts summa cum laude, 1997; MA in History, Western Conn. State U., 1999. Cert. legal asst. Sec. I.B.M., Rye, N.Y., 1968-69; bus. mgr. Redding (Conn.) Country Club, 1973-86; paralegal Koskoff, Koskoff & Bieder, Danbury, Conn., 1986—. Vol., court monitor Children in Placement, Danbury, 1993. Mem. NAFE, ATLA, AAUW, Assn. for Rsch. and Enlightenment, Phi Theta Kappa Honor Soc., Alpha Chi Honor Soc. Avocations: astronomy, astrology, writing, metaphysical study, history. Home: Deer Ridge Townhouse 110 Coalpit Hill Rd Danbury CT 06810-8023

**KEENE, JOHN CLARK,** lawyer, educator; b. Phila., Aug. 17, 1931; s. Floyd Elwood and Marthe (Bussiere) K.; m. Ana Maria Delgado, July 21, 1973; children: Lisa Keene Kerns, John, Suzanna, Katherine, Peter; stepchildren: Carlos, Rene, Mario, Raul, Silvio Navarro, Carmen Peláez. BA, Yale U., 1953; JD, Harvard U., 1959; M in City Planning, U. Pa., 1966. Bar: Pa. 1960. Assoc. Pepper, Hamilton & Scheetz, 1959-64; prof. city and regional planning U. Pa., Phila., 1968—, chmn., 1989-93, univ. ombudsman, 1978-84, chmn. faculty senate, 1998-99; ptnr. Coughlin, Keene & Assocs., Phila., 1981—; vis. prof. U. Paris X, 1991. Fulbright fellow Tunisia, 1985. Trustee ex officio Phila. Mus. Art, 1978-80. Lt. USN, 1953-56. Mem. Am. Inst. Cert. Planners, Merion Cricket Club. Author: (with Robert E. Coughlin) The Protection of Farmland, 1981, Growth Without Chaos, 1987; (with others) Untaxing Open Space, 1976, (with Samuel Hamill) Growth Management in New Jersey, 1989, (with Robert Coughlin and Joanne Denworth) Guiding Growth: Managing Urban Growth in Pennsylvania, 1991, 93, (with Julia Freedgood) Saving American Farmland: What Works, 1997. Real property. Home: 119 Llanfair Rd Ardmore PA 19003-3341 Office: U Pa 127 Meyerson Hall Philadelphia PA 19104

**KEENE, KENNETH PAUL,** lawyer; b. Torrington, Wyo., Oct. 29, 1940; s. Lyndell Franklin and Marion (Morgan) K.; m. Katherine LaHeist Keith Bell, Sept. 10, 1966 (div. May 1992); children: Elizabeth LaHeist Keene Lusby, Kenneth Paul Jr., Susan Morgan. BS, U. Nebr., 1962, JD cum laude, 1965. Bar: Nebr. 1965, Colo. 1968, Ariz. 1989. Shareholder Hecox, Tolley, Keene & Beltz, PC, Colorado Springs, Colo., 1970-94; ptnr. Rothgerber, Johnson & Lyons LLP, Colorado Springs, 1995—. Bd. dirs. Penrose-St. Francis Healthcare Found., Colorado Springs, 199—, also past chmn.; bd. dirs. Cheyenne Mountain Zoo, Colorado Springs, 1997—. Capt. JAGC, U.S. Army, 1965-69. Mem. Colo. Bar Assn., Nebr. Bar Assn., Ariz. Bar Assn., El Paso County Bar Assn. (probate sect., past pres.), Colorado Springs Estate Planning Coun. (past pres.), Cheyenne Mountain Country Club, El Paso Club, Kissing Camels Club. Republican. Estate planning, Estate taxation, Probate. Office: Rothgerber Johnson & Lyons 90 S Cascade Ave Ste 1100 Colorado Springs CO 80903-1677

**KEENEY, E. ANDREW,** lawyer; b. Queens Village, N.Y., Mar. 19, 1951. BA, Drew U., 1973; JD, Am. U., 1976. Bar: Va. 1978, U.S. Ct. Appeals (4th cir.) 1978, U.S. Dist. Ct. (ea. dist.) Va. 1984, D.C. 1988. Ptnr. Baker & Hostetler, Washington; pres. Bob DeGabrielle & Assocs., Corolla, N.C., 1998—; bd. advisors Black's Guide, Fairfax County Va. Bd. Equalization, 1990-92; circut ct. tax case mgmt. exec. com., Fairfax County Va., 1994—. Author: Glossary of Real Estate Terms. Fellow Am. Coll. Mortgage Attys. (D.C. state chmn.); mem. ABA (mem. real estate financing, mgmt. of real estate, construction contracts and architects contracts, comml. fin. svcs., consumer fin. svcs., and credit union coms., Va. chmn. real property, property tax com.), Va. State Bar, D.C. Bar. Office: Bob DeGabrielle & Assoc 821 Ocean Trl Ste 4 Corolla NC 27927-9612

**KEENEY, STEVEN HARRIS,** lawyer; b. Phila., Oct. 1, 1949; s. Arthur Hail and Virginia (Tripp) K.; m. Jean Ashburn, May 10, 1974 (div. Oct. 1986); 1 child, Christian Jeffrey. BA, Trinity Coll., Hartford, Conn., 1971; MA, Hartford Sem. Found., 1973; JD, U. Conn., 1980. Bar: Ky. 1980, U.S. Dist. Ct. (we. dist.) Ky. 1981, U.S. Dist. Ct. (ea. dist.) Ky. 1983. Staff reporter/edn. editor The Hartford Courant, 1971-74; asst. to supt. Hartford Pub. Schs., 1974-77; assoc. Igor Sikorsky & Assocs., Hartford, 1979-80, Brown, Todd & Heyburn, Louisville, 1980-82; ptnr. Barnett & Alagia, Louisville, 1982-88, Keeney & Willock, Louisville, 1988-90; prin. Amerilaw, Louisville, 1990-93; pres. LawTech Svcs. Co., Louisville, 1993—; mng. mem. Trautwein & Keeney PLLC, Louisville, 1993—. Co-author/editor: Death Benefit: A Lawyer Uncovers A 20 Year Pattern of Seduction, 1993, 94, Reader's Digest Today's Best Non-Fiction Vol. 24, 1994; contbr. articles to profl. jours. Bd. dirs. Hospice of Louisville, Inc., 1984-86; exec. dir. Juvenile Justice Pub. Edn. Project, West Hartford, Conn., 1978-80; pres. bd. dirs. Stage One: Louisville Children's Theatre, 1982-83; founding bd. dirs. Ky. Citizens for Arts, Frankfort, 1983; mem. Lebanon (Conn.) Bd. Edn., 1975-80; campaign mgr. Mazzoli 3d C.D. Ky., Jefferson County, 1982, 84; elder 2d Presbyn. Ch., Louisville, 1984-86. Recipient Disting. Contbn. award Nat. Com. for Prevention of Child Abuse, Ky. chpt., 1982, Disting. Svc. award Conn. Assn. Bds. of Edn., 1976, Profl. Achievement for Gen. Reporting Series award Soc. Profl. Journalists, Sigma Delta Chi, Conn. chpt. 1974. Mem. ABA (editl. com. The Tax Lawyer 1984-89), Assn. Trial Lawyers of Am., Ky. Acad. Trial Atty's., Ky. Bar Assn., Louisville Bar Assn., Million Dollar Advocates Forum, Jefferson Club. Democrat. Presbyterian. Avocations: bibliophile, marksman, golf. General civil litigation, General corporate, Bankruptcy. Office: Trautwein and Keeney PLLC 1 Riverfront Plz Ste 510 Louisville KY 40202-2923

**KEENEY, THOMAS CRITCHFIELD,** lawyer; b. Providence, Sept. 1, 1946; s. Barnaby Conrad and Mary Elizabeth (Critchfield) K.; m. Lorraine Ingrid Busch, 1976 (div. 1997); children: Brian Conrad, Alice Linnea. BA, U. Calif., Berkeley, 1973; JD, George Washington U., Washington, D.C., 1976. Bar: R.I. 1976, U.S. Dist. Ct. R.I. 1976, U.S. Supreme Ct. 1980, D.C.

1981, Mass. 1985, U.S. Ct. Appeals (D.C. cir.) 1991. Atty. div. of enforcement litigation Office Gen. Counsel Nat. Labor Rels. Bd., Washington, 1977-81; ptnr. Powers, Kinder & Keeney, Providence, 1981—. Editor R.I. Employment Law Letter, 1996—; editor-in-chief: How to Take a Case before the National Labor Relations Bd., 1995. Sgt. USAF, 1965-69, Vietnam. Mem. ABA (mem. com. on practice and procedure before NLRB), Hope Club, Sakonnett Yacht Club. Labor, Education and schools. Office: Powers Kinder & Keeney 1 Turks Head Pl Ste 1400 Providence RI 02903-2212

**KEEP, JUDITH N.,** federal judge; b. Omaha, Mar. 24, 1944. B.A., Scripps Coll., 1966; J.D., U. San Diego, 1970. Bar: Calif. 1971. Atty. Defenders Inc., San Diego, 1971-73; pvt. practice law, 1973-76; asst. U.S. atty. U.S. Dept. Justice, 1976; judge Mcpl. Ct., San Diego, 1976-80; judge U.S. Dist. Ct. (so. dist.) Calif., San Diego, 1980—, chief judge, 1991-98; judge U.S. Office: US Dist Ct Ct Rm 16 940 Front St Ste 5190 San Diego CA 92101-8917

**KEESEE, ROGER NEAL, JR.,** lawyer; b. Lynchburg, Va., Mar. 5, 1963; s. Roger Neal and June B. (Booth) K.; m. Lisa Marie Keesee, Sept. 2, 1989; children: Nicole, Megan. BS in Acctg. magna cum laude, Va. Tech. U., 1985; JD, Wiliam and Mary Coll., 1988. Assoc. Woods, Rogers & Hazelgrove, Roanoke, Va., 1988-95, ptnr., 1996—. Co-chmn. Roanoke pro-bono hotline Legal Aid Soc., 1996-98; bd. dirs Roanoke Valley Trouble Ctr., 1992-98; trustee, mem. Roanoke Tech. Ednl. Coun., roanoke City Schs., 1992—. Mem. ABA, Va. Bar Assn. (young lawyers exec coun. 1992-98), Roanoke Valley Estate Planning Coun., Order of Coif. Office: Woods Rogers & Hazelgrove PO Box 14125 Roanoke VA 24038-4125

**KEETON, ROBERT ERNEST,** federal judge; b. Clarksville, Tex., Dec. 16, 1919; s. William Robert and Ernestine (Tuten) K.; m. Betty E. Baker, May 28, 1941; children: Katherine, William Robert. BBA, U. Tex., 1940, LLB, 1941; SJD, Harvard U., 1956; LLD (hon.), William Mitchell Coll., 1983, Lewis and Clark Coll., 1988. Bar: Tex. 1941, Mass. 1955. Assoc. firm Baker, Botts, Andrews & Wharton (and successors), Houston, 1941-42, 45-51; assoc. prof. law So. Meth. U., 1951-54; Thayer teaching fellow Harvard U., 1953-54, asst. prof., 1954-56, prof. law, 1956-73, Langdell prof., 1973-79; assoc. dean Harvard, 1975-79; judge Fed. Dist. Ct., Boston, 1979—; Commr. on Uniform State Laws from Mass., 1971-79; trustee Flaschner Jud. Inst., 1979-86; exec. dir. Nat. Inst. Trial Advocacy, 1973-76; ednl. cons., 1976-79; mem. com. on ct. adminstrn. U.S. Jud. Conf., 1985-87, mem. standing com. on rules, 1987-90, chmn., 1990-93. Author: Trial Tactics and Methods, 1954, 2d edit., 1973, Cases and Materials on the Law of Insurance, 1960, 2d edit., 1977, Legal Cause in the Law of Torts, 1963, Venturing To Do Justice, 1969, (with Jeffrey O'Connell) Basic Protection for the Traffic Victim: A Blueprint for Reforming Automobile Insurance, 1965, After Cars Crash: The Need for Legal and Insurance Reform, 1967, (with Page Keeton) Cases and Materials on the Law of Torts, 1971, 2d edit., 1977, Basic Text on Insurance Law, 1971, (with others) Tort and Accident Law, 1983, 2d edit., 1989, (with others) Prosser & Keeton, Torts, 5th edit., 1984, Pocket Part, 1988, (with Alan Widiss) Insurance Law, 1988, Judging, 1990; also articles. Served to lt. comdr. USNR, 1942-45. Recipient Wm. B. Jones award Nat. Inst. Trial Advocacy, 1980; recipient Leon Green award U. Tex. Law Rev., 1981, Francis Rawle award Am. Law Inst.-ABA, 1983, Samuel E. Gates litigation award Am. Coll. Trial Lawyers, 1984. Fellow Am. Bar Found., mem., Am. Acad. Arts and Scis., Am. Bar Assn., Mass. Bar Assn., State Bar Tex., Am. Law Inst., Am. Risk and Ins. Assn., Chancellors, Friars, Order of Coif, Beta Gamma Sigma, Beta Alpha Psi, Phi Delta Phi, Phi Eta Sigma. Office: US Dist Ct 1 Courthouse Way Ste 3130 Boston MA 02210-3005

**KEHL, LARRY BRYAN,** lawyer; b. Cheyenne, Wyo., Nov. 5, 1959; s. Lawrence E. and Ruth A. (Deines) K. BS with honors, U. Wyo., 1982, JD with honors, 1985. Bar: Wyo. 1985, U.S. Dist. Ct. Wyo. 1985, U.S. Ct. Appeals (10th cir.) 1985, Colo. 1986. Law clk. Dist. Ct. (7th dist.) Wyo., Casper, 1985-86; atty. Guy, Williams, White & Argeris, Cheyenne, 1986-92; ptnr. Orr, Buchhammer & Kehl, Cheyenne, 1992—; instr. People's Law Sch., Cheyenne, 1997. Contbr. articles to law jours. Mem. Cheyenne L.E.A.D.S., 1989—, Cheyenne Frontier Days, 1995—. Mem. Assn. Wyo. Def. Counsel, Wyo. Trial Lawyers, Def. Rsch. Inst., C. of C. General civil litigation, Insurance, Personal injury. Home: 1518 Pole Mountain Rd Cheyenne WY 82009-8305 Office: Orr Buchhammer & Kehl 1821 Logan Ave Cheyenne WY 82001-5007

**KEHL, RANDALL HERMAN,** executive, consultant, lawyer; b. Furstenfeldbruck, Federal Republic of Germany, May 18, 1954; came to U.S., 1955; s. Raymond Herman and Annabelle (Fair) K.; m. Sharon Kay Barnes; children: Lindsey Elizabeth, Jessica Anne, Austin Randall. BS, USAF Acad., 1976; MBA, U. N.D., 1980; JD, Pepperdine U., 1983. Bar: N.D. 1983, D.C. 1988, U.S. Supreme Ct. 1990. Commd. 2d lt. USAF, 1976, advanced through grades to maj., 1986, chief civil law, 1983-84, chief criminal law, 1984-85; squadron commdr. Alaska Air Command, Anchorage, 1985, chief def. counsel, 1985-86; dep. base atty. Kirtland AFB, Albuquerque, 1986-89; spl. asst. U.S. atty. U.S. Dept. Justice, Albuquerque, 1986-89; chief energy litigation Office of USAF JAG, Washington, 1989-90; White House fellow, 1990-91; chmn., CEO POD Assocs., Inc., 1992-97; cons., counsel to DESA-office of sec. of def. U.S. Dept. Def., Albuquerque, 1993; prin. Randall H. Kehl Consulting, Albuquerque, 1993-98; chmn. RHK Capital Group Internat., San Antonio, 1997—; pres., CEO Safe Zone Sys., Inc., 1998—; mem. staff Pres.'s Coun. on Competiveness, 1990-91; vice chmn. White House Working group on Commercialization of Fed. Lab. Tech., 1991; chmn. Candeli, Ltd., Kerorioni, Ltd., Rep. of Georgia, 1992-96; adj. instr. law U. Alaska, 1985-86; bd. dirs., counsel Kirtland Fed. Credit Union, Albuquerque; bd. dirs., sec. Triad Comm., Inc., Albuquerque; chmn. bd. POD Assocs., Inc., 1988-90. Asst. scoutmaster Boy Scouts Am., Minot, N.D., 1977-80; tchr. Officers Christian Fellowship, Minot, 1977-80; civic arbitrator Mediation and Conciliation Svc., 1983-86; mem. pvt. sch. bd. Anchorage, 1984-85; mem. Gov.'s Task Force for Utility Corp. Restructuring, 1987; vice-chmn. N.Mex. Gov.-Elect Transition Team, 1994, Gov.'s Bus. Adv. Coun., 1995—; mem. steering com. Rep. Campaigns, 1995—; co-chmn. N. Mex. Character Counts in the Workplace, 1996—; bd. dirs. Kirtland Partnership Com., 1995—, N.Mex. Ctr. for Civic Values, 1997—; dir. Albuquerque Character Counts, 1998—. Mem. ABA, AMA, Albuquerque Acad. Capital Devel. Com. and Assoc. Trustee, The Forman Sch. (capital devel. com.), Tanoan Country Club, Phi Delta Phi. Republican. Presbyterian. Avocations: swimming, skiing, scuba diving, sailing, golf. Office: Ste 415 5100 John D Ryan Blvd San Antonio TX 78245-3534

**KEHOE, JAMES W.,** federal judge; b. 1925. A.A., U. Fla., 1947, LL.B., 1950. Bar: Fla. Assoc. firm Worley, Kehoe & Willard, 1952-55; asst. county solicitor Dade County, Fla., 1955-57; assoc. firm Miltor R. Wasman, 1957-61; judge Civil Record Ct., Miami, 1961-63, 11th Jud. Cir. Ct., Fla., 1963-77, U.S. Ct. Appeals (3d cir.) 1977-79; judge U.S. Dist. Ct. (so. dist.) Fla., 1979—, sr. judge, 1993—. Mem. ABA, Fla. Bar Assn. Office: US Dist Ct 8th Fl Tower 301 N Miami Ave Miami FL 33128-7702

**KEHOE, TERRENCE EDWARD,** lawyer; b. Washington, June 21, 1955; s. Edward Thomas and Dorothy (Dunbar) K.; m. Priscilla Joan O'Brien, Nov. 24, 1984; children: Ryan Edward, Brendan Charles. BA, U. N.C., 1976; JD, Georgetown U., 1981. Bar: Fla. 1981, U.S. Supreme Ct. 1987; bd. cert. criminal appellate lawyer. Assoc. James M. Russ P.A., Orlando, Fla., 1981-85, Haas Boehm Brown Rigdon Seacrest & Fischer P.A., Orlando, 1985-88; pvt. practice Orlando, 1988—. Mem. Nat. Assn. Criminal Def. Lawyers, Fla. Assn. Criminal Def. Lawyers. Criminal, Appellate. Home: 1911 Ivanhoe Rd Orlando FL 32804-5938 Office: 18 W Pine St Orlando FL 32801-2612

**KEHOE, THOMAS JOSEPH,** lawyer; b. N.Y.C., Mar. 12, 1949; s. Francis Xavier and Winifred Agnes Kehoe; m. Peggy Ann Bradley; children: Matthew, Fiona, Gavin. BA in History, Holy Cross Coll., 1971; JD, Hofstra U., 1975. Bar: N.Y. 1975. Assoc. O'Dwyer & Bernstien, N.Y.C., 1975-78; sr. atty. Combustion Engring., Inc., windsor, Conn., 1978-82; counsel Gray Tool Co., Houston, 1982-84; regional cousnel Combustion Engring., London, 1984-86; assoc. gen. counsel ABB Resource Recovery Systems, Windsor, 1987-93; gen. cousnel Electric Boat Corp., Groton, Conn., 1993—. Bd. dirs., pres. Land Heritage Coalition of Glastonbury (Conn.), Inc., 1994-96. Mem. Conn. Bar Assn., N.Y. State Bar Assn., Am. Corp. Counsel Assn., Am. Shipbldg. Assn. (mem. cabinet 1996—). Avocations: coaching soccer and basketball, riding. General corporate, Intellectual property, Contracts commercial. Office: Electric Boat Corp 75 Eastern Point Rd Groton CT 06340-4905

**KEHRLI, DAVID P.,** lawyer; b. Centralia, Ill.; m. Marcia A. Kehrli. BA, Slippery Rock U., 1972; MA, Indiana (Pa.) U., 1975; JD, Western State U., Fullerton, Calif., 1990. Bar: Calif., U.S. Dist. Ct. (ctrl. dist.) Calif. Br. mgr., auditor, credit adminstr. GE Credit Corp., Stamford, Conn., 1974-82; adminstrn. mgr., corp. counsel Amada Leasing Corp., Amada Am., Inc., Buena Park, Calif., 1983—. Mem. Calif. State Bar (bus. law sect. 1993—, litigation sect., 1993-96, internat. law sect. 1997—), Orange County Bar (comml. law and bankruptcy sect. 1993—, corp. counsel sect. 1995—, fin. practice sect. 1996—). Contracts commercial, General corporate, Mergers and acquisitions. Office: Amada Am Inc 7025 Firestone Blvd Buena Park CA 90621-1869

**KEIGHTLEY, JAMES J.,** lawyer; b. 1942. AB, Villanova U.; LLB, Cornell U. Bar: 1967. Now gen. counsel Pension Benefit Guaranty Corp., Washington. Office: Pension Benefit Guaranty Corp 1200 K St NW Washington DC 20005-4025*

**KEIHNER, BRUCE WILLIAM,** lawyer; b. Hackensack, N.J., Sept. 29, 1946; s. Robert V. and Mary T. (Brennan) K.; children: Paul, John, Peter. BA, Rutgers U., 1968; JD, Cornell U., 1971. Bar: N.Y. 1972, Fla. 1982. Atty. Chadbourne & Park, N.Y.C., 1971-75, Bouck Holloway, Albany, N.Y., 1976-78, S.E. Banking Corp., Miami, Fla., 1978-82; ptnr. Blackwell Walker, Miami, 1982-86, Beasley Ollie Downs & Keihner, Miami, 1986-87; sole practitioner Palm Beach, Fla., 1988-96; ptnr. Zeller & Keihner LLP, Palm Beach, 1996—; bd. dirs. Palm Beach Housing Partnership, West Palm Beach, Fla., 1995—. Capt. USAR, 1969-74. General corporate, Real property, Private international. Office: Zeller & Keihner LLP 411 S County Rd # 200 Palm Beach FL 33480-4440

**KEILP, JOE,** lawyer; b. Weehawken, N.J., Aug. 18, 1944; s. Leo and Mary (Pankowitz) K.; m. Leslie Jeanne Skelton, Dec. 31, 1980; 1 child, Joanna Lee. AB in Psychology, Georgetown U., 1965; JD, George Washington U., 1968. Bar: N.J. 1969, U.S. Dist. Ct. D.C. 1969, Ariz. 1973, U.S. Dist. Ct. Ariz. 1971, U.S. Dist. Ct. N.J. 1969, D.C. 1973, U.S. Supreme Ct. 1972, U.S. Ct. Appeals (5th cir.) 1970, U.S. Ct. Appeals (9th cir.) 1972, U.S. Ct. Appeals (D.C. cir.) 1969, U.S. Ct. Fed. Claims, 1995. Atty. examiner U.S. Dept. Justice, Washington, 1970-71; asst. U.S. atty. U.S. Atty.'s Office, Phoenix, 1971-81, chief fraud sect., 1978-81; atty. sole practice Joe Keilp Law Office, Phoenix, 1981-87; ptnr. Jaburg & Wilk, P.C., Phoenix, 1987-91, Dillingham, Keilp & Cross, Phoenix, 1991-93; cert. specialist in criminal law Ariz. Bd. Legal Specialization, 1981—, criminal law adv. commn., 1997—. Mem. Ariz. Attys. for Criminal Justice (bd. govs. 1998—), Nat. Assn. Criminal Def. Lawyers. Criminal, General civil litigation. Office: 1440 E Washington St Phoenix AZ 85034-1109

**KEINER, CHRISTIAN MARK,** lawyer; b. Omaha, Mar. 16, 1953; s. John Frederick Keiner and Geraldine Elizabeth (Smith) Eadie; m. Rosemary Monique White, Nov. 21, 1980; 1 child, Colin MacGregor. BA with high honors, U. Calif., Santa Barbara, 1977; JD with distinction, U. of Pacific, 1980. Bar: Calif. 1980, U.S. Ct. Appeals (9th cir.) 1988, U.S. Supreme Ct. 1991. Assoc. Biddle, Walters, Bukey, Sacramento, 1980-82, Biddle and Hamilton, Sacramento, 1982-92; pvt. practice Sacramento, 1992-98; ptnr. Girard and Vinson, 1998—. Contbr. articles to law jours. Bd. dirs. Calif. Found. for Improvement Employer-Employee Rels., Sacramento, 1994—, Calif. Coun. Sch. Attys., Sacramento, 1996—; instr., mem. labor-mgmt. adv. com. U. Calif. Davis Extension, Sacramento, 1986—. Recipient award for adminstrv. law Am. Jurisprudence, 1979. Mem. ABA (pub. law sect.), Sacramento County Bar (adminstv., pub. and employment law sects.), Sacramento Capitol Club, Harry S. Truman Club (pres. 1992), Order of Coif. Democrat. Catholic. Administrative and regulatory, Appellate, Education and schools. Office: 1006 4th St Ste 701 Sacramento CA 95814-3326

**KEINER, SUELLEN TERRILL,** lawyer; b. Cin., Sept. 29, 1944; d. William A. and Lois (Hamilton) Terrill; m. R. Bruce Keiner Jr., June 15, 1958; children: Scott, Grant, Terrill. Student, Inst. Polit. Studies, Paris, 1964-65; BA, Bryn Mawr Coll., 1966; JD, Georgetown U., 1971. Bar: D.C. 1971, U.S. Supreme Ct. 1975. Fgn. documents analyst CIA, Washington, 1966-67; rsch. analyst Civil Rights divsn. U.S. Dept. Justice, Washington, 1968, 70; law clk. Weyerhaeuser Co., Tacoma, 1968-69, D.C. Superior Ct., Washington, 1971; atty. Terris & Assocs., Washington, 1972-78; asst. solicitor U.S. Dept. Interior, Washington, 1978-81; cons. for natural resources mgmt. Coun. of State Planning Agys., Washington, 1982-84; dir. litigation project Environ. Policy Inst., Washington, 1984-86; sr. atty. Environ. Law Inst., Washington, 1988—. Pres. Crestwood Citizens Assn., Washington, 1982-84. Environmental. Office: Environ Law Inst 1616 P St NW Ste 200 Washington DC 20036-1423

**KEISTER, JEAN CLARE,** lawyer; b. Warren, Ohio, Aug. 28, 1931; d. John R. Keister and Anna Helen Brennan. JD, Southwestern U., 1966. Bar: Calif. 1967, U.S. Supreme Ct. 1972, U.S. Dist. Ct. (so. dist.) Calif. 1988. Legal writer Gilbert Law Summaries, L.A., 1967; instr. Glendale (Calif.) Coll. Law, 1968; pvt. practice Glendale, 1967-70, L.A., Calif., 1970-80, Burbank, Calif., 1987-97, Lancaster, Calif., 1992—, Ventura, Calif, 1997—. Mem. Themis Soc., 1989-97. Recipient Golden Poet award World of Poetry. Mem. Burbank Bar Assn. (sec. 1993), Ventura County Bar Assn., Antelope Valley Bar Assn. Avocations: writing prose and poetry, travel, crochet. Estate planning, Family and matrimonial, Real property.

**KEITH, ALEXANDER MACDONALD,** retired state supreme court chief justice, lawyer; b. Rochester, Minn., Nov. 22, 1928; s. Norman and Edna (Alexander) K.; m. Marion Sanford, April 29, 1955; children: Peter Sanford (dec.), Ian Alexander, Douglas Scott. BA, Amherst Coll., 1950; JD, Yale U., 1953. Assoc. counsel, mem. Mayo Clinic, Rochester, 1955-60; state sen. Olmstead County, St. Paul, 1959-63; lt. gov. State of Minn., St. Paul, 1963-67; pvt. practice, Rochester, 1960-73; ptnr. Dunlap Keith Finseth Berndt and Sandberg, Rochester, 1973-89; assoc. justice Minn. Supreme Ct., St. Paul, 1989-90, chief justice, 1990-98; ret., 1998; of counsel Dunlap & Seeger P.A., Rochester, Minn., 1998—. Sen. del. White House Conf. on Aging, Washington, 1960; U.S. del. UN Delegation for Funding Developing Countries, Geneva, 1966; bd. dirs. Rochester Grad. Edn. Adv. Com., 1988-89, Ability Bldg. Ctr. Inc. 1st lt. USMC, 1953-55, Korea. Named Outstanding Freshman Senator, Minn. Senate, St. Paul. Fax: 507-288-9342. Home: 5225 Meadow Crossing Rd SW Rochester MN 55902-3506 Office: Dunlap & Seeger PA PO Box 549 Rochester MN 55903-0549

**KEITH, DAMON JEROME,** federal judge; b. Detroit, Mich., July 4, 1922; s. Perry A. and Annie L. (Williams) K.; m. Rachel Boone, Oct. 18, 1953; children: Cecile Keith, Debbie, Gilda. BA, W.Va. State Coll., 1943; JD, Howard U., 1949; LLM, Wayne State U., 1956; PhD (hon.), U. Mich., Howard U., Wayne State U., Mich. State U., N.Y. Law Sch., Detroit Coll. Law, W.Va. State Coll., U. Detroit, Atlanta U., Lincoln U., Marygrove Coll., Detroit Inst. Tech., Shaw Coll., Ctrl. State U., Yale U., Loyola Law Sch., L.A., Ea. Mich. U., Va. Union U., Ctrl. Mich. U., Morehouse Coll., Western Mich. U., Tuskegee U., Georgetown U., Hofstra U., DePaul U. Bar: Mich. 1949. Atty. Office Friend of Ct., Detroit, 1952-56; sr. ptnr. firm Keith, Conyers Anderson, Brown & Wahls, Detroit, 1964-67; mem. Wayne County Bd. Suprs., 1958-63; dist. judge U.S. Dist. Ct. (ea. dist.) Mich., 1967-77, chief judge, 1975-77; judge U.S. Ct. Appeals (6th cir.), Detroit, 1977-95, sr. judge, 1995—; mem. Wayne County (Mich.) Bd. Suprs., 1958-63; chmn. Mich. Civil Rights Commn., 1964-67; pres. Detroit Housing Commn., 1958-67; commr. State Bar Mich., 1960-67; mem. Mich. Com. Manpower Devel. and Vocat. Tng., 1964, Detroit Mayor's Health Adv. Com., 1969; rep. dist. judges 6th Cir. Jud. Conf., 1975-77; adv. com. on codes of conduct Jud. Conf. U.S., 1979-86; subcom. on supporting pers. Jud. Conf. Com. on Ct. Adminstrn., 1983-87; chmn. Com. on the Bicentennial of Constn. of Sixth Cir., 1985—; nat. chmn. Jud. Conf. Com. on the Bicentennial of Constn., 1987—; mem. Commn. on the Bicentennial of U.S. Constn., 1990; lectr. Howard U., 1972, Ohio State U. Law Sch., 1992, N.Y. Law Sch., 1992; guest lectr. Howard U. Law Sch., 1981; Bicentennial of Constn. lectr. W.Va. State Coll., 1987; keynote speaker Black Law Students Assn., Harvard Law Sch., 1987. Contbr. articles to profl. jours. Trustee Med. Corp. Detroit; trustee Interlochen Arts Acad., Cranbrook Sch., U. Detroit, Mich. chpt. Leukemia Soc. Am.; mem. Citizen's Adv. Com. Equal Ednl. Opportunity Detroit Bd. Edn.; gen. co-chmn. United Negro Coll. Fund Detroit; 1st v.p. emeritus Detroit chpt. NAACP; mem. com. mgmt. Detroit YMCA, Detroit coun. Boy Scouts Am., Detroit Arts Commn; vice chmn. Detroit Symphony Orch.; vis. com. Wayne State U. Law Sch.; adv. coun. U. Notre Dame Law Sch.; bd. dirs. Detroit Bd. Table, NCCJ; deacon Tabernacle Missionary Bapt. Ch.; chmn. Citizen's Coun. for Mich. Pub. Univs. With AUS, World War II. Recipient Mich. Chronicle outstanding Citizen award, 1960. 64. 74, Alumni citation Wayne State U., 1968, Ann. Jud. award, 1971, Citizen award Mich. State U., Disting. Svc. award Howard U., 1972, Jud. Independence award, 1973, Spingarn medal NAACP, 1974, Fed. Judge of Yr. award, Black Law Students Assn., 1974, award for Outstanding Contbns. to Black Community, Nat. Assn. Black Social Workers, 1974, Judge of Yr. award Nat. Conf. Black Lawyers, 1974, Bill of Rights award Jewish Community Coun., 1977, A. Philip Randolph award Detroit Coalition Black Trade Unionists, 1981, Human Rights Day award B'nai B'rith Women's Coun. Met. Detroit, Robert L. Millender award So. Christian Leadership Conf. Mich. chpt., 1982, Afro-Asian Inst. award Histadrut in Israel, 1982, civil rights lectr. award, Creighton U. Ahmanson Law Ctr., 1983, Nat. Human Rels. award Greater Detroit Roundtable of NCCJ, 1984, Knights of Charity award Pontifical Inst. for Mission Extension, 1986, Disting. Pub. Svc. award Mich. Anti-Defamation League of B'nai B'rith, 1987, Nat. Chpt. award, 1988, Black Achievement award Equitable Fin. Cos., 1987, Menorah award Afro-Asian Inst. Histadrut of Israel, 1988, Dr. George Derry award Marygrove Coll. Detroit, One Nation award The Patriots Found./GM, 1989, 1st Ann. Move Detroit Forward award City of Detroit, 1990, Gov's. Minuteman award Rotary Club Lansing, 1991; named 1 of 100 Most Influential Black Ams. Ebony Mag., 1971-92; Damon J. Keith Elementary Sch. named in his honor Detroit Bd. Edn., 1974; Damon J. Keith Ann. Civic and Humanitarian award established in his honor Highland Park YMCA, 1984; 15th Mich. Legal Milestone The Uninvited Ear presented in honor of The Keith Decision, 1991. Mem. ABA (coun. sect. legal edn. and admission to bar), Nat. Bar Assn. (William H. Hastie award Jud. Coun., 8th Ann. equal Justice award), Mich. Bar Assn. (champion of justice award), Detroit Bar Assn. (pres'. award), Nat. Lawyers Guild, Am. Judicature Soc., Alpha Phi Alpha. Baptist (deacon). Club: Detroit Cotillion. Office: US Ct Appeals US Courthouse 231 W Lafayette Blvd Rm 240 Detroit MI 48226-2779*

**KEITH, JOHN A.C.,** lawyer; b. Washington, Aug. 22, 1946. BA, U. Va., 1968, JD, 1974. Bar: Va. 1975, D.C. 1976. Law clk. Hon. Albert V. Bryan, Jr. U.S. Dist. Ct. (ea. dist.) Va., 1974-75; ptnr. Blankingship & Keith, Fairfax, Va. Fellow Am. Bar Found.; mem. ABA, Am. Counsel Assn., Va. State Bar Assn. (10th dist. com. 1983-86, chmn. 1985-86, chmn. standing com. on legal ethics 1996-97, bar coun. 1991—, exec. com. 1993—, pres.-elect 1997-98, pres. 1998—), Fairfax Bar Assn. E-mail: JKeith@blankeith.com. General civil litigation, Real property, Personal injury. Office: Blankingship & Keith PC 4020 University Dr Ste 312 Fairfax VA 22030-6802*

**KEITHLEY, BRADFORD GENE,** lawyer; b. Nov. 23, 1951; s. Sanderson Irish and Joan G. (Kenneday) K.; m. Ginger W. Wilhelmi, Mar. 26, 1994; children: Paul Michael, Rachel Austin Bernstein. BS, U. Tulsa, 1973; JD, U. Va., 1976. Bar: Va. 1976, Okla. 1978, D.C. 1979. Atty. Office of Gen. Counsel to Sec. USAF, Washington, 1976-78; ptnr. Hall, Estill, Hardwick, Gable, Collingsworth and Nelson, Tulsa, 1978-84; sr. v.p. gen. counsel Arkla, Inc. (now NorAm Energy Corp. divsn. Reliant Energy, Inc.), Shreveport, La., 1984-90; ptnr. head oil and gas practice team Jones, Day, Reavis and Pogue, Dallas, 1990—. Mem. ABA, Fed. Energy Bar Assn., Va. State Bar, Okla. Bar Assn., D.C. Bar Assn., Am. Gas Assn. (mem. legal sect.), Dallas Petroleum Club, Prestonwood Country Club. Oil, gas, and mineral, FERC practice, Federal civil litigation. Home: 12652 Sunlight Dr Dallas TX 75230-1856 Office: Jones Day Reavis & Pogue 2300 Trammell Crow Ctr 2001 Ross Ave Dallas TX 75201-2958

**KEITHLEY, ROGER LEE,** lawyer; b. Macomb, Ill., July 19, 1946; s. Gilbert Lee and Mary Jane (Torrance) K.; m. Karen Sue Metzger, Apr. 1, 1973; children: Roger Livingston, Terrance Christopher, Kathryn Suzanne. BS, U. Ill., 1968; JD, Harvard U., 1973. Bar: Colo. 1973, U.S. Dist. Ct. Colo. 1973, U.S. Ct. Appeals (10th cir.) 1976. Law clk. to justice Colo. Supreme Ct., Denver, 1973-74; trial atty. SEC, Denver, 1974-76; assoc. Morrato, Gueck & Colantuno, Denver, 1976-80; ptnr. Krys, Boyle, Golz & Keithley, Denver, 1980-86, Law, Knous & Keithley, Denver, 1986-90, Law, Keithley & Tuttle, Denver, 1990-93; pvt. practice Roger L. Keithley, P.C., Denver, 1993-98; presiding disciplinary judge Colo. Supreme Ct., 1998—; prof. physics U. Asmara, Eritrea, Ethiopia, 1969-70. With U.S. Army, 1968-70. Mem. ABA (litigation sect., corp. banking and bus. sect., criminal justice sect., mem. and officer various coms.), Colo. Bar Assn., Denver Bar Assn. Securities, Personal injury, Insurance. Home: 5239 E 17th Ave Denver CO 80220-1313

**KELAHER, JAMES PEIRCE,** lawyer; b. Orlando, Fla., Oct. 28, 1951; s. Philip James and Neva Cecelia (Peirce) K. BA, U. Cen. Fla., 1973; JD, Fla. State U., 1981. Bar: Fla. 1981, U.S. Dist. Ct. (mid. dist.) Fla. 1982, U.S. Ct. Appeals (11th cir.) 1983, U.S. Supreme Ct.; cert. civil trial law. Assoc. Law Office of Nolan Carter, P.A., Orlando, 1981-83, Law Office of James Kelaher, P.A., Orlando, 1983-87; ptnr. Kelaher & Wieland, P.A., Orlando, 1987—, Kelaher, Wieland and Hilado, P.A., Orlando, 1996-98, Kelaher Law Offices, P.A., Orlando, 1998—. Contbr. articles to profl. jours. Eagle benefactor Rep. Party. Mem. ABA, ATLA (sustaining), Orange County Bar Assn., Acad. Fla. Trial Lawyers (sec. 1994-95, treas. 1995-96, pres. 1997-98, bd. dirs. coll. diplomates, membership exec. com. bd. trustees Fla. lawyers action group), Ctrl. Fla. Trial Lawyers Assn. (pres. 1992-94). Roman Catholic. Avocations: tennis, golf, snow skiing, fishing. E-mail: jim@kelaherlaw.com. Personal injury, General civil litigation. Office: Kelaher Law Offices 800 N Magnolia Ave Ste 1301 Orlando FL 32803-3255

**KELAKOS, GEORGE M.,** lawyer; b. Boston; s. Michael George and Theresa (Plakias) K. BA, Brandeis U., 1979; JD, U. Denver, 1982. Bar: Colo. 1982, U.S. Dist. Ct. Colo. 1982, U.S. Ct. Appeals (10th cir.) 1985, Mass. 1986, U.S. Dist. Ct. Mass. 1986. Assoc. Inman & Flynn, P.C., Denver, 1982-83, Sterling & Miller, P.C., Denver, 1984-85, Riemer & Braunstein, Boston, 1985-89, Fine & Ambrogne, Boston, 1989-90; partner Cohn & Kelakos LLP, Boston, 1990—. Editor Denver Jour. Iternat. Law and Policy, 1981-82. Mem. ABA, Am. Bankruptcy Inst., Turnaround Mgmt. Assn., Boston Bar Assn., Mass. Bar Assn., Insol Internat., Inter-Pacific Bar Assn. Avocations: martial arts, motorcycle touring, music. Bankruptcy, Private international. Office: Cohn & Kelakos LLP 265 Franklin St Boston MA 02110-3113

**KELEHER, MICHAEL LAWRENCE,** lawyer; b. Albuquerque, Sept. 21, 1934; s. William A. Keleher and Loretta Barrett; m. Margaret Anne Wills, June 10, 1961; children: Anne Barrett, Elizabeth Katherine, Margaret Mary, Mary Ann, Loretta Wills, Michael Wills. BA, U. N. Mex., 1956; MA, NYU, 1958; JD, U. Miss., 1962. Bar: N. Mex. 1962. Atty. Keleher & McLeod PA, Albuquerque, 1962—. Lt. (j.g.) USN, 1956-58. Democrat. Roman Catholic. Estate planning, Probate, Real property. Office: Keleher & McLeod PA 201 3rd St NW Albuquerque NM 87102-3370

**KELEPECZ, BETTY PATRICE,** protective services official, lawyer; b. Santa Monica, Calif., Nov. 13, 1955; d. Andrew J. and Doris L. Giba; m. Steve T. Kelepecz, Sept. 3, 1983. AS, Antelope Valley Coll., 1975; BS in Biology, U. So. Calif., L.A., 1977; JD, Southwestern U., 1990; grad., FBI Nat. Acad., 1992. Bar: Calif. 1990, U.S. Dist. Ct. (ctrl. dist.) Calif. 1991. Microbiologist Rachelle Labs., Long Beach, Calif., 1978-80; police officer I, II, III, background investigator L.A. Police Dept., 1980-85, detective I S.W. Cmty. Police Sta., 1985-86, sgt. I Pacific, 77th and West L.A. patrol divsn., 1986-88, sgt. I ops. South Bur., 1988-89, sgt. II planning and rsch. divsn., 1989-90, lt. I Harbor Cmty. Police Sta., 1990-91, lt. II Ops.-South Bur., 1991, lt. II Office of the Chief of Police, 1991-93, capt. I Harbor Cmty. Police Sta., 1993-95, capt. I Pacific Cmty. Police Sta., 1995-96; owner, prinr. Law Offices of Pheil & Kelepecz, Long Beach, Calif., 1995-99; capt. II West Traffic divsn. L.A. Police Dept., 1996, capt. III Sci. Investigation divsn., 1996-97, comdr. Cmty. Policing Group, 1997, comdr. Ops.-West Bur., 1997—, comdr. Pers. Group, 1998—; spkr., trainer and cons. in field. Recipient Am. Jurisprudence Book award, 1987, Congratulatory cert. Mayor

Riordan, 1997, Affirmative Action Assn. Women Recognition for women leaders and pacesetters, 1997, Congress Racial Equality Calif. commendation, 1997; named Outstanding Young Women of Am., 1988. Mem. ABA, FBI Nat. Acad. Assocs., Internat. Assn. Chiefs Police (com. mem. major city chiefs human resources), Am. Soc. Crime Lab. Dirs., Nat. Assn. Women Law Enforcement Execs. (immediate past pres., charter), Calif. Bar Assn., L.A. County Bar Assn., L.A. County Police Officer's Assn., L.A. Police Command Officer's Assn. (com. mem.), L.A. Women Police Officer's Assn., Police Exec. Rsch. Forum, Rotary Club Westchester, Delta Theta Phi.

**KELL, JOHN MARK,** lawyer; b. Champaign, Ill., June 14, 1951; s. Scott Kenneth and Helen Suzanne (Reger) K.; m. Cynthia Marie Evens, Mar. 3, 1975; children: Christian, Erin, Emily, Ashley, James. BA, U. Mo., Columbia, 1973; JD, St. Louis U., 1978. Bar: Mo. 1978, U.S. Dist. Ct. (ea. dist.) Mo. 1980, U.S. Ct. Appeals (8th cir.) 1985. Assoc. Theodore Hoffman, St. Louis, 1978-82, Miller & McAvoy, St. Louis, 1982-83; ptnr. Kell Custer Weller & Miller, St. Louis, 1983-96, Kell Couglin & Miller, St. Louis, 1996-97, Kell Flach & Miller, St. Louis, 1997-99, Kell & Flach, St. Louis, 1999—; adj. prof. law Webster U., St. Louis, 1995—. Mem. Met. St. Louis Bar Assn., Mo. Assn. Trial Attys. Personal injury, Workers' compensation, Product liability. Office: Kell & Flach 6 Algonquin Wood Saint Louis MO 63122-2013

**KELL, SCOTT K.,** lawyer; b. Lake Worth, Fla., Jan. 11, 1928; s. Scott Kell and Frances (Aborn) Jefferson; m. Virginia Kell, Sept. 30, 1990. BA, Ill. Wesleyan U., 1953; LLB, Lincoln Coll. of Law, Springfield, Ill., 1953. Bar: Ill. 1953, Ohio 1963, Mo. 1967. Pvt. practice, St. Louis, St. Charles, and, Hermann, Mo., 1967—. Mem. Assn. Trial Lawyers Am., St. Louis Met. Bar Assn. Insurance, Criminal, Real property. Office: Barks & Kell 127 E 4th St Hermann MO 65041-1129

**KELL, VETTE EUGENE,** retired lawyer; b. Marengo, Iowa, Oct. 17, 1915; s. Eugene S. and Florence (Vette) K.; m. Alice Eaton, Sept. 3, 1938; 1 son, Michael V. JD, U. Iowa. Bar: Iowa 1940, Ill. 1948. Ptnr. Joslyn, Parker & Kell, Woodstock, Ill., 1948-67, Kell, Conerty & Poehlmann, Woodstock, 1967-84; sr. ptnr. Kell, Nuelle & Loizzo, 1985-97; lectr. Ill. Continuing Edn. Inst. Served to lt. USN, 1942-45, PTO. Mem. Ill. State Bar Assn., Soc. Trial Lawyers, Am. Coll. Trial Lawyers, Internat. Coll. Trial Lawyers. Episcopalian. State civil litigation, General practice, Personal injury. Home: 10431 Deerpath Rd Woodstock IL 60098-7224

**KELLAR, NORMAN,** lawyer; b. N.Y.C., June 6, 1964; s. Samuel Kellar and Rose Standard; m. Tullia P., Sept. 3, 1938 (dec.); children: Laura, Jane, Paul. BA, U. N.C., 1935; LLB, Fordham U. Law Sch., 1938. Bar: U.S. Dist. Ct. (so. and no. dists.) N.Y. 1955, U.S. Supreme Ct. 1970. Pro bono atty. N.Y. State Civil Liberties Union, Hudson Valley, 1970-80, Hudson Vly. Legal Svcs., 1975-85; atty. Town of Esopus, N.Y., 1977—. Mem. N.Y. State Bar Assn. (ho. dels. 1973), Ulster County Bar Assn. (pres. 1973-75). Democrat. Avocations: gardening, orchid growing, farming fruit and dairy. Office: Kellar & Kellar 14 Pearl St Kingston NY 12401-4522

**KELLEHER, D. RING,** lawyer; b. Somerville, Mass., Jan. 4, 1927; s. Jeremiah Michael and Ellen (Ring) K.; children: Johanna, Margaret Mary, Suzanne, Anna Michaela Meehan. LLB, Boston Coll., 1953; LLM, Columbia U., 1972. Pvt. practice Arlington, Mass., 1975—. Avocations: reading, gardening. Criminal, Estate planning, Personal injury. Home and Office: One Chestnut St Arlington MA 02474

**KELLEHER, ROBERT JOSEPH,** federal judge; b. N.Y.C., Mar. 5, 1913; s. Frank and Mary (Donovan) K.; m. Gracyn W. Wheeler, Aug. 14, 1940; children: R. Jeffrey, Karen Kathleen Kelleher King. A.B., Williams Coll., 1935; LL.B., Harvard U., 1938. Bar: N.Y. 1939, Calif. 1942, U.S. Supreme Ct 1954. Atty. War Dept., 1941-42; asst. U.S. atty. So. Dist. Calif., 1948-50; pvt. practice Beverly Hills, 1951-71; U.S. dist. judge, 1971-83; sr. judge U.S. Dist. Ct. 9th Cir., 1983—. Mem. So. Calif. Com. Olympic Games, 1964; capt. U.S. Davis Cup Team, 1962-63; treas. Youth Tennis Found. So. Calif., 1961-64. Served to lt. USNR, 1942-45. Mem. So. Calif. Tennis Assn. (v.p. 1958-64, pres. 1983-85), U.S. Lawn Tennis Assn. (pres. 1967-68), Internat. Lawn Tennis Club U.S.A., Gt. Britain, France, Can., Mex., Australia, India, Israel, Japan, All Eng. Lawn Tennis and Croquet (Wimbledon), Harvard Club (N.Y./So. Calif.), Williams Club (N.Y.), L.A. Country Club, Delta Kappa Epsilon. Home: 15 St Malo Bch Oceanside CA 92054-5854 Office: US Dist Ct 255 E Temple St Ste 830 Los Angeles CA 90012-3334

**KELLEHER, TERENCE L.,** lawyer; b. Bklyn., July 21, 1947; s. Edward F. and Harriett M. (Lane) K.; m. Margaret A. Moylan, May 22, 1976; children: Brian, Catherine, Cristina, Claire. AB, St. Peter's Coll., Jersey City, 1968; JD, Fordham U., 1972. Bar: N.Y. 1973, U.S. Dist. Ct. (so. and ea. dists.) N.Y. 1974, U.S. Ct. Appeals (2d cir.) 1975, U.S. Supreme Ct. 1980. Assoc. Pavia & Harcourt, N.Y.C., 1972-76; ptnr. Twohy, Kelleher & Gallagher, Bklyn., 1976—; bd. dirs. CCC Ins. Co. Ltd., Bermuda, CCC Ins. Corp., Barbados. Bd. dirs. Bklyn. Boys and Girls Club, 1978—, pres., 1994-96; trustee N.Y. Meth. Hosp., Bklyn., 1984—. Capt. M.I., U.S. Army, 1970. Fulbright-Hays tchg. asst., Italy, 1968. Mem. N.Y. State Bar Assn. (exec. com. real property sect. 1992—), Bklyn. Bar Assn., Nassau County Bar Assn. Roman Catholic. Real property, Banking, Contracts commercial. Office: Twohy Kelleher & Gallagher 188 Montague St Brooklyn NY 11201-3609

**KELLEHER, WILLIAM EUGENE, JR.,** lawyer; b. Scranton, Pa., Dec. 7, 1953; s. William E. and Elizabeth Coles (Gates) K.; m. Teresa Marie Iorfido, July 22, 1977. BA in Econs. and Polit. Sci., U. Pitts., 1975; JD, Duquesne U., 1979. Bar: Pa. 1979, U.S. Dist. Ct. (we. dist.) Pa. 1979, U.S. Ct. Appeals (5th cir.) 1989, U.S. Ct. Appeals (3rd cir.) 1990, U.S. Ct. Appeals (11th cir.) 1998, U.S. Supreme Ct. 1992. Assoc. Eckert, Seamans, Cherin & Mellott, Pitts., 1979-86, ptnr., mem., 1987—, adminstr. bankruptcy and creditors rights sect., 1990—; counsel, asst. sec. Brockway (Pa.), Inc., 1984-85; mem. exec. com. Eckert Seamans Cherin & Mellott L.L.C., Pitts., 1995-96. Assoc. editor Duquesne Law Rev., 1978-79. Mem. ABA, ATLA, Pa. Bar Assn., Allegheny County Bar Assn. (bankruptcy and comml. law sect. 1995—, exec. counsel, rules com., ednl. programs com., chmn. 1997), Am. Bankruptcy Inst. (cert.). Avocations: sports, astronomy. Bankruptcy, Contracts commercial, General civil litigation. Home: 3 Green Brier Dr Allison Park PA 15101-1600 Office: Eckert Seamans Cherin & Mellott LLC 600 Grant St Ste 4400 Pittsburgh PA 15219-2702

**KELLER, C. REYNOLDS,** lawyer; b. N.Y.C., Mar. 23, 1938; s. Chauncey A.R. and Frances Alida (Richardson) K. m. Julie C. Heyburn, Dec. 16, 1980; children: Sarah Frances, Chauncey A.R. III, Carolyn Marie, Joseph Martin Gerard. BA cum laude, Princeton U., 1960; LLM, JD, U. Mich., 1963. Bar: Ohio 1963, U.S. Dist. Ct. (no. and ea. dists.) Ohio 1963, Calif. 1974, U.S. Dist. Ct. (no. and ctrl. dists.) Calif. 1974, U.S. Supreme Ct. 1974. Assoc. Weston, Hurd, Fallon, et al, Cleve., 1963-68, ptnr., 1968-92, mng. ptnr., 1988-92; ptnr. Hahn, Loeser & Parks, Cleve., 1992-99; founder Keller & Kehoe LLP, Cleve., 1999—; trustee Horizon Montessori Sch., Cleveland Heights, Ohio, 1970—. Chmn. del. selection process Carter/Mondale Campaign, Ohio, 1980. Fellow Am. Coll. Trial Lawyers; mem. ABA, Cleve. Bar Assn., Ct. Nisi Prius (sgt. 1990—). Avocations: aviation license (commercial/instrument), soccer coach, gardening. General civil litigation. Home: 253 Hawthorne Dr Chagrin Falls OH 44022-3326 Office: Keller & Kehoe LLP 900 Baker Bldg 1940 E Sixth St Cleveland OH 44114-2210

**KELLER, JAMES,** state supreme court justice; b. Harlan, 1942; m. Elizabeth Keller; 2 children. Student, Ea. Ky. U.; JD, U. Ky. Pvt. practice; master commr. Fayette Cir. Ct., 1969-76, judge, 1976-99; justice Ky. Supreme Ct., 1999—. Mem. Ky. Bar Assn., Fayette County Bar Assn. Office: Supreme Ct Ky Ste 200 155 E Main Lexington KY 40507*

**KELLER, JOHN WARREN,** lawyer; b. Niagara Falls, Aug. 6, 1954; s. Joseph and Edith Lillian (Kilvington) K.; m. Sandra D. Hubbard, Dec. 18, 1981; children: Sean, Christopher. BA, Rider U., 1976; JD, Coll. William and Mary, 1979. Bar: Ky. 1980, U.S. Dist. Ct. (ea. dist.) Ky. 1985, U.S. Ct. Appeals (6th cir.) 1988, U.S. Dist. Ct. (we. dist.) Ky. 1988. Staff atty. Appalachian Rsch. & Def. Fund Ky., Inc., Barbourville, 1979-82; assoc. F. Preston Farmer Law Offices, London, Ky., 1982-88; ptnr. Farmer, Keller & Kelley, London, 1988-91, Taylor, Keller & Dunaway, London, 1991—; mem. Fla. Adv. Com. on Arson Prevention, 1990—; chair bd. dirs. Appalachian Rsch. & Def. Fund Ky., 1994-96; founder, chmn. bd. dirs. Ky. Lawyers for Legal Svcs. to the Poor; mem. editl. adv. bd. Ky. West Publ. Group, 1997; bd. mem. Nat. Soc. Ins. Investigators. Contbg. editor: ABA Annotations to Homeowner's Policy, 3rd edit., 1995, ABA Bad Faith Annotations, 2d edit., 1997. Bd. dirs. Christian Ch. in Ky., 1994-98; elder First Christian Ch., London, 1994-97; pres. Access to Justice Found., 1996—. Recipient Access to Justice award Ky. Legal Svcs. Programs, 1995. Mem. ABA (vice chair property ins. law com. 1992-97), Laurel County Bar Assn. (pres. 1992-93), Ky. Bar Assn. (mem. bd. govs. 1996—), The Honorable Order of Ky. Cols. General civil litigation, Insurance. Office: Taylor Keller & Dunaway 1306 W 5th St London KY 40741-1615

**KELLER, MARY GARVEY,** lawyer; b. Milbank, S.D., July 27, 1937; d. Michael Peter and Rose Mary (Ernster) Garvey; m. John Whitworth Keller, Dec. 28, 1957; children: Elizabeth Carlin Keller Bransdorfer, John Whitworth, Thomas Merrick. BA, U. S.D., 1958; JD, U. Minn., 1981. Bar: S.D. 1981, U.S. Dist. Ct. S.D. 1981, U.S. Ct. Appeals (8th cir.) 1981, U.S. Supreme Ct. 1995. Pub. sch. tchr. Chamberlain, S.D., 1964-78; pvt. practice Huron, S.D., 1981—; county prosecutor County of Beadle, Huron, 1985-96; spl. asst. atty. gen. State of S.D., Huron, 1997—. Del. State Dem. Conv., Pierre, Aberdeen, S.D., 1996; del. Nat. Dem. Conv., Chgo., 1996. Mem. Bus. and Profl. Women (local officer 1982—), S.D. Bar Assn., Beadle Bar Assn. (pres., sec.-treas. 1983-85), Beadle County Dems., Beadle County Dem. Women, Nat. Assn. Women Lawyers (area rep. 1996—). Roman Catholic. Avocations: reading crime novels, photography. Office: PO Box 97 351 Wisconsin Ave SW # 103 Huron SD 57350-0097

**KELLER, SHARON FAYE,** state supreme court justice. Judge Tex. Ct. Criminal Appeals. Office: Tex Ct Criminal Appeals PO Box 12308 Austin TX 78711-2308

**KELLER, THOMAS CLEMENTS,** lawyer; b. New Orleans, Dec. 20, 1938; s. Charles Agustus and Mary (Chisolm) K. BA, Tulane U., 1960, JD, 1963; LLM, NYU, 1964. Bar: La. 1963. Assoc. Jones, Walker, Waechter, Poitevent, Carrere & Denegre, New Orleans, 1963-70, ptnr., 1970-98, of counsel, 1998—, exec. dir., 1998—; cons. Hunt Plywood Co., Inc., 1991—; sec. bd. dirs. McIlhenny Co. Bd. dirs. New Orleans Mus. Art, 1982—, pres., 1988-90; bd. dirs. Met. Arts Found., New Orleans. Mem. ABA (sect. on taxation 1970—), La. Bar Assn. (chmn. tax sect. 1978), Metropolitan Club (Washington), Knickerbocker Club (N.Y.C.), Pickwick Club (New Orleans). Democrat. Roman Catholic. Estate taxation, Taxation, general, State and local taxation. Office: Jones Walker Waechter Poitevent Carrere & Denegre 201 Saint Charles Ave Ste 5200 New Orleans LA 70170-5100

**KELLER, WILLIAM D.,** federal judge; b. 1934. BS, U. Calif., Berkeley, 1956; LLB, UCLA, 1960. Asst. U.S. atty. U.S. Dist. Ct. (so. dist.) Calif., 1961-64; assoc. Dryden, Harrington, Horgan & Swartz, Calif., 1964-72; U.S. atty. U.S. Dist. Ct. (cen. dist.) Calif., Los Angeles, 1972-77; ptnr. Rosenfeld, Meyer & Susman, 1977-78; solo practice, 1978-81; ptnr. Mahm & Cazier, 1981-84; judge U.S. Dist. Ct. (cen. dist.) Calif., Los Angeles, 1984—; ptnr. Rosenfeld, Meyer & Susman, Calif., 1977-78; pvt. practice law Calif., 1978-81; ptnr. Hahn & Cazier, Calif., 1981-84. Office: US Dist Ct 312 N Spring St Ste 1653 Los Angeles CA 90012-4718

**KELLERMAN, EDWIN,** lawyer, physician; b. Phila., Feb. 9, 1932. AB, U. Pa., 1954; MD, Northwestern U., 1959; JD, Temple U., 1984. Bar: Pa. 1984, U.S. Dist. Ct. (ea. dist.) Pa. 1984, U.S. Ct. Appeals (3d cir.) 1985, U.S. Ct. Claims 1995; diplomate Am. Bd. Internal Medicine, Am. Bd. Nephrology. Intern Jersey City Med. Ctr., 1959-60; resident Mt. Sinai Hosp., 1962-63, Jackson Meml. Hosp., 1963-64; NIH fellow Hahnemann Med. Coll., 1964-65; pvt. practice medicine N.J., 1965-72; pvt. practice medicine Phila., 1972-86, sole practice health care law, 1984—; cons. in medicine, Social Security Adminstrn., 1979-84. Contbr. to Legal Medicine, 1988, 90, 95. Capt. M.C., U.S. Army, 1960-62. Fellow Am. Coll. Legal Medicine. Health, State civil litigation, Personal injury.

**KELLEY, CHRISTOPHER DONALD,** lawyer; b. Manhasset, N.Y., Nov. 6, 1957; s. Donald Kelley and Audrey (Wuestmann) Raebeck; m. Nancy Nagle, June 27, 1981. BA in History with high honors, Coll. William and Mary, 1978; JD cum laude, N.Y. Law Sch., 1981. Bar: N.Y. 1982, U.S. Dist. Ct. (ea. dist.) N.Y. 1984. Assoc. Twomey Latham & Shea, Riverhead, N.Y., 1981-85; ptnr. Twomey Latham Shea & Kelley, Riverhead, N.Y., 1985—. Chmn. East Hampton (N.Y.) Dem. Com., 1982-86, 87-88, East Hampton Town Zoning Bd. Appeals, 1986-87. Mem. N.Y. Bar Assn. (environ. law sect.), Suffolk County Bar Assn., N.Y. County Bar Assn., Am. Trial Lawyers Assn. Episcopalian. General practice, Environmental, State civil litigation. Home: 727 Accabonac Rd East Hampton NY 11937-1807 Office: Twomey Latham Shea & Kelley 33 W 2nd St Riverhead NY 11901-2701

**KELLEY, JAMES FRANCIS,** lawyer; b. Dec. 30, 1941; s. James O'Connor and Marcella Cecilia (Salb) K.; children: Sarah, Leah, Laurence. AB, Yale U.; JD, U. Chgo. Bars: N.Y. 1967, Tex. 1981. Assoc. Breed, Abbott & Morgan, N.Y.C., 1967-75; dep. gen. counsel United Tech. Corp., Hartford, Conn., 1975-81; sr. v.p., gen. counsel Diamond Shamrock Corp. (name now Maxus Energy Corp.), Dallas, 1981-88; ptnr. Jones, Day, Reavis & Pogue, Dallas and Paris, 1988-93; sr. v.p. law, gen. counsel Georgia-Pacific Corp., 1993—. Gov. Dallas Symphony Assn., 1985-89; bd. dirs. North Tex. Pub. Broadcasting Found., Dallas, 1983-91, mem. exec. com., 1988-91; bd. dirs. Atlanta Symphony Orch., 1994—, mem. exec. com., 1996—, vice chair fin. com., 1996—; bd. dirs. Ga. Trust Hist. Preservation, 1994—; mem. bd. visitors Emory U., 1999—. Mem. ABA, Assn. Gen. Counsel. General corporate, Private international, Mergers and acquisitions. Office: Georgia-Pacific Corp 133 Peachtree St NE Atlanta GA 30303-1808

**KELLEY, JAMES RUSSELL,** lawyer; b. Conneaut, Ohio, Feb. 25, 1948; s. Russell Wynne and Mattie Lou (Robertson) K.; m. Lissa Galloway, Jan. 7, 1984; 1 child, Kathleen Anne. BA, Vanderbilt U., 1970; JD, Emory U., 1975, LLM in Taxation, 1977. Bar: Ga. 1975, U.S. Dist. Ct. (no. dist.) Ga. 1975, U.S. Ct. Appeals (5th cir.) 1975, Tenn. 1977, U.S. Dist. Ct. (mid. dist.) Tenn. 1977, U.S. Ct. Appeals (6th cir.) 1977. Systems analyst Standard Oil of Ohio, Cleve., 1970-72; assoc. Greene, Buckley, DeRieux & Jones, Atlanta, 1975-77; assoc. Dearborn & Ewing, Nashville, 1977-80, ptnr., 1980-90; ptnr. Neal & Harwell, Nashville, 1990—; bd. dirs. Mid-South Comml. Law Inst., Nashville. Author: (with others) Corporations-Formation, 1980; contbg. editor: Norton Bankruptcy Law and Practice, 1987—. Bankruptcy, Corporate taxation, General corporate. Office: Neal & Harwell PLC 2000 1st Union Tower Nashville TN 37219

**KELLEY, MICHAEL EUGENE,** lawyer; b. Creston, Iowa, June 18, 1941; s. Cletus George and Zelphia Ellen (Billingsley) K.; m. Helen Ann Cox Alger, Apr. 14, 1963 (div. Oct. 1974); 1 child, Kurt Allen; m. Georgia Elyse Lunn Aistrope, Oct. 14, 1974; children: Suzanne Elyse Kelley Porter, Michael Keith. AA, S.W. C.C., 1965; BA, Omaha U., 1968; JD, Creighton U., 1971. Bar: Nebr. 1971, Iowa 1971, U.S. Dist. Ct. Nebr. 1971. Trainman, yardmaster Burlington No., Creston, Council Bluffs, Iowa, 1959-71; assoc. Edgar Cook, Atty., Glenwood, Iowa, 1971-73; pvt. practice, Glenwood, 1973-76; gen. counsel Kearney (Nebr.) Mcpl. Airport Corp., 1976—; atty. Mills County, Glenwood, 1972-74; city atty. City of Kearney, 1976—; spkr. in field. Mem. Kearney cabinet Kearney Gideons, ch. asst. sec., 1988-90. With USN, 1960-64. Mem. Internat. Mpls. Lawyers Assn. (Nebr. state chair 1995—), Nebr. State Bar Assn., Buffalo County Bar Assn., Nebr. Gideons (mem. state cabinet, ch. asst. sec. 1990-93), Full Gospel Businessmen's Fellowship Internat. (v.p. 1987-89). Avocations: ichthyology, model trains and villages, shotgun sports. Home: 1203 E 34th St Kearney NE 68847-3226 Office: City of Kearney PO Box 1180 Kearney NE 68848-1180

**KELLEY, SHANE RICHARD,** lawyer; b. Sioux Falls, S.D., July 17, 1960; s. Richard Donald and Catherine Hedvig Kelley; m. Sara Ann Platt, July 8, 1983. BS, U. S.D., 1982, MBA, 1987, JD, 1987. Bar: Minn. 1987, U.S. Dist. Ct. Minn. 1987. Shareholder Popham Haik Schnobrich & Kaufman, Mpls., 1987-97; ptnr. Hinshaw & Culbertson, Mpls., 1997—. Mem. Minn. Bar Assn., Hennepin County Bar Assn. Mergers and acquisitions, General corporate, Contracts commercial. Office: Hinshaw & Culbertson 222 S 9th St Minneapolis MN 55402-3389

**KELLEY, TIMOTHY EDWARD,** state judge; b. Canton, N.Y., Aug. 16, 1954; s. Andrew James and Arlene Ellen (Dishaw) m.; m. Nanette Noland, Mar. 18, 1989. BS, Cornell U., 1976; JD, La. State U., 1983. Bar: La. 1983, Tex. 1991, U.S. Supreme Ct. 1988. Engr. La. Dept. Transp. Devel., Baton Rouge, 1976-78; project engr. Forte & Tablada, Inc., Baton Rouge, 1978-80; cons. engr. Baton Rouge, 1980-83; law clk. to presiding justice La. Supreme Ct., New Orleans, 1983-84; ptnr. Phelps, Dunbar, Marks, Claverie & Sims, Baton Rouge, 1984-93; prin. Timothy E. Kelley, P.L.C., Baton Rouge, 1993-96, Kelley & Guerry L.L.C., Baton Rouge, 1993-96; state dist. ct. judge, 19th judicial dist. ct. State of Louisiana, Baton Rouge, 1997—. Bd. dirs. Greater Baton Rouge YMCA, La. affiliate and Baton Rouge divsn. Am. Heart Assn., pres., 1994-95; mem. Cmty. Fund for Arts, Leadership Baton Rouge Class of 1992. Mem. ABA, Fed. Bar Assn., Baton Rouge Bar Assn., Am. Arbitration Assn. (arbitrator for constrn. industry, cert. mediator), La. Engring. Soc., La. Assn. Def. Counsel, La. Bar Found. (founder), Baton Rouge Area Found., New Orleans Bar Assn., C. of C. La., Greater Baton Rouge C. of C., Baton Rouge Country Club, Baton Rouge City Club, ChamPac (founder). Office: 222 Saint Louis St Rm 623 Baton Rouge LA 70802-5816

**KELLOUGH, WILLIAM C.,** lawyer; b. Tulsa, Dec. 2, 1949; s. Robert B. and Jo M. (Craker) K.; m. Louisa C. Watt, May 22, 1971; children: Sara Louise, Annie Elizabeth, Caroline Alyce. BA, U. Tex., 1972, JD, 1975. Bar: Tex., Okla. Ptnr. Blackstock, Joyce, Blackstock & Montgomery, Tulsa, 1975-80; shareholder Boone, Smith, Davis, Hurst & Dickman, Tulsa, 1980—. Trustee Lorene Cooper Hasbrouck Charitable Trust, Tulsa, 1991—; commr. Tulsa City/County Libr. Sys., 1998—; pres. Gilcrease Mus. Assocs., Tulsa, 1994-95. Recipient Disting. Svc. award Law and You Found., Oklahoma City. Mem. Tex. Bar Assn., Oklahoma Bar Assn., Tulsa County Bar Assn. (named outstanding jr. lawyer 1982). Democrat. Unitarian. Avocations: music, writing. Health, General practice. Home: 1965 E 33d Pl Tulsa OK 74105 Office: Boone Smith Davis et al 500 Oneok Plz Tulsa OK 37410-3000

**KELLUM, NORMAN BRYANT, JR.,** lawyer; b. Maysville, N.C., Aug. 12, 1937; s. Norman Bryant and Dollie Mallard Kellum; m. Ruth Taylor, Nov. 24, 1968. BS, Wake Forest U., 1959, JD, 1965. Bar: N.C. 1965, U.S. Dist. Ct. (ea. dist.) N.C. 1965, U.S. Dist. Ct. (mid. dist.) N.C. 1991, U.S. Ct. Appeals (4th cir.) 1968, U.S. Supreme Ct. 1994. Salesman, mgr. The Southwestern Co., Nashville, summers 1962-68; research asst. N.C. Supreme Ct., Raleigh, N.C., 1965-66; atty. Norman Kellum Jr., New Bern, N.C., 1966-68; ptnr. Beaman & Kellum, New Bern, 1968-75; owner Beaman, Kellum, Hollows & Jones, P.A. and predecessor firms, New Bern, 1975-94; shareholder, pres. Kellum & Jones, New Bern, 1994—. Deacon, trustee First Bapt. Ch., New Bern. 1st lt. U.S. Army, 1960-62; trustee Meredith Coll., 1988-92, 94-97,, chmn., 1996, 97, 99—; bd. visitors Wake Forest U. Sch. Law, 1992—; mem. Craven Regional Med. Ctr. Found., 1997, pres., 1998, 99. Mem. ATLA, N.C. State Bar, N.C. Acad. Trial Lawyers (bd. govs. 1983-87), N.C. Bar Assn., Ea. N.C. Inn Ct. (pres. 1995), Am. Bd. Trial Advs., Wake Forest U. Law Sch. (Alumni of Yr. award 1993). Avocations: travel, boating, golf, gardening. General civil litigation, Personal injury. Office: Kellum & Jones PO Box 866 New Bern NC 28563-0866

**KELLY, ANASTASIA DONOVAN,** lawyer; b. Boston, Oct. 9, 1949; d. Charles A. and Louise V. Donovan; m. Thomas C. Kelly, Aug. 23, 1980; children: Michael, Brian. BA cum laude, Trinity Coll, 1971; JD magna cum laude, George Washington U., 1981. Bar: D.C. 1982, Tex. 1982. Analyst Air Line Pilots Assn., 1971-74; dir. employee benefits Martin Marietta Corp., Bethesda, Md., 1974-81; assoc. Carrington, Coleman, Sloman & Blumenthal, Dallas, 1981-85, Wilmer, Cutler & Pickering, Washington, 1985-90; ptnr. Wilmer, Cutler & Pickering, 1990-95; sr. v.p., gen. counsel, sec. Fannie Mae, Washington, 1995-99; exec. v.p., gen. counsel, sec. Sears, Robuck & Co., 1999—. Named one of Outstanding Young Women of Am., 1980. Mem. ABA (co-chair litigation sects. com. on commercial and bus. litigation), Dallas Bar Assn., Order of Coif. Republican. Roman Catholic. Banking, General corporate. Home: 9 Kensington Dr North Barrington IL 60010 Office: Sears Robuck & Co 3333 Beverly Rd Hoffman Estates IL 60179

**KELLY, BRIAN COLEMAN,** lawyer; b. Portland, Oreg., Oct. 1, 1960; s. John Coleman and Ruthanne (Dwyer) K.; m. Jamie Brasher, June 27, 1990; children: Sean James, Lauren. BS in Engring., Harvey Mudd Coll., 1982; JD, U. of the Pacific, 1985; LLM, George Washington U., 1988. Bar: Nev. 1985, D.C. 1989. Atty. Sandler & Greenblum, Arlington, Va., 1985-86, Naval Rsch. Lab., Washington, 1986-88, Vargas & Bartlett, Reno, 1988-90, Hawkins, Folsom, Muir & Kelly, Reno, 1990—. Republican. Avocations: autos, computers, skiing, sailing. Estate planning, General corporate, Estate taxation. Office: Hawkins Folsom Muir & Kelly 1 E Liberty St Ste 416 Reno NV 89501-2184

**KELLY, CHRISTOPHER EDWARD,** lawyer; b. St. Paul, Aug. 19, 1952; s. Edward Horan and Rose Ann Kelly; m. Jean Anne Neppl, Jan. 25, 1986; children: Jennifer Ann, Kathryn Jean, Brett Christopher. BA, Creighton U., 1974, JD, 1979. Bar: Nebr. 1980, U.S. Dist. Ct. Nebr. 1980. Dep. county atty. Douglas County Atty.'s Office, Omaha, 1980-87; assoc. atty. Young & White Law Offices, Omaha, 1987-89; ptnr. McKenney & Kelly Law offices, Omaha, 1989-94, Fellman, Moylen, Natuig & Kelly, Omaha, 1994—; mem. jud. nominating commn. Nebr. Supreme Ct., Lincoln, 1998—; mem. domestic violence ct. sys. com. Douglas County Cts., Omaha, 1997; mem. foster care rev. bd. State of Nebr., Omaha, 1990—. Mem. sch. bd. Mary Our Queen Grace Sch., Omaha, 1998; mem. Bus. for a Better Omaha, 1993. Mem. Nebr. State Bar Assn., Nebr. County Attys. Assn., Nebr. Criminal Def. Attys. Assn., Nebr. Assn. Trial Attys. Criminal, Juvenile, Family and matrimonial. Home: 3308 S 116th Ave Omaha NE 68144-4542 Office: Fellman Moylan et al 209 S 19th St Ste 100 Omaha NE 68102-1705

**KELLY, D. MICHAEL,** lawyer; b. Roanoke Rapids, N.C., May 25, 1952; s. Garland and Helena C. Kelly; m. Victoria H. Kelly, Aug. 3, 1874 (div. Mar. 1981); m. Bonnie H. Kelly, May 16, 1981; children: Patrick M., Mackenzie C. BA in polit. sci., U. S.C., 1974, JD, 1977. Bar: S.C. 1977. Assoc. Loe & Suggs, Columbia, S.C., 1977-80; shareholder Suggs & Kelly, Columbia, 1981—; chair Combined Health Appeal, S.C., 1992-94. Author: Law of Worker's Compensation, 1992. Bd. dirs. Palmetto Legal Svc., Columbia, 1992—, Mental Health Assn., Columbia. Mem. S.C. Bar Assn. (Lawyer of Yr. 1988, pres. 1999—), S.C. Trial Lawyers Assn. (Pub. Citizen award 1994). Episcopalian. Workers' compensation, Personal injury, Insurance. Office: 1821 Hampton St Columbia SC 29201-3533*

**KELLY, DANIEL GRADY, JR.,** lawyer; b. Yonkers, N.Y., July 15, 1951; s. Daniel Grady and Helene (Coyne) K.; m. Annette Susan Wheeler, May 8, 1976; children—Elizabeth Anne, Brigid Claire, Cynthia Logan. Grad., Choate Sch., Wallingford, Conn., 1969; BA magna cum laude, Yale U., 1973; JD, Columbia U., 1976. Bar: N.Y. 1977, U.S. Dist. Ct. (so. and ea. dists.) N.Y. 1977, Calif. 1986, U.S. Dist. Ct. (cen. dist.) Calif. 1987. Law clk. to judge U.S. Ct. Appeals (2d cir.), N.Y.C., 1976-77; assoc. Davis Polk & Wardwell, N.Y.C., 1977-83; sr. v.p. Lehman Bros., N.Y.C., 1983-85; sr. v.p., gen. counsel Kaufman & Broad, Inc., L.A., 1985-87; ptnr. Manatt, Phelps, Rothenberg & Phillips, L.A., 1987-90, Sidley & Austin, L.A. and N.Y., 1990-99, Davis Polk & Wardwell, N.Y.C. and Menlo Park, 1999—. Mem. editl. bd. Columbia Law Rev., 1975-76. Mem. ABA (com. on law firms), L.A. County Bar Assn. (exec. com. bus. and corps. law sect.). Mergers and acquisitions, Securities, Finance. Office: Davis Polk & Wardwell 450 Lexington Ave New York NY 10017-3911

**KELLY, DAVID ANDREW,** lawyer; b. Elmira, N.Y., Aug. 16, 1964; s. William Daniel and LaQuita Joy Kelly; m. Lisa Cantu, Sept. 15, 1990; children: Anderw, Caitlin. BA in L.Am. Studies, Washington and Lee U., 1985; JD, U. Ga., 1989. Bar: Ga. 1989, Ariz. 1990, U.S. Dist. Ct. Ariz. 1990, U.S. Ct. Appeals (9th cir.) 1995. Assoc. O'Connor Cavanagh, Phoenix, 1996, Lewis and Roca LLP, Phoenix, 1990-95, 96—. Bd. dirs. Found. for Blind Children, Phoenix, 1993—. Labor. Office: Lewis and Roca LLP 40 N Central Ave Phoenix AZ 85004-4424

**KELLY, DENNIS MICHAEL,** lawyer; b. Cleve., May 6, 1943; s. Thomas Francis and Margaret (Murphy) K.; m. Marilyn Ann Divoky, Dec. 28, 1967; children: Alison, Meredith. BA, John Carroll U., 1961-65; JD, U. Notre Dame, 1968. Bar: Ohio 1968. Law clk. U.S. Ct. Appeals (8th cir.), Cleve., 1968-69; assoc. Jones, Day, Reavis & Pogue, Cleve., 1969-75, ptnr., 1975—. Mem. Ohio Bar Assn., Bar Assn. Greater Cleve. Federal civil litigation, General civil litigation, State civil litigation. Office: Jones Day Reavis & Pogue North Point 901 Lakeside Ave E Cleveland OH 44114-1116

**KELLY, EDWARD JOSEPH,** lawyer; b. Scranton, Pa., Oct. 31, 1966; s. Edward Joseph and Jane Elizabeth (Lavelle) K. BA, Duke U., 1988; JD, Boston U., 1991. Bar: N.Y. 1992. Coach Fairfield (Conn.) Preparatory Sch., 1988-91; assoc. Blank Rome Comisky & McCauley, Phila., 1990; ptnr. Kelly Rode & Kelly, LLP, Mineola, N.Y., 1991—; lectr. in field. Cons. Legal Ctr. for Def. of Life, N.Y.C., 1991—. Emery Worldwide Inc. scholar, 1984-88. Mem. N.Y. State Bar Assn., Nassau County Bar Assn., Nassau/Suffolk Trial Lawyers Assn., Nat. Inst. Trial Advocacy, Guild Cath. Lawyers, N.Y. State Trial Lawyers Inst. Republican. Roman Catholic. Avocations: horse raising, golf, hunting, weight training. Federal civil litigation, State civil litigation, Personal injury. Home: 312 E 92nd St New York NY 10128-5438 Office: Kelly Rode & Kelly LLP 330 Old Country Rd Ste 305 Mineola NY 11501-4170 also: 218 Griffing Ave Riverhead NY 11901-3009

**KELLY, EDWIN FROST,** prosecutor; b. Kearney, Nebr., Jan. 3, 1946; s. Edwin F. and Eora Louise (Ludlum) K.; children: Christopher, Summer, Matthew. BA, Wayne (Nebr.) State Coll., 1968; JD, U. Iowa, 1971. Bar: Iowa 1971, U.S. Dist. Ct. (so. dist.) Iowa 1972, U.S. Ct. Appeals (8th cir.) 1975, U.S. Supreme Ct. 1975, U.S. Dist. Ct. (no. dist.) Iowa 1980. Sole practice Fairfield, Iowa, 1971-73; ptnr. Kelly & Morrissey, Fairfield, 1974-91; fed. prosecutor, asst. U.S. atty. U.S. Dist. Ct. (So. Dist.) Iowa, Des Moines, 1991—; prosecutor Jefferson County, Fairfield, 1971-83; lectr. Parsons Coll., 1971-72. Author: Iowa Legal Forms; Creditors Remedies, 1983, 2d rev. edition, 1986, 3d rev. edition, 1990. Chmn. Jefferson County Reps., Fairfield, 1984-85, Iowa Rep. Platform Com., 1988; Rep. nominee for Atty. Gen. of Iowa, 1990. Mem. Masons. Methodist. Avocations: private pilot, golf, sailing. Home: 692 48th St Des Moines IA 50312-1955 Office: US Courthouse Annex 110 E Court Ave Des Moines IA 50309-2044

**KELLY, ERIC DAMIAN,** lawyer, educator; b. Pueblo, Colo., Mar. 16, 1947; s. William Bret and Patricia Ruth (Ducy) K.; children: Damian Charles, Eliza Jane, Valissitie Christina Heeren, Douglas Ray Heeren; m. Sandra Walker, 1996. BA, Williams Coll., 1969; JD, U. Pa., 1975, M of City Planning, 1975; PhD, Union Inst., 1992. Bar: Colo. 1975, U.S. Dist. Ct. 1976, U.S. Tax Ct. 1976, U.S. Ct. Appeals (10th cir.) 1986. Chief citizens' participation unit Region III EPA, Phila., 1971-72; project planner Beckett New Town, N.J., 1972-73; v.p., project mgr. Rahenkamp Sachs Wells & Assocs., Inc., Denver and Phila., 1973-76; sole practice Pueblo, 1976-83; pres. Kelly & Potter, P.C., Pueblo, Albuquerque and Santa Fe, 1983-90; adj. prof. U. Colo. Coll. Architecture and Planning, 1976-90; chmn., prof. Dept. cmty. and regional planning Iowa State U., 1990-95; adj. asst. prof. grad. sch. bus. U. So. Colo., 1986-90; dean coll. architecture and planning Ball State U., 1995-98, prof. urban planning, 1999—; mem. city devel. bd. State of Iowa, 1991-95. Gen. editor Zoning and Land Use Controls, 1995—; author: Enforcing Zoning and Land Use Codes, 1988, Managing Community Growth: Policies, Techniques and Impacts, 1993, Selecting and Retaining Consultants, 1993, Planning, Growth and Public Facilities: A Primer for Public Officials, 1994; editor, prin. author: The Roadtripper, 1969; contbr. articles to profl. planning and legal jours. Mem. adv. bd. Mcpl. Legal Studies Ctr., S.W. Legal Found., 1989—; mem. nat. adv. bd. Rocky Mountain Land Use Inst. Coll. Law U. Denver, 1992—; bd. dirs. Broadway Theatre League, Pueblo, 1976-77, Pueblo Beautiful Assn., 1978-82, Better Bus. Bur., 1988-89; trustee Sangre de Cristo Arts and Conf. Ctr., 1981-87, chmn. 1986; trustee Christ Congl. Ch., 1982-83. With U.S. Army, 1969-71. Named Outstanding Student, Am. Inst. Planners, 1976; recipient Outstanding Faculty award Order of Omega, 1992. Mem. ABA, Am. Inst. Cert. Planners (charter, elected Coll. of Fellows 1999), Am. Planning Assn. (nat. pres., 1997—, chair planning & law divsn. 1996-97, pres. Iowa chpt. 1994-95, amicus curiae com. 1988-94, 95-97, legis. & policy com. 1993-97, Colo. chpt. excellence award 1989), Williams Coll. Alumni Assn. (class sec. 1969-74, regional sec. 1980-82, class agt. 1985-89), Rotary (local dir. 1988-90, dir., pres. Pueblo Rotary Found. 1988-89, v.p. 1988-89, pres. 1989-90, area rep. for dist. gov. 1991-92), Phi Kappa Phi. Democrat. Real property, Land use and zoning (including planning). Home: 2312 W Audubon Dr Muncie IN 47304-2003 Office: Ball State U Coll Architecture Planning Muncie IN 47306-0001

**KELLY, FRANK XAVIER, JR.,** lawyer; b. Jersey City, N.J., Apr. 29, 1948; s. Frank Xavier Sr. and Marie Margaret (Connor) K.; m. Karen Anne Unterwald, Feb. 18, 1973; children: Meaghan, Colleen, Caitlin. AB in Govt. and Econs., Georgetown U., 1970, JD, 1974. Bar: D.C. 1975, U.S. Supreme 1978, U.S. Ct. Appeals (D.C. cir.) 1975, U.S. Ct. Appeals (8th cir.) 1980, U.S. Ct. Appeals (5th cir.) 1981. Law clk. Fed. Power Commnr., Washington, 1972-74; assoc. atty. Gallagher, Boland, Meiburger & Brosnan, Washington, 1974-80; ptnr. Gallagher, Boland & Meiburger, Washington, 1981—. Pres. Potomac Falls Homeowners Assn., Md., 1983-84. Mem. ABA, Fed. Energy Bar Assn., Congressional Country Club (Bethesda, Md.). Roman Catholic. Avocations: golf, tennis, skiing. FERC practice. Office: Gallagher Boland & Meiburger 1023 15th St NW Washington DC 20005-2602

**KELLY, HUGH RICE,** lawyer; b. Austin, Tex., Dec. 16, 1942; s. Thomas Philip and Cecilia Elizabeth (Rice) K.; m. Marguerite Susan McIntosh, Dec. 27, 1971; children: Susan McIntosh, Cecilia Rice. BA, Rice U., 1965; JD, U. Tex., 1972. Bar: Tex. 1972, U.S. Dist. Ct. (so. dist.) Tex. 1974; U.S. Ct. Appeals (5th cir.), U.S. Supreme Ct. 1975. Assoc. Baker & Botts, Houston, 1972-78, ptnr., 1979-84; exec. v.p., gen. counsel Reliant Energy, Inc., Houston Lighting and Power Co. (former, 1984—. 1st lt. U.S. Army, 1966-69. Fellow Tex. Bar Found., Houston Bar Found.; mem. ABA, State Bar Tex., Houston Bar Assn., Coronado Club. Republican. Federal civil litigation, State civil litigation, Public utilities. Home: 1936 Rice Blvd Houston TX 77005-1635 Office: Reliant Energy Inc PO Box 1700 1111 Louisiana Houston TX 77251-1700

**KELLY, JAMES HOWARD, JR.,** lawyer; b. Florence, S.C., Dec. 26, 1942; s. James Howard and Mary Neal (Saunders) K.; m. Louise Rankin, April 5, 1969; children: James Howard III, Elizabeth Rankin. AB in English, Political Sci., Davidson (N.C.) Coll., 1965; JD, Duke U., 1968. Bar: N.C. 1968, U.S. Dist. Ct. (ea., we. and ctrl. dists.) 1972, U.S. Supreme Ct. 1974. Assoc. Hudson Petree Stockton Stockton & Robinson, Winston-Salem, N.C., 1972-76; partner Petree Stockton/Kilpatrick Stockton, Winston-Salem, N.C., 1977—. Capt. U.S. Army, 1969-72, Vietnam. Fellow Am. Coll. Trial Lawyers; mem. Internat. Assn. Defense Counsel (N.C. chpt. pres. 1985-86), Assn. Defense Trial Lawyers. Methodist. Avocations: water sports, automobiles, reading, hiking, dogs. General civil litigation, Insurance, Personal injury. Office: Kilpatrick Stockton LLP 1001 W 4th St Winston Salem NC 27101-2410

**KELLY, JAMES MCGIRR,** federal judge; b. 1928. BS, Wharton Sch., 1951; JD, Temple U., 1957. Law clk. to judge U.S. Ct. Common Pleas, Phila., 1957-58; asst. dist. atty. Phila. County, 1958-60; asst. atty. U.S. Dist. Ct. (ea. dist.) Pa., Phila., 1960-62; master jury selection bd. U.S. Ct. Common Pleas, Phila., 1962-64; pvt. practice law Phila., 1962-83; spl. asst. atty. gen. Commonwealth of Pa., 1965; judge U.S. Dist. Ct. (ea. dist.) Pa., Phila., 1983-95, sr. judge, 1995—. Mem. Pa. Pub. Utility Commn., 1966-77. Served with USN, 1951-53. Office: US Courthouse Independence Mall W #8614 601 Market St Philadelphia PA 19106-1713

**KELLY, JAMES MICHAEL,** lawyer; b. Pitts., May 24, 1947; s. James M. and Catherine C. Kelly; m. Mary J. Armstrong, Dec. 20, 1980; children: Lea Day, Heather Marie. AB, Princeton U., 1969; JD, U. Pitts., 1978. Bar: Mich. 1978, Fla. 1982, U.S. Supreme Ct. 1985, U.S. Ct. Appeals (6th cir.), Ga. 1990. Atty. Chrysler Corp., Highland Park, Mich., 1978-81; corp. counsel Harris Corp., Melbourne, Fla., 1981-87; v.p., gen. counsel, corp. sec. Lanier Worldwide, Inc., Atlanta, 1987—. Editor U. Pitts. Law Rev., 1978. Capt. U.S. Army, 1969-75. Mem. ABA, Am. Assn. Corp. Counsel, Am. Assn. Corp. Secs., Fla. Bar Assn., Ga. Bar Assn., Atlanta Bar Assn., DeKalb County Bar Assn., Assn. 82d Airborne Divsn., Cannon Club. General corporate, Mergers and acquisitions, Contracts commercial. Office: Lanier Worldwide Inc 2300 Parklake Dr NE Atlanta GA 30345-2912

**KELLY, JAMES PATRICK,** lawyer; b. Twin Falls, Idaho, Mar. 25, 1946; s. James Patrick Sr. and Ynes Mary (Alastra) K.; m. Carol Louise White, June 6, 1968; children: Mary Louise, Christopher John. AB, Harvard U., 1968, JD, 1975. Bar: Ga., U.S. Dist. Ct. (no. and so. dists.) Ga., U.S. Ct. Appeals (1st, 5th, 6th and 11th cirs.), U.S. Supreme Ct. Assoc. Kilpatrick & Cody, Atlanta, 1975-80; ptnr. Morris & Manning, Atlanta, 1980-83, Smith, Gambrell & Russell, Atlanta, 1983-85, Asbill, Porter & Churchill, Atlanta, 1985-86; sr. ptnr. Kelly Law Firm, P.C., Atlanta, 1986—. Bd. dirs. Sr. Citizen Services of Met. Atlanta, 1980-83. Served to capt. U.S. Army, 1968-72. Mem. ABA (corp. and banking law sect., health law forum), Ga. Bar Assn., Atlanta Bar Assn., Ga. Acad. Hosp. Attys. (bd. dirs. 1987-89), Am. Health Lawyers Assn. (bd. dirs. 1993—), Lawyers Club Atlanta, Harvard Alumni Assn. (bd. dirs. 1983-84), Harvard Law Sch. Assn. Ga. (v.p. 1988-89, pres. 1989-91), Cochise Club, Harvard Club (pres. 1982-83, bd. dirs. 1990—), Georgian Club, Commerce Club, Capital City Club, Kiwanis (pres.). Episcopalian. Avocations: public speaking, marathon running, travel. Health, General corporate, General practice. Home: 3240 Lemons Ridge Dr NW Atlanta GA 30339-4305 Office: 200 Galleria Pky NW Ste 1510 Atlanta GA 30339-5946

**KELLY, JANET LANGFORD,** lawyer; b. Kansas City, Mo., Nov. 27, 1957. BA, Grinnell Coll., 1979; JD, Yale U., 1983. Bar: N.Y. 1985, Ill. 1989. Law clerk to Hon. James J. Hunter III U.S. Ct. Appeals (3rd cir.), 1983-84; ptnr. Sidley & Austin, Chgo., 1984-89; sr. v.p., sec., gen. counsel Sara Lee Corp., Chgo., 1995-99; exec. v.p. corp. devel., gen. counsel, sec. Kellogg Co., Battle Creek, Mich., 1999—. Sr. editor Yale Law Jour., 1983. Bd. dirs. Am. Arbitration Assn., Constl. Rights Found.; mem. adv. bd. Chgo. Vol. Legal Svcs. Found. General corporate, Securities. Office: Kellogg Co PO Box 3599 1 Kellogg Sq Battle Creek MI 49017*

**KELLY, JOHN BARRY, II,** lawyer; b. Washington, Dec. 17, 1942; s. John Barry and Blanche (O'Brien) K.; m. Elizabeth Ann MacDonald, June 26, 1965; children: Christine, John. BA in Am. History, Cath. U. Am., 1965, JD, 1971. Bar: Fla. 1971, Md. 1972, U.S. Dist. Ct. D.C. 1972, U.S. Ct. Appeals (D.C. cir.) 1972, U.S. Dist. Ct. (no. dist.) Fla. 1987; diplomate advanced advocacy Nat. Inst. Trial Advocacy, 1989-90. Investigator U.S. Civil Svc. Com., Alameda, Calif., 1965-66; law clk. U.S. Dist. Ct. D.C., Washington, 1971-72; assoc. Donahue & Ehrmantraut, Rockville, Md., 1972-75; pvt. practice Rockville, 1975-78; atty., project mgr. Westat, Inc., Rockville, 1978-80; trial atty. Tenn. Valley Authority, Knoxville, 1980-85; ptnr. Law Ctr., Pensacola, Fla., 1986-87, Ray, Kievit & Kelly, Pensacola, 1988—; faculty Fla. Bar (advanced adv. seminars), Gainesville, 1990-94, Labor and Employment Trial Seminar, Fla. Bar, Miami, 1995; spkr. in field. Author: (course book) Labor and Employment Seminars, 1990-95; exec. editor (jour.) Cath. U. Law Rev., 1970. Mem. Leadership Pensacola, Fla., 1992—. Cpl. USMC, 1966-68. Named Gulf Coast's Best Atty., Pensacola (Fla.) News Jour., 1988. Mem. Fla. Bar, D.C. Bar Assn., Escambia/Santa Rosa Bar. Avocations: reading, golfing. Labor, General civil litigation, Civil rights. Office: Kievit Kelly & Odom 15 W Main St Pensacola FL 32501-5927

**KELLY, JOHN J.,** prosecutor. U.S. atty. for N.Mex. U.S. Dept. Justice, Albuquerque, 1993—. Office: US Atty for Dist NMex PO Box 607 Albuquerque NM 87103-0607

**KELLY, JOHN JAMES,** lawyer; b. Rockville Centre, N.Y., July 4, 1949; s. John James Sr. and Eleanor Grace (Vann) K.; m. Clara Sarah Gussin; 1 child, John James III. AB in Govt., Georgetown U., 1971, JD, 1975. Bar: Pa. 1976, D.C. 1979, U.S. Dist. Ct. D.C. 1980, U.S. Claims Ct. 1982, U.S. Ct. Appeals (D.C. cir.) 1980, U.S. Ct. Appeals (fed. cir.) 1982. Law clk. to judge U.S. Dist. Ct., Washington, 1975-77; assoc. Corcoran, Youngman & Rowe, Washington, 1977-80; assoc. Capell, Howard, Knabe & Cobbs, Washington, 1980-83; assoc. Loomis, Owen, Fellman & Howe, Washington, 1983-86; ptnr., 1986-90; v.p., sec., gen. coun. Electronic Industries Alliance, Arlington, VA, 1990-96, exec. v.p., gen. counsel, 1997—; of counsel, Howe, Anderson & Steyer, Washington, 1990—; mem. Jud. Conf., D.C. Cir., Washington, 1983, Jud. Conf. Fed. Cir., Washington, 1988—. Contbr. articles to legal publs. Mem. ABA, D.C. Bar, Pa. Bar Assn., Am. Soc. Assn. Execs. (bd. dirs. legal section 1989-94, chmn. 1992-93), Fed. Bar Assn., Met. Club. Democrat. Roman Catholic. Federal civil litigation, Antitrust, General corporate. Office: Electronic Industries Alliance 2500 Wilson Blvd Arlington VA 22201-3834

**KELLY, KARLA ROSEMARIE,** lawyer; b. Newcastle, Wyo., Jan. 16, 1954; d. Carl Elvin and Elvera Marie (Pettis) Denning; children: Scharlet Lee, Jennifer Lynn. BA in Nursing, Coll. St. Katherine, 1976, RN, 1976; JD, George Washington U, Washington, D.C., 1984. Bar: Va. 1984, U.S. Dist. Ct. (ea. dist.) Va. 1984, U.S. Ct. Appeals (4th cir.) 1984, Calif. 1986, U.S. Dist. Ct. (so. dist.) Calif. 1986, U.S. Ct. Appeals (9th cir.) 1986. Charge nurse Bayshore Comm. Hosp., Pasadena, Tex., 1976-78; lt. USNR, San Diego, 1978-81; assoc. atty. Hirschkop & Grad, Alexandria, Va., 1984-86, Gray, Cary Ames & Frye, San Diego, 1987-92; asst. gen. counsel Scripps Health, San Diego, 1992—; bd. dirs. Gluck Child Care Ctr., La Jolla, Calif., 1993—, Campfire Coun., San Diego, 1995—. Contbr. articles to profl. jours. Mem. ABA, San Diego Bar Assn., Nat. Health Lawyers Assn., Calif. Soc. Healthcare Attys. Republican. Avocation: classical pianist. General corporate, Health. Office: Luce Forward Hamilton and Scripps 600 W Broadway San Diego CA 92101

**KELLY, KATHRYN L.,** lawyer; b. Browns, Ill., July 3, 1929; d. Arthur John Messman and Mary Nola Ankenbrand Messman; m. Robert Dean Kelly, Aug. 7, 1954; children: Gregory Lewis, John Robert, David William. BS in Acctg., U. Ill., 1950, JD, 1953. Bar: Ill. 1954. Editor Supreme Ct. report Commerce Clearing House, Chgo., 1954-56; rsch. asst. Am. Bar Found., Chgo., 1956-60; instr. bus. law North Cen. Coll., Naperville, Ill., 1965-70; pvt. practice Wheaton and Naperville, Ill., 1961—; legal coun. Sun Publs., Inc., Naperville, 1989-91. Bd. dirs. LWF, Naperville, 1962-65; pres. bd. Home and Sch., Naperville, 1965-66, 71-72, Little Friends, Inc., Naperville, 1974-75; bd. trustees Lewis U., Romeoville, Ill., 1994—; legal cons. St. Raphael Cath. ch., Naperville, 1985—. Mem. Ill. Bar Assn., DuPage Bar Assn., Phi Chi Theta. Republican. Roman Catholic. Probate, Estate taxation, General practice. Home and Office: 505 Bernie Ct Naperville IL 60565-1506

**KELLY, KEVIN FRANCIS,** lawyer; b. New Orleans, Apr. 27, 1949; s. Frank J. and Dorothy P. (Paige) K.; m. Jean A. Friedhoff, Dec. 27, 1969; children: Bryan F., Eric W. BA, Gonzaga U., 1970; JD, U. Calif. Berkeley, 1973. Bar: Wash. 1973. Law clk. to Hon. Eugene A. Wright U.S. Ct. Appeals, 9th Cir., Seattle, 1973-74; assoc. Davis, Wright, Todd, Riese & Jones, Seattle, 1974-76; ptnr. Wickwire, Goldmark & Schorr, Seattle, 1976-88, Heller, Ehrman, White & McAuliffe, Seattle, 1988—. Bd. dirs. Big Bros. King County, Seattle, 1985-95, v.p., 1991, pres., 1992; bd. trustees Legal Found. Wash., Seattle, 1994-97, pres., 1997. Mem. Wash. Biotechnology and Biomedical Assn. (bd. dirs. 1996—), Wash. Soc. Hosp. Lawyers, Order of Coif. Avocation: cycling. General corporate, Computer, Biotechnology. Home: 4040 55th Ave NE Seattle WA 98105-4957

**KELLY, LINDA L.,** prosecutor. Atty. U.S. Dept. Justice, Pitts., 1993-99, asst. U.S. atty., 1999—. Office: US Attys Office US Post Office & Courthouse 7th Ave & Grant Street Rm 633 Pittsburgh PA 15219

**KELLY, MARILYN,** state supreme court justice; b. Apr. 15, 1938; m. Richard Stout (dec.). BA, Ea. Mich. U., 1960, JD (hon.); postgrad., U. Paris.; MA, Middlebury Coll., 1961; JD with honors, Wayne State U., 1971. Assoc. Dykema, Gossett, Spencer, Goodnow & Trigg, Detroit, 1973-78; ptnr. Dudley, Patterson, Maxwell, Smith & Kelly, Bloomfield Hills, Mich., 1978-80; owner Marilyn Kelly & Assocs., Bloomfield Hills, Birmingham, Mich., 1980-88; judge Mich. Ct. of Appeals, 1989-96; justice Mich. Supreme Ct., 1997—; tchr. lang., lit. Grosse Pointe Pub. Schs., Albion Coll., Ea. Mich. U.; past mem. rep. assembly, comms. com., family law coun. Mich. State Bar, now co-chair Open Justice Commn. Active Mich. Dem. Party, 1963—. Recipient Disting Alumni award Ea. Mich. U., Disting. Svc. award Mich. Edn. Assn. Mem. NOW, Nat. Assn. Women Judges, Mich. Judges Assn., Soc. Irish-Am. Lawyers, Women Lawyers Assn. (past pres.), Oakland County Bar Assn. (past chair family law com.). Office: Mich Supreme Ct Ste 2000 500 Woodward Ave Detroit MI 48226-3435*

**KELLY, MARK PATRICK,** lawyer; b. Guam, Marianna Islands, Nov. 25, 1951; s. AlexanderJ. and Mary Ann Kelly; m. Patricia Joan O'Doran, Jan. 21, 1988; children: Megan Elizabeth, Patrick. BA in Econs., Loyola U., New Orleans, 1973; JD, Loyola U., 1976. Bar: Fla. 1976, U.S. Dist. Ct. (mid. dist.) Fla. 1977. Law clk. 2d Dist. Ct. Appeals, State of Fla., Lakeland, 1976-77; ptnr. Lopez & Kelly P.A., Tampa, 1977—. Asst. pack leader Boy Scouts Am., Tampa, 1998. Me. Hill County Bar Assn. (exec. com. family law sect. 1996—, treas./sec. family law sect. 1999), Family Law Inn of Tampa (master 1995—, treas. 1996-97). Avocations: flying, SCUBA diving, blue water fishing. State civil litigation, Family and matrimonial, Personal injury. Office: Lopez & Kelly PA 4600 W Cypress St Ste 500 Tampa FL 33607-4024

**KELLY, MICHAEL JOHN,** lawyer; b. N.Y.C., Aug. 9, 1943; s. John E. and Vivian (McNamara) K.; m. JoAnn L. Villamizar, Feb. 2, 1987; 1 child, Shannon. BS in chemistry, Farleigh Dickinson Univ., 1969; JD, Seton Hall Univ., 1976. Bar: N.J. 1976, Conn. 1988, U.S. Ct. Appeals (fed. cir.) 1988, U.S. Supreme Ct. 1992. Rsch. chemist Lever Bros. Co., Edgewater, N.J., 1965-72, patent coord., 1972-76, sr. staff atty., 1976-80; asst. patent counsel Internat Playtex, Stamford, Conn., 1980-81; divsn. patent counsel Am. Cyanamid Co., Stamford, Conn., 1981-92; chief patent counsel Cytec Industries Inc., Stamford, Conn., 1992—; v.p. Cytec Industries Inc., Stamford, 1998—. Mem. N.Y. Intellectual Property Law Assn. (membership chair, 1991-94, dir. 1995-97). Intellectual property, Patent, Trademark and copyright. Office: Cytec Industries Inc 1937 W Main St Stamford CT 06902-4516

**KELLY, MICHAEL JOSEPH,** lawyer; b. Bklyn., Apr. 24, 1947; s. Patrick and Bridget Kelly; m. Sharon Ann Erwin, Aug. 8, 1970; children: Tara Bridget, Liam Patrick, Caitlin Jane, Devon Michael. BA, Syracuse U., 1969; JD, SUNY, Buffalo, 1972. Bar: N.Y. 1972. Assoc. Sam Greene, Syracuse, N.Y., 1972-73; ptnr. Bayer, Dupre & Smith, Rochester, N.Y., 1973-79, Gates & Kelly, Perry, N.Y., 1979-81; pvt. practice, Perry, 1981—; judge Town and Village of Warsaw, N.Y., 1990-91; asst. dist. atty. Wyoming County, Perry, 1991-97. Pres. Arts Coun. Wyoming County, 1983-84. Mem. ABA, N.Y. State Bar Assn. (bd. dirs. grievance com. 1986-92, svc. recognition award 1986, 92), Wyoming County Bar Assn. (pres. 1985-86), Rotary (bd. dirs., pres. Perry 1995-96). Avocations: tennis, biking, music, reading, gardening. General civil litigation, Probate, General practice. Office: 24 Lake St Perry NY 14530-1516

**KELLY, PATRICIA ANN,** lawyer, social welfare administrator; b. Los Gatos, Calif., Nov. 26, 1962; d. John Huse and Catherine Patricia (McIntyre) K.; m. John V. Kellenberg, Aug. 14, 1993; 1 child, Sara Kellenberg. BS, Georgetown U., 1984, JD, 1991; BS, SUNY, Binghamton, 1986. Bar: DC 1991, Md. 1992. Atty. Nat. Ctr. Proscution of Child Abuse, Alexandria, Va., 1992-94; project staff NOW, Washington, 1995-96; atty. Legal Aid Bur., Balt., 1996-97; dep. dir. Md. Ctr. Assault Prevention, Wheaton, 1997—. Office: Md Ctr Assault Prevention 2424 Reedie Dr # 220 Wheaton MD 20902-4652

**KELLY, PAUL DONALD,** lawyer; b. Rochester, N.Y., Sept. 20, 1955; s. Gerard D. and Ruth A. K.; m. Anne E. Alfieri, Nov. 30, 1985; children: Thomas, Alexander, Raymond, John. BA in English, LeMoyne Coll., 1977; JD, U. Albany, 1980. Bar: N.Y. 1981, U.S. Dist. Ct. (no. dist.) N.Y. 1986, U.S. Dist. Ct. (we. dist.) 1988, U.S. Ct. Claims 1989. Asst. counsel N.Y. State Sen. Mary Goodhue, Albany, 1980-81; asst. pub. defender Monroe County Pub. Defender, Rochester, N.Y., 1981-85; assoc. Davidson, Fink, Cook & Gates, Rochester, N.Y., 1985-91; ptnr. Davidson, Fink, Cook, Kelly & Galbraith, Rochester, N.Y., 1992—. Mem. Assn. Trial Lawyers Am., N.Y. State Trial Lawyers Assn., Genesee Valley Trial Lawyers Assn., N.Y. State Bar Assn., Monroe County Bar Assn. (plaintiff's personal injury sect.). Democrat. Roman Catholic. Avocations: family activities, athletics. Personal injury, General civil litigation. Office: Davidson Fink Cook Kelly & Galbraith 28 Main St E Ste 1700 Rochester NY 14614-1915

**KELLY, PAUL JOSEPH, JR.,** judge; b. Freeport, N.Y., Dec. 6, 1940; s. Paul J. and Jacqueline M. (Nolan) K.; BBA, U. Notre Dame, 1963; JD, Fordham U., 1967; m. Ruth Ellen Dowling, June 27, 1964; children—Johanna, Paul Edwin, Thomas Martin, Christopher Mark, Heather Marie. Bar: N.Mex. 1967. Law clk. Cravath, Swaine & Moore, N.Y.C., 1964-67; assoc. firm Hinkle, Cox, Eaton, Coffied & Hensley, Roswell, N.Mex., 1967-71, ptnr., 1971-92; judge U.S. Ct. Appeals (10th cir.), Santa Fe, 1992—; mem. N.Mex. Bd. Bar Examiners, 1982-85; mem. N.Mex. Ho. of Reps., 1976-81, chmn. consumer and public affairs com., mem. judiciary com. Mem. N.Mex. Pub. Defender Bd.; bd. of visitors, Fordham U. Sch. of Law, 1992—; pres. Oliver Seth Inn of Ct., 1993—; pres. Roswell Drug Abuse Com., 1970-71; mem. Appellate Judges Nominating Commn., 1989-92. Pres. Chaves County Young Reps., 1971-72; vice chmn. N.Mex. Young Reps., 1969-71, treas., 1968-69; mem. bd. dirs. Zia council Girl Scouts Am., Roswell Girls Club, Chaves County Mental Health Assn., 1974-77; bd. dirs. Santa Fe Orch., 1992-93, Roswell Symphony Orch. Soc., 1969-82, treas., 1970-73, pres., 1973-75; mem. Eastern N.Mex. State Fair Bd., 1978-83. Mem. ABA, Fed. Bar Assn., State Bar N.Mex. (v.p. young lawyers sect. 1969, co-chmn. ins. sub-com. 1972-73, mem. continuing legal edn. com. 1970-73). Roman Catholic (pres. parish council 1971-76). K.C. Office: US Court Appeals 10th Circuit Federal Courthouse PO Box 10113 Santa Fe NM 87504-6113

**KELLY, PETER MCCLOREY, II,** lawyer; b. Chgo., Mar. 23, 1948; s. John Stephen and Helen (Patterson) K.; m. Susan Barrett, Aug. 17, 1995; children: Peter, Eli, Eamon, Liam. A.B., U. Notre Dame, 1970; J.D. cum laude, Ind. U., 1973. Bar: Ill. 1973. Assoc. McDermott, Will & Emery, Chgo., 1973-78, ptnr., 1979-81; ptnr. Kirkland & Ellis, Chgo., 1981-84, Bell, Boyd & Lloyd, Chgo., 1984-91, Murphy, Smith & Polk, Chgo., 1991-98, Ogletree, Deakins, Murphy, Smith & Polk (formerly Murphy, Wmith & Polk), 1999—; adj. prof. Sch. of Law, Loyola U., Chgo., 1976-84, Ind. U. Law Sch., Bloomington, 1985; speaker to various profl. groups and orgns. Mem. U.S. C. of C. (employee benfits council 1981—), ABA, Ill. Bar Assn., Chgo. Bar Assn. (sec. employee benefits com. 1982-83, vice chmn. employee benefits com. 1983-84, chmn. 1984-85), Midwest Pension Conf. (exec. bd. 1984—), Order of Coif. Pension, profit-sharing, and employee benefits. Home: 1316 Davis St Evanston IL 60201-4104 Office: Ogletree Deakins Murphy Smith & Polk 2 1st Nat Plz Fl 24 Chicago IL 60603

**KELLY, QUENTIN PATRICK,** lawyer; b. New Orleans, Jan. 3, 1959; s. George F. Kelly and Joan (Maxwell) Florez; m. Elizabeth Price Duffy, Jan. 23, 1988 (div.). BSBA, U. New Orleans, 1981; JD, Loyola U., New Orleans, 1987. Bar: La. 1987, U.S. Dist. Ct. (mid., ea. and we. dists.) La. 1987, U.S. Ct. Appeals (5th cir.) 1987, Calif., 1995. Petroleum landman Ken Savage & Assocs., New Orleans, 1981-83; assoc. Chaffe, McCall, Phillips, Toled & Sarpy, New Orleans, 1986, Capitelli & Wicker, New Orleans, 1987-91; asst. dist. atty. Jefferson Parish, 1991—. Contbr. to profl. publs. Mem. ABA, Fed. Bar Assn., La. State Bar Assn., Calif. Bar Assn., Phi Delta Phi. Republican. Roman Catholic. Avocations: tennis, fishing, water skiing, skiing. Criminal, Personal injury. Home: 9924 Hawthorne Ave River Ridge LA 70123-1506

**KELLY, REID BROWNE,** lawyer; b. Kingston, Ont., Can., June 19, 1960; came to U.S., 1965; s. William Browne and Betty Lou (Rowland) K.; m. Debra Lee Carpenter, July 11, 1987. BA magna cum laude, Colo. Coll., 1982; JD, U. Colo., 1985; cert., U. San Diego Inst., Oxford U., Eng., 1985. Bar: Colo. 1986, U.S. Dist. Ct. Colo. 1987, U.S. Ct. Appeals (6th cir.) 1997. Assoc. LaFrance & Assocs., Durango, Colo., 1986-87, Warren, Mundt, Martin & O'Dowd, Colorado Springs, Colo., 1987-93; ptnr. Warren, Mundt & Martin, Colorado Springs, 1993-95; mem. The Kelly Law Firm, L.L.C, Pagosa Springs, Colo., 1996—; co-chair employment law com. El Paso County Bar Assn., Colorado Springs., 1992-94. Named Outstanding Young Men of Am. Colo. Bar Assn., 1987-96. Mem. S.W. Colo. Bar Assn. (sec. Pagosa Springs chpt., sec. local chpt. 1997-99), Pi Gamma Mu. Avocations: Tae Kwon Do, yoga, running, skiing, chess. General civil litigation, Labor,

Civil rights. Office: The Kelly Law Firm LLC 4440 N Pagosa Blvd Pagosa Springs CO 81147-8312

**KELLY, ROBERT F.,** federal judge; b. 1935. BS, Villanova U., 1957; LLB, Temple U., 1960. Pvt. practice law Media, Pa., 1961-62, 64-76, Chester, Pa., 1962-64; law clk. to Hon. Francis J. Catania Ct. Common Pleas, Delaware County, Pa., 1964-72; prothonotary Delaware County, 1972-76; former judge Ct. Common Pleas 32d Jud. Dist. Pa.; judge U.S. Dist. Ct. (ea. dist.) Pa., Phila., 1987—; lectr. law Villanova U. Law Sch. Voluntary defender Delaware County, 1962; chmn. Delaware County Rep. Exec. Com., 1972-76, Subcom. on Libr. Programs; mem. Judicial Coun. com. on Automation and Tech., 1989—. Mem. ABA, Am. Judicature Soc., Pa. Bar Assn., Pa. Trial Judges Assn., Delaware County Bar Assn. (judicial counsel's com. automation and tech., 1989—, chmn. subcom. libr. programs). Office: US Dist Ct 11613 US Courthouse 601 Market St Philadelphia PA 19106-1713

**KELLY, SANDRA M.,** lawyer; b. Parma, Ohio, July 19, 1960; d. Ernest E. and Cynthia B. Maurer; m. Michael W. Kelly, Feb. 14, 1990; children: Kaitlin, Michael, Chelsea. BS, Ohio State U., 1983, MS, 1984; JD, Pepperdine U., 1986. Bar: Ohio 1986, Calif. 1987, D.C. 1987. Lawyer Ray, Robinson, Carle, Davies & Snyder, Cleve., 1986—; mem. adv. bd. Network Leading Law Firms, 1995—. Vol. atty. Hospice of Western Res., Cleve., 1994—. Mem. Maritime Law Assn. Admiralty, Federal civil litigation, General corporate. Office: Ray Robinson Carle Davies and Snyder 1650 East Ohio Gas Bldg Cleveland OH 44114

**KELLY, SHAWN PAUL,** lawyer; b. N.Y.C., Feb. 9, 1952; s. John Donald and Kathleen Marie (O'Leary) K.; m. Carol Ann Baumgarth, Sept. 24, 1989; children: Sean, Ryan. BA, U. Notre Dame, 1974; JD, St. John's Sch. Law, 1977. Bar: N.Y. 1977. Ptnr. Kelly, Rode & Kelly L.L.P., Mineola, N.Y., 1977—; vice-chmn. Nassau, Suffolk (N.Y.) Trial Lawyer's Assn., 1987—. Vol. (pro-bono) Lawyer's Initiative St. Mary's Parish, Manhasset, N.Y., 1998—. Mem. N.Y. Bar Assn., N.Y. State Med. Def. Bar Assn., Nassau Bar Assn. Personal injury, Insurance, Product liability. Office: Kelly Rode & Kelly LLP 330 Old Country Rd Ste 305 Mineola NY 11501-4170

**KELLY, T. CHRISTOPHER,** lawyer; b. Cedar Falls, Iowa, Aug. 12, 1955; s. Ryan and Harriett Kelly. BA, U. Wis., 1977, JD, 1980. Bar: Wis. 1980, U.S. Dist. Ct. (we. and ea. dists.) Wis. 1980, U.S. Ct. Appeals (7th cir.) 1983, U.S. Supreme Ct. 1991. Law clk. Wis. Ct. Appeals, Madison, 1980-82; ptnr. Dewa, Beardin & Kelly, Madison, 1983-86; sole practitioner Kelly Law Offices, Madison, 1987-94; ptner. Thomas, Kelly, Habermehl & Mays, Madison, 1995—; v.p., bd. dirs. Mercados Ltd., Madison, 1991-94; instr. U. Wis. Law Sch., Madison, 1994-97. Mem. Nat. Assn. Criminal Def. Lawyers, Wis. Assn. Criminal Def. Lawyers. Criminal, Labor, Personal injury. Office: Thomas Kelly et al 145 W Wilson St Madison WI 53703-3213

**KELLY, THOMAS MICHAEL,** lawyer; b. Atlanta, Oct. 5, 1958; s. Edward (dec.) and Marie K. AB cum laude, Columbia U., 1979; JD cum laude, Harvard U., 1983. Bar: N.Y. 1985. Law clk. to Hon. Eugene Nickerson U.S. Dist. Ct. (ea. dist.) N.Y., Bklyn., 1983-84; assoc. Debevoise & Plimpton, N.Y.C., 1984-93, ptnr., 1993—. Mem. Assn. of Bar of City of N.Y. Democrat. General corporate, Insurance, Banking. Office: Debevoise & Plimpton 875 3rd Ave Fl 23 New York NY 10022-6256

**KELLY, THOMAS PAINE, JR.,** lawyer; b. Tampa, Fla., Aug. 29, 1912; s. Thomas Paine and Beatrice (Gent) K.; m. Jean Baughman, July 25, 1940; children: Carla (Mrs. Henry Dee), Thomas Paine III, Margaret Jo (Mrs. Jeffrey Holmes). AB, U. Fla., 1935, JD, 1936. Bar: Fla. 1936, U.S. Dist. Ct. (no. dist.) Fla. 1936, U.S. Ct. Appeals (5th cir.) 1936, U.S. Dist. Ct. (mid. dist.) Fla. 1940, U.S. Dist. Ct. (so. dist.) Fla. 1939, U.S. Ct. Appeals (11th cir.) 1983, U.S. Supreme Ct. 1990. Since practiced in Tampa; assoc. McKay, Macfarlane, Jackson & Ferguson, 1939-40; ptnr. McKay, MacFarlane, Jackson & Ferguson, 1940-48; ptnr. Macfarlane, Ferguson, Allison & Kelly, 1948-83, sr. ptnr., 1983-91; of counsel Shear, Newman, Hahn & Rosenkranz, 1992-95; shareholder MacFarlane Ferguson & McMullen, P.A., Tampa, Fla., 1996—. Chmn. Tampa Com. 100, 1960-61; pres. Tampa Citizens' Safety Coun., 1961-62; Bd. dirs. Tampa chpt. ARC, 1955-62, pres., 1958-59; bd. dirs. Boys Clubs Tampa, 1956-67, pres., 1966-67. Col. F.A. AUS, 1940-45. Decorated Silver Star. Fellow Am. Coll. Trial Lawyers, Internat. Acad. Trial Lawyers; mem. Am. Bar Assn., Bar Assn. Hillsborough County, Fla. Bar (chmn. com. profl. ethics 1953-58, chmn. com. ins. and negligence law 1962-63, chmn. fed. rules com. 1969-70). Republican. Federal civil litigation, State civil litigation, Personal injury. Home: 5426 Lykes Ln Tampa FL 33611-4747 Office: McFarlane Ferguson & McMullen PO Box 1531 Tampa FL 33601-1531

**KELLY, TIMOTHY WILLIAM,** lawyer; b. Chgo., Apr. 27, 1953; s. George Raymond and Mary Therese (Kelly) K.; m. Mary Teresa Harms, May 24, 1980; children: Ryan Timothy, Colin Patrick, Kaitlynn Elizabeth. B.S. in Bus. Adminstrn., U. Dayton, 1975, J.D., 1978. Bar: Ill. 1978, U.S. Dist. Ct. (cen., no. dist.) Ill. 1979. Staff counsel Praire State Legal Aid, Bloomington, Ill., 1978-81; felony asst. McLean County Pub. Defenders, Bloomington, 1981-83; assoc. Jerome Mirza & Assocs., Bloomington, 1983-88; asst. prof. polit. sci. Ill. State U., Normal, 1980-83; faculty mem. Ill. Inst. Continuing Legal Edn. Bd. dirs. Bloomington/Normal Day Care Assn., 1982-83; civil actions arbitrator and mediator McLean County, 1996—; lectr. in field. Contbr. articles to profl. jours. Named one of Top Three Attys. in McLean, Bus. to Bus. Mag., 1997. Fellow Ill. Bar Found.; mem. Ill. State Bar Assn. (mem. civil practice and procedure sect. coun. 1992—, chmn. 1998, Allerton house steering com. 1994, 96, 98, tort law sect. coun. 1995—, assembly mem. 1995—), Ill. Trial Lawyers Assn. (mem. bd. managers 1992—, continuing legal edn. com. 1995-96, exec. com. 1996, chmn. ins. law com. 1996-98), Assn. Trial Lawyers of Am., Chgo. Bar Assn., McLean County Bar Assn. (sec. 1984-85), McLean County Inns of Court. Democrat. Roman Catholic. Personal injury. Office: Allison & Kelly 202 N Prospect Rd Bloomington IL 61704-3555

**KELLY, W. MICHAEL,** lawyer; b. Camden, N.J., Apr. 27, 1948; s. Frank Joseph and Catherine (Costello) K.; m. Daniela Adele Lodes, Mar. 23, 1985. children: Amanda Rose. BA magna cum laude, U. Notre Dame, 1970, JD cum laude, 1973. Bar: N.Y. 1975. Ptnr. Breed, Abbott & Morgan, N.Y.C., 1984-93, Whitman, Breed, Abbott & Morgan, N.Y.C., 1993-96, Coudert Brothers, N.Y.C., 1996—. Fellow Am. Coll. Investment Counsel; mem. ABA, N.Y. State Bar Assn., Assn. Bar City N.Y. Finance, General corporate, Sports. Office: Coudert Brothers 1114 Avenue Of The Americas New York NY 10036-7703

**KELLY, WILLIAM FRANKLIN, JR.,** lawyer; b. Houston, Feb. 12, 1938; s. William Franklin and Sara (McAshan) K.; m. Ingrid Leach, Sept. 11, 1965; children: Kristin Adams, Sara McAshan. BA, Stanford U., 1960; LLB, U. Tex., 1963. Bar: Tex. 1965. Assoc. Vinson & Elkins, Houston, 1965-72, ptnr., 1972-97. Served to 1st lt. U.S. Army, 1963-65. Fellow Houston Bar Found; mem. ABA, Tex. Bar Assn., Houston Bar Assn. Episcopalian. Club: Forest (Houston), The Houston. Avocation: sport diving. Securities, General corporate. Home: 600 E Friar Tuck Ln Houston TX 77024-5707 Office: Vinson & Elkins LLP 2300 First City Tower 1001 Fannin St Ste 3300 Houston TX 77002-6706

**KELLY, WILLIAM GARRETT,** judge; b. Grand Rapids, Mich., Nov. 30, 1947; s. Joseph Francis and Gertrude Frances (Downes) K.; m. Sharon Ann Diroff, Aug. 11, 1979; children: Colleen, Joseph, Caitlin, Meaghan and Patricia. BA, U. Detroit, 1970, JD, 1975. Bar: Mich. 1975, U.S. Dist. Ct. (we. dist.) Mich. 1975. Tchr. Peace Corps, Ghana, Republic of West Africa, 1970-72; asst. prosecutor Kalamazoo (Mich.) Prosecutor's Office, 1975-77; atty. Office of Defender, Grand Rapids, 1977-78; judge 62d B Dist. Ct., Kentwood, 1979—; mem. faculty Mich. Jud. Inst., Lansing, 1985—, 2d Nat. Conf. on Ct. Tech., Denver, 1988; chmn.-elect Jud. Conf. State Bar Mich., 1990-91, chair, 1991-92; vice chmn. Nat. Conf. Spl. Ct. Judges, 1990-91, chair 1992-93. Bd. dirs. Nat. Ctr. for State Cts., 1994—; pres. Kentwood Jaycees, 1979-80. Named one of Five Outstanding Young Men of Mich., Mich. Jaycees, 1982. Mem. ABA (chair nat. conf. spl. ct. judges 1992-93), State Bar Mich., Grand Rapids Bar Assn., Cath. Lawyers Assn. Western Mich. (pres. 1987), Mich. Dist. Judges Assn. (pres. 1989). Roman Catholic. Office: 62d B Dist Ct PO Box 8848 4900 Breton Rd SE Kentwood MI 49518-8848

**KELLY, WILLIAM JAMES, III,** lawyer; b. St. Louis, July 26, 1967; s. William James Jr. and Lenore (Bastian) K.; m. Mary McNamara, Dec. 29, 1990; children: Natalie Miles, Katherine Alexandria. BA, Tulane U., 1989; JD, St. Louis U., 1992. Bar: La. 1992, U.S. Dist. Ct. (ea., we. and mid. dists.) La. 1992, U.S. Ct. Appeals (5th cir.) 1994, U.S. Supreme Ct. 1999. Ptnr. Adams and Reese, New Orleans, 1992—. Author articles in field. Mem. ABA (labor and employment planning bd. young lawyers divsn. 1994-96), FBA, La. State Bar Assn., Am. Judicature Soc., Serra Internat. (pres. 1998-00), Sigma Chi (chpt. advisor 1994-98), Alpha Sigma Nu. Roman Catholic. Avocations: skiing, scuba diving, music collecting. Federal civil litigation, State civil litigation, Labor. Office: Adams and Reese 4500 One Shell Sq New Orleans LA 70139-4501

**KELMACHTER, LESLIE DEBRA,** lawyer; b. Bklyn.; d. Meyer and Jean Muraskin (Metcalf) K. BA magna cum laude, SUNY, New Paltz, 1974; JD, Albany Law Sch., 1977. Bar: N.Y. 1978, U.S. Dist. Ct. (no. dist.) N.Y., U.S. Dist. Ct. (ea. dist.) N.Y. 1989, U.S. Dist. Ct. (so. dist.) N.Y. 1995. Atty. Legal Aid Soc., Schenectady, 1977-79; atty., juvenile rights divsn. Legal Aid Soc., N.Y.C., 1979-86; atty., asst. corp. counsel Law Dept., City of N.Y., 1986-90; ptnr. Schneider, Kleinick, Weitz, Damashek & Shoot, N.Y.C., 1990—; co-chair Mealey's Nat. Lead Litigation Conf., 1999. Contbf. author: Decisions, Legal Maplractice, 1995, 96, 97, 98. Participant, fund raiser Race for the Cure, N.Y.C., 1995-98; mem. dinner com. Judges and Lawyers Breast Cancer Alert, N.Y.C., 1998. Mem. ABA (mem. steering com. first women's trial advocacy conf. 1998), Bar Assn. City N.Y. (tort com. 1997—, co-chair jury selection subcom. 1997-98), Met. Women's Bar, N.Y. State Trial Lawyers Inst. (co-chair decisions lectures 1993—, bd. dirs.). State civil litigation, Personal injury, Toxic tort. Office: Schneider Kleinick et al 233 Broadway New York NY 10279-0001

**KELSALL, SAMUEL, V,** lawyer; b. Austin, Tex., Apr. 30, 1963; s. Samuel IV and Edna W. Kelsall. BA in Environ. Sci., U. Denver, 1985; JD, U. San Diego, 1988. Bar: Calif. 1997, U.S. Dist. Ct. (so. dist.) 1989. Mng. ptnr. Law Office Samuel Kelsall V, San Diego, 1989—; exec. trustee Sam Five Enterprises, San Diego, 1992—; trustee Zepter Sport Internat., San Diego, 1993—; gen. counsel, trustee Calif. Properties Fund, San Diego, 1996—; gen. counsel, sec. PinnFund, USA, San Diego, 1995—. Mem. ABA, Am. Corp. Counsel Assn., TMBA (legis./judicial com. 1996—), MBA (legal issues com. 1997—), San Diego County Bar Assn. Banking, Federal civil litigation, General civil litigation. Office: PinnFund USA Ste 100 2051 Palomar Airport Rd Carlsbad CA 92009-1416

**KELSO, DONALD IAIN JUNOR,** lawyer; b. Edinburgh, Scotland, Apr. 8, 1971; came to U.S., 1997; s. Iain Thomas Taylor and Zan K. BA in Jurisprudence, Merton Coll., Oxford, Eng., 1992. Bar: Eng. and Wales 1995, Colo. 1997, U.S. Dist. Ct. Colo. 1998. Solicitor Shakespeares Solicitors, Birmingham, Ala., U.K., 1996-97; assoc. Holme Roberts & Owen LLP, Denver, 1998—. Mem. Colo. Bar Assn., Denver Bar Assn., Lincoln's Inn (Hardwicke scholarship 1993). Avocations: travel, reading, hiking. General civil litigation, Labor, Securities. Office: Holme Roberts & Owen 1700 Lincoln St Denver CO 80203-4500

**KELSO, LINDA YAYOI,** lawyer; b. Boulder, Colo., Mar. 30, 1946; d. Nobutaka and Tai (Inui) Ike; m. William Alton Kelso, June 17, 1968. BA, Stanford U., 1968; MA, U. Wis., 1973; JD, U. Fla., 1979. Bar: Fla. 1980. Assoc. Mahoney, Hadlow & Adams, Jacksonville, Fla., 1979-82; assoc. Commander, Legler, Werber, Dawes, Sadler & Howell, Jacksonville, 1982-86, ptnr., 1986-91; ptnr. Foley & Lardner, Jacksonville, 1992—. Mem. ABA (bus. law sect.), Jacksonville Bar Assn., Phi Beta Kappa, Order of Coif. Avocations: music, gardening, cooking. General corporate, Securities. Office: Foley & Lardner 200 N Laura St Jacksonville FL 32202-3500

**KELSON, RICHARD B.,** lawyer; b. Pitts., Nov. 20, 1946. B in Polit. Sci., U. Pa.; JD, U. Pitts. Atty. Alcoa, Pitts., 1974-77, gen. atty., 1977-83, mng. gen. atty., 1983-84, asst. sec., mng. gen. atty., 1984-89, asst. gen. counsel, 1989-91, sr. v.p. environ. health and safety, 1991-94, exec. v.p. environ., health and safety, 1994-97, exec. v.p., CFO, 1997—. Bd. dirs. Alcoa Found., U. Pitts. Law Sch. Bd. Visitors, Conf. Bd. Coun. Fin. Execs., Pa. Bus. Roundtable; mem. Fin. Exec. Inst. the Officers Conf. Group, The Pvt. Sector Coun.'s CFPs. Mem. ABA, Pa. Econ. League (bd. govs.). Office: Alcoa 201 Isabella St Pittsburgh PA 15212-5858

**KELTNER, CECIL GREEN,** lawyer; b. Ripley, Tenn., Nov. 10, 1919; s. Cecil U. and Elnora V. Keltner; children: Cathy, Howard, Keith, Mardite. BS, Memphis State U., 1947; LLB, U. Memphis, 1967. Bar: Tenn. 1951. Atty. Gatti, Keltner & Bienvenu, Memphis. V.p. Optimist Club, Memphis. Lt. col. U.S. Army, 1948-73. Mem. Tenn. Bar Assn., Tenn. Trial Lawyers Assn., Memphis Bar Assn. Toxic tort, Workers' compensation.

**KEMLER, R(OBERT) MICHAEL,** lawyer; b. Boston, Oct. 25, 1945; s. Charles and Evelyn (Jaffe) K.; m. Deborah Glaser, Aug. 20, 1970 (div. 1980); 1 child, Matthew Alex Kemler Nelson. AB, U. Pa., 1967; JD, Boston Coll., 1970; LLM, U. Pa. (partial fellowship-grad. law student), 1972; post-grad., U. Oxford, Eng., 1970-71. Guest lectr. Hosp. U. Pa., Phila., 1972; atty. law reform health law Community Legal Svcs., Phila., 1973-79; lectr. health law Vallanova (Pa.) Law Sch., 1980; atty. Pub. Interest Law Ctr. of Phila., 1979-80; asst. regional atty. Office of Civil Rights, U.S. Dept. Health & Human Svcs., Phila., 1980-82; asst. dep. pub. advocate N.J. Dept. Pub. Advocate, Trenton, N.J., 1982-87; assoc. litigation dept. Duane, Morris & Heckscher, Phila., 1987-88; of counsel Monaghan & Gold, Phila., 1990-94; pvt. practice health law Phila., 1994—; pvt. practice health law guest lectr. U. Pa. Med. Sch., Phila., 1972—; cons. legal medicine Wood Inst., Coll. Physicians of Phila., 1990-92; guest lectr. forensic psychiatry U. Pa. Sch. Medicine; gen. lectr. in health law field; apptd. mediator U.S. Dist. Ct. (ea. dist.) Pa. 1992—. Author: A Handbook on the Medicaid Boycott and Antitrust, 1981, Mock Medical Malpractice Trial, U. Pa. Med. Sch., 1989, Health Care Reform: Post Election Look at Congress's Unfinished Agenda, 1994, Medical Malpractice Liabilty and the HMO, 1993, Rationing in Health Care, 1998; contbr. articles to profl. jours. Bd. dirs. Pa. Pro Musica, Phila., 1990—; bass II Mendelssohn Club of Phila., 1990; asst. mgr. Pa. Ballet, Phila., 1985-88. Nat. Legal Svc. Corp. rsch. fellow, 1981. Mem. Phila. Bar Assn. (Medico-legal com. 1989—, health law com. 1992), Pa. Soc. Healthcare Attys. Democrat. Avocations: harpsichord, choral singing, yachting, swimming, tennis. Health, Administrative and regulatory, Federal civil litigation. Home: 1914 Waverly St Philadelphia PA 19146-1425 Office: 2207 Chestnut St Fl 2D Philadelphia PA 19103-3010

**KEMP, BARRETT GEORGE,** lawyer; b. Dayton, Ohio, Feb. 22, 1932; s. Barrett M. and Gladys M. (Linkhart) K.; children: Becky A., Barrett George II; m. Shirley, 1997. BSC, Ohio U., 1954; JD, Ohio No. U., 1959. Bar: Ohio 1959. With FBI, 1959-61; mem. B.G. Kemp Law Firm, St. Marys, Ohio, 1961—; law dir. City of St. Marys, 1964-80. Sec., treas. Cmty. Improvement Corp., 1967-79; founder St. Marys Sister City, Inc.; founder, organizer sister city with Ho Kudan-cho, Japan, 1985. Recipient Outstanding Citizen award City of St. Marys, 1973, Builder of Bridges award St. Mary's C. of C., 1995. Mem. Ohio Bar Assn., Auglaize County Bar Assn., Rotary (v.p. 1968, pres. 1979, Lifetime achievement 1997, Four Aves. of Cvs. citation 1999), Masons, Shriners, Scottish Rite. General practice. Office: Ste 203 Cmty First Bank & Trust Bldg Saint Marys OH 45885

**KEMP, JEFFREY WINSLOW,** lawyer; b. Washington, Aug. 31, 1968; s. J. Michael Kemp and Constance Chase; m. Dana Hearne, May 17, 1997. AB, Duke U., 1990; JD, So. Meth. U., 1993. Bar: Tex. 1993, U.S. Dist. Ct. (no. dist.) Tex. 1995, U.S. Dist. Ct. (we. dist.) Tex. 1997. Asst. dist. atty. Harris County Dist. Atty.'s Office, Houston, 1993-95; assoc. Cowles & Thompson, P.C., Dallas, 1995—. Mem. Duke U. Alumni Assn. (mem. adv. admissions com. 1994—), Federalist Soc. Republican. Presbyterian. Avocations: tennis, reading, jogging. Product liability, Professional liability, Personal injury. Home: 2701 Cotton Ct Plano TX 75093-3230 Office: Cowles & Thompson PC 901 Main St Ste 4000 Dallas TX 75202-3793

**KEMP, KATHLEEN NAGY,** lawyer; b. McKeesport, Pa., Mar. 29, 1949; d. Homer Edward and Jeanne Eileen (Wunder) Nagy; m. K. Lawrence Kemp, May 30, 1970 (div.); children: Paul Gregory, Carolyn Elaine. BS, U. Pitts., 1971, JD, 1981. Bar: Pa. 1981, U.S. Dist. Ct. (we. dist.) Pa. 1981, U.S. Ct. Appeals (3rd cir.) 1986, U.S. Tax Ct. 1986, U.S. Supreme Ct. 1986. Ptnr. Kemp & Kemp, New Kensington, Pa., 1982-95; pvt. practice Murrysville, Pa., 1995—. Pres. New Kensington chpt. NOW, 1973; bd. dirs. Easter Seal Soc., New Kensington, 1982; bd. dirs., chmn. Alle-Kiski Symphony, New Kensington, 1989; chmn. Citizen Adv. Bd. Mental Health/Mental Retardation Ctr., New Kensington, 1983; chmn. Official Com. YMCA swim team parents group, 1990; mem. adv. com. Municipality Murrysville Cable Access Channel, 1997—. Mem. Westmoreland Bar Assn. (membership com.), Allegheny Mountain YMCA Master's Swimming Assn. (sec. 1997-99, YMCA Master's Swimming Nat. Champion 1995), New Kensington Area C. of C. (bd. dirs. 1990-95), East Suburban C. of C. (bd. dirs. 1996-98). Avocations: reading, swimming, needle-work. Estate planning, Family and matrimonial, Probate. Home: 2043 Francis Dr Apollo PA 15613-9241 Office: 3925 Reed Blvd Ste 204 Murrysville PA 15668-1848

**KEMP, ROLAND CONNOR,** lawyer; b. Dallas, May 29, 1943; s. William Thomas and Martha Bell (Arney) K.; m. Carol Ann DeRosa, Dec. 12, 1966 (div.); children—Thomas Roland, Patrick Michael. B.A., Baylor U., 1965, postgrad., 1966; J.D., U. Tex.-Austin, 1972. Bar: Tex. 1972, U.S. Dist. Ct. (so. dist.) Tex. 1973, U.S. Ct. Apls. (5th cir.) 1973, U.S. Sup. Ct. 1976. Law clk. U.S. Dist. Ct. So. Dist. Tex., Houston, 1972-74; assoc. Schlanger, Cook, Cohn & Mills, Houston, 1974-76; assoc. Fred Parks & Assocs., Houston, 1977-80; sole practice, Houston, 1980-87; ptnr. Henderson & Kemp, Houston, 1988—. Chmn. bd. dirs. Timberlane Mcpl. Utility Dist., Harris County, Tex., 1973. Served to capt. USAF, 1966-70. Mem. State Bar Tex., Houston Bar Assn., Phi Delta Phi. Office: PO Box 90775 Houston TX 77290-0775

**KEMP, WENDI J.,** lawyer; b. Blue Island, Ill., Nov. 16, 1964; d. John E. and Marjorie C. (VanLaten) K. BS in Edn., Northwestern U., 1986; JD, U. Conn., 1989. Bar: Conn. 1989, U.S. Dist. Ct. Conn. 1992. Atty. Wiggin & Dana, New Haven, 1989-92, Cummings & Lockwood, Hartford, Conn., 1992—. Mem. ABA, Conn. Bar Assn., Young Lawyers Assn., Meriden C. of C. Labor, Education and schools. Office: Cummings & Lockwood City Place I Hartford CT 06103

**KEMPER, JAMES DEE,** lawyer; b. Olney, Ill., Feb. 23, 1947; s. Jack O. and Vivian L. Kemper; m. Diana J. Deig, June 1, 1968; children: Judd, Jason. BS, Ind. U., 1969, JD summa cum laude, 1971. Bar: Ind. 1971. Law clk. U.S. Ct. Appeals (7th cir.), Chgo., 1971-72; mng. ptnr. Ice Miller Donadio & Ryan, Indpls., 1972—. Note editor Ind. U. Law Rev., 1970-71; contbr. articles to profl. jours. Past officer, bd. dirs. Marion County Assn. for Retarded Citizens, Inc., Indpls.; past bd. dirs. Cen. Ind. Easter Seal Soc., Indpls., Crossroads Rehab. Ctr., Inc, Indpls.; pres., bd. govs. Orchard Country Day Sch., Indpls.; mem. bd. Eiteljorg Mus. Native Americans, Butler U. Fellow Ind. Bar Found.; mem. ABA (employee benefit com.), Ind. Bar Assn., The Group, Inc., Midwest Pension Conf., Stanley K. Lacy Leadership Alumni. Pension, profit-sharing, and employee benefits, Health, Corporate taxation. Office: Ice Miller Donadio & Ryan 1 American Sq Indianapolis IN 46282-0001

**KEMPF, DONALD G., JR.,** lawyer; b. Chgo., July 4, 1937; s. Donald G. and Verginia (Jahnke) K.; m. Nancy Kempf, June 12, 1965; children: Donald G. III, Charles P., Stephen R. AB, Villanova U., 1959; LLB, Harvard U., 1965; MBA, U. Chgo., 1989. Bar: Ill. 1965, U.S. Supreme Ct. 1972, N.Y. 1986, Colo. 1992. Assoc. Kirkland & Ellis, Chgo., 1965-70, ptnr., 1971—. Trustee Chgo. Symphony Orch., 1995—, Am. Inns of Ct. Found., 1997—; bd. govs. Chgo. Zool. Soc., 1975—, Art Inst. Chgo., 1984—; bd. dirs. United Charities Chgo., 1985—, chmn. bd., 1991-93. Capt. USMC, 1959-62. Fellow Am. Coll. Trial Lawyers; mem. Am. Econ. Assn., ABA, Chgo. Club, Econ. Club, Univ. Club, Mid-Am. Club, Saddle and Cycle Club (Chgo.), Snowmass (Colo.) Club, Quail Ridge (Fla.) Club, Westmoreland Club. Roman Catholic. General civil litigation, Antitrust, Mergers and acquisitions. Office: Kirkland & Ellis 200 E Randolph Dr Fl 54 Chicago IL 60601-6636

**KEMPF, DOUGLAS PAUL,** lawyer; b. Mpls., July 24, 1954; s. James Dean and Carol Lois (Dahl) K. BA, St. Olaf Coll., 1976; JD, U. Minn., 1980. Bar: Minn. 1980, U.S. Dist. Ct. Minn. 1982, U.S. Ct. Appeals (8th cir.) 1984. Ptnr. Kempf & Kempf Law Office, Bloomington, Minn., 1981—. Mgr. various Rep. campaigns, Bloomington, 1982—; chmn. Senate Dist. 41 Reps., 1991—; mem. Bloomington Planning Commn., 1983-89, chmn., 1988-89; active Leadership Bloomington, 1984-85; co-chmn. Vinter Sprinten Ski Race, Bloomington, 1985—; atty. coach Kennedy High Sch. Mock Trial Team, 1990. Mem. Minn. Bar Assn., Hennepin County Bar Assn., Assn. Trial Lawyers Am., Minn. Trial Lawyers Assn., Minn. Jaycees (legal counsel Charitable Found. 1984-87, Presdl. Medallion 1984), Bloomington Jaycees (pres. 1983-84). State civil litigation, General practice, Real property. Home: 6045 Lyndale Ave S Apt 118 Minneapolis MN 55419-2236

**KEMPS, LOREEN MARIE,** lawyer; b. Phila., May 4, 1966. BA, Drexel U., 1989; JD, Ohio Northern U., 1992. Atty. Emerick & Kemps, Duncansville, Pa., 1992—; atty. part-time Pub. Defenders Office, Duncansville, 1993—; instr. paralegal and continuing edn. program Mt. Aloysius Coll., Cresson, Pa. Mem. ABA. Republican. Avocation: skiing. General practice. Office: 1923 Old Route 220 N Ste B Duncansville PA 16635-8313

**KENDALL, DAVID E.,** lawyer; b. Camp Atterbury, Ind., May 2, 1944. BA, Wabash Coll., 1966; MA, Oxford U., England, 1968; JD, Yale U., 1971. Bar: N.Y. 1974, U.S. Ct. Appeals (5th cir.) 1976, D.C. 1978, U.S. Supreme Ct. 1978, Md. 1993. Law clerk to Mr. Justice Byron R. White U.S. Supreme Ct., 1971-72; mem. Williams & Connolly; adj. prof. Columbia U. Law Sch., 1977-78, Georgetown U. Law Ctr., 1985-95. Note and comment editor Yale Law Jour., 1970-71; author (with Leonard Ross) The Lottery and the Draft, 1970. Rhodes scholar. Mem. N.Y. State Bar Assn. Criminal, General civil litigation. Office: Williams & Connolly 725 12th St NW Washington DC 20005-5901

**KENDALL, GARY WHEELER,** lawyer; b. Alexandria, Va., June 13, 1949; m. George Clayton and Frances Wheeler Kendall; m. Sandra H. Kendall, Feb. 6, 1987. BA, U. Va., 1971; JD, U. Richmond, 1976. Bar: Va. 1976. Atty. Michie, Hamlett, Lowry, Rasmussen and Tweed, P.C., Charlottesville, Va.; instr. U. Va., 1982-85; gen. counsel Va. AFL-CIO. Mem. Va. State Bar Assn. (lectr., continuing edn. program 1988—), Am. bd. of Trial Advocates (bd. dirs. 1989—), Civil Justice Found., Va. Trial Lawyer sAssn. (lectr., continuing edn. program 1988—), The Assn. of Trial Lawyers of Am. (trust adv. com., celotox bankruptcy, labor liaison com.), Phi Alpha Delta. Fax: 804-295-0681. E-mail: gkendall@mhlrt.com. General civil litigation, Product liability, Workers' compensation. Office: Michie Hamlett Lowry Rasmussen and Tweel PC PO Box 298 Charlottesville VA 22902-0298

**KENDALL, JOE,** federal judge; b. Dallas, 1954; m. Veronica Kendall, 1975; children: Drew, Greg, Alan. BBA, So. Meth. U., 1977; JD, Baylor U., 1980. Bar: Tex. 1980, U.S. Ct. Appeals (5th cir.) 1980, U.S. Supreme Ct. 1980; cert. criminal law specialist. Police officer Dallas Police Dept., 1972-78; asst. dist. atty. Dallas County Dist. Attys. Office, 1980-82; pvt. practice Dallas, 1982-86; judge Tex. State Dist. Ct., Dallas, 1987-92, U.S. Dist. Ct. (no. dist.) Tex., Dallas, 1992—. Office: US Dist Ct 1100 Commerce St 16th Fl Dallas TX 75242-1027

**KENDALL, KEITH EDWARD,** lawyer; b. Martins Ferry, Ohio, Aug. 6, 1958; s. Edward Stanley and Mary Louise (Dagan) Kendziorski; m. Elizabeth Ann Kampert, May 25, 1984. BS, Ohio State U., 1980; JD, Ohio No. U., Ada, 1984. Assoc. Brugler & Levin, Lewistown, Pa., 1985-86; staff atty. Keystone Legal Svcs., Lewistown, 1986-87; assoc. Timothy S. Searer Law Office, Lewistown, 1987-90; with Office of Chief Counsel, Pa. State Police, 1990-91; prin. Kendall Law Office, Harrisburg, Pa., 1992—; asst. dist. atty. Mifflin County, Pa., 1987-90; hearing officer Mental Health & Mental Retardation Program, Lewistown, 1987-88; arbitrator Am. Arbitration Assn., 1987—. Mem. ABA, Ohio Bar Assn., Pa. Bar Assn. Democrat. Avocations: golf, skiing, photography. Labor, Workers' compensation,

General practice. Office: Kendall Law Office 3207 N Front St Ste 101 Harrisburg PA 17110-1311

**KENDALL, PAUL F.,** lawyer. Gen. counsel Office of Justice Programs, Washington. Office: Justice Programs 810 7th St NW Washington DC 20001-3718

**KENDALL, PHILLIP ALAN,** lawyer; b. Lamar, Colo., July 20, 1942; s. Charles Stuart and Katherine (Wilson) K.; m. Margaret Roe Greenfield, May 2, 1970; children: Anne, Timothy. BS in Engring., Stanford U., 1964; JD, U. Colo., Boulder, 1969; postgrad., U. Freiburg (Germany), 1965-66. Engr. Siemens Halske, Munich, 1965; ptnr. Kraemer, Kendall & Benson, Colorado Springs, Colo., 1969—; gen. counsel Peak Health Care, Inc., Colorado Springs, 1979-87; bd. dirs. Norwest Banks Colorado Springs. Pres. bd. Colorado Springs Symphony Orch. Assn., 1977-80; bd. dirs. Penrose Hosps., Colorado Springs, 1982-88; pres. bd. Citizen's Goals, Colorado, 1984-86; bd. dirs. Legal Aid Found., Denver, 1988-94, chmn., 1991-93; bd. dirs. Colo. Nature Conservancy, 1996—. Recipient Medal of Distinction-Fine Arts, Colorado Springs C. of C., 1983. Mem. ABA, Colo. Bar Assn. (bd. govs. 1985-88, outstanding young lawyer 1977), El Paso County Bar Assn. (bd. trustees 1983-85), Colorado Springs Estate Planning Coun. Avocations: triathlons, helicopter skiing, marathon swimming, windsurfing, sailing. Estate planning, Probate, Estate taxation. Home: 1915 Wood Ave Colorado Springs CO 80907-6714 Office: Kraemer Kendall & Benson PC 430 N Tejon St Ste 300 Colorado Springs CO 80903-1167

**KENDALL, ROBERT LOUIS, JR.,** lawyer; b. Rochester, N.H., Oct. 13, 1930; s. Robert Louis and Marguerite (Thomas) K.; m. Patricia Ann Palmer, Aug. 13, 1955; children: Linda J., Cynthia J., Janet L. AB cum laude, Harvard U., 1952; JD cum laude, U. Pa., 1955; Diploma in Law, Oxford (Eng.) U., 1956. Bar: Pa. 1957, Ga. 1993. Assoc. Schnader, Harrison, Segal & Lewis, Phila., 1956-65, ptnr., 1966-95; lectr. Temple U. Law Sch., Phila., 1976-77; spl. instr. U. Pa. Law Sch., 1959-62. Contbr. to Antitrust Law Developments, 2d edit. 1984. Bd. dirs. Mann Music Ctr., Inc., Phila., 1971-98, Settlement Music Sch., Phila., Pa., 1984—, Jr. C. of C., Phila., 1962-65; mem. Gladwyne Civic Assn., 1960—, Phila. Orch. Assn., 1983—. Fellow Soc. Values in Higher Edn.; mem. ABA, Pa. Bar Assn., Ga. Bar Assn., Phila. Bar Assn., Atlanta Bar Assn., U. Pa. Law Alumni Assn. (bd. mgrs.), Rotary, Order of Coif (pres. 1979-80), Lawyers Club Atlanta, Harvard Club. Democrat. Episcopalian. Administrative and regulatory, Antitrust, Public utilities. Home: 1208 Hartdale Ln Gladwyne PA 19035-1434 Office: Schnader Harrison Segal 1600 Market St Ste 3600 Philadelphia PA 19103-7240

**KENDRICK, DARRYL D.,** lawyer; b. Eden, N.C., Sept. 27, 1956; s. Harold D. and June (Martin) K.; m. Patricia A. Cook, Sept. 18, 1981; children: Ashlyn Brianna, Kristyn Amanda, Caitlyn Samantha. BSBA, U. N.C., 1978; JD with honors, U. Fla., 1985. Bar: Fla. 1986, U.S. Dist. Ct. (mid. dist.) Fla. 1986. Claims adjuster Nationwide Ins. Co., Orlando and Gainesville, Fla., Houston, 1979-83; pvt. practice Jacksonville, 1987—; mem. Donohoe & Kendrick, Jacksonville, 1991-98; gen. counsel JAZZIZ mag., Gainesville, 1987—. Mem. Fla. Acad. Profl. Mediators, First Coast Trial Lawyers Assn., Fla. Assn. Collection Profls., Jacksonville Bar Assn. Democrat. Lutheran. Avocations: audiophile, racquetball, travel, stein collecting. Personal injury, Family and matrimonial, General practice. Office: 1817 Atlantic Blvd Jacksonville FL 32207-3403

**KENEALLY, KATHRYN MARIE,** lawyer; b. Dayton, Ohio, Apr. 30, 1958; d. William Henry and Joanna Gertrude K.; m. Thomas Marshall, Oct. 16, 1992. BA, Cornell U., 1979; JD, Fordham U., 1982; LLM in Taxation, NYU, 1993. Bar: N.Y., 1983, U.S. Dist. Ct. (so., ea. dists.) N.Y., 1983, U.S. Ct. Appeal (2d, 3d, 11th cirs.), U.S. Tax Ct. Law clk. to Hon. E. R. Neaher U.S. Dist. Ct. (ea. dist.) N.Y., Bklyn., 1982-83; assoc. Skadden Arps Slate Meagher & Flom, N.Y.C., 1983-85; assoc. Kostelanetz Ritholz Tigue & Fink, N.Y.C., 1985-90, ptnr., 1990-93; ptnr. Kostelanetz & Fink, LLP, N.Y.C., 1993—. Columnist The Champion, 1996—; co-author: Practice Under Federal Sentencing Guidelines, 1998; contbr. articles to profl. jours. Mem. practitioners adv. group U.S. Sentencing Commn., 1993—. Mem. ABA, Nat. Assn. Criminal Def. Lawyers (life). Criminal, Federal civil litigation, Taxation, general. Home: 48 Charlotte Pl Hartsdale NY 10530-2602 Office: Kostelanetz & Fink LLP 530 5th Ave New York NY 10036-5101

**KENNADY, EMMETT HUBBARD, III,** lawyer; b. Houston, Dec. 13, 1957; s. Emmett Hubbard Jr. and Ruth Gail (Lewis) K.; m. Monta Kennady, Sept. 21, 1985; children: Jennings Randolph, Emmett Hubbard IV. BA in Theology, Washington and Lee U., 1980, BA in Polit. Sci., 1980; JD, St. Mary's Sch. Law, San Antonio, 1984. Bar: Tex. 1984, U.S. Army Ct. Criminal Appeals 1994, U.S. Ct. Appeals for Armed Forces 1997. Asst. dist. atty. Brazos County Dist. Atty.'s Office, Bryan, Tex., 1985-87; atty. Lawrence, Thornton, Payne, Bryan, 1987-88; sole practitioner College Station, Tex., 1988—; mem. staff St. Mary's Sch. Law. Co-author: Medico-Legal Considerations for Dental Practitioner, 1988; contbr. articles to profl. jours. Mem. College Station City Coun., 1992-98, mayor pro tem, 1996-98; mem. Leadership Brazos, Bryan, 1989-90; judge College Station Bd. Adjustment, 1990-91; mem. College Station Capital Improvement Com., 1989-90; bd. dirs. Bryan-College Station Econ. Devel. Bd., 1997—, Opera and Performing Arts, College Station, 1997—, United Way, Bryan, 1991-96, Arts Coun., College Station, 1990-93. Capt. U.S. Army, 1999. L.B.J. Congl. scholar, 1980. Republican. Baptist. Avocation: flying. Appellate, General civil litigation. Office: 424 Tarrow St College Station TX 77840-7813

**KENNAMER, JOHN HAROLD,** lawyer, rancher; b. McAlister, Okla.; s. Harold E. and Alma L. Kennamer; m. Kaye C. DeVillier, Oct. 7, 1985; 1 child, Cale. BBA, Tex. Christian U., 1964, MBA, 1965; JD, U. Houston, 1972. Bar: Tex. 1972, Colo. 1990. Pvt. practice Houston, 1972-92, Winnie and Baytown, Tex., 1993—. With U.S. Army, 1959-61. Avocations: skiing, rafting, camping, running. Real property. Home: Box 695 412 SH 124 Winnie TX 77665 Office: 1595 N Alexander Dr Baytown TX 77520-5321

**KENNARD, JOYCE L.,** state supreme court justice. Former judge L.A. Mcpl. Ct., Superior Ct., Ct. Appeal, Calif.; assoc. justice Calif. Supreme Ct., San Francisco, 1989—. Office: Calif Supreme Ct 350 Mcallister St San Francisco CA 94102-4712

**KENNARD, WILLIAM EARL,** federal agency administrator, lawyer; b. L.A., Jan. 19, 1957; s. Robert A. and Helen Z. (King) K.; m. Deborah D. Kennedy, Apr. 9, 1984. BA, Stanford U., 1978; JD, Yale U., 1981. Bar: Calif. 1981, D.C. Ct. Appeals 1985, U.S. Ct. Appeals (D.C. cir.) 1994, U.S. Supreme Ct. 1994. Fellow Nat. Assn. Broadcasters, Washington, 1981-82, asst. gen. counsel, 1983-84; assoc. Verner, Liipfert, Bernhard, McPherson & Hand, Washington, 1984-89, ptnr., 1990-93; gen. counsel FCC, Washington, 1993-97, chmn., 1997—. Office: FCC 445 12th St SW Washington DC 20024-2101

**KENNEDY, ANTHONY MCLEOD,** United States supreme court justice; b. Sacramento, July 23, 1936. AB, Stanford U., 1958; student, London Sch. Econs.; LLB, Harvard U., 1961; JD (hon.), U. Pacific, 1988, U. Santa Clara, 1988. Bar: Calif. 1962, U.S. Tax Ct. 1971. Former ptnr. Evans, Jackson & Kennedy; prof. constl. law McGeorge Sch. Law, U. of Pacific, 1965-88; judge U.S. Ct. Appeals (9th cir.), Sacramento, 1976-88; assoc. justice U.S. Supreme Ct., Washington, 1988—; mem. bd. student advisors Harvard Faculty, 1960-61. Fellow Am. Bar Found. (hon.), Am. Coll. Trial Lawyers (hon.); mem. Sacramento County Bar Assn., State Bar Calif., Phi Beta Kappa. Office: US Supreme Ct Supreme Ct Bldg 1 1st St NE Washington DC 20543-0001

**KENNEDY, BRIAN MELVILLE,** lawyer; b. Renfrew, Ont., Can., Oct. 21, 1948; came to U.S., 1956; s. Matthew James and Mary Margaret Kennedy; m. Shelley Allison Gribble, May 6, 1972; 1 child, Shannon Elizabeth. BA magna cum laude, Mich. State U., 1970; JD cum laude, Wayne State U., 1974. Bar: Mich. 1974, U.S. DDist. Ct. (ea. dist.) Mich. 1979, U.S. Ct. Appeals (6th cir.) 1983. Stockbroker 1st of Mich. Corp., Rochester, Mich., 1970-74; chief trial atty. Bay County Prosecutor's Office, Bay City, Mich., 1974-78; ptnr. Patterson, Gruber, Kennedy, Gill & Milster, Bay City, 1979—; instr. criminal law and procedure Delta Coll., Bay City, 1975-77; panelist, presenter, moderator Inst. Continuing Legal Edn., Ann Arbor, Mich., 1983-88; presenter Nat. Bus. Inst., 1992. Contbg. author: How To Try an Automobile Negligence Case, 1992, (course materials) Trial of Wrongful Death Case in Michigan, 1983. Pres. Mich. State U. Young Reps., East Lansing, 1972; Rep. candidate for Mich. Senate, 1978. Mem. Mich. Bar Assn., Bay County Bar Assn. (bd. dirs.), Assn. Trial Lawyers Am., United Way Pillars Club. Presbyterian. Avocations: golf, fishing, reading. Personal injury, State civil litigation, Criminal. Office: PO Box 855 Bay City MI 48707-0855

**KENNEDY, CHARLES ALLEN,** lawyer; b. Maysville, Ky., Dec. 11, 1940; s. Elmer Earl and Mary Frances Kennedy; m. Patricia Ann Louderback, Dec. 9, 1961; 1 child, Mimi Mignon. AB, Morehead State Coll., 1965, MA in Edn., 1968; JD, U. Akron, 1969; LLM, George Washington U., 1974. Bar: Ohio 1969. Asst. cashier Citizens Bank, Felicity, Ohio, 1961-63; tchr. Triway Local Sch. Dist., Wooster, Ohio, 1965-67; with office of gen. counsel Fgn. Agr. and Spl. Programs Div., U.S. Dept. Agr., Washington, 1969-71; ptnr. Kauffman, Eberhart, Cicconetti & Kennedy Co., Wooster, 1972-86, Kennedy, Cicconetti & Knowlton, L.P.A., Wooster, 1986—. Mem. ABA, FBA, ATLA, Ohio State Bar Assn., Ohio Acad. Trial Lawyers, Ohio Assn. Criminal Def. Lawyers, Wayne County Bar Assn., Exch. Club, Lions, Elks, Phi Alpha Delta, Phi Delta Kappa. Republican. State civil litigation, Criminal, Family and matrimonial. Home: 1770 Burbank Rd Wooster OH 44691-2240 Office: Kennedy Cicconetti & Know Ken 558 N Market St Wooster OH 44691-3406

**KENNEDY, COLLEEN MARY,** lawyer; b. Milw., May 26, 1955; d. William Frederick Kennedy and Mary Patricia (Boyle) Radford; m. Thomas J. Kelly, Jr., Apr. 30, 1983; children: Caitlin, Patrick. BA, U. Colo., 1977; JD, Antioch Sch. Law, Washington, 1980. Bar: D.C. 1981, U.S. Dist. Ct. D.C. 1981, U.S. Ct. Appeals (D.C. cir.) 1981. Law clk. to Judge William S. Thompson and Henry Greene, D.C. Superior Ct., Washington, 1980-81; asst. U.S. atty. U.S. Atty.'s Office, Washington, 1981—. Bd. dirs. Montgomery County (Md.) Assn. Retarded Citizens, 1991-96, KEEN (Kids Enjoy Exercise Now), 1995-98. Democrat. Roman Catholic. Avocations: swimming, reading, hiking, skiing. Office: US Atty's Office 555 4th St NW Ste 11846 Washington DC 20001-2733

**KENNEDY, CORNELIA GROEFSEMA,** federal judge; b. Detroit, Mich., Aug. 4, 1923; d. Elmer H. and Mary Blanche (Gibbons) Groefsema; m. Charles S. Kennedy, Jr. (dec.); 1 son, Charles S. III. B.A., U. Mich., 1945, J.D. with distinction, 1947; LL.D. (hon.), No. Mich. U., 1971, Eastern Mich. U., 1971, Western Mich. U., 1973, Detroit Coll. Law, 1980, U. Detroit, 1987. Bar: Mich. bar 1947. Law clk. to Chief Judge Harold M. Stephens, U.S. Ct. of Appeals, Washington, 1947-48; assoc. Elmer H. Groefsema, Detroit, 1948-52; partner Markle & Markle, Detroit, 1952-66; judge 3d Judicial Circuit Mich., 1967-70; dist. judge U.S. Dist. Ct., Eastern Dist. Mich., Detroit, 1970-79; chief judge U.S. Dist. Ct., Eastern Dist. Mich., 1977-79; circuit judge U.S. Ct. Appeals, (6th cir.), 1979—. Mem. Commn. on the Bicentennial of the U.S. Constitution (presdl. appointment). Recipient Sesquicentennial award U. Mich. Fellow Am. Bar Found.; mem. ABA, Mich. Bar Assn. (past chmn. negligence law sect.), Detroit Bar Assn. (past dir.), Fed. Bar Assn., Am. Judicature Soc., Nat. Assn. Women Lawyers, Am. Trial Lawyers Assn., Nat. Conf. Fed. Trial Judges (past chmn.), Fed. Jud. Fellows Commn. (bd. dirs.), Fed. Jud. Ctr. (bd. dirs.), Phi Beta Kappa. Office: US Ct of Appeals US Courthouse 231 W Lafayette Blvd Detroit MI 48226-2700*

**KENNEDY, CORNELIUS BRYANT,** retired lawyer; b. Evanston, Ill., Apr. 13, 1921; s. Millard Bryant and Myrna Estelle (Anderson) K.; m. Anne Martha Reynolds, June 20, 1959; children: Anne Talbot, Lauren K. Mayle. A.B., Yale U., 1943; J.D., Harvard U., 1948. Bar: Ill. 1949, D.C. 1965. Assoc. Mayer Austrian & Platt, Chgo., 1949-54, 55-59; asst. to U.S. atty. Dept. Justice, Chgo., 1954-55; counsel to minority leader U.S. Senate, 1959-65; sr. ptnr. Kennedy & Webster, Washington, 1965-82; of counsel Armstrong, Teasdale, Schlafly & Davis, Washington, 1983-88; public mem. Adminstrv. Conf. U.S., 1972-82, sr. conf. fellow, 1982-90, chmn. rulemaking com., 1973-82; ret., 1988. Contbr. articles to law jours. Fin. chmn. Lyric Opera Co., Chgo., 1954; chmn. young adults group Chgo. Coun. Fgn. Rels., 1958-59; pres. English Speaking Union Jrs., Chgo., 1957-59; trustee St. John's Child Devel. Ctr., Washington, 1965-67, 75-87, pres., 1983-85; exec. dir. Supreme Ct. Hist. Soc., 1984-87. 1st lt., AC U.S. Army, 1942-46. Fellow Am. Bar Found.; mem. Am. Law Inst., ABA (coun. sect. adminstrv. law 1967-70, chmn. sect. 1976-77), Fed. Bar Assn. (chmn. com. adminstrv. law 1963-64). Clubs: Legal Club Chgo., Explorers, N.Y. City, Capitol Hill, Chevy Chase (Md.), Sailing of Chesapeake (Annapolis, Md.), Adventurer's (Chgo.). Administrative and regulatory, Antitrust, Federal civil litigation. Home: 8462 Brook Rd Mc Lean VA 22102-1703

**KENNEDY, DAVID J.,** lawyer; b. N.Y.C., July 11, 1971; s. James Joseph and Anne Veronica (Hearne) K.; m. Aldina Maria Vazao, Apr. 11, 1997. BA, Harvard U., 1993; JD, Yale U., 1997. Bar: Conn. 1997, N.Y. 1998, U.S. Ct. Appeals (2d cir.) 1998. Pub. Interest Law fellow Alliance for Justice, Washington, 1997-98; law clk. to Hon. Kimba M. Wood U.S. Dist. Ct. (so. dist.) N.Y., N.Y.C., 1998—. Mem. grad. rev. bd. Harvard Lampoon, 1993—; contbr. articles to law rev. Contbg. mem. Dem. Nat. Com., Washington, 1995—. Harry S Truman scholar, 1992, Henry Luce scholar, 1993. Roman Catholic. Avocations: cooking, reading, bears. Home: 3235 Cambridge Ave Bronx NY 10463-3622

**KENNEDY, DAVID TINSLEY,** retired lawyer, labor arbitrator; b. Richmond, Va., Mar. 6, 1919; s. David Tinsley and Lilian Brady (Butcher) K.; m. Jean Elizabeth Stephenson, Nov. 26, 1949; children: David T. III, Thomas D., Michael F. JD, U. Va., 1948. Bar: Va. 1948, W.Va. 1949, U.S. Dist. Ct. (so. dist.) W.Va. 1949, U.S. Ct. Appeals (4th cir.) 1963. Atty. Dist. 29, United Mine Workers Am., Beckley, W.Va., 1949-61; ptnr. Kennedy & Vaughan, Beckley, 1962-98; arbitrator Coal Arbitration Svc., Washington, 1970—; emeritus dir. Raleigh County Nat. Bank, Beckley. Mem. Raleigh County Dem. exec. com., 1980-86, chmn., 1986-90. Lt. col. U.S. Army, 1942-46, PTO. Mem. ABA, W.Va. State Bar, Va. State Bar, Assn. Trial Lawyers Am. Roman Catholic. General practice. Home: 102 Mollohan Dr Beckley WV 25801-2135 Office: Kennedy & Vaughan PO Box 1008 Beckley WV 25802-1008

**KENNEDY, GEORGE WENDELL,** prosecutor; b. Altadena, Calif., Aug. 5, 1945; s. Ernest Campbell Kennedy and Mildred (Onstott) Stuckey; m. Janet Lynn Stites, Aug. 3, 1978; children: Campbell, Britton. BA, Claremont Men's Coll., 1968; postgrad., Monterey Inst. Fgn. Studies, 1968; JD, U. So. Calif., 1971; postgrad., Nat. Coll. Dist. Attys., 1974, F.B.I. Nat. Law Inst., 1989. Bar: Calif. 1972, U.S. Dist. Ct. (no. dist.) Calif. 1972, U.S. Ct. Appeals (9th cir.) 1972. Dep. dist. atty. Santa Clara County, San Jose, Calif., 1972-87, asst. dist. atty., 1987-88, chief asst. dist. atty., 1988-90, dist. atty., 1990—. Author: California Criminal Law Practice and Procedure, 1986. Active NAACP, 1989—, police chiefs' assn. Santa Clara County, San Jose, 1990—; chair domestic violence coun. Santa Clara County, San Jose, 1990-92; bd. dirs. Salvation Army, 1993. Recipient commendation Child Advocates of Santa Clara & San Mateo Counties, 1991, Santa Clara County Bd. Suprs., 1992, Valley Med. Ctr. Found., 1992, 93; elected Ofcl. of Yr. award Am. Electronics Assn., 1998. Mem. Nat. Dist. Attys. Assn. (bd. dirs.), Calif. Dist. Attys. Assn. (bd. dirs. 1988-90, officer 1993-97, pres. 1997-98), Santa Clara County Bar Assn., Rotary Club. Avocation: sailing. Office: 70 W Hedding St 5th Flr West Wing San Jose CA 95110

**KENNEDY, HAROLD EDWARD,** lawyer; b. Pottstown, Pa., Oct. 18, 1927; s. Freeman S. and Alice (Brehm) K.; m. Eleanor Henry, Jan. 9, 1960; children: Kathleen, Nancy, Harold, Robert, Ellen, Anne, Susan. Student, Colgate U., 1945-47; LLB, Syracuse U., 1952. Bar: N.Y. 1952, U.S. Dist. Ct. (no. dist.) N.Y. 1954, U.S. Supreme Ct. 1956, U.S. Dist. Ct. (so. dist.) N.Y. 1962. Ptnr. Taylor & Kennedy, Amsterdam, N.Y., 1952-59; sr. assoc. Kissam & Halpin, N.Y.C., 1959-60; vice chmn., gen. counsel, dir. mergers and acquisitions Foster Wheeler Corp., Clinton, N.J., 1960-94, legal advisor, 1994—, also bd. dirs.; bd. dirs. W.I. Refining Ltd., Compass Capital Group. Trustee First Presbyn. Ch., Orange, N.J., 1973-76, St. Barnabas Med. Ctr., 1986—, Kessler Inst. for Rehab., 1987—, vice chmn., 1992—, Union Hosp., 1994—, Beth Israel Hosp., 1996—; bd. visitors Syracuse U. Coll. of Law, 1987—. Served with USAF, 1945-47. Mem. Order of Coif, Baltusrol Golf Club, Sea Pines Country Club, Double Eagle Club. General corporate, Contracts commercial, Private international. Office: Foster Wheeler Corp Perryville Corp Pk Clinton NJ 08809

**KENNEDY, HARVEY JOHN, JR.,** lawyer; b. Barnesville, Ga., Apr. 9, 1924; s. Harvey John and Marisu (Reeves) K.; m. Jean McRitchie King, Apr. 8, 1950; children: Marisu, Jean Gay. LLB, U. Ga., 1949, JD, 1969; diplomate of psychology, Colo. Christian Coll., 1973. Bar: Ga. 1948. Atty. Lamar Electric Membership Corp., Barnesville, Ga., 1948—; county atty. Lamar County, Barnesville, Ga., 1950-52, 58-60; mem. Ga. Indigent Def. Coun., 1958, Ga. Bar Assn. Bd., 1958-59, State Bar of Ga. Bd. Govs. 1980-92; agt. Govt. Appeal Local Bd. 89, 1958; city atty. City of Barnesville, Ga., 1958-65, 83, City of Milner, Ga., 1963-68. Past pres. Barnesville (Ga.) Rotary Club, 1959-60. Capt. U.S. Army, 1942-46, ETO, PTO. Decorated Bronze Star medal and Combat Infantry badge. Mem. ABA, Ga. Trial Lawyers Assn. (v.p. 1972), State Bar Ga., Ga. Assn. Plaintiff's Trial Attys. (v.p. 1968), Am. Legion (comdr. post #25), Moose (32d degree shriner). Democrat. Presbyterian. Avocations: amateur radio, fishing. General practice, Criminal, Family and matrimonial. Office: PO Drawer B 217 Zebulon St Barnesville GA 30204-1126

**KENNEDY, JACK LELAND,** lawyer; b. Portland, Oreg., Jan. 30, 1924; s. Ernest E. and Lera M. (Talley) K.; m. Clara C. Hagans, June 5, 1948; children: James M., John C. Student, U.S. Maritime Commn. Acad., Southwestern U., L.A.; JD, Lewis and Clark Coll., 1951. Bar: Oreg. 1951. Pvt. practice Portland; ptnr. Kennedy & King, Portland, 1971-77, Kennedy, King & McClurg, Portland, 1977-82, Kennedy, King & Zimmer, Portland, 1982-98, Kennedy, Watts, Arellano & Ricks L.L.P., Portland, 1998—; trustee Northwestern Coll. Law, Portland; dir. Profl. Liability Fund, 1979-82. Contbr. articles to legal jours. Mem. bd. visitors Lewis and Clark Coll. With USNR, 1942-46. Recipient Disting. Grad. award Lewis and Clark Coll., 1983. Fellow Am. Coll. Trial Lawyers, Am. Bar Found. (life), Oreg. Bar Found. (charter); mem. ABA (ho. of dels. 1984-88), Oreg. State Bar (bd. govs. 1976-79, pres. 1978-79), Multnomah Bar Assn., City Club, Columbia River Yacht Club. Republican. General civil litigation, Insurance, Personal injury. Office: Kennedy Watts Arellano & Ricks LLP 2600 Pacwest Ctr 1211 SW 5th Ave Portland OR 97204-3713

**KENNEDY, JEANNE ELIZABETH,** lawyer; b. Fargo, N.D., Jan. 29, 1947; d. Richard Bernard and Rosalie Ann (Murphy) Ryan; m. James N. Kennedy, Apr. 20, 1991; children by previous marriage: Margaret, Robbie. AA, Mira Costa Coll., 1970; BA, Calif. State U., San Diego, 1973, MA, 1975; JD, Citrus Belt Law Sch., 1983. Bar: Calif. 1984, U.S. Dist. Ct. (cen. dist.) Calif. 1984. Instr. Victor Valley Coll., Victorville, Calif., 1975-78; project coord. Cropsey Constrn., Adelanto, Calif., 1978-81; assoc. Caldwell & Hansen, Victorville, 1983-86; ptnr. Caldwell & Cropsey, Victorville, 1986-91, Caldwell & Kennedy, Victorville, 1991—. Bd. trustees Victor Elem Sch. Dist., 1983—. Mem. Hi Desert Bar Assn. (bd. dirs. 1984-87, 96-97, treas. 1987-88), San Bernardino County Bar Assn. (bd. dirs. 1993—), Victorville C. of C. (bd. dirs. 1986-92), Victor Valley Bus. and Profl. Women (treas. 1985-86), Soroptimists Internat. of Victor Valley. Republican. Roman Catholic. Avocations: snow skiing, cycling, reading. State civil litigation, Construction, Landlord-tenant. Office: Caldwell & Kennedy 15476 W Sand St Victorville CA 92392-2349

**KENNEDY, JEFF GRANT,** lawyer, educator; b. Mo., Oct. 1, 1954; m. Wynter Linda Morgan, Oct. 4, 1986. BA, S.W. Mo. State U., 1977; JD, U. Mo., Kansas City, 1980. Pres. L.A. Trial Coll., Encino, Calif., 1995—; pvt. practice Westlake Village, Westlake Village, Calif., 1982—; bd. govs. Ventura County Trial Lawyers Assn., Ventura, Calif., 1996-97. Author: Guide to Personal Injury Arbitrators, 1990. Mem. Consumer Attys. Assn. L.A., Optimists (assoc.), Toastmasters (sec. 1996-97). email: www.jgrantkennedy.com. Real property. Office: 141 Duesenberg Dr Ste 10 Westlake Vlg CA 91362-3481

**KENNEDY, JERRY WAYNE,** lawyer; b. Murphy, N.C., Nov. 18, 1947; s. Almon T. and Ruby Mae (McCalla) K.; m. Maura Comerford, July 15, 1978. BA, Birmingham So. Coll., 1970; MA, Am. U., 1977; JD, Samford U., 1984; postgrad., Georgetown U., 1983-84. Bar: Ala. 1985, D.C. 1986. Press sec. Rep. Ronnie Flippo, 5th dist. Ala., 1977-80; chief of staff, legis. dir. Rep. Ben Erdreich, 6th dist. Ala., 1982-86; assoc. Heron, Burchette, Ruckert & Rothwell, Washington, 1987-90; of counsel Tuttle & Taylor, Washington, 1990-94; owner Kennedy Govt. Rels., Washington, 1995—; adj. prof. Sch. Communication, Am. U., Washington, 1979. Assoc. editor Am. Jour. Trial Advocacy, 1982-83. With USAF, 1970-74. Mem. ABA, Ala. Bar Assn., D.C. Bar Assn., Ala. State Soc. (bd. dirs.), Soc. Profl. Journalists (Sigma Delta Chi), Delta Theta Phi. Democrat. Unitarian. Legislative. Home and Office: Kennedy Govt Rels 313 S Carolina Ave SE Washington DC 20003-4213

**KENNEDY, JOHN PATRICK,** lawyer, corporate executive; b. Houston, Oct. 2, 1943; s. Arch R. and Kathryn R. (Delahunty) K.; children: Kathleen, Elizabeth, Christina, Patrick, Lindsay. BA in Econs., U. Kans., 1965, JD, 1967; LLM, U. Mo., 1973, MBA, 1972. Bar: Kans. 1967, Mo. 1968, Ohio 1973, Wis. 1985, U.S. Supreme Ct. 1972, U.S. Dist. Ct. (we. dist.) Mo. 1972, U.S. Dist. Ct. Kans. 1967. Trial atty. Kodas, Gingerich & Stites, Kansas City, Mo., 1967-69; sr. atty. Mobay Chem. Co., Kansas City, 1969-73; v.p., gen. counsel, dir. Scotts & Sons Co., Marysville, Ohio, 1973-84; v.p., sec., gen. counsel Johnson Controls, Inc., Milw., 1984—; small bus. advisor, venture capitalist. Contbr. articles to profl. jours. Served with USAR, 1967-73. Recipient Wall St. Jour. award, 1972, Am. Jurisprudence awards, 1966-67. Mem. ABA, Ohio Bar Assn., Columbus Bar Assn., Wis. Bar Assn., Am. Corp. Counsel Assn. Democrat. Roman Catholic. Antitrust, Administrative and regulatory, Federal civil litigation. Office: Johnson Controls Inc PO Box 591 5757 N Green Bay Ave Milwaukee WI 53209-4408

**KENNEDY, JOSEPH WINSTON,** lawyer; b. Marshalltown, Iowa, June 5, 1932; s. Roy Wesley and Julia Harriet (Plum) K.; m. Barbara B. Bowman, July 11, 1954 (div. June 1982); children: Kimberle Ann, Kamella Lucille; m. Paula Terry Smith, Nov. 24, 1984. BS cum laude, McPherson (Kans.) Coll., 1954; JD with honors, George Washington U., 1958. Bar: Kans. 1958, U.S. Dist Ct. Kans. 1958, U.S. Ct. Appeals (10th cir.) 1976, U.S. Supreme Ct. 1970. Spl. agt. Office of Naval Intelligence, Washington, 1954-58; assoc. Morris, Laing, Evans & Brock, Wichita, Kans., 1958-62; ptnr. Morris, Laing, Evans, Brock & Kennedy, Wichita, 1962—. Chmn. profl. divsn., atty. United Way of the Plains, Wichita, 1990-93. Recipient Best Lawyers in Am. award, 1987, 89-90, 91-92, 93-94, 95-96. Mem. ABA, Kans. Bar Assn. (bd. law examiners 1993—), Wichita Bar Assn. (bd. govs. 1964-66). Federal civil litigation. Office: Morris Laing Evans Brock & Kennedy 200 W Douglas Ave Fl 4 Wichita KS 67202-3013

**KENNEDY, LOAN BUI,** lawyer; b. Saigon, Nov. 18, 1968; d. Chien Tho and Lan Thi Bui; m. William Ronald Kennedy, July 10, 1993; 1 child, Meghan Veronica. BA, Trinity Coll., 1991; JD, U. Conn., 1995. Bar: Conn. 1995. Cons. Andersen Cons., Hartford, 1991-93; corp. counsel United Techs. Corp., Pratt & Whitney, Jupiter, Fla., 1995—. General corporate. Office: UTC Pratt & Whitney 17900 Beeline Hwy Jupiter FL 33478

**KENNEDY, MARC J.,** lawyer; b. Newburgh, N.Y., Mar. 2, 1945; s. Warren G. K. and Frances F. (Levinson) K.; children: Michael L., Kayla R., Shawna D. BA cum laude, Syracuse U., 1967; JD, U. Mich., 1970. Bar: N.Y. 1971. Assoc. Davies, Hardy, Ives & Lawther, N.Y.C., 1971-72, London, Buttenweiser & Chalif, N.Y.C., 1972-73, Silberfeld, Danziger & Bangser, N.Y.C., 1973; counsel Occidental Crude Sales, Inc., N.Y.C., 1974-75; v.p., gen. counsel Internat. Ore & Fertilizer Corp., N.Y.C., 1975-82; asst. gen. counsel Occidental Chem. Corp., Houston, 1982; v.p., gen. counsel Occidental Chem. Agrl. Products Inc., Tampa, Fla., 1982-87; v.p., gen counsel agrl. products group Occidental Chem. Corp., Tampa, 1987-91; assoc. gen. counsel Occidental Chem. Corp., Dallas, 1991—; faculty mentor Columbia Pacific U., Mill Valley, Calif., 1981-88. Contbr. articles to profl. jours. Trustee Bar Harbor Festival Corp., N.Y.C., 1974-87; bd. dirs. Am. Opera Repertory Co., 1982-85; mem. com. planned giving N.Y. Foundling Hosp., 1977-88; Explorer post advisor Boy Scouts Am., 1976-78. Mem. ABA (vice-chmn. com. internat. law liaison young lawyers sect. 1974-75, chmn. sub-com. proposed trade barriers to the importation of products into U.S. 1985-88, vice chmn. corp. counsel com. 1992-93, co-chmn. corp. counsel com. 1993-98), Maritime

Law Assn., N.Y. State Bar Assn., Am. Corp. Counsel Assn. Admiralty, Private international, General corporate. Office: Occidental Chem Corp PO Box 809050 Dallas TX 75380-9050

**KENNEDY, (HENRY) MARK,** former state supreme court judge; b. Greenville, Ala., May 5, 1952; s. D.M. and Marjorie W. Kennedy; m. Peggy W. Kennedy, Dec. 15, 1973; 1 child, Leigh Chancellor. BA, Auburn U., 1973; JD cum laude, Samford U., 1977. Bar: Ala. 1977. Clk. to presiding justice Ala. Ct. Criminal Appeals, 1977, staff atty., 1978; former judge Ala. Cir. Ct., 15th Jud. Cir.; justice Ala. Supreme Ct., Montgomery, until 1999. Mem. ABA, Ala. State Bar, Montgomery County Bar Assn., Ala. Assn. Dist. Judges. Democrat. Baptist. Office: Supreme Court of Alabama 300 Dexter Ave Montgomery AL 36104-3741

**KENNEDY, MICHAEL DEAN,** lawyer; b. Portland, Oreg., Sept. 13, 1952; s. Olywn Edmund Kennedy and Eleanor Frances Smith; m. Lynn Brown, Mar. 1978 (div.); m. Fabian, Mar. 26, 1998; children: Sara, Nathan. BA, Willamette U., 1974, JD, 1978. Bar: Oreg. 1978, U.S. Dist. Ct. Oreg. 1979. Ptnr., now pres. Kennedy Bowles, Portland, 1978—. Mem. ATLA, Oreg. Trial Lawyers, Oreg. Assn. Def. Counsel, Multnomah Bar Assn. Democrat. Avocations: soccer, snow skiing, tennis, golf, reading. General civil litigation, Contracts commercial, Personal injury. Office: Kennedy Bowles PC 1500 SW 1st Ave Ste 920 Portland OR 97201-5823

**KENNEDY, MICHAEL JOHN,** lawyer; b. Spokane, Wash., Mar. 23, 1937; s. Thomas Dennis Kennedy and Evelyn Elizabeth (Forbes) Gordon; m. Pamalee Hamilton, June 14, 1959 (div. July 1968); children: Lisa Marie, Scott Hamilton; m. Eleanore Renee Baratelli, July 14, 1968; 1 child, Anna Rosario. AB in Econs., U. Calif., Berkeley, 1959; JD, U. Calif., San Francisco, 1962. Bar: Calif. 1963, N.Y. 1976, U.S. Ct. Appeals (9th cir. 1963), U.S. Supreme Ct. 1967, U.S. Ct. Appeals (5th cir.) 1975, U.S. Ct. Appeals 2d cir.) 1977, U.S. Ct. Appeals (1st 3d and 4th cirs.) 1979, U.S. Ct. Appeals (3d and D.C. cirs.) 1982. Assoc. Hoberg & Finger, San Francisco, 1962-67; staff counsel Emergency Civil Liberties, N.Y.C., 1967-69; ptnr. Kennedy & Rhine, San Francisco, 1969-76; sole practice N.Y.C., 1976—. Served to 1st lt. U.S. Army, 1963-65. Mem. ABA, N.Y. Criminal Bar Assn., Nat. Assn. Criminal Defenders. Democrat. Roman Catholic. Club: N.Y. Athletic. Criminal, Libel, Civil rights. Home: 1009 5th Ave New York NY 10028-0155 Office: 425 Park Ave New York NY 10022-3506

**KENNEDY, MICHAEL KELLY,** lawyer, state representative; b. New Hampton, Iowa, Oct. 30, 1939; s. William J. and Eileen (Kelly) K.; m. Linda Weiss, Aug. 14, 1964; 1 child, Cara Kennedy Ode. BA, U. Notre Dame, 1961; JD, U. Iowa, 1968. Bar: Iowa 1968. State rep. Iowa, 1969-73. Pres. Sch. Attys., Iowa, 1985; bd. of govs. Iowa Bar, 1986-90; bd. dirs. Homestead Housing, New Hampton, 1996-99; co-chmn. Build in Faith com., New Hampton, 1996-99. Avocations: reading, golf, sports broadcasting. Home: 929 Ash Dr New Hampton IA 50659-1074 Office: Kennedy & Kennedy Kennedy Law Bldg PO Box 406 New Hampton IA 50659-0406

**KENNEDY, NEAL ALLAN,** real estate executive, lawyer, mediator; b. Austin, Tex., Feb. 3, 1961; s. Harold G. and B. Joy (Lauderbach) K.; m. Cheryl L. Maurer, Aug. 20, 1988; children: Kaylyn Elizabeth, Leah Joy. Student, Tex. A&M U., 1979-82; BBA, U. Tex., 1984; JD, So. Meth. U., 1987. Bar: Tex. 1987, U.S. Ct. Appeals (D.C. cir) 1998, U.S. Dist. Ct. (so. dist.) Tex. 1987, (no., ea., we. dists.) Tex. 1988. Assoc. Liddell, Sapp, Zivley, Hill & LaBoon, Houston, 1987-90; sr. assoc. Milgrim, Thomajan & Lee, N.Y.C., 1990-93; counsel Sutherland, Asbill & Brennan, Atlanta, 1993-96; ptnr. Jackson Walker LLP, Austin, 1996-98; v.p. Kennedy & Assocs. Real Estate, Marble Falls, Tex., 1998—; pvt. practice Marble Falls, 1998—; dir., gen. counsel C&N Properties of Tex., LLC, Austin, 1993—; gen. counsel The Western Group, LLC, Marble Falls, 1997—. Editor: Southwestern Law Jour., 1987; co-author: A Summary of Laws Unique to Texas, 1998. Bd. dirs. Windermere Oaks Tennis Village Property Owners' Assn., Spicewood, Tex., 1996-97; gen. counsel Boys and Girls Club at Highland Lakes Inc., 1999—. Mem. ABA, Highland Lakes Lawyers' Assn., Austin/Travis County Bar Assn. Fax: 530-236-6739. E-mail: neal.kennedy@usa.net. Office: 404 Main St Marble Falls TX 78654-5717

**KENNEDY, RICHARD JOSEPH,** lawyer; b. Joliet, Ill., Aug. 31, 1942. BA in Econs., U. Notre Dame, 1964; JD, Northwestern U., 1967. Bar: Ill. 1967, Colo. 1975, U.S. Dist. Ct. Colo. 1976. Assoc. Barr & Barr, Joliet, 1968-69, Schutts & Hutchison, Joliet, 1969-71; atty. Schutts & Schutts, Joliet, 1971-75, Rector, Melat & Wheeler, Colorado Springs, 1975-77; pvt. practice Colorado Springs, 1977—. Bd. dirs. Colorado Springs Osteopathic Found., 1990-97; mem. Skyway subdivisions archtl. control com. Skyway Archtl. Control Com., Colorado Springs, 1988—. Mem. Skyway Assn. (v.p. 1988—), Broadmoor Rotary Club (dir. 1994-97), Notre Dame Club (pres. 1982-83). Roman Catholic. General civil litigation, Personal injury, Probate. Office: 324 S Cascade Ave Colorado Springs CO 80903-3804

**KENNEDY, SHARON LEE,** lawyer; b. Cin., Mar. 15, 1962; d. Milton Dale and Alice Mae (Weingartner) K. BA, U. Cin., 1984, JD, 1991. Police officer Hamilton (Ohio) Police Dept., 1985-89; law clk. Butler County Commn Pleas Ct., Hamilton, 1989-92; sole practice law Hamilton, 1991—; magistrate Butler County, 1995—; judge Butler County Ct. of Common Pleas, Domestic Rels. divsn., 1999—. Exec. bd. Alcohol Drug Addiction Svcs., Hamilton, 1993, Sr. Citizens, Inc., Hamilton, 1995. Republican. Roman Catholic. Home: 5829 Penelope Dr Hamilton OH 45011-2211

**KENNEDY, STEPHEN CHARLES,** lawyer; b. North Tonawanda, N.Y., Sept. 26, 1951; s. Charles Irving and Isabelle Florence Kennedy; m. Jeannie Kay Wilson; children: Darcy, Christine, Paige, Kay. BS, Niagara U., 1979; JD, SUNY, Buffalo, 1983. Environ. affairs and hazardous waste processing Frontier Chem., Niagara Falls, N.Y., 1971-86; sole practitioenr Stephen Kennedy, Atty., Sanborn and Lockport, N.Y., 1987—. Sgt., N.Y. State Air N.G., 1972-78. Real property, Family and matrimonial. Office: 4759 Saunders Settlement Rd Lockport NY 14094-9631

**KENNEDY, STEVEN CHARLES,** lawyer; b. Benson, Minn., Apr. 24, 1959; s. Eugene Thomas and Alvina Dorothy K.; m. Mary Kathryn. BA in Acctg., St. John's U., 1981; JD, U. Va., 1985. Bar: N.Y., Minn. Atty. Cravath, Swaine & Moore, N.Y.C., 1985-87; ptnr. Faegre & Benson, Mpls., 1987—. Dir. Minn. 4-H Found., St. Paul, 1989-96; dir. St. John's U. Alumni Bd., Collegeville, minn., 1991-95. Mem. Mpls. Club. General corporate, Securities. Office: Faegre & Benson 2200 Norwest Ctr Minneapolis MN 55402

**KENNEDY, THOMAS J.,** lawyer; b. Milw., July 29, 1947; s. Frank Philip and June Marian (Smith) K.; m. Cathy Ann Cohen, Nov. 24, 1978; children: Abby, Sarah. BA, U. Wisc., 1969, JD cum laude, 1972. Bar: Wis. 1972, U.S. Dist. Ct. (ea. and we. dists.) Wis. 1972, Ariz. 1981, U.S. Dist. Ct. Ariz. 1981, U.S. Ct. Appeals (7th cir.) 1980, U.S. Ct. Appeals (9th cir.) 1981, U.S. Ct. Appeals (D.C. cir.) 1983, U.S. Supreme Ct. 1984, U.S. Ct. Appeals (11th cir.) 1986. Assoc. Goldberg, Previant, Milw., 1972-79, Brynelson, Herrick, Madison, Wisc., 1979-81; ptnr. Snell & Wilmer, Phoenix, 1981-93, Lewis and Roca, Phoenix, 1993-96, Ryley, Carlock and Applewhite, Phoenix, 1996-99, Ballagher & Kennedy, 1999—. Contbg. editor The Developing Labor Laws, 2d, 3d edits., The Fair Labor Standards Act. Mem. ABA, Ariz. State Bar, State Bar Wisc., Maricopa County Bar Assn. Avocations: tennis, reading, hiking. Labor, Administrative and regulatory.

**KENNEDY, VEKENO,** lawyer; b. Albany, Ga., Feb. 28, 1961; d. Alfred and Algean (Cole) K. BBA, U. San Diego, 1983; JD, Calif. Western Sch. Law, San Diego, 1990. Bar: Calif., U.S. Ct. Appeals (9th cir.), U.S. Dist. Ct. (so. and ctrl. dists.) Calif. Atty. Viviano & Bradley, San Diego, 1991-92, Gibbs, Eppsteiner & Stagg, San Diego, 1993-95, Saxon, Barry, Gardner et al, San Diego, 1995-96; ptnr. Kolod, Wager and Gordon LLP, San Diego, 1997—. Mng. editor California Western Law Rev. and Internat. Law Jour., 1989. Mem. Nat. Assn. Women Lawyers (outstanding woman law grad. 1990). Roman Catholic. Avocations: theater, golf. General civil litigation, Insurance, Product liability.

**KENNELLY, JOHN JEROME,** lawyer; b. Chgo., Dec. 11, 1918; s. Joseph Michael and Anna (Flynn) K.; m. Mary Thomson, Mar. 21, 1949. Ph.B., Loyola U., Chgo., 1939, LL.B., 1941. Bar: Ill. 1941, U.S. Dist. Ct. (no. dist.) Ill. 1941, U.S. Ct. Appeals (7th cir.) 1946, U.S. Supreme Ct. 1956. Sole practice, Chgo., 1946—. Served with USN, 1941-46. Fellow Internat. Acad. Trial Lawyers (past chmn. aviation sect.); mem. Chgo. Bar Assn. (bd. mgrs. 1965-67), Ill. State Bar Assn., ABA (aviation com. chmn. 1981-82), Inter-Am. Bar Assn., Ill. Trial Lawyers Assn. (pres. 1968-69), World Assn. Lawyers, Am. Coll. Trial Lawyers, Internat. Acad. Law and Sci., Internat. Soc. Barristers, Am. Soc. Internat. Law, Am. Bar Found. Clubs: Butterfield Country (Hinsdale, Ill.); Beverly Country (Chgo.). Author: Litigation and Trial of Air Crash Cases, 1969; contbr. articles to profl. jours. Federal civil litigation, State civil litigation, Aviation. Office: 111 W Washington St Ste 1449 Chicago IL 60602-2708

**KENNEY, BRUCE ALLEN,** lawyer; b. Oklahoma City, Apr. 13, 1950; s. Jack H. and Betty J. Kenney; m. Kathryn Sue Burke, July 19, 1975; children: B. Allen, John Burke, Jayne Allyson. B.B.A., U. Okla., 1972, J.D., 1975. Bar: Okla. 1975, Tex. 1975, U.S. Dist. Ct. (so. dist.) Tex. 1975, U.S. Dist. Ct. (no. dist.) Okla. 1986. Sr. atty. Sun Co., Inc., Dallas, 1975-81; sole practice law, Tulsa, 1981—; counsel Kaiser-Francis Oil Co., Tulsa, 1981—. Mem. ABA, Tulsa County Bar Assn., Okla. Bar Assn., State Bar Tex. Methodist. Oil, gas, and mineral, General corporate. Home: 2246 E 26th St Tulsa OK 74114-4215 Office: PO Box 21468 Tulsa OK 74121-1468

**KENNEY, FREDERIC LEE,** lawyer, business executive; b. Detroit, May 22, 1958; s. Frank E. and Beverly A. Kenney; m. Kimberly Kenney, June 27, 1981; children: Thomas, Kyle, Craig. BA summa cum laude, Dennison U., 1980; JD magna cum laude, U. Mich., 1983. Bar: Ill. 1983. Ptnr. Winters, Featherstun, Gaumer, Kenney, Postlewait & Stocks, Decatur, Ill.; bd. dirs. First Nat. Bank, Decatur, Christy-Foltz, Inc., Decatur. Bd. dirs. YMCA, Decatur. Mem. Ill. State Bar Assn., Decatur Bar Assn., Ill. Assn. Def. Trial Counsel. Insurance, General corporate, Real property. Office: Winters Featherstun Gaumer Kenney Postlewait & Stocks PO Box 1760 Decatur IL 62525-1760

**KENNEY, HERBERT KING,** lawyer; b. Muskogee, Okla., Nov. 16, 1947; s. Carl Frederick and Lillian Margaret (King) K.; m. Diane Blinn, July 1, 1975; children: Valerie, Brent, Andrew. BA in Polit. Sci., Rice U., 1970; JD, U. Okla., 1973. Bar: Okla. 1974, Tex. 1988, U.S. Dist. Ct. (we. dist.) 1974, U.S. Ct. Appeals (10th cir.) 1974. Ptnr. Linn & Helms, Oklahoma City, 1974-87; of counsel Kornfeld & Franklin, Oklahoma City, 1987-88; in-house counsel Am. Fidelity Corp., Oklahoma City, 1988-90; litig. sect. chief Resolution Trust Corp., Valley Forge, Pa., 1991-95. With USAR, 1970-76. Mem. ABA, State Bar Tex., Okla. Bar Assn. Republican. Presbyterian. Avocations: computers, amateur radio. General corporate, Contracts commercial, Banking. Home: 4216 NW 146th Ter Oklahoma City OK 73134-1754 Office: Britton Gray and Hill PC 201 Robert S Kerr Ave Oklahoma City OK 73102-4205

**KENNEY, JOHN ARTHUR,** lawyer; b. Oklahoma City, Aug. 3, 1948; s. Jack H. and Betty Jo (Hill) K.; m. Jane Francis, Sept. 4, 1971; children: John Graham, Lauren Elizabeth. BS in Indsl. Engrng. with distinction, U. Okla., 1971, JD, 1975. Bar: Tex. 1975, U.S. Dist. Ct. (so. dist.) Tex. 1976, U.S. Ct. Appeals (5th cir.) 1977, Okla. 1981, U.S. Dist. Ct. Okla. 1981, U.S. Ct. Appeals (10th cir.) 1983. Assoc. Baker & Botts, Houston, 1975-81; shareholder McAfee & Taft, Oklahoma City, 1982—; temp. judge Okla. Ct. of Appeals, atty. appointed panels, Leadership Oklahoma City, 1993; magistrate judge merit selection com. and civil justice reform act adv. com. U.S. Dist. Ct. (we. dist.) Okla. Bd. advisors dept. indsl. engring.; deacon, past trustee Westminster Presbyn. Ch.; dir., pres. Christmas in April, Oklahoma City. Mem. ABA, Okla. Bar Assn. (adminstrn. of justice com. 1990—), Okla. County Bar Assn. (chmn. bench and bar com. 1989-90, Outstanding Mem. 1989, v.p. 1991, bar counsel 1992-96, dir. 1997-98, pres. 1999—), Order of Coif, Tau Beta Pi. Federal civil litigation, State civil litigation, Intellectual property. Office: McAfee & Taft Two Leadership Sq 10th Fl Oklahoma City OK 73102

**KENNICOTT, JAMES W.,** lawyer; b. Latrobe, Pa., Feb. 14, 1945; s. W.L. and Alice (Hayes) K.; m. Margot Barnes, Aug. 19, 1975 (div. 1977); m. Lynne Dratler Finney, July 1, 1984 (div. 1989). AB, Syracuse (N.Y.) U., 1967; JD, U. Wyo., 1979. Bar: Utah 1979. Prin. Ski Cons., Park City, Utah, 1969—; pvt. practice Park City, 1979-87, 89—; ptnr. Kennicott & Finney, Park City, 1987-89; pvt. practice Park City, 1989—; cons. Destination Sports Specialists, Park City, 1984—; judge pro tem Utah 3d Dist. Ct., Park City, 1988—; arbitrator Am. Arbitration Assn., 1989—. Chmn. Park City Libr. Bd. 1987; bd. dirs. Park City Libr., 1985-91, Park City Handicapped Sports, 1988-94, The Counseling Inst., 1993-97, chmn., 1994-95, treas. 1995-96, mem. program com. Gov.'s Commn. on Librs. and Info. Svcs., 1990-91. Mem. Utah Bar Assn., Am. Arbitration Assn. Avocations: skiing, sailing, hiking, cycling, literature. Real property, General civil litigation, Estate planning. Home and Office: PO Box 2339 Park City UT 84060-2339

**KENNY, GEORGE JAMES,** lawyer; b. Jersey City, Feb. 18, 1935; s. George W. and Alice M. Kenny; m. Sandra B. Kenny, Oct. 10, 1959; children: Erin, Michael, Thomas, Patricia, Brendan, Mary, Timothy. BS in Econs., Seton Hall U., 1956; LLB, Rutgers U., 1959. Bar: N.J. 1961, U.S. Dist. Ct. N.J. 1961, U.S. Dist. Ct. (so. and ea. dists.) N.Y., 1991, U.S. Supreme Ct. 1966, N.Y. 1983, U.S. Ct. Appeals (3d cir.) 1987, U.S. Ct. Appeals (4th cir.) 1988; cert. Civil Trial Atty. N.J. Supreme Ct. 1982. Jud. clerkship to Hon. Theodore J. Labrecque N.J. Superior Ct., 1960-61; assoc. Connell, Foley & Geiser, Roseland and Newark, 1961-68; ptnr. Connell, Foley & Geiser, 1968—; adj. faculty Rutgers U. Sch. Law; lectr. in field. Contbr. articles to profl. jours.; editl. bd. N.J. Law Jour., 1984—; author text ins. law; contbr. chpt. book. Trustee Essex County Coll. 1971-78 (chmn. 1973-74), Legal Svcs. Found. Essex County, 1989—; mem. Montclair Zoning Bd. of Adj. 1978-84 (chmn. 1979-84). Fellow Am. Coll. of Trial Lawyers, Am. Bar Found.; mem. ABA (sec. of litigation,co-chmn. 1983-86, 88-91, divsn. dir. 1986-87, coun. mem. 1991—, chmn. ins. coverage litigation com. 1988-91, co-chmn. spl. com. cert. and CLE 1994—), N.J. State Bar Assn. (trustee 1968-69, 89-93, chmn. young lawyers sect. 1967-68, chmn. 1987—, editorial bd. 1969-96), Essex County Bar Assn. (pres. 1981-82, trustee and officer 1974-81), Practicing Law Inst. N.J. Supreme Ct. coms.; Inst. Continuing Legal Edn., Adv. Am. Bd. Trial Advs., Essex Inn of Court (master), Internat. Assn. Def. Counsel. Democrat. Roman Catholic. Avocation: reading. General civil litigation. Office: Connell Foley & Geiser 85 Livingston Ave Ste 15 Roseland NJ 07068-3702

**KENOFF, JAY STEWART,** lawyer; b. L.A., Apr. 29, 1946; s. Charles Kapp and Martha (Minchenberg) K.; m. Pamela Fran Benyas, Sept. 1, 1979 (div. Dec. 1981); m. Luz Elena Chavira, June 9, 1991. AB, UCLA, 1967; MS, U. So. Calif., L.A., 1972; JD, Harvard U., 1970. Bar: Washington 1970, Calif. 1971, U.S. Ct. Appeals (9th cir.) 1974, U.S. Dist. Ct. (so., cen. dists. Calif.) 1974, U.S. Ct. Mil. Appeals 1974. Assoc. Wyman, Bautzer, Rothman & Kuchel, Beverly Hills, Calif., 1974-76, Epport & Delevie, Beverly Hills, 1977-78; ptnr. Bushkin, Gaims, Gaines & Jonas, L.A., 1978-86; prof. Sch. of Law Northrup U., Inglewood, Calif., 1981-85; ptnr. Kenoff & Machtinger, L.A., 1986—; judge pro tem L.A. Mcpl. Ct., 1985—; arbitrator, mediator Ctr. for Comml. Mediation, L.A., 1986—; mediator L.A. Superior Ct., 1987—, mem. settlement panel, 1987—. Author: Entertainment Industry Contracts, 1986; contbg. editor Entertainment Law & Finance. Commdr. USN Navy Judge Adv. Corps, USNR, 1968-91. Mem. Beverly Hills Bar Assn., Harvard-Radcliffe Club. Democrat. Jewish. Avocations: tennis, skiing, movies. Entertainment, Communications, Intellectual property. Office: Kenoff & Machtinger Bldg 1250 1999 Avenue Of The Stars Los Angeles CA 90067-6022

**KENRICH, JOHN LEWIS,** lawyer; b. Lima, Ohio, Oct. 17, 1929; s. Clarence E. and Rowena (Stroh) Katterheinrich; m. Betty Jane Roehll, May 26, 1951; children: John David, Mary Jane, Kathryn Ann, Thomas Roehll, Walter Clarence. BS, Miami U., Oxford, Ohio, 1951; LLB, U. Cin., 1953. Bar: Ohio 1953, Mass. 1969. Asst. counsel B.F. Goodrich Co., Akron, Ohio, 1956-65; asst. sec., counsel W.R. Grace & Co., Cin., 1965-68, v.p. Splty. Products Group divsn., 1970-71; corp. counsel, sec. Standex Internat. Corp., Andover, Mass., 1969-70; v.p., sec. Chemed Corp., Cin., 1971-82, sr. v.p., gen. counsel, 1982-86, exec. v.p., chief adminstrv. officer, 1986-91, ret., 1991. Trustee Better Bus. Bur., Cin., 1981-90; mem. bus. adv. coun. Miami U., 1986-88; mem. City Planning Commn., Akron, 1961-62; mem. bd. visitors Coll. Law U. Cin., 1988-92; mem. area coun. trustees Franciscan Sisters of Poor Found., Cin., 1989-93; bd. govs. Arthritis found. Southwestern Ohio chpt., 1992-95; mem. Com. on Reinvestment City of Cin., 1991-93. 1st lt. JAGC U.S. Army, 1954-56. Mem. Am. Arbitration Assn., Beta Theta Pi, Omicron Delta Kappa, Delta Sigma Pi, Phi Eta Sigma. Republican. Methodist. General corporate. Home and Office: 504 Abilene Trl Cincinnati OH 45215-2515

**KENSINGTON, COSTA NICHOLAS,** lawyer; b. Bristol, Eng., Feb. 7, 1948; came to U.S., 1954; s. Nicholas K. and Moira Esther Georgiou; m. Cheryl Lee Dees; children: C. Ragan, C. Nicholas. JD, Rutgers U., 1972, BA, 1996. Bar: N.Y. 1973. Assoc. Sullivan & Cromwell, N.Y.C., 1973-77, Skadden, Arps, Slate et. al., N.Y.C., 1977-79; ptnr. Kensington & Ressler, LLC, N.Y.C., 1980—. Henry Rutgers scholar Rutgers U., 1969. Mem. U.S.-Cyprus C. of C. (bd. dirs. 1998—), The Univ. Club, County Club Darien. Avocations: golf, tennis. Finance, General corporate, Securities. Home: 366 Mansfield Ave Darien CT 06820-2112 Office: 400 Madison Ave New York NY 10017-1909

**KENT, CYNTHIA STEVENS,** judge; b. Tulsa, July 8, 1954; d. Gerald Lee and Beverly (D'Aquin) Stevens; m. Don W. Kent, May 24, 1975; children: Andrew Stevens, Jarad Lee, Wayne Anthony. Student, Baylor U., 1971-72; BA, U. Houston, 1975; JD, South Tex. Coll. Law, Houston, 1977. Bar: Tex. 1977, U.S. Dist. Ct. (so. dist.) Tex. 1978, (ea. dist.) Tex. 1979. Atty. Barlow/Lacy/Smith/Pollard, Clear Lake City, Tex., 1976-78; sole practitioner Tyler, Tex., 1979, 80-84, 88; assoc., ptnr. Kent and Bauer, Tyler, 1979-80; judge County Ct. at Law No. 2, Smith County, Tyler, 1988, 114th Jud. Dist. Ct., Tyler, 1989—; instr. Tex. Coll. for New Judges, Huntsville, 1985—, Tex. Reg. Jud. Conf., 1986, 87, 88, 91, 92, 93, 94, 95, Tex. Assn. for Ct. Adminstrn., Huntsville, 1990, 91, 92, 93, 94, 95; faculty instr. Nat. Jud. Coll., 1993, 94, 95. Author: County Court at Law Benchbook, 1986; co-author: District Judges Benchbook, 1990; contbr. articles to profl. jours. Den mother Cub Scouts Am., Tyler, 1990; judge Tyler's Teen Ct., 1985—; mem. adv. bd. East Tex. Regional Boy Scouts Am., 1988—, Parent Svcs., Inc., 1989-92; chair 1995 Smith County Nat. Day of Prayer. Recipient Law Enforcement award Tex. SAR, 1990, Judge of Yr. award Tex. State M.A.D.D., 1989, others. Mem. Tex. Bar Assn. (jud. sect. 1984—), Tex. Assn. Ct. Adminstrn. (adv. bd.), Smith County Bar Assn. Republican. Roman Catholic. Office: Smith County Courthouse 114th Jud Dist Ct Tyler TX 75702

**KENT, DALE R.,** lawyer; b. Salt Lake City, Dec. 15, 1949; s. James E. Kent and Elaine (Peterson) Osborne; m. Cynthia Wilson, June 8, 1972; children: Dale Ryan, Jared Wilson, Elizabeth Anne, James Brice, Emily Gene. BS, USAF Acad., 1972; JD, U. Utah, 1975; grad., U. Calif., San Francisco, 1979, Advanced Coll. Adv., Reno, 1981. Bar: Utah 1975, U.S. Dist. Ct. Utah 1975, U.S. Ct. Appeals (10th cir.) 1975, U.S. Supreme Ct. 1979. Sole practice Salt Lake City, 1975—; exec. dir. Murray (Utah) City Devel. Agy., 1971-81, Murray City Redevelopment Agy., 1979-81; asst. atty. City Attys. Office, Murray, 1978-81; judge pro tem Small Claims Ct., Salt Lake City, 1982—. Mem., soloist Salt Lake City Symphonic Choir, 1980-85; scoutmaster Boy Scouts Am., Salt Lake City, 1981—; mem. com. City Planning and Zoning Com., Salt Lake City, 1982-84; chmn. com. Commn. for Redrafting City Ordinances, Centerville, Utah, 1983. Recipient Don Quixote award Nat. Assn. Advancement of Developmentally Disabled, 1979, Dist. Service award 5th cir. Ct. Utah 1983, 84, 85. Mem. ABA, Utah Bar Assn., Assn. Trial Lawyers Am. Republican. Mormon. Lodge: Rotary (bd. dirs. 1984—). Avocations: skiing, squash, running, music, backpacking. State civil litigation, Banking, Consumer commercial. Home: 1467 Hobble Creek Dr Springville UT 84663-2889 Office: 10 E South Temple Salt Lake City UT 84133-1101

**KENT, DON WAYNE,** lawyer; b. Tyler, Tex., May 27, 1952; s. Luther A. and Christine (Starr) K.; m. Cynthia Ann Stevens, May 24, 1975; children: Andrew Stevens, Jarad Lee, Wayne Anthony. BA, Baylor U., 1974; JD, U. Houston, 1976. Bar: Tex. 1976, U.S. Dist. Ct. (so. dist.) Tex. 1977, U.S. Dist. Ct. (ea. dist.) Tex. 1978, U.S. Dist. Ct. (no. dist.) 1981, U.S. Ct. Appeals (5th cir.) 1982, U.S. Supreme Ct. 1983; cert. personal injury trial law Tex. Bd. Legal Specialization, 1986. Assoc. DeLange, Hudspeth et al, Houston, 1976-78, Potter, Guinn, et al, Tyler, 1978-82; ptnr. Barnett, Schofield & Kent, Tyler, 1982-83, Buchanan, Barnett, Schofield & Kent, Tyler, 1983-87, Cowles & Thompson, Tyler, 1987—; Trustee State Bar Tex. Ins. Trust, 1987—. Alt. del. Rep. County Conv., Tyler, 1984, del. 1986; bd. dirs. Country Place Community Assn., Tyler, 1985-86. Mem. ABA, Def. Research Inst., Tex. Bar Assn., Tex. Assn. Def. Counsel, Smith County Bar Assn. (treas. 1983). Republican. Baptist. Lodge: Kiwanis (v.p. Tyler club 1979-80). Avocations: tennis, skeet shooting, hunting. Insurance, Personal injury, Federal civil litigation. Home: RR 4 Box 1038 Tyler TX 75703-9804 Office: One American Ctr Suite 280 909 ESE Loop 323 Tyler TX 75701

**KENT, EDWARD ANGLE, JR.,** lawyer; b. Oakland, Calif., Sept. 8, 1938; s. Edward Angle and Elizabeth (Trowbridge) K.; m. Carmen Salasar, Mar. 17, 1967 (div. 1976); 1 child, Lisa Anne; m. Carol Harrison, Sept. 24, 1983. A.B., Brown U., 1960; postgrad. UCLA, 1961-62; J.D., Stanford U., 1965. Bar: Calif. 1966, U.S. Dist. Ct. (no. dist.) Calif. 1966, U.S. Ct. Appeals (9th cir.) 1966, U.S. Dist. Ct. (ea. dist.) Calif. 1978. Assoc., Leprohn & Leprohn, San Francisco, 1966-67; assoc. Longstreth & Siegel, Menlo Park, Calif., 1967-68; sole practice, Palo Alto, Calif., 1968—; instr. Foothill Jr. Coll. Dist.; Cupertino, Calif., 1970-71, Canada Coll., Redwood City, Calif., 1975. Mem. State Bar Calif., Santa Clara County Bar Assn., Am. Bankruptcy Inst. Bankruptcy, Consumer commercial. Home: 466 5th Ave Redwood City CA 94063-3728 Office: 2501 Park Blvd Ste 100 Palo Alto CA 94306-1925

**KENT, JOHN BRADFORD,** lawyer; b. Jacksonville, Fla., Sept. 5, 1939; s. Frederick Heber and Norma Cleveland (Futch) K.; m. Monett Powers, Dec. 18, 1969; children: Monett, Susan, Sally, Katherine. AB, Yale U., 1961; JD, U. Fla., 1964; LLM in Taxation, NYU, 1965. Bar: Fla., 1964, U.S. Dist. Ct. (mid. dist.) Fla. 1965, U.S. Tax Ct., 1965, U.S. Dist. (so. dist.) Fla., 1981, Neb., 1995, U.S. Ct. Appeals (11th cir.), U.S. Supreme Ct., 1973. Assoc. Ulmer, Murchison, Kent, Ashby & Ball, Jacksonville, 1965-67; ptnr., shareholder Kent, Watts & Durden, P.A. and predecessor firms, Jacksonville, 1967-85; shareholder Carlton, Field, Ward, Emmanuel, Smith, Cutler & Kent, Jacksonville, 1985-88, Kent, Crawford & Gooding, P.A., Jacksonville, 1988—. Jacksonville Legal Aid Soc. (past bd. dirs.), Fla. Cmty. Coll (past pres., trustee), Children's Home Soc. Fla. (past pres., bd. dirs.). Mem. Nat. Assn. Theatre Owners Fla. (bd. dirs., officer 1969—), Rotary (past officer, Paul Harris Fellow). Banking, General corporate, Contracts commercial. Office: Kent Crawford & Gooding PA 225 Water St Ste 900 Jacksonville FL 32202-5142

**KENT, M. ELIZABETH,** lawyer; b. N.Y.C., Nov. 17, 1943; d. Francis J. and Hannah (Bergman) K. AB, Vassar Coll. magna cum laude, 1964; AM, Harvard U., 1965, PhD, 1974; JD, Georgetown U., 1978. Bar: D.C. 1978, U.S. Dist. Ct. D.C. 1978, U.S. Ct. Appeals (D.C. cir.) 1978, U.S. Supreme Ct. 1983, U.S. Dist. Ct. Md. 1985. From lectr. to asst. prof. history U. Ala., Birmingham, 1972-74; assoc. Santarelli and Gimer, Washington, 1978; sole practice Washington, 1978—. Mem. Ripon Soc., Cambridge and Washington, 1968-93; rsch. dir. Howard M. Miller for Congress, Boston, 1972; vol. campaigns John V. Lindsay for Mayor, 1969, John V. Lindsay for Pres., 1972, John B. Anderson for Pres., 1980. Woodrow Wilson fellow 1964-65; Harvard U. fellow 1968-69. Mem. ABA, ACLU, D.C. Bar Assn., Women's Bar Assn., D.C. Assn. Criminal Def. Lawyers, Superior Ct. Trial Lawyers Assn., Nat. Women's Polit. Caucus, Phi Beta Kappa. Republican. Avocations: history, politics. Appellate, Criminal, General civil litigation. Home: 35 E St NW Apt 810 Washington DC 20001-1520 Office: 601 Indiana Ave NW Ste 605 Washington DC 20004-2918

**KENT, SAMUEL B.,** federal judge; b. 1949. BA, U. Tex., 1971, JD, 1975. Pvt. practice Royston, Rayzor, Vickery & Williams, Galveston, Tex., 1975-90; judge U.S. Dist. Ct. (so. dist.) Tex., Galveston, 1990—; adj. prof. bus. and ins. law Tex. A&M U., Galveston, 1981-86, proctor in admiralty, 1976—. Mem. Maritime Law Assn. Office: US Courthouse 601 Rosenberg St Ste 613 Galveston TX 77550-1738

**KENT, STEPHEN SMILEY,** lawyer; b. Reno, July 6, 1952; s. Robert Roe and Muriel (Smiley) K.; m. H. Mayla Walcutt, Dec. 19, 1976; children: Kristopher, Kimberly, Alisa. BS (hons.), U. Nev., 1975; JD, U. of the Pacific, 1980. Bar: Nev. 1980. Law clk. to Hon. William N. Forman Reno, 1980-81; assoc. Vargas & Bartlett, Reno, 1981-86; assoc. Beckley, Singleton, Jemison & List, Reno, 1986-89, shareholder, 1989-97; shareholder Woodburn & Wedge, Reno, 1997—; mem. exec. coun. Nev. State Bar Young Lawyers Assn., Reno, 1987-89; mem. fee dispute com. Nev. State Bar, Reno, 1985-88, mem. ins. com., 1986-87. Co-author: (manuals/seminars) Nevada Uninsured Motorist Insurance, 1985, Controlling Damages, 1991, Enforcing Judgments, 1989, Pretrial Discovery, 1988, Default Judgements, 1994, Insurance Coverage Law in Nevada, 1998. Mem. Neighborhood Adv. Coun., Reno, 1992-98. Mem. ABA (litigation sect.), Internat. Assn. Def. Counsel, Nat. Bd. Trial Advocacy (cert. civil trial advocate), Rotary Club Reno. Fax: 775-688-3088. General civil litigation, Intellectual property, Personal injury. Home: 2815 Columbus Way Reno NV 89503-1848 Office: Woodburn & Wedge 1 East First St PO Box 2311 Reno NV 89505-2311

**KENT, THOMAS EDWARD,** lawyer; b. Chgo., Jan. 29, 1957. BA in Sociology, U. Calif., Berkeley, 1979; JD, U. So. Calif., 1982. Bar: Calif. 1982, U.S. Dist. Ct. (cen. dist.) Calif., U.S. Dist. Ct. (no. dist.) Calif., U.S. Dist. Ct. (so. dist.) Calif., U.S. Ct. Appeals (9th cir.), U.S. Supreme Ct. Assoc. Fierstein & Sturman, L.A., 1982-87, Robinson, Diamant, Brill & Klausner, L.A., 1987-91; sole practitioner L.A., 1991—; Arbitrator L.A. County Bar Dispute Resolution Svcs. Mem. L.A. County Bar Assn., San Fernando Valley Bar Assn., Fin. Lawyers Conf., Bankruptcy Forum. FAX: 818-990-6792. Contracts commercial, Bankruptcy, General civil litigation. Office: 16161 Ventura Blvd # 475 Encino CA 91436-2522

**KENTRIS, GEORGE LAWRENCE,** lawyer; b. Detroit, Nov. 3, 1949; s. Michael Nicholas and Mary (Cassimatis) K.; m. Susan Jo Van Dorn, Nov. 18, 1972; children: Emily Joya, Vanessa, Ann Alexia. BA, Ohio State U., 1971; JD, U. Toledo Coll. Law, 1976. Bar: Ohio 1976, U.S. Dist. Ct. (no. dist.) Ohio 1977, U.S. Supreme Ct. 1980, U.S. Ct. Appeals (6th cir.) 1989. Asst. prosecuting atty. Hancock County Ohio Prosecutors Office, Findlay, Ohio, 1977-85; assoc. Noble, Bryant & Needles, Findlay, 1977-81; pvt. practice Findlay, 1981-87; sr. ptnr. Kentris & Wolph, Findlay, 1987-92; sr. atty. Kentris & Assocs., Findlay, 1992-96; sr. ptnr. Kentris, Brown & Powell, Findlay, 1996-97; pres. Kentris, Brown, Powell & Balega Co., LPA, 1997—; franchisee Taco Bell Corp., Ohio, 1982—; officer, dir. Findlay TV Corp., 1991—. Bd. trustees Am. Cancer Soc. Hancock County, Findlay, 1980—, pres., 1985-86; mem. Hancock County Rep. Exec. Com., 1982—, treas., 1984-86; bd. dirs. Jr. Achievement of Hancock Co., Inc., 1991—. Mem. ABA, ATLA, Ohio Bar Assn., Ohio Acad. Trial Lawyers (trustee 1986-87), Findlay/Hancock County Bar Assn. (cert. grievance com. 1987—, chmn. 1995, sec. 1993, treas. 1980-81). Mem. Greek Orthodox. Avocations: golf, tennis, skiing, softball, sports cars. Personal injury, General civil litigation, Criminal. Office: Kentris Brown Powell & Balega Co LPA 431 E Main Cross St Findlay OH 45840-4822

**KENYON, ARNOLD OAKLEY, III,** lawyer; b. Creston, Iowa, Aug. 15, 1952; s. Arnold O. II and Joy L. (Lawrence) K.; m. Mary Ann Clendenen, Dec. 23, 1972; children: Angela, Joseph, Arnold O. IV. BS, Iowa State U., 1974; JD with honors, U. Iowa, 1977. Bar: Iowa 1977. With Kenyon & Kenyon PC, Creston, 1977-89; ptnr. Steffes Kenyon & Nielsen PC, Creston, 1989-98, Kenyon & Nielsen PC, Creston, 1998—; county atty. Union County Atty.'s Office, Creston, 1979-87, asst. county atty., 1987-89; city atty. City of Creston, 1992—. Chmn. Crestland Betterment Found., 1983-95. Mem. Iowa Trial Attys. Assn. (bd. govs. 1989-91). Avocation: sailing. General civil litigation, Criminal, Personal injury. Home: 1403 Orchard Dr Creston IA 50801-1035 Office: 211 N Maple St Creston IA 50801-2311

**KENYON, DAVID V.,** federal judge; b. 1930; m. Mary Cramer; children: George Cramer, John Clark. B.A., U. Calif.-Berkeley, 1952; J.D., U. So. Calif., 1957. Law clk. presiding justice U.S. Dist. Ct. (cen. dist.) Calif., 1957-58; house counsel Metro-Goldwyn-Mayer, 1959-60, Nat. Theatres and TV Inc., 1960-61; pvt. practice law, 1961-71; judge Mcpl. Ct. L.A., 1971-72, L.A. Superior Ct., 1972-80; judge U.S. Dist. Ct. (cen. dist.) Calif., L.A., 1980—, sr. judge. Office: US Dist Ct 312 N Spring St Rm 2445 Los Angeles CA 90012-4701

**KENYON, ROSEMARY GILL,** lawyer; b. Syracuse, N.Y., May 3, 1954; d. Harry Paul and Josephine McCullough (Sullivan) Gill; m. Douglas Wayne Kenyon, Mar. 15, 1980; children: Mary Patricia, Katharine Anna, Sarah Rose. Student, Saginaw Valley State Coll., 1972-74, U. Mich., 1974; BA magna cum laude, St. Mary's Coll., Notre Dame, Ind., 1976; JD, U. Notre Dame, 1979. Bar: State Bar Mich., Va., N.C. Law clk. to Hon. W. Earl Britt U.S. Dist.; assoc. Butzell, Long, Gust, Klein & VanZile, Detroit, 1979, Christian, Barton, Epps, Brent & Chappel, Richmond, Va., 1979-85; assoc. gen. counsel legal dept. Carolina Power & Light Co., Raleigh, N.C., 1986—. Co-editor: Desk Book on Alternative Dispute Resolution in North Carolina, 1991. Chair nominating com. Commonwealth Girl Scout, Richmond, 1982-83, bd. dirs., 1983-85; bd. dirs. Pines Carolina Girl Scout Coun., 1986-90, 1st v.p., 1990-92, pres., 1992-95; mem. Exec. Women for Healthier Babies Campaign, March Dimes, 1993. Mem. ABA (mem. dispute resolution sect., mem. labor and employment law sect., mem. lit. sect.), N.C. State Bar, N.C. Bar Assn. (mem. coun. corp. counsel sect. 1989-96, chmn. pro bono com. 1991—, mem. commn. status women in legal profession 1991-92, dispute resolution com. 1988-92, dispute resolution sect., mem. coun. 1992-94, mem. Susie M. Sharp Inn Ct. 1992—, vice chair 1994-95, chair 1995-96), Va. State Bar, Va. Bar Assn., Metro. Richmond Women's Bar Assn. (pres. 1983-84), State Bar Mich., Wake County Bar Assn. Democrat. Roman Catholic. Avocations: running, photography, spectator sports, gardening. Labor, General civil litigation. Home: 2105 Royal Oaks Dr Raleigh NC 27615-7122 Office: Carolina Power and Light Co 411 Fayetteville Street Mall Raleigh NC 27601-1748

**KEPLINGER, (DONALD) BRUCE,** lawyer; b. Kansas City, Kans., Feb. 4, 1952; s. Donald Lee and Janet Adelheit (Viets) K.; children: Mark William, Lisbeth Marie, Kristen Michelle, Kailyn Emily, Courtney Nicole; m. Carol Ann Heinz, Apr. 12, 1991. BA with highest distinction, U. Kans., 1974; JD cum laude, So. Meth. U., 1977. Bar: Kans. 1977, U.S. Dist. Ct. Kans. 1977, Mo. 1980, U.S. Ct. Appeals (10th cir.) 1985, U.S. Supreme Ct. 1989. Assoc. Clark, Mize & Linville, Salina, Kans., 1977-79, Blackwell, Sanders et al, Kansas City, Mo., 1979-82; ptnr. Payne & Jones, Overland Park, Kans., 1982-94, Norris & Keplinger, Overland Park, 1994—; master Kansas Inns of Ct.; chmn. Kansas Lawyer Svcs Corp. Contbr. articles to profl. jours. V.p. Friends of Library, Johnson County, Kans., 1980-85; deacon Village Presbyn. Ch., 1982-86. Mem. ABA, Internat. Assn. Def. Counsel, Assn. Def. Trial Attys. (state chmn. 1996—, exec. coun., 1999—), Kans. Bar Assn. (chmn. Kans. lawyer svc. corp. 1992—), Mo. Bar Assn., Kans. Assn. Def. Counsel (bd. dirs. 1990—, pres.-elect 1992-93, pres. 1993-94), Def. Rsch. Inst., Rotary Internat., Hallbrook Country Club. Republican. Avocations: reading, golf. Federal civil litigation, State civil litigation, Personal injury. Office: Norris & Keplinger LLC 6800 College Blvd Ste 630 Overland Park KS 66211-1556

**KEPNER, REX WILLIAM,** lawyer; b. New Castle, Ind., Aug. 5, 1964; s. Thomas Alva Kepner and Nancy Joan Snider Miller; m. Kelly Lee DeYoung, Aug. 13, 1988; children: Kayla, Chad, Travis. BS, Ball State U., Muncie, Ind., 1987; JD, Ind. U., Indpls., 1990; Diploma, Nat. Inst. for Trial Advocacy. Bar: Ind. 1991, U.S. Dist. Ct. (so. dist.) Ind. 1991. Records clk. Marion County Prosecutor's Office, Indpls., 1988-89; tax analyst Ind. Inheritance Tax Divsn., Indpls., 1989-91, Ind. Fiduciary Tax Divsn., Indpls., 1990-91; chief dep. prosecutor Benton County Prosecutor's Office, Fowler, Ind., 1991-96; pvt. practice Fowler, 1991-96; judge Benton County Cir. Ct., 1997—. Vol. fireman Fowler Vol. Fire Dept., 1993—; mem. Child Protection Team, Benton County, Ind., 1991-96; mem. local coord. coun. Benton County, Ind., 1995—. Recipient Achievement in Child Support Enforcement, Ind. State Child Support Divsn., 1991, Rotary Club award. Mem. Ind. STate Bar Assn., Nat. Dist. Atty.'s Assn., Fowler C. of C. (v.p. 1992-95), Benton County Country Club. Avocations: golf, basketball, softball. General practice, Banking, Probate. Office: 706 E 5th St Fowler IN 47944-1556

**KEPPEL, WILLIAM JAMES,** lawyer, educator, author; b. Sheboygan, Wis., Sept. 25, 1941; s. William Frederick and Anne Elizabeth (Cinealis) K.; m. Polly Holmsberg, June 26, 1965; children: Anne Rusert, Timothy, Matthew. BA, Marquette U., 1963; JD, U. Wis., Madison, 1970. Bar: Minn. 1970, U.S. Dist. Minn. 1970, U.s. Ct. Appeals (8th cir.) 1973, U.S. Dist. Ct. (we. dist.) Wis. 1979, U.S. Supreme Ct. 1979, U.S. Ct. Claims 1982. Assoc. Dorsey & Whitney, Mpls., 1970-76, ptnr., 1979-96; assoc. prof. Hamline U. Sch. Law, 1976-79, disting. practioner in residence, 1996—; instr. U. Minn. Law Sch.; adj. prof. William Mitchell Coll. Law, St. Paul; chmn., dir. Legal Advice Clinics, Ltd.; dir. Legal Assistance of Minn., Inc.; head Hennepin County Pub. Defender's Office for Misdemeanors. Author: (with Mc Farland) Minnesota Civil Practice (4 vols.), 1979, 3d edit., 1999, Administrative Practice and Procedure, 1999; co-author, editor: Minnesota Environmental Law Handbook, 2nd edit., 1995; contbr. articles and monographs to legal jours. Lt. USN, 1963-67, Vietnam. Mem. ABA, Minn. Bar Assn. Roman Catholic. Administrative and regulatory, Federal civil litigation, Environmental. Home: 10 Luverne Ave Minneapolis MN 55419-2612 also: Hamline U Sch Law 1536 Hewitt Ave Saint Paul MN 55104-1284

**KEPPELMAN, NANCY,** lawyer; b. Abington, Pa., June 28, 1950; d. H. Thomas and Helene A. (Harrow) Keppelman; m. Michael E. Smerza, Sept. 9, 1978. Student, Oberlin (Ohio) Coll., 1968-70; BA, U. Mich., 1972, JD, 1978; Cert., Inst. for Paralegal Tng., Phila., 1972. Bar: Mich. 1978, U.S. Dist. Ct. (ea. dist.) Mich. 1978, U.S. Tax Ct. 1986. Legal asst. Dykema, Gossett et al, Detroit, 1972-75; assoc. Butzel, Keidan et al, Detroit, 1978-80, Law Offices of Brook McCray Smith, Ann Arbor, Mich., 1980-82, Miller, Canfield et al, Detroit, 1982-89, Stevenson Assocs., Ann Arbor, 1989-90; shareholder/lawyer Stevenson Keppelman Assocs., Ann Arbor, 1991—; condr. seminars in field. Chpt. author, co-editor QDROs, EDROs and Retirement Benefits: A Guide for Michigan Practitioners, 1994; contbr. articles to profl. jours. James B. Angell scholar, U. Mich., 1972. Fellow Mich. State Bar Found.; mem. ABA, State Bar Mich. (mem. taxation coun. 1991-94), Washtenaw County Bar Assn., Women Lawyers Assn. Mich. (bd. dirs., pres. Washtenaw region 1990-93). Avocations: birdwatching, music, hiking. Pension, profit-sharing, and employee benefits, Taxation, general, General corporate. Office: 444 S Main St Ann Arbor MI 48104-2304

**KERA, DAVID J.,** lawyer; b. N.Y.C., Apr. 22, 1929; s. Jacob William and Frances (Cantor) K.; m. Sally Belzer, Feb. 2, 1958; children: Marian H., Caroline E. BA, NYU, 1950; JD, Harvard U., 1955. Bar: N.Y. 1956, D.C. 1971, Va. 1982, U.S. Ct. Appeal (2d cir.) 1966, U.S. Ct. Appeal (D.C. cir.) 1971, U.S. Ct. Appeal (11th cir.) 1990, U.S. Ct. Appeal (fed. cir.) 1982, U.S. Dist. Ct. (so. and ea. dists.) N.Y. 1971, U.S. Dist. Ct. (D.C. dist.) 1971, U.S. Dist. Ct. (ea. dist.) Va. 1997, Ct. of Customs and Patent Appeals 1968, U.S. Supreme Ct. 1971. Atty. Langner Parry, N.Y.C., 1955-65; asst. trademark counsel Bristol-Myers Co., N.Y.C., 1965-71; atty. in pvt. practice various law firms, Washington, 1971-75; spl. asst. to asst. commr. U.S. Patent and Trademark Office, Arlington, Va., 1976-77, adminstrv. trademark judge, mem. trademark trial/appeal bd., 1975-81; mem. firm Oblon, Spivak, McClelland, Maier & Neustadt, P.C., Arlington, 1981—; adj. prof. George Mason U., Arlington, 1990—, Franklin Perice Law Ctr., Concord, 1999; lectr. in field. Contbr. articles to profl. jours. Mem. ABA, Am. Intellectual Property Law Assn., Internat. Trademark Assn. Avocations: boating, photography. Intellectual property. Office: Oblon Spivak McClellan Maier & Neustadt PC 1755 Jefferson Davis Hwy Arlington VA 22202-3509

**KERBY, YALE LELAND,** lawyer; b. Corunna, Mich., Apr. 11, 1925; s. Yalek Harrington and Eltha M. (Bias) K.; m. Grace G. Cutler, June 30, 1956; children: Marla Lynn, Paula Louise, Kevin Yale. BS, Mich. State U., 1949; JD, Ohio No. U., 1952. Bar: Ohio 1952, Mich. 1952, U.S. Dist. Ct. (ea. dist.) Mich. 1958, U.S. Dist. Ct. (no. dist.) Ohio 1964, Tex. 1983, U.S. Dist. Ct. (we. dist.) Tex. Practice Morenci and Adrian, Mich.; judge Mich. (State) dist. Ct. Mich., 1968-78; sole practice Adrian, 1978-83; assoc. E.D. Kincaid, III, Uvalde, Tex., 1983; elected GOP county and regional chmn. Founder Alcohol Info. Ctr., Bixby Hosp., Adrian, Vols. in Probation, Lenawee Traffic Safety Sch., Lenawee Substance Abuse, Inc.; councilman Morenci City, 1960-63. Served with USMC, 1944-46. Mem. ABA, Tex. Bar Assn., Mich. Bar Assn. (life), Am. Judicature Soc., Am. Legion (1st comdr., county commr., dist. chaplain, dist. judge adv.), ADV, Am. Contract Bridge League, Elks, Kiwanis. Personal injury, Probate, Real property. Home: 1245 N Park Sr PO Box 5158 Uvalde TX 78802-5158 Office: 220 E Main St Uvalde TX 78801-5639

**KERIAN, JON ROBERT,** judge; b. Grafton, N.D., Oct. 23, 1927; s. Cyril Robert and Elizabeth Antoinette (Kadlec) K.; m. Sylvia Ann Larson, Dec. 28, 1959; children: John, Ann. PhB, U. N.D., 1955, LLB, 1957, JD, 1971. Bar: N.D. 1957, U.S. Dist. Ct. N.D. 1958, U.S. Ct. Appeals (8th cir.) 1971, U.S. Supreme Ct. 1963. Pvt. practice law Grand Forks, N.D., 1958-61; asst. atty. gen. State of N.D., Bismarck, 1961-67; ptnr. Bosard, McCutcheon, Kerian, Schmidt, Minot, N.D., 1967-80; dist. judge State of N.D., Minot, 1980-92; surrogate judge State of N.D., 1993—; history instr. Bismarck State Coll., 1965-67; asst. city atty. City of Minot, 1968-76; atty. Zoning & Planning Commn., Minot, 1969-76; lectr. in field. Contbr. articles to profl. jours.; editor ABA newsletter, The Judges News, 1990—95. Mem. ABA (bd. editors Judges Jour. 1990-95), Western States Bar Conf. (pres. 1982-83), N.D. Bar Assn. (pres. 1979-80), Nat. Conf. State Trial Judges (exec. com. 1983-89). Home: 1800 8th St SW Minot ND 58701-6410 Office: PO Box 340 Minot ND 58702-0340

**KERLIN, KARLA DIANE,** prosecutor; b. Erie, Pa., July 12, 1964. BS in Psychology, U. Pitts., 1986; JD, Southwestern U., 1990. Dep. dist. atty. L.A. County Dist. Atty.'s Office, L.A. Pres. Gramercy Housing Group, L.A., 1994—. Mem. Women Lawyers Assn. L.A. (treas. 1998—). Democrat. Office: LA County Dist Attys Office 210 W Temple St Los Angeles CA 90012-3210

**KERN, DAVID BERNARD,** lawyer; b. Milw., Aug. 19, 1954; s. Richard Henry and Delores Mary K.; m. Mary Josephine Sturm, July 8, 1978; children: Teresa, Patrick, Michael, Leah. BA with highest hons., Marquette U., 1976; JD with high hons., U. Mich., 1979. Bar: Wis. 1979, U.S. Dist. Ct. (ea. dist. and we. dist.) Wis., 1979, U.S. Ct. Appeals (7th cir.), U.S. Ct. Appeals (10th cir.), U.S. Dist. Ct. (no. dist.) Ill. 1998, U.S. Supreme Ct. Assoc. Quarles & Brady, Milw., 1979-85, ptnr., 1986—. Co-author: Wisconsin Employment Law, 1998; contbg. editor The Developing Labor law, 1986-90. Bd. dirs. Juvenile Diabetes Found., 1993-98. Mem. ABA, State Bar of Wis., Milw. Bar Assn. Roman Catholic. Avocations: fishing, bicycling, photography. Labor. Home: 7525 Kenwood Ave Wauwatosa WI 53213-1710 Office: Quarles & Brady 411 E Wisconsin Ave Ste 2550 Milwaukee WI 53202-4497

**KERN, GEORGE CALVIN, JR.,** lawyer; b. Balt., Apr. 19, 1926; s. George Calvin and Alice (Gaskins) K.; m. Joan Shorell, Dec. 22, 1962; 1 child, Heath. BA, Princeton U., 1947; LLB, Yale U., 1952. Bar: N.Y. 1952. Chief U.S. Info. Ctr., Mannheim, W.Ger., 1947-48; dep. dir. pub. info. Office U.S. Mil. Govt. for Germany, Berlin and Nurnberg, 1948-49; assoc. Sullivan & Cromwell, N.Y.C., 1952-60, ptnr., 1960—; publ. Cub newspaper, Tehachapi, Calif.; bd. dirs. McJunkin Corp., Charleston, W.Va. Lt. USN, 1944-46. General corporate, Mergers and acquisitions, Securities. Home: 830 Park Ave New York NY 10021-2757 Office: Sullivan & Cromwell 125 Broad St Fl 28 New York NY 10004-2489

**KERN, JOHN MCDOUGALL,** lawyer; b. Omaha, Nov. 28, 1946; s. Conard Lee and Agnes Rose (Brink) K.; m. Susan McDougall Kern, Oct. 15, 1977; children: Matthew, Jennifer. BA, Creighton U., 1970; JD cum laude, George Washington U., 1973. Bar: D.C. 1973, Calif. 1980, U.S. Dist. Ct. D.C. 1974, U.S. Dist Ct. (no. dist.) Calif. 1980, U.S. Dist. Ct. (ctrl. dist.) Calif. 1996, U.S. Ct. Appeals (D.C. cir.) 1974, U.S. Ct. Appeals (9th cir.) 1978; bd. cert. specialist in civil trial advocacy, Nat. Bd. Trial Advocacy. Asst. U.S. atty. criminal divsn. Office of U.S. Atty. D.C., Washington, 1973-78; asst. U.S. atty. civil divsn. Office U.S. Atty. No. Dist. Calif., San Francisco, 1978-82; v.p., dir. Crosby, Heafey, Roach & May P.C., San Francisco, Oakland, L.A., 1981—; cons. regents U. Calif., Berkeley, 1988—; faculty Nat. Inst. Trial Advocacy, 1987—; panelist Superior Ct. City and County of San Francisco Early Settlement Program, Superior Ct. Contra Cost County Bench-Bar Settlement Program; del. VI-IX Internat. AIDS Confs., 1991-93; spkr. numerous programs, confs.; lectr. in field. Contbr. abstracts, book chpt., articles to profl. jours. Mem. Am. Bd. Trial Advocates (advocate), Am. Inn of Ct., Assn. Bus. Trial Lawyers, Nat. Inst. Trial Advocacy. Federal civil litigation, State civil litigation, Health. Office: Crosby Heafey Roach & May PC 4 Embarcadero Ctr Ste 1900 San Francisco CA 94111-4191

**KERN, JOHN WORTH, III,** judge; b. Indpls., May 25, 1928; s. John Worth and Bernice (Winn) K.; children: John, Stephen. BA, Princeton U., 1949; LLB, Harvard U., 1952. Bar: D.C. 1953, U.S. Ct. Appeals (D.C. cir.) 1955. With, CIA, 1952-54; law clk. to chief judge U.S. Ct. Appeals D.C. Cir. Ct., 1954-55; asst. U.S. atty. D.C. Dist., Dept. Justice, Washington, 1955-59; assoc. Kilpatrick, Ballard & Beasley, Washington, 1959-65; with Dept. of Justice, Washington, 1965-68; judge D.C. Ct. Appeals, Washington, 1968-84, sr. judge, 1987—; dean Nat. Jud. Coll., Reno, 1984-87. Mem. D.C. Bar. Presbyterian. Office: DC Ct Appeals 500 Indiana Ave NW Washington DC 20001-2138

**KERN, TERRY C.,** judge; b. Clinton, Okla., Sept. 25, 1944; s. Elgin L. Kern and Lora Lee (Miller) Renegar; m. Charlene Heinen, Dec. 26, 1970; children: Lauren, Suzanne, Justin Hunter. BS, Okla. State U., Stillwater, 1966; JD, U. Okla., 1969. Bar: Okla. 1969, U.S. Dist. Ct. (ea. dist.) Okla. 1974, U.S. Dist. Ct. (we. dist.) Okla. 1979, U.S. Dist. Ct. (no. dist.) Okla. 1993, U.S. Ct. Appeals (10th cir.) 1979. Gen. atty. FTC, Washington, 1969-70; ptnr. Fischl, Culp, McMillin, Kern and Chaffin, Ardmore, Okla., 1971-86; founding ptnr., pres. Kern, Mordy and Sperry, Ardmore, 1986-94; dist. judge U.S. Dist. Ct. (no. dist.) Okla., Tulsa, 1994—, chief judge, 1996—. Chmn. bd. dirs. So. Okla. Meml. Hosp., Ardmore, 1989-91; vice chmn. Ardmore Devel. Authority, 1990; v.p. Perry Maxwell Intercollegiate Assn., Ardmore, 1992—. Served with USAR, 1970-75. Fellow Am. Bar Found., Okla. Bar Found. (pres. 1991, Disting. Svc. award 1992); mem. ABA, Am. Bd. Trial Advocates (Okla. chpt.), Okla. Bar Assn., W. Lee Johnson Inn of Ct. (master of bench), U. Okla. Coll. Law Assn. Democrat. Episcopal. Office: US Dist Courthouse 333 W 4th St Tulsa OK 74103-3839

**KERNAN, STEPHEN MICHAEL, SR.,** judge; b. East St. Louis, Ill., Nov. 16, 1947; s. Stephen Curtis and Margaret Rita (Lundy) K.; m. Mary Jane Wurth, June 20, 1968 (div. Aug. 1981); children: Stephen Michael Jr., Ian Patrick, Ara Joseph, Caroline Adrienne; m. Gina H. Noubarian, May 17, 1989. BBA, U. Notre Dame, 1969; JD, Washington U., St. Louis, 1972. Bar: Ill. 1972, U.S. Dist. Ct. (ea. dist.) Ill. 1972, U.S. Ct. Appeals (7th cir.) 1974. Atty. Sam S. Pessin, Belleville, Ill., 1972-74; pub. adminstr. State of Ill., Belleville, 1972-74, assoc. cir. judge, 1974-77, cir. judge, 1977—, chief cir. judge, 1988—; mem. faculty Nat. Jud. Conf., Reno, 1989. Chmn. ct. watchers LWV, Belleville, 1982; pres. Children First Found., Belleville, 1987—; bd. dirs. Camp Ondessonk, Ozark, Ill., 1972-88, St. John's Children's Home, Belleville, 1980-82. 1st lt. U.S. Army, 1973. Mem. Ill. State Bar Assn., Ill. Judges Assn. (instr. seminar 1973-74), East St. Louis Bar Assn., St. Clair County Bar Assn., Chief Judges' Conf., Eagles, Elks. Democrat. Roman Catholic. Avocations: snow skiing, fishing, hunting. Office: Cir Ct St Clair Courthouse Belleville IL 62220

**KERNAN, TINA LYNN,** lawyer; b. Lewiston, Idaho, June 26, 1966; d. Roger William and Patricia Reid; m. Craig Mitchell Kernan, Oct. 16, 1993; children: Emily Alyse, Abigail Kathleen. BA, U. Idaho, 1988, JD, 1993. Bar: Wash. 1993, Idaho 1994, U.S. Dist. Ct. Wash. 1993, U.S. Ct. Appeals (9th cir.) 1993. Atty. Law Offices of David A. Gittins, Clarkston, Wash., 1993—. Mem. alumni bd. Valley Boys and Girls Club, Lewiston, Idaho, 1994—; trustee Tri-State Hosp. Found., Clarkston, 1998—. Mem. Asotin County Bar Assn. (v.p. 1993, pres. 1994). Democrat. Roman Catholic. Avocations: reading, writing, photography. Family and matrimonial, Criminal, General practice. Office: Law Offices David A Gittins 843 7th St Clarkston WA 99403-2021

**KERNEN, WILL,** lawyer; b. Boston, July 4, 1951; s. Judson and Olive (Bardsley) K.; m. Cindy M. Krueger, June 21, 1970; children: Kerry, Kurt, Kyle, Kasey, Kathy. BA, Bridgewater State Coll., 1974; JD, Ohio State U., 1976. Bar: Ohio, U.S. Dist. Ct. (so. dist.) Ohio 1978. Assoc. Lappen & Lilley, Logan Ohio, 1977-78; ptnr. Lappen, Lilley, Kernen & Co., L.P.A., Logan, Ohio, 1978—; law dir. City of Logan, 1978-79; law librarian Hocking County Law Library, 1980-83; acting judge Hocking County Mcpl. Ct., Logan, 1983-87. Bd. mem. Logan-Hocking City Sch. Dist., 1979-83; counsel Hocking County Rep. Party, 1979—. Served with U.S. Army, 1968-71, Germany. Mem. ABA, Ohio Bar Assn., Hocking County Bar Assn. (v.p. 1978-79, pres. 1989—), Jaycees (pres. Logan 1983-84, dist. dir. Ohio 1984-85). General practice, Real property, State civil litigation. Home: 26816 Darl Rd Rockbridge OH 43149-9601 Office: PO Box 388 Logan OH 43138-0388

**KERNER, MICHAEL PHILIP,** lawyer; b. N.Y.C., July 21, 1953; s. Arthur and Rosalind (Mehr) K. BA, Antioch Coll., 1976; JD, Lewis & Clark U., 1979; LLM in Taxation with honors, Golden Gate U., 1995. Bar: Calif. 1980 (cert. specialist personal and small bus. bankruptcy law), U.S. Dist. Ct. (no. and ea. dists.) Calif. 1983, U.S. Ct. Appeals (9th cir.) 1983, U.S. Tax Ct., 1996. Staff atty. U.S. EPA, Washington, 1979-80; asst. regional counsel region 9 U.S. EPA, San Francisco, 1980-83; ptnr. Kerner, Weppner & Rosenbaum, San Francisco, 1983-95; prin. Kerner & Assocs., San Francisco, 1996—; bd. dirs. Solano County Legal Assistance, Vallejo, Calif., 1983-86; arbitrator San Francisco Superior Ct., 1991-94. Editor law rev. and law jours. Mem. San Francisco Trial Lawyers Assn., Solano County Bar Assn., Nat. Assn. Consumer Bankruptcy Attys. Democrat. Jewish. Avocations: windsurfing, snowboarding, road and mountain biking. Estate planning, Taxation, general, Bankruptcy. Office: Kerner & Assocs 240 Stockton St Ste 4 San Francisco CA 94108-5306

**KERNOCHAN, JOHN MARSHALL,** lawyer, educator; b. N.Y.C., Aug. 3, 1919; s. Marshall Rutgers and Caroline (Hatch) K. AB, Harvard U., 1942; JD, Columbia U., 1948. Bar: N.Y. 1949. Asst. dir. Legis. Drafting Research Fund Columbia U., N.Y.C., 1950-51, acting dir., 1951-52, dir., 1952-69, lectr. law, 1951-52, assoc. prof., 1952-55, prof., 1955-77, Nash prof. law, 1977-89, Nash prof. law emeritus, 1990—, exec. dir. Council for Atomic Age Studies, 1956-59, co-chmn., 1960-62, dir. Ctr. Law & Arts (now Kernochon Ctr. Law Media & Arts), 1986—; spl. lectr., 1991—; chmn. bd. Galaxy Music Corp., 1956-89; cons. Temporary State Commn. to Study Organizational Structure of Govt. of N.Y.C., 1953; bd. dirs. E.C.Schirmer Music Co., Inc.; pres. Gaudia Music & Arts, Inc., 1987—. Author: The Legislative Process, 1980; co-author: Legal Method Cases and Materials, 1980; contbr. articles to profl. jours. Mem. civil and polit. rights com. Pres.'s Commn. on Status of Women, 1962-63; dir. emeritus Vol. Lawyers for the Arts; mem. legal and legis. com. Internat. Confedn. Socs. Authors and Composers. Mem. Assn. Bar City of N.Y. Internat. Lit. and Artistic Assn. (mem. d'honneur, internat. exec. com., mem. U.S.A. group), Copyright Soc. U.S.A. (exec. com. 1986-89), Assn. Tchrs. and Rschrs. in Intellectual Property, Com. for Lit. Property Studies. Office: Columbia U Sch Law 435 W 116th St New York NY 10027-7297

**KERNS, DAVID VINCENT,** lawyer; b. Salt Lake City, Jan. 29, 1917; s. Clinton Bowen and Ella Mae (Young) K.; m. Dorothea Boyd, Sept. 5, 1942; children—David V., Clinton Boyd. B.Ph., Emory U., 1937; J.D., U. Fla., 1939. Bar: Fla. 1939, U.S. Dist. Ct. (mid. dist.) Fla. 1939, U.S. Dist. Ct. (so. dist.) Fla. 1978, U.S. Dist. Ct. (no. dist.) Fla., U.S. Ct. Appeals (11th cir.) 1981, U.S. Supreme Ct. 1988. Assoc. Sutton & Reeves, Tampa, Fla., 1939-41, Fowler & White, Tampa, 1945-47; ptnr. Moran & Kerns, Tampa, 1948-49; resident atty. Fla. Road Dept., 1949-53; research asst. Supreme Ct. Fla., 1953-58; dir. Fla. Legis. Reference Bur., 1958-68, Fla. Legis. Service Bur., 1968-71, Fla. Legis. Library Services, 1971-73; gen. counsel Fla. Dept. Adminstrn., 1973-82; mem. Fla. Career Service Commn., 1983-86; spl. master Fla. Senate, 1987-96; legal cons. chief inspector gen. Fla. Gov. Office, 1995-98. Contbr. articles to profl. jours. Served with U.S. Army, 1941-45. Mem. Fla. Govt. Bar Assn. (pres. 1966, J. Ernest Webb Meml. award 1982), Fla. Bar (bd. govs. 1978-84), Tallahassee Bar Assn. (spl. dir. 1993-95). Democrat. Methodist. Home: 418 Vinnedge Ride Tallahassee FL 32303-5140

**KERR, ALEXANDER DUNCAN, JR.,** lawyer; b. Pitts., May 6, 1943; s. Alexander Duncan Sr. and Nancy Greenleaf (Martin) K.; m. Judith Kathleen Mottl, May 25, 1969; children: Matthew Jonathan, Joshua Brandon. BS in Bus., Northwestern U., 1965, JD, 1968. Bar: Ill. 1968, Pa. 1969, U.S. Dist.

Ct. (ea. dist.) Pa. 1969, U.S. Dist. Ct. (no. dist.) Ill. 1969, U.S. Ct. Appeals (3rd and 7th cirs.) 1969, U.S. Supreme Ct. 1969. Assoc. Clark, Ladner, Fontenbaugh & Young, Phila., 1968-69, 73-74; asst. U.S. atty. U.S. Dept. Justice, Chgo., 1974-79; assoc., ptnr. Keck, Mahin & Cate, Chgo., Oak Brook, Ill., 1979-90; shareholder Tishler & Wald, Ltd., Chgo., 1990—. Staff atty. Park Dist. La Grange, Ill., 1985—; active Ill. St. Andrew Soc., North Riverside, 1982—, pres., 1995-97; vestryman, lay reader, chancellor, chalice bearer Emmanuel Episcopal Ch., 1980—; mem. Pack 177, Troop 19, Order of the Arrow, Boy Scouts Am., La Grange, 1980—. With USN, 1969-75. Mem. Am. Legion, DuPage Club, Atlantis Divers. E-mail: adkerrjr@aol.com. Fax: 708-354-1208. Bankruptcy, General civil litigation, General corporate. Home: 709 S Stone Ave La Grange IL 60525-2725

**KERR, BAINE PERKINS, JR.,** lawyer, writer; b. Houston, June 23, 1946; s. Baine Perkins and Mildred Pickett (Caldwell) K.; m. Cynthia Anne Carlisle; children—Dara, Baine. B.A., Stanford U., 1968; M.A., U. Denver, 1976, J.D., 1979. Bar: Colo. 1979, U.S. Dist. Ct. (Colo.) 1979, U.S. Ct. Appeals 1979. Editor-in-chief Place Mag., Palo Alto, Calif. 1971-74; ptnr. Hutchinson, Black, Hill & Cook, Boulder, 1979—; elections supr., Bosnia, 1997; fiction writer. Nat. Endowment Arts fellow 1983; work appeared in Houghton Mifflin Co. Best American Short Stories of 1977; recipient Editor's prize Mo. Review, 1992. Mem. ABA, Colo. Bar Assn., Boulder County Bar Assn. Democrat. Author: Jumping Off Place, 1981, Harmful Intent, 1999; contbr. numerous short stories and articles to periodicals and literary jours.; contbr. legal articles to law reviews. Home: 1215 Spruce St Boulder CO 80302-4818

**KERR, GERALD LEE, III,** lawyer, paralegal educator; b. Mpls., July 7, 1944; s. Gerald L. Kerr Jr. BS, U.S. Naval Acad., 1966; JD, Cath. U., 1972; MPA, Golden Gate U., 1976. Bar: D.C., Va. Atty. Kelberg & Childress, Virginia Beach, Va., 1977-78, Gerald L. Kerr III, P.C., Virginia Beach, 1978—; asst. prof. Tidewater C.C., Virginia Beach, 1977—. Pres., Norfolk Sister City Assn., 1979-81. Served to comdr. JAGC Corps, U.S. Navy, 1966-87. Named to Outstanding Young Men of Am., 1979, 80, 81. Office: 3634 S Plaza Trl Virginia Beach VA 23452-3351

**KERR, J. MARTIN,** lawyer; b. Kansas City, Kans., Apr. 6, 1943; s. James Rolland and Thelma Elizabeth Kerr; m. Shirley Jean Johnson, Jan. 20, 1971 (div. Oct. 1992); children: James Kyle, James Michael; m. Connie Sue David, Aug. 3, 1993. BSBA, Kans. U., 1966; JD, U. Mo., Kansas City, 1970. Bar: Mo. 1970, U.S. Dist. Ct. (we. dist.) Mo. 1970, U.S. Supreme Ct. 1976. Pvt. practice Independence, Mo.; spkr., moderator CLE programs on criminal def., 1980—. Mem. ACLU, Mo. Bar Assn., Mo. Assn. Trial Attys., Mo. Assn. Criminal Def. Lawyers (founding mem., pres. 1983-84, Svc. award 1981). Democrat. Avocations: reading novels, history and political works, jogging, walking. Fax: 816-461-0774. Criminal. Home: 4802 NE Pebble Beach St Lees Summit MO 64064-1323 Office: 400 W Kansas Ave Independence MO 64050-3617

**KERR, STANLEY MUNGER,** investigator, lawyer, educator; b. Des Moines, Sept. 30, 1949; s. Richard Dixon and Arlene Mae (Munger) K.; m. Myrna Anita Hill, May 22, 1971; children—Mila Anee, Tamara Eve. Student Christian Coll. of the Southwest, 1967-69, U. Tex., 1970-71; B.A., Houston-Tillotson Coll., 1975; J.D., U. Tex., 1977. Bar: Tex. 1977. Investigator, City of Austin, Tex., 1981-87; instr. govt. Houston-Tillotson Coll., Austin, 1978-81; sole practice, Austin, 1977-88; mental health atty. Travis County Probate Ct., 1988—. Gen. counsel, bd. dirs. Operation PUSH, Austin, 1979-81; chmn. Community-Police Relations Adv. Council, Austin, 1981-84; precinct chmn. Travis County Democratic Party, Austin, 1978-82; state del. Dem. Party State Conv., Tex., 1976, 78, 80, 82, 84, 86; sr. warden, mem. Bishop Com., St. James Episcopal Ch., Austin, 1972-79, 85—; cons. interracial marriage and children; Minister, Ch. Christ . Mem. State Bar Tex., Austin Black Lawyers Assn., Am. Fedn. State, County, and Mcpl. Employees. Probate, General practice. Home: 1412 Springdale Rd Austin TX 78721-1353 Office: Probate Ct PO Box 1748 Austin TX 78767-1748

**KERRICK, DAVID ELLSWORTH,** lawyer; b. Caldwell, Idaho, Jan. 15, 1951; s. Charles Ellsworth and Patria (Olesen) K.; m. Juneal Casper, May 24, 1980; children: Peter Ellsworth, Beth Anne, George Ellis, Katherine Leigh. Student, Coll. of Idaho, 1969-71; BA, U. Wash., 1972; JD, U. Idaho, 1980. Bar: Idaho 1980, U.S. Dist. Ct. Idaho 1980, U.S. Ct. Appeals (9th cir.) 1981. Mem. Idaho Senate, 1990-96, majority caucus chmn., 1992-94, majority leader, 1994-96. Mem. S.W. Idaho Estate Planning Coun. Mem. ABA, Assn. Trial Lawyers Am., Idaho Bar Assn. (3d dist. pres. 1985-86), Idaho Trial Lawyers Assn., Canyon County Lawyers Assn. (pres. 1985). Republican. Presbyterian. Lodge: Elks. Avocations: skiing, photography. Personal injury, Estate planning, Real property. Office: PO Box 44 Caldwell ID 83606-0044

**KERRIDGE, RONALD DAVID,** lawyer; b. Houston, Mar. 23, 1962; s. Isaac Curtis and Ruth Stewart Kerridge; m. Elisabeth Michele Crook, June 20, 1987 (div. Aug. 1997); children: Merritt Cottrell, Wynne Banning. AB summa cum laude, Princeton U., 1984; JD magna cum laude, Harvard U., 1987. Bar: Tex. 1987, U.S. Tax Ct. 1991. Assoc. Carrington, Coleman, Sloman & Blumenthal, Dallas, 1987-93; ptnr. Sayles & Lidji, Dallas, 1994-96, Hughes & Luce, LLP, Dallas, 1996—. Episcopalian. Corporate taxation, Taxation, general. Office: Hughes & Luce LLP 1717 Main St Ste 1700 Dallas TX 75201-4605

**KERRIGAN, TIMOTHY GEORGE,** lawyer; b. Nashua, N.H., July 3, 1954; s. Joseph M. and Jean D. (Dooley) K.; m. Catherine M. Devine, Oct. 8, 1983; Devin, Miles Dooley, Brennan Patrick. BA, Tufts U., 1977; JD, Antioch Sch. of Law, 1980. Bar: N.H. 1980, U.S. Dist. Ct. N.H. 1982, U.S. Ct. Appeals (1st cir.) 1988. Intern Environ. Affairs Office, Boston, 1977, D.C. Superior Ct., Washington, 1979; law clk. to chief judge U.S. Dist. Ct. N.H., Concord, 1980-82; assoc. Hamblett & Kerrigan, Nashua, N.H., 1982-87, dir. and shareholder, 1988—. Bd. advisors paralegal program River Coll., Nashua, 1987—, chair 1992—. Mem. ABA (torts and ins. practice sect.), N.H. Bar Found. (bd. dirs. 1988—), N.H. Bar Assn. (county gov. 1986-88, gov.-at-large 1988—, mem. com. accepting the Pres.'s Disting. Svc. award 1989), Nashua Bar Assn. (sec. 1984-85), Assn. Defense Trial Attys., No. New england Defense Coun. Insurance, Environmental, General civil litigation. Address: Hamblett & Kerrigan 146 Main St Nashua NH 03060-2731

**KERRIGAN, VANESSA GRIFFITH,** lawyer; b. Newport News, Va., Dec. 8, 1961; d. James William and Joyce (Nichols) Griffith; m. Dennis Francis Kerrigan, Jr., Nov. 21, 1992; 1 child, Patrick James. BA, Coll. William and Mary, 1984, JD, 1991. Bar: Conn. 1991. Atty. corp. hdqrs. United Techs. Corp., Hartford, Conn., 1992-95; asst. cousnel Pratt & Whitney divsn. United Techs. Corp., East Hartford, Conn., 1995—. Mem. bd. editors William and Mary Law Rev., 1989-91. Mem. Glastonbury (Conn.) Rep. Women, 1994—; v.p. Orchard Homeowners Assn., Glastonbury, 1996-98. Mem. ABA, Am. Corp. Counsel Assn. Republican. Roman Catholic. Avocations: skiing, travel, art. Aviation, Contracts commercial, General corporate. Office: Pratt & Whitney 400 Main St # Ms132-12 East Hartford CT 06108-0968

**KERSH, DEWITTE TALMADGE, JR.,** lawyer; b. Balt., June 1, 1930; s. DeWitte Talmadge and Marianna (Snyder) K.; m. Sharon R. Doherty, Aug. 2, 1986; children: DeWitte III, Sarah Anne. BS, Cornell U., 1952, LLB, 1957. Bar: R.I. 1958, N.H. 1991, U.S. Dist. Ct. R.I. 1959, U.S. Dist. Ct. N.H. 1991. Ptnr. Tillinghast, Collins & Graham, Providence, 1965-93; counsel Tillinghast, Licht & Semonoff, Providence, 1993—; adj. instr. Law Sch. Roger Williams U. Bd. dirs. Tanner Meml. Fund, W.V. Found. Fellow Am. Acad. Matrimonial Lawyers; mem. ABA (family law and elder law sects.), R.I. and N.H. Bar Assns. (pro bono svc. 1987-94), N.H. Family Ct. Bench and Bar, ATLA (family law sect.), Rotary (pres. 1989-90). Republican. Unitarian. General civil litigation, Family and matrimonial, Personal injury. Home: PO Box 346 Waterville Valley NH 03215-0346 Office: Tillinghast Licht & Seminoff One Park Row Providence RI 02905

**KERSTETTER, WAYNE ARTHUR,** law educator, lawyer; b. Chgo., Dec. 1, 1939; s. Arthur Edward and Lillian (Asplund) K.; BA, U. Chgo., 1964, JD, 1967. Bar: Ill. 1968. Asst. commr. N.Y. Police Dept., N.Y.C., 1972-73; supt. Ill. Bur. Investigation, Chgo., 1973-76; assoc. dir. Ctr. for Studies in Criminal Justice, U. Chgo., 1976-78; assoc. prof. criminal justice, dept. criminal justice U. Ill.-Chgo., 1978—; sr. rsch. fellow Am. Bar Found., Chgo., 1982-93, fellow, 1993—; cons. U.S. Civil Rights Commn., U. Chgo., ABT Assocs., Univ. Research Assocs., Police Found. Mem. transition team Mayor Washington, Chgo., 1983, Criminal Justice Project of Cook County, 1987. Served with USNR, 1962-64. Rsch. grantee Nat. Inst. Justice, 1976, Chgo. Bar Found., 1979-80, Am. Bar Found., 1983; fellow Ctr. for Studies in Criminal Justice, U. Chgo. Law Sch., 1978-82. Mem. ABA. Office: U Ill 1007 W Harrison St Chicago IL 60607-7135

**KERWIN, MARY ANN COLLINS,** lawyer; b. Oconomowoc, Wis., Oct. 16, 1931; d. Thomas Patrick and Florence Mary (Morris) Collins; m. Thomas Joseph Kerwin, Dec. 27, 1954; children: Thomas, Edward, Gregory, Mary, Anne, Katherine, John, Michael. BA, Barat Coll., 1953; JD, U. Denver, 1986. Bar: Colo. 1987. Tchr. Country Grade Sch., Wheaton, Ill., 1953-54; travel agt. Chgo. Athletic Club, 1954-55; legal intern City Atty.'s Office, Denver, 1985, Dist. Atty.'s Office, Denver, 1985; atty. Kerwin and Assocs., Denver, 1987-92, Decker, DeVoss & O'Malley, P.C., Denver, 1992-93, King Peterson Brown, LLC, Englewood, Colo., 1993-95; assoc. Daniel F. Lynch, P.C., Denver, 1995-99; legal compliance dept. editor United Banks Colo., Inc., Denver, 1988-93. Author: (with others) The Womanly Art of Breastfeeding, 1958, also revised edits., 1963, 81, 87, 91, 97; contbr. articles to profl. jours. Mem. Colo. Breastfeeding Task Force, 1990-93, 96—; adv. bd. St. Luke's Woman's Hosp., Denver, 1986—, Colo. Sudden Infant Death Syndrome Program, 1992-94; sch. bd. Christ the King Sch., Denver, 1970-73; great books leader Jr. and Collegiate Great Books, Denver, 1963-82; marriage spkr. Cath. Archdiocese, Denver, 1965-75; co-founder, bd. dirs. La Leche League Internat., Franklin Park, Ill., 1956—, founder state orgn., 1960—, chmn. bd. 1980-83, sec. 1988-91. Recipient Margaret Burke Disting. Svc. Alumni award Barat Coll., 1999; named One of Ten Outstanding Alumnus Barat Coll., 1988. Mem. Colo. Bar Assn., Colo. Women's Bar Assn., Denver Bar Assn., Colo. Alumnae Assn. (pres. 1968-70), Theresians (pres. 1974-76). Avocations: reading, biking, swimming, tennis, singing. Family and matrimonial, General civil litigation, Probate. Home: 5130 Nassau Cir W Cherry Hl Vlg CO 80110-5129

**KERYCZYNSKYJ, LEO IHOR,** lawyer, county official, educator; b. Chgo., Aug. 8, 1948; s. William and Eva (Chicz) K.; m. Alexandra Irene Okruch, July 19, 1980; 1 child, Christina Alexandra. BA, DePaul U., 1970, BS, 1970, MS in Pub. Svc., 1975; JD, No. Ill. U., 1979; postgrad., U. Ill., Chgo., 1980-82. Bar: Ill. 1981, U.S. Dist. Ct. (no. dist.) Ill. 1981, U.S. Ct. Appeals (7th cir.) 1981, U.S. Tax Ct. 1981, U.S. Ct. Claims 1982, U.S. Ct. Mil. Appeals 1982, U.S. Ct. Appeals (fed. cir.) 1983, U.S. Supreme Ct. 1984. Condemnation awards officer Cook County Treas.'s Officw, Chgo., 1972-75, adminstrv. asst., 1975-77, dep. treas., 1977-87, chief legal counsel, 1987-96, dir. fin. svcs., 1988-96; pvt. practice, 1996-98; adv. Office of Profl. Stds. Chgo. Police Dept., 1998—; adj. prof. DePaul U., Chgo., 1979-95; elected chmn. bd. dirs., Security Fed. Savs. Bank Chgo., 1992-93. Capt. Ukrainian Am. Dem. Orgn., Chgo., 1971. Recipient Outstanding Alumni award Phi Kappa Theta, 1971. Mem. ABA, Ill. State Bar Assn., Ill. Trial Law Assn., Ukrainian Am. bar Assn., Chgo. Bar Assn., Ill. Assn. County Ofcls., Internat. Assn., Clerks, Recorders, Election Ofcls. and Treas., Shore Line Interurban Hist. Soc. (bd. dirs., legal counsel 1987—, pres. and chmn., 1993-98), Theta Delta Phi. Ukrainian Catholic. Home: 2324 W Iowa St Apt 3R Chicago IL 60622-4720 Office: Office Profl Stds 1130 S Wabash Ave Chicago IL 60605-2372

**KESHIAN, RICHARD,** lawyer; b. Arlington, Mass., Aug. 11, 1934; s. Hamayak and Takuhe (Malkesian) K.; m. Jacqueline C. Cannilla, Sept 11, 1965; children: Carolyn D., Richard M.. BS in Bus. Adminstrn., Boston U., 1956, JD, 1958. Bar: Mass. 1958. Pvt. practice law, Arlington, Mass., 1964-71; ptnr. Keshian & Reynolds, P.C., Arlington, 1971—; instr. real estate law Inst. Fin. Edn., 1976-80; instr. bus law George Washington U., Washington, 1961-63; mem. adv. bd. Coop. Bank Concord, Arlington, 1983-86; corporator Bank Five for Savs., Arlington, 1984-91; bd. dirs., gen. counsel Arlington Coop. Bank, 1978-83. Chmn. Arlington Zoning Bd. Appeals, 1972-76; pres. Arlington C. of C., 1976; v.p. Mass. Fedn. Planning Bds., 1978-85; mem. Arlington Contributory Retirement Bd., 1984—. With USMC, 1958-64; maj. Res. ret. Mem. ABA, Mass. Bar Assn., Am. Arbitration Assn. (arbitrator 1975—), Mass. Conveyancers Assn. (bd. dirs. 1996—, chmn. title standards com. 1996—), Mass. Assn. Bank Counsel (pres. 1992-95), Middlesex County Bar Assn. Democrat. Congregationalist. Real property, Probate, Banking. Home: 93 Falmouth Rd W Arlington MA 02474-1007 Office: 1040 Massachusetts Ave PO Box 440 Arlington MA 02476-0052

**KESLER, JOHN A.,** lawyer, land developer; b. Clark County, Ill., Apr. 25, 1923; s. Hal H. and Clara (Hurst) K.; m. Maxine Ruth Weaver, May 13, 1948; children: Nicki Kesler Herrington, Bradley Weaver, John A. II. AB, Ind. State U., 1948; JD, Ind. U., 1951. Bar: Ind. 1951, Ill. 1951. Chief dep. prosecutor County Vigo, Terre Haute, Ind., 1954-58; probate commr. Cir. Ct., 1971-74; mem. ho. reps. Ind. Legis., 1969-73; asst. state atty. County Madison, Edwardsville, Ill., 1985-88; pvt. practice law Terre Haute, 1951—; pres. Wabash Valley Land Developers, Inc., Terre Haute, 1979—. Sgt. U.S. Army, 1943-46. Recipient Legion of Honor; recipient Good Govt. award West Vigo Jaycees, 1971, Civic Svc. award U.S. Jaycees, 1957, award Grand Soc. Sycamores; named Outstanding Pub. Offcl. Terre Haute Jaycees. Mem. Ill. State Bar Assn., Ind. Bar Assn., VFW, Am. Legion, United War Vets. Coun. Vigo County (past commdr.), SAR (pres.), Exchange Club (pres.), Shriners, Terre Haute Exch. Club (pres.), Grand Soc. Sycamores, Grotto. Democrat. Methodist. Avocations: bowling, geneology, reading. Criminal, General civil litigation, General practice. Home: 76 N Thorpe Pl West Terre Haute IN 47885-9162 Office: 219 Ohio St Terre Haute IN 47807-3420

**KESSEL, MARK,** lawyer; b. Krasnik, Poland, June 14, 1941; came to U.S., 1948; s. Leo and Erna (Friedman) K.; m. Elaine Keit, Aug. 28, 1966; children: Greer Kessel Hendricks, Robert W. BA with honors in Econs., CUNY, 1963; JD magna cum laude, Syracuse U., 1966. Bar: N.Y., Calif. Assoc. Shearman & Sterling, N.Y.C., 1971-77, ptnr., 1977—, mng. ptnr., 1990-94; bd. dirs. Heller Fin. Inc., Mus. of City of N.Y. Dir. W.M. Keck Found., L.A., 1985-86; bd. visitors Syracuse U. Coll. Law; ex-officio bd. dirs. San Francisco Psychoanalytic Inst., 1988-90. Capt. JAGC, U.S. Army, 1963-71. Mem. ABA, N.Y. State Bar, Calif. State Bar, Bar Assn. City of N.Y. Avocations: reading, running, tennis. Securities, Mergers and acquisitions, General corporate. Office: Shearman & Sterling 599 Lexington Ave Fl C2 New York NY 10022-6069

**KESSELMAN, STEPHEN EDWARD,** lawyer; b. Heidelberg, Germany, Oct. 5, 1957; s. William and Edith (Moses) K.; m. Alison D. Schecter, May 25, 1996. BS, Cornell U., Ithaca, N.Y., 1978, JD, 1981. Litigation assoc. Rosenman & Colin, N.Y.C., 1981-91; litigation ptnr. Brief, Kesselman, Knapp & Schulman, LLP, N.Y.C., 1991—. Mem. bd. Park Ave Synagogue, N.Y.C., 1998—; com. mem. Assn. Bar of City of N.Y., 1994—. Jewish. Avocation: marathons. Office: Brief Keselman Knapp & Schulman LLP 805 3rd Ave New York NY 10022-7513

**KESSLER, ALAN CRAIG,** lawyer; b. Washington, Sept. 16, 1950; s. Alfred Milton and Josephine (Taub) K.; m. Gail Elaine Strauss, June 16, 1974; children: Stacy Ilana, Mark Jay, Daniel Jordan. BA with honors, U. Del., 1972; JD with honors, U. Md., 1975. Bar: Pa. 1975, U.S. Dist. Ct. (ea. dist.) Pa. 1975, U.S. Ct. Appeals (3d and 6th cirs.) 1975. Assoc. Dilworth, Paxson, Kalish, Levy & Kauffman, Phila., 1975-77, Berger & Montague, P.C., Phila., 1977-81; ptnr. Mesirov, Gelman, Jaffe, Cramer & Jamieson, Phila., 1981-91, Buchanan Ingersoll, P.C., Phila., 1991-99, Wolf, Block, Schorr & Solis-Cohen, 1999—; instr. Inst. for Paralegal Tng., Phila., 1977-96. Fin. com. Dem. City Com. Phila., 1981-84, dep. counsel, 1980-84; chmn. bd. Bldg. Stds. City of Phila., 1983-84, bd. licenses and inspections rev., 1984-91; mem. City Planning Commn., Phila., 1992-97, Presdl. Transition Team, 1992-93; commr. Lower Merion (Pa.) Twp., 1988—, Mayors Commn. Homelessness, 1990—, Mayors Com. on Spl. Svcs. Dist., 1989—; vice-chmn. Pres. Commn. on Risk Assessment and Risk Mgmt., 1993-97; bd. dirs., pres. Randolph Ct. Assn., Phila., 1980-85; bd. dirs., v.p. South St. Neighbors Assn., Phila., 1983-87, Park Towne Pl. Tenants Assn., 1977-79; bd. dirs. Support Ctr. for Child Advs., 1983-94, Phila. Indsl. Devel. Corp.; exec. com. Ctrl. Phila. Devel. Corp., 1989—, Jewish Employment Vocat. Svcs., 1989—, Phila. 2000., Supreme Ct. of Pa. Commn. on CLE, 1999—; mng. trustee Dem. Nat. Com., 1992—. Mem. ABA, Pa. Bar Assn., Phila. Bar Assn. (exec. bd. dirs. young lawyers sect., legis. liaison com., officer various coms.), Racquet Club, Radnor Valley Country Club. Democrat. Jewish. Antitrust, Federal civil litigation. Home: 204 Daisy Ln Wynnewood PA 19096-1654 Office: Wolf Block Schorr & Solis-Cohen 1650 Arch St Fl 22 Philadelphia PA 19103-2029

**KESSLER, EDWARD J.,** lawyer; b. Fall River, Mass., June 3, 1943. BSEE, George Wash. U., 1967, JD, 1970. Bar: Va. 1970, D.C. 1978, Md. 1983, U.S. Dist. Ct. Md. 1983, U.S. Supreme Ct. 1980, U.S. Dist. Ct. (ea. dist.) Va. 1997, U.S. Dist. Ct. D.C. 1998. Assoc. Stevens, Davis, Miller & Mosher, Arlington, Va., 1970-75; ptnr. Stevens, David, Miller & Mosher, Arlington, Va., 1975-76, LeBlanc & Shur, Washington, 1976-79, LeBlanc, Nolan, Shur & Nies, Arlington, 1979-81, Saidman & Sterne, Washington, 1981-82, Saidman, Sterne & Kessler, Washington, 1982-84, Saidman, Sterne, Kessler & Goldstein, Washington, 1984-90, Sterne, Kessler, Goldstein & Fox, Washington, 1990—; adj. prof. law George Mason Univ. Sch. Law, 1996—. Contbr. articles to profl. jours. Mem. ABA, Am. Intellectual Property Law Assn (former chair Japan/U.S study com.). Patent, Trademark and copyright. Office: Sterne Kessler Goldstein & Fox 1100 New York Ave NW Washington DC 20005-3934

**KESSLER, JOAN BLUMENSTEIN,** lawyer. AB in English, U. Mich., 1967, PhD in Speech Communication, 1973; MA in Speech Communication, UCLA, 1969; JD, Loyola U., L.A., 1986. Bar: Calif. 1987. Tchr., debate coach various pub. high schs., 1967-70; instr. dept. speech Monroe C.C., Rochester, N.Y., 1970-71; instr. communication and law Loyola U., Chgo., 1976, asst. prof., 1973-76; assoc. prof. dept. speech communication Calif. State U., Northridge, 1977-83; extern Calif. Ct. Appeal, 1985-86; assoc. Frandzel and Share, Encion, Calif., 1986-90, Gold, Marks, Ring and Pepper, 1990-93; ptnr. Kessler & Kessler, A Law Corp., Century City, Calif., 1993—. Contbr. to profl. jours. Bd. dirs. San Fernando Valley unit Am. Cancer Soc., 1982-83; bd. dirs., chair long-range planning com. St. Vincent's Hosp. Found.; bd. govs. City of Hope, 1989—; mem. advancement coun. U. Mich. Grad. Sch., 1992—. General civil litigation, Contracts commercial, Bankruptcy. Office: Kessler & Kessler 2029 Century Park E Ste 1520 Los Angeles CA 90067-3002

**KESSLER, JUDD LEWIS,** lawyer; b. Newark, Apr. 10, 1938; s. Samuel W. and Ethel S. (Shapiro) K.; m. Marian Osterweis, Jan. 7, 1979 (div. 1986); m. Carol Ann Farris, Oct. 19, 1987; 1 child, Samuel Farris. AB, Oberlin Coll., 1960; LLB, Harvard U., 1963. Bar: N.J. 1963, D.C. 1972, Md. 1989, U.S. Dist. Ct. N.J., U.S. Dist. Ct. D.C., U.S. Dist. Ct. Md., U.S. Ct. Appeals (4th cir.), U.S. Supreme Ct. 1968. Assoc. Toner, Crowley, Woelper and Vanderbilt, Newark, 1963-66; asst. gen. counsel U.S. Agy. for Internat. Devel., Washington, 1966-82; ptnr., chmn. internat. bus. practice group Porter, Wright, Morris & Arthur, Washington, 1982—. Author: (with others) Legal Aspects of Exporting, 1986; contbr. articles to profl. jours. Bd. dirs. Congregation Har Shalom, Potomac, Md., 1998—. Recipient Outstanding Career Achievement award U.S. Agy for Internat. Devel. 1982; named Presdl. Appointment to Sr. Fgn. Svc., 1982. Mem. ABA, Am. Arbitration Assn. (mem. internat. panel arbitrators 1997—), Inter-Am. Bar Assn., Inter-Am. Bar Found. (pres., 1994—), Am. Soc. Internat. Law, Fed. Bar Assn. (chmn. internat. sect. 1983-87, nat. coord. Export Legal Assistance Network 1985—, Pres.'s E Excellence Export Svc. award 1997), Cosmos Club. Government contracts and claims, Private international, Public international. Office: Porter Wright Morris & Arthur 1667 K St NW Washington DC 20006-1605

**KESSLER, KEITH LEON,** lawyer; b. Seattle, July 18, 1947; s. Robert Lawrence and Priscilla Ellen (Allbee) K.; m. Lynn Elizabeth Eisen, Dec. 24, 1980; children: William Moore, Christopher Moore, Bradley Moore, Jamie Kessler. BA in Philosophy, U. Wash., 1969, JD, 1972. Bar: Wash. 1972, U.S. Dist. Ct. (we. dist.) Wash. 1973, U.S. Dist. Ct. (ea. dist. 1992); U.S. Ct. Appeals (9th cir.) 1973, U.S. Supreme Ct. 1975. Law clk. to Hon. Robert Finley Wash. Supreme Ct., Olympia, Wash., 1972-73; ptnr. Kessler, Tegland & Urmston, Seattle, 1973-75, Kessler & Urmston, Seattle, 1975-76, Kessler, Urmston & Sever, Seattle, 1976-77, Kessler & Sever, Seattle, 1977-79; assoc. Stritmatter & Stritmatter, Hoquiam, Wash., 1980-83; ptnr. Stritmatter, Kessler & McCauley, Hoquiam, Wash., 1983-93, Stritmatter Kessler, Hoquiam, Wash., 1993-97, Stritmatter, Kessler, Whelan, Withey, Hoquiam, 1997—; chmn. LAW PAC, Seattle, 1991-93. Editor: Trial Evidence, 1996, author: (with others) Motor Vehicle Accident Litigation Desk Book, 1988, 1995, 97. Pres. Kairos Ctr., Aberdeen, Wash., 1984-86; co-founder Grays Harbor Support Group; bd. dir. Wash. State Head Injury Found., Bellevue, Wash., 1993-96. Recipient Founders award Wash. State Head Injury Found., 1990, Silver award United Way, 1992; Named Trial Lawyer of the Year Wash. State Trial Lawyers, 1994. Mem. Am. Bd. Trial Advocates, (pres. Wash. chpt. 1997), Wash. State Trial Lawyers Assn. (pres. 1990-91), Damage Attys. Round Table, Wash. Trial Attys. Political Forum (chmn. 1993-95), Trial Lawyers for Public Justice (state exec. com. 1994—). Product liability, Personal injury. Office: Stritmatter Kessler Whelan Withey 413 8th St Hoquiam WA 98550-3607

**KESSLER, MARK ALLEN,** political scientist, educator; b. McKeesport, Pa., Jan. 3, 1955; s. Robert and Rae (Alpern) K.; m. Stephanie Weko, Aug. 14, 1983. BA, U. Pitts., 1977; MA, Pa. State U., 1979, PhD, 1985. Prof. politi. sci. Bates Coll., Lewiston, Maine, 1983—, chair polit. sci., 1993-97. Author: Legal Services for the Poor, 1987; co-author: The Play of Power, 1996; contbr. articles to profl. jours. NSF grantee, 1981. Mem. Am. Polit. Sci. Assn., Law and Soc. Assn., Am. Legal Studies Assn. Democrat. Jewish. Home: 241 5th St Providence RI 02906-3763 Office: Bates Coll 174 Pettingill Hall Lewiston ME 04240-6022

**KESSLER, PHILIP JOEL,** lawyer; b. Detroit, Nov. 15, 1947; s. Herbert Jerome and Mary Rita (Bloomgarden) K.; m. Ruth Ann Kessler, Dec. 22, 1968 (div. 1981); children: Herbert Jeffrey, Jennifer Ann; m. Mary Ray Brophy, Jan. 29, 1988. AB in English with distinction, U. Mich., 1969; JD, U. Calif., Berkeley, 1972. Bar: Mich. 1972, U.S. Dist. Ct. (ea. dist.) Mich. 1972, U.S. Ct. Appeals (6th cir.) 1976, U.S. Dist. Ct. (no. dist.) Tex. 1990, U.S. Tax Ct. 1990. Assoc. Butzel Long Gust Klein & Van Zile, Detroit, 1972-79; ptnr. Butzel Long Gust Klein & Van Zile, 1979-82; shareholder Butzel Long (and predecessor firms), 1982—, also bd. dirs.; legal rsch. tchg. fellow Detroit Coll. Law, 1975-77; asst. prof. law 1977-85; lectr. in field; local rules adv. com. U.S. Dist. Ct. for Ea. Dist. Mich., mem. 1991-95, chair 1994-95; life mem. Jud. Conf. U.S. Ct. Appeals for 6th Cir.; bd. dirs. The Beaumont Found., 1995-96, THAW Fund, 1995—. Mem. Founders Soc. Detroit Inst. Arts, 1988—. Fellow Am. Bar Found., Am. Coll. Trial Lawyers, Mich. Bar Found.; mem. Detroit Club, Franklin (Mich.) Hills Country Club. Avocation: golf. Federal civil litigation, General corporate, Antitrust. Home: 25612 Meadowdale St Franklin MI 48025-1101

**KESSLER, RALPH KENNETH,** lawyer, manufacturing company executive; b. N.Y.C., May 23, 1943; s. Ralph G. Kessler and Margaret Gilmore; m. Margaret McQueeney, Oct. 12, 1980; children—Daniel, Anne. BA, St. John's U., 1965, JD, 1968; LLM, NYU, 1972. Bar: N.Y., U.S. Dist. Ct. (so. and ea. dists.) N.Y., U.S. SEC. SEC trial atty. N.Y.C., 1968-72; assoc. Mudge, Rose et al., N.Y.C., 1972-76; sec., asst. gen. counsel Singer Co., Stamford, Conn., 1976-86, v.p., dep. gen. counsel, sec., 1986-88; v.p. legal affairs, sec. TI Group Inc., N.Y.C., 1988-98, sr. v.p. legal affairs, sec., 1998—. Home: 86 Mountain Ave New Rochelle NY 10804-4708 Office: TI Group Inc 375 Park Ave New York NY 10152-0002

**KESSLER, RICHARD PAUL, JR.,** lawyer; b. Latrobe, Pa., July 11, 1945; s. Richard Paul Sr. and Dorothy Henrietta (Comp) K.; m. Kathleen Jane Parker, June 17, 1973 (dec. May 11, 1996); 1 child, Grace Elizabeth. BA, Fairfield (Conn.) U., 1968; JD Emory U., 1971. Bar: Ga. 1971, U.S. Dist. Ct. (no. dist.) Ga. 1973, U.S. Ct. Appeals (5th cir.) 1974, U.S. Ct. Appeals (11th cir.) 1981, U.S. Supreme Ct. 1995. Law clk. to presiding justice U.S. Dist. Ct. (no. dist.) Ga., 1971-73; ptnr. Macey, Wilensky, Cohen, Wittner & Kessler, Atlanta, 1973—; lectr. Practising Law Inst., 1981, 83, Fin. Svc. Corp. Career Conf., Atlanta, 1986, Ga. and Ala. Insts. of Continuing Legal Edn., 1993-95; panelist Credit Union Nat. Assn., Inc. League Attys. Conf., 1980-82, 87, 88-93, ABA, 1990-91; participant Nat. Conf. Commrs. on Uniform State Laws Drafting Com. on U.C.C. Articles, 3, 4, 4A, 1985-90; chair corp. and banking law sect. State Bar Ga., 1995-96. Author: What You Should Know About the New Bankruptcy Code, 1979, Guide To the Bankruptcy Laws: The Bankruptcy Reform Act of 1978, 1979, Guide to the Bankruptcy Laws: The Bankruptcy Reform Act of 1978 (Bankruptcy Code) as Amended by the Bankruptcy Amendments and Federal Judgeship Act of 1984, The Bankruptcy Judges, U.S. Trustees and Family Farmer Bankruptcy Act of 1986; contbr. articles to profl. jours. Banking, Bankruptcy, Consumer commercial. Office: Ste 600 285 Peachtree Center Ave NE Atlanta GA 30303-1234

**KESSLER, STEVEN FISHER,** lawyer; b. McKeesport, Pa., June 29, 1951; s. Robert and Rae (Alpern) K.; m. Susan Joyce Pearlstein, June 3, 1979; children: Matthew, Katie. BA, U. Pitts., 1973, JD, 1976. Bar: Pa. 1976, U.S. Dist. Ct. (we. dist.) Pa. 1976. Staff atty. Neighborhood Legal Services, McKeesport, Pa., 1976-79; solicitor City of McKeesport, 1980-82; sole practice, McKeesport, 1982—; solicitor McKeesport Housing Corp., 1985—; chmn. bd. dirs. McKeesport Devel. Corp., 1984—. Mem. Am. Arbitration Assn. (panel arbitrators 1981—). Democrat. General practice, Probate, Personal injury. Home: 1337 Foxwood Dr Monroeville PA 15146-4436 Office: 332 5th Ave Mc Keesport PA 15132-2616

**KESSLER, SUSAN D.,** lawyer; b. Quantico, Va., Dec. 30, 1961; d. James and Kathryn Kessler; m. Jeffrey Gold, Jan. 6, 1995; 1 child, Vincent Kessler Gold. BA, Ind. U., Bloomington, 1984; student, U. Seville, Spain, 1984; JD, Ind. U., Indpls., 1987; Advanced Law Degree, McGeorge Sch. Law, Salzburg, Austria, 1987. Bar: Ind. 1987. Counsel Philips Petroleum Co., London, 1987-88, Thomson Consumer Electronics, S.A., Paris, 1989-92, Thomson Consumer Electronics, Inc., Indpls., 1992—. Mem. ABA, Ind. Bar Assn., Internat. Women's Soc. Avocations: bicycling, running. Environmental, Contracts commercial, Private international. Office: Thomson Consumer Electronics 10330 N Meridian St Indianapolis IN 46290-1024

**KESSLER, TODD LANCE,** lawyer, consultant; b. N.Y.C., May 26, 1966; s. Arthur Wayne Kessler and Judith Arlene Connolly; m. Regalena Grace Melrose, Dec. 16, 1995. BS in Entrepreneurship, U. Colo., 1988; JD, Thomas Jefferson Sch. Law, 1992; MBA, Chapman U., 1998. Bar: Calif. 1992, U.S. Dist. Ct. (no., so. and ctrl. dists.) Calif. 1992. Advocate Homeless Advocacy Project, San Francisco, 1992-94; chief counsel AKI, Inc., Las Vegas, Nev., 1995-96; atty. Williams & Gilmore, La Jolla, Calif., 1994-95, Ford, Walker, Haggerty & Behar, Long Beach, Calif., 1996-98, Wood, Smith, Henning & Berman, L.A., 1998-99; mediator Constrn. Mediation Only, L.A., 1999—; chief counsel Urban Youth Coalition, 1994—, bd. dirs. Vol. Big Bros. of Am., L.A., 1997—; settlement officer Long Beach Superior Ct., 1998. Mem. ABA, Def. Rsch. Inst., Assn. So. Calif. Def. Counsel. Avocation: sailing. Federal civil litigation, State civil litigation, Construction.

**KEST, JOHN MARSHALL,** lawyer; b. N.Y.C., June 24, 1948; s. Lloyd H. and Doris (McIlwraith) K.; m. Sally Dee Millward, Nov. 24, 1973; children: Kristopher John, Michael Millward, Danielle McIlwraith. BA, Rollins Coll., Winter Park, Fla., 1970; JD, Fla. State U., 1972. Bar: Fla. 1973, U.S. Dist. Ct. (mid. dist.) Fla. 1973, N.Y. 1981. Ptnr. Wooten, Honeywell and Kest, P.A., Orlando, Fla., 1973—. Mem. Aviation Rev. Bd., Orlando; mem. Solicitation Rev. bd., Orlando, 1984. Recipient Acad. Fla. Trial Lawyers Pres.'s award Outstanding Pro Bono Svc., 1989. Mem. ABA, ATLA, Fla. Bar Assn. (bd. cert. civil trial lawyer 1986, 91, 96, chmn. workers' compensation com. 1978—, pres.'s award for pro bono svc. 9th jud. cir. 1996, bd. govs. 1997—), Orange County Bar Assn. (editor-in-chief jour. 1984, v.p., pres.-elect 1990-91, pres. 1991-92, pres. assn. ednl. fund 1991-92, pres. legal aid soc. 1992-93, Guardian ad Litem of Yr. 1989, recipient William E. Trickel Professionalism award 1997), Acad. Fla. Trial Lawyers (chmn. workers' compensation com. 1979—, pres.'s award for outstanding pro bono svc.), Nat. Bd. Trial Advocacy (bd. cert.), Am. Bd. Trial Advs. (pres. 1999), Rotary (past pres. Orlando chpt.), Fla. State U. Coll. Law Alumni Assn. (pres. 1998-99). Democrat. Presbyterian. Personal injury. Home: 1400 Lancaster Dr Orlando FL 32806-2321 Office: Wooten Honeywell & Kest PA 236 S Lucerne Cir Orlando FL 32801-4499

**KESTEN, LINDA ANN,** lawyer; b. Waterbury, Conn.; d. Abraham and Bina K. BA, Tufts U.; JD, U. Conn., 1989. Bar: Conn. 1989, U.S. Dist. Ct. Conn. 1990. Law clerk Attorney Gen. State of Conn., Hartford, 1988-90; assoc. Appleton & Appleton, Hartford, 1990—. Vol. The Law Works for People, Hartford, 1990—. Personal injury, General civil litigation, Family and matrimonial. Office: Appleton & Appleton 100 Pearl St Ste 1210 Hartford CT 06103-4506

**KESTENBAUM, HAROLD LEE,** lawyer; b. Bronx, N.Y., Sept. 27, 1949; s. Murray Louis and Yetta (Weiner) K.; m. Felice Gail Kravit, Aug. 11, 1973; children: Michelle, Benjamin. BA, Queens Coll., 1971; JD, U. Richmond, 1975. Bar: N.Y. 1976, N.J. 1977, U.S. Dist. Ct. (so. and ea. dist.) N.Y. Assoc. Wayne and Reiss, N.Y.C., 1975-76, Natanson, Reich and Barrison, N.Y.C., 1976-77, Goldstein and Axelrod, N.Y.C., 1977-81; pvt. practice N.Y.C. and L.I., 1981—; chmn. of the bd. Franchise It Corp., Bohemia, N.Y., 1984-89; pres., chief exec. officer Mr. Sign Franchising Corp., 1987-89; bd. dirs. Sbarro Inc., Travel Network Ltd.; cons. in field. Mem. ABA, N.Y. Bar Assn., N.J. Bar Assn., Nassau County Bar Assn. Republican. Jewish. Avocations: softball, weight training. Franchising, General corporate, Real property. Office: 585 Stewart Ave Ste 700 Garden City NY 11530-4785

**KESTER, CHARLES MELVIN,** lawyer; b. Batesville, Ark., Jan. 19, 1968; s. Monty Charles and Phyllis Smith Kester; m. Cheryl Goodwin, June 1, 1991. BA in Philosophy summa cum laude, Liberty U., 1991; JD magna cum laude, Georgetown U., 1994. Bar: Ark. 1994, U.S. Dist. Ct. (ea. and we. dists.) Ark. 1995, U.S. Ct. Appeals (8th cir.) 1995, U.S. Supreme Ct. 1998. Law clk. U.S. Ct. Appeals 8th Cir., Fargo, N.D., 1994-95; atty. Lingle Law Firm, Rogers, Ark., 1995-96; pvt. practice law Fayetteville, Ark., 1996—. Editor Georgetown Law Jour., 1993-94; contbr. articles to profl. jours. Mem. Ark. Bar Assn. (appellate practice com. 1997-99, young lawyers sect. adv. coun. 1998-99), Ark. Trial Lawyers Assn. (amicus curiae com. 1997-99), Phi Alpha Delta. Avocations: camping, rock climbing, spelunking. Appellate, Civil rights, Criminal. Home: 13602 White Oak Ln Fayetteville AR 72704-8312 Office: 1160 N College Ave Ste 1 Fayetteville AR 72703-1907

**KETCHAM, RICHARD SCOTT,** lawyer; b. Columbus, Ohio, Jan. 8, 1948; s. Victor Alvin and Dorothy Eloise (Becher) K.; m. Kim Michelle Halliburton, Apr. 7, 1984 (div. 1989); 1 child, Kate Erin; m. Christy M. Canaday, Sept. 9, 1990 (div. 1994). BS, Bowling Green (Ohio) State U., 1970; JD cum laude, Capital U., Columbus, 1974. Bar: Ohio 1974, U.S. Dist. Ct. (so. dist.) Ohio 1979. Asst. pros. atty. Franklin County (Ohio) Pros., Columbus, 1974-79; sr. asst. pros. atty. Franklin County (Ohio) Pros., 1979-84; ptnr. Ketcham & Ketcham, Columbus, 1984—; mem. task force Legal Aid Referral Project, Columbus Bar Assn. Homeless Project, 1989—. Mem. Gov.'s Task Force on Family Violence, 1984-86. Mem. Nat. Assn. Criminal Def. Lawyers, Ohio Assn. Criminal Def. Lawyers (bd. dirs. 1989—, v.p. CLE, sec.), Ctrl. Ohio Assn. Criminal Def. Lawyers (pres. 1994-95), Ohio State Bar Assn., Columbus Bar Assn. (chmn. criminal law com. 1994-95, 95-96), Franklin County Trial Lawyers. Avocations: fishing, basketball, model railroads. Criminal. Home: 1937 Elmwood Ave Columbus OH 43212-1112 Office: Ketcham & Ketcham 50 W Broad St Ste 1416 Columbus OH 43215-5932

**KETCHAND, ROBERT LEE,** lawyer; b. Shreveport, La., Jan. 30, 1948; s. Woodrow Wilson and Attie Harriet (Chandler) K.; m. Alice Sue Adams, May 31, 1969; children: Peter Leland, Marjory Attie. BA, Baylor U., 1970; JD, Harvard U., 1973. Bar: Tex. 1973, Mass. 1973, D.C. 1981. Assoc., ptnr. Butler & Binion, Houston, 1976-85, Washington, 1981-82; shareholder Brodsky & Ketchand, Houston, 1985-88; ptnr. Webster & Sheffield, Houston, 1988-90; atty. pvt. practice, Houston, 1990-92; ptnr. Short & Ketchand, Houston, 1992—; founder, chmn. bd. dirs. Rolling Waters, d/b/a Houston Legal Clinic. Pres. Prisoner Svcs. Com. Houston, 1986; deacon South Houston Bapt. Ch., 1976—; gen. counsel, dir. Houston Met. Ministries, 1986-88; dir. Interfaith Ministries Greater Houston, 1996-98; gen. counsel Houston Bus. Roundtable, 1988—. Lt. USNR, 1973-76. Mem. ABA, Tex. Bar Assn., Houston Bar Assn. (chmn. dispute com. 1989-90). Avocations: reading, family. Federal civil litigation, General civil litigation, State civil litigation. Home: 2707 Carolina Way Houston TX 77005-3423 Office: Short & Ketchand 11 E Greenway Plz Ste 1520 Houston TX 77046-1194

**KETTERER, ANDREW,** state attorney general; b. Trenton, N.J., Jan. 17, 1949; s. Frederic and Loretta (Mehan) K.; m. Susanne Powell, 1978; 1 child, Andrew Powell. BA magna cum laude, Conn. Coll., 1971; JD, Northeastern U., 1974. Former mem. Maine Ho. of Reps.; atty. gen. State of Maine, 1995—. Chmn. Madison Dem. Town Com., Maine, 1980—; del. Somerset County Dem. Com., 1980—, Dem. State Conv., 1980-82; dir., vice chmn. Norridgewock Indsl. Com., 1982; dir. Ctrl. Maine Airport Authority, 1982—; sec., treas. Youth & Family Svcs., Skowhegan, Maine, 1980. Mem. ABA, ATLA, Maine Bar Assn., Somerset County Bar Assn., Norridgecock C. of C. (pres. 1982-83), Elks. Home: 10 Laney Rd Skowhegan ME 04976-9400 Office: Office of Atty General 6 State House Sta Augusta ME 04333-0006

**KEY, SUSAN MONDIK,** lawyer; b. Washington, Pa., Jan. 28, 1964; d. George H. and Donna T. Mondik; m. Abraham L. Key III, Sept. 9, 1989; children: Casey E., Lincoln. BA in English, Washington and Jefferson Coll., 1986, BA in Econs., 1986; JD, U. Pitts., 1989. Lawyer Phillips, Fladowski & McClosey, P.C., Washington, 1990-93, Smider & Watson P.C., Washington, 1993-96, Peacock Keller Ecker & Crothers LLP, Washington, 1996—. Mem. Washington County Bar Assn. (treas. 1994-95, pres. young lwyers divsn. 1998-99), Pa. Bar Assn. (ho. of dels. 1998, young lawyers divsn. zone chair 1998). Estate planning, Probate, General practice. Office: Peacock Keller Ecker & Crothers LLP 70 E Beau St Washington PA 15301-4714

**KEYES, ALLEN E.,** retired judge; b. Marlette, Mich., Feb. 22, 1926; s. Elmer James and Myra Blanche Keyes; m. Roma Janice Turner, Feb. 23, 1952; children: Janice, Barbara, Cheryl, David. AB, Wayne State U., 1951, JD, 1956. Bar: Mich. 1956. Claims adjuster Mich. Mut. Liability Co., Detroit, 1953-55, State Farm Ins., Detroit, 1955-57; sole practitioner gen. law practice, Marlette, 1957-58, 68-75; pros. atty. Sanilac County, Sandusky, Mich., 1958-68; cir. ct. judge State of Mich., Sandusky, 1975-90; mediator St. Clair, Sanilac and Huron Counties, 1990—. Bd. dirs. United Way, Sandusky, 1961-63, Marlette Comty. Hosp., 1968-75. 1st lt. USAF, 1951-53. Recipient Silver Anniversary award Wayne State U., 1981. Mem. Port Huron Golf Club, Mich. Sr. Golf Assn. Avocations: golf, bowling. Home: 3920 Jack Pine Ln Port Huron MI 48060-1578

**KEYKO, DAVID ANDREW,** judge; b. Camden, N.J., Nov. 2, 1946; s. Alexander and Josephine Rosemarie (Bello) K.; m. Carole Anne Cummings, June 29, 1969 (div.). Student, Am. U., 1967; BA, Drew U., 1968; JD, U. Tex., 1971. Bar: N.J. 1971, U.S. Ct. Appeals (3d cir.) 1972, (fed. cir.) 1986, (D.C. cir.) 1987, U.S. Supreme Ct. 1975, U.S. Ct. Mil. Appeals, 1986, U.S. Ct. Claims, 1986, U.S. Tax Ct., 1987. Law sec. Superior Ct. N.J., 1971-72; assoc. Jeffrey Albertson, Pitman, N.J., 1972-73; ptnr. Tomlin, Tomlin & Keyko, Haddonfield, N.J., 1973-75; sr. atty. Keyko & Walker, P.A., West Deptford, N.J., 1975-83; mcpl. judge Winslow Twp., 1982-92, Swedesboro Borough, Gluocester City, Woodbury Heights, Paulsboro, West Deptford, Greenwich Twp., Newfield, Mt. Ephram, Laurel Springs, Elk Twp., National Park, Collingswood, East Greenwich, 1980—; acting mcpl. judge City Camden, 1980—, Franklin Twp., 1976-89, Cherry Hill, 1979—, Berlin Boro, 1980; presiding judge Mcpl. Cts. Camden County, 1986—; adj. prof. Gloucester County Coll., 1978-79; solicitor Woodbury Bd. Health, 1975-78; chmn. dist. fee and ethic com. N.J. Supreme Ct., 1977-80, com. mcpl. judges edn., 1983—, task force on mcpl. ct. improvement, 1983-85, ct. com. on mcpl. Cts., 1983-84. Author: Municipal Court Practice, 1989; contbr. articles to profl. jours. Of counsel Big Bros./Big Sisters of Camden County; mem. implementation com. Gloucester County Family Ct., 1975-76; state legal counsel N.J. Jaycees, 1977-79. Recipient Outstanding Young Lawyer award N.J. Bar, 1983, Peter J. Devine award Camden County Bar, 1982, One of Five Outstanding Young Men N.J., N.J. Jaycees, 1978. Mem. ABA, Nat. Conf. Spl. Ct. Judges, Am. Judges Assn., Am. Judicature Soc., Gloucester County Bar Assn. (past v.p., sec.), Camden County Mcpl. Judges Assn. (pres. 1982-84), Gloucester County Mcpl. Judges Assn. (pres. 1987-89), Am. Acad. Matrimonial Lawyers (charter fellow). Democrat. Roman Catholic.

**KEYS, ROBERT BARR, JR.,** lawyer; b. Trenton, N.J.; s. Robert B. and Evelyn L. K. BA cum laude, Dickinson Coll., 1975, JD, 1978. Bar: Pa. 1978. Assoc. Edward Miller, Esq., Lebanon, Pa., 1978-81; ptnr. Rowe, Enck & Keys, Lebanon, 1982-85; pvt. practice Lebanon, 1985-91; ptnr. Keys and Burkett, Lebanon, 1992—; asst. pub. defender Lebanon County, 1981-82; spl. master in divorce Ct. Common Pleas Lebanon County, 1986—; child law guardian Ct. Common Pleas Lebanon County, 1987-95;. Spl. dep. atty. gen. Commonwealth of Pa., 1993-94; twp. supr. North Cornwall Twp. Lebanon County, 1996, 98; bd. dirs. Internat. Assn. Sports Museums & Halls of Fame, 1998—; gen. counsel Pa. Sports Hall of Fame, 1982—. Mem. Lebanon County Bar Assn. (fee dispute chmn. 1990-98, Clarke Seltzer award 1987, 89). Family and matrimonial, Criminal, Personal injury. Office: Keys and Burkett 250 S 8th St Lebanon PA 17042-6010

**KHALIL, MONA ALI,** lawyer; b. Dhahran, Saudi Arabia, July 25, 1966; d. Ali and Sa'ada (Daoud) K. AB, Harvard U., 1987, AM, 1988; MS in Fgn. Svc., Georgetown U., 1992, JD, 1992. Bar: N.Y. 1993. Legal counsel Saudi Arabian Oil Co. (Saudi Aramco), Dhahran, 1992-93; legal officer UN, N.Y.C., 1993—. Moslem. Avocations: philosophy, diving, billiards, dancing. Office: UN Office of the Legal Counsel S-3420 New York NY 10017

**KHAN, LORI JEAN,** lawyer; b. Hackensack, N.J., Jan. 28, 1959; d. Ronald Malcolm and Patricia Ruth (Jewell) Meyer; m. Arfan M. Khan, Nov. 9, 1980; children: Amanda, Matthew. BS in Fin. summa cum laude, U. New Orleans, 1990; JD summa cum laude, Tulane U., 1994. Bar: Tex. 1995, La. 1997. Asst. buyer Margay Lindsey, N.Y.C., 1978-80; collection mgr. Weiss Jewelers, Morgantown, W.Va., 1982; payroll supr. Metro Properties, Inc., College Station, Tex., 1983-84; mgr. Charlie, College Station, 1984, Casual Corner, College Station, 1985; extern U.S. Dist. Ct. (ea. dist.) La., New Orleans, 1993-94; jud. clk. La. Supreme Ct., New Orleans, 1994-95; assoc. Jackson Walker, L.L.P., Houston, 1995-96, Lanier Yeates, P.C., Houston, 1996—. Mem. Houston Bar Assn., Women's Energy Network, Order of Coif, Omicron Delta Kappa. Roman Catholic. Avocations: reading, gardening, travel. Oil, gas, and mineral, General corporate. Office: Lanier Yeates PC 1100 Louisiana St Ste 2925 Houston TX 77002-5214

**KHOREY, DAVID EUGENE,** lawyer; b. Pitts., Oct. 5, 1959; s. Eugene George and Margaret (Yanyo) K.; m. Jennifer Ann Robinson, Dec. 29, 1983; children: Christopher David, Katherine Ann, Joanna Dale. BA with honors, U. Notre Dame, 1981; JD, Vanderbilt U., 1984. Bar: Mich. 1984, U.S. Dist. Ct. (we. dist.) Mich. 1984, U.S. Ct. Appeals 1989, U.S. Dist. Ct. (ea. dist.) Mich. 1990. Assoc. Varnum, Riddering, Schmidt & Howlett, Grand Rapids, Mich., 1984-89, ptnr., 1989—; instr. seminars Mich. Inst. of Continuing Legal Edn., Nat. Bus. Inst., Stetson Coll., NACUA Conf. Co-author: Developing Labor Law; mem. editl. bd. State Bar Mich. Mem. ABA (labor sect., com. devels. law under the nat. labor rels. act), Indsl. Rels. Rsch. Assn. (chpt. sec. 1995-97). Labor. Office: Varnum Riddering Schmidt & Howlett PO Box 352 Bridgewater Pl Grand Rapids MI 49501-0352

**KIBLER, RHODA SMITH,** lawyer; b. Gainesville, Fla., Mar. 10, 1947; d. Chesterfield and Vivian Lee (Parker) Smith; children: John Vincent Cannon, Parker Smith Cannon. BA, Skidmore Coll., 1972; JD cum laude, Fla. State Univ., 1982. Bar: Fla. 1982. Research asst. to U.S. Senator, Washington, 1967-68; lobbyist Colo. Civil Rights Commn., Denver, 1974-75; intern Fla. Commn. on Human Relations, Tallahassee, 1981-82; atty. Office of Gen. Counsel Dept. Ins., Tallahassee, 1982-84, hosp. cost containment spl. counsel, 1984-86; ptnr. Kibler & Renard, Tallahassee, 1984-86, Ervin, Varn, Jacobs, Odom & Kitchen, Tallahassee, 1986-88; chmn. Global Enterprises, 1988—; del. S.E. U.S. Japan Assn., S.E. U.S. Korea Assn.; del. leader CIS, Republic of Argentina, People's Republic of China; adv. Internat. Telecom. Tenders (privatizations) Econ. Summit; legis. counsel Fla. Assn. HMO's, 1986-87, Fla. Council Internat. Bus. Devel.; vice chmn. HMO Rules Adv. Task Force, Health Policy Council; mem. Ins. Commr's. Task Force on Discrimination in Ins., Tallahassee, 1983-85, Task Force on Elimination of Discrimination in Statutes, Tallahassee, 1984-85; adv. Internat. Govt. Housing, privatization. Vice chmn. U.S. Constitutional Bicentennial Commn. Fla., 1986, 92; mem. exec. com. Statute of Liberty-Ellis Island Centennial Commn., Fla., 1983-86; mem. trade and investment missions to Far East; bd. dirs. Anti-Recidivism Ctr., Denver, 1973-75, United Way Tallahassee, 1985-87, Capital Women's Network, Tallahassee, 1982-86, Big Bend Bus. Exchange; mem. LeMoyne Art Found., Tallahassee, 1984—; state chmn. Overseas Edn. Fund Women, Law, and Devel., 1984-85; mem. S.E. Regional Conf. on Constl. System. Fellow Am. Bar Found.; mem. Am. Judicature Soc., Nat. Inst. Trial Advocacy (diplomate), ABA (mem. sect. adminstrv. law, individual rights and responsibilities, taxation, ins. coms., forum com. internat. health law), Fla. Bar Assn. (chair com. individual rights and responsibilities 1986-87, chair ins. com. 1986, legis. com. Young Lawyers 1984, health law com., internat. law sect., jud. evaluation com. 1984, long-range planning com. 1987—, mem. spl. com. on gen. assembly 1988-89, spl. com. on ho. of dels. 1989—), Tallahassee Bar Assn., Fla. Assn. Hosp. Attys., Fla. Hosp. Assn., LWV, Tallahassee Assn. Women Lawyers, Tallahassee C. of C. (trustee's com. of 100, bd. regents Leadership Tallahassee, legis. affairs), Fla. C. of C. (steering com. internat. bus.), Fla. Women's Network (chair jud. appts. com. 1984-87). Clubs: Capital Tiger Bay, Gov.'s Fla. Econs. (Tallahassee), International. Finance, Administrative and regulatory, Legislative.

**KIBLINGER, CINDY JO,** lawyer; b. Lynchburg, Va., July 27, 1972; d. Robert William Sr. and Susan Jane Kiblinger. BA, Vanderbilt U., 1994; JD, W.Va. U., 1997. Bar: W.Va. 1997, U.S. Dist. Ct. (so. dist.) W.Va. 1997, D.C. 1998. Assoc. James Humphreys & Assocs., L.C., Charleston, W.Va., 1997—. Mem. ATLA, W.Va. Trial Lawyers. E-mail: cjk jfhlaw@aol.com. State civil litigation, Product liability, Personal injury. Home: 304 Saddle Horn Rd Charleston WV 25314-2416 Office: James Humphreys & Assocs LC 707 Virginia St E Charleston WV 25301-2702

**KIDD, JOHN EDWARD,** lawyer, corporate executive; b. Jan. 17, 1936; s. Edward F. and Mary (Feczko) K.; m. Elaine Mitchell, Feb. 23, 1963; children: John Mitchell, David Alan, Cynthia Lorraine. BS in Physics, LeMoyne Coll., 1957; LLB, Georgetown U., 1961. Bar: Va. 1961, U.S. Supreme Ct. 1966, U.S. Tax Ct. 1966, N.Y. 1968, U.S. Ct. Appeals (2d cir.) 1968, U.S. Ct. Appeals (4th cir.) 1968, U.S. Dist. Ct. (so. and ea. dists.) N.Y. 1969, U.S. Dist. Ct. (no. dist.) Calif. 1980, U.S. Ct. Appeals (3d, 5th, 9th, and 11th cirs.) 1981, U.S. Dist. Ct. (ea. dist.) Va. 1993. Patent examiner U.S. Patent Office, Washington, 1957-60; patent advisor USN, Washington, 1960-62; trial atty. Dept. Justice, Washington, 1963-67; counsel to Copyright Office, Washington, 1966-67; spl. counsel Dept. Justice, 1967; assoc. Kenyon & Kenyon, N.Y.C., 1967-70; assoc., ptnr. Pennie & Edmonds, N.Y.C., 1971-85, Anderson, Kill, Olick & Oshinsky, P.C., 1986-91; ptnr. Shea & Gould, 1991-94; sr. ptnr. Rogers & Wells, 1994-99, exec. com., chmn. intellectual property and tech. group, 1996-99; counsel Baseball Hall of Fame, 1995—; referee 9th Jud. Dept. N.Y. Supreme Ct., 1968-69; exec., chmn. bd. E.M. Kidd, Ltd.; chmn. Symposium on Presdl. Patent Reform Commn., 1966; lectr., mem. faculty Practicing Law Inst., 1967, 84-96; mem. Bicentennial Commn. U.S. Claims Ct., 1987-89; guest lectr. Inventor Hall of Fame, 1996-98. Contbr. writings to legal jours. Active United Fund of Westchester, Comty. Fund of Bronxville, Westchester coun. Boy Scouts Am.; trustee LeMoyne Coll. Alumni. Mem. ABA (lectr. 1984-94), ATLA, Am. Intellectual Property Assn., U.S. Trademark Assn., Copyright Soc. Am., N.Y. State Bar Assn. (chmn. spl. com. on patents and trademarks 1982-86), Fed. Cir. Bar Assn., N.Y. Intellectual Property Assn., N.Y. Patent, Licensing Exec. Soc., Assn. of Bar of City of N.Y., Mahopac Country Club, Yale Club, Sky Club, Rockefeller Club, Delta Theta Phi. Federal civil litigation, Patent, Trademark and copyright. Office: Rogers & Wells LLP 200 Park Ave Fl 8E New York NY 10166-0800

**KIDD, PAMELA SUE,** paralegal, private investigator; b. Cleve., June 25, 1960; d. Harold Mathew and Corrine Ann (Miller) K. AS in Sci., So. Coll., Orlando, Fla., 1993; student, Valencia C.C., Orlando, Fla., 1998—. Care taker Home Health Care, Medina, Ohio, Ukiah, Calif., 1976-79; activities coord. Soc. for Handicapped Citizens, Medina, Ohio, 1979-85; photographer Medina, Ohio, Orlando, Fla., 1988-93; asst. to ptnr., paralegal Drage, DeBeaubein, Knight & Simmons, P.A., Orlando, 1991-94; paralegal Jerry H. Jeffrey, P.A., Maitland, Fla., 1995-96; investigator, paralegal Andrews Agy., Orlando, Fla., 1996—, Claims Investigation Agy., Ft. Lauderdale, Fla., 1996—. Vol. Medina County Blood Mobile, Mental Health Drop-In Ctr., Meals on Wheels; Baby DJ Fund fundraiser. Mem. Nat. Assn. Legal Assistants, Fla. Legal Assn., Inc., Pvt. Investigators Assn. Fla., So. Coll. Alumni Com. (pres., v.p.), Greater Orlando Bus. Networking. Avocations: horses, boating, travel, sports, photography. Home: 6341 Edge O Grove Cir Orlando FL 32819-4161 Office: Andrews Agy Inc PO Box 3445 Orlando FL 32802-3445

**KIDDER, FRED DOCKSTATER,** lawyer; b. Cleve., May 22, 1922; s. Howard Lorin and Virgina (Milligan) K.; m. Eleanor (Hap) Kidder; children—Fred D. III, Barbara Anne Donelson, Jeanne Kidder-Appleton. BS with distinction, U. Akron, 1948; JD, Case Western Res. U., 1950. Bar: Ohio 1950, Tex. 1985, U.S. Dist. Ct. (no. dist.) Ohio 1950, U.S. Dist. Ct. (no. dist.) Tex. 1985. Assoc. Arter & Hadden and predecessors, Cleve., 1950-79, ptnr., 1960-79; ptnr. Jones, Day, Reavis and Pogue, Cleve., 1980-89, regional mng. ptnr. Tex., 1985-86; gen. counsel Lubrizol Corp., Cleve., 1989-92, spl. counsel, 1993—. Contbr. articles to profl. jours. Mem. Cleve. Growth Assn., Shaker Heights Citizens Com., Citizens League Cleve.; former pres. Estate Planning Coun.; co-chmn. bd. trustees Lake Erie Coll.; bd. trustees, v.p., Alzheimer's Assn., Cleve.; mem., bd. trustees Cleve. Sight Ctr.; past mem. alumni coun. U. Akron; past. corp. coun. Dallas Mus. Art; past pres. Case Western Reserve U. Law Sch. Alumni Assn.; past chmn. Shaker Heights Recreation Bd. Mem. ABA, Nat. Assn. Corp. Secs., Tex. Bar Assn., Ohio State Bar Assn., State Troopers Ohio (past sec.), Cleve. Bar Assn., Estate Planning Coun. (past pres.), Blue Coats, Soc. Benchers (past chmn.), Tax Club Cleve. (past pres.), Union Club, Pepper Pike Club (sec.), Country Club Cleve., Skating Club, Order of Coif, Ct. of Nisi Prius (former judge), Phi Eta Sigma, Beta Delta Psi, Phi Sigma Alpha, Phi Delta Theta, Phi Delta Phi. General corporate, Mergers and acquisitions, Securities. Office: The Lubrizol Corp 29400 Lakeland Blvd Wickliffe OH 44092-2298

**KIDDOO, JEAN LYNN,** lawyer; b. White Plains, N.Y., Apr. 30, 1953; d. Richard C. and Catherine (Schumann) K.; m. Timothy James Cooney, Aug. 20, 1988. BA, Colgate U., 1975; JD, Cath. U., Washington, 1980. Bar: D.C. 1980, U.S. Dist. Ct. D.C. 1981, U.S. Ct. Appeals (D.C. cir.) 1981, U.S. Supreme Ct. 1984, U.S. Ct. Appeals (2d cir.) 1995, U.S. Ct. Appeals (5th cir.) 1997. Assoc. Bergson, Borkland, Margolis & Adler, Washington, 1980-82, McKenna, Wilkinson & Kittner, Washington, 1982-85, Pepper, Hamilton & Scheetz, Washington, 1985-88; ptnr. Swidler Shereff Berlin & Friedman, LLP, Washington, 1988—. Mem. Fed. Comms. Bar Assn. (pres. 1999—). Administrative and regulatory, Communications, Public utilities. Office: Swidler Shereff Berlin & Friedman LLP 3000 K St NW Fl 3 Washington DC 20007-5109

**KIDWELL, WAYNE L.,** judge; b. Council, Idaho, 1938; m. Shari Linn; children: Vaughn, Blair. BA, U. Idaho, JD. Bar: Idaho 1964, Hawaii, former U.S. Trust Territories. Past atty. law firms, Idaho and Hawaii; past pvt. practice Idaho and Hawaii; past atty. gen. State of Idaho; past majority leader Idaho Ho. of Reps.; past prosecuting atty. Ada County, Idaho; past assoc. dep. atty. gen. Pres. Reagan adminstrn., past liason Dept. Justice U.S. Govt.; past atty. gen. Republic of Marshall Islands; judge Idaho Supreme Ct. Photographer pvt. shows; one-man shows include galleries in Hawaii. Active numerous civic and profl. orgns. Served USMCR, U.S. Army Mil. Police Corps. Office: Idaho Supreme Ct Supreme Ct Bldg PO Box 83720 Boise ID 83720-3720*

**KIEF, PAUL ALLAN,** lawyer; b. Montevideo, Minn., Mar. 22, 1934; s. Paul G. and Minna S. K. BA, U. Minn., 1957, LLB, 1957. Bar: Minn. 1957, U.S. Dist. Ct. Minn. 1964, U.S. Tax Ct. 1968, U.S. Supreme Ct. 1981; cert. criminal trial law specialist Nat. Bd. Trial Advocacy. Gen. practice Bemidji, Minn., 1959—; ptnr. Kief, Fuller, Baer & Wallner, Ltd., Bemidji, Minn., 1973-97; owner Paul A. Kief Law Firm, Bemidji, Minn., 1998—; pub. defender 9th Jud. Dist. Minn., Bemidji, Minn., 1966-98; pub. defender 9th Jud. Dist. Minn., 1966—, chief pub. defender, 1968-94; vol. atty. Minn. Civil Liberties Union; panel atty. Legal Svcs. Northwest Minn. Vice chmn. Beltrami County Planning Commn., 1964-68; chmn. adv. com. Gov.'s Crime Commn., 1971-77; mem. Minn. Task Force on Standards and Goals in Criminal Justice, 1975-76, Crime Victims Task Force, 1985, Jud. Selection Com., 1987, Com. on Criminal Jury Instrn. Guides, 1988-90; bd. dirs. Legal Svcs. Northwest Minn., 1990-96; capt. CAP, 1969—. Served with USAR, USNG, 1958-64. Mem. ABA, ATLA, NACDL, NAt. Bd. Trial Advocacy (cert. crim. law trial specialist 1998), Minn. Bar Assn., Minn. Trial Lawyers

Assn., 15th Dist. Bar Assn. (past sec.), Beltrami County Bar Assn. (past pres.), Lawyer-Pilots Bar Assn., Minn. Assn. Criminal Def. Lawyers. Democrat. Congregationalist. Club: Toastmasters. Criminal, General practice. Office: 514 America Ave NW PO Box 212 Bemidji MN 56619-0212

**KIEFER, KAREN LAVERNE,** lawyer; b. Lancaster, Ohio, Nov. 8, 1952; d. Ray E. and Marilyn L. (Keister) K. BA in Econs., Chatham Coll., 1974; MBA in Fin., George Washington U., 1977; JD in Internat. Law, U. Balt., 1982. Bar: Md. 1987, D.C. 1988, Pa. 1998. Counsel Europe, Israel and Am. Westinghouse Elec. Corp., Balt., 1974-84; mgr. Internat. Ops. Gould Inc., Washington, 1985-87; pvt. practice law Annapolis, Scottdale, Md., Pa., 1987—; founder, owner Mainsail of Annapolis Yacht Chartering, 1979—. Author: Publ. The Cormany Diaries, A Northern Family in the Civil War, 1982. Sponsor U.S. Naval Acad. Midshipmen, Annapolis 1981—91; coach Naval Acad. Sailing Squadron, 1991-97. Mem. ABA, D.C. Bar Assn., Md. Bar Assn., Pa. Bar Assn., Am. Soc. Internat. Law, Am. Mgmt. Assn., Westmoreland County Bar Assn. Avocations: swimming, sailing, music, arts. General corporate, Government contracts and claims, Private international.

**KIEFFER, JAMES MARSHALL,** lawyer; b. Buffalo, June 10, 1940; s. Elveus Francis and Marjorie (Marshall) K.; m. Judith Ann Fee, Aug. 6, 1965; children: Eric Corwin, Knight Darrow. BA, Colgate U., 1962; JD, U. Mich., 1965. Bar: N.Y. 1966, U.S. Dist. Ct. (we. dist.) N.Y. 1969, U.S. Ct. Appeals (2nd cir.) 1980, U.S. Supreme Ct. 1980. Assoc. Ohlin, Damon, Morey, Sawyer & Moot, Buffalo, 1965-72; ptnr. Damon & Morey, Buffalo, 1972-93, Feldman Kieffer and Hermann LLP, Buffalo, 1993—. Bd. dirs. People, Inc., Buffalo, 1972-79. Fellow Am. Coll. Trial Lawyers; mem. ABA, Erie County Bar Assn. (bd. dirs. 1991-94), Western N.Y. Trial Lawyers Assn. (v.p. 1999, pres. elect ), Def. Trial Lawyers Assn. of Western N.Y. (pres. 1991-92), N.Y. State Bar Assn., Def. Rsch. Inst., Buffalo Tennis and Squash Club (sec. 1982-83, 93-96). Avocations: tennis, squash, skiing. Personal injury, General civil litigation, Insurance. Home: 103 Woodbridge Ave Buffalo NY 14214-1623 Office: Feldman Kieffer Hermann LLP The Dun Bldg 110 Pearl St Buffalo NY 14202-4111

**KIEFNER, JOHN ROBERT, JR.,** lawyer, educator; b. Peoria, Ill., May 31, 1946; s. John Robert and Luna Merle (Froment) K.; m. B.C. Clayton, Feb. 14, 1989; 1 child, John William. BA, Johns Hopkins U., 1968; JD, Stetson U., 1971. Bar: Fla. 1971, U.S. Ct. Appeals (D.C. cir.) 1971, U.S. Ct. Appeals (11th cir.) 1981, U.S. Supreme Ct. 1979, U.S. Ct. Mil. Appeals 1971, U.S. Tax Ct. 1981, U.S. Dist. Ct. (no. dist.) Fla. 1971, U.S. Dist. Ct. (mid. dist.) Fla. 1981. Staff atty. SEC, Washington, 1971-74, br. chief, 1974-77, regional trial counsel, 1977-82; mem. Robbins, Gaynor, Burton, Hampp, Burns, Bronstein & Shasteen, St. Petersburg, Fla., 1982-86; ptnr. Riden , Earle & Kiefner, P.A., St. Petersburg, 1986—; adj. prof. law Stetson U., St. Petersburg, 1982—. Past chmn. Combined Fed. Campaign, 1976-77. Capt. U.S. Army, 1968-76. Recipient Cert. of Merit, SEC, 1982; Charles A. Dana scholar, 1970-71. Mem. Fla. Bar Assn., ABA, St. Petersburg Bar Assn., Fla. Acad. Trial Lawyers, Am. Trial Lawyers Assn., Pinella County Trial Lawyers Assn., Fed. Bar Assn., Nat. Assn. Colls. and Univs. (recruitment com.), St. Petersburg Area C. of C., Johns Hopkins U. Alumni Assn., Masons, Shriners. Lutheran. Administrative and regulatory, Federal civil litigation, Securities. Home: 11805 6th St E Saint Petersburg FL 33706-2918 Office: Riden Earle & Kiefner PA 100 2nd Ave S Saint Petersburg FL 33701-4360

**KIELY, DAN RAY,** lawyer, banking and real estate development executive, consultant; b. Ft. Sill, Okla., Jan. 2, 1944; s. William Robert and Leona Maxine (Ross) K.; BA in Psychology, U. Colo., 1966, JD, Stanford U., 1969; children: Jefferson Ray, Matthew Ray. Bar: Colo 1969, D.C. 1970, Va. 1973. Assoc. firm Holme, Roberts and Owen, Denver, 1969-70; pres. DeRand Equity Group, Arlington, Va., 1973-89; pres., chmn. bd. Bankwest Corp. and related banks, Denver.; pres., dir. United Gibralter Corp. Del., Inc., Unocam, Inc., 1987—; ptnr. Starlin & Kiely, P.C., 1989-94; trustee DeRand Real Estate Investment Trust, 1974—; chmn. Pace Holdings, Inc., Washington, 1988-93, Washington Capital Corp., 1989—, Surry Internat., Ltd., 1995—; speaker, lectr. in field. Deacon, McLean (Va.) Bapt. Ch., 1977-80. Served as officer, USAR, 1969-73. Decorated Legion of Merit; cert. property mgr. Mem. ABA, Nat. Bd. Realtors, Inst. Real Estate Mgmt., Nat. Assn. Rev. Appraisers, Internat. Coun. Shopping Ctrs., Nat. Assn. Real Estate Investment Trusts, D.C. Bar Assn., Va. Bar Assn., Colo. Indsl. Bankers Assn. (bd. dirs. 1985-87), The Internat. Inst (cert. valuer). Home: 67 Norwich C West Palm Beach FL 33417-7939

**KIENER, JOHN LESLIE,** judge; b. Ft. Madison, Iowa, June 21, 1940; s. Cyril Joseph and Lucille Olive (Golden) K.; m. Carol Lynn Winston, June 4, 1966; children—Susan, Gretchen. BA cum laude, Loras Coll., 1962; JD, Drake U., 1965. Bar: Iowa 1965, Tenn. 1972, U.S. Supreme Ct. 1974. Practice, Decorah, Iowa, 1965-68; asst. atty. gen. State of Iowa, 1968-72; ptnr. firm Cantor & Kiener, 1972-80; city judge Johnson City (Tenn.), 1975-80; gen. sessions judge, Johnson City, 1980—; continuing edn. tchr., bus. law East Tenn. State U., 1975—. Mem. ABA, Tenn. Bar Assn., Washington County Bar Assn. Republican. Lodges: Rotary, Elks. Avocations: stamp collecting, genealogy. Contbr. articles to profl. jours. Home: 2403 Camelot Cir Johnson City TN 37604-2938 Office: Gen Sessions Ct Downtown Ctr Courthouse 101 E Market St Ste 7 Johnson City TN 37604-5722

**KIENTZ, VAL WILLIAM,** lawyer, mediator; b. New Orleans, Nov. 15, 1953; s. Valentine William and Glenna Arline Kientz; m. Renee Louise Joseph, Feb. 27, 1974. BA magnum cum laude, Angelo State U., San Angelo, Tex., 1981; JD, U. Houston, 1986. Bar: Tex. 1986, U.S. Dist. Ct. (so. dist.) Tex. 1986, U.S. Dist. Ct. (ea. and we. dists.) Tex. 1987, U.S. Ct. Appeals (5th cir.) 1987, U.S. Dist. Ct. (no. dist.) Tex. 1989. Assoc. Law Offices Doug Cherry, Webster, Tex., 1986-88, Pezzolli and Assocs., Dallas, 1988-89, Coackly and Assocs., Dallas, 1989, S. Reed Morgan and Assocs., Houston, 1990; pvt. practice, Houston, 1990—. Precinct chmn. Tex. Dem. Com., Houston, 1995—. Sgt. USAF, 1972-76. Mem. ATLA, Tex. Trial Lawyers Assn. Avocations: Kayaking, fishing, walking. Personal injury, General civil litigation, Alternative dispute resolution. Home: 1116 Wirt Rd Houston TX 77055-6851 Office: 7413 Westview Dr Houston TX 77055-5100

**KIES, DAVID M.,** lawyer; b. N.Y.C., Jan. 25, 1944; s. Saul and Lillian (Schultz) K.; m. Emily Bardack, July 6, 1966 (div. 1985); children: Laura, Adam, Abigail; m. Anne Hayes Monteith, Oct. 7, 1990 (div. 1998); 1 child, Samuel. AB, Haverford Coll., 1965; JD, NYU, 1968. Bar: N.Y. 1968, U.S. Dist. Ct. ( so. dist.) N.Y. 1969, U.S. Ct. Appeals (2d cir.) 1969. Assoc. Sullivan & Cromwell, N.Y.C., 1968-76, ptnr., 1976—; dir. London office Sullivan & Cromwell, 1992-95; dir. Imclone Systems, Inc. Former trustee Haverford Coll. Root Tilden fellow, NYU Law Sch., 1965. Mem. ABA, N.Y. State Bar Assn., Assn. Bar City of N.Y. Democrat. Jewish. Securities, Private international, Mergers and acquisitions. Office: Sullivan & Cromwell 125 Broad St Fl 28 New York NY 10004-2489

**KIESS, STEPHEN DAVID,** lawyer; b. Saginaw, Mich., July 17, 1965; s. James David Kiess and Joyce Anne Carnahan Williams; m. Kimberly Anne Swank. BBA with distinction, U. Mich., 1988; JD, Wake Forest U., 1991. Bar: D.C. 1991. Assoc. Jones, Day, Reavis & Pogue, Washington, 1991-95; ptnr. Everett, Warren, Swindell, Kiess & Jones, Greenville, N.C., 1995—. Mem. editl. staff Wake Forest Law Rev., 1990-91; contbr. articles to law jours. Law faculty scholar Wake Forest U. Law Sch., 1989-91. Mem. N.C. Bar Assn., Pitt County Bar Assn., Pamlico Sailing Club (fleet capt. 1998-99). Episcopalian. Avocations: sailing, fishing, home improvement. General civil litigation, Health, Franchising. Home: 101 Lamont Rd Greenville NC 27858-6408 Office: Everett Warren Swindell Kiess & Jones 200 S Washington St Greenville NC 27858-1116

**KIGHTLINGER, JEFF,** lawyer; b. L.A., July 5, 1959; s. Harry J. and Diane H. K.; m. Diane H., July 30, 1983; children: Elizabeth, Harry, Desmond. BA, U. Calif., Berkeley, 1981; JD, Santa Clara U., 1985. Bar: Calif., Nev., U.S. Dist. Ct., U.S. Ct. Appeals (9th cir.). Dep. city atty. City of Pasadena, Calif., 1985-87; assoc. Knapp, Marsh, Jones & Doran, L.A., 1987-90; lawyer U.S. EPA, Washington, 1990-91; from assoc. to ptnr. Burke, Williams, & Sorenson, L.A., 1991-95; dep. gen. counsel Metro. Water Dist., L.A., 1995—. Office: Metro Water Dist 700 N Alameda St Los Angeles CA 90012-2944

**KIHLE, DONALD ARTHUR,** lawyer; b. Noonan, N.D., Apr. 4, 1934; s. J. Arthur and Linnie W. (Ljunngren) K.; m. Judith Anne, Aug. 18, 1964; children—Kevin, Kirsten, Kathryn, Kurte. B.S. in Indsl. Engring., U. N.D., 1957; J.D., U. Okla., 1967. Bar: Okla. 1967, U.S. Dist. Cts. (we. and no. dists.) Okla. 1967, U.S. Ct. Appeals (10th cir.) 1967, U.S. Supreme Ct. 1971. Asso., Huffman, Arrington, Scheurich & Kincaid, Tulsa, 1967-71, ptnr., 1971-78; shareholder, dir., officer Arrington Kihle Gaberino & Dunn, Tulsa, 1978-97, pres., 1994-97; shareholder, dir. Gable & Gotwals, Tulsa, 1997—. Dist. chmn. Boy Scouts Am., 1983-85, cubmaster, 1986-88, coun. coms., 1988—, campiree chmn., 1990; mem. Statewide Law Day Com., 1982-86, chmn., 1983-85; trustee Brandon Hall Sch., Atlanta, 1991—, chmn., 1995—. Lt. U.S. Army, 1957-59. Recipient Silver Beaver award Boy Scouts Am. Mem. ABA, Okla. Bar Assn. (chmn. constl. bicentennial com. 1986-89), Constitution 200 (exec. com. 1986-89), Tulsa County Bar Assn., So. Hills Country Club, Q Club (scribe 1991—), Tulsa Club (bd. govs. 1987-94, pres. 1992), Order of Coif, Order of Arrow (vigil), Sigma Tau, Phi Delta Phi, Sigma Chi (Tulsa alumni pres. 1995-97). Republican. General corporate, Oil, gas, and mineral, Securities. Home: 4717 S Lewis Ct Tulsa OK 74105-5135 Office: 1000 ONEOK Plz 100 W 5th St Tulsa OK 74103-4240

**KIKOLER, STEPHEN PHILIP,** lawyer; b. N.Y.C., Apr. 24, 1945; s. Sigmund and Dorothy (Javna) K.; m. Ethel Lerner, June 18, 1967; children: Jeffrey Stuart, Shari Elaine. AB, U. Mich., 1966, JD cum laude, 1969. Bar: Ill. 1969, U.S. Dist. Ct. (no. dist.) Ill. 1969, U.S. Ct. Appeals (7th cir.) 1988, U.S. Ct. Appeals (11th cir.) 1994, U.S. Ct. Mil. Appeals 1970, U.S. Supreme Ct. 1994. Assoc. Rosenthal & Schanfield, Chgo., 1969-70, 73-77, shareholder, 1977—; capt. Judge Advocate Gen.'s Corps U.S. Army, 1970-73. Mem. ABA, Am. Land Title Assn., Ill. State Bar Assn., Chgo. Bar. Assn. (real property law com., chmn. mechanics' liens subcom. 1987-89), Lake County Contractors/Devel. Assn. (chmn. com. profl. svcs. 1998—). Construction, Real property, General civil litigation. Home: 2746 Norma Ct Glenview IL 60025-4661 Office: Rosenthal & Schanfield PC 55 E Monroe St Fl 46 Chicago IL 60603-5713

**KILBANE, ANNE L.,** judge; b. Cleve., Sept. 22, 1941; d. Thomas Bryan and Nora (Coyle) K. BA in Chemistry, Seton Hill Coll., Greensburg, Pa., 1963; JD, Cleve. Marshall Coll. Law, 1977. Bar: Ohio 1977, U.S. Dist. Ct. (so. dist.) Ohio 1977, U.S. Dist. Ct. (no. dist.) Ohio 1978), U.S. Ct. Appeals (6th cir.) 1978, U.S. Supreme Ct. 1985. Sr. chemist Dept. of Health City of Cleve., 1963-66; chief brewing chemist, asst. quality control mgr. Carling Brewing Co., Cleve., 1966-71; chemist, plant mgr. Phillips Syrup Corp., Parma, Ohio, 1971-75; asst. to dir. law City of Cleve., 1975-77; assoc. Kilbane & Kilbane, Columbus, Ohio, 1977-78; assoc. Nurenberg, Plevin, Heller, Cleve., 1978-86, ptnr., 1986-99; judge Ohio Ct. of Appeals (8th dist.), Cuyahoga County, Ohio, 1999—; lectr. in field. Mem. Ohio State Bar Assn. (mem. negligence subcom.), Ohio Women's Bar Assn. (founding), Ohio Jud. Conf., Ohio Ct. Appeal Judge's Assn., Cuyahoga County Bar Assn. (appellate sect.), Cleve. Bar Assn. (appellate sect., commn. on women in the law), Nat. Lawyers Assn., 6th Cir. Jud. Conf. (life), Cleve. Marshall Alumnae Assn. (life), Am. Arbitration Assn., Am. Chem. Soc., Delta Theta Phi. Office: Cuyahoga County Ct House 1 W Lakeside Ave Cleveland OH 44113-1023

**KILBANE, THOMAS M.,** lawyer; b. Cleve., Mar. 1, 1953; s. Thomas M. and Kathleen K.; m. Helen Crowley, June 26, 1976; children: Catherine Ann, Patrick Thomas, Michael Crowley. BA magna cum laude, Xavier U., 1974; postgrad., Miami U., Ohio, 1975; JD with highest distinction, John Marshall Law Sch., 1978. Bar: Ill. 1978, Wash. 1980, U.S. Dist. Ct. (no. dist.) Ill. 1978, U.S. Dist. Ct. (we. dist.) Wash. 1980, U.S. Ct. Appeals (5th and 9th cirs.) 1981, U.S. Dist. Ct. (ea. dist.) Wash. 1992. Jud. extern U.S. Dist. Ct. Ill., Chgo., 1977; jud. clk. to presiding justice Ill. Appellate Ct., Chgo., 1978-80; assoc., shareholder Garvey, Schubert & Barer, P.C., Seattle, 1980-85, 86-89; shareholder Ater Wynne LLP, Seattle, 1990—. Editor-in-Chief John Marshall Law Rev., 1977-78. Trustee Queen Anne Cmty. Coun., Seattle, 1983-85; mem. Queen Anne Land Use Rev. Com., 1983-85; mem. branch bd. Sammamish Family YMCA, 1993-95. Chgo. Bar Found. grantee, 1978. Mem. ABA (sect. natural resources, energy, and environment), Wash. State Bar Assn. (environ. and land use law sect.), King County Bar Assn., Alpha Sigma Nu. Environmental, Mergers and acquisitions, Real property. Home: 7551 Madrona Dr NE Bainbridge Is WA 98110-2901 Office: Ater Wynne LLP 601 Union St Ste 5450 Seattle WA 98101-2327

**KILBOURN, WILLIAM DOUGLAS, JR.,** law educator; b. Colorado Springs, Colo., Dec. 9, 1924; s. William Douglas and Clara Howe (Lee) K.; m. Barbara Ruth Neff, Sept. 16, 1950; children: Jonathan VI, Katharine Ann. BA, Yale U., 1949; postgrad., Columbia U., 1949-50, LLB, 1953. Bar: Mass. 1962, Oreg. 1953, Minn. 1974. Acct. Arthur Andersen & Co., 1949-50; assoc. Davies, Biggs, Strayer, Stoel & Boley, Portland, Oreg., 1953-56; asst. prof. law U. Mont., 1956-57; assoc. prof. law U. Mo., 1957-59; prof. law, founding dir. grad. tax program Boston U., 1959-71; prof. law U. Minn., 1971-98, prof. emeritus, 1998—; dir. U. Mont. Tax Inst., 1956; of counsel Palmer & Dodge, Boston, 1964-75, Oppenheimer, Wolff & Donnelly, St. Paul and Mpls., 1980-94; mem. exec. com. Fed. Tax Inst. New Eng., 1966-72; mem. adv. com. Western New Eng. Coll. Tax Inst; vis. prof. law Duke U., 1974-75, U. Tex., 1977, Washington U., St. Louis, 1977; past ednl. advisor Tex. Execs. Inst.; lectr. in 28 states, Mex., the Caribbean, and D.C.; expert witness in field. Editor: Estate Planning and Income Taxation, 1957; contbr. articles to profl. jours. Dist. dir. United Fund, Belmont, Mass., chair fair practices com. Recipient numerous tchg. awards; Kent scholar, Stone scholar Columbia U. Law Sch. Mem. ABA (tax sect., corp. stockholder rels. com. 1962-76, chair subcom. inc. 1968-73), Boston Bar Assn. (chair tax sect. 1967-70), Boston Tax Forum, Boston Tax Coun. Avocations: tennis, botany, landscape gardening. Home: 2681 E Lake Of The Isles Pky Minneapolis MN 55408-1051

**KILBOURNE, GEORGE WILLIAM,** lawyer; b. Berea, Ky., Mar. 29, 1924; s. John Buchanan and Maud (Parsons) K.; m. Helen Spooner, Dec. 25, 1945 (div. 1968); m. Carole Marko, June 12, 1970 (div. 1984); children: Stuart (dec.), Charles; m. Anne F. Lavine, Aug. 19, 1996. Student, Berea Coll., 1941-42, Denison U., 1944; BS in Mech. Engring., U. Mich., 1946; JD, U. Calif., Berkeley, 1951. Bar: Calif. 1952, U.S. Dist. Ct. (no. dist.) Calif. 1952, Ind. 1957, U.S. Appeals (9th cir.). Sole practice Berkeley, 1952-57; assoc. Hays & Hays, Sullivan, Ind., 1957-59, Boyle & Kilbourne, Sullivan, 1961-63, Bernal, Rigney & Kilbourne, Berkeley, 1963-68, Sherbourne & Kilbourne, Pleasant Hill, Calif., 1968-75; sole practice Pleasant Hill and Martinez, Calif., 1975—; lectr. Lincoln Law Sch., San Francisco, 1956-57, John F. Kennedy Law Sch., Orinda, Calif., 1977-78. Served to 2d lt. USMC, 1942-46, PTO. Episcopalian. Lodge: Elks. Avocations: tennis, bowling, outdoors. Environmental, Personal injury, Toxic tort. Office: 661 Augusta Dr Moraga CA 94556-1035

**KILBURN, EDWIN ALLEN,** lawyer; b. Wenatchee, Wash., Apr. 5, 1933; s. Howard L. and Dorothy M. (Allen) K.; m. Penelope P. White, Feb. 7, 1964; children: Penelope Allen, Nancy Kitchen. BA with highest honors, Wash. State U., 1955; JD cum laude, NYU, 1958. Bar: N.Y. 1958, U.S. Supreme Ct. 1963. Assoc. Cravath, Swaine & Moore, N.Y.C., 1958, 62-68; staff, sr. group counsel ITT, N.Y.C., 1968-74, asst. gen. counsel, 1975-80, assoc. gen. counsel, 1981-95, v.p., dir. litigation, corp. policy compliance, 1982-95, ret., 1996; of counsel Stewart and Stewart, Washington, 1996-98, Wallace, King, Marraro & Branson, P.L.L.C., Washington, 1998—. Capt. JAGC, U.S. Army, 1959-62. Root Tilden Scholar. Mem. ABA (antitrust, litigation), Am. Law Inst., Troon Club (Scottsdale, Ariz.), Phi Beta Kappa. Episcopalian. Antitrust, General civil litigation, Alternative dispute resolution. Office: Wallace King Marraro & Branson PLLC 1050 Thomas Jefferson St NW Washington DC 20007-3837

**KILBY, MARCIA ANNETTE,** lawyer; b. Hopewell, Va., May 23, 1967; d. Richard Steven and Louise Brooks K.; m. Michael Anthony Rethwilm, Oct. 12, 1996. BA, Maryville Coll., 1989; JD, U. Louisville, 1994. Bar: Tenn. 1994, Ky. 1995. Regulatory analyst Oak Ridge (Tenn.) Nat. Lab, 1994-99; ptnr. Environ. Regulatory Cons., LLP, Knoxville, Tenn., 1999—. Administrative and regulatory, Environmental. Home: 3365 Nottingham Cir SE Cleveland TN 37323-6100

**KILEY, ANNE CAMPBELL,** lawyer; b. Kalamazoo, July 2, 1964; d. James Francis and Mary Catherine (Brooks) Campbell; m. Jeffrey Thomas Kiley, Apr. 15, 1996. BA with high honors in Econs., U. Mich., 1986, JD cum laude, 1989. Bar: Calif. 1990. Assoc. O'Melveny and Myers, L.A., 1989-91; sr. assoc. Trope and Trope, L.A., 1991—. Mem. L.A. County Bar Assn., Order of the Coif. Office: Trope and Trope 12121 Wilshire Blvd Los Angeles CA 90025-1123

**KILEY, EDWARD JOHN,** lawyer; b. Jersey City, N.J., Sept. 9, 1948; s. Charles Francis and Billee Ruth (Gray) K.; children—Jennie Elizabeth, Leah Anne, Anne Catherine. B.A. in Polit. Sci., Villanova U., 1970; J.D. with honors, George Washington U., 1973. Bar: D.C. 1973, U.S. Supreme Ct. 1982, U.S. Ct. Appeals (D.C., 3d, 5th, 6th and 11th cirs.) 1982, U.S. Dist. Ct. D.C. 1973, U.S. Claims Ct. 1976. Assoc., Grove, Jaskiewicz, Gilliam and Cobert, Washington, 1973-78, ptnr., 1978—; chmn. Transp. Law Inst., U. Denver Law Sch., 1982-90. Contbr. articles to profl. jours. Rep. Loudoun County (Va.) Washington Met. Council Govts., Water Resources Council, 1977-80; mem. Loudoun County Sch. Bd., 1986—. Mem. ABA, Transp. Lawyers Assn. (chmn. com. 1981-90, pres. 1993-94, Disting. Service award 1984). Administrative and regulatory, Antitrust, Labor. Office: Grove Jaskiewicz & Cobert 1730 M St NW Ste 400 Washington DC 20036-4579

**KILGORE, JEFFREY HARPER,** lawyer; b. Prescott, Ariz., Feb. 17, 1948; s. Richard B. Kilgore and Margaret (Poling) Keller; m. Janice Raley, June 7, 1969 (div. June 1980); children: Christopher A., Adam Harper; m. Mary Russell, Jan. 8, 1983; 1 child, Kelsey Love. BA in Banking and Fin., N. Tex. State U., 1970; JD, U. Houston, 1973. Bar: Tex. 1973, U.S. Ct. Appeals (5th cir.) 1975, U.S. Supreme Ct. 1976, U.S. Dist. Ct. (no. dist.) Tex. 1974, U.S. Dist. Ct. (so. dists.) Tex. 1983. Pvt. practice Dallas, Irving and Galveston, Tex., 1973—; cons. toxic tort-benzene leukemia cases, 1983—; mediation/arbitration Kilgore Mediation Ctr., 1997—. Mem. vestry St. Mark Episcopal Ch., Irving, Tex., 1975-78, Trinity Episcopal Ch., Galveston, 1985-88; bd. dirs., trustee Trinity Episcopal Sch., 1998—. Mem. Assn. Trial Lawyers Am., Tex. State Bar Assn. (mem. litigation sec.), Galveston County Bar Assn., Lions (bd. dirs. Irving chpt. 1975-83, bd. dirs. Galveston chpt. 1983-87, named Irving chpt. Outstanding Lion 1983), Mediation Assn. of Galceston County (pres. 1998-99), NASD Regulation Mediator, NASD Regulation Arbitration Bd. Democrat. Avocations: sailing, scuba diving, photography. Personal injury, General civil litigation, Workers' compensation. Office: 2020 Broadway St Galveston TX 77550-4636

**KILGORE, ROBERT MARTIN,** retired lawyer; b. Beckley, W.Va., Jan. 3, 1924; s. Harley Martin and Lois (Lilly) K.; B.S. in Physics, Georgetown U., 1947; postgrad. Columbia, 1947-49; J.D., George Washington U., 1952; m. Helen Hogan, Dec. 14, 1974 (dec. Jul., 1991). Admitted to D.C. bar, 1952, W.Va. bar, 1953; patent examiner U.S. Patent Office, Washington 1951-55, 68-85; counsel Com. on Judiciary, U.S. Senate, 1955-58; asso. firm Powell, Dorsey & Blum, Washington, 1959-61; pvt. practice, Washington, 1961-80; ret., 1985; legal cons. Bd. Vet. Appeals, VA, 1966-67. CD dir. Forest Heights, Md., 1956-58; instr. first aid ARC, 1955-76, first aid chmn. D.C. chpt., 1971-75, instr. sailing, 1972-76; pres. 2d Homeowners Assn., 1973-76, P.T.O. Credit Union, 1980. Served from pvt. to lt. AUS, 1943-46. Registered parliamentarian. Mem. Am., Fed., W.Va., D.C. bar assns., DAV, W.Va. State Soc. (v.p. 1956-58), SAR, Patent Office Soc. (exec. com. 1972-80, pres. 1975-77, chmn. bd. govs. jour. 1977-83, Outstanding Service award 1981), Am. Camillia Soc., Nat. Assn. Parliamentarians (unit pres. 1976-78, state treas.), Am. Inst. Parliamentarians (nat. dir. 1974-75, pres. D.C. chpt. 1974-76), Am. Legion, Am. Judicature Soc., Washington Area Intergroup Assn. (chmn. 1971). Democrat. Baptist. Clubs: George Washington U.; Toastmaster (dist. lt. gov. 1972-74). Home: 3940 Prince William Pkwy # 112 Woodbridge VA 22192-4513

**KILGORE, TERRY LEE,** lawyer; b. Mansfield, Ohio, May 5, 1948; s. Kenneth Burr and Velma (Gatton) K.; m. Renee Mary Bassak, Sept. 16, 1972; children: Todd Lee, Michelle Renee. BA in Polit. Sci. cum laude, Wittenberg U., 1970; JD cum laude, Ohio State U., 1973. Bar: Ohio 1973, U.S. Dist. Ct. (no. dist.) Ohio 1974, U.S. Ct. Appeals(6th cir.) 1975. Ptnr. Weldon, Huston & Keyser, Mansfield, 1973-94. Mem. interprofl. edn. & practice commn.Ohio State U., Columbus, 1978—; chmn. Mansfield Civil Svc. Commn., 1976-85. Mem. ABA, Assn. Trial Lawyers Am., Columbus Ohio Bar Assn., Ohio Bar Assn., Ohio Acad. Trial Lawyers, Liederkranz Club (Mansfield), Marquis, Masons. Republican. Lutheran. Avocations: sailing, skiing. General civil litigation, Criminal, Personal injury. Home: 75 E Kelso Rd Columbus OH 43202-2311

**KILLEEN, HENRY WALTER,** lawyer; b. Buffalo, Aug. 25, 1946; s. Henry W. and Ruth (Dold) K. BA cum laude, Harvard Coll., 1968; postgrad., Stanford U., 1969-70; JD cum laude, SUNY, Buffalo, 1975. Bar: N.Y. 1975, U.S. Dist. Ct. (we. dist.) N.Y. 1975, U.S. Dist. Ct. (no. dist.) N.Y. 1983, U.S. Ct. Appeals (2d cir.) 1981, U.S. Ct. Appeals (4th cir.) 1986. Assoc. Jaeckle, Fleischmann & Mugel, Buffalo, 1975-80, ptnr., 1980-92; ptnr. Harris, Beach & Wilcox, Buffalo, 1992-98, Killeen & Killeen, Orchard Park, N.Y., 1999—. Mem. ABA, N.Y. State Bar Assn., Erie County Bar Assn. (chmn. fed. practice com. 1984-87). Federal civil litigation, Environmental, Libel. Home: 502 Jewett Holmwood Rd East Aurora NY 14052-2149 Office: Killeen & Killeen 1 Grimsby Dr Hamburg NY 14075-3764

**KILLEEN, MICHAEL JOHN,** lawyer; b. Washington, Oct. 5, 1949; s. James Robert and Georgia Winston (Hartwell) K.; m. Therese Ann Goeden, Oct. 6, 1984; children: John Patrick, Katherine Therese, Mary Clare, James Philip. BA, Gonzaga U., 1971, JD magna cum laude, 1977. Bar: Wash. 1977, U.S. Dist. Ct. (we. dist.) Wash. 1979, U.S. Ct. Appeals (9th cir.) 1984, U.S. Supreme Ct. 1990. Jud. clk. Wash. State Ct. Appeals, Tacoma, 1977-79; assoc. Davis Wright Tremaine, Seattle, 1979-85, ptnr., 1985—; dir. Seattle Goodwill Bd., 1987—, sec., 1998—. Author: Guide to Strike Planning, 1985, Newsroom Legal Guidebook, 1996, Employment in Washington, 1998. Mem. Gonzaga Law Bd. Advisors, Spokane, Wash., pres., 1992-96. Mem. ABA, Wash. State Bar Assn., King County Bar Assn. (treas. 1987-89, pres. award 1989). Democrat. Roman Catholic. Labor, Communications, General civil litigation.

**KILLIAN, ROBERT KENNETH, JR.,** judge, lawyer; b. Hartford, Conn., Jan. 29, 1947; s. Robert Kenneth Sr. and Evelyn (Farnan) K.; m. Candace Korper, Oct. 6, 1979; children: Virginia, Carolyn. BA, Union U., 1969; JD, Georgetown U., 1972. Bar: Conn. 1972, U.S. Ct. Appeals (2nd cir.) 1973, D.C. 1974, U.S. Ct. Appeals (D.C. cir.) 1974. Bur. chief Sta. WTIC-AM-FM-TV, Washington, 1969-72; spl. asst. Senator Abe Ribicoff, Washington, 1972-73; ptnr. Gould, Killian, Wynne et al, Hartford, 1972-84; judge Conn. Probate Ct., Hartford, 1984—; ptnr. Killian, Donohue & Shipman, LLC, Hartford, 1985-98, Killian & Donohue, Hartford, 1998—; spl. counsel Lt. Gov. Conn., Hartford, 1985—; mem. exec. com. Conn. Probate Assembly, 1987—, pres.-judge, 1997—; mem. investment adv. coun. State of Conn., 1995—; mem. Jud. Commn. on Attys.' Ethics, 1990—. Author: Basic Probate in Connecticut, 1990, 5th edit., 1995. Regent, U. Hartford; trustee Hartt Sch. Music; chmn. Conn. chpt. March of Dimes, 1986—; bd. dirs. Yeats Drama Found., 1989—; incorporator St. Francis Hosp. and Med. Ctr. Recipient 1st Pl. award New England Conv. Magicians, 1969; named Conn.'s Outstanding Probate Judge, Conn. Probate Assembly, 1990. Mem. ABA, Nat. Conf. Probate Judges, Conn. Bar Assn., Conn. Trial Lawyers Assn., Internat. Brotherhood Magicians, Soc. Am. Magicians (chmn. nat. conv. 1977). Democrat. Roman Catholic. Home: 83 Bloomfield Ave Hartford CT 06105-1007 Office: Killian & Donohue 363 Main St Hartford CT 06106-1885

**KILLION, MAURICE ULRIC,** lawyer; b. Centralia, Ill., June 23, 1953; s. Maurice and Nina Killion; m. Stephanie Bland, Nov. 15, 1979 (dic. Sept. 1982); children: Tyanika Saunders, Maurice III. AA, Kaskaskia Coll., Centralia, Ill., 1974; BS in Econs., Ill. State U., 1976; JD, Capital U., 1979. Bar: Ohio 1980, Ill. 1988, U.S. Dist. Ct. (so. dist.) Ill. 1992, U.S. Ct. Appeals (7th cir.) 1994. Pvt. practice, Centralia, Ill., 1980—; pub. defender Clinton County Pub. Defender Office, Carlyle, Ill., 1987-90; asst. states atty. Marion County State Atty. Office, Salem, Ill., 1988-89; spl. asst. atty. gen. Ofice Ill. Atty. Gen., Springfield, 1992-96. Advisor to inmates Ohio Pub. Defender Assn., Columbus, 1980; advisor Citizens for Fairness, Centralia, 1990-92; mem. Centralia Criminal Justice Com., 1988-94, Centralia Career and Employment Adv. Com., 1998; bd. dirs. People Against Violent Environs.

(PAVE), Centralia, 1992-96. Avocations: reading, travel, golf, computers. Office: PO Box 978 Centralia IL 62801-0978

**KILLORIN, EDWARD WYLLY,** lawyer, tree farmer; b. Savannah, Ga., Oct. 16, 1928; s. Joseph Ignatius and Myrtle (Bell) K.; m. Virginia Melson Ware, June 15, 1957; children: Robert Ware, Edward Wylly, Joseph Rigdon. BS, Spring Hill Coll., Mobile, 1952; LLB magna cum laude, U. Ga., 1957. Bar: Ga. 1956. Pvt. practice in Atlanta, 1957—; ptnr. firm Gambrell, Russell, Killorin & Forbes, 1964-78; sr. ptnr. firm Killorin & Killorin, 1978—; lectr. Inst. Continuing Legal Edn. Ga., 1967—. Adj. prof. law Ga. State U., 1984-87. Chmn., Gov.'s Adv. Com. on Coordination State and Local Govt., 1973, Gov.'s Legal Adv. Council for Workmen's Compensation, 1974-76; bd. regents Spring Hill Coll., 1975-82, trustee, 1981-91. Served with AUS, 1946-47, 52-54. Recipient Disting. Alumnus award Spring Hill Coll., 1972. Mem. Internat., Ga. (chmn. jud. compensation com. 1976-77, chmn. legis. com. 1977-78), Atlanta Bar Assn. (editor Atlanta Lawyer 1967-70, exec. com. 1971-74, chmn. legislation com. 1978-80), D.C. Bar Assn., Am. Judicature Soc., Lawyers Club Atlanta, Atlanta Legal Aid Soc. (adv. com. 1966-70, dir. 1971-74), Nat. Legal Aid and Defender Assn., Internat. Assn. Ins. Counsel (chmn. environ. law com. 1976-78), Atlanta Lawyers Found., Ga. Bar Found. (life), Ga. Def. Lawyers Assn. (dir. 1972-80), Ga. C. of C. (chmn. govtl. dept. 1970-75, chmn. workmen's compensation com. 1979—, Disting. Svc. award 1970-75), Def. Research Inst. (Ga. chmn. 1970-71), Spring Hill Coll. Alumni Assn. (nat. pres. 1972-74), U. Ga. Law Sch. Assn. (nat. pres. 1986-87, Disting. Svc. Scroll 1989), Ga. Forestry Assn. (life, bd. dirs. 1969—, pres. 1977-79, chmn. bd. 1979-81), Am. Forestry Assn., Demosthenian Lit. Soc. (pres. 1957), Sphinx, Blue Key, Gridiron, Phi Beta Kappa, Phi Beta Kappa Assos., Phi Kappa Phi, Phi Delta Phi, Phi Omega. Clubs: Capital City, Peachtree Golf, Commerce, Oglethorpe (Savannah), Highland Country Club (LaGrange). Roman Catholic. Contbr. articles to legal jours. Federal civil litigation, Insurance, General corporate. Home: 436 Blackland Rd NW Atlanta GA 30342-4005 Office: Killorin & Killorin 11 Piedmont Ctr NE Atlanta GA 30305-1769

**KILLORIN, ROBERT WARE,** lawyer; b. Atlanta, Nov. 12, 1959; s. Edward W. and Virgina (Ware) K. AB cum laude, Duke U., 1980; JD, U. Ga., 1983. Bar: Ga. 1984, U.S. Dist. Ct. (no. dist.) Ga. 1984, U.S. Ct. Appeals (11th cir.) 1984. Ptnr. Killorin & Killorin, Atlanta, 1984—. Mem. Atlanta Bar Assn., Ga. Def. Lawyers Assn., State Bar Ga. (chair SCOPE com. 1986, young lawyers sect. legis. affairs com. 1989-91, instr. mock trial program 1989—), Ga. C. of C. (govtl. affairs com.), Internat. Assn. Def. Counsel, 11th Cir. Hist. Soc., Assn. Trial Lawyers Am., Nat. Assn. Underwater Instrs., Nat. Speliological Soc., U. Ga. Pres.'s Club, Explorer's Club. Avocations: forestry, scuba diving, basketball, tennis. General civil litigation, Environmental, Antitrust. Home: 5587 Benton Woods Dr NE Atlanta GA 30342-1308 Office: Killorin & Killorin 5587 Benton Woods Dr NE Atlanta GA 30342-1308

**KILLOUGH, J. SCOTT,** lawyer; b. Feb. 20, 1957; s. Robert G. and M. Joan (Rhinehart) K.; m. Susan Dantonio, Dec. 29, 1984; children: Ian Scott, Courtney Leigh, Robert Andrew. BSBA, Drake U., 1979; MBA, So. Meth. U., 1980; JD, Tex. Tech U., 1985. Bar: Tex., U.S. Dist. Ct. (no., ea. and we. dists.) Tex., U.S. Tax Ct., U.S. Ct. Appeals (5th cir.); CPA, Tex. Assoc. Carr, Evans, Fouts & Hunt, Lubbock, Tex., 1985-89, Pye, Dobbs & Berry, Tyler, Tex., 1989-90; pvt. practice Tyler, 1990—. Mem. Tex. Soc. CPAs, East Tex. Estate Planning Counsel. Baptist. Avocations: camping, hunting, skiing, auto mechanics. Estate planning, General corporate, Taxation, general. Office: 5610 Old Bullard Rd Ste 203 Tyler TX 75703-4360

**KILMER, DOUGLAS AARON,** lawyer; b. Hedgesville, W.Va., Feb. 11, 1952; s. Robert D. and Maxine (Edwards) K. BA, W.Va. U., 1973, JD, 1976. Bar: W.Va. 1976, U.S. Dist. Ct. (so. dist.) W.Va. Staff atty. W.Va. Tax Dept., Charleston, 1976-80, chief enforcement sect., 1980-85, asst. dir. compliance div., 1985-87, dep. gen. counsel, 1987-97; atty. U.S. Dept. Justice, Charleston, 1997—. Mem. W.Va. 4-H All Stars, W.Va. Track & Field Offcls. Mem. Am. Bankruptcy Inst. Presbyterian. Home: 10 Lynn Pl Charleston WV 25314-2105 Office: 2025 US Courthouse 300 Virginia St E Charleston WV 25301-2503

**KILPATRICK, PETER L.,** lawyer; b. Tyler, Tex., May 4, 1959; s. Billy Wayne Kilpatrick and Linda Travene Jones; m. Darlene McWatters; children: Keagon, Ferris. BA, Austin State U., 1981; JD, Tex. Tech. U., 1984. Bar: Tex. 1984, U.S. Dist. Ct. (ea., we., so., and no. dists.) Tex., U.S. Ct. Appeals (5th cir.) 1990. Atty. Foster Lewis Langley Gardner & Banack, San Antonio, 1984-96; ptnr. Jeffers & Banack, San Antonio, 1996—. Avocations: tennis, chess, poker, computers. Home: 29023 Cloud Croft Ln Fair Oaks TX 78015-4748 Office: Jeffers & Banack Inc 745 E Mulberry Ave San Antonio TX 78212-3137

**KILSCH, GUNTHER H.,** lawyer; b. N.Y.C., Jan. 8, 1930; s. Frederick and Toni (Becher) K.; m. Kathryn A. Severance, Mar. 28, 1959; children: Nancy, Peter, Ann, Sarah. AB, Queens Coll./CUNY, 1957; LLB, NYU, 1963. Bar: N.Y. 1964, U.S. Dist. Ct. (so. and ea. dists.) 1966, U.S. Ct. Appeals (2d cir.) 1993; diplomate Am. Bd. Profl. Liability Attys. Assoc. Schaffner D'Onofrio, N.Y.C., 1964-68, John J. Tullman, N.Y.C., 1968-71, Kroll, Edelman & Lanzone, N.Y.C., 1971-73, Martin, Clearwater & Bell, N.Y.C., 1973-75, Montfort, Healy, McGuire & Salley, Mineola, N.Y., 1975-77; mem. firm McAloon & Friedman, P.C., N.Y.C., 1977—. Warden, mem. vestry Christ Ch. Riverdale, Bronx, N.Y. Cpl. AUS, 1953-55. Fellow Am. Bar Found., N.Y. Bar Found.; mem. N.Y. State Bar Assn. (program chmn., lectr. CLE 1970—, mem. House of Delegates 1979-80, 93-94, 98—, chair TORT reparations com. 1992-97, trial lawyers sect. 1978-79), Am. Bd. Trial Advs. (pres. N.Y.C. chpt. 1998, 99). Episcopalian. Avocations: photography, boating, hiking, choir. General civil litigation, Personal injury, Professional liability. Home: 46 Sunnyside Dr Yonkers NY 10705-1731 Office: McAloon & Friedman PC 116 John St New York NY 10038-3300

**KIM, EDWARD K.,** lawyer; b. N.Y.C., 1969. BA, UCLA, 1992; JD, Cornell U., 1995. Bar: N.Y. 1996, Calif. 1998. Assoc. Simpson Thacher & Bartlett, N.Y.C., 1995-97, Dewey Ballantine LLP, L.A., 1997-99, Milbank, Tweed, Hadley & McCloy LLP, L.A., 1999—. Editor Cornell Law Rev., 1995. Mem. ABA. General corporate, Mergers and acquisitions, Securities. Office: Milbank Tweed Hadley & McCloy LLP 601 S Figueroa St Fl 30 Los Angeles CA 90017-5704

**KIM, HELEN BYUNG-SON,** lawyer; b. Santa Barbara, Calif., Apr. 4, 1962; d. Chung Pyo and Chung He K.; m. Richard E. Nathan, May 26, 1991; 1 child, Rebecca J. AB cum laude, Harvard-Radcliffe Coll., 1982; MusM, Juilliard Sch., 1984; JD, Yale U., 1987. Bar: N.Y. 1988, Calif. 1988, U.S. Dist. Ct. (no. so. and ea. dists.) N.Y. 1988. Law clk. U.S. Ct. Appeals (2d cir.), N.Y.C., 1987-88; assoc. Paul, Weiss, Ritland Wharlor & Garrison, N.Y.C., 1989-95; assoc. Sonnenschein Nath & Rosenthal, N.Y.C., 1995-98, ptnr., 1998—. Mem. Korean-Am. Lawyers Assn. Greater N.Y. (pres. 1998—), Asian-Am. Bar Assn. N.Y. (pres. elect 1998—). General civil litigation. Office: Sonnenschein Nath & Rosenthal Ste 2401 1221 Avenue Of The Americas New York NY 10020-1089

**KIM, MICHAEL CHARLES,** lawyer; b. Honolulu, Mar. 9, 1950; s. Harold Dai You and Maria Adrienne K. Student, Gonzaga U., 1967-70; BA, U. Hawaii, 1971; JD, Northwestern U., 1976. Bar: Ill. 1977, U.S. Dist. Ct. (no. dist.) Ill. 1977, U.S. Ct. Appeals (7th cir.) 1981, U.S. Supreme Ct. 1986. Assoc. counsel Nat. Assn. Realtors, Chgo., 1977-78; assoc. Rudnick & Wolfe, Chgo., 1978-83, Rudd & Assocs., Hoffman Estates, Ill., 1983-85; ptnr. Rudd & Kim, Hoffman Estates and Chgo., 1985-87; prin. Michael C. Kim & Assocs., Chgo. and Schaumburg, Ill., 1987-88; ptnr. Martin, Craig, Chester & Sonnenschein, Chgo. and Schaumburg, 1988-91; sr. ptnr. Arnstein & Lehr, Chgo. and Hoffman Estates, 1991—; gen. counsel Assn. Sheridan Condo-Coop Owners, Chgo., 1988—; adj. prof. John Marshall Law Sch., Chgo. Author column Apt. and Condo News, 1984-87; co-author Historical and Practice Notes; contbr. articles to profl. jours. Bd. dirs. Astor Villa Condo Assn., Chgo., 1987-91, treas. 1987-89. Mem. ABA, Chgo. Bar Assn. (chmn condominium law subcom. 1990-92, chmn. real property legis. subcom. 1995-97, vice chmn. real property law com., 1998-99, chmn. real proprty law com. 1999—), Ill. State Bar Assn. (real estate law sect. coun. 1990-94, corp. and securities law sect. coun. 1990-92), Asian Am. Bar Assn. Greater Chgo. Area (bd. dirs. 1987-88, 90-91), Cmty. Assns. Inst. Ill. (bd. dirs. 1990-92, pres. 1992), Coll. Cmty. Assn. Lawyers (bd. govs. 1994-98), Univ. Club (Chgo.). Avocations: squash, photography, travel. General civil litigation, Construction, Real property. Office: Arnstein & Lehr 120 S Riverside Plz Ste 1200 Chicago IL 60606-3910

**KIM, RICHARD KYOBONG,** lawyer; b. N.Y.C., Nov. 11, 1961; s. Wan Hee and Chung Sook (Noh) K.; m. Terri Lynn Schlesinger, Sept. 16, 1990; 1 child, Brandon J.I. AB, Stanford U., 1983; JD, Columbia U., 1986. Bar: Pa. 1987, D.C. 1989. Atty. Fed. Res. Bd., Washington, 1986-89; assoc. Mayer, Brown & Platt, N.Y.C., 1989-93; asst. gen. counsel Nations Bank Corp., Charlotte, N.C., 1993—. Contbr. to book: Guide to Capital Markets, 1993, also articles to profl. jours.

**KIMBALL, CATHERINE D.,** state supreme court justice. Former judge La. Dist. Ct. (18th dist.); now assoc. justice Supreme Ct. of La. Office: 301 Loyola Ave New Orleans LA 70112-1814

**KIMBERLEY, DAVID ALAN,** lawyer, educator; b. Gadsden, Ala., July 13, 1960; s. Richard Hughlun and Sara (Thomas) K.; m. Cynthia Denise Allen, Apr. 8, 1989; children: Kaitlyn Brooke, Andrew Allen. BS, U. Ala., 1982, JD, 1985. Bar: Am. 1985, Ala. 1985, U.S. Dist. Ct. (no. dist.) Ala. 1986. Assoc. Floyd, Keener & Cusimano, Gadsden, Ala., 1985-92; jr. ptnr. Floyd, Keener Cusimano & Roberts, Gadsden, 1992-97; ptnr. Cusimano, Keener, Roberts & Kimberley P.C., Gadsden, 1997—; adj. prof. Gadsden State C.C. Pres. bd. dirs. Cmty. Theatre Gadsden, 1991, Gadsden Symphony Orch., 1997-99. Petty officer USNR, 1997—. Mem. ABA, Nat. Coll. Advocacy (adv.), Ala. Trial Lawyers Assn. (mem. bd. govs. 1988-97, mem. exec. com. 1997—). Democrat. Baptist. Avocations: sailing, tennis, whitewater rafting. General civil litigation, Personal injury, Product liability. Home: 821 Country Club Dr Gadsden AL 35901-5809 Office: Cusimano Keener Roberts & Kimberley PC 153 S 9th St Gadsden AL 35901-3645

**KIMBERLING, JOHN FARRELL,** retired lawyer; b. Shelbyville, Ind., Nov. 15, 1926; s. James Farrell and Phyllis (Casady) K. B of Naval Sci. and Tactics, Purdue U., 1946; AB, Ind. U., 1947, JD, 1950. Bar: Ind. 1950, Calif. 1954. Assoc. Bracken, Gray, DeFur & Voran, 1950-51; assoc. Lillick McHose & Charles, and predecessor firms, 1953-63, ptnr., 1963-86; ptnr. Dewey Ballantine, L.A., 1986-89. Bd. visitors Ind. U. Sch. Law, 1987—; bd. dirs. Ind. U. Found., 1988—. Lt. (j.g.) USNR, 1951-53. Fellow Am. Coll. Trial Lawyers; mem. ABA (charter mem. litigation sect.), State Bar Calif., L.A. Bar Assn., L.A. Jr. C. of C. (past pres.), Beta Theta Pi, Phi Delta Phi. Democrat. Clubs: California, Chancery, Lincoln. Federal civil litigation, State civil litigation, General civil litigation. Home: 1180 Los Robles Dr Palm Springs CA 92262-4124 *My goal in life is and has been to do the very best of which I am capable in my professional life and in helping to make my community a better place in which to work and live.*

**KIMBLE, KELLY JEAN,** lawyer; b. Clarksburg, W.Va., Nov. 25, 1964; d. Richard L. and Patricia Louise (Thomas) K.; 1 child, Davis Jared. BFA, W.Va. U., 1992, JD, 1996. Bar: W.Va. 1996, U.S. Dist. Ct. (so. dist.) W.Va. 1996. Assoc. Kay Casto & Chaney, PLLC, Morgantown, W.Va., 1996—. Mem. ABA, W.Va. Bar Assn., Order of Coif. Avocations: guitar, painting, arts and crafts, sports, biking. General civil litigation, Insurance, Education and schools. Office: Kay Casto & Chaney PLLC 3000 Hampton Ctr Ste C Morgantown WV 26505

**KIMBROUGH, ROBERT AVERYT,** lawyer; b. Sarasota, Fla., Nov. 2, 1933; s. Verman T. and Edith (Averyt) K.; m. Emilie Hudson, Aug. 24, 1957; children: James E., Robert A. Jr. BS, Davidson Coll., 1955; LLB to JD, U. Fla., 1960. Bar: Fla. 1960, U.S. Dist. Ct. Fla. 1962. Pvt. practice, Sarasota, 1960—. Chmn., bd. trustees, Ringling Sch. Art & Design, Sarasota, 1983-85; chmn. Sarasota Welfare Home Inc., 1986-89; pres. Fla. West Coast Symphony, Sarasota, 1986-90. Recipient Champion Higher Edn. in Fla., Ind. Coll. and Univs. of Fla., 1984-85, Alumnus of Yr. award Phi Delta Theta, 1997. Mem. ABA, Fla. Bar, Sarasota County Bar Assn., Sarasota Yacht Club, Kiwanis. Republican. Presbyterian. Avocations: flying, fishing, boating. Estate planning, Probate, Real property. Home: 7100 S Gator Creek Blvd Sarasota FL 34241-9729 Office: 1530 Cross St Sarasota FL 34236-7015

**KIMELMAN, STEVEN,** lawyer; b. Paterson, N.J., Aug. 11, 1946; s. Charles and Pearl K.; m. Isabella Mueller-Mezin, June 18, 1976. BA, Rutgers U., 1968; JD, Rutgers U., Newark, 1972. Bar: N.Y. 1973, U.S. Dist. Ct. (ea. and so. dists) N.Y. 1974, U.S. Ct. Appeals (2d cir.) 1974. Assoc. Fried, Frank, Harris, Shriver & Jacobson, N.Y.C., 1972-74; asst. U.S. atty., chief fraud sect. dept. chief criminal div. U.S. Dept. Justice, Bklyn., 1974-78; ptnr. Gallop, Danson, Kimelman & Clayman, N.Y.C., 1978-84; pvt. practice N.Y.C., 1985-98; ptnr. Arent Fox, N.Y.C., 1998—; lectr. Practising Law Inst., N.Y.C., 1988—;. Mem. ABA, N.Y. State Bar Assn., Nat. Assn. Def. Attys., N.Y. Coun. Def. Lawyers, Fed. Bar Coun., N.Y. State Assn. Criminal Def. Lawyers, N.Y. State Trial Laywers Assn. (bd. dirs.), N.Y. Criminal Bar Assn. Avocations: horseback riding, tennis. Federal civil litigation, State civil litigation, Criminal. Office: Arent Fox 1675 Broadway Fl 25 New York NY 10019-5820

**KIMLER, ANDREW A.,** lawyer; b. Bronx, N.Y., Nov. 1, 1952; s. Lawrence and Sylvia Kimler; m. Cheryl Pamela Waller, Aug. 24, 1986; children: Alexis, Samuel. BA, Queens Coll./CUNY, 1974; JD, Ohio No. U., 1977. Bar: N.Y. 1979, N.J. 1989, U.S. Dist. Ct. (so. dist.) N.Y. 1981, U.S. Dist. Ct. (ea. dist.) N.Y. 1986, U.S. Dist. Ct. N.J. 1989. Sr. assoc. Rothblatt, Rothblatt & Seijas, N.Y.C., 1978-82; asst. publ. mgr. Matthew Bender & Co., N.Y.C., 1982-85; ptnr. Seidman, Maiman, Morenstein & Kimler, N.Y.C., 1985—; officer, bd. dirs. 299 13th St. Housing Corp., Bklyn., 1987—. Co-author: Criminal Defense Techniques, 1984; assoc. editor Ohio No. U. Law Rev., 1975-77; contbr. chpts. to books. Mem. Cmty. Planning Bd., Bklyn., 1994-95; arbitrator Civil Ct., City of N.Y., 1993-95. Mem. PTA (sch. bd. com. 1998—), N.Y. State Bar Assn. (labor and family law sect.), N.Y. State Trial Lawyers Assn., N.Y. County Lawyers Assn. (labor and family law com.). General civil litigation, Labor, Family and matrimonial. Home: 34 Cypress St New City NY 10956-6444 Office: Seidman Maiman Morenstein & Kimler 330 7th Ave Fl 15 New York NY 10001-5010

**KIMM, MICHAEL S.,** lawyer; b. Seoul, July 12, 1963; came to U.S., 1974; s. Chun Teak and Chong Sim K. BA, Fordham U., 1987; JD, Boston U., 1991. Bar: N.J. 1991, N.Y. 1992, U.S. Dist. Ct. N.J. 1991, U.S. Dist. Ct. (so. and ea. dists.) N.Y. 1993, U.S. Ct. Appeals (2nd, 3rd and Fed cirs.) 1994, U.S. Supreme Ct. 1995. Pvt. practice Hackensack, NJ. Mng. editor: Boston U. Internat. Law Jour., 1990-91; contbr. articles to profl. jours. Gen. counsel Korean-Am. Assn. for Rehab. of Disabled, Queens, N.Y., 1992-94. Mem. ABA, N.J. State Bar Assn., N.Y. State Bar Assn. Intellectual property, Federal civil litigation, Trademark and copyright. Office: 170 Broadway Frnt 1 New York NY 10038-4154 also: 505 Main St Hackensack NJ 07601-5900

**KIMMEL, MORTON RICHARD,** lawyer; b. N.Y.C., Nov. 10, 1940; s. Benjamin Bert and Sylvia (Alabaster) K.; m. Marcia Harriet LaPotin, Sept. 10, 1967; children: Wayne Douglas, Michelle Wendy, Karen Paige, Larry Keith. BA, Temple U., 1962; JD, George Washington U., 1965. Bar: Del. 1965, D.C. 1966. Law clk. Del. Superior Ct., Wilmington, 1965-66; ptnr. Kimmel, Carter, Roman & Peltz P.A., Wilmington, 1970—; supr. Del. Justices of the Peace, 1970-72; rep. State Farm Ins. Co., 1968-90, trustee lawyers' fund for client protection, 1985-97; arbitrator and mediator; lectr. in fields of criminal law, ins. law, personal injury law, law office mgmt., trial practice, ethics, professionalism, mediation and arbitration, 1970—. Author: You Can Do It, 1973, Emergency Medicine, 1982, Delaware Arbitration Manual, 1984, The Delaware Bar in the 20th Century, 1994. Mem. ATLA, Am. Bd. Trial Advs., Del. Trial Lawyers Assn., Fedn. Ins. Counsel, Def. Rsch. Inst. (chmn. Del. 1976-77). Democrat. Jewish. Avocations: sports, reading. State civil litigation, Insurance, Personal injury. Office: Kimmel Carter Roman & Peltz PA 913 N Market St Wilmington DE 19801-3019

**KIMMITT, ROBERT MICHAEL,** lawyer, banker, diplomat; b. Logan, Utah, Dec. 19, 1947; s. Joseph Stanley and Eunice L. (Wegener) K.; m. Holly Sutherland, May 19, 1979; children: Kathleen, Robert, William, Thomas, Margaret. BS, U.S. Mil. Acad., 1969; JD, Georgetown U., 1977. Bar: D.C. 1977. Commd. 2d lt. U.S. Army, 1969, advanced through grades to maj., 1982, served in Vietnam, 1970-71; brig. gen. USAR, 1996—; law clk. U.S. Ct. Appeals, Washington, 1977-78; sr. staff mem. NSC, Washington, 1978-83, dep. asst. to Pres. for nat. security affairs and exec. sec. and gen. counsel, 1983-85; gen. counsel U.S. Dept. Treasury, Washington, 1985-87; ptnr. Sidley & Austin, Washington, 1987-89; undersec. for polit. affairs Dept. State, Washington, 1988-91, ambassador to Germany, 1991-93; mng. dir. Lehman Bros., Washington, N.Y.C., 1993-97; sr. ptnr. Wilmer, Cutler & Pickering, Washington, 1997—; U.S. mem. Panel of Arbitrators, Internat. Ctr. for Settlement of Investment Disputes, 1988-89. Bd. dirs. Mannesmann AG, Siemens AG, Allianz Life Ins. Co. N.Am., Big Flower Holdings, United Def. Industries, German Marshall Fund, Atlantic Coun., Mike Mansfield Found., Am. Coun. on Germany, Am. Inst. for Contemporary German Studies, U.S. Group Coun., BMW AG. Decorated Bronze star (3), Purple Heart, Air medal, Vietnamese Cross of Gallantry, German Svc. Cross, German Army Cross in Gold; recipient Arthur Flemming award Downtown Jaycees, 1987, Alexander Hamilton award U.S. Dept. Treasury, 1987, Presdl. Citizens medal, 1991, Def. Disting. Civilian Svc. medal, 1993. Mem. Am. Acad. Diplomacy, Assn. Grads. U.S. Mil. Acad. (trustee 1976-82), Coun. Fgn. Rels. Roman Catholic. Office: Wilmer Cutler & Pickering 2445 M St NW Ste 500 Washington DC 20037-1487

**KIMPORT, DAVID LLOYD,** lawyer; b. Hot Springs, S.D., Nov. 28, 1945; s. Ralph E. and Ruth N. (Hutchinson) K.; m. Barbara H. Buggert, Apr. 2, 1976; children: Katrina Elizabeth, Rebecca Helen, Susanna Ruth. AB summa cum laude, Bowdoin Coll., 1968; postgrad., Imperial Coll., U. London, 1970-71; JD, Stanford U., 1975. Bar: Calif. 1975, U.S. Supreme Ct. 1978. Assoc. Baker & McKenzie, San Francisco, 1975-82, ptnr., 1982-90; ptnr. Nossaman, Guthner, Knox & Elliot, 1990—. Active San Francisco Planning and Urban Rsch., 1978—, The Family, 1987—. Served with U.S. Army, 1968-70. Mem. ABA, San Francisco Bar Assn., Commonwealth Club of Calif., Phi Beta Kappa. Democrat. Episcopalian. Contracts commercial, Real property, Private international. Office: Nossaman Guthner Knox & Elliott 50 California St Fl 34 San Francisco CA 94111-4624

**KINAKA, WILLIAM TATSUO,** lawyer; b. Lahaina, Hawaii, Apr. 4, 1940; s. Toshio and Natsumi (Hirouji) K.; m. Jeanette Louisa Ramos, Nov. 23, 1968; children: Kimberly H., Kristine N.Y. BA in Polit. Sci., Whittier Coll., 1962; MA in Internat. Rels., Am. U., 1964, JD, 1973. Bar: D.C. 1975, U.S. Ct. Appeals (D.C. cir.) 1975, U.S. Dist. Ct. D.C. 1975, U.S. Tax Ct. 1975, U.S. Ct. Mil. Appeals 1975, Hawaii 1976, U.S. Dist. Ct. Hawaii 1976, U.S. Ct. Appeals (9th cir.) 1976. Career trainee CIA, Langley, Va., 1966; legis. asst. Sen. Hiram L. Fong, Washington, 1966-76; assoc. Ueoka & Luna, Wailuku, Hawaii, 1977-85; pvt. practice law Wailuku, Hawaii, 1985—; grand jury counsel 2d Cir. Ct., 1985-86; ct. arbitrator, 1989—; legal cons. Hale Mahaolu Elderly Housing, Kahului, 1976—. Active Dem. Party of Hawaii, Wailuku, 1988-89; pres. Nat. Eagle Scout Assn. of Boy Scouts Am., Wailuku, 1983-91; bd. dirs. Wailuku Main St. Assn., 1988-94, Maui Adult Day Care Ctr., Puunene, 1978—; Maui coun. Boy Scouts of Am., 1983—; pres., bd. dirs. Maui Youth Intervention Program, Inc., 1993—. Mem. Hawaii Bar Assn., Maui Bar Assn., Maui Japanese C. of C., Maui C. of C., Nat. Eagle Scout Assn. (pres. Wailuku 1983-91). United Ch. of Christ. Avocations: scouting, gardening, swimming, poetry writing. Consumer commercial, Family and matrimonial, Landlord-tenant. Home: 639 Pio Dr Wailuku HI 96793-2622 Office: 24 N Church St Ste 207 Wailuku HI 96793-1606

**KINCAID, JAMES LEWIS,** lawyer; b. Carthage, Mo., Oct. 3, 1936; s. Joseph Lewis and Kathryn Lucille (Stein) K.; m. Aloah Ann Burke, Aug. 24, 1958; children: Kathryn, James Lewis Jr., Robert, Michael. AB, Harvard U., 1958, LLB, 1961. Bar: Okla. 1961. Assoc. then ptnr. Huffman, Arrington, Scheurich & Kincaid, Tulsa, 1961-70; ptnr. Conner & Winters, Tulsa, 1971-89; dir. Crowe & Dunlevy, Tulsa, 1989—. Mem. Okla. Bar Assn. General civil litigation, Federal civil litigation. Office: Crowe & Dunlevy 500 Kennedy Bldg Tulsa OK 74103

**KIND, KENNETH WAYNE,** lawyer, real estate broker; b. Missoula, Mont., Apr. 1, 1948; s. Joseph Bruce and Elinor Joy (Smith) K.; m. Diane Lucille Jozaitis, Aug. 28, 1971; children: Kirstin Amber, Kenneth Warner. BA, Calif. State U.-Northridge, 1973; JD, Calif. Western U., 1976. Bar: Calif. 1976, U.S. Dist. Ct. (ea., so., no. dists.) Calif., 1976, U.S. Cir. Ct. Appeals (9th cir.); lic. NASCAR driver, 1987. Mem. celebrity security staff Brownstone Am., Beverly Hills, Calif., 1970-76; tchr. Army and Navy Acad., Carlsbad, Calif., 1975-76; real estate broker, Bakersfield, Calif., 1978—; sole practice, Bakersfield, 1976—; lectr. mechanic's lien laws, Calif., 1983—. Staff writer Calif. Western Law Jour., 1975. Sgt. U.S. Army, 1967-70. Mem. ABA, VFW, Nat. Order Barristers, Rancheros Visitadores. Libertarian. Real property, Insurance, State civil litigation. Office: 4042 Patton Way Bakersfield CA 93308-5030

**KINDLE, JUDITH O.,** court reporter; b. Richlands, Va., Mar. 1, 1941; d. Robert Lee and Juanita Rebecca (Allen) Osborne; m. Hezekiah C. Kindle, Aug. 21, 1960; children: Joel Todd. Cert. paralegal, Nat. Acad. Paralegal Studies, 1991. Cert. legal sec.; cert. legal asst. Legal sec. Sanders & Moore, Kingsport, Tenn., 1960-61; sec. Holston Glass, Kingsport, Tenn., 1961-63, First Nat. Bank Trust Dept, Kingsport, Tenn., 1963-67; sec. clerk Holston Def., Kingsport, Tenn., 1967; legal sec. E. Lynn Minter, Kingsport, Tenn., 1974-75; court reporter Kingsport, Tenn., 1975—; asst. to pres. Kingsport Bar Assn., 1987-92, adv. com. N.E. State Coll., 1997—. Named Sec. of Yr. Kingsport Legal Sec. Assn., 1984. Mem. Liberty Chapter OES, Tenn. Assn. Legal Sec. (parliamentarian 1993, v.p. 1994-95, Continuing Edn. award 1991, 92), Tri-Cities Legal Support Staff Orgn. (pres. 1997—). Avocations: art, singing, needle work, ceramics. Home: 420 Brentwood Dr Kingsport TN 37660-6869

**KINDLER, JEFFREY,** lawyer; b. May 13, 1955. JD, Harvard U., 1980. Bar: D.C. 1980. V.p., sr. counsel GE; sr. v.p., gen. counsel McDonald's Corp., 1996-97; exec. v.p., gen. counsel McDonald's Corp., Oak Brook, Ill., 1997—. Office: McDonalds Corp One Kroc Dr Oak Brook IL 60521*

**KINDRED, ALAN M.,** lawyer; b. Sydney, Australia, Nov. 1, 1952; came to U.S., 1988; s. William N. and Oriel W. Kindred; m. Maureen Prendergast, May 17, 1986; children: Oliver, Caroline. LLB, U. Sydney, 1976, MA, 1979. Bar: N.Y. 1986, Calif. 1988, U.S. Dist. Ct. (ctrl. dist.) Calif. 1988, U.S. Dist. Ct. (no. dist.) Calif. 1989, U.S. Dist. Ct. (so. dist.) Calif. 1991, U.S. Ct. Appeals (9th cir.) 1989, U.S. Ct. Appeals (10th cir.) 1990, NSW, Australia, 1977. Ptnr. Dibbs, Crowther & Osborne, Sydney, 1977-87; barrister-at-law Selborne Chambers, Sydney, 1987-88; assoc. Morgan, Lewis & Bockius, LLP, L.A., 1988-95; ptnr. Shaub & Williams, L.A., 1995-99; sr. counsel Darby & Darby, L.A., 1999—. Author: Enforcing Money Judgments, 1986. Mem. ABA, Internat. Bar Assn., State Bar Calif. (exec. com. internat. law sect. 1998—), Los Angeles County Bar Assn. (exec. com. internat. law sect. 1994—), Australian Am. C. of C. (bd. dirs. 1995—). Avocations: opera, ballet, golf, tennis. Trademark and copyright, Intellectual property, Private international. Office: Darby & Darby 707 Wilshire Blvd Fl 32 Los Angeles CA 90017-3501

**KINDT, JOHN WARREN, SR.,** lawyer, educator, consultant; b. Oak Park, Ill., May 24, 1950; s. Warren Frederick and Lois Jeannette (Woelffer) K.; m. Anne Marie Johnson, Apr. 17, 1982; children: John Warren Jr., James Roy Frederick. AB, Coll. William and Mary, 1972; JD, U. Ga., 1976, MBA, 1977; LLM, U. Va., 1978, SJD, 1981. Bar: D.C. 1976, Ga. 1976, Va. 1977. Advisor to Gov. of Va., 1971-72; congl. asst. to Congressman M. Caldwell Butler, 1972-73; cons. White House staff, 1976-77; asst. prof. U. Ill., 1978-81, assoc. prof., 1981-85, prof., 1985—; cons. 3d UN Conf. on Law of the Sea; lectr. U. Ill. Exec. MBA Program. Author: Marine Pollution and the Law of the Sea, 4 vols., 1986, 2 vols., 1988, 92, Economic Impacts of Legalized Gambling, 1994; contbr. articles to profl. jours. Caucus chmn., del. White House Conf. on Youth, 1970; co-chmn. Va. Gov.'s Adv. Council on Youth, 1971; mem. Athens (Ga.) Legal Aid Soc., 1975-76. Rotary fellow, 1979-80; Smithsonian ABA/ELI scholar, 1981; sr. fellow London Sch. of Econs., 1985-86. Mem. Am. Soc. Internat. Law, D.C. Bar Assn., Va. Bar Assn., Ga. Bar Assn. Home: 801 Brookside Ln Mahomet IL 61853-9545 Office: U Ill 350 Commerce W Champaign IL 61820

**KING, ADRIENNE SEPANIAK,** lawyer; b. Detroit, Nov. 4, 1947; d. Edward Aloysius and Irene (Kapuchinski) Szczepaniak; m. Samuel Pailthorpe King, Jr., Oct. 19, 1974; children: Christopher, Samuel Wilder. BS in Biology, U. Detroit, 1969, JD, 1972. Bar: Hawaii 1972, U.S/ Dist. Ct. Hawaii 1972, Mich. 1973, U.S. Ct. Appeals (9th cir.) 1974. Dep. prosecuting atty. City and County of Honolulu, 1972-75; dep. corp. counsel City Atty's. Office, Honolulu, 1975-85; pvt. practice King & King, Honolulu, 1985-90; chief trials divsn. City Atty's. Office, Honolulu, 1990-93; pvt. practice King & King, Honolulu, 1993—; guest lecturer U. Hawaii Law School, 1997-98. Arbitrator Hawaii's Ct. Annexed Arbitrtion Program, 1987—; chair Chamber Music Hawaii's Fundraiser, 1988-90; chair County of Honolulu Zoning Bd. Appeals, 1989; vice-chancellor Episcopal Diocese Honolulu, 1989-96 (appointed spl. coun. Episcopal Ch. Eccles. Ct. 1996); active Jr. League Honolulu, 1981-87 (chair rummage sale fundraiser, projects com., bd. mem.); chair St. Andrews Episcopal Cathedral Newcomer Com., 1990, Heritage Fundraising Com., 1991, elected governing Bd. Cathedral, 1991-96, elected chair By-laws Revision Com., 1991-96, elected Bd. Workers St. Andrews, 1991-96 (chair 1992-96); elected Diocesan Coun., 1995-96, 1997—; elected Sec. Coun., 1995-99; elected to Spl. Investigating Com. regarding losses in the matter of Episcopal Homes, 1998; mem. Fundraiser Native Hawaiin Legal Corp., 1993-96 (most money raised 1993); sec. Republican 8th Senate Dist., 1994-95 (precinct sec. 1993, pres. 1994-95, v.p. 1995-96); del. to state conventions, 1992-98 (platform com. 1993); alt. del. Republican Nat. Convention in Houston, 1992; vol. Punahou Sch. Theatrical Performances, 1993-98; mem. Ka Iwi Action Coun.1993—; chairperson Women Lawyers for Bush/Quayle, 1992; mem. Team Hawaii Rep. donors cir., 1998. Mem. Hawaii State Bar Assn. (bd. dirs. 1991-92), Consumer Lawyers Hawaii (bd. govs. 1988-90), Hawaii Women Lawyers, Hawaii Assn. Criminal Def. Lawyers (co-founder, bd. dirs. 1987-90, pres. 1989). Republican. Home: 1163 Kaeleku St Honolulu HI 96825-3007 Office: King & King 735 Bishop St Ste 304 Honolulu HI 96813-4819

**KING, BERNARD T.,** lawyer; b. Gouverneur, N.Y., Feb. 28, 1935. BS, Le Moyne Coll., 1956; JD cum laude, Syracuse U., 1959. Bar: N.Y. 1959. Ptnr. Blitman and King, Syracuse, N.Y.; assoc. editor Syracuse Law Rev., 1958-59; lectr. Labor Studies Program, N.Y. State Sch. Indsl. and Labor Rels., Cornell U., 1974; sec. Onondaga County Indsl. Devel. Agy., 1978-81. Mem., bd. dirs. Syracuse Model Neighborhood Corp., 1972-75, Regents, 1973—, sec., 1983—, bd. trustees, 1984-90. vice chmn., bd. trustees, 1988, LeMoyne Coll., 1974-80, v.p. 1977-79, pres., 1979-80; bd. trustees Manlius Pebble Hill Sch. Corp.; mem. United Way Cen. N.Y., 1971-75, bd. dirs., 1981-87; com. mem. 33rd Congl. Dist. Naval Academise Selection Bd., 1980-83. With USAF, 1961-62, Air NG, 1959-65. Recipient Disting. Alumni award LeMoyne Coll., 1979, Whitney M. Seymour award Am. Arbitration Assn., 1986. Fellow Am. Bar Found.; mem. ABA (labor law and employment law com. 1963, chmn. labor and employment sect. 1987-88, co-chmn., subcom. B com. on devel. of law under NLRA 1971-76, sect. del. to ho. of dels., mem. spl. com. on drug crisis, mem. joint com. on employee benefits), Soc. Profls. in Dispute Resolution, Panel of Arbitrators, Am. Arbitration Assn. (bd. dirs. 1988), Onondaga County Bar Assn., N.Y. State Bar Assn. (exec. com., labor law sect. 1976—, chmn.-elect 1979, chmn. 1980-81), Am. Judicature Soc. Labor, Pension, profit-sharing, and employee benefits, Personal injury. Office: Blitman and King 500 S Salina St Ste 1100 Syracuse NY 13202-3397

**KING, CAROLYN DINEEN,** federal judge; b. Syracuse, N.Y., Jan. 30, 1938; d. Robert E. and Carolyn E. (Bareham) Dineen; children: James Randall, Philip Randall, Stephen Randall; m. John L. King, Jan. 1, 1988. A.B. summa cum laude, Smith Coll., 1959; LL.B., Yale U., 1962. Bar: D.C. 1962, Tex. 1963. Assoc. Fulbright & Jaworski, Houston, 1962-72; ptnr. Childs, Fortenbach, Beck & Guyton, Houston, 1972-78, Sullivan, Bailey, King, Randall & Sabom, Houston, 1978-79; circuit judge U.S. Ct. Appeals (5th cir.), Houston, 1979—, chief judge, 1999—. Trustee, mem. exec. com., treas. Houston Ballet Found., 1967-70; trustee, mem. exec. com., chmn. bd. trustees U. St. Thomas, 1988-98; mem. Houston dist. adv. coun. SBA, 1972-76; mem. Dallas regional panel Pres.'s Commn. White House Fellowships, 1972-76, mem. commn., 1977; bd. dirs. Houston chpt. Am. Heart Assn., 1978-79; nat. trustee Palmer Drug Abuse Program, 1978-79; trustee, sec., treas., chmn. audit com., fin. com., mem. mgmt. com. United Way Tex. Gulf Coast, 1979-85. Mem. ABA, Fed. Bar Assn., Am. Law Inst. (coun. 1991—, chmn. membership com. 1997—), State Bar Tex., Houston Bar Assn. Roman Catholic. Office: US Ct Appeals 11020 US Courthouse 515 Rusk St Houston TX 77002-2600

**KING, CHRISTY OLSON,** lawyer, researcher, author; b. Dallas, June 18, 1969; d. Gary Paul and Mary (Nicholson) King; m. Scott Michael Olson, Apr. 22, 1994. BAJ, La. State U., 1989; JD cum laude, Lewis and Clark Coll., 1993. Bar: Oreg. 1993. Atty. DuBoff Dorband Cushing & King, PLLC and predecessor firms, Portland, Oreg., 1994- . Co-author: Deskbook of Art Law, 2d edit., 1993. Vol., Oreg. Humane Soc., 1998—. Avocations: reading, dog obedience, home remodeling. Intellectual property, Trademark and copyright, General corporate. Office: DuBoff Dorband Cushing & King PLLC 6665 SW Hampton St Fl 2D Portland OR 97223-8357

**KING, DAVID PAUL,** lawyer; b. Washington, June 20, 1956; s. Ivan Robert and Alice King. AB, Princeton U., 1977; JD, U. Pa., 1982. Bar: Ga. 1984, U.S. Dist. Ct. (no. and so. dists.) Ga. 1984, U.S. Ct. Appeals (11th cir.) 1984, D.C. 1985, U.S. Dist. Ct. Md. 1987, U.S. Ct. Appeals (4th cir.) 1987, Md. 1991, U.S. Dist. Ct. D.C. 1995. Law clk. to Hon. Alvin B. Rubin, U.S. Ct. Appeals for 5th Cir., Baton Rouge, 1982-83; assoc. Rogers & Hardin, Atlanta, 1983-85, Covington & Burling, Washington, 1985-87; asst. U.S. atty. Dept. Justice, Balt., 1987-90; assoc. Hogan & Hartson, L.L.P., Balt., 1990-92, ptnr., 1992—; adj. prof. U. Md. Law Sch., Balt., 1995—. Mem. ABA, Fed. Bar Assn. (Md. bd. govs.), Md. Bar Assn., D.C. Bar Assn., Ga. Bar Assn., Serjant's Inn. Criminal, Health, General civil litigation. Office: Hogan & Hartson LLP 111 S Calvert St Ste 1600 Baltimore MD 21202-6106

**KING, DAVID ROY,** lawyer; b. N.Y.C., Jan. 5, 1950; s. Joseph S. and Doris (Kagan) K.; m. Eunice Searles, Aug. 22, 1971; children: Mark B., Anna M. BA, U. Pa., 1971; JD, Harvard U., 1974. Bar: Pa. 1974, U.S. Dist Ct. (ea. dist.) Pa. 1974. Assoc. Morgan, Lewis & Bockius LLP, Phila., 1974-81, ptnr., 1981—. Securities, Mergers and acquisitions, Computer. Office: Morgan Lewis & Bockius LLP 1701 Market St Philadelphia PA 19103-2903

**KING, FRANKLIN WEAVER,** lawyer; b. Alexandria, La., Aug. 8, 1942; s. William F. and Helen Kathleen (Weaver) K. BA, U. Ala., 1965; JD, Duke U., 1972. Bar: Calif. 1974. Pvt. practice law, San Francisco, 1974-88, Sacramento, 1988—. Served to lt. col. JAGC, USAFR, 1975-91. Mem. Am. Trial Lawyers Assn., Calif. Trial Lawyers Assn., ABA, Sacramento County Bar Assn., Calif. Bar Assn., Rancho Cordova C. of C. (pres. bd. dirs. 1997), Pi Kappa Phi, Phi Delta Phi. General corporate, Contracts commercial, Bankruptcy. Office: PO Box 2166 Orangevale CA 95662-7432

**KING, GARR MICHAEL,** federal judge; b. Pocatello, Idaho, Jan. 28, 1936; s. Warren I. King and Geraldine E. (Hanlon) Appleby; m. Mary Jo Rieber, Feb. 2, 1957; children: Mary, Michael, Matthew, James, Margaret, John, David. Student, U. Utah, 1957-59; LLB, Lewis and Clark Coll., 1963. Bar: Oreg. 1963, U.S. Dist. Ct. Oreg. 1965, U.S. Ct. Appeals (9th cir.) 1975, U.S. Supreme Ct. 1971. Dep. dist. atty. Multnomah County Dist. Atty.'s Office, Portland, Oreg., 1963-66; assoc. Morrison, Bailey, Dunn, Carney & Miller, Portland, 1966-71; ptnr. Kennedy & King, Portland, 1971-77, Kennedy, King & McClurg, Portland, 1977-82, Kennedy, King & Zimmer, Portland, 1982-98; judge U.S. Dist. Ct. Oreg., Portland, 1998—. Active various pvt. sch. and ch. bds. Served as sgt. USMC, 1954-57. Fellow Am. Coll. Trial Lawyers (regent 1995-98), Am. Bar Found.; mem. ABA, Oreg. Bar Assn., Multnomah County Bar Assn. (pres. 1975), Jud. Conf. 9th Cir. (del.), Northwestern Coll. Law Alumni Assn. (pres.), Multnomah Athletic Club. Democrat. Roman Catholic. Avocations: tennis, reading, gardening. Office: 907 US Courthouse 1000 SW 3rd Ave Portland OR 97204-2930

**KING, HENRY LAWRENCE,** lawyer; b. N.Y.C., Apr. 29, 1928; s. H. Abraham and Henrietta (Prentky) K.; m. Barbara Hope, 1949 (dec. May 1962); children: Elizabeth King Robertson, Patricia King Cantlay, Matthew Harrison.; m. Alice Mary Sturges, Aug. 1, 1963 (div. 1978); children: Katherine Masury King Baccile, Andrew Lawrence, Eleanor Sturges; m. Margaret Gram, Feb. 14, 1981. AB, Columbia U., 1948; LLB, Yale U., 1951. Bar: N.Y. 1952, U.S. Supreme Ct., other fed. cts. 1952. With Davis Polk & Wardwell, N.Y.C., 1951—, ptnr., 1961—, mng. ptnr., chmn., 1982-96. Mng. editor Yale Law Jour., 1951. Trustee, chmn. bd. Columbia U., 1983-95, chmn. emeritus, 1995—; chmn. bd. Columbia Presbyn. adv. coun.; pres. Assn. Alumni Columbia Coll., 1966-68, Alumni Fedn. Columbia U., 1973-75; chmn. Coll. Fund, 1972-73; pres. Yale Law Sch. Assn., 1984-86, chmn., 1986-88; bd. dirs. N.Y. Acad. of Medicine, Citizen's Com. for N.Y.C., Inc., Am. Skin Assn., Fishers Island Devel. Co., Fund for Modern Cts., Vols. of Legal Svc., Inc., Episcopal Charities, Columbia-Cornell Care, Inc.; vestryman Trinity Ch. N.Y., 1991-98; trustee Chapin Sch., 1977-89, Columbia U. Press, 1978-92. Recipient Columbia Alumni medal for conspicuous service, 1968, John Jay award, 1992. Fellow Am. Coll. Trial Lawyers; mem. ABA, Coun. on Fgn. Rels., Am. Law Inst., N.Y. State Bar Assn. (pres. 1988-89), Assn. Bar City N.Y., Am. Judicature Soc., Fishers Island Club, Century Assn., Union Club (N.Y.C.), Jupiter Island Club, Blind Brook Club, Fishers Island Yacht Club. Antitrust, Federal civil litigation, Private international. Home: 115 E 67th St New York NY 10021-5901 also: 61 Links Rd Hobe Sound FL 33455-2318 Office: Davis Polk & Wardwell 450 Lexington Ave New York NY 10017-3911

**KING, HENRY SPENCER, III,** lawyer; b. Charlotte, N.C., Feb. 7, 1941; s, Henry Spencer Jr. and Janie Pauline (Jenkins) K.; m. Ellen Frost Hayne, Aug. 31, 1963; children: Cheryl King Hay, Ann Lunsford King. BA with honors, Furman U., 1963; JD cum laude, U. S.C., 1968. Bar: S.C. 1963. Atty. Butler, Means, Evins & Browne, Spartanburg, S.C., 1968-78; ptnr. King and Hray, Spartanburg, 1978-92; shareholder Leatherwood Walker Todd & Mann, P.C., Greenville & Spartanburg, 1992—; city atty. City of Spartanburg, 1987—. Lt. col. U.S. Army, 1963-65. Mem. ABA, S.C. Bar Assn., Spartanburg Bar Assn., Internat. Assn. Def. Counsel, S.C. Def. Trial Attys. (past bd. dirs.), Def. Rsch. Inst., Spartanburg Country Club (bd. dirs. 1982-86), Rotary Club, Sertoma (Sertoman of Yr. 1978). E-mail: h.king.@lwtmlaw.com. Home: 3 Cateswood Dr Spartanburg SC 29302-3464 Office: Leatherwood Walker Todd & Mann PC 1451 E Main St Spartanburg SC 29307-2245

**KING, IRA THOMAS,** lawyer; b. Florence, Ala., Oct. 15, 1949; s. Ira Puller and Ellen (Maynor) K.; m. Deborah Thomas, Nov. 17, 1973; 1 child, Clifford Thomas. AA, Alvin (Tex.) Jr. Coll., 1973; BA Criminology, Rehab. and Policy Sci., Sam Houston State U., 1974; JD, U. Tex., 1977. Bar: Tex. 1978, U.S. Dist. Ct. (we. dist.) Tex. 1980, U.S. Dist. Ct. (so. dist.) Tex. 1983, U.S. Dist. Ct. (no. dist.) Tex. 1987, U.S. Dist. Ct. (ea. dist.) Tex. 1988. Assoc. Long, Dugger, Burner & Cotten, Austin, Tex., 1978-81; sole practice Austin, 1981-83; assoc. Hearne, Knolle, Lewallen, Livingston & Holcomb, Austin, 1983-86; asst. atty. gen. Tex. Atty. Gen.'s Office, Austin, 1986-87; ptnr. Cowles and Thompson, Dallas, 1987-92, Stephens & King, Dallas, 1993-94, King & Assocs., Dallas, 1994—; lectr. bus. law Austin Community Coll., 1982, estate planning Waddell Reed Fin. Cons., Austin, 1983; chief ins. investigation and rating sect.; cons. for Am. Internat. Group Nat. Alternative Dispute Resolution Program, 1992-93. Advisor Inmate Assistance Project, Austin, 1973-74, Police Action Project, Austin, 1974, observer; mem. adv. bd. Exec. Sec. Sch. Served with U.S. Army, 1967-71. Named one of Outstanding Young Men in Am., 1983. Mem. Tex. Assn. Def. Counsel, Phi Theta Kappa, Alpha Chi. Republican. Methodist. Avocation: martial arts, kayaking. State civil litigation, Insurance. Home: 4225 Stanford Ave Dallas TX 75225-6932 Office: King & Assocs 4311 Oak Lawn Ave Ste 200 Dallas TX 75219-2311

**KING, J. B.,** medical device company executive, lawyer. AB, Ind. U., 1951; LLB, Mich. U., 1954. Bar: Ind. 1954, Mich. 1954. Atty., ptnr. Baker & Daniels, 1954-87; v.p., gen. counsel Eli Lilly and Co., Indpls., 1987-95, Guidant Corp., Indpls., 1995—; bd. dirs. Ind. Corp. Survey Commn., Bank One, Indpls, Indpls. Water Co.; conf. bd. Coun. Chief Legal Officers. Mem. bd. govs. Riley Meml. Assn. Fellow Ind. Bar Found.; mem. ABA, Ind. State Bar Assn., Indpls. Bar Assn., 7th Cir. Bar Assn., Nat. Tax Assn. (com. on multistate taxation), Assn. Gen. Counsel, Ind. Legal Found. (bd. dirs.), Ind. Fiscal Policy Inst. (bd. govs.), Ind. Corp.Survey Commn. Home: 602 Plum Nearly Ln Apt B Wilmington NC 28403-8480 Office: Guidant Corp PO Box 44906 Indianapolis IN 46244-0906

**KING, J. BRADLEY,** lawyer; b. Noblesville, Ind., Sept. 2, 1957; s. Charles Joseph and Marina (Davis) K. BA in History & Polit. Sci. with honors, Ind. U., 1978; JD, Coll. of William and Mary, 1981. Bar: Calif. 1981, Ind. 1985. Pvt. practice cons. to local govts. Indpls., 1982-85; staff atty. Legislative Svcs. Agy., State of Ind., Indpls., 1985-90; asst. corp. counsel, chief lobbyist at gen. assembly City of Indpls., 1990-92; gen. counsel State of Ind. Election Commn., Indpls., 1992—; del. Ind. State Conv., 1998. Sr. warden, vestryman Episcopal Ch. of All Sts., Indpls., 1989-91, 93-96; asst. state party rules Ind. Rep. State Com., Indpls., 1997, chair Ind. presdl. electors meeting, 1996. Named Election Adminstr. of Yr., Ballot Access News, 1997; named to Order of Ky. Cols. Phi Beta Kappa, 1977. Avocations: singing, walking. Office: Ind Election Commn 302 W Washington St Ste E-204 Indianapolis IN 46204-2738

**KING, JACK A.,** lawyer; b. Lafayette, Ind., July 29, 1936; s. Noah C. and Mabel E. (Pierce) K.; m. Mary S. King, Dec. 10, 1960; children: Jeffrey A., Janice D., Julie D. BS in Fin., Ind. U., 1958, JD, 1961. Bar: Ind. 1961. Ptnr. Ball, Eggleston, King & Bumbleburg, Lafayette, 1961-70; judge Superior Ct. 2 of Tippecanoe County, Ind., 1970-78; v.p., assoc. gen. counsel Superior Ct. 2 of Tippecanoe County, 1979, v.p., gen. counsel, asst. sec., 1980-85; v.p., counsel Sentry Ctr. West, 1981-85; asst. gen. counsel Sentry Corp., 1979-85; v.p., gen. counsel, asst. sec. Gt. S.W. Fire Ins. Co., 1980-85, Gt. S.W. Surplus Lines Ins. Co., 1981-85; v.p., gen. counsel Dairyland County Mut. Ins. Co. Tex., 1980-85; v.p. legal, asst. sec. Scottsdale Ins. Co., 1985-95; asst. sec. Nat. Casualty Co., 1985-95; v.p. legal, asst. sec. Scottsdale Indemnity Co., 1992-95; sr. v.p., gen. coun. TIG Excess & Surplus Lines, Inc., 1995-96; v.p. Ariz. Ins. Info. Assn., 1988-96; exec. dir. Ariz. Ins. Guaranty Funds, 1998—; bd. dirs. Countrywide Ins. Co.; cons., mediator and arbitrator, 1996-97; exec. com. Ariz. Joint Underwriting Plan, 1980-81; mem. Ariz. Property & Casualty Ins. Commn., 1985-86, vice-chmn., 1986; mem. Ariz. Study Commn. on Ins., 1986-87, Ariz. Task Force on Ct. Orgn. and Adminstrn., 1988-89; adv. com. Ariz. Ho. Rep. Majority Leaders, 1989, Ariz. Dept. Ins. Fraud Unit, 1997-97. Contbr. to The Law of Competitive Business Practices, 2d edit. Bd. dirs. Scottsdale Art Ctr. Assn., 1981-84. Mem. ABA, Ind. Bar Assn., Maricopa County Bar Assn. General corporate, Insurance. Office: 3443 N Central Ave Ste 1000 Phoenix AZ 85012-2209

**KING, JAMES LAWRENCE,** federal judge; b. Miami, Fla., Dec. 20, 1927; s. James Lawrence and Viola (Clodfelter) K.; m. Mary Frances Kapa, June 1, 1961; children—Lawrence Daniel, Kathryn Ann, Karen Ann, Mary Virginia. BA in Edn., U. Fla., 1949, JD, 1953; LHD (hon.), St. Thomas U., 1992. Bar: Fla. 1953. Assoc. Sibley & Davis, Miami, Fla., 1953-57; ptnr. Sibley Giblin King & Levenson, Miami, 1957-64; judge 11th Jud. Cir. Dade County, Miami, 1964-70; temp. assoc. justice Supreme Ct. Fla., 1965; temp. assoc. judge Fla. Ct. Appeals (2d, 3d and 4th dist.), 1965-68; judge U.S. Dist. Ct. (so. dist.) Fla., Miami, 1970-84, chief judge, 1984-91, sr. judge, 1991—; temp. judge U.S. Ct. Appeals 5th cir., 1977-78; mem. Jud. Conf. U.S., 1984-87, mem. adv. commn. jud. activities, 1973-76, mem. joint commn. code jud. conduct, 1974-76, mem. commn. to consider stds. for admission to practice in fed. cts., 1976-79, chmn. implementation com. for admission attys. to fed. practice, 1979-85, mem. com. bankruptcy legis., 1977-78; mem. Jud. Conf. U.S., 1984-87; mem. Jud. Coun. 11th Cir., 1989-92; pres. 5th cir. U.S. Dist. Judges Assn., 1977-78; chief judge U.S. Dist. Ct. C.Z., 1977-78; long range planning commn. Fed. Judiciary, 1991-95. Mem. state exec. council U. Fla., 1956-59; mem. Bd. Control Fla. Governing State Univs. and Colls., 1964. Served to 1st lt. USAF, 1953-55. Recipient Outstanding Alumnus award U. Fla. Law Rev., 1980. Mem. Fla. Bar Assn. (pres. jr. bar 1963-64, bd. govs. 1958-63, Merit award young lawyer sect. 1967), ABA, Am. Law Inst., Inst. Jud. Adminstrn., Fla. Blue Key, Pi Kappa Tau, Phi Delta Phi. Democrat. Home: 11950 SW 67th Ct Miami FL 33156-4756 Office: US Dist Ct James King Fed Justice Bldg 99 NE 4th St Rm 1127 Miami FL 33132-2139

**KING, JEFFREY P.,** lawyer; b. Austin, Tex., Nov. 8, 1954. BA, Coll. William and Mary, 1976; MBA, Duke U., 1980, JD, 1980. Assoc. Haynes and Boone, Dallas, 1980-87, ptnr., 1988—, chair health care sect., 1993—. Health, General corporate, Non-profit and tax-exempt organizations. Office: Haynes and Boone LLP 901 Main St Ste 3100 Dallas TX 75202-3789

**KING, JENNIFER ELIZABETH,** editor; b. Summit, N.J., July 15, 1970; d. Layton E. and Margery A. (Long) K. BS in Journalism, Northwestern U., Evanston, Ill., 1992. Asst. editor Giant Steps Media, Chgo., 1992-93, assoc. editor Corp. Legal Times, 1993-94, dir. confs., 1994-95, mng. editor Corp. Legal Times, 1995—; acting mng. editor Ill. Legal Times, 1996-97; mng. editor U.S. Bus. Litig., 1997. Office: Corporate Legal Times LLC 3 E Huron St Chicago IL 60611-2705

**KING, KELLEY JONES,** editor. Editor Tex. Bar Jour., Austin. Office: State Bar Tex 1414 Colorado St Ste 312 Austin TX 78701-1627

**KING, LAWRENCE PHILIP,** lawyer, educator; b. Schenectady, N.Y., Jan. 16, 1929; s. Louis D. and Sonia K.; children—David J. Kaufman, Deborah J. King. B.S.S., CCNY, 1950; LL.B., NYU, 1953; LL.M., U. Mich., 1957. Bar: N.Y. 1954, U.S. Supreme Ct. 1963. Atty. Paramount Pictures Corp., N.Y.C., 1955-56; asst. prof. law Wayne State U., 1957-59; asst. prof. NYU, 1959-61, assoc. prof., 1961-63, prof., 1963—, Charles Seligson prof. law, 1979—, assoc. dean Sch. Law, 1973-77; of counsel Wachtell, Lipton, Rosen & Katz, N.Y.C.; cons. Commn. to Study Bankruptcy Law U.S., 1970-73, advisor nat. bankruptcy rev. com., 1996-97; assoc. reporter adv. com. on bankruptcy rules U.S. Jud. Conf., 1968-76, reporter, 1979-83, mem. adv. com. on bankruptcy rules, 1983-92; vis. faculty law Hebrew U., Jerusalem, 1971, 87, 94, Haifa U., 1994, 96, 97, 98, 99, Tel Aviv U., 1987, 94, Temple U. Sch. Law, U. Calif. Law Sch., Berkeley; lectr. Bar Ilan U., U. Stockholm, U. Innsbruck, Fed. Ct. Author: (with R. Duesenberg) Sales and Bulk Transfers Under the U.C.C., 1966, supplement, 1999, (with M. Cook) Creditors Rights, Debtor's Protection and Bankruptcy, Cases and Materials, 1985, 2d edit., 1989, 3d edit., 1997; contbr. articles, book revs. to legal jours.; edtor-in-chief: Collier on Bankruptcy, 1964, 15th edit. rev., 1979—; co-editor-in-chief: Collier Bankruptcy Practice Guide, 1981—. Trustee Village of Saltaire (N.Y.), 1980-84, mayor, 1984-86, acting justice, 1988—. Recipient NYU Law Alumni Achievement award, 1976, NYU Law Alumni 25-Yr. Faculty Svc. award, 1984, legal teaching award, 1993, award Bankruptcy Lawyers divsn. UJA-Fedn., 1984, Man of Yr. award Comml. Law League Am., 1969, Disting. Svc. award Am. Coll. Bankruptcy, 1997. Mem. ABA, N.Y. State Bar Assn., Assn. of Bar of City of N.Y., Nat. Bankruptcy Conf., Am. Law Inst. Office: NYU Sch Law 40 Washington Sq S New York NY 10012-1005

**KING, LAWRENCE R.,** lawyer; b. Quincy, Ill., May 18, 1951; s. J. Leonard and Edna R. King; m. Susan T. Wentz, Sept. 7, 1974; children: Thomas C., Amanda K. BA, U. Mo., 1973; JD, Hamline U., 1976. Bar: Minn. 1976. Assoc. Murnane, Conlin, White & Brandt, St. Paul, 1976-93; ptnr., dir. King & Hatch, P.A., St. Paul, 1993-98; pvt. practice, St. Paul, 1998—; pres. Minn. Def. Lawyers Assn., Mpls., 1991-92. Fellow Am. Bar Found., Internat. Soc. Barristers; mem. ABA, Am. Bd. Trial Advs., Wis. Bar Assn., Minn. State Bar Assn. (bd. govs. 1982-85, 92-93, chmn. young lawyers sect. 1982-83), Ramsey County Bar Assn. Product liability, General civil litigation, Personal injury. Home: 3 Deer Ln North Oaks MN 55127-6407 Office: King & Counsel LLC 1500 Landmark Tower 345 Saint Peter St Saint Paul MN 55102-1211

**KING, MICHAEL HOWARD,** lawyer; b. Chgo., Mar. 10, 1943; s. Warren and Betty (Fine) K.; m. Candice M. King, Aug. 18, 1968; children—Andrew, Julie. B.S. Washington U., St. Louis 1967, J.D. 1970. Bar: Ill. 1970, U.S. Dist. Ct. (no. dist.) Ill. 1970, U.S. Dist. Ct. (ea. dist.) Wis. 1972, U.S. Ct. Appeals (7th cir.) 1974, U.S. Ct. Appeals (5th cir.) 1979, U.S. Supreme Ct. 1975, U.S. Ct. Appeals (3d cir.) 1983, U.S. Tax Ct. 1987, U.S. Ct. Appeals (10th cir.) 1987, U.S. Dist. Ct. (no. dist.) Calif. 1987, U.S. Dist. Ct. Nebr. 1988, U.S. Dist. Ct. (ctrl. dist.) Ill. 1992, U.S. Dist. Ct. (no. dist.) N.Y. 1992, U.S. Ct. Appeals (2nd cir.) 1994. Spl. atty. organized crime, racketeering sect. U.S. Dept. Justice, Washington, 1970-73; asst. U.S. atty. No. Dist. Ill., Chgo., 1973-75; assoc. Antonow & Fink, Chgo., 1976, ptnr., 1977-79; ptnr. Ross & Hardies, Chgo., 1979-95; chmn. Bd. Commr. Office of State Appellate Defender. Co-author Model Jury Instructions in Criminal Antitrust Cases, 1982, Handbook on Antitrust Grand Jury Investigations, 1988. Bd. dirs. Chgo. Youth Ctrs., 1977-82; trustee Cove Sch., 1984-88, the Goodman Theatre, 1993—. Mem. ABA (litigation sect., antitrust sect., criminal practice procedure com.), Ill. Bar Assn., Chgo. Bar Assn. (judiciary com., antitrust com.), Am. Judicature Soc., Fed. Bar Assn., Assn. Trial Lawyers Am., Mid-Am. Club (bd. govs.), Econ. Club, Phi Delta Phi, Alpha Epsilon Pi. Antitrust, Federal civil litigation, Criminal. Home: 2025 Windy Hill Ln Highland Park IL 60035-4233 Office: Ross & Hardies 150 N Michigan Ave Ste 2500 Chicago IL 60601-7567

**KING, PATRICK OWEN,** lawyer; b. L.A., June 27, 1953; s. Owen and Barbara King; m. Dawn Marie Dawson, May 27, 1987; children: Allison Ecklund, Rachel, Aubrey. AA, Santa Monica Coll., 1975; BA, San Diego State U., 1979; JD, Southwestern U., 1982. Bar: Nev. 1994, U.S. Dist. Ct. Nev., U.S. Ct. Appeals (9th cir.), U.S. Supreme Ct. Prosecuting atty. Pierce County Prosecutor, Tacoma, 1982-84; CEO St. Marks Med. Ctr., Tacoma, 1984-94; atty. Bell & Young, Ltd., Las Vegas, 1994-95; pres., pvt. practice Carson City, Nev., 1995—. Advisor to pres. Douglas County C.C., Carson City, 1998. Mem. ABA, ATLA, Am. Health Lawyers Assn., Am. Coll. Legal Medicine, Nev. Trial Lawyers Assn. Avocation: wine growing. Fax: 775-887-7406. Health, General civil litigation, Estate planning. Office: 550 W Washington St Carson City NV 89703-3829

**KING, PETER J.,** lawyer; b. Stowe Township, Pa., June 15, 1938; s. Peter and Mary (Dugan) K.; m. Dolly J. Mauro, Apr. 23, 1960; children: Linda, Carole, Ronald. BA, Duquesne U., 1960, JD, 1963. Bar: Pa. 1963, U.S. Dist. Ct. (we. dist.) Pa. 1963, U.S. Supreme Ct. 1967. Ptnr. Tucker & Arensberg, Pitts., 1964-80; sole practice Pitts., 1980-85; ptnr. King & Kulik, Pitts., 1986-91, King & King, Pitts., 1991—; civil arbitrator U.S. Dist. Ct. for Western Dist. of Pa., 1992—. Editor-in-chief Duquesne U. Law Rev., 1962. Solicitor Montour Sch. Dist., McKees Rocks, Pa., 1969-88. Irishman of Yr. award Knights of Equity, 1980. Mem. Allegheny County Bar Assn. (various offices), Duquesne U. Law Alumni Assn. (officer 1968—, pres. 1989-91), Duquesne U. Alumni Assn. (bd. dirs. 1970-82). Democrat. Roman Catholic. Lodge: Italian Sons and Daus. Am. (past pres. Morningside club). Family and matrimonial, State civil litigation, Criminal. Home: 1441 Duffield St Pittsburgh PA 15206-1320 Office: King & King 919 Maryland Ave Pittsburgh PA 15232-2709

**KING, PETER NELSON,** lawyer; b. Marblehead, Mass., Nov. 1, 1958; s. Robert Paul and Janice Lee K. BA in Internat. Trade and Transp., U. Wash., 1984; JD, Willamette U., 1987; postgrad., Pepperdine U., Malibu, Calif., 1995—. Bar: Calif. 1989, U.S. Supreme Ct. 1993, U.S. Dist Ct. (so. and ctrl. dists.) Calif. 1989, U.S. Ct. Appeals (9th cir.) 1989, Calif. Supreme Ct. 1989; lic. real estate broker, Calif.; lic. yacht capt. USCG. Rsch. atty. South Bay Ct., Torrance, Calif., 1988-89; prosecutor L.A. City Atty.'s Office, 1989-90, dep. city atty., civil liability divsn., 1990-92, dep. city atty., police litigation divsn., 1992-93, gen. counsel Housing Authority of L.A., 1993-94, gen. counsel land use divsn., 1994—. Contbr. articles to profl. jours. Founder Blitzsnell Alpine Athletic Devel. Found., Big Bear, Calif., 1997; dir. Advancement of Alpine Ski Racing. Recipient Excellence in Lawyering recommendation L.A. City Coun., 1996. Mem. ABA, L.A. City Atty's. Assn. (dir. 1994, 95), U.S. Ski Assn. (master Alpine skier/racer), Phi Alpha Delta. Avocations: alpine ski racing, sailing, biking, photography. Home: PO Box 53737 Los Angeles CA 90053-0737 Office: LA City Attorney Attorney's Office 1800 CHE 200 N Main St Los Angeles CA 90012

**KING, ROBERT BRUCE,** federal judge; b. White Sulphur Springs, W.Va., Jan. 29, 1940; m. Julia Kay Doak, Apr. 16, 1965. BA, W.Va. U., 1961; JD, W.Va. Coll. of Law, 1968. Bar: W.Va. 1968, U.S. Dist. Ct. (so. dist.) W.Va. 1968, U.S. Ct. Appeals W.Va. 1968, U.S. Ct. Appeals (4th cir.) 1970, U.S. Dist. Ct. (no. dist.) W.Va. 1972, U.S. Supreme Ct. 1974, U.S. Dist. Ct. (ea. dist.) Ky. 1975, U.S. Claims Ct. 1985, U.S. Tax Ct. 1991. Asst. mgr. Sam Snead All-Am. Golf Course, Sharpes, Fla., summer 1965; rsch. asst. State and Cmty. Planning Office, Office of R&D, W.Va. U., Morgantown, 1966-68; law clk. Chief Judge John A. Field, Jr. U.S. Dist. Ct. (so. dist.) W.Va., Charleston, 1968-69; assoc. Haynes and Ford, Lewisburg, W.Va., 1969-70; asst. U.S. atty. So. Dist. of W.Va., Charleston, 1970-74; assoc. Spilman,

Thomas, Battle and Klostermeyer, Charleston, 1975, ptnr., 1976-77, 81; U.S. atty. So. Dist. of W.Va., Charleston, 1977-81; ptnr. King Allen Guthrie & McHugh, 1981-98; judge U.S. Ct. Appeals (4th cir.), Richmond, Va., 1998—. Mem. Jud. Investigation Commn. of W.Va., 1990-94; vis. com. Coll. of Law of W.Va. U., 1997—. Patrick Duffy Koontz scholar. Fellow Am. Coll. Trial Lawyers; mem. ABA, W.Va. Bar Assn., Kanawha County Bar Assn., Greenbrier County Bar Assn.,U.S. Golf Assn., W.Va. Golf Assn., W.Va. U. Alumni Assn., W.Va. Law Sch. Assn., Fellows of the Am. Bar Found., Jud. Conf. of 4th Cir. Ct. Appeals, Am. Bd. Trial Advocates (W. Va. chpt. pres. 1986-90), Nat. Assn. Criminal Def. Lawyers, Order of the Coif, Pi Sigma Alpha, Phi Alpha Theta. Presbyterian. Office: c/o Fourth Circuit Clk 1100 E Main St Richmond VA 23219-3538*

**KING, ROBERT LEE,** lawyer; b. Vincennes, Ind., June 19, 1946; s. George W. and Nadine E. (Muentzer) K.; children: Jeffrey, Kevin, Allison. Student, U. Denver, 1964-66; BS, Ind. U., 1968; JD, Harvard U., 1972. Bar: Ind. 1973, U.S. Dist. Ct. (no. dist.) Ind. 1973, Fla. 1973. Assoc. English, McCaughan and O'Bryan, Ft. Lauderdale, Fla., 1973-76; ptnr. Andrews, Voorheis, Lehrer & Baggett, Ft. Lauderdale, 1976-86, Birr & King, P.A., Ft. Lauderdale, 1986-96; pvt. practice Ft. Lauderdale, 1997—. Bd. dirs. Playa del Sol Assn., Inc., Ft. Lauderdale, 1978—, sec., 1987-96, treas., 1996-97, v.p., 1997—. Mem. Ind. Soc. CPAs, Ind. U. Alumni Assn. (pres. Ft. Lauderdale chpt. 1976-85, treas. 1986-90), Mensa, Tower Club, Sigma Chi Alumni Assn. (pres. Ft. Lauderdale chpt. 1976, treas. 1987—). Democrat. Methodist. Avocations: basketball, theater. Real property, Probate, General corporate. Office: 2101 N Andrews Ave Ste 200 Fort Lauderdale FL 33311-3934

**KING, ROBERT LEWIS,** lawyer; b. Johnson City, Tenn., June 20, 1950; s. Herbert and Ruth Marie (Dulaney) K. BA, Earlham Coll., 1973; MS, Columbia U., 1974; JD, U. Tenn., 1985. Bar: Tenn. 1986, D.C. 1989. Fgn. corr. AP, Paris, 1971-72; reporter The Miami (Fla.) Herald, 1974-75; polit. editor The Courier-Post, Cherry Hill, N.J., 1975-78; prof. communications East Tenn. State U., Johnson City, 1978-88; mem. Tenn. Legislature, Nashville, 1978-84; sole practice Johnson City, 1986—; mem. adj. faculty journalism Milligan Coll., Tenn.; chmn. criminal law subcom. Tenn. Ho. Reps., 1978-84. Recipient Scripps-Howard Pub. Service citation, 1977, citation 1990 Dist. Judges for Pro Bono Svcs. to Poor. Mem. ABA (Silver Gavel award 1976), Assn. Trial Lawyers Am., Tenn. Trial Lawyers Assn., N.J. Soc. Profl. Journalists (Investigative Reporting award 1976), Am. Health Lawyers Assn. Personal injury, General civil litigation, Health. Home: 1302 Sunset Dr Johnson City TN 37604-3620 Office: PO Box 4055 Johnson City TN 37602-4055

**KING, ROBERT LUCIEN,** lawyer; b. Petaluma, Calif., Aug. 9, 1936; s. John Joseph and Ramona Margaret (Thorson) K.; m. Suzanne Nanette Parre, May 18, 1956 (div. 1973); children: Renee Michelle, Candyce Lynn, Danielle Louise, Benjamin Robert; m. Linda Diane Carey, Mar. 15, 1974 (div. 1981); 1 child, Debra; m. J'an See, Oct. 27, 1984 (div. 1989); 1 child, Jonathan F.; m. Marilyn Collins, June 15, 1991. AB in Philosophy, Stanford U., 1958, JD, 1960. Bar: Calif., N.Y. 1961. Asst. U.S. atty. U.S. Atty's. Office (so. dist.), N.Y.C., 1964-67; assoc. Debevoise & Plimpton, N.Y.C., 1960-64, 67-70, ptnr., 1970—; mng. ptnr. Debevoise & Plimpton, L.A., 1989-95; lectr. Practicing Law Inst., N.Y.C., ABA, Asia/Pacific Ctr. for Resolution of Internat. Bus. Disputes, CPR Inst. for Dispute Resolution. Fellow Am. Coll. Trial Lawyers; mem. ABA, Assn. Bar City N.Y., Calif. Bar Assn. Democrat. Avocation: poetry. State civil litigation, Federal civil litigation, Criminal. Home: 16 Lockwood Rd Scarsdale NY 10583-5302

**KING, RONALD BAKER,** federal judge; b. San Antonio, Aug. 16, 1953; s. Donald Dick and Elaine (Baker) K.; m. Cynthia Sauer, June 7, 1975; children: Karen Elizabeth, Ronald Baker Jr., Kelsey Ann. BA, So. Meth. U., 1974; JD, U. Tex., 1977. Bar: Tex. 1977, U.S. Dist. Ct. (we. dist.) Tex. 1980, U.S. Ct. Appeals (5th cir.) 1981, U.S. Tax Ct. 1985. Briefing atty. Supreme Ct. Tex., Austin, 1977-78; assoc. Foster, Lewis, Langley, Gardner & Banack Inc., San Antonio, 1978-82, ptnr., 1982-88; judge U.S. Bankruptcy Ct. (we. dist.) Tex., San Antonio, 1988—. Mem. Tex. Bar Assn. Presbyterian. Avocations: piano, basketball, tennis, water sports. Home: 1702 Hounds Rise St San Antonio TX 78248-1206 Office: US Bankruptcy Ct PO Box 1439 San Antonio TX 78295-1439

**KING, RONNIE PATTERSON,** lawyer; b. Henderson, N.C., Nov. 25, 1946; s. Gerston Daniel and Ola (Mustian) K.; m. Barbara Hawks, July 22, 1973; children—Wells Patterson, Paige Rose. B.S., N.C. State U., 1969; J.D., U. N.C., 1972. Bar: N.C. 1972, U.S. Dist. Ct. (mid. dist.) N.C. 1975. Asst. dist. atty. N.C. 9th Jud. Dist., 1972-73; ptnr. Burke & King, Roxboro, N.C., 1974; sole practice, Roxboro, 1975—. 1st v.p. N.C. chpt. Arthritis Found., Durham, 1984, pres. 1985, Named Nat. Vol., Arthritis Found., 1981, Kiwanian of Yr., Roxboro Kiwanis, 1974-75. Mem. ABA, N.C. Bar Assn., Person County Bar Assn. (pres. 1982), Assn. Trial Lawyers Am., N.C. Trial Lawyers Assn., Roxboro C. of C. (pres. 1984). Democrat. Methodist. Lodge: Kiwanis (pres. 1978, lt. gov. Carolina's dist. 1980-81). State civil litigation, Personal injury, Criminal. Office: PO Box 738 300 S Main St Roxboro NC 27573-5526

**KING, SAMUEL PAILTHORPE,** federal judge; b. Hankow, China, Apr. 13, 1916; s. Samuel W. and Pauline (Evans) K.; m. Anne Van Patten Grilk, July 8, 1944; children—Samuel Pailthorpe, Louise Van Patten, Charlotte Lelepoki. B.S., Yale, 1937, LL.B., 1940. Bar: D.C., Hawaii bars 1940. Practiced law Honolulu, 1941-42, 46-61, 70-72, Washington, 1942; atty. King & McGregor, 1947-53, King & Myhre, 1957-61; judge 1st Circuit Ct. Hawaii, 1961-70, Family Ct., 1966-70; sr. judge U.S. Dist. Ct. for Hawaii, 1972—, chief judge, 1974-84; Faculty Nat. Coll. State Judiciary, 1968-73, Nat. Inst. Trial Advocacy, 1976, U. Hawaii Law Sch., 1980-84. Co-translator, co-editor: (O. Korschelt) The Theory and Practice of Go, 1965. Served with USNR, 1941-46; capt. Res. ret. Fellow Am. Bar Found.; mem. ABA, Hawaii Bar Assn. (pres. 1953), Order of Coif. Republican (chmn. Hawaii central com. 1953-55, nat. com. 1971-72). Episcopalian. Home: 1717 Mott-smith Dr Apt 2814 Honolulu HI 96822-2850 Office: US Dist Ct 300 Ala Moana Blr Rm C461 Honolulu HI 96850-0461

**KING, SAMUEL PAILTHORPE, JR.,** lawyer; b. Honolulu, June 16, 1947; s. Samuel Pailthorpe Sr. and Anne Van Patten (Grilk) K.; m. Adrienne Caryl Sepaniak, Oct. 19, 1974; children: Christopher E.S., Samuel Wilder II. BS in Econs., Yale U., 1969; JD, U. Colo., 1973. Bar: Hawaii 1974, U.S. Ct. Appeals (9th cir.) 1974, U.S. Supreme Ct., 1978. Ptnr. King & King, Honolulu; arbitrator Court program and AAA, Honolulu, 1985—. vice chancellor Episc. Diocese Honolulu, 1989-93. Mem. Hawaii Assn. Criminal Def. Lawyers (pres. 1988, sec. 1989—, editor monthly newsletter 1989—), Hawaii State Bar Assn. (mem. jud. adminstrn. com.). Republican. Avocations: English change ringing cathedral bells. Home: 1163 Kaeleku St Honolulu HI 96825-3007 Office: 735 Bishop St Ste 308 Honolulu HI 96813-4819

**KING, THOMAS RAY,** lawyer; b. Mpls., May 18, 1940; s. Ray W. and Charlotte Francis K.; m. Jean Kathleen, June 4, 1944; 1 child, Blair Thomas. BA in Psychology, U. Minn., 1964, LLB, 1965. Ptnr. Cox King & Stern, Mpls., 1966-77, Wright, West & Pessner, Mpls., 1977-84; shareholder, chmn. bd. dirs. Fredrikson & Byron, P.A., Mpls., 1984—; dir. Datakey Inc., Burnsville, Minn., 1981—, Sunrise Internat., Mpls., 1993—, Metacom, Inc., Mpls., 1998. Former chmn., exec. com. Fund for Legal Aid Soc., Mpls., 1988—; dir., exec. com. Children's Home Soc., St. Inez, Minn., 1992—; chmn. prospects com. United Way, Mpls., 1992-97. Williams scholar U. Minn., 1958-62. Mem. ABA, Mpls. Athletic Club, North Oaks Golf Club (dir., pres.). Avocations: traveling, golfing, sports, reading, history. Home: 12 Evergreen Ln North Oaks MN 55127-2003 Office: Fredrikson & Byron 900 2nd Ave S Ste 1100 Minneapolis MN 55402-3397

**KING, VICTOR I.,** lawyer, educator; b. Hong Kong, Nov. 12, 1964; s. William tung-Liang and Chi ging (Chu) K. BA in Polit. Sci. with honors, U. Chgo., 1986, MA in Social Sci., 1986; JD, U. Mich., 1989. Bar: Calif. 1990, U.S. Dist. Ct. (ctrl. dist.) Calif. 1991, U.S. Dist. Ct. (ea. dist.) Calif. 1991, U.S. Ct. Appeals (9th cir.) 1991. Assoc. Alschuler, Grossman & Pines, L.A., 1989-90, Ochoa & Sillas, L.A., 1991-95, Bottum & Feliton, L.A., 1996—; adj. faculty mem. Glendale (Calif.) C.C., 1996—. Trustee Glendale C.C., 1997—. Mem. Rotary. E-mail: vking@Botfel.com. Professional liability, General civil litigation, Insurance. Home: 2061 Valderas Dr Glendale CA 91208-1348 Office: Bottum & Feliton 3200 Wilshire Blvd Ste 1500 Los Angeles CA 90010-1333

**KING, WARREN R.,** judge. Grad., Rensselaer Polytech. Inst.; JD, Am. U.; LLM, Yale U. Atty. U.S. Dist. Ct. D.C.; chief grand jury/intake divsn., dep. and acting chief divsn. Superior Ct. Washington; with Office of Improvements in Adminstrn. of Justice U.S. Dept. Justice; assoc. judge Superior Ct. D.C., Washington, 1981-81, U.S. Ct. Appeals (D.C. cir.), Washington, 1991—, D.C. Ct. Appeals, Washington; mem. faculty Antioch Sch. Law, 1975—; mem. staff Atty. Gen.'s task force on violent crime; mem. hearing com. Bd. Profl. Responsibility. With USN. Office: Dist of Columbia Court of Appeals 500 Indiana Ave NW Rm 6000 Washington DC 20001-2131

**KING, WILLIAM H., JR.,** lawyer; b. Richmomd, Va., Nov. 4, 1940. AB, Dartmouth Coll., 1963; LLB, U. Va., 1967; MA (hon.), Dartmouth Coll., 1992. Bar: Va. 1967, Tex. 1993. Mem. McGuire, Woods, Battle & Boothe, Richmond. Fellow Am. Bar Found., Am. Coll. Trial Lawyers; mem. ABA. Product liability, General civil litigation, Toxic tort. Office: McGuire Woods Battle & Boothe One James Ctr Richmond VA 23219-4030

**KING, WILLIAM KIMBLE, JR.,** lawyer; b. Scranton, Pa., Apr. 11, 1946; s. William K. and Shirley Theresa (Tolan) K.; m. Pavinee Phasaphant, Nov. 22, 1974; 1 child, Joseph Kim-Lee. BS in Polit. Sci., U. Scranton, 1968; MS in Human Resource Mgmt., Gonzaga U., 1978, JD, 1981; LLM, U. London, 1983. Bar: Wash. 1981, U.S. Dist. Ct. (ea. and we. dists.) Wash. 1981, U.S. Ct. Appeals (9th cir.) 1985. Commd. USAF, 1968, advanced through grades to col., 1997; law clk. to presiding justice Wash. State Supreme Ct., Olympia, 1981-82; assoc. Davis, Wright & Jones, Seattle, 1983-85; dir. European and aerospace programs trade divsn. Dept. Cmty., Trade and Econ. Devel., Seattle, 1986—. Trustee Seattle World Affairs Coun., 1987, 95. Mem. ABA, Wash. State Bar Assn., Wash. State Biotech. Assn. (bd. dirs.), French-Am. C. of C. (dir. Seattle chpt., pres. 1994-97, 99—), Wash. Aerospace Assn. (bd. dirs. 1996—), Royal Air Force Club (London), U. London Convocation. Office: Dept Cmty Trade & Econ Devel Internat Trade Divsn 2001 6th Ave Ste 2600 Seattle WA 98121-2895

**KING, WILLIAM OLIVER,** lawyer; b. Louisburg, N.C., July 29, 1937; s. James Benjamin and Louise (Rentz) K.; m. Virginia Vann, Aug. 5, 1961; children: William O. Jr., Bradley V. AB in English, U. N.C., 1959; LLB, Wake Forest U., 1964. Bar: N.C., U.S. Dist. Ct. (mid. dist.) N.C. 1964, U.S. Dist. Ct. (eas. dist.) N.C. 1995, U.S. Ct. Appeals (14th cir.), U.S. Ct. Mil. Appeals 1981. Assoc. Mount, White, King, Hutson, Durham, N.C., 1964-85; ptnr. King, Walker, Lambe, Crabtree, Durham, 1985—; judge advocate, N.C., 1990-93. Col. U.S. Army N.G., 1961-98. Mem. Am. Bd. Trial Advocates (pres. 1995-97), N.C. State Bar (pres. 1997-98), N.C. Acad. Trial Lawyers (pres. 1987-88), 14th Jud. Bar (pres. 1985-86). Democrat. Episcopalian. Avocations: golf, biking, photography. Personal injury, Family and matrimonial, Condemnation. Office: King Walker Lambe & Crabtree PO Box 51549 Durham NC 27717-1549

**KINGHAM, RICHARD FRANK,** lawyer; b. Lafayette, Ind., Aug. 2, 1946; s. James R. and Loretta C. (Hoenigke) K.; m. Justine Frances McClung, July 6, 1968; 1 child, Richard Patterson. BA, George Washington U., 1968; JD, U. Va., 1973. Bar: D.C. 1973, U.S. Dist. Ct. D.C. 1974, U.S. Ct. Appeals (8th cir.) 1977, U.S. Supreme Ct. 1977, U.S. Ct. Appeals (5th cir.) 1980; registered fgn. lawyer Law Soc. Eng. and Wales, 1994. Editorial asst. Washington Star, 1964-68, 69-70; assoc. Covington & Burling, Washington, 1973-81, ptnr., 1981—, mng. ptnr. London office, 1996—; lectr. law U. Va., Charlottesville, 1977-90; mem. com. issues and priorities new vaccine devel. Inst. Medicine, NAS, 1983-86, Nat. Adv. Allergy and Infectious Diseases Coun. NIH, 1988-92, adv. bd. World Pharms. Report, 1990-96; mem. World Health Org. Coun. Internat. Orgns. Med. Scis. Working Party Comm. in Pharmacovigilance, 1997—. Articles editor U. Va. law rev., 1972-73; contbr. articles to profl. jours. Treas., mem. parochial ch. coun. St. Peter's Ch. Eaton Sq., London, 1998—. Mem. AAAS, ABA, Brussels Pharm. Law Group, Drug Info. Assn., Food and Drug Law Inst., European Soc. Pharmacovigilance, Food Law Group (U.K.), Soc. Vertebrate Paleontology, European Forum for Good Clin. Practice, Order of the Coif, Reform Club (London). Republican. Episcopalian. Avocation: vertebrate paleontology. Administrative and regulatory, Health. Home: 26 Walpole St, London SW3 4QS, England also: PO Box 7566 Washington DC 20044-7566 Office: Leconfield House, Curzon St, London W1Y 8AS, England also: Covington & Burling PO Box 7566 1201 Pennsylvania Ave NW Washington DC 20044

**KINGSBURY, SUZANNE NELSON,** judge, educator; b. Dayton, Ohio, July 17, 1956; d. Harry Allen and Kae (Williams) N.; m. James Harold Ammons, Dec. 17, 1984. Student in Criminal Justice/Psychology, Calif. State U., 1974-78; JD, U. of the Pacific, Sacramento, 1982. Bar: Calif. 1982, U.S. Dist. Ct. (ea. dist.) Calif. 1983. Lawyer Anderson & Goff, Sacramento, 1982-84, Brodovsky, Brodovsky & Grossfeld, Sacramento, 1984-85; dep. dist. atty. III El Dorado County Dist. Atty., South Lake Tahoe, Calif., 1985-90; dep. pub. defender III El Dorado County Pub. Defender, 1990-96; instr. in law and adminstrn. of justice Lake Tahoe Community Coll., 1988—; judge Superior Ct. El Dorado County, South Lake Tahoe, Calif., 1997—, presiding judge, 1999—; cons. South Lake Tahoe Sexual Assault Response Team, 1985-90; com. mem. Adminstrn. of Justice Adv. Com., Lake Tahoe Community Coll., South Lake Tahoe, 1988—; mem. Lake Tahoe Arson Task Force, 1989-90, South Lake Tahoe Narcotics Enforcement Team, 1988-90. Bd. dirs. South Lake Tahoe Womens Ctr., sec., 1990-91, v.p., 1992-93, pres., 1993-95, co-v.p., 1997. Mem. Calif. Judges Assn. (criminal law and procedure com.), Am. Judges Assn., Rural Judges Assn. Office: Superior Ct State Calif El Dorado County 1354 Johnson Blvd Ste 2 South Lake Tahoe CA 96150-8200

**KINGSLEY, JOHN PIERSALL,** lawyer; b. Catskill, N.Y., Apr. 22, 1938; s. John Willis and Emma (Piersall) K.; children: Jessica Skiba, Matthew Pyms. BA, Drew U., 1960; LLB, Syracuse U., 1963. Bar: N.Y. 1966. Claims person Travelers Ins. Co., Albany, N.Y., 1963-67; examiner Travelers Ins. Co., Hartford, Conn., 1967-68; supr. Travelers Ins. Co., N.Y.C., 1968-69; assoc. J. Richard Williams, Albany, 1969-70, Mahoney & Williams, Esquires, Albany, 1970-74; ptnr. Williams & Kingsley, Esquires, Albany, 1974-77, Harvey and Harvey, Mumford & Kingsley, Esquires, Albany, 1977-87, Kingsley and Towne, Esquires, Albany and Catskill, N.Y., 1987-98; prin. John P. Kingsley P.C., Albany and Catskill, 1999—. Mem. Shaker Mus., Old Chatham, N.Y., 1988—, Columbia County Coaching Assn., 1986—; bd. dirs. Olana Hist. Site, Hudson, N.Y., 1986—. Mem. N.Y. State Bar Assn., Greene County Bar Assn., Capital Dist. Trial Lawyers Assn., Am. Trial Lawyers Assn., Nat. Beagle Club (bd. dirs.), Old Chatham Hunt Club (master of beagle hounds). Avocations: beagling, tennis, hunting, fox hunting. State civil litigation. Office: John P Kingsley PC 329 Main St Catskill NY 12414-1823 also: 18 Computer Dr W Albany NY 12205-1616

**KINGSTON, ANDREW BROWNELL,** lawyer; b. Rochester, N.Y., Dec. 17, 1958; s. James Gregg and Barbara (Humphrey) K.; m. Nancy Kreiling, July 11, 1981; 1 child, Alexander B. BA with honors, U. Va., 1981; JD cum laude, Harvard U., 1987. Bar: Wash. 1987, U.S. Dist. Ct. (we. dist.) Wash. 1988. Tchr. U.S. Peace Corps, Apia, Western Samoa, 1981-83; law clk. to hon. chief judge U.S. Dist. Ct. Hawaii, Honolulu, 1987-88; assoc. Hillis Clark Martin & Peterson, P.S., Seattle, 1988—; pres. bd. student advisors Harvard U. Law Sch., Cambridge, Mass., 1986-87. Mem. Seattle C. of C. (internat. trade devel. com. 1989—). Democrat. Contracts commercial, General corporate.

**KINGTON, JOHN ANTHONY,** lawyer; b. Lakewood, Ohio, Dec. 13, 1953; s. Victor J. and Bette (Romer) K.; m. Martha Boyce, Aug. 22, 1981; children: Ben, Annie, Sarah, Laura. AA, Columbus Internat. Coll., Seville, Spain, 1974; BA, Ohio State U., 1977, JD, 1979. Bar: Ohio 1980. Assoc. Mayer, Terakedis & Blue, Columbus, Ohio, 1980-81, Chester Willcox & Saxbe, Columbus, 1982-87; ptnr. Chester, Willcox & Saxbe, Columbus, 1988—. General corporate, Estate planning, Real property. Office: Chester Willcox & Saxbe 17 S High St Ste 900 Columbus OH 43215-3442

**KINLIN, DONALD JAMES,** lawyer; b. Boston, Nov. 29, 1938; s. Joseph Edward and Ruth Claire (Byrne) K.; m. Donna C. McGrath, Nov. 29, 1959; children: Karen J., Donald J., Joseph P., Kevin S. BS in Acctg., Syracuse U., 1968, MBA, 1970; JD, U. Nebr., 1975. Bar: Nebr. 1976, Ohio 1982, U.S. Supreme Ct. 1979, U.S. Claims Ct. 1982, U.S. Tax Ct. 1982, U.S. Ct. Appeals (5th and fed. cirs.) 1982. Atty. USAF, Mather AFB, Calif., 1976-78; sr. trial atty. Air Force Contract Law Ctr., Wright-Patterson AFB, Ohio, 1978-86, dep. dir., 1986-87; ptnr. Smith & Schnacke, Dayton, Ohio, 1987-89, Thompson, Hine and Flory L.L.P., Dayton, 1989—; mem. adv. bd. Fed. Publs. Inc. Govt. Contract Costs, Pricing & Acctg. Report. Contbr. articles to legal jours. Pres. Forest Ridge Assn., Dayton, 1984-96; sec., gen. counsel U.S. Air and Trade Show, 1994-98, chmn., 1998—; bd. dirs. Nat. Aviation Hall of Fame, 1998—. Mem. ABA (chmn. sect. pub. contract law 1993-94, sec., budget and fin. officer sect., coun. mem., chmn. fed. procurement divsn., vice chmn. acct., cost and pricing com., truth in negotiations com., chmn. cost Acctg. stas. subcom.), Fed. Bar Assn., Ohio Bar Assn., Nebr. Bar Assn., Contracts Appeals Bar Assn. (bd. govs. 1998—). Avocation: travel. Administrative and regulatory, Contracts commercial, Military. Office: Thompson Hine & Flory LLP PO Box 8801 2000 Courthouse Pla NE Dayton OH 45401-8801

**KINNEARY, JOSEPH PETER,** federal judge; b. Cin., Sept. 19, 1905; s. Joseph and Anne (Mulvihill) K.; m. Byrnece Camille Rogers, June 26, 1950. BA, U. Notre Dame, 1928; JD, U. Cin., 1935, U. Cin., 1967; LLD (hon.), U. Cin., 1991. Bar: Ohio 1935, U.S. Supreme Ct. 1960. Pvt. practice in Cin. and Columbus, 1935-61; spl. asst. atty. gen. Ohio, 1937-39; 1st asst. atty. gen., 1949-51, spl. counsel to atty. gen., 1959-61; U.S. atty. So. Dist. Ohio, 1961-66; judge U.S. Dist. Ct. (so. dist.) Ohio, 1966—, chief judge, 1973-75, sr. judge; lectr. law trusts Coll. Law, U. Cin., 1948. Del. Dem. Nat. Conv., 1952. Served to capt. AUS, World War II. Decorated Army Commendation ribbon. Mem. Phi Delta Phi. Roman Catholic. Home: 2440 Northwest Blvd Columbus OH 43221-3868 Office: US Dist Ct 319 US Courthouse 85 Marconi Blvd Columbus OH 43215-2823*

**KINNEY, GREGORY HOPPES,** lawyer; b. Anderson, Ind., July 15, 1947; s. Dalton Roth and Effie Eleanor (Hoppes) K. B.A., Mich. State U., 1969, M.Labor Relations, 1971; J.D., U. Detroit, 1974. Bar: Mich. 1975, U.S. Dist. Ct. (ea. dist.) Mich. 1975, U.S. Ct. Appeals (D.C. cir.) 1975. Labor law editor Bur. Nat. Affairs, Washington, 1974; pension cons. Edward H. Friend & Co., Washington, 1975, The Wyatt Co., Detroit, 1976-84; sole practice, Detroit, 1984-86, Troy, Mich., 1986—. Pension, profit-sharing, and employee benefits. Home and Office: 2725 Charter Dr Apt 212 Troy MI 48083-1331

**KINNEY, RICHARD GORDON,** lawyer, educator; b. Chgo., May 8, 1939; s. Michael James Sr. and Blanche Marie (Gill) K.; m. Katherine Choffen, Dec. 26, 1969; 1 child, Richard Greg. BSEE, U. Ill., 1961; JD, U. Chgo., 1964. Bar: Ill. 1964, U.S. Ct. Customs and Patent Appeals 1975, U.S. Supreme Ct. 1970, U.S. Ct. Appeals (fed. cir.) 1982. With patent dept. Zenith Radio Corp., Chgo., 1963-64, Borg-Warner Corp., Chgo., 1968-73; divsn. patent counsel Baxter Travenol Labs., Inc., Deerfield, Ill., 1973-76; prin. Law Offices of Richard G. Kinney, Chgo. and Merrillville, Ind., 1976-95, 98—; pres. Richard G. Kinney, P.C., 1995-98. Rep. candidate Ill. State Senate, 1976; chmn. 6th Congrl. Dist. Citizens for Goldwater-Miller, 1964. Roman Catholic. Patent, Trademark and copyright, Intellectual property. Office: Richard G Kinney PO Box 11119 Merrillville IN 46411-1119

**KINNEY, STEPHEN HOYT, JR.,** lawyer; b. Albuquerque, Feb. 27, 1948; s. Stephen Hoyt and Harriet May (Gadsden) K.; m. Leslie vanLiew, June 10, 1972; 1 child, Erin. B.S., MIT, 1970; J.D., Harvard U., 1973. Bar: N.Y. 1974, U.S. Dist. Ct. (so. dist.) N.Y. 1974, U.S. Dist. Ct. (ea. dist.) N.Y. 1974, U.S. Dist. Ct. (no. dist.) N.Y. 1978, U.S. Ct. Apls. (2d cir.) 1975, U.S. Supreme Ct. 1982. Programmer, analyst MIT, 1968-70; law clk. N.J. Organized Crime Unit, Trenton, 1972; assoc. Reid & Priest, N.Y.C., 1973-85, sr. atty., 1985-86, ptnr. 1986-98; ptnr. Thelen Reid & Priest LLP, N.Y.C., 1998—. Author, editor: Outline of Arbitration, 1984; contbr. articles to jour. in field. Authored computer programs. Mem. ABA, N.Y. State Bar Assn. Club: MB Yacht (Port Washington, N.Y.). Securities, Contracts commercial, Computer. Office: Thelen Reid & Priest 40 W 57th St Fl 28 New York NY 10019-4001

**KINSER, CYNTHIA D.,** state supreme court justice; b. Pennington Gap, Dec. 20, 1951; d. Morris and Velda (Myers) Fannon; m. H. Allen Kinser, Jr., March 17, 1974; children: Charles Adam, Terah Diane. Student, Univ. of Ga., 1970-71; BA, Univ. of Tenn., 1974; JD, Univ. of Va., 1977. Bar: Va. 1977, U.S. Dist. Ct. (we. dist.) Va. 1977, U.S. Ct. Appeals (4th cir.) 1977, U.S. Supreme Ct. 1988. Law clk. to Judge Glen M. Williams U.S. Dist. Ct., 1977-78; pvt. law practice, 1978-90; commonwealth's atty. Lee County, Va., 1980-83; magistrate judge U.S. Dist. Ct. (we. dist.) Va., Abingdon, 1990-98; justice Va. Supreme Ct., Richmond, 1998—; trustee Chapter 7 Panel, U.S. Bankruptcy Ct., 1979-90. Mem. Va. Bar Assn., Va. Trial Lawyers Assn., Am. Bar Assn. Methodist. Office: Supreme Court PO Box 457 Pennington Gap VA 24277-0457*

**KINSEY, ROBERT STANLEIGH, III,** lawyer; b. Highland Park, Ill., Dec. 31, 1944; s. Robert Stanleigh, Jr. and Jane Kinsey; m. Kathleen Ann Smith, Oct. 14, 1972; children: Jessica, Catlain, Kristoffer. BA, Grinnell Coll., 1967; JD, U. Iowa, 1973. Bar: Iowa 1973, U.S. Dist. Ct. (no. dist.) Iowa 1973, U.S. Dist. Ct. (so. dist.) Iowa 1982, U.S. Ct. Appeals (8th cir.) 1979, U.S. Supreme Ct. 1979. Assoc. Brown, Kinsey & Funnkhouser P.L.C., Mason City, Iowa, 1973—. Mem. Iowa Bar Assn. (mem. workers compensation coun. 1990-91), Iowa Assn. of Workers Compensation Attys. (pres., v.p., sec., treas., bd. dirs. 1978—), Rotary (pres. 1990-91). Democrat. Congregationalist. Avocations: tennis, biking, sailing, travel, reading. Workers' compensation, Personal injury, Civil rights. Office: Brown Kinsey & Funkhouser PLC 214 N Adams Ave Mason City IA 50401-3120

**KINSEY, RONALD C., JR.,** lawyer; b. Washington, June 28, 1942; s. Ronald C. Kinsey; m. Carola Von Wrangel, June 21, 1969 (div. 1996); children: Kyle, Cara. AB, Dartmouth Coll., 1964; JD, U. Wash., 1967. Bar: Wash. 1970, U.S. Dist. Ct. (we. dist.) Wash. 1973. Dep. pros. atty. King County, Seattle, 1970-71; mcpl. legal cons. Assn. of Wash. Cities, Seattle, 1971-81; mcpl. atty. Holt Law Offices, Issaquah, Wash., 1981-83; pvt. practice law Seattle, 1983-89; marine investigator USCG, Seattle, 1989—; chief Coast Guard Casualty Investigations, Seattle, 1996—. Capt. U.S. Army, 1968-70. Mem. Rotary of Univ. Dist., Seattle Yacht Club, Dartmouth Club of Western Wash. Administrative and regulatory, Admiralty, Public international. Home: 4346 NE 58th St Seattle WA 98105-2250

**KINSOLVING, LAURENCE EDWIN,** lawyer; b. St. Maries, Idaho, Dec. 3, 1941; s. C. Edwin and Julie (Blessing) K.; children: Elizabeth, Charles; m. Ruth Barnes, Jan. 1, 1997. BA magna cum laude, Gonzaga U., 1965; JD, Harvard U., 1968. Bar: Fla. 1968, Mass. 1969, U.S. Dist. Ct. (mid. dist.) Fla. 1972, U.S. Ct. Claims 1972, U.S. Tax Ct. 1972, U.S. Ct. Appeals (5th cir.) 1972, U.S. Supreme Ct. 1972. Atty. legal dept. City of Boston, 1968-69; capt. judge adv. gen.'s dept. USAF, 1969-72; from assoc. to ptnr. Macfarlane, Ferguson, Allison & Kelly, Tampa, Fla., 1972-81; ptnr. Rudnick & Wolfe, Tampa, 1981-88; shareholder, chmn. real estate dept. Shackleford, Farrior, Stallings & Evans, PA, Tampa, 1988-91; shareholder, sr. real estate atty. Carlton, Fields, Ward, Emmanuel, Smith and Cutler, PA, Tampa, 1991—. Editor Charter-A Jour. of Gonzaga Thought, 1964-65. Mem. ABA (real property, probate and trust sect., chmn. homeowners and cmty. assns. com. 1995-99), Fla. Bar (real property, probate and trust sect., vice-chmn. condominium and planned devel. com. 1993—, exec. coun. 1993—, chmn. liaison with lenders com. 1995-96, editl. bd. Fla. Bar Jour. and News 1976-77, chmn. 1977-78), Bar Assn. Hillsborough County, Am. Coll. Real Estate Lawyers, Am. Resort Devel. Assn. (chmn. Fed. Legis. com. 1992—), Harvard Club of West Coast Fla. (bd. dirs.), Cmty. Assn. Inst. (charter class of the Coll. of Cmty. Assn. Lawyers), Culbreath Isles Civic Assn. (pres. 1992, 93), Alpha Sigma Nu (del. nat. conv. 1963, v.p. 1965). Republican. Episcopalian. Real property. Office: Carlton Fields Ward Emmanuel Smith & Cutler PA One S Harbour Island Tampa FL 33602

**KINTZELE, JOHN ALFRED,** lawyer; b. Denver, Aug. 16, 1936; s. Louis Richard and Adele H. Kintzele; children: John A., Marcia A., Elizabeth A.; m. Suzanne Hinsberger; stepchildren: William Karp III, Christopher Karp. BS in Bus., U. Colo., 1958, LLB, 1961. Bar: Colo. bar 1961. Assoc.

James B. Radetsky, Denver, 1962-63; pvt. practice law Denver, 1963—; corp. officer, dir. Kintzele, Inc.; rep. 10th cir. U.S. Ct. of Claims Bar. Chmn. Colo. Lawyer Referral Service, 1978-83, Election commr., Denver, 1975-79, 83-86. Mem. ABA, Colo. Bar Assn., Denver Bar Assn., Am. Judicature Soc. Democrat. Roman Catholic. General civil litigation, Personal injury, Workers' compensation. Home: 10604 E Powers Dr Englewood CO 80111-3957 Office: 1317 Delaware St Denver CO 80204-2704

**KINTZER, GAIL ANN,** law educator; b. Willkes-Barie, PA, Sept. 29, 1949; d. Arthur Ralph and Margaret (Slikes) K.; children: Saffron Kintzer Guiralou. JD, U. Fla., 1992; BA, SUNY, Buffalo, 1981. Law clk. for Judge H Emory Widener Jr. U.S. Ct. Appeals (4th cir.), Richmond, Va., 1993-94; legal methods prof. Sch. Law Widener U, Harrisburg, Pa., 1994-96, acting dir. legal methods Sch. Law, 1996-97; assoc. prof., Sch. Law Appalachian, Grundy, VA, 1997—. Contbr. to profl. jours. Mem. Special Edn. Com. Central Dauphin Sch. Dist., Harrisburg, Pa., 1996-97; com. mem. Erie County Dem. Party, Buffalo, 1980-81. Mem. ABA, Assn. Legal Writing Dirs., Order of the Coif. Democrat. Home: HC 61 Box 13-b Grundy VA 24614-9301 Office: Appalachian Sch Law PO Box 2825 Grundy VA 24614-2825

**KINZLER, PETER,** lawyer; b. N.Y.C., Apr. 18, 1943; s. I. George Kinzler and Isabelle (Schlivek) Kinzler Feher; m. Virginia L. Smith, June 20, 1982; children: Samantha, Jason, Valerie, Kit. BA, Trinity Coll., 1964; JD, Columbia U., 1967. Bar: N.Y. 1967. Atty. NLRB, Washington, 1967-69; legis. asst. U.S. Rep. Thomas L. Ashley, Washington, 1969-74; atty. Fed. Trade Commn., Washington, 1974-75; counsel consumer protection & fin./oversight investigations Commerce Com./Ho. of Reps., Washington, 1975-81; minority counsel then staff dir. consumer affairs subcom. Senate Banking Com., Washington, 1981-89, counsel, 1992; legis. dir. Sen. Christopher J. Dodd, Washington, 1989-92; staff dir. subcom. Fin. Instns. Supervision Regulation and Deposit Ins. House Banking Com., Washington, 1993-95; ptnr. Kinzler & Swab, Alexandria, Va., 1995-98; sole practitioner Alexandria, 1998—; pres. Coalition for Auto-Ins. Reform, 1996—. Pres. River Park Mut. Homes, Inc., Washington, 1976, Hollin Hills Swim Club, Alexandria, Va., 1984, Hollin Hills Tennis Club, 1994; v.p. Parent and Assoc. No. Va. Tng. Ctr., Fairfax, 1982; bd. dirs. HALT-Am. for Legal Reform, Washington, 1983-86, Voice of the Retarded, 1994—. Democrat. Avocations: folk music, crafts, tennis. Office: 7310 Stafford Rd Alexandria VA 22307-1807

**KIOK, JOAN STERN,** lawyer; b. N.Y.C., Dec. 19, 1929; d. Milton William and Pauline (Bauer) Stern; children: Paul, Peter. BA, Cornell U., 1951; LLB, Columbia U., 1954. Bar: N.Y. 1955, Colo. 1958, U.S. Dist. Ct. (so. and ea. dists.) N.Y., U.S. Ct. Appeals (2nd cir.) 1961, U.S. Supreme Ct. 1961, 1968-78. Assoc. gen. counsel D.C.37 AFSCME, AFL-CIO, N.Y.C.; sole practitioner N.Y.C., 1978—; gen. counsel Mgr. Employees Assn., N.Y.C., 1980—, Uniformed Sanitation chiefs Assn., N.Y.C., 1988—, EMS Chiefs Assn., N.Y.C., 1986—, Orgn. Staff Analysts, N.Y.C., 1985—, Fire Alarm Dispatchers, N.Y.C., 1988—; chair bd. dirs. MFY Legal Svcs., N.Y.C., 1980-85. Mem. N.Y. County Lawyers Assn. (labor law com. 1975—). Labor. Home: 442 E 20th St New York NY 10009-8120 Office: 26 Broadway New York NY 10004-1703

**KIPP, JOHN THEODORE,** lawyer, rancher; b. Guadalajara, Mex., Apr. 19, 1932; (parents Am. citizens); s. Eugene Harvey and Theresa (Greer) K.; m. Carol Sue Cooke, June 7, 1969; 1 child, John Grant. BBA, U. Tex., 1954, JD, 1958. Bar: Tex. 1958, U.S. Dist. Ct. (no. dist.) Tex. 1962, U.S. Supreme Ct. 1964. Assoc. Gardere & Wynne, and predecessor, Dallas, 1958-63, ptnr., 1964-98, of counsel, 1998—. Past chmn. Dallas County chpt. Am. Heart Assn.; trustee, treas. Dallas Hist. Soc. Lt. USN, 1954-56, Korea; mem. USNR (ret.). Mem. State Bar Tex. (chmn. corp. law com. 1973-75, bus. law sect. 1976-77), Dallas Bar Assn. Avocations: hunting, fishing, ranching, photography. Securities, Mergers and acquisitions, Finance. Home: 5920 Lupton Dr Dallas TX 75225-1629 Office: Gardere & Wynne 1601 Elm St Ste 3000 Dallas TX 75201-4761

**KIPPERMAN, LAWRENCE I.,** lawyer; b. Chgo., Nov. 22, 1941; s. Solomon and Idelle (Goldman) K.; m. Carol A. Kipperman, Jan. 29, 1967 (div. Sept. 1985); children: Anna, Lynne. BA, U. Ill., 1963, JD, 1966; LLM, George Washington U., 1968. Bar: Ill. 1966, U.S. Dist. Ct. (no. dist.) Ill. 1966, U.S. Supreme Ct. 1968, Ohio 1970, U.S. Ct. Appeals (7th cir.) 1973, U.S. Ct. Appeals (8th cirs.) 1986. Atty. NLRB, Washington, 1966-70; assoc. Burke, Haber & Berick, Cleve., 1970-71; assoc. Sidley & Austin, Chgo., 1971-73, ptnr., 1973—; lectr. Ill. Continuing Legal Edn., 1985, Am. Arbitration Assn. Mem. Chgo. Bar Assn., Legal Club Chgo. Jewish. Avocations: Architectural history, baseball, basketball, jazz. Labor. Office: Sidley & Austin 1 First Natl Plz Chicago IL 60603-2003

**KIPPERT, ROBERT JOHN, JR.,** lawyer; b. Detroit, Aug. 29, 1952; s. Robert John Sr. and Jeanne Marcella (DeYonker) K.; m. Dorothy Marie Cunningham, Oct. 28, 1978 (div. June 1988); 1 child, Cristie; m. Kim Denise Katherine Greenman, Feb. 10, 1990. BBA, U. Mich., 1974; JD, Wayne State U., 1977, LLM in Taxation, 1994. Bar: Mich. 1979; CPA. Tax staff acct. Arthur Young & Co., Bloomfield Hills, Mich., 1977-78; tax staff sr., mgr. McEndarffer, Hoke & Bernhard, P.C., Bloomfield Hills, 1978-84; tax supr. Cen. Transport, Inc., Sterling Heights, Mich., 1984-85; tax atty. Chrysler Fin. Corp., Southfield, Mich., 1985-89, mgr. non-income taxes and licensing, 1989-95, staff tax counsel, 1995-99, sr. tax couns., 1999—. Charter pres. Sterling Heights Jaycees. Mem. AICPA, ABA, Mich. Bar Assn., Mich. Assn. CPA's, Am. Arbitration Assn. (panel mem.). Republican. Roman Catholic. Avocations: softball, basketball officiating, music. Corporate taxation, State and local taxation, Taxation, general. Home: 2740 Apache Tr Wixom MI 48393-2122 Office: Chrysler Fin Co LLC 27777 Franklin Rd Southfield MI 48034-2337

**KIRALY, MICHELE ANN,** lawyer; b. Johnstown, Pa., Mar. 15, 1968; d. Joseph John and Ethel Dolores Kiraly. BA, U. Nev., 1990; JD, U. San Diego, 1993. Bar: Nev. 1993. Law clk. to Hon. John McGroarty, Las Vegas, Nev., 1993-94; assic, Pearson Patton Shea Foley & Kurtz, PC, Las Vegas, 1995—. Bd. dirs. Family and Child Treatment of So. Nev., Las Vegas, 1994—. Insurance, Personal injury. Office: Pearson Patton Shea Foley & Kurtz PC 6900 Westcliff Dr Ste 800 Las Vegas NV 89145-0617

**KIRBERGER, ELIZABETH,** lawyer, consultant; b. Tulsa, 1965; d. Robert Earl Jr. and Phyllis Kirberger. BA in Philosophy and English, Wheaton (Ill.) Coll., 1987; JD, Georgetown U., 1990; MPH, Columbia U., 1997. Bar: N.Y. 1991. Law clk. to chief justice Okla. Supreme Ct., Oklahoma City, 1989; dir. contracts Herbert Barrett Mgmt. Inc., N.Y.C., 1990-93; cons. Population Coun., N.Y.C., 1993-94, Columbia U. Ctr. for Study of Human Rights, N.Y.C., 1995, Internat. Planned Parenthood Fedn., N.Y.C., 1996-98, AVSC Internat., N.Y.C., 1998—; pres. Kirberger & Assocs., N.Y.C., 1998—. Editor Georgetown Internat. Environ. Law Rev., 1988-90; contbr. articles to profl. jours. Mem. ABA, N.Y. State Bar Assn., Assn. Bar City N.Y., Am. Immigration Lawyers Assn. E-mail: kirberger@immigration-lawyer.com. Immigration, naturalization, and customs, General practice, Private international. Office: Kirberger & Assocs 611 Broadway Rm 426B New York NY 10012-2608

**KIRBY, LE GRAND CARNEY, III,** lawyer, accountant; b. Dallas, Feb. 25, 1941; s. Le Grand C. and Michie V. (Moore) K.; m. Jane Marie Daniel, June 14, 1958; children: Le Grand C. IV, Kimberli K., Kristina K. BBA, So. Meth. U., 1963, LLB, 1965. Bar: Tex. 1965; CPA, Tex. From staff acct. to ptnr. Arthur Young & Co., Dallas, 1965-80; ptnr., dir. litigation support Arthur Young & Co. (name now Ernst & Young), Dallas, 1983—; dep. chief acct. SEC, Washington, 1980-83; adv. counsel Fin. Reporting Inst., L.A., 1982—. Mem. ABA (acctg. and law com. 1983—), State Bar Tex. (securities com.), Am. Inst. CPA's, Tex. Soc. CPA's, Nat. Assn. Corp. Dirs. (pres. Dallas chpt. 1985-89), D.C. CPA's. Securities, General civil litigation, Federal civil litigation. Office: Ernst & Young LLP Ste 1500 2121 San Jacinto St Dallas TX 75201-6714

**KIRBY, WILLIAM KAY,** lawyer; b. Portland, Oreg., Aug. 17, 1943; s. William Kermit and Myrl Grace (Elsenman) K.; m. Kay M. Wilson-Kirby; 1 child, Miranda. BA in English, Reed Coll., 1965; MA in Polit. Sci., Portland State U., 1973; JD, UCLA, 1973. Bar: Calif. 1973, Wash. 1986. Staff atty. Wash. State Ins. Commr., Olympia, 1990—. Lt. USNR, 1965-69. Mem. Wash. State Bar Assn. (govt.). Office: Office Ins Commr PO Box 40256 Olympia WA 98504-0256

**KIRBY, WILLIAM ROY,** lawyer; b. Concordia, Kans., Sept. 6, 1914; s. Clarence William and Frances (Cleveland) K.; m. Feb. 20, 1949 (dec.); 1 child, Kent Douglas. BS, So. Meth. U., 1979; M of Arts Divinity, U. Chgo., 1981; MBA, U. Kans., 1983. Bar: Kans. 1939, Okla. 1939, U.S. Dist. Ct. Kans. 1939. Assoc. Yancey & Douglas, Oklahoma City, 1939-40; ptnr. Hall, Kirby & Levy, Coffeyville, Kans., 1960-75; pvt. practice, Coffeyville, 1939, 40-41, 46-60, 75—; asst. county atty. Montgomery County, Kans., Independence, Kans., 1947-49, county atty., 1949-53; city atty. City of Coffeyville, 1975; bd. dirs. Condon Nat. Bank, Coffeyville. Comdr. USN, 1941-45. Named to Hall of Fame, Coffeyville Regional Med. Ctr., 1994. Mem. Montgomery County Bar Assn. (pres. 1965), Masons, Shriners, Order of Coif. Republican. Methodist. Avocations: reading, travel. Banking, Estate planning. Home: 1209 W 4th St Coffeyville KS 67337-3301 Office: PO Box 236 Coffeyville KS 67337-0236

**KIRCHER, JOHN JOSEPH,** law educator; b. Milw., July 26, 1938; s. Joseph John and Martha Marie (Jach) K.; m. Marcia Susan Adamkiewicz, Aug. 26, 1961; children: Joseph John, Mary Kathryn. BA, Marquette U., 1960, JD, 1963. Bar: Wis. 1963, U.S. Dist. Ct. (ea. dist.) Wis. 1963, U.S. Ct. Appeals (7th cir.) 1992. Sole practice, Port Washington, Wis., 1963-66; with Def. Research Inst., Milw., 1966-80, research dir., 1972-80; with Marquette U., 1970—, prof. law, 1980—, assoc. dean acad. affairs, 1992-93; chmn. Wis. Jud. Council, 1981-83. Author: (with J.D. Ghiardi) Punitive Damages: Law and Practice, 1981; editor: Federation of Insurance and Corporate Counsel Quarterly; mem. editorial bd. Def. Law Jour.; contbr. articles to profl. jours. Recipient Teaching Excellence award Marquette U., 1986, Disting. Service award Def. Research Inst., 1980, Marquette Law Rev. Editors' award, 1988. Mem. ABA (Robert B. McKay Professor award 1993), Am. Law Inst., Wis. Bar Assn., Wis. Supreme Ct. Bd. of Bar Examiners (vice-chair 1989-91, chair 1992), Am. Judicature Soc., Nat. Sports Law Inst. (adv. com. 1989—), Assn. Internationale de Droit des Assurances, Scribes. Roman Catholic. Office: PO Box 1881 Milwaukee WI 53201-1881

**KIRCHHOFF, BRUCE C.,** lawyer; b. Rochester, Pa., Sept. 23, 1959; s. Peter Olsen and Harriet (Heiden) K.; m. Andrea Jean Brady, June 1, 1985; children: Andrew Christopher, Tyler Michael. BA, Colo. Coll., 1981; JD, U. Denver, 1984; MSc in Mineral Econs., Colo. Sch. Mines, Golden, 1985. Bar: Colo. 1985, U.S. Dist. Ct. Colo. 1996. Gen. atty. Cyprus Amax Minerals Co., Englewood, Colo., 1986-92, Tempe, Ariz., 1992-96; mem. Alfers & Carver, Denver, 1996—; adj. prof. law U. DenverColl. Law, 1997-98. Mem. ABA, Colo. Bar Assn., Denver Bar Assn. Republican. Methodist. Avocations: bicycling, golf, skiing. Fax: 303-592-7680. Oil, gas, and mineral, Contracts commercial, General corporate. Office: Alfers & Carver LLC 730 17th St Ste 340 Denver CO 80202-3513

**KIRCHMAN, CHARLES VINCENT,** lawyer; b. Washington, June 28, 1935; s. Floyd Vincent and Dorothy Johanna (Johnson) K.; m. Erika Ottilie Knoeppel, July 4, 1959; children: Mark C., Eric H., Charles E. BA, U. Md., 1959; JD, George Washington U., 1962. Bar: D.C. 1962, Md. 1970. Security specialist Adj. Gen's. Office U.S. Army, 1962-64; sole practice Washington, 1964-70, Wheaton, Md., 1970-73; ptnr. Andrews & Schick, Waldorf, Md., 1973-77; sole practice Wheaton, Md., 1977-92; ptnr. Kirchman & Kirchman, Wheaton, 1992—. State civil litigation, Probate. Home: 14801 Notley Rd Silver Spring MD 20905-5837 Office: 11141 Georgia Ave Wheaton MD 20902-4637

**KIRCHMAN, ERIC HANS,** lawyer; b. Washington, May 2, 1962; s. Charles Vincent and Erika Ottilie (Knoeppel) K.; m. Hillary Bronkie Hutson, Apr. 19, 1991; children: Erika B., Thomas E. BA, Univ. Md., 1985; JD, Univ. Balt., 1990. Bar: Md. 1990, U.S. Dist. Ct. Md. 1991. Assoc. Hillel Abrams, Rockville, Md., 1990-92; ptnr. Kirchman & Kirchman, Wheaton, Md., 1992—; of counsel Md. Coun. for Gifted and Talented Children, Inc., Silver Spring, 1994. With U.S. Army Reserve, 1985-98. Mem. ATLA, Md. Criminal Def. Attys. Assn., Montgomery County Bar Assn. General practice. Office: Kirchman & Kirchman 11141 Georgia Ave Ste 403 Wheaton MD 20902-4659

**KIRGIS, FREDERIC LEE,** law educator; b. Washington, Dec. 29, 1934; s. Frederic Lee Sr. and Kathryn Alice (Burrows) K.; children: Julianne, Paul Frederic. B.A., Yale U., 1957; J.D., U. Calif.-Berkeley, 1960. Bar: Colo. 1961, D.C. 1964, Va. 1983. Atty. Covington & Burling, Washington, 1964-67; from asst. prof. to prof. law U. Colo., Boulder, 1967-73; prof. law UCLA, 1973-78; prof. law Washington & Lee U., Lexington, Va., 1978—, dir. Frances Lewis Law Ctr., 1978-83, dean law sch., 1983-88. Author: International Organizations in their Legal Setting, 1977, 2d edit. 1993, Prior Consultation in International Law, 1983; contbr. articles to profl. jours. Pres. Maury River Soccer Club, Lexington, 1978-85. Served to capt. USAF, 1961-64. Recipient Deak award 1974; research fellow NATO, Brussels, 1978. Mem. Am. Soc. Internat. Law (v.p. 1985-87, sec. 1994—), Am. Law Inst., Internat. Law Assn. (Am. br.), Am. Jour. Internat. Law (bd. editors 1984-96, 98—), State Bar Va., Order of Coif. Democrat. Presbyterian. Home: 15 Grey Dove Rd Lexington VA 24450-2269 Office: Washington and Lee U Sch of Law Lexington VA 24450

**KIRK, BARBARA M.,** lawyer; d. John E. and Barbara A. Owczarzak; m. Kenneth G. Kirk, Feb. 11, 1984; children: Michael A., Christopher T., Nicole M. BA, Holy Family Coll., 1986; JD, Temple U., 1996. Bar: Pa. 1996, N.J. 1996. Paralegal, sec. Defender Assn. Phila., 1983-89; legal sec. Groen, Laveson, Goldberg & Rubenstone, Bensalem, Pa., 1989-90, paralegal, 1990-96, atty., 1996—. Chairperson Bucks County March of Dimes Salute to Women, 1996-97, 97-98. Mem. ABA, Pa. Bar Assn., Bucks Bar Assn. Avocations: bicycling, reading, boating. Family and matrimonial. Office: Groen Laveson Goldberg & Rubenstone 4 Greenwood Sq Ste 200 Bensalem PA 19020-2053

**KIRK, CASSIUS LAMB, JR.,** lawyer, investor; b. Bozeman, Mont., June 8, 1929; s. Cassius Lamb and Gertrude Violet (McCarthy) K.; AB, Stanford U., 1951; JD, U. Calif., Berkeley, 1954. Bar: Calif. 1955. Assoc. firm Cooley, Godward, Castro, Huddleson & Tatum, San Francisco, 1956-60; staff counsel for bus. affairs Stanford U., 1960-78; chief bus. officer, staff counsel Menlo Sch. and Coll., Atherton, Calif., 1978-81; chmn. Eberli-Kirk Properties, Inc. (doing bus. as Just Closets), Menlo Park, 1981-94; mem. summer faculty Coll. Bus. Adminstrn. U. Calif., Santa Barbara, 1967-73; past mem. adv. bd. Allied Arts Guild, Menlo Park; past nat. vice chmn. Stanford U. Annual Fund; past v.p. Palo Alto C. of C. With U.S. Army, 1954-56. Mem. VFW, Stanford Faculty Club, Order of Coif, Phi Alpha Delta. Republican. Home and Office: 1330 University Dr Apt 52 Menlo Park CA 94025-4241

**KIRK, DENNIS DEAN,** lawyer; b. Pittsburg, Kans., Dec. 13, 1950; s. Homer Standley and Maida Corena (Rouse) K.; 1 child, Dennis Dean II. AA, Hutchinson Cmty. Jr. Coll., 1970; BS with distinction, No. Ariz. U., 1972; JD, Washburn U., 1975. Bar: Kans. 1975, U.S. Dist. Ct. Kans. 1975, D.C. 1977, U.S. Ct. Appeals (D.C. cir.) 1978, U.S. Supreme Ct. 1979, U.S. Ct. Appeals (5th cir.) 1981, U.S. Dist. Ct. Md. 1984, U.S. Tax Ct. 1984, U.S. Claims Ct. 1984, U.S. Ct. Appeals (fed. cir.) 1984, U.S. Ct. Mil. Appeals 1984, Va. 1990, U.S. Ct. Appeals (4th cir.) 1990. Trial atty. ICC, Washington, 1975-77; assoc. Goff, Sims, Cloud & Stroud, Washington, 1977-82; pvt. practice Washington, 1982-90; ptnr. Slocum, Boddie, Murry & Kirk, Falls Church, Va., 1990-93; pvt. practice Falls Church, Va., 1993—; pres. Law Facilites, Inc., Washington, 1982—. Vol. parole and probation officer Shawnee County, Kans., 1983-74; citizens adv. task force group Md. Nat. Park and Planning Commn., 1978-80; citizens task force on gen. plan amendments study Fairfax County coun., Va., 1981-82; active Seven Corners Task Force, Fairfax County, 1981-82, chmn. transp. and housing subcoms.; pres. Seven Springs Tenants Assn., College Park, Md., 1976-80, Ravenwood Park Citizens Assn., 1981-82; dir. Greenwood Homes, Inc., Fairfax County Dept. Housing and Cmty. Devel., 1983—; active Gala Com. Spotlight the Kennedy Ctr., Pres. Adv. Com. on the Arts, 1986-87, Mason Dist. Rep. Com., 1981-91, Fairfax County Young Reps., Fairfax County Rep. Com., 1982—; founding chmn., charter mem. Mason Dist. Jaycees, 1984-86; sec., gen. counsel, bd. dirs. U.S. Assocs. for the Cultural Triangle in Sri Lanka, 1983-90; commr. Consumer Protection Commn., Fairfax County, 1982—, chmn., 1996-97; towing adv. bd. Fairfax County, 1993-97; Ravenwood precinct chmn. Rep. Orgn., Falls Church, Va., 1982-90; bd. dirs. PTA Baileys Elem.Magnet Sch., 1995—, v.p., 1996-97. Named to Honorable Order Ky. Cols. Mem. ABA, NRA (life), Masons (life, Master of Lodge, D.C. Grand Lodge Masons, Valentine Rentzel medal, Grand Sword Bearer 1992), Shriners (life), Tall Cedars (life), Scottish Rite (life), Moose, Royal Arch (life), Phi Kappa Phi, Phi Alpha Delta (life, nat. capital area alumni chpt. justice 1984-86, 94-96). Methodist. Avocation: music. Administrative and regulatory, Federal civil litigation, General practice. Home: 6315 Anneliese Dr Falls Church VA 22044-1620 Office: 5201 Leesburg Pike Ste 1108 Falls Church VA 22041-3268

**KIRK, JOHN MACGREGOR,** lawyer; b. Flint, Mich., Mar. 9, 1938; s. R. Dean and Berenice E. (Mac Gregor) K.; m. Carol Lasko, June 8, 1971; children: John M. Jr., Caroline Dwyer. BA, Washington & Lee U., 1960, LLB, 1962; LLM in Taxation, NYU, 1967. Bar: Mich. 1962, U.S. Ct. Mil. Appeals 1966, U.S. Supreme Ct. 1966, U.S. Tax Ct. 1969, U.S. Dist. Ct. (ea. dist.) Mich. 1982, U.S. Ct. Appeals (6th cir.) 1983. Trial atty. tax divsn. U.S. Dept. Justice, Washington, 1967-72; assoc. Boyer & Briggs, Bloomfield Hills, Mich., 1972-74; ptnr. Butler, Long, Gust, Klein & Van Zile, Detroit, 1975-78; mem. Meyer, Kirk, Snyder & Safford P.L.L.C., Bloomfield Hills, 1978—. Mem., past pres. Friends of Baldwin Pub. Libr., Birmingham, Mich., 1972—. Mem. ABA, State Bar Mich., Oakland County Bar Assn., Detroit Bar Assn., Birmingham Rotary, Walloon Yacht Club (treas., past commodore 1960—). Republican. Presbyterian. Estate planning, Probate, Estate taxation. Home: 4350 Yale Ct Bloomfield Hills MI 48302-1669 Office: Meyer Kirk Snyder and Safford PLLC 100 W Long Lake Rd Ste 100 Bloomfield Hills MI 48304-2773

**KIRK, JOHN ROBERT, JR.,** lawyer; b. Stuart, Va., June 21, 1935; s. John Robert and Mary Elise (Mustaine) K.; children: Karen Louise, Laura Elise, Rebecca Elizabeth. student Rice Inst., 1953-56; BSChemE, U. Tex., 1959; JD, U. Houston, 1966. Bar: Tex. 1966, U.S. Patent and Trademark Office 1967, U.S. Supreme Ct. 1973, U.S. Dist. Ct. (so. dist.) Tex. 1974, U.S. Ct. Claims 1975, U.S. Dist. Ct. (no. dist.) Tex. 1977, U.S. Ct. Appeals (5th cir.) 1980, U.S. Ct. Appeals (11th cir.) 1981, U.S. Ct. Appeals (fed. cir.) 1983. Patent atty. Jefferson Chem. Co., Houston, 1966-69, mgr. patent div., 1969-72; mem. Pravel, Gambrell, Hewitt, Kirk & Kimball, P.C., Houston, 1972-84, ptnr., 1973-84; ptnr. Baker & Kirk, P.C., 1984-87, Baker, Kirk & Bissex, P.C., 1987-90, Kirk & Lindsay, P.C., 1990-93, Jenkens & Gilchrist, 1993—; dir. Nat. Inventors Hall of Fame Found., Inc., 1979-82, 87—, treas., 1983-84, v.p., 1984-86, pres., 1986-87; adv. bd. U. Houston Intellectual Property Law Program, 1991—, Gulf Coast Regional Small Bus. Devel. Ctr., 1994—, Tex. Mfg. Assistance Ctr., Inc., 1995—. Served to lt. USMCR, 1958-60. Fellow Tex. Bar Found., Houston Bar Found, Coll. State Bar Tex., State Bar of Tex. (chmn. intellectual property law sect. 1977-78); mem. ABA (intellectual property law sect. coun. 1990-94, vice chmn. 1994-95, chmn. elect 1995-96, chmn., 1996-97, com. chair 1982-90), Am. Intellectual Property Law Assn., Nat. Counsel Intellectual Property Law Assns. (vice chmn. 1986-87, chmn. 1987-88), commr of Patents Edn. Roundtable (commr. 1987-95), Houston Intellectual Property Law Assn. (pres.-elect 1989-90, pres. 1990-91, bd. govs. 1986-92), Houston Bar Assn., Licensing Execs. Soc., Nat. Inventive Thinking Assn. (adv. dir. 1990—), Inwood Forest Golf Club. Republican. Baptist. Patent, Trademark and copyright, Intellectual property. Office: 1100 Louisiana St Ste 1800 Houston TX 77002-5215

**KIRK, PATRICK LAINE,** lawyer; b. South Bend, Ind., May 12, 1948; s. Jerry W. and Vivian E. (Evans) K.; m. Cheryl A. Ensminger, Dec. 30, 1967; children: Kevin P., Travis S. BA, Valparaiso U., 1970, JD, 1973. Bar: N.Y. 1974, U.S. Dist. Ct. (no. dist.) N.Y. 1977, U.S. Supreme Ct. 1986. Ptnr. Grilli & Kirk, Herkimer, N.Y., 1974-89; asst. dist. atty. Herkimer County, Herkimer, N.Y., 1976-78; chief asst. dist. atty. Herkimer County, 1978-86, 1978-86, dist. atty., 1986-91, county judge and county surrogate, 1992—; acting justice Supreme Ct. of N.Y., 1997—; counsel Herkimer Cen. Sch., 1974-76; asst. counsel Village of Herkimer, N.Y., 1981-89; lectr. Police Tng. Sch., Utica, N.Y., 1979-91, Arson Seminar, 1987, Rape Crisis Tng.; tchr. Herkimer County C.C., 1981; criminal justice com. Nat. Conf. State Trial Ct. Judges. Advisor Law Explorer Post, Herkimer, 1974-76; bd. dirs. Martin Luther Home, Clinton, N.Y., 1980, Herkimer County Drug Task Force; chmn. sect. Mohawk Valley United Fund, Ilion, N.Y., 1985; mem. Arson Task Force, 1986-91. Mem. ABA (N.Y. del. to nat. conf. of spl. court judges 1995), N.Y. State Bar Assn. (jud. adminstrn. com.), Internat. Narcotics Enforcement Officers Assn., Drug Enforcement Assn. N.Y. (v.p. 1990-91), N.Y. State County Judges Assn., N.Y. State Surrogate Judges Assn., Am. Judges Assn., Elks. Republican. Lutheran. Criminal. Home: 840 W German St Herkimer NY 13350-2136 Office: Herkimer County Courthouse Herkimer NY 13350

**KIRK, RICHARD DILLON,** lawyer; b. Washington, Jan. 23, 1953; s. William Edward and Mary Elizabeth (Dillon) K.; m. Bridget Louise Stillwagon, June 27, 1981; children: Catherine Dillon, Suzanne Grace. AB, Georgetown U., 1975; JD, U. Va., 1978. Bar: Del. 1978, U.S. Dist. Ct. Del. 1980, U.S. Ct. Appeals (3rd cir.) 1984, U.S. Supreme Ct. 1984. Law clk. Del. Supreme Ct., Wilmington, 1978-79; assoc. Richards, Layton & Finger, Wilmington, 1979-82; dep. atty. gen. Del. Dept. Justice, Wilmington, 1982-84; assoc. Morris, James, Hitchens & Williams, Wilmington, 1984-86, ptnr., 1987—. Mem. Del. State Bar Assn. (pres. 1993-94, New Lawyers Disting. Svc. award 1988). Democrat. Roman Catholic. Administrative and regulatory, Environmental, General corporate. Office: Morris James Hitchens & Williams 222 Delaware Ave Wilmington DE 19801-1621

**KIRK, ROBERT S.,** lawyer; b. Aima, Mich., June 28, 1946; s. Robert S. and M. Elizabeth Kirk; m. W. Eliza Newell, June 23, 1979; children: Robert S. III, Maximilian Newell. BA, U. Ky., 1969; JD, U. Louisville, 1973. Assoc. Stiles & Fowler, Lansing, Mich., 1973-74; atty. City Nat. Bank of Detroit, 1974-77; assoc. Davidson Gottschell Kohl Secrest Warble & Lynch, Farmington Hills, Mich., 1977-79; gen. counsel Vertac Chem. Corp., Memphis, 1979-80; assoc. Waring Cox, Memphis, 1980-83; ptnr. Waring Cox PLC, Memphis, 1983—; asst. city atty. City of Germantown, 1988-89. Dir., adv. bd. Samuelson Boys Club, 1982-86. Mem. ABA, State Bar of Mich., Tenn. Bar Assn., Memphis Bar Assn., Shelby County Bar Assn., U. Club of Memphis. Real property, Construction, Environmental. Office: Waring Cox PLC 50 N Front St Fl 13 Memphis TN 38103-2126

**KIRKHAM, JOHN SPENCER,** lawyer; b. Salt Lake City, Aug. 29, 1944; s. Elbert C. and Emma (Grayson) K.; m. Janet L. Eatough, Sept. 16, 1966; children: Darcy, Jeff, Kristie. BA with honors, U. Utah, 1968, JD, 1971. Bar: Utah 1971, U.S. Dist. Ct. Utah 1971, U.S. Ct. Appeals (10th cir.) 1990, U.S. Supreme Ct. 1991. Assoc. Senior & Senior, Salt Lake City, 1971-73; ptnr. VanCott, Bagley, Cornwall & McCarthy, Salt Lake City, 1973-92, Stoel Rives LLP, Salt Lake City. Mem. exec. bd. Great Salt Lake coun. Boy Scouts Am., 1987—; mem. Utah Statewide Resource Adv. Coun., 1995-97. Mem. Utah Bar Assn., Utah Mining Assn. (bd. dirs. Salt Lake City chpt. 1987—), Rocky Mountain Mineral Law Found. (trustee 1989-92). Republican. Mormon. Natural resources, Environmental, Real property. Office: Stoel Rives LLP 201 S Main St Ste 1100 Salt Lake City UT 84111-4904

**KIRKLAND, ALFRED YOUNGES, SR.,** federal judge; b. Elgin, Ill., 1917; s. Alfred and Elizabeth (Younges) K.; m. Gwendolyn E. Muntz, June 14, 1941; children: Pamela E. Kirkland Jensen, Alfred Younges Jr., James Muntz. BA, U. Ill., 1941, JD, 1943. Bar: Ill. 1943. Assoc. Mayer, Meyer, Austrian & Platt, Chgo., 1943; sr. ptnr. Kirkland, Brady, McQueen, Martin & Callahan and predecessor firms, Elgin, 1951-73; spl. asst. atty. gen. State of Ill., 1969-73; judge 16th Cir. Ct. Ill., 1973-74; judge U.S. Dist. Ct. (no. dist.) Ill., 1974-79, sr. judge, 1979—; mem. Coun. Practicing Lawyers U. Ill. Law Forum, 1969—, mem. adv. bd., 1972-73, mem. adv. coun. continuing legal edn., 1959-62; chmn. Ill. Def. Rsch. Inst., 1965-66. Outdoor editor: Elgin Daily Courier-News, Kewanee Star-Courier; fishing editor: Midwest Outdoors Mag. Pres. Elgin YMCA, 1963, chmn. bd. trustees, 1995—. 2d lt. inf. AUS, 1943-46. Fellow Am. Coll. Trial Lawyers, Am. Bar Found.; mem. ABA (ho. of dels. 1967-70), Ill. State Bar Assn. (pres. 1968-69), Chgo. Bar Assn., Kane County Bar Assn. (pres. 1961-62), Elgin Bar Assn. (pres. 1951-52), Am. Judicature Soc. (bd. dirs. 1967—), Ill. Bar Found. (bd. dirs. 1961-69), Ill. Def. Counsel (bd. dirs. 1966-69), Soc. Trial Lawyers, Legal Club Chgo., Law Club Chgo., Internat. Assn. Ins. Counsel, Fed. Ins. Counsel,

Assn. Ins. Counsel, Outdoor Writers Assn. Am. (gen. counsel), Assn. Gt. Lakes Outdoor Writers (v.p., bd. dirs.), Ill. C. of C. (bd. dirs. 1969-70), Phi Delta Phi, Sigma Nu. Republican. Congregationalist. Clubs: Elgin Country (pres. 1956), Cosmopolitan Internat. (past pres., judge advocate). Lodges: Elks, Moose. Home: 2421 Tall Oaks Dr Elgin IL 60123-4844

**KIRKLAND, GALEN D.,** lawyer, civil rights advocate; b. N.Y.C., Sept. 18, 1950; s. Elvira (Jonathan) K.; m. Natalie P. Chapman, May 31, 1986. AB, Dartmouth Coll., 1972; JD, U. Pa., 1976. Bar: N.Y. 1978. Assoc. Cowan, Liebowitz & Latman, P.C., N.Y.C., 1976-78; v.p., gen. counsel West Harlem Cmty. Orgn., N.Y.C., 1978-88; exec. dir. N.Y.C. Civil Rights Coalition, 1989-90; dir. polit. devel. Cmty. Svc. Soc., N.Y.C., 1991-93; exec.dir. Advocates for Children of N.Y., Inc., N.Y.C., 1993-98; sole practitioner N.Y.C., 1998-99; 1st dep. dir. of policy devel. Office of N.Y. State Atty. Gen., N.Y.C., 1999—. Pres. Harlem Coun. of Elders, N.Y.C., 1993—; bd. dirs. Cmty. Tng. and Resource Ctr., N.Y.C., 1994—, Lawyers Alliance for N.Y., N.Y.C., 1997—; pres., chmn. bd. Assn. for Neighborhood and Housing Devel., N.Y.C., 1982-86; candidate for state senator Liberal Party, Dem. Primary, 29th Dist. Manhattan, 1985, 86; tenant rep. N.Y.C. Rent Guidelines Bd., 1989-92; mem. exec. bd. Park River Ind. Dems., N.Y.C., 1990—. Recipient award for excellence in edn. Reliance Ins. Group, N.Y.C., 1992, Techrs. Network award, 1992, Achievement award Cmty. Tng. and Resource Ctr., 1998. Mem. Assn. Bar City N.Y., County Lawyers Assn. Methodist. Avocation: volunteer teaching. Real property, Estate planning, General corporate. Office: Office of NY State Atty Gen 120 Broadway Fl 23D New York NY 10271-0002

**KIRKLAND, JOHN C.,** lawyer; b. Omaha, Nebr., Dec. 28, 1963; s. John and Marilou (Witt) K. AB, Columbia U., 1986; JD, UCLA, 1990. Bar: Calif. 1990. Assoc. Cadwalader, Wickersham & Taft, L.A., 1990-97; of counsel Weissmann, Wolff, Bergman, Coleman & Silverman, LLP, Beverly Hills, Calif., 1997—. Bd. dirs. Oaktree Found., Inc. Mem. ABA, L.A. County Bar Assn., Assn. Bus. Trial Lawyers, Beverly Hills Bar Assn. Avocations: hunting, bull riding, opera. General civil litigation. Home: 754 Swarthmore Ave Pacific Palisades CA 90272-4355 Office: Weissmann Wolff Bergman Coleman & Silverman LLP 9665 Wilshire Blvd Ste 900 Beverly Hills CA 90212-2340

**KIRKPATRICK, CARL KIMMEL,** prosecutor; b. Kingsport, Tenn., Aug. 2, 1936; s. Carl Kimmel and Alice (Rowland) K.; m. Barbara G. Kirkpatrick, Aug. 7, 1992; 1 child, Carl Kimmel III. BA, Vanderbilt U., 1959, JD, 1962. Bar: Tenn. 1962, U.S. Dist. Ct. (ea. dist.) Tenn. 1964. Pvt. practice Kingsport, 1962-66; asst. dist. atty. 20th Jud. Dist. Sullivan County, Tenn., 1963-64; dist. atty. gen. 2d Jud. Dist. Tenn., 1966-93; U.S. atty. U.S. Dept. of Justice, Knoxville, Tenn. Recipient Disting. Svc. award Am. Legion, 1979, Community Achievement award Kingsport Times News, 1973, Law Enforcement award Optimist Club, 1973, 79. Mem. Nat. Dist. Attys. Assn. (bd. dirs. 1983-93), Knoxville Bar Assn., Phi Delta Phi. Democrat. Baptist. Avocations: motorcycle riding, sport shooting, gardening. Office: US Attys Office 800 Market St Ste 211 Knoxville TN 37902-2342

**KIRKPATRICK, JAMES W.,** lawyer; b. Buffalo, July 31, 1933; s. Walter Augustine and Bernice M. (Hofreiter) K.; m. Norine A. Callan; children: Kathleen, Michael, Terese, James, Meganne. JD, U. Buffalo, 1959. Bar: N.Y. 1959. Atty. Lipsitz, Green, Fahringer, Roll, Salisbury & Cambria LLP, Buffalo, 1968—. Personal injury. Office: Lipsitz Green Fahringer Roll Salisbury & Cambria LLP 42 Delaware Ave Ste 300 Buffalo NY 14202-3901

**KIRKPATRICK, PAUL L.,** lawyer; b. Butte, Mont., Nov. 26, 1959; s. William M. and Mary Pat (Dowling) K.; m. Kris Kirkpatrick, Apr. 21, 1990; children: Ryan William, Tyler Matthew, Mitchell Leo. BS, Mont. State U., 1982; JD, Gonzaga U., 1986. Bar: Wash., Idaho, Mont. Assoc. Evans Lackie, Spokane, Wash., 1986-88; assoc., ptnr. Morrison & Leveque, Spokane, 1988-96; ptnr. Leveque & Kirkpatrick, Spokane, 1997—. Mem. Def. Rsch. Inst., Wash. State Bar Assn., Idaho State Bar Assn., Mont. State Bar Assn. Office: 1717 S Rustle Rd Spokane WA 99224-2011

**KIRMAN, IGOR,** lawyer; b. Kharkov, Ukraine, Nov. 28, 1970; came to the U.S., 1979; s. Vladimir and Ida Kirman; m. Galina Krasilovksy, Aug. 29, 1998. BA, Yale U., 1993; JD, Columbia U., 1996. Assoc. Sullivan & Cromwell, N.Y.C., 1996—; adv. bd. mem. U.S. L.Am. Aid Found., N.Y.C. Mem. ABA, Assn. of the Bar of the City N.Y. (com. on symposium), Federalist Soc. Mergers and acquisitions, General corporate. Home: 225 W 83rd St Apt 12C New York NY 10024-4960 Office: Sullivan & Cromwell 125 Broad St Fl 28 New York NY 10004-2489

**KIRNA, HANS CHRISTIAN,** lawyer, consultant; b. N.Y.C., Sept. 16, 1956; s. Hans H. and Ingrid D. (Korjus) K.; m. Eileen T. Barrett, June 19, 1993. BA cum laude, Upsala Coll., 1978; MA in Anthropology, New Sch. for Social Rsch., 1982; JD, CUNY, 1986. Indexer H.W. Wilson, Bronx, N.Y., 1986-87; claim counsel Am. Internat. Group, N.Y.C., 1987-94; cons. Willcox, Inc., N.Y.C., 1994-97; broker Guy Carpenter, N.Y.C., 1997-98; sr. claims atty. Risk Enterprise Mgmt. (Zurich Ins.), N.Y.C., 1998—. Author: Sam's Strange Friend, 1994; rschr.: (by Dr. Sid Harring) Crow Dog's Case, 1994; artist: prin. works include painting of Christ and 4 disciples, St. Gabriel and Michael's Orthodox Ch., Stroudsburg, Pa.; composer piano pieces. Active Great Neck (N.Y.) Rep. Club, 1980-81, Congl. Ch. of Manhasset, 1987-96. Mem. Am. Anthrop. Assn. Avocations: artist, collector of art, antiques, runner. Home: 25 Cypress Dr Denville NJ 07834-1709

**KIRSCH, LAURENCE STEPHEN,** lawyer; b. Washington, July 20, 1957; s. Ben and Bertha (Gomberg) K.; m. Celia Goldman, Aug. 19, 1979; children: Rachel Miriam, Max David. BAS, MS, U. Pa., 1979; JD, Harvard U., 1982. Bar: D.C. 1982, U.S. Ct. Appeals (3d cir.) 1983, (5th cir.) 1997, U.S. Dist. Ct. D.C. 1985, U.S. Ct. Appeals (D.C. cir.) 1985, U.S. Supreme Ct. 1987; registered environ. assessor, Calif. 1988. Law clk. to presiding judge Pa. Dist. Ct., Phila., 1982-83; vis. asst. prof. law U. Bridgeport (Conn.) Law Sch., 1983-84; assoc. Cadwalader, Wickersham & Taft, Washington, 1984-90, ptnr., 1991—; chmn. steering coms. Superfund. *Mr. Kirsch is an environmental litigator, counselor and transactional attorney. His litigation victories include three appellate decisions overturning site listings on the National Priorities List, including the first such decision in the history of the Superfund program, and opinions on the interaction of bankruptcy and environmental law. He negotiates with government agencies and private parties, advises on environmental implications of real estate and corporate transactions, and performs environmental assessments. Mr. Kirsch lectures widely on environmental law subjects and taught a law school course on Law, Science and Technology. He was interviewed as an expert in environmental law by CBS News, the MacNeil-Lehrer Report, and numerous radio shows and newspapers.* Editor-in-chief Indoor Pollution Law Report, 1987-91; mng. editor Harvard Environ. Law Rev., 1981-82; contbr. articles to profl. jours. Mem. ABA, Fed. Bar Assn., AAAS, Air Pollution Control Assn. (indoor air quality com.), Environ. Law Inst., Nat. Inst. Bldg. Scis. (indoor air quality com.), Am. Soc. Testing and Measurement (indoor air quality com.), Phi Beta Kappa. Environmental, Administrative and regulatory, Federal civil litigation. Home: 7212 Longwood Dr Bethesda MD 20817-2122 Office: Cadwalader Wickersham & Taft Ste 700 1333 New Hampshire Ave NW Washington DC 20036-1574

**KIRSCH, LYNN,** lawyer; b. New Orleans, Oct. 31, 1964; d. Henry C. and Therese M. ((Guenther) K. BS in Bus. Mgmt., Fla. State U., Panama City, 1992; JD, U. Ariz., 1995. Bar: Nev. 1995, U.S. Dist. Ct. Nev. 1995, U.S. Ct. Fed. Claims 1997, U.S. Ct. Appeals (9th cir.) 1998, U.S. Supreme Ct. 1999. Law clk. U.S. Atty.'s Office, Phoenix, 1993, Slutes, Sakrison, Evan, Grant & Pelander, Tucson, 1993-94, Lionel, Sawyer & Collins, Las Vegas, 1994; judicial extern Fed. Dist. Ct., Tucson, 1994; rsch. asst. U. Ariz., Tucson, 1994-95; law clk. Jacob & Fishbein, Tucson, 1994-95; assoc. Goold, Patterson, DeVore & Rondau, Las Vegas, 1995-97, Curran & Parry, Las Vegas, 1997-99, Bernhard & Leslie, Las Vegas, 1999—; alt. panel mem. So. Nev. Disciplinary Bd., Las Vegas, 1997—; mem. Justice of the Peace pro-tempore panel, Las Vegas Twp., County of Clark. Article editor U. Ariz. Law Rev., 1994-95. Mem. Jr. League of Las Vegas, 1998, State of Nev. Commn. on Postsecondary Edn., 1998. Recipient Cert. Appreciation, U.S. Atty.'s Office, Phoenix, 1993, AmJur award Lawyers Coop. Publ., Tucson, 1993. Mem. ABA (litigation sect.) ATLA, State Bar Nev. (chair young lawyers sect. 1999-2000), Clark County Bar Assn. (trial by peers com., cmty. svc. com.), Nev. Trial Lawyers Assn., So. Nev. Assn. Women Attys. Avocations: horseback riding, hiking, skydiving. General civil litigation, Government contracts and claims, Construction. Office: Bernhard & Leslie 3980 Howard Hughes Pkwy Ste 550 Las Vegas NV 89109-5905

**KIRSCHBAUM, JOEL LEON,** lawyer; b. Miami, Fla., Dec. 14, 1947; s. Jack and Gertrude (Sager) K.; m. Ellen M. Proctor Small, Aug. 23, 1969 (div. Jan. 1984); m. Karin S. Dillon, June 8, 1985; 1 child, Anna N. BS, Fla. State U., 1970; JD, U. Fla., 1973. Bar: Fla. 1973, U.S. Dist. Ct. 1976, U.S. Supreme Ct. 1981. Assoc. Berryhill, Avery et al, Ft. Lauderdale, Fla., 1973-77; ptnr. Esler & Kirschbaum, Ft. Lauderdale, 1977-91, Ruden, Barnett et al, Ft. Lauderdale, 1991-96, Bunnell, Woulfe, Kirschbaum, Keller & McIntyre, Ft. Lauderdale, 1996—. Bd. dirs. Humane Soc. Broward County, Ft. Lauderdale, 1994—. Mem. ABA (vice chairperson trial techniques 1996, legal ethics com., family law sect. 1994—), Fla. Bar Assn. (mem. appellate rules com., mem. family law legis. com., mem. family law rules com. 1977-90, lectr. CLE, family law 1995-96), Broward County Bar Assn. (lectr. family law 1988—). Family and matrimonial. Office: Bunnell Woulfe Kirschbaum Keller & McIntyre 888 E Las Olas Blvd Fort Lauderdale FL 33301-2272

**KIRSCHNER, JONNA DEE KAUGER,** lawyer; b. Oklahoma City, Feb. 24, 1962; d. Michael Paul Kirschner and Yvonne Kauger; m. Bruce John Scambler, June 12, 1992; 1 child, Jay Michael Eduard Kauger Scambler. BA in English, Dartmouth Coll., 1984; JD, Boston Coll., 1987. Bar: Mass. 1987, D.C. 1995, Okla. 1995, Solicitor Supreme Ct. of Eng. and Wales 1994. Congl. inter Rep. Mike Synar, Washington, 1981-82; atty. Boodle Hatfield, London, 1988-90; assoc. Bracewell & Patterson LLP, London, 1990-94, McKinney & Stringer, P.C., Oklahoma City, 1994-97; shareholder, dir. Fuller, Tubb, Pomeroy, Kirschner Bickford & Stokes, Oklahoma City, 1997-99, The Kirschner Law Firm, Oklahoma City, 1999—. Mem. Jr. League, London, 1990-94, Oklahoma City, 1994—. Mem. Am. Women Lawyers in London (founding mem.), Soc. of English and Am. Lawyers, Red Earth, Inc. (dir. 1996—), Dartmouth Club (co-chair 1992-94), Queens Club. Episcopalian. Avocations: Native Am. art, snow skiing, Am. quilts, violin. General corporate, Public international, Securities. Home: 1715 Guilford Ln Oklahoma City OK 73120-1013 Office: The Kirschner Law Firm Bank One Ctr Ste 3300 100 N Broadway Ave Oklahoma City OK 73102-8606

**KIRSCHNER, KENNETH HAROLD,** lawyer; b. Bklyn., Dec. 1, 1953; s. Samuel and Stella K.; m. Andrea Chase, Feb. 8, 1997. BS, Cornell U., 1975; JD, NYU, 1978, LLM, 1981. Bar: N.Y. 1979, U.S. Ct. Appeals (2d, 5th and D.C. cirs.), 1979, U.S. Dist. Ct. (so. and ea. dists.) N.Y., 1979, U.S. Supreme Ct. 1982. Assoc. Kelley Drye & Warren, N.Y.C., 1978-82; assoc. Breed Abbott & Morgan, N.Y.C., 1982-86, ptnr., 1986-93; ptnr. Kelley Drye & Warren LLP, N.Y.C., 1993—; adj. asst. prof. mgmt. NYU, 1988—. Contbr. articles to profl. jours. Labor, General civil litigation, Non-profit and tax-exempt organizations. Office: Kelley Drye & Warren 101 Park Ave Fl 30 New York NY 10178-0062

**KIRSH, SANFORD,** lawyer; b. Chgo., Dec. 5, 1930; s. Paul and Esther (Leniol) K.; m. Edwina R. Edelson, Apr. 15, 1951; children: Lori, David, Cari, Matthew. LLB, Chgo. Kent Coll. Law, 1953. Bar: Ill. 1953, U.S. Dist. Ct. (no. dist.) Ill. 1955; cert. matrimonial arbitrator. Sole practitioner, assoc. Epstein & Wilsey, Chgo., 1953-55; ptnr. Epstein, Wilsey & Kirsh, Chgo., 1955-71; sole practitioner Chgo., 1971-76; ptnr. Kirsh & Berman, Ltd., Chgo., 1976—. Mem. ABA, ATLA, Ill. Bar Assn., Am. Acad. Matrimonial Lawyers (sec., v.p., pres. Ill. chpt. 1983-85). Avocation: golf. Family and matrimonial. Office: Kirsh & Berman Ltd 10 S La Salle St Ste 2424 Chicago IL 60603-1002

**KIRSHBAUM, HOWARD M.,** judge, arbitrator; b. Oberlin, Ohio, Sept. 19, 1938; s. Joseph and Gertrude (Morris) K.; m. Priscilla Joy Parmakian, Aug. 15, 1964; children—Audra Lee, Andrew William. B.A., Yale U., 1960; A.B., Cambridge U., 1962, M.A., 1966; LL.B., Harvard U., 1965. Ptnr. Zarlengo and Kirshbaum, Denver, 1969-75; judge Denver Dist. Ct., Denver, 1975-80, Colo. Ct. Appeals, Denver, 1980-83; justice Colo. Supreme Ct., Denver, 1983-97; arbiter Jud. Arbiter Group, Inc., Denver, 1997—, sr. judge, 1997—; adj. prof. law U. Denver, 1970—; dir. Am. Law Inst. Phila., Am. Judicature Soc., Chgo., Colo. Jud. Inst. Denver, 1979-89; pres. Colo. Legal Care Soc., Denver, 1974-75. Bd. dirs. Young Artists Orch., Denver, 1976-85; pres. Community Arts Symphony, Englewood, Colo., 1972-74; dir. Denver Opportunity, Inc., Denver, 1972-74; vice-chmn. Denver Council on Arts and Humanities, 1969. Mem. ABA (standing com. pub. edn.), Colo. Bar Assn., Denver Bar Assn. (trustee 1981-83), Soc. Profls. in Dispute Resolution. Avocations: music performance; tennis. Office: Jud Arbiter Group Inc 1601 Blake St Ste 400 Denver CO 80202-1328

**KIRTLAND, MICHAEL ARTHUR,** lawyer; b. St. Louis, Oct. 27, 1951; s. John Thornton and Joan Reichert Kirtland; m. Kay Tegman Kirtland, May 17, 1975; children: David Arthur, James Michael. BA, Coe Coll., 1974; MPA, U. Colo., 1981; JD, Faulkner U., 1993. Bar: Ala. 1994, U.S. Dist. Ct. (mid. dist.) Ala. 1994, U.S. Supreme Ct. 1997, U.S. Ct. Appeals (11th cir.) 1998. Commd. 2d lt. USAF, 1974, advanced through grades to lt. col., 1990, retired, 1995; atty. pvt. practice, Montgomery, Ala., 1995—. Editor: Air University Review Index, 1990, Air Power Journal Index, 1992. instr. Laubruch Literacy Coun., Montgomery, 1996—. Mem. ABA, Nat. Assn. Estate Planners & Counsels, Air Force Assn. (life), Retired Officers Assn. Avocations: basketball, officiating. Estate planning, Probate, Estate taxation. Office: 2835 Zelda Rd Montgomery AL 36106-2667

**KIRTLEY, JANE ELIZABETH,** professional society administrator, lawyer; b. Indpls., Nov. 7, 1953; d. William Raymond and Faye Marie (Price) K.; m. Stephen Jon Cribari, May 8, 1985. BS in Journalism, Northwestern U., 1975, MS in Journalism, 1976; JD, Vanderbilt U., 1979. Bar: N.Y. 1980, D.C. 1982, Va. 1995, U.S. Dist. Ct. (we. dist.) N.Y. 1980, U.S. Dist. Ct. D.C. 1982, U.S. Ct. Claims 1982, U.S. Ct. Appeals (4th cir.) 1982, U.S. Ct. Appeals (D.C. cir.) 1985, U.S. Ct. Appeals (10th cir.) 1996, U.S. Ct. Appeals (5th cir.) 1997, U.S. Ct. Appeals (6th cir.) 1998, U.S. Ct. Appeals (6th and 11th cir.) 1998, U.S. Supreme Ct. 1985. Assoc. Nixon, Hargrave, Devans & Doyle, Rochester, N.Y., 1979-81, Washington, 1981-84; exec. dir. Reporters Com. for Freedom of Press, Arlington, Va., 1985—; mem. adj. faculty Am. U. Sch. Comm., 1988-98. Exec. articles editor Vanderbilt U. Jour. Transnat. Law, 1978-79; editor: The News Media and the Law, 1985—, The First Amendment Handbook, 1987, 4th edit., 1995, Agents of Discovery, 1991, 93, 95, Pressing Issues, 1998—; columnist NEPA Bull., 1988—, Virginia's Press, 1991—, Am. Journalism Rev., 1995—, W.Va.'s Press, 1997—, Tenn. Press, 1997—; mem. editl. bd. Govt. Info. Quar., Comm. Law and Policy. Bd. dirs. Student Press Law Ctr., Arlington, Va.; mem. steering com. Libel Def. Resource Ctr., N.Y.C.; adv. bd. Pa. Ctr. for the 1st Amendment, University Park, Freedom Forum 1st Amendment Ctr., Nashville. Mem. ABA, N.Y. State Bar Assn., D.C. Bar Assn., Va. State Bar Assn., Sigma Delta Chi. Home: 724 Franklin St Alexandria VA 22314-4104 Office: Reporters Com 1815 Fort Myer Dr Ste 900 Arlington VA 22209-1817

**KIRTLEY, WILLIAM THOMAS,** lawyer; b. Des Moines, May 12, 1936; s. Clearance Marcellus and Gladys Marjorie Kirtley; m. Mary Diane Foster, Aug. 23, 1958; children: Kyle Benton Kirtley Davis, Kimberly Diane, John Foster. BS in Commerce, U. Iowa, 1958, JD, 1960. Bar: Iowa 1960, Fla. 1977. Ptnr. Williams, Hart, Lavorato & Kirtley, Des Moines, 1968-79; assoc. English, McCaugh & O'Brien, Ft. Lauderdale, Fla., 1979-81; ptnr. Kirk Pinkerton, Sarasota, Fla., 1981-83, Kusic & Kirtley, P.A., Sarasota, 1983-85; sole prin. William T. Kirtley, P.A., Sarasota, 1985—. Trustee Ringling Sch. Art and Design, Sarasota, 1986—, vice chmn., 1993-96, chmn., 1996—. Capt. U.S. Army Res., 1961-67. Mem. Fla. Bar, Sarasota County Bar Assn., The Field Club. Republican. Securities, General corporate, Federal civil litigation. Office: 2940 S Tamiami Trl Sarasota FL 34239-5105

**KIRVEN, TIMOTHY J.,** lawyer; b. Buffalo, Wyo., May 26, 1949; s. William J. and Ellen F. (Farrell) K.; m. Elizabeth J. Adams, Oct. 31, 1970; 1 child, Kristen B. BA in English, U. Notre Dame, 1971; JD, U. Wyo., 1974. Bar: Wyo. Ptnr. Kirven & Kirven, PC, Buffalo, 1974—. Author Rocky Mountain Mineral Law, 1982. Mem. Johnson County Libr. Br., Buffalo. Mem. ABA, Wyo. State Bar (v.p. 1997—), Johnson County Bar Assn., KC (G.K. treas. 1992-96), Western States Bar Conf. (pres.-elect 1997—), Rotary (pres. Buffalo club 1988-89, YEP chmn. 1993—). Home: PO Box C Buffalo WY 82834-0060 Office: Kirven & Kirven PC PO Box 640 Buffalo WY 82834-0640

**KIRWAN, PETER H.,** lawyer; b. San Francisco, Mar. 25, 1949; s. Peter T. and Marilee H. Kirwan; m. Lorena R. Kirwan; children: Emily, Matthew, Brittany. BS, U. Calif., Berkeley, 1981; JD, Santa Clara Law Sch., 1986. Bar: Calif. 1986, U.S. Dist. Ct. (no. dist.) Calif. 1986. Atty. Hege, Fenton, Jones & Appel, San Jose, Calif., 1986—. Avocations: golf, water polo, swimming. Insurance. Home: 220 More Ave Los Gatos CA 95032-1110 Office: Hoge Fenton Jones & Appel 60 S Market St # 1200 San Jose CA 95113-2351

**KIRWIN, KENNETH FRANCIS,** law educator; b. Morris, Minn., May 10, 1941; s. Francis B. and Dorothy A. (McNally) K.; m. Phyllis J. Hills, June 2, 1962; children—David, Mark, Robert. B.A., St. John's U., 1963; J.D., U. Minn., 1966. Bar: Minn. 1966, U.S. Dist. Ct. Minn. 1968, U.S. Ct. Appeals (8th cir.) 1969. Law clk. to assoc. justice Supreme Ct., Minn., 1966-67; assoc. Lindquist & Vennum, Mpls., 1967-70; prof. law William Mitchell Coll. Law, St. Paul, 1970—; staff dir. Uniform Rules Criminal Procedure, 1971-74, reporter, 1982-87; reporter Uniform Victims of Crime Act, 1991-92; adj. prof. U. Minn. Law Sch., 1977, 80; active Minn. Lawyers Profl. Responsibility Bd., 1975-81, Minn. Bd. Continuing Legal Edn., 1975-83. Author: (with Maynard E. Pirsig) Cases and Materials on Professional Responsibility, 1984. Mem. Ramsey County Bar Assn., Minn. State Bar Assn., ABA (mem. standing com. on discipline 1983-89), Am. Law Inst. Home: 1418 Brookshire Ct New Brighton MN 55112-6390 Office: William Mitchell Coll Law 875 Summit Ave Saint Paul MN 55105-3030

**KISER, JACKSON L.,** federal judge; b. Welch, W.Va., June 24, 1929; m. Carole Gorman; children: Jackson, William, John Michael, Elizabeth Carol. B.A., Concord Coll., 1951; J.D., Washington and Lee U., 1952. Bar: Va. Asst. U.S. atty. Western Dist. Va., 1958-61; assoc., then ptnr. R.R. Young, Young, Kiser, Haskins, Mann, Gregory & Young P.C., Martinsville, Va., 1961-82; judge U.S. Dist. Ct. (we. dist.) Va., 1982-93, chief judge, 1993-97, sr. judge, 1997—. Mem. Martinsville City Sch. Bd., 1971-77. With JAGC U.S. Army, 1952-55, capt. Res., 1955-61. Mem. Am. Coll. Trial Lawyers (state com.), Va. Bar Assn. (exec. com.), Va. State Bar, Va. Trial Lawyers Assn., 4th Cir. Jud. Conf. (permanent), Martinsville-Henry County Bar Assn., Order of Coif. Office: US Dist Ct PO Box 3326 700 Main St Danville VA 24543-3326

**KISHEL, GREGORY FRANCIS,** federal judge; b. Virginia, Minn., Jan. 26, 1951. AB, Cornell U., 1973; JD, Boston Coll., 1977. Bar: Minn. 1978, U.S. Dist. Ct. Minn. 1978, U.S. Ct. Appeals (8th cir.) 1978, Wis. 1985, U.S. Dist. Ct. (we. dist.) Wis. 1985. Staff atty. Legal Aid Svc. of N.E. Minn., Duluth, 1978-81; pvt. practice law Duluth, 1981-86; judge U.S. Bankruptcy Ct., St. Paul, 1986—; part-time judge U.S. Bankruptcy Ct., Duluth, 1984-86. Mem. ABA, Nat. Conf. Bankruptcy Judges, Minn. Bar Assn., Wis. State Bar Assn., Polish Geneal. Soc. Minn. (pres. 1996—). Office: US Bankruptcy Ct 316 Robert St N Ste 210 Saint Paul MN 55101-1241

**KISS, ROBERT,** state supreme court justice; s. Matthew J. Sr. and Catherine E. (Schnarr) K.; m. Melinda Lou Ashworth. BA, Ohio State U., 1979, JD, 1982. With firm Gorman, Sheatsley & Co., L.C.; mem. W.Va. Ho. of Dels., 1988-99, chmn. subcom. on ways and means, 1989, vice chair fin. com., chmn. fin. com., 1993, speaker of the house, 1996-99; justice W.Va. Supreme Ct. Appeals, 1999—. Bd. dirs. Beckley Renaissance, Raleigh County Hospice. Bernard Levy scholar, 1980-82. Mem. Fla. State Bar Assn., Ohio Bar Assn., W.Va. Bar Assn., Raleigh County Bar Assn., Beckley Bus. and Profl. Women's Club. Office: W Va Supreme Ct Appeals Capitol Complex Bldg 1 Charleston WV 25305*

**KISSEL, PETER CHARLES,** lawyer; b. Watertown, N.Y., Sept. 29, 1947; s. Laurence Haas and Catherine Cantwell (Weldon) K.; m. Sharon Darlene Murphy, June 14, 1970. AB, Syracuse U., 1969; JD, Am. U., 1972. Bar: D.C. 1973, U.S. Ct. Claims 1976, U.S. Dist. Ct. D.C. 1979, U.S. Ct. Appeals (9th cir.) 1979, U.S. Ct. Appeals (D.C. cir.) 1983, U.S. Ct. Appeals (3d cir.) 1986, U.S. Ct. Appeals (5th cir.) 1988, U.S. Supreme Ct. 1978. Atty.-advisor Fed. Power Commn., Washington, 1972-74; atty. pub. utilities, 1974-77; assoc. O'Connor & Hannan, Washington, 1977-79, ptnr., 1979-87; ptnr. Baller Hammett, Washington, 1987-93; ptnr., CFO, Grammer, Kissel, Robbins, Skancke & Edwards, Washington, 1993—; co-bus. mgr. Energy Law Jour., Washington, 1981, asst. editor, 1982-89, bus. mgr., 1989-92. Contbr. articles to profl. jours. Mem. vestry St. Patrick's Episcopal Ch., Washington, 1975-78, 82-85, 86-90, chmn. ann. fundraising campaign, 1987-89; bd. dirs. Episcopal Caring Response to AIDS Inc., 1988-93, v.p., 1990-91, pres., 1992, mem. exec. com., 1990-93; bd. dirs. PRISM, 1996-97, Foun. of the Energy Law Jour., 1990-92. Recipient Spl. award Fed. Power Commn., 1973. Mem. Bar Assn. D.C., Fed. Energy Bar Assn. (vice-chmn. com. on publs. 1984-85, chmn. com. on hydroelectric regulation 1991-92), Nat. Hydropower Assn., John Sherman Myers Soc. (Washington Coll. Law), Syracuse U. Soc. Fellows, Syracuse U. Washington adv. bd., Phi Kappa Psi. Democrat. Episcopalian. Avocations: gardening, American history, Irish history. FERC practice, Administrative and regulatory, Appellate. Home: 5604 Utah Ave NW Washington DC 20015-1230 Office: Grammer Kissel Robbins Skancke & Edwards 1225 I St NW Ste 1225 Washington DC 20005-5939

**KISSEL, RICHARD OLIVER, II,** lawyer; b. Evansville, Ind., Aug. 30, 1958; s. Richard Oliver and Ethel Marie (Peasae) K.; m. Lynn Ellen Rinehart, June 8, 1988; children: Sarah B., Anne K. BS, Ind. U., 1981, JD, 1985. Bar: Ill. 1985, Mo. 1989, Ind. 1992. Atty. Rooks Pitts & Poust, Chgo., 1985-88, Gallop Johnson & Neuman, St. Louis, 1988-90, Bryan Cave, St. Louis, 1990-92, Dann Pecar Newman & Kleiman, Indpls., 1992—. Bd. dirs. Young Audiences of Ind., Indpls., 1993—; trustee Circle Centre Youth Investment Fund, Indpls., 1994—; trustee Simon Youth Found., Indpls., 1998—. Mem. Woodstock Club. Estate planning, Estate taxation, Taxation, general. Office: Dann Pecar Newman & Kleiman 2300 One American Sq Indianapolis IN 46282

**KITAY, HARVEY ROBERT,** lawyer, investment manager; b. Bklyn., Oct. 16, 1931; s. David and Celia (Sherman) K.; m. Betty Finkelstein, Sept. 3, 1956; children: Robin Ann, William Douglas. BA, NYU, 1953; JD, Harvard U., 1956. Bar: N.Y. 1957. Acct. Peat Marwick Mitchel, N.Y.C., 1956-57; assoc. Law Office Gustave Simons, N.Y.C., 1957-70; ptnr. Kolleeny, Kitay & Hort, N.Y.C., 1970—; mgr. Sahabe Securities Co., Scarsdale, N.Y., 1960—. Mem. ABA, N.Y. State Bar Assn., N.Y. Co. Bar Assn., Assn. of Bar of City of N.Y. Estate planning, Taxation, general, Probate. Home: 38 Montrose Rd Scarsdale NY 10583-1127 Office: Kolleeny Kitay & Hort 22d Fl 114 W 47th St New York NY 10036-1510

**KITCH, EDMUND WELLS,** lawyer, educator, private investor; b. Wichita, Kans., Nov. 3, 1939; s. Paul R. and Josephine (Pridmore) K.; m. Joanne Steiner, Dec. 1, 1966 (div. 1976); 1 child, Sarah; m. Alison Lauter, Jan. 29, 1978; children: Andrew, Whitney. BA, Yale U., 1961; JD, U. Chgo., 1964. Bar: Kans. 1964, Ill. 1966, U.S. Supreme Ct. 1973, Va. 1986. Asst. prof. law Ind. U., 1964-65; mem. faculty U. Chgo., 1965-82, prof., 1971-82; prof., mem. Ctr. Advanced Studies U. Va., Charlottesville, 1982-85, Joseph M. Hartfield prof., 1985—, Sullivan and Cromwell rsch. prof., 1996-99; vis. prof. Bklyn. Law Sch., 1995; Jack N. Pritzger Disting. vis. prof. of law Northwestern U., 1996; spl. asst. solicitor gen. U.S. Dept. Justice, 1973-74; exec. dir. Adv. Com. on Procedural Reform CAB, 1975-76; reporter Com. on Pattern Jury Instruction, Ill. Supreme Ct., 1966-69; mem. com. on pub.-pvt. sector rels. in vaccine innovation Inst. of Medicine, NAS, 1982-85, mem. com. on evaluation polio vaccine, 1987-88. Author: (with Harvey Perlman) Intellectual Property, 5th edit., 1997; Regulation, Federalism and Interstate Commerce, 1981. Contbr. articles to profl. jours. Mem. Va. Bar Assn., Am. Law Inst., Order of Coif, Phi Beta Kappa. Office: U Va Sch Law 580 Massie Rd Charlottesville VA 22903-1738

**KITCHEN, CHARLES WILLIAM,** lawyer; b. July 17, 1926; s. Karl K. and Lucille W. (Keynes) K.; m. Mary Applegate, July 22, 1950; children: Kenneth K., Guy R., Anne Kitchen Campbell. BA, Western Res. U., 1948, JD, 1950. Bar: Ohio 1950, U.S. Dist. Ct. Ohio 1952, U.S. Ct. Appeals (6th cir.) 1972, U.S. Supreme Ct. 1981. Ptnr. Kitchen, Derry & Barnhouse Co., LPA,

Cleve., 1950-97, sr. ptnr., 1972, ret., 1997; life mem., exec. com. 8th Jud. Dist. Ct., 1988-91. Mem. Regional Coun. on Alcoholism, 1981-86, chmn., 1985-86; bd. dirs. Scarbourgh Hall, 1992-94. With A.C., U.S. Army, 1944-45. Fellow Internat. Acad. Trial Lawyers, Am. Coll. Trial Lawyers; mem. ABA (sect. tort and ins. practice, sec. litigation), Am. Arbitration Assn. (panelist 1961-91), Cleve. Assn. Civil Trial Attys. (pres. 1971-72), Ohio Assn. Civil Trial Attys. (pres. 1975-76), Greater Cleve. Bar Assn. (chmn. med.-legal com. 1974-75, chmn. lawyers assistance program 1981-83, chmn. mentor com. 1988-95, jud. campaign com. chmn. 1993-95, ttustee 1984-87), Am. Legion, Order of Coif, Beta Theta Pi, Phi Delta Phi. Presbyterian. State civil litigation, Federal civil litigation. Home: 401 Bounty Way Apt 242 Avon Lake OH 44012-2482

**KITCHEN, E.C. DEENO,** lawyer; b. Tallahassee, May 1, 1942; s. Oscar Edward and Rose (Deeb) K.; m. Patricia Gautier, June 22, 1968; children: Anne-Elizabeth K. Williams, Kimberly Gautier, William Gautier, Deeb-Paul II. JD cum laude, U. Fla., 1967. Bar: 1968, U.S. Dist. Ct. (no. and ctrl. dists.) Fla., U.S. Ct. Appeals (3d and 11th cirs.), U.S. Supreme Ct.; cert. cir. mediator, Fla. Ptnr. Ervin, Varn, Jacobs, Odom & Kitchen, Tallahassee, 1971-88, Kitchen & High, Tallahassee, 1988-93; founding ptnr. Kitchen, Judkins, Simpson & High, Tallahassee, 1993—. Past mem. editl. bd. U. Fla. Law Rev. Chmn. exec. com., Leon County (Fla.) Dem. Party, 1971-73, mem. state exec. com., 1971-75; karate instr., City of Tallahassee. Master Tallahassee Am. Inn of Ct. (charter mem.); fellow Am. Coll. Trial Lawyers, Internat. Soc. Barristers, Am. Bar Found., Fla. Bar Found.; mem. ABA (bd. regents Nat. Coll. Criminal Def., 1981-84, mem. litigation and criminal justice sects.), Am. Bd. Trial Advocates (charter mem. Tallahassee chpt., advocate, pres. 1996), Nat. Assn. Criminal Def. Lawyers, Acad. Fla. Trial Lawyers (bd. dirs. 1983-85, past Eagle sponsor), Florida Bar (bd. cert. trial lawyer 1983, exec. coun. trial lawyers sect. 1980-88, chmn. steering com. trial lawyers sect., trial advocacy program 1982, 88, faculty mem. and lectr. 1979—, faculty mem. advanced trial advocacy program, exec. coun. criminal law sect. 1976-85, chmn. legis. com., chmn. grievance com. 2d Jud. Cir. Fla. 1979-80, mem. 1977-80), Leading Fla. Attys. (adv. bd.), Order of Coif, Phi Kappa Phi, Phi Alpha Delta (past pres.). Avocation: karate (black belt Cuong Nhu Oriental Martial Arts, black belt Isshin-Ryu Karate). Fax: (850) 561-1471. General civil litigation, Criminal, Personal injury. Office: Kitchen Judkins Simpson & High PO Box 10368 Tallahassee FL 32302-2368 and: 1102 N Gadsden St Tallahassee FL 32303-6328

**KITCHENOFF, ROBERT SAMUEL,** lawyer; b. Reading, Pa., June 19, 1959; s. Maxwell Milton and Elizabeth (Marshall) K.; m. Roberta Lucker, Sept. 6, 1987; 1 child, Rachel Sloan. BA, U. Pitts., 1981; JD, Rutgers U., 1986. Bar: Pa. 1985, N.J. 1985, U.S. Dist. Ct. (ea. dist.) Pa. 1987, U.S. Dist. Ct. (mid. dist.) Pa. 1993, U.S. Dist. Ct. N.J. 1990, U.S. Ct. Appeals (3d cir.) 1988, U.S. Supreme Ct. 1993. Law clk. to Hon. M. Palladino Commonwealth Ct. Pa., Allentown, 1986-87; assoc. Kohn, Swift & Graf, P.C., Phila., 1987-95; ptnr. Weinstein, Kitchenoff, Scarlato & Goldman, L.L.C., Phila., 1995—. Recipient Pub. Justice Achievement award Trial Lawyers for Pub. Justice Found., 1997, Human Rights award Am. Immigration Lawyers Assn., 1994. Mem. ABA, Phila. Bar Assn. Avocations: golf, reading, travel. Federal civil litigation, Antitrust. Office: Weinstein Kitchnoff Scarlato & Goldman LLC 1608 Walnut St Ste 1400 Philadelphia PA 19103-5407

**KITCHIN, JOHN JOSEPH,** lawyer; b. Kansas City, Mo., Mar. 23, 1933; s. John Bernard and Delia Clare (White) K.; m. Mary A. Medill, Feb. 15, 1958; children: Teresa M., Nancy J., John T., Barbara A. BA, Rockhurst Coll., 1954; JD cum laude, St. Louis U., 1957. Bar: Mo. 1957. Assoc. Swanson, Midgley Law Firm, Kansas City, 1961-65; ptnr. Swanson, Midgley, Gangwere, Kitchin and McLarney, Kansas City, 1966—, mng. ptnr., 1983—; gen. counsel Nat. Collegiate Athletic Assn. Contbr. articles to profl. jours. Chmn. Kansas City Bd. Liquor Rev.; mem. Avila Coll. Bd. Councillors, Kansas City, 1972-90, pres., 1989-90; trustee Avila Coll., 1991—; mem. Seton Ctr., Inc., Kansas City, 1980—, pres., 1982-88; trustee St. Joseph Health Ctr. Found., 1994—. Capt. USAF, 1957-61. Mem. ABA, Kansas City Bar Assn., Lawyers Assn. of Kansas City, Am. Judicature Soc., Mo. Bar Assn., Nat. Sports Law Inst. (bd. advisors), Sports Lawyers Assn., Serra Club (pres. 1978-79), St. Teresa Acad. Club (pres. 1976-77), Rotary. Democrat. Roman Catholic. Avocations: golfing, travel, reading. Sports, Entertainment, General corporate. Home: 11548 Baltimore Ave Kansas City MO 64114-5554 Office: Swanson Midgely Gangwere Kitchin and McLarney 1500 Commerce Trust Bldg 922 Walnut St Ste 1500 Kansas City MO 64106-1848

**KITE, RICHARD LLOYD,** lawyer, real estate development company executive; b. Chgo., Jan. 26, 1934; s. Leonard Robert and Idelle (Berss) K.; m. Iris Goldberg, Aug. 26, 1984; children—Lawrence, Daniel, Jill. B.S. with highest honors in Bus. Adminstrn. and Acctg., UCLA, 1955, J.D., 1958. Bar: Wis. 1964, Calif. 1959. Sole practice, Beverly Hills, Calif., 1959-64; pres. Marcus Theatres Corp., Milw., 1964-80; pres. Kite Devel. Corp., Milw., 1980—; pres. Kite Investment Corp.; sec.-treas., trustee Regency Investors, 1982-83; v.p., sec., dir., chief legal counsel Marcus Corp., 1964-81; dir. Mid-Continental Bancorp., Milw., Am. Hampton Bank, Milw., Guardian State Bank, Milw., Continental Bank and Trust, Milw., Mid-Am. Bank, Milw. Pres. Variety Club of Wis., 1978-79, bd. dirs., 1964—; sec., bd. dirs. Mt. Sinai Glendale Health Ctr., Milw.; hon. bd. dirs. Ballet Found. Milw., Inc.; bd. govs. Wis. Israel Bonds Com., Milw. Jewish Fedn.; pres., bd. dirs. Wis. chpt., trustee Am. Friends Hebrew U. Mem. Young Pres.'s Orgn., Internat. Council Shopping Ctrs., Order of Coif. Editor UCLA Law Rev., 1957-58. Real property, Personal income taxation, General corporate. Office: 1031 Cove Way Beverly Hills CA 90210-2818

**KITE, WILLIAM MCDOUGALL,** lawyer; b. Buffalo, N.Y., Aug. 25, 1923; s. William Henry and Susanna (McDougall) K.; m. Margaret Maupin Wulsin, Apr. 15, 1950; children: Margaret, William Jr., Thomas, Matthew. AB, Princeton U., 1945; LLB, Harvard U., 1949. Bar: Ohio 1949, U.S. Dist. Ct. (so. dist.) Ohio 1949. Assoc. Cottle, Campbell, Druffel & Hogan, Cin., 1949-56; ptnr. Cohen, Todd, Kite & Stanford, Cin., 1956—; bd. dirs. Midland Co., Cin.; bd. dirs., sec. Camargo Hunt, Inc.; pres., gen. mgr. Camargo Stables, Inc.; mem. pres.'s adv. coun. Berea Coll., 1993—. Mayor City of Indian Hill (Ohio), 1971-75; bd. mem. Cin. Hist. Soc., 1973-82; pres., bd. dirs. Coun. Alcoholism of S.W. Ohio, 1975-77; bd. dirs. Shawn Womack Dance Project, Friends Spl. Treatment Ctr., Children's Hosp.; chmn. bd. dirs. Maple Knoll Hosp. and Home, Cin., 1958-62, Cin. Country Day Sch., 1982-86; pres. Planned Parenthood Assn., Cin., 1978-82; trustee Cin. Country Day Sch. Found.; ruling elder Glendale Indian Hill and Presbyn. Chs.; mem. Bd. Tax Appeals, Indian Hill. Lt. USN, 1942-46, PTO, 1950-52, Korea. Mem. ABA (bd. dirs.), Ohio Bar Assn. (bd. dirs.), Cin. Bar Assn. (diversity com. 1993—). Presbyterian. Avocations: horseback riding, swimming, sailing. General corporate, Estate planning, Securities. Home: 9645 Cunningham Rd Cincinnati OH 45243-1621 Office: Cohen Todd Kite & Stanford 525 Vine St Ste 16 Cincinnati OH 45202-3121

**KITTA, JOHN NOAH,** lawyer; b. San Francisco, Aug. 26, 1951; s. John E. and Norma Jean (Noah) K. BS, U. Santa Clara, 1973, JD, 1976. Bar: Calif. 1976. Asst. mgr. Transamerica Title Co., Dublin, Calif., 1977-78; assoc. Rhodes, McKeehan & Bernard, Fremont, Calif., 1978-79; sr. atty. Rhodes, McKeehan & Bernard, Fremont, 1979—; v.p. Californians Against Fraud, 1996—. Author: Wrongful Discharge...Look Before You Leap, 1990. Commr. Calif. Crime Resistance Task Force, Sacramento; trustee Alameda County Bd. Edn.; del. Dem. Cen. Com., Alameda County, 1980-81, 83-84. Democrat. Real property, General corporate, Personal injury. Home: 2135 Ocaso Camino Fremont CA 94539-5645 Office: 39560 Stevenson Pl Ste 217 Fremont CA 94539-3074

**KITTAY, DAVID R.,** lawyer; b. Mineola, N.Y., Nov. 6, 1952; s. William and Rhoda (Siegelman) K. BA, Brandeis U., 1973; JD, Boston U., 1978. Bar: N.Y. 1979, Md. 1984. Assoc., of counsel Cadwalader, Wickersham & Taft, N.Y.C., 1978-88; ptnr. Liddell, Sapp, Zivley, Hill & Laboon, Houston and N.Y.C., 1988-92; pres. Kittay, Gold & Gershfeld, P.C., N.Y.C. and White Plains, N.Y., 1992—; panel bankruptcy trustee So. Dist. N.Y., N.Y.C., 1989—. Avocation: foreign languages. Bankruptcy, General civil litigation. Office: Kittay Gold & Gershfeld PC 1 Exchange Plz New York NY 10006-3008

**KITTELSEN, RODNEY OLIN,** lawyer; b. Albany, Wis., Mar. 11, 1917; s. Olen B. and Nellie Winifred (Atkinson) K.; m. Pearle M. Haldiman, Oct. 12, 1940; children: Gregory S., James E., Bradley J. PhB, U. Wis., 1939, LLB, 1940. Spl. agt. FBI, Washington, 1940-46; ptnr. Kittelsen, Barry, Ross, Wellington & Thompson, Monroe, Wis., 1946—; dist. atty. Green County, Monroe, 1947-53; pres. State Bar Wis., Madison, 1976-77, 83-85; dir. Wis. Law Found., Madison, 1992—. Pres. Monroe Police and Fire Commn., 1947—; legal counsel X-FBI Inc., Quantico, Va., 1986—; mem. Am. Coll. Trust and Estate Coun., Chgo., 1983—. Recipient Outstanding Citizen award Monroe Jaycees, 1977, Outstanding Svc. award Albany FFA, 1991, Disting. Svc. award U. Wis. Law Sch., 1995, Disting. Svc. award U. Wis. Law Alumni Assn., 1995. Fellow Am. Bar Found., Wis. Bar Assn. (pres. 1976-77, 83-85, Goldberg award 1990), Wis. Bar Found. (pres. 1985). Education and schools, General practice, Probate. Home: 708 26th Ave Monroe WI 53566-1620 Office: 916 17th Ave Monroe WI 53566-2003

**KITTLESON, HENRY MARSHALL,** lawyer; b. Tampa, Fla., May 13, 1929; s. Edgar O. and Ardath (Ayers) K.; m. Barbara Clark, Mar. 20, 1954; 1 dau., Laura Helen. BS with high honors, U. Fla., 1951, JD with high honors, 1953. Bar: Fla. 1953. Ptnr. Holland & Knight, Lakeland and Bartow, Fla., 1955—; mem. adv. bd. Fla. Fed. Savs. & Loan Assn., 1974-86; mem. Fla. Law Revision Commn., 1967-76, vice chmn., 1969-71; mem. Gov.'s Property Rights Study Commn., 1974-75, Nat. Conf. Commrs. Uniform State Laws, 1982—. Mem. council U. Fla. Law Center, 1974-77. Served to maj. USAF, 1953-55. Fellow Am. Bar Found.; mem. ABA (chmn. standing com. on ethic and profl. responsibility 1980-81), Am. Law Inst., Am. Coll. Real Estate Lawyers, Fla. Bar (chmn. standing com. profl. ethics 1965-66, tort litigation rev. commn. 1983-84), Blue Key, Sigma Phi Epsilon, Phi Delta Phi, Phi Kappa Phi, Beta Gamma Sigma, Lakeland Yacht and Country Club. Presbyterian. Real property. Home: 5334 Woodhaven Ln Lakeland FL 33813-2656 Office: Holland & Knight PO Box 32092 92 Lake Wire Dr Lakeland FL 33815-1510

**KITTRELL, PAMELA R.,** lawyer; b. Athens, Ga., June 15, 1965; d. John Edison and Anne (Hagins) K. AB summa cum laude, U. Miami, 1987; JD, U. Mich., 1990. Bar: Fla. 1990, U.S. Dist. Ct. (so. dist.) Fla. 1991, D.C. 1992, Colo. 1994, U.S. Ct. Appeals (11th cir.) 1994, U.S. Dist. CT. (mid. dist.) Fla. 1995. Assoc. Stearns, Weaver, Miller, Weissler, Alhadeff & Sitterson, PA, Miami, 1990-93; sr. assoc. Cooney, Mattson, Lance, Blackburn, Richards & O'Connor, P.A., Ft. Lauderdale, Fla., 1994-98. Mem. Fla. Bar (appellate practice and advocacy sec.), Broward County Bar Assn., Fla. Def. Lawyers Assn. Democrat. Appellate.

**KITTRIE, ORDE F.,** lawyer; b. Washington, Apr. 19, 1964; s. Nicholas N. and Sara Y. Kittrie. BA, Yale U., 1986; JD, U. Mich., 1992. Bar: Md. 1993, D.C. 1995. Legis. asst. U.S. Ho. of Reps., Washington, 1987, press spokesman for congressman, 1988; atty.-advisor for arms and dual-use export controls Office of the Legal Adviser, U.S. Dept. State, Washington, 1993-96, atty.-adviser for nuclear affairs, 1997, sr. atty.-adviser for nuclear affairs, 1997—. Mem. Coun. on Fgn. Rels. Home: 6908 Ayr Ln Bethesda MD 20817-4902 Office: Office of Legal Adviser US Dept State 2201 C St NW Washington DC 20008

**KITZES, WILLIAM FREDRIC,** lawyer, safety analyst, consultant; b. Bklyn., Nov. 24, 1950; s. David Louis and Rhoda Rachel (Feldman) K; m. Sandra Shimasaki, Apr. 7, 1979: children: Justin, Dana. BA, U. Wis., 1972; JD, Am. U., 1975. Bar: D.C. 1977. Legal advisor on product recalls U.S. Consumer Products Safety Commn., Washington, 1975-77, program mgr., 1977-80, regulatory counsel, 1980-81; v.p., gen. mgr. Inst. for Safety Analysis, Rockville, Md., 1981-83; prin. Consumer Safety Assocs., Potomac, Md., Boca Raton, Fla., 1983—; cons. Toro Co., Bloomington, Minn., 1987, Vendo Co., Fresno, Calif., 1987, Nat. Assn. Attys. Gens., Washington, 1987, Arctic Cat, Inc., thief River Falls, Minn., 1995—, Global Furniture, Toronto, Ont., 1997, Product Safety Online, Boca Raton, 1997—. Counsel Friends of Charlie Gilchrist, Montgomery County, Md., 1983; chmn. Fla. Consumers Coun., 1995—. Recipient silver medal for meritorious svc. U.S. Consumer Products Safety Commn., 1976. Mem. Am. Soc. Safety Engrs., Human Factors Soc., System Safety Soc., Nat. Safety Coun., Internat. Consumer Product Health and Safety Orgn. Personal injury. Home and Office: Consumer Safety Assocs 4501 NW 25th Way Boca Raton FL 33434-2506

**KITZMILLER, HOWARD LAWRENCE,** lawyer; b. Shippensburg, Pa., May 6, 1930; s. Franklin Leroy and Emma Corinna (Bedford) K.; m. Shirley Mae Pine, Apr. 4, 1953; children: David Lawrence, Diane May. BA summa cum laude, Dickinson Coll., 1951; JD, Dickinson Sch. of Law, 1954; LLM, George Washington U., 1958. Bar: Pa. 1955, D.C. 1984. Commr. U.S. Ct. Mil. Appeals, Washington, 1958-59; various positions to assoc. gen. counsel FCC, Washington, 1959-80; various positions to sr. v.p. and sec. Washington Mgmt. Corp., 1983—. Editor Dickinson Law Rev., 1954. Deacon, elder Westminster Presbyn. Ch., Alexandria, Va.; bd. dirs. S.E. Fairfax Devel. Corp., Fairfax County, Va., 1977-98, also past pres.; various positions including pres., parents adv. coun., bd. assocs., trustee, investment com. Randolph-Macon Coll., Ashland, Va., 1984-95. Capt. JAGC, U.S. Army, 1955-58. Mem. ABA, FBA, City Club Washington, Masons, Phi Beta Kappa. Republican.

**KIYONAGA, JOHN CADY,** lawyer; b. Atsugi, Japan, Dec. 27, 1953; s. Joseph Yoshio and Bina Mary (Cady) K.; m. Susan Marie Fraser, Dec. 5, 1980 (div. Oct. 1990); children: Joseph Yoshio, Anastasia; m. Nan Catherine Schnell, Sept. 13, 1997. BA, Georgetown U., 1976; JD, MS in Journalism, Columbia U., N.Y.C., 1980. Bar: N.Y. 1981, D.C. 1990, Va. 1990. Assoc. Brown & Wood, N.Y.C., 1980-83; ins. officer Overseas Pvt. Investment Corp., Washington, 1984; ptnr. Kiyonaga & Kiyonaga, Alexandria, Va., 1990—. Contbr. articles and editl. writings to profl. publs. With U.S. Army, 1985-89. Mem. Hispanic Bar Assn. No. Va., Alexandria Bar Assn., Columbia Country Club, Army and Navy Club. Roman Catholic. Avocations: shooting waterfowl and upland game. General civil litigation, Criminal, Private international. Office: Kiyonaga & Kiyonaga 526 King St Ste 213 Alexandria VA 22314-3143

**KJOS, VICTORIA ANN,** lawyer; b. Fargo, N.D., Sept. 17, 1953; d. Orville I. and Annie J. (Tanberg) K. BA, Minot State U., 1974; JD, U. N.D., 1977. Bar: Ariz. 1978. Assoc. Jack E. Evans, Ltd., Phoenix, 1977-78, pension and ins. cons., 1978-79; dep. state treas. State of N.D., Bismarck, 1979-80; freelance cons. Phoenix, 1980-81, Anchorage, 1981-82; asst. v.p., v.p., mgr. trust dept. Great Western Bank, Phoenix, 1982-84; assoc. Robert A. Jensen P.C., Phoenix, 1984-86; ptnr. Jensen & Kjos, P.C., Phoenix, 1986-89; assoc. Allen, Kimerer & LaVelle, Phoenix, 1989-90, ptnr., 1990-91; dir. The Yoga and Fitness Inst., Phoenix, 1994-97; lectr. in domestic relations. Contbr. articles to profl. jours. Bd. dirs. Arthritis Found., Phoenix, 1986-89, v.p. for chpt. devel., 1988-89; bd. dirs. Ariz. Yoga Assn., 1993-95, v.p., 1993-95. Mem. ABA, ATLA, Ariz. Bar Assn. (exec. coun. family law sect. 1988-91), Maricopa Bar Assn. (sec. family law com. 1988-89, pres. family law com. 1989-90, judge pro tem 1989-91), Ariz. Trial Lawyers Assn. Family and matrimonial, Personal injury.

**KLAASEN, TERRY JOHN,** lawyer; b. Detroit, Mar. 11, 1943; s. Gerald and Johanna (Gerding) K.; m. Margo A. Loniewski, June 27, 1992. AB, Calvin Coll., 1965; JD, U. Mich., 1968. Atty., shareholder Bullen, Moilanen, Klaasen & Swan, P.C., Jackson, Mich., 1969—. Bd. dirs. Greater Jackson Habitat for Humanity, Inc. Mem. Jackson County Bar Assn. (pres.1988), Jackson Exchange Club (pres. 1994). Presbyterian. Avocations: skiing, sailing, golf, tennis. Real property, General civil litigation, Estate planning. Office: Bullen Moilanen Klaasen & Swan PLC 402 S Brown St Jackson MI 49203-1426

**KLADNEY, DAVID,** lawyer; b. N.Y.C., Oct. 25, 1948; s. Rubin and Gloria Anita (Serotick) K.; m. Deborah Bayliss, Aug. 20, 1978; children: Mathew Blair, Blythe Nicole. BA in Journalism, U. Nev., 1972; JD, Calif. Western Sch. of Law, 1977. Bar: Nev. 1977, U.S. Dist. Ct. (no. dist.) Nev. 1977. Pvt. practice law Reno, Nev., 1977—; gen. counsel State of Nev. Employees Assn., Carson City, 1977-81; chairperson Truckee Meadows C.C. on Para-Legals; alt. hearing officer Nev. State Pers. Adv. Commn., 1996—. Writer, producer documentary Nevada Connection, 1973. Legal counsel B.U.R.N.S., Inc., 1992—, Make-A-Wish Found. of Nev., Reno, 1984—; chmn. of bd. dirs. Nev. Festival Ballet, Reno, 1984; bd. dirs. Washoe Legal Svcs., Reno, 1978-79; mem. citizen adv. bd., chmn. Mt. Rose, 1994-96, mem., 1996—. With USAR, 1966-72. Mem. ABA, Nev. Bar Assn., Washoe County Bar Assn., Assn. Trial Lawyers Am. (sustaining), Nev. Trial Lawyers Assn. (bd. dirs. 1979-85, Outstanding Svc. award 1985), Nat. Orgn. of Social Security Claimants Representatives, Phi Delta Phi. Avocations: skiing, cycling. State civil litigation, Personal injury, Insurance. Office: 1575 Delucchi Ln Ste 204 Reno NV 89502-8539

**KLAHR, GARY PETER,** lawyer; b. N.Y.C., July 9, 1942; s. Fred and Frieda (Garson) K. Student, Ariz. State U., 1958-61; LL.B. with high honors, U. Ariz., 1964. Bar: Ariz. 1967, U.S. Dist. Ct. Ariz. 1967. Assoc. Brazlin & Greene, Phoenix, 1967-68; sr. ptnr. Gary Peter Klahr, P.C., Phoenix, 1967-68. Asst. editor Ariz. Law Rev., 1963-64; contbr. articles to profl. jours. bd. dirs. CODAMA, 1975-89, pres., 1980-81; bd. dirs. Tumbleweed Runaway Ctr., 1972-76; bd. dirs., corp. sec. Internat. Found. Anti-Cancer Drug Discovery; chmn. Citizens Criminal Justice Commn., 1977-78; co-chmn. delinquency subcom. Phoenix Forward Task force; vol. referee Juvenile Ct., 1969; vol. adult probation officer; vol. counselor youth programs Dept. of Corrections, Phoenix; ex-officio mem., spl. cons. Phoenix Youth Commn.; mem. citizen adv. coun. Phoenix Union H.S. Dist., 1985-90, 95—, co-chmn. 1998—, elected governing bd., 1991-95, v.p., 1992-95, co-chmn. citizens adv. com., 1970-72; mem. rev. bd. Phoenix Police Dept., 1985-94; bd. dirs. Metro Youth Ctr., 1986-87, Svc./Employment/Redevel. (SER) Jobs for Progress, Phoenix, 1985-90, pres., 1986-87, East McDowell Youth Assn., 1992-94; v.p. local chpt. City of Hope, 1985-86; Justice of the Peace pro tem Maricopa County Cts., 1985-89; juvenile hearing officer Maricopa County Juvenile Ct., 1985-89; v.p., co-founder Cmty. Leadership for Youth Devel. (CLYDE); del. Phoenix Together Town Hall on Youth Crime, 1982. Named 1 of 3 Outstanding Young Men of Phoenix Phoenix C. of C., 1969; recipient Disting. Citizen award Ariz. chpt. ACLU, 1976. Mem. ACLU (v.p. ctrl. chpt. Ariz. 1990-95, pres. 1995—, mem. state bd.), Ariz. State Bar (past sec., bd. dirs. young lawyers sect., co-chmn. unauthorized practice com. 1988-89, mem. other coms.), Maricopa County Bar Assn. (past sec., bd. dirs. young lawyers sec., vice-chmn. juvenile practice com. 1998—), Am. Judicature Soc., Jewish Children's and Family Svc., Common Cause, NAACP, Ariz. ConsumersCoun., Phoenix Jaycees, Order of the Coif, Phi Alpha Delta. Democrat. Jewish. Criminal, Juvenile, Personal injury. Office: 917 W Mcdowell Rd Phoenix AZ 85007-1729

**KLAJBOR, DOROTHEA M.,** lawyer, consultant; b. Dunkirk, N.Y., Dec. 2, 1915; d. Joseph M., Sr. and Susan R. (Schrantz) K. Student, George Washington U., 1949-52; JD, Am. U., Washington, 1956. Bar: D.C. 1957. From legal asst., legis. atty., atty., 2d asst. to Chief U.S. Marshal; civil rights compliance officer Dept. of Justice, Washington, 1938-70; supr. Town of Dunkirk, N.Y., 1973-76; mem. N.Y. State Liquor Authority, Buffalo, 1976-80; lawyer, consultant; b. Dunkirk, N.Y., Dec. 2, 1915; d. Joseph M., Sr., and Susan R. (Schrantz) K.; student George Washington U., 1949-52; JD, Am. U., Washington, 1956. Bar: D.C., 1957. From legal asst., legis. atty., atty., 2d asst. to Chief U.S. Marshal, civil rights compliance officer Dept. of Justice, Washington, 1938-70; supr. Town of Dunkirk, N.Y., 1973-76; mem. N.Y. State Liquor Authority, Buffalo, 1976-80. Bd. dirs. Center for Women Govt., Albany, N.Y., 1978-82, Dunkirk Sr. Citizens Ctr., 1983; mem. Chautauqua County Task Force on Aging, 1972-73, Town of Dunkirk Indsl. Devel. Agy., 1972-76, Chautauqua County Planning Bd., 1973-76, No. Chautauqua County Intermcpl. Planning Bd., 1974-76, Chautauqua County Overall Econ. Devel. Planning Bd., 1974-76, Literacy Vols., 1972-76, West Dunkirk Vol. Fire Dept., 1973—; adv. bd. Dunkirk Sr. Citizens, 1974-76; mem. women's divsn. N.Y. State Democratic Com. Mem. Am. Bar Assn. (life), Fed. Bar Assn., D.C. Bar, Women's Bar Assn. D.C. (life), AAUW, Nat. Lawyers Club, Cath. Daus. Am., No. Chautauqua Club Assocs. (life), Dunkirk Hist. Soc. (life), Friends of Rockefeller Art Ctr. SUNY Fredonia, Brooks Meml. Hosp. Aux., Chautauqua County Home Aux., Kappa Beta Pi. Roman Catholic. Clubs: Chautauqua County Dem. Women's (treas. 1974-76), Zonta Internat. (chmn. com. on status of women; Industry Person of Yr. award 1980, Calista Jones award for advancement rights of women 1984), Fredonia Dem. Bd. dirs. Center for Women Govt., Albany, N.Y., 1978-82, Dunkirk Sr. Citizens Ctr., 1983; mem. Chautauqua County Task Force on Aging, 1972-73, Town of Dunkirk Indsl. Devel. Agy., 1972-76, Chautauqua County Planning Bd., 1973-76, No. Chautauqua County Intermcpl. Planning Bd., 1974-76, Chautauqua County Overall Econ. Devel. Planning Bd., 1974-76, Literacy Vols., 1972-76, West Dunkirk Vol. Fire Dept., 1973—; adv. bd. Dunkirk Sr. Citizens, 1974-76; mem. women's divsn. N.Y. State Democratic Com. Recipient Cert. of Appreciation, Chautauqua County Legislature, 1984. Mem. Am. Bar Assn. (life), Fed. Bar Assn., D.C. Bar, Women's Bar Assn. D.C. (life), AAUW, Nat. Lawyers Club, Cath. Daus. Am., No. Chautauqua Club Assocs. (life), Dunkirk Hist. Soc. (life), Friends of Rockefeller Art Ctr. SUNY Fredonia, Brooks Meml. Hosp. Aux., Chautauqua County Home Aux., Kappa Beta Pi. Roman Catholic. Clubs: Chautauqua County Dem. Women's (treas. 1974-76), Zonta Internat. (chmn. com. on status of women; Industry Person of Yr. award 1980, Calista Jones award for advancement rights of women 1984), Fredonia Dem. Home: 91 Forest Pl Fredonia NY 14063-1701

**KLAMER, JANE FERGUSON,** lawyer; b. Lynchburg, Va., Jan. 29, 1954; d. John William Jr. and Marilyn Joyce Ferguson; m. J. Mark Klamer. BA, U. Va., 1976; JD, St. Louis U., 1980. Bar: Mo. 1980, D.C. 1982. Assoc. Mann, Roger & Wittner P.C., St. Louis, 1980-81; atty. St. Louis Redevel. Authority, St. Louis, 1981-82; counsel The May Dept. Stores Co., St. Louis, 1982-88; assoc. gen. counsel Anheuser-Busch Cos., Inc., St. Louis, 1988—. Mem. The Mo. Bar, D.C. Bar, Bar Assn. Met. St. Louis. Real property, Landlord-tenant. Office: Anheuser Busch Cos Inc 1 Busch Pl Saint Louis MO 63118-1852

**KLAPER, MARTIN JAY,** lawyer; b. Chgo., Jan. 12, 1947; s. Carl and Kate F. (Friedman) K.; m. Julia Warner, Nov. 14, 1973. B.S. in Bus. summa cum laude, Ind. U., 1969, J.D. summa cum laude, 1971. Bar: Ind. 1971, U.S. Dist. Ct. (no. and so. dists.) Ind. 1971, U.S. Ct. Appeals (7th cir.) 1972, U.S. Supreme Ct. 1979. Law clk. to justice U.S. Ct. Appeals (7th cir.), 1971-72; ptnr. Ice Miller Donadio & Ryan, Indpls., 1972—. Mem. ABA, Ind. Bar Assn. Labor, Civil rights. Office: Ice Miller Donadio & Ryan 1 Am Sq Box 82001 Indianapolis IN 46282

**KLAPPER, GAIL HEITLER,** lawyer; b. Denver, May 26, 1943; d. Emmett H. and Dorothy (Shwayder) Heitler; m. Jack A. Klapper, June 25, 1965; children: Dana, Stacy, Amy, Lisa. BA in Polit. Sci., Wellesley (Mass.) Coll., 1965; JD, U. Colo., 1968. Bar: Colo. 1968, U.S. Dist. Ct. Colo. 1968. Pvt. practice Denver, 1968-76, 1983—; White House fellow U.S. Dept. of Interior, Washington, 1976-77; exec. dir. Colo. Dept. Regulatory Agencies, Denver, 1977-81, Colo. Dept. Pers., Denver, 1981-82; candidate Colo. atty. gen. ptnr. Klapper Zimmermann, Denver, 1983-86; of counsel Moye, Giles, O'Keefe, Vermeire & Gorrell, Denver, 1986-89; founder, mng. prin. The Klapper Firm, Denver, 1989—; bd. dirs. Norwest Banks of Colo., Houghton Mifflin, Boston, Gold, Inc., Denver, Orchard Trust, Denver. Trustee Wellesley Coll., 1986—, chair, 1993—; founder, bd. dirs. Pub. Edn. Coalition, Denver, 1984-95; bd. dirs. Nat. Jewish Ctr. for Immunology and Respiratory Medicine, Denver, 1986-96, Downtown Denver Partnership, chair, 1996-97. Recipient Leadership Denver Assn. award, 1984, Norlin award U. Colo., 1987, Pub. Svc. award U. Colo. Grad. Sch. Pub. Affairs, 1987; White House fellow, 1976-77. Mem. Colo. Bar Assn., Denver Bar Assn., Colo. Forum (dir.), Colo. Women's Forum (pres. 1980-81), Denver Met. C. of C. (bd. dirs. 1997-98). Democrat. Avocations: marathon running, quarter horses. Administrative and regulatory, Legislative, Private international.

**KLAPPER, MOLLY,** lawyer, educator; b. Berlin, Germany; came to U.S., 1950; d. Elias and Ciporah (Weber) Teicher; m. Jacob Klapper; children: Rachelle Hannah, Robert David. BA, CUNY, MA, 1964; PhD, NYU, 1974; JD, Rutgers U., 1987. Bar: N.J. 1987, U.S. Dist. Ct. N.J. 1987, N.Y. 1989, U.S. Dist. Ct. (so. and ea. dists.) N.Y. 1989, D.C. 1989, U.S. Supreme Ct. 1991, U.S. Ct. Appeals (2d cir.) 1992. Prof. English Bronx C.C., CUNY, 1974-84; law intern U.S. Dist. Ct. N.J., Newark, 1987; law sec. to presiding judge appellate div. N.J. Supreme Ct., Springfield, 1987-88; assoc. Wilson, Elser, Moskowitz, Edelman and Dicker, N.Y.C., 1988-96; adminstrv. law judge Dept. Finance, N.Y.C., 1997—. Author: The German Literary Influence on Byron, 1974, 2d edit., 1975, The German Literary Influence on Shelley, 1975; contbr. to profl. publs. NEH fellow, 1978; grantee Am. Philos. Soc., 1976. Mem. ABA (bankruptcy com.), N.Y. Bar Assn. (bankruptcy com.), D.C. Bar Assn. Avocations: bicycling, skiing, roller skating, walking, hiking. Insurance, General corporate, General civil litigation. Office: Wilson Elser Moskowitz Edelman and Dicker 720 Ft Washington Ave New York NY 10040-3708

**KLAPPER, RICHARD H.,** lawyer; b. White Plains, N.Y., 1954. AB, Hamilton Coll., 1975; MA, Yale U., 1979, JD, 1979. Bar: N.Y. 1981. Ptnr. Sullivan & Cromwell, N.Y.C. Office: Sullivan & Cromwell 125 Broad St Fl 28 New York NY 10004-2489

**KLARFELD, PETER JAMES,** lawyer; b. Holyoke, Mass., Aug. 19, 1947; s. David Nathan and Gloria (Belsky) K.; m. Mary Myrtle, July 7, 1985; children: Peter Marcus (dec.), Mary Elizabeth, Louis Edward. BA, U. Va., 1969, JD, 1973; MA, U. Chgo., 1970. Bar: Va. 1973, D.C. 1975, U.S. Dist. Ct. D.C. 1977, U.S. Dist. Ct. (ea. dist.) Va. 1977, U.S. Supreme Ct. 1977, U.S. Ct. Appeals (4th cir.) 1978, U.S. Ct. Appeals (3rd & 9th cirs.) 1986, U.S. Ct. Appeals (2d cir.) 1998, U.S. Dist. Ct. (ea. dist.) Wis. 1987, U.S. Dist. Ct. (no. dist.) Calif. 1990. Law clk. to Hon. Robert R. Merhige, Jr. U.S. Dist. Ct. (ea. dist.) Va., Richmond, 1973-74; atty., advisor office of legal counsel U.S. Dept. Justice, Washington, 1974-76; ptnr. Brownstein Zeidman & Lore, Washington, 1977-96, Wiley, Rein and Fielding, Washington, 1996—. Editor: Covenants Against Competition in Franchise Agreements, 1992; contbr. articles to profl. jours. Trustee Dalkon Shield Other Claimants Trust, Richmond, 1990-96, chmn., 1991-96. Mem. ABA. Franchising, Antitrust, General civil litigation. Home: 434 E Columbia St Falls Church VA 22046-3501 Office: Wiley Rein & Fielding 1776 K St NW Washington DC 20006-2304

**KLARQUIST, KENNETH STEVENS, JR.,** lawyer; b. Washington, Aug. 18, 1948; s. Kenneth S. and Lois M. (Boening) K.; m. Linda L. Arndt, Sept. 18, 1971; children: Josef, Peter, Jared. AB, Princeton U., 1970; JD, U. Oreg., 1973. Bar: Va. 1974, Oreg. 1975, U.S. Supreme Ct. 1980. Atty. estate tax U.S. Dept. Treasury, Richmond, Va., 1973-76; assoc. McMurry & Nichols, Portland, Oreg., 1976-77, Dahl, Zalutsky, Nichols & Hinson, P.C., Portland, Oreg., 1977-80; shareholder Zalutsky & Klarquist, P.C., Portland, Oreg., 1980—. Dir., past pres. Oreg. Wildlife Heritage Found., Portland, 1981—; dir., treas. KBPS Pub. Radio Found., Portland, 1991-99. Mem. Rotary (Rotarian of Month Portland 1996). Avocation: competitive rowing. Estate planning, Pension, profit-sharing, and employee benefits, Probate. Office: Zalutsky & Klarquist PC 215 SW Washington St Portland OR 97204-2636

**KLASKO, HERBERT RONALD,** lawyer, law educator, writer; b. Phila., Nov. 26, 1949; s. Leon Louis and Estelle Lorraine (Baratz) K.; m. Marjorie Ann Becker, Aug. 27, 1977; children: Brett Andrew, Kelli Lynn. BA, Lehigh U., 1971; JD, U. Pa., 1974. Bar: Pa. 1974, U.S. Dist. Ct. (ea. dist.) Pa. 1974, U.S. Ct. Appeals (3d cir.) 1981. Assoc. Fox, Rothschild, O'Brien & Frankel, Phila., 1974-75; ptnr., chmn. immigration dept. Abrahams & Loewenstein, Phila., 1975-88, Dechert, Price & Rhoads, Phila., 1988—; instr., mem. adv. bd. Inst. for Paralegal Tng., Phila., 1974-81; instr. Temple Law Sch. Grad. Legal Studies, Phila., 1984; adj. prof. Villanova U. Law Sch., Pa., 1985-90. Co-author: (with Matthew Bender and Hope Frye) Employer's Immigration Compliance Guide, 1985; bd. editors: Immigration Law and Procedure Reporter. Exec. committeeman, bd. dirs. Jewish Community Rels. Coun., Phila., 1977—; chmn. exec. com., com. on unprosecuted Nazi war criminals Nat. Jewish Community Rels. Adv. Coun., N.Y.C., 1983-90; v.p. Hebrew Immigrant Aid Soc., Phila., 1977—; pres. Coun. of Tenants Assn., Southeastern Pa., 1980-81. Recipient Legion of Honor award Chapel of Four Chaplains, 1977. Mem. ABA (coordinating com. on immigration), Phila. Bar Assn., Am. Immigration Lawyers Assn. (chmn. Phila. chpt. 1980-82, bd. govs. 1980—, nat. sec. 1984-85, 2d v.p. 1985-86, 1st v.p. 1986-87, pres.-elect 1987-88, pres. 1988-89, exec. com. 1984-90, 96—, gen. counsel, 1996—, Founders award 1999), Am. Immigration Law Found. (bd. dirs. 1987-90). Avocations: politics, sports, traveling, organizations. Immigration, naturalization, and customs. Office: Dechert Price & Rhoads 4000 Bell Atlantic Tower 1717 Arch St Ste 3 Philadelphia PA 19103-2793

**KLASS, MARVIN JOSEPH,** lawyer; b. Sioux City, Iowa, Nov. 6, 1913; s. Isaac L. and Rose (Raskin) K.; m. Merry Gralnek Klass, Mar. 28, 1946; children: Tim, Marilyn Weissman, Susan Karen, Kay Levitt, Kalman. BA, Morningside Coll., 1936, LLD, 1993; LLB, Harvard Law Coll., 1939. Assoc. Stewart and Hatfield, Sioux City, 1946-56; ptnr. Stewart, Hatfield and Klass, Sioux City, 1956-60; sr. ptnr. Klass, Whicher and Mishne, Sioux City, 1960-87, Klass, Hanks, Stoos & Carter, Sioux City, 1987-89, Klass, Stoos, Stoik, Mugan, Villone & Phillips LLP, Sioux City, 1989—; bd. dirs. Shaare Zion Synagogue, Sioux City, 1960—, Sioux City Concert Course, 1974-76; mem. Atty. Disciplinary Com. State Iowa, 1976-80. Civil Svc. com. mem. Sioux City, 1966-68; bd. dirs. Morningside Coll., 1950-70, Sanford Ctr., 1975-86, United Way of Siouxland, 1979-84, Sioux City Schs. Found., Inc., 1989-94. Sgt. U.S. Army, 1942-46. Mem. Iowa Bar Assn. Republican. Jewish. Avocations: tennis, music, reading. General corporate, Estate planning, Probate. Home: 3937 Douglas St Sioux City IA 51104-1443 Office: Klass Stoos Stoik Mugan Villone & Phillips LLP PO Box 327 Sioux City IA 51102-0327

**KLAUSMAN, GLENN,** lawyer; b. Miami Beach, Fla., Feb. 26, 1952; s. Edward and Birdye Klausman; m. Shelley Klausman, Sept. 3, 1989; 1 child, Octavia Rose. AB in Journalism, U. Ga., 1973; JD, Stetson U., 1976. Bar: Fla. 1976, U.S. Supreme Ct. 1977. Asst. pub. defender State of Fla., Office of Pub. Defender, Sanford, 1976, Orlando, 1976-80; assoc. Jacobs & Goodman, Altamonte Springs, Fla., 1981—. Mem. Seminole County Bar Assn. (pres. 1996). Insurance, Personal injury.

**KLAUSNER, JACK DANIEL,** lawyer; b. N.Y.C., July 31, 1945; s. Burt and Marjory (Brown) K.; m. Dale Arlene Kreis, July 1, 1968; children: Andrew Russell, Mark Raymond. BS in Bus., Miami U., Oxford, Ohio, 1967; JD, U. Fla., 1969. Bar: N.Y. 1971, Ariz. 1975, U.S. Dist. Ct. Ariz. 1975, U.S. Ct. Appeals (9th cir.) 1975, U.S. Supreme Ct. 1975. Assoc. counsel John P. McGuire & Co., Inc., N.Y.C., 1970-71; assoc. atty. Hahn & Hessen, N.Y.C., 1971-72; gen. counsel Equilease Corp., N.Y.C., 1972-74; assoc. Burch & Cracchiolo, Phoenix, 1974-78; ptnr. Burch & Cracchiolo, 1978-98; judge pro tem Maricopa County Superior Ct., 1990—, Ariz. Ct. Appeals, 1992—; ptnr. Warner Angle Roper & Hallam, Phoenix, 1998—. Bd. dirs. Santos Soccer Club, Phoenix, 1989-90; bd. dirs., pres. south Bank Soccer Club, Tempe, 1987-88. General civil litigation, Real property, Antitrust. Home: 1390 W Island Cir Chandler AZ 85248-3700 Office: Warner Angel Roper & Hallam 3550 N Central Ave Ste 1500 Phoenix AZ 85012-2105

**KLAY, ANNA NETTIE,** lawyer; b. Palo Alto, Calif., Aug. 27, 1940. BA, U. Colo., Boulder, 1962; JD, Golden Gate Law Sch., 1976. Bar: Calif. 1976. Ptnr. Edson & Klay, Eureka, Calif., 1977-82; atty. Anna N. Klay Law Firm, Eureka, 1982-87, Conrad F. Gulluison Law Firm, Palo Alto, 1987-93; sole practice San Jose, Calif., 1993—. Sec., bd. dirs. 564 Colo. Corp., Palo Alto, 1993—; vol. chaplain Stanford U. Hosp., Palo Alto, 1996—. Democrat. Episcopalian. Avocations: music, opera, gardening. General practice. Office: 95 S Market St Ste 300 San Jose CA 95113-2350

**KLAYMAN, BARRY MARTIN,** lawyer; b. Montclair, N.J., Sept. 26, 1952; s. Max M. and Sylvia (Cohen) K.; m. Anna Kornbrot, June 8, 1975; children: Alison Melissa, Matthew Daniel. BA magna cum laude, Columbia U., 1974; JD cum laude, Harvard U., 1977. Bar: Pa. 1977, U.S. Dist. Ct. (ea. dist.) Pa. 1977, U.S. Ct. Appeals (3d cir.) 1978, Del. 1998. From assoc. to ptnr. Wolf, Block, Schorr & Solis-Cohen LLP, Phila., 1977—. Contbr. articles to profl. jours. Bd. dirs. Akiba Hebrew Acad., 1991—, sec., 1994-95, v.p., 1995-96, 98—, treas. 1996-98; mem. com. on nat. and overseas svcs. Fedn. Jewish Agys., 1991—. Mem. ABA (litig. sect., torts and ins. practice sect.), Del. Bar Assn., Phila. Bar Assn., Pa. Bar Assn., Assn. Trial Lawyers Am., B'nai B'rith Youth Orgn. (bd. dirs. Phila. region 1984—, chmn. 1991-95, mem. internat. youth commn. 1991—, exec. com., 1996—), B'nai B'rith (coun. v.p. 1996-97, mem. Justice Lodge 1992—), Phi Beta Kappa. Federal civil litigation, State civil litigation, Environmental. Office: Wolf Block Schorr & Solis-Cohen LLP 920 King St Ste 300 Wilmington DE 19801-3300

**KLAYMAN, ROBERT ALAN,** lawyer; b. Cin., Apr. 5, 1929; s. Harry Edward and Betty Irene (Lovitch) K.; m. Annette Bell, July 14, 1957; children: Rachel Ann, Emily Susan, Benjamin Harry, Jed Noah. BS, W.Va. U., 1951, LLB, 1954. Bar: D.C. Atty.-office chief counsel IRS, Washington, 1957-60; atty. Office Tax Legis. Counsel, Treasury Dept., Washington, 1960-62, asst. tax legis. counsel, 1962-64, assoc. tax legis. counsel, 1964; assoc. Caplin & Drysdale, Washington, 1964-65, ptnr., 1966-97; dir. tax adv. program Treasury Dept., 1997—; assoc. professorial lectr. George Washington U. Sch. Law, Washington, 1965-72. Contbr. articles to profl. jours. Bd. govs. Beauvoir Sch., Washington, 1976-79; mem. devel. bd. Edmund Burke Sch., Washington, 1982-85. Mem. ABA, Phi Beta Kappa. Democrat. Jewish. Avocations: skiing, sailing, reading, travel. Office: Treasury Dept Rakoczi, ut 1-3 II em 29, 1088 Budapest Hungary

**KLEBANOFF, STANLEY MILTON,** lawyer; b. N.Y.C., Sept. 8, 1926; s. Sam and Fannie (Rothblatt) K.; m. Natalie Lind, Oct. 15, 1944; children: Barbara, Laura, Mitchell, Richard. LLB, Bklyn. Law Sch., 1950. Bar: N.Y. 1950, U.S. Dist. Ct. (ea. and so. dists.) N.Y. 1978, U.S. Supreme Ct. 1960. Ptnr. Klebanoff & Klebanoff, P.C., West Hempstead, N.Y., 1950—; pvt. practice Stanley M. Klebanoff, P.C., West Hempstead, 1990—. Pres. Cambria Heights Jewish Ctr. With U.S. Army, 1945-48, ETO. Mem. Assn. Trial Lawyers Am., N.Y. State Trial Assn., Real Estate Bd. N.Y., Inc., N.Y. County Lawyers, N.Y. State Bar, Nassau County Bar Assn., Masons. Democrat. Jewish. Avocation: sports. Personal injury, Insurance, Real property. Home: 392 Woodfield Rd West Hempstead NY 11552-3046 Office: 392 Woodfield Rd West Hempstead NY 11552-3046

**KLEBE, KURT EDWARD,** lawyer; b. San Rafael, Calif., June 22, 1966; s. Alton S. and Joan G.B. Klebe; m. Elizabeth B. Sexton, Aug. 14, 1993; children: William Benson Sexton Klebe, Nathaniel Hyde Sexton Klebe. BA, Williams Coll., 1988; JD, U. Maine, 1994. Bar: Maine 1995. Tax acct. KPMG Peat Marwick, Portland, Maine, 1993-94, Baker, Newman & Noyes, Portland, 1994-95; lawyer Verrill & Dana, LLP, Portland, 1995—. Trustee Victoria Mansion, Portland, 1994—, Planned Parenthood No. New. Eng., Williston, Vt., 1996—, Falmouth (Maine) Edn. Found., 1999—, Rippleffect, Inc., Portland, Maine, 1999—. Mem. Maine Bar Assn., Maine Estate Planning Coun. Probate, Estate taxation, Estate planning. Office: Verrill & Dana LLP PO Box 586 Portland ME 04112-0586

**KLECKNER, ROBERT GEORGE, JR.,** lawyer; b. Reading, Pa., Mar. 14, 1932; s. Robert George and Elizabeth (Endlich) K.; m. Carol Espie, June 15, 1955; children: Anthony Savage, Susan Duffield. BA, Yale U., 1954; LLB, U. Pa., 1959. Bar: Pa. 1960, N.Y. 1964. Pvt. practice Reading, 1960-63; assoc. Sullivan & Cromwell, N.Y.C., 1963-70; house counsel Goldman, Sachs & Co., N.Y.C., 1970-78; cons. N.Y.C., 1978-80; house counsel Johnson & Higgins, N.Y.C., 1980-97; sr. atty. legal dept. Marsh & McLennan Cos., Inc., N.Y.C., 1997; ret., 1997. 1st lt. USAR, 1955-57, Korea. Mem. ABA, Assn. Bar City N.Y., Berks County (Pa.) Bar Assn., Union Club, Univ. Club, Phi Beta Kappa. Republican. Lutheran. General corporate. Home: 80 East End Ave New York NY 10028-8004

**KLECKNER, SIMONE MARIE,** law librarian; b. Bucharest, Romania, Mar. 7, 1927; came to U.S., 1966; d. George Vrabiescu and Clementa (Cionea) Radian; m. Rudolf Kleckner, Apr. 23, 1960. JD, Bucharest U., 1953; MLS, Columbia U., 1969; LLM, NYU, 1973. Asst. curator NYU Sch. Law Libr., 1969-74; legal libr. UN Dag Hammarskjold Libr., N.Y.C., 1975-86, chief reference and biblio. sect., 1986-87; chief libr. U.S. Ct. Internat. Trade, N.Y.C., 1987-96. Author: International Legal Bibliography, 1983, Settlement of Disputes in International Law Bibliography, 1985; translator Penal Code of the Romanian Social Republic, 1976; lic, 1976; compiler UN Juridical Yearbook, 1974-84. Pres. ad hoc com. Orgn. Romanian Democracy, 1997—. Mem. Am. Soc. Internat. Law, Am. Fgn. Law Assn. Republican. Ea. Orthodox. Avocation: travel. Home: 110 W 69th St New York NY 10023-5116

**KLEFF, PIERRE AUGUSTINE, JR.,** lawyer; b. Washington, Oct. 28, 1942; s. Pierre A. Sr. and Mary Emily (Hayes) K.; m. Cheryl S. Henk, June, 1965 (div.); 1 child, Pierre A. III; m. Rosemarie F. Lockmer, Mar. 17, 1973 (div.); 1 child, Amber Marie. BA, U. Dayton, 1968; JD, No. Ky. State U., 1973. Bar: Ohio, 1973, Tex., 1976, U.S. Ct. Appeals (5th cir.) 1981, U.S. Ct. Mil. Appeals 1974, U.S. Dist. Ct. (we. dist.) Tex., 1979, U.S. Dist. Ct. (no. dist.) Tex. 1993, U.S. Supreme Ct. 1986. Ptnr. Kleff and Assocs. P.C., Killeen, Tex. Mem. Nat. Rep. Orgn., Rep. Orgn. Tex.; alt. del. Rep. Nat. Conv., Detroit, 1980. Served to capt. U.S. Army, 1973-77, lt. col. USAR, 1977-95, ret., 1995. Mem. Tex. Bar Assn., Bell-Lampasas-Mills Counties Bar Assn. (bd. dirs. 1986-89, reporter 1989-90, sec.-treas. 1990-91, pres. 1992-93), Rotary (treas. Killeen club 1984). Roman Catholic. Avocations: weightlifting, boating. Contracts commercial, General practice, Real property. Office: PO Box 11329 Killeen TX 76547-1329

**KLEID, WALLACE,** lawyer; b. Balt., June 25, 1946; s. Max E. and Bess (Hubberman) K.; m. Loryn Sari Lesser, July 1, 1979; children: Micah Saul, Matthew Brett; 1 child by previous marriage, Kathy Jill. BA, U. Md., 1967; JD, U. Md.-Balt., 1971. Bar: Md. 1972, U.S. Dist. Ct. Md. 1972, U.S. Ct. Mil. Appeals 1973, U.S. Supreme Ct. 1975, U.S. Ct. Appeals (4th cir.) 1975, D.C. 1982. Law clk. State's Atty. Baltimore County, Md., 1970-72, asst. state's atty., 1972-77; pvt. practice law, Balt. and Towson, Md., 1972—; ptnr. Floam & Kleid, Balt., Towson, 1985-93; ptnr. Margolis, Pritzker & Epstein, Towson and Annapolis, Md., 1993—; mem. Rape Adv. Commn., Baltimore County, 1974-75, grievance commn., 1982-95, 97—; presenter testimony on rape Md. Gen. Assembly, 1975, presenter on expungements, 1989, presenter on workers compensation, 1993-94; cons. TV program Women and the Law, 1976-77; lectr. in field. Bd. dirs. Colonial Village Neighborhood Assn., Balt., 1969-75, Citizens Dem. Club, Balt., 1972-75; Cheswolde Neighborhood Assn., Balt., v.p., 1981-84, pres., 1984-86, bd. dirs. 1986-89; bd. dirs. Krieger-Schecter Sch., 1990-94; watch commdr. Northwest Citizens Patrol, 1990—; treas. Summit Chase Home Owners Assn., 1996—; commentator, lectr. workmen's compensation audio tape series and continuing legal edn. Md. Inst. for Continuing Profl. Edn. of Lawyers. Sgt. USAR, 1968-74. Recipient Civilian award Balt. County Police Dept., 1975. Mem. ABA (gen. practice sect., vice-chmn., liaison to nat., state, and local bar leaders 1987-88, mem. conf. planning subcom. 1988-89., chmn. subcom. on assocs. employment agreements 1978-88, sr. vice chair litigation subcom. 1993-94), ATLA, FBA, Baltimore County Bar Assn. (lawyer referral com. 1976-78, chmn. ins. trust 1980-87, 91-93, vice chmn. 1988-91, 93-95, entertainment com. 1989-90, mem. bench bar com. 1993-94, 97-98), Balt. City Bar Assn. (workers compensation com., family law com., subcom. on legis.), Md. State Bar Assn. (chmn. spl. com. to establish gen. practice sect. 1984-85, chmn. gen. practice sect. 1985-87, sect. council 1988—, cons. spl. com. on regulation of lawyers' trust and fiduciary accounts 1987, negligence, ins. and worker's compensation sect. coun. 1990—, treas. 1991-93, sec. 1993-94, chmn. 1994-95, contbg. editor family law hotline), Md. Criminal Def. Assn., Nat. Def. Attys. Assn., Md. State Atty.'s Assn., Md. Trial Lawyers Assn., Md. Assn. for Continuing Edn. Lawyers (bd. dirs. 1992—, long range planning com. 1993—), Nat. Dist. Attys. Assn., D.C. Bar Assn., Directory Lit. Attys., Zeta Beta Tau. Democrat. Jewish. Workers' compensation, Family and matrimonial, State civil litigation. Home: 14 Ruby Field Ct Baltimore MD 21209-1559 Office: 405 E Joppa Rd Ste 100 Baltimore MD 21286-5402

**KLEIMAN, BERNARD,** lawyer; b. Chgo., Jan. 26, 1928; s. Isadore and Pearl (Wikoff) K.; m. Gloria Baime, Nov. 15, 1986; children—Leslie, David. B.S., Purdue U., 1951; J.D., Northwestern U., 1954. Bar: Ill. 1954. Practice law in assn. with Abraham W. Brussell, 1957-60; dist. counsel United Steel Workers Am., 1960-65, spl. counsel, 1997—, gen. counsel, 1965-97; ptnr. Kleiman, Cornfield & Feldman, Chgo., 1960-75; prin. B. Kleiman (P.C.), 1976-77, Kleiman, Whitney, Wolfe & Elfenbaum, P.C., 1978—; Mem. collective bargaining coms. for nat. labor negotiations in basic steel, aluminum, tire and can mfg. industries. Contbr. articles to legal jours. Served with U.S. Army, 1946-48. Mem. ABA, Ill. Bar Assn., Chgo. Bar Assn., Cook County Bar Assn. Labor.

**KLEIMAN, MARY MARGARET,** lawyer; b. Norfolk, Va., May 26, 1959; d. William Edward and Patricia Mae Holste; m. David James Kleiman, June 29, 1991; children: Amanda Grace, Amy Elizabeth. BA in History summa cum laude, Marian Coll., Indpls., 1981; JD cum laude, Ind. U., Indpls., 1984. Bar: Ind. 1985, U.S. Dist. Ct. (no. and so. dists.) Ind. 1985. Bailiff, law clk. Marion County Mcpl. Ct., Indpls., 1983-84; counsel Am. Fletcher Nat. Bank (now Bank One, Ind. N.A.), Indpls., 1985-88; assoc. Krieg DeVault Alexander & Capehart, Indpls., 1989-95; ptnr. Krieg Devault Alexander & Capehart, Indpls., 1995—; bd. dirs. Ind. Bus. Devel. Corp., 1994-97. Contbr. articles to profl. jours. Pro bono atty. Cmty. Orgns. Legal Assistance Project, Indpls., 1994—; vol. com. chair, mem. client programs com. Ind. chpt. Nat. Multiple Sclerosis Soc., 1997—; mem. mission com. Castleton United Meth. Ch., Indpls., 1993—, acolyte coord., mem. worship com., 1997—. Recipient Leadership award Nat. Multiple Sclerosis Soc., 1998, Outstanding Vol. award Ind. Ronald McDonald House, 1990; named to Outstanding Young Women in Am., 1981, 87. Mem. Ind. State Bar Assn., Indpls. Bar Assn. (chair printed forms com. 1987), Phi Delta Phi. Democrat. Avocations: gardening, cross-stitch, reading science fiction, calligraphy. E-mail: mmk@kdac.com. Banking, Securities, Contracts commercial. Office: Krieg Devault Alexander & Capehart LLP One Indiana Sq Ste 2800 Indianapolis IN 46204

**KLEIN, ALAN M.,** lawyer; b. Midland, Mich., Dec. 31, 1960; s. Paul Eugene and Judith Ruth Klein. BA with honors, Haverford Coll., 1981; JD cum laude, Harvard U., 1984. Bar: N.Y. 1986. Assoc. Simpson Thacher & Bartlett, N.Y.C., 1984-93, ptnr., 1994—. Contbr. articles to profl. jours. Mem. ABA, Internat. Bar Assn., Union Internat. des Avocats, Assn. Bar of City of N.Y., Phi Beta Kappa. Mergers and acquisitions, Securities. Office: Simpson Thacher and Bartlett 425 Lexington Ave Fl 15 New York NY 10017-3954

**KLEIN, BETH MORRISON,** lawyer; b. Colorado Springs, Colo., May 22, 1961; d. Ralph Bruce and Lois Jean Morrison; m. Connor James Klein. BA, Truman State, 1983; JD, U. Denver, 1987. Bar: Colo., 1988, U.S. Dist. Ct. Colo., 1988, U.S. Ct. Appeals (10th cir.) 1988, Calif., 1996, Tex., 1996, U.S. Dist. Ct. Ky., 1997. Lawyer Long-Jandon, Denver, 1987-93, Gorsuch Kirgis, Denver, 1993, Brownstein Hyatt, Denver, 1993-94; pvt. practice Boulder, Colo., 1994-98. Bd. dirs. Zach Found., Devner, 1993-97. Mem. NITA, Rhone-Brachet Inn Ct. Avocation: formula car racing SCCA-crew. State civil litigation, Product liability, Professional liability.

**KLEIN, COLEMAN EUGENE,** lawyer; b. Chgo., Apr. 8, 1938. BBA, Wayne State U., 1960, JD magna cum laude, 1967. Bar: Mich. 1968, U.S. Dist. Ct. (ea. dist.) Mich. 1968, U.S. Tax Ct. 1968, U.S. Ct. Appeals (6th cir.) 1970, U.S. Supreme Ct. 1989. Ptnr. Shere & Klein, Detroit, 1968-82; pvt. practice Southfield, Mich., 1982—. Contbr. articles to profl. jours. Recipient Disting. Cmty. Svc. award Alzheimer's Assn., Detroit, 1984, 91. Mem. State Bar of Mich., Detroit Bar Assn., Oakland County Bar Assn. Taxation, general, Estate planning, General corporate. Office: 3000 Town Center Ste 2500 Southfield MI 48075-1197

**KLEIN, EDITH MILLER,** lawyer, former state senator; b. Wallace, Idaho, Aug. 4, 1915; d. Fred L.B. and Edith (Gallup) Miller; m. Sandor S. Klein (dec. 1970). BS in Bus., U. Idaho, 1935; tchg. fellowship, Wash. State U., 1935-36; JD, George Washington U., 1946, LLM, 1954; LLD (hon.), U. Idaho, 1998. Bar: D.C. 1946, Idaho 1947, U.S. Supreme Ct. 1954, N.Y. 1955. Pers. spec. Labor and War Depts., Wash., 1942-46; practice law Boise, Idaho, 1947—; judge Mcpl. Ct., Boise, 1947-49; mem. Idaho Ho. Reps., 1948-50, 64-68, Idaho Senate, 1968-82; atty. FCC Wash., 1953-54; FHA N.Y.C., 1955-56. Chmn. Idaho Gov.'s Commn. Status Women, 1964-72, mem., 1965-79, 82-92; mem. Idaho Gov.'s Coun. Comprehensive Health Planning, 1969-76, Idaho Law Enforcement Planning Commn., 1972-82, Nat. Adv. Commn. Regional Med. Programs, 1974-76, Idaho Endowment Investment Bd., 1979-82; trustee Boise State U. Found., Ind., 1973-95; pres. Boise Music Week, 1991-94; bd. dirs. Harry W. Morison Found. Ind., 1978—, St. Alphonsus Regional Med. Ctr. Found., 1982-96; past pres. bd. dirs. Boise Philharm. Assn., Opera Idaho. Named Woman of Yr. Boise Altrusa Club, 1966, Boise C. of C., 1970, Disting. Citizen, Idaho Statesman 1970, Woman of Progress, Idaho Bus. Prof. Women, 1978; recipient Women Helping Women award Soroptomist Club, 1980, Stein Meml. award Y.M.C.A., 1983, Silver and Gold award for Outstanding Svc., U. Idaho, 1985, March of Dimes award to Honor Outstanding Women, 1987, Cert. of Appreciation by Boise Br., AAUW, 1990, Morrison Ctr. Hall of Fame award, 1990, Disting. Cmty. Svc. award Boise Area C. of C., 1995, Lifetime Achievement award Girl Scouts Am., 1996, 50 Yrs. in Law Practice award Idaho State Bar, 1997. Mem. DAR (regent Pioneer chpt. 1991-93). Republican. Congregationalist. Non-profit and tax-exempt organizations. Home: 1588 Lenz Lane PO Box 475 Boise ID 83701-0475 Office: 1400 US Bank Plaza PO Box 2527 Boise ID 83701-2527

**KLEIN, HAROLD S(HERMAN),** justice; b. Yonkers, N.Y., Jan. 14, 1921; s. Bernard and Frances K.; m. Agnes G. Folts, May 24, 1947 (dec. Dec. 1988); children: Kathryn, Christiann, Gretchen, Laura. BA, U. Mich., 1942; JD, Harvard U., 1948. Bar: N.Y. 1949, U.S. Dist. Ct. (so. dist.) N.Y. 1949, U.S. Ct. Appeals (2d cir.) 1951, U.S. Supreme Ct. 1957. Assoc. Dunn & Zuckerman, N.Y.C., 1949-51; asst. to gen. counsel CBS, Inc., N.Y.C., 1951-52; dep. gen. counsel, asst. sec. Columbia Pictures Corp., N.Y.C., 1952-65; exec. asst. to pres. United Artists Corp., N.Y.C., 1965-69; ptnr. Javits Trubin Sillcocks & Edelman, then Trubin Sillcocks Edelman & Knapp, N.Y.C., 1969-75; sole practice, N.Y.C., 1975—; justice, Greenburgh Town, Westchester County, N.Y., 1986—; lectr. Columbia U., NYU, Rutgers U. Law Sch., New Sch. Social Rsch., Ithaca Coll., SUNY-Binghamton, N.Y. County Lawyers Assn.; spl. dep. atty. gen. N.Y. State for Election Frauds Bur., 1969-70; chmn. Cmty. Hosp. At Dobbs Ferry, N.Y., 1985—; Dir. Westchester County Magistrates Assn., Inc., 1993-95, sec. 1996-97, 1st v.p., 1997-98, pres., 1998-99; adv. bd. Columbia Rsch. Ctr. for Arts and Culture, 1995—; trustee Copyright Soc. U.S.A., 1982-85, sec., 1987-88; arbitrator Am. Arbitration Assn., 1960—. Cons. editor Jour. Arts Mgmt., Law and Society Law, 1981—; contbr. articles to profl. jours. Pres. Dance In Edn. Fund, Inc./Steffi Nossen Sch., Scarsdale, N.Y., 1962-83, mem. 1957—; mem. Dobbs Ferry (N.Y.) Bd. Edn., 1974-80, pres., 1977-78; trustee Village Dobbs Ferry, 1980-86; mem. N.Y.C. Mayor's Coun. on Motion Pictures, T.V. and Theatre, 1968-94; nat. chmn. U. Mich. Annual Giving, 1980-87. Ret. col. USAR. Decorated Meritorious Svc. medal; recipient Disting. Alumni Svc. award U. Mich., 1974; Am. Coun. Learned Socs. fellow, 1942. mem. ABA, Fed. Bar Coun. (trustee 1972-82), N.Y. State Bar Assn., Westchester County Bar Assn., Assn. Bar City N.Y., N.Y. County Lawyers Assn., U. Mich. Alumni Assn. (pres. 1985-87), Harvard Club (N.Y.C.), The Ret. Officers Assn. (west chpt., pres., 1998—). Democrat. Unitarian. Office: 36 W 44th St New York NY 10036-8102

**KLEIN, HARRIET FARBER,** judge; b. Elizabeth, N.J., Apr. 30, 1948; d. Melvin Julius and Frances Mildred (Novit) Farber; m. Paul Martin Klein, Sept. 9, 1973; children: Andrew, Zachary. BA with honors, Douglass Coll., New Brunswick, N.J., 1970; JD, Rutgers U., 1973. Bar: N.J. 1973, U.S. Dist. Ct. N.J. 1973. Jud. clk. chancery divsn. Superior Ct. N.J., 1973-74; assoc. Budd, Larner, Kent, Gross, Picillo & Rosenbaum, Newark, 1974-78; ptnr. Greenbaum, Rowe, Smith, Ravin, David & Himmel, Woodbridge, N.J., 1979-98; judge Superior Ct. of N.J., Law Divsn., Essex County, 1998—; mem. N.J. State Bd. Bar Examiners, 1987-90, reader, 1977-87; mem. adv. com. on bar admissions N.J. Supreme Ct., 1987-90; mem. Maplewood (N.J.) Juvenile Conf. Com., 1995-98. Mem. ABA, Essex County Bar Assn. (vice-chmn. com. on status of women in law firms 1988-90, vice-chmn. equity jurisprudence com. 1989-90, co-chmn. com. on women in the profession 1990-92), N.J. Bar Assn. (labor and employment law sect., co-chmn. com. on civil and personal rights 1995-98), Order of Barristers, Phi Alpha Theta.

**KLEIN, HERBERT C.,** lawyer, real estate investor; b. Newark; s. Alfred and Fae (Sackin) K.; m. Jacqueline Krieger, Aug. 3, 1952; 1 child, Roger M. BA, Rutgers U., 1951; JD, Harvard U., 1953; LLM, NYU, 1957. Assoc. McGlynn, Weintraub & Stein, Newark, 1953, Budd, Larner & Kent, Newark, 1956-60; ptnr. Krieger & Klein, Passaic, N.J., 1961-77, Klein & Chester, Clifton, N.J., 1978-82, Klein & Chapman, Clifton, N.J., 1982-92; congressman U.S. Ho. of Reps., Washington, 1993-95; dir. Hannoch & Weisman, Roseland, N.J., 1995-99; ptnr. Nowell, Amoroso, Klein & Bierman, P.A., Hackensack, N.J., 1999—; trustee First Real Estate Investment Trust N.J., Hackensack, 1961—, pres., 1987-92. Assemblyman N.J. Legis., 1972-76, majority conf. chair, 1974-76; trustee Dem. Nat. Com., Washington, 1978-88, 95-96; trustee Beth Israel Hosp., 1973-92 (pres. 1979-81), Rutgers U., 1990-96. 1st Lt. USAF, 1954-56. Jewish. Avocations: golf, travel. Home: 11 Brook Ridge Ct Cedar Grove NJ 07009-1641 Office: Nowell Amoroso Klein & Bierman PA 155 Polifly Rd Hackensack NJ 07601-1749

**KLEIN, HOWARD BRUCE,** lawyer, law educator; b. Pitts., Pa, Feb. 28, 1950; s. Elmer and Natalie (Rosenzweig) K.; m. Lonnie Jean Wilets, Dec. 12, 1977; children: Zachary B., Eli H. Student, Northwestern U., 1968-69; BA, U. Wis., 1972; JD, Georgetown U., 1976. Bar: Wis. 1976, Pa. 1981, U.S. Ct. Appeals D.C., 1978, U.S. Dist. Ct. Pa. 1981, U.S. Ct. Appeals (3rd cir.) 1982, U.S. Supreme Ct. 1983. Law clk. to justice Robert Hansen Wis. Supreme Ct., Madison, 1976-77; asst. atty. gen. dept. justice State of Wis., 1977-80; chief criminal divsn. U.S. Atty.'s Office, Phila., 1980-87; ptnr. Blank, Rome & McCauley, Phila., 1987-96, chmn. litigation dept., 1991-94; prin. Law Offices of Howard Bruce Klein, Phila., 1996—; dir. in house tng. Am. Law Inst.-ABA, 1996—; regional, nat. instr. Nat. Inst. Trial Advocacy, Phila. and Boulder, Colo., 1987—; lectr. introduction to trial advocacy, evidence Temple U., Phila., 1984—; instr. Atty. Gen. Advocacy Inst., Washington, 1983-87; lectr. pub. corruption and trial advocacy; cons. Pa. Valley Neighborhood Assn., 1984—. Contbr. to profl. jours. Advisor Phila. Police Dept. Reform Commn., 1986—; campaign issues dir. Pa. Atty. Gen. campaign, Phila., 1988, 92; bd. dirs. Citizens Crime Commn. Delaware Valley, Phila. Mem. Fed. Bar Assn. (chmn. criminal law com.), Phila. Bar Assn., Wis. Bar Assn., D.C. Bar Assn., U.S. Attys. Alumni Assn. (co-founder, exec. bd.), Vesper Club (Phila.). Democrat. Jewish. Avocations: swimming, basketball, hiking. Criminal, Federal civil litigation. Office: 1700 Market St Ste 2632 Philadelphia PA 19103-3903

**KLEIN, JERRY A.,** lawyer; b. Chillicothe, Mo., Jan. 10, 1937; s. Melvin H. and Gertrude K.; m. Mary Sharon, Apr. 15, 1967; childre; Suzanne Klein Randolph, Jordan M. AB, Washington U., St. Louis, 1961, JD, 1961. Bar: Mo. 1961, U.S. Dist. Ct. (ea. dist.) Mo. 1962, U.S. Ct. Appeals (8th cir.) 1978, U.S. Supreme Ct. 1979. Ptnr. Taub & Klein, St. Louis, 1962-76; prin. Dolgin, Beilenson & Klein, St. Louis, 1977-81; atty. pvt. practice, St. Louis, 1981—. Avocations: golf, racquetball, travel, investments. General civil litigation, Personal injury, Workers' compensation. Office: 7777 Bonhomme Ave Ste 1910 Clayton MO 63105-1911

**KLEIN, JILL,** lawyer, arbitrator; b. L.A., May 7, 1954; d. Gilbert and Julie (Escudero) K. AB, Stanford U., 1976; JD, U. So. Calif., 1979. Bar: Calif. 1979, U.S. Dist. Ct. (cen. dist.) Calif. 1979, U.S. Ct. Appeals (9th cir.) 1979. Adminstrv. judge U.S. EEOC, L.A., 1980-89; pvt. practice atty., arbitrator Beverly Hills, Calif., 1989-98, Pasadena, Calif., 1998—; mem. bd. arbitrators Am. Arbitration Assn., L.A., 1989—, L.A. County Employee Rels. Commn., L.A., 1990—, State Mediation and Conciliation Svc., Sacramento, 1990—, Fed. Mediation and Conciliation Svc., L.A., 1997, City of L.A. Employee Rels. Bd., 1997—. Jewish. Labor, Estate planning, Probate. Office: 2470 Lambert Dr Pasadena CA 91107-2507

**KLEIN, JOEL AARON,** lawyer; b. Red Bank, N.J., Feb. 15, 1949; s. David M. and Sybil (Schwartz) K.; m. Patricia Caliguiri, May 17, 1975; children: Cynthia, Victoria. BA, Duquesne U., 1973, JD, 1979. Bar: Pa. 1979, U.S. Dist. Ct. (we. dist.) Pa. 1979, U.S. Ct. Mil. Appeals 1980, U.S. Ct. Appeals (fed. cir.) 1983. Staff atty. USAF, Ellsworth AFB, S.D., 1979-82, Castle AFB, Calif., 1982-83; sr. ptnr. Klein & Rayl, Pitts., 1984-85; sole practice Pitts., 1985—; adj. prof. U. S.D., Rapid City, 1981; guest lectr. Duquesne U., 1988, Pitts. Pub. Schs., 1988. Mem. Montour Sch. Bd., 1987—; v.p. S. Side Local Devel. Co., Pitts., 1985-87; chmn. Main St. Adv. Bd., Pitts., 1985-87, S. Side Planning Task Force, 1985, S. Side Planning Forum, 1986—. Served to capt. USAF, 1979-83. Mem. Air Force Assn., Assn. Trial lawyers Am., Pa. Trial Lawyers Assn., Pa. Bar Assn., Allegheny County Bar Assn. Democrat. Jewish. State civil litigation, Criminal, Family and matrimonial. Office: 1931 E Carson St Pittsburgh PA 15203-1835

**KLEIN, JUDAH B.,** retired lawyer; b. Bklyn., Feb. 9, 1923; s. Kolman Karl and Gladys Ruth (Edelson)) K.; m. Paula Berk, Nov. 8, 1953; 1 child, Caryn Ann. BS, U. Md., 1947; LLB, Bklyn. Law Sch., 1950. Bar: N.Y. 1951, U.S. Dist. Ct. (so. and ea. dists.) N.Y. Ptnr. Klein & Klein, N.Y.C., 1952-58; gen. counsel Paragon Industries Inc., Mineola, N.Y., 1959-70; pvt. practice, 1970-71; asst. chief counsel, sr. v.p. The Title Guarantee Co., N.Y.C., 1972-79; v.p., gen. counsel LTIC Assoc., Inc., N.Y.C., 1979-93; ret., 1993; lawyer; b. Bklyn., Feb. 9, 1923; s. Kolman Karl and Gladys Ruth (Edelson) K.; m. Paula Berk, Nov. 8, 1953; 1 dau., Caryn Ann. B.S., U. Md., 1947; LL.B., Bklyn. Law Sch., 1950. Bar: N.Y. 1951, U.S. Dist. Ct. (so. and ea. dists.) N.Y. Ptnr. Klein & Klein, N.Y.C., 1952-58; gen. counsel Paragon Industries Inc., Mineola, N.Y., 1959-70; sole practice, 1970-71; asst. chief counsel, sr. v.p. The Title Guarantee Co., N.Y.C., 1972-79; v.p., gen. counsel LTIC Assoc., Inc., N.Y.C., 1979—, ret. Served to 1st lt. U.S. Army, 1943-46, 51-52. Mem. ABA, Assn. Bar City of N.Y., Nassau County Bar Assn., Am. Coll. Real Estate Lawyers, N.Y. State Bar Assn. Jewish. Club: Masons. 1st lt. U.S. Army, 1943-46, 51-52. Mem. ABA, Assn. Bar City N.Y., Nassau County Bar Assn., Am. Coll. Real Estate Lawyers, N.Y. State Bar Assn., Masons. Jewish. Real property, Insurance.

**KLEIN, LINDA ANN,** lawyer; b. N.Y.C., Nov. 7, 1959; d. Gerald Ira Klein and Sandra Florence (Kimmel) Fishman; m. Michael S. Neuren, Sept. 23, 1985. BA cum laude, Union Coll., 1980; JD, Washington & Lee U., 1983. Bar: Ga. 1983, D.C. 1984, U.S. Dist. Ct. (no. and mid. dist.) Ga. 1985, U.S. Ct. Appeals (11th cir.) 1986. Assoc. Nall & Miller, Atlanta, 1983-86, Martin, Cavan & Andersen, Atlanta, 1986-90; ptnr. Martin, Cavan & Andersen, 1990-93, Gambrell & Stolz, 1993—; instr. Nat. Ctr. Paralegal Tng., Atlanta, 1986. Mem. ABA (editor Trial Techniques newsletter 1989, vice-chmn. trial techniques com. 1989-90, chair 1991-92, vice chair fidelity and surety com. 1994-97, mem. coun. tort and ins. practice sect. 1998—, chair ann. meeting 1996-97, ho. of dels. 1998—, exec. coun. nat. conf. of bar pres. 1998—), State Bar of Ga. (vice chair profl. liability com., chair study com. on rules of practice 1987—, bd. govs. 1989—, mem. exec. com. 1992—, sec. 1994-96, pres. 1997-98), Nat. Conf. Bar Pres. (exec. coun. 1998—), Inst. for CLE (chair Ga. br. 1998—), Atlanta Bar Assn. (bd. dirs. Atlanta Coun. on Young Lawyers 1986-89, chair commn. on uniform rules of ct. 1986), Coun. of Superior Cts. Judges (ex-officio uniform rules com.), Phi Alpha Delta, Pi Sigma Alpha. Construction, Personal injury, General civil litigation.

**KLEIN, MARILYN YAFFE,** lawyer; b. Phila.; d. Herman H. and Lillian (Newman) Yaffe; m. Alexander S. Klein Jr. (div.); m. Anthony Stuart Niskanen. BS in BUs., Temple U., JD. Bar: Pa., N.Y. Assoc. counsel Sperey Corp., N.Y.C.; divsn. counsel Unisys PSSD, Blue Bell, Pa.; group counsel Unisys Networks, Woodcliff Lake, N.J., 1989-91; gen. counsel Timeplex, Inc., Woodcliff Lake, N.J., 1991—. Contracts commercial, Intellectual property, Mergers and acquisitions. Office: Timeplex Inc 400 Chestnut Ridge Rd Woodcliff Lake NJ 07675-7604

**KLEIN, MARTIN I.,** lawyer; b. N.Y.C., Nov. 12, 1947; m. Diane Levbarg. B.A., Lehigh U., 1969; J.D., Am. U., 1972. Bar: N.Y. 1973, Fla. 1978, Calif. 1981, D.C. 1981; solicitor Supreme Ct. Eng., 1996—. Mem. profl. staff U.S. Senate Com. on Labor and Pub. Welfare, 1969-72, legis. aide U.S. Senator Jacob K. Javits, 1969-72; ptnr., head creditors' rights dept. Dreyer & Traub, N.Y.C., 1980-93; ptnr., head dept. bankruptcy Shea & Gould, N.Y.C., 1993—; Martin I. Klein, P.C., 1995—; lectr. Am. Law Inst.-ABA Com. on Continuing Profl. Edn., 1975—, The Practising Law Inst., 1975—, Mathematica, 1981—; adj. assoc. prof. law Benjamin Cardozo Sch. Law, Yeshiva U., 1980—; lectr. Columbia U. Sch. Law, 1980—; mem. med. malpractice mediation panel appellate div. Supreme Ct. State N.Y. 1980—; trustee, treas., pres. Cen. Synagogue, N.Y.C., 1986—; arbitrator, N.Y.C. Small Claims Ct. Contbr. articles on fin., real estate and comml. law to profl. jours. Del. White House Conf. on Youth, 1971. Mem. ABA, N.Y. State Bar Assn., Fla. Bar. Assn., Calif. Bar Assn., D.C. Bar Assn., N.Y. County Lawyers Assn. (mem. com. on bankruptcy), Am. Arbitration Assn. (mem. comml. panel). Bankruptcy, Federal civil litigation, General practice. Office: 9 W 57th St Ste 4160 New York NY 10019-2701

**KLEIN, MICHAEL CLARENCE,** lawyer; b. Kearney, Nebr., July 16, 1952; s. Milton N. and Mary E. (Moore) K.; m. Jacqueline A. McGuigan, Aug. 14, 1971; children—Andrew M., Benjamin P., Molly E., Katherine A. B.A., Kearney State Coll., 1974; J.D., U. Nebr., 1977. Bar: Nebr. 1977, U.S. Dist. Ct. Nebr. 1977, U.S. Supreme Ct. 1987. Ptnr., Anderson, Klein, Peterson & Swan, Holdrege, Nebr., 1977—; chmn. 10th Jud. Dist. Mental Health Board, Holdrege, 1981—. Editor Nebr. Law Rev., 1975-77. Bd. dirs. Child Saving Inst., Omaha, Phelps County Community Found., Holdrege, Nebr. Mem. ABA, Nebr. Bar Assn., 10th Jud. Dist. Bar Assn. (sec. 1981-82), Phelps County Bar Assn. (pres. 1981). Republican. Roman Catholic. Lodge: Elks. General practice, Personal injury, Workers' compensation. Home: 820 Hancock St Holdrege NE 68949-2146 Office: Anderson Klein Peterson & Swan 417 East Ave Holdrege NE 68949-2216

**KLEIN, MICHAEL D.,** lawyer; b. Wilkes-Barre, Pa., June 9, 1951. BA magna cum laude, King's Coll., 1973; JD, Dickinson Coll., 1976. Bar: Pa. 1976, U.S. Ct. Appeals (3rd cir.) 1984, U.S. Dist. Ct. (mid. dist.) Pa. 1984, U.S. Dist Ct. (ea. dist.) Pa. 1994. Asst. atty. gen. Commonwealth of Pa., Harrisburg, 1976-82; mgr. corp. affairs, corp. sec. Pa. Am. Water Co., Hershey, 1982-89; ptnr. LeBoeuf, Lamb, Greene & MacRae LLP, Harrisburg, Pa., 1991—. Mem. Pa. Bar Assn., Am. Water Works Assn. Office: LeBoeuf Lamb Greene & MacRae LLP PO Box 12105 200 N 3rd St Ste 300 Harrisburg PA 17101-1511

**KLEIN, MICHAEL ROGER,** lawyer, business executive; b. N.Y.C., Apr. 10, 1942; s. Jesse and Stephanie (Siegel) K.; m. Diane Atkinson, July 4, 1967 (div. June 1974); m. Joan Ilona Fabry, Feb. 19, 1977; children: Nicholas Jesse, Alexander Fabry. BBA, U. Miami, Coral Gables, Fla., 1963, JD, 1966; LLM, Harvard U., 1967. Bar: Fla. 1966, D.C., 1969, U.S. Dist. Ct. (D.C. cir.) 1970, U.S. Supreme Ct., 1970. Asst. prof. law La. State U., Baton Rouge, 1967-69; assoc. Wilmer, Cutler & Pickering, Washington, 1969-74, ptnr., 1974—; pres. Zenith Gallery, Inc., Washington, 1978—; chmn. LePavillon of D.C., Washington, 1983-89, CoStar Group Inc., Bethesda, Md., 1988—; bd. dirs. Perini Corp., SRA Internat. Inc., Comml. Mortgage Exch. LLC, Structured Fin. Assocs. LLC, C-Sport.com LLC. Author: Eminent Domain, 1969; contbr. articles to profl. jours. Trustee Ctr. for Law in the Pub. Interest, L.A., 1975-91, Am. Himalayan Found., 1996—; chmn. bd. trustees Advocates for Pub. Interest, Washington, 1986-89; dir. Support Ctr. of D.C., Inc., 1991-95. Mem. Am. Law Inst. Jewish. General corporate, Federal civil litigation, Banking. Office: Wilmer Cutler & Pickering 2445 M St NW Ste 500 Washington DC 20037-1487

**KLEIN, PAUL E.,** lawyer; b. N.Y.C., Apr. 26, 1934. AB, Cornell U., 1956; JD, Harvard U., 1960. Bar: Mich. 1960, Ill. 1965, N.Y. 1967, U.S. Supreme Ct. 1977, U.S. Ct. Appeals (2d cir.) 1980. Atty. Dow Chem. Co., Midland, Mich., 1960-65; assoc. Gunther & Choka, Chgo., 1965-66; atty. Esso Rsch. & Engring. Co., Linden, N.J., 1966-67; sr. mng. editor Matthew Bender & Co., N.Y.C., 1967-72; assoc. gen. counsel N.Y. Life Ins. Co., N.Y.C., 1972-80, v.p., assoc. gen. counsel, 1980-84; v.p., counsel Huggins Fin. Svcs., Inc., N.Y.C., 1984-86; exec. corp. tax. div. Ernst & Young, N.Y.C., 1986-95; pvt. practice White Plains, N.Y., 1995—; adj. asst. prof. L.I. U., 1972-79, adj. assoc. prof., 1979-80; adj. assoc. prof. acctg. and taxation, Fordham U. at Lincoln Ctr. grad. sch. of bus. adminstrn., 1995—. Former columnist Jour. Real Estate Taxation; writer; editor. Mem. ABA (past chmn. subcom. on life ins. products/ins. cos. com., sect. taxation), Assn. Bar City N.Y. (past chair subcom. on life and health ins. of the com. on ins. law), Assn. Life Ins. Counsel (sec.-treas. 1979-83, bd. govs. 1983-87), N.Y. State Bar Assn. Corporate taxation, Insurance, Pension, profit-sharing, and employee benefits. Office: 58 Midchester Ave White Plains NY 10606-3817

**KLEIN, PAUL IRA,** lawyer; b. Newark, Sept. 30, 1948; s. Alexander and Yolanda (Klein) K.; m. Susan R. Rosenberg, Aug. 8, 1971; 1 child, Joshua. A.B., Rutgers U., 1970; J.D., St. John's U., 1974. Bar: N.Y. 1975, U.S. Dist. Cts. (so. and ea. dists.) N.Y. 1976, U.S. Dist. Ct. (no. dist.) N.Y. 1983, N.J. 1986, U.S. Dist. Ct. N.J. 1986, N.C. 1992, U.S. Dist. Ct. (we. and mid. dists.) N.C. 1992, U.S. Ct. Appeals (4th cir.) 1995. Assoc. Alexander, Ash, Schwartz & Cohen, N.Y.C., 1975-76, Morris & Duffy, N.Y.C., 1976-85; ptnr. Belair, Klein & Evans, N.Y.C., 1985-90, Harris & Klein, South Orange, N.J., 1990-92, Weinstein & Sturges, P.A., Charlotte, N.C., 1993-94, Crews & Klein, P.C., Charlotte, 1995—. Mem. ABA, N.Y. State Bar Assn. (ins. negligence and compensation law sect.), N.C. Bar Assn. (health law, litigation sects.), N.C. Soc. Health Care Attys. (litigation, health law sects.). Jewish. General civil litigation, Health, Personal injury. Home: 4501 Croft Mill Ln Charlotte NC 28226-9222

**KLEIN, PETER WILLIAM,** lawyer, corporate officer, investment company executive; b. Lorain, Ohio, Sept. 22, 1955; s. Warren Martin Klein and Barbara (Lesser) Pomeroy; m. Jennifer Lynn Ungers, Aug. 3, 1984. Student, U. Sussex, 1975-76; BA, Albion Coll., 1976; JD, Cleve. Marshall Coll. Law, 1981; LLM, NYU, 1982. Bar: Ohio 1981, Ill. 1984. Assoc. Guren, Merritt, Feibel, Sogg & Cohen, Cleve., 1982-84, Siegan, Barbakoff, Gomberg & Gordon, Ltd., Chgo., 1984-86; mng. dir., gen. counsel Trivest Inc., Miami, Fla., 1986—. Mem. ABA (taxation sect., corp. sect., banking and bus. law). General corporate, Securities, Corporate taxation. Home: 3618 Palmetto Ave Miami FL 33133-6221 Office: Trivest Inc 2665 S Bayshore Dr Ste 800 Miami FL 33133-5401

**KLEIN, RAYMOND MAURICE,** lawyer; b. Phila., Jan. 31, 1938; s. Maurice J. and Fay (Clearfield) K.; m. Roberta Steinberg, Apr. 8, 1984; children: Seth Grossman, Micah Grossman. AB, Williams Coll., 1959; JD, Harvard U., 1962. Bar: Pa. 1962, Calif. 1968, U.S. Supreme Ct. 1966. Lawyer Fed. Home Loan Bank Bd., Washington, 1963-67; ptnr. Hahn Cazier, L.A., 1967-78; lawyer Klein Law Corp., L.A., 1978-89, 93—; of counsel Davis Wright Tremaine, L.A., 1989-93; lectr. C. of C., Calif., 1988—, Young Pres.' Orgn., Ohio, 1990, Law Sch. for Entrepreneurs, L.A., 1990—; mem. exec. com. Cal Tech/MIT Enterprise Forum. Author: Putting a Lid on Legal Fees: How to Deal Effectively with Lawyers, 1987. Mem. ABA, Calif. State Bar Assn., L.A. Bar Assn. Avocation: tennis. Real property, Mergers and acquisitions, General corporate. Home: 908 Kenfield Ave Los Angeles CA 90049-1405 Office: Cassady & Klein 908 Kenfield Ave Los Angeles CA 90049-1405 *Teach us to number our days, that we may get us a heart of wisdom.*

**KLEIN, ROBERT GORDON,** state supreme court justice; b. Honolulu, Nov. 11, 1947; s. Gordon Ernest Klein and Clara (Cutter) Elliot; m. Aleta Elizabeth Webb, July 27, 1986; children: Kurt William, Erik Robert. BA, Stanford U., 1969; JD, U. Oreg., 1972. Dep. atty. gen. State of Hawaii, 1973, with state campaign spening commn., 1974, with state dept regulatory agys., 1975-78; judge State Dist. Ct. Hawaii, 1978-84; judge cir. ct. State of Hawaii, 1984-92, supreme ct. justice, 1992—. Office: Supreme Ct 417 S King St Honolulu HI 96813-2902

**KLEIN, WILLIAM, II,** lawyer; b. N.Y.C, June 18, 1919; s. Jacob and Gertrude (Bok) K.; m. Faith Zimmer, Oct. 12, 1947 (div. Oct. 1980); children: William L., Nancy J., Margaret A.; m. Sara Griffith, Dec. 31, 1981 (div. Apr. 1991). BA, NYU, 1941; LLB, Yale U., 1943. Bar: N.Y. (2d cir.) 1943, U.S. Supreme Ct. 1968. Assoc. Hays, St. John, Abramson & Heilbron, N.Y.C., 1943-48, ptnr., 1949-58; gen. counsel ABC Internat. TV Co., Inc., N.Y.C., 1959-63; pvt. practice N.Y.C., 1964-68; ptnr. Austrian, Lance & Stewart, P.C., N.Y.C., 1968-78; profl. corp. ptnr. Tenzer, Greenblatt, LLP, N.Y.C., 1978-89, of counsel, 1989—; assoc. gen. counsel Am. Soc. Travel Agts., Assn. Precious Stone Dealers, Composers and Authors Guild, Authors League Am., N.Y.C., 1943-58; counsel to mut. funds, money mgrs., instl. investors, arbitrageurs, in securities derivative and class actions and in bankruptcies, 1964—; lectr. to internat. bankers and corp. execs., Geneva, 1989; mediator Fed. Ct. Mediation Program, U.S. Dist. Ct. (so. dist.) N.Y.; pro bono small claims arbitrator Civil Ct. N.Y. County; judge moot ct. competition N.Y. Law Sch., 1996—. Contbr. articles to legal jours. Mem. ABA, Am. Arbitration Assn., N.Y. State Bar Assn., Assn. of Bar of City of N.Y., NYU Alumni Coun. (bd. dirs.). Federal civil litigation, Mergers and acquisitions, Securities. Home: 120 E 34th St New York NY 10016-4609 *At 2 I got polio. My right leg was three inches short, but I quickly learned that my limp notwithstanding, I must - and I did - use myself fully, creatively, energetically, compassionately and particularly, positively and with good humor. Yesterday is history, tomorrow is mystery, today is a gift. That's why they call it present.*

**KLEINBERG, HOWARD BRUCE,** lawyer; b. Passaic, N.J., Apr. 29, 1962; s. Lewis and Ida Kleinberg; m. Geri Ellen Solomon, Feb. 14, 1991; 1 child: Reid Alexander. AB, Cornell U., 1984; JD, Hofstra U., 1989. Bar: N.Y., 1990, U.S. Dist. Ct. (so., ea. dists.) N.Y., 1991. Jud. law clk. to Hon. Marvin Holland U.S. Bankruptcy Ct., Bklyn., 1989-91; assoc. Moses & Singer, N.Y.C., 1991-95; sr. assoc. Shaw, Licitra, Bohner, Esernio & Schwarz, Garden City, N.Y., 1995—. Mem. ABA, N.Y. State Bar Assn., Nassau County Bar Assn. Bankruptcy, Federal civil litigation, Consumer commercial. Office: Shaw Licitra Bohner Esernio & Schwartz 1010 Franklin Ave Garden City NY 11530-2900

**KLEINBERG, JUDITH G.,** lawyer, children's advocate; b. Hartford, Conn., Jan. 28, 1946; d. Burleigh B. and Ruth (Leven) Greenberg; m. James Paul Kleinberg, Aug. 30, 1970; children: Alexander, Lauren. BA cum laude, U. Mich., 1968; JD, U. Calif., Berkeley, 1971. Atty. pvt. practice, San Francisco, 1971-74; legal affairs reporter comml. and pub. TV, San Francisco, 1974-76; prof. law Mills Coll., Oakland, Calif., 1977-84; chief of staff The Global Fund for Women, Los Altos, Calif., 1987-88; pub. interest atty., non-profit corp. law/orgn. specialist alternative dispute resolution Palo Alto, Calif., 1988-94; exec. dir. Kids in Common: A Children & Families Collaborative, San Jose, Calif., 1994—; chair Am. Promise, Silicon Valley, 1997—; arbitrator/mediator, legal adv. for abortion rights, women and children's rights and environ. groups, Santa Clara County and Calif., 1980—; speaker in field; chair Am.'s Promise - Silicon Valley. Mem. bd. editors Calif. Law Rev., 1969-71. Mem. steering com. lawyers coun. No. Calif. sect. ACLU, bd. dirs., 1990-92; founder, chairperson No. Calif. Friends of Pediat. AIDS Found.; past pres. Com. for Green Foothills; mem. legis. and steering coms. Calif. Coalition for Childhood Immunization, 1995—; mem. Calif. Children's Advs. Roundtable, 1995—; bd. dirs. Palo Alto SAFE, Support Network for Battered Women, 1990-92, Palo Alto Coun. PTAs, Leadership Midpeninsula, 1994-96; pres. Palo Alto Stanford divsn. Am. Heart Assn., 1994-95; v.p. Assn. for Sr. Day Health, 1994-95; founder Safer Summer Project; pres., legal counsel Calif. Abortion and Reproductive Rights Action League, 1980-86. Recipient Calif. Pks. and Recreation Soc. Merit award, 1995, World of People award Girl Scouts Am., Santa Clara County, 1996. Mem. Nat. Assn. Child Advocates, Calif. Women Lawyers (v.p. 1986-88). Juvenile, Non-profit and tax-exempt organizations.

**KLEINBERG, NORMAN CHARLES,** lawyer; b. Phila., July 18, 1946; s. Frank and Mildred Brosnan (Hill) K.; m. Marcia Sue Topperman, Jan. 31, 1971; children—Lauren Blythe, Joanna Leigh. A.B., Tufts U., 1968; J.D., Columbia U., 1972. Bar: N.Y. 1973, U.S. Supreme Ct., U.S. Ct. Appeals (1st, 2d, 3d and 4th cirs.), U.S. Dist. Ct. (so. and ea. dists.) N.Y., U.S. Tax Ct., U.D. Dist. Ct. (ea. dist.) Wis., U.S. Dist. Ct. (no. dist.) Calif., U.S. Dist. Ct. (ea. dist.) Mich. Law clk. to judge U.S. Dist. Ct. (so. dist.) N.Y., N.Y.C., 1972-74; assoc. Hughes Hubbard & Reed, N.Y.C., 1974-80, ptnr., 1980—. Articles editor Columbia Jour. Law and Social Problems, 1971-72. Served to staff sgt. USAR, 1968-74. Fellow Am. Coll. Trial Lawyers; mem. ABA, Fed. Bar Coun., Assn. of Bar of City of N.Y. (com. on state cts. of superior jurisdiction, com. profl. responsibility, com. profl. and judicial ethics, com. on judiciary, coun. on jud. adminstrn.), Internat. Bar Assn., N.Y. State Bar Assn., Def. Rsch. Inst. General civil litigation, Insurance, Antitrust. Home: 460 E 79th St New York NY 10021-1443 Office: Hughes Hubbard & Reed 1 Battery Park Plz Fl 12 New York NY 10004-1482

**KLEINFELD, ANDREW JAY,** federal judge; b. 1945. BA magna cum laude, Wesleyan U., 1966; JD cum laude, Harvard U., 1969. Law clk. Alaska Supreme Ct., 1969-71; U.S. magistrate U.S. Dist. Ct. Alaska, Fairbanks, 1971-74; pvt. practice law Fairbanks, 1971-86; judge U.S. Dist. Ct. Alaska, Anchorage, 1986-91, U.S. Ct. Appeals (9th cir.), San Francisco, 1991—. Contbr. articles to profl. jours. Mem. Alaska Bar Assn. (pres. 1982-83, bd. govs. 1981-84), Tanana Valley Bar Assn. (pres. 1974-75), Phi Beta Kappa. Republican. Office: US Ct Appeals 9th Cir Courthouse Sq 250 Cushman St Ste 3-a Fairbanks AK 99701-4665

**KLEINFELD, DENIS ALAN,** lawyer; b. Chgo., Feb. 10, 1946; s. J. Laurence and Helen Kleinfeld; m. June Kleinfeld; children: Harrison, Jaclene. BS Accountancy, U. Ill., 1967; JD, Loyola U., Chgo., 1970. CPA; Bar: Ill., 1970, Fla., 1983. Atty. IRS, Chgo., 1970-74, Denis Kleinfeld & Assocs., Chgo., 1974-83, Kleinfeld & Assocs., Miami, Fla., 1983-97, Kleinfeld Law Firm, 1997—; of counsel Ten State Street LLP, Alwin M. Tamosins & Ptnrs., Duke Law Firm. Author: Offshore Trusts, 1999; co-author: Estate Planning for Florida Resident, 1994, Practical International Tax Planning, 1999, Structuring Offshore Asset Protection Trusts, 1999; contbr. editor: Offshore Investment Mag.; columnist Jour. Asset Protection, 1999; mem. editl. bd. Offshore Fin. U.S.A. mag.; contbr. articles to profl. jours. Mem. ABA (asset protection com.), Internat. Tax Planning Assn., Soc. Trust and Estate Practitioners, Fla. Bar Assn., Ill. Bar Assn., Am. Assn. Attys.-CPAs, Fla. Soc. CPAs, Estate Planning Coun. Miami. Avocations: sailing, shooting, chess, reading, travel. Office: The Kleinfeld Law Firm Ste 1940 One SE 3d Ave Miami FL 33131

**KLEMANN, GILBERT LACY, II,** lawyer; b. New Rochelle, N.Y., July 26, 1950; s. N. Robert and Rosemary Virginia (Gerard) K.; m. Patricia Louise Hild, June 16, 1973; children: Tricia Rosemary, Gilbert Hild. AB, Coll. Holy Cross, 1972; JD, Fordham U., 1975. Bar: N.Y. 1976, U.S. Dist. Ct. (so. and ea. dists.) N.Y. 1976, Conn. 1988, U.S. Supreme Ct. 1991. Assoc. Chadbourne, Parke, Whiteside & Wolff, N.Y.C., 1975-83; ptnr. Chadbourne & Parke (formerly Chadbourne, Parke, Whiteside & Wolff), N.Y.C., 1983-90; sr. v.p., gen. counsel Fortune Brands, Inc. (formerly Am. Brands Inc.), Old Greenwich, Conn., 1991-97, exec. v.p. strategic and legal affairs, 1998; exec. v.p. corp., mem. bd. dirs. Fortune Brands, Inc. (formerly Am. Brands Inc.), Old Greenwich, 1999—. Editor Fordham Law Rev., 1974-75. Mem. Conn. Bar Assn., Greenwich (Conn.) Country Club, Nassau Club (Princeton, N.J.). Republican. Roman Catholic. Avocation: golf. General corporate, General practice. Home: 25 Hope Farm Rd Greenwich CT 06830-3331 Office: Fortune Brands Inc 1700 E Putnam Ave Old Greenwich CT 06870-1321

**KLEMIN, LAWRENCE R.,** lawyer; b. New Rockford, N.D., Mar. 31, 1945; s. Lawrence R. Klemin and Carol M. (Cook) Roaldson; m. Rita R. DiPalma, Sept. 2, 1970; children: Laura K., Peter L. BA in English, U. N.D., 1967, JD with distinction, 1978. Bar: N.D. 1978, U.S. Dist. Ct. N.D. 1978, U.S. Ct. Appeals (8th cir.) 1987, U.S. Supreme Ct. 1988. Hearing officer N.D. Employment Security Bur., Bismarck, 1971-75; assoc. Atkinson & Dwyer, Bismarck, 1978-81; ptnr. Atkinson, Dwyer & Klemin, Bismarck, 1981-82, Dwyer & Klemin, Bismarck, 1982-86; pres. Lawrence R. Klemin, P.C., Bismarck, 1986-92, Bucklin & Klemin, P.C., Bismarck, 1992-96, Bucklin, Klemin & McBride, P.C., Bismarck, 1996—; pres. Title and Escrow Co., Bismarck, 1988-98, Litigation Svcs., Inc., Bismarck, 1995—; state rep. N.D. legis assembly, 1998—; commr. Nat. Conf. of Commrs. on Uniform State Laws, 1999—; mem. state adv. coun. N.D. Office Adminstrv. Hearings, Bismarck, 1993-98; lectr. on real property law Nat. Bus. Inst., 1989—. Author, editor Civil Practice of North Dakota, 1993—. Bd. dirs. N.D. March of Dimes, Bismarck, 1994—; mem. Corpus Christi Parish Coun., Bismarck, 1996—. With U.S. Army, 1967-70, Vietnam. Mem. State Bar Assn. N.D. (chair adminstrv. law com. 1996-98), N.D. Land Title Assn. (legis. com. 1990-99), Bismarck Mandan C. of C. (bd. dirs. 1996-98), Optimist Internat. (bd. dirs. 1985-86), Elks, Eagles, Am. Legion. Roman Catholic. Avocations: antique auto restoration, astronomy, camping. Administrative and regulatory, General civil litigation, Real property. Home: 1709 Montego Dr Bismarck ND 58501-0856 Office: Bucklin Klemin & McBride PC 400 E Broadway #500 PO Box 955 Bismarck ND 58502-0955

**KLEPPIN, GLENDA LEA,** lawyer; b. Rapid City, S.D., Dec. 5, 1945; d. Glen T. and Leah E. (Armstrong) K.; children: Dawna Kennedy, John Dickson, Deborah Dickson. BS, Brigham Young U., Provo, Utah, 1965, MS, 1966, PhD; JD, U.C. Hastings Sch. Law, San Francisco, 1990. Calif. Bar, 1990; U.S. Dist. Ct., (ctrl. dist.) Calif., 1990; U.S. Supreme Ct., 1994. Faculty Brigham Young U., 1966-68; ednl. diagnostician, 1974-75; tchr., psychologist, adminstr. Shiprock (N.Mex.) Alternative H.S., 1976-78; cons. Bur. Indian Affairs, 1977-80; faculty, dept. chmn. Navajo C.C., Shiprock, N.Mex., 1977-81; bus. and ednl. cons. Farmington, N.Mex., 1978-85; adjunct faculty U. N.Mex., 1981, N.Mex. Highlands U., 1981, N.Mex. State U., Los Cruces, N.Mex., 1982-84, Navajo C.C., Tsaile, Ariz., 1984-85; rsch. asst. Pub. Law Rsch. Inst., San Francisco, 1988-90; tutor Legal Edn. Opportunity Program, San Francisco, 1989; law clk. San Fernando Valley Legal Svcs., Pacoima, Calif., 1989; extern, law clk. L.A. Superior Ct. 9th cir. ct. appeals, Pasadena and Lancaster, Calif., 1989; lawyer pvt. practice, Calif., 1990—. Recipient Elks Club Most Valuable Student scholarship, S.D., 1963, Civil Air Patrol Nat. Bd. Chmn. scholarship, 1963-67, Brigham Young U. scholarship, 1965, Nat. Sci. Found. traineeship, 1968-69, Nat. Def. Edn. Act fellowship, 1969-71, Disting. Svc. award for Cmty. Svc., Jaycees, 1980, Cert.

Spl. Recognition, Jicarilla Headstart Program, 1985. Avocations: travel, crafts, flying, reading. Office: 1502 192nd Ave E Sumner WA 98390

**KLETT, EDWIN LEE,** lawyer; b. Clearfield, Pa., Dec. 8, 1935; s. John L. and Gertrude Elizabeth (Larson) K.; m. Janis Lynn Gibson; children: David, Lauren, Krista, Kirklin, Keenan. BS in Commerce and Finance, Bucknell U., 1957; JD, Dickinson Sch. Law, Carlisle, Pa., 1962. Bar: Pa. 1963, U.S. Dist. Ct. (we. dist.) Pa. 1963, U.S. Ct. Appeals (3d cir.) 1967, U.S. Ct. Appeals (6th cir.) 1985, U.S. Supreme Ct. 1983. Assoc. Eckert, Seamans, Cherin & Mellott, Pitts., 1962, ptnr., 1969; sr. ptnr., chmn. Klett Lieber Rooney & Schorling, Pitts., 1989—; trustee Dickinson Sch. Law, 1982—; mem. civil procedural rules com. Pa. Supreme Ct., 1986—, vice chair, 1989-92, chair, 1993—. Mem. Pa. State Transp. Adv. Bd., Harrisburg, Pa., 1985-88, Rep. State Fin. Com., Harrisburg, 1986-91, Allegheny County Rep. Fin. Com., Pitts., 1987-92. Fellow Internat. Acad. Trial Lawyers, Am. Coll. Trial Lawyers (Pa. state com. 1994—, state chair 1996-98), Am. Bd. Trial Advs., Am. Bar Found., Am. Bar Inst., Pa. Bar Found., Alletheny County Bar Found.; mem. ABA (ho. dels. 1999), Am. Bd. Trial Advs., Acad. Trial Lawyers Allegheny County (bd. govs. 1986-88, pres. 1988-89), Am. Judicature Soc., Allegheny County Bar (bd. govs. 1989-92, 99—, pres.-elect 1999—). Federal civil litigation, State civil litigation, Securities. Home: 151 Ordale Blvd Pittsburgh PA 15228-1525 Office: Klett Lieber Rooney & Schorling 1 Oxford Ct 40th Flr Pittsburgh PA 15219-1407

**KLEWANS, SAMUEL N.,** lawyer; b. Lock Haven, Pa., Mar. 2, 1941; s. Morris and Ruth N. K.; children: Richard Bennett, Ruth Elise, Paul Henry, Margo Ilene. A.B., U. Pa., 1963; J.D., Am. U., 1966. Bar: Va. 1966, U.S. Dist. Ct. (ea. dist.) Va. 1966, U.S. Dist. Ct. D.C. 1967, U.S. Ct. Appeals D.C. 1967, U.S. Ct. Appeals (4th cir.) 1967, U.S. Supreme Ct. 1971. Law clk., U.S. Dist. Ct. Ea. Dist. Va. 1966-67; ptnr. Fried, Fried & Klewans, Springfield, Va., 1970-86; prin. Klewans & Assocs., 1986-91; shareholder/atty. Grad, Logan & Klewans, P.C., 1991—; lectr. No. Va. Inst. Continuing Med. Edn., No. Va. Ctr. Quality and Health Edn. Contbr. articles to profl. jours. Served to 1st lt. JAGC-USAR, 1966-72. Mem. Fairfax County Bar Assn. (ethics and grievance com. 1971-72, mem. 75-76, courts com. 1975-76; jud. selection com. 1979-82, chmn. 1981-82), Va. State Bar (mem. disciplinary bd. 1976-84, vice chmn. 1982-83, chmn. 1983-84, lectr. continuing legal edn., professionalism faculty), Practice Resource Group (lectr.). General corporate, Corporate taxation, Health. Office: 1421 Prince St Alexandria VA 22314-2805

**KLINE, ALLEN HABER, JR.,** lawyer; b. Houston, June 17, 1954; s. Allen H. Sr. and Maude Rose (Brown) K.; m. Barbara Ann Byrd, July 24, 1982; children: Allison Ashley, Allen III. BA, U. Denver, 1976; JD, U. Miami, 1979. Bar: Tex. 1980, U.S. Dist. Ct. (so. dist.) Tex. 1980, U.S. Ct. Appeals (5th cir.) 1980, U.S. Ct. Appeals (11th cir.) 1983, U.S. Supreme Ct. 1985; bd. cert. personal injury trial law Tex. Bd. Legal Specialization. Sole practice Houston, 1980—. Mem. Houston Bar Assn., Coll. of the State Bar of Tex. Club: City Wide (Houston) (life). Avocations: tennis, water, snow skiing. Personal injury, State civil litigation, Admiralty. Office: 440 Louisiana St Ste 2120 Houston TX 77002-4205

**KLINE, DANIEL ADAM,** lawyer, state senator; b. Red Bank, N.J., Oct. 27, 1944; s. Harry and Bertha (Shapiro) K.; m. Laura Gene Middaugh, June 25, 1989; 1 child, Genevieve. BA, Johns Hopkins U., 1968; JD, U. Md., Balt., 1972. Bar: Md. 1972, Miss. 1973, Wash. 1974, U.S. Ct. Appeals (5th cir.) 1973, U.S. Ct. Appeals (9th cir.) 1978. Staff lawyer No. Miss. Rural Legal Svcs., Greenwood, 1972-73, Evergreen Legal Svcs., Seattle, 1973-77; pvt. practice, Seattle, 1977—; mem. Wash. State Senate, Olympia, 1997—. Contbr. articles to Seattle Times and Seattle Post-Intelligencer. Bd. dirs., PAC chair NARAL, Seattle, 1991-97; founding mem., co-chair Wash. Conservation Voters, Seattle, 1991-97. Recipient Benson award Wash. CeaseFire, 1997, Achievement award Mothers Against Drunk Driving, 1998. Mem. Wash. State Trial Lawyers Assn. (legis. steering com. 1989-93, chair civil rights sect. 1993-95). Democrat. Jewish. Avocations: mountain climbing, sea-kayaking, bicycling. Personal injury, Civil rights. Office: 216 1st Ave S Ste 330 Seattle WA 98104-2534

**KLINE, DAVID BENJAMIN,** lawyer, paralegal educator, writer; b. Phila., June 3, 1963; s. Herbert M. and Pearl Kline; m. Beth Renee May, Mar. 10, 1989; children: Allison, Rachael, Jacob, Sam. BA in Journalism, Temple U., 1985; JD, Widener U., 1990. Bar: Pa. 1990, U.S. Dist. Ct. (ea. dist.) Pa. 1990, Md. 1991, U.S. Ct. Appeals (3rd cir.) 1991, U.S. Supreme Ct. 1999; cert. neutral arbitrator Am. Arbitration Assn. Assoc. LaBrum & Doak, Phila., 1990-92, Mayerson, Munsing et al, Norristown, Pa., 1992; ptnr. Ostroff & Kline, P.C., Lansdale, Pa., 1993-98; assoc. Weinstein Goss et al, Lansdale, 1998—; mem. paralegal adv. com. CCA, Washington, 1993-99. Co-author: Emotional Injuries: Law & Practice, 1998; contbr. articles to profl. jours. Active St. Faith Ch., Havertown, Pa., 1997-99; active Montgomery County Bar Pro Bono projects, MARD vol. work. Scottish Rite scholar Temple U., Phila., 1984. Mem. Pa. Bar Assn. (mem. professionalism com. 1993-99), Montgomery County Bar Assn. (chair alt. dispute resolution 1999). Avocations: classic motor vehicles, science fiction, animals, swimming, skiing. Personal injury, Insurance, State civil litigation. Office: Weinstein Goss 311 N Broad St Lansdale PA 19446-2411

**KLINE, JAMES EDWARD,** lawyer; b. Fremont, Ohio, Aug. 3, 1941; s. Walter J. and Sophia Kline; m. Mary Ann Bruening, Aug. 29, 1964; children: Laura Anne Kline, Matthew Thomas, Jennifer Sue. BS in Social Sci., John Carroll U., 1963; JD, Ohio State U., 1966; postgrad., Stanford U., 1991. Bar: Ohio, 1966, N.C., 1989, U.S. Tax. Ct., 1983. Assoc. Eastman, Stichter, Smith & Bergman, Toledo, 1966-70; ptnr. Eastman, Stichter, Smith & Bergman (name now Eastman & Smith), Toledo, 1970-84, Shumaker, Loop & Kendrick, Toledo, 1984-88; v.p., gen. counsel Aeroquip-Vickers, Inc. (formerly Trinova Corp.), Toledo, 1989—; corp. sec. Sheller-Globe Corp., 1977-84; adj. prof. U. Toledo Coll. Law, 1988-94; bd. dirs. Plastic Techs., Inc. Author: (with Robert Seaver) Ohio Corporation Law, 1988. Trustee Kidney Found. of Northwestern Ohio, Inc., 1972-81, pres., 1979-80; bd. dirs. Toledo Botanical Garden (formerly Crosby Gardens), 1974-80, pres., 1977-79; bd. dirs. Toledo Zool. Soc., 1983-96, pres., 1991-93; bd. dirs. Toledo Area Regional Transit Authority, 1984-90, pres., 1987-88; bd. dirs. Home Away From Home, Inc. (Ronald McDonald House NW Ohio), 1983-88; trustee Toledo Symphony Orch., 1981—, St. John's H.S., 1988-91, Ohio Found. Ind. Colls., 1991—; trustee Lourdes Coll., 1988-96, chmn., 1994-96. Fellow Ohio Bar Found.; mem. ABA, Nat. Assn. Corp. Dirs., Ohio Bar Assn. (corp. law com. 1977—, chmn. 1983-86), Toledo Bar Assn., Mfrs. Alliance (chair Law Coun. II 1997—), Toledo Area C. of C. (trustee 1994—), Inverness Club, Toledo Club (trustee 1990-97), Stone Oak Country Club, Ottawa Skeet Club, Answer Club. Roman Catholic. General corporate, Corporate taxation, Securities. Home: 216 Treetop Pl Holland OH 43528-8451 Office: Aeroquip-Vickers Inc 3000 Strayer Rd Maumee OH 43537-9700

**KLINE, JOHN ANTHONY,** state court justice; b. N.Y.C., Aug. 17, 1938; s. Harry and Bertha (Shapiro) K.; m. Fiona Fleming, Dec. 7, 1968 (div. 1977); m. Susan Sward, Nov. 25, 1982 (div.); children: Nicholas Sward, Timothy Sward. BA, Johns Hopkins U., 1960; MA, Cornell U., 1962; LLB, Yale U., 1965. Bar: Calif. 1966, N.Y. 1967, U.S. Supreme Ct. 1971. Assoc. atty. Davis Polk & Wardwell, N.Y.C., 1966-69; staff atty. legal svcs. program OEO, Berkeley, Calif., 1969-70; mng. atty. Pub. Advocates Inc., San Francisco, 1970-75; legal affairs sec. to gov. Calif. Sacramento, 1975-80; judge Superior Ct., San Francisco, 1980-82; presiding justice 1st appelate dist. div. two Calif. Ct. Appeal, 1982—; mem. Calif. Commn. on Jud. Appointments, 1995—; mem. Calif. Jud. Coun. Adv. Commn. Juvenile Law, 1997—. Bd. dirs. San Francisco Lawyers Commn. Urban Affairs, 1972-74, San Francisco Pvt. Industry Coun., 1981-89, Am. Jewish Congress of No. Calif., 1981-85, Youth Svc. Am., 1987-90; chmn. bd. dirs. Golden Gate Kindergarten Assn., 1992—, Youth Guidance Ctr. Improvement Com., 1982-90, San Francisco Conservation Corps, 1984—, Environ. Action Ctr., 1980—. Alfred P. Sloan fellow Cornell U., 1960-62; recipient Ambrose Gherini prize and Sutherland Cup Yale U., 1965. Mem. Calif. Judges Assn. Democrat. Jewish. E-mail: justice.Kline@jud.ca.gov. Office: 350 Mcallister St San Francisco CA 94102-4712

**KLINE, LOWRY F.,** lawyer. Sr. v.p., gen. counsel Coca-Cola Enterprises, Atlanta, now exec. v.p., gen. counsel. Office: Coca-Cola Enterprises 2500 Windy Ridge Pkwy SE Atlanta GA 30339-5677

**KLINE, MICHAEL J.,** lawyer; b. Phila., Nov. 5, 1944. BS summa cum laude, U. Pa., 1966, JD cum laude, 1969. Bar: Pa. 1969, N.J. 1976. Atty. Fox, Rothschild, O'Brien & Frankel, Lawrenceville, N.J. Author: Introduction to Corporate Law, 1978. Gen. counsel Deborah Heart and Lung Ctr. and Deborah Hosp. Found., Browns Mills, N.J., 1976—; pres. Jewish Geriatric Home, Cherry Hill, N.J., 1991-93; pub. mem. Adv. Grad. Med. Edn. Coun. N.J., 1990—. Mem. ABA, Am. Acad. Hosp. Attys., Nat. Assn. Bond Lawyers, N.J. State Bar Assn., N.J. Soc. Hosp. Attys., Mercer County Bar Assn. General corporate, Securities, Health. Office: Fox Rothschild O'Brien & Frankel Princeton Pike Corp Ctr 997 Lenox Dr Bldg 3 Lawrenceville NJ 08648-2317

**KLINE, NORMAN DOUGLAS,** federal judge; b. Lynn, Mass., Dec. 28, 1930; s. Samuel and Ida (Luff) K.; m. Betty Toba Feldman, Feb. 27, 1966; children: Sarah, Samuel. AB, Harvard Coll., 1952, postgrad., 1952-53; JD, Boston U., 1959. Bar: Mass. 1959. Pvt. practice Boston, 1959-60; atty. U.S. Dept. Army, Cleve., 1960; trial atty. FMC, Washington, 1960-72, adminstrv. law judge, 1972-92, chief adminstrv. law judge, 1992—. With U.S. Army, 1953-55. Mem. Fed. Adminstrv. Law Judges Conf. Avocations: classical music, collecting CDs. Office: Fed Maritime Commn 800 N Capitol St NW Washington DC 20573-0001

**KLINE, SIDNEY DELONG, JR.,** lawyer; b. West Reading, Pa., Mar. 25, 1932; s. Sidney D. and Leona Clarice (Barkalow) K.; m. Barbara Phyllis James, Dec. 31, 1955; children: Allison S. McCanney, Leslie S. Davidson, Lisa P. Gallen. BA, Dickinson Coll., 1954, LLD, 1998; JD with honors, The Dickinson Law Sch., 1956, LLD, 1994. Bar: Pa. 1956, U.S. Dist. Ct. (ea. dist.) Pa. 1961, U.S. Supreme Ct. 1967. Assoc. Stevens & Lee, Reading, Pa., 1958-62, ptnr., shareholder, 1963-97, pres., 1977-93, chmn., 1993-97, counsel, 1998—; bd. dirs. Reading Eagle Co. Pres., United Way of Berks County, Reading, 1972-74, campaign chmn., 1986; bd. dirs. Reading Ctr. City Devel. Fund, 1976-98, pres., 1992-97; trustee Dickinson Sch. Law, 1978—, sec., 1988—; trustee Dickinson Coll., 1979—, chmn., 1990-98; bd. dirs. Greater Berks Devel. Fund, 1998—. Served with U.S. Army, 1956-58. Recipient Doran award United Way Berks County, 1978, Richard J. Caron Cmty. Svc. award Caron Found., 1993, Thun Cmty. Svc. award, 1995. Fellow Am. Coll. Trust and Estate Coun., Nat. Soc. Fund Raising Execs. (Outstanding Vol. Fund Raiser Greater Northeastern Pa. chpt. 1992), Pa. Bar Assn., Berks County Bar Assn., Berkshire Country Club (Reading), Moselem Springs Golf Club (Fleetwood, Pa.), The Club at Pelican Bay (Naples, Fla.). Republican. Lutheran. Banking, Probate, Real property. Office: PO Box 679 111 N 6th St Reading PA 19603-0679

**KLINE, TIMOTHY DEAL,** lawyer; b. Oklahoma City, July 16, 1949; s. David Adam and Ruthela (Deal) K.; m. Alyssa Lipp Krysler, Aug. 29, 1985. BA, U. Okla., 1971, JD, 1976. Bar: Okla. 1976, U.S. Dist. Ct. (we. dist.) Okla. 1977, U.S. Ct. Appeals (10th cir.) 1977; cert. in bus. bankruptcy law and consumer bankruptcy Am. Bankruptcy Bd. of Certification. Law clk. to presiding justice U.S. Dist. Ct. (we. dist.) Okla., Oklahoma City, 1976-80; assoc. Linn, Helms, Kirk & Burkett, Oklahoma City, 1980-83; ptnr. Kline & Kline, Oklahoma City, 1983—; adj. prof. law Oklahoma City U., 1980-84, 90. Mem. Am. Coll. Bankruptcy, Okla. County Bar Assn. (pres. 1998-99), Phi Delta Phi. Democrat. Bankruptcy. Office: Kline & Kline 720 NE 63rd St Oklahoma City OK 73105-6405

**KLINEDINST, JOHN DAVID,** lawyer; b. Washington, Jan. 20, 1950; s. David Moulson and Mary Stewart (Coxe) K.; m. Cynthia Lynn DuBain, Aug. 15, 1981. BA cum laude in History, Washington and Lee U., 1971, JD, 1978; MBA in Fin. and Investments, George Washington U., 1975. Bar: Calif. 1979, U.S. Dist. Ct. (so. dist.) Calif. 1979, U.S. Ct. Appeals (9th cir.) 1987. With comml. lending dept. 1st Nat. Bank Md., Montgomery County, 1971-74; assoc. Ludecke, McGrath & Denton, San Diego, 1979-80; ptnr. Whitney & Klinedinst, San Diego, 1980-83, Klinedinst & Meiser, San Diego, 1983-86; mng. ptnr. Klinedinst, Fliehman & McKillop, San Diego, 1986—. Mem. law coun. Washington and Lee U., 1993-97, vice chmn. law campaign, 1991-94; vice chmn. bd. dirs. ARC of San Diego/Imperial, 1991-97; pres. House Corp. Calif. Lamda, Phi Kappa Psi, 1999—. Recipient Disting. Alumnus award Washington and Lee U., 1993. Mem. ABA, Calif. Bar Assn., San Diego Bar Assn., San Diego Def. Lawyers, Washington Soc. (bd. dirs. 1997—), Washington and Lee U. Alumni Assn. (bd. dirs. 1986-90, pres. 1989-90), Washington and Lee U. Club (pres. San Diego chpt. 1980-87), La Jolla Beach and Tennis Club, Fairbanks Ranch Country Club, Phi Kappa Psi. Republican. Episcopalian. Federal civil litigation, State civil litigation. Home: 6226 Via Dos Valles Rancho Santa Fe CA 92067-9999 Office: Klinedinst Fliehman & McKillop 501 W Broadway Ste 600 San Diego CA 92101-3584

**KLINEFELTER, JAMES LOUIS,** lawyer; b. L.A., Oct. 8, 1925; s. Theron Albert and Anna Marie (Coffey) K.; m. Joanne Wright, Dec. 26, 1957 (div.); children: Patricia Anne, Jeanne Marie, Christopher Wright; m. Mary Lynn S. Klinefelter, Aug. 19, 1971; 1 child, Mary Katherine. BA, U. Ala., 1949, LLB, 1951. Bar: Ala. 1951, U.S. Dist. Ct. (no. dist.) Ala. 1959, U.S. Ct. Appeals (11th cir.) 1983. Regional claims rep. State Farm Mut. Auto Ins. Co., Anniston, Ala., 1951-54; ptnr. Burnham & Klinefelter, Anniston, 1954—; Mem. adv. com. Supreme Ct. Ala. Mem. Ala. Dem. Exec. Com., 1964—, chmn. legis. rev. com., 1964—; past chmn. Calhoun County Dem. Exec. Com., 1964—. Lt. (j.g.) USNR, 1943-46. Mem. ABA, Assn. Def. Trial Attys., Ala. Bar Assn. (mem. task force on jud. selection, mem. long-range planning task force), Calhoun County Bar Assn., Ala. Def. Lawyers Assn. (past pres.), Ala. Law Inst. (bd. dirs.), Ala. Sch. Bd. Attys. (past pres.), Internat. Assn. Def. Counsel, Kiwanis (past pres.), Anniston Country Club, Phi Kappa Sigma, Phi Alpha Theta. Avocations: tennis, swimming, reading. General civil litigation, Education and schools, Insurance. Home: 1412 Christine Ave Anniston AL 36207-3924 Office: Burnham & Klinefelter So Trust Nat Bank Bldg PO Box 1618 Anniston AL 36202-1618 *When obligations or obnoxious tasks are accepted gratefully as opportunities, one's life can be turned about, and bitterness and resentment changed into joyful satisfaction. Hard tasks are the food of growth.*

**KLINGLE, PHILIP ANTHONY,** law librarian; b. Bklyn., July 24, 1950; s. Lorin Russell and Therese Margaret (Meehan) K.; m. Rachelle Phyllis Miller, Nov. 20, 1977; children: David Adam, Michael Matthew, Anne Elizabeth. BA, Fordham U., 1971; MA, NYU, 1973; MS, Columbia U., 1976. Asst. reference libr. N.Y. Hist. Soc., N.Y.C., 1973-77; libr. Bklyn. Pub. Libr., 1977-78; reference libr., asst. prof. John Jay Coll. Criminal Justice CUNY, 1978-81; libr. Inst. Jud. Adminstrn. Sch. of Law NYU, 1981-82; sr. law libr. ct. libr. N.Y. State Supreme Ct., S.I., 1982—. Editor: jour. The Literature of Criminal Justice, 1980-81, IJA Report, 1981-82. Mem. ALA, Am. Assn. Law Librs., Law Libr. Assn. Greater N.Y., Libr. Assn. CUNY (mem. exec. coun. 1978-81). Office: NY State Supreme Ct Libr Richmond County Courthouse Staten Island NY 10301

**KLIPSTEIN, ROBERT ALAN,** lawyer; b. N.Y.C., Sept. 23, 1936; s. Harold David and Hyacinth (Levin) K. AB, Columbia U., 1957, JD, 1960; LLM in Taxation, NYU, 1965. Bar: N.Y. 1960, U.S. Supreme Ct. 1964. Practice law, N.Y.C., 1961—; assoc. Saxe Bacon & O'Shea, 1961, Rosenman, Colin, Kaye, Petschek & Freund, 1962-63; law sec. to justice N.Y. County Supreme Ct., 1963-64; assoc. Bernays & Eisner, 1965-70; ptnr. Eisner, Klipstein & Klipstein, 1971-77; ptnr. Danziger, Bangser, Klipstein, Goldsmith, Greenwald & Weiss (name now Bangser Klein Rocca & Blum), 1977-92; counsel Sullivan & Donovan, 1992—; arbitrator City of N.Y. Small Claims Ct., 1971—. Served with U.S. Army, 1960-62. Mem. ABA, N.Y. State Bar Assn., Assn. Bar City of N.Y., N.Y. County Lawyers Assn., Am. Immigration Lawyers Assn., Westchester County Bar Assn., Am. Judges Assn., Phi Alpha Delta. Club: Univ. Glee (N.Y.C.). Probate, Estate taxation, Immigration, naturalization, and customs. Home: 401 E 74th St Apt 6G New York NY 10021-3931 Office: Sullivan & Donovan LLP 415 Madison Ave New York NY 10017-1111

**KLOBASA, JOHN ANTHONY,** lawyer; b. St. Louis, Feb. 15, 1951; s. Alan R. and Virginia (Yager) K.; m. Kathleen L. Davlan, June 15, 1979. BA in Econs., Emory U., 1972; JD, Wash. U., 1975. Bar: Mo. 1975, U.S. Dist. Ct. (ea. dist.) Mo. 1975, U.S. Ct. Appeals (8th cir.) 1976, U.S. Supreme Ct. 1979, U.S. Tax Ct. 1981, U.S. Ct. Appeals (9th cir.) 1990, U.S. Ct. Appeals (10th cir.) 1993. Assoc. Kohn, Shands, Elbert, Gianoulakis & Gilium, St. Louis, 1975-80; ptnr. Kohn, Shands, Elbert, Gianoulakis & Giljum, St. Louis, 1981—. Spl. counsel City of Town and Country, Mo., 1987; spl. counsel City of Des Peres, Mo., 1987, alderman, 1989-91. Mem. ABA, Mo. Bar Assn., Met. St. Louis Bar Assn., Order of Coif, Phi Beta Kappa. Republican. General civil litigation, Probate, Family and matrimonial. Office: Kohn Shands Elbert Gianoulakis & Giljum LLP 1 Mercantile Ctr Fl 24 Saint Louis MO 63101-1643

**KLOCKAU, LORI LEE,** lawyer; b. Ft. Madison, Iowa, Dec. 26, 1953; d. Alan Barret and Joan Louise (Klingelmueller) Cuthbert; m. Terence J. McCormally, Oct. 14, 1972 (div. Apr. 10, 1981); 1 child, John Barry McCormally; m. David W. Klockau, May 5, 1984; 1 child, Sara Beth. BS, U. Iowa, 1980, MA, 1982, JD, 1991. Bar: Iowa 1991. Legal intern Johnson County Atty., Iowa City, 1990-91; atty. Bray & Klockau, P.L.C., Iowa City, 1995—. Editor (newsletter) Iowa Family Law Report, 1991-96. Youth counselor Camp Nauvoo (Ill.), 1973-98; Girl Scout leader Am. Girl Scouts, Iowa City, 1991-98. Mem. ABA (vice chair adoption com. 1998-99, co-chair 1999—), Am. Acad. Adoption Attys. (legis. com. 1998—), Iowa State Bar (Supreme Ct. futures com. 1998—). Democrat. Mem. RLDS Ch. Avocations: gardening, reading, softball, hiking. Family and matrimonial. Office: Bray and Klockau PLC 402 S Linn St Iowa City IA 52240-4929

**KLODOWSKI, HARRY FRANCIS, JR.,** lawyer; b. Pitts., June 18, 1954; s. Harry F. and Nancy (Coll) K.; m. Amy Martha Auslander, Nov. 12, 1983; children: Deborah, Daniel. BA, SUNY, Buffalo, 1976, JD, 1979. Bar: Pa. 1979, U.S. Dist. Ct. (we. dist.) Pa. 1979, U.S. Tax Ct. 1979, U.S. Ct. Appeals (3d cir.) 1979. Assoc., then ptnr. Berkman, Ruslander, Pohl, Lieber & Engel, Pitts., 1979-88; prin. Doepken, Keevican & Weiss, P.C., Pitts., 1988-93, Picadio McCall Kane & Norton, Pitts., 1993-94; pvt. practice, Pitts., 1994—. Assoc. editor Pitts. Legal Jour., 1979—; contbr. articles to profl. jours. Mem. ABA, Pa. Bar Assn., Allegheny County Bar Assn. (chmn. environ. law sect. 1997), Environ. Law Inst. (assoc.), Air and Waste Mgmt. Assn. (chmn. pub. info. com. 1996—), Rivers Club. Avocations: skiing, racquetball. Environmental, Administrative and regulatory, General civil litigation. Home: 615 Sandy Hill Rd Valencia PA 16059-2731 Office: 330 Grant St Ste 3321 Pittsburgh PA 15219-2202

**KLOESS, LAWRENCE HERMAN, JR.,** lawyer; b. Mamaroneck, N.Y., Jan. 30, 1927; s. Lawrence H. and Harriette Adelia (Holly) K.; m. Eugenia Ann Underwood, Nov. 19, 1931; children: Lawrence H. III, Price Mentzel, Branch Donelson, David Holly. AB, U. Ala., 1954, JD, 1956; grad., Air War Coll., 1976; grad. Indsl. Coll. of the Armed Forces, Nat. Def. U., 1977. Bar: Ala. 1956, U.S. dist. Ct. (no. dist.) Ala. 1956, U.S. Ct. Appeals (5th cir.) 1957, U.S. Ct. Mil. Appeals 1971, U.S. Supreme Ct. 1971, U.S. Ct. Appeals (11th cir.) 1981. Sole practice Birmingham, Ala., 1956-60, 62-66; corp. counsel Bankers Fire and Marine Ins. Co., 1961-62; dist. counsel for Ala. Office Dist. Counsel U.S. Dept. Vets. Affairs, Montgomery, 1966-95. Contbr. articles on law to profl. jours. Vice chmn. Salvation Army adv. bd., 1981, mem. bd., 1978-81; mem. nat. conf. bar pres.'s ABA, 1981—; mem. adminstrn. bd. Frazer Meml. United Meth. Ch., 1987-90, 92—; mem. adv. coun. Ret. and Sr. Vol. Program, Montgomery, 1997—. Col. Judge Adv. Gen. USAFR, 1954-86, ret. Bd. dirs., sec. Air Force Judge Adv. Gen. Sch. Found., 1996—. Decorated Legion of Merti, Meritorious Svc. medal with oak leaf cluster, Commendation medal; named Outstanding Judge Advocate USAFR, 1977, 79. Mem. ABA (nat. conf. bar. pres. 1981—), Ala. State Bar Assn. (chmn. editl. adv. bd. Ala. Lawyer 1975-79, editl. bd. 1970-82, character and fitness com. 1975-, chmn. law day com. 1973, chmn. citizen edn. com. 1974, CLE adv. com. 1983), Ala. Law Found. (trustee), Montgomery County Bar Assn. (chmn. law day com. 1972, chmn. state bar liaison com. 1975, chmn. bd. dirs. 1977, bd. dirs. 1979, chmn. and editor Montgomery County Bar Jour., ABA Merit award 1979-80, v.p. 1980, pres. 1981), Fed. Bar Assn. (pres. Montgomery Fed. Bar Assn. 1973), Citizens Conf. on Ala. Ct. (exec. com., sponsor of new jud. article to state constn. 1973), Citizens Conf. on Criminal and Juvenile Justice (mem. staff 1974), Farrah Law Soc., REs. Officers Assn. of U.S. (chpt. pres. 1978, state pres. 1982), Air Force Ret. Judge Adv. Assn., Ret. Officers Assn. (life), Air War Coll. Alumni Assn. (life), Sigma Delta Kappa (pres. U. Ala. chpt.), Theta Chi (Outstanding Alumni award 1976), Montgomery Capital Rotary Club (pres. 1979, Paul Harris fellow), Montgomery Rotary Club (v.p. 1996, pres. 1998), Maxwell-Gunter Officers (Montgomery), Capital City Club, Montgomery Country Club, Blue Gray Cols. Assn., Mystic Soc. (Krewe of phantom host), Hon. Order Ky. Cols., Svc. Corps. of Ret. Execs. Assn. (bd. dirs. 1996—), Ala. Soc. for Cripple Children and Adults (bd. mem.), English Speaking Union (bd. dirs. 1997—). Republican. Home: 7157 Pine Crest Dr Montgomery AL 36117-7413

**KLOSOWSKI, THOMAS KENNETH,** lawyer; b. Little Falls, Minn., June 22, 1961; s. Melvin and Jacqueline Klosowski. BA summa cum laude, St. Cloud (Minn.) State U., 1983; JD cum laude, U. Minn., 1986. Bar: Minn. 1986, U.S. Dist. Ct. Minn. 1986, U.S. Ct. Appeals (8th cir.) 1987, U.S. Dist. Ct. Colo. 1998. Assoc. Dorsey & Whitney, Mpls., 1986-89; assoc., then ptnr. Cosgrove, Flynn & Gaskins, Mpls., 1989—; course dir. Minn. State Bar Assn. product liability courses, 1997; mem. faculty product liability ABA, Boston, 1998. Author: Expert Witnesses, Bench and Bar of Minnesota, 1997. Bd. dirs. Playwright's Ctr., Mpls., 1998—. Mem. ABA, Minn. State Bar Assn., Def. Rsch. Inst. Avocations: downhill skiing, hunting. Product liability, General civil litigation. Office: Cosgrove Flynn & Gaskins 2900 333 S 7th St Minneapolis MN 55402

**KLOSS, WILLIAM DARRELL, JR.,** lawyer; b. Nelsonville, Ohio, Aug. 22, 1963; s. William Darrell and Joanne (Nauman) K. BS, Miami U., 1985; JD, U. Cin., 1988. Bar: Ohio 1988, U.S. Dist. Ct. (so. dist.) Ohio 1988. Pntr. Vorys Sater Seymour & Pease, Columbus, Ohio, 1988—. Mem. Ohio Bar Assn., Columbus Bar Assn., Order of the Coif. Republican. Lutheran. Avocations: golf, skiing, sailing, bicycling, weight-lifting. General civil litigation, Product liability. Home: 3337 Somerford Rd Columbus OH 43221-1436 Office: Vorys Sater Seymour & Pease 52 E Gay St Columbus OH 43215-3161

**KLOTHEN, KENNETH,** lawyer; b. 1951. BA, Swarthmore Coll.; JD, Georgetown U. Gen. counsel Corp. for Nat. and Cmty. Svc., Washington. Mem. ABA. Office: Office Gen Counsel 1201 New York Ave NW Washington DC 20525-0001*

**KLOTSCHE, JOHN CHESTER,** lawyer; b. Milw., June 18, 1942; s. Johannes Martin and Roberta (Roberts) K.; m. Christine Elizabeth Nelson, May 12, 1975; children: Karissa Faith, Jason Martin, Jonathan William. BS, U. Ariz., 1964; JD, U. Wis., 1967. Bar: Wis. 1967, Ill. 1968, U.S. Dist. Ct. (no. dist.) Ill. 1968, U.S. Ct. Appeals (7th cir.) 1970, Tex. 1987, U.S. Supreme Ct. 1987, U.S. Ct. Appeals (5th cir.) 1989, U.S. Dist. Ct. (no. dist.) Tex. 1990, U.S. Ct. Appeals (6th cir.), U.S. Claims Ct., U.S. Tax Ct. Law clk. to presiding justice Wis. Supreme Ct., Madison, 1967-68; assoc. Baker & McKenzie, Chgo., 1968-73, ptnr., 1973-87; ptnr. Baker & McKenzie, Dallas, 1987-93, L.A., 1993-94, Palo Alto, 1994—. Contbr. articles to profl. jours. Named Order of Coif. Mem. ABA, Ill. Bar Assn., Wis. Bar Assn., Tex. Bar Assn., Phi Delta Phi. Corporate taxation, Private international. Office: Baker & McKenzie 660 Hansen Way Palo Alto CA 94304-1044

**KLOTT, DAVID LEE,** lawyer; b. Vicksburg, Miss., Dec. 10, 1941; s. Isadore and Dorothy (Lipson) K.; m. Maren J. Randrup, May 25, 1975. BBA summa cum laude, Northwestern U., 1963; JD cum laude, Harvard U., 1966. Bar: Calif. 1966, U.S. Ct. Claims. 1968, U.S. Supreme Ct. 1971, U.S. Tax Ct. 1973, U.S. Ct. Appeals (Fed. cir.) 1982. Ptnr. Pillsbury, Madison & Sutro, San Francisco, 1966—; mem. tax adv. group to sub-chpt. C J and K, Am. Law Inst.; tchr. Calif. Continuing Edn. of Bar, Practising Law Inst., Hastings Law Sch., San Francisco; bd. dirs. and counsel Marin Wine and Food Soc. Commentator Calif. Nonprofit Corp. Law; bd. dirs. Joan Shorenstein Barone Found. for Harvard, The Phyllis J. Shorenstein Fund for the Asian Art Mus. San Francisco; counsel Drum Found. Mem. ABA (tax exempt fin. com.), Calif. State Bar Assn. (tax sect.), San Francisco Bar Assn., Am.-Korean Taekwondo Friendship Assn. (1st dan-black belt), Harvard Club, Northwestern Club, Olympic Club, City Club San Francisco (founding mem.), Bay Club (charter mem.), Harbor Point Racquet and

Beach Club, Internat. Wine and Food Soc. (bd. dirs., exec. com., bd. govs. Ams.), Beta Gamma Sigma, Beta Alpha Psi (pres. local chpt.). Corporate taxation. Office: Pillsbury Madison & Sutro 235 Montgomery St Ste 1616 San Francisco CA 94104-2902

**KLOZE, IDA IRIS,** lawyer; d. Max and Bertha (Samet) K. A.A., George Washington U., 1944, AB, 1947; LLB, U. Md., 1926; JD, 1967. Bar: Md. 1927, U.S. Supreme Ct. 1949. Sole practice, Balt., 1927-34; dep. collector IRS, Balt., 1934-39; with GAO, 1943-45, War Assets Adminstrn., 1945-49, Labor Dept., 1950-53, FTC Antitrust Divsn., 1956-71; vol. atty. Pro Bono Law Litigation Divsn. Pub. Citizen, Washington, 1972-76; ret. Mem. Mrs. Rosalyn Carter's Com. Mental Health; exec. sec. Commn. for Prevention Infantile Paralysis, Balt., 1940-42; lobbyist Md. Legis., U.S. Congress for Equal Rights Amendment Constitution; rep. Indsl. Coun. Nat. Womens Party, Balt., 1940-42; sec. Citizen's Commn. Md., Balt., 1935-39; trial atty. Fed. Trade Commn., U.S. Anti-Trust Divsn. Mem. ABA, Women's Bar Assn. (v.p. Balt. 1928-32), Profl. Women's Coun. (pres. 1928-33), Nat. Women's Party (lobbyist, co-chmn. campaign com. Md. for re-election FDR for 4th term, legal asst. life mem. 1951—), Fed. Bar Assn. (rec. sec., mem. nat. coun., sec. com. gen. counsels 1951-52).

**KLUGE, WILLIAM FREDERICK,** lawyer; b. Allentown, N.J., Nov. 3, 1950; s. Herbert William and Hertha Meta (Tollner) K.; m. Louise Anne Pleva, Apr. 5, 1974 (div. 1980); m. Tina Marie Swickrath, May 13, 1983; children: Danielle Marie, Tyler William, Jessica Kristen. BA, Alderson-Broaddus Coll., Philippi, W.Va., 1973; JD, Ohio No. U., Ada, 1976. Bar: Ohio 1976, U.S. Dist. Ct. (no. dist.) Ohio, 1977, U.S. Ct. Appeals (6th cir.) 1984, U.S. Supreme Ct. 1986. Prosecutor Lima (Ohio) Law Dirs. Office, 1976-78; ptnr. Rizor, Minnard, Hamman, Kluge & Rizor, Lima, 1979-80, Dugan, Kluge, Donohue & Williams, Lima, 1980-89; sr. ptnr. Kluge, Pitts, Santo & Iseman, Lima, 1989—; pub. defender Lima Pub. Defenders Office, 1982—; mem. Ohio Death Penalty Task Force, Columbus, 1986—, Ohio Supreme Ct. Rule 65 Com., 1987—. Contbr. articles to profl. jours. Mem. Gov.'s Panel on Battered Women, Columbus, 1990—, Ohio Pub. Defender Rules Rev. Com., 1990—. Mem. Ohio Bar Assn., Ohio Assn. Criminal Def. Lawyers (founder, treas. 1989-90, bd. dirs., pres. award 1990, v.p. seminars 1990-91, pres. 1992-93), FOP, Elks. Republican. Methodist. Avocations: basketball, gardening, reading, antiques. Criminal, Education and schools, Probate. Home: 115 Orchard Dr Elida OH 45807-1083 Office: Kluge Pitts Santo & Iseman 124 S Metcalf St Lima OH 45801-4746

**KLUKAS, ELIZABETH ANN,** lawyer; b. Bensenville, Ill., Oct. 26, 1963; d. Karl Edward and Elizabeth Jane (Schueler) K. BA in Econs., BA in History, U. Ill., 1985; JD cum laude, No. Ill. U., 1989. Bar: Ill. 1989, Mo. 1990, U.S. Dist. Ct. (so. dist.) Ill. 1989, U.S. Dist. Ct. (no. dist.) Ill. 1993, U.S. Dist. Ct. (ea. dist.) Mo. 1991, U.S. Ct. Appeals (7th cir.) 1991. Assoc. Heyl, Royster, Voelker & Allen, Edwardsville, Ill., 1989-93, Block, Krockey, Cernugel & Cowgill, Joliet, Ill., 1993—. Mem. ABA, Ill. Bar Assn., Will County Bar Assn. Personal injury, Product liability, General civil litigation. Office: Block Krockey Cernugel & Cowgill 19 W Jefferson St Joliet IL 60432-4390

**KLUNDER, SCOTT ROSS,** lawyer, real estate broker; b. Chgo., Dec. 6, 1948; s. Willard Carl and Dorothy Irene (Ross) K.; m. Rovenna Maria Duncan, Aug. 9, 1998; 1 child, Pike Nelson. BA, Miami U. of Ohio, 1970; JD, Wash. U., 1973. Bar: Mo. 1974, Colo. 1975, Ill. 1981. Prin. Klunder & Assocs., Morton Grove, Ill., 1981—. Prodr., dir. (TV show) Party Line, 1995-97; author: Indian Lore, 1995. Founder, pres. First Party, Morton Grove, 1993-98. Avocations: nature, Native American history, exercise. General practice, General civil litigation, Real property. Home: 5757 N Sheridan Rd Chicago IL 60660-4746 Office: Klunder & Assocs 5945 Dempster St Morton Grove IL 60053-3056

**KLYMAN, ANDREW MICHAEL,** lawyer; b. Boston, Mar. 2, 1953; s. Leo and Beth (Murstein) K.; m. Carol Anne Cioe, May 20, 1984. B.A., U. Mass., 1974; J.D., U. Miami, Coral Gables, Fla., 1977. Bar: Fla. 1977, U.S. Dist. Ct. (so. dist.) Fla. 1981, Mass. 1987. Assoc. Victor Eskenas, P.A., Miami, Fla., 1978; asst. pub. defender, West Palm Beach, Fla., 1978-84; assoc. Cohen, Scherer, Cohn & Silverman, P.A., North Palm Beach, Fla., 1984-86; staff atty. Com. for Pub. Counsel Services, Springfield, Mass., 1986—, atty. in charge, 1990—. Mem. Fla. Bar Assn., Hampden County Bar Assn. Criminal. Home: 267 Northwest Rd Westhampton MA 01027-9542 Office: Com for Pub Counsel Svcs 1145 Main St Springfield MA 01103-2123

**KMIEC, STEVEN GERARD,** lawyer; b. West Allis, Wis., Jan. 28, 1965; s. Marian Ralph and Jeannie Rose K.; m. Kathi Jo Anderson, Oct. 22, 1994; 1 child, Abigail Jo. BA, U. Wis. (Milw.), 1988; JD, Marquette U., 1991. Bar: Wis. 1991, we. and ea. dist. cts. Wis. 1991. Office mgr. Kmiec Law Offices, Milw., 1984-91, atty., 1991—. Presenter Moot Ct. presentation State Bar Wis., West Allis, 1996. Mem. ABA, ATLA, Wis. Acad. Trial Lawyers, Milw. Bar Assn. Roman Catholic. Personal injury, Product liability, Workers' compensation. Office: 3741 W National Ave Milwaukee WI 53215-1050

**KMIOTEK-WELSH, JACQUELINE,** lawyer; b. Bklyn., Dec. 31, 1959; d. Casimir Edward and Anna Catherine Kmiotek; m. James Winfield Welsh III. BA, St. John's U., N.Y.C., 1981, JD, 1983; MBA, NYU, 1991. Bar: N.Y. 1984, U.S. Dist. Ct. (so. and ea. dists.) N.Y. 1984, U.S. Dist. Ct. (we. dist.) N.Y. 1992, U.S. Supreme Ct. 1989. Asst. counsel N.Y. Job Devel. Auth., 1984-85; assoc. Squadron, Ellenoff, Pleasant & Lehrer, N.Y.C., 1985; assoc. atty. N.Y. Power Authority, 1985-86, atty., 1986-90, sr. atty., 1990-99; prin., 1999—. Fellow N.Y. Bar Found., N.Y. State Bar Assn. (mem. Ho. of Dels. 1993-96, exec. com. young lawyers sect. 1993-97, pub. utility law com. 1994—, chair young lawyers sect., com. profl. svc. project on women subcom. 1994-96, chair young lawyers sect. com. on pub. svcs. and pro-bono project on disaster legal assistance 1994-95, mem. 1995-96, mem. com. 1995—, mem. internat. law and practice sect. com. on U.S.-Can. law 1994—, young lawyer divsn. pub. utility law com.), Am. Bar Found., young Lawyers Divsn.; mem. ABA (fellow young lawyers divsn., liaison pub. contract law sect. 1988-90, exec. com. 1988-89, vice-chmn. 1989-91, chmn. 1991—, young lawyers divsn. pub. utility law com., internat. law exec. com. 1989-91, mem. govt. lawyers exec. com. 1990-91, liaison coord. group on energy law 1990-92, coord. group energy law 1992-95, mem. com. sect. of real property, probate & trust law 1995-97, liaison ABA Jour. 1992-95, mem. Ho. of Dels. 1993-96, vice chair bylaws com. govt. and pub. sector lawyer's divsn. 1993-95, vice chmn. young lawyer divn. publs. com. 1995-96, vice chair women in the profession com. 1994-95, judge awards of achievement com. 1992-95, mem. exec. coun. young lawyer's divsn. 1993-95, 4th dist. rep., mem. membership com. sect. real property probate trust law, 1995-96, liaison, 1995-97, vice chair publ. com. 1995-96, mem. editl. bd. sect. pub. utility comm. transp. law 1996—), Fed. Energy Bar Assn., Phi Alpha Delta. Office: NY Power Authority 1633 Broadway New York NY 10019-6708

**KNABE, BRUCE DAVID,** lawyer; b. Cin., Dec. 29, 1967; s. Arthur Tompkins and Peggy Lou K.; m. Christina Marie Schmerber Knabe, Mar. 8, 1997. BA, Miami U., Oxford, Ohio, 1990; JD, Salmon P. Chase Coll. Law, Alexandria, Ky., 1994. Bar: Ohio, Ind. Assoc. atty. McIntosh, McIntosh & Knabe, Cin., 1994—. Mem. Nat. Rifle Assn., Alexandria, Va., 1993, Ohio Farm Bur., Columbus, 1997. Mem. Ohio State Bar Assn., Cin. Bar Assn., Ind. State Bar Assn., Cin. Claims Assn. Republican. Lutheran. Avocations: motocycles, firearms. General civil litigation, Insurance, Probate. Office: McIntosh McIntosh & Knabe 700 Walnut St Ste 200 Cincinnati OH 45202-2015

**KNAPP, DENNIS RAYMOND,** federal judge; b. Buffalo, W.Va., May 13, 1912; s. Amon Lee and Ora Alice (Forbes) K.; m. Helen Ewers Jordan, June 1, 1935; children: Mary F., Margaret Ann, Dennis Raymond. AB, W.Va. Inst. Tech., 1932, LLD, 1972; AM, W.Va. U., 1934, LLB, 1940. Bar: W.Va. 1940. High sch. tchr. Putnam County, W.Va., 1932-35; supt. schs., 1935-37; practiced in Nitro, 1940-56; judge Ct. of Common Pleas, Kanawha County, W.Va., 1957-70; U.S. dist. judge for So. Dist. W.Va., Charleston, 1970-93, sr. judge, 1993—; Vice pres., dir. Bank of Nitro, 1949-70; v.p. Hygeia, Inc., 1968-70. Bd. dirs. Goodwill Industries, Inc., 1968-70; adv. bd. Marshall U., Huntington, W.Va. With AUS, 1944-46. Named Alumnus of Year W.Va. Inst. Tech., 1967. Mem. Am., W.Va. bar assns., W.Va. Jud. Assn., W.Va. Tech. Coll. Alumni Assn. (pres. 1968). Republican. Methodist. Home: 705 Club Ridge Ct Longwood FL 32779-2222 Office: US Courthouse PO Box 2546 Charleston WV 25329-2546

**KNAPP, JAMES IAN KEITH,** judge; b. Bklyn., Apr. 6, 1943; s. Charles Townsend and Christine (Grange) K.; m. Joan Elizabeth Cunningham, June 10, 1967 (div. Mar. 1971); 1 child, Jennifer Elizabeth; m. Carol Jean Brown, July 14, 1981; children: Michelle Christine, David Michael Keith. AB cum laude, Harvard U., 1964; JD, U. Colo., 1967; M in Law in Taxation, Georgetown U., 1989. Bar: Colo. 1967, Calif. 1968, U.S. Supreme Ct. 1983, D.C. 1986, Ohio 1995. Dep. dist. atty. County of L.A., 1968-79; head dep. dist. atty. Pomona br. office, 1979-82; dep. asst. atty. gen. criminal divsn. U.S. Dept. Justice, Washington, 1982-86, dep. assoc. atty. gen., 1986-87, dep. asst. atty. gen. tax divsn., 1988-89, acting asst. atty. gen. tax divsn., 1989, acting dep. chief organized crime sect. criminal divsn., 1989-91, dep. dir., asset forfeiture office criminal divsn., 1991-94; adminstrv. law judge Social Security Adminstrn., 1994—. Editor: California Uniform Crime Charging Standards and Manual, 1975. Vice chmn. Young Reps. Nat. Fedn., 1973-75; pres. Calif. Young Reps., 1975-77; mem. exec. com. Rep. State Ctrl. Com., Calif., 1975-77. Mem. Calif. Bar Assn., D.C. Bar Assn., Dayton Bar Assn. Episcopalian. Avocations: travel; reading. Office: Office of Hearings & Appeals 110 N Main St Ste 800 Dayton OH 45402-1786

**KNAPP, WHITMAN,** federal judge; b. N.Y.C., Feb. 24, 1909; s. Wallace Percy and Caroline Morgan (Miller) K.; m. Ann Fallert, May 17, 1962; 1 son, Gregory Wallace; children by previous marriage—Whitman Everett, Caroline Miller (Mrs. Edward M. W. Hines), Marion Elizabeth. Grad., Choate Sch., 1927; BA, Yale, 1931; LLB, Harvard U., 1934; LLD (hon.), CUNY City Coll., 1992. Bar: N.Y. 1935. With firm Cadwalader, Wickersham & Taft, N.Y.C., 1935-37; dep. asst. dist. atty. N.Y.C., 1937-41; with firm Donovan, Leisure, Newton & Lumbard, N.Y.C., 1941; mem. staff dist. atty. N.Y.C., 1942-50; chief indictment bd., 1942-44, chief, appeal bur., 1944-50; partner firm Barrett Knapp Smith Schapiro & Simon (and predecessors), 1950-72; U.S. dist. judge So. Dist. N.Y., 1972-87, sr. dist. judge, 1987—; spl. counsel N.Y. State Youth Commn., 1950-53; Waterfront Commn. N.Y. Harbor, 1953-54; mem. temp. commn. revision N.Y. State penal law and criminal code, 1964-69; chmn. Knapp Commn. to Investigate Allegations of Police Corruption in N.Y.C., 1969-72; gen. counsel Urban League Greater N.Y., 1970-72. Editor: Harvard Law Rev, 1933-34. Sec. Community Council Greater N.Y., 1952-58; pres. Dalton Schs., N.Y.C., 1950-53, Youth House, 1967-68; Trustee Univ. Settlement, 1945-64, Moblzn. for Youth, 1965-70. Mem. ABA, Am. Law Inst., Am. Bar Found., Am. Coll. Trial Lawyers, Assn. Bar City N.Y. (sec. 1946-49, chmn. exec. com. 1971-72). Office: 1201 US Courthouse 40 Foley Sq New York NY 10007-1502

**KNAUER, JAMES A.,** lawyer; b. Terre Haute, Ind., Sept. 18, 1946; s. Eugene A. and Dorothy R. K.; m. Jill A. Knauer, Apr. 25, 1988. BS, Ind. U., Bloomington, 1968, Ind. U., Indpls., 1972. Bar: Ind. 1972, U.S. Dist. Ct. (so. dist.) Ind. 1972, U.S. Ct. Appeals (7th cir.) 1972, U.S. Supreme Ct. 1977. Assoc. Korger Gardis & Regas, Indpls., 1972-70, mng. ptnr., 1979—; adj. prof. law Ind. U., 1987-88, 90-91; trustee U.S. Bankruptcy panel, 1980-88; pres. bd. dirs. Alpha Tau Omega, Inc., 1997-99; pres. The Lakeridge Group, 1998. Contbr. articles to profl. jours. Served tp capt. U.S. Army, 1971-72. Mem. ABA, ATLA, Comml. Law League of Am., Indpls. Bar Assn., Am. Bankruptcy Inst., Columbia Club, Woodstock Club. Republican. Bankruptcy, Contracts commercial, Federal civil litigation. Office: Kroger Gardis & Regis 900 Bank One Ctr Indianapolis IN 46204

**KNAUER, LEON THOMAS,** lawyer; b. N.Y.C., July 16, 1932; s. Lawrence R. and Loretta M. (Trainor) K.; m. Traude Kunz, Sept. 11, 1976; children: Robert A., Katrine M. BS in Math., Fordham U., 1954; JD, Georgetown U., 1961. Bar: Conn. 1961, D.C. 1961, U.S. Supreme Ct. 1965. Law clk. U.S. Dist. Ct. (D.C.), 1960-61; assoc. Wilkinson, Barker & Knauer LLP, Washington, 1961-68, ptnr., 1968-82; ptnr. Wilkinson Barker Knauer, LLP, Washington, 1982—; instr. Georgetown U. Law Center, 1964-65. Editor: Telecommunications Act Handbook: A Complete Reference for Business, 1996, Telecommunications Act of 1996-A Domestic and International Prospective for Business, 1998. Pres. Catholic Apostolic Mass Media, 1974-76, Knights of Malta, 1979—. Lt. USMC, 1954-57. Recipient award for outstanding legal svc. in media area NAACP, 1973, Officer's Cross for legal svcs. to Austria, 1992. Mem. Fed. Comms. Bar Assn. (editor Comms. Bar Jour. 1960-69, treas. 1980-82, mem. exec. com. 1982-84), Washington Golf and County Club, Cosmos Club Washington, Fordham U. Alumni of Washington (pres. 1982-85). Republican. Roman Catholic. Administrative and regulatory, Private international, Communications. Office: 2300 N St NW #700 Washington DC 20037-1122

**KNEBEL, DONALD EARL,** lawyer; b. Logansport, Ind., May 26, 1946; s. Everett Earl and Ethel Josephina (Hultgren) K.; m. Joan Elizabeth Vest, June 5, 1976 (div. 1980); 1 child, Mary Elizabeth. BEE with highest distinction, Purdue U., 1968; JD magna cum laude, Harvard U., 1974. Bar: Ind. 1974, U.S. Ct. Appeals (7th cir.) 1980, U.S. Ct. Appeals (3rd cir.) 1986, U.S. Ct. Appeals (6th cir.) 1987, U.S. Ct. Appeals (fed. cir.) 1988. Assoc. Barnes, Hickam, Pantzer & Boyd, Indpls., 1974-81; ptnr. Barnes & Thornburg, Indpls., 1981—. Contbr. articles on intellectual property, antitrust and distbn. law to profl. publs. Trustee Indpls. Civic Theatre, 1986-95, chmn., 1988-91, hon. trustee, 1995—. Mem. ABA, Ind. Bar Assn., Indpls. Bar Assn., 7th Cir. Bar Assn., Kiwanis (pres. 1991-92), Columbia Club. Antitrust, Intellectual property, Federal civil litigation. Office: Barnes & Thornburg 11 S Meridian St Indianapolis IN 46204-3506

**KNECHT, TIMOTHY HARRY,** lawyer; b. Flint, Mich., Nov. 6, 1953; s. Wayne Warren and Nancy Jane (Post) K.; m. Linda Marie D'Appolonia, Aug. 14, 1976; children: Nicole Constance, Colleen Lin, Patric Timothy. BA in Econs., Duke U., 1975; JD, Detroit Coll. of Law, 1979. Shareholder Cline, Cline & Griffin, Flint, 1979—. Bd. dirs. Flint Inst. Arts, 1985-91, trustee, 1985-91; bd. dirs. Friends of Modern Art, Flint, 1980-86, Flint Environ. Action Team, 1985-93, treas., 1985-88, pres. 1988-93; legal com. rep., Flint Area Health Fedn., 1986-92; century mem. Boy Scouts Am.; trustee Grand Blanc Cmty. Fund, 1993—, pres., 1998-99; trustee Family Svc. Agy., 1993—, pres., 1998-99. Mem. ABA, Def. Rsch. Inst., Mich. Def. Trial Counsel, Genesee County Bar Assn.(treas. 1986-87, dir. 1988-91, coun. negligence law sect. 1995—), Mich. Bar Assn., Flint Golf Club. Avocations: snow skiing, water sports, sailing, swimming, aviation. Insurance, Personal injury. Home: 5112 Territorial Rd Grand Blanc MI 48439-2049 Office: Cline Cline & Griffin 1000 Mott Foundation Bldg Flint MI 48502-1861

**KNECHT, WILLIAM L.,** lawyer; b. Lock Haven, Pa., Jan. 15, 1946; s. Clair N. and Betty R. (Harter) K.; m. Margaret E. O'Malley, June 10, 1972; children: William E., Jennifer M. BA, Pa. State U., 1967; JD, Dickinson Sch. Law, 1970. Bar: Pa. 1970, U.S. Supreme Ct. 1976, U.S. Tax Ct. 1981, U.S. Dist. Ct. (middle dist.) Pa. 1973, Ct. Common Pleas 1970. Assoc. McCormick, Lynn, Reeder, Nichols & Sarno, Williamsport, Pa., 1973-76; ptnr. McCormick, Reeder, Nichols, Bahl, Knecht & Person, Williamsport, 1976-96, McCormick Law Firm, Williamsport, 1996—; bankruptcy trustee U.S. Justice Dept., Williamsport, Pa., 1978-91. Editor Lycoming Reporter, 1976—. 1st lt. U.S. Army, 1971-73. Mem. ABA, Pa. Bar Assn., Lycoming County Law Assn. (exec. com. 1976—), Lycoming Law Assn. (pres. 1995), Ross Club. Republican. United Ch. of Christ. Avocations: stamps and first day cover collecting. Banking, Bankruptcy, Real property. Home: 253 Lincoln Ave Williamsport PA 17701-2237 Office: McCormick Law Firm PO Box 577 835 W 4th St Williamsport PA 17703-0577

**KNEE, PEGGY SHEAHAN,** lawyer; b. N.Y.C., Apr. 8, 1960; d. Michael Joseph and Alice Teresa (Coleman) Sheahan; m. Lawrence Klestinec, Oct. 17, 1987 (div. June 1989); m. Robert Alan Knee, May 5, 1991; children: Kylie Sheahan, Mollie Hanna. BA, Fordham Coll., 1981, JD, 1984; LLM in Taxation, N.Y. U., 1984. Bar: N.Y. 1985, N.J. 1986, U.S. Dist. Ct. N.J. 1986, Fla. 1992. Assoc. Hannoch Weisman, 1986-87, McCarter & English, Newark, 1987-88; prin. Winne, Banta & Rizzi, Hackensack, N.J., 1988-95; ptnr. Dillon, Bitar & Luther, Morristown, N.J., 1995; counsel Deener, Feingold & Steen, Hackensack, N.J., 1995-96; private practice Oradell, N.J., 1996-97; ptnr. Hartman, Winnicki & Finnerty P.C., Paramus, N.J., 1997-98; prin. Knee Law Firm LLC, Hackensack, 1998—. Contbr. articles to profl. jours. Fellow Am. Coll. Trust and Estate Counsel; mem. N.J. State Bar Assn. (chair real property, probate and trust law sect., chair women in profession sect.), Estate Planning Council No. N.J. (treas. 1998). Republican. Roman Catholic. Probate, Taxation, general, Estate planning. Office: Knee Law Firm LLC Ct Plz N 25 Main St Ste 200 Hackensack NJ 07601-7015

**KNEE, STEPHEN H.,** lawyer; b. Newark, Oct. 15, 1940; s. Simon E. and Mollie (Liest) K.; m. Carole Leibowitz, Feb. 17, 1984; children: Robert A., David E., Dana R. AB, Duke U., 1962; JD, N.Y.U., 1965. Bar: N.J. 1965, N.Y. 1981, U.S. Ct. Appeals (3rd cir.) 1981, U.S. Supreme Ct. 1969, U.S. Dist. Ct. (so. dist.) N.Y. 1999. Law sec. Superior Ct. of N.J., Paterson, 1965-66; ptnr. Stryker, Tams & Dill, LLP, Newark, 1966-98, Saiber, Schlesinger, Satz & Goldstein, LLC, Newark, 1998—. Author: Buying and Selling Businesses, 1996. Trustee N.J. Shakespeare Festival, 1988—, sec.; trustee Jewish Family Services of Metrowest, 1988—. Mem. ABA (com. on negotiated acquistions, subcom. on uniform securities act of state regulation of securities com.), N.J. Bar Assn. (dir. corp. and bus. law sect. 1979—, chmn. 1984-86, program com. 1991-97), Inst. for Continuing Legal Edn. (mem. adv. com. 1980—), Essex County Bar Assn., Am. Coll. Investment Counsel, Nat. Assn. Bond Lawyers. General corporate, Bankruptcy, Finance. Office: Saiber Schlesinger Satz & Goldstein LLC One Gateway Ctr Newark NJ 07102

**KNEISEL, EDMUND M.,** lawyer; b. Atlanta, Feb. 21, 1946; s. John F. and Mary E. (Moore) K.; m. Leslie A. Jones, June 19, 1976; 1 child, Mary Kathleen. AB, Duke U., 1968; JD, U. Ga., 1974. Bar: Ga. 1974, U.S. Dist. Ct. (no. and mid. dists.) Ga. 1976, U.S. Ct. Appeals (4th, 5th, 6th and 11th cirs.) 1976, U.S. Supreme Ct. 1984. Law clk. to Hon. R.C. Freeman U.S. Dist. Ct. (no. dist.) Ga., Atlanta, 1974-76; assoc. Kilpatrick & Cody, Atlanta, 1976-82; ptnr. Kilpatrick Stockton LLP, 1982—. Mng. editor Ga. Law Rev., Athens, 1973-74; contbr. articles to profl. jours. Lt. USNR, 1968-71. Mem. ABA, Lawyers Club Atlanta, Druid Hills Golf Club. Labor, Federal civil litigation, Insurance. Office: Kilpatrick Stockton LLP 1100 Peachtree St NE Ste 2800 Atlanta GA 30309-4501

**KNEPP, VIRGINIA LEE HAHN,** legal assistant; b. South Bend, Ind., Nov. 1, 1946; d. Charles William and Mary Louise (Hunter) Hahn; m. James Patrick Knepp, Apr. 20, 1968; children: Meredith Leigh, Melanie Leigh. BS in Bus., Ind. U., 1971. Legal asst. Hahn, Walz, Knepp & Dvorak, South Bend, Ind., 1983—; mem. Ind. allocation com. for Social Svc. Block Grants. Founder YWCA Women's Shelter, South Bend, 1978; founder, facilitator Women's Support Group, South Bend, 1979-90; vol. coord. Olympic Town Internat./Spl. Olympics, 1984-87, Kids Kingdom, South Bend, 1991, Children's Dispensary, South Bend, 1981-93, adv. coun., 1994, St. Joseph County Scholarship Found., 1990, Am. Cancer Soc., St. Joseph County, 1988-89; bd. dirs. Corvilla Inc., South Bend, 1989-96; treas. Dvorak for State Rep., 1986—, Very Spl. Arts Ind., 1980—, pres., 1995-97, South Bend Heritage Found., 19990-95; active Gov. Bayh Commn., 1991—; chmn. Domestic Violence Prevention and Treatment Coun., Michiana Arts and Sci. Coun.'s Carnival for the Arts; bd. dirs. South Bend Heritage Found., 1991-95. Mem. AAUW, Hoosier Art Patrons, Thalia Sorority (pres. 1988), Ind. Lawyers Aux. Avocations: needlepoint, soccer, tennis. Home: 7849 E Crestwood Way Scottsdale AZ 85250-7625 Office: Hahn Walz Knepp & Dvorak 509 W Washington St South Bend IN 46601-1527

**KNEPPER, KATHLEEN N.,** lawyer; b. Mpls., May 19, 1946; d. John Henry and Helen (Kohlan) Buelow; children: Eric, Zachary. BS with distinction, U. Minn., 1968; JD, DePaul U., Chgo., 1979; LLM in Health Law, St. Louis U., 1995. Bar: Ill. 1979. Atty. Ill. Assn. Sch. Bds., Lombard, 1979-81, Ill. State Bd. Edn., Springfield, 1981-83, Ill. Dept. Nuclear Safety, Springfield, 1983-85, Sangamon County State's Atty.'s Office, Springfield, 1985-95; dep. dir. divsn. legal svcs. Mo. Dept. Social Svcs., Jefferson City, 1995—. Contbr. articles to profl. jours. Pres. bd. Helping Hands, Springfield, 1989-90; pres. Zoning Bd. of Appeals, LaGrange, Ill., 1980-81. Recipient Golden Rule award for exceptional voluntary svc. J.C. Penney, 1990. Unitarian Universalist.

**KNICKERBOCKER, ROBERT PLATT, JR.,** lawyer; b. Hartford, Conn., Sept. 23, 1944; s. Robert P. and Audrey Jane (Stempel) K.; m. Kathleen A. Sakal (div. May 1985); children: Sarah, Abigail, Jonathan; m. Barbara Denise Whinnem, Oct. 3, 1987. BA, Cornell U., 1966; JD, U. Conn., 1969. Bar: Conn. 1969, U.S. Dist. Ct. Conn. 1969, U.S. Ct. Appeals (2d cir.) 1970. Law clk. to presiding justice Conn. Supreme Ct., Hartford, 1968-69; ptnr. Day, Berry & Howard, Hartford, 1969—; mem. State Implementation Plan Regulation Adv. Commn., 1979-90. Chmn. Town Plan and Zoning Commn., Glastonbury, Conn., 1975-79, Glastonbury Bd. Edn., 1982-86. Mem. Conn. Bar Assn., Greater Hartford C. of C. (state legis. com.). Republican. Episcopalian. Nuclear power, Administrative and regulatory, Communications. Office: Day Berry & Howard Cityplace Hartford CT 06103-3499

**KNIGHT, DAVID ARCENEAUX,** lawyer; b. Little Rock, Ark., Aug. 15, 1949; s. Mack and Elsie Teresa K.; m. Janna Riley, Nov. 1, 1995; 1 child, Katherine Riley. BA, Hendrix Coll., 1971; MPA, U. Okla., 1975; JD with high honors, U. Ark., 1978. Bar: Ark., U.S. Dist. Ct. (ea. dist.) Ark. Law clk. U.S. Ct. Appeals (8th cir.), St. Louis, 1978-79; staff atty. SEC, Washington, 1979-81; assoc., sr. ptnr. Rose Law Firm, Little Rock, Ark., 1981-88; exec. v.p., gen. counsel Stephens, Inc., Little Rock, Ark., 1988—. Editor-in-chief Ark. Law Rev., Fayetteville, 1978; adj. prof. U. Ark., Sch. Law, Little Rock, 1983-88. Dir., pres. Ark. Advocates Children & Families, Little Rock, 1992—. 1st lt. USAF, 1971-75. Methodist. Avocations: running, cycling, kayaking, skiing, sailing. Securities, Mergers and acquisitions, General corporate. Office: 111 Center St Little Rock AR 72201-4402

**KNIGHT, EDWARD S.,** lawyer, federal official; b. Amarillo, Tex., Jan. 20, 1951; m. Amy Knight; 1 child, Travis. BA in Latin Am. Studies with honors, U. Tex., Austin, 1973; JD, U. Tex., 1976. Bar: Tex., D.C., Supreme Ct. With Akin, Gump, Strauss, Hauer and Feld, Washington, 1978-82, ptnr., 1982-93; exec. sect., sr. adv. to sec. Treasury U.S. Dept. Treasury, Washington, 1993-94, gen. counsel, 1994-99; exec. v.p., chief legal officer NASD, Washington, 1999—. Mem. ABA, Supreme Ct. Bar Assn., D.C. Bar Assn., Tex. Bar Assn. Office: NADS 1735 K St NW Washington DC 20006-1516

**KNIGHT, FAITH TANYA,** lawyer; b. N.Y.C., Oct. 20, 1969; d. Ernest L. and Marion L. K. AB in Sociology, Dartmouth Coll., 1991; JD cum laude, Tulane U., 1996. Bar: Ga., U.S. Dist. Ct. (no. dist.) Ga. 1997. Assoc. Alston & Bird, Atlanta, 1996-99, Mc Dowell & Butler, 1999—; temp. in house counsel Charter Behavioral Health Svcs., Atlanta, 1998. Mem. Am. Health Lawyers Assn., Ga. Assn. Black Women Attys. Avocations: photography, travel. Health, Administrative and regulatory.

**KNIGHT, JEFFREY LIN,** lawyer, corporation executive; b. Evansville, Ind., Sept. 21, 1959; s. Jack T. and Ruth (Rogers) K.; m. Erin Elizabeth Hostettler, Dec. 18, 1982; children: Kathryn Ruth, Abigail Rebekah, Margaret Rachel, Caroline Elizabeth. BS, U. Evansville, 1981; JD, U. Ind., Indpls., 1984. Bar: Ind. 1984. Assoc. Clark, Statham, McCray, Thomas & Krohn, Evansville, 1984-85, Frank, Collins & Stephens, Evansville, 1985-88; v.p., sec., treas., gen. counsel Pacific Press & Shear, Inc., Mt. Carmel, Ill., 1988-90; gen. mgr. Pacific Press & Shear, Inc., 1991-93; corp. sec., gen. counsel Old Nat. Bancorp, 1993—. Mentor Evansville Vanderburgh Sch. Corp., 1984-87; campaign chmn. Hostettler For Congress Com., 1994, 96, 98. Mem. Ind. Bar Assn., Evansville Bar Assn., Am. Soc. Corp. Secs., Optimists (sec. 1987-88, v.p. 1988-89). Republican. Baptist. Avocations: golf, tennis. General corporate, General civil litigation, General practice. Home: 330 Largo Ct Evansville IN 47712-7616

**KNIGHT, MARGARETT LEE,** lawyer, editor; b. Newtown, Ind., Jan. 3, 1923; d. Charles Oscar and Edna (Pace) Smith; m. Robert Cook Knight, June 20, 1961. LL.B., Ind. U., 1945, J.D., 1965; A.B., Mills Coll., 1953; LL.M., Yale U., 1955. Bar: Ind. 1945. Dep. atty. gen. Ind. Home: 1318 Hoover Ln Indianapolis IN 46260-2832 Office: Atty Gen 219 State Office Bldg Indianapolis IN 46204-2212

**KNIGHT, MONTGOMERY, JR.,** lawyer; b. Atlanta, Nov. 1, 1932; s. Montgomery and Kimberly (Millner) K.; m. Jeraline Seelinger, Aug. 7, 1954; children: Paul, Kimberly Anne. AA, Coll. William and Mary, Norfolk, Va., 1952; AB, Coll. William and Mary, Williamsburg, Va., 1954, JD, 1956. Bar:

Va. 1956, U.S. Ct. Appeals (4th cir.) 1960. Ptnr. Knight, Clarke, Dolph & Rapaport, P.L.C., Norfolk, 1960-98; mem. Hofheimer Nuisbaum P.C., Norfolk, 1998—; life mem. Jud. Conf. of U.S. Ct. Appeals for 4th Circuit. Pres. Norfolk Sports Club, 1966, Chesapeake Athletic Club, 1963; bd. dirs. Norfolk Tides. Fellow Am. Coll. Trust and Estate Counsel (fiduciary litigation com. 1992—). Episcopalian. Avocations: golf, tennis, cars. Estate planning, Taxation, general, Probate. Office: 1700 Dominion Tower 999 Waterside Dr PO Box 3460 Norfolk VA 23514-3460

**KNIGHT, ROBERT HUNTINGTON,** lawyer, bank executive; b. New Haven, Feb. 27, 1919; s. Earl Wall and Frances Pierpont (Whitney) K.; m. Rosemary C. Gibson, Apr. 19, 1975; children—Robert Huntington, Jessie Valle, Patricia Whitney, Alice Isabel, Eli Whitney. Grad., Phillips Acad., Andover, Mass., 1936; B.A., Yale, 1940; LL.B., U. Va., 1947, LLM, 1949. Bar: N.Y. bar 1950. With John Orr Young, Inc. (advt. agy.), 1940-41; asst. prof. U. Va. Law Sch., 1947-49; assoc. firm Shearman & Sterling & Wright, N.Y.C., 1949-55; ptnr. Shearman & Sterling & Wright, 1955-58; dep. asst. sec. def. for internat. security affairs Dept. Def., 1958-61; gen. counsel Treasury Dept., 1961-62; ptnr. firm Shearman & Sterling, N.Y.C., 1962-80, sr. ptnr., 1980-85, of counsel, 1986—; dep. chmn. Fed. Res. Bank N.Y., 1976-77, chmn., 1977-83; counsel to bd. United Technologies Corp., 1974-85; dir. internat. bd. Owens-Corning Fiberglas Corp., 1989—; dir. I-Corps, Nat. Leadership Bank, Mercator, Inc., Citizen Exchange Coun.; mem. Intelsat Arbitration Panel, 1971-91. Bd. dirs. Internat. Vol. Services; chmn. bd. dirs. U. Va. Law Sch. Found., 1970-90; bd. dirs. Asia Found.. Served to lt. col. USAAF, 1941-45. Mem. ABA, Fed. Bar Assn., Internat. Bar Assn., Inter-Am. Bar Assn., Assn. of Bar of City of N.Y., N.Y County Lawyers Assn., Internat. Law Assn., Washington Inst. Fgn. Affairs, Council Fgn. Relations, Pilgrims Club, Links Club, World Trade Ctr Club, River Club (N.Y.C.), Army and Navy Club, Met. Club (Washington), Round Hill Club (Greenwich, Conn.), Ocean Club (Ocean Ridge, Fla.), Farmington Club (Va.). Antitrust, General corporate, Private international. Home: 12 Knollwood Dr Greenwich CT 06830-4733 also: 570 Park Ave New York NY 10021-7370 also: 6767 N Ocean Blvd Ocean Ridge FL 33435-3394 Office: 599 Lexington Ave New York NY 10022-6030

**KNIGHT, TOWNSEND JONES,** lawyer; b. N.Y.C., Aug. 10, 1928; s. Jesse and Marguerite H. (Jones) K.; m. Elise Heck; children: Margaret Knight Dudley, Elise Knight Wallace, Jessica Knight Casoni. BS, Harvard U., 1949; JD, Columbia U., 1952. Bar: N.Y. 1952. Assoc. Curtis, Mallet-Prevost, Colt & Mosle, N.Y.C., 1953-65, ptnr., 1965—. Trustee Audrey Cohen Coll., N.Y.C., 1969—, Cold Spring Harbor (N.Y.) Lab., 1970-76, 82-88, 89-95, hon. trustee, 1995—; dir. Friends Ivory & Sime Trust Co., 1995—. Mem. ABA, N.Y. State Bar Assn., Assn. of Bar of City of N.Y., Downtown Assn., Harvard Club, Cold Spring Harbor Beach Club. Episcopalian. Avocation: photography. Banking, Probate, Private international. Office: Curtis Mallet-Prevost Colt & Mosle 101 Park Ave Fl 34 New York NY 10178-0061

**KNIGHT, W. DONALD, JR.,** lawyer; b. Macon, Miss., May 30, 1941. BA summa cum laude, Miss. State U., 1961; MA, Emory U., 1963; LLB, U. Va., 1967. Bar: Ga. 1967. Ptnr. King & Spalding, Atlanta, 1974; mem. adv. bd. N.Am. Free Trade & Investment Report. Co-author: Structuring Foreign Investment in U.S. Real Estate, 1982; editorial bd.: Va. Law Review; editorial advisory bd.: Tax Mgmt. Internat. Jour., 1981—; contbr. editor: Intertax (internat. tax review). Mem. ABA, Atlanta Bar Assn., Internat. Bar Assn., Internat. Fiscal Assn., Raven Soc., Order of the Coif, Omicron Delta Kappa. Office: King & Spalding 191 Peachtree St NE Ste 40 Atlanta GA 30303-1763

**KNIGHT, WILLIAM COLLINS, JR.,** lawyer; b. St. Louis, Jan. 24, 1938; s. W. Collins and Virginia (Koerner) K.; m. Betty Timberlake, Sept. 30, 1961; children: Elizabeth T. Knight Hubbard, Mary Virginia. BS, U. Ala., 1960, LLB, 1966. Bar: Ala. 1967, U.S. Dist. Ct. (no. and so. dists.) Ala. 1967, U.S. Ct. Appeals (11th and 5th cirs.) 1967. With labor relations dept. Ala. Power Co., Birmingham, 1960-67; adminstrv. ptnr. Burr and Forman and predecessor firm Thomas, Taliaferro, Forman, Burr & Murray, Birmingham, 1967—; adj. prof. Birmingham Sch. Law, U. Ala., 1974-78. Bd. dirs. Highlands Meth. Ch., Birmingham, 1962-64, YMCA, Birmingham, 1968-70, Better Bus. Bur., Birmingham, 1988—, Ala. Found. Hearing and Speech, 1972-75, pres. 1975. Capt. U.S. Army, 1960-62. Mem. ABA (ho. of dels. 1991—), ATLA, Ala. State Bar (adv. com. 1985-86, med. liaison tort reform com. 1985-86), Birmingham Bar Assn. (pres. 1987-88), Internat. Assn. Ins. Counsel, Ala. Def. Lawyers Assn. (prs. 1985-86), Nat. Assn. R.R. Trial Counsel, Am. Arbitration Assn., Redstone Club, Mountain Brook Club. Avocations: outdoor activities, cooking. General civil litigation, Personal injury, Toxic tort. Home: 3364 Hermitage Rd Birmingham AL 35223-2004 Office: Burr & Forman 3100 Southtrust Tower Birmingham AL 35203-5206

**KNISPEL, HOWARD EDWARD,** lawyer; b. Bklyn., Apr. 22, 1959; s. Joseph and Irene K.; m. Marisa Gonzalez, July 5, 1987; children: Jennifer, Stephen. BA, Rochester Inst. Tech., 1981; JD, NYU, 1988. Bar: N.Y. 1989, U.S. Dist. Ct. (so. and ea. dist.) 1990. Assoc. Lipsig, Sullivan & Liapakis, N.Y.C., 1988-89, Fein & Steinberg, Bklyn., 1990-91; pvt. practice N.Y.C., 1991-96, Sunrise, Fla., 1996-98; assoc. Assocs. and Bruce Sheiner, Ft. Myers, Fla., 1998, Feldman, Kramer & Monaco P.C., Hauppauge, N.Y., 1998—; instr. N.Y. Paralegal Sch., N.Y.C., 1994-96; adminstrv. law judge N.Y.C. Taxi Limousine Commn., 1995-96. Bd. dirs. Eisenhower Coll. Alumni Assn., Seneca Falls, N.Y., 1998. Democrat. Jewish. General practice, Family and matrimonial, Bankruptcy. Office: Feldman Kramer & Monaco PC Ste 400 330 Vanderbilt Motor Pkwy Hauppauge NY 11788-5110

**KNOBBE, LOUIS JOSEPH,** lawyer; b. Carroll, Iowa, Apr. 6, 1932; s. Louis C. and Elsie M. (Praeger) K.; m. Jeanette M. Sganga, Apr. 3, 1954; children: Louis, Michael, Nancy, John, Catherine. BSEE, Iowa State U., 1953; JD, Loyola U., L.A., 1959. Bar: Calif. 1960, U.S. Supreme Ct. 1963; U.S. Patent and Trademark Office. Tech. staff Bell Telephone Labs., 1953-54; patent engr. GE, Washington, 1955-56, N.Am. Aviation, Downey, Calif., 1956-59; patent lawyer Beckman Instruments, Fullerton, Calif., 1959-62; co-founder, ptnr. Knobbe, Martens, Olson & Bear, Newport Beach, Calif., 1962—; lectr. Am. Intellectual Property Law Assn., Computer Law Assn., Inc., L.A. Intellectual Property Law Assn., San Diego Bar Assn., Orange County Patent Law Assn.; adj. prof. Sch. Law U. San Diego, 1987—. Co-author: Attorney's Guide to Trade Secrets, 1972, 2d edit., 1996, How to Handle Basic Patent, 1992; contbg. author: Using Intellectual Property Rights to Protect Domestic Markets, 1986; contbr. articles to profl. jours. Bd. dirs. Orange County (Calif.) Performing Arts Ctr., 1975-83, Orange County chpt. Assn. Corp. Growth; past pres. Philaharmonic Soc. Orange County; bd. mem., past v.p. Opera Pacific, Orange County. Fellow Inst. Advancement Engring.; mem. ABA, IEEE (past chmn. Orange County sect., Centennial medal 1984), Am. Intellectual Property Law Assn., Am. Arbitration Soc. (mem. panel neutrals), State Bar Calif., Orange County Bar Assn. (mem. civil mediation panel), Orange County Patent Law Assn., San Diego Patent Law Assn., Licensing Execs. Soc., Santa Ana North Rotary, First Friday Friars, Pacific Club, Balboa Yacht Club, Phi Kappa Phi, Tau Beta Pi, Eta Kappa Nu. Avocations: boating, still and video photography, travel and exploration in Lake Powell, Death Valley, deserts of Arizona and Baja, California. Intellectual property, Patent, Trademark and copyright. Office: 620 Newport Center Dr Fl 16 Newport Beach CA 92660-6420

**KNÖBEL, DAVID HAROLD,** financial advisor, entrepreneur, retired lawyer; b. Beaufort, S.C., Sept. 5, 1951; s. William Harold and Joan (Purdy) K. BA in Polit. Sci., Calif. State U., Long Beach, 1974; postgrad., Cath. U., 1979, Nat. U., San Diego, 1980; JD, Western State U., Fullerton, Calif., 1982. Bar: Ind. 1983, U.S. Dist. Ct. (no. and so. dists.) Ind. 1983, U.S. Tax Ct. 1983, U.S. Ct. Mil. Appeals 1983. Pvt. practice fin. advisor Norco, Calif., 1980—; sole practice law Merrillville, Ind., 1983-96; owner LEC Enterprises Valparaiso, Ind., 1991—; instr. Am. Coll. Paralegal Studies, Detroit, 1984; cons., advisor SCORE, Gary, Ind., 1984-96; bd. dirs. Poma, Inc., Merrillville, Consumer Credit Counseling Soc. of N.W. Ind., Gary, Kairo's of Maine. Pres., v.p. Marlon Home Assn., Cedar Lake, Ind., 1984-88; mem. Kairos Internat. Prison Ministry. 1st lt. USMCR, 1975-77, Res., 1977-94. Mem. Marine Corps Assn., KC. Avocations: antique auto restoration, sailing. Home: 995 3rd St Norco CA 92860-2775

**KNOBLOCH, CHARLES SARON,** lawyer; b. Wayne, Mich., May 11, 1959; s. Faustyn Edwin and Ameaila Caroline (Marquardt) K. BS in Applied Geophysics with honors, Mich. Tech. U., 1980; JD, U. Houston, 1991; Diploma in Internat. Law, Col. William & Mary, Madrid, 1990, U. San Diego, Russia, 1991. Bar: Tex. 1992; cert. patent atty. U.S. Patent & Trademark Office, Coll. of State Bar of Tex., 1994-96. Pvt. practice Houston, 1992—; with DuPont/Conoco, Houston/Jakarta, 1980—; finalist, Outstanding Young Texans, Jaycees, 1993, adv. bd. Tex. Accts. and Lawyers for the Arts, 1997; bd. dirs. Houston Intranet, Inc., 1995. Chair M.D. Anderson Cancer Ctr. Network, Houston, 1997; nominated attendee John Ben Shepperd Pub. Leadership Forum, Austin, Tex., 1995. Recipient Engrg. Excellence award DuPont Engring., Imaging Tech. award, 1996. Mem. Houston Intellectual Property Law Assn., Indonesian Petroleum Assn., Amer. Bar Assn. (corp. law com.). Trademark and copyright, Patent, Intellectual property. Home: Jahorta Pouch PO Box 4569 Houston TX 77210-4569 Office: DuPont Conoco Jakarta Pouch PO Box 4569 Houston TX 77210-4569

**KNOLL, ALAN M.,** lawyer; b. N.Y.C., Dec. 11, 1963; 1 child, Alexander. BA, Bklyn. Coll., 1985; JD, U. Chgo., 1988. Bar: N.Y. 1989. Assoc. Milbank, Tweed, Hadleyn & McCloy, N.Y.C., 1988-93; ptnr. Orrick, Herrington & Sutcliffe, N.Y.C., 1993—. Securities. Office: Orrick Herrington & Sutcliffe LLP 666 5th Ave Rm 203 New York NY 10103-1798

**KNOLL, JEANNETTE THERIOT,** state supreme court justice; b. Baton Rouge; m. Jerold Edward Knoll; children: Triston Kane, Eddie Jr., Edmond Humphries, Blake Theriot, Jonathan Paul. BA in Polit. Sci., Loyola U., 1966, JD, 1969; LLM, U. Va., 1996; studied with Maestro Adler, Mannes Coll. of Music, 1962-63. Criminal defense atty., first asst. dist. atty. Twelfth Jud. Dist. Ct. Avoyelles Parish, 1972-82; gratuitous atty., advisor U.S. Selective Svc., Marksville, La.; judge (3d cir.) U.S. Ct. of Appeal, 1982-93; justice La. Supreme Ct., 1997—; instr. La. Jud. Coll.; chair CLE La. Ct. of Appeal Judges; mem. vis. com. Loyola U. Sch. of Law, Loyola Music Sch.; bd. dirs. Loyola U. Alumni Assn.; former mem. state bd. of La. commn. on law enforcement and criminal justice. Past pres. Bus. and Profl. Women's Club; Marksville C. of C.; active Am. Legion Aux. Recipient scholarship Met. Opera Assn., New Orleans Opera Guild. Office: La Supreme Ct 301 Loyola Ave New Orleans LA 70112-1814*

**KNOPF, AMY SUSAN,** lawyer; b. Utica, N.Y., Aug. 22, 1962; d. Donald and Audrey (Smith) Oshansky; m. Lawrence J. Knopf, June 26, 1988; children: Samuel, Alexa. BA, Brandeis U., 1983; JD, U. Mich., 1986. Bar: Mass. 1986. Atty.-advisor Social Security Adminstrn., Balt., 1986-87; asst. regional counsel Social Security Adminstrn., Boston, 1987—. Mem. Needham Hadassah (v.p. 1996—), Brandeis U. Alumni Admissions Coun. Home: 2 Winslow Rd Needham MA 02492-1140 Office: Social Security Admin Reg I 625 JFK Bldg Boston MA 02203

**KNOPF, BARRY ABRAHAM,** lawyer; b. Passaic, N.J., May 11, 1946; s. Edward and Sonia (Sameth) K.; children: Elisa, Scott. Student, Rutgers U., 1968, JD, 1972. Bar: N.J. 1972, U.S. Dist. Ct. N.J. 1972, U.S. Tax Ct. 1975, U.S. Supreme Ct. 1975, U.S. Ct. Appeals (3d cir.) 1981; cert. civil trial atty. Nat. Bd. Trial Advocacy, N.J. Supreme Ct. Assoc. Cohn & Lifland, Saddle Brook, N.J., 1972-75, ptnr., 1975—; instr. N.J. Inst. for Continuing Legal Edn., 1982—, Nat. Inst. Trial Advocacy, 1989—. Co-author: Professional Negligence, Law of Malpractice in New Jersey, 1979, 2d edit., 1984, 3d edit., 1990, 4th edit., 1996, Personal Injury Litigation Practice in New Jersey, 1990, Civil Trial Preparation, Practical skills Series, 1992, 2d edit., 1996; New Jersey Product Liability Law, 1994. V.p. Temple Beth Tikvah, Wayne, N.J., 1985-93, pres. 1993-95. Personal injury, Federal civil litigation, State civil litigation. Home: 1014 Smith Manor Blvd West Orange NJ 07052-4227 Office: Cohn Lifland Pearlman Herrmann & Knopf Park 80 West 1 Saddle Brook Rochelle Park NJ 07662

**KNOPIK, CHRISTOPHER SCOTT,** lawyer; b. South Bend, Ind., Nov. 8, 1959; s. Walter Michael and Ora Mae (Jones) K.; m. Andrea Kim Cheney, Nov. 12, 1988. BS, Fla. State U., 1980; JD, U. Va., 1983. Bar: Fla. 1983, U.S. Dist. Ct. (middle and so. dists.) Fla., U.S. Ct. Appeals (11th cir.), U.S. Supreme Ct. Law clk. U.S. Dist. Judge Hon. William Terrell Hodges, middle dist., Tampa, Fla., 1983-85; assoc. Holland and Knight, Tampa, Fla., 1985-86; shareholder Stagg, Hardy and Yerrid, Tampa, Fla., 1986-90, Yerrid, Knopik & Valenzuela, Tampa, Fla., 1990-96, Yerrid, Knopik & Mudano, Tampa, 1996—; Bd. cert. civil trial atty. Dir. YMCA of Hillsborough County, Tampa, 1983—, pres. downtown br., 1989-91; vol. Big Bros. of Hillsborough County, Tampa, 1982—; prodr. Tampa Bay Performing Arts Ctr., 1990—. Mem. Fla. Bar Assn., Hillsborough County Bar Assn., Assn. Trial Lawyers Am., Fed. Bar Assn., Am. Inns of Ct., Am. Judicature Soc., Maritime Law Assn., Bay Area Vol. Lawyers Assn., Am. Bd. Trial Advocates. Avocations: health and fitness, politics, reading, travel, sports. General civil litigation, Personal injury, Product liability. Home: 4817 S Sunset Blvd Tampa FL 33629-6416 Office: Yerrid Knopik & Mudano 101 E Kennedy Blvd Ste 2160 Tampa FL 33602-5187

**KNOPP, TIMOTHY JOHN,** lawyer; b. Selden, Kans., Jan. 25, 1958; s. Vincent J. and Juliana B. (Meitl) K.; m. Linda K. Mufich, Aug. 17, 1984; children: Millicent J., Lydia M. Student, Ft. Hays State U., 1976-77; BA, U. Kans., 1980, JD, 1983. Bar: Kans. 1983, U.S. Dist. Ct. Kans. 1983, U.S. Ct. Appeals (10th cir.) 1986, U.S. Ct. Claims, 1987, U.S. Supreme Ct. 1987, Mo. 1991, U.S. Dist. Ct. (we. dist.) Mo. 1992. Assoc. Law Office of Michael P. O'Keefe, Leawood, Kans., 1983-84; ptnr. O'Keefe Knopp & Weishaar, Leawood, 1984-94; pres. Timothy J. Knopp and Assocs., P.A., Overland Park, Kans., 1994—; pro bono atty. Kans. Legal Svcs., Olathe, 1986—. Mem. Kans. Bar Assn., Mo. Bar Assn., Johnson County Bar Assn. Contracts commercial, General practice, General civil litigation. Office: Knopp Law Office PA 6405 Metcalf Ave Ste 420 Overland Park KS 66202-3929

**KNORR, STEPHEN JAMES,** lawyer; b. Youngstown, Ohio, Oct. 1, 1951; s. John Andrew Knorr and Julia Elizabeth Donahue Knorr; m. Anne C. Overesch, Aug. 4, 1979 (div. Dec. 1980); m. Cheryl Jeanine Dickinson, Nov. 7, 1992. Bar: Ill. 1979, U.S. Dist. Ct. (no. dist.) Ill. 1979, U. S. Ct. Appeals (7th cir.) 1980, U.S. Dist. Ct. (no. dist.) Okla., U.S. Dist. Ct. (ea. dist.) Okla. 1993, U.S. Ct. Appeals (10th cir.) 1993. Assoc. Bergson Borkland Margoles & Adler, Washington, 1978, Jenner & Block, Chgo., 1979; law clk. to presiding justice U.S. Dist. Ct., Chgo., 1979-80; mem. staff Fed. Defender Program, Office of Pub. Defender, Chgo., 1980-93; fed. pub. defender Fed. Defender Program, Office of Pub. Defender, Tulsa, 1993—. Mem. Nat. Assn. Criminal Def. Lawyers, Tulsa Criminal Def. Lawyers Assn. (charter), Inns of Ct. (master). Democrat. Roman Catholic. Office: Office Fed Pub Defender Williams Ctr Tower Ste 1225 One W 3d St Tulsa OK 74103

**KNOWLES, EMMITT CLIFTON,** lawyer; b. Pensacola, Fla., Oct. 9, 1951; s. Lawrence Clifton and Emily (Josey) K.; m. Leigh Walton, Jan. 1, 1985; children: Margaret Emily, William Walton. BA magna cum laude, Vanderbilt U., 1973; JD, U. Tenn., 1977. Bar: Tenn. 1978, U.S. Dist. Ct. (ea. dist.) Tenn. 1978, U.S. Ct. Appeals (6th cir.) 1979, U.S. Dist. Ct. (mid. dist.) Tenn. 1980. Law clk. to chief judge U.S. Ct. Appeals (6th cir.), Cin., 1978-79; from assoc. to ptnr. Bass, Berry & Sims, Nashville, 1979—; mem. civil justice reform act adv. group Mid. Dist. Tenn., 1995-97. Editor-in-chief U. Tenn. Law Rev., 1977. Mem. ABA (appellate practice com.), Am. Judicature Soc. (bd. dirs. 1988-92), Tenn. Trial Lawyers Assn., Tenn. Bar Assn. (litigation sect., chair-elect 1990, chair 1991, chair CLE com. 1992-94), Nashville Bar Assn. (bd. dirs. young lawyers divsn. 1985-86, treas. divsn. 1987-88, trustee Meml. Fund 1987-90, bd. dirs., 1st v.p. 1995), Nashville Bar Found. (pres., chmn. 1990-93), Coll. of Law Alumni U. Tenn. (adv. coun. 1992-95), Order of Coif, Master of the Bench, Harry Phillips Am. Inn of Ct., Kiwanis, Masons, Shriners, Phi Beta Kappa. Democrat. Government contracts and claims, Federal civil litigation, State civil litigation. Office: Bass Berry & Sims 2700 1st American Ctr Nashville TN 37238

**KNOWLES, MARJORIE FINE,** lawyer, educator, dean; b. Bklyn., July 4, 1939; d. Jesse J. and Roslyn (Leff) Fine; m. Ralph I. Knowles, Jr., June 3, 1972. BA, Smith Coll., 1960; LLB, Harvard U., 1965. Bar: Ala., N.Y., D.C. Teaching fellow Harvard U., 1963-64; law clk. to judge U.S. Dist. Ct. (so. dist.), N.Y., 1965-66; asst. U.S. atty. U.S. Atty.'s Office, N.Y.C., 1966-67; asst. dist. atty. N.Y. County Dist. Atty., N.Y.C., 1967-70; exec. dir. Joint Found. Support, Inc., N.Y.C., 1970-72; asst. gen. counsel HEW, Washington, 1978-79; insp. gen. U.S. Dept. Labor, Washington, 1979-80; assoc. prof. U. Ala. Sch. Law, Tuscaloosa, 1972-75, prof., 1975-86, assoc. dean, 1982-84; law prof., dean Ga. State U. Coll. Law, Atlanta, 1986-91, law prof., 1986—; cons. Ford Found., N.Y.C., 1973-98, trustee Coll. Retirement Equities Fund, N.Y.C., 1983—; mem. exec. com. Conf. on Women and the Constn., 1986-88; mem. com. on continuing profl. edn. Am. Law Inst.-ABA, 1987-93. Contbr. articles to profl. jours. Am. Council Edn. fellow, 1976-77, Aspen Inst. fellow, Rockefeller Found., 1976. Mem. ABA (chmn. new deans workshop 1988), Ala. State Bar Assn., N.Y. State Bar Assn., D.C. Bar Assn., Am. Law Inst. Office: Ga State U Coll Law University Plz Atlanta GA 30303

**KNOWLES, RICHARD JOHN,** judge; b. Ft. Belvoir, Va., 1956; s. Richard Thomas and Barbara Jane Knowles. BA in English, U. Fla., 1978, JD, 1980. Bar: Colo. 1981, U.S. Dist. Ct. Colo. 1981, N.Mex. 1983, U.S. Dist. Ct. N.Mex. 1983, U.S. Tax Ct., U.S. Ct. Appeals (10th cir.), U.S. Supreme Ct.; specialist criminal law N.Mex Bd. Legal Specialization. Law clk. U.S. Ct. Appeals (10th cir.), Denver, 1981; assoc. Sumners, Miller & Clark, Denver, 1981-82; sole practice Roswell, N.Mex., 1982-83; asst. pub. defender State of N.Mex., Roswell, 1983-84, dist. defender, 1984-86; tng. dir. pub. defenders office State of N.Mex., Albuquerque, 1986-87, dist. defender, 1987-88; pvt. practice Albuquerque, 1988-95; judge U.S. Dist. Ct., Albuquerque. Critic films Roswell Daily Record, 1983-86. Bd. dirs. Counseling Assocs., Inc., Roswell, 1985-86. Named one of Outstanding Young Men Am., 1985. Mem. Colo. Bar Assn., N.Mex. Bar Assn. (criminal law sect., 1984-95, bd. dir. criminal law sect. 1992-95), Albuquerque Bar Assn., Nat. Assn. Criminal Def. Lawyers. Republican. Lodge: Rotary (bd. dirs. Roswell club 1984-86). Avocations: reading, films, writing, bicycling. Office: PO Box 488 Albuquerque NM 87103-0488

**KNOWLTON, KEVIN CHARLES,** lawyer; b. Syracuse, N.Y., Oct. 19, 1957; s. Erwin Leslie and Arlene Grace (Morgan) K.; m. Lois Jean Clair, July 21, 1979; children: Andrew, Keith, Lauren. BA cum laude, Houghton Coll., 1979; JD, Syracuse U., 1982. Bar: Fla. 1982, U.S. Dist. Ct. (mid. dist.) Fla. 1982, U.S. Ct. Appeals (11th cir.) 1982, U.S. Supreme Ct. 1986. Law clk. to judge 2nd Dist. Ct. Appeals, Lakeland, Fla., 1982-85; ptnr. Peterson & Myers P.A., Lakeland, 1985—, mgmt. com. Treas. Phoenix (N.Y.) Rep. Com., 1980-82, Planning Bd., 1980-82, Town of Schroeppel Planning Bd., 1980-82; chmn. bd. dirs. Lakeland Christian Sch.; chmn. pres.'s adv. coun. on excellence Houghton Coll.; chmn. exec. bd. dirs. Lake Morton Cmty. Ch., 1995—, elder; mem. instnl. rev. bd. Lakeland Regional Med. Ctr., mem. ethics com. N.Y. State Regents scholar 1975-79. Mem. ABA, Fla. Bar Assn., Lakeland Bar Assn. (chmn. law day legal forum 1986), Fla. Acad. Healthcare Attys., Am. Health Lawyers Assn., Christian Legal Soc., Houghton Coll. Alumni Assn. (pres. Orlando, Fla. chpt. 1985, 91—), Willson Inn of Ct., Lakeland Yacht and Country Club, Phi Alpha Theta. Avocations: basketball, snow skiing. Health, General civil litigation. Home: 839 Heathercrest Lakeland FL 33813-1240 Office: Peterson & Myers PA 100 E Main St Lakeland FL 33801-4655

**KNOX, JAMES MARSHALL,** lawyer; b. Chgo., Jan. 12, 1944; s. Edwin John and Shirley Lucille (Collett) K.; m. Janine Foster, July 18, 1964; children: Erik M., Christian S. BA, U. Ill., 1968; MA in Libr. Sci., Rosary Coll., 1973; JD, DePaul Coll. of Law, 1979. Bar: Ill. 1979, U.S. Dist. Ct. (no. dist.) Ill. 1979, U.S. Ct. Appeals (7th cir.) 1980. Head reference Northbrook (Ill.) Pub. Libr., 1973-76; asst. dir. hdqrs. Jackson (Miss.) Met. Libr. Sys., 1976-77; assoc., Fishman & Fishman, Ltd., Chgo., 1979-91; prin. Law Office James M. Knox, 1991—; gen. counsel Deerfield (Ill.) Pub. Libr., 1994—. Commr. Evanston Preservation Commn., 1991-98. Mem. ABA, Ill. State Bar Assn., Ill. Trial Lawyer's Assn., Chgo. Bar Assn., U. Ill. Alumni Assn. (dir. 1986-91). Workers' compensation, Personal injury, General practice. Home: 1305 Lincoln St Evanston IL 60201-2334 Office: 3700 Three 1st National Plz Chicago IL 60602

**KNOX, WILLIAM ARTHUR,** judge; b. Fargo, N.D., Jan. 8, 1945. BS, N.D. State U., 1966; JD, U. Minn., 1968. Law specialist USCG, Boston and Juneau, Alaska, 1968-72; prof. U. Mo. Sch. Law, Columbia, 1972-85; magistrate judge U.S. Cts., Jefferson City, Mo., 1985—. Author: (books) Federal Criminal Forms, 1993, Missouri Criminal Practice, 1995. Lt. comdr. USCGR. Office: 131 W High St Jefferson City MO 65101-1557

**KNOX RIOS, DELILAH JANE,** lawyer; b. Springfield, Ohio, Mar. 2, 1954; d. Ralph H. Jones and Charlotte Jane (Epling) Hilbert; m. Ralph Knox, Mar. 2, 1975 (div. 1979); m. Pedro Waldimiro Rios Rodriguez, Dec. 27, 1981; children: Franchesca Amanecer Jane Rios Jones, Mark Anthony Rios Jones. AA in Acctg., San Bernardino Valley Coll., 1976; BS in Law, Western State U., Fullerton, Calif., 1978, JD, 1979. Bar: Calif. 1980, U.S. Dist. Ct. (cen. and so. dists) Calif. 1980, U.S. Dist. Ct. (ea. dist.) Calif. 1989; cert. mediator. Pvt. practice San Bernardino, Calif., 1980-84, Diamond Bar, Calif., 1984-94, Orange County, Calif., 1994—; pro bono judge pro tem, San Bernardino, L.A. Counties. Mem. State Bar Calif., East-West Family Law Coun., L.A. Bar Assn., Diamond Bar C. of C. Avocation: fiction writer. Real property, Family and matrimonial, Bankruptcy. Office: 433 Civic Center Dr W Ste 227 Santa Ana CA 92701-4550 also: 22640 Golden Springs Dr Ste C Diamond Bar CA 91765-2221

**KNUCKEY, KENNETH SCOTT,** lawyer; b. Hawthorne, Calif., May 29, 1963; s. Richard Leland and Grace Marian (Eccles) K.; m. Renate Susanne Bal, Oct. 12, 1996. Student, Tex. Christian U., 1981-84; BS in Fin., U. Ariz., 1987; JD, Coll. William and Mary, 1990. Bar: Tex. 1990, U.S. Dist. Ct. (no. dist.) Tex. 1991, U.S. Dist. Ct. (ea. and so. dists.) Tex. 1993, U.S. Ct. Appeals (5th cir.) 1995, Md. 1998, U.S. Dist. Ct. Md., 1999, Dist. of Columbia, 1999. Staff atty. ENSERCH Corp., Dallas, 1991-92; assoc. Kirkendall & Collins, Houston, 1993-94, Wickliff & Hall P.C., Houston, 1995-98, Semmes Bowen & Semmes, Balt., 1998—. General civil litigation, Contracts commercial, Labor. Office: Semmes Bowen & Semmes 250 W Pratt St Ste 1600 Baltimore MD 21201-2400

**KNUEPFER, ROBERT CLAUDE, JR.,** lawyer; b. Oak Park, Ill., Feb. 23, 1952; s. Robert Claude Sr. and Suzanne (White) K.; m. Nancy Jo Bauderer, Aug. 20, 1977; children: Robert Claude III, Jennifer Jo, Lauren Elizabeth, Joseph James. BA, Denison U., 1974; JD and M in Mgmt., Northwestern U., 1978. Bar: Ill. 1978, U.S. Dist. Ct. (no. dist.) Ill. 1978, U.S. Ct. Appeals (7th cir.) 1980, U.S. Dist. Ct. (no. dist.) Ill. 1983, U.S. Supreme Ct. 1989. Law clk. to hon. judge William J. Bauer U.S. Ct. Appeals (7th cir.), Chgo., 1978-80; asst. U.S. atty. criminal divsn. Office of U.S. Atty., Chgo., 1980-83; assoc. Baker & McKenzie, Chgo., 1983-87, ptnr., 1987-92; mng. ptnr. Baker & McKenzie, Budapest, Hungary, 1992-95; ptnr. Baker & McKenzie, Chgo., 1995—; pres. Am. C. of C., Budapest, 1994-95; chmn., bd. dirs. Nat. Svc. League, Budapest, 1994-95; bd. dirs. Leadershape, Inc., 1986—. Active Chgo. Coun. on Fgn. Rels., 1984—, Hinsdale (Ill.) Plan Commn., 1990-92; chmn. Glen Ellyn (Ill.) Zoning Bd. Appeals, 1983, Hinsdale Village Caucus; chmn. bd. ATO Nat. Frat., Champaign, Ill., 1986-92, nat. pres., 1990-92; chmn. ATO Found., Indpls., 1995—; bd. dirs. Met. Family Svcs. Assn. DuPage County, 1986—, pres., 1997—; founding pres. Budapest City Rotary Club. Mem. ABA, Fed. Bar Assn., Ill. Bar Assn. (corp. and securities sect. coun. 1990, 1996—), Chgo. Bar Assn., DuPage County Bar Assn., Legal Club Chgo., Law Club Chgo., Phi Beta Kappa, Omicron Delta Epsilon, Omicron Delta Kappa. General corporate, Private international, Federal civil litigation. Office: Baker & McKenzie 130 E Randolph St Ste 3500 Chicago IL 60601-6314 also: Baker & McKenzie, Andrassy ut 125, H-1062 Budapest Hungary

**KNUTH, ERIC JOSEPH,** lawyer; b. Detroit, Oct. 25, 1964; s. Harold Joseph and Mary Kay (Werthmann) K.; m. Toni Lynn Yopps, Dec. 19, 1987; children: Cory, Kelsey, Christa. BS, No. Mich. U., 1987; JD cum laude, Thomas Cooley Law Sch., Lansing, Mich., 1990. Bar: Mich. 1991, U.S. Dist. Ct. (ea. and we. dists.) Mich. 1991, U.S. Ct. Appeals (6th cir.) 1992, U.S. Dist. Ct. (ea. dist.) Wis. 1994. Law clk. Reid & Reid Law Firm, Lansing, Mich., 1987-90; rsch. atty. Mich. Ct. of Appeals, Detroit, 1990; atty. Mouw & Celello, Iron Mountain, Mich., 1991-97, Bernstein & Bernstein, 1997-99, Law Offices of Christopher Varjabedian, P.C., 1999—; mem. Cooley-Am. Bar Assn. Nat. Trial Team, Lansing, 1989-90; instr. Thomas Cooley-Legal Methods Course, Lansing, 1990. Recipient Am. Jurisprudence Book award-Advocacy, Lawyers Coop., 1989, Am. Jurisprudence Book award-Sales, 1990, Merit award Gun Control, 1990, Disting. Student award Cooley Law Sch., 1990. Mem. ABA, ATLA, State Bar of Mich., Dickinson

County Bar Assn. Democrat. Roman Catholic. Avocations: volleyball, hunting, softball. Product liability, Personal injury, General civil litigation.

**KNUTSON, SAM HOUSTON,** lawyer; b. San Antonio, Feb. 28, 1955; s. Ocie Lee and Sallye Slaughter Knutson; m. Joanne Villa, Oct. 24, 1993. BSin Edn., S.W. Tex. State U., 1982, MA, 1984; JD, St. Mary's U., San Antonio, 1987. Bar: Tex., U.S. Dist. Ct. (so., no. and we. dists.) Tex., U.S. Dist. Ct. (ea. and we. dists.) Ark., U.S. Dist. Ct. Hawaii, U.S. Ct. Appeals (9th cir.). Atty. Thornton, Summers, Biechlin, Dunham & Brown, Corpus Christi, Tex., 1989-91, Patterson & Assocs., Corpus Christi, Tex., 1991-93, Burns & O'Gormon, San Antonio, 1993-95, Ware, Snow, Fogel, Jackson & Greene, Houston, 1995—; mem. Coll. of State Bar of Tex., Austin, 1993—; organizer Am. Liver Found., Houston, 1998. Contbr. continuing legal and ins. edn. seminars, 1990—. With USN, 1976-80. Mem. Tex. Assn. Def. Counsel, Hawaiian Hist. Soc., Def. Rsch. Inst. Avocations: fencing, history, writing. Personal injury, General civil litigation, Insurance. Office: Ware Snow Fogel Jackson & Greene 1111 Bagby St Fl 49 Houston TX 77002-2551

**KNUTZEN, RAYMOND EDWARD,** federal official, legal consultant; b. Burlington, Wash., July 9, 1941; s. Erwin Edward Knutzen and Lillian Irene (Davis) Mowat; m. Cynthia Louise Neufeldt, Feb. 1, 1969; children: Traci Ann, Michael Edward. AAS with high honors, Everett Community Coll., 1970; BA magna cum laude, Pacific Luth. U., 1971; MA, Wash. State U., 1972. Ret. N.E. La. U., Monroe, 1992; cons. Everett, 1992—; freelance legal cons. Wash., 1992—; spl. dep. U.S. Marshal U.S. Marshal, Seattle, 1994—; dir. pub. safety, chief of police Taholah, Wash., 1994-98. Coord. Ouachita Valley coun. Boy Scouts Am., Monroe, 1979. With USAF, 1962-66, lt. col. USAR, ret. 1994. Law Enforcement Edn. Program grantee Pacific Luth. U., 1970-71. Mem. Internat. Assn. Chiefs of Police, Mensa, acad. Criminal Justice Sci., La. Justice Educators Assn., Blue Key Soc., La. Soc. Criminal Justice and Criminology (state pres. 1990-91), Lambda Alpha Epsilon (chpt. pres. 1971-72), Alpha Phi Sigma (nat. treas. 1971-72), Omicron Delta Kappa, Alpha Kappa Delta. Republican. Lutheran. Home and Office: 1811 Dull Pl Everett WA 98203-1619

**KOBAK, JAMES BENEDICT, JR.,** lawyer, educator; b. Alexandria, La., May 2, 1944; s. James Benedict and Hope (McEldowney) K.; m. Carol Johnson, June 11, 1966; children: James Benedict III, Katherine Jean, Marcie Ann. BA magna cum laude, Harvard U., 1966; LLB, U. Va., 1969. Bar: U.S. Dist. Ct. (so. and ea. dists.) N.Y. 1972, U.S. Supreme Ct. 1977, U.S. Ct. Appeals (2nd cir.) 1973, (5th cir.) 1982, U.S. Dist. Ct. (no. dist.) Calif. 1983, N.J. 1996. Asst. prof. U. Ala., 1969-70; assoc. Hughes Hubbard & Reed, N.Y.C., 1970-77, ptnr., 1977—; lectr. in law U. Va., 1986—; adj. assoc. prof. Fordham U., 1986—. Bd. editors Va. Law Review 1967-69 (assoc. editor 1968-69); contbr. articles to profl. jours., mags., and newspapers. Trustee Morristown-Beard Sch.; pres. bd. trustees N.J. Chamber Music Soc., Montclair, 1988-90. Mem. ABA (antitrust sect., chair intellectual property com.), Assn. Bar City N.Y., N.Y. County Lawyers Assn. (bd. dirs. 1988-93, 95-97, chmn. trade regulation com. 1987-88, chmn. com. on changing trends in the profession 1990-93, chmn. com. on law reform 1994-98, exec. com. 1996-98, libr. com., 1998—), Order of Coif, Am. Law Inst., Adirondack 46ers Club, Keene Valley Country Club (trustee), Harvard Club (N.Y.). Antitrust, Federal civil litigation, Trademark and copyright. Home: 6 Edgehill Rd Llewellyn Park West Orange NJ 07052 Office: Hughes Hubbard & Reed 1 Battery Park Plz Fl 12 New York NY 10004-1482

**KOBAYASHI, BERT TAKAAKI, JR.,** lawyer; b. Honolulu, Feb. 4, 1940; s. Bert Takaaki Sr. and Victoria Ruth (Tsuchiya) K.; m. Harriet Sanae Ishimine, Aug. 11, 1962; children: Christopher T., Jonathan A., Matthew H., Jennifer Sanae. Student, U. Hawaii, 1958-62; BA, Gettysburg (Pa.) Coll., 1962; JD, U. Calif., Hastings, 1965. Bar: Hawaii 1965, U.S. Dist. (fed. dist.) Hawaii 1965. Assoc. Chung, Vitousek, Chuck & Fujimana, Honolulu, 1967-69, Kono, Ariyoshi, Honolulu, 1969-71; sr. ptnr. Kobayashi, Sugita & Goda, Honolulu, 1971—; bd. dirs. First Hawaiian Bank, Honolulu, Bank West Corp., Schuler Homes; exec. com. Bank West Corp. Honolulu; mem. State Jud. Selection Commn., Honolulu, 1985-01, chmn., 1987-89. Mem. ABA, Am. Coll. Trial Lawyers, Hawaii Bar Assn., Assn. Trial Lawyers Am., Am. Bd. Trial Advs., Japah-Hawaii Econ. Coun., Pub. Schools Found. Construction, Real property, State civil litigation. Office: Kobayashi Sugita & Goda 999 Bishop St Ste 2600 Honolulu HI 96813-4430

**KOBDISH, GEORGE CHARLES,** lawyer; b. Casper, Wyo., June 30, 1950; s. Richard Matthew and Jo Earl (Uttz) K.; m. Mary Ellen Griffith, Jan. 24, 1969; children: George Charles, Jr., Kelly Rebecca, Kimberlee Nelle. BBA with honors, U. Tex., 1971, JD, 1974. Bar: Tex. 1974, U.S. Dist. Ct. (no. dist.) Tex. 1975. Asst. atty. gen. State of Tex., Austin, 1974-76; assoc. McCall, Parkhurst & Horton LLP, Dallas, 1976-80, ptnr., 1981—. Bd. dirs. North Dallas Shared Ministries, pres. 1996-98. Mem. Am. Coll. Bond Counsel, Nat. Assn. Bond Lawyers, Tex. Bar Assn., Dallas Bar Assn., Royal Oaks Country Club, Tower Club, Dallas Friday Group, Serra Club of Dallas (bd. dirs., pres. 1998-99), Phi Delta Theta. Roman Catholic. Municipal (including bonds). Home: 9206 Arbor Branch Dr Dallas TX 75243-6308 Office: McCall Parkhurst & Horton LLP 717 N Harwood St Ste 900 Dallas TX 75201-6586

**KOBERT, JOEL A.,** lawyer; b. Newark, Oct. 4, 1943. BA, Norwich U., 1965; JD, Howard U., 1968. Bar: D.C. 1968, N.J. 1971. Atty. U.S. Dept. Justice, Washington, 1968; ptnr. Courter, Kobert, Laufer & Cohen P.C., Hackettstown, N.J.; active Supreme Ct. Ad Hoc Com. on Legal Svcs. 1982-88, Supreme Ct. Com. on Interests and Trust Accts., 1984-86, Supreme Ct. Com. on Computerization of Ct. System, 1984-86; chmn. bd. trustees Interest on Lawyers Trust Accts., 1988-91. Capt. U.S. Army, 1968-70. Reginald Heber Smith fellow, 1970-71. Fellow Am. Bar Found.; mem. ABA (mem. dist XIII ethics com. 1982-86), D.C. Bar, N.J. State Bar Assn. (treas. 1987, sec. 1988, 2d v.p. 1989, 1st v.p. 1990, pres. elect 1991, pres. 1992, bd. trustees 1981-87, bd. trustees N.J. Lawyer, bd trustees N.J. State Bar Found., 1986-93, mem. ops. com. 1985-91, chmn. com. law adminstrn. and econs. 1981-86, mem. membership com., 1986-87, mem. com. fin. and ops. 1990-93, mem. travel com. 1990-93), N.J. League Mcpl. Attys. Office: Courter Kobert Laufer & Cohen PC 1001 County Road 517 Ste 1 Hackettstown NJ 07840-2709

**KOBLENTZ, ROBERT ALAN,** lawyer; b. Columbus, Ohio, Aug. 20, 1946; s. Maurice Charles and Martha (Levelle) K.; m. Kathryn Anderson, Oct. 20, 1973; children: Maureen, Robert. BA, Ohio State U., 1967, JD, 1970. Bar: Ohio 1970, U.S. Dist. Ct. (so. dist.) Ohio 1971, U.S. Supreme Ct. 1992. Legal rsch. Bancroft-Whitney Co., San Francisco, 1970-71; atty. Tracy, DeLibera, Lyons & Collins, Columbus, 1971-78, DeLibera, Lyons, Koblentz & Scott, Columbus, 1978-80, Scott, Koblentz & Binau, Columbus, 1980-86; pvt. practice Columbus, 1986—. Bd. dirs. Friends of WOSU, Columbus, 1982-88, Opera Columbus, 1984-87, Upper Arlington Civic Assn., Columbus, 1988-90. Mem. ABA, Ohio State Bar Assn. (del. family law section 1979—), Ohio Acad. Trial Lawyers (chmn. family law sect. 1983), Columbus Bar Assn. (chmn. family law com. 1976-78), Franklin County Trial Lawyers (pres. 1985-86). Family and matrimonial. Office: 35 E Livingston Ave Columbus OH 43215-5768

**KOBLENZ, MICHAEL ROBERT,** lawyer; b. Newark, Apr. 9, 1948; s. Herman and Esther (Weisman) K.; m. Bonnie Jane Berman, Dec. 22, 1973; children: Adam, Alexander, Elizabeth. B.A., George Washington U., 1969, LL.M., 1974; J.D., Am. U., 1972. Bar: N.J. 1972, D.C. 1973, N.Y. 1980, U.S. Dist. Ct. N.J. 1972, U.S. Dist. Ct. D.C. 1973, U.S. Dist. Ct. (so. dist.) N.Y. 1980, U.S. Ct. Appeals (7th cir.) 1976, U.S. Ct. Claims 1973, U.S. Tax Ct. 1973, U.S. Mil. Ct. Appeals 1974. Atty., U.S. Dept. Justice, Washington, 1972-75; lectr. Am. U., 1975-78; spl. asst. U.S. atty. Office of U.S. Atty., Chgo., 1976-78; atty. Commodity Futures Trading Commn., Washington, 1975-77; spl. counsel, 1977, asst. dir., 1977-78; regional counsel, N.Y.C., 1978-80; assoc. Rein, Mound & Cotton, N.Y.C., 1980-82, ptnr., Mound, Cotton & Wollan (and predecessor firms), 1983—. Contbr. articles to legal jours. Mem. bd. appeals Village of Flower Hill, Manhasset, N.Y., 1983-84, trustee, 1984-86; trustee Village of East Hills, 1988—, Dep. Mayor, 1993-94, Mayor, 1994—; mem. Roslyn Little League, 1991—, bd. dirs., 1992. Recipient Cert. of Appreciation for Outstanding Service U.S. Commodity Futures Trading Commn., 1977. Contracts commercial, Securities, General corporate. Home: East Hills 20 Hemlock Dr Roslyn NY 11576-2303 Office: Mound Cotton & Wollan 1 Battery Park Plz New York NY 10004-1405

**KOBLENZ, N(ORMAN) HERSCHEL,** lawyer; b. Albany, N.Y., Nov. 19, 1934; s. Edmund Akiba and Tillie (Paul) K.; m. Maxine Doris Levy, Aug. 12, 1956; children: Marci, Brian. BA, Cornell U., 1956; JD, Yale U., 1960. Bar: N.Y. 1960, Ohio 1960, U.S. Dist. Ct. (no. and ea. dists.) Ohio 1960, U.S. Ct. Appeals (6th cir.) 1960, U.S. Tax Ct. 1982. Assoc. Hahn Loeser & Parks LLP and predecessor firms, Cleve., 1960-67, ptnr., 1967—, mng. ptnr., 1985-89, exec. ptnr., 1989-91, COO, CFO, 1991-98. Pres. Bur. Jewish Edn. Cleve., 1977-82; mem. exec. com. Park Synagogue, Cleveland Heights, 1986—; trustee Jewish Cmty. Fedn. Cleve., 1997—. Capt. U.S. Army, 1956-57. Recipient Marvin and Milton Kane award Jewish Community Fedn., Cleve., 1972, A.H. Friedland award Bur. Jewish Edn., 1993; named Centerite of Yr. Park Synagogue, 1990. Mem. ABA, Ohio Bar Assn., Cleve. Bar Assn., Lomond Assn. (pres. 1969), Oakwood (South Euclid, Ohio), City (Cleve.). Democrat. Avocation: golf. Taxation, general, General corporate, Health. Home: 18000 S Woodland Rd Cleveland OH 44120-1773 Office: Hahn Loeser & Parks LLP 3300 BP Tower Cleveland OH 44114

**KOBRIN, LAWRENCE ALAN,** lawyer; b. N.Y.C., Sept. 14, 1933; s. Irving and Hortense (Freezer) K.; m. Ruth E. Freedman, Mar. 5, 1967; children: Jeffrey, Rebecca, Debra. AB in History with honors, summa cum laude, Columbia U., 1954, JD, 1957. Bar: N.Y. 1957, U.S. Dist. Ct. (so. dist.) N.Y. 1958, U.S. Dist. Ct. (ea. dist.) N.Y. 1959, U.S. Ct. Appeals (2d cir.) 1959, U.S. Supreme Ct. 1966. Assoc. Cahill, Gordon, Reindel & Ohl, N.Y.C., 1958-59, Arthur D. Emil, N.Y.C., 1959-63; ptnr. Emil & Kobrin, N.Y.C., 1963-79, Milgrim, Thomajan, Jacobs and Lee, N.Y.C., 1979-83, Cahill Gordon & Reindel, N.Y.C., 1984—; bd. govs. Wurzweiler Sch. of Social Work, 1984—, vice-chmn., 1994-98; dir. UMB Bank and Trust Co., 1978-91; dir., treas. The Jewish Week, N.Y.C., 1992-96, chmn., 1996—. Notes editor Columbia U. Law Rev.; contbr. articles to law jours. V.p., assoc. treas., chmn. dist. com. Fedn. Jewish Philanthropies, N.Y.C., 1981-84, com. long range planning, 1985-86, com. inner city, 71-76; chmn. Ramaz Sch., N.Y.C., 1978-83; sec. to bd. Bar Ilan U., N.Y.C., 1972-80; pres. The Jewish Ctr., N.Y.C., 1987-90; dir. N.Y.C.-UJA-Fedn., chmn. communal planning com., 1988-91, chmn. com. on cmty. couns., 1996-98; v.p. Union Orthodox Jewish Congregations, 1968-74, dir., 1962—, chmn. campus com., 1962-66, chmn. Israel com., 1967-72, chmn. pub. com., 1972-78; pres. Massad Camps, 1971-77; mng. editor Tradition, 1961-64, editl. com. 1964—; bd. dirs. Am. Friends Pardes, 1991-96, Histadrut Ivrit, 1991—; pres. Ariel Am. Friends of Midrasha and United Instns., 1991-95, chmn., 1995—; sec. Beth Din of Am., 1994-96, chmn. exec. com., 1997—, exec. com. Orthodox Caucus, 1995—. Kent scholar, Stone scholar. Mem. Am. Coll. Real Estate Lawyers, Coop. Housing Lawyers Group (exec. com. 1972-80), N.Y. atty. gen. adv. com. 1972-80, Assn. Bar City of N.Y. (com. on philanthropic orgns. 1974-79, edn. and law com. 1985-88, com. on legal edn. 1988-91, com. on legal problems of elderly 1991-94), N.Y. County Lawyers Assn. (real property law sect., chmn. 1991-93), Nat. Assn. Coll. and Univ. Attys. (1971-79), N.Y. State Bar Assn. (com. coops and condominiums, com. fgn. investment real estate), Columbia Coll. Alumni Assn. (bd. dirs. 1990—, v.p. 1996-98), The Down Town Assn., Cream Hill Lake Assn., Phi Beta Kappa. Real property, General corporate, Non-profit and tax-exempt organizations. Home: 15 W 81st St New York NY 10024-6022 also: 8 Popple Swamp Rd Cornwall Bridge CT 06754-1135 Office: Cahill Gordon & Reindel 80 Pine St Fl 17 New York NY 10005-1790

**KOBRIN, THOMAS BARSTOW,** lawyer; b. Washington, June 11, 1964; s. Stephen Kobrin and Elizabeth Long; m. Lisa Wilson Brantley, Nov. 3, 1990. BA in History, U. Pa., 1986; MA in History, U. N.C., 1988, JD, 1992. Bar: N.C. 1992, U.S. Dist. Ct. (ea., mid., and we. dists.) N.C. 1993, U.S. Ct. Appeals (4th cir.) 1993. Pvt. practice Greensboro, N.C., 1994—. Mem. Greensboro Bar Assn. (pres. 1998—), Order of Coif. General civil litigation, Labor, Consumer commercial. Home: 1603 Helmwood Dr Greensboro NC 27410-3707 Office: 400 W Market St Ste 500 Greensboro NC 27401-2254

**KOCH, EDNA MAE,** lawyer, nurse; b. Terre Haute, Ind., Oct. 12, 1951; d. Leo K. and Lucille E. (Smith) K.; m. Mark D. Orton. BS in Nursing, Ind. State U., 1977; JD, Ind. U., 1980. Bar: Ind. 1980, U.S. Dist. Ct. (so. dist.) Ind. 1980. Assoc. Dillon & Cohen, Indpls., 1980-85; ptnr. Tipton, Cohen & Koch, Indpls., 1985-93, LaCava, Zeigler & Carter, Indpls., 1993-94, Zeigler Carter Cohen & Koch, Indpls., 1994—; leader seminars for nurses, Ind. U. Med. Ctr., Ball State U., Muncie, Ind., St. Vincent Hosp., Indpls., Deaconess Hosp., Evansville, Ind., others; lectr. on med. malpractice Cen. Ind. chpt. AACCN, Indpls. "500" Postgrad. Course in Emergency Medicine, Ind. Assn. Osteo. Physicians and Surgeons State Conv., numerous others. Mem. ABA, ANA, Ind. State Bar Assn., Indpls. Bar Assn., Am. Soc. Law and Medicine, Ind. State Nurses Assn. Republican. Personal injury, Insurance, State civil litigation. Office: Zeigler Carter Cohen & Koch 8500 Keystone Xing Ste 510 Indianapolis IN 46240-2461

**KOCH, EDWARD RICHARD,** lawyer, accountant; b. Teaneck, N.J., Mar. 25, 1953; s. Edward J. and Adelaide M. K.; m. Cora Susan Koch, Apr. 12, 1997, one child: Edward Peter. BS in Econs. magna cum laude, U. Pa., 1975; JD, U. Va., 1980; LLM in Taxation, NYU, 1986. Bar: N.J. 1980, U.S. Dist. Ct. N.J. 1980, U.S. Tax Ct. 1981, U.S. Ct. Claims 1981. Staff acct. Touche Ross & Co. (now Deloitte & Touche), Newark, 1975-77; assoc. Winne, Banta & Rizzi, Hackensack, N.J., 1980-82; tax atty. Allied Corp. (now Allied-Signal, Inc.), Morristown, 1982-87; asst. v.p. ChemBank (now Chase Manhattan), N.Y.C., 1987-90; tax mgr. Paul Scherer & Co. LLP, N.Y.C., 1990-97, ptnr., 1998—. Vice chmn. law and legis. com. U.S.A. Track and Field, Indpls., 1985-89—, chmn., 1989—, chmn. ins. com., 1984-88, bd. dirs., 1989—; pres. N.J. Athletics Congress, Red Bank, 1986-90; mem. Jury of Appeals, 1988, U.S. Olympic Men's Marathon Trials, Holy Family Sch. Edn. Coun., 1992-96; Olympic Track and Field ofcl., 1996. Mem. AICPA, N.J. Soc. CPAs, Am. Assn. Attys.-CPAs, N.J. State Bar Assn., N.J. Striders Track Club (chmn. 1981-96). Republican. Roman Catholic. Avocations: running, track and field. State and local taxation, Corporate taxation, Personal income taxation. Home: 130 Grant St Haworth NJ 07641-1951 Office: Paul Scherer & Co 335 Madison Ave Fl 9 New York NY 10017-4605

**KOCHANSKI, DAVID MAJLECH,** lawyer; b. Bergen Belsen, Fed. Republic Germany, Jan. 12, 1948; came to U.S., 1949; s. Leon Josef and Maria (Kemp) K.; m. Adrienne Janet Laskowitz, June 6, 1969; children: Michael, Lori. BA, U. Md., 1969, JD, 1973. Bar: Md. 1973, D.C. 1974, U.S. Dist. Ct. Md. 1974, U.S. Supreme Ct. 1977. Ptnr., real estate dept. chair Shulman, Rogers, Gandal, Pordy & Ecker, Rockville, Md., 1973—; lectr. Montgomery Coll.; lectr., adv. bd. Md. Inst. Continuing Profl. Edn. of Lawyers; instr. Savings and Loan League, Fairfax, Va., 1984. Mem. Citizens Adv. Bd., Bethesda and Chevy Chase, Md., 1981; pres. Woodmoor Civic Assn., Silver Spring, 1979; fin. com. Hebrew Home, Rockville, 1985. Mem. ABA, Montgomery County Bar Assn. (chair real estate sect.), Md. Bar Assn. (mem. sect. coun., real property, planning and zoning). Democrat. Real property, Consumer commercial, Banking. Home: 13709 Hobart Dr Silver Spring MD 20904-5463 Office: Shulman Rogers Gandal Pordy & Ecker 11921 Rockville Pike Ste 300 Rockville MD 20852-2743

**KOCHEMS, ROBERT GREGORY,** lawyer; b. Cleve., Aug. 6, 1951; s. Roy George and Virginia Mae (Budniak) K.; m. Georgann Ryan; 1 child, Alane Carin. BA cum laude, John Carroll U., 1973; JD, St. Louis U., 1976. Bar: Pa. 1976, U.S. Dist. Ct. (we. dist.) 1978. Sole practice Mercer, Pa., 1976-81, 88-92; ptnr. Bogaty, McEwen, Sparks, & Kochems, P.C., Mercer, 1981-87, Nelson, Ryan & Kochems, 1992—; asst. pub. defender Mercer County, 1977-88; asst. dist. atty., 1988—; sub-com. chairperson Mercer County Juvenile Ct. Adv. Com., 1986-88. Assoc. editor St. Louis U. Law Jour., 1975-76. Bd. dirs. Transfer Harvest Home Assn., 1986-88. Mem. ABA, Pa. Bar Assn., Mercer County Bar Assn. (sec. 1977-79, bench bar com. 1982, 84). Republican. Roman Catholic. Lodge: KC (advocate 1978-88). Juvenile, Criminal, Family and matrimonial. Home: PO Box 226 Mercer PA 16137-0226

**KOCORAS, CHARLES PETROS,** federal judge; b. Chgo., Mar. 12, 1938; s. Petros K. and Constantina (Cordonis) K.; m. Grace L. Finlay, Sept. 22, 1968; children: Peter, John, Paul. Student, Wilson Jr. Coll., 1956-58; BS, DePaul U., 1961, JD, 1969. Bar: Ill. 1969. Assoc. Bishop & Crawford, 1969-71; asst. atty. Office of U.S. Atty. U.S. Dist. Ct. (no. dist.) Ill., Chgo., 1971-77, judge, 1980—; chmn. Ill. Commerce Commn., Chgo., 1977-79; ptnr. Stone, McGuire, Benjamin and Kocoras, Chgo., 1979-80; adj. prof. trial practice, evening div. John Marshall Law Sch., 1975—; various positions IRS, Chgo., 1962-69. With Army N.G., 1961-67. Mem. Chgo. Bar Assn., Fed. Criminal Jury Instrn. Com. 7th Cir., Beta Alpha Psi. Greek Orthodox. Office: US Courthouse 2588 Dirksen Bldg 219 S Dearborn St Chicago IL 60604-1702

**KOCZAJA, JOSEPH STANLEY,** lawyer, assistant attorney general; b. Lackawanna, N.Y., Apr. 25, 1954; s. Adam R. and Helene C. K.; m. Sharon Margaret Boileau Mar. 25, 1985 (div. Jan. 7, 1992); 1 child, Melissa Marie. BA, SUNY, Buffalo, 1976; MA in Counseling Psychology, Ohio State U., 1978; JD, Syracuse U., 1983. Bar: N.Y. 1984, U.S. Ct. Appeals (2d cir.) 1988, U.S. Supreme Ct. 1990, U.S. Dist. Ct. (no. dist.) N.Y. 1995, U.S. Dist. Ct. (we. dist.) N.Y. 1998, U.S. Bankruptcy Ct. 1998. Confidential law clk. NYS Appellate Divsn., Albany, N.Y., 1983-84, NYS Ct. of Appeals, Albany, 1984-86; asst. atty. gen. Office of the Atty Gen., Albany, N.Y., 1986—. Lay minister St. Matthew's Roman Cath. Ch., Voormeesville, N.Y. Recipient fellowship Ohio State U., 1976-77, Syracuse U., 1980-82. Mem. Phi Beta Kappa. Avocations: travel, hiking, cross country skiing, poetry, mycology. Home: 258 Indian Ledge Rd Voorheesville NY 12186-4312 Office: Office Atty Gen The Capitol Albany NY 12224

**KOEBEL, DELMAR OLIVER,** lawyer; b. Lebanon, Ill., Jan. 30, 1926; s. Oliver J. and Laura A. (Rieger) K.; m. Betty A. Brammeier, July 8, 1950 (dec. 1978); children: Mike, Barbara, Steven, Beth; m. Harriet A. Gould, June 12, 1982. AB, McKendree Coll., 1950; JD, Wash. U., 1953. Bar: Mo. 1953, Ill. 1953. Ptnr. Goldenhersh & Goldenhersh, East St. Louis, Ill., 1953-60; pvt. practice, Lebanon and East St. Louis, 1960-76, Lebanon, 1979—; cir. judge St. Clair County, 1976-79; bd. dirs. Trenton (Ill.) Savs. & Loan Assn.; trustee McKendree Coll., Lebanon, 1972-90. With USN, 1944-46. Mem. ABA, Ill. Bar Assn., St. Clair County Bar Assn., East St. Louis Bar Assn. Republican. Mem. United Ch. Christ. Administrative and regulatory, Probate. Home and Office: 6 Joshua Dr O'Fallon IL 62269-1213

**KOEGEL, WILLIAM FISHER,** lawyer; b. Washington, Aug. 18, 1923; s. Otto Erwin and Rae (Fisher) K.; m. Barbara Bixler, Feb. 2, 1946 (dec. 1968); children: John Bixler, Robert Bartlett; m. Ruth Swan Boynton, June 21, 1969 (dec. 1983); m. Irene Lawrence, Aug. 4, 1984. B.A., Williams Coll., 1944; LL.B., U. Va., 1949. Bar: N.Y. 1950. From assoc. to ptnr. Roger & Wells and predecessor firms, N.Y.C., 1949—, head litigation dept., 1977-88, sr. counsel, 1989—. Chmn. Scarsdale (N.Y.) Republican Town Com., 1965-71; pres. trustees Hitchcock Presbyn. Ch., Scarsdale, 1970-73, 78-79, 82-83. Served with AUS, 1943-45, ETO. Fellow ACTL; mem. ABA, N.Y. State Bar Assn., Bar Assn. City N.Y., Order of Coif. Clubs: Town (Scarsdale) (pres. 1976-77); Sky (N.Y.C.), Williams (N.Y.C.); Shenorock Shore, Fox Meadow Tennis, The Moorings. Federal civil litigation, State civil litigation. Home: 7 Chesterfield Rd Scarsdale NY 10583-1619 Office: Rogers & Wells 200 Park Ave New York NY 10166-0005

**KOEHLER, FRITZ K.,** lawyer; b. Cambridge, Mass., May 3, 1964; s. Hans H.B. and Martha K. Koehler; m. Gabriele Graf, May 20, 1992; children: Justin, Hanna. BA, Stanford U., 1986; JD, U. Calif., Berkeley, 1990, MBA, 1990. Bar: Calif. 1990. Assoc. Brobeck, Phleger & Harrison, Palo Alto, Calif., 1991-93, Fenwick & West, Palo Alto, 1993-96; sr. counsel Merant, PLC, Mountain View, Calif., 1996—. General corporate, Intellectual property, Computer. Office: Merant PLC Law Dept 701 E Middlefield Rd Mountain View CA 94043-4023

**KOEHNKE, PHILLIP EUGENE,** lawyer, consultant; b. Denver, Sept. 3, 1962; s. Eugene and Lorraine Koehnke; m. Diane Koehnke. BS, Colo. State U., 1985; JD, U. Wash., 1992. Bar: Calif., Colo., U.S. Dist. Ct. (ctrl., so. and no. dists.) Calif., U.S. Supreme Ct. Atty. San Diego, 1992—. Bus. editor U. Wash. Sch. Law Pacific Rim Law and Policy Jour., 1992; contbr. articles to profl. jours. Avocations: running, weightlifting, surfing. Construction, Securities, General civil litigation. Office: Tradeway Securities Group Inc 5875 Avenida Encinas Carlsbad CA 92008-4404

**KOELLER, ROBERT MARION,** lawyer; b. Quincy, Ill., Apr. 8, 1940; s. Marion Alfred and Ruth (Main) K.; m. Marlene Meyer, June 1962; children—Kristin, Katherine, Robert. A.B., MacMurray Coll., 1962; LL.B., Vanderbilt U., 1965. Bar: Ind. 1968. Asst. gen. csl. Nat. Homes Acceptance Corp., Lafayette, Ind., 1967-70; gen. csl., sec. Herff Jones Co., Indpls., 1970-74; ptnr. Warren, Snider, Koeller & Warren, Indpls., 1974-76; sole practice, Indpls., 1976—; mem. Coons, Maddox & Koeller, Indpls., 1993-96, Maddox, Koeller Hargett & Caruso, 1996—; dir. various cos. Mem. ABA, Ind. Bar Assn., Indpls. Bar Assn. Republican. Methodist. General corporate, Securities, Computer. Office: Ste 190 7351 Shadeland Station Way Indianapolis IN 46256-3924

**KOELLING, THOMAS WINSOR,** lawyer; b. Jefferson City, Mo., Oct. 10, 1951; s. Oscar Alvin and Helen Louise (Shields) K.;m. Rebecca Ann Nentwig, Nov. 24, 1973; children: Zachary Thomas, Mathew Garret. BS in Criminal Justice Adminstrn., Ctrl. Mo. State U., Warrensburg, 1978; JD, U. Mo., 1981. Bar: Mo. 1981, Colo. 1982, U.S. Dist. Ct. (we. dist.) Mo. 1981, U.S. Dist. Ct. Colo. 1981, U.S. Ct. Appeals (8th cir.) 1982, U.S. Ct. Appeals (10th cir.) 1981, U.S. Supreme Ct. 1992. Assoc. Tinsley, Frantz et al, Lakewood, Colo., 1981-82, Rex Johnson Law Office, Colorado Springs, Colo., 1982-85; ptnr. Koelling & Crawford, P.C., Kansas City, Mo., 1985—; legal advisor Kansas City Ski Club, 1987, Competitors Assn., Kansas City, 1995—; adj. prof. dept. criminal justice and legal studies Mo. Western State Coll., St. Joseph, Mo., 1998—. With USAF, 1972-76. Mem. ABA, Am. Coll. Legal Medicine, Am. Soc. Law, Medicine Ethics, Am. Trial Lawyers Assn., Mo. Assn. Trial Lawyers, Clay County Bar Assn. Roman Catholic. Avocations: snow skiing, fly fishing, backpacking. Personal injury, Professional liability, Toxic tort. Home: 9617 N Campbell St Kansas City MO 64155-2056 Office: Koelling & Crawford PC 5950 N Oak Trfy Ste 202 Kansas City MO 64118-5164

**KOELTL, JOHN GEORGE,** judge; b. N.Y.C., Oct. 25, 1945; s. John J. and Elsie (Bender) K. AB summa cum laude, Harvard U., 1967, JD magna cum laude, 1971. Bar: N.Y. 1972, U.S. Dist. Ct. (so. and ea. dists.) N.Y. 1975, U.S. Ct. Appeals (2d cir.) 1975, U.S. Supreme Ct. 1978, U.S. Ct. Appeals (5th and 11th cirs.) 1981, U.S. Ct. Appeals (4th cir.) 1992, U.S. Dist. Ct. (no. dist.) N.Y. 1982. Law clk. to Judge U.S. Dist. Ct. (so. dist.), N.Y.C., 1971-72; law clk. to Justice Potter Stewart U.S. Supreme Ct., Washington, 1972-73; asst. spl. prosecutor Watergate Spl. Prosecution Force, Dept. Justice, Washington, 1973-74; assoc. Debevoise & Plimpton, N.Y.C., 1975-78, ptnr., 1979-94; judge U.S. Dist. Ct. (so. dist.), N.Y.C., 1994—. Contbr. articles to profl. jours. Mem. ABA (bd. editors jour. 1991-97, vice chmn. securities com. adminstrv. law sect. 1979-81, co-dir. divsn. publs. litigation sect. 1982-84, coun. mem. litigation sect. 1984-87, assoc. editor Litigation jour. 1975-78, exec. editor 1978-80, editor-in-chief 1980-82, chmn. 1st amendment com. 1987-89, chmn. spl. pubs. com. 1989-92, dir. divsn. publs. litigation sect. 1992-93), Coalition for Justice, Assn. Bar N.Y.C. (mem. com. on fed legislation 1976-78, sec. 1978-81, mem. com. profl. and jud. ethics 1981-84, fed. cts. com. 1984-86, chmn. 1986-89, mem. com. on profl. responsibility 1991-94), N.Y. State Bar Assn., N.Y. County Lawyers Assn. (mem. fed. cts. com. 1984-87), Harvard Law Sch. Assn. N.Y. (v.p. 1993-94). Office: US Courthouse 500 Pearl St Rm 1030 New York NY 10007-1316

**KOENIG, RODNEY CURTIS,** lawyer, rancher; b. Black Jack, Tex., Nov. 21, 1940; s. John Henry and Elva Marguerite (Oeding) K.; m. Mary Mishler, May 1, 1993; children: Erik Jason, Jon Todd. BA, U. Tex., 1962, JD with honors, 1969; postgrad., Auburn U., 1965-67. Bar: Tex. 1969, U.S. Dist. Ct. (so. dist.) Tex. 1970, U.S. Ct. Appeals (5th cir.) 1970, U.S. Tax Ct. 1980, U.S. Ct. Mil. Appeals 1986. Ptnr. Fulbright & Jaworski, LLP, Houston, 1969—; lectr. State Bar Tex., various univs., local estate planning councils; asst. prof. Auburn U., 1965-67. Contbr. articles to profl. jours. Pres. Houston Navy League, 1979-81; commr. Battleship Texas Commn.; Houston Saengerbund; bd. dirs. Houston divsn. Am. Heart Assn., Fayette Heritage Mus.; dir. Advanced Estate Planning and Probate Course, 1988; trustee Luck and Loessin Collection Trust, Luth. Found. of the S.W.; active Tex. Luth. U. Corp. With USN, 1962-67; served to capt. JAGC, USNR, 1967-89.

Recipient Fed. Republic of Germany Order of Merit, 1994. Fellow Am. Coll. Trust and Estate Counsel, Coll. State Bar Tex. (charter); mem. ABA, Internat. Acad. Estate and Trust Law (academician), Tex. Judge Adv. Res. Officers Assn., German Texan Heritage Soc. (pres. 1997—), Res. Officers Assn., Sons of Republic of Tex., Wednesday Tax Forum (past chmn.), German Gulf Coast Assn. (pres. 1989-93), Bach Soc. (bd. dirs.), Houston Karneval Verein (prince 1994-95), USS San Jacinto Com. (treas.), Houstonian Club, Houston Ctr. Club, Frisch Auf Valley Country Club, Order of Coif, U.S. Naval Order, Phi Delta Phi, Omicron Delta Kappa. Lutheran. Estate planning, Probate, Estate taxation. Home: 2720 University Blvd Houston TX 77005-3440 Office: Fulbright & Jaworski LLP 1301 Mckinney St Fl 51 Houston TX 77010-3031

**KOENIGS, RITA SCALES,** judge; b. Milw., May 5, 1952; d. John J. and Gertrude M. (Kendall) S. BA, Am. Internat. Coll., 1974; JD, Western New Eng. Coll., 1977. Bar: Mass. 1977, U.S. Dist. Ct. Mass. 1977. Assoc. Joseph & Manganaro, Springfield, Mass., 1977-79, Oberg, Linial & Scales, Springfield, 1979-80; staff trial atty. Mass. Defenders Com., Pittsfield, 1980—; atty.-in-charge Com. for Pub. Counsel Svcs., Pittsfield, 1987-90, Springfield, 1990—; judge Trial Ct. of Commonwealth of Mass. Dist. Ct. Dept., 1990—. Mem. planning bd. and capital outlay com. City of Pittsfield, 1988-90. Office: Pittsfield Dist Ct 24 Wendell Ave Pittsfield MA 01201-6306

**KOEP, RICHARD MICHAEL,** lawyer; b. Mpls., Dec. 4, 1949; s. Clifford Michael and Mary Corrine (Narey) K.; children: Matthew, Theodore, John, Sarah. JD, William Mitchell Coll. Law, 1980. Bar: Colo. 1980, U.S. Dist. Ct. Colo. 1980, Calif. 1981, U.S. Dist. Ct. (cen. dist.) Calif. 1982. Dir. Even, Crandall Wade Lowe & Gates, Woodland Hills, Calif., 1982—. Served with USMC, 1968-70, Vietnam. Mem. Am. Bd. Trial Advocates, So. Calif. Defense Counsel, Ventura County Bar Assn. Roman Catholic. Personal injury. Office: Even Crandall Wade Lowe & Gates 21031 Ventura Blvd Ste 801 Woodland Hills CA 91364-2240

**KOERNER, GREGORY O.,** lawyer; b. N.Y.C., Dec. 6, 1966; s. Richard Martin Koerner and Marianne Glasel; m. Jean Andreuzzi; 1 child, Miles. BA, Colgate U., 1988; JD, NYU, 1995. Investigator Legal Aid Soc., N.Y.C., 1992-94; assoc. Hughes Hubbard & Reed LLP, N.Y.C., 1995—. General practice, Insurance, Personal injury. Office: Hughes Hubbard & Reed LLP 1 Battery Park Plz Fl 12 New York NY 10004-1482

**KOERNER, WENDELL EDWARD, JR.,** lawyer, mediator; b. Mexico, Mo., July 22, 1938; s. Wendell Edward and Dorothy Irene Koerner; m. Mary Jo Maday, Sept. 29, 1973 (dec. Jan. 1998); children: Jennifer L. Wolfe, R. John Maday, Greg S. Maday, Ryan E. Koerner. BS in Indsl. Mgmt., U. Kans., 1960; JD, U. Mo., Columbia, 1968. Bar: Mo. 1968, U.S. Dist. Ct. (we. dist.) Mo. 1968, U.S. Ct. Appeals (8th cir.) 1973, U.S. Dist. Ct. Kans. 1998. Assoc. Brown, Douglas & Brown, St. Joseph, Mo., 1968-71, ptnr., 1972—; vol. legal counsel YWCA, St. Joseph, 1983-92; temple atty. Moila Shrine Temple, St. Joseph, 1993-97; spkr. in field. Bd. dirs. Ecumenical Corp. for Housing Opportunity, St. Joseph, 1997—; vol. in probation and parole The Mo. Bar, 1971-73. Recipient Lon O. Hocker Meml. Trial Lawyer award Mo. Bar Found., 1973. Fellow Am. Coll. Trial Lawyers; mem. Mo. Bar, St. Joseph Bar Assn. (pres. 1985), Mo. Orgn. Def. Lawyers (pres. 1995-96), Am. Bd. Trial Advocates, Masons, Shriners. Mem. Chjistian Ch. (Disciples of Christ). Avocations: golf, fishing. General civil litigation, Personal injury, Product liability. Home: 4005 Miller Rd Saint Joseph MO 64505-1541 Office: Brown Douglas & Brown 120 S 5th St Saint Joseph MO 64501-2130

**KOFF, HOWARD MICHAEL,** lawyer; b. Bklyn., July 25, 1941; s. Arthur and Blanche Koff; m. Linda Sue Bright, Sept. 10, 1966; 1 son, Michael Arthur Bright. B.S., NYU, 1962; J.D., Bklyn. Law Sch., 1965; LL.M. in Taxation, Georgetown U., 1968. Bar: N.Y. 1965, D.C. 1966, U.S. Supreme Ct. 1969, U.S. Ct. Appeals (2d, 3d, 4th, 5th, 7th, 9th and D.C. cirs.), U.S. Dist. Ct. (no. dist.) N.Y. 1981. Appellate atty. Tax Div., U.S. Dept. Justice, Washington, 1965-69; tax supr. Chrysler Corp., Detroit, 1969-70; chief tax counsel Conn. Gen. Life Ins. Co., Hartford, Conn., 1970-77; chief tax counsel Rohm & Haus Co., Phila., 1977-78; ptnr. Dibble, Koff, Lane, Stern and Stern, Rochester, N.Y., 1978-81; pres. Howard M. Koff, P.C., Albany, N.Y., 1981—; lectr. tax matters. Mem. pub. adv. coun. N.Y. State Ethics Commn. Recipient Founders Day award NYU, 1962; Lawyers Coop. award for gen. excellence Lawyers Coop. Pub. Co., 1965. Mem. Fed. Bar Assn. (past pres. Hartford County chpt.), ABA (past chmn. subcom. com. on partnerships tax sect.), Albany County Bar Assn., Estate Planning Council Eastern N.Y., Albany Area C. of C. Republican. Jewish. Clubs: Rotary, Colonie Guilderland N.Y. Editor-in-chief Bklyn. Law Rev., 1964-65; charter mem. editorial adv. bd. Jour. Real Estate Taxation; contbr. articles to legal jours. Corporate taxation, State and local taxation, Personal income taxation. Home: 205 Bentwood Ct W Albany NY 12203-4905 Office: 600 Broadway Albany NY 12207-2205

**KOFFLER, WARREN WILLIAM,** lawyer; b. N.Y.C., July 21, 1938; s. Jack and Rose (Conovich) K.; m. Barbara Rose Holz, June 11, 1959; m. Jayne Audri Goetzel, May 15, 1970; children: Kevin, Kenneth, Caroline. B.S., Boston U., 1959; J.D., U. Calif.-Berkeley, 1962; LLD, NYU, 1972. Bar: D.C. 1962, N.Y. 1963, U.S. Dist. Ct. D.C. 1963, Fla. 1980, Va. 1981, Pa. 1982. Atty. FAA, Washington, 1964; pvt. practice law, Washington, 1964, 78—, Hollywood, Palm Beach, and Miami, Fla., 1978—; atty. Fed. Home Loan Bank Bd., Washington, 1964-66; ptnr. Koffler & Spivack, Washington, 1967-77. Mem. ABA, Inter-Am. Bar Assn., Fed. Bar Assn., D.C. Bar Assn., Fla. Bar Assn., Va. Bar Assn., Assn. Trial Lawyers Am., Brit. Inst. Internat. and Comparative Law, Univ. Club (Washington), Bankers Club (Miami). Administrative and regulatory, Banking, Private international. Office: 11440 Us Highway 1 North Palm Beach FL 33408 also: 1730 K St NW Washington DC 20006-3868

**KOFMAN, STEPHANIE WANK,** lawyer; b. Queens, N.Y., Aug. 3, 1971; d. Jerald Lee and Linda Barbara Wank; m. Ilya S. Kofman, Aug. 18, 1996. AB, Brown U., 1993; JD, Harvard U., 1996. Bar: N.Y. 1997, D.C. 1998, U.S. Dist. Ct. Md. 1997, U.S. Ct. Appeals (4th cir.) 1997. Law clk. Judge Marvin J. Garvis, Balt., 1996-97; assoc. Williams & Connolly, Washington, 1997—. General civil litigation. Office: Williams & Connolly 725 12th St NW Washington DC 20005-5901

**KOGAN, BRUCE IVAN,** law educator; b. N.Y., Nov. 19, 1944; s. Robert and Jeanne S. (Sloane) K.; m. Susan Silver Cohen, Jul. 3, 1966 (div. Oct. 1982); children; Mark J., Matthew J.; m. Jaime Klinger, Aug. 19, 1960. BA in philosophy, Syracuse U., 1967; JD, Dickinson Sch. Law, 1970; LLM in taxation, Georgetown U., 1972. Bar: Pa. 1970, U.S. Ct. Appeals (3rd cir.) 1972, U.S. Tax Ct. 1983. Appellate atty. tax div. U.S. Dept. Justice, Washington, 1970-73; ptnr. Kogan & Smigel, Harrisburg, Pa., 1973-82; law prof. Widener U. Sch. Law, Wilmington, Del., 1982-93; law prof., assoc. dean Roger Williams U., Bristol, R.I., 1993—; mem. R.I. com. on Indigent Litigants, Providence, 1994—; mem. bd. dirs. Legal Aid Soc. R.I., 1994—; exec. com. Del. Tax Int., Wilmington, 1982-93. Contbr. articles to profl. jours. Vice chmn. West Chester Mcpl. Authority West Chester, Pa., 1991-94. With U.S. Army, 1965-67. Mem. ABA (tax sect. com. on stds. of tax practice). Republican. Jewish. Office: Roger Williams U Sch Law Ten Metacom Ave Bristol RI 02809

**KOGAN, GERALD,** state supreme court justice; b. Bklyn., May 23, 1933; s. Morris and Yetta (Weinstein) K.; m. Irene Vulgan, Nov. 17, 1955; children: Robert, Debra, Karen. BBA, JD, U. Miami, Coral Gables, Fla., 1955. Bar: Fla. 1955. Sole practice Miami, Fla., 1955-60, 67-80; asst. state's atty. Dade County, Fla., 1960-67, chief prosecutor homicide and capital crimes sect., 1960-67; judge criminal div. Fla. 11th Jud. Cir. Ct., Miami, 1980-87, adminstrv. judge criminal div., 1984-87; justice Supreme Ct. Fla., Tallahassee, 1987-98, chief justice, 1996-98; adj. prof. law Nova U. Law Sch., U. Miami Sch. Law, Fla. State U. Sch. Law; mem. faculty Am. Acad. Jud. Edn. Served with CIC, AUS, 1955-57. Mem. ABA, Fla. Bar, Dade County Bar Assn. Office: Supreme Ct Fla 500 S Duval St Tallahassee FL 32399-6556

**KOGER, FRANK WILLIAMS,** federal judge; b. Kansas City, Mo., Mar. 20, 1930; s. C.H. and Lelia D. (Williams) K.; m. Jeanine E. Strawhacker, Mar. 19, 1954; children: Lelia Jane, Mary Courtney. AB, Kansas City U., 1951, LLB, 1953; LLM, U. Mo., Kansas City, 1966. Staff judge adv. USAF, Rapid City, S.D., 1953-56; ptnr. Reid, Koger & Reid, Kansas City, 1956-61, Shockley, Reid & Koger, Kansas City, 1961-86; U.S. bankruptcy judge U.S. Dept. Judiciary, Kansas City, 1986—; chief judge 8th Cir. Bankruptcy Appellate Panel, 1997—; adj. prof. law sch. U. Mo., Columbia, 1990—, U. Mo.-Kansas City, 1992—. Author: (manual) Foreclosure Law in Missouri, 1982, Missouri Collection Law, 1983; author, co-editor: Bankruptcy Handbook, 1992; editor: Bankruptcy Law, 1990. Bd. dirs. Jackson County Pub. Hosp., Kansas City, 1974-79, St. Lukes Hosp., Kansas City, 1970—; chair subcom. Jackson County Charter Transition Com., Kansas City, 1978-79. Capt. USAF, 1953-56. Recipient Shelley Peters Meml. award Am. Inst. Banking, Kansas City, 1986. Fellow Am. Coll. Bankruptcy Judges; mem. Nat. Conf. Bankruptcy Judges (dir. 1990-93, sec. 1994-95, pres.-elect 1995-96, pres. 1996-97), Comml. Law League Am. (pres. 1983-84). Avocations: contract bridge, gardening. Office: US Bankruptcy Ct 811 Grand Blvd Kansas City MO 64106-1904

**KOGOVSEK, DANIEL CHARLES,** lawyer; b. Pueblo, Colo., Aug. 4, 1951; s. Frank Louis and Mary Edith (Blatnick) K.; m. Patricia Elizabeth Connell, June 30, 1979; 1 child, Ryan Robert. B.A., U. Notre Dame, 1973; J.D., Columbia U., 1976. Bar: Colo. 1976, U.S. Dist. Ct. Colo. 1976, U.S. Ct. Appeals (10th cir.) 1978, U.S. Supreme Ct. 1983. Asst. atty. gen. Colo. Dept. Law, Denver, 1976-79; campaign mgr. Congressman Kogovsek, Pueblo, 1980, 82; dir. Office Consumer Services, Denver, 1981; mem. firm Fish & Kogovsek, Denver, 1983-84; sr. assoc. Petersen & Fonda, P.C., Pueblo, 1984-89; mem. firm Kogovsek & Higinbotham, P.C., 1989—. Mem. ABA, Colo. Bar Assn., Pueblo Bar Assn. Email: kogo-law@fone.net. Consumer commercial. Home: 584 W Spaulding Ave S Pueblo West CO 81007-1874 Office: 323 S Union Ave Pueblo CO 81003-3429

**KOHL, JACQUELYN MARIE,** lawyer; b. Bloomington, Ind., Nov. 29, 1950; d. George Henry and Betty Louise (Bach) K.; m. Jeffrey James Fisher, Feb. 23, 1973 (div. Apr. 1976). BA in Math., Ind. U., 1972; JD, Thomas M. Cooley Law Sch., 1981. Bar: Ind. 1981, Ill. 1981, U.S. Dist. Ct. (so. dist.) Ind. 1981, U.S. Dist. (no. dist.) Ind. 1982. Assoc. atty. Raskosky & Kohl, Hammond, Ind., 1981-85; ptnr. Raskosky & Kohl, Hammond, 1985—; hearing officer/dir. Unsafe Bldg. Program, Hammond, 1983; dep. prosecutor 31st Jud. Cir., Lake County, Hammond, 1984. Mem. Ind. State Bar Assn., Lake County Bar Assn. Democrat. General practice, Probate, Family and matrimonial. Office: Raskosky & Kohl 5252 Hohman Ave Rm 203 Hammond IN 46320-1599

**KOHL, KATHLEEN ALLISON BARNHART,** lawyer; b. Ft. Leavenworth, Kans., Jan. 11, 1955; d. Robert William and Margaret Ann (Snowden) Barnhart. BS, Memphis State U., 1978; JD, Loyola U., New Orleans, 1982. Bar: La. 1982, U.S. Dist. Ct. (ea. dist.) La. 1982, U.S. Dist. Ct. (no. dist.) Tex. 1985, U.S. Ct. Appeals (5th cir.) 1986, U.S. Ct. Appeals (11th cir.) 1988, U.S. Supreme Ct. 1994. Assoc. Garrity & Webb, Harahan, La., 1982; revenue officer IRS, Dallas, 1984; sr. trial atty. EEOC, Dallas, 1984-86; sr. criminal enforcement counsel U.S. EPA, Dallas, 1986-91, chief water enforcement sect., office regional counsel, 1991-92; dep. dir. criminal enforcement counsel divsn. U.S. EPA, Washington, 1992-93, dir. criminal enforcement counsel divsn., 1993-94; sr. criminal enforcement counsel U.S. EPA, Dallas, 1994—; spl. asst. U.S. atty. (spl. assignment from U.S. EPA), U.S. Atty.'s Office, Montgomery, Ala., 1988-89; vis. instr. Fed. Law Enforcement Tng. Ctr., Glynco, Ga., 1987—; adj. prof. environ. crimes seminar Cornell U. Law Sch., spring 1993, environ. law Sch. Law Tex. Wesleyan U., fall 1998; instr. EPA Nat. Acad., 1997—. Vol. instr. New Orleans Police Acad., 1981. Mem. La. Bar Assn. Office: EPA 1445 Ross Ave Ste 1200 Dallas TX 75202-2733

**KOHLES, DAVID ALLAN,** lawyer; b. Crofton, Nebr., Sept. 8, 1952; s. Albert A. and Pauline (Keiser) K.; m. Patrice C. Fay, Mar. 20, 1982; children: Kristin N., Lindsay F. BA, U. Nebr., 1974; JD, Washington U., St. Louis, 1977. Bar: Wash. 1977, U.S. Ct. Appeals (9th cir.) 1977. Assoc. Wolfstone, Panchot, Bloch & Kelley, Seattle, 1979-81; pvt. practice Seattle, 1981—. Pres. East Lake Cmty. Assn., Seattle, 1977-79, Brierwood Neighborhood Assn., Brier, Wash., 1988-90. Mem. Wash. State Trial Lawyers. Personal injury, Admiralty, Workers' compensation. Office: 2800 Century Sq 1501 4th Ave Seattle WA 98101-3225

**KOHLWEY, JANE ELLEN,** lawyer; b. Milw., Oct. 19, 1957. BS, U. Wis., 1980, JD, 1985. Bar: Wis. 1985, U.S. Dist. Ct. (ea. and we. dists.) Wis. 1985. Assoc. Stoltz Law Office, Columbus, Wis., 1985-86, Miller Rogers & Owens, Portage, Wis., 1986-89; asst. dist. atty. Columbia County Dist. Atty.'s Office, Portage, 1988; pvt. practice, Portage, 1990-98; dist. atty. Columbia County, Wis., 1999—. Juvenile, Criminal. Office: PO Box 638 Portage WI 53901-0638

**KOHM, LYNNE MARIE,** lawyer, educator; b. Albany, N.Y., Aug. 26, 1959; d. James R. and Lois E. (Irwin) Donnelly; m. Joseph A. Kohm, Jr.; children: Joseph A., III, Kathleen Elizabeth. BA in Philosophy, SUNY, Albany, 1980; MA in Theology, Inst. Biblical Studies, 1986; JD, Syracuse U., 1988. Bar: N.Y. 1989, Mass. 1989, D.C. 1990, Fla. 1990, Va. 1994, U.S. Dist. Ct. (no. dist.) N.Y. 1990. Travelling rep. Campus Crusade for Christ, New England, Springfield, Mass., 1981-84; assoc. campus dir. Campus Crusade for Christ, Syracuse U., Syracuse, N.Y., 1984-87; assoc. Evan L. Webster, Groton, N.Y., 1988-89; mng. ptnr. Webster & Kohm, Groton, N.Y., 1989-93; asst. prof. Regent U. Sch. Law, Virginia Beach, Va., 1993—; affiliate atty. Rutherford Inst., Charlottesville, Va., 1990—, Am. Ctr. for Law and Justice, Virginia Beach; participant Alliance Def. Fund's Nat. Litig. Acad. I, June, 1979. Contbr. articles to profl. jours. Acad. citizen mem. Real Estate Appraisers Bd., 1997; bd. mem., sec. Bethany Christian Svcs. of Hampton Roads; bd. mem. Second Wind Dance Co.; presenter Campus Crusade for Christ Internat. Staff Training, Will Seminar, 1997. Mem. Va. State Bar Assn. (bd. govs., family law sec.), Women's Rep. Club, Concerned Women for Am., Christian Legal Soc., Rotary Internat. Republican. Office: Regent U Sch Law 1000 Regent U Dr Virginia Beach VA 23456

**KOHN, DEXTER MORTON,** lawyer; b. Brookline, Mass., Dec. 11, 1921; s. Archibald George and Taurice Wit K.; m. Emily Rose Haas, Dec. 22, 1947; children: Edward H., John D., Roger S. AB, Cornell U., 1943; JD, Boston U., 1949. Bar: Mass.; U.S. Ct. Appeals; U.S. Dist. Ct., U.S. Supreme Ct. Assoc. Sachs and Jacobs, Washington, 1950-54; pvt. practice Law Offices of Dexter M. Kohn, Washington, 1954—. Editor: Boston U. Law Rev., 1948-49. Officer, mem. Woodmont Country Club, bd. govs.; mem. estate planning coun. Washington, 1985—; pres. Montgomery County, Md. Assn. of Country Clubs, 1982-85. Ssgt. Army Air Force, 1943-46. Mem. Bar Assn. of D.C. (bd. govs., chmn. D.C. affairs sect.). Avocations: golf, hiking, securities analysis. Probate, Estate planning, General corporate. Office: 2000 Massachusetts Ave NW Washington DC 20036-1022

**KOHN, HAROLD ELIAS,** lawyer; b. Phila., Apr. 5, 1914; s. Joseph C. and Mayme (Rumm) K.; m. Edith Anderson, Dec. 30, 1946; children: Amy, Ellen, Joseph Carl. AB, U. Pa., 1934, LLB, 1937; LLD (hon.), Temple U., 1990. Bar: Pa. 1938, D.C. 1972. Pres. Kohn, Swift & Graf, P.C., Phila.; spl. counsel transit matters City of Phila., 1952-53, 56-62; counsel to gov. State of Pa., 1972; mem. bd. Southeastern Pa. Transp. Authority, 1972-77; mem. Pa. Jud. Inquiry and Rev. Bd., 1973-77; mem. Pa. Supreme Ct. Continuing Legal Edn. Bd., 1992-97; bd. consultors Villanova U. Law Sch. Trustee Temple U., U. of Arts; bd. dirs. Wilma Theatre, Moss Rehab. Hosp., Phila. Geriatric Ctr.; treas., bd. dirs. Kohn Found.; pres., bd. dirs. Arronson Found., Lavine Found.; past bd. dirs. Phila. Psychiat. Ctr.; trustee, mem. exec. com. Phila. Fedn. Jewish Agys.; past mem. exec. com. United Jewish Appeal; past v.p., bd. dirs. Phila. chpt. ACLU. Mem. ABA, Pa. Bar Assn., Phila. Bar Assn., D.C. Bar Assn., Internat. Acad. Trial Lawyers, Jud. Conf. 3d Cir., Am. Law Inst., Order of Coif, Phi Beta Kappa. Federal civil litigation, Antitrust, Libel. Office: Kohn Swift & Graf PC 1101 Market St Ste 2400 Philadelphia PA 19107-2926 *Died June 14, 1999.*

**KOHN, HENRY,** lawyer; b. St. Louis, May 2, 1917; s. Henry and Hannah (Lederer) K.; m. Anne Frankenthaler, Sept. 23, 1945; children: Margaret, Barbara, Alice. B.A., Yale U., 1939, LL.B., 1942. Bar: Mo. 1942, N.Y. 1946. With Bd. Econ. Warfare, 1942; practice with George Frankenthaler, N.Y.C., 1946-48; pvt. practice N.Y.C., 1949-56; sr. ptnr. Frankenthaler, Kohn, Schneider & Katz, N.Y.C., 1957—; Former pres., dir. Fiduciary Mut. Investing Co., Mercer Fund Inc.; bd. dirs. Meta Health Tech., Inc. Chmn. bd., founder Am. Jewish Soc. for Service; former treas. and bd. dirs. Nat. Jewish Welfare Bd.; bd. dirs. Lavanburg Corner House Found.; pres. Ed. Lee and Jean Campe Found., Sam and Louise Campe Found.; dir., past pres. and chmn. bd. dirs. 92d St. YM-YWHA; former dir. Edison Bros. Stores Inc., Graphic Sci. Inc. Served to capt. AUS, 1942-46. Mem. ABA, N.Y. County Lawyers Assn., Assn. Bar City N.Y., Order of Coif, Phi Beta Kappa. Jewish. Clubs: New York Lawn Bowling, Harmonie, The India House (N.Y.C.). Home: 155 E 72nd St New York NY 10021-4371 also: Strawberry Hill Ackert Hook Rd Rhinebeck NY 12572

**KOHN, JEFFREY IRA,** lawyer; b. N.Y.C., Mar. 10, 1959; s. Howard Sanford and Arlene Vivian (Kostrinsky) K.; m. Martha C. Obler, Aug. 12, 1984; children: Brian Edward, Alexandra Hannah. BS in Indsl. and Labor Rels., Cornell U., 1981; JD, George Washington U., 1984. Bar: N.Y. 1985, U.S. Dist. Ct. (so. and ea. dists.) N.Y. 1985, N.J. 1988, U.S. Ct. Appeals (2d cir.) 1991, U.S. Supreme Ct., 1992, U.S. Ct. Appeals (3d cir.) 1993. Assoc. O'Melveny & Myers, N.Y.C., 1984-92, ptnr., 1992—; adj. prof. N.Y. Law Sch., 1989—, adj. instr. law, 1986-89. Author: (book chpt.) NLRA Law and Policy, 1992; supplemental author: Modern Law of Employment Relations, 1990—. Mem. ABA (employment and labor law com. 1991—). Avocations: tennis, baseball, photography. Labor, Federal civil litigation. Home: 4 Stony Hollow Rd Chappaqua NY 10514-2014 Office: O'Melveny & Myers 153 E 53rd St Fl 53 New York NY 10022-4688

**KOHN, ROBERT,** lawyer; b. Boston, June 27, 1952; s. Lester Jerome Kohn and Barbara Marion Morrill; m. Misa Ninomiya, May 17, 1993; 1 child, Sandra Ninomiya. AB, U. Calif., Berkeley, 1974; JD, Hastings Coll., San Francisco, 1977; MA in Edn., San Francisco State U., 1989. Bar: Hawaii, Calif., Guam, Palau. Staff attorney Calif. Ct. Appeals, Fresno, Calif., 1977-78, Supreme Ct. Republic of Palau, Koror, Palau, 1993-94; assoc. Price, Okamoto, Himeno & Lum, Honolulu, 1995—. Mem. Order of the Coif, Thurston Soc., Hastings Law Jour. General civil litigation, Personal injury. Office: Price Okamoto Himeno & Lum 707 Richards St Ste 728 Honolulu HI 96813-4623

**KOHN, ROBERT ALEXANDER,** lawyer; b. Washington, June 8, 1969; s. Robert and Rose K. BS in Fgn. Svc., Georgetown U., 1991; Diplome des Etudes Juridiques Europeen, et Internat., U. Paris, 1994; JD, Am. U., 1995. Bar: N.Y. 1996, D.C. 1998, Ga. 1998. Assoc. Ward & Assocs., Washington, 1995-97, Troutman Sanders, LLP, Atlanta, 1998—. Mem. ABA, Inter-Am. Bar Assn., Atlanta Hispanic C. of C. (bd. dirs. 1998—), Brazilian-Am. C. of C. Ga. (bd. dirs. 1998—). Private international, General corporate. Office: Troutman Sanders LLP 600 Peachtree St NE Ste 5200 Atlanta GA 30308-2231

**KOHN, SHALOM L.,** lawyer; b. N.Y.C., Nov. 18, 1949; s. Pincus and Helen (Roth) K.; m. Barbara Segal, June 30, 1974; children: David, Jeremy, Daniel. B.S. in Acctg. summa cum laude, CUNY, 1970; J.D. magna cum laude, Harvard U., 1974, M.B.A., 1974. Bar: Ill. 1975, U.S. Dist. Ct. (no. dist.) Ill. 1975, U.S. Ct. Appeals (7th cir.) 1976, U.S. Supreme Ct. 1980, N.Y. 1988, U.S. Dist. Ct. (so. dist.) N.Y. 1988. Law clk. to chief judge U.S. Ct. Appeals (2d cir.), N.Y.C., 1974-75; assoc. Sidley & Austin, Chgo., 1975-80, ptnr., 1980—. Contbr. articles to profl. jours. Mem. exec. com. Adv. Coun. Religious Rights in Eastern Europe and Soviet Union, Washington, 1984-86; bd. dirs. Brisk Rabbinical Coll., Chgo., 1980—. Mem. ABA, Chgo. Bar Assn. Bankruptcy, Federal civil litigation. Office: Sidley & Austin 1 First Natl Plz Chicago IL 60603-2003 also: 875 3rd Ave New York NY 10022-6225

**KOHN, VALORIE,** lawyer; b. May 6, 1952. BA, U. Wis., 1974, MS, 1977; JD, Marquette U., 1988. Bar: Wis. 1988; cert. divorce mediator 1991. Pvt. practice, 1988—; mem. mentor coun. Wis. State Bar, Milw., 1993-96, guardian ad litem com., 1997—, custody com., 1997—. Author: Directory of Service Agencies to Assist Family Law Practitioners Regarding Custody, placement issue, 1997; coord., editor: Family Law Videotape, 1995—. Mem. Milw. Bar Assn. (mem. joint bench/bar famility law com. 1997—). Family and matrimonial. Office: Kohn Family Law Offices SC 8989 N Pt Wash Rd Ste 207 Milwaukee WI 53217-1633

**KOHN, WILLIAM IRWIN,** lawyer; b. Bronx, N.Y., June 27, 1951; s. Arthur Oscar and Frances (Hoffman) K.; m. Karen Mindlin, Aug. 29, 1974; children: Shira, Kinneret, Asher. Student, U. Del., 1969-71; BA with honors, U. Cin., 1973; JD, Ohio State U., 1976. Bar: Ohio 1976, U.S. Dist. Ct. (no. dist.) Ohio 1982, Ind. 1982, U. S. Dist. Ct. (no. and so. dists.) Ind. 1982, D.C. 1992, U.S. Supreme Ct., 1992, Ill. 1994; cert. Bus. Bankruptcy Law Am. Bankruptcy Bd. Cert. Ptnr. Krugliak, Wilkins, Griffith & Dougherty, Canton, Ohio, 1976-82, Barnes & Thornburg, Chgo., 1982—; adj. prof. law U. Notre Dame, Ind., 1984-90. Author: West's Indiana Business Forms, West's Indiana Uniform Commercial Code Forms; contbr. articles to profl. jours. Bd. dirs. Family Svcs., South Bend, 1985-94, Jewish Fedn., Highland Park United Way. Mem. ABA (bus. bankruptcy subcom.), Am. Bankruptcy Inst. (insolvency sect., bd. dirs.), Ill. Bar Assn., Chgo. Bar Assn., Comml. Law League. Banking, Bankruptcy, Contracts commercial. Office: Barnes & Thornburg 2610 Madison Plz 200 W Madison St Chicago IL 60606-3414

**KOJEVNIKOV, BORIS OLEG,** lawyer, foreign legal consultant; b. Rome, Oct. 16, 1950; came to U.S., 1977; s. Oleg Vladimir and Oxana (Artem) K.; m. Irina Maxim Baranova, Aug. 8, 1974; children: Oxana, Oleg. Law Degre, Inst. Fgn. Rels., Moscow, 1972, Cand Legal Scis., 1984. Legal adviser USSR Ministry Fgn. Trade, Moscow, 1972-77, Amtorg Trading Corp., N.Y.C., 1977-82, Comecon, Moscow, 1982-84; dir. legal dept. Chamber Commerce and Industry, Moscow, 1984-91; v.p. Prosystem GmbH, Vienna, 1991-96; v.p., mem. Golubov & Tiagai, N.Y.C., 1996—; arbitrator Internat. Comml. Arbitration ct., Moscow, 1984—, Internat. Arbitration Ctr., Vienna, 1989-94. Author 4 books; contbr. more than 20 articles to U.S., Russian and German periodicals. Fellow Chartered Inst. of Arbitrators; mem. Assn. Bar City N.Y. Avocations: tennis, squash. Contracts commercial, Private international. Office: Golubov & Tiagai PLLC 475 5th Ave Rm 1112 New York NY 10017-6220

**KOKES, ALOIS HAROLD,** lawyer; b. Miami Beach, Fla., Mar. 30, 1955; s. Alois Louis and Margaret Ozier (Muller) K. BA, U. Va., 1977; JD, Vt. Law Sch., 1980. Bar: N.J. 1981, U.S. Dist. Ct. N.J., U.S. Supreme Ct.; cert. criminal trial atty. Jud. clk. to judge hon. Merritt Lane Freehold, N.J., 1979; jud. law clk. Hon. Judges Julia L. Ashbey and Burton L. Fundler, Freehold, N.J., 1980-81; asst. dep. pub. defender Office of Pub. Defender State of N.J., Mays Landing, 1981-86; assoc. Loveland, Garrett, Russell & Young, Ocean City, N.J., 1986-88; ptnr. Smith & Kokes, Ocean City, 1988-94; pvt. practice, 1994—; investigator Dist. I Ethics Com., Northfield, N.J., 1990-94. Bd. dirs. Caring Inc., Pleasantville, N.J., 1988—. Avocations: writing, sports, camping, surfing, coaching. Criminal, General civil litigation, State civil litigation. Home: 1903 W Brigantine Ave Brigantine NJ 08203-2047

**KOKULIS, PAUL NICHOLAS,** lawyer; b. Goffstown, N.H., Mar. 30, 1924; s. Nicholas Paul and Despou (Golias) K.; m. Carolyn Anne Edwards, Sept. 26, 1959; children: Nicholas, Kimberly, Christy Lee, Steven. B-SChemE, Worchester Poly Inst., 1944; LLB, George Washington U., 1950. Bar: D.C. 1950, U.S. Ct. Appeals (fed. cir.)ú 1952, U.S. Supreme Ct. 1954. Engr. Naval Rsch. Lab., Washington, 1944-46; assoc. Cushman, Darby & Cushman, Washington, 1950-54, ptnr., 1954-79, sr. ptnr., 1980—. Mem. editorial bd. Patent World, London, 1985-88. Elder 4th Presbyn. Ch., Washington, 1957—; bd. dirs. Potomac (Md.) Community Ctr., 1981-89; youth coach Potomac Boys Club, 1976-85. Recipient Community Svc. award Potomac Almanac, 1982; named Man of Yr., Potomac C. of C., 1985. Mem. D.C. Bar, Bar Assn. D.C., Am. Intellectual Property Assn., Assn. Indsl. Intellectual Property, Inst. Chartered Patent Agts. (U.K., fgn.), Can. Patent Inst. (fgn.), Christian Legal Soc. Republican. Avocations: youth work, athletics. Patent. Home: 9409 Falls Rd Potomac MD 20854-3917 Office: Cushman Darby & Cushman 1100 New York Ave NW Ste 800E Washington DC 20005-6117

**KOLBACK, KIMBERLY DAWN,** lawyer; b. Rochester, Pa., May 23, 1960; d. James Harry and Patricia Ann Kolback. BA magna cum laude, Pa. State U., 1982; JD, U. Miami, 1986. Bar: Fla. 1986, U.S. Dist. Ct. (so. dist.) Fla., U.S. Ct. Appeals (11th cir.). With Ryder Systems, Inc., Miami, Fla., 1986, Frates, Bienstock & Sheehe, Miami, 1986-87; assoc. Kelley Drye & Warren, N.Y.c., 1987-88, Stuzin & Camner, P.A., Miami, 1988-90; ptnr. Kluger, Peretz, Kaplan & Berlin, P.A., Miami, 1990—. Contbr. articles to profl. jours. Active Am. Cancer Soc., Habitat for Humanity. Mem. ABA, Dade County Bar Assn. (bd. dirs. 1996-98), Vol. Lawyers for the Arts, Phi Alpha Delta, Omicron Delta Kappa, Pi Sigma Alpha. Avocations: flying, guitar. Entertainment, Intellectual property. Office: Kluger Peretz Kaplan & Berlin PA Miami Ctr 201 S Biscayne Blvd Fl 17 Miami FL 33131-4325

**KOLBE, KARL WILLIAM, JR.,** lawyer; b. Passaic, N.J., Sept. 29, 1926; s. Karl William Sr. and Edna Ernestine (Rumsey) K.; m. Barbara Louise Bogart, Jan. 28, 1950 (dec. Aug. 1992); children: Kim E., William B., Katherine B.; m. Patricia L. Coward, Apr. 30, 1994. BA, Princeton U., 1949; JD, U. Va., 1952. Bars: N.Y. 1952, D.C. 1976. Ptnr. Thelen, Reid & Priest, N.Y.C., 1966-92, of counsel, 1993—; dir. Bessemer Trust Co. (N.A.), N.Y.C.,1977-97, Carolinas Cement Co., 1994-98, World Trade Corp.; vice-chmn. The friends of Thirteen Inc. Bd. dirs. N.J. Ballet Co., West Orange, 1970-98, Ocean Liner Mus., 1992—. Served with USN, 1944-46. Mem. ABA (chmn. pub. utility law sect. 1984-85). Republican. Episcopalian. Clubs: Univ. (N.Y.C.); Metro. (Washington). Taxation, general. Home: PO Box 278 111 Old Chester Rd Essex Fells NJ 07021-1625 Office: Thelen Reid & Priest 40 W 57th St New York NY 10019-4001

**KOLBER, RICHARD A.,** lawyer; b. Wantagh, N.Y., Aug. 2, 1961; s. Leonard and Yola Kolber. BA, SUNY, Binghamton, 1983; JD, U. Calif., 1986. Bar: Calif. 1986, U.S. Dist. Ct. (so. and ea. dists.) Calif. 1987. Assoc. Haight, Brown & Bonesteel, Santa Monica, Calif., 1986-88, Barash & Hill, L.A., 1988-93; pvt. practice Law Offices of Richard A. Kolber, L.A., 1993—. Fax: 310-286-2351. E-mail: rkolber@t-nlaw.com. General civil litigation. Office: 2049 Century Park E Ste 755 Los Angeles CA 90067-3172

**KOLBRENER, JONATHAN,** lawyer; b. Newark, Feb. 18, 1957; s. Peter Denker and Sandra Lee (Heller) K. BA, Brandeis U., 1979; JD, Hofstra U., 1982. Bar: N.Y. 1983, U. S. Dist. Ct. (ea. and so. dists.) N.Y. 1983. Assoc. Bower & Gardner, N.Y.C., 1982-85, Sheft and Sheft, N.Y.C., 1986-90, Peter Kolbrener, Garden City, N.Y., 1991-93, Marshall, Conway & Wright, N.Y.C., 1993-94, Kelner & Kelner, N.Y.C., 1996-98, Patric Colligan, Purchase, N.Y., 1998—. Mem. ABA, N.Y. Bar Assn. Avocations: bicycling, running, swimming, skiing. General civil litigation, Insurance, Personal injury. Office: Patric Colligan 2700 Westchester Ave Purchase NY 10577-2554

**KOLE, JANET STEPHANIE,** lawyer, writer, photographer; b. Washington, Dec. 20, 1946; d. Martin J. and Ruth G. (Goldberg) K. AB, Bryn Mawr Coll., 1968; MA, NYU, 1970; JD, Temple U., 1980. Bar: Pa. 1980, N.J. 1994. Assoc. editor trade books Simon & Schuster, N.Y.C., 1968-70; publicity dir. Am. Arbitration Assn., N.Y.C., 1970-73; freelance photojournalist, N.Y.C., 1973-76; law clk. Morgan Lewis & Bockius, Phila., 1977-80; assoc. Schnader, Harrison, Segal & Lewis, Phila., 1980-85; ptnr. Cohen, Shapiro, Polisher, Shiekman & Cohen, Phila., 1985-95; ptnr., chmn. environ. practice group Klehr, Harrison, Harvey, Branzburg & Ellers, 1995-97; pvt. practice, 1997—. Author: Post Mortem, 1974; editor Environmental Litigation, 1991, 99; contbr. numerous articles to gen. interest publs., profl. jours.; past mem. bd. editors New Am. Rev. Mem. Mayor's Task Force on Rape, N.Y.C., 1972-77; adv. Support Ctr. Child Advs., Phila., 1980—; mem. Phila. Vol. Lawyers for the Arts; steering com. Lawyers for Reproductive Rights. Fellow Acad. Advocacy, Am. Bar Found.; mem. ABA (co-chair environ. litigation com., former dir. publs., former coun. mem. sect. litigation, dir. publs., former co-div. dir. substantive areas of litigation, former editor litigation news, former chmn. com. on monographs and unpublished papers, com. spl. pubs.), ATLA. Democrat. Federal civil litigation, State civil litigation, Environmental. Office: 900 Haddon Ave Ste 412 Collingswood NJ 08108-2113

**KOLE, JULIUS S.,** lawyer; b. Chgo., July 27, 1953; s. Jack H. and Ruth (Rakowsky) K.; m. Dorie Elrod, June 27, 1976; children: Ryan, Frederick, Abby. BS in Fin., U. Ill., Chgo., 1975; JD, John Marshall Law Sch., 1978. Bar: Ill. 1978. Asst. pub. defender Cook County Pub. Defender, Chgo., 1978-80; prin. Law Offices of Julius S. Kole, Buffalo Grove, Ill., 1980—. Fellow Ill. State Bar Assn., Lake County Bar Assn. Jewish. Avocations: sports, reading, motorcycling. Real property, Criminal, General corporate. Office: 750 W Lake Cook Rd Ste 135 Buffalo Grove IL 60089-2075

**KOLICK, DANIEL JOSEPH,** lawyer; b. Lakewood, Ohio, May 12, 1950; s. Joseph Frank and Agnes Helen (Lusnak) K. B.A., Holy Cross Coll., 1972; J.D., Case Western Res. U., 1975. Bar: Ohio 1975. Sole practice, North Olmsted, Ohio, 1975-85; ptnr. Kolick & Kondzer, Westlake, Ohio, 1985—; asst. law dir. City of Strongsville, Ohio, 1976—; dir. law Village of Lindale, Cleve., 1975-76. Chmn. North Olmsted Charter Rev. Commn., 1981, 83; mem. council St. Richard's Parish Council, North Olmsted, 1980-82, tchr. Sch. Religion, 1979-81. Mem. Cuyahoga County Bar Assn., Ohio Sch. Bd. Assn., Ohio State Bar Assn., ABA. Roman Catholic. Club: North Olmsted Exchange (trustee, treas. 1977-78). Avocations: softball, basketball, tennis. Administrative and regulatory, State civil litigation, Personal injury. Home: 20686 Wildwood Ln Strongsville OH 44136-5727 Office: Kolick & Kondzer 24500 Center Ridge Rd Ste 175 Westlake OH 44145-5628

**KOLIN, LAWRENCE HOWARD,** lawyer; b. Mar. 19, 1969. BA, Trinity Coll., 1991; JD, U. Miami, Coral Gables, Fla., 1994. Bar: Fla. 1994, U.S. Dist. Ct. (mid. dist.) Fla. 1994, U.S. Dist. Ct. (no. and so. dists.) Fla. 1997, U.S. Supreme Ct. 1998. Atty. Hannah, Estes & Ingram, Orlando, Fla., 1994—. Exec. editor Entertainment & Sports, 1993-94. Recipient Outstanding Guardian Ad Litem, Legal Aid Soc., Orange County, Fla., 1997. Mem. ABA, Fla. Bar Assn. (dist. chmn. entertainment, arts & sports sect. 1998), Am. Inns of Ct. Entertainment, Insurance, General civil litigation. Office: Hannah Estes & Ingram 37 N Orange Ave Orlando FL 32801-2449

**KOLKER, LAWRENCE PAUL,** lawyer; b. Huntington, N.Y., Aug. 1, 1956; s. Justin William and Sondra Geraldine (Budow) K.; m. Emily Diane Porter, June 14, 1981; children: Danielle, Jeremy, Madeline. BA, SUNY, Binghamton, 1978; JD, Bklyn. U., 1983. Bar: N.Y. 1984, U.S. Dist. Ct. (so. and ea. dists.) N.Y. 1984, U.S. Dist. Ct. (we. dist.) Mich. 1992, U.S. Ct. Appeals (2d cir.) 1989, U.S. Ct. Appeals (11th cir.) 1992. Clk. Hon. Henry F. Werker, N.Y.C., 1981-82; asst. corp. counsel N.Y.C. Law Dept., 1983-87; assoc. Hill, Betts & Nash, N.Y.C., 1987-89; ptnr. Wolf, Haldenstein, Adler, Freeman & Herz, LLP, N.Y.C., 1989—. Mem. N.Y. State Bar Assn., Assn. of Bar of City of N.Y. Avocations: carpentry, cooking, guitar, cross-country skiing, tennis. General civil litigation, Securities. Office: Wolf Haldenstein Adler Freeman & Herz LLP 270 Madison Ave New York NY 10016-0601

**KOLKER, SCOTT LEE,** lawyer; b. St. Louis, Dec. 31, 1968; s. Allan E. and Jacquelyn E. Kolker. BSBA, U. Mo., 1991; JD, Wash. U., 1994. Bar: Mo. 1994, Ill. 1995, U.S. Dist. Ct. (ea. dist.) Mo. 1995. Assoc. Holtkamp, Liese et al, St. Louis, 1994-95, Law Offices of Thomas M. Burke, P.C., St. Louis, 1995-99, The Hullverson Law Firm, St. Louis, 1999—. Mem. Bar Assn. Met. St. Louis, Lawyer's Assn. St. Louis (exec. com. 1997—). Personal injury, Workers' compensation. Office: Hullverson Law Firm 1010 Market St Ste 1550 Saint Louis MO 63101-2091

**KOLKEY, DANIEL MILES,** judge; b. Chgo., Apr. 21, 1952; s. Eugene Louis and Gilda Penelope (Cowan) K.; m. Donna Lynn Christie, May 15, 1982; children: Eugene, William, Christopher, Jonathan. BA, Stanford U., 1974; JD, Harvard U., 1977. Bar: Calif. 1977, U.S. Dist. Ct. (ea. dist.) Calif. 1978, U.S. Dist. Ct. (cen. dist.) Calif. 1979, U.S. Ct. Appeals (9th cir.) 1979, U.S. Dist. Ct. (no. dist.) Calif. 1980, U.S. Supreme Ct. 1983, U.S. Dist. Ct. Ariz. 1992, U.S. Dist. Ct. (so. dist.) Calif. 1994. Law clk. U.S. Dist. Ct. judge, N.Y.C., 1977-78; assoc. Gibson Dunn & Crutcher, L.A., 1978-84, ptnr., 1985-94; counsel to Gov., legal affairs sec. to Calif. Gov. Pete Wilson, 1995-98; assoc. justice Calif. Ct. Appeal, 3rd Appellate Dist., Sacramento, 1998—; arbitrator bi-nat. panel for U.S.-Can. Free Trade Agreement, 1990-94; commr. Calif. Law Revision Commn., 1992-94, vice chair, 1993-94, chair, 1994; mem. Blue Ribbon Commn. on Jury Sys. Improvement, 1996. Contbr. articles to profl. pubs. Co-chmn. internat. rels. sect. Town Hall Calif., L.A., 1981-90; chmn. internat. trade legis. subcom., internat. commerce steering com. L.A. Area C. of C., 1983-91, mem. law and justice com., 1993-94; mem. adv. coun., mem. exec. com. Asia Pacific Ctr. for Resolution of Internat. Bus.Disputes, 1991-94; bd. dirs. L.A. Ctr. for Internat. Comml. Arbitration, 1986-94, treas., 1986-88, v.p., 1988-90, pres., 1990-94; assoc. mem. ctrl. com. Calif. Rep. Party, 1983-94, mem. ctrl. com., 1995-98, dep. gen. coun. credentials com., Rep. Nat. Convention, 1992, alt. Calif. Delegation, 1992, Calif. del., 1996; mem. L.A. Com. on Fgn. Rels., 1983-95, Pacific Coun. Internat. Policy, 1999—; gen. counsel Citizens Rsch. Found., 1990-94. Master Anthony Kennedy Inns. of Ct., 1996—. Mem. Am. Arbitration Assn. (panel of arbitrators, arbitrator large complex case dispute resolution program 1993-94), Chartered Inst. Arbitrators, London (assoc. 1986-94), Friends of Wilton Park So. Calif. (chmn. exec. com. 1986-94, exec. com. 1986—). Jewish. Office: Calif Ct of Appeal 3d Appellate Dist 914 Capitol Mall Sacramento CA 95814-4906

**KOLKHORST, KATHRYN MACKAY,** lawyer; b. Richmond, N.Y., Sept. 21, 1949; d. Bernard Edwin and Jane Mackay (Shaw) K.; m. Mark Finks, 1968 (div. 1972); m. William George Ruddy, Mar. 31, 1979; children: Anna Caroll, Elena Jane. Student, Wellsley Coll., 1966-68; BA, So. Conn. State Coll., 1969; postgrad., Yale U., 1975-77; JD, U. Conn., West Hartford, 1977. Bar: Alaska 1979, U.S. Dist. Ct. Alaska 1982. Reporter New Haven Jour. Courier, 1970-75; law clk. to presiding justice Alaska Supreme Ct., Juneau, 1977-78; asst. atty. gen. State of Alaska, Juneau, 1979-85; ptnr. Ruddy, Bradley & Kolkhorst, Juneau, 1986—. Active Juneau Arts Coun., 1979-82, Juneau Symphony, 1980-84; chairperson Juneau Jazz & Classics, 1987—. Mem. Alaska Bar Assn. Democrat. Presbyterian. Office: Ruddy Bradley & Kolkhorst PO Box 34338 Juneau AK 99803-4338

**KOLKO, HANAN B.,** lawyer; b. Rochester, N.Y., June 22, 1960; s. Mordecai J. and Bradliegh A. Kolko; m. Martha E. Hines, June 10, 1994; 1 child, Abe. BA, Cornell U., 1982; JD, U. Mich., 1985. Bar: Ohio, Mich., U.S. Dist. Ct. (ea. dist.) Mich., N.Y., U.S. Dist. Ct. (ea. dist.) N.Y., U.S. Dist. Ct. (so. dist.) N.Y. Assoc. Schwarewald, Rubiner, Cleve., 1985-86, Miller Cohen, Detroit, 1986-89; assoc. Vladeck, Waldman, Elias & Engelhard, N.Y.C., 1989-93, ptnr., 1993—; adj. prof. Cornell U., 1990—. Labor, Pension, profit-sharing, and employee benefits. Office: Vladeck Waldman Elias & Engelhard 1501 Broadway Ste 800 New York NY 10036-5560

**KOLMIN, KENNETH GUY,** lawyer; b. N.Y.C., Oct. 22, 1951; s. Frank William and Edith Kolmin; m. Suzan L. Frumm, Sept. 3, 1978; children—Stephen Todd, Jennifer Dana, Robert Scott. BS summa cum laude, SUNY-Albany, 1973; MS, Syracuse U., 1975, JD cum laude, 1975. Bar: Ill. 1976, U.S. Dist. Ct. (7th dist.) Ill. 1976, U.S. Tax Ct. 1980, U.S. Supreme Ct. 1985; CPA, Ill. Tax cons. Arthur Young and Co., Chgo., 1976-79; atty. Shefsky Saitlin & Froelich, Chgo., 1979-81; ptnr. Rooks Pitts & Poust, Chgo., 1981-84, Schwartz & Freeman, 1984-96, Sonnenschein, Nath & Rosenthal, Chgo., 1996—. Contbr. articles to profl. jours. Mem. ABA, AICPA, Ill. Bar Assn., Ill. Soc. CPAs. General corporate, Taxation, general, Securities. Home: 975 Eastwood Rd Glencoe IL 60022-1122 Office: Sonnenschein Nath & Rosenthal 8000 Sears Tower Chicago IL 60606

**KOLODINSKY, RICHARD HUTTON,** lawyer; b. Perth Amboy, N.J., Aug. 31, 1952; s. William Alexander and Helen (Kulpinsky) K.; m. Betty Mangino, 1975 (div. 1978); m. Alison Kolodinsky, June 20, 1981; 1 child, Chris. BA, Rutgers U., 1974, JD, 1977. Bar: Fla. 1978, N.J., Penn., U.S. Dist. Ct. (no. and mid. dists.) Fla., U.S. Dist. Ct. N.J., U.S. Ct. Appeals (11th cir). Atty. Ctr. Fla. Legal Svc., Daytona Beach, 1977-81; partner Kolodinsky, Berg, Seitz & Tresher, Daytona Beach, 1981—, New Smyrna Beach, 1981—; Fla. Gov.'s appointee to Judicial Nominating Commn., Daytona Beach, 1997. Bd. dirs. Atlantic Ctr. for Arts, New Smyrna Beach, Fla., 1990-94, 98—, Unitarian Universalist Ch., Ormond Beach, Fla., 1991-94; cmty. svc. vol. NAACP, 1992. Mem. Leading Am. Attys., Fla. Bar Assn. (grievance com., bd. mem., chair), Academy Fla. Trial Lawyers (bd. dirs., Eagle Talon), Volusia County Bar Assn. (bd. dirs.). Democrat. Avocations: tennis, sailing. E-Mail: KBSandT@worldnet.att.net. Personal injury, Professional liability, General civil litigation. Office: Kolodinsky Berg Seitz & Tresher 707 E 3rd Ave New Smyrna Beach FL 32169-3101

**KOLODNY, STEPHEN ARTHUR,** lawyer; b. Monticello, N.Y., 1940. BA in Bus. Adminstrn., Boston U., 1963, JD, 1965. Bar: Calif. 1966, U.S. Dist. Ct. (cen. dist.) Calif. 1966; cert. family law specialist. Sole practice L.A., 1966-95; with Kolodny & Anteau, L.A., 1995—; lectr. on family law subjects. Co-author: Divorce Practice Handbook, 1994; author: Evidence ABA Advocate, 1996. Mem. ABA (family law sect., author ABA Advocate), Am. Acad. Matrimonial Lawyers (pres. So. Calif. chpt., bd. govs.), Am. Coll. Family Trial lawyers (founding dir.), Internat. Acad. Matrimonial Lawyers (bd. govs., pres. USA chpt.), Calif. State Bar Assn. (cert. family law specialist, lectr. State Bar panel, CEB programs, mem. family law sect.), Los Angeles County Bar Assn. (lectr., mem. and past chmn. family law sect.), Beverly Hills Bar Assn. (lectr., mem. family law sect.). Family and matrimonial.

**KOLOSTIAN, RICHARD GEORGE, SR.,** judge; b. L.A., Dec. 2, 1931; s. Kalost Der Kolostian and Rose Koumrian; m. Joan R. Gabriel, Aug. 22, 1964; children: Richard Jr., Jon Kalost Der. BBA, Loyola U., 1954, LLB, 1963. Bar: Calif. 1984. Dep. city atty. L.A. City Attys. Office, 1964-68; pvt. practice L.A., 1968-73; ct. commr. L.A. Mcpl. Ct., L.A., 1973-80; judge L.A. Superior Ct., 1980—; supr. judge Van Nuys Dist. of L.A. Superior Ct., 1989-90. Bd. dirs., pres. Vols. Am. Alcohol Program, L.A.; bd. dirs. Salvation Army, L.A. With USAF, 1955-57; scoutmaster Boy Scouts Am., Van Nuys, 1978—. Named Judge of Yr., San Fernando Valley Criminal Bar, 1988, Constitutional Rights Found. of L.A., 1989. Armenian Orthodox. Avocations: woodwork, house maintenance, backpacking, golf. Office: LA Superior Ct 6230 Sylmar Ave Van Nuys CA 91401-2712

**KOLTNOW, H. ROBERT,** lawyer; b. Atlantic City, N.J., Aug. 19, 1929; s. Abraham and Minnie (Golove) K.; m. Carol Siegler, Oct. 28, 1955; children: William, Karen, Sara, Amy. Student, Dickinson Coll., Carlisle, Pa., 1947-50; JD, U. Miami, 1953. Bar: Fla. 1953, U.S. Ct. Appeals (5th cir.) 1967, U.S. Ct. Appeals (11th cir.) 1981, U.S. Dist. Ct. (so. dist.) Fla. 1953, U.S. Supreme Ct. 1968; bd. cert. civil trial lawyer, Fla. Pvt. practice Plantation, Fla.; mem. hearing exam. Fla. real estate commn. State of Fla., Tallahassee, 1970-74; pres., dir. Lawyers Credit Union, Miami, 1991-97, chmn. credit com., 1963-91; adj. prof. legal assts. program Miami Dade C.C., 1975-80, U. Miami, 1980, Briarcliff Coll., 1990-92, Fla. Internat. U., 1987. Mem. Fla. Bar Assn. (chmn. unauthorized practice of law 1960-65, chmn. grievance com. 1966-67, security fund com. 1967-70, legal assts. com. 1975-78). General civil litigation, Probate. Office: 7473 NW 4th St Plantation FL 33317-2204

**KOMAROFF, STANLEY,** lawyer; b. Bklyn, Apr. 1, 1935; s. William Ralph and Fanny (Wein) K.; m. Rosalyn Steinglass, Dec. 25, 1960; children: William Charles, Andrew Steven. BA, Cornell U., 1956, JD, 1958. Bar: N.Y. 1959. Assoc. Proskauer Rose LLP, N.Y.C., 1958-68, ptnr., 1968—, chmn., 1991-99. Mem. rev. and planning coun. N.Y. State Hosp., 1982-92; trustee Beth Israel Med. Ctr., 1984—; bd. dirs. Edmond de Rothschild Found., Club Med, Inc., 1984-95, Overseas Shipholding Group, Inc., Westhampton Beach Performing Arts Ctr.; chmn. ann. fund Cornell U. Law Sch., 1991-93. 1st lt. USAR, 1958. Mem. N.Y. State Bar Assn., Assn. of Bar of City of N.Y., N.Y. County Lawyers Assn., Order of Coif, Sunningdale Country Club, Phi Kappa Phi. General corporate, Private international, Mergers and acquisitions. Home: 910 Park Ave Apt 5-s New York NY 10021-0255 Office: Proskauer Rose LLP 1585 Broadway New York NY 10036-8200

**KOMEN, LEONARD,** lawyer; b. St. Louis, May 31, 1943; s. Meyer and Yetta (Ellman) K.; m. Sandra Gail Cytron, June 8, 1969; children: Douglas Steven, Matthew Todd. BA, U. Mo., 1965, JD, 1970. Bar: Mo. 1970, U.S. Dist. Ct. (ea. dist.) Mo. 1971, U.S. Supreme Ct. 1973, U.S. Ct. Appeals (8th cir.) 1985, U.S. Claims Ct. 1992, U.S. Ct. Appeals (3d cir.) 1995. Assoc. Susman, Willer & Rimmel, St. Louis, 1970-74; assoc. Susman Schermer Rimmel & Parker, St. Louis, 1974-77, ptnr., 1977-80; prin., v.p. Selner, Glaser, Komen, Berger & Galganski, P.C., St. Louis, 1980-96; prin. mgr. Komen, Berger & Cohen, L.C., 1996—; ct.-apptd. trustee, examiner, receiver U.S. Bankruptcy Ct., 1988—. bd. dirs. Zeta Beta Tau Frat. Inc., 1984—, nat. sec., 1989-90, nat. v.p., 1990-92, nat. pres., 1992-94; mem. supervisory bd. Nat. Interfraternity Coun. Legal Advocacy Fund, 1993-98. Pres. Creve Coeur Hockey Club Inc., St. Louis, 1987-88, bd. dirs., 1989-93; coord. Parkway North Hockey Club, 1989-91; pres., bd. dirs. Roswell Messing Edn]. Found., 1989—; bd. dirs. Zeta Beta Tau Centennial Found. 1990-98. Recipient Merit citation Zeta Beta Tau Frat., Inc., 1977, 91, 92. Mem. ATLA, Comml. Law League Am., Met. St. Louis Bar Assn., Lawyers Assn. Jewish. Bankruptcy, General civil litigation, Contracts commercial. Home: 14385 Stablestone Ct Chesterfield MO 63017-2502 Office: Komen Berger & Cohen 222 S Central Ave Ste 1100 Saint Louis MO 63105-3576

**KOMER, MARK EDWARD,** lawyer; b. Norfolk, Va., Jan. 17, 1963; s. Charles S. and Patsy S. Komer; m. Lynn Komer, Sept. 21, 1991; 1 child, Lauren. BA, Ithaca Coll., 1985; JD, U. Va., 1988. Trial lawyer The Roehl Law Firm, Albuquerque, 1988—; mem. consumer adv. bd. N.Mex. Blue Cross Blue Shield, Albuquerque; panelist N.Mex. Med. Rev. Commn., Albuquerque. Mem. ATLA, N.Mex. Trial Lawyers Assn., Albuquerque Bar Assn. Fax: 505-242-0530. E-mail: lawyer@roehl.com. Office: The Roehl Law Firm PC 300 Central Ave SW Albuquerque NM 87102-3298

**KOMEYA, GEOFFREY KIMO SANSHIRO,** lawyer; b. Honolulu, Sept. 12, 1965; s. James Y. and Eileen I. Komeya. BA, U. Hawaii, Honolulu, 1987, MA, 1989; JD, U. Hawaii, 1993. Bar: Hawaii 1993, U.S. Dist. Ct. Hawaii 1993. Law clk. U.S. Dist. Ct. Hawaii, Honolulu, 1993-94; adminstrv. law clk. Supreme Ct. Hawaii, Honolulu, 1994-96; assoc. Cronin, Fried, Sekiya, Kekina & Fairbanks, Honolulu, 1996—; mem. appellate rules com. Supreme Ct. Hawaii, 1997—. Recipient Am. Jurisprudence award, 1991-93. Mem. ABA, Consumer Lawyers Hawaii. Product liability, Personal injury, Insurance. Office: Cronin Fried Sekiya Kekina & Fairbanks 841 Bishop St Ste 1900 Honolulu HI 96813-3962

**KOMIE, STEPHEN MARK,** lawyer; b. Chgo., Jan. 22, 1949; s. Leonard D. and Miriam (Wineberg) K. BA, U. Ariz., 1970, MA in Russian History, 1973; JD, DePaul U., 1976. Bar: Ill. 1976, U.S. Dist. Ct. (no. dist.) Ill. 1976, U.S. Ct. Appeals (7th cir.) 1976, U.S. Ct. Appeals (8th cir.) 1982, U.S. Dist. Ct. (ctrl. dist.) Ill. 1984, U.S. Dist. Ct. (no. dist.) Ind. 1985, U.S. Ct. Appeals (6th cir.) 1989, U.S. Dist. Ct. (ea. dist.) Mich. 1995, U.S. Supreme Ct. 1993. With Komie & Assocs., Chgo., 1976—; prin. Buffalo Grove (Ill.) Law Offices Ltd., 1977-86; prin. Drunken Drivers Def. Lawyers of Ill. Ltd., Chgo., 1982—. Recipient Nat. Pub. Svc. award ATLA, 1994. Mem. ABA (solo practice and small firm practice task force 1990-92, elected mem. criminal justice sect. coun., 1995—), Ill. Bar Assn. (mem. assembly 1985-91, vice chmn. 1988-89, chmn. 1989-90, vice chmn. com. professionalism 1990-91, chair 1991—, bd. govs. 1992-98, 99—, sec. 1997-98), Chgo. Bar Assn. (chmn. criminal law com. 1983-84, def. of prisoners com. 1986-87), Nat. Assn. Criminal Def. Lawyers (parliamentarian 1988-89, 90-91, bd. dirs. 1983-86), Ill. Bar Found. (bd. dirs. 1988-90, 92—), Ill. Attys. for Criminal Justice (treas. 1991-92), Lincoln Inn of Ct., Internat. Bar Assn. (vice-chair family law com.). Criminal, Federal civil litigation, Family and matrimonial. Office: 20 N Clark St Ste 3500 Chicago IL 60602-5088

**KOMOROWSKI, MICHELE,** lawyer; b. Saddle Brook, N.J., Sept. 25, 1967; d. kenneth and Virginia Lee Komorowski; m. Steven Bruce Elliott, Oct. 10, 1997; children: Dillon, Anthony, Elliott. BS, U. Tex., Tyler, 1990; JD, So. Tex. Coll. Law, 1993. Bar: Tex. 1994, U.S. Dist. Ct. (ea. dist.) Tex. 1995. Assoc. Hill & Hill, Longview, Tex., 1993—. Bd. dirs. Women's Ctr. East Tex., Longview, 1997—; fundraiser United Way, Longview, 1998; vol. Habitat for Humanity, Longview, 1998. Mem. ABA, Tex. Trial lawyers Assn., Tex. Criminal Def. lawyers Assn. (bd. dirs. 1996-98), Gregg County Pro Bono Soc., Gregg County Bar Assn. (bd. dirs. 1996-98). Republican. Baptist. Avocation: singing. Criminal, Family and matrimonial, Juvenile. Office: Hill & Hill 211 N Center St Longview TX 75601-7221

**KONDRACKI, EDWARD JOHN,** lawyer; b. Elizabeth, N.J., Sept. 27, 1932; s. John and Catherine Chudio (Saas) K.; m. Barbara Terese Caruso; children: Carol Ann, Maryanne, Christopher. BSEE, N.J. Inst. Tech., 1959; JD with honors, George Washington U., 1963. Bar: Va. 1964, DC 1964, U.S. Dist. Ct. D.C. 1964, U.S. Dist. Ct. (ea. dist.) Va. 1964, U.S. Dist. Ct. (ctrl. dist.) Calif., U.S. Dist. Ct. (so. dist.) Ala., U.S. Dist. Ct. (no. dist.) Fla., U.S. Dist. Ct. (no. dist.) Ga., U.S. Dist. Ct. (we. dist.) La., U.S. Dist. Ct. (ea. dist.) Mich., U.S. Dist. Ct. (no. dist.) Okla., U.S. Dist. Ct. (ea. dist.) Pa., U.S. Dist. Ct. (no. dist.) N.Y., U.S. Dist. Ct. (ea. dist.) Tex., U.S. Dist. Ct. (no. dist.) Tex., U.S. Ct. Appeals (fed. cir.) 1983, U.S. Ct. Claims 1976, U.S. Ct. Customs and Patent Appeals 1976. Patent atty. Gen. Electric Co., Washington, 1959-63; dir. Kerkam, Stowell Kondracki & Clarke, P.C. and predecessor, Arlington, Va., 1963-65; ptnr., 1965—; dir. Patmark Paralegal Svcs., 1975-90; treas. SOC Enterprises, 1998-99. Author: Trademarks-Servicemarks, Use, Usage and Protection, 1990, Proper Use of Trademarks and Servicemarks, 1982, Common Pitfalls Encountered in Patenting Inventions, 1983, Copyright Protection of Computer Software, 1989, Intellectual Property, Rights Acquisition and Protection Conference World Trade Assn. N.J., 1989; contbr. article to Voice of Tech. Served with USN, 1951-55. Mem. ABA, Am. Intellectual Property Law Assn., Internat. Assn. Protection Indsl. Property, Fed. Bar Assn., Va. Bar Assn., Internat. Trademark Assn., Washington Patent Lawyers Club, D.C. Bar Assn. (chmn. com. internat. affairs 1973), Gt. Falls Hist. Soc., Marmota Farm Assn., KC, Tau Beta Pi, Eta Kappa Nu, Omicron Delta Kappa, Phie Eta Sigma. Patent, Trademark and copyright, Private international. Office: 5203 Leesburg Pike Falls Church VA 22041-3401

**KONENKAMP, JOHN K.,** state supreme court justice; b. Oct. 20, 1944; m. Geri Konenkamp; children: Kathryn, Matthew. JD, U. S.D., 1974. Dep. state's atty. Rapid City; pvt. practice, 1977-84; former and presiding judge S.D. Cir Ct. (7th cir.), 1988-94; assoc. justice S.D. Supreme Ct., Pierre, 1994—. Bd. dirs. Alt. Dispute Resolution Com., Adv. Bd. for Casey Family Program. With USN. Mem. Am. Judicature Soc., State Bar S.D., Pennington County Bar Assn., Nat. CASA Assn., Am. Legion. Office: SD Supreme Ct 500 E Capitol Ave Pierre SD 57501-5070*

**KONEZNY, JERYN ANN-HALL,** lawyer; b. St. Paul, Aug. 26, 1970; d. James Ralph Hall and JoAnn Cedarleaf Campbell; m. Ronald Edward Konezny, Oct. 10, 1998. BS in Polit. Sci., U. St. Thomas, St. Paul, 1992; JD, U. Mich., 1994. Bar: Minn. 1994. Atty. Dorsey & Whitney LLP, Mpls., 1994—. Vol. Bus. Ptnrs. Program, Mpls., 1997, Jeremiah Program, Mpls., 1998, Whittier Elem. Sch., Mpls., 1998. Mem. Minn. State Bar Assn. (mem. nonprofit com. 1998), Exec. Womens Golf Assn., Jr. League Mpls. Health, Non-profit and tax-exempt organizations, Mergers and acquisitions. Office: Dorsey & Whitney LLP 220 S 6th St Minneapolis MN 55402-4502

**KONNEY, PAUL EDWARD,** consumer products company executive, lawyer; b. Hartford, Conn., June 24, 1944; s. William Frederick and Dorothy (Dittmer) K.; m. Elizabeth Buhl Wright Temple, July 27, 1968 (div. 1979); m. Barbara Jean Greaves, June 2, 1979; children: Gretchen Blair, Tyler Wingard. AB cum laude, Harvard U., 1966; LLB, U. Pa., 1969. Bar: N.Y. 1973. Law clk. to Hon. Chief Judge William Hastie U.S. Ct. Appeals, Phila., 1969-70; assoc. Debevoise & Plimpton, N.Y.C., 1971-81; v.p., gen. counsel Tambrands Inc., Lake Success, N.Y., 1982-83; v.p., gen. counsel, sec. Tambrands Inc., White Plains, N.Y., 1983-89, sr. v.p., gen. counsel, sec., 1989-93; v.p., gen. counsel Quaker State Corp., Oil City, Pa., 1994; v.p., gen. counsel, sec. Quaker State Corp., Irving, Texas, 1995, sr. v.p., gen. counsel, sec., 1996-98; sr. v.p., gen. counsel., sec. Estee Lauder Cos., Inc., N.Y.C., 1999—; bd. dirs. Taylor & Dodge Inc., N.Y.C.; mem. U.S. Del. US/USSR Legal Exchange, Russia, 1988; mem. internat. policy com. U.S. C of C, Washington, 1989—. Article and book rev. editor U. Pa. Law Rev., 1968-69. Bd. dir. Visiting Nurse Assn., Dallas, 1996—. Mem. U.S. delegation to 1st U.S.-USSR legal seminar. Mem. ABA, Am. Soc. Corp. Secs., NYU Corp. Real Estate Forum (v.p.), U.S. C. of C. (internat. policy com.), Internat. Pub. Rels. Dirs. Roundtable. Episcopalian. Clubs: Harvard (N.Y.C.) (bd. mgrs., past dir. found.). E-Mail: pekonney@aol.com. Fax: 972-868-0407. Office: The Estee Lauder Cos Inc 767 5th Ave New York NY 10153

**KONSELMAN, DOUGLAS DEREK,** lawyer; b. Tampa, Fla., Oct. 3, 1958; s. Derek Konselman and Linda (Horton) Fisher. BA in Biology, U. South Fla., 1981; JD, Loyola U., New Orleans, 1984; LLM, Georgetown U., 1996.

Bar: Fla., 1984, N.J. 1985, N.Y. 1985, D.C. 1985, U.S. Supreme Ct. 1986. Ptnr. Konselman & Co., Washington, 1991-96; mng. ptnr. Konselman & Ptnrs., N.Y.C., 1996—; mem. Practicing Law Inst., N.Y.C., 1985—. Contbr. articles to law jours. Bd. dirs. Boca Raton (Fla.) Mus. Art, 1987, Market Square West, 1995-98. Mem. Am. Corp. Counsel Assn., Am. Soc. Internat. Law, Fgn. Law Soc., Soc. for Internat. Devel., Asia Soc., Mensa. Republican. Presbyterian. Avocations: foreign languages, Russian, French, German. Contracts commercial, Mergers and acquisitions, Pension, profit-sharing, and employee benefits. Office: 801 Pennsylvania Ave NW Washington DC 20004-2615

**KONSTANTY, JAMES E.,** lawyer; b. Jamestown, N.Y., Feb. 26, 1942; s. C. James and Mary B. Konstanty; m. Irene B. Konstanty, June 3, 1977; children: James, Daniel, Jared, Kristin, Michael. BS, Cornell U., 1964; LLB, JD, U. Syracuse, 1967. Bar: N.Y. 1967, U.S. Dist. Ct. (no. dist.) N.Y. 1967. Asst. dist. atty. Otsego County, Oneonta, N.Y., 1970-71; urban renewal atty. Oneonta City, Oneonta, 1971-79; town atty. Oneonta Town Bd., 1970-85; county atty. Otsego County, Cooperstown, N.Y., 1986—; pvt. practice Oneonta, 1969—. Bd. dirs. Salvation Army, Oneonta, 1978-93, Dooley Found., N.Y.C., 1998—, Am. Cancer Soc., Oneonta, 1970-75, Nat. Soccer Hall of Fame, Oneonta, 1995—; chmn. Oneonta Reps., 1972-76; del. Reb. Jud. Conv., Otsego County, 1978—; bd. dirs., coach Oneonta Youth Soccer, 1988-94. Mem. Elks. Avocations: golf, skiing, reading. Personal injury, Estate planning, Municipal (including bonds). Office: 252 Main St Oneonta NY 13820-2510

**KONWINSKI, LISA MICHELE,** lawyer; b. Lansing, Mich., June 29, 1966; d. John Michael and Alita Ruth (Lipsey) K. BA in Polit. Sci. with honors, U. Mich., 1988, JD, 1991. Bar: N.C. 1992. Atty. Moore & Van Allen, Charlotte, N.C., 1992-94; counsel, sr. legis. asst. U.S. Rep. Marcy Kaptur, Washington, 1994-96; rules com. assoc. U.S. Rep. Louise Slaughter, Washington, 1996-97; gen. counsel U.S. Senate Budget Com., Dem. Staff, Washington, 1997—. Democrat. Office: US Senate Budget Com 621 Dirksen Bldg Washington DC 20510-0001

**KOONCE, NEIL WRIGHT,** lawyer; b. Kinston, N.C., July 8, 1947; s. Harold Wright and Edna Earle (Regan) K.; m. Virginia Gayle Evans, Feb. 27, 1993; children: Channing, Carl Younger, Ginny Younger. AB, U. N.C., 1969; JD, Wake Forest U., 1974; postgrad. exec. program, U. Va., 1983. Bar: N.C. 1973, U.S. Dist. Ct. (mid. dist.) N.C. 1975, U.S. Ct. Appeals (4th cir.) 1978, U.S. Supreme Ct. 1981. Atty. Cone Mills Corp., Greensboro, N.C., 1974-81; sr. atty. Cone Mills Corp., Greensboro, 1981-85, asst. gen. counsel, 1985-87, gen. counsel, 1987—, v.p., 1989—, v.p., gen. counsel, corp. sec., 1999—. Bd. dirs. Family and Children's Svcs., Greensboro, 1981-89, S.C. Energy Users Com., Columbia, S.C., 1984-89, Carolina Utility Customer's Assn., Raleigh, 1983-90, 94—, N.C. Found. for Rsch. and Econ. Edn., 1986-87, 93—, Electricity Consumers Resource Coun., Washington, 1987, 92—, vice chmn., 1990, chmn., 1991; bd. dirs. N.C. Citizens for Bus. and Industry, Raleigh, 1991-96, Met. YMCA, Greensboro, 1991-95, Salvation Army Boys and Girls Clubs, Greensboro, 1996—, S.C. Mfrs. Alliance, 1998—, N.C. Textile Mfrs. Assn., 1998—. With AUS, 1970-71. Mem. ABA, N.C. Bar Assn., N.C. Textile Mfrs. Assn., Greensboro Bar Assn., Rotary (sec. 1983-86, bd. dirs. 1985-90, pres. 1988). Democrat. Presbyterian. Administrative and regulatory, General corporate, Personal injury. Home: 200 Irving Pl Greensboro NC 27408-6510 Office: Cone Mills Corp 3101 N Elm St Greensboro NC 27408-3184

**KOONS, STEPHEN ROBERT,** lawyer; b. Elmira, N.Y., Apr. 28, 1948; s. Robert Oscar and Katheryn Elizabeth (Norris) K.; m. Kathleen Marie Brooks Burman, Aug. 24, 1968 (div. July 1991); 1 child, David Robert; m. Laurene Ann Valdez, June 25, 1994; 1 child, Daniel Justin. BS, Fla. State U., 1970, JD, 1973. Bar: Fla. 1973, U.S. Dist. Ct. (so. dist.) Fla. 1974, U.S. Dist. Ct. (mid. dist.) Fla. 1974, U.S. Supreme Ct. 1978; bd. cert. civil lawyer. Asst. atty. gen. State of Fla., West Palm Beach, 1973, asst. state atty., 1975-77; assoc. Weathers & Narkier, West Palm Beach, 1977-78; ptnr. Davis, Rose & Koons, West Palm Beach, 1978-81, Mgee, Jordan, Shuey & Koons, Lake Worth, Fla., 1981-88, Stephen R. Koons, P.A., West Palm Beach, 1988-90, 93-97, Powers & Koons, West Palm Beach, 1990-93, Koons & Volpi, West Palm Beach, 1997—; gen. counsel First Fed. Savs. & Loan, Lake Worth, 1982-87; mem. Criminal Justice Commn., Palm Beach County, 1987-92; bd. dirs., sec. Treasure Pride Probation Svc., Palm Beach County, 1983-95; adj. instr. Fla. Atlantic U., Boca Raton, Fla., 1995-97. Author seminar material. Fedn. chief Indian Guides, YMCA, West Palm Beach, 1977-82; mem. pres.'s cir. Republican Pary of Palm Beach County; chmn. Lake Worth Civil Svc. Bd., 1982-82, 88. Recipient Svc. award Lake Worth Bar Assn., 1985, Pride Probation Svcs., 1991, Lake Worth Civil Svc. Bd., 1992. Mem. Fed. Bar Assn. (pres. Gold Coast chpt. 1988), Acad. Fla. Trial Lawyers (chair pro bono com. 1986—, lectr. continuing legal edn. 1984-95, Svc. award Spkrs. Bur. 1988). Avocations: golf, tennis, skiing, travel. Personal injury, Professional liability, State civil litigation. Office: Koons & Volpi Ste 219 1897 Palm Beach Lakes Blvd West Palm Beach FL 33409-3508

**KOONTZ, GLEN FRANKLIN,** lawyer, historian; b. Martinsville, Va., Jan. 9, 1960; s. Ben Franklin and Ruby Estelle (Hollandsworth) K. BA in History, Wash. and Lee U., 1982, JD, 1987. Assoc. Keller & Heckman, Washington, 1987-92; asst. city atty. City of Richmond, 1992-94; litig. counsel Nat. Assn. Home Builders, Washington, 1994-97; counsel Keller & Heckman, Washington, 1996-97, The Lewis Law Firm, Washington, 1997—. Mem. Va. Bar Assn., Md. State Bar Assn., Federalist Soc., Bar Assn. of the City of Richmond, Alexandria Bar Assn. Criminal, Federal civil litigation, Appellate. Office: The Lewis Law Firm 805 15th St NW Lbby 200 Washington DC 20005-2224

**KOONTZ, LAWRENCE L., JR.,** state supreme court justice; b. Roanoke, Va, Jan. 25, 1940. BS, Va. Polytech. U., 1962. Asst. commonwealth's atty. Roanoke, 1967-68; judge Va. Juvenile & Domestic Rels. Dist. Ct., 1968-76, Va. Cir. Ct. (23rd cir.), 1976-85, Ct. Appeals of Va., 1985-95, Supreme Ct. of Va., 1995—. Mem. ABA. Office: PO Box 687 Salem VA 24153-0687

**KOPEL, DAVID BENJAMIN,** lawyer; b. Denver; s. Gerald Henry and Dolores B. Kopel; m. Deirdre Frances Dolan, Apr. 5, 1987. BA in History, Brown U., 1982; JD, U. Mich., 1985. Bar: Colo. 1986, N.Y. 1986, U.S. Dist. Ct. (ea. and so. dists.) N.Y. 1986, U.S. Ct. Appeals (2d cir.) 1986, U.S. Dist. Ct. Colo. 1988, U.S. Ct. Appeals (10th cir.) 1988, U.S. Supreme Ct., 1991, U.S. Ct. Appeals (D.C. cir.) 1997. Assoc. Sullivan & Cromwell, N.Y.C., 1985-86; asst. dist. atty. Manhattan Dist. Atty., N.Y.C., 1986-88; asst. atty. gen. Colo. State Atty. Gen., Denver, 1988-92; rsch. dir. Independence Inst., Golden, Colo., 1992—; adj. prof. NYU Sch. of Law, 1999—. Mem. Order of Coif. Democrat. Avocations: skiing, ham radio.. Office: Independence Inst Ste 185 14142 Denver West Pkwy Golden CO 80401-3119

**KOPELMAN, IAN STUART,** lawyer; b. Chgo., Oct. 11, 1949; s. Ted and Norma (Hyman) K.; m. Nancy Henriette Stamp, Mar. 18, 1984; children: Meredith Samantha, Jason Lee. BA cum laude, Knox Coll., 1971; JD with distinction, U. Iowa, 1974. Bar: Ill. 1974, U.S. Dist. Ct. (no. dist.) Ill. 1974, U.S. Tax Ct. 1974. Ptnr. Arnstein & Lehr, Chgo., 1979-88; prin. Shefsky & Froelich Ltd., Chgo., 1988-96; ptnr., co-chair employee benefits/exec. compensation group Altheimer & Gray, Chgo., 1996-99; ptnr., chair employee benefits/exec. compensation group Rudnick & Wolfe, Chgo., 1999—; lectr. in field. Contbr. articles to profl. publs. Pres. Chgo.-Knox Coll. Alumni Assn., Chgo., 1978-79. Recipient Commendation award Internat. Acad. Trial Lawyers, 1974, Iowa Acad. Trial Lawyers. Mem. ABA, Ill. State Bar Assn., Chgo. Bar Assn. (chmn. employee benefits com. 1981-82, Commendation award 1986), Profit Sharing Coun. Am. (mem. legal and legis. com. 1990—, bd. dirs. 1997—), Midwest Benefits Coun. (chmn. legal and legis. com. 1991-93), Chgo. Assn. Commerce and Industry, Phi Sigma Alpha, Omicron Delta Kappa. Jewish. Avocations: theater, history, reading, sports. Pension, profit-sharing, and employee benefits, Health, Mergers and acquisitions. Home: 1385 Trapp Ln Winnetka IL 60093-1632 Office: Rudnick & Wolfe 203 N La Salle St Fl 19 Chicago IL 60601-1210

**KOPELMAN, LEONARD,** lawyer; b. Cambridge, Mass., Aug. 2, 1940; s. Irving and Frances Estelle (Robbins) K.; m. Carol Hunsberger. B.A. cum laude, Harvard U., 1962, J.D., 1965. Bar: Mass. 1966. Assoc. Warner & Stackpole, Boston, 1965-73; sr. ptnr. Kopelman and Paige, Boston, 1974—; lectr. Harvard U., 1965—; permanent master Mass. Superior Ct., 1971—; hon. consul gen. of, Finland, Mass., 1975—; U.S. del. Soc. for Internat. Devel.; Chmn. Mass. Jud. Selection Com. for the Fed. Judiciary, 1971—; chief counsel AAUP. Trustee Cathedral of the Pines, 1972; pres. Hillel Found. of Cambridge, Inc., 1973—; trustee Faulkner Hosp., 1974—, Parker Hill Med. Ctr., 1976—; dir. gen. Consular Corps Coll. NEH grantee, 1975. Mem. ABA (exec. coun. 1969—), Mass. Bar Assn. (chmn. mcpl. law sect.), Am. Judges Assn., Mass. C. of C. (pres. 1974-77), Harvard Faculty Club, Algonquin Club (pres.), Harvard Club, Union Club, Hasty Pudding Club, St. Botolph Club. Municipal (including bonds), Private international, Public international. Home: 33 Yarmouth Rd Chestnut Hill MA 02467-2815 Office: Kopelman and Paige 31 St James Ave Boston MA 02116-4101

**KOPF, RICHARD G.,** federal judge; b. 1946. BA, U. Nebr., Kearney, 1969; JD, U. Nebr., Lincoln, 1972. Law clk. to Hon. Donald R. Ross U.S. Ct. Appeals (8th cir.), 1972-74; ptnr. Cook, Kopf & Doyle, Lexington, Neb., 1974-87; U.S. magistrate judge, 1987-92; fed. judge U.S. Dist. Ct. (Nebr. dist.), 1992—. Mem. ABA, ABA Found., Nebr. State Bar, Nebr. State Bar Found. Office: US Dist Ct 586 US Courthouse 100 Centennial Mall N Lincoln NE 68508-3859

**KOPIL, THOMAS EDWARD,** lawyer; b. Perth Amboy, N.J., May 12, 1956; s. Edward F. and Dorothy (Dumansky) K.; m. Carol A. Walsh, May 26, 1979; children: Catherine, Genevieve. AB, Georgetown U., 1978; JD, Rutgers U., 1981. Bar: Pa. 1981, N.J. 1981, U.S. Dist. Ct. (no. dist.) N.J. 1981, U.S. Dist. Ct. (ea. dist.) Pa. 1984, U.S. Ct. Appeals (3d cir.) 1984. Atty. Smith, Stratton, Wise, Heber & Brennan, Princeton, N.J., 1981-84, Blank, Rome, Comisky & McCauley, Phila., 1984-88, Perlberger & Haft, Bala Cynwyd, Pa., 1988-91, Timby & Dillon, Newtown, Pa., 1991—. Fellow Am. Bar Found.; mem. ABA (tort and ins. practice sect., editor-in-chief The Brief 1991-94, chair comms. com. 1994-95, chair civil procedure and evidence com. 1997—, vice chair toxic and hazardous substance and environ. law com. 1988-94), ATLA. Product liability, Personal injury, General civil litigation. Home: 1126 Harvest Rd Cherry Hill NJ 08002-1061 Office: Timby and Dillon 330 S State St Newtown PA 18940-1977

**KOPLAN, ANDREW BENNET,** lawyer; b. Birmingham, Ala., Apr. 12, 1971. Student, U. Sidney (Australia), 1991; BS in Fin. cum laude, Birmingham-Southern Coll., 1993; JD, U. Ala., 1996. Bar: Ala. 1996, Ga. 1997, U.S. Dist. Ct. (so. dist.) Ga., U.S. Dist. Ct. (no. dist.) Ga., U.S. Dist. Ct. (so. dist.) Ala. 1997. Legal intern Ala. Supreme Ct., Montgomery, 1995, Ala. Dept. Fin., Montgomery, 1995; jud. extern U.S. Dist. Ct. (no. dist.) Ala., Birmingham, 1995-96; clk. for Hon. Assoc. Justice Janie Shores Supreme Ct. Ala., Montgomery, 1996-97; assoc. Post & Pond, LLP, Atlanta, 1997-98, Drew, Elkl, & Farnham, LLP, Atlanta, 1998—. Jr. editor: Law & Psychology Rev., 1995-96. Mem. ABA, Ga. Trial Lawyers Assn. Avocations: music, sports, art, cooking, exercising. General civil litigation, Contracts commercial, Entertainment. Office: Drew Eckl & Farnham LLP 880 W Peachtree St NW Ste A Atlanta GA 30309-3847

**KOPP, MARK DAVID,** lawyer; b. Gt. Lakes Naval Base, Ill., Aug. 10, 1962; s. David Charles and Judith Ann Kopp; m. Marjorie Kopp, Nov. 10, 1990; children: Neil Markus, Brock Schliem, Ian. BS, U. Wis., Eau Claire, 1985; JD, U. Wis., Madison, 1988. Bar: Wis., U.S. Dist. Ct. Wis. Ptnr. Consigny Andrews Hemming & Grant S.C., Janesville, Wis., 1988—; bd. dirs. Vis. Nurse Health Care Svcs., Janesville, 1991—. Coach Janesville Youth Football, Youth Baseball Janesville; den leader Boy Scouts Am. Democrat. Methodist. State civil litigation, Municipal (including bonds), Family and matrimonial. Office: Consigny Andrews Hemming & Grant SC 303 E Court St Janesville WI 53545-4008

**KORB, KENNETH ALLAN,** lawyer; b. Boston, Oct. 11, 1932; s. Allan and Mynue (Herbert) K.; m. Jaclyn C. Patricof, June 30, 1962; 1 child, Jason B. BA magna cum laude, Harvard U., 1953, JD cum laude, 1956. Bar: Mass. 1956. Law clk. Supreme Jud. Ct., Mass., 1956-57; assoc. Hutchins & Wheeler, Boston, 1957-60, Kargman & Kargman, Boston, 1960-63; sr. ptnr. Brown, Rudnick, Freed & Gesmer, Boston, 1963-89, Posternak, Blankstein & Lund, Boston, 1990-96; ptnr. Perkins, Smith & Cohen, LLP, Boston, 1996—; lectr. Mass. Continuing Legal Edn., Nat. Coun. Savs. Instns., Oxford Club, Cambridge House-Vancouver, Calgary, Toronto, 1997—, Prospecters & Developers Assn. of Can.; sec., bd. dirs., gen. counsel Safety Ins. Co., 1980—; underwriting mem. Lloyd's of London, 1984—; sec., bd. dirs. Neb-Cell, Inc., 1989-95. Legal columnist The Brookline Citizen, 1990-91; contbr. articles to profl. jours. Internat. pres. Soc. Israel Philatelists, 1974-76, bd. dirs., 1976-80; bd. dirs., treas. Watergate Villas East Condominium U.S.V.I., 1989-95. With USAR, 1956-62. Mem. Mass. Bar Assn. Democrat. Real property, General corporate, Securities. Home: 24 Helene Rd Waban MA 02468-1025 Office: 1 Beacon St Boston MA 02108-3107

**KORCHIN, JUDITH MIRIAM,** lawyer; b. Kew Gardens, N.Y., Apr. 28, 1949; d. Arthur Walter and Mena (Levisohn) Goldstein; m. Paul Maury Korchin, June 10, 1972; 1 sond, Brian Edward. BA with high honors, U. Fla., 1971, JD with honors, 1974. Law clk. to judge U.S. Dist. Ct., 1974-76; assoc. Steel, Hector & Davis, Miami, Fla., 1976-81; ptnr. Steel, Hector & Davis, Miami, 1981-87, Holland and Knight, Miami, 1987—. Author, exec. editor U. Fla. Law Rev., 1973-74. Mem. U. Fla. Law Ctr. Coun., 1980-83; pres. alumni bd. U. Fla. Law Rev., 1983; bd. dirs. Fla. Film & Rec. Inst., 1982-84. Recipient Trail Blazer award The Women's Com. of 100, 1988. Fellow Am. Bar Found.; mem. ABA (sect. alternative dispute resolution, vice chmn. 1994-95, co-chmn. fed. ct. mediation com. 1995), Am. Arbitration Assn. (employment law panel, southeast 1993—), CPR Inst. for Dispute Resolution (nat. panelist 1994—), Dade County Bar Assn. (bd. dirs. 1981-82, treas. 1982, sec. 1983, 3d v.p. 1984, 2d v.p. 1985, 1st v.p. 1986, pres. 1987), Nat. Assn. Women Bus. Owners (adv. coun. 1987-88), Nat. Assn. Bank Women (TV panelist greater Miami chpt. 1987), Fla. Bar Assn. (vice chmn. jud. nominating procedures com. 1982, civil procedure rules com. 1984-89, 93-95), Fla. Bar Found. (subcom. legal assistance for poor 1988-90), Rabbinical Assn. Greater Miami (TV panelist Still Small Voice 1987), Dist. XI Health and Human Svcs. Bd. (gov.'s appointee 1993-95, vice chmn. 1993, 94), Greater Miami C. of C. (com. profl. devel. 1988-90), City Club (bd. dirs. 1988-93), Order of Coif, Phi Beta Kappa, Phi Kappa Phi. General civil litigation, State and local taxation, Labor. Office: Holland & Knight PO Box 015441 701 Brickell Ave Ste 3000 Miami FL 33131-2898

**KORDIK, DANIEL JOSEPH,** lawyer; b. Chgo., May 26, 1959; s. George Joseph and Catherine Theresa (Dujnic) K.; m. Lorraine Ann Randell, June 19, 1982; children: Daniel Joseph Jr., Lindsay Alexis, Ashley Lauren. BS in Acctg., U. Ill., 1981, JD, 1984. CPA; cert. arbitrator; lic. real estate broker. Atty. Brown, James & Rabbit, St. Louis, 1984-87, Bouma, Martin & Charlton, Glen Ellyn, Ill., 1987-89, Caluwaert, Panegasser, Elmhurst, Ill., 1989-94; sole practice Elmhurst, 1994—. Author: (computer disk/text) Flexpractice-Personal Injury Edit., 1991. Mem. bd. Elem. Sch. Dist. 45, Villa Park, Ill. 1988-95, v.p. 1991-94, citizens adv. com. on potential referendum and budget, 1998-99; campaign mgr. Citizens for State Rep. Bob Biggins, 1992; mgr., coach Villa Park Youth Baseball, 1992-97; chmn. edn. adv. com. 40th State Rep. Dist. 1990-92; campaign treas. Rae Rupp Search for Pres., Village of Villa Park, 1993—, planning and zoning commr., 1999—; com. chair Vision 2000, Villa Park, 1994—; mem. ISBA Cmty. Involvement Com., 1991-95, Pub. Rels. Com., 1995-96; Rep. precinct committeeman, York Twp. Precinct 25, 1994—; lector St. Alexander Ch. Mem. Ill. State Bar Assn., DuPage County Bar Assn. Republican. Roman Catholic. Avocations: family, indoor soccer, baseball, politics. State civil litigation, Personal injury, General practice. Home: 550 S Princeton Ave Villa Park IL 60181-2858 Office: 200 N York St Elmhurst IL 60126-2750

**KORDONS, ULDIS,** lawyer; b. Riga, Latvia, July 9, 1941; came to U.S., 1949; s. Evalds and Zenta Alide (Apenits) K.; m. Virginia Lee Knowles, July 16, 1966. AB, Princeton U., 1963; JD, Georgetown U., 1970. Bar: N.Y. 1970, Ohio 1978, Ind. 1989. Assoc. Whitman, Breed, Abbott & Morgan, N.Y.C., 1970-77, Anderson, Mori & Rabinowitz, Tokyo, 1973-75; counsel Armco Inc., Parsippany, N.J., 1977-84; v.p., gen. counsel, sec. Sybron Corp., Saddle Brook, N.J., 1984-88, Hillenbrand Industries Inc., Batesville, Ind., 1989-92; pres. Plover Enterprises, Cin., 1992-95; of counsel Case Law Offices, Cin., 1996-97; pres. Kordons & Co., LPA, Cin., 1998—. Lt. USN, 1963-67. Mem. N.Y. Bar Assn., Ohio Bar Assn., Ind. Bar Assn. Contracts commercial, General corporate, Private international.

**KORDUNER, DAVID JEROME,** lawyer; b. Canoga Park, Calif., Mar. 17, 1961; s. Harold S. and Shirley H. Korduner; m. Joan F. Krimston, Dec. 29, 1991; children: Zachary Asher, Benjamin Micah. BA with honors, U. Calif., Santa Cruz, 1985; MSc, London Sch. Econs./Polit. Sci., 1987; JD, UCLA, 1992. Bar: Calif. 1992, U.S. Dist. Ct. (cen. dist.) Calif. 1992, U.S. Dist. Ct. (so. and ea. dists.) Calif. 1993, U.S. Ct. Appeals (9th cir.) 1997. Assoc. Robie & Matthai, L.A., 1992-95, Russ, August & Kabat, L.A., 1995; assoc. gen. counsel Dirs. Guild of Am., L.A., 1995—. Vol. arbitrator L.A. County Superior and Mcpl. Cts., 1998—. Mem. L.A. County Bar Assn. (vol. fee arbitrator 1997—). Alternative dispute resolution, Entertainment, Labor. Office: Dirs Guild of Am 7920 W Sunset Blvd Los Angeles CA 90046-3300

**KORDUNER, DEBRA LYNN,** lawyer; b. Encino, Calif., Oct. 5, 1955; d. Harold and Shirley (Mantel) K. BA magna cum laude, UCLA, 1976; JD, Loyola Law Sch., 1982. Bar: Calif. 1982. Assoc. Boren & Sloan, L.A., 1983-87, ptnr., 1987-90; sole practice Law Offices Debra L. Korduner, L.A., 1990—. Mem., editor Loyola Law Review. 1980-82. Mem. State Bar of Calif., Women Lawyers of Los Angeles, Los Angeles County Bar Assn. (mem. client relations com. 1984—), Pi Gamma Mu, Pi Sigma Alpha. Democrat. Jewish. General civil litigation. Office: 1900 Avenue Of The Stars Fl 19 Los Angeles CA 90067-4301

**KOREN, EDWARD FRANZ,** lawyer; b. Eustis, Fla., Aug. 6, 1946; s. Edward Franz Sr. and Frances (Boyd) K.; m. Louise Poole, June 19, 1970; children: Daniel Edward, Susan Louise. BSBA, U. Fla., 1971, JD, 1974. Bar: Fla. 1975, U.S. Dist. Ct. (mid. dist.) Fla. 1977, U.S. Supreme Ct. 1980, U. S. Ct. Appeals (11th cir.) 1981, U.S. Tax Ct. 1985, U.S. Ct. Claims 1986. Instr. tax U. Fla., Gainesville, 1974-75; assoc. Holland & Knight, Lakeland, Fla., 1975-79; ptnr. Holland & Knight, Lakeland, 1980—, chmn. trusts and estates dept., 1983—; adj. prof. graduate tax program U. Fla., Gainesville, 1996. Author: Estate and Personal Financial Planning, 1988, 11th edit., 1999; contbr. articles to profl. jours. Capt. U.S. Army, 1971-72. Fellow Am. Coll. Trust and Estates Counsel (mem. estate and gift tax and bus. planning com., bd. regents 1997—), Am. Coll. Tax Counsel, Am. Bar Found.; mem. ABA (real property, probate and trust law sect., mem. exec. coun. 1995—, chmn. marital deduction com. 1991-95), Fla. Bar Assn. (chmn. real property, probate and trust law sect. 1988-89, chmn. tax sect. 1990-91, active various sects. and coms.), Am. Assn. Attys. and CPAs, Fla. Inst. CPAs, Order of the Coif, Tampa Club, Lakeland Yacht and Country Club, Centre Club. Republican. Presbyterian. Probate, Estate planning, Taxation, general. Home: 114 Hickory Creek Dr Brandon FL 33511-8012 Office: Holland & Knight 92 Lake Wire Dr PO Box 32092 Lakeland FL 33802-2092

**KORFF, PHYLLIS G.,** lawyer; b. N.Y.C., 1943. BA, Bklyn. Coll., 1964; EdM, Boston U., 1967; JD, NYU, 1981. Bar: N.Y. 1982. Ptnr. Skaden, Arps, Slate, Meagher & Flom, N.Y.C., 1990. Office: Skadden Arps Slate Meagher & Flom 919 3rd Ave New York NY 10022-3902

**KORIN, JOEL BENJAMIN,** lawyer, educator; b. Phila., Apr. 15, 1945; s. Leon Aaron and Charlotte Sylvia (Snyder) K.; m. Kallen Stillwell, Aug. 11, 1968; children: Saul, Steven. AB, Dickinson Coll., 1967; JD, Rutgers U., 1971. Bar: N.J. 1971, U.S. Ct. Appeals (3d cir.) 1978, U.S. Supreme Ct. 1978. Assoc. Stransky & Poplar, Camden, N.J., 1971-72, James F. Florio, Camden, 1972-73; asst. dep. pub. defender State of N.J., Camden, 1973-74; assoc. Brown, Connery, Kulp, Willie, Purnell & Greene, Camden, 1975-77, ptnr., 1977-82; ptnr. George, Korin, Quattrone, Blumberg and Chant, P.A., Woodbury, N.J., 1982-99; of counsel Kenney and Kearny, Cherry Hill, 1999—; lectr. Rutgers U. Sch. Law, Camden, 1982—. Author: (with others) Clinical Correspondence Course, 1983, (with Steven Selbst) Preventing Malpractice Lawsuits in Pediatric Emergency Medicine, 1999; editor: Pediatric Emergency Care, 1985; contbr. articles to profl. publs. Bd. of Govs. Haddonfield (N.J.) Civic Assn. Fellow Am. Coll. Trial Lawyers, Am. Bd. Trial Advocacy, Am. Inns of Ct.; mem. ABA, N.J. Bar Assn. (bd. trustees 1994—), N.J. Trial Attys. Assn., Assn. Criminal Def. Attys., Woodbury C. of C. Democrat. Jewish. E-mailo: jkorin@kenneylaw.com. Federal civil litigation, State civil litigation, Criminal. Home: 127 N Hinchman Ave Haddonfield NJ 08033-2725 Office: Kenney and Kearney PO Box 5034 220 Lake Dr E Ste 210 Cherry Hill NJ 08034-0421

**KORIN, OFFER,** lawyer; b. Jerusalem, Nov. 24, 1964; came to U.S., 1972; s. Uri and Sarah Korin; m. Michelle L. Korin, Nov. 2, 1991; children: Ariel L., Tahlia E. BA, Ind. U., Bloomington, 1985; JD, Ind. U., Indpls., 1988. Ptnr. Katz & Korin, Indpls., 1994—; mem. seminar faculty Nat. Bus. Inst., Indpls., 1994, Peoples Law Sch., 1992-94, Indpls. Bar Assn., Indpls., 1998; panelist Ind. U. Sch. of Law, Bloomington, 1998. Bd. dirs. Congregation Shaarey Tefilla, Indpls., 1994-96, Jewish Fedn. Greater Indpls., 1997—; bd. dirs. Jewish Cmty. Rels. Coun., Indpls., 1991—, v.p., 1997—. Mem. ABA, ATLA, Ind. State Bar Assn., Ind. Trial Lawyers Assn., Indpls. Bar Assn. Constitutional, Environmental, Estate planning. Office: Katz & Korin PC 10 W Market St Ste 1120 Indianapolis IN 46204-2964

**KORMAN, EDWARD R.,** federal judge; b. N.Y.C., Oct. 25, 1942; s. Julius and Miriam K.; m. Diane R. Eisner, Feb. 3, 1979; children: Miriam M., Benjamin E. B.A., Bklyn. Coll., 1963; LL.B., Bklyn. Law Sch., 1966; LL.M., NYU, 1971. Bar: N.Y. 1966, U.S. Supreme Ct. 1972. Law clk. to judge N.Y. Ct. Appeals, 1966-68; assoc. Paul, Weiss, Rifkind, Wharton and Garrison, 1968-70; asst. U.S. atty. Eastern Dist. N.Y., N.Y.C., 1970-72; asst. to solicitor gen. of U.S., 1972-74; chief asst. U.S. atty. Eastern Dist. N.Y., 1974-78, U.S. atty., 1978-82; ptnr. Stroock & Stroock & Lavan, N.Y.C., 1982-84; prof. Bklyn. Law Sch., 1984-85; U.S. dist. judge Eastern Dist. N.Y., 1985—. Chmn. Mayor's Com. on N.Y.C. Marshals, 1983-85; mem. Temporary Commn. of Investigation of State of N.Y., 1983-85. Jewish. Office: US Dist Ct US Courthouse 225 Cadman Plz E Brooklyn NY 11201-1818

**KORMES, JOHN WINSTON,** lawyer; b. N.Y.C., May 4, 1935; s. Mark and Joanna P. Kormes; m. Frances W. Kormes, Aug. 19, 1978; 1 child, Mark Vincent. BA in Econs., U. Mich., 1955, JD, 1959. Bar: Pa. 1961, D.C. 1961, U.S. Sup. Ct. 1968. With License and Inspection Rev. Bd. Phila., 1972-73; asst. dist. atty. City of Phila., 1973-74, asst. city solicitor, 1974-80; pvt. practice, Phila., 1961—; moot ct. advisor. Mem. staff Re-Elect the Pres. Com., 1972, Rizzo for Mayor Com., 1971, 75, Phila. Flag Day Assn., 1965—. Served with USAF, 1956-57. Recipient N.Y. Intercoll. Legis. Assembly award, 1954; R.I. Model Congress award, 1954, Queens Coll. Speech Guild award; Eminent wisdom fellow Wisdom Hall of Fame. Fellow Lawyers in Mensa (charter), Triple Nine Soc. (elections officer 1992-93, legal officer, new mem. welcome program officer 1993—, com. to revise constitution 1993—, ombudsman 1994—), Internat. Soc. Philos. Enquiry (sr. fellow, pub. Best Telicom. 1986, 87, legal officer 1986-91, mgr. new mem. welcome program 1988-91, v.p. 1990-91); mem. Am. Legion (life mem.), Phila. Bar Assn., Phila. Trial Lawyers Assn., N.Y. State Trial Lawyers Assn., Am. Arbitration Assn., Fed. Bar Assn., Pitts. Inst. Legal Medicine, Assn. Trial Lawyers Am., Intertel, Internat. Platform Assn., Cincinnatus Soc., Top One Percent Soc., Collegium Soc. 99.5 (charter), Poetic Genius Soc. 99.5 (charter), Masons, Shriners, KP, Lions, Delta Sigma Rho. Republican. Family and matrimonial, State civil litigation, Personal injury. Home: 1070 Edison Ave Philadelphia PA 19116-1342 Office: 2nd Fl 1201 Chestnut St Ste 2 Philadelphia PA 19107-4123

**KORN, ALAN IRA,** lawyer; b. Queens, N.Y., Sept. 25, 1948; s. Joseph and Dorothy Korn; m. Rebecca Kropf, June 8, 1975; children: Sara, David S., Aaron C., Joseph D. BA, NYU, 1970; JD, St. John's U., 1974. Bar: N.Y., U.S. Dist. Ct. (ea. dist.) N.Y., U.S. Dist. Ct. (so. dist.) N.Y. 1975, U.S. Supreme Ct. 1994. Assoc. Nathan Cyperstein, Manhattan, 1977-91, Steven L. Sidney, Woodbury, N.Y., 1991—; cons. Met. Youth Symphony Orch., Manhassett, N.Y., 1997—. With U.S. Army, 1970-75. Mem. N.Y.State Bar Assn., Nassau county Bar Assn. Home: 1538 Andrews Ln East Meadow NY 11554-3623

**KORN, MICHAEL JEFFREY,** lawyer; b. Jersey City, Dec. 22, 1954; s. Howard Leonard and Joyce Ellen (Blumenkranz) K.; m. Pamela Ann VanZandt, May 29, 1983; children: David Harold, Suzanne Faye. BA, U. Va., 1976; JD, U. Fla., 1979. Bar: Fla. 1980, U.S. Dist. Ct. (no. and mid. dists.) Fla., U.S. Ct. Appeals (5th and 11th cirs.). Jud. law clk. Fla. 1st Dist Ct. Appeal, Tallahassee, 1980-81; assoc. Boyer, Tanzler & Boyer, Jacksonville, Fla., 1981-84; pvt. practice Jacksonville, 1984-87; ptnr. Prom, Korn & Zehmer, P.A., Jacksonville, 1987—, Korn & Zehmer, P.A., Jacksonville,

1995—; mem. Fla. Appellate Ct. Rules Com., 1990—. Bd. dirs. North Fla. coun. Camp Fire, 1983-86, Jacksonville Jewish Fedn., 1985—, v.p., 1994-99, treas., 1999—; bd. dirs. Youth Leadership Jacksonville, 1989-93; bd. dirs. Jacksonville Cmty. Coun., 1989-94, 96-98, pres., 1995; Mandarin Comty. Club, Jacksonville, 1988-91; cmty. adv. bd. WJCT-TV, Jacksonville, 1996—, vice-chmn., 1998-99. Recipient Young Leadership award Jacksonville Jewish Fedn., 1992. Mem. Fla. Bar (litig, appellate and health law sects.), Jacksonville Bar Assn. (fee arbitration cir. 1987-90, CLE chair 1995-96, 97—), Acad. Fla. Trial Lawyers. Democrat. Jewish. Avocations: recreational basketball, reading, golf. General civil litigation, Appellate, Health. Office: Korn & Zehmer PA Ste 200 6620 Southpoint Dr S Jacksonville FL 32216-0940

**KORN, MONROE J.,** lawyer; b. Bklyn.; widowed Oct. 1991. BBA, U. Miami, 1950; LLB, Bklyn. Law Sch., 1953, LLM, 1957. Bar. N.Y., U. S. Dist. Ct. (D.C. dist.), U. S. Dist. Ct. (ea. and so. dists.) N.Y., U. S. Supreme Ct. Pvt. practice N.Y.C., 1997—; ptnr. King & Korn, N.Y.C., 1959-77. General civil litigation. Home: 32 Graham Rd Scarsdale NY 10583-7265 Office: 630 3d Ave Rm #1400 New York NY 10017-6705

**KORNBERG, JOEL BARRY,** lawyer, emergency physician; b. Bklyn., June 17, 1953; s. Bernard Fred and Ada (Ritterstein) K.; m. Melinda Michelle Kornberg;children: Dana Nicole, Jordan Reid. AB, Boston U., 1975; MD, N.Y. Med. Coll., 1980; JD, Nova U., 1989. Bar: Fla. 1989, D.C. 1990, U.S. Dist. Ct. (so. dist.) Fla. 1989, U.S. Supreme Ct. 1994; cert. mediator, Fla. 1995; cert. Am. Bd. Emergency Medicine, healthcare risk mgr., Fla. Resident Long Island Jewish-Hillside Med. Ctr., New Hyde Park, N.Y., 1980-81; emergency physician Emergency Med. Svcs. Assocs., Inc., Plantation, Fla., 1981-83, Joel B. Kornberg, M.D. P.A., Coral Springs, Fla., 1983-90, EMSA Ltd. Partnership, Plantation, 1990—; med. dir. Dept. Emergency Svcs. Humana Hosp., Pompano Beach, Fla., 1985-92, regional med. dir., 1992-94; pvt. practice Joel Kornberg, M.D., J.D., Boca Raton, Fla., 1989-94; med. dir. dept. emergency medicine Cedars Med. Ctr., Miami, 1993-94; pvt. practice Joel Kornberg MD, JD, Boca Raton, Fla., 1994—; mem. exec. com. Humana Hosp. Cypress, Pompano Beach, 1985-92, corp. counsel med. affairs; risk mgmt. cons. EMSA Ltd. Partnership, Plantation, 1989-94; dir. edn. Voice Billstat, Plantation, 1992-94. Head coach Coral Springs Youth Soccer Assn., 1989—, mgr. North Springs Little League, 1995-97. Fellow Am. Coll. Legal Medicine, Am. Coll. Emergency Physician; mem. ABA, Nat. Health Lawyers Assn., Am. Soc. Law and Medicine, Nat. Bd. Med. Examiners. Avocations: skiing, piano, tennis, baseball, bicycle. Health, Contracts commercial, General corporate. Office: Ste 305C 7301A W Palmetto Park Rd Boca Raton FL 33433-3466

**KORNFELD, JULIAN POTASH,** lawyer; b. Dallas, May 1, 1934; s. Abraham L. and Abbie (Potash) K.; children—Meredith, Nancy. B.B.A., Tex. U., 1955, LL.B., 1957; LL.M. in Taxation, N.Y. U. (1962). Bar: Tex. 1958, Okla. 1963, U.S. Ct. Appeals (10th cir.), U.S. Tax Ct., U.S. Supreme Ct. Assoc. Potash, Cameron, Bernat & Studdard, El Paso, Tex., 1959-61, Mosteller, Fellers et al, Oklahoma City, 1962-63, Mosteller, Andrews et al, Oklahoma City, 1963-68, Andrews, Mosburg, Davis, Elam, Legg & Kornfeld, Oklahoma City, 1968-73; ptnr. Kornfeld, Mcmillin, Phillips & Upp, Oklahoma City, 1973-80, Kornfeld, Lester, Franklin, Renegar & Bryant, Oklahoma City, 1980-82, Kornfeld, Franklin, Renegar & Randall, Oklahoma City, 1982—. Served to 1st lt., Q.M.C. AUS, 1957-59. Mem. Am., Okla., Tex. bar assns. Corporate taxation, Estate taxation, Taxation, general. Home: 3404 Partridge Rd Oklahoma City OK 73120-8907 Office: Kornfeld Renegar & Randall 4100 Perimeter Center Dr Oklahoma City OK 73112-2326

**KORNGOLD, GERALD,** law educator. BA, U. Pa., 1974, JD, 1977. Bar: Pa. Atty. Wolf, Block, Schorr & Solis-Cohen, Phila., 1977-79; asst. prof. to prof. N.Y. Law Sch., N.Y.C., 1979-87, assoc. dean for acad. affairs, 1984-86; prof. Case Western Res. U. Sch. Law, Cleve., 1987—, Everett D. and Eugenia S. McCurdy prof., 1994—, dean, 1997—. Author: Private Land Use Arrangements: Easements, Covenants, and Equitable Servitudes, 1990, (with Paul Goldstein) Real Estate Transactions, 1993. Mem. Am. Law Inst. Office: Case Western Res U Sch Law 11075 East Blvd Cleveland OH 44106-5409*

**KORNREICH, ALIDA J.,** lawyer; b. Warren, Pa., Aug. 3, 1947; d. Myer Arthur and Agne sMildred (Anderson) K.; m. Stephen Dunn, Apr. 2, 1993. BA in Slavic langs., Ind. U., 1969, MS in Edn., 1972; JD, Duquesne U., 1982. Bar: Pa. Bar Assn., U.S. Dist. Ct. (we. dist.) Pa., U.S. Supreme Ct. Asst. county solicitor Allegheny County Law Dept., Pitts., 1982—. Elected com. person Allegheny County Dem. Com., Pitts., 1989-93. Mem. Allegheny County Bar Assn. Avocations: bridge, piano. Office: Allegheny County Law Dept 300 Ft Pitt Commons 445 Fort Pitt Blvd Pittsburgh PA 15219-1318

**KORNREICH, EDWARD SCOTT,** lawyer; b. Bklyn., Apr. 18, 1953; s. Lawrence and Selma (Rosenblatt) K.; m. Shirley Werner, Feb. 28, 1982; children: Mollie, Davida, Lawrence. BA magna cum laude, Columbia U., 1974; JD, Harvard U., 1977. Appellate atty. Legal Aid Soc., N.Y.C., 1977-79; assoc. atty. Rosenman & Colin, N.Y.C., 1979-84; v.p., legal affairs/gen. counsel St. Luke's-Roosevelt Hosp. Ctr., N.Y.C., 1984-87; mem. Garfunkel Wild & Travis P.C., Great Neck, N.Y., 1987-90; ptnr. Proskauer Rose LLP, N.Y.C., 1990—; mem. joint com. on health care decisions near end of life ABA and Hastings Ctr., 1992-95. Trustee Postgrad. Ctr. Mental Health, N.Y.C., 1992—. Mem. Am. Health Lawyers Assn., Assn. of Bar of City of N.Y. (mem. com. on medicine and law 1985-88, chairperson health law com. 1991-94, mem. AIDS com. 1986-97), Phi Beta Kappa. Jewish. Avocations: running (completed N.Y.C. Marathon 1978, 83, 86, 95, 97). Health, Nonprofit and tax-exempt organizations, Contracts commercial. Office: Proskauer Rose LLP 1585 Broadway New York NY 10036-8200

**KORNSPAN, SUSAN FLEISCHNER,** shareholder lawyer; b. N.Y.C., Mar. 5, 1965; d. Leonard Fleischner and Loretta (Hekelman) Brown; m. Scott Alan Kornspan, May 17, 1992. BA, Georgetown U., 1987; JD cum laude, U. Miami, 1990. Bar: Fla. 1990, U.S. Dist. Ct. Md. 1990, D.C. 1990, U.S. Ct. Appeals (D.C. cir.) 1991, U.S. Dist. Ct. (so. dist.) Fla. 1991, U.S. Ct. Appeals (11th cir.) 1991, U.S. Supreme Ct. 1997. Assoc. Piper & Marbury, Washington, 1989-91; assoc. Nason Gildan, West Palm Beach, Fla., 1991-94, shareholder, 1994-96; shareholder Greenberg Traurig, West Palm Beach, Fla., 1997—. Bd. Young Govs. of Govs. Club Palm Beaches, Fla., 1998—. Scholar Young Lawyers Divsn. Fla. Bar, 1988. Mem. ABA, Fla. Bar (mem. jud. evaluation com. 1998—, fee arbitration com. 1998—), Palm Beach County Bar Assn. (client rels. com. 1998—, professionalism com. 1999—). Avocations: tennis, theatre, travel. General civil litigation, Public utilities, Municipal (including bonds). Office: Greenberg Traurig PA 777 S Flagler Dr Ste 300E West Palm Beach FL 33401

**KOROI, MARK MICHAEL,** lawyer; b. Grosse Pointe, Mich., May 22, 1963; s. Remus M. and Eleanor Barbara Koroi. AA, Macomb C.C., Warren, Mich., 1983; BA in Psychology, Wayne State U., 1986; JD, Mich. State U., 1990. Bar: Mich. 1991, U.S. Dist. Ct. (ea. dist.) Mich. 1991. Law clk. Law Offices of Roger Leemis, Southfield, Mich., 1986-88, Samaan, Mashni & Assocs., Dearborn, Mich., 1988-89, Law Offices of Salem Samaan, Plymouth, Mich., 1989-91; atty. Law Offices of Mark Koroi, Plymouth, 1991—; lectr. Mich. Head Injury Alliance, Ann Arbor, 1996. Recipient Prix d'Accessit, French Consulate, Detroit, 1985. Mem. ABA, State Bar Mich. Pentecostal. Avocations: weight lifting, reading. Personal injury, Contracts commercial, General practice. Home: 12131 Champaign Ave Warren MI 48089-1246 Office: 150 N Main St Plymouth MI 48170-1236

**KORRY, ALEXANDRA D.,** lawyer; b. London, 1959; Bar: N.Y. 1988.; AB, Harvard U., 1980; MSc, London Sch. Econs./Polit. Sci., 1981; JD, Duke U., 1986. Ptnr. Sullivan & Cromwell, N.Y.C. Office: Sullivan & Cromwell 125 Broad St Fl 28 New York NY 10004-2489

**KORTENHOF, JOSEPH MICHAEL,** lawyer, educator; b. Kimberly, Wis., Aug. 18, 1927; s. Joseph Arthur and Marie Agnes (Probst) K.; m. Althea Hunting, June 7, 1952; children: Elizabeth Ann, Michael, Amy Jo. BA cum laude, Lawrence U., 1950; JD, U. Mich., 1953. Bar: Mo. 1953, U.S. Ct. Appeals (8th cir.) 1953, U.S. Dist. Ct. (ea. dist.) Mo. 1953. Assoc. Coburn, Storckman & Croft, St. Louis, 1953-60; sr. ptnr. Kortenhof & Ely, St. Louis, 1960—; adj. prof. law Washington U., St. Louis, 1984—. Served with USAF, 1945-47. Recipient award of honor Lawyers Assn. St. Louis, 1990. Fellow Am. Coll. Trial Lawyers, Am. Bd. Trial Advs., Internat. Soc. Barristers; mem. ABA, Mo. Bar Found. (trial lawyer award 1962), St. Louis Bar Assn., Assn. Civil Def. Counsel, Am. Maritime Law Assn., Sigma Phi Epsilon. Democrat. Episcopalian. Admiralty, Federal civil litigation, State civil litigation. Home: 5340 N Kenrick Parke Dr Saint Louis MO 63119-5056 Office: Kortenhof & Ely 1015 Locust St Ste 300 Saint Louis MO 63101-1333

**KORTHALS, CANDACE DURBIN,** lawyer; b. Tampa, Fla., Oct. 3, 1948; d. Robert F. and Geraldine B. Durbin; m. John L. Korthals, June 8, 1968; children: John Kristofor, Kathryn Elizabeth. BA in Internat. Studies, Ohio State U., 1969, BS in Edn., 1970; JD cum laude, Nova U., 1982. Bar: Fla. 1982. Tchr. Palatka (Fla.) Mid. Sch., 1970-72, Dillard H.S., Ft. Lauderdale, Fla., 1974-79; atty. Broward County Pub. Defenders, Ft. Lauderdale, 1982-84, Grimmett & Korthals, Ft. Lauderdale, 1984-90, Gunther & Whittaker, Ft. Lauderdale, 1990-94, Law Office of John Camillo, Ft. Lauderdale, 1994-96, Neale & De Almeida, Ft. Lauderdale, 1999—. Staff mem. Nova Law Rev., 1981, 82. Personal injury, Insurance. Office: Neale & De Almeida 221 W Oakland Park Blvd Fort Lauderdale FL 33311-1757

**KORZEC, REBECCA,** law educator; b. Ulm, Germany, May 24, 1947; d. David and Esther Korzec; m. Louis Schoff Halikman, June 22, 1969 (div. Oct. 1982); 1 child, Ruth Miriam. BA, Gourcher Coll., 1969; JD, Temple U., 1972. Bar: Md., U.S. Dist. Ct. Md., U.S. Ct. Appeals (4th cir.) 1972. Assoc. Venable, Beether and Howard, Balt., 1972-75; lectr. U. Balt., 1975, prof. law, 1975—; fellow Hoffberger Ctr. for Ethics, U. Balt., 1992—, Ctr. for Internat. and Comparative law, 1995—. Pro bono lawyer Md. Vol. Lawyers, 1990—, cons. WMAR/Contact 2 Consumer Protection program. Mem. ABA (uniform comml. code study com.), Md. State Bar Assn. (various coms.), Bar Assn. of Balt. (products liability com., others), Women's Bar Assn., Women's Law Ctr. Avocations: tennis, reading, chess. Office: U Balt Sch Law 1420 N Charles St # Lc411 Baltimore MD 21201-5720

**KORZENIK, SIDNEY S.,** lawyer; b. N.Y.C., Jan. 12, 1909; s. Adolph and Sally (Seiden) K.; m. Emily Faust K., June 23, 1949; children: David, Jeremy, Deborah, Joshua. BA, Harvard U., 1929; MA, Columbia U., 1931; LLB, NYU, 1939. Bar: N.Y., Federal Bar, U.S. Supreme Ct. Pvt. practice N.Y.C., 1946—; with N.Y. State Unemployment Adv. Coun., 1936-41; mem. U.S. Govt. Mgmt.-Labor Textile adv. com.; mem. gen. arbitration coun. of Textile Industry; counsel to various apparel, textile and fur interest orgns., including Nat. Knitted Outerwear Assn., Fedn. Apparel Mfrs., Knitted Textile Assn., Am. Transfer Printing Inst., others; formerly adj. asst. prof. NYU Law Sch.; advisor to govt. textile trade missions; adviser in field. Bd. dirs. Ednl. Found. of Fashion Inst. of Technology, N.Y.C. With U.S. Army, 1941-46. Mem. Phi Beta Kappa. Home: 120 Carthage Rd Scarsdale NY 10583-7202

**KOSAKOW, JAMES MATTHEW,** lawyer; b. New London, Conn., Apr. 12, 1954; s. Leonard Louis and Lois Ann (Rosen) K.; m. Yvonne Manijeh Bokhour, June 4, 1978; 1 child, Jonathan Daniel. BA, Conn. Coll., 1976; JD, Yeshiva U., 1984. Bar: N.Y. 1985, Conn. 1985, D.C. 1985, Fla. 1991, U.S. Dist. Ct. (so. and ea. dists.) 1985, U.S. Tax Ct. 1993. Assoc. Vittoria & Forsythe, N.Y.C., 1986-92, Gregory and Adams, Wilton, Conn., 1992-94; pvt. practice N.Y.C. and Westport, Conn., 1994-97; ptnr. Kove & Kosakow, LLC, 1997—; vice-chancellor Cambridge Theol. Seminary, Carthage, Ill., 1996—; guardian and litem N.Y. County Surrogate's Ct., N.Y.C., 1987—, Norwalk Probate Ct., 1993—; lectr. in field; arbitrator BBB, N.Y.C., 1988-89. Co-author: Handling Federal Estate and Gift Taxes, 1999; contbr. articles to profl. jours. Trustee, bd. dirs. Internat. Nursery Sch., Queens, N.Y., 1987-89; mem. estates & trusts specialty group lawyers divsn. United Jewish Appeal-Fedn. Jewish Philanthropies of N.Y., Inc., 1990-94; commr. Wilton Water Commn., 1995-96, Wilton Fire Commn., 1996—; ptnr. Creative Philanthropic Resources, 1995—; chmn. membership com. Mid-Fairfield Substance Abuse Coalition, 1995-96; dir. Thee Art Tree Source, Inc., 1995—; adv. com. The Unicorn Archive. Mem. N.Y. Bar Assn. (legis. com., trusts and estates sect. 1987—), Conn. Bar Assn. (elder law com.), Fla. Bar (real property, probate and trust law, out-of-state mem. rels. com. 1994—), Assn. of Bar of City of N.Y., Exch. Club (bd. dirs. Wilton club). Estate planning, Probate, Estate taxation. Office: 25 Ford Rd Westport CT 06880-1261 also: 122 E 42d St New York NY 10168

**KOSARIN, JONATHAN HENRY,** lawyer; b. Bklyn., Aug. 13, 1951; s. Lester and Norma (Higger) K.; m. Gayle C. Skarupa, Nov. 27, 1982. BA in History magna cum laude, Syracuse U., 1973; JD, Bklyn. Law Sch., 1976; LLM in Govt. Contract Law, George Washington U., 1984; postgrad., U.S. Army Command and Gen. Staff Coll., 1990, U.S. Army War Coll., 1997. Bar: N.Y. 1977, D.C. 1978, U.S. Supreme Ct. 1980, U.S. Ct. Claims 1981, U.S. Ct. Appeals (Fed. cir.) 1982. Commd. 2d lt. U.S. Army, 1973, advanced through grades to col., 1997; prosecutor trial counsel U.S. Army, Ft. McClellan, Ala., 1977-78; adminstrv. law officer U.S. Army, Ft. McClellan, 1978-79, instr. law, 1979-80; trial atty. contract appeals div. U.S. Army, Washington, 1980-84; contracts atty. U.S. Army Hdqrs., Heidelberg, Fed. Rep. Germany, 1985-87; assoc. gen. counsel, dir. procurement law Fed Home Loan Bank Bd., Washington, 1987-89; assoc. counsel USN, Washington, 1989-94, dep. counsel, 1994—; adj. asst. prof. contract law JAG Sch., Charlottesville, Va., 1988-93, adj. assoc. prof., 1993-95, adj. prof., vice chmn., 1995—; adj. faculty contract law U. Va., 1989—; faculty Fed. Publs. Seminars, 1995—. Vol. info. specialist Smithsonian Instn. Washington, 1993—. Mem. ABA, D.C. Bar Assn., Titanic Hist. Soc., No. Va. Football Ofcls. Assn., Phi Alpha Delta, Phi Beta Kappa, Phi Kappa Phi, Phi Delta Kappa. Democrat. Office: USN Office Of Gen Counsel Washington DC 20350-0001

**KOSHIAN, JACQUELINE MARIE,** judge; b. Niagara Falls, N.Y.; d. John and Alice K.; m. Varkis Baligian, Dec. 1, 1962 (dec. Oct. 1991); children: Lisa J., Jeffrey V. AB, Russell Sage Coll.; LLB, U. Buffalo, 1959. Ptnr. Koshian & Baligian, Niagara Falls, N.Y., 1962-75; deputy corp. counsel City of Niagara Falls, 1964-75; Niagara County estate tax atty. State of N.Y., 1975; city ct. judge State of N.Y., Niagara Falls, 1976-86, supreme ct. justice, 1987—; bd. dirs. Adv. Com. Jud. Ethics, N.Y.C. Bd. trustees Niagara Falls Meml. Med. Ctr., 1996-97. Recipient Disting. Alumni award U. Buffalo Sch. Law, 1996. Office: Supreme Ct Chambers Niagara County Civic Bldg 755 3rd St Niagara Falls NY 14301-1003

**KOSIK, EDWIN MICHAEL,** federal judge; b. 1925. BA, Wilkes Coll., Wilkes-Barre, Pa., 1949; LLB, Dickinson Sch. Law, Carlisle, Pa. Asst. U.S. atty. Pa. State Workmen's Compensation Bd., 1953-58, chmn., 1964-69; pvt. practice law Needle, Needle & Needle, 1958-64; pres. judge 45th Jud. Dist. Ct. Common Pleas, 1979-86; judge U.S. Dist. Ct. (mid. dist.) Pa., Scranton, 1986—, now sr. judge. Office: US Dist Ct US Courthouse PO Box 856 Scranton PA 18501-0856*

**KOSKO, SUSAN UTTAL,** legal administrator; b. N.Y.C., Oct. 8, 1954; d. Sheldon and Jane Louise (Kaufmann) Uttal; m. James J. Kosko, July 6, 1996. BA, Clark U., 1976; cert. paralegal, Inst. Paralegal Tng., Phila., 1978. Legal asst. Winthrop, Stimson, Putnam & Roberts, N.Y.C., 1978-80; legal coord. Schroder Real Estate Corp., N.Y.C., 1980-83; legal asst. supr. real estate svcs. dept. Cravath, Swaine & Moore, N.Y.C., 1983-89; sr. legal asst. real estate dept. Rackemann, Sawyer & Brewster, Boston, 1989-90; sr. legal asst. leasing and real estate depts. Goulston & Storrs, Boston, 1990-97; contracts adminstr. Cabletron Systems, Inc., Rochester, N.H., 1997-99; v.p. ops. Nonpareil Software, New Durham, N.H., 1999—. Mem. Clark U. N.Y. Young Alumni Assn. (steering com.). Democrat. Jewish. Avocations: pottery, piano, photography, cycling, gourmet cooking. Office: Nonpareil Software Inc 39 N Shore Rd New Durham NH 03855-2113

**KOSMOWSKI, AUDRA MICHELE,** lawyer; b. Cleve., Apr. 9, 1968; d. Warren M. and Kathleen T. Krueger; m. Michael F. Kosmowski, 1993. BA in Polit. Sci., John Carroll U., 1990; JD, U. Akron, 1993; postgrad., Case Western Res. U., 1997—. Bar: Pa. 1993, Ohio 1995. Assoc. Evans, Garvey, Lackey & Ochs, Sharon, Pa., 1995—. Tutor Sharon Literacy Coun., 1997-98; mem. Pa. Econ. League, Sharon, 1996—; bd. dirs. Aware, Inc., Sharon, 1997-99. Mem. Ohio Bar Assn., Pa. Bar Assn., Mercer County Commn. for Women (vice chair 1998—). Estate planning, Workers' compensation, General civil litigation. Office: Evans Garvey Lackey & Ochs PO Box 949 19 Jefferson Ave Sharon PA 16146-3342

**KOSSAR, RONALD STEVEN,** lawyer; b. Ellenville, N.Y., May 30, 1948; s. Emanuel and Helen (Panken) K.; m. Sandra Perlman, Aug. 25, 1973. B.A. cum laude, Boston U., 1970; J.D., Am. U., 1973. Bar: N.Y. 1974, D.C. 1974, U.S. Dist. Ct. (no. dist.) N.Y. 1974, U.S. Tax Ct. 1974, U.S. Ct. Appeals D.C. 1974. Tax law specialist Office of Asst. Commr. (Tech.), IRS, Washington, 1973-75; sole practice, Middletown, N.Y., 1976—; dir. Newburgh (N.Y.) Realty Corp., Cornwall Realty Corp., Just-Irv Sales, Inc., Newburgh. Mem. ABA, N.Y. State Bar Assn., Orange County Bar Assn., Middletown Bar Assn., D.C. Bar. Jewish. General practice, General corporate, Real property. Office: 402 E Main St Middletown NY 10940-2516

**KOSSL, THOMAS LEONARD,** lawyer; b. Oshkosh, Wis., Oct. 21, 1952; s. Leonard N. and Elaine M. (Noak) K.; m. Jacqueline E. Saco, Sept. 5, 1981; children: Kenzie, Clayton. AB, U. Chgo., 1974; JD, Georgetown U., 1978, MS in Fgn. Svc., 1994. Bar: D.C. 1979, U.S. Dist. Ct. D.C. 1979, N.J. 1992. Assoc. Daniels, Houlihan and Palmeter, Washington, 1978-80, Arent, Fox, Kintner, Plotkin and Kahn, Washington, 1980-83; asst. corp. counsel, then div. counsel Corning (N.Y.), Inc., 1983-86, assoc. internat. counsel, 1984-86; v.p., gen. counsel, asst. sec. MetPath Inc., Teterboro, N.J., 1986-92; v.p., gen. counsel, sec. Unilab Corp. and MetWest, Inc., Teterboro, 1988-92; assoc. gen. counsel Corning Lab. Svcs., Inc. and MetPath, Inc., Teterboro, 1992-94; pvt. practice Kinnelon, N.J., 1994—; exec. com., policy com. MetPath, Inc., 1988-92. Mem. ABA, Am. Health Lawyers Assn. Health, Private international. Office: 472 Laurel Ln Kinnelon NJ 07405-3122

**KOSTELANETZ, BORIS,** lawyer; b. St. Petersburg, Russia, June 16, 1911; came to U.S., 1920, naturalized, 1925; s. Nachman and Rosalia (Dimschetz) K.; m. Ethel Cory, Dec. 18, 1938; children: Richard Cory, Lucy Cory. B.C.S., N.Y. U., 1933, B.S., 1936; J.D. magna cum laude, St. John's U., 1936, LL.D. (hon.), 1981. Bar: N.Y. 1936; CPA, N.Y. With Price, Waterhouse & Co., C.P.A.'s, N.Y.C., 1934-37; asst. U.S. atty. So. Dist. N.Y.; also confidential asst. to U.S. atty, 1937-43; spl. asst. to atty. gen. U.S., 1943-46; chief war frauds sect. Dept. Justice, 1945-46; spl. counsel com. investigate crime in interstate commerce U.S. Senate, 1950-51; ptnr. Kostelanetz Ritholz Tigue & Fink, N.Y.C., 1946-89, of counsel, 1990-94; of counsel Kostelanetz & Fink, N.Y.C., 1994—; instr. acctg. N.Y. U., 1937-47, adj. prof. taxation, 1947-69; Mem. com. on character and fitness Appellate div. Supreme Ct. N.Y., 1st dept., 1974—, chmn., 1985—. Author: (with L. Bender) Criminal Aspects of Tax Fraud Cases, 1957, 2d edit., 1968, 3d edit., 1980; Contbr. articles to legal, accounting and tax jours. Chmn. Kefauver for Pres. Com. N.Y. State, 1952. Recipient Meritorious Svc. award NYU, 1954, John T. Madden Meml. award, 1969, Pietas medal St. John's U., 1961, medal of honor, 1983, James Madison award, 1988, Torch of Learning award Am. Friends of Hebrew U. Law Sch., 1979, N.Y.U. Presdl. citation, 1990, N.Y. State Bar Assn. Fifty-Yr. Lawyer award, 1990. Fellow Am. Coll. Trial Lawyers, Am. Coll. Tax Counsel, Am. Bar Found.; mem. ABA (coun. sect. taxation 1978-81, ho. of dels. 1984-89), Fed. Bar Assn., Internat. Bar Assn., Soc. King's Inn, Ireland (hon. bencher 1995), N.Y. State Bar Assn., N.Y. State CPAs, N.Y. County Lawyers Assn. (v.p. 1966-69, pres. 1969-71, bd. dirs. 1958-64, 66-69, 71-74, chmn. judiciary com. 1965-69), Assn. of Bar of City of N.Y., NYU Sch. Commerce Alumni Assn. (pres. 1951-52), NYU Alumni Fedn. (pres. 1989-92), St. John's U. Law Sch. Alumni Assn. (pres. 1955-57), India House. General civil litigation, Criminal. Home: 37 Washington Sq W New York NY 10011-9181 Office: Kostelanetz & Fink 530 5th Ave Fl 21 New York NY 10036-5101

**KOSTELNY, ALBERT JOSEPH, JR.,** lawyer; b. Phila., July 11, 1951; s. Albert Joseph and Margaret (Naile) K. BA, U. Pa., 1973, MA, 1974; JD, Fordham U., 1979. Bar: N.Y. 1980, U.S. Dist. Ct. (so. dist.) N.Y. 1983, U.S. Ct. Claims 1983, U.S. Supreme Ct. 1983, U.S. Ct. Internat. Trade 1985, U.S. Ct. Appeals (2d cir.) 1985. Atty. N.Y. State Divsn. Human Rights, N.Y.C., 1980-81, sr. atty., 1981-89, acting chief adminstrv. law judge, 1989-91, adjudication counsel to commr., 1990-98, supr. atty., dir. prosecutions unit, 1998—. Mem. ABA, N.Y. State Bar Assn., N.Y. County Lawyers Assn., Assn. Trial Lawyers Am. Republican. Roman Catholic. Office: NY State Div Human Rights 55 W 125th St New York NY 10027-4516

**KOSTEN, JEFFREY THOMAS,** lawyer; b. Newark, Dec. 20, 1960; s. Richard Warren and Ludwika (Arney) K. Student, London Sch. Econs., 1981-82; BS, BA, U. Pa. Wharton Sch., 1983; JD, U. Pa. Law Sch., 1986. Bar: Pa. 1986, N.J. 1986, U.S. Dist. Ct. N.J. 1986, U.S. Ct. Appeals (3d cir.) 1988, U.S. Dist. Ct. (ea. dist. Pa.) 1990. Law clk to Hon. William M. D'Annunzio Appellate div. Superior Ct. N.J., Flemington, 1986-87; assoc. McCarter & English, Newark, N.J., 1987-88, Ozzard Wharton, Somerville, N.J., 1988-91; counsel, v.p. Nat. Westminster Bancorp., Inc., Jersey City, N.J., 1991-96; ptnr. Stanley, Powers & Matyola, Bridgewater, N.J., 1996—; adj. prof. negotiation & bus., govt. & soc. Rutgers U. Sch. Mgmt., Newark, 1995—. Mem. Assn. Trial Lawyers Am., Somerset County Bar Assn., N.J. State Bar Assn. Banking, General civil litigation, Contracts commercial. Office: Stanley Powers & Matyola 1170 Us Highway 22 Ste 203 Bridgewater NJ 08807-2929

**KOSTOVSKI, SUZANNA,** lawyer; b. Macedonia, Feb. 17, 1962; d. Petre and Todorka Ristovski; m. Petre Kostovski, Aug. 30, 1988; children: Melissa, Richard. BA in Polit. Sci. and Spanish with distinction, Wayne State U., 1982; JD magna cum laude, U. Detroit, 1986. Bar: Mich. 1986, U.S. Dist. Ct. (ea. dist.) Mich. 1986, U.S. Ct. Appeals (6th cir.) 1996, U.S. Supreme Ct. 1999. Rsch. atty. Mich. Ct. Appeals, Detroit, 1986-87, law clk., 1987-88; law clk. Mich. Supreme Ct., Detroit, 1988-89; assoc. atty. Miller Canfield Paddock & Stone, Detroit, 1990-92, S. Allen Early & Assocs., Detroit, 1996—. Mem. Macomb County Bar Assn. Criminal, General civil litigation, Appellate. Office: S Allen Early & Assocs 163 Madison St Ste 229 Detroit MI 48226-2138

**KOSTYO, JOHN FRANCIS,** lawyer; b. Findlay, Ohio, Feb. 9, 1955; s. Albert Robert and Mary Agnes (Welsh) K.; m. Shirley Ann Allgyre, June 9, 1984. BA in Polit. Sci. and Philosophy magna cum laude, John Carroll U., 1978; JD, Case Western Res. U., 1981. Bar: Ohio 1981, U.S. Dist. Ct. (no. dist.) Ohio 1982, U.S. Dist. Ct. (ea. dist.) Mich. 1991, U.S. Supreme Ct. 1991, U.S. Dist. Ct. (so. dist.) Mich. 1992, U.S. Dist. Ct. (we. dist.) Mich. 1992. Assoc. Weasel & Brimley, Findlay, 1981-89; ptnr. Brimley, Kostyo & Elliott, L.P.A., Findlay, 1989-91, Brimley & Kostyo Co., L.P.A., Findlay, 1991, Brimley, Kostyo & Lather Co. L.P.A., 1991-93, Brimley & Kostyo Co. L.P.A., 1993-99; v.p. Mid-Am. Title Agy., Inc., Findlay, Ohio, 1989—; mem. Kostyo & Clark, PLL, Findlay, Ohio, 1999—; lectr. contracts and negotiable instruments U. Findlay, 1981-84, sr. lectr. 1984-96. Mem. ABA (corp. banking and bus. law, litigation div.), Ohio Bar Assn., Toledo Bar Assn., Findlay/Hancock County Bar Assn., Alpha Sigma Nu. Roman Catholic. Clubs: Rockwell Springs Trout. Lodge: Elks, K.C. (4th degree). Avocations: sports, comml. trans., books, theater. State civil litigation, Contracts commercial, General practice. Home: 462 Penbrooke Dr Findlay OH 45840-7472 Office: Kostyo & Clark PLL 1995 Tiffin Ave Ste 312 Findlay OH 45840 also: MidAm Title Agy Inc 100 E Main Cross St Findlay OH 45840-4861

**KOSUB, JAMES ALBERT,** lawyer; b. San Antonio, Jan. 8, 1948; s. Ernest Pete and Lonie (Doege) K.; divorced; 1 child, James Jr.; m. Jane Stevens Cain, Aug. 11, 1979; children: Kathryn, Nicholas (dec.). Student, East Carolina U., 1970, San Antonio Coll., 1971-72; BS, SW Tex. State U., 1974; JD, St. Mary's U., San Antonio, 1977. Bar: Tex. 1978, U.S. Dist. Ct. (we. dist.) Tex. 1980, U.S. Ct. Appeals (5th cir.) 1981, U.S. Dist. Ct. (so. dist.) 1986, U.S. Supreme Ct. 1988, U.S. Dist. Ct. (no. and ea. dists.) Tex. 1990. Ptnr. Kosub & Langlois, San Antonio, 1978-79, Kosub, Langlois & Van Cleave, San Antonio, 1979-83; mng. ptnr. Kosub & Langlois, San Antonio, 1983-86; sr. ptnr. James A. Kosub, San Antonio, 1986-94; pvt. practice Eldorado, Tex., 1994—. Bd. dirs. Judson Ind. Sch. Bd. Trustees, Converse, Tex., 1975-81, Bexar County Fedn. Sch. Bds., San Antonio, 1977-80. Sgt. USMC, 1966-70. Fellow Tex. Bar Found., San Antonio Bar Found.; mem. ABA (EEOC liaison com. San Antonio chpt. 1987-93), San Antonio Bar Assn. (bd. dirs. 1990-92, sec. 1992-93), Fed. Bar Assn. 5th Cir. Bar Assn., Coll. of State Bar of Tex., State Bar of Tex. (coun. labor and employment sect. 1993—, sec. 1997-98, vice chair 1998-99, vice chair 1999—). Episcopalian. Avocations: carpentry, gardening, golf. Labor, Civil rights, Constitutional. Office: 105 S Main Eldorado TX 76936-0460

**KOTADA, KELLY KENICHI,** lawyer; b. Honolulu, Nov. 16, 1962; s. Setsuko (Yoshihara) K. BA, U. Hawaii, 1985; JD, Thomas Cooley Law Sch., Lansing, Mich., 1988. Bar: Hawaii 1988, U.S. Dist. Ct. Hawaii 1988, U.S. Ct. Appeals (9th cir.) 1992. Clk. Mich. Ct. Appeals, Lansing, 1986-87; assoc. Cronin, Fried, Sekiya, Kekina & Fairbanks, Honolulu, 1988-89; law clk. Cir. Ct. of the 1st Cir., Honolulu, 1989-90; assoc. Edmunds, Verga & O'Brien, Honolulu, 1990-91, Law Offices of Ian Mattoch, Honolulu, 1992-95; pvt. practice Honolulu, 1995—; arbitrator Cir. Ct. of 1st Cir., 1995—; vol. judge Honolulu Dist. "Teen" Ct., 1996—; barrister Am. Inns of Ct. IV, Honolulu, 1990-92. Legal counsel Hawaii Jaycees, 1994—. Mem. ABA, ATLA, Hawaii State Bar Assn., Consumer Lawyers Hawaii (instr. "People's Law Sch." 1993-95). Workers' compensation, Personal injury. Office: 900 Fort Street Mall Ste 910 Honolulu HI 96813-3716

**KOTCHER, SHIRLEY J. W.,** lawyer; b. June 6, 1924; m. Harry A. Kotcher; children: Leslie Susan, Dana Anne. BA, NYU; JD, Columbia U. Bar: N.Y. In-house counsel Booth Meml. Med. Ctr., Flushing, N.Y., 1975-83, gen. counsel, 1983-91; v.p., gen. counsel the N.Y. Hosp. Med. Ctr. Queens, 1991-97; advisor health care Borough Pres. Queens, 1978. Author: Hidden gold and Pitfalls in New Tax Law, 1970. Mem. ABA (health law forum com.), Nat. Health Lawyers Assn., Am. Acad. Hosp. Attys., Am. Soc. Law and Medicine, Am. Soc. Health Care Risk Mgmt., Assn. for Hosp. Risk Mgmt. N.Y., Greater N.Y. Hosp. Assn. (legal adv. com. 1976—). Health, Insurance, Personal injury. Office: NY Hosp Med Ctr of Queens Flushing NY 11355

**KOTELMAN, LAURA MARY,** lawyer; b. Chgo., Apr. 5, 1972; d. Robert George and Mary Victoria Kotelman. Student, Am. U., 1992; BA, Lake Forest Coll., 1993; JD, U. Ill., 1997. Bar: Ill. 1997, U.S. Ct. Appeals (7th cir.). Legal asst. Gary J. Rubin & Assocs., Libertyville, Ill., 1993; legis. analyst Ill. Senate Majority Staff, Springfield, 1993-94; law clk. City of Champaign, 1995; govt. affairs asst. U. Ill., 1995-96; summer assoc. Sorling, Northrup et al, Springfield, 1996; program legal specialist Ill. Atty. Gen., Chgo., 1997-98; assoc. counsel Nat. Assn. Ind. Insurers, Des Plaines, Ill., 1998—. Pres. Lake County (Ill.) Young Reps., 1993-94. Mem. ABA, Ill. State Bar Assn., Federalist Soc. (chpt. pres. 1996-97), Phi Delta Phi (chpt. pres. 1995-96, Most Active Chpt. award 1996). Roman Catholic. Legislative, Administrative and regulatory, Insurance. Office: Nat Assn Ind Insurers 2600 S River Rd Des Plaines IL 60018-3203

**KOTLARCHUK, IHOR O. E.,** lawyer; b. Ukraine, July 31, 1943; came to U.S., 1946, naturalized, 1957; s. Emil and Lidia N. (Maceluch) K. BS in Fin., Fordham U., 1965, JD, 1968; LLM, Georgetown U., 1974, MA in Govt., 1982. Bar: N.Y. 1969, D.C. 1972, U.S. Ct. Mil. Appeals, U.S. Tax Ct., U.S. Supreme Ct. Trial atty. criminal sect. tax divsn. U.S. Dept. Justice, Washington, 1973-78, civil sect. tax divsn., 1978-80, fraud sect. criminal divsn., 1984-97, office of enforcement ops. sect. criminal divsn., 1997—, internal security sect. criminal divsn., 1984—; mem. U.S. Dept. Justice's Fgn. Corrupt Practices Act Rev. Com., 1980-81. Served with JAG, U.S. Army, 1969-73, now col. USAR, ret. Decorated Bronze star, Legion of Merit. Mem. ABA, N.Y. State Bar, D.C. Bar Assn., Res. Officers Assn., Phi Alpha Delta. Ukraine Catholic. Address: 205 S Lee St Alexandria VA 22314-3307

**KOTLER, RICHARD LEE,** lawyer; b. L.A., Apr. 13, 1952; s. Allen S. Kotler and Marcella (Fromberg) Swarttz; m. Cindy Jasik, Dec. 9, 1990; children: Kelsey Elizabeth, Charles Max. BA, Sonoma State Coll., 1976; JD, Southwestern U., 1979. Bar: Calif. 1980, U.S. Dist. Ct. (cen. dist.) Cal. 1980; cert. family law specialist. Sole practice Newhall, Calif., 1980-83, 88—; sr. ptnr. Kotler & Hann, Newhall, 1983-88; pvt. practice Law Offices of Richard L. Kotler, Newhall, 1984-86; judge pro temp Municipal Ct., 1981-84, Superior Ct., 1985—. Chmn. Santa Clarita Valley Battered Women's Assn., Newhall, 1983-87; bd. dirs. Santa Clarita Valley Hotline, Newhall, 1981-83. Recipient Commendation award L.A. County, 1983; named SCV Paintball champion. Mem. Santa Clarita Valley Bar Assn. (v.p. 1985—), L.A. Assn. Cert. Family Law Specialists, Los Angeles Astronomy Soc., Newhall Astronomy Club. Avocations: astronomy, classic cars, collecting stamps, precious metals, trout fishing. State civil litigation, Family and matrimonial, Entertainment. Office: B Penthouse 23900 Lyons Ave Santa Clarita CA 91321-2440

**KOTULA, MICHAEL ANTHONY,** lawyer; b. Rockville Centre, N.Y., Aug. 17, 1965; s. Michael Stanley and Rosemary Therese Kotula. BA, Emory U., 1987; JD with honors, George Washington U., 1990. Bar: N.J. 1990, D.C. 1991, N.Y. 1995, U.S. Dist. Ct. N.J. 1990, U.S. Dist. Ct. D.C. 1992, U.S. Dist. Ct. (ea. and so. dists.) N.Y. 1998, U.S. Ct. Appeals (3rd cir.) 1992. Law clk. Hon. Curtis E. von Kann U.S. Superior Ct. (D.C.), Washington, 1990-91; assoc. Carr, Goodson, Lee & Warner, Washington, 1991-94; assoc. Rivkin, Radler & Kremer, Uniondale, N.Y., 1994-98, ptnr., 1998—. Contbg. author: The Law of Liabilities Insurance, 1999; contbr. articles to profl. jours. Recipient Outstanding Advocate award Met. Washington Trial Lawyers Assn., 1990. Mem. N.Y. State Bar Assn. (exec. com. young lawyers sect. 1997—, liaison to the environ. law sect. 1997—). Avocations: running, weightlifting, travel, sports. General civil litigation, Environmental, Insurance. Office: Rivkin Radler & Kremer Eab Plz Uniondale NY 11556-0001

**KOUKLIS, JOHN C.,** lawyer; b. Crete, Greece, Feb. 20, 1940. Car, Kettering U., Flint, Mich., 1962; JD, U. Mich., 1970. Bar: Wash. 1970, U.S. Dist. Ct. (we. dist.) Wash. 1970, U.S. Cupreme Ct. 1997. Ptnr. Davies Pearson P.C., Tacoma, Wash., 1970-89; chief asst. city atty. City of Tacoma, 1989-98; of counsel Davies Pearson PC, Tacoma, 1998—. Pres. Pub. Broadcast Found. S.W. Wash., Tacoma, 1985-95. Lt. USNR, 1963-67. Mem. Wash. State Bar Assn. Avocations: karate, sailing, hiking, travel. Office: Davies Pearson PC 920 S Fawcett Ave Tacoma WA 98402-5606

**KOURAY, ATHENA C.,** lawyer; d. Steven B. and Panagiota (Thomas) Caperonis; m. Christian X. Kouray; children: Steven X., Katina P. BA, Syracuse U., 1941; JD, Albany Law Sch., 1946. Bar: N.Y. Founding ptnr. Kouray & Kouray, Schenectady, N.Y., 1948—. Mem. Schenectady County Comm. Svcs. Bd., 1980-90; bd. dirs. SUNY, Albany, 1981-97. Mem. ATLA, ABA, Schenectady County Bar Assn., Capital Dist. Trial Lawyers Assn. (bd. dirs.), Thoroughbred Owners and Breeder's Assn. Democrat. Greek Orthodox. Avocations: golf, owning and racing Thoroughbred horses. Personal injury, Product liability, Probate. Home: 1962 Village Rd Schenectady NY 12309-5533 Office: Kouray & Kouray 525 State St Schenectady NY 12305-2402

**KOURI, HARRY J., III,** lawyer; b. Wichita, Kans., May 4, 1965; s. Harry Jacob Jr. and Beverly Ann Kouri; m. Annette Mary Humsey, Sept. 21, 1991; children: Erika, Jake, Amanda. BA in Bus. Adminstrn., U. Kans., Lawrence, 1987; JD, Oklahoma City U., 1989. Personal injury, Workers' compensation, General civil litigation. Office: Abel Musser Sokolosky Mares & Kouri 211 N Robinson Ave Ste 600 Oklahoma City OK 73102-7100

**KOURLIS, REBECCA LOVE,** judge; b. Colorado Springs, Colo., Nov. 11, 1952; d. John Arthur and Ann (Daniels) Love; m. Thomas Aristithis Kourlis, July 15, 1978; children: Stacy Ann, Katherine Love, Aristithis Thomas. BA with distinction in English, Stanford U., 1973, JD, 1976; LLD (hon.), U. Denver, 1997. Bar: Colo. 1976, D.C. 1979, U.S. Dist. Ct. Colo. 1976, U.S. Ct. Appeals (10th cir.) 1976, Colo. Supreme Ct., U.S. Ct. Appeals (D.C. cir.), U.S. Claims Ct., U.S. Supreme Ct. Assoc. Davis, Graham & Stubbs, Denver, 1976-78; sole practice Craig, Craig, Colo., 1978-87; judge 14th Jud. Dist. Ct., Denver, 1987-94; arbiter Jud. Arbiter Group, Inc., 1994-95; justice Colo. Supreme Ct., 1995—; water judge divsn. 6, 1987-94; lectr. to profl. groups. Contbr. articles to profl. jours. Chmn. Moffat County Arts and Humanities, Craig, 1979; mem. Colo. Commn. on Higher Edn., Denver, 1980-81; mem. adv. bd. Colo. Divsn. Youth Svcs., 1988-91; mem. com. civil jury instructions, 1990-95, standing com. gender & justice, 1994-97, chair jud. adv. coun., 1997—, chair com. on jury reform, 1996—; co-chair com. on atty. grievance reform, 1997—; mem. long range planning com. Moffat County Sch., 1990; bd. visitors Stanford U., 1989-94, Law Sch. U. Denver, 1997—; bd. trustees Kent Denver Sch., 1996—. Fellow Am. Bar Found., Colo. Bar Found.; mem. Am. Law Inst., Rocky Mountain Mineral Found., Colo. Bar Assn. (bd. govs. 1983-85, mineral law sect. bd. dirs. 1985, sr. v.p. 1987-88), Dist. Ct. Judges' Assn. (pres. 1993-94), N.W. Colo. Bar Assn. (Cmty. Svc. award 1993-94). Office: State Jud Bldg 2 E 14th Ave Rm 415 Denver CO 80203-2115

**KOUTSOGIANE, PHILLIP CHARLES,** lawyer; b. Woonsocket, R.I., Sept. 26, 1944; m. Joyce Ann Hindle, July 28, 1984. BA, Brown U., 1966; JD, Boston U., 1973. Bar: R.I. 1973, Mass. 1973, U.S. Dist. Ct. R.I. 1974, U.S. Supreme Ct. 1980, U.S. Dist. Ct. Mass. 1996. Pvt. practice Woonsocket. 1st lt. U.S. Army, 1968-70. Mem. ABA, R.I. Bar Assn., Pawtucket Bar Assn., Assn. Trial Lawyers Am., R.I. Trial Lawyers. General civil litigation, Personal injury, Probate. Office: Stadium Bldg 313 Woonsocket RI 02895-3024

**KOVACHEVICH, ELIZABETH ANNE,** federal judge; b. Canton, Ill., Dec. 14, 1936; d. Dan and Emilie (Kuchan) Kovachevich. AA, St. Petersburg Jr. Coll., 1956; BBA in Fin. magna cum laude, U. Miami, 1958; JD, Stetson U., 1961. Bar: Fla. 1961, U.S. Dist. Ct. (mid. and so. dists.) Fla. 1961, U.S. Ct. Appeals (5th cir.) 1961, U.S. Supreme Ct. 1968. Rsch. and adminstrv. aide Pinellas County Legis. Del., Fla., 1961; assoc. DiVito & Speer, St. Petersburg, Fla., 1961-62; house counsel Rieck & Fleece Builders Supplies, Inc., St. Petersburg, 1962; pvt. practice law St. Petersburg, 1962-73; judge 6th Jud. Cir., Pinellas and Pasco Counties, Fla., 1973-82, U.S. Dist. Ct. (mid. dist.) Fla., St. Petersburg, 1982-96; chief judge U.S. Dist. Ct. (mid. dist.) Fla., Tampa, 1996—; chmn. St. Petersburg Profl. Legal Project-Days in Court, 1967; chmn. Supreme Ct. Bicentennial Com. 6th Jud. Circuit, 1975-76. prodr., coord. TV prodn. A Race to Judgement. Bd. regents State of Fla., 1970-72; legal advisor, bd. dirs. Young Women's Residence Inc., 1968; mem. Fla. Gov.'s Commn. on Status of Women, 1968-71; mem. Pres.'s Commn. on White House Fellowships, 1973-77; mem. def. adv. com. on Women in Service, Dept. Def., 1973-76; Fla. conf. publicity chmn. 18th Nat. Republican Women's Conf., Atlanta, 1971; lifetime mem. Children's Hosp. Guild, YWCA of St. Petersburg; charter mem. Golden Notes, St. Petersburg Symphony; hon. mem. bd. of overseers Stetson U. Coll. of Law, 1986. Recipient Disting. Alumni award Stetson U., 1970, Woman of Yr. award Fla. Fedn. Bus. and Profl. Women, 1981, ann. Ben C. Willard Meml. award, Stetson Lawyers Assn., 1983, St. Petersburg Panhellenic Appreciation award, 1964, Mrs. Charles Ulrick Bay award, St. Petersburg Rotary award, St. Petersburg Quarterback Club award, Pinellas United Fund award in recognition of concern and meritorious effort, 1968, Woman of Yr. award Beta Sigma Phi, 1970, Am. Legion Aux. Unit 14 Pres. award cmty. svc., 1970, Dedication to Christian Ideals award and Man of Yr. award KC Dists. 20-21, 1972. Mem. ABA, Fla. Bar Assn., Pinellas County Trial Lawyers, Assn. Trial Lawyers Am., Am. Judicature Soc., St. Petersburg Bar Assn. (chmn. bench and bar com., sec. 1969). Office: US Dist Ct 801 N Florida Ave Tampa FL 33602-3849

**KOVACIC, WILLIAM EVAN,** law educator; b. Poughkeepsie, N.Y., Oct. 1, 1952; s. Evan Carl and Frances Katherine (Crow) K.; m. Kathryn Marie Fenton, May 18, 1985. AB with honors, Princeton U., 1974; JD, Columbia U., 1978. Bar: N.Y. 1979. Law clk. to sr. dist. judge U.S. Dist. Ct. Md., Balt., 1978-79; atty. planning office bur. competition FTC, Washington, 1979-82, atty. advisor to commr., 1983; assoc. Bryan, Cave, McPheeters & McRoberts, Washington, 1983-86; prof. George Mason U. Sch. Law, Arlington, Va., 1986-99, George Washington U. Law Sch., 1999—; cons. in field; mem. U.S. Senate Judiciary Subcom. on Antitrust and Monopoly, Washington, 1975-76. Contbr. legal articles to profl. jours. Assoc. Father Ford Found. Columbia U. Cath. Campus Ministry, N.Y.C. 1985—. Harlan Fiske Stone fellow Columbia U., 1976-78. Mem. ABA (antitrust law and pub. contract law sects.), Fed. Bar Assn. Roman Catholic. Avocations: hiking, camping, photography. Home: 7575 Dunquin Ct Clifton VA 20124-1840 Office: George Washington U Law Sch 720 20th St NW Washington DC 20052

**KOVACS, JOHN JOSEPH,** ; b. Elyria, Ohio, Nov. 5, 1947; s. John Joseph and Elizabeth (Fusa) K.; 1 child, Jeffrey Joseph. BA, Borromeo Coll., Ohio, 1969; JD cum laude, Cleve. State U., 1977. Bar: Ohio. Probation officer Ohio Adult Parole Authority, Elyria, 1969-72; dist. supr. Ohio Adult Parole Authority, Cleve., 1972-79; asst. prosecutor Lorain County, Elyria, 1980-83; sole practice Elyria, 1979—; arbitrator Lorain County Common Pleas Court, Elyria, 1979—, mediator, 1991—. Bd. dirs. Elyria Sports Hall Fame, 1986—. Mem. Ohio State Bar Assn., Lorain County Bar Assn., Ohio Acad. Trial Lawyers, Jaycees (bd. dirs., legal counsel, 1981-82). Roman Catholic. Avocations: hiking, tennis, swimming, horseback riding, skiing. Family and matrimonial, Personal injury, Real property. Home: 143 Nottingham Dr Elyria OH 44035-1715 Office: 124 Middle Ave Rm 800 Elyria OH 44035-5650

**KOVACS, PAUL EUGENE,** lawyer; b. Newmark, N.J., June 62, 2644; s. Eugene A. and Mary (Betell) K.; m. Susane, Aug. 3, 1968; children: Paul Scott, Kristin, Karen, John Paul. AA, Monmouth Coll., 1964, BS, 1966; JD, U. Mo., 1969. Ptnr. Brinker Doyen & Kovacs, Clayton, Mo., 1969-97, Armstrong, Teasdale, LLP, St. Louis, 1997—; bd. dirs. Marco Sales, St. Louis, Mercantile Bank, St. Louis; adj. prof. Washington U., St. Louis, 1991-96. Fellow Am. Coll. Trial Lawyers, Internat. Soc. Barristers; mem. ABA, Mo. Bar, County Bar Assn., St. Louis, Mo. Assn. Defence Council, Old Warson Club. Office: Armstrong Teasdale LLP 1 Metropolitan Sq Ste 2600 Saint Louis MO 63102-2740

**KOVACS, WILLIAM LAWRENCE,** lawyer; b. Scranton, Pa., June 29, 1947; s. William Lawrence and Jane Claire (Weiss) K.; m. Mary Katherine Maras, Dec. 2, 1979; children: Katherine Elizabeth, William Lawrence III, Margaret Ellen, Tyler Alexander. BS magna cum laude, U. Scranton, 1969; JD, Ohio State U., 1972. Bar: Pa. 1972, D.C. 1973, U.S. Ct. Appeals (D.C. cir.) 1974, U.S. Supreme Ct. 1976, Va. 1981. Legis. asst., staff atty. Congressman Fred B. Rooney, Washington, 1972-74; chief counsel U.S. Ho. of Reps. Subcom. on Transp. and Commerce, Washington, 1975-77; assoc. Liebert, Short, FitzPatrick & Lavin, Phila., 1977-78; environ., litigation atty. Nat. Chamber Litigation Ctr., Washington, 1979; ptnr. Abrams, Kovacs, Westermeier & Goldberg, Washington, 1980-84, Kovacs & Bury, Fairfax, Va., 1984-85, Jaeckle, Fleischmann & Mugel, Washington, 1986-87, Eckert, Seamans, Cherin & Mellott, Washington, 1987-89, Dunn, Carney, Allen, Higgins & Tongue, Portland, Oreg., 1990, Keller & Heckman, Washington, 1991-97; pres. Clean States Found., Inc., 1997-98; dir. legal affairs Worldwide Sunshine Makers, Inc., Washington, 1997-98; v.p. environ. and regulatory affairs U.S. C. of C., Washington, 1998—. Contbr. articles to profl. jours. Mem. Hazardous Waste Facilities Siting Bd., Richmond, Va., 1984-86; vice chmn., 1984-85, chmn., 1985-86. Mem. ABA (vice chmn. energy resources law com. sect. on torts and ins. practice 1981-83, chmn. 1983-84), U.S. C. of C. (mem. environ. law adv. com. 1986-92). Roman Catholic. Environmental, Administrative and regulatory, Legislative. Home: 9805 Arnon Chapel Rd Great Falls VA 22066-3908 Office: 1615 H St NW Washington DC 20062-0001

**KOWALCZYK, WENDY A.,** lawyer; d. David K. and Barbara E. K. BA, N.Y. State U., 1992; JD, SUNY, 1995. Bar: N.Y. 1996; U.S. Dist. Ct. (no. and we. dists. N.Y.) 1996. Assoc. Law Office of Ronald Benjamin, Binghamton, N.Y., 1995-97, Hogan & Sarzynski, LLP, Binghamton, 1997—. Recipient 1st place award for paper Erie County Intellectual Property Assn., Buffalo, 1994. Mem. ATLA, N.Y. State Bar, Boome County Bar Assn. (young lawyers planning com. 1997—). Avocations: proficient in French, phys. fitness. Office: Hogan & Sarzynski LLP One Marine Midland Pl Binghamton NY 13902

**KOZAK, JOHN W.,** lawyer; b. Chgo., July 25, 1943; s. Walter and Stella (Palka) K.; m. Elizabeth Mathias, Feb. 3, 1968; children: Jennifer, Mary Margaret, Suzanne. BSEE, U. Notre Dame, 1965; JD, Georgetown U., 1968. Bar: Ill. 1968, D.C. 1968. Patent advisor Office of Naval Rsch., Corona, Calif., 1968-69; assoc. Leydig, Voit & Mayer, Ltd. and predecessor firms, Chgo., 1969-74, ptnr., 1974—, chmn. mgmt. com., 1982-91; mem. United Charities Legal Aid Soc., 1989—. Mem. ABA, Am. Intellectual Property Law Assn., Licensing Execs. Soc., Chgo. Intellectual Property Law Assn., Univ. Club (Chgo.), Law Club (Chgo.), Winter Club (Lake Forest, Ill.), Knollwood Club (Lake Forest). Patent, Federal civil litigation, Trademark and copyright. Office: Leydig Voit & Mayer Ste 4900 2 Prudential Pla Chicago IL 60601

**KOZINSKI, ALEX,** federal judge; b. Bucharest, Romania, July 23, 1950; came to U.S., 1962; s. Moses and Sabine (Zapler) K.; m. Marcy J. Tiffany, July 9, 1977; children: Yale Tiffany, Wyatt Tiffany, Clayton Tiffany. AB in Econs. cum laude, UCLA, 1972, JD, 1975. Bar: Calif. 1975, D.C., 1978. Law clk. to Hon. Anthony M. Kennedy U.S. Ct. Appeals (9th cir.), 1975-76; law clk. to Chief Justice Warren E. Burger U.S. Supreme Ct., 1976-77; assoc. Covington & Burling, Washington, 1979-81; asst. counsel Office of Counsel to Pres., White House, Washington, 1981; spl. counsel Merit Systems Protection Bd., Washington, 1981-82; chief judge U.S. Claims Ct., Washington, 1982-85; judge U.S. Ct. Appeals (9th cir.), 1985—; lectr. law U. So. Calif., 1992. Office: US Ct Appeals Ste 200 125 S Grand Ave Pasadena CA 91105-1652

**KOZLIK, MICHAEL DAVID,** lawyer; b. Omaha, Apr. 20, 1953; s. Otto John and Ella Mae (Slightam) K.; m. Emily C. Cunningham, Sept. 30, 1983; children: John E., Caroline C. BS in Bus., Creighton U., 1975, JD, 1979. Bar: Nebr. 1979, U.S. Dist. Ct. Nebr. 1979, U.S. Dist. Ct. Appeals (8th cir.) 1979, U.S. Tax Ct. 1991; CPA, Nebr. Acct. Peat Marwick, Omaha, 1979-84; v.p. fin. Emelco, Omaha, 1984-86; assoc. Nelson Morrow, Omaha, 1986-88; shareholder Schmid Mooney, Omaha, 1988-97, Croker Huck, Omaha, 1997—; mem. Nebr. CPA Ethics Comm., 1984-85, Nebr. CPA Edn. Comm., 1988—. Contbr. articles to mags. Bd. dirs. County Health Dept., Omaha, 1986—, Hugh O'Brien Found., Omaha, 1989—, Nebr. ACC Decathlon. Recipient Leadership Omaha award Omaha C. of C., 1989; named One of Ten Outstanding Young Omahans Jaycees, 1990, 92. Mem. Omaha Bar Assn., Nebr. Bar Assn., Optimists (pres. 1989-90, honor award 1990). Republican. Avocations: hunting, fishing, billiards, geneology. Estate taxation, State and local taxation, General corporate. Home: 5122 Nicholas St Omaha NE 68132-1434 Address: Croker Huck DeWitt Anderson & Gonderinger 1250 Commerical Federal Tower 2120 S 72nd St Omaha NE 68124-2366

**KOZLOWSKI, KIMBERLY FRANCES,** lawyer; b. Berwyn, Ill., Feb. 13, 1968; d. William Roman and Mary Frances K. BSBA, U. Ariz., 1990; JD, DePaul U. Coll. Law, 1994. Bar: Ill. 1994. Staff atty. Mercury Fin. Co., Lake Forest, Ill., 1994-96; asst. v.p., corp. counsel 1st Security Comml. Mortgage, Chgo., 1996—. Mem. ABA, Ill. State Bar Assn., Chgo. Bar Assn. Contracts commercial, General corporate. Office: 1st Security Comml Mortgage 150 S Wacker Dr Ste 1100 Chicago IL 60606-4103

**KRACHT, RICHARD WILLIAM,** lawyer; b. Ford City, Pa., Sept. 16, 1936; s. Joseph August and Emma Louise (Kohler) K.; m. Isabel MacDonald, Apr. 8, 1967; children: Richard J., Ronald A. BS, St. Peter's Coll., Jersey City, 1959; JD, Seton Hall U., 1967. Bar: N.J. 1967, U.S. Dist. Ct. N.J. 1967, U.S. Supreme Ct. 1971. Assoc. Norman Robbins, Woodbridge, N.J., 1967-70, Hutt & Berkow, Woodbridge, 1970-73; ptnr. Dato & Kracht, Woodbridge, 1973-84; pvt. practice, Fords and Iselin, N.J., 1984—; judge Mcpl. Ct., Edison, N.J., 1992—; dir. law Edison Twp., 1991-92; mem. bd. adjustment 1967-70, 1984-89; mcpl. counselor, Woodbridge Twp., 1990-92; atty. Edison Bd. Adjustment, 1976-84, 87-90. Atty. Menlo Oaks Dem. Club, Edison, 1975-77. With U.S. Army, 1959-61. Recipient plaque Woodbridge Bd. Adjustment, 1970, 90, Edison Bd. Adjustment, 1984, 90. Mem. Kiwanis (pres.-elect Edison 1977). Roman Catholic. Real property, Land use and zoning (including planning), Municipal (including bonds). Office: 1100 Green St Iselin NJ 08830-2172

**KRACKE, ROBERT RUSSELL,** lawyer; b. Decatur, Ga., Feb. 27, 1938; s. Roy Rachford and Virginia Carolyn (Minter) K.; m. Barbara Anne Pilgrim, Dec. 18, 1965; children: Shannon Ruth, Robert Russell, Rebecca Anne, Susan Lynn. Student Birmingham So. Coll.; BA, Samford U., 1962; JD, Cumberland Sch. Law, 1965 . Bar: Ala. 1965, U.S. Tax Ct. 1971, U.S. Supreme Ct. 1971; individual practice law Birmingham, Ala., 1965—; pres. Kracke, Thompson & Ellis, 1980—. Deacon Ind. Presbyn. Ch., Birmingham, 1973-76, elder, 1999—, pres. adult choir, 1968—, Housing Agy. Retarded Citizens; pres. Ala. chpt. Nat. Voluntary Health Agys.; mem. exec. com. legal counsel Birmingham Opera Theatre, 1983-95; bd. dirs. Ala. Assn. Retarded Citizens, Jefferson County Assn. Retarded Citizens, 1983-91, pres.-elect, 1994-96, pres. 1996-98, past pres., 1998—; coord. com. mem. Nat. Conv. of the ARC of U.S., 1999—; bd. dirs., founding pres. Birmingham chpt. Juvenile Diabetes Found., bd. dirs. The ARC of Ala., 1996-98, Found. of ARC, 1998—. With USNR, 1955-61. Mem. Birmingham (exec. com., chmn. law libr., law day 1976, history and archives com.), Ala. Bar Assn., ABA (award merit law day 1976), Am. Judicature Soc., Ala. Hist. Assn., So. Hist. Assn., The Club, Phi Alpha Delta (pres. chpt. 1964-65), Rotary (pres. Shades Valley club 1988-89, Paul Harris fellow, sec. dist. 686 1990-91, dist. coord. comm., bd. dir., sec. ednl. found.), Sigma Alpha Epsilon. Editor, Birmingham Bar Bull., 1974—; bd. editors Ala. Lawyer, 1980-86; contbr. articles to profl. publs. General practice, State civil litigation, Insurance. Home: 4410 Briar Glen Dr Birmingham AL 35243-1743 Office: Kracke Thompson & Ellis Lakeview Sch Bldg 808 29th St S Birmingham AL 35205-1004

**KRAEMER, LILLIAN ELIZABETH,** lawyer; b. N.Y.C., Apr. 18, 1940; d. Frederick Joseph and Edmee Elizabeth (de Watteville) K.; m. John W. Vincent, June 22, 1962 (div. 1964). BA, Swarthmore Coll., 1961; JD, U. Chgo., 1964. Bar: N.Y. 1965, U.S. Dist. Ct. (so. dist.) N.Y. 1967, U.S. Dist. Ct. (ea. dist.) N.Y. 1971. Assoc. Cleary, Gottlieb, Steen & Hamilton, N.Y.C., 1964-71; assoc. Simpson Thacher & Bartlett, N.Y.C., 1971-74, ptnr., 1974—; mem. vis. com. U. Chgo. Law Sch., 1988-90, 91-94, 97—. Bd. mgrs. Swarthmore Coll., 1993—. Fellow Am. Coll. Bankruptcy; mem. Lawyers Alliance for N.Y. (bd. dirs. 1996—), Assn. of Bar of City of N.Y. (mem. various coms.), Coun. on Fgn. Rels., N.Y. State Bar Assn., Order of Coif, Phi Beta Kappa. Democrat. Episcopalian. Avocations: travel, reading, word games. Bankruptcy, Banking. Home: 2 Beekman Pl New York NY 10022-8058 also: 62 Pheasant Ln Stamford CT 06903-4428 Office: Simpson Thacher & Bartlett 425 Lexington Ave Fl 15 New York NY 10017-3954

**KRAEMER, LISA RUSSERT,** lawyer; b. Fayetteville, Ark., Dec. 6, 1954; d. William S. and Louise R. (Russert) K.; m. Richard S. Lang, Dec. 30, 1977; children: Jonathan Kraemer Lang, Katherine Kraemer Lang, William Kraemer Lang, Daniel Kraemer Lang. BA, Harvard U., 1976; JD, U. Cin., 1979; M in Conflict Resolution, Antioch U., 1997. Bar: Ohio 1979, U.S. Dist. Ct. (no. dist.) Ohio 1979. Staff atty. FTC, Cleve., 1980-85; assoc. Madorsky & Katz, Cleve., 1985-86; dir. CLE Case Western Law Sch., Cleve., 1986-88; assoc. Thomas and Boles, Chagrin Falls, Ohio, 1988-89; pvt. practice Cleve., 1989—. Contbg. author: Ohio Family Law Handbook-Mediation, 1996. Councilwoman Village of Chagrin Falls, 1989—. Mem. Cuyahoga County Bar Assn., Cleve. Bar Assn. Family and matrimonial. Office: Three Commerce Park Square 23230 Chagrin Blvd Ste 740 Cleveland OH 44122-5525

**KRAEUTLER, ERIC,** lawyer; b. Newark, Oct. 9, 1954; s. John Howard and Marie (Bevere) K.; m. Jacqueline Maykranz, May 18, 1985; children: Matthew John, Caroline Ann. BA, Princeton U., 1976; JD, U. Va., 1980. Bar: Pa., U.S. Dist. Ct. (ea. dist.) Pa., U.S. Ct. Appeals (3rd cir.), U.S. Ct. Appeals (9th cir.). Assoc. Morgan, Lewis & Bockius, LLP, Phila., 1980-84; asst. U.S. atty. U.S. Atty.'s Office, Phila., 1984-87; assoc. Morgan, Lewis & Bockius, LLP, Phila., 1987-90; ptnr. Morgan, Lewis & Bockius, Phila., 1990—; spl. dep. atty. gen. Commonwealth of Pa., 1992-94. Trustee Princeton Tower Club, 1980—; trustee Nat. Multiple Sclerosis Soc., 1993—, sec., 1994-96, vice chmn., 1996-98, chmn., 1998—; mem. Princeton Alumni Coun., 1984-87. Mem. ABA, Fed. Bar Assn., Phila. Bar Assn. Presbyterian. Avocation: running. Federal civil litigation, Criminal, Health. Home: 35 Wellesley Rd Swarthmore PA 19081-1232 Office: Morgan Lewis & Bockius LLP 1701 Market St Philadelphia PA 19103-2903

**KRAFT, C. WILLIAM, JR.,** federal judge; b. Phila., Dec. 14, 1903; s. C. William and Wilhelmina J. (Doerr) K.; m. Frances V. McDevitt, June 27, 1942; 1 child, C. William III. A.B., U. Pa., 1924, LL.B., 1927, J.D., 1930. Bar: Pa. 1927. Trial lawyer Kraft, Lippincott & Donaldson, Media, Pa., 1928-55; dist. atty. Delaware County, Pa., 1944-52; judge U.S. Dist. Ct., Phila., 1955-70; sr. judge U.S. Dist. Ct., 1970—. Mem. ABA, Pa. Bar Assn.

Home and Office: Island House 200 Ocean Lane Dr Apt 602 Key Biscayne FL 33149-1447

**KRAFT, CARL DAVID,** lawyer; b. Elgin, Ill., July 28, 1952; s. Howard David and Edna Leota Kraft; m. Joan Marie Kaps Evans, May 24, 1975 (div. Jan. 1981; m. Kathleen susan Webb, Nov. 19, 1983; children: Matthew A., Andrew W. BA, No. Ill. U., 1974; JD, Washington U., St. Louis, 1977. BAr: Mo. 1977, U.S. Dist. Ct. (ea. dist.) Mo., U.S. Ct. Appeals (8th cir.), U.S. Supreme Ct.; cert. civl trial lawyer. Atty. Richard Edwards Law Office, Clayton, Mo., 1977-78, Evans & Dixon, St. Louis, 1978-85; ptnr. Kraft & Harfst, St. Louis, 1985—. Bd. dirs., pres. Luth. Ministries Assn., St. Louis, 1988-95; evaluator, judge, coahc H.S. Mock Trial, St. Louis, 1983—; sec. Glendale (Mo.) Luth. Ch. Coun., 1996—. Recipient Vol. Lawyer Svc. award Legal Svcs. Eastern Mo., 1984. Mem. ATLA, Mo. Bar Assn., Mo. Assn. Def. Lawyers. Family and matrimonial, Insurance, General civil litigation. Home: 7642 Westmoreland Ave Saint Louis MO 63105-3807 Office: Kraft & Harfst 12901 N 40 Dr Saint Louis MO 63141-8634

**KRAFT, HENRY R.,** lawyer; b. L.A., Apr. 27, 1946; s. Sylvester and Freda (Shochat) K.; m. Terry Kraft, July 21, 1968; children: Diana, Kevin. BA in History, San Fernando Valley State Coll., 1968; JD, U. So. Calif., 1971. Bar: Calif. 1972, U.S. Dist. Ct. (ctrl. dist.) Calif. 1985, U.S. Ct. Appeals (9th cir.) 1998, U.S. Dist. Ct. (so. and no. dists.) Calif 1998. Dep. pub. defender San Bernardino (Calif.) County, 1972-78; pvt. practice, Victorville, Calif., 1979-96; city atty. Victorville, 1987—; of counsel Best Best & Krieger LLP, Victorville, 1996-98; assoc. Parker, Covert & Chidester, Tustin, Calif., 1999—; atty. City of Barstow, Calif., 1980-97; instr. Victor Valley Coll., Victorville, 1986—. Atty. Barstow Community Hosp., 1980-88. Mem. FBA, San Bernardino Bar Assn. (fee dispute com., jud. evaluation com.), High Desert Bar Assn. (pres., v.p., sec. 1979-81), Calif. Soc. Health Care Attys., League Calif. Cities, Am. Arbitration Assn. (panel neutral arbitrators). Democrat. Jewish. Avocations: bicycling, travel, wine enthusiast. Administrative and regulatory, General civil litigation, General practice. Office: Parker Covert & Chidester East Bldg 17862 17th St Ste 204 Tustin CA 92780-2158

**KRAFT, KAREN LORRAINE,** legal administrator; b. North Bergen, N.J.; d. Karl Frederick and Thelma Dorothy (Grasser) K.; children: Gary Karl, Glenn Duane. BA, William Paterson Coll., 1972. Bus. mgr. Ledgermatic, Secaucus, N.J., 1972-80; legal administrn. Evans Hand, west Paterson, N.J., 1980-88, Chapman, Henkoff, Kessler, Peduto & Saffer, Roseland, N.J., 1988—; speaker N.J. State Bar Annual Meeting, Alantic City, 1990, training coord. Assn. Legal Adminstr., N.J., 1994-95. Vol. Klein for Congress, 1992, 94, Clifton Mental Health Program, religious Edn. Tchr. Mem. N.J. State Bar Assn., Assn. of Legal Adminstr. Office: Chapman Henkoff Kessler Peduto & Saffer PO Box F Roseland NJ 07068-0906

**KRAFT, RICHARD LEE,** lawyer; b. Lassa, Nigeria, Oct. 14, 1958; m. Tanya Kraft, July 14, 1984; children: Devin, Kelsey. BA in Fgn. Svc., Baylor U., 1980, JD, 1982. Bar: N.Mex. 1982, U.S. Dist. Ct. N.Mex., U.S. Ct. Appeals, U.S. Supreme Ct. Assoc. Sanders, Bruin & Baldock, Roswell, N.Mex., 1982-87, ptnr., 1987-98; ptnr. Kraft & Stone, LLP, Roswell, 1998—. Vol. lawyer Ea. N.Mex. U. Roswell, 1984—; bd. dirs. Roswell YMCA, 1983-87, Crimestopper, 1991-94; pres. Roswell Mens Ch. Basketball League; participant Roswell Mens Ch. Softball League; asst. chair legal div. United Way Drive, 1990. Recipient Outstanding Contribution award N.Mex. State Bar, 1987. Mem. ABA, N.Mex. Trial Lawyers Assn., N.Mex. Bar Assn. (bd. dirs. young lawyers div. 1983-91, pres. 1986-87, chmn. membership com., bar commr. 1986-87, 91—, pres. 1998-99, Outstanding Young Lawyer award 1990), Chaves County Bar Assn. (chair law day activities, chair ann. summer picnic com., rep. bench and bar com.), Roswell Legal Secs. Assn. (hon.), Roswell C. of C. (participant and pres. Leadership Roswell, exec. dir., bd. dirs. 1991-97), Sertoma (bd. dirs. Roswell club 1989-91). Baptist. General civil litigation, Family and matrimonial, Personal injury. Office: Kraft & Stone LLP 400 N Pennsylvania Ave Ste 1250 Roswell NM 88201-4783

**KRAFT, ROBERT MORRIS,** lawyer; b. Seattle, Sept. 17, 1954; s. Harry Jay and Leatrice Mae Kraft; m. Lori Sue Kraft, Nov. 9, 1985. BA in Bus. Adminstrn., U. Puget Sound, 1976, JD, 1980. Bar: Wash. 1980. Shareholder Levinson, Friedman, Vhugen, Duggan & Bland, Seattle. Mem. Wash. State Bar Assn., Wash. State Trial Lawyers Assn. Personal injury, Product liability, Admiralty. Office: Levinson Friedman Et Al 600 University St Ste 2900 Seattle WA 98101-4174

**KRAHMER, DONALD LEROY, JR.,** lawyer; b. Hillsboro, Oreg., Nov. 11, 1957; s. Donald L. and Joan Elizabeth (Karns) K.; m. Suzanne M. Blanchard, Aug. 16, 1986; children: Hillary, Zachary. BS, Willamette U., 1981, MM, 1987, JD, 1987. Bar: Oreg. 1988. Fin. analyst U.S. Bancorp, Portland, 1977-87; intern U.S. Senator Mark Hatfield, 1978; legis. aide State Sen. Jeannette Hamby, Hillsboro, Oreg., 1981-83, State Rep. Delna Jones, Beaverton, Oreg., 1983; bus. analyst Pacificorp, Portland, 1987; mgr. mergers/acquisitions Pacificorp Fin. Svcs., Portland, 1988-89; dir. Pacificorp Fin. Svcs., 1990; CEO, pres. Atkinson Group, Portland, 1991—; ptnr. Black Helterline, Portland, 1991—; bd. dirs., sec. Marathon Fin. Assocs., Portland, 1989; bd. dirs. Self-Enhancement, Inc.; chmn. Willamette Forum; bd. dirs. Oreg. Entrepreneur Forum, 1993—, editor, 1993, chmn. adv. bd., 1995, chmn. bd., 1998; founder co-chmn. Oreg. Emerging Bus. Initiative, 1997—; bd. dirs. Concordia Univ. Found., 1995-97. Treas. Com. to Re-Elect Jeannette Hamby, 1986; bd. dirs. fin. com./devel. com. Am. Diabetes Assn., Portland, 1990-96; founder Needle Bros., 1994; chmn. Atkinson Grad. Sch. Devel. Com., Salem, 1989-92; Bd. Vis. Coll. Law, Willamette U., 1997—; mem. adv. bd. Ctr. for Law and Entrepreneurship, U. Oreg. Sch. Law, 1997—; founder Conf. of Entrepreneurship, Salem, 1984, chmn. Entrepreneurship Breakfast Forum, Portland, 1993; chmn., founder Oreg. Conf. on Entrepreneurship and Awards Dinner, 1994-99, sr. v.p., 1999—; mem. exec. com., bd. dirs. Cascade Pacific Coun. Boy Scouts Am., 1998—, chmn. cmty. fund. dir., 1997; vice chmn. Govs. Coun. on Small Bus., State of Oreg. Recipient Pub.'s award Oreg. Bus. Mag., 1987, Founders award Willamette U., 1987, award Scripps Found., 1980, Bus. Jour. 40 Under 40 award, 1996. Mem. ABA, Oreg. Bar Assn. (chmn. exec. com., fin. instns. com. sec., exec. com., bus. law sect., chmn. 1999, sec. 1998), Multnomah County Bar Assn., Washington County Bar Assn., Assn. for Corp. Growth, Oreg. Biosci. Assn., Portland Soc. Fin. Analysts, Japan-Am. Soc. Oreg., Assn. Investment Mgmt. and Rsch., City Club, Software Assn. of Oreg., Oreg. Biotech. Assn., Multnomah Athletic Club, Arlington Club. Republican. Lutheran. Mergers and acquisitions, General corporate, Securities. Home: 16230 SW Copper Creek Dr Portland OR 97224-6500 Office: Black Helterline 1200 Union Bank Calif Tower 707 SW Washington St Portland OR 97205-3536

**KRAKAUER, BRYAN,** lawyer; b. East Orange, N.J., June 9, 1956; s. Merril and Celia (Burg) K.; m. Marie A. Poppy, Apr. 28, 1991. AB, Duke U., 1978; JD, U. Chgo., 1981. Bar: Ill. 1982, U.S. Dist. Ct. (N.D.) Ill. 1982. Assoc. Sidley & Austin, Chgo., 1981-89, ptnr., 1989—. Contbr. articles to profl. jours. Mem. ABA (mem. bus. banking com. 1987—). Bankruptcy, Contracts commercial. Office: Sidley & Austin 1 First Natl Plz Chicago IL 60603-2003

**KRAKOWSKI, RICHARD JOHN,** lawyer, public relations executive; b. Meppen, Fed. Republic of Germany, Apr. 3, 1946; came to U.S., 1951, naturalized, 1962; s. Feliks and Maria (Chilinski) K. MBA, DePaul U., 1979; JD, John Marshall Law Sch., 1983. Bar: Ill. 1984. Personnel dir. Andy Frain, Inc., Chgo., 1973-78; pub. rels. dir. Chgo. Health Sys. Agy., 1978-84; assoc. firm Mangum, Smietanka & Johnson, Chgo., 1984-87; asst. atty. gen. Ill. Atty. Gen.'s Ofc., 1987-96; lectr. in field. Co-author: Health Care Financing and Policy Making in Chicago and Illinois, 1982. Fundraising and pub. rels. dir. Cabrini-Green Sandlot Tennis Program, Chgo., 1979-83; sustaining mem. Republican Nat. Com., 1981—. Capt. U.S. Army, 1969-72. Mem. ABA, Nat. Advocates Soc., Ill. Bar Assn., Chgo. Bar Assn., Chgo. Coun. Fgn. Rels., Lyric Opera Guild, Art Inst. Chgo., Chgo. Soc. Polish Nat. Alliance, Publicity Club (Chgo.). Roman Catholic. Home: 1350 N Lake Shore Dr Apt 1215 Chicago IL 60610-5143 Office: Cook County Human Resources Divsn 118 N Clark St Ste 818 Chicago IL 60602-1312

**KRAL, WILLIAM GEORGE,** lawyer; b. Bronx, N.Y., Oct. 16, 1946; s. Michael Abraham and Eleanor Helen (DeFilippo) K.; m. Mary Margaret Schuman, Dec. 28, 1970; children: Marianne, Elizabeth, Emily. BA, Manhattan Coll., 1968; JDL, Bklyn. Law Sch., 1974. Bar: N.Y. 1975, U.S. Supreme Ct. 1981. Assoc. D'Amato, Costello & Shea, N.Y.C., 1974-79; ptnr. Costello & Shea, N.Y.C., 1980-85; founding ptnr. Kral, Clerkin, Redmond & Ryan, N.Y.C., 1985—; founder, pres. Adirondack Alarm Systems Inc., Ticonderoga, N.Y., 1983—; co-founder, dir. N.Y. Home Brew Inc., Floral Park, 1992—, North County Collectibles, Moria, N.Y., 1991—; co-founder Angels Watch Inc., N.Y. With U.S. Army, 1969-70. Republican. Roman Catholic. Avocations: history, chess, antique arms collecting. Insurance, General practice, Personal injury. Office: Kral Clerkin Redmond & Ryan 69 E Jericho Tpke Mineola NY 11501-3197 also: 43 Maple Ave Morristown NJ 07960-7506 also: 170 Broadway New York NY 10038-4154

**KRALICK, RICHARD LOUIS,** lawyer; b. Youngstown, Ohio, Dec. 7, 1933; s. Joseph Martin and Dorothy Louise (Canada) K.; m. Roselle A. Richmond, Sept. 10, 1955; children: Kris Ann, Richard II, Kolleen, Kathleen, Michael. BA, Mich. State U., 1955; JD, U. Mich., 1959. Assoc. Baker, Hammond and Baker, Adrian, Mich., 1960-62; ptnr. Hammond Baker and Kralick, Adrian, 1963—. Chmn. Mich. Girls Tng. Sch., Adrian, 1966-67; bd. dirs. Lenawee County Human Svcs. Coun., 1991-95, Lenawee United Way, 1991—; pres. Lenawee Family Coun. and Children's Svcs., Adrian, 1970-71; bd. dirs. Adrian YMCA, 1969-72, Lenawee Ams. with Disabilities Act Coun., 1993-95; v.p. Goodwill Industries, Adrian, 1972-73; bd. dirs. (LEAH) Lenawee Emergency Affordable Housing. Named Mich. Vol. of Yr. Mich. Family Coun. and Children's Svcs., 1971; recipient Good Willie award Goodwill Industries, Adrian, 1972, Disting. Svc. award Lenawee Cancer Soc., 1973, Crisis Hot Line, Adrian, 1992. Mem. ABA, Lenawee County Bar Assn. (pres. 1968-69), Mich. Trial Lawyers Assn., Mich. Def. Trial Lawyers, Mich. Bar Assn. General civil litigation, Family and matrimonial, Insurance. Home: 5140 Wildwood Dr Manitou Beach MI 49253-9628 Office: Hammond Baker and Kralick Key Bank Bldg PO Box 519 Adrian MI 49221-0519

**KRAM, RICHARD COREY,** lawyer; b. N.Y.C., Oct. 8, 1942; s. Irving Monroe and Florence (Levine) K.; m. Betty Ann Schlesinger, Apr. 4, 1971; children: Benjamin Harry, Eden Lenore. BA in Polit. Sci., Syracuse U., 1964, MA in Polit. Sci., 1972, JD, 1973. Bar: N.Y. 1975, U.S. Dist. Ct. (no. dist.) N.Y. 1975, U.S. Ct. Appeals (2d cir.) 1980, U.S. Supreme Ct. 1982. Assoc. Nottingham Law Firm, Syracuse, N.Y., 1975-76; sole practice Syracuse, 1976—; adj. prof. law Syracuse U., 1987-88, 89-90. Mem. Syracuse James Joyce Soc., 1996—. Fellow Am. Acad. Matrimonial Lawyers (N.Y. chpt. bd. mgr. 1993-97, 99—, v.p. 1997-98), Onondaga County Bar Assn. (bd. dirs. 1984-88, chair family law com. 1997-98). Avocations: reading, aerobics, bicycling, Nordic skiing. Family and matrimonial, General practice. Office: 2001 State Tower Bldg Syracuse NY 13202

**KRAM, SHIRLEY WOHL,** federal judge; b. N.Y.C., 1922. Student, Hunter Coll., 1940-41, CUNY, 1940-47; LLB, Bklyn. Law Sch., 1950. Atty. Legal Aid Soc. N.Y., 1951-53, 1962-71; assoc. Simons & Hardy, 1954-55; pvt. practice law, 1955-60; judge Family Ct., N.Y.C., 1971-83; judge U.S. Dist. Ct. (so. dist.) N.Y., N.Y.C., 1983-93, sr. judge, 1993—. Author: (with Neil A. Frank) The Law of Child Custody, Development of the Substantive Law. Office: US Dist Ct US Courthouse 40 Foley Sq Rm 2101 New York NY 10007-1502

**KRAMER, ANDREW MICHAEL,** lawyer; b. N.Y.C., Nov. 2, 1944; s. Irving and Ida (Kaplan) K.; m. Cheryle Lynn Safran, June 21, 1966; children: Howard, Jennifer; m. Nita Lynne Albert, Mar. 13, 1983; children: Samantha, Stephanie. BA cum laude, Mich. State U., 1966; JD cum laude, Northwestern U., 1969. Bar: Ill. 1969, D.C. 1977, U.S. Ct. Appeals (4th cir.) 1977, U.S. Ct. Appeals (5th cir.) 1972, U.S. Ct. Appeals (6th cir.) 1972, U.S. Ct. Appeals (7th cir.) 1970, U.S. Ct. Appeals (11th cir.) 1982, Ohio 1990. Assoc. firm Seyfarth, Shaw, Fairweather & Geraldson, Chgo., 1969-73; ptnr. Seyfarth, Shaw, Fairweather & Geraldson, Washington, 1974-83, Jones, Day, Reavis & Pogue, Washington and Cleve., 1983—; exec. dir. Ill. Office Collective Bargaining, Springfield, 1973-74. Contbr. articles to profl. jours. Mem. ABA, Chgo. Bar Assn., D.C. Bar Assn., Congressional Country Club (Md.), Standard Club (Chgo.), Firestone Country Club, Union Club (Cleve.), Pepper Pike Club (Cleve.). Labor, Civil rights, Federal civil litigation. Office: Jones Day Reavis & Pogue 51 Louisiana Ave NW Washington DC 20001-2113

**KRAMER, DANIEL JONATHAN,** lawyer; b. Cin., Dec. 20, 1957; s. Milton and Fradie (Ehrlich) K.; m. Judith L. Mogul, June 10, 1984; children: Ilona, Hannah, Joshua. BA magna cum laude, Wesleyan U., Middletown, Conn., 1980; JD, NYU, 1984. Bar: N.Y. 1985, U.S. Dist. Ct. (so. and ea. dists.) N.Y. 1985, U.S. Ct. Appeals (2d cir.) 1989. Assoc. Cravath, Swaine & Moore, N.Y.C., 1985-86; law clk. to Chief Judge Wilfred Feinberg, U.S. Ct. Appeals for 2d Cir., N.Y.C., 1986-87; assoc. Schulte Roth & Zabel LLP, N.Y.C., 1987-92, ptnr., 1993—; mem. pro se discretionary panel U.S. Ct. Appeals for 2d Cir., 1988—. Author: Federal Securities Litigation: Commentary and Forms, A Deskbook for the Practitioner, 1997; contbr. articles to law jours. and newspaper. Bd. dirs. Leukemia Soc., N.Y.C., 1995-98. Mem. ABA, Assn. Bar City N.Y. Federal civil litigation, Professional liability, Securities. Office: Schulte Roth & Zabel LLP 900 3rd Ave Fl 19 New York NY 10022-4774

**KRAMER, DONALD BURTON,** lawyer; b. St. Louis, Oct. 21, 1928; s. Allen Samuel and Mae (Sachar) K.; m. Elaine Ruth Phillips, Sept. 7, 1952; children: Jeffrey Scott, Janet Sue. BBA, Wash. U., St. Louis, 1950, JD, 1952. Bar: Mo., 1952. Assoc. Kramer & Chused, St. Louis, 1954-60; ptnr. Kramer, Chused & Kramer, St. Louis, 1960-73; owner Kramer and Frank, St. Louis, 1974-86; pres. Kramer and Frank, P.C., St. Louis, 1987—. Author: Mastering Commercial Collections, 1991; contbr. articles to profl. jours. Cpl. U.S. Army, 1952-54. Named Outstanding Trustee, Zeta Beta Tau, 1970. Mem. Bar Assn. of Met. St. Louis, Mo. Bar Assn. (chmn. com. unauthorized practice of law 1969-73), Comml. Law League Am. (co-chmn. bankruptcy com. 1977-78, chmn. nominating com., 1985-86, midwest dist., 1982-83, practices com. fair debt collection 1986-88), Nat. Assn. Retail Collection Attys. (founder, pres. 1993-95). Consumer commercial. Office: Kramer & Frank PC 9666 Olive Blvd Ste 450 Saint Louis MO 63132-3080

**KRAMER, EDWARD GEORGE,** lawyer; b. Cleve., July 15, 1950; s. Archibald Charles and Katherine Faith (Porter) K.; m. Roberta Darwin, June 15, 1974. BS in Edn., Kent State U., 1972; JD, Case Western Res. U., 1975. Bar: Ohio 1975, U.S. Dist. Ct. (no. dist.) Ohio 1975, U.S. Ct. Appeals (6th cir.) 1980, U.S. Supreme Ct. 1980. Assoc. dir. The Cuyahoga Plan of Ohio, Cleve., 1975-76; exec. dir. The Housing Advs., Inc., Cleve., 1976—; sr. ptnr. Kramer & Assocs., LPA, Cleve., 1981—; spl. counsel atty. gen. State of Ohio, Columbus, 1983-95; pres. Atty. Svcs., Inc., 1987—, ASI Info. Sys.; dir. Housing Law Clinic, 1989-95; dir. Fair Housing Law Clinic, 1995—; adj. lectr. Cleve. State U., 1991-94, adj. prof., 1994—; alt. consumer rep., FTC, Washington, 1976-77; cons. HUD, Washington, 1978-80, joint select com. sch. desegregation, Ohio Gen. Assembly, Columbus, 1979; mem. visitors com., Case Western Res. U. Sch. Law, Cleve., 1977-83; mem., chmn. Ford Motor Consumer Appeals Bd., 1989-93; bd. advisors Brownstone Pub. Author: How to Settle Small Claims: A Guide to The Use of Small Claims Courts, 1973, (with others) A Guide to Regional Housing Opportunities, 1979, (with Buchanan) Mobile Home Living: A Guide to Consumers' Rights, 1979; contbr. articles to legal jours. Chmn. Ohio Protection and Advocacy System for Developmentally Disabled, Columbus, 1978-80; trustee Muscle Disease Soc., Cleve., 1979-81; sec. Cuyahoga County Housing and Econ. Devel. com., Cleve., 1983—; mem. Cleve. Mayor's Com. on Employment of Handicapped, 1978-79; mem. fair housing adv. bd. John Marshall Law Sch. Named Disting. Recent Grad. Case Western Reserve U. Law Alumni Assn., 1985; Rockefeller Pound fellow. Mem. ABA (sect. on urban state & local govt. law, com. on housing and urban devel., forum on constrn. industry), ACLU (litigation com.), Cleve. Bar Assn. (trustee 1995-98, vice chmn. com. on homeless, chmn., vice-chmn., law sch. liaison), Nat. Audubon Assn., Nat. Employment Lawyers Assn., Practicing Law Inst. (assoc.), Assn. Trial Lawyers Am. (employment rights sect., 2d vice chair, newsletter editor), Assn. Am. Law Schs. (com. on clin. legal edn.), Nat. Trust for Hist. Preservation, Nat. Platform Assn., Planetary Soc., Boat Club Nautica, Palm Beach Club (London), Old River Yacht Club, Cleve. Grays, Masons, Tyrian (worshipful master), Order of Eastern Star (James A Garfield chpt.). Democrat. Mem. United Ch. Christ. Avocations: softball, scuba diving, collecting coins and stamps, chess, reading. Civil rights, Landlord-tenant, Federal civil litigation. Office: Kramer & Assocs LPA 3214 Prospect Ave E Cleveland OH 44115-2614

**KRAMER, EUGENE LEO,** lawyer; b. Barberton, Ohio, Nov. 7, 1939; s. Frank L. and Portia I. (Acker) K.; m. JoAnn Stockhausen, Sept. 19, 1970; children: Martin, Caroline, Michael. AB, John Carroll U., 1961; JD, U. Notre Dame, 1964. Bar: Ohio 1964. Law clerk U.S. Ct. Appeals (7th cir.), Chgo., 1964-65; ptnr. Squire, Sanders & Dempsey, Cleve., 1965-91, Roetzel & Andress, A Legal Profl. Assn., Cleve. and Akron, Ohio, 1992-97; cons. Ohio Constl. Revision Commn., Columbus, 1970-74. Trustee Citizens League Greater Cleve., 1984-90, 93—, Citizens League Rsch. Inst., 1995-97, St. Ann Found., 1990-92, Consultation Ctr. for Diocese of Cleve., 1990-96, Lyric Opera Cleve., 1995—, Regina Health Ctr., 1997—; past pres. HELP Found, Inc., HELP, Inc., Cleve., 1981-92, Playhouse Sq. Assn., Cleve., 1980-84; pres. N.E. Ohio Transit Coalition, 1992—; mem. policy com. Build-Up Greater Cleve. Program, 1982-98, Build-Up Lorain County Program, 1998—; mem. Greater Cleve. Growth Assn. Recipient Disting. Leadership award HELP, Inc., 1986, Pioneer achievement award HELP--Six Chimneys, Inc., 1986, Disting. Svc. award Assn. Retarded Citizens, Cuyahoga County, 1990. Mem. ABA, Ohio State Bar Assn. (chmn. local govt. law com. 1986-90), Akron Bar Assn., Cleve. Bar Assn., The Clifton Club (Lakewood, Ohio, bd. dirs. 1986-89), The Union Club of Cleve. Democrat. Roman Catholic. Avocations: music, theater, sports, travel. Municipal (including bonds), State and local taxation. Home and Office: 1422 Euclid Ave Ste 706 Cleveland OH 44115-2001

**KRAMER, JOHN ROBERT,** law educator, dean. BA, Harvard Coll., 1958; LLB, Harvard Law Sch., 1962. Law clk. U.S. Ct. Appeals (9th cir.), 1962-63; asst. U.S. atty. Washington, 1963-65; pvt. practice Shea & Gardner, Washington, 1966-69; exec. dir. Nat. Coun. on Hunger & Malnutrition, 1969-75; prof. Georgetown U. Law Ctr., 1971-86, assoc. dean, 1976-86; dean Tulane U. Law Sch., 1986-96, prof., 1986—; edn. counsel Com. on Edn. & Labor U.S. Ho. of Reps., 1965-66, cousel Agrl. and Ways & Means Coms., 1975-81, spl. counsel to Thomas Foley, 1981-86; chmn. Law Access, Inc., 1993-96; counsel to parliamentarian on the Dem. Conv., Atlanta, 1988; chmn. Ctr. on Budget and Policy Priorities, 1980—. Pres. Field Found., 1981-91. Recipient Fulbright scholarship, 1958-59. Mem. Am. Assn. Law Schs. (chmn. congl. rels. com. 1976-86). Office: Tulane U Law Sch John Giffen Weinmann Hall 6329 Freret St New Orleans LA 70118-6231

**KRAMER, KENNETH BENTLEY,** federal judge, former congressman; b. Chgo., Feb. 19, 1942; s. Albert Aaron and Ruth (Pokrass) K.; children: Kenneth Bentley, Kelly J. BA magna cum laude in Polit. Sci., U. Ill., 1963; JD, Harvard U., 1966. Bar: Ill. 1966, Colo. 1969. Dep. dist. atty. El Paso County, Colo., Colorado Springs, 1970-72; pvt. practice law Colorado Springs, 1972-78; mem. Colo. Ho. of Reps., 1973-78, 96th-99th Congresses from 5th Colo. Dist., 1978-86; asst. sec. Dept. Army, Washington, 1988-89; assoc. judge U.S. Ct. of Appeals for Vets. Claims, Washington, 1989—. Bd. visitors U.S. Air Force Acad., 1979-86; bd. dirs. Pikes Peak Mental Health Ctr., 1976-78, Mountain Valley chpt. March of Dimes, 1983-85, U.S. Space Found., 1983-91; founder U.S. Space Found.; commr. Nat. Coun. on Uniform State Laws, 1977-78. Capt. U.S. Army, 1967-70. Recipient Disting. Civilian Svc. medal. Mem. Phi Beta Kappa. Office: US Ct Appels for Vets Claims 625 Indiana Ave NW Washington DC 20004-2923

**KRAMER, PAUL R.,** lawyer; b. Balt., June 6, 1936; s. Phillip and Lee (Labovitz) K.; m. Janet Amitin, Sept. 1, 1957; children: Jayne, Susan, Nancy. BA, Am. U., 1959, JD, 1961. Bar: Md. 1961, D.C. 1962, U.S. Supreme Ct. 1965, U.S. Ct. Appeals (6th cir.) 1992, U.S. Dist. Ct. 1963, U.S. Ct. Appeals (4th cir.) 1964, U.S. Ct. Appeals (9th cir.) 1996. Staff atty., dep. dir. Legal Aid Agy. Fed. Pub. Defender's Office, Washington, 1962-63; asst. U.S. atty. Dist. Md., 1963-69; dep. U.S. atty. Md. Balt., 1969-83; exec. bd. Balt. area coun. Boy Scouts Am., 1970-83, adv. counsel to exec. bd., 1983—; instr. U. Md. Sch. Law, 1975-80; assoc. prof. law Villa Julie Coll., 1976-80; assoc. professorial lectr. George Washington U., 1979; instr. Nat. Coll. Dist. Attys., 1979; permanent mem. 4th cir. fed. jud. conf. Mem. ABA, Fed. Bar Assn. (pres. Md. chpt. 1973-74, nat. dep. sec. 1981-82, nat. sec. 1982-83, nat. cir. v.p. 1973-81, 86-87, cir. officer 4th cir. 1992-93, v.p. 4th cir. 1996—, chmn. nat. cir. v.p. 1978-80, nat. coun. 1973—, jud. selection com. 1971-79, 88—, faculty Fed Practice Inst. 1981-86, strategic long range planning com. 1995-96), Md. Bar Assn. (subcom. litig. dist. ct. 1990—), Balt. Bar Assn. (jud. selection com. 1992—, chair judiciary sub-com. on policy 1993-94, chair criminal law com. 1994-95, grievance commn. Md. 1993—, drug ct. com. 1994-95, dist. ct. com. 1990—), Nat. Assn. Criminal Trial Attys., Md. Trial Lawyers Assn., Md. Criminal Def. Atty.'s Assn., U.S. Atty. Alumni Assn., Masons (past master). Criminal, State civil litigation, Federal civil litigation. Office: 231 Saint Paul Pl Baltimore MD 21202-2028

**KRAMER, PHILIP JOSEPH,** lawyer; b. Binghamton, N.Y., May 1, 1936; s. Donald W. and Gladys M. (Dorion) K.; m. Barbara E. Fisher, July, 1960; children: Perry, Donald, Matthew, Sharon. BA, Yale U., 1958; LLB, Cornell U., 1961. Bar: N.Y. 1961, U.S. Dist. Ct. (no. dist.) N.Y. 1961. Assoc. Kramer, Wales & Robinson, Binghamton, 1961-64, ptnr., 1964-78; justice, 6th Jud. Dist. N.Y. Supreme Ct., 1978; ptnr. Kramer, Wales & McAvoy, Binghamton, 1979-84, Kramer, Wales & Wright, Binghamton, 1984-95, Kramer & Kenyon, 1996-98. Pres. Binghamton Local Devel. Agy., 1982-87. Fellow Am. Coll. Trial Lawyers; mem. N.Y. State Bar Assn., Broome County Bar Assn. (pres. 1982). Democrat. Roman Catholic. Avocations: fishing, hunting. Fax: (607) 723-6605. General civil litigation, Environmental, Personal injury. Office: 700 Security Mut Bldg 80 Exchange St PO Box 1865 Binghamton NY 13902-1865

**KRAMER, RAYMOND E.,** judge; b. Phila., Sept. 19, 1953; s. Elwood H. and Ilva L. Kramer; m. Suchada Arriyawat Katakikarn, July 5, 1992; children: Gungsadawn Katatikarn, Parichart Katatikarn. BA, U. Va., 1975; JD, Harvard U., 1978. Bar: Pa. 1978, N.Y. 1979, U.S. Dist. Ct. (so. dist.) N.Y. 1983, U.S. Dist. Ct. (ea. dist.) N.Y. 1991. Staff atty. VISTA Statewide Youth Advocacy Project, Rochester, N.Y., 1978-79; trial atty. Juvenile Rights divsn. Legal Aid Soc. N.Y., Bronx, 1979-83; clin. prof. NYU Law Sch., N.Y.C., 1983-85; adminstrv. law judge N.Y.C. Office Adminstrv. Trials and Hearings, N.Y.C., 1985—. Tutor, East Harlem Tutorial Program, N.Y.C., 1998—. Mem. Assn. Bar City N.Y. Office: NYC Office Adminstrv Trials and Hearings 40 Rector St Fl 6 New York NY 10006-1705

**KRAMER, ROBERT J.,** lawyer; b. Sioux City, S.D., July 22, 1963; s. Robert O. Kramer and Judy K. (Purdy) Wilks; children: Clayton, Courtney. BA, U. Calif., San Diego, 1985; JD magna cum laude, Ariz. State U., 1988. Bar: Ariz. 1988, U.S. Dist. Ct. Ariz. 1988. Assoc. Fennemore Craig, Phoenix, 1988-92, dir., 1994—; assoc. counsel Olin Corp., East Alton, Ill., 1993. Author: (with others) Arizona Environmental Law, 1994, Underground and Aboveground Storage Tank Requirements and Cleanup in Arizona, 1994. Mem. Ariz. State Bar Assn., Maricopa County Bar Assn., ABA (vice chair Environmental Quality subcom. 1996), Order of Coif. Environmental, Natural resources, Real property. Office: Fennemore Craig 3003 N Central Ave Ste 2600 Phoenix AZ 85012-2913

**KRAMER, STEVEN J.,** prosecutor; b. Albany, N.Y., Jan. 26, 1968; s. Sanford and Joanne Kramer. BA, Hobart Coll., 1990; JD, Syracuse U., 1993. Bar: N.Y., 1995, U.S. Dist. Ct. (no. dist.) N.Y., 1996. Asst. atty. gen. State of N.Y., Albany, 1995—. Office: Office Atty Gen The Capitol Albany NY 12224

**KRAMER, WILLIAM DAVID,** lawyer; b. Anniston, Ala., Feb. 2, 1944; s. John Robert and Janice Marian (Dye) K.; m. Johanna Scalzi, Dec. 1, 1973; children: Elizabeth Annemarie, David MacLaren. Student, Case Western Res. U., 1959-60; AB in Govt. with honors magna cum laude, Oberlin Coll., 1965; JD, M in Pub. Adminstrn., Harvard U., 1969. Bar: Mass. 1969, D.C. 1973, U.S. Ct. Appeals (D.C. cir.) 1974, U.S. Dist. Ct. D.C. 1976, U.S. Ct. Appeals (10th cir.) 1978, U.S. Ct. Internat. Trade 1983, U.S. Ct. Appeals (fed. cir.) 1983. Assoc. dir. Gov.'s Com. on Law Enforcement and Adminstrn. Criminal Justice, Boston, 1969-71, dep. dir., 1971-73; assoc. Squire, Sanders & Dempsey, Washington, 1973-79, ptnr., 1979-92; ptnr. Baker & Botts, Washington, 1992—; mem. internat. law sect. D.C. Bar. chmn. bd. dirs. Children's Chorus of Washington, 1995-97, mem. adv. bd., 1997—. Mem. Phi Beta Kappa. Private international, Administrative and regulatory, Legislative. Office: Baker & Botts LLP Ste 1200 1299 Pennsylvania Ave NW Washington DC 20004-2408

**KRAMISH, MARC ERIC,** lawyer; b. Far Rockaway, N.Y., Mar. 11, 1958; s. Daniel Aaron and Rhoda Lucile (Jacobs) K.; m. Kathryn Henry; children: Chelsea, David. BA, U. Fla., 1980; JD, Nova U., 1983. Bar: Fla. 1983. Pvt. practice Ft. Lauderdale, Fla. Asst. to Gov. Bob Graham, Tallahassee, Fla., 1980; del. Citizens Amb. Program. Mem. ABA, Fla. Bar Assn. (trial lawyers sect.), Assn. Trial Lawyers Am., Civil Justice Found., Acad. Fla. Trial Lawyers, Ft. Lauderdale (Fla.) Knights Rugby Football Club (player 1981-83), Am. Motorcyclist Assn. (mem. motorcycle injury litigation group). Avocations: reading, woodworking, motorcycles. Personal injury, Product liability. Home: 5301 NW 67th Ave Fort Lauderdale FL 33319-7223 Office: 2404 NE 9th St Fort Lauderdale FL 33304-3524

**KRAMM, DEBORAH LUCILLE,** lawyer; b. Milw.; d. Hartzell McDonald and Alice Lucille (Johnson) K. Student, Trinity Coll., Deerfield, Ill., 1971-73; BS, Bradley U., 1974; JD, New Eng. Sch. of Law, 1977; postgrad., Georgetown U., 1978. Bar: N.Y. 1982, Ill. 1980, Mass. 1978. Trademark atty. U.S. Trademark Office, Washington, 1977-78; assoc. Hume, Clement, Willian, Brinks & Olds, Chgo., 1978-81; atty. Avon Products, Inc., N.Y.C., 1981-84; atty. Tiffany & Co., N.Y.C., 1981-84, v.p., sec., 1984-85; counsel Am. Brands, Inc., Old Greenwich, Conn., 1986-95; of counsel Rudnick & Wolfe, Washington, 1996—. N.Y. bd. dirs. Nat. Found. for Advancement for Arts, 1987-91; chmn. Martha Graham Guild, 1988—; trustee Martha Graham Ctr. for Contemporary Dance, Inc., N.Y.C., 1989—. Curt Tiege scholar, 1973. Mem. U.S. Trademark Assn. (bd. dirs. 1984-87), Cosmetic, Toiletry and Fragrance Assn. (chmn. trademark com. 1984). General corporate, Trademark and copyright. Office: Rudnick & Wolfe 203 N La Salle St Ste 1500 Chicago IL 60601-1293

**KRAMPF, JOHN EDWARD,** lawyer; b. Glens Falls, N.Y., Sept. 11, 1947; s. Charles Edward and Judith Carolyn (Strempel) K.; children: Alison Seelye, Emily Christine, Charles Alexander; m. Christine Ellen Bancheri, May 2, 1981. BA, Duke U., 1969; JD, U. Pa., 1972. Bar: Pa. 1972, U.S. Ct. Appeals (3d cir.), U.S. Dist. Ct. (ea., we. and mid. dists.) Pa. Assoc. Morgan, Lewis & Bockius LLP, Phila., 1972-79; ptnr. Morgan, Lewis & Bockius, Phila., 1979—. Editor: Employer's Guide to Pennsylvania Labor Laws and Regulations, 1990, Employer's Guide to N.J. Labor Laws and Regulations, 1990, Employer's Guide to Delaware Labor Laws and Regulations, 1989, Federal Employer Relations Laws and Regulations, 1991. Bd. dirs. Gilpin Hall Residential Care Facility, Wilmington, Del., 1978—; mem. bd. visitors Duke U. Coll. Arts and Scis. Mem. ABA, Pa. Bar Assn., Phila. Bar Assn., Nat. Assn. Coll. and Univ. Attys., Nat. Assn. Water Cos. Labor, Pension, profit-sharing, and employee benefits, Civil rights. Office: Morgan Lewis & Bockius LLP 1701 Market St Philadelphia PA 19103-2903

**KRANE, STEVEN CHARLES,** lawyer; b. Far Rockaway, N.Y., Jan. 20, 1957; s. Harry and Gloria (Christle) K.; m. Faith Marston, Oct. 1, 1983; children: Elizabeth Jordan, Cameron Marston. BA, SUNY, Stony Brook, 1978; JD, NYU, 1981. Bar: N.Y. 1982, U.S. Dist. Ct. (so. and ea. dists.) N.Y. 1982, U.S. Ct. Appeals (2d and 6th cirs.) 1987, U.S. Supreme Ct. 1987. Ptnr. Proskauer Rose LLP, N.Y.C.; law clk. to Assoc. Judge Judith S. Kaye N.Y. Ct. Appeals, N.Y.C. and Albany, 1984-85; lectr. in law Columbia U. Sch. Law, N.Y.C., 1989-92; vis. prof. Ga. Inst. of Tech., 1994-96; mem. departmental disciplinary com. Appellate divsn. 1st Jud. dept. Supreme Ct. N.Y., 1996—, spl. trial counsel, 1991-93. Editor articles, NYU Jour. International Law and Politics, 1980-81. Securities Inst. NYU fellow, 1980-81; recipient Vol. Counsel award Legal Aid Soc., 1984. Fellow N.Y. Bar Found.; mem. ABA, Westchester County Bar Assn., N.Y. Bar Assn. (com. on stds. of atty. conduct, chmn. 1999—, com. on profl. ethics 1990-94, spl. com. to rev. the code of profl. responsibility 1992-95, chmn. 1995-99, vice chair spl. com. on future of the profession 1997—, ho. of dels. 1996—, com. on mass disaster response 1997—, com. on multidisciplinary practice and the legal profession 1998-99, exec. com. 1998—, mem.-at-large, exec. com. 1998—, spl. com. on the law gov. firm structure and ops., vice chair 1999—), Assn. of Bar of City of N.Y. (com. on profl. and jud. ethics 1990-93, chmn. 1993-96, sec 1985-88, com. on profl. responsibility, chmn. subcom. provision legal svcs. 1985-88, com. on fed. cts. 1996-99, chmn. del. to N.Y. State Bar Assn. ho. dels. 1997-98), Am. Law Inst., Phi Beta Kappa, Pi Sigma Alpha. Republican. Avocations: military history, meteorology, Boston Red Sox baseball. Federal civil litigation, Sports. Office: Proskauer Rose LLP 1585 Broadway New York NY 10036-8299

**KRANIS, MICHAEL DAVID,** lawyer, judge; b. N.Y.C., Aug. 17, 1955; s. Herbert and Mildred (Swartz) K.; m. Patricia Ann Pagano, Sept. 29, 1989. BA, SUNY, Albany, 1977; JD, Union U., 1980. Bar: N.Y. 1981, U.S. Dist. Ct. (so. and ea. dists.) N.Y. 1983. Law clk. to hon. judge Robert C. William N.Y. Supreme Ct., Monticello, 1980-82; prin. Michael D. Kranis, P.C., Poughkeepsie, N.Y., 1982-88; ptnr. Coombs, Kranis & Wing, Poughkeepsie, 1988-94; sole practitioner Poughkeepsie, 1995—; asst. corp. counsel City of Poughkeepsie, 1983-85, hearing officer, 1985—; adj. prof. D.C. C.C., Poughkeepsie, 1984-87; judge Town of Pleasant Valley, N.Y., 1988-97; gen. counsel Grace Smith House, Inc., Poughkeepsie, 1983-95; adj. prof. Marist Coll., 1993. Mem. exec. com. Dutchess County Rep. Com., Pleasant Valley, 1997, Jud. Nominating Com., Dutchess County, 1987, 97—; mem. exec. com. D.C. Republican Com.; mem. Pleasant Valley Planning Bd., 1984-86; bd. dirs., chmn., vice chmn. Task Force for Child Proection, Inc.; mem. bd. dirs. Dutchess County Economic Devel. Corp. Mem. N.Y. State Bar Assn. (del.), Dutchess County Bar Assn. (pres.,treas., v.p. 1996, pres.-elect 1997, chmn. fee dispute com., chmn. bar endowment, v.p.), Dutchess County Magistrates Assn., N.Y. State Magistrates Assn., Rotary (pres., bd. dirs. Pleasant Valley chpt. 1985-96, Paul Harris fellow 1987). Family and matrimonial, Personal injury, Real property. Office: PO Box 4978 Poughkeepsie NY 12602-4978

**KRANSELER, LAWRENCE MICHAEL,** lawyer; b. Newton, Mass., Oct. 28, 1958; s. Arthur Sheldon and Barbara Joan (Siegel) K.; m. Wendy Kranseler; children: Alex, Jenna. BS in Econs., Boston Coll., 1980; MBA, JD, U. Pa., 1984. Bar: Mass. 1985, U.S. Dist. Ct. Mass. 1985. Assoc. Hale and Dorr, Boston, 1984-89; supervising sr. counsel Hasbro, Inc., Pawtucket, R.I., 1989-95, mng. atty., 1995—; vol. mentor UCAP Mentoring Program. Bd. dirs., mem., vol. Big Brother/Big Sister Assn.; fundraising capt. Am. Heart Assn., Combined Jewish Philanthropies; coach Town of Sharon Baseball, Town of Sharon Soccer. Recipient James E. Shaw Meml. award Pres. Boston Coll., 1980. Mem. ABA, Mass. Bar Assn., Boston Bar Assn., Phi Delta Phi. General practice, General corporate, Mergers and acquisitions. Home: 30 Sentry Hill Rd Sharon MA 02067-1522 Office: Hasbro Inc 1027 Newport Ave Pawtucket RI 02861-2500

**KRASNER, DANIEL WALTER,** lawyer; b. N.Y.C., Mar. 18, 1941; s. Nathan and Rose Krasner; m. Ruth Pollack, Dec. 20, 1964; children: Jonathan, Lisa, Noah, Rebecca. BA, Yeshiva Coll., 1962; LLB, Yale U., 1965. Bar: N.Y. 1966, U.S. Dist. Ct. (so. dist.) N.Y. 1967, U.S. Supreme Ct. 1978. Assoc. Pomerantz Levy Houdek & Block, N.Y.C., 1965-76; sr. ptnr. Wolf Haldenstein Adler Freeman & Herz, N.Y.C., 1977—. Vice chmn. Westchester Day Sch., Mamaroneck, N.Y., 1979-86; v.p., trustee Bd. Jewish Edn., N.Y.C., 1981—. Democrat. Avocations: tennis, golf, sailing. Federal civil litigation, Securities. Office: Wolf Haldenstein Adler Freeman & Herz 270 Madison Ave New York NY 10016-0601

**KRASNOW, JEFFREY HARRY,** lawyer; b. San Francisco, Oct. 7, 1946; s. Clement K. and Winifred (Spandorfer) K.; m. Rita Jane Moore, Mar. 23, 1969; children: Mark Samuel, Daniel Edward. BA, Old Dominion U., 1969; JD, U. Va., 1972. Bar: Va. 1972, W.Va. 1990, U.S. Dist. Ct. (ea. and we. dists.) Va., U.S. Ct. Appeals (4th, 5th and 6th cirs.), U.S. Supreme Ct. Diplomate Ct. Practice Inst.; cert. civil trial specialist. Assoc. Frank N. Perkinson Jr. Esq., Roanoke, Va., 1972-74; ptnr. Perkinson, Krasnow and Perkinson, Roanoke, 1974-77; pvt. practice Roanoke, 1977-82; sr. ptnr. Jeffrey H. Krasnow Esq., Roanoke, 1982-86, Jeffrey H. Krasnow & Assocs., Roanoke, 1987—. Mem. ABA, Assn. Trial Lawyers Am. (sustaining), Va. Trial Lawyers Assn. (sustaining, bd. govs. 1995-99), Va. State Bar (lawyer advt. and solicitation com. 1992-96), Roanoke Bar Assn., Nat. Bd. Trial Advocacy (cert. specialist civil trial advocacy). Fax: 540-982-7680. E-mail: krasnow@aol.com. Personal injury, Professional liability, Product liability. Office: PO Box 120 Roanoke VA 24002-0120

**KRASNOW, JORDAN PHILIP,** lawyer; b. Malden, Mass., May 14, 1944; s. Louis and Roslyn (Packer) K.; children: Laura, Joshua, Abbey, Abigail. AB, Clark U., 1965; JD magna cum laude, Boston U., 1968. Bar: Mass. 1970. Law clk. to Presiding Justice Mass. Superior Ct., Boston, 1968-69; assoc. atty. Peabody & Arnold, Boston, 1969-71; assoc. atty. Gaston Snow & Ely Bartlett, Boston, 1971-75, ptnr., 1975-86; officer, dir. Goulston & Storrs, Boston, 1986—; co-mng. dir., 1994-97; lectr. Mass. Continuing Legal Edn., Boston, 1975-85; adv. com. Boston U. Real Estate Program, 1988—; charter mem. Greater Boston Real Estate Bd.-Real Estate Fin., 1989. Mem. Mayor's Adv. Com. Housing Linkage, Boston, 1984. Recipient Disting. Achievement award B'nai B'rith Realty Unit, 1995. Fellow Mass. Bar Found.; mem. Mass. Bar Assn., Boston Bar Assn., B'nai Brith (trustee realty unit New Eng. chpt.). Jewish. Avocations: travel, sports. Real property, Land use and zoning (including planning), Finance. Home: 94 Beacon St Apt 2 Boston MA 02108-3329 Office: Goulston & Storrs 400 Atlantic Ave Boston MA 02110-3333

**KRATHEN, DAVID HOWARD,** lawyer; b. Phila., Nov. 17, 1946; s. Morris S. and Lillian E. Krathen; m. Francine Ellen Krathen, Oct. 21, 1973; children: Richard, Stefanie, Michael. BBA, U. Miami, 1969, JD, 1972. Bar: Fla. 1972, D.C. 1972, U.S. Supreme Ct. 1976, N.Y. 1984, Colo. 1989. Atty. advisor ICC, Washington, 1972-73; asst. pub. defender 17th Jud. Cir., Ft. Lauderdale, Fla., 1973-74; ptnr. Krathen, Rastatter, Stark & Tarlowe, Ft. Lauderdale, 1978-84; pvt. practice Law Offices David Krathen, P.A., Ft. Lauderdale, 1984—; mem. Fla. Bar Grievance Com. 17 C, 1982-85, 1988-91, vice chmn., 1985, 89-90, chmn. 1990-91; mem. Jud. Adminstrn., Selection and Tenure Com., 1982-85, 4th Dist. Ct. of Appeal Jud. Nominating Commn., 1983-87, chmn. 1986-87; mem. jud. nominating commn. 17th Jud. Cir., 1991-95, chmn., 1994-95; apptd. by Fla. Gov. to State Ethics Commn., 1995-99. Mem. ATLA, Acad. Fla. Trial Lawyers (diplomate), Broward County Bar Assn. (bd. dirs. 1988-89), Broward Med. Assn. (com. joint med. legal 1997—), Broward County Trial Lawyers Assn. (bd. dirs. 1983-84, sec. 1984-85, v.p., 1985-86, pres. 1987-88), Fla. Bar (bd. cert. civil trial lawyer 1984—), Nat. Bd. Trial Advocacy (bd. cert. civil trial advocate 1986—), Am. Bd. Trial Advocacy (advocate 1989—, sec. Ft. Lauderdale chpt. 1991-92, pres.-elect 1993-95, pres. 1995-96). Personal injury, State civil litigation. Office: 888 E Las Olas Blvd Ste 200 Fort Lauderdale FL 33301-2239

**KRAUS, LESLIE JAY,** lawyer; b. Bklyn., Sept. 6, 1943; s. George E. and Sylvia (Hornreich) K.; adopted s. Bobbi (Needleman) K.; m. Susan J. Rosenthal, Dec. 21, 1968; 1 child, Erica. BS, Northeastern U., Boston, 1966; JD, Suffolk U., 1969. Bar: Mass. 1969. Assoc. Cohn, Riemer & Pollack, Boston, 1970; atty. estate tax IRS, Bridgeport, Conn., 1970-71; field atty. NLRB, Mpls., 1971-76; v.p. Indsl. Rels. Assocs., Mpls., 1976-82; pres. Leslie J. Kraus & Assocs., Inc., Edina, Minn., 1982—; instr. U. Minn., Mpls., 1977-94. Co-chmn. YWCA Parent Coun., Mpls., 1985-86; vice chmn. Lake Fellowship of Unitarian Universalists, Excelsior, Minn., 1986-87, chmn. 1987-89; mem. Southview Mid. Sch. Site Coun., 1993-97, chair, 1994. Mem. ABA (labor law and litigation sects), Mass. Bar Assn., Northwest Athletic Club. Unitarian Universalist/Jewish. Labor. Office: Leslie J Kraus & Assocs Inc 4375 Thielen Ave Minneapolis MN 55436-1522

**KRAUS, SHERRY STOKES,** lawyer; b. Richmond, Ky., Aug. 11, 1945; d. Thomas Alexander and Callie (Ratliff) Stokes; m. Eugene John Kraus, Aug. 27, 1966. Student, U. Ky., 1962-64; BS, Roosevelt U., 1966; JD cum laude, Albany Law Sch., 1975; LLM in Taxation, NYU, 1981. Bar: N.Y. 1976, U.S. Dist. Ct. (we. dist.) N.Y. 1976, U.S. Tax Ct. 1986. Law clk. U.S. Tax Ct., Washington, summer 1974; law clk. 4th dept. appellate divsn. N.Y. State Supreme Ct., Rochester, 1975-77; assoc. Nixon, Hargrave, Devans & Doyle, Rochester, 1977-81, 83-84, Harter, Secrest & Emery, Rochester, 1984-86; pvt. practice Rochester, 1986—; faculty grad. tax program Sch. Law, NYU, N.Y.C., 1981-82; prin. tech. adv. to assoc. chief counsel - tech. IRS, Washington, 1983-84; mem. N.Y. State Tax Appeals Adv. Panel on Practice & Procedure, 1998—. Articles editor ABA Tax Articles Periodical, The Tax Lawyer, 1984-88; mng. editor NYU Tax Articles Periodical, NYU Tax Law Rev., 1981-82; lead articles editor Tax Articles Periodical, Albany Law Rev., 1973-75; contbr. articles to profl. jours. David J. Brewer scholar Albany Law Sch., 1973. Mem. ABA, N.Y. State Bar Assn. (tax sect. exec. com. 1984—), Monroe County Bar Assn. (treas. 1990-92), Monroe County Bar Found. (pres. 1994-95), Justinian Soc. Avocations: watercolors, guitar, dulcimer. Corporate taxation, Taxation, general, Personal income taxation. Office: 513 Times Square Bldg Rochester NY 14614-2078

**KRAUS, STEVEN GARY,** lawyer; b. Newark, Aug. 22, 1954; s. Leon Judah Kraus and Rose (Cohen) Turchin; m. Jane Susan Sukoneck, June 29, 1980; children: Adam. AB, Brandeis U., 1976; JD, Rutgers U., 1979. Bar: N.J. 1979, Pa. 1979, U.S. Dist. Ct. N.J. 1979. Jud. law sec. to assignment judge Charles A. Rizzi, Superior Ct. N.J., Camden, 1979-80; assoc. Kavesh & Basile, Vineland, N.J., 1980-81, Bennett & Bennett, West Orange, N.J., 1981-82; pvt. practice, Warren, N.J., 1982—. Mem. ABA, N.J. State Bar Assn. State civil litigation, Insurance, Personal injury. Home: 17 Regent Cir Basking Ridge NJ 07920-1900 Office: 122 Mt Bethel Rd Warren NJ 07059

**KRAUSE, STEVEN MICHAEL,** lawyer; b. Detroit, Feb. 26, 1953; s. Robert A. and Beverly M. (Canner) K.; m. Linda Laskey, Aug. 10, 1975; children: Jay L., Dana M., Morgan C. BA, U. Detroit, 1975; JD, Thomas M. Cooley Law Sch., 1978. Bar: S.C. 1978, U.S. Dist. Ct. S.C. 1979, U.S. Ct. Appeals (4th cir.) 1979, U.S. Supreme Ct. 1982; cert. trial adv. Assoc. Anderson, Kenyon & Epps, Anderson, S.C., 1978-79, Anderson & Epps, Anderson, 1979; ptnr. Anderson, Epps & Krause, Anderson, 1979-80, Epps & Krause, Anderson, 1980-85, Epps, Krause & Nicholson, Anderson, 1985-91, Epps, Krause, Nicholson & Stathakis, Anderson, 1991-94; pvt. practice Law Office of Steven M. Krause, P.A., Anderson, 1995—. Trustee S.C. Alliance Legis. Edn., Columbia, S.C., 1986. Mem. ABA, S.C. Bar Assn., Assn. Trial Lawyers Am. (state rep.), Nat. Assn. Criminal Def. Lawyers, S.C. Trial Lawyers Assn. (bd. govs., pres. 1995-96), Shriners, Phi Alpha Delta. Personal injury, Product liability, Workers' compensation. Home: 216 Brittany Park Anderson SC 29621-1563 Office: Stathakis 207 E Calhoun St Anderson SC 29621-5542

**KRAVETZ, DAVID HUBERT,** lawyer, educator; b. Feb. 2, 1938; s. Philip and Sadie (Winokur) K.; m. Phyllis E. Gouse, Aug. 16, 1984; children: Joel, Peter, Andrew. BBA, U. Mass., 1959; JD, Boston Coll., 1962. Bar: Mass. 1962, U.S. Dist. Ct. Mass. 1965, U.S. Supreme Ct. 1980. Staff atty. FTC, Washington, 1962-63, Boston Legal Aid, 1963-64; ptnr. Widett, Slater & Goldman, P.C., Boston, 1965-84; also dir.; pvt. practice Boston and Lexington, 1984-98; sr. lectr. in law Northeastern U., Boston, 1965-98; adj. asst. prof. bus. law Bentley Coll., Waltham, Mass., 1984-99. Trustee Charles River Acad., Cambridge, 1968-85; chmn. Heart Fund, Lexington, Mass., 1970-72; mem. Lexington Housing Authority, 1984-85. Mem. ABA, ATLA, Comml. Law League Am. (chmn. New Eng. region 1979-80), Mass. Bar Assn., Boston Bar Assn., Masons. Jewish. E-mail: dkravetz38@aol.com. Fax: (561) 495-6949. Consumer commercial, General practice. Home: 7809A Lexington Club Blvd Delray Beach FL 33446-3411

**KRAVITCH, PHYLLIS A.,** federal judge; b. Savannah, Ga., Aug. 23, 1920; d. Aaron and Ella (Wiseman) K. BA, Goucher Coll., 1941; LLB, U. Pa., 1943; LLD (hon.), Goucher Coll., 1981, Emory U., 1998. Bar: Ga. 1943, U.S. Dist. Ct. 1944, U.S. Supreme Ct. 1948, U.S. Ct. Appeals (5th cir.) 1962. Practice law Savannah, 1944-76; judge Superior Ct., Eastern Jud. Circuit of Ga., 1977-79, U.S. Ct. Appeals (5th cir.), Atlanta, 1979-81; judge U.S. Ct. Appeals (11th cir.), 1981—, sr. judge, 1996—; mem. Jud. Conf. Standing Com. on Rules, 1994—. Trustee Inst. Continuing Legal Edn. in Ga., 1979-82; mem. Bd. Edn., Chatham County, Ga., 1949-55; mem. coun. Law Sch., Emory U., Atlanta, 1985—; mem. vis. com. Law Sch., U. Chgo., 1990-93; bd. visitors, Ga. State U. Law Sch., 1994—; mem. regional rev. panel Truman Scholarship Found., 1992—. Recipient Hannah G. Solomon award Nat. Coun. Jewish Women, 1978, James Wilson award U. Pa. Law Alumni Soc., 1992. Fellow Am. Bar Found.; mem. ABA (Margaret Brent award 1991), Savannah Bar Assn. (pres. 1976), State Bar Ga., Am. Judicature Soc. (Devitt award com. 1998—), Am. Law Inst, U. Pa. Law Soc. Office: US Ct Appeals 11th Cir 56 Forsyth St NW # 202 Atlanta GA 30303-2205

**KRAW, GEORGE MARTIN,** lawyer, essayist; b. Oakland, Calif., June 17, 1949; s. George and Pauline Dorothy (Herceg) K.; m. Sarah Lee Kenyon, Sept. 3, 1983. BA, U. Calif., Santa Cruz, 1971; student, Lenin Inst., Moscow, 1971; MA, U. Calif., Berkeley, 1974, JD, 1976. Bar: Calif. 1976, U.S. Dist. Ct. (no. dist.) Calif. 1976, U.S. Supreme Ct. 1980, D.C., 1992. Pvt. practice, 1976—; ptnr. Kraw & Kraw, San Jose, 1988—; Mem. ABA, Nat. Assn. Health Lawyers, Inter-Am. Bar Assn., Union Internationale des Avocats. Pension, profit-sharing, and employee benefits, Private international, General corporate. Office: Kraw & Kraw 333 W San Carlos St Ste 1050 San Jose CA 95110-2735

**KRAW, SARAH KENYON,** lawyer; b. Hartford, Conn., Feb. 25, 1949; d. Edward Harrison and Mary (Beale) Kenyon; m. George Martin Kraw, Sept. 3, 1983. Student, Institut d'Etudes Francaises d'Avignon, France, 1971; BA in English, Wellesley Coll., 1972; JD, U. Calif., Berkeley, 1978. Bar: Calif. 1978. Rsch. analyst Civil Rights Div. U.S. Dept. Justice, Seattle, 1973-74, EEOC, 1974-75; assoc. Beeson, Tayer, Silbert & Bodine, San Francisco, 1979-85, ptnr., 1986-88; ptnr. Kraw & Kraw, San Jose, Calif., 1988—; mem. ednl. program com. Internat. Found. Employee Benefit Plans, 1986, 88, 89, chmn. interns com., 1988, 89; seminar instr. George Meany Found., U. Calif., Berkeley, 1983; lectr. Internat. Found. Employee Benefit Plans Ann. Conf., 1983-98, San Francisco Bar Assn. labor sect. ann. meeting, 1986; bd. dirs. Outreach and Escort, Inc., 1989-92. Mem. ABA, Calif. State Bar (treas. labor and employment law sect. 1988, chmn. 1989, chmn. pension com. 1988, 89, mem. exec. com. 1986-89). Democrat. Pension, profit-sharing, and employee benefits. Office: Kraw & Kraw 333 W San Carlos St Ste 1050 San Jose CA 95110-2735

**KRAWCZAK, KENNETH FRANCIS,** lawyer; b. Saginaw, Mich., Mar. 5, 1951; s. Frank Vincent and Annabelle Kathleen Krawczak; m. Kimberlee Kaye Nelson, Oct. 25, 1986; children: Sarah Krawczak Steed, Joseph, Kerri. BA, We. Coll., Oxford, Ohio, 1974; JD, Ohio State U., 1976. Bar: Ohio 1977. Hearing officer State Employee Compensation Bd., Columbus, Ohio, 1977-78, Ohio Ind. Commn., Toledo, 1978-81; claims atty. Gen. Tire Co., Akron, Ohio, 1981-82; atty. dept. law BP Am. Inc., Cleve., 1982—; pres. Self-Insured Group Ohio, 1998—. Avocation: golf. Workers' compensation, Personal injury, Toxic tort. Home: 19163 Seven Oaks Dr Strongsville OH 44136-7541 Office: BP Am Inc 200 Public Sq # 11U Cleveland OH 44114-2375

**KRAYBILL, J(AMES) ELVIN,** lawyer; b. Lancaster, Pa., Feb. 24, 1948; s. Simon Peter and Mary Jean (Sherer) K.; m. Esther E. Kraybill, June 25, 1971; children: Peter, Sarah, Megan. BA, Eastern Mennonite U., Harrisonburg, Va., 1970; JD, Georgetown U. Law Ctr., Washington, 1973. Bar: Pa. 1973. Assoc. atty. Wenger & Byler, Lancaster, Pa., 1973-77; ptnr. Gibbel, Kraybill & Hess, Lancaster, Pa., 1977—; pres. Lancaster (Pa.) Bar Assn., 1997-98. Estate planning, Probate, Real property. Office: Gibbel Kraybill & Hess 41 E Orange St Lancaster PA 17602-2846

**KREBS, ARNO WILLIAM, JR.,** lawyer; b. Dallas, July 7, 1942; s. Arno W. and Lynette (Linnstaedter) K.; m. Peggy Sharon Stagg, Dec. 17, 1966; 1 child, Kirsten; m. Barbara Lyn Craig, Dec. 28, 1973. B.A., Tex. A&M U., 1964; LL.B., U. Tex., 1967. Bar: Tex. 1967, U.S. Dist. Ct. (so. dist.) Tex. 1968, U.S. Ct. Appeals (5th cir.) 1971, U.S. Ct. Appeals (11th cir.) 1981, U.S. Dist. Ct. (we. and no. dists.) Tex. 1981, U.S. Supreme Ct. 1983, U.S. Dist. Ct. (ea. dist.) Tex. 1984. Assoc. Fulbright & Jaworski, Houston, 1967-75, ptnr., 1975—. Contbr. articles to profl. jours. Mem. Tex. Assn. Def. Counsel, Internat. Assn. Def. Counsel, Houston Bar Assn., ABA, Tex. Aggie Bar Assn., Tex. Bar Found., Houston Bar Found., Tex. A&M U. 12th Man Found. (pres. 1988), Houston Ctr. Club. Lutheran. Insurance, Personal injury, State civil litigation. Office: Fulbright & Jaworski 1301 Mckinney St Fl 51 Houston TX 77010-3031 also: 2200 Ross Ave Ste 2800 Dallas TX 75201-2750

**KREBS, LEO FRANCIS,** lawyer; b. Botkins, Ohio, June 9, 1937; s. Eugene L. and Velma L. K.; m. Paula Anne Calvert, Nov. 4, 1961; children: Matthew, Mark, Thomas, Peter. BA, U. Dayton, 1959; JD, Georgetown U., 1965. Bar: Ohio 1966, U.S. Dist. Ct. (so. dist.) Ohio 1966, U.S. Ct. Appeals (6th cir.) 1974, U.S. Supreme Ct. 1975. Legal dep. Montgomery Probate Ct., 1966-68; assoc. Bieser, Greer & Landis, Dayton, Ohio, 1968-74, ptnr., 1974—. Assoc. editor Georgetown Law Rev., 1964-65. Chmn. fin. com. Holy Angels, 1986-98, former chmn., bd. dirs. parish coun.; former bd. dirs. Cath. Social Svcs. Dayton, 1987-90; former mem. Oakwood YMCA Baseball Commn.; coach YMCA baseball. 1st lt. U.S. Army, 1959-62. Fellow Am. Coll. Trial Lawyers, Ohio State Bar Found.; mem. ABA, Ohio State Bar Assn., Ohio Assn. Trial Attys., Dayton Bar Assn., Phi Delta Phi. Avocations: hiking, tennis. General civil litigation, Personal injury, Probate. Office: Bieser Greer & Landis 6 N Main St Ste 400 Dayton OH 45402-1914

**KREBS, ROBERT ALAN,** lawyer; b. Pitts., Dec. 12, 1958; s. James Arthur and Helen Marie (McGrogan) K.; m. Elizabeth Ann Bedford, Apr. 20, 1985; 1 child, Stephen Vladimir. BA, Pa. State U., 1981; student, U. Exeter, U.K., 1981; JD, Capital U., 1984. Bar: Pa. 1984, D.C. 1989, U.S. Dist. Ct. (ea. dist.) Pa. 1990, U.S. Dist. Ct. (we. dist.) Pa. 1984, U.S. Dist. Ct. (no. dist.) Ohio 1990, U.S. Dist. Ct. (D.C.) 1989, U.S. Ct. Appeals (D.C. cir.) 1989, U.S. Ct. Appeals (3d cir.) 1986, U.S. Supreme Ct. 1988. Assoc. Henderson & Goldberg, Pitts., 1985-87, Messer Shilobod & Crenney, Pitts., 1987-89, Klett Lieber Rooney & Schorling, Pitts., 1989-91, Conte, Melton & D'Antonio, Conway, Pa., 1992—. Articles editor Capital Law Rev., 1983-84. Mem. Pa. Dem. State Com., 37th Dist. (elected 1994, re-elected, 1998), Allegheny County Dem. Com., Pitts., 1991—; vol. Pitts. Ctr. for Grieving Children, 1995, 96. Recipient Am. Jurisprudence award Lawyers Coop. Pub. Co., 1982. Mem. ABA, FBA, D.C. Bar Assn., Pa. Trial Lawyers Assn. (amicus curiae com. 1996—), Allegheny County Bar Assn. (fed. ct. sect. coun. 1996—), Capital U. Law Sch. Alumni Assn. (bd. dirs. 1995—, v.p. 1996—), Western Pa. Trial Lawyers Assn. (bd. govs. 1994—). Democrat. Roman Catholic. Personal injury, Appellate, Consumer commercial. Home: 3235 Comanche Rd Pittsburgh PA 15241-1138 Office: 300 9th St Conway PA 15027-1647

**KREEGER, MARGARET RYAN,** lawyer; b. Torrance, Calif., Apr. 1, 1953; d. Robert Emmett and Margaret Caroline Ryan; m. Withold Udo Kreeger, Sept. 10, 1989; 1 child, Patrick Ryan. BA, U. Calif., Irvine, 1975; JD, U. San Francisco, 1978. Bar: Pa. 1979, Calif. 1981. Trial atty. EEO Commn., Balt., 1978-79, L.A., 1979-85; sr. atty. So. Calif. Edison, L.A., 1985-88; gen. counsel Utility Operation Cons., Pasadena, 1988; counsel Atlantic Richfield Co., L.A., 1989—. Mem. ABA, Calif. Bar Assn., Los Angeles County Bar Assn. Home: 1191 Shorecrest Ln Huntington Beach CA 92648-4162 Office: ARCO 444 S Flower St # 3337 Los Angeles CA 90071-2901

**KREEK, LOUIS FRANCIS, JR.,** lawyer; b. Washington, Aug. 24, 1928; s. Louis F. and Esperance (Agee) K.; m. Gwendolyn Schoepfle, Sept. 12, 1970. BS, MIT, 1948; JD, George Washington U., 1952. Bar: D.C. 1952, U.S. Dist. Ct. D.C. 1952, U.S. Ct. Appeals (D.C. cir) 1952, Ohio 1955, N.Y. 1964, U.S. Dist. Ct. (so. and ea. dists.) N.Y. 1964, N.J. 1972. Patent examiner U.S. Patent Office, Washington, 1948-53; patent atty. Pitts. Plate Glass Co., Washington, 1953-54, Battelle Meml. Inst., Columbus, Ohio, 1954-56, Merck & Co., Inc., Rahway, N.J., 1956-60; divsn. patent counsel Air Reduction Co., Murray Hill, N.J., 1960-63; assoc. Kenyon & Kenyon, N.Y.C., 1963-66; patent atty. Johns-Manville Corp., Manville, N.J., 1967-68; sr. patent atty. Esso Rsch. and Engring. Co., Linden, N.J., 1968-73, ICI Ams. Inc, Wilmington, Del., 1973-85; assoc. Oldham, Oldham & Weber Co. (now Oldham & Oldham Co.), Akron, Ohio, 1985-94, of counsel, 1994—. Mem. ABA, Am. Intellectual Property Law Assn., N.Y. Intellectual Property Law Assn. (assoc.), Cleve. Intellectual Property Law Assn. (bd. dirs. 1991-92), Akron Bar Assn., MIT Alumni Assn. (bd. dirs. fund bd. 1977-80, officers conf. com. 1981-84, chmn. 1983), MIT Club Del. Valley (pres. 1978-80), MIT Club NE Ohio (pres. 1986-89), Am. Diabetes Assn. (bd. dirs. Akron chpt. 1989-90), Akron Roundtable (bd. dirs. 1989-90), Kiwanis (pres. 1989-90, lt. gov. 1992-93). Patent, Trademark and copyright. Home: 2321 Stockbridge Rd Akron OH 44313-4512

**KREGER, MELVIN JOSEPH,** lawyer; b. Buffalo, Feb. 21, 1937; s. Philip and Bernice (Gerstman) K.; m. Patricia Anderson, July 1, 1955 (div. 1963); children: Beth Barbour, Arlene Roux; m. Renate Hochleitner, Aug. 15, 1975. JD, Mid-valley Coll. Law, 1978; LLM in Taxation, U. San Diego, 1988. Bar: Calif. 1978, U.S. Dist. Ct. (cen. dist.) Calif. 1979, U.S. Tax Ct. 1979, U.S. Supreme Ct. 1995; cert. specialist in probate law, trust law and estate planning law, taxation law, Calif. Life underwriter Met. Life Ins. Co.,

Buffalo, 1958-63; bus. mgr. M. Kreger Bus. Mgmt., Sherman Oaks, Calif., 1963-78, enrolled agt., 1971—; pvt. practice North Hollywood, Calif., 1978—. Mem. Nat. Assn. Enrolled Agts., Calif. Soc. Enrolled Agts., State Bar Calif., L.A. Bar Assn., San Fernando Valley Bar Assn. (probate sect., tax sect.). Jewish. Avocations: computers, travel. Probate, Estate planning, Taxation, general. Office: 11424 Burbank Blvd North Hollywood CA 91601-2301

**KREGER, MICHAEL E.,** lawyer; b. San Diego, May 31, 1949; s. Robert Thomas and Gladys Eleanor Kreger; m. Darcy B. McMullen, June 3, 1978; children: Jesse Patrick, Kelly Michael. BA in Lit. cum laude, Claremont McKenna Coll., 1971; JD magna cum laude, Willamette U., 1982. Bar: Oreg. 1982, Alaska 1983, U.S. Dist. Ct. Alaska 1985, U.S. Ct. Appeals (9th cir.) 1987, U.S. Supreme Ct. 1993. Law clk. to James A. Von der Heydt, chief judge U.S. Dist. Ct., Anchorage, 1982-84; atty. Perkins Coie, Anchorage, 1984—. Exec. editor Willamette Law Rev., 1982. Bd. dirs. Anchorage Arts Adv. Com., 1988-92, Anchorage Historic Properties, Inc., 1993-96. Avocations: tennis, reading, woodworking. Construction, Government contracts and claims. Office: Perkins Coie 1029 W 3d Ave Anchorage AK 99501

**KREGER-GRELLA, CHERYL LESLIE,** lawyer; b. Bklyn., Feb. 3, 1950; d. Joseph and Edythe H. (Stein) K.; m. Alexander Vincent Grella, Nov. 6, 1988 (dec. Dec. 1991). BA, Syracuse U., 1972; MA in Spanish, Middlebury Coll., 1973; JD, Bklyn. Law Sch., 1979. Bar: N.Y. 1980, U.S. Dist. Ct. (ea. and so. dists.) N.Y. 1980, U.S. Supreme Ct. 1986, U.S. Ct. Appeals (fed. cir.) 1986. Atty. pvt. practice, Garden City, N.Y., 1981—. Recipient Jewish Lawyers award Jewish Lawyers Nassau County, 1994, cert. Disting. Merit Nassau Acad. Law, Mineola, N.Y., 1986. Mem. ABA, N.Y. State Bar Assn., Nassau County Bar Assn. (chair young lawyers com. 1985-86, speakers bur. 1986—, Pres. award 1986), Jewish Lawyers Assn. (chmn. bd. dirs. 1994-95, pres. 1993-94), , Nat. Wildlife Fund, Nature Conservancy, Ctr. Marine Conservation, Smithsonian Instn. Avocations: travel, reading, tennis, bowling, puzzles. Family and matrimonial, General practice, Probate. Office: 1205 Franklin Ave Garden City NY 11530-1629

**KREIDLER, FRANK ALLAN,** lawyer; b. Cleve., Jan. 20, 1947; s. Emil J. and Dorothy M. K.; m. Mary Ann Kreidler, Oct. 4, 1980; children: Catherine Allison, James Fredrick, Kristine Anne, Kimberly Jaclyn. AA, Palm Beach Jr. Coll., Lake Worth, Fla., 1968; BS, Fla. State U., 1970, JD, 1973. Bar: Fla. 1973, U.S. Dist. Ct. (so. dist.) Fla. 1974, U.S. Tax Ct. 1974, U.S. Ct. Appeals (5th cir.) 1976, U.S. Supreme Ct. 1977, U. S. Ct. Mil. Appeals 1977, U.S. Dist. Ct. (mid. dist.) Fla. 1981, U.S. Ct. Appeals (11th cir.) 1982, U.S. Ct. Fed. Claims 1994; diplomate Congress of Cert. Cir. Mediators. Asst. state atty. 15th Circuit, West Palm Beach, Fla., 1973-75; asst. pub. defender 15th Circuit, Belle Glade, Fla., 1976-78; pvt. practice Belle Glade, 1975-78; city atty. City of Lake Worth, Fla., 1978-82; gen. couns. Lake Worth Utilities Authority, 1980-85; pvt. practice Lake Worth, 1982—; adj. prof. Fla. Atlantic U., Boca Raton, 1984—; mediator Supreme Ct. Fla., Tallahassee, 1989—, U.S. Dist. Ct. Trial Bar (so. dist.) Fla., Miami, 1982—. Chmn. human rights adv. com. Dist. 9 State of Fla., West Palm Beach, 1992-96; chmn. adv. bd. Palm Beach Kidney Assn., West Palm Beach, 1985-87; mem. Criminal Justice Commn. Corrections Task Force, 1995-97, Nat. Com. for Employer Support of Guard and Res., 1998—, Palm Beach County Emergency Shelter Grants Program adv. bd., 1997—; mem. adv. coun. Santaluces H.S., 1995—. Comdr. USNR, 1977—. Recipient Cmty. Svc. award Palm Beach Blood Bank, 1979, Donor of Month award, 1991, Pres.'s award Seminole Booster's Club, 1998. Mem. ABA (mediation com., legis. subcom.), Am. Arbitration Assn., Palm Beach County Seminole Boosters (bd. dirs. 1990—), Leadership Palm Beach, Naval Res. Assn. (pres. Palm Beach chpt. 1991—), Legal Aid Soc., Palm Beach County Bar Assn. (Human Rights Advocacy award 1995), Fla. Bar Assn. (Pro Bono Svc. award 1997). Avocation: 1967 Chrysler. General civil litigation, Administrative and regulatory, Criminal. Office: 1124 S Federal Hwy Lake Worth FL 33460-5244

**KREIG, ANDREW THOMAS,** trade association executive; b. Chgo., Feb. 28, 1949; s. Albert Arthur and Margaret Theresa (Baltzell) K. AB, Cornell U., 1970; MSL, Yale U., 1983; JD, U. Chgo., 1990. Bar: D.C. 1991, Mass. 1991, Ill. 1991. Writer, editor Hartford (Conn.) Courant, 1970-84; media dir. Conn. House Spkr., Hartford, 1984; freelance author, journalist, lectr. Hartford and Chgo., 1985-89; law clk. U.S. Dist. Judge Mark L. Wolf, Boston, 1990-91; assoc. Latham & Watkins, Washington, 1991-93; v.p., comms. dir. Wireless Comms. Assn. Internat., Inc., Washington, 1993-96, v.p., gen. counsel, 1996, pres., 1997—; ethics com. Soc. Profl. Journalists, 1987-90. Author: Spiked: How Chain Management, 1987, 2d edit., 1988; editor Spectrum, 1994—; bd. editors Pvt. & Wireless Cable, 1994—, Wireless Internat., 1996—; contbr. articles to profl. jours. V.p. Residences Market Square, Washington, 1993-98. Ford Found. fellow Yale Law Sch., New Haven, 1982-83. Mem. Fed. Com. Bar Assn. (legis. com.). Home: PH8 701 Pennsylvania Ave NW Washington DC 20004-2608 Office: Wireless Comms Assn Ste 810 1140 Connecticut Ave NW Washington DC 20036-4010

**KREINDLER, PETER MICHAEL,** lawyer; b. 1945. BA, Harvard U., 1967, JD, 1971. Bar: D.C. 1971, N.Y. 1989. Assoc. Hughes, Hubbard & Reed, 1975-77, ptnr., 1977-88; ptnr. Arnold & Porter, 1990-91; sr. v.p., gen. counsel and sec. AlliedSignal, Morristown, N.J., 1992—; sec. Allied-Signal, Morristown, N.J., 1995—. General corporate, General civil litigation. Office: Allied Signal Inc 101 Columbia Rd Morristown NJ 07960-4658*

**KREIS, ELIZABETH SUSAN,** lawyer; b. N.Y.C., Nov. 8, 1963; d. Willi and Emily Rutledge Kreis. BS in Biochemistry, U. Wis., 1986; JD, Ohio State U., 1991. Bar: N.Y. 1991, Conn. 1992, D.C. 1992, Colo. 1994. Biochemist Sandoz Pharm., Basel, Switzerland, 1986-88; pvt. practice Stamford, Conn., 1991-93, Arvada, Colo., 1993—. Mem. ABA, Am. Bus. Women's Assn. (chairperson for spkrs.), Colo. Bar Assn., N.Y. State Bar Assn., Conn. Bar Assn., D.C. Bar Assn., Arvada Garden Club (pres. 1997-98). Family and matrimonial, Consumer commercial, General practice. Home and Office: 9277 W 56th Pl Ste 12 Arvada CO 80002-2158

**KREISBERG, STEVEN E.,** lawyer; b. N.Y.C., Apr. 10, 1942; s. Leo and Lucille (Levy) K.; m. Betsy Fuges, Dec. 7, 1969; children—Jonathan Evan, Daniel Emerson, Juliet Eva. B.A., Dickinson Coll., 1962; J.D., Columbia U., 1967; diploma in criminology Cambridge U., 1968. Bar: N.Y. 1968, Fla. 1973, U.S. Dist. Ct. (so. dist.) Fla. 1980, U.S. Ct. Appeals (4th, 5th and 11th cirs.) 1981, U.S. Supreme Ct. 1997. Criminal def. atty. Legal Aid Soc., N.Y.C., 1968-70; asst. dir. N.J. Office of Juvenile Justice, Trenton, 1970-71; law asst. Civil Ct., N.Y.C., 1972-76; asst. fed. pub. defender, Miami, Fla., 1976-80; sole practice, Miami, 1980—; adj. prof. criminal justice Fla. Internat. U., Miami, 1976. Editor Columbia Jour. Law and Social Problems, 1967. Served as 1st lt. U.S. Army, 1962-64. Harlan Fiske Stone scholar Columbia Law Sch., 1966; Ford Found. scholar Cambridge Inst. Criminology, 1967. Democrat. Jewish. Criminal. Home: 10325 SW 90th St Miami FL 33176-1503

**KREITLOW, SARAMAE M.,** lawyer; b. Iowa City, Iowa, May 9, 1969; d. Frank Lee and Mary Nell Kreitlow. BS in Computer Sci. and Acctg., Quinnipiac Coll., 1992, JD, 1998. Bar: Conn. 1998; CPA, Conn. Revenue examiner State of Conn. Dept. Revenue Svcs., Hartford, 1993-98; law clk. State of Conn., Jud. Br. Legal Rsch., New Haven, 1998-99. Mem. New Haven County Bar Assn., New Haven Young Lawyers Assn., Phi Delta Phi. Avocations: crafts, music, reading. Home: 47 Mary St Ansonia CT 06401-1746

**KREITZMAN, RALPH J.,** lawyer; b. N.Y.C., Nov. 11, 1945; s. Emanuel M. and Hannah G. (Steinhardt) K.; m. Wendy A. Karpel, Nov. 24, 1968; children: Susan Beth, Emily Meg. BS in Acctg., Rider U., 1967; JD cum laude, Bklyn. Law Sch., 1970. Bar: N.Y. 1971, U.S. Dist Ct. (so. dist.) N.Y. 1971, U.S. Dist. Ct. (ea. dist.) N.Y. 1973, U.S. Ct. of Appeals (2nd cir.) 1975, U.S. Supreme Ct. 1976. Assoc. Hughes Hubbard & Reed LLP, N.Y.C., 1970-80; ptnr., chmn. real estate group Hughes Hubbard & Reed LLC, N.Y.C., 1980—. Chair planning bd., mem. archtl. review com. Village of Great Neck. Served with U.S. Army (Res.) 1968-74. Mem. ABA (real property law sect. and com. on fgn. investment in U.S. real estate), N.Y. State Bar Assn. (real property law sect., com. on comml. leases and com. on financings), Assn. of Bar of City of N.Y. (com. on real property law, chair environ. subcom., sublease subcom.). Real property, Private international. Office: Hughes Hubbard & Reed LLP 1 Battery Park Plz New York NY 10004-1482

**KREIZINGER, LOREEN I.,** lawyer, nurse; b. Syracuse, N.Y., Apr. 16, 1959; d. David F. and Blanche L. (Heaney) Mosher; m. Kenneth R. Kreizinger, Aug. 30, 1985; 1 child, Katelyn Rose. Grad. in nursing, Crouse-Irving Meml. Hosp., Syracuse, 1981; BS in Bus. with honors, Nova U., 1987, JD, 1990. Bar: Fla. 1990; RN, N.Y., Fla. Nurse ICU and infants neonatal unit, Syracuse, Ft. Lauderdale, Fla., 1979-86; med. malpractice cons. Krupnick, Campbell et al, Ft.Lauderdale, 1986-90, assoc., 1990-92, of counsel, 1992—; pvt. practice, Ft.Lauderdale, 1992—; instr. adult intensive care Crouse-Irving Meml. Hosp., 1981-82; adj. prof. Nova U., Ft. Lauderdale, 1994—; seminar instr. legal aspects of nursing Fla. Bd. Nursing, 1990-92; guest spkr. TV talk show Med. Malpractice, 1991. Sec., bd. dirs. Shepherd Care Ministries, Hollywood, Fla., 1993, 94; mem. choir 1st Bapt. Ch. Ft. Lauderdale, 1994—. Mem. ABA (law and medicine com. 1990—), FBA, ATLA (spl. L-Trytophen com. 1991-94), Fla. Bar Assn., Fla. Assn. Women Lawyers, Fla. Acad. Trial Lawyers, Broward County Women Lawyers Assn., Broward County Trial Lawyers Assn., Phi Alpha Delta. Republican. Avocations: sailing, snow skiing, rollerblading. Personal injury, General civil litigation. Office: 515 E Las Olas Blvd Ste 1150 Fort Lauderdale FL 33301-2281

**KRELSTEIN, RONALD DOUGLAS,** lawyer; b. Memphis, May 7, 1942; s. Harold R. and Rose K. LLB, Vanderbilt U., 1967. Bar: Tenn. 1967, U.S. Dist. Ct. (we. dist.) Tenn. 1969, U.S. Ct. Appeals (6th cir.) 1970, U.S. Supreme Ct. 1976. Pvt. practice Memphis, 1967-70; asst. pub. defender Shelby County, Memphis, 1970-71; police legal adviser Memphis Police Dept., 1971-74; pvt. practice Memphis, 1974—. Pres. Tenn. Law Enforcement Legal Advisers Assn., 1973-74. Nat. Collegiate Pistol Champion 4 times; holder Disting. Pistol Shot and Disting. Rifleman awards; mem. Christian Bros. H.S. (Memphis) Hall of Fame, 1995—. Avocation: competitive rifle and pistol shooting. General civil litigation, Criminal, Personal injury.

**KREMER, MATTHEW MARKUS,** lawyer, mediator; b. San Antonio, Sept. 27, 1951; s. Donn Clarke Kremer and Shari Adler; m. Judy Lynn Ware, Dec. 30, 1978 (div. June 1985); children: Kailee, Maxwell; m. Mary Ann Wynne, Dec. 6, 1987; 1 child, Raoul. BS, Western State U., 1976; JD, Thomas Jefferson Sch. Law, 1978. Bar: Calif. 1978, U.S. Dist. Ct. (so. dist.) Calif. 1978; cert. specialist family law Calif. State Bd. Legal Specialization. Pvt. practice San Diego, 1978—. Pres. Beth Sholom Synagogue, Chula Vista, Calif., 1982. Mem. Assn. Cert. Family Law Specialists, San Diego County Bar Assn., Rep. Senate Club. Republican. Jewish. Avocations: writing, golf, skiing. Family and matrimonial. Office: 9665 Chesapeake Dr Ste 310 San Diego CA 92123-1352

**KREMIN, DAVID KEITH,** lawyer; b. Chgo.; s. Aaron and Rose (Doane) K. BS, U. Ill., 1977; JD with highest honors, ITT, 1983. Bar: Ill. 1983, U.S. Dist. Ct. (no. dist.) Ill. 1983. Assoc. Lenard, Ring & Assocs., Chgo., Rosenfeld, Rotenberg, et al., Chgo.; ptnr. David K. Kremin & Assocs., P.C., Chgo.; judge advocate Belmont Yacht Club, Chgo.; arbitrator Ill. Cir. Ct., Chgo. Mem. ATLA, Ill. Trial Lawyers Assn., Internat. Bar Assn., Nat. Lawyers Assn., Ill. Bar Assn., Chgo. Bar Assn., Decalogue Soc. Personal injury. Office: David K Kremin & Assocs 77 W Washington St Ste 1720 Chicago IL 60602-2903

**KRESKY, HARRY,** lawyer; b. Sioux Falls, S.D., Sept. 7, 1944; s. Philip Joseph and Beatrice (Greenwald) K.; m. Carolyn Egbert, Sept. 6, 1969 (div. 1977). AB, Columbia Coll., 1966; postgrad., Columbia U., 1966-68, JD, 1971. Bar: N.Y., U.S. Dist. Ct. (so., ea. and no. dists.) N.Y., U.S. Ct. Appeals (2nd, D.C. and 6th cirs.), U.S. Supreme Ct. Assoc. Szold & Brandwen, N.Y.C., 1971-72; pvt. practice law N.Y.C., 1973-80; ptnr. Kresky, Sinawski & Davis, N.Y.C., 1980-81, Kresky, Sinawski & Jollenborg, N.Y.C., 1981-84, Block & Kresky, N.Y.C., 1985-86, Frazier & Kresky, N.Y.C., 1986-87; pvt. practice law N.Y.C., 1987—. Mem. state com., N.Y. county exec. com. Ind. Party, N.Y.C., 1995—; mem. nominations com. Reform Party, 1998. Mem. N.Y. County Lawyers Assn. Avocations: history, dog, philosophy, swimming. General civil litigation, Civil rights, Constitutional. Office: 250 W 57th St #32K New York NY 10107

**KRESS, EDWARD MARSHALL,** lawyer; b. Dayton, Ohio, July 22, 1949; s. David R. and Estele C. K.; m. Marcia EllenSaper, Aug. 3, 1975; children: Jeremy C., Dustin M. Student, Miami U., Oxford, Ohio, 1967-71, Ohio State U., 1974. Bar: Ohio 1974. Ptnr. Porter Wright Morris & Arthur (and predecessor firm), Dayton, Ohio, 1980-85, Smith & Schacke, Dayton, 1985-88; sr. ptnr. Cherensky, Heyman & Kress, PLL, Dayton, 1988—; bd. dirs. Rex Stores Corp., Dayton. Mem. Meadowbrook Country Club. Avocations: coin collecting, skiing, weight training, jocking. Home: 6505 Landsend Ct Dayton OH 45414-5905

**KRESSE, WILLIAM JOSEPH,** lawyer, educator, accountant; b. Evergreen Park, Ill., June 12, 1958; s. Robert Alvin and Ellenmary M. (Mulhall) K. BBA, U. Notre Dame, 1980; JD, U. Ill., 1985, MS, 1996, postgrad., 1997—. Bar. Ill. 1985, U.S. Dist. Ct. (no. dist.) Ill. 1985, U.S. Tax Ct. 1987, U.S. Ct. Appeals (7th cir.) 1989, U.S. Supreme Ct. 1989, U.S. Ct. Mil. Appeals 1990, U.S. Ct. Claims 1993. Acct. Deloitte, Haskins & Sells, Chgo., 1980-82; assoc. Hinshaw, Culbertson, Moelmann, Hoban & Fuller, Chgo., 1985-87; law clk. to sr. judge U.S. Dist. Ct. (no. dist.) Ill., Chgo., 1987-90; assoc. Ross & Hardies, Chgo., 1990, Gleason, McGuire & Shreffler, Chgo., 1991-92; pvt. practice, Chgo., 1992—; corp. sec. Micro Records Co., Evergreen Park, Ill., 1987—, pres. 1995—; arbitrator arbitration program Cook County (Ill.) Cir. Ct., 1990—; mem. faculty St. Xavier U. Sch. Mgmt., Chgo., 1992-96, asst. prof., 1996—; election ctrl. atty. Chgo. Bd. Election Commrs. Author: (with others) Chicago Lawyer's Court Handbook, 1989, 92. Bd. dirs. St. John Fisher Sch. Bd., Chgo., 1988-94, pres., 1993-94; field adv. Met. Tribunal, Archdiocese of Chgo., 1994—; bd. dirs. Hist. Soc. U.S. Dist. Ct. for No. Dist. Ill., 1997—. Mem. ABA, FBA, AICPA, Chgo. Bar Assn. (co-chmn. young lawyer sect. bench/bar rels. com. 1988-89, bd. dirs. young lawyer sect. 1989-91, treas. young lawyer sect. 1991-93), Ill. Bar Assn., 7th Cir. Bar Assn., Hist. Soc. U.S. Dist. Ct. for No. Dist. Ill. (bd. dirs. 1997—), Ill. CPA Soc., Midwest Bus. Adminstrn. Acad., Nat. Lawyers Assn., KC, Elks, Delta Theta Phi. Roman Catholic. Avocations: current events, trivia, politics. General practice, General civil litigation, Probate. Office: 10221 S California Ave Chicago IL 60655-1623 also: St Xavier U 3700 W 103rd St Chicago IL 60655-3105

**KREUSLER-WALSH, JANE ANN,** lawyer; b. Rockville Centre, N.Y., Dec. 9, 1953; d. Richard George and Jane (Conway) Kreusler; m. Michael Patrick Walsh, Aug. 5, 1978; children: Brian Patrick, Erin Elizabeth, Lauren Conway. BA, U. Fla., 1975; JD, Loyola U., 1978. Bar: Fla. 1979, U.S. Supreme Ct. 1982, U.S. Ct. Appeals (11th cir.) 1982, U.S. Ct. Appeals (4th cir.) 1986, U.S. Dist. Ct. (so. dist.) Fla. 1979, U.S. Dist. Ct. (mid. dist.) Fla. 1995. Staff atty. 4th Dist. Ct. Appeals, West Palm Beach, Fla., 1979-80; ptnr. Klein & Walsh, P.A., West Palm Beach, Fla., 1981-93; pvt. practice West Palm Beach, Fla., 1993—; mem. appellate rules com. Fla. Bar, Tallahassee, 1983—, chairperson grievance com., 1986-89, vice chair, 1990-92; mem. jud. nominating com. 4th Dist. Ct. Appeals, West Palm Beach, 1990-94, vice-chair, 1990-92, chair, 1993-94; lectr. in field. Contbr. articles to profl. jours. V.p., bd. dirs. Ctr. for Children in Crisis, West Palm Beach, 1994—; bd. dirs. Legal Aid Soc., Palm Beach County, Fla., 1994—; co-chair fundraiser Legal Aid Soc., Palm Beach County, 1996, 97, Healthy Mothers/Healthy Babies, Palm Beach County, 1994. Recipient Appellate Law award Palm Beach County Legal Aid Soc., 1991, Pres.'s Pro Bono Svc. award Fla. Bar, 1993; named one of 11 Who Shape the Law, Daily Bus. Rev., South Fla., 1997. Mem. ABA, ATLA, Nat. Assn. Women Lawyers, Acad. Fla. Trial Lawyers (bd. dirs. appellate sect.), Fla. Assn. Women Lawyers, Palm Beach County Bar Assn. (chairperson appellate ct. adv. com. 1983-95). Appellate. Office: 501 S Flagler Dr Ste 503 West Palm Beach FL 33401-5913

**KREUTZER, FRANKLIN DAVID,** lawyer; b. Miami, Fla., June 5, 1940; s. Ernst and Elsa (Meitner) K.; m. Judith Sue Jacobs, June 16, 1963; children: Renee Charlotte Kreutzer-Mussman, Jay Ernst. BBA, U. Miami, 1960, JD, 1964. Bar: Fla. 1964, U.S. Dist. Ct. (so. dist.) Fla. 1965, U.S. Ct. Appeals (5th cir.) 1971, U.S. Ct. Appeals (11th cir.) 1982, U.S. Supreme Ct. 1971. Assoc., Shevin, Goodman & Holtzman, 1964-65; ptnr. Wallace & Kreutzer, P.A., 1966-74; pvt. practice, Miami, 1974—; participant White House Seminar on Legal Interns, 1963; spl. asst. atty. gen. State of Fla., 1975-78; spl. counsel to comptroller State of Fla., 1975-78; gen. counsel Democratic Exec. Com. Dade County, 1968-70. Mem. City of Miami Pension & Retirement Bd., 1966-68; chmn. Miami Charter Rev. Bd., 1967-81; mem. Dade County Charter Rev. Commn., 1981-82; spl. master, guardian and atty. ad litem, Cir. Ct., Dade county, 1980—; gen. counsel, clk. of cir. and county cts. Dade County, Fla., 1990—; gen. counsel, clk. of Dade County Met. Commn., 1990—; pres. Greater Miami Hebrew Fla. Loan Assn., 1974-77; pres. Temple Zion, 1977-79, 93—; mem. law commn. Conservative Movement of Judaism, 1989—; mem. law com. Conservative Movement of Judaism, 1989—; regional pres. S.E. region United Synagogue Am., 1980-84, v.p., 1983-85, chmn. council regional presidents, 1983-85; internat. pres. United Synagogue of Conservative Movement, 1985—; internat. v.p. World Coun. of Synagogues, 1985—; internat. v.p., exec. com., bd. dirs. Mercaz Conservative Zionism, 1984—; bd. dirs. Jewish Theol. Sem. of Am., 1985—; exec. com. Synagogue Council of Am., 1985—; mem. exec. com. Am. Israel Pub. Affairs , 1985—; mem. Nat. Jewish Community Rels. Adv. Coun.; mem. Conf. of Pres. of Major Am. Jewish Orgns., 1985—; bd. dirs. Gen. Coun. World Zionist Orgn., 1985—; hon. chmn. bd. dirs. Jewish Nat. Fund, 1989—; pres. South Fla. chpt. Cystic Fibrosis Found., 1970-74; endowment com. U. Miami, 1974—; pres. Fla. Friends of Bar Ilan U., Israel, 1990—; regional pres. Am. Zionist Movement, So. Fla., 1993—. Recipient cert. of appreciation City of Miami, 1968; named to Order Golden Donkey, Dem. Exec. Com. Dade County, 1970. Mem. ABA, Fla. Bar Assn., Fla. Trial Lawyers Assn., Fla. Friends of Bar Ilan (Israel) U. (pres. 1990—), Am. Zionist Movement (pres. Fla. region, mem. nat. bd.), Dade County Trial Lawyers Assn., Dade County Bar Assn., Acad. Trial Lawyers Am., Omicron Delta Kappa, Phi Delta Phi. Democrat. State civil litigation, Insurance, Probate. Home: 3041 NW 7th St Ste 100 Miami FL 33125-4216 Office: 3041 NW 7th St Ste 100 Miami FL 33125-4216 also: Temple Zion Israelite Ctr 8000 Miller Dr Miami FL 33155-4349

**KRIEGER, PAUL EDWARD,** lawyer; b. Fairmont, W.Va., Mar. 30, 1942; s. Paul Julius Krieger and Martha Frances (Graham) Ralph; m. Elizabeth N. Krieger, July 2, 1965; children: Andrew, Thomas. BS in Mining Engring., U. Pitts., 1964; postgrad. Pa. State U., 1964-65; LLB, U. Md., 1968; LLM, George Washington U., 1971. Bar: Md. 1968, D.C. 1973, Tex. 1979, U.S. Patent and Trademark Office, 1970. Faculty research asst. U. Md., 1967-70; assoc. Brumbaugh, Graves, Donohue & Raymond, N.Y.C., 1970-71; ptnr. Lane, Aitken, Dunner & Ziems, Washington, 1971-78; sr. pat. atty. Dresser Industries Inc., Dallas, 1978-79; ptnr. Pravel, Hewitt, Kimball & Krieger, Houston, 1979-98, Fulbright & Jaworski, Houston, 1998—; adj. prof. U. Houston Law Ctr., 1985—. Mem. ABA, Am. Bar Found., Am. Pat. Law Assn., Tex. Bar Found., Tex. Bar Assn., Houston Bar Found., Houston Pat. Law Assn., U.S. Trademark Assn., Lic. Exec. Soc. Patent, Trademark and copyright, Federal civil litigation. Home: 11 Sandalwood Dr Houston TX 77024-7122 Office: Fulbright & Jaworski 1301 Mckinney St Ste 5100 Houston TX 77010-3031

**KRIEGER, SANFORD,** lawyer; b. N.Y.C., Nov. 4, 1943; s. Harry and Ruth Krieger; m. Carol B. Bachenheimer, Aug. 19, 1967; 1 child, Paul Matthew. BA cum laude, Cornell U., 1965; JD cum laude, Harvard U., 1968. Bar: N.Y., U.S. Supreme Ct., U.S. Dist. Ct. (so. dist.) N.Y. Legal adviser to Ethiopian Govt., 1968-70; assoc. Simpson Thacher & Bartlett, N.Y.C., 1970-73; assoc. Fried Frank Harris Shriver & Jacobson, London, 1973-75, ptnr., N.Y.C., 1977—; dir. corps. Mem. ABA, Assn. Bar City of N.Y. General corporate, Securities, Entertainment. Office: Fried Frank Harris Shriver & Jacobson 1 New York Plz Fl 22 New York NY 10004-1980

**KRIEGSMAN, EDWARD MICHAEL,** lawyer; b. Bridgeport, Conn., Oct. 29, 1965; s. Irving Martin and Marlene Sonya (Kates) K.; m. Meryl Gail Dennis, June 11, 1989; children: Barry Alan, David Jacob, Rachel Lynn. BS in Biology, MIT, 1986; JD, U. Pa., 1989. Bar: Pa. 1989, U.S. Patent and Trademark Office 1989, Mass. 1990, U.S. Ct. Appeals (Fed. cir.) 1990, U.S. Dist. Ct. Mass. 1992. Assoc. Finnegan, Henderson, Farabow, et al, Washington, 1989-90; ptnr. Kriegsman & Kriegsman, Framingham, Mass., 1990—. Mem. ABA, Am. Intellectual Property Law Assn., Mass. Bar Assn., Fed. Cir. Bar Assn., Boston Patent Law Assn., South Middlesex Bar Assn. Jewish. Avocations: reading, sports. Patent, Trademark and copyright. Home: 103 Richard Rd Holliston MA 01746-1213 Office: Kriegsman & Kriegsman 883 Edgell Rd Framingham MA 01701-3978

**KRIESBERG, SIMEON M.,** lawyer; b. Washington, June 4, 1951; s. Martin and Harriet M. K.; m. Martha L. Kahn, Jan. 9, 1994. AB, Harvard U., 1973; M in Pub. Affairs, Princeton U., 1977; JD, Yale U., 1977. Bar: D.C. 1977, U.S. Dist. Ct. D.C. 1978, U.S. Ct. Appeals (D.C. cir.) 1978, U.S. Ct. Internat. Trade 1979, U.S. Ct. Appeals (Fed. cir.) 1981, U.S. Supreme Ct. 1982. Assoc. Leva, Hawes, Symington, Martin & Oppenheimer, Washington, 1977-83; sr. counsel internat. trade Sears World Trade Inc., Washington, 1983-85, v.p., gen. counsel, 1985-87; ptnr. Mayer Brown & Platt, Washington, 1987—; professorial lectr. Nitze Sch. Advanced Internat. Studies, Johns Hopkins U., 1991-93; mem. binat. dispute resolution panel under U.S.-Can. Free Trade Agreement, 1990-92; guest scholar Brookings Inst., 1992-93; mem. roster of dispute resolution panelists under NAFTA, 1996—. Mem. editorial adv. com. Internat. Legal Materials, 1991-97; article and book rev. editor Yale Law Jour., 1976-77. Officer or dir. Washington Hebrew Congregation, 1980-94, Jewish Cmty. Coun. Greater Washington, 1986-94, Interfaith Conf. of Met. Washington, 1989—, D.C. Jewish Cmty. Ctr., 1994—, Mid-Atlantic coun. Union Am. Hebrew Congregations, 1994—. Recipient Pro Bono Svc. award Internat. Human Rights Law Group, 1991, Lawrence L. O'Connor medal Sears, Roebuck and Co., 1984. Mem. ABA, Am. Law Inst., Am. Soc. Internat. Law, D.C. Bar. Private international, Administrative and regulatory, Public international. Office: Mayer Brown & Platt 1909 K St NW Washington DC 20006-1101

**KRIKORIAN, VAN Z.,** lawyer; b. Framingham, Mass., Feb. 7, 1960; s. George O. and Agnes A. (Kalousdian) K.; m. Priscilla A. Dodakian, June 1, 1985; children: Ani, Sarah, Lena, George. BA in Internat. Affairs, George Washington U., 1981; JD, Georgetown U., 1984. Bar: Vt. 1985, D.C. 1986, U.S. Tax Ct. 1987, N.Y. 1994, U.S. Ct. Internat. Trade 1996. Law clk. Hon. Jerome Niedermeier U.S. Dist. Ct., civlington, Vt., 1984-85; assoc. Gravel & Shea, Burlington, Vt., 1985-88; dir. govt. and legal affairs Armenian Assembly Am., Washington, 1988-92; counsellor, dep. rep. to UN Rep. of Armenia, N.Y.C., 1992; counsel Patterson, Belknap, Webb & Tyler, LLP, N.Y.C., 1993-98; ptnr. Vedder, Price, Kaufman & Kammhol, 1998—; adj. prof. comml. law St. Michael's Coll., Winooski, Vt., 1987-88. Contbr. more than 20 articles to profl. jours. Ofcl. U.S. del. to Moscow Conf. on Security and Cooperation in Europe, 1991; vice chair fin. com. Dole for Pres., Washington, 1995. Mem. ABA, Assn. of the Bar of the City of N.Y., D.C. Bar Assn., Vt. Bar Assn., U.S.-Armenian Bus. Coun. (chmn. 1996—), Armenian Assembly Am. (trustee, chmn. bd. dirs. 1998—). Private international, Public international. Office: Vedder Price Kaufman & Kammholz 805 3rd Ave New York NY 10022-7513

**KRINSLY, STUART Z.,** lawyer, manufacturing company executive; b. N.Y.C., May 19, 1917; m. Charlotte Wolf, Aug. 18, 1944; children: EllinJane, Joan Susan. BA, Princeton U., 1938; LLB, Harvard U., 1941. Bar: N.Y. 1941. Asst. U.S. atty. So. Dist. N.Y., 1942-45; mem. firm Schlesinger & Krinsly, 1945-57; sec. Sun Chem. Corp., N.Y.C., 1957-65, v.p., gen. counsel, 1965-76, sr. v.p., gen. counsel, 1976-78, exec. v.p., gen. counsel, 1978-82, also bd. dirs.; sr. exec. v.p., gen. counsel Sequa Corp., N.Y.C., 1982—; also bd. dirs.; bd. dirs. Chock Full O'Nuts Corp. Mem. Beach Point Club, Princeton Club N.Y. General corporate. Home: 1135 Greacen Point Rd Mamaroneck NY 10543-4612 Office: Sequa Corp 200 Park Ave Fl 44 New York NY 10166-0005

**KRISLOV, MARVIN,** lawyer; b. Balt., Aug. 24, 1960; s. Joseph and Evelyn (Moreida) K.; m. Amy Ruth Sheon, Aug. 25, 1993; children: Zachary Jacob, Jesse Harris. BA in Econs. summa cum laude, Yale U., 1982; BA/MA in Modern History, Oxford (Eng.) U., 1985; JD, Yale U., 1988. Bar: Calif. 1988, D.C. 1989, Mich. 1999. Law clk., Judge M.H. Patel U.S. Dist. Ct. (no. dist.) Calif., San Francisco, 1988-89; trial atty. U.S. Dept. Justice, Civil Rights Divsn., Washington, 1989-93; spl. asst. U.S. atty. U.S. Atty.'s Office, Washington, 1989-90; spl. counsel Office of Counsel to the Pres., Washington, 1993-94, asst. counsel, 1994, assoc. counsel, 1995-96; dep. solicitor U.S. Dept. Labor, Washington, 1996-98, acting solicitor, 1997-98; v.p., gen. counsel U. Mich., Ann Arbor, 1998—; adj. prof. law, George Washington U. Law Sch., Washington, 1991-93. Alderman, New Haven Bd. Aldermen, 1982-83. Rhodes scholar, 1983. Phi Beta Kappa. Office: U Mich 4010 Fleming Adminstrn Bldg Ann Arbor MI 48109-1340

**KRISTENSEN, DEBORA KATHLEEN,** lawyer; b. Bellevue, Pa., Aug. 17, 1965; d. Robert Alan and Kathleen Mary Dimino; m. Ronald Mark Kristensen, Mar. 16, 1991; 1 child, Andrew Daniel. BA in psychology, U. Calif., Berkeley, 1987; JD, Santa Clara U., 1990. Bar: Calif. 1990, Wash. 1991, Idaho 1996, U.S. Dist. Ct. (no. dist.) Calif. 1990, U.S. Dist. Ct. (we. dist.) Wash. 1991, U.S. Dist. Ct. (ea. dist.) Wash. 1992, U.S. Dist. Ct. (ctrl. dist.) Calif. 1993, U.S. Dist. Ct. Idaho 1996. Law clk. Santa Clara County Dist. Atty.'s Office, San Jose, Calif., 1989; assoc. Davis Wright Tremaine LLP, Seattle, 1990-96; ptnr. Davis Wright Tremaine LLP, Boise, 1997-98, ptnr.-in-charge, 1998—; legal svcs. coord. Downtown Emergency Svcs. Ctr., Seattle, 1992-96; founding mem. Idaho Supreme Ct. media/cts. com., 1998-99. Author: LDRC 50-State Survey on Employment Libel Law, 1998-99, LDRC 50-State Survey on Employment Privacy Law, 1998-99. Vol. atty. King County Guardian Ad Litem Program, Seattle, 1990-96; 1st Amendment lobbyist, Idaho Press Club, Boise, 1996—; chair planning com., Leadership Boise, 1998-99; co-chair Winner's Choice Gala Dinner/Auction, Bishop Kelly Found., Boise, 1998. Mem. Idaho State Bar (pub. info. com. 1998—), Idaho Women Lawyers, Inc. (bd. mem. 1996—), Women and Children's Alliance (Tribute to Women & Industry award 1998), Idaho Newspaper Found. (selection com. for Max Dalton Open Govt. award 1998—), New Girls' Network, Idaho State Broadcasters Assn. (assoc. bd. mem. 1998—), City Club of Boise, Boise Area C. of C. Avocations: volleyball, swimming, water and snow skiing, travel. General civil litigation, Constitutional, Libel. Office: Davis Wright Tremaine LLP 877 W Main St Ste 604 Boise ID 83702-5858

**KRISTOL, DANIEL MARVIN,** lawyer; b. July 7, 1936; s. Abraham Louis and Pearl Cecile (Oltman) K.; m. Katherine Fairfax Chinn, Nov. 4, 1968; children: Sarah Douglas, Susan Fairfax. BA, U. Pa., 1958, LLB, 1961. Bar: Del. 1961, U.S. Dist. Ct. Del. 1962. Assoc., ptnr. Killoran & VanBrunt, Wilmington, Del., 1961-76; dir. Prickett, Jones, Elliott & Kristol, Wilmington, 1976—; ptnr. predecessor Prickett, Ward Burt & Sanders, Wilmington, 1976—; pub. defender Ct. Common Pleas, Wilmington, 1966-69; asst. solicitor City of Wilmington, 1970-73; spl. counsel Div. Housing State of Del., 1972-87, gen. counsel Del. State Housing Authority, 1973—. With USAR, 1964-67. Mem. ABA, Del. State Bar Assn. (chmn. real and personal property com. 1974-78, chmn. world peace through law com. 1980-81), Am. Coll. Real Estate Lawyers, Wilmington Country Club, Greenville Country Club, Mill Reef Club (Antigua, W.I.), Wilmington Club. Republican. Jewish. Contracts commercial, Landlord-tenant, Real property. Office: PO Box 1328 Wilmington DE 19899-1328

**KRITCHEVSKY, BARBARA ANN,** law educator; b. Teaneck, N.J., Feb. 8, 1955; d. David and Evelyn (Sholtes) K. BA, Middlebury Coll., 1977; JD, Harvard U., 1980. Bar: Pa. 1980, U.S. Dist. Ct. (ea. dist.) Pa. 1980, U.S. Ct. Appeals (6th cir.) 1992. Assoc. Drinker Biddle & Reath, Phila., 1980-83; prof. U. Memphis, 1983—. Mem. Phi Beta Kappa. Office: U Memphis 3715 Central Ave Memphis TN 38152-0001

**KRITSELIS, WILLIAM NICHOLAS,** lawyer; b. Sault Sainte Marie, Mich., Apr. 5, 1931; s. Nicholas William and Theodora G. (Gianacopoulos) K.; m. Elaine John Jennings, Sept. 1, 1963; 1 child, Nicholas William. BA, Mich. State U., 1959; JD, Ohio No. U., 1962. Bar: Mich. 1962, U.S. Dist. Ct. (we. dist.) Mich. 1963, U.S. Supreme Ct. 1966, U.S. Dist. Ct. (ea. dist.) Mich. 1968. Asst. prosecutor Ingham County, Lansing, Mich., 1963-64, chief criminal div., 1964-65; sole practice Lansing, 1965—. Pres. Holy Trinity Greek Orthodox Ch., Lansing, 1977; lifetime mem. NAACP, Lansing. Served with USN, 1951-55. Recipient Outstanding Atty. of Yr. award Ingham County Bar Assn., 1992. Fellow State Bar Mich. Found; mem. ABA, Fed. Bar Assn., Mich. Bar Assn. (med.-legal com. 1978-81, negligence com. 1982-85), Assn. Trial Lawyers Am. (lectr. product liability), Mich. Trial Lawyers Assn. (lectr. on construction, R.R. and product liabilty, bd. govs. 1978—), Lansing Trial Lawyers Assn. (pres. 1966-70), Am. Judicature Soc., Lawyers for Pub. Justice, Am. Arbitration Assn., Mich. State Alumni Assn., Mich. State U. Pres. Club. (East Lansing). Fax: 517-372-1031. Personal injury, Insurance, Federal civil litigation. Office: 2827 E Saginaw St Lansing MI 48912-4239

**KRITZER, GLENN BRUCE,** lawyer; b. Newark, June 13, 1947; s. Julius B. and Ethyl (Rosenthal) K.; m. Gisela Musa, Nov. 20, 1983; children: Rebecca, Gary. Student, Lehigh U., 1965-67; BA with distinction, U. Wis., 1969; JD, NYU, 1972. Bar: N.Y. 1973, U.S. Dist. Ct. (so. dist.) N.Y. 1974, U.S. Dist. Ct. (ea. dist.) N.Y. 1975, U.S. Ct. Appeals (2d cir.) 1975, Calif. 1977, Fla. 1980, U.S. Ct. Appeals (5th cir.) 1980, U.S. Dist. Ct. (so. dist.) Fla. 1981, U.S. Ct. Appeals (11th cir.) 1981, U.S. Dist. Ct. (trial bar) Fla. 1982, U.S. Supreme Ct. 1985, U.S. Dist. Ct. (ea. dist.) Wis. 1985, U.S. Ct. Appeals (7th cir.) 1986, U.S. Dist. Ct. (mid. dist.) Fla. 1990. Examining atty. N.Y.C. Dept. Investigation, 1972-73, dep. dir. bur. city marshals, 1973-74, dir. bur. city marshals, 1974-76, spl. asst. dist. atty., 1975, spl. asst. corp. counsel, 1976; assoc. Herzfeld & Rubin P.C., N.Y.C., 1976-77; asst. U.S. atty. Office of U.S. Atty. (ea. dist.) N.Y., 1977-79, Office of U.S. Atty. (so. dist.) Fla., 1979-82; pvt. practice Miami, 1982—. Mem. Nat. Assn. Criminal Def. Lawyers, Fla. Assn. Criminal Def. Lawyers (bd. dirs. Miami chpt.), Fed. Bar Assn., Asst. U.S. Attys. Assn., Dade County Bar Assn. Criminal, Insurance, Personal injury. Office: 799 Brickell Plz Ste 700 Miami FL 33131-2805

**KRITZER, PAUL ERIC,** media executive, communications lawyer; b. Buffalo, May 5, 1942; s. James Cyril and Bessie May (Biddlecombe) K.; m. Frances Jean McCallum, June 20, 1970; children: Caroline Frances, Erica Hopkins. BA, Williams Coll., 1964; MS in Journalism, Columbia U., 1965; JD, Georgetown U., 1972. Bar: U.S. Supreme Ct. 1978, Wis. 1980. Reporter, copy editor Buffalo Evening News, 1964, 69, 70; instr. English Augusta (Ga.) Coll., 1968-69; law clk. Office of FCC Commr., Washington, 1971, MCI, Washington, 1972; counsel U.S. Ho. of Reps., Washington, 1972-77; assoc. counsel Des Moines Register & Tribune, 1977-80; editor, pub. Waukesha (Wis.) Freeman, 1980-83; legal v.p., sec. Jour. Communications Inc., Milw., 1983—; bd. dirs. Jour. Communications, Inc., Milw. Trustee Carroll Co., Waukesha, 1981-89; producer Waukesha Film Festival, 1982; bd. dirs. Des Moines Metro Opera, Inc., 1979-80; bd. dirs. Milw. Youth Symphony Orch., 1992—, pres. 1994-97; bd. dirs. Milw. Symphony Orch., 1997—; bd. dirs. United Performing Arts Fund, 1994-97. With U.S. Army, 1965-68. Presbyterian. Avocations: bridge, gardening. Home: 211 Oxford Rd Waukesha WI 53186-6263 Office: Jour Communications Inc 333 W State St PO Box 661 Milwaukee WI 53201-0661

**KRIVICICH, JOHN AUGUSTINE,** lawyer; b. Chgo., Feb. 28, 1955; s. Anthony and Andirana K.; m. Ilona Mae Berry, July 28, 1984; children: James, Peter, Laura. BS in Journalism, Northwestern U., 1976; JD cum laude, U. Ill., 1980. Bar: Ill. 1980, U.S. Dist. Ct. (no. dist.) Ill. 1980, U.S. Ct. Appeals (7th cir.) 1981, U.S. Dist. Ct. (ctrl. dist.) Ill. 1993. Assoc. Reuben & Proctor, Chgo., 1980-84; assoc. Baker & McKenzie, Chgo., 1985-93, ptnr., 1993-96; ptnr. Donohue, Brown, Mathewson & Smyth, Chgo., 1996—. Firefighter Western Springs (Ill.) Dept. Fire and EMS, 1994-96; mem. bd. appeals Zoning Bd. Western Springs, 1996—. Mem. ABA, Def. Rsch. Inst., Ill. Bar Assn. Product liability, General civil litigation, Alternative dispute resolution. Office: Donohue Brown Mathewson & Smyth 140 S Dearborn St Chicago IL 60603-5202

**KRIVOSHIA, ELI, JR.,** lawyer; b. Midland, Pa., Apr. 20, 1935. BA, U. Pitts., 1957; LLB, Harvard U., 1960. Bar: 1961. Assoc., Thorp, Reed & Armstrong, Pitts., 1960-69, ptnr., 1970-83; gen. Counsel Nat. Steel Corp., 1983-95, pvt. practice, Pitts., 1995—. Mem. Allegheny County Bar Assn., ABA, Pa. Bar Assn. Antitrust, Contracts commercial, General corporate.

**KRIVOY, CLARA,** lawyer; b. Caracas, Venezuela, Sept. 26, 1969; came to U.S., 1992; d. Saul and Ruth Krivoy; m. Daniel Grunberg, Feb. 27, 1996. JD, U. Catolica Andres Bello, Caracas, 1992; M Comparative Jurisprudence, NYU, 1993, LLM in Trade Regulation, 1994. Law clk. Superior Civil, Comml. and Adminstrv. Ct., Caracas, 1991-92; internat. assoc. Cleary Gottlieb Steen & Hamilton, N.Y.C., 1994-95; assoc. Robinson Silverman Pearce Aronsohn & Berman LLP, N.Y.C., 1996—; point person for liaison UN Coun. on Internat. Affairs, 1997—. Mem. Assn. Bar City N.Y. (com. fgn. and comparative law 1996—), N.Y. State Bar Assn., Am. Fgn. Law Assn. Private international, General corporate, Banking. Office: Robinson Silverman et al Ste 572 1290 Avenue Of The Americas Fl 33 New York NY 10104-3300

**KROCK, KENNETH MICHAEL,** lawyer; b. Houston, July 21, 1971. BBA in Mgmt., Tex. A&M U., 1993; JD, U. Houston, 1996. Bar: Tex. 1996, U.S. Dist. Ct. (so. dist.) Tex. 1996, U.S. Ct. Appeals (5th cir.) 1997, D.C. 1999. Assoc. Nelkin & Nelkin, Houston, 1996—. Mem. ABA, State Bar Tex., D.C. Bar, Phi Delta Phi. General civil litigation, Civil rights, Labor. Office: Nelkin & Nelkin PC 5417 Chaucer Dr Houston TX 77005-2629

**KROCKER, JAN,** judge; b. Washington, May 10, 1949; d. Walter and Bonita Smith; m. Dan Krocker; two children. JB, U. Tex., 1971, JD, 1980. Bd. cert. in criminal law, 1993. News and media rels. specialist U. Tex., San Antonio, 1972-78; asst. dist. atty. Harris County Dist. Atty.'s Office, Houston, 1981-90; sole practice law Houston, 1990-94; judge 184th Dist. Ct., Houston, 1995—. Spkr. Crimestoppers Internat. Conf., 1993; vol. Timbergrove Nat. Baseball League, Stephens Ministry. Republican. Presbyn. Office: 184th Dist Ct 301 San Jacinto St Houston TX 77002-2022

**KROEMER, JOHN ALBERT,** lawyer; b. Macon, Ga., Nov. 13, 1943; s. Robert H. and Louise E. (Bode) K.; m. Sarah E. Borsch, June 23, 1979; 1 child, Laura Beth. B in Indsl. Engring., Ga. Inst. Tech., 1966; JD, U. Conn., 1970. Bar: Conn. 1970, Tex. 1979, U.S. Dist. Ct. (no., so., ea. and we. dists.) Tex. 1980, U.S. Ct. Appeals (5th, 9th, 11th and 4th cirs.) 1980, U.S. Supreme Ct. 1980, Ga. 1981. Trial atty. Antitrust Divsn. U.S. Dept. Justice, Atlanta and Dallas, 1970-79; ptnr. Vetter, Bates, Tibbals, Lee & DeBusk, Dallas, 1980-85, Matthews, Kroemer & Johnson, Dallas, 1985-88, Maloney & Smith, Dallas, 1989-95; with Hill & Metzger, Dallas, 1996-97; mem. Prager, Metzger & Kroemer, PLLC, Dallas, 1998—. Fellow Tex. Bar Found.; mem. Tex. Bar Assn., Dallas Bar Assn. Republican. Methodist. General civil litigation, Antitrust. Office: Prager Metzer & Kroemer PLLC 2626 Cole Ave Ste 900 Dallas TX 75204-4033

**KROENER, WILLIAM FREDERICK, III,** lawyer; b. N.Y.C., Aug. 27, 1945; s. William Frederick Jr. and Barbara (Mitchell) K.; m. Evelyn Somerville Bibb, Sept. 3, 1966; children: William F. IV (dec.), Mary Elizabeth, Evangeline Alberta, James Mitchell. AB, Yale Coll., 1967; JD, Stanford U., 1971, MBA, 1971. Bar: Calif. 1972, N.Y. 1979, D.C. 1983. Assoc. Davis Polk & Wardwell, N.Y.C. and London, 1971-79, ptnr., N.Y.C., 1979-82, Washington and N.Y.C., 1982-94; gen. counsel Fed. Deposit Ins. Corp., Washington, 1995—; lectr. law sch. Stanford (Calif.) U., 1993-94, George Washington U. Law Sch., Washington, 1994—, Washington Coll. Law, Am. U. Law Sch., Washington, 1996—. Mng. editor Stanford Law Rev., 1970-71. Mem. governing bd. St. Albans Sch., 1991-95; mem. finance com. Protestant/Episcopal Cathedral Found. (Wash. Nat. Cathedral), 1992-95; mem. bd. visitors Stanford U. Law Sch., 1983-92, mem. dean's adv. coun., 1992-93, nat. chair Stanford Law Fund, 1990-92; dir. and gen. counsel Kenwood Citizens Assn., Inc., 1993-94. Mem. ABA, Am. Law Inst., Assn. of Bar of City of N.Y., N.Y. Law Inst., Yale Club, Kenwood Golf Club. Republican. Episcopalian. Home: 6412 Brookside Dr Chevy Chase MD 20815-6649 Office: FDIC 550 17th St NW Washington DC 20429-0001

**KROGH, HARLAN B.,** lawyer, shareholder; b. Yreka, Calif., May 29, 1960; m. Mary Beth Krogh; 1 child, Josh. BS in Bus., Mont. State U., 1982; JD, Gonzaga U., 1987. Bar: Mont. 1987, U.S. Dist. Ct. Mont. 1987, 9th Cir. Ct. Appeals, 1994. Law clk., Judge James F. Battin U.S. Dist. Ct., Billings, Mont., 1987-89; shareholder Moulton, Bellingham, Longo & Mather, Billings, Mont., 1989—. Bd. trustees Dist. 2 Sch. Bd., Billings, 1995-98; bd. mem. Cmty. Crime Control, Billings, 1991-94; mem. ch. coun. Luth. Ch. Good Shepherd, Billings, 1993-96; pres., mem. bd. Big Sky State Games, 1995—; mem. bd., pres., Centennial Yount Found., 1996—; pres. Midland Roundtable, 1994-95. Recipient Disting. Alumni award Mont. State U., 1996. Mem. Mont. State Bar Assn. Avocations: golfing, skiing, coaching youth sports. General civil litigation, Personal injury, Sports. Office: Moulton Bellingham Longo & Mather 27 N 27th St Ste 1900 Billings MT 59101-2343

**KROGH, RICHARD ALAN,** lawyer; b. Des Moines, Mar. 30, 1949; s. Harold Christian and Bess Alberta (Cummins) K.; m. Christina Lynn Hayes, Sept. 4, 1976; children: Michael Steven, Douglas Alan. BA in Geography, U. Kans., 1973; JD, Washburn U., 1987. Bar: Kans. 1987, U.S. Dist. Ct. Kans. 1987. Commd. 2d lt. USMC, 1973, advanced through grades to capt., 1978; assignments in inf., communications and logistics USMC, Vietnam, 1968-69; resigned USMC, 1981; with claims dept. St. Paul Fire & Marine Ins. Co., Overland Park, Kans., 1982-84; assoc. Law Offices George L. Catt, Lawrence, Kans., 1987-89; pvt. practice Lawrence, 1989—; child support enforcement atty. Kans. Dept. Social and Rehab. Svcs., Ottawa, 1987—. Cubmaster, counselor law explorer post, counselor Pelathe dist. Heart of Am. coun. Boy Scouts Am., 1985-89. Decorated Air medal with two oak leaf clusters. Mem. ABA, Kans. Bar Assn., Douglas County Bar Assn., Kans. Trial Lawyers Assn., Order of Arrow, Lions Club. Republican. Lutheran. Avocation: antique collecting and restoring. Criminal, Personal injury, General civil litigation. Home: 2405 Sequoia Ct Lawrence KS 66047-2642 Office: 700 Massachusetts St Ste 306 Lawrence KS 66044-6604

**KROHN, GARY JOHN,** lawyer; b. Seattle, Oct. 8, 1958; s. Rolland G. and Helen M. (Willman) K.; m. Stacie E. Hearst, Sept. 4, 1993; 1 child, Garrison. BBA, U. Wash., 1982, JD, 1985. Bar: Wash. 1995, U.S. Dist. Ct. (we. dist.) Wash. 1986, U.S. Tax Ct. 1987, U.S. Ct. Appeals (9th cir.) 1989. Rule 9 intern Driano & Sorenson, Seattle, 1984-85; assoc. Treece, Richdale, Malone, Corning & Abbott, P.S., Seattle, 1985-93, ptnr., 1993—. Contbr. articles to profl. jours. Mem. Order of Barristers. Real property, Contracts commercial, General civil litigation. Office: Treece Richdale 1718 NW 56th St Seattle WA 98107-5227

**KROLL, ARTHUR HERBERT,** lawyer, educator, consultant; b. N.Y.C., Dec. 2, 1939; s. Abraham and Sylvia Kroll; m. Lois Handmacher, June, 1964; children: Douglas, Pamela. BA, Cornell U., 1961; LLB cum laude, St. John's U., 1965; LLM in Taxation, NYU, 1969. Bar: D.C. Assoc. Patterson, Belknap, Webb & Tyler, N.Y.C., 1965-72, ptnr., 1972-1990; ptnr. Pryor, Cashman, Sherman & Flynn, N.Y.C., 1990-95; CEO KST Consulting Group, Inc.; adj. prof. U. Miami Sch. Law, NYU; lectr. numerous confs.; mem. adv. bd. Bur. Nat. Affairs Tax Mgmt., Inc., Practising Law Inst. Tax Adv. Bd., U. Miami Inst. Estate Planning, Bus. Laws, Inc.; mem. adv. com. NYU Ann. Inst. on Fed. Taxation. Author Executive Compensation, 3 vols., Compensating Executives; monthly newsletter Family Bus. Profl.; mem. bd. contbg. editors and advisers Corporate Taxation; mem. editl. adv. bd. Jour. Compensation and Benefits. Mem. ABA (subcom. exec. compensation), Am. Pension Conf. (mem. steering com.). Pension, profit-sharing, and employee benefits, Corporate taxation, Probate. Office: KST Consulting Group Inc 50 1/2 E 64th St New York NY 10021-7306

**KROLL, BARRY LEWIS,** lawyer; b. Chgo., June 8, 1934; s. Harry M. and Hannah (Lewis) K.; m. Jayna Vivian Leibovitz, June 20, 1956; children: Steven Lee, Joan Lois Kroll Dolgin, Nancy Maxine Kroll Richardson. A.B. in Psychology with distinction, U. Mich., 1955, J.D. with distinction, 1958. Bar: Ill. 1958. Since practiced in Chgo.; assoc. firm Jacobs & McKenna, 1958-66, Epstein, Manilow & Sachnoff, 1966-68, Schiff, Hardin, Waite Dorschel & Britton, 1968-69; partner firm Wolfberg & Kroll, 1970-74, Kirshbaum & Kroll, 1972-74; of counsel Jacobs, Williams & Montgomery, Ltd., 1973-74; partner Jacobs, Williams & Montgomery Ltd., 1974-85, Williams & Montgomery Ltd., 1985—; faculty John Marshall Law Sch., Chgo., 1969-73; atty. for petitioner in U.S. Supreme Ct. decision Escobedo vs Ill., 1964, guest lectr. before groups, 1964—; mem. legal and legis. com. Internat. Franchise Assn., 1976-80. Asst. editor: Mich. Law Rev, 1957-58. Chmn. Park Forest Bd. Zoning Appeals, 1971-78. Served to capt. AUS, 1959-62. Named Outstanding Young Man Park Forest Jr. C. of C., 1966. Mem. Ill. Bar Assn., Chgo. Bar Assn. (chmn. legis. com. 1974-75), Ill. Appellate Lawyers Assn. (treas. 1978-79, sec. 1979-80, pres. 1981-82), Bar Assn. 7th Fed. Circuit, Order of Coif, Tau Epsilon Rho, Alpha Epsilon Pi. Jewish (trustee congregation 1966-70, 72-75, 90—, pres. men's club 1965-66). State civil litigation, Insurance, Appellate. Home: 1440 N State Pky Chicago IL 60610-1564 Office: Williams & Montgomery 20 N Wacker Dr Chicago IL 60606-2806

**KROLL, JEFFREY JOSEPH,** lawyer; b. Chgo., Feb. 24, 1964; s. Lawrence Stanley and Bernadine Joanne (Jurek) K. BSc in Fin./Econs., DePaul U., 1987, JD, 1990. Bar: Ill., U.S. Dist. Ct. (no. dist.) Ill. Assoc. Robert A. Clifford & Assocs., Chgo., 1990—; adj. prof. law DePaul U., Chgo., 1992—; lectr. in field; participant symposium of the future civil jury system in the U.S., Charlottesville, Va., 1992; mem. Ill. Supreme Ct. subcom. on selection and adminstrn. on juries, 1993; mem. host com. 9th Ann. meeting, Am. Inns of Ct., 1993. Mem. Chgo. Inn of Ct., 1989—, Ravenswood Community Coun., Chgo., 1990. Mem. ABA (long range planning group on civil justice system improvements, 1993, litigation sect., tort and ins. policy sect., co-program dir. sect. litigation ann. meeting 1995, mem. pub. rels. com. sect. tort and ins. practice 1993—), ATLA (mem. exec. com. product liability sect. 1994), Ill. State Bar Assn. (chair admiralty and maritime sect. 1995—), Ill. Trial Lawyers Assn. (med. malpractice com. 1992-93, pub. com. 1992-93, bd. advocates, 1993-94, amicus curiae com. 1993—), Chgo. Bar Assn. (lectr. 1992, pub. affairs com. 1993—, mem. core group CBA/YLS health and hosp. law com. 1995—), DePaul Law Devel. Com., Southwest Bar Assn. Chgo. Personal injury, Product liability. Office: Clifford Law Offices PC 120 N La Salle St Fl 3100 Chicago IL 60602-2493

**KROLL, MARTIN N.,** lawyer; b. N.Y.C., Nov. 30, 1937; s. Jack and Ruth (Strassman) K.; m. Rita Evangeline Grossman, Aug. 14, 1965; children: Spencer, Jonathan, Evan. BA, Cornell U., 1959; JD, U. Pa., 1963. Sr. ptnr. Kroll, Levy, Baron & Feinstein, N.Y.C., 1972-80, Snow, Beeker, Kroll, Klaris & Kraus, N.Y.C., 1980-86, Kroll, Moss and Kroll, LLP, Garden City, N.Y., 1987—; reciever Chrysler Bldg., N.Y.C., 1975-77; village atty. Village of East Hills (N.Y.), 1988-95; counsel Town of North Hempstead, 1987—, counsel Econ. Devel. Agy. Town of North Hempstead, 1992—; pres. Jewish Lawyers Assn. of Nassau County, N.Y., 1980. Vice chmn. Nassau County Republican Party, Westbury, N.Y., 1986—. Recipient Torch of Liberty, B'Nai Brigh-ADL, 1982; named Master Builder Conf. of Jewish Educators, 1990. Mem. ABA, N.Y. State Bar Assn., Nassau County Bar Assn. Federal civil litigation, General civil litigation, Municipal (including bonds). Office: Kroll Moss & Kroll 400 Garden City Plz Garden City NY 11530-3322

**KROLL, MILTON PAUL,** lawyer; b. Paterson, N.J., Feb. 6, 1914; s. Samuel and Edna (Keller) K.; m. Beatrice Rappaport, Apr. 4, 1941; children: Stephen R., Barbara S. BA, W.Va. U., 1934; JD, Harvard U., 1937. Bar: D.C. 1938, N.J. 1938, D.C. 1948, U.S. Supreme Ct. 1973. Atty. SEC, Washington, 1940-48, asst. gen. counsel, 1948-52, assoc. gen. counsel, 1952-53; ptnr. Freedman, Levy, Kroll & Simonds, Washington, 1961—; lectr. George Washington U. Sch. Law., 1952-59; lectr. symposia in U.S., Brazil, China, Japan; cons. Am. Law Inst. fed. securities code project and corp. governance project; mem. legal adv. com. N.Y. Stock Exch., 1978—, chmn., 1992—. Mem. adv. bd. BNA Securities Regulation and Law Report; mem. editorial adv. bd. Insights; contbr. articles to profl. jours. Class agt. Harvard U. Law Sch. Fund, 1974-80. 1st lt. AUS, 1943-46, ETO. Decorated Bronze Star. Mem. ABA (mem. adv. com., mem. fed. regulation com.), D.C. Bar Assn., Am. Law Inst., Harvard Club, Phi Beta Kappa. Jewish. General corporate, Securities. Home: 3411 Woolsey Dr Bethesda MD 20815-3924 Office: Freedman Levy Kroll & Simonds 1050 Connecticut Ave NW Ste 825 Washington DC 20036-5366

**KROLL, SOL,** lawyer; b. Russia, Aug. 10, 1918; m. Ruth Saslow; children: Gerald, Judy, Elise, Elliott. LLB, St. John's U., 1942. Bar: N.Y. 1942, U.S. Supreme Ct. 1956. Former U.S. counsel to Assn. Francaise des Socs. D'Assurances Transports; former mem. com. of interfraud task force N.Y. Ins. Dept. *Mr. Kroll has been listed in Who's Who in Law, Who's Who in New York, and Who's Who in United States.* Contbr. articles on Am. ins. law to various ins. mags. Mem. ABA, Fed. Bar Assn., N.Y. State Bar Assn., Internat. Assn. Ins. Counsel, Industry Adv. Com. on Ins.; bd. govs. Internatl. Ins. Soc. Insurance. Home: 600 Cantitoe St Bedford NY 10506-1107 Office: 110 E 59th St New York NY 10022-1304

**KRONAU, KATHLEEN MARIE,** lawyer; b. Ames, Iowa, Aug. 11, 1954; m. Roger William Kronau, Oct. 7, 1989; children: Kathryn Michelle, Kimberly Marie. BS, BA, U. Del., 1976; MS, U. N.C., 1981; JD, Washington and Lee U., 1981. Bar: Va. 1981. Atty. Norfolk So. Corp., 1981-89; asst. city atty. City of Roanoke, Va., 1990-95; assoc. counsel Shenandoah Life Ins. Co., Roanoke, 1995-98, v.p., gen. counsel, sec., 1998—. Office: Shenandoah Life Ins Co 2301 Brambleton Ave SW Roanoke VA 24015-4701

**KRONE, NORMAN BERNARD,** commercial real estate developer, lawyer; b. Memphis, Sept. 13, 1938; s. Irving and Eva (Sauer) K.; m. Norma Lee Moon; children: John, Christine, David. LLB, Stetson U., 1964. Bar: Fla. 1964, U.S. Dist. Ct. (mid. dist.) Fla. 1965, U.S. Ct. Appeals (7th cir.) 1968. Atty. Lifsey & Johnston, Tampa, Fla., 1964-65; pvt. practice Tampa, Fla., 1965-66; property mgmt. atty. Ford Motor Co., Dearborn, Mich., 1966-67; audit mgr. Montgomery Ward & Co., Chgo., 1967-68, corp. real estate mgr., 1968-75; exec. v.p. Momtgomery Ward Properties Corp., Chgo., 1970-75; from v.p. to sr. v.p. Walgreen Co., Deerfield, Ill., 1975-85; pres., CEO The Hausman Cos., Cleve., 1987—; trustee Internat. Coun. Shopping Ctrs., N.Y.C., 1976-79; dir. Myers Industries, Lincoln, Ill., 1976-83; mem. adv. bd. Commerce Exch. Bank, Beachwood, Ohio, 1997—; instr. Intercoun. Shopping Ctrs.-Inst. Profl. Devel. Author, editor: The Lease and Its Language, 1996; contbr. articles to mags. Acting judge City of Tampa, 1964-66; bd. dirs. Met. Housing and Planning Coun., Chgo., 1977-80. Mem. Beachwood C. of C. (pres. 1996), Acacia Country Club (bd. dirs. 1997—). Avocations: flying, woodworking, golf. Home: 8650 Hunting Hill Dr Mentor OH 44060-7858 Office: The Hausman Cos 2101 Richmond Rd Beachwood OH 44122-1390

**KRONE, PAULA H.,** lawyer; b. N.Y.C., Dec. 11, 1953; d. Ben and Goldie (Glass) K. BA cum laude, SUNY, New Paltz, 1974; MS in Secondary Edn., SUNY, 1978; JD, Fordham U., 1992. Bar: N.J. 1992, N.Y. 1993, Ga. 1994. Tchr. Middletown (N.Y.) Pub. Sch., 1974-78; computer programmer IBM Corp., Pough Keepsie, N.Y., 1978-81; systems engr. IBM Corp., N.Y.C., 1981-82; systems programmer Merril Lynch & Co., N.Y.C., 1982-83; systems programming mgr. CBS, Inc., N.Y.C., 1983-85; cons., computer systems N.Y.C., 1985-87; tech. support mgr. Equitable Life, Leonia, N.J., 1987-93; pro bono atty. Legal Aid Soc. N.Y., N.Y.C., 1993; atty. Law Office Paula H. Krone, Atlanta, 1994—; adj. prof. John Marshall Law Sch., Atlanta, 1997; adj. paralegal instr. DeKalb Tech. Inst., Clarkston, Ga., 1994-96. Lay cantor The Temple, Atlanta, 1997. Mem. ABA, Atlanta Bar Assn. (tech. com. 1996-97), Lawyers Club Atlanta, State Bar Ga. (chair mgmt. info. sys. com. 1996-98). Jewish. Avocations: singing, tennis. Computer, Trademark and copyright, Intellectual property.

**KRONMAN, ANTHONY TOWNSEND,** law educator, dean; b. 1945; m. Nancy I. Greenberg, 1982. B.A., Williams Coll., 1968, Ph.D., 1972; J.D., Yale U., 1975. Bar: Minn. 1975, N.Y. 1983. Assoc. prof. U. Minn., 1975-76; asst. prof. U. Chgo., 1976-79; vis. assoc. prof. Yale U. Law Sch., New Haven, 1978-79, prof., 1979—, Edward J. Phelps prof. law, 1985—, dean, 1994—. Editor: (with R. Posner) The Economics of Contract Law, 1979 (with F. Kessler and G. Gilmore) Cases and Materials on Contracts, 1986; past mem. editorial bd. Yale Law Jour.; author: Max Weber, 1983, The Lost Lawyer, 1993. Danforth Found. fellow, 1968-72. Fellow ABA, Am. Acad. Arts and Scis.; mem. Selden Soc., Conn. Bar Assn. (Cooper fellow), Coun. on Fgn. Rels. Office: Yale U Law Sch PO Box 208215 New Haven CT 06520-8215

**KRONMAN, CAROL JANE,** lawyer; b. Passaic, N.J., Mar. 25, 1944; d. Robert M. and Helen (Harris) K.; children: Audrey Jane, Heather Sue. AB, Cornell U., 1965; MA, Columbia U., 1966; JD, Yeshiva U., 1980. Bar: N.Y. 1981, N.J. 1981, Fla. 1981, U.S. Dist. Ct. N.J. 1981, U.S. Dist. Ct. (so. dist.) N.Y. 1984, U.S. Supreme Ct. 1990, U.S. Dist. Ct. (ea. dist.) N.Y. 1991. Asst. prof. William Paterson Coll., Wayne, N.J., 1967-69; treas. Capital Theatre Inc., N.J., 1977-83; coord. paralegal studies Montclair State Coll., N.J., 1982-83, prof., 1982-85; ptnr. Kronman & Kronman P.A., Totowa, N.J., 1981-85; ptnr. N.J. office Max E. Greenberg, Cantor & Reiss, South

Hackensack, N.J., 1986-89; of counsel Budd, Larner, Gross, Rosenbaum, Greenberg & Sade, 1989-90; gen. counsel office of Mayor Office of Constrn. City of N.Y., 1991-94; lectr. N.J. Inst. for Continuing Legal Edn., 1987, Constrn. Failure and Disaster Super conf. Conf. Mgmt. Corp., N.Y.C., 1988; assoc. Hosp. Joint Diseases, N.Y.C. Author: Different Types of Contracts, 1987; pub. The Kronman Letter, Update for Insurance and Bond Providers, Producers and Users, 1995—; contbr. articles to profl. jours. Recipient Svc. award in engring. and industry Am. Orgn. Rehab. through Tng. Fedn., 1993, Svc. award in real estate and constrn., 1994, Spl. Recognition award Profl. Women in Constrn., 1993; noted for Spl. Presentation for Committment to Excellence in Rsch., Hosp. for Joint Diseases, N.Y. Hosp. Mem. Orgn. Rehab. through Tng. (bd. dirs. real estate and constrn. industry divsn., nat. bd. dirs., Svc. award), N.J. Bar Assn., N.Y. State Bar Assn., Fla. Bar Assn., Stern Coll. Profl. Women in Constrn. (bd. dirs.). Construction, Probate, State civil litigation. Home: 2 Sutton Pl S Apt 3A New York NY 10022-3070 Office: 1040 1st Ave Ste 124 New York NY 10022-2902

**KRONZEK, CHARLES MICHAEL,** lawyer; b. Pitts., Feb. 11, 1954; s. Morris and Shirley (Gorin) K.; divorced; children: Allison F., Jill L. BS, Geneva Coll., Pitts., 1991; JD, Mich. State U., 1994. Bar: Mich. 1995. Sr. ptnr. Kronzek & Cronkright PLLC, Lansing, Mich., 1994—. Family and matrimonial, Criminal, Personal injury. Home: 2034 Hamilton Rd Apt 204 Okemos MI 48864-2156 Office: 4601 W Saginaw Hwy Ste 100 Lansing MI 48917-2741

**KROTOSZYNSKI, RONALD JAMES, JR.,** law educator; b. Corpus Christi, Tex., Nov. 3, 1967; s. Ronald James and Barbara Carol (Jamison) K. BA, MA in Philosophy, Emory U., 1987; JD, LLM in Internat. and Comparative Law, Duke U., 1991. Bar: Ga. 1991, U.S. Ct. Appeals (11th cir.) 1991, U.S. Ct. Appeals (4th cir.). Law clk. to Judge Frank M. Johnson, Jr. Montgomery, Ala., 1991-91; assoc. Covington & Burling, Washington, 1992-95; asst. prof. law Ind. U., Indpls., 1995-99, Paul Bean Rsch. Fellow, assoc. prof., 1999—. Contbr. articles to law jours. Page Miss. del. Dem. Nat. Conv., 1984. Grimes fellow Ind. U.,1996-97. Mem. ABA (vice chmn. publs. com. adminstrv. law sect. 1996—). Roman Catholic. Avocations: hiking, theater, wine. Office: Ind U Sch Law 735 W New York St Indianapolis IN 46202-5222

**KROUSE, GEORGE RAYMOND, JR.,** lawyer; b. Atlantic City, Sept. 30, 1945; s. George R. and Viola (Rogers) K.; m. Susan Naylor, Aug. 7, 1967; children: Geoffrey, Alison. AB cum laude, Brown U., 1967; JD with distinction, Duke U., 1970. Bar: N.Y. 1971, U.S. Ct. Mil. Appeals 1971, U.S. Dist. Ct. (so. and ea. dists.) N.Y. 1975. Assoc. Simpson Thacher & Bartlett, N.Y.C., 1970-71, 75-78, ptnr., 1978—. Articles editor Duke Law Jour. Mem. bd. visitors Sch. Law, Duke U., Durham, N.C., 1986-92, chmn., 1997—; mem. nat. devel. coun. Duke U., 1994—. Capt. USAF, 1971-75. Recipient Air Force Commendation medal, 1973, Meritorius Svc. medal 1975. Mem. ABA, N.Y. State Bar Assn., Assn. of Bar of City of N.Y. (com. on corps. 1985-88, com. art law 1990-93), Order of Coif, Montclair Golf Club. Avocation: golf. Securities, Finance, General corporate. Home: 4 Erwin Park Montclair NJ 07042-3018 Office: Simpson Thacher & Bartlett 425 Lexington Ave Fl 15 New York NY 10017-3954

**KROVATIN, GERALD,** lawyer; b. 1952. BA, Columbia U., 1974; JD, Rutgers U., 1977. Bar: N.J. 1977. Ptnr. Arseneault & Krovatin, Chatham, N.J.; adj. faculty crim. trial seminar Rutgers Sch. Law, Newark, 1987-90. Mem. N.J. State Bar Assn., Assn. Criminal Def. Lawyers N.J. (trustee 1995-99). General civil litigation, Criminal. Office: Arseneault & Krovatin 560 Main St Chatham NJ 07928-2119

**KRSUL, JOHN ALOYSIUS, JR.,** lawyer; b. Highland Park, Mich., Mar. 24, 1938; s. John A. and Ann M. (Sepich) K.; m. Justine Oliver, Sept. 12, 1958; children: Ann Lisa, Mary Justine. BA, Albion Coll., 1959; JD, U. Mich., 1963. Bar: Mich. 1963. Assoc. Dickinson Wright PLLP, 1963-71; ptnr. Dickinson Wright PLLP, Detroit, 1971—. Asst. editor: U. Mich. Law Rev, 1962-63; editorial bd. ABA Jour., 1996—. Recipient Disting. Alumnus award Albion Coll., 1984; Sloan scholar, 1958-59; Fulbright scholar, 1959-60; Ford. Found. grantee, 1964. Fellow Am. Bar Found. (life, chmn. Mich. chpt. 1988-89); mem. ABA (sect. gen. practice, chmn. 1989-90, exec. coun. 1984-91, ho. of dels. 1979—, chmn. standing com. on membership 1983-89, tort and ins. practice sect., exec. coun. 1991-94, chmn. fin. com. 1993-94, bd. govs. 1991—, exec. com. 1993-94, 96—, treas. 1996—), Detroit Bar Assn. (dir. 1971-80, pres. 1979-80), Detroit Bar Assn. Found. (dir. 1971-84, pres. 1979-80), State Bar Mich. (commr. 1973-83, pres. 1982-83), Mich. State Bar Found. (trustee 1982-83, 85—, chmn. fellows 1986-87), Fellows of Young Lawyers Am. Bar (bd. dirs. 1977-86, chmn. bd. 1984-86, pres. 1983-84), Am. Judicature Soc. (dir. 1971-79, exec. com. 1973-74), Nat. Conf. Bar Pres. (exec. coun. 1986-89), Am. Bar Endowment (bd. dirs. 1996—), Am. Bar Ins. Cons. Inc. (bd. dirs. sec. 1988-95), Sixth Cir. Jud. Conf. (life), Orchard Lake Country Club, Detroit Club, Phi Beta Kappa, Omicron Delta Kappa, Phi Eta Sigma, Delta Tau Delta. Antitrust, General corporate. Home: 7094 Huntington Dr Sawyer MI 49125-9319 Office: Dickinson Wright PLLC 500 Woodward Ave Ste 4000 Detroit MI 48226-3416

**KRUCKS, WILLIAM NORMAN,** lawyer; b. Chgo., Oct. 28, 1949; s. William and Lorraine (Rauland) K.; m. Linda C. Robertson; children: Kathryn Leigh, Greta Anne, Laura Elizabeth. BA, Tulane U., 1972; JD, U. Miss., 1976. Bar: Ill. 1976, Miss. 1976, U.S. Dist. Ct. (no. dist.) Ill. 1976, U.S. Dist. Ct. (no. dist.) Miss. 1976, U.S. Ct. Appeals (5th and 7th cirs.) 1976, U.S. Supreme Ct. 1980, U.S. Dist. Ct. (cen. dist.) Ill. 1984. Assoc. Rooks, Pitts and Poust, Chgo., 1976-83; founding ptnr. Freeborn & Peters, Chgo., 1983—; chmn., gen. counsel, bd. dirs., corp. sec. Rauland Borg Corp. Editor Miss. Law Jour., 1974-76; contbr. articles to law jours. Atty. Chgo. Vol. Legal Svcs., 1982—. Named Outstanding Young Man Am., U.S. Jaycees, 1976; recipient Dean Robert T. Farley award U. Miss., 1977. Mem. Ill. Self-Insured Assn., Def. Rsch. Inst., Chgo. Assn. Commerce and Industry, Nat. Coun. Self-Insured, Beter Govt. Assn., Am. Jud. Soc., Tulane U. Alumni Assn., U. Miss. Alumni Assn., ABA, Ill. Bar Assn., Chgo. Bar Assn., Miss. Bar Assn., Workers Compensation Lawyers Assn., Legal Club Chgo., Union League Club (Chgo.), Chgo. Yacht Club, Phi Delta Phi, Sigma Nu. Republican. Methodist. Labor, Workers' compensation, State civil litigation. Home: 920 Sunset Rd Winnetka IL 60093-3623

**KRUEGER, JAMES A.,** lawyer; b. Sept. 21, 1943; s. A.A. and Margaret E. (Hurley) K.; m. Therese Eileen Connors, Aug. 2, 1968; 1 child, Colleen. BA cum laude, Gonzaga U., 1965; JD, Georgetown U., 1968; LLM, NYU, 1972. Bar: Wash. 1969, U.S. Supreme Ct. 1972, U.S. Tax Ct. 1972, U.S. Dist. Ct. (we. dist.) Wash. 1980, U.S. Ct. Appeals (9th cir.) 1982. Mem. staff U.S. senator from Wash., 1967-68; assoc. Kane, Vandeberg & Hartinger, Tacoma, 1972-76; ptnr. Kane, Vandeberg, Hartinger & Walker, Tacoma, 1976-90; shareholder Vandeberg Johnson & Gandara, Tacoma, 1990—; spl. dist. counsel Wash. State Bar Assn., 1984-94; adj. prof. law, U. of Puget Sound, 1974-76. Contbr. chpt. to Representing the Close Corporation, 1979, Partnership Agreements, 1981, Planning for the Small Business Enterprise, 1982, The Partnership Handbook, 1984. Chmn. bd. Cath. Cmty. Svcs. of Pierce and Kitsap Counties, 1983-84; bd. dirs. United Way of Pierce County, 1973-82, 99—. Capt. U.S. Army, 1968-72. Decorated Bronze star. Mem. ABA, Wash. State Bar Assn. (spl. dist. counsel), Tacoma-Pierce County Bar Assn. Roman Catholic. General corporate, General civil litigation, Estate planning. Office: 1201 Pacific Ave Ste 1900 Tacoma WA 98402-4315

**KRUEGER, JEFFREY W.,** lawyer; b. Galesburg, Ill., June 30, 1960; s. Robert A. and Carol W. (West) K.; m. Jen E. Valente; children: Nicholas, Eric, Kyle, Elise. BS, Bowling Green State U., 1982; JD, Case Western Reserve U., 1985. Bar: Ohio 1985, U.S. Dist. Ct. (no. dist.) Ohio 1985, U.S. Dist. Ct. (so. dist.) Ohio 1986, U.S. Ct. Appeals (6th cir.) 1990. Atty. examiner Ohio Dept. Taxation, Columbus, 1985-86; staff atty. Jones, Day, Reavis & Pogue, Cleve., 1986-88; atty. Jerome & Smith, Cleve., 1989-92, Wegman, Hessler, Vanderburg & O'Toole, Cleve., 1992—. Bd. govs. Safely Home, Inc., Bedford, Ohio, 1995—. Appellate, General civil litigation, Consumer commercial. Office: Wegman Hessler Vanderburg & O'Toole 6055 Rockside Woods Blvd Cleveland OH 44131-2301

**KRUEGER, STUART JAMES,** lawyer; b. Stillwater, Minn., July 10, 1950; s. Robert Biele and Gretchen Mary (Luebke) K.; m. Charlene Lorraine Hughes, Dec. 18, 1971; children: Wiatt, Louis. BS, U. Wis., River Falls, 1972; JD, U. Wis., 1977. Bar: Wis. 1977, U.S. Dist. Ct. (we. dist.) Wis. 1977. Atty. Gaylord, Bye & Rodli, S.C., River Falls, 1977-82, Bye, Krueger & Goff, S.C., River Falls, 1982-94, Rodli, Beskar, Boles & Krueger, S.C., River Falls, 1995—. Scoutmaster Boy Scouts Am., River Falls. Mem. State Bar Wis., Wis. Acad. Trial Lawyers, Assn. Trial Lawyers Am. Avocations: hunting, fishing, canoeing, woodworking. Personal injury, General civil litigation, Professional liability. Home: N8644 1020th St River Falls WI 54022-4623 Office: Rodli Beskar Boles and Krueger SC PO Box 138 River Falls WI 54022-0138

**KRUEGER, WILLIAM JAMES,** lawyer; b. Bemidji, Minn., July 15, 1953; s. Clarence Erwin and Mary Louise (Marose) K.; children: Benjamin William, Elizabeth Mary; m. Laurie S. Jacobson, Aug. 20, 1993. BA, St. John's U., Collegeville, Minn., 1975; JD, William Mitchell Coll. Law, 1980. Bar: Minn. 1980, U.S. Dist. Ct. Minn. 1981, U.S. Ct. Appeals (8th cir.) 1981, U.S. Supreme Ct. 1987. Pvt. practice New Brighton, Minn., 1980-81; owner Horvei & Krueger P.A., Roseville, Minn., 1981-88, Horvei, Gubbe & Krueger P.A., Roseville, Minn., 1988-95; pvt. practice New Brighton, Minn., 1995—. With U.S. Army, 1971-75. Mem. ABA, Minn. Bar Assn., Assn. Trial Lawyers Am., Minn. Trial Lawyers Assn. Avocations: hunting, fishing. Federal civil litigation, State civil litigation, Personal injury. Office: 888 W Country Rd D Ste 205 New Brighton MN 55112

**KRUEGER, WILLIAM WAYNE, III,** lawyer; b. Houston, Apr. 2, 1960; s. William Wayne Jr. and Ida Graciela (Preciado) K.; m. Lydia Scott Blocker, Nov. 25, 1989; children: Christopher Wayne, Elizabeth Ashley, Sarah Whitney. BA in Acctg., Tex. A&M U., 1984; JD, Baylor U., 1985. Bar: Tex. 1986, U.S. Dist. Ct. (ea., we., so., and no. dist.) Tex., U.S. Ct. Appeals (5th cir.), U.S. Supreme Ct. Assoc. Clark, West, Keller, Butler & Ellis, Dallas, 1985-87, Fanning, Harper & Martinson, Dallas, 1987-91; sr. assoc. Ludlum & Ludlum, Austin, Tex., 1991-93; shareholder Wright & Greenhill P.C., Austin, 1993-95; ptnr. Fletcher & Springer L.L.P., Austin, 1995—; Contbr. articles to profl. jours. Vol. Legal Aid, Austin, 1993—, Habitat for the Humanities, Austin, 1993—. Mem. ABA, State Bar Tex. (adv. bd. evidence com. 1996-97), Tex. Assn. Def. Counsel, State Bar Coll. Law, Tex. Young Lawyers Assn., Austin Young Lawyers Assn., Am. Judicature Soc., Travis County Bar Assn., Knights of Columbus, Phi Delta Phi. Roman Catholic. Avocations: family, jogging, reading. Insurance, Municipal (including bonds), Civil rights. Office: Fletcher & Springer LLP 823 Congress Ave Ste 510 Austin TX 78701-2429

**KRUG, MICHAEL STEVEN,** lawyer; b. St. Paul, Feb. 23, 1956. BA, Johns Hopkins U., 1978; JD, U. Minn., 1982. Bar: Minn. 1982, U.S. Dist. Ct. Minn. 1983. Ptnr. Krug & Zupke, St. Paul, 1984—. Workers' compensation, Personal injury, Product liability. Office: Krug & Zupke 1021 Bandana Blvd E Ste 226 Saint Paul MN 55108-5109

**KRUG, ROB ALAN,** lawyer, real estate broker; b. Munich, Fed. Republic of Germany, May 11, 1951; came to U.S., 1952; s. Robert Anthony Krug and Dolores Hope (Deihm) Webb; m. Suzanne M. Heller, Nov. 6, 1976 (div. June 1985); m. Billye Sue Davis, July 24, 1987. BA, Gettysburg (Pa.) Coll., 1973; postgrad., John Marshall Law Sch., 1974-75; JD, U. Balt., 1976. Bar: Pa. 1977, U.S. Dist. Ct. (mid. dist.) Pa. 1978. Assoc. Wiley, Schrack & Benn, Dillsburg, Pa., 1977-78; sr. assoc. Wiley & Benn, Dillsburg, 1978-80; sole practice Dover, Pa., 1981—; pres. Bill Geltz Realty, York, Pa., 1986—, Hart & Homes Real Estate, Inc., 1988—; pres., broker Hart & Homes, Inc., York, 1986—. Coach Dillsburg Area Soccer Club, 1979—, York Youth Soccer League, 1987—; officer Luth. Brotherhood Br., York, 1983. Mem. ABA, Pa. Bar Assn., York County Bar Assn.(com. mem.), York C. of C. Democrat. Lutheran. Club: York Soccer (coach 1986-88). Avocations: soccer, photography, racquetball. Family and matrimonial, Real property, Probate. Home: 743 Davis Rd Stewartstown PA 17363-8033 Office: 53 E Canal St PO Box 155 Dover PA 17315-0155 also: 4 S Main St Stewartstown PA 17363-4066

**KRUGER, FRANCES PETRONELLE,** lawyer; b. Sasolburg, South Africa, July 14, 1967; came to U.S., 1993; d. Paul du Plessis and Gina (Claassen) K. LLB, U. Orange Free State, South Africa, 1990; LLM, Georgetown Law Ctr., Washington, 1994. Bar: South Africa 1992, N.Y.C. 1996. Assoc. Hofmeyer Inc., Johannesburg, South Africa, 1991-93; sr. assoc. Trinity Assocs., Greenwich, Conn., 1994-96, The Sloane Group, Greenwich, Conn., 1997-98; v.p. mktg., dir. legal affairs Innovative Marble & Tile Inc., Hauppauge, N.Y., 1998—. Avocations: sailing, skiing, diving, hiking. Office: Innovative Marble & Tile 130 Motor Pkwy Hauppauge NY 11788-5107

**KRULEWICH, LEONARD M.,** lawyer; b. N.Y.C., Jan. 10, 1947; s. Wallace and Maxine K.; m. Helen Dworetzky, Sept. 2, 1973; children: Sara Heide, David Samuel. BA, Hofstra U., 1969; JD, Suffolk U., 1972; LLM, Boston U., 1977. Bar: Mass. 1972, U.S. Dist. Ct. Mass. 1972, N.Y. 1973, U.S. Supreme Ct. 1979, U.S. Ct. Appeals (1st cir.) 1984. Assoc. Cohn, Riemer & Pollack, Boston, 1974-78; ptnr. Krulewich & Arnowitz, Boston, 1979-81, Karger, Krulewich & Arnowitz, Boston, 1981-87; of counsel Silverman & Kudisch, Boston, 1987-89; pvt. practice Boston, 1989—. Mem. ABA, Mass. Bar Assn., Boston Bar Assn., Comml. Law League Am. (bd. govs., pres. N.E. region 1981-82), Comml. Law Found. (1st v.p.). Avocations: tennis, cooking, running. Bankruptcy, State civil litigation, Consumer commercial. Office: 50 Staniford St Boston MA 02114-2517

**KRULEWITCH, BETH LEE,** lawyer; b. Chgo., Dec. 19, 1956; d. Lawrence and Carol Lee Krulewitch; m. David Scott Kaplan, Feb. 27, 1998; children: Carolin Michelle Kaplan, Noah Joseph Kaplan. BA, U. Colo., 1980, JD, 1987. On-air reporter Sta. KOCO-TV, Oklahoma City, 1980, Sta. WTNH-TV, New Haven, Conn., 1980-81; prodr. TV news Sta. KBTV-KUSA-TV, Denver, 1981-83; prodr. promotions Sta. KCNC-TV, Denver, 1983-84; trial atty. Colo. Pub. Defenders Office, Denver, 1987-92, appellate atty., 1992-98; trial atty., appellate atty. The Leventhal Law Firm, Denver, 1998—. Author: (screenplay) The Burden of Truth, 1996; appellate editor: Colorado Trial Lawyers—Trial Talk. Mem. Nat. Assn. Criminal Def. Lawyers (Champion of Justice 1998), Colo. Criminal Def. Bar Assn. (bd. dirs. 1994—), Colo. Assn. Trial Lawyers. Appellate, Personal injury, Criminal. Office: The Leventhal Law Firm 950 S Cherry St Ste 600 Denver CO 80246-2665

**KRULL, CURTIS JAY,** lawyer; b. Sibley, Iowa, Aug. 22, 1952; s. Ivan Donald and Phyllis Ann (Ackerman) K.; m. Cris Ann Miller, Aug. 23, 1985; children: Jason Curtis, Joshua Andrew. BA, Northwestern Coll., 1974; JD, Drake U., 1985. Bar: Iowa 1985, U.S. Dist. Ct. (so. dist.) Iowa 1989, U.S. Dist. Ct. (no. dist.) Iowa 1994, U.S. Ct. Appeals (8th cir.) 1990; cert. criminal def. trial lawyer Nat. Bd. Trial Adv. Law clk. to Hon. Schlegel Iowa Ct. Appeals, Des Moines, 1985-86; asst. Polk County atty. Polk County Atty.'s Office, Des Moines, 1986-88; ptnr. Roehrick, Hulting, Krull & Blumberg, P.C., 1988—. Mem. Iowa Assn. Criminal Def. Lawyers (bd. dirs. 1992-93), Blackstone Inn of Ct. (master of bench 1998—). Avocations: distance running, golf, coaching son's activities and sports. Federal civil litigation, Personal injury, Criminal. Office: Roehrick Hulting Krull & Blumberg PC 505 5th Ave Ste 535 Des Moines IA 50309-2320

**KRUPANSKY, ROBERT BAZIL,** federal judge; b. Cleve., Aug. 15, 1921; s. Frank A. and Anna (Lawrence) K.; m. Marjorie Blaser, Nov. 13, 1952. BA, Western Res. U., 1946, LLB, 1948, JD, 1968. Bar: Ohio 1948, Supreme Ct. Ohio 1948, Supreme Ct. U.S 1948, U.S. Dist. Ct. (no. dist.) Ohio 1948, U.S. Ct. Appeals (6th cir.) 1948, U.S. Ct. Customs and Patent Appeals 1948, U.S. Customs Ct. 1948, ICC 1948. Pvt. practice law Cleve., 1948-52; asst. atty. gen. State of Ohio, 1951-57; mem. Gov. of Ohio cabinet and dir. Ohio Dept. Liquor Control, 1957-58; judge Common Pleas Ct. of Cuyahoga County, 1958-60; sr. ptnr. Metzenbaum, Gaines, Krupansky, Finley & Stern, 1960-69; U.S. atty. U.S. Dist. Ct. (no. dist.) Ohio, Cleve., 1969-70, U.S. dist. judge, 1970-82; judge, now sr. judge U.S. Ct. Appeals (6th cir.), Ohio, 1982—; spl. counsel Atty. Gen. Ohio, 1964-68; adj. prof. law Case Western Res. U. Sch. Law, 1969-70. 2d lt. U.S. Army, pilot USAAC, 1942-46; col. USAF Res. ret. Mem. ABA, Fed. Bar Assn., Ohio Bar Assn., Cleve. Bar Assn., Cuyahoga County Bar Assn., Am. Judicature Soc., Assn. Asst. Attys. Gen. State Ohio. Office: US Ct Appeals US Courthouse 201 Superior Ave E Ste 328 Cleveland OH 44114-1201*

**KRUPKA, ROBERT GEORGE,** lawyer; b. Rochester, N.Y., Oct. 21, 1949; s. Joseph Anton and Marjorie Clara (Meteyer) K.; children: Kristin Nicole, Kerry Melissa. BS, Georgetown U., 1971; JD, U. Chgo., 1974. Bar: Ill. 1974, Colo. 1991, D.C., 1991, Calif. 1998, U.S. Dist. Ct. (no. dist.) Ill. 1974, U.S. Dist. Ct. (ea. dist.) Wis. 1974, U.S. Ct. Appeals (7th cir.) 1976, U.S. Supreme Ct. 1978, U.S. Dist. Ct. (cen. dist.) Ill. 1980, U.S. Dist. Ct. (no. dist.) Calif. 1980, U.S. Dist. Ct. (ctrl. and so. dists.) Calif. 1999, U.S. Ct. Appeals (4th and fed. cirs.) 1982, U.S. Ct. Appeals (6th cir.) 1985, U.S. Ct. Appeals (1st, 2d, 3d, 5th, 8th, 9th, 10th and 11th dists.) 1999. Assoc. Kirkland & Ellis, Chgo., 1974-79, ptnr., 1979—. Author: Infringement Litigation Computer Software and Database, 1984, Computer Software, Semiconductor Design, Video Game and Database Protection and Enforcement, 1984. Mem. bd. trustees Francis W. Parker Sch., 1987-98, pres., 1994-97. Mem. ABA (chmn. sec. com. 1982-88, chmn. div. 1988-90, 98—, coun. 1994-97), Computer Law Assn., U.S. Patent Quar. Adv. Bd., Am. Intellectual Property Law Assn. (chmn. subcom. 1988—), Mid-Am. Club, Chgo. Club. Roman Catholic. Federal civil litigation, Trademark and copyright, Patent. Office: Kirkland & Ellis 200 E Randolph St Fl 54 Chicago IL 60601-6636

**KRUSE, CHARLES THOMAS,** lawyer; b. Tulsa, Sept. 26, 1963; s. Joseph Daniel and Judith Sue (Holleman) K.; m. Jennifer Jones, May 20, 1989; 1 child, Charles Thomas Jr. BA, Emory U., 1985; JD, Vanderbilt U., 1989. Bar: Tex. 1989, U.S. Dist. Ct. (so. dist.) Tex. 1990, U.S. Ct. Appeals (5th and 8th cirs.) 1991; bd. cert. civil trial law Tex. Bd. Legal Specialization. Law clk. to Hon. Ricardo H. Hinojosa U.S. Dist. Ct. (so. dist.) Tex., McAllen, Tex., 1989-90; assoc. Fulbright & Jaworski, Houston, 1990-91; ptnr. McDade & Fogler, Houston, 1992-95; counsel to ptnr. King & Spalding, Houston, 1995—. Contbr. articles and papers to profl. publs. Bobby Jones scholar U. St. Andrews, 1985-86. Fellow Tex. Bar Found., Houston Bar Found.; mem. ABA, Houston Bar Assn., Houston Young Lawyer Assn. Republican. Roman Catholic. General civil litigation, FERC practice, Environmental. Home: 10622 S Evers Park Dr Houston TX 77024-5528 Office: King & Spalding 1100 Louisiana St Ste 3300 Houston TX 77002-5217

**KRUSE, JOHN ALPHONSE,** lawyer; b. Detroit, Sept. 11, 1926; s. Frank R. and Ann (Nestor) K.; m. Mary Louise Dalton, July 14, 1951; children: Gerard, Mary Louise, Terence, Kathleen, Joanne, Francis, John, Patrick. BS, U. Detroit, 1950, JD cum laude, 1952. Bar: Mich. bar 1952. Ptnr. Alexander, Buchanan & Conklin, Detroit, 1952-69, Harvey, Kruse, PC, Detroit, 1969—; Guest lectr. U. Mich., U. Detroit, Inst. Continuing Legal Edn.; city atty. Allen Park, Mich., 1954-59; twp. atty., Van Buren Twp., Mich., 1959-61. Co-founder Detroit Cath. Radio. Past pres. Palmer Woods Assn.; mem. pres.'s cabinet U. Detroit; mem. product liability adv. coun. Providence Hosp.; bd. dirs. Providence Hosp. Found. Legatus. Named one of 5 Outstanding Young Men in Mich., 1959, Outstanding Alumnus, U. Detroit Sch. Law, 1989, Humanitarian award Neuromuscular Inst. 1988. Mem. Detroit Bar Assn., State Bar Mich. (past chmn. negligence sect.), Assn. Def. Trial Counsel (bd. dirs. 1966-67), Am. Judicature Soc., Internat. Assn. Def. Counsel, Equestrian Order of the Holy Sepulchre, Cath. Campaign for Am. Roman Catholic. Club: Detroit Golf (past pres.). Insurance, State civil litigation, Personal injury. Home: 5569 Hunters Gate Dr Troy MI 48098-2342 Office: 1050 Wilshire Dr Ste 320 Troy MI 48084-1526 *Start each day with a simple petition - Lord help me to do your will today. End each day in thanks for his divine guidance. Prayer is to the soul as exercise is to the body. Neglect neither!.*

**KRUSE, PAMELA JEAN,** lawyer; b. Miami, Fla., June 3, 1950; d. Robert Emil and Irma G. Kruse. BS, Mich. State U., 1973, MA, 1975, PhD, 1979; JD, U. Mich., 1985. Bar: Mich. 1986. Grad. asst. Mich. State U., East Lansing, 1976-77, asst. intramural dir., 1977-79, labor rels. rep., 1979-81, asst. dir. labor rels., 1981-82; resident mgr. 719 Oakland, Ann Arbor, Mich., 1982-83; rsch. asst. Law Sch. U. Mich., Ann Arbor, 1982-85; jud. clk. U.S. Dist. Ct. (we. dist.) Mich., 1985-86; assoc. Clary, Nantz, Wood, Hoffius, Rankin & Cooper, Grand Rapids, Mich., 1986-91; with Village Bike Shops, 1991—. Bd. dirs. Babe Zaharias Golf Tournament, Am. Cancer Soc., 1987-91. Recipient Gold and Silver medals U.S. Pan Am. Team, Winnipeg, Man., Can., 1967, Silver medal U.S. Olympic Team, Mexico City, 1968; holder world records swimming 400 meters freestyle, 1967, 200 meters freestyle, 1967, 440-yard freestyle, 1966; inducted to Greater Fort Lauderdale Sports Hall of Fame, 1979. Mem. ABA, State Bar Mich. (exec. coun. young lawyers sect. 1987-90), Grand Rapids Bar Assn. (chairperson, exec. bd. dirs. young lawyers sect. 1987-91), Mich. Pub. Employer Labor Rels. Assn. (bd. dirs. 1981-82, chmn. manual revision com. 1982), Mich. State U. Alumni Assn. (1st v.p., bd. dirs. 1988-89), U.S. Olympians, Phi Delta Kappa, Kappa Alpha Theta. Labor.

**KRUSOR, MARK WILLIAM,** lawyer; b. Topeka, Nov. 6, 1951; s. William Albert and Gladys Eleanor (Lyon) K.; m. Carolyn Kay Gish, May 19, 1973 (div. Aug. 1984); 1 dau., Bethany Ellen; m. Teresa D. Garcia, Aug. 1, 1986. BA, Washburn U., 1973, JD, 1976. Bar: Kans. 1976, U.S. Dist. Ct. Kans. 1976. Assoc. Christenson, Mathews & Taylor, Winfield, Kans., 1976-79; ptnr. Mathews, Taylor & Krusor, Winfield, 1979—; instr. Southwestern Coll., Winfield, 1978-86, Cowley County C.C. and Winfield State Hosp. and Tng. Ctr., 1981, 82, 84, 85, 86, St. John's Coll., Winfield, 1984; pres. adv. com. Kans. Dept. Corrections Winfield Pre-release Ctr., 1986. Chmn. bd. trustees Winfield Pub. Library, 1981, 82; pres. bd. dirs. Winfield Child Care Ctr., 1979; chmn. drive Winfield United Way, 1978; pres. Holy Name Parish Coun., Winfield, 1981; county chmn. Allegrucci for Congress com., Winfield, 1978; treas. Citizens Com. for Merit Selection of Judges, Winfield, 1984; mem. resident rights com. Winfield State Hosp. and Tng. Ctr., 1980-82; mem. adv. com. Winfield State Hosp., 1982-90, Kans. Dept. Corrections-Winfield Ctr., 1984-90; pres. Winfield Pub. Sch. Found. Mem. ABA, Kans. Bar Assn., Kans. Trial Lawyers Assn. (bd. govs. 1983-87), Cowley County Bar Assn. (sec.-treas. 1978, v.p. 1979, pres. 1980), Washburn Law Sch. Assn., Kans. Hist. Soc., Cowley County Hist. Soc., Jaycees, Optimists (pres. 1980-81), Elks, KC. Democrat. Roman Catholic. State civil litigation, Criminal, Family and matrimonial. Home: 7 Braid Hills Dr Winfield KS 67156-6303 Office: Mathews Taylor & Krusor First Nat Bank Bldg Winfield KS 67156

**KRUTTER, FORREST NATHAN,** lawyer; b. Boston, Dec. 17, 1954; s. Irving and Shirley Krutter. BS in Econs., MS in Civil Engring., MIT, 1976; JD cum laude, Harvard U., 1978. Bar: Nebr. 1978, U.S. Supreme Ct. 1986, N.Y. 1991. Antitrust counsel Union Pacific R.R., Omaha, 1978-86; sr. v.p. law, sec. Berkshire Hathaway Group, Omaha, 1986—. Co-author: Impact of Railroad Abandonments, 1976, Railroad Development in the Third World, 1978; author: Judicial Enforcement of Competition in Regulated Industries, 1979; contbr. articles Creighton Law Rev. Mem. ABA, Phi Beta Kappa, Sigma Xi. Administrative and regulatory, General corporate, Insurance.

**KRYGER, JON DAVID,** lawyer; b. Boise, Idaho, Nov. 18, 1940; s. Arthur and Frances (Grismer) K.; m. DeEtta Anne LeFor, Aug. 31, 1962; children: Kristin, Kelley, Erin, Kevin. BA, St. Martins Coll., 1962; JD, Willamette U., 1965. Bar: Oreg. 1965, U.S. Dist. Ct. Oreg. 1966. Hearing referee Worker's Compensation Bd., Salem, Oreg., 1966-68; pvt. practice Albany, Oreg., 1968—; ptnr. Kryger, Alexander, Egan & Elmer, P.C., Albany, Oreg., 1989—. Editor: Oregon State Bar Practice Manual on Worker's Compensation, 1975, Oregon State Bar CLE Worker's Compensation Practice Manual, 1980. Mem. Oreg. State Bar (sect. on Worker's Compensation pres. 1980-81), Oreg. Worker's Compensation Atty.'s Assn. (pres. 1980-81), Oreg. Trial Lawyers Assn. (pres. 1986-87), Linn County Bar Assn. (pres. 1973-74). Republican. Roman Catholic. Avocations: running, fishing, golfing. Personal injury, Workers' compensation. Home: 7225 NW Fawnridge Dr Albany OR 97321-9317 Office: Kryger Alexander Egan & Elmer PC PO Box 279 Albany OR 97321-0083

**KRYGOWSKI, WALTER JOHN,** lawyer; b. Detroit; s. Walter Robert and Joann Virginia Krygowski. BA, Oakland U., 1992; JD, U. Dayton, 1996. Bar: Ohio 1996, U.S. Dist. Ct. (so. dist.) Ohio 1996, U.S. Ct. Appeals (6th cir.) 1998. Law clk. Banc One Corp., Dayton, Ohio, 1995; contract atty. Dwight D. Brannon & Assocs., Dayton, 1996-99; ast. city atty. City of Dayton, 1999—; arbitrator Montgomery County Ct. Common Pleas-Compulsory Arbitration, Dayton, 1996—. Mem. Ohio State Bar Assn., Dayton Bar Assn., Ohio Acad. Trial Lawyers. Roman Catholic. Fax: 937-885-4998.

E-mail: chanelka@aol.com. Municipal (including bonds), Contracts commercial. Home: 4037 Loyala Chase Ln Dayton OH 45424-8004 Office: City of Dayton Law Dept 101 W 3d St PO Box 22 Dayton OH 45401

**KRYLOV, NIKOLAI,** lawyer; b. Moscow, July 4, 1958; s. Boris and Halina Krylov; m. Mrina Krylov, July 16, 1985; 1 child, Nikolai Jr. JD, Moscow U., 1983; LLD, Russian Acad. Scis., Moscow, 1990; JD, Yale U., 1994. Bar: Russia 1983, N.Y. 1995. Prof. law Inst. State and Law, Russian Acad. Scis., 1983-90; scholar Columbia U. Sch. Law, N.Y.C., 1990-91; assoc. Paul Weiss Rifkind Wharton & Garrison, N.Y.C., 1992, 94-95, Cadwalader Wickersham & Taft, N.Y.C., 1995—. Author: Membership in the UN, 1986, On the Equilibrum of Femida, 1986, Law Making in International Law, 1990. Mem. Yale Club. General corporate, Private international. Office: Cadwalader Wickersham Taft 100 Maiden Ln New York NY 10038-4818

**KRZYZANOWSKI, RICHARD L(UCIEN),** lawyer, corporate executive; b. Warsaw, Poland, Mar. 25, 1932; came to U.S., 1967, naturalized, 1972; s. Andrew and Mary K.; children: Suzanne, Peter, Christine. BA, U. Warsaw, 1956; ML, U. Pa., 1960; PhD, U. Paris, 1962. Bar: Pa. With Crown Cork & Seal Co., Inc., Phila., 1967—, dir., exec. v.p. gen. counsel, 1990—. Trustee John Paul II Found., Vatican, Rome, Italy; exec. trustee, founder Krzyzanowski Found., Phila. Public international, Private international, General corporate. Office: Crown Cork & Seal Co Inc 1 Crown Way Philadelphia PA 19154-4599

**KUBICEK, THEODORE LINCOLN,** writer, lawyer; b. Cedar Rapids, Iowa, Nov. 6, 1919; s. Fred H. and Mary (Bruna) K.; m. Margaret Elizabeth Zimmerman, June 20, 1941; children: Mary Jen Damrow, David W., John F. BA, U. Iowa, 1941, JD, 1942. Bar: Iowa 1942, U.S. Dist. Ct. (no. dist.) Iowa 1952. Spl. agt. FBI, 1942-46; chief exec. officer, chmn. bd. dirs. Bohemian Savs. & Loan Assn., Cedar Rapids, 1969-77; pvt. practice law Cedar Rapids, 1946-86, legal writer, 1986—; adj. tchr. Kirkwood Community Coll., Cedar Rapids, 1983-87. Author: You and Your Estate, 1988, Your Worldy Possessions, 1992; contbr. articles to profl. jours. Mem. ABA, Linn County Bar Assn. (Disting. Svc. award 1985), Iowa State Bar Assn. Republican. Presbyterian. Avocations: golf, music, reading. Home: 3866 Belden Ct NE Cedar Rapids IA 52402-2569

**KUBICZKY, STEPHEN RALPH,** lawyer; b. North Braddock, Pa., Oct. 8, 1947; s. Stephen Ralph and Helen (Kish) K. BS, U. Notre Dame, 1969, MS, 1977; JD, Northwestern U., 1972. Bar: Ill. 1972, U.S. Dist. Ct. (no. dist.) Ill. 1972, U.S. Ct. Claims 1978, U.S. Tax Ct. 1978, U.S. Ct. Appeals (7th cir.) 1979. Assoc. Altheimer & Gray, Chgo., 1973-75, 77-80, ptnr., 1980-91, counsel, 1991-92; pvt. practice Riverside, Ill.; chmn. planning com., materials author Ill. Inst. Continuing Legal Edn., 1983, 94, 87-88, 93, 97; pub. witness Pres.'s Commn. on Pension Policy, 1981. Vol. coord. Ill. state Bush/Quayle '92 Presdl. campaign; pres. Riverside Twp. Regular Rep. Orgn., 1994-98; trustee Triton Coll., 1995—. Mem. ABA, Ill. State Bar Assn. (chmn. employee benefits sect. 1981-83, sect. coun. fed. taxation sect. 1980-84, contbr. newsletter 1980-85), Chgo. Bar Assn. (chmn. fed. taxation com. divsn. D 1982-83, mem. exec. coun. taxation com. 1980-83, chmn. continuing legal edn. 1987-88), Midwest Benefits Coun., Wigmore Club (exec. com. 1992-96), Henry Wade Rogers Soc., Ill. Cmty. Coll. trustees Assn. (sec. 1999—, chmn. north suburban region 1998-99). Pension, profit-sharing, and employee benefits. Office: PO Box 86 Riverside IL 60546-0086

**KUBLER, FRANK LAWRENCE,** lawyer; b. Pensacola, Fla., July 4, 1957; s. Frank Martin and Esther Helen (Flora) K. AA, Miami-Dade Jr. Coll., 1978; BS in Mech. Engring., U. Miami, Coral Gables, Fla., 1981, BA in History, 1982, JD, 1986. Bar: Fla. 1986, U.S. Cir. Ct. (11th cir) 1988, U.S. Cir. Ct. (fed. cir.) 1989, U.S. Patent Office 1987. Assoc. Dominik, Stein, Saccocio, Reese, Colitz & Van der Wall, Miami Lakes, Fla., 1986-90; pres. Law Office of Frank L. Kubler, Miami Lakes, 1990—; cons. Oltman, Flynn & Kubler, Ft. Lauderdale, Fla., 1990-96, ptnr., 1996—. Mem. Inter-Am. Law Rev., 1985. Mem. Patent Law Assn. South Fla. (v.p. 1993-94, pres. 1994-95), Mensa, Rotary (dir. 1992-94, chmn. scholarship com. 1994-95), Tau Beta Pi. Intellectual property. Office: 915 Middle River Dr Ste 415 Fort Lauderdale FL 33304-3561

**KUBO, EDWARD HACHIRO, JR.,** prosecutor; b. Honolulu, July 9, 1953; s. Edward H. and Rose M. (Coltes) K.; children: Diana K., Dawn M., Edward H. III. BA in Polit. Sci., U. Hawaii, 1976; JD, U. San Diego, 1979. Bar: Hawaii 1979. Dep. pros. atty. Honolulu City Prosecutor's Office, 1980-83, 85-90; assoc. Carlsmith & Dwyer, Honolulu, 1983-85; asst. U.S. atty. U.S. Atty.'s Office, Honolulu, 1990—; instr. Honolulu Police Dept. Acad., Waipahu, Hawaii, 1986-89; lectr. U.S. Dept. Justice, Lincoln, Neb., 1997, Pearl Harbor Police Acad., 1995, Western State Vice Investigators Assn. Conf., Houston, 1997, Las Vegas, 1998; spkr. teleconf. U.S. Dept. Justice Violence Against Women Act, 1998, Hawaii Bar Assn. H.S. Mock trial adv., 1996-98. Co-author: Concurrent Jurisdiction for Cilil RICO, 1987. Recipient Nat. Art medal (France), 1992, Cert. of Appreciation, U.S. Immigration and Naturalization Svc., 1992, Drug Enforcement Adminstrn., 1997, Plaque of Appreciation, U.S. Border Patrol, 1995, cert. appreciation Bureau Alcohol, Tobacco & Firearms, 1999. Mem. Hawaii Bar Assn., Order of Barristers.

**KUBY, RONALD L.,** lawyer; b. Cleve., July 31, 9156; s. Donald Joseph Kuby and Ruth Miller; m. Marilyn Vasta; 1 child, Emma Sojourner. BA, U. Kans., 1979; JD magna cum laude, Cornell U., 1983. Assoc. Kunstler & Kuby, N.Y.C., 1994-95, Law Office William M. Kunstler, N.Y.C., 1984-94; ptnr. Law Office Ronald L. Kuby, N.Y.C., 1996—. Contbr. articles to profl. jours. Mem. adv. bd. N.Y. Civil Liberties Union, 1999—. Recipient Thurgood MArshall award N.Y. City Bar Assn., 1998. Communist. Office: 740 Broadway Fl 5 New York NY 10003-9518

**KUCZWARA, THOMAS PAUL,** postal inspector, lawyer; b. Dec. 21, 1951; s. Stanley Leo and Eleanore (Pawelko) K.; m. Diana Lynn Rychtarczyk, Sept. 8, 1979; 1 child, Paul Stanley. BA, Loyola U., Chgo., 1973; JD, U. S.C., 1976. Bar: Ill. 1976, U.S. Dist. Ct. (no. dist.) Ill. 1982. Assoc. Doria Law Offices, Chgo., 1977-78; asst. corp. counsel City of Chgo., 1978-80; asst. city atty. City of Aurora, Ill., 1980-82; postal insp. U.S. Postal Inspection Svc., Salt Lake City, 1982-85; regional insp. atty. cen. region U.S. Postal Inspection Svc., Chgo., 1985—. Mem. St. Bartholomew's Parish Coun., Chgo., 1978; vol. atty. Lawyers for Creative Arts, 1978. Ill. state scholar, 1969. Mem. Sierra Club, Pi Sigma Alpha. Roman Catholic. Office: US Postal Inspection Svc Ops Support Group 222 S Riverside Plz # 1250 Chicago IL 60606-6100

**KUDER, ARMIN ULRICH,** lawyer; b. Phila., Nov. 14, 1935; s. David Dennis and Ethel Rose (Strasburger) K.; m. Patricia A. Hipple, June 28, 1959 (div. Mar. 1968); children: Carlyn Elizabeth, Eric David, Keith Ulrich; m. Adrienne A. Allison, Aug. 25, 1989. AB, Lafayette Coll., 1956; LLB, Harvard U., 1959. Bar: D.C. 1959, Md. 1987, U.S. Ct. Mil. Appeals 1962, U.S. Dist. Ct. Md. 1968. Assoc. Coles & Goertner, Washington, 1963-65, Mehler, Smollar et al., Washington, 1965-67; ptnr. Smollar & Kuder, Washington, 1967-68, Kuder, Sherman et al., Washington, 1968-78, Kuder, Smollar & Friedman P.C., Washington, 1978—; lectr. continuing legal edn., various locations. Chmn. Nat. Health Agencies, NCAC, 1977-78, Ctr. Marine Conservation, Washington, 1981-83, NIMH human subjects rev. panel, 1978-83, Hyde Sch., Bath, Maine, 1984-87; vice chmn. Arthritis Found., Atlanta, 1979-80, 90-92, chmn., 1992-94; pres. Arthritis and Rhuematism Internat., 1996-98, treas., 1998—; mem. steering group The Bond and Joint Decade, Lund, Sweden, 1999—; chmn. New Art Assn., Washington, 1986-87; sec. Combined Health Appeal, Washington, 1984. Served to lt. comdr. JAGC, USNR, 1959-63. Fellow Am. Acad. Matrimonial Lawyers, Internat. Acad. of Matrimonial Lawyers; mem. ABA, D.C. Bar Assn. (trustee client security fund 1984-92, chmn. 1991-92, hearing com. chmn. bd. on profl. responsibility 1985-91), Md. Bar Assn. State civil litigation, Family and matrimonial, Health. Office: Kuder Smollar & Friedman PC 1925 K St NW Washington DC 20006-1105

**KUDRAVETZ, DAVID WALLER,** lawyer; b. Sumter, S.C., Feb. 2, 1948; s. George and Barbara (Waller) K.; m. Eleanor McCrea Snyder, June 21, 1969; 1 child, Julia McCrea. BS, U. Va., 1971, JD, 1974. Bar: Va. 1974, U.S. Tax Ct. 1974; CPA, Va. Assoc. Robert M. Musselman, Charlottesville, Va., 1974; ptnr. Carwile & Kudravetz, Charlottesville, Va., 1975-78, McClure, Callaghan & McCallum, Charlottesville, Va., 1979-81, McCallum & Kudravetz, P.C., Charlottesville, Va., 1982—; instr. fed. income taxation U. of Va. Sch. Continuing Edn., 1975-79. Mem. AICPA, Va. State Bar Assn., Charlottesville-Albemarle Bar Assn., Am. Assn. Atty.-CPAs, Va. Soc. CPAs. Personal income taxation, Estate planning, Real property. Home: PO Box 162 Earlysville VA 22936-0162 Office: McCallum & Kudravetz PC 250 E High St Charlottesville VA 22902-5178

**KUEHLING, ROBERT WARREN,** lawyer, accountant; b. Madison, Jr. Aug. 31, 1952; s. Warren Ernest and Mary Alice (Jenkins) K.; m. Susan Mary O'Brien, July 8, 1978; children—Megan Ann, Jeffrey Robert. B.B.A., U. Wis., J.D., 1976. Bar: Wis. 1977, U.S. Dist. Ct. (we. dist.) Wis. 1977; C.P.A. Ptnr. Kuehling & Kuehling, Madison, 1977—. Probate, Real property. Office: Kuehling & Kuehling 131 W Wilson St Ste 501 Madison WI 53703-3268

**KUEHN, BARBARA JEAN,** lawyer; b. Frankfurt, Germany, May 10, 1952; parents U.S. citizens; d. Robert Adolf Kuehn and Lucy Elvira Miele; 1 child, Joanne Stephanik. AA, Coll. San Mateo, 1982; JD, San Francisco U., 1985. Bar: Calif. 1991. Family law atty. Anderlini, Guheen, Finkelstein & Emerick, 1991-92; pvt. practice Burlingame, Calif., 1992—. Active Nat. Womens Polit. Caucus, 1992-96, v.p. San Mateo caucus, 1993. Mem. ABA, Calif. Women Lawyers (life, bd. govs. 1993-97, sec. 1994-95, 1st v.p. 1995-96, Pres. award 1994), State Bar Calif. (Wiley W. Manuel Pro Bono Legal Svcs. award 1994), Barristers San Mateo County Bar Assn. (pres. 1993, 94, Barrister of Yr. San Mateo County 1993, 94, 95), Delta Theta Phi (dean 1984-85). Democrat. Roman Catholic. Fax: 650-373-2072. E-mail: bbqnesq@earthlink.net. Family and matrimonial. Office: 433 Airport Blvd Ste 319 Burlingame CA 94010-2010

**KUEHNE, BENEDICT P.,** lawyer; b. Merced, Calif., Mar. 24, 1954; s. Ben and Jean T. K. B.A. cum laude, U. Miami, 1974; J.D. cum laude, 1977; postgrad., Fla. Atlantic U., 1979-81. Bar: Fla. 1977, D.C. 1978, U.S. Dist. Ct. (so. and mid. dists.) Fla. 1977, U.S. Dist. Ct. (so. dist.) Ala. 1983, U.S. Ct. Appeals (5th cir.) 1977, U.s. Ct. Appeals (4th cir.) 1980, U.S. Ct. Appeals (7th and 11th cir.) 1981, U.S. Ct. Appeals (9th and D.C. cirs.) 1982, U.S. Ct. Appeals (2nd cir.) 1984, U.S. Supreme Ct. 1981. Asst. atty. gen. State of Fla., West Palm Beach, 1977-79; spl. asst. state atty. 15th Jud. Cir., 1978-90; sr. assoc. Bierman, Sonnett Shohat & Sale, P.A., Miami and Ft. Lauderdale, Fla., 1980-87; ptnr. Sonnet Sale & Kuehne, P.A., 1987-93, Sale & Kuehne, P.A., 1993—; adj. instr. law U. Miami, 1987-88, Miami Dade Cmty. Coll., 1987-89; lectr. in field. Contbr. articles to profl. jours. Cmty. organizer United Way, 1987; mem. adv. bd. U. Miami Moot Ct., 1987-90; bd. dris. Dem. Forum, Fla., 1987—, Legal Svcs. Greater Miami, Inc., 1992-98; gen. counsel Fla. Young Dems., 1986-87, pres., 1986-87; pres. Dade County Young Dems., Fla., 1982-83, bd. dirs., 1983-84; spl. counsel Biden for Pres. Campaign, 1987; dep. counsel Dade County Democratic Exec. Com., 1989-95; mem. exec. com. Alliance for Ethical Govt., 1998—. Named one of Outstanding Young Mem of Am., 1980, 82. Mem. Fla. Bar Assn. (exec. coun. criminal law sect., chair 1994-95, chair criminal cert. com. 1990-93, appelate cert. com. 1995—, chair-elect coun. sects. 1999—), Fla. Criminal Def. Attys. Assn. (chmn. brief bank com., Cert. of Merit 1984), Pub. Interest Law Bank (Award of Merit 1984), Dade County Bar Assn. (pres. 1998-99), Fla. Assn. Criminal Def. Lawyers (charter mem., bd. dirs., pres. 1990-91), Greater Miami Jewish Fedn. (atty.'s divsn.), U. Miami Iron Arrow Honor Soc., Metro-Miami Action Plant Trust (parliamentarian 1998—), Nat. Eagle Scout Orgn., U. Miami Law Alumni Assn. (pres. 1992-93, Thomas Davison svc. award 1985, 98), U. Miami Gen. Alumni Assn. (bd. dirs. 1987, pres. 1995—, Outstanding Law Alumnus award 1989, Outstanding Svc. award 1989, bd. trustees 1994—98), Coconut Grove Assn. (bd. dirs. 1982—). Criminal, Immigration, naturalization, and customs, Administrative and regulatory. Home: PO Box 113405 Miami FL 33111-3405 Office: Sale & Kuehne PA 100 SE 2nd St Ste 3550 Miami FL 33131-2150

**KUEMMEL, JOSEPH KENNETH,** lawyer; b. San Francisco, May 13, 1945; s. Kenneth Joseph and Elizabeth (Beudoin) K.; m. Sharon Eileen O'Hara, June 20, 1970; children: Daniel, Michael, Kevin. BS, Marquette U., 1967; JD, U. Wis., 1970. Bar: Wis. 1970, U.S. Dist. Ct. (ea. and we. dists.) Wis. 1970, U.S. Supreme Ct. 1978. Atty. Eisenbers & Assocs., Madison, Wis., 1970-75; partner Klein, Kuemmel & Schmidt S.C., Madison, 1975-80, Kuemmel & Beilke S.C., Madison, 1980-86; pvt. practice Madison, 1986—. Baseball and soccer coach, Madison, 1985—; mem. spl. need com. Queen of Peace Sch., Madison, 1989. Mem. Wis. Bar Assn., Dane County Bar Assn. Republican. Roman Catholic. Avocations: travel, G-scale trains, guitar playing, sword collecting. Family and matrimonial, Criminal, Personal injury. Office: 900 John Nolen Dr Ste 220 Madison WI 53713-1477

**KUENY, BERNARD E., III,** lawyer; b. Phila., Feb. 23, 1961; s. Bernard E., Jr. and Dorothy P. Kueny; m. Ellen Hatch, Aug. 30, 1986; children: Bernard V., Claire M., Patrick H., John F. BA, Coll. of the Holy Cross, Worcester, Mass., 1983; JD, St. Louis U., 1986. Bar: Pa. 1986, N.J. 1988, U.S. Supreme Ct. 1990, U.S. Ct. Appeals (3rd cir.) 1990, U.S. Dist. Ct. (ea. dist.) Pa. 1987, U.S. Dist. Ct. N.J. 1989. Assoc. Sweeney & Sheehan, Phila., 1986-91, Kelley, Jasons, McGuire & Spinell, Phila., 1991-95, Magazzu & Spezial, Vineland, N.J., 1995-96, Speziali, Greenwald, Kueny & Hawkins, P.C., Voorhees, N.J., 1996—. Bd. govs. St. Joseph's Preparatory Sch., Phila., 1986—. Recipient Everett Hullverson award St. Louis U., 1986. Mem. Pa. Bar Assn., Phila. Bar Assn., Def. Rsch. Inst. Roman Catholic. Toxic tort, Product liability, Insurance. Home: 129 Whitney Ln Richboro PA 18954-1079 Office: Speziali Greenwald Kueny & Hawkins 2 Echelon Plz Ste 135 Voorhees NJ 08043-2315

**KUH, RICHARD HENRY,** lawyer; b. N.Y.C., Apr. 27, 1921; s. Joseph Hellmann and Fannie Mina (Rees) K.; m. Joyce Dattel, July 31, 1966; children: Michael Joseph, Jody Ellen. BA, Columbia Coll., 1941; LLB magna cum laude, Harvard U., 1948. Bar: N.Y. 1948, U.S. Dist. Ct. (so. dist.) N.Y. 1948, U.S. Dist. Ct. (ea. dist.) N.Y. 1967, U.S. Supreme Ct. 1968. Assoc. firm Cahill, Gordon & Reindel, 1948-53; asst. dist. atty. N.Y. County Dist. Attys. Office, 1953-64, dist. atty., 1974; pvt. practice law N.Y.C., 1966-71; ptnr. firm Kuh, Goldman, Cooperman & Levitt, N.Y.C., 1971-73, Kuh, Shapiro, Goldman, Cooperman & Levitt, P.C., N.Y.C., 1975-78, Warshaw Burstein Cohen Schlesinger & Kuh, N.Y.C., 1978—; adj. prof. NYU Law Sch. Author: Foolish Figleaves, 1967; mem. bd. editors: Harvard Law Rev, 1947-48; mem. adv. bd.: Contemporary Drug Problems, 1975—, Criminal Law Bull, 1976—; contbr. articles to popular and profl. jours. Trustee Temple Israel, N.Y.C., 1975-84, Grace Ch. Sch., 1981-85. With U.S. Army, 1942-45, ETO. Walter E. Meyer Research and Writing grantee, 1964-65. Mem. ABA (chair criminal justice sect. 1983-84, chair spl. com. on evaluation jud. performance 1983-90, ho. dels. 1988-93, mem. jud. evaluation adv. com. Nat. Ctr. State Cts. 1990-91, chair 1st nat. conf. gun violence 1994), Assn. Bar City N.Y., Am. Bar Found., Harvard Law Sch. Assn. N.Y. (trustee 1989-92), Harvard Club (mem. admissions com. 1998—), Phi Beta Kappa. Democrat. Jewish. Federal civil litigation, State civil litigation, Criminal. Home: 14 Washington Pl New York NY 10003-6609 Office: 555 5th Ave New York NY 10017-2416

**KUHLMANN, FRED MARK,** lawyer, business executive; b. St. Louis, Apr. 9, 1948; s. Frederick Louis and Mildred (Southworth) K.; m. Barbara Jane Nierman, Dec. 30, 1970; children: F. Matthew, Sarah Ann. AB summa cum laude, Washington U., St. Louis, 1970; JD cum laude, Harvard U., 1973. Bar: Mo. 1973. Assoc. atty. Stolar, Heitzmann & Eder, St. Louis, 1973-75; tax counsel McDonnell Douglas Corp., St. Louis, 1975-82, corp. asst. sec., 1977-88, corp. counsel fin. matters, 1982-87, assoc. gen. counsel, 1984-87, staff v.p., 1985-87; exec. v.p. McDonnell Douglas Health Systems Co. div. McDonnell Douglas Corp., Hazelwood, Mo., 1987-88, pres., 1988-89; pres. McDonnell Douglas Systems Integration Co. div. McDonnell Douglas Corp., Hazelwood, Mo., 1989-91; v.p., gen. counsel, sec. McDonnell Douglas Corp., St. Louis, 1991-92, sr. v.p. adminstrn., gen. counsel, sec., 1992-95, sr. v.p., gen. counsel, 1995-97; of counsel Bryan Cave, St. Louis, 1997-99; pres. Sys. Svc. Enterprises, St. Louis, 1999—; bd. dirs. Republic Health Corp., Dallas, 1988-90; mem. governing bd. Luth. Med. Ctr., 1989-95, chmn., 1990-92. Bd. dirs. Luth. Charities Assn., 1982-91, sec. 1984-86, chmn. 1986-89; elder Lutheran Ch. of Resurrection, 1977-80; mem. Regents Coun. Concordia Sem., 1981-84; chmn. cub scout pack 459 Boy Scouts Am., 1984-86; bd. dirs. Luth. High Sch. Assn., 1978-84, 91-97, pres. 1992-97, long range planning com. 1990-92, chmn. alumni assn. 1981; chmn. north star dist. Boy Scouts Am., 1990-93; bd. dirs. Mcpl. Theatre Assn., St. Louis, 1991—; chmn. long range planning com. St. Paul's Luth. Ch., 1988-91, 98—, pres., 1996-97; bd. dirs., mem. exec. com. United Way of Greater St. Louis, 1994-97, chmn. Vanguard divsn., 1994-97; mem. amb. coun. Luth. Family and Children's Svcs. of St. Louis, 1998—. Recipient Disting. Leadership award Luth. Assn. for Higher Edn., 1981. Mem. ABA, Mo. Bar Assn., Bar Assn. Met. St. Louis, Bellerive Country Club, Phi Beta Kappa, Omicron Delta Kappa. Republican. Avocations: tennis, golf, racquetball. Corporate taxation, Pension, profit-sharing, and employee benefits, Mergers and acquisitions. Home: 1711 Stone Rdg Trails Dr Saint Louis MO 63122-3546 Office: Sys Svc Enterprises 795 Office Pkwy Saint Louis MO 63141-7137

**KUHN, GRETCHEN,** lawyer; b. San Antonio, June 11, 1951; d. Charles Louis and Evelyn (Patterson) K.; m. Dennis Norman Carnes, Oct. 29, 1977. BA, Rice U., Houston, 1973; JD, U. Tex., 1976. Bar: Colo. 1977. Land rep. Chevron U.S.A., Inc., Denver, 1976-80; atty, area landman Dome Petroleum Corp., Denver, 1980-81; atty., landman Hunt Oil Co., Denver and Dallas, 1981-87; ptnr. Kuhn & Carnes, Denver, 1987-91; shareholder Kuhn, Carnes & Anderson P.C., Denver, 1991—; pres. The Rockport-Essex Co., Denver, 1987—; v.p. H-3 USA for Poland, Denver. Mem. devel. com. Colo. Women's Found., Denver, 1987—; mem. Colo. Lawyers for Arts. Mem. ABA, Colo. Bar Assn., Denver Bar Assn., Colo. Petroleum Assn., Am. Assn. Petroleum Landmen, Rocky Mountain Mineral Law Found. (past trustee), Denver Art Mus. Democrat. Oil, gas, and mineral, Real property, General corporate. Home: 766 Downing St Denver CO 80218-3429 Office: 1525 17th St Denver CO 80202-1201

**KUHN, JAMES E.,** judge; b. Hammond, La., Oct. 31, 1946; s. Eton Percy and Mildred Louise (McDaniel) K.; m. Cheryl Aucoin, Dec. 27, 1969; children: James M., Jennifer L. BA, Southeastern La. U., 1968; JD, Loyola U. of South, 1973. Bar: La. 1973, Colo., 1995, U.S. Supreme Ct. 1978. Asst. dist. atty. 21st Jud. Dist. La., 1980-90; judge 21st Jud. Dist. Ct., Livinston, St. Helena, Tangipahoa, 1990-95; judge Ct. Appeals (1st cir.) Baton Rouge, 1995—; instr. history, govt. and criminal justice Southeastern La. U., Hammond, 1991—; mem. appellate ct. performance and standards com. La. Supreme Ct.; lectr. in field. Founder For Our Youth; past bd. dirs. La. Coun. Child Abuse, past sec.-treas. Conf. of Ct. Appeal Judges for State of La. Recipient Am. Jurisprudence award Loyola Law Sch. Mem. ABA, La. State Bar Assn. (Professionalism and Quality of Life com.), 21st Jud. Bar Assn., Livingston Parish Bar Assn., Delta Theta Phi. Home: 253 W Oak Ponchatoula LA 70454

**KUHN, JEFFREY CRAIG,** lawyer, educator; b. Cleve., Feb. 6, 1956; s. Gerald Russell and Greta Jean (Sawitke) K.; m. Joanie Christopher, Feb. 2, 1979; children: Jeana Marie, Jerrod Joseph, Jenny Rose, Jacob Tyler. BS, Bowling Green (Ohio) State U., 1978; JD, Cleveland Marshall Sch. Law, 1982. Bar: Ohio 1983, Mich. 1996, U.S. Dist. Ct. (mo. dist.) Ohio, 1996. Assoc. Cassidy & Mottl, Parma Heights, Ohio, 1982-86, ptnr., 1987-92; assoc. legal counsel The Toledo (Ohio) Hosp., 1992-96; asst. gen. counsel ProMedica Health Sys., Toledo, 1996—; adj. prof. U. Findlay, Ohio, 1995-97; ethics com. Toledo Hosp., 1997—; institutional review bd. Toldedo Hosp., 1997—, Flower Hosp., 1997—, Childrens Med. Ctr., 1997—; gen. counsel, corp. v.p. legal svcs., sec. ProMedica Health Sys. and subs. corps., 1998—. Coach hockey, baseball. Recipient Am. Jurisprudence Book award criminal law Lawyers Cooperative, 1980. Mem. ABA, Ohio Bar Assn., Mich. Bar Assn., Toledo Bar Assn., Phi Sigma Alpha. Republican. Office: ProMedica Health Sys 2142 N Cove Blvd Toledo OH 43606-3895

**KUHNS, THOMAS O.,** lawyer; b. Patterson, N.J., Sept. 10, 1955; s. Ray Kier and Florence Elizabeth K.; m. Amy Kuhns, Sept. 5, 1981; children: Ben, Peter, Betsy, Paul. BA, Lafayette Coll., Easton, Pa., 1977; JD, Northwestern U., Chgo., 1980. Bar: Ill. 1980; U.S. Supreme Ct. 1985; U.S. Ct. Appeals (3rd cir.) 1981, U.S. Ct. Appeals (4th cir.) 1993, U.S. Ct. Appeals (5th cir.) 1988, U.S. Ct. Appeals (7th cir.) 1985, U.S. Ct. Appeals (8th cir.) 1989. Law clk. to Honorable James Hunter III U.S. Ct. Appeals for 3rd Cir., Phila., 1980-81; with Kirkland & Ellis, Chgo. Exec. editor: Northwestern Univ. Law Rev., 1979-80. Recipient Pro Bono award Protection and Advocacy Soc., Chgo., 1996. Federal civil litigation, Antitrust, Toxic tort. Office: Kirkland & Ellis 200 E Randolph St Chicago IL 60601-6436

**KUHRAU, EDWARD W.,** lawyer; b. Caney, Kans., Apr. 19, 1935; s. Edward E. and Dolores (Hardman) K.; m. Janiece Christal; children: Quentin, Clayton. BA, U. Tex., 1960; JD, U. So. Calif., 1965. Bar: Calif. 1966, Wash. 1968, Alaska 1977. With Perkins Coie (and predecessor firms), Seattle, 1968—, ptnr., 1973—. Editor-in-chief Wash. Real Property Deskbook; contbr. articles to profl. jours. With USAF, 1955-58. Mem. ABA, Wash. Bar Assn., Am. Coll. Real Estate Lawyers, Pacific Real Estate Inst. (pres., founding trustee), Order of Coif, Seattle Yacht Club. Real property, Banking, Finance. Office: Perkins Coie 1201 3rd Ave Fl 40 Seattle WA 98101-3029

**KUHRT, RICHARD LEE,** lawyer; b. Newark, Apr. 24, 1959; s. William Donald and Phyllis Alta (Norton) K.; m. Karen Ruth Dunkle. BA, Hope Coll., 1981; JD, Seton Hall U., 1984. Bar: N.J. 1984. Assoc. Joseph A. Ginarte, Newark, 1984-85; ptnr. Kuhrt & Femia, Elizabeth, N.J., 1985—; atty. adviser Frank H. Morrell Moot Ct., Irvington, N.J., 1985-92. Mem. Three Bridges Reformed Ch. (elder). Mem. ABA, N.J. Bar Assn. (speaker 1987—, fed. practice com. 1987—), Essex and Union County Bar Assn., Assn. Trial Lawyers Assn. (Plaintiff's Trial Acad.), N.J. Trial Lawyers Assn., Essex County Inns. of Ct., ACLU, Patrick J. McNally Civic Assn. Democrat. Avocations: reading, sports. Personal injury, Workers' compensation, Criminal. Office: Kuhrt & Femia 40 Parker Rd Ste 110 Elizabeth NJ 07208-2148

**KUKLIN, ANTHONY BENNETT,** lawyer; b. N.Y.C., Oct. 9, 1929; s. Norman B. and Deane (Cable) K.; m. Vivienne May Hall, Apr. 4, 1964; children: Melissa, Amanda. AB, Harvard U., 1950; JD, Columbia U., 1953. Bar: N.Y. 1953, D.C. 1970. Assoc. Dwight, Royall, Harris, Koegel & Caskey, N.Y.C., 1955-61; assoc. Paul, Weiss, Rifkind, Wharton & Garrison, N.Y.C., 1961-69, ptnr., 1969-95, counsel, 1995—; lectr. in Law, Columbia Law Sch., 1997—; bd. dirs. Chgo. Title & Trust Co., Chgo. Title Ins. Co., 1986-96. Contbr. articles to legal jours. Mem. ABA (chmn., sec. real property, probate and trust law 1987-88), Internat. Bar Assn. (chmn. div. one 1985-88), N.Y. State Bar Assn. (chmn. sect. real property 1981-82), Assn. of Bar of city of N.Y., Am. Coll. Real Estate Lawyers (pres. 1981-82), Anglo-Am. Real Property Inst. (chmn. 1989), Am. Coll. Constrn. Lawyers. Real property. Home: 22 Pryer Ln Larchmont NY 10538-4022 Office: Paul Weiss Rifkind Wharton & Garrison Ste # 4200 1285 Ave of Ams Fl 22 New York NY 10019-6065

**KULESZA, JOSEPH DOMINICK, JR.,** lawyer; b. Wilmington, Del., Oct. 18, 1961; s. Joseph Dominick Sr. and Mary Ann (Newell) K.; m. Linda Ann George, July 26, 1986; children: Joseph Dominick III, Thomas D. BA, St. Joseph's U., 1983; paralegal cert., U. Del., 1985; JD, Widener U., 1987. Bar: Del. 1987. Jud. intern Justice of Peace Cts., Wilmington, 1978, law clk., 1983; paralegal Jacobs and Crumplar P.A., Wilmington, 1984-86; asst. supr. Bank of N.Y. (Del.), Newark, 1985-87; pvt. practice Wilmington, 1987—. Mem. ABA, Del. Bar Assn., Del. Trial Lawyers Assn., Delta Theta Phi. Democrat. Roman Catholic. Avocations: golf, racquetball, swimming. Family and matrimonial, General civil litigation, General practice. Office: Agostini Levitsky Isaacs & Kulesza 824 N Market St Wilmington DE 19801-3024

**KULINSKY, LOIS,** lawyer; b. Chgo., Mar. 17, 1946; d. Ben Albert and Florence Sylvia (Barth) Kay; m. Fred Martin Kulinsky, Sept. 4, 1967 (div. 1980); 1 child, Jeffrey. BS, U. Minn., 1967; MAT, U. Chgo., 1970; JD, Ill. Inst. Tech., 1980. Bar: Ill. 1980, U.S. Dist. Ct. (no. dist.) Ill. 1980, U.S. Supreme Ct. 1995. Tchr. Chgo. Pub. Schs., 1967-70, Maine Twp. Schs., Des Plaines, Ill., 1971-80; atty. John P. Biestek & Assocs., Arlington Heights, Ill., 1980-83; pvt. practice Wheeling, Ill., 1983—. Mem. Ill. Bar Assn., Chgo. Bar Assn., Lake County Bar Assn. Avocations: photography, art. Family and matrimonial, General practice, Probate. Office: 395 E Dundee Rd Ste 200 Wheeling IL 60090-7003

**KULLER, JONATHAN MARK,** lawyer; b. Paterson, N.J., Jan. 2, 1951; George and Muriel (Kaplan) K.; m. Mardi Risa Adelman, Oct. 8, 1977; children: Brett Louis, Devin Howard. BS, Livingston Coll., 1972; JD, Rutgers U., 1976. Bar: N.J. 1976, U.S. Dist. Ct. N.J. 1976, U.S. Supreme Ct. 1985. Law clk. to presiding judge N.J. Superior Ct., Hackensack, 1976-77; assoc. Miller & Platt, Paterson, 1977-78; ptnr. Markus, Kuller & Cohen, Parsippany, N.J., 1978-87, Blaustein & Wasserman, Woodbridge, N.J., 1987-98; spl. counsel L'Abbate, Balkan, Colavita & Contini, L.L.P., Livingston, N.J., 1998—. Mem. N.J. Bar Assn., Middlesex County Bar Assn., Comml. Law League Am. Democrat. Jewish. Avocation: tennis. Contracts commercial, Bankruptcy, Real property. Office: L'Abbate Balkan Et Al 7 Regent St Ste 711 Livingston NJ 07039-1617

**KULONGOSKI, THEODORE RALPH,** state supreme court justice; b. Nov. 5, 1940; married; 3 children. BA, U. Mo., 1967, JD, 1970. Bar: Oreg., Mo., U.S. Dist. Ct. Oreg., U.S. Ct. Appeals (9th cir.). Legal counsel Oreg. State Ho. of Reps., 1973-74; founding and sr. ptnr. Kulongoski, Durham, Drummonds & Colombo, Oreg., 1974-87; deputy dist. atty. Mulnomah County, Oreg., 1992—. State rep. Lane County (Oreg.), 1974-77, state senator, 1977-83; chmn. Juvenile Justice Task Force, 1994, Gov.'s Commn. Organized Crime; mem. Criminal Justice Coun.; exec. dir. Met. Family Svc., 1992; dir. Oreg. Dept. Ins. and Fin., 1987-91. Mem. Oreg State Bar Assn., Mo. Bar Assn. Office: Oreg Supreme Ct 1163 State St Salem OR 97310-1331

**KUMBLE, STEVEN JAY,** lawyer; b. July 3, 1933; m. Barbara Kumble (div.); children: Charles Todd, Roger Glenn; m. Peggy Basten Vandervoort. BA, Yale U., 1954; JD, Harvard U., 1959; LLD (hon.), L.I. U., 1990. Bar: N.Y. 1960. Ptnr. Finley, Kumble, Wagner, Underberg, Manley & Casey, N.Y.C., 1968-87; of counsel Summit Rovins & Feldesman, N.Y.C., 1988-90; chmn. bd. dirs. Lincolnshire Mgmt., Inc., N.Y.C., 1985—. Vice chmn. bd. dirs. L.I.U., Greenvale, N.Y., 1984—, chm., 1982-94; trustee bd. Gov.'s Com. on Scholastic Achievement, N.Y.C., 1981—. 1st lt. U.S. Army, 1955-57. Mem. Assn. of Bar of City of N.Y., Phi Beta Kappa, Yale Club. Avocations: skiing, golf. General corporate, Real property. Office: Lincolnshire Mgmt 780 3rd Ave 40th Fl New York NY 10017-2024

**KUMMER, RICHARD EDWARD, JR.,** lawyer; b. Newark, June 3, 1948; s. Richard Edward and Fleurette Lydia (Raymond) K. BA, SUNY, Stony Brook, 1970; JD, N.Y. Law Sch., N.Y.C., 1974. Bar: N.Y.1975, N.J. 1981; U.S. Ct. Appeals (2d cir.) 1975, U.S. Ct. Appeals (3d cir. 1986), U.S. Supreme Ct. 1987. Law clk. to presiding judge U.S. Dist. Ct. N.J., Newark, 1974-76; assoc. Skadden, Arps, Slate, Meagher & Flom, N.Y.C., 1976-79; ptnr. Carella, Byrne, Bain & Gilfilian, Roseland, N.J., 1979-85, Kummer, Knox, Naughton & Hansbury, Parsippany, N.J., 1985—. Contbr. articles to profl. jours. Mem. Fed. Bar Assn. N.J., N.J. State Bar Assn., Morris County Bar Assn., Morris County C. of C. Repubican. General civil litigation, Environmental. Office: Kummer Knox Naughton & Hansbury 229 Cherry Hill Rd Parsippany NJ 07054-1107

**KUMP, KARY RONALD,** lawyer; b. Provo, Utah, Apr. 27, 1952; s. Ronald and Ann (Thomas) K.; m. Terri Renee Farley, Sept. 24, 1980; children: Kasey Ronald, Kyle Thomas, Kristopher Lewis, Kolby Lawrence, Karson Jack. AA, Rio Hondo Coll., 1972; BA, U. Calif., Fullerton, 1976; JD, Western State U., Fullerton, 1980; cert. trial advocacy, Hastings Law Sch., 1982. Bar: Calif. 1982, Utah 1995, U.S. Dist. Ct. (ctrl. dist.) Calif. 1982, (no. and so. dists.) Calif. 1985. Assoc. William G. Kellen & Assocs., Riverside, Calif., 1980-83, Kellen & Luchs, Riverside, 1983-84; ptnr. Luchs, Kump & Milelich, Riverside, 1984-85, Carter & Kump, Riverside, 1985-87; sole practice Riverside, 1987-90; ptnr. Kump & Kennedy, 1990-98, Kump & Earven, 1998-99, Law Offices of Farley & Kump, LLP, Carpinteria, Calif., 1999—; panel atty. Lawyer Referral Svc., Riverside, 1982—, Coll. Legal Clinic, Riverside, 1984—, Montgomery Ward Legal Svcs. Plan, Riverside, 1986—; judge pro tem Riverside Mcpl. Ct.; arbitrator Riverside Superior Ct.; mediator 4th Dist. Ct. Appeals; hearing officer City of Riverside. Exec. post advisor Boy Scouts Am. Mem. ABA, State Bar Calif. (bd. govs., Svc. Contbn. award 1984), Riverside Bar Assn. (panel atty. 1982, co-chair pub. bar rels., fee arbitrator, mediator client rels.), Assn. Trial Lawyers Am., Santa Barbara Bar Assn., Inland Empire Bankruptcy Forum, Ventura/Santa Barbara Trial Lawyers Assn. Republican. Mormon. Avocations: golf, tennis, fishing, scuba diving. E-mail: kary@j.farley.com. Personal injury, Bankruptcy, State civil litigation. Office: PO Box 937 1056 Eugenia Pl Carpinteria CA 93014

**KUNDA, PRESTON B.,** lawyer; b. Waukegan, Ill., Nov. 20, 1964; m. F. Arlene Houze, Dec. 19, 1992. BA in History, Trevecca Nazarene Coll., Nashville, 1991; JD, John Marshall Law Sch., Atlanta, 1995. Bar: Ga. 1995, U.S. Dist. Ct. (no. and ctrl. dists.) Ga. Pvt. practice Marietta, Ga., 1996—; bd. dirs. Stupid PC, Inc., Norcross, Ga. Served with U.S. Army, 1985-88, Germany. Mem. Sports Lawyers Assn. Republican. Mem. Ch. of the Nazarene. Avocations: classic cars, computers. General corporate, Real property, Sports. Office: 1626 Frederica Rd Ste 202 Saint Simons Island GA 31522-2526

**KUNDINGER, MATHEW HERMANN,** lawyer, author, entrepreneur; b. Wuerzburg, Fed. Republic Germany, Aug. 7, 1955; s. Joseph and Erika (Endres) K. MSME, Inst. Tech., Wuerzburg-Schweinfurt, 1982; PhD, Greenwich U., 1990; JD, U. West Los Angeles Sch. Law, 1991. Bar: Calif. 1991. Sales rep. Michelin Tire Corp., Karlsruhe, Fed. Republic Germany, 1977; trainee Mercedes-Benz, Wuerzburg, Fed. Republic Germany, 1983; sales/project engr. Gerhard Schubert Machinery, Crailsheim, W.Ger., 1983-84; tech. support mgr. F&E Hedman-LA, Inc., L.A., 1984-87; gen. mgr. Diamond Copy Products, Gardena, Calif., 1987; pres. 140 Plus Mgmt. Cons., Inc., L.A., 1985-90; pvt. practice L.A., 1991—; prin. Am.-German Legal Svcs., Santa Monica, Calif., 1996—. Author: California Here I Come, 1987. Avocations: writing. E-mail: agls@linkline.com. Private international, Consumer commercial, Contracts commercial. Home and Office: PO Box 34793 Los Angeles CA 90034-0793

**KUNE, BERNARD JACK,** lawyer, retired judge; b. Washington, Sept. 30, 1924; s. Isador M. and Emma Kune; m. Mina Kune, Jan. 30, 1950; children: Sandra J., Cheryl M., Jeffrey D. BA, George Washington U., 1948, JD, 1950; BBA, Benjamin Franklin U., 1956. Bar: D.C., U.S. Ct. Appeals (D.C. cir.), U.S. Dist. Ct. D.C. Trial atty. U.S. Govt., Washington, 1951-73; judge U.S. Govt., Washinton, 1973, Providence, 1973-81, Tampa, Fla., 1981-87; mediator State of Fla., Tampa, 1988-96, Boynton Beach, 1996—. Sgt. U.S. Army, 1945-46. Mem. ABA. Home: 7709 Rockford Rd Boynton Beach FL 33437-2521

**KUNERT, PAUL CHARLES,** lawyer; b. Hankinson, N.D., Jan. 14, 1935; s. Harry Firdinand Kunert and Mary Bernice Sisson; m. Sandra Kathryn Rood, Nov, 19, 1962 (dec. June 1994); children: Melissa, Kathryn, Miles Joseph; m. Paricia Joan McGraw, Oct. 11, 1997. Student, St. John's U., 1954-55; BA, U. Minn., 1956, JD cum laude, 1960. Bar: Minn. 1962, U.S. Dist. Ct. Minn. 1972. Assoc. Robins, Davis & Lyons, St. Paul, 1961-66; ptnr. Sahr, Kunert & Tambornino, Mpls., 1967-96, Kunert, Kambornino & Kuhar, Mpls., 1996—. Mem. Minn. Trial Lawyers Assn., Minn. Def. Lawyers Assn., Hennepin County Bar Assn. General civil litigation, Insurance. Office: Kunert Tambornino & Kuhar 2505 Centre Village 431 S 7th St Minneapolis MN 55415-1821

**KUNKEL, DANIEL JAMES,** lawyer; b. Cleve., Nov. 20, 1961; s. James A. and Sue Counts K.; m. Maggie Mechtild Burghardt, Sept. 25, 1987. BA, U. Wis., 1988; JD, U. San Diego, 1993. Bar: Calif. 1993, Hawaii 1994, N.Mex. 1994, U.S. Dist. Ct. Hawaii 1994, Colo. 1995, Minn. 1995, D.C. 1995, U.S. Ct. Appeals (9th cir.) 1995. Law clk. Honolulu Corp. Coun., 1993-94, deputy corp. coun., 1994-95; jud. clk. Supreme Ct. Hawaii, Honolulu, 1995-97; staff atty. McCorriston Miho Miller Mukai, Honolulu, 1997-98, assoc., 1999—. Democrat. Avocations: jogging, swimming, hiking. Insurance, Federal civil litigation, State civil litigation. Home: 3933A Koko Dr Honolulu HI 96816-4306 Office: McCorriston Miho Miller Mukai PO Box 2800 Honolulu HI 96803-2800

**KUNKEN, KENNETH JAMES,** lawyer; b. Mineola, N.Y., July 15, 1950; s. Leonard Yale and Judith Mae Kunken. BS, Cornell U., 1973, MA, 1977; MEd, Columbia U., 1976; JD, Hofstra U., 1982. Bar: U.S. Dist. Ct. (ea. and so. dist.) N.Y. 1983, U.S. Supreme Ct. 1997, U.S. Ct. Appeals (fed. cir.) 1997. Vocat. rehab. counselor Human Resources Ctr., Albertson, N.Y., 1977-79; asst. dist. atty. Nassau County Dist. Attys. Office, Mineola, N.Y., 1982-96; dep. bur. chief N.C. Dist. Atty. Office, Mineola, 1997—; Instr. Nat. Inst. of Trail Advocacy, Hempstead, N.Y., 1993—. Recipient Judge Thomas E. Ryan award Nassau County Ct. Officers Benevolent Assn., 1996. Mem. N.C. Bar Assn., Hofstra U. Sch. of Law Alumni (adv. com. 1993-96). Office: Nassau County Dist Attys Office 262 Old Country Rd Mineola NY 11501-4251

**KUNKLE, WILLIAM JOSEPH, JR.,** lawyer; b. Lakewood, Ohio, Sept. 3, 1941; s. William Joseph and Georgia (Howe) K.; m. Sarah Florence Nesti, July 11, 1964; children: Kathleen Margaret, Susan Mary. BA, Northwestern U., Evanston, Ill., 1963; Jd, Northwestern U., 1969. Bar: Ohio 1969, U.S. Dist. Ct. (no. dist.) Ill. 1969, Ill. 1969, U.S. Ct. Appeals (7th cir.) 1991, U.S. Supreme Ct. 1991. Process control engr. Union Carbide Corp., Cleve., 1964-65; prodn. supr. Union Carbide Corp., Greenville, S.C., 1965-66; assoc. Hauxhurst, Sharp, Mollison & Gallagher, Cleve., 1969-70; asst. pub. defender Cook County Pub. Defender, Chgo., 1970-73; asst. states atty. Cook County States Atty., Chgo., 1973-85; ptnr. Phelan, Cahill & Quinlan, Ltd., Chgo., 1985-96, Cahill, Christian & Kunkle, LTD., Chgo., 1996—; chmn. The Ill. Gaming Bd., 1990-93; dep. spl. outside counsel U.S. Ho. Reps., Washington, 1988-89; adj. prof. I.I.T. Chgo. Kent Sch. Law, 1980-84; instr. Nat. Inst. for Trial Advocacy, Chgo., 1978-82, 86; lectr. Nat. Coll. Dist. Attys., Houston, Denver, Chgo., Atlanta, Louisville, 1978-85, Nat. Law Enforcement Inst., San Francisco, Portland, Atlanta, Pitts., Boston, St. Louis, Chgo., 1983-85; 1st asst. states atty. of Cook County, 1983-85; spl. state's atty. 18th Jud. Cir., DuPage County, 1995—. Contbg. author: Punishment Prosecutor's Viewpoint, 1983, 1989, Trial Techniques Compendium, Nat. College of Dist. Attys. (2d, 3rd, 4th, 5th, 6th eds.). Recipient Disting. Faculty award Nat. Coll. Dist. Attys., 1980, Award for Prosecution Svc. Chgo. Assn. Commerce & Industry, 1981. Fellow Am. Coll. Trial Lawyers, ABA; mem. Internat. Soc. Barristers, Nat. Dist. Attys. Assn. (bd. dirs. 1984-85), Assn. Govt. Attys. in Capital Litigation (pres. 1983-84), Chgo. Bar Assn. (bd. mgrs. 1983-84), Ill. State Bar Assn. (LAWPAC trustee 1989-95), Internat. Assn. Gaming Attys., Chgo. Crime Commn. Republican. Avocations: golf, softball, carpentry, motorcycling. General civil litigation, Criminal, Personal injury. Office: Cahill Christian & Kunkle Ltd 224 S Michigan Ave Ste 1300 Chicago IL 60604-2589

**KUNNEL, JOSEPH MATHEW,** lawyer; b. Ernakulam, Kerala, India, May 3, 1963; came to U.S., 1991; s. Matthew and Annakutty Kunnel; m. Valsamma Thottumkal, Jan. 19, 1989; children: Nicole Ann, Jimmy M., Megan E. B.Com., U. Kerala, India, 1983; LLB, U. Gulberga, Karnataka, India, 1987; LLM, Widener U., Wilmington, Del., 1993. Bar: Pa. 1994. Pvt. practice Kerala, 1987-91; ptnr. Pasquarella & Kunnel, Phila., 1994—. Pres Malayalee Assn. of Phila., 1997—. Mem. ABA, Pa. Bar Assn. (exec. com. minority bar), Phila. Bar Assn., Am. Immigration Lawyers Assn., Dist. Bar Assn. Kerala (sec. 1988-90). Avocations: reading, writing, travel. Immigration, naturalization, and customs, Personal injury, Workers' compensation. Office: Pasquarella & Kunnel 1401 Walnut St Philadelphia PA 19102-3128

**KUNTZ, CHARLES POWERS,** lawyer; b. L.A., May 7, 1944; s. Walter Nichols and Katherine (Powers) K.; m. June Emerson Moroney, Dec. 23, 1969; children: Michael Nicholas, Robinson Moroney, Katie Moroney. AB with honors, Stanford U., 1966, JD, 1969; LLM, NYU, 1971. Bar: Calif. 1970, N.Y. 1970, U.S. Dist. Ct. (no. dist.) Calif. 1970, U.S. Ct. Appeals (9th cir.) 1970, U.S. Supreme Ct. 1979. Staff atty. project for urban affairs Office Econ. Opportunity, N.Y.C., 1969-71; dep. pub. defender Contra Costa County Pub. Defender's Office, Martinez, Calif., 1971-75; assoc. Treuhaft, Walker & Brown, Oakland, Calif., 1976-78; ptnr. Hirsch & Kuntz, San Rafael, Calif., 1979-85; pvt. practice San Rafael, 1985-89; ptnr. Coombs & Dunlap, Napa, Calif., 1989—. Mem. ABA, Calif. Attys. Consumer Justice, Napa County Bar Assn. General civil litigation, Insurance, Personal injury. Home: 1271 Monticello Rd Napa CA 94558-2019 Office: Coombs & Dunlap 1211 Division St Napa CA 94559-3372

**KUNTZ, JOEL DUBOIS,** lawyer; b. Dennis, Mass., Feb. 5, 1946; s. Paul Grimley Kuntz and Harriette (Hunter) Ainsworth; m. Karan Judd, June 29, 1968; children: Matthew Christopher, Kristin Lara. BA, Haverford Coll., 1968; JD, Yale U., 1971; LLM in Taxation, NYU, 1980. Bar: Conn. 1972, Oreg. 1974. Assoc. Stoel, Rives, Boley, Jones & Grey, Portland, Oreg., 1974-79, ptnr., 1979-94; v.p., gen. counsel Entek Internat. LLC, Lebanon, Oreg., 1994—. Co-author: (with James S. Eustice) Federal Income Taxation of S Corporations, 1982, 3d edit., 1993; (with James S. Eustice, Charles S. Lewis III and Thomas P. Deering) Tax Reform Act of 1986: Analysis and Commentary, 1987; (with Robert J. Peroni) U.S. International Taxation, 1992. Capt. USMC, 1971-74. Mem. Am. Coll. Tax Counsel, Internat. Fiscal Assn. Democrat. Corporate taxation, Personal income taxation, General corporate. Home: 3910 Lakeview Blvd Lake Oswego OR 97035-5549 Address: PO Box 39 Lebanon OR 97355-0039

**KUNTZ, WILLIAM FRANCIS, II,** lawyer, educator; b. N.Y.C., June 24, 1950; s. William Francis I and Margaret Evelyn (Brown) K.; m. Alice Beal, May 20, 1978; children: William Thaddeus, Katharine Lowell, Elizabeth Anne. AB, Harvard U., 1972, AM, 1974, JD, 1977, PhD, 1979. Bar: N.Y. 1978. Assoc. Shearman & Sterling, N.Y.C., 1978-86; mem. Milgrim, Thomajan & Lee, N.Y.C., 1986-94; ptnr. Seward & Kissel, N.Y.C., 1994—; assoc. prof. Bklyn. Law Sch., 1987—. Author: Criminal Sentencing, 1988. Bd. dirs. MFY Legal Svcs., Inc., N.Y.C., 1984-90, Boys Brotherhood Republic, N.Y.C., 1986-90, Habitat for Humanity, N.Y.C., 1987-90; chmn. Resources for Children with Spl. Needs, N.Y.C., 1986-89; mem. N.Y. Civilian Complaint Rev. Bd., 1987—, chmn., 1994. Mem. ABA, N.Y. State Bar Assn., N.Y. County Lawyers Assn. (bd. dirs. 1991-96), Assn. of Bar of City of N.Y. (chmn. mcpl. affairs com. 1992-95, judiciary com.), Bklyn. Bar Assn. (judiciary com. 1995—), Met. Black Bar Assn. Democrat. Roman Catholic. Office: Seward & Kissel 1 Battery Park Plz Fl 21 New York NY 10004-1485

**KUNTZ, WILLIAM HENRY,** lawyer, mediator; b. Indpls., Feb. 27, 1954; s. Herman William and Ethel Cleora (Stangle) K. BA in Chemistry, Purdue U. at Indpls., 1984; MS in Chemistry, Purdue U., Indpls., 1986; JD, Ind. U., Indpls., 1989. Bar: Ind. 1989, U.S. Dist. Ct. (so. and no. dists.) Ind. 1989, U.S. Patent Office 1992, U.S. Supreme Ct. 1993. Assoc. Urdal, Tarvin and Alexander, P.C., Connersville, Ind., 1989-90; dep. prosecutor County of Fayette, Connersville, 1990, chief dep. prosecutor, 1991-92; pvt. practice Indpls., 1992-94; chief dep. prosecutor Fayette County, Connersville, 1995-98; with Baker and Bodwell, P.C., Connersville, Ind., 1999—. Mem. ABA, Nat. Bar Assn., Ind. State Bar Assn. (bd. dirs. ADR sect. 1997—), Indpls. Bar Assn. (chmn. legal awareness com. 1996, chmn. law student liaison com. 1996), Fayette County Bar Assn. (sec.-treas. 1989-90), Marion County Bar Assn., Ind. Trial Lawyers Assn., Ind. Assn. Mediators (sec. 1993-94, 97—, pres.-elect 1994-95, pres. 1995-96), Soc. Profls. in Dispute Resolution, Acad. Family Mediators, Purdue U. Indpls. Sch. Sci. Alumni Bd. (v.p. 1998—). Home: 2065 Lick Creek Dr Indianapolis IN 46203-4922 Office: Bader and Bodwell PC County of Fayette 621 N Central Ave Ste 1 Connersville IN 47331-2012

**KUNZ, MICHAEL E.,** legal administrator; b. Bristol, Pa., Feb. 13, 1943; s. Frank John Kunz and Mary Margaret Corrigan; m. Marleen Agnes Senkarik, Aug. 10, 1963; children: Catherine, Mary Ann, Joanne, Lisa. BS, St. Joseph's U., 1970, MBA, 1980. Dep. clk. U.S. Dist. Ct. (ea. dist.) Pa., Phila., 1962-75, chief dep. clk., 1976-79, clk. of the ct., 1979—. Contbr. articles to profl. jours. Active adv. bd. Coll. Bus. Adminstrn., St. Joseph's U., Phila., 1990—. Recipient Bartholomew A. Sheehan award St. Joseph's U. Law Alumni, 1987, Dir.'s Outstanding Leadership award Adminstrv. Office U.S. Cts., 1992; named for Outstanding Leadership, Fed. Cts. Com. Phila. Bar, 1989. Mem. Am. Judicature Soc., Fed. Cts. Clks. Assn., Capitol Historical Soc., Hist. Soc. USDC, EDPA (sec.). Office: US Dist Ct 2609 US Courthouse Philadelphia PA 19106

**KUPCHAK, KENNETH ROY,** lawyer; b. Forrest Hills, Pa., May 15, 1942; s. Frank V. and Anne B. (Ruzanic) K.; m. Patricia K. Geer, Jan. 27, 1967; children: Lincoln K., Robinson K. AB, Cornell U., 1964; BS, Pa. State U., 1965; JD in Internat. Affairs, Cornell U., 1971. Bar: Hawaii 1971, U.S. Dist. Ct. Hawaii 1971, U.S. Supreme Ct. 1988. Meteorology staff U. Hawaii, Honolulu, 1968; ptnr. Damon Key Leong Kupchak & Hastert, Honolulu, 1971—, also bd. dirs.; chief minority counsel 8th legis. Hawaii Ho. of Reps., Honolulu, 1974-75, legis. coord. Hawaii State Assn. Counties, Honolulu, 1988; bd. dirs. Fletcher Constrn. Co., N.Am. Ltd., Dinwiddie constrn. Co., San Francisco, Fletcher Gen. Ltd., Seattle; adj. prof. William S. Richardson Sch. of Law, U. Hawaii, 1993; mem. Honolulu Common Fgn. Rels., 1995—; vice chair bd. counselors Mid-Pacific Inst., 1993-95; bd. trustees Mid-Pacific Inst., 1995—, chmn. personnel com., vice chmn. edn. com.; lectr. on constrn. law. Co-author: Fifty State Construction Lien and Bond Laws, 1992, The Design/Build Process, 1997, A State-By-State Guide to Architect, Engineer and Contractor Licensing, 1998, A State-By-State Guide to Construction and Design Law, 1998; contbr. articles to profl. jours. Chair agenda com. C.Z.M. Statewide Adv. Com., Hawaii, 1980-92; pres., bd. dirs. Hawaii Cmty. Svc. Coun., Honolulu, 1982-88; trustee Moanalua Gardens Found., 1985-88, Operation Raleigh (N.C.) U.S.A., 1986-90; bd. dirs., chair program com. Hawaii Nature Ctr., 1989—; chair Hawaii State Commn. on Korean and Vietnam War Meml., 1992-95. Capt. USAF, 1964-68, Vietnam. Centennial fellow Pa. State U., 1996. Fellow Am. Coll. Constrn. Lawyers; mem. ABA (constrn. industry forum, dispute resolution steering com. 1994—, chair 1998—), Hawaii Bar Assn., Internat. Bar Assn., Am. Arbitration Assn. (panel arbitrators), USAF Assn. (v.p. Hawaii chpt. 1994-97), Cornell Law Alumni Assn. (exec. com. 1990-93), Cornell Club Hawaii (bd. dirs., chair scholarship com. 1994—), Oahu Country Club, Volcano Golf and Country Club. Avocations: lacrosse, hiking, photography. Construction, Real property, Land use and zoning (including planning). Office: 1600 Pauahi Tower 1001 Bishop St Honolulu HI 96813-3429

**KUPFERBERG, LLOYD SHERMAN,** lawyer; b. Chgo., May 11, 1931; s. Emanuel and Lillian (Chalfen) K.; m. Barbara Jean Behr, July 22, 1956; children: Susan, Janis, Peter. BA, U. Wis., 1953; JD, Harvard U., 1956. Bar: Ill. 1956, U.S. Dist. Ct. (no. dist.) Ill. 1960, U.S. Ct. Appeals (7th cir.) 1964, U.S. Supreme Ct. 1975. Assoc. atty. Lederer, Livingston, Kahn & Adsit, Chgo., 1960-63; ptnr. Schwartz, Cooper, Kolb & Gaynor (now Schwartz, Cooper, Greenberger & Krauss, Chartered), Chgo., 1963—; bd. dirs. TK Group, Inc., Rockford, Ill. Pres. 113 caucus High Sch. Dist., Highland Park, Ill., 1972; commr. Traffic Commn., Highland Park, 1975-83. Mem. Ill. State Bar Assn., Chgo. Bar Assn., Std. Club, Birchwood Club (pres. 1978-80), Longboat Key Club. Jewish. Avocations: swimming, baseball cap collecting. General corporate, Estate planning. Home: 800 Deerfield Rd Apt 206 Highland Park IL 60035-3548

**KUPIETZKY, MOSHE J.,** lawyer; b. N.Y.C., May 17, 1944; s. Jacob Harry and Fanny (Dresner) K.; m. Arlene Debra Usdan, June 22, 1966; children: Jay, Jeff, Jacob. BBA cum laude, CCNY, 1965; LLB, Harvard U., 1968, JD magna cum laude, 1968. Bar: N.Y. 1969, Calif. 1970. Law clerk to Hon. William B. Herlands U.S. Dist. Ct., N.Y.C., 1968-69; assoc. Mitchell Silberberg & Knupp, L.A., Calif., 1969-74; ptnr. Mitchell Silberberg & Knupp, L.A., 1974-80; ptnr., prin. Hayutin Rubinroit Praw & Kupietzky, L.A., 1980-87; ptnr. Sidley & Austin, L.A., 1987—. Bd. dirs. Nat. Inst. Jewish Hospice, Beverly Hills, Calif., 1986—; mem. bd. advisors Graziadio Sch. Bus. and Mgmt. Pepperdine U., L.A., 1996-98. Mem. ABA, Beverly Hills Bar Assn., L.A. County Bar Assn. Contracts commercial, General corporate. Office: Sidley & Austin 555 W 5th St Ste 4000 Los Angeles CA 90013-3000

**KUPPERMAN, HENRY JOHN,** lawyer; b. N.Y.C., May 18, 1957; s. Ben J. and Roma M. (Ash) K.; m. Rebecca Beauchamp, 1990; 1 child, Jonathan Andrew. BA, Johns Hopkins U., 1978; JD, St. John's U., 1982. Bar: N.Y. 1983, U.S. Ct. Appeals (3d cir.) 1983, Pa. 1984, Calif. 1987, U.S. Ct. Appeals (9th cir.) 1987, U.S. Supreme Ct. 1988; cert. fraud examiner. Student law clk. to judge U.S. Dist. Ct., N.Y.C., 1981-82; law clk. to chief judge U.S. Dist. Ct., Wilmington, Del., 1982-83; assoc. Drinker, Biddle & Reath, Phila., 1984-86; assoc. Brobeck, Phleger & Harrison, L.A., 1986-89, ptnr., 1990-93; gen. counsel, dir. West Coast ops. The Investigative Group, Internat., Inc., L.A., 1994—. Mem. ABA (co-chmn. subcom. on fed. local procedure 1986-88), Calif. Bar Assn. L.A. Bar Assn., Beverly Hills Bar Assn. Jewish. Criminal, Intellectual property, Private international. Office: The Investigative Group Internat Inc 725 S Figueroa St Ste 2400 Los Angeles CA 90017-5424 also: Kroll Assocs 300 S Grand Ave Ste 1300 Los Angeles CA 90071-3123

**KUPPERMAN, LOUIS BRANDEIS,** lawyer; b. Augusta, Ga., Dec. 16, 1946; s. Herbert Spencer and Mollie (Kleven) K.; children: David Evan, Robert Dennis; m. Eileen Spadafina, Oct. 24, 1992. BS, Fairleigh Dickinson U., 1972; JD, Bklyn. Law Sch., 1975. Bar: Pa. 1975, U.S. Dist. Ct. (ea. dist.) Pa. 1978, U.S. Ct. Appeals (3d cir.) 1978, U.S. Supreme Ct. 1982. Jud. law clk. to Judge Jacob Kalish Ct. of Common Pleas of Phila. County, 1975-76, jud. law clk. to Judge Eugene Gelfand, 1976-77; corp. counsel Health Corp. Am., Wayne, Pa., 1977-78; ptnr. Dilworth, Paxson, Kalish & Kauffman, Phila., 1978-86; mem. firm, chmn. real estate dept. Baskin Flaherty Elliott & Mannino, P.C., Phila., 1986-90; ptnr., vice chmn. environ. law dept. Obermayer, Rebmann, Maxwell & Hippel, Phila., 1990—; lectr. Pa. Bar Inst. Author: Real Estate Tax Assessment Appeals, 1987. Chancellor's del. to Phila. Fairleigh Dickinson U., 1983, 86. Recipient Disting. Alumnus award Fairleigh Dickinson U., 1983. Mem. ABA, Pa. Bar Assn., Phila. Bar Assn., (chmn. real estate litigation com. 1983-85), Pyramid Club of Phila. General civil litigation, Real property, Environmental. Home: 80 Delancy Ct Phoenixville PA 19460-5741 Office: Obermayer Rebmann Maxwell & Hippel 1 Penn Ctr 19th Fl 1617 John F Kennedy Blvd Philadelphia PA 19103-1821

**KUPPERMAN, STEPHEN HENRY,** lawyer; b. New Orleans, Sept. 17, 1953; s. Abraham Bernard and Jo-Ellyn (Levy) K.; m. Mara Rothstein, Oct. 18, 1980; children: Zachary Hart, Shane Levi, Jake Benjamin. BA, Duke U., 1974; JD, Tulane U., 1977. Bar: La. 1977, U.S. Dist. Ct. (ea. dist.) La. 1977, U.S. Dist. Ct. (mid. dist.) La. 1978, U.S. Dist. Ct. (we. dist.) La. 1981, U.S. Ct. Appeals (5th cir.) 1977, U.S. Ct. Appeals (11th cir.) 1982, U.S. Supreme Ct. 1980. Assoc. Stone Pigman Walther Wittmann & Hutchinson, New Orleans, 1977-81, ptnr., 1981—; adj. prof. Tulane Law Sch., 1988—; mem. Tulane Law Rev., 1975-77, adv. bd., 1992—. Articles editor Tulane Law Rev., 1976-77, mem. 1975-76; contbr. articles to law revs., profl. jours. Bd. dirs. Goodwill Industries, 1980-87, mem. adv. bd. 1987-91; bd. dirs. Jewish Family Svcs., New Orleans, 1978-93, treas. 1986, v.p. 1987-88, pres., 1988-90; bd. dirs. Jewish Fedn., New Orleans, 1989-93, 95—, treas. 1991-93; adv. bd. mem. Jewish Endowment Found., New Orleans, 1979—; mem. adv. bd. Tulane Continuing Legal Edn. Program, 1983—, B'nai B'rith Anti-Defamation League S. Ctrl. Region, 1987—, vice-chmn., 1991-95, chmn. 1995-99; mem. Young Leadership Cabinet United Jewish Appeal, 1990-92; bd. dirs. Touro Infirmary Found., 1998—, Touro Synagogue, New Orleans, 1991—, sec. 1995-97, v.p. 1997-99. Mem. ABA, La. Bar Assn. (continuing legal edn. com. 1986-88, disciplinary conduct com. 1995—), New Orleans Bar Assn. (mem. Inn of Ct. 1994—), Fed. Bar Assn. (bd. dirs. New Orleans chpt. 1989-94), Securities Industry Assn., Order of Coif. Democrat. Jewish. Securities, State civil litigation, Federal civil litigation. Office: Stone Pigman Walther Wittmann & Hutchinson 546 Carondelet St Ste 100 New Orleans LA 70130-3588

**KURFIRST, LEONARD STANLEY,** lawyer; b. Chgo., Oct. 10, 1959; s. Leonard Richard and Margaret Josephine Kurfirst; m. Sally Gordon, Sept. 26, 1987; children: Kyle, Kelsy. BA, Stanford U., 1981; JD cum laude, Ind. U., 1984. Bar: Ill. 1984, U.S. Dist. Ct. (no. dist.) Ill. 1984. Assoc. Hinshaw & Culbertson, Chgo., 1984-86; assoc. Wildman, Harrold, Allen & Dixon, Chgo., 1986-92, ptnr., 1992-95; ptnr. Hickey, Driscoll, Kurfirst, Patterson & Melia, Chgo., 1995—. Editor De Paul Jour. Health Care Law, 1998. Commr. Traffic and Safety Commn., Village of Western Springs, Ill., 1993—; coach Am. Youth Soccer Orgn., Western Springs, 1998. Mem. ABA, Ill. Bar Assn., Chgo. Bar Assn. (chmn. med./legal rels. com. 1995-96). Avocations: softball, basketball, coaching. Health, Construction, General civil litigation. Office: Hickey Driscoll Kurfirst Patterson & Melia 77 W Washington St Ste 800 Chicago IL 60602-2804

**KURLAND, PAUL CARL,** lawyer, educator; b. Bklyn., May 28, 1946; s. Marvin and Beatrice (Marmer) K.; m. Phyllis Pfeffer, Sept. 1, 1968; children: Joshua Ethan, Abigail Sara. BA, Bklyn. Coll., 1967; JD, NYU, 1970. Bar: N.Y. 1971, U.S. Ct. Appeals (2d cir.) 1971, U.S. Dist. Ct. (so. and ea. dists.) N.Y. 1972, U.S. Supreme Ct. 1974. Assoc. Cahill, Gordon & Reindel,

N.Y.C., 1970-73, Emil, Korbin, Klein & Garbus, N.Y.C., 1973-77; ptnr. Kurland and Scheiman, N.Y.C., 1977-79, Baer, Marks & Upham, N.Y.C., 1979-85, Snow, Becker & Krauss, P.C., N.Y.C., 1986—; mem. faculty Nat. Inst. Trial Advocacy, 1980—, faculty trial techniques course Hofstra U., 1980—, Emory U., 1982-91, Cardozo Law Sch., 1987—; arbitrator U.S. Dist. Ct. (ea. dist.) N.Y., Am. Arbitration Assn. Pres. Manhasset (N.Y.) Dem. Club; mem. Nassau County Dem. Com.; bd. dirs. World Hunger Yr.; bd. dirs. Sing Out mag. Mem. ACLU, ABA, Assn. Bar City of N.Y. Federal civil litigation, State civil litigation. Home: 142 Hemlock Rd Manhasset NY 11030-1216 Office: Snow Becker & Krauss PC 605 3rd Ave Fl 25 New York NY 10158-0125

**KUROWSKI, CHARLES EDWARD,** lawyer; b. Washington, Pa., Sept. 26, 1952; s. Albert J. and Anna (Sleziak) K. BA, Geneva Coll., Beaver Falls, Pa., 1974; M in Sociology, Duquesne U., 1977, JD, 1980. Bar: Pa. Pvt. practice Canonsburg, Pa. Mem. Washington County Dem. Com., 1988—. Mem. Am. Legion, T.P.A., Polish Am. Citizens and Benefits Club, Pulaski-Slovak-Bears Club, Pulaski Literary Soc., Polish Am. Congress, Alpine VFW Club, Moose, Elks, Eagles, White Eagles. Avocation: remodeling real estate. Family and matrimonial, Consumer commercial, Construction. Office: 12 N Jefferson Ave Canonsburg PA 15317-1306

**KURRELMEYER, LOUIS HAYNER,** retired lawyer; b. Troy, N.Y., July 26, 1928; s. Bernhard and Lucy Julia (Hayner) K.; m. Phyllis A. Damon, June 14, 1952 (div. 1973); children: Ellen Laura, Louis Hayner, Nancy Snow; m. Martina Sophia Kluis, June 14, 1975. AB, Columbia U., 1949, LLB, 1953; MA in Econs., U. N.Mex., 1950. Bar: N.Y. 1953, D.C. 1968. Assoc. Debevoise, Plimpton, Lyons & Gates, N.Y.C., 1953-66; ptnr. Hale Russell & Gray, N.Y.C., 1967-75, counsel, 1976-85; counsel Winthrop, Stimson, Putnam & Roberts, Washington, 1985-96, ret. 1996. Author: The Potash Industry, 1951; contbr. to CPLR Forms and Guidance for Lawyers, 1963. U.S. panelist U.S.-Can. Free Trade agreement, 1989-92; asst. transp. adminstr. City of N.Y., 1966-67; v.p. Emerson Sch., N.Y.C., 1960-64, chmn., 1964-69; bd. dirs. Rice Meml. H.S., South Burlington, Vt., 1992-95; mem. Prudential Com. Fire Dist. No. 1, Shelburne, Vt., 1977-90, chmn., 1977-84; mem. Shelburne Sewer Commn., 1990-93, chmn., 1991-93, interim mgr., 1992-93; bd. commrs. Chittenden County Transp. Authority, 1991-97, treas., 1992-96; mem. Shelburne Selectboard, 1995. Decorated Knight 1st class Royal Swedish Order of North Star. Mem. ABA, D.C. Bar Assn. Private international, Aviation, Federal civil litigation. Home: 364 Clearwater Rd Shelburne VT 05482-7724

**KURRUS, THOMAS WILLIAM,** lawyer; b. Carmel, N.Y., May 13, 1947; s. Theo Hornsby and Jean Ellen (Cumming) K.; m. Desiree Ann Ross, Mar. 25, 1989. BS magna cum laude, U. Fla., 1975, JD, 1979. Bar: Fla. 1980, U.S. Dist. Ct. (no. dist.) Fla. 1980, U.S. Ct. Appeals (5th cir.) 1980, U.S. Dist. Ct. (mid. dist.) Fla. 1981, U.S. Ct. Appeals (11th cir.) 1981, U.S. Ct. Appeals (4th cir.) 1984, U.S. Supreme Ct. 1984. Assoc. Law Firm Larry G. Turner, Gainesville, Fla., 1981-83; ptnr. Turner, Kurrus & Griscti, Gainesville, 1983-88; prin. Law Offices of Thomas W. Kurrus, Gainesville, 1988—; mem. Fla. Supreme Ct. commn. on jury instructions, 1995. Contbr. articles to profl. jours. Mem. ACLU (Gainesville chpt. legal panel chmn. 1999), Nat. Assn. Criminal Defense Lawyers (Fla. chpt. bd. dirs., chmn. continuing legal edn. com., local legis. laison, pres. award 1993, appreciation award 1998). Avocations: fishing, art, horses. Criminal, Personal injury, General civil litigation. Office: PO Box 838 Gainesville FL 32602-0838

**KURTZ, ANDREA SLOANE,** lawyer; b. Ridgewood, N.J., July 13, 1970; d. Sheldon Francis and Alice Kaufman Kurtz. AB cum laude, Smith Coll., 1992; JD cum laude, U. Iowa, 1995. Bar: Iowa 1995, N.C. 1997. Staff atty. Youth Law Ctr., Des Moines, 1995-97, Ctrl. Carolina Legal Svcs., Lexington, N.C., 1997—; self defense instr. Forsyth Tech. C.C., Winston-Salem, N.C., 1998—; guardian ad litem Guardian ad Litems Office, Lexington, 1997—; task force mem. family law task force N.C. Legal Svcs., Raleigh, 1998—. Active Adolescent Pregnancy Prevention Adv. Bd., Des Moines, 1996-97; bd. dirs. United Action for Youth, Iowa City, 1987-88. Mem. 21st Jud. Dist. Bar Assn., Davidson County Bar Assn. Avocation: Aikido. Office: Ctrl Carolina Legal Svcs Inc PO Box 1574 Lexington NC 27293-1574

**KURTZ, CHARLES JEWETT, III,** lawyer; b. Columbus, Ohio, May 13, 1940; s. Charles Jewett, Jr. and Elizabeth Virginia (Gill) K.; m. Linda Rhoads, Mar. 18, 1983. BA, Williams Coll., 1962; JD, Ohio State U., 1965. Bar: Ohio 1965, D.C. 1967, U.S. Dist. Ct. (so. dist.) Ohio 1967, U.S. Dist. Ct. (no. dist.) Ohio 1976, U.S. Ct. of Appeals (6th cir) 1992. Law clk. to justice Ohio State Supreme Ct., Columbus, 1965-67; assoc. Porter, Wright, Morris & Arthur, Columbus, 1967-71, ptnr., 1972—, mng. ptnr. litigation dept., 1988-91, mem. directing ptnrs. com., 1988-89; mem. faculty Ohio Legal Ctr. Inst. Trustee Ballet Met., Columbus, 1990-94; vestry St. Albans Episcopal Ch., 1986-89. Mem. ABA, Am. Arbitration Assn. (mem. panel comml. arbitrators), Ohio Bar Assn. (mem. workers' compensation com.), Columbus Bar Assn. (sustaining mem.), Columbus Bar Found., Columbus Def. Assn. (pres. 1976), Athletic Club, Columbus Country Club, Capital Club. General civil litigation, Condemnation, Contracts commercial. Office: Porter Wright Morris & Arthur 41 S High St Ste 2800 Columbus OH 43215-6194

**KURTZ, HARVEY A.,** lawyer; b. Baraboo, Wis., July 9, 1950; s. Walter R. and Henrietta M. (Hinze) K.; m. Yvonne Larme, Jan. 28, 1978; children: Benjamin L., Leah L. BA, U. Wis., 1972; JD, U. Chgo., 1975. Bar: Wis. 1975, U.S. Dist. Ct. (ea. dist.) Wis. 1980. Atty. Whyte & Hirschboeck S.C., Milw., 1975-89, shareholder, 1981-89; ptnr. Foley & Lardner, Milw., 1989—. Mem. ABA, State Bar of Wis. Assn., Milw. Bar Assn. (chmn. employee benefits sect. 1993-94), Greater Milw. Employee Benefit Coun., Wis. Retirement Plan Profls. (pres. 1987-88), Internat. Pension and Employee Benefits Lawyers Assn., Kiwanis, Phi Beta Kappa. Pension, profit-sharing, and employee benefits. Home: 3927 N Stowell Ave Milwaukee WI 53211-2461 Office: Foley & Lardner Firstar Ctr 777 E Wisc Ave Milwaukee WI 53202

**KURTZ, JEROME,** lawyer, educator; b. Phila., May 19, 1931; s. Morris and Renee (Cooper) K.; m. Elaine Kahn, July 28, 1956; children: Madeleine, Nettie Kurtz Greenstein. BS with honors, Temple U., 1952; LLB magna cum laude, Harvard U., 1955. Bar: Pa. 1956, N.Y. 1981, D.C. 1982; CPA, Pa. Assoc. Wolf, Block, Schorr & Solis-Cohen, Phila., 1955-56, 57-63; ptnr. Wolf, Block, Schorr & Solis-Cohen, 1963-66, 68-77; tax legis. counsel Dept. Treasury, Washington, 1966-68; commr. IRS, 1977-80; ptnr. Paul, Weiss, Rifkind, Wharton & Garrison, 1980-90; prof. law NYU, 1991—, dir. grad. tax program, 1995-98; instr. Villanova Law Sch., 1964-65, U. Pa., 1969-74; vis. prof. law Harvard U., 1975-76; mem. adv. group to commr. IRS, 1976. Editor: Harvard Law Rev, 1953-55; contbr. numerous articles to profl. jours. Pres. Ctr. Inter-Am. Tax Adminstrn., 1980; bd. dirs. Common Cause, 1984-90, chmn. fin. com., 1985-88; bd. dirs. Nat. Capitol Area ACLU, 1990-91; mem. adv. bd. NYU Tax Inst., 1988-97, Little, Brown Tax Practice Series, 1994-96. Recipient Exceptional Service award Dept. Treasury, 1968, Alexander Hamilton award, 1980. Mem. ABA (chmn. tax shelter com. 1982-84), N.Y. Bar Assn. (exec. com. tax sect. 1981-82), Pa. Bar Assn., Phila. Bar Assn. (chmn. tax sect. 1975-76), Assn. of the Bar of the City of N.Y. (chmn. tax coun. 1993-95), Am. Law Inst. (cons. fed. inc. tax project taxation of pass through entities), Am. Coll. Tax Counsel, Beta Gamma Sigma. Corporate taxation, Taxation, general, Personal income taxation. Home: 17 E 16th St New York NY 10003-3116 Office: NYU Sch Law 40 Washington Sq S New York NY 10012-1005

**KURY, FRANKLIN LEO,** lawyer; b. Sunbury, Pa., Oct. 15, 1936; s. Barney and Helen (Witkowski) K.; m. Elizabeth Heazlett, Sept. 14, 1963; children: Steven, David, James. Bar: Pa. 1962. Atty. Pa. Dept. Justice, Harrisburg, 1961-62; ptnr. Kury & Kury, Sunbury, 1963-80, Tive, Hetrick & Pierce, Harrisburg, 1981-82, Reed, Smith, Shaw & McClay, Harrisburg, 1983—. Mem. Pa. Ho. of Reps., Harrisburg, 1967-72, Pa. Senate, Harrisburg, 1973-80; del. at large Dem. Nat. Conv., San Francisco, 1984; bd. dirs. Pa. Environ. Coun., Hawk Mountain Sanctuary Assn. 1st lt. USAR, 1962-66. Mem. Am. Immigration Lawyers Assn., Pa. Bar Assn. (chmn. environ. sect. 1984, 1st award for Outstanding Contbn. to Profession of Environ. Law Practice 1993), Polish Nat. Alliance. Democrat. Avocation: golf. Environmental, Administrative and regulatory, Real property. Office: Reed Smith Shaw & McClay PO Box 11844 213 Market St Ste 900 Harrisburg PA 17101-2108

**KURYK, DAVID NEAL,** lawyer; b. Balt., Aug. 24, 1947; s. Leon and Bernice G. (Fox) K.; m. Alice T. Lehman, July 8, 1971; children—Richard M., Robert M., Benjamin A. B.A., U. Md., 1969; J.D., U. Balt., 1972. Bar: Md. 1972, U.S. Dist. Ct. Md. 1973, U.S. Ct. Mil. Appeals 1973, D.C. 1974, U.S. Ct. Appeals (4th cir.) 1974, U.S. Supreme Ct. 1976, U.S. Ct. Appeals (Fed. cir.) 1982. Assoc. Harold Buchman, Esq., Balt., 1970-76; sole practice, Balt., 1976—. Served to sgt. USAF, 1967-73. Mem. ABA (products, gen. liability and consumer law com. 1976—, com. auto law 1977), Md. State Bar Assn., Bar Assn. Balt. City, Assn. Trial Lawyers Am., U. Balt. Alumni Assn., Zeta Beta Tau. Democrat. Jewish. Mem. bd. editors Md. Bar Jour., 1973-76. Personal injury, State civil litigation, Contracts commercial. Home: 11200 5 Springs Rd Lutherville MD 21093-3520 Office: Am Bldg 231 E Baltimore St Ste 702 Baltimore MD 21202-3446

**KURZ, JERRY BRUCE,** lawyer; b. Chgo., June 21, 1949; s. Jack and Delores Estelle (Koss) K.; 1 child, Matthew Hall. B.S., U. Okla., 1971; J.D., No. Ill. U., 1979. Bar: Ill. 1980, U.S. Dist. Ct. (no. dist.) Ill. 1980, U.S. Ct. Appeals (7th cir.) 1980, U.S. Tax Ct. 1980, U.S. Dist. Ct. (cen. dist.) Ill. 1983, U.S. Ct. Appeals (11th cir.) 1986, U.S. Supreme Ct. 1984. Tchr., counselor, Chgo. Pub. Schs., 1972-79; ptnr. Hall & Kurz, Chgo., 1980—; owner Arena Football League and Gridiron Enterprises, Inc., owner of worldwide rights to Arena Football; dir. Met. Football League, Chgo., 1983—, Free Agt. Scouting Combine, Chgo., 1983—, Minor Profl. Football Assn., 1980—; gen. counsel Arena Football League; gen. counsel Arena Football, U.S. and Europe. Served to capt. U.S. Army, 1968-69, Vietnam. Inducted into Minor Semi-pro Football Hall of Fame, 1987, Arena Football Hall of Fame. Mem. ABA, Nat. Assn. Criminal Def. Lawyers, Chgo. Bar Assn., Assn. Trial Lawyers Am., Phi Alpha Delta. Democrat. Jewish. Avocations: football, swimming, hockey, travel. Criminal, Sports, Entertainment. Home: 3117 Knollwood Ln Glenview IL 60025-2646 Office: Hall & Kurz 900 W Jackson Blvd # 5W Chicago IL 60607-3024

**KURZ, MARY ELIZABETH,** lawyer; b. Scranton, Pa., May 13, 1944; m. William H. Bright III. Student, U. Paris, Sorbonne, summer 1965; BA in French magna cum laude, Marywood Coll., 1966; postgrad., U. Md., 1966-67, U. N.C., 1967, U. Wis., 1969; JD with honors, U. Md., 1971. Bar: Md. 1972, D.C. 1978, Mont. 1982, Mich. 1988, Tex. 1994, N.C. 1996, U.S. Dist. Ct. (we. dist.) Mich., U.S. Supreme Ct., U.S. Ct. Appeals (4th, 6th, D.C. cirs.), U.S. Dist. Ct. Md., U.S. Dist. Ct. Mont. Law clk. to presiding justice Ct. Spl. Appeals Md., 1971-72; asst. atty. gen. criminal div. State of Md., 1972-74, asst. legis. officer to gov., 1974-75; asst. atty. gen. representing U. Md. State of Md., College Park, 1975-82; legal counsel U. Mont., Missoula, 1982-87; gen. counsel, v.p. legal affairs Mich. State U., East Lansing, 1987-94; vice chancellor and gen. counsel Tex. A&M U. System, 1994-96; gen. coun. N.C. State U., Raleigh, 1996—; speaker numerous confs. and profl. meetings; mem. Commn. to Study Sovereign Immunity, 1975. Mem. staff Md. Law Rev. Reginald Heber Smith fellow, 1969. Mem. ABA, Nat. Assn. Coll. and Univ. Attys. (mem. numerous coms., chmn. com. site selection 1985-86, chmn. com. continuing legal edn. 1986-89, bd. dirs. 1985-88, 2d v.p. 1989-90, 1st v.p. 1990-91, pres.-elect 1991-92, pres. 1992-93) . Education and schools, Labor, General practice. Home: 102 King George Loop Cary NC 27511-6334 Office: NC State U 3rd Fl Holladay Hall Raleigh NC 27695

**KURZ, THOMAS PATRICK,** lawyer; b. Stevens Point, Wis., Dec. 26, 1951; s. Edward Albert and Bertha Marie (Schmidt) K.; m. Debra Kay Gentz, Jan. 6, 1979; children: Natalie Jean, Thomas Patrick Jr. BA, U. Wis.-Madison, 1974; JD, Georgetown U., 1977. Bar: Wis. 1977, U.S. Dist. Ct. (ea. dist.) Wis. 1977, Ill. 1982, Tex. 1989. Assoc. Foley & Lardner, Milw. and Madison, 1977-82; atty. A.E. Staley Mfg. Co., Decatur, Ill., 1982-85; corp. counsel Staley Continental, Inc., Rolling Meadows, Ill, 1985-88; gen. counsel, asst. sec. Sysco Corp., Houston, 1988—. Mem. Georgetown Law Jour., 1975-76, editor, 1976-77. Recipient Eagle Scout award Samoset coun. Boy Scouts Am., 1967; Wis. honors scholar, 1970. Fellow Tex. Bar Found.; mem. ABA, Ill. Bar Assn., Wis. Bar Assn., State Bar Tex., Phi Beta Kappa. Roman Catholic. General corporate, Contracts commercial, Securities. Home: 20010 Sky Hollow Ln Katy TX 77450-5218 Office: Sysco Corp 1390 Enclave Pkwy Houston TX 77077-2099

**KURZBAN, IRA JAY,** lawyer; b. Bklyn., May 9, 1949; s. Benjamin and Irene (Weiss) K.; m. Magda Montiel Davis, Apr. 15, 1989; children: Kathryn Montiel Davis, Paula Lindsay Davis, Magda Marie Davis, Sadie Bethany Kurzban, Benjamin Kurzban. BA magna cum laude, Syracuse U., 1971; MA, U. Calif., Berkeley, 1973, JD, 1976; hon. fellow, U. Pa. Law Sch., 1987. Bar: Calif. 1976, Fla. 1976, U.S. Dist. Ct. (no. dist.) Calif., 1976, U.S. Dist. Ct. (so. dist.) Fla., 1976, U.S. Ct. Appeals (5th cir.) 1978, U.S. Ct. Appeals (11th cir.) 1981, U.S. Supreme Ct. 1980. Ptnr. Kurzban, Kurzban, Weinger & Tetzeli P.A., Miami, Fla., 1977—; Fla. counsel Nat. Energy Civil Liberties Com., 1979-98; gen. counsel Am. Immigration Lawyers Assn., 1992-93; adj. prof. immigration and nationality law U. Miami Sch. of Law, 1979—, Nova Southeastern Law Sch., 1982—; instr. polit. sci. U. Calif. Berkeley, 1973; mem. civil justice adv. com. U.S. Dist. Ct. (so. dist.) Fla., 1993-94; mem. certification com. in immigration and univ. law Fla. Bar, 1994-96; lectr. in field. Author: Kurzban's Immigration Law Sourcebook: A Comprehensive Outline and Reference Tool, 6th edit., 1998; contbr. articles to profl. jours. Founder Berkeley Law Found. Recipient Tobias Simon pro bono svc. award Fla. Supreme Ct., 1982, Trial Lawyer of Yr. award Trial Lawyers for Public Justice, Carol King award Nat. Lawyers Guild, 1996; Polit. Sci. Dept. fellow U. Calif., Berkeley, 1971, Kent fellow Danforth Found., 1974-77, Law and Society fellow U. Calif., Berkeley, 1975-76. Fellow Am. Immigration Law Found. (hon.); mem. Am. ABA (chair refugee legal assistance com. 1983-84, mem. immigration coord. com. 1991-93), Immigration Lawyers Assn. (pres. so. Fla. chpt. 1980-81, nat. pres. 1987, Jack Wasserman award for excellence in federal litigation 1983, Human Rights award 1992), Am. Inns of Ct. Civil rights, Immigration, naturalization, and customs, Public international. Office: Kurzban Kurzban Weinger & Tetzeli PA 2650 SW 27th Ave Miami FL 33133

**KURZER, MARTIN JOEL,** lawyer, litigation communication consultant; b. May 6, 1938; s. Louis and Clare (Steinberg) K.; m. Karen Sue Zinn, Sept. 17, 1945; children: Sandra Lois, Jody Renee (dec.). BBA, U. Wis., Milw., 1960; JD cum laude, Marquette U., 1968; LMM in Taxation, U. Miami, 1971. Bar: Wis. 1968, Fla. 1968; cert. master practitioner neuro linguistic programming. Assoc. Blackwell, Walker, Fascell & Hoehl, Miami, Fla., 1968-72, jr. ptnr., 1973-77, gen. ptnr., 1978-90; of counsel Matzner, Ziskind, Hermelee & Jaffe, 1990-91; pvt. practice, 1991—, litigation comm. cons., 1996—; dir. legal svcs. Miami Heart Rsch. Inst., 1992-96; adj. pof. law, grad. tax dept. U. Mami, 1976-80; lectr. seminars and orgns. Author monthly column Health Notes, 1986; contbr. articles to profl. jours. Sales com. Elizabeth Arden Golf Classic Am. Cancer Soc., Miami, 1984-86. Capt. USAR, 1960-69. Mem. Greater Miami Tax Inst. (sec. 1979, treas. 1980, 1st v.p. 1981, pres. 1982), Am. Assn. Atty.-CPAs (dir. 1978—, treas. 1981-82, sec. 1982-83, v.p. 1983-84, 1st v.p. 1984-85, pres.-elect 1986-87, pres. 1987-88), Am. Soc. Trial Cons., Nat. Health Lawyers Assn., Healthcare Fin. Mgmt. Assn., Fla. Assn. Atty.-CPAs (dir. 1975—, v.p. 1975-81, exec. v.p. 1981-87, 92—), South Fla. Employee Benefits Coun. (sec. 1979-80), Fla. Bar Assn. (chmn. com. on rels. with Fla. Inst. CPAs 1981-82, health law com., chmn. travel programs com. 1986), State Bar Wis., Nat. Health Lawyers Assn., Fla. Assn. Hosp. Attys., Fla. Inst. CPAs, Miami Club, Miami Shores Country Club (adminstrn. bd. 1976). Jewish. Avocations: golf, travel, collecting 1950's music. Taxation, general, Health, General corporate. Home and Office: 1951 NE 191st Dr Miami FL 33179-4353

**KURZMAN, ROBERT GRAHAM,** lawyer, educator; b. N.Y.C., July 3, 1932; s. Benjamin E. and Betty Kurzman; m. Carol Ellis, Aug. 26, 1956; children: Marc, Nancy, Amy. BA, Hofstra U., 1954; JD, Cornell U., 1957. Bar: N.Y. 1959, U.S. Supreme Ct. 1964, U.S. Dist. Ct. (no., so., ea. and we. dists.) N.Y. 1964. Assoc., Wynn, Blattmachr & Campbell, N.Y.C., 1959-63; ptnr. Leaf, Kurzman, Deull & Drogin, N.Y.C., 1963-79, Goldschmidt, Fredericks, Kurzman & Oshatz, 1979-82, Kurzman, Eisenberg, Singer, Midler, Lever & Corbin (now Kurzman & Eisenberg), White Plains, N.Y., 1982—; adj. prof. law NYU; dir. Stratton Industries, Inc.; acting city ct. judge City of New Rochelle (N.Y.), 1981. Adv. bd. So. Meth. U. Sch. Law, Estate Planning Inst.; coordinator estates and trusts paralegal program Manhattanville Coll., 1974-75; pres. West Putnam council Boy Scouts Am., 1981; trustee, pres., Temple Israel; former chmn. New Rochelle Republican Com. Capt. USAR, 1957-59. Recipient Silver Beaver award Boy Scouts Am., Silver Antelope award; named Man of Yr., New Rochelle B'nai B'rith, 1977. Fellow Am. Coll. Probate Counsel; mem. ABA, N.Y. State Bar Assn., Assn. Bar City N.Y., Westchester Bar Assn. Clubs: Ridgeway Country (White Plains, N.Y.); Masons; Cornell of N.Y.C. (pres.). Author: (with Rita Gilbert) Paralegals and Successful Law Practice, 1981; contbr. articles profl. jours. Probate, Estate taxation, Family and matrimonial. Home: 166 Tewksbury Rd Scarsdale NY 10583-6036 Office: 1 N Broadway White Plains NY 10601-2310

**KURZWEIL, BETTE GRAYSON,** lawyer; b. Newark, July 10, 1947; d. Sidney and Joan (Rosenman) Grayson; children: Jeremy Scott, Cynthia Joan. BA in History with honors, NYU, 1969; JD, Bklyn. Law Sch., 1977. Bar: N.J. 1977. Tchr. Newark Bd. Edn., 1969, Boston Bd. Edn., 1970-71; social worker Mt. Sinai Hosp., N.Y.C., 1971-74; pvt. practice Springfield, N.J.; mem., chmn. Fee Arbitration in Union County, Union, N.J., 1984-92. V.p. membership program Hadassah, Millburn, N.J., 1985-89; treas. The Hoopsters, 1997—; dir. Internat. Youth Orgn. Recipient Women of Excellence awrad Union County Commn. on the Status of Women, 1998. Mem. Women Lawyers in Union County (treas., sec., v.p., pres. 1980-92), Union County Bar Assn. (activities com. 1984-89). Family and matrimonial, Real property, Land use and zoning (including planning). Office: 140 Mountain Ave Springfield NJ 07081-1725

**KURZWEIL, VIVIANNE V.,** lawyer; b. Miami, Fla., Nov. 12, 1964; d. Oscar J. and Vivian Vila; m. Scott F. Feder, July 21, 1984 (div. Oct. 1989); m. Adam B. Kurzweil, Sept. 5, 1992; children: Kristina R., Michael A. BBA, Southern Meth. U., 1986; JD, U. Miami, 1991. Bar: Fla. 1991. Asst. state attorney Office of the State Attorney, Miami, 1991—. Mem. Jr. League Miami. Office: Office of the State Attorney 1350 NW 12th Ave Miami FL 33136-2102

**KUSHEL, GLENN ELLIOT,** lawyer; b. Bklyn., May 5, 1945. BME, CUNY, 1968; MSME, Columbia U., 1970; JD, Seton Hall U., 1974; LLM, NYU, 1978; cert., Coll. Fin. Planning, 1987. Bar: N.J. 1974, N.Y. 1977, U.S. Supreme Ct. 1978. Mem. tech. staff Bell Telephone Labs., Whippany, N.J., 1968-71; cost engr. Exxon Resource and Engr. Co., Florham Park, N.J., 1971-72; dep. atty. gen. State of N.J., Trenton, 1974-76; assoc. Rosenman and Colin, N.Y.C., 1976-81; sole practice Bklyn., 1981—; mem. N.Y. State Bd. Arbitrators, 1995—. assoc. mem. malpractice panel N.Y. State Supreme Ct., Kings County, 1986-90. Atomic Energy Commn. fellowship, 1968. Mem. Pi Tau Sigma, Tau Beta Pi. Avocations: skiing, running, financial planning. State civil litigation, Insurance, Personal injury. Office: 67 Wall St Ste 2411 New York NY 10005-3101

**KUSHNER, GORDON PETER,** lawyer; b. Calgary, Alta., Can., Nov. 3, 1966; came to U.S., 1984; s. H. Peter and V. Marlene (Shatilla) K.; m. Patti A. Yakich, Aug. 10, 1991; children: Brantley Peter, Katerina Mari. BA summa cum laude, U. N.D., 1988; JD cum laude, U. Dayton, 1991. Bar: Ohio 1991, U.S. Dist. Ct. (so. dist.) Ohio 1991. Atty. Dinsmore & Shohl, Cin., 1991-94; atty. internat. ops. LensCrafters Internat., Inc., Cin., 1994-95; corp. atty. Structural Dynamics Rsch. Corp., Milford, Ohio, 1995—; dir. Rite Track Equipment Svcs., Inc., Cin., 1994-95; mem. Vision Coun. of Can., Toronto, Ont., 1994-95; spkr. U. Cin. Law Sch., 1993. Author: (newsletter) Cincinnati Small Business Newsletter, 1993; contbr. articles to profl. jours. Mem. Big Bros. and Big Sisters, Dayton, 1990-91; dir. Housing Network of Hamilton County, Cin., 1993-94; coach Lakota Sports Orgn., West Chester, Ohio, 1997—. Recipient Yale in Can. Outstanding Can. award Yale U. Can. Alumni Assn., 1990. Mem. ABA, Ohio Bar Assn., Cin. Bar Assn. (presenter NAFTA seminar 1992), Phi Alpha Delta, Phi Beta Kappa. General corporate, Intellectual property, Private international. Home: 1409 Moore Pl SW Leesburg VA 20175-5809 Office: Structural Dynamics Rsch Corp 2000 Eastman Dr Milford OH 45150-2712

**KUSMA, KYLLIKKI,** lawyer; b. Tartu, Estonia, Dec. 8, 1943; came to U.S., 1951, naturalized, 1958; d. August and Helju (Traat) K.; B.F.A., Ohio U., 1966; M.A. (Vets. Rehab. Adminstrn. fellow), Ohio State U., 1967; J.D., Ohio No. U., 1976; M.L.T., Georgetown U., 1980. Bar: Ohio 1977, D.C. 1978. Speech and hearing therapist Lima (Ohio) Meml. Hosp., 1967-70, Tipp City (Ohio) Schs., 1970-74; atty.-adv. Office Chief Counsel, IRS, Washington, 1977-81; v.p., asso. tax counsel Security Pacific Nat. Bank, Los Angeles, 1981-83; ptnr. Brownstein Zeidman & Lore, Washington, 1983-95, Ernst & Young LLP, Columbus, Ohio, 1995—; instr. Wright State U., 1972-76. Author: (with others) Mortgage-Backed Securities Special Update: REMICs, 1988. Vol. local civic, polit. activities; contbr. articles to profl. jours. Mem. ABA, Columbus Bar Assn., Ohio Bar Assn., D.C. Women's Bar Assn., Phi Kappa Phi. Democrat. Corporate taxation, Personal income taxation, Pension, profit-sharing, and employee benefits. Office: Ernst & Young LLP 10 W Broad St Ste 2300 Columbus OH 43215-3400

**KUSSEL, WILLIAM FERDINAND, JR.,** lawyer; b. Norway, Mich., July 30, 1957; s. William F. and Mitzi (Markus) K.; m. Maria Salas, July 26, 1995. BS, St. Norbert Coll., 1979; JD, Southwestern U., 1984. Bar: Calif. 1985, D.C. 1985, Minn. 1986, Wis. 1989. Law clk. Wis. Cir. Ct., Marinette, 1982; law extern L.A. Dist. Atty.'s Office, 1983; pros. Menominee Indian Reservation, Keshena, Wis., 1986-92; program atty. Menominee Indian Tribe Wis., Keshena, 1992—. Mem. ABA, Calif. Bar Assn., Minn. Bar Assn., D.C. Bar Assn., Wis. Bar Assn. Avocations: photography, snowmobiling, boating, motorcycling. Office: Menominee Indian Tribe Office Program Atty PO Box 910 Keshena WI 54135-0910

**KUTCHER, ROBERT A.,** lawyer; b. N.Y.C., Dec. 27, 1950; s. Joseph L. and Renee M. (Durben) K.; m. Renee Bauchat, Oct. 29, 1985; children: J.C. Rosenbloom, Skylar Rosenbloom, Andrea Kutcher, Jessica Kutcher. BS, Cornell U., 1972; JD cum laude, Loyola U., New Orleans, 1975; postgrad., Tulane U., 1975-77. Bar: N.Y. 1976, La. 1976, U.S. Dist. Ct. (ea., we. and mid. dists.) La., U.S. Ct. Appeals (5th and 11th cirs.) 1976, U.S. Supreme Ct. 1976. Law clk. U.S. Dist. Ct. (ea. dist.) La., New Orleans, 1975-77; assoc. Bronfin & Heller, New Orleans, 1977-82; ptnr. Bronfin, Heller, Steinberg & Berins, New Orleans, 1982-96, Chopin, Wagar, Cole, Richard, Reboul & Kutcher, LLP, Metairie, 1996—; mem. La. Atty. Disciplinary Bd., 1993-99, chmn. 1999—. Contbr. articles to profl. publs. Bd. dirs. Jewish Community Ctr., New Orleans, 1983—, treas., 1986-89, v.p., 1989-91, pres., 1991—; bd. dirs. south cen. region Anti-Defamation League, New Orleans, 1985—, vice chmn., 1988-91, chmn., 1991—, mem. nat. civil rights com., nat. legal affairs com.; chmn. state adv. com. U.S. Civil Rights Commn., 1990—. Mem. Fed. Bar Assn. (bd. dirs. New Orleans chpt. 1984-91, pres. 1991), N.Y. Bar Assn., 5th Cir. Bar Assn., Orleans Parish Bar Assn. Republican. Federal civil litigation, Antitrust, Contracts commercial. Home: 12 Swan St New Orleans LA 70124-4405 Office: Chopin Wagar Cole Richard Reboul & Kutcher LLP 3850 N Causeway Blvd Ste 900 Metairie LA 70002-8130

**KUTCHIN, EDWARD DAVID,** lawyer; b. Bklyn., Sept. 1, 1953; s. Melvin and Maxine (Lampert) K.; m. Jill C. Pollack, Aug. 18, 1979. BA, Muhlenberg Coll., 1975; JD, New Eng. Sch. Law, 1978; LLM in Taxation, Boston U., 1981. Bar: Mass. 1978, U.S. Dist. Ct. Mass 1978, U.S. Tax Ct. 1978, U.S. Ct. Appeals (1st cir.) 1978. Law clk. Atty. Gen.'s Advocacy Inst. U.S. Dept. Justice, Washington, 1977; assoc. Law Offices Robert Smith, Boston, 1978-81, Kline & Gordon, Boston, 1981-85; ptnr. Lapping & Kutchin, Boston, 1985-88, Kutchin & Rufo, P.C., Boston, 1988—. Mem. exec. com. Merrimack Valley Jewish Fedn., 1996—; chmn. Muhlenberg Coll. New Eng. Regional Alumni Assn., 1995—. Mem. ABA, Mass. Bar Assn., Boston Bar Assn. Democrat. Jewish. Avocations: tennis, soccer, jogging, weightlifting, travel. General corporate, General civil litigation. Home: 9 Blueberry Hill Rd Andover MA 01810-5001 Office: Kutchin & Rufo PC 175 Federal St Boston MA 02110-2210

**KUYKENDALL, FREDERICK THURMAN, III,** lawyer; b. Mobile, Ala., July 16, 1954; s. Frederick Thurman Jr. and Peggy Eileen (Stacey) K.; m. Nancy Carol McKinnon; children: Frederick Thurman IV, Amalee Bowman. BA, U. Ala., 1976; JD, Samford U., 1981. Bar: Ala., U.S. Dist. Ct. (no. and so. dists.) Ala., U.S. Ct. Appeals (1st, 3d, 5th and 11th cirs.). Of counsel Garndner, Middlebrooks et al., Mobile, Pensacola, Ala., Fla., 1981—; bd. dirs. Lawyers Com. for Civil Rights Under Law, Washington,

1995—, Trial Lawyers for Pub. Justice, Washington, 1995—; mem. adv. panel Nat. Labor Rels. Bd., Washington, 1994—;. Mem. ATLA, Ala. Trial Lawyers Assn. Democrat. Avocations: sailing, running, fly fishing. Personal injury, Product liability, Environmental. Office: Kuykendall & Assocs River Route 427 Magnolia Springs AL 36555

**KVINTA, CHARLES J.,** lawyer; b. Hallettsville, Tex., Feb. 16, 1932; s. John F. and Emily (Strauss) K.; m. Margie N. Brenek, Oct. 9, 1954; children—Charles, Sherri, Kenneth, Christopher. BA in Govt., U. Tex., 1954, LLB, 1959. Bar: Tex. 1959. Atty. Tex. Hwy. Dept., Yoakum, Tex., 1959-61; ptnr. Gaus & Kvinta, Yoakum, 1962-67, Kvinta, Young & Frietsch, Yoakum, 1975—, Kvinta & Kvinta, attys., 1986—; exec. v.p. First State Bank, Yoakum, 1968-74, atty., 1975—; city atty. City of Yoakum, 1980—. Co-founder Bluebonnet Youth Ranch, Yoakum, 1968, bd. trustees Yoakum Ind. Sch. Dist.; bd., pres., Yoakum Ind. Sch. Dist.; judge Lavaca County. Served to 1st lt. U.S. Army, 1954-56. Recipient Outstanding Community Service award Sons of Herman, 1984, Outstanding Service award Bluebonnet Youth Ranch, 1975, Outstanding Service award Yoakum Little League, 1982, Outstanding Service award Yoakum Lions, 1982, Paul Gustwick Outstanding Community Service award, 1986, Tex. Rd. Hand award for Outstanding Support Tex. Highway Tex. Dept. Transp. Mem. Tex. Bar Assn., Am. Legion. Democrat. Roman Catholic. Family and matrimonial, Probate, Real property. Home: 713 Coke St Yoakum TX 77995-4415 Office: Kvinta & Kvinta Attys 403 W Grand Ave Yoakum TX 77995-2617

**KWESKIN, EDWARD MICHAEL,** lawyer; b. Stamford, Conn., June 26, 1946; s. Sydney C. and Ethel (Jaffe) K.; m. Helen S. Truss, Aug. 17, 1969; children: Abigail, Adam. BA, U. Pa., 1968; JD with honors, George Washington U., 1971. Bar: Conn. 1971, U.S. Dist. Ct. Conn. 1971, U.S. Ct. Appeals (2d cir.) 1971, Pa. 1971, U.S. Dist. Ct. (ea. dist.) Pa. 1971, U.S. Supreme Ct. 1979. Staff atty. Cmty. Legal Svcs., Phila., 1971-73; assoc. Wofsey Rosen Kweskin & Kuriansky, Stamford, 1973-79, ptnr., 1979—; spl. master family law Superior Ct., State of Conn., 1995—; bd. dirs. Curtain Call, Inc., 1999—. Commr. Sixth Taxing Dist., Norwalk, Conn., 1993—; coach Little League 1990-95; pres. Temple Sinai, Stamford, 1994-96. Mem. ABA (mem. family law sect.), Conn. Bar Assn. (mem. exec. com. family law sect. 1997—), Stamford-Norwalk Regional Bar Assn. (past pres., past family law chmn.), U. Pa. Alumni Club of Fairfield County (pres. 1973-77, chmn. secondary sch. com. 1992—). Family and matrimonial, General civil litigation, Real property. Home: 3 Plant Ct Norwalk CT 06853-1824 Office: Wofsey Rosen Kweskin & Kuriansky 600 Summer St Stamford CT 06901-1490

**KYHOS, THOMAS FLYNN,** lawyer; b. Cheverly, Md., May 13, 1947. B.A. in Econs., DePauw U., 1969; J.D., Cath. U., 1973. Bar: Md. 1974, D.C. 1974, U.S. Tax Ct. 1974, U.S. Supreme Ct. 1978. sole practice, Washington, 1974—; pres. First Oxford Corp., Washington, 1976—. Mem. ABA, Md. Bar Assn., D.C. Bar Assn. Taxation, general. Home: 5714 Massachusetts Ave Bethesda MD 20816-1929 Office: 3528 K St NW Washington DC 20007-3503

**KYLE, AMY LYNN,** lawyer; b. N.Y.C., Dec. 10, 1958; d. John Dean and Dorothy (Roscoe) K.; m. Alfred Otis Rose, May 10, 1986; children: Sarah Lynn, William Kyle. AB, Princeton U., 1980; JD, Columbia U., 1983. Bar: Mass. 1983. Assoc. Bingham Dana, LLP, Boston, 1983-89, ptnr., 1989—. Contbr. articles to profl. jours. Banking, Contracts commercial, Finance. Office: Bingham Dana LLP 150 Federal St Boston MA 02110-1713

**KYLE, RICHARD HOUSE,** federal judge; b. St. Paul, Apr. 30, 1937; s. Richard E. and Geraldine (House) K.; m. Jane Foley, Dec. 22, 1959; children: Richard H. Jr., Michael F., D'Arcy, Patrick G., Kathleen. BA, U. Minn., 1959, LLB, 1962. Bar: Minn. 1962, U.S. Dist. Ct. Minn. 1992. Atty. Briggs & Morgan, St. Paul, 1963-68, 1970-92; solicitor gen. Minn. Atty. Gen. Office, St. Paul, 1968-70; judge U.S. Dist. Ct., St. Paul, 1992—. Pres. Minn. Law Rev., Mpls., 1962. Mem. Minn. State Bar Assn., Ramsey County Bar Assn. Republican. Episcopal. Office: US Dist Ct Federal Courts Bldg 316 Robert St N Saint Paul MN 55101-1495

**KYRIAZIS, ARTHUR JOHN (ATHANASIOS IOANNIS KYRIAZIS),** lawyer; b. Thessaloniki, Greece, Nov. 2, 1958; came to U.S., 1960; s. George A. and Elpis (Halkedis) K.; m. Maria M. Zissimos, Aug. 31, 1986; children: Cassandra Hope, Michael John, George Athanasios II. AB, Harvard U., 1981; postgrad, Pepperdine U., 1982-83; JD cum laude, Temple U., 1985; postgrad., U. Pa., 1998—. Bar: Pa. 1985, U.S. Dist. Ct. (ea. dist.) Pa. 1985, U.S. Bankruptcy Ct. (ea. dist.) Pa. 1985, U.S. Bankruptcy Ct. N.J., 1986, U.S. Dist. Ct. N.J. 1986, Calif. 1987, U.S. Dist. Ct. (ea. dist.) Calif. 1988, U.S. Ct. Appeals (3d cir.) 1991, U.S. Supreme Ct. 1994. Assoc. Cardillo & Corbett, N.Y.C., 1983; law clk. to Hon. Norma J. Shapiro U.S. Dist. Ct. (ea. dist.) Pa., 1984; assoc. Needleman Needleman Carey Stein & Kratzer, 1984-85; law clk. to Hon. James Gardner Colins Commonwealth Ct. Pa., Phila., Harrisburg, 1985-86; assoc. Rawle & Henderson, Phila. and Marlton, N.J., 1987-88, Lesser & Kaplin and predecessor firm, Phila., Blue Bell, Pa. and Marlton, N.J., 1988-89; prin. Kyriazis & Assocs., Phila., Cherry Hill, N.J. and Delaware County, Pa., 1989—; arbitrator Phila. Ct. Common Pleas, 1988—, Delaware County Ct. Common Pleas, 1993—; pro bono counsel Am. Assn. Univ. Students, 1989—. Author: (with H. Caldwell) Unchecked Discretion: The Buck Stops Here: Is There a Fourth Amendment at the International Borders of the United States, 1993, Whittier Law Rev. Pa. co-coord. Dukakis for Pres., 1987-88; del. Nat. Fin. Com., Dem. Conv., Atlanta, 1988, 1982 Dem. Mid-Term Conv., Phila.; mem. Young Lawyers for Dukakis, Hellenic Am. for Dukakis, Pa., 1987-88; founder Am. Assn. Univ. Students, Cambridge, Mass. and Phila., 1978-79, pres., 1990—; v.p. Hercules-Spartan Phila. chpt. 26 Am. Hellenic Progressive Edn. Assn., 1989-90, pres., 1990-91, bd. govs., 1987—; treas., shrager Common Pleas Judge, 1999. Mem. ATLA, ABA (young lawyers div., litigation and bus. law sect., bus., real estate sects.), Am. Hellenic Lawyers Assn. (treas. 1992-94), Phila. Bar Assn. (exec. com. young lawyers sect. 1988-90, fin. sec. exec. com. 1990, sec. exec. com. 1989, co-chmn. law related edn. com. 1988—, mem. bar edn. found. com. 1988—, mem. Bill Rights 200 coms., mem. fed. cts. 200 com., chmn. debate com. and mock trial 1987—, debate dir. fed. cts. 200 nat. high sch. debate tournament 1990—), Camden County Bar Assn. (young lawyers, pub. benefits, debtor-creditor relations), Pa. Bar Assn. (litigation, young lawyers jud. administrn.), N.J. Trial Lawyers Assn., Pa. Trial Lawyers Assn., Am. Arbitration Assn. (comml. arbitrator 1988—), State Bar Calif. (litigation, intellectual property, entertainment), Hellenic-Am. Lawyers Assn. (treas. 1992-96), Am. Assn. Univ. Students (legal counsel 1989—), Coll. Admissions Inst. Am. (adv. bd. 1992—), Hellenic Univ. Club (bd. trustees), Harvard Club (N.Y., Washington), Penn Club (N.Y.), Maxwell Football Club, Nat. Press Club, Harvard-Radcliffe Club Phila. (schs. com.), Maxwell Football Club, Penn Faculty Club. Republican. Greek Orthodox. General civil litigation, Criminal, Entertainment. Office: 1806 Garrett Rd Lansdowne PA 19050-1005 also: Woodland Falls Corp Park 336 Bay Ave Ste 503 Ocean City NJ 08226

**KYROS, KONSTANTINE WILLIAM,** lawyer, consultant; b. Mar. 24, 1971. BA, U. Mass., 1993; JD, Boston U., 1996. Bar: Mass., U.S. Ct. Appeals (1st cir.). Ptnr. Law Offices of K. William Kyros, P.C., Boston, 1996—; pres. Lawyer Views, Boston, 1997—. Prodr. (film) Art Direction, 1992. Mem. Mass. Bar Assn., Phi Beta Kappa. Computer, Entertainment. Office: Lawyer Views 35 Bay State Rd Boston MA 02215-2121

**KYTE, SUSAN JANET,** lawyer; b. Riverhead, N.Y., Nov. 17, 1956; d. Bruce Whiteman Kyte and Barbara Jean (Clark) Goldberg. BA cum laude, Southampton Coll. divsn. L.I. U., 1978; JD, Capital U., 1984. Bar: Ohio, 1984. Assoc. atty. Matan & Smith, Columbus, Ohio, 1984-90; econ. devel. dir. City of Columbus, 1990-91; chief counsel, legis. dir. Ohio Sec. State, Columbus, 1991-95; pvt. practice Columbus, 1996—; del. Am. Coun. Young Polit. Leaders, Columbus, 1997; mgr. Drake for Congress, 1998. Vice-chair Franklin County Rep. Party, Columbus, 1992—, chair doorbbell blitz, 1988-90; founder, 1st pres. Ohio Rep. Womens Campaign Fund, Columbus, 1994—, treas., 1997—; bd. dirs. Actors Theater, Columbus, 1996—; vol. Rinehart for State Treas., Columbus, 1982, Rinehart for Mayor of Columbus, 1983, Race for the Cure, Columbus, 1995—; coord. Franklin County coalitions Voinovich for Senate, Columbus, 1988, co-chair, 1997—; treas. Keep Ohio Working Ballot Issue Commn., 1997, Every Child Counts Ballot Issue Commn., 1998, Deters for Ohio's Future, 1998—; legal counsel Teater for Mayor, 1999; treas. Tanner for City Coun., 1999; co-mgr. Browell for Judge, Columbus, 1997—; policy com. Pryce for Congress, Columbus, 1992, 94; coord. Taft for Sec. of State, Columbus, 1990; trustee Cap City Young Rep., 1984-96; active Com. for 2000, 1993; asst. legal counsel Young Rep. Nat. Fedn., 1993-95; rep. Renews Congrl. Adv. Com., D.C., 1995, 97; v.p. Columbus Literacy Coun., Columbus, 1984-92; chair comm. com. Oktoberfest, Columbus, 1992-96; steering com. Kaleidoscope Conf. for Women, Columbus, 1994—. Mem. Nat. Fedn. Ind. Businesses, Assn. Polit. Cons., Ohio State Bar Assn., Coun. Govt. Ethics Lawyers, Ohio C. of C. (polit. affairs com. 1996—). Republican. Lutheran. Avocations: cooking, travel, reading, politics. Office: 57 E Gay St Ste 300 Columbus OH 43215-3103

**LAATSCH, GARY KENNETH,** lawyer; b. Chgo., Oct. 7, 1954. BA cum laude, Augustana Coll., 1976; JD, Loyola U., Chgo., 1979. Bar: Ill. 1979, U.S. Dist. Ct. (no. dist.) Ill. 1979. Ptnr. Pavalon, Gifford, Laatsch & Marino, Chgo., 1979—. Personal injury. Office: Pavalon Gifford Et Al 2 N Lasalle St Chicago IL 60602-3702

**LAB, CHARLES EDWARD,** lawyer; b. Findlay, Ohio, Dec. 21, 1952; s. Eugene G. and Estella E. L.; m. Cynthia A. Bank, June 4, 1977; children; Stephanie J., Ashley V. BA, Purdue U., 1975; JD, Ill. Inst. Tech., 1979. Bar: Ill. 1979, U.S. Dist. Ct. (no. dist.) Ill. 1979. Assoc. James L. Elsesser & Assocs., Chgo., 1979-81, Galowich & Galowich, Joliet, Ill., 1981; atty. pvt. practice, Minooka, Ill., 1982—. Trustee Village of Shorewood (Ill.), 1985-89; deacon St. John Luth. Ch., Joliet. Mem. Ill. State Bar Assn. Republican. Lutheran. Avocations: music, golf, martial arts. Appellate, Personal injury, Real property. Office: PO Box 911 Minooka IL 60447-0911

**LABAJ, PAMELA JOAN,** Lawyer; b. Newark, N.J., Oct. 3, 1963; d. Edward Joseph and Joan Mary L. BA in Comms., Montclair State U., 1985; JD, Widener U., 1989. Bar: N.J., 1990, N.Y., 1991, Pa., 1992, U.S. Dist. Ct. N.J. 1990, U.S. Dist. Ct. (so. dist.) N.Y. 1997, U.S. Ct. Appeals (3rd cir.) 1997, U.S. Supreme Ct. 1997. Jud. clk. N.J. Supreme Ct., Jersey City, 1990; lawyer Comml. Union Ins., Florham Park, N.J., 1991, Bivona Cohen Kunzman et al., Warren, N.J., 1991-93, Curtis, Mallet-Prevost, N.Y., N.J., 1993—. Officer Essex County Women Lawyers. Mem. Fed. Bar Assn., N.Y. State Bar Assn., N.J. State Bar Assn., N.J. Cares. Avocations: golf, scuba diving. Home: 751 Evergreen Pkwy Union NJ 07083-8731 Office: Curtis Mallet Prevost Colt & Mosle 1 Gateway Ctr Ste 403 Newark NJ 07102-5311 also: 101 Park Ave New York NY 10178-0002

**LABAY, EUGENE BENEDICT,** lawyer; b. El Campo, Tex., July 20, 1938; s. Ben F. and Cecelia M. (Orsak) L.; m. Katherine Sue Ermis, Dec. 29, 1962; children: Michael, Joan, John, Paul, David, Patrick, Steven. BBA, St. Mary's U., San Antonio, 1960; JD, St. Mary's U., 1965. Bar: Tex. 1965, U.S. Dist. Ct. (we. dist.) Tex. 1968, U.S. Dist. Ct. (no. dist.) Tex. 1973, U.S. Dist. Ct. (ea. dist.) Tex. 1986, U.S. Ct. Appeals (5th cir.) 1968, U.S. Ct. Appeals (11th cir.) 1981, U.S. Supreme Ct. 1980. Briefing atty. Supreme Ct. Tex., Austin, 1965-66; assoc. Cox & Smith Inc., San Antonio, 1966-71, ptnr., 1972-83, v.p., 1972-94; pvt. practice, 1994—. Contbr. articles to profl. jours. Served to 1st lt. U.S. Army, 1960-62. Mem. ABA, State Bar Tex. (chmn. sect. internat. law 1979-80), San Antonio Bar Assn., Fed. Bar Assn., Am. Judicature soc., Cath. Lawyers Guild San Antonio, KC (coun. grand knight 1982-83), Phi Delta Phi. State civil litigation, Oil, gas, and mineral, Environmental. Home: 31720 Post Oak Trl Boerne TX 78015-4133 Office: PO Box 15244 112 W Craig Pl San Antonio TX 78212-3416

**LABE, ROBERT BRIAN,** lawyer; b. Detroit, Sept. 2, 1959; s. Benjamin Mitchell and Gloria Florence (Wright) L.; m. Mary Lou Budman, Nov. 12, 1989; two children: Bridget and Katherine. BA with high honors, Mich. State U., 1981; JD, Wayne State U., 1984; LLM, Boston U., 1985. Bar: Mich. 1984, U.S. Dist. Ct. Mich. 1985, U.S. Tax Ct. 1985. Assoc. Weingarden & Hauer, P.C., Bingham Farms, Mich., 1988-92, shareholder, 1992-94; prin. Robert B. Labe, P.C., Southfield, Mich., 1994—; adj. prof. taxation and estate planning Walsh Coll., Troy, Mich., 1990-92; lectr. and presenter in field. Author: Research Edge-Taxation Guide, 1994, Bus. Succession Planning, 1996, Family Limited Liability Cos. and Limited Partnerships, 1998; mem. publ. adv. bd. Inst. Continuing Legal Edn. U. Mich., 1993—; contbr. articles to profl. jours. Bd. dirs. Oakland Bar Adams Pratt Found. Avocations: tennis, spectator sports. General corporate, Estate taxation, Estate planning. Office: Robert B Labe P C 2000 Town Ctr Ste 1780 Southfield MI 48075-1254

**LABIN, THOMAS S.,** lawyer, town justice; b. Buffalo, Dec. 7, 1940; s. Samuel and Esther A. Labin; m. Joanne Green, Jan. 20, 1968; children: Tracy A., Wendy A., Lisa C., Julie B. BS, Canisius Coll., Buffalo, 1962; JD, U. St. John, Buffalo, 1966. Bar: N.Y. 1966, U.S. Dist. Ct. (we. dist.) N.Y. 1968. Ptnr. Labin & Buffomante, Buffalo, 1972—; town justice Town of Marilla, N.Y., 1974—. Trustee Buffalo Sem., 1998-95. Fellow Am. Acad. Matrimonial Lawyers. Democrat. Roman Catholic. Avocations: golf, swimming, reading. Family and matrimonial. Home: 11937 Liberia Rd East Aurora NY 14052-9579 Office: Labin & Buffomante 531 Farber Lakes Dr Williamsville NY 14221-5773

**LABOVITZ, PRISCILLA,** lawyer; b. Lynn, Mass., May 4, 1946; d. Jack Oscar and Barbara Helene (Small) L.; m. Joseph Cirincione, June 25, 1978; children: Amy Labovitz Cirincione, Peter Vincent Labovitz Cirincione. BA, Wellesley Coll., 1968; JD, Northeastern U., 1972. Bar: Mass. 1973, U.S. Ct. Appeals (D.C. cir.) 1983. Ptnr. Geller, Miller, Taylor, Weinberg & Labovitz, Cambridge, Mass., 1973-78; assoc. Bastone & Kaplan, Boston, 1978-81, Law Offices of Jan Pederson, Washington, 1981, Paul Shearman Allen & Assocs., Washington, 1982-84; pvt. practice law Washington, 1988—. Contbr. articles to profl. jours. Literacy and homeless vol. Mem. NOW, Am. Immigration Lawyers Assn., Amnesty Internat. (legis. coord. 1990-96). Immigration, naturalization, and customs. Office: 6856 Eastern Ave NW Ste 354 Washington DC 20012-2165

**LABUDDE, ROY CHRISTIAN,** lawyer; b. Milw., July 21, 1921; s. Roy Lewis and Thea (Otteson) LaB.; m. Anne P. Held, June 7, 1952; children: Jack, Peter, Michael, Susan, Sarah. AB, Carleton Coll., 1943; JD, Harvard U., 1949. Bar: Wis. 1949, U.S. Dist. Ct. (ea. and we. dists.) Wis. 1950, U.S. Ct. Appeals (7th cir.) 1950, U.S. Supreme Ct. 1957. Assoc. Michael, Best & Friedrich, Milw., 1949-57, ptnr., 1958—; dir. DEC-Inter, Inc., Milw. Western Bank, Western Bancshares, Inc., Superior Die Set Corp., Aunt Nellie's Farm Kitchens, Inc. Bd. dirs. Wis. Hist. Soc. Found.; chmn., bd. dirs. Milw. div. Am. Cancer Soc. Served to lt. j.g. USNR, 1943-46. Mem. Milw. Estate Planning Coun. (past pres.), Wis. Bar Assn., Wis. State Bar Attys. (chmn. tax sch., bd. dirs. taxation sect.), Univ. Club, Milw. Club, Milw. Country Club. Republican. Episcopalian. General corporate, Estate planning, Personal income taxation. Home: 4201 W Stonefield Rd Mequon WI 53092-2771 Office: Michael Best & Friedrich 100 E Wisconsin Ave Ste 3300 Milwaukee WI 53202-4108

**LACAPRUCIA, CYNTHIA MARIE,** lawyer; b. Hartford, Conn., Feb. 2, 1962; d. Patrick J. and Ann Marie (Hayes) LaC.; m. Thomas E. Taylor III, Aug. 29, 1992. BA, Western Conn. State U., 1984; JD, CUNY, 1990. Bar: N.Y. 1991, Conn. 1990. Fundraiser Conn. Citizen Action Group, Hartford, Conn., 1982-87; staff atty. N.Y.C. Dept. of Housing Preservation and Devel., 1990-94, MFY Legal Svcs., Inc., N.Y.C., 1994-97, Juvenile Rights divsn. Legal Aid Soc., N.Y.C., 1997—. Mem. Nat. Abortion Rights Action League, N.Y.C., Co-op Am. Mem. NOW. Democrat. Unitarian Universalist. Avocation: competitive figure skating. Home: 70 LaSalle St Apt 21B New York NY 10027 Office: Legal Aid Soc Juvenile Rights Divsn 60 Lafayette St New York NY 10013-4048

**LACASSE, JAMES PHILLIP,** lawyer; b. Delta, Colo., Oct. 21, 1948; s. Kyndall and Elizabeth Ann (Harrington) L.; m. Lynda Diane Manly, June 17, 1978; 1 child, Laura Elizabeth. BS in Acctg. with distinction, Ariz. State U., 1970; JD, Coll. of William and Mary, 1973. Bar: Va. 1973. Tax staff Arthur Andersen & Co., Washington, 1973-75; corp. tax coordinator Continental Telecom Inc., Atlanta, 1975-78; internat. tax mgr. R.J. Reynolds Co., Winston-Salem, N.C., 1978-83, western hemisphere treas., 1983-84; sr. tax counsel Sea-Land Corp., Iselin, N.J., 1984-86; dir. taxes Am. Pres. Cos., Ltd., Oakland, Calif., 1986-95; dir. fin. N.Am. Am. Pres. Cos., Ltd., Memphis, 1995-98; CFO Lykes Lines Ltd. LLC, Tampa, Fla., 1998—. Mem. Downtown Crisis Ctr. Winston-Salem, 1983, bd. pilot commrs. Bays of San Francisco, San Pablo and Suisun; chairperson social ministry com. St. John's Lutheran Ch., Summit, N.J., 1986; deacon Piedmont Community Ch. Named one of Outstanding Young Men of Am. U.S. Jaycees, 1983. Mem. ABA, Va. Bar Assn., Tax Execs. Inst. Avocations: jogging, skiing, travel. Corporate taxation. Home: 904 Anchorage Rd Tampa FL 33602 Office: Lykes Lines Ltd LLC 401 E Jackson St Tampa FL 33602-5233

**LACER, ALFRED ANTONIO,** lawyer, educator; b. Hammonton, N.J., Feb. 14, 1952; s. Vincent and Carmen (Savall) L.; m. Kathleen Visser, June 15, 1974; children: Margaret, James, Matthew. BA in Polit. Sci., Gordon Coll., 1974; JD, Cath. U. Am., 1977. Bar: Md. 1977, U.S. Dist. Ct. Md. 1980, U.S. Ct. Appeals (4th cir.) 1980, U.S. Supreme Ct. 1997. Law clk. to Honorable Joseph A. Mattingly, Sr. Cir. Ct. St. Mary's County, Leonardtown, Md., 1977-78; ptnr. Lacer, Sparling, Dewsford & Reynolds PA and predecessors, Lexington Park, Md., 1978-99; county atty. St. Mary's County, Md., 1999—; adj. prof. bus. law Fla. Inst. Tech., Patuxent, Md., 1989-92, 95—; vis. instr. St. Mary's Coll. of Md., 1988, 91; mem. bd. edn. St. Mary's County (Md.) Pub. Schs., 1989-94, pres., 1991-92; mem. inquiry panel Atty. Grievance Commn. of Md., 1984-90. Bd. dirs. St. Mary's Hosp., Leonardtown, 1982-88, v.p., 1985-88; bd. dirs. So. Md. Cmty. Action, Inc., Hughsville, Md., 1982-84, St. Mary's County Tech. Coun., 1997—. Mem. ABA, Md. Bar Assn. (com. on jud. appointments 1982-85), St. Mary's County Bar Assn. (v.p. 1979-80, pres. 1980-81). Episcopalian. General civil litigation, Contracts commercial, General corporate. Office: Lacer Sparling Densferd & Reynolds PA 22335 Exploration Dr Ste 2030 Lexington Park MD 20653-2015

**LACEY, HENRY BERNARD,** lawyer; b. Aurora, Colo., Nov. 30, 1963; s. Leonard Joseph and Colleen Trece (Ryan) L. BS, Ariz. State U., 1988, JD, 1991. Bar: Ariz. 1991, Oreg. 1996; U.S. Dist. Ct. Ariz. 1991, U.S. Ct. Appeals (9th cir.) 1992, U.S. Dist. Ct. Oreg. 1999. Jud. law clk. to Hon. Cecil F. Poole U.S. Ct. Appeals 9th Cir., San Francisco, 1991-92; assoc. Kimball & Curry, P.C., Phoenix, 1992-93; atty. Law Office of Henry B. Lacey, Phoenix and Portland, Oreg., 1993-94, 97—; vis. fellow Natural Resources Law Inst. Northwestern Sch. Law, Lewis and Clark Coll., Portland, Oreg., 1994-95; atty. Wilenchik & Bartness, P.C., Phoenix, 1996-97; counsel/environ. group adv. bd. dirs. Coalition to Reform the Ctrl. Ariz. Project, Phoenix, 1993; vol. lawyer Land and Water Fund of the Rockies, Boulder, Colo., 1993—; vol. lawyer Portland Audubon Soc., 1996—; bd. dirs. Brite, Inc., Phoenix. Gen. counsel Maricopa County, Ariz. Dem. Party, 1992-94. Mem. ATLA, Order of Coif, Phi Delta Phi. Roman Catholic. Avocations: hiking, bicycling, reading, photography. Natural resources, Consumer commercial, General civil litigation. Home: 6515 SE 17th Ave Portland OR 97202-5523 Office: PO Box 82582 Portland OR 97282-0582

**LACH, JOSEPH ANDREW,** lawyer; b. Wilkes-Barre, Pa., Oct. 26, 1949; s. Joseph and Catherine (Pavelko) L.; m. Barbara Jean Lach, July 29, 1972; children: Elizabeth Ann, Joseph Robert. BA in Psychology, Lafayette Coll., 1971; JD, Pa. State U., 1977. Bar: Pa. 1977, U.S. Dist. Ct. (mid. dist.) Pa., U.S. Ct. Appeals (3d cir.), U.S. Supreme Ct. Assoc. Lenahan & Dempsey, Scranton, Pa., 1977-81; prin. Hourigan, Klugerr & Quinn, Wilkes-Barre, 1981-94, mng. prin., 1994—. Mem. ethics com. Good Samaritan Regional Med. Ctr., Pottsville, Pa., 1988—, Mercy Hosp., Wilkes-Barre, 1991—; pres. bd. dirs. Wyoming Valley Montessori Sch., Kingston, Pa., 1994—; trustee Mercy Health Care Ctr., Nanticoke, Pa., 1991-95; bd. dirs. Little Flower Manor, Wilkes-Barre, 1996—. Mem. ABA, Pa. Bar Assn. (mem. ho. of dels. 1991—), Psi Chi. Democrat. Roman Catholic. General civil litigation, Personal injury, Product liability. Office: Hourigan Kluger & Quinn 700 Mellon Bank Ctr Wilkes Barre PA 18701

**LACHCIK, NANCY LOU MARSHALL,** lawyer; b. Biloxi, Miss., July 25, 1957; d. Joseph John and Ruth Elaine (Glidden) Marshall; m. Joseph A. Lachcik. AA, St. Clair County Community Coll., 1977; BA, U. Mich., 1979; JD, Thomas M. Cooley Law Sch., 1982. Bar: Mich. Assoc. firm Dietrich & Cassavaugh, Port Huron, Mich., 1983—; atty., referee St. Clair County Probate Ct., Port Huron, 1984—. Deaconess 1st Congregational Ch., Port Huron, 1975-77; campaign worker William T. Fischer for County Commr., 1983. Mem. ABA, Mich. Bar Assn., St. Clair County Bar Assn., St. Clair County Council for Prevention of Child Abuse and Neglect, Women Lawyers Assn. (Blue Water region treas.), Assn. Trial Lawyers Am., Phi Theta Kappa. Republican.

**LACKEY, S. ALLEN,** lawyer, petroleum company executive. BBA, U. Miss., 1963, JD, 1968. Bar: Miss. 1968. CEO, pres., legal gen. counsel Shell Oil Co., Houston, v.p., gen. counsel, 1988—. Office: Shell Oil Co 910 Louisiana St Houston TX 77002-4916

**LACKLAND, JOHN,** lawyer; b. Parma, Idaho, Aug. 29, 1939. A.B., Stanford U., 1962; J.D., U. Wash., 1964; master gardener, Colo. State U., 1996. Bar: Wash. 1965, U.S. Dist. Ct. (we. dist.) Wash. 1965, (ea. dist.) Wash. 1973, U.S. Ct. Appeals (9th cir.) 1965, Conn. 1981, U.S. Dist. Ct. Conn. 1983, U.S. Supreme Ct. 1973, U.S. Dist. Ct. (so. dist.) N.Y. 1988. Assoc. firm Lane Powell Moss & Miller, Seattle, 1965-69; asst. atty. gen. State of Wash., Seattle, 1969-72; asst. chief State of Wash. (U. Wash. div.), 1969-72; v.p., sec., gen. counsel Western Farmers Assn., Seattle, 1972-76, Fotomat Corp., Stamford, Conn., 1976-80; ptnr. Leepson & Lackland, 1981-88, Lackland and Nalewaik, 1988-92; pvt. practices Westport, Conn., 1992-94; prin. Lackland Assocs., Grand Junction, Colo., 1994—. Bd. dirs. Mercer Island (Wash.) United Ch., 1967-70, pres. bd. dirs., 1970; mem. land use plan steering com. City of Mercer Island, 1970-72; bd. dirs. Mercer Island Sch. Dist., 1970-73, v.p. bd. dirs., 1972, pres. 1973; trustee Mid-Fairfield Child Guidance Ctr., 1982-84, Norfield Congl. Ch., 1982-84; bd. dirs. Grand Junction Symphony Orch., 1995—.

**LA COUR, LOUIS BERNARD,** lawyer; b. Columbus, Ohio, Aug. 12, 1926; s. Louis and Cleo (Carter) La C.; m. Jane Lee McFarland, Mar. 24, 1950; children: Lynne Denise, Avril Rose, Cheryl Celeste. BA, Ohio State U., 1951; LLB, Franklin U., 1961; JD, Capital U., Columbus, 1967. Bar: Ohio 1962. Land commr. U.S. Dist. Ct. (so. dist.) Ohio, Columbus, 1981, spl. master, 1983-87; spl. counsel City of Columbus Atty.'s Office, 1986—. Contbr. articles to profl. jours. Cons. NAACP, N.Y.C., 1975-80; mem. Greater Columbus Arts Coun., Model State Legis. Com.; sec. Mid-Ohio Regional Planning Commn., Columbus, 1978; vice-chmn. Columbus Civic Ctr. Commn., 1979; mem. rural zoning commn. Franklin County, 1994; mem. Ohio Elected Ofcls. Commn.; mem. Franklin Soil and Water Conservation Dist. Mem. ABA, Columbus Bar Assn., Am. Planning Assn. (task force), Ohio Elected Ofcls. Commn., The Capital Club (spl. com.), New Albany C.C., Franklin Soil and Water Conservation, Sigma Pi Phi, Lambda Boulé. Democrat. Roman Catholic. Avocations: tennis, cooking, theatre, jazz. Home: 1809 N Cassady Ave Columbus OH 43219-1520 Office: 500 S Front St Ste 1140 Columbus OH 43215-7619

**LACOVARA, KIRSTEN MARIE,** lawyer; b. Phila., July 15, 1965; d. William Albert L. and Sheila Anne Maher. BA in English, U. Mass., 1987; JD, Suffolk U., 1990. Bar: Mass. 1990, R.I. 1993, N.Y. 1999, U.S. Dist. Ct. Mass. 1992, U.S. Dist. Ct. R.I. 1994, U.S. Ct. Appeals (1st cir.) 1994, U.S. Supreme Ct. 1995. Pvt. practice Winchester, Mass., 1990-92; contract atty. Warner & Stackpole, Boston, 1991-92; assoc. Peabody & Arnold, Boston, 1992-95; ptnr. Cetrulo & Capone LLP, Boston, 1995—. Mem. ABA, FBA, R.I. Bar Assn., N.Y. Bar Assn., N.Y.C. Bar Assn. Federal civil litigation, State civil litigation, Criminal. Office: Cetrulo & Capone LLP 53 State St Boston MA 02109-2804

**LACOVARA, MICHAEL,** lawyer; b. Bklyn., Oct. 21, 1963; s. Philip Allen and Madeline Estelle (Papio) L.; m. Carla J. Foran, Sept. 9, 1989; children: Claire Elizabeth, Edward Christopher. BA, U. Pa., 1984; MPhil, Cambridge (U.K.) U., 1985; JD, Harvard U., 1988. Law clk. Hon. Stephen Reinhardt, L.A., 1988-89; assoc. Sullivan & Cromwell, N.Y.C., 1989-96, ptnr., 1997—. Bd. dirs. Lower Manhattan Cultural Coun., N.Y.C., 1995—, chair, 1998. Thouron Found. fellow, 1984. Mem. ABA, Assn. of Bar of City of N.Y., Phi Beta Kappa. Democrat. Roman Catholic. Home: 131 5th Ave Apt 401 New York NY 10003-1012 Office: Sullivan & Cromwell 125 Broad St Fl 28 New York NY 10004-2489

**LACOVARA, PHILIP ALLEN,** lawyer; b. N.Y.C., July 11, 1943; s. P. Philip and Elvira Lacovara; m. Madeline E. Papio, Oct. 14, 1961; children: Philip, Michael, Christopher, Elizabeth, Karen, Daniel, Andrew. AB magna cum laude, Georgetown U., 1963; JD summa cum laude, Columbia U., 1966. Bar: N.Y. 1967, D.C. 1974, U.S. Supreme Ct. 1970. Law clk. to presiding justice U.S. Ct. Appeals D.C. Cir., 1966-67; asst. to solicitor gen. U.S. Washington, 1967-69; assoc. Hughes Hubbard & Reed, N.Y.C., 1969-71; ptnr. Hughes Hubbard & Reed, N.Y.C. and Washington, 1974-88; v.p., sr. counsel GE, Fairfield, Conn., 1988-90; mng. dir, gen. counsel Morgen Stanley & Co., N.Y.C., 1990-93; ptnr. Mayer, Brown & Platt, N.Y.C. and Washington, 1993—; spl. counsel to N.Y.C. Police Commr., 1971-72; dep. solicitor gen. U.S. Dept. Justice, Washington, 1972-73; counsel to spl. prosecutor Watergate Spl. Prosecution Force, 1973-74; lectr. law Columbia U.; adj. prof. Georgetown U. Law Ctr.; vis. lectr. various colls., univs.; mem. Jud. Conf. D.C. Circuit, 1973—; chmn. commn. on admissions and grievances U.S. Ct. Appeals for D.C. Circuit, 1980-86; spl. counsel U.S. Ho. of Reps. Com. on Standards Ofcl. Conduct, 1976-77; chmn. bd. trustees Public Defender Service for D.C., 1976-81; sec. exec. com. bd. visitors Columbia U. Sch. Law; pres. Columbia U. Sch. Law Alumni Assn., 1986-88; bd. govs. D.C. Bar, 1981-84, gen. counsel, 1985-87, pres., 1988-89, mem. legal ethics com., 1976-81, chmn. code subcom., 1977-81. Contbr. articles to profl. jours. Co-chair, Washington Lawyers Com. for Civil Rights Under Law, 1982-84; mem. D.C. Jud. Nomination Commn., 1981-86; bd. dirs. Legal Aid Soc. of N.Y.C., 1992—. Fellow Am. Coll. Trial Lawyers; mem. ABA (ho. of dels. 1978-89, vice-chmn. sect. individual rights and responsibilities 1985-87, 89-91, chmn. 1991-92), Am. Law Inst., Practicing Law Inst. (trustee), Cath. Interracial Coun. N.Y., Lawyers Com. for Human Rights (trustee 1991—), Legal Aid Soc. N.Y.C. (bd. dirs. 1992—), 1925 F St. Club, Lotos Club, Knights of Malta. Roman Catholic. Administrative and regulatory, Federal civil litigation, Securities. Home: 1137 Smith Ridge Rd New Canaan CT 06840-2333 Office: 1675 Broadway New York NY 10019-5820

**LACY, ELIZABETH BERMINGHAM,** state supreme court justice; b. 1945. BA cum laude, St. Mary's Coll., Notre Dame, Ind., 1966; JD, U. Tex., 1969; LLM, U. Va., 1992. Bar: Tex. 1969, Va. 1977. Staff atty. Tex. Legis. Coun., Austin, 1969-72; atty. Office of Atty. Gen., State of Tex., Austin, 1973-76; legis. aide Va. Del. Carrington Williams, Richmond, 1976-77; dep. atty. gen. jud. affairs div. Va. Office Atty. Gen., Richmond, 1982-85; mem. Va. State Corp. Commn., Richmond, 1985-89; justice Supreme Ct. Va., Richmond, 1989—. Office: Va Supreme Ct PO Box 1315 Covington VA 23218-1315*

**LACY, ROBINSON BURRELL,** lawyer; b. Boston, May 7, 1952; s. Benjamin Hammett and Jane (Burrell) L. AB, U. Calif., Berkeley, 1974; JD, Harvard U., 1977. Bar: N.Y. 1978, U.S. Dist. Ct. (so. and ea. dists.) N.Y. 1979, U.S. Dist. Ct. (we. dist.) N.Y. 1992, U.S. Ct. Appeals (2d cir.) 1983, U.S. Ct. Appeals (10th cir.) 1990, U.S. Supreme Ct. 1986. Law clk. to judge U.S. Dist. Ct. (so. dist.) N.Y., N.Y.C., 1977-78; law clk. to chief justice Warren Burger U.S. Supreme Ct., Washington, 1978-79; assoc. Sullivan & Cromwell, N.Y.C., 1979-85, ptnr., 1985—. Mem. ABA, Assn. of Bar of City of N.Y., N.Y. State Bar Assn. Bankruptcy, Federal civil litigation. Office: Sullivan & Cromwell 125 Broad St Fl 28 New York NY 10004-2489

**LACY, STEVEN C.,** lawyer; b. Everett, Wash., Dec. 2, 1950; s. James Edward and Mae Lacy; m. Debra Janifer Smith, Nov. 10, 1972; children: Steven James, Sommer Ann, Brooke Miel, Stephanie Marie. BA in Spanish, Brigham Young U., 1975; JD, U. Utah, 1979. Bar: Wash. 1980, U.S. Dist. Ct. (ea. dist.) Wash. 1980, U.S. Dist. Ct. (we. dist.) Wash. 1982. Assoc. Law Offices of Lowell Sperline, East Wenatchee, Wash., 1980-82; ptnr. Sperline & Lacy, Inc., P.S., East Wenatchee, 1982-84; pvt. practice East Wenatchee, 1984-86; co-owner, ptnr. Lacy & Kane, P.S., East Wenatchee, 1986—. Councilman City of east Wenatchee, 1992-98, mayor, 1998—. Mem. Wash. State Bar Assn. (bd. dirs., treas. family law exec. com. 1983-86), Wash. State Trial Lawyers Assn. (Eagle mem. 1980—). Republican. Mem. Ch. of Jesus Christ of Latter Day Saints. Avocations: golf, tennis, gardening. General civil litigation, Civil rights, Pension, profit-sharing, and employee benefits. Home: 1018 N Fairview Pl East Wenatchee WA 98802-4494 Office: Lacy and Kane PS 222 Eastmont Ave East Wenatchee WA 98802-5306

**LADAR, JERROLD MORTON,** lawyer; b. San Francisco, Aug. 2, 1933. AB, U. Wash., 1956; LLB, U. Calif., Berkeley, 1960. Bar: Calif. 1961, U.S. Supreme Ct. 1967. Law clk. to judge U.S. Dist. Ct. (no. dist.) Calif., 1960-61; asst. U.S. atty. San Francisco, 1961-70; chief criminal div., 1968-70; mem. firm MacInnis & Donner, San Francisco, 1970-72; prof. criminal law and procedure U. San Francisco Law Sch., 1962-83; pvt. practice San Francisco., 1970—; ptnr. Ladar & Ladar, San Francisco, 1994—; lectr. Hastings Coll. Law, Civil and Criminal Advocacy Programs, 1985—; chair pvt. defender panel U.S. Dist. Ct. (no. dist.) Calif., 1980-90; ct. apptd. chair stats. and tech. subcom. Fed. Civil Justice Reform Act Com. (no. dist.) Calif., 1990-95; ct. apptd. mem. Fed. Ct. Civil Local Rules Revision Com. (no. dist.) Calif., 1994—; ct. apptd. chmn. Criminal Local Rules Revision Com. (no. dist.) Calif., 1991—; mem. continuing edn. of bar criminal law adv. com. U. Calif., Berkeley, 1978-83, 89—; panelist, mem. nat. planning com. ABA Nat. Ann. White Collar Crime Inst., 1996—; ct. apptd. mem. Local Disciplinary Rule com., 1998—. Author: (with others) Selected Trial Motions, California Criminal Law Procedure and Practice, 1986, Direct Examination-Tips and Techniques, 1982, Collateral Effects of Federal Convictions, 1997: Insult Added to Injury: The Fallout From Tax Conviction, 1997; co-author: Criminal Trial Tactics, 1985. Trustee Tamalpais Union High Sch. Dist., 1968-77, chmn. bd., 1973-74; mem. adv. com. Nat. PTA Assn., 1972-78; apptd. mem. criminal justice act com. U.S. Ct. Appeals (9th cir). Fellow Am. Bd. Criminal Lawyers; mem. ABA, San Francisco Bar Assn. (editor in Re 1974-76), State Bar Calif. (pro-tem disciplinary referee 1976-78, vice chmn. pub. interest and edn. com. criminal law sect., mem. exec. com. criminal law sect. 1980-87, editor Criminal Law Sect. News 1981-87, chmn. exec. com. 1983-84), Am. Inns. of Ct. (exec. com. 1994-97), Fed. Bar Assn. (panelist), Nat. Sentencing Inst. (contbr.). Federal civil litigation, Criminal, State civil litigation. Office: 507 Polk St Ste 310 San Francisco CA 94102-3339

**LADD, JEFFREY RAYMOND,** lawyer; b. Mpls., Apr. 10, 1941; s. Jasper Raymond and Florence Marguerite (DeMarce) L.; m. Kathleen Anne Crosby, Aug. 24, 1963; children: Jeffrey Raymond, John Henry, Mark Jasper, Matthew Crosby. Student, U. Vienna, Austria; BA, Loras Coll.; postgrad., U. Denver; JD, Ill. Inst. Tech. Bar: Ill. 1973, U.S. Dist. Ct. 1973. V.p. mktg. Ladd Enterprises, Des Plaines, Ill., 1963-66; v.p. mktg. and fin. Ladd Enterprises, Crystal Lake, Ill., 1966-70; ptnr. Ross & Hardies, Chgo., 1973-81, Boodell, Sears, et al., 1981-86, Bell, Boyd & Lloyd, Chgo., 1986—; spl. asst. atty. gen. for condemnation State of Ill., 1977-82. Named Chgo. City Club's 1995 Citizen of Yr. Mem. ABA, Chgo. Bar Assn., Nat. Assn. Bond Lawyers, Ill. Assn. Hosp. Attys., Am. Acad. Hosp. Attys., Crystal Lake Jaycees (Disting. Svc. award), Crystal Lake C. of C. (past pres.), Econ. Club, Legal Club, Union League Club, Bull Valley Golf Club, Woodstock Country Club, Alpha Lambda. Roman Catholic. Avocations: golf, hunting, fishing, tennis, skiing. General corporate, Health, Municipal (including bonds). Office: Bell Boyd & Lloyd 3 First National Pla 70 W Madison St Ste 3300 Chicago IL 60602-4284

**LADDAGA, BETH JANE,** lawyer; b. Beaufort, S.C., Sept. 29, 1953; d. Philip Covert and Leone (Ford) Goodlove; m. R. Charles May, May 20, 1977 (div. Apr. 1978); 1 child, Amanda; m. Lawrence A. Laddaga, Nov. 12, 1983; 1 child, Rachel. BA, Coll. Charleston, 1993; JD, U. S.C., 1996. Bar: S.C. 1996, U.S. Ct. Appeals (4th cir.) 1996. Assoc. Ness, Motley, Loadholt, Richardson & Poole, Charleston, S.C., 1996—. Contbr. articles to profl. jours. Mem. ABA, ATLA, S.C. Bar Assn., S.C. Trial Lawyers Assn. (products liability subcom.), S.C. Women Lawyers Assn., Phi Kappa Phi, Phi Delta Phi. Product liability, Personal injury, Federal civil litigation. Office: Ness Motley Loadholt Richardson & Poole 174 E Bay St Ste 100 Charleston SC 29401-2133

**LADDAGA, LAWRENCE ALEXANDER,** lawyer; b. New Hyde Park, N.Y., Aug. 12, 1957; s. Carmine Michael and Adeline (Lauricella) L.; m. Beth Jane Goodlove, Nov. 12, 1983; children: Amanda May, Rachel. BA cum laude, U. S.C., 1978, JD, 1981. Bar: S.C. 1981, U.S. Dist. Ct. S.C. 1981, U.S. Ct. Appeals (4th cir.) 1981, U.S. Tax Ct. 1982, U.S. Supreme Ct. 1989. Assoc. Wise & Cole, P.A., Charleston, S.C., 1981-83; founding shareholder, sr. ptnr. Laddaga Drachman & Garrett PA, Charleston, 1983—; adj. asst. prof. dept. health adminstrn. and policy MUSC, Charleston, 1999—. Bd. dirs., 1st v.p. Charleston chpt. Am. Cancer Soc., 1987-88. Fellow Healthcare Fin. Mgmt. Assn. (advanced mem., bd. dirs. 1991-94, sec., v.p. 1991-95, pres. 1997-98), S.C. Bar Assn. (chairperson health care law com. 1995-97), Charleston County Bar Assn., Am. Health Lawyers Assn., S.C. Health Alliance, Order Ky. Cols., Kiwanis, Elks, Masons, Phi Beta Kappa. Health, Contracts commercial. Home: 1391 Madison Ct Mount Pleasant SC 29466-7961 Office: 300 W Coleman Blvd Ste 205 Mount Pleasant SC 29464-5641

**LADSON, M. BRICE,** lawyer; b. Moultrie, Ga., Jan. 18, 1952; s. John E. and Margaret (Brice) L.; m. Anna Montgomery, Aug. 15, 1976; children: M. Brice Jr., Laurie Marie. BA, Emory U., 1974, JD, 1977. Ptnr. Bonhan, William & Levy, Savannah, Ga., 1977-96, Ladson, Odom & Des Roches, Savannah, 1996-98, Ladson & Suthers, Savannah, 1998—. Mem. ABA, ATLA, Ga. Bar Assn., Ga. Trial Lawyers Assn. Federal civil litigation, State civil litigation, Personal injury. Home: 537 Star Creek Rd Richmond Hill GA 31324-6141 Office: Ladson & Suthers Drayton St Ste 401 Savannah GA 31401

**LADWIG, PATTI HEIDLER,** lawyer; b. Harleysville, Pa., Aug. 28, 1958; d. L. Donald and Joan E. (Wright) Heidler; m. Manfred Friedrich Ladwig, July 30, 1983; 1 child, Brittney Nichole. BA in Psychology, U. Miami, 1980, JD, 1988. Bar: Fla. 1988, U.S. Dist. Ct. (so. dist.) Fla. 1988. Assoc. atty. Taplin, Howard & Shaw, West Palm Beach, Fla., 1988-92; ptnr. Shaw, St. James, & Ladwig, West Palm Beach, Fla., 1992, St. James & Ladwig, P.A., West Palm Beach, Fla., 1992-93; pvt. practice Patti Heidler Ladwig, P.A., West Palm Beach, 1993—; bd. dirs. Cmty. Assns. Inst., West Palm Beach, First Wellington, Inc.; mem. condominium and planned devel. com., real property, probate and trust law sect. Fla. Bar. Pres., bd. dirs. Treasure Coast Communities Assn., West Palm Beach, 1990—, Pine Lake Condominium Assn. Inc., Pembroke Pines, Fla., 1986-88; mem. community appearance com. ACME Improvement Dist., Wellington, Fla., 1990—, Condominium Owners Fla., 1991—, Fedn. Mobile Home Owners Fla., 1990—; del. Fla. Legis. Action Com., 1989-91. Mem. Fla. Bar Assn. (bus. law sect., mem. condominium and planned devel. com. real property, probate and trust law sect.). Lutheran. Real property, Estate planning. Office: Ste 1317 12765 W Forest Hill Blvd Wellington FL 33414-4782

**LADY, JAMES EDWARD,** lawyer; b. Richmond, Va., Sept. 29, 1960; s. Terrell Calvin and Carol Lehman L.; m. Mary Pauline McAlister, Sept. 11, 1993; children: James Edward, Grace McAlister. BA in Polit. Sci., The Citadel, 1982; postgrad., Exeter (Eng.) U., 1988; JD, Coll. William and Mary, 1989. Bar: Va. 1989, S.C. 1990, U.S. Dist. Ct. S.C. 1991, U.S. Ct. Appeals (4th cir.) 1991, U.S. Supreme Ct. 1991. Law clk. 9th Circuit Ct. Va., Fairfax, 1989-90; assoc. Haynsworth, Marion, McKay & Guerard, LLP, Columbia and Charleston, S.C., 1990-97, ptnr., 1998—. Chmn. parish coun. St. Mary's Ch., Charleston, 1995-98; bd. dirs. Charitable Soc. Charleston, 1996—. 1st lt. U.S. Army, 1982-85. Mmem. Nat. Assn. R.R. Trial Counsel (exec. com. 1998—), Sertoma (v.p. Charleston 1995-96). Republican. Roman Catholic. Avocations: sports fan, golf. Appellate, General civil litigation, Land use and zoning (including planning). Office: Haynesworth Marion Et Al 134 Meeting St Fl 4 Charleston SC 29401-2224

**LAFFITTE, HECTOR MANUEL,** federal judge; b. Ponce, P.R., Apr. 13, 1934; s. Miguel and Gilda (Colomer) L.; m. Nydia M. Rossy, June 13, 1958; children: Yasmin, Hector W., Bernice M., Walter M., Giselle M. BA, Interamerican U., 1955; LLB, U. P.R., 1958; LLM, Georgetown U., 1960. Bar: U.S. Dist. Ct. P.R. 1959, U.S. Ct. Appeals (1st cir.) 1959, Supreme Ct. P.R. 1959, U.S. Mil. Appeals 1960, U.S. Supreme Ct. 1976. Assoc. Hartzell, Fernandez & Novas, 1959-64; pvt. practice law, 1965-66; ptnr. Nachman, Feldstein, Laffitte, & Smith, 1966-69, Laffitte & Dominguez, 1970-83; judge U.S. Dist. Ct. P.R., 1983—; advisor on labor practice and procedures Govt. of U.S. V.I., 1970. Mem. Gov.'s Adv. Com. on Jud. Appointments, 1977-83, Gov.'s Adv. Com. on Labor Policy, 1977-83; mem. Civil Rights Commn. of P.R., 1969-72; mem. magistrate judges com. of Jud. Conf., 1992. Mem. ABA, Fed. Bar Assn., Am. Arbitration, Assn. of Labor Rels. Practitioners, Inst. Jud. Adminstrn. Office: Federico Degatau Fed Bldg CH-142 150 Carlos Chardon Ave Hato Rey PR 00918-1757

**LAFILI, ELLEN YOST See YOST, ELLEN G.**

**LAFOLLETTE, ERNEST CARLTON,** lawyer; b. Buffalo, Aug. 12, 1934; s. John and Mary Esther (Schramm) LaF.; m. Marcy Eleanore Freeman, June 16, 1979; children: Andre Michael, David Steven; children from previous marriage—Karen Yvonne, Brian Clark, Ernest Claud, Leah Ann. B.A. cum laude, Alfred U., 1956; J.D. summa cum laude, Syracuse Law Sch., 1959; LLM in Taxation U. Bridgeport, 1987; Bar: N.Y. 1959, Pa. 1964, Conn. 1978, U.S. Ct. Appeals (2d cir.) 1984, U.S. Supreme Ct. 1985, U.S. Dist. Ct. (so. dist.) N.Y. 1990, U.S. Tax Ct. 1991. Law clk. chief justice, N.Y. Supreme Ct., Rochester, 1959; div. atty. GE, King of Prussia, Pa., Bridgeport, Conn., 1962-70; prof. law Albany Law Sch., 1970-73; supr. attys. NLRB, Washington, 1973-75; labor rels. counsel Norlin Corp., N.Y.C., 1975-78; pvt. practice, Fairfield, 1978—. Capt., U.S. Army. Mem. ABA, Assn. Trial Lawyers Am., Conn. Bar Assn., Justinian Soc., Order of Coif. Editor-in-chief Syracuse Law Sch. Rev., 1959. Labor, Corporate taxation, State civil litigation. Office: 1432 Post Rd Fairfield CT 06430-5930

**LAFOND, THOMAS JOSEPH,** lawyer; b. Chgo., Feb. 25, 1941; s. Charles J. and Marie F. (Lane) LaF.; m. Karen Kent, June 13, 1964; children: Julia, Jennifer, Laura, Susan. BSBA, John Carroll U., 1963; JD, Case Western Res. U., 1966. Assoc. Henderson, Quail, Schneider & Smeltz, Cleve., 1968-75; ptnr. Schneider, Smeltz, Ranney & LaFond, Cleve., 1975—. Pres. Citizens League, Cleve., 1984-86; grad. Leadership Cleve., 1985. Capt. U.S. Army, 1966-68. Mem. ABA, Ohio State Bar Assn., Cleve. Bar Assn. (bd. trustees 1983-86, chmn. young lawyers 1972, ethics com. 1979, profl. trends com. 1982, pres. 1991—). General practice, Family and matrimonial, State civil litigation. Office: Schneider Smeltz Ranney & LaFond 1111 Superior Ave E Ste 1000 Cleveland OH 44114-2568

**LAFONT, WILLIAM HAROLD,** lawyer,farmer; b. Plainview, Tex., May 14, 1940; s. Harold Matthews and Jane Powell L.; m. Susan Chandler, 1961 (div. Oct. 1964); m. Ellie Agnus Dardis, Dec. 27, 1984; children: Christopher Chapman, Emily, Christopher Lafont, Nicole Smock, Matthew. BBA, U. Tex., 1961, JD, 1964. Bar: Tex. 1964, Am. Bar, Ctrl. Plains Bar. Ptnr. Lafont, Tunnell & Formby, Plainview, Tex., 1964—; pres. Ctrl. Plains, Plainview, 1980-82. Pres. Plainview C. of C., Plainview, 1964—, Optimist Club, Plainview, 1975. Mem. Toastmasters Internat. (pres. 1964-78), YMCA (dir. 1998—), Plainview Country Club (pres. 1998—). Democrat. Methodist. General civil litigation, Banking, Criminal. Home: 310 Mesa Cir Plainview TX 79072-6508 Office: Lafont Tunnell Formby Lafont Skaggs Bldg 701 Broadway St Fl 1 Plainview TX 79072-7353

**LA FORCE, PIERRE JOSEPH,** lawyer; b. Berlin, N.H., Mar. 29, 1936; s. F. Maurice and Marie R. (Montminy) La F. AB, St. Anselm Coll., 1957; JD, Georgetown U, 1960. Bar: D.C. 1960, U.S. Supreme Ct. 1972, U.S. Ct. Appeals (D.C. Cir.) 1960, (6th Cir.) 1976, (9th Cir.) 1984, Fed. Cir. 1966. Assoc. Hogan & Hartson, D.C., 1960-69; ptnr. Wilkinson, Cragun & Barker, D.C., 1970-82, Baenen, Timme, D.C., 1982-84, Wilkinson, Barker, Knauer LLP, D.C., 1984—. Mem. ABA, D.C. Bar Assn., Barristers, Univ. Club. Republican. Roman Catholic. Avocations: tennis, squash. Federal civil litigation, Administrative and regulatory, Private international. Office: Wilkinson Barker Knauer LLP 2300 N St NW Ste 700 Washington DC 20037-1122

**LAFOREST, LANA JEAN,** lawyer, real estate broker; b. Providence, Apr. 14, 1952; d. Harold Joseph Ecker and Nettie Jean (Starks) Page; children: Timothy Charles, Tisha DeAnne. AA in Humanities and Social Scis., Niagara County C. C., 1989; BA in English Lit. magna cum laude, Buffalo State Coll., 1990, MA in English Lit., 1999; JD, SUNY Buffalo Sch. Law, 1994; doctoral student, SUNY, Buffalo, 1994—. Lic. real estate broker. Property mgr. Personal Income Property Mgmt., Lockport, 1976—; sales assoc. John F. Collins Realty, Lockport, 1979-83, Town Crier Clark Nodine Realty, Lockport, 1983-90, McKnight, Hogan & Noonan, Lockport, 1990-91, H. Potter Realty, Lockport, 1991-93; advocate Family Court Resource Project Haven House, 1994—; advocate domestic violence clinic U. Buffalo Law Sch., 1994; pvt. practice East Amherst, N.Y., 1994—; owner, operator Custom Crafts by Lana, Lockport, 1975-79; adv. domestic violence clinic U. Buffalo Law Sch., 1994. Editor: (lit. mag.) Writer's Revue, 1989; corr. Union-Sun and Jour., summer 1989. Girl scouts coord. Niagara County Coun. Girl Scouts, Sanborn, N.Y., 1978-84; clover clan 4-H club leader Niagara County Coop. Extension, Lockport, 1984-87; with Project Dandelion, Neighborhood Legal Svcs., 1994—. Mem. ABA, MLA, N.Y. State Bar Assn., Niagara Linguistics Soc., Nat. Assn. Realtors, Univ. Buffalo Law Sch. Alumni Assn., Buffalo State Coll. Alumni Assn., Niagara County Community Coll. Alumni Assn., U. Buffalo Assn. Women Law Students, Erie County Bar Assn., Women's Bar Assn. Erie County, Phi Alpha Delt. Avocations: writing, sewing, gourmet cooking, painting. Fax: 716-668-7103. E-mail: Lana@unforgettable.com. Family and matrimonial, Real property, Probate.

**LAFORTE, GEORGE FRANCIS, JR.,** lawyer; b. Oak Lawn, Ill., Dec. 15, 1970; s. George Francis and Nancy Ruth (Avery) LaF. BS, No. Ill. U., 1992; JD, John Marshall Law Sch., Chgo., 1996. Bar: Ill. 1996. Assoc. Bishop, Rossi & Scarlati, Ltd., Oakbrook Terrace, Ill., 1996—; of counsel Law Offices George F. LaForte, Olympia Fields, Ill., 1996—; adminstrv. hearing officer Village of Frankfort, Ill., 1997-98. Mem. ABA, Ill. Bar Assn., DuPage County Bar Assn (arbitrator 1997—). Republican. Roman Catholic. Avocation: sports. General civil litigation, Personal injury, Labor. Office: Bishop Rossi & Scarlati Ltd 2 Transam Plaza Dr Ste 200 Oakbrook Terrace IL 60181-4296

**LAGDAMEO-HOGAN, MARIA-ELENA,** lawyer; b. Manila, Jan. 18, 1969; came to U.S., 1983; d. Antonio Manuel and Maria-Linda (Floirendo) Lagdameo; m. Brian F. Hogan, Dec. 13, 1996. BA in Govt., Smith Coll., Northampton, Mass., 1990; JD, Bklyn. Law Sch., 1993; LLM in Internat. Trade & Bus. Law, Fordham U., N.Y.C., 1996. Bar: N.J. 1994, N.Y. 1996. Assoc. Franklin Lakes, N.J. Private international, Real property, Communications. Home: 908 Mohawk Rd Franklin Lakes NJ 07417-2837

**LAGLE, JOHN FRANKLIN,** lawyer; b. Kansas City, Mo., Jan. 22, 1938; s. Ernest J. and Hilda B. L.; m. Nina E. Weston, Aug. 1, 1959; m. Diana G. Fogle, July 14, 1962 (dec. 1992); children—Robert, Gregory. BBA, UCLA, 1961, JD, 1967. Bar: Calif. 1967, U.S. Dist. Ct. (no. dist.) Calif. 1967. Assoc. Hindin, McKittrick & Marsh, Beverly Hills, Calif., 1967-70, Macco Corp., Newport Beach, Calif., 1970, Rifkind & Sterling, Beverly Hills, 1971; mem. Fulop & Hardee, and predecessor Fulop, Rolston, Burns & McKittrick, Beverly Hills, 1971-82; ptnr. Leff & Stephenson, Beverly Hills, 1983; sole practice, Los Angeles, 1984; ptnr. Barash & Hill (formerly Wildman, Harrold, Allen, Dixon, Barash & Hill), Los Angeles, 1985-91; pvt. practice, L.A., 1992—, ptnr. Barbosa Garcia, 1998—; arbitrator Am. Arbitration Assn.; arbitrator NASD Regulation, Inc. Served with U.S. Army, 1961-63. Mem. ABA, Am. Arbitration Assn. (arbitrator), Calif. Bar Assn., Los Angeles County Bar Assn. Republican. Contbr. to Practice Under the California Corporate Securities Law of 1978. Real property, Securities, General corporate. Office: 16750 Marquez Ave Pacific Palisades CA 90272-3240 also: 801 S Grand Ave Los Angeles CA 90017-4613

**LAGOS, JAMES HARRY,** lawyer; b. Springfield, Ohio, Mar. 14, 1951; s. Harry Thomas and Eugenia (Papas) L.; m. Nike Daphne Pavlatos, July 3, 1976. BA cum laude, Wittenberg U., 1970; JD, Ohio State U., 1972. Bar: Ohio 1973, U.S. Dist. Ct. (so. dist.) Ohio 1973, U.S. Tax Ct. 1975, U.S. Supreme Ct. 1976, U.S. Ct. Appeals (6th cir.) 1979. Asst. pros. atty. Clark County, Ohio, 1972-75; ptnr. Lagos & Lagos, Springfield, 1975—; mem. Springfield Small Bus. Coun., past chmn., 1977—, Ohio Small Bus. Coun., 1980—, past chmn., vice chmn.; past pres., v.p. Nat. Small Bus. United, 1982—; del. Small Bus. Nat. Issues Conf., 1984; del. Ohio Gov.'s Conf. on Small Bus., 1984, resource person regulatory and licensing reform com., 1984. Bd. dirs., past pres. Greek Orthodox Ch., 1974—; mem. coun. Greek Orthodox Diocese of Detroit, 1985-86; past chmn. Clark County Child Protection Team, 1974-82; past chmn. Clark County Young Rep. Club, past pres., sec., treas., 1968-76, chmn. Ohio del. to White Ho. Conf. on Small Bus., 1985-86, del. to White Ho. Conf. on Small Bus., 1995. Staff sgt. Ohio Air N.G., 1970-76. Recipient Dr. Melvin Emanuel award West Ctrl. Ohio Hearing and Speech Assn., 1983, Medal of St. Paul the Apostle, Greek Orthodox Archdiocese North and South Am., 1985, Disting. Svc. award Springfield-Clark County, 1977; named one of Outstanding Young Men of Am., 1978, Small Bus. Adv. Yr., U.S. Sma.. Bus. Adminstrn., 1991. Mem. Am. Hellenic Inst. (pub. affairs com. 1979—, bd. dirs.), Am. Hellenic Ednl. Progressive Assn. (past treas.), Rsch. Inst. Small and Emerging Bus. (bd. dirs. 1993—), C. of C. (past bd. dirs.), Jaycees (past chmn. several coms. 1973-89, Spoke award 1974), Ohio State Bar Assn., Clark County Bar Assn. (past sec., exec. com. 1973—), West Ctrl. Ohio Hearing and Speech Assn. (bd. dirs., pres., v.p. 1973-84), Alpha Alpha Kappa, Phi Eta Sigma, Tau Pi Phi, Pi Sigma Alpha. Personal injury, Family and matrimonial, Criminal. Home: 2023 Audubon Park Dr Springfield OH 45504-1113 Office: Lagos & Lagos 1 S Limestone St Ste 1000 Springfield OH 45502-1294

**LAGUEUX, RONALD RENE,** federal judge; b. Lewiston, Maine, June 30, 1931; s. Arthur Charles and Laurette Irene (Turcotte) L.; m. Denise Rosemarie Boudreau, June 30, 1956; children: Michelle Simone, Gregory Charles, Barrett James. AB, Bowdoin Coll., 1953; LLB, Harvard U., 1956. Assoc. then ptnr. Edwards and Angell Law Firm, Providence, R.I., 1956-68; assoc. justice Superior Ct. State of R.I., Providence, 1968-86; judge U.S. Dist. Ct., Providence, 1986—; chief judge, 1992—; exec. counsel to Gov. Chafee, R.I., 1963-65. Rep. candidate for U.S. Senate, 1964; corporator R.I. Hosp., Providence, 1965—; solicitor Southeastern New Eng. Province United Way, 1957-68. Mem. ABA, Bowdoin Coll. Alumni Council (past v.p., pres.), Am.-French Geneal. Soc. Home: 90 Greenwood Ave Rumford RI 02916-1934 Office: US Dist Ct 1 Exchange Ter Providence RI 02903-1720

**LAHOUD, NINA JOSEPH,** lawyer, international organization assistant; b. Littleton, N.H., July 10, 1956; d. Joseph and Loretta Lahout. Student, Smith Coll., 1975-76; BA, Harvard U., 1978; JD, U. Pa., 1981; postgrad., Am. U., Cairo, 1982. Bar: N.Y. 1981. Assoc. Shearman & Sterling, N.Y.C., 1982-83; legal advisor Office of the Force Comdr., UN Interim Force in Lebanon, Naqoura, 1983-86; dep. legal advisor UN Transition Assistance Group in Namibia, Windhoek, 1989-90; sr. legal officer UN Transitional Authority in Cambodia, Phnom Penh, 1992-93; spl. asst. to asst. sec.-gen. for mgmt. and coordination UN Peace Forces in the Former Yugoslavia, Zagreb, Croatia, 1995-96; legal officer Office of Legal Affairs, UN Hdqrs., N.Y.C., 1986-93, sr.legal officer, 1993-97; spl. asst. to asst. sec.-gen. for planning and support Dept. Peacekeeping Ops., UN Hdqrs., N.Y.C., 1997-98, spl. asst. to under-sec.-gen. for peacekeeping ops., 1998—. Contbr. articles to profl. jours. Mem. Assn. Bar City N.Y. (com. on internat. human rights 1987-90, com. on internat. law 1996—), Internat. Law Assn. (human rights com. 19837), Am. Soc. Internt. Law, U. Pa. Law Sch. Alumni Assn., Harvard U. Alumni Assn. Office: Un Hdqrs Dept Peacekeeping Ops One Un Plz Rm S-3727A New York NY 10017

**LAIDLAW, ANDREW R.,** lawyer; b. Durham, N.C., Aug. 28, 1946. BA, Northwestern U., 1969; JD, U. N.C., 1972. Bar: Ill. 1972. Chair exec com., mem. Seyfarth, Shaw, Fairweather & Geraldson, Chgo.; CEO Seyfarth Shaw, Fairweather & Geraldson, Chicago. Contbr. articles to profl. jours. Mem. ABA (antitrust and securities law coms. 1982—), Barristers. Contracts commercial. Office: Seyfarth Shaw Fairweather & Geraldson Mid Continental Plz 55 E Monroe St Ste 4200 Chicago IL 60603-5863

**LAING, ROBERT SCOTT,** lawyer; b. Chgo., Aug. 7, 1952; s. Robert Bruce and Mary Edith (Lindsay) L. BA magna cum laude, Fla. Technol. U., 1973; JD, U. Fla., 1976. Bar: Fla. 1977, U.S. Dist. Ct. (so. dist.) Fla. 1978. Asst. pub. defender Pub. Defender's Office, Bartow, Fla., 1975-76, Vero Beach, Fla., 1976; asst. states atty. State's Atty.'s Office, West Palm Beach, Fla., 1976-77; pvt. practice West Palm Beach, 1977—. Contbr. numerous articles to profl. jours. Bd. dirs. Gainesville Cultural Commn., Fla., 1974-75; Fla. Dem. committeeman, Lakeland, 1976; mem. City Utilities Bd., Vero Beach, Fla., 1976. Mem. Assn. Trial Lawyers Am., Fla. Bar Assn. (chmn. gen. practice sect. 1980-81, chmn. fed. practice com. criminal law sect. 1982-83), ABA (vice chmn. criminal practice com. 1983-85, gen. practice sect., chmn.

1985-86), Acad. Fla. Trial Lawyers, Palm Beach County Bar Assn. (mem. cir. ct. criminal adv. com. charter), Palm Beach County Criminal Def. Lawyers Assn., Am. Judicature Soc., West Palm Beach Eagles (charter chpt. v.p. 1988-89), Phi Delta Kappa (nat. parliamentarian 1981-82, 83-84, nat. long range planning com. 1983-85, pres., capliph 1992-93), Moose (life mem., life legionnaire 1976—), Elks (treas. 1987-88, chaplain 1994-95). Consumer commercial, Contracts commercial, Personal injury. Office: Laing Law Bldg 2072 S Military Trl West Palm Beach FL 33415-6441

**LAIRD, EDWARD DEHART, JR.,** lawyer; b. Pitts., July 14, 1952; s. Edward D. Sr. and Miriam (Hellman) L.; m. Ellen Armstrong, July 30, 1977; children: Megan, Edward, Peter. BA, SUNY, Oswego, 1974; JD, Western New Eng. Sch. Law, 1977. Bar: N.Y. 1978, U.S. Dist. Ct. (no. dist.) N.Y. 1978, U.S. Dist Ct. (so. dist.) N.Y. 1989, U.S. Dist. Ct. Vt. 1995, U.S. Ct. Appeals (2d cir.) 1985, U.S. Supreme Ct. 1986. Shareholder Carter, Conboy, Case, Blackmore, Napierski & Maloney, P.C., Albany, N.Y., 1977—; instr. legal rsch. and writing Western New Eng. Sch. Law, Springfield, Mass., 1976-77. Master Am. Inns Ct. Albany Law Sch. chpt.; mem. ABA, N.Y. State Bar Assn., Albany County Bar Assn., Def. Rsch. Inst., Def. Rsch. Inst. of Northeastern N.Y. General civil litigation, Personal injury, Insurance. Office: Carter Conboy Case Blackmore Napierski & Maloney PC 20 Corporate Woods Blvd Ste 8 Albany NY 12211-2362

**LAIT, HAYDEN DAVID,** lawyer; b. Bangor, Maine, Dec. 18, 1947; s. Saul and Marion (Pepper) L.; m. Kay Scruggs, Mar. 10, 1982; children: Erin Middleton, David Middleton. BBA, U. Okla., 1969; JD, Memphis State U., 1975. Bar: Tenn., U.S. Dist. Ct. (we. dist.) Tenn. Pvt. practice Memphis, 1975—; instr. constitutional law Shelby State Coll., Memphis, 1977-78; vol. U.S. Peace Corps, Kuala Lumpur, Malaysia, 1969-71; pres. Memphis State U. Law, Alumni Nat. Chpt., 1988. Dir. Shelby Residential & Vocat., Memphis, 1987—. Mem. Memphis Bar Assn., Memphis Trial Lawyers (bd. govs. 1977), Tenn. Trial Lawyers, Am. Trial Lawyers. Personal injury, Family and matrimonial, General practice. Office: 99 N 3rd St Memphis TN 38103-2306

**LAITINEN, SARI K.M.,** lawyer; b. Mikkeli, Finland, July 5, 1966; d. Leevi A. and Liisa M. Laitinen. Student, U. Jyväskylä, Finland, 1986-87; BA, Hamline U., 1991, JD, 1993. Bar: Minn., D.C. Lay judge, clk. City Ct. of Mikkeli, summers 1990-91; atty. King & Spalding, Atlanta, 1996, Lindquist & Vennum PLLP, Mpls., 1993-95, 96—. Mem. staff Hamline Law Rev., 1992. Bd. dirs. Twin Cities chpt. Finlandia Found., 1997—; founding mem. Finnish Trade Steering Com., Mpls., 1997—. Finnish Found. for Econ. Edn. grantee, 1992. Mem. Phi Beta Kappa. Avocations: opera. Email: slaitinen@lindquist.com. Finance, General corporate, Securities. Office: Lindquist & Vennum PLLP 4200 IDS Ctr Minneapolis MN 55402

**LAKE, DAVID ALAN,** investments lawyer; b. El Campo, Tex., Jan. 15, 1938; s. Cortus L. and Ottis W. (Noland) L.; m. Shirley L. Hill, Dec. 20, 1966; children: Joel, Jonathan, Jeffrey Kyle, Kristi. BA, Baylor U., 1960; BD, Southwestern Seminary, 1963; JD, So. Methodist U., 1966. Bar: Tex. 1966. Lawyer Nickerson & Lake, Pittsburg, Tex., 1966-68; pvt. practice Tyler, Tex., 1967—; gen. ptnr. Colonial Manor, Tyler, 1968-90, Golden Manor, Pittsburg, 1968-82; pres. Gardendale, Inc., Jacksonville, Tex., 1973-93, Am. Health Svcs., Inc., Tyler, 1977—, N.E. Tex. Contracting Co., Tyler, 1982—; sec., bd. dirs. Sunset Care Ctr., Jacksonville, 1973-79; chmn. bd. dirs. Cypress Bank, Fed. Savs. Bank, Pittsburg. Bd. dirs. Way of Life, Inc., Tyler, 1972-75, Smith County Heart Assn., Tyler, 1974-75; bd. dirs., chmn. Smith County Red Cross, Tyler, 1972-77; bd. dirs., Sunday sch. tchr. 1st Bapt. Ch., Tyler, 1972—; bd. dirs., v.p. Tex. Health Care Assn., 1975-76; trustee East Tex. Bapt. U., Marshall, 1993—. Mem. Tex. and Smith County Bar Assn., Baylor Univ. Devel. Coun., Jacksonville Jaycees (bd. dirs. 1965-66), Petroleum Club, Emerald Bay club, Lee Booster Club (pres. 1977-78), Rotary Internat. (Paul Harris fellow 1990—, bd. dirs. South Tyler chpt. 1971-74, pres. 1978-79). Avocations: reading, fishing, hunting. Banking, Health, Real property. Home: 815 Pinedale Pl Tyler TX 75701-9645 Office: 120 E South Town Dr Tyler TX 75703-4728

**LAKE, I. BEVERLY, JR.,** state supreme court justice; b. Raleigh, N.C., 1934; s. I. Beverly, Sr. and Gertrude L.; m. Susan Deichmann Smith; children: Lynn Elizabeth, Guy, Laura Ann, I. Beverly III. Student, Mars Hill Coll., 1951; BS, Wake Forest U., 1955, JD, 1960. Bar: N.C. Pvt. practice, 1960-69, 76-85; asst. atty. gen. State of N.C., 1969-74, dep. atty. gen., 1974-76; Gov.'s legis. liason, chief lobbyist, 1985; judge Superior Ct., 1985-91; assoc. justice N.C. Supreme Ct., 1992—. chmn. bd. trustees Ridge Rd. Bapt. Ch., 1968-69; mem. N.C. Senate, 1976-80, chmn. Senate Judiciary Com.; Rep. nominee Gov. N.C., 1979-80; del. Rep. Nat. Convention, 1980; Rep. state fin. chmn., mem. ctr. com., mem. exec. com., 1980-82; N.C. eastern chmn. Reagan-Bush Campaign, 1984; bd. visitors Wake Forest U. Sch. Law, 1995—; bd. vis. Southeastern Bapt. Theol. Sem. Intelligence staff officer U.S. Army, 1956-58; capt. USAR, 1960-68; col. N.C. State Militia, 1989-92. Mem. AMVETS, N.C. Bar Assn., Wake County Bar Assn., Assn. Interstate Commerce Commn. Practitioners, Navy League, Am. Legion, Masons, Shriners, Phi Alpha Delta. Office: NC Supreme Ct PO Box 1841 Raleigh NC 27602-1841

**LAKE, SIM,** federal judge; b. Chgo., July 4, 1944; s. Simeon T. Jr. and Helen (Hupka) L.; m. Carol Illig, Dec. 30, 1970; children: Simeon Timothy IV, Justin Carl. BA, Tex. A&M, 1966; JD, U. Tex., 1969. Bar: Tex. 1969, U.S. Dist. Ct. (so. dist.) Tex. 1969, U.S. Ct. Appeals (5th cir.) 1969, U.S. Supreme Ct. 1976. From assoc. to ptnr. Fulbright & Jaworski, Houston, 1969-70, 72-88; judge U.S. Dist. Ct. (so. dist.) Tex., Houston, 1988—. Past editor Houston Lawyer. Capt. U.S. Army., 1970-71. Fellow Tex. Bar Found., Houston Bar Assn., State Bar Tex., Am. Law Inst. Office: US Courthouse 515 Rusk Ave Rm 9535 Houston TX 77002-2605

**LAKIN, JOHN FRANCIS,** lawyer; b. Chelsea, Mass., Nov. 21, 1960; s. Kenneth and Nancy Lakin; m. JoAnne Lanza, Oct. 6, 1990; children: Joy, Justin. AB, Boston Coll., 1983; JD, Mass. Sch. Law, Andover, 1990. Bar: Mass. 1990, U.S. Ct. Appeals (1st cir.) 1991, U.S. Dist. Ct. Mass. 1991, U.S. Supreme Ct. 1994. Adjuster Liberty Mut. Ins. Co., Boston, 1983-84; law clk. Marchese & Barnes, Revere, Mass., 1984-90, assoc., 1990—. Mem. ABA, Assn. Trial Lawyers Am., Mass. Acad. Trial Attys., Mass. Bar Assn. (mock-trial tchr. 1990-91), Mass. Criminal Def. Lawyers. Democrat. State civil litigation, Criminal, Personal injury. Office: Broadhurst Lakin & Lakin One Elm Sq Andover MA 01810-3714 also: 19 Beacon St Boston MA 02108-2821

**LAKO, CHARLES MICHAEL, JR.,** lawyer; b. Bridgeport, Conn., July 26, 1947; s. Charles Michael and Helen Rose (Martin) L.; m. Robin W. Lako, Aug. 26, 1972; children: Charles Michael, Christopher Martin. AA, Broward C.C., 1971; BBA, Fla. Atlantic U., 1972; JD cum laude, John Marshall Law Sch., 1977. Bar: Ga. 1977, Fla. 1990, U.S. Dist. Ct. (no. and so. dists.) Ga. 1977, U.S. Tax Ct., 1977, U.S. Supreme Ct. 1990, Fla. 1990. Stockbroker Reynolds Securities, Boca Raton, Fla., 1972-73; sole practice Fla. & Ga., 1977—; adj. prof. law Indian River C.C. and Indian River C.C. Acad. of Law, Ft. Pierce, Fla.; cert. mediator Fla. Supreme Ct., Cir. and County Cts.; arbitrator complex litigation Atlanta Superior Cts. With USNR, 1966-72. Mem. ABA, Fla. Bar Assn., Ga. Bar Assn., Sigma Delta Kappa. Democrat. Roman Catholic. General civil litigation, Personal injury, Probate. Office: 611 S Federal Hwy Ste F Stuart FL 34994-2925 also: Wachovia Bldg Ste 815 Decatur GA 33030

**LALLA, THOMAS ROCCO, JR.,** lawyer; b. Bronxville, N.Y., July 23, 1950; s. Thomas R. and Vincie Catherine (Cremona) L. BA, Fordham U., 1972; JD, Temple U., 1975. Bar: N.Y. 1986, U.S. Dist. Ct. (so. dist.) N.Y. 1978. Asst. dist. atty. Office of Dist. Atty. Westchester County, White Plains, N.Y., 1975-81; assoc. Buchman & O'Brien, N.Y.C., 1981-85, ptnr., 1985-91; mng. ptnr. Buchman Buchman & O'Brien, N.Y.C., 1986-90; gen. counsel Austin, Nichols & Co., Inc., N.Y.C., 1991—. Mem. ABA, N.Y. State Bar Assn. Republican. Episcopalian. Avocations: running, swimming, cycling. General corporate, Contracts commercial. Office: Austin Nichols & Co Inc 156 E 46th St New York NY 10017-2632

**LALLI, MICHAEL ANTHONY,** lawyer; b. N.Y.C., Sept. 14, 1955; s. Joseph and Maria (Magnacca) L.; m. Marigrace Ann Esposito, May 19, 1979; children: Elena Marie, Marissa Ann. BA, Fordham Coll., 1976, JD, 1979; LLM, NYU, 1984. Bar: N.Y. 1980, U.S. Dist. Ct. (so. dist.) N.Y. 1981. Assoc. counsel Equitable Life Assurance Soc. U.S., N.Y.C., 1979-85; sr. tax atty. Texaco, Inc., White Plains, N.Y., 1985—; mem. moot ct. bd. 1977-79. Mem. Fordham Urban Law Jour., 1977-79. Mem. ABA, N.Y. State Bar Assn., Phi Beta Kappa, Pi Sigma Alpha. Roman Catholic. Pension, profit-sharing, and employee benefits, Taxation, general, Corporate taxation. Home: 16 Thomas St Scarsdale NY 10583-1031 Office: Texaco Inc 2000 Westchester Ave White Plains NY 10650-0002

**LALLY-GREEN, MAUREEN ELLEN,** judge, law educator; b. Sharpsville, Pa., July 5, 1949; d. Francis Leonard and Charlotte Marie (Frederick) Lally; m. Stephen Ross Green, Oct. 5, 1979; children: Katherine Lally, William Ross, Bridget Marie. BS, Duquesne U., 1971, JD, 1974. Bar: Pa. 1974, D.C., U.S. Dist. Ct. (we. dist.) Pa. 1974, U.S. Ct. Appeals (3d cir.) 1974, U.S. Supreme Ct. 1978. Atty. Houston Cooper, Pitts., 1974-75, Commodity Futures Trading Commn., Washington, 1975-78; counsel Westinghouse Electric Corp., Pitts., 1978-83; adj. prof. law Duquesne U., Pitts., 1983-86, 1986—; apptd. justice Superior Ct. Pa., 1998—; fed. dist. ct. arbitrator; mem. criminal procedure rules com. Supreme Ct. Pa., 1994-97; dir. European Union Law Conf., Dublin, 1995-97, Intellectual Law Conf., Italy, 1997; mem. panel Disciplinary Bd. of Commonwealth of Pa. Chair Cranberry Twp. Zoning Hearing Bds., Pa., 1983—; counsel Western Pa. Ptnrs. of Ams., 1987—, pres. 1993-95, bd. dirs., 1995—; active Elimination of World Hunger Project, 1977—; mem. Bishop's Com. on Dialogue with Cath. Univs.; co-chair Millenium com. Duquesne U., 1997—. Fellow Kellogg Found. (for Ptnrs. of Ams.), 1990-92. Mem. Pa. Bar Assn. (ethics com. 1987-94, commn. on women in the law 1994—), Allegheny County Bar Assn. (women in law com., professionalism com., ethics com., sec. bd. dirs. 1992-94, 94—), Duquesne U. Alumni Assn. (bd. dirs. 1982-89, sec. 1988-89, gov. of bd. 1995—), Duquesne U. Law Alumni Assn. (bd. dirs. 1987—, treas. 1991—, v.p. 1992—). Republican. Roman Catholic. Avocations: children's activities, sports. Office: 2701 Grant Bldg 330 Grant St Pittsburgh PA 15219-2202

**LALOR, DANIEL KEVIN,** judge; b. Catskill, N.Y., June 14, 1944; s. Edward and Anna (O'Grady) L.; m. Susan Munn, Aug. 18, 1968; children: Atticus Edward, Becket Colin, Clement Munn. AB, Georgetown U., 1966, JD, 1969. Bar: N.Y. 1969, U.S. Dist. Ct. (no. and so. dists.) N.Y., D.C. 1974, Fla. 1977, U.S. Supreme Ct. 1978. Atty. Met. Life Ins. Co., N.Y.C., 1969-72; ptnr. law firm Meadow Ruf and Lalor, P.C., Catskill, 1972-87; pub. defender Greene County, Catskill, 1972-76, 1st asst. dist. atty., 1978-88, dist. atty., 1988-90, family, country and surrogate ct. judge, 1991—; counsel Village of Catskill, 1972-80, Village of Coxsackie, 1983-88, Town of Greenville, 1980, Rheedlen Found. Recipient McCahill medal, 1969. Mem. ABA, Greene County Bar Assn. (sec. 1975, treas. 1976, v.p. 1977, pres. 1978), Nat. Dist. Attys. Assn., N.Y. State Bar Assn., Nat. Legal Aide and Defenders Assn., N.Y. State Defenders Assn. (bd. dirs. 1973-78), D.C. Bar Assn., Assn. of Bar of City of N.Y., Fla. Bar Assn., Royal Cork Yacht Club, Elks. Roman Catholic. Home: 58 William St Catskill NY 12414-1419 Office: County Courthouse 320 Main St Catskill NY 12414-1816

**LALOR, EDWARD DAVID DARRELL,** labor and employment arbitrator, lawyer; b. Madison, Wis., Jan. 29, 1944; s. Edward Richard and Viola (Byrne) Lalor; adult adopted mother: Helen Rose (Litney) Pribble; m. Paula Sue Tompkins, Aug. 12, 1978; children. BBA, U. Wis., 1966, JD, 1969. Bar: Wis., 1969, Minn., 1980, U.S. Dist. Ct. (we. dist.) Wis., 1969, U.S. Supreme Ct., 1979. Gen. atty. NLRB, Kansas City, Mo., Kans., 1969-80; atty. advice divsn., advice br. NLRB, Washington, 1973-74; trial specialist NLRB, Kansas City, 1977-80; arbitrator labor and employment, pres. Pribble Arbitration and Mediation Svcs., Inc., Mpls., 1980-85; arbitrator, pres. Pribble Arbitration and Mediation Svcs., Inc., St. Cloud, Minn., 1985-95; CEO, pres., arbitrator Lalor Arbitration and Mediation, Inc., St. Cloud, Minn., 1995—; mcpl. judge City Countryside (Kans.), 1979-80; mem. arbitration panels Fed. Mediation and Conciliation Svc., 1982—, Am. Arbitration Assn., 1984—, Nat. Mediation Bd., 1991—, Iowa Pub. Employment Rels. Bd., 1983—; pvt. panel EDDL Case Corp. and I.A. Machinists and Aerospace Workers Local 2525, Fargo, N.D., 1985—; full-day moderator in arbitration, labor and employement law discrimination, alt. dispute resolution, evidence and family law programs Minn. Continuing Legal Edn., 1989—; labor and employment arbitrator Minn. Cts. Alt. Dispute Resolution, 1994—. Contbr. articles to profl. jours. Mem. Minn. Dem. Farm Labor State and Congl. Dist. Ctrl. Com., 1981—, Minn. State Platform Commn., Dem. Farm Labor Party, 1984-85, chmn. senate dist., 1984-85, fundraiser, initiator, co-founder Dr. Guy Stanton Ford Ednl. Found., 1964-69; co-founder Westport Free Health Clinic, Kansas City, Mo., 1970-80; active coun. Land of Lakes coun. Girl Scouts, Minn., 1985—, lifetime mem. adult leader mem.; active Leadership Coun. So. Poverty Ctr., Habitat for Humanity Internat. Ptnrs. Coun.; coach Girls Youth Basketball League, St. Cloud, 1992—; bd. dirs. St. Cloud Symphony Orch., 1992-94; chair New Voter registration Drives Senate Dist. 59, 1981-85, Stearns-Benton County Senate Dist.17, 1989-91; historian Lalor Clan for the Ams.; host family for Irish polit. prisoners children's holiday, 1996—; mem. Internat. Hearing Found. Mem. ABA (labor and employment law sects. 1978—), Fed. Bar Assn. (labor and employment law sects. 1974—), Minn. Bar Assn. (labor and employment law sects. 1980—, mock trial program judge 1989-93), Nat. Youth Sports Coaches Assn. (cert.), Wis. Bar Assn. (labor and employment law sects. 1969—), Internat. Indsl. Rels. Assn., Soc. Profls. in Dispute Resolution Internat., Indsl. Rels. Rsch. Assn., EDDL Internat., Theta Delta Chi Internat. Roman Catholic. Avocations: reading, family history, fishing, stock investing. Office: Lalor Arbitration & Mediation Inc 1220 N Thirteenth Saint Cloud MN 56303

**LALUMIA, MATTHEW PAUL,** lawyer; b. Passaic, N.J., July 28, 1953; s. Matthew Joseph Lalumia and Josephine Kathleen DeRosa; m. Carol Blanch Mundorf, May 6, 1984. BA, Princeton U., 1975; PhD, Yale U., 1981; JD, U. Md., 1992. Bar: Md. 1992, U.S. Dist. Ct. Md. 1993. Prof. Trinity Coll., Hartford, Conn., 1982-83; guest prof. Princeton (N.J.) U., 1983-84; prof. Goucher Coll., Balt., 1984-89; law clk. Md. Supreme Ct. Appeals, Annapolis, 1992-93; atty. Law Office of William Beale, Balt., 1993-94, Turnbull, Wase & Lyons, Towson, Md., 1994-95, Mudd, Harrison & Burch, Towson, 1996—. Author: Victorian Realism and Politics, 1983; contbr. articles to mags. Chmn. Md. Commn. on Hist. and Artistic Property, Annapolis, 1994—. Paul Mellon fellow Yale U., 1978. Mem. Bar Assn. Md., Bar Assn. Balt. County, Order of Coif, Phi Beta Kappa. Avocations: fencing, carpentry, history. Probate, Estate planning, General civil litigation. Home: 7002 Wardman Rd Baltimore MD 21212-1636 Office: Mudd Harrison & Burch 105 W Chesapeake Ave Ste 300 Towson MD 21204-4762

**LAMARI, JOSEPH PAUL,** lawyer, mediator; b. Taunton, Mass., Feb. 20, 1955; s. Paul B. and Rosa D'Emilia L.; m. Lisa Carol moore, Aug. 10, 1980; children: Joseph P. Jr., Charles C. BA in Sociology, Randolph-Macon Coll., 1977; JD, Campbell U., 1980. Ptnr. Lamari & Schwartz, Rockville, Md., 1981-87; atty. pvt. practice, Rockville, Md., 1987—; facilitator, mediator Montgomery County Cir. Ct., Rockville, Md., 1997—. Pres. Lido Civic Club, Washington, 1991. Democrat. Roman Catholic. Personal injury, Family and matrimonial, Criminal. Office: 414 Hungerford Dr Ste 404 Rockville MD 20850-5116

**LAMARR, JACK PAUL,** lawyer; b. Key West, Fla., June 29, 1927; s. Queen and Jack LaMarr; m. Sylvia LaMarr; children: Lisa, Barbara LaMarr-Dirienzo. BA in Polit. Sci., Fla. State U., Tallahassee, 1952; JD, U. Miami, 1962. Bar: D.C., Fla., U.S. Ct. Appeals (D.C. cir.), U.S. Supreme Ct. De. clk. Circuit Ct., 1957-62; asst. pub. defender Broward County Pub. Defender's Office; atty. Clk. of Circuit Ct. and for Broward County; propr. Law Offices of Jack P. LaMarr, P.A., Ft. Lauderdale, Fla., 1965—. Pres. City Coun. of Plantation, Fla.; Dem. nominee for Fla. Ho. of Reps., 1964; spl. attache State Legislature for Broward County. Mem. ABA, ATLA, D.C. Bar, Fla. Bar, Broward County Bar Assn., Assn. Fla. Trial Lawyers, Am. Arbitration Assn., Am. Judicature Soc., Knights of Malta. Office: 2601 E Oakland Park Blvd Fort Lauderdale FL 33306-1606

**LAMB, BRUCE DOUGLAS,** lawyer; b. Miami, Fla., Mar. 21, 1955; s. Jean Altman and Irene Gloria Lamb; married, July 31, 1981; 1 child, Alison Marie. BA, U. South Fla., 1977; JD, Fla. State U., 1980, MA, 1981. Bar: Fla. 1981. Staff atty. Dept. Profl. Regulation, Tallahassee, Fla., 1981-83, sr. atty., 1983-88, gen. counsel, 1988; chief atty. Dept. Profl. Regulation, Tampa, Fla., 1988-91; assoc. Shear Newman Hahn & Rosenkranz PA, Tampa, 1991-92, shareholder, 1992—. Contbr. articles to profl. jours. Mem. Fla. Bar Assn. (treas. health law sect. 1998—, exec. coun.). Avocation: scuba. Administrative and regulatory, General civil litigation, Health. Office: Shear Newman Hahn & Rosenkranz PA 201 E Kennedy Blvd Ste 1000 Tampa FL 33602-5173

**LAMB, KEVIN THOMAS,** lawyer; b. Quincy, Mass., Nov. 14, 1956; s. John Phillip and Kathleen Elaine (O'Brien) L. BA, Washington and Lee U., 1978, JD, 1982. Bar: Va. 1982, D.C. 1988, Mass. 1990. Law clk. to presiding justice U.S. Bankruptcy Ct. (we. dist.) Va., Lynchburg, 1982-84; atty. U.S. Dept. Justice, Los Angeles, 1984-85; assoc. Jones, Day, Reavis & Pogue, Los Angeles, 1985-86, Ballard, Spahr, Andrews & Ingersoll, Washington, 1986-89; assoc. Testa, Hurwitz & Thibeault, Boston, 1989-91, ptnr., 1992—. Mem. ABA (com. on cons. fin. svcs., subcom. on securities products, com. on bus. bankruptcy), FBA, Am. Bankruptcy Inst. (com. on legis.), Comml. Law League Am., Fin. Lawyers Conf. Bankruptcy, Contracts commercial. Office: Testa Hurwitz & Thibeault High St Tower 125 High St Fl 22 Boston MA 02110-2725

**LAMB, MARGARET WELDON,** lawyer; b. Arlington, Mass., June 26, 1935; d. Hubert Weldon and Lydia Cazneau (Baker) L. BA, U. Denver, 1959; JD, Boston Coll., 1964. Bar: Mass. 1964, N.M. 1969. Pvt. practice Taos County, N.Mex., 1971-76; dist. atty. N.Mex. 8th Jud. Dist., Taos, 1978-80; pvt. practice specializing in aviation adminstrv. law, 1981-98; with Sunshine Aviation Safety Studies, 1989—; air safety investigator, writer, flight instr., 1981—; faculty assoc. Johns Hopkins Univ. Ctr. for Inquiry Rsch. and Policy, 1994—. Contbr. articles on aviation safety to profl. publs. Mem. AIAA, Am. Meteorol. Soc., Aerospace Med. Assn., Lawyer-Pilots Bar Assn., Nat. Assn. Flight Instrs., NTSB Bar Assn. Achievements include research into microscale mountain weather and aircraft crashes. Aviation. Home and Office: PO Box 650 Questa NM 87556-0650

**LAMBE, JAMES PATRICK,** lawyer; b. Washington, June 4, 1952; s. John Joseph and Patricia Ann (Job) Lambe; m. Marie Barbara Giardino, May 21, 1977; children: Katherine Mary, Joseph Patrick. AB with distinction, U. Mich., 1974; JD, U. Ill., 1977. Bar: Calif. 1977, U.S. Dist. Ct. (ea. dist.) Calif. 1977, U.S. Ct. Appeals (9th cir.) 1978, U.S. Supreme Ct. 1981, U.S. Dist. Ct. (ctrl. dist.) Calif. 1983, D.C. 1985; cert. specialist in criminal law State Bar Calif. Bd. Legal Specialization; cert. specialist in criminal trial advocacy Nat. Bd. Trial Advocacy. Assoc. Wagner & Wagner, Fresno, Calif., 1978-79, Parichan, Renberg, Crossman & Harvey, Fresno, 1979; claims atty. CIGNA Corp., Fresno, 1979-85; dep. city atty. City of Fresno, 1985-86; dep. pub. defender County of Fresno, 1986—; cons., author Continuing Edn. of the Bar, U. Calif./State Bar Calif., Berkeley, 1992—. Cons. to books: California Criminal Law Procedure and Practice, update, 1992, 2d edit., 1994, 3d edit., 1996, 4th edit., 1998, California Criminal Law Forms Manual, 1995, update, 1999; co-author: (book chpt.) California Criminal Law Procedure and Practice, 4th edit., 1998. Mem. Vols. in Parole. Mem. Calif. Attys. for Criminal Justice, Calif. Pub. Defenders Assn., D.C. Bar, Fresno County Bar Assn. (bd. dirs. 1998—), State Bar Calif. (conf. of dels. 1996—), Phi Alpha Delta. Democrat. Avocation: distance running. Office: Fresno County Pub Defenders Office 2220 Tulare St Ste 300 Fresno CA 93721-2104

**LAMBERT, DALE JOHN,** lawyer; b. Lethbridge, Alberta, Can., Mar. 1, 1946; s. Theron M. and Verl (Johansen) L.; m. Janice Noreen Clitheroe, July 29, 1975; children: Kristin, Kimberly, Tamara. BS, Brigham Young U., 1970; JD, U. Utah, 1973. Bar: Utah 1973, U.S. Dist. Ct. Utah 1975, U.S. Supreme Ct 1991, U.S. Ct. Appeals (10th cir.) 1976. Legis. asst. Congressman Gunn McKay, Washington, 1973-75; dir. Christensen Jensen P.C., Salt Lake City, 1978—. Contbr. articles to profl. jours.; presenter legal seminars. Bd. trustees Dixie State Coll., St. George, Utah, 1983-93; state chmn. Utah State Dem. Party, 1979-81, chmn. platform com., 1982, chmn. state conv., 1983. Recipient Golden Key award Gov.'s Commn. on Employment, 1978; named one of Outstanding Young Men of Am., Jr. C. of C., 1979. Fellow Am. Coll. Trial Lawyers; mem. Internat. Assn. of Def. Counsel, ABA (litigation sect.), Utah State Bar Assn. (litigation sect.), Def. Rsch. Assn. (Utah chair 1989-90), Internat. Assn. Def. Counsel. Mormon. Avocations: golf, teaching, traveling. General civil litigation, Civil rights, Personal injury. Home: 2563 Maywood Dr Salt Lake City UT 84109-1657 Office: Christensen & Jensen 50 S Main St Ste 1500 Salt Lake City UT 84144-0103

**LAMBERT, GARY ERVERY,** lawyer; b. Providence, Oct. 27, 1959; s. Ervery Eldege and Melitta (Hirsch) L.; m. Lori Keller, Apr. 22, 1995; 1 child, Katherine Elizabeth. BS in Chemistry and Biology, Valparaiso (Ind.) U., 1981; JD with honors, Drake U., 1984. Bar: Iowa 1984, Mass. 1986, U.S. Ct. Mil. Appeals 1986, U.S. Dist. Ct. Mass. 1987, U.S. Ct. Appeals (1st cir.) 1987, U.S. Patent and Trademark Office 1993, U.S. Ct. Appeals (fed. cir.) 1996. Litigator Gallagher & Gallagher, P.C., Boston, 1987-89; owner Law Office of Gary Lambert, Boston, 1989-93; ptnr. Lambert & Garrison, P.C., Boston, 1993—; intellectual property judge advocate, hdqs. USMC, 1997—. Capt. USMC, 1984-87, Japan. Mem. Boston Bar Assn., Boston Patent Law Assn., Am. Intellectual Property Assn., Marine Corps Res. Officers Assn. (life), NRA (life). Republican. Lutheran. Patent, Trademark and copyright, Intellectual property. Home: 32 Columbia Ave Nashua NH 03064-1601 Office: Lambert & Garrison 92 State St Boston MA 02109-2004

**LAMBERT, GEORGE ROBERT,** lawyer, realtor; b. Muncie, Ind., Feb. 21, 1933; s. George Russell and Velma Lou (Jones) L.; m. Mary Virginia Alling, June 16, 1956; children: Robert Allen, Ann Holt, James William. BS, Ind. U., Bloomington, 1955; JD, IIT Chgo.- Kent Coll. Law, Coll. Law, 1962. Bar: Ill. 1962, U.S. Dist. Ct. (no. dist.) Ill. 1962, Iowa 1984, Pa. 1988, Ind. 1999. V.p., gen. counsel, sec. Washington Nat. Ins. Co., Evanston, Ill., 1970-82; v.p., gen. counsel Washington Nat. Corp., Evanston, 1979-82; sr. v.p., sec., gen. counsel Life Investors Inc., Cedar Rapids, Iowa, 1982-88; v.p., gen. counsel Provident Mut. Life Ins. Co., Phila., 1988-95; pres. Lambert Legal Consulting, Inc., Wilmington, Del., 1995—; realtor Coldwell Banker, North Palm Beach, Fla., 1996—, Cressy and Everett, Inc., South Bend, Ind., 1999—. Alderman Evanston City Coun., 1980-82. Served to lt. USAF, 1955-57. Mem. Ill. State Bar Assn., Iowa Bar Assn., Pa. Bar Assn., Assn. of Life Ins. Counsel (past pres.), St. Joseph County Bar Assn., Nat. Assn. Realtors, Ind. Assn. Realtors, Greater South Bend-Mishawaka Assn. Realtors, Inc. General corporate, Insurance, Estate planning. Home: 915 Deep Wood Dr Mishawaka IN 46544-6746 Office: 332 N Ironwood Dr South Bend IN 46615-2555

**LAMBERT, JOSEPH EARL,** state supreme court chief justice; b. Berea, Ky., May 23, 1948; s. James Wheeler and Ruth (Hilton) L.; m. Debra Hembree, June 25, 1983; children: Joseph Patrick, John Ryan. BS in Bus. and Econs., Georgetown Coll., 1970; JD, U. Louisville, 1974; completed sr. appellate judges seminar, NYU Sch. Law, 1987. Bar: Ky. 1974. Staff Sen. John Sherman Cooper U.S. Senate, Washington, 1970-71; law clk. to judge U.S. Dist. Ct., Louisville, 1974-75; ptnr. Lambert & Lambert, Mt. Vernon, Ky., 1975-87; justice Supreme Ct. Ky., Frankfort, 1987-98, chief justice, 1998—; chmn. Jud. Form Retirement Commn., 1996—. Mem. Bd. Regents Eastern Ky. U., Richmond, 1988-92. Recipient Disting. Alumni award U. Louisville Sch. Law, 1988. Mem. Ky. Bar Assn. Republican. Baptist. Office: State of Ky State Capitol Bldg Office Chief Justice Room 231 Frankfort KY 40601

**LAMBERT, KIM ANITA,** lawyer. BA, Rosary Coll., 1982; JD, Loyola U., Chgo., 1985. Bar: Ill. 1985, Calif. 1988. Assoc. Rudnick & Wolfe, Chgo., 1985-88, 97—, Bartko, Zankel, Tarrant & Miller, San Francisco, 1988-97; mem. Coun. of Franchise Suppliers, 1992—. Editor newsletter The Franchise Lawyer, 1996-99; assoc. editor Franchise Law Jour., 1990-96. Mem. ABA (governing com. forum on franchising 1999—), State Bar Calif. (chair, mem. franchise law com. 1992-95). Franchising. Office: Rudnick & Wolfe 203 N Lasalle St Ste 1800 Chicago IL 60601-1210

**LAMBERT, LYN DEE,** library media specialist, law librarian; b. Fitchburg, Mass., Jan. 5, 1954; m. Paul Frederick Lambert, Aug. 11, 1979; children: Gregory John, Emily Jayne, Nicholas James. BA in History, Fitchburg State Coll., 1976, MEd in History, 1979; JD, Franklin Pierce Law Ct., 1983;

MLS, Simmons Coll., 1986. Law libr. Fitchburg Law Libr., Mass. Trial Ct., 1985-96; media specialist libr. Samoset Sch., Leominster, Mass., 1996—; instr. paralegal studies courses Fisher Coll., Fitchburg, 1989-94, Anna Maria Coll., Paxton, Mass., 1995—, Atlantic Union Coll., Lancaster, Mass., 1995—, pre-law coll. courses Fitchburg State Coll., 1995—; tech. com. City of Leominster Shc., Net Day Participant and trainer/leader, Leominster H.S., Northwest, Johnny Appleseed, Fall Brook, Southeast and Samoset. Mem. Am. Legion Band, Fitchburg, 1959—, Westminster (Mass.) Town Band, 1965—; appt. to Mass. Strategic Plan Com. for delivery of libr. svcs. among multi-type librs. within the commonwealth. Recipient Community Leadership award Xi Psi chpt. Kappa Delta Pi-Fitchburg State Coll. chpt., 1993. Mem. ALA, Am. Assn. Law Librarians (copyright com. 1987-89, publs. rev. com. 1990-92, state, ct. and county law librs. spl. interest sect. publicity com. 1993—), Law Librarians New Eng. (conf. com. 1988), Mass. Libr. Assn. (edn. chair 1991-93, freedom of info. com., legislation com.), New Eng. Libr. Assn., New Eng. Microcomputer Users Group (profl. assoc.), North Cen. Mass. Libr. Alliance (newsletter editor 1990—), Spl. Libr. Assn., Beta Phi Mu, Phi Alpha Delta, Phi Delta Kappa (newsletter editor Montachusett chpt. 1998—). Avocations: singing, guitar, clarinet, hiking, camping. Office: Samoset Libr Media Ctr 100 DeCicco Dr Leominster MA 01453

**LAMBERTH, ROYCE C.,** federal judge; b. 1943. BA, U. Tex., 1965, LLB, 1967. With civil dir. U.S. Atty's. Office, Wasshington, 1974-77, asst. chief, 1977-78; chief U.S. Atty's. Office, 1978-87; judge U.S. Dist. Ct. (D.C. dist.), Washington, 1987—. Capt. (j.a.g.) U.S. Army, 1967-74. Mem. ABA (chmn. armed svcs. and vets. affairs com. sect. adminstrv. law 1983-83), Fed. Bar Assn. (chmn. fed. litigation sect. 1986—), Jud. Conf. D.C. Cir. (arrangements com. 1985, D.C. Bar., D.C. Bar Assn. (Cert. Appreciatio 1977), State Bar Tex. Office: US Dist Ct 333 Constitution Ave NW Washington DC 20001-2802

**LAMBORN, DANIEL G.,** lawyer, district attorney, educator; b. San Jose, Calif., 1956; s. Howard Merle and Kathryn Mary Lamborn; m. Denise Alsup; children: Lauren Michelle, Philip Stephen, Alyssa Kathryn. BA, U. Calif., Davis, 1979; JD, U. Calif., San Diego. Bar: Calif., U.S. Dist. Ct. (so. dist.) Calif. Dep. dist. atty. Office of Dist. Atty., San Diego, 1983—; adj. prof. trial advocacy Calif. Western Sch. Law, San Diego, 1994—; insr. Nat. Coll. Dist. Attys., Columbia, S.C., 1996—. Mem. San Diego Dist. Attys. Assn. (named Prosecutor or Yr. 1993). Republican. Mem. Ch. Assembly of God. Avocations: golf, softball, tennis. Office: Office of Dist Atty 330 W Broadway Ste 1100 San Diego CA 92101-3827

**LAMBORN, LEROY LESLIE,** law educator; b. Marion, Ohio, May 12, 1937; s. LeRoy Leslie and Lola Fern (Grant) L. AB, Oberlin Coll., 1959; LLB, Western Res. U., 1962; LLM, Yale U., 1963; JSD, Columbia U., 1973. Bar: N.Y. 1965, Mich. 1974. Asst. prof. law U. Fla., 1965-69; prof. Wayne State U., 1970-97, prof. emeritus, 1997—; vis. prof. State U., Utrecht, 1981. Author: Legal Ethics and Professional Responsibility, 1963; contbr. articles on victimology to profl. jours. Mem. Am. Law Inst., Nat. Orgn. Victim Assistance (bd. dirs. 1979-88, 90-91), World Soc. Victimology (exec. com. 1982-94). Home: Apt 2502 1300 E Lafayette St Detroit MI 48207-2924 Office: Wayne State U Law Sch Detroit MI 48202

**LAMEL, LINDA HELEN,** professional society executive, former insurance company executive, former college president, lawyer; b. N.Y.C., Sept10, 1943; d. Maurice and Sylvia (Abrams) Treppel; 1 child, Diana Ruth Sands. BA magna cum laude, Queens Coll., 1964; MA, NYU, 1968; JD, Bklyn. Law Sch., 1976. Bar: N.Y. 1977, U.S. Dist. Ct. (3d dist.) N.Y. 1977. Mgmt. analyst U.S. Navy, Bayonne, N.J., 1964-65; secondary sch. tchr. Farmingdale Pub. Sch., N.Y., 1965-73; curriculum specialist Yonkers Bd. Edn., N.Y., 1973-75; program dir. Office of Lt. Gov., Albany, N.Y., 1975-77; dep. supt. N.Y. State Ins. Dept., N.Y.C., 1977-83; pres., CEO Coll. of Ins., N.Y.C., 1983-88; v.p. Tchr.'s Ins. and Annuity Assn., N.Y.C., 1988-96; exec. dir. Risk and Ins. Mgmt. Soc., N.Y.C., 1997—. Contbr. articles to profl. jours. Campaign mgr. lt. gov.'s primary race, N.Y. State, 1974; v.p. Spencer Ednl. Found. Mem. ABA (tort and ins. sect. com. chmn. 1985-86), N.Y. State Bar Assn. (exec. com. ins. sect. 1984-88), Assn. of Bar of City of N.Y. (chmn. med. malpractice com. 1989-91, ins. law com. 1997—), Am. Mgmt. Assn. (ins. and risk mgmt. council), Fin. Women's Assn., Assn. Profl. Ins. Women (Woman of Yr. award 1988), Bklyn, Law Sch. Alumni Assn., Phi Beta Kappa Assocs. (v.p. 1992—).

**LAMIA, CHRISTINE EDWARDS,** lawyer; b. Hollywood, Fla., Dec. 8, 1962. BS in Comms., Fla. State U., 1984; JD, Mercer U., 1987. Lawyer Byrd & Murphy, Ft. Lauderdale, 1987-92, Abel, Bond et al, Sarasota, Fla., 1992-97, Becker & Poliakoff, Sarasota, 1997—. General civil litigation, Construction. Office: Becker & Poliakoff 630 S Orange Ave Sarasota FL 34236-7504

**LAMISON, ERIC ROSS,** lawyer; b. Akron, Aug. 3, 1970; s. Donald Ross and Linda Marie (Alexander) L. BS in Physiology, Mich. State U., 1992; JD magna cum laude, U. Mich., 1995. Bar: Calif. 1995, U.S. Dist. Ct. (ctrl. dist.) Calif. 1996, U.S. Ct. Appeals (9th cir.) 1998, U.S. Dist. Ct. Ariz. 1998, U.S. Dist. Ct. (no. dist.) Calif. 1998, U.S. Ct. Appeals (Fed. cir.) 1999, U.S. Patent Office 1999. Assoc. Kirkland & Ellis, L.A., 1995—. Mem. Order of the Coif. General civil litigation, Intellectual property, Patent. Office: Kirkland and Ellis 300 S Grand Ave Ste 3000 Los Angeles CA 90071-3140

**LAMM, CAROLYN BETH,** lawyer; b. Buffalo, Aug. 22, 1948; d. Daniel John and Helen Barbara (Tatakis) L.; m. Peter Edward Halle, Aug. 12, 1972; children: Alexander P., Daniel E. BS, SUNY Coll. at Buffalo, 1970; JD, U. Miami (Fla.), 1973. Bar: Fla., 1973, D.C., 1976, N.Y. 1983. Trial atty. frauds sect. civil div. U.S. Dept. Justice, Washington, 1973-78, asst. chief comml. litigation sect. civil div., 1978, asst. dir., 1978-80; assoc. White & Case, Washington, 1980-84, ptnr., 1984—; mem. Sec. State's Adv. Com. Pvt. Internat. law, 1988-91; arbitrator U.S. Panel of Arbitrators, Internat. Ctr. Settlement of Investment Disputes, 1995—. Mem. bd. editors Can./U.S. Rev. Bus. Law, 1987-92; mem. editorial adv. bd. Inside Litigation; contbg. editor: Internat. Arbitration Law Rev., 1997—; contbr. articles to legal publs. Mem. Mayor's Commn. on Violence Against Women. Fellow Am. Bar Found.; mem. ABA (chmn. young lawyers divsn., rules and calendar com., chmn. house membership com., chmn. assembly resolution com., sec. 1984-85, chmn. internat. litigation com. coun. 1991-94, sect. litigation, ho. dels. 1982—, nomination com. 1984-87, chair 1995-96, past D.C. Cir. mem., standing com. fed. judiciary 1992-95, chmn. com. scope and correlation of work 1996-97, commn. on multidisciplinary practice), Am. Arbitration Assn. (arbitrator, com. on fed. arbitration act), Fed. Bar Assn. (chmn. sect. on antitrust and trade regulation), Bar Assn. D.C. (bd. dirs., sec.), D.C. Bar (pres. 1997-98, bd. govs. 1987-93, steering com. litigation sect.), Am. Law Inst., Women's Bar Assn. D.C., Am. Soc. Internat. Law, Am. Indonesian C. of C. (bd. dirs.), Am. Uzbekistan C. of C. (bd. dirs., sec., gen. counsel), Am. Turkish Friendship Coun. (bd. dirs., chair), Nat. Women's Forum, Columbia Country Club. Democrat. Federal civil litigation, Administrative and regulatory, Private international. Home: 2801 Chesterfield Pl NW Washington DC 20008-1015 Office: White and Case 601 13th St NW Washington DC 20005-3807

**LAMME, KATHRYN ANNE,** lawyer; b. Dayton, Ohio, Aug. 7, 1946; d. Herschel R. and Lola G. (Recknor) L.; m. James V. Johnson, Sept. 3, 1982; children: Anna R. Tucker, Molly E. Raske. AB, Cornell U., 1968; MSW, U. Mich., 1971; JD, U. Dayton, 1980. Bar: Ohio 1980, U.S. Ct. Appeals (6th cir.) 1986, U.S. Dist. Ct. (so. dist.) Ohio 1980. Assoc. Turner Granzow & Hollenkamp, Dayton, 1980-83, ptnr., 1983-98; corp. v.p., sec., dep. gen. counsel The Standard Register Co., Dayton, 1998—. Bd. advisors U. Dayton Scho. Law, 1992—; pres., trustee Bldg. Bridges Inc., Dayton, 1995—. Mem. ABA, Dayton Bar Assn. (trustee 1995-96), Lawyers Club. General corporate, Labor, Mergers and acquisitions. Office: Standard Register Co 600 Albany St Dayton OH 45408-1442

**LAMME, THOMAS ROBERT,** lawyer; b. Houston, Nov. 25, 1967; s. Charles Lindas and Lucy Lee Lamme; m. Gine Elise Muehr, Nov. 23, 1996. BA, Dartmouth Coll., 1990; JD, U. Houston, 1993. Bar: Tex. 1993, U.S. Dist. Ct. (so. dist.) Tex. 1994. Tax cons. Arthur Andersen LLP, Houston, 1994-96; assoc. Brown, Parker & Leahy LLP, Houston, 1996—. Adv. bd. Odyssey House Tex., Inc., Houston, 1998—. Mem. Houston Young Lawyers Assn., State Bar of Tex. Avocations: writing, screenwriting, recreational sports. General corporate, Securities, Taxation, general. Office: Brown Parker & Leahy LLP 1200 Smith St Ste 3600 Houston TX 77002-4596

**LAMMERT, THOMAS EDWARD,** lawyer; b. Pitts., Mar. 26, 1947; s. John Albert and Gladys Irene (Miller) L.; m. Anita N. Kelm, Sept. 25, 1976; children: Brian, Andrew. BS, U. Pitts, 1969; JD, U. Akron, 1976. Bar: Ohio 1976, Fla 1983, U.S. Ct. Appeals (6th cir.) 1983, U.S. Supreme Ct., 1982. Assoc. Guy, Mentzer & Towne, Akron, Ohio, 1976-84, ptnr., 1984-85; ptnr. Guy, Lammert & Towne, Akron, 1985—. Mem. ABA, Ohio State Bar Assn., Fla. Bar Assn., Stark County Bar Assn., Akron Bar Assn., City Club. Republican. Bankruptcy, Contracts commercial, General civil litigation. Office: Guy Lammert & Towne 2210 1st National Towers Akron OH 44308

**LAMON, HARRY VINCENT, JR.,** lawyer; b. Macon, Ga., Sept. 29, 1932; s. Harry Vincent and Helen (Bewley) L.; m. Ada Healey Morris, June 17, 1954; children: Hollis Morris, Kathryn Gurley. BS cum laude, Davidson Coll., 1954; JD with distinction, Emory U., 1958. Bar: Ga. 1958, D.C. 1965. Of counsel Troutman Sanders LLP, Atlanta, 1995—; adj. prof. law Emory U., 1960-79. Contbr. articles to profl. jours. Mem. adv. bd. Metro Atlanta Salvation Army, 1963-97, chmn., 1975-79, life mem., 1997—, mem. nat. adv. bd., 1976-96, chmn. 1991-93, emeritus, 1996—; mem. Adv. Coun. on Employee Welfare and Pension Benefit Plans, U.S. Dept. Labor, 1975-79; mem. Employee Benefits Reporter adv. bd. Bur. Nat. Affairs; mem. bd. visitors Davidson Coll., 1979-89; trustee, pres. So. Fed. Tax Inst., Inc., 1965—; trustee Am. Tax Policy Inst., Inc., 1989-96, Embry-Riddle Aero U., 1989—, Cathedral of St. Philip, Atlanta, 1989-95. 1st lt. AUS, 1954-56. Recipient Others award Salvation Army, 1979, Centennial honoree, 1990. Fellow Am. Bar Found. (life), Am. Coll. Trust and Estate Counsel, Am. Coll. Tax Counsel, Internat. Acad. Estate and Trust Law, Ga. Bar Found. (life); mem. ABA, FBA, Atlanta Bar Assn. (life), Am. Bar Retirement Assn. (bd. dirs. 1989-96, pres. 1994-95), Am. Law Inst. (life), Am. Employee Benefits Conf., So. Employee Benefits Conf. (pres., 1972, hon. life mem.), State Bar Ga. (chmn. sect. taxation 1969-70, vice chmn. comm on continuing lawyer competency 1982-89), Am. Judicature Soc., Atlanta Tax Forum, Lawyers Club Atlanta, Nat. Emory U. Law Sch. Alumni Assn. (pres. 1967), Practicing Law Inst., ALI-ABA Inst., CLUs Inst., Kiwanis Club Atlanta (hon. mem.; pres. 1974), Peachtree Racket Club (pres. 1986-87), Atlanta Coffee House Club, Capital City Club, Peachtree Club, Cosmos Club, Univ. Club (Washington), Phi Beta Kappa, Omicron Delta Kappa, Phi Delta Phi, Phi Delta Theta (chmn. nat. comty. svc. day 1969-72, legal commr. 1973-76, prov. pres. 1976-79). Episcopalian. Taxation, general, Pension, profit-sharing, and employee benefits, Estate planning. Home: 4415 Paces Battle NW Atlanta GA 30327-3023 Office: Troutman Sanders LLP 600 Peachtree St NE Ste 5200 Atlanta GA 30308-2231

**LAMONACA, JOSEPH MICHAEL,** lawyer, pilot; b. Phila., Feb. 25, 1962; 1 child, Debra; married; children: Jennifer, Jessica. JD, Widener U., 1990. Bar: Pa., U.S. Ct. Appeals (3d cir.), U.S. Dist. Ct. (ea. dist.) Pa. Cert. Aircraft Owners and Pilots Assn., Nat. Transp. Safety Bd. Pvt. practice Chadds Ford, Pa.; comml. pilot Flight Safety Internat.; apptd. safety counselor FAA. Mem. ABA (family law sect.), Pa. Bar Assn. (family law sect.), Lawyer Pilot Bar Assn., NTSB Bar Assn., AOPA (panel lawyer). Roman Catholic. Aviation, Family and matrimonial. Home: 304 Darwin Dr Newark DE 19711-6645 Office: G&M Bldg Ste 303 Chadds Ford PA 19317

**LAMONICA, P(AUL) RAYMOND,** lawyer, academic administrator, educator; b. Baton Rouge, June 10, 1944; s. Leonard and Olivia (Frank) L.; m. Dianne Davis, Aug. 23, 1971; children: Drew, Neal, Leigh. BA, La. State U., 1965, MA, 1966, JD, 1970. Bar, La. 1970. Law clk. to chief judge U.S. Dist. Ct. (we. dist.) La., 1970-71; assoc. Hebert, Moss & Graphia, Baton Rouge, 1971; judge pro tem 19th Jud. Dist. Ct., East Baton Rouge Parish, 1979; prof. La. State U. Law Sch., Baton Rouge, 1973-86; exec. counsel to La. Gov., 1983-84; U.S. atty. for mid. dist. La., 1986-94; vice chancellor, prof. law La. State U., Baton Rouge, 1994-97; counsel La. Ho. of Reps., 1976-79, 80-83. Fellow Am. Bar Found.; mem. ABA, La. Bar Assn. (bd. govs. 1979). Republican. Roman Catholic. Office: La State U 416 LSU Law Ctr Baton Rouge LA 70803-0001

**LAMORENA, ALBERTO C., III,** territory supreme court justice; b. Agana, Guam, Nov. 29, 1949; s. Alberto Tominez and Fe Grata (Cristobal) L. Student, St. Louis U., 1967-69; BA in Polit. Sci., U. Ill., 1971; postgrad., U. Tex., 1974; JD, Drake U., 1977. Bar: Guam 1978, Dist. Ct. Guam 1978, Dist. Ct. No. Marianas 1980, U.S. Ct. Appeals (9th cir.) 1981. Assoc. Kearney Lee Hammer P.C., Agana, 1977-80; pvt. practice Agana, 1980-85; ptnr. Lamorena and Ingles P.C., Agana, 1985-88; presiding judge Superior Ct. of Guam, Agana, 1988—; spl. judge Supreme Ct. of Commonwealth of No. Mariana Islands, 1995—; mem. Guam Legislature, Agana, 1979-88, chmn. ways and means com., vice chmn. crimimal justice com., 1979-83, minority leader, 1987-88; advisor Filipino Community of Guam, 1979-88, Ilocano Community of Guam, 1979-88; chmn. Guam Legal Svcs., 1983-85, bd trustees; assoc. prof. U. Guam, 1986-89; chmn. Judicial Coun. Guam, nat. judicial leader, Guam bd. examiners, public defender; pres., founder, Pacific Judicial Coun., 1991—; chmn. criminal justice automation commn., 1991—; judicial rep. Commn. on Self Determination. Chmn. bd. trustees Guam Legal Svcs., 1983-85. Mem. ABA (judicial adminstrn. divsn.), Am. Judges Assn., Conf. Chief Justices, Guam Bar Assn., Fed. Bar Assn., Am. Judicature Soc., Pacific Jud. Coun. (founder, pres.), South Pacific Judicial Conf. Pacific Inst. Judicial Administrn., Supreme Ct. Rules Commn. (Guam),. Office: Judicial Ctr 120 W Obrien Dr Agana GU 96910-5174*

**LAMOTHE, ARTHUR J.,** lawyer; b. Augusta, Maine, June 20, 1962; s. Roland J. and Kathleen A. (Small) L., Sept. 29, 1990; children: Joel T., Matthew G., Kimberlee A. JD, U. Maine, 1987. Bar: Maine 1987, U.S. Dist. Ct. Maine 1987, U.S. Ct. Appeals (1st cir.) 1998. In-house atty. Cen. Maine Power Co., Augusta, 1987-90; assoc. Friedman & Babcock, Portland, Maine, 1990-97; pvt. practice Brunswick, Maine, 1997—. Bd. dirs. Big Bros./Big Sisters, Portland, 1994-97, Brunswick, 1997—; co-chair Communities of MerryMeeting Bay Bus. Assn. Mem. ABA, Maine State Bar Assn., Cumberland Bar Assn., Bath-Brunswick Bar Assn., Phi Beta Kappa. General practice, General civil litigation, Workers' compensation. Office: PO Box 425 Brunswick ME 04011-0425

**LAMPERT, MICHAEL A.,** lawyer; b. Queens, N.Y., Nov. 25, 1951; s. Jack and Bernice Claire Lampert. BA, SUNY, Albany, 1973; JD, Harvard U., 1976. Bar: N.Y. 1977, D.C. 1977, N.J. 1987, U.S. Dist. Ct. (so., ea. and no. dists.) N.Y., U.S. Ct. Appeals (2d, 3d and 4th cirs.), U.S. Supreme Ct. Assoc. Paul, Weiss, Rifkind, Wharton & Garrison, N.Y.C., 1976-87; assoc, ptnr. St. John, Oberdorf, Williams, Newark, 1987-90; ptnr. McManimon and Scotland, Newark, 1990-96, Saul, Ewing, Remick & Saul, Princeton, 1996—; adj. lectr. Cardozo Law Sch., N.Y.C., 1978-80. Bd. editors N.J. Lawyer, 1995—; author: (with others) Federal Practice in New Jersey. Mem. ABA (sect. litigation), N.J. Bar Assn. (past chair fed. practice sect.), SUNY-Albany Alumni Assn. (dir., pres. 1973-85). Federal civil litigation, General civil litigation, State civil litigation. Home: 1115 Irving Ave Westfield NJ 07090-1662 Office: Saul Ewing Remick & Saul 214 Carnegie Ctr Ste 202 Princeton NJ 08540-6237

**LAMPERT, MICHAEL ALLEN,** lawyer; b. Phila., May 6, 1958; s. Arnold Leonard and Marilyn (Sternberg) L.; m. Angela Gallicchio, Dec. 6, 1987; 1 child, David Max. AB in Econs. cum laude, U. Miami, Coral Gables, Fla., 1979, postgrad., 1980; JD, Duke U., 1983; LLM in Taxation, NYU, 1984. Bar: Fla. 1983, D.C. 1984, Pa. 1984, U.S. Tax Ct. 1984, U.S. Ct. of Appeals for the Armed Forces 1995; bd. cert. tax lawyer, Fla. Bar. Assoc. Cohen, Scherer, Cohn & Silverman, P.A., North Palm Beach, Fla., 1984-88; instr. div. continuing edn. Fla. Atlantic U., Boca Raton, 1988—; prin. Jacobson & Lampert, P.A., Boca Raton, 1988-91; pvt. practice West Palm Beach, 1991—. Mem. editl. bd. Southeastern Tax Alert, 1993-97, mem. editl. bd. Sales and Use Tax Alert, 1997—. Instr., trainer, chpt. vice-chair, bd. dirs. ARC, Palm Beach County, Fla.; bd. dirs. Jewish Fedn. Palm Beach County, 1989-91, 97—; bd. dirs. Jewish Family and Children's Svc. Palm Beach County, 1988—, treas., 1991-94, pres., 1997-99; pres. Jewish Residential and Family Svc., Inc., 1997—; commr. Commn. for Jewish Edn.-Palm Beach chpt., 1997-99; mem. nat. planned giving com. Weismann Inst., Israel. Recipient Young Leadership award, 1988, Safety award ARC, 1989, Cert. of Merit, Am. Radio Relay League, West Palm Beach Club, 1988, Cert. of Appreciation for Leadership, ARC Disaster Svcs., Palm Beach County, 1989, Disaster Svc. award, 1994, Human Resources award, 1993, Tax Law award Legal Aid Soc. of Palm Beach County and Palm Beach County Bar Assn., 1993, Young Leadership award Jewish Fedn. of Palm Beach County, 1998. Mem. Palm Beach Tax Inst. (pres., bd. dirs.), Fla. Bar (exec. coun., tax sect.), Palm Beach County Bar Assn. (chair bus. and corp. continuing legal edn. com. 1989-90, chair legal asst. com. 1988-91, Tax Law award 1993), Legal Aid Soc. of Palm Beach County, Inc. Avocations: aquatics, amateur radio, running. Estate planning, Taxation, general. Office: Ste 900 1655 Palm Beach Lakes Blvd West Palm Beach FL 33401-2211

**LAMSON, WILLIAM MAXWELL, JR.,** lawyer; b. Laramie, Wyo., June 28, 1943; s. William Maxwell Lamson and Neville A. Troutman; m. Michaela A. Wright; children: Kelly, Bill, Jill, Katie. BA, Wayne State Coll., 1965; JD, U. Nebr., 1969. Bar: Nebr. 1969, U.S. Ct. Appeals (8th cir.) 1973. Assoc. Kennedy, Holland, Omaha, 1969-74, ptnr., 1974—. Fellow Am. Coll. Trial Lawyers; mem. ABA, Nebr. Bar Assn., Omaha Bar Assn., Def. Rsch. Inst. Avocations: reading, golf. Federal civil litigation, General civil litigation. Office: Lamson Dugan & Murray 10306 Regency Parkway Dr Ste 1 Omaha NE 68114-3748

**LANA, ANTHONY J.,** lawyer; b. Buffalo, Dec. 18, 1967; s. Joseph and Josephine Lana. BA, Canisius Coll., 1989; JD, U. Arkon, 1992. Ptnr. Eoannou & Lane, Buffalo, 1995—. Mem. Nat. Trial Lawyers Assn., Nat. Criminal Def. Lawyers Assn., N.Y. State Defenders Assn., Erie County Bar Assn. Office: Cornell Mansion 484 Delaware Ave Buffalo NY 14202-1304

**LANAM, LINDA LEE,** lawyer; b. Ft. Lauderdale, Fla., Nov. 21, 1948; d. Carl Edward and Evelyn (Bolton) L. BS, Ind. U., 1970, JD, 1975. Bar: Ind. 1975, Pa. 1979, U.S. Dist. Ct. (no. and so. dists.) Ind. 1975, U.S. Supreme Ct. 1982, Va. 1990. Atty., asst. counsel Lincoln Nat. Life Ins. Co., Ft. Wayne, Ind., 1975-76, 76-78; atty., mng. atty. Ins. Co. of N.Am., Phila., 1978-79, 80-81; legis. liaison Pa. Ins. Dept., Harrisburg, 1981-82, dep. ins. commr., 1982-84; exec. dir., Washington rep. Blue Cross and Blue Shield Assn., Washington, 1984-86; v.p. and sr. counsel Union Fidelity Life Ins. Co., Am. Patriot Health Ins. Co., etc., Trevose, Pa., 1986-89; v.p., gen. counsel, corp. sec. The Life Ins. Co. Va., Richmond, 1989-97, sr. v.p., gen. counsel, corp. sec., 1997-98, also bd. dirs.; v.p., chief counsel state rels. Am. Coun. Life Ins., Washington, 1999—; chmn. adv. com. health care legis. Nat. Assn. Ins. Commrs., 1985-87, chmn. long term care, 1986-87, mem. tech. resource com. on cost disclosure and genetic testing, 1993-98; mem. tech. adv. com. Health Ins. Assn. Am., 1986-89; mem. legis. com. Am. Coun. Life Ins., 1994-96, mem. market conduct com., 1997-98. Contbr. articles to profl. jours. Pres. Phila. Women's Network, 1980-81; chmn. city housing code bd. appeals Harrisburg, 1985-86. Mem. ABA, Richmond Bar Assn. Republican. Presbyterian. General corporate, Legislative, Insurance. Office: Am Coun Life Ins 1001 Pennsylvania Ave NW Washington DC 20004-2505

**LANCASTER, JOAN ERICKSON,** state supreme court justice; b. 1954. BA magna cum laude, St. Olaf Coll., Northfield, Minn., 1977; spl. diploma in social studies, Oxford U., 1976; JD cum laude, U. Minn., 1981. Atty. LeFevere, Lefler, Kennedy, O'Brien & Drawz, Mpls., 1981-83; asst. U.S. atty. Dist. Minn., Mpls., 1983-93; shareholder Leonard, Street and Deinard, Mpls., 1993-95; dist. ct. judge 4th Jud. Dist., Mpls., 1995-98; assoc. justice Minn. Supreme Ct., 1998—. Office: Minn Supreme Ct 25 Constitution Ave Saint Paul MN 55155*

**LANCASTER, KENNETH G.,** lawyer; b. Stafford Springs, Conn., Dec. 6, 1949; s. Talbot Augustin and Helen Collier (McRae) L.; m. Margaret Jane Royer, Aug. 25, 1973; children—Kimberly Jane, John Talbot, Christopher Andrew. BA, U. Miami, 1971, JD, 1974. Bar: Fla. 1974, U.S. Dist. Ct. (so. dist.) Fla. 1975, U.S. Dist. Ct. (mid. dist.) Fla. 1976. Adminstr. Met. Dade County, Miami, Fla., 1971-73; assoc. Robert A. Spiegel, Coral Gables, Fla., 1973-78; sole practice, South Miami, Fla., 1978-80; ptnr. Clark, Dick & Lancaster, P.A., South Miami, 1980-87; ptnr. King, Leavy & Lancaster, P.A., South Miami, 1987—; cons. 1st City Bank Dade County, Miami, 1983-84; dir. U. Miami Bus. Sch. Bd. dirs., v.p. U. Miami Hall Fame, Coral Gables, 1984—, mem. endowment com., 1982—; mem. Atty.'s Title Ins. Fund, 1982—. Mem. ABA, Fla. Bar Assn., Dade County Bar Assn. (Disting. Service award 1984), Dade County Attys. Real Property Coun., Hurricane Club/U. Miami (bd. dirs .1984—, pres. 1996-97). Estate planning, Probate, Real property. Home: 10241 SW 141st St Miami FL 33176-7005 Office: King Leavy & Lancaster 5975 Sunset Dr Ste 301 Miami FL 33143-5198

**LANCASTER, MIRIAM DIEMMER,** lawyer; b. Brunswick, Ga., Dec. 17, 1957; d. Edward H. and Barbara Alice (Smith) Diemmer; m. Wayne A. Lancaster, Aug. 22, 1981; 1 child, Caitlin Allyn. BA, U. Ga., 1979, JD, 1982. Bar: Ga. 1982, U.S. Ct. Appeals (11th cir.) 1984, U.S. Dist. Ct. (so. dist.) Ga. 1982, U.S. Dist. Ct. (no. dist.) Ga. 1987. Assoc. Wiseman, Blackburn & Futrell, Savannah, Ga., 1982-89; ptnr. Wiseman, Blackburn & Futrell, Savannah, 1989—; asst. city atty. City of Savannah. Ga., 1984--. Sec. Downtown Devel. Authority, Savannah, 1982—, Devel. Authority Savannah, 1982—; bd. dirs. Savannah Runaway Home, 1988—, chmn. 1989; bd. dirs. Marshlands Found., 1990—. Mem. ABA, State Bar Ga., Savannah Bar Assn., Savannah Jaycees (treas. 1985-86), Altrusa Club (2d v.p. 1988-89, 1st v.p. 1989—). Federal civil litigation, Civil rights. Office: Wiseman Blackburn & Futrell 240 W Broughton St Savannah GA 31401-3214

**LANCASTER, RALPH IVAN, JR.,** lawyer; b. Bangor, Maine, May 9, 1930; s. Ralph I. and Mary Bridget (Kelleher) L.; m. Mary Lou Pooler, Aug. 21, 1954; children: Mary Lancaster Miller, Anne, Elizabeth, Christopher Peoples, John, Martin. AB, Coll. Holy Cross, 1952; LLB, Harvard U., 1955; LLD (hon.), St. Joseph's Coll., 1991. Bar: Maine 1955, Mass. 1955. Law clk. U.S. Dist. Ct. Dist. Maine, 1957-59; ptnr. firm Pierce Atwood, Portland, Maine, 1961—; mng. ptnr. Pierce Atwood, 1993-96; ind. counsel In Re Herman apptd. by spl. divsn. D.C. Ct. Appeals, 1998—; condr. trial advocacy seminar Harvard U.; lectr. U. Maine; chmn. merit selection panel U.S. Magistrate for Dist. of Maine, 1982, 88; bd. visitors U. Maine Sch. Law, 1991-96, chair, 1991-93; spl. master by appointment U.S. Supreme Ct. in State of N.J. vs. State of Nev. et al, 1987-88; mem. 1st Ctr. Adv. Com. on Rules, 1991-96, legal adv. bd. Martindale Hubbell, 1990—; represented U.S. in Gulf of Maine in World Ct. at The Hague, 1984. Former mem. Diocese of Portland Bur. Edn. With U.S. Army, 1955-57. Mem. Maine Jud. Coun., Am Coll. Trial Lawyers (chmn. Maine 1974-79, bd. regents 1982-87, treas. 1985-87, pres. 1989-90), Maine Bar Assn. (pres. 1982), Cumberland County Bar Assn., Canadian Bar Assn. (hon.). Republican. Roman Catholic. Federal civil litigation, State civil litigation, Insurance. Home: 162 Woodville Rd Falmouth ME 04105-1120 Office: 1 Monument Sq Portland ME 04101-4033

**LANCE, ALAN GEORGE,** state attorney general; b. McComb, Ohio, Apr. 27, 1949; s. Cloyce Lowell and Clara Rose (Wilhelm) L.; m. Sheryl C. Holden, May 31, 1969; children: Lisa, Alan Jr., Luke. BA, S.D. State U., 1971; JD, U. Toledo, 1973. Bar: Ohio 1974, U.S. Dist. Ct. (no. dist.) Ohio 1974, U.S. Ct. Mil. Appeals 1974, Idaho 1978, U.S. Supreme Ct. 1996. Asst. pros. atty. Fulton County, Wauseon, Ohio, 1973-74; ptnr. Foley and Lance, Chartered, Meridian, Idaho, 1978-90; prin. Alan G. Lance, Meridian, 1990-94; rep. Idaho Ho. of Reps., Boise, 1990-94, majority caucus chmn., 1992-94; atty. gen. State of Idaho, 1995—. Capt. AUS, 1974-78. Mem. Nat. Assn. Attys. Gen. (vice chair conf. western attys. gen. 1998, chmn. 1999), Ohio Bar Assn., Idaho Bar Assn., Idaho Trial Lawyers Assn., Meridian C. of C. (pres. 1983), Am. Legion (judge adv. 1981-90, assoc. judge adv. 1997—, state comdr. 1988-89, alt. nat. exec. com. 1992-94, nat. exec. com. 1994-96, chmn. nat. fgn. rels. commn. 1996-97, ex-officio mem. nat. POW/MIA com. 1996—, nat. comdr. 1999—), Elks. Republican. Avocation: fishing. Home: 1370 Eggers Pl Meridian ID 83642-6528 Office: PO Box 83720 Boise ID 83720-3720

**LANCIONE, BERNARD GABE,** lawyer; b. Bellaire, Ohio, Feb. 3, 1939; s. Americus Gabe and June (Morford) L.; m. Rosemary C., Nov. 27, 1976; children: Amy, Caitin, Gillian, Bernard Gabe II, Elizabetta Marie. BS, Ohio U., 1960; JD, Capitol U., 1965. Bar: Ohio 1965, U.S. Dist. Ct. (so. dist.) Ohio 1967, U.S. Supreme Ct., 1969, U.S. Ct. Appeals (4th cir.) 1982, U.S. Dist. Ct. (no. dist.) Ohio, 1989. Pres. Lancione Law Office, Co., L.P.A., Bellaire, Ohio, 1965-87, mng. atty. Cichon Lancione Co., L.P.A., St. Clairsville, Ohio, 1982-85, of counsel Ward, Kaps, Bainbridge, Maurer, Bloomfield and Melvin, Columbus, Ohio, 1987-88; Ohio Asst. Atty. Gen., Columbus, 1988-91; sole practice, 1991—; spl. counsel Ohio Atty. Gen.'s Office, 1991-95; solicitor Bellaire City (Ohio), 1968-72; asst. prosecutor County of Belmont (Ohio), 1972-76; legal counsel Young Democrats Am., 1971-73; pres. Young Dems. of Ohio, 1970-72; pack com. chmn. Pack 961, Westerville, Ohio Cub Scouts of Am., 1992-93. Mem. ABA, Ohio State Bar Assn., Assn. Trial Lawyers Am., Ohio Acad. Trial Lawyers (award of merit 1972). Democrat. Roman Catholic. Personal injury, General practice, Family and matrimonial. Home: 1108 Acillom Dr Westerville OH 43081-1104 Office: 647 Park Meadow Rd # E Westerville OH 43081-2878

**LANCKTON, ARTHUR VAN CLEVE,** lawyer; b. New London, Conn., Sept. 7, 1942; s. Arthur Leroy and Catherine Alison (Nicol) L.; m. Alice Elizabeth Keidan, Aug. 31, 1967; children: Benjamin E., Samuel F. BA cum laude, Yale U., 1964; JD cum laude, Harvard U., 1967. Bar: Mass. 1967, U.S. Dist. Ct. Mass. 1968, U.S. Tax Ct. 1969, U.S. Ct. Appeals (1st cir.) 1982, U.S. Supreme Ct. 1986. Atty., dir. Harvard Law Sch. Community Legal Assistance Office, Cambridge, Mass., 1967-71; teaching fellow Harvard Law Sch., Cambridge, 1970-71; dep. gen. counsel Mass. Exec. Offices of Human Svcs., Boston, 1971-75; gen. counsel Dept. of Pub. Welfare, Boston, 1975-78; assoc. Bingham, Dana & Gould, Boston, 1978-83; assoc. Craig and Macauley, Boston, 1983-85, ptnr., 1985—. Democrat. Jewish. Health, Insurance, General civil litigation. Office: Craig and Macauley 600 Atlantic Ave Ste 2900 Boston MA 02210-2215

**LANDAU, FELIX,** lawyer; b. Hof/Salle, Germany, June 29, 1947; came to U.S., 1950; s. Fiszel and Ursula (Wahncau) L.; m. Kay Ellen Krutza, Aug. 10, 1979; children: Erik Lloyd, Kelly Anne, Kristine Marie. BS, U. Colo., 1969; MA, U. Northern Colo., 1972; JD cum laude, Gonzaga U., 1982. Bar: Wash. 1983, Wis. 1988. Assoc. Liebman, Conway, Olejniczak and Jerry, S.C., Green Bay, Wis., 1987-90; pvt. practice, Bellevue, Wash., 1990—. Assoc. editor Gonzaga U. Law Rev., 1981-82; founder, head coach Bellevue Eagles Track and Cross County Team. Capt. USAF, 1983-87. Mem. ABA, Wash. Bar Assn., Wash. State Trial Lawyers Assn. (Eagle mem., chmn. Eastside roundtable 1995-98), East King County Trial Lawyers Assn., Wis. Bar Assn., Phi Delta Phi. Avocations: sports, golf, basketball, tennis, jogging, coaching USA Track and Field and Cross Country Running. General civil litigation, Family and matrimonial, Personal injury. Office: 14670 NE 8th St Bellevue WA 98007-4127

**LANDAU, JAMES KENNETH,** lawyer; b. Ann Arbor, Mich., Sept. 4, 1960; s. Burton Joseph and Ellen Elizabeth (Segal) L.; m. Amy Maude Grabino; children: Emily Phylicia, Jessica Ann. BA, U. Mich., 1982; JD, Boston U., 1985. Bar: Pa. 1985, N.Y. 1987, U.S. Dist. Ct. (so. and ea. dists.) N.Y. 1988, U.S. Dist. Ct. (no. and we. dists.) N.Y. 1995, U.S. Ct. Appeals (2d cir.) 1995. Atty. Rubin, Glickman & Steinberg, Lansdale, Pa., 1985-86, Sharfman, Shanman, Poret & Siviglia, N.Y.C., 1987-89, Brown, Raysman, Millstein, Felder & Steiner, N.Y.C., 1989-97, Rosen & Reade, LLP, N.Y.C., 1997—. Recipient Silver Shingle Alumni award Boston U. Sch. Law, 1986. Mem. Assn. Bar City N.Y., Securities Industry Assn. (mem. compliance and legal div.). Federal civil litigation, Appellate, State civil litigation. Office: Rosen & Reade LLP 757 3rd Ave Fl 6 New York NY 10017-2049

**LANDAU, MICHAEL B.,** law educator, musician, author; b. Wilkes-Barre, Pa., July 3, 1953; s. Jack Landau and Florence (Rabitz) Simon. BA, Pa. State U., 1975; JD, U. Pa., 1988. Vis. prof. law Dickinson Sch. Law, Pa. State U., Carlisle; assoc. Cravath, Swaine and Moore, N.Y.C., 1988-90, Skadden, Arps, N.Y.C., 1990-92; assoc. prof. Coll. Law Ga. State U., Atlanta, 1992-99, prof. law, 1999—; pres., founder Balloon-A-Grams of N.Y., N.Y.C., 1981-86, N.Y. Singing Telegrams, 1981-86; vis. prof. law U. Ga. Law Sch.;, 1998; guest lectr. Johannes Kepler U., Linz, Austria, summer 1994, 95, 96. Contbr. articles to law jours. on copyright, art, patent, entertainment law. Mem. ABA, N.Y. State Bar Assn., Internat. Bar Assn., Vol. Lawyers for Arts, Am. Fedn. Musicians, Am. Intellectual Property Law Assn., Copyright Soc. U.S. Am., Phi Kappa Phi, Omicron Delta Epsilon. Democrat. Avocations: photography, jazz guitar, jazz piano. Office: Ga State U Coll Law University Pla Atlanta GA 30303

**LANDAU, WALTER LOEBER,** lawyer; b. New Orleans, Sept. 9, 1931; s. Walter Loeber and Mae (Wilzin) L.; m. Barbara Jane Gordon, June 23, 1954; children: Donna Hardiman, Blair Trippe, Gordon Loeber. BA, Princeton U., 1953; LLB, Harvard U., 1956. Bar: N.Y. 1956, U.S. Dist. Ct. (so. dist.) N.Y. 1962, U.S. Supreme Ct. 1971. Assoc. firm Sullivan & Cromwell, N.Y.C., 1959-65, ptnr., 1966-98, sr. counsel, 1999—. Trustee Reece Sch., N.Y.C.; mem. Met. Opera Assn.; bd. dirs., treas. Opera Orch. N.Y., bd. dirs. N.Y.C. Opera; bd. dirs., sec. Manhattan Theatre Club. Fellow Am. Bar Found.; mem. ABA, N.Y. State Bar Assn., Assn. Bar City N.Y., Am. Law Inst. Republican. Securities, General corporate, Mergers and acquisitions. Office: Sullivan & Cromwell 125 Broad St Fl 28 New York NY 10004-2489

**LANDAY, ANDREW HERBERT,** lawyer; b. N.Y.C., Mar. 8, 1920; s. Max and Ida Rose (Fox) L.; m. Carolyn Anne Greco, Aug. 22, 1962; children: Vincent, Mark, James, Roseanne. BA, UCLA, 1946, Mt. Angel Sem., Oreg., 1950; MS, Columbia U., 1953; JD, Southwestern U., 1964. Bar: Calif. 1964, U.S. Dist. Ct. (cen. dist.) Calif. 1964, U.S. Tax Ct. 1965, U.S. Ct. Appeals (9th cir.) 1966, U.S. Supreme Ct. 1971. Sole practice L.A., 1964-68; ptnr. Rozner, Yorty, Landay, Gibbs, Hodges, Bernstein & Wagner, L.A., Calif., 1968-73, Bernstein, Wagner, Hodges & Landay, Beverly Hills, Calif., 1974-78; of counsel H. Bradley Jones, Inc., Beverly Hills, 1978-89; arbitrator Calif. Superior Ct., L.A., 1979—; judge pro-tem, arbitrator Santa Monica (Calif.) Mcpl. Ct., 1971-98, L.A. Mcpl. Ct., 1971-98, Culver Mcpl. Ct., 1988-98, Malibu Mcpl. Ct., 1988-98; mem. security com. Superior Ct., L.A., 1995-97. Bd. dirs. Santa Monica Rep. Club, 1983-91. With AUS, 1942-46. Mem. L.A. County Bar Assn. (mcpl. cts. com. 1977-78, cts. com. 1992—), Am. Judicature Soc., L.A. County Lawyers Club (chmn. profl. ethics and unauthorized practice com. 1968-70, 77-78, bd. govs. 1988—, pres.-elect 1999—), KC, Am. Legion, Phi Alpha Delta. Roman Catholic. Probate, Estate taxation, Estate planning. Office: 322 12th St Santa Monica CA 90402-2014 also: 225 Broadway Ste 1210 San Diego CA 92101-5028

**LANDE, DAVID STEVEN,** lawyer; b. N.Y.C., Aug. 1, 1944; s. Jerome J. and Selma (Segal) L.; m. Fern Margolis, Aug. 17, 1975; children: Jill, Jeffrey, Jerome J. BS, Cornell U., 1966; JD, NYU, 1969. Bar: N.Y. 1969, U.S. Dist. Ct. (so. dist.) N.Y. 1971, U.S. Dist. Ct. (ea. dist.) N.Y. 1971, U.S. Supreme Ct. 1976. Aide Office of Mayor, N.Y.C., 1967-69; assoc. Javits & Javits, N.Y.C., 1970-71, Kreindler, Relkin, Olick & Goldberg, N.Y.C., 1971-74; pvt. practice N.Y.C., 1974—; apptd. chmn. N.Y.C. Loft Bd., 1994-96; commr., vice-chmn. N.Y.C. Civil Svc. Commn., 1996—. Contbr. articles to profl. jours. Dist. leader 69th A. Dist. South N.Y.C. Reps., 1975-94; mem. state com. N.Y. Reps., Albany, 1976-94. Recipient Meritorious Service to Nation award U.S. Selective Service System, 1976. Mem. N.Y. State Bar Assn. (chmn. subcommittee auditing attys. trust accounts; com. on profl. discipline, 1987-93). Jewish. Probate, General practice. Office: 305 Madison Ave New York NY 10165-0006

**LANDE, ROGER L.,** lawyer; b. Lake Mills, Iowa, Nov. 7, 1936; s. Carl Johann and gladys Kathryn (Schmidthuber) L.; m. Sarah Dunkerton, Aug. 20, 1960; children: Margaret Ann Lande Minor, Roger Christopher. BA, U. Iowa, 1961, JD, 1961. Bar: Iowa 1961. Pres., CEO Stanley, Lande & Hunter, Muscatine, Iowa, 1961—. Mem. editl. bd. U. Iowa Jour. Corp. Law, 1976-98. Bd. dirs. Iowa Law Sch. Found., Iowa City, 1989—; mem. Iowa State Bd. Regents, 1996—; chair Iowa Assn. Bus. and Industry, 1991-92; bd. dirs. Muscatine Devel. Corp., 1990—. Mem. Iowa State Bar Assn. (pres. 1981-82, bd. govs. 1977-79), Rotary, Union League Club Chgo., Outing Club, Davenport Des Moines Club. General corporate. Office: Stanley Lande & Hunter 301 Iowa Ave Ste 400 Muscatine IA 52761-3881

**LANDES, ANGELA HOCHMEISTER,** lawyer; b. Evansville, Ind., Apr. 9, 1958; d. John Louis and Ruth Mae (Kirsch) Hochmeister; m. R. Steven Landes, Oct. 1, 1994. BS, James Madison U., 1980; JD, U. Richmond, 1983. Bar: Va. 1983, U.S. Dist. Ct. (ea. dist.) Va. 1983, U.S. Dist. Ct. (we. dist.) Va. 1984. Assoc. James D. Parker, Hampton, Va., 1983-84, Hatmaker & Dinsmore, Harrisonburg, Va., 1984-85, Law Office David J. Hatmaker, Harrisonburg, 1985-87; pvt. practice Harrisonburg, 1987-94; asst. Commonwealth's atty. Harrisonburg/Rockingham County, 1994—; spl. justice for commitment hearings Gen. Dist. Ct., Harrisonburg, 1986-94; adj. prof. James Madison U., Harrisonburg, 1984-85, 92, Blue Ridge C.C., Weyers Cave, Va., 1988-93. Bd. dirs. Big Bros. and Big Sisters, Harrisonburg, 1984, com. chmn. 1985-87, sec., 1987-88; treas. Area C Reherd Acres Homeowners Assn., Harrisonburg, 1984-89, pres., 1990-91, bd. dirs., 1992-94; bd. dirs. Blue Ridge Legal Svcs., 1989-93, com. chmn., 1991-93, v.p., 1992, 93; mem. ch. coun. St. Stephen's United Ch. of Christ, 1990-93, 97-98, treas., 1997, v.p., 1998, pres. ch. coun., 1992, 93. Mem. ABA, Harrisonburg/Rockingham County Bar Assn. (sec.-treas. 1987-88, com. chmn. 1994), ATLA, Va. Trial Lawyers Assn., Va. Bar Assn., Va. State Bar. Home: 48 Maple Hill Ln Weyers Cave VA 24486-2434 Office: Office of Commonwealths Atty 53 Court Sq Ste 210 Harrisonburg VA 22801-3720

**LANDES, ROBERT NATHAN,** lawyer; b. N.Y.C., Dec. 24, 1930; s. Joseph William and Gertrude Ann (Sindeband) L.; m. Phyllis Markman, Apr. 16, 1964; children: Lucy Ann Harrop, Kathy Jill Braddock, Jeffrey Mark. A.B., Columbia U., 1952, LL.B. (Harlan Fiske Stone scholar), 1954. Bar: N.Y. 1954. Assoc. Shearman & Sterling, N.Y.C., 1957-61; asst. gen. counsel, v.p. U.S. Industries, Inc., N.Y.C., 1961-73; exec. v.p., gen. counsel, sec. McGraw-Hill, N.Y.C., 1974-95; bd. dirs. and vice chmn. Greenwich House, Inc. Editor: Columbia Law Rev, 1953-54; contbr. corp. counsel column N.Y. Law Jour., 1986-87. Bd. trustees Lawyers Com. for Civil Rights Under the Law, 1993—; bd. dirs. Lawyers Alliance for New York; bd. dirs. Town Hall. Served as lt. (j.g.) USNR, 1954-57. Mem. ABA, N.Y. State, N.Y. County Bar Assns., Assn. Bar City N.Y. (com. corp. law 1978-81, sec., corp. law depts, 1985-88, internat. law com. 1981-84), Mag. Pubs. Assn. (chmn. legal affairs com. 1977-82, chmn. AAP lawyers com. 1983-85), Columbia Coll. Alumni Assn. (v.p., bd. dirs. 1974-76, 86-90), Soc. Columbia Grads., (pres., bd. dirs. 1985-88), Columbia Law Sch. Alumni Assn. (treas. 1994—), Vineyards Country Club (Naples, Fla.), Pelham Country Club, (N.Y.), The Club at Pelican Bay (Naples.). Democrat. General corporate, Mergers and acquisitions, Securities. Home: 1192 Park Ave New York NY 10128-1314 Office: 45 Rockefeller Plz Fl 20 New York NY 10111-2099

**LANDES, WILLIAM M.,** law educator; b. 1939. AB, Columbia U., 1960, PhD in Econs., 1966. Asst. prof. econs. Stanford U., 1965-66; asst. prof. U. Chgo., 1966-69; asst. prof. Columbia U., 1969-72; assoc. prof. Grad. Ctr., CUNY, 1972-73; now prof. U. Chgo. Law Sch.; founder, chmn. Lexecon Inc., 1977-98, chmn. emeritus, 1998—; mem. bd. examiners GRE in Econs., ETS, 1967-74. Mem. Am. Econ. Assn., Am. Law and Econ. Assn. (v.p. 1991-92, pres. 1992-93), Mont Pelerin Soc. Author: (with Richard Posner) The Economic Structure of Tort Law, 1987; editor: (with Gary Becker) Essays in the Economics of Crime and Punishment, 1974; editor Jour. Law and Econs., 1975-91, Jour. Legal Studies, 1991—. Office: U Chgo Sch Law 1111 E 60th St Chicago IL 60637-2776 also: Lexecon Inc 332 S Michigan Ave Chicago IL 60604-4434

**LANDFIELD, RICHARD,** lawyer; b. Chgo. Jan. 16, 1941; s. Joseph D. and Donna (Mayberg) L.; m. Ilona Kiraldi, Aug. 6, 1965; children: Anne, Katharine, Sarah. BA Amherst Coll., 1962; LLB cum laude, Harvard U., 1965. Bar: N.Y. 1966, D.C. 1972. Assoc. Breed, Abbott & Morgan, N.Y.C., 1965-66, 1969-72, Washington, 1972-75; ptnr. Dunnells, Duvall & Porter, 1975-79, Landfield, Becker & Green, Washington, 1979-89, Breed, Abbott & Morgan, 1989-92, Landfield & Becker, Chartered, 1992-94; shareholder Sanders, Schnabel, Brandenburg & Zimmerman, P.C., 1995-97; ptnr. Berliner, Corcoran & Rowe, L.L.P., 1997—. Bd. dirs. Carlson Holdings Corp., 1984-89; gen. counsel The European Inst. Active numerous Amherst Coll. alumni groups; lawyers com. The Washington Opera, 84-86, 87—, trustee, Holton-Arms Sch., Bethesda, Md., 1984-86, 87-96, chmn. bldgs., grounds com., 1985-91, chmn. fin. com., 1993-95, past pres. Parents' Assn., trustee emeritus, 1996—. 1st lt. U.S. Army, 1966-69. Decorated Army Commendation medal; John W. Simpson Law fellow Amherst, 1963. Mem. ABA, N.Y. State Bar Assn. Republican. Clubs: Met. (Washington), Kenwood Country (Bethesda, Md.). General corporate, Private international, Real property. Home: 5101 Baltan Rd Bethesda MD 20816-2309 Office: Berliner Corcoran & Rowe LLP 1101 17th St NW Ste 1100 Washington DC 20036-4798

**LANDIN, DAVID CRAIG,** lawyer; b. Jamestown, N.Y., Aug. 1, 1946; s. David Carl and Rita Mae (Felthaus) L.; m. Susan Ann Gregory, July 11, 1970; children: Mary Stuart, Alexander Craig, David Reed. BA, U. Va., 1968, JD, 1972. Bar: Va. 1972, Pa. 1991, Tex. 1992, U.S. Supreme Ct. 1979. Ptnr. McGuire, Woods & Battle, Richmond, Va., 1972-95, mgr. of product liability and litigation mgmt. group, 1987-95; gen. counsel Va. Assn. Ind. Schs., 1989—, Coun. for Religion in Ind. Schs., 1990—; ptnr. Hunton & Williams, Richmond, Va., 1995—; pres. The Landin Cos., 1994—. Trustee Va. Law Found., 1981—, v.p. 1986-87, pres. 1987-88; trustee St. Anne's Belfield Sch., Charlottesville, Va., 1984—, chmn. trusteeship com., 1985-87, exec. com. 1985—, sec. 1988—; mem. long-range planning com. Ch. Schs. of Episcopal Diocese Va., 1988-91; chmn. ctrl. Va. chpt. Nat. MS Soc., 1995-96. With USAR, 1968-74. Fellow Va. Law Found. (DRI Exceptional Performance award 1988); mem. ABA, Va. Bar Assn. (chmn. young lawyers sect. 1979-80, chmn. com. on Issues of State and Nat. Importance 1982-90, chmn. judiciary com. 1990-95, exec. com. 1994—, pres. 1999—), Va. Assn. Def. Attys. (regional v.p. 1982-84, pres. 1987-88, chmn. long range planning com. 1990—), Charlottesville-Albemarle Bar Assn. (sec., treas. 1975-77, chmn. young lawyers sect. 1975-78), Richmond Bar Assn., Def. Rsch. Inst., Country Club Va., Commonweath Club. Roman Catholic. Avocations: squash, tennis. Federal civil litigation, Personal injury, Environmental. Home: 310 Oak Ln Richmond VA 23226-1639 Office: Hunton & Williams East Tower PO Box 1535 Richmond VA 23218-1535

**LANDOLFI, JOHN LOUIS,** lawyer; b. Niles, Ohio, Nov. 15, 1963; s. Gregory A. and Antonette Landolfi; m. Christina Ann Masdea; 1 child, John Gregory. BA, Westminster Coll., Pa., 1986; JD, Ohio State U., 1989. Bar: Ohio 1989, U.S. Dist. Ct. (no. and so. dists.) Ohio 1989, U.S. Ct. Appeals (6th cir.) 1991. Ptnr. Vorys, Sater, Seymour and Pease, LLP, Columbus, Ohio, 1989—. Devel. bd. mem. Children's Hosp., Columbus, 1996—; bd. mem. Am. Cancer Soc., Columbus, 1997—, Ohio State U. Student Loan Found., Columbus, 1998—. Recipient Disting. Svc. award Columbus Jr. C. of C., 1998. Mem. ABA, Ohio State Bar Assn., Columbus Bar Assn. (past chair admissions com. 1996-98, chair professionalism com. 1998), Ohio State U. Alumni Assn. (Williaim Oxley Thompson award 1998). Office: Vorys Sater Seymour & Pease LLP 52 E Gay St Columbus OH 43215-3161

**LANDON, WILLIAM J.,** intelligence officer; b. Menno, S.D., June 23, 1939; s. Helmuth Samuel and Violet A. (McPherson) Neuharth. LLB, Blackstone Sch. Law, 1962, JD, 1968; AA in Bus. Mgmt., Coastline C.C., 1984. Criminal investigator Internat. Acad. Police Sci., Oklahoma City, Southwestern Inst. Criminology, Lawton, Okla.; criminal investigator, intelligence officer ASI divsn. Internat. Investigators and Police, St. John, N.B., Can., 1964-94; intelligence officer, analyst Internat. Investigators & Police, Rapid City, S.D., 1990—. Sponsor Robin Anne Syperda Benedict meml. scholarship Calif. State U., Fullerton, 1990—. With USMC, 1957-65. Mem. Internat. Assn. Criminal Intelligence Analysts, Internat. Investigators Police Assn., Internat. Assn. Law Enforcement Intelligence Analysts, Assn. Former Intelligence Officers, Am. Soc. Criminology, Nat. Mil. Intelligence Assn. Avocations: martial arts, music.

**LANDRETH, KATHRYN E.,** prosecutor. U.S. atty. Dept. Justice, Las Vegas, 1993—. Office: US Attys Office 701 E Bridger Ave Ste 600 Las Vegas NV 89101-5554*

**LANDRON, MICHEL JOHN,** lawyer; b. Santurce, P.R., June 15, 1946; s. Francis Xavier and Francisca (Carretero) Healy; m. Carol McQuade, Apr. 22, 1989; children: Micahel Francis, Ryan McQuade. BA, Lehman Coll., 1968, postgrad., 1969-73; JD, Fordham U., 1977. Bar: N.Y. 1978, U.S. Dist. Ct. (so. dist.) N.Y. 1978, U.S. Dist. Ct. (ea. dist.) N.YU. 1978. Asst. atty. gen. Office of Atty. Gen., N.Y. State Dept. Law, N.Y.C., 1978-80; enforcement atty. N.Y. Stock Exch., N.Y.C., 1980-81; pvt. practice Bklyn., 1981-82, 84—; mem. Leaf, Duell, Drogin P.C., N.Y.C., 1982-84; gen. counsel Rockcom, Inc., 1985-87; adminstrv. law judge City of N.Y., 1987; cousnel Berger and Paul, N.Y.C., 1984-85; assoc. area counsel Digital Equipment Corp., 1988-89; adj. instr. N.Y. Law Sch., Ramapo Coll.; master arbitrator, Am. Arbitration Assn., U.S. Dist. Ct. (ea. dist.) N.Y.; mediator U.S. Dist. Ct. (ea. dist.) N.Y.; guest lectr. Lehman Coll.; cons. in field; arbitrator Civil Ct. N.Y.C., No Fault Ins. Panel State of N.Y., Nat. Assn. Securities Dealers, Inc.; arbitrator, mem. arbitration appeals panel Am. Arbitration Assn. Author: Conflicts of Law, 1992; (with others) Personal Injury: Actions, Defenses and Damages, 1992, Choice of Law; contbr. chpts. to books, articles to profl. jours. Mem. N.Y. State Bar Assn. (com. to cooperate with law revision commn.), Assn. Arbitrators City of N.Y., Am. Judges Assn., KC, Phi Alpha Delta (Disting. Svc. award 1977). Republican. Roman Catholic. Avocations: music, reading, sports. General practice, Trademark and copyright, General civil litigation. Office: Ste 2002 254 Canal St New York NY 10013-3501

**LANDRY, BRENDA MARGUERITE,** lawyer; b. New Iberia, La.. BS in Bus. Edn., U. Southwestern La., 1971; MS in Econs., U. So. Miss., 1973; JD, Loyola U., 1985. Bar: La. 1985, Tex. 1993, Fla. 1991. Assoc. Barham & Churchill, New Orleans, 1985-88, Elkins & Assocs., New Orleans, 1989-91; sr. staff atty. The Coastal Corp., Houston, 1993—. Mem. Am. Corp. Counsel Assn., Tex. Bar Assn., La. Bar Assn., Fla. Bar Assn. General corporate, Securities, Pension, profit-sharing, and employee benefits. Office: The Coastal Corp 9 Greenway Pla Houston TX 77046-0995

**LANDRY, FRANCES LEGGIO,** lawyer; b. Baton Rouge, Aug. 11, 1908; d. George and Josephine (Loicano) Leggio; m. Jules F. Landry, Aug. 9, 1934; 1 child, Frances Harriet Landry Borghardt. BA, La. State U., 1926, JD, 1934. Bar: La. 1934. Ptnr. Landry & Landry, Baton Rouge, 1934-90; sole practice Baton Rouge, 1990—; atty. to assist tax collector East Baton Rouge Parish, 1940-46; lectr. law sch. La. State U., Baton Rouge, 1942-43. Mem. Baton Rouge Beautification Com., 1963-66; pres. bd. control East Baton Rouge Library, 1964-84, hon. mem. 1984—; bd. dirs. Lafayette Gallery, Baton Rouge, 1969—; past v.p. West Baton Rouge Parish Mus.; past mem. bd. dirs. Anglo-Am. Mus., Baton Rouge; hon. mem. bd. dirs. La. State U. Art Mus. Mem. ABA (past chmn. membership com.), La. Bar Assn., Baton Rouge Bar Assn., Inter-Am. Bar Assn., Cath. Daus. Am., Equestrian Order of Holy Sepulchre, Women's Club (past pres.), Quota (past internat. pres.). Avocations: historical preservation, art galleries. Home: 2036 Lake Hills Pky Baton Rouge LA 70808-1453 Office: 348 Lafayette St Baton Rouge LA 70801-1206

**LANDRY, JOEL DANIEL, II,** lawyer; b. Washington, Oct. 18, 1963; s. Joel Daniel and Mary Ann (DiMario) L.; m. Lisa Roseann Giuliano, Oct. 24, 1993. BA, U. R.I., 1986; JD, New Eng. Sch. Law, 1989. Bar: R.I., 1989; U.S. Dist. Ct. R.I., 1990. Spl. asst. atty. gen. State of R.I., Providence, 1989-90; asst. city solicitor City of Providence, 1990-92; pvt. practice Providence, 1990—; ptnr. Voccola & Landry Law Offices; Bd. dirs. DiMario Motors, Inc., Providence. Vice chmn. Providence Water Supply Bd., 1992—. Mem. ABA, Am. Trial Lawyers Assn., Order Sons of Italy in Am., Nat. Italian Am. Bar Assn., Justinian Law Soc. (bd. dirs. 1994). Roman Catholic. Home: 16 Lladnar Dr Lincoln RI 02865-4013 Office: Voccola & Landry 454 Broadway Ste 201 Providence RI 02909-1650

**LANDRY, MICHAEL W.,** lawyer; b. Lafayette, La., Jan. 23, 1967; s. John Wayne and Eva Jane (Hebert) L.; m. Jeannie Hsuman Cheng, June 5, 1993. BS in Chem. Engring., La. State U., 1989, JD, 1992. Bar: La. 1992, U.S. Dist. Ct. (ea., mid., we. dists.) La., U.S. Ct. Appeals (5th cir.). Assoc. The Onebane Law Firm, Lafayette, 1992-95, Cooper & Woodruff, Abbeville, La., 1995-98, Briney & Foret, Lafayette, La., 1998—. Mem. ABA, La. State Bar Assn., La. Assn. Def. Counsel, Lafayette Parish Bar Assn. Democrat. Roman Catholic. Avocations: cooking, reading, water sports, tennis. General civil litigation, Workers' compensation, Personal injury. Office: Briney & Foret 413 Trauls St Lafayette LA 70505

**LANDRY, WALTER JOSEPH,** lawyer; b. Willswood, La., Jan. 23, 1931; s. John Theodore and Lelia Lucille (Peltier) L.; m. Carolyn Margaret Kruschke, Nov. 24, 1962; children: Celeste, John, Joseph, Catherine, Walter Jr., James. BSME, U. Notre Dame, 1952; JD, Tulane U., 1958; MA, Am. U., 1969, PhD, 1975. Bar: La. 1958, U.S. Supreme Ct. 1961. Legis. asst. to U.S. Sen. Russell B. Long, Washington, 1956-57, pvt. practice law, New Orleans, 1958-61; foreign service officer Dept. State, 1961-70; mem., action officer U.S. del. to San Jose Conf., Am. Conv. on Human Rights, 1969; ptnr. Landry, Poteet and Landry, Lafayette, La., 1974-79, Poteet & Landry, 1979-90; Futures Broker, 1990-99, U.S. Patent Office, 1999—; asst. prof. U. Southwestern La., 1970-74; chmn. U.S. Lang. Policy Conf., Chgo., 1983; pres. Fedn. Am. Cultural and Lang. Communities, Inc., 1984—. Editor: La. Donkey, 1977-79; contbr. articles to profl. jours. Mem. Lafayette Parish Dem. Exec. Com., 1971—, chmn., 1976-83; mem. Dem. State Central Com. La., 1971—, past state co-chmn. affirmative action, 1975-76; counsel Bill of Rights Com. La. Constnl. Conv., 1973-74; del. Dem. Nat. Mid-Term Conf., 1974, 78, alt. del. Dem. Nat. Conv., 1980; organizer La. Assn. Parish Dem. Exec. Coms., 1976-77, pres., 1977-78; chmn. Dem. Caucus, 7th Congl. Dist. La., 1985-87. Maj. USMCR, Korea. Mem. Internat. Rels. Assn. of Acadiana (pres. 1974-75), ABA (chmn. internat. law working group 1971-76), Internat. Good Neighbor Council (organizer, pres. Acadiana chpt. 1978-81), Think Tank for Nat. Self Determination (vol.1994—). Intellectual property, Public international, Patent. Home and Office: 1817 N Quinn St Ste 209 Arlington VA 22209-1308

**LANDSBERG, BRIAN KEITH,** law educator; b. Sacramento, Oct. 27, 1937; s. Morris and Dorothy K. Landsberg; m. Dorothy S. Landsberg, June 11, 1967; children: Elizabeth, Rachel, Joshua. BA, U. Calif., Berkeley, 1959, LLB, 1962; cert. African law, U. London, 1963. Bar: Calif. 1963, U.S. Ct. Appeals (4th cir.) 1969, U.S. Ct. Appeals (9th cir.) 1970, D.C. 1972, U.S. Ct. Appeals (7th and 10th cirs.) 1972, U.S. Ct. Appeals (8th and D.C. cirs.) 1975, U.S. Ct. Appeals (3rd cir.) 1977, U.S. Ct. Appeals (2nd cir.) 1979, U.S. Ct. Appeals (5th cir.) 1980. Atty. U.S. Dept. Justice, Washington, 1964-86, chief edn. sect., civil rights divsn., 1969-74, chief appellate sect., civil rights divsn., 1974-86, acting dep. asst. atty. gen. civil rights divsn., 1993-94; prof. law McGeorge Sch. Law, Sacramento, 1986—; mem. ethics com. D.C. Bar Assn., Washington, 1981-84; dir. Civil Rights Divsn. Assn., Washington, 1992—; vis. prof. law U. Calif., Berkeley, 1995, 97; trustee Lawyers Com. for Civil Rights Under Law, Washington, 1996—. Author: Enforcing Civil Rights, 1997; contbr. articles to profl. jours. Mem. Pub. Access Programming Task Force, Sacramento, 1992; bd. mem. Jewish Cmty. Rels. Coun., Sacramento, 1993—, chair, 1998-99; bd. mem. Aids Housing Alliance, Sacramento, 1993-95; mem. exec. bd. Congregation B'nai Israel, v.p., 1996-98. With USNR, 1954-62. Summer fellow NEH, Washington, 1979. Mem. ABA, Order of Coif. Democrat. Jewish. Office: McGeorge Sch law 3200 5th Ave Sacramento CA 95817-2799

**LANDY, BURTON AARON,** lawyer; b. Chgo., Aug. 16, 1929; s. Louis J. and Clara (Ernstein) L.; m. Eleanor M. Simmel, Aug. 4, 1957; children: Michael Simmel, Alisa Anne. Student, Nat. U. Mex., 1948; B.S., Northwestern U., 1950; postgrad. scholar, U. Havana, 1951; J.D., U. Miami, 1952; postgrad. fellow, Inter-Am. Acad. Comparative Law, Havana, Cuba, 1955-56. Bar: Fla. 1952. Practice law in internat. field Miami, 1955—; ptnr. firm Ammerman & Landy, 1957-63, Paul, Landy, Beiley & Harper, P.A. and predecessor firm, 1964-94, Steel Hector & Davis, 1994-97; ptnr. firm, chmn. Internat. Practice Group Akerman, Senterfitt & Eidson, P.A., 1997—; lectr. Latin Am. bus. law U. Miami Sch. Law, 1972-75; also internat. law confs. in U.S. and abroad; mem. Nat. Conf. on Fgn. Aspects of U.S. Nat. Security, Washington, 1958; mem. organizing com. Miami regional conf. Com. for Internat. Econ. Growth, 1958; mem. U.S. Dept. Commerce Regional Export Expansion Council, 1969-74, mem. Dist. Export Council, 1978—; mem. U.S. Sec. State Adv. Com. on Pvt. Internat. Law; dir. Fla. Council Internat. Devel., 1977—, chmn. 1986-87, 99; mem. U. Miami Citizens Bd., 1977—; chmn. Fla. del. S.E. U.S.-Japan Assn., 1980-82; mem. adv. com. 1st Miami Trade Fair of Ams., 1978; dir., v.p. Greater Miami Fgn. Trade Zone, Inc., 1978—; mem. organizing com., lectr. 4 Inter-Am. Aviation Law Confs.; bd. dirs. Inter-Am. Bar Legal Found.; participant Aquaculture Symposium Sci. and Man in the Ams., Mexico City, Fla. Gov's Econ. Mission to Japan and Hong Kong, 1978; mem. bd. exec. advisors Law and Econs. Ctr.; mem. vis. com., internat. adv. bd. U. Miami Sch. Bus.; mem. internat. fin. council Office Comptroller of Fla.; founding chmn. Fla.-Korea Econ. Coop. Com., 1982—, Southeast U.S.-Korea Econ. Com., 1985—; chmn. Expo 500 Fla.-Columbus Soc., 1985-87; founding co-chmn. So. Fla. Roundtable-Georgetown U. Ctr. for Strategic and Internat. Studies, 1982-85; chmn. Fla. Gov.'s Conf. on World Trade, 1984—; gen. counsel Fla. Internat. Bankers Assn.; dir., former gen. counsel Fla. Internat. Ins. and Reins. Assn., chmn.

Latin Am. Carribbean Bus. Promotion Adv. Counc. to U.S. Sec. of Commerce and Aid Adminstr; appointee Fla. Internat. Trade and Investment Coun.; mem. steering com. Summit of Ams., 1994—, co-chair post summit planning com.; strategic planning com. Mayor Miami Dade County Internat. Trade Commn. Contbg. editor Econs. Devel. Lawyers of the Ams., 1969-74; contbr. numerous articles to legal jours. in U.S. and fgn. countries. Chmn. City of Miami Internat. Trade and Devel. Com., 1984-86; chmn. internat. task force Beacon Coun. of Dade County, Fla., 1985, dir., chmn., 1991—; bd. dirs., exec. com. Internat. Comml. Dispute Resolution Ctr., Miami Internat. Arbitration and Mediation Inst.; chmn. Comml. Dispute Resolution Ctr. for the Ams., Miami, 1995—; apptd. by Gov. of Fla. to Internat. Currency and Barter Commn., 1986; lectr. U. Miami Inter-Ban course for Latin Am. bankers; steering com. Summit of the Americas, Miami, 1994, co-chair post Summit Planning Com., 1994; co-chair mayor Miami-Dade County Strategic Planning for Internat. Trade, 1998—; co-chair strategic planning com. Mayor of Miami Dade County Internat. Trade Commn. With JACGC, USAF, 1952-54, Korea; to maj. Res. Named Internat. Trader of Yr., Fla. Council Internat. Devel., 1980, Bus. Person of Yr., 1986; recipient Pan Am. Informatica Comunicaciones Expo award, 1983, Lawyer of Americas award U. Miami, 1984, Richard L. McLaughlin award Fla. Econ. Devel. Coun., 1993; named hon. consul gen. Republic of Korea, Miami, 1983-88, State of Fla., 99—, recipient Heung-in medal (Order of Diplomatic Service), 1986, Ministerial Citation, Min. of Fgn. Affairs, 1988; apptd. Hon. consul Ft. Lauderdale, Fla., 1991-98; apptd. Hon. consul gen. State of Fla., 1999—. Fellow ABA Found. (chmn. com. arrangements internat. and comparative law sect. 1964-65, com. on Inter-Am. affairs of ABA 1985-87); mem. Inter-Am. Bar Assn. (asst. sec.-gen. 1957-59, treas. 11th conf. 1959, co-chmn. jr. bar sect. 1963-65, mem council 1969—, exec. com. 1975—, pres. 1982-84, Diploma de Honor 1987, William Roy Vallance award 1989), Spanish Am. Bar Assn., Fla. Bar Assn. (vice chmn. adminstrv. law com. 1965, vice chmn. internat. and comparative law com. 1967-68, chmn. aero. law com. 1968-69), Dade County Bar Assn. (chmn. fgn. laws and langs com. 1964-65), Internat. Ctr. Fla. (World Trade Ctr., pres. 1981-82), World Peace Through Law Ctr., Miami Com. Fgn. Relations, Inst. Ibero Am. Derecho Aero., Am. Soc. Internat. Law, Council Internat. Visitors, Am. Fgn. Law Assn. (pres. Miami 1958), Bar of South Korea (hon. mem.), Greater Miami C. of C. (bd. govs. 1986—), Colombian-Am. C. of C. (bd. dirs. 1986—), Peruvian-Am. C. of C. (bd. dirs.), Norwegian Am. C. of C. (bd. dirs.), Phi Alpha Delta. Private international, Banking, General corporate. Home: 605 Almeria Ave Coral Gables FL 33134-5602 Office: One SE Third Ave 28th Flr Miami FL 33131

**LANDY, LISA ANNE,** lawyer; b. Miami, Fla., Apr. 20, 1963; d. Burton Aaron and Eleonora Maria (Simmel) L. BA, Brown U., 1985; JD cum laude, U. Miami, 1988. Bar: Fla. 1988, U.S. Dist. Ct. (so. dist.) Fla. 1988. Atty. Paul, Landy, Beiley & Harper, P.A., Miami, Fla., 1988-94; atty. Steel Hector & Davis, Miami, Fla., 1994-97, ptnr., 1996-97; ptnr. Akerman Senterfitt & Eidson P.A., Miami, 1997—. Bd. dirs. Miami City Ballet, 1992-97, pres., 1996; bd. dirs. Women in Internat. Trade, Miami, 1992—, pres., 1994; bd. dirs. Orgn. Women in Internat. Trade, 1994—, v.p., 1997, 98, pres. 1998—. Mem. ABA, Inter-Am. Bar Assn. (asst. sec. 1997—). Avocations: sports, arts, fluent in Spanish, French. Private international, Trademark and copyright, Contracts commercial.

**LANE, ARTHUR ALAN,** lawyer; b. N.Y.C., Dec. 2, 1945; s. George and Delys L.; m. Jane Ficocella, Dec. 30, 1972; 1 child, Eva B. BA, Yale U., 1967; JD, Columbia U., 1970, MBA, 1971. Bar: N.Y. 1971. Assoc. Webster, Sheffield, Fleischmann, Hitchcock & Brookfield, N.Y.C., 1971-72; asst. to div. counsel Liggett & Myers, Inc., N.Y.C., 1973; assoc. Wickes, Riddell, Bloomer, Jacobi & McGuire, N.Y.C., 1974-78, Morgan, Lewis & Bockius, N.Y.C., 1979; ptnr. Eaton & Van Winkle, N.Y.C., 1980—, DeForest & Duer, N.Y.C., 1994—; counsel Lamb & Barnosky, Melville, 1999—. Mem. ABA, Assn. of Bar of City of N.Y. Avocation: gardening. Banking, General corporate, General practice. Home: 103 Brooksite Dr Smithtown NY 11787-4456 Office: DeForest & Duer 90 Broad St Fl 18 New York NY 10004-2276

**LANE, BRUCE STUART,** lawyer; b. New London, Conn., May 15, 1932; s. Stanley S. and Frances M. (Antis) L.; m. Ann Elizabeth Steinberg, Aug. 10, 1958; children: Sue Ellen, Charles M., Richard I. Student, Boston U., 1948-49; AB magna cum laude, Harvard U., 1952, JD, 1955. Bar: Ohio 1955, D.C. 1966, U.S. Ct. Claims 1960, U.S. Tax Ct. 1961, U.S. Supreme Ct. 1961. Assoc. Squire, Sanders & Dempsey, Cleve., 1955-59; sr. trial atty. tax div. Dept. Justice, Washington, 1959-61; tax atty. Dinsmore, Shohl, Barrett, Coates & Deupree, Cin., 1961-65; sec., asst. gen. counsel corp. and tax matters Communications Satellite Corp., Washington, 1965-69; v.p., gen. counsel Nat. Corp. Housing Partnerships, Washington, 1969-70; pres. Lane and Edson P.C., Washington, 1970-89; ptnr. Kelley Drye & Warren, Washington, 1989-93, Peabody & Brown, Washington, 1993-99, Nixon Peabody LLP, Washington, 1999—. Co-editor-in-chief Housing and Devel. Reporter; author publs. and articles on tax, partnership and real estate. Incorporator, bd. dirs., past pres. D.C. Inst. Mental Health; past chmn. citizens Com. sect. 5 Chevy Chase, Md.; past mem. Montgomery County Hist. Preservation Commn., Md.; mem. chmn. coun. Crow Canyon Archeol. Ctr., Cortez, Colo. Maj. JAG, USAR, 1952-68. Mem. ABA, Am. Law Inst., Am. Coll. Real Estate Lawyers (pres. 1986-87), Anglo-Am. Real Property Inst., Phi Beta Kappa. Corporate taxation, Real property, Alternative dispute resolution. Home: 3711 Thornapple St Chevy Chase MD 20815-4111 Office: Nixon Peabody LLP 1255 23rd St NW Ste 800 Washington DC 20037-1125

**LANE, CHARLOTTE,** lawyer; b. 1948. AB, Marshall U.; JD, W.Va. U. Bar: W.Va. 1972. Chmn. W.Va. Pub. Svc. Commn. Mem. W.Va. Bar Assn. (pres.-elect). Public utilities, Government contracts and claims. Office: PO Box 812 Charleston WV 25323-0812*

**LANE, DOMINICK V.,** lawyer; b. South Amboy, N.J., Mar. 18, 1961; s. Lister Ray and Marie L. AA in Criminal Justice, San Diego Miramar Coll., 1982; BA in Polit. Sci., U. San Diego, 1985; JD, Calif. Western U., 1988. Bar: Calif. 1989, U.S. Dist. Ct. (so. dist.) Calif. 1989, U.S. Dist. Ct. (ctrl. and no. dists.) Calif. 1990, U.S. Dist. Ct. Ariz. 1996. Assoc. Rutledge, Hathaway, Harris & Newman, L.A., 1990-94; trial atty. Farmers Ins. Co., Aiken, D'Angelo, & Banner, San Diego, 1994-97; trial atty. Richardson, Bambrick, Cermak & Fair, San Diego, 1997-98; supervising atty. Richardson, Bambrick, Cermak & Fair, Costa Mesa, Calif., 1998—; arbitrator San Diego Superior Ct., 1995—. Bd. dirs. Crime Victims Fund, San Diego, 1997; vol. L.A. Mission, 1993-94. Mem. San Diego County Bar Assn. Avocations: music, tennis, golf, travel. Fax: 714-424-0861. Entertainment, Insurance, Trademark and copyright. Office: Richardson Bambrick Cermak & Fair PO Box 25191 Santa Ana CA 92799-5191

**LANE, FRANK JOSEPH, JR.,** lawyer; b. St. Louis, May 10, 1934; s. Frank Joseph and Virginia Laurette (Hausman) L.; m. Margaret Ann Dwyer, Mar. 2, 1957; children: Mary, Stephen, Thomas, Michael. BS in Commerce, St. Louis U., 1956, JD, 1956; LLM, Georgetown U., 1960; grad. Parker Sch. Internat. Law, Columbia U., 1970, cert., Coll. Fin. Planning, Denver, 1988. Bar: Mo. 1956, U.S. Dist. Ct. (ea. dist.) Mo. 1956, U.S. Ct. Appeals (8th cir.) 1960, U.S. Supreme Ct. 1959, U.S. Ct. Mil. Appeals, 1957. Ptnr. Goldenhersh, Goldenhersh, Fredericks, Newman & Lane, St. Louis, 1960-64, Lane & Leadlove, St. Louis, 1964-66, Dill & Lane, St. Louis, 1978-79; counsel Ralston Purina Co., St. Louis, 1966-78; mem. pres.'s adv. bd., 1967-69; of counsel Petrolite Corp., St. Louis, 1979-83; v.p., trust officer Gravois Bank, St. Louis, 1983-85; regional v.p., trust officer Merc Bank N.A., St. Louis, 1985-89; of counsel Dill, Wamser, Bamvakais & Newsham PC, St. Louis, 1989—; instr. internat. law St. Louis U., 1979. Bd. dirs. Met. St. Louis Sewer Dist., 1965-73, chmn., 1968-69; mem. St. Louis Regional Commerce & Growth Assn. environ. com., 1978-82; mem. planned giving com. Am. Heart Assn., St. Louis, 1986-88, St. Louis Soc. for Crippled Children, 1991; bd. dirs. Midwestern Braille Vols., Inc., chmn., 1995—; atty. St. Louis Geneal. Soc., 1996—; pres. Ozark Cmties. Coun. St. Louis County, 1964-65. Capt. U.S. Army JAGC, Pentagon, 1957-60. Mem. Mo. Bar Assn., Met. St. Louis Bar Assn. (chmn. rels. with law schs. com. 1961-62, enrollment com. 1962-63, chmn. office practice com. 1963-64, elected admissions com. 1967), Estate Planning Coun. St. Louis, Rotary (bd. dirs. Crestwood, Mo. chpt. 1988-89), KC (grand knight 1964-66, adv. West County 1983-90, Webster Groves 1991—). Republican. Roman Catholic. Avocations: oil painting, golf, travel, investment analysis. Estate planning, Estate taxation, Probate. Home: 520 Lering Dr Ballwin MO 63011-1588 Office: 9939 Gravois Rd Saint Louis MO 63123-4211

**LANE, GARY M.,** lawyer; b. Fairfield, Iowa, Oct. 12, 1944; m. Gerda C. Lane; children: Matthew P., Stephen W. BA, U. Iowa, 1967, JD with distinction, 1969. Bar: Iowa 1969, U.S. Dist. Ct. (so. dist.) Iowa 1969, U.S. Dist. Ct. (no. dist.) Iowa 1977. Asst. county atty. Scott County, Davenport, Iowa, 1969-78; ptnr. Wehr, Berger, Lane & Stevens and predecessors, Davenport, Iowa, 1969—; bd. dirs., past pres. HELP, Legal Svcs. Corp., Davenport, Iowa, 1972—; founding dir., past pres. Legal Svcs. Corp. Iowa, Des Moines, 1977-93. Pres. Davenport Diocesan Lay Coun., Iowa, 1980-82; trustee Quad City Symphony Orch., Davenport, 1980-89; pres. Marriage and Family Counseling Svc., Davenport, 1985-87; chmn. Davenport Neighborhood Task Force, 1991; pres. bd. Assumption H.S., 1994-96. Fellow Iowa Acad. Trial Lawyers; mem. ATLA (Disting. Mem. award 1989), Iowa Trial Lawyers Assn. (bd. govs. 1980-88, Outstanding Key Mem. 1988), Iowa Bar Assn., Scott County Bar Assn. General civil litigation, Personal injury, Alternative dispute resolution. Office: Wehr Berger Lane & Stevens Ste 900 Kahl Bldg 326 W 3d St Davenport IA 52801

**LANE, TOM CORNELIUS,** lawyer; b. Borger, Tex., Dec. 8, 1948; s. Aubrey G. and Barbara Ellen (Cook) L.; m. Nanette Marie Betts, Jan. 25, 1969; children: Trevor C., Tom Cornelius Jr. BBA in Mktg., Tex. A&M U., 1971; JD, U. Tulsa, 1988. Bar: Okla. 1988, U.S. Dist. Ct. (no. dist.) Okla. 1988, U.S. Dist. Ct. (ea. dist.) Okla. 1995, U.S. Supreme Ct. 1996, U.S. Ct. Mil. Appeals, 1989. Sales mgr. Sears, North Platte, Nebr., 1972-76, Motorola C&E, Laredo, Tex., 1976-79; gen. mgr. Autophone of Laredo, Inc., 1979-81; owner Laredo Comms., Inc., 1981-85; from clk. to atty. W.C. "Bill" Sellers, Inc., Sapulpa, Okla., 1987-95; prin. Tom C. Lane, Sr. & Assocs., Sapulpa, 1995—; atty. Ea. Okla. Legal Aid, Tulsa, 1990—. City commr. City Counsel, Sapulpa, 1992; fin. chmn. Boy Scouts Am., Sapulpa, 1993. With USN, 1985-92. Recipient Silver Key award ABA, Tulsa, 1988, Appreciation award Fraternal Order of Police, Sapulpa, 1992. Mem. Am. Trial Lawyers Assn. (membership com. 1993-94), Okla. Trial Lawyers Assn. (membership com.), ABA, 1995, Lions Club Internat., Masons. Democrat. Baptist. Avocations: working with youth groups, hunting, fishing, working with wood. General civil litigation, Labor, Personal injury. Office: Tom C Lane Sr & Assocs PO Box 384 Sapulpa OK 74067-0384

**LANE, WILLIAM ARTHUR,** lawyer; b. Nashville, Sept. 16, 1958; s. Thomas Jennings Lane and Nancy Eleanor (Shirley) Boyd; m. Brenda Diane Kinamon, Dec. 5, 1981; children: Charles Thomas, John Ross. BS, Mid. Tenn. State U., 1980; JD, Nashville U., 1984. Bar: Tenn. 1986, U.S. Dist. Ct. (mid. dist.) Tenn. 1986, U.S. Ct. Appeals (6th cir.) 1986, U.S. Supreme Ct. 1990. Pvt. practice law Smyrna, Tenn., 1987-94, Murfreesboro, Tenn., 1994—; atty. Travelers Ins. Co., Nashville, 1990-91, U.S.F.&G Ins. Co., Nashville, 1991-92, Willis-Corroon Adminstrv. Svcs. Corp., 1992-94. Mem. Tenn. Bar Assn., Nashville Bar Assn., Assn. Trial Lawyers Am., Masons, Shriners, Sigma Delta Kappa. Baptist. Avocations: golf, hunting, shooting. Family and matrimonial, Criminal, Personal injury. Office: Stahlman Bldg 211 Union St Ste 902 Nashville TN 37201-1579

**LANEY, JOHN THOMAS, III,** federal judge; b. Columbus, Ga., Mar. 27, 1942; s. John Thomas Jr. and Leila (Davis) L.; m. Louise Pierce, Nov. 23, 1974; children: Thomas Whitfield, Elizabeth Davis. AB, Mercer U., 1964, JD magna cum laude, 1966. Bar: Ga. 1965, U.S. Dist. Ct. (mid. dist.) Ga. 1966, U.S. Ct. Appeals (5th cir.) 1966, U.S. Ct. Mil. Appeals 1967, U.S. Ct. Appeals (11th cir.) 1981. Assoc. Swift, Pease, Davidson & Chapman, Columbus, 1970-73; ptnr. Page, Scrantom, Harris & Chapman, Columbus, 1973-86; judge mid. dist. Ga. U.S. Bankruptcy Ct., Columbus, 1986—. Co-editor-in-chief Mercer Law Rev., 1965-66; contbr. articles to profl. jours. Former pres., dir. Metro. Boys Club of Columbus. Capt. U.S. Army, 1966-70. Mem. ABA (judge adminstrv. divsn. Nat. Conf. Fed. Trial Judges), State Bar Ga. (chmn. gen. practice and trial sect. 1983-84, chmn. state disciplinary bd. 1984-85), Am. Judicature Soc., Nat. Conf. Bankruptcy Judges, Columbus Bar Assn., Inc. (pres. 1985-86), Rotary. Presbyterian. Office: US Bankruptcy Ct 1 Arsenal Pl 901 Front Ave Ste 309 Columbus GA 31901-2797

**LANFORD, NORMAN EUGENE,** judge; b. Houston, Feb. 10, 1948; s. Charles Edward and Juanita (O'Farrell) L.; m. Diane Woods, Sept. 1977 (div. 1978). BA cum laude, Rice U., 1969; JD, U. Chgo., 1972; postgrad. in jud. studies, U. Nev., 1986—. Bar: Tex. 1972, U.S. Dist. Ct. (so. dist.) Tex. 1973, U.S. Ct. Mil. Appeals 1973, U.S. Ct. Appeals (5th cir.) 1973, U.S. Supreme Ct. 1976; cert. in criminal law Tex. bd. Legal Specialization. Assoc. Baker & Heard, Houston, 1972-74; sole practice Houston, 1974-84; judge 339th Dist. Ct. Harris County, Houston, 1985—. Mem. ABA, State Bar Tex., Houston Bar Assn. Republican. Methodist. Home: 10399 Fm 2325 Wimberley TX 78676-4112 Office: 339th Dist Ct 301 San Jacinto St Houston TX 77002-2022

**LANG, GEORGE EDWARD,** lawyer; b. Peekskill, N.Y., Apr. 7, 1932; s. George Louis and Florence (Sheehan) L.; m. Rose Marie Corrao, June 8, 1953; children: G. Vincent Lang, Kathleen M. Lang. AB, U. Notre Dame, 1954, JD, 1955. Bar: Ky. 1955, U.S. Dist. Ct. Ky. 1956. City atty. Munfordville, Ky., 1958-85, Bonnieville, Ky., 1958-85; atty. Hart County, Munfordville, 1962-70; hearing officer Ky. Workmen's Compensation Bd., Munfordville, 1971-79; master commr. Hart Cir. Ct., Munfordville, 1984—; pres. South Ctr. Ky. Broadcasting Co., Munfordville, 1984-88; v.p. Cub Run (Ky.) Industries, 1986-90. Pres. Munfordville Indsl. Found., 1968-90; bd. dirs. Mammoth Cave (Ky.) Devel. Assn., 1972—; chmn. Hart County Dem. Party, Munfordville, 1972-78. Mem. Ctrl. Ky. Wildlife Fedn. (pres. 1962-64), Munfordville Lions Club (pres. 1966-68), Horse Cave Rotary Club (v.p. 1968-69). Roman Catholic. Office: PO Box 366 Munfordville KY 42765-0366

**LANG, GORDON, JR.,** retired lawyer; b. Evanston, Ill., July 27, 1933; s. Gordon and Harriet Kendig Lang; m. Clara Bates Van Derzee, Sept. 26, 1970; children: Elizabeth K., Gordon III, Harriet B. BA, Yale U., 1954; MA in History, U. Ariz., 1958; LLB, Harvard U., 1960. Bar: Ill. 1960. Assoc. Gardner, Carton & Douglas, Chgo., 1960-67, ptnr., 1967-98, ret., 1998; cons., 1999—. Dir. North Side Boys' Clubs, Chgo., 1961-67, Yale Scholarship Trust Ill., 1966-69, pres., 1967; mem. Assocs. Rush-Presbyn.-St. Luke's Med. Ctr., Chgo., 1962—, Assocs. Northwestern U., Evanston, 1970—; dir. Chgo. Youth Ctrs., 1967—, pres., 1982-84; trustee Chgo. Latin Sch. Found., 1978—, pres., 1995—; trustee Groton (Mass.) Sch., 1982-93; dir. United Way of Chgo., 1984-90, United Way/Crusade of Mercy (Met. Chgo.), 1989-95. 1st lt. USAF, 1955-57. Mem. ABA (sect. bus. law), Ill. State Bar Assn., Chgo. Bar Assn. (mem. corp. law com. 1975-98, mem. fin. instns. com. 1985-98), Chgo. Club (former dir. and sec.), Econ. Club Chgo. (former dir. and sec.), Onwentsia Club, Racquet Club Chgo., Chgo. Commonwealth Club, Yale Club Chgo. (former dir., past pres.). Republican. Episcopalian. Avocations: golf, skiing, hiking. General corporate, Securities, Finance. Home: 1520 N Astor St Chicago IL 60610-1610 Office: Gardner Carton & Douglas 321 N Clark St Ste 3400 Chicago IL 60610-4717

**LANG, JOHN ERNEST,** lawyer; b. Arkansas City, Kans., Dec. 27, 1936; s. Ernest R. and Ruth (Evans) L.; m. Joleen C. Jilka, Nov. 22, 1959; children: Jill Kay Lang Gobble, Jeffrey R. BS, U. Kans., 1958; JD, Washburn U., 1962. Bar: Kans. 1962, U.S. Dist. Ct. Kans. 1962, U.S. Ct. Appeals (10th cir.) 1969. Mcpl. judge City of Wamego, Kans., 1967-78; county atty. Pottawatomie County, Kans., 1967-70, county counselor, 1977—; sole practitioner Wamego, 1961—; bd. dirs. First Nat. Bank, Wamego. Trustee The Stormont Found., Topeka, 1989-95; trustee Wamego City Hosp., 1969-89, chmn. bd. trustees, 1988-89; chair Gov.'s Com. on Instnl. Mgmt. and Comty. Mental Health, Topeka, 1974-80; mem. Gov.'s Adv. Com. on Criminal Adminstrn., Topeka, 1970-72. With USAR, 1956-62. Mem. Kans. Bar Assn., Pottawatomie County Bar Assn. Democrat. Methodist. Avocation: golf. Office: PO Box 2 Wamego KS 66547-0002

**LANG, JULES,** lawyer; b. Basel, Switzerland, Aug. 30, 1938; came to U.S., 1941; s. Simon and Regina (Fisch) L.; m. Barbara Diane Gottheil, Aug. 28, 1960; 1 child, Erik. BA, U. Conn., 1960; JD with distinction, U. Mich., 1963; LLM, NYU, 1968. Bar: Conn. 1963, U.S. Dist. Ct. Conn. 1964, U.S. Tax Ct. 1964, U.S. Ct. Appeals (2d cir.) 1967, U.S. Supreme Ct. 1969. Ptnr. Lepofsky, Lepofsky & Lang, Norwalk, Conn., 1963—; state trial referee, 1985—, special master, U.S. Dist. Ct. Conn., 1988—. Mem. Norwalk Bd. Edn., 1969-75, chmn. 1973, Norwalk Bd. Estimate and Taxation, 1977-83, chmn. 1979; trustee Conn. Comty.-Tech. Colls., 1977—; pres. Goodman Found., Norwalk, 1988—. Mem. Am. Judicature Soc., Assn. Trial Lawyers Am., Greater Norwalk Community Council. Democrat. Jewish. General practice, Real property, General civil litigation. Office: Lepofsky Lepofsky and Lang 7-9 Isaac St Norwalk CT 06850-4102

**LANG, SUSAN GAIL,** lawyer; b. New Orleans, Nov. 18, 1954; d. Laurence Young and Gail (Groetsch) Compagno. BA cum laude, U. Southwestern La., 1975; JD cum laude, Loyola U. Sch. Law, 1986. Bar: La. 1986, U.S. Dist. Ct. (ea. dist.) La. 1986, U.S. Dist. Ct. (mid. dist.) La. 1993. Assoc. Barham & Churchill, New Orleans, 1986-88, Naquin & Ourso, New Orleans, 1988-91, Barham & Assocs., New Orleans, 1991-92; in-house counsel Agy. Rent-A-Car, Inc., New Orleans, 1992-93; sole practice New Orleans, 1993—. Mem. ABA, Assn. Women Attys., La. State Bar Assn., New Orleans Bar Assn. General civil litigation, Insurance, Personal injury. Office: 530 Natchez St Ste 250 New Orleans LA 70130-2790

**LANG, THOMAS FREDERICK,** lawyer; b. Elyria, Ohio, Jan. 12, 1944; s. Carl Frederick and Martha (Hagedorn) L.; m. Marilyn March, June 1, 1968; children: Thomas F. Jr., Sarah, Anne. BS, U. Pa., 1966, MBA, 1968; JD, Fla. State U., 1974. Bar: Fla., U.S. Dist. Ct. (mid. dist.) Fla., U.S. Ct. Appeals (5th and 11th cir.), U.S. Supreme Ct. Assoc. Maguire, Voorhis & Wells, Orlando, Fla., 1975-77; ptnr. Jones & Bishop, Orlando, 1978-79, Swann & Haddock, Orlando, 1979-88, Bryant, Miller, Olive, Lang & Krupenbacher, Orlando, 1988, Parker, Johnson, Owen, Lang & Kruppenbacher, Orlando, 1989, Honigman Miller Schwartz & Cohn, Orlando, 1990-94, Allen, Lang, Morrison & Carotto, P.A., 1994—; instr. U. Cen. Fla.-Allied Legal Svcs., 1978; gen. counsel Orlando Lions Profl. Soccer, 1988—; mediator Mcpl. Securities Rules Bd.; commr. Fla. Pub. Rels. Commn., 1977-79. Pres. U. Ctrl. Fla. Boosters, 1989-90; chmn. Orange County Civic Facilities Authority, 1990-98; mem. secondary sch. com. U. Pa.; sr. warden Cathedral Ch. St. Luke, 1982-83, 92, 93, 94; bd. dirs. Red Cross Ctrl. Fla.; chmn. Weekends of Greater Orlando, Ct. of Array, Diocese of Ctrl. Fla.; del. 72nd Gen. Conv. Episcopal Ch. U.S.; trustee U. Pa. Officer USN, 1968-72. Mem. Nat. Assn. Bond Lawyers, Greater Orlando C. of C. (dir.), Fla. Citrus Sports Assn., Downtown Orlando Athletic Club, Orlando Touchdown Club. Episcopalian. Avocations: reading, sports, travel, photography. Municipal (including bonds), Sports, Entertainment. Office: Allen Lang Morrison & Curotto PA 105 E Robinson St Ste 201 Orlando FL 32801-1622

**LANGBERG, BARRY BENSON,** lawyer; b. Balt., Nov. 24, 1942; s. Nathan and Marion (Cohen) L.; m. Vickie Williams, Mar. 27, 1978 (div. 1987); children: Mitchell, Marie, Elena. BA, U. San Francisco, 1964, JD, 1968. Bar: Calif. 1971, U.S. Dist. Ct. (cen. dist.) Calif. 1971, U.S. Supreme Ct. 1974, U.S. Tax Ct. 1976. Dep. pub. defender Los Angeles County, 1971-72; assoc. Trope & Trope, L.A., 1972-74, Hayes & Hume, Beverly Hills, Calif., 1974-85; pres. David Jamison Carlyle Corp., L.A., 1979-84; ptnr. Hayes, Hume, Petas & Langberg, L.A., 1985-89; atty. Barry B. Langberg & Assocs., L.A., 1989-97; ptnr. Bronson, Bronson & McKinnon, L.A., 1997—; prof. Mid-Valley Coll. Law, L.A., 1972-82; lectr. U. So. Calif., 1980. Mem. ABA. Democrat. Avocations: sailing, baseball. General civil litigation, Entertainment, Libel. Office: Bronson Bronson & McKinnon 3415 S Sepulveda Blvd Ste 1200 Los Angeles CA 90034-6014

**LANGE, C. WILLIAM,** lawyer; b. St. Louis, June 15, 1946; s. Carl W. and Marion M. (Guenther) L.; m. Catherine L. Janowiak, June 7, 1981; children: Courtney Anne, Carl William IV. BA, Westminster Coll., 1968; MBA, St. Louis U., 1972; JD, Oklahoma City U., 1974. Bar: Mo. 1975, U.S. Dist. Ct. Mo. 1975, U.S. Ct. Appeals (8th cir.) 1986. With claims dept. MFA Ins. Cos., Columbia, Mo., 1968-71; ptnr. Lange & Lange, Cuba, Mo., 1976-81; pvt. practice Cuba, 1981-88; ptnr. Lange & Lange, Cuba, 1989—; pros. atty. Crawford County (Mo.), 1979-80; city atty. City of Cuba, 1978-80, 82-88; prof. mgmt. Maryville U., St. Louis, 1974—; instr. East Central Coll., Union, Mo., 1975. Mem. Crawford County Child Welfare Adv. Com., 1979-88, pres. 1984-86; mem. Crawford County Child Abuse and Neglect Team, 1981-90; treas. Sixteenth Senatorial Dist. Rep. Com., 1993-94. Served with Air N.G., 1967-74. Mem. ABA, Mo. Bar Assn., 42d Jud. Cir. Bar Assn., St. Louis Met. Bar Assn., Cuba C. of C. Presbyterian. Lodges: Optimists. General practice, Family and matrimonial, General corporate. Home: PO Box 88 Cuba MO 65453-0088 Office: Lange and Lange Attys PO Box 280 Cuba MO 65453-0280

**LANGE, GEORGE WILLARD, JR.,** lawyer, trust banker; b. West Bend, Wis., Dec. 29, 1949; s. George W. and Ruth I. (Stobbe) L.; m. Joan Elizabeth Koeln, June 26, 1971; children: Matthew Ryan, Aaron Michael. BA, Southeast Mo. State U., 1972; JD, St. Louis U., 1977; postgrad., Southwestern Sch. Banking, 1981. Bar: Mo. 1977; cert. trust and fin. advisor; accredited estate planner. Assoc. Law Office Thomas Green, St. Louis, 1977-79; trust officer Merc. Bank, N.A., St. Louis, 1979-84; sr. v.p., trust officer Mark Twain Bank, St. Louis, 1984-87; v.p., sr. trust officer Am. Pioneer Savs. Bank, Orlando, Fla., 1987-90; sr. v.p., trust officer, mgr. Bancorp Trust Co. N.A., Naples, Fla., 1990-94; pres., COO, dir. Marshall & Ilsley Trust Co. Fla., Naples, 1994-97; mng. dir. State St. Global Advisors, N.A., Naples, Fla., 1997—; mem. adv. dir. S.W. Fla. Bus. Hall of Fame. Bd. dirs. Mental Health Assn. of Collier County, 1990-95, treas., 1992, v.p., 1993, prs., 1994; bd. dirs. Mental Health Assn. St. Louis, 1980-82, treas., 1981; bd. dirs. Mental Health Assn. Mo., 1981-82, United Arts Coun. Collier County, 1991—, v.p., 1991-92, pres., 1992-95; mem. Friends of Eldison Collier Men, chair, 1996; trustee Bonita Springs Firefighter's Retirement Fund. Lt. col. N.G., 1971-94. Mem. ABA (com. adminstrn. and distbn. of trusts, chmn. com. fiduciary issues of holding closely held bus. in trust), Mo. Bar Assn., Soc. Am. Mil. Engrs., Res. Officers Assn., Corp. Fiduciaries Assn. S.W. Fla., Rotary (Paul Harris fellow), Estate Planning of Naples, Collier Athletic Club, Naples Area C. of C. (pres. club, chair edn. com. 1991-93), Leadership Collier, Leadership S.W. Fla., Leadership Lee County), Fla. Bankers Assn. (trust divsn., vice chmn. legis. com. 1994-95, chair 1995-97, pres. 1998-99, exec. com., mem. state govtl. rels. com.), S.W. Fla. C. of C. (trustee rep. 1992—), Fla. C. of C. (Leadership Fla.), Atty. for Closing-Held Enterprises, DeBough Soc. St. Louis U. (hon. v.p.), Fla. Bank Pac (bd. dirs.), Leadership Fla., Phi Alpha Delta, Sigma Tau Gamma. Home: 3770 Catbrier Ct Bonita Springs FL 34134-7929 Office: State St Global Advisors 4851 Tamiami Trl N Ste 401 Naples FL 34103-3024

**LANGE, JOSEPH JUDE MORGAN,** lawyer; b. San Diego, June 30, 1961; s. Roy Oliver and Edith Ann Lange; m. France-Helen Marina Russman, Mar. 31, 1995; 1 child, Michaela Jeannette. BA in econs. cum laude, UCLA, 1983; JD, Loyola U., 1986. Bar: Calif. 1986, U.S. Dist. Ct. (ctrl. and so. dists.) Calif., U.S. Ct. Claims. Jud. extern Appellate divsn. L.A. Superior Ct., 1984; extern U.S. Dept. Justice, L.A., 1984; law clk. Lewis, D'Amato Brisbois & Bisgara, L.A., 1985-87, assoc., 1987-88; assoc. Lebovits & David, L.A., 1988-91, ptnr., 1991-93; pvt. practice L.A., 1993—. Mem. ATLA, L.A. County Bar Assn. (fee arbitrator 1997-99), Consumer Attys. Calif., Consumer Attys. L.A., Assn. Bus. Trial Lawyers, Lawyers Against Hunger. Avocations: karate (Black Belt), inline skating, underwater photography, skiing. General civil litigation, Professional liability, Personal injury. Office: 1880 Century Park E Ste 900 Los Angeles CA 90067-1698

**LANGE, WILLIAM MICHAEL,** lawyer; b. Hammond, Ind., Oct. 9, 1946; s. William Frederick L.; m. Nancy A. White; 1 child, William Robert. BA, Ind. U., 1968; JD, George Washington U., 1974. Bar: D.C. 1975, Colo. 1977, U.S. Ct. Appeals (D.C. cir.) 1975, U.S. Ct. Appeals (10th cir.) 1977, U.S. Ct. Appeals (5th cir.) 1981, U.S. Ct. Appeals (8th cir.) 1984, U.S. Supreme Ct. 1982, U.S. Ct. Appeals (3d cir.) 1988, U.S. Ct. Appeals (7th cir.) 1989, U.S. Ct. Appeals (6th cir.) 1989, U.S. Ct. Appeals (2d cir.) 1997. Assoc., Wolf & Case, Washington, 1974-75, J.R. Wolf, Washington, 1975-76; atty. Colo. Interstate Gas Co., Colorado Springs, Colo., 1976-79, sr. atty., 1979-82, gen. atty., 1982-84, asst. gen. counsel, 1984-87; asst. gen. counsel The Coastal Corp., 1985-87; assoc. gen. counsel ANR Pipeline Co, 1986-87; pvt. practice, Washington, 1987; asst. gen. counsel Consumers Energy Co.; gen. counsel Mich. Gas Storage Co., 1987—. Lt. (j.g.) USN, 1968-71; Vietnam. Democrat. Episcopalian. FERC practice, Federal civil litigation, General corporate. Office: 1016 16th St NW Washington DC 20036-5703

**LANGENBAHN, JAY RICHARD,** lawyer; b. Covington, Ky., Apr. 25, 1950; s. John William and Ruth Marion (Grefer) L.; m. Sally Ann Strother, Aug. 17, 1973; children—Jeffrey R., Alison Taaffe. B.S. in Acctg., U. Ky., 1972; J.D., Samuel P. Chase Coll. Law, Covington, Ky., 1976. Bar: Ohio

1976, Ky. 1983. Assoc. McIntosh, McIntosh & Knabe, Cin., 1977-78, Lindhorst & Dreidame, Cin., 1978—. Mem. Cin. Bar Assn., Ohio Bar Assn., Ky. Bar Assn., ABA. Home: 622 Watchcove Ct Cincinnati OH 45230-3777 Office: 312 Walnut St Ste 2300 Cincinnati OH 45202-4030

**LANGENHEIM, ROGER ALLEN,** lawyer; b. Seward, Nebr., Feb. 21, 1935; s. Elmer L. and Esther L. (Gerkensmeyer) L.; BS, U. Nebr., 1957, LLB, 1960; m. Susan C. McMichael, Aug. 31, 1963; children: Ann Elizabeth, Mark Allen, Sara Ann. Admitted to Nebr. bar, 1960, Mo. bar, 1960; asso. firm Stinson, Mag, Thomson, McEvers & Fizzell, Kansas City, Mo., 1960-66; v.p., gen. counsel Black, Sivalls & Bryson, Inc., Kansas City, Mo., 1966-70; internat. atty. Dresser Industries, Inc., Dallas, 1970-71; group counsel Petroleum & Mineral Group, Houston, 1971-75; v.p., gen. counsel Oilfield Products Group, Houston, 1975-80; v.p., gen. counsel Magcobar Group, Houston, 1980-85; assoc. gen. counsel Dresser Industries Inc., Houston, 1985-87, sr. assoc. gen. counsel, 1987-94, staff v.p., assoc. gen. counsel, 1994-98. Mem. ABA, Nebr. Bar Assn., Mo. Bar Assn., Order of Coif. Republican. Roman Catholic. Editor U. Neb. Law Rev., 1958-59. General civil litigation, Contracts commercial, Private international. Home: 6172 Haley Ln Fort Worth TX 76132-3875

**LANGER, BRUCE ALDEN,** lawyer; b. N.Y.C., Mar. 17, 1953; s. Samuel S. and Yvette Langer. BA summa cum laude with distinction, Boston U., 1975; JD cum laude, Boston U. Sch. Law, 1978. Bar: N.Y. 1979, U.S. Dist. Ct. (so. and ea. dist.) N.Y. 1979, U.S. Tax Ct. 1979, U.S. Ct. Appeals (2d cir.) 1983., U.S. Supreme Ct. 1985. Law clk. to presiding chief justice U.S. Bankruptcy Ct. (ea. dist.) N.Y., summers 1976-77; with Breed Abbott & Morgan, N.Y.C., 1978-81, White & Case, N.Y.C., 1981-84, Fishman Forman & Landau, N.Y.C., 1984-85, Fishman Forman and Langer, 1985-86, Paradise & Alberts, N.Y.C., 1986-89; pvt. practice, N.Y.C., 1989—. Editor Boston U. Law Rev., 1977-78. Contbg. author: Pensions and Investments, 1979; contbr. articles to profl. jours. Harold C. Case Presdl. scholar, 1974-75. Mem. Phi Beta Kappa, Phi Alpha Theta. Federal civil litigation, State civil litigation, Bankruptcy. Office: 1500 Broadway New York NY 10036-4015

**LANGER, CARLTON EARL,** lawyer; b. Cleve., Nov. 4, 1954; s. Warren Dexter and Florence (Thompson) L.; m. Rita Lennox, Apr. 30, 1983; children: Christopher Colin, Deanna Faith. BA, Albion Coll., 1976; JD, Cleve. State U., 1979; MBA, Case Western Res. U., 1980. Bar: Ohio 1979, Fla. 1980, U.S. Dist. Ct. (no. dist.) Ohio 1979. Assoc. Vanik, Monroe, Zucco, Donahue & Scanlon, Cleve., 1979-80; atty. Nat. City Bank (subs. of Nat. City Corp.), Cleve., 1980-83; chief counsel, v.p. and sec. Ohio Citizens Bank (subs. Nat. City Corp.), Toledo, 1983-87; v.p., sr. atty., asst. sec. Nat. City Corp., Cleve., 1987-94, sr. v.p., chief counsel, 1994—. Trustee, asst. sec. Goodwill Industries of Greater Cleve., Inc., 1988—; trustee, sec. Goodwill Industries of Greater Cleve. Found., Inc., 1991—; chmn. Ledgewood Christian Ch. Mem. ABA, Ohio Bar Assn., Fla. Bar Assn., Cleve. Bar Assn., Am. Soc. Corp. Secs. (treas. Ohio regional group 1999—). Avocations: woodworking. Securities, General corporate, Mergers and acquisitions. Home: 9000 Kinsman Rd Novelty OH 44072-9638 Office: Nat City Bank 1900 E 9th St Cleveland OH 44114-3484

**LANGER, SHARON LYNNE,** lawyer; b. Miami, Fla., Feb. 16, 1947; d. Ralph and Edith Grossman; children: Lester Langer, June 16, 1968; children: Deborah Deitz, Stephanie, Jon. B of Edn., U. Miami, 1969, JD, 1979. Bar: Fla. 1983, U.S. Dist. Ct. (so. dist.) Fla. 1983. Atty. Dillon & Langer, Miami, Fla., 1979-84, pvt. practice, Miami, Fla., 1984-86; dir. Dade County Legal Aid, Miami, Fla., 1986—. Chair Coral Gables (Fla.) Hist. Preservation Bd., 1993—; vice chair Met. Dade Domestic Violence Oversight Bd., Miami, 1994—. Fellow Family Law Inns of Ct.; mem. Fla. Bar Assn. (bd. govs. 1998—), Fla. Assn. Women Lawyers, Dade County Bar Assn. Office: Legal Aid 123 NW 1st Ave Ste 117 Miami FL 33128-1897

**LANGFORD, JAMES JERRY,** lawyer; b. Birmingham, Ala., May 19, 1933; S. N.B. and Margaret Elizabeth (Fuller) L.; m. Mary Elizabeth Fryant, Mar. 21, 1958; children: Jan Carol Langford Hammett, Joel Fryant L. BS, U. So. Miss., 1955; JD, U. Miss., 1970. Bar: Miss. 1970, U.S. Dist. Ct. (no. and so. dists.) Miss. 1970, U.S. Ct. Appeals (5th cir.) 1971, U.S. Ct. Appeals (11th cir.). Agt. Met. Life Ins. Co., Jackson, Miss., 1957-58; sales rep. Employers Mut. of Wausau, Jackson, 1958-64; v.p. Reid-McGee Ins. Co., Jackson, 1964-67; from assoc. to sr. ptnr., mng. ptnr. Wells Marble & Hurst, Jackson, 1970-97, sr. ptnr., 1997—. Editor-in-chief Miss. Law Jour., 1969-70. Active U.S. Naval Inst., Annapolis, Md. 1st lt. U.S. Army, 1955-57. Fellow. Miss. Bar Found.; mem. ABA, Fed. Bar Assn. (pres. Miss. chpt. 1981-82),Fdn. Ins. and Corp. Counsel, Nat. Assn. RR Trial Counsel, Miss. Bar Assn., Miss. Def. Lawyers Assn. (pres. 1992-93), Def. Rsch. Inst., Country Club Jackson, Phi Delta Phi, Omicron Delta Kappa, Pi Kappa Alpha. Presbyterian. Avocations: military history, baseball. Insurance, Product liability, General civil litigation. Home: 12 Plum Tree Ln Madison MS 39110-9620 Office: Wells Marble & Hurst PO Box 131 Jackson MS 39205-0131 *People respect honesty, trustworthiness, hard work and sincerity. Do what you truly want to do for your vocation, for that is the secret of happiness in a business career.*

**LANGFORD, TIMOTHY ANDREW,** lawyer, farmer; b. Union City, Tenn., Nov. 17, 1955; s. Alvie Dee and Mary Eva Langford; m. Karen Shipley, July 17, 1983; children: Andrea, Mary Evelyn, Amy. BS, Murray (Ky.) State U., 1977; JD, U. Ky., 1980. Bar: Ky. 1980, U.S. Dist. Ct. (we. dist.) Ky., U.S. Dist. Ct. (we. dist.) Tenn. County atty. Fulton County, Hickman, Ky., 1988-89; commonwealth atty. State of Ky., Hickman, 1989—. Mem. Masons. Home: 8574 State Rd 1128 Hickman KY 42058 Office: 227 Clinton St Hickman KY 42050-1307

**LANGS, EDWARD F(ORREST),** lawyer; b. Detroit, Jan. 26, 1941; s. John W. and Elizabeth (Stark) L.; m. Dorothy Morrall, May 15, 1965; children—Katherine Elizabeth, June Anna. A.B., U. Mich., 1962, J.D., 1965. Bar: Mich. 1966, U.S. Dist. Ct. (ea. dist.) Mich. 1968, U.S. Ct. Appeals (6th cir.) 1973, U.S. Supreme Ct. 1973. Assoc. McInally, Brucker, Newcombe, Wilke & DeBona, Detroit, 1965-68; staff atty. Chrysler Fin. Corp., Detroit, 1968-69; assoc. McClintock, Fulton, Donovan and Waterman, Detroit, 1969-73; with Burroughs Corp., Detroit, 1973—, mng. atty., 1975-77, legal dir., 1977—; lectr. on computer law Practising Law Inst., Computer Law Assn., Mich. Tech. Conf., Boston Bar Assn., Am. Law Inst., ABA. Recipient Concerned Citizens award City of Grosse Pointe Park (Mich.), 1982. Mem. Detroit Bar Assn., ABA, Computer Law Assn. (sec./treas., dir.), Mich. Bar Assn. (computer law sect. elected council). Episcopalian. Clubs: Detroit Athletic, Econs. of Detroit, Renaissance (Detroit). Contracts commercial, Antitrust. Office: Burroughs Pl Detroit MI 48202

**LANGTON, JEFFREY H.,** judge; b. Hamilton, Mont., Apr. 22, 1953; s. Richard L. and N. Louise (Mittower) L.; m. Patricia L. Stanbery, June 17, 1978 (div. Feb. 1999); children: Melanie, Matthew, Stephen, Thomas. BA in history with high honors, U. Mont., 1975, JD, 1978. Bar: Mont. 1978, U.S. Dist. Ct. Mont. 1978. Assoc. Schultz Law Firm, Hamilton, 1978-82; pvt. practice Hamilton, 1982-92; dist. judge 21st Dist. Ct., Hamilton, 1993—; bd. clin. visitors Law Sch., U. Mont., Missoula, 1993—; Montant Sentence Review Divsn., 1998—. Author: The Victor Story, 1985. Bd. dirs. Victor Heritage Mus., 1990-95. Named Man of Yr. Victor Booster Club, 1988, 93. Mem. ABA (Mont. del. 1994—), Mont. Bar Assn., Mont. Judges Assn. Presbyterian. Avocations: Montana history, fly fishing, environmental issues. Home: 2975 Mittower Rd Victor MT 59875-9542 Office: 21st Jud Dist 205 Bedford St Hamilton MT 59840-2853

**LANGWORTHY, LUCINDA MINTON,** lawyer; b. Paris, Jan. 3, 1956; came to U.S. 1958; d. Wilfred Max Mortimer and Florence (Schrey) Minton; m. John Alan Langworthy, Feb. 17, 1989; children: Alan Frederick David, Gary Paul, Maxwell Carr. Student, Univ. Coll., Buckingham, Eng., 1977; BA in Biology and English, Bucknell U., 1978; JD, George Washington U., 1981. Bar: D.C. 1981, U.S. Dist. Ct. D.C. 1984, U.S. Ct. Appeals (D.C. cir. 1986). Jud. clk. Atomic Safety and Licensing Bd. Panel, U.S. NRC, Washington, 1981-83; assoc. Hunton & Williams, Washington, 1983-90, counsel, 1990—. Mem. ABA, Prettyman-Leventhal Am. Inn of Ct. Administrative and regulatory, Environmental, Nuclear power. Office: Hunton & Williams 1900 K St NW Washington DC 20006-1110

**LANGWORTHY, ROBERT BURTON,** lawyer; b. Kansas City, Mo., Dec. 24, 1918; s. Herman Moore and Minnie (Leach) L.; m. Elizabeth Ann Miles, Jan. 2, 1942; children: David Robert, Joan Elizabeth Langworthy Tomek, Mark Burton. AB, Princeton U., 1940; JD, Harvard U., 1943. Bar: Mo. 1943, U.S. Supreme Ct 1960. Practiced in Kansas City, 1943—; assoc., then mem. and v.p. Linde, Thomson, Langworthy, Kohn & Van Dyke, P.C., 1943-91; pres., mng. shareholder Blackwood, Langworthy & Schmelzer, P.C., Kansas City, Mo., 1991-96; mng. mem. Blackwood & Langworthy, LC, Kansas City, Mo., 1996—; lectr. on probate, law sch. CLE courses U. Mo., Kansas City. Mem. bd. editors Harvard Law Rev., 1941-43; contbr. chpts. to Guardian and Trust, Powers, Conservatorships and Nonprobate Desk Books of Mo. Bar. Mem. edn. appeal bd. U.S. Dept. Edn., 1982-86; commr. Housing Authority Kansas City, 1963-71, chmn., 1969-71; chmn. Bd. Election Commrs. Kansas City, 1973-77; chmn. bd. West Ctrl. area YMCA, 1969—; mem. bd. Mid-Am. region YMCA, 1970-83, vice chmn., 1970-73, chmn., 1973-78; pres. Met. Bd. Kansas City (Mo.) YMCA (now YMCA of Greater Kansas City), 1965, bd. dirs., 1965—, mem. nat. bd. 1971-78, 79-83; bd. dirs. YMCA of the Rockies, 1974—, bd. sec., 1994—; chmn. bd. trustees Sioux Indian YMCAs, 1983—; bd. dirs. Armed Svcs. YMCA, 1984-85; pres. Met. Area Citizens Edn., 1969-72; chmn. Citizens Assn. Kansas City (Mo.), 1967, bd. dirs., 1995-96; bd. dirs. Project Equality Kans.-Mo., 1967-80, pres., 1970-72, treas., 1972-73, sec., 1973-76; 1st v.p. Human Resources Corp. Kansas City, 1969-71, 72-73, bd. dirs., 1965-73; hon. v.p. Am. Sunday Sch. Union (now Am. Missionary Fellowship), 1965—; vice chmn. bd. trustees Kemper Mil. Sch., 1966-73; U.S. del. YMCA World Coun., Buenos Aires, 1977, Estes Park, Colo., 1981, Nyborg, Denmark, 1985; bd. dirs. Mo. Rep. Club, 1960—; del., mem. platform com. Rep. Nat. Conv., 1960; Rep. nominee for U.S. Congress, 1964; mem. gen. assembly Com. on Representation Presbyn., 1991-97, moderator, 1993-94; commr. to gen. assembly Presbyn. Ch., 1984, mem. gen. assembly com. on location of hdqs. 1984-87; moderator Heartland Presbyn., 1984. Lt. (j.g.) USNR, 1943-46, capt. Res. ret. Mem. ABA, Kansas City Bar Assn. (chmn. probate law com. 1988-90, living will com. 1989-91), Mo. State Bar (chmn. probate and trust com. 1983-85, chmn. sr. lawyers com. 1991-93), Lawyers Assn. Kansas City, Harvard Law Sch. Assn. Mo. (v.p. 1973-74, pres. 1974-75, 85-87), Univ. Club (Kansas City). Presbyterian (elder). Probate, Estate planning, Nonprofit and tax-exempt organizations. Home: 616 W 69th St Kansas City MO 64113-1937 Office: 1220 Washington St Ste 300 Kansas City MO 64105-2245

**LANIO, KIMBERLEY DIGIACOBBE,** lawyer, legal recruiter; b. Pitts., Aug. 7, 1968; d. August Jerome and Bonnie Lee DiGiacobbe. BS, U. R.I., 1990; MBA, U. Pitts., 1991, JD, 1994. Bar: Tex., Pa. Atty. Westinghouse Electric Co., Pitts., 1994-95, Jenkens & Gilchrist, Dallas, 1995-96; v.p. Assoc. Counsel of Am., Dallas, 1996—. Avocations: running, reading, skiing, golf. Office: Assoc Counsel Am 2911 Turtle Creek Blvd Ste 300 Dallas TX 75219-6243

**LANKOWSKY, ZENON P.,** lawyer. V.p., gen. counsel, sec. CVS, Inc., Woonsocket, R.I. Office: CVS Inc One CVS Dr Woonsocket RI 02895*

**LANSING, MARK ALEXANDER,** lawyer; b. Grants Pass, Oreg., July 18, 1957; s. Ronald Bert and Jewel Anne (Beck) L.; m. Jeanne Nelson Marshall, Aug. 17, 1985; children: Jade M., Matt X., Shan S. BA, U. Oreg., 1979; JD, U. Wash., 1987. Bar: Oreg. 1988. Sports editor Ctrl. Oregonian, Prineville, Oreg., 1979-81; asst. export mgr. Columbia Grain, Portland, Oreg., 1981-84; assoc. Myrick, Seagraves et al, Grants Pass, 1988-89; ptnr. Sloan & Lansing, Grants Pass, 1989-98; pvt. practice Grants Pass, 1998—. Bd. dirs., pres. Rogue Recovery Programs, Grants Pass, 1989-96; bd. dirs. YMCA, 1992-94, United Way of Josephine County, Grants Pass., 1991-95. Mem. ABA, Oreg. State Bar Assn., Josephine County Bar Assn. (pres. 1992). Democrat. Avocation: bicycling. Personal injury, Contracts commercial, Civil rights. Office: Sloan and Lansing 242 NW E St Grants Pass OR 97526-2046

**LANTIER, BRENDAN JOHN,** lawyer; b. Rockville Centre, N.Y., July 6, 1948; s. James David and Jane Veronica (O'Connor) L.; m. Karyn Lainis, May 14, 1994. BA, U. Notre Dame, 1970; JD, Syracuse U., 1974. Bar: N.Y. 1975, U.S. Dist. Ct. (so. and ea. dists.) N.Y. 1975, U.S. Supreme Ct. 1979. Asst. dist. atty., dep. bur. chief Kings County Dist. Atty., Bklyn., 1974-83; atty., ptnr. McAloon & Friedman, N.Y.C., 1983—. Mem. N.Y. State Med. Def. Bar Assn. Personal injury. Home: 245 E 93rd St Apt 26J New York NY 10128-3967 Office: McAloon & Friedman 116 John St New York NY 10038-3300

**LANZA, CHRISTOPHER F.,** lawyer; b. Winthrop, Mass., Feb. 15, 1965; s. Francis M. Lanza and Carlie Jean Martin; m. Aleida Delgado, Nov. 1, 1997. BA, U. Mass., 1989; JD, Nova U. Bar: Fla., Mass. Atty. Hoffman Larin and Agnetti PA, Miami, Fla., 1994—. Named to Order of Barristers, 1993. Mem. Dade County Bar Assn., Coral Reef Yacht Club. Democrat. Roman Catholic. Personal injury, Workers' compensation, General civil litigation. Home: 15520 SW 85th Ave Miami FL 33157-2131 Office: Hoffman Larin & Agnetti PA 909 N Miami Beach Blvd Ste 201 Miami FL 33162-3722

**LANZA, ROBERT JOHN,** lawyer; b. N.Y.C., June 10, 1957; s. Joseph John and Rose (LaGatta) L.; m. Ana Fatima Abraido; 1 child, Anthony Joseph. BA, Baruch Coll., 1982; JD, Yeshiva U., 1985; LLM, NYU, 1986. Bar: N.Y. 1986, Calif. 1986, U.S. Dist. Ct. (all dists.) Calif. 1986, U.S. Ct. Appeals (9th cir.) 1987. Assoc. Morgan Lewis & Bockius, Calif., 1986-89, N.Y., 1986-89; from assoc. to ptnr. Marcus Montgomery Wolfson PC, N.Y.C., 1989—; sec. com. on mcpl. affairs N.Y. City Bar Assn., N.Y.C., 1992. Contbg. author: California Labor Law, 1989. Cpl. USMC, 1974-79. Avocations: boxing, hiking. Federal civil litigation, Labor. Address: 20 Exchange Pl Fl 35 New York NY 10005-3201

**LAPAN, ROGER DON,** lawyer; b. Galva, Ill., Nov. 5, 1929; s. Donald Robert and Dorothy Lillian (Ericson) L.; m. Jacqueline F. Lapan, June 22, 1957; children—Lori, Bradley, Roberta, Eric. B.S. in Econs., Ill. State U., 1951; J.D., Northwestern U., 1958. Bar: U.S. Dist. Ct. (so. dist.) Ill. 1958. Asst. Ill. atty. gen., Springfield, 1958-83; asst. states atty., McLean County, Bloomington, Ill., 1960-63; sole practice, Bloomington, 1963—; lectr. W/C Seminars of Ill., Bloomington, 1980—. Served to capt. USAF, 1951-55. Methodist. Workers' compensation, Real property. Office: 237 E Front St Bloomington IL 61701-5211

**LA PETINA, GARY MICHAEL,** lawyer; b. Chgo., Apr. 25, 1955; s. Nicholas J. and Mildred E. (Roth) La P.; m. Donna M. Kulisz, Oct. 9, 1982; children: Patrick James, Nicole Elizabeth. BS, Loyola U., Chgo., 1977; JD, John Marshall Law Sch., Chgo., 1980. Bar: Ill. 1980. Staff atty. Internat. Assn. Lions Clubs, Oak Brook, Ill., 1982-87, gen. counsel, 1987—. Mem. ABA, Lions. Roman Catholic. Avocations: collectibles, sporting events, reading. General corporate, Insurance. Home: 2 S 030 Bristol Ln Warrenville IL 60555 Office: Internat Assn Lions Clubs 300 W 22nd St Oak Brook IL 60523-8815

**LAPIN, ANDREW WILLIAM,** lawyer; b. Chgo., Feb. 2, 1953; s. Robert Allan and Elaine (Muhlrad) L.; m. Debra Nan Goldberg, July 7, 1979; children: Lauren Elyse, Marisa Anne. BA, Ind. U., 1975; JD, John Marshall Law Sch., 1978. Bar: Ill. 1978, U.S. Dist. Ct. (no. dist.) Ill. 1978. Pvt. practice law, Chgo., 1978-79, 81-87; assoc. Tash & Slavitt, Ltd., Chgo., 1979-81; of counsel Siegan, Barbakoff & Gomberg, Chgo., 1987-89, Lapin & Assocs., Chgo., 1989—; lectr. Nat. Assn. Govt. Guaranteed Lenders. Author: Closing and Funding the SBA Loan. Mem. ABA, Chgo. Bar Assn. (real property com., real property fin. subcom.), Ill. Bar Assn., Chgo. Mortgage Attys. Assn. Real property, Contracts commercial, Franchising. Office: Lapin & Assocs 300 W Washington St Ste 707 Chicago IL 60606-1720

**LAPIN, HARVEY I.,** lawyer; b. St. Louis, Nov. 23, 1937; s. Lazarus L. and Lillie L.; m. Cheryl A. Lapin; children: Jeffrey, Gregg. BS, Northwestern U., 1960, JD, 1963. Bar: Ill. 1963, Fla. 1980, Wis. 1985; cert. tax lawyer, Fla.; CPA, Ill. Atty. Office Chief Counsel, IRS, Washington, 1963-65; trial atty. Office Regional Counsel, IRS, Washington, 1965-68; assoc., then ptnr. Fiffer & D'Angelo, Chgo., 1968-75; pres. Harvey I. Lapin, P.C., Chgo., 1975-83; mng. ptnr. Lapin, Hoff, Spangler & Greenberg, Chgo., 1983-88, Lapin, Hoff, Slaw & Laffey, Chgo., 1989-91; ptnr. Gottlieb and Schwartz, Chgo., 1992-93; prin. Harvey I. Lapin & Assocs., P.C., Northbrook, Ill., 1993—; instr. John Marshall Law Sch., 1969—; facility adv. lawyers asst. program Roosevelt U., Chgo.; mem. cemetery adv. bd. Ill. Comptroller, 1974-96. Asst. editor Fed. Bar Jour., 1965-67; contbg. editor Cemetary and Funeral Business and Legal Guide; contbr. articles to profl. jours. Mem. ABA, Fla. Bar Assn. (Fla. cert. tax specialist), Wis. Bar Assn., Ill. Bar Assn., Chgo. Bar Assn. (chmn. tax exempt orgns. subcom., sect. taxation 1988-90). Jewish. Corporate taxation, General corporate. Office: Harvey I Lapin & Assocs PC PO Box 1327 Northbrook IL 60065-1327

**LAPIN, JEFFREY BRENT,** lawyer; b. Kansas City, Mo., Dec. 31, 1970; s. Arthur Edward and Bonnie Dubinsky Lapin. BA, U. Kans., 1993; JD with distinction, U. Nebr., 1997. Bar: Kans., Nebr. Law clk. Friedman Law Offices, Lincoln, Nebr., 1995-97; atty. Friedman Law Offices, Lincoln, 1998—. Tchr. Cmty. Legal Edn. Program, Lincoln, 1997. Recipient Corpus Juris Secundum award in property West Pub., Creighton Coll. Law, 1995; scholar U. Nebr., Lincoln, 1997. Mem. ATLA, Kans. Bar Assn., Nebr. Bar Assn., Nebr. Assn. Trial Lawyers. Republican. Avocations: computers, golf. E-mail: jlapin@friedmanlaw.com. Fax: 402-476-8364. Office: Friedman Law Offices 633 S 9th St Lincoln NE 68508-2807

**LAPIN, ROBERT E.,** lawyer; b. Houston, July 10, 1960; s. Jack and Susan K. Lapin; m. Eve S. Lapin, June 25, 1989; children: Oliver, Elliott, Alec. BA in English Lit. with honors, Stanford U., 1982; JD with honors, U. Tex., 1985. Bar: Tex. 1985, U.S. Dist. Ct. (so. dist.) Tex. 1986, U.S. Ct. Appeals (5th cir.) 1986. Lawyer Hill, Parker, Franklin, Cardwell & Jones, Houston, 1985-91, Carrigan, Lapin & Landa, 1991—; panel atty. Ill. Office State Appellate Defender, 1998—; asst. pub. defender, felony divsn. Office of Macon County Pub. Defender, 1999—. Pres. Houston chpt. Am.-Jewish Com., 1997-99; pres. Jewish Comty. Ctr., Houston 1999—; mem. Leadership Houston, Class VII, 1988-89. Fellow Coll. of State Bar Tex. General civil litigation, Personal injury, Product liability. Office: Carrigan Lapin & Landa 500 Dallas St Ste 2600 Houston TX 77002-4802

**LAPINE, FELIX VICTOR,** lawyer; b. Poznan, Poland, Mar. 25, 1941; came to U.S., 1951; s. Otto Karl and Bronislawa Lapping; children: Misha, Edward, Andrei, Maximillian. BA, U. Rochester, 1964; LLB, Syracuse U., 1967, JD, 1969. Bar: N.Y. 1969, U.S. Dist. Ct. (we. and no. dists.) N.Y. 1972, U.S. Ct. Appeals (2d cir.) 1977. Asst. dist. atty. Monroe County, Rochester, N.Y., 1969-72; ptnr. Napier & Lapine, Rochester, 1972-78; pvt. practice, Rochester, 1978—. Recipient R.C. Napier award Criminal Def. League, 1992. Mem. Monroe County Bar Assn. (Charles F. Crimi award 1994). Avocation: managing a semi-professional soccer team (finalist U.S. Amateur Cup, 1995). Criminal, General civil litigation. Office: 1 E Main St Ste 711 Rochester NY 14614-1807

**LAPINSKI, ALEXANDER J.,** lawyer; b. Exeter, Pa., Apr. 6, 1932; s. Alexander F. and Maryanna (Orzechowski) L. BA in Liberal Arts, St. John's U., 1955; LLB, Bklyn. Law Sch., 1962; LLM, NYU. Bar: N.Y. 1962, U.S. Dist. Ct. (ea. dist.) N.Y. 1964, U.S. Dist. Ct. (so. dist.) N.Y. 1966, U.S. Ct. Appeals (2nd cir.) 1966, U.S. Supreme Ct. 1967, U.S. Tax Ct. 1994. Ctrl. office supr. N.Y. Tel. Co., N.Y.C., 1957-62; pvt. practice Elmhurst, N.Y., 1962—; project coord. law sch. devel., deferred giving dir. Hofstra U. Law Sch., Hempstead, N.Y., 1968-70. Mem., pres., bd. govs. 30th A.D. Dem. Club, Maspern, N.Y., 1969-73; vice chair county law Queens County Dem. Party, 1971-73; candidate N.Y.C. Coun., Dem. Primary, 1973. 1st lt. USMC, 1955-57. Mem. ABA, N.Y. State Bar Assn., N.Y. State Tax Lawyers Assn., Queens County Bar Assn., Marine Corps Res. Officers Assn., Res. Officers Assn. Democrat. Roman Catholic. Avocation: golf. General practice, Family and matrimonial, General corporate. Office: 78-20 Woodside Ave Elmhurst NY 11373

**LA PLATA, GEORGE,** federal judge; b. 1924; m. Frances Hoyt; children: Anita J. La Plata Rard, Marshall. AB, Wayne State U., 1951; LLB, Detroit Coll. Law, 1956. Pvt. practice law, 1956-79; judge Oakland County (Mich.) Cir. Ct., Pontiac, 1979-85, U.S. Dist. Ct. (ea. dist.) Mich., Ann Arbor, 1985-96; spl. litigation counsel Allan Miller, P.C., Mich., 1996—; prof. Detroit Coll. Law, 1985-86. Trustee William Beaumont Hosp., 1979—, United Found., 1983—. Served to col. USMC, 1943-46, 52-54. Mem. ABA, Oakland County Bar Assn., Hispanic Bar Assn. Lodge: Optimists. Office: Allan Miller PC 370 E Maple Rd Fl 4 Birmingham MI 48009-6303

**LAPORTE, CLOYD, JR.,** lawyer, retired manufacturing executive; b. N.Y.C., June 8, 1925; s. Cloyd and Marguerite (Raeder) L.; m. Caroline E. Berry, Jan. 22, 1949; children—Elizabeth, Marguerite, Cloyd III. AB, Harvard U., 1946, JD, 1949. Bar: N.Y. 1949. Assoc. mem. firm Cravath, Swaine & Moore, N.Y.C., 1949-56; dir. adminstrn. Metals div. Olin Corp., N.Y.C., 1957-66; legal counsel Dover Corp., N.Y.C., 1966-93, sec., 1971-93. 2d lt. A.C. AUS, WWII. Mem. Harvard Club (N.Y.C.). General corporate. Home: Gipsy Trail Club Carmel NY 10512

**LAPPAS, SPERO THOMAS,** lawyer; b. Danbury, Conn., Oct. 20, 1952; s. Tom John and Alexandria (Manolakes) L.; m. Josephine Wahrendorf, Nov. 8, 1981 (div. 1986); 1 child, Thom Spero; m. Julie Marie Waugh, July 12, 1986 (div. 1995); 1 child, Alexandria Julia. BA cum laude, Allegheny Coll., Meadville, Pa., 1974; JD cum laude, Dickinson Sch. Law, Carlisle, Pa., 1977. Bar: Pa. 1977, U.S. Dist. Ct. (mid. dist.) Pa. 1977, U.S. Ct. Appeals (3rd cir.) 1980, U.S. Supreme Ct. 1991. Assoc. Law Office of Arthur Kusic, Harrisburg, Pa., 1977-79; atty. Kusic & Lappas, P.C., Harrisburg, 1979-84; pvt. practice Harrisburg, 1984-85; ptnr. Stefanon & Lappas, Harrisburg, 1985-88; prin. Law Offices Spero T. Lappas, Harrisburg, 1988—. Mem. ATLA, Pa. Bar Assn., Dauphin County Bar Assn., Pa. Assn. Criminal Def. Lawyers, Mensa, Am. Hellenic Edni. and Progressive Assn. Criminal, General civil litigation, Civil rights. Office: 205 State St Harrisburg PA 17101-1130

**LAPPEN, TIMOTHY,** lawyer, investor; b. L.A., Dec. 26, 1947; s. Chester Irwin and Jon Tyroler (Irmas) L.; children: Amy Elizabeth, Jay Robert, Tyler Lewis. AB, U. Calif., Berkeley, 1972; JD, UCLA, 1975. Bar: Calif. 1975, U.S. Dist. Ct. (no. dist.) Calif. 1975, U.S. Ct. Appeals (9th cir.) 1975. Assoc. Lillick, McHose & Charles, San Francisco, 1975-77; ptnr. Lappen & Lappen, L.A., 1977-84; of counsel Jeffer, Mangels, Butler & Marmaro, L.A., San Francisco, 1984—; pres. Lappen Realty and Investment Corp., Santa Monica, Calif., 1987—; bd. dirs., sec. Dee Constrn. Co., L.A., 1968—. Bd. dirs., pres. Santa Monica Protective Assn., Calif., 1981-90, pres. 1991-93; bd. dirs. L.A. Regional Food Bank, 1988-95, pres., 1992-93; founder, bd. dirs. chmn. Lawyers Against Hunger, 1994—; trustee Sch. Law UCLA, 1990-94, pres. 1992; mem. bd. advisors Am. Acad. for Dance and Kindred Arts, 1995-99; mem. Chancellor's Assocs. UCLA, 1980-90; exec. coms. L.A. County D.A.'s Office, 1993—, D.A.R.E., 1992-95; mem. Calif. Lexington Group, L.A. World Affairs Coun. Mem. ABA, Calif. Bar Assn., L.A. County Bar Assn., Century City Bar Assn. General corporate, Real property. Office: Jeffer Mangels Butler & Marmaro # 1000 2121 Avenue of the Stars Los Angeles CA 90067

**LARA, ART B., JR.,** lawyer; b. Dallas, Mar. 5, 1948; s. Arthur Benjamin Sr. and Barbara Ann Lara; m. Carole Lynn Bremer, July 18, 1969; children: Zachary G., Matthew. B. BBA, West Tex. State U., 1970; JD, Tex. Tech. U., 1973. Bar: Tex., U.S. Dist. Ct. (no. dist.) Tex. Trial atty. Dept. Justice, Washington, 1973-74; asst. dist. atty. Office of the Dist. Atty., El Paso, Tex., 1974-77; pvt. practice Amarillo, Tex., 1977-85, 98—; ptnr. Buckner Lara & Swindell, Amarillo, Tex., 1985-98. Elder Westminster Presbyn. Ch., Amarillo; former bd. dirs. Cath. Family Svcs. of the Diocese of Amarillo, Inc., 1982-96. Mem. ATLA, Tex. Bar Assn., Amarillo Bar Assn., Hispanic C. of C. General civil litigation, Family and matrimonial, Personal injury. Office: Ste 240 1616 S Kentucky St Bldg D Amarillo TX 79102-2252

**LARDENT, ESTHER FERSTER,** lawyer, legal consultant; b. Linz, Austria, Apr. 23, 1947; came to U.S., 1951; d. William and Rose (Seidweber) Ferster; m. Dennis Robert Lardent, July 27, 1969 (div. Dec. 1981). BA, Brown U., 1968; JD, U. Chgo., 1971. Bar: Ill. 1972, U.S. Dist. Ct. Ill. 1972, Mass. 1975, U.S. Dist. Ct. Mass. 1975. Civil rights specialist Office of Civil Rights U.S. HEW, Chgo., 1971-72; staff dir. individual rights ABA, Chgo., 1972-74; staff atty., supr. Cambridge (Mass.) Problem Ctr., 1975-76; exec. dir. Vol. Lawyers Project Boston Bar Assn., 1977-85; legal and policy cons. Santa Fe and Washington, 1985—; cons. Ford Found., Washington, 1990—;

vis. prof. U. N.Mex. Sch. Law, Albuquerque, 1985; cons. Nat. Vets. Legal Svcs. Program, Washington, 1991—; vis. scholar ethics program Boston U. Sch. Law, 1991-92; reporter ABA/Tulane Law Sch., New Orleans, 1988-90; pres. pro bono inst. Georgetown U. Law Ctr., 1996—. Contbr. articles to profl. jours. Recipient Founders' award Phila. Bar Assn., 1991, Outstanding Pub. Interest Adv. award Nat. Assn. Pub. Interest Law, 1992. Mem. ABA (Ho. of Dels. 1991—, cons. 1974-76, legal cons. postconviction death penalty 1987-96, legal cons. law firm pro bono project 1989-96), Nat. Legal Aid and Defenders Assn. (bd. dirs. 1990—), D.C. Bar (spl. advisor pub. svc. activities review com. 1990—), U. Chgo. Law Sch. (vis. com. 1992—).

**LARDNER, CYNTHIA MARIE-MARTINOVICH,** lawyer; b. Detroit, Sept. 20, 1959; m. Michael Lardner, Nov. 5, 1994. BA in Journalism, Mich. State U., 1981; JD magna cum laude, U. Detroit, 1984. Bar: Mich. 1984, U.S. Dist. Ct. (ea. dist.) Mich. 1984. Assoc. Pepper Hamilton & Scheetz, Detroit, 1984-86; pvt. practice law St. Clair Shores, Mich., 1986-89; asst. v.p., atty. NBD Bank NA, Detroit, 1989-93; pvt. practice law Detroit, 1993—; legal writing instr. U. Detroit, 1985-89; bus. law instr. Walsh Coll., Troy, Mich., 1986-87; bd. mem. Mich. State Bar Jour., Lansing, 1992—; bus. law instr. Macomb C.C., Fraser, Mich., 1994—. Contbr. chpt. to book and articles to profl. jours. Budget adminstrn. and fiscal planning com. City of Ferndale, Mich., 1988-90. Mem. State Bar Mich., Macomb County Bar Assn. Banking, Contracts commercial. Office: 729 Meldrum St Detroit MI 48207-4323

**LAREMONT, ANITA WEBB,** lawyer; b. Canton, Ohio, Aug. 18, 1954; m. Quentin F. Smith; children: Jamaal, Imani. BA magna cum laude, Mt. Holyoke Coll., South Hadley, Mass., 1976; JD, NYU, N.Y.C., 1979. Bar: N.Y. 1980. Assoc. Milbank, Tweed, Hadley & McCloy, N.Y.C., 1979-82; assoc. counsel N.Y. State Urban Devel. Corp., N.Y.C., 1982-85, sr. counsel, 1985-88, dep. gen. counsel, 1988-95; acting gen. counsel, sr. v.p. N.Y. Job Devel. Authority, N.Y.C., 1994-96; sr. v.p., legal and gen. counsel Empire State Devel. Corp., N.Y.C., 1995—; gen. counsel, sr. v.p. N.Y. Job Devel. Authority, N.Y.C., 1996—. Mem. ABA, Assn. Bar City N.Y. (com. on govt. lawyers 1995—, com. on minorities in profession 1993—). General corporate, Government contracts and claims. Office: Empire State Devel Corp 633 3rd Ave New York NY 10017-6706

**LARIMER, DAVID GEORGE,** federal judge; b. Rochester, N.Y., Mar. 3, 1944; s. John and Mary (Sullivan) L.; m. Karen Moore, July 29, 1967; children: Amy, Beth, John. BA, St. John Fisher Coll., 1966; JD, Notre Dame U., 1969. Bar: N.Y. 1970, D.C. 1971. Law clk. to Hon. Joseph C. McGarraghy U.S. Dist. Ct. (D.C. dist.), 1969-70; asst. U.S. atty. U.S. Dept. Justice, Washington, 1970-73, Rochester, 1973-75; with Beckerman, Davidson, Cook & Fink, Rochester, 1975-78, Lapine & Larimer, 1978-79; chief appellate law asst. Supreme Ct. (4th Dept.), Rochester, 1979-81; mem. firm Greisberger, Zicari, McConville, Cooman & Morin, Rochester, 1982-84; U.S. magistrate U.S. Dist. Ct., Rochester, 1983-87; judge U.S. Dist. Ct. (west dist.) N.Y., Rochester, 1987—, chief judge, 1996—; law instr. St. John Fisher Coll., Rochester, 1979-81. Office: US Dist Ct 100 State St 250 US Courthouse Rochester NY 14614

**LARIO, FRANK M., JR.,** lawyer, judge; b. Phila., July 1, 1937; s. Frank M. and Marie Ann (Mandarino) L.; m. Kathleen A. Cowan, July 1, 1961; children—Michael James, Kathleen Marie, Frank M. III. A.B. cum laude, Georgetown U., 1959; postgrad. Harvard U., 1959; J.D. cum laude, Rutgers U., 1962. Bar: N.J. 1962, U.S. dist. ct. N.J. 1963, U.S. Ct. Apls. (3d cir.) 1978, U.S. Sup. Ct. 1969. Law sec. to Assoc. Justice Vincent S. Haneman, N.J. Sup. ct. 1962-63; ptnr. Lario, Nardi & Gleaner, Haddonfield, N.J. 1973-93; mcpl. judge Borough of Magnolia (N.J.), 1969-93; mcpl. judge Borough of Audubon Park (N.J.), 1970-93; mcpl. judge Borough of Woodlynne (N.J.), 1971-76; mcpl. judge Borough of Bellmawr (N.J.), 1976-93; superior ct. judge, State of N.J., 1993—. Instr. estate planning Inst. Continuing Legal Edn., 1962-69, instr. legal ethics, 1973-78; mem. com. on mcpl. cts. N.J. Supreme Ct., 1980-92; mem. Supreme Ct. Com. on Character, 1983-92. Mem. alumni senate Georgetown U., 1981—; bd. govs. Georgetown U., 1978-81. Mem. ABA, N.J. Bar Assn. (chmn. mcpl. cts. of N.J. com. 1978-81), Camden County Bar Assn. (bd. mgrs. 1973-76, chmn. immigration and naturalization com. 1974-83, long range planning com. 1976-78, sec. 1979-80, treas. 1980-81, v.p. 1982-83, pres. 1984-85), Camden County Mcpl. Judges Conf. (sec. 1975, pres. 1976-77), Rutgers U. Law Sch. Alumni Assn. (chmn. scholarship com. 1971-82), Rutgers U. Law Sch. Alumni Assn. South Jersey (chancellor 1968-69, bd. mgrs. 1970-82), Georgetown U. Alumni Assn. (gov. 1976—), Men of Malvern (assoc. capt. 1968—). Clubs: Vesper (Phila.); Tavistock Country (Haddonfield); Union League of Phila.; KC; Georgetown U. Alumni South Jersey (pres. 1970-72). Assoc. editor: Rutgers Law Rev., 1961-62. General practice, General corporate, Probate. Office: Hall of Justice 101 S Fifth St Camden NJ 08103-4001

**LARISON, BRENDA IRENE,** law librarian; b. Springfield, Ill., Apr. 3, 1949; d. Richard Wayne and Corabell Marie (Bea) L.; 1 child, Alyce Sherbenou. BA, U. Ill., 1971; MA, Sangamon State U., Springfield, 1977; MLS, U. Mich., 1980. Corp. libr. ADP Network Svcs., Ann Arbor, Mich., 1978-86; legis. rsch. law libr. State of Ill., Springfield, 1986-91; libr. Supreme Ct. Ill., Springfield, 1992—; del. White House Conf. on Librs., 1990; midwest coord. Nat. Conf. State Legislatures, Denver, 1987-91; mem. state agy. libr. bd. State of Ill. Libr., Springfield, 1988-90. Literacy vol. Lincoln Land C.C., Springfield, 1992-95; vol. coord. Lincoln Meml. Gardens, Springfield, 1993-94. Mem. Am. Assn. Law Librs., Chgo. Assn. Law Librs., Spl. Librs. Assn. (bd. dirs. Ill. chpt. 1989-90). Avocations: gardening, birding, cycling. Office: Supreme Ct Ill Supreme Ct Bldg Springfield IL 62701

**LARKIN, LEO PAUL, JR.,** lawyer; b. Ithaca, N.Y., June 19, 1925; s. Leo Paul and Juanita (Wade) L. AB, Cornell U., 1948, LLB, 1950. Bar: N.Y. 1950, U.S. Dist. Ct. (so. dist.) N.Y. 1951, U.S. Supreme Ct. 1967. Assoc., ptnr., sr. counsel Rogers & Wells and predecessor firms, N.Y.C., 1950—. Served with U.S. Army, 1943-45. Mem. ABA, Fed. Bar Coun., Univ. Club, Sky Club, Delta Phi, Phi Beta Kappa, Phi Kappa Phi, Theta Delta Phi. Antitrust, Federal civil litigation, Libel. Home: 200 E 66th St Apt B-1804 New York NY 10021-6728 Office: Rogers & Wells 200 Park Ave Ste 5200 New York NY 10166-0005

**LARMOYEUX, CHRISTOPHER MASON,** lawyer; b. Jacksonville, Fla., June 4, 1954; s. Louis John and Helen (Crandall) L.; m. Leigh T. Larmoyeux, Nov. 23, 1985; children: Christopher Mason, Nash Thorpe, Camille Maureen. BA, U. Fla., 1976; JD, U. Notre Dame, 1979; postgrad., Kings Coll., London, 1977-78. Bar: Fla. 1979, Colo. 1991, U.S. Dist. Ct. (so. dist.) Fla. 1979, U.S. Ct. Appeals (11th cir.) 1979. Atty./assoc. Montgomery, Lytal, Reiter, West Palm Beach, Fla., 1979-85; patnr. Montgomery, Searcy & Denney, West Palm Beach, 1985-89, Montgomery & Larmoyeux, West Palm Beach, 1989—. V.p. Palm BeEach Cultural Coun.; co-chair Children's Cultural Coun. of Palm Beac County, West Palm Beach, Fla.; hon. trustee Armory Arts Ctr., West Palm Beach, 1989—; treas. Palm Beach Cultural Coun., West Palm Beach, 1995—; mem. Palm Beach Opera Assn., 1989—; mem. fin. bd. Rosarian Acad., West Palm Beach, 1996—. Mem. ATLA, ABA, Fla. Bar, Palm Beach County Bar Assn., Acad. Fla. Trial Lawyers, Am. Bd. Trial Advocates. Democrat. Roman Catholic. Avocations: swimming, golf, gardening, reading. Office: 147 Armenia Union Rd Sharon CT 06069

**LARO, DAVID,** judge; b. Flint, Mich., Mar. 3, 1942; s. Samuel and Florence (Chereton) L.; m. Nancy Lynn Wolf, June 18, 1967; children: Rachel Lynn, Marlene Ellen. BA, U. Mich., 1964; JD, U. Ill., 1967; LLM, NYU, 1970. Bar: Mich. 1968, U.S. Dist. Ct. (ea. dist.) Mich. 1968, U.S. Tax Ct. 1971. Ptnr., Winegarden Booth Shedd and Laro, Flint, Mich., 1970-75; sr. ptnr. Laro and Borgerson, Flint, Mich., 1975-86; prin. David Laro, P.C., Flint, 1986-92; apptd. judge U.S. Tax Ct., Washington, 1992—; of counsel Dykema Gossett, Ann Arbor, Mich., 1989-90; pres., chief exec. officer Durakon Industries, Inc., Ann Arbor, 1989-91, chmn., Lapeer, Mich., 1991—; chmn. Republic Bank, 1986—, vice chmn. Republic Bancorp, Inc., Flint, 1986—; instr. Nat. Inst. Trial Advocacy, vis. prof. U. San Diego Law Sch., adj. prof. law Georgetown Law Sch., 1994—; cons. lectr. on tax reform and litigation in Moscow Harvard U., 1997, Ga. State U., 1998. Regent U. Mich., Ann Arbor, 1975-81; mem. Mich. State Bd. Edn., 1982-83; chmn. Mich. State Tenure Commn., 1972-75; commr. Civil Svc. Commn., Flint, Mich., 1984—. Mem. Am. Coll. Tax Counsel, State Bar Mich., Phi Delta Phi. Republican. Office: US Tax Ct 400 2nd St NW Rm 217 Washington DC 20217-0002

**LAROCCA, NICHOLAS JOSEPH,** lawyer, financial planner; b. Union City, N.J., Oct. 4, 1913; s. Giovanni and Gaetana (Satriano) LaR.; m. Cabiria LaRocca, Aug. 11, 1940; 1 child, Susan. BS, Fordham U., 1934; JD, NYU, 1937. Bar: N.J. 1937, U.S. Supreme Ct. 1957. Ptnr. Joseph & Feldman, Ft. Lee, N.J.; bd. dirs., counsel Bergen Trust Co., Jersey City, 1950-70. Mem. N.J. Senate, Trenton, 1982-83, N.J. Assembly, Trenton, 1984-85; mem. SSS, Union City; bd. dirs. Palisade Gen. Hosp., North Bergen, N.J., 1970-90, Mt. Moriah Cemetery, Fairview, N.J., 1980—; mem. N.J. Commn. on Status of Women, Trenton, N.J. Monorail Commn., Trenton. Sgt. USCG, 1943-47. Mem. N.J. Bar Assn., Hudson County Bar Assn., DAV, Am. Legion, North Hudson Lawyers Club (pres. 1976-77). Democrat. Roman Catholic. Avocations: reading, gardening. Estate planning, General corporate. Home: 309 23d St Union City NJ 07087-4520 Office: Joseph & Feldman Parker House Fort Lee NJ 07024

**LA ROSA, LILLIAN J.,** lawyer; b. Stoneham, Mass.; d. Anthony and Antonia La Rosa; m. Peter T. Toland. BA, Mt. Holyoke Coll., 1978; JD, Am. U., Washington, 1981. Bar: Mass. 1982, U.S. Ct. Appeals (1st cir.) Mass. Atty. Serra & Flynn, Boston, 1982-85, Busa & Sohechner, Woburn, Mass., 1985-87, Abelson & Cohen, Framingham, Mass., 1987-88, Mannoz Marino, Winchester, Mass., 1988-91; atty. in pvt. practice Winchester, 1990—. Mem. Mass. Bar Assn., Justinian Law Soc., Winchester Rotary Club. Democrat. Methodist. Family and matrimonial, State civil litigation, Probate. Office: 540 Main St Ste 6 Winchester MA 01890-2940

**LAROSE, KEITH VERNON,** lawyer; b. Jacksonville, N.C., Apr. 11, 1953; s. Barton I. and Helen (Zuckor) LaR.; m. Shelley Ann Garbut, Dec. 10, 1978; children: Stephanie Paula, Michael Scott. BS in Journalism, Northwestern U., 1975; JD magna cum laude, Syracuse U., 1978. Bar: N.Y. 1979, U.S. Dist. Ct. (so. and ea. dist.) N.Y. 1979. Legal cons. Fred C. Hart Assocs., N.Y.C., 1978-80; ptnr. Moran, Spiegel, Pergament & Brown, Poughkeepsie, N.Y., 1980-88, Petito and LaRose, Poughkeepsie, 1989-95, LaRose & LaRose, Poughkeepsie, 1996—. Fellow Assn. Trial Lawyers Am.; mem. N.Y. State Trial Lawyers Assn., N.Y. State Bar Assn., Dutchess County Bar Assn. (membership chmn. 1985-86). Avocations: tennis, sailing, skiing. Personal injury, Environmental, Product liability. Office: LaRose and LaRose 12 Raymond Ave Poughkeepsie NY 12603-2354

**LAROSE, LAWRENCE ALFRED,** lawyer; b. Lowell, Mass., Oct. 26, 1958; s. Alfred M. and Rita B. (Plunkett) L.; m. Janet G. Yedwab, Aug. 12, 1984. BA summa cum laude, Tufts U., 1980; JD magna cum laude, Georgetown U., 1983. Bar: N.Y. 1984. Assoc. Sullivan & Cromwell, N.Y.C., 1983-85, 87-90, Melbourne, Australia, 1985-87; assoc. Cadwalader, Wickersham & Taft, N.Y.C., 1990-92, ptnr., 1993—; vis. fellow Faculty of Law, U. Melbourne, 1986-87. Contbr. articles to profl. publs. Mem. ABA, N.Y. State Bar Assn., N.Y. County Lawyers Assn., Assn. Bar City N.Y., Am. Soc. Internat. Law, Georgetown U. Nat. Law Alumni Bd. (exec. com., sec.), Down Town Assn. in City of N.Y., Phi Beta Kappa. Avocations: art collecting, art history. General corporate, Private international, Mergers and acquisitions. Office: Cadwalader Wickersham & Taft 100 Maiden Ln New York NY 10038-4818

**LAROSILIERE, JEAN DARLY MARTIN,** lawyer; b. Port-au-Prince, Haiti, Feb. 4, 1963; came to U.S. 1976; s. Bernadotte Larosiliere and Lucitania Soline St. Dic Lysius; m. Valerie Lynette Yearwood, Aug. 20, 1988. AB, Fairfield U., 1985; JD, Tulane U., 1988; LLM, Georgetown U., 1990. Bar: Mass. 1989, U.S. Dist. Ct. Mass. 1989, U.S. Ct. Appeals (D.C. cir.) 1989, N.J. 1990, U.S. Dist. Ct. N.J. 1990. Grad. teaching fellow Georgetown U. Law Ctr., Washington, 1988-90; asst. U.S. atty. U.S. Dept. Justice, U.S. Atty.'s Office, Newark, 1990—; adj. prof. law Seton Hall U., Newark, 1992—. Editor Nat. Black Law Jour., 1988. Mem. ABA, Nat. Bar Assn., Garden State Bar Assn. Democrat. Roman Catholic. Avocations: sports, music, reading. Home: 14 Homestead Way Rockaway NJ 07866-4816 Office: US Attys Office 970 Broad St Newark NJ 07102-2506

**LA ROSSA, JAMES M(ICHAEL),** lawyer; b. Bklyn., Dec. 4, 1931; s. James Vincent and Marie Antoinette (Tronolone) La R.; m. Dominique Bazin-Thall, Aug. 11, 1998; children: James M., Thomas, Nancy, Susan. B.S., Fordham U., 1953, J.D., 1958. Bar: N.Y. 1958, U.S. Dist. Ct. N.Y. 1961, U.S. Supreme Ct. 1969. Pvt. practice law N.Y.C., 1958-62, 67-74, 76—; asst. U.S. atty. Eastern Dist. N.Y., Bklyn., 1962-65; ptnr. firm Lefkowitz & Brownstien, N.Y.C., 1965-67, La Rossa, Shargel & Fishetti, N.Y.C., 1974-76, La Rossa, Brownstein & Mitchell, N.Y.C., 1980-82, La Rossa, Axenfeld & Mitchell, N.Y.C., 1982-84, La Rossa, Cooper, Axenfeld, Mitchell & Bergman, N.Y.C., 1984-85, 86-98; now ptnr. Larossa & Ross, N.Y.C.; participant Debate on Legal Ethics Criminal Cts. Bar Assn. Queens County, N.Y., 1978, Criminal Trial Advocacy Workshop, Harvard U. Law Sch., 1978. Author: White Collar Crimes: Defense Strategies, 1977, Federal Rules of Evidence in Criminal Matters, 1977, White Collar Crimes, 1978. Served to 1st lt. USMC, 1953-55. Recipient Guardian of Freedom award B'nai B'rith, 1979, Career Achievement awardN.Y. Coun. Def. Lawyers, 1996. Mem. ABA, N.Y. State Bar Assn. (Criminal Law Practitioner of Yr. 1990), Fed. Bar Counsel, Assn. Bar City N.Y. Office: LaRossa & Ross 41 Madison Ave New York NY 10010-2202

**LARROCA, RAYMOND G.,** lawyer; b. San Juan, P.R., Jan. 5, 1930; s. Raymond Gil and Elsa Maria (Morales) L.; m. Barbara Jean Strand, June 21, 1952 (div. 1974); children—Denise Anne Sheehan, Gail Ellen, Raymond Gil, Mark Talbot, Jeffrey William. B.S.S., Georgetown U., 1952, J.D., 1957. Bar: D.C. 1957, U.S. Supreme Ct. 1960. Assoc., Kirkland, Fleming, Green, Martin & Ellis, Washington, 1957-64; ptnr. Kirkland, Ellis, Hodson, Chaffetz & Masters, Washington, 1964-67, Miller, Cassidy, Larroca & Lewin, Washington, 1967—. Served with arty. U.S. Army, 1948-49, to 1st lt., inf., 1952-54. Mem. ABA, D.C. Bar, Bar Assn. D.C., The Barristers. Republican. Roman Catholic. Clubs: Congl. Country (Potomac, Md.); University (Washington). Criminal, Federal civil litigation, Private international. Office: 2555 M St NW Ste 500 Washington DC 20037-1302

**LARSEN, DANIEL PATRICK,** lawyer; b. Milw., July 2, 1968; s. Richard Allen and Elaine Ann Larsen; m. Janet Knauss, Aug. 15, 1998. BS, U. Wis., 1990; JD, Lewis and Clark Coll., 1994. Bar: Oreg. 1994. Jud. clk. to Judge Robert E. Jones Fed. Dist. Ct., Portland, Oreg., 1994-96; assoc. Ater Wynne LLp, Portland, 1996—. Contbr. articles to profl. jours. Mem. Oreg. State Bar (chair membership svcs. com. to New Lawyers divsn. 1996—), Owen M. Panner Am. Inns of Ct. General civil litigation. Office: Ater Wynne LLP 222 SW Columbia St Portland OR 97201-6600

**LARSEN, DAVID COBURN,** lawyer, educator; b. Honolulu, Mar. 20, 1944; s. Harold Samuel and Eugenia Bowen (Coburn) L.; m. Pamela Ann Magee, Aug. 1, 1970; 1 child, Jennifer M. BA with honors, U. Va., 1965, MA, 1966; JD, UCLA, 1974. Bar: Calif. 1974, Hawaii 1975. Assoc. Cades Schutte, Honolulu, 1974-80, ptnr., 1980—; tchr. U. Hawaii Law Sch., Honolulu, 1975-79, U. Hawaii Cont. Edn., 1980—. Author: Who Gets It When You Go, 1982, 2d edit. 1987, You Can't Take It With You, 1986. Lt. USN, 1967-70. Ford Found. fellow 1966. Estate planning, Estate taxation, Probate. Office: Cades Schutte PO Box 939 1000 Bishop St Honolulu HI 96808

**LARSEN, DIRK HERBERT,** lawyer, magistrate; b. Minot, N.D., Jan. 3, 1931; s. Norman Herbert and Inez Lockman (Leighton) L.; m. Connie Grace McIver, Nov. 21, 1959; children: Kim, Kyle, Kary. BS, U. Mont., 1952, LLB, 1956. Bar: Mont. 1956, U.S. Dist. Ct. Mont. 1959, U.S. Ct. Appeals (9th cir.) 1959, U.S. Ct. Mil. Appeals 1961, U.S. Supreme Ct. 1961. Practice, Great Falls, Mont., 1956—; mem. Larsen and Gliko, 1972-79, Larsen and Neill, 1979-96, Larsen Law Firm P.L.L.C., 1997—; U.S. commr., 1961-71; magistrate U.S. Dist. Ct. Mont., 1971-88; legal officer Mont. Air N.G., 1958-80. Active mem. Cascade County Hist. Soc., 1998-99. Lt. col. USAFR, 1952-80. Decorated Air Force Commendation medal. Mem. Cascade County Bar Assn. (pres. 1973-74), Mont. Bar Assn. Clubs: Optimists (pres. club 1968-70), Toastmasters (pres. 1960-61); Elks (Great Falls). Author: Montana Collection Law, 1982, Successful Judgement Collection in Montana, 1998. Consumer commercial, General practice, Probate. Office: Ste 2J 121 4th St N Great Falls MT 59405

**LARSEN, LYNN BECK,** lawyer; b. Salt Lake City, Feb. 26, 1945. BA magna cum laude, U. Utah, 1969; MS, U. Wash., 1971; JD with honors, George Washington U., 1975. Bar: Va. 1975, U.S. Dist. Ct. (ea. dist.) Va. 1975, D.C. 1976, U.S. Dist. Ct. D.C. 1976, U.S. Ct. Appeals (4th and D.C. cirs.) 1976, U.S. Claim Ct. 1977, Calif. 1978, U.S. Dist. Ct. (cen. dist.) Calif. 1978, U.S. Dist. Ct. (so. dist.) Calif. 1979, U.S. Ct. Appeals (9th cir.) 1979, U.S. Dist. Ct. (no. and ea. dists.) Calif. 1981, Utah 1983, U.S. Dist. Ct. Utah 1983, U.S. Ct. Appeals (fed. cir.) 1983, U.S. Ct. Appeals (10th cir.) 1988. Engr. Boeing Co., Seattle, 1969-70; engring analyst CIA, Washington, 1971-73, contracting officer, 1973-74; ptnr. Wickwire, Gavin & Gibbs, P.C., Washington, Los Angeles and Salt Lake City, 1974-86, Larsen & Stewart, Salt Lake City, 1986-94, McKay, Burton & Thurman, 1995—; chmn. legal adv. com. Associated Gen. Contractors Calif. 1983, Associated Gen. Contractors Utah. Contbr. articles to profl. jours. Mem. Phi Beta Kappa. Mormon. Construction, Government contracts and claims, General civil litigation. Office: McKay Burton & Thurman 10 E South Temple Ste 600 Salt Lake City UT 84133-1192

**LARSEN, PAUL EDWARD,** lawyer; b. Rock Springs, Wyo., Jan. 5, 1964; s. Otto E. and Linda K. (Wright) L.; m. Dawn Jannette Griffin, June 25, 1986; 1 child, Quinne Caitlin. BA, U. Oreg., 1986, JD, 1989. Bar: Nev. 1989, U.S. Dist. Ct. Nev. 1989, U.S. Ct. Appeals (9th cir.) 1994. Atty. Lionel, Sawyer & Collins, Las Vegas, Nev., 1989—, chmn. land use and planning divsn., 1995—; gen. counsel Nev. State Democrats, 1996, corp. for solar tech. and renewable resources, 1995-96. Author, editor: Nevada Environmental Law Handbook, 1991, 1st edit., 2d edit., 3rd edit.; contbg. author: Nevada Gaming Law, 2d edit., 1995; contbr. articles to profl. jours. Pres., dir. Desert Creek Homeowners Assn., Las Vegas, 1994-95; atty. Clark County Pro-Bono Project, Las Vegas, 1989-95, Nev. Dem. Party, Las Vegas, 1994. Mem. ABA (vice chair com. natural resources pub. lands sect. 1993-95, bd. dirs. young lawyers divsn. natural resources com. 1992-95, atty. young lawyers divsn. program 1989-90), Nev.-Am. Inns of Ct., Nev. Assn. Gaming Attys., Internat. Assn. Gaming Attys. Avocations: scuba diving, golf, fishing. Administrative and regulatory, Constitutional, Entertainment. Office: Lionel Sawyer and Collins 300 S 4th St Ste 1700 Las Vegas NV 89101-6053

**LARSEN-HILL, DI LYN,** paralegal; b. Pocatello, Idaho, Feb. 25, 1955; d. Alvin Julius and Ellen Beth (Barnes) Larsen; m. Edward Michael Hill, July 23, 1983. BA in English and Journalism, Idaho State U., 1979. Sec. U.S. Sen. Frank Church, Pocatello, 1973-74; reporter Blackfoot (Idaho) Morning News, 1979-81, The Observer, La Grande, Oreg., 1981-84; pub. rels. specialist Ea. Oreg. U., La Grande, 1984-90; paralegal Mautz Baum & O'Hanlon, La Grande, 1990—. Mem. La Grande City Coun., 1986—, mayor, 1993-94; pres. League of Oreg. Cities, 1995, treas., 1994, bd. dirs., 1992-96; mem. sml. cities adv. coun. Nat. League of Cities, 1995-97, pub. safety policy com., 1996, steering com. planning nat. conf., 1996; mem. strategies com. Union-Wallowa-Umatilla Counties. Recipient 3d place for investigative reporting Oreg. Newspaper Pubs. Assn., 1983, Pacific N.W. Excellence in Journalism award, 3d place social issues reporting, Sigma Delta Chi, 1983, 3d place in comprehensive coverage, 1983, 3d place sci. and health news and features, 1982. Mem. League of Oreg. Cities Past Pres. Orgn. (charger, chair), Soroptimist Internat. (pres. 1990), Oreg. Trail Toastmasters. Democrat. Home: 1305 O Ave La Grande OR 97850-2430

**LARSON, BRUCE ROBERT,** lawyer, educator; b. Whittier, Calif., Jan. 14, 1955; s. Robert Edward and Ruth Marie (Peterson) L.; m. Judith Elaine Sword, Oct. 30, 1982; children: Seth Julius, Gregory Bruce. BA magna cum laude, Gustavus Adolphus Coll., 1977; JD cum laude, U. Minn., 1980. Bar: Minn. 1980, U.S. Dist. Ct. Minn. 1980, U.S. Ct. Appeals (8th cir.) 1980, Ga. 1986. Immigration officer U.S. Immigration & Naturalization Svc., Mpls., 1977-81; atty. Bd. Immigration Appeals U.S. Dept. Justice, Washington, 1981-85; assoc. Powell, Goldstein, Frazer & Murphy, Atlanta, 1986-89, ptnr., 1990-96; ptnr. Littler, Mendelson, Atlanta, 1996-98; hon. consul of Sweden Atlanta, Ga., 1996—; ptnr. Paul, Hastings, Janofsky, Walker, Atlanta, 1998-99, Flippin, Densmore, morse, Rutherford & Jessee, Roanoke, Va., 1999—; adj. prof. immigration law U. Ga., 1991—; legal advisor Tonka Babe Ruth Baseball League, Minnetonka, Minn., 1980-81. Asst. organist Apostles Luth. Ch., Atlanta, 1986—, mem. coun., 1994-96, pres. 1995; coach Tonka Babe Ruth and Little Leagues, Minnetonka, 1973-81; bd. govs., Scandinavian Am. Found. Ga., Atlanta, 1992—, chmn., 1993-97; bd. dirs. Scandinavian Festival, Inc., 1994-96; asst. dir. Masterworks Chorale, Atlanta, 1988-95; bd. dirs. Swedish Coun. of Am., 1998—, bd. advs. Atlanta Internat. Museum, 1997-99. Recipient Cert. of Merit, U.S. Atty. Gen., 1982-85. Mem. Am. Immigration Lawyers Assn. (chpt. pres. 1991-93, nat. bd. govs.), Swedish-Am. C. of C., Australian-Am. C. of C., Vasa Order of Am., Iota Delta Gamma. Republican. Avocations: music, tennis, bridge, baseball. Immigration, naturalization, and customs, Private international, Labor. Office: Flippin Densmore Morse Rutherford & Jessee 1800 First Union Tower Roanoke VA 24006

**LARSON, BRYAN A.,** lawyer; s. Byron Ancedus and Betty Marilyn Larson; m. Kathy Larson; children: Aaron, Adam, Conor, Kaden, Sara, Aubrey. BA, Brigham Young U., 1980, JD, 1983. Bar: Utah 1983. Assoc. Christensen, Jensen & Powell, Salt Lake City, 1983-86, McKay, Burton & Thurman, Salt Lake City, 1986-91; ptnr. Larson, Jenkins & Halliday, Salt Lake City, 1991-95, Larson, Kirkham & Turner, Salt Lake City, 1995-99, Larson, Turner, Fairbanks and Dalby, Salt Lake City, 1999—. Editor newsletter Backtalk, 1995. Mem. ALTA (mem. polit. action com. 1991—), Utah Bar Assn. (com. chmn. 1990-92), Utah Trial Lawyers Assn. (polit. action com. 1991—), Order of Barristers. Mem. LDS Ch. Avocations: boating, snow skiing. Personal injury, Insurance. Office: Larson Turner Fairbanks & Dalby 4516 S 700 E Ste 100 Salt Lake City UT 84107-8319

**LARSON, DAVID CHRISTOPHER,** lawyer; b. Spencer, Iowa, Sept. 4, 1955; s. Leonard and Margaret Rozanne Larson; m. Carol Ann Kuntz, Sept. 17, 1983. BS in Constrn. Engring., Iowa State U., 1978; JD, Creighton U., 1981. BAr: Iowa 1981, U.S. Patent Office 1981, U.S. Dist. Ct. (no. dist.) Iowa 1981, U.S. Ct. Appeals (8th cir.) 1981. Law clk. Henderson & Sturm, Omaha, 1981; ptnr. Stoller & Larson, Spriti Lake, Iowa, 1981-84; pvt. practice, 1984-98; alt. dist. assoc. judge Iowa Jud. Dist. 3A, 1983-98, dist. assoc. judge, 1998—. Mem. Iowa State Bar Assn. (com. on patents, trademarks and copyrights 1982-86), Iowa Judges Assn., Dist. 3A Bar Assn. (pres. 1983-84), DIckinson County Bar Assn. (chmn. Am. citizen com. 1982-83, pres. 1983-84), Iowa Patent Law Assn., Iowa Great Lakes C. of C. (amb. 1982-86), Okoboji Yacht Club (trophy chmn. 1984-88, bd. dirs. 1987—), Kiwanis (chmn. fin. com. 1983, bd. dirs. 1984, pres. 1987), Masons, Order Eastern Star. Republican. Methodist. Office: PO Box 246 Spirit Lake IA 51360-0246

**LARSON, EDWARD,** state supreme court justice. Justice Kans. Supreme Ct., Topeka, 1995—. Office: Kans Supreme Ct 301 W 10th Rm 388 Topeka KS 66612

**LARSON, ERIK NILS,** lawyer, public defender; b. Oakland, Calif., Sept. 14, 1964; s. Rodney Randall and Corinne Weiss (Edmonson) L. BA, U. Calif., Berkeley, 1987; JD, U. San Francisco, 1995. Bar: Calif. 1995. Sole practitioner San Francisco, 1995-97; dep. state pub. defender Office of State Pub. Defender, San Francisco, 1997—. Capt. U.S. Army Res., Gulf War. Pub. Interest Law scholar, 1995. Mem. Calif. Pub. Defenders Assn. Avocations: surfing, sharpshooting. Office: Office of State Pub Defender 221 Main St Fl 10 San Francisco CA 94105-1925

**LARSON, GLORIA ANN CORDES,** lawyer; b. Rosewell, N.Mex., Apr. 15, 1950; d. Harry N. and Rogene (Corn) Cordes; m. Daniel W. Macklin, Nov. 8, 1975 (div. 1982); m. Allen R. Larson, Dec. 20, 1987. Student, Trinity Coll., 1970-71; BA, Vassar Coll., 1968-72; JD, U. Va., 1977. Bar: Va. 1978, Mass. 1989. Dir. statewide legal svcs. for elderly Legal Svcs. Corp., Richmond, Va., 1977-79; program advisor funeral rule FTC, Washington, 1979-81, legal counsel to commr., 1981-88; ptnr. Larson, Curry & Larson, Hyannis, Mass., 1988-98, Foley, Hoag & Eliot LLP, Boston, 1999—; dep. dir. Bur. Consumer Protection, FTC, Washington, 1989-91; sec., Exec. Office Consumer Protection and Bus. Regulation; sec. Exec. Office Econ.

Affairs Commonwealth of Mass., Boston, 1993-96. Contbr. articles to profl. jours. Chair bd. dirs. Mass. Conv. Ctr. Authority. Named One of Outstanding Young Women in Am., 1979; recipient Outstanding Svc. award FTC, 1991, Wonder Woman award Mass. Women's Polit. Caucus, Outstanding Women Bus. Leaders, New Eng. Coun., 1995, Pinnacle award Grtr. Boston C. of C., 1999. Mem. ABA, Va. Bar Assn. (chmn. com. on legal needs of elderly 1978-82), Mass. Bar Assn., U. Va. Law Women Club. (pres. 1976-77). Republican. Home: 30 Main St Yarmouth Port MA 02675-1618 Office: Foley Hoag & Eliot LLP One Post Office Sq Boston MA 02109

**LARSON, GREGORY SCOTT,** lawyer; b. Fargo, N.D., Oct. 1, 1959; s. Harold Vernon Larson and Ilene Mabel Pederson. BA, Moorhead State, 1983; JD, U. N.D. Sch. Law, 1986. Bar: Calif. 1989. Assoc. James Marinos Law Firm, San Diego, 1989—. Office: James S. Marinos APC 111 Elm St Fl 3 San Diego CA 92101-2692

**LARSON, JERRY LEROY,** state supreme court justice; b. Harlan, Iowa, May 17, 1936; s. Gerald L. and Mary Eleanor (Patterson) L.; m. Debra L. Christensen; children: Rebecca, Jeffrey, Susan, David. BA, State U. Iowa, 1958, JD, 1960. Bar: Iowa. Partner firm Larson & Larson, 1961-75; dist. judge 4th Jud. Dist. Ct. of Iowa, 1975-78; justice Iowa Supreme Ct., 1978—. Office: Supreme Ct Iowa PO Box 109 Des Moines IA 50319-0001

**LARSON, JOHN WILLIAM,** lawyer; b. Detroit, June 24, 1935; s. William and Sara Eleanor (Yeatman) L.; m. Pamela Jane Wren, Sept. 16, 1959; 1 dau., Jennifer Wren. BA with distinction, honors in Economics, Stanford, 1957; LLB, Stanford U., 1962. Bar: Calif. 1962. Assoc. Brobeck, Phleger & Harrison, San Francisco, 1962-68, ptnr., 1968-71, 73—, CEO, mng. ptnr., 1988-92, chmn. of firm, CEO, 1993-96; asst. sec. Dept. Interior, Washington, 1971-73; exec. dir. Natural Resources Com., Washington, 1973; counsellor to chmn. Cost of Living Coun., Washington, 1973; faculty Practising Law Inst. Mem. 1st U.S.-USSR Joint Com. on Environment; mem. bd. visitors Stanford U. Law Sch., 1974-77, 85-87, 95-96; pres. bd. trustees The Katherine Branson Sch., 1980-83. With AUS, 1957-59. Mem. ABA, Calif. Bar Assn., San Francisco C. of C. (bd. dirs., chmn. 1996), Bay Area Coun., Calif. Acad. Sci., San Francisco Partnership, Bay Area Life Scis. Alliance, Order of Coif, Pacific Union Club, Burlingame Country Club, Bohemian Club. General corporate, Mergers and acquisitions, Securities. Home: PO Box 349 Ross CA 94957-0349 Office: Brobeck Phleger & Harrison Spear St Tower 1 Market Plz Ste 341 San Francisco CA 94105-1420

**LARSON, LINDA R.,** lawyer; b. Seattle, Jan. 18, 1954; d. Raymond O. and Ilah B. L. BA in History magna cum laude, U. Wash., 1975, JD, 1978. Bar: Wash. 1979, U.S. Dist. Ct. (we. dist.) Wash. 1982, U.S. Ct. Appeals (9th cir.) 1986, U.S. Dist. Ct. Nebr. 1993, U.S. Dist. Ct. Idaho 1994. Staff counsel U.S. Senate Appropriations Com., Washington, 1978-79; staff atty. and spl. asst. dep. adminstr. NOAA, Washington, 1979-81; assoc. Syrdal, Danelo, Klein, Myre & Woods, Seattle, 1981-88; shareholder Heller Ehrman White & McAuliffe, Seattle, 1988—. Co-author: Washington Environmental Law and Practice, 1997; comments editor Wash. Law Rev., 1977-78; contbr. articles to profl. jours. Trustee Ronald McDonald Childrens Charities We. Washington, Kirkland, 1993-98, Seattle Pub. Libr., Seattle, 1997—; trustee, pres. Seattle Children's Mus., 1992-98; chair Hist. Schs. Taskforce, Seattle, 1997-98; bd. dirs. City Seattle Landmarks Preservation Bd., 1983-89. Mem. ABA, Seattle-King County Bar Assn., Wash. Women Lawyers, Rocky Mt. Mineral Found., Rainier Club. Democrat. Land use and zoning (including planning), Environmental, Federal civil litigation. Office: Heller Ehrman White & McAuliffe 701 5th Ave Ste 6100 Seattle WA 98104-7098

**LARSON, MARK ADAM,** lawyer; b. Steubenville, Jan. 14, 1964. BA, U. Pitts., 1986; JD, U. Akron, 1994. Bar: Pa. 1994, U.S. Dist. Ct. (we. dist.) Pa. 1994. Surety underwriter Chubb Ins., Pitts. and Washington, 1986-89; paralegal Burns, White & Hickton, Pitts., 1989-92; law clk. Magistrate judge C. Laurie U.S. Dist. Ct. No. Dist. Ohio, Cleve., 1993; law clk. Burns, White & Hickton, Pitts., 1993-94, Bowes & Grefenstette, P.C., Pitts., 1994-95; pvt. practice law McKeesport, Pa., 1994-95; of counsel Adams, Myers & Baczkwsoki, McKeesport, 1995; asst. dist. atty. Allegheny County, Pa., 1995—. Recipient Clark Boardman Callaghan Book award Clark Boardman Callaghan Pub. Co., Deerfield, Ill., 1994. Mem. Pa. Bar Assn., Pa. Dist. Atty's. Assn., Allegheny County Bar Assn. Criminal. Office: 401 Courthouse Pittsburgh PA 15219

**LARSON, MARK EDWARD, JR.,** lawyer, educator, financial advisor; b. Oak Park, Ill., Dec. 16, 1947; s. Mark Edward and Lois Vivian (Benson) L.; m. Patricia Jo Jekerle, Apr. 14, 1973; children: Adam Douglas, Peter Joseph, Alex Edward, Gretchen Elizabeth. BS in Acctg., U. Ill., 1969; JD, Northwestern U., 1972; LLM in Taxation, NYU, 1977. Bar: Ill. 1973, N.Y. 1975, D.C. 1976, Minn, 1982, Tex. 1984, U.S. Dist. Ct. (no. dist.) Ill. 1973, U.S. Dist. Ct. (so. dist.) N.Y. 1975, U.S. Ct. Appeals (2d cir.) 1975, U.S. Ct. Appeals (7th cir.) 1976, U.S. Dist. Ct. D.C. 1977, U.S. Ct. Appeals (D.C. cir.) 1977, U.S. Dist. Ct. Minn. 1982, U.S. Ct. Appeals (8th cir.) 1982, U.S. Tax Ct. 1976, U.S. Supreme Ct. 1976; CPA, Ill. Acct. Deloitte & Touche (formerly Haskins & Sells), N.Y.C., Chgo., 1973-81; atty., ptnr. Larson, Perry & Ward and former firms, Chgo., 1981—; prin. Winfield Fin. Svcs. and affiliates, Chgo., 1986—; adj. prof. U. Minn., Mpls., 1982-83, Aurora (Ill.) U., 1990—; program chair CFP Edn. Program No. Ill. U., Chgo., 1996—. Contbr. articles to profl. jours. Mem. ABA, AICPA, AHLA, Am. Assn. Atty.-CPAs. Corporate taxation, Securities, Private international. Office: 1212 S Naper Blvd Ste 119 Naperville IL 60540-7349

**LARSON, OLIVE ELIZABETH,** lawyer; b. Newark, N.J., Jan. 24, 1955; s. Joseph N. and Barbara W. (Paterson) L.; m. Jeffrey S. Larson, Sept. 14, 1991; 1 child, Allegra J. AB cum laude, Boston Coll., 1976; MS in Taxation, Bentley Coll., 1982; JD cum laude, Suffolk U., 1988. Bar: Mass. 1988, U.S. Tax Ct. 1989, U.S. Dist. Ct. Mass. 1989. Tax mgr. Gen. Cinema Corp., Chestnut Hill, Mass., 1977-84, Barry Wright Corp., Newton, Mass., 1984-86; sr. tax. cons. Digital Equipment Corp., Acton, Mass., 1986-88; prin. Olive E. Larson, Boston, 1988-96, Friedman & Atherton, Boston, 1996—; cons. in field. Mem. Boston Bar Assn. Avocations: photography, music, art. Family and matrimonial, Taxation, general, Entertainment. Home: 25 Way To The River Rd West Newbury MA 01985-1217 Office: Friedman & Atherton Exchange Pl 53 State St Boston MA 02109-2804

**LARSON, PAUL MARTIN,** lawyer; b. Tacoma, June 8, 1949; s. Charles Philip and Margeret (Kobervig) L.; m. Kristina Simonson, June 19, 1971; children: Kristin Ilene, Paul Philip, Erika Louise. AB, Stanford U., 1971; JD, Gonzaga U., 1974. Bar: Wash. 1975, U.S. Dist. Ct. (we. dist.) Wash. 1975, U.S. Dist. Ct. (ea. dist.) Wash. 1978, U.S. Ct. Appeals (9th cir.) 1981. Assoc. Hoff & Cross, Tacoma, 1975-76; ptnr., prin. Brooks & Larson, P.S., Yakima, Wash., 1976-87; ptnr. Bogle & Gates, Yakima, 1987-93, Larson & Perkins, 1994—. Author: (with others) Commercial Law Deskbook, 1981. Pres. Cardio & Pulmonary Inst., Yakima, 1981; bd. dirs. Yakima YMCA, 1981-98, Yakima Youth Commn., 1989-93, Yakima Valley chpt. ARC, 1990-93; bd. dirs. Sisters of Providence Med. Ctr.-Yakima Found., 1986-96, pres., 1992-93. Fellow ABA (standing com. lawyer's responsibility for client protection 1984-89); mem. Wash. State Bar Assn. (spl. dist. counsel, 1985-96, pres. corp. bus. and banking sect. 1987-88, chmn. unauthorized practice of law task force 1995-96), Yakima Estate Planning Coun. (pres. 1981), Rotary. Avocations: tennis, fishing. Contracts commercial, Estate planning, Real property. Office: Larson & Perkins PO Box 550 Yakima WA 98907-0550

**LARSON, PETER L.,** legal assistant, investigator; b. Chgo., June 24, 1941; s. Allan M. and Harriet G. (Lans) L.; m. Carole J. Dierking, Feb. 4, 1961; children: Lori, Lance, Lynn, Lee. Assoc. Bus. Adminstrn., Muskegon Bus. U., 1961. South Tex. area mgr. So. Detectives, Inc., Houston, 1976-78; pres. Confidential Investigation Agy., Houston, 1978-85; sr. legal asst. Leger, Coplen & Jefferson, PC, Houston, 1985—; pres. Tex. Inc. Citizens' Property Rights Orgn., Houston. Chmn. Tri-County Foster Parents, Muskegon, 1974; committeeman Boy Scouts Am., Ravenna, Mich., 1972. Staff sgt. USAF, 1961-64. Mem. ATLA (paralegal affiliate), Nat. Assn. Legal Assts. (cert.), Nat. Assn. Legal Investigators (cert., Editor/Pubs. award 1994), Tex. Bd. Legal Specialization (L.A. divsn. stds. cert. civil, personal injury). Avocations: photography/videography, stamps, antique woodworking tools, target pistols, art. Home: 10135 Prospect Hill Dr Houston TX 77064-5439 Office: Tex Citizen Property Rights Org 5847 San Felipe St Ste 2440 Houston TX 77057-3009

**LARSON, THOMAS ROY,** lawyer; b. Kansas City, Mo., May 30, 1950; s. Roya A. and Virginia (Effertz) L.; m. Jane Strub, Sept. 2, 1972; children: Bryan, James, Elizabeth, John. BA, U. Kans., 1972; JD, Washburn U., 1974. Bar: Mo. 1975, U.S. Dist. Ct. (we. dist.) Mo. 1975, U.S. Dist. Ct. (ea. dist.) Mo. 1996, U.S. Ct. Appeals (8th cir.) 1982, U.S. Ct. Appeals (10th cir.) 1996. Assoc. Morris & Larson, Kansas City, 1974-80, shareholder/dir., 1980-89; ptnr. Watson & Marshall, Kansas City, 1990-94, chmn. dept. litigation, 1994; pres. Larson & Larson P.C., Kansas City, 1995—; instr. Rockhurst Coll., Kansas City, 1980-83. Chmn. Visitation Sch. Bd., Kansas City, 1988. Mem. Nat. Propane Def. Assn., Def. Rsch. Inst., Mo. Bar Assn., Kansas City Met. Bar Assn. (com. chair 1975-83—). Republican. Roman Catholic. Product liability, General civil litigation, Appellate. Office: Larson and Larson PC 2345 Grand Blvd Ste 2110 Kansas City MO 64108-2656

**LA RUE, EDWARD RICE,** lawyer; b. Toledo, June 19, 1964; s. Carl Forman and Jane Stevens La R.; m. Beth Nicole Zanelli, May 22, 1993; 1 child, Elizabeth Connell. AB, U. Mich., 1986; JD, Case We. Res. U., 1991. Bar: Ohio 1992, U.S. Dist. Ct. (no. dist.) Ohio 1996. Legal asst. Jones, Day, Reavis & Pogue, Cleve., 1986-88; asst. pros. atty. City of Cleve., 1992-96; mng. ptnr. Edward R. La Rue Atty. Atty.-at-law, Cleve., 1996—; guest trial tactics advisor Case We. Res. U. Sch. Law, Cleve., 1993-98. Founder, bd. dirs. Nature League Mus. Nat. History, Cleve., 1997—. Mem. ABA, Ohio Bar Assn., Cuyahoga Criminal Def. Lawyers Assn. Avocations: reading, sports. Criminal, Constitutional, General civil litigation. Home: 3623 Townley Rd Shaker Heights OH 44122-5119 Office: 526 Superior Ave NE The Leader Bldg Ste 1050 Cleveland OH 44114

**LARUE, PAUL HUBERT,** lawyer; b. Somerville, Mass., Nov. 16, 1922; s. Lucien H. and Germaine (Choquet) LaR.; m. Helen Finnegan, July 20, 1946; children: Paul Hubert, Patricia Seward, Mary Hogan. PhB, U. Wis., 1947, JD, 1949. Bar: Ill. 1955, Wis. 1949, U.S. Supreme Ct. 1972. Instr. polit. sci. dept. U. Wis., 1947-48; mem. staff Wis. Atty. Gen., 1949-50; trial atty., legal advisor to commr. FTC, 1950-55; pvt. practice Chgo.; mem. Chadwell & Kayser, Ltd., 1955-90; ptnr. Vedder, Price, Kaufman & Kammholz, 1990-93; of counsel, 1993-99; spkr. profl. meetings; mem. Com. Modern Cts. in Ill., 1964; mem. Ill. Com. Constl. Conv., 1968, Better Govt. Assn., 1966-70;. Contbr. articles to profl. jours. Mem. lawyers com. Met. Crusade of Mercy, 1967-68, United Settlement Appeal, 1966-68; apptd. pub. mem. Ill. Conflict of Interest Laws Commn., 1965-67. With AUS, 1943-45, ETO; capt. JAGC, USAFR, 1950-55. Fellow Ill. Bar Found. (life); mem. ABA (mem. coun. sect. antitrust law 1980-83, chmn. Robinson-Patman Act com. 1975-78), Ill. State Bar Assn., Chgo. Bar Assn. (chmn. antitrust com. 1970-71), Wis. State Bar, Rotary. Roman Catholic. Fax: 847-825-3363. E-mail: phlarue@msn.com. Antitrust, Federal civil litigation, Alternative dispute resolution. Home and Office: 250 Cuttriss Pl Park Ridge IL 60068

**LARZELERE, KATHY LYNN HECKLER,** paralegal; b. Sellersville, Pa., Dec. 4, 1955; d. Harold Tyson and Hannah Ruth (Wile) Heckler; m. Lawrence Sollanek, Nov. 1984 (div.); m. Loel Harry Larzelere, Aug. 27, 1992; 1 stepdaughter, Lindsie M. AAS magna cum laude, Columbus State C.C., 1991. From sales person to dept. mgr. Macy's New York, North Wales, Pa., 1977-83; store mgr. Bathtique, Wilmington, Del., Towson, Md., 1983-86; customer svc. person Marshall Fields, Chgo., 1987; word processor Franklin County Children Svcs., Columbus, Ohio, 1988-89; legal sec., paralegal M. Cohen and Assocs., Columbus, 1989-94; paralegal Calig and Handelman LPA, Columbus, 1994-97, Weltman, Weinberg & Reis, Columbus, 1997—. Author: (poetry) American High School Poets, 1973. Ward coord. Amelia Salerno for City Coun., Columbus, 1993. Mem. award Phi Theta Kappa. Mem. Nat. Fedn. Paralegal Asns., Paralegal Assn. Cen. Ohio (writer newsletter The Citator, co-chair student outreach com. 1994-95, chair 1995-97, 1st v.p. 1995-97, pres. 1997-99, mem. adv. bd. 1999—, chair student outreach com. 1999—), Columbus Bar Assn. (assoc.). Lutheran. Avocations: handcrafts, reading, walking, watercolor painting, counted cross-stitch. Home: 2119 Kingsglen Dr Grove City OH 43123-1252 Office: Weltman Weinberg & Reis 175 S 3rd St Ste 900 Columbus OH 43215-5177

**LASAK, JOHN JOSEPH,** lawyer; b. Moosic, Pa., Jan. 18, 1944; s. Frank J. and Ann (Grudzinski) L.; m. Julilee Werteen, Mar. 17, 1973; children: Jennifer Ann, James Michael, Jessica Lee, Jill Emily. AB cum laude, U. Pa., 1965; JD, Harvard U., 1968. Bar: Pa. 1968. Assoc. Crumlish & Kania, Phila., 1968, Kania & Garbarino, Rosemont, Pa., 1971-76; ptnr. Kania & Garbarino, Bala Cynwyd, Pa., 1977-82, Kania, Lindner, Lasak & Feeney, Bala Cynwyd, 1982—. Vice chmn. Haverford Twp. Planning Commn., 1983; mem. Radnor Twp. (Pa.) Zoning Bd., 1985-92, 94—, vice chmn., 1987-91, 96, chmn., 1992, 97; mem. Radnor Twp. Planning Commn., 1993; co-chmn. Delaware County Transition Coun., 1995-98. Mem. ABA, Pa. Bar Assn., Phila. Bar Assn., Harvard-Radcliffe Club (Phila.), St. Albans Club (Newtown Square, Pa.), Phi Beta Kappa. Republican. Roman Catholic. General corporate, Real property. Office: 2 Bala Plz Ste 525 Bala Cynwyd PA 19004-1501

**LA SALLE, LAWRENCE JOSEPH,** judge; b. N.Y.C., Aug. 21, 1951; s. Louis and Iris LaS.; m. Larancelle Annette Hinton, Mar. 30, 1955; children: Lisa, Lawrence Jr. BA, Fordham U., 1975; JD, Cleve. State U., 1978. Bar: Ohio 1978, U.S. Dist. Ct. (so. dist.) Ohio 1985. Staff atty. Southeast Ohio Legal Svcs., Zanesville, 1982-85, Ohio Dept. Taxation, Columbus, 1985-87; adminstrv. law judge Ohio Bd. Tax Appeals, Columbus, 1987—. Home: 3140 Norwood St Columbus OH 43224-4243 Office: Ohio Bd Tax Appeals 30 E Broad St Columbus OH 43215-3414

**LASAROW, WILLIAM JULIUS,** retired federal judge; b. Jacksonville, Fla., June 30, 1922; s. David Herman and Mary (Hollins) L.; m. Marilyn Doris Powell, Feb. 4, 1951; children: Richard M., Elisabeth H. BA, U. Fla., 1943; JD, Stanford U., 1950. Bar: Calif. 1951. Counsel judiciary com. Calif. Assembly, Sacramento, 1951-52; dep. dist. atty. Stanislaus County, Modesto, Calif., 1952-53; pvt. practice law L.A., 1953-73; bankruptcy judge U.S. Cts., L.A., 1973-94; chief judge U.S. Bankruptcy Ct., Central dist., Calif., 1978-90; judge Bankruptcy Appellate Panel 9th Fed. Cir., 1980-82; fed. judge U.S. Bankruptcy Ct., L.A., 1973; faculty Fed. Jud. Ctr. Bankruptcy Seminars, Washington, 1977-82. Contbg. author, editor legal publs.; staff: Stanford U. Law Review, 1949. Mem. ABA, Am. Coll. Bankruptcy, Am. Bankruptcy Inst., Nat. Conf. Bankruptcy Judges, Los Angeles County Bar Assn., Wilshire Bar Assn., Blue Key, Phi Beta Kappa, Phi Kappa Phi. Home: 11623 Canton Pl Studio City CA 91604-4164

**LASCARA, DOMINIC PAUL,** lawyer; b. Portsmouth, Va., July 9, 1958; s. Vincent Edward Sr. and Antoinette Marie Lascara; m. Shadi Raha, May 14, 1988; children: Michael Dominic, Danielle Marie. BSBA magna cum laude, Old Dominion U., 1981; JD, Coll. William and Mary, 1986. Bar: Va. 1986, U.S. Bankrupcy Ct. (ea. dist.) 1987. Mgr. The Atlete's Foot, Virginia Beach, Va., 1975-80, Aamco Transmissions, Portsmouth, 1980-82; ptnr. Roy Larsen Romm & Lascara, P.C., Chesapeake, Va., 1986—. Mem. Tidewater Bankruptcy Bar Assn., Chesapeake Bar Assn., Kiwanis Club Gt. Bridge (pres. 1994). Roman Catholic. Real property, Bankruptcy, General corporate. Home: 829 Loch Island Dr Chesapeake VA 23320-9284 Office: Roy Larsen Romm Lascara PC 109 Wimbledon Sq Ste A Chesapeake VA 23320-4945

**LASEE, MARK EDWARD,** lawyer; b. Burbank, Calif., Mar. 12, 1957; m. Jean A. Lasee, July 24, 1982. BSBA, U. Wis., 1979; JD, Hamline U., 1983. Bar: Minn. 1983, U.S. Dist. Ct. Minn. 1983, Ariz. 1986, U.S. Dist. Ct. Ariz. 1986. Assoc. Thomsen Nybeck Johnson Bouquet and Van Valkenburg, Edina, Minn., 1983-86; ptnr. Shull, Rolle, Watland & Kalyna, Phoenix, 1986-92, Watland, Allen & Lasee PLLC, Phoenix, 1992—. Mem. Kiwanis (pres. Metroctr. chpt. 1994-95). Avocation: sailing. Contracts commercial, Real property, State civil litigation. Office: Watland Allen & Lasee PLLC 393 E Palm Ln Phoenix AZ 85004-1532

**LASH, RICHARD ANTHONY,** lawyer; b. Radford, Va., Jan. 17, 1961; s. Thomas Nicholas and Anne Carol (Devonald) L.; m. Kathleen Marie Davis, June 21, 1986; children; Carolina Portia, Margaret Electra, Robert Michael, Stephanie Perdita, Virginia Grace. AB, Coll. of William & Mary, 1983; diploma in internat. and comparative law, U. San Diego, 1985; JD, George Mason U., 1986; LLM in Internat. and Comparative Law, George Washington U., 1991. Bar: Md. 1986, U.S. Ct. Appeals (D.C. cir.) 1987, U.S. Dist. Ct. Md. 1987, U.S. Dist. Ct. D.C. 1987, U.S. Dist. Ct. (ea. dist.) Va. 1987, D.C. 1987, U.S. Bankruptcy Ct. 1987, U.S. Ct. Internat. Trade 1988, U.S. Ct. Appeals (fed. cir.) 1988, U.S. Supreme Ct. 1992. Rsch. asst. George Mason U., Arlington, Va., 1984-85; claims specialist USDA, Washington, 1985-86; atty. Buonassissi, Henning, Campbell & Moffet, P.C., Fairfax, Va., 1986—. Co-author (with James E. Byrne): Actions & Remedies: Partnerships and Corporations, 1985. Del. Rep. State Conv., Virginia Beach, Va., 1980; bd. dirs., sec., treas. Ashton Housing Corp., 1991-93. Mem. ABA, Va. State Bar Assn., Md. State Bar Assn., D.C. Bar Assn., Fairfax Bar Assn., am. Soc. Internat. Law, George Mason U. Alumni Assn. (bd. dirs. 1987—, v.p. 1990-91, pres. 1992-93), Holy Trinity Sch. Home Sch. Assn. (bd. dirs. 1994—, pres. elect 1994—), Georgetown Club, Phi Kappa Tau, Delta Theta Phi (bailiff 1984-85, tribune 1985-86). Episcopalian. Avocation: classical studies. General civil litigation, General corporate, Public international. Home: 3009 2d St N 1711 N Edgewood St Arlington VA 22201-4037 Office: Buonassissi Henning Campbell & Moffett PC 11350 Random Hills Rd Ste 600 Fairfax VA 22030-7430

**LASHLEY, CURTIS DALE,** lawyer; b. Urbana, Ill., Nov. 3, 1956; s. Jack Dale and Janice Elaine (Holman) L.; m. Tamara Dawn Yahnig, June 14, 1986. BA, U. Mo., Kansas City, 1978, JD, 1981. Bar: Mo. 1981, U.S. Dist. Ct. (we. dist.) Mo. 1981, U.S. Tax Ct. 1982, U.S. Ct. Appeals (8th cir.) 1992. Assoc. Melvin Heller, Inc., Creve Coeur, Mo., 1982; ptnr. Domjan & Lashley, Harrisonville, Mo., 1983-86; asst. gen. counsel Mo. Dept. Revenue, Independence, 1986-89, assoc. gen. counsel, 1989-92, sr. counsel, 1992—, adminstrv. hearing officer, 1995—; spl asst. atty. gen., 1986—; spl. asst. prosecutor Jackson County, Mo., 1990—; city atty., Adrian and Strasburg, Mo., 1985-86. V.p. Cass County Young Reps., Harrisonville, 1985. Mem. ABA, Kiwanis (treas. Harrisonville chpt. 1985-86, Harrisonville Disting. Svc. award 1985), NRA, Phi Alpha Delta. Republican. Presbyterian. Office: Mo Dept Revenue 16647 E 23rd St S Independence MO 64055-1922

**LASHLEY, LENORE CLARISSE,** lawyer; b. N.Y.C., June 3, 1934; d. Leonard Livingston and Una Ophelia (Laurie) L.; children: Donna Bee-Gates, Michele Bee, Maria Bee. BA, CUNY, 1956; MSW, U. Calif., Berkeley, 1970, MPH, 1975; JD, U. Calif., San Francisco, 1981. Bar: Calif. 1981. Atty. W.O.M.A.N., Inc., San Francisco, 1982-84; pvt. practice San Francisco Law Office, 1984-87; dep. dist. atty. Monterey Dist. Atty., Salinas, Calif., 1987-89; trial atty. State Bar of Calif., L.A., 1989; dep. dist. atty. L.A. Dist. Atty., 1989; dep. city atty. Office of City Atty., L.A., 1989—; chair, bd. dirs. St. Anthony's Dining Room, San Francisco, 1986-87; sec., bd. dirs. NAAC, Monterey, 1987-88; bd. dirs. Childrens Home Soc., Oakland, Calif., 1966-68. Recipient Cert. of Merit, Nat. Assn. Naval Officers, 1987. Mem. L.A. County Bar Assn. (del. to state bar 1992, 93). Roman Catholic. Avocations: running, reading, animal welfare, volunteer work with people with AIDS. Office: City Atty LA 200 N Main St Ste 1700 Los Angeles CA 90012-4110

**LASHMAN, L. EDWARD,** arbitrator, mediator, consultant; b. New Orleans, June 6, 1924; s. L. Edward and Edith Ruth (Deutsch) L.; m. Elizabeth Gitt Fichman, June 6, 1948 (dec. Aug. 1984); children: Deborah, Rebekah, David W. (dec. Feb. 1993), Judith; m. Joyce Blicher Schwartz, July 25, 1987. Student, U. N.C., 1940-42, Tulane U., 1942-43. Ptnr. Caire Assocs., New Orleans, 1946-51; with CIO and AFL-CIO, 1951-67; asst. to sec., dir. cong. liason HUD, Washington, 1967-69; mng. ptnr. Urban Housing Assocs., Denver, 1969-70; v.p. U. Mass., 1970-75; dir. external affairs, sr. planning counselor Harvard U., Cambridge, Mass., 1975-89; sec. adminstrn. and fin. Commonwealth of Mass., Boston, 1989-91, chmn. bd. regents pub. higher edn., 1986-88; chmn. Mass. Housing Fin. Agy., Boston, 1977-79, Commonwealth Land Bank, Boston, 1975-77; acting exec. dir. Mass. State Lottery, 1999. Mem. exec. com. Denver County Dem. Party, 1952-64; chmn. Colo. Urban League, Denver, 1961-63; acting COO (pro bono) Judge Baker Children's Ctr., Boston, 1993-94; dir. Nat. Housing Conf., Washington, 1969-75; v.p. Handel & Haydn Soc., Boston, 1982-84. With U.S. Army, 1943-46, ETO. Mem. Am. Arbitration Assn., Mass. Assn. Mediation Programs, Norfolk and Suffolk County Superior Ct. Mediation Panels, Joint Labor Mgmt. Com. Mediation Panel. Avocations: fly fishing, cooking, photography. Home and Office: 236 Conant Rd Weston MA 02493-1654

**LASHMAN, SHELLEY BORTIN,** judge; b. Camden, N.J., Aug. 18, 1917; s. William Mitchell and Anna (Bortin) L.; m. Ruth Horn, Jan. 3, 1959; children: Karen E. Lashman Hall, Gail A. McBride, Mitchell A., Christopher R. BS, William and Mary Coll., 1938; postgrad., Columbia U., 1938, 39; JD, U. Mich., 1946. Bar: N.Y. 1947, N.J. 1968. Judge N.J. Workers Compensation, 1981—. With USNR, 1940-70. Mem. Atlantic County Bar Assn., Am. Judges Assn., Atlantic County Hist. Soc., Am. Judicature Soc., Ret. Officers Assn., U.S. Navy League, Fleet Res. Assn., USS Yorktown CV-5 Club, Mil. Order World Wars. Republican. Fax: 609-441-3161. Home: 1209 Old Zion Rd Egg Harbor Township NJ 08234-7667 Office: Atlantic County Office Bldg 1333 Atlantic Ave Atlantic City NJ 08401

**LASKER, MORRIS E.,** judge; m. Helen M. Schubach; 4 children. BA magna cum laude Harvard U., 1938; LLB, JD Yale U., 1941. Bar: N.Y. 1941. Atty. Nat. Def. Com., U.S. Senate, 1941-42, Battle, Fowler, Jaffin & Kheel, 1946-68; fed. judge, U.S. Dist. Ct. (so. dist.) N.Y., 1968-94; fed. judge, U.S. Dist. Ct., Boston, Mass., 1994—; bd. dirs. Vera Inst. Justice. Contbr. articles to profl. jours. Maj. U.S. Army, 1942-46. Recipient Learned Hand medal Fed. Bar Coun., Edward Weinfeld award N.Y. County Lawyers Assn. Mem. ABA, Assn. of Bar of City of N.Y. (exec. com. 1985-89). Avocations: gardening, reading, history, English and American literature. Office: US Dist Ct US Courthouse 1 Courthouse Way Boston MA 02210-3002

**LASKEY, JAMES HOWARD,** lawyer; b. N.Y.C., Dec. 19, 1953; s. Herbert M. and Mina (Yohalem) L.; m. Mary C. Jacobson, Oct. 1, 1983; children: Michael Henry, Kevin Connor, Katherine Anne. BS, MIT, 1975; JD, Yale U., 1978. Bar: N.J. 1978, U.S. Tax Ct. 1982. Law sec. to Hon. Sidney M. Schreiber N.J. Supreme Ct., Newark, 1978-79; atty. antitrust divsn. U.S. Dept. Justice, Washington, 1979-82; assoc. Rosen, Gelman & Weiss, Newark, 1982-84; assoc. Norris, McLaughlin & Marcus, Somerville, N.J., 1984-86, ptnr., 1986—. Contbr. articles to profl. jours. Mem. mgmt. com. RideWise Raritan Valley, Somerville, N.J., 1993—. Mem. ABA (mem. antitrust sect., pub. utility law sects.), N.J. State Bar Assn. (chair pub. utility law sect. 1997-98), Somerset County C. of C. (bd. dirs. 1997—), Fed. Comms. Bar Assn., Yale Law Sch. N.J. Alumni Assn. (pres.). Administrative and regulatory, Antitrust, Public utilities. Office: Norris McLaughlin & Marcus 721 Rt 202-206 PO Box 1018 Somerville NJ 08876

**LASKY, DAVID,** lawyer, corporate executive; b. N.Y.C., Nov. 12, 1932; s. Benjamin and Rebecca (Malumed) L.; m. Phyllis Beryl Sumper, Apr. 14, 1957; children—Jennifer Lee, Robert Barry. BA, Bklyn. Coll., 1954; LLB, Columbia U., 1957. Bar: N.Y. 1957. Atty. N.Y.C. R.R. Co., 1957-62; with Curtiss-Wright Corp., N.Y.C., 1962—, corp. counsel, 1966-67, gen. counsel, 1967-93, v.p., 1972-80, sr. v.p., 1980-93, sec., 1989-93, pres., 1993-99, chmn., 1995—; bd. dirs. Primex Technologies, Inc. Chmn. zoning bd. appeals, Ramapo, N.Y., 1968-72; dir., v.p. Oak Trail Homeowners Assn., 1987-90. Mem. ABA (chmn. com. corp. gen. counsel 1992-93), N.Y. Bar Assn., Phi Beta Kappa. Contracts commercial, General corporate, Securities. Office: 1200 Wall St W Ste 501 Lyndhurst NJ 07071-3680

**LA SORSA, WILLIAM GEORGE,** lawyer, educator; b. Lancaster, Pa, Apr. 30, 1945; s. Francis Peter and Madge Marian (Hanson) L.; m. Linda Kay Chappell, Dec. 8, 1973. BA, Marquette U., 1967; JD, U. Tulsa, 1973. Bar: Okla. 1974, U.S. Dist. Ct. (no. dist.) Okla. 1976, U.S. Ct. Appeals (10th cir.) 1976, U.S. Supreme Ct. 1977, U.S. Ct. Mil. Appeals 1985. Asst. dist. atty. Tulsa County Dist. Atty.'s Office, Tulsa, 1974-80; assoc. Howard & Rapp, Tulsa, 1980-81, Gene C. Howard & Assocs., Tulsa, 1981-82; ptnr. Howard, La Sorsa & Widdows, Tulsa, 1982-85, La Sorsa & Weber, Tulsa, 1985-87, La Sorsa, Weber & Miles, P.C., Tulsa, 1987-93; shareholder Corbitt, La Sorsa, Rineer & Zacharias, P.C., 1993-96, Jones, Givens, Gotcher & Bogan, P.C., Tulsa, 1996—; spl. prosecutor Tulsa County Dist. Atty.'s Office, 1996-97; adj. prof. Tulsa Jr. Coll., 1978-83, Langston U., 1983-84. Capt. U.S. Army, 1969-72, Vietnam; lt. col. USAR, ret. Fellow Am. Bar Found., Okla. Bar Found. (trustee), Tulsa County Bar Found. (charter), ABA (litigation and family law sects.); mem. Okla. Bar Assn. (bd. govs. 1994-96, family law sect., exec. com.), ATLA, Okla. Trial Lawyers Assn., Tulsa County Bar Assn. (chmn. fee arbitration com. 1992-93), Am. Inns. of Ct. (master, Hudson-Hall-Wheaton chpt.), Lions Club Internat. (pres. Brookside chpt. 1986-87),

Porsche Club Am. (pres. War Bonnet region 1981-82). Republican. Roman Catholic. Family and matrimonial, General civil litigation, Criminal. Office: Jones Givens Gotcher & Bogan PC 15 E 5th St Ste 3800 Tulsa OK 74103-4309

**LASSAR, SCOTT R.,** lawyer; b. Evanston, Ill., Apr. 5, 1950; s. Richard Ernest and Jo (Ladenson) L.; m. Elizabeth Levine, May 22, 1977; children: Margaret, Kate. B.A., Oberlin Coll., 1972; J.D., Northwestern U., 1975. Bar: Ill. 1975. Former dep. chief spl. prosecutions divsn. no. dist. Office U.S. Atty., Chgo.; former ptnr. Keck, Mahin & Cate, Chgo.; now U.S. atty. North Dist. Dept. Justice, Chgo. Office U.S. Atty., Chgo. Criminal. Office: US Attys Office 219 S Dearborn St Chicago IL 60604-1702*

**LASSETER, EARLE FORREST,** lawyer; b. Gadsden, Ala., Dec. 26, 1933; s. Thomas Hobart and Mildred (Williamson) L.; m. Sally Elizabeth Bork, Sept. 2, 1961; children: Sally Fernald, David Forrest. BS, Auburn U., 1957; LLB, U. Ala., 1966. Bar: Ala. 1966, Ala. Supreme Ct. 1966, U.S. Ct. Military Appeals 1970, U.S. Dist. Ct. D.C. 1971, U.S. Ct. Internat. Trade 1971, D.C. 1972, U.S. Supreme Ct. 1972, Ga. 1987, Ga. Supreme Ct. 1988, U.S. Ct. Appeals Ga. 1988, U.S. Dist. Ct. (no. and mid. dists.) Ga. 1988, U.S. Ct. Vet. Appeals 1992, U.S. Ct. Claims 1994. Commd. U.S. Army, 1958, advanced through grades to col., 1987; dep. staff judge adv. Hdqs. 1st Cav. Divsn., Republic of Vietnam, 1968-69; exec. officer Hdqs. U.S. Army Europe, Heidelberg, Germany, 1969-70; dep. staff judge adv. U.S. Army, Berlin, 1970-72; student Command and Gen. Staff Coll., Ft. Leavenworth, Kans., 1972; staff judge adv. 82d Airborne Divsn., Ft. Bragg, N.C., 1972-75; legal advisor Mil. Assistance Command and Am. Embassy, Taipei, Taiwan, 1975-77; staff judge adv. U.S. Army Mil. Police Sch., Ft. McClellan, Ala., 1977-79, U.S. Army Inf. Ctr., Ft. Benning, Ga., 1979-83; student U.S. Army War Coll., Carlisle Barracks, Pa., 1983; staff judge adv. U.S. Army Forces Command, Ft. McPherson, Ga., 1983-87; ret., 1987; ptnr. Pope, McGlamry, Kilpatrick & Morrison, Atlanta, Columbus, Ga., 1988—. Contbr. articles to profl. jours. Pres. Ft. Benning Sch. Bd., 1980-82. Col. U.S. Army. Decorated Purple Heart, Bronze Star with Oak Leaf Cluster, Legion of Merit, Meritorious Svc. medal with two Oak Leaf Clusters; recipient Air medal, Master Parachutists Wings, Taiwan. Mem. ABA (chmn. 1991-92, bd. govs. 1996—, treas. 1999—), Ga. State Bar (bd. govs. 1995—), Ala. State Bar, Ala. Trial Lawyers Assn., Ga. Trial Lawyers Assn., Army-Navy Country Club (Arlington, Va.), Army-Navy Club (Washington), Green Island Country Club. Avocations: golf, tennis, running. Personal injury, General civil litigation, Product liability. Home: 6855 Ranch Forest Dr Columbus GA 31904-2428 Office: Pope McGlamry et al PO Box 943 318 11th St Columbus GA 31902

**LASSMAN, IRO RICHARD,** lawyer; b. Munich, Germany, May 21, 1946; came to U.S., 1949; s. Walter Zev and Eva (Biologrod) L.; m. Gail Ellen Hecker, June 9, 1967; children: Hannah, Eli. BA in Psychology, U. Wash., 1968; JD, Gonzaga U., 1976. Bar: Wash. 1976, U.S. Dist. Ct. (ea. dist.) Wash. 1976, (we. dist.) Wash. 1982, U.S. Ct. Appeals (9th cir.) Wash. 1980. Mng. atty. Spokane (Wash.) Legal Svcs., 1976-80; atty. gen. Commonwealth of the No. Mariana Islands, Saipan, 1980-82; assoc. atty. Gaines Law Firm, Seattle, 1982-83, Alexander & Assocs., Seattle, 1989-90; sr. atty. Great Am. Ins. Co., Seattle, 1983-89, 90-92; pvt. practice Bergman, Gibbs & Lassman, Seattle, Wash., 1992—. With U.S. Army, 1969-71. General civil litigation, Insurance, Personal injury. Office: Bergman Gibbs & Lassman 2420 One Union Square Seattle WA 98101

**LASTER, GAIL W.,** lawyer. BA, Yale U.; JD, NYU. Law clk. to Judge Mary Johnson Lowe U.S. Dist. Ct. (so. dist.) N.Y., 1983-85; staff atty. Pub. Defender Svc. D.C., 1985-90; counsel com. labor and human resources, subcom. labor U.S. Senate, 1990-92; counsel subcom. antitrust, monopolies and bus. rights U.S. Senate on Judiciary, 1992-94; dir. govtl. rels., counsel Legal Svcs. Corp., 1994—; gen. counsel U.S. Dept. Housing and Urban Devel., Washington, 1997—. Office: Dept Housing and Urban Devel 451 7th St SW Washington DC 20410-0002

**LASTER, J. TRAVIS,** lawyer; b. Beirut, Nov. 10, 1969; s. James H. and Madlon T. L.; m. Rebecca G. Wells, May 22, 1993. AB summa cum laude, Princeton U., 1991; JD, U. Va., 1995, MA in Govt., 1996. Bar: Va. 1995, Del. 1996. Law clk. to Hon. Jane R. Ruth U.S. Ct. Appeals, Wilmington, Del., 1995-96; assoc. Richards, Layton & Finger, Wilmington, 1996—. Editor U. Va. Law Rev., 1993-94, mem. articles rev. bd., 1994-95; contbr. articles to profl. jours. Recipient Alumni Assn. award U. Va., 1995. Mem. Order of Coif. General corporate, State civil litigation, Federal civil litigation. Office: Richards Layton & Finger One Rodney Sq Wilmington DE 19801

**LASTER MAYS, ANITA,** lawyer, accountant; b. Cleve., Oct. 19, 1964; d. Charles Lee and Evelyn Madeline (Brooks) L.; m. Kurt LaSalle Mays, June 22, 1996; children: Christin Imani, Courtney Malik, Cory Jamaal. BA in Acctg. and MIS, Ohio State U., 1986; JD, Cleve. State U., 1992. Bar: Ohio 1992. Mgmt. trainee State Savs. Bank, Columbus, Ohio, 1986-87; fin. sys. analyst Met. Health Med. Ctr., Cleve., 1987-94; asst. city prosecutor City of Cleve., 1994-96; dir. ops. Cleve. Clk. Cts., 1996—. Mem. Black Women's Polit. Action Com., Cleve., 1997. Baptist. Avocations: reading, sewing, coin collecting. Home: 3022 Albion Rd Cleveland OH 44120-2706

**LASTRA, CARLOS MARIANO,** lawyer; b. N.Y.C., Aug. 29, 1967; s. Carlos Gerardo andMercedes (Caridad) L.; m. Sheri Lynn Turnbow, Apr. 5, 1997. BA, U. Miami, 1989, JD, 1992. Bar: Fla. 1992, D.C. 1994, U.S. Ct. Appeals (fed. cir.) 1994, U.S. Ct. Appeals (11th cir.) 1993, U.S. Dist. Ct. (so. dist.) Fla. 1993, U.S. Dist. Ct. (mid. dist.) Fla. 1993. Law clk. Dade Ct. Ct. Judge Leonard M. Rivkind, Miami, 1990; intern Law Offices of Janet Reno, Miami, 1992; asoc. atty. Law Offices of Richard H. Ferro, Miami, 1992-95, of counsel, 1995—; sole practice law Miami, 1993—; spl. asst. pub. defender Dade County Pub. Defender's Office, Miami, 1996—. Mem. ABA, ATLA. Home: 698 NE 69th St Miami FL 33138-5704 Office: 2828 Coral Way Ste 306 Miami FL 33145-3214

**LATCHUM, JAMES LEVIN,** federal judge; b. Milford, Del., Dec. 23, 1918; s. James H. and Ida Mae (Robbins) L.; m. Elizabeth Murray McArthur, June 16, 1943; children: Su-Allan, Elizabeth M. A.B. cum laude, Princeton U., 1940; J.D., U. Va., 1946. Bar: Va. 1942, Del. 1947. Assoc. Berl, Potter & Anderson, Wilmington, 1946-53; partner Berl, Potter & Anderson, 1953-68; judge U.S. Dist. Ct. Del., Wilmington, 1968-73; chief judge U.S. Dist. Ct. Del., 1973-83, sr. judge, 1983—; New Castle County atty. Del. Hwy. Dept., 1948-50; asst. U.S. atty., 1950-53; atty. Del. Interstate Hwy. Div., 1955-62, Delaware River and Bay Authority, 1962-68. Chmn. New Castle County Democratic Com., 1953-56, Wilmington City Com., 1959-63. Served to maj. Insp. Gen. Corps AUS, 1942-46, PTO. Mem. ABA, Del. Bar Assn., Va. Bar Assn., Order of Coif, Sigma Nu Phi. Presbyn. Clubs: Wilmington, Univ. Office: US Dist Ct 844 N King St # 34 Wilmington DE 19801-3519

**LATHAM, WELDON HURD,** lawyer; b. Bklyn., Jan. 2, 1947; s. Aubrey Geddes and Avril (Hurd) L.; m. Constantia Beecher, Aug. 8, 1948; children: Nicole Marie, Brett Weldon. BA, Howard U., 1968; JD, Georgetown U., 1971, postgrad., 1975-76. Bar: D.C. 1972, U.S. Ct. Appeals (D.C. cir.) 1972, U.S. Ct. Mil. Appeals 1974, U.S. Ct. Claims 1975, U.S. Supreme Ct. 1975, Va. 1981, U.S. Ct. Appeals (fed. cir.) 1988. Mgmt. coms. Checchi & Co., Washington, 1968-71; atty. Covington & Burling, Washington, 1971-73; sr. atty. Fed. Energy Adminstrn., Washington, 1974; asst. gen. counsel Exec. Office Pres. Office Mgmt. and Budget The White House, Washington, 1974-76; atty. Hogan & Hartson, Washington, 1976-79; gen. dep. asst. sec. HUD, Washington, 1979-81; v.p., gen. counsel Sterling Sys., Inc. subs. PRC.; exec. asst., counsel to chmn., CEO, assoc. gen. counsel Planning Rsch. Corp., McLean, Va., 1981-86; mng. ptnr. Reed, Smith, Shaw & McClay, McLean, Va., 1986-91; sr. ptnr. Shaw, Pittman, Potts & Trowbridge, Washington, 1992—; adj. prof. Howard U. Law Sch., Washington, 1972-82; guest prof. U. Va., Charlottesville, 1976-90; mem. Va. Govs. Bus. and Industry Adv. Com. on Crime Prevention, 1983-85, Va. Govs. Regulatory Reform Adv. Bd., 1982-84; chmn. task force SBA, 1982; legal counsel Md. Mondale for Pres. Campaign, 1984; gen. counsel Nat. Coalition Minority Bus., 1993—. Columnist Minority Bus. Entrepreneur Mag., 1991—; mem. editl. bd. Washington Bus. Jour., 1985-87. Washington steering com. NAACP Legal Def. Fund, 1975-95, Fairfax County Airports Adv. Com., 1987-88; bd. dirs., gen. counsel Northern Va. Minority Bus. and Profl. Assn., 1985-92; trustee Va. Commonwealth U., Richmond, 1986-90, George Mason U., Fairfax, Va., 1990-94; bd. dirs. Washington Urban League, 1986-90, U. D.C. Found., 1982-87, Washington Coun. Lawyers, 1973, Profl. Svcs. Coun., 1983-88, Minority Bus. Enterprise Legal Def. and Edn. Fund, 1989-91, Wash. Hosp. Ctr. Found., 1996-98; appointee Greater Washington Bd. Trade, Blue Ribbon Task Force on Home Rule, 1985-86, bd. dirs., exec. com., chmn. regional affairs com., corp. sec. Greater Wash. Bd. Trade, 1990-95; adv. bd. First Union Nat. Bank, 1995—; civilian aide Sec. Dept. of Army, 1995—; active Clinton Small Bus. Adminstrn. Nat. Adv. Coun., 1993—, Burger King Corp. Diversity Action Coun., 1996-98, Md. Econ. Devel. Commn., 1996-98, Gov. Bd. Transition Team, 1995, Dem. Nat. Com., 1996, Platform Drafting Com., 1996; prin. coun. for Excellence in Govt., 1989—; mayor D.C. Internat. Ins. Adv. Commn., 1994-95; chmn. D.C. Mayors Bus. Adv. Coun., 1994-96; vice-chmn. Dem. Bus. Coun. DNC, 1994—; co-chmn. UNCF Sportsfest Fundraiser, 1994; hon. vice-chmn. Clinton-Gore Campaign, 1996, Metro. Washington Airports Authority, 1997—; bd. govs. Joint Ctr. Polit. and Econ. Studies, 1998—; gen. counsels Honors Program Office Sec. Capt. USAF, 1973-74. Recipient SES Effective Mgr. award HUD, 1980, Nat. Assn. for Equal Achievement Opportunity in Higher Edn. award, 1987. Mem. ABA (vice-chmn. subcom. pub. contract law sect. 1988-93), Fed. Bar Assn., Nat. Bar Assn., D.C. C. of C. (gen. counsel 1979), State Va. Bar Assn., Washington Bar Assn., Bar Assn. D.C., Nat. Contract Mgmt. Assn., Econ. Club Washington. General corporate, Administrative and regulatory, Government contracts and claims. Home: 7004 Natelli Woods Ln Bethesda MD 20817-3924 Office: Shaw Pittman Potts & Trowbridge 2300 N St NW Fl 5 Washington DC 20037-1172

**LATHROP, MITCHELL LEE,** lawyer; b. L.A., Dec. 15, 1937; s. Alfred Lee and Barbara (Mitchell) L.; children: Christin Lorraine Newlon, Alexander Mitchell, Timothy Trewin Mitchell. BSc, U.S. Naval Acad., 1959; JD, U. So. Calif., 1966. Bar: D.C. 1966, Calif. 1966, U.S. Supreme Ct. 1969, N.Y. 1981; registered environ. assessor, Calif.; cert. arbitrator, ARIAS-US. Dep. counsel L.A. County, Calif., 1966-68; with Brill, Hunt, DeBuys and Burby, L.A., 1968-71; ptnr. Macdonald, Halsted & Laybourne, L.A. and San Diego, 1971-80; sr. ptnr. Rogers & Wells, N.Y.C., San Diego, 1980-86; sr. ptnr., exec. com. Adams, Duque & Hazeltine, L.A., San Francisco, N.Y.C., San Diego, 1986-94, firm chmn., 1992-94; sr. ptnr. Luce, Forward, Hamilton & Scripps, San Diego, N.Y.C., San Francisco, L.A., Chgo., 1994—; presiding referee Calif. Bar Ct., 1984-86, mem. exec. com., 1981-88; lectr. law Calif. Judges Assn., Practicing Law Inst. N.Y., Continuing Edn. of Bar, State Bar Calif., ABA, others. Author: State Hazardous Waste Regulation, 1991, Environmental Insurance Coverage, 1991, Insurance Coverage for Environmental Claims, 1992; mem. editl. bd. Def. Counsel Jour., 1997—; editl. bd. Y2K advisor Jour. Ins. Coverage. Western Regional chmn. Met. Opera Nat. Coun., 1971-81, v.p., mem. exec. com., 1971—, now chmn.; trustee Honnold Libr. at Claremont Colls., 1972-80; bd. dirs. Music Ctr. Opera Assn., L.A., sec., 1974-80; bd. dirs. San Diego Opera Assn., 1980—, v.p., 1985-89, pres.-elect, 1993, pres., 1994-96; bd. dirs. Met. Opera Assn., N.Y.C.; mem. nat. steering coun. Nat. Actors Theatre, N.Y. Mem. ABA, N.Y. Bar Assn., Fed. Bar Assn., Fed. Bar Council, Calif. Bar Assn., D.C. Bar Assn., San Diego County Bar Assn. (chmn. ethics com. 1980-82, bd. dirs. 1982-85, v.p. 1985), Assn. Bus. Trial Lawyers, Am. Intellectual Property Law Assn., Assn. So. Calif. Def. Counsel, Los Angeles Opera Assos. (pres. 1970-72), Soc. Colonial Wars in Calif. (gov. 1970-72), Order St. Lazarus of Jerusalem, Friends of Claremont Coll. (dir. 1975-81, pres. 1978-79), Am. Bd. Trial Advocates, Judge Advocates Assn. (dir. Los Angeles chpt. 1974-80, pres. So. Calif. chpt. 1977-78), Internat. Assn. Def. Counsel, Brit. United Services Club (dir. Los Angeles 1973-75), Mensa Internat., Calif. Soc., S.R. (pres. 1977-79), Calif. Club (Los Angeles), Valley Hunt Club (Pasadena, Calif.), Met. Club (N.Y.C.), The Naval Club (London), Phi Delta Phi. Republican. General civil litigation, Intellectual property, Insurance. Home: 455 Silver Gate Ave San Diego CA 92106-3327 Office: Luce Forward Hamilton and Scripps 600 W Broadway Fl 26 San Diego CA 92101-3311 also: Citicorp Ctr 153 E 53rd St Frnt 26 New York NY 10022-4611

**LATHROP, ROGER ALAN,** lawyer; b. Fairfield, Iowa, Aug. 24, 1951; s. Melvin G. and Naomi Rose (Liles) L.; m. Cynthia Lee Topping, Aug. 14, 1971; 1 son, Benjamin Alan. B.S., U. No. Iowa, 1972; J.D., U. Iowa, 1976. Bar: Iowa 1976, U.S. Dist. Ct. (no. and so. dists.) Iowa 1976. Constrn. laborer Stewart Constrn. Co., Fairfield and Iowa City, 1969-71; mgmt. trainee Osco Drug Co., Waterloo, Iowa, 1971-72; traffic mgr. Waterloo Industries, 1972; assoc. Betty, Neuman & McMahon, Davenport, Iowa, 1976-79, ptnr., 1979—; instr. bus. law Scott Community Coll., Bettendorf, Iowa, 1976, Blackhawk Community Coll. Moline, Ill., 1977. Mem. Iowa State Bar Assn. (interprofl. rels. com. 1991—, totic litigation com. 1991—), Scott County Bar Assn. (pres. 1987-88, exec. council 1978—), ABA, Iowa Def. Counsel Assn., Def. Research Inst. (product liability and ins. law coms.), Iowa Acad. Trial Lawyers, Iowa Assn. Trial Lawyers, Assn. Trial Lawyers Am., Internat. Assn. Def. Counsel (product liability and toxic torts com. 1989—), U. Iowa Alumni Assn. Club: Pentacrest Soc. (Iowa City). Methodist. Federal civil litigation, State civil litigation, Personal injury. Home: 3433 Maple Glen Dr Bettendorf IA 52722-2898 Office: Betty Neuman & McMahon 600 Union Arc Bldg Davenport IA 52801

**LATIMER, STEPHEN MARK,** lawyer; b. Bklyn., July 15, 1939; s. Ted and Martha (Goldberg) L.; m. Judith R. Shulman, June 3, 1964 (dec. Mar. 29, 1984); 1 child, Gary. BA, Tufts U., 1961; JD, NYU, 1968. Bar: N.Y. 1968, N.J. 1979, U.S. Dist. Ct. (so. dist.) N.Y. 1970, U.S. Dist. Ct. (ea. dist.) N.Y. 1972, U.S. Dist. Ct. N.J. 1979, U.S. Dist. Ct. (we. dist.) N.Y. 1984, U.S. Dist. Ct. (no. dist.) Tex. 1992, U.S. Ct. Appeals (2d cir.) 1974, U.S. Ct. Appeals (3rd cir.) 1981, U.S. Ct. Appeals (5th cir.) 1986, U.S. Supreme Ct. 1975. Clk. Burke & Parsons, N.Y.C., 1966-67; mng. clk. Otterbourg, Steindler, Houston & Rosen, N.Y.C., 1967-68; assoc. Otterbourg, Steindler, Houston & Rosen, 1968-69, Halpern, Schivitz, Scholer and Steingut, N.Y.C., 1969-71; dir. supervised pre-trial release project N.Y. Lawyers Com. for Civil Rights Under Law, N.Y.C., 1972-73; dir. cmty. devel. and law reform Bronx Legal Svcs., N.Y.C., 1973-79; acting mng. atty. Bronx Legal Svcs., 1974; dir. litigation Camden (N.J.) Regional Legal Svcs., Inc., 1979-81, acting dir., 1981-82; statewide litigation coord. Legal Svcs. of N.J., New Brunswick, 1982-84; sr. litigation atty. Prisoners' Legal Svcs. of N.Y., N.Y.C., 1984-94; asst. dep. pub. defender N.J. Pub. Defender, Newark, 1994-95; ptnr. Loughlin & Latimer, Hackensack, N.J., 1995—; lectr. Rutgers U. Law Sch., 1975-90. Contbr. articles to profl. jours. Trustee ACLU of N.J., 1982— (exec. com. 1984—), N.J. Assn. Correction, 1986—, Planned Parenthood of Middlesex County, 1981-85. Lt. USN, 1961-66, USNR, 1966-68. Instr. U.S. Marine Acad., Kings Point, N.Y., 1964-66/. Mem. N.J. Bar Assn. (vice chmn. individual rights 1998—). Civil rights, Criminal. Home: 120 Floyd Ave Bloomfield NJ 07003-5610 Office: Loughlin & Latimer 131 Main St Hackensack NJ 07601-7140

**LATIMER, TIMOTHY B.,** lawyer; b. Lincoln Park, Mich., Sept. 1, 1958; s. Thomas C. and Ruth M. (Stewart) L.; m. Dewana Darlene Alexander, May 14, 1983; children: Nicholas, Megan. BS, Beth Coll., 1980; JD, Memphis State U., 1984. Bar: Tenn. 1984. Atty. Uttey & Latimer, P.C., Jackson, Tenn., 1984—; bd. dirs. Carl Perkins Exch. Club Child Abuse Ctr.; trustee Bethel Coll., McKenzie, Tenn., 1991—. Mem. Jackson Exch. Club. Bankruptcy, Real property, General practice. Office: Uttey & Latimer PC 425 E Baltimore St Jackson TN 38301-6387

**LATOVICK, PAULA R(AE),** lawyer, educator; b. Detroit, Feb. 17, 1954; d. Raymond and Marjorie Camille (Peters) L.; m. William P. Weiner, Aug. 17, 1985; children: Jeffrey Devon, Robert Stirling. BA in Personnel with high honor, Mich. State U., 1976; JD cum laude, U. Mich., 1980, LLM, 1999. Bar: Mich. 1980, U.S. Dist. Ct. (ea. dist.) Mich. 1980, U.S. Dist. Ct. (we. dist.) Mich. 1981, U.S. Ct. Appeals (6th cir.) 1985. Assoc. Fraser, Trebilcock, Davis & Foster P.C., Lansing, Mich., 1980-86, ptnr., 1986-92, chmn. hiring com., 1987-92, chmn. govt. law dept., 1988-90; assoc. prof. Thomas M. Cooley Law Sch., 1992-97, prof., 1998—; adj. prof. Thomas M. Cooley Law Sch., Lansing, 1984-86. Head advisor law explorers Boy Scouts Am., Lansing, 1982-84; mem. Capitol Area Women's Network, Lansing, 1984-95; v.p. YWCA, Lansing, 1988, pres., 1989-91, chmn. bldg. com., 1989-91; rec. sec. Friends of Kresge Art Mus., 1992-93, corr. sec., 1993-94, 1st v.p., 1994-95, pres., 1995-96; treas. Cub Scouts Pack 107, Boy Scouts Am., 1998—. Named One of Outstanding Young Women of Am., 1985. Fellow Mich. State Bar Found.; mem. NOW, Mich. Bar Assn. (mem. young lawyers exec. coun. 1984-86, mem. com. character and fitness dist. F 1991—, subcom. chairperson 1994—), Women Lawyers Assn. Mich., Ingham County Bar Assn. (chairperson hist. com. 1984-87, mem. young lawyers bd. 1981-84, pres. 1983, mem. com. on jud. qualifications 1990-93, bd. dirs. 1990-92), Thomas M. Cooley Legal Authors Soc., U. Mich. Alumni Assn. (life), Mich. State U. Alumni Assn., Zonta (rec. sec. local club 1985-86, chmn. membership com. 1988-89). Democrat. Roman Catholic. Office: Thomas M Cooley Law Sch 217 S Capitol Ave Lansing MI 48933-1503

**LATTA, THOMAS ALBERT,** lawyer; b. Tulsa, Nov. 3, 1931; s. Albert Lloyd and Myrtle Irene (Lay) L.; m. Shirley Elaine Glauser, June 20, 1965 (div. 1985); children: Thomas Albert, John Montgomery, Shannon Elaine. Student, Carnegie Mellon U., 1949-52; BA, U. Tex., 1955; JD, U. Tulsa, 1959. Bar: Okla. 1959, Ariz. 1964, D.C. 1965, Calif. 1974. Pvt. practice San Francisco, 1974-97, Phoenix, 1975-97; dir., shareholder Wentworth & Lundin, P.A., Phoenix, 1975-86, San Francisco, 1980-84; of counsel Whitehead, Porter & Gordon LLP, San Francisco, 1997—; mem. Ariz. Bd. Accountancy, Phoenix, 1979-83. Capt. JAGC, USAR, 1959-60. Avocation: sailing. Securities, General corporate, Finance. Office: Whitehead Porter & Gordon 220 Montgomery St Ste 1850 San Francisco CA 94104-3419

**LATTINVILLE, ROBERT HENRY,** lawyer, educator; b. Kansas City, Mo., Feb. 8, 1963; s. Henry Elmer and Marie Anna Lattinville. BS, U. Mo., 1985; MBA, St. Louis U., 1987; JD, Ind. U., 1990. Bar: Mo. 1990, Ill. 1991. Assoc. Lewis, Rice & Figersh, St. Louis, 1990-95; ptnr. Stinson, Mag & Fizzell, St. Louis, 1995—; bd. dirs. St. Louis Sports Commn., 1997—; contract adivsor Nat. Football League Players Assn., 1990—, Can. Footbnall League Players Assn., 1992—. Bd. dirs. Mary Grove Home for Abused Children, St. Louis, 1997—, Cardinal Glennon Children's Hosp., St. Louis, 1997—. Mem. Mo. Bar Assn. (chmn. sports and entertainment com. 1997—). Avocations: water sports, running, golf. Sports, General corporate, Intellectual property. Home: 8411 Kingsbury Blvd Clayton MO 63105-3629 Office: Stinson Mag & Fizzell 100 S 4th St Saint Louis MO 63102-1800

**LAU, EUGENE WING IU,** lawyer; b. Canton, China, Sept. 23, 1931; came to U.S., 1939; s. Eugene K. F. and Ann (Leung) L.; m. Dierdre Florence, July 20, 1962; children: Elyse M., Jennifer M. AB, U. Mich., 1953; LLB, Yale U., 1960. Bar: Hawaii 1960, U.S. Supreme Ct. 1965. Dep. Pros. Attys. Office, Honolulu, 1960-63; pvt. practice Honolulu, 1963-67, 73—; v.p. Hawaii Corp., Honolulu, 1967-73; del. People to People Legal Del. to China, 1987; mem. Commn. on Manpower and Full Employment, Honolulu, 1965-67. With U.S. Army, 1954-55. Mem. ABA, Hawaii Bar Assn., Punahou Tennis Club (Honolulu). Real property, Contracts commercial, Finance. Home: 3079 La Pietra Cir Honolulu HI 96815-4736 Office: 1188 Bishop St Ste 1912 Honolulu HI 96813-3308

**LAU, JEFFREY DANIEL,** lawyer; b. Honolulu, May 2, 1948; s. Daniel B.T. and Evelyn (Yee Quil) L.; m. Susan Tilden, June 1, 1974; 1 child, Daniel Prescott Tilden. BSBA in Econs., Lehigh U., 1970; MBA in Fin., Temple U., 1973; JD, U. Calif., San Francisco, 1977. Bar: Hawaii, U.S. Dist. Ct. Hawaii, U.S. Ct. Appeals (9th cir.) 1978. Legis. asst. to U.S. Senator Hiram L. Fong, Washington, 1971-72; law clk. to presiding justice U.S. Dist. Ct. Hawaii, Honolulu, 1975, U.S. Ct. Appeals (9th cir.), Honolulu, 1976; assoc. Frank D. Padgett, Honolulu, 1977-80; ptnr. Chung, Lau, MacLaren and Lau, Honolulu, 1980-81, Fong and Miho, Honolulu, 1981-84; shareholder, v.p. Oliver, Lau, Lawhn, Ogawa & Nakamura, Honolulu, 1985—; bd. dirs., asst. corp. sec. Fin. Factors, Ltd., Honolulu, Fin. Realty, Ltd., Honolulu; bd. dirs., corp. sec. Grand Pacific Life Ins., Ltd., 1984—; apptd. ct. arbitrator State of Hawaii, 1987—. Served to capt. U.S. Army, 1972-74. Mem. ABA, Assn. Trial Lawyers Am., Hawaii State Bar Assn. (del. to Hawaii Congress on Small Bus. 1994—), Lehigh U. Alumni Assn. Hawaii (pres.), Hawaii Soc. Corp. Planners (dir. 1997—). Mem. United Ch. of Christ. Avocations: skiing, volleyball, softball; coaching youth soccer, basketball and baseball. E-mail: ollon@gte.net. Banking, General civil litigation, Real property. Office: Ocean View Ctr 707 Richards St Ste 600 Honolulu HI 96813-4623

**LAU, MARY APPLEGATE,** lawyer; b. Washington, Dec. 17, 1952; d. Robert Lee and Barbara Edith (Pressler) Applegate; m. James Victor Lau, Apr. 1, 1982; 1 child, Chelsea Nicole. BA magna cum laude, Mich. State U., 1974; JD with honors, Fla. State U., 1976. Bar: Fla. 1977, U.S. Dist. Ct. (mid. dist.) Fla. 1977, U.S. Ct. Appeals (11th cir.) 1977. Assoc. atty. Holland and Knight, Tampa, Fla., 1977-82, ptnr., 1982-86; shareholder Lau, Lane, Pieper, Conley & McCreadie, P.A., Tampa, 1986—. Mem. Fed. Bar Assn., (treas. Tampa Bay chpt. 1993), Hillsborough County Bar Assn. Republican. Roman Catholic. Federal civil litigation, Labor, Bankruptcy. Office: Lau Lane Pieper Conley & McCreadie PA 100 S Ashley Dr Tampa FL 33602-5360

**LAUCHENGCO, JOSE YUJUICO, JR.,** lawyer; b. Manila, Philippines, Dec. 6, 1936; came to U.S., 1962; s. José Celis Sr. Lauchengco and Angeles (Yujuico) Sapota; m. Elisabeth Schindler, Feb. 22, 1968; children: Birthe, Martina, Duane, Lance. AB, U. Philippines, Quezon City, 1959; MBA, U. So. Calif., 1964; JD, Loyola U., L.A., 1971. Bar: Calif. 1972, U.S. Dist. Ct. (cen. dist.) Calif. 1972, U.S. Ct. Appeals (9th cir.) 1972, U.S. Supreme Ct. 1975. Banker First Western Bank/United Calif. Bank, L.A., 1964-71; assoc. Demler, Perona, Langer & Bergkvist, Long Beach, Calif., 1972-73; ptnr. Demler, Perona, Langer, Bergkvist, Lauchengco & Manzella, Long Beach, 1973-77; sole practice Long Beach and L.A., 1977-83; ptnr. Lauchengco & Mendoza, L.A., 1983-92; pvt. practice L.A., 1993—; mem. commn. on jud. procedures County of L.A., 1979; tchr. Confraternity of Christian Doctrine, 1972-79; counsel Philippine Presdl. Commn. on Good Govt., L.A., 1986. Chmn. Filipino-Am. Bi-Partisan Polit. Action Group, L.A., 1978. Recipient Degree of Distinction, Nat. Forensic League, 1955. Mem. Criminal Cts. Bar Assn., Calif. Attys. Criminal Justice, Calif. Pub. Defenders Assn., Philippine-Am. Bar Assn., U. Philippines Vanguard Assn. (life), Beta Sigma. Roman Catholic. Lodge: K.C. Avocations: classical music, opera, romantic paintings and sculpture, camping, shooting. Federal civil litigation, Personal injury, Criminal. Office: 3545 Wilshire Blvd Ste 247 Los Angeles CA 90010-2388

**LAUDERDALE, KATHERINE SUE,** lawyer; b. Wright-Patterson AFB, Ohio, May 30, 1954; d. Azo and Helen Ceola (Davis) L. BS in Polit. Sci., Ohio State U., 1975; JD, NYU, 1978. Bar: Ill. 1978, U.S. Dist. Ct. (no. dist.) Ill. 1978, Calif. 1987. Assoc. Schiff, Hardin & Waite, Chgo., 1978-82; dir. bus. and legal affairs Sta. WTTW-TV, Chgo., 1982-83, gen. counsel, 1983—, also v.p., sr. v.p., gen. counsel legal and bus. affairs, 1993—; acting sr. v.p. Prodn. Ctr., 1994; sr. v.p. New Ventures, 1995—. Mem. Lawyers Com. for Harold Washington, Chgo. 1983; bd. dirs. Midwest Women's Ctr., Chgo., 1985-94; active Chgo. Coun. Fgn. Rels., 1981—, mem. fgn. affairs com., 1985—; mem. adv. bd. Malcolm X Coll. Sch. Bus., 1996—. mem. ABA, Chgo. Bar Assn. (bd. dirs. TV Prodns., Inc. 1986—), Lawyers for Creative Arts (bd. dir. 1984—, v.p. 1998—), ACLU (bd. dirs. 1987-94), Nat. Acad. TV Arts and Scis., NYU Law Alumni Assn. Midwest (mem. exec. bd. 1982—), The Ohio State U. Pres.'s Nat. Adv. Coun. on Pub. Affairs (Chgo. com., 1994—), The U. Chicago Women's Bd., 1996—. Democrat. Entertainment, General corporate. Office: Sta WTTW-TV 5400 N Saint Louis Ave Chicago IL 60625-4680

**LAUE, BRANT MITCHELL,** lawyer; b. Hanover, Kans., June 24, 1961; s. Lester Clayton and Leanna (Jandera) L. BA summa cum laude, Oral Roberts U., 1983; JD magna cum laude, Cornell U., 1986. Bar: Mo. 1987; U.S. Ct. Appeals (8th cir.) 1988, U.S. Ct. Appeals (9th cir.) 1988, U.S. Ct. Appeals (10th cir.) 1990, U.S. Ct. Appeals (4th cir.) 1992; U.S. Dist. Ct. (we. dist.) Mo. 1989, Kans. 1995, U.S. Ct. Appeals (7th cir.) 1997. Law clk. to judge U.S. Ct. Appeals (8th cir.), Pierre, S.D., 1986-87; assoc. Stinson, Mag & Fizzell, Kansas City, Mo., 1987, 1988-92; spl. asst. to asst. atty. gen. Civil Div. U.S. Dept. Justice, Washington, 1987-88; assoc. Rouse, Hendricks, German, May & Shank, P.C., Kansas City, Mo., 1992-93, shareholder, 1993-97; shareholder Shank, Laue & Hamilton, P.C., Kansas City, Mo., 1997—. Mem. ABA, Order of Coif, Phi Kappa Phi. Republican. Lutheran. Avocation: ranching. Office: Shank Laue & Hamilton PC 2345 Grand Blvd Ste 1600 Kansas City MO 64108-2638

**LAUER, ANDREW JAY,** lawyer; b. Queens, N.Y., Aug. 2, 1967; s. Elias and Ilse Susan L.; m. Aleeza S. Lauer, Nov. 22, 1989; children: Jennifer

Amanda, David Aaron, Ashley Beth, Elias. BA in Acctg. and Econ., CUNY, 1988; JD, Bklyn. Law Sch., 1991. Bar: N.Y. 1991, N.J. 1991, U.S. Dist. Ct. (eas. and so. dists.) N.Y., U.S. Dist. Ct. N.J., U.S. Supreme Ct. Asst. dist. atty. Kings County, Bklyn., 1991-95; asst. gen. counsel Deloitte & Touche U.S.A., LLP, N.Y.C., 1995—. Primary editor Bklyn. Jour. Internat. Law, 1990-91; editor Queens Coll. Law Jour. Mem. ABA, N.Y. State Bar Assn. General civil litigation, Labor, Workers' compensation. Office: Deloitte & Touche USA LLP Office of Gen Counsel 1633 Broadway New York NY 10019

**LAUER, ELIOT,** lawyer; b. N.Y.C., Aug. 17, 1949; s. George and Doris (Trenk) L.; m. Marilyn Steinberg, June 5, 1977; children: Tamar Rachel, Ilana Jennifer, Michael Jonathan, Samuel Geoffrey. BA, Yeshiva U., 1971; JD cum laude, Fordham U., 1974. Bar: D.C. 1975, N.Y. 1975, U.S. Dist. Ct. (so. and ea. dists.) N.Y. 1975, U.S. Ct. Appeals (2d cir.) 1975, U.S. Supreme Ct. 1984. Assoc. Curtis, Mallet-Prevost, Colt & Mosle, N.Y.C., 1974-82, ptnr., 1982—. Counsel Keren-Or Inc., N.Y.C., 1985—; bd. dirs. Hebrew Acad. Long Beach, N.Y., 1985—, Young Israel Lawrence, Cedarhurst, N.Y., 1984—. Mem. ABA, N.Y. State Bar Assn., Assn. of Bar of City of N.Y., Fed. Bar Council, Am. Arbitration Assn. (arbitrator 1979—), Nat. Futures Assn. (arbitrator 1983—). Republican. Federal civil litigation, Criminal. Office: Curtis Mallet-Prevost Colt & Mosle 101 Park Ave Fl 34 New York NY 10178-0061

**LAUFER, JACOB,** lawyer; b. Munich, Feb. 28, 1949; came to the U.S., 1951; s. Moritz and Felicja (Pruszanowska) L.; m. Clara G. Schwabe, Jan. 27, 1983; children: Samara, Aviva, Mia. BS, CUNY, 1971; JD cum laude, Fordham U., 1974. Bar: N.Y. 1975, D.C. 1975, U.S. Ct. Appeals (2d cir.) 1975, U.S. Dist. Ct. (so. and ea. dists.) N.Y. 1976, U.S. Ct. Appeals (5th cir.) 1979, U.S. Supreme Ct. 1980, U.S. Ct. Appeals (3d cir.) 1985, U.S. Ct. Appeals (D.C. cir.) 1994. Spl. atty. Organized Crime and Racketeering Sect., U.S. Dept. Justice, 1974-77; asst. U.S. atty. So. Dist. N.Y., N.Y.C., 1977-79; of counsel Bartels, Pykett & Aronwald, White Plains, N.Y., 1979-81; ptnr. Bornstein & Laufer, N.Y.C., 1981-85, Laufer & Karish LLP, N.Y.C., 1986—. Mem., contbr. Fordham Law Rev., 1973-74. Mem. D.C. Bar Assn., Bklyn. Bar Assn., Assn. Bar City of N.Y (com. criminal advocacy 1998—). Democrat. Jewish. Avocation: reading. General civil litigation, Criminal, Entertainment. Office: Laufer Halberstam & Karish LLP 165 Broadway Fl 37 New York NY 10006-1404 *Notable cases include: Pavelic & LeFlore vs. Marvel Entertainment Group; and Allen vs. National Video, Inc.*

**LAUGHEAD, JAMES MARSHALL,** lawyer; b. San Antonio, Oct. 12, 1959; s. George J. and Margaret R. L.; m. Lisa Ott Laky, Nov. 7, 1987; children: James Marshall Jr., George Jackson. BA with highest honors, U. Tex., 1981, JD with high honors, 1984. Bar: Tex. 1984. Atty. Graves, Dougherty, Hearon & Moody, Austin, Tex., 1984—. Assoc. editor: Tex. Law Review. Mem. ABA, State Bar Tex., Travis County Bar Assn., Chancellors, Order of Coif, Phi Beta Kappa. General corporate, Securities, Computer. Office: Graves Dougherty Hearon & Moody 515 Congress Ave Ste 2300 Austin TX 78701-3503

**LAUGHLIN, DREW ALAN,** lawyer; b. McKeesport, Pa., Feb. 28, 1952; s. Edward Stanley L. and Delores Easton Weiler; m. Susan Kuykendall, May 26, 1974; childre: Philip, Abigail; m. Linda Lucas, May 21, 1988; 1 child, Katherine. BA, U. Va., 1974; JD, U. S.C., 1977. Bar: S.C., 1977, U.S. Dist. Ct. S.C., 1978, U.S. Ct. Appeals (4th, 1986, 5th, 1983, and 11th cirs.). Atty. Bowen, Cooper, Beard & Smoot, Hilton Head Island, S.C., 1977-84, Bowen, Smoot & Laughlin, Hilton Head Island, S.C., 1984-86, Qualey, Laughlin & Qualey, Hilton Head Island, S.C., 1986-87, McNair Law Firm, P.A., Hilton Head Island, S.C., 1987-90, Laughlin & Bowen, Hilton Head Island, S.C., 1990—. Pres. Hilton Head Plantation, Property Owner's Assn, 1996; chmn. Hilton Head Island Planning Commn., 1994-96, Hilton Head Island Corridor Revs. Com., 1992-94; commr. Hilton Head Island Pub. Svc. Dist., 1998—. Avocations: music, golf. General civil litigation, Construction, Real property. Home: 6 Oyster Reef Cv Hilton Head Island SC 29926-1800 Office: Laughlin & Bowen PO Drawer 21119 Hilton Head SC 29925-1119

**LAUGHLIN, JAMES HAROLD, JR.,** lawyer; b. Charleston, W.Va., July 18, 1941; s. James Harold and Pearl Ruby L; m. Eleanor Blackford Watson, II, Aug. 3, 1968; children: C. Michelle, Jeanette C., Cheryl Adele. BS in Chem. Engring., W.Va. U., 1964; JD, Am. U., 1968. Bar: D.C. 1968, Va. 1969. Atty. Am. Cyanamid Co., Wayne, N.J., 1968-70, Xerox Corp., Rochester, N.Y., 1971-77; ptnr. Benoit, Smith & Laughlin, Arlington, Va., 1977-93, Lane & Mittendorf, LLP, Washington, 1993-97, Shook, Hardy & Bacon, LLP, Washington, 1997-99, Antonelli Terry Stout & Kraus, LLP, 1999—. Mem. ABA, Am. Intellectual Property Law Assn. (bd. dirs. 1976-79, treas. 1982-85, councilman 1993-94), Va. State Bar (chmn. PTC sect. 1982-83), Nat. Coun. Patent Law Assns. (Va. del. 1983—), Nat. Inventors Hall of Fame Found. (bd. dirs. 1988-93, pres. 1991-92). Patent, Federal civil litigation, Legislative. Office: 1300 N Seventeenth St Arlington VA 22209

**LAUGHLIN-SCHOPIS, SUSAN KAY,** public defender; b. Jackson, Mich., Mar. 10, 1957; d. Joseph Hadley and Lillian Grace Laughlin; m. Robert O. Schopis Jr., May 20, 1995; 1 child, Nicholas Laughlin. BA in Journalism, Ohio State U., 1979, JD, 1982. Bar: Ohio 1982, U.S. Dist. Ct. (so. dist.) Ohio 1983. Atty. Franklin County Pub. Defender, Columbus, Ohio, 1983—; asst. adj. prof. Ohio State U. Coll. Law, Columbus, 1987. Active homeless project Our Lady of Victory Cath. Ch., Marble Cliff, Ohio, 1996—. Mem. Nat. Assn. Criminal Def. Lawyers, Ohio Assn. Criminal Def. Lawyers. Democrat. Roman Catholic. Avocations: opera, backpacking/hiking, travel, church. Office: Franklin County Pub Defender 373 S High St Fl 12 Columbus OH 43215-4591

**LAUGHTER, RON D.,** lawyer; b. Detroit, Oct. 4, 1948; s. Harry Brookshire and Patsy Ruth (Coles) L.; m. Barbara Jane Morrison, Aug. 1, 1969; children: Heather Elizabeth, Shannon Marie. BS, Mich. State U., 1970; JD cum laude, T.M. Cooley Law Sch., 1980. Bar: Mich. 1980. Registered rep. Conn. Gen. Ins. Corp., Grand Rapids, Mich., 1972-73; dir. planned giving Am. Cancer Soc., Lansing, Mich., 1973-80; exec. dir. Mich. State U. Found., East Lansing, 1980-90; chief oper. officer Growth Design Corp., Milw., 1990—; pres. Univ. Rsch. Park, Inc., 1989-90; mem. bd. gov's. T.M. Cooley Law Sch., 1988—. Author: Planned Giving Guidebook, 1980. Treas. Family and Child Services, Lansing, Mich., 1981-88; mem. Capitol Enterprise Forum, Mich. Tech. Coun. Mem. ABA, Mich. Bar Assn., Ingham County Bar Assn. (real property law com.), Council for Advancement and Support of Edn., Mich. State U. Pres.'s Club. Avocations: golf, boating, woodworking, sport fishing. Home: 325 Sunrise Dr Salem SC 29676-3444 Office: Growth Design Corp 828 N Broadway Ste 700 Milwaukee WI 53202-3658

**LAUKENMANN, CHRISTOPHER BERND,** lawyer; b. Aug. 15, 1962. BA, Duke U., 1984, JD, 1988, LLM, 1988. Bar: Ga. 1989, Calif. 1990, D.C. 1990, U.S. Dist. Ct. (ctrl. dist.) Calif. 1990, U.S. Ct. Appeals (9th cir.) 1990. Assoc. Kilpatrick & Cody, Atlanta, Washington, 1988-89; assoc. Loeb & Loeb, L.A., 1989-91, Hancock, Rothert & Bunshoft, L.A., San Francisco, 1996—, Washington Mutual, 1996—. Asst. editor: (book) Doing Business in Japan, 1995; contbr. articles to profl. jours. Mem. ABA (state bar corp. law depts. exec. com., corps. com. legis. liaison), Directory of Japanese Speaking Attys. in the U.S. Avocations: languages (German, French, Japanese). General civil litigation, General corporate, Private international. Office: Washington Mutual 9200 Oakdale Ave Fl 7 Chatsworth CA 91311-6528

**LAULICHT, MURRAY JACK,** lawyer; b. Bklyn., May 12, 1940; s. Philip and Ernestine (Greenfield) L.; m. Linda Kushner, Apr. 4, 1965; children: Laurie Hasten, Pamela Hirt, Shellie Davis, Abigail Herschmann. BA, Yeshiva U., 1961; LLB summa cum laude, Columbia U., 1964. Bar: N.Y. 1965, N.J. 1968, U.S. Supreme Ct. 1976. Legal staff Warren Commn., Washington, 1964; law clk. Hon. Harold R. Medina U.S. Ct. Appeals, 1964-65; assoc. Kaye, Scholer, Fierman, Hays & Handler, N.Y.C., 1965-68; ptnr. Lowenstein, Sandler, Brochin, Kohl & Fisher, Newark, N.J., 1968-79, Pitney, Hardin, Kipp & Szuch, Florham Park, N.J., 1979—. Mem. N.J. Consumer Affairs Adv. Com., 1991-93; N.J. Commn. on Holocaust Edn., 1991—, chmn. 1992-95; pres. Jewish Edn. Assn., 1981-84, Jewish Fedn. Metro West, 1996-99; chmn. Cmty. Rels. Com., 1988-91.; exec. comm. Coun. of Jewish Fedn., 1996-99. Recipient Julius Cohn Young Leadership award Jewish Fedn. Metrowest, 1976. Mem. ABA, N.J. State Bar Assn. (dist. X ethics com. 1986-89, bd. editors N.J. Law Jour. 1986-93), N.J. Lawyer Mag. (chmn. 1993-95). Democrat. Avocations: Jewish studies, communal activities. Antitrust, General civil litigation, Intellectual property. Home: 18 Crestwood Dr West Orange NJ 07052-2004 Office: Pitney Hardin Kipp & Szuch PO Box 1945 200 Campus Dr Ste 1 Florham Park NJ 07932-1007

**LAURA, ANTHONY JOSEPH,** lawyer; b. Bklyn., July 15, 1961; s. Andrew J. and Edda V. (DePaola) L.; m. Rosemary B. Marino, Sept. 21, 1986; children: Diana Marie, Amanda Rose. BA, Yale U., 1983; JD, Fordham U., 1986. Bar: N.J. 1986, U.S. Dist. Ct. N.J. 1986, N.Y. 1987, U.S. Dist. Ct. (so. dist.) N.Y. 1987, U.S. Ct. Appeals (3rd cir.) 1993. Assoc. atty. Kelley Drye and Warren, N.Y.C., 1986-87, Morristown, N.J., 1987-89, Parsippany, N.J., 1989-97; ptnr. Reed, Smith, Shaw & McClay, Newark, 1997—; bd. trustee Cmtys. on Cable, Summit, N.J., 1994-97, chair budget rev. com. United Way Summit, New Providence, N.J., 1995—. Township committeeman Rep. Com. Union County, Berkeley Hts., N.J., 1994—; trustee Runnells Specialized Hosp. Found., 1996-98. Mem. N.J. State Bar Assn. (vice chair product liability and toxic tort sect. 1997—), The Mory's Assn., Park Ave Club (membership com. 1994-96), Yale Club Ctrl. N.J. Avocation: golf. General civil litigation, Product liability, Toxic tort. Office: Reed Smith Shaw & McClay 1 Riverfront Plz Fl 2 Newark NJ 07102-5470

**LAURANS, JONATHAN LOUIS,** lawyer; b. Hartford, Conn., Apr. 1, 1965. BA in Polit. Philosophy, U. Dallas, 1987; MA in Pub. Adminstrn., Midwestern U., 1989; MD, Washburn U., 1992. Assoc. Niewald, Waldeck & Brown, Kansas City, Mo., 1992-94; pvt. practice Kansas City, Mo., 1994—, Shawnee Mission, Kans., 1994—. Mem. Mo. Bar Assn., Kans. Bar Assn. Criminal, General practice. Office: 819 Walnut St Ste 204 Kansas City MO 64106-1810

**LAURENCE, STEVEN LAMAR,** lawyer; b. Oakdale, La., June 22, 1952; s. Cecil and Mary Laurence; m. Kathy Denise Holton, Sept. 2, 1978; children: Meredith Erin, Beth, Ryan. AA, Pensacola Jr. Coll., 1977; BS, Fla. State U., 1979; JD, U. Ark., 1982. Asst. state atty. State Atty. 18th Jud. Cir., Sanford, Fla., 1983-85; ptnr. Cleveland, Bridges, Laurence, Sanford, 1985-90, Fisher, Laurence, Deen & Fromang, Altamonte Springs, Fla., 1990—. Bd. dirs. Ctrl. Fla. Soap Box Derby, Sanford, 1985—, ctrl. Fla. Golden Age Games, sanford, 1985—. Served with U.S. Army, 1972-75. Mem. Orange County Bar Assn., Seminole County Bar Assn., Ctrl. Fla. criminal Lawyers, Seminole County Family Law Assn. Avocation: coaching Little League baseball, girls softball and Pop Warner football. Family and matrimonial, Criminal, Probate. Office: Fisher Laurence et al 101 S Wymore Rd Ste 337 Altamonte Springs FL 32714-4313

**LAURENSON, EDWIN CHARLES,** lawyer; b. Akron, Ohio, Mar. 4, 1949; s. Paul Rider and Elizabeth Brooks L.; m. Margaret Conley Findlay McLaughlin, Feb. 13, 1982; 1 child, Lydia Betsy Brooks. BA, Amherst Coll., 1972; JD, Yale U., 1975. Law clk. to Hon. William K. Thomas Cleve., 1975-77; assoc. Skadden, Arps, Slate, Meaghan & Flom, N.Y.C., 1977-79; assoc. Paul, Wiess, Rifkind, Wharton & Garrison, N.Y.C., 1980-83, 86-89, prin. atty., 1990-96, securities counsel, 1996—; assoc. Berman Engel P.C., Boston, 1983-86. Contbr. articles to profl. jours. Pres. Unitarian Soc. Westchester, Hastings-on-Hudson, N.Y., 1997-99; coun. mem. Inst. Religion in Age of Sci., Portsmouth, N.H., 1997—. Democrat. Avocations: philosophy, religion, science, theater. Securities, Mergers and acquisitions, Finance. Home: 3 Burnside Pl Hastings Hdsn NY 10706-3016 Office: Paul Weiss Rifkind Wharton & Garrison 1285 Avenue of the Americas New York NY 10706

**LAURIE, GERALD TENZER,** lawyer; b. St. Paul, Jan. 22, 1942; s. Hyman and Leona (Smith) L.; m. Joellyn Kronick, Mar. 12, 1968; children: Ian, Eben, Joshua. BA, U. Minn., 1964, JD, 1967. Bar: Minn. 1967, U.S. Dist. Ct. Minn. 1967, U.S. Ct. Appeals (fed. cir.) 1987. Spl. asst. atty. gen. Minn. Atty. Gen. Office, St. Paul, 1968-70; ptnr. Lapp, Laure, Libra, Abramson & Thomson, Chartered, Mpls., 1970—. Contbr. articles in field to legal jours. Mem. City of New Hope Indsl. Commn.; chmn. New Hope Liquor Commn. Mem. ABA, Assn. Trial Lawyers Am., Minn. Bar Assn. (cert. civil litigation specialist), Minn. Trial Lawyers Assn. (bd. govs. 1983-89), Hennepin County Bar Assn., Mpls. Athletic Club. Avocations: reading, swimming, biking. General civil litigation, Personal injury. Office: Lapp Laurie Libra Abramson & Thomson Chartered One Financial Plz Minneapolis MN 55402

**LAURIE, ROBIN GARRETT,** lawyer; b. Mobile, Ala., June 10, 1956; s. George and Margaret Eloise (Garrett) L.; m. Deborah Dockery; children: Elizabeth Anne, Robin Garrett. AA, Marion (Ala.) Mil. Inst., 1976; BS in Bus., U. Ala., Tuscaloosa, 1978; JD, U.Ala., Tuscaloosa, 1988. Bar: Ala. 1988, U.S. Dist. Ct. (no., mid. and so. dists.) Ala. 1988, U.S. Ct. Appeals (11th cir.) 1988. Lawyer, ptnr. Balch & Bingham, Montgomery, Ala., 1988—. Lead articles editor Ala. Law Rev., 1986-88. Recipient Outstanding Svc. award Ala. Law Rev., 1988. Mem. ABA, Ala. State Bar, Montgomery County Bar Assn., Montgomery Rotary Club, Order of the Coif. Methodist. Avocations: flying small airplanes, fishing, hunting. General civil litigation, Administrative and regulatory, Public utilities. Office: Balch & Bingham PO Box 78 Montgomery AL 36101-0078

**LAURIE, RONALD SHELDON,** lawyer; b. San Francisco, June 30, 1942; s. Charles M. and Mimosa (Ezaoui) L.; m. Mina Heshmati, June 1, 1986. BS in Indsl. Engring., U. Calif., Berkeley, 1964; JD, U. San Francisco, 1968. Bar: Calif. 1969, U.S. Ct. Appeals (9th cir.) 1969, U.S. Patent Office 1969, U.S. Supreme Ct. 1971, U.S. Ct. Appeals (fed. cir.) 1972. Programmer, sys. engr. Lockheed Missiles & Space Co., Sunnyvale, Calif., 1960-64; patent atty. Kaiser Aluminum & Chem. Co., Oakland, Calif., 1968-70; ptnr. Townsend and Townsend, San Francisco, 1970-88, Irell & Manella, Menlo Park, Calif., 1988-91, Weil, Gotshal & Manges, Menlo Park, 1991-94, McCutchen, Doyle, Brown & Emersen, San Francisco, 1994-98; chmn. McCutchen Computers and Software Industry Group, 1995-98; ptnr. Skadden, Arps, Meagher & Flom, Palo Alto, Calif., 1998—; co-chair Skadden Arps' Computer and Info. Tech. Group, 1998—; lectr. computer law Stanford U. Law Sch., 1993-94; advisor NAS, U.S. Copyright Office and U.S. Patent and Trademark Office, Washington, Office Tech. Assessment, U.S. Congress, World Intellectual Property Orgn., Geneva; lectr. patent law U. Calif., Berkeley, 1999—; permanent faculty World Law Inst., 1996—. Co-editor: International Intellectual Property, 1992; contbr. articles to profl. jours. Mem. Internat. Intellectual Property Assn. (exec. com.), State Bar Calif. (past mem. exec. com. intellectual property sect.), Computer Law Assn. (bd. dirs.). Avocation: vintage auto racing. Computer, Patent, Mergers and acquisitions. Home: 107 Acacia Ave Belvedere CA 94920-2309 Office: Skadden Arps Meagher & Flom 525 University Ave Palo Alto CA 94301-1903

**LAURINO, ROBERT DENNIS,** prosecutor; b. Orange, N.J., Feb. 26, 1951; s. Henry Michael and Constance Jeanette (Conti) L. BA, Villanova U., 1973; MA, Rutgers U., 1974; JD, Seton Hall U., 1979. Bar: N.J. 1979, N.Y. 1985, U.S. Dist. Ct. N.J. 1979, U.S. Dist. Ct. (so. and ea. dists.) N.Y. 1985, U.S. Ct. Appeals (3d cir.) 1985, U.S. Supreme Ct. 1985; cert. criminal atty., N.J. Law clk. to presiding justice Superior Ct. N.J., Newark, 1979-80; asst. prosecutor Essex County, Newark, 1980—. Editor Seton Hall U. Law Rev., 1978-79, author, 1978. Mem. N.Y. State Bar Assn. Office: Essex County Cts Bldg Newark NJ 07102

**LAUTENSCHLAGER, PEGGY ANN,** prosecutor; b. Fond du Lac, Wis., Nov. 22, 1955; d. Milton A. and Patsy R. (Oleson) L.; m. Rajiv M. Kaul, Dec. 29, 1979 (div. Dec. 1986); children: Joshua Lautenschlager Kaul, Ryan Lautenschlager Kaul; m. William P. Rippl, May 26, 1989; 1 child, Rebecca Lautenschlager Rippl. BA, Lake Forest Coll., 1977; JD, U. Wis., 1980. Bar: Wis., U.S. Dist. Ct. (we. dist.). Pvt. practice atty. Oshkosh, Wis., 1981-85; dist. atty. Winnebago County Wis., Oshkosh, 1985-88; rep. Wis. Assembly, Fond du Lac, 1988-92; U.S. atty. U.S. Dept. of Justice, Madison, Wis., 1992—; apptd. mem. Govs. Coun. on Domestic Violence, Madison, State Elections Bd., Madison; bd. dirs. Blandine House, Inc. Active Dem. Nat. Com., Washington, 1992-93; com. Wis., 1989-92. Named Legislator of Yr., Wis. Sch. Counselors, 1992, Legislator of Yr., Wis. Corrections Coalition, 1992. Mem. Wis. Bar Assn., Dane County Bar Assn., Western Dist. Bar Assn., Fond du lac County Bar Assn., Phi Beta Kappa. Avocations: gardening, house renovation, sports, cooking. Home: 1 Langdon St Apt 211 Madison WI 53703-1326

**LAUTENSCHLAGER, TRACY HAUB,** lawyer; b. Mpls., Sept. 19, 1961; d. George Joseph and Mildred Mary (Allred) Haub; m. Mark Russell Lautenschlager, Sept. 28, 1985; children: Kyle George, Amy Katherine. BA in Bible and Music, Fla. Bible Coll., 1982; JD, Nova U., 1988. Bar: Fla. 1988, U.S. Dist. Ct. (so. dist.) Fla. 1989, U.S. Ct. Appeals (11th cir.) 1990, U.S. Supreme Ct. 1992. Asst. county atty. Broward County Atty. Office, Ft. Lauderdale, Fla., 1988—. Avocation: classical pianist. Office: Broward County Attys Office 320 Terminal Dr Fort Lauderdale FL 33315-3608

**LAVALLEE, GEORGE,** lawyer; b. Massapequa, N.Y., July 6, 1934; s. George E. and Denise Lavallee; m. Margaretta C. Mullen, June 14, 1960; children: Keith, Denise, Karen. BBA, St. John's U., LLB. Spl. agt. FBI, 1960-65; asst. dist. atty. Nassau County, N.Y., 1965-70; of counsel Officers Assn. Nassau County Police, Mineola Custodian Assn., Syosett Fire Dist. Sgt. U.S. Army, 1954-55, Korea. Mem. N.Y. State Bar Assn., FBI Assn. Republican. Roman Catholic. Avocations: tennis, golf, racquetball. Home: 4 W Gate Farmingdale NY 11735-3160

**LAVALLEY, FREDERICK J. M.,** lawyer; b. May 23, 1947; m. Christine Dengler. AB, Stanford U., 1969; JD, U. Pa., 1972. Bar: Pa. 1972. Ptnr. Morgan, Lewis & Bockius, Phila. Trustee Francis W. Sullivan Found., J.R. Grundy Found. Mem. Phila. Club. Office: Morgan Lewis & Bockius 1701 Market St Philadelphia PA 19103-2903

**LAVECCHIA, JOHN B.,** lawyer; b. Newark, Feb. 4, 1932; s. Nicholas and Mary (Boylan) L.; m. Emma Louise Cahill, Feb. 2, 1957; children: John, Emy, Michael, Catherine, Elizabeth, Vincent, Nicholas. BA, Princeton U., 1954; LLB, Columbia U., 1957. Bar: N.J. 1957, U.S. Dist. Ct. N.J. 1957. Assoc. Connell, Foley & Geiser LLP, Newark, 1957-65; ptnr. Connell, Foley & Geiser LLP, Roseland, N.J., 1965—; mem. Supreme Ct. Fee Arbitration Com., 1978-79; mem. Essex dist. Supreme Ct. Ethics Com., 1981-86. With N.J. N.G., 1957. Harlan Fiske Stone scholar Columbia U., 1957. Fellow Am. Coll. Trial Lawyers; master William J. Brennan Inn Ct.; diplomate Am. Bd. Trial Advs.; mem. ABA, Fed. Ins. and Corp. Counsel, N.J. State Bar Assn., Trial Attys. N.J., Essex County Bar Assn. Avocations: golf, cross-country skiing, platform tennis. General civil litigation, Insurance, Environmental. Home: PO Box 172 Dorset VT 05251-0172 Office: Connell Foley & Geiser LLP 85 Livingston Ave Roseland NJ 07068-3702

**LAVELLE, BETTY SULLIVAN DOUGHERTY,** legal professional; b. Omaha, Nov. 12, 1941; d. Marvin D. and Marie C. Sullivan; children from previous marriage: Clayton B. Dougherty, Lance A. Dougherty; m. James S. LaVelle, 1986; 1 child, Lindsay L. A of Pre-Law, U. Nebr., 1960; student, U. Colo., 1964-66; BA in Philosophy, Metro State Coll., 1979; cert. legal assistant, U. San Diego, 1979. Teaching asst. Metro State Coll., Denver, 1978; paralegal Holland and Hart, Denver, 1979-85; litigation paralegal Rothgerber, Appel, Powers and Johnson, Denver, 1985-88; pres. Vivant, Inc., Boulder, 1987—; owner, adminstr. Homestead Group Home for Elderly, Longmont, 1987-92; ptnr. LaVelle & McMillan, Boulder, 1989-90; water law and litigation paralegal Moses, Wittemyer, Harrison and Woodruff, P.C., Boulder, 1990—; mediator domestic relations 20th Jud. Dist., Boulder, 1984-85. Contbr. articles to profl. jours. Vol. legal aid Thursday Night Bar, Denver Bar Assn., 1979-86, paralegal coordinator, panelist, speaker, 1983-85; sr. paralegal Boulder County Legal Svcs., 1988-89; mediator landlord/tenant project City of Boulder, 1983-87; coach, trainer Ctr. for Dispute Resolution, Denver and Boulder, 1984-86; vol. Shelter for Homeless, Boulder, 1988. Recipient cert. U. Denver Coll. Law, 1981, Hoagland award Colo. Bar Assn., 1984. Mem. Colo. Bar Assn., Soc. Profls. in Dispute Resolution, Rocky Mountain Paralegal Assn. (mem. adv. bd. 1980-81, bd. dirs. 1983-85, 94-96, rep. to Colo. Bar Assn. 1994-96, dir. pro bono svcs. 1984-85). Republican. Avocations: vol. legal services for the indigent, computer applications. Home: 1660 Bradley Ct Boulder CO 80303-7300

**LAVELLE, BRIAN FRANCIS DAVID,** lawyer; b. Cleve., Aug. 16, 1941; s. Gerald John and Mary Josephine (O'Callagahan) L.; m. Sara Hill, Sept. 10, 1966; children: S. Elizabeth, B. Francis D., Catherine H. BA, U. Va., 1963; JD, Vanderbilt U., 1966; LLM in Taxation, N.Y.U., 1969. Bar: N.C. 1966, Ohio 1968. Assoc. VanWinkle Buck, Wall, Starnes & Davis, Asheville, N.C., 1968-74, ptnr., 1974—; lectr. continuing edn. N.C. Bar Found., Wake Forest U. Estate Planning Inst., Hartford Tax Inst., Duke U. Estate Planning Inst. Contbr. articles on law to profl. jours. Trustee Carolina Day Sch., 1981-92, sec., 1982-85; bd. dirs. The Salvation Army, Western N.C. Community Found., 1986— (sec. 1987-90); bd. advs. U.N.C. Annual Tax Inst., 1981—. Capt. JAG USAF, 1966-67. Mem. ABA, N.C. Bar Assn. (v.p. 1997—, bd. govs. 1979-82, councillor tax sect. 1979-83, councillor estate planning law sect. 1982-85), Am. Coll. Trust and Estate Counsel (state chmn. 1982-85, regent 1984-90, lectr. continuing edn.), N.C. State Bar (splty. exam. com. on estate planning and probate law 1984-90, chmn. 1990-91, cert. 1987). Episcopalian. Clubs: Biltmore Forest Country. Lodge: Rotary (Asheville). Probate, Estate planning, Taxation, general. Home: 45 Brookside Rd Asheville NC 28803-3015 Office: 11 N Market St PO Box 7376 Asheville NC 28802-8506

**LAVELLE, CHARLES JOSEPH,** lawyer; b. Louisville, Aug. 31, 1950; s. James Ronald and Mary Elizabeth (Logan) L.; m. Donna Kay Mulligan, Jan. 21, 1978. BS with high honors, U. Notre Dame, 1972; JD, U. Ky., 1975; LLM in Taxation, NYU, 1977. Bar: Ky. 1975, U.S. Dist. Ct. (wes. dist.) Ky. 1977, U.S. Tax Ct. 1977, U.S. Claims Ct. 1986, U.S. Ct. Appeals (6th and Fed. cirs.) 1986, U.S. Supreme Ct. 1989. Assoc. Greenebaum Doll & McDonald PLLC, Louisville, 1977-82, mem., 1982—; chmn. bar liaison cen. region IRS, Cin., 1989, sec., 1997, bar liaison southeast region IRS; mem. Regional Counsel Adv. Group, Cin., 1988-89. Contbr. articles to profl. jours. Bd. dirs. Ky. Ctr. Pub. Issues, 1992-94; mem. steering com. Ky. Coalition for Edn., 1993-94; mem. Ky. Ltd. Liability Co. Legislation Drafting Com., 1993-94; mem. planning com. Ky. Conclave on Legal Edn., 1995. Secondary Sci. Tng. grant NSF, U. Ga., 1967, rcsh. grantee NSF, U. Notre Dame, 1969. Mem. ABA (tax sect.), Ky. Bar Assn. (chmn. tax sect. 1992-93), Louisville Bar Assn. (chmn. tax com. 1983, 84, vice chmn., treas. tax com. 1980-82), U. Ky. Law Alumni Assn. (bd. dirs. 1986—, pres. 1989-90, treas. 1987-90, 90—), Ky. C. of C. (bd. dirs. 1991—, exec. com. 1997—, chair pub. policy com. 1997-98, health ins. task force, tax com.), Rotary (bd. dirs. 1991-93, 95-97, treas. 1995-97, dist. conf. chair 1994), Notre Dame Club (pres. 1984-86, chmn. 1986-88, Ky. Man of Yr. 1990), Leadership Ky. (vice chmn. membership svcs. 1995-98, alumni bd. dirs. 1992-92, pres. alumni 1993-94, bd. dirs. 1993-98, exec. com. 1995-98). Corporate taxation, Taxation, general. Office: Greenebaum Doll & McDonald PLLC 3300 National City Tower Louisville KY 40202

**LAVELLE, JOSEPH P.,** lawyer; b. Scranton, Pa., Sept. 7, 1957; s. Patrick Leo and Anne M. (Antal) L.; m. Kathy A. Mlodzienski, Aug. 14, 1982; children: Remy, Joseph, Taylor. BS in Physics, Wilkes Coll., 1979; JD summa cum laude, U. Pitts., 1982. Bar: D.C. 1982, U.S. Ct. Appeals (Fed. cir.) 1982, U.S. Patent and Trademark Office 1982, U.S. Ct. Appeals (3d, 2d and 6th cir.). Assoc. Howrey & Simon, Washington, 1982-90, ptnr., 1991—; adj. prof. Georgetown U. Law Ctr., 1995—. Editl. bd. ABA Antitrust Law Developments, III, 1992; contbr. articles to profl. jours.; mng. editor U. Pitts. Law Rev., 1981-82. Mem. ABA, AAAS, Am. Phys. Soc., Order of the Coif. Republican. Antitrust, Patent, Federal civil litigation. Office: Howrey & Simon 1299 Pennsylvania Ave NW Ste 1 Washington DC 20004-2420

**LAVELLE, WILLIAM AMBROSE,** lawyer, judge; b. Athens, Ohio, Jan. 18, 1925; s. Francis Anthony and Belle Elizabeth (Schloss) L.; m. Marion Halen Yanity, Aug. 7, 1954; children: Frank A., John P., Lydia E., Amy M. BBA, Ohio U., 1949; JD, Ohio State U., 1952. Bar: Ohio 1952, U.S. Dist. Ct. (so. dist.) Ohio 1952. Sr. ptnr. Lavelle Law Offices, Athens, Ohio, 1952-91; judge probate/juvenile divsn. Athens County Common Pleas Ct., 1991-94; assigned judge Supreme Ct. of Ohio, 1994—; pvt. practice estate planning, trusts, probate, 1994—; former solicitor City of Nelsonville, Villages of Albany, Chauncey, Coolville, Glouster, Trimble and Zaleski; counsel Margaret Creek Conservancy Dist., L-Ax Water Distbn. Co., Sunday Creek and Hollister Water Assns.; instr. wills, trusts, estate planning Ohio U., Athens, 1991-99; mem. commn. on cert. as atty. specialists Supreme Ct. Ohio, 1994—. Former chmn. Athens County and Ohio Dem. Party; former mem. Dem. Nat. Com.; chmn. Athens County Bd. Elections, 1967-80; chmn. pers. rev. bd. State of Ohio, 1983-91; trustee, chmn. trustees Ohio U., 1975-81; mem. parish fin. com., parish coun., sch. bd., diocesan bd. lay consultors St. Paul's Cath. Ch., Athens. Served with inf. U.S. Army, 1943-46, ETO, PTO. Mem. ABA, Ohio State Bar Assn. (bd. govs. probate and trust law sect. 1993—, coun. of dels. 1986-89), Athens County Bar Assn. (past pres.), Nat. Acad. Elder Law Attys., Ohio Horse Coun., Tenn. Walking Horse Breeders and Exhibitors Assn., Walking Horse Owners Assn., Athens Symposiarch Club (past pres.), Athens Cotillion Club, Athens Country Club, Athens Rotary Club, VFW, Am. Legion, Sons of Union Vols., Ohio U. Green and White Club, KC (3d and 4th deg.), St. Francis Soc. Avocation: breeding, raising, riding and driving Tennessee Walking Horses. Home: 39 Cable Ln Athens OH 45701-1304 Office: 207 Columbus Rd Ste B Athens OH 45701-1335

**LAVENDER, JAY LAWRENCE,** lawyer; b. Wellston, Ohio, Jan. 21, 1949; s. Elbert Jack and Alma Edith (Davis) L.; m. Joy Annette Landis, May 27, 1982; children: Courtney Jaye, Derek Blake. BA, Otterbein Coll., 1971; JD, Capital U., 1982. Bar: Ind. Sole practice Warsaw, Ind., 1982—. Home: 104 Southfield Rd Winona Lake IN 46590-1718 Office: 116 N Buffalo St Warsaw IN 46580-2728

**LAVENDER, ROBERT EUGENE,** state supreme court justice; b. Muskogee, Okla., July 19, 1926; s. Harold James and Vergene Irene (Martin) L.; m. Maxine Knight, Dec. 22, 1945; children—Linda (Mrs. Dean Courter), Robert K., Debra (Mrs. Thomas Merrill), William J. LL.B., U. Tulsa, 1953; grad., Appellate Judges Seminar, 1967, Nat. Coll. State Trial Judges, 1970. Bar: Okla. bar 1953. With Mass. Bonding & Ins. Co., Tulsa, 1951-53, U.S. Fidelity & Guaranty Co., Tulsa, 1953-54; asst. city atty. Tulsa, 1954-55, practice, 1955-60; practice Claremore, Okla., 1960-65; justice Okla. Supreme Ct., 1965—, chief justice, 1979-80; guest lectr. Okla. U., Oklahoma City U., Tulsa U. law schs. Republican committeeman, Rogers County, 1961-62. Served with USNR, 1944-46. Recipient Disting. Alumnus award U. Tulsa, 1993. Mem. ABA, Okla. Bar Assn., Rogers County Bar Assn., Am. Judicature Soc., Okla. Jud. Conf., Phi Alpha Delta (hon.). Methodist (adminstrv. bd.). Club: Mason (32 deg.). Home: 2910 Kerry Ln Oklahoma City OK 73120-2507 Office: US Supreme Ct Okla Rm 1 State Capitol Oklahoma City OK 73105

**LAVERTY, SARAH GRACE,** lawyer; b. Ann Arbor, Mich., May 13, 1971; d. Robert Eric and Suzanne Beth Laverty; m. Richard Lawrence Alonzo, Aug. 8, 1998. BA, Albion Coll., 1993; JD, U. Mich., 1996, MHSA, 1998. Bar: Mich. Atty. Miller, Canfield, Paddock & Stone, Ann Arbor, 1996—. Fax: 734-747-9076. E-mail: mcpsshark@aol.com. and laverty@millercanfield.com. Office: Miller Canfield Paddock & Stone 101 N Main St Ste 700 Ann Arbor MI 48104-1481

**LAVERY, LIAM BURGESS,** lawyer; b. Homestead AFB, Fla., Apr. 26, 1967; s. William John and Barbara Burgess Lavery; m. Yazmin Fatima Mehdi, Aug. 20, 1994. AB in Philosophy, Harvard U., 1989; JD, U. Mich., 1994. Bar: Wash. 1994. Assoc. Preston Gates & Ellis LLP, Seattle, 1994—. Avocations: running, lawyers league basketball. Intellectual property, Computer. Office: Preston Gates & Ellis LLP 701 5th Ave Ste 5000 Seattle WA 98104-7078

**LAVES, ALAN LEONARD,** lawyer; b. Austin, Tex., June 17, 1960; s. Benard and Cecile (Perry) Laves; m. Joan Riley, 1987; children: Susan, Sarah, Jacob. BSEE, MIT, 1982; JD with honors, U. Tex., 1985. Bar: Tex. 1985. Assoc. Akin, Gump, Strauss, Hauer & Feld, LLP, Dallas, 1985-94, ptnr., 1994—. Contbr. articles to profl. jours. Banking, Mergers and acquisitions, Finance. Office: Akin Gump Strauss Hauer & Feld 1700 Pacific Ave Ste 4100 Dallas TX 75201-4675

**LAVES, BENJAMIN SAMUEL,** lawyer; b. Bklyn., Aug. 2, 1946. BBA, Temple U., 1968; JD, Am. U., 1971. Bar: N.J. 1971, U.S. Dist. Ct. 1971. Intern Select Com. U.S. Senate, Washington, 1969; atty. Newark-Essex Joint Law Reform Project, N.J., 1971-74; dep. pub. advocate N.J. Dept. Mental Health, Newark, 1974-83, Rate Counsel Pub. Advocate, Newark, 1983-84; pvt. practice West Orange, N.J., 1984—, 1996—. Active Essex County Estate Planning Coun. Bd. dirs. N.J. Maclaw, 1987—. Mem. ABA (gen. practice, econs. law sects.), N.J. State Bar Assn. (real property, probate and trust law sect., taxation sect.), Essex County Bar Assn. (chair computer/Internet com. 1999-00, chmn. gen. practice com. 1987-89), Essex County Estate Planning Coun., Inc., Tax Commn. Estate planning, Estate taxation, Probate. Office: 200 Executive Dr Ste 130 West Orange NJ 07052-3303

**LAVEY, JOHN THOMAS,** lawyer; b. Somerville, Mass., Oct. 19, 1932; s. Francis Paul and Theresa Maria (Ronzio) L.; m. Catherine Louise Gallager, Aug. 5, 1961; children: Margaret Ann, Elizabeth Mary, Mark Alexis. BS in Polit. Sci., Holy Cross Coll., 1954; LLB, New Eng. Law Sch., 1957. Atty. NLRB, Washington, 1961-63, Ft. Worth, 1963-66; assoc. McMath, Leatherman, Woods & Youngdahl, Little Rock, 1966-69; ptnr. Walker, Kaplan, Lavey, Hollingworth & Mays, Little Rock, 1969-71, Lavey, Harmon & Burnett, Little Rock, 1971-90, Lavey & Burnett, Little Rock, 1991—. 1st lt. USMC, 1958-60. Mem. Ark. Bar Assn., Assn. Trial Lawyers Am., Ark. Trial Lawyers Assn. Democrat. Roman Catholic. Avocations: jogging, boating. Civil rights, Federal civil litigation, Labor. Home: 501 N Bryan St Little Rock AR 72205-2703 Office: Lavey & Burnett 904 W 2nd St Little Rock AR 72201-2102

**LAVIGNE, LAWRENCE NEIL,** lawyer; b. Newark, June 30, 1957; s. Daniel S. and Alice M. (Melon) L.; m. Benjie Panesh, Oct. 12, 1980; children: Gabriel A., Derek N. BA, Franklin & Marshall Coll., 1979; JD, Seton Hall U., 1982. Bar: N.J. 1982, U.S. Dist. Ct. N.J. 1982, U.S. Ct. Appeals (3d cir.) 1986, U.S. Supreme Ct. 1986, N.Y. 1989. Assoc. Shanley & Fisher, P.C., Newark, 1982-83; ptnr. Hanlon & Lavigne (and predecessor firm), Edison, N.J., 1983—; instr. Am. Inst. Paralegal Studies, Mahwah, N.J., 1985-88. Mem. ABA (litigation sect.), N.J. Bar Assn. (product liability com.), Middlesex County Bar Assn., Trial Attys. N.J., N.J. Def. Assn., Assn. Trial Lawyers Am., Somerset Bar Assn., Worrall F. Mountain Inn of Court (barrister 1991-93). Republican. Jewish. Avocations: tennis, music, computers. State civil litigation, Federal civil litigation, Personal injury. Office: Hanlon Lavigne Topchik 10 Parsonage Rd Ste 200 Edison NJ 08837-2429

**LAVIGNE, PETER MARSHALL,** environmentalist, lawyer, consultant; b. Laconia, N.H., Mar. 25, 1957; s. Richard Byrd and D. Jacquiline (Cobleigh) L.; m. Nancy Gaile Parent, Sept. 20, 1979. BA, Oberlin Coll., 1980; MSL cum laude, Vt. Law Sch., 1983, JD, 1985. Bar: Mass. 1987. History tchr. Cushing Acad., Ashburnham, Mass., 1983-84; rsch. writer Environ. Law Ctr., Vt., 1985; lobbyist Vt. Natural Resources Coun., Montpelier, 1985; exec. dir. Westport (Mass.) River Watershed Alliance, 1986-88, Merrimack River Watershed Coun., West Newbury, 1988-89; environ. cons. Mass., N.H., Vt., and Oreg., 1990—; N.E. coord. Am. Rivers, Washington, 1990-92; dir. river leadership program River Network, Portland, Oreg., 1992-95; dir. spl. programs River Network, Portland, 1995-96; dep. dir. For the Sake of the Salmon, Portland, 1996-97; pres. Watershed Cons., Portland, 1997—; adj. prof. Antioch New Eng. Grad. Sch., Keene, N.H., 1991-92, Portland State U., 1997—; mem. Portland Willamette River Task Force, 1997—; chair adv. bd. Cascadia Times, Portland, 1995—, Amigos Bravos, Taos, N.Mex., 1993—; trustee Rivers Coun. Washington, Seattle, 1993-98; bd. dirs. Alaska Clean Water Alliance, 1995-98, acting pres. 1997-98; adv. bd. River CPR, 1998—; Watershed adv. group Natural Resources Law Ctr. U. Colo., 1995-96; coastal resources adv. bd. Commonwealth of Mass., Boston, 1987-91; bd. dirs. Oreg. Watershed Advisors, 1998-99; adj. assoc. prof. Portland State U., 1997—; Watershed Mgmt. Profl. program dir., Portland State U., 1999—; pres. Cascadia Times Rsch. Fund, 1998—. Co-author: Vermont Townscape, 1987; contbr. articles to profl. jours. Dir. Mass. League of Environ. Voters, Boston, 1988-92; mem. steering com. N.H. Rivers Campaign, 1988-92; co-founder, co-chair New England Coastal Campaign, 1988-92; EMT South Royalton (Vt.) Vol. Rescue Squad, 1982-86; dir., chairperson Vt. Emergency Med. Svcs. Dist. 8, Randolph, 1984-86; co-founder, v.p. Coalition for Buzzards Bay, Bourne, Mass., 1987; housing renewal commn. City of Oberlin, Ohio, 1980-81; mem. properties com. First Unitarian Ch., 1995; mem. Willamette River task Force, City of Portland, Oreg., 1997—. Recipient Environ. Achievement award Coalition for Buzzards Bay, 1988; land use rsch. fellow Environ. Law Ctr., Vt. Law Sch., 1984-85; Mellon found. rsch. grantee Oberlin Coll., 1980. Mem. Natural Resources Def. Coun., Pacific Rivers Coun., River Alliance of Wis., Rivers Coun. Wash., Idaho Rivers United, League of Conservation Voters, Amigos Bravos, Glen Canyon Inst. Democrat. Unitarian-Universalist. Avocations: sea kayaking, mountaineering, woodwork, reading, photography. E-mail: watershed@igc.org. Fax: (503) 232-2887. Home: 3714 SE 11th Ave Portland OR 97202-3724 Office: Watershed Cons PO Box 42162 Portland OR 97242-0162

**LAVILLE, DANIEL MICHAEL,** lawyer; b. Columbus, Ohio, Jan. 28, 1951. BS, Ohio State U., 1973; JD, U. Notre Dame, 1978. Bar: Mich. 1978. Pvt. practice Dowagiac, Mich., 1978-82; asst. U.S. atty. Dept. Justice, Grand Rapids, Mich., 1982-99; clk. U.S. Bankruptcy Ct., Grand Rapids, 1999—. Office: US Attys Office 299 Ford Federal Bldg Grand Rapids MI 49503

**LAVIN, BARBARA HOFHEINS,** lawyer; b. Buffalo, Feb. 27, 1934; m. Charles V. Lavin, June 19, 1954; children: Laurel, Michael, Peter, Robert. BA, Cornell U., 1955; MA in Tchg., Jacksonville U., 1970; JD, U. Richmond, 1989. Bar: Va. 1991, U.S. Ct. Appeals (4th cir.) 1991, U.S. Dist. Ct. (ea. dist.) Va. 1991, U.S. Bankruptcy Ct. 1991. Asst. prin. Greenwich (Conn.) H.S., 1976; owner, pres. Greenwich Real Estate Co., 1977; owner, broker Lavin Realty, Suffolk, Va., 1978; adj. faculty Tidewater C.C., Suffolk, 1982, Paul D. Camp C.C., Suffolk, 1982; pvt. practice Portsmouth, Va.; mediator Va. Mediation Network, 1994—. Active Jr. League, Soc. Mayflower Descendants. Mem. Va. Bar Assn., Portsmouth Bar Assn., Family Law Orgn. Greater Hampton Rds., Portsmouth Bar Assn. (pub. rels. bd. 1996), DAR, Va. Women Attys. Assn. (pres. 1988), Phi Alpha Delta. Republican. Episcopalian. Avocations: figure skating, boating. Family and matrimonial, General practice, Alternative dispute resolution. Office: 301 Columbia St Portsmouth VA 23704-3714

**LAVINE, HENRY WOLFE,** lawyer; b. Phila., Apr. 21, 1936; s. Samuel Phillips and Sarah Pamela (Leese) L.; m. Meta Landreth Doak, Feb. 20, 1960 (div. Feb. 1980); children: Lisa, Lindsay; m. Martha Putnam Cathcart; children: Samuel Putnam, Gwenn Cathcart. BA, U. Pa., 1957, JD, 1961. Assoc. Squire, Sanders & Dempsey L.L.P., Cleve., 1961-70; ptnr. Squire, Sanders & Dempsey L.L.P., Washington, 1970-85, mng. ptnr. Washington office, 1985-91, sr. mng. ptnr., 1991—; dir. Greater Washington Bd. of Trade. Trustee Fed. City Coun., Washington; bd. assocs. Gallaudet U.; mem. The Bretton Woods Com. Mem. Siasconset Casino Club, Met. Club. General corporate, Private international. Office: Squire Sanders & Dempsey 1201 Pennsylvania Ave NW PO Box 407 Washington DC 20044-0407

**LA VINE, ROBERT L.,** lawyer; b. San Francisco, Dec. 24, 1929; s. Jack and Fay L.V.; m. Betty Ann La Vine, June 2, 1951; 1 child, Barbara. BS, U. Calif., 1952; JD, U. Calif. (Hastings), 1959. Bar: Calif., 1959; CPA, Calif. Ptnr. La Vine & Shain, San Francisco, 1961—. Capt. U.S. Army, 1952-54. Mem. San Francisco Bar. Assn., San Francisco Lawyers Club. Fax: 415-777-0222. General corporate, Real property, Taxation, general. Office: 5 3rd St Ste 415 San Francisco CA 94103-3205

**LAVITT, KATHY A.,** lawyer; b. N.Y.C., Apr. 28, 1963; d. Mel S. and Wendy L.; m. Kerry Leeds Griffith, June 27, 1992; 1 child, Ian Leeds Griffith. BA, Brown U., 1985; JD, U. Utah, 1991. Bar: Utah, 1991. Assoc. Giauque, Crockett, Bendinger & Peterson, Salt Lake City, 1991-95; atty. Intermountain Health Care, Inc., Salt Lake City, 1995—. Mem. ABA, Am. Acad. Healthcare Attys., Salt Lake County Bar Assn. (mem. exec. com. 1995-96), Utah State Bar. Health, Labor, Antitrust. Office: Intermountain Health Care 36 S State St Ste 2200 Salt Lake City UT 84111-1401

**LAVORATO, LOUIS A.,** state supreme court justice; s. Charles Lavorato; m. Janis M. Lavorato; children: Cindy, Natalie, Anthony, Dominic. BS in Bus. Adminstrn., Drake U., 1959, JD, 1962. Judge Iowa Supreme Ct., Des Moines, 1986—; sole practice Des Moines, 1962-79; judge Iowa Dist. Ct., Des Moines, 1979-86; justice Iowa Supreme Ct., Des Moines, 1986—. Office: Iowa Supreme Ct St Capitol Bldg Des Moines IA 50319-0001*

**LAW, ELLEN MARIE,** lawyer; b. Bklyn., Aug. 15, 1960; d. Michael Vincent and Marylee (Secker) Tepedino. BS in Acctg. and Banking, Wheeling Coll., 1982; JD, Hofstra U., 1985. Bar: Fla. 1986, N.Y. 1986, Trial Bar Fed. Dist. Ct. (so. dist.) Fla. Assoc. Allen & Allen, Baldwin, N.Y., 1985-86; pvt. practice Boca Raton, Fla., 1986—. Mem. N.Y. Bar Assn., Fla. Bar Assn., Fla. Assn. Women Lawyers, Internat. Assn. Fin. Planners, Boca Raton C. of C. Immigration, naturalization, and customs, Bankruptcy, Personal injury. Office: 1300 N Federal Hwy Boca Raton FL 33432-2801

**LAW, JOHN MANNING,** retired lawyer; b. Chgo., Dec. 5, 1927; s. Fred Edward and Elisabeth (Emmons) L.; m. Carol Lufkin Ritter, May 14, 1955; children: John E., Lucy L., Frederick R., Beth K. Student, U. Chgo., 1944-45, St. Ambrose Coll., 1945; BA, Colo. Coll., 1948; JD, U. Colo., 1951. Bar: Colo. 1951, Ill. 1952, U.S. Ct. Appeals (10th cir.) 1954, U.S. Supreme Ct. 1989. Atty. trust dept. Harris Bank, Chgo., 1951-52; assoc. Dickerson, Morrissey, Zarlengo & Dwyer, Denver, 1952-57; ptnr. Law, Nagel & Clark, Denver, 1958-84, Law & Knous, Denver, 1984-93; ret.; mem. law com. Colo. Bd. Law Examiners, 1971-81, Colo. Ofcls. Compensation Commn., 1985-89. Mem. Moffatt Tunnel Commn., Denver, 1966-90. Capt. USNR, 1945-77, ret. Fellow Colo. Bar Found. (charter); mem. ABA (chmn. 1975, mem. com. legal assistance to mil. pers. 1973-77), Colo. Bar Assn. (bd. govs. 1968-71), Denver Bar Assn. (trustee 1971-74), Internat. Soc. Barristers, Denver Country Club. Republican. Presbyterian. Insurance, State civil litigation, Federal civil litigation. Home: 3333 E Florida Ave Unit 35 Denver CO 80210-2541

**LAW, MICHAEL R.,** lawyer; b. Rochester, N.Y., Nov. 30, 1947; s. George Robert and Elizabeth (Stoddart) L.; m. Cheryl Heller.; BS, St. John Fisher Coll., 1969; JD, U. Louisville, 1975. Bar: N.Y. 1976, U.S. Supreme Ct. 1982. Assoc. Wood, P.C., Rochester, N.Y., 1976-77; pvt. practice Rochester, 1977-78; assoc. Sullivan, Peters, et al, Rochester, 1978-80; ptnr., 1980-81, Phillips, Lytle, Hitchcock, Blaine & Huber, Rochester, 1982—. Mem. exec. com. Camp Good Days and Spl. Times, Rochester, 1984—; bd. dirs. Vol. Legal Svcs. Project, 1995-98. Served with USAR, 1968-74. Mem. ABA (trial law sect., trial techniques com., editor 1986 Trial Techniques, alternate dispute resolution ocm. 1995—), N.Y. State Bar Assn. (trial sect., ins. negigence com.), N.Y. State Trial Lawyers (bd. dirs.), Monroe County Bar Assn. (judiciary com. 1981-88, personal injury com. 1988, chmn. 1999—, profl. responsibility com. 1996—), Genesee Valley Trial Lawyers Assn. (treas. 1992-93, pres.-elect 1993-95, pres. 1995-98). Republican. Roman Catholic. State civil litigation, Federal civil litigation, Personal injury. Home: 3373 Elmwood Ave Rochester NY 14610-3425 Office: Phillips Lytle Hitchcock Blaine & Huber 1400 First Federal Plz Rochester NY 14614-1981

**LAW, ROGER ALAN,** lawyer; b. Grand Rapids, Mich., July 25, 1933; s. R. Dale and Esther S. (Johnson) L.; m. June B. Howe, Dec. 29, 1956; children: David, Diane Smith, James, Charles. BS, U. Mich., 1954, LLB, 1957. Bar: Mich. 1957, U.S. Dist. Ct. (we. dist.) Mich. 1957. Ptnr. Law, Weathers & Richardson, Grand Rapids, 1957-92. Mem. Mich. Bar Assn., Grand Rapids Bar Assn. (pres. 1983-84). Avocations: piano, golf, mathematics, billiards. General corporate, Estate planning, Real property. Home and Office: 4311 Ottawa Trl Shelby MI 49455-8018

**LAW, THOMAS HART,** lawyer; b. Austin, Tex., July 6, 1918; s. Robert Adger and Elizabeth (Manigault) L.; m. Terese Tarlton, June 11, 1943 (div. Apr. 1956); m. Jo Ann Nelson, Dec. 17, 1960; children: Thomas Hart Jr., Debra Ann. AB, U. Tex., 1939, JD, 1942. Bar: Tex. 1942, U.S. Supreme Ct. 1950. Assoc. White, Taylor & Chandler, Austin, 1942; assoc. Thompson, Walker, Smith & Shannon, Ft. Worth, 1946-50; ptnr. Tilley, Hyder & Law, Ft. Worth, 1950-67, Stone, Tilley, Parker, Snakard, Law & Brown, Ft. Worth, 1967-71; pres. Law, Snakard, Brown & Gambill, P.C., Ft. Worth, 1971-90; of counsel Law, Snakard & Gambill, P.C., Ft. Worth, 1990—; gen. counsel Gearhart Industries, Inc., Ft. Worth, 1960-88, Tarrant County Jr. Coll. Dist. Chmn. Leadership Ft. Worth, 1974-90; bd. regents U. Tex. System, 1975-81, vice chmn., 1979-81. Lt. USNR, 1942-46. Recipient Nat. Humanitarian award Nat. Jewish Hosp./Nat. Asthma Ctr., 1983; named Outstanding Young Man, City of Ft. Worth, 1950, Outstanding Alumnus, Coll. of Humanities, U. Tex., 1977, Outstanding Citizen, City of Ft. Worth, 1984, Bus. Exec. of Yr., City of Ft. Worth, 1987, Blackstone award for contbns. field of law Ft. Worth Bar Assn., 1990, Disting. Alumnus U. Tex., 1992. Fellow Am. Bar Found., Tex. Bar Found., Am. Coll. Probate Counsel, Tarrant County Bar Found. (founding chmn.); mem. Ft. Worth C. of C. (pres. 1972), Mortar Bd., Phi Beta Kappa, Omicron Delta Kappa, Pi Sigma Alpha, Delta Sigma Rho, Phi Eta Sigma, Delta Tau Delta. Democrat. Presbyterian. Clubs: Ft. Worth (bd. govs. 1984-90), Century II (bd. govs. to 1985), River Crest Country, Exchange (pres. 1972), Steeplechase. Lodge: Rotary (local club pres. 1960). Avocation: numismatics. General civil litigation, Education and schools, Probate. Home: 6741 Brants Ln Fort Worth TX 76116-7201 Office: Law Snakard & Gambill 3200 Bank One Tower 500 Throckmorton St Fort Worth TX 76102-3859

**LAWATSCH, FRANK EMIL, JR.,** lawyer; b. Avenel, N.J., May 11, 1944; s. Frank Emil and Jessie Margaret L.; m. Deanna Conover, May 25, 1969; children: Amanda, Abigail, Frank. BA, Colgate U., 1966; JD, Cornell U., 1969. Bar: N.Y. 1969, Pa. 1992, N.J. 1993. Assoc. Shearman & Sterling, N.Y.C., 1969-78; sr. v.p., gen. counsel, sec. Midlantic Corp., Edison, N.J., 1978-91; sr. v.p., gen. counsel PNC Bank Corp., Pitts., 1991-92; ptnr. Gibbons, Del Deo, Dolan, Griffinger & Vecchione, Newark, 1993-99; exec. v.p., sec., gen. counsel Nat. Discount Brokers Group, Inc., Jersey City, N.J., 1999—. Mem. ABA, N.J. Bar Assn., Pa. Bar Assn., Assn. of Bar of City of N.Y., Am. Soc. Corp. Secs. Episcopalian. General corporate, Securities, Mergers and acquisitions. Home: 11 The Fairway Montclair NJ 07043-2533 Office: Nat Discount Brokers Group Inc 10 Exchange Pl Ste 37 Jersey City NJ 07302-3975

**LAWHON, SUSAN HARVIN,** lawyer; b. Houston, Oct. 10, 1947; d. William Charles and Ruth Helen (Beck) Harvin; m. Robert Ashton, July 25, 1970 (dec. Dec. 1992); children: Bryan Ashton, Harvin Griffith. AB, Smith Coll., Northampton, Mass., 1970; MEd, U. Tex., 1973; JD, U. Houston, 1990. Bar: Tex. 1990, U.S. Dist. Ct. (so. dist.) Tex. 1991, U.S. Ct. Appeals (5th cir.) 1993. Tchr. Nat. Cathedral Sch., Washington, 1970-71, Austin (Tex.) Ind. Sch. Dist., 1973-74, Spring Branch Ind. Sch. Dist., Houston, 1974-76; sr. assoc. Fulbright & Jaworski, LLP, Houston, 1990—. Editor-in-chief: Houston Jour. Internat. Law, 1989-90. Mem. devel. coun. Tex. Children's Hosp., Houston, 1986—; mem. devel. bd. U. Tex. Health Sci. Ctr., Houston, 1984-87; sponsor Children's Fund, Inc., Houston, 1979-87; bd. dirs. Houston Child Guidance Ctr., 1977-80, Bo's Place, Inc., Tex., 1997—, treas., v.p., pres. bd. dirs.; bd. dirs., treas., fin. v.p. Jr. League Houston, 1984-86; docent Bayou Bend, 1977-84. Mem. ABA, State Bar Tex., Houston Bar Assn., Houston Country Club, Houston Ctr. Club, U. Tex. Club, Smith Coll. Club (Houston) (Seven Coll fund rep. 1982-87). Episcopalian. Federal civil litigation, General civil litigation, State civil litigation. Home: 6222 Holly Springs Dr Houston TX 77057-1137 Office: Fulbright & Jaworski LLP 1301 Mckinney St Ste 5100 Houston TX 77010-3031

**LAWINGER, JANE M.,** lawyer; b. Dodgeville, Wis., Feb. 5, 1960; d. William Nicholas and Helena Theresa (Salzmann) L. BS in Criminal Justice, U. Wis., Platteville, 1984; JD, DePaul U., 1991. Ill. 1991, Wis. 1992, U.S. Dist. Ct. (so. dist.) Ill. 1991, U.S. Ct. Appeals (7th cir.) 1991. Pvt. practice, Vandalia, Ill., 1991—; spl. asst. atty. gen. State of Ill., Vandalia, 1994—. Family and matrimonial, Criminal, Workers' compensation. Home: 130 W Madison St Vandalia IL 62471-2323 Office: PO Box 240 106 S 5th St Vandalia IL 62471-2702

**LAWIT, JOHN WALTER,** lawyer; b. Phila., Aug. 13, 1950; s. Alfred and Marilyn Jane (Balis) L.; children: Andrew Alejandro, Samuel Martin, Ivan Luis (twins). Student, U. Bridgeport, 1968-70; B of Univ. Studies, U. N.Mex., 1972; JD, Franklin Pierce Law Ctr., Concord, N.H., 1977. Bar: Pa. 1978, N.Mex. 1980, Tex. 1992, U.S. Dist. Ct. (ea. dist.) Pa. 1978, U.S. Dist. Ct. N.Mex. 1980. Investigator Franklin Pierce Law Ctr., 1976-77; social researcher Commun. Svc. Coun., Concord, 1977-78; sole practitioner N.Y.C., 1978-79; atty., assoc. McCallister, Fairfield, Query, Strotz & Stribling, Albuquerque, 1979-80; sole practitioner Albuquerque, 1980—; adj. prof. immigration law U. N.Mex. Sch. Law, 1983, 84, 88; spl. immigration counsel U. N.Mex., Albuquerque, 1987—; U.S. immigration judge US. Dept. Justice, 1985; apptd. mem. N.Mex. Internat. Trade/Investment Coun., 1984-87, N.Mex. Border Commn., 1982-86; hon. cons. atty. Ministry Fgn. Affairs Republic of Mex., 1983; lobbyist, author, drafter N.Mex. Immigration & Nationality Law Practice Act. Presenter in field. Founder, profl. cons. Jewish Family Svcs. of Albuquerque, 1988—; bd. dirs., pres. Rainbow House Internat. Adoption, Belen, N.Mex., 1987—; v.p. N.Mex. Refugee Assn., Albuquerque, 1979-84; bd. dirs. N.Mex. Civil Liberties Union, 1988-90; mem. adv. bd. Healing the Children, Albuquerque, 1989—; bd. dirs. Inst. for Spanish Arts, 1994—. Recipient Disting. Svcs. award Cath. Social Svcs., 1988. Mem. N.Mex. State Bar (chair internat. and immigration lawyers sect. 1990-91, bd. dirs. 1988-90), Albuquerque Bar Assn., Am. Immigration Lawyers Assn. (nat. chair 1988-89), El Paso Assn. Immigration and Nationality Lawyers. Avocations: biking, travel, whitewater rafting, hiking, cross-country skiing. Fax: 505-244-1834. E-mail: jwlúsh@hotmail.com. Immigration, naturalization, and customs. Office: 900 Gold Ave SW Albuquerque NM 87102-3043 also: 320 Galisteo St Ste 202 Santa Fe NM 87501-2642

**LAWLER, RICHARD ALLEN,** lawyer; b. Somerville, N.J., June 12, 1954; s. John W. and Marie A. Lawler; m. Donna M. Brady, Jan. 9, 1988. BA, Colo. State U., 1976; JD, U. Colo., 1988. Bar: Colo. 1989, U.S. Dist. Ct. Colo. 1990. Pvt. practice, Boulder, Colo., 1990-94, Lakewood, Colo., 1995—. Fire chief St. Mary's Glacier (Colo.) Vol. Fire Dept., 1996—. Landlord-tenant, Family and matrimonial, Criminal. Office: 2575 S Wadsworth Blvd Lakewood CO 80227-3218

**LAWLER, THOMAS ALBERT,** lawyer; b. Eldora, Iowa, June 10, 1946; s. Lewis W. and Mary C. (Schafer) L.; m. Elaine E. Bruch, June 29, 1968; children: Erin Elizabeth, Loretta Mary. BA, St. Ambrose U., 1968; JD, Cath. U. Am., 1971. Bar: Iowa 1972, U.S. Dist. Ct. (no. and so. dists.) Iowa 1974, U.S. Tax Ct. 1985, U.S. Supreme Ct., 1990, U.S. Ct. Appeals (10th cir.) 1998. Pvt. practice Greene, Iowa, 1972-73; atty., asst. to acct. O's Gold Seed Co., Parkersburg, Iowa, 1972-73; ptnr. Klinkenborg, Lawler, Hansmann & Mansheim, Parkersburg, 1973-85; pvt. practice Parkersburg, 1985—; lectr. on taxation and fin. planning for agr. at State Agrl. Acad., Nizhni, Nougorod, Russia, 1995. Author: Iowa Legal Forms, Probate, 1991; Income Tax Consequences of Real Estate Leasing, 1995; contbr. articles to profl. jours. Atty. City of Parkersburg, 1973-91, City of New Hartford, Iowa, 1973—, City of Stout, Iowa, 1973-91, City of Aredale, Iowa, 1981—, Parkersburg Hist. Soc., 1973—; active Parkersburg Econ. Devel. Mem. ABA, Iowa Bar Assn.(chair agrl. law sect.), Am. Agrl. Law Assn. (pres. citizen adv. panel IRS midwest dist.), Butler County Bar Assn., 2A Bar Assn., Parkersburg C. of C. (pres. 1979-80, Citizen of Yr. 1983), Rotary. Democrat. Roman Catholic. Avocations: gardening, reading, woodworking. Probate, Taxation, general, Real property. Home: 1301 Wemple St Parkersburg IA 50665-2028 Office: 601 Coates St Parkersburg IA 50665

**LAWN, TIMOTHY REGIS,** lawyer; b. Phila., Nov. 23, 1962; s. John Joseph and Carolyn Marie (McTamney) L.; m. Arlene Patricia Lawn, Apr. 5, 1991; children: Joshua, Daniel, John, Maureen. BS in Acctg. cum laude, Spring Garden Coll., 1984; JD cum laude, Widener U., 1989. Bar: Pa. 1989, U.S. Dist. Ct. (ea. dist.) Pa. 1990. Assoc. O'Brien & Ryan, Plymouth Meeting, Pa., 1989-96, Litvin, Blumberg, Matusow & Young, Phila., 1996—; adj. faculty Montgomery County C.C. Chmn. bd. dirs. Dave Palmer Meml. Found., Phila., 1992—. Recipient Am. Jurisprudence awards (2), 1989. Mem. ATLA, ABA, Pa. Bar Assn., Phila. Bar Assn., Pa. Trial Lawyers Assn., Phila. Trial Lawyers Assn. General civil litigation, Personal injury, Product liability. Office: Litvin Blumberg Matusow & Young 1339 Chestnut St Fl 18 Philadelphia PA 19107-3520

**LAWNICZAK, JAMES MICHAEL,** lawyer; b. Toledo, Sept. 11, 1951; m. Christine Nielsen, Dec. 31, 1979; children: Mara Katharine, Rachel Anne, Amy Elizabeth. BA, U. Mich., 1974, JD, 1977. Bar: Mich. 1977, Ill. 1979, Ohio 1989. Law clk. to the Honorable Robert E. DeMascio U.S. Dist. Ct. (ea. dist.) Mich., Detroit, 1977-79; assoc. Levy and Erens, Chgo., 1979-83; assoc. then ptnr. Mayer, Brown & Platt, Chgo., 1983-88; ptnr. Calfee, Halter & Griswold, LLP, Cleve., 1988—. Contbg. author: Collier on Bankruptcy, 15th rev. edit., 1997—. Mem. Chgo. Bar Assn. (subcom. on bankruptcy 1983-88), Cleve. Bar Assn. (bankruptcy com.). Banking, Bankruptcy, Contracts commercial. Home: 14039 Fox Hollow Dr Novelty OH 44072-9773 Office: Calfee Halter & Griswold 800 Superior Ave E Ste 1400 Cleveland OH 44114-2688

**LAWRENCE, BETTY TENN,** lawyer; b. Memphis, Tenn., Feb. 3, 1949; d. William Harvey and Margaret Amrhein Lawrence. AB, Rollins Coll., 1971; JD, Duke U., 1983. Bar: N.Y. 1984, N.C. 1986. Curator Pack Meml. Pub. Libr., Asheville, N.C., 1974-80; assoc. Davis Polk and Wardwell, N.Y.C., 1983-86; pvt. practice Asheville, 1986—. Mem. Preservation Soc. Asheville and Burcombe Co., Asheville, 1976—, v.p. 1978-80, pres. 1986-89; Commr. Hist. Resources Commn. of Asheville and Buncombe County, 1978-80, 86-92, 94—, chair, 1999. Mem. N.C. Bar Assn. Probate, Estate planning, Environmental. Home and Office: 142 Hillside St Asheville NC 28801-1206

**LAWRENCE, EDWARD JACK, III,** lawyer; b. Beaumont, Tex., Sept. 23, 1949; s. Edward Jack and Nelda Rae (McClure) L. BA in Govt., Lamar U., 1971; JD, U. Houston, 1988. Bar: U.S. Dist. Ct. (ea. dist.) Tex. 1993, U.S. Supreme Ct. 1995. Atty. East Tex. Legal Svcs., Beaumont, 1989; pvt. practice Beaumont, 1990—. Bd. dirs. ACLU, Beaumont, 1978—, Clean Air and Water Orgn., 1996—. Mem. Tex. Bar Assn., Jefferson County Bar Assn. Democrat. Methodist-Unitarian. Avocations: golf, tennis, poetry, astronomy, guitar. Criminal, Family and matrimonial, Education and schools. Home and Office: 5570 Winfree St Beaumont TX 77705-5939

**LAWRENCE, GERALD, JR.,** lawyer; b. Phila., Jan. 10, 1968; s. Gerald and Rita Katherine (Duffy) L.; m. Andrea Stewart, Jan. 8, 1994. BSBA, Georgetown U., 1990; JD, Villanova U., 1993. Bar: Pa. 1993, U.S. Dist. Ct. Pa. 1994, U.S. Ct. Appeals (3d cir.) 1994. Atty. Elliott Reihner Siedzikowski & Egan, Blue Bell, Harrisburg, Scranton, Pa. and Woodbury, N.J., 1992-97; counsel Aetna U.S. Healthcare, Inc., Blue Bell, 1997—; counsel Del. County Dem. Party, 1996-98; Del. County counsel to Pa. Dem. Party Victory, 1996. Interviewer Georgetown Alumni Admission Program, 1992—; bd. dirs. James A. Finnegan Found., 1995—; v.p. Georgetown Club Phila., 1996.; treas. Del. County Dem. Party, 1998; mem. Dem. State Com., 1998; treas. Southeastern Caucus Pa. Dem. State Com., 1998; chair Radnor Twp. Dem. Com., 1998—. Mem. ABA, ATLA, Pa. Bar Assn. (mem. judicial selection and adminstrn. com., mem. commn. to rev. and evaluate jud. campaign advt. guidelines 1996), Phila. Bar Assn. State civil litigation, Federal civil litigation. Home: 349 Oak Ter Wayne PA 19087-5205 Office: Aetna US Healthcare Law Dept (U194) 980 Jolly Rd Blue Bell PA 19422-1904

**LAWRENCE, JAMES KAUFMAN LEBENSBURGER,** lawyer; b. New Rochelle, N.Y., Oct. 8, 1940; s. Michael Monet and Edna (Billings) L.; m. George-Ann Adams, Apr. 5, 1969; children: David Michael, Catherine Robin. AB, Ohio State U., 1962, JD, 1965. Bar: Ohio. 1965, U.S. Dist. Ct. (so. dist.) Ohio 1971, U.S. Ct. Appeals (6th cir.) 1971, U.S. Ct. Appeals (4th cir.) 1978. Field atty. NLRB, Cin., 1965-70; ptnr. Frost & Jacobs LLP, Cin., 1970—; adj. prof. econs. dept. and Coll. Law, U. Cin., 1975— (outstanding adj. faculty award 1998), Ohio State U. Coll. Law, 1995—, Xavier U., 1995—, McGregor Sch., Antioch U., 1993-98; master Potter Sewart Inn of Ct., Cin., 1987—, treas., 1988-90, The Coll. of Labor and Employment Lawyers, 1999—; tchg. fellow Harvard Negotiation Project, 1991; chmn. adv. panel on appointment of magistrate judges U.S. Dist. Ct. for So. Dist. Ohio, 1993—. Contbr. articles to profl. jours. Mem. nat. coun. Ohio State U. Coll. Law, 1974—; mem. steering com. Leadership Cin., 1985-89; mem. Seven Hills Neighborhood Houses, Cin., 1973-95, pres., 1992-94; bd. dirs. Beechwood Home, Cin., 1983-86; mem. adv. bd. Emerson Behavioral Health Svcs., 1990-95, chmn., 1995; chmn. Labor Dept., 1978-89, Franciscan Hosp. Devel. Coun., 1995—, chmn., 1996-97; trustee Ctr. for Resolution of Disputes, Inc., 1988-91, treas., 1990-91; mem. Ohio Gov.'s Ops. Improvement Task Force, 1991. Mem. ABA, Cin. Bar Assn. (chmn. labor law com. 1979-82, comm. adv. com. 1994-96, alternative dispute resolution com. 1996—), Ohio Bar Assn. (vice chmn. labor and employment law sect. 1987-90, chmn. 1990-92), Indsl. Rels. Rsch. Assn. (bd. govs. 1977-80), Alumni Assn. Coll. Law Ohio State U. (pres. 1984-85), Soc. Profls. in Dispute Resolution, Cincinnatus Assn. (pres. 1985-86), Collaborative Law Inst. (steering com. 1996—), Soc. Profls. in Dispute Resolution, Univ. Club. Avocations: collecting movie posters, biking. Labor, Alternative dispute resolution. Home: 3300 Columbia Pkwy Cincinnati OH 45226-1044 Office: Frost & Jacobs LLP 2500 PNC Ctr 201 E 5th St Ste 2500 Cincinnati OH 45202-4182

**LAWRENCE, JOHN KIDDER,** lawyer; b. Detroit, Nov. 18, 1949; s. Luther Ernest and Mary Anna (Kidder) L.; m. Jeanine Ann DeLay, June 20, 1981. AB, U. Mich., 1971; JD, Harvard U., 1974. Bar: Mich. 1974, U.S. Supreme, 1977, D.C. 1978. Assoc. Dickinson, Wright, McKean & Cudlip, Detroit, 1973-74; staff atty. Office of Judge Adv. Gen., Washington, 1975-78; assoc. Dickinson, Wright, McKean, Cudlip & Moon, Detroit, 1978-81; ptnr. Dickinson, Wright, Moon, VanDusen & Freeman, Detroit, 1981-98, Dickinson Wright, PLLC, Detroit, 1998—. Exec. sec. Detroit Com. on Fgn. Rels., 1988—; trustee Ann Arbor (Mich.) Summer Festival, Inc., 1990—; patron Founders Soc. Detroit Inst. Arts, 1979—. With USN, 1975-78. Mem. AAAS, ABA, Am. Law Inst., Fed. Bar Assn., State Bar Mich., D.C. Bar Assn., Am. Judicature Soc., Internat. Bar Assn., Am. Hist. Assn., Detroit Club, Detroit Athletic Club, Econ. Club Detroit, Phi Eta Sigma, Phi Beta Kappa. Democrat. Episcopalian. Banking, Mergers and acquisitions, Private international. Office: Dickinson Wright PLLC 500 Woodward Ave Ste 4000 Detroit MI 48226-3416

**LAWRENCE, MATTHEW RUSSELL,** lawyer; b. Grand Forks, N.D., Feb. 1, 1971; s. M.O. and E.R. Lawrence; m. Esther-Marie Smith, Apr. 24, 1999. BA, U. Ga., 1993; JD, Ga. State U., 1996. Bar: Ga. 1996, U.S. Dist. Ct. (mid. dist.) Ga. 1996. Atty. Young, Thagard, Hoffman, Scott & Smith, Valdosta, Ga., 1996—; adj. prof. Valdosta State U., 1998—. Youth soccer coach YMCA, Valdosta, 1996-97. Mem. Ga. Assn. Criminal Def. Lawyers, Valdosta Bar Assn., Lawyers Club Valdosta, Valdosta Area Sigma Alpha Epsilon Alumni Assn. (pres.), Lowndes County C. of C. Insurance, General civil litigation, Criminal. Office: Young Thagard Hoffman Scott & Smith 801 Northwood Park Dr Valdosta GA 31602-1393

**LAWRENCE, RICHARD DEAN,** lawyer; b. Jefferson City, Mo., Sept. 20, 1944; s. Charles Eugene and Edith Lucille (Moore) L.; m. Diana H. McIntyre, Aug. 13, 1967; children: Jennifer, Daniel, Michael, David, Lindsay. AA, U. Cin., 1964, BA, 1967; JD with honors, J.D. Chase Coll. Law, 1971. Bar: Ohio 1971, Ky., 1989, U.S. Dist. Ct. Ohio, U.S. Ct. Appeals. Founder, ptnr., pres. Gustin & Lawrence, 1971—; ptnr., pres. Lawrence, Linder & McGrath, Cin., 1991—; guest lectr. Chase Coll. Law, 1983-87, Ohio Trial Practice Inst., Cin., 1975-77; speaker med. malpractice Ohio Acad. Trial lawyers, Cin. Bar Assn., Ky. Bar Assn. Pres. Washington Hills Assn., Cin., 1977-78; bd. dirs. Hamilton Mut. Ins. Co.; past deacon Pleasant Ridge Presbyn. Ch.; past mem. adminstrv. bd. United Meth. Ch. of Milford. Mem. ABA, Ohio Bar Assn., Cin. Bar Assn., Assn. Trial Lawyers Am., Ky. Bar Assn. , No. Ky. Bar Assn., Hamilton County Trial Lawyers Assn., Ohio Acad. Trial Lawyers, Ky. Acad. Trial Attys. State civil litigation, Personal injury. Office: Plz Level Ste 120 50 E Rivercenter Blvd Covington KY 41011-1683

**LAWRENCE, STEVEN THOMAS,** lawyer; b. Sacramento, Calif., Feb. 28, 1968; s. Thomas George and Sharon Lee L.; m. Jodi Lynd Hipps, Aug. 8, 1993. BS, Calif. State U., Sacramento, 1990; JD, U. Pacific, 1994. Fin. cons. Govt. Fin. Strategies, Inc., Sacramento, 1990-91; jud. clk. Ariz. Ct. Appeals, Phoenix, 1994-95; dep. county atty. Maricopa County Atty.'s Office, Phoenix, 1995-96; assoc. atty. Felix & Holohan, Phoenix, 1996-98; assoc. gen. counsel JDA Software Group, Inc., Phoenix, 1998—. Parish chancellor Episc. Diocese of Ariz., Phoenix, 1996—. Mem. ABA, Maricopa County Bar Assn. Republican. Avocations: golf, physical fitness, training hunting dogs. Home: 801 W Glenn Dr Phoenix AZ 85021-8638 Office: JDA Software Group Inc 11811 N Tatum Blvd Bldg Ste2000 Phoenix AZ 85028-1614

**LAWRENCE, THOMAS EUGENE,** judge; b. Dallas, Mar. 2, 1949; s. Thomas Usry and Clara Elizabeth (Peel) L.; m. Mickey Jo Lindgren, Mar. 18, 1978. BA, Chapman U., 1971; JD, South Tex. Coll., Houston, 1980. Bar: U.S. Dist. Ct. (so. dist.) Tex. 1981, U.S. Ct. Appeals (5th cir.) 1981. Gen. mgr. Marine Pollution Control Inc., Houston, 1975-77, Peterson Maritime, Inc., Houston, 1977-79; atty. Texaco, Inc., Houston, 1980-82; judge Harris County, Houston, 1983—; chmn. ad hoc coms. Justice of the Peace and Constable Assn. Tex., 1989, justice of the peace sect. State Bar Tex., 1989, State Commn. Jud. Conduct, Austin, Tex., 1996-97; mem. desk rev. com. Tex. Justice Ct. Tng. Ctr., Austin, 1985-87; presiding judge Harris County Justice of the Peace, 1989-90; spkr. in field. Contbr. articles to profl. jours. Adv. bd. mem. Roseate, Inc., Houston, North Harris County Jr. League, Houston, 1994-96; mem. North Harris Montgomery C.C. Found., Houston; trustee Mercer Arboretum Found., Houston, 1991-92; organizer Teen Ct. Program, 1991—; chmn. flaming arrow dist. Sam Houston coun. Boy Scouts Am., Houston, 1995. Lt. USCG, 1971-75. Named Boss of Yr., Am. Bus. Women's Assn., 1989, Vol. of Month, Houston Northwest C. of C., April 1997; recipient Meritorious Svc. award Houston Apt. Assn., 1989, Liberty Bell award North Harris Montgomery C.C. Dist., 1992, Scholars award, 1993; Judge Tom Lawrence Day proclaimed by City of Humble, 1992. Fellow Tex. Bar Found.; mem. Am. Judicature Soc., Tex. Bar Assn., Houston Bar Assn. (alternate dispute resolution com.), Houston Northwest and Northeast Harris County Bar Assns., Tex. Justice Ct. Tng. Ctr. (faculty, legal), Houston Northwest C. of C., Rotary (Paul Harris fellow). Republican. Presbyterian. Avocations: golfing, reading, computers. Office: 121 W Main St Humble TX 77338-4383

**LAWS, GORDON DERBY,** lawyer; b. Dallas, Feb. 1, 1949; s. Wilford Derby and Ruby (Whiteleather) L.; m. Barbara Ruth Hill, May 9, 1974; children: Gordon Derby Jr., Stephen Richard, Ruthanne. BA in Econs., Brigham Young U., 1973, JD, 1976. Bar: Utah 1976, Tex. 1986, U.S. Supreme Ct. 1981, U.S. Ct. Appeals (5th cir.) 1982, U.S. Dist. Ct. (we. dist.) Tex. 1987, U.S. Dist. Ct. (so. dist.) Tex. 1991. Trial atty. U.S. Justice Dept., Washington, 1976-81; asst. U.S. atty. Western Dist. Tex., San Antonio, 1981-87, asst. chief, civil divsn., U.S. atty., 1985-87; assoc. Gary, Thomasson, Hall & Marks, Corpus Christi, Tex., 1987-89; ptnr./mem. Gary, Thomasson, Hall & Marks, 1989—; mem. exec. com. Gary, Thomasson, Hall & Marks,1994—. Bishop Ch. of Jesus Christ of Latter Day Saints, Corpus Christi, 1990-95. Avocations: reading, camping. Personal injury, Product liability, General civil litigation. Home: 4158 Eagle Dr Corpus Christi TX 78413-2024 Office: Gary Thomasson Hall & Marks 210 Carancahua Ste 500 PO Box 2888 Corpus Christi TX 78403-2888

**LAWS, JAMES TERRY,** lawyer; b. Greenville, S.C., Mar. 14, 1952; s. James Talmadge and Alma Dell (Ledford) L.; m. Lynn Marie Watson, June 6, 1973; children: Courtney Marie, Jourdan Elizabeth. BA, U. S.C., 1974, JD, 1977. Bar: S.C. 1977, U.S. Dist. Ct. S.C. 1978, U.S. Ct. Appeals (4th cir.) 1979, U.S. Supreme Ct. 1984. Ptnr. Laws & Daniel, Greenville, 1977-81, Laws, Daniel & Stewart, Greenville, 1981, Riley, Riley, Laws & Stewart, Greenville, 1982-86, Nelson, Mullins, Riley & Scarborough, Greenville, 1987—; pres., chmn. Travelers Rest (S.C.) Devel. Corp., 1980—, Marietta Mgmt. and Holding, Greenville, 1985—. Bd. dirs. Stroud Mem. Hosp., Marietta, S.C., 1978—; dem. precinct pres., Marietta, 1978-82, 1986—, county v.p., Greenville, 1982—; mem. 300 for Greenville, 1986—; traveling ambassador Hdqrs. for Recruitement, Greenville, 1986—, bd. dirs., 1987—; bd. dirs. Greenville County Recreation Commn., Meals on Wheels, Greenville; chmn. Travelers Rest Great Towns Com., 1980-82. Named Young Businessman of the Yr., N. Greenville Area Econ. Devel. Group., 1985. Mem. ABA, S.C. Bar Assn., Greenville County Bar Assn., Internat. Platform Assn., Greenville C. of C., Travelers Rest Jaycees (pres. 1983, Jaycee of the Yr. award 1981). Lodges: Rotary, Lions (local pres. 1979), Masons. Avocations: alpine skiing, sailing. Federal civil litigation, State civil litigation, Real property. Home: 106 S Warwick Rd Gul SC 24609 Office: Nelson Mullins Riley & Scarborough 24th Floor Daniel Bldg PO Box 10084 Greenville SC 29603-0084

**LAWSON, A. PETER,** lawyer. AB, Dartmouth Coll., 1968; JD, Columbia U., 1971. Bar: N.Y. 1971, Ill. 1979. Assoc. Sullivan & Cromwell, 1971-78; sr. counsel Baxter Internat., 1978-79; various positions Motorola Corp., 1979-89, corp. v.p., asst. gen. counsel, 1989-95, sr. v.p., asst. gen. counsel, 1995-96, sr. v.p., sec., gen. counsel, 1996-98, exec. v.p., gen. counsel, sec., 1998—. Office: Motorola Inc 1303 Algonquin Rd Schaumburg IL 60196*

**LAWSON, BEN F.,** lawyer, international legal consultant; b. Marietta, Okla., Feb. 7, 1939; s. Woodrow W. and Lennie L. (McKay) L.; m. Diane W. Lawson; children: Nicole, Michael C. BBA, U. Houston, 1965, JD, 1967. Bar: Tex. 1967. Atty. Monsanto/Burmah Oil, Houston, 1967-72; mgr. internat. acquisitions Oxy (formerly Cities Svc. Co.), Houston, 1972-78; gen. atty. Damson Oil Corp., Houston, 1978-81; gen. counsel, v.p. Newmont Oil Co., Houston, 1981-86; pvt. practice internat. law Houston, 1986—; cons. internat., 1987—. Contbr. numerous articles to profl. jours. Staff sgt. USAF, 1959-65. Fellow Houston Bar Found.; mem. ABA, Am. Corp. Counsel Assn. (chmn. oil and gas com. 1986-87). Republican. Avocations: fishing, antiques. Private international, Mergers and acquisitions, Oil, gas, and mineral. Address: 3027 Bernadette Ln Houston TX 77043-1302

**LAWSON, CHRISTOPHER PATRICK,** lawyer; b. Independence, Mo., Mar. 20, 1970; s. Joel Craig and Linda Michelle Lawson, Aug. 14, 1992. BS, Baker U., 1992; JD, M Health Svcs. Adminstrn., U. Kans., 1996. Bar: Kans. 1996, U.S. Dist. Ct. Kans. 1996. V.p. Individual Support Sys., Inc., Topeka, 1995-97; legal rsch. assoc. Kans. Health Inst., Topeka, 1996-97; assoc. Davis, Unrein, Hummer, McCallister, Biggs & Head, L.L.P., Topeka, 1997—; seminar presenter Med. Ednl. Svcs., Inc., Topeka, 1998. Author: (monograph) Understanding Health Data Privacy Issues, 1997. Mem. Am. Health Lawyers Assn. Avocations: basketball, scuba diving, fishing. General civil litigation, Health, General corporate. Home: 1545 SW Chelsea Dr Topeka KS 66604-2484 Office: Davis Unrein Hummer Et Al 100 E 9th St Topeka KS 66601

**LAWSON, JACK WAYNE,** lawyer; b. Decatur, Ind., Sept. 23, 1935; s. Alva W. and Florence C. (Smitley) L.; m. Sarah J. Hibbard, Dec. 28, 1961; children: Mark, Jeff. BA in Polit. Sci., Valparaiso U., 1958, JD, 1961. Bar: Ind. 1961, U.S. Supreme Ct. 1970, U.S. Dist. Ct. (no., so. dists.) Ind. 1991, Ind. Supreme Ct., Appellate Cts. 1991. Ptnr. Beckman, Lawson LLP, Ft. Wayne, Ind., 1961-84; sr. ptnr. Beckman, Lawson LLP, Ft. Wayne, 1984—; seminar presenter and writer Ind. CLE Forum, Indpls., 1970—, Nat. Health Lawyers Assn., Washington, 1986. Editor-in-chief Indiana Real Estate Transactions; contbr. articles to profl. jours. Mem. Ft. Wayne C. of C., 1975—; small claims ct. judge, Allen County, Ind., 1963-67. Mem. Am. Coll. Real Estate Lawyers. Republican. Lutheran. Avocations: sailing, teaching religious seminars, antique consulting. General corporate, Real property, Land use and zoning (including planning). Office: Beckman Lawson LLP 800 Standard Federal Plaza PO Box 800 Fort Wayne IN 46801-0800

**LAWSON, JANE ELIZABETH,** lawyer; b. Washington, July 30, 1965; d. Benn and Ada Ruth (Clotfelter) L. BA, Ga. State U., 1988, JD, 1991. Internal ops. coord. Sandy Springs Assocs., Atlanta, 1986-88; pvt. practice law Atlanta, 1991-93; legal svc. specialist Capstone Legal Staffing, Chgo., 1994—; arbitrator Fulton County Superior Ct., Atlanta, 1992-93. Guardian ad litem Atlanta Vol. Lawyers Found., 1992-94. Mem. Chgo. Bar Assn. (law office tech. com. 1994—), Atlanta Bar Assn., State Bar of Ga., D.C. Bar Assn. Office: Capstone Legal Staffing 2 N La Salle St Ste 950 Chicago IL 60602-3785

**LAWSON, MICHAEL,** magistrate; b. Erie, Pa., Feb. 22, 1954; s. Judge and Audrey Marie Lawson; children: Hillary, Meghan. BA in Psychology, Edinboro U., 1977; MA in Counseling and Psychology, Ashland U., 1980; JD, U. Toledo, 1987. Bar: Ohio 1988, Pa. 1997. Magistrate Sandusky County Ct. Common Pleas, Fremont, Ohio, 1994—; corp. counsel Deerfield Behavioral Health, Erie, Pa., 1995—. Home: 45 W Virginia Ave Apt 1 Vermilion OH 44089-2800 Office: PO Box 110 Sandusky OH 44871-0110

**LAWSON, SUSAN COLEMAN,** lawyer; b. Covington, Ky., Dec. 4, 1949; d. John Clifford and Louise Carter Coleman; m. William Henry Lawson, June 6, 1980; 1 child, Philip. BA, U. Ky., 1971, JD, 1979. Bar: Ky. 1979. Ptnr. Lawson & Lawson, P.S.C., Harlan, 1995—; atty. Stoll, Keenon & Park, Lexington, Ky., 1979-80; atty., Harbert Constrn. Co., Middlesboro, Ky., 1980-81; ptnr. Buttermore, Turner, Lawson & Boggs, P.S.C., Harlan, Ky., 1981-94. Elder 1st Presbyn. Ch., Pineville, Ky., 1986—. Mem. ABA, Ky. Bar Assn., Harlan County Bar Assn. (pres. 1983), Order of Coif. Democrat. Avocations: tennis, golf. General civil litigation, General corporate, General practice. Home: 511 W Kentucky Ave Pineville KY 40977-1307

**LAWSON, THOMAS SEAY, JR.,** lawyer; b. Montgomery, Ala., Oct. 30, 1935; s. Thomas Seay and Rose Darrington (Gunter) L.; m. Sarah Hunter Clayton, May 27, 1961; children: Rose Gunter, Gladys Robinson, Thomas Seay III. AB, U. Ala., 1957, LLB, 1963. Bar: Ala. 1963, U.S. Supreme Ct. 1969. Law clk. to chief judge U.S. Dist. Ct. (no. dist.) Ala., 1963-64; assoc. Steiner, Crum & Baker, Montgomery, 1964-68; ptnr. Capell, Howard, Knabe & Cobbs P.A., Montgomery, 1968-98; asst. dist. atty. 15th jud. cir. of Ala., 1969-70; ptnr. Cappell & Howard, P.C., Montgomery, 1999—; mem. lawyers adv. com. U.S. Ct. Appeals, 5th cir. 1978, 11th cir. 1979-82. Pres. The Lighthouse, 1978-79. Lt. USNR, 1957-60. Fellow Ala. Law Found.; mem. ABA, FBA, Ala. State Bar (pres. young lawyers sect. 1970-71), Montgomery County Bar Assn. (pres. 1980), Am. Judicature Soc., 11th Cir. Hist. Soc. (pres. 1999—), Soc. of Pioneers of Montgomery (pres. 1983), Farrah Law Soc. (pres. 1986-88, Outstanding Alumnus award U. Ala. student chpt. 1989), Montgomery Inn of Ct. (master bencher, bd. dirs. 1989-93, chancellor 1991, pres. 1992-93, emeritus 1994—), Ala. Law Inst. (bd. dirs. 1986—), Ala. Law Sch. Found. (trustee 1985—), Montgomery Country Club, Capital City Club (Montgomery). Episcopalian. General civil litigation, Administrative and regulatory, Alternative dispute resolution. Home: 1262 Glen Grattan Dr Montgomery AL 36111-1402 Office: Capell & Howard PC PO Box 2069 150 S Perry St Montgomery AL 36102-2069

**LAWSON, WILLIAM HOMER,** lawyer; b. Champaign, Ill., Jan. 15, 1953; s. Joel Smith and Grace Colgate (Rumbough) L.; m. Laurie Anne Millikan, Nov. 24, 1979; children: William S., Amy R., Bradley C. B.A., Trinity Coll., Hartford, Conn., 1974; J.D., Stanford U., 1977. Bar: Hawaii, 1977. Assoc. Cades, Schutte, Honolulu, 1977-79; sole practice, Honolulu, 1979—. Mem. Assn. Trial Lawyers Am., ABA, Hawaii Bar Assn., Consumer Lawyers of Hawaii. Federal civil litigation, State civil litigation, Personal injury. Office: 1188 Bishop St Ste 2902 Honolulu HI 96813-3312

**LAWSON, WILLIAM THOMAS, III,** lawyer, accountant; b. Phila., June 30, 1955; s. William Thomas Jr. and Norma Marie (DiGiuseppe) L.; m. Mary Ellen T. Lazauskas, Oct. 17, 1987. BS in Acctg., Villanova U., 1977, JD, 1980. Bar: Pa. Supreme Ct. 1980, U.S. Dist. Ct. (ea. dist.) Pa. 1983, U.S. Ct. Appeals (3d cir.) 1983, U.S. Supreme Ct. 1993. Law clk. to Hon Francis L. Van Dusen U.S. Ct. Appeals (3d cir.), Phila., 1979; assoc. Edward J. Morris, P.C., Phila., 1980-83; pvt. practice Phila., 1983—; solicitor Parkside (Pa.) Fire Commn., 1982—; mem. Fed. Criminal Justice Act Panel, Phila., 1989—. Mem. ABA, Phila. Bar Assn., Justinian Soc., Beta Gamma Sigma, Phi Kappa Phi. Avocations: scuba diving, reading, fishing. Criminal, State civil litigation, Contracts commercial. Office: 1420 Walnut St Ste 1000 Philadelphia PA 19102-4010

**LAWSON-JOWETT, MARY JULIET,** lawyer; b. Mobile, Ala., May 26, 1959; d. William Max Lawson and Perina Juliet (Barich) Franc; m. Adam Geoffrey Jowett; 1 child, Caitlin Victoria Jowett. BA, U. Miss., 1981, JD, 1987. Bar: Miss. 1988, U.S. Dist. Ct. (no. and so. dists.) Miss. 1988. Tchr. Ocean Springs (Miss.) Sch. System, 1981-85; atty. Ronald W. Lewis & Assocs., Oxford, Miss., 1988-89; ptnr. occupl. hearing loss and hand-arm vibration syndrome Scruggs, Millette, Lawson, Bozeman & Dent, P.A., Pascagoula, Miss., 1989—; gen. practice, civil rights and employment law Juliet Jowett, P.A., 1997—; cons. Occupational Hearing Loss, P.A., 1989-96. Contbr. articles to profl. jours. Mem. Walter Anderson Players, Ocean Springs, 1973-96. Mem. ABA, ATLA (chmn. occupational hearing loss litigation group 1990-94), Miss. Trial Lawyers Assn. (editor 1990-92), Magnolia Bar Assn. Democrat. Roman Catholic. Avocations: reading, golf, horseback riding, gardening, acting. General civil litigation, Labor, Personal injury. Office: Juliet Jowett PA PO Office Drawer 1625 1016 La Fontaine St Ocean Springs MS 39564-4934

**LAWTON, ERIC,** lawyer, photographer, visual artist, writer; b. N.Y.C., Apr. 9, 1947; s. Leo and Vira L.; m. Gail Schenbaum, July 15, 1989; children: Rebecca Nicole, Alexandra Rose. AB, UCLA, 1969, photographic studies, 1980-81; JD, Loyola U., Los Angeles, 1972. Bar: Calif. 1972, U.S. Dist. Ct. (cen. dist.) Calif. 1974, U.S. Ct. Appeals (9th cir.) 1973, U.S. Supreme Ct. 1976. Assoc. West & Girardi, Los Angeles, 1972-76; pvt. practice Los Angeles, 1976—; of counsel Mahoney, Coppenrath, Jaffe & Pearson, 1997—; guest lectr. UCLA Law Sch., 1986; instr. visual arts dept. UCLA Ext.; AV rating Martindale-Hubbell. One-man shows include L.A. Children's Mus., 1980-81, Am. Film Inst., 1981, Marc Richards Gallery, L.A., 1986, U. Art Gallery Calif. State U. Northridge, 1987, John Nichols Gallery, Santa Paula, Calif., 1988, Gallery at 817, L.A., 1991, Pacific Asia Mus., Pasadena, Calif., 1993; exhibited in group shows at Stockholm Art Fair, Sweden, 1986, Francine Ellman Gallery, 1986-87, Artists' Soc. Internat. Gallery, San Francisco, 1986-87, Fla. State U. Fine Arts Gallery and Mus., Tallahassee, 1988, Silvermine Gallery, Stamford, Conn., 1988, City Hall of West Hollywood, 1988, others; group show P.L.A.N Spring Street Gallery, L.A., 1995, Christie's, Beverly Hills, Calif., 1998, Finegood Gallery, L.A., 1999; spl. film photographer in The Last Day, 1979, Chiva, Getting on in Style, 1980, Child's Play, 1981, others; multi-media prodns. include The Power, 1979, The Tie That Binds, 1981, Large-Screen Photographic Slide Montage with performance of Los Angeles Philharm. Orch. at Hollywood Bowl, 1986, Floating Stone performance, Japan Am. Theater, L.A., 1987, Pacific Asia Mus., 1993, Rejoice Performance at Thousand Oaks Performing Arts Ctr., 1998 (multi-media prodr. and digital visual performance), others; represented in permanent collections including Bibliotheque Nationale, Paris, N.Y. Pub. Libr., L.A. Children's Mus., Westwood Nat. Bank, Gibralter Savs., L.A., Mobius Soc., L.A., Western Bank, Internat. Photography Mus., Oklahoma City, Condon & Forsyth, others; photographer, co-author The Soul of the World, 1993, The Soul Aflame, 1999; spl. assignment White House photographer, 1983; record album covers include Gyuto Monks, Tibetan Tantric Choir, Jungle Suite; poster Japanese Boats; contbr. photographs to books, newspapers and mags. including, N.Y. Times Mag., Fortune Mag., Conde Nast Traveler Mag., Comm. Arts. Mag., Am. Photo Mag., Chgo. Tribune, Variety, Gente (Italy), Dukas Femina (Switzerland), The World of Photography (China), Popular Photography, Pan Am Mag., Travel & Leisure Mag., U.S. News Mag., Time, Newsweek, Nat. Geographic, Harper & Row Books, Harcourt Brace Books, Holt, Rinehart & Winston books, John Wiley & Sons Books, others; world-wide advtsg. campaign Iridium, 1998; ann. report Tenn. Valley Authority, 1997; author: (short stories anthologies) Soul Moments, 1997, The Art of Pilgrimage, 1998. Active organizing com., citizens adv. and cultural and fine arts adv. commns. XXIII Olympic Games, Los Angeles, 1983-84; mem Cultural and Fine Arts Adv. Commn, 1983-84. Recipient award Fla. Nat. '88, Artquest awards, 1987, 88, 1st Prize Sierra Mag. Photo Contest, 1990, Award of Excellence for Photography, Communication Arts Mag., 1994; named one of top 40 photographers Internat. Photography Congress, 1988, winner Am. Photo Mag. 3rd Ann. Photography Contest, 1994. Mem. ABA, Consumer Atty. Assn. L.A., Consumer Atty. Assn. Calif., L.A. County Bar Assn. Avocations: swimming, music, skiing, world traveling, Karate (1st degree black belt). State civil litigation, Personal injury, Construction. Office: Ste 2480 2049 Century Park East Los Angeles CA 90067-3126

**LAWTON, THOMAS EDWARD, JR.,** lawyer; b. Boston, Sept. 13, 1947; s. Thomas Edward and Margaret (Callahan) L.; m. Ronnie Arlene Zwickel Klein, Aug. 30, 1970 (div. Jan. 1995); children: Joshua Thomas, Jared Aran; m. Paula Marie St. Jean, Feb. 21, 1998. BA, Hofstra U., 1970; JD, St. John's U., 1974. Bar: Mass. 1974, Fla. 1979, U.S. Dist. Ct. Mass. Atty. Quincy, Mass., 1974-78, Nigro, Pettepit & Lucas, Wakefield, Mass., 1978-84, White, Inker & Aronson, Boston, 1984-91, Malik, Lawton & DiCicco, Boston, 1991-98; propr. Law Offices of Thomas E. Lawton, Jr., Boston and Lowell, 1998—; guest lectr. Suffolk Univ., 1989—, Boston Coll. Sch. Law, 1989-90, N.E. Sch. Law., 1992; faculty Mass. Continuing Leg. Edn. Inc., Boston, 1989—. Contbr. articles to profl. jours. Bd. dirs. Keystone Hall, Nashua, N.H., 1995—. Fellow Am. Acad. Matrimonial Lawyers (bd. mgrs.); mem. Boston Bar Assn. (sect. chair, 1991-93). Avocations: hiking, fishing, bicycling. Family and matrimonial. Office: 10 Bridge St Lowell MA 01852-1201

**LAWYER, DAVID JAMES,** lawyer; b. Chgo., Mar. 28, 1961; s. Cornelius Bernard and Margaret (Leamy) L.; m. Jean Elizabeth Lawyer, July 23, 1983; children: Brandon David, Caitlin Elizabeth, Dylan Thomas. BA in Govt.,

St. John's U., Collegeville, Minn., 1982; JD, Seattle U., 1986. Bar: Wash., 1986, U.S. Dist. Ct. (we. dist.) Wash., 1986, U.S. Ct. Appeals (9th cir.), 1995. Ptnr. Inslee, Best, Doezie & Ryder, Bellevue, Wash., 1986—. Vol. Vol. Legal Svcs., Seattle, 1991—, Eastside Literacy Coun., 1993—; gen. counsel, pro bono Kids Voting, Wash., Bellevue, 1994—. Mem. Wash. State Bar Assn., King County Bar Assn., Ea. King County Bar Assn. (trustee 1991-95, Oustanding Trustee award, 1994). Roman Catholic. Avocations: baseball, music, theater, coaching youth athletics, writing. State civil litigation, Civil rights, Constitutional. Home: 15116 NE 67th Pl Redmond WA 98052-4739 Office: Inslee Best Doezie & Ryder PS PO Box c-90016 777 108th Ave NE Ste 1900 Bellevue WA 98004-5144

**LAWYER, VIVIAN JURY,** lawyer; b. Farmington, Iowa, Jan. 7, 1932; d. Jewell Everett Jury and Ruby Mae (Schumaker) Brewer; m. Verne Lawyer, Oct. 25, 1959; children: Michael Jury, Steven Verne. Tchr.'s cert. U. No. Iowa, 1951; BS with honors, Iowa State U., 1953; JD with honors, Drake U., 1968. Bar: Iowa 1968, U.S. Supreme Ct. 1986. Home econs. tchr. Waukee High Sch. (Iowa), 1953-55; home econs. tchr. jr. high sch. and high sch., Des Moines Pub. Schs., 1955-61; pvt. practice law, Des Moines, 1972-95; chmn. juvenile code tng. sessions Iowa Crime Commn., Des Moines, 1978-79, coord. workshops, 1980; assoc. Lawyer, Lawyer & Assocs., Des Moines, 1981-98; co-founder, bd. dirs. Youth Law Center, Des Moines, 1977-93; mem. com. rules of juvenile procedure Supreme Ct. Iowa, 1981-87, adv. com. on costs of ct. appointed counsel Supreme Ct. Iowa, 1985-88; trustee Polk County Legal Aid Svcs., Des Moines, 1980-82; mem. Iowa Dept. Human Svcs. and Supreme Ct. Juvenile Justice County Base Joint Study Com., 1984—. Mem. Iowa Task Force permanent families project Nat. Coun. Juvenile and Family Ct. Judges, 1984-88; mem. substance abuse com. Commn. Children, Youth and Families, 1985—; co-chair Polk County Juvenile Detention Task Force, 1988. Editor: Iowa Juvenile Code Manual, 1979, Iowa Juvenile Code Workshop Manual, 1980; co-editor: 1987 Cumulative Supplement, 1993 supplement, Iowa Academy of Trial Lawyers Trial Handbook; author booklet in field, 1981. Mem. Polk County Citizens Commn. on Corrections, 1977. Iowa Dept. Social Svcs. grantee, 1980. Mem. Purple Arrow, Phi Kappa Phi, Omicron Nu. Republican. Juvenile, Personal injury. Home: 5831 N Waterbury Rd Des Moines IA 50312-1339 Office: 427 Fleming Building Des Moines IA 50309-4011

**LAY, DONALD POMEROY,** federal judge; b. Princeton, Ill., Aug. 24, 1926; s. Hardy W. and Ruth (Cushing) L.; m. Miriam Elaine Gustafson, Aug. 6, 1949; children: Stephen Pomeroy (dec.), Catherine Sue, Cynthia Lynn, Elizabeth Ann, Deborah Jean, Susan Elaine. Student, U.S. Naval Acad., 1945-46; BA, U. Iowa, 1948, JD, 1951; LLD (hon.), Mitchell Coll. Law, 1985. Bar: Nebr. 1951, Iowa 1951, Wis. 1953. Assoc. Kennedy, Holland, DeLacy & Svoboda, Omaha, 1951-53, Quarles, Spence & Quarles, Milw., 1953-54, Eisenstatt, Lay, Higgins & Miller, 1954-66; judge U.S. Ct. Appeals (8th cir.), 1966—, chief judge, 1980-92, senior judge, 1992—; faculty mem. on evidence Nat. Coll. Trial Judges, 1964-65, U. Minn. Law Sch., William Mitchell Law Sch.; mem. U.S. Jud. Conf., 1980-92. Mem. editorial bd.: Iowa Law Rev., 1950-51; contbr. articles to legal jours. With USNR, 1944-46. Recipient Hancher-Finkbine medal U. Iowa, 1980. Fellow Internat. Acad. Trial Lawyers; mem. ABA, Nebr. Bar Assn., Iowa Bar Assn., Wis. Bar Assn., Am. Judicature Soc., Assn. Trial Lawyers Am. (bd. govs. 1963-65, Jud. Achievement award), Order of Coif, Delta Sigma Rho (Significant Sig award 1986, Herbert Harley award 1988), Phi Delta Phi, Sigma Chi. Presbyterian. Office: US Ct Appeals 8th Cir 316 Robert St N Ste 560 Saint Paul MN 55101-1461

**LAYDEN, CHARLES MAX,** lawyer; b. Lafayette, Ind., Nov. 10, 1941; s. Charles E. and Elnora M. (Parvis) L.; m. Lynn D. McVey, Jan. 28, 1967; children: David Charles, Kathleen Ann, John Michael, Daniel Joseph. BA in Indsl. Mgmt., Purdue U., 1964; JD, Ind. U., 1967. Bar: Ind. 1967, U.S. Dist. Ct. (no. and so. dists.) Ind. 1967, U.S. Ct. Appeals (7th cir.) 1970. U.S. Tax Ct. 1986. Assoc. Vaughan & Vaughan, Lafayette, 1967-70; ptnr. Vaughan, Vaughan & Layden, Lafayette, 1970-86, Layden & Layden, Lafayette, 1986—. Chmn. profl. div. United Way Lafayette, 1986. Mem. ABA, Ind. Bar Assn., Tippecanoe County Bar Assn. (pres. 1994-95), Am. Bd. Trial Advs. (charter mem. Ind. chpt. 1984—), Ind. Trial Lawyers Assn. (bd. dirs. 1983—). Republican. Roman Catholic. Avocations: photography, classic cars, flying. Federal civil litigation, State civil litigation, Personal injury. Home: 2826 Ashland St West Lafayette IN 47906-1510 Office: Layden & Layden PO Box 909 Lafayette IN 47902-0909

**LAYDEN, LYNN MCVEY,** lawyer; b. Mpls., June 15, 1941; d. David Hugh and Adelyn Martha (Dvorak) McVey; m. Charles Max Layden, Jan. 28, 1967; children: David Charles, Kathleen Ann, John Michael, Daniel Joseph. LBA, Carleton Coll., Northfield, Minn., 1963; JD, Ind. u., 1967. Bar: Ind. 1967, U.S. Dist. Ct. (so. and no. dists.) 1967. Assoc. Vaughan, Vaughan & Layden, Lafayette, Ind., 1967-86; ptnr. Layden & Layden, Lafayette, Ind., 1986—; guardian ad litem Superior Ct. III-Juvenile Ct., Lafayette, 1986-96. Pres. devel. coun. Ivy Tech. State Coll., 1993—; pres. bd. trustees West Lafayette Sch. Corp., 1988-95. Mem. ABA, Ind. Bar Assn., Tippecanoe County Bar Assn., Order of Coif, Phi Beta Kappa. Home: 2826 Ashland St West Lafayette IN 47906-1510 Office: Layden & Layden Bank 1 Bldg Ste 712 Lafayette IN 47901

**LAYMAN, DAVID MICHAEL,** lawyer; b. Pensacola, Fla., July 28, 1955; s. James Hugh and Winifred (Smith) L. BA with high honors, U. Fla., 1977, JD with honors, 1979. Bar: Fla. 1980. Assoc. Gunster, Yoakley, Criser & Stewart, West Palm Beach, Fla., 1980-83; assoc. Wolf, Block, Schorr & Solis-Cohen, West Palm Beach, 1983-87, ptnr., 1987-88; shareholder Shapiro and Bregman P.A., 1988-91, Greenberg, Traurig, Hoffman, Lipoff, Rosen & Quentel, P.A., West Palm Beach, Fla., 1991-93, Prom, Korn & Zehmer, P.A., Jacksonville, Fla., 1993-94, Mahoney Adams & Criser, P.A., Jacksonville, Fla., 1994-96, Greenberg, Traurig, Hoffman, Lipoff, Rosen & Quentel P.A., West Palm Beach, Fla., 1996—; mem. Attys. Title Ins. Fund. Contbg. editor U. Fla. Law Rev.; contbr. articles to profl. jours. Del. Statewide Rep. Caucus, Orlando, Fla., 1986; mem. Blue Ribbon Zoning Rev. Com., West Palm Beach, 1986; bd. dirs., pres. Palm Beach County Planning Congress, 1984-89; trustee South Fla. Sci. Mus., 1994-96; bd. dirs., sec., v.p. Ronald McDonald House, Jacksonville, 1994-96, Cultural Coun. of Greater Jacksonville; bd. dirs. Home Safe of Palm Beach County Inc., 1996-97. Named one of Outstanding Young Men in Am., 1980. Mem. ABA, Fla. Bar Assn. (bd. govs. young lawyers divsn. 1989-91), Palm Beach County Bar Assn. (pres. young lawyers sect. 1987-88), Fla. Blue Key, Palm Beach County Gator Club (pres., bd. dirs.), Omicron Delta Kappa, Sigma Chi, Phi Kappa Phi. Episcopalian. Real property, Landlord-tenant. Office: 777 S Flagler Dr Ste 310E West Palm Beach FL 33401-6161

**LAYTON, GARLAND MASON,** lawyer; b. Boydton, Va., Aug. 20, 1925. LLB, Smith-Deal-Massey Coll. Law, 1952; LLD, Coll. of William and Mary, 1962. Bar: Va. 1951, U.S. Dist. Ct. (ea. dist.) Va. 1961, U.S. Supreme Ct. 1968. Sole practice Virginia Beach, Va., 1952—; of house counsel Layton & Layton Enterprises, Inc. Served with USMC, 1940-45, PTO. Mem. ABA, Fed. Bar Assn., Nat. Lawyers Club, Va. Beach Bar Assn. Democrat. Methodist. Real property, Administrative and regulatory, General corporate. Office: 4809 Baybridge Ln PO Box 5211 Virginia Beach VA 23471-0211

**LAZAR, DALE STEVEN,** lawyer; b. Cleve., Aug. 16, 1952; s. Donald S. and Mary J. (Zavada) L.; m. Deborah S. Gorecki, Apr. 28, 1979; children: Stephen, Kevin, Vanessa. BS with distinction, Cornell U., 1974, JD, 1977. Bar: D.C. 1977, U.S. Patent and Trademark Office 1978, U.S. Claims Ct. 1979, U.S. Ct. Appeals (D.C. cir.) 1979, U.S. Supreme Ct. 1993. Assoc. Cushman Darby & Cushman Intellectual Property Group Pillsbury Madison & Sutro LLP, Washington, 1977-82, ptnr., 1982—, mng. ptnr., 1989-93; lectr. in field. Mem. Am. Intellectual Property Assn., D.C. Bar Assn., IEEE, Cornell Club Washington (pres. 1989-92), Tau Beta Pi, Eta Kappa Nu. Avocations: swimming, tennis, snow skiing, computers. Patent, Trademark and copyright, Computer. Office: Cushman Darby & Cushman 9th Flr East Tower 1100 NY Ave NW Washington DC 20005-3934

**LAZAR, RAYMOND MICHAEL,** lawyer, educator; b. Mpls., July 16, 1939; s. Simon and Hessie (Teplin) L; children: Mark, Deborah. BBA, U. Minn., 1961, JD, 1964. Bar: Minn. 1964, U.S. Dist. Ct. Minn. 1964. Spl. asst. atty. gen. State of Minn., St. Paul, 1964-66; pvt. practice Mpls., 1966-72; ptnr. Lapp, Lazar, Laurie & Smith, Mpls., 1972-86; ptnr., officer Fredrikson & Byron P.A., Mpls., 1986—; lectr. various continuing edn. programs, 1972—; adj. prof. law U. Minn., Mpls., 1983—. Fellow Am. Acad. Matrimonial Lawyers; mem. ABA (chair divorce laws and procedures com. family law sect. 1993-94), Minn. Bar Assn., Hennepin County Bar Assn. (chair family law sect. 1978-79). Family and matrimonial, State civil litigation. Home: 1201 Yale Pl Minneapolis MN 55403-1901 Office: Fredrikson & Byron PA 1100 Internat Centre 900 2nd Ave S Minneapolis MN 55402-3314

**LAZAROW, MARTIN SIDNEY,** lawyer, accountant; b. Schenectady, N.Y., July 10, 1937. BS, SUNY, Albany, 1968, MS, 1969; LLB, JD, Albany Law Sch., 1966. CPA; Bar: N.Y. 1966, U.S. Dist. Ct. (no. dist.) N.Y. 1966, U.S. Tax Ct. 1967, U.S. Ct. Appeals (2d cir.) 1994. Mem. acctg. faculty Bus. Sch., SUNY, Albany; counsel to Com. on Taxation N.Y. State Senate, Albany; counsel to Zoning Bd. Appeals Town of Clifton, N.Y., town justice; sole practitioner Clifton Park. With U.S. Army, 1956-59, France. Mem. numerous profl. orgns. Taxation, general, Real property, General corporate. Office: PO Box 284 Barney Rd Clubhouse Clifton Park NY 12065

**LAZARUS, BRUCE I.,** restaurant and hotel management educator; b. Pitts.; s. Arnold H. and Belle Lazarus. BS, Pa. State U., 1975; JD, U. Pitts., 1980. Bar: Pa. 1980. Ops. analyst ARA Services, Phila., 1976-77; legal intern Pa. Human Relations Commn., Pitts., 1978-79; food service dir. Martin's Run Life Care, ARA Services, Phila., 1980-81; asst. dir. dept. nutrition Bryn Mawr (Pa.) Hosp., ARA Services, 1981-84; assoc. prof. restaurant and hotel mgmt. Purdue U., West Lafayette, Ind., 1984-96, prof. emeritus, 1996—; Council Hotel, Restaurant and Instnl. Edn. (membership com. 1984—, paper rev. com. 1988—). Contbr. articles to profl. pubs. Nat. Inst. Food Service Industry grantee, 1986, Internat. Franchise Assn., 1987; recipient Mary Mathew award for Outstanding Undergraduate teaching Consumer anf Family Svcs., 1993, Purdue Univ. award Outstanding Undergraduate Teaching, 1993. Mem. ABA, Ind. Bar Assn., Pa. Bar Assn., Nat. Restaurant Assn., Phi Kappa Phi. Office: Purdue U 1266 Stone Hall Lafayette IN 47907-1266

**LAZOR, JOHN ADAM,** lawyer, composer; b. L.A., Nov. 4, 1965; s. Edward Bena and Dorothy (Bzouch) L.; m. Pamela Daphne, Feb. 15, 1997. BS, Stanford U., 1987; JD, U. Mich., 1992. Bar: Calif. 1992. Sole practitioner L.A., 1992-98; staff atty. Levitt & Quinn, L.A., 1997—; sec. Family Law Indigent Paternity Panel, L.A., 1993—; mem. Family Support South, L.A., 1994—. Mem. State Bar Calif., Los Angeles County Bar Assn. Christian. Avocations: bicycling, scuba diving, various sports, musical performances. Family and matrimonial, Probate.

**LAZZARO, CLIFFORD EMANUEL,** lawyer; b. Bklyn., Apr. 29, 1959; s. Emanuel Clifford and Nicoletta (Giametta) L.; m. Maria Coffinas, June 8, 1986. BA, NYU, 1981; JD, Touro Law Sch., 1985. Bar: N.J. 1988, U.S. Dist. Ct. N.J. 1988. Asst. prosecutor Essex County Prosecutor Office, Newark, 1988-92; ptnr. Farco & Lazzaro, P.C., 1992—. Mem. N.J. State Bar Assn., Trial Lawyers Assn. Am., Essex County Bar Assn., N.Y. State Bar Assn. (assoc.), Nat. Italian-Am. Bar Assn., Am. Hellenic Ednl. Progressive Assn., Masons, Delta Theta Phi. Democrat. Roman Catholic. Avocations: skiing, weight training, theatre. Criminal, Personal injury, Real property. Office: Farco & Lazzaro PC 744 Broad St Bldg 1801 Newark NJ 07102-3805

**LEA, LOLA STENDIG,** lawyer; b. N.Y.C., Sept. 20, 1934; d. Hershel and Sophie (Golub) Stendig; m. Robert M. Lea, Sept. 12, 1953 (div. Apr. 1976); 1 child, Jennie. B.A. cum laude, NYU, 1954; LL.B., Yale U., 1957. Bar: N.Y. 1958, Maine 1989. Law clk. to U.S. dist. judge So. Dist. N.Y., 1957-59, asst. U.S. atty., 1959-61; assoc. C.C. Davis, N.Y.C., 1961-67; mem. firm Davis & Cox, N.Y.C., 1967-71, Lea, Goldberg & Spellun (P.C.), N.Y.C., 1971-77, Trubin, Sillcocks, Edelman & Knapp, N.Y.C., 1977-80; counsel Parker & Duryee, 1983-86, mem., 1987-88; spl. counsel to N.Y. 1st dept. joint interprofl. com. Drs. and Lawyers, 1972-78; lectr. Practising Law Inst., N.Y.C., 1969-70, 74, 79; spl. mediator Med. Malpractice Mediation part Supreme Ct. N.Y., 1971-80; chmn. N.Y. State Commn. Investigation, 1981-83; mem. parole bd. State of Maine, 1999—. Fellow Am. Bar Found., N.Y. Bar Found.; mem. N.Y. Bar Assn. (del. 1972-77, 87-88, mem. exec. com. 1976-77), Assn. Bar City N.Y. (chmn. grievance com. 1978-80, chmn. medicine and law com. 1969-71, chmn. spl. com. on drug laws 1986-88, mem. other coms.), N.Y. County Lawyers Assn. (dir. 1978-81). Federal civil litigation, General civil litigation, General corporate. Home and Office: 22 Arnold Rd Freeport ME 04032-6025 also: 529 5th Ave New York NY 10017-4608

**LEA, LORENZO BATES,** lawyer; b. St. Louis, Apr. 12, 1925; s. Lorenzo Bates and Ursula Agnes (Gibson) L.; m. Marcia Gwendolyn Wood, Mar. 21, 1953; children—Victoria, Jennifer, Christopher. BS, MIT, 1946; JD, U. Mich., 1949; grad. Advanced Mgmt. Program, Harvard U., 1964. Bar: Ill. 1950. With Amoco Corp. (formerly Standard Oil Co. Ind.), Chgo., 1949—, asst. gen. counsel, 1963-71, assoc. gen. counsel, 1971-72, gen. counsel, 1972-78, v.p., gen. counsel, 1978-89. Trustee Village of Glenview (Ill.) Zoning Bd., 1961-63, Cmty. Found. Collier Country; bd. dirs. Chgo. Crime Commn., 1978—, Midwest Council for Internat. Econ. Policy, 1973—, Chgo. Bar Found., 1981—, Chgo. Area Found. for Legal Services, 1981—; bd. dirs. United Charities of Chgo., 1973—, chmn., 1985—. Served with USNR, 1943-46. Mem. ABA, Am. Petroleum Inst., Am. Arbitration Assn. (dir. 1980—), Ill. Bar Assn., Chgo. Bar Assn., Assn. Gen. Counsel, Order of Coif, Law Club, Econs. Club, Legal, Mid-Am. (Chgo.), Glen View, Wyndemere, Hole-In-The-Wall, Sigma Xi. Republican. Mem. United Ch. of Christ. General corporate, Antitrust, Administrative and regulatory.

**LEACH, JAMES GLOVER,** lawyer; b. Panama City, Fla., Jan. 26, 1948; s. Milledge Glover and Thelma Louise (Hamilton) L.; m. Judith A. Leach, Feb. 26, 1972 (div. 1987); children: Allison, Arica; m. January Parker, Dec. 1997. AS, Gulf Coast Coll., 1968; BA, Duke U., 1970; MBA, Ga. State U., 1974, MI, 1976; JD, Drake U., 1989. Bar: Iowa 1990; CPCU 1977, CLU 1978. Bank officer Bank South, Atlanta, 1972-75; asst. v.p. Johnson & Higgins, Atlanta, 1975-78; pres. Nat. Gen. Ins. Co., St. Louis, 1978-85, AOPA Svc. Corp., St. Louis, 1985-87, Kirke-Van Orsdel Specialty, Des Moines, 1987-89, Gallagher Specialty, St. Louis, 1990-92; prin., dir., counsel Pauli & Co. Inc., St. Louis, 1992-93; sr. v.p. and gen. counsel Am. Safety Ins., Atlanta, 1993-98; vice chair, gen. counsel, dir. Unistar Fin. Svc. Corp., Dallas, 1998—; cons. McDonnell Douglas, St. Louis, 1987; dir. Gateway Ins. Co., St. Louis, 1992; corp. assembly Blue Cross/Blue Shield, St. Louis, 1991-92. Contbr. articles to profl. jours. 1st lt. USAF, 1970-72, Korea. Avocations: pilot, golf. General corporate, Insurance, General civil litigation. Home: 7 Shadow Ridge Ct Frisco TX 75034-6849 Office: Unistar Fin Svc Corp 4635 Mcewen Rd Dallas TX 75244-5308

**LEACH, RUSSELL,** judge; b. Columbus, Ohio, Aug. 1, 1922; s. Charles Albert and Hazel Kirk (Thatcher) L.; m. Helen M. Sharpe, Feb. 17, 1945; children: Susan Sharpe Snyder, Terry Donnell, Ann Dunham Samuelson. B.A., Ohio State U., 1946, J.D., 1949. Bar: Ohio 1949. Clk. U.S. Geol. Survey, Columbus, 1948-49; reference and teaching asst. Coll. Law, Ohio State U., 1949-51; asst. city atty. City of Columbus, 1951, 53-57, city atty., 1957-63, presiding judge mcpl. ct., 1964-66; ptnr. Bricker & Eckler, 1966-88, chmn. exec. com., 1982-87; judge Ohio Ct. Claims, 1988—. Commr., Columbus Met. Housing Authority, 1968-74; chmn. Franklin County Republican Com., 1974-78. Served with AUS, 1942-46, 51-53. Named One of 10 Outstanding Young Men of Columbus, Columbus Jaycees, 1956, 57. Mem. ABA, FBA, Ohio Bar Assn. (coun. of dels. 1970-75), Columbus Bar Assn. (pres. 1973-74, Svc. medal 1993), Am. Judicature Soc., Pres.' Club Ohio State U., Am. Legion, Delta Theta Phi, Chi Phi. Presbyterian. Home: 1232 Kenbrook Hills Dr Columbus OH 43220-4968 Office: Ohio Ct Claims 65 E State St Ste 1100 Columbus OH 43215-4213

**LEACH, SYDNEY MINTURN,** lawyer; b. Tuscaloosa, Ala., Dec. 13, 1951; s. Randall Peck and Jean (Key) L.; m. Catherine Louise Aertker, Mar. 31, 1984 (div. July 1986). Cert., U. Ala., 1975, BEE, 1975; JD, U. Va., 1978. Bar: U.S. Patent Office 1978, Tex. 1979, U.S. Dist. Ct. (so. dist.) Tex. 1979, U.S. Dist Ct. (no. and ea. dists.) Tex. 1991, U.S. Ct. Apepals (4th cir.) 1980, U.S. Ct. Appeals (fed. cir.) 1985, U.S. Supreme Ct. 1986. Ptnr. Honigman, Miller, Schwartz & Cohn, Houston, 1992—, Arnold, White & Durkee, Hosuton, 1978-92. Author: How to Sue in Small Claims Court, 1984, Tenants Rights, 1985; editor Current Aspects of Licensing Technology, 1981, Your Case in Traffic Court, 1984, Patent Law Handbook, 1987, 88, 89, 90. Mem. steering com. campaign Judge Sheila Jackson Lee, Houston, 1984, Judge Lamar McCorkle, Houston, 1986-88, Judge Joseph "Tad" Halbach, 1992. Named one of Outstanding Young Men of Am., 1980-82, 85-86; recipient Disting. Alumnus award U. Ala. Coll. Engring, Disting. Fellow U. Ala. Elec. Engring. Dept., 1992. Fellow Houston Bar Found., Tex. Bar Found.; mem. ABA (Young Lawyers Assn. liaison to patent sect.), Tex. Young Lawyers Assn. (treas. 1984-85, bd. dirs. 1983-85, 1986-88), Houston Young Lawyers Assn. (bd. dirs. 1981-82, Outstanding Service award 1982, 83), Am. Intellectual Property Law Assn., U. Ala. Alumni Assn. (pres. Houston chpt. 1980, 83), Capstone Engring. Soc. (bd. dirs. 1982-88). Republican. Baptist. Club: Houstonian, Univ. (Houston). Lodge: Rotary. Patent, Trademark and copyright, Federal civil litigation. Office: Honigman Miller et al PO Box 262389 Houston TX 77207-2389

**LEACH, TERRY RAY,** lawyer, judge; b. Ft. Worth, Apr. 6, 1949; s. Herbert W. and Catherine A. (Flanary) L.; m. Dixie Gail Day, Jan 8, 1972; children: Michelle Rene, David Richard, Jennifer Anne. BS in Indsl. Engring., Tex. Tech U., 1971, JD with honors, 1975. Bar: Tex. 1975, U.S. Dist. Ct. (no. dist.) Tex. 1976. Engr. Southwest Bell Telephone, San Antonio, 1970; assoc. Whitley, Boring & Morrison, Bedford, Tex., 1975-76; ptnr. Evans, Leach & Ames, Hurst, Tex., 1976-82; sr. ptnr. Leach & Ames P.C., Hurst, 1982—; judge City of Bedford, 1979-93, City of Lakeside, Tex., 1984—, Halton City, Tex., 1986-94; lectr. real estate law Tarrent County Jr. Coll., Hurst, 1980-81; instr. bus. law Tarrent County Jr. Coll., Hurst, 1991-96. Mem. Hurst Zoning Bd. Adjustment, 1985-88, Hurst Planning and Zoning Commn., 1988-93, Hurst Found. Com., 1986; deacon Frist Bapt. Ch., Colleyville, 1997; bd. dirs. N.E. Tarrant County Community Trust, 1987-93. Mem. ABA, Tex. Bar Assn., N.E. Tarrant County Bar Assn. (pres. 1980-81), Coll. State Bar Tex., Tex. Bd. Specialization (cert., estate planning and probate law coms. 1989—). Probate, Estate taxation, Estate planning. Office: Leach & Ames PC 1236 Southridge Ct Ste 101 Hurst TX 76053-4283

**LEACHMAN, BERNARD D., JR.,** lawyer; b. Louisville, Feb. 22, 1938; s. Bernard D. Sr. and Katherine (Grief) L.; m. Rita Simonetti, Dec. 23, 1967; children: Bernard D. III, Carmen M., Jonathan A., James C. AB, U. Louisville, 1959, LLB, JD, 1962. Bar: Ky. 1962. Sole practitioner Louisville, 1965—. Contbr. articles to legal jours. Polit. campaigns and party worker Dem. Party, Jefferson County, Ky., 1970s, 1980s; trustee Monticello Pl. Assn., Jefferson County, 1996—. Mem. Ky. Bar Assn., Ind. State Bar Assn., Louisville Bar Assn., Ind. Bar Found. Christian. Avocations: golf, travel, fitness, reading. Office: 410 W Chestnut St Ste 564 Louisville KY 40202-2323

**LEACHMAN, RUSSELL DEWITT,** lawyer; b. Amarillo, Tex., Aug. 8, 1965; s. William D. and Alexia (Hall) L.; m. Margaret Feuille, July 8, 1989; children: William Benton, Richard Boone. BA in Polit. Sci., Tex. Tech. U., 1986, JD, 1990. Bar: Tex. 1990, U.S. Dist. Ct. (we. dist.) Tex. 1992, U.S. Dist. Ct. (no. dist.) Tex. 1994, U.S. Dist. Ct. (ea. dist.) Tex. 1998, U.S. Ct. Appeals (5th cir.) 1994. Asst. dist. atty. 34th Judicial Dist. Tex., El Paso, 1990-92; atty. Leachman & Escobar LLP, El Paso, 1992-94, Diamond Rash Gordon & Jackson, El Paso, 1994—. Dir. El Paso Young Lawyers Assn. Mock Trial Competition, El Paso, 1990-95; mem. Ducks Unltd. Area Com., El Paso, 1991—. Mem. Lodge 130 (mason), Phi Gamma Delta, Delta Theta Phi, Delta Phi Epsilon, Phi Rho Pi, Pi Sigma Alpha. Methodist. General civil litigation, Criminal. Office: Diamond Rash Gordon & Jackson PC 300 E Main Dr Fl 7 El Paso TX 79901-1372

**LEADER, ROBERT JOHN,** lawyer; b. Syracuse, N.Y., Oct. 14, 1933; s. Henry John and Dorothy Alberta (Schad) L.; m. Nancy Bruce, Sept. 23, 1960; children—Henry, William, Catherine, Thomas, Edward. A.B., Cornell U., 1956; J.D., Syracuse U., 1962. Bar: N.Y. 1963. Assoc. Ferris, Hughes, Dorrance & Groben, Utica, N.Y., 1962-64; ptnr. Cole Leader & Elmer, Gouverneur, N.Y., 1964-66; ptnr. Case & Leader, Gouverneur, 1966—;sec. North Country Hosps. Inc., 1972—; atty. Village of Hermon (N.Y.), 1968—, Town of Gouverneur, 1967-94, Town of Pitcairn (N.Y.), 1974—, Town of Edwards, 1974—, Town of Rossie, 1985—, Town of Fowler, 1978—; corp. counsel Village of Gouverneur, 1973—; counsel Gouverneur Ctrl. Sch. Dist., 1980—; bd. dirs. Gouverneur Savs. and Loan. Trustee Edward John Noble Hosp., Gouverneur, 1972—, chmn. bd., 1979-81; trustee North Country Hosps., Inc., Gouverneur, 1972—, Gouverneur Library, 1973-83; trustee Gouverneur Nursing Home Co., Inc., 1972—, past pres. 1979-81; Republican chmn. Town and Village of Gouverneur, 1969-72; del. N.Y. State Jud. Conv., 1981—. Served to capt. USAF, 1956-59. Mem. Rotary (pres. 1988-89). Roman Catholic. State civil litigation, General practice, Construction. Home: 187 Rowley St Gouverneur NY 13642-1220 Office: 107 E Main St Gouverneur NY 13642-1408

**LEAKE, LARRY BRUCE,** lawyer; b. Asheville, N.C., May 19, 1950; s. A.E. and Ann (McDevitt) L. BA, U. N.C., 1971, JD, 1974. Ptnr. Uzzell and Dumont, Asheville, 1974-80, Harrell & Leake, Asheville, 1980—. Chmn. 11th Congl. Dist. YD, 1974-77; nat. committeeman Young Dems. of N.C., 1977-79, pres. 1979-80; gen. counsel Young Dems. of Am., 1981-83; state sen. N.C., 1979-80; mem. State Goals and Policy Bd., N.C., 1978-84, Commn. on the Future, N.C., 1981-83; mem. N.C. State Bd. of Elections, 1993-97, chmn., 1997—,. Named 1 of 10 Outstanding Young Democrats N.C., 1977; recipient Ella Grasso award, Outstanding Young Democrat in Am., 1983, Order of Long Leaf Pine, Gov. James B. Hunt, 1981. Mem. Phi Beta Kappa. Presbyterian. Avocations: bowling, spectator sports, tennis. General civil litigation, Insurance, Personal injury. Home: 16 Ridgeway Dr Mars Hill NC 28754-9707 Office: Harrell & Leake 701 BB&T Plz Asheville NC 28801

**LEAPHART, W. WILLIAM,** state supreme court justice; b. Butte, Mont., Dec. 3, 1946; s. Charles William and Cornelia (Murphy) L.; m. Barbara Berg, Dec. 30, 1977; children: Rebecca, Retta, Ada. Student, Whitman Coll., 1965-66; BA, U. Mont., 1969, JD, 1972. Bar: Mont. 1972, U.S. Dist. Ct., U.S. Ct. Appeals (9th cir.) 1975, U.S. Supreme Ct. Law clk. to Hon. W.D. Murray U.S. Dist. Ct., Butte, 1972-74; ptnr. Leaphart Law Firm, Helena, Mont., 1974-94; justice Mont. Supreme Ct., Helena, 1995—. Home: 510 Dearborn Ave Helena MT 59601-2761 Office: Mont Supreme Ct Justice Bldg 215 N Sanders StRoom 315 Helena MT 59620

**LEAR, RICHARD EDWIN,** lawyer; b. Keene, N.H., Mar. 10, 1958; s. Robert Charles and Jean (Davis) L.; m. Teresa Jeanne Vasquez, Oct. 17, 1987; children: Charles Edwin II, Courtney Elizabeth, Caroline Elise, Cathleen Erin, Christina Ellen. BA, U. N.H., 1980; JD, Washington & Lee U., 1983. Bar: N.H. 1983, U.S. Ct. Appeals (4th cir.) 1985, U.S. Dist. Ct. D.C. 1986, U.S. Dist. Ct. Md. 1987, U.S. Dist. Ct. (ea. dist.) Va. 1992, U.S. Dist. Ct. (we. dist.) Va. 1992. Law clk. U.S. Bankruptcy Ct. Ea. Dist. Va., Alexandria, 1983-85; assoc. Hazel, Beckhorn & Hanes, Fairfax, Va., 1985-87; ptnr. Hazel & Thomas, Washington, 1987-94, Holland & Knight LLP, Washington, 1994—. Vol. asst. basketball coach, Hayfield Secondary Sch., Fairfax County, Va., 1992-99. Mem. Am. Bankruptcy Inst., No. Va. Bankruptcy Bar Assn., Phi Beta Kappa. Avocation: coaching youth sports. E-mail: rlear@hklaw.com. Bankruptcy, Federal civil litigation. Office: Holland & Knight LLP 2100 Pennsylvania Ave NW Washington DC 20037-3295

**LEAR, S. MICHAEL,** lawyer; b. Cleve., Dec. 31, 1962; s. Ronald F. and Paula A. Lear; m. Colleen A. Mackensen, July 21, 1990; children: Melissa, Shannon, Meghan. BA, Ohio State U., 1985; JD, Case Western Res. U., 1988. Bar: Ohio 1989. Assoc. Zukerman & Daiker Co., Cleve., 1996—. General civil litigation, Criminal, Banking. Office: Zuckerman & Daiker Co 2000 E 9th St Ste 700 Cleveland OH 44115-1301

**LEARD, DAVID CARL,** lawyer; b. Hartford, Conn., Dec. 9, 1958. BA, Bucknell U., 1981; JD, U. Conn., 1984. Bar: Conn. 1984, U.S. Dist. Ct. Conn. 1985. Assoc. Podorowsky and Wladimer, Hartford, 1985; assoc. Manasse, Slaiby & Leard, Torrington, Conn., 1985-88, ptnr., 1989—; lectr. legal studies Northwestern Conn. Community Coll., Winsted, 1991-92. Contbr. articles to profl. jours. Dir., past pres. Winchester (Conn.) Land Trust, 1988-93; chmn. allocations com. United Way Torrington, 1989—. Mem. Conn. Bar Assn. (workers compensation sect.), Nat. Orgn. Social

Security Claimants Reps. Personal injury, Workers' compensation, General civil litigation. Office: Manasse Slaiby & Leard PO Box 1104 249 Winsted Rd Torrington CT 06790-2958

**LEARY, MARY LOU,** prosecutor. Interim U.S. atty. Washington; acting dir. cmty. oriented policing svcs. U.S. Dept. Justice. Office: US Dept Justice Cmty Oriented Policing Svcs 1100 Vermont Ave NW Washington DC 20530*

**LEARY, THOMAS BARRETT,** lawyer; b. Orange, N.J., July 15, 1931; s. Daniel and Margaret (Barrett) L.; m. Stephanie Lynn Abbott, Dec. 18, 1954, June 3, 1991; children: Thomas A., David A., Alison Leary Estep. AB, Princeton U., 1952; JD magna cum laude, Harvard U., 1958. Bar: N.Y. 1959, Mich. 1972, D.C. 1983. Assoc. White & Case, N.Y.C., 1958-68, ptnr., 1968-71; atty.-in-charge antitrust Gen. Motors Corp., Detroit, 1971-77, asst. gen. counsel, 1977-82; ptnr. Hogan & Hartson, Washington, 1983—. Served to lt. USNR, 1952-55. Mem. ABA. Antitrust, Administrative and regulatory, Federal civil litigation. Office: Hogan & Hartson Columbia Sq 555 13th St NW Ste 800W Washington DC 20004-1109

**LEATH, WILLIAM JEFFERSON, JR.,** lawyer; b. Oakland, Calif., Sept. 9, 1945; s. William and Margaret (Jeffreys) L.; children: Catherine, Zoe, Eugenia, Susanne. BA, U. N.C., 1967; diplome, U. Lyon (France), 1966; JD, George Washington, 1971. Bar: D.C. 1971, Md. 1972, S.C. 1975. Atty. U.S. Internat. Trade Commn., Washington, 1971-73; ptnr. Plaia & Leath, Wheaton, Md., 1973-74, Barnwell, Whaley, Patterson, Charleston, S.C., 1974-80, Young, Clement, Rivers, Tisdale, Charleston, 1980-98, Leath, Bouch & Crawford, LLP, Charleston, 1998—. Chmn. Charleston City Rep. Party, 1981; pres. Charleston Neighborhood Assn., 1982. Mem. ABA, Charleston County Bar Assn. (chmn. legal med. com. 1988—), Maritime Law Assn., S.C. State Bd. Archtl. Examiners (vice chmn.), Southeastern Admiralty Law Inst., Internat. Assn. Def. Counsel. Episcopalian. Fax: 843-937-0606. E-mail: wjleath@leathbouchlaw.com. General civil litigation, Construction, Admiralty. Home: 125 Tradd St Charleston SC 29401-2419 Office: Leath Bouch & Crawford LLP PO Box 59 134 Meeting St Charleston SC 29401-2224

**LEATHERBURY, GREGORY LUCE, JR.,** lawyer; b. Mobile, Ala., Feb. 11, 1947; s. Gregory L. and Florence (Greaves) L.; m. Susan Thames, June 13, 1969; children: Gregory L. Leatherbury III, Clifton Thames Leatherbury. BA, U. Ala., Tuscaloosa, 1969, JD, 1972; LLM in Taxation, NYU, 1973. Bar: Ala. 1973, U.S. Dist. Ct. (so. dist.) Ala. 1973. Atty. Hand Arendall, L.L.C., Mobile, 1973-98, Foley, Ala., 1998—. Mem. Mobile Estate Planning Coun., 1986—. Mem. Am. Coll. Mortgage Counsel, Rotary (pres. 1992, Paul Harris fellow 1992). Episcopalian. Avocations: fishing, hunting, scuba diving, skiing. General corporate, Estate planning, Real property. Home: 29512 Canal Rd Orange Beach AL 36561-4407 Office: Hand Arendall LLC PO Box 1231 Foley AL 36536-1231

**LEATHERS, STEPHEN KELLY,** lawyer; b. West Palm Beach, Fla., June 17, 1956; s. Edward Kelly Leathers and Dorothy Lou Bledsoe Bendele; m. Evelyn Margarite Moore, Sept. 9, 1990. JD, Western State U., Irvine, Calif., 1996. Bar: Calif. 1997, U.S. Dist. Ct. (ctrl. dist.) Calif. 1997. Sheriff's investigator Live Oak Sheriff's Dept., George West, Tex., 1980-82; chief investigator Shavano Park (Tex.) Police, 1982-83; ins. gen. agt. B&B Mktg., San Antonio, Tex., 1986-89; atty. in pvt. practice, Mission Viejo, Calif., 1996—. Mem. Pier group Scripps Instn. Oceanography, 1992—, Diamond Club, San Diego, 1992—, Zool. Soc., 1992—; supporter L.A. Mission, 1994—. Mem. ATLA, Orange County Bar Assn., Fed. Bar Assn., Nat. Assn. Criminal Def. Lawyers, Calif. Attys. for Criminal Justice, Consumer Attys. of Calif., Orange County Trial Lawyers Assn., Internat. Game Fish Assn., NRA (Calif. state steering com. 1991), ACLU, Lawyers 2d Amendment Soc. Avocations: fishing, hunting, shooting, reading. Criminal, Constitutional, Personal injury. Office: 25801 Obrero Dr Ste 4 Mission Viejo CA 92691-3141

**LEATZOW, MILLICENT ANNE (PENNY LEATZOW),** lawyer; b. Oak Park, Ill., Sept. 26, 1941; d. Fredric Charles Sr. and Mildred Ruth (Swenson) Muntwyler; m. Victor Bruce Leatzow Jr., July 25, 1964; children: Victor Bruce III, Dan Michael. BA in Edn., Bradley U., 1964; postgrad., U. Colo., 1970-74; JD, U. Mont., 1984. Bar: Mont. 1984. Paralegal McGarvey, Lence & Heberling, Kalispell, Mont., 1980-84; sole practitioner M. Penny Leatzow, Kalispell, 1985—; pro bono legal counselor Agy. on Aging, Kalispell, 1987—; speaker on aging topics, Alzheimers, women's issues. Mem. State Bar Mont., Nat. Guardianship Assn., Order Eastern Star, Daus. of the Nile, Phi Delta Phi. Republican. Avocations: summer water sports, sewing, crafts, travel. Bankruptcy, Family and matrimonial, General practice. Office: 111 S Main St Kalispell MT 59901

**LEAVITT, JEFFREY STUART,** lawyer; b. Cleve., July 13, 1946; s. Sol and Esther (Dolinsky) L.; m. Ellen Fern Sugerman, Dec. 21, 1968; children: Matthew Adam, Joshua Aaron. AB, Cornell U., 1968; JD, Case Western Res. U., 1973. Bar: Ohio 1973. Assoc. Jones, Day, Reavis & Pogue, Cleve., 1973-80, ptnr., 1981—. Contbr. articles to profl. jours. Trustee Bur. Jewish Edn., Cleve., 1981-93, v.p. 1985-87; trustee Fairmount Temple, Cleve., 1982—, v.p. 1985-90, pres., 1990-93; trustee Citizens League Greater Cleve., 1982-89, 92-94, pres., 1987-89; trustee Citizens League Rsch. Inst., Cleve., 1989-98, Great Lakes Region of Union Am. Hebrew Congregations, 1990-93; mem. bd. gov. Case Western Res. Law Sch. Alumni Assn., 1989-92; sec. Kulas Found., 1986-88, 93—, asst. treas., 1989-92. Mem. ABA (employee benefits coms. 1976—), Nat. Assn. Pub. Pension Attys., Midwest Pension Conf. Jewish. Pension, profit-sharing, and employee benefits, Personal income taxation, Non-profit and tax-exempt organizations. Home: 25961 Annesley Rd Cleveland OH 44122-2437 Office: Jones Day Reavis & Pogue N Point 901 Lakeside Ave E Cleveland OH 44114-1116

**LEAVITT, MARTIN JACK,** lawyer; b. Detroit, Mar. 30, 1940; s. Benjamin and Annette (Cohen) L.; m. Janice C. (McCreary); children: Michael J., Paul J., David A., Dean N., Keleigh R. LLB Wayne State U., 1964. Bar: Mich. 1965, Fla. 1967. Assoc. Robert A. Sullivan, Detroit, 1968-70; officer, bd. dirs. Law Offices Sullivan & Leavitt, Northville, Mich., 1970—, pres., 1979—; bd. dirs. Tyrone Hills of Mich., Premiere Video, Inc., Menlo Tool Co., Inc., others. Lt. comdr. USNR, 1965-68. Detroit Edison Upper Class scholar, 1958-64. Mem. ABA, Mich. Bar Assn., Fla. Bar Assn., Transp. Lawyers Assn., ICC Practitioners, Meadowbrook Country Club, Huron River Hunting & Fishing Club (past pres.), Rolls Royce Owners Club (bd. dirs.). Jewish. General corporate, Labor, Federal civil litigation. Office: Sullivan and Leavitt PC PO Box 5490 Northville MI 48167-5490

**LEAVITT, MYRON E.,** judge. Justice Nev. Supreme Court, Carson City. Office: Supreme Ct Capitol Complex 201 S Carson S Carson City NV 89710-0001*

**LEAVY, EDWARD,** judge; m. Eileen Leavy; children: Thomas, Patrick, Mary Kay, Paul. AB, U. Portland, 1950, LLB, U. Notre Dame, 1953. Dist. judge Lane County, Eugene, Oreg., 1957-61, cir. judge, 1961-76; magistrate U.S. Dist. Ct. Oreg., Portland, 1976-84, judge, 1984-87, cir. judge U.S. Ct. Appeals (9th cir.), 1987-97, sr. judge, 1997—. Office: US Ct Appeals Pioneer Courthouse 555 SW Yamhill St Ste 232 Portland OR 97204-1323

**LEB, CLARA SILVIA,** lawyer; b. Cernowitz, Ukraine, July 5, 1939; came to the U.S., 1974; d. Naftalie Bleiweiss and Sendel Jeanette Bleiweiss-Coslover; m. Laszlo Vasile Leb, Dec. 7, 1963; 1 child, Ellen Susan Leb Benz. Diploma in law, U. Parhon, Bucharest, Romania, 1960; JD, Northeastern U., 1985. Bar: Mass. 1985, U.S. Dist. Ct. Mass. 1987. Legal counsel Govt. Confs. in Romania, Suceava, 1960-64, Braila, 1964-67, Bucharest, 1967-70; asst. dir. pers. Ctrl. Bur. Stats., Jerusalem, 1972-74; atty. Gould & Ettenberg, Worcester, Mass., 1985—. Mem. Mass. Bar Assn., Worcester County Bar Assn. Family and matrimonial, Probate. Office: Gould & Ettenberg 370 Main St Worcester MA 01608-1731

**LEBARON, CHARLES FREDERICK, JR.,** lawyer; b. Grand Rapids, Mich., Oct. 8, 1949; s. Charles Frederick and Barbara Jean (Day) LeB.; m. Elizabeth Ann Zwickert, Aug. 12, 1978; children: Ann Saunders, Katherine Clark, Eve Zwickert, John Frederick. AA, Grand Rapids Jr. Coll., 1969; AB, U. Mich., 1971, AMLS, 1973; JD summa cum laude, Ind. U., 1980. Bar: Ill. 1980, U.S. Dist. Ct. (no. dist.) Ill. 1980, U.S. Ct. Appeals (7th cir.) 1981. Dir. Georgetown Library, Jenison, Mich., 1974-77; law clk. to cir. judge U.S. Ct. Appeals (7th cir.), Chgo., 1980-82; assoc. Mayer, Brown & Platt, Chgo., 1982-84; atty. Centel Corp., Chgo., 1984-85, staff atty., 1985-86; corp. counsel Acco World Corp., Northbrook, Ill., 1986-88; assoc. Keck, Mahin & Cate, Chgo., 1988-89, ptnr., 1989-94; ptnr. Ross & Hardies, Chgo., 1994—. Trustee Clarendon Hills Pub. Library, Ill., 1985-89. Recipient Dyer-Ives Found. award, 1972. Mem. Order of Coif, Legal Club Chgo., Law Club Chgo. Republican. Episcopalian. Contracts commercial, General corporate, Communications. Home: 114 S Prospect Ave Clarendon Hills IL 60514-1423 Office: Ross & Hardies 150 N Michigan Ave Ste 2500 Chicago IL 60601-7567

**LEBEDOFF, JONATHAN GALANTER,** federal judge; b. Mpls., Apr. 29, 1938; s. Martin David and Mary (Galanter) L.; m. Sarah Sargent Mitchell, June 10, 1979; children: David Shevlin, Ann McNair. BA, U. Minn., 1960, LLB, 1963. Bar: Minn. 1963, U.S. Dist. Ct. Minn. 1964, U.S. Ct. Appeals (8th cir.) 1968. Pvt. practice Mpls., 1963-71; judge Hennepin County Mcpl. Ct., State Minn., Mpls., 1971-74; dist. ct. judge State of Minn., Mpls., 1974-91; U.S. magistrate judge U.S. Dist. Ct., Mpls., 1991—; mem. Gov.'s Commn. on Crime Prevention, 1971-75; mem. State Bd. Continuing Legal Edn.; mem. Minn. Supreme Ct. Task Force for Gender Fairness in Cts., mem. implementation com. of gender fairness in cts.. Jewish. Avocations: reading (biographies, history), family, bridge. Office: 300 S 4th St Minneapolis MN 55415-1320

**LEBEDOFF, RANDY MILLER,** lawyer; b. Washington, Oct. 16, 1949; m. David Lebedoff; children: Caroline, Jonathan, Nicholas. BA, Smith Coll., 1971; JD magna cum laude, Ind. U., 1975. Assoc. Faegre & Benson, Mpls., 1975-82, ptnr., 1983-86; v.p., gen. counsel Star Tribune, Mpls., 1989—; asst. sec. Star Tribune Cowles Media Co., Mpls., 1990—; Bd. dirs. Milkweed Editions, 1989-96. Bd. dirs. Minn. Opera, 1986-90, YWCA, 1984-90, Planned Parenthood Minn., 1985-90, Fund for Legal Aid Soc., 1988-96—, Abbott-Northwestern Hosp., 1990-94. Mem. Newspaper Assn. Am. (legal affairs com. 1991—), Minn. Newspapers Assn. (bd. dirs. 1995—). Home: 1738 Oliver Ave S Minneapolis MN 55405-2222 Office: Star Tribune 425 Portland Ave Minneapolis MN 55488-0002

**LEBLANC, J. BURTON, IV,** lawyer; b. Baton Rouge, La., Jan. 24, 1964; s. Jules Burton III and Nancy Sue (Chesson) LeB.; m. Jean Ann McKernan, Aug. 11, 1989; children: Mary Margaret, Lauren Elizabeth, Lilly Ann. BA in Polit. Sci., La. State U., 1987; JD, Loyola U., 1990. Bar: La. 1990, Tex. 1992, U.S. Dist. Ct. (middle, ea. and we. dists.) La. 1991, U.S. Supreme Ct., 1998. Atty. Friedman/McKernan & Gold, Baton Rouge, 1990-94, Ness, Motley et al, Baton Rouge, Charleston, 1994-96; ptnr. LeBlanc, Maples & Waddell, LLC, Baton Rouge, New Orleans, 1996—; lectr. in field; featured on TV and radio. Mem. La. Trial Lawyers Assn. (bd. govs. 1996—), Assn. of Trial Lawyers of Am. Avocations: tennis, fishing, snow skiing. Toxic tort, Product liability, Environmental. Office: LeBlanc Maples and Waddell LLC 5353 Essen Ln Ste 420 Baton Rouge LA 70809-0500

**LEBLANC, RICHARD PHILIP,** lawyer; b. Nashua, N.H., Aug. 5, 1946; s. Ronald Arthur and Jeanette G. (Chomard) LeB.; m. Doris Julie Lavoie, May 25, 1968; children: Justin D., Renée M., Anne-Marie. AB summa cum laude, Coll. of the Holy Cross, 1968; JD cum laude, Harvard U., 1972. Bar: Maine 1972, U.S. Dist. Ct. Maine 1972. Assoc. Bernstein, Shur, Sawyer & Nelson, Portland, Maine, 1972-75, shareholder, 1976-95; ptnr. LeBlanc & Young, Portland, 1995—; mem. Probate Law Revision Commn., Augusta, Maine, 1975-80; mem. probate rules and forms adv. com. Maine Supreme Ct. Pres. United Way Greater Portland, 1982-84; trustee Cleverus H.S., Portland, 1982-88; bd. dirs. Habitat for Humanity, Portland, 1984-92, Cumberland County Affordable Housing Venture, Portland, 1987-94, Maine Spl. Olympics, 1988-94, United Way Found. of Greater Portland, 1997—. Fellow Am. Coll. Trust and Estate Counsel; mem. ABA, Maine Bar Assn., Maine Estate Planning Coun. Democrat. Roman Catholic. Probate, Estate planning, Estate taxation. Home: 142 Longfellow St Portland ME 04103-4027 Office: LeBlanc & Young PO Box 7950 Portland ME 04112-7950

**LEBLANC, SAM A., III,** lawyer; b. Nov. 12, 1938; m. Noelle Engler; children: Sam A. IV, Raoul, Marcel. BA, Georgetown U., 1960; LLB, Tulane U., 1963, LLM in Energy and Environ. Law, 1991. Ptnr. Adams & Reese, New Orleans. Mem. ways and means com. La. State Rep., Dist. 86, 1972-76, mem. jud. B com., mem. natural resources com., 1972-76, chmn. com. on civil law and procedure, 1976-80; mem. Gov.'s Adv. Com. to the Consumer Protection Divsn., Gov.'s Adv. Com. on Milk Pricing and Regulation; liaison officer La. State Adv. Coun. on Drug Abuse and Edn. to House of Reps.; commr. Regional Transit Authority, 1980-83, chmn., 1983-84; bd. dirs. Tulane Hosp., 1991—, World Trade Ctr., 1991—; mem. Downtown Devel. Dist., 1998, Aubudon Cup. Gifts Campaign, 1998; chmn. adv. com. Tulane Cancer Ctr., 1998, chmn. corp. gifts com., 1998. Mem. ABA, La. Bar Assn. (sec. treas. young lawyer's sect. 1969, vice chmn. 1969, bd. govs. 1970, Outstanding Young Lawyer award 1976), Orleans Parish Bar Assn., Union Internat. de Avocats, New Orleans C. of C. (bd. dirs., exec. com. 1979-80, bd. dirs. 1996-97, v.p. chmn., govtl. affairs com. 1992-94, exec. cabinet 1991—), Met. Young Lawyers Assn. (pres. 1971-73), Order of the Coif. Avocations: flying, tennis, skiing, golf, jogging. Office: Adams and Reese 4500 One Shell Sq New Orleans LA 70130

**LEBLANG, SKIP ALAN,** lawyer; b. Phila., Jan. 14, 1953; s. Morton and Leah LeB.; m. Beth Siegel, Nov. 27, 1977; children: Kaitlyn Alexa, Chelsey Jenna. BA magna cum laude, U. Pitts., 1974; JD, U. San Diego, 1977. Bar: Pa. 1977, U.S. Dist. Ct. (we. dist.) Pa. 1977, D.C. 1980, N.Y. 1980, U.S. Dist. Ct. (so. and ea. dists.) N.Y. 1980. Jud. clk. Pa. Ct. Common Pleas, Pitts., 1977-78; atty. FTC, N.Y.C., 1978-81; asst. corp. counsel law dept. City of N.Y., 1981-84; assoc. Kramer, Dillof, N.Y.C., 1984-87; pvt. practice law N.Y.C., 1987—, 1987—; mem. faculty N.E. regional seat Nat. Inst. Trial Advocacy, Hofstra U., Uniondale, N.Y., 1984-98; mem. faculty advanced trial program Law Sch., Hofstra U., 1984-93, ABA/USTA Trademark Trial Advocacy Inst., 1993; spkr. in field. Author: Police Misconduct, 1981, Emergency Vehicle Liability, 1981, Sidewalks and Roadways, 1981. Co-dir. Coalition to Save Hempstead Harbor, Sea Cliff, N.Y., 1987-98, pres., 1998—; mem. Environ. Leaders Network, Hicksville, N.Y., 1988; mem. adv. com. Internat. Environ. Conf., Hofstra U., 1990; pres. Coalition, 1998—. Recipient award of merit N.Y. State Gov., 1990. Mem. ATLA, N.Y. State Trial Lawyers Assn., Pa. Bar Assn., Assn. of Bar of City of N.Y., Million Dollar Advocates Forum (elected life mem.). Avocations: family, running, basketball, skiing, fly fishing. Fax: (212) 287-5813. Personal injury, Insurance, General civil litigation. Office: 325 Broadway Ste 401 New York NY 10007-1112

**LEBOVITS, MOSES,** lawyer; b. Munich, Mar. 30, 1951; came to U.S., 1951.; BA cum laude, UCLA, 1972, JD, 1975. Bar: Calif. 1975. Assoc. Butler, Jefferson & Fry, L.A., 1973-80; pvt. practice L.A., 1980-82; ptnr. Lebovits & David, L.A., 1982—; adj. prof. aviation law Sch. Law Southwestern U., 1981-83; mem. arbitration panel (labor dispute) Reynolds Aluminum Torrance Can Plant, 1981—; arbitrator Superior Ct. County of L.A., 1979—. Mem. Moot Ct. Exec. Bd. of Judges, 1974-75, Spl. Panel for Referrals for Spl. Litigation Needs of Dependent Children of the Superior Ct., L.A. County, Juvenile Dept., 1980—; mem. fed. cts. and practice com. L.A. County, 1982-84, del., 1982. 1st pl. winner So. Calif. Moot Ct. Tournament, 1975. Mem. ABA, Am. Bd. Trial Advocates, State Bar of Calif. (conf. dels. 1982), L.A. Trial Lawyers Assn. (bd. govs. 1982-85), Consumer Attys. Calif. (bd. govs. 1994—), Nat. Order of Barristers, Am. Bd. Trial Lawyers. General civil litigation, Professional liability, Product liability. Office: Lebovits & David 2049 Century Park E Los Angeles CA 90067-3101

**LEBOW, MICHAEL JEFFREY,** lawyer; b. Detroit, Apr. 4, 1956; s. David and Thelma (Shainack) L.; m. Deby Fay Muskovitz, Dec. 23, 1978. BA, Wayne State U., 1978; JD, Detroit Coll. Law, 1981. Bar: Mich. 1982, D.C. 1986, U.S. Dist. Ct. (ea. dist.) Mich. 1982; diplomate Nat. Bd. Trial Advocacy; cert. civil trial specialist. Litigation assoc. Kemp Klein Endelman & Beer, Birmingham, Mich., 1982-83; sole practice Southfield, Mich., 1983-85; ptnr. Lebow & Tobin, Birmingham, 1985-86, Gropman, Lebow & Tobin, Birmingham, 1986-89, Lebow & Tobin, Birmingham, 1989—; state coord. Nat. Bd. Trial Advocacy, 1994—, mem. bd. law examiners, 1993—, bd. dirs. Contbr. articles to profl. jours. Bd. dirs. Mich. Com. Human Rights, Oak Park, 1976—. Mem. ABA (Excellence Nat. Appellate Advocacy award 1981), Mich. Bar Assn., Am. Inns of the Ct. (barrister Oakland County chpt.), Mto Guzzi Nat. Owners Assn. Jewish. Club: Mich. Handball Assn. Avocations: handball, motorcycle collecting, 1950's jazz. General civil litigation, Criminal. Office: Lebow & Tobin PLLC 31420 Northwestern Hwy Ste 120 Farmington MI 48334-2500

**LEBRATO, MARY THERESA,** lawyer, psychologist; b. Ft. Wayne, Ind., June 13, 1950; d. Joseph James and Veronica (Adamonis) L. BA, U. Dayton, 1971; MA, U. Ala., Tuscaloosa, 1973, PhD, 1975; JD, Lincoln Law Sch., 1986. Bar: Calif. 1986; lic. psychologist, Calif. Psychologist Ala. Dept. Mental Hygiene, Tuscaloosa, 1975, Calif. Dept. Health, Eldridge, Calif., 1975-77; chief statewide evaluation devel. svcs. Calif. Dept. Health, Eldridge, 1977-79; dir. evaluation Oakland Perinatal Health Project, Calif. Dept. Health, Sacramento, 1979-81; coord. Maternal, Child and Adolescent Health, Sacramento, 1981-82; dir. sexual harassment in employment project Calif. Commn. on Status of Women, Sacramento, 1982-85; chief long range planning Calif. Dept. Devel. Svcs., Sacramento, 1985-88; staff counsel Calif. State Lottery, Sacramento, 1988-91. Co-author (with Marilyn Pearman) Sexual Harassment Investigators Guidebook, 1984; author, editor: Help Yourself: A Manual for Dealing with Sexual Harassment, 1986. Adv. bd. mem. Calif. State Pers. Bd., Appeals Div. Adv. Com., 1987-91; bd. mem. Sacramento Rape Crisis Ctr., 1988. Recipient fellowships in psychology NIMH, U. Ala., Tuscaloosa, 1971, 72, 73, teaching asst. in psychology U. Ala., Tuscaloosa, 1974-75. Mem. APA, ABA, Am. Assn. on Mental Deficiency, Calif. State Bar Assn., Calif. State Psychol. Assn., Calif. Women Lawyers, Sacramento County Bar Assn., Women Laywers Sacramento (bd. mem., chair del. com. 1989, chair scholarship 1990). Avocations: horse breeding, art. Home: 335 Del Wes Ln Rio Linda CA 95673-2031

**LECHNER, ALFRED JAMES, JR.,** judge; b. Elizabeth, N.J., Jan. 7, 1948; s. Alfred J. and Marie G. (McCormack) L.; m. Gayle K. Peterson, Apr. 3, 1976; children: Brendan Patrick, Coleman Thomas, Mary Kathleen. BS, Xavier U., Cin., 1969; JD, U. Notre Dame, 1972. Bar: N.J. 1972, U.S. Dist. Ct. N.J. 1972, N.Y. 1973, U.S. Dist. Ct. (so. and ea. dists.) N.Y. 1974, U.S. Ct. Appeals (2d cir.) 1974, U.S. Supreme Ct. 1975, U.S. Ct. Appeals (3d cir.) 1980. Assoc. Cadwalader, Wickersham & Taft, N.Y.C., 1972-75, MacKenzie, Welt & Duane, Elizabeth, 1975-76, MacKenzie, Welt, Duane & Lechner, Elizabeth, 1976-84; judge Superior Ct. State N.J., 1984-86, U.S. Dist. Ct. N.J., 1986—. Note and comment editor Notre Dame Law Rev., 1972; contbr. articles to legal jours. Mem. Union County (N.J.) Adv. Bd. Cath. Cmty. Svcs., 1981-83, chmn., 1982. Lt. col. USMCR. Fellow Am. Bar Found.; mem. Assn. Fed. Bar of State N.J., Friendly Sons of St. Patrick (pres. 1982), Union County Club. Office: US Dist Ct Martin Luther King Jr Fed Bldg PO Box 999 Newark NJ 07101-0999

**LECHTMAN, MICHAEL LOWELL,** lawyer; b. St. Paul, Feb. 15, 1947; s. Hy M. and Beatrice C. Lechtman; m. Lidia L. Epelbaum, Dec. 29, 1973; children: Deborah, Daniel. BA, U. Minn., 1969; JD, U. Miami, 1974. Bar: Fla. 1974, U.S. Dist. Ct. (so. dist.) Fla. 1975, U.S. Ct. Appeals (5th cir.) 1979, U.S. Ct. Appeals (11th cir.) 1981, U.S. Supreme Ct. 1979. Asst. city atty. City of North Miami Beach, Fla., 1974-75; pvt. practice North Miami Beach, 1975—; city prosecutor, North Miami Beach, 1974-75, pub. defender, 1975-77, mediator, 1977-80. Author: Shapiro's Plan, 1997, Shapiro's Revenge, 1998. 1st lt. U.S. Army, 1969-71. Mem. Fla. Bar Assn., North Dade Bar Assn., Optimists. Avocations: writing, golf, hockey. Family and matrimonial, Professional liability, Personal injury. Office: 17001 NE 6th Ave North Miami Beach FL 33162-2408

**LECKIE, GAVIN FREDERICK,** lawyer, banker; b. Cambridge, Eng., Dec. 31, 1958; came to U.S., 1987; s. Frederick Alexander and Alison Elizabeth (Wheelwright) L.; m. Elizabeth Anne O'Donnell, Aug. 15, 1987. BA in Law, Cambridge U., 1981, MA, 1985; LLM, U. Ill., 1988. Bar: N.Y. 1990, U.S. Tax Ct. 1992; solicitor Eng. and Wales, 1984. Articled clk. Lawrence Graham, London, 1982-84, solicitor, 1984-87; assoc. Milbank, Tweed, Hadley & McCloy, N.Y.C., 1988-98; v.p. Chase Manhattan Bank, N.Y.C., 1998—. Mem. ABA, N.Y. State Bar Assn., Law Soc. Eng. and Wales, Soc. Trusts and Estates Practitioners. E-mail: gavin.leckie@chase.com. Corporate taxation, Estate taxation, Private international. Home: 226 Highbrook Ave Pelham NY 10803-2203 Office: Chase Manhattan Bank 1211 Ave of Americas New York NY 10036

**LE CLAIR, DOUGLAS MARVIN,** lawyer, educator, judge; b. Montreal, Nov. 13, 1955; s. Lawrence M. and Joan B. Le Clair; m. Debra L. Garland, Oct. 12, 1985. BA, Loyola U., 1977; JD, Southwestern U., 1980; peace officer cert., Mesa C.C. Law Enforcement Acad., 1985; cert. theology, min., Kino Religious Inst., 1994; Juris Canonica Licentiae, St. Paul U., 1998; M in Canon Law, U. Ottawa (Can.), 1998; cert. theology, min., Kino Religious Inst., 1994. Bar: Ariz. 1982, U.S. Dist. Ct. Ariz. 1983, U.S. Ct. Appeals (9th cir.) 1983, U.S. Tax. Ct. 1987, U.S. Ct. Claims 1987, U.S. Supreme Ct. 1987; ordained deacon Roman Cath. Ch., 1995. Pvt. practice Mesa, Ariz., 1983—; mem. faculty law & acctg. Sterling Sch., Phoenix, Ariz., 1992-96; judge Tribunal of Diocese, Phoenix, 1998—. Author: Le Clair/Morgan Income Tax Organizer, 1982-83; prodn. editor Computer Law Jour., 1979-80. Res. officer Mesa Police Dept., 1984-92. Named One of Outstanding Young Men Of Am., 1979. Mem. ABA, Ariz. Bar Assn., Maricopa County Bar Assn., Internat. Platform Assn., Southwestern Student Bar Assn. (exec. bd. 1978-79), Southwestern U. Tax Law Soc., Mesa C. of C., Delta Theta Phi, Phi Alpha Theta. Corporate taxation, General corporate, State and local taxation. Office: 400 E Monroe St Phoenix AZ 85004-2336

**LECLAIR, PAUL LUCIEN,** lawyer; b. Plainfield, N.J., Oct. 6, 1962; m. Rebecca J. Leclair. BA, U. Scranton, 1984; JD, Georgetown U., 1987. Bar: N.Y. 1988, U.S. Dist. Ct. (so., ea., no. and we. dists.) N.Y. 1988, U.S. Supreme Ct. 1992. Assoc. Nixon Hargrave Devans & Doyle, Rochester, N.Y., 1987-91, Frontier Corp., Rochester, 1991-93; ptnr. Wolford & Leclair LLP, Rochester, 1993—. Bd. dirs. Habitat for Humanity, Rocheser, 1988-91, Big Bros.-Big Sisters, Rochester, 1993—. Recipient spl. svc. award U.S. Dist. Ct. for Western Dist. N.Y., 1997. Mem. N.Y. State Bar Assn., Monroe County Bar Assn. (co-chmn. membership com. 1987—), Rochester Inns of Ct. (programming co-chmn. 1996—), Alpha Sigma Nu. Federal civil litigation, General civil litigation, State civil litigation. Office: Wolford & Leclair LLP 16 E Main St Rochester NY 14614-1808

**LECLERE, DAVID ANTHONY,** lawyer; b. New Orleans, Sept. 5, 1954; s. Paul Richard and Rosalee (Cefalu) LeC.; m. Karen Menzie; children: David II, Michael Joshua, Jacob Gunter, Benjeman Joseph. BA, La. State U., 1978, JD, 1979. Bar: La. 1979, U.S. Dist. Ct. (mid. dist.) La. 1979, U.S. Dist. Ct. (ea. dist.) 1982, U.S. Dist. Ct. (we. dist.) La. 1983, U.S. Ct. Appeals (5th cir.) 1984. Assoc. Perrault & Uter, Baton Rouge, 1979-81, jr. ptnr., 1981-83; ptnr. Perrault, Uter & LeClere, Baton Rouge, 1983-87, Schwab & LeClere, Baton Rouge, 1987-90; of counsel Powers, Vaughn & Clegg, Baton Rouge, 1990-91; ptnr. Duplechain & LeClere, Baton Rouge, 1991-93; pvt. practice David A. LeClere, A Profl. Law Corp., Baton Rouge, 1993—; asst. bar examiner. Assoc. chmn. East Baton Rouge Parish Notary Pub. Exam Com., 1982, chmn. dispute resolution com.; asst. State Bar Examiner; prof. paralegal studies La. State U. Mem. ABA, La. State Bar Assn., Comml. Law League of Am., Baton Rouge Bar Assn. Republican. Roman Catholic. Avocations: hunting, hiking, camping, gardening, gourmet cooking. Federal civil litigation, Health, Probate. Office: 8338 Summa Ave Ste 302 Baton Rouge LA 70809-3669

**LECOCKE, SUZANNE ELIZABETH,** lawyer; b. Nuremburg, Germany, Nov. 3, 1958; came to U.S., 1959; d. Frank Joseph and Carolyn Elizabeth (Partain) L. BS magna cum laude, U. Tex., 1981; JD, U. Houston, 1987. Bar: Tex. 1987, U.S. Dist. Ct. (so. and no. dists.) Tex. 1987, U.S. Ct. Appeals (5th and fed. cirs.) 1992, U.S. Dist. Ct. (no. dist.) Calif. 1993. Supr. systems support Southwestern Bell Telephone, San Antonio, 1981-82; engr. Mitre Corp., Houston, 1982-84; law clk. to judges DeAnda, Bue and Hoyt U.S. Dist. Ct. (so. dist.) Tex., Houston, 1986-89; assoc. Liddell, Sapp, Zivley, Hill & Laboon, Houston, 1989-91, Arnold, White & Durkee, Houston, 1991-96. Co-author: Patent Law Handbook, 1992-93, 93-94, 94-95, 95-96, 96-97. Mem. ABA, Am. Intellectual Property Law Assn., Tex. Bar Assn., Houston Intellectual Property Law Assn., Houston Young Lawyers Assn., Mensa Soc., Upsilon Pi Epsilon. Roman Catholic. Avocations: tennis, workouts, back-packing, outdoor activities, reading. Patent, Trademark and copyright, Antitrust.

**LECOMPTE, CHARLES MARTIN,** lawyer, sole practice; b. Springfield, Mo., Dec. 3, 1943; s. John Henry and Louise LeC.; m. Judith Diane, Oct. 8, 1988 (div. Feb. 1996). BS in Econs. and Bus., Drury Coll., 1965; JD, U. Ark., 1970. Asst. pros. atty. Pros. Atty.'s Office, Springfield, 1970-72, pros. atty., 1973-75; pvt. practice Springfield, 1975—. Pvt. USM, 1969. Mem. Elks. Republican. Episcopalian. Avocation: golf. Bankruptcy, Criminal, Family and matrimonial. Home: 7588 E FM Rd 748 Rogersville MO 65742

**LEDBETTER, JOSEPH MICHAEL,** lawyer, accountant; b. Jonesboro, Ark., Oct. 12, 1953; s. John Paul and Joyce Mayo Ledbetter; m. Deborah Gail Lawson, Nov. 29, 1984; 1 child, Mitchell Joseph. BS in Acctg., Ark. State U., 1989; JD, U. Memphis, 1994. Bar: Tenn., Ark., U.S. Dist. Ct. (we. dist.) Tenn., U.S. Dist. Ct. (ea. dist.) Ark.; CPA, Ark., Tenn. Auditor, staff acct. Jones & Co., Ltd., CPA's, Jonesboro, 1989-92; assoc. atty. Ledbetter & Caldwell, Jonesboro, 1995-97; pvt. practice Jonesboro, 1997—. Mem. ABA, AICPA, Am. Soc. CPA (N.W. chpt.), Ark. Bar Assn., Tenn. Trial Lawyers Assn., Memphis Bar Assn. Avocations: trout fishing, woodworking, water-sports, snow skiing. General civil litigation, Estate planning, Personal injury. Office: 201 W Washington Ave Jonesboro AR 72401-2840

**LEDBETTER, MELISA GAY,** lawyer; b. Cocoa Beach, Fla., May 24, 1966; d. Vernon T. and Susan L. Michelsen; m. David Lee Ledbetter, Sept. 6, 1997. BA, Am. U., 1988; JD, George Mason U., 1996. Bar: Va. 1996, U.S. Dist. Ct. (ea. and we. dists.) Va. 1997. Atty. Brault, Palmer, Grove, Zimmerman, White & Hims, Fairfax, Va., 1996-97, Litten & Sipe, LLP, Harrisonburg, Va., 1997—. Mem. Def. Rsch. Inst, Harrisonburg/Rockingham Bar Assn., Harrisonburg Jr. Women's Club. General civil litigation, Insurance. Office: Litten & Sipe 410 Neff Ave Harrisonburg VA 22801-3434

**LEDBETTER, MICHAEL RAY,** lawyer; b. San Bernardino, Calif., June 13, 1956; s. Raymond Leonard and Anna Laura Ledbetter; m. Diane Elizabeth Burger, Jan. 16, 1987 (div. Aug. 1991); 1 child, Lauren Ann; m. Diane Lorraine Errick, June 30, 1993. BA, U. Calif., Irvine, 1978; JD, U. So. Calif., 1981. Bar: Calif. 1981, U.S. Dist. Ct. (ctrl. dist.) Calif. 1982, U.S. Dist. Ct. (ea. dist.) Calif. 1992, U.S. Ct. Appeals (9th cir.) 1990, U.S. Supreme Ct. Assoc. atty. Roger J. Rosen Law Office, L.A., 1981-83; dep. pub. defender Office of Pub. Defender, Santa Barbara, Calif., 1983-90; sr. dep. counsel Office of County Counsel, Santa Barbara, 1990—; bd. dirs. Calif. Joint Powers Ins. Authority, La Palma, 1992-94, 96—. Contbg. editor: California County Counsels Benchbook, 1996, 97, 98. Mem. City Coun., City of Carpinteria, Calif., 1990-94, 96—, mayor, 1991-93. Mem. Optimists Club of Carpinteria. Avocations: music (keyboards), computers, automobiles. Home: 1453 Camellia Cir Carpinteria CA 93013-1608 Office: Office of County Counsel 105 E Anapamu St Rm 201 Santa Barbara CA 93101-6060

**LEDEBUR, LINAS VOCKROTH, JR.,** retired lawyer; b. New Brighton, Pa., June 18, 1925; s. Linas Vockroth and Mae (McCabe) L.; m. Conne Ryan, July 3, 1969; children: Gary W., Sally, Nancy, Sandra. Student, Geneva Coll., Beaver Falls, Pa., 1943, 45-46, Muhlenberg Coll., Allentown, Pa., 1943-44; J.D., U. Pitts., 1949. Bar: Pa. 1950. Assoc., then ptnr. Ledebur, McClain & Ledebur, New Brighton, 1950-63; trust mktg. mgr. Valley Nat. Bank Ariz., Phoenix, 1963-72; ptnr. Ledebur & Ledebur, New Brighton, 1972-76; sr. v.p., mgr. state trust div. Fla. Nat. Banks Fla., Inc., Jacksonville, 1976-81; sr. v.p. Fla. Nat. Bank, Jacksonville, 1977-81; pres. Northeastern Trust Co. Fla., N.A., Vero Beach, 1982-86; exec. v.p. PNC Trust Co. Fla., N.A., 1986-87; sole practice Beaver, Pa., 1987-96; master in divorce Beaver County, Pa., 1990-96; ret., 1996; instr. bus. law Geneva Coll., 1951-52, 88-90; past pres. Ctrl. Ariz. Estate Planning Coun. Chmn. Beaver County chpt. Nat. Found.-March of Dimes, Pa., 1950-63; chmn. com. corrections Pa. Citizens Assn., 1958-63; bd. dirs., counsel Beaver County Mental Health Assn., 1962-63; bd. dirs. Maricopa County chpt. ARC, Ariz. 1968-72. Served with USMC, 1943-45, 51-53. Mem. ABA, Pa. Bar Assn. Family and matrimonial. Home: 652 Bank St Beaver PA 15009-2728

**LEDERBERG, VICTORIA,** judge, former state legislator, lawyer; b. Providence, July 7, 1937; d. Frank and Victoria (Marzilli) Santopietro; m. Seymour Lederberg, 1959; children: Tobias, Sarah. AB, Pembroke Coll., 1959; AM, Brown U., 1961, PhD, 1966; JD, Suffolk U., 1976, LLD (hon.), 1995. Mem. R.I. Ho. of Reps., 1975-82, chmn. subcom. on edn., fin. com., 1975-82; subcom. on mental health, retardation and hosps. and health, spl. legis. commns. pub. sch. funding and funding handicapped edn. programs; chmn. nat. adv. panel on financing elem. and secondary edn. Washington, 1979-82; mem. R.I. State Senate, 1985-91, chmn. fin. com. subcom. on social svcs., 1985-89, dep. majority leader, 1989-91; prof. psychology R.I. Coll., 1968-93; pvt. practice Providence, 1977-93; justice R.I. Supreme Ct., Providence, 1993—, chmn. com. on judicial performance evaluation, 1993—, mem. com. jud. edn., 1993—, chmn. com. on user-friendly cts., 1994-97. Trustee Brown U., 1983-89, com. on biomed. affairs, 1999—; trustee Roger Williams U., 1980—, vice chmn. corp., dir. Sch. Law, Butler Hosp., 1985-93, aslo sec. of corp. USPHS fellow physiol. psychology, 1964-66. Mem. ABA, New Eng. Psychol. Assn., R.I. Bar Assn., Am. Judicature Soc., Nat. Assn. Women Judges, Sigma Xi. Office: 250 Benefit St Providence RI 02903-2719

**LEDERER, GERARD LAVERY,** association executive; b. Phila., Apr. 18, 1958; s. Thomas John and Rita Lavery Lederer; m. Sara Denise Trujillo, Aug. 30, 1981; children: Sara Isabella, Gabriel Lavery. BA, Haverford Coll., 1980; JD, Temple U., 1983. Cert. assn. exec. Chief dep. commr. Voting and Registration Commn., Phila., 1982-84; gen. counsel U.S. Conf. of Mayors, Washington, 1985-89; exec. dir. U.S. Telephone Assn., Washington, 1989-95; v.p. Bldg. Owner and Mgrs. Assn., Washington, 1995—; chair Nat. Real Estate Orgns., 1997—. Co-author: Wired for Profit, 1998. Committeeman Phila. Dem. Party, 1976-85, state committeeman, 1980-82. Roman Catholic. Avocations: raising kids, golfing, scuba diving. Office: Bldg Owners and Mgr Assn 1201 New York Ave NW Ste 300 Washington DC 20005-3917

**LEDERER, KAREN F.,** lawyer; b. N.Y.C., Sept. 28, 1954. BA, U. Wis., 1975; JD, SUNY, Buffalo, 1978. Bar: N.Y. 1979, U.S. Dist. Ct. (so. and ea. dists.) N.Y. 1979. Atty. N.Y.C. Dept. Consumer Affairs, 1978-80, Weil Gotshal & Manges, N.Y.C., 1980-82, N.Y.C. Corp. Counsel's Office, N.Y.C., 1982-86; ptnr. Parker, Chapin, Flatlau & Klimpl, LLP, N.Y.C., 1986—. Mem. Assn. of Bar of City of N.Y. (consumer affairs com.). Administrative and regulatory, Federal civil litigation, State civil litigation. Office: Parker Chapin Flatlau & Klimpl LLP Ste 1700 1211 Avenue Of The Americas New York NY 10036-8735

**LEDERER, MAX DONALD, JR.,** lawyer; b. Plattsburgh, N.Y., June 21, 1960; s. Max Donald and Mary Lilian (Adie) L. BA magna cum laude, Marshall U., Huntington, W.Va., 1982; JD, U. Richmond, 1985. Bar: Pa. 1986, U.S. Army Ct. Mil. Rev. 1986. Commd. 2d lt. U.S. Army, 1982-86, advanced through grades to capt., 1987—; def. counsel Ft. Sill, Okla., 1986-87; command judge advocate CP Red Cloud, Korea, 1987-88; sr. trial counsel Combined Field Army, 1989; chief adminstrv. law div. Combined Field Army- 2d armored div. (forward), 1989-90; command judge adv. Op. Desert Storm 2d armored div. (forward), 1991; officer-in-charge Bremerhaven Legal Ctr., Fed. Republic of Germany, 1991-92; gen. counsel European Stars and Stripes, 1992-96, gen. mgr., 1996—. Fellow ABA, Pa. Bar Assn. Avocation: running. Home: 4850 Middleton Dr Lockport NY 14094-1616 Office: Dept Def European Stars and Stripes Unit 29480 Box 126 APO AE 09211-0126

**LEDERLEITNER, JOSEPH BENEDICT,** lawyer; b. Chgo., Sept. 3, 1922; s. Steve and Lottie Lederleitner; m. Elaine M. Meyer, Sept. 29, 1952; children: Terry, Tom, Kathy (dec.), Rob, Mary Ellen, Bill, Peg, John. BS in Polit. Sci., Northwestern U., 1947, JD, 1950. Bar: Ill. 1951, Ill. Supreme Ct. 1951, U.S. Dist. Ct. (no. dist.) Ill. 1952, U.S. Ct. Appeals (7th cir.) 1952, U.S. Supreme Ct. 1954. Digester Callaghan Law Pub., Chgo., 1951-52; atty. Wyatt Jacobs, Chgo., 1952-62; asst. gen. counsel Fed. Res. Bank, Chgo., 1962-63; atty. Jas. A. Dooley Assocs., Chgo., 1963-64; atty., dir. Pretzel & Stouffer, Chartered, Chgo., 1964—; div. instr. John Marshall Law Sch., Chgo., 1968-75. Mem. Supreme Ct. com. that drafted pattern of civil jury instructions, 1957-65; adv. bd., gen. counsel Lite Opera Works, Chgo., 1986—; bd. dirs. Northwest Suburban Montessouri Sch., 1965-72. Named Owen L. Coon Found. scholar, 1947-50. Mem. ABA (vice-chmn. Appellate Advocacy 1986-87), Chgo. Bar Assn., Internat. Platform Assn. Republican. Roman Catholic. General civil litigation, Personal injury. Home: 200 Ferndale Ct Prospect Heights IL 60070-2801 Office: Pretzel & Stouffer Chartered One S Wacker Dr Ste 250 Chicago IL 60606

**LEDGERWOOD, THOMAS L.,** lawyer; b. Pomeroy, Wash., Oct. 27, 1952; s. William Troy and Ann Marie (Roueche) L.; m. Carlyn Louise Davis, June 16, 1979; children: Troy Allen, Kevin Thomas. BA in Polit. Sci., Wash. State U., 1975; JD, U Puget Sound, 1979. Bar: Wash. 1979, U.S. Dist. Ct. (we. dist.) Wash. 1979, U.S. Dist. Ct. (ea. dist.) Wash. 1981. Assoc. Mann, King, Anderson, Bingham & Scraggin, Tacoma, 1979-80, Irwin, Friel, Myklebust, Clarkston, Wash., 1983-85; ptnr. Anderson, Ledgerwood & Anderson, Tacoma, 1980-83; pvt. practice, Clarkston, 1985—. Mem. Wash. State Bar Assn., Asotin County Bar Assn. (pres. 1985), Wash. State Trial Lawyers Assn., Wash. Assn. Criminal Def. Lawyers. General practice, Criminal, Personal injury. Office: 827 5th St Clarkston WA 99403-2633

**LEDONNE, EUGENE,** lawyer; b. Fairmont, W.Va., May 22, 1963; s. Eugene and Mary (Retton) LeD.; m. Lisa M. Parlato, Sept. 2, 1995. BSME, W.Va. U., 1985, MBA, 1986; JD, Am. U., 1991. Bar: Pa. 1991, N.Y. 1998. Lawyer Sughrue Mion Zinn Macpeak & Seas, Washington, 1991-92, Westinghouse Elec. Co., Balt., 1993-95, McAulay Nissen Goldberg & Hand, N.Y.C., 1995—. Mem. ABA, Am. Intellectual Property Law Assn., N.Y. Intellectual Property Law Assn. Intellectual property, Patent, Trademark and copyright. Home: 45 Lenox Rd Summit NJ 07901 Office: McAulay Nissen Goldberg & Kiel & Hand LLP 261 Madison Ave Fl 12 New York NY 10016-2303

**LEE, BRIAN EDWARD,** lawyer; b. Oceanside, N.Y., Feb. 29, 1952; s. Lewis H. Jr. and Jean Elinor (Andrews) L.; m. Eleanor L. Barker, June 5, 1982; children: Christopher Martin, Alison Ruth, Danielle Andrea. AB, Colgate U., 1974; JD, Valparaiso U., 1976. Bar: N.Y. 1977, U.S. Dist. Ct. (so. and ea. dists.) N.Y. 1978, U.S. Ct. Appeals (2nd cir. 1992). Assoc. Marshall, Bellofatto & Callahan, Lynbrook, N.Y., 1977-80, Morris, Duffy, Ivone & Jensen, N.Y.C., 1980-84; sr. assoc. Ivone, Devine & Jensen, Lake Success, N.Y., 1984-85, ptnr., 1985—. Pres., trustee Trinity Christian Sch. of Montville Inc., N.J., 1985—, also track coach. Mem. ABA, N.Y. State Bar Assn., N.Y. County Lawyers Assn., Christian Legal Soc. Republican. Baptist. General civil litigation, Product liability, Personal injury. Home: 292 Jacksonville Rd Pompton Plains NJ 07444-1511 Office: Ivone Devine & Jensen 2001 Marcus Ave Lake Success NY 11042-1024

**LEE, DAN M.,** retired state supreme court justice; b. Petal, Miss., Apr. 19, 1926; s. Buford Aaron and Pherbia Ann (Camp) L.; m. Peggy Jo Daniel, Nov. 27, 1947 (dec. 1952); 1 child, Sheron Lee Anderson; m. Mary Alice Gray, Sept. 30, 1956; 1 child, Dan Jr. Attended, U. So. Miss., 1946; LLB, Jackson Sch. Law, 1949; JD, Miss. Coll., 1970. Bar: Miss. 1948. Ptnr. Franklin & Lee, Jackson, Miss, 1948-54, Lee, Moore and Countiss, Jackson, Miss., 1954-71; county judge Hinds County, 1971-77; cir. judge Hinds-Yazoo Counties, 1977-82; assoc. justice Miss. Supreme Ct., Jackson, 1982-87, presiding justice, 1987-95, chief justice, 1995-98; ret., 1998; of counsel Dogan & Wilkinson, PLLC, Jackson, 1999. With U.S. Naval Air Corps, 1944-46. Mem. ABA, Hinds County Bar Assn., Miss. State Bar Assn., Aircraft Owners and Pilots Assn., Am. Legion, VFW, Kiwanis Internat. Baptist.

**LEE, DENNIS PATRICK,** lawyer, judge; b. Omaha, Feb. 12, 1955; s. Donald Warren and Betty Jean (O'Leary) L.; m. Rosemarie Bucchino, July 28, 1979; children: Patrick Michael, Katherine Marie, Megan Elizabeth. BA, Creighton U., 1977, JD, 1980. Bar: Nebr. 1980, U.S. Dist. Ct. Nebr. 1980, U.S. Ct. Appeals (8th cir.) 1980, Iowa 1990. Assoc. Thompson Crounse & Pieper, Omaha, 1980-84; ptnr. Lee Law Offices, Omaha, 1984-87, Silverman, Lee & Crounse Law Offices, 1987-94, Lee Bucchino & Lee Law Offices, 1994—; atty. Nebr. State Racing Commn., Lincoln, 1984-87, commr. 1988—, chmn., 1991—; adminstrv. law judge, State of Nebr., 1985-87; lectr. Creighton U., Omaha, 1982-85. Author: Law of Conservatorships, 1981: Legal Aspects of Equine Veterinary Practice, 1984, Planning Opportunities with Living Trusts in Nebraska, 1995; others. Trustee Holy Name Cath. Ch., Omaha, 1980-84; chmn. nat. enforcement officers com. Nat. Assn. State Racing Commrs., Lexington, Ky., 1984-87; commr. Nebr. State Racing Commn., 1988—. Mem. ABA, Nat. Assn. Trial Attys., Comml. Law League Am., Nebr. State Racing Commn. (chmn. 1991), Assn. Racing Commrs. Internat. (treas. 1996—), Nebr. Bar Assn., Omaha Bar Assn. (chmn. conservatorship com. 1981—), Nebr.-Iowa Referees Assn. (v.p. 1981-88), Omaha C. of C. (Outstanding Young Omahan 1993). Administrative and regulatory, State civil litigation, Consumer commercial. Home: 14767 Burt Dr Omaha NE 68154-1944 Office: Lee & Bucchino 12165 W Center Rd Ste 52 Omaha NE 68144-3974

**LEE, DONALD JOHN,** federal judge; b. 1927. AB, U. Pitts., 1950; LLB, Duquesne U., 1954. Bar: Pa. Supreme Ct. 1955; U.S. Supreme Ct. 1984. Assoc. George Y. Meyer and Assocs., 1954-57; law clk. to Hon. Rabe F. Marsh Jr. U.S. Dist. Ct., Pa., 1957-58; assoc. Wilner, Wilner and Kuhn, 1958-61; ptnr. Dougherty, Larrimer & Lee, Pitts., 1961-84, 86-88; judge Ct. Common Pleas of Allegheny County, Pa., 1984-86, 88-90, U.S. Dist. Ct. (we. dist.) Pa., Pitts., 1990—; councilman Borough of Green Tree, 1961-63, solicitor, 1963-84, 86-88; spl. asst. atty. gen. Office of Atty. Gen. Commonwealth of Pa., 1963-74; spl. legal counsel Home Rule Study Commn., Municipality of Bethel Park and Borough of Green Tree, 1973-74, City of Pitts., 1978-80, various municipalities, 1970-86; chmn. Home Rule Charter Transition Com. Bethel Park, 1978. Mem. ad hoc com. Salvation Army. With USN, 1945-47. Mem. ABA, Allegheny County Bar Assn., St. Thomas More Legal Soc., Ancient Order of Hibernians, Woodland Hills Swim Club, Gaelic Arts Soc., Tin Can Sailors. Office: US Dist Ct 7th Grant St Rm 916 Pittsburgh PA 15219

**LEE, HENRY,** lawyer; b. N.Y.C., Dec. 18, 1952; s. Tong Shong and Toy (Wong) L. BA, Bklyn. Coll., 1973; JD, U. Iowa, 1977. Bar: Calif. 1979, N.Y. 1980, N.J. 1993. Research atty. Calif. Ct. Appeal, San Bernardino, 1977-78; assoc. Mendes & Mount, N.Y.C., 1980-85, ptnr., 1985-91; legal cons. Am. law Peruvian pvt. corps., 1991-92; of counsel Mendes & Mount, N.Y.C., 1992-95, ptnr., 1996-98; ptnr. Mendes & Mount, L.A., 1998—. Note editor Jour. Corp. Law, U. Iowa Coll. Law, 1976-77. Insurance, Personal injury, Professional liability. Office: Mendes & Mount LLP 725 S Figueroa St Fl 19 Los Angeles CA 90017-5524

**LEE, IN-YOUNG,** lawyer; b. In-Cheon, Kyonggi-do, Korea, Dec. 5, 1952; came to U.S. 1978; s. In-Seok and Hyun-Bo (Rim) L.; m. Young-Lae Hong, July 1, 1978; children: Casey K., Brian K. LLB, Seoul Nat. U., Korea, 1975; LLM, Harvard U., 1980; JD, UCLA, 1983. Bar: Ill. 1983, N.Y. 1987, D.C. 1989, U.S. Ct. Internat. Trade. Assoc. Baker & McKenzie, Chgo., 1983-86, Marks & Murase, N.Y.C., 1986-87, Baker & McKenzie, N.Y.C., 1987-91; ptnr. Marks & Murase, N.Y.C., 1991-96, McDermott, Will & Emery, N.Y.C., 1996—; gen. counsel Korean C. of C. and Industry in USA, Inc., 1993—, Assn. Korean Fin. Instns. Am., Inc. Articles editor Pacific Basin Law Jour. Presbyterian. Avocations: fishing, golf. Contracts commercial, Banking, Private international. Office: McDermott Will & Emery 50 Rockefeller Plaza New York NY 10020-1605

**LEE, JEROME G.,** lawyer; b. Chgo., Feb. 23, 1924; m. Margo B. Lee, Dec. 23, 1947; children: James A., Kenneth M. BSChemE, U. Wis., 1947; JD, NYU, 1950. Bar: N.Y. 1950, U.S. Supreme Ct. 1964. Assoc. firm Jeffery, Kimball, Eggleston, N.Y.C., 1950-52; assoc. firm Morgan, Finnegan, Durham & Pine, N.Y.C., 1952-59; ptnr. Morgan, Finnegan, Pine, Foley & Lee, N.Y.C., 1959-86; sr. ptnr. Morgan & Finnegan, N.Y.C., 1986-95, of counsel, 1995—; lectr. in field. Author: (with J. Gould) Intellectual Property Counseling and Litigation, 1988, USPTO Proposals to Change Rule 56 and the Related Rules Regarding a Patent Applicant's Duty of Candour, Patent World, 1992; contbr. articles to legal jours. in patent and trademark litigation splty. Fellow Am. Bar Found.; mem. ATLA, ABA (mem. coun. Intellectual Property Law sect., chmn. com. fed. practice and procedure, chmn. com. Ct. of Appeals Fed. Cir., chmn. com. on ethics and profl. responsibility, stds. com., mem. fed. cir. adv. com. 1992-97), Am. Intellectual Property Law Assn. (bd. dirs. 1984-90, pres. 1991, Am. Judicature Soc., Internat. Fedn. Indsl. Property Attys., Found. for Creative Am. (bd. dirs.), N.Y. Bar Assn., Assn. of Bar of City of N.Y., N.Y. County Bar Assn., N.Y. Patent, Trademark and Copyright Law Assn. (bd. dirs. 1975-80, pres. 1981), others. Patent, Trademark and copyright, Federal civil litigation. Home: 3328 Sabal Cove Ln Longboat Key FL 34228-4157 Office: Morgan & Finnegan 345 Park Ave Fl 22 New York NY 10154-0053

**LEE, LANSING BURROWS, JR.,** lawyer, corporate executive; b. Augusta, Ga., Aug. 27, 1919; s. Lansing Burrows and Bertha (Barrett) L.; s. Natalie Krug, July 4, 1943; children: Melinda Lee Clark, Lansing Burrows III, Bothwell Graves, Richard Hancock. BS, U. Va., 1939; postgrad., U. Ga. Sch. Law, 1939-40; JD, Harvard U., 1948. Bar: Ga. 1947. Corp. officer Ga.-Carolina Warehouse & Compress Co., Augusta, 1957-89, pres., CEO; co-owner Ga.-Carolina Warehouse; pvt. practice, Augusta. Chmn. bd. trustees James Brice White Found., 1962—; sr. warden Episcopal Ch., also chancellor, lay min.; sr. councillor Atlantic Coun. U.S.; bd. dirs. Med. Coll. Ga. Found. Capt. USAAF, 1942-46. Fellow Am. Coll. Trust and Estate Counsel; mem. Ga. Bar Found., Harvard U. Law Sch. Assn. Ga. (pres. 1966-67), Augusta Bar Assn. (pres. 1966-67), Soc. Colonial Wars Ga., State Bar Ga. (former chmn. fiduciary law sect.), U.S. Supreme Ct. Hist. Soc., U. Va. Thomas Jefferson Soc. Alunni, Internat. Order t. Luke the Physician, Augusta Country Club, Harvard Club Atlanta, President's Club Med. Coll. Ga. General corporate, Estate planning, Probate. Home: 2918 Bransford Rd Augusta GA 30909-3004 Office: First Union Bank Bldg 699 Broad St Ste 904 Augusta GA 30901-1448

**LEE, LAURENS CONWAY,** judge; b. Fort Valley, Ga., Apr. 11, 1958; s. Milledge Bruce and Valeria Virginia (Brown) L.; m. Kimberly Denise Peeler, May 30, 1986; children: Laurens C. Jr., Kimberly Valeria Virginia. BSc, Ga. Coll., 1981; JD, Mercer U., 1984. Bar: Ga., U.S. Dist. Ct. (mid. dist.) Ga. 1984. Assoc. Robert E. Lanyon, Atty., Fort Valley, Ga., 1984-85; asst. dist. atty. Ogeechee Cir. D.A.'s Office, Statesboro, Ga., 1985-86; asst. pub. def. Houston County Pub. Defenders Office, Perry, Ga., 1986-87; assoc. Hebert L. Wells, Atty., Perry, 1987-88; pvt. practice Fort Valley, Ga., 1988—; pub. defender Twiggs County Bd. of Commrs., Jeffersonville, Ga., 1988—; chief magistrate Peach County Magistrate Ct., Fort Valley, 1995—; juvenile judge pro-tem Peach County Juvenile Ct., 1994—. Mem. Downtown Devel. Authority, Fort Valley, 1990-92; atty. Peach Area Habitat for Humanity, Fort Valley, 1990-95, Peach County C. of C., Fort Valley, 1989. Mem. State Bar of Ga., Peach-Crawford Bar Assn., Crawford-Peachs Sons Confederate Vets. Baptist. Avocations: basketball, horseback riding, old cars, reading, politics. Office: 112A S Camellia Blvd Fort Valley GA 31030-3013

**LEE, LAURIE NEILSON,** lawyer; b. Portland, Oreg., Jan. 22, 1947; d. Duncan Reese and Lilian (Schwichtenberg) Neilson; m. Douglas Caldwell, Sept. 13, 1968 (div. Aug. 1987); children: Jessica, Ashley; m. Alan M. Lee, Jan. 1, 1988; stepchildren: Erin Lee, Sam Lee. BA, U. Oreg., 1969; JD, Lewis & Clark Coll., 1980. Bar: Oreg. 1980, U.S. Dist. Ct. Oreg. 1980. Assoc. Urbigkeit, Hinson & Abele, Oregon City, Oreg., 1980-85, Gleason, Scarborough, McNeese, O'Brien & Barnes, P.C., Portland, Oreg., 1985-88; ptnr. Bullivant, Houser, Bailey, Pendergrass & Hoffman, Portland, 1989-94, Foster Pepper & Shefelman, Portland, 1994—; spkr. legal seminars Oreg. State Bar, 1984-86, 88, 90, 92, 93, 94, 95, Oreg. Law Inst., 1989, Oreg. Soc. CPAs, 1986-90, 92, 95, Nat. Bus. Inst., 1990, Portland Tax Forum, 1991. Contbr. articles to profl. jours.; contbg. author: Administering Trusts in Oregon, 1994. Mem. activities coun. Portland Art Mus., 1989-91, Nature Conservancy, Portland, 1990; bd. dirs. The Dougy Ctr., Portland, 1989-91; mem. N.W. Planned Giving Roundtable, 1992—; past chair, past sec., com. mem. exec. com. estate planning and adminstrn. sect. Oreg. State Bar, Lake Oswego, 1982-88. Fellow Am. Coll. Trust and Estate Coun.; mem. ABA, Oreg. Women Lawyers (charter), Estate Planning Coun. Portland Inc. (bd. dirs. 1992—, chair planning com. 22d Ann. Estate Planning Seminar 1992, sec. 1995), Oreg. State Bar, Multnomah County Bar Assn. Estate planning, Probate, Estate taxation. Office: Foster Pepper & Shefelman 1 Main Pl 101 SW Main St Fl 15 Portland OR 97204-3292

**LEE, LESLIE STAEHLE,** lawyer; b. Bay Saint Louis, Miss., Mar. 21, 1962; d. Charles F. and Vicky Ann Staehle; m. Joseph Thomas Lee, May 13, 1995; 1 child, John. BA in Polit. Sci., U. Miss., 1983, JD, 1986. Bar: Miss. Spl. asst. atty. gen. Office of Atty. Gen., State of Miss., Jackson, 1989—. Mem. Miss. Bar Assn. E-mail: 71461.162@compuserve.com. Home: 130 Dogwood Trl Brandon MS 39047-8600 Office: State of Miss Office of Atty Gen 450 High St Fl 5 Jackson MS 39201-1006

**LEE, LEWIS SWIFT,** lawyer; b. Dallas, Nov. 19, 1933; '. Lenoir Valentine and Margaret Louise (Clendon) L.; m. Frances Ann Childress, Mar. 16, 1956; children: Frances Ann Lee Webb, Lewis S. Jr., George Childress, Lenoir Valentine Lee II. AB, U. South, 1955; postgrad., Washington & Lee U., 1954-55; MA, Emory U., 1956, JD, 1960. Bar: Fla. 1960, U.S. Dist. Ct. (so. and mid. dists.) Fla., U.S. Ct. Appeals (5th and 11th cirs.). Trainee Citizens & So. Nat. Bank, Atlanta, 1956, 58-59; assoc. Adair, Ulmer, Murchison, Kent & Ashby, Jacksonville, Fla., 1960-63; shareholder Ulmer, Murchison, Ashby & Ball, Jacksonville, 1963-95; of counsel LeBoeuf, Lamb, Greene & MacRae, LLP, Jacksonville, 1996—; gen. counsel Fla. Rock Industries, Inc., Jacksonville, 1972—, FRP Properties, Inc., Jacksonville, 1989—; dir. Fla. Sch. Book Depository, Jacksonville, 1990—. 1st lt. AUS, 1956-58. Mem. ABA, Jacksonville Bar Assn., Ponte Vedra Inn & Club, Timuquana Country Club, Fla. Yacht Club, The River Club, The Heritage Club. Republican. Episcopalian. Avocations: hiking, skiing, swimming, hunting, travel. General corporate, Mergers and acquisitions, Probate. Home: 3733 Ortega Blvd Jacksonville FL 32210-4347 Office: LeBoeuf Lamb Greene & MacRae LLP 50 N Laura St Ste 2800 Jacksonville FL 32202-3634

**LEE, MARILYN (IRMA) MODARELLI,** law librarian; b. Jersey City, Dec. 8, 1934; d. Alfred E. and Florence Olga (Koment) Modarelli; m. Alfred McClung Lee III, June 8, 1957 (div. July 1985); children: Leslie Lee Ekstrand, Alfred McClung IV, Andrew Modarelli. BA, Swarthmore (Pa.) Coll., 1956; JD, Western New Eng. Sch. of Law, 1985. Bar: Mass. 1986. Claims rep., supr. region II Social Security Adminstrn., Jersey City, 1956-59; law libr. County of Franklin, Greenfield, Mass., 1972-78; head law libr. Mass. Trial Ct., Greenfield, 1978—; mem. Franklin County Futures Lab Project (Mass. Cts.), 1994—. /hmn. Franklin County (Mass.) Regional Tech., Turners Falls, 1974-76, Sch. Bldg. Com., 1974-76; mem. Franklin Regional Planning Bd., 1988-98, mem. exec. bd., 1992-95; clk. Franklin County Tech. Sch., 1976-81; vice chmn. Greenfield Planning Bd., 1987-95; mem. Greenfield Sch. Bldg. Com., 1995—; mem. Greenfield C.C. Found., 1990—, Franklin Regional Transp. Com., 1992—; moderator All Souls Unitarian Ch., 1996—, asst. treas., 1997-98, treas., 1998—; mem. alumni coun. Swarthmore Coll., 1994-97. Mem. Mass. Bar Assn., Franklin County Bar Assn. (chmn. lawyer referral com. 1992-94, 97-99, vice chmn. 1994-97, chmn. libr. com. 1992—), Law Librs. of New Eng. (treas. 1993-97), Am. Assn. Law Librs. (mem. state ct. and county law librs. sect. 1972—, chair bylaws com. 1997-98), Greenfield Charter (commn. clk. 1979-83). Avocations: swimming, gardening. Office: Mass Trial Ct Franklin Law Libr 425 Main St Greenfield MA 01301-3313

**LEE, MICHAEL GREGORY,** lawyer; b. Berkeley, Calif., June 23, 1951; s. General and Lucy Elizabeth Lee; m. Patricia Anne Spears, Aug. 10, 1974; children: Jared Ahmad, Derrek Jordan. AA, Contra Costa Coll., San Pablo, Calif., 1972; BA, U. Calif., Davis, 1976, JD, 1979. Bar: Calif., U.S. Dist. Ct. (ea., no., and ctrl. dists.) Calif., U.S. Ct. Appeals (9th cir.). Dep. solicitor Calif. Agrl. Labor Rels. Bd., Sacramento, 1979-87; staff counsel II Calif. Sec. State, Sacramento, 1987, Calif. State Water Resources Control Bd., Sacramento, 1987-88; supervising dep. atty. gen. Calif. Dept. Justice, Sacramento, 1988—. Mem. 100 Black Men of Sacramento, Inc., 1996—; mgr., coach Northgate PeeWee League, Sacramento, 1987, Nat. Pony Baseball, Sacramento, 1988-91, Pocket Little League, Sacramento, 1992-98. Fellow U. Calif., 1976-79; recipient Donor's award Calif. State Employees' Campaign, 1991-98, Tournament Team Mgr. award Pocket Little League, 1996, Tournament Coach award Natomas Pony Baseball, 1991. Democrat. Baptist. Office: Calif Dept Justice 1300 I St Rm 1050-34 Sacramento CA 95814-2919

**LEE, MICHAEL HAL,** lawyer; b. L.A., Oct. 12, 1955; s. Martin M. and Rose M. Lee. BA, UCLA, 1977; JD cum laude, Suffolk U., 1980; LLM, London Sch. Econs., 1984; grad. barrister program with honors, Inns of Ct.

Sch. Law, London, 1987. Bar: Calif. 1980, Mass. 1982, Eng. and Wales 1987. Dep. pub. defender City of L.A., 1981; assoc. Garber & Garber, L.A., 1984-86; barrister at law Chambers of R. Thwaites, Queen's Counsel, London, 1990—; pvt. practice Inglewood, Calif., 1993—. Author: Bermuda I's Borodino, 1983. Mem. ACLU, NAACP, Amnesty Internat., B'nai Brith Youth Orgn. (internat. pres. 1973-74). Criminal, Private international, Public international. Office: 467 S Market St Inglewood CA 90301-2309

**LEE, PATRICIA MARIE,** lawyer; b. Memphis, Mar. 17, 1964; d. Robert Edwin and Aida Rachel (de Leon) L.; children: Hanaisabel Lee Brownsell, André P. Steenkamp. BA, U. Tampa, 1987; JD, Stetson U., 1992. Bar: Fla. 1992, U.S. Dist. Ct. (mid. dist.) Fla. 1992, U.S. Ct. Appeals (11th cir.) Fla. 1994. Clk. U.S. Secret Svc., Tampa, Fla., 1984-85; adminstrv. asst. NCCJ, Tampa, 1986-88; law clk. Terry & Dittmar P.A., Tampa, 1990, Annis, Mitchell P.A., Tampa, 1990-91; assoc. Blasingame, Forisz, P.A., St. Petersburg, Fla., 1992-93, Goodman & Neckvasil, P.A., Safety Harbor, Fla., 1993; pvt. practice St. Petersburg, 1993—. Editor (book chpt.) Nursing and the Working Mother, 1997. Barrister Carakaris Inns. of Ct. Democrat. Roman Catholic. E-mail: leeplaw@intnet.net. Family and matrimonial, Personal injury, Labor. Office: 538 1st Ave N Saint Petersburg FL 33701-3702

**LEE, RICHARD DIEBOLD,** law educator, legal publisher; b. Fargo, N.D., July 31, 1935; s. Sidney Jay and Charlotte Hannah (Thompson) L.; m. Patricia Ann Taylor, June 17, 1957; children—Elizabeth Carol, Deborah Susan, David Stuart. B.A. with distinction, Stanford U., 1957; J.D., Yale U., 1960. Bar: Calif. 1961. U.S. Dist. Ct. (no. dist.) Calif. 1961, U.S. Ct. Appeals (9th cir.) 1961. Dep. atty. gen. Office of Atty. Gen., Sacramento, 1960-62; assoc. McDonough, Holland, Schwartz, Allen & Wahrhaftig, Sacramento, 1962-66, ptnr., 1966-69; asst. dean U. Calif. Sch. Law, Davis, 1969-73, assoc. dean, 1973-76; assoc. prof. law Temple U. Sch. Law, Phila., 1976-77, vis. prof., 1975-76, prof., 1977-89; dir. profl. devel. Baker & McKenzie, Chgo., N.Y.C., 1981-83; dir. Am. Inst. for Law Tng., Phila., 1985-89; dir. profl. devel. Morrison & Foerster, San Francisco, 1989-93; dir. Continuing Edn. of the Bar, Berkeley, 1993-97; mem. Grad. and Profl. Fin. Aid Coun., Princeton, N.J., 1974-80; trustee Law Sch. Admission Council, Washington, 1976-78; mem. internat. adv. com. Internat. Juridical Org., Rome, 1977-88; mem. bd. advisors Lawyer Hiring and Tng. Report, Chgo., 1983-95; vis. prof. law sch. law Golden Gate U., San Francisco, 1988-89. Author: (coursebook) Materials on Internat. Efforts to Control the Environment, 1977, 78, 79, 80, 84, 85, 87. Co-editor: Orientation in the U.S. Legal System annual coursebook, 1982-92. Contbr. articles to profl. jours. Bd. dirs. Lung Assn. of Sacramento-Emigrant Trails, 1962-69, pres., 1966-68; bd. dirs. Sacramento County Legal Aid Soc., 1968-74, pres., 1971-72; chmn. bd. overseers Phila. Theol. Inst., 1984-88, bd. overseers, 1979-80, 84-88; mem. bd. of council Episcopal Community Services, Phila., 1984-88; trustee Grace Cathedral, San Francisco, 1989—, chair bd. trustees, 1992-95; mem. bd. visitors John Marshall Law Sch., Chgo., 1989-93; trustee Grad. Theol. Union, Berkeley, 1991—, vice-chair, 1994—. Mem. ABA (chmn. various coms., spl. cons. on continuing legal edn. MacCrate Task Force on Law Schs. and the Profession: Narrowing the Gap 1991-93, standing com. on specialization, 1998—), State Bar Calif. (chair standing com. on minimum continuing legal edn. 1990-92, com. mem. 1990-93), Bar Assn. San Francisco (legal ethics com., conf. of delegates, 1987—), Profl. Devel. Consortium (chair 1991-93), Am. Law Inst. Democrat. Episcopalian. Club: Yale (N.Y.C., San Francisco). Home and Office: 2001 Sacramento St Ste 4 San Francisco CA 94109-3342

**LEE, RICHARD H(ARLO),** lawyer; b. Glen Falls, N.Y., June 5, 1947; s. Donald D. and Jeanne M. (Uthus) L.; m. Mary Ahearn, June 10, 1972; children: Christine Marie Ahearn Lee, Andrea Elizabeth Ahearn Lee. BS with honors, Mich. State U., 1972; JD magna cum laude, Ariz. State U., 1976. Bar: Ariz. 1977, U.S. Ct. Appeals (6th cir.) 1977, U.S. Dist. Ct. Ariz. 1978, U.S. Ct. Appeals (9th cir.) 1981. Law clk. to Judge George Edwards U.S. Ct. Appeals (6th cir.) Ohio, Cin., 1976-77; assoc. Sparks & Siler, Scottsdale, Ariz., 1977-78; assoc. Murphy & Posner, Phoenix, 1979-82, ptnr., 1983-86; assoc. Storey & Ross, Phoenix, 1986-88; prin. McDaniel & Lee, Phoenix, 1989-91, Law Office of Richard H. Lee, Phoenix, 1982—; of counsel Martin & Patterson, Ltd., 1992-98, Martin & Assocs., 1998-99, Lee & Manoil, 1999—. Comment and notes editor Ariz. State U. Law Jour., 1975-76; bd. editors Maricopa County Lawyer, 1990-91. Chmn. Ariz. Canal Diversion Channel task force City of Phoenix, 1985-86, mem. exec. com. citizens bond com., 1975, chmn. solid waste bond com., 1987-88, mem. bond adv. com., 1988—, 1975 Bond com. City of Phoenix, 1975; state committeeman Ariz. Dems., Phoenix, 1983-84; mem. adv. com. City of Phoenix Neighborhood Orgn. Divsn., 1974-75; vol. VISTA Crow Indian Tribe, Crow Agy., Mont., 1969-71; bd. dirs. Valley of the Sun Sch. and Habilitation Ctr., 1991-95, treas., 1992-93, chair fin. com., 1993-94. Mem. Ariz. Bar Assn. (chmn. com. on CLE bankruptcy sect. 1985-87, chmn. bankruptcy sect. 1987-88), Maricopa County Bar Assn., Ariz. State U. Coll. Law Alumni Assn. (pres. 1981), Ariz. State U. Alumni Assn. (bd. dirs. 1981-82), Kappa Sigma. Bankruptcy, Real property, General civil litigation. Home: 331 W Orangewood Ave Phoenix AZ 85021-7249 Office: PO Box 7749 Phoenix AZ 85011-7749

**LEE, ROBERT EDWARD, JR.,** lawyer; b. Bklyn., Feb. 6, 1941; s. Robert E. and Edna C. (Koerber) L.; m. Janet A., July 12, 1975; children: Kristen A., Robyn E. B.A. summa cum laude, Niagara U., 1962; LL.B., St. John's U., 1967. Bar: N.Y. 1967, N.J. 1975. Assoc. Lee & Lee and predecessor firms, N.Y.C., 1967-72, jr. ptnr., 1972-78, sr. ptnr., 1978-97, pres., 1997—; assoc. Snevily, Ely & Williams, Westfield, N.J.; instr. St. Francis Coll., 1975-76. Served to 1st lt. U.S. Army, 1963-65. Mem. ABA, N.J. State Bar Assn., Bklyn. Bar Assn., Cath. Lawyers Guild (past pres.). Republican. Roman Catholic. Clubs: Lawyers of Bklyn. (past pres.); KC (Westfield, N.J.). Banking, Probate, Real property. Home: 1230 Christine Cir Scotch Plains NJ 07076-2629 Office: Lee & Lee 233 Broadway New York NY 10279-0001

**LEE, ROTAN EDWARD,** lawyer, entrepreneur; b. Phila., Oct. 18, 1948; s. Rotan and Bessie (Hart) L. BA with high honors, U. Md. Eastern Shore, Princess Anne, 1971; JD with high honors, Antioch Sch. Law, Washington, 1979. Bar: Pa. 1979, U.S. Dist. Ct. (ea. dist.) Pa. 1980. Sr. legal asst. to congl. office U.S. Ho. of Reps., Washington, 1978-79; chief legal counsel to subcom. Small Bus. Com., U.S. Ho. of Reps., Washington, 1978-79; pres. Alcon/Unified Internat., Inc., 1975-79; sr. project mgr. energy and small scale tech. Mark Battle & Assocs., Inc., 1979-82; dir., chief counsel Minority Bus. Legal Def. and Edn. Fund, Washington, 1979-85; founding ptnr. Burrell, Waxman, Donaghy & Lee, Phila., 1985-88; ptnr. Fox, Rothschild, O'Brien & Frankel, Phila., 1988-94; sr. exec. v.p., COO, dir. RMS Techs., Inc., Marlton, N.J., 1994-96; ptnr. Sherr, Joffe & Zuckerman, P.C., West Conshohocken, Pa., 1994—; vice chmn. Genesis Teleserv Corp., West Conshohocken, 1996—; affiliate prof. Sch. Bus. and Mgmt., Temple U., Phila., 1995, adj. prof. Coll. Edn., 1993-94; chmn. bd. dirs. Phila. Gas Works, 1994-97, Talleyrand Atlantic, LLC, 1997; dir. law, pub. policy, edn., strategic planning and energy Mellon Bank Corp., Mellon PSFS; speaker in field. Contbr. articles to profl. jours. Bd. dirs. Urban League Phila., 1989, Phila. Child Guidance Ctr., 1995-96, Phila. Orch. Assn., 1991-94; chmn. Cultural Diversity Inst., 1991-95; mem. Bd. Edn., Sch. Dist. Phila., pres., 1992-94. Recipient Paul Porter award Antioch Sch. Law, 1976-79, Learned Hand award Am. Jewish Com., 1993, Brotherhood/Sisterhood Cmty. award NCCJ, 1995, others; Rose Walt scholar, 1969-71. Mem. Beta Kappa Chi, Alpha Kappa Mu, Sigma Tau Delta. General corporate, Finance, Municipal (including bonds). Address: Ste 320 One Bala Ave Bala Cynwyd PA 19004-0800

**LEE, THOMAS DONGHO,** lawyer; b. Seoul, Republic of Korea, June 9, 1940; came to U.S., 1969; s. Kwan S. and Ko B. (Wee) L.; m. Donna Inja, May 15, 1969; children: James C., Benjamin C. LLB, Seoul Nat. U., 1962; JD, N.Y. Law Sch., 1978. Bar: N.Y. 1979, U.S. Dist. Ct. (ea. and so. dists.) N.Y. 1980, U.S Supreme Ct. 1984. In-house counsel Riba Industry Co., Ltd., Seoul, 1963-67, Lotte Korea, N.Y.C., 1969-74; prin. Law Offices Thomas Dongho Lee, N.Y.C., 1979—; of counsel Dow, Lohnes & Albertson, N.Y.C., 1990-91, Winthrop, Stimson, Putnam & Robertson, 1991—; counsel Korea Ctrl. Daily News, 1979—, Korea Devel. Bank, 1994—, Korea Semiconductor Industry Assn., 1992—, Samsung Electronics Co., Ltd., 1993—, Korea Telecom., 1992—, Export Import Bank of Korea, 1986—, Korea Automobile Mfrs. Assn. Contbr. articles to profl. jours. Mem. Korean Am. Lawyers Assn. (pres. 1987-88), Nissequogue Golf Club, Seoul Nat. U. Law Sch. Alumni Assn. (pres. 1986-88). Finance, Contracts commercial, Private international. Home: 2345 S Bentley Ave Apt 101 Los Angeles CA 90064-1953 Office: Winthrop Stimson Putnam & Robertson 1 Battery Park Plz Fl 31 New York NY 10004-1490

**LEE, TOM STEWART,** judge; b. 1941; m. Norma Ruth Robbins; children: Elizabeth Robbins, Tom Stewart Jr. BA, Miss. Coll., 1963, JD cum laude, U. Miss., 1965. Ptnr. Lee & Lee, Forest, Miss., 1965-84; pros. atty. Scott County, Miss., 1968-71; judge Scott County Youth Ct., Forest, 1979-82; mcpl. judge City of Forest, 1982; judge U.S. Dist. Ct. (so. dist.) Miss., Jackson, 1984-96, chief judge, 1996—. Asst. editor: Miss. Law Jour. Deacon, Sunday sch. tchr. Forest Bapt. ch.; pres. Forest Pub. Sch. Bd., Scott County Heart Assn.; bd. visitors Miss. Coll. Law Sch.; lectr. Miss. Coll., 1993. Served to capt. USAR. Named one of Outstanding Young Men Am. Mem. Miss. Bar Assn., Scott County Bar Assn., Hinds County Bar Assn., Fed. Bar Assn., Fed. Judges' Assn., 5th Cir. Jud. Coun., Forest Jaycees (past pres., Disting. Service award), Ole Miss. Alumni Assn. (pres.), Miss. Coll. Alumni Assn. (bd. dirs.), Am. Legion. Office: US Dist Ct 245 E Capitol St Ste 110 Jackson MS 39201-2414

**LEE, VICTORIA,** lawyer; b. Bklyn., June 12, 1956; d. Leroy and Betty Lee; m. Otto H. Chu, May 30, 1983; children: Alexa, Jonathan. BA, Vassar Coll., 1978; JD, U. Pa., 1981. Atty. civil rights divsn. U.S. Dept. Justice, Washington, 1981-84; atty. Wall Gotshal & Mayer, N.Y.C., 1985; v.p. Chu Investment Coun., Pitts., 1993-97; atty. Thorp Reed & Armstrong, Pitts., 1997—. Contracts commercial, General civil litigation. Office: Thorp Reed Armstrong One River Front Pittsburgh PA 15212

**LEE, WILLIAM CHARLES,** judge; b. Ft. Wayne, Ind., Feb. 2, 1938; s. Russell and Catherine (Zwick) L.; m. Judith Anne Bash, Sept. 19, 1959; children: Catherine L., Mark R., Richard R. AB, Yale U., 1959; JD, U. Chgo., 1962. Bar: Ind. 1962. Ptnr. Parry, Krueckeberg & Lee, Ft. Wayne, 1963-69, chief dep., 1966-69; U.S. atty. No. Dist. Ind., Ft. Wayne, 1970-73; ptnr. Hunt, Suedhoff, Borror, Eilbacher & Lee, Ft. Wayne, 1973-81; U.S. dist. judge U.S. Dist. Ct. (no. dist.) Ind., Ft. Wayne, 1981—; instr. Nat. Inst. Trial Advocacy; lectr. in field. Co-author: Business and Commercial Litigation in Federal Courts, 1998; author: Volume I Federal Jury Practice and Instructions, 1999; contbr. to numerous publs. in field. Co-chmn. Fort Wayne Fine Arts Operating Fund Drive, 1978; past bd. dirs., v.p., pres. Fort Wayne Philharm. Orch.; past bd. dirs., v.p. Hospice of Fort Wayne, inc.; past bd. dirs. Fort Wayne Fine Arts Found., Fort Wayne Civic Theatre, Neighbors, Inc., Embassy Theatre Found.; past bd. dirs., pres. Legal Aid of Fort Wayne, Inc.; past mem. chm. coun., v.p. Trinity English Lutheran Ch. Coun.; past trustee, pres. Fort Wayne Cmty. Schs., 1978-81, pres., 1980-81; trustee Fort Wayne Mus. Art, 1984-90; past bd. dirs., pres. Fort Wayne-Allen County Hist. Soc. Griffin Scholar, 1955-59; chmn. Fort Wayne Cmty. Schs. Scholarship Com.; bd. dirs. Arts United of Greater Fort Wayne, Fort Wayne Ballet. Weymouth Kirkland scholar, 1959-62; named Ind. Trial Judge of Yr., 1988. Fellow Am. Coll. Trial Lawyers, Ind. Bar Found.; mem. ABA, Allen County Bar Assn., Ind. State Bar Assn., Fed. Bar Assn., Seventh Cir. Bar Assn., Benjamin Harrison Am. Inn of Ct., North Side High Alumni Assn. (bd. dris., pres.), Fort Wayne Rotary Club (bd. dirs.), Phi Delta Phi (past bd. dirs., 1st pres.). Republican. Lutheran. Office: US Dist Ct 2145 Fed Bldg 1300 S Harrison St Fort Wayne IN 46802-3495

**LEE, WILLIAM GENTRY,** lawyer; b. St. Louis, Apr. 2, 1944; s. Gentry and Wilma (Elliott) L.; m. Carter Kerr, Aug. 9, 1969; children: William Gentry Jr., Kathryn Carter. BA cum laude, Harvard U., 1966; JD, U. Okla., 1969. Bar: Okla. 1969, Tex. 1972. Assoc. Vinson & Elkins, Houston, 1973-81, ptnr., 1981—; mem. com. on revision of corp. laws bus. law sect. State Bar of Tex., 1975—. Editor: Okla. Law Rev., 1967-69; contbr. articles to profl. jours. Adminstrv. bd. mem. Cho-Yeh Camp and Conf. Ctr., Livingston, Tex., 1990-94; deacon 1st Presbyn. Ch. of Houston, 1979-83, elder, 1984—. Capt. U.S. Army JAGC, 1969-73. Named to Order of Coif U. Okla., 1969. Mem. Allegro, Houston Club, Houston Ctr. Club, River Oaks Country Club, Kiwanis (bd. dirs. 1993-95). Republican. Avocations: tennis, golf. Securities, General corporate, Mergers and acquisitions. Home: 3665 Overbrook Ln Houston TX 77027-4127 Office: Vinson & Elkins LLP 2300 First City Tower 1001 Fannin St Houston TX 77002-6760

**LEE, WILLIAM JOHNSON,** lawyer; b. Oneida, Tenn., Jan. 13, 1924; s. William J. and Ara (Anderson) L.; student Akron U., 1941-43, Denison U., 1943-44, Harvard U., 1944-45; J.D., Ohio State U., 1948. Bar: Ohio 1948, Fla. 1962. Research asst. Ohio State U. Law Sch., 1948-49; asst. dir. Ohio Dept. Liquor Control, chief purchases, 1956-57, atty. examiner, 1951-53, asst. state permit chief, 1953-55, state permit chief, 1955-56; asst. counsel, staff Hupp Corp., 1957-58; spl. counsel City Attys. Office Ft. Lauderdale (Fla.), 1963-65; asst. atty. gen. Office Atty. Gen., State of Ohio, 1966-70; adminstr. State Med. Bd. Ohio, Columbus, 1970-85, also mem. Federated State Bd.'s Nat. Commn. for Evaluation of Fgn. Med. Schs., 1981-83; Mem. Flex 1/Flex 2 Transitional Task Force, 1983-84; pvt. practice law, Ft. Lauderdale, 1965-66; acting municipal judge, Ravenna, Ohio, 1960; instr. Coll. Bus. Adminstrn., Kent State U., 1961-62. Mem. pastoral relations com. Epworth United Meth. Ch., 1976; chmn. legal aid com. Portage County, Ohio, 1960; troop awards chmn. Boy Scouts Am., 1965; mem. ch. bd. Melrose Park (Fla.) Meth. Ch., 1966. Mem. Exptl. Aviation Assn. S.W. Fla., Franklin County Trial Lawyers Assn., Am. Legion, Fla., Columbus, Akron, Broward County (Fla.) bar assns., Delta Theta Phi, Phi Kappa Tau, Pi Kappa Delta. Served with USAAF, 1943-46. Editorial bd. Ohio State Law Jour., 1947-48; also articles. Administrative and regulatory, General practice, Health. Home: Apple Valley 704 Country Club Dr Howard OH 43028-9530

**LEE, WILLIAM MARSHALL,** lawyer; b. N.Y.C., Feb. 23, 1922; s. Marshall McLean and Marguerite (Letts) L.; m. Lois Kathryn Plain, Oct. 10, 1942; children: Marsha (Mrs. Stephen Derynck), William Marshall Jr., Victoria C. (Mrs. Larry Nelson). Student, U. Wis., 1939-40; BS, Aero. U., Chgo., 1942; postgrad., UCLA, 1946-48, Loyola U. Law Sch., L.A., 1948-49; JD, Loyola U., Chgo., 1952. Bar: Ill. 1952, U.S. Supreme Ct., 1972. Thermodynamicist Northrop Aircraft Co., Hawthorne, Calif., 1947-49; patent agt. Hill, Sherman, Meroni, Gross & Simpson, Chgo., 1949-51, Borg-Warner Corp., Chgo., 1951-53; ptnr. Hume, Clement, Hume & Lee, Chgo., 1953-72; pvt. practice Chgo., 1973-74; ptnr. Lee and Smith (and predecessors), Chgo., 1974-89, Lee, Mann, Smith, McWilliams, Sweeney & Ohlson, Chgo., 1989—; ind. expert intellectual property Barrington, Ill., 1999—; cons. Power Packaging, Inc. Speaker and contbr. articles on legal topics. Pres. Glenview (Ill.) Citizens Sch. Com., 1953-57; v.p. Glenbrook High Sch. Bd., 1957-63. Lt. USNR, 1942-46, CBI. Recipient Pub. Svc. award Glenbrook High Sch. Bd., 1963. Mem. ABA (chmn. sect. intellectual property law 1986-87, sect. fin. officer 1976-77, sect. sec. 1977-80, sect. governing coun. 1980-84, 87-88), Ill. Bar Assn., Chgo. Bar Assn., 7th Fed. Cir. Bar Assn., Am. Intellectual Property Law Assn., Intellectual Law Assn. Property Chgo., Licensing Execs. Soc. (pres. 1981-82, treas. 1977-80, trustee 1974-77, 80-81, 82-83, internat. del. 1980—), Phi Delta Theta, Phi Alpha Delta. Republican. Patent, Trademark and copyright, Antitrust. Office: 84 Otis Rd Barrington IL 60010-5128

**LEEBRON, DAVID WAYNE,** dean, law educator; b. Phila., Feb. 12, 1955. BA, Harvard U., 1976, JD, 1979. Bar: N.Y. 1982, Pa. 1981, Hawaii 1980. Law clk. Judge Shirley Hufstedler, L.A., 1979-80; assoc. Cleary, Gottlieb, Steen & Hamilton, N.Y.C., 1981-83; prof. Sch. Law NYU, 1983-89; prof. Sch. Law Columbia U., N.Y.C., 1989—, dean, 1996—. Office: Columbia U Sch Law 435 W 116th St New York NY 10027-7297

**LEECH, NOYES ELWOOD,** lawyer, educator; b. Ambler, Pa., Aug. 1, 1921; m. Louise Ann Gallagher, Apr. 19, 1954; children: Katharine, Gwyneth. AB, U. Pa., 1943, JD, 1948. Bar: Pa. 1949. Assoc. Dechert, Price & Rhoads (and predecessors), Phila., 1948-49, 51-53; mem. faculty law sch. U. Pa., Phila., 1949-57; prof. U. Pa., 1957-78, Ferdinand Wakeman Hubbell prof. law, 1978-85, William A. Schnader prof. law, 1985-86, prof. emeritus, 1986—. Co-author: The International Legal System, 3d edit., 1988; gen. editor: Jour. Comparative Bus. and Capital Market Law, 1978-86. Mem. Order of Coif, Phi Beta Kappa. Office: U Pa Law Sch 3400 Chestnut St Philadelphia PA 19104-6204

**LEED, ROGER MELVIN,** lawyer; b. Green Bay, Wis., July 15, 1939; s. Melvin John and Veronica Sarah (Flaherty) L.; m. Jean Ann Burg, Mar. 1967; children: Craig, Maren, Jennifer. AB, Harvard U., 1961; JD cum laude, U. Mich., 1967. Bar: Wash. 1967, U.S. Dist. Ct. (we. dist.) Wash. 1968, U.S. Ct. Appeals (9th cir.) 1969, U.S. Supreme Ct. 1973. Law clk. Wash. Supreme Ct., Olympia, 1967-68; assoc. Perkins, Coie et al, Seattle, 1968-70; ptnr. Schroeter, Goldmark et al, Seattle, 1970-77; sole practice Seattle, 1977—; adj. prof. law U. Puget Sound, Tacoma, 1974-77. Editor Shorelines Mgmt., the Wash. Experience, 1972. Pres. Cen. Seattle Community Council Fedn., 1972, Wash. Environ. Council, 1980-82; bd. dirs. Allied Arts, Seattle, 1971-72, Downtown Human Services Council, Seattle, 1985-92. Mem. Wash. State Bar Assn., Seattle-King County Bar Assn., Assn. Trial Lawyers Am. Clubs: Met. Dem., Washington Athletic. Environmental, State civil litigation, Federal civil litigation. Office: 2003 Western Ave Ste 600 Seattle WA 98121-2161

**LEEHEY, PAUL WADE,** lawyer; b. Johnson AFB, Japan, Sept. 9, 1954; s. Donald James and Sara Aileen (Britton) L.; m. Gail Marie Krafft, Aug. 8, 1987; children: Whitney Kaileen, Shara Michele, Wade Jarik. BA in Polit. Sci./Sociology, Loyola U. L.A., 1976; JD, U. San Diego, 1979. Bar: Calif. 1980, U.S. Dist. Ct. (so. dist.) Calif.; cert. specialist family law, State Bar of Calif. Bd. of Legal Specializations. Pvt. practice law Fallbrook, Calif., 1980—. Past pres., mem. Fallbrook chpt., Am. Heart Assn., 1988, dir. San Diego chpt., 1990-95; v.p. Zion Luth. Ch., 1996—. Mem. Calif. Bar Assn., San Diego County Bar Assn., San Diego Trial Lawyers Assn., Bar Assn. No. San Diego County, Fallbrook C. of C., Rotary (Fallbrook Village chpt., sec. 1989—). Democrat. Avocations: skiing, volleyball, mountain biking. Family and matrimonial, Pension, profit-sharing, and employee benefits, General civil litigation. Office: 205 W Alvarado St Fallbrook CA 92028-2002

**LEEKLEY, JOHN ROBERT,** lawyer; b. Phila., Aug. 27, 1943; s. Thomas Briggs and Dorothy (O'Hora) L.; m. Karen Kristin Myers, Aug. 28, 1965 (dec. Mar. 1997); children: John Thomas, Michael Dennis; m. Gerry Lee Gildner, June 5, 1999. BA, Boston Coll., 1965; LLB, Columbia U., 1968. Bar: N.Y. 1968, Mich. 1976. Assoc. Curtis, Mallet-Prevost, Colt & Mosle, N.Y.C., 1968-69, Davis Polk & Wardwell, N.Y.C., 1969-76; asst. corp. counsel Masco Corp., Taylor, Mich., 1976-77, corp. counsel, 1977-79, v.p., corp. counsel, 1979-88, v.p., gen. counsel, 1988-96; sr. v.p., gen. counsel Masco Corp., Taylor, 1996—. Bd. visitors Columbia U. Law Sch., N.Y.C., 1994-96; mem. Freedom Twp. Bd. Tax Appeals, 1984-85. Mem. ABA (com. long range issues affecting bus. practice 1976-96), Mich. State Bar Assn. Democrat. Roman Catholic. Avocations: Percheron horse breeding, hunting, fishing, outdoor activities. Office: Masco Corp 21001 Van Born Rd Taylor MI 48180-1300

**LEEMON, JOHN ALLEN,** lawyer; b. Hoopeston, Ill., Jan. 12, 1928; ss. Allen Wallace and Eva Carol (Merritt) L.; m. Sally Paul Pierce, July 14, 1951; children: John Paul, Lisa Ann Johnson. BS, U. Ill., 1950, LLB, 1952. Bar: Ill. 1952, U.S. Dist. Ct. (no. dist.) Ill. 1958, U.S. Tax Ct. 1985. Pvt. practice Savanna, Ill., 1952-54, Mt. Carroll, Ill., 1969-95; ptnr. Eaton & Leemon, Mt. Carroll, Ill., 1954-55, Eaton, Leemon & Rapp, Mt. Carroll, Ill., 1966-69, Leemon, Weinstine, Shirk & Mellott PC, Mt. Carroll, Ill., 1995-97, Leemon & Kane, Mt. Carroll, Ill., 1997—; spl. asst. atty. gen. Ill. Atty. Gen., 1969-76. Mem. Ill. State Bar Assn. (negligence coun. 1961-66, grievance com. inquiry divsn. 1967-70), Carroll County Bar Assn., Whiteside County Bar Assn. Avocations: golf, fishing, hunting. State civil litigation, Family and matrimonial, Probate. Office: Leemon & Kane PO Box 112 102 1/2 E Market St Mount Carroll IL 61053-1108

**LEEPER, HAROLD HARRIS,** arbitrator; b. Kansas City, Mo., July 29, 1916; s. Truman Elmer and Bess Mayburn (Harris) L.; m. Maribelle Potts, Sept. 21, 1941; children: Robert Chester, Marilyn Anne. BSBA, U. Mo., 1937; JD, Oklahoma City U., 1956. Bar: Okla. 1957, U.S. Supreme Ct. 1969. Regional pers. officer VA, Oklahoma City, 1946-52; state adminstrv. officer IRS, Oklahoma City, 1952-56; pers. officer FAA, Oklahoma City, 1956-63; from hearing officer to chief hearing officer FAA, Washington, 1963-71; adminstrv. law judge Social Security Adminstrn., Dallas, 1971-73; freelance labor mgmt. arbitrator Dallas, 1974—. Pres. Way Back House, Inc., Dallas, 1975-77, bd. dirs., 1997—; chmn. pers. com. Wesley Rankin Community Ctr., Dallas, 1989-95, scoutmaster Boy Scouts of Am., SD, OK, VA. 1st lt. U.S. Army, 1943-46, lt. col. Res. ret. Mem. Fed. Bar Assn. (pres. Dallas chpt. 1982-83), Nat. Acad. Arbitrators (regional chmn. 1990-92), Mil. Order World Wars (comdr. D.C. chpt. 1969-70), Mason, Shriner. Democrat. Methodist. Avocations: golf, sailing, flying, church activities. Home and Office: 6256 Glennox Ln Dallas TX 75214-2144

**LEESON, SUSAN M.,** state judge. Law clerk U.S. 9th Cir. Ct. of Appeals; Tom. C. Clark judicial fellow U.S. Supreme Ct.; prof. polit. sci., assoc. prof. law Willamette U., Salem, Oreg.; judge Oreg. Ct. Appeals, 1993-98, Oreg. Supreme Ct., 1998—. Former mem. Oreg. Criminal Justice Coun., Marion-Polk Local Govt. Boundary Commn. Office: Supreme Ct Bldg 1163 State St Salem OR 97310-1331*

**LEEVIRAPHAN, AMERIC (ERIC LEEVIRAPHAN),** lawyer, sole practitioner; b. Stillwater, Okla., Nov. 3, 1963; s. Manoon and Rosalinda Leeviraphan; m. Suzanne Neely, Oct. 27, 1990; children: Eric Austin, Katelyn Marie. B in Bus. Adminstrn., U. Okla., 1986, JD, 1990. Atty. Lyle R. Nelson, P.C., Oklahoma City, 1990-94; sole practitioner Oklahoma City, 1994—. Banking, Bankruptcy, Civil rights. Office: 204 N Robinson Ave Oklahoma City OK 73102-6803

**LEFCO, KATHY NAN,** law librarian; b. Bethesda, Md., Feb. 24, 1949; d. Ted Lefco and Dorothy Rose (Fox) Harris; m. Stephen Gary Katz, Sept. 2, 1973 (div. May 1984); m. John Alfred Price, Nov. 24, 1984 (dec. Jan. 1989). BA, U. Wis., 1971; MLS, U. Wis., Milw., 1975. Rsch. asst. Ctr. Auto Safety, Washington, 1971-73; asst. to dir. Ctr. Consumer Affairs, Milw., 1973-74; legis. libr. Morgan, Lewis & Bockius, Washington, 1976-78; dir. library Mulcahy & Wherry, Milw., 1978; paralegal Land of Lincoln Legal Assistance, Springfield, Ill., 1979-80; reference and interlibrary loan libr. So. Ill. U. Sch. Medicine, Springfield, 1980; reader svcs. libr. Wis. State Law Library, Madison, 1981-83; ref. libr. Mudge Rose Guthrie Alexander & Ferdon, N.Y.C., 1983-85; sr. legal info. specialist Cravath, Swaine & Moore, N.Y.C., 1985-86; asst. libr. Kaye, Scholer, Fierman, Hays & Handler, N.Y.C., 1986-89; head libr. Parker Chapin Flattau & Klimpl, N.Y.C., 1989-94; dir. libr. svcs. Winston & Strawn, Chgo., 1994—. Author: (with others) Mobile Homes: The Low-Cost Housing Hoax, 1973. Mem. Chgo. Assn. Law Librs., Am. Assn. Law Librs. Democrat. Jewish. Avocations: biking, backgammon, politics. Home: 5445 N Sheridan Rd Apt 808 Chicago IL 60640-7457 Office: Winston & Strawn 35 W Wacker Dr Ste 4200 Chicago IL 60601-1695

**LEFEBVRE, ALAN J.,** lawyer; b. Akron, Colo., Mar. 17, 1953; s. Vern L. and Adeline V. (Molacek) L.; m. Eileen Helen Buhmann, Feb. 26, 1987; 1 child, Rachel Elisabeth. BA in Polit. Sci. with high honors and departmental distinction, U. Calif., Santa Barbara, 1975; JD, U. San Francisco, 1978. Bar: Calif. 1978, Nev. 1979, U.S. Dist. Ct. Nev. 1979, U.S. Ct. Appeals (9th cir.) 1979, U.S. Supreme Ct. 1992, U.S. Dist. Ct. (cen. dist.) Calif. 1994. Law clk. 8th Jud. Dist. Ct., Las Vegas, Nev., 1978-79; assoc. Jolly, Urga & Wirth, Las Vegas, 1979-80; assoc., ptnr. Beckley, Singleton, DeLanoy Jemison & List, Las Vegas, 1980-89; sr. ptnr. Lefebvre & Barron, Las Vegas, 1989—. Mem. Nev. Commn. on Jud. Discipline, Carson City, 1991—. Mem. Internat. Assn. Def. Counsel. Republican. Roman Catholic. Avocations: boating, French horn, classical music. General civil litigation, Construction. Office: 1404 S Jones Blvd Las Vegas NV 89146-1231

**LEFEBVRE, ALBERT PAUL CONRAD,** lawyer; b. Biddeford, Maine, Apr. 11, 1930; s. Leonide J. and Cesarine M. (Nadeau) L.; m. Celine Marguerite Therrien, Nov. 25, 1950; children: Albert Paul, Michelle Claire. BSL, Georgetown U., 1959; JD, George Washington U., 1967. Bar: D.C. 1969, Maine 1983. Various positions U.S. govt., Washington, 1955-82; pvt. practice Biddeford, 1983—; columnist Biddeford-Saco Courier, Biddeford, 1990—. Bd. dirs. York-Cumberland Assn. for Handicapped, Saco, Maine, 1984—; elected to Biddeford City Charter Revision Commn., 1986-89; chmn. Biddeford Rep. City Commn., 1991—; mem. Voters Registration Bd., Biddeford, 1991. With USAF, 1951-54, Korea. Mem. VFW (quartermaster 1986-92), Am. Legion (vice-commdr. 1990-92), Elks Club (trustee 1985), Lions Club, Assn. of Former Intelligence Officers. Republican. Avocations: public service, ethics, cut wood, walking, travel. General practice, Probate, Real property. Home and Office: 579 Sagamore Ave Unit 33 Portsmouth NH 03801-5569

**LEFEVRE, DAVID E.**, lawyer, professional sports team executive; b. Cleve., Oct. 25, 1944; s. Fay A. and Mary (Eaton) LeF. BA, Yale U., 1966; JD, U. Mich., 1971. Bar: N.Y., U.S. Dist. Ct. (so. and ea. dists.) N.Y. Assoc. Reid & Priest, N.Y.C., 1971-78, ptnr., 1979-92; owner Houston Astros Baseball Club, 1979-84, Cleve. Indians Baseball Club, 1984-86; dir. Tampa Bay Lightning, NHL; bd. dirs. TDC (USA), Inc., NHL Pension Soc.; chmn. bd. dirs. Chertsey Corp.; bd. govs. NHL, 1992—; bd. dirs. Fla. Sports Found., 1996—. Bd. dirs. Tampa Downtown Partnership; vol. Peace Corps, Uruguay, 1966-68. Recipient Spl. award Tampa Sports Club.; named Hon. Alumnus, Cleve. State U., 1985. Mem. ABA, Sports Lawyers Assn., Canyon Club (pres. Armonk, N.Y. 1986—), Alexis de Tocqueville Soc., Univ. Club of Tampa. General corporate, Entertainment, Private international. Also: 303 E 57th St New York NY 10022-2947

**LEFFLER, MICHAEL D.**, lawyer; b. Racine, Wis., May 25, 1963; s. Clark David and Joyce Elaine L.; m. Kathryn Lynne Leffler, AUg. 27, 1994; children: David Michael, Alyssa Marie. BS, Marquette U., 1985, JD, 1988. Bar: Wis. 1988. Atty. Capwell-Berthelsen, S.C., Racine, 1988-89, Daniel P. Kondos Law Offices, Milw., 1989—. Mem. ATLA, Wis. Acad. Trial Lawyers, Milw. Bar Assn. (mediation com. 1997-98), Marquette Club Milw. (bd. dirs.). Personal injury. Home: PO Box 17452 Milwaukee WI 53217-0452 Office: Danile P Kondos Law Offices 407 W Silver Spring Dr Milwaukee WI 53217-5048

**LEFKOWITZ, ALAN ZOEL**, lawyer; b. Pitts., Dec. 1, 1932; s. Curtis and Lily Rose Lefkowitz; m. Francine Marcia Kaplan, Feb. 5, 1956; children: Curtis Robert, Gail Ann, David Edward. AB, U. Pitts., 1953; JD, U. Mich., 1955. Bar: Pa. 1956, U.S. Supreme Ct. 1959, U.S. Ct. Appeals (3d cir.), U.S. Dist. Ct. (we. dist.) Pa., U.S. Tax Ct. Assoc. Kaplan, Finkel & Roth, Pitts., 1955-72; mng. ptnr. Kaplan, Finkel, Lefkowitz, Roth & Ostrow, Pitts., 1972-82, Finkel Lefkowitz Ostrow & Woolridge, Pitts., 1982-88; ptnr., head corp. sect. Tucker Arenberg, P.C., Pitts., 1988-93; dir. Kabala & Geeseman, Pitts., 1993-99; adj. prof. arts and law Heinz Sch. Pub. Policy and Adminstrn./ Carnegie Mellon Un.; sec. TPC Comm., Inc., Pitts., 1970-91, Computer Rsch., Inc., Pitts., 1969-92, Star-Tron Tech., Inc., Pitts., 1986-92. Mem. Pitts. Coun. Internat. Visitors; trustee United Jewish Fedn. Pitts., 1964-68, Rodef Shalom Congregation, Pitts., 1962-64, 90-98; bd. dirs., treas., v.p. Jewish Family and Childrens Svcs., Pitts., 1967-68; bd. dirs. Family Resources, 1986—, U.S. Counter-Intelligence Corp. With U.S. Army, 1956-59. Mem. ABA, Internat. Assn. Fin. Planners (Pitts. chpt. v.p. ethics regulation), Internat. Assn. Jewish Lawyers, Pa. Bar Assn., Allegheny County Bar Assn. (chair arts law sect., coun. corp. sec.), Photoimagers Guild, Acad. Arts and Scis. (photography sect., bd. dirs. 1994—), Silver Eye Ctr. for Photography (trustee, sec.). Avocations: photography, theatre. General corporate, Mergers and acquisitions, Securities. Office: Kabala & Geeseman The Waterfront 200 1st Ave Ste 4 Pittsburgh PA 15222-1575

**LEFKOWITZ, HOWARD N.**, lawyer; b. Utica, N.Y., Oct. 28, 1936; s. Samuel I. and Sarah Lefkowitz; m. Martha Yelon, June 16, 1958; children: Sarah, David. BA, Cornell U., 1958; LLB, Columbia U., 1963. Bar: N.Y. 1963. Ptnr. Proskauer Rose LLP, N.Y.C., 1963—; tri-bar opinion com., editl. subcom. Editor Columbia Law Rev., 1963; author: New York LLC and LLP Forms and Practice Manual, Data Trace, 3d edit. 1999; co-author: New York and Delaware Business Entities: Choice, Formation, Operation, Financing and Acquisitions West, 1997. Lt. (j.g.) USN, 1958-61. Kent scholar Columbia U. Law Sch. Fellow Am. Coll. Investment Counsel; mem. ABA (mem. ltd. liability entity subcom. of bus. sect. 1993—), Assn. of Bar of City of N.Y. (chmn. com. on corp. law 1990-93, com. on corp. law 1997—), N.Y. County Lawyers Assn. (chmn. com. on comm. entertainment and arts-related law 1983-86), Pvt. Investment Fund Forum (charter). Contracts commercial, General corporate. Office: Proskauer Rose LLP 1585 Broadway New York NY 10036-8200

**LEFKOWITZ, IVAN MARTIN**, lawyer; b. Winston-Salem, N.C., Jan. 4, 1952; s. Ernest W. and Matilda C. (Center) L.; m. Fern Deutsch, Apr. 14, 1972; children: Aaron M., Shira B. BBA, U. Cen. Fla., 1973; JD, U. Miami, 1979, LLM Estate Planning, 1980. Bar: Fla. 1979, U.S. Dist. Ct. (mid. dist.) 1980, U.S. Tax. Ct. 1980; CPA, Fla. Sr. acct. Alexander Grant & Co. CPA, Orlando, Fla., 1974-76; assoc. Gray, Harris & Robinson P.A., Orlando, 1980-82; pvt. practice, Orlando, 1982-88; ptnr. Lefkowitz & Miner, P.A., Orlando, 1988-93; sr. ptnr. Lefkowitz & Bloom, P.A., Orlando, 1993—; adj. prof. Am. Coll., Denver, 1984-90, Mgmt. Inst., U. Cen. Fla., Orlando, 1988—; sec., dir. Employee Benefits Coun. Fla., 1987-89, pres., 1990. Bd. dirs. U. Ctrl. Fla. Found., Orlando, 1981-96; bd. dirs., pres. Nat. Kidney Found. Ctrl. Fla., Orlando and Tampa, 1984-91; mem. governing bd. Princeton Hosp., Orlando, 1997-98. Mem. Ctrl. Fla. Estate Planning Coun., Holocaust Meml. Resource and Edn. Ctr. Ctrl. Fla. Democrat. Corporate taxation, Estate planning, Pension, profit-sharing, and employee benefits. Office: 430 N Mills Ave Orlando FL 32803-5746

**LEFKOWITZ, JEROME**, lawyer; b. N.Y.C., Mar. 24, 1931; s. Jack and Sue (Horowitz) L.; m. Myrna Judith Weishaut, Aug. 12, 1956; children: Jay, Mark, Miriam, Alan. Student, Jewish Theol. Sem., N.Y.C., 1948-51; BA, NYU, 1952; JD, Columbia U., 1955. Bar: N.Y. 1955, U.S. Dist. Ct. (so. and ea. dists.) N.Y. 1990. Asst. atty. gen. N.Y. State Dept. of Law, Albany, 1958-60; counsel, dep. commissioner N.Y. State Dept. of Labor, N.Y.C., Albany, 1960-67; dep. chmn., mem. N.Y. Pub. Rels. Bd., Albany, 1967-87; adj. faculty Albany Law Sch. Columbia U., N.Y.C., Albany, 1968-89; dep. counsel Civil Svc. Employment Assn., Albany, 1987—; cons. State of Mich., 1969, State of Hawaii, 1970, State of Pa., 1976, State of Mass., 1978. Author: Public Employee Unionism In Israel, 1971; editor: Public Sector Labor & Employment Law, 1988, 2d edit., 1998, The Evolving Process--Collective Negotiations In Public Employment, 1985. Chmn. community rels. com. Albany Jewish Fedn., 1980-84, 86-87; pres. Massad Hebrew Speaking Camps. Mem. N.Y. State Bar Assn. (chmn. com. on pub. sector labor rels. 1975-79, chmn. com. on legis. 1980-83, chmn. labor law sect. 1991-92). Republican. Avocations: tennis, skiing, reading, history. Home: 54 Maxwell St Albany NY 12208-1639 Office: Civil Svc Employment Assn 143 Washington Ave Albany NY 12210-2303

**LEFTWICH, JAMES ASBURY, JR.**, lawyer, entrepreneur; b. Chesapeake, Va., Dec. 11, 1962; s. James Asbury and Eleaner (Otto) L.; m. Renee Doreen Frey, Sept. 11, 1993; children: Logan Alexander, Austin Reid. BS, James Madison U., 1985; JD, U. Richmond, 1988. Bar: Va. 1988, U.S. Dist. Ct. 1988, U.S. Bankruptcy Ct. 1988. Assoc. atty. Basnight, Creekmore, Wright, Jones, Kinser and successors, Chesapeake, Va., 1988-95; ptnr. Basnight, Kinser & Leftwich, P.C., Chesapeake, 1996—. Bd. dirs. Chesapeake Care Free Clinic, 1995—, Am. Cancer Soc., Chesapeake/Portsmouth, Va., 1994-98; mem. Va. Inst. Polit. Leadership at U. Va., 1996—. Mem. Chesapeake Bar Assn. (pres. 1999), Va. Bar Assn., Hampton Roads Family Law Assn., Great Bridge Jaycees (pres. 1992), Deep Creek Ruritan Club (sec. 1997, treas. 1998, v.p. 1999). Avocations: family, tennis, golf. Health, Family and matrimonial. Office: Basnight Kinser & Leftwich 308 Cedar Lakes Dr Chesapeake VA 23322-8343

**LEGER, WALTER JOHN, JR.**, lawyer; b. New Orleans, Nov. 11, 1951; s. Walter John Sr. and Mildred Veronica (Brown) L.; m. Catherine Ann Buras, Aug. 4, 1973; children: Walter John III, Rhett Michael, Elizabeth Catherine. BA, La. State U., 1973; JD, Tulane U., 1976. Bar: La. 1976, U.S. Dist. Ct. (ea. dist.) La. 1976, U.S. Dist. Ct. (ea. dist.) La. 1976, U.S. Dist. Ct. (we. dist.) La. 1978, U.S. Ct. Appeals (5th and 11th cirs.) 1981, U.S. Supreme Ct. 1981, U.S. Dist. Ct. (mid. dist.) La. 1989. Assoc. Phelps, Dunbar, Marks, Claverie & Smith, New Orleans, 1976-78; ptnr. George & George, New Orleans, 1978-79; sr. ptnr. Leger & Mestayer, New Orleans, 1979—; pres. CBL Barge Co., 1979—; lectr. law Tulane U. 1983-85, U. New Orleans, Para-Legal Inst., 1987-88; adv. bd. dirs. First Nat. Bank of St. Bernard, Chalmette, La.; bd. dirs. Bergeron Marine Svc., Inc., New Orleans, Ryan Marine, Inc., Pearlington, Miss. Chmn. March of Dimes, Met. New Orleans and Southeastern La., 1980-84; adv. com. bd. commrs. Port of New Orleans, 1986-88; bd. dirs. St. Bernard Community Coll. Found., Chalmette, La., 1986-92; bd. dirs., vice chmn. Nunez Community Coll., Chalmette, 1992—; adv. counsel St. Bernard Parish Home Rule Charter Commn., 1988, econ. devel. commn., 1989—, pers. bd., 1990—, chmn. Appointments Rev. Bd; Disting. fellow Govt. Leadership Inst., U. New Orleans. Named one of People to Watch in 1982 New Orleans Mag., 1982. Mem. ABA, Fed. Bar Assn., Assn. Trial Lawyers Am., La. Trial Lawyers Assn. (pres.'s adv. council 1982-88, bd. govs. 1988—, exec. com. 1991—), Miss. Trial Lawyers Assn., Maritime Law Assn., Southeastern Admiralty Law Inst., La. State U. Fedn. (pres.-elect St. Bernard chpt. 1986-87), St. Bernard Council C. of C. (chmn. 1986, 92—), New Orleans/River Region C. of C. (bd. dirs. 1986—, vice-chmn. bd. dirs. 1987-88), Omicron Delta Kappa. Democrat. Roman Catholic. Avocations: jogging, sailing, tennis. Admiralty, Personal injury, Federal civil litigation. Home: 20 Carolyn Ct Arabi LA 70032-1955 Office: Leger & Mestayer 600 Carondelet St New Orleans LA 70130-3511

**LEGG, BENSON EVERETT**, federal judge; b. Balt., June 8, 1947; s. William Mercer Legg and Beverly Mason; m. Kyle Prechtl Legg; children: Jennifer, Charles, Matthew. AB magna cum laude, Princeton U., 1970; JD, U. Va., 1973. Bar: Md. 1973. Law clk. to Hon. Frank A. Kaufman, Balt., 1973-74; assoc. Venable, Baetjer & Howard, Balt., 1975-81, ptnr., 1982-91; judge U.S. Dist. Ct., Dist. Md., Balt., 1991—; spl. reporter appeals com. and standing com. on rules of practice and procedure Ct. Appeals Md., 1983-85; faculty mem. nine day intensive trial advocacy program Md. Inst. Continuing Profl. Edn. for Lawyers, Inc., 1987, program on appellate advocacy, 1988; lectr. and panelist in field. Mem. editl. bd. Va. Law Rev., 1973-74; contbr. articles to profl. jours. Bd. dirs. Ctrl. Md. chpt. ARC, 1979-88, past chpt. gen. counsel; mem. adv. bd. Nat. Aquarium in Balt., 1987—; trustee Balt. Zoo. Mem. ABA (bus. torts litigation com. 1987), Md. State Bar Assn., Inc. (chmn. econs. of litigation com. 1981-82), Bar Assn. Balt. City (vice chmn. CLE com. 1986-87, chmn. 1987-88, exec. coun. 1987-88, judiciary com. 1989-90), The Serjeant's Inn Law Club, Order of Coif. Office: US Dist Ct 101 W Lombard St Ste 340 Baltimore MD 21201-2605

**LEGG, MICHAEL WILLIAM**, lawyer, executive recruiter; b. Detroit, Sept. 1, 1952; s. Howard Wesley and Mary Elizabeth (Lucas) L. AA, Oakland Community Coll., 1972; BS, U. Detroit, 1975; JD, Mich. State U., 1979. Bar: Mich. 1980, U.S. Ct. Appeals (6th cir.) 1991, U.S. Supreme Ct. 1986. Assoc. Berry, Hopson, Francis, Mack and Seifman, Detroit, 1980-82; corp. counsel Compuware Corp., Birmingham, Mich., 1982-85, product mgr. law systems div., 1985-89, sr. cons. law office mgmt. adv. svcs. group, 1989-90; pvt. practice law, 1991-92; sales, acct. mgr. Compuware Corp., Farmington, 1992-94, mgr. of spl. projects, corp. recruiting, 1994—; adj. prof. bus. economics, Walsh Coll., Troy, Mich., 1992—. Rep. dist. chmn., Mich., 1983-88, presdl. elector, 1984, nat. conv. del., 1984, 88; bd. dirs. Wayne County Neighborhood Legal Services, 1987-89, Mich. Youth in Govt., 1985-86, Sixty-Plus Legal Clinic, 1985-86; mem. Blue Ribbon Citizens Task Force Wayne County, 1986-87, Oakland County Exec.'s Spl. Privatization Commn., 1986; mem. bd. canvassers Clarenceville Sch. Bd., 1985. Mem. ABA (dist. rep. Young Lawyers div. 1980-91), Mich. Bar Assn. (commr. 1985-87, 91-94, chmn. Young Lawyers sect. 1985-86, chair Rep. Assembly, chair 1993-94), Livonia Bar Assn. (pres. 1985-86). Mem. Ch. of Christ. Computer, General corporate. Home: 21714 Roosevelt Ave Farmington Hills MI 48336-4943 Office: Compuware Corp 31440 Northwestern Hwy Farmington MI 48334-2564

**LEGG, REAGAN HOUSTON**, lawyer; b. Kaufman, Tex., Nov. 18, 1924; s. Edward and Mary Alta (Coon) L.; m. Norma Jean Eden, July 16, 1949 (div. 1976); children: John, Ellen, Emily, Reagan Houston. BBA, U. Tex., Austin, 1947, LLB, 1948. Bar: Tex. 1948, U.S. Dist. Ct. (we. dist.) Tex. 1951, U.S. Dist. Ct. (no. dist.) Tex. 1957, U.S. Ct. Appeals (5th cir.) 1960, U.S. Supreme Ct. 1961. County atty. Midland County, Tex., 1951-55; ptnr. Legg, Saxe & Baskin, Midland, Tex., 1955-79, Legg, Aldridge & Carr, Midland, 1980-84; pvt. practice law Midland, 1984-89, Kaufman, Tex., 1989—. Trustee Midland Coll., 1971-86, pres bd., 1972-75; bd. dirs. Permian Basin Regional Planning Commn., 1977-86; pres. Leadership Midland, 1978-80, Tex. C.C. Trustees and Adminstrs., 1980-81, Nat. Assn. C.C. Trustees, 1982-83. With USN, 1942-46. Named Boss of Yr., Midland Legal Secs. Assn., 1969; recipient M. Dale Ensign Leadership award Assn. C.C. Trustees, 1977. Fellow Tex. Bar Found.; mem. ABA, Tex. Bar Assn. (chmn. com. group legal svcs. 1968-74), Midland C. of C. (bd. dirs. 1968-73, 78-81), Midland County Bar Assn. (pres. 1967-68), Kaufman C. of C. (bd. dirs. 1993-99), Cedar Creek Country Club, Masons. Democrat. Methodist. Federal civil litigation, State civil litigation, General corporate. Office: PO Box 227 Kaufman TX 75142-0227

**LEGG, WILLIAM JEFFERSON**, lawyer; b. Enid, Okla., Aug. 20, 1925; s. Garl Paul and Mabel (Gensman) L.; m. Eva Imogene Hill, Dec. 16, 1950; children: Melissa Lou, Eva Diane, Janet Sue. Grad., Enid Bus. Coll., 1943; student, Pittsburg State U., 1944; BBA, U. Tex., Austin, 1946; JD, U. Tulsa, 1954. Bar: Okla. 1954, U.S. Supreme Ct., U.S. Ct. Appeals (10th cir.), U.S. Dist. Ct. (we. dist.) Okla. With aviation sales Phillips Petroleum Co., 1946-48; atty. Marathon Oil Co., 1954-61; pvt. practice Oklahoma City, 1962—; ptnr. Andrews Davis Legg Bixler Milsten & Price, Inc. and predecessor firms, Oklahoma City, 1962—, pres., 83-86, also dir., 1973-77, 80-81, 83-86, 90, sec., 1975-80, 82-83, 90; sr. counsel, 1991—; adj. prof. law Oklahoma City U., 1975-80; lectr. Okla. U. Law Sch., 1986; bd. dirs., v.p. internat. oil cos., Turkey, Australia, Brunei, 1967-82; bd. dirs., gen. counsel N.J. Natural Resources Co., 1986-91; bd. dirs. Skillpath Seminars, Kansas City, Mo., 1994-98; lectr. energy seminars; rsch. fellow Southwestern Legal Found., Dallas, 1989—, mem. CLE adv. bd., 1998—. Contbr. articles to profl. jours. Ordained Reorganized Ch. of Jesus Christ of Latter Day Saints, 1964, dist. pres., 1975-80, br. pres., 1986-91, evangelist, 1993—; mem. legal com. Okla. Gov.'s Energy Adv. Coun., 1973, Okla. Blue Ribbon Com. on natural gas well allowables, 1983; trustee Am. Inst. Discussion, 1962-88, chmn., 1969-72, now mem. exec. com., counsel; trustee Jenkins Found. Rsch., sec., 1975-81; trustee Restoration Trails Found., 1975; trustee Graceland Coll., Lamoni, Iowa, 1986—, mem. exec. com., chmn. bus. affairs com., 1988-98, mem. investment com., 1998—; trustee Met. Lib. Endowment Trust, 1986-99, treas. 1988-99, chmn. investment com. With USN, 1943-46, lt. (j.g.) USNR, 1946-66. Mem. ABA, Okla. Bar Assn. (past com. chmn.), Oklahoma County Bar Assn. (past com. chmn.), Internat. Assn. Energy Econs., Econ. Club Okla., Men's Dinner Club, Petroleum Club. Oil, gas, and mineral, Administrative and regulatory, State and local taxation. Home: 3017 Brush Creek Rd Oklahoma City OK 73120-1855 Office: Andrews Davis Legg Bixler Milsten & Price Inc 500 W Main St Ste 500 Oklahoma City OK 73102-2275

**LEGLER, MITCHELL WOOTEN**, lawyer; b. Alexandria, Va., June 3, 1942; s. John Clarke and Doris (Wooten) L.; m. Harriette Dodson; children: John Clarke, Dorothy Trumbull, Harriette Holland. BA in Polit. Sci. with honors, U. N.C., 1964; JD, U. Va., 1967. Bar: Va. 1967, Fla. 1967. Pres. Commander, Legler, Werber, Dawes, Sadler & Howell, Jacksonville, Fla., 1976-91; mng. ptnr. Foley & Lardner, Jacksonville, 1991-95; chmn. Fla. Bar Consumer Protection Law Com. Editorial bd. Va. Law Rev., 1966-67. Mem. Va. Bar Assn., Fla. Bar Assn. (lectr. continuing legal edn.), Order of Coif, Phi Beta Kappa, Phi Eta Sigma, Delta Upsilon, Delta Theta Phi. Bankruptcy, Contracts commercial, General corporate. Office: 300A Wharfside Way Jacksonville FL 32207-8153

**LEH, CHRISTOPHER MARSHALL**, lawyer; b. Boulder, Colo., Aug. 28, 1962; s. James and Ann Leh; m. Natalie Hanlon; children: Madeline, Eleanor. AB, Princeton U., 1985; JD, NYU, 1989. Bar: Colo. 1989; U.S. Dist. Ct. Colo. 1990, U.S. Dist Ct. (13th) Colo., 1989; U.S. Ct. Appeals (10th cir.) 1991, U.S. Ct. Appeals (9th cir.) 1995. Law clk. to Hon. Alfred A. Arraj U.S. Dist. Ct. Colo., Denver, 1989-90; assoc. Davis, Graham & Stubbs LLC, Denver, 1990-95; assoc. Caplan and Earnest LLC, Boulder, Colo., 1995-98, mem., 1999—. Contbr. to profl. jours. Recipient Deak award Am. Soc. Internat. Law, 1989, JILP award NYU Jour. of Internat. Law & Politics, 1989. Mem. ABA, Colo. Bar Assn., Denver Bar Assn.,Boulder County Bar Assn. (employment law sect. chair 1996-98), Faculty of Federal Advocates, 13th Jud. Dist. Bar Assn. Presbyterian. Labor, Federal civil litigation, State civil litigation. Office: Caplan and Earnest LLC 2595 Canyon Blvd Ste 400 Boulder CO 80302-6737

**LEHAN, JONATHAN MICHAEL**, judge; b. Los Angeles, Apr. 25, 1947; s. Bert Leon and Frances (Shapiro) L.; m. Annett Jean Garrett, Aug. 1, 1970; children: Joshua Michael, Melanie Janine. BA, Calif. State U., Fullerton, 1968; JD, Calif. Western Sch. Law, 1971. Bar: Calif. 1972, U.S. Dist. Ct. (no. dist.) Calif. 1973, U.S. Supreme Ct. 1975. Law clk. to presiding and assoc. justice Calif. Dist. Ct. Appeals, San Bernardino, 1971-73; dep. dist. atty. Mendocino County, Ukiah, Calif., 1973-76; coast asst. dist. atty. Mendocino County, Fort Bragg, Calif., 1976-83; sole pratice Fort Bragg, 1983-84; ptnr. Lehan & Kronfeld, Fort Bragg, 1984-90; judge Mendocino County Superior Ct., Ft. Bragg, 1990—; instr. Barstow C.C., Calif., 1972, Mendocino C.C., Ukiah, 1974-75, Coll. Redwoods, Ft. Bragg, 1981-82; seminar faculty Calif. Jud. Coll., U. Calif., Berkeley, 1993; faculty Calif. Judges Assn. Mid-Year Conf., 1998; contbr. Calif. Drunk Driving Law, Kuwatch, 1995. Bd. dirs. Salmon Restoration Assn., Fort Bragg, Gloriana Opera Co., Mendocino, Mendocino Art Ctr. Editor Calif. Western Sch. Law Law Rev., 1971. Mem. ABA, Mendocino County Bar Assn. (pres. 1989), Phi Delta Phi, Mendocino C. of C. (bd. dirs.). Democrat. Avocations: violinist, violist, Mendocino string quartet. Office: Mendocino Superior Ct 700 S Franklin St Fort Bragg CA 95437-5464

**LEHMAN, JEFFREY SEAN**, dean, law educator; b. Bronxville, N.Y., Aug. 1, 1956; s. Leonard and Imogene (McAuliffe) L.; m. Diane Celeste Becker, May 20, 1979; children: Rebecca Colleen, Jacob Keegan, Benjamin Emil. AB, Cornell U., 1977; M of Pub. Policy, U. Mich., 1981, JD, 1981. Bar: D.C. 1983, U.S. Ct. Appeals (fed. cir.) 1984, U.S. Ct. Appeals (D.C. cir.) 1987, U.S. Supreme Ct. 1987. Law clk. to chief judge U.S. Ct. Appeals (1st cir.), Portland, Maine, 1981-82; law clk. to assoc. justice U.S. Supreme Ct., Washington, 1982-83; assoc. Caplin & Drysdale, Chartered, Washington, 1983-87; asst. prof. U. Mich. Law Sch., Ann Arbor, 1987-92, prof., 1992-93, prof. law and pub. policy, 1993—, dean, 1994—; vis. prof. Yale U., 1993, U. Paris II, 1994. Co-author: Corporate Income Taxation, 1994; editor-in-chief: Mich. Law Rev., 1979-80. Foster parent Arlington County Dept. Human Svcs., 1983-87; trustee Skadden Fellowship Found., 1995—. Henry Bates fellow, 1981. Mem. ABA, Am. Law Inst., Order of Coif. Democrat. Jewish. Office: U Mich Law Sch 324 Hutchins Hall Ann Arbor MI 48109

**LEHMAN, KENNETH WILLIAM**, lawyer; b. N.Y.C., Dec. 4, 1956. Student, City of London Poly., 1977; AB summa cum laude, Hamilton Coll., 1978; JD, U. Va., 1981. Bar: N.Y. 1982, U.S. Dist. Ct. (we. dist.) N.Y. 1982, Maine 1986, U.S. Dist. Ct. Maine 1986. Assoc. Nixon, Hargrave, Devans & Doyle, Rochester, N.Y., 1981-85; asst. atty. gen. Maine Dept. of Atty. Gen., Augusta, Maine, 1986-92; ptnr. Bernstein, Shur, Sawyer & Nelson, Portland, Maine, 1992—; vis. instr. Univ. New England Coll. Osteopathic Med., Biddeford, Maine, 1991—. Bd. dir. Congregation Bet Ha'am, Portland, 1987—, Cerebral Palsy Assn. Greater Portland, 1992-94, Am. Lung Assn. of Maine, Augusta, 1993-99. Recipient Cert. of Award Maine Citizens Against Sexual Abuse, 1990. Mem. Maine State Bar Assn., Maine Bar Found. (fellow, dir. 1990-96, 97—), Maine Vol. Lawyer's Project (chair 1990—), Phi Beta Kappa. Health, General civil litigation, Administrative and regulatory. Home: 28 Newell Ridge Rd Cumberlnd Center ME 04021-9349 Office: Bernstein Shur Sawyer & Nelson PO Box 9729 Portland ME 04104-5029

**LEHMAN, LARRY L.**, state supreme court justice. Judge Wyo. County Ct., 1985-88, Wyo. Dist. Ct. (2nd dist.), 1988-94; justice Wyo. Supreme Ct., Cheyenne, 1994-98, chief justice, 1998—. Office: Supreme Court Bldg Cheyenne WY 82002-0001*

**LEHMAN, LEONARD**, lawyer, consultant; b. Bklyn, July 5, 1927; s. Samuel and Marcy (Dolgenas) L.; m. Imogene McAuliffe, June 11, 1954; children—Jeffrey, Toby, Amy, Zachary. B.A., Cornell U., 1949; J.D., Yale U., 1952. Bar: N.Y. 1953, U.S. Supreme Ct. 1969, D.C. 1979, U.S. Ct. Internat. Trade 1981, U.S. Ct. Appeals (fed. cir.) 1982. Atty.-advisor U.S. Tax Ct., Washington, 1952-55; sole practice, N.Y.C., 1955-63; sr. counsel Office Tax Legis. Counsel, U.S. Dept. Treasury, Washington, 1963-65; asst. to chief counsel U.S. Customs Service, 1965-67, dep. chief counsel, 1968-71, asst. commr. 1971-79; ptnr. Barnes, Richardson and Colburn, N.Y.C., Washington and Chgo., 1979-89, counsel, 1989-95; mem. industry functional adv. com. on customs/trade policy U.S. Dept. Commerce, 1989-95. Recipient U.S. Treasury Meritorious Service award, 1971, Exceptional Service award, 1979; U.S. Customs Honor award, 1977. Mem. ABA (standing com. on customs law 1974-80, chmn. 1980, customs and tariff com., adminstrv. law sect. 1971-88, vice chmn. 1981-83, chmn. 1984-88), Phi Beta Kappa, Phi Kappa Phi. Contbr. articles to profl. jours. Private international, Immigration, naturalization, and customs, Administrative and regulatory. Home and Office: 18 Rich Branch Ct North Potomac MD 20878-2461

**LEHMAN, RICHARD LEROY**, lawyer; b. Johnstown, Pa., Feb. 4, 1930; s. John S. and Deliah E. (Chase) L.; m. Lucia M. Ragnone; children: Ann Laurie, Leslie Ann, Lucia Marie. AB in Social Work, U. Ky., 1957; LLB, U. Detroit, 1960. Bar: Mich. 1961, U.S. Dist. Ct. (ea. dist.) Mich. 1961, U.S. Ct. Appeals (6th cir.) 1961. Pvt. practice Detroit; ptnr. Garan, Lucow, Miller, Lehman, Seward & Cooper, 1961-79; pres. Home Bldg. Plan Svc., Inc., Portland, Oreg., 1979-82; pres., gen. counsel Matvest Inc., Farmington Hills, Mich., 1980-86; pres. Xi Industries, Flint, Mich., 1982-86; ptnr. Lehman & Valentino, P.C., Bloomfield Hills, Mich., 1986—; pres. Premiere Packaging, Inc., Flint, 1987-91, chmn., CEO, 1990-98; vis. lectr. U. Detroit Law Sch., 1970-74, also Inst. Continuing Legal Edn. Mem. exec. com. pres.'s cabinet U. Detroit, 1975-79; mem. Old Newsboys Goodfellow Fund Detroit, 1966—, bd. dirs., 1975-78. 1st lt. AUS, 1947-53. Recipient Algernon Sydney Sullivan Medallion U. Ky., 1957; fellow U. Ky. Mem. Mich. Bar Assn., Genesee County Bar Assn. (mem. bench and bar com. 1975-78), U. Ky. Alumni Assn., U. Detroit Law Sch. Alumni Assn. (dir. 1970-77, pres. 1974-75), U. Detroit Alumni Assn., 6th Cir. Jud. Conf. (life), Pine Lake Country Club (bd. dirs. 1991-96, pres. 1994-95), K.C., Am. Legion, VFW. Roman Catholic. Avocations: golf, downhill skiing, carpentry. General civil litigation, Personal injury, Insurance. Home: 4052 Waterwheel Ln Bloomfield Hills MI 48302-1870 Office: Lehman & Valentino PC 1411 S Woodward Ave Bloomfield Hills MI 48302-0546

**LEHOUILLIER, PATRIC JAYMES**, lawyer; b. San Diego, Feb. 8, 1948; s. Leo Clarence and Barbara (Selacek) LeH.; m. Alice Honey, May 28, 1966 (div. May 1986); children: Frank Dean, Joel Patrick. Student, San Diego State Coll., 1973-74; JD, Syracuse U., 1974. Bar: N.Y. 1975, U.S. Dist. Ct. (so. and ea. dists.) N.Y. 1975, U.S. Ct. Appeals (2d cir.) 1975, Colo. 1977, U.S. Dist. Ct. Colo. 1977, U.S. Ct. Appeals (10th cir.) 1977, U.S. Supreme Ct. 1985. Spl. asst. atty. gen. Office of State Prosecutor, N.Y.C., 1974-76; dep. dist. atty. 10th Jud. Dist., Pueblo, Colo., 1976-77; ptnr. Barash & LeHouillier now called LeHouillier, Erler & Nolan, Colorado Springs, Colo., 1978—; bd. dirs. Pikes Peak Legal Service, Colorado Springs, 1981-86; lectr. legal seminars. Contbr. articles to law jours. Bd. dirs. Urban League Pikes Peak Region, Colorado Springs, 1980—, Pikes Peak area campfire, Colorado Springs, 1984—; chmn. El Paso City Dem. Party, Colorado Springs, 1985-87. Mem. ABA, Assn. Trial Lawyers Am., Colo. Bar Assn., Colo. Trial Lawyers Assn., Order of Coif. Democrat. Roman Catholic. Avocations: marathon running, bicycling. State civil litigation, Federal civil litigation, Personal injury. Office: LeHouillier Erler & Nolan 90 S Cascade Ave Ste 1430 Colorado Springs CO 80903-1680

**LEHR, DENNIS JAMES**, lawyer; b. N.Y.C., Feb. 7, 1932; s. Irwin Allen and Teeny (Scofield) L.; m. Enid J. Auerbach, June 10, 1956; children—Austin Windsor, Bryant Paul, Amy Lynn. BA, NYU, 1954, LLM, 1961; LLB, Yale U., 1957. Bar: N.Y. 1959, D.C. 1967. Atty. Allstate Ins. Co., N.Y.C., 1958-59; atty. Regional Office SEC, N.Y.C., 1959-61; assoc. Borden and Ball, N.Y.C., 1961-63; atty. Office Spl Counsel Investment Co. Act Matters SEC, Washington, 1963-64; assoc. chief counsel Office Comptroller Currency U.S. Treasury Dept., Washington, 1964-67; assoc. Hogan & Hartson, Washington, 1967-69, ptnr., 1969-94, of counsel, 1994—; bd. advs. So. Meth. U. Grad. Sch. Banking; adj. prof. Georgetown Law Sch., 1964-68; legal adv. com. Nat. Ctr. on Fin. Svcs., U. Calif.; lectr. Practicing Law Inst.; adv. coun. Banking Law Inst.; pub. mem. Adminstrv. Conf. of the U.S. Bd. contbrs. Fin. Services Law Report. Contbr. articles to profl. jours. Mem. ABA (coun. mem. sect. bus. law, former chmn. com. on Long Range Issues Affecting Bus. Law Practice, former chmn., com. on devels. in investment svcs.). Banking, Finance, Securities. Office: Hogan and Hartson 555 13th St NW Ste 800E Washington DC 20004-1161

**LEHRER, JULIUS MARSHALL**, lawyer; b. Chgo., Feb. 7, 1921; s. Charles I. and Etta (Zuckerman) L.; m. Dorothy Levitan, Mar. 16, 1968. BA, U. Chgo., 1942, JD, 1948. Pvt. practice Chgo., 1948—. Pres.

Adolf Kraus B'nai B'rith, Chgo. With U.S. Army, 1943-47. Mem. Chgo. Bar Assn. (chmn. lawyer referral 1990), Am. Legion (sr. vice comdr. Highland Park, Ill. unit 1990-91). Probate, Family and matrimonial. Office: 205 W Randolph St Ste 2222 Chicago IL 60606-1814

**LEIBEL, STEVEN K.,** lawyer; b. N.Y.C., Sept. 21, 1956; s. Bernard and Sylvia (Zavder) L.; m. Julie Oberdorfer, May 16, 1987; children: Lauren Molly, Michelle, Jonathan. BA, Queens Coll., 1977; JD, Emory Law Sch., 1980. Police Officers Standards and Tng. certification, 1986. Trial atty. Nat. Labor Rels. Bd., Atlanta, 1980-86; pvt. practice Atlanta, 1987—; host WGST Radio, Atlanta, 1988-90. V.p. B'nai B'rith Gate City Lodge, Atlanta, 1985-90; police officer Gwinnett County Sheriff's Dept., Atlanta, 1986-89; pres. Home Pk. Bus. Assn., Atlanta, 1989-90; mem. Leadership Sandy Springs, Atlanta, 1989-90; reserve police officer Duluth Police Dept., 1990—. Mem. ABA, Atlanta Bar Assn., Atlanta Lawyers Club, Sandy Springs C. of C., Masonic Lodge (Mableton, Ga.), Ga. Trial Lawyers Assn. Republican. Avocations: skiing, swimming. Office: PO Box 93506 Atlanta GA 30377-0506

**LEIBOLD, ARTHUR WILLIAM, JR.,** lawyer; b. Ottawa, Ill., June 13, 1931; s. Arthur William and Helen (Cull) L.; m. Nora Collins, Nov. 30, 1957; children: Arthur William III, Alison Aubry, Peter Collins. AB, Haverford Coll., 1953; JD, U. Pa., 1956. Bar: Pa. 1957. With Dechert, Price & Rhoads, Phila., 1956-69, ptnr., 1965-69; ptnr. Dechert, Price & Rhoads, Washington, 1972-97; gen. counsel Fed. Home Loan Bank Bd. and Fed. Savs. & Loan Ins. Corp., Washington, 1969-72, Fed. Home Loan Mortgage Corp., 1970-72; lectr. English St. Joseph's Coll., Phila., 1957-59. Contbr. articles to profl. publs. Mem. Pres. Kennedy's Lawyers Com. Civil Rights, 1963, Adminstrv. Conf. U.S., 1969-72; bd. dirs. Marymount Coll. Va., 1974-75; Mem. Phila. Com. 70, 1965-74, Fellowship Commn. Mem. ABA (mem. ho. dels. 1967-69, 79-88, treas. 1979-83, mem. fin. com., mem. bd. govs. 1977-83), Fed. Bar Assn. (mem. nat. coun. 1971-80), D.C. Bar Assn., Phila. Bar Assn., Am. Bar Found. (treas. 1979-83), Am. Bar Ret. Assn. (dir. 1978-83), Am. Bar Endowment (bd. dirs. 1984-97, pres. 1995-97), Internat. Bar Assn., Phila. Country Club (Gladwyne, Pa.), Chester River Yacht & Country Club (Chestertown, Md.), Skating Club Phila., Orpheus Club (Phila.), Order of the Coif, Phi Beta Kappa. Republican. Roman Catholic. Administrative and regulatory, Banking. Home: 900 N Randolph St Apt 727 Arlington VA 22203-4068 Office: Dechert Price & Rhoads 1775 Eye St NW Ste 1100 Washington DC 20006-2402

**LEIBOW, RONALD LOUIS,** lawyer; b. Santa Monica, Calif., Oct. 4, 1939; s. Norman and Jessica (Kellner) L.; m. Linda Bengelsdorf, June 11, 1961 (div. Dec. 1974); children: Jocelyn Elise, Jeffrey David, Joshua Aaron; m. Jacqueline Blatt, Apr. 6, 1986. AB, Calif. State U., Northridge, 1962; JD, UCLA, 1965. Bar: Calif. 1966, U.S. Dist. Ct. (cen. dist.) Calif. 1966, U.S. Dist. Ct. (no., so. and ea. dists.) Calif. 1971. Spl. asst. city atty. City of Burbank, Calif., 1966-67; from assoc. to ptnr. Meyers, Stevens & Walters, L.A., 1967-71; ptnr. Karpf, Leibow & Warner, Beverly Hills, Calif., 1971-74, Volk, Newman Gralla & Karp, L.A., L.A., 1979-81, Spector & Leibow, L.A., 1982-84, Stroock & Stroock & Lavan, L.A., 1984-94; ptnr. Kaye, Scholer, Fierman, Hays & Handler, L.A., 1994-97, mng. ptnr., 1996, 97; lectr. law UCLA, 1968-69; asst. prof. Calif. State U., Northridge, 1969-71. Contbr. articles to profl. jours. Pres. Jewish Cmty. Ctr., Greater L.A., 1983-86; v.p. Jewish Cmty. Ctr. Assn. N.Am., N.Y.C., 1988—; v.p. Jewish Fedn. Cmty., Greater L.A., 1988—, chair planning and allocations com., 1998—. Mem. ABA (bus. bankruptcy com.), Phi Alpha Delta. Avocations: writing, tennis, skiing, travel. Bankruptcy, Contracts commercial, Finance. Office: Kaye Scholer Fierman Hays & Handler 1999 Avenue Of The Stars Fl 16 Los Angeles CA 90067-6022

**LEIBOWITT, SOL DAVID,** lawyer; b. Bklyn., Feb. 18, 1912; s. Morris and Bella (Small) L.; BA, Lehigh U., 1933; LLB, Harvard U., 1936; m. Ethel Leibowitt, June 18, 1950 (dec. Aug. 1985); m. Babs Lee Dec. 28, 1986. Bar: N.Y. 1937, Conn. 1970. Pvt. practice, N.Y.C., 1937-84, Stamford, Conn., 1970-78, Milford, Conn., 1978-79; gen. counsel New Haven Clock and Watch Co., 1955-59, pres., 1958-59; pres. Diagnon Corp., 1981-83, vice chmn., 1983-86; chmn. Card Tech. Corp., 1983-85; dir. Data Card Internat. Corp., Hevant, Eng., 1977-79. Pres. Ethel and David Leibowitt Found.; dir. Am. Com. for Weizmann Inst. Sci.; mediator family law Supreme Ct. State Fla. 15th Jud. Ct., 1990—; arbitrator Am. Arbitration Assn., Fla.; chmn. Israel Cancer Assn. USA; dir. Am. Assocs., Ben-Gurion U., 1999. Recipient Human Relations award Anti-Defamation League, 1969, Ethel Leibowitt Fund Johns Hopkins U. Sch. Medicine, Meml. award Anti-Defamation League, 1971, Tikvah award Israel Cancer Assn., 1995. Mem. ABA, Assn. Bar N.Y.C., N.Y. State bar Assn, Anti-Defamation League (commr.), Am. Soc. for Technion U. (mem. bd., v.p., Conn. pres.), Lotos Club, Harvard Club (N.Y.C.), Banyon Country Club (West Palm Beach, Fla.). General corporate.

**LEIBOWITZ, MARK A.,** lawyer; b. N.Y.C., Jan. 22, 1950; s. Philip and Muriel Shirley Leibowitz; m. Cara Nusinov, July 27, 1974; children: Joan, Jonathan. BA, Syracuse U., 1972; JD, U. Miami, 1975. Bar: Fla. 1975, U.S. Dist. Ct. (so. dist.) Fla. 1976, Colo. 1994. Lawyer Wolfson & Diamond, Miami Beach, Fla., 1976-82, Wolpe & Leibowitz, Miami, Fla., 1982—. Mem. Fla. Bar Assn. (evaluation com. 1995—), Dade County Bar Assn. (com. on professionalism 1997—). Avocations: skiing, hiking, golf. Personal injury, Professional liability, State civil litigation. Office: Wolpe & Leibowitz LLP 19 W Flagler St Ste 320 Miami FL 33130-4400

**LEIBOWITZ, MARVIN,** lawyer; b. Phila., Jan. 24, 1950; s. Aaron and Etheln (Kashoff) L.; m. Faye Rebecca Liepack, Nov. 12, 1983; children: Cheryl Renée, Ellen Paulette. BA, Temple U., 1971, postgrad., 1971-72; JD, Widener U., 1976. Bar: Pa. 1977, N.J. 1977, U.S. Dist. Ct. N.J. 1977, U.S. Dist. Ct. (we. dist.) Pa. 1980. Atty.-advisor SSA, Pitts., 1977-95, sr. atty., 1995—; quality assurance reviewer Office of Program and Integrity Revs., 1997; pvt. practice Pitts., 1979—. Committeeman Phila. Dem. Com., 1973-77. Pa. State Scholar Pa. Higher Edn. Assistance Agy., Harrisburg, 1967-71; recipient U.S. Dept. Health and Human Svcs. citation, 1994. Mem. Nat. Treasury Employees Union (regional steward 1982—), Pa. Bar Assn., Allegheny County Bar Assn. Democrat. Jewish. Administrative and regulatory, Bankruptcy, Workers' compensation. Home: 6501 Landview St Pittsburgh PA 15217-3000

**LEIBOWITZ, NADINE S.,** lawyer; b. Bklyn., Dec. 26, 1969; d. Mel and Frieda Leibowitz. BSBA cum laude, SUNY, Albany, 1991; JD, Bklyn. Law Sch., 1994; student, Tel Aviv Law Sch., summer 1992. Bar: N.Y., N.J., Fla., U.S. Dist. Ct. (ea. dist.) N.Y., U.S. Dist. Ct. (so. dist.) N.Y. Assoc. Weiner & Millo, N.Y.C., 1993-94, Fischer Bros., N.Y.C., 1995-97, Caruso, Spillane, Contrastano & Ulaner, N.Y.C., 1997—. Mem. ABA, City of N.Y. Bar Assn. Avocations: sports, art, writing. Workers' compensation, Real property, Pension, profit-sharing, and employee benefits. Home: 200 E 36th St Apt 12A New York NY 10016-3648 Office: Caruso Spillane Constantino & Ulaner 132 Nassau St Fl 12 New York NY 10038-2400

**LEIBOWITZ, PAUL H.,** lawyer; b. N.Y.C., June 13, 1947. BBA, Denver U., 1970, JD, 1973. Bar: Colo. 1974. Various State of Colo., 1974-84; ptnr. Hahn, Leibowitz & Assocs., Denver, 1984—. Mem. Workers' Compensation Edn. Assn., Colo. Bar Assn. (family law sect.). Avocations: cycling, golf. Workers' compensation, Family and matrimonial, Personal injury. Office: Hahn Leibowitz & Assocs 1337 Delaware St Denver CO 80204-2704

**LEIBSLE, ROBERT CARL,** lawyer; b. L.A., May 15, 1946; s. Robert D. and Helen (ryan) L.; m. Susan Elizabeth Tully; children: Scott, Elizabeth, Eric, Hillary. BS, No. Ill. U., 1968; JD, Marquette U., 1972. Bar: Wis. 1972, U.S. Dist. Ct. (we. and ea. dists.) Wis. 1972, U.S. Supreme Ct. 1972. Intern edn. sect. civil rights div. U.S. Dept. Justice, Washington, 1971; assoc. Godfrey, Neshek and Worth, Elkhorn, Wis., 1973-76; ptnr. Godfrey, Neshek, Worth & Leibsle, S.C., Elkhorn, 1976—; lectr. State Bar Wis., Madison, 1992. Contbr. articles to profl. publs. Capt. U.S. Army, 1972-73. Recipient Outstanding Achievement award U.S. Dept. Justice, 1971. Mem. ABA (subcom. adaptation of bus. law accord to real estate transactions 1992—), State Bar Wis. (communication com. 1984-88, assistance for lawyers com. 1990—, standard form legal opinion com. chmn. 1990—), Walworth County Bar Assn. (pres. 1989-90, chmn. legal aid com. 1973-74). Avocations: woodworking, skiing. Environmental, Land use and zoning (including planning), Real property. Home: 429 Edgewood Ave Elkhorn WI 53121-1209 Office: Godfrey Neshek Worth & Leibsle PO Box 260 11 N Wisconsin St Elkhorn WI 53121-1737

**LEIDNER, SUZANNE CAROLYN,** lawyer; b. Summit, N.J., Feb. 7, 1942; d. Preston P. and Elvera D. (Meiele) Burnett; m. Edmund W. Arthur, Mar. 17, 1961 (div. 1966); m. Joel D. Leidner, Dec. 24, 1966; 1 child, David C. BS, UCLA, 1970; JD, Peoples Coll. of Law, L.A., 1979. Bar: Calif. 1980. Assoc. Weiser, Kane, Ballmer & Berkman, L.A., 1980-82; ptnr., pres. Leidner & Leidner, L.A., 1982—. Mem. ABA, Calif. Bar Assn., Los Angeles County Bar Assn. (past chmn. social security sect.), Nat. Lawyers Guild, Nat. Orgn. Social Security Claims Reps. Democrat. Jewish. Avocations: art, folk art collecting, gardening. Office: 4622 Hollywood Blvd Los Angeles CA 90027-5408

**LEIGHTON, GEORGE NEVES,** retired federal judge; b. New Bedford, Mass., Oct. 22, 1912; s. Antonio N. and Anna Sylvia (Garcia) Leitao; m. Virginia Berry Quivers, June 21, 1942; children: Virginia Anne, Barbara Elaine. AB, Howard U., 1940; LLB, Harvard U., 1946; LLD, Elmhurst Coll., 1964; LL.D., John Marshall Law Sch., 1973, Southeastern Mass. U., 1975, New Eng. U. Sch. Law, 1978; LLD, Loyola U., Chgo., 1989, R.I. Coll., 1992. Bar: Mass. 1946, Ill. 1947, U.S. Supreme Ct. 1958. Ptnr. Moore, Ming & Leighton, Chgo., 1951-59, McCoy, Ming & Leighton, Chgo., 1959-64; judge Circuit Ct. Cook County Ill., 1964-69, Appellate Ct. 1st Dist., 1969-76; U.S. dist. judge No. Dist. Ill., 1976-86; sr. dist. judge U.S. Dist. Ct., No. Dist. Ill., 1986-87; of counsel Earl L. Neal & Assocs., 1987—; adj. prof. John Marshall Law Sch., Chgo., 1965—; commr., mem. character and fitness com. for 1st Appellate Dist., Supreme Ct. Ill., 1955-63, chmn. character and fitness com., 1961-62; joint com. for revision Ill. Criminal Code, 1959-63; chmn. Ill. adv. com. U.S. Commn. on Civil Rights, 1964; mem. pub. rev. bd. UAW, AFL-CIO, 1961-70; Asst. atty. gen. State of Ill., 1950-51; pres. 3d Ward Regular Democratic Orgn., Cook County, Ill., 1951-53; v.p. 21st Ward, 1964. Contbr. articles to legal jours. Bd. dirs. United Ch. Bd. for Homeland Ministries, United Ch. of Christ, Grant Hosp., Chgo.; trustee U. Notre Dame, 1979-83, trustee emeritus, 1983—; bd. overseers Harvard Coll., 1983-89. Capt., inf. AUS, 1942-45. Decorated Bronze Star.; Recipient Civil Liberties award Ill. div. ACLU, 1961; named Chicagoan of Year in Law and Judiciary Jr. Assn. Commerce and Industry, 1964. Fellow ABA (chmn. coun. 1976, mem. coun. sect. legal edn. and admissions to bar); mem. NAACP (chmn. legal redress com. Chgo. br.), Am. Coll. Trial Lawyers, John Howard Assn. (bd. dirs.), Chgo. Bar Assn., Ill. Bar Assn. (joint com. mem. for revision jud. article 1959-62, sr. counselor 1997), Nat. Harvard Law Sch. Assn. (mem. coun.), Howard U. Chgo. Alumni Club (chmn. bd. dirs.), Phi Beta Kappa. Office: Earl L Neal & Assocs 111 W Washington St Ste 1700 Chicago IL 60602-2711

**LEIGHTON, ROBERT JOSEPH,** state legislator; b. Austin, Minn., July 7, 1965; s. Robert Joseph Sr. and JoAnn (Mulvihill) L. BA, U. Minn., 1988; JD, U. Calif., Berkeley, 1991. Minn. state rep. Dist. 27B, 1995—. Presdl. and Waller scholar U. Minn., 1988. Mem. ABA, Minn. Bar Assn., Minn. Trial Lawyers Assn., Phi Beta Kappa. Home: 1007 9th St NW Austin MN 55912-2047 Office: Leighton Meany Cotter & Enger 601 N Main St Austin MN 55912-3319

**LEIKEN, EARL MURRAY,** lawyer; b. Cleve., Jan. 19, 1942; s. Manny and Betty G. L.; m. Ellen Kay Miner, Mar. 26, 1970; children: Jonathan, Brian. BA magna cum laude, Harvard U., 1964, JD cum laude, 1967. Asst. dean, assoc. prof. law Case Western Res. U., Cleve., 1967-71; ptnr. Hahn, Loeser, Freedheim, Dean & Wellman, Cleve., 1971-86, Baker & Hostetler, Cleve., 1986—; adj. faculty, lectr. law Case Western Res. U., 1971-86. Pres. Shaker Heights (Ohio) Bd. Edn., 1986-88, Jewish Community Ctr., Cleve., 1988-91, Shaker Heights Family Ctr., 1994-97. Named one of Greater Cleve.'s 10 Outstanding Young Leaders, Cleve. Jaycees, 1972; recipient Kane award Cleve. Jewish Community Fedn., 1982. Mem. ABA, Greater Cleve. Bar Assn. (chmn. labor law sect. 1978). Labor, Federal civil litigation, State civil litigation. Home: 20815 Colby Rd Cleveland OH 44122-1903 Office: Baker & Hostetler 3200 Nat City Ctr 1900 E 9th St Ste 3200 Cleveland OH 44114-3475

**LEIKIN, MITCHELL,** judge; b. Chgo., July 31, 1921; s. Irving and Fannie Leikin; m. Evelyn Leikin, Aug. 10, 1952; children: Jerrold Blair, Robin Cheryl. BS, U. Ill., 1943; JD, DePaul U., 1949. Judge Cir. Ct. of Cook County, Chgo. Cmdr. USNR, 1943. Mem. North Suburban Bar Assn. (pres. 1966), Decalogue Soc. Lawyers (bd. dirs.). Home: 8909 Kolmar Ave Skokie IL 60076-1835 Office: Cir Ct of Cook County Daley Ctr 1502 Chicago IL 60602

**LEIMAN, EUGENE A.,** lawyer; b. N.Y.C., June 6, 1914; s. Irving and Jean (Schwartz) L.; m. Betty Ann Mitchell, Nov. 15, 1949. BA, CCNY, 1934; JD, NYU, 1936. Bar: N.Y. 1936, U.S. Dist. Ct. (so. dist.) N.Y. 1946, U.S. Supreme Ct. 1947, U.S. Ct. Appeals (2d cir.) 1947, U.S. Dist. Ct. (ea. dist.) N.Y. 1957, U.S. Ct. Mil. Appeals 1990. Pvt. practice N.Y.C., 1936-38; asst. dist. atty. Dist. Attys. Office N.Y. County, N.Y.C., 1938-57; adj. prof. NYU, N.Y.C., 1957-79; of counsel Mound, Cotton & Wollan, N.Y.C., 1957—. Composer musical shows. Capt. USAF, 1942-46. Mem. ABA, Maritime Law Assn., N.Y. State Bar Assn., Assn. of Bar of City of N.Y. (chmn. com. admiralty, memorials and entertainment 1947—). Avocations: composing and playing music. Insurance, Personal injury, Federal civil litigation. Office: Mound Cotton & Wollan One Battery Park Pla New York NY 10004

**LEINEN, AMY LYNN,** lawyer; b. Denison, Iowa, Aug. 3, 1971; d. Lawrence Thomas and Judith Phyllis L. BA in Psychology and Orgnl. Comm., Creighton U., 1993; JD, U. Iowa, 1996. Bar: Ariz. 1996, U.S. Dist. Ct. Ariz. 1996. Atty. Snell & Wilmer, Phoenix, 1996—; com. mem. Med.-Legal Liaison Com., Phoenix, 1997—. Mem. ABA, Ariz. State Bar, Ariz. Assn. Def. Counsel (exec. com. mem. young lawyers divsn. 1997—, sec. 1997-98, publ. chair 1998—), Ariz. Women's Lawyer Assn., Maricopa County Bar Assn. (vol. tchr. H.S. tchg. program 1997—). Roman Catholic. Health, Professional liability, Personal injury. Office: Snell & Wilmer 400 E Van Buren St Phoenix AZ 85004-2223

**LEINENWEBER, HARRY D.,** federal judge; b. Joliet, Ill., June 3, 1937; s. Harry Dean and Emily (Lennon) L.; m. Lynn Morley Martin, Jan. 7, 1987; 5 children; 2 stepchildren. AB cum laude, U. Notre Dame, 1959; JD, U. Chgo., 1962. Bar: Ill. 1962, U.S. Dist. Ct. (no. dist.) Ill. 1967. Assoc. Dunn, Stefanich, McGarry & Kennedy, Joliet, Ill., 1962-65, ptnr., 1965-79; city atty. City of Joliet, 1963-67; spl. counsel Village of Park Forest, Ill., 1967-74; spl. prosecutor County of Will, Ill., 1968-70; spl. counsel Village of Bolingbrook, Ill., 1975-77, Will County Forest Preserve, 1977; mem. Ill. Ho. of Reps., Springfield, 1973-83, chmn. judiciary I com., 1981-83; ptnr. Dunn, Leinenweber & Dunn, Joliet, 1979-86; fed. judge U.S. Dist. Ct. (no. dist.) Ill., Chgo., 1986—; bd. dirs. Will County Bar Assn., 1984-86, State Jud. Adv. Coun., 1973-85, sec. 1975-76; tchr. legis. process seminar U. Ill., Chgo., 1988—; mem. U. Ill. Inst. Govt. and Pub. Affairs Nat. Adv. Com., 1998—. Bd. dirs. Will County Legal Assistance Found., 1982-86, Good Shepard Manor, 1981—, Am. Cancer Soc., 1981-85, Joliet (Ill.) Montessori Sch., 1966-74; del. Rep. Nat. Conv., 1980; precinct committeeman, 1966-86; mem. nat. adv. com. U. Ill. Inst. Govt. and Pub. Affairs, 1998—. Recipient Environ. Legislator Golden award. Mem. Will County Bar Assn. (mem. jud. adv. coun., 1973-85, sec. 1975-76, bd. dirs. 1984-86), Nat. Conf. Commrs. on Uniform State Laws (exec. com. 1991-93, elected life mem. 1996), The Law Club of Chgo. (bd. dirs. 1996-98). Roman Catholic. Office: US Dist Ct 219 S Dearborn St Ste 1946 Chicago IL 60604-1801

**LEINEWEBER, ROBERT J.,** lawyer; b. Portland, Oreg., Apr. 12, 1953; s. James John and Mary Alice Dee L.; m. Robin Ellen Yorde, June 30, 1979; children: Henry, Samuel, Charles, John. BA, U. Oreg., 1976; JD, U. Hamline, 1980. Bar: Minn. 1980, Oreg. 1981, U.S. Dist. Ct. Oreg. 1988. Dep. dist. atty. Multnomah County, Portland, 1981-87, 89—; assoc. Williams, Fred., Stark, Portland, 1987-89. Den leader Boy Scouts Am., Wilsonville, Oreg., 1993; coach Babe Ruth Baseball, Wilsonville, 1993, West Linn Soccer, Wilsonville, 1994, 95. Recipient Disting. Svc. medal Portland Police Bur., 1995. Democrat. Roman Catholic. Office: Multnomah County Dist Atty 1021 SW 4th Ave Ste 600 Portland OR 97204-1110

**LEINOFF, ANDREW MORRIS,** lawyer; b. Paterson, N.J., Mar. 28, 1950; s. Benjamin B. and Rhoda Leinoff; m. Ellen Judith Cohen, Aug. 19, 1973; children: Paul, Alexis, Max. BA, Ohio State U., 1971; JD, U. Miami, 1974. Bar: Fla. 1974, U.S. Dist. Ct. (so. dist.) Fla. 1975, U.S. Ct. Appeals (5th cir.) 1975; cert. matrimonial and family lawyer. Assoc. Adams, Beeabe, Wood, Shuir & Mampson, P.A., Miami, Fla., 1974-75, Storace, Idri & Hauser, Miami, 1975-77; ptnr. Marks, Aronovitz & Leinoff, Miami, 1978-88; pvt. practice, Coral Gables, Fla., 1988—. Fellow Am. Acad. Matrimonial Lawyers (frequent lectr., pres. Fla. chpt. 1989-99); mem. ABA, Fla. Bar, Dade County Bar Assn., Am. Inns Ct. (master chpt. 181), Phi Delta Phi. Fax: 305-665-2555. Family and matrimonial. Office: 1500 San Remo Ave Ste 206 Coral Gables FL 33146-3047

**LEINWAND, HARRIS DONALD,** lawyer; b. Mt. Vernon, N.Y., Dec. 5, 1944; s. Isidor E. and Florence M. Leinwand; 1 child, Joseph Gabriel. BA, U. Pitts., 1965; JD, Cornell U., 1968. Bar: N.Y. 1969, U.S. Dist. Ct. (so. and ea. dists.) N.Y. 1970, U.S. Ct. Appeals (2d cir.) 1982. Ptnr. Leinwand Maron Hendler & Krause, N.Y.C., 1973-80; pvt. practice N.Y.C., 1980—. Bankruptcy. Office: 750 3rd Ave New York NY 10017-2703

**LEISURE, PETER KEETON,** federal judge; b. N.Y.C., Mar. 21, 1929; s. George S. and Lucille E. (Pelouze) L.; m. Kathleen Blair; Feb. 27, 1960; children: Lucille K. (dec.), Mary Blair, Kathleen K. B.A., Yale U., 1952; LL.B., U. Va., 1958. Bar: N.Y. 1959, U.S. Supreme Ct. 1966, D.C. 1979, U.S. Dist. Ct. Conn. 1981. Assoc. Breed, Abbott & Morgan, 1958-61; asst. U.S. atty. So. Dist. N.Y., 1962-66; partner firm Curtis, Mallet-Prevost, Colt & Mosle, 1967-78; ptnr. Whitman & Ransom, N.Y.C., 1978-84; judge U.S. Dist. Ct. So. N.Y., New York, NY, 1984—. Bd. dirs. Retarded Infants Svcs., 1968-78, pres., 1971-75; bd. dirs. Community Coun. of Greater N.Y., 1972-79, Youth Consultation Svcs., 1971-78; trustee Ch. Club of N.Y., 1973-81, 87-90; mem. jud. ethics com. Jud. Conf., 1990-93, fin disclosure com. Fellow Am. Bar Found., Am. Coll. Trial Lawyers; mem. ABA, Am. Law Inst., Fed. Judges Assn., Am. Judges Assn., D.C. Bar Assn., Fed. Bar Coun. (trustee, v.p. 1973-78), Bar Assn. City of N.Y., Nat. Lawyers Club (hon.). Office: US Dist Ct 1910 US Courthouse 500 Pearl St New York NY 10007-1316

**LEITCH, RYAN L.,** lawyer; b. Ft. Wayne, Ind., July 18, 1962; s. Richard D. and Nancy E. L.; m. Amy L. Kilfoil, June 6, 1987; children: Jessica, Matthew, Jake, Hannah. BS in Fin., Ind. U., 1984, JD, 1987. Bar: U.S. Dist. Ct. (so. dist.) Ind. 1987. Assoc. Hunt & Suedhoff, Ft. Wayne, 1987-89; assoc. Riley, Bennett & Egloff, Indpls., 1989-95, ptnr., 1995—. Bd. dirs. N. Willow Farms, Inc., Indpls., 1996-98, pres., 1998; mem. devel. com., bd. dirs. Prevent Child Abuse Ind., Indpls., 1988. Mem. ABA, Ind. State Bar Assn., Indpls. Bar Assn. Republican. Avocations: golfing, coaching sports. E-mail: rleitch@rbelaw.com. Estate planning, Probate, General civil litigation. Office: Riley Bennett & Egloff One American Sq Box 82035 Indianapolis IN 46282

**LEITER, JOHN M.,** lawyer; b. Marietta, Ga., July 14, 1951; s. Henry David and Lilo (Schwartzchild) L.; m. Mary Clayton, May 8, 1976; children: Jonathan, Elizabeth, Kristin. BA, Emory U., 1973; JD, U. S.C., 1978. Bar: S.C. 1978, Ga. 1978, U.S. Dist. Ct. S.C. 1978, U.S. Dist. Ct. (no. dist.) Ga. 1978, U.S. Ct. Appeals (4th and 5th cirs.), U.S. Supreme Ct. Assoc. Harmon, Smith & Bridges, Atlanta, 1978-82, Lawn & Leiter, Myrtle Beach, S.C., 1982-87; ptnr. Leiter & Tall, Myrtle Beach, 1988-92; pvt. practice Myrtle Beach, 1992-94; prin. Leiter and Snook, P.A., 1994—; intern World Peace Through Law Conf., Manila, 1977. Bd. dirs. Myrtle Beach Housing Authority, 1987—. David Means scholar, 1977. Mem. ABA, S.C. State Bar Assn., Ga. State Bar Assn., Horry County Bar Assn. (pres. 1995). Federal civil litigation, State civil litigation, General civil litigation. Office: PO Box 7516 Myrtle Beach SC 29577-0108

**LEITER, RICHARD ALLEN,** law librarian, law educator; b. Sacramento, Mar. 21, 1952; s. Lionel and Lois Rose Leiter; m. Wendy Ellin Werges, Dec. 30, 1978; children: Madeline Rose, Anna Joy, Rebecca Hope. BA in Anthropology and Religious Studies with honors, U. Calif., Santa Cruz, 1976; JD, Southwestern U., 1981; M of Libr. and Info. Sci., U. Tex., 1986. Libr. asst. Irell & Manella, L.A., 1977-78; libr. Hopkins, Mitchell & Carley, San Jose, Calif., 1982-84; head of reference Law Sch., U. Tex., Austin, 1984-86; pub. svcs. libr. Law Sch., U. Nebr., Lincoln, 1986-88; head libr. Littler, Mendelson, Fastiff & Tichy, San Francisco, 1988-91; dir. law libr., assoc. prof. law Regent U. Sch. Law, Virginia Beach, Va., 1991-94; assoc. prof. law Howard U. Sch. Law, A.M. Daniels Law Libr., Washington, 1994-98, dir. law libr., 1994—; assoc. dean, prof. Howard U., Washington, 1998—; mem. Westlaw Acad. Adv. Bd., 1990-93; sec. bd. dirs. StoneBridge Sch., 1993-94; mem. adv. bd. Oceana Publs., Inc., 1994—. Editor: (book sect.) Yellow Pads to Computers, 1986, 91; author: (bibliography) New Frontiers of Forensic & Demonstrative Evidence, 1985; editor: Automatome, 1987-89, The Spirit of Law Librarianship, 1991, National Survey of State Laws, 1993, 2d edit., 1997; (with A. White) Concordance of Federal Legislation, 1999; editor Southwestern U. Law Review; contbr. articles to profl. jours. Mem. adv. com. StoneBridge Ednl. Found. Mem. ABA, Assn. Computing Machinery, Am. Soc. Info. Sci., Am. Assn. Law Librs. (so. chpt., automation and sci. devel. spl. interest sect. 1986—, chair 1989-90, indexing of periodical lit. adv. com. 1990-91, chair 1990-91, mem. spl. com. to promote development of resources for legal info. cmty. 1994-96, recruitment com. 1995-97, chair rsch. com. 1998—), San Francisco Pvt. Law Librs. (steering com. 1989), Consortium Southeast Law Librs. (vice chair), Scribes. Avocations: bicycling, reading, backpacking. Home: 2830 Woodlawn Ave Falls Church VA 22042-2011 Office: Howard U Daniel Law Libr 2900 Van Ness St NW Washington DC 20008-1100

**LEITNER, DAVID LARRY,** lawyer; b. Bklyn., Feb. 20, 1956; s. Sol and Beatrice (Brodsky) L.; m. Jana L. Grady, Sept. 11, 1983; children: Morgan Blaire, Gabriel Rand. Student, SUNY, Brockport, 1974-75; BA, SUNY, Stony Brook, 1976; JD, U. Iowa, 1979. Bar: Iowa 1979, U.S. Dist. Ct. (no. and so. dists.) Iowa 1979, U.S. Ct. Appeals (2d, 7th and 8th cirs.) 1980, U.S. Tax Ct. 1981, U.S. Supreme Ct. 1994; CPCU. Asst. atty. various counties, Iowa, 1979-81; assoc. Cooper, Sinnard & Cooper, Forest City, Iowa, 1981-83; sole practice Forest City, 1983; atty. Grinnell (Iowa) Mut. Reins. Co., 1983-86, Allied Group Inc. Co., Des Moines, 1986-87; with Davis, Grace, Horvath, Gonnerman and Rowenhorst, Des Moines, 1987-89; pvt. practice Des Moines, 1990—; judicial hospitalization referee Winnebago County, Ia., 1983. Author: Lawyers Guide to LawPro, 1999, Lawyers Guide to Casemap, 1999, Juris for Lawyers, 1999; co-author: Automobile Accident Law and Practice, 1988; editor Tort and Ins. Law Jour., 1988-92, Truck Accident Litigation and Insurance: Tobacco and Litigation Insurance; Managed Care Liability; editor: Employment Discrimination Litigation, 1999; contbr. articles to profl. jours.; contbg. author: No Fault and Uninsured Motorist, 1992; editor-in-chief Insurance Coverage Litigation, 1998. Mem. ABA (speaker, mem. tort and ins. practice sect., com. chair), Iowa Bar Assn. (bridge gap com., Mason Ladd award com.), Assn. Trial Lawyers, Am. Trial Lawyer Assn., Soc. Chartered Property and Casualty Underwriters, Def. Rsch. Inst. Jewish. Avocations: photography, furniture bldg. General civil litigation, Personal injury, Insurance. Office: 5850 NW 62d Ave Johnston IA 50131-1537

**LEITNER, GREGORY MARC,** lawyer; b. Chattanooga, Apr. 19, 1957; s. Paul Revers and Suzanne Joy Leitner; m. Sheryl Leitner; children: Gregory Marc, Ashley Meredith. BA cum laude, Memphis State U., 1978; JD, U. Tenn., Knoxville, 1980. Bar: Tenn. 1981, U.S. Dist. Ct. (ea. dist.) 1981, U.S. Ct. Appeals (6th cir.) 1983, U.S. Ct. Appeals (11th cir.) 1988. Ptnr. Leitner, Warner, Moffitt, Williams, Dooley, Carpenter & Napolitan, Chattanooga, 1986—. Mem. ABA, Tenn. Bar Assn., Pi Sigma Alpha, Phi Delta Phi. Republican. Methodist. Avocations: politics, international politics, history. Federal civil litigation, Environmental. Home: 6259 Forest Trl Signal Mountain TN 37377-2807

**LEITNER, PAUL REVERE,** lawyer; b. Winnsboro, S.C., Nov. 11, 1928; s. W. Walker and Irene (Lewis) L.; m. Jeannette C. Card, Mar. 16, 1985; children by previous marriage: David, Douglas, Gregory, Reid, Cheryl. AB, Duke U., 1950; LLB, McKenzie Coll., 1954. Bar: Tenn. 1954; cert. civil trial specialist Nat. Bd. Trial Advocacy and Tenn. Commn. on CLE and Specialization. Pvt. practice law Chattanooga, 1954; assoc. firm Leitner, Warner, Moffitt, Williams, Dooley, Carpenter & Napolitan and predecessor firms,

1952-57, ptnr., 1957—; Tenn. chmn. Def. Rsch. Inst., 1978-89. Bd. dirs. Family Service Agy., 1957-63, Chattanooga Symphony and Opera Assn., 1986-89, sec., 1987-89; mem. Chattanooga-Hamilton County Community Action Bd.; mem. Juvenile Ct. Commn., Hamilton County, 1955-61, chmn., 1958-59; chmn. Citizens Com. for Better Schs.; mem. Met. Govt. Charter Commn. Served with U.S. Army, 1946-47. Named Young Man of Yr. Chattanooga Area, 1957. Fellow Am. Coll. Trial Lawyers, Tenn. Bar. Found, Chattanooga Bar Found. (founding); mem. ABA, Tenn. Bar Assn., Jaycees (Chattanooga, pres. 1956-57), Fed. Ins. Corp. Counsel, Internat. Assn. Def. Coun., Trial Attys. Am., Tenn. Def. Lawyers Assn. (pres. 1975-76), Am. Bd. Trial Advs. (advocate), U.S. Sixth Cir. Jud. Conf. (life). Methodist. Federal civil litigation, State civil litigation, Personal injury. Home: Augusta Dr Lookout Mountain TN 37350

**LEITZKE, RANDY LEE,** law firm executive, accountant; b. Seattle, car, June 16, 1958; s. Harold A. and Eloise C. Leitzke; m. Janice K. Oswald, Apr. 12, 1980; children: Danielle, Robin, Jamie. BA in Bus. Adminstrn., U. Wash., 1980, MBA, 1984. CPA, Wash. Fin. adminstr. GTE, Stamford, Conn., 1980-83; mgr. fin. planning and cost acctg. Fairchild Semicondr. Corp., Puyallup, Wash., 1984-87; CFO, ESCA Corp., Bellevue, Wash., 1987-94; exec. dir. Lane Powell Spears Lubersky LLP, Seattle, 1994—. Mem. Am. Mgmt. Assn., Fin. Execs. Inst., Wash. Soc. CPA's. Office: Lane Powell Spears Lubersky LLP 1420 5th Ave Ste 4100 Seattle WA 98101-2375

**LEKISCH, PETER ALLEN,** lawyer; b. Midland, Tex., Jan. 7, 1941; m. Ellen M. Wierenga; 1 child, Jennifer L. Bar: Alaska 1969, Calif. 1969, U.S. Dist. Ct. Alaska 1969. Law clk., assoc., ptnr. Robinson, McCaskey, et al., Anchorage, 1967-75; atty., ptnr. Hoge and Lekisch APC, Anchorage, 1975—. Dir. Arctic Winter Games Team Alaska, Fairbanks, 1990; mem. Downtown Anchorage com., 1996; bd. dirs. Amateur Sports Authority, Anchorage, 1986. Mem. ABA, Am. Coll. Real Estate Attys., Am. Arbitration Assn. (arbitrator 1976—), Alaska Bar Assn., Calif. Bar Assn. Avocations: cross-country skiing, bicycle racing, photography. Consumer commercial, General corporate, Real property. Office: 441 W 5th Ave Ste 500 Anchorage AK 99501-2340

**LEMANN, THOMAS BERTHELOT,** lawyer; b. New Orleans, Jan. 3, 1926; s. Monte M. and Nettie E. (Hyman) L.; m. Barbara M. London, Apr. 14, 1951; children: Nicholas B., Nancy E. A.B. summa cum laude, Harvard U., 1949, LL.B., 1952; M.C.L., Tulane U., 1953. Bar: La. 1953. Assoc. Monroe & Lemann, New Orleans, 1953-58, ptnr., 1958-98; of counsel Liskow & Lewis, New Orleans, 1998—; bd. dirs. B. Lemann & Bro., Mermentau Mineral and Land Co., So. States Land & Timber Corp., Avrico Inc.; advisory bd. dirs. Riviana Foods. Contbr. articles to profl. publs. Mem. council La. State Law Inst., sec. trust adv. com.; chmn. Mayor's Cultural Resources Com., 1970-75; pres. Arts Coun. Greater New Orleans, 1975-80, bd. dirs.; mem. vis. com. art museums Harvard U., 1974-80; trustee Metairie Park Country Day Sch., 1956-71, pres., 1967-70, New Orleans Philharmonic Symphony Soc., 1956-78, Flint-Goodridge Hosp., 1960-70, La. Civil Service League, pres., 1974-76, New Orleans Mus. Art, 1986-92; bd. dirs. Zemurray Found., Hever Found., Parkside Found., Azby Fund, Azby Art Fund, Greater New Orleans Found., Arts Coun. New Orleans, Musica da Camera. Served with AUS, 1944-46, PTO. Mem. ABA, La. Bar Assn. (bd. govs. 1977-78), New Orleans Bar Assn., Assn. Bar City N.Y., Am. Law Inst., Soc. Bartolus, Phi Beta Kappa. Jewish. Clubs: New Orleans Country, Wyvern (New Orleans). Probate, Estate taxation, Estate planning. Home: 6020 Garfield St New Orleans LA 70118-6039 Office: Liskow & Lewis 701 Poydras St Ste 5000 New Orleans LA 70139-5099

**LEMBERG, FREDERIC GARY,** lawyer; b. Los Angeles, Sept. 25, 1944; s. Jack and Rose (Zuckerman) L.; m. Sharon Lee Probst; children: William Derek, Carren Lynn, Serena Melody. BS, Ariz. State U., 1966, JD, 1971. Bar: Ariz. 1971, U.S. Dist. Ct. Ariz. 1971, U.S. Ct. Appeals (9th cir.) 1977. Ptnr. Pollock & Lemberg, Phoenix, 1971-73, Lemberg, Green, Lester & Walsh, Phoenix, 1973-76, Mallin & Lemberg, Phoenix, 1980-83, Fannin, Terry & Lemberg, P.A., Phoenix, 1983-88, Quarles & Brady & Fannin, Phoenix, 1988—. Mem. ABA, Ariz. Bar Assn., Maricopa County Bar Assn., Assn. Trial Lawyers Am. General civil litigation, Real property. Office: Quarles Brady & Fannin 1 E Camelback Rd Ste 470 Phoenix AZ 85012-1659

**LEMBERIS, THEODORE THOMAS,** lawyer, educator; b. LaPorte, Ind., Sept. 15, 1948; s. Thomas Theodore and Helen N. (Pappas) L.; m. Renna T. Theodorakas, Nov. 13, 1978; children: Eleni, Stephanie. BA, Purdue U., 1972; MPA, Roosevelt U., 1978; JD, John Marshall Law Sch., Chgo., 1982. Bar: Ill. 1982, U.S. Dist. Ct. (no. dist.) Ill. 1982. Sys. analyst Metro. Reclamation, Chgo., 1979-82; pub. defender Cook County, Chgo., 1982-85; assoc. Hinshaw & Culberson, Chgo., 1985-86; ptnr. Keck, Mahin & Cate, Chgo., 1986-94; prof. law Chgo.-Kent Law Sch., 1994-95; ptnr. Arstein & Lehr, Chgo., from 1995, Smith, Lodge & Schneider, Chartered, Chgo.; adj. prof. Chgo.-Kent Law Sch., 1995—. Contbr. articles to profl. jours. Mem. Ill. Bar Assn. (sect. counsil mem.). Greek Orthodox. Avocations: tennis, horseback riding. Fax: 312-853-3127. Private international, Contracts commercial. Office: Smith Lodge Schneider 300 S Wacker Dr Ste 1700 Chicago IL 60606-6632

**LEMIRE, JEROME ALBERT,** lawyer, geologist, consultant; b. Cleve., June 4, 1947; s. George A. and Matilda (Simon) L.; m. Sandra Marsick, Oct. 1, 1976; children: Laura, Lesley, Thomas. BS in Geology, Ohio State U., 1969, MS in Geology, 1973, JD, 1976. Bar: Ohio 1976; cert. fin. planner. Geologist United Petroleum Co., Columbus, Ohio, 1976-77; assoc. Brownfield, Bowen & Bally, Columbus, 1977-79; land mgr. POI Energy Inc., Cleve., 1979-81; cons. Jefferson, Ohio, 1981-83; v.p. Carey Resources Inc., Jefferson, 1984-86; pres. Lemire & Assocs Inc., Jefferson, 1986—; cons. in field. Vice chmn. Tech. Adv. Coun., Columbus, 1984-84; solicitor Village of Jefferson. Served to 1st lt. U.S. Army, 1970-72. Mem. VFW, Ohio Bar Assn., Ashtabula County Bar Assn., Rotary. Oil, gas, and mineral, Environmental, General corporate. Home: 838 N State Route 46 Jefferson OH 44047-9785

**LEMLE, ROBERT SPENCER,** lawyer; b. N.Y.C., Mar. 6, 1953; s. Leo Karl and Gertrude (Bander) L.; m. Roni Sue Kohen, Sept. 5, 1976; children: Zachary, Joanna. AB, Oberlin Coll., 1975; JD, NYU, 1978. Bar: N.Y. 1979. Assoc. Cravath, Swaine & Moore, N.Y.C., 1978-82; assoc. gen. counsel Cablevision Sys. Corp., Woodbury, N.Y., 1982-84, v.p., gen. counsel, 1984-86, sr. v.p., gen. counsel, sec., 1986-94, exec. v.p., gen. counsel, sec., 1994—; bd. editors Cable TV and New Media Law and Fin., N.Y.C., 1983—, bd. dirs. Cablevision Systems Corp., 1988—. Bd. trustees L.I. Children's Mus., 1990—, pres., 1996—; bd. trustees Oberlin Coll., 1996—. Mem. ABA, N.Y. State Bar Assn. Avocation: real estate. General corporate, Entertainment. Office: Cablevision Systems Corp 1111 Stewart Ave Bethpage NY 11714-3581

**LEMLY, THOMAS ADGER,** lawyer; b. Dayton, Ohio, Jan. 31, 1943; s. Thomas Moore and Elzabeth (Adger) L.; m. Kathleen Brame, Nov. 24, 1984; children: Elizabeth Hayden, Joanna Marsden, Isabelle Stafford, Kate Brame. BA, Duke U., 1970; JD with honors, U. N.C., 1973. Bar: Wash. 1973, U.S. Dist. Ct. (we. dist.) Wash. 1973, U.S. Ct. Appeals (9th cir.) 1975, U.S. Supreme Ct. 1980. Assoc. Davis Wright Tremaine, Seattle, 1973-79, ptnr., 1979—. Contbg. editor Employment Discrimination Law, 1984-87, 94—; editor Wash., Oreg., Alaska and Calif. Employment Law Deskbooks, 1987—. Chmn. Pacific Coast Labor Conf., Seattle, 1983; trustee Plymouth Congregational Ch., 1980-84, Seattle Opera Assn., 1991—. Mem. ABA (labor employment law sect. 1975—, subcom. chmn. 1984-90, govt. liaison com. 1982—), Seattle-King County Bar Assn. (chmn. labor sect.), Assn. Wash. Bus. (trustee 1992—, chmn. human resources coun. 1993—, chmn. employment law task force 1987-93), U. N.C. Bar Found. (bd. dirs. 1973-76), Seattle Duke Alumni Assn. (pres. 1979-84), Order of Coif, Wash. Athletic Club (Seattle), Rotary. Republican. Presbytarian. Labor, General civil litigation. Home: 1614 7th Ave W Seattle WA 98119-2919 Office: Davis Wright Tremaine 2600 Century Sq 1501 4th Ave Ste 2600 Seattle WA 98101-1688

**LEMMON, HARRY THOMAS,** state supreme court justice; b. Morgan City, La., Dec. 11, 1930; s. Earl and Gertrude (Blum) L.; m. Mary Ann Vial; children: Andrew, Lauren, Roslyn, Carla, Jake, Patrick. BS, Southwestern La. Inst., 1952; LLB cum laude, Loyola U., New Orleans, 1963. Atty. firm Vial, Vial & Lemmon, Hahnville, La., 1963-70; judge Court Appeals 4th Cir., 1970-80; assoc. justice Supreme Ct. La., New Orleans, 1980—; vis. prof. law La. State U. Law Ctr., Tulane U. Sch. Law.; adj. faculty Loyola U. Sch. Law, New Orleans. Chmn. La. Jud. Coll. With U.S. Army. Office: Supreme Ct of La 301 Loyola Ave New Orleans LA 70112-1814*

**LEMOINE, GANO D., JR.,** lawyer, pharmacist; b. Cottonport, La., Apr. 2, 1938; s. Gano D. and Therese D. Lemoine; m. Carolyn Y. Lemoine, July 13, 1963; children: Gano D. III, Jean Louis. BS in Pharmacy, U. Houston, 1960; LLB, JD, Tulane U., 1964. Bar: U.S. Dist. Ct. (mid. and ea. dists.) La. 1964, U.S. Dist. Ct. (we. dist.) La. 1988, U.S. Ct. Appeals (5th cir.) 1981, U.S. Supreme Ct. 1981; registered pharmacist, La. Sr. ptnr. Andrus, Boudreaux, Lemoine & Tonore, Lafayette, 1987—; pres. Cottonport Bank, 1985, v.p., 1981-84, bd. dirs.; pres. Lemoine Contracting and Antique Co., 1979-81; mem. plaintiff's steering com. La. Breast Implant Litig., 1992—. Pres. St. Mary's Sch. Bd., 1979-81. Mem. ABA, La. Bar Assn., Avoyelles Parish Bar Assn. (past pres. 1972), Am. Soc. Pharm. Law, La. Pharm. Assn., Nat. Assn. Retail Druggists, Am. Pharm. Assn., Am. Bankers Assn., Am. Coll. Legal Medicine, ATLA (pharm. and toxic tort com.), La. Trial Lawyers Assn., Grand Lake Gun and Rod Club (pres. 1980-81), Cottonport Svc. Club, Sigma Alpha Epsilon. Democrat. Roman Catholic. Avocations: tennis, horseback riding, swimming, golfing, hunting. Personal injury, Product liability, Admiralty. Home: PO Box 639 1733 Horseshoe Dr Cottonport LA 71327-3537 Office: Andrus Boudreaux Lemoine & Tonore 416 W Main St Lafayette LA 70501-6728

**LEMON, WILLIAM JACOB,** lawyer; b. Covington, Va., Oct. 25, 1932; s. James Gordon and Elizabeth (Wilson) L.; m. Barbara Inez Boyle, Aug. 17, 1957; children: Sarah E. Lemon Ludwig, William Tucker, Stephen Weldon. BA, Washington & Lee U., 1957, JD, 1959. Bar: Va. 1959. Assoc. Martin, Martin & Hopkins, Roanoke, Va., 1959-61; ptnr. Martin, Hopkins & Lemon, Roanoke, 1962—. Trustee Washington and Lee U., Lexington, Va., 1988-97, North Cross Sch., Roanoke, 1995—; pres. Specific Reading and Learning Difficulties Assn. Shedd Early Learning Ctr., 1985-86, George C. Marshall Found., Lexington, Va., 1997—. With U.S. Army, 1952-54. Mem. Va. Bar Assn., Roanoke Bar Assn. (pres. 1982-83), Va. State Bar, Shenandoah Club. Presbyterian. Avocations: farming, hunting, travel. Health, Real property, Probate. Office: Martin Hopkins Lemon First Union Tower 10 S Jefferson St Ste 1000 Roanoke VA 24011-1314 also: PO Box 13366 Roanoke VA 24033-3366

**LEMONS, KEITH DAVID,** lawyer; b. Plainview, Tex., Jan. 14, 1954; s. Walter Warren and Wilma Ruth (Wykes) L.; m. Pamela Jo Grantham, Aug. 13, 1977; children: Chad Grantham, Amber Leigh. BA, Baylor U., 1976, JD, 1978. Bar: Tex. 1978. Pvt. practice law Plainview, 1978-83; assoc. Stokes & Fields, Amarillo, Tex., 1983-86; ptnr. Segers & Lemons, Ft. Worth, 1986-90, Keith D. Lemons & Assocs., Ft. Worth, 1991--. Chmn. South Plains Child Welfare Bd., Lubbock, Tex., 1981-82. Mem. Assn. Trial Lawyers Am., Tex. Trial Lawyers Assn., Tarrant County Trial Lawyers, State Bar of Tex. Republican. Baptist. General civil litigation, Personal injury, Pension, profit-sharing, and employee benefits. Office: Keith D Lemons & Assocs 1119 Pennsylvania Ave Fort Worth TX 76104-2121

**LENARD, GEORGE DEAN,** lawyer; b. Joliet, Ill., Aug. 26, 1957; s. Louis George and Jennie (Helopoulos) L.; m. Nancy Ilene Sundquist, Nov. 11, 1989. BS, Ill. State U., 1979; JD, Thomas Cooley Law Sch., 1984. Bar: Ill. 1984, U.S. Dist. Ct. (no. dist.) Ill. 1984, U.S. Ct. Appeals (6th cir.) 1998, U.S. Supreme Ct. 1990, Mich. 1998, Ariz. 1999. Asst. states atty. Will County States Attys. Office, Joliet, 1984-88; pvt. practice law Joliet, 1988—. Mem. ABA, ATLA, Nat. Assn. Criminal Def. Lawyers, Ill. State Bar Assn., Chgo. Bar Assn., State Bar Ariz., State Bar Mich., Phi Alpha Delta (Isaac P. Christiancy chpt.). Avocation: golf. Criminal, Constitutional. Office: 81 N Chicago St Ste 206 Joliet IL 60432-4383

**LENEAVE, CORTNEY SCOTT,** lawyer; b. Lavonia, Mich., May 25, 1961; s. C. Wayne and A. Anita (Johnson) L.; m. Kristen E. Hill, Aug. 15, 1987; children: Sarah, Sam, Kathryn. BA in Pol. Sci., U. Minn., 1983; JD, William Mitchell Law Sch., 1987. Bar: Minn. 1987, U.S. Dist. Ct. Minn. 1988. Law clk. Hennepin County Dist. Ct., Mpls., 1987-88; assoc. Meagher & Geer, Mpls., 1988-95; ptnr. Hunegs, Stone, Koenig & LeNeave, Mpls., 1995—; arbitrator Am. Arbitration Assn., Mpls., 1994—; designated legal counsel United Transp. Union. Hockey/soccer coach Wayzata Youth Hockey/Plymouth Soccer Assn., 1994—. Mem. ABA, ATLA, Minn. Bar Assn., Minn. Trial Lawyers Assn. Avocations: golf, hockey. Product liability. Office: Hunegs Stone Koenig LeNeave 1650 Internat Ctr 900 2d Ave S Minneapolis MN 55402

**LENGA, J. THOMAS,** lawyer; b. Toledo, Dec. 16, 1942; s. Casimir M. and Rose C. (Sturniolo) L.; children by previous marriage: Christina M., John Thomas Jr., Peter M. BA, U. Toledo, 1965, JD, 1968. Bar: Mich. 1968, Ohio 1968. Mem. Dykema Gossett PLLC, Detroit, 1972-96; mem Clark Hill P.L.C., Detroit, 1996—; mem. com. on std. jury instrns. Mich. Supreme Ct.; advocate Am. Bd. of Trial Advocates. Capt. JAGC, U.S. Army, 1968-72. Named Disting. Alumnus, Coll. Law, U. Toledo, 1987. Fellow Am. Coll. Trial Lawyers; mem. ABA, Detroit Bar Assn. (pres. 1989-90), State Bar Mich. (bd. commrs. 1992—, treas. 1995-96, v.p. 1996-97, pres.-elect 1997-98, pres. 1998-99), Internat. Assn. Def. Counsel. Product liability, General civil litigation. Office: Clark Hill PLC 500 Woodward Ave Ste 3500 Detroit MI 48226-3435

**LENGA, ROBERT ALLEN,** lawyer; b. Cleve., Jan. 2, 1938; s. Alexander Richard and Florence Gertrude Lenga; m. Nancy Ann Dobina, Oct. 6, 1968; children: Jennifer Ann, Kenneth Robert. BA, Bowling Green State U., 1960; JD, Case Western Res. U., 1964. Bar: Ohio 1965, U.S. Dist. Ct. (no. dist.) Ohio 1966. Mem. Harrington Hoppe & Mitchell Ltd., Youngstown, Ohio, 1966—. Pres. Poland (Ohio) Bd. Edn., 1988-91; trustee Mahoning Shenango Estate Planning Coun., Youngstown, Ohio, 1996-98. Mem. Ohio State Bar Assn. (bd. govs. estate planning trust and probate sect. 1985-91, 97—), Mahoning County Bar Assn. (pres. 1990-91), Rotary Club (Paul Harris fellow 1997). Estate planning, Probate, General corporate. Office: Harrington Hoppe Mitchell Ltd 1200 Mahoning Bank Bldg Youngstown OH 44503

**LENIHAN, ROBERT JOSEPH, II,** lawyer; b. Detroit, Jan. 16, 1947; s. Robert J. and Rita M. (O'Rourke) L.; m. Ann Carolyn Kelly, July 3, 1971; children: Robert J. III, James K. BS, Xavier U., 1969; JD cum laude, Wayne State U., 1972. Bar: Mich. 1972, U.S. Dist. Ct. (ea. dist.) Mich. 1972, U.S. Dist. Ct. (we. dist.) Mich. 1974, U.S. Ct. Appeals (6th cir.) 1986. Ptnr. Lenihan & Plese, Birmingham, Mich., 1972-85; sr. ptnr., prin. Colombo & Colombo, Bloomfield Hills, Mich., 1986-96; prin., ptnr. Harness, Dickey & Pierce, P.L.C., Troy, Mich., 1997—. Served to lt. col. USAR, 1973-93. Mem. ABA, Mich. Bar Assn., Oakland County Bar Assn., Fed. Bar Assn., Order of Barristers, Detroit Boat Club (pres. 1985-86), Renaissance Club. Avocations: golf, carpentry, reading, boating. General corporate, Intellectual property, Federal civil litigation. Office: Harness Dickey & Pierce PLC 5445 Corporate Dr Ste 400 Troy MI 48098-2683

**LENKOV, JEFFREY MYLES,** lawyer; b. Montreal, Que., Can., July 10, 1965; came to U.S., 1980; s. Abraham Leo and Ellen (Wolkove) L. BA, McGill U., Montreal, 1987; JD, No. Ill. U., 1991. Bar: Calif. 1991, U.S. Ct. Appeals (9th cir.) 1991. Teaching asst. No. Ill. U., DeKalb, 1989-90; assoc. Bishop, Barry, Howe, Haney & Ryder, L.A., 1992—. Contbg. author: Remedies in Arbitration, 1990. Mem. ABA, Los Angeles County Bar Assn., Beverly Hills Bar Assn., Assn. Def. Counsel, Landau Lawyers. Avocations: American classical literature, anthropology, hockey, computers. Entertainment, Trademark and copyright, Insurance. Office: Bishop Barry Howe Haney & Ryder 1901 Avenue Of The Stars Los Angeles CA 90067-6001

**LENOFF, MICHELE MALKA,** lawyer; b. Balt., Apr. 10, 1961; d. Israel and Dina (Munz) Drazin; m. Steven Lenoff, Sept. 23, 1984; children: Michael Monroe, Jonathan David, Joseph Nathan, Rachel Lauren. BA cum laude, Bar-Ilan U., Ramat Gan, Israel, 1979; MA in Clin. Psychology, U. Md., 1981; JD cum laude, Nova U., 1986. Bar: Fla. 1987, U.S. Dist. Ct. (so. dist.) Fla. 1991. Therapist Rosewood Hosp., Balt., 1981-82; psycologist Young Adult Inst., N.Y., 1982-83; law clk. Md. Pub. Defender's Office, Balt., 1984; law clk. to presiding justice Fla. Cir. Ct., Ft. Lauderdale, 1985; assoc. McCune & Hiaasen, Ft. Lauderdale, 1985-88; ptnr. Lenoff & Lenoff P.A., Deerfield Beach, Fla., 1988—; of counsel Law Office of Robert T. Carlilie, Deerfield Beach, 1988-91, G. Ware Cornell Jr., Ft. Lauderdale, Fla., 1988-90; adj. prof. Howard Community Coll., Columbia, Md., 1981-82; legal rsch. and writing instr. Nova U. Ctr. for the Study of Law, Ft. Lauderdale, 1988-89. Mem. Nova Law Rev., 1985-86. Goodwin fellow Nova U., 1986. Mem. ABA, Fla. Bar Assn. Republican. Jewish. Probate, Estate planning, Real property. Office: Lenoff & Lenoff 1761 W Hillsboro Blvd Ste 405 Deerfield Beach FL 33442-1563

**LENOX, ROGER SHAWN,** lawyer; b. Prescott, Ark., June 27, 1961; s. Ollie and Mae Lenox; m. Patricia Mickens; children: Mariah, Maya. BSN cum laude, U. Ala., Huntsville, 1987; JD, U. Mich., 1991. Bar: Tex. 1992, D.C. 1993, U.S. Ct. Appeals (D.C. cir.) 1993, U.S. Dist. Ct. (no., so., ea. and we. dists.) Tex. 1994, U.S. Ct. Appeals (5th cir.) 1995; RN, Ala. Summer assoc. Dykema Gossett, Detroit, 1989-90; assoc. Fulbright & Jaworski, L.L.P., Dallas, 1991-95; pvt. practice Law Office of Roger S. Lenox, Dallas, 1995—. Firm rep. Dallas Black C. of C., 1992-95, The Sci. Place, Dallas, 1993-95; spkr. Greater Tex. chpt. Nat. Assn. Pediatric Nurse Practitioners and Assocs., 1995; atty. mentor for Criminal Cts. Day, Youth Leadership Dallas, 1994; Career Day spkr. Dallas Bus. Magnet H.S., 1993. Lt. (j.g.) USN, 1987-91. Recipient Faculty Award for Clin. Excellence, U. Ala., Huntsville, 1987, Nat. Collegiate Nursing award U.S. Achievement Acad., 1987; U. Mich. Law Sch. Clarence Darrow scholar, 1988-91. Mem. ABA, Tex. Bar, D.C. Bar, Dallas Bar Assn., J.L. Turner Legal Assn., Sigma Theta Tau. Avocations: travel, water skiing, biking, automotive mechanics. Criminal, Personal injury, Professional liability. Home: 842 Clear Fork Dr Dallas TX 75232-2004 Office: PO Box 222128 Dallas TX 75222-2128

**LENTZ, HAROLD JAMES,** lawyer; b. Hackensack, N.J., Feb. 22, 1947; s. Harold John and Winifred (Fallon) L.; m. Susan Pope, June 22, 1974; 1 son, Miles. BArch, U. Nebr., 1971; M in Bldg. Constrn., U. Fla., 1974; JD, Stetson U., 1983. Bar: Fla. 1984; lic. architect, Fla., Ga., Colo., Tex.; cert. gen. contractor, Fla. Atty. Pilot Corp., Palm Harbor, Fla., 1983-88; prin. H. James Lentz & Assocs., P.A., Palm Harbor, 1988-94; shareholder Lentz & Fair P.A., Palm Harbor, 1994—. Mem. ABA, Fla. Bar Assn., Colo. Bar, D.C. Bar, Am. Arbitration Assn. (mem. panel 1987—), Am. Inst. Constructors, AIA, Trial Advocacy Soc., Nat. Coun. Archtl. Registration Bds., Gargoyle, Phi Kappa Phi, Sigma Lambda Chi. Roman Catholic. Avocations: golf, snow skiing. Construction, General civil litigation. Office: Lentz & Fair PA 35111 US Hwy 19 N Ste 302 Palm Harbor FL 34684-1934

**LENTZ, MARY A.,** lawyer, educator; b. Cleve., May 17, 1942; d. Edward G. and Agnes D. (O'Brien) L. BA, Ursuline Coll., Cleve., 1964; MA, Georgetown U., 1968; JD, Cleve. State U., 1973. Bar: Ohio 1973, Pa. 1984, U.S. Dist. Ct. (no. and ea. divsns.) Ohio 1974, U.S. Ct. Appeals (6th dist.) 1975, U.S. Ct. Appeals (D.C. cir.) 1986, U.S. Supreme Ct. 1977; cert. secondary tchr., Ohio. Tchr. Cleve. Pub. Schs., 1965-74; legal counsel Ohio State Dept. Edn., Columbus, 1974-76; asst. pros. atty. criminal divsn. Cuyahoga County, Cleve., 1976-78; atty., ptnr. Weston, Hurd, Fallon, Paisley & Howley, Cleve., 1978-92; atty. in pvt. practice Cleve., 1992-95; ptnr. Walter & Haverfield, Cleve., 1995-99; chief atty. office civil rights U.S. Dept. Edn., Cleve., 1999—; lectr. and presenter in field. Editor Ohio Sch. Jour., 1977—; author quar. periodical Pvt. Sch. Law Digest, 1982-89. Dir. Sch. Safety and Security Acad., Cuyahoga C.C., Cleve., 1997-99; dir. Inst. for Sch. Resource and Security Officers, Ashland (Ohio) U., 1998—. Recipient Master Tchr. award Jennings Found., 1970, Appreciation award Westlake Police Dept., 1996, Appreciation award Cuyahoga County C.C., 1997, Appreciation award Cleve. Pub. Schs. Divsn. Safety and Security, 1997. Mem. ABA, Ohio State Bar Assn., Greater Cleve. Bar Assn., Geauga (Ohio) Bar Assn., Pa. Bar Assn., D.C. Bar ASsn. Education and schools, General civil litigation, Labor. Office: US Dept of Education Bank One Ctr 600 Superior Ave E Ste 750 Cleveland OH 44114

**LENZI, ALBERT JAMES, JR.,** lawyer; b. Chgo., Feb. 15, 1955; s. Albert Joseph Sr. and Helen Lenzi; adopted children: April Lynn Sorensen, Sean Patrick Sorensen. Student, U.S. Naval Acad., 1972-74; BA, Loyola U., Chgo., 1976; JD, U. of the Pacific, 1979. Bar: Calif. 1979, U.S. Dist. Ct. (ea. dist.) Calif. 1982, U.S. Supreme Ct. 1990. Asst. prof. law Wilamette U., Salem, Oreg., 1979-80; assoc. Thompson Mayhew & Michel, Sacramento, 1980-81, Goldstein, Barceloux & Goldstein, Chico, Calif., 1981-82, Brislain & Zink, Chico, 1982-84; ptnr. Brislain, Zink & Lenzi, Chico, 1984-94, Zink & Lenzi, Chico, 1994—. Served with USN, 1972-74. Mem. ABA, Calif. Trial Lawyers, Consumer Attys. Calif. (bd. mem. 1997-98), Calif. Bar Assn., Chico Kiwanis Club (pres. 1998-99). Democrat. Roman Catholic. Avocations: bowling, reading. Personal injury, Workers' compensation, Insurance. Office: Zink & Lenzi 20 Independence Circle Chico CA 95973

**LEON, ROLANDO LUIS,** lawyer; b. Ponce, P.R., Oct. 18, 1952; s. Luis Manuel and Patricia (Cruz) L.; m. Janet Williams, May 20, 1994; children: Brandon Alexandre, Bryan Christopher, Lauren Patricia. BA in Govt., U. Tex., Arlington, 1972; JD, Tex. Tech. U., 1975; MS in Pub. Adminstrn., Golden Gate U., 1979. Bar: Tex. 1976, U.S. Ct. Mil. Appeals 1977, U.S Dist. Ct. (we., so. dists) Tex. 1981, U.S. Ct. Appeals (5th cir.) 1985; cert. in personal injury and civil trial law Tex. Bd. Legal Specialization, 1985; cert. civil trial advocacy Nat. Bd. Trial Advocacy, 1990. Ptnr. Thornton, Summers, Biechlin, Dunham & Brown LC, Corpus Christi, Tex., 1980—. Editor: Tex. Tech. U. Law Rev., 1974-75. Lt. USN, 1976-80. Mem. ABA, Tex. Bar Assn., Assn. Trial Lawyers Am. General civil litigation, Insurance, Personal injury. Office: Thornton Summers Biechlin Dunham & Brown 600 American Bank Plz 711 N Carancahua St Corpus Christi TX 78475-1120

**LEONARD, ARTHUR J.,** lawyer; b. Pitts., Feb. 7, 1950; s. Thomas and Edith L.; m. Michelle L., June 25, 1983; children: Brian, Tara. BA, Westminster Coll., New Wilmington, Pa., 1971; JD, Duquesne U., Pitts., 1975. Ptnr. Robb Leonard & Mulvihill, Pitts., 1975—. Personal injury, Insurance, Real property. Office: Robb Leonard & Mulvihill 2300 One Mellon Pittsburgh PA 15219

**LEONARD, BRIAN FRANCIS,** lawyer; b. Rolla, N.D., Jan. 27, 1948; s. Howard Francis and Millie Mae (Olson) L.; m. Martha Ellen Ziff, May 11, 1945;children: Sarah, Emily, Brian. BA, U. N.D., 1970; JD, U. Minn., 1973. Bar: Minn. 1973, U.S. Dist. Ct. Minn. 1973, U.S. Ct. Appeals (8th cir.) 1976, U.S. Supreme 1981. Assoc. O'Neill, Burke, O'Neill, Leonard and O'Brien, Ltd., St. Paul, 1973-78, ptnr., 1978-94; ptnr. Leonard, O'Brien, Wilford Spencer and Gale, Ltd., Mpls., 1994—; bus. law instr. adult extension St. Paul TV I, 1978—; adj. prof. U. Minn. Law Sch., 1989—. Bd. dirs. Minn. Literacy Coun., 1993-99. Mem. ABA, Minn. Bar Assn. (bankruptcy sect.), Ramsey County Bar Assn., St. Paul Jaycees (bd. dirs. 1975-79), Rotary club (chmn. com. St. Paul chpt.1985). Republican. Roman Catholic. Bankruptcy, Consumer commercial, Banking. Home: 1532 Tamberwood Trl Saint Paul MN 55125-3362 Office: 100 S 5th St Ste 1200 Minneapolis MN 55402-1216

**LEONARD, EDWIN DEANE,** lawyer; b. Oakland, Calif., Apr. 22, 1929; s. Edwin Stanley and Gladys Eugenia (Lee) L.; m. Judith Swatland, July 10, 1954; children: Garrick Hillman, Susanna Leonard Hill, Rebecca Leonard McCauley, Ethan York. BA, The Principia, 1950; LLB, Harvard U., 1953; LLM, George Washington U., 1956. Bar: D.C. 1953, Ill. 1953, N.Y. 1957. Assoc. Davis Polk Wardwell Sunderland & Kiendl, N.Y.C., 1956-61; ptnr. Davis Polk & Wardwell, N.Y.C., 1961—. Trustee the Brearley Sch., N.Y.C., 1980-90. Served to 1st lt. JAGC, 1953-56. Mem. ABA, N.Y. Bar Assn., N.Y. County Bar Assn., Assn. of Bar of City of N.Y. (chmn. various coms.), Millbrook Equestrian Ctr. (pres.). General corporate, Mergers and acquisitions, Securities. Home: Conklin Hill Rd PO Box 213 Stanfordville NY 12581-0213 Office: Davis Polk & Wardwell 450 Lexington Ave New York NY 10017-3911

**LEONARD, JEFFREY S.,** lawyer; b. Bklyn., Sept. 14, 1945; m. Maxine L. Bortnick, Dec. 28, 1967; children: Deborah, Jennifer. AB in History, U. Rochester, 1967; JD, U. Ariz., 1974. Bar: Ariz. 1974; U.S. Dist. Ct. Ariz. 1974, U.S. Ct. Appeals (9th cir.) 1974, U.S. Supreme Ct. 1985. Law clk. to judge U.S. Dist. Ct. Ariz., 1974-75. Mem. editorial bd. Ariz. Law Rev., 1973-74. Mem. Order of Coif. E-mail: jslphx@lck.net. Federal civil litigation, State civil litigation. Office: Leonard Collins & Kelly PC Two Renaissance Sq 40 N Central Ave Ste 2500 Phoenix AZ 85004-4405

**LEONARD, MICHELLE NAHON,** lawyer; b. Springfield, Mo., Dec. 7, 1962; d. Paul Graffius and Sharon Kay Nahon; m. Patrick Joseph Leonard, Feb. 10, 1954. BA, S.W. Mo. State U., 1986; JD, U. Tulsa, 1992. Bar: Mo. 1992, D.C. 1994, U.S. Dist. Ct. (we. dist.) Mo. 1992, U.S. Ct. Appeals (8th cir.) 1992. Sec. U.S. Congress, Washington, 1986; adminstrv. asst. S.W. Mo. State U., Springfield, 1987-89; assoc. Greene & Curtis, Springfield, Mo., 1992-94; asst. fed. pub. defender Office of Fed. Pub. Defender, Springfield, 1994—. Mem. ABA, Fed. Defenders Assn., Mo. Assn. Criminal Def. Attys., Springfield Met. Bar Assn. (bd. dirs.). Republican. Avocations: tennis, golf, reading, spending time with family, my dogs. Office: Office Fed Pub Defender 1949 E Sunshine St Ste 3-104 Springfield MO 65804-1607

**LEONARD, TIMOTHY DWIGHT,** judge; b. Beaver, Okla., Jan. 22, 1940; s. Dwight and Mary Evelyn Leonard; m. Nancy Louise Laughlin, July 15, 9167; children: Kirstin Dione, Ryan Timothy, Tyler Dwight. BA, U. Okla., 1962, JD, 1965; student, Mil. Naval Justice Sch., 1966. Bar: Okla. 1965, U.S. Dist. Ct. (no. and we. dists.) Okla. 1969, U.S. Ct. Appeals (10th cir.) 1969, U.S. Supreme Ct. 1970. Asst. atty. gen. State of Okla., 1968-70; mem. Okla. Senate, 1979-88; ptnr. Blankenship, Herrold, Russell et al, Oklahoma City, 1970-71, Trippet, Leonard & Kee, Beaver, 1971-88; of counsel Huckaby, Fleming et al, Oklahoma City, 1988-89; U.S. atty. Western Dist. Okla., 1988-92; judge U.S. Dist. Ct. (we. dist.) Okla., 1992—; guest lectr., tchr. Oklahoma City U., 1988-89; mem. U.S. Atty. Gen.'s Adv. Com., 1990-92, chmn. office mgmt. and budget subcom., 1990-92. Co-author: 4 Days, 40 Hours, 1970. Rep. Party candidate for lt. gov. of Okla.; minority leader Okla. State Senate, 1985-86; White House mil. aide, Washington, 1966-67; ex officio mem. Okla. State Fair Bd., Oklahoma City, 1987-90; mem. Gov.'s Coun. on Sports and Phys. Edn., Oklahoma City, 1987-89; mem. Donna Nigh Found., Edmond, Okla., 1987-9. Lt. USN, 1965-68. Named Outstanding Legislator, Okla. Sch. Bd. Assn., 1988. Mem. ABA, Okla. Bar Assn., Phi Alpha Delta, Beta Theta Pi. Republican. Presbyterian. Avocations: basketball, running, reading. Office: US Courthouse 200 NW 4th St Ste 5012 Oklahoma City OK 73102-3031

**LEONARD, WILL ERNEST, JR.,** lawyer; b. Shreveport, La., Jan. 18, 1935; s. Will Ernest and Nellie (Kenner) L.; m. Maureen Laniak; children—Will Ernest III, Sherry Elizabeth, Robert Scott, Stephen Michael, Christopher Anthony, Colleen Mary, Leigh Alison. BA, Tulane U., 1956, LLB, 1958; LLM, Harvard U., 1966. Bar: La. 1958, D.C. 1963, U.S. Supreme Ct. 1963. Announcer sta. WVUE-TV, New Orleans, 1958-60; legislative asst. to U.S. Senator Russell B. Long, 1960-65; profl. staff mem. com. fin. U.S. Senate, 1966-68; mem. Internat. Trade Commn. (formerly U.S. Tariff Commn.), 1968-77, chmn., 1975-76; ptnr. Ablondi, Foster, Sobin & Davidow, Washington, 1996—; Congl. staff fellow Am. Polit. Sci. Assn., 1965-66. Private international, Public international, Administrative and regulatory. Home: 7324 Bradley Blvd Bethesda MD 20817-2130 Office: Ablondi Foster Sobin & Davidow 1150 18th St NW Ste 9th Washington DC 20036-3816

**LEONE, DENNIS DEAN,** lawyer; b. Kingston, N.Y., June 2, 1970; s. Dennis Frank and Karen Jean (Natale) L. BBA, U. Miami, 1992, JD, 1995. Bar: Fla. 1995, U.S. Dist. Ct. (so., no. and mid. dists.) Fla. 1996. Assoc. Schulte Blum & Joblove, Miami, Fla., 1995-96, Blum Perlman & Cherdacil, Miami, Fla., 1996-97, Genovese Lichtman Joblove & Battista, Miami, Fla., 1997—. Mem. ABA (forum on franchising), Dade County Bar Assn. General civil litigation, Franchising. Home: 426 Santander Ave Apt 2 Coral Gables FL 33134-6543 Office: Genovese Lichtman Joblove & Battista 100 SE 2d St Ste 3300 Miami FL 33131

**LEONE, LOUIS ANTHONY,** lawyer, mediator; b. Montclair, N.J., Jan. 6, 1956; s. Anthony and Anne Leone; m. Joan O'Brien; children: Antonella, Alyssa. BA, Am. U., Washington, 1978; JD, Pepperdine U., 1981. Bar: Calif., U.S. Dist. Ct. (no., ctrl. and ea. dists.) Calif. Lawyer Stubbs, Hittig & Leone, San Francisco; mediator U.S. Dist. Ct., San Francisco, 1996—; bd. dirs. San Romon Valley Edn. Found., Danville, Calif. Author (booklet) Student to Student Sexual Harrassment-What Now, 1996. Mem. San Francisco Bar Assn., Contra Costa Bar Assn., Alameda County Bar Assn. Education and schools, General civil litigation, Civil rights. Office: Stubbs Hittig and Leone 1450 Maria Ln Ste 310 Walnut Creek CA 94596-5391

**LEONE, STEPHAN ROBERT,** lawyer; b. Patterson, N.J., Aug. 24, 1939; s. Esterino Brando and Hilda (DeRose) L.; m. Diane Buzzard, June 1959 (div. June 1969); children: Cheryl Alice, Debra Grace; m. Judith Gibson, Nov. 27, 1971. BA, Columbia U., 1961; JD, Yeshiva U., 1988. Bar: N.J. 1989, U.S. Dist. Ct. N.J. 1989, N.Y. 1989, U.S. Dist. Ct. (so. dist.) N.Y. 1989, D.C. 1989. Ptnr. Bathgate, Wegener, Dugan & Wolf, Newark and Lakewood, N.J., 1988-97; mng. mem. Carluccio, Leone, Dimon, Doyle & Sacks, LLC, Toms River, N.J., 1997—. Chmn. Ocean County Dem. Fin. Com., 1991—; trustee Ocean County Coll. Found., 1973—. Recipient Disting. Svc. award Brick Jaycees, 1962; named Man of Yr. Brick Twp. C. of C. 1976. Mem. AMA, N.J. Bar Assn., Ocean County Bar Assn., Toms River Country Club. Avocations: skiing, sailing, tennis. Condemnation, General civil litigation, Real property. Office: Carluccio Leone Dimon Doyle & Sacks LLC 9 Robbins St Toms River NJ 08753-7628

**LEONG, LINDA S.,** lawyer; b. Hong Kong, July 14, 1957. JD, Hunphrey's Sch. Law, 1991. Legal sec. Strauss, Neibauer, Anderson & Ramirez, Modesto, Calif., 1980-90; law clk. Lamb & Michael, Modesto, Calif., 1990-91, ptnr., 1991—. Mentor Stansilaus County Yourth Ct., Modesto, 1997-98. Mem. ABA, Calif. Bar Assn. Avocations: golf, reading, ballroom dancing. Bankruptcy, Consumer commercial, Contracts commercial. Office: Lamb & Michael 1314 G St Modesto CA 95354-2422

**LEONHARDT, FREDERICK WAYNE,** lawyer; b. Daytona Beach, Fla., Oct. 26, 1949; s. Frederick Walter and Gaetane Larua Leonhardt; m. Victoria Ann Cook, Dec. 27, 1975; children: Ashley Victoria, Frederick Whitaker. BA, U. Fla., 1971, JD, 1974. Bar: Fla. 1974, N.C. 1984, D.C. 1985; cert. real estate lawyer, Fla. Gen. cousnel Fla. Ho. of Reps., 1974-75; ptnr. Cobb, Cole and Bell, Daytona Beach, 1975-79; pres. Leonhardt & Upchurch, 1979-87; ptnr. Holland & Knight, Orlando, Fla., 1987-93, Gray, Harris & Robinson, Orlando, Melbourne, Tallahassee, 1993—. Chmn. bd. dirs. Orlando/Orange County Compact, 1989-90, Orlando/Orange County Civic Facilities Authority, 1998—; founder Leadership Daytona Beach; grad. Leadership Fla., mem. bd. regents, 1995—, chmn. state program, 1997-98, chair-elect 1999; active Leadership Ctrl. Fla., Leadership Orlando; past chmn. Ctrl. Fla. Sports Commn., bd. dirs., 1992-98; mem. Orange County Civic Facilities Authority, 1998—; bd. dirs. Orlando/Orange County Conv. and Visitors Bur.; founder VCARD; past gen. campaign mgr. Volusia County United Way; bd. dirs. Celebration Health Found., Ctr. for Drug Free Living, Prevent Blindness Fla. Mem. ABA (chmn. stae and local govt. law sect. 1997-98, editor sect. newsletter 1991-94), Orange and Volusia Counties Bar Assn., Greater Orlando C. of C. (chmn. 1991-92), Daytona Beach Area C. of C. (pres. 1985), Fla. C. of C. (bd. dirs. 1984-90, 93—), Phi Alpha Delta, Delta Chi. Real property, Administrative and regulatory, Contracts commercial. Office: Gray Harris & Robinson PA PO Box 3068 201 E Pine St Ste 1200 Orlando FL 32801-2798

**LEONIE, ANDREW DRAKE, III,** judge, lawyer; b. Loma Linda, Calif., Dec. 13, 1952; s. Andrew and Norma Lou Leonie; m. Jamie Lorraine Chism, June 16, 1995; children: Andrew, Aaron. BS, Western Ill. U., 1972; MA, U. Ill., 1974; JD, St. Mary's U., 1977; postgrad., Andrews U., 1998—. Assoc. Smith, McIleran, Lauderdale & Jones, Weslaco, Tex., 1977-79; ptnr. Jones, Marsh, Rodriguez, Welch & Leonie, McAllen, Tex., 1980-85; asst. atty. gen. Atty. Gen. Tex., Dallas, 1987-95; pvt. practice Dallas, 1995-96; judge, family law ct. master 1st Jud. Region Tex., Dallas, 1995—; mediator Christian Conciliation Svc., McAllen, Tex., 1984—; advisor Tex. Senate Com. on Family Law Issues, 1996. Contbr. article to profl. jour., chpt. to book. Mem. exec. com. Rockwall (Tex.) Rep. Party, 1989-98; commr. planning and zoning commn. City of Rockwall, 1990-92. Recipient Pro Bono award Rockwall County Bar Assn., 1995. Mem. Tex. Bar Assn. (vice chair mcpl. judges sect.), Dallas Bar Assn. (mem. judiciary com., ethics com. 1994—), Christian Legal Soc., Rotary (pres. Rockwall (Tex.) Breakfast Club). Republican. Episcopalian. Avocations: running, gardening, religious history. Home: 4617 Lakepointe Ave Rowlett TX 75088 Office: First Jud Region Tex George Allen Civil Cts Bldg 600 Commerce St Rm 4110 Dallas TX 75202-4616

**LEON-SOTOMAYOR, JOSE RAFAEL,** lawyer, engineer, educator; b. Ponce, P.R., Aug. 27, 1930; s. Jose León and Olga Sotomayor; m. Carmen D. Ribas-Rivera, Dec. 11, 1954; children—Jose R., Teresa, Allen L., Carlos J., Carmen L., Candida M., David A., Juan E., Glorimar, Carmen D., Olga G. BSME, U. P.R., 1954; JD magna cum laude, Catholic U. of P.R., 1970. Bar: P.R. 1970, U.S. Dist. Ct. P.R. 1973, U.S. Supreme Ct., 1985, U.S. Ct. Mil. Appeals, 1987. Pvt. practice, Ponce, 1970—; assoc. prof. Sch. of Law, Cath. U. of P.R., Ponce, 1977-93, prof., 1993-99; spl. cons., v.p. fin. affairs, 1977-84; cons. and lectr. in law. Author: Casebook on Notarial Law, 1984; Puerto Rico Real Property Law Manual, 1984, Family Law in Puerto Rico. Contbr. articles to profl. jours. V.p., bd. trustees, Ponce Med. Sch. Found., 1979-93; legal cons. Com. on Civil Legislation, Ho. of Reps. of Legislature P.R., 1982-84. Capt. USAF. Decorated Knight Equestrian Order Holy Sepulcher Jerusalem. Recipient Am. Jurisprudence award, 1970; P.R. Bar Assn. award, 1970, Ponce Bar Assn. award, 1970, Outstanding Alumni award Cath. U. P.R., 1983. Mem. Assn. Trial Lawyers Am., ASME, P.R. Bar Assn., Acad. Arts, History and Archaeology P.R., Coll. Engrs. and Surveyors P.R., Deportivo de Ponce (treas. 1975-77, v.p. 1977-78), Ponce Yacht & Fishing Club, William's Shooting Club, KC, Phi Delta Kappa, Phi Alpha Delta, Nu Sigma Beta. Republican. Roman Catholic. Probate, Real property, Family and matrimonial. Home: 334 St 2 La Rambla Ponce PR 00731 Office: Marvesa Bldg Office Ste 201 Rambla Ponce PR 00731

**LEONTSINIS, GEORGE JOHN,** lawyer; b. St. Louis, Feb. 23, 1937; s. John Peter and Lula (Lorandos) L.; m. Patricia Marie Demetrulias, July 9, 1967; children: Anne Marie, Michelle Lynne. BSBA, Washington U., St. Louis, 1958, JD, 1961; LLM, NYU, 1964. Bar: Mo. 1961. Ptnr. Greensfelder, Hemker & Gale, P.C., St. Louis, 1964—. Bd. dirs. Ahepa Apts., St. Louis, 1985-95, Citizens for Modern Transit, St. Louis, 1988-96, Citizen's com. high speed rail Chgo.-St. Louis Corridor, Springfield, Ill., 1992-96. Capt. U.S. Army, 1961-63. Mem. Am. Hellenic Ednl. and Profl. Assn., Racquet Club. Avocation: tennis. Contracts commercial, General corporate, Private international. Office: Greensfelder Hemker & Gale P C 10 S Broadway Saint Louis MO 63102-1712

**LEOPOLD, MARK F.,** lawyer; b. 1950; s. Paul F. and Corinne (S.) L.; m. Jacqueline Rood, June 9, 1974; children: Jonathan, David. BA, Am. U., Washington, 1972; JD, Loyola U., 1975. Bar: Ill. 1975, U.S. Dist. Ct. (no. dist.) Ill. 1975, Fla. 1976, U.S. Ct. Appeals (7th cir.) 1976, U.S. Ct. Appeals (8th cir.) 1979. Assoc. McConnell & Campbell, Chgo., 1975-79; atty. U.S. Gypsum Co., Chgo., 1979-82, sr. litigation atty., 1982-84; sr. litigation atty. USG Corp., Chgo., 1985-87, corp. counsel, 1987, sr. corp. counsel, 1987-89; asst. gen. counsel G.D. Searle & Co., 1989-93, Household Internat., Inc., Prospect Heights, Ill., 1993—; adv. bd. Roosevelt U. Legal Asst. Program, 1994—; legal writing instr. Loyola U. Sch. Law, Chgo., 1978-79. Pres., bd. dirs. Internat. Policyholders Assn., 1992-93; del. candidate Rep. Nat. Conv., 1996; mem. Lake County Study Commn. II, Waukegan, Ill., 1989-90; commr. Lake County, Waukegan, 1982-84, Forest Preserve, Libertyville, Ill., 1982-84, Pub. Bldg. Commn., Waukegan, 1980-82; chmn. Deerfield Twp. Rep. Cen. Com., Highland Park, Ill., 1984-86, officer, 1981-89; vice chmn. Lake County Rep. Cen. Com., Waukegan, 1982-84; bd. dirs. Am. Jewish Com., Chgo., 1988-91. Recipient Disting. Svc. award Jaycees, Highland Park, 1983. Mem. ABA, (antitrust com. 1976—, litigation com. 1980—, torts and ins. practice com. 1989—), Pi Sigma Alpha, Omicron Delta Kappa. Republican. Antitrust, Federal civil litigation, Product liability. Office: Household Internat 2700 Sanders Rd Prospect Heights IL 60070-2701

**LEPELSTAT, MARTIN L.,** lawyer; b. Bklyn., Apr. 10, 1947; s. Larry and Nana (Citrin) L.; m.. Audrey A. Fireman, Jan. 18, 1975; children: Rachel M., Michael H. BBA, CCNY, 1968; JD, Cornell U., 1971; MBA, U. Mich., 1970; LLM, NYU, 1976. Bar: N.J. 1978, N.Y. 1972, Fla. 1972. Tax cons. Touche Ross, N.Y.C., 1971-73; assoc. Weil, Gotshal & Manges, N.Y.C., 1973-78, Greenbaum, Rowe, Smith, Woodbridge, N.J., 1978—. Bd. dirs. Winston Towers 300 Assn., Inc., Cliffside Park, N.J., 1978-86. Fellow Am. Coll. of Trust and Estate Counsel, 1991—; mem. ABA (tax and real estate probate com.), N.J. State Bar Assn., Middlesex County Bar Assn. (pres. tax com. 1987-88, pres. probate com. 1986-87, trustee 1988-92), Fla. Bar Assn. Estate planning, Corporate taxation, Estate taxation. Home: 20 Snoden Ln Watchung NJ 07060-6253 Office: Greenbaum Rowe Smith PO Box 5600 Woodbridge NJ 07095-0988

**LEPP, GERALD PETER,** lawyer; b. Milw., Sept. 26, 1932; s. William Harris and Ida (Mendelson) L.; m. Sept. 8, 1963; children: Rebecca Anne, Michael Niels. BA, U. Wis., 1954; JD, Harvard U., 1959; LLM, NYU, 1973. Bar: Wis. 1959, D.C. 1962, N.Y. 1963, U.S. Supreme Ct. Assoc. counsel Continental Grain Co., N.Y.C., 1969-78, dir. of arbitration, 1987—; gen. counsel Cobec (USA) Brazilian Trading Co., Inc., N.Y.C., 1978-80; mng. atty. Gerald P. Lepp, N.Y.C., 1980-86; counsel to Nourse & Bowles, N.Y.C., 1986-87; dir. arbitration Continental Grain Co., N.Y., 1987-92; ADR adminstr., U.S. Dist. Ct. (ea. dist.) N.Y., Bklyn., 1992—. Contbr. articles to profl. jours. 1st Lt. USAR, 1954-56. Mem. ABA, Am. Fgn. Law Assn. (bd. dirs. 1987-89, v.p. 1989), Assn. of Bar of City of N.Y. (inter-Am. affairs com. 1989-90), Internat. Bar Assn., Maritime Law Assn. U.S. (arbitration com. 1986—), Lawyers for the Arts (vol. 1991—). Avocation: squash. Federal civil litigation, Private international.

**LERACH, RICHARD FLEMING,** lawyer; b. Pitts., Oct. 26, 1940; s. Richard E. and Evelyn (Fleming) L.; m. Judith Ifft, June 29, 1963; children: Mollie Lerach Gannon, Richard I. BBA, U. Pitts., 1962, LLB, 1965. Bar: N.Y. 1966, Pa. 1969. Atty. USX Corp., Pitts., 1968-76, gen. atty., 1976-85, sr. gen. atty., 1985-98, asst. gen. counsel, 1998—; dir. Pitts. Home Savs. Bank, 1990—. Federal civil litigation, State civil litigation, Toxic tort. Home: 796 Flint Ridge Rd Pittsburgh PA 15243-1101 Office: USX Corp 600 Grant St Rm 1515 Pittsburgh PA 15219-2702

**LERER, NEAL M.,** lawyer; b. Chelmsford, Mass., June 20, 1954; m. Rose P. Meegan, July 28, 1991; 1 child, Benjamin Joseph. BA, Brown U., 1976; JD, Duke Law Sch., 1979. Bar: Mass. 1979, U.S. Dist. Ct. Mass. 1980, U.S. Ct. Appeals (1st cir.) 1991. Ptnr. Martin, Magnuson, McCarthy & Kenney, Boston, 1980-96; mng. atty., pvt. practice Chelmsford, Mass., 1996—; corporator Lowell (Mass.) 5 Cents Savings Bank, 1985—. Co-author: Personal Injury and Death, 1980, Damages in Massachusetts, 1990, Personal Injury Litigation in Massachusetts, 1991, Premises Liability, 1994. Reader Recording for the Blind, Cambridge, Mass., 1987-94; bd. dirs. Goodwin Fund; officer Town of Chelmsford Scholarship Fund; dir. Town of Chelmsford Scholarship Com. Mem. Mass. Bar Assn. (ins. com.), Mass. Bar Found., Greater Lowell Bar Assn., Brown Club of Boston (bd. dirs., co-pres. 1998—). General civil litigation, Personal injury, Insurance. Office: 56 Central Sq Chelmsford MA 01824-3055

**LERMAN, KENNETH BRIAN,** lawyer; b. N.Y.C., Mar. 3, 1961; s. Robert Allan and Ellen Lerman. BA in Bus. Mgmt. and Govt., Clark U., 1983; JD, Emory U., 1986. Bar: Conn. 1987, U.S. Dist. Ct. Conn. 1987, Fla. 1997. Assoc. Siegel, O'Connor, Schiff, Zangari & Kainen, Hartford, Conn., 1986-88; pvt. practice Kenneth B. Lerman, P.C., Windsor, Conn., 1988—; counsel Conn. chpt. Sickle Cell Disease Assn. of Am., 1991—. Co-founder, v.p. Wadsworth Atheneum Art Club, Hartford, 1990-93; mem. exec. com. Hartford chpt. Anti-Defamation League, 1993—; founder, coach, pres. Lacrosse team Clark U., 1981-83. Mem. ABA, Fla. Bar Assn., Conn. Bar Assn., Hartford County Bar Assn., New Eng. Intercollegiate Lacrosse Assn. (v.p., dir. club divsn. 1983). General corporate, Real property, Securities. Office: 651 Day Hill Rd Windsor CT 06095-1719

**LERNER, ALAN JAY,** lawyer; b. Scranton, Pa., July 29, 1949; s. Jack and Dorothy Rene (Golob) L.; m. Mary Alicia Kincaid, Nov. 9, 1979; children—Hailey, Joan; m. Estelle Fields, Dec. 21, 1970 (div. Apr. 1978); children—Sonia, Bernadette. B.A. in Polit. Sci. cum laude, San Fernando Valley Coll., 1971; J.D. magna cum laude, U. Toledo, 1974. Bar: Mont. 1974, U.S. Dist. Ct. Mont. 1975, U.S. Ct. Appeals (9th cir.) 1975, U.S. Supreme Ct. 1984. Assoc. Crowley Law Firm, Billings, Mont., 1974-75, Hartelius & Lewin, Great Falls, Mont., 1975-76; ptnr. Richter & Lerner, 1976-81; sole practice, Bigfork, Mont., 1981-88; sole practice Kalispell, Mont., 1988—. Author U. Toledo Law Rev., 1973, editor, 1974. Author: (novel) Spare Parts, 1980. Teaching fellow U. Toledo, 1973; Ohio State Bar scholar, 1972, PAD Nat. scholar, 1973. Mem. Assn. Trial Lawyers Am., Mont. Trial Lawyers Assn., Mont. Bar Assn., N.W. Mont. Bar Assn. Democrat. Jewish. Insurance, Personal injury, State civil litigation. Home: 88 Stafford St Kalispell MT 59901-2729 Office: 2450 Us Hwy 93 S Kalispell MT 59901-7532

**LERNER, HARRY,** lawyer, consultant; b. Easton, Pa., Jan. 24, 1939; s. Albert I. and Shirley (Kraus) L.; m. Sherryl Adrienne Blumin, Nov. 18, 1962; 1 child, Michelle Hope. BA, Cornell U., 1960; JD, NYU, 1963. Bar: N.Y. State 1963, N.J. 1966. Assoc. Otterbourg, Steindler, Houston & Rosen, N.Y.C., 1964-65, Robert Greenberg, West New York, N.J., 1965-67; asst. house counsel Ronson Corp., Bridgewater, N.J., 1967-71; asst. to gen. counsel Ronson Corp., 1971-75, sec., corp. counsel, 1975-82; corp. law cons., 1982—; v.p. Investors and Lenders Ltd., 1988-89. Served with U.S. Army, 1963-64. Mem. N.J. Bar Assn., Zeta Beta Tau. General corporate, Contracts commercial.

**LERNER, MAX KASNER,** lawyer; b. N.Y.C., Dec. 27, 1916; s. Louis Lerner and Beckie Kasner; m. Lila Schachner, Oct. 5, 1943; children: Helene, Beth. LLB, Bklyn. Law Sch., 1939. Bar: N.Y. 1940, U.S. Supreme Ct. 1952. Author: ABA Journal of Limitations Imposed on Radio and TV, 1949. Commdg. officer U.S. Army, 1942-46, POW. Trademark and copyright, Probate, Criminal. Home: 350 1st Ave New York NY 10010-4902

**LERNER, STEVEN PAUL,** lawyer; b. Bklyn., Nov. 9, 1958; s. Lloyd J. and Arline May (Solomon) L.; m. Donna Lynn Borges, Sept. 9, 1984; children: Kaitlin Olga, Colin Lane, Cody Layton. BA, L.I. U., 1980; JD, Syracuse U., 1983. Bar: N.Y. 1984, U.S. Dist. Ct. (ea. and so. dists.) N.Y. 1984, U.S. Ct. Appeals (2d cir.) 1984. Assoc. Robert & Schneider, Hempstead, N.Y., 1983-86; ptnr. Robert, Lerner & Robert, Rockville Centre, N.Y., 1986—. Advisor, sponsor Nassau County Rep. Com., Mineola, N.Y., 1990—; sponsor Suffolk County Rep. Com., Riverhead, N.Y., 1992—; vice chmn. budget com. Baldwin (N.Y.) Ednl. Assembly and Baldwin Bd. Edn., 1994; mem., lectr. Nassau/Suffolk Health Sys. Agy., N.Y., 1994. Mem. ABA, Nassau Bar Assn., Suffolk Bar Assn., Kings Bar Assn., Nassau Acad. Law (lectr. 1987—), Nat. Acad. Elder Care Attys. Jewish. Avocations: golf, all sports, my children. General practice, Probate, Pension, profit-sharing, and employee benefits. Home: 1854 Longfellow St Baldwin NY 11510-2336 Office: Robert Lerner & Robert 100 Merrick Rd Ste 508W Rockville Centre NY 11570-4880

**LESAGE, TRACY ROCHELLE,** lawyer; b. Upland, Calif., Mar. 16, 1969; d. Thomas Raphael and Barbara Jean (Douglas) McKinney; m. Robert W. LeSage, Jan. 14, 1995; 1 child, Taylor W. BA, UCLA, 1991; JD, Western State U., Fullerton, Calif., 1995. Bar: Calif. 1996, U.S. Dist. Ct. (ctrl. dist.) Calif. 1997, U.S. Ct. Appeals (9th cir.) 1998. Assoc. atty. Elder & Manning LLP.C., Santa Ana, Calif., 1999—. Contbr. to Western State U. Law Rev., 1994. Mem. ATLA, Orange County Bar Assn., William P. Gray Legion Lex Inns of Ct. Avocation: golf. Personal injury. Office: Elder & Manning LLP 1912 N Broadway Ste 210 Santa Ana CA 92706-2621

**LESAR, JAMES HIRAM,** lawyer; b. Lawrence, Kans., May 23, 1940; s. Hiram Henry and Rosa Lee (Berry) L.; m. May Siang Lim, Aug. 31, 1968; 1 child, Jennifer Claire. BA, U. Ill., 1962, postgrad., 1962-64; JD, U. Wis., 1969. Bar: Wis. 1969, U.S. Ct. Appeals (D.C. cir.) 1971, D.C. 1972, U.S. Dist. Ct. D.C. 1972, U.S. Ct. Appeals (6th cir.) 1973, U.S. Supreme Ct. 1974, U.S. Ct. Appeals (5th and 11th cirs.) 1981, U.S. Ct. Claims 1986, U.S. Ct. Appeals (1st cir.) 1987, U.S. Dist. Ct. Md. 1990, U.S. Ct. Appeals (4th cir.) 1990. Atty. Com. to Investigate Assassinations, Washington, 1970-74; pvt. practice Washington, 1976—; part-time atty. Fensterwald & Assocs., Washington, 1980-85; v.p. Assassination Archives and Rsch. Ctr., Washington, 1985-91, pres., 1991—. Mem. Am. Soc. Access Profls. Avocations: reading, basketball, bowling. Administrative and regulatory. Office: Assassination Archives and Rsch Ctr 1003 K St NW Ste 204 Washington DC 20001

**LESHER, STEPHEN HARRISON,** lawyer; b. Tucson, Dec. 31, 1953; s. Robert Overton and June Ruth (Huffer) L. BA, U. Vt., 1975; JD, U. Ariz., 1978. Bar: Ariz. 1978, U.S. Dist. Ct. Ariz. 1978, U.S. Ct. Appeals (9th cir.) 1991. Assoc. Lesher & Kimble PC, Tucson, 1978-79; ptnr. Lesher, Clausen & Borodkin PC, Tucson, 1980-83, Lesher & Borodkin PC, Tucson, 1983-91, Lesher & Williams, Tucson, 1991-93, Lesher & Lesher, Tucson, 1993-99, Kimble, Lesher, Corradini & Toone, Tucson, 1999—. Mem. ABA, Am. Bd. Trial Advocates, Def. Rsch. Inst., Tucson Country Club. Republican. Avocations: computers. Insurance, General civil litigation, Appellate. Home: 5667 N Via Salerosa Tucson AZ 85750-1154 Office: Kimble Lesher Corradini & Toone 5151 E Broadway Blvd Tucson AZ 85711-3705

**LESHY, JOHN D.,** lawyer, legal educator, government official; b. Winchester, Ohio, Oct. 7, 1944; s. John and Dolores (King) L.; m. Helen M. Sandalls, Dec. 15, 1973; 1 child, David Alexander. AB cum laude, Harvard U., 1966, JD magna cum laude, 1969. Trial atty. Civil Rights Divsn. Dept. Justice, Washington, 1969-72; atty. Natural Resources Def. Coun., Palo Alto, Calif., 1972-77; assoc. solicitor energy and resources Dept. Interior, Washington, 1977-80; prof. law Ariz. State U., Tempe, 1980—; spl. counsel to chair Natural Resources Com. U.S. Ho. Reps., Washington, 1992-93; solicitor (gen. counsel) Dept. Interior, 1993—; cons. Calif. State Land Commn., N.Mex. Atty. Gen., Western Govs. Assn., Congl. Rsch. Svc., Ford Found.; mem. com. Onshore Oil & Gas Leasing, NAS Nat. Rsch. Coun., 1989-90; vis. prof. Sch. Law U. San Diego, 1990. Author: The Mining Law: A Study in Perpetual Motion, 1987, The Arizona State Constitution, 1993; co-author Federal Public Land and Resources Law, 3d edit., 1992; contbr. articles, book chpts. to profl. jours., environ. jours. Bd. dirs. Ariz. Ctr. Law in Pub. Interest, 1981-86, Ariz. Raft Adventures, 1982-92; mem. Gov.'s Task Force Recreation on Fed. Lands, 1985-86, Gov.'s Task Force Environ. Impact Assessment, 1990, City of Phoenix Environ. Quality Commn., 1987-90. Robinson Cox vis. fellow U. Western Australia Law Sch., Perth, 1985, rsch. fellow U. Southampton, Eng., 1986; Ford Found. grantee, Resources for the Future grantee. Democrat. Avocations: piano, hiking, whitewater rafting, photography. Office: Department of the Interior Solicitor 1849 C St NW Washington DC 20240-0002

**LESKINEN, STEVE PETER,** lawyer; b. Gardner, Mass., Aug. 6, 1953; s. Allan Oliver and Grace Esther (Rawson) L.; m. Karen Mae Shoemaker, June 11, 1976; children: Michael, Kristina, Amanda; m. Sharon Getz, May 17, 1997; 1 child, Shane. BA, Bucknell U., 1975; JD, U. Pa., 1978. Bar: Pa. 1978. Law clk. Fayette County Ct., Uniontown, Pa., 1978-79; pvt. practice Uniontown, 1979—; ptnr. Leskinen & Cook, Uniontown, 1980—; marina cons. Leskinen Enterprises, Inc., Uniontown, 1983—; solicitor Fayette County Domestic Rels. Office, Uniontown, 1979-94, Wharton Twp., 1982—, Ohiopyle Borough, 1989—; asst. dist. atty. Fayette County Dist. Atty.'s Office, Uniontown, 1991—. Recipient postgrad. scholarship NCAA, Bucknell U., 1975; named Acad. All-Am., Coll. Sports Info Dirs. Assn., Bucknell U., 1975. Mem. Fayette County Bar Assn. (pres. 1991, chmn. rules com. 1986-90), Pa. Bar Assn., Pa. Trial Lawyers Assn. Democrat. Avocations: golf, snow skiing, water skiing, canoeing, bicycling. Personal injury, Probate, Land use and zoning (including planning). Office: 55 E Church St Uniontown PA 15401-3530

**LESLIE, RICHARD MCLAUGHLIN,** lawyer, educator; b. Chgo., Oct. 31, 1936; s. Richard S. and Belle (McLaughlin) L.; m. Nancy Elizabeth Lomax; children: Saralynn, Richard W., Lance T. BA, U. Fla., 1958; JD, U. Mich., 1961. Bar: Ill. 1961, Fla. 1962, U.S. Dist. Ct. (no. dist.) Ill., U.S. Dist. Ct. (so. and mid. dists.) Fla., U.S. Ct. Appeals (5th cir.), U.S. Ct. Appeals (11th cir.), U.S. Supreme Ct. 1970. Assoc. Jacobs & McKenna, Chgo., 1961-63, Louis G. Davidson, Chgo., 1963; assoc., then ptnr. Shutts & Bowen, Miami, Fla., 1964—; adj. prof. trial advocacy program U. Miami Law Sch., 1979-89. Chmn. bd. trustees Plymouth Congl. Ch., Miami, 1978. Capt. USAR, 1961-67. Mem. ABA (com. chmn. torts and ins. practice sect. 1980, 88, 93, elect. to counsel 1998—), Fla. Def. Lawyers Assn. (pres. 1987), Fedn. Ins. and Corp. Counsel (v.p. 1987, bd. dirs. 1988-93), Dade County Bar Assn. (bd. dirs. 1987-90, 94-97, 99—), Maritime Law Assn. U.S. (arrangements com.), Fla. Bar Assn. (admiralty com.), Ill. Bar Assn., Average Adjustors Assn., Phi Delta Theta, Delta Theta Phi, Miami City Club, Riviera Country Club

(Coral Gables, Fla.). Avocations: tennis, skiing, travel. Admiralty, General civil litigation, Personal injury. Home: 4116 Pinta Ct Coral Gables FL 33146-1119 Office: Shutts & Bowen Miami Ctr 201 S Biscayne Blvd Miami FL 33131

**LESLIE, ROBERT LORNE,** lawyer; b. Adak, Alaska, Feb. 24, 1947; s. J. Lornie and L. Jean (Conelly) L.; children—Lorna Jean, Elizabeth Allen. B.S., U.S. Mil. Acad., 1969; J.D., Hastings Coll. Law, U. Calif.-San Francisco, 1974. Bar: Calif. 1974, D.C. 1979, U.S. Dist. Ct. (no. dist.) Calif. 1974, U.S. Ct. Claims 1975, U.S. Tax Ct. 1975, U.S. Ct. Appeals (9th and D.C. cirs.), U.S. Ct. Mil. Appeals 1980, U.S. Supreme Ct. 1980. Commd. 2d lt. U.S. Army, 1969, advanced through grades to maj., 1980; govt. trial atty. West Coast Field Office, Contract Appeals, Litigation Div. and Regulatory Law Div., Office JAG, Dept. Army, San Francisco, 1974-77; sr. trial atty. and team chief Office of Chief Trial Atty., Dept. Army, Washington, 1977-80 ; ptnr. McInerney & Dillon, Oakland, Calif., 1980—; lectr. on govt. contracts CSC, Continuing Legal Edn. Program; lectr. in govt. procurement U.S. Army Materiel Command. Col. USAR. Decorated Silver Star, Purple Heart. Mem. ABA, Fed. Bar Assn., Associated Gen. Contractors, The Beavers. Government contracts and claims, Construction, Contracts commercial. Office: Ordway Bldg Fl 18 Oakland CA 94612-3610

**LESMAN, MICHAEL STEVEN,** lawyer; b. N.Y.C., May 26, 1953; s. Herman and Estelle (Levy) L.; m. Gail R. Grossman, May 26, 1980; children: Adam, Laura. BA magna cum laude, CUNY, 1975; JD, Bklyn. Law Sch., 1982. Bar: N.Y. 1983. From assoc. to supervising atty. Jacobowitz & Lysaght, N.Y.C., 1983-88; atty. of record, mng. atty. Jacobowitz, Garfinkel & Lesman, N.Y.C., 1989—; staff counsel Am. Internat. Cos., N.Y.C., 1989—. Mem. ABA, N.Y. State Bar Assn., N.Y. County Lawyers Assn., Def. Rsch. Inst., N.Y. State Trial Lawyers Assn. State civil litigation, Personal injury, Insurance. Office: Jacobowitz Garfinkel & Lesman 7 Hanover Sq New York NY 10004-2616

**LESNICK, IRVING ISAAC,** lawyer; b. Bronx, Dec. 23, 1932; s. George L. and Sadie (Rovner) L.; m. Sheila H. Chorney, June 5, 1954; children: Charles Schorr, Grace. BA, Columbia U., 1954; LLB, Yale U., 1959. Bar: N.Y. 1960, Fla. 1982, U.S. Dist. Ct. (so. and ea. dists.) N.Y. 1961, U.S. Dist. Ct. (so. and middle dists.) Fla. 1983. Assoc. Poletti, Friedin, Prashker & Harnett, N.Y.C., 1959-60; assoc. Koeppel, Sommer, Lesnick & Martone, P.C. and predecessor firms, Mineola, N.Y., 1961, ptnr., 1962-81; pvt. practice Garden City, N.Y. and Boca Raton, Fla., 1981-86; ptnr. Dryer & Traub, Garden City, N.Y. and Boca Raton, Fla., 1986-88; v.p. Harnett, Lesnick & Ripps, P.A., Boca Raton, 1988—; spl. prof. Hofstra U. Co-author: The Law of Life and Health Insurance, 1988; contbr. articles to profl. publs. With U.S. Army, 1954-56. Mem. ABA, N.Y. State Bar Assn., Fla. Bar Assn., Assn. of Bar of City of N.Y., Yale Club. Democrat. Jewish. Insurance, General corporate, Administrative and regulatory. Office: Harnett Lesnick & Ripps PA 150 E Palmetto Park Rd Ste 500 Boca Raton FL 33432-4834

**LESOURD, NANCY SUSAN OLIVER,** lawyer, writer; b. Atlanta, Aug. 22, 1953; d. Carl Samuel and Jane (Meadows) Oliver; m. Jeffrey Alan LeSourd, Oct. 18, 1986; children: Jeffrey Luke, Catherine Victoria. BA in Polit. Sci., Agnes Scott Coll., 1975; MA in History, Edn., Tufts U., 1977; JD, Georgetown U., 1984. Bar: Pa. 1985, D.C. 1986, Va. 1992, Fed. Cir. Ct. Appeals., 1988, U.S. Claims Ct., 1988. Instr. Newton (Mass.) High Sch., 1976-78, The Stony Brook (N.Y.) Sch., 1978-81; assoc. Gammon and Grange, Washington, 1984-88; ptnr. Gammon and Grange, P.C., 1988—; mgr. Marshall-LeSourd L.L.C., 1996—; legal commentator (radio shows) UPI News, Washington, 1985-91, Focus on the Family (Washington corr.), Colorado Springs, Colo., 1987-94; legal columnist Christian Mgmt. Rev., Downers Grove, Ill., 1987-90; spkr. numerous confs. Author: No Longer The Hero, 1992; editor: Georgetown Law Jour., 1982-84; contbr. articles to profl. jours. Bd. dirs. Arlington County Equal Employment Opportunity Commn., 1985. William Robertson Coe fellow SUNY, Stony Brook, 1978. Mem. D.C. Bar Assn., Va. Bar Assn., Christian Legal Society (bd. dirs. 1990-93). Republican. Intellectual property, Non-profit and tax-exempt organizations, General corporate. Home: 2624 New Banner Ln Herndon VA 20171-2659 Office: Gammon and Grange PC 8280 Greensboro Dr Fl 7 Mc Lean VA 22102-3807

**LESSEN, LARRY LEE,** federal judge; b. Lincoln, Ill., Dec. 25, 1939; s. William G. and Grace L. (Plunkett) L.; m. Susan Marian Vaughn, Dec. 5, 1964; children: Laura, Lynn, William. BA, U. Ill., 1960, JD, 1962. Bar: Ill. 1962, U.S. Dist. Ct. (ctrl. dist.) Ill. 1964, U.S. Bankruptcy Ct. 1964, U.S. Tax Ct. 1982, U.S. Ct. Appeals (7th cir.) 1981, U.S. Supreme Ct. 1981. Law clk. to presiding justice U.S. Dist. Ct., 1962-64; asst. state's atty. State of Ill., Danville, 1964-67; mng. ptnr. Sebat, Swanson, Banks and Lessen, Danville, 1967-85; judge U.S. Bankruptcy Ct., Danville, 1973-85, U.S. Magistrate, Danville, 1973-84; chief judge U.S. Bankruptcy Ct., Springfield, Ill., 1985-93; U.S. bankruptcy judge Springfield divsn., 1993—. Mem. ABA, FBA, Sangamon County Bar Assn., Vermilion County Bar Assn, Nat. Conf. Bankruptcy Judges (bd. govs. 1994-97), Am. Bankruptcy Inst., Lincoln-Douglas Inn of Cts. Office: US Bankruptcy Ct 235 U S Courthouse 600 E Monroe St Springfield IL 62701-1626

**LESSER, HENRY,** lawyer; b. London, Feb. 28, 1947; came to U.S., 1976; s. Bernard Martin and Valerie Joan (Leslie) L.; m. Jane Michaels, June 29, 1969. BA with honors, Cambridge (Eng.) U., 1968, MA with honors, 1972; LLM, Harvard U., 1973. Bar: Eng. 1969, N.Y. 1977, U.S. Dist. Ct. (so. and ea. dists.) N.Y. 1977, Calif. 1984, U.S. Dist. Ct. (cen. dist.) Calif. 1984. Pvt. practice London, 1969-71; assoc. Spear & Hill, N.Y.C. and London, 1974-75, Webster & Sheffield, N.Y.C. and London, 1976-77; assoc. Wachtell, Lipton, Rosen & Katz, N.Y.C., 1977-80, ptnr., 1980-83; ptnr. Gibson, Dunn & Cutcher, L.A., 1983-87, Fried, Frank, Harris, Shriver & Jacobson, L.A., 1987-91, Irell & Manella, L.A., 1991-97, Heller, Ehrman, White & McAuliffe, Palo Alto, Calif., 1997—; lectr. law Oxford (Eng.) U., 1968-69, Cambridge U., 1970-71, UCLA, 1989. Editor-in-chief (bi-monthly) Corporate Governance Adviser; contbr. articles to profl. publs. Harkness fellow Commonwealth Fund, N.Y., 1971. Mem. ABA, Internat. Bar Assn., Calif. Bar Assn. (chmn. corps. com. 1990-91, vice chmn. bus. law sect. exec. com. 1993-94), Am. Law Inst., Assn. Bar City N.Y. Avocations: running, golf. Securities, General corporate, Mergers and acquisitions. Office: Heller Ehrman White & McAuliffe 525 University Ave Ste 800 Palo Alto CA 94301-1922

**LESSER, JOAN L.,** lawyer; b. L.A.. BA, Brandeis U., 1969; JD, U. So. Calif., 1973. Bar: Calif. 1973, U.S. Dist. Ct. (cen. dist.) Calif. 1974. Assoc. Irell and Manella LLP, L.A., 1973-80, ptnr., 1980—; mem. planning com. Ann. Real Property Inst., Continuing Edn. of Bar, Berkeley, 1990-96; speaker at profl. confs. Trustee Windward Sch.; grad. Leadership L.A., 1992; bd. dirs. L.A. chpt. Legion Lex. Mem. Orgn. Women Execs. (past pres., bd. dirs.), Order of Coif. General corporate, Finance, Real property. Office: Irell and Manella LLP 1800 Avenue Of The Stars Los Angeles CA 90067-4276

**LESSER, MARGO ROGERS,** legal consultant; b. Oklahoma City, Aug. 30, 1950; d. William Wright and Velma June (Clark) Rogers; m. George Robert Lesser, Apr. 25, 1982; children: Scott Robert, Kira Michelle. AB, Cornell U., 1972; JD, Georgetown U., 1975. Bar: D.C. 1975, Mich. 1990, U.S. Ct. Claims 1976, U.S. Tax Ct. 1979, U.S. Ct. Appeals (fed. cir.) 1982, U.S. Supreme Ct. 1979. Law clk. to Hon. judge Oscar Davis U.S. Appellate Ct. Claims, Washington, 1975-76; assoc. Covington & Burling, Washington, 1976-81; asst. prof. Wayne State U. Law Sch., Detroit, 1981-88; legal cons. Birmingham, Mich., 1988—; exec. dir. Ind. Dir. Found., Detroit, 1990—. Co-author: Michigan Corporation Law and Practice, 1990, supplements through 1999; assoc. editor Internat. Soc. Barristers Quar., 1988—; contbr. articles to profl. jours. Mem. ABA, Mich. Bar (co-reporter Bus. Corp. Act subcom., law sect. 1986-97, reporter ad hoc limited liability co. rev. com. 1991—). Avocations: family, tennis, sailing. Home and Office: 1044 N Glenhurst Dr Birmingham MI 48009-1111

**LESSER, WILLIAM MELVILLE,** lawyer; b. N.Y.C., Jan. 26, 1927; s. Sydney Edward and Hattie (Wolf) L.; m. Laura Helen Schwartz, Oct. 3, 1953; children: Robin, Debra, Nancy. BS, NYU, 1949, JD, 1958. Bar: N.Y. 1959, U.S. Dist. Ct. (so. and ea. dists.) N.Y. 1969. Sr. ptnr. Lesser Popick & Rutman, N.Y.C., 1959-96; with Verner Simon LLP, N.Y.C., 1996—; lawyer; b. N.Y.C., Jan. 26, 1927; s. Sydney Edward and Hattie (Wolf) L.; m. Laura Helen Schwartz, Oct. 3, 1953; children: Robin, Debra, Nancy. BS, NYU, 1949, JD, 1958. Bar: N.Y. 1959, U.S. Dist. Ct. (so. and ea. dists.) N.Y. 1969. Sr. ptnr. Lesser Popick & Rutman, N.Y.C., 1959-96; with Verner, Simon & Rocha, PC, N.Y.C., 1996—. Treas., bd. dirs. Assn. Help Retarded Children, N.Y.C. chpt., 1961-67; chmn. Environ. Control Commn., Town of New Castle, N.Y., 1969-81. Served with USN, 1945-46, PTO. Mem. ABA, Assn. Trial Lawyers Am., N.Y. State Trial Lawyers Assn., Assn. Trial Lawyers City of N.Y., Am. Soc. Law and Medicine. Jewish. Treas., bd. dirs. Assn. Help Retarded Children, N.Y.C. chpt., 1961-67; chmn. Environ. Control Commn., Town of New Castle, N.Y., 1969-81. With USN, 1945-46, PTO. Mem. ABA, ATLA, N.Y. State Trial Lawyers City of N.Y., Am. Soc. Law and Medicine. Jewish. Insurance, Personal injury, State civil litigation. Home: 70 Taconic Rd Millwood NY 10546-1124 Office: Verner Simon LLP 24 E 38th St New York NY 10016-2564

**LESSMAN, ROBERT EDWARD,** lawyer; b. Chgo., July 8, 1947; s. Edward W. and Mary R. (O'Connor) L.; m. Sarah Powers, June 19, 1972; children: Kathleen M., Timothy R. BA, St. Norbert Coll., De Pere, Wis., 1969; JD, Loyola U., Chgo., 1972. Bar: Ill. 1972, U.S. Dist. Ct. (no. dist.) Ill. 1972, U.S. Ct. Appeals (7th cir.) 1972. Law clk. to presiding justice U.S. Dist. Ct. (no. dist.) Ill., Chgo., 1972-73; litigation atty. Chgo. & Northwestern Ry. Co., 1973-74; assoc. Diver, Brydges, Bollman, Grach & Quade, Waukegan, Ill., 1974-78; ptnr. Diver, Bollman, Grach, Quade & Lessman, Waukegan, 1978-83, Hall, Holmberg, Roach, Johnston, Fisher & Lessman, Waukegan, 1983-89; assoc. gen. counsel The Pepper Cos., Inc., Barrington, Ill., 1989-93; gen. counsel Pepper Constrn. Co., Barrington, 1993—, v.p., 1995—; asst. corp. counsel City of Waukegan, 1977-81; gen. counsel Waukegan Port Dist., 1985-89. Mem. ABA, Ill. State Bar Assn., Chgo. Bar Assn. Roman Catholic. Avocations: sailing, photography, mountaineering. Construction. Office: Pepper Constrn Co 411 Lake Zurich Rd Barrington IL 60010-3179

**LESSY, ROY PAUL, JR.,** lawyer; b. Wallingford, Pa., Feb. 27, 1944; s. Roy Paul and Ruth W. Lessy; m. Ellen Mauck, Jan. 24, 1970 (dec. Dec. 1994); children: Rose-Ellen, Anne, Page. BA, Franklin and Marshall U., 1966; JD, George Washington U., 1969; postgrad., Harvard U., 1979. Bar: D.C. Atty.-advisor Office of Sec. U.S. Treasury Dept., Washington, 1969-72; dep. chief hearing counsel U.S. Nuclear Regulatory Commn., Washington, 1972-82; atty. and counsel Morgan, Lewis & Bockius, Washington, 1983-86; ptnr. Akin, Gump, Strauss, Hauer & Feld, Washington, 1986—; mem. lawyers steering com. Nuclear Energy Inst. (formerly Atomic Indsl. Forum), Washington, 1984—. Author: Casenote on Federal Jurisdiction, 1969. Trustee St. Margaret's Sch., Va., 1995—. Mem. ABA (lectr. Am. Law Inst. 1984—), Fed. Energy Bar Assn., Phi Delta Phi. Nuclear power, Federal civil litigation, Antitrust. Home: 8605 Fenway Dr Bethesda MD 20817-2709 Office: Akin Gump Strauss Hauer & Feld Ste 400 1333 New Hampshire Ave NW Washington DC 20036-1564

**LESTELLE, TERRENCE JUDE,** lawyer; b. New Orleans, May 31, 1949; s. August Jr. and June Rose (Pays) L.; m. Andrea Sucherman, Sept. 21, 1975; children: Evan Pays, Nicole Jessica. BA, Tulane U., 1971; JD, Loyola U., 1974; LLM, U. London, 1976. Bar: La. 1974, U.S. Dist. Ct. (ea. dist.) La. 1974, U.S. Ct. Appeals (5th cir.) 1981, U.S. Dist. ct. (we. dist.) La. 1977, U.S. Dist. Ct. (mid. dist.) La. 1979, U.S. Ct. Appeals (11th cir.) 1981, U.S. Supreme Ct. 1983, Miss. 1990, Colo. 1990, U.S. Dist. Ct. (so. and no. dist.) Miss. 1990. Law clk. to Hon. James A. Comiskey U.S. Dist. Ct. D.C., New Orleans, 1974-75, law clk. to Hon. Frank Summers, 1975; assoc. Deutsch, Kerrigan & Stiles, New Orleans, 1975, Lemle, Kelleher, Kohlmeyer, Dennery , Hunley, Moss & Frilot, New Orleans, 1976-78; ptnr. Law Firm of Amato & Creeley, Gretna, La., 1978-81; prin. Law Office of Terrence J. Lestelle, New Orleans, 1981-84; ptnr. Lestelle & Lestelle, New Orleans, 1984—. Admiralty, General civil litigation, Personal injury.

**LESTER, ANDREW WILLIAM,** lawyer; b. Mpls., Feb. 17, 1956; s. Richard G. and Marion Louise (Kurtz) L.; m. Barbara Regina Schmitt, Nov. 22, 1978; 1 child, Susan Erika. Student, Ludwig-Maximilians Univ., Munich, 1975-76; BA, Duke U., 1977; MS in Fgn. Service, JD, Georgetown U., 1981. Bar: Okla. 1981, D.C. 1985, Tex. 1990, U.S. Supreme Ct. 1992, Colo. 1995. Cons. Dresser Industries, Inc., Washington, 1979-81; assoc. Conner & Winters, Tulsa, 1981-82; asst. atty. City of Enid, Okla., 1982-84; ptnr. various law firms Enid, Oklahoma City, 1984-96; ptnr. Lester, Loving & Davies P.C., Edmond, 1996—; adj. prof. Okla. City Univ. Sch. of Law; lectr. in field; U.S. magistrate judge Western Dist. Okla., 1988-96; constl. law specialist Ctrl. and East European Law Initiative, ABA, Ukraine, Belarus and Moldova, 1993. Author: Constitutional Law and Democracy, 1994; contbr. book revs. and articles to profl. jours. Intern Office of Senator Bob Dole, Washington, 1977-78; mem. transition team EEOC Office Pres.-Elect Reagan, Washington, 1980-81; chmn. Enid Police Civil Service Commn., 1985-87; bd. dirs. Enid Habitat for Humanity, 1986-88, Booker T. Washington Community Ctr., Enid, 1987-90; mem. Martin Luther King, Jr. Holiday Commn. of Enid, 1988-91; deacon First Bapt. Ch. of Oklahoma City. Fellow Okla. Bar Found.; mem. Okla. Bar Assn., D.C. Bar Assn., Tex. Bar Assn., Colo. Bar Assn., Okla. Assn. Mcpl. Attys. (bd. dirs. 1987-91, 94-98, gen. counsel 1987-88, pres. 1988-90), Oklahoma County Bar Assn., Def. Rsch. Inst. (govt. liability com.), Federalist Soc. (vice chmn. civil rights practice group 1996—, pres. Ctrl. Okla. chpt. 1996-99). Republican. Avocations: German language, cartography. Civil rights, Constitutional, General civil litigation. Office: Lester Loving & Davies PC 1505 Renaissance Blvd Edmond OK 73013-3018

**LESTER, DAVID S.,** lawyer, educator; b. Bklyn., Dec. 13, 1955; s. Robert Louis and Rita (Skib) L.; m. Donna Daun, Nov. 17, 1979; children: Randon, Erin. BS, Bklyn. Coll., CUNY, 1977; JD, NYU, 1980. Bar: N.Y. 1981. Assoc. atty. Weil, Gotshal & Manges, N.Y.C., 1980-81, Cooperman & Levitt PC, N.Y.C., 1981-86; ptnr. Cooperman, Levitt Winkoff Lester & Newman, P.C., N.Y.C., 1987—; adj. prof. real estate transactions Touro Law Sch., Huntington, N.Y., 1990—. Mem. law rev. NYU Sch. Law, 1978. Mem. Phi Beta Kappa. Avocations: piano, tennis, golf. Health, Real property, General corporate. Home: 5 Arleigh Rd Great Neck NY 11021-1308 Office: Cooperman Levitt et al 1129 Northern Blvd Manhasset NY 11030-3022

**LESTER, KEN HARRISON,** lawyer; b. Wilson, N.C., Apr. 4, 1941; s. Lonnie H. and Polly Lester; m. Rose Nell Bruorton, Nov. 26, 1964; children: Kris, Ken Jr., Kelli. BA, U. S.C., 1964, JD, 1966. Bar: S.C. 1966. Ptnr. Lester & Jones, Columbia, S.C. Fellow Acad. Matrimonial Lawyers; mem. Am. Coll. Family Trial Lawyers, S.C. Trial Lawyers Assn. (bd. govs., mem. various coms.), Richland Co. Bar. Assn. (family law com), Lexington Co. Bar Assn., Beaufort Co. Bar Assn.. Family and matrimonial. Office: Lester & Jones 1716 Main St Columbia SC 29201-2820 also: 1 Professional Dr Port Royal Beaufort SC 29935

**LETSON, WILLIAM NORMAND,** lawyer; b. N.Y.C., Mar. 24, 1930; s. Benjamin Hugle and Ellen (Skon) L.; m. Barbara C. Briggs, Jan. 22, 1956 (div. May 1980); children—Benjamin B., Katherine L., William C.; m. Brenda Powell, Oct. 10, 1981 (div. Oct. 1995). A.B. cum laude, Harvard U., 1952, J.D. magna cum laude, 1955. Bar: Ohio 1955, N.Y. 1956, D.C. 1973, Pa. 1975. Assoc. Shearman & Sterling, N.Y.C., 1955-62; ptnr. Letson, Letson & Kightlinger, Warren, Ohio, 1962-71; gen. counsel U.S. Dept. Commerce, Washington, 1971-73; v.p., gen. counsel, sec. Westinghouse Electric, Pitts., 1973-76; ptnr. Schiff, Hardin & Waite, Washington, 1977-79, Letson, Griffith, Woodall & Lavelle, Warren, Ohio, 1979-86; ptnr. Letson & Jarrett, Warren, 1986-95; ptnr. Letson, Griffith, Woodall Lavelle & Rosenberg, L.P.A., 1995—; dir. HON Industries, Muscatine, Iowa, 1977-94. Mem. Pres. Commn. on Personnel Interchange, Washington, 1976-80; mem. U.S.-USSR Sci. and Tech. Commn., Washington, 1972-73; mem. State Com. to Elect Clarence Brown Gov., 1982; mem. law sch. adv. com. U. Akron, 1981—. Mem. ABA, Ohio State Bar Assn., Warren Area C. of C. (dir. 1984-87). Republican. Episcopalian. Clubs: Duquesne, Fox Chapel (Pitts.); Metropolitan (Washington); Trumbull Country, Buckeye (Warren). Avocations: skiing, sailing, fly fishing, tennis, golf. General corporate, Pension, profit-sharing, and employee benefits, Estate planning. Home: 930 Fairway Dr NE Warren OH 44483-5640 Office: Letson Griffith Wooddall Lavelle & Rosenberg LPA PO Box 151 155 S Park Ave Warren OH 44482

**LETTOW, CHARLES FREDERICK,** lawyer; b. Iowa Falls, Iowa, Feb. 10, 1941; s. Carl Frederick and Catherine (Reisinger) L.; m. Sue Lettow, Apr. 20, 1963; children: Renee, Carl II, John, Paul. BS in Chem. Engring., Iowa State U., 1962; LLB, Stanford U., 1968. Bar: Calif. 1969, Iowa 1969, D.C. 1972, Md. 1991. Law clk. to Hon. Ben C. Duniway U.S. Ct. Appeals (9th cir.), San Francisco, 1968-69; law clk. to Hon. Warren E. Burger U.S. Supreme Ct., Washington, 1969-70; counsel Council on Environ. Quality, Washington, 1970-73; assoc. Cleary, Gottlieb, Steen & Hamilton, Washington, 1973-76, ptnr., 1976—; pres. Busy Way Farms, Inc., 1989—. Contbr. articles to profl. jours. Trustee Potomac Sch., McLean, Va., 1983-90, chmn. bd. trustees, 1985-88. 1st lt. U.S. Army, 1963-65. mem. ABA, Am. Law Inst., D.C. Bar Assn., Iowa Bar Assn., Order of Coif. Club: University. Federal civil litigation, Environmental. Office: 2000 Pennsylvania Ave NW Washington DC 20006-1812

**LETTS, J. SPENCER,** federal judge; b. 1934. BA, Yale U., 1956; LLB, Harvard U., 1960. Commd. U.S. Army, 1956, advanced through grades to capt., resigned, 1965; pvt. practice law Fulbright & Jaworski, Houston, 1960-66, Troy, Malin, Loveland & Letts, L.A., 1973-74, Hedlund, Hunter & Lynch, L.A., 1978-82, Latham & Watkins, L.A., 1982-85; gen. counsel Teledyne, Inc., 1966-73, 75-78, legal cons., 1978-82; judge U.S. Dist. Ct. (cen. dist.) Calif., L.A., 1986—. Contbr. articles to profl. jours. Mem. ABA, Calif. State Bar, Tex. State Bar, L.A. Bar Assn., Houston Bar Assn. Office: US Dist Ct 312 N Spring St Ste 243J Los Angeles CA 90012-4704

**LETWIN, JEFFREY WILLIAM,** lawyer; b. Pitts., Nov. 26, 1953; s. Myron Harvey and Phyllis Harriet (Unatin) L.; m. Roberta Lee Rosenbloom, July 24, 1983; 1 child, S. Ari; stepchildren: Andrew B. Filipek, Amanda H. Filipek. BA in History and Lit., U. Pitts., 1975; JD, Am. U., 1979. Bar: Pa. 1980, D.C. 1980. Staff atty. Dept. Justice, Washington, 1979-80; assoc. Gilloti, Goldberg & Capristi, Pitts., 1980-83, Finkel, Lefkowitz & Ostrow, Pitts., 1983-85, Rosenberg & Kirshner, Pitts., 1986-94, Doepken Keevican & Weiss, Pitts., 1994—; lectr. Pa. Bar Inst., 1983, 87, 88; mem. Pitts. High Tech. Council, 1985—, Enterprise Group, Pitts., 1985—; arbitrator N.Y. Stock Exch. Bd. dirs. Holocaust Commn., Pitts., 1983—, Jewish Family and Children's Svc., Pitts., 1983-86, Cmty. Coll. Allegheny County Found.; bd. dirs. United Jewish Fedn., Pitts., 1984-86, 98—, chmn. young bus. and profl. divsn., 1985-87, chmn. exec. and profl. divsn. 1987-88; mem. Young Leadership Cabinet USA, 1984-87; participant Leadership Pitts., 1989—; chmn. Holocaust Commn. of Greater Pitts., 1991-94, Pitts. Israel C. of C. 1991-97; commr. City of Pitts. Planning Commn., 1996—; bd. dirs. Pitts. Film Office, 1996—, Leadership Pitts., Jewish Assn. on Aging, 1997— ; v.p. C.C. of Allegheny County Edn. Found., 1996—; mem. exec. com. United Jewish Fedn., 1997—. Named one of Outstanding Young Men in Am., 1985; recipient Stark Young Leadership award, 1989. Mem. ABA, Pa. Bar Assn., D.C. Bar Assn., Alleghany County Bar Assn. (bus., banking, and comml. sect., continuing legal edn. com.), Nat. Assn. Securities Dealers (arbitrator). Democrat. Jewish. Avocations: golf, tennis, films. Securities, General corporate, Real property. Office: Doepken Keevican 5800 USX Tower Pittsburgh PA 15219

**LEUCHTMAN, STEPHEN NATHAN,** lawyer; b. Detroit, Oct. 14, 1945; s. Alexis C. and Frances J. (Boucher) L.; m. Jacque Ward, Nov. 29, 1991; children: Stephen, John II, Lucinda. BA, U. Mich., 1967, JD, 1970. Bar: Mich. 1970, Calif. 1993, U.S. Dist. Ct. (ea. and so. dists.) Mich. 1970, U.S. Ct. Appeals (6th cir.) 1982. Assoc. Eggenberger, Eggenberger, McKinney & Weber, Detroit, 1970-75, Tyler & Canham, Detroit, 1975-80; ptnr. Sommers, Schwartz, Silver & Schwartz, Southfield, 1980-97; founding ptnr. Trowbridge Law Firm, P.C., Detroit, 1997—. Contbr. articles to profl. jours. Mem. ABA, ATLA, Am. Bd. Trial Advocates, Million Dollar Advocates Forum, Consumer Attys. of Calif., Mich. Bar Assn., Calif. Bar Assn. Democrat. Avocations: writing, golf, travel. Personal injury, State civil litigation, Civil rights. Home: 241 Strathmore Rd Bloomfield Hills MI 48304-3667 Office: Trowbridge Law Firm PC 1380 E Jefferson Ave Detroit MI 48207-3104

**LEUNG, JACQUELINE JORDAN,** lawyer; b. Fargo, N.D., May 1, 1950; d. Leonard Albert and Mary Patricia Anderson; m. Simon Y. Leung, Aug. 28, 1993; 1 child, Zachary Steven Jordan. BS, Mont. State U., 1988; JD, U. Minn., 1991. Bar: Calif. 1991, U.S. Dist. Ct. (all dists.) Calif. 1991, U.S. Ct. Appeals (9th cir.) 1991. Lawyer Boornazian, Jensen & Garthe, Oakland, Calif., 1991—. Mem. Assn. Def. Counsel, Alameda County Bar Assn., Def. Rsch. Inst. Insurance, Appellate. Office: Boornazian Jensen & Garthe PO Box 12925 Oakland CA 94604-2925

**LEUZZI, PAUL WILLIAM,** corporate lawyer; b. Rochester, N.Y., July 4, 1953; s. Paul W. and Marie (Cumbo) L.; m. Helen M. Wanderlingh, May 21, 1983; children: Alexandria, Derek, Ricky. BS, Syracuse U., 1975, SUNY, 1975; JD, N.Y. Law Sch., 1978. Conn. 1979, N.Y. 1980, Patent and Trademark Office 1979, CAFC 1982. Patent atty. Am. Cyanamid Co., Stamford, Conn., 1978-81; patent counsel Union Carbide Corp., Danbury, Conn., 1981-90, mng. patent counsel, 1990-97, assoc. patent counsel, 1997—. Contbr. articles to profl. jours., including Jour. Proprietary Rights, Jour. Law and Tech., Jour. Patent Office Soc. Mem. ABA, Am. Intellectual Property Law Assn. Avocations: skiing, camping, fishing. Intellectual property, Patent. Home: 10 Kent Rd Newtown CT 06470-1785 Office: 39 Old Ridgebury Rd # 3267 Danbury CT 06810-5108

**LEV, AVI MEIR,** lawyer; b. L.A., Mar. 28, 1956. BA, U. Calif., L.A., 1977; JD, U. Oreg., 1980. Computer. Office: 350 North St # 403 Boston MA 02113-2114

**LEVAL, PIERRE NELSON,** federal judge; b. N.Y.C., Sept. 4, 1936; s. Fernand and Beatrice (Reiter) L. B.A. cum laude, Harvard U., 1959, J.D. magna cum laude, 1963. Bar: N.Y. 1964, U.S. Ct. Appeals 2d Circuit 1964, U.S. Dist. Ct. So. Dist. N.Y 1966. Law clk. to Hon. Henry J. Friendly, U.S. Ct. Appeals, 1963-64; asst. U.S. atty. So. Dist. N.Y., 1964-68, chief appellate atty., 1967-68; assoc. firm Cleary, Gottlieb, Steen & Hamilton, N.Y.C., 1969-74; ptnr. firm, 1973-75; 1st asst. dist. atty. Office of Dist. Atty., N.Y. County, 1975-76; chief asst. dist. atty. Office of Dist. Atty., 1976-77; U.S. dist. judge So. Dist. N.Y., N.Y.C., 1977-93; judge U.S. Ct. of Appeals (2d cir.), N.Y.C., 1993—. Contbr. articles to profl. jours. Served with U.S. Army, 1959. Mem. Am. Law Inst. (council), Assn. Bar City N.Y., N.Y. County Lawyers Assn. Office: US Courthouse 40 Foley Sq New York NY 10007-1502*

**LE VAN, NOLAN GERALD,** lawyer, consultant; b. Tulsa, July 10, 1934; s. Nolan Guinn and Mary (Bel) Le V.; m. Sara Nell Ashworth, Jan. 5, 1957; children: Mary Elizabeth Le Van Riley, Nolan Guy, Marthe Nell. BA, So. Meth. U., 1956; JD, La. State U., 1962. Bar: La. 1962, U.S. Ct. Appeals (5th cir.) 1963. Ptnr. Smitherman, Lunn, Shreveport, La., 1962-71, Breazeale Sachse, Baton Rouge, 1982-84; prof. law La. State U., Baton Rouge, 1971-82; gen. counsel Fidelity Nat. Bank, Baton Rouge, 1985; spl. counsel Kean, Miller, Baton Rouge, 1989—; mng. dir. The Le Van Co., Baton Rouge, Black Mtn., N.C., 1986—. Author: Louisiana Wills & Trusts, 1982, Lawyers Lives Out of Control, 1993, Survival Guide for Business Families, 1998; editor-in-chief La. Law Rev., 1962. Pres. Baton Rouge Symphony, 1978; bd. trustees Presbyn. Found., Louisville, Ky., 1996—. Lt. U.S. Coast Guard Res., 1956-73. Fellow Am. Coll. Trust & Estate Counsel (former regent); mem. Internat. Acad. Estate & Trust Law (academician 1978—), La. Bar Assn., N.C. Bar Assn. Democrat. Avocations: hiking, travel, music, literature. Estate planning. Office: The Le Van Co 101 West St Black Mountain NC 28711-3166

**LEVANDER, ANDREW JOSHUA,** lawyer; b. N.Y.C., Aug. 15, 1953; s. Seymour S. and Ellenore B. L.; m. Carol A. Loewenson, Sept. 18, 1983; children: Samuel, Benjamin. BA summa cum laude, Tufts U., 1973; JD, Columbia U., 1977. Bar: N.Y. 1978, D.C. 1978, U.S. Supreme Ct., U.S. Ct. Appeals (2d, 3d, 7th and D.C. cirs.), U.S. Dist. Ct. (so. and ea. dists.) N.Y. Law clk. Judge Wilfred Feinberg, U.S. Ct. Appeals, N.Y.C., 1977-78; asst. Solicitor Gen.'s Office, U.S. Dept. Justice, Washington, 1978-81; asst. U.S. atty. U.S. Attys. Office, N.Y.C., 1981-85; ptnr. Shereff, Friedman, Hoffman & Goodman, N.Y.C., 1985-98; assoc. ind. counsel Washington, 1987; ptnr. Swidler, Berlin, Shereff, Friedman, N.Y.C., 1998—; bd. dirs. Swidler, Berlin, Shereff & Friedman, mem. exec. com., 1990-98. Co-author: The Prosecution and Prevention of Computer and High Technology Crime, 1986, Settling Commercial Litigation, 1999; contbr. articles to profl. jours. Chmn. scholar com. Westside Youth Soccer League, N.Y.C., 1996—. Mem. ABA (litig. com. 1997—), Bar Assn. City of N.Y. (securities regulation com. 1997—). Avocations: tennis, travel, coaching. General civil litigation, Criminal, Securities. Office: Swidler Berlin Shereff Friedman 919 3d Ave New York NY 10022

**LEVANDER, HAROLD POWRIE, JR.,** lawyer; b. St. Paul, Aug. 28, 1940; s. Harold and Iantha (Powrle) L.; m. Carla Ann August, Nov. 15, 1969; children: Eric, Wade, Laura. BA in Polit. Sci., Gustavus Adolphus Coll., 1962; JD, Harvard U., 1965. Bar: Minn. 1965. Ptnr. LeVander Gillen Miller Anderson & Kuntz, St. Paul, 1965-88, Maun & Simon, St. Paul, 1988—; chmn., pres. Ford Commn., Minn. Del. Nat. Rep. Conv., Kansas City, 1976; chmn. St. Paul Area ARC, 1985-87, bd. govs., 1988-94; mem. Gov.'s Coun. Red River Valley Flood Control, 1997. Named one of Outstanding Young Men of Am., U.S. Jaycees, 1972. Mem. ABA, Dakota County Bar Assn. (pres. 1983-86), Nat. Rural Electric Coop. Assn. (region 6 rep. lawyer's com. 1986-88, 1993-96). Lutheran. Avocations: public speaking, tennis, squash, hunting, politics. Public utilities. Home: 8086 Somerset Knls Saint Paul MN 55125-2362 Office: Maun and Simon 2000 Midwest Plaza Bldg W 801 Nicollet Ave Minneapolis MN 55402-2500

**LEVEL, KURT ALAN,** lawyer, judge; b. Merriam, Kans., Oct. 14, 1966; s. Dale A. and Martha June (Saine) L.; m. Elaine D. Woodford, May 25, 1991; 1 child, Madeline. BA in Comm. Studies with honors, U. Kans., 1989, JD, 1992. Bar: Kans, 1992, U.S. Dist. Ct. Kans., 1992, Mo., 1993, U.S. Ct. Appeals (10th cir.), 1993, U.S. Dist. Ct. (we. dist.) Mo., 1993. Lawyer Fisher, Patterson, Sayler & Smith, Overland Park, Kans., 1992-95, Robert G. Herndon PA, Overland Park, 1995-97; ptnr. Herndon & Level Chartered, Overland Park, 1998—; mcpl. judge pro tem City of Fairway, Kans., 1994—, City Roeland Park, Kans., 1997—. Mem. Kans. Trial Lawyers Assn. (mem. jr. bd. gov. 1995-96), Delta Tau Delta. Republican. Methodist. Personal injury, Labor, General civil litigation. Office: Herndon & Level Chartered 8655 College Blvd Overland Park KS 66210-1835

**LEVENSON, ALAN BRADLEY,** lawyer; b. Long Beach, N.Y., Dec. 13, 1935; s. Cyrus O. and Jean (Kotler) L.; m. Joan Marlene Levenson, Aug. 19, 1956; children: Scott Keith, Julie Jo. AB, Dartmouth Coll., 1956; BA, Oxford U., Eng., 1958, MA, 1962; LLB, Yale U., 1961. Bar: N.Y. 1962, U.S. Dist. Ct. D.C. 1964, U.S. Ct. Appeals (D.C. cir.) 1965, U.S. Supreme Ct. 1965. Law clk., trainee div. corp. fin. SEC, Washington, 1961-62, gen. atty., 1962, trial atty., 1963, br. chief, 1963-65, asst. dir., 1965-68, exec. asst. dir., 1968, dir., 1970-76; v.p. Shareholders Mgmt. Co., L.A., 1969, sr. v.p., 1969-70, exec. v.p., 1970; ptnr. Fulbright & Jaworski, Washington, 1976—; lectr. Cath. U. Am., 1964-68, Columbia U., 1973; adj. prof. Georgetown U., 1964, 77, 79-81, U.S. rep. working party OECD, Paris, 1974-75; adv. com. SEC, 1976-77; mem. adv. bd. Securities Regulation Inst., U. Calif., San Diego, 1973—, vice chmn. exec. com., 1979-83, chmn., 1983-87, emeritus chmn., 1988—; mem. adv. coun. SEC Inst., U. So. Calif., L.A., Sch. Acctg., 1981-85; mem. adv. com. Nat. Ctr. Fin. Svcs., U. Calif.-Berkeley, 1985-89; mem. planning com. Ray Garrett Ann. Securities Regulation Inst. Northwestern U. Law Sch.; mem. adv. panel to U.S. compt.-gen. on stock market decline, 1987, panel of cons., 1989—; mem. audit adv. com. GAO, 1992—. Mem. bd. editl. advisors U. Iowa Jour. Corp. Law, 1978—; Bur. Nat. Affairs adv. bd. Securities Regulation and Law Report, 1976—; bd. editors N.Y. Law Jour., 1976—; bd. advisors, corp. and securities law advisor Prentice Hall Law & Bus., 1991-95; contbr. articles to profl. jours.; mem. adv. bd. Banking Policy Report. Recipient Disting. Service award SEC, 1972; James B. Richardson fellow Oxford U., 1956. Mem. ABA (adv. com., fed. regulation securities com., task force rev. fed. securities laws, former chair subcom. on securities activities banks), Fed. Bar Assn. (emeritus mem. exec. com. securities law com.), Am. Law Inst., Practicing Law Inst. (nat. adv. com. 1974, adv. com. ann. securities reg. inst.), AICPA (pub. dir., bd. dirs. 1983-90, fin. com. 1984-90, chmn. adv. coun. auditing standards bd. 1979-80, future issues com. 1982-85), Nat. Assn. Securities Dealers (corp. fin. com. 1981-87, nat. arbitration com. 1983-87, gov.-at-large, bd. govs. 1984-87, exec. com. 1986-87, long range planning com. 1987-90, chmn. legal adv. bd. 1988-93, spl. com. governance and structure 1989-90, numerous adv. coms.). Securities, Banking. Home: 12512 Exchange Ct S Potomac MD 20854-2431 Office: Fulbright & Jaworski LLP 801 Pennsylvania Ave NW Washington DC 20004-2615

**LEVENTHAL, HOWARD G.,** lawyer; b. N.Y.C., Aug. 15, 1946; BA cum laude, CCNY, 1968; JD, NYU, 1971. Bar: N.Y. 1971, U.S. Ct. Appeals (2d cir.) 1972, U.S. Dist. Ct. (ea. and so. dists.) N.Y. 1973, U.S. Supreme Ct. 1975. Assoc. Cahill, Gordon & Reindel, N.Y.C., 1971-75, Arrow, Silverman & Parcher, N.Y.C., 1975-76; sr. law asst. Supreme Ct. State N.Y., N.Y.C., 1976-80, law sec. to Justice Hortense W. Gabel, 1981-87, spl. referee; bd. dirs., v.p., sec. Park Reservior Housing Corp., Bronx, 1974—; bd. dirs., Kingsbridge-Riverdale-Van Cortlandt Devel. Corp., Bronx, 1986—; treas. Law Secs. and Law Assts. Collegium. Author: Charges to the Jury and Requests to Charge in a Criminal Case, 1983, Byer's Civil Motions, rev. edit., 1994, Byer's Civil Motions; contbr. articles to profl. jours. Mem. Law Secs. and Law Assts. Assn. (treas.), Law Secs. Assn. (dir.), Sigma Alpha. State civil litigation, Criminal, Family and matrimonial.

**LEVETOWN, ROBERT ALEXANDER,** lawyer; b. Bklyn., July 20, 1935; s. Alfred A. and Corinne L. (Cohen) L.; m. Roberta S. Slobodkin, Oct. 18, 1959. Student, U. Munich, Fed. Republic Germany, 1954-55; AB, Princeton U., 1956; LLB, Harvard U., 1959. Bar: D.C. 1960, N.Y. 1982, Va. 1984, Pa. 1985. Assoc. Pierson, Ball & Dowd, Washington, 1960-62; asst. U.S. atty. Washington, 1962-63; atty. Chesapeake & Potomac Telephone Cos., Washington, 1963-66, gen. atty., 1966-68, gen. solicitor, 1968-73, v.p., gen. counsel, 1975-83; exec. v.p., gen. counsel Bell Atlantic, 1983-91, vice chmn., 1991-92, also bd. dirs., 1989-92; chmn. H.R. com. Telecom NZ, 1995-99. Mem. ABA (vice chmn. comm. com., pub. utility law sect. 1986-93), Washington Met. Corp. Counsels' Assn. (bd. dirs. 1981-83), Nat. Legal Ctr. (legal adv. coun. 1986-92). Republican. Jewish. Home: 6418 E Caron Dr Paradise Valley AZ 85253-1856

**LEVI, DAVID F.,** federal judge; b. 1951. BA, Harvard U., MA, 1973; JD, Stanford U. Bar: Calif. 1983. U.S. atty. ea. dist. State of Calif., Sacramento, 1986-90; judge U.S. Dist. Ct. (ea. dist.) Calif., 1990—; chmn. task force on race, religious and ethnic fairness U.S. Ct. Appeals (9th cir.), 1994-97, mem. jury com., 1993-95. Adv. com. on Civil Rules, 1994—; vis. com. U. Chgo. Law Sch., 1995-98. Mem. Am. Law Inst., Milton L. Schwartz Inn of Ct. (pres. 1992-95). Office: 501 I St Rm 14-230 Sacramento CA 95814-7300

**LEVIE, MARK ROBERT,** lawyer; b. Chgo., Sept. 2, 1951; s. Harold M. and Muriel L.; m. Gail M., Aug. 19, 1973; children: Melissa, Allison, David. BA, U. Ill., 1973; JD, Harvard U., 1976. Bar: Calif. 1978, U.S. Dist. Ct. (no. dist.) Calif. 1978. Clk. to presiding justice U.S. Ct. Appeals (9th cir.), San Francisco, 1976-77; assoc. Orrick, Herrington & Sutcliffe, San Francisco, 1977-82, ptnr., 1983—. Mem. ABA (sub-com. on securitization of assets, fin. task force), State Bar of Calif., San Francisco Bar Assn. Avocations: golf, reading. General corporate, Securities, Finance. Office: Orrick Herrington & Sutcliffe 400 Sansome St San Francisco CA 94111-3143

**LEVIN, A. LEO,** law educator, retired government official; b. N.Y.C., Jan. 9, 1919; s. Issaachar and Minerva Hilda (Shapiro) L.; m. Doris Feder, Dec. 28, 1947; children—Allan, Jay Michael. BA, Yeshiva Coll., 1939; JD, U. Pa., 1942; LLD (hon.), Yeshiva U., 1960, NY Law Sch., 1980, Quinnipiac Coll., 1995; PhD (hon.), Bar-Ilan U., Israel, 1990. Bar: N.Y. 1947, U.S. Supreme Ct. 1982. Instr., then asst. prof. law U. Iowa, 1947-49; law faculty U. Pa., Phila., 1949-69, 70-89, Meltzer prof. law, 1987-89, Meltzer prof. emeritus, 1989—, vice provost, 1965-68; v.p. for acad. affairs Yeshiva U., N.Y.C., 1969-70; dir. Fed. Jud. Ctr., Washington, 1977-87; chmn. Pa. State Legis. Reapportionment Commn., 1971-73; founding dir. Nat. Inst. Trial Advocacy, 1971-73; conf. coord. Nat. Conf. on Causes of Popular Dissatisfaction with Adminstrn. of Justice (Pound Conf.); chmn. bd. cert. Circuit Execs., 1977-87; mem. adv. bd. Nat. Inst. Corrections, 1977-87. Author: (with Woolley) Dispatch and Delay: A Field Study of Judicial Administration in Pennsylvania, 1961; (with Cramer) Problems on Trial Advocacy, 1968; editor: (with Schuchman and Yablon) Cases on Civil Procedure, 1992, Supplement, 1997. Hon. trustee Bar Ilan U., Ramat Gan, Israel, 1967—; hon. pres. (former pres.) Jewish Publ. Soc. Am. Served to 1st lt. USAF, 1942-46, ETO. Recipient Mordecai Ben David award Yeshiva U., 1967, Disting. Svc. award U. Pa. Law Sch. Alumni, 1974, Bernard Revel award Yeshiva Coll., 1963, Justice award Am. Judicature Soc., 1995; White lectr. La. U., 1970, Jeffords lectr., N.Y. Law Sch., 1980, Murrah Lectr. U. Pa. Law Sch., 1989. Fellow Am. Acad. Arts and Scis.; mem. Am. Law Inst., Am. Judicature Soc. (pres. 1987-89), Order of Coif (nat. pres. 1967-70). Jewish. Office: U Pa Law Sch 3400 Chestnut St Philadelphia PA 19104-6204

**LEVIN, ALLEN JAY,** lawyer; b. Bridgeport, Conn., May 27, 1932; s. Simon H. and Adele Miriam (Rossinoff) L.; m. Judith Ann Rubinstein, Aug. 18, 1957 (div. 1987); children: Jennifer Suzanne, Miriam Adele, David Newmark, Michael Aaron; m. Gabrielle Hasson-Azar, Feb. 24, 1995. BA, NYU, 1954; postgrad., Boston U., 1954-55; JD, U. Miami, 1957. Bar: Fla. 1957, Conn. 1958, U.S. Dist. Ct. Conn. 1960, U.S. Dist. Ct. (so. dist.) Fla. 1962, U.S. Dist. Ct. (mid. dist.) Fla. 1969, U.S. Ct. Appeals (11th cir.) 1981, U.S. Supreme Ct. 1972. Small claims ct. judge County of Charlotte, Punta Gorda, Fla., 1962-72; legal counsel Port Charlotte-Charlotte Harbor (Fla.) Fire Control Dist., 1965-86; mcpl. judge City of North Port, Fla., 1973-76, city atty., 1977-87; pvt. practice Charlotte, Fla. Mem. ABA, Fla. Bar Assn. (probate law com. real property probate and trust law sects.), Charlotte County Bar Assn., Port Charlotte-Charlotte County C. of C., Port Charlotte-Charlotte County Bd. Realtors (assoc.), Elks, Kiwanis (youth svcs. chmn. Port Charlotte club 1986—, pres. 1998-99). Avocation: stamp collecting. Probate, Real property, Estate planning. Home: 125 Graham St SE Pt Charlotte FL 33952-9153 Office: 3440 Conway Blvd Ste 1A Pt Charlotte FL 33952-7050

**LEVIN, ALLEN JOSEPH,** lawyer; b. Lewistown, Pa., Jan. 17, 1948; s. Norman Lewis and Dorothy Sanford (Herbster) L.; m. Mary Gwendolyn McAdoo, Aug. 14, 1974. Cert., Ecole d'art Americaines, Fontainebleau, France, 1968; BA, Dickinson Coll., 1969; JD, Dickinson Sch. Law, 1974. Bar: Pa. 1974, U.S. Supreme Ct., U.S. Ct. Appeals (3d cir.), U.S. Dist. Ct. (mid. dist.) Pa. Assoc. Brugler & Levin Law Offices, Lewistown, 1974-80, ptnr., 1980—; counsel Mifflin County Ind. Devel. Corp., Lewistown, 1978—, Mifflin County Ind. Devel. Authority, Lewistown, 1980—; pres. Pa. Sch. Bd. Solicitors Assn., Harrisburg, 1989; v.p., assoc. gen. counsel Pocono Mountain R.R., Scranton, Pa., 1994-96; pres. Lewistown Ctrl. R.R. Co., Mt Union Connecting R.R. Co. Pres. Greater Lewistown Corp., 1983-95, v.p., 1995—. Recipient Outstanding Svc. to Edn. award Pa. Sch. Bds. Assn., 1989. Mem. Pa. Bar Assn., Mifflin County Bar Assn. (pres. 1992-93), Juniata Valley C. of C. (pres. 1983-85), Rotary Club Lewistown, Elks (# 663). Jewish. Avocations: fishing, reading. General corporate, Real property, Family and matrimonial. Home: 9 N Grand St Lewistown PA 17044-2040 Office: Brugler & Levin 10 S Wayne St Lewistown PA 17044-8112

**LEVIN, ARNOLD SAMPSON,** lawyer; b. Lorain, Ohio, Dec. 10, 1909; s. Morris and Mina (Kaufman) L.; m. Harriet Jacobs, Jan. 21, 1977. JD, Ohio State U., 1934. Bar: Ohio 1934, U.S. Dist. Ct. (no. dist.) Ohio 1935, U.S. Ct. Appeals (6th cir.) 1950, U.S. Ct. Claims 1950, U.S. Supreme Ct. 1958. Ptnr. Levin & Levin, Lorain, 1934-42, 46-64, Levin & Durfee, Lorain, 1965-81; sole practice Lorain, 1981-92, Sheffield Lake, Ohio, 1992—; acting mcpl. judge, Lorain, 1948. Served to 1st lt. USAF, 1942-46. Mem. ABA, Ohio Bar Assn., Lorain County Bar Assn., Assn. Trial Lawyers Am., Ohio Acad. Trial Lawyers, VFW. Lodges: Masons, B'nai B'rith. Personal injury, Probate, Real property. Office: 5555 E Lake Rd Lorain OH 44054-1904

**LEVIN, CHARLES LEONARD,** state supreme court justice; b. Detroit, Apr. 28, 1926; s. Theodore and Rhoda (Katzin) L.; children: Arthur, Amy, Fredrick. B.A., U. Mich., 1946, LL.B., 1947; LL.D. (hon.), Detroit Coll. of Law, 1980. Bar: Mich. 1947, N.Y. 1949, U.S. Supreme Ct. 1953, D.C. 1954. Pvt. practice law N.Y.C., 1948-50, Detroit, 1950-66; ptnr. Levin, Levin, Garvett & Dill, Detroit, 1951-66; judge Mich. Ct. Appeals, Detroit, 1966-73; assoc. justice Mich. Supreme Ct., 1973-96; mem. Mich. Law Revision Commn., 1966. Trustee Marygrove Coll., 1971-77, chmn., 1971-74; mem. vis. coms. to Law Schs., U. Mich., U. Chgo., 1977-80, Wayne State U. Mem. Am. Law Inst. Office: Mich Supreme Ct 500 Woodward Ave Fl 20 Detroit MI 48226-5498*

**LEVIN, DAVID ALAN,** lawyer; b. Cheverly, Md., Nov. 16, 1947; s. Jacob Solomon and Elaine (Astrin) L.; m. Pamela Evelyn Ruff, Sept. 18, 1976; 1 child, Michael Brian. BS, U. Md., 1968, JD, 1972. Bar: Md. 1972, U.S. Ct. Appeals (4th cir.) 1975. Ptnr. Levin & Levin, Langley Park, Md., 1972-75, O'Malley, Miles, Largo, Md., 1975-84, Wharton, Levin, Ehrmantraut, Klein & Nash, Annapolis, Md., 1984—. Fellow Am. Coll. Trial Lawyers. Personal injury. Office: Wharton Levin Ehrmantraut Klein & Nash PO Box 551 104 West St Annapolis MD 21404-0551

**LEVIN, DAVID HAROLD,** lawyer; b. Pensacola, Fla., Nov. 19, 1928. A.B., Duke U., 1949; J.D., U. Fla., 1952. Bar: Fla. 1952. Asst. county solicitor Escambia County (Fla.), 1952; sr. ptnr. Levin, Middlebrooks, Thomas, Mitchell, Green, Echsner, Proctor & Papantonio, P.A., Pensacola; chmn. 1st Jud. Circuit Fla. Jud. Nominating Commn., 1976-78; chmn. Fla. Pollution Control Bd., 1971-74. Chmn., Escambia County Cancer Crusade, 1963-65; pres. Escambia County unit Am. Cancer Soc., 1964-65; bd. dirs. W. Fla. Heart Assn., 1966-69; chmn. United Jewish Appeal Escambia County, 1967-68; former mem. human rights commn. W. Fla. Hosp. Mem. Fla. Alumni Assn. (pres. chpt. 1960), U. Fla. Alumni Assn. (dist. v.p. 1961-62), Blue Key. Recipient Good Govt. award Pensacola Jaycees, 1972; Service award Fla. Council for Clean Air, 1974; Francis Marion Weston award Audubon Soc., 1974; commendation Gov. Fla., 1974. mem. Am. Acad. Matrimonial Lawyers (pres. Fla. chpt. 1987-88). Family and matrimonial, State civil litigation, Personal injury. Home: 3632 Menendez Dr Pensacola FL 32503-3133 Office: Levin Middlebrooks Thomas et al PO Box 12308 Pensacola FL 32581-2308

**LEVIN, EDWARD M.,** lawyer, government administrator; b. Chgo., Oct. 16, 1934; s. Edward M. and Anne Meriam (Fantl) L.; children from previous marriage: Daniel Andrew, John Davis; m. Margot Aronson, Apr. 4, 1993. BS, U. Ill., 1955; LLB, Harvard U., 1958. Bar: Ill. 1958, U.S. Supreme Ct. 1968. Mem. firm Ancel, Stonesifer, Glink & Levin and predecessors, Chgo., 1958, 61-68; draftsman Ill. Legis. Reference Bur., Springfield, 1961; spl. asst. to regional adminstr. HUD, Chgo., 1968-71, asst. regional adminstr. community planning and mgmt., 1971-72; asst. dir. Ill. Dept. Local Govt. Affairs, Chgo., 1973-77; of counsel Holleb, Gerstein & Glass, Ltd., Chgo., 1977-79; chief counsel Econ. Devel. Adminstrn., U.S. Dept. Commerce, Washington, 1979-85, 97—; sr. fellow Nat. Gov's. Assn., 1985-86; sr. counsel U.S. Dept. Commerce, Washington, 1987-96; lectr. U. Ill., 1972-73, adj. assoc. prof. urban scis., 1973-79; lectr. Loyola U., 1976-79, No. Va. law Sch., 1988. Assoc. editor Assistance Mgmt. Jour., 1990-95; contbr. articles to profl. jours. Mem. Ill. Nature Preserves Com., 1963-68, Northea. Ill. Planning Commn., 1974-77, Ill.-Ind. Bi-State Commn., 1974-77; bd. dirs. Cook County Legal Assistance Found., 1978-79, D.C. Appleseed Ctr., 1994—; mem. Ill. divsn. ACLU, 1965-68, 77-79, v.p., 1977-78; chmn. ABA fed. assistance com., 1995-96. With AUS, 1958-60. Recipient Lincoln award Ill. Bar Assn., 1977. Mem. FBA (chmn. fed. grants com. 1991-95), Nat. Grants Mgmt. Assn. (bd. dirs. 1988-92, Pres.'s award 1994), Appleseed Found. (bd. dirs., mem. exec. com. 1994—). Home: 3201 Porter St NW Washington DC 20008-3212 Office: 14th & Constitution Ave NW Washington DC 20230-0001

**LEVIN, EVANNE LYNN,** lawyer; b. L.A., Nov. 6, 1949; d. Marshall Levin and Rose (Tolchin) Levin Albert; m. Jeffrey Neal Oliver, Sept. 5, 1992 (div. Dec. 1996). BA in Polit. Sci. cum laude, UCLA, 1971; JD, Loyola Law Sch., L.A., 1974. Bar: Calif. 1995; lic. real estate broker, Calif. Assoc. Ervin, Cohen & Jessup, Beverly Hills, Calif., 1977-78, Mason & Sloane, L.A., 1978-82; atty. Orion Pictures Corp., L.A., 1982-84; sr. dir. TV prodn. legal affairs Twentieth Century Fox Film Corp., Beverly Hills, 1986-89; of counsel Weinberg, Zipser, Arbiter & Heller, L.A., 1990; v.p., gen. counsel Zodiac Entertainment, Studio City, Calif., 1991-95; prin., owner Law Offices of Evanne L. Levin, L.A., 1995—; instr. personal mgmt. pub. and music career courses The Learning Network, 1985-86; spkr. in field. Contbr. articles to profl. publs.; columnist L.A. Women in Music Newsletter,1 986-88. Bd. dirs. Hollywood Women's Coalition, 1985-86, arts festival, 1985. Mem. L.A. County Bar Assn. (vols. in parole, exec. bd. Intellectual Property sect.), Beverly Hills Bar Assn. (former bd. govs., barristers bd. govs., founding mem./co-chair com. for arts, entertainment law com., del. to state bar and ABA convs.), Women in Entertainment Law, L.A. Women in Music (bd. dirs. 1986-88, adv. com.), Calif. Copyright Conf. Avocations: scuba diving, personal weight training, collecting kaleidoscipes, travel. Fax: 818-788-2255; e-mail:evlevin@hotmail.com. Entertainment, Intellectual property, General corporate. Office: 1901 Avenue Of The Stars Los Angeles CA 90067-6001

**LEVIN, EZRA GURION,** lawyer; b. Bklyn., Feb. 10, 1934; s. Harry and Bertha (Lebendiger) L.; m. Batya Ann Schaefer, June 19, 1960; children: Zachary Abraham, Ayala Deborah Levin-Kruss. AB, Columbia U., 1955; postgrad., U. Chgo., 1955-56; LLB, Columbia U., 1959. Bar: N.Y. 1961. Assoc., then ptnr. Marshall, Bratter, Greene, Allison & Tucker, N.Y.C., 1961-79; ptnr. Kramer Levin Naftalis & Frankel LLP, N.Y.C., 1979—; bd. dirs. Kaiser Aluminum Corp., MAXXAM, Inc., Houston; adj. prof. sociology Columbia U., 1973-77, 87, 93; adj. faculty U. Conn. Law Sch., 1970-73; vis. prof. U. Wis. Law Sch., 1967, 98. Contbr. articles to profl. jours. Mem.-at-large Jewish Cmty. Rels. Coun., N.Y.C., 1983—, v.p., 1994—; vice chmn. Coalition for Soviet Jewry, N.Y.C., 1984-93, co-chair, 1994—; counsel Am. Friends Sarah Herzog Meml. Hosp.-Jerusalem, Inc., N.Y.C., 1975—; sec., bd. dirs. Scholarship, Edn. and Def. Fund for Racial Equality, N.Y.C., 1961-70; founding chair Solomon Schechter High Sch. of N.Y., 1992-96, trustee 1992—. Mem. ABA, Law and Society Assn., Columbia Coll. Alumni Assn. (bd. dirs., v.p.). Avocation: tennis. General corporate, Securities, Mergers and acquisitions. Office: Kramer Levin Naftalis & Frankel LLP 919 3rd Ave New York NY 10022-3902

**LEVIN, HERVEY PHILLIP,** lawyer; b. Oct. 22, 1942; s. Julius L. and Gertrude (Cohen) L.; m. Madeleine J. Raskin, Sept. 22, 1970; children: Arianne, Nicole, David. BBA, U. Mich., 1964, MBA, 1968; JD, DePaul U., 1969. Bar: Ill. 1969, Tex. 1979, U.S. Dist. Ct. (no. dist.) Ill. 1970, U.S. Ct. Appeals (5th cir.) 1981, U.S. Ct. Appeals (7th cir.) 1971, U.S. Supreme Ct. 1972. Assoc. Potts Randall & Horn, Chgo., 1970-71; assoc., jr. ptnr. Mehlman, Ticho, Addis, Susman, Spitzer, Randall, Horn & Pyes, Chgo., 1971-75; pvt. practice Chgo., 1975-78, Dallas, 1979—; dir. Leedal Inc., Chgo.; cons. in workers' compensation, occupational disease and gen. practice. Bd. dirs. Solomon Schecter Acad. of Dallas, 1979—, Cong. Shearith Israel, Dallas, 1981-88, Am. Jewish Congress, Dallas, 1980-85, Nat. Assn. Mortgage Planners, 1995—. Named Ky. Col. Mem. ABA (workers compensation com. torts and ins. practices sect., chmn. 1989-90, sr. vice-chair 1990—, coun. mem. torts and ins. practices sect. 1995-98, various adminstrv. coms., torts and ins. practices sect. 1990—, liaison to Internat. Assn. Indsl. Accident Bds. and Comms. 1989—, cons. labor stds. subcom., house edn. and labor com., U.S. Congress, chmn. solo and small firm practices com. 1994-95), Ill. Bar Assn., Tex. Bar Assn., Dallas Bar Assn., Chgo. Bar Assn. E-mail: hervey@airmail.net. Fax: 972-733-3269. General practice, Workers' compensation, Real property. Office: 6918 Blue Mesa Dr Ste 115 Dallas TX 75252-6140

**LEVIN, JEFFREY L.,** lawyer; b. Bklyn., Aug. 10, 1950; s. Lester E. and Evelyn S. L.; m. Diane S. Levin, Apr. 4, 1976; children: Michael, Allison. BS in Acctg., SUNY, Buffalo, 1972; JD, St. John's U., 1975. Bar: N.Y.; U.S. Dist. Ct. (no., so. and ea. dists.) N.Y. Asst. corp. counsel City of Mt. Vernon, N.Y., 1977-78, City of Long Beach, N.Y., 1978-79; assoc. Bruckman Bernstone & Goldman, N.Y.C., 1980-82; ptnr. Law Offices of Jeffrey L. Levin, N.Y.C. and Port Chester, N.Y., 1982—. Bd. dirs. Temple Israel Cmty. Hebrew H.S., White Plains, N.Y., 1997—, Scarscale Little League, N.Y., 1997—. General practice, Real property, Private international. Home: 16 Ridgedale Rd Scarsdale NY 10583-7313 Office: Law Offices Jeffrey L Levin 10 Midland Ave Port Chester NY 10573-4927

**LEVIN, MARSHALL ABBOTT,** judge, educator; b. Balt., Nov. 22, 1920; s. Harry Oscar and Rose (DeLaviez) L.; m. Beverly Edelman, Aug. 6, 1948; children: Robert B., Susan R. Lieman, Burton H. BA, U. Va., 1941; JD, Harvard Law Sch., 1947. Bar: Md. 1947, U.S. Dist. Ct. Md. 1947, U.S. Ct. Appeals (4th cir.) 1950, U.S. Supreme Ct. 1953. Bill drafter, legis. asst. Dept. Legis. Reference, Annapolis, Md., 1948-49; rsch. asst. Workers Compensation Commn., 1951, police magistrate, 1951-55, magistrate housing ct., 1955-58; ptnr. Levin & Levin, Balt., 1947-66; pvt. practice Balt., 1966-68; ptnr. Edelman, Levin, Levy & Rubenstein, Balt., 1968-71; judge cir. ct. City of Balt., 1971-87, judge for asbestos litigation, 1987-97; lectr. nationally on toxic torts, complex litigation, asbestos; lectr. Nat. Conf. on Child Abuse, 1976; dir. Legal Aid Soc., Balt., 1979-81; chmn. jud. bd. sentencing State of Md., 1979-83, chmn. sentencing guidelines bd., 1983-87; instituted One Trial/One Day jury system, Balt., 1983; adj. prof. mass torts, legal & ethical studies grad. sch. U. Balt., 1979-90; charter mem. faculty coun., coord. and faculty general jurisdiction, current issues in civil litigation Nat. Jud. Coll., 1980—; mem. vis. faculty trial advocacy workshop Harvard Law Sch. Contbr. articles to law revs. Mem. Jud. Disability Commn., 1980-87; chmn. Mass Tort Litigation Com., 1991-95. NEH fellow, 1976. Mem. ABA (vice chmn. mass tort and litigation com.), Md. State Bar Assn. (Leadership award 1984), Balt. City Bar Assn. (commendation 1982). Home: 6106 Ivydene Ter Baltimore MD 21209-3522

**LEVIN, MICHAEL DAVID,** lawyer; b. Chgo., Oct. 11, 1942; s. Joseph F. and Libbie (Landman) L.; children: Victoria, David, Elizabeth, Emma, Madeline; m. Carol A. McErlean, Oct. 10, 1993. AB, U. Mich., 1964, JD, 1967. Bar: Ill. 1967. Assoc. Arnstein, Gluck, Weitzenfeld & Minow, Chgo., 1967-73, ptnr., 1973-81; ptnr. Latham & Watkins, Chgo., 1982-95; sr. v.p., sec. & gen. counsel Sears Roebuck & Co., Hoffman Estates, Ill., 1996-98; ptnr. Latham & Watkins, 1998—. Mem. ABA, Chgo. Bar Assn. (chmn. securities law 1982-83), Met. Club. Republican. Jewish. General corporate, Securities. Office: Sears Roebuck & Co 5800 Sears Tower Chicago IL 60684-0001

**LEVIN, MICHAEL HENRY,** lawyer; b. Phila., Nov. 24, 1942; s. Benjamin and Beatrice G. (Jackson) L.; m. Nora Jean Bieler, Jan. 5, 1966; children: Jeremy Ben, Daniel Hirsch. BA summa cum laude, U. Pa., 1964; MLitt, Oxford U., 1970; JD cum laude, Harvard U., 1969. Bar: D.C. 1970, U.S. Ct. Appeals (8 cirs.) 1970-77, U.S. Supreme Ct. 1973. Atty. appellate ct. br. NLRB, Washington, 1969-71; spl. asst. Office of Solicitor U.S. Dept. Labor, Washington, 1971-72; counsel for appellate litigation OSHA, U.S. Dept. Labor, Washington, 1972-77; dep. dir. Task Force on Workplace Safety and Health, The White House, Washington, 1977-78; legis. aide U.S. House, Senate, Washington, 1978-79; dir. regulatory reform staff U.S. EPA, Washington, 1979-88; counsel Nixon, Hargrave, Devans & Doyle, Washington, 1988-95; ptnr. McGuire, Woods, Battle & Boothe, LLP, Washington, 1995—; vis. lectr. on regulation Harvard, Columbia, Va. univs., 1976-89; chair task force on market approaches Clean Air Working Group, Washington, 1989-90; mem. nat. adv. panel U.S. Office Tech. Assessment, Washington, 1990-92. Contbr. articles to profl. jours. Thouron fellow to Oxford, U. Pa., Phila., 1964-66, Congl. fellow U.S. Civil Svc. Commn., Washington, 1978-79; recipient Gold medal EPA, 1982. Mem. ABA (vice-chmn. environ. values com. 1988-90), Air and Waste Mgmt. Assn. (govt. affairs com. 1989-96, co-chmn. strategic environ. planning subcom. 1991-92, sec. legal com. 1993-94, vice-chmn. legal-liability com. 1994-96, chmn. 1996-99), D.C. Bar Assn., Phi Beta Kappa. Administrative and regulatory, Environmental, Finance. Office: McGuire Woods Battle Et Al Ste 1200 1050 Connecticut Ave NW Washington DC 20036-5317

**LEVIN, MICHAEL JOSEPH,** lawyer; b. Detroit, Feb. 1, 1943; s. Bayre and Lydia Ruth (Kahn) L.; m. Adah Hanson, Aug. 3, 1974; children: Andrew, Stephen. BA, Johns Hopkins U., 1964; JD, U. Mich., 1967. Bar: Mich. 1968, N.Y. 1973. Assoc. Milbank, Tweed, Hadley & McCloy, N.Y.C., 1971-86; ptnr. Boyle, Vogeler & Haimes, N.Y.C., 1986-93, Sutherland, Asbill & Brennan, N.Y.C. and Washington D.C., 1993-97; of counsel Menaker & Herrmann LLP, N.Y.C., 1997—. Served to lt. col. USMCR, 1963-90. Mem. Mich. Bar Assn., N.Y. State Bar Assn., Assn. of Bar of City of N.Y. General civil litigation, Bankruptcy. Office: Menaker & Herrmann LLP 10 E 40th St Fl 43 New York NY 10016-0354

**LEVIN, RICHARD BARRY,** lawyer; b. Chgo., Nov. 26, 1956; s. Stanley H. and Dorothy Louise (Goldman) L. BS, U. New Orleans, 1981; JD, La. State U., 1984. Bar: La. 1984, U.S. Dist. Ct. (ea. and middle dist.) La. 1984, U.S. Ct. Appeals (5th cir.) 1984, U.S. Supreme Ct. 1990. Law clk. to judge La. Dist. Ct., New Orleans, 1984-85; ptnr. Goldman & Levin, New Orleans, 1985-93, Levin Law Offices, New Orleans, 1993—. Bd. dirs. Temple Sinai, New Orleans, 1987—, Jewish Children's Regional Svcs., 1988—. Mem.

ABA (dist. rep. 1990—), La. Bar Assn., New Orleans Bar Assn. (sec.-treas. young lawyers sect. 1987-88, vice-chair 1988-89, chair-elect 1989-90, chair 1990-91, chmn. law day legal clinics 1987, mem. pub. rels. com. 1987—, bd. dirs.). Republican. Avocations: golf, bowling, sailing, reading, tennis. General civil litigation, Consumer commercial, Family and matrimonial. Office: Levin Law Offices 1515 Poydras St Ste 2010 New Orleans LA 70112-3762

**LEVIN, ROGER MICHAEL,** lawyer; b. N.Y.C., Oct. 20, 1942; s. Harold F. and Blanche M. (Tarr) L. BA in Polit. Sci., U. Chgo., 1964; MA with distinction in polit. sci., U. Calif.-Berkeley, 1966; JD, NYU, 1969. Bar: N.Y. 1970, D.C. 1982, U.S. Dist. Ct. (so. and ea. dists.) N.Y., 1971, U.S. Ct. Appeals (2d cir.) 1971, U.S. Ct. Appeals (D.C. cir.) 1979, U.S. Customs Ct. 1974, U.S. Tax Ct. 1981, U.S. Ct. Customs and Patent Appeals 1974, U.S. Supreme Ct. 1974. Personal asst. to U.S. rep. Dept. State, Quang Nam Province, South Vietnam, 1966; asst. to dir. Nr. East/South Asia Bur. Office Internat. Security Affairs, Office Sec. of Def., Washington, 1967; mng. ptnr. Levin & Weissman, N.Y.C., 1982—; lawyer; b. N.Y.C., Oct. 20, 1942; s. Harold F. and Blanche M. (Tarr) L. B.A. in Polit. Sci., U. Chgo., 1964; Fulbright scholar U. Sri Lanka, 1964-65; M.A. with distinction in Polit. Sci. (Woodrow Wilson fellow), U. Calif.-Berkeley, 1966; J.D., NYU, 1969. Bar: N.Y. 1970, D.C. 1982, U.S. Dist. Ct. (so. and ea. dists.) N.Y., 1971, U.S. Ct. Appeals (2d cir.) 1971, U.S. Ct. Appeals (D.C. cir.) 1979, U.S. Customs Ct. 1974, U.S. Tax Ct. 1981, U.S. Ct. Customs and Patent Appeals 1974, U.S. Supreme Ct. 1974. Personal asst. to U.S. rep. Dept. State, Quang Nam Province, South Vietnam, 1966; asst. to dir. Nr. East/South Asia Bur., Office Internat. Security Affairs, Office Sec. of Def., Washington, 1967; mng. ptnr. Levin & Weissman, N.Y.C., 1982— . Named Best Oralist, Jessup Internat. Law Moot Ct. Regional Competition NYU, 1969. Research editor NYU Jour. Internat. Law and Politics. Rsch. editor NYU Jour. Internat. Law and Politics. Fulbright scholar U. Sri Lanka, 1964-65; Woodrow Wilson fellow U. Calif.-Berkeley, 1966; named Best Oralist, Jessup Internat., Law Moot Ct. Regional Competition, NYU, 1969. Federal civil litigation, General corporate, Labor. Office: 15 E 90th St New York NY 10125-0001

**LEVIN, RONALD MARK,** law educator; b. St. Louis, May 11, 1950; s. Marvin S. and Lois (Cohn) L.; m. Anne Carol Goldberg, July 29, 1989. BA magna cum laude, Yale U., 1972; JD, U. Chgo., 1975. Bar: Mo. 1975, D.C. 1977. Law clk. to Hon. John C. Godbold U.S. Ct. Appeals, 5th cir., 1975-76; assoc. Sutherland, Asbill & Brennan, Washington, 1976-79; asst. prof. law Washington U., St. Louis, 1979-80, assoc. prof. law, 1980-85, prof. law, 1985—, assoc. dean, 1990-93; cons. Adminstrv. Conf. U.S., 1979-81, 93-95. Co-author: Administrative Law and Process, 4th edit., 1997, State and Federal Administrative Law, 2d edit., 1998. Chair senate coun. Washington U., 1988-90. Mem. ABA (chair-elect, sect. adminstrv. law and regulatory practice 1999-2000), Assn. Am. Law Sch. (chair sect. adminstrv. law 1993, chair sect. legis. 1995). Home: 7352 Kingsbury Blvd Saint Louis MO 63130-4142 Office: Wash Univ Sch Law Campus Box 1120 Saint Louis MO 63130

**LEVIN, ROY C.,** lawyer; b. Boston. BSE, San Francisco State U., 1974; JD, McGeorge U., 1991. Bar: Calif. 1991. Mgr. GE Med. Sys., Burlingame, Calif., 1975-88; assoc. Bernheim Gutierrez Levin & McCready, Dixon, Calif., 1992—. Workers' compensation, Personal injury, Consumer commercial. Office: Bernheim Gutierrez Levin & McCready 255 N Lincoln St Dixon CA 95620-3238

**LEVIN, SIMON,** lawyer; b. Newark, Aug. 4, 1942; m. Barbara Leslie Lasky, Dec. 21, 1989; children: David, Jennifer Menken, Yale, Michael, Jacob. BS cum laude, Lehigh U., 1964; JD, NYU, 1967, LLM in Taxation, 1974. Bar: N.J. 1967, U.S. Tax Ct. 1971, U.S. Ct. Claims 1972, N.Y. 1980. Assoc. Shanley & Fisher, Newark, 1970, Hannoch Weisman, Newark, 1970-73; ptnr. Robinson, Wayne, Levin, Riccio & La Sala, Newark, 1973-88; mem., co-chmn. tax dept. Sills Cummis Radin Tischman Epstein & Gross, Newark, 1988—; civillian aide to Sec. Army for N.J., 1992-95; mem. N.J. Dept. Treasury Transition Team for Gov. Christine Todd Whitman, 1993-94; mem. treas. adv. group N.J. Dept. of Treasury, 1995—; lectr., panelist numerous orgns. Co-author: Taxation Investors in Securities and Commodities, 1983, 2d edit., 1984, supplement, 1986, Estate Planning and Administration in New Jersey, 1987; contbr. articles to profl. jours. Trustee, mem. exec. com. Jewish Comty. Found., MetroWest, Whippany, N.J., pres., 1979-83; trustee, mem. exec. com. Israel Bond Campaign MetroWest, Livingston, N.J., chmn., 1988-89; trustee Monmouth Healthcare Ctr. Found., 1997—, N.J. Vietnam Vets. Meml. and Edn. Ctr. Found., Holmdel, 1994—. Capt. U.S. Army, 1968-69, Vietnam. Recipient Cohn Leadership award Jewish Fedn. MetroWest, 1982, Endowment Achievement award Coun. Jewish Fedns., 1986, N.J. Meritorious Svc. medal, 1995. Fellow Am. Coll. Tax Counsel; mem. ABA, N.J. Bar Assn. (chmn. commodities sect. 1982-86), Essex County Bar Assn. (chmn. sect. taxation 1974-76), Monmouth County Bar Assn., Phi Delta Phi. Avocations: tennis, skiing, politics, opera, community service. Taxation, general, State and local taxation, Estate taxation. Office: Sills Cummis Radin Tischman Epstein & Gross 1 Riverfront Plz Fl 10 Newark NJ 07102-5401

**LEVIN, WILLIAM EDWARD,** lawyer; b. Miami, Fla., June 13, 1954; s. Harold A. and Phyllis (Wolfson) L.; m. Mary Catherine Egan, June 25, 1994; 1 child: Sean Alexander. Student, Conn. Coll., 1972-74; BA, Emory U., Atlanta, 1976; JD, U. Miami, 1979. Bar: Fla. 1979, Calif. 1982; lic. real estate broker, Calif. Distbr. N.Y. Times, Atlanta, 1975-76; legis. intern Congressman William Lehman, Washington, 1974; law clk. Superior Ct. Hillsborough County, Tampa, Fla., 1974; legal asst./law clk. U. Miami Sch. Law, 1977-78; law clk. Shevin, Shapo & Shevin, Miami, 1977-79; assoc. Law Offices of John Cyril Malloy, Miami, 1979-82; assoc./ptnr. Flehr, Hohbach, Test, Albritton & Herbert, San Francisco, 1982-87; ptnr. Cooper, White & Cooper, San Francisco, 1987-88; pvt. practice trademark and copyright law San Francisco, 1988-92, Irvine, Calif., 1993-96; broker/sole proprietor Levin Realty, San Francisco, 1987-92; of counsel Goldstein & Phillips, San Francisco, 1988-91, Hawes & Fischer, Newport Beach, Calif., 1992-93, Gauntlett & Assocs., Irvine, Calif., 1995-96; mng. partner Levin & Gluck, Laguna Beach, Calif., 1996-97; mng. ptnr. Levin & Hawes, Laguna Beach, Calif., 1997—; co-chmn. trademark com. San Francisco Patent & Trademark Assn., 1985-86; moot ct. judge Giles Rich Moot Ct. Competition, San Francisco, 1986; ofcl. arbitrator Am. Arbitration Assn., 1987-96; mem. exec. com. L.A. Complex Inns of Ct., 1994-96; lectr. in field. Author: Trade Press Protection, 1996; mem. editorial bd. Trademark World, London, 1987-90, Trademark Reporter, 1987-89, 93—, Trademark Reporter Task Force, 1994-97, San Francisco Atty., 1986-89; contbr. articles to profl. jours. Adminstrv. bd. Californians for Missing Children, San Francisco, 1989-92, Hebrew Inst. Law, San Francisco, 1986-88; atty's. steering com. Jewish Cmty. Fedn., San Francisco, 1987-88; fin. com. Temple Emanu-el, San Francisco, 1985-86; bd. dirs. Ctr. 500, Orange County Performing Arts Ctr. Support Group, 1996, Anti-Defamation League Orange county and Long Beach Region, 1998—; trustee Shir Ha Ma'lot Temple, 1997—. Mem. ABA, Internat. Trademark Assn., Orange County Bar Assn., Orange County Patent Law Assn., Am. Intellectual Property Law Assn. Democrat. Jewish. Avocations: biking, skiing, gardening. Trademark and copyright, Federal civil litigation.

**LEVINE, ALAN,** lawyer; b. Middletown, N.Y., Jan. 17, 1948; s. Jacques and Florence (Tananbaum) L.; m. Nancy Shapiro, June 7, 1971; children: Emily Jane, Malcolm Andrew. BS in Econs., U. Pa., 1970; JD, NYU, 1973. Bar: N.Y. 1974, U.S. Dist. Ct. (so. dist.) N.Y. 1974, U.S. Dist. Ct. (ea. dist.) N.Y. 1980, U.S. Tax Ct. 1980, U.S. Ct. Appeals (2d cir.) 1975. Law clk. U.S. Dist. Ct. (so. dist.) N.Y., N.Y.C., 1973-75; asst. U.S. atty, U.S. Attys. Office, so. dist. N.Y., Dept. Justice, N.Y.C., 1975-80; assoc. Kronish, Lieb, Weiner & Hellman, N.Y.C., 1980-82, mem., 1982—, co-mng. ptnr., 1997—. Chmn. bd. Park Ave. Synagogue, N.Y.C., 1993—; bd. dirs. Jewish Theol. Sem. Rabbinical Sch.; bd. dirs. MYF Legal Svcs., Inc., 1990-93. Law chmn. N.Y. County Rep. Com., 1991-93. Recipient Atty. Gen. Dirs. award U.S. Dept. Justice, 1980, Torch of Learning award Am. Friends Hebrew U., 1995. Fellow Am. Bar Found., Am. Coll. Trial Laywers; mem. ABA (ho. of dels. 1983-84, chmn. spl. com. youth edn. for citizenship, 1988-91, vice chmn. white collar crime com. 1996—), N.Y. State Bar Assn. (chmn. com. on citizenship edn. 1979-84, ho. of dels. 1982-84, award of achievement 1984). Republican. Jewish. Club: Sunningdale Country (bd. trustees 1988-90 Scarsdale, N.Y.); Mask and Wig (Phila.). Federal civil litigation, Criminal. Home: 1185 Park Ave New York NY 10128-1308 Office: Kronish Lieb Weiner & Hellman 1114 Avenue Of The Americas New York NY 10036-7703

**LEVINE, BERYL JOYCE,** former state supreme court justice; b. Winnipeg, Man., Can., Nov. 9, 1935; came to U.S., 1955; d. Maurice Jacob and Bella (Gutnik) Choslovsky; m. Leonard Levine, June 7, 1955; children: Susan Brauna, Marc Joseph, Sari Ruth, William Noah, David Karl. BA, U. Man., Winnipeg, 1965; JD with distinction, U. N.D., 1974. Bar: N.D. 1974. Assoc. Vogel, Branther, Kelly, Knutson, Weir & Bye, Ltd., Fargo, N.D., 1974-85; justice N.D. Supreme Ct., Bismarck, 1985-1996; chmn. jud. planning com. Joint Procedure Com., Bismarck. Bd. dirs. Fargo Youth Commn., 1974-77, Hospice of Red River Valley, Fargo; chmn. Gov.'s Commn. of Children at Risk, 1985, co-chair N.D. Gender Fairness Com. Named Outstanding Woman in N.D. Law, U. N.D. Law Women's Caucus, 1985, ABA Comm. on Margaret Brent award, 1996. Mem. Cass County Bar Assn. (pres. 1984-85), N.D. State Bar Assn., Burleigh County Bar Assn., Order of Coif.

**LEVINE, DAVID ETHAN,** lawyer; b. Niagara Falls, N.Y., Feb. 28, 1955; s. Morree Morell Levine and Marbud Juel (Gagen) Prozeller; m. Ann Lee Ruhlin, May 23, 1981. BS in Bus., Miami U., 1977; JD, Capital U., 1981. Bar: N.Y. 1982, U.S. Dist. Ct. (we. dist.) N.Y. 1982. Assoc. Grossman, Levine and Civiletto, Niagara Falls, 1981-89, Cummings and Levine, Niagara Falls, 1989-92; pvt. practice Niagara Falls, 1992—. V.p. Buffalo Area Recreational Cyclists, Inc., 1995. Mem. N.Y. State Bar Assn., Niagara Falls Bar Assn. Unitarian Universalist. Avocations: skiing, photography, bicycling, camping. Probate, Workers' compensation, Real property. Home: 22 Hemlock Dr Grand Island NY 14072-3315 Office: PO Box 922 669 Main St Niagara Falls NY 14301-1701

**LEVINE, DAVID I.,** lawyer; b. Queens, N.Y., 1966. BA in History, Binghamton U., 1987; JD, NYU, 1990. Bar: N.Y. 1990, N.J. 1990, U.S. Dist. Ct. N.J. 1990, U.S. Dist. Ct. (so. and ea. dists.) N.Y. 1993. Asst. dist. atty. Queens (N.Y.) Dist. Attys. Office, 1990-97; atty. pvt. practice, Mineola, N.Y., 1997—. Mem. Queens County Bar Assn., Nassau County Bar Assn., Criminal Cts. Bar Assn., N.Y. Law Sch. Alumni Assn. (dir. 1996—). Criminal, General practice, Real property. Office: 1565 Franklin Ave Ste 200 Mineola NY 11501-4808

**LEVINE, GLENN STUART,** lawyer, consultant; b. Phila., Mar. 13, 1961; s. Stanley A. and Binney Levine. BA, U. Va., 1983; JD, U. Miami, 1989. Bar: Va. 1989, U.S. Dist. Ct. (ea. dist.) Va., U.S. Dist. Ct. Md. Assoc. Tyler, Bartl, Burke & Albert, Alexandria, Va., 1989-92, Protas & Spivok, Bethesda, Md., 1992-93; ptnr. Levine & Levine, P.C., Washington, 1993-96; comml. law liaison ABA, Sofia, Bulgaria, 1996-97; Cen. and East European Law Initiative fellow ABA, Washington, 1997-98; ABA advisor S.E. European Cooperative Initiative U.S. State Dept., Washington, 1998—; mem. adv. bd. U.S.-Bulgaria Trade Coun., Washington, 1997—; chair hi-tech bus. com. Reston (Va.) C. of C., 1994-95; bd. dirs. Performing Arts Assn., Alexandria, Va., 1984-86. Contbr. articles to profl. jours. Mem. rsch. staff Rep. Nat. Com., Washington, 1983-84. Office: ABA-CEELI 740 15th St NW Fl 8 Washington DC 20005-1022

**LEVINE, HAROLD,** lawyer; b. Newark, Apr. 30, 1931; s. Rubin and Gussie (Lifshitz) L.; children: Brenda Sue, Linda Ellen Levine Gersen, Louise Abby, Jill Anne Levine Lipari, Charles A., Cristina Gussie, Harold Rubin II; m. Cristina Cervera, Aug. 29, 1980. BS in Engring., Purdue U., 1954; JD with distinction, George Washington U., 1958. Bar: D.C. 1958, Va. 1958, Mass. 1960, Tex. 1972, U.S. Patent Office 1958. Naval arch., marine engr. U.S. Navy Dept., 1954-55; patent examiner U.S. Patent Office, 1955-58; with Tex. Instruments, Inc., Attleboro, Mass., 1959-77; asst. sec. Tex. Instruments, Inc., Dallas, 1969-72, asst. v.p. and gen. patent counsel, 1972-77; ptnr. Sigalos & Levine, Dallas, 1977-93; prin. Levine & Majorie LLP, Dallas, 1994—; chmn. bd. Vanguard Security, Inc., Houston, 1977—; chmn. Tex. Am. Realty, Dallas, 1977—; lectr. assns., socs.; del. Geneva and Lausanne (Switzerland) Intergovtl. Conf. on Revision, Paris Pat. Conv., 1975-76. Editor George Washington U. Law Rev., 1956-57; mem. adv. bd. editors Bur. Nat. Affairs, Pat., Trdmk. and Copyright Jour.; contbr. chpt. to book and articles to profl. jours. Mem. U.S. State Dept. Adv. Panel on Internat. Tech. Transfer, 1977. Mem. ABA (chmn. com. 407 taxation pats. and trdmks. 1971-72), Am. Patent Law Assn., Dallas Bar Assn., Assn. Corp. Pat. Csl. (sec.-treas. 1971-73), Dallas-Ft. Worth Patent Law Assn., Pacific Indsl. Property Assn. (pres. 1975-77), Electronic Industries Assn. (pres. pat. com. 1972), NAM, Southwestern Legal Inst. on Patent Law (planning com. 1971-74), U.S. C. of C., Dallas C. of C., Kiwanis, Alpha Epsilon Pi, Phi Alpha Delta. Republican. Jewish. Intellectual property, Trademark and copyright, Patent. Office: Levine and Majorie LLP 12750 Merit Dr Ste 1000 Dallas TX 75251

**LEVINE, HERBERT,** lawyer; b. June 5, 1924; s. Barnet and Mollie (Morris) L.; m. Parl H. Kahn, Mar. 30, 1946; children: Barbara, Susan, Deborah, Steven. BBA, U. Wis., 1950, JD, 1950. Bar: Wis. 1950, U.S. Dist. Ct. (ea. dist.) Wis. 1950. Pvt. practice Milw., 1950-66; assoc. Bernstein, Wessel & Lewis, Milw., 1967-75; shareholder Stupar, Schuster & Cooper S.C., Milw., 1976—; instr. Am. Inst. Banking, Milw., 1964-88 ; lectr. Marquette U., 1968-79, Milw. Bd. Realtors, 1961. Pres. Bayside PTA, Wis., 1965-66; active Indian Guides, Bayside, Wis., 1972-73. Sgt. USAAF, 1943-46. Mem. Wis. Bar Assn., Milw. Bar Assn. Contracts commercial, General corporate, Real property. Home: 9055 N King Rd Milwaukee WI 53217-1848 Office: Stupar Schuster & Cooper SC 633 W Wisconsin Ave Milwaukee WI 53203-1918

**LEVINE, HOWARD ARNOLD,** state supreme court justice; b. Mar. 4, 1932; m. Barbara Joan Segall, July 25, 1954; children: Neil Louis, Ruth Ellen, James Robert. BA, Yale U., 1953, LLB, 1956; LLD (hon.), Union U., 1994. Bar: N.Y. 1956. Asst. in instrn., research asso. in criminal law Yale Law Sch., 1956-57; asso. firm Hughes, Hubbard, Blair, Reed, N.Y.C., 1957-59; practiced in Schenectady, 1959-70; asst. dist. atty. Schenectady County, N.Y., 1961-66, dist. atty., 1967-70; judge Schenectady County Family Ct., 1971-80; acting judge Schenectady County Ct., 1971-80; adminstrv. judge family cts. N.Y. State 4th Jud. Dist., 1974-80; asso. justice appellate div. 3d dept. N.Y. State Supreme Ct., 1982-93; asso. judge N.Y. Ct. of Appeals, 1993—; vis. lectr. Albany Law Sch., 1972-81; mem. N.Y. Gov.'s Panel on Juvenile Violence, N.Y. State Temp. Commn. on Child Welfare, N.Y. State Temp. Commn. on Recodification of Family Ct. Act, N.Y. State Juvenile Justice Adv. Bd., 1974-80; mem. ind. rev. bd. N.Y. State Div. for Youth, 1974-80; mem. rules and adv. com. on family ct. N.Y. State Jud. Conf., 1974-80. Contbr. articles to law revs. Bd. dirs. Schnecatady County Child Guildance Ctr., Carver Community Ctr., Freedom Forum of Schnectady. Mem. ABA, Am. Law Inst., N.Y. State Bar Assn. (chmn. spl. com. juvenile justice), Assn. Family Ct. Judges State N.Y. (pres. 1979-80). Home: 2701 Rosendale Rd Niskayuna NY 12309-1300 Office: County Jud Bldg 612 State St Schenectady NY 12305-2112

**LEVINE, JACK ANTON,** lawyer; b. Monticello, N.Y., Dec. 23, 1946; s. Milton and Sara (Sacks) L.; m. Eileen A. Garsh, Sept. 7, 1974; children: Matthew Aaron, Dara Esther. BS with honors, SUNY, Binghamton, 1968; JD with honors, U. Fla., 1975, LLM in Taxation, 1976. Bar: Fla. 1975, U.S. Ct. Appeals (11th cir.) 1981, U.S. Tax Ct., 1982. Tax atty. legis. and regulations divsn. Office chief counsel IRS, Washington, 1977-81; assoc. Holland & Knight, Tampa, Fla., 1981-83, ptnr., 1984—; lectr. in field. Contbr. articles to profl. jours. Mem. ABA, Fla. Bar Assn. (sect. taxation exec. coun. 1984—, chmn. ptnrship. com. 1985-88, chmn. taxation regulated public utilities com. 1988-92, co-chmn. corps. and tax-exempt orgns. com. 1992—, bd. cert. in tax law 1984—). Democrat. Jewish. Avocations: golf, reading, traveling. Corporate taxation, Taxation, general, Personal income taxation. Home: 10905 Carrollwood Dr Tampa FL 33618-3903 Office: Holland & Knight 400 N Ashley Dr Ste 2300 Tampa FL 33602-4322

**LEVINE, JAMES HOWARD,** lawyer; b. Chattanooga, Apr. 8, 1970; s. Howard I. and Mary Jane Levine; m. Jill Keegan, Aug. 8, 1998. BA, Yale U., 1992; JD, Tulane U., 1997. Bar: Tenn. 1997. Legal asst. Arnold & Porter, Washington, 1992-94; assoc. Baker Donelson, Bearman & Caldwell, Chattanooga, 1997—. Mng. editor Tulane Environ. Law Jour., 1996-97. Mergers and acquisitions, Securities, General corporate. Home: 805 Mount Vernon Cir Chattanooga TN 37405-2944 Office: Baker Donelson Bearman & Caldwell 1800 Republic Ctr 633 Chestnut St Chattanooga TN 37450-4000

**LEVINE, JEFFREY BARRY,** lawyer; b. Detroit, Jan. 13, 1949; s. Jack Morris and Blanche (Kaufman) L. BA, Wayne State U., 1971, JD cum laude, 1974; LLM in Taxation, NYU, 1975. Bar: Mich. 1974, U.S. Dist. Ct. (ea. dist.) Mich. 1977, U.S. Ct. of Appeals (6th cir. 1979), U.S. Tax Ct. 1981. Assoc. Thomas W. Kimmeryl P.C., Bloomfield Hills, Mich., 1974-78; chief counsel DeLoren Motor Co., Bloomfield Hills, 1978; assoc. Rubenstein, Isaacs, Lax & Bordman, Southfield, Mich., 1978-82; ptnr. Hyman, Gurwin, Nachman, Friedman & Winkelman, Southfield, 1982-88; assoc. Carson, Fischer & Potts, Birmingham, Mich., 1988-91; of counsel Rubenstein, Isaacs, Haroutunian & Sobel, Southfield, 1991-92; shareholder Rubenstein, Plotkin P.C., Southfield, 1992—; spkr. orgns. of attys. and pub. accts. on taxation and bus. law. issues. Taxation, general, General corporate, Construction. Office: Rubenstein Plotkin PC 2000 Town Ctr Ste 2700 Southfield MI 48075-1318

**LEVINE, JEROME LESTER,** lawyer; b. Los Angeles, July 20, 1940. m. Maryanne Shields, Sept. 13, 1966; children: Aron Michael, Sara Michelle. BA San Francisco State U., 1962; JD, U. Calif., 1965. Bar: Calif. 1966, U.S. Supreme Ct., 1986. Dir. operational svcs., assoc. dir. Western Ctr. on Law and Poverty, Los Angeles, 1968-72; assoc. Swerdlow, Glikbarg & Shimer, Beverly Hills, Calif., 1972-77; ptnr. Lans Feinberg & Cohen, L.A., 1977-79, Albala & Levine, L.A., 1980-83, Neiman Billet Albala & Levine, L.A., 1983-90, Levine & Assocs., L.A., 1991—; lectr. in law U. So. Calif. Law Ctr., Loyola U. Sch. Law. Mem. ABA, L.A. County Bar Assn., Beverly Hills Bar Assn., Assn. Bus. Trial Lawyers, Fed. Bar Assn., Nat. Indian Gaming Assn. (co-chair Law and Legis. Com.), Internat. Assn. Gaming Lawyers (editorial bd. Indian Gaming Mag.). Federal civil litigation, State civil litigation, General corporate. Office: 2049 Century Park E Ste 710 Los Angeles CA 90067-3109

**LEVINE, JULIUS BYRON,** lawyer, legal educator; b. Waterville, Maine, Feb. 8, 1939; s. Lewis Lester and Celia G. (Gurewitz) L.; m. Diane Groner, Aug. 26, 1965 (div.); children—Rachel A., Sarah L.; m. 2d Susan M. Ginns, Sept. 7,. 1980 (div.); 1 child, James G. A.B. summa cum laude, Harvard U., 1960, J.D. cum laude, 1964; Ph.D., Oxford U., Eng., 1969. Bar: Maine 1963, Mass. 1964, U.S. Ct. Appeals (1st cir.) 1964. Law clk. U.S. Dist. Ct. Maine, Portland, 1964-65; ptnr., of counsel Levine, Brody & Levine, Boston and Waterville, 1963-80, of counsel Levine, Bishop & Levine, Boston and Waterville, 1980—; assoc. prof. law Boston U., 1969-72, prof. law, 1972—; master Superior Ct. Mass., Boston, 1972—, coordinator jud. intern program, 1979—; asst. dist. atty. Norfolk County, Mass., 1976; lectr. New Eng. Law Inst.-Mass. Continuing Legal Edn., Boston, 1977-93 , Nat. Coll. Probate Judges, Williamsburg, Va., 1979-82. Author: Discovery: A Comparison between English and American Civil Discovery Law with Reform Proposals, 1982, Winning Trial Advocacy, 1989; co-author: Supplements to Massachusetts Pleading and Practice, 1981. Faculty editor Probate Law Jour., 1985-89; legal editor Nat. Coll. Probate Judges Newsletter, 1979-82. Contbr. to legal jours. and books. Chmn. Citizens for Better Urban Renewal Plan, Waterville, 1962-63; mem. No. Kennebec Valley Regional Planning Commn., 1966-68, Maine Com. to Select Rhodes Scholars, 1971—; co-chmn. Aspinwall Hill Neighborhood Assn., Brookline, Mass., 1974-76; v.p. Ellis (South End) Neighborhood Assn., Boston, 1980-82, 87-88, bd. dirs., 1986-92, pres. 1989-90; chmn. Mass. Victims of Crime, Boston, 1983—; legal dir. Nat. Victims of Crime, Washington, 1983-85 . John Harvard scholar Harvard U., 1957-59; Rhodes scholar Oxford U., 1960-61, 67-69. Mem. ABA (mem. adv. council real property, probate and trust sect. 1972-81, contbg. editor jour. of litigation sect. 1974-77), Phi Beta Kappa, Omicron Chi Epsilon. Club: Mt. Auburn (Watertown, Mass.). Lodge: Masons. Condemnation, Criminal, Personal injury. Home: 1443 Beacon St Brookline MA 02446-4707 Office: Boston Univ Law Sch 765 Commonwealth Ave Boston MA 02215-1401

**LEVINE, KIMBERLY ANNE,** lawyer; b. Bklyn., Aug. 6, 1967; d. Fred Howard and Miriam Carol (Cohen) L. BS, Cornell U., 1989; JD, B.N. Cardozo Sch. Law, N.Y.C., 1993. Bar: N.Y. 1994, U.S. Dist. Ct. (ea. dist.) N.Y. 1996, U.S. Dist. Ct. (so. dist.) N.Y. 1996, U.S. Ct. Appeals (2d cir.) 1999, U.S. Supreme Ct. 1999. Asst. dir. of representation Office of Collective Bargaining, N.Y.C., 1989-91; counsel, asst. to dir. Conf. of Presidents of Major Am. Jewish Orgns., N.Y.C., 1995-96; assoc. civil litigation Karp, Silver, Glinkenhouse & Floumanhaft, Far Rockaway, N.Y., 1996-97; assoc. employment litigation Milman & Heidecker, Lake Success, N.Y., 1997—; adv. bd. Cornell U. Hillel Alumni Bd., 1995—;. Advisor Neve Yerushalayim Coll., N.Y.C. and Jerusalem, Israel, 1993—; tutor Bible studies Aish Ha Torah, N.Y.C., 1997—. Recipient Pres.'s prize Met. Squash Rackets Assn., N.Y.C., 1992; named High Ranking Amateur U.S. Squash Rackets Assn., 1990, 91. Fellow Hashevaynu (cons. 1995—); mem. Neve Yerushalayim Coll. Alumni Assn. (Alumni of Yr. 1995). Avocations: tennis, squash, softball. Labor, Federal civil litigation, State civil litigation. Office: Milman & Heidecker 3000 Marcus Ave Ste 3w3 New Hyde Park NY 11042-1009

**LEVINE, LAURENCE HARVEY,** lawyer; b. Cleve., Aug. 23, 1946; s. Theodore and Celia (Chaikin) Levine; m. Mary M. Conway, May 13, 1978; children: Abigail, Adam, Sarah. BA cum laude, Case Western Res. U., 1968; JD, Northwestern U., 1971. Bar: Ill. 1971, U.S. Dist. Ct. (no. dist.) Ill. 1972, U.S. Ct. Appeals (6th, 7th, 10th and D.C. cirs.), U.S. Ct. Claims 1997. Law clk. to presiding judge U.S. Ct. Appeals (6th cir.), Detroit, 1971-72; assoc. Kirkland & Ellis, Chgo., 1972-76; ptnr. Latham & Watkins, Chgo., 1976—. Bd. editors Northwestern Law Rev., 1968-71. Mem. ABA, Chgo. Bar Assn., Mid-Am. Club. Environmental, Administrative and regulatory, Federal civil litigation. Office: Latham & Watkins Sears Tower Ste 5800 Chicago IL 60606-6306

**LEVINE, MARILYN MARKOVICH,** lawyer, arbitrator; b. Bklyn., Aug. 9, 1930; d. Harry P. and Fannie L. (Hymowitz) Markovich; m. Louis L. Levine. June 24, 1950; children: Steven R., Ronald J., Linda J. Morgenstern. BS summa cum laude, Columbia U., 1950; MA, Adelphi U., 1967; JD, Hofstra U., 1977. Bar: N.Y. 1978, U.S. Dist. Ct. (so. and ea. dists.) N.Y. 1978, D.C. 1979, U.S. Supreme Ct. 1982. Sole practice Valley Stream, N.Y., 1978—; contract arbitrator bldg. svc. industry, N.Y.C., 1982—; panel arbitrator retail food industry, N.Y.C., 1980—; arbitrator N.Y. dist. cts., Nassau County, 1981—; mem. Nat. Acad. Arbitrators, 1992—. Panel arbitrator Suffolk County Pub. Employee Relations Bd., 1979—, Nassau County Pub. Employee Relations Bd., 1980—, Nat. Mediation Bd., 1986—; mem. adv. council Ctr. Labor and Industrial Relations, N.Y. Inst. Tech., N.Y., 1985—; counsel Nassau Civic Club, 1978—. Mem. ABA, N.Y. State Bar Assn., D.C. Bar Assn., Nassau County Bar Assn., N.J. Bd. Mediation (panel arbitrator), Am. Arbitration Assn. (arbitrator 1979—), Fed. Mediation Bd. (arbitrator 1980—). Labor, Alternative dispute resolution. Home and Office: 1057 Linden St Valley Stream NY 11580-2135

**LEVINE, MELDON EDISES,** lawyer, former congressman; b. Los Angeles, June 7, 1943; s. Sid B. and Shirley B. (Blum) L.; children: Adam Paul, Jacob Caplan, Cara Emily. AB, U. Calif., Berkeley, 1964; MPA, Princeton U., 1966; JD, Harvard U., 1969. Bar: Calif. 1970, D.C. 1972. Assoc. Wyman, Bautzer, Rothman & Kuchel, 1969-71; legis. asst. U.S. Senate, Washington, 1971-73; ptnr. Levine Krom & Unger, Beverly Hills, Calif., 1973-77; mem. Calif. Assembly, Sacramento, 1977-82, 98th-102d Congresses from 27th Calif. dist., Washington, 1983-93; ptnr. Gibson, Dunn & Crutcher, L.A., 1993—. Author: The Private Sector and the Common Market, 1968; contbr. articles to various publs. Mem. governing bd. U.S.-Israel Sci. and Tech. Commn., So. Calif. chpt. NAACP Legal Def. Fund; mem. amateur baseball team Hollywood Stars, 1971—. Mem. Calif. Bar Assn., Los Angeles Bar Assn. Office: Gibson Dunn & Crutcher 2029 Century Park E Ste 4000 Los Angeles CA 90067-3032

**LEVINE, MELVIN CHARLES,** lawyer; b. Bklyn., Nov. 12, 1930; s. Barnet and Jennie (Iser) L. BCS, NYU, 1952; LLB, Harvard U., 1955. Bar: N.Y. 1956, U.S. Supreme Ct. 1964. Assoc. Kriger & Haber, Bklyn., 1956-58, Black, Varian & Simons, N.Y.C., 1959; sole practice N.Y.C., 1959—; devel. multiple dwelling housing; dir. Am. Ort; mem. housing ct. adv. coun. N.Y. State Unified Ct. Sys.; mem. ind. dem. jud. screening panel N.Y.C civil ct. judges. Trustee Jewish Ctr. of the Hamptons. Recipient N.Y. Ort Scholarship Fund Cmty. Achievement award. Mem. N.Y. County Lawyers Assn. (civil ct. practice sect., civil ct. com., housing ct. com., uniform housing ct. rules com., liaison to Assn. Bar City of N.Y. on selection of housing, civil and criminal ct. judges, com. on jud., task force on tort reform, civil ct. practice sect. disting. svc. award), Assn. Bar of City of N.Y. (adj. mem. jud.

com.). Democrat. Jewish. Real property, Landlord-tenant, State civil litigation. Home: 146 Waverly Pl New York NY 10014-3848 Office: 271 Madison Ave Ste 1404 New York NY 10016-1001

**LEVINE, NED J.,** lawyer; b. N.Y.C., Aug. 8, 1947; s. Leo and Ethel (Posner) L.; m. Marian Friedenreich, Aug. 10, 1969; children: Jonathan, Ely. AB, SUNY, Binghamton, 1968; JD, U. Pa., 1971. Bar: Pa. Law clerk Hon. Paul Chalpin, Phila., 1971-72; atty. Defender Assn., Phila., 1972-75, unit chief mental health, 1975—. Bd. dirs. Jewish Fedn. Phila., human svcs. adv. com., 1977; past pres. Pearlmen-Schecter Day Sch., Bala Cynwyd, Pa., 1990-92. Mem. Phila. Bar Assn. (past chair disabilities), Mental Health Assn. Southeastern Pa. (bd. dirs.), Prisoners Family Welfare Assn. (past treas.). Office: Defender Assn Phila 70 N 12th St Philadelphia PA 19107-2821

**LEVINE, ROBERT JEFFREY,** lawyer; b. Miami Beach, Fla., Nov. 27, 1956; s. I. Stanely and Elaine (Martz) L. BSBA, U. Fla., 1978; JD, George Washington U., 1981. Bar: Fla. 1981, U.S. Dist. Ct. (so. dist.) Fla. 1981, U.S. Ct. Appeals (5th and 11th cirs.) 1981, U.S. Supreme Ct. 1986. Assoc. Barron, Lehman & Cardenas, Miami, 1981-82; ptnr. Haves & Levine, Miami, 1982-83; pvt. practice law Miami, 1983-85; ptnr. Toland & Levine, 5, 1985-90, Levine & Geiger, P.A., Miami, 1990-94, Levine & Ptnrs., P.A., Miami, 1994—. Mem. Fla. Bar Assn., Assn. Trial Lawyers Am., Acad. Fla. Trial Lawyers. Avocations: diving, fishing, skiing, golf, tennis. Insurance, General civil litigation. Home: 136 Rosales Ct Coral Gables FL 33143-6547 Office: Levine & Ptnrs PA 1110 Brickell Ave Fl 7 Miami FL 33131-3132

**LEVINE, RONALD JAY,** lawyer; b. Bklyn., June 23, 1953; s. Louis Leon and Marilyn Priscilla (Markovich) L.; m. Cindy Beth Israel, Nov. 18, 1979; children: Merisa, Alisha. BA summa cum laude, Princeton U., 1974; JD cum laude, Harvard U., 1977. Bar: N.Y. 1978, U.S. Dist. Ct. (so. and ea. dists.) N.Y. 1978, D.C. 1980, N.J. 1987, U.S. Supreme Ct. 1982, U.S. Ct. Apeals (2d cir.) 1983, N.J. 1987, U.S. Dist. Ct. N.J. 1987, U.S. Dist. Ct. (we. dist.) N.Y. 1991, U.S. Ct. Appeals (3d cir.) 1991, Pa. 1995. Assoc. Phillips, Nizer, Benjamin, Krim & Ballon, N.Y.C., 1977-80; Debevoise & Plimpton, N.Y.C., 1980-84; assoc. Herrick, Feinstein, N.Y.C., 1984-85, ptnr., 1985—; gen. counsel Greater N.Y. Safety Council, N.Y.C., 1979-81; arbitrator Small Claims Ct. of Civil Ct. of City of N.Y., 1983-85. Mem. Site Plan Rev. Adv. Bd., West Windsor, N.J., 1986, planning bd., 1987. Mem. ABA (litigation sect.), N.Y. State Bar Assn. (chmn. com. on legal edn. and bar admission 1982-92, com. on profl. discipline 1989-90), N.J. State Bar Assn. (product liability com. 1991—, profl. responsibility com. 1992-96), Assn. of Bar of City of N.Y. (coun. jud. adminstrn. 1994-95, com. on profl. responsibility 1980-83, com. on legal assistance 1983-86, product liability com. 1987-91, trustee career devel. awards 1989-90), Phi Beta Kappa. Product liability, General civil litigation, Environmental. Home: 6 Arnold Dr Princeton Junction NJ 08550-1521 Office: Herrick Feinstein 2 Park Ave New York NY 10016-5675

**LEVINE, RONALD RAYMOND,** lawyer; b. Ithaca, N.Y., June 3, 1961; s. Ronald R. and Jean M. Levine; m. Carole Elizabeth Baran, Aug. 6, 1988; children: Nicholas, Michael. BS, Cornell U., 1984; JD, Harvard U., 1987. Bar: N.Y. 1987, Colo. 1989. Assoc. Hughes Hubbard & Reed, N.Y.C., 1987-89; assoc. Davis, Graham & Stubbs, LLP, Denver, 1989-93, ptnr., 1993—. Bd. dirs. Children's Mus. Denver, 1993—, Adoption Options, 1999—. Mergers and acquisitions, Securities. Office: Davis Graham & Stubbs LLP 370 17th St Ste 4700 Denver CO 80202-5682

**LEVINE, SAMUEL MILTON,** lawyer; b. Syracuse, N.Y., Feb. 24, 1929; s. Joseph and Sophie Levine; m. Leona Miller, Sept. 9, 1950; children: Judith, Donald, Gary. BBA, Syracuse U., 1950; JD, Bklyn. Law Sch., 1953. Bar: N.Y. 1953, U.S. Supreme Ct. 1960, U.S. Dist. Ct. (ea. and so. dists.) N.Y. 1962. Assoc. Law Office of William S. Miller, Esq., N.Y.C., 1954-62, Law Office of Ferdinand I. Haber, Esq., Mineola, N.Y., 1958-62; pvt. practice Nassau County, N.Y., 1962-65; counsel English, Cianciulli, Reisman & Peirez, 1962-65; supt. of real estate Nassau County, 1965-84; pvt. practice Garden City, N.Y., 1984—; lobbyist for handicapped; pres. bd. of judges Dist. Ct. Nassau County; lectr. in field. Contbr. articles to profl. jours. Past chmn. Sch. Aid Coun. L.I., Citizens Com. for Elmont Schs., N.Y.; former counsel, trustee Temple Bnai Israel, Elmont; former bd. visitors Pilgrim State Hosp.; treas., counsel N.Y. State Coun. Orgns. for Handicapped; past pres. Nassau County Epilepscy Found.; former chmn. Health and Welfare Coun. Nassau County; former mem. Nassau-Suffolk Health Sys. Agy.; del. White House Conf. on Children and Youth, 1960; candidate N.Y. State Senate, 1964; Dem. candidate Dist. Ct. Judge, 1985; candidate N.Y. State Supreme Ct., 1990; counsel Health Advs., Voice for Handicapped, Fedn. Parent Orgns., League of Voters for Handicapped. With U.S. Army, 1948. Recipient Adv. of Yr. award L.I. Coun. Fedn. Parents Orgns., 1978. Mem. Nat. Acad. Elder Law Attys., N.Y. State Bar Assn., Nassau County Bar Assn. (former chmn. social svc. and health law com., legis. com.), Syracuse U. Alumni Club, Kiwanis, Knights of Pythias, B'nai B'rith. General practice, Real property, Estate planning. Home: 711 Shore Rd Apt 2E Long Beach NY 11561-4707

**LEVINE, SANFORD HAROLD,** lawyer; b. Troy, N.Y., Mar. 13, 1938; s. Louis and Reba (Semegren) L.; m. Margaret R. Appelbaum, Oct. 29, 1967; children—Jessica Sara, Abby Miriam. A.B., Syracuse U., 1959, J.D., 1961. Bar: N.Y. 1961, U.S. Dist. Ct. (no. dist.) N.Y. 1961, U.S. Dist. Ct. (we. dist.) N.Y. 1979, U.S. Dist. Ct. (ea. and so. dists.) N.Y. 1980, U.S. Ct. Appeals (2d cir.) 1962, U.S. Supreme Ct. 1967. Law asst. to assoc. judge N.Y. Ct. Appeals, Albany and to justice N.Y. Supreme Ct., 1962-66; law asst. to assoc. judge N.Y. Ct. Appeals, Albany, 1964; asst. counsel N.Y. State Temporary Commn. on Constl. Conv., N.Y.C., 1966-67; assoc. counsel SUNY System, Albany, 1967-70, dep. univ. counsel, 1970-78, acting counsel, 1970-71, acting univ. counsel, 1978-79, univ. counsel and vice chancellor legal affairs, 1979-97, svc. prof. Sch. of Edn., dir. program in edn. and law, 1997—; adj. prof. Sch. of Edn. State U. N.Y., Albany, 1992-97; mem. paralegal curriculum adv. com. Schenectady County Community Coll., 1975—. Fellow Am. Bar Found., N.Y. Bar Found., State Acad. for Public Adminstrn.; mem. ABA (ho. dels. 1987-89), N.Y. State Bar Assn., Albany County Bar Assn., Nat. Assn. Coll. and Univ. Attys. (exec. bd. 1979-82, bd. dirs. 1982-89, pres. 1986-87), Am. Soc. Pub. Adminstrn., Am. Health Lawyers Assn. Editorial bd. Syracuse U. Law Rev., 1960-61; editorial adv. bd. Jour. Coll. and Univ. Law, 1977-81. Education and schools. Home: 1106 Godfrey Ln Schenectady NY 12309-2712

**LEVINE, SOLOMON L.,** lawyer; b. N.Y.C., Aug. 7, 1923; s. Louis and Sonia (Zaleznik) L.; m. Rhea Starr Levine, Dec. 18, 1948 (dec.); children: Lisbeth S., Stephen E. BBA, CCNY, 1948; JD, N.Y. Law Sch., 1953. Bar: N.Y. 1954. Pvt. practice N.Y.C., 1954—. Mem. ABA, Queens County Bar Assn. Contracts commercial, Real property.

**LEVINE, STEVEN B.,** lawyer; b. Malden, Mass., Mar. 8, 1956; s. Harry Saul and Edythe (Betty) Levine; m. Laurie A. Jacobs, June 9, 1985; children: Zachary, Hannah, Sarah. AB magna cum laude, Harvard Coll., 1978, JD cum laude, 1981. Bar: Mass. 1981, U.S. Dist. Ct. Mass. 1982, U.S. Ct. Appeals (1st cir.) 1982. Assoc. Brown, Rudnick, Freed & Gesmer, Boston, 1981-89, shareholder, 1989—; adj. prof. Boston U., 1996-98. Contbr. articles to profl. jours. Mem. ABA, Boston Bar Assn. Avocations: basketball, cycling, hiking, reading. Bankruptcy, Contracts commercial, Finance. Home: 36 Bellevue Rd Swampscott MA 01907-1517 Office: Brown Rudnick Freed & Gesmer One Financial Ctr Boston MA 02111

**LEVINE, STEVEN JON,** lawyer; b. N.Y.C., Sept. 27, 1942; s. Irving I. and Freda S. (Silverman) L.; m. Linda Jane Silberman, Apr. 23, 1967; 1 child, Lawrence Alan. BS, Syracuse U., 1964; JD, St. John's U., 1966; MA, CCNY, 1973; LLM, NYU, 1978. Bar: N.Y. 1967. Assoc. Augustin J. San Filippo & Steven Jon Levine, PC, predecessor, N.Y.C., 1968-78; mem. Vittoria & Forsythe and predecessor, N.Y.C., 1978-93, Levine & Zelman, 1993—; arbitrator N.Y. County Civil Ct. Panel, 1980-93; asst. csl. N.Y. State Senate Judiciary Com., 1977. *Steven Jon Levine has been a practicing attorney for over 25 years. Mr. Levine's firm, Levine & Zelman, provides representation in the areas of matrimonial/family law, real estate, trusts and estates and civil litigation. He is also an experienced arbitrator and mediator. Mr. Levine writes a monthly legal column and hosted the weekly radio program, "Radio Lawyer". He produced and narrated the audio cassette program "Coping with Separation and Divorce" and co-authored "Divorce Q&A: Answers to Questions About Divorce, Equitable Distribution, Maintenance, Custody and Child Support".* Author: of legal column Tomorrow newspaper; co-author: Divorce Q & A: Answers to Questions about Divorce, Equitable Distribution, Maintenance, Custody and Child Support; host weekly radio law program Sta. WVOX, 1990-91; creator, narrator: (audio cassette program) Coping with Separation and Divorce. Committeeman, Bronx County, 1970-76; bd. dirs. Jewish Conciliation Bd. Am., 1973-93. Mem. ABA, N.Y. State Bar Assn., Westchester County Bar Assn., Assn. Bar City N.Y. (sect. vice chmn. matrimonial com. 1977-80), Am. Arbitration Assn. (no-fault, comml. panels 1975-88). Family and matrimonial, Personal injury, General practice. Office: 50 Main St Ph White Plains NY 10606-1901 also: Levine & Zelman 630 5th Ave New York NY 10111-0100

**LEVINE, STEVEN MARK,** lawyer; b. N.Y.C., Feb. 1, 1956; s. Arthur Morton and Selma (Aber) L.; m. Patricia Mary Petersilia, Sept. 2, 1990; children: Caitlin, Ryan. BA, Clark U., 1978; JD, George Washington U., 1981. Bar: D.C. 1981, Md. 1987, Va. 1994, U.S. Dist. Ct. D.C. 1982, U.S. Dist. Ct. Md. 1985, U.S. Dist. Ct. (ea. dist.) Va. 1995, U.S. Ct. Appeals (D.C. cir.) 1982, U.S. Ct. Appeals (1st cir.) 1991, U.S. Ct. Appeals (2d cir.) 1986, U.S. Ct. Appeals (3d cir.) 1987, U.S. Ct. Appeals (4th cir.) 1983. Atty. Wilson, Elser, Moskowitz, Edelman & Dicker, Washington, 1981-93; prin. The Law Office of Steven M. Levine, Washington, 1993—; bd. dirs. SOC Enterprises, Inc., Arlington, Va., 1994—. Contbr. chpt. to book. Officer of Election, Arlington County Bd. Elections, Arlington, Va., 1990-97. Democrat. Jewish. General civil litigation, Civil rights, Personal injury. Home: 2631 S Grant St Arlington VA 22202-2519 Office: 2000 L St NW Ste 803 Washington DC 20036-4913

**LEVINE, THOMAS JEFFREY PELLO,** lawyer; b. Santa Monica, Calif., Mar. 6, 1952; s. Allan Lester and Shirley Elaine (Pello) L.; m. Margaret Louise Adlon, Aug. 27, 1977; children: Marissa, Matthew, Molly. Student, U. Denver, 1970-71, Calif. State U., Northridge, 1971-73, Uppsala U., Sweden; BA, Calif. State U., Sacramento, 1974; JD, Southwestern U., 1977; student, Yale U., 1999. Bar: Calif. 1977, U.S. Dist. Ct. (cen. dist.) Calif. 1978. Partner Levine & Levine, L.A., 1977-83; staff atty. Fed. Deposit Ins. Corp., Newport Beach, Calif., 1983-85; v.p., assoc. counsel Imperial Bank, Inglewood, Calif., 1985-88; v.p., counsel Community Bank, Pasadena, Calif., 1988; gen. counsel, sr. v.p., sec. Calif. Commerce Bank, Banamex USA Bancorp, L.A., 1988—; legal affairs com. mem. Calif. Bankers Assn., San Francisco, 1990—; chmn. Am. Bankers Assn. Bank Counsel Com. 1993-97. Dir. Angelino Heights Historic Preservation Assn., L.A., 1985-95; sec., dir. Carroll Ave. Restoration Found., L.A., 1979-87; dir. Wilshire C. of C., L.A., 1982. Mem. L.A. County Bar Assn. Jewish. Avocations: running, golf, Aztec history, historic preservation. Banking, Consumer commercial, Private international. Office: Banamex USA Bancorp 2029 Century Park E Fl 42 Los Angeles CA 90067-2901

**LEVINE, WALTER DANIEL,** lawyer, accountant; b. Paterson, N.J., July 19, 1941; s. Samuel M. and May (Zaretzky) LeV.; m. Joy Herman, Dec. 24, 1964 (div. 1972); children: Lee Jason, Stephen Ian; m. Ellen R. Ignatoff, Feb. 12, 1976; children: Elissa Whitney, Evan Harris. BA, Rutgers U., 1962; JD, Temple U., 1965; BS, Fairleigh Dickinson U., 1967. Bar: N.J. 1965. Assoc. Gutkin & Miller, Newark, 1965-72; ptnr. firm Gutkin Miller Shapiro Berson, Millburn, N.J., 1972-78; sole practice Fairfield, N.J., 1978-88; sr. ptnr. Friedman LeVine & Brooks, Florham Park, N.J., 1988-91; sole practice Florham Park, 1991—; sec., dir. Tekimage Inc., Florham Park, 1986—; pres., dir. Macet Corp., Florham Park, 1988—. Author: Prentice Hall Tax Reports, 1971. Bd. dirs., v.p. Men's Club, Congregation B'nai Jeshurun, 1991, pres., 1993-95; coach, mgr. Livingston (N.J.) Am. Little League, 1988-95. Mem. N.J. Bar Assn., Passaic County Bar Assn. (chmn. tax com. 1989), K.P. (chancellor-comdr. Passaic chpt. 1987). Democrat. Jewish. Avocations: sports autographs, sports memorabilia. Taxation, general, Probate, Estate planning. Home: 345 Walnut St Livingston NJ 07039-5011 Office: 23 Vreeland Rd Florham Park NJ 07932-1510

**LEVINGS, THERESA LAWRENCE,** lawyer; b. Kansas City, Mo., Oct. 24, 1952; d. William Youngs and Dorothy (Neer) Frick; m. Darryl Wayne Levings, May 25, 1974; children: Leslie Page, Kerry Dillon. BJ, U. Mo., 1973; JD, U. Mo., Kansas City, 1979. Bar: Mo. 1979, U.S. Dist. Ct. (we. dist.) Mo. 1979, U.S. Ct. Appeals (8th cir.) 1982, U.S. Ct. Appeals (10th cir.) 1986, U.S. Dist. Ct. (ea. dist.) Mo. 1989. Copy editor Kansas City Star, 1975-78; law clk. to judge Mo. Supreme Ct., Jefferson City, 1979-80; from assoc. to ptnr. Morrison & Hecker, Kansas City, 1980-94; founding ptnr. Badger & Levings, L.C., Kansas City, 1994—; mem. fed. practice com. U.S. Dist. Ct. (we. dist.), 1990-95; mem. fed. adv. com. U.S. Ct. Appeals (8th cir.), 1994-97. Leadership grad. Kansas City Tomorrow; account exec. United Way; bd. dirs. Jr. League, Housing Info. Ctr. Mem. Mo. Bar (bd. govs. 1990—, young lawyers coun. 1982-89, chair 1988-89, Pres. award 1989, Outstanding Svc. award young lawyers coun. 1985, 86), Assn. Women Lawyers Greater Kansas City (pres. 1986-87, Woman of Yr. 1993), Lawyers Assn. Greater Kansas City (bd. dirs. young lawyers sect. 1982-83), Kansas City Met. Bar Assn. (chair civil practice and procedure com. 1988-89, chair fed. practice com. 1990-91). Avocations: antiques, history, cooking. Federal civil litigation, Insurance, Product liability. Office: Badger & Levings LC 1101 Walnut St Kansas City MO 64106-2134

**LEVINSON, DAVID LAWRENCE,** lawyer; b. Bklyn., Jan. 9, 1945; s. Herman and Bertha (Fuchs) L.; m. Marjorie Joan Friedman, June 18, 1967; children: Andrew, Joshua, Lauren. BA, Bklyn. Coll., 1966; JD, Bklyn. Law Sch., 1969. Bar: N.Y. 1969, U.S. Dist. Ct. (so. dist.) N.Y. 1971, U.S. Supreme Ct. 1976. Asst. dist. atty. N.Y. County Dist. Atty.'s Office, N.Y.C., 1969-73; ptnr. law firm Rider, Weiner & Loeb, P.C., Newburgh, N.Y., 1973-80; ptnr. Levinson, Zeccola, Reineke, Ornstein & Selinger, P.C., 1980—. Pres. Monroe (N.Y.) Temple of Liberal Judaism, 1981-83; justice Town of Woodbury, 1978—, Village of Tuxedo Park; mem. Zoning Bd. Appeals, 1977-78; atty. Village of Monroe Planning Bd., 1988—, Village of Goshen Zoning Bd. Appeals, 1988—, Village of Goshen, 1989—; mem. Orange County Charter Rev. Commn., 1985. Mem. Orange County Bar Assn. (mem. judiciary com. 1980-90, mem. grievance com. 1983-88, bd. dirs. 1988—, pres. 1993), N.Y. State Bar Assn., Newburgh Bar Assn., Lions Club (publicity com. 1983-84), Woodbury Cmty. Assn. State civil litigation, Family and matrimonial, Criminal. Home: 4 Jones Dr Highland Mills NY 10930-2710 Office: Levinson Zeccola Reineke & Ornstein PC 11 Abrams Rd Central Valley NY 10917-4101

**LEVINSON, KENNETH LEE,** lawyer; b. Denver, Jan. 18, 1953; s. Julian Charles and Dorothy (Milzer) L.; m. Shauna Titus, Dec. 21, 1986. BA cum laude, U. Colo., 1974; JD, U. Denver, 1978. Bar: Colo. 1978, U.S. Ct. Appeals (10th cir.), 1978. Assoc. atty. Balaban & Lutz, Denver, 1979-83; shareholder Balaban & Levinson, P.C., Denver, 1984—, pres., 1994—. Contbr. articles to profl. jours. Pres., Dahlia House Condominium Assn., 1983-85, bd. dirs., 1991-94; intern Reporters Com. for Freedom of the Press, Washington, 1977; atty. grievance hearing bd., 1988—; jr. varsity volleyball coach Good Shepherd Cath. Sch., 1992-95. Recipient Am. Jurisprudence award Lawyers Co-op, 1977, 3d Place award Rocky Mountain Fiction Writers Mystery Novel Contest, 1994. Mem. Colo. Bar Asn. (profl. liability com. 1991-94), Denver Bar Assn., Denver Law Club. General practice, Insurance, General civil litigation.

**LEVINSON, KENNETH S.,** lawyer, corporate executive; b. Mineola, N.Y., Oct. 27, 1947; s. Max Leonard and Eva (Klamen) L.; m. Laura R. Levinson, Sept. 14, 1969 (div. 1981); 1 child, Barbara Ann Schmidt; m. Jerelyn E. Jarmacz, Feb. 6, 1982; children: Alexander T., Brianna F., Joshua K. BA in Polit. Sci. with distinction, U. Wis., 1969; JD with honors, George Washington U., 1975; LLM in Taxation, Georgetown U., 1978. Bar: D.C. 1975, Va. 1975, U.S. Ct. Claims 1976, U.S. Dist. Ct. (D.C. dist.) 1976, U.S. Tax Ct. 1976, U.S. Ct. Appeals (D.C. cir.) 1976, U.S. Supreme Ct. 1979. Atty., advisor Office Chief Counsel Interpretative div. IRS, Washington, 1975-78, reviewer, asst. br. chief Office Chief Counsel, 1978-79; sr. tax atty. Pepper, Hamilton & Scheetz, Washington, 1979-81; v.p., mng. tax dir. Marriott Corp., Bethesda, Md., 1981-85, v.p. internat. project fin., 1985-90; v.p. tax Northwest Airlines, Inc., Eagan, Minn., 1990-92; v.p. tax, risk mgmt., ins. Northwest Airlines, Inc., St. Paul, 1992-94, v.p. fin. and planning cargo/charter divsn., 1994-96, v.p. tax, risk mgmt. and ins., 1996—; adj. prof. Georgetown U. Law Ctr., Washington, 1978-86; asst. sec., v.p. various Marriott Corp. subs., Bethesda, 1981-90; v.p. Wings Holdings, Inc./N.W. Airlines Corp., 1990—; v.p. tax N.W. Airlines, Inc., 1990—, v.p. various subs.; cons., pres. The Chechhi Group, Beverly Hills, Calif., 1990—; bd. dirs. City Harbour Hotel, Ltd., London. Contbr. articles to profl. jours. Bd. dirs. Minn. Taxpayers Assn., Mpls. Lt. USN, 1969-72. Mem. ABA (subcom. chair 1978-84), D.C. Bar, Va. State Bar, Tax Execs. Inst. (bd. dirs. Minn. chpt. 1999—), Washington Tax Group, Air Transport Assn., Internat. Air Transport Assn. (chair taxation com. 1991, vice chmn. 1999, chair ins. com. 1994, chair internat. risk mgrs. forum 1995, 98—), Nat. Taxpayers Assn. (bd. dirs. 1999—). Avocations: golf, art appreciation/collection, boating, equestrian show jumping, skiing. Finance, Aviation. Home: 401 Peavey Ln Wayzata MN 55391-1534 Office: Northwest Airlines Inc Dept A 4450 5101 Northwest Dr Dept A4450 Saint Paul MN 55111-3027

**LEVINSON, PAUL HOWARD,** lawyer; b. N.Y.C., Nov. 9, 1952; s. Saul and Gloria (Samson) L.; m. Susan Norine Morley, May 29, 1983; children: Lauren Hope, David Ross. BA in Sociology, Northwestern U., 1973; JD, Columbia U., 1977. Bar: N.Y. 1978; U.S. Dist. Ct. (so. and ea. dist.) N.Y. 1983, U.S. Dist. Ct. (no. dist.) N.Y. 1992; U.S. Ct. Appeals (2d cir.) 1986, U.S. Ct. Appeals (3rd cir. 1987), U.S. Supreme Ct. 1986. Asst. dist. atty., supervising sr. trial atty. Kings County, Bklyn., 1977-84; assoc. Blodnick, Schultz & Abramowitz, P.C., Lake Success, N.Y., 1984-85; ptnr. Leavy, Rosensweig & Hyman and predecessor firms, N.Y.C., 1985—. Trustee Cmty. Synagogue, Rye, N.Y., 1996—; mem. adv. coun. parks and recreation Village of Rye Brook, N.Y., 1994-97. Harlan Fiske Stone scholar. Mem. ABA, N.Y. State Bar Assn., Assn. of Bar of City of N.Y. (com. on criminal justice ops. and budget 1992-94, com. on criminal cts. 1995—, chmn. subcom. on the N.Y.C. civilian complaint rev. bd., moderator), Bklyn. Bar Assn. (continuing legal edn. seminars in criminal trial advocacy and matrimonial practice), Columbia Law Sch. Alumni Assn., Northwestern U. Entertainment Alliance East (treas. 1998—), Northwestern U. Alumni Assn., Sierra Club. Democrat. Jewish. Club: Northwestern U. Alumni of N.Y.C. Avocations: tennis, skiing, swimming. General civil litigation, Criminal, Entertainment. Home: 312 Betsy Brown Rd Rye Brook NY 10573-1901 Office: Leavy Rosensweig & Hyman 11 E 44th St Fl 10 New York NY 10017-3666

**LEVINSON, PETER JOSEPH,** lawyer; b. Washington, June 11, 1943; s. Bernard Hirsh and Carlyn Virginia (Krupp) L.; m. Nanette Susan Segal, Mar. 30, 1968; children: Sharman Risa, Justin David. AB in History cum laude, Brandeis U., Waltham, Mass., 1965; JD, Harvard U., 1968. Bar: Hawaii 1971, U.S. Supreme Ct. 1975. Summer supr. Harvard Legal Aid Bur., Cambridge, Mass., 1968; research asst. Harvard Law Sch., 1968-69; teaching fellow Osgoode Hall Law Sch., York U. (Can.), 1969-70, research assoc., 1969-70, asst. prof., 1970-71; dep. atty. gen. State of Hawaii, 1971-75; vis. fellow Harvard U., 1976-77; ptnr. Levinson and Levinson, Honolulu, 1977-79; spl. asst. to dir. Office Program Support, Legal Services Corp., Washington, 1979; cons. Select Commn. on Immigration and Refugee Policy, Washington, 1980-81; minority counsel subcom. on immigration, refugees and internat. law com. on judiciary, U.S. Ho. of Reps., Washington, 1981-85, minority counsel subcom. monopolies and comml. law, 1985-89, minority counsel subcom. econ. and comml. law, 1989-95, counsel com. on judiciary, 1995—. Trustee, Hawaii Jewish Welfare Fund, 1972-75, chmn. fund drive, 1972; trustee Temple Emanu-El, Honolulu, 1973-75; mem. alumni admissions council Brandeis U., 1978-82. Recipient award of merit United Jewish Appeal, 1974. Mem. Hawaii State Bar Assn. (chmn. standing com. on continuing legal edn. 1972, chmn. standing com. on jud. adminstrn. 1979), ABA, Am. Judicature Soc. Contbr. articles to profl. jours. Office: B353 Rayburn House Office Bldg Washington DC 20515-0001

**LEVINSON, STEVEN HENRY,** state supreme court justice; b. Cincinnati, OH, June 8, 1946. BA with distinction, Stanford U., 1968; JD, U. Mich., 1971. Bar: Hawaii 1972, U.S. Dist. Ct. Hawaii 1972, U.S. Ct. Appeals (9th cir.) 1972. Law clk. to Hon. Bernard H. Levinson Hawaii Supreme Ct., 1971-72; pvt. practice Honolulu, 1972-89; judge Hawaii Cir. Ct. (1st cir.), 1989-92; assoc. justice Hawaii Supreme Ct., Honolulu, 1992—. Staff mem. U. Mich. Jour. Law Reform, 1970-71. Active Temple Emanu-El. Mem. ABA (jud. adminstrn. divsn. 1989—), Hawaii State Bar Assn. (dir. young lawyers divsn. 1975-76, dir. 1982-84), Nat. Jud. Coll. (state jud. leader 1991—), Am. Judges Assn., Am. Judicature Soc. Jewish. Office: Supreme Ct of Hawaii Ali'iōlani Hale 417 S King St Honolulu HI 96813-2902

**LEVIT, JAY J(OSEPH),** lawyer; b. Phila., Feb. 20, 1934; s. Albert and Mary Levit; m. Heloise Bertman, July 14, 1962; children: Richard Bertman, Robert Edward, Darcy Francine. AB, Case Western Res. U., 1955; JD, U. Richmond, 1958; LLM, Harvard U., 1959. Bar: Va. 1958, D.C. 1961, U.S. Supreme Ct. 1961. Trial atty. U.S. Dept. Justice, Washington, 1960-64; sr. atty. Gen. Dynamics Corp., Rochester, N.Y., 1965-67; ptnr. Stallard & Levit, Richmond, Va., 1968-77, Levit, Mann & Halligan, Richmond, 1978—; instr. U. Mich. Law Sch., Ann Arbor, 1964-65; adj. assoc. prof. U. Richmond Law Sch., 1974-77; adj. lectr. Va. Commonwealth U., Richmond, 1970-85; lectr. in field. Contbg. editor The Developing Labor Law-Bur. Nat. Affairs, 1974—. Mem. ABA (labor com.), Va. Bar Assn. (labor com.), Fed. Bar Assn. (labor com.). Avocations: art collecting, jogging, swimming, travel. General civil litigation, Labor, Pension, profit-sharing, and employee benefits. Home: 419 Dellbrooks Pl Richmond VA 23233-5559 Office: Levit Mann & Halligan 1301 N Hamilton St Richmond VA 23230-3959 also: Levit Mann & Halligan 127 Thompson St Ashland VA 23005-1511

**LEVIT, VICTOR BERT,** lawyer, foreign representative, civic worker; b. Singapore, Apr. 21, 1930; s. Bert W. and Thelma (Clumeck) L.; divorced; children: Carson, Victoria; m. Margery K. Blum, Oct. 26, 1996. A.B. in Polit. Sci. with great distinction, Stanford, 1950; LL.B., Stanford U., 1952. Bar: Calif. 1953. Assoc. Long & Levit, San Francisco and Los Angeles, 1953-55, ptnr., 1955-83; mng. ptnr. Long & Levit, San Francisco and L.A., 1971-83; ptnr. Barger & Wolen, San Francisco, L.A. and Newport Beach, 1983—; assoc. and gen. legal counsel U.S. Jaycees, 1959-61; legal counsel for consul gen. Ethiopia for San Francisco, 1964-71; hon. consul for Ethiopia for San Francisco, Ethiopia, 1971-76; guest lectr. Stanford U. Law Sch., 1958—, Haile Selassie I Univ. Law Sch., 1972-76; mem. com. group ins. programs State Bar Calif., 1980—; Mem. Los Angeles Consular Corps, 1971-77; mem. San Francisco Consular Corps, 1971-77, vice dean, 1975-76; Grader Calif. Bar Exam., 1956-61; del. San Francisco Mcpl. Conf., 1955-63, vice chmn., 1960, chmn., 1961-63. Author: Legal Malpractice in California, 1974, Legal Malpractice, 1977, 2d edit., 1983; Note editor: Stanford Law Rev., 1952-53; legal editor: Underwriters' Report, 1963—; Contbr. articles to legal jours. Campaign chmn. San Francisco Aid Retarded Children, 1960; mem. nat. com. Stanford Law Sch. Fund, 1959—; mem. Mayor's Osaka-San Francisco Affiliation Com., 1959-65, Mayor's Com. for Mcpl. Mgmt., 1961-64; mem. San Francisco Rep. Country Cen. Com., 1956-63; assoc. mem. Calif. Rep. Cen. Com., 1956-63, 70-72; campaign chmn. San Francisco Assemblyman John Busterud, 1960; bd. dirs. San Francisco Comml. Club, 1967-70, San Francisco Planning and Urban Renewal Assn., 1959-60, San Francisco Planning and Urban Renewal Assn. Nat. Found. Infantile Paralysis, 1958, Red Shield Youth Assn., Salvation Army, San Francisco, 1960-70, bd. dirs. NCCJ, San Francisco, 1959—, chmn., No. Calif., 1962-64, 68-70; mem. nat. bd. dirs., 1964-75; bd. dirs. San Francisco Tb and Health Assn., 1962-70, treas., 1964, pres., 1965-67; bd. dirs. San Francisco Assn. Mental Health, 1964-73, pres., 1968-71; mem. com. Nat. Assn. Mental Health, 1969-71; trustee United Bay Area Crusade, 1966-74, Ins. Forum San Francisco; bd. visitors Stanford Law Sch., 1969-75; mem. adv. bd. Jr. League San Francisco, 1971-75. Named Outstanding Young Man San Francisco mng. editors San Francisco newspapers, 1960, One of Five Outstanding Young Men Calif., 1961. Fellow ABA (chmn. profl. liability com. for gen. practice sect. 1979-81, council gen. practice sect. 1982-86, sec.-treas. gen. practice sect. 1986-87); mem. San Francisco Bar Assn. (chmn. ins. com. 1962, 73, chmn. charter flight com. 1962-66), State Bar Calif. (com. on group ins. programs 1980—, chmn. gen. practice sect. 1988—), Consular Law Soc., Am. Arbitration Assn. (arbitrator), World Assn. Lawyers (chmn. parliamentary law com. 1976—), Am. Law Inst. (adviser restatement of law governing lawyers 1985—), Internat. Bar Assn., San Francisco Jr. C. of C. (dir. 1959, pres. 1958), U.S. Jaycees (exec. com. 1959-61), Jaycees Internat. (life, senator), Calif. Scholarship Fedn., U.S. C. of C. (labor com. 1974-76), San Francisco C. of C. (dir.), Phi Beta Kappa, Order of Coif, Pi Sigma Alpha. Clubs: Commercial (San Francisco) (dir.); Commonwealth (quar. chmn.), California Tennis; World Trade; Bankers. Insurance, Federal civil litigation, State civil litigation. Home: 2063 Broadway St San Francisco CA 94115-1537 Office: Barger & Wolen 650 California St Fl 9 San Francisco CA 94108-2702

**LEVIT, WILLIAM HAROLD, JR.,** lawyer; b. San Francisco, Feb. 8, 1938; s. William Harold and Barbara Janis Kaiser L.; m. Mary Elizabeth Webster, Feb. 13, 1971; children: Alison Jones Baumler, Alexandra Bradley, Laura Elizabeth Fletcher, Amalia Elizabeth Webster, William Harold, III. BA magna cum laude, Yale U., 1960; MA Internat. Rels., U. Calif., Berkeley, 1962; LLB, Harvard U., 1967. Bar: N.Y. 1968, Calif. 1974, Wis. 1979. Fgn. service officer Dept. State, 1962-64; assoc. Davis Polk & Wardwell, N.Y.C., 1967-73; assoc. ptnr. Hughes Hubbard & Reed, N.Y.C., L.A., 1973-79; sec. and gen. counsel Rexnord Inc., Milw., 1979-83; ptnr., dir., chair internat. practice group Godfrey & Kahn, Milw., 1983—; substitute arbitrator Iran-U.S. Claims Tribunal, The Hague, 1984-88; lectr. Practicing Law Inst., ABA, Calif. Continuing Edn. of Bar, State Bar of Wis. Contbr. to: Mergers and the Private Antitrust Suit: The Private Enforcement of Section 7 of the Clayton Act, 1977. Bd. dirs. Wis. Humane Soc., 1980-90, pres., 1986-88; bd. dirs. Vis. Nurse Corp., Milw., 1980-90, chmn., 1985-87; bd. dirs. Vis. Nurse Found., 1986-95, chmn., 1989-91; bd. dirs. Aurora Health Care Inc., 1988-93, Wis. Soc. to Prevent Blindness, 1981-91, Columbia Coll. Nursing, 1992—, vice chair, 1998—, Aurora Health Care Ventures, 1993—, chmn., 1998—; adv. bd. Med. Coll. Wis. Cardiovasc. Rsch. Ctr., 1994—, chmn., 1999—; rep. Assn. Yale Alumni, 1976-79, 81-84, 90-93; pres. Yale Club So. Calif., 1977-79; mem. neutral advisor panel and franchise, Yr. 2000 and ins. panels CPR Inst. for Dispute Resolution. Ford Found. fellow U. Pa., 1960-61, NDEA fellow U. Calif., Berkeley, 1961-62. Mem. ABA (com. on corp. counsel litigation sect.), Am. Soc. Corp. Secs. (pres. Wis. chpt. 1982-83, dir. 1981-92), Am. Arbitration Assn. (comml. panel 1977—, internat. panel 1997—), Assn. Bar City N.Y., State Bar Calif. (com. on continuing edn. of bar 1977-79), Los Angeles County Bar Assn. (ethics com. 1976-79), State Bar Wis. (dir. internat. bus. transactions sect. 1985-92, dist. 2 bd. attys. profl. responsibility com. 1985-94, chmn. 1993-94), Bar Assn. 7th Cir. (bd. govs. 1999—), Am. Br. Internat. Law Assn., Nat. Assn. Security Dealers (panel arbitrators 1988—), Chartered Inst. Arbitrators (assoc., London), N.Y. Stock Exch. (panel arbitrators 1988—), N.Am. Coun. London Ct. of Internat. Arbitration, Am. Soc. Internat. Law, Inst. Jud. Adminstrn., Milw. Club, Milw. Athletic Club, Town Club, Phi Beta Kappa. E-mail: whlevit@gklaw.com. Federal civil litigation, State civil litigation, Antitrust. Office: 780 N Water St Ste 1500 Milwaukee WI 53202-3512

**LEVITAN, DAVID M(AURICE),** lawyer, educator; b. Tver, Lithuania, Dec. 25, 1915; (parents Am. citizens); m. Judith Morley; children: Barbara Lane Levitan, Stuart Dean Levitan. BS, Northwestern U., 1936, MA, 1937; PhD, U. Chgo., 1940; JD, Columbia U., 1948. Bar: N.Y. 1948, U.S. Dist. Ct. (so. dist.) N.Y. 1948, U.S. Supreme Ct. 1953. Various U.S. Govt. adminstrv. and advisory positions with Nat. Youth Adminstrn., Office Price Adminstrn., War Prodn. Bd., Fgn. Econ. Adminstrn. Supreme Hdqrs. Allied Expeditionary Force, and Cen. European div. Dept. State, 1940-46; cons., sec. joint-com. of 5th and 6th coms., 2d Gen. Assembly, dir. com. of experts for establishing adminstrv. tribunal UN, 1946-47; cons. pub. affairs dept., producer series of pub. affairs programs on TV and radio ABC, 1946-53; pvt. practice N.Y.C., 1948-66; counsel Hahn & Hessen, N.Y.C., 1966-68, ptnr., 1968-86; counsel Hahn & Hessen, 1986-96; instr. U. Chgo., 1938-41; adj. prof. public law Columbia U., 1946-65; adj. prof. John Jay Coll. Criminal Justice, CUNY, 1966-75; adj. prof. polit. sci. Post Coll., 1964-66; adj. prof. law Cardozo Sch. Law, 1978-82; pvt. practice, 1996—; asst. to Ill. state adminstr. Nat. Youth Adminstrn., chief budget sect., Washington, 1940-41; mgmt. analyst Office of Price Adminstrn., 1941; spl. asst. to chmn. War Prodn. Bd., 1942-43; chief property control divsn. Fgn. Econ. Adminstrn., Washington, 1944-45; with U.S. Group of Control Coun. for Germany at SHAEF, London, 1944; advisor Ctrl. European divsn. U.S. Dept. State, 1945; cons. UN, 1946-47, Sect. Joint Com. 5th and 6th Coms., 1946-47, 2d session of 1st Gen. Assembly, 1946-47; dir. Com. of Experts on Establishment of Adminstrn. Tribunal, 1946-47; cons. pub. affairs dept. ABC, 1946-53. Contbr. articles to legal jours. Mem. Nassau County (N.Y.) Welfare Bd., 1965-69; chmn. Planning Bd., Village of Roslyn Harbor, N.Y., 1965-66; chmn. Bd. of Zoning Appeals, Village Roslyn Harbor, 1967-86. Recipient Demobilization award Social Sci. Rsch. Coun., 1946-48. Fellow Am. Coll. Trust and Estate Counsel; mem. ABA, Am. Polit. Sci. Assn., Am. Soc. Internat. Law, Am. Law Inst., Assn. Bar City N.Y. Probate, Estate taxation, Constitutional. Home: 103 NE 19th Ave Deerfield Beach FL 33441-6106

**LEVITAN, KATHERINE D.,** lawyer; b. Vienna, Austria, July 8, 1933; came to U.S. 1938, naturalized 1942; d. Otto and Hedweega (Saltzer) Lenz; m. Leonard Levitan, Sept. 12, 1952; children—Joel, Jeffrey, Debbie, Diane. B.A. cum laude, N.Y.U. 1952, J.D. cum laude, 1955, LL.M. in Criminal and Family Law, 1977. Bar: N.Y. 1956, U.S. Dist. Ct. (ea. dist.) N.Y. 1972, U.S. Supreme Ct. 1974. Tchr. bus. law N.Y. Inst. Tech., Old Westbury, 1968-69; assoc. Bennett Reiss, Great Neck, N.Y., 1969-70, Malone and Dorfman, Freeport, N.Y., 1970-71; sole practice, Jericho, N.Y., 1971-80; practice with assocs., Mineola, N.Y., 1980—; also lectr.; assoc. prof. Hofstra Law Sch. Bd. dirs., legal counsel For Our Children and Us, Inc., Nassau chpt. ACLU, 1975—; mem. Nassau County Democratic Com., 1969—, law guardian adv. panel 2d dept. Human Rights Adv. Commn. Nassau County; past pres. Nassau chpt. N.Y. Civil Liberties Union. Mem. Nassau Bar Assn. (grievance com., martim com.), Nassau/Suffolk Women's Bar Assn. (past pres., legal counsel), Nassau Civil Liberties Union, L.I. Women's Network, Acad. Matrimonial Lawyers, Contbr. articles to profl. publs. Family and matrimonial, Civil rights, General practice. Home: PO Box 846 New Lebanon NY 12125-0846 Office: 83 Prospect St Huntington NY 11743-3306

**LEVITAN, LARA MARIE,** lawyer; b. Mpls., July 9, 1969; d. Alexander Allen and Lucy Kerr (Abbe) L. BA cum laude, Macalester Coll., 1991; JD, NYU, 1994. BAR: N.Y. 1995, Ill. 1996, U.S. Dist. Ct. (no. dist.) Ill. 1996, U.S. Ct. Appeals (7th cir.) 1996. Law clk. to Hon. David Coar U.S. Dist. Ct. (no. dist.) Ill., Chgo., 1994-96; assoc. McDermott, Will & Emery, Chgo., 1996—. Editor: NYU Jour. Internat. Law and Politics, 1994-95. Bd. dirs. Just the Beginning Found., Chgo., 1995—; alumni coord. Macalester Coll. Alumni Admissions Chgo., 1994—. Judge Galgay fellow N.Y.U. Sch. of Law, 1992. Mem. ABA, Ill. State Bar Assn., N.Y. State Bar Assn., Chgo. Bar Assn. (co-chair bar rels. com. 1999—). Home: 1658 N Claremont Ave Chicago IL 60647-5313 Office: McDermott Will & Emery 227 W Monroe St Ste 3100 Chicago IL 60606-5096

**LEVITAN, ROGER STANLEY,** lawyer; b. Washington, Jan. 31, 1933; s. Simon Wolfe and Bessie (Abramson) L.; m. Maria Anneli Stennius, May 27, 1975 (div. 1980); 1 child, Mark Howard; m. Laurel Lynn Allen, July 9, 1982; 1 child, Brandon Wolfe. BS in Econs., U. Pa., 1954; JD, Columbia U., 1957. Bar: D.C. 1957, U.S. Ct. Appeals (D.C. cir.) 1957, Ariz. 1976. Tax specialist, reorgn. br. IRS, Washington, 1957-62; atty. McClure & Trotter, Washington, 1962-65; assoc. ptnr. Main Lafrentz, Washington and N.Y.C., 1970-72; dir. taxes U.S. Industries, Inc., N.Y.C., 1972-73; asst. tax counsel Am. Home Products Co., N.Y.C., 1973-75; ptnr., Bilby & Shoenhair, P.C., Tucson, 1976-89; ptnr. Snell & Wilmer, Tucson, 1989-90; ptnr. Molloy, Jones & Donohue P.C., Tucson, 1991-92; counsel Hecker, Phillips & Zeeb, 1992—; lectr. Am. Law Inst., State Bar Ariz. Legal counsel Tucson Community Found., 1981—. Contbr. articles to profl. jours. Mem. ABA (chmn. ann. report com. 1965-67, continuing legal edn. com. 1969-70), Ariz. Bar Found., State Bar Ariz. (chmn. sect. taxation 1987-88, mem. tax specialization adv. bd., 1991-93). General corporate, Taxation, general, Estate planning. Home: 727 E Chula Vista Rd Tucson AZ 85718-1028 Office: 405 W Franklin St Tucson AZ 85701-8209

**LEVITSKY, ASHER SAMUEL,** lawyer; b. Wilkes-Barre, Pa.; s. Boris H. and Lillian F. L.; m. Iris S. Wolfe, Feb. 2, 1973 (div. 1994); children: Joshua, Lily. BA, Cornell U., 1965; JD, NYU, 1968. Bar: N.Y. 1968, D.C. 1970. Assoc. Powers & McNiff, N.Y.C., 1968-70; assoc. Busby Rivkin Sherman & Levy, N.Y.C., 1970-78, prin., 1978-82; pvt. practice, N.Y.C., 1982-85; ptnr. Levitsky Cohen & McAleenan, N.Y.C., 1986-89; ptnr. Esanu Katsky Korins & Siger, LLP, N.Y.C., 1989-90, of counsel, 1990—. Trustee Congregation Kehilath Jeshurun, N.Y.C., 1990—. Mem. Order of Coif. Avocations: cooking, travel. E-mail: alevitsk@ekks.com. Securities, Contracts commercial, General corporate. Office: Esanu Katsky Korins & Siger 605 3d Ave New York NY 10158

**LEVITT, SIDNEY BERNARD,** lawyer; b. Bklyn., Mar. 23, 1920; s. Abraham and Becky (Turetsky) L.; m. Lillian Cohen, June 18, 1950; children: Kenneth Ross, Jeffrey Alan. BA, Bklyn. Coll., 1942; LLB, Bklyn. Law Sch., 1948, JD, 1967; LLM in Labor Law, NYU, 1953. Bar: N.Y. 1949, U.S. Dist. Ct. (ea. and so. dists.) N.Y., U.S. Tax Ct., U.S. Supreme Ct. Pvt. practice law Seagate, N.Y.; small claims arbitrator N.Y. Civil Ct. Active Boy Scouts Am., Planning Bd.; instr. ARC. Capt. U.S. Army, 1942-46. Mem. Bklyn. Bar Assn., Jewish War Vets. USA, Knights Pythias. Republican. Jewish. General practice, Probate, Real property. Office: 4310 Beach 43d St Seagate NY 11224-1032

**LEVY, ALAN M.,** lawyer; b. Milw., Nov. 10, 1940; s. Sam and Emma (Gold) L.; m. Tee Gee Azine, Mar. 3, 1964; children: Shawn, Joshua, Pamela, Jonathan. AB, U. Chgo., 1963, JD, 1965. Bar: Wis. 1965, Ill. 1982, U.S. Ct. Appeals (2d, 5th, 6th, 7th, 8th, 9th and 10th cirs.) 1968, U.S. Dist. Ct. (ea. dist.) Wis. 1965, (no. dist.) Ill. 1982, (so. dist.) Ill. 1969, U.S. Supreme Ct. 1980. Ptnr. Goldberg, Previant, Uelman, Gratz, Miller et al, Milw., 1965-82; sr. legal counsel, dir. plan devel./compliance Central States, S.E. and S.W. Areas Pension Fund, Chgo., 1982-85; assoc. O'Neil, Cannon & Hollman, S.C., Milw., 1985-91, Lindner & Marsack, S.C., Milw., 1991—; bd. incorporators Commonwealth Mutual Savs. Bank, Milw., 1977-82; adj. prof. labor law U. Wis., Milw., 1974—. Contbr. articles to profl. jours. Chmn. U. Chgo. Alumni Schs. Com., Milw., 1987—; trustee Congregation Emanu-El B'Ne Jeshurun, Milw., 1978-82, 86-92; campaign co-chmn. Urban Day Sch., Milw., 1988; active ACLU, Milw., 1966-82. Named Page scholar, U. Chgo., 1961, Iron Mask, 1961-64. Mem. ABA (labor law sect. 1967—), Wis. Bar Assn. (labor law sect. chmn. 1979-80), Ill. Bar Assn., Iron Mask Soc., U. Chgo. Alumni Assn. of Milw. (chmn. 1996-98), U. Chgo. Alumni Assn. (bd. govs.). Labor, Pension, profit-sharing, and employee benefits, Municipal (including bonds). Office: Lindner & Marsack SC 411 E Wisconsin Ave Ste 1000 Milwaukee WI 53202-4416 *Notable cases include: Phillips vs. Alaska HERE Pension Fund, 11 EBC 1929 W.D. Wash., 1989, which involved class action regarding eligibility criteria as structural defect in a multiemployer pension fund; I-Mark Industries, Inc., et al vs. Arthur Young & Co., et al, 148 Wis. 2d 605, 436 N.W. 2d 311, 1989, which involved third party borrower's liability to plaintiff lender for malpractice by defendant acct.; Teamster's Local 348 Health and Welfare Fund, et al vs. Kohn Beverage Co., 749 F. 2d 315 6th Cir., 1984, which involved the enforcement of benefit fund contribution obligations regardless of union activity; Loran W. Robbins, et al vs. The Pepsi-Cola Met. Bottling Co., et al, 7 EBC 2033 N.D. Ill. 1986, which involved the withdrawal liability obligations to multiemployer pension fund; Wardle vs. Cen. States, S.E. and S.W. Areas Pension Fund, 627 F. 2d 820 7th Cir., 1980, which involved the right to jury trial and standard of rev. in pension benefit claim; Inland Trucking Co. vs. NLRB, 440 F. 2d 562 7th Cir., 1971, which involved the use of replacement employees during single employer lock-out.*

**LEVY, COLEMAN BERTRAM,** lawyer; b. New Haven, Conn., May 9, 1939; s. Samuel and Esther Levy; m. Judith S. Siegal; children: Perry, Dean, Matthew and Evan. BA, U. Conn., 1961, MA in Psychology, 1962, JD, 1966. Bar: Conn. 1966, U.S. Dist. Ct. Conn. 1966, N.Y. 1967, U.S. Dist. Ct. (so. dist.) N.Y. 1967, U.S. Supreme Ct. 1976. Ptnr. Levy & Droney, P.C., Farmington, Conn., 1971—. Fax: 860-676-3200. E-mail: clevy@idlaw.com. Real property, Mergers and acquisitions, Finance. Office: Levy & Droney PC 74 Batterson Park Rd Farmington CT 06032-2565

**LEVY, DAVID,** lawyer, insurance company executive; b. Bridgeport, Conn., Aug. 3, 1932; s. Aaron and Rachel (Goldman) L. BS in Econs., U. Pa., 1954; JD, Yale U., 1957. Bar: Conn. 1958, U.S. Supreme Ct. 1963, D.C. 1964, Mass. 1965, N.Y. 1971, Pa. 1972; CPA, Conn. Acct. Arthur Andersen & Co., N.Y.C., 1957-59; sole practice Bridgeport, 1959-60; specialist tax law IRS, Washington, 1960-64; counsel State Mut. Life Ins. Co., Worcester, Mass., 1964-70; assoc. gen. counsel taxation Penn Mut. Life Ins. Co., Phila., 1971-81; sole practice Washington, 1982-87; v.p., tax counsel Pacific Life Ins. Co., Newport Beach, Calif., 1987—. Author: (with others) Life Insurance Company Tax Series, Bureau National Affairs Tax Management Income Tax, 1970-71. Mem. adv. bd. Tax Mgmt., Washington, 1975-90, Hartford Inst. on Ins. Taxation, 1990-97; bd. dirs. Citizens Plan E Orgn., Worcester, 1966-70. With AUS, 1957. Mem. ABA (vice-chmn. employee benefits com. 1980-86, ins. cos. com. 1984-86, torts and ins. practice sect., subcom. chair ins. cos. com. tax sect. 1994—), Assn. Life Ins. Counsel, AICPA, Beta Alpha Psi. Jewish. Corporate taxation, Insurance, Taxation, general.

**LEVY, DAVID,** lawyer; b. Atlanta, July 7, 1937; s. Meyer and Elsie (Reisman) L.; m. Diane L. Lerner; children: Jeffrey Marc, Robert William, Danielle Beth, Margo Shaw; stepchildren: Mitchell S. Haber, Cort A. Haber. BA, Emory U., 1959, LLB, 1961; LLM, Georgetown U., 1964. Bar: Ga. 1961. Atty. SEC, Washington, 1961-65; assoc., partner Arnstein, Gluck, Weitzenfeld & Minow, Chgo., 1965-71; partner Kaler, Karesh & Frankel, Atlanta, 1971-73; exec. v.p. adminstrn., counsel, dir. Nat. Svc. Industries, Inc., Atlanta, 1973—; also bd. dirs. Nat. Service Industries, Inc., Atlanta. Mem. Am., Ga. bar assns. General corporate. Office: Nat Svc Industries Inc 1420 Peachtree St NE Atlanta GA 30309-3002

**LEVY, HERBERT MONTE,** lawyer; b. N.Y.C., Jan. 14, 1923; s. Samuel M. and Hetty D. L.; m. Marilyn Wohl, Aug. 30, 1953; children: Harlan A., Matthew D., Alison Jill. BA, Columbia, 1943, LLB, 1946. Bar: N.Y. 1946, U.S. Dist. Ct. (so. dist.) N.Y. 1946, U.S. Ct. Appeals (2d cir.) 1949, U.S. Dist. Ct. (ea. dist.) N.Y. 1949, U.S. Supreme Ct. 1951, U.S. Ct. Appeals (10th cir.) 1956, U.S. Tax Ct. 1973, U.S. Ct. Appeals (4th cir.) 1988. Assoc. Rosenman, Goldmark, Colin & Kaye, 1946-47, Javits & Javits, 1947-48; staff counsel ACLU, 1949-56; pvt. practice, 1956-64; ptnr. Hofheimer, Gartlir, Hofheimer, Gottlieb & Gross, 1965-69; pvt. practice, N.Y.C., 1969—; bd. dirs. Music Outreach; faculty N.Y. County Lawyers Assn.; past lectr. Practising Law Inst. Exec. com. on law and social action Am. Jewish Congress, 1961-66; trustee Congregation B'nai Jeshurun, 1987-98, chmn. bd. trustees 1988-91, gen. counsel bd. trustees, 1991-92. Mem. Fed. Bar Coun. (past trustee), Bar Assn. City N.Y., N.Y. County Lawyers Assn., 1st Amendment Lawyers Assn. Democrat. Author: How to Handle an Appeal (Practising Law Inst.), 1968, 3d rev. edit., 1999; contbr. articles to profl. jours. Appellate, General civil litigation, Constitutional. Home: 285 Central Park W Apt 12W New York NY 10024-3006 Office: 60 E 42nd St Ste 4210 New York NY 10165-4299

**LEVY, JONATHAN TODD,** lawyer; b. Milw., June 1, 1970; s. Alan M. and Tee Gee Levy; m. Donna Lam, June 7, 1997. BA, U. Vt., 1992; JD, U. Wis., 1995. Bar: Fla. 1995, Wis. 1995, U.S. Dist. Ct. (mid. dist.) Fla. 1995. Atty. Shapiro Law Group, Bradenton, Fla., 1995-98, Rosenthal & Weissman, PA, West Palm Beach, Fla., 1998—. Mem. ATLA, Acad. Fla. Trial Lawyers (bd. dirs. young lawyers sect. 1995—). Personal injury, Pension, profit-sharing, and employee benefits, Product liability. Office: Rosenthal & Weissman PA 1645 Palm Beach Lakes Blvd West Palm Beach FL 33401-2204

**LEVY, LEONARD JOEL,** lawyer, comedian, actor; b. Balt., Dec. 13, 1949; s. Sol and Gertrude Sylvia Levy; m. Shelley Harriet Moskin, Dec. 30, 1972; children: Gershon David, Jason Daniel. BA, U. Md., 1971; JD, Catholic U. Am., 1976; LLM, Georgetown U., 1981. Bar: D.C. 1979, Md. 1985. Atty., hearing examiner U.S. Merit Sys. Protection Bd., Falls Church, Va., 1975-85; pvt. practice, Rockville, Md., 1985-94; gen. counsel Counter Tech., Inc., Bethesda, Md., 1994—. Author: My Neighborhood, 1995, World's Longest Book of the World's Shortest Poems, 1997; contbr. articles to law jours. Precinct chmn. Montgomery County Dem. Com., 1994—; mem. Upcounty Adv. Bd., Montgomery County, Md., 1996-97; mem. Gaithersburg (Md.) Bd. Appeals, 1997—. With USAR, 1971-77. Jewish. Avocations: comedy, acting, writing. General corporate, Labor. Home: PO Box 7732 Gaithersburg MD 20898-7732 Office: Counter Tech Inc 4733 Bethesda Ave Ste 200 Bethesda MD 20814-5246

**LEVY, MARK ALLAN,** lawyer; b. Cambridge, Mass., May 31, 1939; s. Robert A. and Muriel (Goldman) L.; m. Ellen Grob, Oct. 2, 1966; children: Abigail R., Eric V.R. AB, Harvard U., 1961; LLB, Columbia U., 1964, MBA, 1965. Bar: N.Y. 1964, Mass. 1965. Assoc. Parker, Chapin, Flattau & Klimpl, N.Y.C., 1965-68; sr. ptnr. Stroock & Stroock & Lavan, N.Y.C., 1968—. Contbr. articles to profl. jours. Former mem. Planning Bd. Town of Greenburgh, N.Y. Mem. N.Y. State Bar Assn., Columbia Law Sch. Alumni Assn. (former dir.). Corporate taxation, Personal income taxation, Real property. Home: 60 Highridge Rd Hartsdale NY 10530-3605 Office: Stroock & Stroock & Lavan 180 Maiden Ln New York NY 10038-4925

**LEVY, ROBERT MORRIS,** judge. BA, Harvard Coll., 1971; JD, NYU, 1975. Bar: N.Y., U.S. Dist. Ct. (so. and ea. dists.) N.Y., U.S. Ct. Appeals (D.C. and 2nd cirs.), U.S. Supreme Ct. Staff atty. juvenile rights divsn. Legal Aid Soc., N.Y.C., 1976-77; staff atty. mental health law project N.Y. Civil Liberties Union, N.Y.C., 1977-80, dir. mental health law project, 1980-85, sr. staff atty., 1985-92; gen. counsel N.Y. Lawyers for the Pub. Interest, N.Y.C., 1992-93; U.S. magistrate judge Ea. Dist. N.Y., Bklyn., 1995—; advisor on jud. reform in the Republic of Georgia, Ctrl. and East European Law Initiative ABA, 1998; adj. prof. Bklyn. Law Sch., 1989—, NYU, 1991—, Columbia U., 1993—. Author: (with V. Rosenthal) Rights of Nursing Home Residents in New York, 1984, (with L. Rubenstein) Rights of People with Mental Disabilities, 1996. Bd. dirs. NYU Pub. Interest Law Found., N.Y.C., 1980-82; mem. Gov.'s Task Force on Advocacy, N.Y., 1988-91; mem. adv. bd. Protection and Advocacy Svcs. for the Mentally Ill, N.Y.C., 1991-93; vol. factfinding missions Human Rights Watch, No. Ireland and Romania, 1990, 91, 92, 93. Mem. Fed. Bar Coun. (2nd cir. cts. com. 1998—), Assn. Bar of the City of N.Y. (com. on internat. human rights 1995-98). Fax: 718-260-2647. E-mail: RobertM.Levy@nyed.uscourts.gov. Office: 225 Cadman Plz E # 621 Brooklyn NY 11201-1818

**LEVY, SAMUEL ROBERT,** lawyer; b. Bklyn., Nov. 25, 1931; s. Martin and Bertha (Freeman) L.; m. Gloria Waldman, Oct. 12, 1963; children: Robin C., Marlene F. AB, NYU, 1952, LLB, 1954. Bar: N.Y. 1954, U.S. Supreme Ct. 1961, U.S. Dist. Ct. (ea. dist.) N.Y. 1957, U.S. Dist. Ct. (so. dist.) N.Y. 1957, U.S. Tax Ct. 1961, U.S. Ct. Claims, 1961. Jr. ptnr. Levy-Levy, Bklyn., 1957-58; pvt. practice, Bklyn., 1959—; notary pub., Kings County, N.Y., 1956—. Capt. Clarendon Dem. Club, Bklyn., 1960-62. With U.S. Army, 1954-56. Mem. N.Y. State Bar Assn., NYU Alumni Assn., NYU Law Alumni Assn., Automobile Assn. Am., Nat. Geog. Soc. Jewish. Taxation, general, Real property, Pension, profit-sharing, and employee benefits. Home and Office: 1845 Ocean Ave Brooklyn NY 11230-7711

**LEVY, STEPHEN JEFFREY,** lawyer; b. N.Y.C., Oct. 19, 1961; s. Harry Levyand Sandra Wohlgemuth; m. Caroline Kane, Mar. 17, 1996; 1 child: Maya Alexandra Levy. BS, Cornell U., 1983; JD, Boston U., 1986. Assoc. Schnapp & Cordover, Bklyn., 1986-90; ptnr. Schnapp & Levy, Bklyn., 1991-95; of counsel Williams & Geiger, Bklyn., 1996—. Office: Schnapp & Levy 26 Court St Ste 2400 Brooklyn NY 11242-1124

**LEVY, STEVEN BARRY,** lawyer; b. Chgo., Sept. 3, 1954; s. Robert and Beverly (Rouzin) L.; children: Rachel, Karen, Stephanie, Kimberly. BA, U. Ill., 1975; JD, IIT, 1978. Bar: Ill. 1979, Fla. 1980, U.S. Dist. Ct. (no. dist.) Ill. 1979, U.S. Ct. Appeals (7th cir.) 1979, U.S. Dist. Ct. (so. and mid. dists.) Fla. 1980, U.S. Ct. Appeals (10th and 11th cirs.) 1980, U.S. Supreme Ct. 1993. Pvt. practice Chgo., 1983—; Apptd. Ill. Supreme Ct. com. on profl. responsibility, 1996-98, Ill. Supreme Ct. rules com., 1998-2000. Contbr. articles to profl. publs. Founding mem. DuPage County Chpt. Am. Inns of Ct. Mem. Ill. State Bar Assn. (mem. editl. bd. Bar Jour. 1996-99, standing com. on contng. legal edn. 1997-99), Fla. Bar Assn., Du Page County Bar Assn. (editor-inchief Bar Jour. 1995-99, recipient 20th ann. Lawyer of Yr. award, 2nd ann. Professionalism award). General civil litigation, Professional liability, Personal injury. Office: 40 Shuman Blvd Ste 151 Naperville IL 60563-8464

**LEW, RONALD S. W.,** federal judge; b. L.A., 1941; m. Mamie Wong; 4 children. BA in Polit. Sci., Loyola U., L.A., 1964; JD, Southwestern U., 1971. Bar: Calif. 1972. Dep. city atty. L.A. City Atty's. Office, 1972-74; ptnr. Avans & Lew, L.A., 1974-82; commr. fire and police pension City of L.A., 1976-82; mcpl. ct. judge County of L.A., 1982-84, superior ct. judge, 1984-87; judge U.S. Dist. Ct. (cen. dist.) Calif., L.A., 1987—; Bar: Calif. 1971. Mem. World Affairs Council of L.A., 1976—, Christian Businessmen's Com. of L.A., 1982—; active Com. of 100, Chinese Am. Heart Coun., Friends of the Mus. Chinese Am. History. 1st lt. U.S. Army, 1967-69. Recipient Vol. award United Way of L.A., 1979, cert. of merit L.A. Human Relations Commn., 1977, 82. Mem. Am. Judicature Soc., Calif. Assn. of Judges, So. Calif. Chinese Lawyer's Assn. (charter mem. 1976, pres. 1979), Chinese Am. Citizens Alliance, San Fernando Valley Chinese Cultural Assn., Delta Theta Phi. Office: US Dist Ct 312 N Spring St Los Angeles CA 90012-4701

**LEWAND, F. THOMAS,** lawyer; b. San Diego, July 24, 1946; s. Barbara (Boening) L.; m. Kathleen Sullivan, Aug. 3, 1968; children: Thomas, Kevin, Kristen, Carrie. BA, U. Detroit, 1968; JD, Wayne State U., 1970. Bar: Mich. 1970, U.S. Dist. Ct. (ea. dist.) 1970. Law clk. to presiding justice U.S. Ct. Appeals (6th cir.), Detroit, 1970; commr. Oakland County, Pontiac, Mich., 1978-80; chief of staff to Gov. J. Blanchard Lansing, Mich., 1982-83; ptnr. Jaffe, Raitt & Heuer, Detroit, 1970-92, Bodman, Longley & Dahling, Detroit, 1992—; trustee Gov. Blanchard Found., Lansing, 1982—, U. Detroit Mercy, 1996—; bd. dir. Met. Realty Corp., Detroit, 1988—. Campaign mgr. Gov. James J. Blanchard, MIch., 1978; chmn. Mich. Dems., 1989-91. Mem. State Bar Mich., Nat. Assn. Bond Lawyers. Municipal (including bonds), Government contracts and claims, General corporate. Office: Bodman Longley & Dahling 100 Renaissance Ctr Fl 34 Detroit MI 48243-1001

**LEWAND, KIMBERLY ELLEN,** lawyer; b. L.A., July 23, 1966; d. Kevin O'Reilly and Jeanne Lewand. BA, UCLA, 1998; JD, Pepperdine U., 1992. Bar: Calif. 1992, U.S. Dist. Ct. (ctrl. dist.) Calif. 1992, U.S. Ct. Appeals (9th cir.) 1994. Atty. Graham & James LLP, L.A., 1993-96, Demetriou, Del Guercio, Springer & Moyer LLP, L.A., 1996-98, Cheaten-Brown Assocs., L.A., 1998—. Mem. editl. bd. Environ. Liability, Enforcement and Penalty Reporter, 1997-98, Calif. Environ. Law and Remediation Reporter, 1998—; contbr. articles to profl. jours. Mem. legal com. Heal the Bay, L.A., 1997—; vol. Coalition for Clean Air, L.A., 1991—. Mem. ABA (natural resources sect.), State Bar Calif. (environ. sect.), Los Angeles County Bar Assn. (exec. com. environ. sect. 1997—). Environmental, Land use and zoning (including planning), Natural resources. Office: Chatten-Brown and Assocs 10951 W Pico Blvd Fl 3D Los Angeles CA 90064-2126

**LEWANDOWSKI, ALEX MICHAEL,** lawyer; b. St. Louis, Nov. 16, 1946; s. Alexander Simon and Ida Margerite L.; m. Patricia L., July 6, 1968 (div. June 1983); m. Kim L. Rode, Oct. 27, 1990; children: Michael, Andrew, Michelle. BA, Ctrl. Meth. Coll., 1968; JD, U.Mo., 1972, LLM, 1976. Bar: Mo., U.S. Dist. Ct. (we. dist.) Mo., U.S. Dist. Ct. Kans., U.S. Ct. Appeals (5th, 8th, 10th, 11th and D.C. cirs.), U.S. Supreme Ct. V.p., dir. Dysart Taylor Lay Lweancoroski & Cotter, Kansas City, Mo., 1972-96; atty. pvt. practice, Kansas City, Mo., 1997—. Editor The Transp. Lawyer, 1992-93. Non-voting dir., legal cons. Deaf Hope, Inc., Kansas City, 1994—, Global Youth Devel., Inc., Kansas City, 1998—. Sgt. U.S. Army, 1969-70, Vietnam. Mem. Mo. Bar Assn. (chair aviation, transp. com. 1991-93), Transp. Lawyers Assn. (pres. 1994-95), Alpha Phi Omega. Independent. Lutheran. Avocations: travel, reading, movies, family. Transportation, General civil litigation, Contracts commercial. Office: 9249 Ward Pkwy Kansas City MO 64114-3335

**LEWIN, JEFFREY DAVID,** lawyer; b. Mpls., Feb. 11, 1945; s. Harry Davidson and Leota Rose (Seitz) L.; m. Eva Gertrud Sonnenberg, Dec. 21, 1971; children: Eric, Peter. BA with honors, Stanford U., 1967; JD, Calif. Western U., 1975. Bar: Calif. 1976, U.S. Supreme Ct. 1979. Trial atty. antitrust div. U.S. Dept. Justice, Chgo., 1975-76; assoc., then ptnr. Sullivan, Jones & Archer, San Diego, 1976-82; ptnr. Sullivan, Hill, Lewin Rez & Engel, San Diego, 1983—; lectr., instr. continuing edn. of bar NITA, San Diego, 1985—. Contbr. articles to profl. publs. Trustee Calif. Western Sch. Law, San Diego, 1981—; lawyer del. 9th Cir. Jud. Conf., San Diego, 1982-84. Mem. ABA, San Diego County Bar Assn., Harvard Club San Diego (bd. dirs. 1990-93). Antitrust, Federal civil litigation, State civil litigation. Office: Sullivan Hill Lewin Rez & Engel 550 W C St Ste 1500 San Diego CA 92101-3570

**LEWIN, ROSS ALLEN,** lawyer; b. Chgo., Apr. 2, 1955; s. Herbert Martin and Gertrude Anne (Gordon) L.; m. Nancy Deborah Feldman, May 18, 1986; children: Gina, Gabriel. BA, Trinity Coll., 1977; JD, Yale Law Sch.,

1982. Bar: N.J. 1983, U.S. Dist. Ct. N.J. 1983, U.S. Ct. Appeals, U.S. Supreme Ct. Law clerk Justice Alan Handler N.J. Supreme Ct., Trenton, N.J., 1982-83; deputy atty. gen. Atty. Gen. N.J., Trenton, N.J., 1983-89; deputy chief counsel Gov. of N.J., Trenton, N.J., 1989-90; assoc. Jamieson Moore Peskin & Spicer, Princeton, N.J., 1990-93, ptnr., 1993—; dir. Legal Svcs. of N.J., Iselin, 1996—, Mercer County Legal Aid Soc., Trenton, 1992-96. Contbr. articles to profl. jours. Mem. Yale Law Sch. Assn. of N.J. (pres. 1996-97, v.p. 1995-96). Environmental, Insurance, General civil litigation. Office: Jamieson Moore Peskin & Spicer 300 Alexander Park Princeton NJ 08540-6396

**LEWIN, WERNER SIEGFRIED, JR.,** lawyer; b. San Francisco, Apr. 13, 1954; s. Werner Siegfried and Libby (Lewis) L.; married. BS, Cornell U., 1975; JD, U. Calif., Hastings, 1980. Bar: Calif. 1980. Assoc. Lynch, Loofbornraow et al, San Francisco, 1980-82, Rudy Rapoport & Holden, San Francisco, 1982-86, Hanson, Bridgett, Marcus, Vlahos & Rudy, San Francisco, 1986-87; prin. Werner S Lewin Jr., Esq., Novato, Calif., 1987—; founder, pres. Attorney Assistance, San Francisco Bay Area, 1987—. General practice. Office: Atty Assistance Co Hdqs 55 Cavalla Cay Novato CA 94949-5341

**LEWIS, ALBERT B.,** lawyer; b. N.Y.C., Oct. 16, 1925; m. Sara Anne Lewis, Apr. 10, 1949 (dec. 1985); children: David, Eric, Jonathan; m. Leila Stein, Oct. 6, 1987. BA, Bklyn. Coll., 1948; LLB, St. John's U., 1954. Bar: N.Y. 1954, U.S. Dist. Ct. (so. and ea. dists.) N.Y.; CPA, N.Y. Sec. to Hon. James S. Brown N.Y. Supreme Ct, Kings County, N.Y., 1962-67; mem. N.Y. State Senate, Albany, 1967-78; supt. N.Y. Ins. Dept., N.Y.C., 1978-83; ptnr. Bower & Gardner, N.Y.C., 1983—. Author: Danger: Insurance Fraud in Progress, 1987. With U.S. Army, 1944-46. Mem. N.Y. State Bar Assn., Bklyn. Bar Assn., Assn. Bar City of N.Y., N.Y. State Soc. CPA. Home: 1025 5th Ave New York NY 10028-0134 Office: Bower & Gardner 110 E 59th St New York NY 10022-1304

**LEWIS, ALEXANDER INGERSOLL, III,** lawyer; b. Detroit, Apr. 10, 1946; s. Alexander Ingersoll Jr. and Marie T. (Fuger) L.; m. Gretchen Elsa Lundgren, Aug. 8, 1970; children: Jennifer L., Katherine F., Elisabeth M., Alexander Ingersoll IV. BA with honors, Johns Hopkins U., 1968; JD cum laude, U. Pa., 1971. Bar: Md. 1972, U.S. Dist. Ct. Md. 1972, U.S. Ct. Appeals (4th cir.) 1975, U.S. Supreme Ct. 1976, D.C. 1982. Assoc. Venable, Baetjer & Howard, LLP, Balt., 1972-75, 78-80, ptnr., 1981—, sr. ptnr., head estate and trust practice group, 1993—; asst. atty. gen. State of Md., Balt., 1975-77; cons. subcom. on probate rules, standing com. on rules and procedures Md. Ct. Appeals, 1976—; mem. Md. Gov.'s Task Force to Study Revision of Inheritance and Estate Tax Laws, 1987-88; lectr. Md. Inst. Continuing Profl. Edn. Lawyers, 1978—, Nat. Bus. Inst., 1986-87, 92—, Cambridge Inst., 1986-90, Nat. Law Found., 1988—. Contbr. articles to legal jours. Vice chmn. Md. Gov.'s Task Force on Long-Term Fin. Planning for Disabled Individuals, 1990-94. 1st lt. U.S. Army, 1972. Fellow Am. Coll. Trust and Estate Counsel; mem. ABA, Md. Bar Assn. (chmn. probate reform and simplification com. estates and trusts coun. 1984-86, sec. 1987-88, chmn. 1989-90, com. on laws 1994-98), D.C. Bar Assn., Bar Assn. City Balt., Balt. Estate Planning Coun., Johns Hopkins Club. Republican. Roman Catholic. Avocations: canoeing, camping, tennis. Estate planning, Estate taxation, Probate. Home: 922 Army Rd Ruxton MD 21204-6703 Office: Venable Baetjer & Howard LLP 1800 Two Hopkins Plz Baltimore MD 21201

**LEWIS, ALVIN BOWER, JR.,** lawyer; b. Pitts., Apr. 24, 1932; s. Alvin Bower Sr. and Ethel Weidman (Light) L.; m. Elizabeth Therese O'Shea; children: Alvin B. III, Judith W., Robert B. II. BA, Lehigh U., 1954; LLB, Dickinson Sch. Law, 1957. Bar: Pa. 1957, U.S. Dist. Ct. (mid. and ea. dists.) Pa. 1958, U.S. Ct. Appeals (3d cir.) 1958, D.C. 1979. Ptnr. Lewis & Lewis, Lebanon, Pa., 1957-66, Lewis, Brubaker, Whitman & Christianson, Lebanon, 1967-76; spl. counsel, acting chief counsel, dir. select com. on assassinations of M.L. King, and J.F. Kennedy U.S. Ho. of Reps., Washington, 1976-77; ptnr. Lewis & Kramer, Phila., 1977-78, Hartman, Underhill & Brubaker, Lancaster, Pa., 1979-95, Sprague & Lewis, Ltd., Lancaster, 1995-99, Stevens & Lee, Lancaster, 1999—; dist. atty. County of Lebanon, Pa., 1962-70; chmn. Gov.'s Justice Commn., Pa., 1969-74; mem., chmn. Pa. Crime Commn., Pa., 1979-85. Fin. chmn., mem. exec. com. Rep. County Com., Lebanon, 1959-76; chmn. Lancaster City Rep. Com., 1994—; bd. dirs., chmn. adv. com., mem. nominating com. Urban League Lancaster County, 1986-91; chmn. Lehigh U. Scholar-Athletes Fund Drive, 1990-94. Recipient Furtherance of Justice award Mercyhurst Coll., 1979, Dist. Service award Ho. of Reps. Pa., 1982, Award of Distinction Pa. Senate, 1982, Outstanding Service award Gov. and Atty. Gen. Pa., 1974. Mem. ABA, Pa. Bar Assn. Lancaster County Bar Assn. (chmn. trial law sect. 1995—), Preservation Fund Pa., Inc., Lebanon County Bar Assn. (pres. 1974-76, bd. dirs. 1982-90), Nat. Dist. Attys. Assn. (bd. dirs. 1966-68), Pa. Dist. Attys. Assn. (officer, pres., bd. dirs. 1964-68). Lutheran. Lodge: Masons. Avocations: pilot, small airplanes. State civil litigation, Federal civil litigation, General corporate. Office: Stevens & Lee One Penn Sq Lancaster PA 17602-1594

**LEWIS, CLYDE A.,** lawyer; b. Hoquiam, Wash., June 20, 1913; s. J.D. Clyde and Loretta C. (Adelsperger) L.; m. Helen M. Judge, Sept. 22, 1936 (dec. Sept. 1985); m. Patricia Davis Judge, Oct. 1, 1988; children: Clyde A., John E. AB, U. Notre Dame, 1934; JD, Harvard U., 1939. Bar: N.Y. 1940, U.S. Supreme Ct. 1959. Mem. Lewis, Roger & Kudrie, P.C. and predecessor firms, Plattsburgh, N.Y. Comdr. in chief VFW, 1949-50, also served as sr. and jr. vice comdr. in chief, mem. nat. legis. com. Maj. USAAF, 1942-45. Decorated DFC with 2 oak leaf clusters, Air medal with 4 oak leaf clusters; recipient Croix de Guerre, France; invested Knight of Malta. Mem. ABA, N.Y. State Bar Assn., U.S. Strategic Inst., Def. Orientation Conf. Assn., Notre Dame Alumni Assn., Harvard Alumni Assn., Am. Legion. Clubs: Capitol Hill, K.C., Elks. Republican. Roman Catholic. Home: 93 Lighthouse Rd Plattsburgh NY 12901-7018 Office: 53 Court St Plattsburgh NY 12901-2834

**LEWIS, DANIEL EDWIN,** lawyer; b. Goshen, Ind., May 2, 1910; s. Daniel Arthur and Emma (Williams) L.; m. Annette Jean Fewell, July 28, 1934; children: Daniel E., Nancy Jean Haswell. A.B., Hanover (Ind.) Coll., 1932; M.S., Ind. U., 1939; J.D., Valparaiso U., 1949. Bar: Ind. 1949. Tchr. secondary schs., Ind., 1932-43; dir. indsl. relations Allis-Chalmers, LaPorte, Ind., 1943-55; ptnr. Newby, Lewis & Kaminski, LaPorte, after 1955, now of counsel. Treas., Health Care Fedn., 1982; pres. LaPorte Bd. Edn., 1952-55; vice chmn. Pottawatomie County Boy Scouts Am., 1963-69; pres. United Fund, 1957-65; chmn. LaPorte County ARC, 1948-49; pres. LaPorte YMCA, 1960-62; pres. LaPorte County Family Service, 1975-77; pres. LaPorte County Human Relations Bd., 1967-68. Recipient Alumni Achievement award Hanover Coll., 1965; inducted into the Football Hall of Fame, LaPorte. Fellow Ind. State Bar Found.; mem. ABA, Ind. State Bar Assn., LaPorte City and County Bar Assn., Soc. Profls. in Dispute Resolution, Kiwanis (Kiwanian of Yr. 1989), Elks (Elk of Yr. 1987), Masons. Presbyterian. Author: (fiction) At the Crossroads, 1980; So It Comes to Arbitration, 1982. Died Oct. 15, 1997. General practice, Labor, Probate. Office: 916 Lincolnway La Porte IN 46350-3412

**LEWIS, DAVID JOHN,** lawyer; b. Zanesville, Ohio, Feb. 4, 1948; s. David Griff and Barbara Ann (Hoy) L.; m. Susan G. Smith; 1 child, Ann Elizabeth. BS in Fin., U. Ill., 1970, JD, 1973. Bar: Ill. 1973, D.C. 1974. Law clk. to Judge Philip W. Tone U.S. Dist. Ct. For North Dist. Ill., Chgo., 1973-74; assoc. Sidley & Austin, Washington, 1974-80, ptnr., 1980—; comml. arbitrator Am. Arbitration Assn. Mem. ABA. Federal civil litigation, Alternative dispute resolution, Product liability. Office: Sidley & Austin 1722 I St NW Washington DC 20006-3795

**LEWIS, DAVID ROBERT,** lawyer; b. Bklyn., Dec. 5, 1958; s. Finley and Elaine Mildred (Cohen) L. BA, SUNY, Stony Brook, 1980; JD, Yeshiva U., 1983. Bar: N.Y. 1984, U.S. Dist. Ct. (so. and ea. dists.) N.Y. 1988. Law clk., assoc. Norman Perlman, Esquire, N.Y.C., 1983-84; assoc. Epstein, Newman & Lubitz, Esquires, Bronx, N.Y., 1984-88; ptnr. Bender & Lewis, Esquires, Bronx, N.Y., 1988-90, Lewis & Lewis, Esquires, Bronx, N.Y., 1990-94; assoc. Pulvers, Pulvers, Thompson & Kutner, N.Y.C., 1995—. Mem. ABA, N.Y. State Bar Assn., N.Y. State Trial Lawyers Assn., Assn. Trial Lawyers Am. Jewish. Avocations: baseball, music. Personal injury, Product liability, Insurance. Home: 1 Rosalie Ct Plainview NY 11803-1400 Office: Pulvers Pulvers Thompson & Kutner PC 110 E 59th St New York NY 10022-1304

**LEWIS, EDWIN LEONARD, III,** lawyer; b. Phila., Nov. 24, 1945; s. Edwin Leonard Jr. and Nancy (Hoffman) L.; m. Elisabeth C. Bacon, Oct. 6, 1984; children: Katharine Bacon, Caroline Huffington. BA, Lafayette Coll., 1967; JD, Temple U., 70. bar: Pa. 1970, Ill. 1995. Assoc. MacElree, Platt & Harvey, West Chester, Pa., 1970-73; asst. gen. counsel Fidelity Mut. Life, Phila., 1973-76; sr. atty. Atlantic Richfield Co., Phila., 1976-83; v.p. law Wells Fargo Alarm Svcs., King of Prussia, Pa., 1983-91; v.p., gen. counsel, sec. Borg Warner Protective Svcs., Parsippany, N.J., 1991-95, Borg Warner Security Corp., Chgo., 1995-97; pres. Atlantic Legal Found., N.Y.C., 1998—; pub., editor Science in the Courtroom Review, 1998. Capt. M.I., USAR, 1970-76. Mem. Am. Corp. Counsel Assn., Phila. Bar Assn. Avocations: marathon running, tennis, golf, sailing. General corporate, Mergers and acquisitions, Product liability. Home: 59 Delafield Island Rd Darien CT 06820-6012 Office: Atlantic Legal Found 205 E 42d St New York NY 10017

**LEWIS, FELICE FLANERY,** lawyer, educator; b. Plaquemine, La., Oct. 5, 1920; d. Lowell Baird and E. Elizabeth (Lee) Flanery; m. Francis Russell Lewis, Dec. 22, 1944. BA, U. Wash., 1947; PhD, NYU, 1974; JD, Georgetown U., 1981. Bar: N.Y. 1982. Dean L.I. Univ., Liberal Arts & Scis., Bklyn., 1974-78; assoc. Harry G. English, Bklyn., 1983-85, 91—; adj. prof., polit. sci. L.I. Univ., Bklyn., 1983—. Author: Literature, Obscenity and Law, 1976; co-editor: Henry Miller, Years of Trial & Triumph, 1962-64, 1978. General practice, Probate, Constitutional. Home: 28 Whitney Cir Glen Cove NY 11542-1316 Office: Harry G English 7219 3rd Ave Brooklyn NY 11209-2131

**LEWIS, GERALD JORGENSEN,** judge; b. Perth Amboy, N.J., Sept. 9, 1933; s. Norman Francis and Blanche M. (Jorgensen) L.; m. Laura Susan McDonald, Dec. 15, 1973; children by previous marriage: Michael, Marc. AB magna cum laude, Tufts Coll., 1954; JD, Harvard U., 1957. Bar: D.C. 1957, N.J. 1961, Calif. 1962, U.S. Supreme Ct. 1968. Atty. Gen. Atomic, La Jolla, Calif., 1961-63; ptnr. Haskins, Lewis, Hugent & Newnham, San Diego, 1963-77; judge Mcpl. Ct., El Cajon, Calif., 1977-79, Superior Ct., San Diego, 1979-84; assoc., justice Calif. Ct. of Appeal, San Diego, 1984-87; dir. Fisher Scientific Group, Inc., 1987-98, Bolsa Chica Corp., 1991-93, Gen. Chem. Group, Inc., 1996—; of counsel Lathan & Watkins, 1987-97; adj. prof. evidence Western State U. Sch. Law, San Diego, 1977-85, exec. bd., 1977-89; faculty San Diego Inn of Ct., 1979—, Am. Inn of Ct., 1984—. Cons. editor: California Civil Jury Instructions, 1984. City atty. Del Mar, Calif., 1963-74, Coronado, Calif., 1972-77; counsel Comprehensive Planning Orgn., San Diego, 1972-73; trustee San Diego Mus. Art, 1986-89; bd. dirs. Air Pollkution Control Dist., San Diego County, 1972-76. Served to lt. comdr. USNR, 1957-61. Named Trial Judge of Yr. San Diego Trial Lawyers Assn., 1984. Mem. Am. Judicature Soc., Soc. Inns of Ct. in Calif., Confrerie des Chevaliers du Tastevin, Order of St. Hubert (knight comdr.), Friendly Sons of St. Patrick, The Irisn 50 Aztec Big 50, Bohemian Club, La Jolla Country Club (dir. 1980-83), Prophets, The K Club (County Kildare). Republican. Episcopalian. Home: 6505 Caminito Blythefield La Jolla CA 92037-5806 Office: Latham & Watkins 701 B St Ste 2100 San Diego CA 92101-8197

**LEWIS, JOHN MICHAEL,** lawyer; b. N.Y.C., May 22, 1946; s. Martin J. and Ursula Urdang Dewitz; m. Cindy S. Sexton, Feb. 12, 1977; children: Michael, David, Madeline. BA, Dartmouth Coll., 1967; JD, Columbia U., 1973. Bar: N.Y. 1974, U.S. Dist. Ct. (no. dist.) Ohio 1974, U.S. Dist. Ct. (so. dist.) N.Y. 1976, U.S. Ct. Appeals (2d cir.) 1977, N.H. 1982, U.S. Dist. Ct. N.H. 1982, U.S. Dist. Ct. (ea. dist.) N.Y. 1982, Maine 1983, U.S. Dist. Ct. Maine 1988, U.S. Ct. Appeals (1st cir.) 1989. Tchr. Stockbridge (Mass.) Sch., 1968-70; law clk. U.S. Dist. Ct. (no. dist.) Ohio, Cleve., 1973-74; asst. regional atty. EEOC, Phila., 1974-76; atty. Proskauer Rose Goetz & Mendelsohn, N.Y.C., 1976-82; pres. Borofsky Lewis & Amodeo-Vickery, Portsmouth, N.H., 1982—, also bd. dirs.; Chmn. N.H. State Bd. Edn., 1997—; bd. dirs. Lamprey Health Care, Newmarket, N.H. Bd. dirs. Oyster River Sch. Bd., Durham, Madbury Lee, N.J., 1992-95. Fulbright scholar, Grenoble, France, 1968. Mem. N.H. Bar Assn., N.H. Trial Lawyers Assn. General civil litigation, Personal injury, Workers' compensation. Office: Borofsky Lewis & Amodeo-Vickery 2204 Woodbury Ave Newington NH 03801-2817

**LEWIS, JOSEPH KENNETH,** lawyer; b. St. Joseph, Mo., Dec. 3, 1953; s. Joseph Kenneth and Gloria Mae (Beckwith) L.; m. Deborah Fontana, Dec. 27,. 1996. BBA, U. Mo., Kansas City, 1977, JD, 1980. Acct. Thompson Hayward Chem. Co., Kansas City, Kans., 1976-77; asst. atty. Jackson County, Mo., 1980-81; assoc. atty. Morris & Foust, Kansas City, Mo., 1981-84; sr. ptnr. Herron & Lewis, Kansas City, Mo., 1984—. Chmn. U. Mo. Dean's Fin. Com., 1979-80, Mo. Air NG United Way Dr., Rosecrans, 1976. NAmed one of Outstanding Young Men Am., U.S. C. of C., 1985. Mem. Mo. Bar Assn., Kansas City Met. Bar Assn. (vol. atty project 1982—, mar media and pub. info. com.), Mo. Assn. Trial Attys. (cir. ct. com. 1985—), Am. Trial Lawyers Assn., Nat. Orgn. Tax Experts, Phi Alpha Delta, Phi Kappa Phi. Republican. Avocations: musician, softball, gardening. Home: 12600 W 130th Overland Park KS 66213 Office: Herron & Lewis Attys 4739 Belleview Ave Ste 300 Kansas City MO 64112-1364

**LEWIS, KIRK MCARTHUR,** lawyer; b. Schenectady, N.Y., Jan. 3, 1957; s. David MacArthur and Eleanor Burrows (Smith) L.; m. Barbara Jean Lewis, June 12, 1982; children: John Christopher, Kerry Elizabeth. BS, Cornell U., 1979; JD, Syracuse U., 1985. Bar: N.Y. 1986, U.S. Dist. Ct. (no. dist.) N.Y. 1988, U.S. Dist. Ct. (ea. dist.) N.Y. 1991, U.S. Ct. Appeals (2d cir.) 1989. Jud. clk to Hon. Conrad K. Cyr U.S. Dist. Ct. Maine, Bangor, 1985-87; assoc. DeGraff, Foy, Holt, Harris, Mealey & Kunz, Albany, N.Y., 1987-93, ptnr., 1998—; gen. counsel Schenectady Assn. Retarded Citizens, 1999—. Bd. dirs., v.p., pres. Schenectady (N.Y.) Assn. for Retarded Citizens, 1990-98. Mem. ABA, N.Y. State Bar Assn. General civil litigation, Environmental, Product liability. Home: 30 Washington Rd Scotia NY 12302-2413 Office: Schidy ARC PO Box 2236 Schenectady NY 12301-2236

**LEWIS, MARILEA WHATLEY,** judge; b. Waco, Tex., Aug. 2, 1953; d. Thomas Howard and Della Frank (Shannon) Whatley; m. Danny Glen Lewis, Mar. 5, 1983; children: Thomas Hunter, Sheridan Frances. BA, Baylor U., 1975, JD, 1978. Bar: Tex. 1978; cert. Tex. State Bar Bd. of Legal Specialization. Assoc. Blassingame & Osburn, Dallas, 1978-80; asst. Atty. Gen. Tex., Dallas, 1980; ptnr. Bradley & Schellhammer, Dallas, 1980-83, Bradley & Lewis, Dallas, 1983-86; master, referee, magistrate 305th Dist. Ct., Dallas, 1986-92; assoc. judge 330th Dist. Ct., Dallas, 1992—. Bd. dirs., mem. Women's Guild United Cerebral Palsey, Dallas; mem. Jr. League, Dallas, 1990—; active La Fiesta de la Seis Banderas. Rsch. fellow Southwestern Legal Found. Fellow Tex. Bar Found.; mem. DAR, Tex. Acad. Family Law Specialists, Coll. of State Bar, State Bar Tex., Dallas Bar Assn. Republican. Episcopalian. Office: 330th Dist Court 600 Commerce St Dallas TX 75202-4616

**LEWIS, MARK RUSSELL, SR.,** lawyer; b. Cin., Oct. 21, 1946; s. John Russell and Lillian (Hilgeman) L.; m. Tana Tillotson, Dec. 14, 1968 (div. Mar. 1974); m. Sharon R. Sullivan (div. Aug. 1994); children: Mark R. II, John C. BS in Engring., U. Cin., 1969, JD, 1973. Bar: Ohio 1973, Fla. 1975. Law clk. to presiding justice U.S. Ct. Appeals (6th cir.), Cin., 1973-75; assoc. Harrison, Greene, Mann, Rowe, Stanton & Mastry, St. Petersburg, Fla., 1975-77; sole practice St. Petersburg, 1977—; tchr. continuing edn. St. Petersburg Jr. Coll., 1984-86; atty. City of So. Pasadena, Fla., 1977-79. Author: Legalese, 1984, Fundamentals of Buying and Selling Real Estate, 1987, An Introduction to Trusts, 1999; contbr. articles to law jours. Atty. Pinellas County Child Protection Team, St. Petersburg, 1982—. Mem. ABA, Fla. Bar Assn. Republican. Avocation: tennis. Real property, Probate, General corporate. Office: 3131 66th St N Ste A Saint Petersburg FL 33710-3115

**LEWIS, MYRON BRUCE,** lawyer, accountant; b. Washington, Sept. 3, 1957; s. Phillip S. and Bessie Cardash Lewis. BBA, George Washington U., 1979, JD, 1984, LLM, 1991. Bar: Md. 1991; CPA, D.C., Md. Acct. Arthur Andersen & Co., CPA's, Washington, 1979-81; pvt. practice, Bethesda, Md., 1991—; owner, mgr. Bruce Lewis PC, CPA, Bethesda, 1991—. Mem. Md. Bar Assn., Montgomery County Bar Assn. Estate taxation, Taxation, general, Personal income taxation. Office: 7101 Wisconsin Ave Ste 1012 Bethesda MD 20814-4805

**LEWIS, R. FRED,** state supreme court justice; b. Beckley, W.Va., Dec. 14, 1947; m. Judith Lewis, 1969; children: Elle, Lindsay. Grad. cum laude, Fla. So. Coll., 1969; JD cum laude, U. Miami, 1972; grad., U.S. Army A.G. Sch. Pvt. practice Miami; justice Fla. Supreme Ct., 1998—. contbr. pubs. Continuing Edn. Legal Program. Bd. dirs. Miami Children's Hosp.; inventory atty. The Fla. Bar. NCAA postgrad. grantee, 1969. Mem. Omicron Delta Kappa, Psi Chi, Sigma Alpha Epsilon. E-mail: supremecourt@mail.flcourts.org. Address: 500 S Duval St Tallahassee FL 32399-1925*

**LEWIS, RICHARD M.,** lawyer; b. Gallipolis, Ohio, Dec. 11, 1957; s. Denver E. and Mary Esther (Mobley) L.; m. Cheryl F. Hickman (div.); m. Diane K. Williams, Apr. 26, 1986. BA in Polit. Sci., Ohio State U., 1979; JD, Capital U., 1982. Bar: Ohio 1982, U.S. Dist. Ct. (so. dist.) Ohio 1984, U.S. Supreme Ct. 1986, U.S. Ct. Appeals (6th cir.) 1999; cert. civil trial advocacy Nat. Bd. Trial Advocacy. Pvt. practice law, 1982-83; assoc. Mary Bone Kunze, Jackson, Ohio, 1983-85; pvt. practice law Jackson, 1985-86; ptnr. Ochsenbein, Cole & Lewis, Jackson, 1986-96, Cole & Lewis, Jackson, 1996—; lectr. in field; expert witness. Mem. ABA, Assn. Trial Lawyers Am., Ohio State Bar Assn., Jackson County Bar Assn. (past pres.), Ohio Acad. Trial Lawyers (bd. trustees 1993—, budget com. 1993-94, supreme ct. screening com. 1994, vice-chairperson family law com. 1994-95, chairperson-elect family law com. 1995—, chairperson family law com. 1995-96, exec. com., chair mem. com. 1996-97, co-chair regional CLE seminars 1997, exec. com. 1998-99, chair ADOPT task force 1998). General civil litigation, Family and matrimonial, Personal injury. Home: 603 Reservoir Rd Jackson OH 45640-8714 Office: Cole and Lewis 295 Pearl St Jackson OH 45640-1748

**LEWIS, ROBERT LEE,** lawyer; b. Oxford, Miss., Feb. 26, 1944; s. Ernest Elmo and Johnice Georgia (Thirkeld) L.; children: Yolanda Sherice, Robert Lee Jr., Dion Terrell, Viron Lamar, William Lovell. BA, Ind. U., 1970, JD, 1973; M in Pub. Service, West Ky. U., 1980. Bar: Ind. 1973, Ky. 1979, U.S. Ct. Claims, U.S. Ct. Internat. Trade, U.S. Tax. Ct., U.S. Ct. Mil. Appeals, U.S. Ct. Appeals (fed. cir.), U.S. Supreme Ct. Sole practice Evansville, Ind., 1973-75, Gary, Ind., 1980—; atty., army officer U.S. Army, Ft. Knox, Ky., 1975-78; appellate referee Ind. Employment Security Div., Indpls., 1978-80. Mem. adv. com. Vincennes (Ind.) U., 1983—; bd. dirs. Opportunities Industrialization Ctr., Evansville, 1973-75. Served to sgt. JAGC, USMC, 1962-66, Vietnam, sgt. U.S. Army, 1975-78, lt. col. USAR. Named Ky. Col. Mem. ABA, Ind. Bar Assn., Ky. Bar Assn., Nat. Bar Assn., Ind. Bd. Realtors, Ind. U. Alumni Assn., Phi Alpha Delta. Methodist. Criminal, Family and matrimonial, Personal injury. Home and Office: 2148 W 11th Ave Gary IN 46404-2306

**LEWIS, RONALD WAYNE,** lawyer; b. Buffalo, Wyo., May 13, 1943; s. George Weber and Marianne (Parsons) L.; m. Lisa Scruggs; children: Stephen Lee, Joshua Byron, Kristopher Byron, Katherine Byron. AB, Dartmouth Coll., Hanover, N.H., 1965; MAT in French, Harvard U., 1969; JD, U. Miss., Oxford, 1978. Bar: Miss. 1978, U.S. Dist. Ct. (no. dist.) Miss. 1978, U.S. Ct. Appeals (5th cir.) 1979, U.S. Dist. Ct. (so. dist.) Miss. 1985, U.S. Supreme Ct. 1990, U.S. Claims Ct. 1991. Pvt. practice Oxford, 1978-81; assoc. Hill, Lewis & Bell, Oxford, 1981-83, Hill & Lewis, Oxford, 1983-86, Holcomb, Dunbar, Connell, Chaffin & Willard, Oxford, 1986-88; pvt. practice Oxford, 1988—; CJA criminal def. tng. coord. No. Jud. Dist., Miss., 1991—, CJA panel rep. to nat. confs., 1995-99. Mem. Lafayette County Dem. Exec. Com., Oxford, 1985-96, chmn., 1987-91; bd. dirs. ACLU of Miss., 1989-90, Miss. Assn. for Children with Learning Disabilities, 1990-91. Mem. ABA, ATLA, Nat. Assn. Criminal Def. Lawyers, Miss. Trial Lawyers, Miss. Bar, Lafayette County Bar Assn., Am. Inn. of Ct. Ill. (bencher). Labor, Civil rights, Criminal. Office: PO Box 207 607 S Lamar Blvd Oxford MS 38655-4428

**LEWIS, STEPHEN C.,** prosecutor. U.S. atty. Dept. Justice, Tulsa, 1993—. Office: US Attys Office Page Belcher Fed Bldg 333 W 4th St Ste 3460 Tulsa OK 74103-3880

**LEWIS, TIMOTHY K.,** federal judge; b. 1954. BA, Tufts U., 1976; JD, Duquesne U., 1980. Asst. dist. atty. Allegheny County Dist. Attys. Office, Pa., 1980-83; asst. U.S. atty. U.S. Attys. Office (we. dist.) Pa., 1983-91; fed. judge U.S. Dist. Ct. (we. dist.) Pa., 1991-92; fed. judge U.S. Ct. Appeals (3d cir.), Pitts., 1992-99, ret., 1999; vis. com. mem. U. Chgo. Law Sch., 1993-96. Former bd. dirs. Ctr. Victims Violent Crime; former mem. Aid Citizen Enterprise. Mem. Pa. Bar Assn. (del. to PBA ho. of dels. 1989-91), Allegheny County Bar Assn. (mem. jud. com. 1988-90, mem. profl. ethics com., mem. planning com., chmn. subcom. minorities in law of planning com., mem. nominating com., mem. fin. com., mem. minorities mentor program, mem. women in law com., fed. ct. sect.), Homer S. Brown Bar Assn., The Boule, Alpha House (former bd. dirs.). Office: US Ct of Appeals 3rd Cir 219 US Courthouse 7th Ave and Grant St Pittsburgh PA 15219

**LEWIS, WILLIAM HENRY, JR.,** lawyer; b. Durham, N.C., Nov. 12, 1942; s. William Henry Sr. and Phyllis Lucille (Phillips) L.; m. Jo Ann Whitsett, Apr. 17, 1965 (div. Sept. 1982); 1 child, Kimberly N.; m. Peyton Cockrill Davis, Nov. 28, 1987. Student, N.C. State U., 1960-63; AB in Polit. Sci., U. N.C., 1965, JD with honors, 1969. Bar: Calif., D.C., U.S. Dist. Ct. (cen. dist.) Calif., U.S. Ct. Appeals (D.C. cir., 2nd and 5th cirs.), U.S. Supreme Ct. Assoc. Latham & Watkins, Los Angeles, 1969-74; exec. officer Calif. Air Resources Bd., Los Angeles and Sacramento, Calif., 1975-78; dir. Nat. Com. on Air Quality, Washington, 1978-81; counsel Wilmer, Cutler & Pickering, Washington, 1981-84; ptnr. Morgan, Lewis & Bockius LLP, Washington, 1984—, mgr. nat. environ. practice, 1999—; spl. advisor on environ. policy State of Calif., L.A. and Sacramento, 1975; lectr. Law Sch. U. Va., 1993—. Bd. dirs. For Love of Children, Inc., Washington, 1985-95, pres., 1987-91; bd. dirs. Advs. for Families, Washington, 1985-87, Hillandale Homeowners Assn., Washington, 1986-87, Thurgood Marshall Ctr. Trust, Washington, 1989-95; mem. EPA Clean Air Act Adv. Com., 1994—; chmn. bd. dirs., co-founder The Montpelier Found., 1998—. Mem. ABA. Environmental, Federal civil litigation. Home: 3900 Georgetown Ct NW Washington DC 20007-2127 also: 18454 Monteith Farm Rd Gordonsville VA 22942-7560 Office: Morgan Lewis & Bockius LLP 1800 M St NW Washington DC 20036-5802

**LEWIS, WILMA ANTOINETTE,** prosecutor, former federal agency administrator; b. Santurce, P.R.. BA with distinction, Swarthmore Coll., 1978; JD, Harvard U., 1981. Assoc. Steptoe & Johnson, Washington, 1981-1986; asst. U.S. atty. civil divsn. U.S. Atty.'s Office, Washington, 1986-1993; assoc. solicitor divsn. gen. law U.S. Dept. Interior, 1993-95, inspector gen., 1995-98; U.S. atty. Dept. Justice, Washington, 1998—; mem. civil justice reform act adv. group U.S. Dist. Ct. D.C., mem. adv. com. on local rules; adj. faculty mem. George Washington U. Nat. Law Ctr.; mem. faculty Coll. Trial Advocacy. Mem. Phi Beta Kappa. Office: US Atty's Office Judiciary Ctr 555 4th St NW Washington DC 20001-2733

**LEWITUS, MARLA BERMAN,** lawyer; b. N.Y.C.; d. Myron P. and Roslyn Berman. BS, Georgetown U., 1981; JD, NYU, 1985. Bar: N.Y. 1986. Corp. assoc. Parker Chapin Flattau & Klimpl, N.Y.C., 1985-91; sr. counsel Primerica Corp., N.Y.C., 1991-93; asst. gen. counsel Travelers Group Inc. (formerly Primerica Corp.), N.Y.C., 1993-98; assoc. gen. counsel Citigroup Inc. (formerly Travelers Group Inc.), N.Y.C., 1998-99; sr. v.p., gen. counsel Travelers Life & Annuity, Hartford, Conn., 1999—. Mem. Phi Beta Kappa. Securities, General corporate, Mergers and acquisitions.

**LEYHANE, FRANCIS JOHN, III,** lawyer; b. Chgo., Mar. 29, 1957; s. Francis J. and Mary Elizabeth (Crowley) L.; m. Diana M. Urizarri, May 8, 1982; children: Katherine, Francis J. IV, Joseph, Brigid Rose, James Matthew. BA, Loyola U., Chgo., 1977, JD, 1980. Bar: Ill. 1980, U.S. Dist. Ct. (no. dist.) Ill. 1980, U.S. Ct. Appeals (7th cir.) 1986. Assoc. Condon, Cook & Roche, Chgo., 1980-87; ptnr. Condon & Cook, Chgo., 1988-98, Boyle & Leyhane, Ltd., Chgo., 1998—. Contbr. articles to profl. jours. Mem. Sch. bd. Immaculate Conception Parish, Chgo., 1993-96. Fellow Ill. Bar Found.; mem. Appellate Lawyers Assn. Ill., Ill. State Bar Assn. (mem. assembly 1987-90), Chgo. Bar Assn., Blue Key. Appellate, Insurance, State civil litigation. Office: Boyle & Leyhane Ltd 9924 S Walden Pkwy Chicago IL 60643-1806

**LEZAMIZ, JOHN T.,** lawyer; b. Boise, Idaho, Sept. 12, 1952; s. Sid and Luchy L.; children: Brett, Luke, Jodi. BA, Coll. Idaho, 1974; JD, U. Idaho, 1977. Legal clerk Idaho Supreme Ct., Boise, 1977-78; assoc. Hepworth, Lezamiz & Hohnhorst, Twin Falls, Idaho, 1978-80, ptnr., 1980—. Fellow. Am. Coll. Trial Lawyers, Am. Inns. Ct.; mem. Am. Bd. Trial Advocacy (treas.), Idaho Trial Lawyers Assn. Personal injury, Insurance, Product liability. Office: Hepworth Lezamiz & Hohnhorst PO Box 389 Twin Falls ID 83303-0389

**LI, BENJAMIN MIN,** lawyer; b. China, Jan. 8, 1956; came to U.S., 1986.; m. Shasha Liu, Jan. 1, 1986; children: Alexader, Janelaine. LLM, Wuhan U., 1986, Temple U., 1988; JD, Washburn U., 1992. Immigration, naturalization, and customs, Private international, General practice. Office: 4912 Park Rd Charlotte NC 28209-3506

**LI, DONNA DONGLI,** lawyer; b. China, Nov. 24, 1956; came to U.S., 1984; d. Dulie and Kewu (Wu) L.; m. Jianguo Tang, Aug. 1, 1986; children: Anna Tang, Lisa Tang. BA, Beijing 2d Fgn. Lang. Inst., 1982; MA, U. Notre Dame, 1987; JD, Albany Law Sch., 1996. Bar: N.Y. 1996. Assoc. Kaye, Scholer, Fierman, Hays & Handler, LLP, N.Y.C., 1996-98, Winthrop, Stimson, Putnam & Roberts, N.Y.C., 1998—. Mem. Assn. Bar City N.Y. (mem. Asian affairs com. 1997—), Justinian Soc. E-mail: lid@winstim.com. Finance, General corporate, Private international. Office: Winthrop Stimson et al One Battery Park Plz New York NY 10004

**LI, REBECCA JIA,** lawyer; b. Chengdu, China, June 28, 1968; came to U.S., 1990; d. Ying Li. BS, Beijing U., 1990; MA, U. Chgo., 1993, JD, 1996. Bar: N.Y. 1996. Assoc. Sullivan & Cromwell, Hong Kong, 1997-98, N.Y.C., 1996-97, 98—. Mem. Bar Assn. City of N.Y. (mem. various coms.). Finance, Securities, Private international. Office: Sullivan & Cromwell 125 Broad St Fl 28 New York NY 10004-2489

**LIA, JAMES DOUGLAS,** lawyer; b. Utica, N.Y., Sept. 26, 1939; s. Vito Sebastian and Emma (Rotundo) Lee. BA, Syracuse U., 1962; JD, Stanford U., 1965. Bar: Calif. 1966, U.S. Dist. Ct. (no. and so. dists.) Calif. 1966, U.S. Ct. Appeals (9th cir.) 1966, Mich. 1982. Assoc. Law Office of A.C. Zief, San Francisco, 1965-72; ptnr. Law Office of Lia & Combs, San Francisco, 1972-77; pvt. practice San Francisco, Prescott, Mich., 1977-82; corp. counsel Farm Credit Banks, Saginaw, Mich., 1983-86; pvt. practice L.A., 1986—. Mem. Lions. Fax: (562) 596-3294. E-mail: cheezio@earthlink.net. Personal injury, General practice, Family and matrimonial. Office: 3662 Katella Ave Ste 117 Los Alamitos CA 90720-3174

**LIACOS, PAUL JULIAN,** retired state supreme judicial court chief justice; b. Peabody, Mass., Nov. 20, 1929; s. James A. and Pitsa K. (Karis) L.; m. Maureen G. McKean, Oct. 6, 1954; children: James P., Diana M., Mark C., Gregory A. AB magna cum laude, Boston U. Coll. Liberal Arts, 1950; LLB magna cum laude, Boston U., 1952; LLM, Harvard U., 1953; diploma, Air Command and Staff Sch., 1954; LLD, Suffolk U., 1984, New Eng. Sch. Law, 1985; LHD (hon.), Salem State Coll., 1988; LLD, Northeastern U., 1991, Boston U., 1996. Bar: Mass. 1952, U.S. Dist. Ct. Mass. 1954, U.S. Ct. Mil. Appeals 1955, U.S. Ct. Appeals (1st cir.) 1971, U.S. Supreme Ct. 1980. Ptnr. firm Liacos and Liacos, Peabody, Mass., 1952-76; prof. law Boston U., 1952-76, adj. prof. law, 1976-89; assoc. justice Mass. Supreme Jud. Ct., 1976-89, chief justice, 1989-96; Disting. lectr. on law U.S. Mil. Acad., West Point, N.Y., 1972; lectr. Suffolk U. Sch. Law, 1978-79; U.S. Constn. Bicentennial lectr. Boston Pub. Libr., 1987; cons. on staffing and pers. Atty. Gen. of Mass., 1974-75; lectr. on criminal evidence Boston Police Acad., 1963-64; reporter New Eng. Conf. on Def. of the Indigent, Harvard Law Sch., 1963; reader and cons. on legal manuscripts Little, Brown & Co., Boston, 1968-76; editl. cons. Warren, Gorham & Lamont, 1968-69; mem. State Ethics Commn., 1998—; mem. steering com. Lawyers Com. for Civil Rights under Law, Boston, 1969-72; chmn. com. on discrimination in the cts. Conf. of Chief Justices, 1993-96. Author: Handbook of Massachusetts Evidence, 6th edit., 1994, supplement, 1998, 98; contbr. articles in field to legal jours.; book rev. editor Boston U. law Rev., 1952. Trustee Suffolk U., Boston, 1993—; trustee, mem. exec. com. Chamberlayne Sch. and Jr. Coll., Boston, 1982-84; trustee Anatolia Coll., Salonika, Greece, 1980—, exec. com., 1986-89; hon. trustee Deree-Pierce Colls., Athens, 1976—; corp. mem. MIT, 1989-96. Named Man of Yr. Boston U. Law Sch., 1952, Man of Yr. Alpha Omega, 1977, Mem. Colleguum Disting. Alumni Boston U. Coll. Liberal Arts, 1974; recipient Disting. Pub. Svc. award Boston U. Alumni, 1980, Allied Profl. award Mass. Psychol. Assn., 1987, Man of Vision award Nat. Soc. to Prevent Blindness, 1988, State Bill of Rights award Nat. Assn. Criminal Def. Lawyers, 1988, Good Neighbor award Mishkan Tefila Brotherhood, 1990, Founders' award Lawyers Com. for Civil Rights Under the Law, Boston Bar Assn., 1993, citation of jud. excellence Boston Bar Assn., 1995, Ehrman award Mass. Crime and Justice Found., 1996, award Fed. Bar Assn., 1996, Mass. Jud. Conf. award, 1996, Social Law Libr. award, 1996. Mem. ABA (jud. cert. of appreciation 1994), ATLA (editor 1968-73, Outstanding State Appellate Judge 1982), Mass. Bar Assn. (criminal law com. 1964-66), Essex County Bar Assn., Peabody Bar Assn., Greater Lowell Bar Assn. (hon.), Harvard Law Sch. Assn., Mass. Supreme Jud. Ct. Hist. Soc. (chmn. 1996—), Boston U. Law Sch. Alumni Assn. (Silver Shingle award 1977), Phi Beta Kappa. Democrat. Mem. Greek Orthodox Ch.

**LIAPIS, GEORGIA P.,** lawyer; b. Chgo., Feb. 2, 1970. BBA cum laude, Loyola U., Chgo., 1992; JD, Mass. Sch. Law, 1996. Bar: Mass. 1996. Law clk. Peter F. Geraci Law Office, Chgo., 1991-92; auditor Lake Shore Bank, Chgo., 1992-92; law clk., atty. Law Office Christos C. Biotos, Somerville, Mass., 1995-97; pvt. practice Boston, 1997—; v.p., exec. bd. AXION, Boston, 1996—; v.p., co-founder Hellenic Bus. Network, Boston, 1997—. Mem. Women's Bar Assn., Mass. Bar Assn., Boston Bar Assn., Golden Key. Avocations: reading, public speaking, dancing, tennis, running. Real property, Personal injury. Home: 9448 W Loomis Rd # 4 Franklin WI 53132-9666 Office: 220 Lewis Wharf Boston MA 02110-3927

**LIBBY, GENE ROGER,** lawyer; b. Portland, Maine, Oct. 31, 1951; s. Leon and Doris (Jordan) L.; m. Mary J. Kerry, July 25, 1970; children: Jessica, Katie, Matthew, Lindsay. BS in Econs., U. So. Maine, 1974; JD, U. Maine, 1978. Bar: Maine 1978, U.S. Dist. Ct. Maine 1978. Ptnr. Cervizzi & Libby, Scarborough, Maine, 1978-79; asst. dist. atty. York County State of Maine, Alfred, 1979-80, dep. dist. atty. York County, 1980-81, dist. atty. York County, 1981-85; ptnr., gen. counsel, loss prevention officer Verrill & Dana, Kennebunk, Maine, 1986—; bd. dirs. Sentencing Options, Portland, Maine. Mem. Maine Hwy. Traffic Safety Commn., 1982-83, Gov.'s Group on Child Abuse & Neglect, Maine, 1984; pres. Maine Prosecutor's Assn., 1984-85; chmn. York County Budget Com., 1993-97. Mem. ABA, Maine Bar Assn., York County Bar Assn., Assn. Trial Lawyers Am., Nat. Assn. Criminal Def. Lawyers, Maine Trial Lawyers Assn. Democrat. Roman Catholic. Avocations: hockey, racquetball, jogging. E-mail: GRL@verdan.com. Criminal, General civil litigation, Personal injury. Office: Verrill & Dana Lafayette Ctr PO Box 147 Kennebunk ME 04043-0147

**LIBER, JOHN (DOUGLAS),** lawyer; b. Salem, Ohio, Aug. 23, 1938; m. Nancy Bergren, Aug. 30, 1959; children: John R. II, Craig, Shannon. BS, Purdue U., 1960; JD, Ohio State U., 1963. Bar: Ohio 1963. Ptnr. Manchester, Bennett, Powers & Ullman, Youngstown, Ohio, 1963-72, Spangenberg, Shibley & Liber, Cleve., 1972—. Bd. dirs. Partnership for a Safer Cleve. Recipient Spangenberg award Cleve. Acad. Trial Attys., 1987. Fellow Am. Bar Found., Am. Bd. Trial Advocates, Am. Coll. Trial Lawyers, Internat. Soc. Barristers, Ohio Bar Found.; mem. Cleve. Acad. Trial Lawyers, Ohio Acad. Trial Lawyers (pres. 1985-86), Assn. Trial Lawyers Am. (bd. govs. 1987—), Shaker Heights (Ohio) Country Club, Wilderness Country Club (Naples, Fla.), Cleve. Bar Assn. (pres.), Ohio Met. Bar Assn. (pres.). General civil litigation, Personal injury. Office: Spangenberg Shibley & Liber 1900 E 9th St Ste 2400 Cleveland OH 44114-3498

**LIBERMAN, DAVID ISRAEL,** lawyer; b. St. Louis, June 26, 1965; s. Samuel and Myrna Rae L.; m. Linda May Fitts, Apr. 21, 1996; 1 child, Hannah Rose. Student, Am. Coll. Switzerland, Leysin, 1986; BA, Colo. Coll., 1987; JD, U. Colo., 1993. Bar:Colo. 1993, U.S. Dist. Ct. Colo. 1994. Advtsg. acct. exec. Intermountain Jewish News, Denver, 1988-89; bus. reporter The Denver Bus. Jour., 1989; legal asst. Natural Resources Law Ctr., Boulder, Colo., 1991; law clk. Native Am. Rights Fund, Boulder, 1991-93; assoc. MacDougall Law Office, Colorado Springs, Colo., 1994-99; asst. city atty. City of Thornton, Colo., 1999—. Contbr. articles to profl. jours., newspapers. Wilderness counselor Camp Nebagamon for Boys, Lake Nebagamon, Wis., 1985, 87, 88; counselor Developmental Disabilities Ctr., Boulder, Colo., 1989-90; commr. El Paso County (Colo.) Bd. Planning, 1996-99. Mem. Colo. Bar Assn., Spl. Dist. Assn., El Paso County Bar Assn. (mem. professionalism com. 1998-99), Temple Shalom Men's Club (treas. 1997-99). Democrat. Jewish. Avocations: family, hiking, sports, skiing. General civil litigation, Real property, Appellate. Office: City of Thornton 9500 Civic Center Dr Thornton CO 80229-4300

**LIBERMAN, KEITH GORDON,** lawyer; b. St. Louis, Aug. 2, 1956; s. Maurice Pierce and Doris (Gordon) L.; children: Danni Elaine, Jacob August, Caleb Samuel; m. Nancy Homsher. BS, Tulane U., 1978; JD, U. Mo., 1982. Bar: Mo. 1982, U.S. Dist. Ct. (we. dist.) Mo. 1982, U.S. Dist. Ct. (ea. dist.) Mo. 1983, U.S. Supreme Ct. 1987. Assoc. Wolff & Frankel, Clayton, Mo., 1984-85; counsel Wolff & Mass, Clayton, 1985-86; pvt. practice, St. Louis, 1986—; chmn. Law Related Edn. Commn., St. Louis, 1987-88. Author: (column) Professional Ethics and Methods of Practice Committee, 1987-89, chmn., 1990-94. Treas. Jay Nixon for U.S. Senate Com., 1987-88. Mem. ATLA, Bar Assn. Metro. St. Louis. Democrat. Jewish. Avocation: tennis. Personal injury, Criminal. Office: 7912 Bonhomme Ave Ste 214 Saint Louis MO 63105-3512

**LIBERMAN, SCOTT A.,** lawyer; b. Knoxville, Tenn., Jan. 19, 1966; m. Ann M. Liberman; 1 child, Andrea S. BS in Pub. Policy, Ind. U., 1988; JD, U. Dayton, 1991. Bar: Ohio 1992, U.S. Dist. Ct. (so. dist.) Ohio 1992, U.S. Ct. Appeals (6th cir.) 1993. Law clk. McHugh & McHugh, Dayton, Ohio, 1989-92; assoc. McHugh & McHugh, Dayton, 1992-93; assoc. Altick & Corwin Co., LPA, Dayton, 1993-98, shareholder, 1998—; spkr. in field. Chmn. Centerville/Washington Twp. Bicentennial Commn., 1993-96; com. mem. Washington Twp. Bd. Zoning Appeals, 1997—. Mem. Ohio State Bar Assn., Dayton Bar Assn., Comml. Law League, Jr. C. of C. (pres. 1993-94). Consumer commercial, Real property, General corporate. Office: Altick & Corwin Co LPA 1700 One Dayton Ctr Dayton OH 45402-2024

**LIBERT, DONALD JOSEPH,** lawyer; b. Sioux Falls, S.D., Mar. 23, 1928; s. Bernard Joseph and Eleanor Monica (Sutton) L.; m. Jo Anne Murray, May 16, 1953; children: Cathleen, Thomas, Kevin, Richard, Stephanie. B.S. magna cum laude in Social Scis., Georgetown U., 1950, LL.B., 1956. Bar: Ohio. From assoc. to ptnr. Manchester, Bennett, Powers & Ullman, Youngstown, Ohio, 1956-65; various positions to v.p., gen. counsel and sec. Youngstown Sheet & Tube Co., 1965-78; assoc. group counsel LTV Corp., Youngstown and Pitts., 1979; v.p. and gen. counsel Anchor Hocking Corp., Lancaster, Ohio, 1979-87; pvt. practice Lancaster, 1987—. Served to lt. (j.g.) USN, 1951-54. Mem. Ohio Bar Assn. (former chmn. sr. lawyers com.), Fairfield County Bar Assn. (mem. alt. dispute resolution com.), Lancaster Country Club, Rotary. Republican. Roman Catholic. Administrative and regulatory, Antitrust, General corporate. Office: 127 W Wheeling St Lancaster OH 43130-3737

**LIBERTH, RICHARD FRANCIS,** lawyer; b. Bklyn., Mar. 1, 1950; s. S. Richard and Frances J. (Falconer) L.; m. Lisa M. Feenick, June 8, 1974; children: Andrew R., Erica M. BS in Bus. Adminstrn., U. Denver, 1972; JD, Bklyn. Law Sch., 1976. Bar: N.Y. 1977, U.S. Dist. Ct. (so. and ea. dists.) N.Y. 1981, U.S. Dist. Ct. (no. dist.) N.Y. 1991. Staff atty. Mental Health Legal Svcs., Poughkeepsie, N.Y., 1976-78; sr. asst. dist. atty. Rockland County Dist. Attys. Office, N.Y.C., 1978-81; prin. Drake, Sommers, Loeb, Tarshis & Catania, Newburgh, N.Y., 1981—; atty. Fraternal Order of Police Lodge #957. Dir. Legal Aid Soc. Orange County, Goshen, N.Y., 1982-84, Orange County Cerebral Palsy Assn., Goshen, 1986-89; mem. Rep. Nat. Com., Washington, 1990—; Rep. chmn. Town of Woodbury, 1997—. Mem. N.Y. Bar Assn., Newburgh Bar Assn. (pres. 1991), Orange County Bar Assn. (v.p. 1995, pres. 1997), Woodbury Lions Club (Central Valley, N.Y.) (past pres.). Avocations: golf, tennis, reading, collecting. Product liability, General civil litigation. Home: 50 Buena Vista Ter Central Valley NY 10917-3515 Office: Drake Sommers Loeb Tarshis & Catania One Corwin Ct Newburgh NY 12550

**LIBERTY, ARTHUR ANDREW,** judge; b. Oak Park, Ill., Nov. 7, 1954; s. Arthur and Patricia (Horton) L.; m. G. Jean Liberty, Nov. 22, 1980; children: Rebecca, Rachael. BS, Regents Coll., Albany, 1983; JD with honors, Ill. Inst. Tech., Chgo., 1987. Bar: Ill. 1987, U.S. Dist. Ct. (no. dist.) Calif. 1988, U.S. Dist. Ct. (no. dist.) Ill., 1992, U.S. Dist. Ct. (cen. dist.) Ill., 1995, U.S. Ct. Appeals (7th cir.) 1992, U.S. Ct. Appeals (9th cir.) 1989. Asst. dist. counsel U.S. Immigration and Naturalization Service, San Francisco, Chgo., 1987-88, 91-92; sector counsel U.S. Border Patrol, Livermore, Calif., 1988-91; ptnr. Azulay & Azulay, Chgo., 1992-95; pvt. practice Chgo. and Joliet, Ill., 1995-97; U.S. adminstrv. law judge Office of Hearings and Appeals, Detroit, 1997-98; chief U.S. adminstrv. law judge Office of Hearings and Appeals, Evansville, Ind., 1998—; spl. asst. U.S. atty. ea. dist. Calif., Fresno, 1988-91; instr. law and legal procedure Fed. Law Enforcement Tng. Ctr., Artesia, N.Mex., 1989-91. Contbr. articles to profl. books. Office: Office of Hearings and Appeals US Court House Rm 272 101 NW Martin L King Jr Evansville IN 47708-1989

**LIBNER, MAURICE ALAN,** lawyer; b. Ann Arbor, Mich., Mar. 20, 1953; s. Robert and Ruth (Garfunkel) L.; m. Sharon C. Bouchard, July 13, 1980; 1 child, Dena. BS, MIT, 1974; JD cum laude, Boston U., 1977. Bar: Maine 1977, U.S. Dist. Ct., Maine, 1977. Ptnr. McTeague Higbee, Libner, MacAdam, Case & Watson, Topsham, Maine, 1977-95; pvt. practice Brunswick, 1995—. Contbr. articles to profl. jours. Mem. Assn. Trial Lawyers Am. (Maine chpt., Maine bd. govs. 1991-93), Maine Bar Assn. Democrat. Jewish. Office: PO Box G Brunswick ME 04011-0831

**LICATA, ARTHUR FRANK,** lawyer; b. N.Y.C., June 16, 1947. BA in English, Le Moyne Coll., 1969; postgrad., SUNY, Binghampton, 1969-71; JD cum laude, Suffolk U., 1976. Bar: Mass. 1977, N.Y. 1985, U.S. Ct. Appeals (1st cir.) 1977, U.S. Dist. Ct. Mass. 1977, admitted Frank B. Murray, Jr. Inns of Ct. 1990-92. Assoc. Parker, Coulter, Daley & White, Boston, 1977-82; pvt. practice Arthur F. Licata P.C., Boston, 1982—; prin. Ardlee Internat. Trading Co., Ea. and Ctrl. Europe and Russia, 1989—; del. White House Conf. on Trade and Investment in Ctrl. Europe, Cleve., 1995; lectr. Mass. Continuing Legal Edn., Boston, 1982-90, mem. trial adv. com., 1984-88; mem. working group on drinking and drunk driving Harvard Sch. Pub. Health Ctr. for Health Comms., 1986; spkr. Conv. Nat. Fedn. Paralegal Assns., Boston, 1987; del. U.S.-People's Republic of China Joint Session on Trade, Investment and Econ. Law, Beijing, 1987; co-sponsor Estonian legal del. visit to Mass. and N.H. correctional instns., 1990; Boston host former Soviet legal del. visit, 1989; legal advisor Czech Anglo-Am. Bus. Inst., Prague, Czech Republic, 1989—, Russian Children's Fund, 1992-94, Estonia Acad. for Pub. Safety, 1992-94; adv. bd. Ford Found.'s Legal Resource Ctr., Czech Republic, 1994-96; participant U.S.-Russian Investment Symposium, Harvard U., 1997, spkr. Harvard Law Sch., 1997. Panel mem. sta. WBZ TV, Boston; contbr. articles to profl. jours. U.S. Del. 6th People to People Juvenile Justice Program to USSR, Moscow, 1989; legal advisor Mass. chpt. MADD, Plymouth County, 1984-87; mem. State Adv. Com. Med. Malpractice, Boston, 1985; bd. dirs. Boston Ctr. for the Arts, 1990-94; mem. profl. adv. bd. Mass. Epilepsy Assn., 1986-93; counsel state coord. commn. MADD, Mass., 1984-86. Recipient Outstanding Citizen award Mothers Against Drunk Driving, 1986. Fellow Mass. Bar Found.; mem. ABA, ATLA, Mass. Bar Assn. (bd. dirs., young lawyers sect. 1979-80, 21st Century Club 1984), Mass. Acad. Trial Attys. (bd. dirs. 1991-99, exec. com. 1997-99), Nat. Bd. Trial Advocacy (bd. cert. civil trial advocate 1992—. Avocation: travel. Fax: (617) 523-7743. E-mail: Licata@worldnet.att.net. Personal injury, General civil litigation, Private international. Office: Fed Res Plz 600 Atlantic Ave 27th Fl Boston MA 02210-2211

**LICATESI, ANTHONY JOSEPH,** lawyer; b. Bklyn., Mar. 9, 1963; s. Thomas and Marianna L.; m. Caryn Gail Navarro, Sept. 5, 1988; children: Danielle, Thomas, Michael. BS, NYU, 1984; JD, Hofstra U., 1987. Bar: N.Y. 1988. Litigating ptnr. Rubin & Licatesi, PC, Garden City, N.Y., 1989—; guest lectr. Am. Arbitration Assn., Garden City, 1998, N.Y. State Chiropractic Coun., 1988—, N.Y. State Chiropractic Assn., 1988—. Mem. N.Y. State Trial Lawyers, Nassau County Bar Assn. Personal injury, Real property, Banking. Office: Rubin and Licatesi PC 600 Old Country Rd Garden City NY 11530-2001

**LICCARDO, SALVADOR A.,** lawyer; b. San Francisco, Mar. 15, 1935; s. Samuel and Rosalie (Pizzo) L.; m. Laura Liccardo, Nov. 21, 1959; children—Laura, Kathleen, Paul, Rosalie, Sam. B.A., U. Santa Clara, 1956, J.D., 1961. Bar: Calif. 1962, U.S. Ct. Appeals (9th cir.) 1962, U.S. Supreme Ct. 1966. Sole practice law, San Jose, Calif., 1962-65; ptnr. Caputo & Liccardo, San Jose, 1965-76; pres./officer Caputo, Liccardo, Rossi & Sturges, P.C., San Jose, 1976-82; pres. Caputo, Liccardo, Rossi, Sturges & McNeil, P.C., San Jose, 1982—; mem. Santa Clara County Joint Com. of Bench and Bar on Ct. Reorgn.; lectr. in field. Editor-in-chief Jour. Calif. Trial Lawyers Assn., 1981. Contbr. articles to profl. jours. Founder, bd. dirs., officer Trial Lawyers for Pub. Justice, Washington, 1983—, pres. 1989-90 ; pres. bd. regents Bellermine Prep. Coll., San Jose, 1982—; mem. bd. fellows U. Santa Clara. Served to 1st lt. U.S. Army, 1956-58. Recipient Cert. of Appreciation for Service as Judge Pro Tem Santa Clara County Superior Ct., 1982-84; Michael Shallo award in polit. sci. U. Santa Clara, 1956, Silver medal for outstanding student, 1956. Fellow Internat. Acad. Trial Lawyers; mem. Inner Circle of Advocates, Am. Bd. Trial Advocates, Assn. Trial Lawyers of Am., ABA, Calif. Trial Lawyers Assn. (bd. dirs. 1976-82, 87—), Am. Bd. Profl. Liability Attys. Democrat. Roman Catholic. Club: Civic. State civil litigation, Personal injury, Product liability. Office: Caputo Liccardo Rossi Sturges & McNeil 1960 The Alameda Fl 2D San Jose CA 95126-1441

**LICCIONE, MAUREEN T.,** lawyer; b. N.Y.C., Sept. 4, 1953; m. Kenneth F. Lindahl Jr., Nov. 27, 1981; children, Elizabeth Rogan Lindahl, Emily Nelson Lindahl. BA, Siena Coll., Loudonville, N.Y., 1975; JD, St. John's U., 1981. Bar: N.Y. 1982, U.S. Dist. Ct. (ea. and so. dists.) N.Y. 1982. Legis. aide N.Y. State Senate, 1972-78; student legal specialist City of N.Y., N.Y.C., 1978-81, asst. corp. counsel, 1981-85; ptnr. Twomey, Latham, Shea & Kelley, Riverhead, N.Y., 1985—. Mem. N.Y. State Bar Assn., Suffolk County Bar Assn. General practice, General civil litigation, Environmental. Office: Twomey Latham Shea & Kelley 33 W 2nd St # 398 Riverhead NY 11901-2701 also: 400 Townline Rd Hauppauge NY 11788-2838

**LICHT, RICHARD A.,** lawyer; b. Providence, Mar. 25, 1948; s. Julius M. Licht and Irene (Lash) Olson; m. Roanne Sragow; children: Jordan David, Jeremy Michael, Jaclyn Rose. AB cum laude, Harvard U., 1968, JD cum laude, 1972; LLM in Taxation, Boston U., 1975. Law clk. to chief justice R.I. Supreme Ct., Providence, 1973-74; ptnr. Letts, Quinn & Licht, Providence, 1974-84; mem. R.I. Senate, Providence, 1975-84, chmn. judiciary com. and rules com., 1984; lt. gov. State of R.I., Providence, 1985-89; ptnr. Tillinghast, Licht & Semonoff, Providence, 1989—; former chmn. R.I. Commn. on Racial, Religious and Ethnic Harrassment, Dr. Martin Luther King Jr. Holiday Commn., State Energy and Tech. Study Commn. rules com.; chmn. Coun. of State Govt., Intergovtl. Affairs Com., Nat. Focus Team, Bd. Gov. Higher Edn.; bd. regents Elem. and Secondary Edn.; mem. Pub. Telecom. Authority R.I., Univ. R.I. Found., Community Coll. R.I. Found. Bd. dirs., mem. corp. Roger Williams Hosp.; advisor Community Prep. Sch.; corporator Roger Williams Hosp.; trustee Save the Bay, Inc., Emma Pendleton Bradley Hosp.; bd. dirs. Temple Emanuel, Providence, Jewish Fedn. R.I., Samaritans; chmn. Small Bus. Adv. Council, Task Force on Teenage Suicide Prevention, CD Civil Preparedness Adv. Council, Urban League R.I., 1980-82, John Hope Settlement House, 1976-81; chair Am. Cancer Soc. Ball, 1989, Jewish Fedn. R.I. Passage to Freedom, 1989; chair R.I. chpt. Anti-Defamation League; mem. Women and Infants Corp., Dorcas Place, PARI, UNITAM, NCLG task force of Youth Suicide Prevention, Jewish Home for the Aged of R.I., bd. govs. for the handicapped; active YWCA of Greater R.I., Vols. in Action, Inc., Big Sister Assn. of R.I., Big Bros. R.I.; coordinator vols. gubernatorial campaigns Frank Licht, 1968, 70; active Jewish Community Ctr., Providence, 1975-83, East Side Sr. Citizens Ctr., 1975-76, R.I. Youth Guidance Ctr., Inc., 1987, Block Island Conservancy, Inc., Notre Dame Health Care Corp., 1987; Dem. candidate for U.S. Senate, 1988; chmn. ann. campaign Meeting Street Sch., 1990-91, mem. steering com. for capital fund drive, 1989-92; mem. corp. Womens and Infants Hosp. Named an Outstanding Young Man of R.I., R.I. Jaycees, 1979; recipient David Ben Gurion award State of Israel Bonds, 1977, Outstanding Pub. Service award Temple Torat Yisrael, 1985, Disting. Services to the Hispanic Community award Casa Puerto Rico, 1985, Hon. Pub. Service award Meeting St. Sch., 1986, Recognition award R.I. Day Care Dirs. Assn., 1986, award of Appreciation Child Care/Human Services, 1986, Govtl. Services award Ocean State Residences for the Retarded, 1987. Mem. R.I. Bar Assn., Hosp. Assn. R.I. (bd. dirs. 1997). Democrat. Office: Tillinghast Licht & Semonoff One Park Row Providence RI 02903

**LICHTEN, RACHEL GORDON,** lawyer; b. Phila., Nov. 2, 1971; d. Joshua Hessel and Marilyn (Weiss) Gordon; m. Jason Brett Lichten, May 25, 1997. BA, Brandeis U., 1993; JD, U. Pa., 1996. Bar: Pa. 1996, N.J. 1996, U.S. Dist. Ct. (ea. dist.) Pa. 1996, U.S. Dist. Ct. N.J. 1996, U.S. Ct. Appeals (3d cir.) 1996, N.Y. 1999, U.S. Dist. Ct. (so. and ea. dists.) N.Y. 1999. Assoc. Fox, Rothschild, O'Brien & Frankel, LLP, Phila., 1996-98, Sonnenschein Nath & Rosenthal, N.Y.C., 1998—. Avocations: in-line skating, travel, reading. General civil litigation, Labor. Office: Sonnenschein Nath & Rosenthal 1221 Ave of Americas New York NY 10020

**LICHTENSTEIN, ELISSA CHARLENE,** legal association executive; b. Oct. 23, 1954; d. Mark and Rita (Field) L. AB cum laude, Smith Coll., Northampton, Mass., 1976; JD, George Washington U., 1979. Bar: D.C. 1980, U.S. Dist. Ct. (D.C. dist.) 1980, U.S. Ct. Appeals (D.C. cir.) 1980. Law clk. U.S. EPA, Washington, 1978-79; staff dir. ABA, Washington, 1979—, assoc. dir. pub. svcs. divsn., 1981-85, dir., 1985—. Editor, contbr.: Common Boundary/Common Problems: The Environmental Consequences of Energy Production, 1982, Exit Polls and Early Election Projections, 1984, The Global Environment: Challenges, Choices and Will, 1986, (newsletter) Environ. Law; co-editor, contbr. The Environ. Network; co-editor: Determining Competency in Guardianship Proceedings, 1990, Due Process Protections for Juveniles in Civil Commitment Proceedings, 1991, Environmental Regulation in Pacific Rim Nations, 1993, The Role of Law in the 1992 UN Conference on Environment and Development, 1992, Trade and the Environment in Pacific Rim Nations, 1994, Public Participation in Environmental Decisionmaking, 1995, Endangered Species Act Reauthorization: A Biocentric Approach, 1996, Sustainable Development in the Americas: The Emerging Role of the Private Sector, 1996, Environmental Priorities in Southeast Asian Nations, 1997, numerous others. Mem. Nat. Trust for Hist. Preservation. Named Outstanding Young Woman of Am., 1982. Mem. ABA, NAFE, Am. Soc. Assn. Execs., Washington Coun. Lawyers, Assn. Women in Comms., Inc., Environ. Law Inst. (assoc.), Met. Washington Environ. Profls. (pres. 1986-96), D.C. Bar Assn., Greater Washington Soc. Assn. Execs. Democrat. Jewish. Office: ABA Div Pub Svcs 740 15th St NW Fl 8 Washington DC 20005-1022

**LICHTENSTEIN, NATALIE G.,** lawyer; b. N.Y.C., Sept. 17, 1953; d. Abba G. and Cecile (Geffen) L.; m. Willard Ken Tom, June 10, 1979. AB summa cum laude, Radcliffe Coll., 1975; JD, Harvard U., 1978. Bar: D.C. 1978. Atty., advisor U.S. Dept. Treasury, Washington, 1978-80; prin. counsel World Bank, Washington, 1980-94, chief counsel East Asia and Pacific divsn. Legal Dept., 1995—; adj. prof. Chinese law Georgetown U., Washington, 1982-86. Contbr. articles on Chinese and Vietnamese law to profl. jours. Public international.

**LICHTENSTEIN, ROBERT JAY,** lawyer; b. Phila., Jan. 23, 1948; s. Irving M. and Marjorie J. (Weiss) L.; m. Sandra Paley, Aug. 14, 1971; children: David P., Kate. BS in Econs., U. Pa., 1969; JD, U. Pitts., 1973; LLM in Taxation, NYU, 1974. Bar: Pa. 1974, U.S. Tax Ct. 1978, U.S. Dist. Ct. (ea. dist.) Pa. 1979, U.S. Ct. Appeals (3rd cir.) 1982, U.S. Ct. Appeals (4th cir.) 1987. Ptnr. Saul, Ewing, Remick & Saul, 1978-88; assoc. Morgan, Lewis & Bockius, Phila., 1974-78, ptnr., 1988—; dir. Maritrans Inc.; instr. Main Line Paralegal Inst., Wayne, Pa., 1984-87, Paralegal Inst., Phila., 1987-90; adj. prof. law Villanova U. Sch. Law, 1991—, U. Pa. Sch. of Law, 1999—. Trustee Temple Brith Achim, King of Prussia, Pa., 1986-91. Mem. ABA, Pa. Bar Assn., Phila. Assn. Democrat. Avocations: skiing, tennis, reading. Taxation, general, Pension, profit-sharing, and employee benefits, Corporate taxation. Office: Morgan Lewis Bockius LLP 1701 Market St Philadelphia PA 19103-2903

**LICHTER-HEATH, LAURIE JEAN,** law educator; b. Bklyn., Mar. 13, 1951; d. Irving and Beatrice (Gelber) Lichter; m. Donald Wayne Heath, Feb. 28, 1981; children: Michele Samuel, Adam Ryan, Jason Charles. BS with honors, U. Tenn., Knoxville, 1972; JD, John Marshall Law Sch., 1975; postgrad. NYU, 1978; LLM, Georgetown U., 1979. Bar: Ill. 1975, D.C. 1977, N.Y. 1980, Nev. 1981. Law clk. D.C. Ct. Appeals, Washington, 1975-77; atty. enforcement div. SEC, Washington, 1977-78; lectr. NYU Sch. Continuing Edn. in Law and Taxation, 1980-81; atty. govt. relations asst. Met. Life Ins. Co., N.Y.C., 1978-81; assoc. atty. Miller & Daar, Reno, Nev. 1981; legal cons. Stockton, Calif., 1981-84; asst. prof. U. Pacific, Stockton, 1984-92, assoc. prof., 1992-93, cons. 1993—; cons. Kulisch & Koller Consulting, LLC, 1997—. adj. prof. U. S.D., 1998—. Instr., YMCA, Knoxville, 1969-72; leader Concerned Parents, Stockton, Calif., 1984. Mem. Coalition to Stop Food Irradiation; guest lectr. on Ethics U. Pacific Alumni Assn. U. Ill. fellow, 1972; presenter seminar Starting a New Bus. City of Stockton Bus. Devel. Program, 1985-88, seminars on sexual harassmant, 1992, 93. Co-author: Labor Management Relations in Changing Environment, 1991, 96; contbr. papers and articles to Am. Bus. Law Jour., and Labor Law Jour.; presenter in field. Mem. ABA, Nev. Bar Assn., N.Y. Bar Assn. D.C. Bar Assn., Ill. Bar Assn.

**LICKE, WALLACE JOHN,** lawyer; b. Bemidji, Minn., Jan. 23, 1945; s. George John and Lois (Sanford) L.; m. Martha Miriam Eddy, Dec. 19, 1969; children: Loriann, Paul. BA, U. Minn., 1967, MA, 1970, JD cum laude, 1973. Bar: Minn. 1973, U.S. Dist. Ct. Minn. 1973, U.S. Ct. Appeals (8th cir.) 1981, U.S. Supreme Ct. 1981. Instr. Itasca Community Coll., Grand Rapids, Minn., 1968—; assoc. Helgesen, Peterson, Engberg & Spector Attys. at Law (now Peterson, Engberg & Peterson), Mpls., 1972-75; sec., gen. counsel Blandin Paper Co. and Blandin Sales Corp. subs. Upm-Kymmene, Grand Rapids, 1975—; bd. dirs. Vol. Atty. Program Super Bd., Judy Garland Children's Mus.; chmn. bus. retention and expansion strategies program U. Minn.; mem. panel of arbitrators Am. Arbitration Assn. Mem. bd. editors Minn. Law Rev. Bd. dirs., pres. hon. bd. dirs. Itasca County Family YMCA, Grand Rapids; bd. dirs., v.p., pres. Itasca County unit Am. Cancer Soc.; bd. dirs., pres. Myles Reif Performing Arts Ctr.; chmn., sec. post com. computer-small bus. explorer post Boy Scouts Am.; adult leader 4-H program Agrl. Extension Svc., U. Minn., St. Paul; area rep. Minn. awareness project Minn. Internat. Ctr./World Affairs Ctr.; mem. Bass Brook Twp. (Minn.) Econ. Devel. Com.; mem. promotion and prospecting com. Itasca Devel. Corp.; trustee Grand Rapids area community found.; chmn. coop. solutions adv. bd., Grand Rapids, Minn.; bd. dirs. Judy Garland Children's Mus., Grand Rapids, Minn. Recipient William Spurgeon III award Boy Scouts Am., 1988; NDEA Title IV fellow, 1967, Paul Harris fellow. Mem. ABA (com. mem.), Fed. Bar Assn., Minn. Bar Assn. (del., planning com.), Itasca County Bar Assn. (past sec., pres.), Minn. 15th Dist. Bar Assn. (com. mem.), Am. Corp. Counsel Assn. (charter), Am. Soc. Corp. Secs., Grand Rapids C. of C. (chmn. com., bd. dirs.), Rotary (bd. dirs., pres., sec. Grand Rapids, dist. rep.), Order of Ski U Mah, Phi Beta Kappa. E-mail: john.licke@upm-kymmene.com. General corporate, Labor, General practice. Office: Blandin Paper Co 115 SW 1st St Grand Rapids MN 55744-3699

**LIDSKY, ELLA,** law librarian; b. Wilno, Poland; came to U.S. 1962; d. Leib and Sheina (Izygzon) Cwik; m. Alexander Lidsky, Feb. 20, 1963 (dec. Mar., 1996); 1 son, David Abraham. B.A., Pedagogical Inst. Odessa, USSR; M.S., Columbia U., 1966; M.A., 1973. Cert. Russian and Hebrew lang. tchr. Tchr. high sch., Poland, 1948-1951, elem. sch. Israel, 1961-62; asst. cataloger Tchrs. Coll., Columbia U., N.Y.C., 1966-68; cataloger Fairleigh Dickinson U., Teaneck, N.J., 1968-69, asst. dir. tech. services, Madison, N.J., 1973-84; head cataloger Ramapo Coll., Mahwah, N.J., 1971-73; asst. libr. U.S. Ct. Internat. Trade Law Libr., 1985—. Mem. Am. Assn. Law Libraries, Law Librarians of Greater N.Y., N.Y. Tech. Services Librarians, N.J. Law Librarians Assn. Democrat. Jewish. Avocations: music, travel. Office: US Ct Internat Trade One Federal Pla New York NY 10007

**LIDSTONE, HERRICK KENLEY, JR.,** lawyer; b. New Rochelle, N.Y., Sept. 10, 1949; s. Herrick Kenley and Marcia Edith (Drake) L.; m. Mary Lynne O'Toole, Aug. 5, 1978; children: Herrick Kevin, James Patrick, John Francis. AB, Cornell U., 1971; JD, U. Colo., 1978. Bar: Colo. 1978, U.S. Dist. Ct. Colo. 1978. Assoc. Roath & Brega, P.C., Denver, 1978-85, Brenman, Epstein, Raskin & Friedlob, P.C., Denver, 1985-86; shareholder Brenman, Raskin & Friedlob, P.C., Denver, 1986-94; mem. Friedlob Sanderson Raskin Paulson & Tourtilott, LLC, Denver, 1995-98, Norton Lidstone, LLC, Englewood, Colo., 1998—; adj. prof. U. Denver Coll. Law, 1985—; speaker in field various orgns.; fluent in Spanish. Editor U. Colo. Law Rev., 1977-78; co-author: Federal Income Taxation of Corporations, 6th edit.; contbg. author: Legal Opinion Letters Formbook, 1996; contbr. articles to profl. jours. Served with USN, 1971-75, with USNR, 1975-81. Mem. ABA (Am. Law Inst.), Colo. Bar Assn., Arapahoe County Bar Assn., Denver Assn. Oil and Gas Title Lawyers. General corporate, Securities, Mergers and acquisitions. Office: Norton Lidstone LLC 5445 Dtc Pkwy Ste 850 Englewood CO 80111-3076

**LIEB, CHARLES HERMAN,** lawyer; b. N.Y.C., July 21, 1907; s. Herman and Belle (Levy) L.; m. Maron Hatton, Nov. 29 1933. BS, U. Pa., 1927; LLB cum laude, Fordham U., 1930. Bar: N.Y. 1931, Conn. 1959. Assoc. Paskus, Gordon & Hyman, N.Y.C., 1931-39, ptnr., 1940-52, sr. ptnr., 1952-87; of counsel White & Case, N.Y.C., 1987-91, retired; past dir. John Wiley & Son, Inc., N.Y.C.. Served to 1st lt. ordinance corps AUS, 1942-45. Mem. ABA, N.Y. State Bar Assn., N.Y. County Bar Assn., Conn. Bar Assn., Copyright Soc. U.S.A. Clubs: Players, Harmonie (N.Y.C.); Aspetuck Valley Country (Weston, Conn.). Contbr. articles to profl. jours. Trademark and copyright, General corporate, General practice.

**LIEB, JOHN STEVENS,** lawyer; b. N.Y.C., Jan. 31, 1911; s. Hermann Johan and Evelyn Viola (Walls) L.; m. Helena Ann Warne, Sept. 18, 1942; children—Thomas (dec.), William. B.S. in Elec. Engring., NYU, 1936; J.D., Marquette U., 1948; B.A., U. Ariz., 1982; M.A., 1984. Bar: Wis. 1948; U.S. Dist. Ct. (ea. dist.) Wis. 1948, U.S. Ct. Customs and Patent Appeals 1953, U.S. Ct. Appeals (3d cir.) 1969, U.S. Ct. Appeals (Fed. cir.) 1982; registered patent agent U.S. Patent and Trademark Office, 1948; registered prof. engr., Wis. Patent atty. Allis-Chalmers, West Allis, Wis., 1948-57, corp. law atty., 1957-63, asst. gen. atty., 1963-64, gen. atty., asst. sec., 1964-71; examiner in chief Bd. Appeals, U.S. Patent Office, Washington, 1971-73; of patent counsel Richard R. Mybeck, Scottsdale, Ariz., 1983—; bd. dirs. Allis-Chalmers; lectr. patent law Marquette U. Law Sch., 1955; lectr. math. Pima Community Coll., Tucson, Ariz., 1985. Bd. dirs. Allis Chalmers Found., Milw., 1977-79. Author: (with Colleran and Jordan) Sketches of the Ordnance Research and Development Center in World War II, 1946; contbr. articles to profl. jours. Pres. Wauwatosa Bd. Edn., Wis., 1962-64; pres. Friends of Green Valley Library, Ariz., 1983; bd. dirs. Tucson Urban League, 1985. Served to maj. AUS, 1941-46; Mem. IEEE (sr.; life), ABA (life), Wis. Bar Assn., Am. Soc. Corp. Secs. (life sr.), N.Y. Acad. Scis., Am. Intellectual Property Law Assn., Patent Office Soc., Am. Hist. Assn., Hist. Sci. Soc., OAH, AAAS, Delta Upsilon, Phi Alpha Theta. Republican. Episcopalian. Antitrust, Patent, Trademark and copyright. Home: 525 S Anaheim Hills Rd # 211 Anaheim CA 92807-4721

**LIEBAU, JUDD ALAN,** lawyer, athlete agent; b. Independence, Kans., June 9, 1961; s. Kenneth R. and Nancy J. Liebau; m. Amy Jo Weller, Oct. 26, 1996. AD, Cowley County C.C., Arkansas City, Kans., 1992; BBA in Fin., Washburn U., Topeka, 1994, JD, 1997. Bar: Kans. 1997, U.S. Dist. Ct. Kans. 1997. Asst. baseball coach Washburn U., 1994-97; assoc. atty. Boyer, Donaldson & Stewart, LLP, Wichita, 1997—. Avocations: hunting, fishing, softball, golf. Sports, General civil litigation, General practice. Office: Boyer Donaldson & Stewart 1030 First Nat Bank Bldg Wichita KS 67202

**LIEBBE, MICHAEL WILLIAM,** lawyer; b. Muscatine, Iowa, Nov. 27, 1946; s. William Ernest and Joslyn Delee (Jones) L.; m. Vicki Jo Miller, June 10, 1972; 1 child, Ann Hazel. BBA, U. Iowa, 1968, JD, 1971. Bar: Iowa 1971, U.S. Dist. Ct. (no., so. dists.) Iowa 1971, U.S. Ct. Appeals (8th cir.) 1973, U.S. Supreme Ct. 1976, U.S. Dist. Ct. (cen. dist.) Ill. 1980. Dir. H.E.L.P. Legal Aide, Davenport, Iowa, 1971-75; pvt. practice law Davenport, 1975-78, 80—; 1st asst. Scott County Atty.'s Office, Davenport, 1979; cons. Family Resources, Davenport, 1975—. Chmn. Davenport Dem. Com., 1975; active Davenport CSC, 1987. Named Citizen of Yr. Quad City chpt. Nat. Assn. Social Workers, 1976. Mem. Iowa Assn. Worker Compensation Lawyers (bd. dirs. 1998). Personal injury, Workers' compensation. Office: 116 E 6th Davenport IA 52803-5502

**LIEBERMAN, ELLEN,** lawyer; b. N.Y.C., Oct. 19, 1939; d. George Warren Seplow and Daisy Pearl Derfner; m. Morris S. Zedeck, Mar. 4, 1989; children: Lisa Rachel Lieberman, Andrea Lynn Lieberman. BS cum laude, Columbia U., 1964; JD cum laude, Pace U., 1980. Bar: N.Y., 1981. Assoc. Willkie Farr & Gallagher, N.Y.C., 1980-88; assoc. Debevoise & Plimpton, N.Y.C., 1988-89, counsel, 1989—. Contbr. chpts. to books and articles to profl. jours. Fellow Am. Bar Found., N.Y. Bar Found.; mem. ABA (bus. law sect. 1983—, sect. legal edn. and admission to the bar 1987—, v. chair com. on state regulation securities 1999—, sec. com. on state regulation securities 1987—, co-chair/chair subcom. on state takeover laws 1990-96, co-chair subcom. on CLE and publs. 1995—, ho. of dels. 1996-97, 99), N.Y. State Bar Assn. (bus. law sect. 1983—, mem. com. on legal edn. and admission to the bar 1983—, chair com. on legal edn. and admission to the bar 1987-90, 95-98, mem. com. on profl. ethics 1990-96, mem. spl. com. on lawyer advt. and referral svc. 1993-97, mem. fin. com. 1996—, ho. of dels. 1996—, mem. exec. com. 1997—, co-chair spl. com. rev. proposed bridge-the-gap program 1997, co-chair spl. com. to rev. MCLE proposal 1998—, mem. com. on securities regulation 1998—), Phi Beta Kappa. Securities, Antitrust. Office: Debevoise & Plimpton 875 3rd Ave Fl 23 New York NY 10022-6256

**LIEBERMAN, EUGENE,** lawyer; b. Chgo., May 17, 1918; s. Harry and Eva (Goldman) L.; m. Pearl Naomi Feldman, Aug. 3, 1947; children: Mark, Robert, Steven. LLB, DePaul U., 1940, JD, 1941. Bar: Ill. 1941, U.S. Supreme Ct. 1963. Mem. firm Jacobs and Lieberman, 1954-60; sr. ptnr. Jacobs, Lieberman and Aling, 1960-74; spl. hearing officer U.S. Dept. Justice, 1967-78; hearing officer Ill. Pollution Control Bd., 1973—; pvt. practice Chgo. Contbr. articles to profl. jours. With U.S. Army, 1942-45. Recipient 1st in State award Moot Ct. Championship, 1940, gold award Philatelic Exhbn., Taipei, 1981, gold award World Philatelic Exhbn., Melbourne, 1984, Meritorious Svc. medal, bronze arrowhead award, others. Mem. Ill. State Bar Assn. (sr. counselor 1991), Chgo. Bar Assn., Appellate Lawyers Assn., Chgo. Philatelic Soc. (pres. 1964-68), Ill. Athletic Club. Appellate, Environmental, Family and matrimonial. Home: 801 Leclaire Ave Wilmette IL 60091-2065

**LIEBERMAN, JOEL M.,** lawyer; b. Vineland, N.J., Dec. 31, 1943; s. Bernard F. and Evelyn L.; m. Amy, Dec. 24, 1967; children: Michael, Brett. BS, L.I. U., 1965. Bar: Pa. 1970, U.S. Dist. Ct. Pa. 1970, U.S. Ct. Appeals (3d cir.) 1970, U.S. Supreme Ct. 1974. Atty. Silver & Silver, Phila., 1970-72, Gekoski & Bogdanoff, Phila., 1972-78; mng. atty. Allen Rothenberg, Phila., 1978-81; atty. pvt. practice, Phila., 1981—. Personal injury, Insurance. Office: 1801 Market St Ste 606 Philadelphia PA 19103-1606

**LIEBERMAN, MARC R(OBERT),** lawyer, director; b. Chgo., Dec. 6, 1956; s. David Lee Lieberman and Margit (Wirth) Johnson; m. Lucinda Kuzmi, Oct. 10, 1987. AB, Ind. U , 1980; JD, DePaul U., 1983. Bar: Ariz. 1983, U.S. Dist. Ct. Ariz. 1983, U.S. Ct. Appeals (9th cir.) 1983, D.C. 1985. Assoc. Eaton Lazarus & Dodge, Ltd., Phoenix, 1983-88, prin., dir., 1988—. Mem. joint task force Jewish Fedn. of Greater Phoenix, 1988—. Mem. Maricopa County Bar Assn. Avocations: scuba diving, skiing. Administrative and regulatory, General civil litigation, General corporate. Office: Lieberman Dodge & Sendrow Ltd 410 N 4442 St #290 3550 N Central Ave Fl 18 Phoenix AZ 85012-2105

**LIEBERMAN, MARK JOEL,** lawyer; b. Chgo., Apr. 12, 1949; s. Eugene and Pearl Naomi (Feldman) L.; children: Amy, Kevin. BA, DePaul U., 1971, JD, 1974. Bar: Ill. 1974, Calif. 1980, Tex. 1989. House counsel Mercantile Fin. Corp., Chgo., 1974-80; sr. atty. Assocs. Comml. Corp., Chgo., 1981-84; v.p., asst. gen. counsel Assocs. Comml. Corp., Dallas, 1984—. Mem. ABA, Calif. State Bar Assn. Republican. Jewish. Avocation: woodcarving. Office: Assocs Comml Corp 300 E Carpenter Fwy Irving TX 75062-2727

**LIEBERMAN, NANCY ANN,** lawyer; b. N.Y.C., Dec. 30, 1956; d. Elias and Elayne Hildegrade (Fox) L.; m. Mark Ellman. BA summa cum laude, U. Rochester, 1977; JD, U. Chgo., 1979; LLM in Taxation, NYU, 1981. Bar: N.Y. 1980. Intern White House, Washington, 1975; law clk. Hon. Henry A. Politz U.S. Ct. Appeals (5th cir.), Shreveport, La., 1979-80; assoc. Skadden Arps Slate Meagher & Flom, N.Y.C., 1981-87, ptnr., 1987—; bd. dirs. Rite Aid Corp. Bd. trustees U. Rochester, 1994—. Recipient McGill prize, 1977; N.Y. State Regents' scholar, 1973. Mem. ABA, Assn. Bar City N.Y., Coun. Fgn. Rels., Phi Beta Kappa. Republican. Jewish. Contracts commercial, General corporate. Home: 935 Park Ave # 7A New York NY 10028-0212 Office: Skadden Arps Slate Meagher & Flom LLP 919 3rd Ave New York NY 10022-3902

**LIEBERSON, JAY B.,** lawyer; b. Phila., Jan. 7, 1956; s. Martin and Vivian L.; m. Lisa R. Patton, Nov. 27, 1982; children: David Martin, Anne Elizabeth. BA, Temple U., 1976; JD, Dickinson U., 1979. Bar: Pa. 1979, U.S. Dist. Ct. (ea. dist) Pa. 1980. Exec. dir. domestic rels. Schuylkill Co., Pottsville, Pa., 1979-80, sr. staff atty. legal aid, 1980-81; assoc. Curtin & Heefner, Morrisville, Pa., 1981-84; pvt. practice Yardley, 1984—. Pres. scholar Temple U., 1976. Mem. Pa. Bar Assn. (mem. various coms.), Bucks County Bar Assn. (mem. various coms.), Phi Beta Kappa, Phi Alpha Delta. Democrat. Jewish. Avocation: Civil War enthusiast. Family and matrimonial, Personal injury, General practice. Office: 301 Oxford Valley Rd Ste 303A Yardley PA 19067-7709

**LIEBES, CINDY ANN,** lawyer; b. N.Y.C., Sept. 24, 1957; d. Harold and Doris (Fagan) L.; m. Richard Paul Lindsey. BS, Trenton State Coll., 1979; JD, Samford U., 1984. Bar: N.J. 1984, U.S. Dist. Ct. N.J. 1984, Ala. 1985, Ga. 1987. Officer probation dept. Middlesex County, New Brunswick, N.J., 1979-81; law clk. to presiding justice Ala. Supreme Ct., Montgomery, 1984-85, U.S. Dist. Ct. (no. dist.) Ala., 1985-86; atty. FTC, Atlanta, 1986—. Assoc. editor Cumberland Law Rev., 1983. Active So. Crescent, Atlanta. Mem. ABA, Southside Theater Guild. Jewish. Office: FTC 60 Forsyth St SW Ste Sm35 Atlanta GA 30303-8801

**LIEBHABER, JACK MITCHELL,** lawyer; b. Great Neck, N.Y., Apr. 6, 1958; s. Leslie and Lois Betty (Peiser) L.; 1 child, Brandon Matthew. BA, SUNY, Binghamton, 1980; JD, Pepperdine U., 1983. Bar: Calif. 1984. Pvt. practice, 1983-86; assoc. Spray, Gould & Bowers, L.A., 1986-93; shareholder Robinson, Di Lando & Whitaker, L.A., 1993—. Avocations: running, reading, theater, basketball, golf. Personal injury, State civil litigation, Insurance. Home: 10577 Cheviot Dr Los Angeles CA 90064-4351 Office: Robinson DiLando & Whitaker 800 Wilshire Blvd Ste 1300 Los Angeles CA 90017-2665

**LIEBMAN, LANCE MALCOLM,** law educator, lawyer; b. Newark, Sept. 11, 1941; s. Roy and Barbara (Trilinsky) L.; m. Carol Bensinger, June 28, 1964; children: Jeffrey, Benjamin. BA, Yale U., 1962; MA, Cambridge U., 1964; LLB, Harvard U., 1967. Bar: D.C. 1968, Mass. 1976, N.Y., 1995. Asst. to Mayor Lindsay, N.Y.C., 1968-70; asst. prof. law Harvard U., 1970-76, prof., 1976-91, assoc. dean, 1981-84; dean, Lucy G. Moses prof. law Columbia U. Sch. Law, N.Y.C., 1991-96, prof., dir. Parker Sch. Fgn. Law, 1996—, Williams S. Beinecke prof. law; dir. designate Am. Law Inst., 1998—. Successor trustee Yale Corp., 1971-83. Office: Columbia U Sch Law 435 W 116th St New York NY 10027-7297

**LIEBMAN, RONALD STANLEY,** lawyer; b. Balt., Oct. 11, 1943; s. Harry Martin and Martha (Altgenug) L.; m. Simma Liebman, Jan. 8, 1972; children: Shana, Margot. BA, Western Md. Coll., Westminster, 1966; JD, U. Md., 1969. Bar: Md. 1969, U.S. Dist. Ct. Md. 1970, U.S. Ct. Appeals (4th cir.) 1972, D.C. 1977, U.S. Dist. Ct. D.C. 1982, U.S. Ct. Appeals (D.C. cir.) 1982, U.S. Ct. Appeals (5th cir.) 1985, U.S. Ct. Appeals (2nd cir.) 1988, U.S. Ct. Appeals (9th cir.) 1992, U.S. Dist. Ct. (no. dist.) Calif. 1994, U.S. Supreme Ct. 1995, U.S. Ct. Appeals (7th cir.) 1996, U.S. Dist. Ct. (ea. dist.) Tex. 1999. Law clk. to chief judge U.S. Dist. Ct. Md., 1969-70; assoc. Melnicove, Kaufman & Weiner, Balt., 1970-72; asst. U.S. atty. Office of U.S. Atty., Dept. Justice, Balt., 1972-78; ptnr. Sachs, Greenebaum & Tayler, Washington, 1978-82, Patton Boggs, L.L.P., Washington, 1982—. Author: Grand Jury, 1983; co-editor: Testimonial Privileges, 1983. Recipient spl. commendation award U.S. Dept. Justice, 1978. Mem. ABA, D.C. Bar Assn., Md. Bar Assn., Sergeants Inn Club (Balt.). Criminal, Federal civil litigation, State civil litigation. Office: Patton Boggs LLP 2550 M St NW Ste 500 Washington DC 20037-1350

**LIEN, JOHN DONOVAN,** lawyer; b. LaCrosse, Wis., Dec. 30, 1943; s. Arthur Marvin and Alverda (Larson) L.; m. Kathleen McHenry, June 17, 1967 (div. Mar. 1983); m. Molly Warner, Apr. 2, 1983. BA, U. Wis., 1965; JD, Harvard U., 1968. Bar: Wis. 1968, Ill. 1972, U.S. Dist. Ct. (no. dist.) Ill. 1972, U.S. Ct. Appeals (7th cir.) 1977. Assoc. Wilson & McIvaine, Chgo., 1972-77, ptnr., 1978-86; ptnr. Antonow & Fink, Chgo., 1986-88, Foley & Lardner, Chgo., 1988—. Trustee Village of Winnetka, Ill., 1997—, Winnetka Libr. Dist., 1985-93. Capt. USAF, 1968-72. Republican. Methodist. General civil litigation. Home: 921 Pine St Winnetka IL 60093-2021 Office: Foley & Lardner One IBM Plz Chicago IL 60611

**LIEN, WALLACE WAYNE,** lawyer, land use consultant; b. McMinnville, Oreg., Aug. 19, 1949; s. Allen John and Elaine Eulala (Spafford) L.; m. Neala Georgene King, Mar. 14, 1966 (div. 1972); children: Stephen Brian, Wallace Wayne Jr.; m. Janet Kathleen MacInnes, Aug. 20, 1977; children: Elizabeth Andrea, Alexis Anne, Michael Allen. AS, Chemeketa Community Coll.; BS with honors, Oreg. Coll. Edn.; JD, Willamette U. Bar: Oreg. 1979, U.S. Supreme Ct. 1985. Ptnr. Lien, Lien & Hobson, Keizer, Oreg., 1979-81; asst. county counsel Marion County, Salem, Oreg., 1981-82; chief legal counsel Polk County, Dallas, Oreg., 1982-83; instr. Chemeketa Community Coll., Salem, 1980-85; ptnr. Paulus, Rhoten & Lien, Salem, 1983-86; sole practice Salem, 1986—. Mem. bd. dirs. Oreg. Econ. Inst., Portland, 1985; pres. Oreg. Community Coll. Student Assn., Salem, 1972-73; mem. Oreg. Bd. Edn., Salem, 1972. Western Interstate Commn. Higher Edn. scholar, U.S. Govt., 1976; recipient Col. Robertson award Willamette U., 1978, first pl. moot ct. award Willamette Law Sch., 1977. Mem. ABA, Oreg. State Bar Assn. (exec. com. real estate and land use sect.), Marion County Bar Assn., Chemeketa Alumni Assn. Republican. Lodge: Elks. Avocations: water skiing, youth sports coaching and adminstrn., theater, writing. E-mail address: manager@lienlaw.com. Land use and zoning (including planning), Real property. Home: 1004 Crescent Dr NW Salem OR 97304-2702 Office: 1775 32d Pl NE Salem OR 97303

**LIETZAU, WILLIAM KENDALL,** career officer, lawyer; b. Annapolis, Md., Nov. 9, 1960; s. Karl Ernest and Janice Mae L.; m. Diane Michelle, May 19, 1984; children: Rachel Anne, Zachary Thomas. BS, U.S. Naval Acad., 1983; JD, Yale U., 1989; LLM, U.S. Army JAG Sch., 1995. Bar: Conn. 1989, Ct. Mil. Appeals 1990, U.S. Supreme Ct. 1995. Rifle co. comdr. USMC, Kaneohe Bay, Hawaii, 1984-87; spl asst. U.S. atty. USMC, Jacksonville, N.C., 1989-91; lt. col. USMC, 1995; chief prosecutor Camp Lejeune, N.C., 1991-92; chief def. counsel Iwakuni, Japan, 1992-93, dep. sta. judge adv., 1993-95; head law armed conflict br. Navy JAG, Washington, 1996-97; dep. legal counsel to chmn. Joint Chiefs Staff Washington, 1997-99; chief mil. judge Atlantic cir., 1999—; adj. prof. Georgetown U., Washington, 1998—; spkr. Contbr. articles to profl. jours. Mentor Glasgow Mid. Sch., Fairfax, Va., 1997—; U.S. del. Ottawa conv. Banning Landmines, Terrorist Bombing Conv., Nuc. Terrorism Conv., Rome Treaty Internat. Criminal Ct., Hague Cultural Property Protocol. Recipient Major Gen. Pugh award, 1995; named Career Mil. Lawyer of the Yr. Judge Adv. Assn., 1998. Avocations: running, biking, lifting. Home: 9366 Tovito Dr Fairfax VA 22031-3825 Office: Navy-Marine Corps Trial Judiciary Washington Navy Yard 1014 N St SE Ste 250 Washington DC 20374-5016

**LIEUWEN, JOHN N.,** lawyer; b. Berkeley, Calif., Aug. 19, 1951; s. Edwin and Marian R. (Whitehead) L. BA, U. Calif., Berkeley, 1973; JD, Hastings Coll., 1976; LLM in Taxation, NYU, 1977. Bar: Calif. 1977, N.Mex. 1978, U.S. Tax Ct. 1980. Ptnr. Laflin, Lieuwen, Tucker, Pick, Heer & Neerken, P.A., Albuquerque, 1978—. Mem. ABA, Calif. Bar Assn., N.Mex. State Bar. Democrat. Avocations: fishing, skiing. Corporate taxation, Pension, profit-sharing, and employee benefits, Estate taxation. Office: 6400 Uptown Blvd NE Albuquerque NM 87110-4204

**LIFLAND, JOHN C.,** federal judge; b. 1933. BA, Yale U., 1954; LLB, Harvard U., 1957. Pvt. practice law, 1957-59; law sec. to Hon. Thomas F. Meaney U.S. Dist. Ct. N.J., 1959-61; mem. firm Stryker, Tams & Dill, 1961-88; dist. judge U.S. Dist. Ct. N.J., Newark, 1988—; mem. N.J. State Bd. Bar Examiners, 1968-77. 1st lt. U.S. Army, 1958. Fellow Am. Bar Found., Assn. Fed. Bar (v.p. 1986—), N.J. State Bar Assn., Essex County Bar Assn.; mem. ABA (antitrust sect. publs. com., books editor/co-editor Antitrust Law Jour. 1981-87), Clearwater Seim Club, Essex Club, Harvard Law Sch. Assn. Office: US Dist Ct M L King Fed Bldg & Cthouse PO Box 999 Newark NJ 07101-0999

**LIFSCHULTZ, PHILLIP,** financial and tax consultant, accountant, lawyer; b. Oak Park, Ill., Mar. 5, 1927; s. Abraham Albert and Frances Rhoda (Siegel) L.; m. Edith Louise Leavitt, June 27, 1948; children: Gregory, Bonnie, Jodie. BS in Acctg., U. Ill., 1949; JD, John Marshall Law Sch., 1956. Bar: Ill. 1956; CPA, Ill. Tax mgr. Arthur Andersen & Co., Chgo., 1957-63; v.p. taxes Montgomery Ward & Co., Chgo., 1963-78; fin. v.p., contr. Henry Crown & Co., Chgo., 1978-81; prin. Phillip Lifschultz & Assocs., Chgo., 1981—; exec. dir. Dodi Orgn., 1987-90; v.p. Altra Travel, Northbrook, Ill., 1975—; pres. Great Lakes Shoe Co., Bannockburn, Ill., 1996—. Mem. adv. coun. Coll. Commerce and Bus. Adminstrn. U. Ill., Urbana-Champaign, 1977-78; chmn., Civic Fedn. Chgo., 1980-82; chmn. adv. bd. to Auditor Gen. of Ill., 1965-73; project dir. Exec. Service Corps of Chgo., Chgo. Bd. Edn. and State of Ill. projects, 1980-87. With U.S. Army, 1945-46. Mem. Ill. Bar Assn., Chgo. Bar Assn., Am. Inst. CPA's, Ill. CPA Soc., Am. Arbitration Assn. (comml. panel 1983-94), Nat. Retail Merchants Assn. (chmn. tax com. 1975-78), Am. Retail Fedn. (chmn. taxation com. 1971), Standard Club. Home and Office: 442 Kelburn Rd Apt 123 Deerfield IL 60015-4370

**LIFTIN, JOHN MATTHEW,** lawyer; b. Washington, June 25, 1943; children: Eric, Hilary. AB, U. Pa., 1964; LLB, Columbia U., 1967. Bar: N.Y.. 1967, D.C. 1974, U.S. Dist. Ct. D.C. 1975, U.S. Ct. Appeals (D.C. cir.) 1975, U.S. Supreme Ct. 1980. Assoc. Sullivan & Cromwell, N.Y.C., 1967-71; spl. counsel to chmn. SEC, Washington, 1971-72, assoc. dir. market reg. div., 1972-74; ptnr. Rogers & Wells, Washington, 1974-85; pres. Quadrex Securities Corp., N.Y.C., 1985-87; sr. v.p., gen. counsel Kidder, Peabody Group Inc., N.Y.C., 1987-96, Prudential Ins. Co. Am., Newark, 1998—; mem. adv. bd. securities regulation and law reports Bur. Nat. Affairs, Inc., Washington, 1979—; cons. in field. Contbr. articles on securities law to profl. jours. Mem. ABA (chmn. com. on fed. regulation securities), Univ. Club. Securities, General corporate. •

**LIGGETT, LUTHER LEROY, JR.,** lawyer; b. Marysville, Ohio, Mar. 1, 1956; s. Luther L. and Kathryn O. Liggett; m. Anne Liggett, June 25, 1983; children: Luther Alex, Katherine Ann. BA, George Washington U., 1978, JD, 1981. Bar: Ohio 1981. Atty. Liggett Law Offices, Marysville, 1981-83; asst. atty. gen. Ohio Atty. Gens. Office, Columbus, 1983-91; atty. Bricker & Eckler, Columbus, 1991—; mem. Futures Task Force, Hocking Coll., Nelsonville, Ohio. Democrat. Greek Orthodox. Avocations: politics, geology, stamps, coins, refinishing. E-mail: lligg@be.bricker.com. Fax: 614-227-2390. Construction, Government contracts and claims, Legislative. Office: Bricker & Eckler 100 S Third St Columbus OH 43215-4291

**LIGGIO, CARL DONALD,** lawyer; b. N.Y.C., Sept. 5, 1943. AB, Georgetown U., 1963; JD, NYU, 1967. Bar: N.Y. 1967, D.C. 1967, Wis. 1983, Ill. 1998. Cons. Arent, Fox, Kintner, Plotkin & Kahn, Washington, 1968-69; assoc. White & Case, N.Y.C., 1969-72; gen. counsel Arthur Young & Co., N.Y.C., 1972-89, Ernst & Young, N.Y.C., 1989-94; ptnr. Dickinson, Wright, Moon, Van Dusen & Freeman, Chgo., 1995-97, of counsel, 1998-99; CFO, gen. counsel Tempico, Inc., 1998—; of counsel McCullough, Campbell & Lane, 1999—; mem. Brookings Civil Justice Reform Task Force, 1988—. Mem. editl. bd. Rsch. in Acctg. Jour.; contbr. articles to profl. jours. Trustee Fordham Prep. Sch. Mem. ABA, Am. Corp. Counsel Assn. (chmn.

bd. dirs. 1984, mem. exec. com. 1982-95), Am. Judicature Soc. (bd. dirs. 1988-92), Coll. Law Mgmt., N.Y. State Bar Assn., Wis. Bar Assn., Ill. Bar Assn., D.C. Bar Assn. General corporate, General civil litigation, Securities. Home: 233 E Walton St Chicago IL 60611-1510 Office: 401 N Michigan Ave Chicago IL 60611-4255

**LIGHT, ALFRED ROBERT,** lawyer, political scientist, educator; b. Dec. 14, 1949; s. Alfred M. Jr. and Margaret Francis (Asbury) L; m. Mollie Sue Hall, May 25, 1977; children: Joseph Robert, Gregory Andrew. Student, Ga. Inst. Tech., 1967-69; BA with highest honors, Johns Hopkins U., 1971; PhD, U. N.C., 1976; JD cum laude, Harvard U., 1981. Bar: D.C. 1981, Va. 1982. Tax clk. IRS, 1967; lab technician Custom Farm Svcs. Soils Testing Lab, 1968; warehouse asst. State of Ga. Mines, Mining and Geology, 1970; clk.-typist systems mgmt. div., def. contract adminstrv. Def. Supply Agy., Atlanta, 1971; rsch. and teaching asst. dept. polit. sci. U. N.C., Chapel Hill, 1971-74; rsch. asst. Inst. Rsch. in Social Sci., 1975-77; program analyst Office of Sec. Sef., 1974; asst. prf. polit. sci., rsch. scientist Ctr. Energy Rsch. Tex. Tech. U., Lubbock, 1977-78; rsch. asst. grad. sch. edn. Harvard U., 1978-79; assoc. Butler, Binion, Rice, Cook & Knapp, Houston, summer 1980; Bracewell & Patterson, Washington, summer 1980, Hunton & Williams, Richmond, Va., 1981-89; of counsel, 1989-93, 95-96; assoc. prof. St. Thomas U. Sch. Law, Miami, Fla., 1989-93; prof., 1993—; interim dean, 1993-94; bd. advisors Toxics Law reporter, Bur. Nat. Affairs, Washington, 1987—. Contbr. articles to profl. jours. Charter mem. West BRoward Cmty. Ch. Capt. USAR, 1971-85. Grantee NSF, Inst. Evaluation Rsch., U. Mass., Ctr. Energy Rsch., Tex. Tech. U., 1977-78; recipient Julius Turner award Am. Polit. Sci. Assn., 1977. Mem. ABA (vice-chmn.) tort and ins. practice sect. 1988-97, nat. res. and environ. sect. 1993-95, chmn. 1995—), Fed. Bar. Assn., Va. Bar Assn., Richmond Bar Assn., Phi Beta Kappa, Phi Eta Sigma. Democrat. Home: 1042 Woodfall Ct Fort Lauderdale FL 33326-2832 Office: St Thomas U Sch Law 16400 NW 32nd Ave Opa Locka FL 33054-6459

**LIGHT, RUSSELL JEFFERS,** lawyer; b. Dallas, Sept. 8, 1949; s. Marion Russell and Isabel (Jeffers) L.; m. Mary Louise Allen, July 20, 1979; children: Erin, Brendan, Justin. BA, So. Meth. U., 1971, JD, 1975. Bar: Tex. 1976. Instr. legal writing So. Meth. U., Dallas, 1975-76; briefing atty. to assoc. justice Ct. of Civil Appeals, Austin, Tex., 1976-77; law clk. U.S. Dist. Ct., Ft. Worth, 1977-78; atty. Union Pacific Resources Co., Ft. Worth, 1978—; chmn. air task force of subcom. on environment and health law Am. Petroleum Inst., 1987-89. Author: (poetry) Nirvana, 1971 (recipient Dallas Poetry award 1971); actor, dir. (film) A Child's Garden, 1971 (recipient D.W. Griffith award 1971). Mem. Calif. Coun. Environ. and Econ. Balance, Dallas Bar Environ. Com. Mem. ABA (vice chmn. air com. natural resources sect. 1987-93, environ. controls corp. banking sect. 1987-89), Tex. Mid-Continent Oil and Gas Assn. (environ. law com.), Ft. Worth Petroleum Club, Ridglea Country Club, Ft. Worth Club. Environmental, General corporate. Home: 3705 Streamwood Rd Fort Worth TX 76116-9316 Office: Union Pacific Resources Co PO Box 7 Fort Worth TX 76101-0007

**LIGHT, WILLIAM RANDALL,** lawyer; b. Lynchburg, Va., Sept. 11, 1958; s. John Leftwich and Patricia (Wilson) L.; m. Lisa Burcher, Apr. 27, 1991; children: William Randall II, Madeline Gibson. BA, Emory and Henry Coll., 1980; JD, Nova U. Bar: Va. 1985, U.S. Dist. Ct. (we. dist.) Va. 1985, U.S. Ct. Appeals (4th cir.), U.S. Supreme Ct. Assoc. Killis T. Howard, a profl. corp., Lynchburg, 1984—; spl. justice Commonwealth of Va. 24th Jud. Dist., Lynchburg, 1987—; adj. prof. Lynchburg Coll., 1989, 91. Bd. dirs. Lynchburg Mental Health Assn.; vice chmn. Rep. com. City of Lynchburg, 1986-90, acting chmn., 1990-91; vestry St. Paul Episcopal Ch., Ecclesiastical Coun. Episcopal Diocese of Southwestern Va. Maj. Va. Def. Force. Mem. ABA, Lynchburg Bar Assn. (v.p. young lawyers sect. 1984-88, pres. 1989-90), Va. Trial Lawyers Assn., Amherst County-Nelson County Bar Assn., Masons (Master 1991), Phi Alpha Delta. Republican. Episcopalian. Criminal, General practice, Personal injury. Home: 1804 Mobile Rd Lynchburg VA 24503-2434 Office: Killis T Howard PC 712 Court St PO Box 99 Lynchburg VA 24505-0099

**LIGHTER, LAWRENCE,** lawyer; b. Bklyn., Sept. 13, 1935; s. Abe and Frances (Laufer) L.; m. Gloria Rita Stiefel, June 28, 1959; children: Adam, Todd, Eric. BS in Acctg., Bklyn. Coll., 1956; JD, NYU, 1960. Bar: N.Y. 1962. Staff atty. S.E.S.A.C., N.Y.C., 1961-65; house counsel Mills Music Inc., N.Y.C., 1965-68; N.Y. counsel Capitol Records, N.Y.C., 1969-70; pvt. practice N.Y.C., 1970—; guest lectr. St. John's U., Queens, N.Y., Five Towns Coll., Seaford, N.Y., NYU, N.Y.C., and others. Legal editor: (ency.) Encyclopedia of The Music Business, 1984. Entertainment, Intellectual property, Contracts commercial. Office: 488 Madison Ave Fl 8 New York NY 10022-5702

**LIGHTSTONE, RONALD,** lawyer; b. N.Y.C., Oct. 4, 1938; s. Charles and Pearl (Weisberg) L.; m. Nancy Lehrer, May 17, 1973; 1 child, Dana. AB, Columbia U., 1959; JD, NYU, 1962. Atty. CBS, N.Y.C., 1967-69; assoc. dir. bus. affairs CBS News, N.Y.C., 1969-70; atty. NBC, N.Y.C., 1970; assoc. gen. counsel Viacom Internat. Inc., N.Y.C., 1970-75; v.p., gen. counsel, sec. Viacom Internat. Inc., 1976-80; v.p. bus. affairs Viacom Entertainment Group, Viacom Internat., Inc., 1980-82, v.p. corp. affairs, 1982-84, sr. v.p., 1984-87; exec. v.p. Spelling Entertainment Inc., L.A., 1988-91, CEO,, 1991-93; chmn. Multimedia Labs. Inc., 1994-97; CEO, pres. New Star Media Inc., 1997-99, vice chmn., 1999—. Lt. USN, 1962-66. Mem. ABA (chmn. TV, cable and radio com.), Assn. of Bar of City of N.Y., Fed. Comm. Bar Assn. General corporate, Entertainment.

**LIGHTY, FREDRICK W.,** lawyer; b. Danville, Pa., Mar. 18, 1967; s. Raymond G. and Geraldine A. (Brill) L. BA, Lycoming Coll., 1989; JD, Widener U., 1992. Bar: Pa. 1992, U.S. Dist. Ct. (mid. dist.) Pa. 1993, U.S. Ct. Appeals (3d cir.) 1993, U.S. Ct. Internat. Trade 1995. Private practice Harrisburg, Pa., 1995—; dir. Enviroquest, Inc., Harrisburg, 1995—. Personal injury, Consumer commercial, Private international. Office: PO Box 60312 Harrisburg PA 17106-0312

**LIGORANO, MICHAEL KENNETH,** lawyer; b. Morristown, N.J., July 24, 1954; s. Michael Thomas and Virginia J. Ligorano; m. Debra Ann Baumann, Aug. 12, 1978. BA cum laude, Rutgers U., Newark, 1975; JD, Western New Eng. Law Sch., Springfield, Mass., 1978. Bar: N.J. 1978, U.S. Dist. Ct. N.J. 1978, Fla. 1980, U.S. Ct. Appeals (3d cir.) 1980, U.S. Tax Ct. 1980, U.S. Supreme Ct. 1985, N.Y. 1990; lic. real estate sales N.J. Assoc. Charles M. Lee, Washington, N.J., 1978-79; assoc. Hogan Folk Mahon & Simms, Flemington, Somerville, N.J., 1979-82, ptnr., 1982-83; ptnr. Mahon Moeller & Ligorano, Flemington, 1983-84, Schaff Motiuk et al, Flemington, Trenton, 1984-87, Ligorano & Sozansky P.C., Flemington, 1987-98, Archer & Greiner, P.C., Flemington, Princeton, 1998—; atty. Mine Hill Twp. Bd. Adjustment, 1978-88; asst. Hunterdon County counsel, 1979-82; legal counsel Hunterdon County Bd. Recreation Commrs., 1980—; atty. Alexandria Twp. Bd. Adjustment, 1983-84; spl. counsel Solid Waste, Hunterdon County, 1984; atty. Readington Twp. Planning Bd., 1985-91, Readington Twp., 1991-96, Clinton Twp., 1996, Clinton Twp. Planning Bd., 1997—, Glen Gardner Bd. Edn., 1996—; spl. title counsel High Bridge Bd. Edn., 1996; mem. Dist. XIII Ethics Com., 1987-91, chair, 1990-91; mem. Dist. XIII Fee Arbitration Com., 1991—; mem. N.J. Supreme Ct. Complementary Dispute Resolution Project, 1995—; instr. N.J. Inst. Continuing Legal Edn., 1995-97; adv. bd. Summit Bank, 1990-92, First Cmty. Bank, 1992—. Environ. commr. Denville Twp., 1973-75; legis. aide N.J. Assembly, 1974-75; mem. N.J. Natural Areas Coun., 1983-84; mem. Glen Gardner Bd. Health, 1993-95; bd. dirs. HHunterdon chpt. ARC, 1982-84, Glen Gardner Youth Ctr., 1988-90; mem. Hunterdon County Rep. Com., 1983-97; mem. Leukemia Soc. of Am. Team in Tng. Alaska Marathon, 1997, San Diego Marathon, 1999; adv. bd. ARC, 1994—. Mem. N.J. State Bar Assn. (gen. coun. 1993-94, sects. on land use, real property, probate and trust, dispute resolution), N.Y. State Bar Assn. (sect. on real property, probate and trust), The Fla. Bar (sect. on land use, real property, probate and trust), Am. Immigration Lawyers Assn., Hunterdon County Bar Assn. (sec. 1991-92, v.p. 1992-93, pres. 1993-94, trustee 1994-97, equity settlement panel 1994—, chair com. on professionalism 1996—), Hunterdon C. of C. (bd. dirs. 1981-86), Hunterdon/Somerset Realtors Assn., Nat. Geneology Soc. Avocations: geneology, long distance running. Real property, Immigration, naturalization, and customs, Municipal (including bonds). Office: Archer & Greiner PC 100 Main St Flemington NJ 08822-1413

**LIJOI, PETER BRUNO,** lawyer; b. Suffern, N.Y., Sept. 2, 1953; s. Salvatore and Josephine (Gentile) L.; m. Christine Louise Confroy, Aug. 19, 1978; children: Jonathan Peter, Christopher Andrew. BA in History and Econs., Montclair State Coll., 1975; postgrad. in urban planning, Rutgers U., 1975-76; JD, Pace U., 1979; postgrad., Harvard U., 1992. Bar: N.J. 1981, N.Y. 1988. Rsch. intern N.J. Dept. Edn., Trenton, 1976; intern Office U.S. Atty., N.Y.C., 1977-78; energy coord. Rockland County, 1979-80; dep. dir., of counsel Pvt. Industry Coun., Pearl River, N.Y., 1980-91; pvt. practice law Summit, N.J., 1981—; dir., counsel County of Rockland Indsl. Devel. Agy., 1981-95; v.p., gen. counsel Rockland Econ. Devel. Corp., Pearl River, 1990-91; cons. U.S. Dept. Energy, Washington, 1980; mem. program of instrn. for lawyers Law Sch., Harvard U., 1992; legal counsel and land acquisition mgr. K. Hovnanian Cos. North Jersey, Inc., 1993-95, K. Hovnanian Cos. Northeast, Inc., 1995—. Guest writer The Bond Buyer. Bd. dirs. Rockland County coun. Girl Scouts U.S., 1982-92; pres. Washington Elem. Sch. PTA, Summit, 1986—; mem. Summit Planning Bd., desegregation grant adv. com. Summit Bd. Edn., 1992—. Mem. ABA, N.J. Bar Assn., N.Y. Bar Assn., Union County Bar Assn., Assn. Trial Lawyers Am., Nat. Assn. Bond Lawyers. Roman Catholic. Avocations: running, coaching youth soccer. Environmental, Real property, Finance. Home: 124 Canoe Brook Pky Summit NJ 07901-1436 Office: 110 Fieldcrest Ave Edison NJ 08837-3620

**LIKE, STEVEN,** lawyer; b. Vincennes, Ind., Sept. 5, 1956; s. Cameron Keith and Sharon Lee (Smith) L.; m. Jane Elizabeth Lambert, June 2, 1979; children: Brandon, Christopher, Stephanie. BA in Econs., DePauw U., 1978; JD cum laude, Ind. U., 1981. Bar: Ind. 1981, Mich. 1984, U.S. Dist. Ct. (no. and so. dists.) Ind. 1981, U.S. Ct. Appeals (7th cir.) 1986. Assoc. Warrick, Weaver & Boyn, Elkhart, Ind., 1981-85, ptnr., 1986—. Editor newsletter Warrick, Weaver & Boyn, 1984-88. Bd. dirs. United Way Elkhart County, 1982-88; bd. dirs. Assn. for Disabled of Elkhart County, 1984-91, pres., 1989. Mem. ABA, Ind. Bar Assn., Mich. Bar Assn., Elkhart City Bar Assn., Rotary, Lions. Republican. Roman Catholic. Avocations: boating, fishing, golf, travel. General corporate, Labor, Pension, profit-sharing, and employee benefits. Office: 307 S Main St Elkhart IN 46516-3119

**LILE, LAIRD ANDREW,** lawyer; b. Troy, Ohio, Feb. 7, 1960; s. Levi W. and Nancy N. (Nicholl) L.; m. Laurie Detrick, Aug. 1, 1981. BBA, Coll. William and Mary, 1981; JD, Ohio No. U., 1984; LLM in Estate Planning, U. Miami, 1987. Bar: Fla. 1984. Pvt. practice. Author: Powers of Appointment, 1988. Bd. dirs., mem. adv. bd. Children's Home Soc., Naples, 1988-90; bd. dirs., pres. Carver Fin. Com., Naples, 1989-90; bd. dirs. Collier City Edn. Found., 1990-95. Mem. Masons. Republican. Avocation: scuba diving. Estate planning, Probate, Estate taxation. Office: Ste 106 3033 Riviera Dr Naples FL 34103-2746

**LILES, RUTLEDGE RICHARDSON,** lawyer; b. Miami, Fla., Jan. 30, 1942; s. Rutledge Person and Kathryn (Richardson) L.; m. Noel Doepke, Dec. 28, 1963; children: Ashley Faye, Hillary Lynn, Stacey Noel. BA, Fla. State U., 1964; JD, U. Fla., 1966. Bar: Fla. 1966, U.S. Dist. Ct. (mid. dist.) Fla. 1967, U.S. Supreme Ct. 1972, U.S. Dist. Ct. (no. and so. dists.) Fla. 1978; bd. cert. civil trial lawyer. Pres. Liles, Gavin & Costantino, Jacksonville, Fla., 1991—; bd. of govs. Fla. Bar, 1981-87, pres.-elect 1987-88, pres. 1988-89. Mem. Jacksonville U. Council, 1966-88; trustee Episcopal High Sch. of Jacksonville, 1986-89, U. Fla. Coll. Law Ctr. Assn., 1981-89. Recipient Pres.'s award Fla. Bar, 1986. Fellow ABA (house dels. 1988-91, 93-94), Am. Coll. Trial Lawyers, Internat. Soc. Barristers; mem. ATLA, Acad. Fla. Trial Lawyers, Jacksonville Bar Assn. (pres. 1976-77), Fla. Blue Key, Am. Bd. Trial Advocates, Fla. Jud. Qualifications Commn., Fed. Jud. Nomination Commn. Democrat. Personal injury, Securities, General civil litigation. Home: 1013 Maple Ln Jacksonville FL 32207-4010 Office: Liles Gavin & Costantino One Enterprise Ctr 225 Water St Ste 1500 Jacksonville FL 32202-5148*

**LILJEQUIST, JON LEON,** patent lawyer; b. Chgo., Apr. 24, 1936; s. Leon Rogner and Muriel Alice (Staples) L.; m. Bonnie Ann Barrow, Aug. 20, 1960; children: Lisa Jean, Laura Kirsten, Lars Christian. BSME, U. Ill., 1958; JD, Loyola U., Chgo., 1964. Bar: Ill. 1964, U.S. Dist. Ct. (no. dist.) Ill. 1964, U.S. Patent Office 1964, U.S. Ct. Appeals (D.C. cir.) 1980; registered profl. engr., Ill., Fla. Design engr. Outboard Marine Corp., Waukegan, Ill., 1958-60; instr. engring. U. Ill., Chgo., 1960-63, prof. in structural engring., undergrad. law, 1964—, patent cons., 1984—; assoc. Hofgren, Wegner, et al, Chgo., 1963-64, Darbo, Robertson et al, Arlington Heights, Ill., 1964-66; patent counsel Appleton Electric Co., Chgo., 1966-86; owner, pres. Timark Co., Mt. Prospect, Ill., 1969-76; legal and engring. cons. Hannafan & Handler, Chgo., 1985—, Dressler, Goldsmith, Shore, Sutker & Milnamow, Chgo., U. South Fla., Tampa, Leydig, Voit and Mayer, 1988. Patentee in field. Recipient Silver Circle award U. Ill., Chgo., 1983, 86. Mem. Licensing Execs. Soc., Soc. Univ. Patent Adminstrs., Patent Law Assn. Chgo. Patent, Trademark and copyright. Home and Office: 5770 Pine Tree Dr Sanibel FL 33957-2304

**LILLARD, JOHN FRANKLIN, III,** lawyer; b. Cheverly, Md., Aug. 2, 1947; s. John Franklin Jr. and Madeline Virginia (Berg) L.; m. Shannon Leslie Oliver, June 1, 1991 (div.). Bar: N.Y. 1972, D.C. 1974, Md. 1975. Assoc. Donovan, Leisure, Newton & Irvine, N.Y.C., 1971-74; trial atty. civil div. Dept. Justice, Washington, 1976-77; ptnr. Lillard & Lillard, Washington, 1977—; instr. Dale Carnegie Course, 1988—. Vice chair Village Coun. Friendship Heights, Chevy Chase, Md., 1975-77; candidate U.S. Congress from 5th dist. Md., 1981; chair Am. Solar Energy Assn.; founding mem. Nat. Adv. Coun. Ctr. for Study of the Presidency, 1970—, Md. State Adv. Bd. on Spl. Tax Dists., 1976-77, alcoholic beverage adv. bd. Montgomery County, 1977-79; chair Eisenhower Centennial Meml. Com., 1990—. Recipient Eastman award Am. Arbitration Assn., 1971. Mem. Md. Bar Assn., Prince George's County Bar Assn., Anne Arundel County Bar Assn., Met. Club (Washington), Tred Avon Yacht Club (Oxford, Md.), Marlborough Hunt Club. Republican. Episcopalian. Federal civil litigation, General practice. Office: 8 Loudon Ln Annapolis MD 21401-1219

**LILLEHAUG, DAVID LEE,** lawyer; b. Waverly, Iowa, May 22, 1954; s. Leland Arthur and Ardis Elsie (Scheel) L.; m. Winifred Sarah Smith, May 29, 1982; 1 child, Kara Marie. BA summa cum laude, Augustana Coll., Sioux Falls, S.D., 1976; JD cum laude, Harvard U., 1979. Bar: Minn. 1979, U.S. Dist. Ct. Minn. 1979, D.C. 1981, U.S. Ct. Appeals (8th cir.) 1981, U.S. Dist. Ct. D.C. 1982. Law clk. to presiding judge U.S. Dist. Ct. Minn., Mpls., 1979-81; assoc. Hogan & Hartson, Washington, 1981-83, 84-85; issues aide, exec. asst. to Walter Mondale, Washington, 1983-84; assoc. Leonard, Street & Deinard, Mpls., 1985-87, ptnr., 1988-93, 98—; U.S. atty. Dist. of Minn., 1994-98. Candidate U.S. Senate, 1999—. Mondale Policy Forum fellow U. Minn., 1990-91. Mem. ABA, Minn. Bar Assn. (past chair constrn. law sect., Author's award 1990). Lutheran. Avocations: fishing, racquetball. Home: 6701 Parkwood Ln Edina MN 55436-1735

**LILLY, JOHN RICHARD, II,** prosecutor; b. Phila., July 20, 1962; s. John Richard Sr. and Elizabeth Anne (Brown) L.; children: John Richard III, Cameron Lewis. BA, Geoge Washington U., 1987; JD, U. Balt., 1991. Bar: Md. 1992, U.S. Dist. Ct. Md. 1995, U.S. Ct. Mil. Appeals 1994. Law clk. 7th Jud. Cir. Md., Upper Marlboro, 1991-92; asst. state's atty. State's Atty.'s Office Prince George's County Md., Upper Marlboro, 1992-98; asst. atty. gen. Md. Atty. Gen.'s Office, Balt., 1998—; co-founder Prince George's County Task Force on Environ. Crimes, Upper Marlboro, 1994. Comments editor U. Balt. Jour. Environ. Law. Chmn. Oakland Mills Village Bd., Columbia, Md., 1990-92; pres. St. Stephen's Area Civic Assn., Crownsville, Md., 1994-95. Lt. USNR, 1988—. Mem. Anne Arundel Bar Assn. Avocations: tennis, sailing, reading, photography. Home: 1306 Eva Gude Dr Crownsville MD 21032-2102 Office: Md Atty Gen's Office Environ Crimes Unit 2500 Broening Hwy Baltimore MD 21224-6601

**LILLY, THOMAS JOSEPH,** lawyer; b. Bklyn., Feb. 17, 1931; s. Frank A. and Mary Ellen (Kelly) L.; m. Margaret Mary Doherty, June 28, 1959; children: Thomas J., Mary Jo, Joseph, Sean. BA, St. John's Coll., 1953; JD, Fordham U., 1961; LLM, NYU, 1967. Bar: N.Y. 1962, U.S. Dist. Ct. (ea. and so. dists.) N.Y. 1963, U.S. Ct. Appeals (2d cir.) 1965. Dir. rsch. Office and Profl. Employees Internat. Union AFL-CIO, N.Y.C., 1960-62; asst. U.S. atty. U.S. Dist. Ct. (ea. dist.) N.Y., Bklyn., 1962-66; ptnr. Doran, Colleran, O'Hara, Pollio & Dunne, N.Y.C., 1966-79, Quinn & Lilly, P.C., N.Y.C. and Garden City, N.Y., 1979-89; pvt. practice Garden City, 1989—; adj. prof. N.Y. State Indsl. and Labor Rels. Sch., Cornell U., 1980-81; arbitrator U.S. Dist. Ct. (ea. dist.) N.Y.; mem. Nassau County Pub. Employment Rels. Bd. With USN, 1953-57. Mem. ABA, N.Y. Bar Assn., Nassau County Bar Assn., Sea Cliff Yacht Club. Labor, Pension, profit-sharing, and employee benefits, Civil rights. Home: 136 8th Ave Sea Cliff NY 11579-1308 Office: 300 Garden City Plz Garden City NY 11530-3302 also: 950 3rd Ave New York NY 10022-2705

**LIM, JOSEPH EDWARD,** lawyer; b. Manila, Dec. 4, 1955; s. Protacio Jose Lim and Ellen Belle Galang; m. Blesilda Ladines; children: Joseph, Meilin. BS in Agribus., U. The Philippines, Laguna, 1978; MBA, U. The Philippines, Diliman, 1984; JD, U. Balt., 1992. Bar: Md. 1992. Agribus. specialist Tech. Resource Ctr., Makati, The Philippines, 1978-80; divsn. mgr. Coop. Found. the Philippines, Quezon City, 1980-82; mktg. officer Nat. Home Mortgage Corp., Makati, 1982-86; with U.S. Army, Md., 1986-90; law clk. Md. State Atty.'s coord., Balt., 1990-91; claims examiner Injured Workers Ins., Towson, Md., 1991-92; adminstrv. judge Office Employee Appeals, Washington, 1993-95, 98—; pvt. practice, 1995—. Editor Agribus. Newsletter, 1977. Mem. Md. Trial Lawyers Assn., Nature Conservancy. Avocations: Chow dog breeding, photography, martial arts, writer. Administrative and regulatory, General civil litigation, General practice. Home: 2018 Summit Ave Baltimore MD 21237-1334 Office: Office Employee Appeals 717 14th St NW Washington DC 20005-3200

**LIMBAUGH, STEPHEN NATHANIEL,** federal judge; b. Cape Girardeau, Mo., Nov. 17, 1927; s. Rush Hudson and Bea (Seabaugh) L.; m. DeVaughn Anne Mesplay, Dec. 27, 1950; children—Stephen Nathaniel Jr., James Pennington, Andrew Thomas. B.A., S.E. Mo. State U., Cape Girardeau, 1950; J.D., U. Mo., Columbia, 1951. Bar: Mo. Prosecuting atty. Cape Girardeau County, Mo., 1954-58; judge U.S. Dist. Ct. (ea. and we. dists.) Mo., St. Louis, 1983—. Served with USN, 1945-46. Recipient Citation of Merit for Outstanding Achievement and Meritorious Service in Law, U. Mo., 1982. Fellow Am. Coll. Probate Counsel, Am. Bar Found.; mem. ABA (ho. of dels. 1987-90), Mo. Bar Assn. (pres. 1982-83). Republican. Methodist. Office: US Dist Ct 1114 Market St Rm 315 Saint Louis MO 63101-2038

**LIMBAUGH, STEPHEN NATHANIEL, JR.,** state supreme court judge; b. Cape Girardeau, Mo., Jan. 25, 1952; s. Stephen N. and Anne (Mesplay) L.; m. Marsha Dee Moore, July 21, 1973; children: Stephen III, Christopher K. BA, So. Meth. U., 1973, JD, 1976; LLM, U. Va., 1998. Bar: Tex. 1977, Mo. 1977. Assoc. Limbaugh, Limbaugh & Russell, Cape Girardeau, 1977-78; pros. atty. Cape Girardeau County, Cape Girardeau, 1979-82; shareholder, ptnr. Limbaugh, Limbaugh, Russell & Syler, Cape Girardeau, 1983-87; cir. judge 32d Jud. Cir., Cape Girardeau, 1987-92; judge Supreme Ct. Mo., Jefferson City, 1992—. Mem. ABA, State Bar Tex., Mo. Bar. Office: Supreme Ct Mo 207 W High St Jefferson City MO 65101-1516

**LINCOLN, MICHAEL POWELL,** lawyer; b. Pitts., Feb. 14, 1953; s. Herbert Kennedy and Ann (Dearing) L.; m. Marsha Laurene Fletcher Sochor, Oct. 19, 1979 (div. May 1988); children: Craig Fletcher, Megan Ann, Colby Patrick. BA in Polit. Sci., So. Conn. State Coll., New Haven, 1978; JD, U. Bridgeport, 1981. Bar: Conn. 1981, U.S. Dist. Ct. Conn. 1981, N.C. 1985, U.S. Dist. Ct. N.C. 1985, Ga. 1986. Mail rm. clk. Conn. Nat. Bank, Bridgeport, Conn., 1971-72; part-time bartender Surfside Café, Fairfield, Conn., 1974-78; part-time sales rep. Joyce Beverage, 7-Up, Norwalk and Watertown, Conn., 1976-81; assoc. Anthony F. Slez, Jr., Westport, Conn., 1981-83, Chan, Mitchell & Slez, Danbury, Conn., 1982-83; ptnr. Slez & Lincoln, Westport, 1983-84; assoc. Nelson W. Taylor III, Morehead City, N.C., 1984-86; ptnr. Edmundson & Lincoln, Emerald Isle, N.C., 1986—. With USMC, 1972-74. Republican. Avocations: golf, bodybuilding, basketball, nutrition. Real property, Estate planning, Criminal. Home: PO Box 4130 2414 Ocean Dr Emerald Isle NC 28594-6529 Office: Edmundson & Lincoln PO Box 4130 8204 Emerald Dr Unit 5 Emerald Isle NC 28594

**LIND, JON ROBERT,** lawyer; b. Evanston, Ill., July 4, 1935; s. Robert A. and Ruth (Anderson) L.; m. Jane Langfitt, Aug. 29, 1959; children: Jon Robert Jr., Elizabeth Neal, Susan Porter. AB, Harvard U., 1957, LLB, 1960; diploma in comparative law, Cambridge (Eng.) U., 1961. Bar: Ill. 1961. Assoc. Isham, Lincoln & Beale, Chgo., 1961-68, ptnr., 1968-88; ptnr. McDermott, Will & Emory, Chgo., 1988-96, of counsel, 1997—. Atty. Winnetka (Ill.) Park Dist., 1973-78; bd. dirs. Swedish-Am. Mus. Ctr., 1988-96. Mem. ABA, Chgo. Bar Assn., Harvard U. Alumni Assn. (sec. 1970-73), Econ. Club Chgo., Law Club Chgo. Securities, Banking, General corporate. Home: 644 Walden Rd Winnetka IL 60093-2035 Office: McDermott Will & Emery 227 W Monroe St Ste 3100 Chicago IL 60606-5096

**LINDAMOOD, JOHN BEYER,** lawyer; b. Columbus, Ohio, Jan. 18, 1941; children: Jennifer, J. Brad. AB, DePauw U., 1963; JD, Western Res. U., 1966. Bar: Ohio 1966, U.S. Dist. Ct. (no. dist.) Ohio 1968, U.S. Ct. Appeals (6th cir.) 1984, U.S. Supreme Ct. 1986. Assoc. Carson, Vogelgesang & Sheehan, Canton, Ohio, 1966-71; ptnr. Vogelgesang, Howes & Lindamood, Canton, 1971-79, Vogelgesang, Howes, Lindamood & Brunn, Canton, 1979—. Editor Western Res. Law Rev., 1965-66. Pres. Canton Exch. Club, 1970; v.p. Canton Jaycees, 1970-71; pres. Stark County Bar Assn., Canton, 1989-90. Fellow Ohio State Bar Found.; mem. ABA, Def. Rsch. Inst., Ohio State Bar Assn. (exec. com. 1982-85), Ohio Assn. Civil Trial Attys. Insurance, General civil litigation, Product liability. Office: Vogelgesang Howes Lindamood & Brunn 400 Tuscarawas St W Canton OH 44702-2018

**LINDAUER, ERIK D.,** lawyer; b. Bklyn., Oct. 1, 1956; s. Albert and Dinah (Epner) L.; m. Lisa Diamond, Aug. 16, 1981; children: Jacob, Samuel. BA, SUNY, Albany, 1978; JD, SUNY, Buffalo, 1981. Bar: N.Y. 1982, U.S. Dist. Ct. (ea. dist.) N.Y. 1982, U.S. Dist. Ct. (so. dist.) N.Y. 1982. Assoc. Sullivan & Cromwell, N.Y.C., 1981-89, ptnr., 1989—. Banking, Bankruptcy, Contracts commercial. Home: 37 Seminole Way Short Hills NJ 07078-1216 Office: Sullivan & Cromwell 125 Broad St Fl 28 New York NY 10004-2489

**LINDBERG, CHARLES DAVID,** lawyer; b. Moline, Ill., Sept. 11, 1928; s. Victor Samuel and Alice Christine (Johnson) L.; m. Marian J. Wagner, June 14, 1953; children: Christine, Breta, John, Eric. AB, Augustana Coll., Rock Island, Ill., 1950; LLB, Yale U., 1953. Bar: Ohio 1954. Assoc. Taft, Stettinius & Hollister, Cin., 1953-61, ptnr., 1961-85; mng. ptnr. Taft, Stettinius & Hollister, 1985-98, ptnr., 1999—; dir. Cin. Bengals Profl. Football Team, Gibson Greetings, Inc., Knowlton Constrn. Co., Market Max Inc.; chmn. bd. dirs. Schonstedt Instrument Co., 1994-97. Editor Nat. Law Jour., 1979-90. Bd. dirs. Taft Broadcasting Co., Cin., 1973-87, Dayton Walther Corp., 1986-87; bd. dirs. Augustana Coll., 1978-87, 91-99, sec., 1981-82, vice-chmn., 1982-83, chmn., 1983-86; pres. Cin. Bd. Edn., 1971, 74, Zion Luth. Ch., Cin., 1966-69; chmn. policy com. Hamilton County Rep. Com., 1981-90; mem. exec. com. Ohio Rep. Fin. Com., 1989-90; trustee Greater Cin. Ctr. Econ. Edn., 1976-91, pres., 1987-89, chmn., 1989-91; chmn. law firm divsn. Fine Arts Fund, 1985; trustee Pub. Libr. Cin. and Hamilton County, 1982—, pres., 1989, 96. Mem. Ohio Bar Assn., Cin. Bar Assn., Greater Cin. C. of C. (trustee 1985, exec. com., vice chmn. govt. and cmty. affairs com. 1989-91), Ohio Libr. Trustees Assn. (bd. dirs. 1986-87), Ohio C. of C. (bd. dirs. 1988-89), Queen City Club (sec. 1989-91), Commonwealth Club, Comml. Club (sec. 1994-96), Cin. Country Club, Optimists. General corporate, Mergers and acquisitions. Office: 1800 Firstar Tower 425 Walnut St Cincinnati OH 45202-3923

**LINDBERG, GEORGE W.,** federal judge; b. Crystal Lake, Ill., June 21, 1932; s. Alger Victor and Rilla (Wakem) L. BS, Northwestern U., 1954, JD, 1957. V.p., legal counsel John E. Reid & Assocs., Chgo., 1955-68; ptnr. Franz, Franz, Wardell & Lindberg, Crystal Lake, 1968-73; comptr. State of Ill., Springfield, 1973-77; dep. atty. gen. State of Ill., Chgo., 1977-78; justice Ill. Appellate Ct., Elgin, 1978-89; dist. judge U.S. Dist. Ct. (no. dist.) Ill., Chgo., 1989—; chmn. Ill. House Com. on Judiciary, Com. on Ethics, Springfield, 1970-73. Holder numerous govt. offices, 1966—. Office: US Dist Ct 219 S Dearborn St Ste 1460 Chicago IL 60604-1705

**LINDE, MAXINE HELEN,** lawyer, business executive, private investor; b. Chgo., Sept. 2, 1939; d. Jack and Lottie (Kroll) Stern; B.A. summa cum laude, UCLA, 1961; J.D., Stanford U., 1967; m. Ronald K. Linde, June 12, 1960. Bar: Calif. 1968. Applied mathematician, reseach engr. Jet Propulsion Lab., Pasadena, Calif., 1961-64; law clk. U.S. Dist. Ct. No. Calif., 1967-68;

mem. firm Long & Levit, San Francisco, 1968-69, Swerdlow, Glikbarg & Shimer, Beverly Hills, Calif., 1969-72; sec., gen. counsel Envirodyne Industries, Inc., Chgo., 1972-89; pres. The Ronald and Maxine Linde Found., 1989—; vice chmn. bd., gen. counsel Titan Fin. Group, LLC, Chgo., 1994-98. Mem. bd. visitors Stanford Law Sch., 1989-92, law and bus. adv. coun., 1991-94, dean's adv. coun. 1992-94. Mem. Order of Coif, Phi Beta Kappa, Pi Mu Epsilon, Alpha Lambda Delta. General corporate.

**LINDER, HARVEY RONALD,** lawyer, arbitrator, mediator; b. Pitts., July 23, 1949; s. Charles Joseph and Rose (Ruben) L.; m. Reva Rebecca Vertman, Aug. 14, 1971; children: Zalman F., Seth A. BA, Duquesne U., 1971, JD, 1975. Bar: Pa. 1975, U.S. Dist. Ct. (we. dist.) Pa. 1975, U.S. Supreme Ct. 1979. Legal intern Dist. Atty.'s Office, Pitts., 1974-75; asst. mgr. arbitration U.S. Steel, Pitts., 1975-80, mgr. labor rels., 1980-81; supt. employee rels. U.S. Steel, Clairton, Pa., 1981-83; corp. dir. employee rels. U.S. Steel Agri-Chemicals, Atlanta, 1984-86; corp. dir. law and human resources LaRoche Industries Inc., Atlanta, 1986-88, v.p., gen. counsel, 1988-96; v.p., gen. counsel Orion Mgmt. Svcs. Inc., 1996-97, SED Internat., Inc., 1997-99; arbitrator, mediator, 1996—; pres. A.C.I.R.A., 1987-90. Contbr. poetry and photography to Duquesne Literary Mag., 1968-74. Exec. cons. Jr. Achievement, Pitts., 1978-83; head coach Atlanta Jewish Cmty. Ctr., Dunwoody, Ga., 1984—, bd. dirs., 1991—; pres. B'nai Torah Synagogue, 1995-97, Hunter's Woods Homeowners' Assn., Dunwoody, 1986-87; commr. Baseball & Soccer Leagues; bd. dirs. Atlanta Jewish Fedn., 1995-96. Steel fellow Am. Iron and Steel Inst., 1977-85. Mem. ABA, Allegheny County Bar Assn., Indsl. Rels. Rsch. Assn., Duquesne U. Law Sch. Alumni Assn. (bd. dirs. 1980-84), B'nai B'rith (local v.p. 1975-80), Amer-Israel C. of C. (bd. dirs. 1993—). Democrat. Avocations: coaching, collecting books and sports memorabilia. General corporate, Alternative dispute resolution, Contracts commercial. Home: 365 Waters Bend Way Alpharetta GA 30022-8014

**LINDER, VIRGINIA LYNN,** state judge; b. Cañon City, Colo., Apr. 20, 1953; d. Irene D. Linder. BS in Polit. Sci., So. Oreg. State U., 1975; JD, Willamette U., 1980. Bar: Oreg., U.S. Dist. Ct. Oreg. 1981, U.S. Ct. Appeals (9th cir.) 1981, U.S. Supreme Ct. 1983. Asst. atty. gen. Oreg. Dept. Justice, Salem, 1980-83, atty. in charge edn. sect., gen. counsel, 1983-84, asst. solicitor gen., 1984-86, solicitor general, 1986-97; judge Oreg. Ct. Appeals, Salem, 1997—; presenter, spkr., panelist in fields of women's law, constnl. law, family and juvenile law, capital cases, other topics; adj. law prof. Willamette U., 1998—, U. Oreg. Law Sch., 1988; mem. Oreg. Judicial Dept. exec. com.; mem. appellate ct. tech. com., 1997—; mem. Coun. on Ct. Procedures, 1997—; mem. Appellate Cts. Settlement Conf. com., 1994; mem. Ho. Task Force on Oreg. Appellate Ct. Sys;., 1993-94; apptd. Oreg. Appellate Ct. rules com., 1990, 92-93; mem. 9th Cir. Death Penalty Task Force, 1988-91. Prin. author minority report Videotape Ct. Reporting Evaluation com., trial level, 1990, appellate level, 1991. Judge Nat. We the People (Bill of Rights) H.S. Competition, Washington, 1993; judge state-wide h.s. We the People Competition, Oreg. Law Related Edn. Program, 1992, 93; trial practice instr./judge, Willamette U., 1983—. Recipient Outstanding Alumna award, So. Oreg. State Coll., 1987; recipient Cmty. award YWCA Tribute to Outstanding Women, 1991; recipient merit award Oreg. Gay and Lesbian Lawyers Assn., 1996. Mem. Nat. Assn. Attys. Gen. (state specialist group providing amicus support and expertise on 8th amendment issues), Oreg. State Bar (exec. com. constnl. law sect., chair appellate practice sect. 1994-95, vice chair 1993-94, chair-elect 1994-95), Oreg. Women Lawyers (bd. mem. 1997—, exec. com. mem.), Marion County Bar Assn. (Law Practices Career Day host 1991, 92), Willamette Inns of Ct. Office: Oreg Ct Appeals 300 Justice Bldg 1162 Court St NE Salem OR 97310-1320

**LINDHOLM, DONALD WAYNE,** lawyer; b. Des Moines, Dec. 12, 1937; s. Rudolf William and Hazel Marie (Yoder) L.; m. E. DeAnne Wilson, Feb. 4, 1962; children: Dawn DeRae, Dow William. LLB, U. Ariz., 1966. Bar: Ariz. 1966, U.S. Dist. Ct. Ariz. 1966, U.S. Claims Ct. 1975, U.S. Ct. Appeals (9th cir.) 1988. Asst. city atty. City of Phoenix, 1966-74; ptnr. Flynn, Kimerer, Thinnes, Derrick & Lindholm, Phoenix, 1974-78; shareholder Donald W. Lindholm, P.C., Phoenix, 1978-81; counsel Treon, Warnicke & Roush, Phoenix, 1981; owner Capt. Jack's Landing Channel Island Harbor, Oxnard, Calif., 1982-85; shareholder Burch & Cracchiolo, P.A., Phoenix, 1985—. Fellow Ariz. Bar Found.; mem. ABA (family law section), Assn. Trial Lawyers Am., Nat. Inst. Mcpl. Law Officers (zoning and planning com.), State Bar of Ariz. (family law section, cert. specialist in domestic relations bd. of legal specialization), Ariz. Trial Lawyers Assn., Maricopa County Bar Assn. (family law sect.). Avocations: mountain biking, hiking, skiing, flying. Family and matrimonial, General civil litigation. Office: Burch and Cracchiolo PA 702 E Osborn Rd Ste 200 Phoenix AZ 85014-5234

**LINDLEY, JAMES DAVID,** lawyer; b. Paterson, N.J., May 24, 1948; s. Arthur Gugler and Dorothy Virgene (Roberts) L.; m. Jane Elizabeth Rosenberg, Aug. 22, 1971 (div. Aug. 1994); children: Maya Rachel, Joseph Samuel; m. Anita Martha Lemaire, June 30, 1996. BS in Acctg., U. N.C., 1973, PhD in Mktg., 1983; JD, Suffolk U., 1989. Bar: Mass. 1990, U.S. Dist. Ct. Mass. 1991, U.S. Bankruptcy Ct. 1991, U.S. Ct. Appeals (1st cir.) 1992, U.S. Supreme Ct. 1994. Sr. assoc. Antell & Assocs., Boston, 1990-96; pvt. practice law Boston, 1996—; asst. prof. Ohio U., Athens, 1978-84; assoc. prof. Suffolk U., Boston, 1984-89, Bentley Coll., Waltham, Mass., 1989-93. Fellow Nat. Employment Lawyers Assn., Univ. Club. Avocations: gardening, home repair, travel. Federal civil litigation, State civil litigation, Civil rights. Home: 120 Bynner St Jamaica Plain MA 02130-1043 Office: 33 Mount Vernon St Boston MA 02108-1420

**LINDQUIST, DONALD AUGUST,** lawyer; b. New Orleans, Sept. 28, 1924; s. Owen Henry and Anne (Grimes) L.; m. Fran C. Gorton, June 6, 1953; children: Christine Lindquist Smith, Catherine Lindquist Partridge, Donald C., Mary Fran Rosamond. BS, Mcht. Marine Acad., 1945; LLB, JD, Loyola U., New Orleans, 1951. Bar: U.S. Ct. Mil. Appeals, 1952, U.S. Supreme Ct. 1952, La. 1953, U.S. Dist. Ct. (ea. and mid. dists.) La. 1953, U.S. Ct. Appeals (5th cir.) 1953. Ptnr. Chaffe McCall Phillips Toler Sarpy, New Orleans, 1953—; mem. judge Fed. Ct. Disciplinary Bd., 1983-88; former lectr. naval R & D, Tulane U. Adv. editor Tulane Maritime Law Jour. Bd. dirs. New Orleans Acad.; lectr. on prostate cancer at med. schs. and clins.; mem. permanent adv. bd. Tulane Admiralty Inst. Ensign USN, 1945-48, 51-52; comdr. USNR (ret.). Mem. ABA, La. Bar Assn., New Orleans Bar Assn. (past chmn. fed. ct. com.), Bar City N.Y., Maritime Law Assn. U.S (membership com.), Assn. Average Adjusters, Comité Maritime Internat., Mil. Order Fgn. Wars (bd. dirs.), Metairie Country Club, Bienville Club, Delta Theta Phi. Republican. Roman Catholic. Avocations: golf, hunting and fishing, sailing, travel, reading. Fax: 504-585-7075. Admiralty. Office: Chaffe McCall Et Al 2300 Energy Ctr 1100 Poydras St New Orleans LA 70163-1101

**LINDQUIST-KLEISSLER, ARTHUR,** lawyer; b. East Orange, N.J., Feb. 19, 1954; s. Joan Ahern; m. Kathy Lindquist-Kleissler, Aug. 1, 1976; children: Danielle, Nichole, Brent. BA, Drew U., 1976; JD, U. Denver, 1979. Bar: Colo. 1976. Assoc. Solomon, Zimmerman, Schwartz, Denver, 1979-81; mng. ptnr. Solomon Lindquist-Kleissler, Denver, 1981-95, Lindquist-Kleissler, Cooper & Moore, Denver, 1995-98, Lindquist-Kleissler & Cooper, Denver, 1988—; charter mem. Faculty of Fed. Advocates, Denver. Bankruptcy, Federal civil litigation, General civil litigation. Office: Lindquist-Kleissler & Cooper 950 S Cherry St Ste 710 Denver CO 80246-2665

**LINDSAY, GEORGE PETER,** lawyer; b. Bklyn., Feb. 22, 1948; s. Charles Joseph and Marie Antionette (Faraone) L.; m. Sharon Winnett, Sept. 8, 1973; children: William Charles, Kimberly Michelle. BA, Columbia U., 1969; JD, Harvard U., 1973. Bar: N.Y. 1974, Mass. 1985, U.S. Dist. Ct. (so. dist.) N.Y. 1974, U.S. Ct. Appeals (2d cir.) 1975. Assoc. White & Case, N.Y.C., 1973-82; ptnr. Miller, Wrubel & Dubroff, N.Y.C., 1982-83, Sullivan & Worcester LLP, N.Y.C., 1983—. Mem. ABA, Assn. Bar City of N.Y., N.Y. State Bar Assn. Banking, Finance, Contracts commercial. Office: Sullivan & Worcester LLP 767 3rd Ave New York NY 10017-2023

**LINDSAY, REGINALD CARL,** lawyer; b. Birmingham, Ala., Mar. 19, 1945; s. Richard and Louise L.; cert. U. Valencia (Spain), 1966; A.B. in Polit. Sci. with honors, Morehouse Coll., 1967; J.D., Harvard U., 1970; m. Cheryl E. Hartgrove, Aug. 15, 1970. Admitted to Mass. bar, 1970, U.S. Dist. Ct. Mass. 1971, U.S. Ct. Appeals (1st cir.) 1971; assoc. firm Hill & Barlow, 1970-75, 78-79, partner, 1979-93; judge U.S. Dist. Ct. Mass., Boston, 1994—; arbitrator, mem. comml. arbitration panel Am. Arbitration Assn., 1994—; commr. Mass. Dept. Pub. Utilities, Boston, 1975-77; pres. adv. bd. Mus. of Nat. Center of Afro-Am. Artists, 1975-81, v.p., 1981—; trustee Thompson Islands Edn. Center, Boston, 1975-81; bd. dirs. United Way of Mass. Bay, 1981-84, Morgan Meml. Goodwill Industries, Boston, 1992—, Ptnrs. for Youth with Disabilities, Boston; mem. Nat. Consumer Law Ctr. (bd. dirs.), Mass. Commn. on Jud. Conduct, 1982-88; trustee Newton (Mass.) - Wellesley Hosp. Recipient Ruffin-Fenwick Trailblazer award Harvard Black Law Students Assn., 1994, recipient, Amanda V. Houston Community Svc. Awd., Boston Coll., 1998. Mem. Am., Nat., Mass., Boston (council 1977—, Citation of Jud. Excellence 1999) Bar Assns., Pi Sigma Alpha. Democrat. Office: 1 Courthouse Way Ste 5130 Boston MA 02210-3007

**LINDSEY, EDWARD HARMAN, JR.,** lawyer; b. Atlanta, Dec. 5, 1958; s. Edward Harman and Mary Dennard Lindsey; m. Elizabeth Green, Dec. 30, 1988; children: Harman, Zack, Charlie. BA, Davidson Coll., 1981; JD, U. Ga., 1984. Bar: Ga. 1984, U.S. Ct. Appeals (11th cir.) 1984, U.S. Dist. Ct. (so., mid., and no. dists.) Ga. 1984. Assoc. McClure Ramsey & Dickerson, Toccoa, Ga., 1984-87, Savell & Williams, Atlanta, 1987-90; ptnr. Goodman, McGuffey, Aust & Lindsey, Atlanta, 1990—. Bd. dirs. Atlanta Vol. Lawyers Found., 1997—. Mem. ABA, State Bar Ga., Atlanta Bar Assn., Atlanta Lawyers Club. General civil litigation, Insurance, Personal injury. Office: Goodman McGuffey Aust & Lindsey 2100 Tower Pl 3340 Peachtree Rd NE Atlanta GA 30326-1000

**LINDSEY, HUBERT ROLANE,** judge; b. Jacksonville, Fla., July 15, 1933; s. Hubert Rush and Martha Mae (Johnson) L.; m. Elma Jean Bryan, Oct. 17, 1958; 1 child, Susan. BA, U. fla., 1957; JD, U. Fla., 1966. Bar: Fla. 1966; U.S. Dist. Ct. (so. dist.) Fla. 1968; U.S. Ct. Appeals (5th cir.) 1968; U.S. Supreme Ct. 1975. Tchr., English Duval County Sch. System, Jacksonville, 1958-61; asst. mgr. Fla. Nat. Bank, Jacksonville, 1961-64; assoc. Farish & Farish, West Palm Beach, Fla., 1966-79; pvt. practice West Palm Beach, 1979-86; cir. judge Fla. Judiciary, West Palm Beach, 1986—. Mem. Fla. Bar Assn., Palm Beach County Bar Assn., Fla. Trial Lawyers Assn., ABA. Avocations: gardening, travel, carpentry. Office: Palm Beach County Courthouse 300 N Dixie Hwy West Palm Beach FL 33401-4640

**LINDSEY, LORI DAWN,** lawyer; b. Dallas, Apr. 12, 1972; d. Marion Glenn and Judy Jo Lindsey. BA summa cum laude, U. Okla., 1994, JD with highest honors, 1997. Bar: Okla. 1998. Law clk., legal intern, atty. Norman, Edem, McNaughton & Wallace, Oklahoma City, 1995-98; assoc. Pray, Walker, Jackman, Williamson & Marlar, Oklahoma City, 1998-99; law clk. for U.S. Dist. judge Vicki Miles-LaGrange Wester Dist. Okla., 1999—. Mem. ABA, ATLA, Okla. Trial Lawyers Assn. Avocations: tennis, puzzles. General civil litigation, Personal injury, General practice. Office: US Dist Ct Western Dist of Okla 200 NW 4th St Rm 5011 Oklahoma City OK 73102

**LINDSEY, THOMAS KENNETH,** lawyer, administrator; b. Radford, Va., Oct. 29, 1959; s. Joseph F. and Clare (LaCross) L.; m. Kathryn L. Gordon, Aug. 16, 1985. Student, Yale U., 1978-79; BS in Bus. Econs., Miami U., Oxford, Ohio, 1982; JD, So. Meth. U., 1985. Bar: Ohio 1986, U.S. Dist. Ct. (so. dist.) Ohio 1986, U.S. Ct. Appeals (6th cir.) 1988, U.S. Supreme Ct. 1991, Ill. 1991. Trial prosecutor Office Columbus City Atty., 1986, chief appellate prosecutor, 1988-91; assoc. Robert J. Behal Co., L.P.A., Columbus, Ohio, 1987; asst. city atty. City of Urbana, Ill., 1991-95, City of Columbus, 1995-96; with Franklin County Prosecuting Atty. Office, Columbus, 1996-98; chief dep. Franklin County Clk. of Cts., Columbus, 1998—. Mem. Ohio Bar Assn. (criminal justice com. 1989), Columbus Bar Assn. Republican. Roman Catholic. Avocations: sports, gardening. Office: Franklin County Clk of Cts 369 S High St 3d Fl Columbus OH 43215-4516

**LINE, WILLIAM GUNDERSON,** lawyer; b. July 19, 1927; s. William Harrison and Lulu Mae (Gunderson) L.; m. Laura C. Line; children: Nancy Line Jacobs, Lindsey Line Natvig, Katherine Line Rasmussen, Julie Ann Line Bailey, Ashley E. Student, Nebr. State Tchrs. Coll., 1943-44; BSL, U. Nebr., 1948, JD, 1950. Bar: Nebr. 1950, U.S. Dist. Ct. Nebr. 1950, U.S. Supreme Ct. 1965. County atty. Dodge County, Nebr., 1955-59; ptnr. Kerrigan, Line & Martin, Fremont, Nebr., 1962-95; lectr. Nebr. State Patrol Tng. Camp, Ashland, 1959. Bd. dirs. Nebr. Civil Liberties Union, 1971-75. Mem. Nebr. Bar Assn., Dodge County Bar Assn. (pres. 1967), Phi Alpha Delta. Republican. Episcopalian. General practice, Family and matrimonial, Criminal. Office: PO Box 410 33 W 4th St Fremont NE 68026-0410

**LINEBAUGH, DANIEL BRUCE,** lawyer; b. Youngstown, Ohio, Dec. 15, 1955; s. Clyde Albert Linebaugh and Wilma Ellen (Mackall) Connolley; m. Joan Renee Jackson, June 3, 1983; children: Sara, Christopher, Carolyn, Alex. BA in Speech Comms., Youngstown State U., 1978; JD, South Tex. Coll. Law, Houston, 1985. Bar: Tex. 1985, U.S. Dist. Ct. (so. and ea. dists.) Tex., U.S. Ct. Appeals (5th cir.), U.S. Supreme Ct. Claims rep. Employers Ins. Tex., Houston, 1979-83; legal asst. Michael Phillips, P.C., Houston, 1983-85, atty., 1985-86; atty. Glenn Vickery & Assocs., Baytown, Tex., 1987-92; ptnr. Vickery & Linebaug, Baytown, 1992—. Mem. ATLA, Tex. Bar Assn., Houston Bar Assn., East Harris County Bar Assn., Tex. Trial Lawyers Assn. (assoc. dir. 1991-92, dir. 1992—). Baptist. Personal injury, Product liability, Insurance. Office: Vickery & Linebaugh 1300 Rollingbrook St Ste 601 Baytown TX 77521-3846

**LINEBAUGH, KENT B.,** lawyer; b. Provo, Utah, Sept. 22, 1934; s. Glade Carleton and Thora Hawkins Linebaugh; m. Sherron Evelyn Bird, Jan. 12, 1962; children: Catherine, Mark B., Kent B. Jr., Elizabeth, Sarah. BS, U. Utah, 1958, JD, 1961. Bar: Utah 1961, U.S. Dist. Ct. Utah 1961, U.S. Ct. Appeals (10th cir.) 1969, U.S. Supreme Ct. 1995. Atty. Jones, Waldo, Holbrook & McDonough, Salt Lake City, 1965-70; gen. counsel Terracor, Salt Lake City, 1970-74; atty. Johnson & Linebaugh, Salt Lake City, 1974-76, Jardine, Johnson & Baldwin, Salt Lake City, 1976-78, Jardine, Johnson & Dunn, Salt Lake City, 1978—; pres. young lawyers sect. Utah State Bar, Salt Lake City, 1969-70; pres., dir. Olympus Farms, Salt Lake City, 1981—. With USAF, 1962-65. Mem. A. D. Anderson Inn of Ct. (past pres.). Mem. LDS Ch. Avocation: breeding and raising quarter horses. General civil litigation, Personal injury, Equine. Home: 3000 Connor St Apt 3 Salt Lake City UT 84109-2463 Office: Jardine Linebaugh & Dunn 370 E South Temple Ste 400 Salt Lake City UT 84111-1255

**LINEBERGER, PETER SAALFIELD,** lawyer; b. Akron, Ohio, Mar. 9, 1947; s. Walter F. Jr. and Mary Robinson (Saalfield) L.; children: Katherine Ann, Mary Elizabeth; m. Constance Meyers, Mar. 12, 1988. BA in English, Williams Coll., 1969; JD, Gonzaga U., 1976. Bar: Mont. 1976, Wash. 1994, U.S. Dist. Ct. Mont. 1977, U.S. Dist. Ct. (ea. dist.) Wash. 1994. Legal intern Witherspoon, Kelly, Davenport, O'Toole, Spokane, 1975; law clk. Mont. Supreme Ct., Helena, 1976; assoc. Landoe, Gary, Bozeman, Mont., 1977-78; ptnr. Landoe, Brown, Planalp, Komers & Lineberger, Bozeman, Mont., 1979-83, Lineberger & Davis, Bozeman, Mont., 1984-85, Lineberger & Harris, P.C., Bozeman, Mont., 1986-88, Lineberger, Walsh & McKenna, P.C., Bozeman, Mont., 1989-94; atty. sole practitioner Peter S. Lineberger, Spokane, 1994—; city atty. Town of West Yellowstone, Mont., 1978-94; chmn. Gallatin County Legal Svcs. Com., Bozeman, 1985-89, chmn. Mont. Child and Family Law Sect., 1993-94. Lt. USNR, 1969-72. Mem. ABA (mem. family law sect. 1987—), Wash. State Bar Assn. (mem. family law sect., exec. com. 1998—), Am. Acad. Matrimonial Lawyers, Gallatin County Bar Assn., Mont. City Attys. Assn. (pres. 1983), Spokane County Bar Assn. (vol. lawyers program adv. com. 1996—, chmn. 1998-99). Avocations: fly fishing, skiing. Family and matrimonial, General civil litigation, Real property. Office: 422 W Riverside Ave Ste 518 Spokane WA 99201-0302

**LINGELBACH, ALBERT LANE,** lawyer; b. N.Y.C., July 19, 1940; s. Robert Lane and Sarah (Lewis) L.; m. Ann Norton, July 31, 1965; children: Albert Lane, Charity Ann. BS, U. Pa., 1962, LLB, 1965. Bar: N.Y. 1967, U.S. Tax. Ct. 1984. Assoc. Jackson & Nash, LLP, N.Y.C., 1965-72, ptnr., 1972—. Co-chmn. Port Washington (N.Y.) Cmty. Chest Fund Drive, 1972-73, bd. dirs. 1973-74, sec. 1974-75, v.p. 1975-76, exec. v.p. 1976-78, pres. 1978-80; elder Roslyn Presbyn. Ch. Mem. ABA (com. on significant new devels. in probate and trust law practice 1983-87), Assn. Bar of City of N.Y. (mem. com. on trusts estates and surrogates ct. 1980-83), N.Y. State Bar Assn., Am. Coll. Trust and Estate Counsel, Estate Planning Coun. N.Y.C. (dir. 1998-99), Univ. Club (N.Y.C.), Southport (Maine) Yacht Club. Estate planning, Probate, Estate taxation. Home: Ketch Lady Ann PO Box 472 Port Washington NY 11050-0104 Office: Jackson & Nash 330 Madison Ave Rm 1800 New York NY 10017-5095

**LINGL, JAMES PETER,** lawyer; b. Appleton, Wis., Dec. 19, 1946; s. Peter Lawrence and Barbara (Verstegen) L.; children: Jason, Julie, Jameson. Student, Loyola U., Rome, 1967-68; BA, Rockhurst Coll., 1969; JD, U. Wis., 1975. Bar: Wis. 1975, U.S. Dist. Ct. (we. dist.) Wis. 1975, Calif. 1977, U.S. Dist. Ct. (cen. dist.) Calif. 1977. Ptnr. Bowman & Lingl, Depere, Wis., 1975-77, Taylor, Churchman & Lingl, Camarillo, Calif., 1977-83; prin. James P. Lingl & Assocs., Camarillo, 1983—. Author 8 pieces legis. State of Calif., 1987-90; chief editor Community Assn. Ref. Guide, 1990. Mem. Calif. Legis. Action Com., 1988-90; advisor Calif. Assembly Housing Com., 1989; bd. dirs. Boys and Girls Club, Camarillo, 1977-89, pres. 1986, adv. bd., 1989—; bd. dirs. Camarillo Arts Council, 1984—, Make-a-Wish, Ventura, Calif., 1985-89; bd. dirs. Channel Islands chpt. Community Assns. Inst., 1987—, pres., 1989, chief editor ref. guide and newsletter, 1990. Recipient Am. Jurisprudence award Bancroft-Whitney, 1975. Mem. Ventura County Trial Lawyers Assn. (bd. dirs. 1983-84), Ventura County Bar Assn. (various offices 1981-86). Democrat. Roman Catholic. Lodge: Rotary (bd. dirs. Camarillo 1982-83). Avocations: sailing, golf. Alternative dispute resolution, Legislative. Office: 1200 Paseo Camarillo Ste 170 Camarillo CA 93010-6085

**LINK, DAVID THOMAS,** lawyer, university administrator; b. 1936. B.S. magna cum laude, U. of Notre Dame, 1958, J.D., 1961; postgrad., Georgetown U., 1965-66. Bar: Ohio 1961, Ill. 1966, Ind. 1975, U.S. Supreme Ct. Trial atty., Office of Chief Counsel, IRS, 1961-66; ptnr., Winston, Strawn, Smith & Patterson, Chgo., 1966-70; prof., U. Notre Dame Law Sch., Notre Dame, Ind., 1970—, dean, 1975—; cons. to GAO; mem. Ind. Gov's Com. on Individual Privacy; mem. pres.' task force on New Methods for Improving the Quality of Lawyers' Services to Clients; chair Ind. State Ethics Commn., 1988-90; acad. coun., provost's adv. com., athletic affairs, acad. affairs, faculty affairs coms. of bd. of trustees U. Notre Dame; founding pres., vice chancellor U. Notre Dame, Perth, Aus., 1990-92, bd. trustees, bd. govs. Iterim dir. U. Notre Dame Ctr. for Civil and Human Rights; chair World Law Inst. Served to lt. comdr. USN. Mem. Soc. for Values in Higher Edn., ABA (council on sci. and tech., com. on advt., sect. on legal edn., com. on professionalism 1993-97). Author: (with Soderquist) Law of Federal Estate and Gift Taxation, Vol. 1, 1978, Vol. 2, 1980. Office: U Notre Dame Law Sch Notre Dame IN 46556*

**LINK, GARY STEVEN,** lawyer; b. Higginsville, Mo., June 7, 1949; s. Donald Ray and Aileen Margaret (Neher) L.; m. Nona Ann Lindsey, Jan. 3, 1970 (div. 1980); 1 child, Jennifer Megan; m. Kathleen Annette Stewart, June 19, 1982 (div. 1996); children: Amy Leigh Morgan, Benjamin Stewart Morgan, Jessica Catherine. BA in Polit. Sci., Colo. State U., 1971; JD, U. Denver, 1974. Bar: Colo. 1974. Lawyer, sole practice Gary S. Link, Atty. at. Law, Colorado Springs, 1974—. Participant fundraising Am. Cancer Soc., Colorado Springs, 1991. With USAR, 1970-76. Recipient scholarship Hewlett-Packard, Colorado Springs, 1967, El Paso County Sheriffs Assn., 1967. Mem. Colo. Bar Assn., El Paso County Bar Assn. Democrat. Methodist. Avocations: golf, reading, travel to Mexico. Criminal, Probate, Juvenile. Office: Gary S Link Atty at Law 716 E Fontanero St Colorado Springs CO 80907-7743

**LINK, GEORGE HAMILTON,** lawyer; b. Sacramento, Calif., Mar. 26, 1939; s. Hoyle and Corrie Elizabeth (Evans) L.; m. Betsy Leland; children—Thomas Hamilton, Christopher Leland. AB, U. Calif., Berkeley, 1961; LLB, Harvard U., 1964. Bar: Calif. 1965, U.S. Dist. Ct. (no., ea., ctrl. and so dists.) Calif. 1965, U.S. Ct. Appeals (9th cir.) 1965. Assoc. Brobeck, Phleger & Harrison, San Francisco, 1964-69, ptnr., 1970—; mng. ptnr. Brobeck, Phleger & Harrison, L.A., 1973-93; mng. ptnr. firmwide Brobeck, Phleger & Harrison, 1993-96; chmn. Pacific Rim Adv. Coun., 1992-95. Bd. regents U. Calif., 1971-74; trustee Berkeley Found., Jr. Statesmen Am.; bd. govs. United Way, 1979-81; trustee, v.p. Calif. Hist. Soc., 1987—. Fellow Am. Bar Found.; mem. ABA, Calif. Bar Assn., L.A. Bar Assn., U. Calif. Alumni Assn. (pres. 1972-75), Calif. Club, Bohemian Club, Jonathan Club. Republican. Methodist. Office: Brobeck Phleger & Harrison 550 S Hope St Los Angeles CA 90071-2627

**LINK, JAMES S.,** lawyer; b. Pasadena, Calif., Aug. 19, 1954; s. Marion T. and Adelaide C. Link; m. Pamela Mary Taylor, Jan. 8, 1977; children: Ross, Justin, Nicholas, Adam. BA, U. San Francisco, 1976; JD, Southwestern U., 1980. Bar: Calif. 1980, U.S. Cir. Ct. (9th cir.) 1982, U.S. Supreme Ct. 1985. Cert. specialist appellate law Calif. State Bar Assn., 1998. Atty. Spray, Gould & Bowers, L.A., 1980-81, Murchison & Cumming, L.A., 1981-84; atty., shareholder, dir. Spray, Gould & Bowers, L.A., 1984-91; pvt. practice, 1991—. Asst. baseball coach L.A. Pks. and Recreation, 1997, 98. Mem. Calif. State Bar (legis. sub-com 1995), L.A. County Bar Assn. (appellate ct. com.). Appellate, Insurance. Office: 215 N Marengo Ave Fl 3 Pasadena CA 91101-1504

**LINK, ROBERT JAMES,** lawyer, educator; b. Washington, May 25, 1950; s. Robert Wendell and Barbara Ann (Bullock) L.; m. Cheryl Ann Brillante, Apr. 22, 1978; children: Robert Edward, Holden James. BA, U. Miami, 1972, JD, 1975. Bar: Fla. 1975, U.S. Dist. Ct. (mid. dist.) Fla. 1980, U.S. Ct. Appeals (5th cir.) 1980, U.S. Ct. Appeals (11th cir.) 1981, U.S. Supreme Ct. 1984, U.S. Dist. Ct. (no. dist.) Fla. 1989. Asst. pub. defender City of Miami, Fla., 1975-78, City of Jacksonville, Fla., 1978-82; ptnr. Greenspan, Goodstein & Link, Jacksonville, 1982-84, Goodstein & Link, Jacksonville, 1984-85; pvt. practice, Jacksonville, 1985-88; assoc. Howell, Liles & Milton, Jacksonville, 1988-89; ptnr. Pajcic & Pajcic P.A., 1990—; guest instr. U. Miami, 1976, U. Fla., 1979-88, Stetson U. Law Sch., 1984, Jacksonville U., 1987-88, U. North Fla., 1991. Atty. legal panel ACLU, Jacksonville, 1982-88. Mem. Fla. Bar Assn. (chmn. com. for representation of indigents criminal law sect. 1980, cert. criminal trial lawyer 1989), Jacksonville Bar Assn. (criminal law sect.), Nat. Assn. Criminal Def. Lawyers (vice-chmn. post conviction com. 1990), Fla. Pub. Defender Assn. (death penalty steering com. 1980-82, instr. 1979-89). Democrat. Methodist. Avocations: sailing, fishing, diving, softball. Criminal, Personal injury, Product liability. Home: 3535 Carlyon St Jacksonville FL 32207-5836 Office: 1900 Independent Sq Jacksonville FL 32202-5013

**LINKER, RAYMOND OTHO, JR.,** lawyer; b. Charlotte, N.C., Jan. 18, 1946; s. Raymond Otho Sr. and Frances (Baucom) L.; m. Nola Grady Jenning, June 24, 1969; 1 child, John Raymond. BS in Chem. Engring., N.C. State U., 1968; JD, Georgetown U., 1972. Bar: N.C. 1972, U.S. Dist. Ct. (we. dist.) N.C. 1972, U.S. Patent Trademark Office 1972. From assoc. to ptnr. Bell, Seltzer, Park & Gibson, Charlotte, 1972—; group leader Alston & Bird. Mem. N.C. Bar Assn., Am. Intellectual Property Assn. (chair inventor issues com.), Carolinas Patent, Trademark and Copyright Law Assn. (past pres.). Presbyterian. Patent, Trademark and copyright, Computer. Office: Alston & Bird LLP 1211 E Morehead St Charlotte NC 28204-2816

**LINKLATER, WILLIAM JOSEPH,** lawyer; b. Chgo., June 3, 1942; s. William John and Jean (Connell) L.; m. Dorothea D. Ash, Apr. 4, 1986; children: Erin, Emily. BA, U. Notre Dame, 1964; JD, Loyola U., 1968. Bar: Ill. 1968, U.S. Dist. Ct. (no. dist.) Ill. 1968, U.S. Ct. Appeals (7th cir.) 1971, U.S. Supreme Ct. 1971, U.S. Ct. Appeals Washington, 1978, U.S. Ct. Appeals Washington 1978, Calif. 1981, U.S. Dist. Ct. (cen. dist.) Calif. 1981, U.S. Tax Ct. 1982, U.S. Dist. Ct. (no. dist.) Calif. 1983, U.S. Dist. Ct. (ea. dist.) Mich. 1989, U.S. Ct. Appeals (6th cir.) 1990, U.S. Dist. Ct. Hawaii, 1992. Atty. Fed. Defender Project, Chgo.; assoc. Baker & McKenzie, Chgo., 1968-75, ptnr., 1975—. Contbr. articles to profl. jours. Mem. ABA (past co-chmn. com. on internat. criminal law criminal justice sect., mem. criminal practice and procedure com. antitrust sect., mem. criminal justice sect.), FBA, Ill. Bar Assn., 7th Cir. Bar Assn., Chgo. Bar Assn. ( v.p. 1998-99, bd. mgrs. 1997-98, past v.p. jud. candidates evaluation com., chmn. large law firm com., 2d v.p. 1998-99, 1st v.p. 1999—, pres.-elect), Internat. Inst., Calif. Bar Assn., Colo. Bar Assn., Am. Coll. Trial Lawyers, Am. Bd. Criminal Lawyers, Chgo. Inn of Ct., Wong Sun Soc. San Francisco (internat. proctor),

Alpha Simga Nu. Criminal, Antitrust, Federal civil litigation. Office: Baker & McKenzie 1 Prudential Plz Ste 3000 Chicago IL 60601

**LINKNER, MONICA FARRIS,** lawyer; b. Detroit, Dec. 2, 1947; d. Bernard and Madelyn (Lederer) Farris; m. Robert V. Linkner, Dec. 27, 1967 (div. May 1973); 1 child, Joshua Morgan Linkner; m. Dennis J. Dlugokinski, June 4, 1984; 1 child, Matthew Scott Dlugokinski. Student, U. Mich., 1965-67; BA magna cum laude, Wayne State U., 1972, JD, 1977. Bar: Mich. 1977, U.S. Dist. Ct. (ea. dist.) Mich. 1977, U.S. Ct. Appeals (6th cir.) 1985. Asst. to reporter State of Mich. Standard Criminal Jury Instrns. Com., Detroit, 1973-74; clin. student atty. Wayne State Univ. Employment Discrimination, Detroit, 1977; clk. Mich. Ct. Appeals, Detroit, 1977-78; assoc. Lampert, Fried & Levitt, PC, Birmingham, Mich., 1978-80, Lopatin, Miller, Freedman, et. al., Detroit, 1980-88; pvt. practice Berkley, Mich., 1988—; prin. atty. Adoption Law Ctr., P.C., 1993—. Editor: Winning Final Arguments, 1985, contbr. articles to profl. jours. Advocate Parents for Pvt. Adoption, Lathrup Village, Mich., 1990—; vol. tchr. Peoples Law Sch., Detroit, 1985, Women's Prison Legal Edn. Project, Ypsilanti, Mich., 1975-77. Mem. ATLA, ACLU, Am. Acad. Adoption Attys. (trustee 1995-99), Mich. Trial Lawyers Assn. (sustaining; handicappers law reform advocate 1988-90, chair amicus curae com. 1988-94), State Bar (family law sect. adoption com.), 1995—, Disability Rights Bar Assn., Women Lawyers Assn. Mich., S.C. Trial Lawyers Assn., Family Tree (pres.), Amnesty Internat., Phi Beta Kappa, Alpha Lambda Delta. Avocations: hiking, sailing, cooking, reading. Immigration, naturalization, and customs. Office: 3250 Coolidge Hwy Berkley MI 48072-1634

**LINKS, ROBERT DAVID,** lawyer; b. San Francisco, Aug. 25, 1949; s. Milton Arnold and Roslyn (Morris) L.; m. Robyn Taidy Chew, July 22, 1984 (div.); 1 child, Alexis Jade. AB in Journalism, U. Calif., Berkeley, 1971; JD, UCLA, 1974. Bar: Calif. 1974, U.S. Dist. Ct. (no. dist.) Calif. 1974, U.S. Ct. Appeals (9th cir.) 1979, U.S. Supreme Ct. 1978. Assoc. Jacobs, Blanckenburg, May & Colvin, San Francisco, 1974-79; ptnr. Colvin Martin & Links, 1979-85; assoc. Harold S. Dobbs, 1985; assoc. Dobbs, Berger, Molinari, Casalnuovo, Vanelli & Nadel, 1985-86, ptnr., 1986-89; ptnr. Dobbs, Berger, Molinari, Vanelli, Nadel & Links, 1989-94; spl. counsel Berger, Nadel & Vannelli; student intern, Justice Mathew O. Tobriner, Calif. Supreme Ct., 1973. Editor: Toward Social Change, 1971, California Civil Practice Civil Rights Module, 1994—; author: Follow the Wind, 1995. Bd. dirs. San Francisco-Bay area chpt. Am. Jewish Com., 1982—. Mem. Calif. Bar Assn., San Francisco Bar Assn., San Francisco Trial Lawyers Assn., Lake Merced Golf and Country Club, Phi Beta Kappa. Democrat. Avocations: golf, photography, creative writing. E-mail: bolinks@lmi.net. Education and schools, General civil litigation. Office: Berger Nadel & Vannelli 650 California St Fl 25 San Francisco CA 94108-2702

**LINN, BRIAN JAMES,** lawyer; b. Seattle, July 8, 1947; s. Bruce Hugh and Jeanne De V. (Weidman) L.; m. Renee Diane Mousley; children: Kelly, Kareem, Kari. BA in Econs., U. Wash., 1972; JD, Gonzaga Sch. Law, 1975. Bar: Wash. 1975, U.S. Supreme Ct. 1979. Mng. atty. Legal Svcs. for Northwestern Pa., Franklin, 1975-76; staff atty. The Nat. Ctr. for Law and the Handicapped, 1976-78, U. Notre Dame Law Sch., South Bend, Ind., 1976-78; pvt. practice, Seattle, 1978—; lectr. Seattle U., 1980-85. Chmn. civil and legal rights subcom. Gov.'s Com. on Employment of the Handicapped, 1981-87; arbitrator King County Superior Ct., 1981—, judge pro tem, 1989—. Editor Gonzaga Law Rev., 1974-75. Mem. Wash. State Devel. Disabilities Planning Council, 1980-83; trustee Community Service Ctr. for the Deaf and Hard of Hearing, Seattle, 1982-84; chmn. legal rights task force Epilepsy Found. Am., 1979-81; mem. Witness for Peace Delegation, Nicaraqua, 1993. Served with U.S. Army, 1967-69; Vietnam. Mem. Wash. State Bar Assn. (chair world peace through law sect. 1990-91, spl. dist. counsel 1991-95), Omicron Delta Epsilon. Democrat. Methodist. Hon. editor DePaul Law Rev., 1978; contbr. articles to profl. jours. General civil litigation, Civil rights, Juvenile. Home: 9716 S 204th Ct Kent WA 98031-1400 Office: 245 SW 152nd St Seattle WA 98166-2307

**LINN, RICHARD,** lawyer; b. Bklyn., Apr. 13, 1944; s. Marvin and Enid (Rowe) L.; m. Patricia Madden, Aug. 8, 1966; children: Sandra Joan, Deborah Anne. BEE, Rensselaer Poly. Inst., 1965; JD, Georgetown U., 1969. Bar: Va. 1969, D.C. 1970, N.Y. 1994, U.S. Dist. Ct. (ea. dist.) Va. 1969, U.S. Dist. Ct. D.C. 1970, U.S. Ct. Appeals (4th cir.) 1970, U.S. Ct. Appeals (D.C. cir.) 1970, U.S. Ct. Appeals (fed. cir.) 1982, U.S. Supreme Ct. 1994. Patent examiner U.S. Patent and Trademark Office, Washington, 1965-68; patent agt. Office Naval Rsch., Washington, 1968-69; assoc. Brenner, O'Brian, Guay & Connors, Arlington, Va., 1969-71, Stepno & Neilan, Arlington, 1971-72; ptnr. Stepno, Schwab & Linn, Arlington, 1972-74; pvt. practice Washington, 1974-77; ptnr. Wender, Murase & White (name changed to Marks & Murase), Washington, 1977, mng. ptnr. Washington office, 1982-97; ptnr. Foley & Lardner, Washington, 1997—. Mem. ABA, Am. Intellectual Property Law Assn., Va. Bar Assn. (founding bd. govs. Intellectual Property sect. 1971), Rensselaer Washington Alumni Assn. (chmn. 1972). Avocations: cycling, swimming, restoring classic cars. Patent, Trademark and copyright, Federal civil litigation. Office: Foley & Lardner Washington Harbor 3000 K St NW Ste 500 Washington DC 20007-5143

**LINNAN, JAMES DANIEL,** lawyer; b. Olean, N.Y., Nov. 29, 1946; s. William Martin and Genevieve (Toohey) L.; m. Pamela LaFalce, June 5, 1971; 1 child, Brigid Mary. B.S., Northeastern U., Boston, 1969; J.D., Albany Law Sch., 1972. Bar: N.Y. 1973, U.S. Dist. Ct. (No. Dist.) N.Y. 1973, U.S. Dist. Ct. Vt. 1976, U.S. Ct. Appeals (2d Cir.) 1976, U.S. Supreme Ct. 1978. Spl. litigation counsel City of Albany, N.Y., 1976—; assoc. law firm Garry, Cahill & Edmunds, Albany, 1973-76; sole practice law, Albany, 1976-84; ptnr. law firm Linnan, Shea & Flannery, Albany, 1984-86, Linnan, Bacon & Shea, Albany, 1987—. Founder, pres., v.p. Northeastern Family and Children's House, Inc., 1981; mem. Albany County Democratic Com., 1976—. Mem. Assn. Trial Lawyers Am., N.Y. State Bar Assn., N.Y. Trial Lawyers, Capital Dist. Trial Lawyers. Democrat. Roman Catholic. Personal injury, State civil litigation, Federal civil litigation. Home: 41 Euclid Ave Albany NY 12203-1809 Office: Linnan Bacon & Meyer 61 Columbia St Albany NY 12210-2736

**LINOWITZ, SOL MYRON,** lawyer; b. Trenton, N.J., Dec. 7, 1913; s. Joseph and Rose (Oglenskye) L.; m. Evelyn Zimmerman, Sept. 3, 1939; children: Anne, June, Jan, Ronni. AB, Hamilton Coll., 1935; JD, Cornell U., 1938; LLD (hon.), Allegheny Coll., Amherst Coll., Bucknell U., Babson Inst., Brandeis U., Colgate U., Curry Coll., Dartmouth Coll., Elmira Coll., Georgetown U., Hamilton Coll., Hebrew Union Coll., Ithaca Coll., Marietta Coll., Johns Hopkins U., Oberlin Coll., St. John Fisher Coll., St. Lawrence U., Jewish Theol. Sem., Washington U., St. Louis, U. Miami, Muskingum Coll., Notre Dame U., U. Pacific, U. Pa., Rutgers U., Pratt Inst., Rider Coll., Roosevelt U., Chapman Coll., U. Mich., Govs. State U., U. Mo., Syracuse U.; LHD (hon.), Am. U., Loyola U., U. Rochester, Yeshiva U., U. Judaism, Wooster Coll.; PhD (hon.), U. Haifa. Bar: N.Y. 1938. Asst. gen. counsel OPA, Washington, 1942-44; ptnr. Sutherland, Linowitz & Williams, 1946-58, Harris, Beach, Keating, Wilcox & Linowitz, Rochester, N.Y., 1958-66; chmn. Nat. Urban Coalition, 1970-76; chmn. bd. dirs., chmn. exec. com., gen. counsel Xerox Corp., 1958-66; chmn. bd. dirs. Xerox Internat., 1966; sr. ptnr. Coudert Bros., 1969-84, sr. counsel, 1984-94; ambassador to OAS, 1966-69; negotiator Panama Canal treaties, 1977-78; spl. Middle East negotiator for Pres. Carter, 1979-81; chmn. Am. Acad. of Diplomacy, 1984-89; co-chmn. Inter-Am. Dialogue, 1981-92; pres. Fed. City Coun., 1974-78; chmn. Pres. Commn. World Hunger, 1978-79; bd. dirs., co-founder Internat. Exec. Svc. Corps; chmn. State Dept. Adv. Com. on Internat. Orgns., 1963-66. Author: The Betrayed Profession, 1994, (memoir) The Making of a Public Man, 1985, This Troubled Urban World, 1974; contbr. articles to profl. jours. Trustee Hamilton Coll. (life), Cornell U. (emeritus), Johns Hopkins U. (emeritus), Am. Assembly; chmn. bd. overseers, bd. dirs. Jewish Theol. Sem., 1971-79. Lt. USNR, 1944-46. Recipient Presdl. Medal of Freedom, 1998. Fellow Am. Acad. Arts and Scis.; mem. Am. Assn. for UN (pres. N.Y. State), Rochester Assn. for UN (pres. 1952), Rochester C. of C. (pres. 1958), ABA, N.Y. Bar Assn., Rochester Bar Assn. (v.p. 1949-50), Am. Assn. UN (bd. dirs.), Council on Fgn. Relations, Order of Coif, Phi Beta Kappa, Phi Kappa Phi. Private international, Public international. Office: Acad for Ednl Devel 1875 Connecticut Ave NW Washington DC 20009-5728

**LINSCOTT, MICHAEL S.,** lawyer; b. Oklahoma City, Apr. 22, 1959; s. Gilbert Leroy and Anita Joan (Silver) L.; m. Lynda Carole Burris, May 26, 1959; children: Michael James, Thomas Mason, Matthew Burris, Carolyn Tyree. BS, Okla. U., 1984; JD, U. Tulsa, 1991. Atty. Liddell, Sapp, Zivley, Hill & LaBron, LLP, Dallas, 1991-97, Logan & Lowry LLP, Vinita, Okla., 1997—. Mem. ABA, FBA, Okla. Bar Assn., Craig County Bar Assn. (law day chair), Lions Club (officer). Avocations: chess, fishing, hunting, golf. State civil litigation, Insurance, Federal civil litigation. Office: Logan & Lowry LLP 101 S Wilson St Vinita OK 74301-3729

**LINSTEDT, WALTER GRIFFITHS,** lawyer, banker; b. Turlock, Calif., Mar. 16, 1933; s. Daniel Henry and Wanda Mae (Griffiths) L.; m. Kathleen Dawson, Apr. 1956 (div. 1977); children: Adam, Laurel, Pamela; m. MaryLou Campbell, Apr. 29, 1978. BA, Stanford U., 1955; JD, U. Calif., San Francisco, 1960. Bar: Calif. 1961, Ill. 1976. Counsel Calif. Pub. Utilities Commn., San Francisco, 1960-63; assoc. Erskine & Tulley, San Francisco, 1963-66; v.p., assoc. gen. counsel Crocker Bank, San Francisco, 1966-74; ptnr. Macdonald, Halsted & Laybourne, L.A., 1974-76; v.p., assoc. gen. counsel Continental Ill. Nat. Bank and Trust Co. Chgo., 1976-88; asst. gen. counsel Bank of Am., L.A., 1988-99; trustee Calif. Indian Legal Svcs., San Francisco, 1968-75, 860 Lake Shore Dr. Trust, Chgo., 1985-88. Avocations: tennis, photography. Banking, Contracts commercial, Real property. Home: 3600 Yorkshire Rd Pasadena CA 91107-5433

**LINTON, JACK ARTHUR,** lawyer; b. N.Y.C., May 29, 1936; s. Paul Phillip and Helen (Feller) L.; m. Nancy A., Sept. 1, 1957; children: Ann Deborah Linton Wilmot, James Paul, John Michael. BA, Albright Coll., 1958; JD, NYU, 1961, LLM in Taxation, 1966. Bar: Pa. 1962, N.Y. 1963, U.S. Tax Ct. 1966, U.S. Dist. Ct. (ea. dist.) Pa. 1978, U.S. Ct. Appeals, 1984. Assoc. DeLong, Dry & Binder, Reading, Pa., 1961-63; asst. ho. counsel Bob Banner Assocs., Inc., N.Y.C., 1963-66; ptnr. DeLong, Dry, Cianci & Linton, Reading, 1967-70, Williamson, Miller, Murray & Linton, Reading, 1970-72, Gerber & Linton, P.C., Reading, 1972-88, Linton, Giannascoli, Barrett & Distasio, P.C., Reading, 1989-97, Linton, Giannascoli, Distasio & Adams, PC, Reading, 1997-98, Linton, Distasio, Adam & Kauffman, PC, Reading, 1998—; solicitor Reading Parking Authority, 1967-76, City of Reading, 1980-96; bd. dirs. The Group, Inc., Small Bus. Coun. Am., Inc., chmn. polit. action com., 1988—, numerous med. profl. corps., Reading area; lectr. nat. seminars on tax problems for small bus.; co-founder, mem. Estate Planning Coun. Berks County, 1978—. Editor Tax Law Rev., 1965-67; contbr. articles to profl. jours. Pres. Berks County Mental Health Assn., 1968-69, Reading Jewish Community Ctr., 1980-82; mem. Mental Health/Mental Retardation Bd. Berks County, 1974-80; treas., bd. dirs. Reading-Berks Youth Soccer League, 1982-85; bd. dirs. Gov. Mifflin Sch. Dist., Shillington, 1985-93. Kenneson fellow NYU Sch. Law, 1965-67. Mem. ABA (mem. personal svc. orgn. com., tax sect. 1981—, chairperson task force for repeal top-heavy rules 1987-89, vice chmn. personal svc. orgn. com. 1990-92, chmn. personal svc. orgn. com. 1992-94), Pa. Bar Assn., Berks County Bar Assn. (treas. 1969-72), Berks County C. of C. (mem. nat. affairs com.). Democrat. Jewish. Avocations: sports, reading. Estate taxation, Pension, profit-sharing, and employee benefits, Estate planning. Office: Linton Distasio Adams & Kauffman PC PO Box 461 1720 Mineral Spring Rd Reading PA 19602-2231

**LINXWILER, JAMES DAVID,** lawyer; b. Fresno, Calif., Apr. 9, 1949; s. George Edwin and Stella Ruth (Schmidt) L.; m. Robyn Kenning, July 12, 1986; children: Elizabeth Ann, John Edwin, Jeffrey David. BA, U. Calif., Berkeley, 1971; JD, UCLA, 1974. Bar: D.C. 1976, U.S. Dist. Ct. Alaska 1976, U.S. Dist. Ct. (D.C. cir.) 1976, Alaska 1977, U.S. Ct. Appeals (9th cir.) 1977, U.S. Supreme Ct. 1988. Lawyer U.S. Dept. Interior, Washington, 1974-76, Cook Inlet Region, Inc., Anchorage, 1976-78, Sohio Petroleum Co., Anchorage, 1978-81; shareholder Guess & Rudd, Anchorage, 1981—; spkr. seminars on environ. and natural resources law. Contbr. chpts. to book, articles to profl. jours. Chmn. Alaska Coalition Am. Energy Security, 1986-87, Alliance Arctic Nat. Wildlife Refuge Com., 1986-87; bd. dirs. Commonwealth North, 1993-99, pres., 1999—. Mem. ABA, FBA, Alaska Bar Assn. (chmn., exec. com. nat. resources sect. 1988-93), D.C. Bar Assn. Democrat. Oil, gas, and mineral, Environmental, Administrative and regulatory. Home: 2407 Loussac Dr Anchorage AK 99517-1272 Office: Guess & Rudd 510 L St Ste 700 Anchorage AK 99501-1959

**LIONE, JOHN GABRIEL, JR.,** lawyer; b. Bayonne, N.J., Mar. 26, 1949; s. John Gabriel and Marjorie (Hartwell) L.; m. Wendy A. Lione, June 8, 1974; children: Ryan Wesley, Kacey Lyn. BA in Govt., Georgetown U., 1971; JD, U. Tex., 1974. Bar: Tex. 1974; bd. cert. in comml. real estate law, Tex. Asst. city atty. City of Houston Legal Dept., 1974-80; regional counsel Coldwell Banker Real Estate, Houston, 1980-83; assoc. atty. Babb & Hanna, Austin, Tex., 1983-95; prin. atty. Lione & Lee, P.C., Austin, 1985—. Avocations: golf, jogging, basketball. Real property, State civil litigation, General corporate. Office: Lione & Lee PC 3921 Steck Ave Ste A119 Austin TX 78759-8647

**LIOZ, LAWRENCE STEPHEN,** lawyer, accountant; b. N.Y.C., Sept. 24, 1945; s. William and Irma (Berkshn) L.; m. Carol Renee Skolnik, Nov. 20, 1971; children: Adam Russell, Randall Eric. BS, SUNY, Albany, 1967; JD, SUNY, Buffalo, 1970; LLM in Taxation, NYU, 1975. Bar: N.Y.; CPA, N.Y. Mgr. Ernst & Whinney, N.Y.C., 1970-79; dir. tax affairs Azcon Corp., N.Y.C., 1979-82; mgr. Deloitte Haskins & Sells, N.Y.C., 1982-83, ptnr., 1983-84; ptnr. Deloitte Haskins & Sells, Woodbury, N.Y., 1984-87, Margolin, Winer & Evens L.L.P., Garden City, N.Y., 1987—; speaker various tax seminars, 1986—. Contbr. articles on tax to profl. jours. Pres. Rolling Wood Civic Assn., Roslyn, N.Y., 1983—; trustee Flower Hill (N.Y.) Assn., 1985-87, Village of Flower Hill, 1987-92; treas. Roslyn Sch. Dist., 1986-99. Mem. ABA, AICPAs, N.Y. State Bar Assn., N.Y. State Soc. CPAs (chmn. fed. tax com. Nassau chpt. 1989-92, exec. bd. 1992—). Jewish. Avocations: skiing, golf. Home: 84 Knollwood W Roslyn NY 11576-1319 Office: Margolin Winer & Evens LLP 400 Garden City Plz Fl 5 Garden City NY 11530-3323

**LIPCON, CHARLES ROY,** lawyer; b. N.Y.C., Mar. 20, 1946; s. Harry H. and Rose Lipcon; m. Irmgard Adels, Dec. 1, 1974; children: Lauren, Claudia. BA, U. Miami, 1968, JD, 1971. Bar: Fla. 1971, U.S. Dist. Ct. (so. dist.) Fla. 1971, U.S. Ct. Appeals (5th cir.) 1972, U.S. Supreme Ct. 1976, U.S. Ct. Appeals (D.C. cir.) 1980, U.S. Dist. Ct. (so. dist.) Tex. 1982, U.S. Ct. Appeals (11th cir.) 1994, U.S. Dist. Ct. Colo. 1999. Pvt. practice Miami, Fla., 1971—; lectr. U. Miami Sch. Law. Author: Help for the Auto Accident Victim, 1984, Seaman's Rights in the United States When Involved in An Accident, 1989; contbr. articles to profl. jours. Named Commodore of High Seas, Internat. Seaman's Union. Mem. ABA, ATLA, Fla. Bar Assn., Fla. Trial Lawyers Assn., Dade County Bar Assn., Dade County Trial Lawyers, Fla. Admiralty Trial Lawyers Assn. Admiralty, Personal injury, Federal civil litigation. Office: 2 S Biscayne Blvd Ste 2480 Miami FL 33131-1803

**LIPEZ, KERMIT V.,** federal judge, former state supreme court justice. Former judge Maine Superior Ct.; assoc. justice Supreme Jud. Ct. of Maine, Portland, 1994-98; judge U.S. Ct. Appeals (1st cir.) Maine, Portland, 1998—. Office: 156 Federal St Portland ME 04101-4152

**LIPFORD, ROCQUE EDWARD,** lawyer, corporate executive; b. Monroe, Mich., Aug. 16, 1938; s. Frank G. and Mary A. (Mastromarco) L.; m. Marcia A. Griffin, Aug. 5, 1966; children: Lisa, Rocque Edward, Jennifer, Katherine. BS, U. Mich., 1960, MS, 1961, JD with distinction, 1964. Bar: Mich. 1964, Ohio 1964. Instr. mech. engring. U. Mich., 1961-63; atty. Miller, Canfield, Paddock & Stone, Detroit, 1965-66; asst. gen. counsel Monroe Auto Equipment Co., 1966-70, gen. counsel, 1970-72, v.p., gen. counsel, 1973-77; v.p., gen. counsel Tenneco Automotive, 1977-78; ptnr. firm Miller, Canfield, Paddock & Stone, Detroit, 1978—, mng. ptnr., 1988-91; bd. dirs. La-Z-Boy Chair Co., Monroe Bank & Trust, Q.E.D. Environ. Systems, Ferrous Environ. Recycling Corp. Mem. Mich. Bar Assn., Legatus, Knights of Malta, North Cape Yacht Club, Monroe Golf and Country Club, Otsego Ski Club, Ocean Reef Club, Tau Beta Pi, Pi Tau Sigma. Antitrust, General corporate, Estate planning. Home: 1065 Hollywood Dr Monroe MI 48162-3045 Office: Miller Canfield Paddock & Stone 214 E Elm Ave Ste 100 Monroe MI 48162-2682

**LIPNACK, MARTIN I.,** lawyer; b. Bklyn., Apr. 6, 1936. BA, Bklyn. Coll., 1957, JD, 1960. Bar: N.Y. 1961, Colo. 1989, Fla. 1973, U.S. Supreme Ct. 1970. Ptnr. Applebaum & Eisenberg, Liberty, N.Y., 1968-73; asst. counsel Am. Title Ins. Co., Miami, Fla., 1973-74; ptnr. Schnur & Lipnack, Ft. Lauderdale, Fla., 1974-85; pvt. practice Ft. Lauderdale, 1985—; pres. Dispute Resolution Consultants, Inc.; cert. civil mediator, Fla.; mediator U.s. Dist. Ct. (so. dist.) Fla., Fla. Dept. Ins. Mediation; lectr. Dispute Resolution Isnt., Nova Southeastern U. V.p., dist. chmn. Hudson Del. council Boy Scouts Am., Middletown, N.Y.; pres. Temple Beth Israel, Ft. Lauderdale; bd. dirs. Humanitarian Found. Ft. Lauderdale, Jewish Community Ctr., Jewish Fedn. Greater Ft. Lauderdale. Fellow Am. Coll. Civil Trial Mediators; mem. ABA, Fla. Bar Assn., N.Y. State Bar Assn., Broward County Bar Assn., Soc. Profls. in Dispute Resolution, Fla. Acad. Profl. Mediators, Acad. Fla. Trial Lawyers. Alternative dispute resolution, Contracts commercial, Insurance. Home: 7421 SW 20th St Fort Lauderdale FL 33317-4918 Office: 7027 W Broward Blvd Fort Lauderdale FL 33317-2208

**LIPNICK, STANLEY MELVIN,** lawyer; b. Washington, Nov. 14, 1934; s. Max and Cecilia (Hollins) L.; m. Judith Sara Berman, Nov. 19, 1961; children: Stuart, Laura Gail. B.A., Columbia Coll., N.Y.C., 1956; J.D. with honors, George Washington U., 1960. Bar: D.C. 1960, Colo. 1967, Ill. 1968, Fla. 1983. Law clk. U.S. Ct. Appeals, Washington, 1960-61; trial atty. FTC, Washington, 1961-66; assoc. Ireland, Stapleton, Pryor & Holmes, Denver, 1966-68; ptnr. Arnstein & Lehr, Chgo. and West Palm Beach, 1968—. Mem. ABA. General civil litigation, Antitrust. Office: Arnstein & Lehr 120 S Riverside Plz Rm 1200 Chicago IL 60606-3910

**LIPPES, GERALD SANFORD,** lawyer, business executive; b. Buffalo, Mar. 23, 1940; s. Thomas and Ruth (Landsman) L.; m. Sandra Franger; children: Tracy E., David S., Adam F. Student, U. Mich., 1958-61; JD, U. Buffalo, 1964. Bar: N.Y. 1964. Sr. ptnr. Lippes, Silverstein, Mathias & Wexler, Buffalo, 1964—; sec., dir., gen. counsel Mark IV, Industries, Inc., Amherst, N.Y., 1969—; chmn. Del. Photographic Products, Buffalo, 1970-88, Ingram Micro-D, Buffalo, 1982-86, Abels Bagels, Inc., Buffalo, 1972-75; bd. dirs. Mark IV Industries, Inc., Amherst, N.Y., Gilbraltar Steel Corp., Buffalo Nat. Health Care Affiliates, Inc., The Wolf Group, Inc., Reciprocal, Inc. Bd. dirs. Buffalo Fine Arts Acad., Kaleida Health Sys.; U. Buffalo Found., U. Buffalo Coun., N.Y. State Arts Coun. Recipient Disting. Alumni award U. Buffalo Law Sch., Nat. Conf. of Christians and Jews Citation award 1997, Jaeckle award SUNY, Buffalo; named Entrepreneur of Yr., 1993. Mem. N.Y. State Bar Assn., Erie County Bar Assn., Am. Soc. Corp. Secs. General corporate, Mergers and acquisitions, Securities. Office: Lippes Silverstein Mathias & Wexler 28 Church St Buffalo NY 14202-3908

**LIPPES, RICHARD JAMES,** lawyer; b. Buffalo, Mar. 18, 1944; s. Thomas and Ruth (Landsman) L.; m. Sharon Richmond, June 4, 1972; children: Amity, Joshua, Kevin. BA, U. Mich., 1966; JD cum laude, SUNY-Buffalo, 1969. Bar: N.Y. 1970, U.S. Dist. Ct. Md. 1970, U.S. Ct. Appeals (4th cir.) 1970, U.S. Ct. Appeals (2d cir.) 1971, U.S. Dist. Ct. (we. dist.) N.Y. 1971, U.S. Dist. Ct. (no. dist.) N.Y. 1973, U.S. Dist. Ct. (so. dist.) N.Y. 1985. Clk. Arnold & Porter, 1967, Hodgson, Russ, Andrews, Woods & Goodyear, 1968-69; clk. to presiding justice U.S. Ct. Appeals, Balt., 1970; exec. dir. Ctr. for Justice Through Law, Buffalo, 1971; pvt. practice law, Buffalo, 1971-77; ptnr. Moriarity, Allen, Lippes & Hoffman, Buffalo, 1977-79, Allen & Lippes, Buffalo, 1979—; lectr. SUNY, Buffalo, 1978, 79; lead counsel and spl. environ. counsel for hazardous waste, mass toxic tort cases. Contbr. articles to profl. jours. Chmn. Atlantic chpt. Sierra Club, 1980-83; chmn. Buffalo chpt. Am. Jewish Com., 1986-88; chmn. lawyers com. Niagara Frontier chpt. N.Y. Civil Liberties Union, 1971, chpt. chair, 1972-74; chmn. City of Buffalo Environ. Mgmt. Commn., 1987-96; bd. dirs. N.Y. State Preservation League; also gen. counsel; chmn. City of Buffalo Task Force, 1986-87; pres. Erie County Preservation Coalition, 1998—; various others. Recipient Am. Jurisprudence award, 1968; Urban and Environ. Law fellow, 1969. Mem. ABA, N.Y. State Bar Assn., Erie County Bar Assn. (former chmn. pub. interest law com., former chmn. prepaid legal svcs. com.). Democrat. Environmental, Personal injury.

**LIPPINCOTT, WALTER EDWARD,** law educator; b. Bronxville, N.Y., Aug. 15, 1959; s. Walter Edwin and Helen (Patterson) L.; m. Andrea Pratt, July 30, 1983; children: Brittany Marie, Matthew. BS, Roger Williams Coll., 1981; JD, Western New Eng. Coll., 1984; MS, Fla. Inst. Tech., 1995. Bar: Conn. 1984, D.C. 1985. Prosecutor State of Conn. Judicial Dept., Hartford, 1990-93; prof. Naugatuck Valley Cmty. Tech. Coll., Waterbury, Conn., 1993—, U. Conn., Storrs, 1996-97. Lt. col. U.S. Army, 1985-90, USAR, 1990—. Mem. ABA, Conn. Bar Assn., D.C. Bar Assn. Home: 613 Highland Ave Torrington CT 06790-4410

**LIPPOLDT, DARIN MICHAEL,** lawyer; b. Okarche, Okla., Aug. 24, 1965; s. David Thomas and Barbara Faye Lippoldt; m. Mary Allison Wolfle, Sept. 23, 1995. BBA, St. Mary's U., San Antonio, 1987, JD, MA, 1995. Bar: Tex. 1995. Assoc. Matthews & Branscomb, P.C., San Antonio, 1995-96, Fulbright & Jaworski LLP, San Antonio, 1996—. Mem. San Antonio Bar Assn. (sec. 1997—, treas. 1996-97), San Antonio Young Lawyers Assn., St. Mary's U. Alumni Assn. (dir. 1997—). Securities, Mergers and acquisitions, General corporate. Home: 502 Woodcrest Dr San Antonio TX 78209-2939 Office: Fulbright & Jaworski LLP 300 Convent St Ste 2200 San Antonio TX 78205-3714

**LIPSEY, HOWARD IRWIN,** law educator, justice, lawyer; b. Providence, Jan. 24, 1936; s. Harry David and Anna (Gershman) L.; children: Lewis Robert, Bruce Stephen. AB summa cum laude, Providence Coll., 1957; JD, Georgetown U., 1960. Bar: R.I. 1960, U.S. Dist. Ct. R.I. 1961, U.S. Supreme Ct. 1972. Assoc. Edward I. Friedman, 1963-67, Kirshenbaum & Kirshenbaum, 1967-82; ptnr. Abedon, Michaelson, Stanzler, Biener, Skolnik & Lipsey, 1972-83; ptnr. Lipsey & Skolnik, Esquires, Ltd., Providence, 1983-93; assoc. justice R.I. Family Ct., 1993—; lectr. trial tactics Nat. Coll. Adv., 1986, U. Bridgeport Law Sch., Yale U., U. Denver Law Sch., Suffolk U. Law Sch., 1987—; adj. prof. U. Houston Law Sch., 1994-98; adj. prof. family law Roger Williams U. Law Sch., 1996—. Bd. editors Georgetown U. Law Jour. Served to capt. JAGC, USAR, 1960-71. Fellow Am. Coll. Trial Lawyers, Am. Acad. Matrimonial Lawyers; mem. ABA (chair trial advocacy inst., 1994-97, coun. mem. 1995—, chmn. family cts. com., bd. editors: Fairshare, Family Advocate), R.I. Bar Assn., Assn. Trial Lawyers Am. Clubs: B'nai B'rith (Anti-Defamation League). Contbg. author: Valuation and Distribution of Marital Property, 1984. Fax: 401-458-5360. Office: RI Family Ct 1 Dorrance Plz Providence RI 02903-3922

**LIPSHULTZ, LEONARD L.,** lawyer; b. Cleve., Dec. 19, 1922; s. Albert and Sylvia Lipshultz; m. Anna Smith, Feb. 12, 1943; children: Stanley, Gary, Frank, Mark. AA, Am. U., 1953, BS, 1954; JD, Washington Coll. Law, 1956. Bar: Md. 1956, D.C. 1956, U.S. Dist. Ct. D.C. 1956, U.S. Dist. Ct. Md. 1959, U.S. Ct. Appeals (D.C. cir.) 1959, U.S. Ct. Appeals (4th cir.) 1976, U.S. Supreme Ct. 1979. With Lipshultz and Hone Chartered, Silver Spring, Md.; legal counsel Prince George's County Boys and Girls Club, Md., 1962—; arbitrator Health Claims Arbitration Office, Md. Pres. Langley Park (Md.) Civic Assn., 1984-86, Langley Park Boys and Girls Club, 1970-74. With U.S. Army, 1944-45. Mem. ABA (sect. on ins., negligence and compensation, litigation), Bar Assn. of D.C., Def. Rsch. Inst. (products liability com.), Md. Assn. Def. Trial Counsel, Assn. for Advancement of Automotive Medicine. Avocations: camping, fishing. Product liability, Insurance, Personal injury. Home: 8256 New Hampshire Ave Silver Spring MD 20903-3423 Office: Lipshultz and Hone Chartered 8630 Fenton St Silver Spring MD 20910-3806

**LIPSHUTZ, ROBERT MURRAY,** lawyer; b. Phila., Jan. 13, 1948; s. Saul William and Esther Mollie (Litten) L.; m. Laurel Sprung, June 15, 1975; 1 child, Jonathan. BA, Johns Hopkins U., Balt., 1969; JD, NYU, 1972. Bar: Pa. 1972, U.S. Dist. Ct. (ea. dist.) Pa. 1977, U.S. Ct. Appeals (3d cir.) 1977, U.S. Supreme Ct. 1978. Asst. dist. atty. Dist. Atty.'s Office, Phila., 1972-77, 79-82; assoc. Malis, Tolson & Malis, Phila., 1977-79, Small and Margolin, P.C., Phila., 1982-89, Manchel, Lundy & Lessin, Phila., 1989-92, Liss and Tintenfass, P.C., Phila., 1992-95, Stephen J. Margolin & Assocs., L.L.C., 1995; pvt. practice, 1995—; Condr. seminars in field. Author: Pennsylvania Personal Injury Complaints, 1994. Fundraiser Jewish Fedn. of Phila., 1991—. Mem. Masons. Consumer commercial, Personal injury, Criminal.

Office: Two Penn Ctr Plz Ste 200 1500 John F Kennedy Blvd Philadelphia PA 19102-1721

**LIPSKY, BURTON G.,** lawyer; b. Syracuse, N.Y., May 29, 1937; s. Abraham and Pauline (Leichtner); m. Elaine B. Mannheimer, July 27, 1967; 1 child, Erika S., m. Carol S. Samberg, Feb. 4, 1973; 1 child, Andrew H. BBA, U. Mich., 1959; JD summa cum laude, Syracuse U., 1962. Bar: N.Y. 1962, U.S. Sup. Ct. 1967. Trial atty. U.S. Dept. Justice, Washington, 1962-67; assoc. Kaye, Scholer, Fierman, Hays & Handler, N.Y.C., 1967-72; ptnr. Delson & Gordon, N.Y.C., 1972-87, Lipsky & Stout, N.Y.C., 1991-96; pvt. practice, N.Y.C., 1996—. Mem. bd. visitors Syracuse U. Coll. of Law, 1989—; sec.-treas., dir. Robert Mapplethorpe Found., Inc., 1988—. Mem. ABA, N.Y. Bar Assn., Order of Coif, Justinian Soc., Am. Contract Bridge League (life master). Corporate taxation, Estate taxation, Personal income taxation. Office: 805 3rd Ave New York NY 10022-7513

**LIPSMAN, RICHARD MARC,** lawyer, educator; b. Bklyn., Aug. 17, 1946; s. Abraham W. and Ruth (Weinstein) L.; m. Geri A. Russo, 1979; children: Eric, Dara Briana. BBA, CCNY, 1968; JD, St. John's U., Jamaica, N.Y., 1972; LLM in Taxation, Boston U., 1976. Bar: N.Y. 1973, Mass. 1975, U.S. Dist. Ct. (ea. and so. dists.) N.Y. 1977, U.S. Supreme Ct. 1978, U.S. Tax Ct. 1979; CPA, N.Y., Mass. Tax atty. Arthur Young & Co., N.Y.C., 1972-74; assoc. Gilman, McLaughlin & Hanrahan, Boston, 1974-76, Lefrak, Fischer & Meyerson, N.Y.C., 1976-77; ptnr. Tarnow, Landsman & Lipsman, N.Y.C., 1978; pvt. practice N.Y.C., 1979—; adj. faculty Baruch Coll. CUNY, 1984-86, curriculum specialist Rsch. Found. CUNY, 1977-78; adj. faculty Pratt Inst., Bklyn., 1974, Queensboro Coll., Bayside, N.Y., 1978-80. Author, producer book/cassette program Learning Income Taxes, 1978—. Mem. ABA, AICPA, N.Y. State Bar Assn., Assn. of the Bar of the City of N.Y., N.Y. State Soc. CPA's. Jewish. Taxation, general, General civil litigation, Private international.

**LIPSON, BARRY J.,** lawyer, columnist; b. N.Y.C., May 30, 1938; s. Sidney J. and Irene (Abrams) L.; m. Lois J., June 7, 1975; children: Steven J., David J. BS in Econs., U. Pa., 1959; JD, Columbia U., 1962; LLM in Trade Regulation, NYU, 1968; postgrad. in law, Oxford U., 1982, Harvard U., 1984. Bar: N.Y. 1962, Pa. 1970, U.S. Supreme Ct. 1967. Dep. asst. atty. gen. State of N.Y., 1963-64, asst. atty. gen., 1964-67; assoc. counsel, asst. sec. Block Drug Co., Inc. and Reed & Carrick, 1968-69; asst. sec., counsel, trade regulation counsel Koppers Co., Inc., Pitts., 1969-81; v.p., gen. counsel, sec. Elkem Metals Co., Pitts., 1982-85; head of corp. divsn. Weisman, Goldman, Bowen & Gross, Pitts., 1985—; adj. settlement judge U.S. Dist. Ct. (we. dist.) Pa., 1995—, arbitrator, 1995—; arbitrator, master Pa. Ct. Common Pleas, Allegheny County, 1970—; arbitrator, mediator Am. Arbitration Assn., 1978—, Better Bus. Bur., 1986—; mediator Arbitration Forums, Inc., 1993—, EEOC, 1997—; guest lectr. George Washington U., 1979-83; mem. Bus. Roundtable Lawyers Adv. Com., 1978-82; mem. Pa. C. of C. Antitrust Adv. Com., 1978-85; nat., internat. lectr. on antitrust, trade regulations and legal compliance at legal and bus. seminars; mem. indsl. functional adv. com. on internat. stds. U.S. Dept. Commerce and Office of U.S. Trade Rep., 1980-88. Mem. editl. bd., columnist Pitts. Legal Jour., 1992—, Pitts. Neighbors, 1993-94, Lawyers Jour., 1999—; columnist Corplaw Commentaries, 1985—; contbg. editor N.Y. Law Jour., 1965-67, Antitrust Law Jour., 1982, L.A. Daily Jour. Report, 1983, 86, The Practical Lawyer's Manual on Trade Regulation, 1985, Pa. Law Jour.-Reporter, 1985-87, Small Bus. Legal Report, 1986, Pitts. Bus. Times, 1986-87, Antitrust for Bus., 1989, Allegheny Bus. News, 1991-92, Advising Small Bus., 1992—; founding editor Sherman's Summations, 1979-82; interviewee Off the Bench and Off the Cuff, 1987; contbr. articles to profl. jours. Vice chmn. Pitts. chpt. ACLU, 1977-78, 93-94, bd. dirs., 1972—, chmn. legal com., 1975-77; bd. dirs. Pa. ACLU, 1977-84, 91-94, nat. biennial del., 1995; pres. Allegheny County Transit Coun., 1996-97, legis. chair, 1993-94, v.p., 1994-96, chief counsel, 1995-99, exec. com., 1993-99; mem. adv. panel Southwestern Pa. Regional Planning Commn., 1993-98; pres. Beth Samuel, 1990-92; dir. United Synagogue, Western Pa. Region, 1989-97; organizer, mem. steering com. Nat. Conf. Peacemaking and Conflict Resolution, 1996-97. Lt. comdr. JAGC, USNR, 1965-75. Mem. ABA (chmn. monopolization taskforce 1976-79, chmn., lectr. monopolization program 1978, chmn. monopolization subcom. 1979-82, vice chmn. Sherman Act com. 1979, chmn. antitrust compliance counseling taskforce 1979-82, faculty Nat. Inst. 1980), Allegheny County Bar Assn. (founding mem., chmn. antitrust and class action com. 1980-82, chair Unauthorized Practice of Law Com. 1998—, vice chmn. hdqs. com. 1983-85, alt. dispute resolution com. 1992—, tel-law com. 1993—, twinning com. 1993—, ADR Players 1995—, writer ACBA Players 1997—), Am. Corp. Counsel Assn. (founding Western Pa. chpt., dir. sec. 1984-86), Fed. Bar Assn. (3d cir. v.p. 1998—, pres. Western Pa. chpt. 1994-98, v.p. nat. del. Pitts. chpt. 1987-93, democracy devel. initiative 1990—, nat. rules com. 1993-95, nat. membership com. 1995-98, antitrust and trade regulation sect., govt. contracts sect., gen. counsels sect., internat. law sect., Nat. Spl. Recognition award 1995), Boy Scouts Am. (com. chair greater Pitts. coun. 1995-98, troop com. chair 1993-97, commr.), Am. Legion (judge adv., former post adjutant), Forty and Eight (Chevaux 1994-96), Kiwanis (pres. Pitts. chpt. 1991-92, chmn. Bill of Rights project 1990-91, internat. del., dir., Kiwanian of Yr. 1990-91, Internat. Meritorious award 1990-91), Masons (32d degree, dir. Doric Hall Assn. 1990-97), Royal Arch Masons (most excellent high priest 1994), Royal and Select Master Masons (chaplain 1995-96), Scottish Rite (Princes of Jerusalem Line 1996—, high priest 1999, Comdr., Legion of Honor 1999, judge advocate 1994—, King Cyrus ritual team), Odd Fellows, Elks (presiding justice, leading knight 1996-97), Shriners (former Syria Temple luncheon club 1993, Syria asst. solicitor, pres., chmn. Heinz Hall spectacular, pres. West Hills Caravan 1997, judge advocate legion of honor, Oriental guide ritual team), Tall Cedars, Grotto (ritual team). General corporate, Antitrust, Private international. Home: 102 Christler Ct Moon Township PA 15108-1359

**LIPSON, MYER JACK,** lawyer; b. Munich, Germany, July 4, 1946; came to U.S., 1949; s. Sundel and Rachel (Bendalin) L.; m. Beth Rubin, June 22, 1969; children: Shane, Shelby. BBA, U. Tex., 1968, JD, 1972. Bar: Tex. 1972, U.S. Dist. Ct. (we. dist.) Tex. 1975. Asst. dist. atty. 34th and 205th Jud. Dist., El Paso, Tex., 1972-74; ptnr. Lipson, Dallas & Weiser P.C., El Paso, Tex., 1974—. Pres., bd. dirs. B'nai Zion Synagogue, El Paso, 1985-86, El Paso Holocaust Mus., 1989-92, El Paso Tennis Club, 1988, B'nai Brith, El Paso, 1978. Recipient Cert. of Merit, El Paso C.C., Cert. of Merit, El Paso Adult Probation Dept.; named to Soc. of Fellows, Anti Defamation League, 1987, Tree of Life award Jewish Nat. Fund, 1995. Mem. ABA, Tex. Trial Lawyers Assn., El Paso Young Lawyers Assn. (dir., v.p. 1973-80), El Paso Bar Assn. (dir.). Avocation: tennis. General civil litigation, Contracts commercial, Real property. Office: Lipson Dallas and Weiser PC 1444 Montana Ave El Paso TX 79902-5659

**LIPSON, ROGER RUSSELL,** lawyer; b. Lynn, Mass., May 24, 1937; s. Abraham Abel and Sally G. L.; m. Alberta Lois Grossman, Aug. 29, 1965; 1 child: Andrew Barry. AB, Boston U., 1958, LLM, 1990; JD, New Eng. Sch. Law, Boston, 1962. Bar: Mass. 1963, U.S. Dist. Ct. Mass. 1964, U.S. Tax Ct. 1990, U.S. Ct. Appeals (1st cir.) 1990, U.S. Supreme Ct. 1994. Assoc. Law Offices of Solomon Sandler, Gloucester, Mass., 1963-64, Goldman & Goldman, Lynn, Mass., 1964; pvt. practice, Lynn, Mass., 1965-71; atty. Neighborhood Legal Svcs., Lynn, Mass., 1971-72; exec. dir., gen. counsel Town of Brookline (Mass.) Rent Control Bd., 1972-87; assoc. Israel & Goldenberg, Boston, 1987-91; mem. Goldenberg, Walters & Lipson, P.A., Brookline, Mass., 1991—. Mem. Lynn City Dem. Com., 1970-72; assoc. mem. Brookline Town Dem. Com., 1992—; bd. dirs. Neighborhood Legal Svcs., Inc., 1969-71, pres., 1970-71. With USAR, 1960-66. Recipient Disting. Svc. award Lynn Jaycees, 1971, Recognition award New Eng. Realty Lodge, B'nai B'rith, Boston, 1976, 79. Mem. Mass. Bar Assn. (property sect., landlord-tenant subcom.), Mass. Conveyancers Assn., Temple Israel Brotherhood (pres. 1992-96), Rotary (pres. 1997-98, Paul Harris award 1999). Avocations: cooking, travel, guitar. Real property, Landlord-tenant, General practice. Home: 622 Chestnut Hill Ave Brookline MA 02445-4154 Office: Goldenberg Walters & Lipson PA 7 Harvard St Ste 220 Brookline MA 02445-7379

**LIPTON, JACK PHILIP,** lawyer; b. N.Y.C., Apr. 23, 1952. BA, UCLA, 1973; MA, Calif. State U., Northridge, 1975; PhD, U. Calif., Riverside, 1979; JD, U. Ariz., 1988. Bar: Calif., 1989. Faculty Humboldt State U., Arcata, Calif., 1979-80, Union Coll., Schenectady, N.Y., 1980-85, U. Ariz., Tucson, 1985-88; clk. U.S. Ct. Appeals, Phoenix, 1988-89; assoc. Irell & Manella, L.A., 1989-92; pvt. practice law $, Beverly Hills, Calif., 1992-98; ptnr. Burke, Williams & Sorensen, LLP, L.A., 1998—. Contbr. articles to profl. jours. Mem. APA. General civil litigation, Education and schools, Labor. Office: Burke Williams & Sorensen 611 W 6th St Fl 25 Los Angeles CA 90017-3101

**LIPTON, MATTHEW CONAN,** lawyer; b. Little Rock, Mar. 15, 1966; s. James M. and Carolyn R. Lipton; m. Catherine F. Lux (div.); m. Martha MacDonald, Dec. 10, 1994; children: Teresa Sais, Marie Sais. BA in Psychology, Johns Hopkins U., 1988; JD, So. Meth. U., 1991. Bar: Tex. 1991. Assoc. atty. Godwin & Carlton, Dallas, 1991-94, Looper, Reed, Mark & McGraw, Dallas, 1994-96; v.p. adminstrn. and devel., gen. counsel Inova Health, Inc., Dallas, 1996-97; sole practitioner Dallas, 1997-98; pres., CEO, gen. cousnel Abitis Pharms., Dallas, 1997—; shareholder Browning & Lipton, P.C., Dallas, 1998—. Avocations: golf, reading. Health. Home: 3810 Wooded Creek Dr Dallas TX 75244-4750 Office: Browning & Lipton PC 370 Founders Sq 900 Jackson St Dallas TX 75202-4436

**LIPTON, PAUL R.,** lawyer, educator; b. N.Y.C., June 18, 1945; s. Maurice and Lorraine Lipton; m. Marjorie Yourman, June 16, 1968; children: Melissa, Lindsay. BA, Pa. State U., 1967; JD, Washington U., St. Louis, 1970. Bar: N.Y. 1972, Fla. 1973, U.S. Supreme Ct. 1975. Asst. dist. atty. Dist. Atty. of Nassau County, Mineola, N.Y., 1971-72; assoc. Snyder, Young & Stern, Miami, Fla., 1972-78; ptnr. Paul R. Lipton, P.A., Miami, 1978-87, Fine, Jacobson, P.A., Miami, 1987-92, Weaver, Kuven, Weaver & Lipton, P.A., Ft. Lauderdale and Miami, 1992-94, Bedzow, Korn, Brown & Lipton, P.A., Miami, 1994-99, Greenberg Traurig P.A., Miami, 1999—; adj. prof. Nova U. Sch. Law, 1990—; spkr. in field. Bd. dirs. Journey Inst., 1998; co-chair 11th Cir. Commn. on Professionalism, 1998—; com. Fed. Ct. Peer Rev., 1998—. Mem. Fla Bar (standing com. on professionalism), North Dade Bar Assn. (pres. 1980). Avocations: music, writing, riflery, guitar. Federal civil litigation, State civil litigation. Office: Greenberg Traurig PA 1221 Brickell Ave Miami FL 33131

**LIPTON, ROBERT STEPHEN,** lawyer; b. Malone, N.Y., Apr. 19, 1942. BS in Aerospace Engring., U. Mich., 1964; postgrad., U. Wash., 1965-66; JD, Temple U., 1972. Bar: U.S. Patent and Trademark Office 1970, Pa. 1972, U.S. Dist. Ct. (ea. dist.) Pa. 1973, U.S. Ct. Appeals (fed. cir.) 1982. Wind tunnel test engr. The Boeing Co., Seattle, 1965-67; patent adminstr. The Boeing Co., Phila., 1967-70, patent agt., 1970-72, patent atty., 1972-75; pvt. practice law Media, Pa., 1975-84; ptnr. Lipton, Weinberger & Husick, Media, 1984—. Mem. ABA, Pa. Bar Assn., Delaware County Bar Assn., Phila. Intellectual Property Law Assn., Am. Intellectual Property Law Assn., Am. Helicopter Soc. Patent, Contracts commercial, Computer. Office: Lipton Weinberger & Husick 201 N Jackson St Media PA 19063-2902

**LIPTON, WILLIAM,** lawyer; b. Newark, Dec. 9, 1928; m. Sharon Lee Levine; children: Marc, Craig, Judy, Eric. BA, Wayne State U., 1950, MA, 1953; LLB, Detroit Coll. Law, 1958. Bar: Mich. 1958. Ptnr. Lipton, Papista & Garfinke, Detroit, 1959-75; sr. ptnr. Lipton Papista, Cohen & Alt, Southfield, Mich., 1975-91, Lipton & Lipton, Southfield, 1991—. Cpl. U.S. Army, 1953-55. Mem. ATLA, Mich. Trial Lawyers Assn. Personal injury. Office: Lipton & Lipton 18930 W 10 Mile Rd # 300 Southfield MI 48075-2618

**LIRETTE, DANNY JOSEPH,** lawyer; b. Houma, La., Sept. 21, 1948; s. Alexander Jean and Ouida (Pellegrin) L.; m. Carolyn Roe, Dec. 12, 1981; children—Dana L., Lauren E., Aimee C. B.S. in Polit. Sci., La. State U., 1970, J.D., 1974. Bar: La. 1974, U.S. Dist. Ct. (ea. dist.) La. 1974, U.S. Ct. Appeals (5th cir.) 1974. Ptnr. St. Martin & Lirette, Houma, 1974-79; sole practice, Houma, 1979-83; ptnr. St. Martin, Lirette & Gaubert, Houma, 1983—. Mem. La. Trial Lawyers Assn. (gov. 1979-80, 84-85), ABA, La. Bar Assn., Order of Coif, Phi Kappa Phi. Democrat. Roman Catholic. Admiralty, Personal injury. Home: 2242 Eliza Beaumont Ln Baton Rouge LA 70808-2210 Office: St Martin Lirette & Gaubert 3373 Little Bayou Black Dr Houma LA 70360-2840

**LISHER, JAMES RICHARD,** lawyer; b. Aug. 28, 1947; s. Leonard B. and Mary Jane (Rafferty) L.; m. Martha Gettelfinger, June 16, 1973; children: Jennifer, James Richard II. AB, Ind. U., 1969, JD, 1975. Bar: Ind. 1975, U.S. Dist. Ct. (so. dist.) Ind. 1975. Assoc. Rafferty & Wood, Shelbyville, Ind., 1976, Rafferty & Lisher, Shelbyville, 1976-77; dep. prosecutor Shelby County Prosecutor's Office, Shelbyville, 1976-78; ptnr. Yeager, Lisher & Baldwin, Shelbyville, 1977-96; pvt. practice, Shelbyville, 1996—; pros. atty. Shelby County, Shelbyville, 1983-95, pub. defender, 1995—. Speaker, faculty advisor Ind. Pros. Sch., 1986. Editor: (seminar manual) Traffic Case Defenses, 1982. Bd. dirs. Girls Club of Shelbyville, 1979-84, Bears of Blue River Festival, Shelbyville, 1982-98; pres. Shelby County Internat. Rels. Coun., 1997-99. Recipient Citation of Merit, Young Lawyers Assn. Mem. Nat. Assn. of Criminals, State Bar Assn. (bd. dirs.), Ind. Pub. Defender Assn., Ind. State Bar Assn. (bd. dirs. young lawyer sect 1979-83, bd. dirs. gen. practice sect. 1996-98, treas. 1997-98, vice-chmn. 1998-99), Shelby County Bar Assn. (sec./treas. 1986, v.p. 1987, pres. 1988, Ind. Pros. Attys. Assn. (bd. dirs. 1985-95, sec./treas. 1987, v.p. 1988, pres. 1990), Masons, Elks, Lions. Democrat. General practice, Probate, Criminal. Home: 106 Western Trce Shelbyville IN 46176-9765 Office: 407 S Harrison St Shelbyville IN 46176-2170

**LISHER, JOHN LEONARD,** lawyer; b. Indpls., Sept. 19, 1950; s. Leonard Boyd and Mary Jane (Rafferty) L.; m. Mary Katherine Sturmon, Aug. 17, 1974. B.A. with honors in History, Ind. U., 1975, J.D., 1975. Bar: Ind. 1975. Dep. atty. gen. State of Ind., Indpls., 1975-78; asst. corp. counsel City of Indpls., 1978-81; assoc. Osborn & Hiner, Indpls., 1981-86; ptnr. Osborn, Hiner & Lisher, 1986—. Vol. Mayflower Classic, Indpls., 1981—; pres. Brendonwood Common Inc.; asst. vol. coord. Marion County Rep. Com., Indpls., 1979-80; vol. Don Bogard for Atty. Gen., Indpls., 1980, Steve Goldsmith for Prosecutor, Indpls., 1979, 83, Sheila Suess for Congress, Indpls., 1980. Recipient Outstanding Young Man of Am. award Jaycees, 1979, 85, Indpls. Jaycees, 1980. Mem. ABA, Ind. Bar Assn., Indpls. Bar Assn. (membership com.), Assn. Trial Lawyers Am., Ind. U. Alumni Assn., Hoosier Alumni Assn. (charter, founder, pres.), Ind. Trial Lawyers Assn., Ind. Def. Lawyers Assn., Ind. U. Coll. Arts and Scis. (bd. dirs. 1983-92, pres. 1986-87), Wabash Valley Alumni Assn. (charter), Founders Club, Presidents Club, Phi Beta Kappa, Eta Sigma Phi, Phi Eta Sigma, Delta Xi Alumni Assn. (charter, v.p., sec., Delta Xi chpt. Outstanding Alumnus award 1975, 76, 79, 83), Delta Xi Housing Corp. (pres.), Pi Kappa Alpha (midwest regional pres. 1977-86, parliamentarian nat. conv. 1982, del. convs. 1978-80, 82, 84, 86, trustee Meml. Found. 1986-91. Presbyterian. Avocations: reading; golf; jogging; Roman coin collecting. State civil litigation, Insurance, Personal injury. Home: 5725 Hunterglen Rd Indianapolis IN 46226-1019 Office: Osborn Hiner & Lisher PC 8500 Keystone Xing Ste 480 Indianapolis IN 46240-2460

**LISI, MARY M.,** federal judge. BA, U. R.I., 1972; JD, Temple U., 1977. Tchr. history Prout Meml. High Sch., Wakefield, R.I., 1975-76; law clerk U.S. Atty., Providence, R.I., 1976, Phila., 1976-77; asst. pub. defender R.I. Office Pub. Defender, 1977-81; asst. child advocate Office Child Advocate, 1981-82; also. pvt. practice atty. Providence, 1981-82; dir. office ct. appointed spl. advocate R.I. Family Ct., 1982-87; dep. disciplinary counsel office disciplinary counsel R.I. Supreme Ct., 1988-90, chief disciplinary counsel, 1990-94; U.S. Dist. judge 10th Dist. Ct., Providence, R.I., 1995—; mem. Select Com. to Investigate Failure of R.I. Share and Deposit Indemnity Corp., 1991-92. Recipient Providence 350 award, 1986, Meritorious Svc. to Children of Am. award, 1987. Office: Fed Bldg and US Courthouse 1 Exchange Ter Rm 113 Providence RI 02903-1720

**LISMAN, ERIC,** publishing executive, lawyer. V.p. and gen. counsel Cahners Pub. Co., sr. v.p., gen. counsel; v.p., gen. counsel Advanstar Holdings Inc., 1998—. *

**LISS, JEFFREY F.,** lawyer, educator; b. Balt., June 10, 1951; s. Solomon and Gertrude (Nadich) L.; m. Susan Michelson, July 30, 1972; children: Joanna M., Harrison S. BA, U. Mich., 1972, MA, JD, 1975. Bar: D.C. 1975, Md. 1981. Jud. law clk. U.S. Dist. Ct., Washington, 1975-77; from assoc. to ptnr. Wald, Harkrader & Ross, Washington, 1977-85; ptnr. Piper & Marbury, Washington, 1985—, COO, 1997—; adj. prof. U. Mich. Law Sch., 1996, Georgetown Law Sch., 1985—, Am. U. Sch. Law, 1978-85. Co-author: Remedies in Business Torts Litigation, 1992. Bd. dirs. Washington Lawyers Com. for Civil Rights, Washington, 1992-98; pro bono counsel numerous orgns., Washington, 1977—; treas., Friends of Lt. Gov. Kathleen Kennedy Townsend, Md.; mem. adv. bd. D.C. Bar Found., 1992—. Fellow Am. Bar Found.; mem. Center Club (Balt.), D.C. Cir. Hist. Soc. (bd. dirs.), Balt. Symphony Orchestra. Democrat. Jewish. Avocations: baseball, reading, piano. General civil litigation, Environmental, Intellectual property. Office: Piper & Marbury 1200 19th St NW Fl 7 Washington DC 20036-2430

**LISS, MATTHEW MARTIN,** lawyer; b. Oak Park, Ill.. BS in Acctg., BS in Fin., Southern Ill. U., 1991, MS in Acctg., 1994, JD, 1994. Bar: Ill. 1994, Ga. 1998. Assoc. Phillip G. Neal and assocs., Chgo., 1994-95; v.p. and gen. counsel Innovative Health Svcs., Inc., St. Petersburg, Fla., 1995-98; with Swift, Currie, McGhee and Hiers, L.P., Atlanta, 1998-99, Wagner, Johnston & Rosenthal, P.C., Atlanta, 1999—. Fax: 404-261-6779. Real property, Estate taxation, Contracts commercial. Home: 4184 Nashoba Dr NE Roswell GA 30075-1667 Office: Wagner Johnston & Rosenthal PC Ste 1200/ Tower Place 100 3340 Peachtree St Atlanta GA 30326

**LISS, NORMAN,** lawyer; b. New York, May 7, 1932; m. Sandra Hirsch, Feb. 28, 1959. BS, NYU, 1952, LLB, 1955. Bar: N.Y. 1955, U.S. Dist. Ct. (so. dist.) N.Y. 1961, U.S. Dist. Ct (ea. dist.) N.Y. 1962. Assoc. Booth, Lipton & Lipton, New York, 1956-57, Seymour Detsky, New York, 1957-58; pvt. practice New York, 1958—; cons. to Portugal Re-Cultural Events in U.S.; represented Norway in N.Y. proceedings to clear records of sailors arrested during 900th anniversary of Leif Ericson Voyage; jour. chair UJA Trial Lawyers USCG Acad. Law Day, 1987, 89, 94, 98. Contbr. articles to profl. jours. Chmn. Bronx County Bar div. United Jewish Appeal, Hist. Documents Exhbn., Operation Sail, 1986, USCG Acad. Law Day, 1987, 89; chmn. devel. Ellis Island Restoration Commn.; counsel N.Y. State Statue of Liberty Centennial Com., Mayor's Handicapped Citizens Adv. Bd., N.Y.C., Coun. on Arts; mem. Bronx County 350 Commn., N.Y.C. Commn. for Presdl. Conv.; rep., counsel N.Y.C. Com. on Bicentennial of U.S. Constitution; cons. Soc. Congl. Medal of Honor; commd. lt. col. N.Y. Guard Judge Advocate Gen. Unit. Recipient Disting. Humanitarian award Inst. of Applied Human Dynamics, Meritorious Pub. Svc. award USCG, 1989; named Man of Yr. Am. Jewish Congress, Man of Yr. Kinneret Sch., 1985. Mem. ABA, N.Y. Bar Assn., Bronx County Bar Assn., Am. Arbitration Assn. (panel arbitrators), Assn. Trial Lawyers Am., Law Day Outreach Com., NYU Alumni Assn. (adv. coun.). General practice, General civil litigation, Education and schools. Home: 2727 Palisade Ave Bronx NY 10463-1018 Office: 200 W 57th St New York NY 10019-3211

**LISTER, STEPHANIE JOYCE,** lawyer; b. Spokane, Wash., July 5, 1962; d. David L. and Donna J. Johnson; m. James D. Lister, July 19, 1996; 1 child, Hailey J. BA, Gonzaga U., Spokane, 1984, JD, 1987. Bar: Wash. Dep. prosecutor Kootenai County Prosecutors Office, Coeur d'Alene, Idaho, 1987; asst. U.S. atty. Dept. of Justice, Ea. Dist. Wash., Spokane, 1987—. Office: US Atty's Office PO Box 1494 Spokane WA 99210-1494

**LISTER, THOMAS EDWARD,** lawyer; b. Columbus, Ohio, Apr. 19, 1948; s. Richard Elwyn and Jean (Nelson) L.; m. Sarah Gray Robinson, July 25, 1970; children—Matthew Thomas, Joshua Capps. B.A., DePauw U., 1970; J.D., U. Wis.-Madison, 1973. Bar: Wis. 1973, U.S. Dist. Ct. (we. dist.) Wis. 1973. Vice-pres. Coll. Mktg. & Research Corp., Indpls., 1969-70; staff criminal appeals unit Wis. Dept. Justice, 1971-73; ptnr. Sherman, Stutz & Lister, Black River Falls, Wis., 1973-83; dist. atty. Jackson County, Wis., Black River Falls, 1975-80, corp. counsel, 1975-78; mem. firm Stutz & Lister, S.C., Black River Falls, 1983—. Guest lectr. U. Wis., Madison, 1988; pres. Wis. Global Tech. Ltd., 1992—; chmn. ThermoSense Co., LLC, 1998—. Chmn. S.W. Council on Criminal Justice, 1979-82; mem. Wis. Council on Criminal Justice, 1982-83, Wis. County Forest Adv. Council, 1982-84; bd. dirs. Tri-County Community Mental Health, Alcohol and Drug Abuse Bd., 1976-82, Black River Falls Youth Hockey, 1983-84; co-founder, dir. Black River Falls Area Found., 1986-88; chmn. Mayor's Commn. Golf Course Expansion Fundraising, 1988-90, Wazee Lake Recreation Commn., 1991—; commencement spkr. Black River Falls H.S., 1992; mem. com., judge All-Am. City Finalist Competition, Charlotte, N.C., 1992; chmn. adminstrv. coun. United Meth. Ch., Black River Forest, 1992-93, bldg. commn., co-chair fundraising, 1992-94; cmty. rels. com. Wis. Dept. Corrections, 1993—. Mem. ABA, Assn. Trial Lawyers Am., Wis. Acad. Trial Lawyers (bd. dirs. 1984-90), Wis. Bar Assn., Tri-County Bar Assn. (pres. 1991-92), Black River Falls C. of C. (bd. dirs.). Lodge: Rotary (bd dirs., pres.-elect youth exchange officer); Black River Recreation Assnn. Skyline Golf Club (pres. 1993). Personal injury, State civil litigation, Workers' compensation. Home: RR 4 Box 310B Black River Falls WI 54615-9207 Office: Stutz & Lister SC PO Box 370 Black River Falls WI 54615-0370

**LITANT, WILLIAM T. G.,** communications professional; b. Bklyn., May 11, 1951; s. Irving and Raquel (Shafran) L.; m. Michele Order, June 8, 1980; children: Josiah, Micah. BFA, Emerson Coll., Boston, 1973; cert. in teaching, Northeastern U., Boston, 1976. Cert. tchr. secondary English, Mass. Media specialist Raytheon Co., Cambridge, Mass., 1973-76; dir. pub. rels. Mus. Transp., Boston, 1976-82; pub. affairs cons. Mass. Bay Transp. Authority, Boston, 1982-84, Mass. Dept. Pub. Works, Boston, 1984-86; dir. comms. and publs. Mass. Bar Assn., Boston, 1986—. Editor: Mass. Court Journalists Handbook, 1996; editor-in-chief: Lawyers Jour. newspaper; supervising editor Mass. Law Rev., Sect. Revue. Mem. Am. Soc. Assn. Execs., Nat. Assn. Bar Execs., Soc. for Profl. Journalists, New Eng. Press Assn., BSA Club (pres. 1978—). Avocations: flying, photography, motorcycling. Home: 276 Reed Farm Rd Boxboro MA 01719-1615 Office: Mass Bar Assn 20 West St Boston MA 02111-1204

**LITCH, JOHN MICHAEL,** lawyer; b. Detroit, Oct. 14, 1927; m. June E. Meyers, June 21, 1953; children: Brian M., Nancy A. Student, Detroit Coll. Law, 1951; LLB, Detriot U., 1957, JD, 1968. Mng. ptnr. Litch, Gordon & Assocs., Center Line, Mich., 1952—. Cpl. USAF, 1946-48. Mem. Mich. State Bar Assn., Macomb Probate Bar Assn., Macomb Fin. Planning and Probate Assn. Estate planning, Probate, Real property. Office: Litch Gordon & Assocs 26224 Van Dyke Ave Center Line MI 48015-1220

**LITCHFIELD, ROBERT LATTA, JR.,** lawyer; b. Tucson, Apr. 6, 1949; s. Robert Latta Sr. and Mary Wyatt (Palmer) L.; m. Suzanne Kay Zerby, Dec. 29, 1971; children: Melissa Marie, Robert Latta III, Paul Andrew, James Ryan. BS, West Point Acad., 1971; MA, Miami U., 1977; JD, McGeorge Sch. Law, 1980. Bar: Oreg. 1980, U.S. Dist. Ct. Oreg. 1980, Calif. 1981, U.S. Dist. Ct. (ea. dist.) Calif. 1985. Assoc. Hershner, Hunter, Miller, Moulton & Andrews, Eugene, Oreg., 1980-83; pvt. practice Eugene, 1983-85; assoc. Felderstein, Rosenberg & McManns, Sacramento, 1985-86, Felderstein, Rosenberg, McManns, Diepenbrock, Wulff, et al., Sacramento, 1986-87; pvt. practice Grass Valley, Calif., 1987—; adv. bd. Truckee River Bank, Grass Valley, 1992-94; radio talk show host KNCO Radio, Grass Valley, 1991-92. Author: The Man Who Had No Wings, 1977. Mem. adv. bd. Salvation Army, Grass Valley, 1991-94; team leader marriage encounter group Westminster Presbyn. Ch., Eugene, 1984—, deacon and elder, 1983-85; candidate Nev. County Superior Ct. Judge, 1996. Capt. USAF, 1971-77. Named Atty. of Yr., Consumer Bus. Rev., 1995. Mem. Nevada County Bar Assn., Tea Bag Tax Revolt (founder, chmn. 1990-94), Make a Difference, Inc. (bd. dirs. 1992-94), Angelian Soc. (founder, chmn. 1992—), Nevada County Gideons (pres. 1995). Republican. Avocations: scuba diving, writing, woodworking, Christian family enrichment. Estate planning, General civil litigation, Real property. Office: 210 Magnolia Ave # 1 Auburn CA 95603-4823

**LITKE, JENNIFER HOLLAND,** lawyer; b. Tulsa, May 12, 1971; d. Tommy Lee and Janet Kay (Bromert) Holland; m. Stephen Walter Litke, Sept. 6, 1997. BA, U. Tulsa, 1993, JD with honors, 1996. Bar: Okla. 1996, U.S. Dist. Ct. (no. dist.) Okla. 1996, Tex. 1997. Assoc. Lipe, Green, Trump & Dreyer, Tulsa, 1996-97, Bourland, Kirkman, Seidler & Evans, Ft. Worth, 1997-98, Blaies & Hightower, Ft. Worth, 1998—. Author: Grace v. Foster: Oklahoma's Public Policy Exception to the Employment-At-Will Doctrine, 1995. Recipient Am. Jurisprudence awards U. Tulsa Coll. of Law, 1994-96. Mem. ABA, Okla. Bar Assn., State Bar Tex., Ft. Worth-Tarrant County Young Lawyers Assn. (dir. 1998, treas. 1999), Phi Delta Phi. Democrat.

Roman Catholic. Avocations: outdoor activities, cooking, golf, reading. General civil litigation. Home: 3632 Hilltop Rd Fort Worth TX 76109-2711 Office: Blaies & Hightower 301 Commerce St Ste 1501 Fort Worth TX 76102-4115

**LITMAN, HARRY PETER,** lawyer, educator; b. Pitts., May 4, 1958; s. S. David and Roslyn M. (Margolis) L. BA, Harvard U., 1981; JD, U. Calif., Berkeley, 1986. Bar: Calif. 1987, U.S. Ct. Appeals (D.C. cir.) 1987, Pa. 1988, D.C. 1989, U.S. Ct. Appeals (9th cir.) 1990, U.S. Dist. Ct. (so. dist.) Tex. 1992, U.S. Supreme Ct. 1992, U.S. Dist. Ct. (ea. and we. dists.) Pa. 1993, U.S. Ct. Appeals (7th cir.) 1994, U.S. Dist. Ct. (ea. dist.) Va. 1997. Prodn. asst. feature films N.Y.C., 1980-82; newsman, clk. baseball desk AP, N.Y.C., 1982-83; sports reporter AP, 1983-86; law clk. to Hon. Abner J. Mikva U.S. Ct. Appeals (D.C. cir.), 1986-87; law clk. to Hon. Thurgood Marshall U.S. Supreme Ct., Washington, 1987-88, law clk. to Hon. Anthony M. Kennedy, 1989; asst. U.S. atty., dep. chief appellate sect. Dept. Justice, San Francisco, 1990-92; dep. assoc. atty. gen. Dept. Justice, Washington, 1992-93, dep. asst. atty. gen., 1993-98; U.S. atty. Western Dist. of Pa., 1998—; adj. prof. Boalt Hall Sch. Law U. Calif., Berkeley, 1990-92, Georgetown U. Law Ctr., 1996-99. Editor-in-chief Calif. Law Rev., Vol. 73; author various articles. Presdl. scholar, 1976. Mem. Pa. Bar Assn., State Bar Calif., D.C. Bar, Order of Coif. Office: 63 US Courthouse Pittsburgh PA 15219

**LITMAN, RICHARD CURTIS,** lawyer; b. Phila., May 2, 1957; s. Benjamin Norman and Bette Etta (Saunders) L.; m. Cheryl Lynn Goldstein, May 28, 1989; children: Amanda Rose, Jessica Brooke, Daniel Grant, Victoria Grace. BS, Union Coll., 1973; JD cum laude, U. Miami, 1979; LLM in Patent and Trade Regulation, George Washington U., 1980; M of Forensic Sci., Antioch Sch. Law, 1981. Bar: D.C. 1979, Fla. 1979, Pa. 1979, Va. 1980, Md. 1984, U. Ct. Appeals (fed. cir.), U.S. Patent and Trademark Office, U.S. Supreme Ct. Pvt. practice Arlington, Va., 1983—; instr. continuing legal edn.; organizer, dir. James Monroe Bank; host radio program Great Ideas!. Host Great Ideas! radio program; Contbr. articles to profl. jours. Fellow Food and Drug Law Inst., 1979-80; named Small Bus. of Yr. Arlington C. of C., 1995. Mem. ABA, Fed. Bar Assn., Am. Acad. Forensic Scis., Am. Intellectual Property Law Assn., Arlington County Bar Assn., Masons (32d degree Scottish Rite), Shriners. Intellectual property, Patent, Trademark and copyright. Office: Litman Law Offices Ltd Patent Law Bldg 3717 Columbia Pike Arlington VA 22204-4255

**LITMAN, ROSLYN MARGOLIS,** lawyer, educator; b. N.Y.C., Sept. 30, 1928; d. Harry and Dorothy (Perlow) Margolis; m. S. David Litman, Nov. 22, 1950; children: Jessica, Hannah, Harry. BA, U. Pitts., 1949, JD, 1952. Bar: Pa. 1952. Practiced in Pitts., 1952—; ptnr. firm Litman, Litman, Harris & Brown, P.C., 1952—; adj. prof. U. Pitts. Law Sch., 1958—; permanent del. Conf. U.S. Circuit Ct. Appeals for 3d Circuit; past chair dist. adv. group U.S. Dist. Ct. (we. dist.) Pa., 1991-94, mem. steering com. for dist. adv. group, 1991—; chmn. Pitts. Pub. Parking Authority, 1970-74; mem. curriculum com. Pa. Bar Inst., 1986—, bd. dirs., 1972-82. Recipient Roscoe Pound Found. award for Excellence in Tchg. Trial Advocacy, 1996, Disting. Alumnus award U. Pitts. Sch. Law, 1996; named Fed. Lawyer of Yr., We. Pa. Chpt. FBA, 1999. Mem. ABA (del., litigation sect., anti-trust health care com.), ACLU (nat. bd. dirs., Marjorie H. Matson Civil Libertarian award Greater Pitts. chpt. 1999), Pa. Bar Assn. (bd. govs. 1976-79), Allegheny County Bar Assn. (bd. govs. 1972-74, pres. 1975), Allegheny County Acad. Trial Lawyers (charter), United Jewish Fedn. (cmty. rels. com., co-chair ch./state com.), Order of Coif. General practice, Federal civil litigation, State civil litigation. Home: 5023 Frew St Pittsburgh PA 15213-3829 Office: 3600 One Oxford Centre Pittsburgh PA 15219

**LITT, H. ALLEN,** lawyer; b. Phila., Oct. 18, 1949; s. Jerome and Lillian (Stern) Lipschutz; m. Leslie Orloff; children: David, Michael, Samantha. BA, Temple U., 1971, JD, 1975. Bar: Pa. 1975, U.S. Dist. Ct. (ea. dist.) Pa. 1979, U.S. Ct. Appeals (3d cir.) 1981. Atty. Pa. Dept. Pub. Welfare, Phila., 1975-77; assoc. Laurence Ring Assocs., Phila., 1977-80, Jerome Taylor, P.C., Phila., 1980-84; pvt. practice Phila., 1984—. Co-author manual: Agent's Guide to Child Support, 1976. Mem. ABA, Phila. Bar Assn., Pa. Trial Lawyers Assn., Phila. Trial Lawyers Assn., White Manor Country Club. Republican. Jewish. Avocations: golf, tennis, softball. Personal injury, General civil litigation. Office: 1515 Market St Ste 504 Philadelphia PA 19102-1905

**LITTEER, HAROLD HUNTER, JR.,** lawyer; b. Rochester, N.Y., Nov. 13, 1943; s. Harold Hunter and Winifred Gladys (Gemming) L.; m. Kathleen May Dool, July 14, 1964; children: Harold H. III, Raymond J. BS, Empire State Coll., 1988; JD, Syracuse U., 1990. Bar: N.Y. 1991. Ptnr. Murray & Litteer, Batavia, N.Y., 1991—. Town justice Town of Wheatland, Scottsville, N.Y. Mem. ABA, N.Y. State Bar Assn., N.Y. State Defenders Assn., Lions. Democrat. Baptist. Avocations: golf, fishing, sports, music. General practice, Criminal, Personal injury. Home: 460 Armstrong Rd Mumford NY 14511 Office: 3184 State St Caledonia NY 14423-1222

**LITTELL, RICHARD GREGORY,** lawyer; b. Hartford, Conn., Feb. 7, 1931; s. Elliot Manning and Lilyan Ruth (Stiegel) L.; m. Barbara Anne Diggs, Mar. 31, 1962 (div. Dec. 1983); children: John Gregory, Susan Anne. BA, Cornell U., 1953; JD, Harvard U., 1956. Bar: D.C., Calif., N.Y. Asst. gen. counsel Civil Aeronautics Bd., Washington, 1967-69, assoc. gen. counsel, 1969-71, gen. counsel, 1973-74; gen. counsel Postal Rate Commn., Washington, 1971-73; ptnr. Dickstein, Shapiro & Morin, Washington, 1974-80, Bishop, Cook, Purcell & Reynolds, Washington, 1980-90; pvt. practice Washington, 1990—. Author: Endangered and Threatened Species, 1992; contbr. numerous articles to profl. publs. Chmn. Air Pollution Adv. Com., Met. Washington Coun. of Govts., 1965-67. Mem. Cosmos Club, Nat. Press Club, Belle Haven Country Club. Avocations: flyfishing, tennis. Public utilities, Aviation, Environmental. Home: 613 S Fairfax St Alexandria VA 22314-3833 Office: 1220 19th St NW Ste 400 Washington DC 20036-2438

**LITTERAL, DANIEL PACE,** lawyer; b. Washington, Aug. 10, 1955; s. Kelley Litteral and Kathleen Margaret Olson; m. Katherine Hedwig Madson, Jan. 22, 1977 (div. Oct. 1998); 1 child, Jennifer Erin. BA, Wake Forest U., 1976; JD with honors, U. N.D., 1981. Bar: Md. 1981, U.S. Dist. Ct. Md. 1982. Lawyer, prin. Litteral & Litteral Chartered, Silver Spring, Md., 1981-84, Rockville, Md., 1984-88; pvt. practice law Rockville, 1988—; adj. lectr. U. N.D., Grand Forks, 1980-81; lectr. Coll. Bd., Phila., 1997, Assn. Ind. Md. Schs., Potomac, 1998. Author (monthly column) Leisure Living, 1996—, (profl. newsletter) Pvt. Ednl. Newsletter, 1998. Capt. U.S. Army/USAR, 1976-83. Mem. Md. State Bar Assn., Montgomery County Bar Assn. Avocation: private pilot. Education and schools, Estate planning, General civil litigation. Office: 932 Hungerford Dr Ste 23A Rockville MD 20850-1752

**LITTLE, F. A., JR.,** federal judge; b. 1936; m. Gail Little; children: Sophie, Sabrina. BA, Tulane U., 1958, LLB, 1961. Assoc. Chaffe, McCall, Phillips, Toler & Sarpy, New Orleans, 1961-65, Gold, Little, Simon, Weems & Bruser, Alexandria, La., 1965-69; pres. Gold, Little, Simon, Weems & Bruser, Alexandria, 1968-84; judge U.S. Dist. Ct. (we. dist.) La., Alexandria, 1984-96, chief judge, 1996—; mem. fin. disclosure com. U.S. Cts., 1987-97. Fellow Am. Bar Found., Am. Coll. Trust and Estate Coun., La. Bar Found.; mem. La. State Law Inst. Coun. Office: US Dist Ct PO Box 1031 Alexandria LA 71309-1031

**LITTLE, WILLIAM DUNCAN, III,** state government lawyer; b. Anniston, Ala., Sept. 25, 1952; s. William Duncan and Elizabeth (Marvin) L.; m. Mary Lillian Owens, Apr. 4, 1981; children: William, Mary Margaret. BA in History, U. Ala., 1974, JD, 1979. Bar: Ala., U.S. Dist. Ct. (mid., so., no. dists.) Ala., U.S. Ct. Appeals (11 cir.). Assoc. atty. Frank W. Riggs, P.A., Montgomery, Ala., 1979-81; asst. atty. gen. State of Ala., Montgomery, 1981—. Episcopal. Home: 7830 Butler Mill Rd Montgomery AL 36105-3608 Office: Ala Atty Gen's Office 11 S Union St Montgomery AL 36130-2103

**LITTLEFIELD, ROY EVERETT, III,** association executive, legal educator; b. Nashua, N.H., Dec. 6, 1952; s. Roy Everett and Mary Ann (Prestipino) L.; m. Amy Root; children: Leah Marie, Roy Everett IV, Christy Louise. BA, Dickinson Coll., 1975; MA, Catholic U. Am., 1976, PhD, 1979. Aide U.S. Senator Thomas McIntyre, Democrat, N.H., 1975-78, Nordy Hoffman, U.S. Senate Sergeant-at-arms, N.H., 1979; dir. govt. rels. Nat. Tire Dealers and Retreaders Assn., Washington, N.H., 1979-84; exec. dir. Svc. Sta. and Automotive Repair Assn., Washington, N.H., 1984—; exec. v.p. Svc. Sta. Dealers of Am., 1994—; cons. Internat. Tire and Rubber Assn., 1984; mem. faculty Cath. U. Am., Washington, 1979—. Author: William Randolph Hearst: His Role in American Progressivism, 1980, The Economic Recovery Act, 1982, The Surface: Transportation Assistance Act, 1984; editor Nozzle mag.; contbr. numerous articles to legal jours. Mem. Nat. Dem. Club, 1978—. Mem. Am. Soc. Legal History, Md. Hwy. User's Fedn. (pres.), Nat. Hwy. User's Fedn. (sec.), Nat. Capitol Area Transp. Fedn. (v.p.), N.H. Hist. Soc., Kansas City C. of C., Capitol Hill Club, Phi Alpha Theta. Roman Catholic. Home: 1707 Pepper Tree Ct Bowie MD 20721-3021 Office: 9420 Annapolis Rd Ste 307 Lanham Seabrook MD 20706

**LITTLEJOHN, KENT OSCAR,** lawyer; b. Terre Haute, Ind., Oct. 3, 1945; s. Elmer O. and Evelyn P. (Shawver) L.; m. Brenda K. Swisher Littlejohn, Apr. 2, 1966; children: Douglas, Jessica Spurgeon, Gregory. BS in Bus. Adminstrn., Ind. State U., 1966; JD, Ind. U., 1969. Bar: U.S. Supreme Ct. Nebr. 1969, U.S. Dist. Ct. Nebr. 1969, U.S. Tax Ct. 1972, U.S. Ct. Appeals 1972, U.S. Ct. Claims, 1977. Assoc. Baird, Holm, McEachen, Pedersen, Hamann & Strasheim, Omaha, 1969-72, ptnr., 1972—, mng. ptnr., 1991—; dir. Great Plains Fed. Tax Inst., Lincoln, Nebr., 1972—, Nebr. Continuing Legal Edn. Svc., Lincoln, Nebr., 1975-84, Section of Taxation Nebr. Bar Assn., Lincoln, 1977, 89. Fellow Am. Coll. Tax Counsel, Nebr. State Bar Found., Nebr. Bar Assn., Omaha Bar Assn. Taxation, general, Estate planning, Corporate taxation. Office: Baird Holm McEachen Pedersen Hamann & Strasheim 1500 Woodmen Tower Omaha NE 68102

**LITTMAN, DAVID BERNARD,** lawyer; b. Plainfield, N.J., Oct. 16, 1949; s. Alexander and Muriel Roslyn (Block) L.; m. Deborah Joy Fields, Nov. 9, 1980; 1 child, Alexandra Ellen Pauline. AB, Lafayette Coll., 1970; JD, Rutgers U., 1973. Bar: N.J. 1974, U.S. Dist. Ct. N.J. 1974, U.S. Supreme Ct. 1983. Assoc. Winetsky & Winetsky, Linden, N.J., 1973-76; sole practice Linden, 1976—; mcpl. pub. defender Scotch Plains Twp., NJ, 1999—. Mem. ABA, N.J. Bar Assn., Union County Bar Assn., Linden Bar Assn. (pres. 1977-80), N.J. Trial Lawyers, Masons (sec. Highland Park lodge 1979-86, treas. 1987—). Democrat. Jewish. General practice, Criminal, Family and matrimonial. Home: 1557 Ashbrook Dr Scotch Plains NJ 07076-2854 Office: 129 N Wood Ave Linden NJ 07036-4227

**LITTON, RANDALL GALE,** lawyer; b. Idaho Falls, Idaho, July 13, 1939; s. Ralph John and Inez Evelyn (Petersen) L.; m. Sandra Byrne, Aug. 19, 1961 (div. 1993); children: Sean B., Stephanie L., Emily R. BSEE, U. Idaho, 1961; LLB, George Washington U., 1965. Bar: Mich. 1965, U.S. Dist. Ct. (ea. dist.) Mich. 1966, U.S. Dist. Ct. (we. dist.) Mich. 1967, U.S. Ct. Appeals (6th cir.) 1971, U.S. Ct. Appeals (8th cir.) 1979, U.S. Ct. Appeals (Fed. cir.) 1984, U.S. Ct. Appeals (7th cir.) 1993, U.S. Supreme Ct. 1993. Examiner U.S. Patent Office, Washington, 1962-64; ptnr. Price, Heneveld, Cooper, DeWitt & Litton, Grand Rapids, Mich., 1965—. Mem. ABA, Mich. Bar Assn. Presbyterian. Avocations: hunting, fishing, skiing. Federal civil litigation, Patent, Trademark and copyright. Office: Price Heneveld CoopeR DeWitt & Litton 695 Kenmoor Ave SE Grand Rapids MI 49546-2375

**LITVACK, SANFORD MARTIN,** lawyer; b. Bklyn., Apr. 29, 1936; s. Murray and Lee M. (Korman) L.; m. Judith E. Goldenson, Dec. 30, 1956; children—Mark, Jonathan, Sharon, Daniel. BA, U. Conn., 1956; LLB, Georgetown U., 1959. Bar: N.Y. 1964, D.C. 1979. Trial atty. antitrust div. Dept. Justice, Washington, 1959-61; asst. atty. gen. Dept. Justice, 1980-81; asso. firm Donovan, Leisure, Newton & Irvine, N.Y.C., 1961-69; ptnr. Donovan, Leisure, Newton & Irvine, 1969-80, 81-86, Dewey, Ballantine, Bushby, Palmer & Wood, N.Y.C., 1987-91; sr. exec. v.p., chief of corp. ops. The Walt Disney Co., Burbank, Calif., 1991—, also bd. dirs. Bd. dirs. Bet Tzedek. Fellow Am. Coll. Trial Lawyers; mem. ABA, Fed. Bar Coun., N.Y. State Bar Assn. (sec. antitrust sect. 1974-77, chmn. antitrust sect. 1985-86), Va. Bar Assn., Calif. Inst. of Arts (bd. dirs.), Am. Arbitration Assn. (bd. dirs.). Federal civil litigation, General civil litigation. Office: The Walt Disney Co 500 S Buena Vista St Burbank CA 91521-0004

**LITWAK, GLENN TOD,** lawyer; b. N.Y.C., Mar. 10, 1954; s. Sanford and Nettie (Fisher) L. BA in Polit. Sci. and Comms., Queens Coll./CUNY, 1976; JD, Santa Clara U., 1979. Bar: Calif. 1980, U.S. Dist. Ct. (so., ea., ctrl and no. dists.) Calif., U.S. Ct. Appeals (9th cir.); lic. real estate broker, Calif. Assoc. Daigneault, Abel & Daigneault, Torrance, Calif., 1980-83; sr. assoc. Wolfe, Hecht, Riskin, Eisenhart & Smith, L.A., 1983-90; sole practitioner Beverly Hills, Caif., 1990; assoc. gen. counsel Splty. Restaurants Corp., Anaheim, Calif., 1990-93; assoc. Law Offices of Richard Schtiller, Beverly Hills, 1993-95; founding mem. Law Offices of Litwak, Havkin & Babos, Beverly Hills, 1995—. Mem. Beverly Hills Bar Assn. (entertainment law sect.), Los Angeles County Bar ASsn. (vol. arbitrator), State Bar Calif. (litigation and intellectual property sects.), Calif. Lawyers for the Arts (referral and arbitration panel 1998—). Avocations: skiing, bicycle riding. General civil litigation, Entertainment, Intellectual property. Office: Litwak Havkin & Babos 315 S Beverly Dr Ste 200 Beverly Hills CA 90212-4310

**LITWIN, BURTON LAWRENCE,** entertainment industry executive, theatrical producer, lawyer; b. N.Y.C., Jan. 1, 1931; s. Samuel G. and Eleanore (Kos) L.; m. Dorothy Beth Lefkowitz, Nov. 18, 1956; children: Richard Seth, Robert Aron, Kenneth David. BA, Washington and Lee U., 1951; LLB, NYU, 1953. Bar: N.Y. 1954, U.S. Dist. Ct. (so. dist.) N.Y. 1958, U.S. Ct. Appeals (2d cir.) 1964. Assoc. Wilzin and Halperin, N.Y.C., 1956-64; ptnr. DaSilva and Litwin, N.Y.C., 1964-65; sole practice, N.Y.C., 1965-67; v.p., dir. bus. affairs Belwin-Mills Pub. Corp., N.Y.C., 1967-74, v.p., gen. mgr., counsel, 1975-86; pres., CEO Newcal Properties and Prodns., Ltd., Newcal Music Co., Dobbs Ferry, N.Y., 1986—; bd. dirs. Nat. Teaching Aids, Inc., Garden City Park, N.Y. Producer: (theatrical works) Sophisticated Ladies, N.Y.C., Tokyo, Paris, Moscow, Leningrad, L.A., Washington 1980—, Poppy, London, 1982-83, Stardust, N.Y.C., 1986—. Pres. Temple Beth Abraham, Tarrytown, N.Y., 1982-83; bd. dirs. Creative Arts Rehab. Ctr., N.Y.C., 1983-84. Served to sgt. U.S. Army, 1953-55. Recipient Tony award nomination League of N.Y. Theatres, 1982; ann. Image award NAACP, 1982, Outer Critics Circle award, 1987, Ivor Novello award nomination Brit. Acad. Songwriters, Composer and Authors, 1983. Mem. ASCAP (bd. appeals 1981-83, adv. com. 1985-87), N.Y. State Bar Assn., Copyright Soc. USA, League of Am. Theatres and Producers., Friars Club, B'nai B'rith. Avocations: photography, traveling, golf, tennis. Home and Office: Newcal Properties and Prodns 12 Crescent Ln Dobbs Ferry NY 10522-3204

**LIU, ALBERT JINGION,** lawyer; b. Louisville, May 15, 1967; s. Pinghui Victor and Chiameng Judy L. BA in East Asian Studies, Ind. U., 1989; JD, U. Oreg., 1992. Bar: Wash., Ky. Pvt. practice Louisville, 1996—. Unitarian. Criminal.

**LIU, DIANA CHUA,** lawyer; b. N.Y.C., Mar. 23, 1961; d. Donald and Emilie Chua Liu. BA, Johns Hopkins U., 1983; JD, Cornell U., 1986. Bar: Pa. 1986, U.S. Dist. Ct. (ea. dist.) Pa. 1986. Assoc. Montgomery, McCracken, Walker & Rhoads, Phila., 1986-88; assoc. Wolf, Block, Schorr and Solis-Cohen, Phila., 1988-94, ptnr., 1994—; participant legal leadership summit Am. Corp. Counsel Assn., Washington, 1996-97; lectr. law U. Pa. Law Sch., Phila., 1998. Mem. Asian Am. Women's Coalition, Phila., 1986—, pres., 1990; bd. dirs. Big Bro./Big Sister Assn., Phila., 1989—; mem. Johns Hopkins U. Second Decade Soc., Balt., 1993—, nat. chair, 1997. Named 40 under 40 Phila. Bus. jour., 1995. Mem. Nat. Asian Pacific Am. Bar Assn. Ptnrs. Network, Asian Am. Bar Assn. Del. Valley (pres. 1999), Pa. Bar Assn. (ho. of dels. 1991-97), Phila. Bar Assn. (bd. govs. 1996-98). Real property, Contracts commercial, General corporate. Office: Wolf Block Schorr & Solis-Cohen LLP 111 S 15th St Ste 1200 Philadelphia PA 19102-2678

**LIVADARY, PAUL JOHN,** lawyer; b. L.A., Oct. 6, 1937; s. John Paul and Helen (Loomis) L.; m. Betsy Gregory, Oct. 12, 1974 (div. 1990); children: Sarah Elizabeth, Catherine Carter, Emily Elene, John Matthew. BA in Econs., Stanford U., 1959; LLB, U. Calif., Berkeley, 1964. Bar: Calif. 1965, U.S. Dist. Ct. Calif. 1965. Assoc. O'Melveny & Myers, L.A., 1965-75; ptnr. Parker, Milliken, Clark, O'Hara & Samuelian, L.A., 1975-93; pvt. practice L.A., 1993—. Bd. dirs. Children's Hosp. of L.A., 1982-93, Greater L.A. Zoo Assn., 1989—; founder, bd. trustees Pasadena Waldorf Sch., Altadena, Calif., 1978-92; bd. trustees Republican Assocs., L.A., 1970-92. 1st lt. U.S. Army, 1959-61. Mem. Valley Hunt Club. Estate planning, Probate, Estate taxation. Office: 2029 Century Park E Ste 437 Los Angeles CA 90067-2905

**LIVAUDAIS, MARCEL, JR.,** federal judge; b. New Orleans, Mar. 3, 1925; m. Carol Black; children: Julie, Marc, Durel. BA, Tulane U., 1945, JD, 1949. Bar: La. Assoc. Boswell & Loeb, New Orleans, 1949-50, 52-56; ptnr. Boswell Loeb & Livaudais, New Orleans, 1956-60, Loeb & Livaudais, 1960-67, 71-77, Loeb Dillon & Livaudais, 1967-71; U.S. magistrate, 1977-84; judge U.S. Dist. Ct. (ea. dist.) La., New Orleans, 1984-96, sr. judge, 1996—. Mem. Am. Judicature Soc. Office: US Dist Ct C-405 US Courthouse 500 Camp St New Orleans LA 70130-3313

**LIVELY, PIERCE,** federal judge; b. Louisville, Aug. 17, 1921; s. Henry Thad and Ruby Durrett (Keating) L.; m. Amelia Harrington, May 25, 1946; children: Susan, Katherine, Thad. AB, Centre Coll., Ky., 1943; LL.B., U. Va., 1948. Bar: Ky. 1948. Individual practice law Danville, Ky., 1949-57; mem. firm Lively and Rodes, Danville, 1957-72; judge U.S. Ct. Appeals (6th cir.), Cin., 1972—, chief judge, 1983-88, sr. judge, 1988-97, ret., 1997; Mem. Ky. Commn. on Economy and Efficiency in Govt., 1963-65, Ky. Jud. Advisory Com., 1972. Trustee Centre Coll. Served with USNR, 1943-46. Mem. ABA, Am. Judicature Soc., Order of Coif, Raven Soc., Phi Beta Kappa, Omicron Delta Kappa. Presbyterian.

**LIVERGOOD, ROBERT FRANK,** prosecutor; b. Akron, Ohio, Dec. 20, 1957; s. Robert Burton and Rita Veronica (Haidnick) L.; m. Sandra Anne Ko, Aug. 5, 1983; children: Robert Santos, Jacob Christopher, Sarah Nicole. BA, St. Louis U., 1981, M in Health Adminstrn., 1983, JD, 1988. Bar: Mo. 1988, Ill. 1989, U.S. Dist. Ct. (ea. dist.) Mo. 1989, U.S. Dist. Ct. (so. dist.) Ill. 1989. Dir. market rsch. St. Joseph's Hosp. Kirkwood, Mo., 1983-85; assoc. Husch & Eppenberger, St. Louis, 1988-90; asst. prosecuting atty. Office of the Prosecutor, Clayton, Mo., 1990—. Editor St. Louis U. Law Jour., 1986-87, mng. editor, 1987-88. Vol. lawyer Voluntary Lawyers Program, St. Louis, 1988-90; spkr. St. Louis (Mo.) County and Mcpl. Police Acad., 1993-94. Mem. ABA, Ill. State Bar Assn., Bar Assn. Met. St. Louis. Avocations: martial arts, amateur radio. Office: Office of the Prosecutor 100 S Central Ave Clayton MO 63105-1732

**LIVINGSTON, ANN CHAMBLISS,** lawyer; b. Mpls., July 25, 1952; d. Johnston Redmond and Patricia A. Livingston. BA, Trinity U., San Antonio, 1974; JD, St. Mary's U., San Antonio, 1979. Bar: Tex. 1979, U.S. Ct. Appeals (5th cir.) 1981, U.S. Patent and Trademark Office, 1986, Ct. Appeals (fed. cir.) 1988. Briefing atty. Supreme Ct. of Tex., Austin, 1979-80; assoc. Groce, Locke & Hebdon, San Antonio, 1980-85; ptnr. Gunn, Lee & Jackson, San Antonio, 1985-89; assoc. Baker, Mills & Glast, San Antonio, 1989-90, Baker & Botts, San Antonio, 1990—. Exec. editor St. Mary's U. Law Jour., 1978-79. Mem. Tex. Bar Assn., Phi Delta Phi. Patent, Trademark and copyright, Computer. Home: 1201 Loop 165 Dripping Springs TX 78620-4725 Office: Baker & Botts 98 San Jacinto Blvd Ste 1600 Austin TX 78701-4078

**LIVINGSTON, DOUGLAS MARK,** lawyer; b. Lawton, Okla., Nov. 2, 1945; s. Oscar Calloway and Irene (Norton) L.; m. Vicki Sue Ratts, Dec. 21, 1969; children: Lisa Marie, Stephen Mark, Anna Lee, Micah James. BS, Okla. Christian Coll., 1967; MPH, U. Okla., 1969, JD, 1980; MEd, Wayne State U., 1981; Grad., USAF War Coll., 1994, U.S. Army War Coll., 1998. Bar: Okla. 1980, U.S. Dist. Ct. (we. dist.) Okla. 1987, U.S. Army Ct. Mil. Rev. 1989, U.S. Ct. Appeals for Armed Forces 1995, U.S. Ct. Appeals (fed. cir.) 1995, U.S. Supreme Ct. 1999. Intern Cleveland County Dist. Atty., Norman, Okla., 1979-80; gen. counsel, dir. Delphi Devel., Ltd., Norman, 1980-81; gen. counsel Pepco Devel., Inc., Norman, 1981-85, Pepco, Inc., Norman, 1981-85; owner, ptnr. Payne, Livingston & Harold, P.C., Oklahoma City, 1985-86, Livingston Law Office, Norman, 1986-92, 93-94; staff atty. U.S. Dept. of Army, Ft. Sill, Okla., 1992-93, labor atty., 1994—; ptnr. Concord Investments, Ltd., Norman, 1982-88; team dir. 33d judge adv. gen. detachment, Oklahoma City, 1988-91, 29th judge adv. gen. detachment, Tulsa, 1991-93; staff judge adv. 4003d U.S. Army Garrison, Ft. Chaffee, Ark., 1993-95, 122nd USAR Command, North Little Rock, Ark., 1995; comdr. 1st Legal Support Orgn., San Antonio, 1995-98; staff judge adv. 90th Regional Support Command, North Little Rock, Ark., 1998—. Editor coll. newspaper Talon, 1966; note editor Am. Indian Law Rev., 1979-80. Bd. dirs. Big Bros./Big Sisters, Norman, 1983-85, Rock Creek Youth Camp, Norman, 1985-94; Rep. precinct chmn., Oklahoma City, 1971. Capt. U.S. Army, 1973-77; col. USAR. Named one of Outstanding Young Men of Am., 1973. Mem. Okla. Bar Assn., Fed. Bar Assn., Cleveland County Bar Assn., Res. Officers Assn., Assn. U.S. Army., Sr. Army Res. Comdr.'s Assn., U.S. Army JAG Sch. Alumni Assn., U.S. Army War Coll. Alumni Assn. Mem. Ch. of Christ. Avocations: family activities, reading, running. Home: 911 S Lahoma Ave Norman OK 73069-4509 Office: Office of Staff Judge Adv Building 462 Fort Sill OK 73503

**LIVINGSTON, EDWARD MICHAEL,** lawyer; b. Gardner, Mass., Aug. 31, 1948; s. Elmer Harris and Pearl Alice (Gonyeo) L.; m. Dianne Mary Collette, Feb. 6, 1971; children: Erica Linda, Gregory Edward, James Michael. BS in Mech. and Aerospace Engring., U. Mass., 1970; MBA, U. Wyo., 1974; JD, U. Miami, 1978. Bar: Fla. 1978, U.S. Dist. Ct. (mid. dist.) Fla. 1978, U.S. Ct. Appeals (11th cir.) 1978, U.S. Patent Office, U.S. Ct. Appeals (fed. cir.) 1989. Assoc. Glass, Schultz, Weinstein & Moss, P.A. (name now Holland and Knight), 1978-79, Levine & Cohen, Orlando, Fla., 1979-80; ptnr. Livingston, Blau & Rutter, Orlando, 1980-81, Stanley, Lovett, Livingston & Whitacre, Orlando, 1981-86, Livingston & Whitacre, Winter Park, Fla., 1986-89; prin. Edward M. Livingston, P.A., Winter Park, 1989—; probation counselor, Cheyenne, Wyo., 1972-75. V.p. Homeowners Assn., Orlando, 1979-81; coach Little League Baseball, Orlando, 1981; leader Boy Scouts Am., 1989-93. Lt. Col. USAFR, 1970-96. Mem. ABA, Am. Intellectual Property Law Assn., Orange County Bar Assn., Winter Park Jaycees, Beta Gamma Sigma, Omicron Delta Kappa. Democrat. Roman Catholic. Avocations: flying, all sports, golf, boating. Patent, Trademark and copyright, General corporate. Office: 628 Ellen Dr PO Box 1599 Winter Park FL 32790-1599

**LIVINGSTON, JUDITH A.,** lawyer; b. N.Y.C., Sept. 28, 1954. BA magna cum laude, SUNY, Stony Brook, 1976; JD, Hofstra U., 1979. Bar: N.Y. 1980, U.S. Dist. Ct. (so. and ea. dists.) N.Y. 1991, U.S. Supreme Ct. Ptnr. Kramer, Dillof, Tessel, Duffy & Moore, N.Y.C. Named one of 50 Top Women Lawyers Nat. Law Jour., 1998. Fellow Internat. Acad. Trial Lawyers; mem. ABA, N.Y. State Trial Lawyers Assn. (bd. dirs. 1988—), Women's Bar Assn. N.Y. State, Met. Women's Bar Assn., Am. Bd. Trial Advocates (bd. dirs.), Inner Cir. Advocates. Personal injury, General civil litigation. Office: Kramer Dillof Tessel Duffy & Moore 233 Broadway New York NY 10279-0001*

**LIVINGSTON, MARY COUNIHAN,** lawyer; b. Providence, Apr. 22, 1952; d. William J. Jr. and Lois C. Counihan; m. D. Dunbar Livingston, July 7, 1984; children: Schuyler M., Samuel D. BA and MA in English with honors, Brown U., 1974; JD, Villanova U., 1977. Bar: R.I. 1977, Mass. 1980, U.S. Dist. Ct. Mass. 1980, U.S. Ct. Appeals (1st cir.) 1980. Law clk. hon. Joseph R. Weisberger R.I. Supreme Ct., Providence, 1977-79; counsel New Eng. Fin., Boston, 1979—, 2d v.p., 1998—; bd. dirs. R.I., Mass. and N.H. Life and Health Assns. Trustee Lincoln Sch., Providence, 1987-89; mem. fin. com. and bldg. com. Nahant (Mass.) Village Ch., 1998—. Avocation: tennis. Computer, Insurance, Intellectual property. Office: New Eng Fin 501 Boylston St Boston MA 02116-3706

**LIVINGSTON, RANDALL MURCH,** lawyer; b. New Britain, Conn., May 2, 1949; s. William Toliver and Elizabeth (Murch) L.; m. Kathleen Anne Lord, Feb. 28, 1986; children: Heather Ann, Emma Siobhan, Rachel Erin, Nora Searlait. BA, Williams Coll., 1971; MA, U. Mich., 1972; JD, Vt. Law Sch., 1982. Bar: Colo. 1983, U.S. Dist. Ct. Colo. 1983, U.S. Ct. Appeals (10th cir.) 1984, U.S. Ct. Appeals (9th cir.) 1985. Law clk. to Hon. Donald J. Porter U.S. Dist. Ct. for S.D., Pierre, 1982-83; assoc. Calkins, Kramer, Grimshaw & Harring, P.C., Denver, 1983-88, ptnr., 1989-92; with Bailey, Harring & Peterson, P.C., Denver, 1993—. Editor: Vt. Law Rev., 1981-82.

Mem. ABA, Colo. Bar Assn., Denver Bar Assn. Democrat. Avocations: opera, fly fishing. General civil litigation. Office: Bailey Harring & Peterson 1660 Lincoln St Ste 3175 Denver CO 80264-3102

**LIVOLSI, FRANK WILLIAM, JR.,** lawyer; b. Stamford, Conn., June 6, 1938; s. Frank Sr. and Rose M. Livolsi. BA, Pa. Mil. Coll., 1962; JD, Fordham U., 1965. Bar: Ct. 1968. Ptnr. Melzer & Livolsi, Stamford, 1970—. Served to capt. U.S. Army, 1965-67, Vietnam. General practice, State civil litigation. Home: 155 Thornwood Rd Stamford CT 06903-2616 Office: 1035 Washington Blvd Stamford CT 06901-2204

**LLORENTE, ALEX JERONIMO,** educator, lawyer; b. Havana, Cuba, Aug. 20, 1959; came to US 1965; s. Carlos O. L. and Aida Rodriguez; m. Evelyne N. Havan, July 2, 1988; children: Ariel, Adrian. BA, U. South Fla., 1978, MA in Econs., 1980; MBA in Acctg., U. Houston, 1983; JD, Western State U., 1994. Bar: Calif. 1995. CPA Tex., 1984. Tax auditor IRS, Tampa, Fla., 1979-81; assoc. prof. Brazosport Coll., Lake Jackson, Tex., 1982-84; prof. Saddlebrook Coll., Mission Viejo, Calif., 1984—; pvt. practice Laguna Hills, Calif., 1995—. Office: 2 Mareblu Ste 114 Aliso Viejo CA 92656-3014

**LLOYD, ALEX,** lawyer; b. Atlantic, Iowa, Aug. 13, 1942; s. Norman and Ruth (R.) L.; m. Jacqueline Roe, Aug. 24, 1963; children: Erin, Andrea, John, Peter. BA in Econs., Colby Coll., 1964; LLB, Law Sch., Yale U., 1967. Bar: Conn., U.S. Dist. Ct. (Conn.), U.S. Ct. Appeals (2d cir.), U.S. Tax Ct., U.S. Supreme Ct. Assoc. Shipman & Goodwin, 1967-72, ptnr., 1972—, chmn. mgmt. com., 1985-96; bd. dirs. Hartford Hosp., Conn. Health System, Inc., Conn. Bar Found., VNA Health Care, Inc.,, Vis. Nurse and Home Care, Inc. Recipient Charles J. Parker award Conn. Bar Assn., Dist. Svc. award Conn. Legal Svcs. Fellow Am. Bar Found., Conn. Bar Found.; mem. ABA, Am. Soc. of Hosp. Attys., Conn. Bar Assn. Avocations: golf, boating, fishing, raquet sports, piano. General corporate, Health, Corporate taxation. Office: Shipman & Goodwin 1 American Row Hartford CT 06103-2833

**LLOYD, CHARLES ALLEN,** lawyer; b. Hickory, N.C., Mar. 27, 1944; s. Charles Edward and Maude (Shuford) L.; m. Cheryl Ann Taylor, Aug. 20, 1966; children: Susan Taylor, Rebecca Ann. BA, Davidson Coll., 1966; JD, U. N.C., 1969. Bar: N.C. 1969, U.S. Dist. Ct. (ea., mid. and we. dists.) N.C. 1970, U.S. Ct. Appeals (4th cir.) 1972, U.S. Supreme Ct. 1974; bd. cert. specialist in criminal law. Law clk. to presiding chief judge U.S. Dist. Ct. for Eastern Dist. N.C., Clinton, 1969-70; asst. atty. gen. Office of N.C. Atty. Gen., Raleigh, 1970-74; ptnr. Smith, Patterson, Follin, Curtis, James & Harkavy, Greensboro, N.C., 1974-87, Carrington & Lloyd, Greensboro, 1987-88; pvt. practice Greensboro, 1988—; lectr. continuing legal edn. seminars, 1982—. Mem. ABA, N.C. Bar Assn. (chmn. criminal justice sect. 1986-88), Nat. Criminal Def. Lawyers Assn., Greensboro Criminal Def. Lawyers Assn. (pres. 1981, 88, 94). Avocation: running. Criminal. Home: 5300 Sequoia Ct Greensboro NC 27455-2184 Office: 301 S Greene St Ste 100 Greensboro NC 27401-2660

**LLOYD, FRANCIS LEON, JR.,** lawyer; b. Winchester, Va., Dec. 1, 1955; s. Francis Leon Sr. and Jeannette Marie (Dove) L.; m. Myra Denise DuBose, Sept. 18, 1982. BA in English and French, U. Richmond, 1978; JD, U. Va., 1981. Bar: Va. 1981, Tenn. 1982, U.S. Dist. Ct. (ea. dist.) Tenn. 1982, U.S. Ct. Appeals (6th cir.) 1984. Assoc. Herndon, Coleman, Brading & McKee, Johnson City, Tenn., 1981-86, ptnr., 1987-88; of counsel The Taylor Group, Ltd., Johnson City, 1983; law clk. to judge U.S. Dist. Ct. (ea. dist.) Tenn., Knoxville, 1988-98; assoc. London & Amburn, P.C., Knoxville, 1998—. Bd. dirs. Assn. Retarded Citizens Washington County, Inc., Johnson City, 1982-88. Avocations: literature, music, hiking. Home: 8804 Regent Ln Knoxville TN 37923-1640 Office: London & Amburn PC 1716 W Clinch Ave Knoxville TN 37916-2408

**LLOYD, LEONA LORETTA,** judge; b. Detroit, Aug. 6, 1949; d. Leon Thomas and Naomi Mattie (Chisolm) L.; 1 stepson, Joseph Andersen. BS, Wayne State U., 1971, JD, 1979. Bar: Mich. 1981, U.S. Dist. Ct. (ea. dist.) 1981, U.S. Supreme Ct. 1988, U.S. Cir. Ct. (6th cir.) 1983. Speech, drama tchr. Detroit Bd. Edn., 1971-75; instr. criminal justice Wayne State U., Detroit, 1981; sr. ptnr. Lloyd and Lloyd, Detroit, 1982-92; prin. asst., corp. counsel City Detroit Law Dept., 1992-94; judge 36th Dist. Ct., Detroit, 1994—. Co-author, dir. (gospel musical) Freedom Song, 1991. Wayne State U. scholar, 1970, 75; recipient Fred Hampton Image award, 1984, Kizzy Image award, 1985, Nat. Coalition of 100 Black Women Achievement award, 1986, Community Svc. award Wayne County exec. William Lucas, 1986, Merit Black Law Student Assn. cert. U. Detroit, 1986, Spirit of Detroit award, 1991, Martin Luther King Keep This Dream Alive award, 1995, Special Tribute award State of Mich., 1995, Resolution award County of Wayne, 1995, Appreciation cert. City of Detroit, 1995, Bar Assn. award, 1995, B'nai B'rith Barristers award, 1995, Testimonial Resolution award Detroit City Coun., 1995, Woman of Yr. award African Am. Awards Coun., 1996, African Am. Sheroes award Drusilla Farwell Mid. Sch., 1997; named to Black Women Hall of Fame. Mem. ABA, NARAS, Wolverine Bar Assn., Mich. State Bar, Mary McLeod Bethune Assn. Office: 421 Madison St Ste 3067 Detroit MI 48226-2358

**LLOYD, ROBERT W.,** lawyer; b. Daytona Beach, Fla., Jan. 9, 1965; s. Robert Frederick and Sandra DeArmas Lloyd; m. Sherri Ingle Fowler, June 8, 1996. BA, U. Fla., 1987, JD, 1990. Bar: Fla. 1991, U.S. Dist. Ct. (mid. dist.) Fla. 1991, U.S. Dist. Ct. (so. dist.) Fla. 1992, U.S. Ct. Appeals (11th cir.) 1994. Atty. Cobb Cole & Bell, Daytona Beach, Fla., 1991—; legal counsel Daytona Beach Chamber, 1996-98. Chmn. Bethune-Cookman Bd. Counselors, Daytona Beach, 1995, 97; pres. Crime Stoppers of Volusia, Daytona Beach, 1997-98; pres.-elect Futures Edn. Found., Daytona Beach, 1998. Mem. Civil League Halifax Area, Rotary Club Daytona Beach (bd. dirs. 1996—), Daytop Fla. (bd. dirs. 1996—), Mission United (sec. 1992—). Avocation: kayaking. Labor. Home: 6210 Shoreline Dr Port Orange FL 32127-5967 Office: Cobb Cole & Bell 150 Magnolia Ave Daytona Beach FL 32114-4346

**LOATS, J. TIMOTHY,** lawyer, educator, arbitrator; b. Colo., July 14, 1954. BA summa cum laude, George Williams Coll., Downers Grove, Ill., 1975; JD, U. Notre Dame, 1978. Bar: Ill. 1978, U.S. Dist. Ct. Ill. 1978. Atty. Graney & Gerstein, P.C., Chgo., 1976-79, Scheele, Serkland & Boyle, Ltd., Chgo., 1979-81; founder, owner Fox Valley Legal Clinic, Aurora, Ill., 1981-90; ptnr. Alschuler, Funkey, Loats & Pilmer, P.C., Aurora, 1990-94, mng. ptnr., 1992-94; sole practitioner Aurora, 1995—; instr. employment law Waubonsee C.C., 1992—, Aurora U., 1985—; arbitrator 16th Jud. Cir., Kane, Ill., 1995—, 18th Jud. Cir., DuPage, Ill., 1989—. Contbr. articles to profl. jours. Bd. dirs. United Way of Aurora Area, 1995—, pres., 1996-97; bd. dirs. Cities in Schs. Aurora 2000, Inc., 1993—, pres., 1993-94; bd. dirs. Mut. Ground, Inc., 1990-93, Family Counseling Svc., 1983-85, Aurora Interfaith Food Pantry, 1982-85; bd. dirs. Big Bros./Big Sisters of So. Kane and Kendall County, 1985-87, chmn., 1986. Paul Harris fellow Rotary Internat. Mem. ABA (vice chmn. workers compensation com. 1994—), Ill. State Bar Assn., Kane County Bar Assn. (labor and employment law com., chair workers compensation com. 1992—), DuPage County Bar Assn., Ill. Workers Compensation Bar Assn., Rotary Club of Fox Valley Villages (pres. 1988-89). Workers' compensation. Office: 330 N Broadway Aurora IL 60505-2642

**LOBAUGH, LESLIE E., JR.,** lawyer, holding company executive. AB, Santa Clara U., 1967; JD, Georgetown U., 1970. Bar: Calif. Assoc. Holdberg, Finger, Brown & Abramson, 1971-75; staff atty. Pacific Lighting, 1975-77, sr. counsel, 1977-82, asst. gen. counsel, 1982-85, assoc. gen. counsel, 1985-86; v.p., gen. counsel Pacific Enterprises, 1986—, So. Calif. Gas Co., 1986—. Office: Pacific Enterprises 555 W 5th St Los Angeles CA 90013-1010

**LOBDELL, HENRY RAYMOND,** lawyer; b. Seoul, Korea, Dec. 29, 1961; s. LeRoy C. and Kyung Wha (Lee) L. Student, Wash. State U., 1979-80; BA, U. Wash., 1983; postgrad., U. Hawaii, 1985; JD, Lewis and Clark Coll., Portland, Oreg., 1986. Bar: Hawaii 1987, U.S. Dist. Ct. Hawaii 1987. Law clk. Honorable Wan Be Chang Cir. Cts. of State of Hawaii, Honolulu, 1986-87, law clk. Honorable Patrick K.S.L. Yim, 1987-88; sr. assoc. Law Offices of Ian L. Mattoch, Honolulu, 1988-90; ptnr. Kawamura & Lobdell, Honolulu, 1990-92, Kawamura Lobdell & Stern, Honolulu, 1992-94, Kawamura & Lobdell, Honolulu, 1994-96, Kawamura Lobdell & Moniz, Honolulu, 1996—; cons. Duncan Inc., Aiea, Hawaii, 1986—, Profl. Bus. Svcs., Aiea, 1990—; chmn. Hypersearch Ltd., Inc., Costa Mesa, Calif., 1993-95. Vol. Hawaii Make a Wish, Honolulu, 1988-90, Prevent Child Abuse, Honolulu, 1989-90. Mem. ABA, ATLA, Hawaii State Bar Assn., Hawaii Trial Lawyers Assn. Avocations: skiing, kayaking, tennis, volleyball, sailing. Insurance, Personal injury, Consumer commercial. Office: Kawamura Lobdell & Moniz Penthouse 1221 Kapiolani Blvd Honolulu HI 96814-3503

**LOBEL, MARTIN,** lawyer; b. Cambridge, Mass., June 19, 1941; s. I. Alan and Dorothy W. L.; m. Geralyn Krupp, Mar. 15, 1981; children: Devra Sarah, Rachel Melissa, Hannah Krupp. AB, Boston U., 1962, JD, 1965; LLM, Harvard U., 1966. Bar: Mass. 1965, D.C. 1968, U.S. Supreme Ct. 1968. Ptnr. Lobel & Lobel, Boston, 1965-66; asst. prof. law U. Okla., Norman, 1967; Congl. fellow, Washington, 1968; legis. asst. to Senator William Proxmire, 1968-72; ptnr. Lobel, Novins & Lamont, Washington, 1972—; lectr. Law Sch. Am. U., Washington, 1972—; resellers referee, U.S. Dist. Ct., Wichita; chmn. Tax Analysts, 1972—. Chmn. tax notes/tax analysts. Mem. ABA, Mass. Bar Assn., D.C. Bar Assn. (chmn. consumer affairs com. 1976-77, chmn. steering com. on antitrust and consumer affairs sect.), Order of Coif, Harvard Club (Washington), Boston U. Club (Washington). Contbr. articles to legal jours. Administrative and regulatory, Federal civil litigation, Legislative. Home: 4525 31st St NW Washington DC 20008-2130 Office: Lobel Novins & Lamont 1275 K St NW Ste 770 Washington DC 20005-4048

**LOBENHERZ, WILLIAM ERNEST,** container company/association executive, lawyer; b. Muskegon, Mich., June 22, 1949; s. Ernest Pomeroy and Emajean (Krautheim) L.; children: Jessica Anne, Rebecca Jean, Christopher William, Andrew William. BBA, U. Mich., 1971; JD cum laude, Wayne State U., 1974. Bar: Mich. 1974. Legal counsel Mich. Legis. Services Bur., Lansing, Mich., 1974-77; legal legis. cons. Mich. Assn. of Sch. Bds., Lansing, 1977, asst. exec. dir. for legal legis. affairs, 1977-79; asst. v.p. state and congl. relations Wayne State U., Detroit, 1979-81, assoc. v.p. state relations, 1981-82, v.p. govtl. affairs, 1982-87; assoc. Dykema Gossett, Lansing, Mich., 1987-89; pres., CEO, Mich. Soft Drink Assn., Lansing, 1989—, MSDA Svc. Corp., Lansing, 1997—; guest lectr. in govtl. affairs, Wayne State U., U. Mich., U. Detroit; referee Mich. Tax Tribunal, 1993-97. Contbr. chpt. Mich. Handbook for School Business Officials, 1979, 2nd edit., 1980; also articles to profl. jours. and mags. Mem. govtl. affairs com. New Detroit Inc., 1984-87, chmn. state subcom. of govtl. affairs com., 1986-87; chmn. ind. schs. campaign Greater Metro Detroit United Fund Torch Dr., 1979, chmn. Colls. and Univs. campaign, 1980; bd. dirs. Mich. Epilepsy Ctr., 1991-97, Coun. for Mich. Pub. Univs., 1991—, Tourism Industry Coalition of Mich., vice-chair, 1998—. Recipient Book award Lawyer's Coop. Pub. Co., 1973, Outstanding Svc. award Mich. Assn. for Marriage and Family Therapy, 1992, 95, Silver scholar key Wayne State U. Law Sch., 1974. Mem. Mich. Bar Assn., NAACP, Coun. for Advancement and Support of Edn. (Mindpower citation 1982), Mich. Delta Found. (bd. dirs. 1977-97, sec. 1981-84, v.p. 1987-88), Greater Metro Detroit C. of C. (contact interviewer bus. attraction and expansion coun. 1984-86), City Club. Home: 605 Glenmoor Rd Apt 1B East Lansing MI 48823-3925 Office: Mich Soft Drink Assn 634 Michigan Nat Towers Lansing MI 48933

**LOBL, HERBERT MAX,** lawyer; b. Vienna, Austria, Jan. 10, 1932; s. Walter Leo and Minnie (Neumann) L.; m. Dorothy Fullerton Hubbard, Sept. 12, 1960; children: Peter Walter, Michelle Alexandra. AB magna cum laude, Harvard U., 1953, LLB cum laude, 1959, Avocat honoraire, 1993. Bar: N.Y. 1960, U.S. Tax Ct. 1963, French Conseil Juridique 1973; French avocat, mem. Paris bar, 1992, avocat hon., 1993. Assoc. Davis, Polk & Wardwell, N.Y.C., 1959-60; assoc. counsel to Gov. Nelson Rockefeller, Albany, N.Y., 1960-62; assoc. Davis, Polk & Wardwell, N.Y. and Paris, 1963-69, ptnr., Paris, 1969-92, sr. counsel, 1993—; lectr. law Columbia U., N.Y.C., 1993-95; supervisory bd. mem. CII-HB Internationale, Amsterdam, Holland, 1977-82. Gov. Am. Hosp. Paris, 1981-83, 88-93; trustee Am. Libr., Paris, 1969-81, Nantucket (Mass.) Cottage Hosp., 1996—. Served to 1st lt. USAF, 1954-56, Berlin. Fulbright scholar U. Bonn, Germany, 1954. Mem. Am. C. of C. (bd. dirs. France 1988-90), Univ. Club, Harvard Club (N.Y.). Private international, Corporate taxation. Address: PO Box 2488 Nantucket MA 02584-2488 also: PO Box 118 Rye NY 10580-0118 also: Davis Polk & Wardwell 450 Lexington Ave New York NY 10017-3911

**LOCH, ROBERT ANTHONY,** lawyer; b. Pitts., Jan. 18, 1964; s. Richard A. and Barbara Ann (Rogers) L. BA, Pa. State U., 1986; JD, U. Pitts., 1989. Bar: Pa. 1989, U.S. Dsit. Ct. (we. dist.) Pa. 1989. Lawyer Robb, Leonard & Mulvihill, Pitts., 1989—. Mem. Phi Beta Kappa. Insurance, Municipal (including bonds), Workers' compensation. Office: Robb Leonard & Mulvihill 2300 One Mellon Bank Ctr Pittsburgh PA 15219

**LOCHHEAD, ROBERT BRUCE,** lawyer; b. St. Louis, June 20, 1952; s. Angus Tulloch and Matilda Evangeline (Thurman) L.; m. KLynn Walker, June 21, 1974; children: Robert, Richard, Cynthia, Melinda, Rebekah, Elizabeth. BA, Brigham Young U., 1975; JD, Columbia U., 1978. Bar: D.C. 1979, Utah 1980, U.S. Dist. Ct. Utah 1980, U.S. Ct. Appeals (10th cir.) 1980, U.S. Supreme Ct. 1986. Law clk. to judge U.S. Ct. Appeals (10th cir.) Salt Lake City, 1978-79; assoc. Hogan & Hartson, Washington, 1979-80, Larsen, Kimball, Parr & Crockett, Salt Lake City, 1980-82; shareholder Parr, Waddoups Brown, Gee & Loveless, Salt Lake City, 1982—; judge pro tem Small Claims Ct., Salt Lake City, 1985-88; mem. panel of arbitrators U.S. Bankruptcy Ct., Dist. Utah, 1995—. Harlan Fiske Stone scholar, 1976-78. Mem. ABA, Am. Bankruptcy Inst. Mormon. Bankruptcy, Federal civil litigation, Contracts commercial. Home: 492 N Flint St Kaysville UT 84037-9777 Office: Parr Waddoups Brown Gee & Loveless 185 S State St Ste 1300 Salt Lake City UT 84111-1537

**LOCHRIDGE, IAN JAMES,** lawyer; b. New York, N.Y., Nov. 15, 1950; s. Campbell David Lochridge and Jean Elizabeth (Brownlow) Berasaluce; 1 child, Collin James. BA, U. Ill., 1976; JD, DePaul U., 1979. Bar: Ill. 1979, U.S. Dist. Ct. (no. dist.) Ill. 1979, U.S. Ct. of Appeals (7th cir.) 1979, U.S. Supreme Ct. 1986. Law clerk to presiding justice U.S. Dist. Ct. (no. dist.), Chgo., 1979, Ill. Appellate Ct., Chgo., 1980-81; assoc. Garretson & Santora, Chgo., 1981-86, ptnr., 1986—; cons. Adoptive Parent's Guild, Cath. Charities, 1981-84, Village Mgr. Assn., Oak Park, 1982—; commr. Liquor Control Bd., Oak Park, 1986—. Bd. dirs. United Village Party, 1980-82, T.O.P. Party, 1982-86. Mem. ABA, Ill. Bar Assn., Chgo. Bar Assn., Appellate Lawyers Assn., Defense Research Inst. Avocation: white water canoeist. Office: Garretson & Santora 33 N Dearborn St Chicago IL 60602-3102

**LOCHRIDGE, LLOYD PAMPELL, JR.,** lawyer; b. Austin, Tex., Feb. 3, 1918; s. Lloyd Pampell and Franklyn (Blocker) L.; m. Frances Potter, Jan. 23, 1943; children: Anne, Georgia, Lloyd P. III, Patton G., Hope N., Frances P. AB, Princeton U., 1938; LLB, Harvard U., 1941. Bar: D.C. 1942, Tex. 1945, U.S. Ct. Appeals (5th cir.), U.S. Supreme Ct. Assoc. Law Office Vernon Hill, Mission, Tex., 1945-46; ptnr. Hill & Lochridge, Mission, Tex., 1946-49, Hill, Lochridge & King, Mission, Tex., 1949-59, McGinnis, Lochridge & Kilgore, Austin, 1959—. Mem. adv. bd. Salvation Army, Austin, 1962—; mem. vestry Ch. Good Shepherd, Austin, 1968-73; trustee Austin Lyric Opera, 1986—. Comdr. USNR, 1941-46, ETO. Mem. ABA (bd. govs. 1989-92), State Bar Tex. (pres. 1974-75), Travis County Bar Assn. (pres. 1970-71), Hidalgo County Bar Assn. (pres. 1954-55). Episcopalian. Avocations: tennis, squash, sailing. Federal civil litigation, General civil litigation, Oil, gas, and mineral. Office: McGinnis Lochridge & Kilgore 1300 Capitol Ctr 919 Congress Ave Ste 1300 Austin TX 78701-2499

**LOCK, JOHN RICHARD,** lawyer; b. Baton Rouge, Dec. 24, 1941; s. John Henry Lock and Julia (Hooker) Sturdivant; m. Sidney Brient, Dec. 28, 1965; children: Julia Corrine, Elizabeth Ann. BBA, Tex. A&M U., 1964; JD, U. Tex., 1967. Bar: Tex. 1967, U.S. Tax Ct. 1973, U.S. Dist. Ct. (we. dist.) Tex. 1974, U.S. Ct. of Appeals (5th cir.), U.S. Supreme Ct.; CPA, Tex. Atty. John Lock & Assocs., Austin, Lock & Virr, P.C., Austin. Mem. ABA, AICPA, Travis County Bar Assn., State Bar Assn. of Tex. (cert. estate planning, probate law, and tax law), Tex. Soc. of CPAs. Estate planning, Personal income taxation, Estate taxation. Home: 4300 Avenue G Austin TX 78751-3818 Office: Lock & Virr PC 221 W 6th St Ste 1540 Austin TX 78701-3472

**LOCKE, JOHN HOWARD,** lawyer; b. Berryville, Va., Sept. 4, 1920; s. James Howard and Mary Elizabeth (Hart) L.; m. Frances Rebecca Cook, Feb. 23, 1946; children: Anne Locke Evans, Nancy Locke Curlee, Rebecca Locke Leonard. BS, U. Richmond, 1941; LLB, U. Va., 1948. Bar: Va. 1948. Ptnr., Gentry, Locke, Rakes & Moore, Roanoke, Va., ret. 1985. Apptd. Hearing Officer Supreme Ct. Va., 1987; founder, pres. Big Bros., Roanoke, 1960. With USN, 1942-46. Fellow Am. Coll. Trial Lawyers, Internat. Soc. Barristers (pres. 1970); mem. ABA, Va. State Bar, Va. Bar Assn., Roanoke City Bar Assn. (pres. 1970-71), Internat. Assn. Ins. Counsel, 4th Cir. Jud. Conf., Omicron Delta Kappa, Raven Soc. Presbyterian. Club: Shenadoah (Roanoke, Va.). Personal injury, Federal civil litigation, State civil litigation.

**LOCKE, LAURENCE S.,** lawyer, consultant; b. N.Y.C., Apr. 29, 1917; s. Lee Levy and Nettie Samuels; m. Eleanor G., Dec. 21, 1939 (div. Dec. 1970); children: Nancy Meyer, James, David; m. Maryel F., Dec. 4. 1970. AB, Harvard U., 1939, LLB, 1942. Bar: Mass. 1942, U.S. Dist. Ct. Mass. 1943. Ptnr. Horovitz, Petkun & Locke, Boston, 1946-72, Petkun & Locke, Boston, 1972-78; prin. Laurence Locke & Assocs., Boston, 1978-85, Laurence Locke & Assocs. (a Wynn & Wynn law firm), Boston, 1985-92; instr. Boston Coll. Sch. Law, 1969-75. Author: Massachussets' Worker's Compensation Law, 1968; also articles. Pres. New Eng. Am. Jewish Congress, Boston, 1965-69; chmn. Survey Commn. on Weston (Mass.) Schs., 1959-63; officer Jobs with Peace Ednl. Found., Boston, 1983-97, NAt. Priorities Project, North Hamptin, Mass., 1996—. Served to 2d lt. USAAF, 1941-45. Fellow Mass. Bar Found.; mem. Mass. Bar Assn. (chmn. workmens compensation com. 1973-76, law practice sect. 1976-78), Assn. Trial Lawyers Am. (sec.-treas. 1946-63, chmn. workmens compensation sect. 1963-64, 70-71), Boston Bar Assn. Jewish. Avocations: activism, performing arts. Workers' compensation.

**LOCKE, WILLIAM HENRY,** lawyer; b. Eagle Pass, Tex., Nov. 14, 1947; s. William Henry and Genevieve (Moss) L.; children: William Henry III, Elizabeth Madeleine. AA with honors, Del Mar Coll., 1967; BA, U. Tex., 1969, JD with honors, 1972. Bar: Tex. 1972; cert. in real estate law. Exec. dir. The Kleberg Law Frim, Corpus Christi, Tex., 1972—; co-dir. advanced real estate law course State Bar of Tex., 1986-87. Author: Seizure of Lender's Collateral Under Drug Enforcement Laws, 1990, Contractual Indemnity in Texas, 1991, Civil Forfeiture Actions, 1993, Shifting of Risk: Contractual Provisions for Indemnity, Additional Insureds, Wavier of Subrogation and Exculpation, 1995, Texas Foreclosure Manual, 1995, Risk Management: Through Contractual Provisions for Indemnity, Additional Insureds Waiver of Subrogation, Releases and Exculpation, 1997, Sales Contracts: A Framework for Risk Allocation, 1998; contbg. author: Texas Construction Law, 1988. Chmn. Corpus Christi Planning Commn., 1984-85, Corpus Christi Airport Zoning Commn., 1985; bd. dirs., sec. Leadership Corpus Christi, 1984-85; pres. Palmer Drug Abuse Program, Corpus Christi, 1985-87, pres.-elect. 1996; treas. St. James Episcopal Elem. Sch., 1987-91. Fellow Tex. Bar Found. (life), Tex. Coll. Real Estate Law (dir. 1990-99), Coll. Law of State Bar Tex.; mem. ABA, Corpus Christi Bar Assn. (pres. 1987-88), Rotary (bd. dirs. Corpus Christi 1987-88, sec. 1989, Disting. Svc. Above Self award 1985, Corpus Christi merit award 1987), Beta Theta Pi. Democrat. Episcopalian. E-mail: blocke@kleberg.com. Fax: 361-693-8600. Real property, Contracts commercial, Finance. Office: The Kleberg Law Frim 800 N Water St Ste 900 Corpus Christi TX 78401-2020

**LOCKETT, TYLER CHARLES,** state supreme court justice; b. Corpus Christi, Tex., Dec. 7, 1932; s. Tyler Coleman and Evelyn (Lemond) L.; m. Sue W. Lockett, Nov. 3, 1961; children: Charles, Patrick. AB, Washburn U., 1955, JD, 1962. Bar: Kans. 1962. Pvt. practice law Wichita, 1962—; judge Ct. Common Pleas, 1971-77, Kans. Dist. Ct. 18th Dist., 1977-83; justice Supreme Court Kans., Topeka, 1983—. Methodist. Office: Kans Supreme Ct 374 Kansas Judicial Ctr Topeka KS 66612-1502

**LOCKHART, GREGORY GORDON,** lawyer; b. Dayton, Ohio, Sept. 2, 1946; s. Lloyd Douglas and Evelyn (Gordon) L.; m. Paula Louise Jewett, May 20, 1978; children: David H., Sarah L. BS, Wright State U., 1973; JD, Ohio State U., 1976. Bar: Ohio 1976, U.S. Dist. Ct. (so. dist.) Ohio 1977, U.S. Ct. Appeals (6th cir.) 1988, U.S. Supreme Ct. 1993. Legal advisor Xenia and Fairborn (Ohio) Police Dept., 1977-78; asst. pros. atty. Greene County Prosecutor, Xenia, 1978-87; ptnr. DeWine & Schenck, Xenia, 1978-82, Schenck, Schmidt & Lockhart, Xenia, 1982-85, Ried & Lockhart, Beavercreek, Ohio, 1985-87; asst. U.S. atty. So. Dist. of Ohio, Columbus, 1987-89, Dayton, 1989—; adj. prof. Coll. Law U. Dayton, 1990—, Wright State U., Dayton, 1979—. Co-author: Federal Grand Jury Practice, 1996. Pres. Greene County Young reps., Xenia, 1977-79. With USAF, 1966-70; Vietnam. Mem. Fed. Bar Assn. (chpt. pres. 1994-95), Dayton Bar Assn., Kiwanis (pres. 1983-84, lt. gov. 1986-87), Jaycees (pres. 1976-79), Am. Inns of Ct. (master of bench emeritus). Methodist. Avocations: golf, tennis, hiking, camping. Office: US Attorney Federal Bldg 200 W 2d St Rm 602 Dayton OH 45402

**LOCKLEAR, W. ROSS,** lawyer; b. Quantico, Va., July 22, 1950; m. Estelle H., June 27, 1981. BBA, Va. Commonwealth U., 1976; JD, Coll. William and Mary, 1980. Bar: Va. 1980, U.S. Dist. Ct. (ea. dist.) Va. 1981, U.S. Ct. Appeals (5th cir.) 1981, U.S. Supreme Ct. 1986. Pvt. practice W. Ross Locklear, P.C., Stafford. Mem. Lions. Family and matrimonial, General practice, General civil litigation. Office: 385 Garrisonville Rd Ste 110 Stafford VA 22554-1545

**LOCKLIN, KEVIN LEE,** lawyer; b. Pitts., Dec. 26, 1954; s. Thomas Murray and Dorothy (Tingler) L.; m. Tara McCarthy, Oct. 14; children: Kelly Meghan, Caitlin Marie, Devan Moira. BA, Franklin and Marshall Coll., 1977; JD, George Mason Law Sch., 1981. Bar: Va. 1981. Jud. law clk. 31st Jud. Cir., Prince William, Va., 1981; jud. law clk. to Hon. Oren R. Lewis U.S. Dist. Ct., Alex, Va., 1981-82; ptnr., trial atty. Slenker, Brandt, Jennings & Johnston, Fairfax, Va., 1982-92; with J.E. Flournoy P.C., Manassas, Va., 1992—; bd. dirs. Va. Young Lawyers, Richmond. Pres. Jaycees, Annandale, Va., 1986. Recipient Spl. Achievement award U.S. Dept. of Justice, 1981. Mem. Va. Assn. Def. Lawyers (bd. dirs. 1990-92), No. Va. Def. Lawyers (bd. dirs. 1991—, pres. 1990), No. Va. Young Lawyers (pres. 1986), Internat. Assn. Def. Coun. Republican. Methodist. General civil litigation, Personal injury. Office: J E Flournoy PC 9117 Church St Manassas VA 20110-5434

**LOCKSHIN, LORI,** lawyer, prosecutor; b. North Miami Beach, fla., Sept. 23, 1965; d. Donald Herman and Lynn (Goldberg) L. BS in Advt., U. Fla., 1986, JD, 1989. Bar: Fla. 1989, U.S. Dist. Ct. (mid. dist.) Fla. 1989. Asst. state atty. State Atty.'s Office, Ocala, Fla., 1990—; lectr., facilitator Fla. Pros. Attys. Assn., Tallahassee, 1993—; facilitator Nat. Coll. Dist. Attys., Houston, 1994—; lectr. on domestic violence, trial advocacy, other subjects. Mem. Leadership Ocala, 1993-94, Advanced Leadership, 1994; bd. dirs. Temple Beth Shalom, also sec.; bd. dirs. Ret. Sr. Vol. Program, Ocala Arts and Scis. Coalition. Recipient Domestic Violence Shelter recognition, Clin. Advocacy Ctr. recognition, 1998. Jewish. Avocations: horseback riding, whitewater rafting. Office: State Atty Office 19 NW Pine Ave Ocala FL 34475-6620

**LOCKYER, BILL,** state attorney general; b. Oakland, Calif., May 8, 1941; 1 child, Lisa. BA in Polit. Sci., U. Calif., Berkeley; cert. in sec. tchg., Calif. State U., Hayward; JD, U. of the Pacific. Past tchr. San Leandro, Calif.; Mem. Calif. State Assembly, 1973; state senator State of Calif., 1982; pres. pro tem, chmn. senate rules com., chmn. senate jud. com. Calif. State Senate, 1994-98; atty. gen. State of Calif., 1999—; active San Leandro Sch. Bd., 1968-73. past chair Alameda County Dem. Ctrl. Com. Named Legislator of Yr. Planning and Conservation League, 1996, Calif. Jour., 1997,. Office: Office of Atty Gen 1300 I St Ste 1740 Sacramento CA 95814-2919

**LODDERS, RONALD R.,** lawyer; b. Missoula, Mont., Apr. 29, 1948; s. Richard Denison and Georgia Dell (Wendt) L.; m. Dianne Kaye Pugh, May 18, 1968 (div. Sept. 1993); 1 child, Justin Richard. BA in Philosophy, U. Mont., 1970, JD, 1973. Bar: Mont. 1973. Law clk. U.S. Dist. Ct., Butte, Mont., 1973-74; assoc. Crowley, Haughey, Hanson, Toole & Dietrich, Billings, Mont., 1974-79, ptnr., 1979—. Mem. ABA, Mont. Bar Assn., Mont. Def. Trial Lawyers Assn., Internat. Def. Trial Lawyers Assn. Avocation: kayaking. Personal injury, Product liability, Insurance. Office: Crowley Haughey Hanson Toole & Dietrich 490 N 31st St Billings MT 59101-1256

**LODGE, EDWARD JAMES,** federal judge; b. 1933. BS cum laude, Coll. Idaho, 1957; JD, U. Idaho, 1969. With Smith & Miller, 1962-63; probate judge Canyon County, Idaho, 1963-65; judge Idaho State Dist. Ct., 1965-88; U.S. bankruptcy judge State of Idaho, 1988; dist. judge, chief judge U.S. Dist. Ct. Idaho, 1989-99; mem. Ninth Cir. Jud. Coun., 1997-98; chair Chief Dist. Judges for Ninth Cir., 1998-99. Recipient Kramer award for excellence in jud. adminstrn.; named three time All-Am., disting. alumnus Coll. Idaho, Boise State U., Professionalism award Idaho State Bar, 1997; named to Hall of Fame Boise State U., Coll. Idaho. Mem. Idaho Trial Lawyer Assn., Idaho State Bar Assn. (Professionalism award 1997), U.S. Fed. Judges Assn., Boise State Athletic Assn., Elks Club. Office: US Dist Ct MSC 040 550 W Fort St Fl 6 Boise ID 83724-0101

**LODICO, YVONNE C.,** lawyer, consulatant; b. Phila., Nov. 12, 1957; d. Lawrence Lodico and Joann (Lee) Sohn; 1 child, Sebastian Karl Lodico Konecsay. MIPA, Columbia U., N.Y.C., 1983; JD, Am. U., Washington, 1989; LLM, NYU, 1994. Liaison officer UN, Luanda, Angola, 1992-93; legal advisor, pol. officer UN, N.Y.C., 1989-92; legal adv. UN, Maputo, Mozambique, 1994-95, N.Y.C., 1995-96; dir. Galileo Inst. for Global Coop., N.Y.C., 1997—; legal officer, asst. to dir. UN Angola, 1995-96; lectr. human rights law U. Melbourne. Recipient award N.Y. State Bar Assn. Mem. ABA, UN Assn., N.Y.C. Bar Assn., Internat. Bar Assn. Episcopal. Avocations: cinema, running, painting. Home: 21 W 88th St Apt 4 New York NY 10024-2551

**LODWICK, MICHAEL WAYNE,** lawyer; b. New Orleans, Sept. 21, 1946; s. Frank Tillman Jr. and Grace Evelyn (Hilty) L.; children: Sarah Peirce, Jane Durborow, Elizabeth Hilty; m. Mary League, June 15, 1991. BA, La. State U., 1968; MA, Tulane U., 1972, PhD, 1976; JD, Loyola U., New Orleans, 1981. Bar: La., U.S. Dist. Ct. (ea. dist.) La. 1981, U.S. Ct. Appeals (5th cir.) 1981, U.S. Ct. Appeals (D.C. cir.) 1982, U.S. Ct. Appeals (11th cir.) 1986, U.S. Ct. Appeals (9th cir.) 1990, U.S. Ct. Appeals (2d cir.) 1996, U.S. Ct. Appeals (4th cir.) 1996, U.S. Supreme Ct., 1987, Calif. 1990, U.S. Dist. Ct. (ctrl., no. and so. dists.) Calif. 1990. Instr. to asst. prof. Tulane U., New Orleans, 1976-78; assoc. Barham & Churchill, New Orleans, 1981-83; assoc. O'Neil, Eichin & Miller, New Orleans, 1983-87, ptnr., 1987-89; ptnr. Fisher & Porter, 1989-97, Porter, Groff & Lodwick, 1997—. Editor, co-founder and pub. Plantation Soc. in Americas jour., 1979-83, 86—; editor-in-chief Loyola Law Rev., 1980-81; contbr. articles to profl. jours. Mem. New Orleans Symphony Chorus, 1985-89, Pacific Chorale, 1989—. Tulane U. fellow, 1970-72; recipient Loyola U. Law Rev. Honor award, 1981, Loyola Law Alumni award, 1981. Mem. ABA, La. State Bar Assn., State Bar Calif., Fed. Bar Assn., Assn. Transp. Law, Logistics and Policy, Maritime Law Assn. U.S. Admiralty, Insurance, General civil litigation. Home: 20241 Seashell Cir Huntington Beach CA 92646-4436 Office: Porter Groff & Lodwick 110 Pine Ave Fl 11 Long Beach CA 90802-4430

**LOE, BRIAN ROBERT,** lawyer; b. Denver, Dec. 28, 1954; s. Robert and Adah L.; m. Deborah Dedman, May 20, 1978. BA, U. Calif., San Diego, 1977; JD, Am. U., 1981. Bar: D.C. 1981, Va. 1982, U.S. Dist. Ct. (ea. dist.) Va. 1982, U.S. Dist. Ct. D.C. 1982, U.S. Ct. Appeals (4th cir.) 1982, U.S. Supreme Ct. 1986, Fla. 1987, U.S. Dist. Ct. (mid. dist.) Fla. 1989, U.S. Ct. Claims 1990. Pvt. practice Falls Church, Va., 1982-87, Lake Mary, Fla., 1988—. Family and matrimonial, Real property, State civil litigation. Office: 3074 W Lake Mary Blvd # 136 Lake Mary FL 32746-6024

**LOEB, LEONARD L.,** lawyer; b. Chgo., Mar. 30, 1929. BBA, U. Wis., 1950, JD, 1952. Bar: Wis. 1952, U.S. Supreme Ct. 1960. Sole practice Milw., 1952—; ptnr. Loeb & Herman, Milw.; faculty family mediation inst. Harvard Law Sch.; lectr. family law Marquette U., U. Wis., Madison; cons. revisions Wis. Family Code Wis. Legislature; mem. com. for review of initiatives in child support State of Wis.; Concordia Coll. (Wis.) Paralegal Adv. Bd. Author: Systems Book for Family Law; contbr. articles to profl. jours. Served to col. JAGC, USAF, 1952-53. Fellow Am. Bar Found., Am. Acad. Matrimonial Lawyers (past charter pres. Wis. chpt., pres. nat. chpt.); mem. ABA (past chmn. family law sect., del. to ho. of dels.), Wis. Bar Assn. (pres. 1999—), Wis. Bar Found. (bd. dirs.), Milw. Bar Assn. (past chmn. family law sect., past pres.). E-mail: lloeb@loebherman.com. Family and matrimonial. Office: Loeb & Herman 111 E Wisconsin Ave Ste 1125 Milwaukee WI 53202-4868*

**LOEFFLER, ROBERT HUGH,** lawyer; b. Chgo., May 27, 1943; s. Julius and Faye (Fink) L.; m. Jane Canter, Sept. 6, 1970; children: James Benjamin, Charles Edward. AB magna cum laude, Harvard Coll., 1965; JD cum laude, Columbia U., 1968. Bar: N.Y. 1969, U.S. Ct. Appeals (2d cir.) 1969, D.C. 1970, U.S. Ct. Appeals (D.C. cir.) 1972, U.S. Supreme Ct. 1976, U.S. Ct. Appeals (9th cir.) 1981, U.S. Ct. Appeals (Fed. cir.) 1992. Law clk. to Hon. Harold R. Medina U.S. Ct. Appeals, 1968-69; assoc. Covington & Burling, Washington, 1969-76; assoc., ptnr. Isham, Lincoln & Beale, Washington, 1976-79; mng. ptnr. Morrison & Foerster, Washington, 1980-89, sr. ptnr., 1990—. Chmn. consumer com. Muskie presdl. campaign, 1972. Mem. ABA (vice chmn. energy law com. adminstrv. law sect. 1980-85), Am. Intellectual Property Law Assn., Fed. Energy Bar Assn. (chmn. oil pipeline regulation), Columbia Law Sch. Assn. (pres. Washington chpt. 1993—, nat. v.p. 1994—), Univ. Club, Std. Club, Harvard Club (N.Y.C.). Patent, FERC practice, Federal civil litigation. Home: 2607 36th Pl NW Washington DC 20007-1414 Office: Morrison & Foerster Ste 5500 2000 Pennsylvania Ave NW Washington DC 20006-1831

**LOENGARD, RICHARD OTTO, JR.,** lawyer; b. N.Y.C, Jan. 28, 1932; s. Richard Otto and Margery (Borg) L.; m. Janet Sara Senderowitz, Apr. 11, 1964; children: Maranda C., Philippa S.M. AB, Harvard U., 1953, LLB, 1956. Bar: N.Y. 1956, U.S. Dist. Ct. (so. dist.) N.Y. 1958. Assoc. Fried, Frank, Harris, Shriver & Jacobson, predecessor firms, N.Y.C., 1956-64, ptnr., 1967-97; of counsel Fried, Frank, Harris, Shriver & Jacobson, N.Y.C., 1997—; dep. tax legis. counsel, spl. asst. internat. tax affairs U.S. Dept. Treasury, Washington, 1964-67; mem. Commerce Clearing House, Riverwoods, Ill. Editl. bd. Tax Transaction Libr., 1982-94; contbr. articles to profl. publs. Fellow Am. Coll. Tax Counsel; mem. ABA, N.Y. State Bar Assn. (exec. com. tax sect. 1984—, sec. 1994-95, vice chair 1995-97, chair 1997-98), Assn. Bar City N.Y. Taxation, general. Office: Fried Frank Harris Shriver & Jacobson 1 New York Plz New York NY 10004-1980

**LOEVINGER, LEE,** lawyer, science writer; b. St. Paul, Apr. 24, 1913; s. Gustavus and Millie (Strouse) L.; m. Ruth Howe, Mar. 4, 1950; children: Barbara L., Eric H., Peter H. BA summa cum laude, U. Minn., 1933, JD, 1936. Bar: Minn. 1936, Mo. 1937, D.C. 1966, U.S. Supreme Ct., 1941. Assoc. Watson, Ess, Groner, Barnett & Whittaker, Kansas City, Mo., 1936-37; atty., regional atty. NLRB, 1937-41; with antitrust div. Dept. Justice, 1941-46; ptnr. Larson, Loevinger, Lindquist & Fraser, Mpls., 1946-60; assoc. justice Minn. Supreme Ct., 1960-61; asst. U.S. atty. gen. charge antitrust div. Dept. Justice, 1961-63; commr. FCC, 1963-68; ptnr. Hogan & Hartson, Washington, 1968-85; of counsel Hogan & Hartson, 1986—; v.p., dir. Craig-Hallum Corp., Mpls., 1968-73; dir. Petrolite Corp., St. Louis, 1978-83; U.S. rep. com. on restrictive bus. practices Orgn. for Econ. Coop. and Devel., 1961-64; spl. asst. to U.S. atty. gen., 1963-64; spl. counsel com. small bus. U.S. Senate, 1951-52; lectr. U. Minn., 1953-60; vis. prof. jurisprudence U. Minn. (Law Sch.), 1961; professorial lectr. Am. U., 1968-70; chmn. Minn. Atomic Devel. Problems Com., 1957-59; mem. Adminstrv. Conf. U.S., 1972-74; del. White House Conf. on Inflation, 1974; U.S. del. UNESCO Conf. on Mass Media, 1975, Internat. Telecomms. Conf. on Radio Frequencies, 1964, 66. Author: The Law of Free Enterprise, 1949, An Introduction to Legal Logic, 1952, Defending Antitrust Lawsuits, 1977, Science As Evidence, 1995; author first article to use term: jurimetrics, 1949; contbr. articles to profl. and sci. jours.; editor, contbr.: Basic Data on Atomic Devel. Problems in Minnesota, 1958; adv. bd. Antitrust Bull., Jurimetrics Jour. Served to lt. comdr. USNR, 1942-45. Recipient Outstanding Achievement award U. Minn., 1968; Freedoms Found. award, 1977, 84. Fellow Am. Acad. Appellate Lawyers; mem. ABA (del. of sci. and tech. sect. to Ho. of Dels. 1974-80, del. to joint conf. with AAAS 1974-76, co-chair 1990-93, liaison 1984-90, 93-98, chmn. sci. and tech. sect. 1982-83, coun. 1986-89, standing com. on nat. conf. groups 1984-90), AAAS, Minn. Bar Assn., Hennepin County Bar Assn., N.Y. Acad. Sci., D.C. Bar Assn., FCC Bar Assn., Broadcast Pioneers, U.S. C. of C. (antitrust coun. 1980-94), Am. Arbitration Assn. (comml. panel), Atlantic Legal Found. (adv. coun.), Cosmos Club (pres. 1990), City Club (Washington), Phi Beta Kappa, Sigma Xi, Delta Sigma Rho, Sigma Delta Chi, Phi Delta Gamma, Tau Kappa Alpha, Alpha Epsilon Rho. Fax: 202-637-5910. Antitrust, Appellate, Intellectual property. Home: 5600 Wisconsin Ave Apt 17D Chevy Chase MD 20815-4414 Office: Hogan & Hartson 555 13th St NW Ste 800E Washington DC 20004-1161 *With age I come increasingly to believe that life is, and should be,a learning experience. This involves a peculiar paradox: Ignorance increases faster than knowledge, as each new fact or principle opens new frontiers for intellectual exploration. Thus, with greater learning comes intellectual humility and skepticism. So, after reaching 75 I am less certain of anything than at 25 I was of everything.*

**LOEW, JONATHAN L.,** lawyer; b. Chgo., May 24, 1956; s. Andrew and Rita L.; m. Margarite Primozich, Sept. 8, 1950; children: Zachary, Vanessa, Jacob. BA in Philosophy, Ripon Coll., 1978; JD, DePaul U., 1981. Bar: Ill. 1982, U.S. Dist. Ct. (no. dist.) Ill. 1982, U.S. Ct. Appeals (7th cir.) 1991, U.S. Supreme Ct. 1993. Assoc. Maryniak & Steere, Chgo., 1982-83, Berman, Fagel, Haber, Maragos & Abrams, Chgo., 1983-86; assoc., ptnr. Spitzer, Addis, Susman & Krull, Chgo., 1986-98; ptnr. Katz, Randall & Weinberg, Chgo., 1998—. Contbr. articles to profl. jours. Mem. Chgo. Bar Assn., Appellate Lawyers Assn. Appellate, Contracts commercial. Office: Katz Randall & Weinberg 333 W Wacker Dr Chicago IL 60606-1220

**LOEWINGER, KENNETH JEFFERY,** lawyer; b. Washington, Sept. 22, 1945; s. Myron Arthur and Lenore (Kopf) L.; m. Margaret Irene Krol, May 5, 1978. BA, Georgetown U., 1967, JD, 1971. Bar: U.S. Dist. Ct. D.C. 1971, U.S. Ct. Mil. Appeals 1972, U.S. Ct. Appeals (D.C. cir.) 1972, U.S. Supreme Ct. 1979. Law clk. to judge D.C. Superior Ct., Washington, 1971-72; law clk. to presiding judge D.C. Ct. Appeals, Washington, 1972-74; sr. ptnr. Loewinger, Brand & Kappstatter, Washington, 1975-95, Loewinger & Brand, PLLC, Washington, 1995—; pres. N.Am. Title and Escrow Co., Inc.; mem. D.C. Superior Ct., 1976—; mem. adv. com. U.S. Bankruptcy Ct., 1985-86. Author: Loewinger on Landlord and Tenant, 1986. Commr. Housing Prodn. Com., D.C., 1986-87. Mem. ABA, D.C. Bar Assn., Supreme Ct. Hist. Soc. Landlord-tenant, Real property, Bankruptcy. Office: Loewinger & Brand 471 H St NW Washington DC 20001-2617

**LOFFREDO, PASCO FRANK,** lawyer; b. Providence, Apr. 22, 1950; s. Pasco and Adeline (Pitocchi) L.; m. Caroline M. Crudele, Jan. 15, 1993; children: Bethany, Amy. BA, Bethany Coll., 1972; JD, New Eng. Sch. of Law, 1976. Bar: R.I. 1976, U.S. Dist. Ct. R.I. 1977, Mass. 1979, U.S. Dist. Ct. Mass. 1979. Sole practice Cranston, R.I., 1976-79, Providence, 1986-88; ptnr. Chaika & Loffredo, Cranston, 1979-85, Loffrede & Scott, Cranston, 1991—. Mem. adv. bd. Providence (R.I.) Foster Grandparents Program, 1983—; bd. dirs. R.I. Div. Mediation Council, Providence, 1984—. Mem. ABA, R.I. Bar Assn., R.I. Trial Lawyers Assn. (com. on state and fed. legis.). Democrat. Roman Catholic. Avocations: farming, politics, reading. Real property, Personal injury, Family and matrimonial. Office: 946 Park Ave Cranston RI 02910-2708

**LOFLIN, THOMAS FRANKLIN, III,** lawyer; b. Hendersonville, N.C., Nov. 22, 1942; s. Thomas Franklin and Mary Anne (Turner) L.; m. Anne Frye, May 31, 1969; 1 dau., Jocelyn Ann. B.A., Davidson Coll., 1964; J.D. with high honors, U. N.C., 1970. Bar: N.C. 1970, U.S. Dist. Ct. (mid. and we. dists.) N.C. 1970, U.S. Dist. Ct. (ea. dist.) N.C. 1971, U.S. Ct. Appeals (4th cir.) 1971, U.S. Supreme Ct. 1973. Ptnr. Spaulding & Loflin, Durham, N.C., 1970-71; ptnr. Loflin & Loflin and predecessors, beginning with Loflin, Anderson & Loflin, Durham, 1972—; adj. prof. U. N.C. at Chapel Hill Sch. Law, 1971; bd. dirs. N.C. Civil Liberties Union Legal Found., Inc., 1975-78, 80-81, mem. legal com., 1978—. Pres. Durham chpt. N.C. Civil Liberties Union, 1976-85. Served to 1st lt. U.S. Army, 1965-67. Morehead Found. fellow, 1967-70. Mem. Nat. Assn. Criminal Def. Lawyers, Assn. Trial Lawyers Am., ABA, N.C. Acad. Trial Lawyers, N.C. Bar Assn., Durham County Bar Assn., Order of Coif, Phi Beta Kappa, Omega Delta Kappa. Democrat. Editor-in-chief N.C. Law Rev., 1969-70. Criminal, Personal injury, Civil rights. Home: 2726 Circle Dr Durham NC 27705-5727 Office: 123 Orange St Durham NC 27701-3316

**LOFSTROM, MARK D.,** lawyer, educator, communications executive; b. Mpls., May 11, 1953; s. Dennis E. and Dorothy Dee (Schreiber) L. BA in Art History, Carleton Coll., 1979; MBA, Columbia U., 1989; JD, U. Hawaii, 1992. Bar: Hawaii 1992, Minn. 1995. Pub. rels. asst. Honolulu Acad. Arts, 1979, pub. rels. rep., 1980-84, pub. rels. officer, 1984-87; law clk. Kiefer Oshima Chun Fong and Chung, Honolulu, 1990-91; assoc. Cades Schutte Fleming & Wright, Honolulu, 1991-95; pvt. practice Law Offices of Mark D. Lofstrom, Mpls., 1995—; instr. internat. bus. law/bus. law for accts. U. Hawaii Coll. Bus., 1995-96; instr. art law U. Hawaii summer session, 1995-96; organizer artists and writers exhbn., 1981; coord. rep. program Carleton Coll. Alumni Assn., Hawaii, 1984-87; co-editor and mktg. assoc. Pacific Telecomms. Coun., 1988-92, intern East-West Ctr., 1992. Editor mag. on preservation; exec. editor U. Hawaii Law Rev., 1991-92; co-editor: (newsletter) Pacific Comm. Coun. Procs., 1990-92; bd. editors Hawaii Bar Jour., 1992—; contbr. articles on current exhbns., intellectual property, art, and internat. law. Sec., bd. dirs. Arts Coun. Hawaii, 1985-86, chmn. ways and means com., 1986-87, pres. bd. dirs.; bd. dirs. Hawaii Alliance for Arts Edn., 1994-95, chmn.-elect, 1995-97; mem. St. Mathias Twp. Comprehensive Devel. Plan Com., 1997-99. Recipient NCR Stakeholders award, 1988, legal rsch. and writing award Hawaii State Bar Assn. Young Lawyers Div., 1991. Mem. ABA, Hawaii State Bar Assn. (sec. internat. law sect. 1994, chair internat. law sect. 1995-96), Minn. Bar Assn. General corporate, Private international, Trademark and copyright. Office: PO Box 3605 Minneapolis MN 55403-0605 also: PO Box 27 Brainerd MN 56401-0027

**LOFTUS, THOMAS DANIEL,** lawyer; b. Nov. 8, 1930; s. Glendon Francis and Martha Helen (Wall) L. BA, U. Wash., 1952, JD, 1957. Bar: Wash. 1958, U.S. Ct. Appeals (9th cir.) 1958, U.S. Dist. Ct. Wash. 1958, U.S. Ct. Mil. Appeals 1964, U.S. Supreme Ct. 1964. Trial atty. Northwestern Mut. Ins. Co., Seattle, 1958-62; sr. trial atty. Unigard Security Ins. Co., Seattle, 1962-68, asst. gen. counsel, 1969-83, govt. rels. counsel, 1983-89; of counsel Groshong, LeHet & Thornton, 1990-98; mem. Wash. Commn. on Jud. Conduct (formerly Jud. Qualifications), 1982-88, vice-chmn., 1987-88; judge pro tem Seattle Mcpl. Ct., 1973-81; mem. nat. panel of mediators Arbitration Forums, Inc., 1990—. Sec., treas. Seattle Opera Assn., 1980-91; pres., bd. dirs. Vis. Nurse Svcs., 1979-88; pres., v.p. Salvation Army Adult Rehab. Ctr., 1979-86; nat. committeeman Wash. Young Rep. Fedn., 1961-63, vice-chmn, 1963-65; pres. Young Reps. King County, 1962-63; bd. dirs. Seattle Seafair, Inc., 1975; bd. dirs., gen. counsel Wash. Ins. Coun., 1984-86, sec., 1986-88, v.p., 1988-90, Am. Mediation Panel of Mediators, 1990-96; bd. dirs. Arson Alarm Found., 1987-90; bd. visitors Law Sch. U. Wash., 1993—. 1st lt. U.S. Army, 1952-54, col. Res., 1954-85. Fellow Am. Bar Found.; mem. Am. Arbitration Assn. (nat. panel arbitrators 1965—), Am. Arbitration Forums, Inc. (nat. panel arbitrators 1992), Nat. Assn. Security Dealers (bd. arbitrators 1997—), Am. Mediation Panel, Wash. Bar Assn. (gov. 1981-84), Seattle King County Bar Assn. (sec., trustee 1977-82), ABA (ho. of dels. 1984-90), Internat. Assn. Ins. Counsel, U.S. People to People (del. Moscow internat. law-econ. conf. 1990), Def. Rsch. Inst., Wash. Def. Trial Lawyers Assn., Wash. State Trial Lawyers Assn., Am. Judicature Soc., Res. Officers Assn., Judge Advocate Gen.'s Assn., Assn. Wash. Gens., U. Wash. Alumni Assn., Coll. Club Seattle, Wash. Athletic Club, Masons, Shriners, English Spkg. Union, Ranier Club, Pi Sigma Alpha, Delta Sigma Rho, Phi Delta Phi, Theta Delta Chi. Republican. Presbyterian. Insurance, Personal injury, Alternative dispute resolution. Home: 3515 Magnolia Blvd W Seattle WA 98199-1841 Office: Coll Club Bldg 505 Madison St Ste 300 Seattle WA 98104-1198

**LOGAN, FRANCIS DUMMER,** lawyer; b. Evanston, Ill., May 23, 1931; s. Simon Rae and Frances (Dummer) L.; m. Claude Riviere, Apr. 13, 1957; children: Carolyn Gisele, Francis Dummer. B.A., U. Chgo., 1950; B.A. Juris, Oxford U., 1954; LL.B., Harvard U., 1955. Bar: N.Y. 1956, Calif. 1989. Assoc. Milbank, Tweed, Hadley & McCloy, N.Y.C., 1955-64; ptnr. Milbank, Tweed, Hadley & McCloy, N.Y.C. and L.A., 1965-96, chmn., 1992-96. Mem. vis. com. U. of Chgo. Coll.; bd. dirs. Pasadena Symphony Orchestra. Mem. Calif. State Bar, Coun. on Fgn. Rels., Am. Law Inst., Pacific Coun. on Internat. Policy, N.Y. State Bar. Banking. Home: 1726 Linda Vista Ave Pasadena CA 91103-1132

**LOGAN, JAMES KENNETH,** lawyer, former federal judge; b. Quenemo, Kans., Aug. 21, 1929; s. John Lysle and Esther Maurine (Price) L.; m. Beverly Jo Jennings, June 8, 1952; children: Daniel Jennings, Amy Logan Sliva, Sarah Logan Sherard, Samuel Price. A.B., U. Kans., 1952; LL.B. magna cum laude, Harvard, 1955. Bar: Kans. 1955, Calif. 1956. Law clk. U.S. Cir. Judge Huxman, 1955-56; with firm Gibson, Dunn & Crutcher, L.A., 1956-57; asst. prof. law U. Kans., 1957-61, prof., dean Law Sch., 1961-68; ptnr. Payne and Jones, Olathe, Kans., 1968-77; judge U.S. Ct. Appeals (10th cir.), 1977-98; pvt. practice Olathe, 1998—; Ezra Ripley Thayer tchg. fellow Harvard Law Sch., 1961-62; vis. prof. U. Tex., 1964, Stanford U., 1969, U. Mich., 1976; sr. lectr. Duke U., 1987, 91, 93; commr. U.S. Dist. Ct., 1964-67; mem. U.S. Judicial Conf. Adv. Com. Fed. Rules of Appellate Procedure, 1990-97, chair, 1993-97. Author: (with W.B. Leach) Future Interests and Estate Planning, 1961, Kansas Estate Administration, 5th edit., 1986, (with A.R. Martin) Kansas Corporate Law and Practice, 2d edit., 1979, The Federal Courts of the Tenth Circuit: A History, 1992; also articles. Candidate for U.S. Senate, 1968. Served with AUS, 1947-48. Rhodes scholar, 1952; recipient Disting. Service citation U. Kans., 1986, Francis Rawle award ABA-ALI, 1990. Mem. ABA, Kans. Bar Assn., Phi Beta Kappa, Order of Coif, Beta Gamma Sigma, Omicron Delta Kappa, Pi Sigma Alpha, Alpha Kappa Psi, Phi Delta Phi. Democrat. Presbyterian. Appellate, General corporate, Estate planning.

**LOGAN, SAMUEL PRICE,** lawyer; b. Lawrence, Kans., Dec. 26, 1964; s. James Kenneth and Beverly Jo (Jennings) L. BA magna cum laude, Duke U., 1987; JD, U. Kans., 1990. Bar: Mo. 1990, U.S. Dist. Ct. (we. dist.) Mo. 1990, Kans. 1991, U.S. Dist. Ct. Kans. 1991, U.S. Ct. Appeals (10th cir.) 1994. Assoc. Spencer Fane Britt & Browne, Kansas City, Mo., 1990-95, Stinson, Mag & Fizzell, P.C., Kansas City, 1995—. Mem. Kans. Bar Assn., Kansas City Met. Bar Assn., Lawyers Assn. Kansas City, Order of Coif. Democrat. Presbyterian. Avocations: golf, reading, music. General civil litigation, Federal civil litigation, Antitrust. Home: 5604 Cherry St Kansas City MO 64110-2722 Office: 153 W 151st St Ste 110 Olathe KS 66061-5300

**LOGAN, SHARON BROOKS,** lawyer; b. Easton, Md., Nov. 19, 1945; d. Blake Elmer and Esther N. (Statum) Brooks; children: John W. III, Troy Blake. BS in Econs., U. Md., 1967, MBA in Mktg., 1969; JD, U. Fla., 1979. Bar: Fla. 1979. Ptnr. Raymond Wilson, Esq., Ormond Beach, Fla., 1980, Landis, Graham & French, Daytona Beach, Fla., 1981, Watson & Assocs., Daytona Beach, 1982-84; prin. Sharon B. Logan, Esq., Ormond Beach, 1984—; legal advisor to paralegal program Daytona Beach Community Coll., 1984—. Sponsor Ea. Surfing Assn., Daytona Beach, 1983—, Nat. Scholastic Surfing Assn., 1987—; bd. dirs. Ctr. for Visually Impaired, Daytona Beach, 1991—; mem. Fla. Supreme Ct. Hist. Soc. Recipient Citizenship award Rotary Club, 1962-63; Woodrow Wilson fellow U. Md., 1967. Mem. ABA, Fla. Bar Assn. (real property and probate sect., cert. real estate atty. 1996), Volusia County Bar Assn. (bd. dirs.), Volusia County Real Property Council, Inc. (bd. dirs. 1987—, sec. 1987-88, v.p. 1988-89, pres. 1989-90, sec. 1990-91, 91-97, pres., 1997-98), Ducks Unlimited, Mus. Arts and Scis., Volusia County Estate Planning Council, Daytona Beach Area Bd. Realtors, Ormond Beach C. of C., Gator Club, Halifax Club, Tomoka Oaks Country Club, Daytona Boat Club, Md. Club, Univ. Ctr. Club (Tallahassee), Beech Mountain County Club, Beta Gamma Sigma, Alpha Lamba Delta, Phi Kappa Phi, Omicron Delta Epsilon, Delta Delta Delta (Scholarship award 1964), Sigma Alpha Epsilon. Democrat. Episcopalian. Avocations: cooking, sewing, golf, tennis, aerobics. Office: Sharon B Logan Esq 180 Vining Ct PO Box 4258 Ormond Beach FL 32175-4258

**LOGAN, THOMAS JOSEPH,** lawyer; b. Washington, Iowa, Aug. 13, 1951; s. John A. and Rhea (Buck) L.; m. Jean E. Wolf, Aug. 11, 1973; children: Abigail E., Grant T. BA, Drake U., 1973, JD, 1976. Bar: Iowa 1976, U.S. Dist. Ct. (no. and so. dists.) Iowa 1976. Assoc. Hopkins & Heubner, Des Moines, 1976-78; ptnr., dir. Hopkins & Heubner P.C., Des Moines, 1979—. Elder Presbyn. Ch. Mem. ABA, Def. Rsch. and Trial Lawyers, Iowa Bar Assn. (exec. coun. 1979-87), Polk County Bar Assn. (pres. Jr. bar assn. 1984-85), Iowa Def. Counsel Assn., Blackstone Inn of Ct. Democrat. Club: Des Moines Golf. Federal civil litigation, State civil litigation, Personal injury. Office: Hopkins & Huebner PC 2700 Grand Ave Ste 111 Des Moines IA 50312-5215

**LOGINOV, WILLIAM ALEX,** lawyer; b. N.Y.C., July 27, 1963; s. Alex and Geraldine Helen (Ely) L. AB in Engring., Dartmouth Coll., 1985; student, Leningrad (U.S.S.R.) State U., 1983; Jd, Cornell U., 1988. Bar: N.H. 1988, U.S. Dist. Ct. N.H. 1989, Mass. 1989, U.S. Patent and Trademark Office 1990. Rsch. asst. Thayer Sch. of Engring. Dartmouth Coll., Hanover, N.H., 1984-85; assoc. Sulloway, Hollis & Soden, Concord, N.H., 1988-89, Wolf, Greenfield & Sacks, P.C., Boston, 1989—; lect. Boston U.; legal counsel Gamma Delta Chi Corp., Hanover, 1988—. Inventee in field. Mem. Mass. Bar Assn., N.H. Bar Assn. (com. on cooperation with other professions), Gamma Delta Chi Corp. (bd. dirs., v.p., controller, 1986—). Republican. Avocations: skiing, sailing, flying, antique collecting and restorating, investing. Patent, Trademark and copyright. Office: Wolf Greenfield & Sacks PC 600 Atlantic Ave Boston MA 02210-2211

**LOGSDON, HAROLD L.,** lawyer; b. Oklahoma City, Okla., Oct. 8, 1940; s. Jasper Zelmer and Nellie (Modjeski) L.; m. Sharon R. Seward, Nov. 23, 1962 (div. June 1987); 2 children; m. Martha J. Stewart, June 7, 1991. BA, U. Okla., 1962, JD, 1964. Bar: Okla. 1964. Assoc. Shutler, Baker & Simpson, Kingfisher, Okla., 1967-70; ptnr. Shutler, Baker, Simpson & Logsdon, Kingfisher, Okla., 1970-85, Baker Logsdon & Schulte, Kingfisher, Okla., 1985—. Pres. Kingfisher Libr. Bd., 1988. Capt. U.S. Army, 1964-67. Mem. ABA, Okla. Bar Assn., Kingfisher C. of C., Kiwanis (pres. Kingfisher chpt. 1983). Democrat. Avocation: dogs. General practice, Banking, Public utilities. Home: PO Box 822 Kingfisher OK 73750-0822 Office: Baker Logsdon & Schulte 302 N Main St Kingfisher OK 73750-2799

**LOGSDON, RICHARD RALPH,** lawyer, mediator; b. Hamilton, Ohio, Mar. 18, 1948; s. Richard M. and Rose Marie (Kitchner) L.; m. Susan Frances Crane, Sept. 15, 1973; 1 child, Stephen Gregory. BA, U. Cin., 1970; JD, Fla. State U., 1973. Bar: Fla. 1973, U.S. Dist. Ct. (mid. dist.) Fla. 1975. Asst. state atty. State of Fla., Clearwater, Fla., 1973-76; ptnr. DeVlaming & Logsdon, Clearwater, Fla., 1976-77; owner Richard R. Logsdon, Clearwater, Fla., 1978—. Trustee Samaritan Ctr., Clearwater, 1992; vestryman Calvary Episcopal Ch., Indian Rocks Beach, Fla., 1995—; family law mediator State of Fla., Clearwater, 1994—. Recipient Achievement in Civil Procedure and Fed. Jurisdiction award Am. Juris Prudence, 1973. Republican. Episcopalian. Avocations: fishing, scuba diving, tennis. Office: 1423 S Fort Harrison Ave Clearwater FL 33756-2002

**LOGSDON, VALERIE MEAD,** lawyer; b. Washington, Nov. 17, 1958; d. Hugh David Logsdon and Myrna (Rees) Fulton. BA, San Francisco State U., 1987; JD, Hastings U., 1992. Bar: Calif. 1992. Corp. lawyer Fed. Emergency Mgmt. Agy., Miami, Fla., 1993-95; mgr. Fed. Emergency Mgmt. Agy., San Francisco, 1995-97; dir. granting svcs. Sierra Club Found., San Francisco, 1997—; dir. Internat. Comm. Lawyers for Tibet, Berkeley, Calif., 1996—. Mem. Commonwealth Club. Episcopalian. Avocations: hiking, birdwatching. Office: Sierra Club Found 220 Sansome St Ste 1100 San Francisco CA 94104-2321

**LOIS, DALE JOSEPH,** lawyer; b. Tarrytown, N.Y., Nov. 2, 1960; s. Eugene and Ellen Edna Lois. BA, Siena Coll., Loudonville, N.Y., 1983; JD, NYU, 1990. Bar: N.Y. 1990, Conn. 1990. Assoc. Whitman Breed Abbott & Morgan, Greenwich, Conn., 1990-94, Rosenman & Colin, LLP, N.Y.C., 1994-95, Epstein Fogarty Cohen & Selby, Greenwich, 1995-96, Martin Law Group, Stamford, Conn., 1996-98; ptnr. Martin, Lois & Gasparrini LLC, Stamford, 1998—. Editor N.Y. Law Sch. Law Rev., 1988-90. Recipient Cert. of Achievement, Moot Ct., N.Y. Law Sch. Mem. N.Y. State Bar Assn., Conn. Bar Assn., Reg. Bar Assn. Contracts commercial, General corporate, Real property. Office: Martin Lois & Gasparrini LLC 1177 Summer St Stamford CT 06905-5572

**LOISEAU, RICHARD,** lawyer; b. Arvida, Quebec, Can., Sept. 3, 1955; came to U.S., 1977; s. Phil and Alma (Michel) L.; m. Melitta Elena Mueller, Sept. 3, 1988; 1 child, Klaus J. BS in Chemistry, Morris Brown Coll., 1982; MBA, Cleve. State U., 1985, JD, 1991. Bar: Ind. 1991, U.S. Dist. Ct. (no. and so. dists.) Ind. 1991, U.S. Ct. Appeals (7th cir.) 1991. Chemist Std. Oil of Ohio, Cleve., 1982-86; ops. analyst British Petroleum, p.l.c., Cleve., 1987-90; staff atty. Eli Lilly and Co., Indpls., 1991-93; prin. Richard Loiseau,

P.C., 1993—. Co-inventor 3-methylpyridine. Mem. ABA, Internat. Law Soc. (Internat. Law Moot Ct. award 1991), Ind. State Bar Assn., Marion County Bar Assn., Indpls. Bar Assn., Omicron Delta Kappa. Avocations: reading, tennis. Consumer commercial, Immigration, naturalization, and customs, General civil litigation. Home: 5539 Central Ave Indianapolis IN 46220-3074

**LOKEN, JAMES BURTON,** federal judge; b. Madison, Wis., May 21, 1940; s. Burton Dwight and Anita (Nelson) L.; m. Caroline Brevard Hester, July 30, 1966; children: Kathryn Brevard, Kristina Ayres. BS, U. Wis., 1962; LLB magna cum laude, Harvard U., 1965. Law clk. to chief judge Lumbard U.S. Ct. Appeals (2d Cir.), N.Y.C., 1965-66; law clk. to assoc. justice Byron White U.S. Supreme Ct., Washington, 1966-67; assoc. atty. Faegre & Benson, Mpls., 1967-70, ptnr., 1973-90; gen. counsel Pres.'s Com. on Consumer Interests, Office of Pres. of U.S., Washington, 1970; staff asst. Office of Pres. of U.S., Washington, 1970-72; judge U.S. Ct. Appeals (8th cir.), St. Paul, 1991—. Editor Harvard Law Rev., 1964-65. Mem. Minn. State Bar Assn., Phi Beta Kappa, Phi Kappa Phi. Avocations: golf, running. Office: Cir Cts Appeals 8th Cir Warren E Burger Bldg 316 Robert St N Saint Paul MN 55101-1495 Office: US Courthouse 300 S 4th St Ste 11W Minneapolis MN 55415-2249*

**LOLLI, DON R(AY),** lawyer; b. Macon, Mo., Aug. 9, 1949; s. Tony and Erma naomi (Gerlich) L.; m. Deborah Jo Mrosek, May 29, 1976; children: Christina Terese, Joanna Elyse, Anthony Justin. BA in Econs., U. Mo., 1971, JD, 1974. Bar: Mo. 1974, U.S. Dist. Ct. (we. dist.) Mo. 1974, U.S. Dist. Ct. (ea. dist) Mo. 1996, U.S. Dist. Ct. Kans. 1998, U.S. Ct. Appeals (8th cir.) 1976, U.S. Ct. Appeals (10th cir.) 1979, U.S. Ct. Appeals (3rd cir.) 1992, U.S. Supreme Ct. 1979, U.S. Tax Ct. 1981. Assoc. Beckett & Steinkamp, Kansas City, Mo., 1974-79; mem. Swanson, Midgley, Gangwere, Kitchin & McLaney, LLC, 1997—; lectr. CLE seminar U. Mo. Sch. Law, Kansas City, 1984, 89. Vol. coach Visitation Sch. Mem. ABA, Mo. Bar Assn., Kansas City Bar Assn., Lawyers Assn. Kansas City, U. Mo. Alumni Assn., Beta Theta Pi (asst. Tiedman Inn 1973-74, Merit cert. 1974), Kansas City 611 Club. Roman Catholic. Federal civil litigation, State civil litigation, Contracts commercial. Home: 645 W 62nd St Kansas City MO 64113-1501 Office: Swanson Midgley Gangwere Kitchin & McLarney LLC 922 Walnut St Ste 1500 Kansas City MO 64106-1848

**LOMBARD, BENJAMIN G.,** lawyer; b. Milw., Sept. 29, 1967; s. Michael A. and Judith A. (Toor) L. BA, Northwestern U., 1989; JD, Cornell U., 1992. Assoc. Jones, Day, Reavis & Pogue, Cleve., 1992-96, Reinhart Boemer, Van Deuren, Norris & Rieselbach, Milw., 1996—. Mem. Milw. Bar Assn., State Bar Wis., Order of the Coif, Phi Beta Kappa. Securities, Mergers and acquisitions, General corporate. Office: Reinhart Boerner Van Deuren et al 1000 N Water St Milwaukee WI 53202-6648

**LOMBARD, JOHN CUTLER,** lawyer; b. Berkeley, Calif., Oct. 9, 1918; s. Norman and Ellen (McKeighan) L.; m. Dorothy Brandt, July 9, 1946; children: Lawrence, John, David, Laurie. BA, Principia U., 1946; JD, Northwestern U., 1949. Assoc. Jones, Birdseye & Grey, Seattle, 1950-60; ptnr. Hamley & Lombard, Seattle, 1960-70, Day, Taylor, Lombard & Kiefer, Seattle, 1970-85; pvt. practice Seattle, 1985—; mem. com. Jud. Counsel, 1980-84. Trustee King County Mcpl. League, 1980-84. With USAF, 1941-45. Decorated D.F.C., 5 Air medals, presdl. citation. Mem. Seattle King County Bar Assn. (chmn. probate com. 1975-76, chmn. lawyer referral com. 1989-90), Rainier Club. Avocations: golf, skiing, bridge, playing piano. Estate planning, Probate, General practice. Home: 3003 26th Ave W Seattle WA 98199-2821

**LOMBARD, JOHN JAMES, JR.,** lawyer; b. Phila., Dec. 27, 1934; s. John James and Mary R. (O'Donnell) L.; m. Barbara Mallon, May 9, 1964; children: John James, William M., James G., Laura K., Barbara E. BA cum laude, LaSalle Coll., Phila., 1956; JD, U. Pa., 1959. Bar: Pa. 1960. Assoc., Obermayer, Rebmann, Maxwell & Hippel, Phila., 1960-65, ptnr., 1966-84, fin. ptnr., 1980-84; ptnr. Morgan, Lewis & Bockius, LLP, Phila., 1985—, mgr. personal law sect., 1986-90, vice chair personal law sect., 1990-92, chair, 1992—; sec., dir. Airline Hydraulics Corp., Phila., 1969—; mem. adv. com. on decedents estates laws Joint State Govt. Commn., 1992—, mem. subcom. on powers of atty., 1993—; co-chair So. Jersey Ethics Alliance, 1993-97. Bd. dirs. Redevel. Authority Montgomery County, Pa., 1980-87, Gwynedd-Mercy Coll., Gwynedd Valley, Pa., 1980-89, LaSalle College High Sch., Wyndmoor, Pa., 1991-97. Recipient Treat award Nat. Coll. Probate Judges, 1992. Mem. ABA (chmn. com. simplification security transfers 1972-76, chmn. membership com. 1972-82, mem. council real property, probate and trust law sect. 1979-85, sec. 1985-87, div. dir. probate div. 1987-89, chair elect 1989-90, chair 1990-91, co-chair Nat. Conf. Lawyers & Corp. Fiduciaries), Pa. Bar Assn. (ho. of dels. 1979-81), Phila. Bar Assn. (chmn. probate sect. 1972), Am. Coll. Trust and Estate Counsel (editor Probate Notes 1983, bd. regents 1986-91, mem. exec. com. 1988-91, elder law com. 1993—), Internat. Acad. Estate and Trust Law (exec. com. 1984-88, 90—), Am. Bar Found., Internat. Fish and Game Assn. Clubs: Union League (Phila.); Ocean City (N.J.) Marlin and Tuna, Ocean City Yacht. Co-author: Durable Power of Attorney and Health Care Directives 1984, 3d edit. 1994; contbr. articles to profl. jours. Probate, Estate planning, Estate taxation. Office: Morgan Lewis & Bockius LLP 1701 Market St Philadelphia PA 19103-2903

**LOMBARDI, CURTIS JAY,** lawyer; b. San Antonio, Oct. 14, 1952; s. Ciriaco Jay and Mary Elizabeth (Moore) L. BA in Sociology with distinction, U. Wash., 1976, BA in Polit. Sci. with distinction, 1976; MPA, U. Puget Sound, 1979; JD, U. N.Mex., 1984. Bar: U.S. Dist. Ct. N.Mex. 1985, N.Mex. 1985, U.S. Dist. Ct. (no. dist.) Ark. Detention counselor Pierce County Juvenile Ct., Tacoma, 1977-79; presdl. mgmt. intern SBA, Washington, 1979-81; maj. subcontract adminstr. Sperry Flight Systems, Albuquerque, 1981-82; pvt. practice, Albuquerque, 1985—; judge advocate Gen.'s Sch., U.S. Dept. of Army. Vice-chairperson, bd. dirs. Carrie Tingley Childrens Hosp., Albuquerque, 1985-87; chmn. bd. dirs. Carrie Tingley Childrens Found., Albuquerque, 1985-87; active Dem. Nat. Conv., San Francisco, 1984. With USNR, 1970-71. Mem. Assn. Trial Lawyers Am., Nat. Contract Mgmt. Assn., N.Mex. Bar Assn., N.Mex. Trial Lawyers Assn., Anglefire Country Club. Avocations: sailing, water and snow skiing, golf, hiking, river rafting. General civil litigation, Construction, General corporate. Office: 4550 Eubank Blvd NE Ste 107 Albuquerque NM 87111-2565

**LOMBARDI, DAVID ENNIS, JR.,** lawyer, lecturer, mediator; b. Mar. 5, 1940; s. David E. and Ruth Harriet (Harrison) L.; m. Susanna C. Woodbury, June 20, 1970; children: Sara Ennis, Eric David. BA, U. Calif., Berkeley, 1962; postgrad., U. Florence, Italy, 1964; JD, Yale U., 1966. Bar: Calif. 1966. John woodman Ayer fellow at law U. Calif., Berkeley, 1963; assoc. Brobeck, Phleger & Harrison, San Francisco, 1967-73; adj. prof. bus. law U. Md., NATO Hdqrs., Belgium and Italy, 1974-75; sr. atty. Crown Zellerbach Corp., San Francisco, 1975-76; sr. ptnr. Lombardi & Lombardi, San Francisco, 1976-83, Steinhart & Falconer, San Francisco, 1983-92; spl. counsel Bianchi, Engel, Keegin & Talkington, San Rafael, Calif., 1992—; chief cir. mediator U.S. Ct. Appeals (9th cir.), San Francisco, 1992—; lectr. bus. litigation U. Md.; negotiation, mediation U. Calif. Sch. Law, Davis, U. San Francisco Sch. Law, U. Santa Clara Sch. Law, Stanford Law Sch., U. Wash. Sch. Law, U. Cairo Faculty of Law, Sch. Law Nat. U. India, Coll. Law U. Calcutta, others; mem. chancellor's com. for univ. affairs U. Calif. 1962-63; cons. on law reform and mediation for Ministry of Justice, Egypt, India, Israel, Hawaii, others; mem. alumni adv. com. U. Calif., 1968-69. Trustee Head Royce Sch., 1983-86, San Domenico Sch., 1986-90, Kentfield Schs. Found., 1985-90. Mem. ABA, Calif. Bar Assn. (prin. referee Calif. State Bar Ct. 1977-86), San Francisco Bar Assn., Am. Soc. Internat. Law, Yale U. Law Sch. Alumni Assn. (pres. No. Calif. 1989—), Pacific-Union Club, Olympic Club. General civil litigation, Alternative dispute resolution. Home: 1650 Lake St San Francisco CA 94121-1343 Office: US Ct Appeals PO Box 193939 San Francisco CA 94119-3939

**LOMBARDI, DAVID RICHARD,** lawyer; b. Bremerton, Wash., Mar. 27, 1949; s. Richard Caesar and Virginia Elizabeth (Smallridge) L.; m. Judith Ann Rummell, June 1, 1974; children: Rebecca, Katherine. BA, Stanford U., 1971; JD, U. Santa Clara, 1976. Bar: Idaho 1976, U.S. Dist. Ct. Idaho 1976, U.S. Ct. Appeals (9th cir.) 1985; cert. civil trial specialist. Ptnr. Langroise, Sullivan & Smylie, Boise, Idaho, 1976-84; of counsel Holland & Hart, Langroise & Sullivan, Boise, 1984-85; ptnr. Imhoff & Lynch, Boise, 1985-90, Givens Pursley, LLP, Boise, 1990—. Mem. Def. Rsch. Inst., Am. Inns of Ct. Roman Catholic. Avocations: fly fishing, skiing, performing and visual arts. General civil litigation, Personal injury, Health. Office: Givens Pursley LLP Ste 200 277 N 6th St Boise ID 83702-7720

**LOMBARDI, DENNIS M.,** lawyer; b. L.A., May 15, 1951; s. Peter Joseph and Jean (Nelson) L.; m. Suan Choo Lim, Jan. 9, 1993; children: Alexis Jeanne, Erin Kalani. BA, U. Hawaii, 1974; JD summa cum laude, U. Santa Clara, 1977. Bar: Calif. 1977, U.S. Dist. Ct. Hawaii, 1981. Assoc. Frandzel & Share, Beverly Hills, Calif., 1977-79; pvt. practice Capistrano Beach, Calif., 1979-81; ptnr. Case, Bigelow & Lombardi, Honolulu, 1982—. Real property, Land use and zoning (including planning), Environmental. Office: Case Bigelow & Lombardi 737 Bishop St Fl 26 Honolulu HI 96813-3201

**LOMBARDI, FREDERICK MCKEAN,** lawyer; b. Akron, Ohio, Apr. 1, 1937; s. Leonard Anthony and Dorothy (McKean) L.; m. Margaret J. Gessler, Mar. 31, 1962; children: Marcus M., David G., John A., Joseph F. BA, U. Akron, 1960; LLB, Case Western Res., 1962. Bar: Ohio 1962, U.S. Dist. Ct. (no. and so. dists.) Ohio 1964, U.S. Ct. Appeals (6th cir.) 1966. Prin., shareholder Buckingham, Doolittle & Burroughs, Akron, 1962—, chmn. comml. law and litigation dept., 1989-99. Bd. editors Western Res. Law Rev., 1961-62. Trustee, mem. exec. com., v.p. Ohio Ballet, 1985-93; trustee Walsh Jesuit H.S., 1987-90; life trustee Akron Golf Charities, NEC World Series of Golf; bd. mem. Summa Health Sys. Found., Downtown Akron Partnership, St. Hilary Parish Found. Mem. Ohio Bar Assn. (coun. of dels. 1995-97), Akron Bar Assn. (trustee 1991-94, v.p., pres.-elect 1997-98, pres. 1998-99), Case Western Res. U. Law Alumni Assn. (bd. govs. 1995-98), Case Western Res. Soc. Benchers, Fairlawn Swim and Tennis Club (past pres.), Portage Country Cub (fin. com.), Pi Sigma Alpha. Democrat. Roman Catholic. General civil litigation, Contracts commercial, Construction. Office: Buckingham Doolittle & Burroughs 50 S Main St Akron OH 44308-1828

**LOMBARDI, VALENTINO DENNIS,** lawyer; b. Providence, Feb. 5, 1943; s. Joseph and Angelina (DiDonato) L.; m. Linda Ann Dardeen, Sept. 5, 1966; children: Valerie Lynn, Nicole Maria, Joseph Thomas. AB, Providence Coll., 1966; JD, Suffolk U., 1971. Bar: R.I. 1971, U.S. Dist. Ct. R.I. 1971. Sole practice Providence, 1971—; legal counsel dept. labor and tng. State of R.I., 1978—, dept. social and rehabilitative services, 1972-73, dept. corrections, 1973-76, chief legal counsel, 1976-78; assoc. judge mcpl. ct. Town of North Providence, R.I., 1986—. Chmn. businessman's athletic club YMCA, Providence, 1976-80; bd. dirs. and sec. Iannotiti Scholarship Fund. Mem. Providence Coll. Alumni Assn. (class agt. 1981—). Democrat. Roman Catholic. Lodge: Sons of Italy (treas. 1985—, 1st v.p. 1997—). Avocations: golf, running, sports spectating. Real property, Family and matrimonial. Home: 11 Stephanie Dr Providence RI 02904-2913 Office: 128 Dorrance St Providence RI 02903-2814

**LOMBARDO, MICHAEL JOHN,** lawyer, educator; b. Willimantic, Conn., Mar. 25, 1927; s. Frank Paul and Mary Margaret (Longo) L.; children: Nancy C., Claire M. BS, U. Conn., 1951, MS, 1961, JD, 1973. Bar: Conn. 1974, U.S. Dist. Ct. Conn. 1975, U.S. Supreme Ct. 1979, U.S. Ct. Appeals (2d cir.) 1980. Div. controller Jones & Laughlin Steel Corp., Willimantic, 1956-67; adminstrv. officer health ctr. U. Conn., Hartford, 1968-69; dir. adminstrv. svcs. South Central Community Coll., New Haven, 1969-70; asst. dir. adminstrn. Norwich (Conn.) Hosp., 1970-77; asst. atty. gen. State of Conn., Hartford, 1977-92; pvt. practice, Willimantic, 1992—; adj. asst. prof. U. Hartford, 1961-70; adj. prof. bus. Old Dominion U., 1973-81; adj. lectr. in law and bus. Ea. Conn. State U., 1973—, disting. adj. faculty, 1990. Vol. Windham Ctr. (Conn.) Fire Dept. Sgt. U.S. Army, 1945-46, 1st lt. USAFR, 1951-53, col. USAFR, 1953-87, col. USAF ret., 1987. Decorated Air Force Meritorious Svc. medal, 1980; named Disting. Mil. Grad., U. Conn., 1950. Mem. AAUP, VFW, ATLA, Internat. Platform Assn., Retired Officers Assn., Conn. Bar Assn., Windham County Bar Assn., Assn. Trial Lawyers Am., Mensa Internat., Am. Legion, Lions (bd. dirs. Willimantic chpt. 1960-64). Personal injury, State civil litigation, Condemnation. Home: 35 Oakwood Dr Windham CT 06280-1520 Office: 6 Storrs Rd Ste 2 Willimantic CT 06226-4006

**LOMBARDO TROSTORFF, DANIELLE MARIA,** lawyer, educator; b. Buffalo, Dec. 31, 1951; d. Daniel M. and D. Anne (Bezer) Lombardo; m. Alexander Peter Trostorff, June 30, 1984; children: Alexander Peter Jr., Lauren. BS, Cornell U., 1972; MSW, Washington U., St. Louis, 1976, JD, 1977. Bar: N.Y. 1978, D.C. 1978, U.S. Dist. Ct D.C. 1979, U.S. Ct. Appeals (D.C. cir.) 1980, La. 1981, U.S. Dist. Ct. (ea. dist.) La. 1981, U.S. Ct. Appeals (5th and 11th cirs.) 1981, U.S. Dist. Ct. (mid. and we. dists.) La. 1983. Legal asst. Michael LoPinto, Atty., Ithaca, N.Y., 1973; intern Pub. Defender's Office State of Ill., Belleville, 1974; legal asst. hon. judge Betty Friedlander, Ithaca, summer 1975; with personal trust new bus. dept. Irving Trust Co., N.Y.C., 1977-78; staff atty., acting mng. atty. family law unit Neighborhood Legal Svcs., Washington, 1978-80; trial atty. Office of Corp. Counsel spl. litigation sect. Commonwealth of D.C., 1980-81; ptnr. Donna D. Fraiche, 1981-84; chairperson health law sect. Broadhurst, Brook, Mangham & Hardy, New Orleans, 1984-87; ptnr. Brook, Morial, Cassibry, Fraiche & Pizza, New Orleans, 1987-91; shareholder Locke Purnell Rain Harrell, New Orleans, 1991-99; ptnr. Locke Liddell & Sapp, LLP, New Orleans, 1999—; ptnr., chairperson Healthcare Practice Group; adj. prof. health care law Tulane U. Sch. Pub. Health and Tropical Medicine, New Orleans, 1989-93. Contbr. articles to profl. jours. Mem. adv. bd. Agenda for Children, New Orleans, 1990—; co-pres. Child Abuse Coun. of Greater New Orleans, 1989-90; past pres. Greater New Orleans Women's Healthcare Exec. Network. Mem. Am. Coll. Healthcare Execs. (regent's adv. coun. La.), La. Soc. Hosp. Attys. of La. Hosp. Assn. (pres. 1983-85), Cornell U. Alumni Assn. (chairperson admissions network 1989—). Health, Administrative and regulatory. Office: Locke Liddell & Sapp LLP 601 Poydras St Ste 2400 New Orleans LA 70130-6029

**LOMHOFF, PETER GEORGE,** lawyer; b. N.Y.C., Jan. 21, 1945. BA, Reed Coll., 1966; MA, U. Chgo., 1970; postgrad., Harvard U., 1970-71; JD, U. Calif. at Berkeley, 1974. Bar: Calif. 1974, U.S. Dist. Ct. (no. dist.) Calif. 1974, U.S. Ct. Appeals (9th cir.) 1974. Law clk. Judge William T. Sweigert, U.S. Dist. Ct. (no. dist.) Calif., San Francisco, 1975-77; assoc. Law Office John Diaz Coker, Pittsburg, Calif., 1974-75; instr. Lincoln U. Sch. Law, San Francisco, 1977-80; atty. pvt. practice, Oakland, Calif., 1977—; speaker in field. Contbr. to profl. handbooks. Democrat. Civil rights, Personal injury, Elder. Office: 1 Kaiser Plz Ste 1725 Oakland CA 94612-3681

**LOMONTE, DOUGLAS EDWARD,** lawyer; b. Riverhead, N.Y., Oct. 21, 1966; s. Anthony F. and Constance F. LoMonte; m. Valerie A. LoMonte, Jan. 16, 1993. BA in History, Trinity Coll., Hartford, Conn., 1988; JD, U. Conn., Hartford, 1991; MS in Taxation, U. New Haven, 1999. Bar: Conn. 1991, U.S. Dist. Ct. Conn. 1991. Atty. Wake See Dines & Byrniczka, Westport, Conn., 1991—; clk. Bd. of Fin., Town of Westport, 1992—. Mem. KC. Contracts commercial, Taxation, general, Pension, profit-sharing, and employee benefits. Offce: Wake See Dines & Bryniczka 27 Imperial Ave Westport CT 06880-4303

**LOMP, PETER VINCENT,** prosecutor, educator; b. Rockville Centre, N.Y., Apr. 24, 1967; s. Raymond and Elena (Conway) L. BA in Criminal Justice, C.W. Post Coll./L.I. U., 1989; JD, Touro Coll. Law, Huntington, N.Y., 1992. Bar: N.Y. 1992. Sole practitioner Melville, N.Y., 1992-93; asst. dist. atty. Queens County Dist. Atty.'s Office, Kew Gardens, N.Y., 1993—; tchr. Queens Dist. Atty.'s Sch. Anti-Violence Program, Far Rockaway, N.Y., 1997-98. Roman Catholic. Avocations: baseball, skiing, billiards, reading, exercise. Home: 505 Ann Ln Wantagh NY 11793-1403 Office: Queens County Dist Atty 12501 Queens Blvd Kew Gardens NY 11415-1514

**LOMURRO, DONALD MICHAEL,** lawyer; b. N.Y.C., Dec. 9, 1950; s. Joseph George and Mildred (De Rosa) L.; m. Patricia Kanis, Aug. 18, 1974; children: Donna Marie, Jonathan Herbert, Richard Patrick, Stephanie Lynne. BA, Rutgers U., 1973; JD, MBA, U. S.D., 1976. Bar: N.J. 1976, S.D. 1976, N.Y. 1983. Assoc. Levchuk & Halleran, Freehold, N.J., 1976-78; pvt. practice Freehold, 1978-80; ptnr. Lomurro & Eastman, Freehold, 1980-88, Lomurro, Davison, Eastman & Munoz, Freehold, 1988—. Candidate N.J. Assembly, 1985; chmn. Greater Freehold YMCA, 1989-91; commr. Monmouth County Park Commn., 1986-88. Mem. N.J. Bar Assn. (Outstanding Profl. Achievement award young lawyers divsn. 1985, cert. trial attys. sect., trustee 1990-97, chmn. 1998—), ATLA, Monmouth County Bar Assn. (trustee 1983-85, 91-94). Democrat. Roman Catholic. Criminal, Professional liability, Personal injury. Home: 365 E Freehold Rd Freehold NJ 07728-9017 Office: Lomurro Davison Eastman & Munoz Monmouth Exec Ctr 100 Willow Brook Rd Bldg 1 Freehold NJ 07728-2879

**LONABAUGH, ELLSWORTH EUGENE,** lawyer; b. San Diego, Feb. 24, 1923; s. Alger Wellman and Marion G. (Bailey) L.; m. Carol W. Marr, Dec. 29, 1949 (div. June 1965); children: Marr, Ellsworth, Carol; m. Jean LaValle Miterenga, Dec. 29, 1967; 1 child, Jason. JD, U. Colo., 1950. Bar: Wyo. 1950, Tex. 1951, U.S. Dist. Ct. (so. dist.) Tex. 1951, U.S. Dist. Ct. (fed. dist.) Wyo. 1953, U.S. Ct. Appeals (10th cir.) 1963, U.S. Supreme Ct. 1971. Assoc. Williams & Thornton, Galveston, Tex., 1951-53; ptnr. Lonabaugh & Lonabaugh, Sheridan, Wyo., 1953-71; sr. ptnr. various law firms, Sheridan, 1971-79; sr. ptnr. Lonabaugh & Riggs, Sheridan, 1980-98, of counsel, 1998—; mem. uniform state laws commn. State of Wyo., 1963-77; city atty. City of Sheridan, 1957; mem. Wyo. Ho. of Reps., Cheyenne, 1955-56, 67-71. Commr. Wyo. Bar, 1972-74. Staff sgt. U.S. Army, 1942-45, ETO. Decorated Bronze Star; recipient Spl. 76 award Sheridan County Commrs., 1976. Mem. Am. Bar Found. (life), Sheridan County Bar Assn. (pres. 1960-61), Sheridan County C. of C. (pres. 1974-75, named Man of Yr., 1975), Am. Legion, DAV, Sheridan Country Club (sec. 1955-59, Phi Delta Phi, Rotary (pres. local chpt. 1972-73), Elks, Shriners. Republican. Episcopalian. Avocations: golf, sports. Fax: 307-672-2230. Insurance, Real property, Estate planning. Office: Lonabaugh & Riggs 50 E Loucks St Ste 110 Sheridan WY 82801-6334

**LONARDO, CHARLES HENRY,** lawyer; b. Providence, June 23, 1955; s. Pasco and Viola (Tomasso) L.; 1 child, Matthew. BS in Broadcast Journalism cum laude, Syracuse U., 1977, JD, 1981. Bar: R.I. 1981, Mass. 1981, U.S. Dist. Ct. R.I. 1982, Mo. 1984, U.S. Dist. Ct. (we. dist.) Mo. 1985. Assoc. Connors & Kilguss, Providence, 1981-84; gen. counsel Monkem Co. Inc., Joplin, Mo., 1984; sole practice Joplin, 1984—; coordinator R.I. course SMH Bar Rev., Boston, 1981-84; bd. dirs. Legal Aid Western Mo., Kansas City, 1985-91. Mem. Mo. Bar (com. family law), Phi Delta Phi, Order of Barristers. Republican. Roman Catholic. Lodge: Kiwanis. Avocations: officiating basketball and soccer, running, weightlifting, cooking. Family and matrimonial, Consumer commercial, Criminal. Home: 1310 Starlite Dr Joplin MO 64801-1454 Office: 211 Main Ste 320 Joplin MO 64801-2368

**LONDON, DAVID L.,** lawyer; b. N.Y.C., Mar. 3, 1967; s. Jack and Charlotte (Lord) L.; m. Penelope London, June 18, 1994. BA, Yale U., 1989, JD, 1993. Bar: N.Y. 1994, U.S. Dist. Ct. (so. and ea. dists.) N.Y. 1995, Colo. 1997, U.S. Dist. Ct. Colo. 1997, U.S. Tax Ct. 1998. Jud. clk. to Hon. John C. Lifland, U.S. Dist. Ct. for N.J., Newark, 1993-94; assoc. Simpson Thacher & Bartlett, N.Y.C., 1994-97, Hogan & Hartson LLP, Denver, 1997—. Mem. Colo. lawyers com. Housing Task Force, Denver, 1997—. E-mail: DLLondon@hhlaw.com. General civil litigation. Office: Hogan & Hartson LLP 1200 17th St Ste 1500 Denver CO 80202-5840

**LONDON, IRA D.,** lawyer; b. N.Y.C., July 9, 1931; s. Murray M. and Janet (Weiss) Lichtenstein; m. Phyllis I. Kagel, May 30, 1956; children: Roberta Silverstein, Elyssa Weitzer, Suzanne Corbin. BA in English, NYU, 1956; JD, Bklyn. Law Sch., 1960. Bar: N.Y. 1960. Asst. dist. atty. Kings County Dist. Attys. Office, Bklyn., 1962-67; pvt. practice, N.Y.C., 1967—; instr., lectr. Harvard Law Sch., Cardozo Law Sch., Yeshiva U., N.Y.C., 1983—, Hofstra U., Hempstead, N.Y., 1984—, Nat. Criminal Def. Coll., Macon, Ga., 1986—; lectr. various nat. and state bar assns. Author: Intra Family Homicide: The Battered Family, 1987. Cpl. U.S. Army, 1953-55. Fellow Am. Bd. Criminal Lawyers (pres. 1990); mem. ABA (def. function com. 1988—), N.Y. State Bar Assn. (exec. com. 1990—), Kings County Criminal Bar Assn. (bd. dirs. 1986-89), Nat. Assn. Criminal Def. Lawyers (bd. dirs. 1986-91), N.Y. State Assn. Criminal Def. Lawyers (v.p. 1986-94, pres. 1995-96), L.I. Mens Tennis League (pres. 1987-89), Lawrence Tennis Club (pres. 1971). Criminal, General civil litigation. Office: 475 Park Ave S New York NY 10016-6901

**LONDON, JACK EDWARD,** lawyer; b. Hartford, Conn., Feb. 3, 1949; s. Irving Walter and Lillian (Gottlieb) L.; m. Trina June Fiedler, July 3, 1983; children: Sarah, Marissa. BBA, U. Miami, 1971, JD cum laude, 1974. Bar: Fla., 1974, U.S. Dist. Ct (so. dist.) Fla. 1975, U.S. Ct. Appeals (5th cir.) 1975, U.S. Ct. Appeals (11th cir.) 1981. Ptnr. Mills, Hodin & London P.A., Miami, Fla., 1979-81, Mills & London P.A., Miami, 1981-83; sole practice Hollywood, Fla., 1983-87; ptnr. London & Gamberg, Hollywood, 1987—. Atty., mem. bus. adv. council Meed Project, Miami, 1986—; bd. dirs. Vietnam Vets. Leadership Program, Fla., 1983-84. Mem. ABA, Fla. Bar Assn., Assn. Trial Lawyers Am., Acad. Fla. Trial Lawyers (civil rules com. 1989—, prepaid legal svcs. com. 1989—), Broward County Trial Lawyers Assn., South Broward Bar Assn., Vietnam Vets of Fla. (1st v.p. 1984), Vietnam Vets. of Am. (bd. dirs., atty. 1982-84, 1st v.p. Broward chpt.), Phi Kappa Phi. Avocations: tennis, golf, racquetball. State civil litigation, Consumer commercial, Personal injury. Office: 4651 Sheridan St Ste 300 Hollywood FL 33021-3427

**LONDON, JAMES HARRY,** lawyer; b. Balt., Dec. 12, 1949; s. Frank and Coral Marie (Calongne) L.; children: Frank T., Charles J. BS, U. Tenn., 1971, JD, 1974. Bar: Tenn. 1974, U.S. Dist. Ct. (ea. dist.) Tenn. 1974, U.S. Ct. Mil. Appeals 1975, U.S. Tax Ct. 1976. Law clk. to judge Joe D. Duncan State Tenn. Criminal Ct., 1971-74; assoc. Bond, Carpenter & O'Connor, Knoxville, Tenn., 1979-80; ptnr. Hogin, London & Montgomery, Knoxville, 1980-91, London Amburn & Thomforde, Knoxville, 1991—; nominated to White House to be fed. dist. judge, 1991; mem. hearing com. Bd. of Profl. Responsibility Tenn. Supreme Ct., 1991-95. Chmn. Bd. Deacons Lake Forest Presbyn. Ch., 1984, clk. of Session, 1985; active state and local Rep. politics. Served to capt. JAGC, USAF, 1974-79. Mem. ABA, Tenn. Bar Assn. (chmn. interdisciplinary rels. com. 1995-96), Knoxville Bar Assn. (chmn. citizenship com. 1983-89), Am. Legion (comdr. post #126 1983-85). Avocations: fishing, hunting, tennis. Personal injury, Insurance, State civil litigation. Home: 700 Kenesaw Ave Knoxville TN 37919-6661 Office: London & Amburn PC 1716 W Clinch Ave Knoxville TN 37916-2408

**LONERGAN, KEVIN,** lawyer; b. Racine, Wis., Oct. 2, 1954; s. Ralph and M. Janet L.; m. Elizabeth Ison, Oct. 10, 1981; children: Lindsey, Kristen, Emily, Marc. BS, USAF Acad., 1976; JD, U. Wis., 1979. Bar: Wis. 1979, U.S. Dist. Ct. (we. dist.), Wis. 1979; cert. Nat. Bd. Trial Advocates. Commd. 2nd lt. USAF, 1976, med. retirement, 1977; asst. dist. atty. Eau Claire County, Eau Claire, Wis., 1979-81; assoc. Thompson, Parke & Heim, Ltd., LaCrosse, Wis., 1981-82; ptnr., v.p. Herrling, Clark, Hartzheim & Siddall, Ltd., Appleton, Wis., 1982—; apptd. ct. commr. Outagamie County, 1994—; host (TV program) You and the Law, 1988—; regular guest WHBY "Open Line" Radio show, 1995—. Bd. dirs. Eau Claire Kinship Program, 1981; bd dirs., v.p., pres. Casa Clare Half-Way House, Appleton, 1984-87; mem. United Way Cabinet, 1988, 90. Mem. ATLA, Wis. Acad. Trial Lawyers (bd. dirs. 1991—, treas. 1996, sec. 1997, v.p. 1998, pres. elect 1999), Outagamie County Bar Assn. (sec. 1992-93, v.p. 1993-94, pres. 1994-95). Roman Catholic. Avocations: family, physical fitness. Personal injury, Product liability, Insurance. Home: 44 N Crestway Ct Appleton WI 54913-9510 Office: Herrling Clark Hartzheim & Siddall 800 N Lynndale Dr Appleton WI 54914-3017

**LONG, ANDRE EDWIN,** law educator, lawyer; b. San Francisco, Dec. 28, 1957; s. Edwin John and Anna (Suss) L.; m. Michele Jean Dubinsky, Oct. 4, 1986; children: Christian Andre, Katrina Marie. BA, U. Pacific, 1979; MBA, Golden Gate U., 1981; JD, Southwestern U., 1982. Bar: Hawaii 1984, D.C. 1990, U.S. Ct. Appeals (9th cir.) 1984. Legal counsel Pure Water, Ltd., Manama, Bahrain, 1982-84; pvt. practice Honolulu, 1984-85; sr. contracts negotiator Litton Data Systems Corp., Van Nuys, Calif., 1985-87; contracts mgr. Eaton, Am. Nucleonics Corp., Westlake Village, Calif., 1987-92; owner, broker A. Long Realty, Walnut Creek, Calif., 1989—; asst. prof. contract law Air Force Inst. Tech., Dayton, 1992-99; atty. Dept. of Navy, Office of Gen. Counsel, Tucson, 1999; assoc. counsel Navy Office of Gen. Counsel, China Lake, 1999—; bd. dirs. Canyon Ranch Assn., Camarillo; mediator Arbitration Forums Inc., 1989—; lectr. Tech. Tng. Corp., 1991-92; instr. Oxnard Coll., 1990-92, George Washington U. Law Sch. Author: U.S.

Immigration and Visa Laws Made Simple, 1985, 2d edit., 1991, Government Contract Law, 1995, 96, 98, 99, Negotiating Government Contracts, 1996; editor: The Clause, 1995—; editor Contract Mgmt. Jour., 1998—. Fellow Nat. Contract Mgrs. Assn.; mem. Hawaii Bar Assn., D.C. Bar Assn., Aircraft Owners and Pilots Assn., Bd. Contracts Appeals Bar Assn. (chmn. publs. com. 1995—, bd. govs. 1997—). Avocations: scuba diving, snow skiing, sailing, flying. Office: NAWCWD Code 770000 12458 Presilla Rd Camarillo CA 93012

**LONG, CHARLES THOMAS,** lawyer; b. Denver, Dec. 19, 1942; s. Charles Joseph and Jessie Elizabeth (Squire) L.; m. Susan Rae Kircheis, Aug. 9, 1967; children: Brian Christopher, Lara Elizabeth, Kevin Charles. BA, Dartmouth Coll., 1965; JD cum laude, Harvard U., 1970. Bar: Calif. 1971, U.S. Dist. Ct. (cen. dist.) Calif. 1971, U.S. Ct. Appeals (9th cir.) 1975, D.C. 1980, U.S. Dist. Ct. D.C. 1981, U.S. Ct. Claims 1995. Assoc. Gibson, Dunn & Crutcher, Los Angeles, 1970-77, ptnr., 1977-79; ptnr. Gibson, Dunn & Crutcher, Washington, 1979-83; dep. gen. counsel Fed. Home Loan Bank Bd., Washington, 1984-85; ptnr. Jones, Day, Reavis & Pogue, Washington, 1985-98; grad. tchg. asst. hist. dept. George Washington U., 1998—; Bar: Calif. 1971, U.S. Dist. Ct. (ctrl. dist.) Calif. 1971, U.S. Ct. Appeals (9th cir.) 1975, D.C. 1980, U.S. Dist. Ct. 1981, U.S. Ct. Fed. Claims 1995. Contbr. articles to profl. jours. Mem. Chesapeake Bay Maritime Mus., Friends of the Nat. Maritime Mus., Greenwich, Eng.; pres. Leigh Mill Meadows Assn., Great Falls, Va., 1980. Served to lt. USNR, 1965-67. Mem. ABA, Calif. Bar Assn., D.C. Bar Assn., Coun. for Excellence in Govt., Women in Housing and Fin., Dartmouth Lawyers Assn., Herrington Harbour Sailing Assn. (sec.-treas. 1996), Navy Records Soc. (London), U.S. Naval Inst., Chesapeake Bay Maritime Mus., Friends of the Nat. Maritime Mus. (Greenwich, Eng.), Westwood Country Club (Vienna, Va.). Republican. Methodist. Avocations: sailing, photography, computers, naval history. Banking, Securities, General corporate.

**LONG, CLARENCE DICKINSON, III,** lawyer; b. Princeton, N.J., Feb. 7, 1943; s. Clarence Dickinson and Susanna Eckings (Larter) L.; children: Clarence IV, Andrew, Amanda, Victoria, Stephen. BA, Johns Hopkins U., 1965; JD, U. Md., 1971; postgrad., Judge Adv. Gen.'s Sch., 1979-80. Bar: Ct. Appeals Md. 1972, U.S. Dist. Ct. D.C. 1972, U.S. Ct. Mil. Appeals 1975, U.S. Supreme Ct. 1976, N.C. 1978, U.S. Ct. Claims 1982, U.S. Ct. Appeals (fed. cir.) 1990. Asst. state's atty. Balt., 1973-74; trial atty., trial team chief Office Chief Trial Atty. Contract Appeals Divsn., U.S. Army, Washington, 1980-84; chief atty. Def. Supply Svc., Washington, 1984-87; trial team chief contract appeals divsn. U.S. Army, Washington, 1987-92; sr. atty. Sec. Air Force, Office of Gen. Counsel, Washington, 1992—. Lt. col. U.S. Army. Decorated Silver Star, Soldier's medal, Bronze Star, Purple Heart (2), Meritorious Svc. medal (2), Army Commendation medal (2), Cross of Gallantry with gold star, Combat Infantryman's badge, Legion of Merit. Mem. D.C. Bar Assn., N.C. Bar Assn., BCA Bar Assn. (bd. govs.), Federalist Soc. Federalist Soc. Home: PO Box 640 Bowling Green VA 22427-0640

**LONG, JAMES JAY,** lawyer; b. Pitts., Jan. 23, 1959; s. James E. and Barbara E. (Holsberg) L.; m. Tamara Rae Beer, Sept. 7, 1985. AB, U. Chgo., 1981; JD magna cum laude, U. Minn., 1984. Bar: Ill. 1984, U.S. Dist. Ct. (no. dist.) Ill. 1984, Minn. 1988, U.S. Dist. Ct. Minn. 1989. Atty. Winston & Strawn, Chgo., 1984-87; assoc. Briggs & Morgan, St. Paul, 1987-91, shareholder, 1991—. Contbr. articles to profl. jours. Mem. St. Paul Jaycees (v.p. 1989-90, pres. 1993-94), Order of Coif. Democrat. Avocations: travel, sports, horse racing. General civil litigation, Antitrust, Franchising. Office: Briggs & Morgan 2400 IDS Center 80 S 8th St Ste 2400 Minneapolis MN 55402-2157

**LONG, JEROME ALLEN,** lawyer; b. Menomonie, Wis., Aug. 22, 1946; s. Joseph Allen Long and Vivienne Irene Chaffee; m. Kathleen Mae Bradford, July 22, 1978; children: Joseph Edward Robert, Bradford Allen, Jessie Lynn. BS, U. Wis., Stevens Point, 1975; JD, Marquette U., 1978. Bar: Wis. 1978, U.S. Dist. Ct. (ea. and we. dists.) Wis. 1978; cert. trial and defense counsel Army Courts Martial. Asst. dist. atty. Marinette (Wis.) County, 1978-81, Rock County, Janesville, Wis., 1981-84; dist. atty Polk County, Balsam Lake, Wis., 1984-85; litigation atty. Wausau (Wis.) Ins. Cos., 1985-89; pvt. practice Hinkfuss Assoc. Attys., Green Bay, Wis., 1989-95, Green Bay, 1995-98; ptnr. Long & Mancoske Assoc. Attys., Green Bay, 1998, Kasdorf, Lewis & Swietlik, S.C., Wausau, 1998—; lectr. in mil. law U. Wis., Oshkosh, 1997, adj. prof. mil. sci., 1998. Lt. col. Wis. Army Nat. Guard, Madison, 1983—; commr., coach Allouez Anchors Soccer Club, Green Bay, Wis., 1997—. With U.S. Navy, 1964-72, Vietnam. Mem. ABA, ATLA. Roman Catholic. Avocations: soccer, fishing, camping. Workers' compensation, Pension, profit-sharing, and employee benefits, Military. Office: Kasdorf Lewis & Swietlik SC 2100 Stewart Ave Ste 230 Wausau WI 54401-1707

**LONG, JESSE PAUL,** lawyer; b. Punxsutawney, Pa., Mar. 22, 1912; s. Jesse C. Long and Florence E. Shadle; m. June 28, 1939; children: David W., Sarah Long O'Brien. BA, U. So. Calif., L.A., 1933; JD, Dickinson Sch. Law, 1935. Bar: Pa. 1935, Pa. Superior Ct. 1936, U.S. Dist. Ct. (we. dist.) Pa., U.S. Ct. Appeals (3rd cir.) 1945, U.S. Ct. Claims 1954, U.S. Tax Ct. 1969, Commonwealth Ct. Pa. 1971, U.S. Dist. Ct. (mid. dist.) Pa. 1971. Pvt. practice law Punxsutawney, 1935—; pres. Punxsutawney Bank/Keystone Nat. Bank, 1971-74. General practice, Probate, Estate taxation. Home and Office: 246 W Mahoning St Punxsutawney PA 15767-1919

**LONG, LUCINDA PARSHALL,** lawyer; b. Salisbury, Md., Dec. 5, 1946; d. George Richard and Sara (Freeman) L.; 1 child, Joseph Geschlecht. BA, Mary Washington Coll., 1968; MA, Johns Hopkins U., 1970, PhD, 1977; JD, Rutgers U., Newark, 1984. Bar: N.J. 1984. Assoc. prof. Montclair (N.J.) State U., 1972-84; assoc. Lowenstein, Sandler, Roseland, N.J., 1985-90; sr. v.p., gen. counsel Valley Nat. Bank, Wayne, N.J., 1991—. Author: (monograph) Some Second Thoughts About Court Administrators, 1978; contbr. articles to legal publs. Bd. dirs., sec., v.p., pres. 1st Unitarian Ch., Orange, N.J., 1987—; bd. dirs. Leni-Lenape coun. Girl Scouts U.S.A., 1997—. Mem. ABA, N.J. Bar Assn., N.J. Corp. Counsel Assn. (bd. dirs., com. chmn. 1996—), N.J. Bank Lawyers Coun. (chmn. 1995—). Avocations: travel, reading, antiques. Banking, Contracts commercial, Real property. Home: 20 Birch St West Orange NJ 07052-4534 Office: Valley Nat Bank 1455 Valley Rd Ste 4 Wayne NJ 07470-8448

**LONG, MARY BETH,** lawyer, diplomat; b. Clearfield, Pa., Aug. 20, 1963; d. Kenneth Ralph and Betsy (Diehl) L. BA, Pa. State U., 1985. Exec. asst. Petra Internat. Bank, Washington, 1985-86; fgn. svc. officer Dept. State, Washington, 1986—. Mem. ABA (Nat. Negotiation award 1994, Southeastern Negotiation award 1996), NAFE, Phi Alpha Delta, Phi Beta Kappa. Methodist. Avocations: reading, international travel, music, painting. Home: 1600 N Oak St Apt 1026 Arlington VA 22209-2766 Office: Dept State 23rd And C Sts Washington DC 20520-0001

**LONG, NICHOLAS TROTT,** lawyer; b. Bethlehem, Pa., Jan. 24, 1947; s. John Cuthbert and Mary Catherine (Parsons) L.; m. Abigail Brooks, Oct. 11, 1981; 1 child, Gabriel Parsons Brooks Long. BA, Cornell U., 1968; JD, Columbia U., 1972. Bar: Pa., R.I. Asst. dist. atty. Phila., 1972-73, pvt. practice, 1973-77, 92—; asst. pub. defender State of R.I., Providence, 1977-79; gen. counsel U. R.I., Kingston, 1979-86; chief asst. A.G. civil divsn. State of R.I., 1987-90, spl. prosecutor and counsel to the atty. gen., 1987-91, counsel to commn. of higher edn., 1992—; ednl. cons. Co-author: The Legal Deskbook for Administrators of Independent Colleges and Universities, 1993, rev., 1999, Managing Liability and Overseas Programs, 1999; author: Strategic Legal Planning: The College and University Legal Audit, 1998. Bd. dirs. Internat. Inst. R.I., Providence, 1990—, 1st v.p., 1997—; pres. Sakonnet Preservation Assn., Little Compton, R.I., 1994-98, bd. dirs., 1985—. Mem. Nat. Assn. Coll. and Univ. Attys. Avocations: sailing, theatre. E-mail: www.ntlong.com. General practice, Education and schools, Labor. Office: Ste 2400 One Bank Boston Plz Providence RI 02903

**LONG, PATRICK DAVID,** lawyer; b. Middletown, Ohio, Jan. 4, 1951; s. John Clarence and Marilyn (Greenfield) L.; m. Jennifer Rapp, Aug. 16, 1975; children: James, Erin, Zachry. BA in Speech and English, Western Ky. U., 1973; postgrad. U. Ky., 1974-75; JD, U. Dayton, 1977. Bar: Ohio 1977. Assoc. Tracy & Tracy, Franklin, Ohio, 1977-82; ptnr. Tracy & Long, Franklin, 1982-85; pvt. practice, Franklin, 1985—; contact atty. Pub. Children Services Assn., 1983—. Mem. Warren County Dem. Central Com., 1976-82; pres. Franklin Area Community Services, 1983—; mayor Village of Carlisle, Ohio, 1986—. Editor Jour. Honors Bull., 1973. Mem. ACLU (cooperating atty. 1980—), ABA, Warren County Bar Assn., Ohio Bar Assn., Cin. Bar Assn., C. of C.(pres. Franklin Area chpt. 1986-87), Lions, Rotary. Avocation: amateur radio. Office: 8 E 5th St Franklin OH 45005-2403

**LONG, REGINALD ALAN,** lawyer, educator; b. Pitts., Jan. 9, 1960; s. William Bryant and Betty (Holmes) L.; m. Lisa D. Love, Apr. 26, 1987; children: Reginald Alan Jr., Bryant A. BS, California (Pa.) State Coll., 1981; MBA, Fordham U., 1990; JD, N.Y. Law Sch., 1996. Bar: N.Y. 1997, N.J. 1998, U.S. Dist. Ct. (no. dist.) N.J. 1998. Sys. analyst Pa. Dept. Transp., Harrisburg, 1981-84; bus. analyst Pa. Blue Shield, Camp Hill, 1984-87; assoc. dir. TIAA-CREF, N.Y.C., 1987-98; ptnr. Love and Long, L.L.P., Newark, 1997—; adj. prof. real estate Rutgers U. Grad. Sch. Bus., Newark, 1998—. Mentor Youth Emergency Ctr., Newark, 1987; counselor, vol. Youth Crisis Ctr., Newark, 1987; mem. Bro. to Bro. Mentor Program, East Orange, N.J., 1998. Mem. ABA, N.Y. Bar Assn., Omega Psi Phi (Man of Yr. award 1993). Avocations: winemaking, basketball, golf. Real property, Probate, Contracts commercial. Home: 338 Warwick Ave South Orange NJ 07079-2445 Office: Love & Long LLP 108 Washington St Newark NJ 07102-3024

**LONG, ROBERT ELLIOTT,** lawyer; b. Brownwood, Tex., July 25, 1947; s. Robert Hanover and Peggy (Edwards) L.; m. Susan robins, July 6, 1974; 1 child, Robert Edwards. BA in Govt., Fla. So. Coll., Lakeland, 1969; JD, Coll. William and Mary, 1974. Bar: Va., U.S. Dist. Ct. (ea. dist.) Va. 1975, U.S. Ct. Appeals (4th cir.) 1975, U.S. Supreme Ct. 1975. Prin. Robert E. Long & Assocs., Ltd., Hampton, Va., 1974—. Den leader Boy Scouts Am., Hampton, 1991-95; pres. Hampton Hist. Soc., 1980. Served to capt. U.S. Army, 1969-71, Vietnam. Mem. Hampton Bar Assn. (officer 1976), Kiwanis, Masons. Republican. Episcopalian. Avocations: boating, fishing, art collecting. General civil litigation, Libel, Personal injury. Office: Robert E Long & Assocs Ltd 12 W Queens Way Hampton VA 23669-4012

**LONG, SUSAN,** lawyer; b. Safford, Ariz., Sept. 18, 1963. BA in Polit. Sci., U. Nev., 1987; JD, U. of the Pacific, 1992. Bar: Calif. 1992, U.S. Dist. Ct. (cen. dist.) 1993. Assoc. Cooksey Howard Martin & Toolen, Costa Mesa, Calif., 1997—. Mem. L.A. County Bar Assn., Orange County Bar Assn. General civil litigation, Construction, Insurance. Office: Cooksey Howard Martin & Toolen 535 Anton Blvd Costa Mesa CA 92626-1947

**LONG, THAD GLADDEN,** lawyer; b. Dothan, Ala., Mar. 9, 1938; s. Lindon Alexander and Della Gladys (Pilcher) L.; m. Carolyn Wilson, Aug. 13, 1966; children: Louisa Frances, Wilson Alexander. AB, Columbia U., 1960; JD, U. Va., 1963. Bar: Ala. 1963, U.S. Dist. Ct. (no. dist., so. dist., mid. dist.) Ala., U.S. Ct. Appeals (11th cir., 5th cir.), U.S. Supreme Ct. Assoc. atty. Bradley, Arant, Rose & White, Birmingham, Ala., 1963-70; ptnr. Bradley, Arant, Rose & White, Birmingham, 1970—; adj. prof. U. Ala., Tuscaloosa, 1988—, Samford U., Birmingham, 1999—, Cumberland Law Sch., 1999—. Co-author: Unfair Competition Under Alabama Law, 1990, Protecting Intellectual Property, 1990; mem. editl. bd. The Trademark Reporter; contbr. articles to profl. jours. chmn. Columbia U. Secondary Schs. Com. Ala. Area, 1975—, Greater Birmingham Arts Alliance, 1977-79; trustee, treas. Birmingham Music Club; trustee Oscar Wells Trust for Mus. Art, Birmingham, 1983—, Canterbury Meth. Found., 1993—, sec., 1993—; chmn. Entrepreneurship Inst. Birmingham, 1989; vice chmn., trustee Sons Revolution Found., Ala., 1994—; pres. Birmingham-Jefferson Hist. Soc., 1995-97; trustee Birmingham Music Club Endowment, 1995—; mem. Birmingham Com. Fgn. Rels. Mem. U.S. Patent Bar, Internat. Trademark Assn., Am. Law Inst., Ala. Law Inst., Birmingham Legal Aid Soc., Ala. Bar Assn. (chmn., founder bus. torts and antitrust sect.), Biotechnology Assn. of Ala., Inc. (sec. 1998—), U. Va. Law Alumni (chmn. Birmingham chpt. 1984-89), S.R. (pres. 1994-95), Gen. Soc. S.R. (gen. solicitor 1994—), Am. Arbitration Assn., Order of the Coif, Omicron Delta Kappa. Republican. Methodist. Avocations: travel, writing, table tennis. Antitrust, Intellectual property, General civil litigation. Home: 2880 Balmoral Rd Birmingham AL 35223-1236 Office: Bradley Arant Rose & White 2001 Park Pl Ste 1400 Birmingham AL 35203-2736

**LONG, VICTOR EARL,** lawyer; b. Syracuse, N.Y., Apr. 3, 1954; s. William E. and Ernestine G. Long; m. Jemma M. Long, Dec. 29, 1983; children: James Joshua, William Matthew. BS, Johns Hopkins U., 1976; JD, Northeastern U., 1979. Atty. U.S. Dept. Labor, Washington, 1979-84, U.S. Dept. Justice, Washington, 1984-86, D.C. Corp. Counsel, Washington, 1986-90; atty., ptnr. Koonz, McKenney & Johnson, Washington, 1990-96; ptnr. Regor, Halperin & Lung, Washington, 1996—. Patentee. Pres., bd. dirs. Friendship House Assn., Washington, 1995-96, 98—; treas. Friendship Charter Sch., Washington, 1998—; pres. Friendship Cmty. Devel. Corp., Washington, 1998. Personal injury, Product liability. Home: 1331 K St SE Washington DC 20003-4407 Office: Regan Halperin & Long 900 19th St NW Washington DC 20006-2105

**LONG, VIRGINIA,** state supreme court justice; m. Jonathan D. Weiner; 3 children. Grad., Dunbarton Coll. of Holy Cross; JD, Rutgers U., 1966. Dep. atty. gen. State of N.J.; assoc. Pitney, Hardin, Kipp and Szuch; dir. N.J. Divsn. Consumer Affairs, 1975; commr. N.J. Dept. Banking, 1977-78; judge N.J. Superior Ct., 1978-84; judge Appellate Divsn. N.J. Superior Ct., 1984-95, presiding judge, 1995-99; assoc. justice Supreme Ct. N.J., 1999—. Office: Supreme Ct NJ PO Box 970 Trenton NJ 08625*

**LONGDEN, ROBERT EDWARD, JR.,** lawyer; b. Jersey City, July 18, 1949; s. Robert Edward and Eileen (Kelly) L.; m. Joanna R. Longden, June 2, 1979; children: Timothy Charles, Carolyn Mary. BA, Boston Coll., 1971; JD, Suffolk U., 1975. Bar: Mass. 1975, U.S. Dist. Ct. Mass. 1975. Ptnr. Bowditch & Dewey, Worcester, Mass., 1975—. Pres. Elm Park Ctr. for Early Childhood Edn., Worcester, 1989-91, Worcester County Bar Found., 1995-96, trustee; fellow Mass. Bar Found. Mem. Worcester County Bar Assn. (exec. com. 1990—, pres . 1994-95). Real property, General corporate. Office: Bowditch & Dewey 311 Main St Worcester MA 01608-1552

**LONG-EBERHARDT, CORDOVA JACQUELINE,** paralegal; b. Dec. 21, 1941; d. William S. Sr. and Imogene Hammock Lewis; m. James E. Long Sr., Nov. 6, 1965 (dec.); children: James E. Long Jr., Kelly S. Lewis; m. Edward Eberhardt, Dec. 23, 1994. AS, Duff's Bus., 1990. Paralegal Ford and Council, Pitts., 1990-93, Carl Browning Jr., Pitts., 1993—. Acting chmn. bd. Grandparents Rearing Grandchildren, 1996. With USWAC, 1960-62. Democrat. Baptist. Office: Carl H Brown Jr 515 Court Pl Pittsburgh PA 15219-2002

**LONGER, WILLIAM JOHN,** lawyer; b. Vinton, Iowa, Oct. 20, 1951; s. Hal Owen and Patricia Diane (Milroy) L.; m. Deborah Ann Dagenais, Aug. 7, 1976; 1 child, Kathryn Johanna. BA, Valparaiso U., 1974, JD, 1977. Bar: U.S. Dist. Ct. (no. dist.) Ind. 1978. Assoc. John D. Breclaw & Assocs., Griffith, Ind., 1977-79; sole practice Hobart, Ind., 1979—; judge Hobart (Ind.) City Ct., 1992—; dep. pros. atty., Lake County, Ind., 1982-91; asst. city atty., Hobart, Ind., 1986-87; instr. bus. law Calumet Coll., Hammond, Ind., 1978-79; atty. Sch. City Hobart, 1988—. V.P. Hobart Family YMCA, 1985-86, pres. 1987-88. Mem. ABA, Ind. Bar Assn., Lake County Bar Assn., Hobart Bar Assn. (pres. 1985, sec. 1983-84), Hobart C. of C. (pres. 1986). Methodist. Lodge: Rotary. General practice, Probate, Real property. Home: 514 N Lake Shore Dr Hobart IN 46342-5016 Office: 651 E 3rd St Hobart IN 46342-4419

**LONGFELDER, LAWRENCE LEE,** lawyer; b. Seattle, Feb. 23, 1944; s. Harlow J. and Nancy Jane (Nicholson) L.; m. Christine Doucet, Mar. 25, 1978. BA in Polit. Sci., Whitman Coll., 1966; JD, U. Wash., 1970. Bar: Wash. 1971, U.S. Dist. Ct. (we. dist.) Wash. 1971, U.S. Dist. Ct. (ea. dist.) Wash. 1974, U.S. Dist. Ct. (so. dist.) Calif. 1983, Idaho 1994, U.S. Dist. Ct. Idaho 1994. Assoc. Miracle & Pruzan, Seattle, 1971-73; ptnr. Sullivan, Morrow & Longfelder, Seattle, 1973-79; prin., ptnr. Morrow, Longfelder, Tinker & Kidman, Seattle, 1979-83; pres., prin. Longfelder Tinker Kidman Inc., P.S., Seattle, 1983—. Pres. Forgotten Children's Fund, Seattle, 1984—; mem. bd. adjustment City of Seattle, 1978-81. Mem. ABA, Seattle-King County Bar Assn., Wash. State Bar Assn., Wash. Trial Lawyers Assn., Assn. Trial Lawyers Am., Columbia Tower, Seattle Club. Personal injury, General civil litigation, Professional liability. Office: Longfelder Tinker Kidman Inc PS 101 Stewart St Ste 1010 Seattle WA 98101-1048

**LONGHI, VINCENT J.,** lawyer; b. N.Y.C., Apr. 16, 1916; s. Joseph and Rosa (Zitani) L.; m. Gabrielle Gold, Nov. 13, 1943; children: Jaime Gold, Gabrielle Jr. LLD, St. Lawrence U., 1946. Ptnr. Longhi & Loscalzo, N.Y.C., 1952-80; prin. V.J. Longhi P.C., N.Y.C., 1980-97; pres. V.J. Longhi Assoc., N.Y.C., 1997—. Author: (plays) Two Fingers of Pride, 1955, Climb the Greased Pole, 1968, The Lincoln Mask, 1972, (book) Woody, Cisco and Me, 1997. Rep. candidate for congress, Bklyn. With Merchant Marine, 1943-45. Mem. N.Y. State Bar Assn., N.Y. State Trial Lawyers Assn., D.C. Bar Assn. Office: VJ Longhi Assoc 277 Broadway Ste 1600 New York NY 10007-2001

**LONGHOFER, RONALD STEPHEN,** lawyer; b. Junction City, Kans., June 30, 1946; s. Oscar William and Anna Mathilda (Krause) L.; m. Elizabeth Norma McKenna; children: Adam, Nathan, Stefanie. BMus, U. Mich., 1968, JD, 1975. Bar: Mich. 1975, U.S. Dist. Ct. (ea. dist.) Mich., U.S. Ct. Appeals (6th cir.), U.S. Supreme Ct. Law clk. to judge U.S. Dist. Ct. (ea. dist.) Mich., Detroit, 1975-76; ptnr. Honigman, Miller, Schwartz & Cohn, Detroit, 1976—, chmn. litigation dept., 1993-96. Co-author: Mich. Court Rules Practice-Evidence, 1998, Courtroom Handbook on Michigan Evidence, 1997, Michigan Court Rules Practice, 1998, Courtroom Handbook on Michigan Civil Procedure, 1998; editor Mich. Law Rev., 1974-75. Served with U.S. Army, 1968-72. Mem. ABA, Detroit Bar Assn., Fed. Bar Assn., U. Mich. Press Club, Order of Coif, Phi Beta Kappa, Phi Kappa Phi, Pi Kappa Lambda. State civil litigation, Federal civil litigation. Home: 46401 W Main St Northville MI 48167-3035 Office: Honigman Miller Schwartz & Cohn 2290 1st National Bldg Detroit MI 48226

**LONGLEY, CHRISTOPHER QUENTIN MORI,** lawyer; b. Mpls., May 23, 1961; s. Robert William and Frances Margaret (Heil) L.; m. Nancy Mori, Dec. 13, 1985; children: Christopher Hideo, Mariko Ann Frances, Charles Stratton. BA, St. Thomas U., 1987; JD, William Mitchell Coll. of Law, 1992. Bar: Minn. Staff asst. Senator Rudy Boschwitz, St. Paul, 1980-81; fundraiser Congressman Arlen Erdahl, Osseo, Minn., 1982; legis. asst. Senator Rudy Boschwitz, Washington (D.C.), 1982-83; fin. dir. People for Boschwitz, Mpls., 1984-89; cons. Longley & Assoc., St. Paul, 1986-96; chief devel. officer St. Thomas Acad., St. Paul, 1989-92; assoc. Hessian, McKasy & Soderberg, P.A., Mpls., 1992-94; pes. Quantum Comms. Group, Inc., Eden Prairie, Minn., 1994-96; pres., CEO Quantum Wireless Solutions, Inc., Bloomington, Minn., 1996-97; v.p., COO Internet Fin. Svcs., LLC, Mpls.; bd. dirs. QAI Corp., St. Paul, Newtel, Ltd., QWSI, Inc. Bd. dirs. Welcome Neighbor Time Savers, Inc., Indian Head coun. Boy Scouts Am.; co-founder Rep. Victory Club PAC. Named Outstanding Young American, OYM, Inc., N.Y., 1986. Mem. U.S. Supreme Ct. Bar Assn., Minn. State Bar, Ramsey County Bar. Home: 726 Summit Ave Saint Paul MN 55105-3440 Office: Internet Fin Svcs 510 Marquette Ave Ste 206 Minneapolis MN 55402-1134

**LONGO, AMY L.,** lawyer. BSN, Creighton U., 1970, JD, 1979. Bar: Nebr. 1979. Ptnr. Ellick, Jones, Buelt, Blazek & Longo, Omaha; mem. moot ct. bd., adj. asst. prof. law Coll. Medicine, U. Nebr., 1987—. Fellow Am. Bar Found.; mem. ABA (del. 1993), Nebr. State Bar Assn. (pres.-elect, ho. dels. 1984—, chair 1996), Omaha Bar Assn. Office: Ellick Jones Buelt Blazek & Longo 8805 Indian Hills Dr Ste 280 Omaha NE 68114-4077*

**LONGO, RONALD ANTHONY,** lawyer; b. Schenectady, N.Y., Nov. 17, 1952; s. Vito Frank and Frances (Scardamaglia) L.; m. Susan Fraioli, Nov. 15, 1980; children: Kristen, John Michael. BS, Cornell U., 1974; JD, Pace U., 1980. Bar: N.Y. 1981, U.S. Dist. Ct. (so. dist.) N.Y. 1984, U.S. Supreme Ct. 1984. Asst. dir. labor rels. Onondaga County, Syracuse, N.Y., 1974-75; dir. employee rels. Ardsley (N.Y.) Sch. Dist., 1975-80; assoc. Plunkett & Jaffe, White Plains, N.Y., 1980-86, ptnr., 1986-93; ptnr. Keane & Beane, P.C., White Plains, N.Y., 1993—; dep. town atty. Town of Clarkstown, New City, N.Y., 1985—; adj. assoc. prof. Iona Coll., New Rochelle, N.Y., 1982-90; adj. prof. L.I. U., Brookville, N.Y., 1986-88; instr. labor rels. studies program Cornell U., 1991-92. Author: (with others) Public Sector Labor and Employment Law, 1988, 98. Mem. ABA, N.Y. State Bar Assn., N.Y. State Pub. Employer Labor Rels. Assn. (sec., treas. 1979-81, pres. 1982-83, Disting. Svc. award 1983). Labor, Education and schools. Office: Keane & Beane PC 1 N Broadway Ste 700 White Plains NY 10601-2310

**LONGOBARDI, JOSEPH J.,** federal judge; b. 1930; m. Maud L.; 2 children: Joseph J. III, Cynthia Jean. BA, Washington Coll., 1952; LLB, Temple U., 1957. Deputy atty. Gen. State Del., Wilmington, 1959-61, tax appeal bd., 1973-74; ptnr. Longobardi & Schwartz, Wilmington, 1964-72, Murdoch, Longobardi, Schwartz & Walsh, Wilmington, 1972-74; judge Superior Ct. State of Del., Wilmington, 1974-82; vice chancellor Ct. Chancery, State Del., Wilmington, 1982-84; federal judge U.S. Dist. Ct. Del., Wilmington, 1984-97, chief judge, 1989-96, sr. judge, 1997—; assoc. editor Temple Law Rev. Recipient Paul C. Reardon award Nat. Ctr. for State Cts., 1981, S.S. Shull Meml. awrd for excellence in legal rsch. and writing. Office: US Dist Ct 844 N King St # 40 Wilmington DE 19801-3519

**LONGSTAFF, RONALD E.,** federal judge; b. 1941. BA, Kans. State Coll., 1962; JD, U. Iowa, 1965. Law clk. to Hon. Roy L. Stephenson U.S. Dist. Ct. (so. dist.) Iowa, 1965-67, clk. of ct., 1968-76, U.S. magistrate judge, 1976-91; fed. judge U.S. Dist. Ct. (so. dist.) Iowa, Des Moines, 1991—; assoc. McWilliams, Gross and Kirtley, Des Moines, 1967-68; adj. prof. law Drake U., 1973-76. Mem. Iowa State Bar Assn. (chmn. spl. commn. to revise Iowa exemption law 1968-70, mem. adv. com. 8th cir. ct. appeals 1988—). Office: US Dist Ct 422 US Courthouse 123 E Walnut St Des Moines IA 50309-2035

**LONGSTREET, SUSAN CANNON,** lawyer; b. Washington, July 18, 1944; d. Price Watkins and Martha Virginia (Cannon) L.; m. Harrison Fargo McConnell II, Sept. 4, 1965 (div. July 1974); 1 child, Catherine Dianne. Student, Duke U., 1964; BA in Econs., George Washington U., 1968; JD, Coll. of William and Mary, 1984. Of counsel Shaw, Pittman, Potts & Trowbridge, Washington, 1984—. Mem. ABA, Va. State Bar Assn., D.C. Bar Assn. Real property, Contracts commercial. Home: 5831 Berkshire Ct Alexandria VA 22303-1630 Office: Shaw Pittman Potts & Trowbridge 2300 N St NW Fl 5 Washington DC 20037-1172

**LONNER, JONATHAN ARI,** lawyer; b. N.Y.C., May 26, 1969; m. Leora Tanenbaum. BA, U. Pa., 1991; JD, Northwestern U., 1994. Bar: N.Y. 1995, Calif. 1997. Assoc. Skadden Arps Slate Meagher & Flom, N.Y.C., 1994-96, Franklin Weinrib Rudell & Vassallo P.C., N.Y.C., 1997—. Entertainment. Office: Franklin Weinrib Rudell & Vassallo PC 488 Madison Ave New York NY 10022-5702

**LOOBY, TIMOTHY JOHN,** lawyer; b. Chgo., Dec. 19, 1953; s. George John and Coletta Marie (Buttliere) L.; m. Evelyn Ann Ayers, Sept. 13, 1980; children: Maureen, Bridget, Ann Ayers. BS, Bemidji State U., 1976; JD, U. Minn., 1982. Bar: Minn., U.S. Dist. Ct. Minn., U.S. Supreme Ct. Capitol reporter Legis. Assocs., St. Paul, 1982-83; ptnr. Melchert, Hubert, Sjodin, PLLP, Waconia, Minn., 1983—; atty. coach State Bar Assn. Mock Trial Lawyers, Waconia, 1983—. Coach Waconia Cmty. Edn./Recreation, 1991—; dir., bd. dirs. Sch. Dist. # 110 Found., Waconia, 1996—. Recipient Golden Apple award Waconia C. of C., 1997. Mem. ABA (mem. family law sect.), Minn. State Bar Assn. (mem. family law sect.), Minn. Eighth Dist. Bar Assn. (past pres.), Waconia Lions Club. Family and matrimonial. Home: 216 Sunset Blvd Waconia MN 55387-1227 Office: Melchert Hubert Sjodin PLLP 121 W Main St Ste 200 Waconia MN 55387-1023

**LOOMIE, EDWARD RAPHAEL,** lawyer; b. N.Y.C., Aug. 18, 1918; s. Leo Stephen Loomie and Loretta F. Murphy; widowed; children: Christine, Paul. AB, Columbia U., 1940, JD, 1942. Pvt. practice; pres. Internat. Copyrights Inc., Resources Plus Inc. Mem. 7th Regiment Vets. Assn. (v.p.). Real property, Probate, General corporate.

**LOOMIS, WENDELL SYLVESTER,** lawyer; b. Houston, July 17, 1926; s. Wendell S. and Lily Holstein (Brammer) L.; m. Joan E. Springer, June 14,

1949; children: Mina Loomis Norris, Marcia, Constance Loomis Pulido, Susan, Tamara Leigh; m. Charlotte White Metcalf, Mar. 13, 1983. BBA, U. Tex., 1951; JD, U. Houston, 1960. Bar: Tex. 1959, U.S. Dist. Ct. (so. dist.) Tex. 1960, U.S. Dist. Ct. (we. dist.) Tex. 1965, U.S. Dist. Ct. (no. dist.) Tex. 1967, U.S. Ct. Appeals (5th cir.) 1970, U.S. Supreme Ct. 1977. Ptnr. Lemmon and Loomis, Ins., 1957-59; pvt. practice Houston, 1959-82, 87—; pres. Loomis & McKenney, P.C., 1986-87; dir. numerous corps. With USAAF, 1945-46. Mem. ABA, Internat. Bar Assn., Am. Judicature Soc., Comml. Law League Am., Am. Arbitration Assn. (arbitrator), State Bar Tex., Houston Bar Assn., Masons. Republican. Mem. Disciples of Christ Ch. General practice, Contracts commercial, General civil litigation. Office: 4138 Laverock Rd Spring TX 77388-5739

**LOONEY, CULLEN ROGERS,** lawyer; b. Edinburg, Tex., July 22, 1946; s. James Cullen and Margaret (Montgomery) L.; m. Carol Lynn Smith, June 22, 1969; children: Lorin Connor, William Kelley, Courtney Lynn. BBA, U. Tex., 1968, JD, 1973. Bar: Tex. 1973. Lawyer Kelley, Looney, Alexander & Sawyer, Edinburg, 1973-87; pvt. practice Edinburg, 1987—; mgr. Edinburg Improvement Assn., 1988—; pres., chmn. bd. Security State Bank, Pharr, Tex., 1989-96; bd. dirs. Tex. A&I Citrus Adv. Bd., Weslaco, Tex., Rio Grande Valley Sports Authority, South Tex. Higher Edn. Authority, Tower Club, Edinburg Indsl. Found. Mem. Tex. House Reps., Austin, 1977-81. 1st lt. U.S. Army. Named Exec. of Yr. Profl. Secs. Internat., 1983. Mem. Tex. State Bar Assn., Hidalgo County Bar Assn., Tex. Bar Found., Edinburg Rotary, Tex. Cowboys, Phi Delta Phi, Sigma Chi. Democrat. Episcopalian. Oil, gas, and mineral, Probate. Office: PO Box 118 Edinburg TX 78540-0118

**LOONEY, ROBERT DUDLEY,** lawyer; b. Tishomingo, Okla., Mar. 25, 1919; s. M.A. and Helen (Dudley) L.; m. Caroline Ambrister, Dec. 19, 1941; children: Caroline H. Hill, Robert D., John A. BA, Okla. U., 1941, LLB, 1943. Bar: Okla. 1942, U.S. dist. ct. Okla., 19, U.S. ct. apls. (10th Cir.) Okla., 1946. Sr. ptnr. Looney Nichols et al, Oklahoma City, 1942—; prof. law Oklahoma City U. Sch. Law, 1971-73; lectr. U. Okla. Sch. Law. Mem. exec. bd. Wesleyan Youth Inc., 1958-97. Served with USCGR, 1942-45. Fellow Am. Coll. Trial Lawyers, Internat. Coll. Trial Lawyers, Internat. Acad. Trial Lawyers; mem. Oklahoma County Bar Assn. (dir.), ABA, Okla. Bar Assn., Oklahoma City Rotary (pres. 1961-62, dist. gov. internat. 1964-65), Masons. Presbyterian. General civil litigation, Insurance, Product liability. Home: 2617 NW 58th St Oklahoma City OK 73112-7103 Office: 528 NW 12th St Oklahoma City OK 73103-2407

**LOONEY, WILLIAM FRANCIS, JR.,** lawyer; b. Boston, Sept. 20, 1931; s. William Francis Sr. and Ursula Mary (Ryan) L.; m. Constance Mary O'Callaghan, Dec. 28, 1957; children: Willam F. III, Thomas M., Karen D., Martha A. AB, Harvard U., JD. Bar: Mass. 1958, D.C. 1972, U.S. Supreme Ct. 1972, U.S. Dist. Ct. (ea. dist.) Mich. 1986. Law clk. to presiding justice Mass. Supreme Jud. Ct., 1958-59; assoc. Goodwin, Procter & Hoar, Boston, 1959-62; chief civil divsn. U.S. Attys. Office, 1964-65; ptnr. Looney & Grossman, Boston, 1965-94, sr. counsel, 1995—; asst. U.S. atty. Dist. Mass., 1962-65; spl. hearing officer U.S. Dept. Justice, 1965-68; mem. Mass. Bd. Bar Overseers, 1985-91, vice-chmn., 1990-91; corp. mem. Greater Boston Legal Svcs., Inc., 1994—. Mem. Zoning Bd. of Appeals, Dedham, Mass., 1971-74; bd. dirs. Boston Latin Sch. Found., 1981-85, pres. 1981-84, chmn. bd. dirs., 1984-86; trustee Social Law Libr., 1994-97; chmn. ADR adv. com. U.S. Dist. Ct., 1998—. Fellow Am. Coll. Trial Lawyers (state com. 1996—); mem. Mass. Bar Assn. (co-chmn. standing com. lawyers responsibility for pub. svc. 1987-88, chmn. fed. ct. adv. com. Alternative Dispute Resolution 1998—), Boston Bar Assn. (pres. 1984-85, coun. mem. 1985-90, chmn. sr. lawyers sect. 1992-94, Maguire award for professionalism 1995), Nat. Assn. Bar Pres.'s, Boston Latin Sch. Assn. (pres. 1980-82, life trustee 1982—, man of yr. 1985), USCG Found. (bd. dirs. 1987—), Norfolk Golf Club, Harvard Club, New Seabury Golf Club. Democrat. Roman Catholic. General civil litigation, Criminal, Constitutional. Home: 43 Coronation Dr Dedham MA 02026-6230 Office: 101 Arch St Fl 9 Boston MA 02110-1130

**LOOPER, DONALD RAY,** lawyer; b. Ft. Worth, Sept. 4, 1952; s. Rudolph Winnard and Margie Lee (Nix) L.; m. Cara Shoen, Oct. 17, 1992; children: Scott Aaron, Cory Michael, Jonathan Reed, L. Quinn. BBA with honors, U. Tex., Austin, 1974, M in Profl. Acctg., 1976; JD cum laude, U. Houston, 1979. Bar: Colo. 1979, Tex. 1981; cert. arbitrator. Assoc. Cohen, Brame, Smith & Krendl, Denver, 1979-81; dir. Reynolds, Allen & Cook, Houston, 1981-85, head tax sect., 1984-85; dir. Looper, Reed, Mark & McGraw, Houston, 1985—; lectr. Houston Soc. CPA's, 1984; acquisition negotiations in Europe, Asia, U.S. and OPEC Countries, 1987—. Coach national champion Women's Softball Team, Houston, 1981-90. Named one of Outstanding Young Men Am., 1980, 84. Mem. ABA, Tex. Bar Assn. (seminar speaker 1983-85, divorce tax com. 1985-86, lectr. tax sect. 1983-86), Houston Bar Assn. (tax sect. coun. 1985-87), Phi Delta Phi (province pres. 1984-86). Republican. Presbyterian. Avocations: tennis, softball, backpacking, coaching. Corporate taxation, Public international. Home: 23 Mott Ln Houston TX 77024-7315 Office: Looper Reed Mark & McGraw 1300 Post Oak Blvd Ste 2000 Houston TX 77056-8000

**LOOTS, ROBERT JAMES,** lawyer; b. Havelock, Iowa, Mar. 6, 1931; s. John William and Anna Mary Loots; m. Mary Esther Ladd, June 28, 1954; children: James Mason, Margaret Mary, Catherine Ann. BA, U. Iowa, 1953, JD, 1958. Bar: Wis. 1958, Iowa 1959. Assoc. Burlingame, Gibbs & Roper, Milw., 1958-63; ptnr. Gibbs, Roper & Fifield, Milw., 1963-75, Gibbs, Roper, Loots & Williams, Milw., 1975-96; shareholder von Briesen, Purtell & Roper, Milw., 1996—. Editor Iowa Law Rev. Pres. Wis. United Meth. Found., Sun Prairie, 1991. Lt. (j.g.) USNR, 1953-56. Fellow Am. Coll. Trust and Estate Counsel; mem. ABA, Wis. Bar Assn., Milw. Bar Assn., Milw. Estate Planning Coun. (pres. 1982), Order of Coif, Phi Delta Phi, Univ. Club Milw. Republican. Methodist. Avocations: sailing, gardening, foreign travel, reading, classical music. Estate planning, General corporate, Mergers and acquisitions. Office: von Briesen Purtell & Roper SC 411 E Wisconsin Ave Milwaukee WI 53202-4461

**LOPACKI, EDWARD JOSEPH, JR.,** lawyer; b. Bklyn., June 4, 1947; s. Edward Joseph and Lillian Jane (Wallace) L.; m. Crystal May Miller, June 21, 1969; children: Edward Joseph III, Elizabeth Jane. BA in sociology, Villanova U., 1971; JD, Vt. Law Sch., 1980. Bar: Fla. 1981, U.S. Dist. Ct. (mid. dist.) Fla. 1983, U.S. Ct. Appeals (11th cir.) 1986. Mgmt. trainee Bankers Trust Co., N.Y.C., 1968-72; counselor N.J. State Employment Svcs., Red Bank, 1972-77; pvt. practice Bradenton, Fla., 1981—; adj. prof. of law Nova U., Ft. Lauderdale, Fla., 1981, Manatee C.C., Bradenton, Fla., 1994-96. Mem. Fla. Ind. Living Coun., 1996—, dist. VI adv. coun. Fla. Dept. Health and Rehabilitative Svcs., 1988-92, Manatee County Health Care Adv. Bd., 1993—, Manatee County Coun. on Access for the Disabled, 1994—, Suncoast Ctr. for Ind. Living, 1995—; pres. Cen. Soccer Assn., 1981-82; mem. De Soto Boys Club, 1982-87, sec., 1986-87; chmn. edn. com. Manatee Area c. of C., 1983; mem. Manatee Area Youth Soccer Assn., 1981-82, Manatee Coun. on Aging, 1986-87, Boys' Club Manatee County, 1986-87; bd. dirs. Manatee County G.T. Bray Little League Est, 1988-89. Mem. Nat. Orgn. Social Security Claimants Reps., Manatee County Bar Assn. (bd. dirs. 1988-89), KC (advocate 1984-85, 88-91), Lions (pres. Manatee River 1985-86, treas. 1987-88, 90-91, sec. 1988-89, Lion of Yr. award 1988, 94). Democrat. Roman Catholic. Avocations: running, photography. Probate, Estate planning, Pension, profit-sharing, and employee benefits. Home: 6612 27th Avenue Dr W Bradenton FL 34209-7405 Office: 5515 21st Ave W Ste C Bradenton FL 34209-5601

**LOPATIN, ALAN G.,** lawyer; b. New Haven, Conn., May 25, 1956; s. Paul and Ruth (Rosen) L.; m. Debra Jo Engler, May 17, 1981; children: Jonah Adam, Asa Louis. BA, Yale U., 1978; JD, Am. U., 1981. Bar: D.C. 1981, U.S. Supreme Ct. 1985. Law clk. FMC, Washington, 1980-81; counsel com. on post office and civil service U.S. Ho. of Reps., Washington, 1981-82, counsel com. on budget, 1982-86, dep. chief counsel, 1986-87, counsel temp. joint com. on deficit reduction, 1986, dep. gen. counsel com. on post office and civil svc., 1987-90, gen. counsel com. on edn. and labor, 1991-94; pres. Ledge Counsel, Inc., Washington, 1994—; exec. dir. Nat. and Cmty. Svc. Coalition, 1995—; ptnr. Valente Lake Lopatin & Schulze, Washington, 1998—; mem. presdl. task force Health Care Reform, Washington, 1993. Mem. ABA, D.C. Bar Assn., Nat. Assn. Thrift Savs. Plan Participants (pres. 1999—), Nat. Dem. Club, Yale Club (bd. dirs. Washington chpt.). Democratic. Jewish. Legislative, Labor, Pension, profit-sharing, and employee benefits. Home: 4958 Butterworth Pl NW Washington DC 20016-4354 Office: Valente Lake Lopath & Schulze 1900 L St NW Ste 610 Washington DC 20036-5032

**LOPEZ, DAVID,** lawyer; b. N.Y.C., May 9, 1942; s. Damaso and Carmen (Gonzalez) L.; A.B., Cornell U., 1963; J.D., Columbia U., 1966; m. Nancy Mary Cea, Aug. 29, 1964; children—David, Jonathan. Bar: N.Y. State 1966. Assoc. firm Leon, Weill & Mahoney, N.Y.C., 1966-67, Bressler & Meislen, N.Y.C., 1967-70; individual practice law, N.Y.C., 1970—; chmn. bd. A.T.I. Adv. Svcs., Inc., 1979—; dir. Nancy Lopez, Inc., Southampton, N.Y. Mem. Am. Bar Assn., N.Y. State Bar Assn., Suffolk County Bar Assn. Federal civil litigation, General corporate, Mergers and acquisitions. Office: 171 Edge of Woods Rd PO Box 323 Southampton NY 11969-0323

**LOPEZ, DAVID TIBURCIO,** lawyer, educator, arbitrator, mediator; b. Laredo, Tex., July 17, 1939; s. Tiburcio and Dora (Davila) L.; m. Romelia G. Guerra, Nov. 20, 1965; 1 child, Vianei López Robinson. *Wife Romelia G. López came with her family from Mexico speaking Spanish, enrolled in U.S. schools, and graduated valedictorian of her class. She has been office manager for López law firm in Houston for more than 20 years. Daughter Vianei López Robinson is an accomplished lawyer and a popular actress and dancer in civic theater productions in Abilene, Texas. Vianei and her husband, N. Keith Robinson, Jr., M.D., a very well-regarded internist in private practice, collect art and fine wines. Father, Tiburcio López, was born in 1902 in Mexico and lives in Laredo, Texas.* Student, Laredo Jr. Coll., 1956-58; BJ, U. Tex., 1962; JD summa cum laude, South Tex. Coll. Law, 1971. Bar: Tex. 1971, U.S. Dist. Ct. (so. dist.) Tex. 1972, U.S. Ct. Appeals (5th cir.) 1973, U.S. Dist. Ct. (we. dist.) Tex. 1975, U.S. Ct. Claims 1975, U.S. Ct. Appeals (fed. cir.) 1975, U.S. Supreme Ct. 1976, U.S. Dist. Ct. (ea. dist.) Tex. 1978, U.S. Ct. Appeals (11th cir.) 1981, U.S. Ct. Appeals (9th cir.) 1984; cert. internat. com. arbitrator Internat. Ctr. for Arbitration; mediator tng. Atty.-Mediator Inst. Reporter Laredo Times, 1958-59; cons. Mexican Nat. Coll. Mag., Mexico City, 1961-62; reporter Corpus Christi (Tex.) Caller-Times, 1962-64; state capitol corr. Long News Svc., Austin, Tex., 1964-65; publs. dir. Interam. Regional Orgn. of Workers, Mexico City, 1965-67; nat. field rep. AFL-CIO, Washington, 1967-71; publs. dir. Tex. chpt. AFL-CIO, Austin, 1971-72; pvt. practice Houston, 1971—; adj. prof. U. Houston, 1972-74, Thurgood Marshall Sch. Law, Houston, 1975-76; mem. adv. com. nat. Hispanic ednl. rsch. project One Million and Counting Tomas Rivera Ctr., 1989-91; mem. adv. bd. Inst. Transnat. Arbitration; charter mem. Resolution Forum Inc.; mem. adv. bd. South Tex. Ctr. Profl. Responsibility; mem. nat. panel of neutrals JAMS/ENDISPUTE, 1996—. *Before graduating first in his law school class in 1971, David T. López was a prize-winning journalist in Texas and public relations executive in Mexico. His litigation experience includes civil rights, employment, international venture and intellectual property cases. Trained as a mediator and international commercial arbitrator, he was appointed in 1996 as a panelist by J*A*M*S/Endispute. He has worked in Latin America, travelled extensively in Europe, Asia and the Middle East, and written and lectured at professional seminars in English and Spanish on international labor issues, dispute resolution, and cross-cultural negotiation and communication.* Bd. dirs. Pacifica Found., N.Y.C., 1970-72, Houston Community Coll., 1972-75; mem. bd. edn. Houston Ind. Sch. Dist., 1972-75. With U.S. Army. Mem. ABA (co-chair sub.-com. NAFTA dispute resolution, chair sub-com. atty. fees in appeals), FBA, ATLA, Tex. Bar Assn. (dir. State Bar Coll., task force on rules of civil procedures), Houston Bar Assn., Internat. Bar Assn., Interam. Bar Assn., Bar of U.S. Fed. Cir., Mex.-Am. Bar Assn., Inter-Pacific Bar Assn., Tex.-Mex. Bar Assn. (chair labor com.), Hispanic Bar Assn., World Assn. Lawyers (chair com. on law and the handicapped), Am. Judicature Soc., Indsl. Rels. Rsch. Assn.,a, Sigma Delta Chi, Phi Alpha Delta. Democrat. Roman Catholic. Federal civil litigation, Labor, Private international. Home: 28 Farnham Ct Houston TX 77024 Office: 3900 Montrose Blvd Houston TX 77006-4908

**LOPEZ, FLOYD WILLIAM,** lawyer; b. Albuquerque, Sept. 7, 1952; s. J. Joseph and Eleanor (Marron) L.; m. Susan Templeton, Dec. 27, 1980; children: Kathleen, Melinda, Michael, Carolyn, Owen. BA in English and Spanish, Amherst Coll., 1974; JD, U. N.Mex., 1982. Bar: N.Mex. 1982, U.S. Dist. Ct. N.Mex. 1983, U.S. Ct. Appeals (10th cir.) 1983. Senate intern N.Mex. Legis., Santa Fe, 1979; messenger Modrall, Sperling, Roehl, Harris & Sisk, Albuquerque, 1979; pvt. practice in constn. Albuquerque, 1979; legal extern Marron & McKinnon, Albuquerque, 1979-81; law clk. to judge Edwin L. Mechem U.S. Dist. Ct., Albuquerque, 1982-84; counsel Gov.s Organized Crime Prevention Commn., Albuquerque, 1984-86; asst. county atty. County of Bernalillo, Albuquerque, 1991—; pvt. practice Albuquerque, 1985—; mem. ethics com. Bernalillo County; analyst N.Mex. Senate, 1993. Mem. Albuquerque Bar Assn. (bd. dirs. 1990-93), Legal Aid Soc. (bd. dirs. 1990-94, Pro Bono award 1986-89). Democrat. Roman Catholic. Avocations: skiing, golf. General civil litigation, Criminal, General practice. Office: 110 2nd St SW Ste 204 Albuquerque NM 87102-3339

**LOPEZ, RAMON ROSSI,** lawyer; b. Vallejo, Calif., Aug. 14, 1950; s. Louis and Katherine Rita (Rossi) L.; m. Jamie Gray, May 26, 1973; children: James Louis, Matthew Ramon, Scott Nicholas, Katherine Joan. BS, Loyola U., L.A., 1972, JD, 1978. Bar: Calif. 1979, U.S. Dist. Ct. (so. dist.) Calif. 1979. Sales rep. Eaton Labs., L.A., 1972-75; claims rep. Chubb/Pacific Indeminity, L.A., 1975-78; assoc. Cummins, White, Robinson & Robinson, L.A., 1979-80, Robinson & Robinson, Newport Beach, Calif., 1981-82; ptnr. Barth & Lopez, Newport Beach, 1982-87, Barth, Lopez & Hodes, Newport Beach, 1987-90, Lopez & Hodes, Newport Beach, Calif., 1991—. Bd. dirs. Newport Nat. Little League, 1988, Our Lady Queen of Angels Sch., 1989-90, Am. Youth Soccer Assn., 1988—. Mem. Assn. Trial Lawyers Am., Calif. Trial Lawyers Assn., L.A. Trial Lawyers Assn., Orange County Bar Assn., Consumer Lawyers Calif. (plaintiffs steering com., breast implant litigation, plaintiff exec./mgmt. com., diet drugs litigation, bd. mem.), Balboa Bay Club. Democrat. Roman Catholic. General civil litigation, Personal injury, Insurance. Home: 5 Canyon Ct Newport Beach CA 92660-5918 Office: Lopez Hodes Restaino Milman & Skikos 450 Newport Center Dr Fl 2 Newport Beach CA 92660-7617

**LOPREST, FRANK JAMES JR.,** lawyer; b. N.J., Oct. 6, 1960; s. Frank James and Jane Ann (Stables) L.; m. Theresa Beth Moser, May 10, 1997. AB, Cornell U., 1982; postgrad., NYU, 1984; JD, U. Notre Dame, 1989. Bar: Calif. 1989, N.Y. 1991. Law clk. to Hon. David G. Larimer U.S. Dist. Ct. (we. dist.) N.Y., Rochester, 1989-90; assoc. Paul, Hastings, Janofsky & Walker, L.A., 1990-92; special asst. U.S. atty. U.S. Dist. Ct. (so. dist.) N.Y., N.Y.C., 1992—. First Lt. U.S. Army, 1984-85. Roman Cath. Office: Office US Atty State Dept 100 Church St New York NY 10007-2601

**LOPRETE, MICHAEL D.,** lawyer; b. Newark, June 1, 1932; s. D. Michael Loprete and Josephine C. Tuttle; m. Nancy Jane Murchison, July 9, 1960; children: Michael D. Jr., Christopher Scott, Gregory Andrew. AB in Econs., Princeton U., 1954; JD, Columbia U., 1959. Bar: N.J. 1960, D.C. 1980, N.Y. 1980. Assoc. McCarter & English, Newark, 1959-64; ptnr. Mattson, Madden, Polito & Loprete, Newark, 1965-77; corp. atty. AT&T, N.Y.C. and Washington, 1977-81; ptnr. Porzio, Bromberg & Newman, Morristown, N.J., 1981-85, Gibbons, Del Deo Dolan, Griffinger & Vecchione, Newark, 1985—; vice chmn. N.J. Supreme Ct. Dist. Ethics Com., Newark, 1993-97; mediator U.S. Dist. Ct. (N.J.) Mediation Panel, 1995—; adv. Am. Bd. Trial Advs. With U.S. Army, 1954-56, ETO. Fellow Am. Coll. Trial Lawyers, Am. Bar Found. General civil litigation, Environmental, Intellectual property. Office: Gibbons Del Deo Dolan Griffinger & Vecchione 1 Riverfront Plz Newark NJ 07102-5401

**LORBERBAUM, RALPH RICHARD,** lawyer; b. Chattanooga, May 19, 1948; s. Leonard and Caroline (Sadacca) L.; m. Jodie Center, June 20, 1971; children: Jennifer, Scott, Julie. BBA, U. Ga., 1970; JD, Emory U., 1973. Bar: Ga. 1973, U.S. Dist. Ct. (no. dist.) Ga. 1974, U.S. Supreme Ct. 1979, U.S. Ct. Appeals (5th and 11th cirs.) 1981, U.S. Dist. Ct. (so. dist.) Ga. 1989. Asst. dist. atty. Chatham County Dist. Atty. Assn., Savannah, Ga., 1974-75; assoc. Smith & Portman, P.C., Savannah, 1975-77, Ashman & Zipperer, P.C., Savannah, 1977-89; ptnr. Zipperer & Lorberbaum, P.C., Savannah, 1989—; bd. dirs. Center Bros., Savannah. 1st lt. U.S. Army, 1973. Mem. Am. Bd. Trial Advocates (assoc.), Maritime Law Assn. (proctor), Assn. Trial Lawyers Am., Ga. Trial Lawyers Assn., Southeastern Admiralty Law Inst., Savannah Trial Lawyers Assn. (pres.). Admiralty, Personal injury, Workers' compensation. Office: Zipperer & Lorberbaum PC 200 E Saint Julian St Savannah GA 31401-2700

**LORD, BARBARA JOANNI,** public official, lawyer; b. Bay Shore, N.Y., Aug. 7, 1939; d. Theodore and Doris Aileen (Smith) Joanni; m. Robert Wilder Lord, June 24, 1967. BA, U. Miami, 1961; JD, NYU, 1966. Bar: N.Y. 1967, Fla. 1978, U.S. Supreme Ct. 1991. Asst. editor A.M. Best Co., N.Y.C., 1961-64; contract analyst Guardian Life Ins. Co., N.Y.C., 1964-66; legal trainee N.Y. State Liquor Authority, 1966-67, atty., 1967-70, sr. atty., 1970-80, assoc. atty., 1980—, sec., 1979—. Mem. ABA, N.Y. State Bar Assn., Fla. Bar Assn., Order Eastern Star. Office: N Y State Liquor Authority 11 Park Pl New York NY 10007-2801

**LORDI, KATHERINE MARY,** lawyer; b. Jersey City, Mar. 24, 1949; d. Peter G. and Hilde E. (Illy) L. AB, Trinity Coll., Washington, 1971; JD, Fordham U., 1975. Bar: N.J. 1975, U.S. Supreme Ct. 1983, U.S. Dist. Ct. N.J. 1975, U.S. Ct. Appeals (3d cir.) 1989. Law clk. Friedman & D'Allessandro, East Orange, N.J., 1974-75, assoc., 1975-76; pvt. practice, Bloomfield, N.J., 1976—; adj. instr. Coll. St. Elizabeth, Convent Station, N.J., 1978-86, adj. prof., 1986—; legal adviser Mcpl. Ct. Clks. Assn., 1977-84. Trustee, Cath. Family and Community Services, 1980—, v.p. 1986—; adv. bd. Acad. St. Elizabeth, Convent Station, N.J., 1980-84; mem. Essex County Adv. Bd. Status of Women, 1983-92, chmn., 1985-88, co-chair, 1990-92; trustee New Sch. for Arts, 1988-89, League for Family Svc. of Bloomfield and Glen Ridge, 1986—, pres. 1990-92. Notes editor: Fordham Urban Law Jour., 1974-75. Fellow Royal Soc. for Encouragement of Arts, Mfrs. and Commerce; mem. ABA, N.J. Bar Assn., Essex County Bar Assn., Bloomfield Lawyers Club (pres. 1983-84), Bloomfield C. of C. (trustee 1986-94, v.p. legis. 1990-94). Roman Catholic. General practice. Office: 54 Fremont St Bloomfield NJ 07003-3428

**LORENZ, WILLIAM JOSEPH,** lawyer; b. Independence, Iowa, Aug. 19, 1952; s. Clair Henry and Maxine Ellen (Donohue) L. BA, U. No. Iowa, 1975; JD, Drake U., 1980. Bar: Iowa 1980, U.S. Dist. Ct. (no. dist.) Iowa 1980, U.S. Dist. Ct. (so. dist.) Iowa 1980, U.S. Ct. Appeals (8th cir.) 1982, U.S. Supreme Ct. 1992. Asst. county atty. Black Hawk County, Waterloo, Iowa, 1980-81; assoc. Harrison, Brennecke, Moore, Smaha & McKibben, Marshalltown, Iowa, 1981-85; ptnr. Welp, Harrison, Brennecke & Moore, Marshalltown, Iowa, 1986—; bd. dirs. Pride, Inc., Marshalltown, 1982-83; city atty. City of Laurel, Iowa, 1986—. Bd. dirs. Marshalltown Football League, Inc., 1983-87, Marshalltown Girls Softball Assn., 1985—, Big Bros. and Big Sisters Marshall County, Inc., Marshalltwon, 1988—, Vol. Lawyers Project, 1994—; advisor Marshalltown Tennis Assn., 1986—. Recipient Disting. Dirs. award Marshalltown Football League, 1987; named Boss of Yr. Marshall County Legal Secs. Assn., 1988. Fellow Iowa State Bar Found.; mem. ABA, Iowa State Bar Assn. (chmn. criminal law sect. 1995-96, chmn. ann. meeting com. 1998—), Marshall County Bar Assn. Roman Catholic. Avocations: tennis, golf. General civil litigation, Criminal, General practice. Home: 1006 W State St Marshalltown IA 50158-5649 Office: PO Box 618 Marshalltown IA 50158-0618

**LORENZEN, DONALD ROBERT,** lawyer; b. Chgo., Aug. 29, 1964. BS in Computer Sci., Loyola U., Chgo., 1986; JD, U. Mich., 1991. Bar: Ill. 1991, Minn. 1993, Colo. 1993. Sr. cons. Andersen Cons., Chgo., 1986-88; assoc. Sidley & Austin, Chgo., 1991-93; assoc. Holleb & Coff, Chgo., 1993-98, ptnr., 1999—. Mem. ABA, Ill. Bar Assn., Chgo. Bar Assn., Healthcare Info. Mgmt. Sys. Soc., Food and Drug Law Inst., Regulatory Affairs Profl. Soc. Health, Computer, Intellectual property. Office: Holleb & Coff 55 E Monroe St Ste 4100 Chicago IL 60603-5896

**LORENZO, NICHOLAS FRANCIS, JR.,** lawyer; b. Norfolk, Va., Nov. 22, 1942; s. Nicholas and Jean W. L.; m. Patricia C. Connare, Sept. 7, 1968; children: Nicholas Michael, Matthew Christopher. BA, St. Francis Coll., 1964; JD, Duquesne U., 1968. Bar: Pa. 1968, U.S. Dist. Ct. (we. dist.) Pa. 1969, U.S. Supreme Ct. 1976, U.S. Dist. Ct. (mid. dist.) Pa. 1977, U.S. Ct. Appeals (3rd cir.) 1983. Pres. Lorenzo and Lundy, P.C., Punxsutawney, 1979-81, Nicholas F. Lorenzo, Jr. P.C., Punxsutawney, 1981-90, successor firm Lorenzo and Gianutto, P.C., 1990-98, Lorenzo & Gianvito, P.C., 1999—; instr. Sch. Continuing Edn., Pa. State U., 1969-73. Bd. dirs. Punxsutawney Area Hosp., 1972-74; mem. parish coun. S.S.C.D. Roman Cath. Ch., 1978-84, pres., 1979-84; bd. dirs. dist. coun. Boy Scouts Am., 1982-84. Mem. ABA, ATLA, Jefferson County Bar Assn. (v.p. 1980-82, pres. 1982-84), Pa. Bar Assn., Pa. Bar Inst. (bd. dirs. 1988-94), Pa. Trial Lawyers Assn. (bd. govs), West Pa. Trial Lawyers Assn., Nat. Bd. Trial Advocacy (civil cert.). Republican. Club: Punxsutawney Country. Lodges: K.C., Elks, Eagles, Rotary (pres. Punxsutawney 1973). Personal injury, General civil litigation, Workers' compensation. Home: 180 Monticello Dr Punxsutawney PA 15767-2614 Office: 410 W Mahoning St Punxsutawney PA 15767-1908

**LORIA, MARTIN A.,** lawyer; b. N.Y.C., Apr. 11, 1951; s. Daniel Bernard and Estelle Miriam (Barasch) L.; m. Carol Berkowitz, June 3, 1973; children: Alyson, Marissa. BA, SUNY, Albany, 1972; JD, Suffolk U., 1975. Bar: Mass. 1975, U.S. Dist. Ct. Mass. 1976, U.S. Supreme Ct. 1979. Atty. New Eng. states counsel Lawyers Title Ins. Corp., Boston, 1979-82; ptnr. Adelson, Golden & Loria, P.C., Boston, 1983—. Mem. ABA, Mass. Bar Assn., Boston Bar Assn., Mass. Conveyancers Assn. (pres. 1991, bd. dirs. 1988—), Abstract Club (bd. dirs.). Real property, Banking. Office: Adelson Golden Loria & Simons PC Two Center Plz Boston MA 02108

**LORING, EMILIE,** lawyer; b. Bklyn., May 29, 1923; d. Henry L. and Helen K. Smith; m. Len Loring, Mar. 24, 1948 (dec. Apr. 1991); children: Wendy Rightmire, Judith A. BA with high honors, Swarthmore Coll., 1944; MA with honors, U. Mont., 1963, JD with high honors, 1973. Bar: Mont., U.S. Dist. Ct. Mont., U.S. Ct. Appeals (D.C., 9th and 10th cirs.), U.S. Supreme Ct.; also Blackfeet Tribal Ct., Confederated Salish and Kootenai Tribal Ct., Tribal Ct. of Ft. Belknap Indian Cmty., Tribal Ct. of Chippewa Cree Tribe. Instr. U. Mont., Missoula, 1966-67, 69-70; legal intern NLRB, Seattle, 1972; ptnr. Hilley & Loring, Great Falls, Mont., 1973-92; sole practitioner Missoula, 1992—. Mem. state bd. dirs ACLU of Mont., 1988-94; mem. Mont. state adv. com. U.S. Commn. on Civil Rights, 1988-91; pub. mem. State Bd. Cosmetology, 1987-88. Mem. State Bar Mont., Western Mont. Bar Assn. (Disting. Atty. award 1995), Cascade County Bar Assn., Mont. Legal Svcs. Assn. (bd. dirs., pres. 1991-92). Labor, Education and schools, Administrative and regulatory. Office: 500 Daly Ave Missoula MT 59801-4413

**LORY, LORAN STEVEN,** lawyer; b. Phoenix, July 11, 1961; s. Marvin and Lee (Shain) L.: m. Diane Tabachman, Aug. 4, 1984. JD, Thomas Jefferson Sch. Law, 1984. Bar: Calif., U.S. Dist. Ct. (so. dist.) Calif., U.S. Dist. Ct. Ariz. Legal documentation coord. Ernest W. Hahn Co., Inc., San Diego, 1984-86; pvt. practice San Diego, 1986—. Mem. Juvenile Justice Bar Assn. Avocations: golf, tennis, boating. General civil litigation, Insurance, Juvenile. Address: 1335 Hotel Cir S Ste 209 San Diego CA 92108-3408

**LOSCALZO, ANTHONY JOSEPH,** lawyer; b. Bklyn., May 13, 1946; s. Frank Anthony and Frances (Puliatti) L.; m. Kathryn Mary Pica, Aug. 4, 1973. BBA, St. John's U., 1967, JD, 1969. Bar: N.Y. 1969, Fla. 1971, U.S. Dist. Ct. (so. and ea. dists.) N.Y. 1973, U.S. Ct. Appeals (2d cir.) 1975, U.S. Supreme Ct. 1975. Ptnr. Loscalzo & Loscalzo, P.C., N.Y.C., 1981—. Mem. ABA, Assn. Trial Lawyers Am., Fla. Bar Assn., N.Y. State Trial Lawyers Assn., N.Y. State Bar Assn. State civil litigation, Personal injury, Workers' compensation. Office: Loscalzo & Loscalzo PC 14 E 4th St Apt 408 New York NY 10012-1141

**LOSEY, MARY A.,** lawyer; b. E. St. Louis, Ill., May 5, 1960; d. Raymond and Rose Crawford; m. Douglas E. Losey, Mar. 18, 1978; children: Christopher Crawford, Clarissa Renee. BA, DePaul U., 1982; JD, La. State U., 1985. Bar: Wis., Ill. Assoc. Hyatt Legal Svcs., Niles, Ill., Pomper & Assocs., Chgo.; ptnr. Law Office Losey & Harrold, Kenosha, Wis. Family and matrimonial, Bankruptcy. Office: Law Office Losey & Harrold 1025 67th St Kenosha WI 53143-1307

**LOSEY, RALPH COLBY,** lawyer; b. Daytona Beach, Fla., May 26, 1951; s. George Spar and Alix (Colby) L.; m. Molly Isa Friedman, July 7, 1973; children: Eva Merlinda, Adam Colby. Student, Inst. European Studies, Vienna, Austria, 1971; BA, Vanderbilt U., 1973; JD cum laude, U. Fla., 1979. Bar: Fla. 1980, U.S. Dist. Ct. (mid. dist.) Fla. 1980. Assoc. Subin, Shams, Rosenbluth & Moran, Orlando, Fla., 1980-84; ptnr. Katz, Kutter, Haigler, Alderman, Bryant & Yon, P.A., Orlando, Fla., 1984—. Author: Laws of Wisdom, 1994, Your Cyber Rights and Responsibilities: Using the Internet, 1996; contbr. articles to profl. jours. Pres. Sch. of Wisdom, Fla. Mem. Fla. Bar Assn., Orange County Bar Assn., Computer Law Assn. Democrat. Avocations: computers, golf, music, philosophy, reading. State civil litigation, Computer, Federal civil litigation. Home: 1661 Woodland Ave Winter Park FL 32789-2774 Office: Katz Kutter Haigler Alderman Bryant & Yon PA PO Box 4950 Orlando FL 32802-4950

**LOTITO, JOSEPH DANIEL,** lawyer; b. Corato, Italy, Apr. 26, 1912; came to U.S., 1916; s. Thomas and Dolores (Zucaro) L.; m. Lucille Teresa Rizzo, Feb. 17, 1945; children: Joseph Jr., Patricia, Paul. BS, St. John's U., 1935, B of Law, 1937, LLM, 1940. Bar: N.Y., Washington. Pres., mgr. Homeland Realty Corp., Bklyn., 1938-41; atty. pvt. practice, Bklyn., 1941, 54-59; contracts & adminstrv. clk. War Dept., Washington, 1942; contracts analyst Dept. Def., Washington, 1946-47; adjudicator, atty. VA, Washington, 1947-54; acct. Garan Elecs., Inc., Hackensack, N.J., 1959-68; sr. editor Prentice-Hall, Englewood Cliffs, N.J., 1968-77; dir. Garan Elecs., 1964-68; trustee, v.p., gen. counsel Rivervale at Holiday Farm Condo. Assn., Apt. Section, Inc., River Vale, N.J., 1997—. Staff sgt. USAF, 1942-46. Mem. Cmty. Assns. Inst., KC. Roman Catholic. Avocations: computers, travel, museums, chemistry, foreign languages. General civil litigation, General practice, State and local taxation. Home and Office: 521 Piermont Ave Apt 212 River Vale NJ 07675-5717

**LOTITO, NICHOLAS ANTHONY,** lawyer; b. Neptune, N.J., June 19, 1949; s. Nicholas and Grace (Pascazio) L. BA, Emory U., 1971; JD, U. Va., 1975. Bar: Ga. 1975, U.S. Dist. Ct. (no. dist.) Ga., U.S. Ct. Appeals (4th, 5th, 11 cirs.). Atty. FTC, Atlanta, 1975-76; trial atty. Antitrust Div. U.S. Dept. Justice, Atlanta, 1976-82; of counsel Fierer & Westby, Atlanta, 1983-89; ptnr. Davis, Zipperman, Kirschenbaum & Lotito, Atlanta, 1989—. Contbr. articles to profl. jours. Mem. NACDL, ABA (criminal and antitrust sects.), Atlanta Bar Assn. (task force mcpl. ct. reform 1986), Ga. Assn. Criminal Def. Lawyers (immediate past pres., exec. com., chmn. amicus com.). Democrat. Avocations: sports, writing. E-mail: nick@dzkl.com. Antitrust, Criminal. Home: 1055 Alta Ave NE Atlanta GA 30307-2512 Office: Davis Zipperman Kirschenbaum & Lotito 918 Ponce De Leon Ave NE Atlanta GA 30306-4212

**LOTKIN, ADAM H.,** lawyer; b. Balt., May 3, 1971; s. Ralph Louis and Pauline Barton Lotkin. BA, Lafayette Coll., 1993; JD cum laude, Howard U., 1996. Bar: Calif. 1996, U.S. Dist. Ct. (so. dist.) Calif. 1996. Assoc. Ault Deuprey & Gorman, San Diego, 1996-97, White Gentes & Garcia, APC, San Diego, 1997—. Assoc. mng. editor Howard U. Law Jour., 1995-96. Mem. Assn. So. Calif. Def. Counsel, Calif. State Bar, San Diego Bar Assn., San Diego Def. Lawyers, San Diego Barristers Club. Avocations: soccer, golf, basketball, bodysurfing, traveling. State civil litigation, Personal injury, Insurance. Office: White Gentes & Garcia 550 W C St Ste 950 San Diego CA 92101-8569

**LOTSTEIN, JAMES IRVING,** lawyer; b. Steubenville, Ohio, Jan. 27, 1944; s. Jack and Dorothy (Nach) L.; m. Paulette L. Gutcheon, June 25, 1972; children: Melissa A., Amanda J. BSBA, Northwestern U., 1965; JD, U. Conn., 1968. Bar: Conn. 1969, U.S. Ct. Appeals (2d cir.) 1971, U.S. Supreme Ct. 1972. From assoc. to ptnr. Hoppin, Carey & Powell, Hartford, Conn., 1969-86; ptnr. Cummings & Lockwood, Hartford, 1986—, ptnr.-in-charge, 1988-95. Author: An Introduction to the Connecticut Business Corporation Act, 1994, Ten Things You Can Do Now to Prepare for the New Connecticut Business Corporation Act, New Connecticut Business Corporation Act Sourcebook, New Indemnification Provisions of the Conneticut Business Corporation Act, 1997. Trustee Conn. Pub. Broadcasting, Inc., Conn. Policy and Econ. Coun., Inc., 1990, exec. com., 1995—, Conn. Pub. Broadcasting, Inc.; mem. Sec. of State's bus. adv. com. State of Conn.; active Am. Coll. Investment Counsel. 1st lt. JAGC, USAR, 1968-74. Mem. ABA (chmn. dirs. and officers task force, mem. corp. laws com. 1992), Conn. Bar Assn. (chmn. mcpl. law and govtl. svc. com. 1981—, chmn. bus. law sect. 1990-92, co-chmn. Conn. bus. corp. act task force 1993—). Banking, General corporate, Mergers and acquisitions. Office: Cummings & Lockwood City Pl I Hartford CT 06103

**LOTT, LESLIE JEAN,** lawyer; b. Louisville, Nov. 12, 1950; d. Emmett Russell Jr. and Allene (Barbee) L.; m. Michael T. Moore, Dec. 28, 1977; children: Michael T. Jr., Emmett Russell Lott. BA, U. Fla., 1972, JD, 1974; postgrad., Escuela Libre de Derecho, Mexico City, 1973. Bar: Fla. 1974, D.C. 1975, U.S. Ct. Appeals (fed. cir.) 1975, N.Y. 1977, U.S. Dist. Ct. (so. dist.) Fla. 1981, U.S. Dist. Ct. (so. dist.) Trial Bar 1981, U.S. Dist. Ct. (mid. dist.) Fla. 1995. Trademark examiner U.S. Patent and Trademark Office, Arlington, Va., 1974-76; assoc. Pennie & Edmonds, N.Y.C., 1976-80, Hassan Mahassni/Burlingham, Underwood & Lord, Jeddah, Saudi Arabia, 1978-79, Floyd, Pearson, Stewart, Richman, Greer, Weil & Zack, Miami, Fla., 1981-83; pvt. practice Leslie J. Lott & Assocs., P.A., Coral Gables, Fla., 1983-94; ptnr. Lott & Friedland, P.A., Coral Gables, 1994—; judge Moot Ct., Trial Advocacy U. Miami, 1981, 82, 84, 85, 87; lectr. continuing legal edn., 1987—. Editor So. Dist. Digest, 1981-84; contbr. articles to profl. jours. Trustee U. Fla. Law Ctr. Assn., 1998—, St. Stephens Episcopal Day Sch., 1998—. Recipient Am. Jurisprudence Book Award in Fed. Practice, 1973. Mem. Internat. Trademark Assn. (chmn. com. 1986-88, 97—, bd. dirs. 1993-94), Am. Intellectual Property Law Assn., Fla. Bar Assn. (chmn. 1983—), Exec. Counc. Bus. Law Sec., 1991-93, South Fla. Patent Law Assn., mem. CPR/INTA Panel of Distinguished neutrals for the Resolution of Trademark Disputes, 1994—. Trademark and copyright, Federal civil litigation, Intellectual property. Office: Lott & Friedland PA 255 Alhambra Cir Ste 555 Coral Gables FL 33134-7404

**LOTT, VICTOR H., JR.,** lawyer; b. Mobile, Ala., Aug. 15, 1950. BA cum laude, U. of the South, 1972; JD, U. Ala., 1975. Bar: Ala. 1975, U.S. Dist. Ct. (so. dist.) Ala., U.S. Ct. Appeals (5th and 11th cirs.). Ptnr. Adams and Reese LLP, Mobile, Ala. Founding editor Ala. Law and Psychology Rev., 1974-75. Mem. ABA, Ala. State Bar Assn. (pres.-elect 1997-98, bar commr. 1987—, chmn. sect. on oil, gas and mineral law 1986-87, chmn. disciplinary commn. 1989—, exec. com. 1991-92), Mobile Bar Assn., Ala. Law Inst., Phi Delta Phi. E-mail: lottvh@arlaw.com. Banking, General corporate, Real property. Office: Adams and Reese LLP PO Box 1348 4500 One St Louis Centre Mobile AL 36633*

**LOTTER, CHARLES ROBERT,** corporate lawyer, retail company legal executive; b. 1937; married. BA, St. Johns U., 1959, JD, 1962; LLM, NYU, 1969. With anti-trust div. U.S. Dept. Justice, 1962-65; with Revere Copper & Brass, Inc., 1965-69, Del E. Webb Corp., 1969-70, Louis O. Kelso, 1970-71; with J.C. Penney, Dallas, 1971—, sr. v.p., 1987—; sec., gen. counsel, 1987-93, exec. v.p., 1993; v.p., sec. JCP Realty, Inc.; sec. J.C. Penney Properties, Inc., J.C. Penney Funding Corp. With USAFR, 1962-64, lt. USNR, 1964-70. Office: J C Penney Co Inc 6501 Legacy Dr Plano TX 75024-3698

**LOTVEN, HOWARD LEE,** lawyer; b. Springfield, Mo., Apr. 8, 1959; s. Isadore and Gytel (Tuchmeier) L.; m. Charlotte Lotven. BA, Drake U., 1981; JD, U. Mo., Kansas City, 1984. Bar: Mo. 1984, U.S. Dist. Ct. (we. dist.) Mo. 1984. Pvt. practice Kansas City, 1984—; asst. prosecutor City of Kansas City, 1985; prosecutor City of Harrisonville (Mo.), 1989-91, atty., 1989-91. Mem. B'nai B'rith Dist. II, 1977-97; vol. Hunger Project, 1985—; judge Mo. State H.S. Moot Ct. Competition, 1992; Hyde Park Crime Patrol, 1985-91, Hyde Park Assn. Zoning and Planning Commn., 1993-97; vol. Heartland United Way, 1995. Mem. ABA, Mo. Bar Assn. (young lawyer's coun. 1986-88, lectr. 1987-90, criminal law com. 1989—, gen. practice law com. 1990—, co-chair criminal law com. 1991-92, exec. coun. gen. practice law com. 1993—, Law Day spkr. 1986, 96, lectr. 1987-90, 92, 97), Kansas City Bar Assn. (mcpl. cts. com., Vol. Atty. Project, 1992—, Vol. Atty. Project award winner 1994), House Rabbit Soc., Delta Theta Phi, Omicron Delta Kappa, others. Democrat. Jewish. Avocation: sports. General civil litigation, Criminal, Municipal (including bonds). Office: PO Box 15055 Kansas City MO 64106-0055

**LOTWIN, STANFORD GERALD,** lawyer; b. N.Y.C., June 23, 1930; s. Herman and Rita (Saltzman) L.; m. Judy Scott, Oct. 15, 1994; children: Lori Hope, David. BS, Bklyn. Coll., 1951, LLB, 1954, LLM, 1957. Bar: N.Y. 1954, U.S. Supreme Ct. 1961, Pa. 1986. Ptnr. Tenzer, Greenblatt LLP, N.Y.C., 1987—; of counsel Frankfurt, Garbus, Klein & Selz, N.Y.C., 1983-87. Served with U.S. Army, 1954-56. Fellow Am. Acad. Matrimonial Lawyers (bd. of mgrs. 1984—); mem. N.Y. State Bar Assn. (family law sect.), N.Y. County Trial Lawyers (lectr. 1980—), Internat. Acad. Matrimonial Attys. Family and matrimonial. Office: 405 Lexington Ave New York NY 10174-0002

**LOTZER, GERALD BALTHAZAR,** lawyer; b. Moorehead, Minn., May 28, 1951; s. Clem B. and Erna (Jeschke) L.; m. Nancy Louise Martin, June 1, 1974; children: Jonathan, Benjamin. BA, U. North Tex., 1973; JD, Baylor U., 1988. Bar: Tex. 1988, U.S. Dist. Ct. (no. dist.) Tex. 1988. Supr. br. Liberty Mut., Dallas, 1974-80; supr. home office Trinity Universal, Dallas, 1980-82; supr. region Comml. Union Ins. Co., Dallas, 1982-86; dir. Fanning, Harper & Martinson, Dallas, 1994—. Mem. Tex. Bar, Dallas Bar Assn. Insurance, Product liability, General civil litigation. Office: Fanning Harper & Martinson Preston Commons West 3d Fl 8117 Preston Rd Ste 300 Dallas TX 75225-6375

**LOUBE, IRVING,** lawyer, corporation executive; b. Winnepeg, Can., Dec. 19, 1918; s. Samuel and Alice (Chasin) L.; m. Shirley P. Lombardero, Feb. 22, 1922; children: Garrett David, Suzanne Adrienne. AB, U. Calif., Berkeley, 1941, JD, 1951. Bar: Calif. 1951, U.S. Dist. Ct. (no. dist.) Calif., U.S. Ct. Apls. (9th cir.). Assoc., Harold Strom, 1952-53; ptnr. Loube & Rounseville, 1954-60, Loube & Lewis, 1961-66, Loube, Lewis & Blum, 1967-72, Loube, Lewis, Lowen & Albers, 1973-80, Loube, Lewis, Lowen, Albers & Klein, 1981-82; sr. ptnr. Loube, Lewis, Lowen, Klein & Lando, 1983—; bd. dirs. Convalescent Hosp. Honolulu, Park Marino Health Ctr., Loube & Loube, Calif., Found. for Cardiac Rsch., Diversified Health Svcs., Van Nuys Psychiat. Hosp. Mem. Calif. Bar Assn., County Alameda Bar Assn. Republican. Jewish. Clubs: St. Francis Yacht, Waikiki Yacht, The Family, Richmond Yacht. Real property, General corporate, State civil litigation. Address: 312 San Rafael Ave Belvedere CA 94920-2334

**LOUBET, JEFFREY W.,** lawyer; b. Mt. Vernon, N.Y., May 12, 1943; s. Nathaniel R. and Joan (Fleischer) L.; m. Susan Maria Thom, Aug. 29, 1972 (div. Dec. 1997); 1 child, Thom Carlyle; m. Yvonne Phelps, Feb. 26, 1998. BA, Colgate U., 1965; JD, St. John's U., 1968; LLM in Taxation, N.Y. U., 1970. Bar: N.Y. 1968, U.S. Tax Ct. 1969, U.S. Dist. Ct. (so. dist.) N.Y. 1969, N.Mex. 1976, U.S. Dist. Ct. N.Mex. 1977. Assoc. Poletti, Freidin, Prashker, Feldman & Gartner, N.Y.C., 1969-76; ptnr. Modrall, Sperling, Roehl, Harris & Sisk, Albuquerque, 1976-94; counsel Rodey, Dickason, Sloan, Akin & Robb, Albuquerque, 1994—; lectr. N.Mex. Estate Roundtable, Albuquerque, 1979—; vis. prof. Estate and Gift Tax U. N.Mex., Albuquerque, 1988-89. Contbr. articles to profl. jours. Mem. Lovelace Respiratory Rsch. Inst. Estate Planning Adv. Coun., 1993—; mem. adv. bd. on charitable giving Albuquerque Cmty. Found., 1995—; bd. dirs. Wheels Mus. Masters World Record Holder, high hurdles and decathlon. Fellow Am. Coll. Trust and Estate Counsel (mem. estate and gift com.); mem. ABA (chair N. Mex. property tax com.), N.Mex. Estate Planning Coun., Greater Albuquerque C. of C. (chair tax task force, 1992, chair state govt. com., 1993), YMCA (mem. bd. dirs.). Avocations: track & field, skiing, fly fishing. Estate planning, State and local taxation, Taxation, general. Home: PO Box 3754 Albuquerque NM 87190-3754 Office: Rodey Dickason Sloan Akin & Robb PO Box 1888 Albuquerque NM 87103-1888

**LOUDERMILK, JOEY M.,** insurance corporation executive, corporate lawyer; b. 1953. BS, Ga. State U., 1975; JD, U. Ga., 1978. Pvt. practice law Columbus, Ga., 1978-83; sr. v.p., sr. counsel Am. Family Corp., Columbus, Ga., 1983—, now sr. v.p., gen. counsel, corp. sec., 1991—. Office: Am Family Corp 1932 Wynnton Rd Columbus GA 31999-0001

**LOUGEE, DAVID LOUIS,** lawyer; b. Worcester, Mass., Mar. 20, 1940; s. Laurence H. and Erma Virginia (MacAllister) L.; m. Mary Anne Strebb, July 15, 1979; children: Adam, Sara, Barbara, Laurence. AB, Bates Coll., 1962; LLB, Duke U., 1965. Bar: Mass. 1965. Mng. ptnr. Mirick, O'Connell, DeMallie & Lougee, Worcester, 1965—, Woodward White, The Best Lawyers in Am.; bd. dirs. Commonwealth Bio Ventures, Inc., Meridian Med. Technologies, Inc., BioVentures Investors, BiVentures Mgmt. Corp., Little Harbor Capitol, LLC, VIALOG Corp. General corporate, Securities, Mergers and acquisitions. Home: 78 Ridge Rd Hardwick MA 01037 Office: 1700 Bank of Boston Tower Worcester MA 01608

**LOUGHRIDGE, JOHN HALSTED, JR.,** lawyer; b. Chestnut Hill, Pa., Oct. 30, 1945; s. John Halsted Sr. and Martha Margaret (Boyd) L.; m. Amy Claire Booe, Aug. 3, 1980 (div. Apr. 1995); 1 child, Emily Halsted. AB, Davidson Coll., 1967; JD, Wake Forest U., 1970. Bar: N.C. 1970, U.S. Dist. Ct. 1970, U.S. Ct. Mil. Appeals 1986. Divsn. head, v.p., counsel Wachovia Mortgage Co., Winston-Salem, N.C., 1971-79; sr. v.p., counsel Wachovia Bank, Winston-Salem, N.C., 1980—; mem. Article V drafting com. N.C. Gen. Statutes Commn. UCC. Mem. cabinet, chair profl. divsn. United Way Forsyth County, 1994. Col. JAGC, USAR, 1970—. Mem. ABA (corp., banking and bus. law sect. 1971—), N.C. Bar Assn. (internat. law com. 1984—, fin. instns. com. 1985—, real property sect. governing coun. 1988-91, bus. law sect. 1971—, corp. counsel sect. 1989—, governing coun. 1992-98, treas., 1999—, real property curriculum com. 1990-93, bus. law curriculum com. 1999—), N.C. State Bar, N.C. Coll. of Advocacy, Forsyth County Bar Assn., Am. Corp. Counsel Assn. (v.p., bd. dirs. N.C. chpt. 1988-98, comml. law com. 1996—), Mortgage Bankers Assn. of Am. (legal issues com. 1982—, fin. affiliates com. 1988—), Res. Officers Assn. (chpt. pres. 1996-97, sec. 1997—), Union League (Phila.), Twin City Club (sec. and gov. 1990—, pres. 1997-99), Forsyth Country Club, Phi Delta Phi, Phi Delta Theta. Republican. Presbyterian. Avocations: golf, tennis. General corporate, Banking, Private international. Home: 615 Arbor Rd Winston Salem NC 27104-2331 Office: Wachovia Bank 100 N Main St Winston Salem NC 27101-4047

**LOUNSBURY, STEVEN RICHARD,** lawyer; b. Evanston, Ill., July 26, 1950; s. James Richard and Reba Janette (Smith) L.; m. Dianne Louise Daley, Apr. 16, 1983; children: Jimson, Cody, Richard. BA, U. Calif., Santa Barbara, 1973; JD, U. West L.A., 1977. Bar: Calif. 1979, U.S. Dist. Ct. (cen. dist.) Calif. 1979, Oreg. 1997. Pvt. practice L.A., 1979-83; contract atty. FAA, L.A., 1981; trial atty. Hertz Corp., L.A., 1983-86; mng. counsel 20th Century Ins. Co., Woodland Hills, Calif., 1986-94; mng. atty. Lounsbury and Assocs., Brea, Calif., 1986-94; sr. trial atty. Bollington, Lounsbury and Chase, Brea, 1994—; asst. county counsel Coos County, Cocquille, Oreg., 1999—; arbitrator Orange County Superior Ct., Santa Ana, Calif., 1992-99. Dir. internat. rels. Rotary Internat., Venice-Marina Club, Calif., 1980-81; dir. L.A. Jr. C. of C., 1981-82. Mem. ABA, Calif. Bar Assn., Oreg. Bar Assn., Calif. House Counsel (bd. dirs., chmn. membership 1993-94). Avocations: snow skiing, music, travel. Insurance, Personal injury, State civil litigation. Office: Coos County Office Legal Counsel 4504 Upper Camas Rd Camas Valley OR 97416

**LOU PENDÁS, LUZARDO,** lawyer; b. Pinar del Rio, Cuba, Aug. 3, 1965; came to U.S., 1971, naturalized; s. Tomá0s Eloy and Rosa Caridad Pendás; m. Ada Guardado, Feb. 12, 1994. BSBA, U. Ctrl. Fla., 1988; JD, St. Thomas U., Miami, Fla., 1996. Bar: Fla. 1997, U.S. Dist. Ct. (mid. dist.) Fla. 1997. Pres. Atlantic Investment Net, Inc., Orlando, Fla., 1986-91; right-of-way specialist II, Fla. Dept. Transp., Bartow, 1992; v.p. Baron's Pollner Corp., Orlando, 1993-94; law clk., then assoc. Hightower & Rudd, Miami, 1995-97; assoc. Rogers, Dowling, Fleming & Coleman, P.A., Orlando, 1997—. Mem. Orlando Civic Facilities Authority, 1988-94, Orlando Dist. II Adv. Com., Orlando oning Bd., 1991-92, Orlando Nominating Bd., 1998—, Horizon 2000, City of Orlando, 1998—; bd. dirs. USO, Orlando, 1998—; candidate for Orlando City Coun., 1992, for Orange County Commn. from dist. III, 1998. Republican. Baptist. Avocation: politics. General civil litigation, Insurance. Office: Rogers Dowling Et Al 34 E Pine St Orlando FL 32801-2608

**LOURIE, ALAN DAVID,** federal judge; b. Boston, Mass., Jan. 13, 1935. AB, Harvard U., 1956; MS, U. Wis., 1958; PhD, U. Pa., 1965; JD, Temple U., 1970. Bar: Pa. 1970. Chemist Monsanto Co., St. Louis, 1957-59; lit. scientist, chemist, patent agt. Wyeth Labs., Radnor, Pa., 1959-64; counsel Smith Kline Beechum Corp., Phila., 1964-90, successively as patent agt., atty., dir. corp. patents, asst. gen. counsel, v.p. corp. patents; cir. judge U.S. Ct. Appeals (fed. cir.), Washington, 1990—; mem. Judicial Conf. Com. on Financial Disclosure, 1990-98; mem. U.S. del. to Diplomatic Conf. on Revision of Paris Conv. for Protection of Indsl. Property, 1982, 84; vice chmn. industry functional adv. com. to U.S. Trade Rep. and Dept. Commerce, 1987-90; chmn. U.S. group of U.S.-Japan Bus. Coun. Task Force on Patents. Bd. visitors Law Sch., Temple U. Mem. ABA, Phila. Patent Law Assn. (pres. 1984-85), Am. Intellectual Property Law Assn. (bd. dirs. 1982-85), Assn. Corp. Patent Counsel (treas. 1987-89), Pharm. Mfrs. Assn. (chmn. patent com. 1981-86), Am. Chem. Soc., Cosmos Club, Harvard Club Washington. Office: US Ct Appeals Fed Cir 717 Madison Pl NW Washington DC 20439-0002

**LOUSBERG, PETER HERMAN,** lawyer; b. Des Moines, Aug. 19, 1931; s. Peter J. and Otillia M. (Vogel) L.; m. JoAnn Beimer, Jan. 20, 1962; children: Macara Lynn, Mark, Stephen. AB, Yale U., 1953; JD cum laude, U. Notre Dame, 1956. Bar: Ill. 1956, Fla. 1972, Iowa 1985; cert. mediator, Iowa. Law clk. to presiding justice Ill. Appellate Ct., 1956-57; asst. states atty. Rock Island County, Ill., 1959-60; ptnr. Lousberg, Kopp, Kutsunis and Weng, P.C., Rock Island, Ill.; opinion commentator Sta. WHBF, 1973-74; lectr., chmn. Ill. Inst. Continuing Edn.; lectr. Ill. Trial Lawyers seminars; chmn. crime and juvenile delinquency Rock Island Model Cities Task Force, 1969; chmn. Rock Island Youth Guidance Coun., 1964-69; mem. adv. bd. Ill. Dept. Corrections Juvenile Divsn., 1976; Ill. commr. Nat. Conf. Commrs. Uniform State Laws, 1976-78; treas. Greater Quad City Close-up Program, 1976-80; mem. nominations commn. U.S. Senate Judicial Nominations Commn. Ctrl. Dist., Ill., 1995; bd. visitors No. Ill. U. Coll. Law. Contbr. articles to profl. jours. Bd. dirs. Rock Island Indsl.-Comml. Devel. Corp., 1977-80; bd. govs. Rock Island Cmty. Found., 1977-82. 1st lt. USMC, 1957-59. Fellow Am. Bar Found. (rsch. adv. com., chair 1993-96, Ill. chair of fellows 1995—), Am. Coll. Trial Lawyers, Ill. Bar Found. (bd. dirs. 1986-93, chmn. fellows 1987-88); mem. ABA (ho. of dels. 1990-93, com. on client protection 1997—), Am. Law Inst., Ill. State Bar Assn. (bd. govs. 1969-74, 88-94, chmn. spl. survey com. 1974-75, com. on mentally disabled 1979-80, spl. com. on professionalism 1986-87, task force on professionalism 1987-89, atty.'s fees 1988, bd. dirs. 1989—, pres. 1992-93, pres./chair bd. Mutual Ins. Co. 1993-94), Rock Island Bar Assn., Assn. Trial Lawyers Am., Ill. Trial Lawyers Assn. (bd. mgrs. 1974-78), Am. Judicature Soc., Nat. Legal Aid and Defenders Assn. (regional coord. 1989-90), Ill. Inst. Continuing Legal Edn. (bd. dirs. 1980-83, chmn. 1981-82), Lawyers Trust Fund Ill. (bd. dirs. 1984-88), Fla. Bar Assn. (chmn. out-of-state practitioners com. 1985-86), Rock Island C. of C. (treas. 1975, pres. 1978), Quad Cities Coun. of C. of C. (1st chmn. 1979-80), Notre Dame Club, Quad Cities Club, Rotary (bd. dirs. Quad Cities). Roman Catholic. General civil litigation, Family and matrimonial, Contracts commercial. Home: 5281 Isla Key Blvd S Apt 404 Saint Petersburg FL 33715-1683 Office: 322 16th St Rock Island IL 61201-8626

**LOVE, JEFFREY BENTON,** lawyer; b. Houston, Oct. 4, 1949; s. Benton Fooshee and Margaret (McKean) L.; m. Katherine Brownlee, Dec. 30, 1972; children: Benton Fooshee III, Elizabeth Houston. BA, Vanderbilt U., 1971; JD, U. Tex., 1976. Bar: Tex. 1976. Assoc. Liddell, Sapp, Zivley, Hill & LaBoon, L.L.P., Houston, 1976-81, ptnr., 1982—, adv. dir., 1990—, vice chmn. bd. dirs. nominating com. 1992—; dir. Tex. Commerce Bank-Houston regional adv. bd., Kinark Corp., 1985-88, St. Luke's Episc. Hosp., 1989-96; hon. consul gen. Sweden in Tex., 1983-89, U. Tex. Devel. Bd., 1991—; mem. com. for Tex. campaign U. Tex., 1992—; assoc. mem. bd. visitors U. Tex. M. D. Anderson Cancer Ctr., 1991—; chmn. Harris County Fin. Com. Re-Election Campaign, Tex. Supreme Ct. Justice Tom Phillips, 1995-96; dir. exec. com. Houston Grand Opera. Pres. Sunrisers Houston Breakfast Assn., Houston, 1979; dir. exec. com. Houston Grand Opera Assn., Houston, 1979-86; dir., chmn. Children's Fund, Inc., Houston, 1981-82; bd. dirs. Tex. Bus. Hall of Fame Found., 1985—, chmn. bd. dirs., 1987, awards com. 1992—; bd. dirs. March of Dimes, Houston, 1989—, chmn. 1989, bd. nominations com. 1992—; adv. dir. Eileen McMillin Blood Ctr., Meth. Hosp.; bd. govs., exec. com., sec. The Forum Club, 1987-92, The Hospice Tex. Med. Ctr. Cap. Campaign, 1991, St. John Divine Episcopal Ch. Cap. Campaign, 1992; bd. dirs., exec. com. Nat. Conf. Christians and Jews, Inc., 1987-90; mem. devel. council Tex. Children's Hosp., 1987—; mem. adv. bd. Covenant House Tex., 1988—; Houston Internat. Festival: co-chmn., Mayor's Gala, 1993, mem. underwriters com. Houston Ballet Ball, 1992; bd. dirs., mem. exec. com. Houston Youth Symphony & Ballet, 1990—, pres., 1992-93, chmn., emcee 1993 Cultural Leader of Yr. Dinner; hon. chair Lupus Disease Benefit, 1992. Recipient Outstanding Young Texas Ex award U. Tex. Ex Students Assn., 1988, 5 Outstanding Young Houstonian awards Houston Jr. C. of C., 1988, 5 Outstanding Young Texan awards Tex. Jaycees, 1988; named one of Outstanding Young Men in Am., U.S. Jaycees, 1980, 81; decorated Knighthood of Royal Order of North Star King Carl XVI Gustaf of Sweden, 1989, Hon. Family of Yr., Child Advocates, Inc., 1991. Mem. ABA, Houston C. of C., Houston Bar Assn., Tex. Bar Assn., Swedish Am. Trade Assn. (bd. dirs. 1983—), Swedish Am. C. of C., U. Tex. Law Alumni Assn. (bd. dirs. 1981—, nat. pres., chmn. exec. com. 1986-87), Phi Delta Theta Alumni Assn. Episcopalian. Clubs: River Oaks, Allegro, Houston. Immigration, naturalization, and customs, General corporate. Home: 3744 Inwood Dr Houston TX 77019-3002 Office: Liddell Sapp Zivley Hill & LaBoon LLP 600 Travis St 3400 Chase Tower Houston TX 77002-3095

**LOVE, JENNIFER STEPHENS,** lawyer; b. Indpls., May 21, 1971; d. Robert Wayne and Susan Ann Stevens; m. Matthew Stephens Love, June 19, 1993; 1 child, Emma Stephens. BA, Ind. U., 1993, JD, 1996. Bar: Ind. 1996, U.S. Dist. Ct. (so. dist.) Ind. 1996, U.S. Ct. Appeals (7th cir.) 1997. Atty. Price & Findling, Indpls., 1996-97, Findling, Garau, Germano & Pennington, P.C., Indpls., 1997—. Scholar Ind. U. Sch. Law, 1994. Mem. ATLA, Am. Inns. of Ct., Ind. Trial Lawyers Assn., Ind. State Bar Assn., Indpls. Bar Assn. Personal injury, General civil litigation. Office: Findling Garau Garmano & Pennington PC 151 N Delaware St Ste 1515 Indianapolis IN 46204-2522

**LOVE, MARK STEVEN,** lawyer; b. Phila., July 20, 1950; s. Allen and Florence (Botkiss) L.; m. Joyce Elaine Greer, Mar. 24, 1973; children: Stephanie, Valerie. BS in Biochemistry, Pa. State U., 1972; JD, Temple U., 1976. Bar: Pa. 1976, U.S. Dist. Ct. (mid. dist.) Pa. 1977, U.S. Supreme Ct. 1980. Law clk. to presiding justice Northampton County Ct. of Common Pleas, Easton, Pa., 1976-77; assoc. Mervine, Brown, Newman, Williams & Mishkin, Stroudsburg, Pa., 1977-85; ptnr. Miller & Love, Mt. Pocono, Pa., 1986-91. Solicitor Polk Twp. Suprs., Monroe County, Pa., 1981-87, Tunkhannock Twp. Suprs., Monroe County, 1981-88, Borough of Mt. Pocono, 1986-88, asst. solicitor Monroe County, 1988–. Named one of Outstanding Young Men Am., 1985. Mem. ABA, Pa. Bar Assn., Northampton County Bar Assn., Monroe County Bar Assn., Assn. Trial Lawyers Am., Pa. Trial Lawyers Assn. Democrat. Jewish. Personal injury, Criminal. Home: PO Box 690 Tannersville PA 18372-0690 Office: PO Box 349 Tannersville PA 18372-0349

**LOVE, MICHAEL KENNETH,** lawyer; b. Richmond Height, Mo., Oct. 2, 1951; s. Clarence Kenneth and Helen (Schlapper) L.; m. Gloria Pia Miccioli, Sept. 8, 1979; children: Claire Pia, Patrick Kenneth. BS in Forestry, U. Mo., 1974; JD, George Washington U., 1977. Bar: Va. 1977, D.C. 1978, Md. 1981. Asst. dir. model procurement code project ABA, Washington, 1977-80; assoc. Wickwire, Gavin & Gibbs, P.C., Vienna, Va., 1980-84; ptnr. Wickwire, Gavin & Gibbs, P.C., Vienna, 1984-86, Smith, Pachter, McWhorter & D'Ambrosio, Vienna, 1986-94; corp. counsel Info. Sys. and Networks, Inc., Bethesda, 1994-95; sr. atty. Epstein, Becker & Green, Washington, 1995-98; rsch. fellow Logistics Mgmt. Inst., McLean, Va., 1998—. Contbr. articles to profl. publs. Vice chair D.C. Procurement Reform Task Force. Mem. ABA (chmn. subcontracting and constrn. com. 1984-92, constrn. com. 1990-91, chair constrn. divsn. 1993-94, mem. coun. 1994-97, chmn. fed. divsn. 1997-98), D.C. Bar Assn., Md. Bar Assn., Va. Bar Assn. Government contracts and claims, Construction. Office: Logistics Mgmt Inst 2000 Corporate Ridge McLean VA 22102-7805

**LOVE, SCOTT ANTHONY,** lawyer; b. Houston, Dec. 30, 1969; s. Robert Allen and Louisa Ann Love. BA in History with honors, U. Houston, 1997, JD, 1993. Bar: U.S. Dist. Ct. (so. dist.) Tex., U.S. Dist. Ct. (ea. dist.) Tex. Law clk. Abraham, Watkins, Nichols & Friend, Houston, 1995-97; assoc. Duckett, Bouligny & Collins, L.L.P., El Campo, Tex., 1997-99, Wojciechowski & Assocs., P.C., Houston, 1999—. Mem. Ducks Unltd., El Campo, 1997—. Mem. Houston Young Lawyers Assn., Houston Bar Assn., Wharton County Bar Assn., Tex. Assn. of Def. Counsel. Republican. Avocations: weight lifting, softball, reading. Personal injury, Insurance, General civil litigation. Home: 3015 Brookdale Dr Kingwood TX 77339 Office: Wojciechowski & Assocs PC PO Box 1567 2 Northpoint Dr Houston TX 77060

**LOVE, WALTER BENNETT, JR.,** lawyer; b. Monroe, N.C., Nov. 14, 1921; s. Walter B. and Pearl (Hamilton) L.; m. Elizabeth Cannon, Dec. 28, 1951; children: Elizabeth Sheldon Love Sturges, Walter Bennett III, Linda Louise Love Talmadge. BS in Commerce, U. N.C., 1942, JD, 1949; Indsl. Coll. Armed Services, 1972. Bar: N.C. 1949, Fed. bar 1949. Ptnr. Love and Love, Monroe, N.C., 1949-52; pvt. practice, 1952-54, 92-99; sr. ptnr. Love and Milliken, 1958-92, attys. for City of Monroe; ptnr. Love & Hutaff PLLP, 1999—. Bd. dirs. Nat. Bd. Am. Cancer Soc., 1969-82, pres. N.C. div., 1984, chmn. bd., 1985; chmn. bd. trustees Cen. United Meth. Ch., 1977-86, 90-92, lay leader, 1986-89; trustee United Meth. Found. for Western N.C. Conf., 1988—, Union county Found., 1989—; past pres. Union County Hist. Soc.; past sec. bd. trustees, Ellen Fitzgeral Hosp. and Union Mem. Hosp.; life mem. bd. adv. The Methodist Home, Inc. Col. USAFR, WWII and Korea. Decorated with Disting. Unit citation. Mem. ABA, N.C. Bar Assn. (estate planning and fiduciary law com. 1988), 20th Jud. Dist. Bar Assn. (past pres.), Union County Bar Assn. (past pres.), Carolinas Geneological Soc. Clubs: Rolling Hills Country, Tower, Lions (past pres. and zone chmn. Monroe). Probate, Real property, Estate planning. Home: 217 Ridgewood Dr Monroe NC 28112-6365 Office: PO Box 278 Monroe NC 28111-0278

**LOVE, WILLIAM ALLAN,** lawyer, educator; b. Phila., June 19, 1959; s. Norman and Arlene (Basiches) L.; m. Sari Rose Perlman, Aug. 28, 1988; children: Meranda Beth, Gary Isaac. BA in Criminal Justice, Temple U., 1982; JD, Thomas M. Cooley, 1987. Bar: Pa. 1988, N.J. 1989, U.S. Dist. Ct. (ea. dist.) Pa. 1988, U.S. Dist. Ct. N.J. 1989. Clk. Shop N Bag Market, Phila., 1977-83; police officer U.S. Dept. Def., Phila., 1983-84; admissions counselor Thomas Cooley Law Sch., Lansing, Mich., 1985-87; assoc. Mark Koral Assocs., Phila., 1988-90; pvt. practice Phila., 1990—; instr. C.C. Phila., 1992—; panel arbitrator Phila. Ct. Common Pleas, 1990—. Fundraiser Gary Love Cancer Rsch. Fund, Phila., 1985—. Mem. Am. Soc. Criminology, Phila. bar Assn. (faculty, planner continuing edn. 1995), Pa. Bar Assn. Republican. Jewish. Avocations: music, reading, cars. Juvenile, Criminal. Office: 1218 Chestnut St Ste 600 Philadelphia PA 19107-4814

**LOVELESS, A. SCOTT,** lawyer, consultant; b. Ely, Nev., Oct. 13, 1951; s. George K. Loveless and Esther (Hopkins) Stoddard; m. Cheri Anderson, Nov. 22, 1974. BA in German, Brigham Young U., 1975, JD, 1978. Bar: D.C. 1979, U.S. (D.C. dist.) Dist. Ct. 1979. Atty. Wigman & Cohen, Arlington, Va., 1979, Sughrue, Rothwell, Mion, Zinn & Macpeak, Washington, 1979-80; pvt. practice McLean, Va., 1980-81; atty., advisor Office of the Solicitor, Dept. of the Interior, Washington, 1981-90, Office of the Solicitor, Salt Lake City Field Office, 1991—. Office: 125 S State St Ste 6201 Salt Lake City UT 84138-1180

**LOVELESS, GEORGE GROUP,** lawyer; b. Baldwinsville, N.Y., Sept. 16, 1940; s. Frank Donald and Mayme (Lont) L.; m. Shirley Morrison, Nov. 27, 1965; children: Michael, Peter. BS, Cornell U., 1962, MBA, 1963; JD, U. Md., 1968. Bar: Pa. 1969, U.S. Dist. Ct. (ea. dist.) Pa., U.S. Ct. Appeals (3d cir.). Ptnr. Morgan, Lewis & Bockius LLP, Phila., 1968—. With USAFR, 1963-68. Republican. Presbyterian. E-mail: GGL1@cornell.edu. Banking, General corporate, Bankruptcy. Home: 11 Rose Valley Rd Media PA 19063-4217 Office: Morgan Lewis & Bockius LLP 1701 Market St Philadelphia PA 19103-2903

**LOVELESS, RALPH PEYTON,** lawyer; b. Birmingham, Ala., Apr. 8, 1936; s. Ralph Peyton Sr. and Arbrette Inez (Loveless) Anderson; m. Mary Katherine Rushing, Dec. 30, 1957; children: Laura Katherine, Linda Arbrette. BS, U. Ala., 1957, LLB, 1959. Bar: Ala. 1959, U.S. Dist. Ct. (so. dist.) Ala. 1959, U.S. Dist. Ct. D.C. 1969, U.S. Ct. Appeals (5th cir.) 1966, U.S. Supreme Ct. 1969, U.S. Ct. Appeals (11th cir.) 1981. Assoc. Caffey, Gallalee & Caffey, Mobile, Ala., 1959-63; ptnr. Caffey, Gallalee, Edington & Loveless, Mobile, Ala., 1963-67; atty. Fed. Trade Commn., Washington, 1967-69; asst. dist. atty. Mobile County, Ala., 1969-71; assoc. Marr & Friedlander, Mobile, 1971-72; ptnr. Marr, Friedlander & Loveless, Mobile, 1972-74; pvt. practice Mobile, 1974-79; ptnr. Loveless & Banks, Mobile, 1979-91, Loveless, Banks & Lyons, Mobile, 1991-96, Loveless & Lyons, Mobile, 1996—; mcpl. judge Citronelle, Ala., 1990-91, Bayou La Batre, Ala., 1990-94; bd. dirs. Ala. Law Sch. Found., Tuscaloosa. Co-author: FTC Staff Report on Automobile Warranties, 1969. Bd. dirs. Mobile Track and Field Assn., 1960-67; pres. Am. Field Svc., Mobile, 1965-67; mem. County Dem. Exec. Com., Mobile, 1962-67. Mem. ABA, Ala. Bar Assn., Ala. Trial Lawyers Assn. (exec. com. 1983-87), Ala. Law Inst. (partnership law adv. com.), U. Ala. Nat. Alumni Assn. (pres., exec. com. 1985-90), Civitan Club, U.S. Power Squadron. Methodist. Avocations: boating, travel, reading. General practice, Contracts commercial, Real property. Home: 4100 Woodhill Cir Mobile AL 36608-2431 Office: Loveless and Lyons 3103 Airport Blvd Ste 668 Mobile AL 36606-3660

**LOVELL, CARL ERWIN, JR.,** lawyer; b. Riverside, Calif., Apr. 12, 1945; s. Carl Erwin and Hazel (Brown) L.; m. Danna I. Wale; children: Carl Erwin III, Timothy C., Tishia R., Ashley P., Garrett T. BA, Vanderbilt U., 1966, JD, 1969. Bar: Nev. 1969, D.C. 1971, U.S. Supreme Ct. 1973. Jr. editor Land and Water Law Rev., 1973-89; instr. bus. law U. Nev., Las Vegas, Clark County C.C.; city atty. City of N. Las Vegas, 1970-73; elected city atty. City of Las Vegas, 1973-77; v.p., sec.-treas., legal counsel Circus Circus Hotels, Inc., Las Vegas, 1977-83; sr. ptnr. Lovell, Bilbray & Potter, Las Vegas, 1984-89; pvt. practice Las Vegas, 1989—; v.p., dir. Air Nev. Airlines, Inc.; chmn. Nat. Inst. Mcpl. Law Officers Consumer Protection Adv. Com., 1973-77, Nev. Crime Commn. Bd., 1974-77; U.S. rep. to China Internat. Trade and Law Talks, 1987; arbitrator, AAA, 1989—. Bd. dirs., v.p. BBB, 1983-91; chmn. NCCJ; pres. Clark County Young Dems., 1971-72; bd. dirs. Nat. Kidney Found.; pres., trustee Nev. Donor Network, Inc., 1992-96. With USAF, 1966-68. Mem. ABA, ATLA, Nev. State Bar, Nev. Trial Lawyers Assn., Elks (justice Las Vegas chpt. 1985-88). General corporate, Administrative and regulatory, Personal injury. Office: 2801 S Valley View Blvd Ste 1B Las Vegas NV 89102-0116

**LOVELL, CHARLES C.,** federal judge; b. 1929; m. Ariliah Carter. BS, U. Mont., 1952, JD, 1959. Assoc. Church, Harris, Johnson & Williams, Great Falls, Mont., 1959-85; judge U.S. Dist. Ct. Mont., Helena, 1985—; chief counsel Mont. Atty Gen.'s Office, Helena, 1969-72. Served to capt. USAF, 1952-54. Mem. ABA, Am. Judicature Soc., Assn. Trial Lawyers Am. Office: US Dist Ct PO Box 10112 Helena MT 59626-0112

**LOVERDI, ROSEMARY J.,** lawyer; b. Camden, N.J., Sept. 2, 1968. BS, Rutgers U., 1990, JD, 1993. Bar: Pa. 1993, N.J. 1993, U.S. Dist. Ct. N.J. 1993, U.S. Dist. Ct. (ea. dist.) Pa. 1994. Assoc. Dilworth Paxson LLP, Phila., 1993—. Mem. Phila. Bar Assn., Camden County Bar Assn., Pa. Bar Assn., N.J. State Bar Assn. Real property, General corporate. Office: Dilworth Paxson LLP 3200 Mellon Bank Ctr 1735 Market St Philadelphia PA 19103-7501

**LOVING, DEBORAH JUNE PIERRE,** lawyer, real estate broker; b. Omaha, Jan. 21, 1953; d. Thomas Eukis and June (Dawson) L.; children: La Shaun, Ronald, Mignion. BA, Mills Coll., 1977; JD, U. Iowa, 1979. Bar: Hawaii 1987, U.S. Dist. Ct. (no. dist.) Calif. 1987, U.S. Dist. Ct. Hawaii 1987, U.S. Ct. Mil. Appeals 1987; lic. real estate broker, Calif.; tchg. credential Calif. C.C. Pvt. practice, Oakland, Calif., 1987—; real estate developer, Cancun, Mex. and U.S., 1991—; officer, bd. dirs. Cmty. Based Developers, Oakland, 1992—; mem. adv. bd. Bayview Med. Group, Vallejo, Calif., 1995—. Mem. Oxford Club. Avocations: sailing, travel, tennis, art. Admiralty, Contracts commercial, Entertainment. Office: 3911 Harrison St Oakland CA 94611-4536

**LOVING, SUSAN BRIMER,** lawyer, former state official; m. Dan Loving; children: Lindsay, Andrew, Kendall. BA with distinction, U. Okla., 1972, JD, 1979. Asst. atty. gen. Office of Atty. Gen., 1983-87, 1st asst. atty. gen., 1987-91; atty. gen. State of Okla., Oklahoma City, 1991-94; ptnr. Lester, Loving & Davies, Edmond, Okla., 1994—; Master Ruth Bader Ginsburg Inn of Ct., 1995-97. Vice chmn. Pardon and Parole Bd., 1995; mem. Gov.'s Commn. on Tobacco and Youth, 1995-97; bd. dirs. Bd. for Freedom of Info., Okla. Inc., Legal Aid of West Okla., Okla. Com. for Prevention of Child Abuse; mem. med. steering com. Partnership for Drug Free Okla., Inst. for Child Advocacy, 1996-97. Recipient Nat. Red Ribbon Leadership award Nat. Fedn. Parents, Headliner award, By-liner award Okla. City and Tulsa Women in Comm., First Friend of Freedom award, Freedom of Info., Okla., Dir. award Okla. Dist. Attys. Assn. Mem. Okla. Bar Assn. (past chmn. adminstrv. law sect., mem. ho. dels. 1996—, chmn. adminstrn. of justice com., chmn. profl. responsibility commn., task force on professionalism and civility 1999—, Spotlight award 1997), Phi Beta Kappa. Administrative and regulatory, Civil rights, General practice. Office: Lester Loving & Davies PLLC 1505 Renaissance Blvd Edmond OK 73013-3018

**LOW, ANDREW M.,** lawyer; b. N.Y.C., Jan. 1, 1952; s. Martin Laurent and Alice Elizabeth (Bernstein) L.; m. Margaret Mary Stroock, Mar. 31, 1979; children: Roger, Ann. BA, Swarthmore Coll., 1973; JD, Cornell U., 1976. Bar: Colo. 1981, U.S. Dist. Ct. Colo. 1981, U.S. Ct. Appeals (10th cir.) 1986. Assoc. Rogers & Wells, N.Y.C., 1977-81; assoc. Davis, Graham & Stubbs, Denver, 1981-83, ptnr., 1984—. Editor: Colorado Appellate Handbook, 1984, 94. Pres. Colo. Freedom of Info. Coun., Denver, 1990-92, Colo. Bar Press Com., 1989, appellate practice subcom. Colo. Bar Assn. Litigation Coun., 1994—; bd. dirs. CLE in Colo., Inc., 1993-96; trustee 9 Health Fair, Denver, 1988—; mem. Colo. Sup. Ct. Joint Commn. on Appellate Rules, 1993—. Avocations: skiing, golfing, fly-fishing. General civil litigation, Libel, Appellate. Office: Davis Graham & Stubbs 370 17th St Ste 4700 Denver CO 80202-5682

**LOW, TERRENCE ALLEN,** lawyer, sole practice, woodworker; b. Calif., Jan. 24, 1950; s. William H. Low and Elisabeth Ann Steiger; m. Jean Siminitis, 1982; children: Alexandra E. Low and Tucker A.J. Low. BA, U. Pa., 1981; JD, Vt. Law Sch., 1984. Bar: Mass. 1985, U.S. Dist. Ct. Mass. 1985, U.S. Ct. Appeals (1st cir.) 1996. Assoc. Pellegrini & Selly, P.C., Springfield, Mass., 1984-92; pvt. practice, Springfield, 1992—; tchr. Mass. Cont. Legal Edn., Mass. 1996—. Chmn. Hist. Dist. Commn., Longmeadow, 1995—. Mem. ATLA (adv. 1997), Mass. Acad. Trial Lawyers, Hampden County Bar Assn. Avocations: rare book collecting, woodworking. Personal injury, Workers' compensation, General civil litigation. Office: Rosen Greenhut Catuogno & Low 244 Bridge St Springfield MA 01103-1410

**LOWE, E(DWIN) NOBLES,** lawyer; b. Minturn, Ark., Oct. 4, 1912; s. James A. and Ether (Nobles) L.; m. Catherine McDonald, June 9, 1934 (div. 1959); children: Nancy, Edwin N.; m. Margaret Breece, Dec. 1, 1961; 1 son, James W. A.B., U. Ark., 1932, LL.B., 1934; postgrad., Harvard U. Bus. Sch. Advanced Mgmt. Program, 1950; JD, U. Ark., 1976. Bar: Ark. 1934, N.Y. 1936, U.S. Ct. Appeals (2d cir.) 1938, D.C. 1975, U.S. Ct. Internat. Trade 1979, U.S. Supreme Ct. 1942. Mem. staff Ark. Bond Refunding Bd., 1934; with legal dept. Electric Bond & Share Co., N.Y.C., 1934-35; assoc. mng. atty., ptnr. Reid & Priest, 1935-43; gen. counsel Westvaco Corp. (formerly W.Va. Pulp & Paper), N.Y.C., 1943-77; dir. pub. rels. Westvaco Corp., 1944-48, dir. govt. affairs, 1944-76, sec., 1947-66, v.p., 1966-77; spl. ptnr. Gadsby & Hannah, N.Y.C., 1978-79; mem. firm Lowe & Knapp, N.Y.C., 1979-84; sole practice N.Y.C., 1985-86, Carmel, N.Y., 1986—; gen. counsel Photography in the Fine Arts, 1957-68; sec., dir. Fund for Modern Cts., N.Y., 1974—; counsel, dir. Photographic Adminstrs., Inc., 1995—. Trustee (life) Clinton Hall Assn., 1956—, pres., 1966-69, 85-90; dir. Putnam County Alliance, counsel dir., 1990-99; dir. Putnam County Arts Coun., 1992—; fellow Am. Bar Found. Recipient Disting. Alumni cert. U. Ark., 1972, 50 Yr. Practice Adminstr. Judice award Fellows of Am. Bar Found., 1985, CLE Spl. award Am. Law Inst.-ABA, 1985, Practice Law Inst. Seligson CLE award, 1986, Disting. Svc. award U. Maine, Pulp and Paper Found., 1990, Disting. Svc. award N.Y. chpt. Am. Corp. Counsel Assn.; Eagle Scout Boy Scouts Am., 1928; decorated Order of the Arrow Boy Scouts Am., 1928. Mem. ABA ( bus. law sect., founder corp. law com. 1955, emeritus 1979—, sr. lawyers divsn. coun. 1992-99, book pub. com. 1990-95, chmn. 1991-95, Experience mag. 1990—, chmn. 1995-97), Am. Arbitration Assn. (hon. exec. com. 1968—, chmn. 1972-77, chmn. bd. 1977-79), Am. Law Inst. (life mem.), N.Y. State Bar Assn., Practicing Law Inst. (trustee 1966-86, pres. 1972-79, chmn. 1979-86, chmn. emeritus 1986—), Gen. Counsel Assn., Dut ch Treat Club. (gov., sec. 1992—), Assn. Bar City N.Y. (past v.p., exec. chmn.), World Soc. Ekistics (v.p., exec. com. UN rep. NGO), Univ. Club (past v.p. coun., chmn. club activities, charter revision com.), Sigma Nu. Methodist. General corporate, Probate, Real property. Home and Office: The Knoll Gypsy Trail Rd Carmel NY 10512

**LOWE, JAMES ALLEN,** lawyer; b. L.A., Apr. 23, 1946; s. Fitzhugh Lee and Dorothy Helen (Van Kirk) L.; m. Francis Elaine Pirnat, June 6, 1967 (div. Aug. 1979); children: David T., Michael D.; m. Sandra Sue Larson, May 31, 1984 (dec. June 1988); children: Tammy Foulke, Robert, Krueger; m. Caroline Margaret Gellrick, June 6, 1992; children: Bryce Otsuka, Cardene Otsuka, Brent Otsuka. BA, U. Colo., 1968, JD, 1970. Bar: Colo. 1971, Ct. Mil. Appeals 1971, U.S. Dist. Ct. (10th cir.) 1988, U.S. Dist. Ct. (fed. cir.) 1989, U.S. Supreme Ct. 1993. Judge adv. USAF, 1971-75; chief deputy dist. atty. Dist. Attys. Office, Pueblo, Colo., 1975-80; atty. Sobol & Sobol, Denver, 1980-82, pvt. practice, Denver, 1982-95; ptnr. Lowe & Meyer, Denver, 1996—. Lt. col. USAF, 1971-95. Republican. Avocations: skiing, hiking.

**LOWE, JAMES ALLISON,** lawyer, educator; b. Cleve., July 15, 1945; s. Allison S. and Betty B. (Bernstein) L.; m. Jacalyn S. Scholss, June 24, 1967 (div.); children: David, Joseph, Jeremiah; m. Teresa L. DiPuccio, Aug. 13, 1989; 1 child, Alison. BA, U. Pa., 1967; JD cum laude, Cleve. State U., 1972. Bar: Ohio 1972, U.S. Dist. Ct. (no. dist.) Ohio 1973, U.S. Ct. Appeals (6th cir.) 1981, U.S. Supreme Ct. 1979; cert. civic trial adv. Nat. Bd. Trial Advocacy. Assoc. Berkman, Gordon & Kancelbaum, Cleve., 1972-74; sole practice Cleve., 1974-76; ptnr. Sindell, Lowe & Guidubaldi Co., L.P.A., Cleve., 1976-96, Lowe Eklund Wakefield Co., LPA, Cleve., 1996—; instr. law Cleve. State U., 1974-77, Case Western Res. U., 1979-92. Author: Products Liability Litigation: Pretrial Practice, 1988, Product Liability in Ohio After Tort Reform, 1988. Active Jewish Community Fedn.; fellow Roscoe Pound Found. Fellow Am. Coll. Trial Lawyers; mem. ABA, Assn. Trial Lawyers Am. (chmn. products liability adv. com., chmn. products liability sect., dir. products liability sect.), Ohio Acad. Trial Attys. (chmn. products liability sect. 1987-89, trustee 1990—), Ohio Bar Assn., Cleve. Acad. Trial Attys. (bd. dirs. 1988—, v.p. 1990—), Greater Cleve. Bar Assn., Attys. Info. Exch. Group. Personal injury, Federal civil litigation, Product liability. Office: Lowe Eklund Wakefield Co LPA 610 Skylight Office Tower 1660 W 2nd St # 1660 Cleveland OH 44113-1454

**LOWE, JOHN STANLEY,** lawyer, educator; b. Marion, Ohio, May 11, 1941; s. John Floyd and Florence (Andrews) L.; m. Jacquelyn Taft, Jan. 15, 1968; children: Sarah Staley, John Taft. BA, Denison U., 1963; LLB, Harvard U., 1966. Bar: Ohio 1966, Okla. 1980, U.S. Supreme Ct. 1972, Tex. 1989. Adminstrv. officer Govt. of Malawi, Limbe, 1966-69; assoc. Emens, Hurd, Kegler & Ritter, Columbus, Ohio, 1970-75; assoc. prof. law U. Toledo, Ohio, 1975-78; prof. law U. Tulsa, 1978-87, So. Meth. U., Dallas, 1987—; vis. prof. U. Tex., Austin, 1983; disting. vis. prof. natural resources law U. Denver, 1987; disting. vis. prof. U. N.Mex., 1996. Author: Oil and Gas Law in a Nutshell, 1983, 3d edit., 1995; editor: Cases and Materials on Oil and Gas Law, 1986, 3d edit., 1998; editor Internat. Petroleum Transactions, 1993, others. Trustee, sec., mem. exec. com. Rocky Mountain Mineral Law Found.. Recipient Outstanding Law Rev. Article award Tex. Bar Found., 1988, 96. Mem. ABA (chair natural resources, energy and environ. law 1992-93), Am. Arbitration Assn. (nat. energy panel), Southwest Legal Found. (treas., mem. exec. com. adv. bd. Internat. Oil and Gas Edn. Ctr.). Episcopalian. Avocation: sailing. Home: 3526 Greenbrier Dr Dallas TX 75225-5003 Office: So Meth U 3315 Daniel Ave Dallas TX 75275-0001

**LOWE, LOUIS ROBERT, JR.,** lawyer; b. Indpls., May 30, 1937. BSCE, Purdue U., 1959; LLD, Ind. U., 1967. Bar: U.S. Dist. Ct. (so. dist.) Ind. 1967, U.S. Tax Ct. 1977; lic. profl. engr. Engr. Clyde Williams and Assocs., Indpls., 1960-64, Ind. Hwy Needs Study, Indpls., 1966-67; ptnr. Lowe, Gray, Steele & Darko, Indpls., 1967—. Contbr. articles to profl. jours. Sec. English Speaking Union, Indpls., 1967—; trustee Hanover Coll.; elder Second Presbyn. Ch. Fellow Indpls. Bar Found.; mem. Ind. Bar Assn., Purdue U. Alumni Assn., Indpls. Purdue Assn. (pres. 1968-69), Contemporary Club (pres. 1986-87), Columbia Club (bd. dirs. 1993-96), Columbia Club Found. (pres. 1995-97), Gyro Club (bd. dirs. 1982-85). Securities, Construction, Probate. Home: 535 Pine Dr Indianapolis IN 46260-1452 Office: Bank One Tower Ste 4600 Indianapolis IN 46204-5146

**LOWE, MARY JOHNSON,** federal judge; b. N.Y.C., June 10, 1924; m. Ivan A. Michael, Nov. 4, 1961; children: Edward H. Lowe, Leslie H. Lowe, Bess J. Michael. BA, Hunter Coll., 1952; LLB, Bklyn. Law Sch., 1954; LLM, Columbia U., 1955; LLD, CUNY, 1990. Bar: N.Y. 1955. Pvt. practice law N.Y.C., 1955-71; judge N.Y.C. Criminal Ct., 1971-72; acting justice N.Y. State Supreme Ct., 1972-74; judge Bronx County Supreme Ct., 1974; justice N.Y. State Supreme Ct., 1977, 1st Jud. Dist., 1978; judge U.S. Dist. Ct. (so. dist.) N.Y., 1978-91, sr. judge, 1991—. Recipient award for outstanding service to criminal justice system Bronx County Criminal Cts. Bar Assn., 1974, award for work on narcotics cases Asst. Dist. Attys., 1974. Mem. Women in Criminal Justice, Harlem Lawyers Assn., Bronx Criminal Lawyers Assn., N.Y. County Lawyers Assn., Bronx County Bar Assn., N.Y. State Bar Assn. (award for outstanding jud. contbn. to criminal justice Sect. Criminal Justice 1978), NAACP, Nat. Urban League, Nat. Council Negro Women, NOW. Office: US Dist Ct 40 Foley Sq New York NY 10007-1502

**LOWE, RALPH EDWARD,** lawyer; b. Hinsdale, Ill., Nov. 24, 1931; s. Charles Russell and Eva Eleanor (Schroeder) L.; m. Patricia E. Eichhorst, Aug. 23, 1952; children: John Stuart, Michael Kevin, Timothy Edward. BA, Depauw U., 1953; LLB, U. Ill., 1956. Bar: Ill. 1956, U.S. Dist. Ct. (no. dist.) Ill. 1957, Ga. 1974, U.S. Dist. Ct. (no. dist.) Ga. 1980, S.C. 1990. Assoc. Ruddy & Brown, Aurora, Ill., 1956-58; ptnr. Lowe & Richards, Aurora, 1959-62, Vincent, Lowe & Richards, Aurora, 1963-71; pvt. practice, Aurora and Atlanta, 1974-85; prin. Lowe & Steinmetz, Ltd., Aurora and Atlanta, 1985-91; pvt. practice, Aurora, Ill., 1972-74, 92—; chmn. Inter-Am. Devel. Corp., Ill., 1965-67. Real property, Administrative and regulatory, Probate. Office: 407 W Galena Blvd Aurora IL 60506-3946

**LOWE, ROBERT CHARLES,** lawyer; b. New Orleans, July 3, 1949; s. Carl Randall and Antonia (Morgan) L.; m. Theresa Louise Acree, Feb. 4, 1978. 1 child, Nicholas Stafford. BA, U. New Orleans, 1971; JD, La. State U., 1975. Bar: La. 1975, U.S. Dist. Ct. (ea. dist.) La. 1975, U.S. Ct. Appeals (5th cir.) 1980, U.S. Dist. Ct. (we. dist.) La. 1978, U.S. Supreme Ct. 1982. Assoc. Sessions, Fishman, Rosenson, Boisfontaine, and Nathan, New Orleans, 1975-80, ptnr., 1980-87; ptnr. Lowe, Stein, Hoffman, Allweiss and Hauver, 1987—. Author: Louisiana Divorce, 1984; mem. La. Law Rev., 1974-75; contbr. articles to profl. jours. Mem. ABA, La. State Bar Assn. (chmn. family law sect. 1984-85), La. Assn. Def. Counsel, New Orleans Bar Assn. (chmn. family law sect. 1991-92), La. State Law Inst., La. Trial Lawyers Assn., Order of Coif, Phi Kappa Phi. Republican. State civil litigation, Family and matrimonial, General practice. Home: 9625 Garden Oak Ln River Ridge LA 70123-2005 Office: 701 Poydras St Ste 3600 New Orleans LA 70139-7735

**LOWE, ROBERT STANLEY,** lawyer; b. Herman, Nebr., Apr. 23, 1923; s. Stanley Robert and Ann Marguerite (Feese) L.; m. Anne Kirtland Selden, Dec. 19, 1959; children: Robert James, Margaret Anne. AB, U. Nebr., 1947, JD, 1949. Bar: Wyo. 1949. Ptnr. McAvoy & Lowe, Newcastle, 1949-51, Hickey & Lowe, Rawlins, 1951-55; county and pros. atty. Rawlins, 1955-59, pvt. practice, 1959-67; assoc. dir. Am. Judicature Soc., Chgo., 1967-74; gen. counsel True Oil Co. and affiliates, 1974-98, of counsel, 1998-99; bd. dirs. Hilltop Nat. Bank, Casper, sec., 1981—; legal adv. divsn. Nat. Ski Patrol Sys., 1975-88; city atty. City of Rawlins, 1963-65; atty., asst. sec. Casper Mountain Ski Patrol, 1988—. Chmn. Casper C. of C. Military Affairs Com., 1995—; mem. Wyo. Ho. of Reps., 1952-54; bd. dirs. Vols. in Probation, 1969-82; leader lawyer del. to China, People to People, 1986; mem. Wyo. Vets. Affairs Commn., 1994—, chmn., 1996—; mem. legis. com. United Vets. Coun. Wyo., 1993—; trustee Troopers Found., Inc., 1994—, pres., 1994—; pres. Casper WWII Commemorative Assn., 1995-96, Navy League Wyo. Coun. (pres. 1997—). Recipient Dedicated Community Worker award Rawlins Jr. C. of C., 1967, Yellow merit star award Nat. Ski Patrol System, 1982, 85, 87, 88, Small Bus. Administrate Vet. Advocate award, 1998, Disting. Svc. award Disabled Am. Vets. Dept., 1994. Fellow Am. Bar Found. (life); mem. VFW (life mem.; post adv. 1991-96, nat. aide-de-camp 1993-94, 98-99, judge adv. dist. 3 Dept. Wyo., 1994—, mil. order of cootie grand judge adv. 1994—), ABA (sec. jud. adminstrn. divsn. lawyers conf., exec. com. 1975-76, chmn. 1977-78, chmn. judicial qualification and selection com. 1986-93, coun. jud. adminstrn. divsn. 1977-78, mem. com. to implement jud. adminstrn. stds. 1978-83, Ho. of Dels. state bar del. 1978-80, 86-87, state del. 1987-93, Assembly del. 1980-83, mem. standing com. on the fed. judiciary 1997-99, ad hoc com. state justice initiatives 1997-99), Am. Judicature Soc. (dir. 1961-67, 85-89, bd. editors 1975-77, Herbert Harley award 1974), Wyo. State Bar (chmn. com. on cts. 1961-67, 77-87), Nebr. State Bar Assn., Ill. State Bar Assn., D.C. Bar, Inter-Am. Bar Assn., Selden Soc., Inst. Jud. Adminstrn., Rocky Mountain Oil and Gas Assn. (legal com. 1976-99, chmn. 1979-82, 90-91), Rocky Mountain Mineral Law Found. (trustee 1980-94), Am. Law Inst. (life), Order of Coif, Delta Theta Phi (dist. chancellor 1982-83, chief justice 1983-93, assoc. justice 1993—; Percy J. Power Meml. award 1983, Gold Medallion award 1990), Casper Rotary Club (pres. 1985-86), Casper Rotary Found. (dir., sec. 1990—). Mem. Ch. of Christ, Scientist. Banking, General corporate, Oil, gas, and mineral. Home and Office: 97 Primrose Casper WY 82604-4018 Office: 5905 CY Avenue Casper WY 82604

**LOWE, ROY GOINS,** lawyer; b. Lake Worth, Fla., Apr. 8, 1926; s. Roy Sereno and May (Goins) L.; A.B., U. Kans., 1948, LL.B., 1951. Admitted to Kans. bar, 1951; gen. practice, Olathe, 1951—; mem. firm Lowe, Farmer, Bacon & Roe and predecessor, 1951—. Served with USNR, 1944-46. Mem. Bar Assn. State Kans., Johnson County Bar Assn., Am. Legion, Phi Alpha Delta, Sigma Nu. Republican. Presbyn. Probate, Oil, gas, and mineral, Real property. Home: 701 W Park St Olathe KS 66061-3137 Office: Colonial Bldg Olathe KS 66061

**LOWELL, H. BRET,** lawyer; b. N.Y., Aug. 5, 1953; s. Stanley and Elaine Lowell; m. Holly Ross, June 20, 1982; 1 child, Michael Stuart. BS in Econs., SUNY, Buffalo, 1975; JD, Georgetown U., 1978. Bar: D.C. 1978, U.S. Dist. Ct. D.C. 1979, U.S. Ct. Appeals (D.C. cir.) 1979. Assoc. Brownstein Zeidman and Lore, Washington, 1978-85; ptnr. Brownstein & Zeidman, Washington, 1985-96, Rudnick & Wolfe, Washington, 1996—. Author: Regulation of Buying and Selling a Franchise, 1983, 1997, Franchising, 1989, Franchise Sales and Full Agreement Compliance, 1990, Multiple-Unit Franchising: The Key to Rapid System Growth, 1991; coord. (book) Survey of Foreign Laws Affecting International Franchising, 1982; editor Franchise Law Jour., 1984-88. Mem. ABA (forum on franchising, governing com. 1988-97, chair 1992-95, gen. practice sect., co-chair franchise law com. 1989-92), Internat. Bar Assn., N.Am. Securities Adminstrs. Assn. (franchise advisor 1989—). Franchising, Contracts commercial, Trademark and copyright. Office: Rudnick & Wolfe Penthouse Ste 1201 New York Ave NW Washington DC 20005-3917

**LOWELL, ROLAND M.,** lawyer; b. Three Rivers, Mich.; m. Ruby Ellon Lowell. BA, Kalamazoo Coll., 1969; JD, Vanderbilt U., 1972. Bar: Tenn. 1972, U.S. Ct. Appeals (6th cir.) 1975, U.S. Supreme Ct. 1976, U.S. Dist. Ct. (mid. dist.) Tenn. 1984, U.S. Dist. Ct. (we. dist.) Tenn. 1992. Ptnr. Ludwick & Lowell, Nashville, 1984-87, Lowell & Bradley, Nashville, 1987-91; atty., of counsel Leitner Warner Moffitt Dooley Carpender & Napolitan, Nashville, 1991-95; atty. Bruce Weathers Corley Dughman & Lyle, Nashville, 1995—. Mem. Am. Moving and Storage Assn. (agt.), Am. Process Agts. (agt.). Transportation, General civil litigation, General corporate. Office: Bruce Weathers Corley et al 20th Fl Ste 2075 First American Center Nashville TN 37238

**LOWENBRAUN, SOLOMON M.,** lawyer; b. N.Y.C., Feb. 1, 1921; s. Harry and Mary L.; m. Florence M. Grossman, Aug. 7, 1945; children: Dale Lowenbraun Boyle, Cathy Lowenbraun McKeon, Leslie Lowenbraun Weitzman. BS in Social Sci., CCNY, 1941; JD, Fordham U., 1949. Bar: N.Y. 1950, U.S. Dist. Ct. (so. dist.) N.Y. 1950, U.S. Dist. Ct. (ea. dist.) N.Y.

1953, U.S. Supreme Ct. 1978. Atty. pvt. practice, N.Y.C., 1950—. Lt. comdr. USNR, 1942-45. Mem. N.Y. State Bar Assn., Queens County Bar Assn. Jewish. General civil litigation, General practice, Personal injury. Home: 16625 Powells Cove Blvd Beechhurst NY 11357-1545 Office: 122 E 42d St New York NY 10168

**LOWENFELS, LEWIS DAVID,** lawyer; b. N.Y.C., June 9, 1935; s. Seymour and Jane (Phillips) L.; m. Fern Gelford, Aug. 15, 1965; children: Joshua, Jacqueline. BA magna cum laude, Harvard U., 1957, LLB, 1961. Bar: N.Y. 1961; lic. corp. and securities atty. Ptnr. Tolins & Lowenfels, N.Y.C., 1967—; adj. prof. Seton Hall U. Law Sch; lectr. Practicing Law Inst., Southwestern Legal Found., U. Minn. Fed. Bar Assn., 1972; pub. gov. Am. Stock Exch., 1993-96. Co-author: Securities Fraud and Commodities Fraud, 6 vols., 1999; contbr. articles to profl. jours. With USAR, 1957-63. Mem. ABA (fed. regulation of securities com. 1978—, lectr.), N.Y. County Lawyers Assn. (securities and exchanges com. 1974—), Phi Beta Kappa, Harvard Club. Avocations: reading, writing, athletics. Securities, General corporate. Office: Tolins & Lowenfels 12 E 49th St New York NY 10017-1028

**LOWENHAUPT, CHARLES ABRAHAM,** lawyer; b. St. Louis, May 19, 1947; s. Henry Cronbach and Cecile (Koven) L.; m. Rosalyn Lee Sussman, Dec. 28, 1969; children: Elizabeth Anne, Rebecca Jane. BA cum laude, Harvard U., 1969; JD magna cum laude, U. Mich., 1973. Bar: Mo. 1973, U.S. Dist. Ct. (ea. dist.) Mo. 1975, U.S. Ct. Appeals (8th cir.) 1975, U.S. Tax Ct. 1975, U.S. Ct. Claims 1975, U.S. Supreme Ct. 1987. Law clk. to presiding justice U.S. Tax Ct., Washington, 1973-75; ptnr. Lowenhaupt, Chasnoff, Armstrong & Mellitz, St. Louis, 1977-94; mem. adv. faculty Inst. for Pvt. Investors, 1991-93; mem. Lowenhaupt & Chasnoff, LLC, St. Louis, 1994—; emeritus mem. adv. faculty Inst. for Pvt. Investors, St. Louis, 1995—; speaker Nat. Assn. Ind. Schs., St. Louis Assn. Legal Assts., Washington U. Bus. Sch., Inst. for Pvt. Investors, numerous others; mem. adv. bd. dirs. Textile Mus., Washington. Bd. dirs. Ctrl. West End Assn., Inc., St. Louis, 1976-80, Temple Emanuel, St. Louis, 1982-89, Butterfly Ho., St. Louis, sec., 1995—; Craft Alliance St. Louis, 1987-90, Helicon Found., San Diego, 1989—, St. Louis Met. Assn. for Philanthropy, 1997—; bd. dirs. St. Louis Regional Med. Ctr. Found., 1993—, chmn. bd. dirs., 1995-98, Crown Ctr., St. Louis sect., Nat. Coun. Jewish Women, 1994-96; bd. dirs. St. Louis Zoo Found., 1993-99, sec., 1995-98; mem. St. Louis Zool. Subdist. commn., 1989-92; bd. govs. Clements Libr. Assocs., U. Mich., 1997—; mem. St. Louis Cmty. Sch. Assn., 1981-89; pres. Assn. St. Louis U. Librs., Inc., 1982-83; mem. exec. com. U.S.-China C. of C. Midwestern Regional Office. Mem. ABA (tax section, estate and gift section, real property section, probate and trust law, task force legal financial planning, chmn. generation-skipping transfer tax subcom., estate and gift tax com. tax sect. 1995—), Mo. Bar Assn. (tax section, probate and trust section), Bar Assn. of Met. St. Louis (tax section, real property and development sect.), Order of the Coif, St. Louis Estate Planning Coun., Mo. Athletic Club, Harvard Club of N.Y.C., Noonday Club, Harvard Club of St. Louis (pres. 1991-92, chmn. schs. and scholarshop com. 1989-91). Estate planning, Estate taxation, Personal income taxation. Home: 801 S Skinker Blvd Saint Louis MO 63105-3228 Office: Lowenhaupt & Chasnoff LLC 10 S Broadway Ste 600 Saint Louis MO 63102-1733

**LOWER, PHILIP EDWARD,** lawyer; b. Parsons, W.Va., Sept. 16, 1949; s. Edward J. and Helen Mae (Kelley) L.; m. Susan Deborah Jacobs, June 4, 1972; children: Shelley Leah, Jeremy Joseph. BS, U.S. Mil. Acad., 1971; JD, U. of the Pacific, 1978; LLM in Environ. Law, George Washington U., 1995; A, Govt. Insts., 1998. Bar: Calif. 1979, U.S. Ct. Mil. Appeals 1981. Commd. 2d lt. U.S. Army, 1971, advanced through grades to lt. col., 1989; chief prosecutor, asst. U.S. atty. U.S. Army, Ft. Meade, Md., 1978-81; dep. chief internat. law U.S. Army in Europe, Heidelberg, Fed. Republic Germany, 1982-85; instr. U.S. Army Command and Gen. Staff Coll., Ft. Leavenworth, Kans., 1985-88; chief. adminstrv. law III Corps, Ft. Hood, Tex., 1988-89; staff judge adv. 1st Cav. Div., Ft. Hood, 1989-90; staff judge advocate 1st Cavalry Div. on Operations Desert Shield/Desert Storm, Saudi Arabia, 1991; legal advisor Nat. Def. U., Ft. McNair, Washington, 1991-94; environ. atty.-advisor Chem. and Biol. Def. Command, Aberdeen Proving Ground, Md., 1994-98; atty.-advisor, program mgr. chem. demilitarization Aberdeen Proving Ground, Edgewood Arsenal, Md., 1999—; ret., 1998. Author: Operational Law, 1987; editor: Military Law, 1985-88; contbr. articles to legal jours. Mem. ABA, FBA, Calif. Bar Assn., Environ. Law Inst., Assn. U.S. Army. Democrat. Jewish. Home: 12607 Brunswick Ln Bowie MD 20715-2214

**LOWERY, TIMOTHY J.,** lawyer; s. Martin B. and Rita Lowery. BA in English Lit., U. Ill., 1982; JD, Ill. Inst. Tech., 1985. Bar: Ill., U.S. Dist. Ct. (no. dist.) Ill., U.S. Ct. Appeals (7th cir.). Owner Lowery & Assocs., LLC, Chgo.; pvt. practice Chgo. Mem. ABA (transp. sect.), Ill. State Bar Assn., Ill. Assn. Def. Trial Counsel, Def. Rsch. Inst. (trucking law subcom.), Trucking Industry Def. Assn. Personal injury, Transportation. Office: Lowery & Assocs 333 W Wacker Dr #680 Chicago IL 60606-1225

**LOWERY, WILLIAM HERBERT,** lawyer; b. Toledo, June 8, 1925; s. Kenneth Alden and Drusilla (Pfanner) L.; m. Carolyn Broadwell, June 27, 1947; children: Kenneth Latham, Marcia Mitchell. PhB, U. Chgo., 1947; JD, U. Mich., 1950. Bar: Pa. 1951, U.S. Supreme Ct. 1955. Assoc. Dechert Price & Rhoads, Phila., 1950-58, ptnr., 1958-89, mng. ptnr., 1970-72; mem. policy com., chmn. litigation dept., 1962-68, 81-84; of counsel Dechert Price & Rhoads, Phila., 1989—; counsel S.S. Huebner Found. Ins. Edn., Phila., 1970-89; faculty Am. Conf. of Legal Execs., Pa. Bar Inst.; permanent mem. com. of visitors U. Mich. Law Sch. Author: Insurance Litigation Problems, 1972, Insurance Litigation Disputes, 1977. Pres. Stafford Civic Assn., 1958; chmn. Tredyffrin Twp. Zoning Bd., Chester County, Pa., 1959-75; bd. dirs. Paoli (Pa.) Meml. Hosp., 1964-89, chmn., 1972-75; bd. dirs. Main Line Health, Radnor, Pa., 1984-89; permanent mem. Jud. Conf. 3d Cir. Ct. Served to 2d lt. USAF, 1943-46. Mem. ABA (chmn. life ins. com. 1984-85, chmn. Nat. Conf. Lawyers and Life Ins. Cos. 1984-88), Order of the Coif, Royal Poinciana Golf Club (bd. dirs. 1997—, sec. 1997—), Phi Gamma Delta, Phi Delta Phi. Insurance, Federal civil litigation, Health. Home: 2777 Gulf Shore Blvd N Apt 4-s Naples FL 34103-4360 Office: Dechert Price & Rhoads 4000 Bell Atlantic Tower 1717 Arch St Ste 3 Philadelphia PA 19103-2793

**LOWES, ALBERT CHARLES,** lawyer; b. Oak Ridge, Mo., Dec. 1, 1932; s. Guy Everett and Lillian Bertina (Tuschhoff) L.; m. Peggy Rae Watson, Aug. 27, 1960; children: Danita Rae, Albert Charles II, Kurt Brandon. Student, Cape State Coll., 1954-56; JD, U. Mo., 1959. Bar: Mo. 1959, U.S. Dist. Ct. (ea. dist.) Mo. 1959, U.S. Ct. Appeals (8th cir.) 1971. With Buerkle, Lowes, Beeson & Ludwig, Jackson, Mo., 1959-84; ptnr. Lowes & Drusch, Cape Girardeau, 1984—; atty. City of Jackson, 1960-62. Staff sgt. USMC, 1950-54, Korea. Mem. ABA, Mo. Bar Assn., Internat. Assn. Ins. Counsel, VFW (judge adv. dept. Mo.1962-64, 67-68, state judge adv. 1997-98), Masons, Shriners, Elks. Democrat. Lutheran. Avocations: reading, history, legal fields. Insurance, Personal injury, Criminal. Office: Lowes & Drusch 2913 Independence St Cape Girardeau MO 63703-8320

**LOWINGER, FREDERICK CHARLES,** lawyer; b. Chgo., July 18, 1955; s. Alexander I. and Muriel (Rosencranz) L.; m. Lynn T. Wollins, July 12, 1981; Lauren, Daniel, Stephen. BS in Acctg., U. Pa., 1977, MS in Acctg., 1977; JD, U. Chgo., 1980. Bar: Ill. 1982. Clk. U.S. Ct. Appeals (D.C. cir.), Washington, 1980-81, U.S. Supreme Ct., Washington, 1981-82; assoc. Sidley & Austin, Chgo., 1982-87, ptnr., 1988—. Dir. Jewish Vocat. Svc., Chgo., 1993-98. Mem. The Law Club. Avocations: golf, skiing. Mergers and acquisitions, General corporate. Office: Sidley & Austin 1 First Natl Plz Chicago IL 60603-2003

**LOWINGER, LAZAR,** lawyer; b. Antwerp, Berchem, Belgium, Nov. 7, 1934; came to U.S., 1954; s. Julius and Maria (Gilburd) L.; m. Audrey Schwelling, Aug. 15, 1965; children—Jeffrey Paul, Brian Marc. Student Boston U., 1956-57, Sir Geo. Williams Coll., 1957-59; J.D., New England Sch. Law, 1962. Bar: Mass. 1964, U.S. Dist. Ct. Mass. 1965. Sole practice, Brookline, Mass., 1964—. Served with U.S. Army, 1954-56. Recipient Mem. of Honour award Cuban Bar in Exile, Miami, Fla., 1971. Mem. Mass. Bar Assn. (chmn.), Assn. Trial Lawyers Am., Mass. Acad. Trial Attys. Clubs: Hazel Hotchkiss Wightman Tennis Ctr. (Weston, Mass.). Fluent in Romanian, Spanish, Italian, Jewish, French. General practice, Criminal, Personal injury. Home: 305 Woodcliff Rd Newton MA 02461-2127 Office: 850 Boylston St Ste 312 Chestnut Hill MA 02467-2402

**LOWN, BRADLEY MERRILL,** lawyer; b. Hartford, Conn., Mar. 18, 1958; children: Frances, Abigail. BA in History, Harvard U., 1981; JD, U. Maine, 1985. Bar: N.H. 1985, Maine 1987. Ptnr. Boynton & Waldron, Portsmouth, N.H., 1993—. Active Portsmouth Sch. Bd., 1989-93; sec. Portsmouth Hist. Soc., 1995—, now pres. Mem. Nat. Trial Lawyers Assn., Harvard Club N.H. (pres. 1996-99). General civil litigation, Real property, Personal injury. Office: Boynton & Waldron 82 Court St Portsmouth NH 03801-4473

**LOWNDES, JOHN FOY,** lawyer; b. Jan. 1, 1931; s. Charles L. B. and Dorothy (Foy) L.; m. Rita Davies, Aug. 18, 1983; children: Elizabeth Anne, Amy Scott, John Patrick, Joseph Edward, Jennifer Susanne. BA, Duke U., 1953, LLB, 1958. Bar: Fla. 1958. Pvt. practice Daytona Beach, Fla., 1958, Orlando, Fla., 1959-69; sr. ptnr., chmn. bd. dirs. Lowndes, Drosdick, Doster, Kantor & Reed, P.A., Orlando, 1969—; mem. dean's adv. coun. Coll. Bus. Adminstrn. U. Cen. Fla.; bd. dirs. First Union Nat. Bank Fla., Fla. Housing Fin. Corp.; mem. Fla. Constl. Rev. Commn., 1998. former chmn. bd. trustees Orlando Mus. Art, Winter Park Meml. Hosp.; bd. visitors Duke U. Capt. USMCR, 1953-55. Republican. Real property, General corporate. Home: 1308 Green Cove Rd Winter Park FL 32789-2549 Office: Lowndes Drosdick Doster Kantor & Reed 215 N Eola Dr Orlando FL 32801-2095

**LOWRY, DAVID BURTON,** lawyer; b. Bronxville, N.Y., Nov. 6, 1943; s. Burton S. and Virginia Evelyn (Ford) L. BA, U. Ariz., 1966, JD, 1969. Bar: Ariz. 1969, Oreg. 1973. Legal aid atty. Tucson and Coolidge, Ariz. and Hillsboro, Oreg.; asst. atty. gen. Oreg.; dep. dist. atty. Marion County, Oreg.; dep. pub. defender Mohave County, Ariz.; pvt. practice Portland, Oreg., 1989—. Mem. Oreg. State Bar Assn., Ariz. State Bar Assn., Am. Mgmt. Assn., Assn. Trial Lawyers Am., Alpha Delta Sigma, Phi Alpha Delta, Alpha Sigma Phi. Republican. Pension, profit-sharing, and employee benefits, Civil rights, Personal injury. Home: 13490 SW Genesis Loop Tigard OR 97223-3959

**LOWRY, DONALD MICHAEL,** retired lawyer; b. Milw., 1929. LLB, Marquette U., 1953, PhB. Bar: Wis. 1953, Ill. 1961. Underwriter CNA Lloyd's of Tex.; sr. v.p., gen. counsel Am. Casualty Co., Reading, Pa., CNA Life & Annuity Co., Continental Assurance Co., Nat. Fire Ins. Co., Hartford, Conn., Transcontinental Ins., Transportation Ins. Co., Valley Forge Ins. Co., Valley Forge Life Ins. Co., Continental Casualty Co. Inc.; v.p., sec. CNA Fin. Corp., 1958-98, ret., 1998. Office: CNA Fin Corp CNA Plaza Chicago IL 60685

**LOWRY, EDWARD FRANCIS, JR.,** lawyer; b. L.A., Aug. 13, 1930; s. Edward Francis and Mary Anita (Woodcock) L.; m. Patricia Ann Palmer, Feb. 16, 1963; children: Edward Palmer, Rachael Louise. Student, Ohio State U., 1948-50; AB, Stanford U., 1952, JD, 1954. Bar: Ariz. 1955, D.C. 1970, U.S. Supreme Ct. 1969. Camp dir. Quarter Circle V Bar Ranch, 1954; tchr. Orme Sch., Mayer, Ariz., 1954-56; trust rep. Valley Nat. Bank Ariz., 1958-60; pvt. practice, Phoenix, 1960—; assoc. atty. Cunningham, Carson & Messinger, 1960-64; ptnr. Carson, Messinger, Elliott, Laughlin & Ragan, 1964-69, 70-80, Gray, Plant, Mooty, Mooty & Bennett, 1981-84, Eaton, Lazarus, Dodge & Lowry Ltd., 1985-86; exec. v.p., gen. counsel Bus. Realty Ariz., 1986-93; pvt. practice, Scottsdale, Ariz., 1986-88; ptnr. Lowry & Froeb, Scottsdale, 1988-89, Lowry, Froeb & Clements, P.C., Scottsdale, 1989-90, Lowry & Clements P.C., Scottsdale, 1990, Lowry, Clements & Powell, P.C., Scottsdale, 1991—; asst. legis. counsel Dept. Interior, Washington, 1969-70; mem. Ariz. Commn. Uniform Laws, 1972—, chmn., 1976-88; judge pro tem Ariz. Ct. Appeals, 1986, 92-94; mem. Nat. Conf. Commrs. on Uniform State Laws, 1972-97, life mem., 1997—. Chmn. Coun. of Stanford Law Socs., 1968; bd. dirs. Scottsdale Prevention Inst., 1999—; vice chmn. bd. trustees Orme Sch., 1972-74, treas., 1981-83; trustee Heard Mus., 1965-91, life trustee, 1991—, pres., 1974-75; bd. visitors Stanford Sch. Law; magistrate Town of Paradise Valley, Ariz., 1976-83, town councilman, 1998—, mayor, 1998—; juvenile ct. referee Maricopa County, 1978-83. Capt. USAF, 1956-58. Fellow Ariz. Bar Found. (founder); mem. ABA, Maricopa County Bar Assn., State Bar Ariz. (chmn. com. uniform laws 1979-85), Stanford Law Soc. Ariz. (past pres.), Scottsdale Bar Assn. (bd. dirs. 1991—, v.p. 1991, pres. 1992-95), Ariz. State U. Law Soc. (bd. dirs.), Delta Sigma Rho, Alpha Tau Omega, Phi Delta Phi. Estate planning, Real property, Probate. Home: 7600 N Moonlight Ln Paradise Valley AZ 85253-2938 Office: Lowry Clements & Powell PC 2901 N Central Ave Ste 1120 Phoenix AZ 85012-2731 also: 6900 E Camelback Rd Ste 1040 Scottsdale AZ 85251-2444

**LOWRY, HOUSTON PUTNAM,** lawyer; b. N.Y.C., Apr. 1, 1955; s. Thomas Clinton Falls and Jean Allen (Day) L.; m. Kathryn Santoro Curtiss. BA, Pitzer Coll., 1976; MBA, U. Conn., 1980; JD cum laude, Gonzaga U., 1980; LLB in Internat. Law, U. Cambridge, Eng., 1981. Bar: Conn. 1980, U.S. Dist. Ct. Conn. 1981, U.S. Tax Ct. 1982, U.S. Ct. Mil. Appeals 1982, U.S. Ct. Appeals (1st, 2d, 5th, 11th cirs.) 1982, U.S. Ct. Claims 1984, D.C. 1985, U.S. Ct. Appeals (4th, 6th, 7th, 9th, fed., D.C. cirs.) 1985, U.S. Ct. Appeals (3d, 8th, 10th cirs.) 1986, U.S. Supreme Ct., N.Y. 1989. Law clk. to Judge William M. Acker, Jr. U.S. Dist. Ct., Birmingham, Ala., 1982-83; assoc. Tarlow, Levy & Droney, Farmington, Conn., 1983-88; prin. Tarlow, Levy & Droney, P.C., Farmington, Conn., 1989-93, Brown & Welsh P.C., Meriden, Conn., 1993—; mem. adj. faculty internat. trade law and internat. comml. arbitration U. Conn. Law Sch., 1990-95; mem. adv. com. internat. law Sec. of State. Fellow Chartered Inst. Arbitrators; mem. ABA (various coms.), Conn. Bar Assn. (various coms.), Am. Soc. Internat. Law, Inter-Am. Bar Assn. (various coms.), Internat. Law Assn., Am. Law Inst., Hon. Soc. Gray's Inn, Hartford Club. General civil litigation, Private international, Contracts commercial. Office: Brown & Welsh PC PO Box 183 530 Preston Ave Meriden CT 06450-4893

**LOWRY, ROBERT DUDLEY,** lawyer; b. Washington, Apr. 12, 1949; s. Robert Newton and Mary (Dudley) L.; m. Becky Jo Kangas, Aug. 3, 1974; children: Samuel Robert, Joseph Houston. BA in Biology, U. Oreg., 1971, postgrad., 1971-73, JD, 1980. Bar: Oreg. 1980, U.S. Dist. Ct. Oreg. 1980, U.S. Claims Ct. 1987, U.S. Supreme Ct. 1991, U.S. Ct. Appeals (9th cir.) 1991, U.S. Ct. Appeals (fed. cir.) 1992. Law clk. Oreg. Supreme Ct., Salem, 1980-81; ptnr. Jaqua & Wheatley, Eugene, 1981-91; prin. Robert D. Lowry, Atty. at Law, Eugene; past chmn. Regional Trauma Adv. Bd., Oreg.; legal counsel Boy Scouts Am., Eugene, 1984—, March of Dimes; past chair Lawyer Reps. to 9th Cir. Jud. Conf., U.S. Cts. Dist. Oreg.; vice chair Lawyers Reps. Jud. Conf. U.S. Cts. for 9th Cir. Mem. ABA (chmn. joint state med.-legal com. 1988-89), ATLA, Lane County Bar Assn. (chmn. fed. ct. com. 1985-88, med. legal com. 1986-87), Oreg. Assn. Def. Counsel, Def. Rsch. Inst., Nat. Health Lawyers Assn., Phi Delta Phi. Democrat. Episcopalian. Insurance, Health, Federal civil litigation. Home: 2875 Emerald St Eugene OR 97403-2504 Office: PO Box 12010 975 Oak St Ste 790 Eugene OR 97401-3121

**LOWTHER, CHARLES MICHAEL,** lawyer; b. Detroit, Apr. 7, 1945; s. Russell J. and Ruth Jean (Herweyer) L.; m. Dianna Jean Clarke, Mar. 23, 1974; children: Lisa M., Charles M., Joseph R., Robert C., Michael-Paul. BA, Mich. State U., 1967; JD, Wayne State U., 1971, LLM, 1977. Bar: Mich. 1971, U.S. Dist. Ct. (ea. dist.) Mich. 1975, U.S. Ct. Appeals (6th cir.) 1975. Asst. prosecutor Oakland County, Pontiac, Mich., 1971-73; asst. city atty. City of Royal Oak (Mich.), 1973-78, city atty., 1982-91; asst. corp. counsel Bank of the Commonwealth, Detroit, 1977-78; assoc. Jenkins & Nystrom, Southfield, Mich., 1978-82, Brian Smith & Assocs., Troy, Mich., 1991-92; ptnr. Lowther & Schneider, Southfield, 1992—; city atty. City of Romulus, Mich., 1978-82, City of Berkeley, 1995—. Contbr. articles to profl. jours. Chmn. Oakland County Mcpl. Law Commn., Pontiac, 1989-90. Mem. Mich. Bar Assn. (chmn. pub. corp. sect. 1991—), Oakland County Bar Assn. (employment law com. 1992—), South Oakland Bar Assn. Roman Catholic. Labor, Municipal (including bonds). Home: 1846 Oakshire Ave Berkley MI 48072-1283 Office: Lowther & Schneider 28575 Greenfield Rd Ste 201 Southfield MI 48076-7158

**LOWTHER, PATRICK ALAN,** lawyer; b. Winona, Minn., Oct. 20, 1951; s. Myron Roy and Elizabeth Frie L.; m. Robin Walz, 1973 (div. 1975); m. Michal M. Anderson, Sept. 27, 1977; children: Emily, Alison, Ian. BA in Polit. Sci., Winona State U., 1976; JD, William Mitchell Coll. Law, 1980. Bar: Minn. 1980, U.S. Dist. Ct. Minn. 1982, U.S. Supreme Ct. 1987. Assoc., asst. city atty. Hauser & Schmid, Sleepy Eye, Minn., 1981-83; assoc. Parris Law Offices, Hector, Minn., 1983-85; sr. ptnr. Meuller, Lowther & Vickery, Sleepy Eye, 1985-99, Pat Lowther Law Firm, PLC, Sleepy Eye, 1999—, Mueller-Lowther Law Firm, New Ulm, Minn., 1999—. Mem. Ch. coun. Trinity Luth. Ch., Sleepy Eye, 1986-98; basketball coach Sleepy Eye Elem. Sch., 1992—. Mem. Minn. State Bar Assn. (cert. civil trial specialist, mock trial judge/atty. coach 1991—). Avocation: tae kwon do (2d degree black belt), fast pitch softball. Fax: 507-794-3400. E-mail: lowtherp@prairie.lakes.com. Family and matrimonial, Personal injury, Real property. Office: Mueller-Lowther Law Firm PLC 512 2nd St N New Ulm MN 56073-1745 also: Pat Lowther Law Firm PLC 134 2nd Ave SE Sleepy Eye MN 56085-1604

**LOWTHER, THOMAS EDWARD,** lawyer; b. St. Louis, Aug. 14, 1936; s. Noel Edward and Catherine Virginia (Polliham) L.; m. Lois Duggins, Dec. 28, 1963; children: Nancy, Sandra, Patricia, Susan. LLB, Wash. U., St. Louis, 1962. Bar: Mo. 1962. Assoc. The Stolar Partnership, St. Louis, 1962, ptnr., 1967—. Recipient Disting. Alumnus award Washington U. Sch. Law, 1997. Avocations: travel, trout fishing. General corporate, Finance, Contracts commercial. Office: The Stolar Partnership 911 Washington Ave Ste 7 Saint Louis MO 63101-1243

**LOYD, WARD EUGENE,** lawyer, state legislator; b. Henderson, Ky., Feb. 8, 1943; s. Ward Beecher Loyd and Maxine Watkins; m. Suzanne Keeler, Dec. 29, 1966; children: Katherine Marie, Keele Suzanne. BA, Southwestern Coll., 1965; JD with honors, Washburn U., 1968. Bar: Kans. 1968, U.S. Dist. Ct. Kans. 1968, U.S. Ct. Appeals (10th cir.) 1969. Pvt. practice, Garden City, Kans., 1968—; mem. Kans. Ho. of Reps., 1998—; gen. counsel Garden City Urban Renewal Agy., 1969-75, Garden City Pub. Sch. Sys., 1972-91, Garden City C.C., 1971—, S.W. Kans. Area Cooperative, Ensign, 1995—; mem. Kans. Supreme Ct. Stds. Com., Topeka, 1980; bd. dirs. Western State Bank, Garden City. Comments editor Washburn Law Jour., 1967-68. City commr. City of Garden City, 1985-89, 90-94, 97, mayor, 1986, 88; mem. Cmty. Congl. Ch. Garden City; past bd. mem., past pres. Cmty. Day Care Ctr.; past mem. Kans. League Municipalities. Recipient Award of Merit, Garden City Area C. of C., 1992. Fellow Kans. Bar Found.; mem. Nat. Assn. Sch. Bds. (coun. sch. attys.), Kans. Bar Assn. (mem. ethics com. 1978-82), S.W. Kans. Bar Assn. (pres. 1986-88, sec. 1992-93, dir.), Kans. Sch. Attys. Assn. (regional dir. 1980-84), Kans. Assn. Def. Counsel, Finney County Bar Assn., Garden City C. of C. (bd. dirs. 1990-92), Phi Alpha Delta (justice 1968). Republican. General practice, General civil litigation, Education and schools. Home: 1304 Cloud Cir Garden City KS 67846-3525 Office: Loyd & Maudlin Law Office LLC PO Box 834 118 W Pine St Garden City KS 67846-5444

**LOZANO, RUDOLPHO,** federal judge; b. 1942. BS in Bus., Ind. U., 1963, LLB, 1966. Mem. firm Spangler, Jennings, Spangler & Dougherty. P.C., Merrillville, Ind., 1966-88; judge U.S. Dist. Ct. (no. dist.) Ind., Hammond, 1988—. With USAR, 1966-73. Mem. ABA, Ind. State Bar Assn., Def. Rsch. Inst. Office: US Dist Ct 205 Fed Bldg 507 State St Hammond IN 46320-1503

**LUBBEN, DAVID J.,** lawyer; b. Cedar Rapids, Iowa, 1951. BA, Luther Coll., 1974; JD, U. Iowa, 1977. Bar: Minn. 1977. Ptnr. Dorsey & Whitney, Mpls., to 1993; gen. counsel UnitedHealth Group, Minnetonka, Minn., 1993—. General corporate, Securities. Office: UnitedHealth Group 9900 Bren Rd E Minnetonka MN 55343-9664*

**LUBER, THOMAS J(ULIAN),** lawyer; b. Louisville, Feb. 16, 1949; s. John J. and Martha E. (Cotton) L.; m. Dorothy Ann Carter, Dec. 19, 1975; children: Katharine Ann, Allison Julia. BS in Acctg., U. Louisville, 1972, JD with honors, 1976; LLM in Taxation, NYU, 1977. Bar: Ky. 1976. Agt. IRS, Louisville, 1972-73; assoc. Fahey & Gray, Louisville, 1977-79; from assoc. to ptnr. Wyatt, Tarrant & Combs and predecessor firms, Louisville, 1979—, chmn. tax sect., 1983—; lectr. U. Louisville, 1978-80; speaker in field; bd. advisors Jour. Multistate Taxation. Contbr. articles to profl. jours. Bd. dirs. Univ. Pediatrics Found., Louisville, Univ. Ob-gyn. Found., Louisville, Assumption High Sch., Louisville. With USAF, 1967-69. Mem. ABA, Ky. Bar Assn. (chmn. tax sect. 1983-84), Louisville Bar Assn., Ky. Inst. Fed. Taxation (mem. planning com. 1981—, chmn. 1984—), Jefferson Club, Big Spring Country Club. Democrat. Roman Catholic. Avocations: hiking, working out. Taxation, general, State and local taxation, General corporate. Home: 2324 Saratoga Dr Louisville KY 40205-2021 Office: Wyatt Tarrant & Combs 2800 Citizens Plz Louisville KY 40202-2898

**LUBERDA, GEORGE JOSEPH,** lawyer, educator; b. N.Y.C., Apr. 27, 1930; s. Joseph George and Mary Loretta (Koslowski) L. Bar: D.C. 1959, U.S. Ct. Appeals (D.C. cir.) 1959, Mich. 1970, Mo. 1973. Washington rep. Ford Motor Co., Washington, 1955-59; atty. FTC, Washington, 1960-64; trial atty. Antitrust Div. Dept. Justice, Washington, 1965-69; sr. atty. Bendix Corp., Mich., 1970-71; assoc. Butzel, Long, Gust, Klein & Van Zile, Detroit, 1972; antitrust counsel Monsanto Co., St. Louis, 1973-88; assoc. Herzog, Crebs and McGhee, 1988-93; ptnr. Luberda & Carp, St. Louis, 1993—; adj. prof. St. Louis U., 1985-96. Mem. Mo. Bar Assn., Bar Assn. Met. St. Louis. Republican. Roman Catholic. Antitrust, General civil litigation, General corporate. Home: 716 Ridgeview Circle Ln Ballwin MO 63021-7810 Office: Luberda & Carp 225 S Meramec Ave Ste 325 Saint Louis MO 63105-3511

**LUBIN, DONALD G.,** lawyer; b. N.Y.C., Jan. 10, 1934; s. Harry and Edith (Tannenbaum) L.; m. Amy Schwartz, Feb. 2, 1956; children: Peter, Richard, Thomas, Alice Lubin Spahr. BS in Econs., U. Pa., 1954; LLB, Harvard U., 1957. Bar: Ill. 1957. Ptnr. Sonnenschein Nath & Rosenthal, Chgo., 1957—, chmn. exec. com., 1991-96; bd. dirs., mem. exec. com. McDonald's Corp., Molex, Inc., Daubert Industries Inc., Charles Levy Co., Tennis Corp. Am. Former mem. Navy Pier Redevel. Corp., Highland Park Cultural Arts Commn.; life trustee, former chmn. bd. Highland Park Hosp., Ravinia Festival Assn.; trustee, mem. exec. com. Rush-Presbyn.-St. Luke's Med. Ctr.; life trustee Chgo. Symphony Orch.; bd. dirs., v.p. Ronald McDonald House Charities, Inc., Chgo. Found. for Edn.; former dir. Smithsonian Inst., Washington; pres., bd. dir. The Barr Fund; former bd. dirs., v.p., sec. Ragdale Found.; bd. govs. Art Inst. Chgo., Chgo. Lighthouse for the Blind; mem. citizens bd. U. Chgo.; mem. coun. Children's Meml. Hosp.; former bd. overseers Coll. Arts and Sci., U. Pa.; dir. Nat. Mus. Am. History, Washington. Woodrow Wilson vis. fellow. Fellow Am. Bar Found., Ill. Bar Found., Chgo. Bar Found.; mem. ABA, Ill. Bar Assn., Chgo. Bar Assn., Law Club Chgo., Chgo. Hort. Soc. (past bd. dirs.), Econ. Club, Comml. Club (former sec., mem. civic com.), Chgo. Club, Std. Club, Lakeshore Club, Beta Gamma Sigma. General corporate. Home: 2269 Egandale Rd Highland Park IL 60035-2501 Office: Sonnenschein Nath & Rosenthal 233 S Wacker Dr Ste 8000 Chicago IL 60606-6342

**LUBIN, STANLEY,** lawyer; b. Bklyn., May 7, 1941; children: David Christopher, Jessica Nicole; m. Barbara Ann Lubin. AB, U. Mich., 1963, JD with honors, 1966. Bar: D.C. 1967, Mich. 1968, U.S. Ct. Appeals (D.C. cir.) 1967, U.S. Ct. Appeals (6th cir.) 1968, U.S. Supreme Ct. 1970, Ariz. 1972, U.S. Ct. Appeals (9th cir.) 1976, U.S. Ct. Appeals (fed. cir.) 1985. Atty. NLRB, Washington, 1966-68; asst. gen. counsel UAW, Detroit, 1968-72; assoc. Harrison, Myers & Singer, Phoenix, 1972-74, McKendree & Tountas, Phoenix, 1975; ptnr. McKendree & Lubin, Phoenix and Denver, 1975-84; shareholder Treon, Warnicke & Roush, P.A., 1984-86; pvt. practice, Law Offices Stanley Lubin, Phoenix, 1986-95, The Law Offices of Stanley Lubin, P.C., 1996-98, Lubin & Enoch, P.C., 1999—; mem. Ariz. Employment Security Adv. Coun., 1975-77. Active ACLU, dir. Ariz. chpt. 1974-81; mem. Ariz. State Cen. Com. Dem. Party, 1973-78, 84—; vice-chmn. Ariz. State Dem. Party, 1986-91, 1993-99, sec., 1991-92, mem. state exec. com., 1986-99, Ariz. Dem. Coun., 1987-99, chmn., 1988-93, Thomas Jefferson Forum, 1987—, chmn. 1988-93. Mem. ABA, State Bar Ariz., Maricopa County Bar Assn., Indsl. Rels. Rsch. Assn., Ariz. Indsl. Rels. Assn. (exec. bd. 1973—, pres. 1979-80, 84). Club: University. Co-author: Union Fines and Union Discipline Under the National Labor Relations Act, 1971. Labor, Entertainment, Administrative and regulatory. Home: 7520 N 9th Pl Phoenix AZ 85020-4138 Office: 2702 N 3rd St Ste 3020 Phoenix AZ 85004-4607

**LUCAS, CRAIG JOHN,** lawyer; b. Ogden, Utah, Mar. 15, 1962; s. Frank James and Joan (Christensen) L. BS, Weber State U., 1985; JD, U. Idaho, 1988. Bar: Nev. 1989, D.C. 1992, U.S. Dist. Ct. Nev. 1990, U.S. Ct. Appeals (9th cir.) 1990. Legis. intern Utah House Majority Leader, Salt Lake City, 1984; Congl. intern U.S. Senate, Washington, 1984; legal intern Idaho Prosecuting Atty. Assn., Boise, 1987; law clk. to Hon. Miriam Shearing 8th Dist. Ct., Las Vegas, 1988-90; from assoc. gen. counsel to chief assoc. counsel State Indsl. Ins. System, Las Vegas, 1990-91; pvt. practice Las Vegas, 1992—. Ctrl. com. mem. Rep. Party, Clark County, Nev., 1990-92, conv. del., 1990. Mem. Federalist Soc., Nev. Trial Lawyers Assn. Church of Jesus Christ of Latter-day Saints. Avocations: travel, hiking, skiing. Personal injury, Workers' compensation. Office: 715 S 4th St Las Vegas NV 89101-6706

**LUCAS, ROBERT FRANK,** lawyer; b. Beacon Falls, Conn., Nov. 11, 1935; s. Otto F. and A. Helen (Schuster) L.; m. Regina Abbiati, July 16, 1960; children: Robert Frank Jr., David R., Jennifer J. AB, Bates Coll., Lewiston, Maine, 1956; JD, Boston U., 1959. Bar: Mass. 1960, U.S. Dist. Ct. Mass. 1962, U.S. Supreme Ct. 1973. Trial atty. Boston Legal Aid Soc., 1960-63; prin. Nigro, Pettepit & Lucas, Wakefield, Mass., 1963—; mem. standing list of masters Mass. Superior Ct., Cambridge, 1979—. Chmn. City of Melrose (Mass.) Bd. of Appeals, 1982—; trustee Melrose High Sch. Permanent Scholarship Fund, 1979—; lay leader 1st United Meth. Ch., Melrose, 1979-82; active Rep. City Com., Melrose, 1980-84. Sgt. USAR, 1959-63. Mem. ABA, Mass. Bar Assn. (bd. dels. 1980-83, exec. com. 1993, chmn. fee arbitration bd. 1983-84, 20th Century Club 1985, Cert. of Appreciation 1988, Community Svc. award 1989), Middlesex County Bar Assn. (bd. dirs. 1986—), 1st Dist. Ea. Middlesex Bar Assn. (pres. 1987-88), Bellevue Golf Club, Masons (dist. dep. grand master 1982-83). Avocations: music, choral singing, youth sports. General civil litigation, Personal injury, Probate. Home: 20 Pilgrim Rd Melrose MA 02176-3019 Office: Nigro Pettepit & Lucas 649 Main St Wakefield MA 01880-5216

**LUCAS, ROBERT MARK,** lawyer; b. Lebanon, Pa., Sept. 9, 1959; s. Robert Lee and Elizabeth Anne (Frymyer) L.; m. Anna Frances Pena, Oct. 1, 1988; children: Kyle Scott, Dorothy Elizabeth, Anna Christine. BA, U. Del., 1981; JD, U. Va., 1984. Bar: Pa. 1984, U.S. Dist. Ct. (we. dist.) Pa. 1984. Assoc. Eckert Seamans Cherin & Mellott, Pitts., 1984-85, Cohen & Grigsby, Pitts., 1985-89, Kirkpatrick & Lockhart, Pitts., 1989-92; environ. counsel Beazer East, Inc., Pitts., 1993-98; gen. counsel, sec. Union Switch and Signal, Inc., Pitts., 1998—. Soccer coach Upper St. Clair Athletic Assn., 1997—; Big Brave YMCA Indian guides and Indian princesses programs. Mem. Am. Corp. Counsel Assn., Pa. Bar Assn. Democrat. Roman Catholic. General practice, Contracts commercial. Office: Union Switch & Signal Inc 1000 Technology Dr Pittsburgh PA 15219-3104

**LUCAS, STEVEN MITCHELL,** lawyer; b. Ada, Okla., Jan. 19, 1948; s. John Dalton and Cherrye (Smith) L.; m. Lori E. Seeberger; children: Steven Turner, Brooke Elizabeth, Sarah Grace. BA, Yale U., 1970; JD, Vanderbilt U., 1973. Bar: D.C. 1973, U.S. Ct. Mil. Appeals 1974, U.S. Dist. Ct. D.C. 1979, U.S. Ct. Appeals (D.C.) 1979, U.S. Supreme Ct. 1979. Assoc. Shaw, Pittman, Potts & Trowbridge, Washington, 1978-82, ptnr., 1983-92; ptnr., head fin. instns. practice Wiley, Rein & Fielding, Washington, 1992-93, Winston & Strawn, Washington, 1993-97; pvt. practice Washington, 1997—; cons. on internat. rels., Rockefeller Found., N.Y.C., 1978, mem. negotiating team Panama Canal Treaty, Washington, 1975-77, legal adviser Dept. Def. Panama Canal negotiations working group. Editor in chief Vanderbilt U. Jour. Transnational Law, 1972-73. Capt. JAGC, U.S. Army, 1974-77. Mem. ABA, FBA (chmn. internat. law com. 1978-80, Outstanding Com. Chmn. award 1979), Inter-Am. Bar Assn., Am. Soc. Internat. Law, Army-Navy Country Club (Arlington, Va.), Yale Club (N.Y.C.), Army and Navy Club (Washington). Republican. Episcopalian. Banking, Private international, Securities. Home: 1001 Jigger Ct Annapolis MD 21401-6832 Office: 1730 K St NW Ste 304 Washington DC 20006-3839

**LUCCHESE, DAVID ROSS,** lawyer; b. San Jose, Calif., July 25, 1944; s. Salvador Francis and Natalie (Ross) L.; m. Joan. M. Lucchese, Feb. 28, 1987; children: Jon, Ben, Sevda, Elise. BA, U. Calif., Berkeley, 1966; JD, U. Calif., Davis, 1969. Bar: Calif. 1972, U.S. Dist. Ct. (no. dist.) Calif. 1972, U.S. Ct. Appeals (9th cir.) 1972. Cons. Assembly Majority Cons., Sacramento, 1969-71; adminstrv. asst. Sen. Peter Behr, Sacramento, 1971-72; dep. dist. atty. Alameda County Dist. Attys. Office, Oakland, Calif., 1972-75; sr. ptnr. Anderson, Galloway & Lucchese, Inc., Walnut Creek, Calif., 1975—. Mem. Am. Bd. Trial Advocates, No. Calif. Assn. Def. Counsel (bd. dirs. 1992-93), Def. Rsch. Inst., Calif. Med.-Legal Com. General civil litigation, Personal injury, Professional liability. Home: 1718 Rockspring Pl Walnut Creek CA 94596-6164 Office: Anderson Galloway & Lucchese 1676 N California Blvd Ste 500 Walnut Creek CA 94596-4183

**LUCCHESI, LIONEL LOUIS,** lawyer; b. St. Louis, Sept. 17, 1939; s. Lionel Louis and Theresa Lucchesi; m. Mary Ann Wheeler, July 30, 1966; children: Lionel Louis III, Marisa Pilar. BSEE, Ill. Inst. Tech., 1961; JD, St. Louis U., 1969. Bar: Mo. 1969. With Emerson Electric Co., 1965-69; assoc. Polster, Polster & Lucchesi, St. Louis, 1969-74, ptnr., 1974—; city atty. City of Ballwin (Mo.), 1979-85, 92—. Alderman City of Ballwin, 1977-79, mem. Zoning Commn., 1971-77. Served to lt. USN, 1961-65. NROTC scholar, 1957-61; recipient Am. Jurisprudence award St. Louis U., 1968-69. Mem. ABA, ATLA, Am. Patent Law Assn., St. Louis Met. Bar Assn., (exec. com., pres.-elect 1984, pres. 1985-86), Newcomen Soc. N.Am., Forest Hills Club, Rotary (pres.-elect St. Louis 1991-92, pres. 1992-93). Republican. Roman Catholic. E-mail: llucches@patpro.com. Patent, Trademark and copyright, Federal civil litigation. Office: 763 S New Ballas Rd Saint Louis MO 63141-8704

**LUCCHI, LEONARD LOUIS,** lawyer; b. Alexandria, Va., Jan. 29, 1958; s. Alvin and Rita (Berman) L.; m. Brenda Lee Beitzell, June 22, 1985. BA, Johns Hopkins U., 1980; JD, U. Md., 1983. Bar: Md. 1983, D.C. 1985, U.S. Dist. Ct. Md. 1984, U.S. Supreme Ct. 1989. Assoc. Wolman Gushee and Newman, Upper Marlboro, Md., 1983-87; ptnr. Wolman and Lucchi, Upper Marlboro, Md., 1988-95; dir. legis. affairs Prince George's County, Md., 1996—. Mem. ATLA, Nat. Assn. County Intergovtl. Rels. Officers, Nat. Italian-Am. Bar Assn., Md. Bar Assn., Md. Trial Lawyers Assn., Md. Criminal Def. Attys. Assn., Prince George's County Bar Assn. (legis. chmn. 1988-95). Legislative, Personal injury, Administrative and regulatory. Home: 12608 Safety Turn Bowie MD 20715-1902 Office: 4000 Mitchellville Rd # 426 Bowie MD 20716-3104

**LUCCHINO, LAWRENCE,** sports team executive, lawyer; b. Pitts., Sept. 6, 1945; s. Dominic A. and Rose (Rizzo) L. A.B. cum laude, Princeton U., 1967; J.D., Yale U., 1972. Bar: Calif. and Pa. 1973, D.C. 1975. Counsel Impeachment Inquiry, House Judiciary Commn., Washington, DC, 1974; assoc. Williams & Connolly, Washington, 1975-79, ptnr., 1979—; sec., bd. dirs., gen. counsel Washington Redskins Football Club, 1978-85; bd. dirs., gen. counsel Balt. Orioles Baseball Club, from 1979, v.p., 1982-88, pres., CEO, 1988-93; CEO San Diego Padres Baseball Club, 1994—; bd. dirs. Army Times, Springfield, Va. Trustee Nat. Found. on Counseling, Princeton, N.J., 1984—; bd. dirs. Nat. Aquarium Natl., Balt. Symphony, Princeton Electronic Bd., Babe Ruth Mus. Mem. ABA. Democrat. Roman Catholic. Office: San Diego Padres PO Box 2000 San Diego CA 92112-2000 also: Williams & Connolly 725 12th St NW Washington DC 20005-3901

**LUCE, GREGORY M.,** lawyer. Bar: D.C., Va., Md. With Jones, Day, Reavis & Pogue, Washington. Mem. ABA, Am. Health Lawyers Assn. (bd. dirs. 1996—), Va. State Bar (past chair, mem. bd. govs. health law sect.). Health, Administrative and regulatory, Federal civil litigation. Office: Jones Day Reavis & Pogue 51 Louisiana Ave NW Washington DC 20001-2113

**LUCERO, CARLOS,** federal judge; b. Antonito, Colo., Nov. 23, 1940; m. Dorothy Stuart; 1 child, Carla. BA, Adams State Coll.; JD, George Washington U., 1964. Law clk. to Judge William E. Doyle U.S. Dist. Ct., Colo., 1964-65; pvt. practice Alamosa, Colo.; sr. ptnr. Lucero, Lester & Sigmund, Alamosa, Colo.; judge U.S. Ct. Appeals (10th cir.), 1995—; mem. Pres. Carter's Presdl. Panel on Western State Water Policy. Bd. dirs. Colo. Hist. Soc., Santa Fe Opera Assn. of N.Mex. Recipient Outstanding Young Man of Colo. award Colo. Jaycees, Disting. Alumnus award George Washington U.; Paul Harris fellow Rotary Found. Fellow Am. Coll. Trial Lawyers, Am. Bar Found., Colo. Bar Found. (pres.), Internat. Acad. Trial Lawyers, Internat. Soc. Barristers; mem. ABA (mem. action com. to reduce ct. cost and delay, mem adv. bd. ABA jour., mem. com. on the availability of legal svcs.), Colo. Bar Assn. (pres. 1977-78, mem. ethics com.), San Luis Valley Bar Assn. (pres.), Nat. Hispanic Bar Assn., Colo. Hispanic Bar Assn. (profl. svc. award), Colo. Rural Legal Svcs. (bd. dirs.), Order of the Coif. Office: US Ct Appeals 1823 Stout St Denver CO 80257-1823

**LUCIANI, THOMAS RICHARD,** lawyer; b. Niagara Falls, N.Y., Apr. 15, 1952; s. Richard Edward and Anne Katherine L.; m. Theresa Ellen O'Brien, May 25, 1984; children: Jon, Tara, Stephanie, Dominic. BA, Columbia U., 1974; JD, Gonzaga U., 1978. Bar: Wash. 1979, U.S. Dist. Ct. (ea. dist.) Wash. 1979, U.S. Ct. Appeals (9th cir.) 1988. Dep. pros. atty. Spokane (Wash.) County Prosecutor, 1979-83; assoc. Underwood--Campbell, Spokane, 1983-85; pvt. practice Spokane, 1985-95; ptnr. Stamper, Rubens, Stocker & Smith, Spokane, 1995—. Mem. Wash. State Trial Lawyers Assn., Wash. State Def. Trial Lawyers. General civil litigation, Insurance, Personal injury. Office: Stamper Rubens Stocker & Smith PS 720 W Boone Ave Ste 200 Spokane WA 99201-2560

**LUCIVERO, LUCRETIA M.,** lawyer; b. Brooklyn, N.Y., Oct. 9, 1962; d. Luigi and Marta (Amato) L. BA, St. Joseph's Coll., 1984; JD, Touro Law Sch., 1987. Bar: N.Y. 1991, U.S. Dist. Ct. (ea. dist.) N.Y. 1991. Pvt. practice Law Offices of Lucretia M. Lucivero, Miller Place, N.Y., 1989—. Mem. Smithtown (N.Y.) Rep. Club, 1995—. Mem. Suffolk County Bar Assn., Columbian Lawyers Assn. Personal injury, Estate planning, Probate. Office: 565 Route 25A Miller Place NY 11764-2600

**LUCKEY, ALWYN HALL,** lawyer; b. Biloxi, Miss., Oct. 3, 1960; s. Toxie Hall and Joy Evelyn (Smith) L.; m. Jeanne Elaine Carter, Aug. 4, 1984; children: Laurel McKay, Taylor Leah. BA in Zoology, U. Miss., 1982, JD, 1985. Bar: Miss. 1985, U.S. Dist. Ct. (so. and no. dist.) Miss. 1985, U.S. Ct. Appeals (5th cir.) 1985. Assoc. Richard F. Scruggs, Pascagoula, Miss., 1985-88; shareholder Richard F. Scruggs, Pascagoula, 1988—, Asbestos Group PA, 1988-93; prin. Alwyn H. Luckey, Atty. at Law, Ocean Springs, Miss., 1993—; v.p., bd. dirs. Marine Mgmt., Inc., Ocean Springs, Miss., 1987—. Author: Mississippi Landlord Tenant Law, 1985. Deacon First Presbyn. Ch., Ocean Springs, 1989; chmn. Dole for Pres. com., Jackson County, 1988. Mem. Am. Trial Lawyers Assn., Miss. Bar Assn., Miss. Trial Lawyers Assn., Jackson County Bar Assn., Jackson County Young Lawyers Assn. (v.p.), Ocean Springs Yacht Club, Bienville Club, Treasure Oak Country Club. Avocations: tennis, boating, traveling. Personal injury, Product liability. Office: PO Box 724 Ocean Springs MS 39566-0724

**LUCKMAN, GREGG A.,** lawyer; b. Manhasset, N.Y., Dec. 26, 1967; s. Jerry and Lesley Luckman; m. Dara Susan Weintraub, May 3, 1998. BA in Polit. Sci., Am. U., 1989; JD, Whittier Coll., 1992; MBA in Fin., Hofstra U., 1995. Bar: N.Y. 1992. Legis. asst. Congressman Robert J. Mrazek, Washington, 1988; law clk. Calif. Dept. Health-Food and Drug Divsn., L.A., 1992; lawyer various firms, N.Y.C., 1993-96; pvt. practice law Great Neck, N.Y., 1996-99; ptnr. Schwartz, Schlussel & Luckman, Great Neck, 1999—. Vol. lawyer Vol. Lawyers for the Arts, N.Y.C., 1996—; mentor W.T. Clarke Middle Sch., Westbury, N.Y., 1997—; spkr. Profl. Spkrs. Bur., Roslyn, N.Y., 1998. Recipient Pro Bono award Vol. Lawyers for the Arts, N.Y.C., 1998. Mem. NARAS, ABA, N.Y. State Bar Assn., Nassau County Bar Assn. (spkr. 1996—). Avocations: golf, tennis. E-mail: gregglaw@aol.com. Fax: 516-829-3993. Entertainment, Real property, General corporate. Office: Ste 306 1010 Northern Blvd Great Neck NY 11021-5306

**LUCYK, GREGORY E.,** lawyer; b. St. Louis, Mar. 6, 1950; s. Elias Alexander and Ann Goldak; m. Eugenia Hardy Hutcheson, Jan. 19, 1991; 1 child, James Gregory. BS in polit. sci., Northeastern U., 1973; JD, Temple U., 1976. Bar: Pa. 1976, Va. 1980, U.S. Supreme Ct. 1985. Law clerk Supreme Ct. Pa., Phila., 1976-77; staff atty. Cmty. Legal Svcs., Phila., 1977-79; mnging. atty. Va. Poverty Law Ctr., Richmond, Va., 1979-84; asst. atty. gen. Office of Atty. Gen., Richmond, Va., 1984-90, sr. asst. atty. gen., 1990-94, sr. asst. atty. gen., chief litigation divsn., 1994—; adj. prof. criminal justice Va. Union U., 1998—; adv. coun. Nat. Legal Svcs., Washington, 1997-98. Editor: Virginia Reporter, 1980-82. Pres. Fan Dist. Tenants' Assn., Richmond, Va., 1981-83; dir. Va. Housing Coal., 1982-84. Avocations: music, British car restoration. Office: Office Atty Gen 900 E Main St Richmond VA 23219-3513

**LUDEMANN, CATHIE JANE,** lawyer; b. Glen Ridge, N.J., Jan. 30, 1948; d. Blair Edward and Marie Elizabeth (Blum) L. BA in Econs., Douglass Coll., 1970; MBA in Fin., Fairleigh Dickinson U., 1975; JD, Seton Hall Law Sch., 1986. Bar: N.J. 1986. Mgmt. positions Prudential Ins. Co., Newark, 1970-83; rsch. asst. Seton Hall Law Sch., Newark, 1983-84; atty. Barry D. Berman, Esq., West Orange, N.J., 1984-87, Sala & Caposela, Esqs., Clifton, N.J., 1987-89; sole practitioner Pompton Plains, N.J., 1989—. Editor Law Sch. Newspaper, 1985-86. Commr., Planning Bd., City of Clifton, 1982-86; commr. bd. of adjustment, Twp. of Pequannock, N.J., 1993; v.p., treas. Richfield Village Tenants Assn., Clifton, 1979-82. Mem. N.J. State Bar Assn. Avocations: antiques and collectibles, book collecting, old movies, Big Band music. Real property, Probate, Elder. Home: 105 Newark Pompton Tpke Bldg C Unit 14 D Pequannock NJ 07440-1638 Office: 287 Boulevard Pompton Plains NJ 07444-1726

**LUDEMANN, DOREEN ANN,** lawyer; b. Oshkosh, Nebr., Oct. 15, 1956; d. Edward Donald and Gwendolyn Margaret Ludemann; m. Clifford Jay Shapiro, June 3, 1990; children: Robert Andrew Shapiro, Amy Elizabeth Shapiro. BA, Creighton U., 1978; postgrad., Friedrich-Wilhelms-U. Bonn, Germany, 1978-79; JD, Columbia U., 1982. Bar: Tex., 1982, Calif., 1985. Assoc. Butler & Binion, Houston, 1982-85, Thelen, Marrin, Johnson & Bridges, San Francisco, 1985-88; atty. Pacific Gas and Electric Co., San Francisco, 1988-98; sr. atty. PG&E Corp., San Francisco, 1998—. Chmn. Rockridge Parks Com., Oakland, Calif., 1993-95; classroom vol. Oakland Pub. Schs., 1996-98, Piedmont (Calif.) Pub. Schs., 1998—. Fulbright scholar Friedrich-Wilhelms-U. Bonn, 1978-79. Mem. Bar Assn. San Francisco. General corporate, Finance. Home: 8 Pala Ave Piedmont CA 94611-3739 Office: PG&E Corp Spear Tower One Market Ste 400 San Francisco CA 94105

**LUDGUS, NANCY LUCKE,** lawyer; b. Palo Alto, Calif., Oct. 28, 1953; d. Winston Slover and Betty Jean Lucke; m. Lawrence John Ludgus, Apr. 8, 1983. BA in Polit. Sci. with honors, U. Calif., Berkeley, 1975; JD, U. Calif., Davis, 1978. Bar: Calif. 1978, U.S. Dist. Ct. (no. dist.) Calif. 1978. Staff atty. Crown Zellerbach Corp., San Francisco, 1978-80, Clorox Co., Oakland, Calif., 1980-82; staff atty. Nat. Semiconductor Corp., Santa Clara, Calif., 1982-85, corp. counsel, 1985-92, sr. corp. counsel, asst. sec., 1992—. Contbr. articles to profl. jours. Mem. ABA, Am. Corp. Counsel Assn., Calif. State Bar Assn., Santa Clara County Bar Assn., Phi Beta Kappa. Democrat. Avocations: travel, jogging, opera. Contracts commercial, General corporate, Pension, profit-sharing, and employee benefits. Office: Nat Semiconductor Corp 1090 Kifer Rd # 16135 Sunnyvale CA 94086-5301

**LUDLUM, JAMES S.,** lawyer; b. Elk City, Okla., Jan. 15, 1952; s. James Norman and Dorothy Blanche (Standifer) L.; 1 child, Michael James. JD, Baylor U., 1974. Bar: Tex. 1974, U.S. Dist. Ct. (so., ea., we. and no. dists.) Tex. 1974, U.S. Ct. Appeals (5th cir.) 1974, U.S. Supreme Ct. 1974. Litigator Ludlum & Ludlum, Austin, 1974-84, litigation chief, 1984-87, chief exec., 1987—; gen. counsel Tex. Police Assn., Austin, 1991—; mem. nat. adv. bd. govtl. programs AON Spl. Group, Richmond, Va., 1988—; chmn., CEO, Am. News Svc. Corp., 1996—. Contbr. articles to profl. jours. Chmn. Amtrac Com.-Austin C. of C., 1970-78; vice chmn., mem. Police Retirement Bd., Austin, 1981-88. Named Def. Litigator of the Yr., So. Transport Group, 1990, 91, 93. Mem. ABA, Tex. Bar Assn., Tex. Assn. Def. Counsel, Def. Rsch. Inst., Travis County Bar Assn., The Defense Rsch. Inst. Mem. Ch. of Christ. Avocations: tennis, swimming, aviating, public speaking, writing professional articles. Federal civil litigation, State civil litigation, Civil rights. Office: Ludlum & Ludlum Enterprize Plz 13915 Burnet Rd Austin TX 78728-6517

**LUDTKE, DAVID ALLEN,** lawyer, educator; b. Lakota, N.D., Jan. 14, 1939; s. Reinhold H. and Ruggie (Christopherson) L.; m. Jeanne Charlson (div.); children: Mark, Linda, Tom; m. Marilyn Jean Hergenradev, Nov. 20, 1988. AB, Harvard U., 1961; JD, U. Mich., 1968. Assoc. Hogan & Hartson, Washington, 1969-72; from assoc. prof. and full prof. Coll. of Law U. Nebr., Lincoln, 1972-86; ptnr. Rembolt, Ludtke & Berger, Lincoln, 1986-95; adj. prof. U. Nebr. Coll. of Law, 1986—. Author: (with others) Estate Planning for Farmers and Ranchers, 1986, 3d edit., 1995, Family Business Organizations, 2d edit., 1996. Mem. Great Plains Fed. inst., Nebr., 1972—. Lt. USN, 1961-66, Vietnam. Democrat. Lutheran. Taxation, general, General corporate, Estate planning. Home: 3 Forestview Cir Lincoln NE 68522-1828 Office: Rembolt Ludtke & Berger 1201 Lincoln Mall Lincoln NE 68508-2822

**LUDWIG, EDMUND VINCENT,** federal judge; b. Phila., May 20, 1928; s. Henry and Ruth (Viner) L.; children: Edmund Jr., John, Sarah, David. AB, Harvard U., 1949, LLB, 1952. Assoc. Duane, Morris & Heckscher, Phila., 1956-59; ptnr. Barnes, Biester & Ludwig, Doylestown, Pa., 1959-68; judge Common Pleas Ct., Bucks County, Pa., 1968-85, U.S. Dist. Ct. (ea. dist.), Phila., 1985—; faculty Pa. Coll. of the Judiciary, 1974-85; presenter Villanova (Pa.) U. Law Sch., 1975-80, lectr., 1984-97; vis. lectr. Temple Law Sch., 1977-80; clin. assoc. prof. Hahnemann U., Phila., 1977-85; mem. Pa. Juvenile Ct. Judge's Commn., 1978-85; chmn. Pa. Chief Justice's Ednl. Com., 1984-85; pres. Pa. Conf. State Trial Judges, 1981-82; co-chmn. 3d cir. task force on counsel for ind. litigants in civil cases, 1998. Contbr. articles to profl. jours. Chmn. Children and Youth Adv. Com., Bucks County, 1978-83; mem. Pa. Adv. Com. on Mental Health and Mental Retardation, 1980-85; founder, bd. dirs. Today, Inc., Newtown, Pa., 1971-85, Probation Vols., Bucks County, 1971-81; bd. dirs. New Directions for Women, Del. Valley, 1988—; mem. Pa. Joint Coun. Criminal Justice, Inc., 1979-80; mem. Joint Family Law Council Pa., 1979-85; vice chmn. Human Services Council Bucks County, 1979-81; mem. Com. to Study Unified Jud. System Pa., 1980-82, Pa. Legislative Task Force on Mental Health Laws, 1986-87; chmn. Juvenile Justice Alliance, Phila., 1992—; co-chmn. Doylestown (Pa.) Revitalization Bd., 1993-96; mem. 3d cir. task force on equal treatment in the cts., 1995-97; chmn. Doylestown (Pa.) Hist. Soc., 1995—. Recipient Disting. Svc. award Bucks County Corrections Assn., 1978, Spl. Svc. award Big. Bros., 1989, Humanitarian award United Way Bucks County, 1980, Founder's award Vol. Svcs., 1982, Spl. award Bucks County Juvenile Ct., 1985, Humanitarian award Ctrl. Bucks County C. of C., 1994; Wasserstein Pub. Interest fellow Harvard Law Sch., 1996-97. Mem. ABA, Pa. Bar Assn. (chmn. com. legal svcs. to disabled 1990-92), Phila. Bar Assn. (pro bono pub. award 1998), Fed. Bar Assn. (hon.), Harvard Club (N.Y.C. and Phila., v.p. 1979-80), Harvard Law Sch. Assn. (exec. com. 1993—), Fed. Judges Assn. (bd. dirs. 1998—, mem. chmn. 1999—), U.S. Jud. Conf. (com. on ct. adminstrn. and case mgmt.), Am. Law Inst. Office: 12614 US Courthouse Independence Mall W 601 Market St Philadelphia PA 19106-1713

**LUDWIG, SCOTT EDWARD,** lawyer; b. Pitts., Mar. 9, 1958; s. David W. and Kathryn (Scofield) L.; m. Kathy Lansdell, May 28, 1983. BS in Acctg., U. Ala., 1980, JD, 1983; LLM in Taxation, U. Fla., 1984. Bar: Ala. 1983, U.S. Dist. Ct. (no. dist.) Ala. 1984, U.S. Ct. Appeals (11th cir.) 1985. Assoc. Watts, Salmon, Roberts, Manning & Noojin, Huntsville, Ala., 1983-88, Bradley, Arant, Rose & White, Huntsville, 1988—. Assoc. editor Am. Jour. Tax Policy. Mem. Huntsville Econ. Devel. Com.; bd. dirs. Hosp. Hospitality House Huntsville, Inc., 1987—, Hospice Huntsville, Inc., 1988—, v.p.; mem. Huntsville Mus. Art Assn., Huntsville Historic Found., Small Bus. Devel. Com., Huntsville, Free Enterprise Com., Huntsville, Botanical Garden Soc., Huntsville. Richard B. Stephens scholar, 1984. Mem. ABA, Ala. Bar Assn. (state tax com.), Anderson Soc., Bench and Bar, Mortar Bd., Southeastern Tax Inst. (planning com.), Fed. Tax Clinic (planning com.), Jason's, Beta Alpha Psi, Delta Sigma Pi, Beta Gamma Sigma. Corporate taxation, Estate planning, General corporate. Office: Bradley Arant Rose & White 200 Clinton Ave W Ste 900 Huntsville AL 35801-4900

**LUGBILL, ANN,** lawyer; b. P.R., Jan. 9, 1954. BA, Kalamazoo (Mich.) Coll., 1976; JD, U. Va., 1980. Bar: Ohio 1980, D.C. 1999, U.S. Dist. Ct. (so. dist.) Ohio 1981, U.S. Ct. Appeals (6th cir.) 1983, U.S. Supreme Ct. 1997, U.S. Dist. Ct. (no. dist.) Ohio 1998, U.S. Dist. Ct. D.C. 1999. Atty. U.S. Dept. of Labor, Cin., 1980-82; assoc. Kohn & Helmer, 1982-83, James B. Helmer Jr. Atty.'s, 1983-87; shareholder Helmer, Lugbill, Martins & Morgan Co. and predecessor firm, Cin., 1988-98; counsel Manley, Burke, Lipton & Cook, Cin., 1999—. Author: (with Helmer) Representing the Terminated Employee in Ohio, 1990, 2d edit., 1997; (with Helmer, Neff) False Claims Act: Whistleblower Litigation, 1994. Pres. Oakley Residents Assn., Cin., 1982-85; bd. dirs. City of Cin. Cable Communications Bd., 1983-85; trustee Talbert House, Cin., 1983—, v.p., 1987-89, pres., 1989-91. Mem. AFL-CIO (mem. lawyers coordinating com.), Nat. Employment Lawyers Assn. (Ohio bd. dirs.), Cin. Bar Assn. (grievance com. 1993—), Ohio Bar Assn., Fed. Bar Assn., Greater Cin. Women Lawyers Assn., Hamilton County Trial Lawyers Assn. (charter), Potter Stewart Am. Inn Ct. (Master Emeritus), Cincinnatus Assn. Federal civil litigation, General civil litigation, Labor. Office: Manley Burke Lipton & Cook 225 W Court St Cincinnati OH 45202-1052

**LUGO, IVONNE T.,** lawyer; b. Santurce, P.R., Sept. 4, 1949; d. Jose Angel Lugo and Maria Teresa Sandin; divorced; children: Stephen, Eric, Jennifer. Diploma, U. P.R., 1969; BA, Fordham U., 1980; JD, Yale U., 1983. Bar: N.Y. 1984. Assoc. Chadbourne & Parke, N.Y.C., 1983-87; spl. counsel Am. Stock Exch., N.Y.C., 1987—; Mentor N.Y.C. Partnership, 1992-94. Mem. ABA, N.Y. County Lawyers Assn., P.R. Bar Assn., Hispanic Nat. Bar Assn. Democrat. Roman Catholic. Avocations: body building, dancing. Office: Am Stock Exch Inc 86 Trinity Pl New York NY 10006-1817

**LUIKENS, THOMAS GERARD,** lawyer. JD, U. Ariz., 1976. Bar: Ariz. 1976, U.S. Dist. Ct. Ariz. 1976, U.S. Ct. Appeals (9th cir.) 1999. Assoc. Murphy & Storey, Phoenix, 1980-82; ptnr. Storey & Ross, Phoenix, 1980-82; prin. Law Offices of Thomas Luikens, Phoenix, 1982-90; of counsel Ayers & Brown, P.C., Phoenix, 1990—. Mem. ABA, Assn. Trial Lawyers Am., Maricopa County Bar Assn., State Bar of Ariz. General civil litigation, Contracts commercial, Personal injury. Office: Ayers & Brown PC 4227 N 32nd St Ste 100 Phoenix AZ 85018-4754

**LUITJEN, MARK RANDAL,** judge; b. McAllen, Tex., July 30, 1955; s. Douglas Merle and Norma Joy (George) L.; m. Dawna Lynn Crabb, Nov. 7, 1981; children: Cassidy Chea, Schedel Baker. BBA, Trinity U., 1976; JD, St. Mary's U., 1980. Bar: Tex. 1980, U.S. Dist. Ct. (we. dist.) Tex. 1992. Assoc. McDonald Karam Naranjo & Guyer, San Antonio, 1980-81; pvt. practice San Antonio, 1981-82; asst. criminal dist. atty. Bexar County Criminal Dist. Atty.'s Office, San Antonio, 1982-98; dist. judge 144th Jud. Dist. Ct. Bexar County, San Antonio, 1998—. Contbr. articles to profl. publs. Mem. Assn. Govt. Attys. in Capital Litig. (pres. 1996-97), Coastal Conservation Assn. Tex. (v.p. 1996-98, pres. 1999), Shriners, Masons. Avocations: antique map collecting, antique car restoration, fishing, hunting. Office: Bexar County Justice Ctr 300 Dolorosa Ste 3054 San Antonio TX 78205-3005

**LUKAS, JOSEPH FRANK,** paralegal; b. Bronx, N.Y., Mar. 24, 1952; s. Francis Joseph and Theresa (Beaumont) L.; m. Jane Elizabeth Roberts, Dec. 23, 1989; 1 child, Matthew Joseph. AA, Fulton-Montgomery C.C., Johnstown, N.Y., 1972; BA, L.I. U., Southampton, N.Y., 1974, Miss. U. for Women and Men, Columbus, 1993. Cert. Miss. Assn. Legal Assts. Paralegal Webb, McLaurin & O'Neal, Tupelo, Miss., 1990-94; ind. paralegal Thorne & Assocs., Tupelo, 1994-96; paralegal Roger M. Tubbs, Atty. at Law, 1996—. Mayoral candidate Guntown, Miss., 1992; justice ct. judge candidate No. Dist. Lee County, Miss. Mem. ATLA (paralegal divsn.), Nat. Assn. Legal Assts. Republican. Avocations: photography, reading, swimming, landscaping. Home: PO Box 444 Tupelo MS 38802-0444 Office: Thorne & Assocs 210 W Main St Tupelo MS 38804-3954

**LUKEY, JOAN A.,** lawyer; b. Malden, Mass., Dec. 28, 1949; d. Philip Edward and Ada Joan (Roberti) L.; m. Philip Davis Stevenson. BA magna cum laude, Smith Coll., 1971; JD cum laude, Boston Coll., 1974. Bar: Mass. 1974, U.S. Dist. Ct. Mass. 1975, U.S. Ct. Appeals (1st cir.) 1976, U.S. Supreme Ct. 1985. Assoc. Hale & Dorr, Boston, 1974-79, jr. ptnr., 1979-83, sr. ptnr., 1983—. Mem. Joint Bar Com. on Judicial Appointments, Mass., 1985-87, steering com. Lawyers' Com. for Civil Rights Under the Law, Boston, 1987-90. Fellow Am. Coll. Trial Lawyers (mem. state com. 1993—, chair 1997-99, first cir. rules adv. com. 1997, chair 1998—); mem. ABA,

Mass. Bar Assn., Boston Bar Assn. (chair litigation sect. 1990-92, mem. coun. 1987-90, v.p. 1998-99, pres.-elect 1999—), Women's Bar Assn. Mass., Boston Club. Federal civil litigation, State civil litigation, Labor. Office: Hale & Dorr 60 State St Boston MA 02109-1816

**LULICH, STEVEN,** lawyer, consultant; b. Astoria, N.Y., Apr. 21, 1952; s. Steve and Rose L.; m. Michele Lulich, 1978 (div. Nov. 1987); m. Linda Christina, Feb. 17, 1994; children: Steven, Jordan, Tasha. BA, SUNY, 1978; JB, Nova Law Ctr., Ft. Lauderdale, Fla. Lic. real estate broker, Fla.; cert. bldg. contractor, Fla. Pvt. practice Sebastian, Fla. Mem. Fla. Bar Assn., Italian Am. Club, Elks Club. Real property, Probate, Professional liability. Office: 1069 Main St Sebastian FL 32958-8627

**LUMBARD, ELIOT HOWLAND,** lawyer, educator; b. Fairhaven, Mass., May 6, 1925; s. Ralph E. and Constance Y. L.; m. Jean Ashmore, June 21, 1947 (div.); m. Kirsten Dehner, June 28, 1981 (div.); children: Susan, John, Ann, Joshua Abel, Marah Abel. BS in Marine Transp., U.S. Mcht. Marine Acad., 1943-46; BS in Econs., U. Pa., 1949; JD, Columbia U., 1952. Bar: N.Y. 1953, U.S. Supreme Ct. 1959, Pa. 1983. Assoc. Breed, Abbott and Morgan, N.Y.C., 1952-53; asst. U.S. atty. So. Dist. N.Y., 1953-56; assoc. Chadbourne, Parke, Whiteside & Wolff, N.Y.C., 1956-58; ptnr. Townsend & Lewis, N.Y.C., 1961-70; ptnr. Spear and Hill, N.Y.C., 1970-75; ptnr. Lumbard and Phelan, P.C., N.Y.C., 1977-82, Saul, Ewing, Remick & Saul, N.Y.C., 1982-84; pvt. practice law, N.Y.C., 1984-86; ptnr. Haight, Gardner, Poor & Havens, N.Y.C., 1986-88; pvt. practice law, N.Y.C., 1988-92, ret.; chief counsel N.Y. State Commn. Investigation, 1958-61; spl. asst. counsel for law enforcement to Gov. N.Y., 1961-67; organizer N.Y. State Identification and Intelligence Sys., 1963-67; chair Oyster Bay Conf. on Organized Crime, 1962-67; criminal justice cons. to Gov. Fla. and other states, 1967; chief criminal justice cons. to N.J. Legis., 1968-69; chmn. com. on organized crime N.Y.C. Criminal Justice Coordinating Coun., 1971-74; organizer schs. of criminal justice at SUNY Albany and Rutgers, Newark; mem. departmental disciplinary com. First Dept., N.Y. Supreme Ct., 1982-88; trustee bankruptcy Universal Money Order Co., Inc., 1977-82, Meritum Corp., 1983-89; spl. master in admiralty Hellenic Lines Ltd., 1984-86; chmn. Palisades Life Ins. Co. (former Equity Funding subs. 1974-75); bd. dir. RMC Industries Corp.; chair Am. Maritime History Project, Inc., Kings Point, N.Y., 1996—; lectr. trial practice NYU Law Sch., 1963-65; mem. vis. com. Sch. Criminal Justice, SUNY-Albany, 1968-75; adj. prof. law and criminal justice John Jay Coll. Criminal Justice, CUNY, 1975-86; arbitrator Am. Arbitration Assn. and N.Y. Civil Ct.-Small Claims Part, N.Y. County; mem. Vol. Master Program U.S. Dist. Ct. (so. dist.) N.Y. Contbr. articles to profl. jours. Bd. dirs. Citizens Crime Commn. N.Y.C., Inc., Big Bros. Movement, Citizens Union; trustee Trinity Sch, 1964-78, N.Y.C. Police Found., Inc., 1971-92, chmn., 1971-74, emeritus. Lt. j.g. USNR, 1943-52. Recipient First Disting. Svc. award Sch. Criminal Justice, SUNY-Albany, 1976. Mem. Assn. Bar City N.Y., N.Y. County Lawyers Assn., ABA, N.Y. State Bar Assn., Maritime Law Assn., Down Town Assn. Club. Republican. State civil litigation, Bankruptcy, Federal civil litigation. Home: 39B Apple Ln Hollis NH 03049-6311

**LUMBARD, JOSEPH EDWARD, JR.,** federal judge; b. N.Y.C., Aug. 18, 1901; s. Joseph Edward and Martha Louise (Meier) L.; m. Polly Poindexter, Sept. 4, 1929; children: Abigail, Thomas. A.B. cum laude, Harvard U., 1922, LL.B., 1925, LL.D., 1970; LL.D., William Mitchell Coll., U. Bridgeport, Northwestern U., N.Y. Law Sch., Columbia U.; S.J.D. (hon.), Suffolk U. Asst. U.S. atty. So. Dist. N.Y., 1925-27; spl. asst. atty. gen. N.Y. State, in Queens Sewer investigation and prosecution of Maurice E. Connelly, 1928-29; mem. firm Fogarty, Lumbard & Quel, 1929-31; asst. to William J. Donovan in bankruptcy inquiry conducted by Assn. Bar City N.Y. and others, 1929; asst. U.S. atty. charge criminal div. So. Dist. N.Y., 1931-33; mem. firm Donovan, Leisure, Newton, Lumbard & Irvine (and predecessor firms), 1934-53; spl. asst. atty. gen. N.Y. State, in Drukman murder prosecutions, 1936; def. counsel U.S. vs. Standard Oil and 23 oil cos., 1937-38; spl. asst. atty. gen. N.Y. State charge Election Frauds Bur., 1943; justice Supreme Ct. N.Y. State, June-Dec. 1947; U.S. atty. So. Dist. N.Y., 1953-55; U.S. circuit judge 2d Circuit, 1955—; chief judge U.S. Court Appeals, 2d Circuit, 1959-71. Contbr. to law jours. Bd. overseers Harvard, 1959-65; trustee William Nelson Cromwell Found. Jud. fellow Am. Coll. Trial Lawyers; mem. ABA (chmn. spl. com. minimum standards for criminal justice 1964-68, Gold medal 1968), N.Y. State Bar Assn. (Gold medal 1969), Assn. Bar City N.Y., S.R. Republican. Unitarian. Clubs: Country (Fairfield); Harvard, Century (N.Y.C.). Home: 490 Hillside Rd Fairfield CT 06430-2140 *Died June 3, 1999.*

**LUMPKIN, DOUGLAS BOOZER,** lawyer; b. Birmingham, Ala., Aug. 31, 1964; s. Robert Franklin and B. Faye (Boozer) L.; m. Julia Ann Lumpkin, June 24, 1995. BA, Birmingham-Southern Coll., 1987; JD, U. Ala., 1990. Bar: Fla. 1990. Atty. Dickinson & Gibbons, Sarasota, Fla., 1990-93; atty., ptnr. Lutz, Webb & Bobo, Sarasota, Fla., 1993—. Bd. mem. Teen Ct., Sarasota, Fla., 1993-95; pres. Ala. Alumni Assn., Sarasota, Fla., 1997—. Health, Personal injury. Office: Lutz Webb & Bobo One Sarasota Tower 5th Fl 2 N Tamiami Trl Sarasota FL 34236-5574

**LUMPKIN, GARY LEONARD,** judge; b. Sentinel, Okla.; m. Barbara Lumpkin; 1 child. Student, Northwestern State Coll., Alva, Okla., 1964-65; BS, Soutwestern State Coll., Weatherford, Okla., 1968; JD, U. Okla., 1974. Bar: Okla. 1974. Staff atty. Okla. Dept. Consumer Affairs, 1974-75; asst. dist. atty. to 1st asst. dist. atty. Marshall County, Okla., 1976-82, assoc. dist. judge, 1982-85; dist. judge 20th Jud. Dist., Divsn. II, Marshall County, Okla., 1985-89; judge Okla. Ct. Criminal Appeals, Oklahoma City, 1989—, vice-presiding judge, 1991-92, 99—, presiding judge, 1993-94; USMC res. judge Navy-Marine Ct. Criminal Appeals, 1994-98; pres. Okla. Jud. Conf., 1989; past mem. sentencing and release policy com. created by Senate Bill 432 of 42d legislature; rep. Ct. Criminal Appeals on Truth in Sentencing Policy Adv. Commn.; mem. Okla. Supreme Ct. com. on uniform civil jury instrns. and ct. liaison to Ct. of Criminal Appeals uniform criminal jury instrn. com. With USMC, 1968-71; col. USMCR, Vietnam, ret. Mem. Okla. Bar Assn. (past chair criminal law com., mem. law related edn. com.), Okla. Bar Found., Okla. County Bar Assn., Marshall County Bar Assn., William J. Holloway Jr. Am. Inns of Ct. (pres.-elect, chair program com. 1992, pres. 1993, William J. Holloway Jr. Professionalism award 1999), VFW, Marine Corps Res. Officers Assn. Baptist. Office: Okla Court Criminal Appeals State Capitol Bldg Rm 230 Oklahoma City OK 73105

**LUMSDEN, DIANA J.,** lawyer; b. Framingham, Mass., Sept. 15, 1950. BA with honors, U. Conn., 1972; JD, Suffolk U., 1978. Bar: Mass. 1978, U.S. Ct. Appeals (1st cir.) 1980, U.S. Dist. Ct. Mass. 1980. Pvt. practice Boston, 1978-80; ptnr., lawyer Nissen & Lumsden, Boston, 1980-93; pres., lawyer Lumsden & Inge, P.C., Boston, 1993—; chmn. personal injury curriculum adv. com. Mass. Continuing Legal Edn., Boston, 1990-95. Co-author: Damages in Massachusetts Litigation, 1998. Avocations: running, photography, reading, cooking. Product liability, Personal injury. Office: Lumsden & Inge PC PO Box 340 Boston MA 02117-0340

**LUNA, BARBARA CAROLE,** financial analyst, accountant, appraiser; b. N.Y.C., July 23, 1950; d. Edwin A. and Irma S. (Schub) Schlang; m. Dennis Rex Luna, Sept. 1, 1974; children: John S., Katherine E. BA, Wellesley Coll., 1971; MS in Applied Math. and Fin. Analysis, Harvard U., 1973, PhD in Applied Math. and Fin. Analysis, 1975. CPA; cert. gen. real estate appraiser Calif. Orgn. Real Estate Appraisers, valuation analyst Nat. Assn. Cert. Valuation Analysts, fraud examiner Assn. Cert. Fraud Examiners, mgmt. cons. Inst. Mgmt. Consultants; accredited sr. appraiser Am. Soc. Appraisers, bus. valuation Am. Inst. CPAs. Investment banker Warburg Paribas Becker, L.A., 1975-77; cons./mgr. Price Waterhouse, L.A., 1977-83; sr. mgr. litigation Pannell Kerr Forster, L.A., 1983-86; nat. dir. litigation cons. Kenneth Leventhal & Co., L.A., 1986-88; ptnr. litigation svcs. Coopers & Lybrand, L.A., 1988-93; sr. ptnr. litigation svcs. White, Zuckerman, Warsavsky, Luna & Wolf, Sherman Oaks, Calif., 1993—. Wellesley scholar, 1971. Mem. AICPA, Assn. Bus. Trial Lawyers (com. on experts), Am. Soc. Appraisers, Nat. Appraisal Inst., Assn. Cert. Valuation Analysts, Assn. Cert. Real Estate Appraisers, Appraisal Inst., Assn. Cert. Fraud Examiners, Inst. Mgmt. Cons., Calif. Soc. CPAs (steering com. L.A. litigation svcs. com. econ. damages common interest mem. svcs. com., fraud common interest mem. svcs. com., bus. valuation common interest mem. svcs. com.), Am. Bd. Forensic Accts. and Examiners. Avocations: golf, swimming. Home: 18026 Rodarte Way Encino CA 91316-4370

**LUND, DANIEL P.,** lawyer; b. N.Y.C., Aug. 15, 1940; s. Adolph and Esther (Sinn) L.; m. Marilan Murdock, Feb. 20, 1967. AB cum laude, Princeton U., 1962; LLB, Columbia U., 1965. Bar: N.Y. 1965, U.S. Dist. Ct. D.C. 1974, U.S. Dist. Ct. (so. dist.) N.Y. 1974, U.S. Ct. Appeals (2d cir.) 1975. Sr. ptnr. Krass & Lund, N.Y.C., 1979—. General corporate, General civil litigation. Office: Krass & Lund 419 Park Ave S New York NY 10016-8410

**LUND, JAMES LOUIS,** lawyer; b. Long Beach, Calif., Oct. 4, 1926; s. G. Louis and Hazel Eunice (Cochran) L.; m. Jo Alvarez, Aug. 5, 1950; 1 son, Eric James. Student Stanford U., 1943; B.A. in Math., U. So. Calif., 1946; postgrad. Grad. Sch. Annapolis, 1949; J.D., Southwestern U., 1955; postgrad. Sch. Law., U. So. Calif., 1956. Bar: Calif. 1955, U.S. Dist. Ct. (cen. dist.) Calif. 1955, U.S. Ct. Apls. (9th cir.) 1955, U.S. Tax Ct. 1955, U.S. Supreme Ct. Spl. agt., U.S. Govt., 1950-52; gen. mgr. Pacific ops., gen. counsel Holmes & Narver, Inc., Los Angeles, 1952-66; exec. v.p. Calif. Fabricators, Oakland and Honolulu, 1966-67; sr. ptnr. James Lund Law Firm, Beverly Hills, Tehran, London and Tokyo, 1967-83; pres., founder Fortres Mgmt. Co.; ptnr. Lund & Lund, 1983—. Served to lt. comdr. USNR, 1943-46, 48-50. Mem. ABA, SAR, Los Angeles County Bar Assn., Internat. Bar Assn., Inter-Am. Bar Assn., Asia Pacific Lawyers Assn., Les Ambassadeurs Club (London). Construction, Private international, Real property. Office: 20th Fl 1901 Ave of The Stars Los Angeles CA 90067-6001

**LUND, THEODORE ANTON,** lawyer; b. Boston, June 4, 1963; s. Helge Erik and Diane L. BA, Bowdoin Coll., 1985; JD, Boston U., 1990. Bar: Mass. 1990, U.S. Dist. Ct. Mass. 1991. Assoc. Choate, Hull & Stewart, Boston, 1990-96, Lodaey & Grossman, Boston, 1996-97; ptnr. Fausett, Gaeta & Lund, Boston, 1998—. Mem. Boston Bar Assn. Avocations: photography, skiing, windsurfing. General civil litigation. Office: Fausett Baeta & Lund 21 School St Fl 3D Boston MA 02108-4305

**LUNDBACK, STAFFAN BENGT GUNNAR,** lawyer; b. Stockholm, Sweden, Mar. 23, 1947; came to U.S., 1965; s. B. Holger and Ingrid (Fjellstrom) L.; m. Lee Craig, June 14,1969; children: Hadley Elizabeth, Erik Burchfield. Student, U. Stockholm, 1966-67; BA, U. Rochester, 1970; JD, Boston U., 1974. Bar: N.Y. 1975, Fla. 1983. Assoc. Nixon, Hargrave, Devans & Doyle, Rochester, N.Y., 1974-83; ptnr. Nixon, Hargrave, Devans & Doyle, Rochester, 1983—; bd. dirs. Scandinavian Seminar, Amherst, Mass.; chmn. Scanamerican Properties, Inc., Atlanta, 1989—. Mem. Swedish-Am. C. of C. (sec., bd. dirs. 1994—), Genesee Valley Club, Country Club of Rochester, Phi Beta Kappa. Avocations: music, literature, sports, current events, photography, golf. General corporate, Banking, Real property. Office: Nixon Hargrave Devans & Doyle PO Box 1051 One Clinton First Sq Rochester NY 14603

**LUNDE, ASBJORN RUDOLPH,** lawyer; b. S.I., N.Y., July 17, 1927; s. Karl and Elisa (Andenes) L. AB, Columbia U., 1947, LLB, 1949. Bar: N.Y. 1949. Since practiced in N.Y.C.; with Kramer, Marx, Greenlee & Backus and predecessors, 1950-68, mem., 1968—. Bd. dirs., v.p. Orch. da Camera, Inc., 1964—; bd. dirs. Sara Roby Found., 1971—, Clarion Concerts in Columbia County, 1999—. Fellow Met. Mus. Art (life); mem. ABA, N.Y. State Bar Assn., Assn. Bar City N.Y., Met. Opera Club, East India Club (London). Art collector, donor paintings and sculptures to Met. Mus. Art, N.Y.C., Nat. Gallery Art, Washington, Mus. Fine Arts, Boston, Clark Art Inst., Williamstown, Mass., others. Contracts commercial, General corporate, Private international. Home and Office: 135 LaBranche Rd Hillsdale NY 12529-5713

**LUNDEEN, BRADLEY CURTIS,** lawyer; b. Karlstad, MN, Nov. 16, 1958; s. Curtis W. and LaVonne M. (Oistad) L.; m. Kristina Ogland, May 18, 1984 (div. Dec. 1991); 1 child, Jonathan B. BA, Moorhead State U, 1980; JD cum laude, William Mitchell Coll. Law, 1984. Bar: Minn. 1984, Wis. 1984. Assoc. Gwin, Gilbert, Gwin, Mudge & Porter, Hudson, Wis., 1984, Gilbert, Mudge & Porter, Hudson, 1985; ptnr. Gilbert, Mudge, Porter & Lundeen, Hudson, 1986-92; lawyer, shareholder Mudge, Porter & Lundeen S.C., Hudson, 1992-94, Mudge, Porter, Lundeen & Seguin S.C., Hudson, 1995—. Bd. dirs. Hudson Rotary, 1990-91, Bank St. Croix, Hudson, Wis., 1987-94, St. Croix Valley Employers Assn., 1996—. Mem. St. Croix Valley Bar Assn., St. Croix Valley Employers Assn., Masons, Shriners. Lutheran. Avocations: golf, skiing, travel, computers and cooking. Workers' compensation, Pension, profit-sharing, and employee benefits, Labor. Home: 318 Saint Annes Pkwy Hudson WI 54016-8075 Office: Mudge Porter Lundeen & Seguin SC 110 2nd St Hudson WI 54016-1504

**LUNDGREN, GAIL M.,** lawyer; b. Tacoma, Wash., June 14, 1955; d. Arthur Dean and Vera Martha (Grimm) L. AB cum laude, Vassar Coll., 1977; JD cum laude, U. Puget Sound (now Seattle U. Law Sch.), 1980. Bar: Wash. 1981. Legal intern Reed, McClure, Moceri & Thonn, Seattle, 1979, Burges & Kennedy, Tacoma, Wash., 1979-80, Lee, Smart, Cook, Martin & Patterson, P.S., Inc., Seattle, 1980-81; assoc. Lee, Smart, Cook, Martin & Patterson, P.S., Inc., Seattle, Wash., 1981-92; prin. Law Offices Gail L. Weber, Bothell, Wash., 1992-95, Tom Chambers & Assocs., 1995-99; lawyer Law Offices of Kirk Bernard, Seattle, 1999—. Vestry com. Queen Anne Luth. Ch., 1983-86, v.p. congregation, 1988, 89, mem. worship and music com., 1982-83, 84-86, parish edn. com., 1983-84. Recipient Am. Jurisprudence Book award in Criminal Procedure, Corps. and Bus. Planning, 1980. mem. ABA, Fed. Bar Assn., Wash. State Trial Lawyers Assn., Order of Barristers, Wash. State Vassar Club (chmn. alumni admissions 1983-85, rep. 1986-92). Democrat. Avocations: scuba diving, tennis, classical music, needlepoint, stitchery. General civil litigation, Personal injury, Product liability. Office: Law Offices of Kirk Bernard 83 S King St Seattle WA 98104-3852

**LUNDQUIST, WEYMAN IVAN,** lawyer; b. Worcester, Mass., July 27, 1930; s. Hilding Ivan and Florence Cecilia (Westerholm) L.; m. Joan Durrell, Sept. 15, 1956 (div. July 1977); children—Weyman, Erica, Jettora, Kirk; m. Kathryn E. Taylor, Dec. 28, 1978; 1 child, Derek. BA magna cum laude, Dartmouth Coll., 1952; LLB, Harvard U., 1955. Bar: Mass. 1955, Alaska 1961, Calif. 1963, Vt. 1994. Assoc. Thayer, Smith & Gaskill, Worcester, 1957-60; atty. U.S. Attys. Office, Mass. and Alaska, 1960-62; assoc. Heller, Ehrman, White & McAuliffe, San Francisco, 1963-65, ptnr., 1967—; counsel, v.p. State Mut. Life Ins. Co., Worcester, 1965-67; vis. prof. environ. studies Dartmouth Coll., Hanover, N.H., 1980, 84, bus. sch., 1997, vis. scholar, 1994-97, adj. prof. Amos Tuck Bus. Sch., Dartmouth Coll., 1997—; program chmn. 1990 Moscow Conf. on Law and Bilateral Econs. Rels.; mem. U.S. adv. com. Alaska/Can./Soviet No. Justice Conf., 1993-94, N.Y., San Francisco Cutting Edge Lawyer Liability Programs, 1989; bd. dirs. U. Press New England, 1997, adv. dir.; bd. dirs. West Coast Magnetics, Stockton, Calif. Author: (fiction) The Promised Land, 1987, (nonfiction) The Art of Shaping the Case, 1999; contbr. articles to profl. jours. Trustee Natural Resources Def. Coun., 1982-91. Recipient CPR Significant Achievement award, 1987. Fellow ABA (founder and chmn. litigation sect. 1978-79, chmn. Soviet Bar Assn. liaison com. 1986, co-chmn. spl. com. for study discovery abuse 1976-83, spl. com. on tort liability sys. 1981-84, superfund 301e study group advisor to U.S. Congress, 1983), Am. Coll. Trial Lawyers; mem. Dartmouth Lawyer's Assn. (founding mem.), Am. Antiquarian Soc. (councillor), Assn. Life Ins. Coun., U.S. Supreme Ct. Hist. Soc., No. Dist. Hist. Soc., Dartmouth Lawyers Assn., Swedish Am. C. of C. (pres., bd. dirs. western U.S. 1982-89). Avocations: squash, skiing, writing. Federal civil litigation, State civil litigation, Environmental. Home: 16 Occum Rdg Hanover NH 03755-1410 Office: Heller Ehrman White & McAuliffe PO Box 888 Norwich VT 05055-0888

**LUNDREGAN, WILLIAM JOSEPH,** lawyer; b. Peabody, Mass., Nov. 8, 1940; s. William J. and Suzanne G. (Hichens) L.; m. Jane T. Lundregan, July 15, 1967; children: Catherine S., William J., Anne T. BS in BA, Boston Coll., 1962, LLB, 1967. With office of tax counsel United Shoe Machinery Corp., Boston, 1967; atty. tax dept. Arthur Young & Co., Boston, 1967-69; first asst. clk. magistrate First Dist. Ct. of Essex, Salem, Mass., 1969-74; ptnr. Welch & Lundregan, Salem, Mass., 1974-88, Lundregan Law Offices, Salem, Mass., 1974—; corporator, trustee, bd. investment Salem Five Cents Savs. Bank; gen. counsel Essex County Retirement Bd., treas.; gen. counsel Salem Contributory Retirement Bd., Salem Housing Authority, Beverly Housing Authority, 1988—. Bd. dirs. North Shore Cath. Charities, Peabody; trustee, pres. Salem Atheneum; pres., dir. Boys and Girls Club, Salem; city solicitor City Salem. 1st lt. U.S. Army, 1962-64. Mem. Mass. Bar Assn., Salem Bar Assn., Essex County Bar Assn. (exec. com.), Rotary (bd. dirs., pres. 1985-86), Corinthian Yacht Club (membership com.). Roman Catholic. Administrative and regulatory, Estate planning, General practice. Home: 11 Faye Cir Marblehead MA 01945-3714

**LUNDSTROM, GILBERT GENE,** banker, lawyer; b. Gothenburg, Nebr., Sept. 27, 1941; s. Vernon G. and Imogene (Jackett) L.; m. Joyce Elaine Ronin, June 26, 1965; children: Trevor A., Gregory G. BS, U. Nebr., 1964, JD, 1969; MBA, Wayne State U., 1966. Bar: U.S. Dist. Ct. (1st dist.) Nebr. 1969, Nebr. 1969, U.S. Ct. Appeals (5th cir.) 1970, U.S. Ct. Appeals (10th cir.) 1971, U.S. Ct. Appeals (8th cir.) 1974, U.S. Ct. Appeals (3d cir.) 1986. Ptnr. Woods & Aitken, Lincoln, Nebr., 1969-93; pres. and CEO First Fed. Lincoln Bank, 1994—, First Lincoln Bancshares Inc., a Delaware Corp.; part-time faculty law sch. U. Nebr.-Lincoln, 1970-74; dir. First Fed. Lincoln Bank, TMS Corp. of Ams., First Fin. Corp.; bd. dirs. Sahara Enterprises, Inc., Sahara Coal Co., Chgo.; dir., vice chmn. Fed. Home Loan Bank Topeka, 1996-98, 99—. Bd. dirs. Folsom Children's Zoo, Lincoln, 1979-83, St. Elizabeth Hosp. Found.; dir. Nat. Coun. Fed. Home Loan Banks. Fellow Nebr. State Bar Assn.; mem. ABA, ATLA, Lincoln Bar Assn., Nebr. Bar Assn., Newcomer Soc. U.S., bd. dirs. Heartland Cmty. Bankers Assn. Republican. Methodist. Club: Country Club of Lincoln, Firethorn County Club. Lodge: Masons, Scottish Rite (33 degree). Home: 9519 Firethorn Ln Lincoln NE 68520-1459 Office: First Fed Lincoln 1235 N St Lincoln NE 68508-2083

**LUNDSTROM, THOMAS JOHN,** lawyer; b. Ashland, Dec. 21, 1954; s. Martti Albert and Shirley Dorothy (Carlson) L. BS, U. Wis., 1978; JD, Ohio No. U., 1981; LLM in Environ. Law, U. San Diego, 1996. Bar: Ohio, Va., U.S. Dist. Ct. (ea. dist.) Va., U.S. Ct. Appeals (4th cir.). Commd. ensign USN, 1983, advanced through grades to lt. comdr., 1988; staff comdr. naval surface Atlantic fleet USN, Norfolk, Va., 1983-84, staff judge adv. U.S. forces Lebanon, 1983, legal svc. office Norfolk def. counsel, 1984-86; staff judge adv. comdr. U.S. forces Caribbean USN, Key West, Fla., 1986-87; staff judge adv. USS Coral Sea USN, 1987-89; def. counsel Va. State Pub. Defender, Portsmouth, 1989-91; asst. counsel Office of Gen. Counsel of Navy, Norfolk, 1991-93; counsel Marine Corps Logistics Base, Barstow, Calif., 1993-97; sr. assoc. counsel Naval Air Sys. Command, Patuxent River, Md., 1997—; wine steward Williamsburg (Va.) Inn, 1990-93. Big brother Big Bros. Am., Norfolk, 1989-92; Navy outreach mentor Lusby H.S., 1998. Avocations: golf, sailing, camping, cooking, wines. Office: Naval Air Sys Command Office of Counsel Attn: Air 7.7.5 Patuxent River MD 20670

**LUNDT, ERIC L.,** lawyer; b. N.Y.C., July 20, 1965; s. Rudy Oscar and Susan Robin (Cagan) L. BBA, U. Miami, Coral Gables, Fla., 1987, JD, 1990. Bar: Fla. 1990, U.S. Ct. Appeals (11th cir.) 1994, U.S. Dist. Ct. (so. dist.) Fla. 1994, U.S. Dist. Ct. (mid. dist.) 1995, U.S. Supreme Ct. 1995, U.S. Dist. Ct. (no. dist.) Fla. 1997. Summer assoc. Daniels & Hicks P.A., Miami, 1988-90; law clk. U.S. Dist Ct. Fla., Miami, 1990-92; adj. prof. Miami-Dade C.C., 1991-92; assoc. Kelly, Black, Black, Byrne & Beasley, P.A., Miami, 1992-97, Heinrich Gordon Hargrove Weihe & James, P.A., Ft. Lauderdale, 1997—. Cons., rev. editor West Ednl. Pub., St. Paul, 1992-93. Vol. coord. Health Crisis Network, Miami, 1995. Mem. ABA, Dade County Bar Assn. (dir. young lawyers sect. 1994-97, cert. of merit 1994), Fla. Bar (exec. com. on eminent domain 1993-96, appellate practice and advocacy sect. 1994-96), Broward County Bar Assn. (young lawyers exec. com. 1997-98). Avocations: tennis, travel, oenology. General civil litigation, Product liability, Appellate. Office: Heinrich Gordon Hargrove Weihe & James PA 500 E Broward Blvd Ste 1000 Fort Lauderdale FL 33394-3087

**LUNDY, SHEILA EDWARDS,** lawyer; b. Balt., Nov. 29, 1954; d. James Morris and Christine Anne E.; children: Tiffany D., Christopher R. BA, U. Balt., 1978, JD, 1991. Bar: U.S. Ct. Appeals Md. 1992, U.S. Dist. Ct. Md. 1994. Adminstrv. specialist BWI Airport, Md. Aviation Adminstrn., Balt., 1988-91, risk mgmt. specialist, 1991-92; staff atty. Md. Office Atty. Gen., Glen Burnie, 1992-94, asst. atty. gen., 1994—; faculty The Md. Inst. for Continuing Profl. Edn. of Lawyers, 1999. Mem. Mt. St. Josephs H.S. Mother's Club, Balt., 1997—. Mem. Am. Inns of Ct., Md. Bar Assn. (mem. lawyer counseling com. 1998—), Paca-Brent Joint Inn of Ct., Anne Arundel County Bar Assn. (mem. com. 1994—, bd. trustees 1999), U. Balt. Alumni Assn., Paca-Brent Inn of Ct. (bd. dirs. 1999), Monumental Bar Assn. Democrat. Roman Catholic. Avocations: gardening, reading, old movies.

**LUNGREN, JOHN HOWARD,** law educator, oil and gas consultant, author; b. Chgo., Feb. 11, 1925; s. Charles Howard and Edna Hughes (Edwards) L.; m. Phyllis Joan Jolidon, Dec. 12, 1953 (div.); 1 son, John Eric; m. Susan Jeanette Whitfield, Sept. 22, 1984. B.A., Beloit Coll., 1948; J.D., Marquette U., 1952; M.A., U. Wis.-Milw., 1974. Bar: Wis. 1952, Ill. 1975, Kans. 1980. Assoc. gen. counsel A. O. Smith Corp., 1964-74; gen. atty. Clark Oil & Refining Corp., 1954-64; prof. law Lewis U., Glen Ellyn, Ill., 1975-80; assoc. prof. law Washburn U. Sch. Law, Topeka, 1980-85; practice, Chgo., from 1977; with Turner & Boisseau Ltd., Wichita, Kans., 1985-88; of counsel Lungren and Whitfield-Lungren, Wichita, 1987—; cons. oil and gas; Kans. rep. legal com. Interstate Oil Compact. Chmn., Milwaukee County Republican Party, 1966-70; justice of peace, Wauwatosa, Wis., 1964-68. Served with USN, 1943-46. Mem. ABA, Ill. Bar Assn., Wis. Bar Assn., Kans. Bar Assn., Wichita Bar Assn.

**LUNGSTRUM, JOHN W.,** federal judge; b. Topeka, Kans., Nov. 2, 1945; s. Jack Edward and Helen Alice (Watson) L.; m. Linda Eileen Ewing, June 21, 1969; children: Justin Matthew, Jordan Elizabeth, Alison Paige. BA magna cum laude, Yale Coll., 1967; JD, U. Kans., 1970. Bar: Kans. 1970, Calif. 1970, U.S. Dist. Ct. (ctrl. dist.) Calif., U.S. Ct. Appeals (10th crct.). Assoc. Latham & Watkins, L.A., 1970-71; ptnr. Stevens, Brand, Lungstrum, Golden & Winter, Lawrence, Kans., 1972-91; U.S. Dist. judge Dist. of Kans., Kansas City, Kans., 1991—; lectr. law U. Kans. Law Sch., 1973—; mem. faculty Kans. Bar Assn. Coll. Advocacy , Trial Tactics and Techniques Inst., 1983-86; chmn. Douglas County Rep. Ctrl. Com., 1975-81; mem. Rep. State Com.; del. State Rep. Convention, 1968, 76, 80. Chmn. bd. dirs. Lawrence C. of C., 1990-91; pres. Lawrence United Fund, 1979; pres. Independence Days Lawrence, Inc., 1984, 85, Seem-to-be-Players, Inc., Lawrence Rotary Club, 1978-79; bd. dirs. Lawrence Soc. Chamber Music, Swarthout Soc. ( corp. fund-raising chmn.); mem. Lawrence Art Commn., Williams Scholarship Fund, Lawrence League Women Voters, Douglas County Hist. Soc.; bd. trustees, stewardship chmn. Plymouth Congl. Ch.; pres. Lawrence Round Ball Club; coach Lawrence Summertime Basketball; Vice chmn. U. Kans. Disciplinary Bd.; bd. govs. Kans Sch. Religion; bd. dirs. Kans. Day Club, 1980, 81. National Merit scholar, Yale Nat. scholar. Fellow Am. Bar Found.; mem. ABA (past mem. litigation and ins. sect.), Douglas County Bar Assn., Johnson County Bar Assn., Wyandotte County Bar Assn., Kans. Bar Assn (vice chair legislative com., subcom. litigation, mem. continuing legal edn. com.), U Kans. Alumni Assn. (life), Phi Beta Kappa, Phi Gamma Delta, Phi Delta Phi. Avocations: basketball, hiking, skiing. Office: US Courthouse 500 State Ave Kansas City KS 66101-2403

**LUNING, THOMAS P.,** lawyer; b. St. Louis, Oct. 11, 1942. AB magna cum laude, Xavier U., 1964; JD, Georgetown U., 1967. Bar: D.C. 1968, Ill. 1968. Law clk. to Hon. Spottswood W. Robinson III and to ct. U.S. Ct. Appeals (D.C. cir.), 1967-68; atty. Schiff Hardin & Waite, Chgo. Mng. editor Georgetown Law Jour., 1966-67. Mem. ABA, Ill. State Bar Assn., Chgo. Bar Assn., 7th Cir. Bar Assn., Chgo. Coun. Lawyers. Antitrust, General civil litigation, Insurance. Office: Schiff Hardin & Waite 6600 Sears Tower Chicago IL 60606

**LUNSFORD, JEANNE DENISE,** lawyer, educator; b. Huntington, W.Va., Feb. 20, 1952; d. Harold D. and Dorothy (Jones) Lunsford. BS, W.Va. U., 1974; JD, Okla. City U., 1977; MBA, U. Tex., El Paso, 1984. Bar: Tex. 1979, W.Va. 1977, U.S. Dist. Ct. (we. dist.) Tex. 1980, U.S. Supreme Ct. 1983. Staff atty. W.Va. State Tax Dept., Charleston, 1977-78; in-house counsel El Paso Natural Gas Co., 1978-85; staff atty. City Atty. Office, El Paso, 1985-89; prof. law Calif. State Polytechnic U., Pomona, 1989—; law lectr. U. Tex., El Paso, 1991-92, UCLA Ext., 1997—; cons. El Paso Exploration Co., Houston, 1985. Fellow Tex. Bar Found.; mem. ABA, Tex. State Bar Assn., W.Va. State Bar Assn., El Paso Women's Bar Assn. (v.p., pres. 1979-81). Education and schools, Banking, General corporate. Office: Calif State Poly U FRL Dept 3801 W Temple Ave Pomona CA 91768-2557

**LUNT, JENNIFER LEE,** lawyer; b. Big Springs, Tex., July 18, 1965; d. John Daleton and Karen Adele (Olson) L. BS, Auburn U., 1986; JD, U. Ala., 1989, MLS, 1990. Bar: Ala. 1989, U.S. Ct. Appeals (11th cir.) 1990, U.S. Dist. Ct. (mid. dist.) Ala. 1991, U.S. Dist. Ct. (no. dist.) Ala. 1993, U.S. Supreme Ct. 1997. Rsch. asst. Supreme Ct. Ala., Tuscaloosa, 1988-90; cons. Gorham, Waldrep, Stewart, Kendrick & Bryant P.C., Birmingham, 1990; pvt. practice Montgomery, Ala., 1991—; legal asst. adv. bd. Auburn U., Montgomery, 1994—. Rsch. editor: Law and Psychology Rev., 1988-89. Mem. ABA (mem. planning bd. young lawyers divsn. com. on women in the profession 1997—), Ala. State Bar (mem. com. on small firms and solo practitioners 1995—), Montgomery County Bar Assn. (law libr. com. 1997—). Criminal, Family and matrimonial, General civil litigation. Office: 207 Montgomery St Ste 224 Montgomery AL 36104-3528

**LUONG, PHONG MINH,** lawyer; b. Saigon, Vietnam, May 24, 1969; s. Ham Minh and Loi Ho thi Luong; m. Jacqueline Anne Paul, May 18, 1996. BA, Marycrest Coll., 1991; JD, William Mitchell Coll. Law, St. Paul, 1995; postgrad., Temple U. ext., Japan, 1994. Bar: Minn. 1995, U.S. Dist. Ct. Minn. 1995, U.S. Dist. Ct. (ea. dist.) Wis. 1995. Law clk. Price & Bruns Ltd., New Brighton, Minn., 1992-93, Reinhardt & Anderson, St. Paul, 1993-94, Am. Express, Tokyo, 1994; assoc. Yaeger, Jungbauer, Barczak & Roe, Mpls., 1994—. Head coach Little League, St. Paul, 1992, 94. Mem. Nat. Asian-Pacific ABA. Roman Catholic. Avocations: golf, cooking, travel, volleyball. Personal injury, Labor, General civil litigation. Home: 1791 Riverwood Dr Burnsville MN 55337-5306 Office: Yaeger Jungbauer Barczak & Roe 701 4th Ave S Ste 1400 Minneapolis MN 55415-1816

**LUONGO, STEPHEN EARLE,** lawyer; b. Phila., June 15, 1947; s. Alfred Leopold and Dorothy West L.; m. Louise Anne Cipriani, Aug. 12, 1972; children: Peter James, Richard Stephen, Michael Paul. BS, U. Pa.; JD, Temple U. Bar: Pa. 1972, U.S. Dist. Ct. (ea. dist.) Pa. 1972. Assoc. atty. Blank, Rome, Comisky & McCauley, Phila., 1972-79, ptnr., 1979—, mem. mgmt. com., 1992—, co.-chmn. corp. dept., 1988-93, mem. exec. com., 1995—; bd. dirs. Genesis Health Ventures, Inc., Kennett Suare, Pa., 1985—. Solicitor Merion Pk. Civic Assn., 1990-93. Mem. ABA, Am. Acad. Hosp. Attys., Pa. Bar Assn., Phila. Bar Assn., Nat. Assn. Coll. and Univ. Attys. Lodge: Order of Sons of Italy. General corporate, Health. Home: 215 Winding Way Merion Station PA 19066-1217 Office: Blank Rome Comisky & McCauley One Logan Sq Philadelphia PA 19103-6998

**LUPERT, LESLIE ALLAN,** lawyer; b. Syracuse, N.Y., May 24, 1946; s. Reuben and Miriam (Kaufman) L.; m. Roberta Gail Fellner, May 19, 1968; children: Jocelyn, Rachel, Susannah. BA, U. Buffalo, 1967; JD, Columbia U., 1971. Bar: N.Y. 1971. Ptnr. Orans Elsen & Lupert, N.Y.C., 1971—. Contbr. articles to profl. jours. Mem. ABA, N.Y. State Bar Assn. (trial lawyers sect.), Assn. of Bar of City of N.Y. (com. fed. legislation 1977-80, profl. and jud. ethics com. 1983-86, com. on fed. cts. 1986-89, 95-96), Phi Beta Kappa. Federal civil litigation, Criminal, State civil litigation. Office: Orans Elsen & Lupert 1 Rockefeller Plz New York NY 10020-2102

**LUPINO, JAMES SAMUEL,** lawyer; b. Mpls., Oct. 23, 1952; s. Rocco and Marie (Furlong) L.; m. Diane Schaefer, May 14, 1983. BS, Augustana Coll., 1974; JD, Hamline U., 1977. Bar: Fla. 1977, Minn. 1977, U.S. Dist. Ct. (so. dist.) Fla. 1977, U.S. Dist. Ct. Minn. 1977, Colo. 1997. Assoc. Thomson, Nordby & Peterson, St. Paul, 1976-77; counsel Lone Star Industries, Greenwich, Conn., 1977-79; sole practice Coral Gables, Fla., 1980-86; ptnr. Storace & Lupino, Miami, Fla., 1986-87, 91-93, Storace, Lupino & Middelthon, Miami, 1987-91, Storace, Lupino, Gregg & Casey, Miami, 1993-95, Hershoff, Lupino, DeFoor & Gregg, Miami, 1995—. Mem. ABA, Fla. Bar Assn., Minn. Bar Assn., Assn. Trial Lawyer Am., Miami C. of C, Kiwanis. Republican. Roman Catholic. Avocations: family, skiing, scuba, football. General corporate, Personal injury, Contracts commercial. Office: Hershoff Lupino DeFoor & Gregg 90130 Old Hwy Tavernier FL 33070-2348

**LUPKIN, JONATHAN DANIEL,** lawyer; b. N.Y.C., Feb. 6, 1968; s. Stanley Neil and Anne Rachel Lupkin; m. Michelle Ilene Gitlitz, June 10, 1990; children: Shira, Arielle, Leora, Ilana. BA, Columbia U., 1989, JD, 1992. Bar: N.Y. Law clk. hon. Edward R. Korman U.S. Dist. Judge Ea. Dist. N.Y., Bklyn., 1992-93; assoc. Kramer Levin Naftalis & Frankel, N.Y.C., 1993-96, Solomon, Zauderer, Ellenhorn, Frischer & Sharp, N.Y.C., 1996—. Staff mem. Columbia Law Rev., 1990-91, notes and comments editor, 1991-92. Harlan Fiske Stone scholar Columbia U. Sch. Law, N.Y.C., 1990, 92. Mem. Assn. of the Bar of the City of N.Y. (sec. com. on criminal advocacy 1995-97, com. on the judiciary 1998—), Soc. Sachems (sr.). Jewish. Avocations: reading, tropical fish. E-mail: jlupkin@szefs.com. Fax: 212-956-4068. Office: Solomon Zauderer Ellenhorn Frischer & Sharp 45 Rockefeller Plz New York NY 10111-0100

**LUPKIN, STANLEY NEIL,** lawyer; b. Bklyn., Mar. 27, 1941; s. David B. and Sylvia (Strassman) L.; m. Anne Rachel Fischler, June 3, 1962; children: Jonathan Daniel, Deborah Eve. BA, Columbia Coll., 1962; LLB, NYU, 1966. Bar: N.Y. 1966, U.S. Dist. Ct. (so. and ea. dists.) N.Y. 1970, U.S. Ct. Appeals (2d cir.) 1970, U.S. Supreme Ct. 1971. Asst. dist. atty., sr. trial atty., chief indictment bur. N.Y. County Dist. Atty.'s Office, N.Y.C., 1966-71; asst. commr. City of N.Y., 1966-71; 1st dep. commr., commr. Dept. Investigation, N.Y.C., 1978-82; ptnr. Litman, Asche, Lupkin, Gioiella & Bassin, N.Y.C., 1982-96; sr. mng. dir., counsel Decision Strategies/Fairfax Internat., L.L.C., N.Y.C., 1996—; mem. faculty Nat. Coll. Dist. Attys., Houston, 1974-75, FBI Nat. Acad., Quantico, Va., 1980-82; chmn. com. on criminal justice ops. Assn. of Bar of City of N.Y., 1982-85. Co-author book: Anatomy of A Municipal Franchise: N.Y.C. Bus Shelter Program, 1973-79, 4 vols., 1981. Trustee, counsel Solomon Schechter Sch. of Queens, Flushing, N.Y., 1974—; mem. secondary schs. com. admissions office Columbia Coll., N.Y.C., 1987—. With USAR, 1963-69. Mem. N.Y. State Bar Assn. (chmn. com. on def. 1985—, chmn. com. on prosecution 1977-85, exec. com. criminal justice sect. 1977—, Prosecutor of Yr. 1981), N.Y. State Assn. Criminal Def. Lawyers, Nat. Assn. Criminal Def. Lawyers, N.Y. Criminal Bar Assn., Am. Corp. Counsel Assn., Soc. Columbia Grads. (v.p. 1989-98, dir. 1989—), Internat. Assn. Ind. Pvt. Sector Insps. Gen. Avocations: classical music, Talmudic law. Criminal, General civil litigation, Administrative and regulatory. Office: Decision Strategies/Fairfax Internat LLC 505 Park Ave Fl 7 New York NY 10022-1106

**LURENSKY, MARCIA ADELE,** lawyer; b. Newton, Mass., May 4, 1948. BA magna cum laude, Wheaton Coll., 1970; JD, Boston Coll. Law Sch., 1973. Bar: Mass. 1973, D.C. 1990, U.S. Dist. Ct. (we. dist.) Wis. 1978, U.S. Dist. Ct. Mass. 1974, U.S. Ct. Appeals (1st cir.) 1974, U.S. Ct. Appeals (3d cir.) 1982, U.S. Ct. Appeals (4th cir.) 1984, U.S. Ct. Appeals (5th cir.) 1995, U.S. Ct. Appeals (8th cir.) 1985, U.S. Ct. Appeals (9th cir.) 1976, U.S. Ct. Appeals (10th cir.) 1995, U.S. Ct. Appeals (11th cir.) 1982, U.S. Ct. Appeals (fed. cir.) 1989, U.S. Claims Ct. 1989, U.S. Supreme Ct. 1979. Atty. U.S. Dept. Labor, Washington, 1974-90, Fed. Energy Regulatory Commn., U.S. Dept. Energy, Washington, 1990—. Mem. Phi Beta Kappa. Office: Fed Energy Regulatory Commn 888 1st St NE Washington DC 20426-0002

**LURVEY, IRA HAROLD,** lawyer; b. Chgo., Apr. 6, 1935; s. Louis and Faye (Grey) L.; m. Barbara Ann Sirvint, June 24, 1962; children: Nathana, Lawrence, Jennifer, Jonathan, David, Robert. BS, U. Ill., 1956; MS, Northwestern U., 1961; JD, U. Calif., Berkeley, 1965. Bar: Calif. 1965, Nev. 1966, U.S. Dist. Ct. (cen. dist.) Calif. 1966, U.S. Tax Ct. 1966, U.S. Ct. Appeals (9th cir.) 1966, U.S. Supreme Ct. 1975. Law clk. to hon. justices Nev. Supreme Ct., Carson City, 1965-66; from assoc. to ptnr. Pacht, Ross, Warne, Bernhard & Sears, Inc., 1966-84; predecessor firm Shea & Gould, L.A.; founding ptnr. Lurvey & Shapiro, L.A., 1984—; lectr. legal edn. programs; mem. Chief Justice's Commns. on Ct. Reform, Weighted Caseloads; mediator family law L.A. Superior Ct. Editor Community Property Jour., 1979-80, Primary Consultant CFL 2d, 1994; columnist Calif. Family Law Monthly; contbr. articles to profl. jours. Former chmn. L.A. Jr. Arts Ctr.; past pres. Cheviot Hills Homeowners Assn.; exec. v.p., counsel Hillel Acad. Sch., Beverly Hills, Calif., 1977—. With U.S. Army, 1957-58. Fellow Am. Acad. Matrimonial Lawyers (pres. So. Calif. chpt. 1991-92, mem. nat. bd. govs. 1992-94), Internat. Acad. Matrimonial Lawyers; mem. ABA (chair family law sect. 1996-97, liaison family law to sr. lawyers' divsn. 1998—, exec. com. 1991-97, governing coun. 1986—, fin. officer 1991-92, chmn. support com., chmn. CLE, chmn. policy and issues com., vice chmn. com. arbitration and mediation, bd. of editors Family Adv. mag.), Calif. Bar Assn. (editor jour. 1982-85, chmn. family law sect. 1986-87, exec. com. family law sect. 1982-88, specialization adv. bd. family law 1979-82), L.A. County Bar Assn. (chmn. family law sect. 1981-82, exec. com. family law 1989-92), Beverly Hills Bar Assn. (chmn. family law sect. 1976-77). Family and matrimonial, State civil litigation, Entertainment. Home: 2729 Motor Ave Los Angeles CA 90064-3441 Office: Lurvey & Shapiro Ste 1550 1333 Beverly Green Drive Los Angeles CA 90035-1018

**LUSK, TRACY BLAINE,** lawyer; b. Princeton, W.Va.; s. Tracy Norman Lusk and Delores Ann Yarborough; m. Carrie Wynne Catron, Feb. 20, 1985; children: Joshua Aaron, Zachary Blaine. BA in Polit. Sci., BA in Speech, Concord Coll., 1984; JD, U. Dayton Law Sch., 1987. Atty. Feuchtenberger, Barringer, Princeton, 1987-88; prosecutor McDowell County, Welch, W.Va., 1988-90; chief pub. defender McDowell County Pub. Defender 8th Cir., Welch, 1990-97; sole practice law Princeton, 1997—. Mem. Order Eastern Star, Shriners, Masons. Presbyn. Avocations: coach Little League baseball, coach Pee Wee football, teaching Sunday Sch. Home: PO Box 6 Princeton WV 24740-0006 Office: 200 1/2 S Walker St Princeton WV 24740-2747

**LUSKIN, ROBERT DAVID,** lawyer; b. Chgo., Jan. 21, 1950; s. Bert L. and S. Ruth (Katz) L.; m. Fairlea A. Sheehy, Aug. 23, 1975; children: Peter Duncan, Charles Cassimer. BA magna cum laude, Harvard U., 1972, JD magna cum laude, 1979; postgrad., Oxford (Eng.) U., 1972-75. Bar: D.C. 1979, U.S. Ct. Appeals (1st, 4th, 5th, 6th, 7th, 8th, 9th, 11th, D.C. cirs.) 1979, U.S. Supreme Ct., 1983. Law clk. to Hon. Louis F. Oberdorfer U.S. Dist. Ct. for D.C., Washington, 1979-80; spl. counsel organized crime racketeering sect. U.S. Dept. Justice, Washington, 1980-82; ptnr. Onek, Klein & Farr, Washington, 1982-89, Powell, Goldstein, Frazer & Murphy, Washington, 1989-93, Comey, Boyd & Luskin, Washington, 1993—; lectr. in law U. Va. Sch. Law, 1992—. Rhodes scholar, 1972-75. Mem. ABA (chmn. RICO Forfeitures and Civil Remedies com. 1986-94, vice chmn. task force on forfeitures), Harvard Law Sch. Assn. Washignton (pres.). Criminal, Federal civil litigation. Home: 3244 38th St NW Washington DC 20016-3729 Office: Comey Boyd & Luskin Ste 420 1025 Thomas Jefferson St NW Washington DC 20007-5201

**LUSTIG, DAVID CARL, III,** lawyer; b. Walden, N.Y., July 6, 1954; s. David Carl, Jr. and Violet (Rosenblum) L.; m. Debra Silver, Aug. 13, 1977; children: David, Evan. BS magna cum laude, Syracuse U., 1975; JD, Hofstra U., 1978. Bar: N.Y. 1979, U.S. Dist. Ct. (so. dist.) N.Y. 1979, U.S. Dist. Ct. (ea. dist.) N.Y. 1979, U.S. Ct. Appeals (2d cir.) 1986, U.S. Supreme Ct. 1993. Assoc. Esau J. Mishkin, Garden City, N.Y., 1978-79, Arye & Kors, P.C., N.Y.C., 1979-84; ptnr. Arye, Kors, Lustig & Sassower, N.Y.C., 1984—. lectr. in field. Mem. ATLA, N.Y. State Trial Lawyers Assn. (bd. dirs.), N.Y. County Lawyers Assn., Am. Bd. Trial Advocates. Personal injury, State civil litigation, Federal civil litigation. Office: Arye Kors Lustig & Sassower 20 Vesey St New York NY 10007-2913

**LUSTIG, DOUGLAS JAMES,** lawyer; b. Rochester, N.Y., July 19, 1949; s. Abraham and Ilene (Liberman) L.; m. Karen Ann Schiff, Aug. 17, 1975; children: Benjamin, JoEllen, Lindsay. BS, Syracuse (N.Y.) U., 1971; JD, Bklyn. Law Sch., 1974. Bar: N.Y. 1975, U.S. Dist. Ct. (we. dist.) N.Y. 1975, U.S. Supreme Ct. 1984. Assoc. Laverne, Sortino & Hanks, Rochester, 1975-79; ptnr. Laverne, Sortino, Hanks & Lustig, Rochester, 1979-84; sole practice Rochester, 1984-94; ptnr. Saperston & Day PC, 1997—; past pres. Jewish Family Svc., Rochester; v.p. Helping People With AIDS; mem. U.S. panel of trustees We. Dist. N.Y., Bankruptcy Ct., 1983—; lectr. N.Y. State Bar Assn., Monroe County Bar Assn., Nat. Bus. Inst. Pres. Jewish Family Svc. of Rochester, Inc. Mem. ABA, N.Y. State Bar Assn., Monroe County Bar Assn., Yates County Bar Assn., Nat. Assn. Bankruptcy Trustees, Comml. Law League, Am. Bankruptcy Inst., Irondequoit Country Club. Republican. Jewish. Fax: 716-325-5458. E-mail: dlustig@saperstonday.com. Bankruptcy, Consumer commercial, Real property. Home: 17 S Pittsford Hill Ln Pittsford NY 14534-2896 Main Office: 800 First Federal Plz Rochester NY 14614-1916 Branch Office: 100 E Main St Penn Yan NY 14527-1668

**LUSTIG, NORMAN I.,** lawyer; b. N.Y.C., Nov. 18, 1938; married; 3 children. BA, U. Fla., 1959; MA, Mich. State U., 1966; JD, U. Calif., Berkeley, 1968. Bar: Calif. 1969, U.S. Dist. Ct. (no. dist.) Calif. 1969, U.S. Dist. Ct. (cen. dist.) Calif. 1972, U.S. Dist. Ct. (ea. dist.) Calif. 1974, U.S. Ct. Appeals (9th cir.) 1997. Atty. Safeway Stores Inc., Oakland, Calif., 1969-70; asst. counsel The Regents of U. Calif., Berkeley, 1970-77; labor counsel Crown-Zellerbach Corp., San Francisco, 1977-87; adminstrv. law judge (ad hoc) Calif. Agrl. Labor Rels. Bd., Sacramento, 1977-85; pvt. practice Lafayette, Calif., 1987—. With USAFR, 1963-69. Mem. ABA. Civil rights, General civil litigation, Labor. Office: PO Box 1506 Lafayette CA 94549-1506

**LUTHER, DEBORA GAYLE,** lawyer; b. L.A., July 9, 1956; d. Richard Karel and Charlene Marie van der Weyde; m. Christopher Mark Luther, Oct. 8, 1994. BA, U. Calif., Davis, 1977; JD, U. Puget Sound, 1985. Bar: Calif. 1985, U.S. Ct. Appeals (9th cir.) 1990. Trial atty. U.S. Dept. Justice, Washington, 1985-89; asst. U.S. atty. ea. dist. Calif., Office of U.S. Atty., Sacramento, 1989—. Vol. rape crisis counselor Montgomery County, Rockville, Md., 1988-89. Recipient Am. Jurisprudence award in adminstrv. law Lawyers Coop. Pub. Co., 1985. Office: Office US Atty 501 I St Ste 10-100 Sacramento CA 95814-7300

**LUTHER, DONALD WILLIAM,** lawyer; b. Glendale, Calif., Mar. 16, 1964; s. Donald Harry and Jean Ellen Luther; m. Stephanie Anne Vincent, Nov. 16, 1996. BSME, Clemson U., 1987; JD, Ga. State U., 1995. Bar: Ga. 1995. Design engr. NOK, Inc., LaGrange, Ga., 1987-89; project engr. Selmix/Wilshire Corp., Norcross, Ga., 1989-93; atty. King & Spalding, Atlanta, 1995-97; assoc. Bovis Kyle & Burch LLC, Atlanta, 1997—. Mem. Atlanta Lit. Soc. General corporate, Intellectual property. Home: 481 Lakeshore Dr NE Atlanta GA 30307-1747 Office: Bovis Kyle & Burch LLC 53 Perimeter Ctr E Atlanta GA 30346-2294

**LUTHEY, GRAYDON DEAN, JR.,** lawyer; b. Topeka, Sept. 18, 1955; s. Graydon Dean Sr. and S. Anne (Murphy) L.; m. Deborah Denise McCullough, May 26, 1979; children: Sarah Elizabeth, Katherine Alexandra. BA in Letters with highest honors, U. Okla., 1976, JD, 1979; Fellow in Theology, Oxford (Eng.) U., 1976. Bar: Okla. 1979, U.S. Ct. Appeals (10th cir.) 1979, U.S. Dist. Ct. (no., we. and ea. dists.) Okla. 1980, U.S. Supreme Ct. 1982. Assoc. Jones, Givens, Gotcher, Bogan & Hilborne, Tulsa, 1979-84, ptnr., 1984-92, also bd. dirs.; ptnr. Hall, Estill, Hardwick, Gable, Golden & Nelson, Tulsa, 1992—, also bd. dirs.; adj. assoc. prof. U. Tulsa, 1985-87, adj. prof., 1987—; vis. fellow in theology Keble Coll., Oxford (Eng.) U., 1976; presiding judge Okla. Temporary Ct. Appeals, 1992-93; mem. Okla. Supreme Ct. Rules Com., 1992—. Bd. dirs. Tulsa Ballet, 1987—; chmn. Tulsa Pub. facilties Authority, 1990-93; trustee Episcopal Theol. Sem. of S.W., 1991-99, exec. com., 1992-99; vice chmn. Univ. Hosps. Authority, 1993-94, chmn. 1994-98, sec., 1998-99; chancellor Episcopal Diocese Okla., 1986—; mem. State of Okla. Futures Auth., 1998—. Nat. Merit scholar U. Okla., 1973. Fellow Am. Bar Found.; mem. ABA, Okla. Bar Assn. (chmn. continuing legal edn. com. 1989-91), Tulsa County Bar Assn. (bd. dirs. 1983-89, Disting. Svc. award 1988), Am. Inns of Ct. (barrister), Summit Club, Golf Club Okla., Beta Theta Pi, Phi Beta Kappa, Omicron Delta Kappa. Federal civil litigation, State civil litigation, Securities. Office: Hall Estill Hardwick Gable Golden & Nelson 320 S Boston Ave Ste 400 Tulsa OK 74103-3704

**LUTRINGER, RICHARD EMIL,** lawyer; b. N.Y.C., Feb. 4, 1943; s. Emil Vincent Lutringer and Alice Hamilton Rich; m. Dagmar Bonitz, May 1, 1970 (div. 1980); m. Clarinda Higgins, Oct. 11, 1980; children: Emily, Eric. AB, Coll. of William and Mary, 1964; JD in Internat. Affairs, Cornell U., 1967; MCL, U. Chgo., 1969. Bar: N.Y. 1972, U.S. Dist. Ct. (so. dist.) N.Y. 1972. Assoc. Whitman & Ransom, N.Y.C., 1971-80, ptnr., 1980-94; ptnr. Morgan, Lewis & Bockius LLP, N.Y.C., 1994—. Vice pres. N.Y.-N.J. Trail Conf., N.Y.C., 1976-80; pres. German-Am. Roundtable, Inc., 1998—. Mem. ABA, Internat. Bar Assn., Assn. of Bar of City of N.Y. (chmn. com. fgn. and comparative law 1990-93), Am. Fgn. Law Assn. (pres. 1989-93, treas. 1986-89), European-Am. C. of C. (vice chair trade com. 1992—), German-Amer. C of C, Inc., Philadelphia (mem. bd. dirs., 1999—). Avocations: sailing, hiking, skiing. Contracts commercial, General corporate, Private international. Home: 101 Compo Rd S Westport CT 06880-5007 Office: Morgan Lewis & Bockius LLP 101 Park Ave New York NY 10178-0060

**LUTTER, CHARLES WILLIAM, JR.,** lawyer; b. Kenosha, Wis., July 12, 1944; s. Charles William and Eva (Kuyawa) L.; m. Carol Hamilton Ewing, July 13, 1974; children: Charles William III, Scott. BS, U. Wis., 1966; postgrad., U. Tex., 1972; JD, St. Mary's U., 1976. Bar: Tex. 1976, U.S. Dist. Ct. (no. dist.) 1977, U.S. Dist. Ct. (so. dist.) 1981, U.S. Dist. Ct. (we. dist.) 1985, U.S. Ct. Appeals (5th and 11th cir.) 1981. Gen. atty. fin. SEC, Atlanta, 1976-80; chief regulations br. SEC, Houston, 1980-83; ptnr. Byrnes & Martin, Houston, 1983-84, Martin, Shannon & Drought, Inc., San Antonio, 1984-87; sr. corp. atty. LaQuinta Motor Inns, Inc., San Antonio, 1987-90; v.p., assoc. gen. counsel, sec. United Svcs. Advisors, Inc., 1991-93; v.p., spl. counsel, sec. United Svcs. Advisors, Inc., San Antonio, 1993-95, legal/operational cons., 1995—; counsel to trust and ind. trustees ICON Funds, 1996—, Lindbergh Funds, 1999—; mem. planning com. Ann. Securities Regulation Conf., SEC, Tex. Securities Bd., State Bar Tex., U. Tex. Law Sch., 1986—; mem. initial exec. com. San Antonio Tech. Adv. Group, 1985-87; mem. target '90 Goals for San Antonio Sci. and Tech. Venture Task Force, 1985-90, exec. com. for forum on entrepreneurship, 1985-87; mem. estate planning coun. Southwest Found. Biomed. Rsch., San Antonio, 1987—; mem. U. Tex. Health Sci. Ctr. Estate Planning Coun., 1998—; arbitrator Nat. Assn. Securities Dealers, N.Y. Stock Exch., Mcpl. Securities Rulemaking Bd. Contbr. articles to profl. jours. Bd. dirs. Boysville, San Antonio, 1989—, mem. exec. com., 1995—, pres., 1999; scout leader Alamo Area coun. Boy Scouts Am., 1988—. Capt. USAF, 1966-71. Decorated Air medal (6). Mem. ABA, State Bar Tex. (securities and investment banking com. 1984—, ad hoc subcom. on securities activities of banks 1987-89, subcom. on rules of fair practce for Tex. broker-dealers 1990), Internat. Assn. for Fin. Planning (bd. dirs. and regulatory coord. San Antonio chpt. 1987-98), Investment Co. Inst. (SEC rules com. 1993-95), San Antonio Bar Assn., San Antonio Bar Found., U. Wis. Alumni Assn., Air Force Assn., John M. Harlan Soc., Kiwanis, Phi Delta Phi. Securities, General corporate, Administrative and regulatory. Office: 103 Canyon Oaks Dr San Antonio TX 78232-1305 also: care US Global Investors 7900 Callaghan Rd San Antonio TX 78229-2327

**LUTTER, PAUL ALLEN,** lawyer; b. Chgo., Feb. 28, 1946; s. Herbert W. and Lois (Muller) L. BA, Carleton Coll., 1968; JD, Yale U., 1971. Bar: Ill. 1971, U.S. Tax Ct. 1986. Assoc. Ross & Hardies, Chgo., 1971-77, ptnr., 1978—. Co-author: Illinois Estate Administration, 1993. Dir. ACLU of Ill., Roger Baldwin Found.; pres., dir. Howard Brown Health Ctr.; chmn.'s coun. Design Industries Found. Fighting AIDS, Chgo. Mem. ABA, Chgo. Bar Assn. Estate planning, Probate, Personal income taxation. Home: 2214 N Magnolia Ave Chicago IL 60614-3104 Office: Ross & Hardies 150 N Michigan Ave Ste 2500 Chicago IL 60601-7567

**LUTTIG, J. MICHAEL,** federal judge; b. 1954. BA, Washington and Lee U., 1976; JD, U. Va., 1981. Asst. counsel The White House, 1981-82; law clk. to Judge Antonin Scalia U.S. Ct. of Appeals D.C. Cir., 1982-83; law clerk to chief justice Warren Burger Supreme Ct. of U.S., 1983-84, spl. asst. to chief justice Warren Burger, 1984-85; assoc. Davis Polk & Wardwell, 1985-89; prin. dep. asst. atty. gen., office of legal counsel U.S. Dept. of Justice, 1989-90, asst. atty. gen., office of legal counsel, counselor to atty. gen., 1990-91; judge U.S. Cir. Ct. (4th cir.), McLean, Va., 1991—. Mem. Nat. Adv. Com. of Lawyers for Bush, 1988, Lawyers for Bush Com., 1988. Mem. ABA, Va. Bar Assn., D.C. Bar Assn. Office: US Ct of Appeals 4th cir US Courthouse 401 Courthouse Sq Fl 9 Alexandria VA 22314-5704

**LUTTRELL, WILLIAM HARVEY,** lawyer; b. Compton, Ga., Apr. 19, 1952; s. William Anderson and Yolanda L.; m. Nancy Jean Luttrell, Apr. 14, 1973; children: Jennifer Marie, Jason Michael. BA cum laude, U. Colo., 1986; JD, U. Denver, 1996. Bar: Calif., 1997, U.S. Dist. Ct. (ctrl. dist.) Calif. 1997. Electrician, foreman IBEW Local 441, Santa Ana, Calif., 1976-83; project mgr. Simmons Elec. Corp., Denver, Colo., 1983-88, Action Elec., Santa Anna, Calif., 1988-90, Sasco Elec., Cerritos, Calif., 1990-94; contractor, owner Foxx Elec., Denver, 1994-96; constrn. cons. W.H. Luttrell & Assocs., Monarch Beach, Calif., 1996—; lawyer pvt. practice, Monarch Beach, 1997—; cons., advisor M.C. Consultants, Carlsbad, Calif., 1996—, JN Consulting Co., Orange County, Calif., 1996—. Mem. ABA, Orange County Bar Assn., L.A. County Bar Assn., William P. Gray Legion Lex Inn of Court, Golden Key. Democrat. Avocations: cycling, triathalon, Dalmatians breeding. Construction, Personal injury, General practice. Office: W H Luttrell & Assocs 15 Monarch Bay Plz Ste 601 Monarch Beach CA 92629-3424

**LUTZ, JAMES GURNEY,** lawyer; b. Cin., Sept. 18, 1933; s. Arthur Harold and Frances (Gurney) L.; children: Monica, Susan. JD, U. Cin., 1960. Bar: Ohio 1960, U.S. Dist. Ct. (so. dist.) Ohio 1961, U.S. Ct. Appeals (6th cir.) 1961, U.S. Tax Ct. 1975, U.S. Supreme Ct. 1975. Ptnr. Barbour, Kinpel & Allen, Cin., 1960-68; chief counsel E.C. Industries Inc., Cin., 1968-71; sr. ptnr. Lutz Cornetet & Albrinck, Cin., 1971—; pres., mem. bd. dirs. Motivation Dynamics Inc., Cin., 1978-85. Advisor, staff Hamilton County Vocat. Schs., Cin., 1968; advisor U. Cin. Coll., 1970-75; mem. adv. counsel Wyoming (Ohio) Bd. Edn., 1972-75; mem. bd. Ohio Pvt. Industry Coun., Columbus, 1975; gen. counsel S.W. Ohio Autistic Assn., Cin., 1980—. Mem. ABA, Am. Trial Lawyers Assn., Ohio State Bar Assn., Cin. Bar Assn. Avocations: psychology, computer science. Franchising, General civil litigation, Personal injury. Office: Lutz Cornetet & Albrinck 130 Tri County Pkwy Cincinnati OH 45246-3289

**LUTZ, JOHN SHAFROTH,** lawyer; b. San Francisco, Sept. 10, 1943; s. Frederick Henry and Helena Morrison (Shafroth) L.; m. Elizabeth Boschen, Dec. 14, 1968; children: John Shafroth, Victoria. BA, Brown U., 1965; JD, U. Denver, 1971. Bar: Colo. 1971, U.S. Dist. Ct. Colo. 1971, U.S. Ct. Appeals (2d cir.) 1975, D.C. 1976, U.S. Supreme Ct. 1976, U.S. Dist. Ct. (so. dist.) N.Y. 1977, U.S. Tax Ct. 1977, U.S. Ct. Appeals (10th cir.) 1979, N.Y. 1984, U.S. Ct. Appeals (9th cir.) 1990, U.S. Dist. Ct. (no. dist.) Calif. 1993. Trial atty. Denver regional office U.S. SEC, 1971-74; spl. atty. organized crime, racketeering sect. U.S. Dept. Justice, So. Dist. N.Y., 1974-77; atty. Kelly, Stansfield and O'Donnell, Denver, 1977-78; gen. counsel Boettcher & Co., Denver, 1978-87, Kelly, Stansfield and O'Donnel, Denver, 1987; spl. counsel, 1987-88, ptnr., 1988-93; of counsel LeBoeuf, Lamb, Greene and Mac Rae, L.L.P., 1993-94, ptnr. 1995—; spkr. on broker, dealer, securities law and arbitration issues to various profl. orgns. Contbr. articles to profl. jours. Bd. dirs. Cherry Creek Improvement Assn., 1980-84, Spalding Rehab. Hosp., 1986-89; chmn., vice-chmn. securities sub sect. Bus. Law Sect. of Colo. Bar, 1990, chmn., 1990-91. Lt. (j.g.), USNR, 1965-67. Mem. ABA, Colo. Bar Assn., Denver Bar Assn., Am. Law Inst., Securities Industry Assn. (state regulations com. 1982-86), Nat. Assn. Securities Dealers, Inc. (nat. arbitration com. 1987-91), St. Nicholas Soc. N.Y.C., Denver Law Club, Denver Country Club, Denver Athletic Club (dir. 1990-93), Rocky Mountain Brown Club (founder, past pres.), Racquet and Tennis Club. Republican. Episcopalian. Securities, Contracts commercial. Office: LeBoeuf Lamb Greene MacRae LLP 633 17th St Ste 2000 Denver CO 80202-3620

**LUTZ, RANDALL MATTHEW,** lawyer; b. New Brunswick, N.J., June 1, 1945; s. Ralph P. and Gertrude (Goodman) L. BS with honors, U. Md., 1967, JD, 1970. Bar: Md. 1970, U.S. Dist. Ct. Md. 1970, U.S. Ct. Appeals (4th cir.) 1970, U.S. Supreme Ct. 1970. Assoc. Burke, Gerber & Wilen, Balt., 1970-75; asst. atty. gen. State of Md., 1975-84; dir. criminal enforcement U.S. EPA, Washington, 1984-87; ptnr. Kaplan, Heyman, Greenberg, Engleman & Belgrade, Balt., 1987-90, Smith, Somerville & Case, LLC, Balt., 1990-98, Hodes, Ulman, Pessin & Katz, PA, Towson, Md., 1998—; lectr. in field. Author: (column) Environmental Law jour.,1987-88. Mem. dist. cabinet Balt. area coun. Boy Scouts Am., 1974-75. Mem. ABA, Md. Bar Assn., Balt. Bar Assn., Nat. Health Lawyers Assn., Health Facilities Assn. Health, Environmental, General corporate. Office: Hodes Ulman Pessin & Katz PA 901 Dulaney Valley Rd Towson MD 21204-2600

**LUTZKER, ELLIOT HOWARD,** lawyer; b. Flushing, N.Y., Feb. 22, 1953; s. Stanley Lawrence and Mildred (Goldberg) L.; m. Jill Leslie Simon, Aug. 24, 1975; children: Stacey, Amanda. BA, SUNY, Stony Brook, 1974; JD, N.Y. Law Sch., 1978. Bar: N.Y. 1979, Fla. 1979, U.S. Dist. Ct. (so. and ea.

dists.) N.Y. 1979. Atty. SEC, N.Y.C., 1978-81; assoc. Bachner, Tally, Polevoy, Misher & Brinberg, N.Y.C., 1981-85; ptnr. Snow Becker Krauss P.C., N.Y.C., 1985—. Mem. ABA (corp., banking law div.). Jewish. Avocations: reading, sports. Securities, General corporate. Home: 15 Kevin Ct Jericho NY 11753-1308 Office: Snow Becker Krauss PC 605 3rd Ave Fl 25 New York NY 10158-0125

**LYBECK, KEVIN LEE,** lawyer; b. Havre, Mont., May 23, 1959; s. Harold Lybeck and Marilyn Joanne (Thielman) Willman; m. Susan Clyatt Lybeck, July 3, 1982; children: Erik Christopher, Jason Michael. BA, Mont. State U., 1982; JD, Gonzaga U., 1985. Bar: U.S. Dist. Ct. (we. dist.) Wash. 1986. Atty. The Gaines Law Firm, P.S., Seattle, 1986-96; corp. sec. Contractors Bonding & Ins. Co., Seattle, 1990—, sr. v.p., 1995—; spkr. in field. Contbr. chpts. to books. Mem. ABA (vice-chmn. FSLC 1995—), Wash. State Bar Assn. Avocations: reading, swimming, baseball, basketball. Surety, Construction. Office: Contractors Bonding & Ins Co 1213 Valley St Seattle WA 98109-4428

**LYBECKER, MARTIN EARL,** lawyer; b. Lincoln, Nebr., Feb. 11, 1945; s. Earl Edward and Jeanette Frances (Kiefer) L.; m. Andrea Kristine Tollefson, Dec. 27, 1969; children: Carl Martin, Neil Anders. BBA, U. Wash., 1967, JD, 1970; LLM in Taxation, NYU, 1971; LLM, U. Pa., 1973. Bar: Wash. 1970, D.C. 1972, Pa. 1982. Atty. investment mgmt. div. SEC, Washington, 1972-75, assoc. dir. div., 1978-81; assoc. prof. SUNY, Buffalo, 1975-78; ptnr. Drinker Biddle & Reath, Washington, 1981-87, Ropes & Gray, Washington, 1987—; adj. prof. Georgetown U., Washington, 1974-75, 80-81; vis. assoc. prof. Duke U., Durham, N.C., 1977-78. Contbr. articles to law revs. Fellow U. Pa. Ctr. for Study of Fin. Instns., 1971-72. Mem. ABA (mem. subcom. on investment cos. and investment advisers, mem. subcom. on securities activities of banks, mem. com. on fed. regulation of securities bus. law sect., chairperson com. on devels. in investment svcs. bus. law sect., co-chair com. on long-range planning, mem. subcom. on bank holding co. activities and subcom. on trust and investment svcs. of com. of banking bus. law sect.), Am. Law Inst., Univ. Club Washington. Securities, Banking, General corporate. Home: 2806 Daniel Rd Bethesda MD 20815-3149 Office: Ropes & Gray 1301 K St NW Ste 800E Washington DC 20005-7008

**LYDON, DEBORAH RUTH,** lawyer, educator; b. Cin., June 7, 1955; d. Harry James Lydon Sr. and Georgia Ruth Peele; m. Michael Vernon Meister, Apr. 7, 1990; children: Lauren Lydon Meister, Matthew James Lydon Meister. B Gen. Studies, U. Cin., 1977, JD, 1981. Bar: Ohio 1981, Ky. 1991, U.S. Dist. Ct. (so. dist.) Ohio 1981, U.S. Dist. Ct. (ea. and we. dists.) Ky. 1991, U.S. Dist. Ct. (no. dist.) Ohio 1992, U.S. Ct. Appeals (8th cir.) 1982, U.S. Ct. Appeals (6th cir.) 1985, U.S. Supreme Ct. 1993. Assoc. Dinsmore & Shohl, Cin., 1981-88, ptnr., 1988—; adj. faculty U. Cin. Coll. Law, 1986—; med. mgmt. cons. Indsl. Health Svc., Inc., Cin., 1973-81. Author: Law of Medical Practice in Ohio, 1989, (book supplements) Law of Medical Practice in Ohio, 1990-95; contbr. numerous articles to law publs. Pres. adv. bd. Cin. Drug and Poison Info. Ctr., 1990-92. Mem. ABA, Ohio Bar Assn., Ohio Assn. Civil Trial Attys., Def. Rsch. Inst., Soc. Ohio Hosp. Attys. Avocations: bicycling, boating, travel. General civil litigation, Health, Personal injury. Office: Dinsmore & Shohl 1900 Chemed Ctr 255 E 5th St Cincinnati OH 45202-4700

**LYERLA, BRADFORD PETER,** lawyer; b. Savanna, Ill., Aug. 2, 1954; s. Ralph Herbert and Nancy Lee (Nelson) L.; m. Marilyn Wyse, Aug. 18, 1979; 3 children. BA, U. Ill., 1976, JD, 1980. Bar: Ill. 1980, U.S. Dist. Ct. (no. dist.) Ill. 1980, U.S. Dist. Ct. (no. dist.) Ind. 1982, U.S. Dist. Ct. (no. dist.) Calif. 1991, U.S. Dist. Ct. (ctrl. dist.) Ill. 1991, U.S. Ct. Appeals (7th cir.) 1983, U.S. Ct. Appeals (fed. cir.) 1991, U.S. Supreme Ct. 1995. Ptnr. Ryndak & Lyerla, Chgo.; lectr. on litigation and intellectual property law. Author publications in field; editor U. Ill. Law Rev., 1978-80. Bd. dirs. North Suburban Bd. of the Heartland Alliance, Wilmette, Ill., 1987-96, pres. 1993-94; bd. dirs. Traveler's and Immigrant's Aid, Chgo., 1991-95; bd. dirs., sec. Youth Svcs. Project, Inc., Chgo., 1987-91; mem. U. Ill. Pres.'s Coun.; founding mem. Cribbett Soc., U. Ill. Coll. Law; mem. Saints Faith Hope and Charity, Winnetka, Ill. Recipient John Powers Crowley Justice award People's Uptown Law Ctr., 1989. Fellow Am. Bar Found.; mem. ABA (editor litigation sect. intellectual properties litigation newsletter 1990—, mem. intellectual property sect. com. on unfair competition litigation), Ill. Bar Assn. (sect. coun. mem. gen. practice sect. 1984-85, intellectual property sect. 1989—, co-editor intellectual property newsletter 1989-95, chair 1996-97), Am. Intellectual Property Law Assn. (mem. antitrust and fed. lit. com.), Federalist Soc., Intellectual Property Law Assn. Chgo. (trade & internat coms.), Lakeshore Athletic Club, Michigan Shores Club, Wilmette Club, Phi Beta Kappa, Phi Kappa Phi. Patent, Federal civil litigation, Computer. Office: Ryndek & Lyerla 30 N Lasalle St Ste 2630 Chicago IL 60602-2506

**LYLE, PHILLIP E.,** lawyer; b. Sioux City, Iowa, Dec. 23, 1941; s. Raymond E. and Lucille A. Lyle; m. Charlotte C. Lyle, Aug. 31, 1975; children: Sean Patrick, Michael Owen. JD, U. S.D., 1968. Bar: Colo. 1968. Dep. dist. atty. Adams County, Brighton, Colo., 1968-77; pvt. practice Denver, 1977-98, Littleton, Colo., 1998—. Mem. Colo. Bar Assn., Columbine Country Club (v.p. 1994-95, bd. dirs. 1992-95). Office: 1800 W Littleton Blvd Littleton CO 80120-2021

**LYMAN, CURTIS LEE, JR.,** lawyer; b. Albion, N.Y., Dec. 8, 1952; s. Curtis Lee and Evelyn M. (Lake) L.; m. Vicki D. Bongiovanni, Oct. 21, 1978. B.A., Hiram Coll., 1974; J.D., Case Western Res. U., 1977. Bar: N.Y. 1979. Ptnr. Lyman & Lyman, Albion, N.Y., 1979-85; 1st asst. dist. atty. Orleans County, 1979-85; atty. Town of Albion, 1980-85; county counsel Orleans Indsl. Devel. Agy., 1981-85; gen. counsel Albion Cen. Sch. Dist., 1983-85; assoc. Merrill, Lynch, Pierce Fenner & Smith, Palm Beach, Fla., 1985-88; v.p. Chase Bank of Fla., 1988-92; pres. Raymond James Trust Co., St. Petersburg, 1992—. Pub. Trust and Estates Mag. Mem. giving com. Hanley-Hazelden Ctr., Palm Beach, 1988-92; chmn. planned giving tech. adv. com. Palm Beach Community Chest; bd. dirs. Goodwill of Suncoast Inc. Found., 1992—, ARC, Tampa Bay, 1992—; mem. planned givine com. United Way Pinellas County, 1992—. Mem. ABA, N.Y. State Bar Assn., Orleans County Bar Assn. (pres. 1982), Lawyers-Pilots Bar Assn., Aircraft Owners and Pilots Assn., Albion Area C. of C. (pres. 1979-80), Masons, Kiwanis, Albion Town Club (sec. 1978-79, Buffalo Ski Club, Tampa Club. Republican. Presbyterian. Banking, Estate planning, Probate. Office: 1 Progress Plz Ste 150 Saint Petersburg FL 33701-4335 Address: 9300 Oak St NE Saint Petersburg FL 33702-2652

**LYMAN, NATHAN MARQUIS,** lawyer; b. Albion, N.Y., Oct. 18, 1955; s. Curtis Lee St. and Evelyn Myra (Lake) L.; m. Gail Therese Boehm, June 25, 1983; children: Laura Therese, Elizabeth Ashley, Catherine Lee. BA cum laude, Hiram Coll., 1977; JD cum laude, Syracuse U., 1980. Bar: N.Y. 1981, U.S. Dist. Ct. (we. dist.) N.Y. 1981, U.S. Dist. Ct. (no. and ea. dists.) N.Y. 1985, U.S. Ct. Appeals (D.C. cir.) 1985, U.S. Dist. Ct. (so. dist.) N.Y. 1989, U.S. Ct. Appeals (2nd cir.) 1989. Ptnr. Lyman & Lyman LLC, Albion, 1981-92; pvt. practice Albion, 1992—; ptnr. Softstar Computer, Albion, 1983—, P&L Energies, 1987-90; gen. counsel Otter Creek Chem. Corp., 1987—, Barden & Robeson Corp., 1985—, Barden Homes of Ind., Inc., 1996—, Milo Corp., 1987—; asst. dirs. atty. County of Orleans, Albion, 1983-85, dist. attys., 1985; v.p. Interstate Pay Phone, Albion, 1985-87; adj. prof. law Syracuse Coll. Law, 1990. Contbr. articles to profl. jours. Fireman Albion Fire Dept., 1981-85; trustee Village of Albion, 1982-85; town atty. Town of Albion, 1984-88, 90-95, Village of Holley, 1996—; pres. Albion Community Devel. Corp., 1990-95; atty. Village of Holly, 1996—; mem. Nat. Ski Patrol, Buffalo, 1984-91; del. jud. nominating com. Buffalo Reps., 1985, 90. Mem. ABA, N.Y. State Bar Assn., Orleans County Bar Assn., Greater Albion C. of C. (pres. 1987-89, bd. dirs. 1982-99), Albion Town Club (pres. 1991-94, bd. dirs. 1994-95), Orleans County C. of C., Rotary (Albion bd. dirs. 1987-90, treas. 1988, sec. 1989, pres.-elect 1992-93, pres. 1993-94, v.p. 1994-95, Paul Harris fellow 1997), Soc. of Erie Canal, Pi Gamma Mu. Republican. Presbyterian. Avocations: tennis, skiing, computers. Computer, Private international, General civil litigation. Home: 3505 Butts Rd Albion NY 14411-9708 Office: Lyman & Lyman 51 N Main St Albion NY 14411-1296 *Notable cases include: Yerkovich vs. Pierce, 85 CV 826 NDNY which obtained 1.58 million recovery for wrongful abduction of a child. Client was the founder of Child Find, Inc.; child was missing for 10 yrs.*

**LYNCH, CRAIG M.,** lawyer; b. Santa Monica, Calif., Jan. 19, 1958; s. Kevin Gary and Edwina Chase Lynch; m. Margaret Michelle Greene, May 19, 1984; 1 child, Sean. BA, Loyola Marymount, L.A., 1979, JD, 1979. Bar: Calif. 1982, U.S. Dist. Ct. (ctrl. and ea. dists.) Calif. 1983, U.S. Ct. Appeals (9th cir.) 1983, U.S. Dist. Ct. (so. dist.) Calif. 1984, U.S. Supreme Ct. 1993, U.S. Dist. Ct. (no. dist.) Calif. 1997. Atty. Goldberg, Fisher & Quirk, Bakersfield, Calif., 1983-85; owner Lynch Devel. Co., Bakersfield, 1985-90; atty. Fachin & McCartney, Bakersfield, 1990-92; atty., corp. counsel Tri-Valley Corp., Bakersfield, 1992-93; atty., ptnr. Lynch & Lynch, Bakersfield, 1993—. Roman Catholic. General civil litigation, Oil, gas, and mineral, Real property. Home: 10913 Craigton Ct Bakersfield CA 93311-3569 Office: Lynch & Lynch 4800 Easton Dr Ste 114 Bakersfield CA 93309-9424

**LYNCH, CRAIG TAYLOR,** lawyer; b. Miami, Fla., Apr. 26, 1959; s. Glenn James and Faith Rowland (Folsom) L. BS, Fla. State U., 1981; JD, U. N.C., Chapel Hill, 1986. Bar: N.C. 1986, U.S. Dist. Ct. (we. dist.) N.C. 1986, U.S. Ct. Appeals (4th cir.) 1992. Analyst Ford Motor Co., Charlotte, N.C., 1981-82, zone mgr., 1982-83; assoc. Parker, Poe, Adams & Bernstein, Charlotte, 1986-93, ptnr., 1994—, chmn. recruiting com., 1996—. Author: A Marketing Plan for Basketball, 1981. Vol. Lawyers Program, Charlotte, 1986—. Named to Charlotte Bus. Jour. Forty Under Forty, 1995. Mem. ABA (real property sect.), Nat. Multiple Sclerosis Soc. (fundraising com. chmn. Greater Carolinas chpt. 1992-93, bd. dirs. 1993—, chmn. 1995-98, Young Profl. Vol. of Yr. 1993), N.C. State Bar Assn., N.C. Bar Assn., Mecklenburg County Bar Assn., Fla. State U. Alumni Assn. (bd. dirs. 1987—), Fla. State U. Alumni Club Charlotte (pres. 1990-93, mem. comml. bd. realtors local region 1997—), Charlotte Chamber Leadership Sch., Tower Club Charlotte, Beta Gamma Sigma, Phi Delta Phi. Avocations: photography, running, water skiing, sports, golf, traveling. Contracts commercial, Real property, General civil litigation. Office: Parker Poe Adams & Bernstein LLP 2500 Charlotte Plz Charlotte NC 28244

**LYNCH, JAMES EDWARD,** lawyer; b. Tampa, Fla., Aug. 5, 1951; s. John Thomas and Dorothy Bridget (Crosson) L.; m. Eileen Marie Baumgardner, Jan. 11, 1975; children: James Edward, Jr., Carolyn Marie. BA, LaSalle Coll., 1973; JD, Del. Law Sch., 1978. Bar: Pa. 1978, U.S. Dist. Ct. (ea. dist.) Pa. 1983, U.S. Supreme Ct. 1984, U.S. Ct. Appeals (3d cir.) 1984, U.S. Tax Ct. 1986, N.J. 1987, U.S. Dist. Ct. N.J. 1987, U.S. Dist. Ct. (cen. dist.) Pa. 1988. Ter. mgr. Clairol, Inc., N.Y.C., 1973-75; assoc. Ettinger, Silverman, Balka & Levy, Phila., 1978-80; ptnr. Lynch & Lynch, Bensalem, Pa., 1980-82, Kardos & Lynch, Newtown, Pa., 1982-87, Keane & Lynch, Newtown, 1987-88; prin. Law Offices James E. Lynch, 1988—. Mem. ABA, Pa. Bar Assn., Bucks County Bar Assn., Phila. County Bar Assn., Upper Makefield Businessmen's Assn., Lower Bucks C. of C., Men of La Salle (bd. dirs.), Upper Makefield Soccer Assn. (bd. dirs.), Upper Makefield Baseball League (bd. dirs.), Gradu-Eights Club, Lions, Phi Alpha Delta. Republican. Roman Catholic. General corporate, General practice, Personal injury. Home: 115 Overlook Ave Washington Crossing PA 18977-1203 Office: Luxembourg Corp Ctr 503 Corporate Dr W Langhorne PA 19047-8011 also: 130 Durand Ave Trenton NJ 08611-3210

**LYNCH, JOHN EDWARD, JR.,** lawyer; b. Lansing, Mich., May 3, 1952; s. John Edward and Miriam Ann (Hyland) L.; m. Brenda Jayne Clark, Nov. 16, 1984; children: John E. III, Robert C., David B., Patrick D., Jacqueline E. AB, Hamilton Coll., 1974; JD, Case Western Res. U., 1977. Bar: Conn. 1978, Ohio 1980, U.S. Dist. Ct. (no. dist.) Ohio 1980, U.S. Ct. Appeals (6th cir.) 1980. Assoc. Thompson, Weir & Barclay, 1977-78; law clk. U.S. Dist. Judge, Cleve., 1978-80; assoc. Squire, Sanders and Dempsey, Cleve., 1980-86, ptnr., 1986-96; v.p., gen. counsel, sec. Caliber System, Inc., Akron, Ohio, 1996-98; sr. v.p. gen. couns. BP America, Inc., 1998-99; assoc. gen. counsel Upstream Western Hemisphere BP Amoco, 1999—; master bencher Am. Inns of Ct. Found., 1987-98; mem. civil justice reform act adv. group U.S. Dist. Ct. (no. dist.) Ohio. Del. Hamilton Coll. Alumni Coun., 1992-97, regional chair alumni admissions, 1993—; trustee The Cath. Charities Corp., 1995-97; mem. Cuyahoga County Rep. Exec. Com., Cleve., 1984—; mem. Seton Soc. St. Vincent Hosp. Fund. Roman Catholic. Avocations: golf, jogging. Antitrust, General civil litigation, Construction. Home: 918 Peachwood Bend Dr Houston TX 77077-1555 Office: BP Amoco 501 Westlake Park Blvd Houston TX 77079-2607

**LYNCH, JOHN JAMES,** lawyer; b. Evergreen Park, Ill., Aug. 22, 1945; s. John J. and Agnes (Daly) L.; m. Kathleen Russell, Aug. 15, 1970; children: Kerry, Elizabeth, Erin. BA, St. Mary of the Lake Sem., 1967; MA in Philosophy, DePaul U., 1970, JD, 1973. Bar: Ill. 1973, U.S. Dist. Ct. (no. dist.) Ill. 1973, U.S. Ct. Appeals (7th cir.) 1976. Assoc. McKenna, Storer, Rowe, White & Haskell, Chgo., 1973-75; ptnr. Haskell & Perrin, Chgo., 1975—. Mem. ABA, Ill. State Bar Assn., Chgo. Bar Assn., Fedn. Ins. & Corp. Counsel. General civil litigation, Insurance, Professional liability. Office: Haskell & Perrin 200 W Adams St Ste 2600 Chicago IL 60606-5284

**LYNCH, JOHN JOSEPH,** lawyer; b. Mt. Pleasant, Mich., Jan. 31, 1936; s. Edward N. Lynch and Dorothy K. Botsford; m. Sandra Claire Nunneley, Feb. 4, 1941; children: James, Michael, Patrick, Katherine. BS, John Carroll U., 1960; JD, U. Mich., 1963. Ptnr. Lynch Gallagher Lynch & Martineau, Mt. Pleasant, Mich., 1963—; arbitrator Am. Arbitration Assn., U.S. Dist. Ct. (we. dist.) Mich., 1980; referee Cir. Ct., Mt. Pleasant, 1963-68. Bd. dir. C.M. Cmty. Hosp., Mt. Pleasant, 1965-80, Broomfield Fund., Mt. Pleasant, 1968-75. With USN, 1955-57. Recipient Plaque Am. Arbitration Assn., 1983, C.M. Cmty. Hosp., 1996. Mem. Mich. Oil and Gas Assn. (legal com.), Assn. Irish Am. Attys. Avocations: fly fishing, hunting, fishing, diving. Oil, gas, and mineral, Real property, Administrative and regulatory. Office: Lynch Gallagher Lynch & Martineau 555 N Main St Mount Pleasant MI 48858-1651

**LYNCH, JOHN PETER,** lawyer; b. Chgo., June 5, 1942; s. Charles Joseph and Anne Mae (Loughlin) L.; m. Judy Godvin, Sept. 21, 1968; children: Julie, Jennifer. AB, Marquette U., 1964; JD, Northwestern U., 1967. Bar: Ill. 1967, U.S. Ct. Appeals (7th cir.) 1979, U.S. Ct. Appeals (5th cir.) 1976, U.S. Supreme Ct. 1979. Ptnr. Kirkland & Ellis, Chgo., 1973-76, Hedlund, Hunter & Lynch, Chgo., 1976-82, Latham, Watkins, Hedlund, Hunter & Lynch, Chgo., 1982-85, Latham & Watkins, Chgo., 1985—. Mem. vis. com. Northwestern U. Law Sch. Served as lt. USN, 1968-71. Mem. ABA, Ill. Bar Assn., Assn. Trial Lawyers Am., Order of Coif, City Club, Exec. Club, Met. Club. Notes and Comments editor Northwestern U. Law Rev., 1967. Antitrust, Public international, Federal civil litigation. Home: 439 Sheridan Rd Kenilworth IL 60043-1220 Office: Latham & Watkins Ste 5800 Sears Tower Chicago IL 60606

**LYNCH, KEVIN G.,** lawyer; b. L.A., Sept. 18, 1933; s. Kenneth G. and Ysabel M. Lynch; m. Edwina Martin, Dec. 22, 1956 (div. May 1991); children: Craig, Brenda, Laura Radanovich, Brian, Maureen. BS, Loyola U., 1955; JD, Southwestern U., 1960. Bar: Calif. 1961, U.S. Dist. Ct. (ctrl. dist.) Calif. 1961, U.S. Supreme Ct. 1973. Dep. city atty. L.A. City Atty., 1961-63; assoc. Dryden, Harrington & Swartz, L.A., 1963-64; ptnr., assoc. Lewis, Varni & Ghirardelli, San Fernando, Calif., 1964-80; ptnr. Lynch & Freytag, Encino, Calif., 1981-90, Lynch and Lynch, San Fernando, Calif., 1991—. Mem. C. of C. (dir., counsel). Republican. Roman Catholic. Avocations: civil war history and weapons, traditional jazz, wine collecting. State civil litigation, Personal injury, Probate. Office: Lynch and Lynch 501 S Brand Blvd Ste 5 San Fernando CA 91340-4932

**LYNCH, LORETTA B.,** prosecutor; b. Durham, N.C., May 21, 1959; s. Lorenzo Lynch. Grad., Harvard Coll., 1981; JD, Harvard U., 1984. Litigation assoc. Cahill, Gordon & Reindel, 1984-90; with Office of U.S. Atty. for Ea. Dist. of N.Y., 1990—; chief L.I. offices, 1994-98; chief asst. U.S. States Attys., 1998—; U.S. atty. ea. dist. N.Y. U.S. Dept. Justice, Bklyn., 1999—. Avocations: reading, tennis. Office: US Courthouse 147 Pierrepont St Brooklyn NY 11201*

**LYNCH, LUKE DANIEL, JR.,** lawyer; b. Bklyn., Mar. 28, 1945; s. Luke Daniel and Marjorie Carol (Thien) L.; m. Nancy G. Ott, Sept. 19, 1970; children: Luke D. III, Bettina Anne. BA cum laude, Yale U., 1966; JD, Harvard U., 1969. Bar: N.Y. 1969, U.S. Dist. Ct. (so. dist.) N.Y. 1970. Assoc. Shearman & Sterling, N.Y.C., 1969-78; spl. asst. U.S. Treasury Dept., Washington, 1978-79, assoc. gen. counsel, 1979-82; gen. counsel Chrysler Corp Loan Guaranty Bd., Washington, 1981-82; ptnr. D'Amato & Lynch, P.C., N.Y.C., 1983—. Mem. ABA. Avocation: golf. Banking, General corporate, Insurance. Office: D'Amato & Lynch 70 Pine St Fl 41 New York NY 10270-0110

**LYNCH, NEIL L(AWRENCE),** state supreme court justice; b. Holyoke, Mass., June 26, 1930. A.B. sum laude, Harvard U., 1952, LL.B., 1957. Bar: Mass. 1952. Assoc. firm. Hale Sanderson Byrnes & Morton, Boston, 1957-65; gen. counsel Mass. Port Authority, 1965-76; assoc. Herilhy and O'Brien, Boston, 1976-79; chief legal counsel to gov. State of Mass., 1979-81; assoc. justice Supreme Jud. Ct. Mass., 1981—; mem. Airport Operators Council Internat., 1965-76, chmn., 1974-75; adj. prof. law, legal writing and environ. law New Eng. Law Sch., 1968-74, assoc. prof. corp. law and evidence, 1974-76. Served to 1st lt. USAF, 1952-54. Mem. ABA (pub. contracts com. pub. contract law sect. 1975-76), Boston Bar Assn., Mass. Bar Assn. Office: Mass Supreme Jud Ct Pemberton Sq 1300 New Courthouse Boston MA 02108*

**LYNCH, PATRICK,** lawyer; b. Pitts., Nov. 11, 1941; s. Thomas Patrick and Helen Mary (Grimes) L.; m. M. Linda Maturo, June 20, 1964; children: Megan, Kevin, Colin, Brendan, Erin, Brian, Liam, Eamonn, Kilian, Caitlin, Ryan, Declan, Cristin, Mairin, Sean. BA in Philosophy, Loyola U., L.A., 1964, LLB, 1966. Bar: Calif. 1967, U.S. Dist. Ct. (cen., so., no. and ea. dists.) Calif., U.S. Ct. Appeals (9th cir.), U.S. Supreme Ct. Ptnr. O'Melveny & Myers, Los Angeles, 1966—; panelist PLI Annual Antitrust Law Inst., 1982-98. Bd. editors Matthew Bender Fed. Litigation Guide Reporter. Fellow Am. Coll. Trial Lawyers; mem. L.A. County Bar Assn. Office: O'Melveny & Myers 400 S Hope St Los Angeles CA 90071-2899

**LYNCH, PAUL PATRICK,** corporate lawyer; b. New Castle, Pa., Oct. 6, 1951; s. Francis Joseph and Josephine Ann (Peluso) L.; m. Marcia Lee Magno, May 21, 1982; children: Jessica Ann, Jennifer Marie. BA, Washington & Jefferson Coll., 1973; JD, U. Pitts., 1991. Bar: Pa. 1991, U.S. Dist. Ct. (we. dist.) Pa. 1991, U.S. Ct. Appeals (3d and 4th cirs.) 1996. Spl. agt. IRS, Detroit, 1973-80; pres. Lynch Bros. Investments, Inc., New Castle, 1980—; bd. dirs. First Nat. Bank Pa., Hermitage, FNB Corp., Hermitage, St. Francis Hosp. New Castle, Westfield Behavior Health Sys., New Castle. Mem. Greater New Castle C. of C. (dir.), Lawrence County Hist. Soc. (dir. 1996—), Wolves Club, Scottish Rite Freemasons. Democrat. Roman Catholic. Avocations: golf, tennis, travel. Probate, General corporate. Home: 11 Victoria Dr Neshannock PA 16105-1229 Office: Lynch & Gallito 2625 Wilmington Rd New Castle PA 16105-1529

**LYNCH, ROBERT BERGER,** lawyer; b. LaCrosse, Wis., June 10, 1931; s. Jan P. and Eve (Berger) L.; m. Iris D. Healy; children: Jan Fredrick Lynch, Jerry Wayne Coggins. BS, U.S. Merchant Marine Acad., 1955; JD, U. of the Pacific, 1967. Bar: Calif. 1969, U.S. Supreme Ct. 1972. Engr. Aeroject Gen. Corp., Sacramento, Calif., 1955-61, proposal mgr., 1961-63, asst. contract adminstrn. mgr., 1963-66, contract adminstrn. mgr., 1967-70; pvt. practice law Rancho Cordova, Calif., 1969—; instr. bus. law Solano Community Coll., 1977-79, San Joaquin Delta Coll., 1978-79; mediator family law panel Sacramento Superior Ct.; mcpl. ct. (traffic) pro tem judge, Sacramento. Active various charity fund-raising campaigns in Sacramento, Calif., 1966-68; mem. mission com. St. Clements Episcopal Ch., Rancho Cordova, Calif., 1967-68; trustee Los Rios Cmty. Coll. Dist., Calif., 1971-79. With USCG, 1949-51, USNR 1951-80, Nat. Guard 1988-91, Maj. AUS, ret. Mem. IEEE, Calif. Wildlife Fedn., Internat. Turtle Club, Marines Meml. Assn., Am. Legion, Mensa. Family and matrimonial, Probate, General practice. Office: 10615 Coloma Rd Rancho Cordova CA 95670-3939

**LYNCH, SANDRA LEA,** judge; b. Oak Park, Ill., July 31, 1946; d. Bernard Francis and Eugenia Tyus (Shepherd) L.; married; 1 child, Stephen Lynch Bowman. AB in Philosophy, Wellesley Coll., 1968; JD cum laude, Boston U., 1971. Bar: Mass. 1971, U.S. Supreme Ct. 1974-75. Law clk. to Hon. Raymond J. Pettine U.S. Dist. Ct., Providence; asst. atty. gen. Commonwealth of Mass., Boston, 1974; gen. counsel Mass. Dept. Edn., Boston, 1974-78; ptnr. Foley, Hoag & Eliot, Boston, 1978-95; judge 1st cir. U.S. Ct. Appeals, Boston, 1995—. Contbr. articles to profl. jours. Past co-chair leading industries com. Greater Boston C. of C. Recipient Distinguished Alumnae award Boston U. Law Sch., 1993, Wellesley Coll., 1997, Disting. Svc. award Planned Parenthood, 1991. Mem. ABA, Nat. Assn. Women Judges, Mass. Bar Assn., Boston Bar Assn. (pres. 1992-93), Women's Forum. Office: US Ct Appeals One Courthouse Way Ste 8710 Boston MA 02210-3010

**LYNCH, THOM,** lawyer; b. N.Y.C., Dec. 15, 1957; s. Joseph and Rebecca (Saeger) Lynch; m. Danielle Cassaro, May 31, 1992; 1 child Mark Joseph. AB, Princeton U., 1979; JD, Columbia U., 1982. Bar: N.Y. 1983, U.S. Dist. Ct. N.Y. (so. dist.) 1997. Assoc. Polk, Howard & Levin, N.Y.C., 1982-92; ptnr. Lynch, Zoltar & Werik, Bronx, 1992—. Mem. ABA, N.Y.C. Bar Assn. General practice, Pension, profit-sharing, and employee benefits. Office: Lynch Zoltar & Werik 169 Revere Ave Bronx NY 10465-3322

**LYNCH, TIMOTHY CRONIN,** lawyer; b. Washington, Mar. 14, 1969. BA cum laude, Loyola Coll., Balt., 1991; JD, U. Md., 1995. Bar: Md. 1995, Va. 1996, DC 1999, U.S. Dist. Ct. (ea. and we. dists.) Va., U.S. Dist. Ct. Md., U.S. Ct. Appeals (4th cir.). Law clk. to hon. J. James McKenna Cir. Ct. for Montgomery County Md., Rockville, 1995-96; assoc. Shulman, Rogers, Gandal, Vorday & Ecker, Rockville, 1996-97, Scanlan, Rosen & Shar, Balt., 1997—. General civil litigation, Personal injury, Securities. Office: Scanlan Rosen & Shar LLC 26 South St Baltimore MD 21202-3215

**LYNCH, TIMOTHY JEREMIAH-MAHONEY,** lawyer, educator, theologian, realtor, writer; b. June 10, 1952; s. Joseph David and Margaret Mary (Mahoney) L.m. on private internat. law U.S. State Dept., Washington; mem. Dead Sea Scrolls Rsch. Project, 1998; mem. author and writers group on multi-vol. transl. series classical works from late Roman, medieval near eastern, patristic and early Christian ch. periods Princeton U., 1998, Cath. U. Am., 1998, U. Calif., Berkely, 1998; rsch. prof. Old and New Testamen bibl. lit. commentary, 1998. *Over twenty years as a top-notch commercial industrial real estate investor, manager, broker and developer. Major achievements include financing venture capital, large scale investments and developments in hotel shopping center markets and through use of applying long-range capital through refinancing of existing mortgages principals net yields. Leading consultant and speaker on business and economic issues that are influenced by Federal Government policies. Also leading expert on corporate governance and speaker issues affecting corporate directors and shareholders.* Author: (10 vol. manuscript) History of Ecumenical Doctrines and Canon Law of Church; editorial bd. Internat. Tax Jour., 1993; author: Publishers National Endowment for Arts and Humanities Classical Translations: Latin, Greek, and Byzantine Literary Texts for Modern Theological-Philosophical Analysis of Social Issues; Essays on Issues of Religious Ethics and Social, Public Policy Issues, 1995, 96, others; editorial bd. Internat. Tax Jour., 1993, Melrose Press: Internat. Firm; contbr. articles to profl. jours. Dir., vice chmn. Downtown Assn. San Francisco; councillor, dir. Atlantic Coun. U.S., 1984—; corp. counsel, chmn. spl. arbitrator's tribunal on U.S.-Brazil trade, fin. and banking rels. Inter-Am. Comml. Arbitration Commn., Washington; chmn. nat. adv. com. U.S.-Mid. East rels. U.S. Mid. East Policy Coun., U.S. State Dept., Washington, 1989—; mem. Pres. Bush's Adv. Commn. on Econ. and Public Policy Priorities, Washington, 1989; mem. conf. bd. Mid. East Policy Coun., U.S. State Dept., Washington, 1994—; elected mem. Coun. of Scholars U.S. Libr. Congress, Washington; bd. dirs. Internat. Diplomacy Coun., San Francisco Opera, Ballet, Symphony Assns. Recipient Cmty. Svc. honors Mayor Dianne Feinstein, San Francisco, 1987, Leadership awards St. Ignatius Coll. Prep., 1984, Calif.'s Gold State award, 1990, AU-ABA Achievement award, 1990, Medal of Honor Order Internat. Ambs. Com. U.S. State Dept. and Foreign Svc. Inst., Washington D.C., World Lifetime Achievement award, Induction 20th Century Millenium Hall Fame and Dist. Leadership Hall Fame Am. Acad. Achievement, 1998, award Superior Talent in Bus. and Arts, Century Dist. Acheivement award, Am. Acad. Achievement, 1998, Internat. Cultural award, 1997, Presdl. Seal Honor, 1997, Decree Internat. Cultural Letters, 1997; named Civic Leader of Yr., Nat. Trust for Hist. Preservation, 1988, 89; named to Presdl. Order of Merit, 1991., Induction U.S. Lib. Congress 500 Leaders of Influence Hall Fame, 1998, Noble Installation Orders of Knighthood Royal British Legions by Queen Elizabeth

II, 1998. Fellow World Jurist Assn., World Assn. Judges (Washington); mem. ATLA, Internat. Bar Assn. (various coms., internat. litigation, taxation, labor issue), Am. Arbitration Assn. (panelist, internat. decree), Am. Fgn. Law Assn. (various coms.), Am. Soc. Ch. History, Am. Inst. Archaeology (Boston), Pontifical Inst. Medieval Studies (Toronto, Can.), Am. Hist. Assn., Am. Philol. Assn., Inst. European Law, Medieval Acad. Am., U.S. Supreme Ct. Hist. Soc. (presdl. seal of honor, cultural diploma honor), J Canon Law Soc. U.S., Nat. Planning Assn., Nat. Assn. Scholars (Eminent Scholar of Yr. 1993), Netherlands Arbitration Inst. (mem. Gen. Panels of Arbitrators, mem. Permanent Ct. Arbitration), Calif. Coun. Internat. Trade (GATT com., tax com., legis. com.), Practicing Law Inst., Am. Fgn. Law Assn. (mem. editl. bd. Working Groups on Rsch. Jour. for Legal systems of Africa, Mid. East, Latin Am., EEC and Soviet Union), U.S.-China Bus. Coun. (export com., GATT com., banking and fin. com., import com.), Bay Area Coun. (corp. mem.), Nat. Acad. Conciliators (Spl. award), Internat. Bar (mem. U.S. Group on Model on Insolvency Corp. Acts), Ctr. Internat. Comml. Arbitration, Comml. Club (various positions), Am. Venture Capital Assn., Pacific Venture Capital Assn., Am. Soc. Internat. Law, Washington Fgn. Law Soc., Asia-Pacific Lawyers Assn., Soc. Profls. in Dispute Resolution, British Inst. Internat. and Comparative Law, Internat. Law Assn. (U.S. br.), Commercial Bar Assn. of United Kingdom (London), Inter-Pacific Bar Assn. (Tokyo; mem. arbitration intellectual property, consitutional taxation, labor, legal groups), Inst. European Law Faculty of Laws (United Kingdom), Urban Land Inst. Internat., Mid. East Inst. (Am.-Arab Affairs Coun.), Inter-Am. Bar Assn., 1987—, Calif. Trial Lawyers Assn., Ctr. Reformation Rsch. (co-chmn. Calif. State Com. on U.S-Mid. East Econ. and Polit. Rels.), Soc. Biblical Lit., Am. Acad. Arts and Letters, Am. Acad. Religion, World Lit. Acad., Coun. Scholars, Am. Com. on U.S.-Japan Rels., Japan Soc. No. Calif., Pan-Am. Assn. San Francisco, Soc. Indsl./Office Realtors, Assn. Entertainment Lawyers London, Royal Chartered Inst. Arbitrators (London), Soc. Indsl. and Office Realtors, Urban Land Inst., San Francisco Realtors Assn., Calif. Realtors Assn., Coun. Fgn. Rels., Chgo. Coun. Fgn. Rels., Conf. Bd., San Francisco Urban and Planning Assn., U.S. Trade Facilitation Coun., Asia Soc., Am. Petroleum Inst., Internat. Platform Assn., San Francisco C. of C. (bus. policy com., pub. policy com., co-chmn. congl. issues study group), Am. Inst. Diplomacy, Overseas Devel. Coun. (Mid. East, Russian Republics, Latin Am. studies group), Internat. Vis. Ctr. (adv. bd.), Fin. Execs. Inst., Nat. Assn. Corp. Dirs., Heritage Found. (bd. dirs.), Archaeological Inst. Am. (fellow coun. near east studies, Egyptology), Am. Literature Judicature Soc., Soc. of Biblical, Nat. Assn. Indsl. and Office Properties, World Literary Acad. (Cambridge, Eng.), Am. Acad. Arts & Letters, Am. Acad. Religion, Pres. Club, Nat. Assn. Bus. Economists, Villa Taverna Club, Palm Beach Yacht Club, Pebble Beach Tennis Club, Calif. Yacht Club, Commonwealth Club, City Club San Francisco, British Bankers Club, London, San Diego Track Club (registered athlete), Crow Canyon Country Club (bd. dirs.), Western Venture Capital Assn., Am. Venture Capital Assn., Authors Guild, Internat. Pen Soc., diplomate-delegate World Econ. Summit Conf., Paris, 1998, IOSECC Conf. Internat. Org. Securities Conf., Paris, 1998. Republican. Roman Catholic; Clubs: Crow Canyon Country Club, The Players. Avocations: theater, social entertainment events, opera, ballet, fine arts. Public international, General corporate. Home: 501 Forest Ave Palo Alto CA 94301-2631 Office: 540 Jones St Ste 201 San Francisco CA 94102-2008

**LYNCH, VICTOR K.,** lawyer; b. Latrobe, Pa., Sept. 9, 1929; s. Victor E. and Helen (Kamerer) L.; m. Jane Louise Sutherland, June 11, 1951 (div. 1970); children: G. Michael, Janet L. Mutschler, Steven J., David J., Thomas S., Victoria A. BS in Sanitary Engring., Pa. State U., 1951; LLD, Duquesne U., 1958. Bar: Pa. 1959. Design engr., constrn. insp. The Chester Engrs., Pitts., 1953-54, project engr., 1954-58; assoc. Burgwin, Ruffin, Perry & Pohl, Pitts., 1958-62; ptnr. Ruffin, Perry, Springer, Hazlett & Lynch, Pitts., 1962-70; assoc. Litman, Litman, Harris & Specter, P.A., Pitts., 1971-74, Lynch, Lynch, Carr & Kabala, Pitts., 1974-78; ptnr. Lynch and Lynch, Pitts., 1978—. Recipient Bedell award Water Pollution Control Fedn., 1973. Mem. Water Pollution Control Assn. of Pa. (Sludge Shoveler's award 1970, Johnny Clearwater award 1971), Pa. Soc. Profl. Engrs. Municipal (including bonds). Home: 1000 Grandview Ave Pittsburgh PA 15211-1362 Office: 702 Times Bldg 336 4th Ave Pittsburgh PA 15222-2004

**LYNCHESKI, JOHN E.,** lawyer; b. Throop, Pa., Sept. 10, 1945; s. John W. and Laura B. (Oshetski) L.; m. Kathy D. Penhale, Aug. 26, 1967; children: John H., Marc E., Kristin E. BA in Econs., Cornell U., 1967; JD, U. Pitts., 1970. Bar: Pa. 1970, Fla. 1974, U.S. Supreme Ct. 1982, U.S. Ct. Appeals (3d cir.) 1970, U.S. Dist. Ct. (we. and mid. dists.) Pa. 1970. Assoc. Reed Smith Shaw & McClay, Pitts., 1970-71, 74-81; USN judge advocate Gen. Corps, Pensacola, Fla., 1971-74; dir. Manion Alder & Cohen, Pitts., 1981-84, Alder Cohen & Grigsby, Pitts., 1984-89; dir., chmn. labor and employment group and healthcare group Cohen & Grigsby, PC, Pitts., 1989—, exec. com., 1989—; bd. vis. Robert Morris Coll. Sch. Mgmt., 1997-98; health adv. bd. U. Pitts. Sch. Law, 1996—; steering com. Law Fellows Sch. Law, 1992-98. Pres. Allegheny Beaver United Soccer, Pitts., 1986-94; bd. dirs., legal coun. Jaycees, Pa., 1977-78, pres., Upper St. Clair, 1976-77. Lt. USNR. Mem. Am. Arbitration Assn. (nat. panel), Tri-State Employers Assn., Pa. Bar Assn. (labor law com., health care law com.), Fla. Bar Assn. (labor law sect.), Allegheny County Bar Assn. (labor and employment law sect., health law sect.) Am. Health Lawyers Assn. (labor, OHSA & human resources com.), Soc. Hosp. Attys. of Western Pa., Pa. Soc. Healthcare Attys., Health Exec. Forum S.W. Pa., Soc. for Human Resource Mgmt., Am. Soc. on Aging, Am. Hosp. Assn. Am. Soc. for Healthcare Risk Mgmt., Am. Soc. for Healthcare Human Resources Adminstrn. (nat. spkrs. bur.), W.Va. Healthcare Human Resources Assn., Federalist Soc., Indsl. Rels. Rsch. Assn., West Pa. chpt. Pitts. Human Resources Assn., West Pa. Working Together Consortium Health Initiative, Western Pa. Soccer Coaches Assn. (sec., bd. dirs. 1987-95), Pa. Soccer Coaches Assn., Nat. Soccer Coaches Assn., Pa. West Soccer Assn. (bd. dirs., exec. com., dir. classic league), Tri-State Referees Assn, Chartiers County Club (bd. dirs., pres., sec., legal adv., greens chmn.), Sewickley Heights Golf Club. Roman Catholic. Avocations: soccer, golf, hunting, fishing, outdoors. Civil rights, Health, Labor. Office: Cohen & Grigsby PC 11 Stanwix St 15th Flr Pittsburgh PA 15222-1312

**LYNN, BARBARA MICHELE,** lawyer; b. Binghamton, N.Y., Sept. 19, 1952; d. Stanley Donald and Nelda Ruth (Brounstein) Golden; m. Michael Paige Lynn, Aug. 12, 1973; children: Tara Paige, Whitney Reed. BA with distinction, U. Va., 1973; JD summa cum laude, So. Meth. U., 1976. Bar: U.S. Dist. Ct. (no. dist.) Tex. 1976, U.S. Ct. Appeals (5th and 11th cirs.) 1981, U.S. Dist. Ct. (we. dist.) Tex. 1983, U.S. Dist. Ct. (ea. dist.) Tex. 1986, U.S. Dist. Ct. (so. dist.) Tex. 1991, U.S. Supreme Ct. 1987. Assoc. Carrington, Coleman, Sloman & Blumenthal, Dallas, 1976-83, ptnr., 1983—; instr. Nat. Inst. Trial Advocacy, 1979—; mem. exec. com. Carrington, Coleman, Dallas, 1984-99; dean search com. So. Meth. U. Law Sch., 1988-89, exec. bd., 1998—; commr. Dallas County Grand Jury, spring 1989. Bd. dirs. Am. Jewish Congress, Dallas, 1983—, co-pres., 1992-94; panelist The Dallas County Cmty. Coll. Dist. Hearing Panel, 1985—. Master Higginbotham Inn of Ct.; fellow Am. Coll. Am. Coll. Trial Lawyers; mem. ABA (chmn. comml. litigation 1989-91, dir. of divs. 1992-93, coun. litigation sect. 1993-96, sect. chair 1998-99), Am. Bar Found., Dallas Assn. Young Lawyers, Dallas Bar Assn. (bd. dirs. 1985-88), Tex. Bar Found., Dallas Bar Found. General civil litigation, Federal civil litigation, State civil litigation. Office: Carrington Coleman Sloman & Blumenthal 200 Crescent Ct Ste 1500 Dallas TX 75201-1848

**LYNN, GEORGE GAMBRILL,** lawyer; b. Birmingham, Ala., Mar. 3, 1946; s. Henry Sharpe and Fariss (Gambrill) L.; m. Gabriella Hulsey, Aug. 30, 1969 (div. Aug. 1980); children: Gabriella Hansell, George Gambrill Jr. AB, Princeton U., 1968; JD, U. Va., 1974. Bar: Ala. 1974. Law clk. to Hon. Walter P. Gewin U.S. Ct. Appeals 5th Cir., Tuscaloosa, Ala., 1974-75; assoc., ptnr. Cabaniss, Johnston, Gardner, Dumas & O'Neal, Birmingham, 1975-84; ptnr. Maynard, Cooper & Gale, Birmingham, 1984—. Mem. Ala. com. U.S. Civil Rights Commn., Birmingham, 1988-92; chmn. State of Ala. Ballet, Birmingham, 1989-95. Lt. (j.g.) USN, 1968-71, Vietnam. Mem. ABA, Ala. State Bar Assn. (chmn. sect. on antitrust and bus. torts 1988-89), Birmingham Bar Assn., Birmingham Rotary (trustee 1999—). Republican. Episcopalian. Avocations: tennis, travel. Antitrust, General civil litigation. Home: 2712 Lockerbie Cir Birmingham AL 35223-2904 Office: Maynard Cooper & Gale 2400 Amsouth/Harbert Pla 1901 6th Ave N Birmingham AL 35203-2618

**LYNN, LESLIE ROBIN,** lawyer; b. Nov. 24, 1970; m. Thomas D. Lynn. BS in Math., Tufts U., 1992; JD, Cornell U., 1995. Bar: N.Y. 1996. Assoc. Kaye, Scholer, Fierman, Hays & Handler LLP, N.Y.C., 1995—. Mem. Assn. of the Bar of the City of N.Y. (sec. com. tax. corp. 1996—). Taxation, general. Office: Kaye Scholer et al 425 Park Ave New York NY 10022-3506

**LYNN, ROBERT PATRICK, JR.,** lawyer; b. N.Y.C., Nov. 17, 1943; s. Robert P. and Marie (Madeo) L.; m. Maria T. Zeccola, Nov. 18, 1967; children—Robert P. III, Stephanie M., Kerry Elizabeth. B.A., Villanova U., 1965; J.D., St. John's U., Bklyn., 1968. Bar: N.Y. 1969, U.S. Dist. Ct. (ea. dist.) N.Y. 1975, U.S. Ct. Appeals (1st cir.) 1978, U.S. Ct. Appeals (2d cir.) 1975, U.S. Supreme Ct. 1978. Clk., then assoc. Leboeuf, Lamb & Leiby, N.Y.C., 1966-69; dep. town atty. Town of North Hempstead, Manhasset, N.Y., 1969-71; assoc. Sprague Dwyer Aspland & Tobin, Mineola, N.Y., 1971-75, ptnr., 1975-76; ptnr. Lynn & Ledwith, Garden City, N.Y., 1976-92; spl. prosecutor Inc. Village of Bayville, 1975-76. Bd. dirs. Cath. Charities, 1971-89, chmn., 1982; vice chmn. Diocese of Rockville Centre Family Life Ctr., 1978-82. Mem. Nassau County Bar Assn., Suffolk County Bar Assn., N.Y. State Bar Assn. Roman Catholic. Clubs: Wheatley Hills Golf Club (East Williston, N.Y.); Lloyd Neck Bath (Lloyd Harbor, N.Y.), La Romana Country Club (Dominican Rep.). Federal civil litigation, State civil litigation, Antitrust. Home: 10 Seaforth Ln Huntington NY 11743-9788 Office: 330 Old Country Rd Ste 103 Mineola NY 11501-4143 also: GV269 Casade Campo La Romana Dominican Republic

**LYNNE, SEYBOURN HARRIS,** federal judge; b. Decatur, Ala., July 25, 1907; s. Seybourn Arthur and Annie Leigh (Harris) L.; m. Katherine Donaldson Brandau, June 16, 1937 (dec. Mar. 1997); 1 dau., Katherine Roberta (dec. Nov. 1988). BS, Ala. Poly. Inst., 1927; LLB, U. Ala., 1930, LLD, 1973. Bar: Ala. 1930. Pvt. practice law Decatur, Ala., 1930-34; judge Morgan (Ala.) County Ct., 1934-41, 8th Jud. Cir. Ct. Ala., 1941-42; judge U.S. Dist. Ct. (no. dist.) Ala., 1946—, chief judge, 1953-73, sr. judge, 1973—. Lt. col., JAGC, U.S. Army, 1942-46. Decorated Bronze Star; named to Ala. Acad. Honor, 1978. Mem. Ala. Bar Assn. (Award of Merit 1989), ABA, Blue Key, Scabbard and Blade, Pi Kappa Alpha, Phi Kappa Phi, Phi Delta Phi, Omicron Delta Kappa, Alpha Phi Epsilon. Democrat. Baptist. Clubs: Kiwanian (dist. gov. Ala. dist. 1938), Univ. of Ala. A. Office: US Dist Ct 419 US Courthouse 1729 5th Ave N Birmingham AL 35203-2000

**LYON, BRUCE ARNOLD,** lawyer, educator; b. Sacramento, Sept. 24, 1951; s. Arnold E. and Arlene R. (Cox) L.; m. Patricia J. Gibson, Dec. 14, 1974; children: Barrett, Andrew. AB with honors, U. Pacific, 1974; JD, U. Calif.-Hastings Coll. Law, 1977. Bar: Calif. 1977, U.S. Dist. Ct. (ea. and no. dists.) Calif. 1977. Ptnr. Ingoglia, Marskey, Kearney & Lyon, Sacramento, 1977-84; sole practice, Auburn, Calif., 1984-91; ptnr. Robinson, Robinson & Lyon, Auburn, Calif., 1991—; counsel Placer Savs. Bank, Auburn, 1987—; instr. in law Sierra Coll., Rocklin, Calif., 1983—. Mng. editor Comment, A Jour. of Communications and Entertainment Law, 1974. Contbr. articles to trade publs. Dir. Auburn Cmty. Found. Mem. State Bar Calif., ABA (liaison student div. 1974), Calif. Trial Lawyers Assn., Placer County Bar Assn., Sacramento County Bar Assn., Thurston Soc., Mensa, Internat. Platform Assn., Order of Coif., Calif. League of Savings Inst. (atty's. com.), Native Sons of the Golden West. Contracts commercial, Real property, State civil litigation. Office: Robinson Robinson & Lyon One California St Auburn CA 95603

**LYON, JAMES BURROUGHS,** lawyer; b. N.Y.C., May 11, 1930; s. Francis Murray and Edith May (Strong) L. BA, Amherst Coll., 1952; LLB, Yale U., 1955. Bar: Conn. 1955, U.S. Tax Ct. 1970. Asst. football coach Yale U., 1953-55; assoc. Murtha, Cullina, Richter and Pinney (and predecessor), Hartford, Conn., 1956-61, ptnr., 1961-96, counsel, 1996—; mem. adv. com., lectr. and session leader NYU Inst. on Fed. Taxation, 1973-86; mem. IRS Northeast Key Dist.'s Exempt Orgns. Liaison Group, Bklyn., 1993—. Mem. editl. bd. Conn. Law Tribune, 1988—. Chmn. 13th Conf. Charitable Orgn. NYU Inst. on Fed. Taxation, 1982; trustee Kingswood-Oxford Sch., West Hartford, Conn., 1961-91, hon. trustee, 1991—, chmn. bd. trustees, 1975-78; mem. exec. com., chmn. Amherst Coll. Alumni Coun., 1963-69; trustee Old Sturbridge Village, Mass., 1974—, chmn. bd. trustees, 1991-93; trustee Ella Burr McManus Trust, Hartford, 1980—, Ellen Battell Stoeckel Trust, Norfolk, Conn., 1994—, Hartford YMCA, 1985—, St. Francis Found., 1991—, Watkinson Libr., 1990—; trustee Wadsworth Atheneum, Hartford, 1968-93, pres., 1981-84, hon. trustee, 1993—; sec. bd. trustees Horace Bushnell Meml. Hall, Hartford, 1993—, trustee, 1994—; corporator Inst. Living, 1981—, Hartford Hosp., 1975—, St. Francis Hosp., Hartford, 1976—, Hartford Pub. Libr., 1979—; bd. dirs. Conn. Policy and Econ. Com., Inc., 1991—; mem. Conn. adv. com. New Eng. Legal Found., 1991—; bd. vis. Hartford Art Sch., 1995—. Recipient Eminent Svc. medal Amherst Coll., 1967, Nathan Hale award Yale Club Hartford, 1982, Disting. Am. award No. Conn. chpt. Nat. Football Found. Hall of Fame, 1983, Community Svc. award United Way of the Capital Area, 1986. Fellow ABA (mem. exempt orgn. com., co-chairperson subcom. on mus. and other cultural orgns. sect. of taxation 1988—), Am. Coll. Tax Counsel; mem. Am. Law Inst., Connecticut State Srs. Golf Assn., Hartford Golf Club, Yale Club, Union Club N.Y.C., Dauntless Club (Essex, Conn.), Wianno Club (Osterville, Mass.), Mory's Assn. (New Haven), Yale Golf Club, Univ. Club Hartford (pres. 1976-77), Phi Beta Kappa. Corporate taxation, Personal income taxation, State and local taxation. Office: 185 Asylum St Hartford CT 06103-3408

**LYON, PHILIP K(IRKLAND),** lawyer; b. Warren, Ark., Jan. 19, 1944; s. Leroy and Maxine (Campbell) L.; children by previous marriage: Bradford F., Lucinda H., Bruce P., Suzette P., John P., Martin K., Meredith J.; m. Jayne Carol Jack, Aug. 12, 1982. JD with honors, U. Ark., 1967. Bar: Ark. 1967, U.S. Supreme Ct. 1970, Tenn. 1989. Sr. ptnr., dir. ops. House, Wallace, Nelson & Jewell, P.A., Little Rock, 1967-86; pres. Jack, Lyon & Jones, P.A, Little Rock & Nashville, 1986—; instr. bus. law, labor law, govt. bus. and collective bargaining U. Ark., Little Rock, 1969-72, lectr. practice skills and labor law, U. Ark. Law Sch., 1979-80; bd. dirs. Southwestern Legal Found., 1978—; editorial bd. dirs. Entertainment Law & Fin., 1993—. Author: Ark. Employment Law Desk Book, 1997; co-author: Schlei and Grossman Employment Discrimination Law, 2d edit., 1982; editor-in-chief: Ark. Law Rev., 1966-67, bd. dirs., 1978-93, v.p., 1990-92; editor: Ark. Employment Law Letter, 1995-97, Ark. Employment Law Ctr., 1998—. Inaugural fellow Coll. Labor and Employment Lawyers, 1996; mem. ABA (select com. liason office fed. contract compliance programs 1982—, select com. liason EEOC 1984—, select com. immigration law, forum com. entertainment and sports industries), Ark. State C. of C. (bd. dirs. 1984-88), Greater Little Rock C. of C. (chmn. community affairs com. 1982-84, minority bus. affairs 1985-89), Ark. Bar Assn. (chmn. labor law com. 1977-78, chmn. labor law sect. 1978-79, chmn. lawyers helping lawyers com. 1988-94), Tenn. Bar Assn. (labor sect., lawyers helping lawyers com. 1989—), Nashville Bar Assn. (entertainment law com., lawyers concerned for lawyers com., employment law com.), Pulaski County Bar Assn., Country Music Assn., Acad. of Country Music, Nashville Entertainment Assn., Nashville Songwriters Assn. Internat., Copyright Soc. of South, Capitol Club. Recipient Golden Gavel award Ark. Bar Assn., 1978, Writing Excellence award Ark. Bar Found., 1980. Labor, Civil rights, Entertainment. Home: 350 Ardsley Pl Nashville TN 37215-3247 also: 17 Heritage Park Cir North Little Rock AR 72116-8528 Office: Jack Lyon & Jones PA 11 Music Cir S Ste 202 Nashville TN 37203-4335 also: Jack Lyon & Jones PA 425 W Capitol 3400 TCBY Tower Little Rock AR 72201 *One of the true secrets of success is to concentrate your efforts—for if you apply these efforts everywhere at once then you will accomplish very little anywhere.*

**LYON, ROBERT CHARLES,** lawyer; b. Southampton, N.Y., July 2, 1953; s. Charles and Harriet L.; m. Maureen Griffin, Sept. 1, 1979; children: Christopher Charles, Sean Robert, Katherine Joy. BBA with highest hons., Hofstra U., 1976; JD, So. Meth. U., 1979. Bar: Tex. 1980, U.S. Dist. Ct. (no. dist.) Tex. 1982, U.S. Ct. Appeals (5th cir.) 1984, U.S. Supreme Ct. 1992; bd. cert. personal injury trial law, Tex. Bd. Legal Specialization. Assoc. Lyon & Smith, Mesquite, Tex., 1979-83; ptnr. Lyon & Lyon, Mesquite and Rowlett, Tex., 1983-91; pvt. practice Rowlett, 1991—; sec. Starlight Candles, Ltd., Bloomington, Minn., 1996—, TPR Ltd., Edina, 1996—. Coach soccer, T-ball, baseball Rockwall YMCA, 1987-94; den leader Cub Scouts, Rockwall, 1990-91. Mem. ABA, ATLA, Tex. Trial Lawyers Assn. (assoc. dir. 1991—), State Bar Tex. (adminstrn. of the rules of evidence com. 1998—), Dallas Trial Lawyers Assn. (bd. dirs. 1990-92, treas. 1992-93, sec. 1993-94, v.p. 1994-95, pres. elect 1995-96, pres. 96-97), Dallas Bar Assn. (judiciary com. and fee dispute com. 1998-99), Mesquite Bar Assn., Rockwall County Bar Assn. (pres. 1990-91), Patron Ducks Unltd. Democrat. E-mail: attybob@msn.com. Personal injury, Product liability. Office: 3301 Century Dr # A Rowlett TX 75088-7511

**LYONS, CHAMP, JR.,** judge; b. Boston, Dec. 6, 1940; m. Emily Lee Oswalt, 1967; children—Emily Olive, Champ III. A.B., Harvard U., 1962; LL.B., U. Ala., 1965. Bar: Ala. 1965, U.S. Supreme Ct. 1973. Law clk. U.S. Dist. Ct., Mobile, Ala., 1965-67; assoc. Capell, Howard, Knabe & Cobbs, Montgomery, Ala., 1967-70; ptnr. Capell, Howard, Knabe & Cobbs, 1970-76, Helmsing, Lyons, Sims & Leach, Mobile, 1976-98; legal advisor Hon. Fob James, Jr. Gov. State Ala., 1998; assoc. justice Supreme Ct. of Ala., Montgomery, 1998—; mem. adv. commn. on civil procedure Ala. Supreme Ct., 1971-98, chmn., 1985-98. Author: Alabama Practice, 1973, 3d edit., 1996; contbr. articles to law jours. Mem. ABA, Ala. Bar Assn., Mobile Bar Assn. (pres. 1991), Am. Law Inst., Ala. Law Inst., Farrah Law Soc., Harvard U. Alumni Assn. (S.E. regional dir. 1988-91, v.p.-at-large 1992-94, 1st v.p. 1994-95, pres. 1995-96). Home: PO Box 1033 Point Clear AL 36564-1033 Office: Supreme Ct of Ala 300 Dexter Ave Montgomery AL 36104-3741

**LYONS, CHARLES MALAHER,** lawyer; b. Coronado, Calif., Apr. 18, 1938; s. Charles Malaher and Ruth Eleanor Lyons; m. Kathleen Anne Ford, June 29, 1963; children: Kristin Ann, Charles M. AB in Polit. Sci., Brown U., 1960; JD, Suffolk U., 1967. Bar: Mass. 1967, U.S. Dist. Ct. Mass. 1968, Conn. 1969. Casualty-fire underwriter Travelers Ins. Co., Boston, 1962-64; ct. officer U.S. Ct. Appeals (1st cir.), Boston, 1964-67; trial atty. Continental Ins. Co., Boston, 1967-68; counsel Hartford (Conn.) Steam Boiler Inspection and Ins. Co., 1968—; chmn. law com. Am. Nuclear Insurers, West Hartford, Conn., 1990—. Mem. 5th Dist. Rep. Com., West Hartford, 1980-85. 1st lt. USMC, 1960-62. Mem. Am. Ins. Assn. (mem. law and regulation com. 1984—, mem. govt. affairs com. 1984—), Ins. Assn. Conn. (mem. govt. rels. com. 1975—). Roman Catholic. Avocation: travel. Insurance, Health, Labor. Home: 82 Crestwood Rd West Hartford CT 06107-3410 Office: 1 State St Hartford CT 06102-8900

**LYONS, FRANCIS XAVIER,** lawyer; b. Evanston, Ill., Apr. 1, 1962; s. Thomas George and Ruth Frances (Tobin) L.; m. Mary Patricia Rotunno, Apr. 25, 1992. BA in History, U. Minn., 1984; JD, Loyola U., Chgo., 1988. Bar: Ill. 1988, U.S. Dist. Ct. (no. dist.) Ill. 1989, U.S. Dist. Ct. (ctrl. dist.) Ill. 1990, U.S. Ct. Appeals (D.C. cir.) 1994. Asst. atty. gen., gen. law divsn. Ill. Atty. Gen.'s Office, Chgo., 1988-93, asst. atty. gen. environ. control div., 1993-94; trial atty. environ. and natural resources divsn. Environ. Enforcement Sect., U.S. Dept. Justice, Washington, 1994—. Mem. 45th Ward Regular Dem. Orgn., Chgo., 1988-94; mem. Young Dems. Cook County, Chgo., 1990-91; mem. steering com. Dem. Leadership for 21st Century, Chgo., 1992-93. Capt. USAR. ret. Recipient Special Achievement and Commendation award U.S. Dept. Justice. Mem. ABA, Ill. Bar Assn. Chgo. Bar Assn., Cath. Lawyers Guild Chgo., Delta Tau Delta, Phi Alpha Delta. Office: US Dept Justice Environ Enforcement Sect PO Box 7611 Washington DC 20044-7611

**LYONS, GEORGE SAGE,** lawyer, oil industry executive, former state legislator; b. Mobile, Ala., Oct. 1, 1936; s. Mark, Jr. and Ruth (Kelly) L.; m. Elsie Crain, Feb. 5, 1960; children: George Sage, Amelia C. B.A. in Econs, Washington and Lee U., Lexington, Va., 1958; LL.B., U. Ala., 1960. Bar: Ala. 1960. Assoc. Lyons, Pipes & Cook, Mobile, 1963-66; ptnr. Lyons, Pipes & Cook, 1966-82, sr. ptnr., 1982-87; pres. Lyons, Pipes & Cook, P.C., 1987-95, LPC Oil Co., Inc., 1988—, Amelia Land Co., Inc., 1978—; chmn., dir. Crain Oil Co., Inc., Guntersville, Ala., 1975—; commr. Ala. Dept. Revenue, 1996; dir., CFO, Ala. Dept. Fin., 1996-97; dir. Jordan Industries, Inc., State Docks; mem. exec. com. Ala. Petroleum Coun.; mem. Tenn.-Tombignee Waterway Devel. Authority, 1966-70, 91-95; chmn. Ala. Commn. on Higher Edn., 1971-78; dir. Ala. Dept. Fin., 1996—; commr. Ala. Dept. Revenue, 1996. Trustee 11th cir. Hist. Soc. Served to capt., JAGC U.S. Army, 1960-62. Decorated Army Commendation medal. Fellow Am. Bar Found., Nat. Assn. Bond Lawyers, Coun. Ala. Law Inst., Farrah Law Soc. (trustee); mem. Am., Ala., Mobile County bar assns., Mid-Continent Oil and Gas Assn. (dir. Ala.-Miss. div.), Maritime Law Assn. U.S., Omicron Delta Kappa, Phi Delta Phi. Episcopalian. General practice, General civil litigation, General corporate. Home: 107 Carmel Dr E Mobile AL 36608-2479 Office: 5 Itacon St Mobile AL 36670-0414

**LYONS, KEVIN W.,** prosecutor; b. Peoria, Ill., Sept. 16, 1956; s. William C. and Mary Belle (Harrison) L. BA, Judson Coll., 1977; JD, Drake U., 1981. Bar: Ill. 1981, U.S. Dist. Ct. (cen. dist.) Ill. 1984, U.S. Ct. Appeals (7th cir.) 1984. Law clk. Iowa Atty. Gen.'s Office, Des Moines, 1979-80; law clk. to chief judge 10th cir. Ill. Trial Ct., Peoria, 1980; pvt. practice Peoria, 1981-88, asst. pub. defender, 1981-88; state's atty. Peoria County, 1988—; asst. pub. defender County of Peoria, 1981-88. Trustee Village of Hanna City, Ill., 1981-82, Farmington (Ill.) Bd. of Edn. Dist. #324, 1981-91; trustee Judson Coll., Elgin, Ill., 1986—; pres. Farmington Dist. Bd. of Edn., 1987-89. Mem. ABA, Ill. Bar Assn., Peoria County Bar Assn., Christian Legal Soc. Baptist. Avocations: golfing, writing. Office: States Attys Office Peoria County Courthouse Peoria IL 61602-1499

**LYONS, NANCE,** lawyer; b. Boston, Mar. 8, 1943; d. Dr. Timothy F.P. and Ann (Doherty) Lyons. BA, Boston Coll., Newton, Mass., 1964; JD cum laude, Suffolk U., 1977. Bar: Mass. 1977, U.S Dist Ct. Mass. 1977. Legis. and adminstrv. asst. to Sen. Edward M. Kennedy Washington, 1967-70; sole practice Boston, 1977-86; atty. Comras & Jackman, Boston, 1986-90; sole practice Boston, 1990—; with Bar Overseers Disciplinary Hearing Panel, 1987-93; active Joint Bar Com. on Jud. Appts., 1991-93; lectr. in field. Contbr. articles to profl. jours. Spl. corp. counsel City of Boston, 1977-82; asst. commr. Addiction Svcs. Agy., N.Y.C., 1972-73. Mem. Am. Trial Lawyers Assn., Mass. Acad. Trial Attys. (gov. 1987—, legislation com. 1990-96, mem. exec. com. 1994—, chair employment rights com. 1994—, women's com. 1994—), Mass. Assn. Women Lawyers (dir. 1983-89, 91-94, chair legis. com. 1984-89), Mass. Bar Assn. (legis. subcom. civil litigation sect. 1985-87, alt. dispute resolution com. 1988), Boston Bar Assn. (vol. lawyers project 1977—). Democrat. General civil litigation, General practice, Labor. Office: 11 Beacon St Ste 605 Boston MA 02108-3002 *Notable cases include: Drinkwater vs. School Committee of Boston, 550 NE 2nd 385 Mass., 1990, which resulted in a unanimous decision of the highest court that a valid affirmative action plan is not an affirmative defense to a charge of reverse discrimination.*

**LYONS, PATRICE ANN,** lawyer; b. Albany, N.Y., Feb. 16, 1942; d. James Sarsfield and Mary (O'Brien) L.; m. Robert E. Kahn, Sept. 13, 1980. BA, Pace U., 1963; MA, Syracuse U., 1966; JD, Georgetown U., 1969. Bar: N.Y. 1970, D.C. 1988, U.S. Supreme Ct. 1978. Examiner U.S. Copyright Office Libr. of Congress, Washington, 1969-71; sr. atty. Libr. of Congress, 1976-87; asst. legal officer UN Ednl. Sci. and Cultural Orgn., Paris, 1971-76; ptnr. Haley, Bader & Potts, Washington, 1987-90; pvt. practice Washington, 1991—. Mem. ABA, N.Y. Bar Assn., Computer Law Assn., Copyright Soc. of the USA, Fed. Bar Assn. Trademark and copyright, Communications, Computer.

**LYONS, PAUL VINCENT,** lawyer; b. Boston, July 19, 1939; s. Joseph Vincent and Doris Irene (Griffin) L.; m. Elaine Marie Hurley, July 13, 1968; children: Judith Marie, Maureen Patricia, Paula Anne, Joseph Hurley. BS cum laude, Boston Coll., 1960; MBA, NYU, 1962; JD, Suffolk U., Boston, 1968. Bar: Mass. 1968, U.S. Cir. Ct. (1st cir.) 1969, U.S. Supreme Ct. 1991. Div. adminstrn. mgr. Pepsi-Cola Co., N.Y.C., 1962-64; mem. bus. faculty Burdett Coll., Boston, 1964-68; atty. NLRB, Boston, 1968-73; assoc. Foley, Hoag & Eliot, Boston, 1973-77, ptnr., 1978—; mem. faculty Boston U., 1972-74. Mem. Town Meeting, Milton, Mass., 1986—, mem. pers. bd., 1994—. Lt. U.S. Army, 1960-62. Mem. ABA, Mass. Bar Assn., Boston Bar Assn. Labor, Education and schools. Office: Foley Hoag & Eliot 1 Post Office Sq Ste 1700 Boston MA 02109-2170

**LYONS, RICHARD NEWMAN, II,** lawyer; b. Dixon, Ill., Nov. 1, 1947; s. Richard Newman and Mary Lorraine Lyons; m. Jo Ellen Lionberger, July 1, 1972; children: Richard Newman III, Anne Lewis,. BA in Polit. Sci., U. Colo., 1969; JD, U. Mo., Kansas City, 1977. Bar: Mo. 1977, Colo. 1979, U.S. Dist. Ct. Colo. 1979, U.S. Ct. Appeals (10th cir.) 1980. Law clk. to Hon. Russell G. Clark U.S. Dist. Ct. (we. dist.) Mo., 1977-79; ptnr. Bernard, Lyons & Gaddis, Longmont, Colo., 1979—. Vice chair Center Rev. Commn., Longmont, 1987; mem. Landmark Designation com., Longmont, 1980-84. 2d lt. U.S. Army, 1971-74. Mem. Boulder County Bar Found. (pres. 1998), U. Colo. Alumni Assn. (pres. Longmont chpt.), Rotary (bd. dirs.). Democrat. Episcopalian. General corporate, Education and schools, Administrative and regulatory. Home: 1135 Purdue Dr Longmont CO 80503-3634 Office: Bernard Lyons & Gaddis PC 515 Kimbark St Longmont CO 80501-5549

**LYTAL, SCOTT LEE,** lawyer; b. Booneville, Ms., Sept. 5, 1950; m. Sherri C., June 9, 1991. BS, U. Tenn., 1972, JD, 1976. Bar: Tenn. 1976, U.S. Dist. Ct. (ea. dist.) Tenn. 1977, U.S. Dist. Ct. (mid. dist.) Tenn. 1980, U.S. Ct. Appeals (6th cir.) 1982. Staff atty. Rural Legal Svcs. Tenn., Oak Ridge, 1976-79; mng. atty. Rural Legal Svcs. Tenn., Cookeville, Tenn., 1980-83; assoc. Law Offices John Poteet, Cookeville, 1984-85; sr. atty. Law Offices Lytal & Kimball, Cookeville, 1986-87, Law Offices Lytal & Hardin, Cookeville, 1988-91, Law Offices Lytal & Lovelette, Cookeville, 1992-94; pvt. practice Cookeville, 1995—; city judge Town of Monterey, Tenn., 1985-88. Mem. Putnam County Bar Assn., Upper Cumberland Trial Lawyers Assn., Cookeville Jaycees (Outstanding Pres. 1986). Avocation: restoring antique corvettes. Family and matrimonial. Office: 165 S Lowe Ave Cookeville TN 38501-3523

**LYTTON, WILLIAM B(RYAN),** lawyer; b. St. Louis, Aug. 22, 1948; s. William Bryan and Josephine (Lamy) L.; m. Christine Mary Miller; children—William Bryan IV, Laura Miller. A.B., Georgetown U., 1970; J.D., Am. U., Washington, 1973. Bar: D.C. 1973, U.S. Ct. Appeals (7th cir.) 1975, U.S. Supreme Ct. 1978, Pa. 1979, U.S. Dist. Ct. (ea. dist.) Pa. 1979, U.S. Ct. Appeals (3d cir.) 1979. Legal counsel, legis. asst. U.S. Senator Charles H. Percy, 1973-75; asst. U.S. atty. U.S. Dist. Ct. (no. dist.) Ill., Chgo., 1975-78; asst. U.S. atty. U.S. Dist. Ct. (ea. dist.) Pa., 1978-83, dep. chief spl. prosecutions div., 1980, dep. chief criminal div., 1980, chief criminal div., 1980-81, 1st asst. U.S. atty., 1981-83; ptnr. Kohn, Savett, Klein & Graf, P.C., Phila., 1983-87, 87-89; chief counsel, staff dir. Phila. Spl. Investigation Commn., 1985-86; dep. spl. counsellor to Pres. of U.S., Washington, 1987; v.p., gen. counsel GE Aerospace, King of Prussia, Pa., 1989-93; v.p., assoc. gen. counsel Martin Marietta & Lockheed Martin, 1993-95; sr. v.p., gen. counsel Internat. Paper, Purchase, N.Y., 1996—. Contbr. articles to profl. jours. Committeeman Republican Party, Chester County, Pa.; mem. Easttown Twp. Bd. Suprs., 1990-95. Mem. ABA, Am. Corp. Counsel Assn. (bd. dirs. 1997—). Criminal, Libel. Office: Internat Paper Co Two Manhattanville Rd Purchase NY 10577

**MA, ALAN WAI-CHUEN,** lawyer; b. Hong Kong, Apr. 20, 1951; s. Pak Ping and Oi Quon (Hung) M.; m. Carrie Pak, Mar. 17, 1993. BBA, U. Hawaii, 1975; MBA, Chaminade U., 1981; JD, Golden Gate U., 1983. Bar: Hawaii 1984, U.S. Dist. Ct. Hawaii 1984, U.S. Ct. Appeals (9th cir.) 1986, U.S. Supreme Ct. 1989. Ptnr. Oldenberg & Ma, Honolulu, 1984-90; prin. Law Offices Alan W.C. Ma, Honolulu, 1990-95; counsel Goodsill Anderson Quinn & Stifel, Honolulu, 1995—; adj. prof. law U. Hawaii, Honolulu, 1988—. Co-editor: New Waves for Foreign Investors, 1990. Recipient Outstanding Vol. award Hawaii Cmty. Svc. Coun., 1990. Mem. ABA, Am. Immigration Lawyers Assn. (chpt. chair 1993-94), Internat. Bar Assn., Inter-Pacific Bar Assn., U.S. Japan Vols. Assn. (bd. dirs. 1989—), Overseas Chinese Am. Assn. (bd. dirs. 1993-94). Avocation: tennis. Immigration, naturalization, and customs. Office: Goodsill Anderson et al 1800 Alii Pl 1099 Alakea St Honolulu HI 96813-4511

**MAAS, FRANK,** judge; b. N.Y.C., June 10, 1950; s. Herbert N. and Vera (Neu) M.; m. Sidney L. Maas, June 22, 1980; children: Edward, Arthur. BA, Harpur Coll./SUNY, Binghamton, 1972; JD, NYU, 1976. Assoc. Curtis, Mallet-Prevost, Coit & Mosle, N.Y.C., 1976-78; asst. U.S. atty. So. Dist. N.Y., N.Y.C., 1980-86; ptnr. Phillips, Lytle, Hitchcock, Blaine & Huber, N.Y.C., 1986-95; 1st dep. commr. N.Y.C. Dept. Investigation, 1995-99; U.S. magistrate judge So. Dist. N.Y., N.Y.C., 1999—; dep. commr., spl. counsel N.Y.C. Dept. Bus. Svcs., 1995-99. Mem. Coun. on Jud. Admisntrn. (assoc. of the bar 1997—), N.Y. State Bar Assn. (comml. and fed. litigation sect. 1984—), Fed. Bar Coun. Office: US Courthouse 40 Center St Rm 431 New York NY 10007-1502

**MACADAM, JAMES JOSEPH,** lawyer; b. Somerville, Mass., June 13, 1951; s. James Joseph MacAdam and Constance Joan (O'Brien) Oleson; m. Marijo Lado, July 7, 1977; children: Michaela, Jaisa. BS, Northeastern U., Boston, 1976, JD, 1980. Bar: Mass. 1980, Maine 1981, U.S. Dist. Ct. Maine 1982, U.S. Ct. Appeals (1st cir.) 1985, U.S. Supreme Ct. 1996. Ptnr. McTeague, Higbee, MacAdam, Case, Watson & Cohen, Topsham, Maine, 1981—; counsel Maine State Bldg. Trades, 1994—. Bd. dirs. Skating Club Boston, 1992-96. Mem. ATLA, Maine Trial Lawyers Assn., Maine Bar Assn. Democrat. Roman Catholic. Avocations: watersports, skiing, family. Personal injury, Workers' compensation, Labor. Office: McTeague Higbee et al 4 Union Park Topsham ME 04086-1731

**MACAN, WILLIAM ALEXANDER, IV,** lawyer; b. Boston, Nov. 21, 1942; s. William A. and Carol (Whitten) M.; m. Jane Mitchell Ahern, Sept. 3, 1965; children: Sandra Jane, William Andrew. BS, Haverford Coll., 1964; LLB, U. Pa., 1967. Bar: Pa. 1968, U.S. Tax Ct. 1970, N.Y. 1999. Law clk. to judge U.S. Tax Ct., Washington, 1967-69; assoc. firm Morgan, Lewis & Bockius, Phila., 1969-76; ptnr. Morgan, Lewis & Bockius L.L.P., 1976—; lectr. legal instns., seminars. Author publs. on tax-oriented equipment leasing, other tax subjects. Mem. ABA, Pa. Bar Assn., Phila. Bar Assn. Republican. Presbyterian. Corporate taxation, Personal income taxation, Finance. Office: Morgan Lewis & Bockius LLP 101 Park Ave Fl 44 New York NY 10178-0060 also: 1701 Market St Philadelphia PA 19103-2903

**MACAULAY, CHRISTOPHER TODD,** lawyer, consultant; b. Halifax, N.S., Can., Aug. 16, 1959; came to U.S., 1974; s. Douglas G. and Shirley Macaulay; m. Kimberly Ann Foster, June 17, 1989. BS in Acctg. cum laude, Villanova U., 1981; JD, U. Colo., 1985. Bar: Colo. 1985, U.S. Dist. Ct. Colo. 1985. Pvt. practice Law Office of Christopher Macaulay, Denver, 1985-87; assoc. Cortez, Friedman & Coombe, P.C., Denver, 1987-93; ptnr. Cortez, Friedman, P.C., Denver, 1993; assoc. McKenna & Cuneo, Denver, 1993—; spl. cons. bd. law examiners Colo. Supreme Ct., Denver, 1987—. Mem. Colo. Bar Assn., Colo. Trial Lawyers Assn., Assn. Trial Lawyers Am., Denver Bar Assn. Federal civil litigation, General civil litigation, State civil litigation. Office: McKenna & Cuneo 370 17th St Ste 4800 Denver CO 80202-5648

**MACAULEY, WILLIAM FRANCIS,** lawyer; b. Boston, Sept. 12, 1943; s. Bernard Joseph and Mary Louise (Dolan) M.; m. Sheila Rose Hubbard, June 29, 1968; children: Jennifer, Douglas, Leiha, Brian. AB, U. Wash., 1966; JD, Boston U., 1969. Bar: Mass. 1969, U.S. Dist. Ct. Mass. 1970, U.S. Ct. Appeals (1st cir.) 1977, U.S. Dist. Ct. R.I. 1979, U.S. Tax Ct. 1982, U.S. Dist. Ct. Conn. 1983. Assoc. Craig & Craig, Boston, 1970-74; prin. Tyler, Reynolds & Craig, Boston, 1975-78; sr. ptnr. Craig and Macauley, Boston, 1979—. Contbr. articles to profl. jours. Trustee Boston U., The Raymond Found., The Craig Found., Boston; gov. Concord Mus. Mem. ABA, Mass. Bar Assn., Boston Bar Assn. (aviation com. 1980—, appellate com. 1984—). Bankruptcy, Federal civil litigation, State civil litigation. Home: 55 Buttricks Hill Rd Concord MA 01742-5314 Office: Craig and Macauley Profl Corp 600 Atlantic Ave Ste 2900 Boston MA 02210-2215

**MACBAN, LAURA VADEN,** lawyer; b. Winston-Salem, N.C., Dec. 19, 1963; d. Donald Edward Ridenour and Constance Carrington Whitehead; m. Barry Allistair MacBan, Oct. 7, 1995. Student, U. Calif. (Santa Barbara), 1981-83; BS in Econs. magna cum laude, U. Ariz., 1985, JD cum laude, 1988. Bar: Ariz. 1988. Law clerk Haralson, Kinerk & Morey, Tucson, 1986-87, Bilby & Shoenhair, P.C., Tucson, 1987-88; assoc. Snell & Wilmer, Tucson, 1988-92, Law Office Robert Hooker, Tucson, 1992-93, Cavett & Kaucher, Tucson, 1993-97; ptnr. MacBan Law Offices, Tucson, 1997—; founding mem., v.p. 20/30 Women's Club, Ariz. Chpt., 1987-88. Mem. campaign com. for Jim Kolbe, Tucson, 1988-90; v.p. City Magistrates Merit Selection Commn., Tucson, 1992-97; chairperson Ariz. State Bar Trial Practice Sect., 1998—; pres. Tucson Def. Bar, 1998—. Mem. ABA (exec. coun. 1995—), Ariz. Women Lawyers Assn., Pima County Bar Assn. (social com. 1994-95), Morris K. Udall Inn of Ct. Republican. Episcopalian. Professional liability, Personal injury, General civil litigation. Office: MacBan Law Offices 1 S Church Ave Ste 2040 Tucson AZ 85701-1620

**MACBETH, LYNN ELLEN,** lawyer; b. Bethlehem, Pa., Mar. 21, 1955; d. James Bart MacBeth and Dolores Lucille (Baab) Fredericks; m. Stephen J. Scholze, June 3, 1978 (div. Oct. 1983); 1 child, Zachary; m. James M. Kelly, Jan. 15, 1988; children: Barney, Toby. BA in English, Chatham Coll., 1977; JD, U. Pitts., 1982. Bar: Pa. 1983, U.S. Dist. Ct. (we. dist.) Pa. 1983. Assoc. Koegler & Tomlinson, Pitts., 1983-88, Weiler & Weiler, Pitts., 1989-92, Pillar Mulroy & Ferber, Pitts., 1992-97; law clk. Ct. Common Pleas Allegheny County, Pitts., 1986-88; mediator Family Mediation Coun. We. Pa., Pitts., 1993—, bd. dirs., sec., 1997—. Author: (manuals) Effective Family Law Practice, 1996, Child Custody in Pennsylvania: the Substantive Law for Mediators, 1997, Paralegals in Family Law Practice, 1997, Probate: Beyond the Basics, 1997. Vol. Children's Hosp. Pitts., 1995-96. Mem. ABA, Allegheny County Bar Assn. Avocations: French language and culture, cooking. Family and matrimonial, Estate planning, Alternative dispute resolution. Home: 211 Highland Rd Pittsburgh PA 15235-3010 Office: 1 Oxford Ct Ste 1500 Pittsburgh PA 15219-1407

**MACCARONE, JOSEPH THOMAS,** lawyer; b. Hackensack, N.J., Nov. 12, 1952; s. Carmelo William and Josephine (Scillia) M.; m. Judith Polakowski, Jan. 31, 1980; children: Joseph, Lauren. BA, Rutgers U., 1974; JD, New England U., 1979. Acct. rep. Burroughs Corp., Bloomfield, N.J., 1974-75; ptnr. Maccarone and Farhi, Esqs., Lodi, N.J., 1981—; atty. Borough of Lodi, 1986. Trustee Lodi Bd. Edn., 1975-76; dir. Boys and Girls Club of Lodi, Inc., 1984-87, pres. 1986-87. Recipient Outstanding Pub. Service award League to Reform Our Community, 1975; named one of Outstanding Young Men of Am. , U.S. Jaycees, 1975, 78, 85, 86. Mem. Bergen County Bar Assn., N.J. Bar Assn., Lodi C. of C. Lodge: Rotary (pres. Lodi chpt. 1985-86). Office: Maccarone & Farhi 335 Passaic Ave Lodi NJ 07644-1525

**MACCARTHY, TERENCE FRANCIS,** lawyer; b. Chgo., Feb. 5, 1934; s. Frank E. and Catherine (McIntyre) MacC.; m. Marian Fulton, Nov. 25, 1961; children—Daniel Fulton, Sean Patrick, Terence Fulton, Megan Catherine. B.A. in Philosophy, St. Joseph's Coll., 1955; J.D., DePaul U., 1960. Bar: Ill. 1960, U.S. Dist. Ct. (no. dist.) Ill. 1961, U.S. Ct. Appeals (7th cir.) 1961, U.S. Supreme Ct. 1966. Assoc. prof. law Chase Coll. Law, Cin., 1960-61; law clk. to chief judge U.S. Dist. Ct., 1961-66; spl. asst. atty. gen. Ill., 1965-67; exec. dir. Fed. Defender Program, U.S. Dist. Ct. (no. dist.) Ill., Chgo., 1966—; mem. nat. adv. com. on criminal rules; 7th cir. criminal jury instrn. com.; chmn. Nat. Defender Com.; chmn. bd. regents Nat. Coll. Criminal Def.; faculty Fed. Jud. Ctr., Nat. Coll. Criminal Def., Nat. Inst. Trial Advocacy, U. Va. Trial Advocacy Inst., Harvard Law Sch. Trial Advocacy Program, Western Trial Advocacy Inst., Northwestern U., U. Ill. Defender Trial Advocacy course, Nat. Criminal Def. Coll., Loyola U. Trial Advocacy Program; lectr. in field. Contbr. articles on criminal law to profl. jours. Bd. dirs. U.S.O. Served as 1st lt. USMC, 1955-57. Recipient Nat. Legal Aid and Defender Assn./ABA Reginald Heber Smith award, 1986, Alumni Merit award St. Joseph Coll., 1970, Cert. of Distinction USO, 1977, Harrison Tweed Spl. Merit award Am. Law Inst./ABA, 1987, Bill of Rights award Ga. chpt. ACLU, 1986, William J. Brennan award U. Va., 1989, Alumni Svc. award DePaul U. Coll. Law, 1994, Ann. Significant Contbns. award Calif. Attys. for Criminal Justice; named to Outstanding Young Men of Am., 1970. Mem. ABA (past chmn. criminal justice sect., ho. of dels., bd. govs.), Ill. Bar Assn., Chgo. Bar Assn., 7th Cir. Bar Assn., Nat. Assn. Criminal Def. Lawyers (Disting. Svc. award 1993), Nat. Legal Aid and Defender Assn., Nat. coll. Criminal Def. (chair), Union League of Chgo. (pres.). Democrat. Roman Catholic. Office: US Dist Ct No Dist Ill 55 E Monroe St Ste 2800 Chicago IL 60603-5802

**MACCHIA, VINCENT MICHAEL,** lawyer; b. Bklyn., Dec. 30, 1933; s. Vincent and Lina Rose (Celli) M.; m. Irene Janet Audino, Feb. 27, 1965; children: Lauren, Michele, Michael. BS, Fordham U., 1955, LLB, 1958; LLM, NYU, 1967. Bar: N.Y. 1958. Assoc., Bernard Remsen Millham & Bowdish, N.Y.C., 1959-60; atty. Equity Corp., N.Y.C., 1961-63, Pfizer Inc., N.Y.C., 1964, Trans World Airlines, Inc., N.Y.C., 1964-66; mem. Gifford, Woody, Palmer & Serles, N.Y.C., 1966-85, Townley & Updike, N.Y.C., 1985-90; of counsel Smith, Don, Alampi, Scalo & D'Argenio, Ft. Lee, N.J., 1990-91; counsel Tenzer, Greenblatt, LLP, N.Y.C., 1991—; dir. Hudson Rev., Inc. With USAR, 1958-64. Mem. ABA, N.Y. State Bar Assn. Republican. Roman Catholic. Mem. editorial staff Fordham Law Rev., 1956-58. Corporate taxation, Estate taxation, Personal income taxation. Home: 4 Greentree Dr Scarsdale NY 10583-7014

**MACCOLL, J. A.,** lawyer; b. Evanston, Ill., July 29, 1948. BA, Princeton U., 1970; JD, Georgetown U., 1973. Bar: Md. 1974, U.S. Dist. Ct. Md. 1974, U.S. Ct. Appeals (4th cir.) 1974. Asst. U.S. atty. Dist. Md., 1978-81; ptnr. Piper & Marbury; v.p., gen. counsel U.S. Fidelity & Guaranty Corp., Balt., 1987-91, sr. v.p., gen. counsel, 1991-94, exec. v.p. dept. human resource, gen. counsel, 1994—; exec. v.p., gen. counsel The St. Paul Cos., Inc., Balt., 1989—. Editor-in-chief Georgetown Law Jour., 1972-73. Office: The St Paul Cos Inc LA 0300 6225 Centennial Way Baltimore MD 21209-3653

**MACDONALD, ANGELO GERARD,** prosecutor; b. Detroit, July 24, 1958; s. Lorraine MacDonald; m. Mary Pia Garofalo, July 2, 1994. BA, U. Mich., 1981; JD, Villanova U., 1986. Bar: N.Y., N.J., U.S. Dist. Ct. (ea. and so. dists.), U.S. Ct. Appeals for the Armed Svcs., U.S. Tax Ct., U.S. Ct. Internat. Trade. Asst. dist. atty. Office of the Dist. Atty. Bronx County, N.Y.C., 1986—. Recipient award of valor NYNEX, N.Y.C. Avocations: travel, sports. Home: 124 W 60th St Apt 42H New York NY 10023-7458 Office: Bronx County Dist Attys Office 198 E 161st St Rm 508 Bronx NY 10451-3506

**MACDONALD, DAVID ROBERT,** lawyer, fund administrator; b. Chgo., Nov. 1, 1930; s. James Wear and Frances Esther (Wine) M.; m. Verna Joy Odell, Feb. 17, 1962; children: Martha, Emily, David, Rachel, Rebecca. B.S., Cornell U., 1952; J.D., U. Mich., 1955. Bar: Ill. 1955, Mich. 1955, D.C. 1983. Practiced in Chgo., 1957-74; mem. firm Kirkland, Ellis, Hodson, Chaffetz & Masters, Chgo., 1957-62, ptnr., 1962; ptnr. Baker & McKenzie, Chgo., 1962-74, 77-81; asst. sec. of Treasury for enforcement, ops. and tariff affairs Dept. Treasury, Washington, 1974-76; undersec. of Navy, 1976-77; dep. U.S. Trade Rep., 1981-83; ptnr. Baker & McKenzie, Chgo., 1983-96; bd. dirs. Chgo. City Bank and Trust Co., Mestek, Inc. (N.Y. Stock Exch.). Pres. David R. Macdonald Found., 1996—. Mem. ABA, D.C. Bar Assn., Chgo. Assn. Commerce and Industry (bd. dirs. 1977-81), Order of Coif, Econ. Club (Chgo.), Cosmos Club (Washington). Home: 6605 Radnor Rd Bethesda MD 20817-6324 Office: 815 Connecticut Ave NW Washington DC 20006-4004

**MACDONALD, KIRK STEWART,** lawyer; b. Glendale, Calif., Oct. 24, 1948; s. Bruce Mace and Phyllis Jeanne MacDonald. BSCE, U. So. Calif., 1970; JD, Western State U., 1982. Bar: Calif. 1982, U.S. Dist. Ct. (cen. dist.) Calif. 1982, U.S. Ct. Appeals (9th cir.) 1982, U.S. Dist. Ct. (no. dist.) Calif. 1984, U.S. Dist. Ct. (so. dist.) Calif. 1985, U.S. Dist. Ct. (ea. dist.) Calif. 1987. Dist. engr. Pacific Clay Products, Corona, Calif., 1971-76, Nat. Clay Pipe Inst., La Mirada, Calif., 1976-82; ptnr. Gill and Baldwin, Glendale, Calif., 1982—. Mem. ABA, L.A. County Bar Assn., Water Environ. Assn., Calif. Water Environ. Assn. Avocations: travel, woodworking. Construction, General civil litigation, Contracts commercial. Office: Gill and Baldwin 130 N Brand Blvd Fl 4 Glendale CA 91203-2646

**MACDONALD, LENNA RUTH,** lawyer; b. Providence, July 16, 1962; d. Arthur Robert and Laina Ruth (Weake) M.; m. Robert Christopher Carew, Sept. 18, 1993. BA, Brown U., 1984; postgrad., London Sch. Econs., 1984-85; JD, Emory U., 1988. Bar: Ohio 1988, R.I., 1989, Mass. 1992, Ky. 1996. Assoc. Smith & Schnacke, Dayton, Ohio, 1988-89, Edwards & Angell, Providence, 1989-91, McDermott, Will & Emery, Boston, 1991-93; asst. gen. counsel, group mgr. BANC ONE N.H. Asset Mgmt. Corp., Manchester, 1993-96, BANK ONE CORP., Louisville, 1996-98; real estate counsel Vencor, Inc., Louisville, Ky., 1998-99; prin. legal counsel Commonwealth Industries, Inc., Louisville, 1999—. mem. Mass. Bar Assn., R.I. Bar Assn., Ky. Bar Assn., Am. Friends London Sch. Econs., Phi Alpha Delta. Republican. Episcopalian. Avocations: sailing, pottery. Contracts commercial, General corporate. Home: 1802 Devondale Dr Louisville KY 40222-4128 Office: Commonwealth Industries Inc Citizens Plz 19th Fl 500 W Jefferson St Louisville KY 40202-2823

**MACDONALD, PETER DAVID,** lawyer; b. Ft. Snelling, Minn., Aug. 30, 1946; s. Alexander Colin and Marie (Peterson) MacD.; m. Kathleen Bourke, Dec. 27, 1969; children: Bourke, Evan. BA in Econs., U. Mont., 1969; MS in Urban Planning, U. Ariz., 1972, JD, 1975. Bar: Ariz. 1976. Planning counsel, dep. city atty. City of Salinas, Calif., 1977-82; city atty. City of Gonzales, Calif., 1980-82, City of Pleasanton, Calif., 1982-88; pvt. practice, Pleasanton, 1988—. Mem. Calif. Bar Assn., Bay Area City Attys. Assn. (pres. 1984), Ea. Alameda County Bar Assn. (pres. 1997), U.S. C. of C., Pleasanton C. of C. (pres. 1992), Rotary (pres. 1998). E-mail: petemacd@ix.netcom.com. Environmental, Land use and zoning (including planning). Home: 5258 Crestline Way Pleasanton CA 94566-5410 Office: 400 Main St Ste 210 Pleasanton CA 94566-7371

**MACDONALD, RICHARD BARRY,** lawyer; b. Hartford, Conn., Aug. 15, 1950; s. Robert James and Margie Juanita (Backes) MacD.; m. Barbara Arlene Breighner, Dec. 15, 1979; children: Miles Trevor, Morgan Michelle. AA, Manchester (Conn.) Community Coll., 1974; BA, Colo. Coll., 1976; JD, Willamette U., 1979. Bar: Oreg. 1979, Pa. 1980, U.S. Dist. Ct. (ea. and cen. dists.) Pa. 1983, U.S. Supreme Ct. 1985. Assoc. Krank, Gross & Casper, Lancaster, Pa., 1981-84; pvt. practice Lancaster, 1984—; ct. appointee to provide criminal def. work for adults and juveniles Lancaster County Common Pleas; co-chair LBA tech. com.; barrister W. Nensel Brown Inn. of Ct. Bd. dirs. Boy Scouts Law and Politics Explorers, Lancaster, 1984-85; elected Rep. committeeman, 1988; chairperson adminstrv. bd., mem. long-range planning steering com. area Meth. ch.; chmn. bd. dirs. Covenant Child Care Ctr. Sgt. USAF, 1968-71, Vietnam. Mem. PACDL, Lancaster County Bar Assn. (fin. com., law office econ. com., del. young lawyers div. 1983-86), Phi Delta Phi. Libertarian. Methodist. Avocations: sports, chess, reading, travel, cultural activities. Criminal, Juvenile, General practice. Home: 2669 Beech Ln Lancaster PA 17601-2267

**MACDONALD, THOMAS COOK, JR.,** lawyer, mediator; b. Atlanta, Oct. 11, 1929; s. Thomas Cook and Mary (Morgan) MacD.; m. Gay Anne Everiss, June 30, 1956; children: Margaret Anne, Thomas William. B.S. with high honors, U. Fla., 1951, LL.B. with high honors, 1953. Bar: Fla. 1953; cert. mediator Supreme Ct. Fla. and U.S. Dist. Ct. (mid. dist.) Fla. Practice law Tampa, 1953—; mem. firm Shackleford, Farrior, Stallings & Evans, 1953-97; mem. Cook, Bell & MacDonald, Tampa, 1997—, mediator, 1997—; spl. counsel Gov. of Fla., 1963, U. Fla., 1972—; del. 5th cir. Jud. Conf., 1970-81; mem. adv. com. U.S. Ct. Appeals (5th cir.), 1975-78, (11th cir.), 1988-93; mem. Fla. Jud. Qualifications Commn., 1983-88, vice chmn., 1987, chmn., 1988, gen. counsel, 1997—; mem. judicial nominating com. Fla. Supreme Ct., 1995-99. Mem. Fla. Student Scholarship and Loan Commn., 1963-67; bd. dirs. Univ. Cmty. Hosp., Tampa, 1968-78, Fla. West Coast Sports Assn., 1965-80, Hall of Fame Bowl Assn., 1989-93, Jim Walter Corp., 1979-87; mem. Hillsborough County Pub. Edn. Study Commn., 1965; lic. lay eucharistic min. Episcopal Ch., 1961—; chancellor Episcopal Diocese of S.W. Fla., 1990-93, ch. atty. for ecclesiastical ct., 1998—; bd. dirs. U. Fla. Found., 1978-86, Shands Tchg. Hosp., U. Fla., 1981-95; counsel Tampa Sports Authority, 1983-94. Recipient George Carr award FBA, 1991, Herbert Goldburg award Hillsborough County Bar Assn., 1995. Fellow Am. Coll. Trial Lawyers (chmn. state com. 1990-91), Am. Bar Found., Fla. Bar (chmn. com. profl. ethics 1966-70, bd. govs. 1970-74, bar mem. Supreme Ct. com. on stds. conduct governing judges 1976, Presdl. award of merit 1995); mem. ABA (com. on ethics and profl. responsibility 1970-76), Am. Law Inst. (life), 11th Cir. Hist. Soc. (trustee 1982-95, pres. 1989-95), U. Fla. Nat. Alumni Assn. (pres. 1973), Phi Kappa Phi, Phi Delta Phi, Fla. Blue Key, Kappa Alpha. Episcopalian. General civil litigation, Education and schools, Alternative dispute resolution. Home: 1904 S Holly Ln Tampa FL 33629-7004 Office: 100 N Tampa St Ste 2100 Tampa FL 33602-5809

**MACDOUGALL, GORDON PIER,** lawyer; b. Bethlehem, Pa., May 31, 1930; s. Curtis Daniel and Elizabeth (Pier) MacD. AB, U. Mich., 1952; postgrad., Columbia U., 1952-55. Bar: Wis. 1955, N.Y. 1958, D.C. 1960. Atty. N.Y. Cen. R.R. Co., N.Y.C., 1957-59; assoc. LaRoe, Winn & Moerman, Washington, 1959-66; pvt. practice, Washington, 1966—; spl. asst. atty. gen. Commonwealth Pa., Washington, 1971-78; asst. counsel Pa. Pub. Utility Commn., Washington, 1975-80. Named Disting. Hoosier Gov. Edgar D. Whitcomb, Inpls., 1972. Mem. Assn. Transp. Law, Logistics and Policy, Transp. Lawyers Assn., Maritime Adminstrv. Bar Assn., Transp. Research Forum (gen. counsel). Administrative and regulatory, Public utilities, Transportation. Home: 2000 N St NW Washington DC 20036-2336 Office: 1025 Connecticut Ave NW Washington DC 20036-5405

**MACDOUGALL, MALCOLM EDWARD,** lawyer; b. Denver, Jan. 26, 1938; s. Malcolm W. and Helen (Harlow) MacD.; m. Phyllis R. Pomrenke, Dec. 20, 1959; children: Barry Malcolm, Christopher Scott (dec.). BS, Colo. State U., 1959; LLD, U. Colo., 1962. Bar: Colo. 1962, U.S. Dist. Ct. Colo. 1962. Law clk. to judge U.S. Ct. Appeals (10th cir.), Denver, 1962-63; atty. Denver Water Bd., 1963-65; assoc. Saunders, Snyder and Ross, Denver, 1965-68; gen. counsel Golden Cycle Corp., Colorado Springs, Colo., 1968-71; ptnr. Geddes, MacDougall and Worley, P.C., Colorado Springs, 1971-91; sole practitioner MacDougall Law Office, Colorado Springs, 1991-99; shareholder MacDougall, Woodridge & Worley, PC, Colorado Springs, 1999—; bd. dirs. Park State Bank. Mem. Colo. Bar Assn. Republican. E-mail: mailbox@macdougalllaw.com. State civil litigation, Real property. Office: 102 N Cascade Ave Ste 400 Colorado Springs CO 80903-1435

**MACDOUGALL, PRISCILLA RUTH,** lawyer; b. Evanston, Ill., Jan. 20, 1944; d. Curtis Daniel and Genevieve Maurine (Rockwood) MacDougall; m. Lester H. Brownlee, July 5, 1987. BA, Barnard Coll., 1965; grad. with honors, U. Paris, 1967; JD, U. Mich., 1970. Bar: Wis. 1970, Ill. 1970. Asst. atty. gen. State of Wis., 1970-74; instr. Law Sch. and undergrad. campuses U. Wis., 1973-75; staff counsel Wis. Edn. Assn. Council, Madison, 1975—; instr. Columbia Coll., Chgo., 1988—; litigator, writer, speaker, educator women's and children's names and women's rights and employment issues. Mem. ABA, Wis. State Bar (founder sect. on individual rights and responsibilities, chairperson, 1973-75, 78-79), Legal Assn. Women Wis. (co-founder). Author: Married Women's Common Law Right to Their Own Surnames, 1972; (with Terri P. Tepper) Booklet for Women Who Wish to Determine Their Own Names After Marriage, 1974, supplement, 1975; The Right of Women to Name Their Children, 1985; contbr. articles to profl. jours. Labor, Civil rights, Family and matrimonial. Home: 502 Engelhart Dr Madison WI 53713-4742 Office: 33 Nob Hill Dr Madison WI 53713-2198

**MACEL, STANLEY CHARLES, III,** lawyer; b. Wilmington, Del., Dec. 5, 1938; s. Stanley C. Macel and Dorothy Katherine (Armstrong) Lloyd; m. Jennifer Sue Bird, Sept. 29, 1965; children: Stanley C. IV, Jeffrey J. BA, U. Del., 1963; JD, Temple U., 1972. Bar: Del. 1972, U.S. Dist. Ct. Del. 1973, U.S. Ct. Appeals (3d cir.) 1974, U.S. Ct. Appeals (Fed. cir.) 1991. Adminstr. Ct. of Chancery State of Del., Wilmington, 1968-72; assoc. Connolly, Bove, Lodge & Hutz, Wilmington, 1972-78, ptnr., 1978—. Capt. USAF, 1963-67. Barenkopf scholar Temple U. Law Sch., 1971. Mem. ABA, Del. Bar Assn. Federal civil litigation, General civil litigation, Intellectual property. Home: 22 Peirce Rd Wilmington DE 19803-3726 Office: Connolly Bove Lodge & Hutz 1220 N Market St Fl 10 Wilmington DE 19801-2552

**MACEY, SCOTT J.,** lawyer; b. San Francisco, Nov. 8, 1946; s. Arthur A. Macey and Miriam (Sherman) Breit; m. Virginia Kathleen Dodge Shrodo, Mar. 14, 1966 (div. 1978); children: Benjamin Scott, Pamela Michelle; m. Linda Sandborg, Feb. 10, 1990; children: Benjamin, Joshua, Sarah. Student, U. Calif., Santa Barbara, 1965-66; BA magna cum laude, U. San Francisco, 1969; postgrad., San Jose State U., 1969-72; JD summa cum laude, Santa Clara U., 1975. Bar: Calif. 1975, N.J. 1980, U.S. Ct. Appeals (2d cir.) 1979. Assoc. Parker, Milliken, Clark & O'Hara, L.A., 1975-77; gen. atty. AT&T, N.Y.C., 1977-86; exec. v.p., gen. counsel AT&T Actuarial Scis. Assocs., Inc.,

Somerset, N.J., 1986-98; sr. cousnel Actuarial Scis. Assocs., Inc., 1998—; chmn. industry com. Employee Retirement Income Security Act of 1974 (ERISA), Washington; mem. Bur. of Nat. Affairs Pension Reporter Adv. Bd., Washington. Contbr. articles to legal jours., also other mags. and publs. Vol. various polit. campaigns; com. mem. United Fund, Somerset; youth activity counselor Cath. Youth Assn. Mem. ABA (chmn. fiduciary subcom. labor law sect.), N.J. Assn. Corp. Counsel (past chmn. labor law com.). Avocations: gardening, reading, sports, raising animals. General corporate, Labor, Mergers and acquisitions. Home: 11 Sugar Mill Rd Belle Mead NJ 08502-3803 Office: AT&T Actuarial Scis Assocs Inc 270 Davidson Ave Fl 7 Somerset NJ 08873-4140

**MACFADYEN, JOHN ARCHIBALD, III,** lawyer; b. Bethleham, Pa., Dec. 7, 1948; s. John Archibald Jr. and Nancy (Gerrish) MacF.; children: James C., Alexander L., Christopher G.; m. B. Jean Rosiello. AB, Harvard Coll., 1970; JD, Boston U., 1974. Bar: R.I. 1974, Mass. 1974, U.S. Dist. Ct. R.I. 1975, U.S. Supreme Ct. 1978, U.S. Ct. Appeals (1st cir.) 1983. Staff atty. Office of Pub. Defender, Providence, 1975-81; assoc. Vetter & White, Providence, 1981-83; sole practitioner Providence, 1983—; lectr. Law Seminars Internat., Seattle, 1991. Co-author: R.I. Criminal Procedure, 1988. Fellow Am. Coll. Trial Lawyers, Am. Acad. Appellate Lawyers; mem. R.I. Bar Assn. (lectr. 1989—), R.I. Bd. Bar Examiners, Barrister, Am. Inns. of Ct. Criminal, General civil litigation. Office: The Remington Bldg 91 Friendship St Providence RI 02903-3837

**MACFARLAN, JOHN HOWARD,** lawyer; b. Miami, Fla., Apr. 10, 1963. BA, Mars Hill Coll., 1985; JD, Stetson U., 1988. Bar: N.C. 1988. Assoc. McKeever, Edwards, Davis & Hays, Murphy, N.C., 1992—. Mem., musical dir. Licklog Players, 1993—. Capt. JAG, USAF, 1988-91. Mem. N.C. Trial Lawyers Assn. Mem. N.C. Trial Lawyers Assn., Phi Delta Phi. Avocations: music, acting, swimming. Real property, Criminal, Family and matrimonial. Office: McKeever Edwards Davis PO Box 596 Murphy NC 28906-0596

**MACFARLANE, MAUREEN ANNE,** lawyer; b. Boston, May 19, 1965; d. Joseph Alexander and Lorraine Anne (Walsh) MacF. BA magna cum laude, Boston Coll., 1986, MA in English, 1999; JD, Boston U., 1989, MS in Journalism, 1990. Bar: Mass. 1989, U.S. Dist. Ct. Mass. 1990, U.S. Ct. Appeals (D.C. and 1st cirs.) 1990, U.S. Supreme Ct. 1993. Law clk. to presiding justice Mass. Ct. Appeals, Boston, 1989-90; assoc. Widett Slater & Goldman P.C., Boston, 1990-92, Hutchins, Wheeler & Dittmar, P.C., Boston, 1992-95; atty. Lucash, Gesmer & Updegrove, LLP, Boston, 1995-98, Boston Sch. Dept., Office Legal Advisor, 1998—. Writer Mass. Lawyers Weekly, Boston, 1988-89. Sec. Boston Liturgical Dance Ensemble, Chestnut Hill, Mass., 1989—; leader Boston Mayor's Youth Leadership Corp., Boston, 1991-92; exec. com. Boston U. Sch. Law Alumni, 1993—; bd. dirs. Autism Found., 1997—; spl. events chair McMullen Mus. Coun., 1997—. Mem. ABA, Mass. Bar Assn., Boston Bar Assn. (YLS steering com. 1991-94). State civil litigation, Federal civil litigation, Intellectual property. Office: Boston Sch Dept Office Legal Advisor 26 Court St Boston MA 02108-2505

**MACGILL, HUGH C.,** dean. BA, Yale U.; LLB, U. Va. Dean U. Conn. Sch. Law, Hartford. Office: U Conn Sch Law 55 Elizabeth St Hartford CT 06105-2213*

**MACGOWAN, EUGENIA,** lawyer; b. Turlock, Calif., Aug. 4, 1928; d. William Ray and Mary Bolling (Gilbert) Kern; m. Gordon Scott Millar, Jan. 2, 1970; 1 dau., Heather Mary. A.B., U. Calif., Berkeley, 1950; J.D., U. Calif., San Francisco, 1953. Bar: Calif. 1953; cert. family law specialist Calif. State Bar Bd. Legal Specialization. Research atty. Supreme Ct. Calif., 1954, Calif. Ct. Appeals, 1955; partner firm MacGowan & MacGowan, Calif., 1956-68; pvt. practice, San Francisco, 1968—. Bd. dirs. San Francisco Speech and Hearing Center, San Francisco Legal Aid Soc., J.A.C.K.I.E. Mem. Am., Calif., San Francisco bar assns., Queen's Bench. Clubs: San Francisco Lawyers, Forest Hill Garden. Family and matrimonial. Office: 1 Sansome St Ste 1900 San Francisco CA 94104-4448

**MACGREGOR, MEICHELLE R.,** lawyer; b. Bronx, N.Y., May 23, 1967. BA in Gen. Lit., SUNY, Binghamton, 1989; JD, Bklyn. Law Sch., 1994. Bar: N.Y., N.J., U.S. Dist. Ct. (so. dist.) N.Y., U.S. Dist. Ct. (ea. dist.) N.Y. Law clk. to hon. Bernard J. Fried Supreme Ct., State of N.Y., 1994-96; assoc. Cowan Liebowitz and Latman, P.C., N.Y.C., 1994—. Assoc. mng. editor Bklyn. Jour. Internat. JLaw, 1993-94. Scholarship Bklyn. Law Sch., 1992-93, 93-94. General civil litigation, Intellectual property. Office: Cowan Liebowitz Latman PC 1133 Avenue Of The Americas New York NY 10036-6710

**MACILROY, JOHN WHITTINGTON,** lawyer; b. Natchez, Miss., Jan. 15, 1946; s. John Cunnington and Mildred (Whittington) MacI.; m. Linda Susan Pierson, Apr. 11, 1987; 1 child, Jeffrey Lee Walters. BA, Yale U., 1968; MPA, Harvard U., 1980; JD, U. Va., 1974; postgrad., Princeton U., 1970. Bar: Va. 1975, U.S. Dist Ct. Va. (ea. and we. dists.) 1976, U.S. Ct. Appeals (4th cir.) 1976. Asst. atty. gen. Office of the Atty. Gen., Commonwealth of Va., Richmond, 1975-77; legis. counsel and spl. asst. to Sen. Byrd U.S. Senate, Washington, 1977-80; legis. counsel and gen. atty. Union Pacific Corp., Omaha, 1980-85; sr. mem. nat. outreach faculty Lesley Coll., Cambridge, Mass., 1985—; cons., exec. asst. for policy Commonwealth of Va., Richmond, 1985-88; cons. faculty U. Va., 1989—; v.p., counsel Va. Mfrs. Assn., 1988-90, pres., CEO, 1990—; mem. sci. and tech. task force, 1994-95; adv. com. Va. Adminstrv. Code Commn., 1995—; adv. com. U. Va., 1995—; vice-chmn. Coun. of State Mfrs., 1998—, chmn., 1998-99; mem. exec. com. Nat. Indsl. Coun., 1996-97, vice-chmn., 1998—. Creator exec. seminars and acad. programs. Bd. dirs. Blue Ridge Leadership Conf., 1995-97. Lt. (j.g.) USNR, 1968-71. Named War Meml. scholar, 1964, Rhodes scholarship candidate 1972, Nat. Merit scholar, 1963. Mem. ABA, Va. State Bar Assn., Am. Mgmt. Assn. (assoc.), U. Va. Alumni Assn. (life), Assn. of Yale Alumni (at-large del. 1997-98), Magna Carta Soc., Harvard Faculty Club (Cambridge), S.C. Yacht Club, (Hilton Head, S.C.), Mory's Assn. (New Haven), Commonwealth Club, Yale Club (N.Y.C.). Episcopalian. Home: 3001 Stony Lake Dr Apt 1B Richmond VA 23235-6813

**MACIOCE, FRANK MICHAEL,** lawyer, financial services company executive; b. N.Y.C., Oct. 3, 1945; s. Frank Michael and Sylvia Maria (Morea) M.; children: Michael Peter, Lauren Decker, Theodore Kenneth; m. Helen Latourette Duffin, July 9, 1988. BS, Purdue U., 1967; JD, Vanderbilt U., 1972. Bar: N.Y. 1973, U.S. Dist. Ct. (so. dist.) N.Y. 1973, U.S. Ct. Appeals (2d cir.) 1975, U.S. Supreme Ct. 1976. Mem. law dept. Merrill Lynch, Pierce, Fenner & Smith Inc., N.Y.C., 1972-80, v.p., 1978-88, 1st v.p., 1988— ; mgr. corp. law dept. Merrill Lynch & Co., Inc., N.Y.C., 1980-93, asst. gen. counsel, 1982—; gen. counsel investment banking group, 1993-95, ops., svcs. and tech. counsel, 1995—, sec. of audit, compensation and nominating coms. bd. dirs., 1978-83, sec. exec. com., 1981-83; mng. dir. Merrill Lynch Overseas Capital, N.V., Netherlands Antilles, 1980-85; sec., dir. Merrill Lynch Employees Fed. Credit Union, N.Y.C., 1978-82; dir. Merrill Lynch Pvt. Capital Inc., N.Y.C., 1981-87, Enhance Fin. Services Inc, N.Y.C., 1988-92; mem. fin. planning adv. bd. Purdue U., 1996—. Served with U.S. Army, 1969-70. Mem. ABA, Assn. of Bar of City of N.Y. (computer law com.), General corporate, Securities, Computer. Home: 22 Essex Rd Summit NJ 07901-2802 Office: Merrill Lynch & Co Inc N Tower World Fin Ctr New York NY 10281-1334

**MACIOLEK, JOHN RICHARD,** lawyer; b. Boston, June 7, 1963; s. Richard D. and Eleanor A. Maciolek; m. Elizabeth Irene Giardini, June 5, 1993; children: Hannah, Ashleigh, Sydney. BA, Boston Coll., 1986, JD, 1990. Bar: Mass. 1990. Ptnr. Berg and Laipson, Worcester, Mass., 1990—. Mem. Natock Conservation Commn., 1994-97. Avocations: tennis, skiing. Condemnation, General civil litigation. Office: Berg and Laipson 34 Mechanic St Ste 202 Worcester MA 01608-2493

**MACIONE, KYLE PRITCHETT,** pharmaceutical company executive, lawyer; b. Jackson, Miss., Dec. 28, 1963; s. Joe and Annette (Pritchett) M.; m. Beatriz Huarte, Sept. 17, 1993; 1 child, Robert Huarte Macione. BA in Accountancy, U. Miss., 1986; MA in Accountancy, U. Ala., 1987; JD, Washington & Lee U., 1991. Bar: Tenn., 1991, Va., 1992, U.S. Dist. Ct. (we. dist.) Va., U.S. Dist. Ct. (ea. dist.) Tenn., 1992, U.S. Dist. Ct. Appeals (6th cir.), 1992; CPA, Miss. CPA tax dept. KPMG Peat Marwick, Jackson, 1988; assoc. atty. Elliott Lawson & Pomrenke, Bristol, Va., 1992-96; corp. counsel King Pharm., Inc., Bristol, Tenn., 1996—; exec. v.p. investor rels. King Pharms., Inc., Bristol, Tenn., 1998—. mem. Bristol Ballet Company Bristol Va.-Tenn., 1993-95, treas., 1994-95, bd. dirs., 1996—; mem., bd. dirs. Main St. Bristol, 1997-98. Mem. Nat. Investor Rels. Inst., Va. State Bar, Va. Bar Assn., Tenn. Bar Assn., Miss. Soc. CPAs, Bristol Va. Bar Assn. (sec., treas. 1993-94), Bristol Tenn. Bar Assn., Beta Alpha Psi, Beta Gamma Sigma. Home: 142 E Main St Abingdon VA 24210-2835 Office: King Pharm Inc 501 5th St Bristol TN 37620-2304

**MACIVOR, CATHERINE J.,** lawyer; b. Royal Oak, Mich., Aug. 17, 1960; d. Angus Stewart and Hazel (Arnold) M. BA magna cum laude, Boston U., 1983; JD, U. Miami, 1989. Bar: Fla. 1992. Atty. Richard & Richard, P.A., Miami, 1990-94; pvt. practice Miami, 1994-96, Franklin & Marbin, P.A., North Miami Beach, 1996—. tem. Fla. Bar (family law sect., appellate law sec.), DAR. Episcopal. Avocations: swimming. Appellate, Family and matrimonial, General civil litigation. Office: Franklin and Marbin Citicentre Ph 2 290 NW 165th St N Miami Beach FL 33169-6457

**MACK, DEBRA K.,** lawyer; b. New Orleans, Mar. 29; d. Willie Bell Mack and Dorothy (Maples) Watson. BA, Dillard U., 1976; JD, Loyola Law Sch., 1979. Bar: La. 1979. Recreational asst. New Orleans Recreation Dept., 1973-79; pub. defender Orleans Indigent Defender Program, New Orleans, 1979-81; staff atty. Larry P. Williams Law Firm, New Orleans, 1979-81; part-time instr. bus. law Ga. State U., Atlanta, 1982; spl. agt. atty. FBI, Newark, 1985-89; supervisory spl. agt., atty. FBI, Washington, 1989—; part-time instr. bus. law Dillard U., New Orleans, 1981; EEO counselor FBI, Newark, 1986—; legal advisor FBI, Newark, 1986—; gen. police instr. FBI, 1986—; target selection interviewer FBI, 1986—, mem. speaker's bur. Mem. Coalition of Black Women, Newark, 1989, Urban League Phila. Mem. Nat. Bar Assn., La. Bar Assn., Garden State Bar Assn., Assn. Black Women Lawyers, Nat. Orgn. Black Law Enforcement. Democrat. Avocations: travel, reading, jogging, movies, plays. Office: FBI 600 Arch St Fl 8 Philadelphia PA 19106-1675

**MACK, JENNIFER,** judicial clerk; b. Williamsport, Pa., Aug. 13, 1942; d. Harvey Clifford and Mildred Conover (Forman) Wallace; m. Michael Lee Mack, June 10, 1968. BFA, San Francisco Art Inst., 1970. Payroll clk. San Francisco Superior Ct., 1973-75, sr. legal process clk., 1975-80, asst. ct. clk., 1980-85, ct. clk., 1985—; v.p. San Francisco Women's Art Gallery, 1997. Mem. San Francisco Bar Assn. Avocations: bead stringing, printmaking. Home: 929 Hayes St San Francisco CA 94117-2514 Office: San Francisco Superior Ct 575 Polk St San Francisco CA 94102-3333

**MACK, JULIA COOPER,** judge; b. Fayetteville, N.C., July 17, 1920; d. Dallas L. and Emily (McKay) Perry; m. Jerry S. Cooper, July 30, 1943; 1 dau., Cheryl; m. Clifford S. Mack, Nov. 21, 1957. B.S., Hampton Inst., 1940; LL.B., Howard U., 1951. Bar: D.C. 1952. Legal cons. OPS, Washington, 1952-53; atty.-advisor office gen. counsel Gen. Svcs. Adminstrn., Washington, 1953-54; trial appellate atty. criminal div. Dept. Justice, Washington, 1954-68; civil rights atty. Office Gen. Counsel, Equal Employment Opportunity Commn., Washington, 1968-75; assoc. judge Ct. Appeals, Washington, 1975-89; sr. judge DC Ct. of Appeals, Washington, 1989—. Mem. Am., Fed., Washington, Nat. Bar Assns., Nat. Assn. Women Judges. Home: 1610 Varnum St NW Washington DC 20011-4206 Office: DC Ct Appeals 6th Fl 500 Indiana Ave NW Washington DC 20001-2131

**MACK, THEODORE,** lawyer; b. Ft. Worth, Mar. 5, 1936; s. Henry and Norma (Harris) M.; m. Ellen Feinknopf, June 19, 1960; children: Katherine Norma, Elizabeth Ellen, Alexandria. AB cum laude, Harvard U., 1958, JD, 1961. Bar: Tex. 1961, U.S. Supreme Ct. 1971, U.S. Ct. Appeals (5th cir.) 1967, U.S. Ct. Appeals (11th cir.) 1981, U.S. Dist. Ct. (no. dist.) Tex. 1961, U.S. Dist. Ct. (we. dist.) Tex. 1968, U.S. Dist. Ct. (so. dist.) Tex. 1968, U.S. Dist. Ct. (ea. dist.) Tex. 1999. Assoc. Mack & Mack, Ft. Worth, 1961-62, ptnr., 1963-70; dir., pres., v.p., treas., ptnr. Renfro, Mack and Hudman, P.C. and predecessors, Ft. Worth, 1970-93; spl. counsel Brackett & Ellis, P.C. and predecessors, Ft. Worth, 1993—. Trustee Ft. Worth Country Day Sch., 1976-82; bd. dirs. Beth-El Congregation, 1964-73, 75-78, pres. 1975-77; bd. dirs. Jewish Fedn. Ft. Worth, 1965-72; mem. Leadership Ft. Worth, 1973-74; bd. dirs. Sr. Citizens Ctrs., Inc., 1969-81, Family and Individual Svcs., 1981-84, Presbyn. Night Shelter Tarrant County, Inc., 1992-97; pres. Harvard Law Sch. Assn. Tex., 1976-77. Fellow Tex. Bar Found. (life); mem. Tex. Bar Assn., ABA, Tarrant County Bar Assn., Bar Assn. 5th Cir. Ct., Colonial County Club, Ft. Worth Club, City Club, Harvard Club (N.Y.C., Boston). Democrat. Jewish. Bankruptcy, Antitrust, Federal civil litigation. Home: 2817 Harlanwood Dr Fort Worth TX 76109-1226 Office: 100 Main St Fort Worth TX 76102-3009

**MACK, WAYNE A.,** lawyer; b. Chambersburg, Pa., Jan. 31, 1961; s. Wayne A. and Carol (Irwin) M.; m. L. Suzanne Forbis; children: Courtney L., Stephanie E., Ashley C., Audrey G., Carolina H. BS magna cum laude, Temple U., 1982; JD cum laude, U. Pa., 1986. Bar: Pa. 1986, U.S. Dist. Ct. (ea. dist.) Pa. 1986, U.S. Ct. Appeals (3d cir.) 1986, U.S. Supreme Ct. 1995, U.S. Ct. Appeals (4th cir.) 1997. Assoc. Duane, Morris & Heckscher, Phila., 1986-94, ptnr., 1995—. Mem. ABA (forum com. on franchising, sect. bus. law, com. on bus. and corp. litigation), Pa. Bar Assn., Phila. Bar Assn., Nat. Health Lawyers Assn., Order of Coif, Beta Gamma Sigma. Antitrust, Franchising, Federal civil litigation. Home: 415 Foothill Dr Blue Bell PA 19422-3113 Office: Duane Morris & Heckscher One Liberty Pl Philadelphia PA 19103

**MACKAMAN, DONALD HAYES,** lawyer; b. Des Moines, Oct. 29, 1912; s. Frank Hindes and Eva (Hayes) M.; children: Linda, Bert, Donald Jr. BA, Drake U., 1933, JD, 1935. Sec., v.p., gen. counsel Campbell Taggart, Inc., Dallas, 1933-77; of counsel Gardere & Wynne, Dallas, 1977—. Mem. Order of Coif, Phi Beta Kappa. Office: Gardere & Wynne 1601 Elm St Ste 3000 Dallas TX 75201-4761

**MACKAUF, STEPHEN HENRY,** lawyer; b. Gulfport, Miss., Mar. 7, 1945; s. Walter Scott and Rose Evelyn (Berkowitz) M. AB cum laude, U. Miami, Coral Gables, Fla., 1965; JD, Columbia Law Sch., 1968. Bar: Fla. 1969, N.Y. 1970, U.S. Dist. Ct. (so. dist.) N.Y. 1970. Assoc. Kelley Drye & Warren, N.Y., 1968-70; assoc. Gair, Gair & Conason, N.Y., 1970-78, ptnr, 1978-90; ptnr. Gair, Gair, Conason, Steigman & Mackauf, N.Y., 1990—. Co-author: Obstetrical-Neonatal Malpractice, 1984, Failures in Anesthesia Care, 1985; editor: Hospital Liability, 1986; co-author: Failure to Diagnose Fetal Distress, 1998. Mem. Assn. Trial Lawyers Am., Assn. of Bar of City of N.Y., N.Y. State Trial Lawyers Assn. Personal injury. Office: 80 Pine St Fl 34 New York NY 10005-1702

**MACKAY, JOHN WILLIAM,** lawyer; b. Highland Pk., Mich., May 28, 1954; s. John Alexander and Edythe Mae (Bucholz) M.; 1 child, William James. BS, Ea. Mich. U., 1979; JD, UCLA, 1982. Bar: Fla. 1983, U.S. Dist. Ct. (mid. and so. dists.) Fla. 1983, U.S. Ct. Appeals (11th cir.) 1983, U.S. Supreme Ct. 1990; cert. civil trial lawyer, Fla. Pvt. practice Tampa, Fla.; adv. bd. Hillsborough County Law Library, Tampa, Fla., 1995—. Mem. First Amendment Lawyers Assn., Acad. Fla. Trial Lawyers, ATLA. Constitutional, Criminal, Personal injury. Office: John W MacKay PA 201 S Westland Ave Tampa FL 33606-1743

**MACKENZIE, CHARLES ALFRED,** lawyer; b. Houston, Sept. 20, 1965; s. Charles Lester and Glenda Faye M.; m. Gretchen Hartberg, Aug. 5, 1989; children: Katherine Ann, James Andrew. BA, Baylor U., 1987, MA, 1988, JD, 1991. Bar: Tex. 1991; bd. cert. civil appellate law Tex. Bd. Legal Specialization. Atty. 10th Ct. Appeals, Waco, Tex., 1991-94; assoc. Haley & Davis, Waco, Tex., 1994—; grader Tex. Bd. Law Examiners, Waco, 1996—; lectr. law Baylor U., Waco, 1991-92. Mem. ABA (young lawyers divsn. citizen edn.), Waco-McLennan County Young Lawyers Assn. (v.p. 1998-99, sec. 1997-98), Abner V. McCall Am. Inn of Ct. (organizing com. 1997). Baptist. Avocation: photography. Fax: 254-776-6823. E-mail: Alfred.Mackenzie@worldnet.att.net. Appellate, General civil litigation. Office: Haley & Davis 510 N Valley Mills Dr Ste 600 Waco TX 76710-6078

**MACKENZIE, CHARLES RUDD,** lawyer; b. Boston, Dec. 19, 1964; s. Alan Eno MacKenzie and Susan Taylor Menges. BA, Bowdoin Coll., 1987; JD, Western New Eng. Coll., 1993; MSEL cum laude, Vt. Law Sch., 1994. Rsch. dir. Senator Chafee Com., Cranston, R.I., 1988; fgn. policy aide U.S. Senator John Chafee, Washington, 1989-90; ptnr. Sayegh & MacKenzie, Hopewell Junction, N.Y., 1995; pvt. practice law Hastings on Hudson, N.Y., 1995—; bd. dirs. VFP Internat. Vol. Svc., Belmont, Vt. Mem. West Chester County Bar Assn., Yonkers Lawyers Assn. Office: 135 Southside Ave Hastings Hdsn NY 10706-2207

**MACKEY, DIANE STOAKES,** lawyer; b. Laverne, Minn., Mar. 28, 1937; d. Homer R. and Astrid Stoakes; children: Benjamin, Stuart, Sarah. BS, Northwestern U., 1958; JD, U. Ark., 1978. Bar: Ark. 1978, U.S. Dist. Ct. (ea. dist.) Ark. 1978, U.S. Ct. Appeals (8th cir.) 1978. Law clk. to Chief Judge G. Thomas Eisele U.S. Dist. Ct. (ea. dist.) Ark., Little Rock, 1978-80, asst. U.S. atty., 1980-83; ptnr. Friday Eldredge & Clark, Little Rock, 1983—; adj. prof. U. Ark. Sch. Law, Little Rock; co-chair fed. practice com., ea. dist. Ark. Author: Review of Year's Cases, 1978, Stone V. Powell, Not As We Like It, 1977, The Emergency Medical Treatment and Active Labor Act: An Act Undergoing Judicial Development, 1997; editor-in-chief U. Ark.-Little Rock Law Jour. Trustee, past pres., bd. trustees Ark. Children's Hosp., Little Rock, 1992-96; chair Good Shepherd Retirement Ctr., Little Rock; mem. commn. on ministry Diocese of Ark., 1987-99; mem., officer Jr. League, Little Rock; bd. dirs. United Way, 1996—, U. Ark.-Little Rock Found., 1997—. Fellow Ark. Bar Found., Am. Bar Found.; mem. ABA, Ark. Bar (chair environ. com. 1991-93, health law com. 1995—), Ark. Bar Assn., Pulaski County Bar Assn., Am. Law Inst. Administrative and regulatory, Environmental, Health. Home: 3404 Cedar Hill Rd #3 Little Rock AR 72202-1913 Office: Friday Eldredge & Clark 400 W Capitol Ave Little Rock AR 72201-3436

**MACKEY, LEONARD BRUCE,** lawyer, former diversified manufacturing corporation executive; b. Washington, Aug. 31, 1925; s. Stuart J. and Margaret B. (Browne) M.; m. Britta Beckhaus, Mar. 2, 1974; children—Leonard B., Cathleen C., Wendy F. B.E.E., Rensselaer Poly. Inst., 1945; J.D., George Washington U., 1950. Bar: D.C. 1951, N.Y. 1954. Instr. elec. engring. Rensselaer Poly. Inst., Troy, N.Y., 1946-47; patent examiner U.S. Patent Office, Washington, 1947-50; atty. Gen. Electric Co., Schenectady and N.Y.C., 1953-60; dir. licensing, asst. sec. ITT, N.Y.C., 1960-73; v.p., gen. patent counsel, dir. licensing ITT, 1973-90; of counsel Davis Hoxie Faithfull & Hapgood, N.Y.C., 1990-93; cons. licensing and tech. transfer Sarasota, Fla., 1994—. Mem. Recreation Commn., Rye, N.Y., 1966-67; mem. Planning Commn., 1967-70, 72-75, city councilman, 1970-71. Served with USNR, 1943-45; to lt. 1951-53. Mem. ABA (coun. mem., intellectual property law sect. 1989-93), Am. Intellectual Property Law Assn. (bd. mgrs. 1968-70, pres. 1982-83), Licensing Execs. Soc. U.S.A. (pres. 1978), Licensing Execs. Soc. Internat. (pres. 1986), Eta Kappa Nu, Am. Yacht Club (sec. 1968-70), N.Y. Yacht Club, Masons, Apawamis. Republican. Presbyterian. Office: 219 S Orange Ave Sarasota FL 34236-6801

**MACKEY, STEVEN R.,** lawyer; b. Enid, Okla., Nov. 10, 1950; s. Emil R. and Ruby M.; m. Vickie L. Cousins, May 13, 1983; children: Jason, Paige. BS in Bus., Okla. State U., 1972; JD, Notre Dame U., 1976. Bar: Okla. 1976, Tex. 1990. Assoc. Fellers, Snider et al, Okla. City, 1976-77, Sneed, Long et al, Tulsa, Okla., 1980-81; assoc. gen. counsel Weeks Petroleum, Westport, Conn., 1981-83; lawyer pvt. practice, Tulsa, 1983-84; regional atty. Kaiser Aluminum, Tulsa, 1984-85; v.p., gen. counsel, sec. Helmerich & Payne, Inc., Tulsa, 1986—. Bd. dirs. Tulsa chpt. Am. Heart Assn., 1996-99. Capt. U.S. Army, 1977-80. Fellow Tulsa County Bar Found.; mem. Tulsa County Bar Assn. (sec. mineral law sect. 1999-00, pres. elect 1998-99, pres. 1999—, Pres. award 1992-93, Disting. Pres. award 1993-94, Golden Rule award 1995). Republican. Roman Catholic. Avocations: Judo (2d degree black belt), reading, running. General corporate, Oil, gas, and mineral, Real property. Office: Helmerich & Payne Inc 1579 E 21st St Ste 748 Tulsa OK 74114-1303

**MAC'KIE, PAMELA S.,** lawyer; b. Jackson, Miss., Jan. 2, 1956; d. Charles Edward and Betty Jo (Moore) Spell; children: John Greene IV, Ann Katherine. BS, Delta State U., Cleveland, Miss., 1978; JD, U. Miss., Oxford, 1984. Bar: Miss. 1984, Fla. 1986. Assoc. Cummings & Lockwood, Naples, Fla., 1985-93; prin. Pamela S. Mac'Kie, P.A., Naples, 1993-95, pres., 1995—. Pres. Naples Better Govt., 1992-95; pres.-elect Women's Rep. Club, Naples, 1994; county commr. Collier County Bd., Naples, 1994—; dir. Youth Haven, 1992, YMCA, 1993, Collier County Women's Polit. Caucus, 1992—. Recipient Pro Bono award Fla. Bar, 1990, Leadership Collier of C., Naples, 1991. Recipient Pro Bono award Fla. Bar, 1990; grad. Leadership Collier, Naples, 1991, Leadership S.W. Fla., 1995. Republican. Episcopalian. Real property. Office: 838 Neapolitan Way # 15 Naples FL 34103-3119

**MACKIEWICZ, EDWARD ROBERT,** lawyer; b. Jersey City, July 2, 1951; s. Edward John and Irene Helen (Rakowicz) H. BA, Yale U., 1973; JD, Columbia U., 1976. Bar: N.J. 1976, U.S. Dist. Ct. N.J. 1976, N.Y. 1977, U.S. Dist. Ct. (so. and ea. dist.) N.Y. 1977, D.C. 1978, U.S. Dist. Ct. D.C. 1978, U.S. Ct. Appeals (D.C. cir.) 1978, U.S. Ct. Appeals (3d cir.) 1980, U.S. Supreme Ct. 1980, Md. 1984, U.S. Ct. Claims 1984, U.S. Ct. Appeals (4th cir.) 1986, U.S. Dist. Ct. Md. 1990. Assoc. Carter, Ledyard & Milburn, N.Y.C., 1976-77, Covington & Burling, Washington, 1977-82; counsel for civil rights litigation solicitor's office U.S. Dept. Labor, Washington, 1982-83; sr. assoc. Jones, Day, Reavis & Pogue, Washington, 1983-85; gen. counsel Pension Benefit Guaranty Corp., Washington, 1985-87; of counsel Pierson, Ball & Dowd, Washington, 1987-89; ptnr. Reed Smith Shaw & McClay, Washington, 1989; gen. counsel Masters, Mates & Pilots Benefit Plans, Linthicum Heights, Md., 1989-92; of counsel Steptoe & Johnson, L.L.P., Washington, 1992-98, ptnr., 1999—; mem. adv. coun. Sec. of Labor's ERISA, 1991-93; profl. lectr. in law Nat. Law Ctr., George Washington U., 1993—. Mem. Am. Coun. Young Polit. Leaders (del. to Australia 1985), Univ. Club, Yale Club. Pension, profit-sharing, and employee benefits, Labor, Bankruptcy. Home: 3001 Veazey Ter NW Apt 1032 Washington DC 20008-5406 Office: 1330 Connecticut Ave NW Washington DC 20036-1704

**MACKINNON, CATHARINE A.,** lawyer, law educator, legal scholar, writer; d. George E. and Elizabeth V. (Davis) MacKinnon. BA in Govt. magna cum laude with distinction, Smith Coll., 1969; JD, Yale U., 1977, PhD in Polit. Sci., 1987. Vis. prof. Harvard U., Stanford U., Yale U., others, Osgoode Hall, York U., Canada, U. Basel, Switzerland; prof. of law U. Mich., 1990—; long term vis. prof. U. Chgo., 1997—. Author: Sexual Harassment of Working Women, 1979, Feminism Unmodified, 1987, Toward a Feminist Theory of the State, 1989, Only Words, 1993, Sex Equality, 1999; co-author: In Harm's Way, 1997. Office: U Michigan Law School Ann Arbor MI 48109-1215

**MACKRIDES, WILLIAM CHARLES,** lawyer; b. Darby, Pa., Sept. 28, 1953; s. William and Louise Martinelli Mackrides; m. Nancy Carol Reagan, Oct. 11, 1955; children: Daniel Gary, Nicholas William. BS in Acctg., Villanova U., 1975; JD, Loyola U., New Orleans, 1979. Bar: Supreme Ct. Pa. 1980, U.S. Dist. Ct. (ea. dist.) Pa. 1980, Supreme Ct. 1984, U.S. Dist. Ct. Colo. 1997. Ptnr. Cericola, Breen & Mackrides, Drexel Hill, Pa., 1980-81; pvt. practice law Springfield, Pa., 1981-82; ptnr. Moss and Mackrides, Media, Pa., 1982—. Editor Edgmont Times, 1997—. V.p., bd. dirs. Rose Tree Media Edn. Found., Delaware County Children's Camp Assn., Inc.; past pres. Okehocking Hills Civic Assn.; fundraiser Cmty. Dispute Settlement Program, Inc., Abilitech, Inc., others; v.p. Edgmont (Pa.) Rep. Party, 1997—; mem. Edgmont Twp. Planning Commn., 1997—, chmn. 1998-99; supr. Edgemont Twp.; bd. dirs., chmn. adv. coun. Goodwill Industries; bd. dirs. Pvt. Industry Coun./Delaware County Office of Employment and Tng.; mem. Delaware County Civil Justice Adv. Com.; supr. Edgemont Township, 1999—. Mem. Pa. Trial Lawyers Assn., Pa. Bar Assn. (chmn. vendors and purchasers com. real property divsn., asst. sect. real property, probate and trust divsn. 1998—, officer, mem. coun.), Delaware County Bar Assn. (chmn. dist. justice com., past chmn. civil rights com., pub. rels. com., bar membership directory com., entertainment com., others, editor legal jour. 1984, dir. 1991-93, 95-97), Delaware County Estate Planning Coun., Trust Counselors Network, Inc. (pres. 1993-94), Gentleman's Com. Dressage Devon, Guy G. DiFuria Inn Ct. Roman Catholic. Avocations: art, woodworking, sports, sporting clays, exercise. Real property, Probate, Personal injury. Office: Moss and Mackrides 755 N Monroe St Media PA 19063-2569

**MACLAUGHLIN, HARRY HUNTER,** federal judge; b. Breckenridge, Minn., Aug. 9, 1927; s. Harry Hunter and Grace (Swank) MacL.; m. Mary Jean Shaffer, June 25, 1958; children: David, Douglas. BBA with distinction, U. Minn., 1949, JD, 1956. Bar: Minn. 1956. Law clk. to justice Minn. Supreme Ct.; ptnr. MacLaughlin & Mondale, MacLaughlin & Harstad, Mpls., 1956-72; assoc. justice Minn. Supreme Ct., 1972-77; U.S. sr. dist. judge Dist. of Minn., Mpls., 1977—; part-time instr. William Mitchell Coll. Law, St. Paul, 1958-63; lectr. U. Minn. Law Sch., 1973-86; mem. 8th Cir. Jud. Council, 1981-83. Bd. editors: Minn. Law Rev, 1954-55. Mem. Mpls. Charter Commn., 1967-72, Minn. State Coll. Bd., 1971-72, Minn. Jud. Council, 1972; mem. nat. adv. council Small Bus. Adminstrn., 1967-69. Served with USNR, 1945-46. Recipient U. Minn. Outstanding Achievement award, 1995; named Best Fed. Dist. Ct. Judge in 8th Cir., Am. Lawyer mag., 1983. Mem. ABA, Minn. Bar Assn., Hennepin County Bar Assn., Beta Gamma Sigma, Phi Delta Phi. Congregational. Office: US Dist Ct 684 US Courthouse 110 S 4th St Minneapolis MN 55401-2205

**MACLEAN, BABCOCK,** lawyer; b. N.Y.C., Jan. 26, 1946; s. Charles Chalmers and Lee Selden (Howe) MacL.; m. Cynthia Gannon, Feb. 15, 1983. BA, Yale U., 1967; MA, Columbia U., 1970; JD, Case Western Res. U., 1975; LLM in Taxation, NYU, 1987. Bar: Ohio 1975, N.Y. 1983. Assoc. Hadley, Matia, Mills & MacLean, Cleve., 1976-77, mem., 1977-83; tax editor Research Inst. Am., N.Y.C., 1983-85; assoc. Robinson Brog, N.Y.C., 1985-86, mem., 1987—; adj. asst. prof. taxation Pace U., N.Y.C., 1983-84; adv. bd. Rsch. Inst. Am., 1992-97. Mem. ABA (sect. taxation), N.Y. State Bar Assn. (sect. taxation), Assn. Bar City N.Y., Yale Club, St. Anthony Club, N.Y. Yacht Club, Seawanhaka Corinthian Yacht Club, St. Andrew's Soc. State of N.Y., Pilgrims of the U.S. Republican. Episcopalian. Corporate taxation, Personal income taxation, Taxation, general. Home: 77 W 55th St New York NY 10019-4910 Office: Robinson Brog Ste 31L 1345 Avenue Of The Americas New York NY 10105-0144

**MACLEAN, JOSEPH CURRAN,** lawyer; b. Detroit, Mar. 19, 1961; s. Lawrence V. and Mary (O'Shea) M.; m. Diane McPherson, June 25, 1987; children: Lawrence, Lauren, Mara. BA, Mich. State U., 1983; MBA, U. Detroit, 1987; JD, U. Detroit/Mercy, 1995. Bar: Mich. 1995, U.S. Dist. Ct. (ea. dist.) 1995. Supr. cash mgmt. Primark Corp., Detroit, 1983-87; mgr. investor rels. Primark Corp., Reston, Va., 1987-88, MCN Corp., Detroit, 1988-90; claim mgr. North Pointe Ins. Co., Southfield, Mich., 1990-94; v.p. claims North Pointe Ins. Co., Southfield, 1994—. Copyright claims info. sys., 1995. Named to Frank Murphy Honor Soc. U. Detroit/Mercy, 1995; recipient dean's scholarship, 1992-95. Mem. ABA, State Bar of Mich., Fed. Bar Assn. Avocations: athletics, computer program design. General civil litigation, Insurance. Office: North Pointe Ins Co 28819 Franklin Rd Ste 300 Southfield MI 48034-1656

**MACLEOD, NORMAN,** lawyer, public speaker; b. Edinburgh, Scotland, Apr. 26, 1938; came to U.S., 1965; s. Neil and Mary Elizabeth MacLeod; m. Dianne Cecilia Sachko; 1 child, Alexander Neil Sachko. Student, Leeds (Eng.), 1957-58; grad., Coll. Law, Guildford, Eng., 1961. Bar: Calif. 1970; solicitor, Eng. and Wales. Solicitor Ware, Warner & Knowles, York, Eng., 1961-62, Williams & James, London, 1962-63, Marshall & Co., London, 1963-65, Pierron & Morley, London, 1968-69; paralegal Bacigalupi, Elkus & Rosenberg, San Francisco, 1965-68; assoc. Williams, Van Joesen & Brigham, San Francisco, 1970-71; pvt. practice, San Francisco, 1971—. Mem. Calif. State Bar, Bar Assn. San Francisco, Law Doc. Eng. and Wales, Nat. Spkrs. Assn. Avocations: acting, history, banquet speaking. Family and matrimonial, Probate, Personal injury. Office: 381 Bush St Ste 200 San Francisco CA 94104-2809

**MACNAUGHTON, ANN L.,** lawyer; b. Lansing, Mich., Sept. 25, 1948; d. John Frederick and Elizabeth Ann (Hackett) MacNaughton. BA, U. Houston, 1972, JD, 1976, MBA, 1980. Bar: Tex. 1977, Colo. 1985. Atty. Aminoil U.S.A., Inc., Houston, 1977-79; assoc. Sowell, Ogg & Hinton, Houston, 1980-81; counsel Superior Oil Co. and Mobil Oil Corp., Houston, Tex., Denver and Richmond, Va., 1981-88; sr. assoc. Vinson & Elkins, Houston, 1988-92; prin. Law Offices of Ann L. MacNaughton, Houston, 1992—; pres. Paragon Dispute Resolution, Inc., Houston, 1993—; gen. counsel Paragon Syst. Design, Inc., Houston, 1994—; dir. dispute resolution strategies Arthur Andersen LLP, Houston, 1998—; cons. Mobil Oil Corp., Dallas, 1992-98, State of Alaska, Juneau, 1994-95, Exxon USA, 1995-98. Bd. dirs. Houston Repertory Theatre, 1994—, Cmty. Ptnrs., 1988-91. Mem. ABA (co-chair subcom. litig. sect. environ. com.'s 1994—, co-chair internat. law sect., cross-cultural dispute resolution task force), State Bar of Tex. (co-chair environ. law sect. task force 1993—, chair corp. counsel sect. 1996-97), Tex. Accts. and Lawyers Arts (bd. dirs. 1996—), U.H. Exec. MBA Alumni Orgn. (bd. dirs. 1999—). Avocations: backpacking, trekking, dancing, skiing, writing. Office: 1301 Mckinney St Ste 500 Houston TX 77010-3029

**MACNISH, JAMES MARTIN, JR.,** judge; b. Richmond Heights, Mo., Sept. 3, 1935; s. James Martin and Virginia May (Kleissle) M.; m. Harriette Anne Rost, Aug. 29, 1964; children: Eleanore Miles, Margaret Calhoun. AB, Washington U., St. Louis, 1958; JD, Washington U., 1964. Bar: Mo. 1964, U.S. Dist. Ct. (ea. dist.) Mo. 1964, Kans. 1967, U.S. Dist. Ct. Kans. 1967, U.S. Ct. Appeals (10th cir.) 1969, U.S. Supreme Ct. 1971. Assoc. Stein & Seigel, St. Louis, 1964-67; pvt. practice Topeka, Kans., 1967-77; judge City of Topeka Mcpl. Ct., 1973-77; dist. judge 3d Jud. Dist. Ct. Kans., 1977—; assigned judge Kans. Ct. Appeals, 1986—, Kans. Supreme Ct., 1990—; mem. Kans. Sentencing Commn., 1989-97. Bd. regents Washburn U., Topeka, 1971-85, chmn., 1974-75, vice chmn., 1981-82. Capt. USMC, 1958-61. Mem. ABA, Kans. Bar Assn., Mo. Bar Assn., Topeka Bar Assn., St. Louis Bar Assn., Am. Judicature Soc., Washburn U. Law Sch. Assn. (hon. life), Phi Delta Phi, Sigma Chi. Republican. Office: Shawnee County Courthouse Topeka KS 66603

**MACO, PAUL STEPHEN,** securities and exchange administrator; s. Paul and Rose Mary (McFadden) M.; m. Lisa M. Griglack, Aug. 23, 1997; 1 child, Claire Fiona. BA, Lehigh U., 1974; JD, NYU, 1977. Ptnr. Mintz, Levin, Cohn, Ferris, Glovesky & Popeo, Boston, 1988-94; instr. law Morin Ctr. for Internat. Banking LAw Boston U., 1992-96, 99—; atty. fellow Office of Gen. Counsel SEC, Washington, 1994, dir. Office of Mcpl. Securities, 1995—; adj. assoc. prof. Wash. Coll. of Law of American U., 1999—; adj. assoc. prof. Washington Coll. Law Am. U., 1999. Author: (with others) Bond Markets, Law and Regulation, 1999; bd. editors Jour. of Mcpl. Fin.; bd. editl. advisors Internat. Jour. of Bonds. Dir. Traditions for Tomorrow, Inc. Mem. ABA (co-reporter disclosure rules of counsel 1994), Nat. Assn. Bond Lawyers (dir. 1989-92, chair spl. com. on securities laws and disclosure 1987-89). Office: Office of Mcpl Securities SEC 450 5th St NW Washington DC 20549-0001

**MACRAE, CAMERON FARQUHAR, III,** lawyer; b. N.Y.C., Mar. 21, 1942; s. Cameron F. and Jane B. (Miller) MacR.; m. Ann Wooster Bedell, Nov. 30, 1974; children: Catherine Fairfax, Ann Cameron. AB, Princeton U., 1963; LLB, Yale U., 1966. Bar: N.Y. 1966, D.C. 1967, U.S. Dist. Ct. (so. dist.) N.Y. 1975. Atty.-advisor Office of Gen. Counsel to Sec. Air Force, Washington, 1966-69; assoc. Davis, Polk & Wardwell, N.Y.C., 1970-72; dep. supt. and counsel N.Y. State Banking Dept., N.Y.C., 1972-74; sr. ptnr. LeBoeuf, Lamb, Greene & MacRae, N.Y.C., 1975—. Trustee, sec. St. Andrew's Dune Ch., 1982—; hon. chmn. Clear Pool Inc., 1990-94. Capt. USAF, 1966-69. Mem. Assn. of Bar of City of N.Y. (past mem. securities regulation com., banking law com.), D.C. Bar Assn. Republican. Episcopalian. Clubs: Racquet and Tennis, Union (N.Y.C.), Meadow (v.p., bd. govs.), Bathing Corp., Shinnecock Hills Golf (Southampton), Cottage (Princeton, N.J.). Note and comment editor Yale Law Jour., 1965-66. Banking, Contracts commercial, Private international. Office: LeBoeuf Lamb Greene & MacRae 125 W 55th St New York NY 10019-5369

**MACRI, MARCANTONIO DOMINIC,** lawyer; b. Englewood, N.J., Oct. 2, 1967; s. Dominic and Maria Josephine Macri; m. Michelle Marie Limbardo, Sept. 12, 1998. BA, Rutgers U., Newark, 1990; postgrad., Mich. State U., Detroit, 1991-92; JD, Seton Hall U., 1994. Bar: N.J. 1994, U.S. Dist. Ct. N.J. 1994, N.Y. 1995, U.S. Dist. Ct. (ea., we., so., no. dists.) N.Y. 1995, U.S. Tax Ct. 1995, U.S. Ct. Appeals (3d cir.) 1995, D.C. 1997. Atty. Leanza & Agrapidis, P.C., Hackensack, N.J., 1992-99, Sokolich & Macri, Fort Lee, N.J., 1999—. Vice chmn. Zoning Bd. Adjustment, Ft. Lee, N.J., 1998. Mem. Bergen County Bar Assn. Roman Catholic. General civil litigation. Office: Sokolich & Macri 1223 Anderson Ave Fort Lee NJ 07024-1756

**MACWILLIAMS, MICHAEL BROUGHTON,** lawyer; b. Balt., Oct. 17, 1966; s. Roger W. and Bette Burk (Broughton) MacW. BSME, Va. Tech. U., 1989; JD, U. Balt., 1994. Tech. rep. ARCO Chem. Co., Chgo., 1989-91; assoc. Goodell, DeVries, Leecy & Gray, Balt., 1994—. Mem. Md. State Bar Assn. (tech. task force 1997—). Avocation: sailboat racing. E-mail: mbm@gdlglaw.com. Home: 606 Woodbine Ter Towson MD 21204-4251 Office: Goodell DeVries Leech & Gray One South St 20th fl Baltimore MD 21202

**MACY, JOHN PATRICK,** lawyer; b. Menomonee Falls, Wis., June 26, 1955; s. Leland Francis and Joan Marie (LaValle) M. BA, Carroll Coll., 1977; JD, Marquette U., 1980. Bar: Wis. 1980, U.S. Dist. Ct. (we. and ea. dists.) Wis. 1980, U. S. Ct. Appeals (7th cir.) 1980. Assoc. Hippenmeyer Reilly Arenz Molter Bode & Gross, Waukesha, Wis., 1980-83; ptnr. Arenz Molter Macy & Riffle, S.C., Waukesha, 1983--; lectr. in field. Mem. ABA, Waukesha County Bar Assn. (chair 1995-96). Republican. Roman Catholic. Municipal (including bonds), State and local taxation, Land use and zoning (including planning). Home: 4839 Hewitts Point Rd Oconomowoc WI 53066-3320 Office: Arenz Molter Macy & Riffle SC 720 N East Ave Waukesha WI 53186-4800

**MACY, RICHARD J.,** state supreme court justice; b. Saranac Lake, N.Y., June 2, 1930; m. Emily Ann Macy; children: Anne, Patty, Mark. BS in Bus., U. Wyo., 1955, JD, 1958. Pvt. practice Sundance, Wyo., 1958-85; justice Wyo. Supreme Ct., Cheyenne, 1985—; Crook County atty., 1970-85; mem. Nat. Conf. Commrs. on Uniform State Laws, 1982—. Mem. Sigma Chi (Nat. Outstanding Sig award 1986). Office: Wyo Supreme Ct Supreme Ct Bldg Cheyenne WY 82002-0001*

**MADDEN, EDWARD GEORGE, JR.,** lawyer; b. Newark, Feb. 21, 1924; s. Edward and Catherine (Mahon) M.; m. Mary B. Haveron, June 20, 1959; children: Maurica, Margaret, Thomas, Mary, Jane. BS, St. Peter's Coll., 1950; JD, U. Mich., 1953. Bar: N.J. 1954, U.S. Dist. Ct. N.J. 1954, U.S. Ct. Appeals (3d cir.) 1981, U.S. Supreme Ct. 1959. Assoc. McCarter & English, Newark, 1954-56, Donohue & Donohue, Nutley, N.J., 1956-61; ptnr. Troast, Mattson & Madden, Newark, 1961-65, Mattson & Madden, Newark, 1965—; mem. N.J. State Legislature, 1960-62. With USN 1943-46. Fellow Am. Bar Found.; mem. ABA, N.J. Bar Assn. (trustee, treas. 1972-78), Essex County Bar Assn. (trustee 1971-75), Internat. Assn. Def. Counsel, Transp. Lawyers Assn. Democrat. Roman Catholic. State civil litigation, Insurance, Transportation. Office: One Gateway Ctr Newark NJ 07102

**MADDEN, JEROME ANTHONY,** lawyer; b. Memphis, Aug. 24, 1948; s. Bernard Clark and Virginia Ann (Golas) M.; m. Cynthia S. Madden, June 27, 1992; 1 child, Clark John. BA, The Franciscan U. Steubenville, Ohio, 1971; JD summa cum laude, U. Dayton, 1978. Bar: Ohio 1978, D.C. 1979, U.S. Dist. Ct. D.C. 1979, U.S. Ct. Appeals (D.C. cir.) 1980, U.S. Ct. Claims 1984, U.S. Ct. Appeals (Fed. cir.) 1984, U.S. Supreme Ct. 1984, U.S. Ct. Appeals (7th and 11th cirs.) 1987, U.S. Ct. Appeals (4th and 5th cirs.) 1988, U.S. Ct. Appeals (9th cir.) 1991, U.S. Ct. Appeals (2d & 10th cirs.) 1992, U.S. Ct. Appeals (1st cir.) 1993. Law clk. to chief justices O'Neill and Leach Ohio Supreme Ct., Columbus, 1978-79; assoc. Cadwalader, Wickersham & Taft, Washington, 1979-85; sr. trial counsel U.S. Dept. Justice, Washington, 1985-91; counsel, then acting sr. counsel, then supervisory counsel FDIC Appellate Litigation Sect., Comml. Litigation Unit, Washington, 1991-98; trial atty. U.S. Dept. Justice, Comml. Litigation Br., Washington, 1998—. Editor-in-chief U. Dayton Law Rev., 1977-78. Served with USMCR, 1970-76. Mem. D.C. Bar Assn. Roman Catholic. Avocations: golf. Home: 1502 Powells Tavern Pl Herndon VA 20170-2831 Office: US Dept of Justice 1100 L St NW Washington DC 20005-4035

**MADDEN, JOHN DALE,** lawyer; b. Lansing, Mich., May 17, 1957; s. Dale Ernest and Catherine Louise (Schneider) M. BA, Davidson Coll., 1979; JD, Wake Forest U., 1983. Bar: N.C. 1983, U.S. Dist. Ct. (ea. dist.) N.C. 1983, U.S. Dist. Ct. (mid. dist.) N.C. 1988, U.S. Supreme Ct. 1996, U.S. Ct. Appeals (4th cir.) 1998, U.S. Dist. Ct. (we. dist.) N.C. 1998. Assoc. Smith Anderson Blount Dorsett Mitchell & Jernigan, Raleigh, N.C., 1983-90, ptnr., 1990—. Mem. ABA, N.C. Bar Assn., Wake County Bar Assn. (pres. young lawyers div. 1987-88), Phi Delta Theta (chpt. advisor N.C. State U. 1988-92), U. N.C. Inn Ct. Republican. Roman Catholic. Avocations: running, golf, softball, travel. General civil litigation, Insurance, Personal injury. Home: 2613 Wells Ave Raleigh NC 27608-1945 Office: Smith Anderson Blount Dorsett Mitchell & Jernigan 2500 1st Union Capitol Ctr Raleigh NC 27601

**MADDEN, JOHN PATRICK,** lawyer; b. N.Y.C., Sept. 9, 1945; s. Eugene Patrick and Eileen Mary (Gaughan) M.; m. Sally Williams, Apr. 21, 1984; children: Samuel, Christopher. BCE, Manhattan Coll., 1967; MSCE, NYU, 1969; JD, St. John's U., 1978. Bar: U.S. Patent Office 1978, N.Y. 1979, N.J. 1982, U.S. Dist. Ct. (so. and ea. dists.) N.Y. 1982, U.S. Dist. Ct. N.J. 1982, U.S. Supreme Ct. 1985; cert. internat. arbitrator, constrn. panelist, comml. mediator, D.O.D. instr. Law clk., assoc. Buckley, Treacy, Shaffel Mackey & Abbate, N.Y.C., 1977-80; cons. Contractors Consulting Svcs. Inc., Greatneck, N.Y., 1980-81; ptnr. Madden, Sciarra & Muirhead, N.Y., N.J., 1981-82, Canfield, Venusti, Madden & Rossi, Manhattan, N.Y., 1983—; lectr. in field. Contbr. articles to profl. jours. V.p. N.Y.C. Jaycees, 1975-95. ROTC USAF, 1963-65. Mem. ABA (pub. contract law sect., forum com. on constrn. industry), London Ct. Internat. Arbitration, Swiss Arbitration Assn., Am. Trial Lawyers Assn., N.Y. State Bar Assn., N.Y. State Trial Lawyers Assn., Assn. of Bar of City of N.Y., Nat. Arts Club. Construction, Government contracts and claims, Private international. Office: Canfield Venusti Madden & Rossi 230 Park Ave Rm 2525 New York NY 10169-2599

**MADDEN, PALMER BROWN,** lawyer; b. Milw., Sept. 19, 1945; m. Susan L. Paulus, Mar. 31, 1984. BA, Stanford U., 1968; JD, U. Calif., Berkeley, 1973. Bar: Calif. 1973, U.S. Dist. Ct. (no. dist.) Calif. 1973, U.S. Supreme Ct. 1982. Ptnr. McCutchen, Doyle Brown & Enersen, Walnut Creek, 1985-98; prin. ADR Svcs., Alamo, Calif., 1999—; mem. State Bar Bd. Govs., 1997—. Chair bd. govs. Continuing Edn. of the Bar, 1997; judge pro tem Contra Costa Superior Ct., 1991—; pres. Contra Costa Coun., 1995, Kennedy-King Found., 1994. Mem. Contra Costa County Bar Assn. (pres. 1996-97). Democrat. Episcopalian. General civil litigation. Office: ADR Svcs PMB # 230 107F Alamo Plz Alamo CA 94507-1549

**MADDEN, PAUL ROBERT,** lawyer; b. St. Paul, Nov. 13, 1926; s. Ray Joseph and Margaret (Meyer) M.; m. Rosemary R. Sorel, Aug. 7, 1974; children: Margaret Jane, William, James Patrick, Derek R. Sorel, Lisa T. Sorel. Student, St. Thomas Coll., 1944; AB, U. Minn., 1948; JD, Georgetown U., 1951. Bar: Ariz. 1957, Minn. 1951, D.C. 1951. Assoc. Hamilton & Hamilton, Washington, 1951-55; legal asst. to commr. SEC, Washington, 1955-56; assoc. Lewis and Roca, Phoenix, Ariz., 1957-59, ptnr., 1959-90; ptnr. Beus, Gilbert & Morrill, Phoenix, 1991-94; ptnr. Chapman and Cutler, Phoenix, 1994-97; of counsel Gallagher & Kennedy, 1997—; bd. dirs. Mesa Air Group, Inc., Phoenix, chmn., 1998—. Sec. Minn. Fedn. Coll. Rep. Clubs, 1947-48; chmn. 4th dist. Minn. Young Rep. Club, 1948; nat. co-chmn. Youth for Eisenhower, 1951-52; mem. Ariz. Rep. Com., 1960-62; bd. dirs. Found. Jr. Achievement Ctrl. Ariz., Cath. Community Found., Phoenix, Heritage Hills Homeowners Assn., St. Joseph the Worker; past bd. dirs. Camelback Charitable Trust, The Samaritan Found., Phoenix; past bd. dirs., past. pres. Ariz. Club, Phoenix, 1990-93; past bd. dirs., past chmn. Found. for Sr. Living; past bd. dirs., vice chmn., Cen. Ariz. chpt. ARC; past bd. dirs., vice chmn., Cen. Ariz. chpt. ARC; past bd. dirs., past pres. Jr. Achievement Cen. Ariz., Inc.; mem. nat. bd. vis. U. Ariz. Law Sch. With USNR, 1946-48. Mem. ABA, Ariz. Bar Assn., Maricopa County Bar Assn., Fed. Bar Assn., Fedn. Ins. Counsel, Phi Delta Phi. Clubs: The Barristers (Washington), Arizona. E-mail: PRM@gknet.com. General corporate, Insurance, Securities. Home: 5847 N 46th St Phoenix AZ 85018-1234 Office: Mesa Air Group Inc 410 N 44th St Ste 700 Phoenix AZ 85008-7608 also: Gallagher & Kennedy PA 2600 N Central Ave Fl 20 Phoenix AZ 85004-3050

**MADDEN, WILLIAM LEE, JR.,** lawyer; b. Hastings, Nebr., Mar. 13, 1948. BA with distinction, Stanford U., 1970; JD, Cornell U., 1973. Bar: Mont. 1974, U.S. Dist. Ct. Mont. 1974, U.S. Ct. Appeals (9th cir.) 1975. Assoc. Towe, Neely & Ball, Billings, Mont., 1973-75; ptnr. Goetz & Madden, Bozeman, Mont., 1975—, Goetz Madden & Dunn, P.C., Bozeman, 1981-98; pvt. practice William Madden, Jr., P.C., Bozeman, 1998—. Bd. dirs. Cinnabar Found., Bozeman. Mem. ABA, Am. Arbitration Assn., Assn. Trial Lawyers Am., Mont. Trial Lawyers Assn., Mont. State Bar Assn., Mont. Contractors Assn. (assoc. mem.), Gallatin County Bar Assn. Bankruptcy, General civil litigation, Construction. Office: William Madden Jr PC 945 Technology Blvd Ste 102 Bozeman MT 59718-6859

**MADDOX, ALVA HUGH,** state supreme court justice; b. Andalusia, Ala., Apr. 17, 1930; s. Christopher Columbus and Audie Lodella Maddox; m. Virginia Roberts, June 14, 1958; children: Robert Hugh, Jane Maddox. AB in Journalism, U. Ala., Tuscaloosa, 1952, JD, 1957. Bar: Ala. 1957. Law clk. to Judge Aubrey Cates, Ala. Ct. Appeals, Montgomery, 1957-58; field examiner Chief Atty.'s Office, VA, Montgomery, 1958-59; law clk. to Judge Frank M. Johnson, U.S. Dist. Ct., Montgomery, 1959-61; pvt. practice, Montgomery, 1961-65; cir. judge, spl. cir. judge Montgomery Cir. Ct., 1963, asst. dist. atty., 1964; legal advisor to govs. including George C. Wallace, Lurleen B. Wallace, Albert P. Brewer, State of Ala., Montgomery, 1965-69; assoc. justice Supreme Ct. Ala., Montgomery, 1969—; mem. adv. bd. JUSTEC Rsch. Author: Alabama Rules of Criminal Procedure, 1991, supplements, 1992—. Founder youth jud. program YMCA, Montgomery, 1979, also mem. metro. bd. dirs. 2d lt. USAF, 1952-54, col. USAF Res. ret. Recipient Man of Yr. award YMCA, 1988, Disting. Program Svc. award, 1989. Mem. ABA, Ala. Bar Assn. (Jud. award of merit 1997), Inst. Jud. Adminstrn., Christian Legal Soc. (bd. dirs.), Federalist Soc. (bd. dirs.), Hugh Maddox Inn of Ct. Montgomery (charter, founding), Ala. Law Inst., Am. Jud. Soc., Kiwanis (past bd. dirs. Montgomery), Am. Inns of Ct. (bd. dirs.). Democrat. Baptist. Office: Supreme Ct Ala 300 Dexter Ave Montgomery AL 36104-3741

**MADDOX, NANCY MCCRAINE,** lawyer; b. Greenwood, Miss., Apr. 3, 1950; d. Bill F. and Helen M. Maddox; m. John Kenneth Pieralisi, Sept. 25, 1976 (div. Aug. 1989). BA, U. Memphis, 1972; JD, U. Miss., 1991. Bar: Miss. 1991, U.S. Ct. Appeals (5th cir.) 1991, U.S. Dist. Ct. (no. and so. dists.) Miss. 1991, Tenn. 1998. Assoc. Holcomb Dunbar, Southaven, Miss., 1991-98, Myers & Assocs., Hernando, Miss., 1999—. Bd. dirs. Miss. Coun. Sch. Bd. Attys., 1998—. Methodist. Federal civil litigation, Civil rights, State civil litigation. Office: Myers & Assocs 140 W Center St Hernando MS 38632-2218

**MADDUX, PARKER AHRENS,** lawyer; b. San Francisco, May 23, 1939; s. Jackson Walker and Jeanette Ahrens M.; m. Mathilde G.M. Landman, Mar. 20, 1966; 1 child, Jackson Wilhelmus Quentin. AB, U. Calif., 1961; JD, Harvard U., 1964. Bar: Calif. 1965, U.S. Dist. Ct. (no. so., ea., ctrl. dist.) Calif. 1965, U.S. Ct. Appeals (9th cir.) 1972, U.S. Ct. Claims, 1974, N.Y. 1981, U.S. Supreme Ct. 1982, Assoc., Pillsbury Madison & Sutro, San Francisco, 1965-72, ptnr., 1973-97; dir. litigation Tandem Computers Inc., Cupertino, Calif., 1997—; lectr. in field. Fulbright fellow, 1964-65. Mem. ABA, Calif. Bar Assn., San Francisco Bar Assn., Harvard Club (N.Y.C.). Republican. Unitarian. Contbr. articles to profl. jours. Antitrust, General civil litigation, Securities. Office: Tandem Computers Inc 10435 N Tantau Loc 200-16 Cupertino CA 95014

**MADERA, CARMEN SORIA,** lawyer; b. Paracale, Philippines, July 28, 1937; came to U.S. 1976; d. Florentino Lauce and Carmen (Soria) M. B.Lit., U. Santo Tomas, Manila, 1958; LLB, Manuel L. Quezon U., Manila, 1968; B.Commerce in Bus. Adminstrn., U. New Orleans, 1980. Bar: La. 1990, U.S. Dist. Ct. (ea. and middle dist.) La. 1990. Consumer/mkt. rschr. Colgate-Palmolive Philippines, Makati, 1958-59; info. writer Dept. Commerce & Industry, Manila, 1962-63, info. editor, 1964-65, comml. analyst, 1966-68; fgn. trade analyst Dept. Trade, Manil, 1969-70; supervising info. officer Dept. Trade, Industry & Tourism, Manil, 1971-73; chief trade info. and export tng. sect. Bur. of Fgn. Trade, Manil, 1974-75; asst. comml. attache Philippine Consulate Gen., New Orleans, 1976-84; pvt. practice law New Orleans, 1990—; legal cons. Presdl. Mgmt. Staff, Manila, 1972-75, Presdl. Staff on spl. projects, 1984; editorial cons. Neda, Philippine Vols. Agy., Manila, 1984. Mng. editor DCI Trade Winds, 1970; editor-in-chief Export Advisor, 1973. Philippine Bur. Fgn. Trade study grantee, 1975, 76. Mem. ABA, La. State Bar Assn., Fgn. Rels. Assn., New Orleans Filipino-Am. Lions (Svc. award 1991). Roman Catholic. Family and matrimonial, Immigration, naturalization, and customs, Consumer commercial. Home: 5505 Bundy Rd Apt 170 New Orleans LA 70127-3007

**MADISON, TRINA SHAUNALDREA,** lawyer; b. Tallahassee, Oct. 9, 1962; d. Frederick Madison Roberts and Marian Harris; m. Christopher C. Hill. BA, Smith Coll., 1990; Cert. in Musicology, U. Chgo., 1993; JD, Northwestern U., Evanston, Ill., 1996. Tax return processor Amalgamated Bank, Chgo., 1992-93; legal intern Shorebank Corp., Chgo., summer 1994; jud. clk. Cook County Cir. Ct., Chgo., 1994; intern Lawyers for Creative Arts, Chgo., 1994-95; legal cons. Phoenix Animation, Lombard, Ill., 1995; prodn. intern Faded Denim Prodns., Chgo., 1995-96; assoc. Michael Best Friedrich, Madison, WI, 1996—. Mem. Arts Censorship Project, ACLU, N.Y.C., 1995, Harper Ct. Arts Coun., Chgo., 1995. Recipient Grad. fellowship U. Chgo., 1990, grant Northwestern Law Sch., 1994, scholarship Baker & McKenzie, Chgo., 1994. Mem. ABA, Black Entertainment and Sports Lawyers Assn., Ctr. for Black Music Rsch., Nat. Acad. Recording Arts & Scis., Alpha Kappa Alpha. Democrat. Roman Catholic. Avocations: writing poetry, classical guitar, reading, travelling. E-mail: trinamadison@looksmart.com. Office: Michael Best & Friedrich 3 S Pinckney St Madison WI 53703-2866

**MADORY, RICHARD EUGENE,** lawyer; b. Kenton, Ohio, May 14, 1931; s. Harold Richard and Hilda (Strictland) M.; m. Barbara Jean Madory, Sept. 25, 1955; children—Richard Eugene, Terry Dean, Michael Wesly. B.S. in Edn., Ohio State U., 1952; J.D., Southwestern U., 1961. Bar: Calif., 1961, U.S. Ct. Mil. Appeals, U.S. Supreme Ct., U.S. Dist. Ct. (cen. dist.) Calif. With firm Madory, Booth, Zell & Pleiss, Santa Ana, Calif., 1962—, now pres., v.p., sec.-treas. lectr. Continuing Edn. of Bar State of Calif. Served to col. USMC. Fellow Am. Coll. Trial Lawyers; mem. ABA, Orange County Bar Assn., Los Angeles County Bar Assn., So. Calif. Def. Counsel Assn., Am. Bd. Trial Advs., Nat. Bd. Trial Advocacy. Personal injury, State civil litigation, Insurance. Office: 17822 17th St Ste 205 Tustin CA 92780-2152

**MADOW, JAMES SHELDON,** lawyer, publisher; b. Lynn, Mass., Mar. 12, 1952; s. Sumner and Sylvia Madow; m. Juliana E. Bonicalzi, Feb. 15, 1986; 1 child, Daniel Lee. BA in Philosophy, Harvard Coll., 1973; JD cum laude, U. Mich., 1983. Bar: Calif. 1983. Assoc. Titchell, Maltzman, Mark et al., San Francisco, 1984-86, Griffinger, Levinson, Freed et al., San Francisco, 1987-91; pvt. practice San Rafael, Calif., 1991—. Author: (comic books) Boots, Vol. 1, 1997, Human Drama, 1979. Mem. Marin County Bar Assn. General civil litigation. Office: Law Offices of James S Madow 1120 Nye St Ste 300 San Rafael CA 94901-2945

**MADRID, ANDRES N.,** lawyer; b. Manila, The Philippines, Feb. 16, 1962; m. Maria Madrid. BSEE, GM Inst., 1985; JD, SUNY, Buffalo, 1991. Bar: N.Y. 1992, U.S. Dist. Ct. (so. dist.) N.Y. 1997, U.S. Ct. Appeals (D.C. cir.) 1997, U.S. Dist. Ct. (we. dist.) N.Y. 1997. Engr. GM, Rochester, N.Y., 1980-88; assoc. Dewey Ballantine, N.Y.C., 1991-94, McAulay Fisher et al, N.Y.C., 1995-97, Schwegman, Lundberg et al, Mpls., 1997-98, Cohen Pontani et al, N.Y.C., 1998—. Mem. Am. Intellectual Property Law Assn., Fed. Cir. Bar Assn. (amicus com.). Patent, Trademark and copyright, Federal civil litigation. Office: Cohen Pontani Lieberman Pavane 551 5th Ave Rm 1210 New York NY 10176-0091

**MADRID, PATRICIA ANN,** state attorney general, lawyer; b. Las Cruces, N.Mex., Sept. 25, 1946; d. Charles and Virginia (Fitch) M.; m. L. Michael Messina, May 2, 1975; children: Giancarlo Anthony, Elizabeth Jennifer. BA in English and Philosophy, U. N.Mex., 1969; JD, 1973; cert. Nat. Jud. Coll., U. Nev., 1978. Bar: N.Mex. 1973. Ptnr. Messina, Madrid & Smith, P.A., Albuquerque, 1984-88; atty. gen. State of N.Mex., 1999—. Editor N.Mex. Law Rev., 1972-73. Bd. mem. Fechin Art Inst., Taos, N.Mex.; Dem. nominee Lt. Gov. N.Mex., 1994. Hon. Commdr. award U.S. Air Force,

1979, Award of yr., Albuquerque Bus. and Profl. Women; named Outstanding Young Women of Am., 1980-81; recipient Gov's award Outstanding N.Mex. Women, 1993. Mem. Hispanic Women's Coun. of N.Mex. (bd. dirs. 1989), Mex. Am. Legal Def. and Ednl. Fund (bd. dirs. 1989). Office: Atty Gen's Office PO Box 1508 Santa Fe NM 87504-1508

**MADSEN, BARBARA A,** state supreme court justice. Justice Washington Supreme Ct., Olympia.

**MADSEN, GEORGE FRANK,** lawyer; b. Sioux City, Iowa, Mar. 24, 1933; s. Frank O. and Agnes (Cuhel) M.; m. Magnhild Norstog; 1 child, Michelle Marie. BA, St. Olaf Coll., 1954; LLB, Harvard U., 1959. Bar: Ohio 1960, Iowa 1961, U.S. Dist. Ct. (no. and so. dists.) Iowa, U.S. Ct. Appeals (8th cir.), U.S. Supreme Ct. 1991. Trainee Cargill, Inc., Mpls., 1954; assoc. Durfey, Martin, Browne & Hull, Springfield, Ohio, 1959-61; assoc., then ptnr. Shull, Marshall & Marks, Sioux City, 1961-85; ptnr. Marks & Madsen, Sioux City, 1985-97, Marks, Madsen & Hirsohbach, Sioux City, 1998—. Author, editor: Iowa Title Opinions and Standards, 1978; contbg. author: The American Law of Real Property, 1991. Sec., bd.dirs. Sioux City Boys Club, 1969-76; mem. Sioux City Zoning Bd. Adjustment, 1963-65; past pres. Morningside Luth Ch., Sioux City; active Iowa Mo. River Preservation and Land Use Authority, 1992—, pres., 1997—. Lt. USAF, 1954-56. Fellow Iowa State Bar Found.; mem. ABA, Iowa Bar Assn., Woodbury County Bar Assn., St. Olaf Coll. Alumni Assn. (past pres. Siouxland chpt.), Nat. Wildlife Assn., Mont. Wildlife Assn., Rocky Mountain Elk Found., Pheasants Forever, Phi Beta Kappa (past pres. Siouxland chpt.), Rotary Internat. Avocations: skiing, hunting, swimming, reading. Real property, General corporate, Contracts commercial. Office: PO Box 3226 Sioux City IA 51102-3226

**MADSEN, STEPHEN STEWART,** lawyer; b. Spokane, Wash., Oct. 13, 1951; s. H. Stephen Madsen and Sarah Pope (Stewart) Ruth; m. Rebecca Wetherill Howard, July 28, 1984; children: Stephen Stewart Jr., Lawrence Washington, Christina Wetherill, Benton Howard. BA, Harvard U., 1973; JD, Columbia U., 1980. Bar: N.Y. 1981, U.S. Dist. Ct. (so. dist.) N.Y. 1981, U.S. Ct. Appeals (6th cir.) 1983, U.S. Ct. Appeals (8th cir.) 1985, U.S. Ct. Appeals (2d, 7th and D.C. cirs.) 1994, U.S. Supreme Ct., 1996. Law clk. to presiding judge U.S. Ct. Appeals (2d cir.), N.Y.C., 1980-81; assoc. Cravath, Swaine & Moore, N.Y.C., 1981-88, ptnr., 1988—. Bd. visitors Columbia U. Sch. Law, 1991—; bd. govs. Hill-Stead Mus., 1995—; mem. vestry St. Bartholomew's Ch., 1995—. Mem. ABA, N.Y. State Bar Assn. (exec. com. antitrust law sect. 1998—), New York County Lawyers Assn., London Ct. Internat. Arbitration. General civil litigation, Antitrust. Office: Cravath Swaine & Moore Worldwide Pla 825 8th Ave Fl 38 New York NY 10019-7475

**MADU, LEONARD EKWUGHA,** lawyer, human rights officer, newspaper columnist, politician, business executive; b. Ibadan, Nigeria, Mar. 17, 1953; came to U.S., 1977; s. Luke E. and Grace (Dureke) M.; m. Jaculine Stephanie Turner, June 4, 1980; children: Christine, Oscar. BA, Marshall U., 1980; JD, U. Tenn., 1988; MA, Sch. Internat. Svc., Am. U. Rsch. assoc. Lamberts Publs., Washington, 1980-82; data specialist Govt. Employees Ins. Co., Washington, 1982-85; law intern Knoxville (Tenn.) Urban League, 1986-88; cons. Morris Brown Coll., Atlanta, 1988; staff atty. East Carolina Legal Svc., Wilson, N.C., 1989-90; cons. youth devel. Nat. Crime Prevention Coun., Washington, 1990; contract compliance officer Walters State C.C., Morristown, Tenn., 1990; examiner Dept. of Human Svc., Nashville, 1990-93; human rights officer Human Rights Commn., Nashville, 1993—; pres. Panafrica, Nashville, 1994—; CEO Madu and Assoc. Internat. Bus. Cons., 1996—; with Bus. Forum & Banquet, 1994—; polit. cons. Embassy of Nigeria, Washington, 1995; cons. Embassy of Sierra Leone, Washington, 1995, Healthcare Internat. Mgmt. Co., 1996—; bd. dirs. Peace and Justice Ctr., Nashville. Editor: African Nations Handbook, 1994, Directory of African Universities and Colleges, 1994; editor-in-chief Panafrican Digest, 1994, Panafrican Jour. of World Affairs, 1994; columnist Met. Times, Nashville, 1991—, The African Herald, Dallas, 1995—, U.S./African Voice, Balt., 1995—, African Sun Times, 1995—, The Nigerian and African, 1995—, The African Press, N.Y. Co-chmn. Clergy and Laity Concerned, Nashville, 1992—; mem. curriculum and character com. Met. Sch. Bd., Nashville, 1994—; co-coordinator The Haitian Project, 1991-94; vice chmn. Nigerian Network Leadership awards N.Y., 1996; chmn. Internat. Women's Expo, Knoxville, Tenn., 1996; co-chairperson Miss Nigeria Internat. Beauty Pageant, Washington, 1995, Miss Africa Internat. Beauty Pageant, Nashville, 1996, Igbo Union Chieftaincy Coronation Ceremony, Nashville, 1995; chmn. Nigerian Patriotic Front, 1997—; coord. United Nigeria Congress Party, 1997—, Southeast U.S.; recruiter internat. students Tenn. State U., 1998—. Recipient World Hunger Devel. Program award Marshall U., 1978, 79, Hall of Nations scholar Am. U., 1980, 82, Mary Strohbel award United Way, 1994, 95, Non-profit Vol. award Nat. Conf. of Christians and Jews, 1994. Mem. NAACP, U.S. Com. on Fgn. Rels., Soc. Profl. Journalists, UN Assn., Orgn. African Natonals (pres. 1994). Avocations: reading, traveling, soccer, ping-pong, tennis. Office: Panafrica 1016 18th Ave S Nashville TN 37212-2105

**MADVA, STEPHEN ALAN,** lawyer; b. Pitts., July 27, 1948; s. Joseph Edward and Mary (Zulick) M.; m. Bernadette A. McKeon; children: Alexander, Elizabeth. BA cum laude, Yale U., 1970; JD, U. Pa., 1973. Bar: Pa. 1973, U.S. Dist. Ct. (ea. dist.) Pa. 1975, U.S. Ct. Appeals (3d cir.) 1976, U.S. Ct. Appeals (11th cir.) 1987, U.S. Supreme Ct. 1985, N.Y. 1990. Asst. defender Defender Assn. Phila., 1973-75, fed. defender, 1975-77, also bd. dirs., 1985—; assoc. Montgomery, McCracken, Walker & Rhoads, Phila., 1977-81, ptnr., 1981—, mem. mgmt. com., 1993—, chmn. litigation sect., 1993—. Bd. dirs. Ctrl. Phila. Devel. Corp., 1995—. Fellow Am. Coll. Trial Lawyers; mem. ABA, Internat. Assn. Def. Counsel, Pa. Bar Assn., Phila. Bar Assn. (fed. cts. com.), Def. Rsch. Inst., Hist. Soc. Pa., Yale Alumni Assn. (schs. com.), Yale Rowing Assn., Union League of Phila. Democrat. Avocations: tennis, distance running, opera, classical music. Federal civil litigation, Product liability, Toxic tort. Home: 2055 Lombard St Philadelphia PA 19146-1314 Office: Montgomery McCracken Walker & Rhoads 123 S Broad St Fl 24 Philadelphia PA 19109-1099

**MAEDER, GARY WILLIAM,** lawyer; b. Los Angeles, Dec. 21, 1949; s. Clarence Wilbur and Norma Jean (Buckbee) M.; m. Sue Ellen; children: Stephen Gregory, Charlene Michelle. BA, UCLA, 1971, JD, 1975; student, Fuller Seminary, 1971-72. Bar: Calif. 1975. Assoc. Kindel & Anderson, Los Angeles, 1975-82, ptnr., 1982-96; shareholder Heller Ehrman White & McAuliffe, Los Angeles, 1996—. Author: God's Will for Your Life, 1973, 76, 91. Elder adult edn. St. John's Presbyn. Ch., Los Angeles, 1981-86, 94-96; mem. adv. bd. Christian Legal Soc. Los Angeles, 1975—; bd. dirs. Christian Conciliation Svc. of L.A., 1983-88. Mem. Los Angeles County Bar Assn. (state & local tax com.), Christian Legal Soc. (bd. dirs. 1989-92), Order of Coif, Phi Beta Kappa. Corporate taxation, Personal income taxation, State and local taxation.

**MAES, PETRA JIMENEZ,** state supreme court justice; widowed; 4 children. BA, U. N.Mex., 1970, JD, 1973. Bar: N.Mex. 1973. Pvt. pratice law Albuquerque, 1973-75; rep., then office mgr. No. N.Mex. Legal Svcs., 1975-81; dist. judge 1st Jud. Dist. Ct., Santa Fe, Los Alamos, 1981-98; chief judge, 1984-87, 92-95. Active S.W. coun. Boy Scouts Am., mem. dist. coms.; presenter pre cana St. John's Cath. Ch.; bd. dirs. Nat. Ctr. on Women and Family Law; chairperson Tri-County Gang Task Force; mem. Gov.'s Task Force on Children and Families, 1991-92; mem. adv. com. Santa Fe County Jail, 1996. Mem. N.Mex. Bar Assn. (elderly law com. 1980-81, alternative dispute resolution com. 1987-92, code of jud. conduct com. 1992—, juvenile cmty. corrections svcs. com. chairperson), Hispanic Women's Coun. (charter). Office: Supreme Court of New Mexico PO Box 848 Santa Fe NM 87504-0848

**MAFFEI, ROCCO JOHN,** lawyer; b. Portland, Maine, Nov. 23, 1949; s. Rocco and Grace Marie (Bartlett) M; m. Susan Marie Farrell, June 23, 1973; children: Rocco Francis, Christopher Matthew. BA in History, Trinity Coll., 1972; JD, U. Maine, 1975. Bar: Maine 1975, Mass. 1975, U.S. Dist. Ct. Maine 1975, Ohio 1977, U.S. Ct. Claim 1980, U.S. Supreme Ct. 1980, Minn. 1981, U.S. Dist. Ct. Minn. 1981. Ptnr. Briggs & Morgan Law Firm, St. Paul, 1980-83, Hart & Bruner Law Firm, Mpls., 1983-85; v.p. gen. counsel Computing Devices Internat., Bloomington, Minn., 1985-98; assoc. gen. counsel Lockheed Martin Tactical Def. Sys., Eagan, Minn., 1999—; adj. prof. law William Mitchell Sch. Law, St. Paul, 1982—, Air Force Inst. Tech., 1983—. Contbr. articles to profl. jours. Capt. USAF, 1975-80; col. USAFR. Fellow Nat. Contract Mgmt. Assn. (bd. advisors, pres. Twin Cities chpt. 1985-86, regional v.p. 1990-91, Charles J. Delaney award 1986); mem. ABA (chmn. com. pub. contract law sect. 1984-88, 93—), Fed. Bar Assn., Minn. Bar Assn., Huber Hts. Jaycees (Jaycee of Yr. 1978). Republican. Roman Catholic. Avocation: long distance running. Government contracts and claims, Private international, General corporate. Home: 1161 Tiffany Cir N Saint Paul MN 55123-1871 Office: Lockheed Martin Tactical Defense Sys PO Box 64525 Saint Paul MN 55164-0525

**MAFFEO, VINCENT ANTHONY,** lawyer, executive; b. N.J., Jan. 22, 1951; s. Michael Anthony and Marie M.; BA summa cum laude, Bklyn. Coll., 1971; JD, Harvard U., 1974; m. Debra, Dec. 16, 1972. Admitted to N.Y. State bar, 1975, Calif. bar, 1982, Va. 1988, D.C. 1988, Mich. 1994; assoc. firm Simpson Thacher & Bartlett, N.Y.C., 1974-77; legal counsel Communications Systems div. ITT, Hartford, Conn., 1977-79, v.p., gen. counsel Bus. Communications div., Des Plaines, Ill., 1979-80, asst. counsel Western region, 1980-83, group counsel ITT Europe, Inc., 1983-86, v.p. gen. coun. ITT Defense Inc., 1987-91, v.p., gen. coun. ITT Automotive, Inc., 1992-95; sr. v.p., gen. counsel ITT Industries, Inc., 1995—. Served to lt. Judge Adv. Gen. Corps, USNR, 1975. Mem. Am. Bar Assn., Calif. State Bar, N.Y. State Bar Assn., Phi Beta Kappa. Office: ITT Industries Inc 4 W Red Oak Ln Ste 2 White Plains NY 10604-3617

**MAGARIAN, EDWARD BRIAN,** lawyer; b. Oxford, Miss., Feb. 14, 1964; s. Edward O. and Sandra M. Magarian; m. Donna F. Magarian, May 27, 1989; children: Brian, Hannah. BA, Georgetown U., 1986, JD, 1989. Bar: Minn. 1990, U.S. Dist. Ct. Minn. 1990, U.S. Ct. Appeals (8th cir.) 1990. Law clk. 8th cir. U.S. Ct. Appeals, 1989-90; ptnr. Dorsey & Whitney, LLP, Mpls., 1990—; spl. asst. city atty. City of Mpls., 1992; guest lectr. Coll. St. Thomas, Mpls., 1995; lectr. Corp. Counsel Symposium, Mpls., 1996-97. Sr. editor The Georgetown Law Rev., 1989; editor: Criminal Procedures Project The Georgetown Law Jour., 1989. Mem. Order of Coif. Avocation: running. Criminal, General civil litigation, Labor. Office: Dorsey & Whitney LLP 220 S 6th St Ste 2200 Minneapolis MN 55402-1498

**MAGAVERN, JAMES L.,** lawyer; b. Buffalo, Feb. 1, 1933; s. Samuel D. and Gertrude (Lewis) M.; m. 1955; children: David, William, Margareg, Samuel. Student, Dartmouth Coll., 1951-54; LLB, U. Buffalo, 1959. Bar: N.Y. 1969, U.S. Dist. Ct. (we. and so. dists.) N.Y., U.S. Ct. Appeals (2nd cir.), U.S. Supreme Ct. Dep. asst., then asst. atty. gen. State of N.Y., Albany, 1959-62; ptnr. Magavern & Magavern, Buffalo, 1962-66, 77-78, 80—; asst. and assoc. prof. law SUNY, Buffalo, 1966-71, adj. prof. law, 1972—; county atty. Erie County, Buffalo, 1972-76; counsel to state comptroller State of N.Y., 1979-80; legal cons. planning and devel. Collaborative Internat.-USAID, South Korea, 1974; co-counsel Commn. on Eminent Domain, State of N.Y., 1971. Contbr. articles to profl. jours. Past bd. dirs. Friendship House, Lackawanna, Community Music Sch., Legal Aid Buffalo, Buffalo and Erie County YMCA, Buffalo Hearing and Speech Ctr.; mem. N.Y. Commn. on Govt. Integrity, 1987-90; chmn. panel to rev. Code of Ethics City of Buffalo, 1986-87; mem. Erie County Fiscal Adv. Commn.; m. Citizens Adv. Coun. to Pub. Svc. Commn., 1976-79; chmn. Buffalo Stadium Design Adv. Com., 1984; former co-chmn. Citizens Coun. Human Rels.; bd. dirs. health care plan Buffalo Zool. Soc.; chair City of Buffalo Charter Revision Commn., 1998-99. With U.S. Army, 1954-56. Mem. ABA, N.Y. State Bar Assn., Erie County Bar Assn. (pres. 1982-83), Assn. Asian Studies (chmn. com. on Asian law 1978-80). Republican. Unitarian. Health, General civil litigation, Municipal (including bonds). Office: Magavern & Magavern 1100 Rand Bldg Buffalo NY 14203-1992

**MAGEE, JOHN B.,** lawyer; b. Seattle, Aug. 4, 1944; s. John B. and Kathryn Rose (Allan) M.; m. Susan Beilby, Dec. 23, 1969; 1 child, Elizabeth. BA, Pomona Coll., 1966; JD, U. Wash., 1972; LLM, Georgetown U., 1977. Bar: Wash. 1972, D.C. 1977. Assoc. Miller & Chevalier, Chartered, Washington, 1977-79, mem., 1980—. Mem. U. Wash. Law Rev., 1972. Mem. ABA, Am. Law Inst., Columbia Country Club, Washington Athletic Club, Met. Club, Order of Coif. Corporate taxation. Office: Miller & Chevalier 655 15th St NW Ste 900 Washington DC 20005-5799

**MAGEE, THOMAS HUGH,** lawyer; b. Rochester, N.Y., Aug. 15, 1943; s. Edward Charles and Jane Kathleen (Cranmer) M.; m. Judith Joy Stone, Oct. 2, 1982; 1 child, Michael Julian. BSME, U. Rochester, N.Y., 1965; JD, Syracuse U., 1973. Bar: N.J. 1974, U.S. Dist. Ct. N.J. 1974, U.S. Ct. Appeals (D.C. cir.) 1975, N.Y. 1981, U.S. Supreme Ct. 1978, U.S. Patent and Trademark Office. Sr. patent counsel RCA Corp., Princeton, N.J., 1973-86, GE/RCA Licensing Operation, Princeton, 1986-88; sr. counsel E.I. duPont de Nemours & Co., Wilmington, Del., 1988—. Lt. USN, 1965-70, Capt. USNR (ret.), 1991. Navy commendation medal with combat V, Vietnam, 1969. Mem. Am. Intellectual Property Law Assn. (com. chair 1974—), Phila. Intellectual Property Law Assn. (com. chmn. 1974—), N.J. Patent Law Assn., Justinian hon. law soc., Phi Alpha Delta. Republican. Presbyterian. Avocations: tennis, handball, coin-collecting. Intellectual property, Patent, Antitrust. Home: 721 Severn Rd Wilmington DE 19803-1724 Office: E I duPont de Nemours & Co Barley Mill Plz BMP 11-1126 Wilmington DE 19880

**MAGEL, LARRY NEAL,** legal administrator; b. Chgo., Sept. 2, 1941; s. Irving and Ida Magel; m. Joanna Blumberg, Aug. 2, 1976; children: Marla, Lauren, David. BS in Acctg., Roosevelt U., 1967. Cert. Data Processing Mgmt. Assn. Dir. MIS, Winston & Strawn, Chgo., 1968-70; v.p. CT Law Tech., N.Y.C., 1970-78; legal adminstr. Katten Muchin Zavis, Chgo., 1978-80; exec. dir. Simpson Thacher & Bartlett, N.Y.C., 1980—. Vice pres. Grand Street Settlement, N.YC., 1996—. Fellow Coll. Law Practice Mgmt.; mem. Assn. Legal Adminstrs. Office: Simpson Thacher & Bartlett 425 Lexington Ave Fl 15 New York NY 10017-3954

**MAGER, SCOTT ALAN,** lawyer, educator; b. Tallahassee, Fla., Jan. 2, 1962; s. Gerald and Curly Mager. BA, U. Fla., 1984; JD, Nova Shepard Broad Law Ctr., 1988. Bar: Fla., U.S. Dist. Ct. (so. dist.) Fla., U.S. Ct. Appeals (4th, 5th, 11th cirs.), U.S. Tax Ct. Ptnr. Mager & Gaffney, Ft. Lauderdale, Fla., 1988-89; pvt. practice Ft. Lauderdale, 1989-90; assoc. Cooney, Ward, Lesher & Damon, West Palm Beach, Fla., 1990-91, Weinstein, Zimmerman & Nussbaum, Tamarac, Fla., 1991-92; prin. Law Office of Scott Mager, Ft. Lauderdale, Fla., 1993—; lectr. colls., high schs.; lectr. legal topics. Contbr. numerous articles to profl. jours. Mem. ABA (appellate practice sect., profl. responsibility sect., young lawyers sect., bus./litigation sect., gen. practice sect.), Acad. Fla. Trial Lawyers (bd. dirs., Amicus Curiae briefwriter, dir. appellate practice sect., chair continuing legal edn. com., chair publs. com.), Broward County Trial Lawyers Assn., Broward County Bar Assn., Palm Beach County Bar Assn. (appellate rules com., speaker's bur.). General civil litigation. Office: Kluger Peretz Kaplan & Berlin Pit Barnet Bank Tower 1 E Broward Blvd Ste 1701 Fort Lauderdale FL 33301-1865

**MAGETTE, KURT ROBERT,** lawyer; b. Ahoskie, N.C., July 23, 1958; s. Raymond Williams and Patricia M.; m. Susan Denise Mahoney, Sept. 3, 1983; children: Ross, Reid, Brenna. AB magna cum laude, Duke U., 1980; JD cum laude, Northwestern U., 1983. Bar: Va. 1983, U.S. Tax Ct. 1985, U.S. Ct. Appeals (4th cir.) 1984; CPA, Ill. Ptnr. McGuire, Woods, Battle & Boothe, Richmond, Va., 1983-94; assoc. gen. counsel RF&P Corp., Richmond, 1994-95; shareholder LeClair Ryan, Richmond, 1995—; adj. prof. law Coll. of William and Mary, 1987—, Va. Commonwealth U., 1984, 85, 86. Contbr. to profl. publs. Mem. ABA (taxation sect.), Va. State Bar Assn., Va. Bar Assn. Avocation: golf. Taxation, general, Corporate taxation, Personal income taxation. Office: LeClair Ryan 707 E Main St Richmond VA 23219-2814

**MAGGIOLO, ALLISON JOSEPH,** lawyer; b. New River, N.C., Aug. 29, 1943; s. Allison and Florence Celeste (Vago) M. Cert., U. Paris-Sorbonne, 1965; AB, Brown U., 1966; JD, U. Louisville, 1975. Bar: Ky. 1976, U.S. Dist. Ct. (we. dist.) Ky. 1981. Ops. mgr., stockbroker Bache & Co., Louisville, 1970-73; ptnr. Reisz, Blackburn, Manly & Treitz, Louisville, 1976-78, Greenebaum Boone Treitz Maggiolo & Brown, Louisville, 1978-91, Wyatt, Tarrant & Combs, Louisville, 1991—; workshop panelist Fin. Adv. Coun., 1994; panelist Seminar on Defaulted Bond Issues, 1987-89, Bond Counsel and the Corp. Trustee, 1990-92, Defaults and Workouts, 1993. Author: Indenture Trustee Liability and Defaulted Bond Issues, 1987, Minimizing Indenture Trustee Liability and Defaulted Bond Issues, 1991, Bond Default Resolution, 1993; co-author: The legal Aspects of Doing International Business in Kentucky, 1990. Exec. com. Louisville Com. Fgn. Rels., 1979—, chmn., 1991-96; bd. dirs. Ky. Opera, Louisville, 1978-91, mem. hon. coun., 1991—; bd. dirs. Ky. Show, Louisville, 1980-88. 1st lt. U.S. Army, 1966-69, Vietnam. Decorated Bronze Star. Mem. Internat. Bar Assn., Nat. Assn. Bond Lawyers, Bond Attys. Workshop (planning com. 1991-93), Pendennis Club, Wynn Stay Club, Jefferson Club. Municipal (including bonds), Banking, Finance. Office: Wyatt Tarrant & Combs Citizens Plz Louisville KY 40202

**MAGGIPINTO, V. ANTHONY,** lawyer; b. Tucson, Apr. 15, 1943; s. William Vito and Elizabeth Maria (Rice) M.; m. Maria Teresa Zequeira, Aug. 31, 1976; children: Marshall Albert Nicholas, Spencer William Jonathan. AB cum laude, Southampton Coll., 1970; JD, Fordham U., 1976. Bar: Fla. 1977, N.Y. 1978, U.S. Dist. Ct. (ea. and so. dists.) N.Y. 1979, U.S. Ct. Appeals (2d cir.) 1980. Asst. to pres. Interpub. Group of Cos., N.Y.C., 1965-66; asst. dean of admission Southampton (N.Y.) Coll., 1971-73; investigative aide N.Y. State Com. on Jud. Conduct, N.Y.C., 1974-76; asst. state atty. Dade County State Atty., Miami, Fla., 1977-78; asst. dist. atty. Suffolk Dist. Atty., Hauppage, N.Y., 1978-80; asst. county atty. Suffolk County Atty., Hauppauge, 1980-84; sole practice Riverhead and St. James, N.Y., 1982—; mem. spl. coms. on discovery, civil litigation U.S. Dist. Ct. (ea. dist.) N.Y., Bklyn., 1983-90, 95—, arbitrator, 1986—, Civil Justice Reform Act adv. group, 1990-95, chair jury task force, 1993—, commendation U.S. Dist. Ct., 1997. Mem. appeals bd. SSS, 1982—, vice chmn., 1986-97, chmn., 1997—. Served with submarine svc. USN, 1961-65. Recipient Disting. Alumni award L.I. U., 1990. Mem. N.Y. State Bar Assn. (exec. com. real property sect. 1997—, Suffolk County Bar Assn., Fla. Bar, U.S. Naval Inst., Navy League (judge advocate L.I. coun. 1990—), Southampton Coll. Alumni Assn. (bd. dirs., exec. com. 1997—). Republican. Roman Catholic. Club: Nissequogue (N.Y.) Golf (counsel 1980—, bd. govs.). Avocations: hiking, horseback riding. General civil litigation, General corporate, Probate. Office: 1212 Roanoke Ave Riverhead NY 11901-2740

**MAGHIAR, LIVIA L.,** lawyer; b. Bucharest, Romania, May 4, 1964; came to the U.S., 1980; d. Liviu Nicolae and Sandra Lucia Maghiar; m. Michael James Andrews, Oct. 10, 1992. BS in Fin. with honors, NYU, 1987; JD cum laude, Vt. Law Sch., 1990. Bar: N.Y. Assoc. Brown & Wood LLP, N.Y.C., 1990-96, Dorsey & Whitney LLP, N.Y.C., 1996-97; counsel TIAA-CREF, N.Y.C., 1997—. Republican. Avocations: travel, hockey, foreign languages. Finance, General corporate, Securities. Office: TIAA-CREF 730 3rd Ave New York NY 10017-3206

**MAGIDSOHN, HERMAN EDWARD,** lawyer; b. Detroit, Dec. 7, 1936; s. Harry and Barbara M.; m. Leslie Marcia Krimton, July 12, 1970; children: Blair H., Heather B., Allison A. BA, U. Mich., 1959; BBA, U. Miami, 1961; JD, Southwestern U., 1970. Bar: U.S. Dist. Ct. (ctrl. dist.) Calif. 1971, U.S. Ct. Appeals (9th cir.) 1971. Assoc. Mansell & Giddens, L.A., 1971-73, Coleman & Coleman, L.A., 1973-75; pvt. practice Encino, Calif., 1975—. General civil litigation, Contracts commercial, Workers' compensation. Office: Law Offices of Herman E Magdsohn 15720 Ventura Blvd Ste 418 Encino CA 91436-4709

**MAGILL, FRANK JOHN,** federal judge; b. Verona, N.D., June 3, 1927; s. Thomas Charles and Viola Magill; m. Mary Louise Timlin, Nov. 22, 1955; children: Frank Jr., Marguerite Connolly, R. Daniel, Mary Elizabeth, Robert, John. BS in Fgn. Service, Georgetown U., 1951, LLB, 1955; MA, Columbia U., 1952. Ptnr. Nilles, Hansen, Magill & Davies, Ltd., Fargo, N.D., 1955-86; judge U.S. Ct. Appeals (8th cir.), Fargo, 1986—. Chmn. fin. disclosure com. U.S. Jud. Conf., 1993-98. Fellow Am. Coll. Trial Lawyers; mem. N.D. Bar Assn. (chmn. legis. com. 1975), Cass County Bar Assn. (pres. 1970). Republican. Avocations: tennis, sailing, skiing. Fax: 701 297-7255. Home: 501 7th St S Fargo ND 58103-2761 Office: Quentin N Burdick US Courthouse 655 1st Ave N Ste 320 Fargo ND 58102-4932

**MAGNER, MICHELE GERALYN,** lawyer; b. Jacksonville, Ill., Nov. 5, 1951; d. Paul Joseph and Mary Helena (Winters) m. Student, U. Calif., Berkeley, 1972; BA, Knox Coll., 1973; JD, Washington U., St. Louis, 1977. BAr: Ill. 1977. Assoc. Arnstein & Lehr, Chgo., 1977-82, ptnr., 1982-85; ptnr. Rudnick & Wolfe, Chgo., 1985-90; of counsel Mayer, Brown & Platt, Chgo., 1992-98, Rudnick & Wolfe, Chgo., 1998—. Mem. Chgo. Bar Assn., River Club, Order of Coif. Democrat. Roman Catholic. Avocation: classical music. Real property, Landlord-tenant. Office: Rudnick & Wolfe 203 N La Salle St Ste 1500 Chicago IL 60601-1293

**MAGNESS, MICHAEL KENNETH,** lawyer, management consultant; b. Tarentum, Pa., July 19, 1948; s. Kenneth Wilcox and Carolyn Frances (Harding) M.; m. Carolyn Marie Wehmann, Oct. 24, 1981; children: Sarah Elisabeth, Andrew Alexander, Peter Frederick. AB in History, Case Western Res. U., 1970, JD, 1973. Bar: Ohio 1973. Asst. dean Case Western Res. Law Sch., Cleve., 1973-76; dir. placement svcs. NYU Sch. Law, N.Y.C., 1976-82; exec. dir. Martindale Svcs. Inc., N.Y.C., 1982-84; v.p. Human Resource Svcs., Inc., N.Y.C., 1984-86; ptnr. Magness & Wehmann, N.Y.C., 1986-97; exec. v.p. Robinson Lerer Sawyer Miller, N.Y.C., 1994-96; dir. corp. comm. Hildebrandt, Inc., Somerset, N.J., 1997—. Prodr.: (videotape) Brief Encounters, 1980; cons. (videotape) Beyond the Resume, 1980; editor: Your New Lawyer, 1992; contbr. articles to profl. jours. Pres. Hudson St. Owners Corp., N.Y.C., 1984-97; mem. vis. com. Case Western Res. U. Law Sch., 1984—, mem. alumni coun., 1989-91, univ. coun., 1993-95, chair vis. com., 1995-97. Fellow Am. Bar Found.; mem. ABA (sec. on legal edn., gen. practice sect., law practice mgmt. sect., mem. publs. bd. 1992-95, mem. edn. bd. 1994-97, chmn. profl. competence com., chmn. career planning com. young lawyers divsn.), Nat. Assn. for Law Placement (pres. 1980-81), Nat. Law Firm Mktg. Assn., Case Western Res. Alumni Assn. N.Y. (pres. 1988-90), Phi Delta Phi, Phi Gamma Delta. Democrat. Episcopalian. Avocations: travel, hiking, bicycling. Office: Hildebrandt Inc 200 Cottontail Ln Somerset NJ 08873-1231

**MAGNUSON, PAUL ARTHUR,** federal judge; b. Carthage, S.D., Feb. 9, 1937; s. Arthur and Emma Elleda (Paulson) M.; m. Sharon Schultz, Dec. 21, 1959; children—Marlene Peterson, Margaret (dec.), Kevin, Kara. BA, Gustavus Adolphus Coll, 1959; JD, William Mitchell Coll., 1963; DLL (hon.), Wm. Mitchell Coll., 1991. Bar: Minn. 1963, U.S. Dist. Ct. Minn. 1968. Asst. registrar William Mitchell Coll. of Law, 1959-60; claim adjuster Agrl. Ins. Co., 1960-62; clk. Bertie & Bettenberg, 1962-63; ptnr. LeVander, Gillen, Miller & Magnuson, South St. Paul, Minn., 1963-81; judge U.S. Dist. Ct. Minn., St. Paul, 1981—, chief judge, 1994—; jurist-in-residence Hamline U., 1985, Augsberg Coll., 1986, Bethel Coll., 1986, Concordia Coll., St. Paul, 1987, U. Minn., Morris, 1987; instr. William Mitchell Coll. Law, 1984-92, Corcordia Coll., Moorhead, 1988, St. John's U., 1988, Coll. of St. Benedict, 1988; mem. judicial conf. com. on adminstrn. of Bankruptcy System, 1987-96, chmn. 1993-96; mem. judicial conf. com. on Internat. Judicial Rels., 1996—, chair, 1999—; mem. com. on dist. judges edn. Fed. Judicial Ctr., 1998—. Mem. Met. Health Bd., St. Paul, 1970-72; legal counsel Ind. Republican Party Minn., St. Paul, 1979-81. Recipient Disting. Alumnus award Gustavus Adolphus Coll., 1982. Mem. Minn. State Bar Assn., 1st Dist. Bar Assn. (pres. 1974-75), Dakota County Bar Assn., Am. Judicature Soc., Fed. Judges Assn. (bd. dirs. 1993—, treas. 1997—).

**MAGNUSON, ROGER JAMES,** lawyer; b. St. Paul, Jan. 25, 1945; s. Roy Gustaf and Ruth Lily (Edlund) M.; m. Elizabeth Cunningham Shaw, Sept. 11, 1982; children: James Roger, Peter Cunningham, Mary Kerstin, Sarah Ruth, Elizabeth Camilla, Anna Clara, John Edlund, Britta Kristina. BA, Stanford U., 1967; JD, Harvard U., 1971; BCL, Oxford U., 1972. Bar: Minn. 1973, U.S. Dist. Ct. Minn. 1973, U.S. Ct. Appeals (8th, 9th, 10th cirs.) 1974, U.S. Supreme Ct. 1978. Chief pub. defender Hennepin County Pub. Defender's Office, Mpls., 1973; ptnr. Dorsey & Whitney, Mpls., 1972—; dean Oak Brook Coll. of Law and Govt. Policy, 1995—. Author: Shareholder Litigation, 1981, Are Gay Rights Right., The White-Collar Crime Explosion, 1992, Informed Answers To Gay Rights Questions, 1994; contbr. articles to profl. jours. Elder, Straitgate Ch., Mpls., 1980—. Mem. Christian Legal Soc., White Bear Yacht Club. Republican. Federal civil litigation, Libel, Criminal. Home: 625 Park Ave Saint Paul MN 55115-1663 Office: Dorsey & Whitney LLP 220 S 6th St Ste 1700 Minneapolis MN 55402-4502

**MAGUIRE, AMELIA REA,** lawyer; b. Port Arthur, Tex., Mar. 13, 1952; d. William Freeland III and Ruth Jackson (Friend) Rea; m. Jose A. Galabert-Navia, June 26, 1992. BA in Edn., U. Fla., 1975; JD with honors, Fla. State U., 1986. Bar: Fla. 1987. Fiscal asst. Naval Ships Sys. Command Office of Ocean Engring., Washington, 1971-72; amendment clk., rsch. asst. Office of the Clk. Fla. Ho. of Reps., Tallahassee, 1977-79; ind. contractor, realtor assoc. J.B. Steelman, Inc., Orlando, Fla., 1979-81; state coord. Coastal Plains Regional Commn., Fla., 1981; dir. Office of Local Govt. Liaison Office of the Gov., Tallahassee, 1981-83; inspector gen. Fla. Dept. of Commerce, Tallahassee, 1983, dep. sec. of commerce, 1983, asst. sec. of commerce, 1983-87; ptnr. Holland & Knight LLP, Miami, Fla., 1987—; mem. Edward Ball Eminent Scholar Chair in Internat. Law Selection Com., 1989-94. State field desk coord. Jim Williams for Gov., Winter Pk., Fla., 1978; fundraiser Buddy MacKay for U.S. Senate, 1980; Escambia County coord. Jimmy Carter for Pre., Pensacola, 1980; chmn. Econ. Devel. Transition Task Force, 1990-91, growth policy com. Gov.'s Commn. for Govt. by the People, 1991-92; mem. Metro-Dade Ad Hoc Com. on Exec., Legis. and Adminstrv. Structure, 1996—; mem. Fla. Internat. Affairs Commn., 1994-96; mem. exec. com. Western Hemispheric Summit, 1994; mem. Fla.'s 3d Environ. Land Mgmt. Study Com., 1992-93, Leadership Fla. Class XVI, 1997-98; mem. housing com. We Will Rebuild, Dade County, Fla., 1992-93; chmn. Econ. Devel. Transition Task Force, 1990-91; bd. dirs. Internat. Trade and Econ. Devel. Bd., Enterprise Fla., Inc., 1996—, Found. for Fla.'s Future, 1996—, Prevent Blindness Fla., 1996—, Sail Miami 2000, Inc., 1996—. Mem. ABA, ACLU (lawyers coun. 1992—), Fla. Bar., Caribbean Law Inst., St. Thomas U. Inns of Ct., Dade County Bar Assn., Greater Miami C. of C. (chmn. Tallahassee Initiative 1991-92, chmn. legis. affairs com. 1991-94, bd. govs. 1992-95, trustee 1997—), Jr. League of Miami, Phi Delta Phi. Avocations: travel, politics, golf, reading, writing. Home: 2715 Toledo St Coral Gables FL 33134-4857 Office: Holland & Knight 701 Brickell Ave Ste 3000 Miami FL 33131-2898

**MAGUIRE, KEVIN JEROME,** lawyer; b. Amarillo, Tex., Jan. 14, 1963; s. Michael Francis and Rhea Marie (Crane) M.; m. Kerry Lucille Sowden, Apr. 6, 1991; children: Morgan Kimberly, Patrick McCoy, Mary Rhea. BA, U. Okla., 1985; JD, So. Meth. U., 1988. Bar: Tex. 1988, U.S. Dist. Ct. (no., so. ea. and we. dists.) Tex. 1989, U.S. Ct. Appeals (5th cir.) 1989. Assoc. Strasburger & Price, L.L.P., Dallas, 1988-96, ptnr., 1996—; mem. Jesuit Alumni Exec. Bd., Dallas, 1996—. Mem. ABA, Dallas Bar Assn. (legal ethics com. 1990-93), Lawyers Alliance for Justice in Ireland. Roman Catholic. Product liability, General civil litigation. Home: 4245 Westway Ave Dallas TX 75205-3725 Office: Strasburger & Price LLP 901 Main St Ste 4300 Dallas TX 75202-3714

**MAHALLATI, NARGES NANCY,** lawyer, consultant; b. Balt., Jan. 19, 1964; d. Salaheddin and Leona Harriet (Hazen) M. BS, Georgetown U., 1985, JD, 1988. Bar: N.Y. 1989, D.C. 1991, U.S. Dist. Ct. (no., we. and ea. dists.) N.Y. 1990, U.S. Dist. Ct. (so. dist.) N.Y. 1989. Atty. Fed. Res. Bank of N.Y., N.Y.C., 1988-90; assoc. Arnold & Porter, Washington, 1990-93; gen. counsel HTR, Inc., Rockville, Md., 1993-95, MicroStrategy, Vienna, Va., 1995-97; pres. NextPoint Cons., Vienna, Va., 1997—. Pres. Gifts for the Homeless, Inc., Washington, 1991-92, treas., 1992-93, bd. dirs., 1991—. Computer, Intellectual property, General corporate.

**MAHAN, (DANIEL) DULANY, JR.,** lawyer, real estate developer; b. Hannibal, Mo., Dec. 22, 1914; s. D. Dulany and Sarah (Marshall) M.; m. Eleanor F. Bethea, Sept. 14, 1948 (div. 1953). AB, U. Mo., Columbia; J.D., Harvard U., 1940. Assoc., Office of George M. Clark, N.Y.C., 1940-42; asst. atty. FTC, Washington, 1948-51; assoc. Adams & James, N.Y.C., 1951-68; assoc. Kurnick & Hackman, N.Y.C., 1968—; ptnr. Tall Pines Estates Devel., Jacksonville, Fla., 1971—. Served with U.S. Army, 1942-46. Mem. ABA, Internat. Bar Assn., World Assn. Lawyers, N.Y. Bar Assn., Fed. Bar Assn. Republican. Clubs: Harvard (N.Y.C.); Nat. Lawyers (Washington). General corporate, Taxation, general. Home: 98 Ralph Ave White Plains NY 10606-3609 Office: 450 Park Ave # 2305 New York NY 10022-2605

**MAHAN, JAMES CAMERON,** lawyer; b. El Paso, Tex., Dec. 16, 1943; m. Eileen Agnes Casale, Jan. 13, 1968; 1 child, James Cameron Jr. BA, U. Charleston, 1965; JD, Vanderbilt U., 1973. Bar: Nev. 1974, U.S. Dist. Ct. Nev. 1974, U.S. Ct. Appeals (9th cir.) 1975, U.S. Tax Ct. 1980, U.S. Supreme Ct. 1980. Assoc. Lee & Beasey, Las Vegas, Nev., 1974-75; mem. firm John Peter Lee Ltd., Las Vegas, 1975-82; sr. ptnr. Mahan & Ellis, Chartered, Las Vegas, 1982-99; dist. ct. judge 8th judicial dist. Nevada, Las Vegas, 1999. With USN, 1966-69. General civil litigation, Contracts commercial, Real property. Office: 200 S 3rd St Las Vegas NV 89155-0001

**MAHAR, ELLEN PATRICIA,** law librarian; b. Washington, Jan. 15, 1938; d. Richard A. and Lina Mahar. BA, St. Joseph Coll., Emmitsburg, Md., 1959; MLS, U. Md., 1968. Asst. librarian Covington & Burling, Washington, 1971-73, libr. dir., 1978-92; librarian Shea & Gardner, Washington, 1974-78; mgr. info. ctr. Assn. Comml. Real Estate, Herndon, Va., 1992-94; head libr. Caplin & Drysdale Chtd., Washington, 1994—. Co-editor: Legislative History of the Securities Act of 1933 and the Securities Act of 1934, 11 vols., 1973. Mem. Am. Assn. Law Libraries, Spl. Libraries Assn., Law Librarians' Soc. Washington. Office: Caplin & Drysdale Chtd 1 Thomas Cir NW Fl 12 Washington DC 20005-5894

**MAHER, DAVID WILLARD,** lawyer; b. Chgo., Aug. 14, 1934; s. Chauncey Carter and Martha (Peppers) M.; m. Jill Waid Armagnac, Dec. 20, 1954; children: Philip Armagnac, Julia Armagnac. BA, Harvard, 1955, LLB, 1959. Bar: N.Y. 1960, Ill. 1961. Pvt. practice Boston, N.Y.C., 1958-60; assoc. Kirkland & Ellis, and predecessor firm, 1960-65, ptnr., 1966-78; ptnr. Reuben & Proctor, 1978-86, Isham, Lincoln and Beale, 1986-88, Sonnenschein, Nath & Rosenthal, Chgo., 1988—; gen. counsel BBB Chgo. and No. Ill.; lectr. DePaul U. Sch. Law, 1973-79, Loyola U. Law Sch., Chgo., 1980-84; chmn. policy oversight com. Internet. Mem. vis. com. U. Chgo. Div. Sch., 1986—. 2d lt. USAF, 1955-56. Fellow Am. Bar Found. (life); mem. ABA, Am. Law Inst., Ill. Bar Assn., Wis. State Bar, Chgo. Bar Assn., Chgo. Lit. Club, Union League Club, Tavern Club. Roman Catholic. Trademark and copyright, Patent, Computer. Home: 311 W Belden Ave Chicago IL 60614-3817 Office: Sonnenschein Nath & Rosenthal 233 S Wacker Dr Ste 8000 Chicago IL 60606-6342

**MAHER, EDWARD JOSEPH,** lawyer; b. Cleve., Sept. 18, 1939; s. Richard Leo and Lucile (Thompson) M.; m. Marilyn K. Maher, Oct. 8, 1966; children: Richard A., David C., Michael E, Colleen Therese. B.S., Georgetown U., 1961, LL.B., 1964; student U. Fribourg, Switzerland, 1959-61. Bar: Ohio 1964, U.S. dist. ct. (no. dist.) Ohio 1964. Assoc., Sweeney, Maher & Vlad, Cleve., 1964-71; sole practice, Cleve., 1971—. Pres. parish council St. Raphael's Ch., Bay Village, Ohio, 1983-84; former adv. bd. Catholic Family and Children's Services; adv. bd. Cath. Youth Orgn., 1973-79, pres., 1975-76; chmn. Elyria Cursillo Ctr., 1974-75; lay del. to Ohio Cath. Conf., Diocese of Cleve., 1973-75; chmn. adv. bd. Cath. Social Services of Cuyahoga County, 1978-79; trustee Cath. Charities Corp., 1977—, treas., 1979, sec., 1981, 1st v.p., 1983, gen. chmn. campaign, 1983, 84, pres., 1985-86; pres. Diocesan adv. bd. Cath. Youth Orgn., 1980-82; team capt. United Way Services Agy. Team Group, 1981, nominating com., 1983; mem. Tabor House, The Consultation Ctr. of the Diocese of Cleve., pres., 1992-94; mem. bd. regents St. Ignotius High Sch., 1997—. Recipient Cardinal Robert Bellarmine S.J. award St. Ignatius High Sch., 1990, Cath. Man of the Year award, 1995. Mem. ABA, Ohio Bar Assn., Cuyahoga County Bar Assn., Cleve. Bar Assn., Cath. Lawyers Guild Cleve. (pres. 1970). Clubs: Irish Good Fellowship (pres.), First Friday of Cleve. (pres. 1990). Personal injury, Probate, Insurance. Office: 1548 Standard Bldg Cleveland OH 44113

**MAHER, FRANCESCA MARCINIAK,** air transportation executive, lawyer; b. 1957. BA, Loyola U., 1978, JD, 1981. Ptnr. Mayer, Brown & Platt, Chgo., 1981-93; sr. v.p., gen. counsel, sec. UAL Corp., Elk Grove Village, Ill., 1993—. Active YMCA Metro. Chgo. Mem. Ill. Humane Soc. (pres. 1996-98). Securities, General corporate, Administrative and regulatory. Office: UAL Corp PO Box 66100 Chicago IL 60666-0100

**MAHER, GARY LAURENCE,** lawyer; b. Summit, N.J., Dec. 19, 1965; s. William J. and Eileen B. (Galen) M.; m. Dana V. Dombroski, Nov. 11, 1994; 1 child, Brian J. BA in Psychology, U. Pa., 1988; JD, Rutgers U., Camden, 1992. Bar: N.J. 1992, Pa. 1992, U.S. Dist. Ct. N.J. 1992. Law clk. to Hon. Ross R. Anzaldi and Hon. Edward J. Toy, Superior Ct. of N.J., Elizabeth, 1993-94; assoc. Mandell & Selesner P.C., Red Bank, N.J., 1994-95; sr. litigation assoc. Shain, Schaffer & Rafanello, P.C., Bernardsville, N.J., 1995—. Mem. N.J. State Bar Assn. (mem. banking law sect.), Geneal. Soc. West Fields; trustee Geneal. Soc. N.J., 1995—. Avocations: music, inline skating. Banking, General civil litigation, Municipal (including bonds). Office: Shain, Schaffer & Rafanello 150 Morristown Rd Ste 105 Bernardsville NJ 07924-2626

**MAHER, MICHAEL J.,** lawyer; b. Chgo., Jan. 15, 1957; s. Cyril John and Margaret Jean Maher; m. Karen S. Maher; 1 child, Olivia Noel. Bar: Ill., Fla., Calif. Atty. Ill. Atty. Gen., Chgo., 1985-88, Ill. Polit. Control Bd., Chgo., 1988-90, McKenna & Storer, Chgo., 1990—. Contbr. articles to profl. jours. Sgt. USMC, 1975-78. Environmental. Home: 213 N Delaplaine Rd Riverside IL 60546-2066 Office: McKenna & Storer 200 N Lasalle St Fl 30 Chicago IL 60601-1014

**MAHER, PATRICK JOSEPH,** lawyer; b. Dallas, Feb. 20, 1956; s. Louis Joseph and Mary Elizabeth Maher; m. Catharine M. McCormack, June 15, 1996. BS in Econs. summa cum laude, Santa Clara U., 1978; JD with high honors, U. Tex., 1981. Bar: Tex. 1981, Calif. 1984. Law clk. to Hon. Joseph T. Sneed Calif. Ct. Appeals (9th cir.), San Francisco, 1981-82; assoc. Gardere & Wynne, Dallas, 1982-84, Morrison & Foerster, San Francisco, 1984-94; ptnr. Shannon, Gracey, Ratliff & Miller L.L.P., Ft. Worth, 1994—. Contbr. articles to profl. jours. Bd. dirs. Chisolm Trail chpt. ARC, Ft. Worth, 1998—; bd. trustees U. Dallas. Mem. ABA (mem. labor and employment sect.), Tarrant County Bar Assn. (chair labor and employment law sect. 1997-98), Rotary, Order of Coif, Phi Beta Kappa. Roman Catholic. Avocations: running, reading mystery novels and history books. Labor. Office: Shannon Gracey Ratliff & Miller LLP 500 Throckmorton St Ste 1600 Fort Worth TX 76102-3803

**MAHER, STEPHEN TRIVETT,** lawyer, educator; b. N.Y.C., Nov. 21, 1949; s. William John and Jean Dorothy (Trivett) M.; m. Sharon Leslie Wolfe, Nov. 22, 1981; children: Meaghan Wolfe, Caitlin Wolfe. BA, NYU, 1971; JD, U. Miami, Coral Gables, Fla., 1975. Bar: Fla. 1975, U.S. Dist. Ct. (so. dist.) Fla. 1976, D.C. 1979, U.S. Dist. Ct. (no. dist.) Fla. 1979, U.S. Supreme Ct. 1980, U.S. Ct. Appeals (5th and 11th cirs.) 1981, U.S. Dist. Ct. (so. dist.) Fla. 1982, U.S. Dist. Ct. (mid. dist.) Fla. 1983. Assoc. Chonin & Levey, Miami, 1975; staff atty. Legal Svcs. of Greater Miami, Inc., 1975-81; assoc. Finley, Kumble, Wagner et al, Miami, 1981-84; dir. clin. program Sch. of Law U. Miami, Coral Gables, 1984-90, assoc. prof. law Sch. of Law, 1984-92; pvt. practice Stephen T. Maher, P.A., Miami, Fla., 1992—; mem. Fla. Bar/Fla. Bar Found. Joint Commn. on Delivery Legal Svcs. to the Indigent, Tallahassee, 1990-91, chair, organizer Seventh Adminstrv. Law Conf., Tallahassee, 1990, Conf. on the Fla. Constn., 1995; cons. on in-house legal edn. Contbr. articles to profl. jours. Fellow Fla. Bar Found. (life, bd. dirs. 1984-91); mem. ABA, Fla. Bar (chair adminstrv. law sect. 1993-94, chair coun. of sects. 1996-97), Dade County Bar Assn. Administrative and regulatory, General civil litigation, Civil rights. Home: 1015 Sevilla Ave Miami FL 33134-6328 Office: 1500 Miami Ctr 201 S Biscayne Blvd Miami FL 33131-4332

**MAHLMAN, HENRY CLAYTON,** lawyer; b. Bismarck, N.D., Aug. 12, 1930; s. Henry C. and Adelaide Dorothy (Albers) M.; m. Patricia C. Menzies, Feb. 16, 1957; children: Kirsten, Karen. BSC, U. N.D., 1952, LLB, 1956. Bar: N.D. 1956, Colo. 1978, U.S. Dist. Ct. Colo. 1978, U.S. Ct. Appeals (10th cir.) 1978. Atty. Solicitor's Office, U.S. Dept. Labor, Kansas City, Mo., 1956-61; dep. regional atty. Solicitor's Office, U.S. Dept. Labor, San Francisco, 1965-69; atty.-in-charge Solicitor's Office, U.S. Dept. Labor, Denver, 1961-65, assoc. regional solicitor, 1969—. Sgt., U.S. Army, 1952-54, Korea. Office: US Dept Labor Solicitor's Office 1999 Broadway Ste 1600 Denver CO 80202-5716

**MAHNK, KAREN,** law librarian, legal assistant; b. Bklyn., July 13, 1956; d. James V. and Mary M. (Jones) Mascari; 1 child, Adam Eugene. Student, Baruch Coll., 1974-75, Miami-Dade Community Coll., 1986-89, St. Thomas U., 1994; cert. in criminal justice, St. Thomas U., 1997; postgrad., Fla. State U., 1998. Asst. libr. Mershon, Sawyer et al, Miami, Fla., 1976-79; libr., legal asst. Steel Hecton & Davis, Miami, 1980-84; libr. Valdes-Fauli, et al, Miami, 1984-94, Pub. Defender's Office, 11th Jud. Cir., Miami, 1994—; asst. coord. Broward County Multi-Family Devel. Recycling Program, 1990-91. Chair ways and means com. Palm Cove Elem. PTO, 1993-94; active vol. Broward County Guardian Ad Litum Program, 1989-92. Mem. ABA (assoc. stat., family law sect., law libr. affiliate), Am. Assn. Law Librs., Southeastern Assn. Law Librs., South Fla. Assn. Law Librs. (bd. dirs. 1988-89, chair constn. and bylaws commn. 1988-91, sec. 1983-84, v.p.-elect 1986-88, nominating com. 1992, sec. 1993-95, chair union list com. 1995—), Spl. Librs. Assn. Democrat. Baptist. Avocations: painting, sailing, chess. Office: 1320 NW 14th St Ste 313 Miami FL 33125-1609

**MAHON, ELDON BROOKS,** federal judge; b. Loraine, Tex., Apr. 9, 1918; s. John Bryan and Nola May (Muns) M.; m. Nova Lee Groom, June 1, 1941; children: Jana, Martha, Brad. BA, McMurry U., 1939; LLB, U. Tex., 1942; LLD (hon.), McMurry U., 1974; HHD (hon.), Tex. Wesleyan U., 1990. Bar: Tex. 1942. Law clk. Tex. Supreme Ct., 1945-46; county atty. Mitchell County, Tex., 1947; dist. atty. 32d Jud. Dist. Tex., 1948-60, dist. judge, 1960-63; v.p. Tex. Electric Service Co., Ft. Worth, 1963-64; mem. firm Mahon Pope & Gladden, Abilene, Tex., 1964-68; U.S. atty. U.S. Dist. Ct. (no. dist.) Tex., Ft. Worth, 1968-72, judge, 1972-89, sr. judge, 1989—; com. on the budget Judicial Conf. the U.S., 1975-83, 5th cir. judicial coun., 1984-89. Pres. W. Tex. council Girl Scouts U.S.A., 1966-68; former trustee McMurry U.; past bd. dirs. Harris Meth. Hosp. With USAAF, 1942-45. Named an Outstanding Tex. Prosecutor, Tex. Law Enforcement Found., 1957; recipient Disting. Alumnus award McMurry U., 1987. em. ABA, FBA, Ft.-Worth-Tarrant County Bar Assn. (Silver Gavel award 1998), Am. Judicature Soc., Dist. and County Attys. Assn. Tex. (pres. 1954-55), Tex. Bar Found. (life, Samuel Pessarra outstanding jusrist award 1998). Methodist. Office: US Courthouse 501 W 10th St Ste 502 Fort Worth TX 76102-3643

**MAHONEY, F. STEVEN,** company executive, lawyer; b. Dover, N.J., Sept. 20, 1958; s. Frank and Margaret M.; m. Lucinda Olsen; children: Ryan, Tyler, Kyle, Sean. BS, Pa. State U., 1979; JD, U. San Francisco, 1985. Bar: Calif. 1985, Tex. 1986, Alaska 1991, U.S. Tax Ct. 1985. Mgr. collection control Zilog Inc., San Jose, Calif., 1983-86; dir. taxes Advanced Nuc. Fuels Inc., Seattle, 1986-88; sr. tax Exxon Corp., Houston, 1988-89; tax compliance mgr. Lyondell Corp., Houston, 1989-90; mng. tax counsel Atlantic Richfield Co., L.A., 1990-96; v.p. tax, gen. tax officer ARCO Alaska Inc., Anchorage, 1996-98; v.p. tax ARCO Pipeline, Anchorage, 1998—. Dir. Am. Diabetes Assn., Anchorage, 1993—, Performing Arts Ctr., Anchorage, 1995—; mem. exec. bd. western area coun. Boy Scouts Am. Mem. ABA. Taxation, general, General corporate, Corporate taxation. Home: PO Box 200429 Anchorage AK 99520-0429 Office: ARCO 700 G St Anchorage AK 99501-3446

**MAHONEY, KATHLEEN MARY,** lawyer; b. Methuen, Mass., Oct. 24, 1954; d. Joseph Patrick and Beatrice Evelyn (Blackington) M.; m. Mark Dennis Schmitt, May 26, 1979; children: Alexis Anne Schmitt, Brynne Elizabeth Schmitt. BA, Keene (N.H.) State Coll., 1976; JD, Syracuse (N.Y.) U., 1979. Bar: Minn. 1979, U.S. Dist. Ct. Minn. 1980, U.S. Ct. Appeals (8th cir.) 1985, U.S. Supreme Ct. 1988. Instr. Sch. of Law Hamline U., St. Paul, 1979-80; law clk. to hon. justice Douglas K. Amdahl Minn. Supreme Ct., St. Paul, 1980-81; law clk. to hon. judge Neal P. McCurn U.S. Dist. Ct. (no. dist.) N.Y., Syracuse, 1981-83; spl. asst. atty. gen. Atty. Gen.'s Office State of Minn., St. Paul, 1983-89; assoc. Oppenheimer, Wolff & Donnelly, St. Paul, 1989-91, sr. assoc., 1991-93; ptnr., 1994—, chair labor and employment practice group, 1995-97; mng. ptnr. St. Paul, 1997—; cons. George Banzhaf Co., Milw., 1979-80; adj. prof. Hamline U. Sch. of Law, 1987-89. Mem. Dist. 621 Study Adv. Com., Shoreview, Minn., 1989-91, chair, 1991-93; mem. Turtle Lake Sch. Adv. Com., Shoreview, 1988-96; mem. exec. com., bd. dirs. Voyageurs Regional Nat. Park Assn., 1993-95; mem. Class of '93; bd. dirs. St. Paul Vol. Ctr., 1994—; leader Girl Scouts Am., 1993—; mem. Leadership St. Paul. Mem. ABA, Minn. Bar Assn., Ramsey County Bar Assn. Environmental, Antitrust, Labor. Office: Oppenheimer Wolff & Donnelly First Bank Building Ste 1700 Saint Paul MN 55101

**MAHONY, KAREN ELIZABETH,** law office administrator; b. Buffalo, N.Y., Mar. 21, 1963; d. Stanley and Joyce (Buckenroth) Urbanski; m. Mark D. Mahony, Mar. 24, 1990; children: Meghan, Matthew. BA in Polit. Sci., SUNY, Buffalo, 1986. Legis. asst. N.Y. State Senate, Albany, 1987; supr. legal adminstr. Erie County Attys. Office, Buffalo, N.Y., 1988—. Vol. Erie County Dem. Orgn., Buffalo, 1988—. Office: Erie County Attys Office 69 Delaware Ave Rm 300 Buffalo NY 14202-3862

**MAHOOD, JAMES EDWARD,** lawyer; b. Sewickley, Pa., Feb. 2, 1948; s. James Calvin and Pauline (DeShields) M.; m. Beth Ann Leuenberger, July 12, 1985. BA, Bard Coll., 1971; JD, U. Pitts., 1974. Bar: Pa. 1974. Atty. Neighborhood Legal Svcs., Pitts., 1974-76, mng. atty., 1976-80; assoc. Wilder & Miller, P.C., Pitts., 1980-83, ptnr., 1983-87; ptnr. Wilder & Mahood, P.C., Pitts., 1987-92, Wilder, Mahood & Crenney, Pitts., 1992—. Co-author: Pennsylvania Family Law Practice and Procedure Handbook, 1986, 2nd edit., 1989. Fellow Am. Acad. Matrimonial Lawyers (cert. matrimonial arbitrator and mediator); mem. ABA, Pa. Bar Assn. (coun., family law sect. 1989-92, treas. 1993-94, sec. 1994-95, 2nd vice chair 1995-96, chair elect 1997-98, chair 1998-99, mem. code of evidence com.,1997—), Allegheny County Bar Assn. (coun., family law sect. 1986-89, 90-93, 94-97, civil rules com., pub. svc. com.), Joint Family Law Coun. Pa. (adv. com. to jt. state gov. commn. on adoption law 1997—), Neighborhood Legal Svcs. Assn. (bd. dirs. 1993—, treas. 1994-95, pres. 1996-98). Avocation: American and world history. Family and matrimonial. Office: Wilder Mahood & Crenney 816 Frick Bldg 437 Grant St Pittsburgh PA 15219-6192

**MAI, HAROLD LEVERNE,** retired judge; b. Casper, Wyo., Apr. 5, 1928. BA, U. Wyo., 1950, JD, 1952. Bar: Wyo. 1952, U.S. Supreme Ct. 1963. Sole practice, Cheyenne, Wyo., 1953-62, 67-71; judge Juvenile Ct., Cheyenne, 1962-67; U.S. bankruptcy judge, Cheyenne, 1971-93, ret., 1993. Mem. ABA, Wyo. Bar Assn., Laramie County Bar Assn., Nat. Conf. Bankruptcy Judges.

**MAI, MARK F.,** lawyer; b. Concord, Calif., Dec. 9, 1960; s. Klaus L. and Helen M. Mai; m. Catherine Ogden Hall, Apr. 9, 1988; children: Patrick H., Claire C., Martha G. BBA, U. Notre Dem, 1983; JD, U. Tex., 1986. Bar: Tex. Assoc. Baker, Brown, Skarmen & Parker, Houston, 1986-91; corp. counsel Cooper Industries Inc., Houston, 1991-96, sr. corp. counsel, 1996—. Active Houston Harvest, 1990-91; dir. Houston Fun Raisers, 1995, 96. Recipient Key to City, South Bend, Ind., 1983. Mem. ABA, State Bar of Tex., Friars. Avocations: travel, sailing, camping. General corporate, Mergers and acquisitions, Antitrust. Office: Cooper Industries Inc 600 Travis St Ste 5600 Houston TX 77002-2909

**MAICHEL, JACK J.,** lawyer; b. Butte, Mont., Apr. 17, 1952; s. E.D. and Jacqueline Maichel. BA, U. Puget Sound, 1978, JD, 1983. Bar: Wash., U.S. Dist. Ct. (we. dist.) Wash. Assoc. Burgess Fitzer, P.S., Tacoma, 1983—. Mem. Wash. State Bar Assn., Wash. Def. Trial Lawyers (mem. legis. com. 1998—). Avocations: golf, skiing. Personal injury, Product liability, General civil litigation. Office: Burgess Fitzer PS 1501 Market St Ste 300 Tacoma WA 98402-3333

**MAIDMAN, STEPHEN PAUL,** lawyer; b. Hartford, Conn., Feb. 8, 1954; s. Harry and Roslyn (Mandell) M. AB summa cum laude, Bowdoin Coll., 1976; MBA, U. Pa., 1979, JD, 1980. Bar: Pa. 1980, Mass. 1996, U.S. Dist. Ct. (ea. dist.) Pa. 1980, U.S. Ct. Appeals (3d cir.) 1980, U.S. Dist. Ct. Mass. 1996, U.S. Ct. Appeals (1st cir.) 1996, U.S. Supreme Ct. 1997. Assoc. Drinker, Biddle & Reath, Phila., 1980-81; atty. IBM Corp., Boca Raton, Fla., 1981-84; atty. IBM Corp., N.Y.C., 1984-85, staff atty., 1985-87; staff atty. IBM Corp., Rye Brook, N.Y., 1987-88; lab. counsel IBM Corp., Poughkeepsie, N.Y., 1988-92; site counsel IBM Corp., Hopewell Junction, N.Y., 1992-95; pvt. practice Springfield, Mass., 1996—. Co-class agt., fund dir. Bowdoin Coll. Alumni Fund; counselor Hugh O'Brian Youth Found., Western Mass. Leadership Seminar, 1996—. Mem. Mass. Bar Assn., Hampden County Bar Assn., Nat. Assn. Criminal Def. Lawyers. Avocations: reading, stamp collecting, running, biking, black Labradors. Computer, Criminal, General practice. Home: 7 Chateau Margaux Bloomfield CT 06002-2153 Office: 1145 Main St Ste 417 Springfield MA 01103-2123

**MAIER, JOHN, III,** lawyer; b. Newark, Feb. 2, 1933; s. John and Emily (Stein) M.; m. Judith Laurel Kelly, July 6, 1963 (div. Dec. 1995); children: David John, Christiane Laurel; m. Barbara Ann Baldwin, Oct. 12, 1996. BSME, Newark Coll. Engring., 1954, MSME, 1957; LLB, Rutgers U., 1960. Bar: N.Y., Fla., D.C., U.S. Patent Office. Assoc. Stockel & Stickel, Newark, 1960-61; patent atty. Western Elec., Kearney, N.Y., 1961-63; patent atty./patent counsel Foster Wheeler, Livingston, N.J., 1963-72; pvt. practice Kingston, N.Y., 1972—. Patentee on arc cutting. Democrat. Methodist. Avocations: home shopping, travel. Patent, Trademark and copyright, Municipal (including bonds). Office: 326 Wall St Kingston NY 12401-3820

**MAIER, PETER KLAUS,** lawyer, business executive; b. Wurzburg, Germany, Nov. 20, 1929; came to U.S., 1939, naturalized, 1945; s. Bernard and Joan (Sonder) M.; m. Melanie L. Stoff, Dec. 15, 1963; children: Michele Margaret, Diana Lynn. BA cum laude, Claremont McKenna Coll., 1949; JD, U. Calif., Berkeley, 1952; LLM in Taxation, NYU, 1953. Bar: Calif. 1953, U.S. Supreme Ct. 1957; cert. specialist in taxation law, Calif. Atty. tax div. U.S. Dept Justice, Washington, 1956-59; pvt. practice tax law San Francisco, 1959-81; prof. law Hastings Coll. Law, U. Calif., San Francisco, 1967-95; vis. prof. U. Calif. Boalt Sch. Law, Berkeley, 1988-98, Stanford U. Sch. Law, 1996-98; pres. Maier & Siebel, Inc., Larkspur, Calif., 1981—; mng. dir. U.S. Trust Co. NA, San Francisco, 1998—; chmn. Fromm Inst. for Lifelong Learning, U. San Francisco, 1997—; pres. John B. Huntington Found., 1996—. Author books on taxation; contbr. articles to profl. jours. Chmn. Property Resources Inc., San Jose, Calif., 1968-77; pres. Calif. Property Devel. Corp., San Francisco, 1974-81; pres. John B. Huntington Found., Larkspur, 1997—. Capt. USAF, 1953-56. Mem. San Francisco Bar Assn. (chmn. sect. taxation 1970-71), Order of Coif. Taxation, general. Home: PO Box 836 Belvedere CA 94920-0836 Office: Maier & Siebel Inc 80 E Sir Francis Drake Blvd Larkspur CA 94939-1709

**MAILANDER, WILLIAM STEPHEN,** lawyer; b. Dover, N.J., July 25, 1958; s. William Stephen and Doris Elizabeth (Post) M.; m. Judith Gay Burrows, May 20, 1989 (div. 1993). BA, NYU, 1984; JD, Temple U., 1988. Bar: Pa. 1988, N.J. 1991, D.C. 1996; U.S. Ct. Vets. Appeals 1991, U.S. Ct. Appeals (fed. cir.) 1993, U.S. Supreme Ct. 1994. Staff atty. Bd. Vets. Appeals, Washington, 1988-90, Coast Guard Chief Counsel, Washington, 1990-91, VA Gen. Counsel, Washington, 1991-93; asst. gen. counsel Paralyzed Vets. Am., Washington, 1993—; faculty continuing legal edn. seminars, various cities, 1993—. Contbr. articles to profl. jours. With USMC, 1976-79. Decorated Navy Achievement medal. Mem. FBA (chair membership vets. law sect. 1993-94, editor newsletter 1996—). Avocations: reading, running. Administrative and regulatory, Federal civil litigation, General corporate. Office: Paralyzed Vets Am 801 18th St NW Washington DC 20006-3517

**MAILO, TOETAGATA ALBERT,** territory attorney general; b. Utulei, Am. Samoa; married; 2 children. BA, Brigham Young U., 1972, JD, 1976. Bar: Hawaii 1977, Samoa 1977. Asst. atty. gen. Am. Samoa, 1977-79; pvt. practice, 1979-89, 93-97; legal counsel Gov. of Am. Samoa, 1989-92; atty. gen. Am. Samoa, Pago Pago, 1997—. Mem. Hawaii State Bar Assn., Am. Samoa Bar Assn. Office: Office of Attorney General PO Box 7 Pago Pago AS 96799-0007*

**MAIN, PHILIP DAVID,** lawyer, probate judge; b. New Britain, Conn., Apr. 10, 1936; s. George Lawrence Main and Nancy Elia; m. Patricia Ann Baker, Sept. 10, 1960; children: Linda S. Irwin, William G. Main. BA in History, Bates Coll., 1958; LLB, George Washington U., 1961. Bar: Conn. 1962. Staff attorney CIGNA, Bloomfield, Conn., 1961-63; partner Pease & Main, Simsbury, Conn., 1963—; judge Granby (Conn.) Probate Ct., 1990—. Tour com. chmn., Granby. Mem. Granby Lions Club (pres. 1966—). Real property, Probate. Office: Pease & Main PO Box 544 Simsbury CT 06070-0544

**MAINOR, W. RANDALL,** lawyer; b. Overton, N.Y., Dec. 9, 1941; s. William B. and Vera H. Mainor; m. Leslie Anne Sullivan, Sept. 4, 1964; children: Jarrod, Emily, Bradley. BA, Brigham Young U., 1969; JD, Am. U., 1972. Spl. agt. FBI, Washington, 1972-74; asst. dist. atty. Clark County Dist. Atty., Las Vegas, 1974-75; sole practitioner Las Vegas, 1975-93; atty., ptnr. Mainor & Harris, Las Vegas, 1993—. Mem. ATLA, Nev. Trial Lawyers Asn., Million Dollar Advocacy Forum. Democrat. Mormon. Avocations: golf, spectator sports. Personal injury, Product liability. Office: Mainor & Harris 530 S 6th St Las Vegas NV 89101-6946

**MAINS, STEVE ALAN,** lawyer, arbitrator, mediator; b. Ft. McClellan, Ala., Oct. 2, 1946; s. Charles H. and Gwendolyn M.; 1 child, Ursula. BS, Ind. U., 1968; JD, Ind. U., Indpls., 1973; Internat. law cert., City of London Poly., 1970. Bar: Ind. 1974, Colo. 1979, Calif. 1989, U.S. Dist. Co. (so. dist.) Ind. 1974, U.S. Dist. Ct. Colo. 1979, U.S. Ct. Appeals (10th cir.) 1990. Sole practitioner Indpls., 1974-78; ptnr. Roper, Mains, & Cobb, Boulder, Colo., 1978-87; of counsel Dorr Carson Sloan & Birney, Denver and Boulder, 1989—, JAMS/ENDispute Colo. Regional Office, Denver, 1995—. With U.S. Army, 1968-70. Mem. Fed. Bar Assn. (pres. Colo. chpt. 1994-95), Computer Law Assn. (dir. 1982-87), Colo. Bar Assn., Boulder County Bar Assn. Avocation: music. General civil litigation, Trademark and copyright, Intellectual property.

**MAIO, F. ANTHONY,** lawyer; b. Passaic, N.J., Mar. 30, 1937; s. Anthony J. and Santina (Sciarra) M.; m. Maureen Margaret McKeown, Dec. 30, 1960; children: Christopher, Duncan, Todd. BSME, Stevens Inst. Tech., 1959; LLB cum laude, Boston Coll., 1968. Bar: Wis. 1968, D.C. 1971. Engr., project mgr. Hazeltine Corp., Greenlawn, N.Y. and Avon, Mass., 1959-64; project mgr. Raytheon Corp., Portsmouth, R.I., 1964-65; atty. Foley & Lardner, Milw., 1968-70; ptnr. Foley & Lardner, Washington, 1971-86; ptnr. Foley & Lardner, Milw., 1986-97, ptnr., gen. counsel, 1997—. Editor Boston Coll. Law Rev., 1967-68. Dir. Arthritis Found., Milw., 1986-88, ARC, Milw., 1986-94. Mem. Order of Coif, Milw. Yacht Club (dir. 1989-95), Naples Sailing & Yacht Club. Avocations: boating, fishing. Office: Foley & Lardner Firstar Ctr 777 E Wisconsin Ave Ste 3800 Milwaukee WI 53202-5367

**MAIOCCHI, CHRISTINE,** lawyer; b. N.Y.C., Dec. 24, 1949; d. George and Andreina (Toneatto) M.; m. John Charles Kerecz, Aug. 16, 1980; children: Charles George, Joan Christine. BA in Polit. Sci., Fordham U., 1971, MA in Polit. Sci., 1971, JD, 1974; postgrad., NYU, 1977—. Bar: N.Y. 1975, U.S. Dist. Ct. (so. and ea. dists.), N.Y. 1975, U.S. Ct. Appeals (2nd cir) 1975. Law clk. to magistrate U.S. Dist. Ct. (so. dist.) N.Y., N.Y.C., 1973-74; atty. corp. legal dept. The Home Ins. Co., N.Y.C., 1974-76; asst. house counsel corp. legal dept. Allied Maintenance Corp., N.Y.C., 1976; atty. corp. legal dept. Getty Oil Co., N.Y.C., 1976-77; v.p., mgr. real estate Paine, Webber, Jackson & Curtis, Inc., N.Y.C., 1977-81; real estate mgr. GK Techs., Inc., Greenwich, Conn., 1981-85; real estate mgr., sr. atty. MCI Telecom. Corp., Rye Brook, N.Y., 1985-93; real estate and legal cons. Wallace Law Registry, 1994-96; sr. assoc. counsel Met. Transp. Authority, 1996—. Bd. dirs. LWV, Dobbs Ferry, N.Y., 1988. Mem. ABA, Nat. Assn. Corp. Real Estate Execs. (pres. 1983-84, treas. 1985-86, bd. dirs. 1995—), Indsl. Devel. Rsch. Coun. (program v.p. 1985, Profl. award 1987), N.Y. Bar Assn., Women's Bar Assn. Manhattan, The Corp. Bar (sec. real estate divsn. 1987-89, chmn. 1990-92), Jr. League Club, Dobbs Ferry Women's Club (program dir. 1981-92, 94-96, publicity dir. 1992-94). Avocations: sports, theatre, gardening. Real property. Home: 84 Clinton Ave Dobbs Ferry NY 10522-3004

**MAISEL, MARGARET ROSE MEYER,** lawyer; b. Manila, Philippines, Dec. 5, 1937; came to U.S., 1952; d. Paul Emil and Conchita (De La Riva) Meyer; m. Donald F. Maisel, Dec. 31, 1956; children: Vicky Colemere, Leslie Otero, Kristi Langford. BA, St. Mary's U., 1965, JD, 1971. Bar: Tex. 1971, U.S. Dist. Ct. (we. dist.) Tex. 1973. Atty., shareholder Tinsman-Houser, San Antonio, 1971-84, 85—; chmn. Tex in indsl. accident bd. State of Tex., 1984-85. Mem., adv. bd. Santa Rosa Health Care, San Antonio, 1993-94; bd. trustees St. mary's Univ., San Antonio, 1988-89; chmn. Santa Rosa Health Care Found., San Antonio, 1994—. Recipient Outstanding Law Alumnus St. Mary's U., 1989; named Outstanding Lawyers Bexar County Womens Bar. Fellow Tex. Bar Found., San Antonio Bar Found. (bd. dirs.); mem. San Antonio Trial Lawyers (bd. dirs.), Tex. Trial Lawyers (bd. dirs.). Roman Catholic. Avocations: antiques, reading, travel. Personal injury, Workers' compensation, Pension, profit-sharing, and employee benefits. Home: 1402 Fortune Hl San Antonio TX 78258-3201 Office: Tinsman Houser Inc 700 N Saint Marys St Ste 1400 San Antonio TX 78205-3511

**MAISTER, DAVID HILTON,** consultant; b. London, July 21, 1947; came to U.S., 1973; s. Alfred and Bertha (Spanglett) M. BS in Soc. Sci., U. Birmingham, Eng., 1968; MSc, London Sch. Econs., 1971; DBA, Harvard U., 1976. Asst. prof. U. B. C., Can., 1976-78; assoc. prof. Harvard Bus. Sch., Mass., 1979-85; pres. Maister Assocs., Boston, 1985—; cons. to profl. svc. firms. Author: The Owner Operator, 1975, The Motor Carrier Industry, 1977, The Domestic Airline Industry, 1977, Management of Owner Operator Fleets, 1979, Cases in Operations Management, 2 vols., 1982, Professional Service Firm Management, 1987, Success Strategies for the Design Professions, 1987. Home and Office: Maister Assocs PO Box 946 Boston MA 02116-3040

**MAITLAND, GUY EDISON CLAY,** lawyer; b. London, Dec. 28, 1942; (mother Am. citizen); s. Paul and Virginia Francesca (Carver) M. BA, Columbia U., 1964; JD, N.Y. Law Sch., 1968. Bar: N.Y. 1969, U.S. Dist. Ct. (so. and ea. dists.) N.Y. 1969, U.S. Ct. Appeals (2d and D.C. cirs.) 1969. Assoc. Burlingham, Underwood & Lord, N.Y.C., 1969-74; admiralty counsel Union Carbide Corp., N.Y.C., 1974-76; exec. v.p., gen. counsel, dir. Liberian Svcs., Inc., N.Y.C. and Reston, Va., 1976-89, pres., 1990—; del. UN Conf. on Trade and Devel., Manila, 1979, Belgrade, 1983; participant London Conf. on Limitation of Maritime Liability, 1976; mem. legal com. Internat. Maritime Orgn. (UN) London, 1980—; del. UN Conf. on Law of the Sea, 1976-82, London UN Maritime Law Conf., 1984; co-founder The Admiralty-Fin. Forum, N.Y.C., 1986; exec. v.p. Internat. Registries, Inc. Contbr. articles on maritime law, U.S. shipping policy. Del. Rep. Nat. Conv., Kansas City, 1976; sec. N.Y. Rep. County Com., 1976-87, vice chmn., 1988—; co-chmn. Citizens for Reagan, N.Y. State, 1979-80; trustee Am. Mcht. Mariine Mus. Found. at U.S. Mcht. Marine Acad., King's Point, Nat. Maritime Hist. Soc., N.Y. Maritime Coll. at Ft. Schuyler Found., Inc.; bd. dirs. Coast Guard Found.; del. Un Geneva Conf. on Arrest of Vessels, 1999; mem. Ctr. for Seafarers Rights; mem. adv. com. Am. Maritime History Project. Named Outstanding Young Man of Am. U.S. Jaycees, 1975; hon. del Rep. Nat. Conv., Dallas, 1984. Mem. ABA, Assn. of Bar of City of N.Y. (chmn. admiralty com. 1982-85), Maritime Law Assn. U.S. (chmn. com. on intergovtl. orgns. 1987-95), Ctr. for Seafarer's Rights Seamen's Ch. Inst. (bd. dirs. 1995—), Maritime Assn. Port of N.Y. (dir. 1984-87, 98—). Admiralty. Office: Internat Registries Inc Exec Pres 12 E 49th St New York NY 10017-1028

**MAIWURM, JAMES JOHN,** lawyer; b. Wooster, Ohio, Dec. 5, 1948; s. James Frederick and Virginia Anne (Jones) M.; m. Wendy S. Leeper, July 31, 1971; children: James G., Michelle K. BA, Coll. Wooster, 1971; JD, U. Mich., 1974. Bar: Ohio 1974, D.C. 1986, Md. 1987, N.Y., 1987. Ptnr. Squire, Sanders & Dempsey, Cleve. and Washington, 1974-90; ptnr., group head Crowell & Moring, Washington, 1990-98; ptnr. Squire, Sanders & Dempsey, Washington, 1998-99; pres., CEO ICF Kaiser Internat., Inc., Fairfax, Va., 1999—. Contbr. articles to profl. jours. Bd. trustees Davis Meml. Goodwill Industries, 1996—. Mem. ABA, D.C. Bar Assn., Leadership Washington, Econ. Club Washington, George Mason U. Century Club (bd. dirs. 1994-95, 97-98, chair tech. resource alliance 1995-99). General corporate, Securities, Mergers and acquisitions. Home: 9419 Brian Jac Ln Great Falls VA 22066-2002 Office: ICF Kaiser Internat Inc 9300 Lee Hwy Fairfax VA 22031-1200

**MAIZEL, SAMUEL RUVEN,** lawyer; b. Paterson, N.J., Apr. 9, 1955; s. Solomon S. and Anita M. Maizel; 1 child, Andrew Chapin. BS, U.S. Mil. Acad., 1977; MA, Georgetown U., 1983; JD, George Washington U., 1985. Commd. 2d lt. U.S. Army, 1977, advanced through grades to lt. col., 1996; infantry officer U.S. Army, Ft. Campbell & Washington, 1977-82; criminal trial lawyer U.S. Army, Frankfort, Germany, 1986-90, Dhahran, Saudi Arabia, 1986-90; trial atty. U.S. Dept. Justice, Washington, 1991-96; of counsel Pachulski, Stang, Ziehl & Young P.C., L.A., 1997—. Mem. editl. bd. Calif. Bankruptcy Jour.; editor Electronic Bankruptcy Newsletter Dept. Justice; contbr. articles to profl. jours. Decorated Bronze Star, Meritorious Svc. medal with oak leaf cluster, Army Commendation medal with oak leaf cluster, Army Achievement medal, S.W. Asia Svc. medal, Nat. Def. Svc. medal with bronze svc. star, Army Svc. ribbon, Overseas Svc. ribbon, Kingdom of Saudi Arabia Liberation of Kuwait medal Kingdom of Saudi Arabia, 1991, Liberation of Kuwait medal Govt. Kuwait, 1992. Mem. ABA (chair working group on healthcare insolvency issues), FBA (newsletter editor 1997-98, treas. 1998), Am. Bankruptcy Inst. (contbg. editor jour.), Am. Health Lawyers Assn. Bankruptcy, Health, General civil litigation. Office: Pachulski Stang Ziehl & Young PC Ste 1100 10100 Santa Monica Blvd Los Angeles CA 90067-4100

**MAJERS, ELIZABETH LOUISE,** lawyer; b. Chgo., Sept. 25, 1958; m. Roger Daniel Majers Bonds; children: Katelyn Christine Majers, Kellyanne Louise Majers. BS, U. Ill., 1979; JD, Ind. U., 1982. Bar: Tex. 1982, Ill. 1983; CPA, Ill. Tax atty. Exxon Co., U.S.A., Houston, 1982-83; assoc. Chapman and Cutler, Chgo., 1983-90, ptnr., 1990-92, mng. ptnr., 1992-97; ptnr. McDermott, Will & Emery, Chgo., 1998—; spkr. in field, 1983—. Fellow Am. Coll. Investment Counsel (past pres. 1995-97, pres., v.p. 1993-95, trustee 1991—). Avocations: golf, cooking, photography, travel. Finance. Office: McDermott Will & Emery 227 W Monroe St Ste 3100 Chicago IL 60606-5096

**MAJOR, ALICE JEAN,** lawyer; b. Denver; m. Kent H. Major, Feb. 16, 1997; children: David, Thomas, Kassie, Samantha, Cameron. BS in Bus., U. Colo., 1984, MBA, 1986; JD, U. Kans., 1987. Bar: Mo. 1987, Kans. 1988, U.S. Dist. Ct. Kans. 1988, Colo. 1990, U.S. Dist. Ct. Colo. 1991, U.S. Ct. Appeals (3d cir.) 1993, U.S. Supreme Ct. 1994. Atty. Legal Aid of Western Mo., Kansas City, 1987-88, Spencer, Fane, Britt & Browne, Kansas City, 1988-91; mcpl. and county atty. City and County of Denver, 1991—; spkr. Colorado Springs mtg. Colo. County Attys. Assn., 1992. Vol. Denver Dumb Friends League, Denver, 1996—. Recipient miscellaneous ribbons and awards for paintings. Mem. Alfred A. Arraj Inn of Ct. (barrister mem.). Avocations: art, skiing, fishing. Office: City Attys Office City and County of Denver 1437 Bannock St Rm 353 Denver CO 80202-5375

**MAJOR, HUGH GEOFFREY,** lawyer; b. L.A., May 22, 1955; s. Robert Allen and Patricia Ann Major; m. Debra Olga Palmini, July 3, 1976; 1 child, Dale Geoffrey. AS in Criminology, City Coll. of San Francisco, 1979; BA in Pub. Adminstrn., Golden Gate U., 1981, JD, 1993. Bar: Calif. 1993, U.S. Dist. Ct. (so., cen., and no. dists.) Calif. 1994, U.S. Ct. Appeals (fed., 1st, 3d, 4th, 5th, 6th, 7th, 8th, 9th, 10th, and 11th cirs.) 1994, U.S. Tax Ct. 1996, U.S. Supreme Ct. 1997. Pvt. practice San Francisco, 1988—, Hugh G. Major, Pvt. Investigator, San Francisco, 1988—. Pres. br. 259 Italian Cath. Fedn., San Francisco, 1997-98. Sgt. U.S. Army, 1974-77. Recipient Wiley W. Manuel award for pro bono legal svcs. State Bar of Calif., 1994. Mem. ABA, Bar Assn. San Francisco (Outstanding Vol. in Pub. Svc. award 1997, Vol. of the Month 1998), Supreme Ct. Hist. Soc., Olympic Club (life). Avocations: collecting wine, restoring classic cars. Estate planning, Family and matrimonial, Probate. Office: 1255 Post St Ste 935 San Francisco CA 94109-6720

**MAKEL, DENNIS MICHAEL,** lawyer; b. Waynesburg, Pa., Mar. 3, 1956; s. John Joseph and Lucille Eleanor (Buday) M.; m. Donna Annette Martin, Oct. 2, 1992; children: Lea Celene Bentz, Dennae Leanne. BA, Washington and Jefferson Coll., 1978; JD, Duquesne U., 1982. Bar: Pa. 1984, U.S. Dist. Ct. (we. dist.) Pa. 1997, U.S. Ct. Appeals (3d cir.) 1997. Law clk. to J. David L. Gilmore Washington County Ct. Common Pleas, Washington, Pa., 1984-86, asst. dist. atty., 1986-93; sch. dist. and mcpl. solicitor Washington and Greene Counties, Washington, Pa., 1993—. Bd. dirs. Law Libr. Com., Washington County, 1986-90; trustee Fredericktown (Pa.) Area Pub. Libr., 1986-89, Bethlehem-Ctr. Edn. Found., Fredericktown, 1995-97; mem. Centerville Borough Bicentennial Com., Centerville, Pa., 1995-96. Mem. Pa. State Assn. Twp. Solicitors, Pa. Sch. Bd. Solicitors Assn., Pa. Borough Solicitors Assn., Masons, Scottish Rite. Democrat. Roman Catholic. Avocations: travel, coin collecting, military history reading. Home: 163 Clare Dr Washington PA 15301-6639 Office: PO Box 4193 Washington PA 15301-1117

**MAKIYAMA, HIROE RUBY,** lawyer, writer; b. Tokyo, Sept. 29, 1964; d. Shizuo and Chika (Kojima) Otomi; m. Yoshimichi Makiyama. BA, Internat. Christian U., 1987; JD, Mich. State U., 1991. Bar: N.Y., Conn. 1993. TV dir. Tokyo Broadcasting Sys., 1987-88; assoc. Marks & Murase, N.Y.C., 1991-93; in-house atty. Warner Bros., Burbank, Calif., 1993, Shochiku Co., Ltd., Tokyo, 1993-95; mgr. legal office Polygram K.K., Tokyo, 1995-96; pvt. practice, 1997—; interpreter, spkr. Vol. Lawyer for the Arts, N.Y.C., 1996. Author: How to Become a Classy Lady, 1997, 1001 Ways to Say I Love You, 1998. Mem. Sommelier Soc. Am. (cert.), Le Vintage Club (pres. 1993—). Entertainment. Address: Jeing & Assocs 809 Montgomery St 2d Fl San Francisco CA 94133-5108

**MAKOWSKI-RIVERA, DONNA,** lawyer, educator; b. Chgo., Oct. 11, 1954; d. Charles J. and Jean V. (Kriaucinuas) M. BA with honors, U. Ill., Chgo., 1976; JD, John Marshall Sch. Law, 1983. Bar: Ill. 1984, U.S. Dist. Ct. (no. dist.) Ill. 1984, U.S. Ct. Appeals (7th cir.) 1984. Mgr. Jewel Food Corp., Chgo., 1972-76; tchr. fgn. lang. U. Ill., Chgo., 1976-77, Chgo. Pub. Schs., 1976-83; course/seminar coordinator John Marshall Law Sch., Chgo., 1983-84; sole practice, Chgo., 1984—; mem. Mayor's Adv. Com. on Women's Affairs, Chgo., 1984—; of counsel John De Leon, Chgo. pro bono advocate Chgo. Vol. Legal Services. Aide Sen. Carroll Dem. Orgn., Chgo., 1981-82. Fellow Kosciusko Found., N.Y., 1983. Mem. ABA, Ill. Bar Assn., Chgo. Bar Assn. (sec. young lawyers div. 1982-83), Women's Bar Assn., Ill. Trial Lawyers Assn., Advocates Soc. Phi Kappa Phi, Phi Delta Phi. Roman Catholic. Fax: 312-554-8780. Criminal, Real property. Office: 53 W Jackson Blvd Ste 1644 Chicago IL 60604-3798

**MAKRICOSTAS, DEAN GEORGE,** lawyer; b. Weirton, W.Va., July 4, 1968; s. George James and Eugenia Makricostas; m. Eugenia Nikki Frangos, Dec. 28, 1997. BA, W.Va. U., 1990; JD, Thomas M. Cooley, 1996. Bar: W.Va. 1997, U.S. Dist. Ct. (no. and so. dists.) W.Va. 1997. Gen. laborer Weirton (W.Va.) Steel Corp., summer 1987; computer sci. asst. W.Va. U., Morgantown, 1988-90; sales and lease cons. Biggio Ford Lincoln Merwry & Toyota, Steubenville, Ohio, 1991-93; clk. Galloway & Taylor Law Office, Weirton, W.Va., 1996-97; ptnr. Gurrera Taylor & Makricostas, Weirton, W.Va., 1997—. Mem. Am. Hellenic Ednl. Program Am., Weirton, 1986—; mem., consel All Saints Greek Orthodox Ch., Weirton, 1995—. Mem. ATLA, W.Va. Trial Lawyers Assn., W.Va. Bar Assn., Hancock County Bar Assn., Elks. Avocations: youth activities, hockey, public interest groups. General civil litigation, Personal injury, General practice. Home: Country Club Estates 104 Sherry Ct Weirton WV 26062-9666 Office: Law Offices of Gurrera Taylor & Makricostas 3401 Pennsylvania Ave Weirton WV 26062-3922

**MALACH, HERBERT JOHN,** lawyer; b. N.Y.C., Aug. 3, 1922; s. James J. and Therese (Lederer) M.; m. Patricia Sweeny, Sept. 12, 1953 (dec. 1972); children: Therese, Herbert John, Helen. A.B., Iona Coll., 1951; J.D., Columbia U., 1955. Bar: N.Y. 1957, D.C. 1958, U.S. Dist. Ct. D.C. 1958, U.S. Dist. Ct. (ea. and so. dists.) N.Y. 1958, U.S. Ct. Mil. Appeals 1958, U.S. Ct. Appeals 2d cir.) 1960, U.S. Supreme Ct. 1961, U.S. Dist. Ct. (no. and we. dists. N.Y.) 1988, U.S. Ct. Appeals (fed. cir.) 1988, U.S. Tax Ct. 1988. Pvt. practice N.Y.C., 1957-72, New Rochelle, N.Y., 1960—; lectr. bus. law Iona Coll., New Rochelle, 1957-59, asst. to pres. for community svcs., 1959-62. Vice chmn., exec. dir. Iona Coll. Westchester County Law Enforcement Inst.; spl. counsel N.Y. State Temporary Commn. on Child Welfare; mem. Westchester County Youth Adv. Coun., 1969-73; mem. Law Enforcement Planning. Agy., New Rochelle, 1968-69; adv. counsel Westchester Police Youth Officers Assn.; mem. Westchester County Child Abuse Task Force; mem. New Rochelle Narcotics Guidance Coun., 1972-75; adv. coun. New Rochelle Salvation Army, 1976-79; legal adviser East-End Civic Assn.; law guardian Westchester County Family Ct.; referee New Rochelle City Ct.; arbitrator Civil Ct., Bronx; arbitrator Supreme and County Ct., Westchester. Bd. dirs. Art Inst., Iona Coll., mem. adv. bd. radio activities, adv. bd. criminal justice Iona Coll., bd. dirs. Westchester County Youth Shelter; hon. dep. sheriff Westchester County. Served with AUS, 1942-46. Recipient Patrick B. Doyle award for outstanding service, 1969, William B. Cornelia Founders award, 1976 (both Iona Coll.). Mem. Am. (family law sect.), N.Y. State (com. child welfare, com. family ct.), Bronx County (com. family ct.), Westchester County, New Rochelle Bar Assns., Am. Judicature Soc., N.Y. County Lawyers Assn. (family ct. com.), Criminal Cts. Bar Assn. Westchester County, Am. Fedn. Police, Internat. Narcotic Enforcement Officers Assn., Internat. Acad. Criminology, Am. Acad. Polit. and Social Sci., Am. Profl. Soc. on Abuse of Children, Law Guardians Assn. Westchester County (pres. 1987-89, dir. 1989-90), Am. Psychology-Law Soc., Internat., N.Y. State, Bergen County chiefs of police, Nat. Assn. Coun. for Children, Nat. Sheriffs Assn., Am. Soc. Internat. Law, Iona Coll. Alumni Assn., Inc. (pres., chmn. bd. dirs. 1958-60, 62-64, 72-74, 74-76, dir. 1954-58, 68-72, 76-86, v.p. 1966-68). Family and matrimonial, Juvenile. Address: 1273 North Ave #4H BLG1 New Rochelle NY 10804-2702

**MALAK, PAUL JOHN,** lawyer; b. Wilkes-Barre, Pa., Jan. 4, 1967; s. Paul and Sylvia (Yurkon) M.; m. Lisa Cogley, June 20, 1998. BA, Dickinson Coll., 1989; JD, Duquesne U., 1992. Bar: Pa. 1992, W.Va. 1993, U.S. Dist. Ct. (so. dist.) W.Va. 1993, U.S. Dist. Ct. (we. dist.) Pa. 1995, U.S. Dist. Ct. (mid. dist.) Pa. 1996, U.S. Ct. Appeals (3d and 4th cirs.) 1996, U.S. Ct. Appeals (D.C. and fed. cirs.) 1997. Jud. law clk. Ct. of Common Pleas, Washington, Pa., 1992-93; counsel BTLL, Inc., Shavertown, Pa., 1993-95; atty. Egler-Garrett, Pitts., 1995—; chmn., gen. counsel MALCO, Inc., Shavertown, 1997—. Contbr. articles to profl. jours. Roman Catholic. Avocations: art collecting, international travel, opera, auto racing. General corporate, Mergers and acquisitions, General civil litigation. Home: 130 S 22d St Pittsburgh PA 15203 Office: MALCO Inc 2086 Chase Rd Shavertown PA 18708-9771

**MALANCA, ALBERT ROBERT,** lawyer, mediator; b. Tacoma, Apr. 25, 1927; s. Albert and Caroline (Mencarelli) M.; m. Jeannine Marian O'Halloran, June 13, 1952 (dec. Sept. 1993); children: Rand (dec.), Gina M., Warren A.; m. Glenna Lee Bradley-House, Jan. 1, 1994; 1 child, Chaise. BA, U. Wash., 1949, JD, 1950. Bar: Wash., U.S. Dist. Ct. (we. and ea. dists.) Wash., U.S. Supreme Ct. Assoc. Goodwin Eastvold & Hicks, Tacoma, 1951-54; ptnr. Goodwin Hicks & Malanca, Tacoma, 1954-55, Goodwin Hicks Malanca & Hager, Tacoma, 1955-57, Carnahan Gordon & Goodwin, Tacoma, 1957-60, Gordon Goodwin Sager Hicks & Thomas, Tacoma, 1960-62, Gordon Goodwin Sager & Thomas, Tacoma, 1962-66, Gordon Sager Honeywell Malanca & Peterson, Tacoma, 1966-68, Gordon Honeywell Malanca Peterson & Johnson, Tacoma, 1968-70, Gordon Thomas Honeywell Malanca Peterson O'Hern & Johnson, Tacoma, 1970-76, Gordon Thomas Honeywell Malanca Peterson & O'Hern, Tacoma, 1976-85; sr. ptnr. Gordon Thomas Honeywell Malanca Peterson & Daheim, Tacoma, 1985—; mediator and arbitrator, Tacoma/Seattle, 1985—. Author, speaker legal seminars. Patron, Tacoma Art Mus., 1998. Fellow Am. Coll. Trial Lawyers (state chmn. 1985-86), Am. Bar Found. (life); mem. ABA, Wash. State Bar Assn., Fed. Bar Assn. (pres. 1980-81), Tacoma-Pierce County Bar Assn. (trustee 1975-77). Episcopalian. Avocations: boating, skiing, fishing, hunting, golf. General civil litigation, Securities, Antitrust. Home: 8915 N Harborview Dr Apt 101 Gig Harbor WA 98332-2179 Office: Gordon Thomas Honeywell Malanca Peterson & Daheim 1201 Pacific Ave Ste 2200 Tacoma WA 98402-4314

**MALARCHICK, TIMOTHY PAUL,** lawyer; b. Hermiston, Oreg., Sept. 24, 1959; s. Mike and Yvonne (Grace) M.; m. Charlotte McMaster, May 31, 1986; children: Nathan, Adam, Kendall. BA, U. Idaho, 1984, JD, 1987. Bar: Wash. 1987, Idaho 1989, U.S. Dist. Ct. (we. dist.) Wash. 1990, U.S. Dist. Ct. (ea. dist.) Wash. 1987, U.S. Dist. Ct. Idaho 1989. Assoc. Evans, Craven & Lackie, Spokane, Wash., 1987-90, Burgess, Fitzer, Leighton & Phillips, Tacoma, Wash., 1990-94; pvt. practice Tacoma, 1994—. Mem. ABA, Tacoma Bar Assn., Pierce County Bar Assn., Wash. Def. Trial Lawyers Assn. Presbyterian. Avocations: family, sports, music. Insurance. Home: 2611 52nd Ave NW Gig Harbor WA 98335-7641 Address: Timothy Malarchick & Assoc 4423 Point Fosdick Dr NW #310 Gig Harbor WA 98335-1794

**MALASPINA, MARK J.,** lawyer; b. Waterbury, Conn., Oct. 7, 1957; s. Domenic F. and Pauline E. (Ariola) M.; m. Teresa Fox, June 8, 1980; children: Lauren, Robert, Martin, Paul. BA summa cum laude, Fairfield U., 1979; JD, Yale U., 1982. Bar: Conn. 1982, U.S. Dist. Ct. Conn. 1983. Assoc. Carmody & Torrance, Waterbury, 1982-88, ptnr., 1989—; mem. U.S. C. of C. Energy and Natural Resources Com., Washington, 1992—. Mem. Gov. Rowland Transition Team, Hartford, Conn., 1994-95; dir., sec./treas. Gov.'s Inauguration Com., Waterbury, Conn., 1994-95; dir., sec. Gov.'s Exec. Chambers Conservancy, Hartford, 1995—; bd. dirs., sec. Father Nadolny Good News Fund, inc., 1994—; mem. adv. bd. Waterbury Spirit Profl. Baseball Club. Mem. ABA, Conn. Bar Assn. (exec. com. pub. utility law sect. 1992—), Waterbury Bar Assn. (treas. 1989-92. Republican. Roman Catholic. Avocations: organist, amateur sports, writing. General corporate, Insurance, Construction. Office: Carmody & Torrance LLP 50 Leavenworth St Waterbury CT 06702-2112

**MALATESTA, MARY ANNE,** lawyer; b. Wapakoneta, Ohio, Aug. 7, 1954; d. Leo J. Jr. and Ellen E. (Kelly) M. BA in English, Ohio State U., 1976; JD, U. Colo., 1979. Bar: Colo. 1979, U.S. Dist. Ct. Colo. 1979, U.S. Ct. Appeals (9th cir.) 1989, U.S. Ct. Appeals (10th cir.) 1990, U.S. Dist. Ct. Ariz. 1992. Dep. dist. atty. 1st Jud. Dist., Golden, Colo., 1979-84; assoc. Tilly & Graves, P.C., Denver, 1985-88, shareholder, 1988-93; asst. atty. gen. Office Atty. Gen. State of Colo., Denver, 1994—; mem. faculty Nat. Inst. Trial Advocacy, South Bend, Ind., 1989-90, asst. team leader, 1990-93, team leader, 1994—; lectr. U. Denver, 1990, 91, 97—; guest faculty U. Colo., 1992—; organizer Victims of Violence seminar; mem. faculty Am. Bd. Trial Advocates seminar, 1992, Domestic Violence Prosecution Tng. Course, 1994, Child Advocates Tng. Course, 1996; mem. Am. Inns of Ct. Judge William E. Doyle Inn, 1994—, Women's Leadership Forum, 1996—. Founder, mem. Facio ut Des, Denver, 1987-94. Mem. Colo. Bar Assn., Denver Bar Assn. (professionalism com. 1990—, co-chair professionalism com. 1994—), Colo. Women's Bar Assn. Avocations: hiking, horseback riding, spectator sports. General civil litigation, Product liability, Criminal. Office: Office of Atty Gen 1525 Sherman St Fl 5 Denver CO 80203-1700

**MALAWSKY, DONALD N.,** lawyer; b. Milw., Dec. 5, 1935; s. Joseph and Anna (Brill) M.; m. Teresa Koncick, Apr. 2, 1995; 1 child, Douglas. BS, U. Wis., 1959, JD, 1961. Bar: Wis. 1961, U.S. Supreme Ct. 1969, N.Y. 1974, U.S. Dist. Ct. (so. and ea. dists.) N.Y. 1974, U.S. Dist. Ct. D.C. 1974. Staff atty. SEC, Denver, 1962-67; various pos. SEC, N.Y.C., 1968-81, regional adminstr., 1981-84; sr. v.p. N.Y. Stock Exchange, 1984-87; 1st v.p., asst. gen. counsel Merrill Lynch & Co. Inc., N.Y.C., 1987—; adj. prof. law N.Y. Law Sch., 1981—. Served to 1st lt. U.S. Army, 1961-62. Mem. ABA, Wis. Bar Assn., Fed. Bar Assn., D.C. Bar Assn. Democrat. Jewish. Administrative and regulatory, Securities. Home: 4 Walnut Ct Warren NJ 07059-5339 Office: Merrill Lynch & Co 222 Broadway New York NY 10038-2510

**MALCHESKI, KIM,** lawyer; b. San Rafael, Calif., Nov. 24, 1953; s. Henry Thomas and Meryle (Rogers) M. BA, U. Ariz., 1975, JD, 1979. Bar: Calif. 1981, U.S. Ct. Appeals (9th cir.) 1981, U.S. Supreme Ct. 1984. Editor Nat. Lawyers Guild, N.Y.C., 1979-80, San Francisco, 1981-82; ptnr. Donaldson, Malcheski, Parker, San Francisco, 1982-85, Malcheski, Parker, Randolph, San Francisco, 1985-88, Malcheski & Parker, San Francisco, 1988-90; pvt. practice San Francisco, 1990—; mem. nat. exec. com. Nat. Lawyers Guild, N.Y.C., 1979-80, mem. exec. bd., San Francisco, 1981-82. Mem. Calif. Attys. for Criminal Justice, Bernal Heights Bar Assn. (pres. 1990-95). Avocation: film noir. Appellate, Criminal, Juvenile. Office: PO Box 40105 San Francisco CA 94140-0105

**MALEDON, MICHAEL BRIEN,** lawyer; b. Mishawaka, Ind., Dec. 9, 1970; m. Lesley Crandall, Feb. 7, 1998. BA in Fin. and Acctg., U. Ariz., 1993; JD magna cum laude, U. Notre Dame, 1996. Atty. Snell & Wilmer, LLP, Phoenix, 1996—. Securities, General corporate, Mergers and acquisitions. Office: Snell & Wilmer LLP One Arizona Center Phoenix AZ 85004

**MALEE, THOMAS MICHAEL,** lawyer; b. Omaha, May 25, 1947. BA, Carroll Coll., 1970; JD, U. Mont., 1975. Bar: Mont. 1975, U.S. Dist. Ct. Mont. 1975, U.S. Ct. Appeals (9th cir.) 1986, U.S. Supreme Ct. 1988. Staff atty. State of Mont. Legis. Counsel, Helena, Mont., 1975-76; asst. atty. gen. State of Mont. Dept. Revenue, Helena, 1976; pvt. practice Seattle, Tacoma area, Wash., 1977-78, Helena, 1979-82, Billings, Mont., 1982—. Mem. State Bar of Mont. (ins. com. 1988—). Roman Catholic. Avocations: skiing, fitness. Federal civil litigation, Personal injury, General civil litigation. Office: 1109 N 22nd St Ste 103A Billings MT 59101-0253

**MALESKI, CYNTHIA MARIA,** lawyer; b. Natrona Heights, Pa., July 4, 1951; d. Richard Anthony and Helen Elizabeth (Palovcak) M.; m. Andrzej Gabriel Groch, Aug. 7, 1982; 1 child, Elizabeth Maria. BA summa cum laude, U. Pitts., 1973; student U. Rouen (France), 1970; JD, Duquesne U., 1976. Bar: Pa. 1976, U.S. Dist. Ct. (we. dist.) Pa. 1976, U.S. Supreme Ct. 1980, U.S. Ct. Appeals (3d cir.) 1984. Indsl. rels. adminstr. Allegheny Ludlum Industries, Inc., Brackenridge, Pa., 1972-74; law clk. Conte, Courtney, Tarasi & Price, Pitts., 1974, Paul Hammer, Pitts., 1974-76; sole practice Natrona Heights, Pa., 1978-92, 95—; ins. commnr. Penna, 1992—; mem. Gov.'s cabinet, 1992—; v.p., regulatory coun. Highmak Blue Cross/ Blue Shield, 1995—; assoc. dir. pers. Mercy Hosp., Pitts., 1976-77, dir. legal affairs, 1977-81, gen. counsel, 1981-92; spl. master Allegheny County Ct. Common Pleas, 1989; bd. dirs. legal adv. bd. Cath. Health Assn., 1980-82; gen. counsel, vice chmn. nat. assembly of reps. Nat. Confedn. Am. Ethnic Groups, 1980—; health law cons. and lectr. Co-author: The Legal Dimensions of Nursing Practice (Nurses' Book of Month Club award 1982), 1982; contbr. articles to publs. Corp. sec., pres. Duquesne U. Tamburitzans, Pitts.; vice chmn. Czechoslovak room com. Nationality Rooms Program, U. Pitts., 1983; bd. dirs. ARC S.W. Penn. Chpt., 1996—; elected mem. Allegheny County Dem. Com., 1986-89; candidate for del. Dem. Nat. Conv. 20th Pa. Congl. Dist., 1984; chmn. Com. to Re-elect U.S. Congressman Doug Walgren, 1982; Ethnic Com. for Pa. Atty. Gen., 1980, Ethnic Com. for Judge Peter Paul Olszewski, 1983; U.S. del 4th Slovak World Congress, 1981; mem. adv. bd. Children's and Youth Services, Allegheny County, 1984—; mem. Allegheny-Keshi Hist. Soc., 1995—; soloist, speaker various groups, Pitts. Slovakians. Scholar U. Rouen, 1970; Allegheny Ludlum Industries scholar, 1969-73; Andrew Mellon scholar, 1969; tuition scholar U. Pitts., 1969-73; tuition remission grantee Duquesne U., 1975, 76; recipient acad. excellence award Duquesne U., 1976, Disting. Alumnus, 1993; Mem. ABA, Am. Soc. Hosp. Attys., Nat. Health Lawyers Assn., Women Execs. in State Govt. (mem. nat. bd. 1994), Soc. Hosp. Attys. of Hosp. Assn. Pa. (v.p.), Soc. Hosp. Attys. Western Pa., Pa. Bar Assn. (commn. on women, 1996—, exec. women's coun.), Allegheny County Bar Assn., Slavic Edn. Assn. (nat. treas. 1981-86), St. Thomas More Soc. (bd. govs. 1980—), First Cath. Slovak Union, 1st Cath. Slovak Women's Assn., Phi Beta Kappa. Roman Catholic. Health, State civil litigation, General practice. Home: 137 Oak Manor Dr Natrona Heights PA 15065-1949 Office: Ins Dept 1326 Strawberry Sq Harrisburg PA 17120-0046

**MALETZ, HERBERT NAAMAN,** federal judge; b. Boston, Oct. 30, 1913; s. Reuben and Frances (Sawyer) M.; m. Catherine B. Loebach, May 8, 1947; 1 child, David M. (dec.). AB, Harvard U., 1935, LLB cum laude, 1939. Bar: Mass. 1939, D.C. 1952. Rev. atty. Mktg. Laws Survey, WPA, Washington, 1939-41; mem. staff Truman com. U.S. Senate, 1941-42; trial atty. anti-trust divsn. Dept. Justice, 1946-50; assoc. to chief counsel Office of Price Stabilization, 1950-53; law assoc. to Charles P. Clark, 1954-55; chief counsel anti-trust subcom., judiciary com. U.S. House of Reps., 1955-61; trial commr. U.S. Ct. Claims, Washington, 1961-67; judge U.S. Ct. Internat. Trade, N.Y.C., 1967-87; sr. judge U.S. Dist. Ct. Md., Balt., 1982—; vis. judge with various fed. cts., including U.S. Ct. Customs and Patent Appeals, U.S. Cts. of Appeals for the 1st and 2nd Cirs., U.S. Dist. Cts. for Mass., N.H., Maine, R.I., Ea. Dist. N.Y., Ea. Dist. N.C., Cen. Dist. Calif., So. Dist. Calif.; vis. judge U.S. Dist. Md., 1987—. Served with AUS, 1942-46; lt. col. Res. Office: US Dist Ct Md 101 W Lombard St Baltimore MD 21201-2626

**MALIA, GERALD ALOYSIUS,** lawyer; b. Blakeley, Pa., Aug. 6, 1933; s. Anthony Francis and Mary Agnes (Kelly) M.; m. Mary Catherine Carolan, June 27, 1959; children: Mary Catherine Malia Higgins, Carolan Elizabeth Malia Taylor, Elizabeth Kelly, Gerald Anthony. BS, St. Peter's Coll., Jersey City, 1954; JD, Georgetown U., 1958, LLM, 1959. Bar: D.C. 1959, U.S. Ct. Appeals (D.C. cir.) 1959, U.S. Supreme Ct. 1964. Law clk. Chief Judge A. Hood D.C. Ct. Appeals, Washington, 1959-60; from assoc. to ptnr. Ragan & Mason, Washington, 1961-92; counsel Kirlin, Campbell & Keating, Washington, 1993—; adj. prof. Georgetown U. Law Ctr., Washington, 1973—; Disting. lectr. Cath. U. Law Sch., Washington, 1979—; vis. prof. World Maritime U., Malmo, Sweden, 1992—; del. Jud. Conf., Washington, 1994—; industry prof. Webb Inst., N.Y.C., 1996—. Author: Maritime Law: The Need for a Comprehensive Maritime Code, 1983; editor Georgetown Law Jour., 1958. 1st lt. U.S. Army, 1954-56. Mem. ABA, Maritime Adminstrv. Bar Assn. (pres.), Maritime Law Assn., Cosmos Club, Congressional Country Club. Roman Catholic. Avocation: golf. Admiralty, Private international. Office: Kirlin Campbell & Keating 1660 L St NW Washington DC 20036-5603

**MALIK, JOHN STEPHEN,** lawyer; b. Bryn Mawr, Pa., Sept. 15, 1958; s. John and Mary M. (Pisko) M. BA, St. Joseph's U., 1980; JD, Del. Law Sch., 1983. Bar: Del. 1984, Pa. 1984, U.S. Dist. Ct. Del. 1984, N.J. 1985, U.S. Ct. Appeals (3d cir.) 1990, U.S. Supreme Ct. 1989. Adj. faculty Widener U., Wilmington, 1984-86; sole practice Wilmington, 1985—. Mem. ATLA, Am. Judicature Soc., Nat. Assn. Criminal Def. Lawyers, Del. Assn. Criminal Def. Lawyers, Del. Bar Assn. Democrat. Roman Catholic. Criminal. Office: 100 E 14th St Wilmington DE 19801-3210

**MALIK, THOMAS WARREN,** lawyer; b. Chgo., Mar. 2, 1948; s. Russell R. and Virginia L. M.; m. Karen L. Coy, June 21, 1975. BA, Northwestern U., 1970; JD, Duke U., 1973. Bar: Ill. 1973, U.S. Dist. Ct. (no. dist.) Ill. 1973, U.S. Ct. Appeals (7th cir.) 1973, U.S. Supreme Ct. 1976. Gen. counsel, asst. gen. counsel, atty. Sun Elec. Corp., Chgo., 1973-78; atty. Trans Union Corp., Lincolnshire, Ill., 1978-79; pvt. practice, Barrington and Wauconda, Ill., 1979—; arbitrator Cir. Ct. Cook County, Chgo., 1995—, Cir. Ct. 19th Jud. Cir., Waukegan, Ill., 1995—. Mem. Ill. Bar Assn., Lake County Bar Assn., Chgo. Bar Assn. General civil litigation, Probate, Real property. Office: 211 S Main St Wauconda IL 60084-1827

**MALINA, MICHAEL,** lawyer; b. Bklyn., Mar. 20, 1936; s. William and Jean (Kutlowitz) M.; m. Anita May Oppenheim, June 22, 1958; children: Rachel Lynn, Stuart Charles, Joel Martin. AB, Harvard U., 1957, LLB, 1960. Bar: N.Y. 1961, U.S. Dist. Ct. (so. and ea. dists.) N.Y. 1962, U.S. Ct. Appeals (2d, 3d, 4th, 9th, and D.C. cirs.) 1965, U.S. Supreme Ct. 1965, U.S. Tax Ct. 1991. Assoc. Kaye, Scholer, Fierman, Hays & Handler, N.Y.C., 1960-69, ptnr., 1969—. Contbr. articles to profl. jours. Mem. ABA (antitrust sect.), N.Y. State Bar Assn. (chmn. antitrust sect. 1998-99), Assn. Bar City N.Y. (profl. ethics com. 1985-88), Phi Beta Kappa. Democrat. Jewish. Antitrust, Federal civil litigation. Home: 12 Innes Rd Scarsdale NY 10583-7110 Office: Kaye Scholer Fierman Hays & Handler 425 Park Ave New York NY 10022-3506

**MALINOWSKI, ANDREA V.,** lawyer; b. Wilkes-Barre, Pa., Feb. 8, 1960; d. Henry S. and Elizabeth (Prieto) Malinowski; m. Randall Henzes; children: Jason, Ryan, Lindsay. BS in Chemistry, Pa. State U., 1982; JD, Temple U., 1987. Bar: Pa. 1987, U.S. Ct. Appeals (3d and D.C. cirs.) 1988, U.S. Dist. Ct. (ea. dist.) Pa. 1989, U.S. Supreme Ct. 1997. Chemist Union Camp Corp., Princeton, N.J., 1982-84; atty. E.I. duPont de Nemours, Wilmington, Del., 1987—. Environmental, Patent. Office: DuPont Co 1007 Market St Wilmington DE 19898-0001

**MALKIN, CARY JAY,** lawyer; b. Chgo., Oct. 6, 1949; s. Arthur D. and Perle (Slavin) M.; m. Lisa Klimley, Oct. 27, 1976; children: Dorothy R., Victoria S., Lydia R. BA, George Washington U., 1971; JD, Northwestern U., 1974. Bar: Ill. 1974, U.S. Dist. Ct. (no. dist.) Ill. 1974. Assoc. Mayer, Brown & Platt, Chgo., 1974-80, ptnr., 1988—. Chmn. spl. events com. Mental Health Assn., 1984-85; mem. steering com. Endowment Campaign of the Latin Sch. of Chgo., 1990-91, trustee, 1991—, v.p. 1992-98, chmn. capital campaign, 1995-98; mem. exec. com. Friends of Prentice Women's Hosp., 1991-92; bd. dirs. SOS Children's Village Ill., 1992-96; mem. M.S. Weiss fund bd. Children's Meml. Hosp., 1989-93; mem. Graziano Fund bd. Children's Meml. Hosp., 1993-96; mem. steering com. Founder's Coun. Field Mus., 1995—, chmn. steering com., 1999—, bd. trustees, 1999—. Mem. Chgo. Club, Saddle and Cycle Club, Arts Club, Standard Club, Order of the Coif, Phi Beta Kappa. Banking, General corporate, Finance. Home: 233 E Walton St Chicago IL 60611-1510 Office: Mayer Brown & Platt 190 S La Salle St Ste 3100 Chicago IL 60603-3441

**MALKIN, MICHAEL M.,** lawyer; b. New Haven, Nov. 1, 1944; s. Eli B. and Gladys (Pollak) M.; children: Andrea, Lisa, Daniel. BA, U. N.Mex., 1966; JD, NYU, 1969. Bar: N.Y. 1970, U.S. Dist. Ct. (so. dist.) N.Y. 1971, U.S. Dist. Ct. (ea. dist.) N.Y. 1971, U.S. Ct. Appeals (2d cir.) 1972, U.S. Supreme Ct. 1984. Assoc. Weil, Lee & Bergin, N.Y.C., 1970-76; assoc. Weil, Guttman & Davis, N.Y.C., 1976-77, ptnr., 1977-82; ptnr. Weil, Guttman, Davis & Malkin, N.Y.C., 1982-86, Weil, Guttman & Malkin, N.Y.C., 1986-95, Weil, Guttman & Malkin, LLP, N.Y.C., 1995—; judge Giles Sutherland Rich Moot Ct. Competition, N.Y.C., 1982; arbitrator Civil Ct. of City N.Y., 1984-88. Mem. editl. bd. Trademark Reporter, 1973-75, 88-90, contbg. editor, 1974-75. Mem. N.Y. State Bar Assn., U.S. Trademark Assn., Phi Delta Phi, Alpha Epsilon Pi. Trademark and copyright, Non-profit and tax-exempt organizations, Antitrust. Office: Weil Guttman & Malkin LLP 60 E 42nd St Rm 4210 New York NY 10165-4299

**MALLETT, CONRAD LEROY, JR.,** state supreme court chief justice; b. Detroit, Oct. 12, 1953; s. Conrad LeRoy and Claudia Gwendolyn (Jones) M.; m. Barbara Straughn, Dec. 22, 1984; children: Alex Conrad, Mio Thomas, Kristan Claudia. BA, UCLA, 1975; MPA, U. So. Calif., 1979, JD, 1979. Bar: Mich. 1979. Legal asst. to congressman Detroit, 1979-80; dep. pol. div. Dem. Nat. Com., Washington, 1980-81; assoc. Miller, Canfield, Paddock & Stone, Detroit, 1981-82; legal counsel, dir. to gov. State of Mich., Lansing, 1983-84; sr. exec. asst. to Mayor City of Detroit, 1985-86; ptnr. Jaffe, Raitt, Heuer & Weiss, Detroit, 1987-90; justice Mich. Supreme Ct., Lansing, 1990—, chief justice, 1997—. Mem. NAACP, Kappa Alpha Psi. Democrat. Roman Catholic. Avocations: writing, fiction. Office: Supreme Ct Office 2d Fl Law Bldg PO Box 30052 Lansing MI 48909-7552

**MALLEY, J. WALLACE, JR.,** lawyer; b. Washington, Nov. 1, 1947; m. Margaret Allen, July 29, 1972; children: Sean, Colin, Brian. BA, Duke U., 1969; JD, Georgetown U. Law Ctr., 1972. Bar: D.C. 1973, U.S. Ct. Mil. Appeals 1973, Vt. 1976, U.S. Dist. Ct. Vt. 1976, U.S. Ct. Appeals (D.C. cir.) 1985, U.S. Ct. Appeals (8th cir.) 1986, U.S. Ct. Appeals (2d cir.) 1981, U.S. Supreme Ct. 1985. Staff judge advocate USN, Washington, 1972-76; dept. state's atty. Bennington County, Bennington, Vt., 1976; from asst. atty. gen. to chief dep. atty. gen. Office of the Atty. Gen., Montpelier, Vt., 1976—; Toll fellow Coun. of State Govts., 1997; mem. sound sci. com. Coun. of State Govts., 1999; model rules of profl. conduct com. Vt. Supreme Ct. Com., Montpelier, 1995-96; chair Legis. Solid Waste Commn. Pres. Montpelier PTO, 1982-84; bd. dirs. Montpelier Little League, 1990. Lt. USNR, 1972-76. Mem. Vt. Bar Assn. Avocations: singing, gospel music, acting, sailing, railroads. Office: Office of Atty Gen 109 State St Montpelier VT 05609-0001

**MALLIA, MICHAEL PATRICK,** lawyer; b. Galveston, Tex., Aug. 1, 1946; s. Simon A. Mallia, Jr. and Aleta Jo (Wooten) Benson; m. Katherine Mae Sandberg, June 6, 1970 (div. Feb. 1986); m. Marianne Haggar, Feb. 11, 1989; 1 child, Lindsay. BS, Lamar State Coll. Tech., 1968; JD, South Tex. Coll., 1973. Bar: Tex. 1973; bd. cert. Nat. Bd. Trial Advocacy, Personal Injury Trial Law, Civil Trial Law. Atty. Law Offices of Dan Ryan, Houston, 1973-75, Law Office of Michael P. Mallia, Houston, 1975-80; atty., ptnr. Barnhart, Mallia & Cochran, Houston, 1981-89, Mallia & Jacobs, Houston, 1989—; chmn. dist. 4H23 grievance com. State Bar Tex. With U.S. Army, 1969-71. Fellow Houston Bar Found.; mem. Trial Lawyers for Pub. Justice (sustaining founder), Tex. Trial Lawyers, Assn. Trial Lawyers Am., Houston Trial Lawyers Assn. (bd. dirs. 1991-93, pres.-elect 1993-94, pres. 1994-95), Houston Trial Lawyers Found. (Vol. of Yr. 1997-98, bd. dirs. 1992—, pres. 1995-96), Delta Theta Phi (dean 1972-73). Avocations: sailing, snow skiing, running. State civil litigation, Federal civil litigation, Personal injury. Office: Mallia & Jacobs 440 Louisiana St Ste 1100 Houston TX 77002-1635

**MALLIOS, GEORGE JAMES,** lawyer; b. Newport News, Va., Mar. 25, 1949; s. George J. and Rose Marie (Jaramillo) M.; m. Mary Janis Bagby, Aug. 14, 1971 (div. May 1979); children: Jason James, Jessica Erin; m. Cynthia Sue Grosse, Aug. 12, 1983 (dec.); 1 child, Kathryn Alexis; m. Karen A. Mallies, Feb. 1993; Children: Jordan, Hannah. BA in Polit. Sci., U. Mo., St. Louis, 1975; JD, U. Tex., 1979. Bar: Tex. 1979; U.S. Dist. Ct. (we. and ea. dists.) Tex. Ptnr. Law Offices of H.J. Blanchard, Austin, Tex., 1979-81, Kuhn, Mallios & Doyle P.C., Austin, 1981-85; lead ptnr. Mallios & Doyle P.C., Austin, 1985-88, Mallios & Associates, Austin, 1988—; mem. Dalkon Shiled Plaintiff com., 1986-87. Treas. "Doc" Blanchard for Tex. R.R. Commn., Austin, 1980, Terry Davis for City Council, Austin, 1983, Juan Duran for Justice of Peace, Austin, 1983. Mem. ABA, Capitol Area Trial Lawyers Assn., Tex. Trial Lawyers Assn., Association of Trial Lawyers of Am., Order of Barristers. Avocations: playing trumpet, jogging. Personal injury, Federal civil litigation, State civil litigation. Office: Mallios & Assocs PC 1607 West Ave Austin TX 78701-1531

**MALLORY, EARL K.,** lawyer, contractor; b. Birmingham, Ala., Oct. 26, 1950; s. Robert W. and Voncile C. Mallory; m. Robin Smerda, Aug. 13, 1988; children: Sarah, Marissa. BS in Elem. Edn., Auburn U., 1973; JD, Nova U., 1993. Bar: Fla. 1993, U.S. Dist. Ct. (so. and mid. dists.) Fla. 1994, Colo. 1997. Contractor M Squre Framing Co., Vero Beach, Fla., 1980-84; project mgr. Arthur Rutenberg Corp., Clearwater, Fla., 1984-85, Hoffman Group of Fla., Pompano, Fla., 1985-86; v.p. Jennings Constrn., Miami, Fla., 1986-88; cons. Mallory & Assocs., Miami, Fla., 1988-90; law clk. James B. Denman, P.A., Ft. Lauderdale, Fla., 1990-93; pvt. practice Jupiter, Fla., 1993—. Mem. ABA, ATLA, Acad. Fla. Trial Lawyers, Palm Beach County Trial Lawyers Assn., Palm Beach County Bar Assn. (dir. 1999—), Kiwanis (dir., v.p. Jupiter-Tequesta chpt. 1993—). Avocations: pilot, surfing, hunting, fishing. General civil litigation, Personal injury, Aviation. Office: PO Box 8858 Jupiter FL 33468-8858

**MALLOY, MARTIN GERARD,** lawyer; b. Phila., Oct. 2, 1949; s. Martin Joseph and Mary Rita (Hannigan) M.; m. Cheryl Leigh Weber, Oct. 15, 1982; children: Martin Gerard Jr., Justine F. BS, La Salle U., Phila., 1971; JD, Widener U., 1975. Bar: Pa. 1976, U.S. Dist. Ct. (ea. dist.) Pa. 1976, U.S. Ct. Appeals (3d cir.) 1992, U.S. Supreme Ct. 1992. Asst. city solicitor City of Phila. Law Dept., 1976-81; ptnr. La Brum & Doak, Phila., 1981-86; sr. assoc. Wilson, Elser, Moskowitz, Edelman & Dicker, Phila., 1986-90; ptnr. Mylotte, David & Fitzpatrick, Phila., 1990—; mem. com. Am. Ireland Fund; counsel J. Wood Platt Scholarship Alumni Assn., Phila., 1980-82. Baseball coach YMCA, Ardmore, Pa., 1988-91; coach Narberth Soccer League, Merion, Pa., 1988-91, Narberth Baseball League, 1991—, Penn Valley Basketball League, 1993—, Lower Merion Soccer Club, 1995—; mem. exec. com. Merion Cub Scout Pack, 1991-95, scoutmaster, 1993-95; bd. dirs. Narberth Athletic Assn., 1996—, St. Margaret Athletic Com.; commr. Main Line Girls Basketball Assn. J. Wood Platt scholar La Salle Coll., 1967. Mem. Pa. Bar Assn., Phila. Bar Assn. (lectr. on worker's compensation 1984—), Pa. Claims Assn., Phila. Workers Compensation Claims Assn. (editor newsletter 1984-85), Nat. Coun. Self-Insureds, Pa. Self Insurers' Assn., Am. Arbitration Assn., Brehon Law Soc., Ireland C. of C. in U.S. Republican. Roman Catholic. Avocations: golf, coaching youth, reading. General civil litigation, Insurance, Workers' compensation. Home: 3 Hampden Ave Narberth PA 19072-2309

**MALLOY, MICHAEL JOSEPH,** lawyer; b. Phila., Dec. 31, 1950; s. Martin Joseph and Mary Rita (Hannigan) M.; m. Rosemary Elizabeth Dilworth, Aug. 30, 1975; children: Caroline Rose, Michael David, Brian Patrick, Sean Martin. B.S., Villanova U., 1972; J.D., Widener Coll., 1976. Bar: Pa. 1976, U.S. Ct. Appeals (3d cir.) 1982, U.S. Supreme Ct. 1986. Sole practice, Media, Pa., 1976—; minor trial atty. Office of Pub. Defender, Media, 1976-79, maj. trial atty., 1979-81, chief maj. trial unit, 1981-90; lectr. law Del. County Community Coll., 1977-80. Mem. ATLA, Pa. Bar Assn., Phila. Bar Assn., Delaware County Bar Assn., Fed. Bar Assn., Pa. Criminal Def. Assn., Nat. Legal Aid and Defender Assn., Brehon Irish Law Soc. Republican. Roman Catholic. Criminal, Personal injury, Workers' compensation. Home: 100 Maple Ave Narberth PA 19072-2413 Office: 10 Veterans Sq Media PA 19063-3103

**MALLOY, MICHAEL P.,** lawyer; b. Providence, July 18, 1959; s. Judge Edward Francis and Patricia Marie Malloy; m. Jamie Marie Azzara, Aug. 20, 1983; children: Christofer, Nicholas, Michael, Cara. BA summa cum laude, Boston Coll., 1981, JD cum laude, 1984. Assoc. Drinker Biddle & Reath LLP, Phila., 1984-93, ptnr., 1993—, ptnr., head investment mgmt. group. Coach numerous childrens athletics teams. Mem. ABA, Phila. Bar Assn. (co-chair investment com.). Avocations: tennis, paddle tennis, racketball. General corporate, Finance, Mergers and acquisitions. Office: Drinker Biddle & Reath LLP One Logan Square 18th and Cherry Sts Philadelphia PA 19103-6996

**MALLOY, MICHAEL PATRICK,** law educator, author, consultant; b. Haddon Heights, N.J., Sept. 23, 1951; s. Francis Edward and Marie Grace (Nardi) M.; divorced; 1 child, Elizabeth; m. Susie Pieratos, Jan., 1992; children: Michael Emil, Nicholas Charles. BA magna cum laude (scholar), Georgetown U., 1973, PhD, 1983; JD (scholar), U. Pa., 1976. Bar: N.J. 1976. Rsch. assoc. Inst. Internat. Law and Econ. Devel., Washington, 1976-77; atty. advisor Office Fgn. Assets Control Dept. Treasury, Washington, 1977-80, Office of Comptroller of Currency, Washington, 1981; spl. counsel SEC Washington, 1981-82; asst. prof. N.Y. Law Sch., N.Y.C., 1982-83; spl. asst. Office of Gen. Counsel U.S. Dept. Treasury, Washington, 1985; assoc. prof. Seton Hall U. Sch. Law, Newark, 1983-86, prof., assoc. dean, 1986-87; prof. Fordham U. Sch. Law, N.Y.C., 1987-96, dir. grad. studies, 1990-94; prof. U. of Pacific McGeorge Law Sch., 1996—, dir. JD concentration in internat. legal studies, 1999—; law lectr. Morin Ctr. Banking and Fin. Law Studies Boston U. Sch. Law, 1986-90, 95-96; vis. prof. U. Salzburg, Austria, 1999—; cons. bank regulation and pvt. internat. law matters. Author: Corporate Law of Banks (2 vols.), 1988, Economic Sanctions and U.S. Trade, 1990, The Regulation of Banking, 1992, Banking Law and Regulation, 3 vols., 1994, Fundamentals of Banking Regulation, 1998, International Banking, 1998, Banking and Financial Services Law, 1999, Hornbook on Banking Regulation, 1999; contbr. articles, revs. and comments to profl. jours. Recipient Spl. Achievement award Dept. Treasury, 1982. Mem. Am. Soc. Internat. Law (exec. council 1986-89), Internat. Law Assn. (com. chair Am. br. 1995-97), Hegel Soc. Am., L'Association des Auditeurs et Anciens Auditeurs de l'Academie de Droit International de la Haye, Phi Beta Kappa. Office: U of Pacific McGeorge Sch Law 3200 5th Ave Sacramento CA 95817-2705

**MALM, JOHN JOSEPH,** lawyer; b. Key West, Fla., May 27, 1966; s. Joseph Howard and Maren Lou Malm; m. Sara Marie Cunningham, Aug. 13, 1988; children: Anders Joseph, Gunnar William. BA, Augusta Coll., 1988; JD, Valparaiso U., 1993. Bar: Ill., U.S. Dist. Ct. (no. dist.) Ill. Mktg. asst. IBM, Moline, Ill., 1987-88; ops. mgr. Cahners Exposition Group, Stamford, Conn., 1988-90; assoc. atty. Clausen Miller P.C., Chgo., 1992-97; ptnr. Stime & Malm, Wheaton, Ill., 1997—. Chmn. Rainbow Place Pre-sch., Glen Ellyn, Ill., 1994-97. Mem. ISBA, CBA. Avocations: photography, home improvement, skiing. Personal injury, Estate planning, General practice. Home: 546 Forest Ave Glen Ellyn IL 60137-4150 Office: Stime & Malm 610 W Roosevelt Rd Ste C2 Wheaton IL 60187-2304

**MALM, ROGER CHARLES,** lawyer; b. Hot Springs, S.D., July 8, 1949; s. Harry Milton and Angeline Mae (Johnson) M.; m. Sandra M. Metz, July 15, 1972; children: Andrew, Elliott, Nicholas. BA, St. Olaf Coll., 1971; JD, U. N.D., 1974. Bar: N.D. 1974, Ariz. 1975, Minn. 1980, U.S. Dist. Ct. N.D. 1974, U.S. Dist. Ct. Ariz. 1976, U.S. Ct. Appeals (9th cir.) 1981, U.S. Supreme Ct. 1981, U.S. Ct. Appeals (8th cir.) 1982, U.S. Dist. Ct. Minn. 1985, U.S. Claims Ct. 1985, U.S. Tax Ct. 1988. Ptnr. Brink, Sobolik, Severson, Malm & Albrecht, P.A., Hallock, Minn., 1980—; county atty. Kittson County, Minn., 1995—; pres. N.W. Minn. County Atty.'s Coun. Hospice dir. Kittson County Hospice, Inc., 1984—; bd. dirs. Cmty. Theatre, Hallock, 1987—, Greater Grand Forks Cmty. Theater, 1991-95. Mem. ABA, Ariz. Bar Assn., N.D. Bar Assn., Minn. Bar Assn. (mem. bd. govs. 1993—), Am. Acad. Hosp. Attys., Norwest Minn. Atty.'s Coun. (pres.). Lutheran. Avocations: skiing, sailing. General civil litigation, General practice, Health. Office: Brink Sobolik Severson Malm & Albrecht PO Box 790 Hallock MN 56728-0790

**MALM, SCOTT,** lawyer. BA magna cum laude, Brigham Young U., 1975, JD, 1978. Bar: Calif. 1978, U.S. Dist. Ct. (ea. dist.) Calif. 1978, U.S. Claims Ct. 1991, U.S. Supreme Ct., 1994, U.S. Dist. Ct. (no. dist.) Calif. 1998; cert. Nev. 2d Jud. Dist. 1986. Assoc. Steinheimer, Riggio, Haydel & Mordaunt, Stockton, Calif., 1978-84, prin., 1984—; judge pro tem San Joaquin County Mcpl. Ct.; arbitrator San Joaquin County Superior Ct.; spkr. and presenter in field. Contbr. articles to profl. jours. Mem. San Joaquin County Bar Assn. (chair mandatory fee arbitration com. 1983-87, chair client rels. com. 1988-89, mem. bus. litig. sect. 1997—), Tuolumne County Bar Assn. Fax: 209-464-9165. Labor, Contracts commercial, General civil litigation. Office: 400 E Main St Ste 600 Stockton CA 95290-0299

**MALMAN, MYLES HENRY,** lawyer; b. N.Y.C., Feb. 27, 1947; 010s. Louis M. and Pearl (Wolff) M.; m. Jill A. Saperstein, Aug. 9, 1997. BA, Fairleigh Dickinson U., 1967; JD, N.Y. Law Sch., 1974. Bar: N.Y. 1975, U.S. Dist. Ct. (so. and ea. dists.) N.Y. 1975, Fla. 1988,, Pa. 1993, U.S. Dist. Ct. (ea. dist.) Pa. 1993, U.S. Ct. Appeals (3d cir.) 1993, U.S. Dist. Ct. (so. dist.) Fla. 1993, U.S. Ct. Appeals (3d cir.) 1993, U.S. Ct. Appeals (11th cir.) 1994, U.S. Dist. Ct. (mid. dist.) Fla. 1995, U.S. Ct. Appeals (2d cir.) 1995. Asst. dist. atty., sr. trial atty. New York County, N.Y.C., 1974-84; spl. counsel to U.S. atty. for so. dist. Fla., U.S. Dept. Justice, Miami, 1984-89, dep. 1st asst. U.S. atty., 1989-92; ptnr. Hornsby & Whiserand, Miami, 1988-89, Kohn Nast & Graf, P.C., Miami, 1992-94, Lehtinen O'Donnell Malman Vargas & Reiner, Miami, 1995-96; pvt. practice, North Miami, Fla., 1996—; testified before Congress re FBI and Drug Enforcement Agy. merger, Washington, 1993. With U.S. Army, 1967-69, Vietnam. Avocation: cycling. Criminal, Federal civil litigation, Sports. Office: 12955 Biscayne Blvd Ste 202 North Miami FL 33181-2021

**MALMSHEIMER, ROBERT WILLIAM,** lawyer, educator; b. Babylon, N.Y., June 26, 1963; s. Robert G. and Mona Malmsheimer; m. Mary Beth Lynett, July 30, 1988; children: Taylor A., R. Jack. B of Landscape Architecture, SUNY Environ. Sci./Forestry, 1986; PhD, 1999; JD, Albany U., 1989. Bar: N.Y. 1990. Atty. Bagley, Lynett and Saia, Buffalo, N.Y., 1989-95; vis. prof. natural resource law SUNY Coll. of Environtl. Sci. and Forestry, Syracuse, 1995-99; asst. prof. environ. and natural resource law and policy SUNY Coll. of Environ. Sci. and Forestry, Syracuse. V.p., bd. dirs. Friends of Beaver Lake Nature Ctr., Lysander, N.Y. C. Eugene Farnsworth fellowship SUNY Coll. of Environtl. Sci. and Forestry, 1997, Joachim fellow SUNY Coll. Environ. Sci. and Forestry, 1998. Avocations: hiking, skiing, fishing. Fax: 315-470-6915. E-mail: rwmalmsh@mailbox.syr.edu. Natural resources, Environmental. Home: 134 Lincklaen St Cazenovia NY 13035-9779 Office: SUNY ESF One Forestry Dr 107 Marshall Hall Syracuse NY 13210-1716

**MALONE, DANIEL ROBERT,** lawyer; b. El Paso, Tex., Feb. 18, 1960; s. Orba Lee and Margaret Ann (Pounds) M. BBA, Baylor U., 1983, JD, 1986. Bar: Tex. 1986, U.S. Dist. Ct. (we. dist.) Tex. 1988, U.S. Ct. Appeals (5th cir.) 1989. Assoc. Hicks Ray McChristian P.C., El Paso, 1987-90; ptnr., shareholder Malone & Davie P.C., El Paso, 1991-96, Malone Law Firm, P.C., El Paso, 1997—. Mem. Baylor Devel. Coun., 1996—. Fellow Tex. Bar Found. (trustee 1993-94); mem. State Bar Tex. (bd. dirs., exec. com. 1992-95), Tex. Young Lawyers Assn. (pres. 1993-94), El Paso Young Lawyers Assn. (pres. 1991-92), Baylor Law Alumni (bd. dirs. 1996—). Federal civil litigation, State civil litigation, Labor. Home: 712 Wellesley Rd El Paso TX 79902-2422 Office: Malone Law Firm 300 E Main Dr Ste 1100 El Paso TX 79901-1356

**MALONE, DAVID ROY,** state senator, university administrator; b. Beebe, Ark., Nov. 4, 1943; s. James Roy and Ila Mae (Griffin) M.; m. Judith Kaye Huff, June 20, 1965 (div. Feb. 1990); 1 child, Michael David. BSBA, U. Ark., 1965, JD, 1969, MBA, 1982. Bar: Ark. 1969, U.S. Dist. Ct. (we. dist.) Ark. 1969, U.S. Tax Ct. 1972, U.S. Ct. Appeals (8th cir.) 1972, U.S. Supreme Ct. 1972. Pvt. practice Fayetteville, Ark., 1969-72; atty. City of Fayetteville, 1969-72; asst. prof. bus. U. Ark., Fayetteville, 1972-76, asst. dean law, 1976-91; mem. Ark. Ho. of Reps., 1980-84, Ark. Senate, 1984—; exec. dir. U. Ark. Found., 1991—; chair senate edn. com.; bd. dirs. Bank of Elkins, S.W. Edn. Devel. Lab., Austin, Tex., 1988-94; legal adv. coun. So. Regional Edn. Bd., Atlanta, 1991—. Contbr. articles to profl. jours.; bd. dirs. Ark. Law Rev.,

1978-92; contbg. author U. Ark. Press, 1989. Mayor City of Fayetteville, 1979-80; mem. Jud. Article Task Force, Little Rock, 1989-91; chair Motor Voter task force, 1994-95; bd. dirs. Music Festival Ark., 1989-91, Washington County Hist. Soc., 1993-96; chmn. bd. Walton Arts Ctr. Found., 1994—; chmn. bd. dirs. Washington County Law Libr., 1970-84; chmn. Ark. Tuition Trust Authority, 1997-99. Recipient Svc. award Ark. Mcpl. League, 1980, Disting. Service award U. Ark., 1988, Lucas Svc. award, Ark. Alumni Assn., 1998. Mem. Ark. Bar Assn. (ho. of dels. 1977-81, award of merit 1980, exec. 1981-82, Outstanding Lawyer-Citizen award 1990), Washington County Bar Assn., Ark. Inst. Continuing Legal Edn. (bd. dirs. 1979-88), Fayetteville C. of C. (bd. dirs. 1984—), Ark. Genealogy Soc. (bd. dirs. 1990—). Democrat. Methodist. Avocations: genealogy, stamp collecting. Home: 2848 Club Oak Dr Fayetteville AR 72701-9168 Office: PO Box 1048 Fayetteville AR 72702-1048

**MALONE, MICHAEL GLEN,** lawyer; b. L.A., Apr. 12, 1943; s. Thomas Daniel and Virginia (Shupe) M.; m. Susan Cornelia Pierson, May 9, 1970 (div. Nov. 1987); m. Linda Kay Thomson, Dec. 26, 1987. Student, U. So. Calif., 1960-61; BS, U.S. Naval Acad., 1965; JD, U. Calif., San Francisco, 1974. Bar: Calif. 1974, U.S. Dist. Ct. (no. dist.) Calif. 1974, U.S. Ct. Mil. Appeals 1979, U.S. Supreme Ct. 1979. Commd. 2d lt. U.S. Marine Corps, 1965, advanced through grades to lt. col., 1980, served in Republic of Vietnam, USS Coral Sea; appellate mil. judge U.S. Navy-Marine Corps Ct. of Mil. Rev., Washington, 1981-83; ret. U.S. Marine Corps, 1986; assoc. Littler, Mendelson, Fastiff & Tichy, San Francisco, 1986-88; staff atty. for SAFECO Ins. Co. Law Offices of James D. Biernat, Foster City, Calif., 1988-97, Law Offices of Donald J. Deshaw, Foster City, 1998-99; mng. atty. Law Offices of Carol L. Ventura, 1999—. Dir. USA Football Rugby Union. Mem. ABA, Assn. Trial Lawyers Am., Bar Assn. San Francisco, Marin County Bar Assn., Sonoma County Bar Assn., Napa County Bar Assn. Republican. Avocation: rugby. Personal injury, General civil litigation, Environmental. Office: Law Offices Donald J Deshaw 120 Montgomery St Ste 1725 San Francisco CA 94104-4320

**MALONE, ROBERT GERARD,** lawyer; b. St. Paul, Jan. 30, 1952; s. Richard Thomas and Elizabeth Marie Malone; m. Debra Phyllis See, July 30, 1988; children: Caitlin, Laura. BA, U. Minn., 1974; JD, William Mitchell Coll. Law, 1978. Bar: Minn. 1978, U.S. Dist. Ct. Minn. 1979, U.S. Ct. Appeals (8th cir.) 1989, U.S. Ct. Appeals (7th cir.) 1993; cert. criminal law specialist Nat. Bd. Trial Advocacy, 1990-95. Pvt. practice law St. Paul, 1978-82, 89—; assoc. Joseph S. Friedberg Chartered, Mpls., 1982-89. Named Leading Minn. Atty., Am. Rsch. Corp., 1996-97, Minn. Top Lawyers, Mpls./St. Paul Mag., 1998. Criminal. Office: Capital Ctr Rm 780 St Paul MN 55102

**MALONE, STEVEN C.,** lawyer; b. Clinton, Mass., May 21, 1949; s. Loran Murray Jr. M. and Dorothy Supernor; m. Linda Carol Sellers; children: Matthew, Douglas, Erin. BA in History cum laude, U. Mass., 1971; JD, Boston Coll., 1976. Bar: Mass., U.S. Dist. Ct. Mass., U.S. Ct. Appeals (1st cir.). Atty. Neville & Segalini, Cambridge, Mass., 1976-84, pvt. practice, Lexington, Mass., 1984-89, Segalini & Neville, Waltham, Mass., 1989—. Avocations: running, fitness, squash, hiking, camping. General civil litigation, Insurance, Personal injury. Office: Segalini & Neville 411 Waverley Oaks Rd Ste 320 Waltham MA 02452-8450

**MALONE, THOMAS WILLIAM,** lawyer; b. Seattle, Sept. 16, 1946; s. James Edward and Marie Cecilia (Anderson) M.; m. Drexel Cox, June 19, 1978; children: Jason, Cary, Jane Marie. BA, U. Wash., 1968, JD, 1972; MBA, Golden Gate U., 1982. Bar: Wash. 1972, U.S. Ct. Appeals (9th cir.) 1972, U.S. Tax Ct. 1980, U.S. Ct. Claims 1981, U.S. Supreme Ct. 1980. Prin. Treece Richdale Malone, P.S., Seattle, 1973—. Pres. Seattle Marine Bus. Coalition, 1983-86; bd. dirs. Ballard Cmty. Hosp., 1982-91, North Seattle C.C. Found., 1989—, chmn. 1992-93, Ballard Cmty Hosp. Found., 1991—; bd. dirs. Swedish Med. Ctr.-Ballard Found., 1991-95; chmn. bd. dirs. Ballard Cmty. Hosp., 1986-88; mem. bd. dirs. Swedish Health Systems, 1992—; vice chair Swedish Health Systems, 1995, chair 1996-99; chmn. City of Seattle Fair Campaign Practices Commn., 1986-92; mem. Bd. Ethics City of Seattle, 1986-92; chair City of Seattle Ethics and Elections Com., 1992; trustee Seattle C.C., 1997—, chmn. 1998—. Mem. ABA, Wash. Bar Assn., Seattle-King County Bar Assn., Ballard C. of C. (pres. 1981-84). General corporate, Estate planning, Taxation, general. Office: Treece Richdale Malone PS PO Box 70467 1718 NW 56th St Seattle WA 98107-5218

**MALONE, WILLIAM GRADY,** retired lawyer; b. Minden, La., Feb. 19, 1915; s. William Gordon and Minnie Lucie (Hortman) M.; m. Marion Rowe Whitfield, Sept. 26, 1943; children: William Grady, Gordon Whitfield, Marion Elizabeth, Helen Ann, Margaret Catherine. BS, La. State U., 1941; JD, George Washington U., 1952. Bar: Va. 1952, U.S. Supreme Ct 1971. Statis. analyst Dept. Agr., Baton Rouge, 1941; investigator VA, Washington, 1946-59; legal officer, dep., gen. counsel, asst. gen. counsel VA, 1959-79; pvt. practice law Arlington, Va., 1979-97. Editor: Fed. Bar News, 1972-73. Pres. Aurora Hills Civic Assn., 1948-49; spl. asst. to treas. Com. of 100, 1979-81, chmn., 1982-83; pres. Children's Theater, 1968-69; trustee St. George's Episc. Ch., 1979—; chmn. Arlington County Fair Assn., 1979-83. Lt. col. AUS, 1941-46, ETO. Decorated Legion of Merit; recipient Disting. Svc. award, 1979, 3 Superior Performance awards, 1952-72, Outstanding Alumni award George Washington Law Sch., 1978. Mem. Fed. Bar Assn. (pres. D.C. chpt. 1970-71, nat. pres. 1978-79), Va. Bar Assn., Arlington County Bar Assn., Nat. Lawyers Club (dir.), Arlington Host Lions, Ft. Myer Officers Club. Family and matrimonial, Personal injury, Probate. Home: 224 N Jackson St Arlington VA 22201-1253 Office: 2060 14th St N Ste 310 Arlington VA 22201-2513 *Success is not measured by dollars accumulated but by service to others.*

**MALONEY, FRANK,** judge, lawyer; b. Worcester, Mass., Nov. 20, 1927; s. Francis James and Dora Marie (Berthiaume) M.; children: Catharine Frances, Edward James. BA, U. Tex., Austin, 1953, LLB, 1956. Bar: Tex. 1956, U.S. Supreme Ct. 1962, Mass. 1969. Asst. dist. atty. Travis Co., Austin, Tex., 1956-60; chief Law Enforcement div. Atty. Gen. State of Tex., Austin, 1960-61; ptnr. Stayton, Maloney, Hearne & Babb, Austin, 1961-79; owner Frank Maloney & Assocs., P.C., Austin, 1979-90; judge Tex. Ct. Criminal Appeals, Austin, 1991-96; vis. judge Trial and Appelate Tex. Cts., 1996—; of counsel Sheinfeld, Maley & Kay, 1996—; adj. prof. law U. Tex. Sch. of Law, 1962-85, 97—. Co-author: (with Stumberg) Criminal Law and Administration, 1964. Capt. U.S. Army, 1946-51. Fellow Tex. Bar Found.; mem. ABA, Nat. Assn. Criminal Def. Lawyers (pres. 1987-88), Mass. Bar Assn., Tex. Bar Assn., Tex. Criminal Def. Lawyers Assn. (pres. 1971-72), Am. Bd. Trial Advocates, Am. Bd. Criminal Lawyers, Travis County Bar Assn. Home: 1414 Wathen Ave Austin TX 78703-2528 Office: 301 Congress Ave Ste 1400 Austin TX 78701-4041

**MALONEY, JOHN T., JR.,** lawyer; b. Washington, Jan. 16, 1959; s. John T. and Thelma I. Maloney; m. Cataryn D. Wayne, May 23, 1987; 1 child, Trinity. BA in Am. Studies, U. Calif., Santa Cruz, 1983; JD, Coll. William and Mary, 1987. Bar: Hawaii 1987. Assoc. Cades Schutte et al, Honolulu, 1987-93; ptnr. D'Amato Maloney & Lonborg, Honolulu, 1994—; pub. spkr. on benefits issues, 1994, 96, 98. Exhibited in group shows, 1993, 95, 97, 98. Mem. Hawaii Tax Rev. Commn., 1995-97. Recipient juror's awards for paintings, 1996, 97. Mem. Order of Coif. Avocation: painting. Pension, profit-sharing, and employee benefits. Office: D'Amato Maloney & Lonborg 707 Richards St Ste 516 Honolulu HI 96813-4623

**MALONEY, JOHN WILLIAM,** retired lawyer; b. Santa Barbara, Calif., Dec. 6, 1930; s. John Joseph and Mildred (Brunenmeyer) m. Jean Anderson, Nov. 18, 1966; children: Patrick Maloney, Cynthia Maloney. BA in Econs., U. Calif., Santa Barbara, 1953; JD, UCLA, 1958. Bar: Calif. 1959, U.S. Dist. Ct. (no., ctrl., ea., so. dists.) Calif. 1959. Assoc. Fogel McInery, Santa Monica, Calif., 1959-62; ptnr. Rhodes Barnard & Maloney, Santa Monica, 1963-82, Rhodes, Maloney et al., Santa Monica, 1983-88; prin. Maloney & Mullen, Santa Monica, 1989-96; ptnr. Real Estate Investors. Capt. U.S. Army, 1953-55. Mem. Bel Air Bay Club, Riviera Tennis Club, Bear River Club. Republican. Roman Catholic. Avocations: fly fishing, duck hunting, golf, tennis. State civil litigation, Family and matrimonial, Personal injury.

**MALONEY, MARYNELL,** lawyer; b. Hutchinson, Kans., Jan. 14, 1955; d. Robert Edgar and Marian Ellen (Benson) Baker; m. Michael D. Maloney, Nov. 30, 1977; children: Michelle M., Erica O., Dennis Jr. BA, Oberlin Coll., 1975; MA, Trinity U., San Antonio, 1978; JD, St. Mary's U., San Antonio, 1980. Cert. by Tex. bd. of legal specialization. Assoc. Law Offices Pat Maloney, P.C., San Antonio, 1981-82; ptnr., owner Maloney & Maloney, San Antonio, 1982—. Bd. dirs. San Antonio Internat. Keyboard Competition, 1988-90; bd. govs. St. Peters/St. Joseph's Children's Home, San Antonio, 1989-92. Mem. ACLU (bd. dirs. 1990—, v.p. 1995-96, Tex. chpt. 1992—, SACLU 1990—), Am. Trial Lawyers Assn., State Bar Tex., Tex. Trial Lawyers Assn. (assoc. bd. dirs. 1989-90, bd. dirs. 1991—, chair coun. local leadership 1990-92, cert. personal injury trial law), San Antonio Bar Assn., San Antonio Trial Lawyers Assn. (pres. 1991-92). Democrat. Avocations: reading, writing, film. Personal injury, State civil litigation, Civil rights. Office: Maloney & Maloney PC 2000 Milam 115 E Travis San Antonio TX 78205

**MALONEY, PATRICK, SR.,** lawyer; b. Dallas, Tex., Aug. 9, 1924; s. James Edward and Flora Agnes (Kessler) M.; m. Olive Boger, May 20, 1950; children: Patricia, Pat Jr., Michael, Janice, Tim. BJ, U. Tex., 1948, LLB, 1950. Bar: Tex. 1950, U.S. Dist. Ct. (we. dist.) Tex. 1955, U.S. Supreme Ct. 1951; cert. civil law and personal injury trial law, Tex. Bd. Legal Specialization, civil trial advocacy Nat. Bd. Trial Advocacy. 1st asst. trial chief Dist. Atty.'s Office, San Antonio, Tex., 1950-53; pvt. practice Law Offices of Pat Maloney P.C., San Antonio, 1953—; moderator, founder annual seminar Anatomy of a Lawsuit, St. Mary's U., San Antonio; frequent lectr. throughout U.S. in areas of product liability and personal injury law. Author: Winning the Million Dollar Law Suit, 1980; co-author: Trials and Deliberations: Inside the Jury Room, 1992. With USMC, 1942-45, PTO. Recipient Warhorse award So. Trial Lawyers Assn., 1992. Fellow Law Sci. Acad. Am., Am. Bd. Trial Advocates (pres. inner circle of trial advocates) mem. ATLA, Internat. Soc. Barristers, Internat. Acad. Trial Lawyers, San Antonio Trial Lawyers Assn. (co-founder, pres. 1967, 72, bd. dirs. 1967-73,) San Antonio Bar Assn., State Bar of Tex., Tex. Trial Lawyers Assn. (director emeritus). Democrat. Roman Catholic. Achievements include 1977 personal injury verdict awarding his client $26,510,800.00. At that time the largest personal injury verdict in the history of the U.S. He has obtained verdicts and settlements in excess of a million dollars more than fifty times. General civil litigation, Oil, gas, and mineral, Personal injury. Office: 239 E Commerce St San Antonio TX 78205-2923

**MALONEY, ROBERT B.,** federal judge; b. 1933. BBA, So. Meth. U., 1956, postgrad., 1960. Asst. dist. atty. County of Dallas, 1961-62; ptnr. Watts, Stallings & Maloney, 1962-65, Maloney, Miller & McDowell, 1966-75, Maloney & McDowell, 1976-78, Maloney & Hardcastle, 1979-80, Maloney & Maloney, 1981-84; assoc. judge Tex. Ct. Appeals (5th cir.), Tex., 1983-85; judge U.S. Dist. Ct. (no. dist.) Tex., Dallas, 1985—. State rep., Austin, Tex., 1973-82. Mem. Tex. Bar Assn. Office: US Dist Ct 1100 Commerce St Rm 15e26 Dallas TX 75242-1027

**MALONEY, ROBERT E., JR.,** lawyer; b. San Francisco, Sept. 17, 1942; s. Robert E. and Mara A. (Murphy) M.; children: Michael, Sarah, Paul. BA magna cum laude, U. Portland, 1964; JD summa cum laude, Willamette U., Salem, Oreg., 1967. Bar: Oreg., Wash., U.S. Dist. Ct. Oreg., U.S. Dist. Ct. (we. dist.) Wash., U.S. Dist. Ct. (ea. dist.) Wash., U.S. Ct. Appeals (9th cir.). Ptnr. Lane Powell Spears Lubersky, Portland, 1967—; bd. dirs., sec. Norm Thompson Outfitters, Inc., Portland, 1981—, Capital Credit Inc., 1996—; chmn. bd. visitors Willamette U. Law Sch., 1993-95, bd. dirs. emeritus, 1998—; past chair, mem. exec. com. Portland Trial Dept.; lawyers del. 9th Cir. Jud. Conf., 1995-97. Bd. dirs., Oreg. chpt. Multiple Sclerosis Soc.; judge pro tem Multnomah County Cir. Ct., 1994—; vice chair fin. com., bd. dirs. Oreg. Lawyers Against Hunger. Mem. ABA (co-chair products liability com., trial practice com. 1990-94), Nat. Assn. R.R. Trial Counsel, Fedn. Ins. Corp. Counsel, Oreg. Assn. Def. Counsel (bd. dirs. 1987-94, sec. 1991-92, v.p. 1993-94, pres. 1994), Fed. Bar Assn. (exec. com. Oreg. divsn. 1988-96, pres. 1994-95), Multnomah Athletic Club. Republican. Roman Catholic. General civil litigation, Product liability, Condemnation. Office: Lane Powell Spears Lubersky 520 SW Yamhill St Ste 800 Portland OR 97204-1383

**MALONEY, VINCENT JOHN,** lawyer, social worker, psychotherapist; b. Bryn Mawr, Pa., June 21, 1949; s. Vincent John and Mary Margaret (Lavelle) M.; m. Kathaleen Joanne Carpenter, Dec. 3, 1988; children: Kimberly Kenny, Jennifer Kenny. BA, U. Mich., 1972, MSW, 1976; JD, Wayne State U., 1987. Bar: Mich. 1987, Colo. 1992; cert. social worker; registered clin. social worker. Camp dir. Hemophilia of Mich., Ann Arbor, 1976-77; clin. supr. Cornerstone Counseling, Belleville, Mich., 1978-84; psychotherapist Community Care Svcs., Belleville, 1984-87; assoc. atty. Hyman, Gurwin Nachman Gold and Alterman, Southfield, Mich., 1987-88; pvt. practice Farmington Hills, Mich., 1988—; mem. Com. to Establish Friend of the Ct. Guidelines for Custody Disputes, State Ct. Adminstrv. Office, 1990-91; field instr. U. Mich. Sch. Social Work, 1978-85. Co-author: Consumer Guide to Divorce, 1990. Mem. State Bar Colo., Nat. Assn. Social Workers, State Bar Mich. (family law sect.). Family and matrimonial, Personal injury, Juvenile. Office: 30445 Northwestern Hwy Ste 200 Farmingtn Hls MI 48334-3175

**MALOOF, FARAHE PAUL,** lawyer; b. Boston, Feb. 10, 1950; s. Farahe and Emily Suzanna (Puchy) M.; m. Brigitte Lucienne DeLugre; children: Alexandre F., Melissa F. BS, Georgetown U., 1975, JD, 1978. Bar: D.C. 1978, Va. 1981, Md. 1990. Assoc. Corcoran & Rowe, Washington, 1978-82; ptnr. Berliner & Maloney, Washington, 1982-84; internat. legal counsel Advocacia Oliveira Ribeiro, Sao Paulo, Brazil, 1984-85; sole practice Washington, 1985-86; prin. Maloof & Assocs., Washington, 1986-97; of counsel Haas & Anderson, P.C., McLean, Va., 1997—; lectr. Am. U., Washington, 1984-85, Internat. Law Inst., Washington, 1986-87. Active Reagan-Bush campaign, Washington, 1984, Frank Wolf re-election campaign, Arlington, Va., 1986, Bush-Quayle campaign, Washington, 1988. Served to cpl. USMC, 1968-70, Vietnam. Mem. ABA, Va. Bar Assn., D.C. Bar Assn. (litigation and corps. sects.), Fed. Bar Assn. (immigration law sect.), Georgetown U. Alumni Assn. (co-chmn. 1983-84). Republican. Roman Catholic. Avocations: tennis, water skiing. General corporate, Real property, Immigration, naturalization, and customs. Home: 1506 Dewberry Ct Mc Lean VA 22101-5629

**MALOON, JERRY L.,** trial lawyer, physician, medicolegal consultant; b. Union City, Ind., June 23, 1938; s. Charles Elias and Bertha Lucille (Crevis-ton) M.; children: Jeffrey Lee, Jerry Lee II. BS, Ohio State U., 1960, MD, 1964; JD, Capital U. Law Sch., 1974. Intern Santa Monica (Calif.) Hosp., 1964-65; tng. psychiatry Ctrl. Ohio Psychiat. HOsp., 1969, Menninger Clinic, Topeka, 1970; clin. dir. Orient (Ohio) Devel. Ctr., 1967-69, med. dir., 1971-83; assoc. med. dir. Western Electric, Inc., Columbus, 1969-71; cons. State Med. Bd. Ohio, 1974-80; pvt. practice law Columbus, 1978—; pres. Jerry L. Maloon Co., L.P.A., 1981—; medicolegal cons., 1972—; pres. Maloon, Maloon & Barclay Co., L.P.A., 1990-95; guest lectr. law and medicine Orient Devel. Ctr. and Columbus Devel. Ctr., 1969-71; dep. coroner Franklin County (Ohio), 1978-84. Dean's coun. Capital U. Law Sch. Capt. M.C., AUS, 1965-67. Fellow Am. Coll. Legal Medicine, Columbus Bar Found.; mem. AMA, ABA, ATLA, Ohio Bar Assn., Columbus Bar Assn., Ohio Trial Lawyers Assn., Columbus Trial Lawyers Assn., Ohio State U. Alumni Assn., U.S. Trotting Assn., Am. Profl. Practice Assn., Ohio State U. Pres.'s Buckeye Club. Personal injury, Professional liability, Health. Home: 2140 Cambridge Blvd Upper Arlngtn OH 43221-4104 Office: 1335 Dublin Rd Ste 100A Columbus OH 43215-7007

**MALORZO, THOMAS VINCENT,** lawyer; b. Rome, N.Y., Jan. 10, 1947; s. Helen Adeline (Grande) M.; m. Catherine Marie Healy, Dec. 28, 1968; children: Amy, Craig, Mary, Thomas Jr. BA, Walsh U., Canton, Ohio, 1969; JD, Cleve. State U., 1979. Bar: Ohio 1979, U.S. Dist. Ct. (no. dist.) Ohio 1980, U.S. Patent Office 1980, Tex. 1981, U.S. Dist. Ct. (no. dist.) Tex. 1981, U.S. Ct. Appeals (7th cir.) 1994, U.S. Dist. Ct. (ea. dist.) Tex., 1998. Environ. regulations analyst Diamond Shamrock Corp., awdlas, 1979-81; ind. counsel, agt. Southwestern Life Ins. Co., Dallas, 1981-83; staff atty. NCH Corp., Irving, Tex., 1983-89; gen. counsel Wormald US, Inc., Dallas, 1989-90; patent atty. Otis Engring. Corp., Carrollton, Tex., 1990-93; pvt. practice Addison, Tex., 1993-95; ptnr. Falk, Vestal & Fish LLP, 1995—; pvt. practice Dallas, Tex., 1996-97; of counsel Bennett & Weston P.C., 1997—; asst. prof. law Dallas/Ft. Worth Sch. Law, Irving, Tex., 1990-92. Dist. com. Circle 10 Boy Scouts Am., Dallas, 1985—; first aid team ARC, Cleve., 1972-80. Recipient Dist. Award of Merit, Boy Scouts Am., 1990, Silver Beaver award Boy Scouts Am., 1997. Mem. State Bar Tex. (chmn. trademark com. intellectual property sect. 1989). Intellectual property, General corporate, General civil litigation. Office: Bennett & Weston PC 10670 N Central Expy Ste 200 Dallas TX 75231-2100

**MALOUF, EDWARD WAYNE,** lawyer; b. Dallas, Oct. 14, 1957; s. Edward Malouf and Marie Moossy; m. Marianne M. Walder, Feb. 11, 1984; children: Natalie, Anastasia, Monica. BA in English, St. Mary's U., San Antonio, 1980, JD, 1986; MA in Social Scis., U. Chgo., 1987. Bar: Tex. 1987, U.S. Ct. Appeals (5th cir.) 1990, U.S. Supreme Ct. 1990, U.S. Dist. Ct. (no. dist.) Tex. 1991. Tchr. Bishop Lynch High Sch., Dallas, 1983; briefing atty. to Justice Blair Reeves Ct. Appeals (4th cir.), San Antonio, 1986-87; atty. Brock & Kelfer, P.C., San Antonio, 1987-89, Milgrim, Thomajan & Lee, Dallas, 1989, Hutchison, Boyle, Brooks & Fisher, Dallas, 1989-91; pvt. practice Dallas, 1991—. Editor, writer Air Force News Svc., 1981. Chmn. bd. of advocates St. Mary's U. Sch. of Law, 1985. Mem. State Bar Tex. (jour. com. 1988-92), Nat. Order of Barristers (E. Davila Jr. award for Excellence in trial advocacy 1986). General civil litigation, Personal injury. Office: 2651 N Harwood St Ste 360 Dallas TX 75201-1560

**MALOVANY, HOWARD,** lawyer; b. Dayton, Ohio, July 6, 1950; m. Cynthia Jane Shilt, Sept. 18, 1976. BA, Ohio State U., 1972; JD, U. Toledo, 1977; MBA, U. Dayton, 1985. Bar: Ohio 1977, Ill. 1997. Staff atty., asst. sec. Nat. Cash Register Corp., Dayton, 1977-85; counsel Outboard Marine Corp., Waukegan, Ill., 1985-89, asst. sec., counsel, 1989-96; asst. sec., sr. counsel William Wrigley Jr. Co., Waukegan, 1996-98, sec., gen. counsel, 1998—. Securities, Mergers and acquisitions, General corporate. Office: William Wrigley Jr Co 410 N Michigan Ave Chicago IL 60611-4213

**MALZAHN, MARK WILLIAM,** lawyer; b. Milw., Nov. 26, 1956; s. Henry William and Rose Ann M.; m. Barbara Jayne Malzahn, Sept. 22, 1979; children: Anna, Joseph, Andrew. BA, St. Cloud State U., 1979; JD, Hamline U., 1983. Bar: Minn. 1983, Wis. 1992, U.S. Dist. Ct. Minn. 1984, U.S. Ct. Appeals (8th cir.) 1984, U.S. Tax Ct. 1984. Ptnr. Edwards & Malzahn, Anoka, Minn.; arbitrator Am. Arbitration Assn. Host, prodr., dir. (pub. access show) Legal Look, 1988—. Mem. Assn. Trial Lawyers Am., Minn. Trial Lawyers Assn. Personal injury. Office: Edwards & Malzahn 229 Jackson St Ste 105 Anoka MN 55303-2254

**MAMALIAN, PAUL,** lawyer; b. Beirut, Lebanon, June 30, 1969; s. Berge and Rosalie (Keushkerian) M. BA, George Washington U., 1991, JD, 1994. Bar: Calif. 1994, D.C. 1997. Atty. Sallie Mae, Washington, 1994-98, Reed Smith Shaw & McClay LLP, Washington, 1998—. Bd. dirs. Nat. Kidney Found., Washington, 1997—; chmn. bd. Thrive, Washington, 1995-97. Office: Reed Smith Shaw & McClay LLP 1301 K St NW Ste 100 Washington DC 20005-3317

**MAMAT, FRANK TRUSTICK,** lawyer; b. Syracuse, N.Y., Sept. 4, 1949; s. Harvey Sanford and Annette (Trustick) M.; m. Kathy Lou Winters, June 23, 1975; children: Jonathan Adam, Steven Kenneth. BA, U. Rochester, 1971; JD, Syracuse U., 1974. Bar: D.C. 1976, U.S. Ct. Appeals (D.C. cir.) 1976, Fla. 1977, U.S. Supreme Ct. 1979, US. Dist. Ct. (ea. dist.) 1983, U.S. Ct. Appeals (6th cir.) 1983, Mich. 1984, U.S. Dist. Ct. (no. dist.) Ind. 1984. Atty. NLRB, Washington, 1975-79; assoc. Proskauer, Rose, Goetz & Mendelsohn, Washington, N.Y.C. and L.A., 1979-83; assoc. Fishman Group, Bloomfield Hills, Mich., 1983-85, ptnr., 1985-87; sr. ptnr. Honigman, Miller, Schwartz and Cohn, 1987-94; pres., CEO Morgan Daniels Co., Inc., West Bloomfield, Mich., 1994—; ptnr. Clark Klein & Beaumont, P.L.C., Detroit, 1995-96; ptnr. Clark Hill, P.L.C., Detroit, 1996—, mem. exec. com., 1999—; bd. dirs. Mich. Food and Beverage Assn., Air Conditioning Contractors of Am., Air Conditioning Contractors of Mich., Associated Builders and Contractors, Am. Subcontractors Assn., Mich. Mfrs. Assn. Labor Counsel. Gen. counsel Rep. Com. of Oakland County, 1986—; chmn. Constrn. Code commn. Mich., 1993—; bd. dirs. 300 Club, Mich., 1984-90; pres. 400 Club, 1990-93, chmn., 1993—; mem. Associated Gen. Contractors Labor Lawyers Coun.; mem. Rep. Nat. Com. Nat. Rep. Senatorial Com., Presdl. Task Force, Rep. Labor Coun., Washington; city dir. West Bloomfield, 1985-87; pres. West Bloomfield Rep. CLub, 1985-87; fin. com. Rep. Com. of Oakland County, 1984-93; pres. Oakland County Lincoln Rep. Club, 1989-90; bd. dirs. camping svcs. and human resources com. YMCA, 1989-93, Anti-Defamation League, 1989—; vice chmn. Lawyers for Reagan-Bush, 1984; v.p. Fruehauf Farms, West Bloomfield, Mich., 1985-88; mem. staff Exec. Office of Pres. of U.S. Inquiries/Comments, Washington, 1981-83. Mem. ABA, FBA, Mich. Bar Assn., Fla. Bar Assn. (labor com. 1977—), Mich. Bus. and Profl. Assn., Am. Acad. Constrn. and Labor Attys. (exec. dir. 1998—), Am. Subcontractors Assn. (Southeastern Mich., bd. dirs.), Founders Soc. Detroit Bar Assn., Oakland County Bar Assn., B'nai B'rith (v.p. 1982-83, trustee 1987-88, bd. dirs. Detroit Barristers unit 1983-91, pres. 1985-87), Oakpointe Country Club, Detroit Soc. Clubs, Skyline Club, Fairlane Club, Renaissance Club. Labor, Administrative and regulatory, General civil litigation. Office: Clark Hill PLC 500 Woodward Ave Ste 3500 Detroit MI 48226-3435 also: Morgan Daniels Co Inc 5484 Crispin Way Rd West Bloomfield MI 48323-3402

**MANAHAN, JAMES HINCHON,** lawyer; b. Medilia, Minn., Aug. 27, 1936; s. Cecil James and Ruth Pearl (Hinchon) M.; m. Suzanne Colette Laurendeau, June 14, 1958 (div. 1975); children: Theodore, Corinne, Matthew, Anne; m. Vanda Botts Hedges, Jan. 30, 1989. AB, Harvard U., 1958, JD, 1961. Bar: Minn. 1961, U.S. Dist. Ct. Minn. 1961, U.S. Ct. Appeals (8th cir.) 1962, U.S. Supreme Ct. 1971, Hawaii 1989, Colo. 1990. Ptnr. Farrish, Zimmerman, Johnson & Manahan, Mankato, Minn., 1962-72, Manahan & Bluth, Mankato, 1972—; asst. prof. mass comm. law and law enforcement Mankato State U., 1970-82; pub. defender Blue Earth County, 1980—; apptd. by Minn. Supreme Ct. to Lawyers Trust Account Bd., 1983-91, and Bd. Legal Certification, 1992-98. Chair Common Cause in Minn., 1974-75; sec. Mankato Police CSC, 1971-76; bd. dir.s Mankato LWV, 1976-78, 95—; sec.-treas. Mankato Area NOW, 1977-79; precinct chair Democratic Farm Labor Party, Mankato, 1976-78, conv. del., 1976, 78, 82, 84, 88, 98. Fellow Am. Bar Found. (life); mem. Minn. Bar Assn. (CLE lectr., 1966, 78, 82, 89, 90, 91, 92, 93, pres. 6th cist. Bar Assn. 1974-75, chair Criminal Law Sect. 1977-78, chair com. human rights 1981-83), ABA (exec. coun. Sect. Individual Rights and Responsibilities 1978-84, chair com. freedom of speech and press 1980-82, news editor Human Rights mag. 1979-92), Minn. Trial Lawyers Assn. (bd. dirs. 1990-99), Acad. Cert. Trial Lawyers of Minn. (dean 1987-88), ACLU, Minn. Civil Liberties Union (pres. 1998—), Nat. Bd. Trial Advocacy (cert. civil and criminal trial specialists 1982—), Am. Acad. Matrimonial Lawyers (pres. Minn. chpt. 1991-92, nat. bd. 1990-96). Family and matrimonial, Criminal, Personal injury. Home: 253 Arrowhead Trl Cleveland MN 56017-9776 Office: Manahan & Bluth PO Box 287 Mankato MN 56002-0287

**MANATT, SCOTT,** lawyer; b. Corning, Ark., Feb. 25, 1943; m. Sharon Manatt, Jan. 19, 1973; children: Scott Jr. (dec.), Yvette, Mitzi. BS in Bus. Adminstrn., U. Ark., JD. Bar: Ark., U.S. Dist. Ct. (ea. dist.) Ark., U.S. Ct. Appeals (8th cir.), U.S. Supreme Ct. Mem. Govs. Emergency Svcs. Adv. Bd. 1st lt. U.S. Army, 1965-67. Avocations: flying, fishing, photography, hunting, collecting. Federal civil litigation, State civil litigation, Bankruptcy. Home: PO Box 473 Corning AR 72422-0473

**MANCINI, ROSE C.,** lawyer; b. Chgo.; m. James G. Alviti, May 21, 1988; 3 children. JD, Ill. Inst. Tech., 1980; BS in Psychology, U. Ill., 1997. Bar: Ill. 1980. Asst. regional counsel Prudential Ins. Co. of Am., Chgo., 1981-85; v.p., gen. counsel Household Fin. Corp. and subs., 1985—, Household Automotive Fin. Corp., Prospect Hts., Ill., 1995—. Mem. Am. Fin. Svcs. Assn. Consumer commercial, General corporate. Office: Household Auto Fin Corp 2700 Sanders Rd Prospect Heights IL 60070-2701

**MANCUSO, ANTHONY O.,** lawyer; b. Springfield, Ohio, Aug. 3, 1961. BA in Econs., U. Dayton, 1983; JD, Ohio State U., 1986. Bar: Ohio 1986, U.S. Dist. Ct. (so. dist.) Ohio. Bailiff/law clk. Judge Deborah Pryce, Columbus, 1985-87; asst. city atty. City of Columbus, 1987-89; ptnr. Riddell & Mancuso, Columbus, 1989-97; chief atty. Mancuso & Assocs., Columbus, 1997—; faculty Am. Inst. Paralegal Studies; lectr. Parkside Lodge Weekend Seminars; lectr. in field; host Lay It on the Line, radio talk show. Past trustee Berliner Action Team for Softball. Ohio Bar Assn., Columbus Bar

Assn. (judiciary com.). Personal injury, Consumer commercial, Criminal. Office: Mancuso & Assocs 135 N Hamilton Rd Columbus OH 43230-2601

**MANDEL, DAVID MICHAEL,** lawyer; b. N.Y.C., Dec. 20, 1951; s. Seymour and Henrietta (Gersoni) M.; m. Alice Elizabeth Stanley, June 10, 1973; 1 child, Michael Stanley. BA, Yale U., 1973; JD, Harvard U., 1976. Bar: Mass. 1977, U.S. Dist. Ct. Mass. 1978, U.S. Ct. Appeals (1st cir.) 1979, U.S. Supreme Ct. 1982. Clk. Judge Murray I. Gurfein, N.Y.C., 1976-77; assoc. Ropes & Gray, Boston, 1977-1985, ptnr., 1985—. Mem. ABA (Labor and Employment sect.), Mass. Bar Assn. (Labor and Employment sect.), Sudbury (Mass.) Pers. Bd. (chair 1988-94). Labor. Office: Ropes & Gray One International Pl Boston MA 02110

**MANDEL, JOSEPH DAVID,** academic administrator, lawyer; b. N.Y.C., Mar. 26, 1940; s. Max and Charlotte Lee (Goodman) M.; m. Jean Carol Westerman, Aug. 18, 1963; children: Jonathan Scott, Eric David. AB, Dartmouth Coll., 1960, MBA, 1961; JD, Yale U., 1964. Bar: Calif. 1965. Law clk. U.S. Ct. Appeals, 9th crct., L.A., 1964-65; lectr. law U. So. Calif. Law Ctr., L.A., 1965-68; assoc. atty. Tuttle & Taylor, L.A., 1965-69, mem., 1970-82, 90-91, of counsel, 1984-90; vice chancellor UCLA, 1991—, lectr., 1993; v.p., gen. counsel, sec. Natomas Co., San Francisco, 1983; mem. Calif. Legal Corps, 1993—; bd. dirs. Legal Rsch. Network, Inc., 1993—. Pres. Legal Aid Found., L.A., 1978-79; trustee Southwestern U. Sch. Law, 1982, UCLA Pub. Interest Law Found., 1981-82, L.A. County Bar Found., 1974-79, 82, Coro Found., 1989-92, UCLA Armand Hammer Mus. Art and Cultural Ctr., 1995—, Geffen Playhouse, Inc., 1995-98; trustee Coro So. Calif. Ctr., 1985-92, bd. dirs. pub. coun., 1989-94, cmty. v.p., 1992-94; mem. L.A. Bd. Zoning Appeals, 1984-90, vice chmn., 1985-86, 89-90, chmn., 1986-87; mem. L.A. City Charter Reform Commn., 1996-99; bd. dirs. Western Justice Ctr. Found., 1989—, v.p., 1992-95, 1st v.p., 1995-97, sr. v.p., 1997—; bd. dirs. Harvard Water Polo Found., 1990-96; bd. advisors Pub. Svc. Challenge Nat. Assn. for Pub. Interest Law, 1990—; bd. govs. Inner City Law Ctr., 1991—; mem. Blue Ribbon Screening Com. to Select Insp. Gen., L.A. Police Commn., 1999; mem. bd. overseers Inst. for Civil Justice, RAND, 1999—. Recipient Maynard Toll award Legal Aid Found. of L.A., 1991, Shattuck-Price award L.A. County Bar Assn., 1993, West Coast Liberty award Lambda Legal Def. and Edn. Fund, 1994, Cmty. Achievement award Pub. Coun., 1996. Mem. State Bar Calif. (legal svcs. trust fund commn. 1985-87, chmn. 1985-86), Yale U. Law Sch. Assn. (exec. com. 1983-88, 90-96, v.p. 1986-88, chmn. planning com. 1990-92, pres. 1992-94, chmn. exec. com. 1994-96), mem. alumni Coun. Dartmouth Coll., 1992-95, Dartmouth Coll. Assn. Alumni (exec. com. 1997—). Democrat. Jewish. Home: 15478 Longbow Dr Sherman Oaks CA 91403-4910 Office: UCLA Office of the Chancellor 2135 Murphy Hl Los Angeles CA 90095-0001

**MANDEL, MARTIN LOUIS,** lawyer; b. L.A., May 17, 1944; s. Maurice S. and Florence (Byer) M.; m. Duree Dunn, Oct. 16, 1982; 1 child, Max Andrew. BA, U. So. Calif., 1965, JD, 1968; LLM, George Washington U., 1971. Bar: Calif. 1969, U.S. Dist. Ct. (cen. dist.) Calif. 1972, U.S. Ct. Claims, 1971, U.S. Tax Ct. 1971, U.S. Supreme Ct. 1972. With office of gen. csl. IRS, Washington, 1968-72; ptnr. Stephens, Jones, LaFever & Smith, L.A., 1972-77, Stephens, Martin & Mandel, 1977-79, Fields, Fehn, Feinstein & Mandel, 1979-83; sr. v.p., gen. counsel Investment Mortgage Internat., Inc., 1983-84; ptnr. Feinstein, Gourley & Mandel, 1984-85, Mandel & Handin, San Francisco, 1985—; pres. The Mandel Group, 1988—; gen. counsel L.A. Express Football Club, 1983-85; instr. corps. U. West L.A., 1973-83. Mem. ABA, L.A. County Bar Assn., L.A. Athletic Club, Phi Delta Phi. Entertainment, General corporate. Office: 1510 Fashion Island Blvd San Mateo CA 94404-1596

**MANDEL, MAURICE, II,** lawyer, educator; b. Hollywood, Calif.; s. Maurice and Wynne Mary Mandel. BSBA, U. So. Calif., 1971, MEd, 1972; JD, Western State U., 1979. Bar: Calif. 1980, U.S. Dist. Ct. (ctrl. dist.) Calif. 1982, U.S. Ct. Appeals (fed. and 9th cirs.) 1983, U.S. Dist. Ct. (we. dist.) Tenn. 1987, U.S. Dist. Ct. Ariz. 1990, U.S. Dist. Ct. (so. dist.) Calif. 1991, U.S. Supreme Ct. 1991, U.S. Ct. Appeals (5th cir.) 1995; cert. level I ski instr. PSIA Nat. Acad. 1998, child specialist 1999, settlement officer, USDC-CDCa. Tchr. Orange County (Calif.) Sch. Dist., 1972-82; pvt. practice law Newport Beach, Calif., 1982—; fed. settlement officer CDCA, 1998—; instr. Coastline C.C., 1987-95, prof., 1995—, Coastline C.C. Acad. Senate, Coastline C.C. Parlimentarian 1996-99; prof. law Irvine (Calif.) U. Coll. of Law, 1994—; instr. Orange County Bar Assn. Coll. of Trial Advocacy, 1994—; instr. Orange County Bar Assn. Mandatory Continuing Legal Edn., 1992—, Bear Mountain Calif. Ski Sch., 1996—, Ziet Maros, 1998—; FBA/OCC Mandatory Continuing Legal Edn. provider, 1994—, COURSE Vail Co. Alpine World Cup Finals, 1997, Alpine World Championships, 1999. Counselor Troy Camp, 1969-72; chmn. Legal Edn. for Youth, 1984-86; active Ctr. Dance Alliance, Orange County, 1986—; JOC racing dir. So. Cal, 1998—; mem. Friends Am. Ballet Theatre, Opera Pacific Guild, Opera Pacific Bohemians, Calypso Soc., World Wildlife Found., L.A. County Mus. Art, Newport Beach Art Mus., Met. Mus. Art, Laguna Beach Mus. Art, Smithsonian Instn., Friend of Ballet Pacifica, Friends of Joffrey Ballet; assoc. U.S. Ski Team, 1975—; com. assoc. U.S. Olympics, 1988—; 100th Olympics vols., 1996; F.I.S. vol., 1997—, COURSE Alpine World Cup Finals, Vail, Colo., 1997, Alpine World Championships, 1999; mem. alumni and scholarship com. Beverly Hills H.S.; Opera Pacific Bohemians, Friends of Ballet Pacifica. Recipient cert. of appreciation U.S. Dist. Ct., L.A., 1985, Thwarted Thwart award Newport Harbor C. of C., 1989, Tovarich award Kirov Ballet, 1989, 92, Perostroika award Moscow Classical Ballet, 1988-89, 94, Skrisivi Nogi award Bolshoi Ballet, 1990, Marinskii Dance award St. Petersburg, 1993; ABT Romeo & Juliet, 1996, Thwarted Thwart award Newport Harbor, 1996; Ziet Maros award Moscow Classical Ballet, 1998, 2nd Place award JOC Slalom, 1998. Mem. ABA, ATLA, Assn. Bus. Trial Lawyers, Federal Bar Assn., (founding pres. Orange Country chpt. 1986, nat. del. 1988-90, founder criminal indigent def. panel 1986, mem. numerous other coms., nat. chpt. activity award 1987, nat. membership award 1987, chpt. svc. award 1989, nat. regional membership chmn. 1990, spl. appointee nat. membership com. 1991), Calif. Bar Assn. (Pro Bono awards 1985-89), Pres.'s Coun. (founder 1996—), Orange County Bar Assn. (legal edn. for youth com. 1982-90, chmn, 1985, fed. practice com., sports com., mandatory fee arbitration com. 1985—, lawyer's referral svc. com. 1984—, Merit award 1986), Orange County Bar Found. (trustee 1984-87), Women Lawyers of Orange County, U.S. Supreme Ct. Hist. Soc., 9th Jud. Cir. Hist. Soc., Am. Inns of Ct., Calif. Trial Lawyers Assn., Calif. Employee Lawyers Assn., Plaintiff Employee Lawyers Assn., Employees Rights Coun., Bar Leaders Coun. Dist. 8, Amicus Publico, U. So. Calif. Alumni Assn., Mensa, Cougar Club of Am., So. Calif. Cougar Club, San Diego Cougar Club, So. Calif. Jaguar Owners Assn. Club: Balboa Yacht. Avocations: skiing, yachting, tennis. Civil rights, Federal civil litigation, Constitutional. Home: PO Box 411 Newport Beach CA 92662-0411 Office: 160 Newport Center Dr Ste 260 Newport Beach CA 92660-6969

**MANDEL, PATRICIA C.,** lawyer; b. N.Y.C., July 20, 1935; d. Herman C. Heyman and Alice Marks; m. Frederick H. Mandel, Aug. 18, 1955; children: Hillary, Lisa, Kevin. BA, CUNY, 1956; MA, NYU, 1965. Ptnr. Mandel & Mandel, N.Y.C., 1976—. Family and matrimonial, Real property, Probate. Home: 415 E Sr 5 New York NY 10022 Office: Mandel & Mandel 12 W 37th St New York NY 10018-7404

**MANDEL, REID ALAN,** lawyer; b. Mpls., Mar. 31, 1954; s. Irwin A. and Sandra Harriet (Fink) M.; m. Jeanne Claire Smith, Aug. 29, 1981. BA, Yale U., 1977; JD, NYU, 1980. Bar: Minn. 1981, Ill. 1981, U.S. Dist. Ct. (no. dist.) Ill. 1981, U. S. Tax Ct. 1981. Law clk. to justice Supreme Ct. Minn., St. Paul, 1980-81; assoc. Katten, Muchin & Zavis, Chgo., 1981-87, ptnr., 1987--; adj. prof. LLM program John Marshall Sch. Law. Contbr. articles to profl. jours. Mem. Chgo. Vol. Legal Svcs.; bd. dirs., past chmn. Chgo. Lawyers Com. for Civil Rights Under Law, 1985—. Mem. ABA, Chgo. Bar Assn. Jewish. Contracts commercial, Taxation, general, Personal income taxation. Office: Katten Muchin & Zavis 525 W Monroe St Ste 1600 Chicago IL 60661-3693

**MANDEL, SUSAN L.,** lawyer; b. Bklyn., Apr. 12, 1958; d. Henry and Libby (Dershowitz) M.; m. Michael Flaks, Aug. 23, 1981; children: Samuel, Keith. BA, Bklyn. Coll., 1978; cert., Stratford Acad., 1978; JD, Hofstra U., 1981. Bar: N.Y., U.S. Dist. Ct. (ea. and so. dist.) N.Y. Asst. dist. atty. Kings County Dist. Atty., Bklyn., 1981; hearing officer N.Y. State Dept. Social Svc., N.Y.C., 1985; pvt. practice appellate atty. Bklyn., 1985-97; adminstrv. trial atty. N.Y.C. Bd. Edn., Bklyn., 1993-98, supervising atty., 1998—; part-time hearing officer, N.Y.C., Bklyn., 1987-93. Mem. Bklyn. Bar Assn. Office: NYC Bd Edn Office Legal Svc 110 Livingston St Brooklyn NY 11201-5004

**MANDELBAUM, BARRY RICHARD,** lawyer; b. Newark, N.J., Dec. 30, 1936; s. Irving and Henrietta (Brown) M.; children: Kenneth, Lisa; m. Leslie Alexander, Oct. 30, 1983. BA, Colgate U., 1958; LLB, Columbia U., 1961. Bar: N.J. 1961, U.S. Dist. Ct. N.J. 1961. Assoc. Irving Mandelbaum, Newark, 1961-63; ptnr. Mandelbaum, Mandelbaum & Gold, Newark, 1963-79; mng. prin. Mandelbaum, Salsburg, Gold, Lazris, Discenza & Steinberg, P.A., West Orange, N.J., 1979—; bd. dirs. Warwick Ins. Co., Castle Group Inc., Commander Realty Corp., pres. bd. dirs. Growth Bank, Growth Fin. Corp., Castle Group, Inc. Atty., v.p. Mental Health Assn. of East Orange, N.J., 1964—. Mem. ABA, Essex County Bar Assn., N.J. Bar Assn., Phi Beta Kappa. Real property, Land use and zoning (including planning), General corporate. Home: 8 Byron Rd Caldwell NJ 07006-4204 Office: Mandelbaum Salsburg Gold Lazris Discenza & Steinberg 155 Prospect Ave Ste 108 West Orange NJ 07052-4204

**MANDELBAUM, SAMUEL ROBERT,** lawyer; b. N.Y.C., June 9, 1951; s. Alvin J. and Florence (Geller) M.; m. Erica Gottfried Mandelbaum, Sept. 27, 1980; children: Lia, Ben. BA, SUNY, 1973; student, Columbia U., 1974-75; JD, Vermont Law Sch., 1977; LLM, Georgetown U., 1995. Bar: Fla. 1979, N.Y. 1985, U.S. Dist. Ct. (mid. dist.) 1979, U.S. Dist. Ct. (so. dist.) 1983, U.S. Ct. Appeals (11th cir.) 1981, U.S. Ct. Appeals (4th cir.) 1984, U.S. Supreme Ct. 1982. Sr. asst. atty. gen. Atty. Gen's. Office, Tampa, Fla., 1981-82; ptnr. Smith, Williams & Bowles, Tampa, Fla., 1986-95, Becker & Poliakoff, P.A. (formerly Anderson & Orcutt, P.A.), Tampa, Fla., 1996—; adj. prof. law Stetson U. Coll. of Law, De Land, Fla., 1995—; editor, trial section Fla. Bar Jour., Tallahassee, 1988—. Fund distbr. com. mem. United Way, Tampa, Fla., 1991—. Recipient Outstanding Svc. to Ct. Arbitration Program award U.S. Dist. Ct. Fla., Tampa, 1991. Mem. Fla. Bar Assn. (exec. coun. internat. sect.), Hillsborough County Bar Assn. (chmn. internat. sect.), Davis Island Yacht Club, Rotary Club. Avocations: sailing, golf, jogging, photography. General civil litigation, Contracts commercial, Insurance. Office: Anderson & Orcutt PA 401 E Jackson St Fl 24 Tampa FL 33602-5233

**MANDELKER, LAWRENCE ARTHUR,** lawyer; b. N.Y.C., Dec. 2, 1943; s. Murray and Sally (Levine) M.; m. Carolyn Anne Bareish, Oct. 4, 1970; children—Daniel H., Benjamin E. B.A., Queens Coll., CUNY, 1964; J.D., NYU, 1968. Bar: N.Y. 1968, Pa. 1981, U.S. Dist. Ct. (so. and ea. dists.) N.Y. 1973, U.S. Dist. Ct. (ea. dist.) Wis. 1980, (no. dist.) N.Y., 1995, U.S. Ct. Appeals (2d cir.) 1979, U.S. Ct. Appeals (9th cir.) 1989. Law sec. N.Y.C. Civil Ct., 1970-71, N.Y. State Supreme Ct., 1972; mem. Kantor, Davidoff, Wolfe, Mandelker & Kass, P.C.; mem. com. character and fitness 9th Jud. Dist., Coun., N.Y. State Athletic Commn., 1995—; bd. dirs. NYU Law Alumni Assocs. Mem. Lewisboro Bd. Assessment Rev., N.Y., 1979—, chmn., 1984—; chmn. Lewisboro Bd. Ethics. Served as staff sgt. USAR, 1968-74. Mem. Assn. Bar City N.Y. Federal civil litigation, State civil litigation, Legislative. Home: 206 Todd Rd Katonah NY 10536-2410 Office: Kantor Davidoff Wolfe Mandelker & Kass PC 51 E 42nd St New York NY 10017-5404

**MANDELL, JOEL,** lawyer; b. Hartford, Conn., July 1, 1939; s. Max Edward and Harriet (Shafer) M.; m. Ellen Solomon, Aug. 23, 1964; children: Peter, Ross, Jason. BA, U. Conn., 1961, JD, 1966. Bar: Conn. 1966, U.S. Dist. Ct. Conn. 1967, U.S. Supreme Ct. 1971. Ptnr. Rosenthal, Clayman & Mandell, Hartford, 1966-72; prin. Levy & Droney, Farmington & West Hartford, Conn., 1972—; mem. adv. bd. First Am. Title Ins. Co., Hartford, 1984—. Bd. dirs. Farmington Valley Jewish Congregation, Simsbury, Conn., 1980-83; mem. State of Conn. Title Ins. Task Force, 1989-90; selectman Town of Simsbury, 1993—; mem. Town of Simsbury Charter Revision Commn., 1990-92, Simsbury Housing Authority, 1992-93. Mem. Conn. Bar Assn. (ho. of dels. 1983-86, real estate exec. com. 1978—, chmn. 1995-97), New Eng. Land Title Assn. (panel mem. 1991—, bd. dirs. 1996—), KP (chancellor comdr. 1981-82), Conn. Assn. Real Estate Profls. (panel mem. 1991, real estate exch. panel moderator 1996), Real Estate Exch., Am. Legion Simsbury. Real property. Office: Levy & Droney PC 74 Batterson Park Rd Farmington CT 06032-2565

**MANDELL, MITCHELL GREGORY,** lawyer; b. Bklyn., Sept. 20, 1960; s. Gary Victor and Geraldine Sherry (Loeffler) M.; m. Monica Lisa Nozyce, Aug. 28, 1988. BA, Rutgers U., 1982; JD, Boston U., 1985. Bar: N.Y. 1986, N.J. 1987, U.S. Dist. Ct. (so. and ea. dists.) N.Y. 1986, U.S. Dist. Ct. N.J. 1987, U.S. Ct. Appeals (2d cir.) 1987, U.S. Supreme Ct. 1989, U.S. Ct. Appeals (11th cir.) 1994, Pa. 1996, U.S. Dist. Ct. (no. dist.) N.Y. 1996, U.S. Dist. Ct. (we. dist.) N.Y. 1999. Assoc. Zane & Rudofsky, N.Y.C., 1985-87; founding ptnr. Sutton, Mandell & Sutton, N.Y.C., 1988-93; ptnr. Pollack & Green, N.Y.C., 1993—; chmn. seminar The Range of Impairment After Traumatic Brain Injury, N.Y.C., 1989; dir. Naked Angels, project ALS. Founder, Mus. Advt.; adv. counsel Am. Acad. Children's Entertainment; bd. dirs. Naked Angels. Mem. ABA, N.Y. State Bar Assn., Assn. Trial Lawyers Am., N.Y. State Trial Lawyers., Am. Arbitration Assn. (comml. arbitrator). Avocations: basketball, baseball, cigars. General civil litigation, Trademark and copyright, Bankruptcy. Office: Pollack & Greene LLP 757 3rd Ave New York NY 10017-2013

**MANDLER, THOMAS YALE,** lawyer; b. Chgo., Oct. 26, 1946; s. Martin and Florence (Hurovitz) M.; m. Cathy Jane Buchbinder, June 29, 1969; children: Lisa Beth, Amy Lyn, Jason Scott. BA, U. Wis., 1968; JD, U. Ill., 1971. Bar: Ill. 1972, U.S. Dist. Ct. (no. dist.) Ill. 1972, U.S. Ct. Appeals (7th cir.) 1972, U.S. Supreme Ct. 1976. Assoc. Goldberg, Weigle Mallin & Gitles, Chgo., 1971-74; ptnr., assoc. Jenner & Block, Chgo., 1974-85; ptnr. Arvey, Hodes, Costello, Chgo., 1985-88, Schwartz & Freeman, Chgo., 1988—. Author: Analysis of a Typical Employment Handbook, 1988, How Employers Can Minimize Employment Discrimination, 1998, Understanding the Negotiaion Process, 1987, How to Hire, Manage and Terminate Employees, 1999; mem. U. Ill. Law Rev., 1969-71; assoc. and charter editor Discipline and Discharge in Arbitration, 1998—. Pres. Sch. Dist. 113 Caucus, Highland Park, Ill., 1996-97; chmn. Highland Park Human Relations Commn., 1987-88, Highland Park Hosp. Jr. Bd., 1980-82, chmn., 1993-94; bd. dirs. Ill. Inst. Continuing Legal Edn., Chgo., 1982-95, mem. exec. com., 1988-95. Recipient Iron Cross award U Wis., 1968. Mem. ABA, Chgo. Bar Assn. Labor, General corporate. Office: Schwartz & Freeman 401 N Michigan Ave Ste 1900 Chicago IL 60611-4238

**MANEKER, MORTON M.,** lawyer; b. N.Y.C., Nov. 14, 1932; s. Arthur and Estelle (Hochberg) M.; m. Roberta S. Wexler, 1985; children: Meryl Colle, Amy Jill, Marion Kenneth. A.B., Harvard U., 1954, LL.B., 1957. Bar: N.Y. State 1957. Assoc. Shearman & Sterling, N.Y.C., 1957-62; trial atty. antitrust div. Dept. Justice, 1962-63; ptnr. Proskauer Rose LLP, N.Y.C., 1963-94. Trustee Beth Israel Hosp., N.Y.C., 1977—. Mem. Am. Law Inst., N.Y. State Bar Assn., Harvard Club (N.Y.C.), Harmonie Club. Jewish. Antitrust, Federal civil litigation, State civil litigation. Home: 30 E 65th St New York NY 10021-7005

**MANELLA, NORA M.,** federal judge. BA in Italian with highest honors, Wellesley Coll., 1972; JD, U. So. Calif., 1975. Bar: Calif. 1976, U.S. Ct. Appeals (5th cir.) 1976, D.C. Ct. Appeals 1978, U.S. Dist. Ct. (ctrl., so., no. and ea. dists.) 1980-81, U.S. Ct. Appeals (9th cir.) 1982. Law clk. to Hon. John Minor Wisdom U.S. Ct. Appeals (5th cir.), New Orleans, 1975-76; legal counsel Subcom. on Constn., Senate Com. on Judiciary, Washington, 1976-78; assoc. O'Melveny & Myers, Washington and L.A., 1978-82; asst. to U.S. Atty. U.S. Dept. Justice, L.A., 1982-90; trial asst. major crimes, 1982-85; dep. chief, criminal complaints U.S. Dept. Justice, L.A., 1986-87, chief criminal appeals, 1988-90; judge L.A. Mcpl. Ct., 1990-92; justice pro tem Calif. Ct. Appeals (2nd dist.), 1992; judge L.A. Superior Ct., 1992-93; U.S. atty. (ctrl. dist.) Calif. U.S. Dept. Justice, L.A., 1994-98; judge U.S. Dist. Ct. (cen. dist.) Calif., L.A., 1998—; instr. U.S. Atty. Gen. Advocacy Inst., 1984-86, Calif. Jud. Coll., 1992-93; mem. Atty. Gen.'s Adv. Com., 1994-95. Mem. editl. bd. State Bar Criminal Law Newsletter, 1991-92. Mem. adv. bd. Monroe H.S. and Govt. Magnet, 1991-94; acad. specialist USAID Delegation, 1993; judge L.A. Times Cmty. Partnership Awards, 1993; bd. councilors Law Sch. U. So. Calif., 1996—. Mem. Am. Law Inst., Calif. Judges Assn., Nat. Assn. Women Judges, Calif. Women Lawyers, Women Lawyers of L.A., Order of the Coif. Office: US Dist Ct 312 N Spring St Los Angeles CA 90012-4701

**MANEY, MICHAEL MASON,** lawyer; b. Taihoku, Japan, Aug. 13, 1936; s. Edward Strait and Helen M. M.; m. Suzanne Cochran, Oct. 22, 1960; 1 child, Michele. B.A., Yale U., 1956; M.A., Fletcher Sch. Law and Diplomacy, Tufts U., 1957; LL.B., U. Pa., 1964. Bar: N.Y. 1966, D.C. 1977. Case officer CIA, 1957-61; law clk. Justice John Harlan, Supreme Ct. U.S., Washington, 1964-65; asso. Sullivan & Cromwell, N.Y.C., 1965-70, ptnr., 1971-77, 81—; mng. ptnr. Sullivan & Cromwell, Washington, 1977-81; law fellow Salzburg Seminar in Am. Studies, 1967; bd. overseers Fletcher Sch. Law and Diplomacy. Trustee, Am. Found. for the Blind, Inc.; mem. bd. overseers, U. Pa. Law Sch. 1st lt. USAF. Mem. ABA, Am. Law Inst., Am. Coll. Trial Lawyers, N.Y. State Bar Assn., Union Club, Down Town Assn., Madison Beach Club, Madison Country Club, Met. Opera Club. E-mail: maney@sullcrom.com. Banking, Bankruptcy, Federal civil litigation. Home: 1220 Park Ave New York NY 10128-1733 also: 48 Neptune Ave Madison CT 06443-3210 Office: Sullivan & Cromwell 125 Broad St Fl 28 New York NY 10004-2489

**MANG, DOUGLAS ARTHUR,** lawyer; b. Little Falls, N.Y., Mar. 25, 1942; s. Willard D. and Mary L. (Murray) M.; m. Nora Ladeane Geren; 1 child, Brittany Nandeana. BS, Cornell U., 1964; LLB, Syracuse U., 1967. Bar: N.Y. 1971, Fla. 1971, U.S. Dist. Ct. (no. dist.) Fla. 1977, U.S. Ct. Appeals (5th and 11th cirs.) 1981, U.S. Dist. Ct. (mid. dist.) Fla. 1982, U.S. Supreme Ct. 1988. Atty. Mut. Life Ins. Co., N.Y.C., 1971-73; asst. gen. counsel Am. Gen. Capital Mgmt., N.Y.C., 1973-77; gen. counsel Fla. Dept. of Ins., Tallahassee, 1977-79; ptnr. Mang & Stowell PA, Tallahassee, 1979-86, Mang Law Firm PA, Tallahassee, 1986—. Served to 1st lt. U.S. Army, 1968-70, Vietnam. Mem. Assn. Trial Lawyers Am., Fla. Def. Lawyers Assn., Tiger Bay Club, Fla. Econs. Club, Rotary. Methodist. Avocations: sailing, golf. Administrative and regulatory, Federal civil litigation, Insurance. Office: Mang Law Firm PA 660 E Jefferson St Tallahassee FL 32301-2582

**MANGANO, LOUIS,** lawyer; b. Passaic, N.J., Sept. 19, 1939; s. Salvatore and Mary Mangano; m. Arlene M. Triolo, Sept. 20, 1964; children: Kenneth L., Eileen M., Louis M., Michael S. BS in Bus. Adminstrn., Seton Hall U., 1970; MA in Criminal Justice, John Jay Coll., 1973; JD, Seton Hall U., 1979. Bar: N.J. 1981, U.S. Dist. Ct. N.J. 1981, U.S. Supreme Ct. 1985. With Elmwood Park (N.J.) Police Dept., 1966-83; pvt. practice atty. Elmwood Park, 1981—; adj. prof. Fairleigh Dickinson U., Rutherford, N.J., 1973-75, Jersey City (N.J.) State Coll., 1973-75; asst. prof. William Paterson Coll., Wayne, N.J., 1983-84; adv. bd. mem. Berkeley Coll., West Paterson, N.J., 1983—. Trustee, pres. Elmwood Park (N.J.) Bd. Edn., 1980-83, 89-93. With U.S. Army, 1959-61. Mem. Bergen County Bar Assn. General practice. Office: PO Box 305 395 River Dr Elmwood Park NJ 07407-1622

**MANGIA, ANGELO JAMES,** lawyer; b. Bklyn., Mar. 12, 1954. AB in Govt. cum laude, Georgetown U., 1975; JD, St. John's U., 1978. Bar: N.Y. 1979, U.S. Dist. Ct. (so. and ea. dists.) N.Y. 1979, U.S. Ct. Appeals (2d cir.) 1985. Asst. atty. Town of North Hempstead, N.Y., 1979-81; assoc. Ain, Libert & Weinstein, Garden City, N.Y., 1981; atty. Town of North Hempstead, N.Y., 1982; counsel senate com. on crime State of N.Y., 1983-85, counsel senate com. on banks, 1985-88; chief counsel to majority N.Y. State Senate, 1989-94; managing dir. Sandler, O'Neill & Ptnrs., L.P., N.Y., 1995—. Mem. bd. editors N.Y. Law Jour., 1994-96. Recipient Outstanding Work in Field of Criminal Justice Legis. award N.Y. State Bar Assn., 1985, Disting. Svc. award Civil Trial Inst./St. John's Law Sch., 1987, Luther Gulick award for Outstanding Achievement in Pub. Svc. Long Island U., 1992; Toll fellow, 1991. Mem. ABA, Nassau County Bar Assn., Coun. of State Govts. (exec. com., intergovernmental affairs com., internat. task force, legal affairs task force, legis./exec. staff task force 1989-94), Nat. Conf. of State Legislatures. Office: 2 World Trade Ctr Fl 104 New York NY 10048-0996

**MANGINO, MATTHEW THOMAS,** lawyer; b. New Castle, Pa., Oct. 3, 1962; s. Thomas Michael and Connie (Frigone) M.; m. Juliann Galmarini, Aug. 6, 1988. BA, Westminster Coll., 1985; JD, Duquesne U., 1988. Bar: Pa. U.S. Dist. Ct. (we. dist.) Pa., U.S. Ct. Appeals (3d cir.), U.S. Supreme Ct. Jud. clk. Hon. Francis X. Caiazza, New Castle, 1988-89; asst. pub. defender County of Lawrence, New Castle, 1989; pvt. practice New Castle, 1990—; dist. atty. Lawrence County, 1998—; chmn. New Castle Airport Authority, 1990-92; solicitor County of Lawrence, New Castle, 1992-96; instr. Pa. State U., 1992—; legal cons. O.J. Simpson Trial, Sta. WBZY-AM, New Castle, 1995; bd. dirs. Allied Human Svcs.; seminar plan mem. on gang violence Pa. Bar Inst., 1996; guest lectr. Westminster Coll.; participant White House Conf. on Sch. Safety, 1998. Prodr. TV program Gang Violence Curbing the Epidemic, 1996; columnist, New Castle News, 1989-90; host TV program Lawrence County's Most Wanted; contbr. chpt. to book, article to profl. jours.; guest numerous TV news programs. Mem. campaign staff Dukakis for Pres., Pitts., 1988; del. Dem. Nat. Conv., Atlanta, 1988; com. mem. Lawrence County Econ. Devel. Corp.; sec. Lawrence County Bd. Assistance, New Castle; bd. dirs. Family Ctr. of Lawrence County, Lawrence County chpt. ARC; mem. Leadership Lawrence County, 1997, Lawrence County Pride; trustee Western Pa. Youth Devel. Ctrs. Mem. ABA (vice chmn. law and media com. 1996-97), Pa. Bar Assn. (state exec. bd. young lawyers divsn. 1994-97, jud. selection and reform com., co-chair spl. project on gang violence 1996-97), Pa. Dist. Atty.'s Assn., Lawrence County Bar Assn., Lawrence County C. of C. (bd. dirs. 1990), Wolves (bd. dirs., pres. 1996-97), Kiwanis. Roman Catholic. Avocations: golf, writing, reading. Criminal, Real property, General practice. Office: 312 N Jefferson St New Castle PA 16101-2222

**MANGLER, ROBERT JAMES,** lawyer; b. Chgo., Aug. 15, 1930; s. Robert H. and Agnes E. (Sugrue) M.; m. Geraldine M. Delich, May 2, 1959; children: Robert Jr., Paul, John, Barbara. BS, Loyola U., Chgo., 1952, MA, 1983; JD, Northwestern U., 1955. Bar: Ill. 1958, U.S. Dist. Ct. (no. dist.) Ill. 1959, U.S. Supreme Ct. 1976, U.S. Ct. Appeals (7th cir.) 1980. Author: (with others) Illinois Land Use Law, Illinois Municipal Law. Village atty., prosecutor Village of Wilmette, 1965-93; mcpl. prosecutor City of Evanston, 1963-65; chmn. Ill. Traffic Ct. Conf., 1977—; pres. Ill. Inst. Local Govt. Law; mem. home rule attys. com. Ill. Mcpl. League. Mem. ABA (chmn. adv. com. traffic ct. program), Nat. Inst. Mcpl. Law Officers (past pres.), Ill. Bar Assn. (former chmn. traffic laws and ct. com.), Chgo. Bar Assn. (former chmn. traffic ct. seminar, former chmn. traffic laws com.), Caxton Club, Phi Alpha Delta. Municipal (including bonds), General practice.

**MANGUM, JOHN K.,** lawyer; b. Phoenix, Mar. 7, 1942; s. Otto K. and Catherine F. Mangum; m. Deidre Jansen, Jan. 10, 1969; children: John Jansen, Jeffery Jansen. Student, Phoenix Coll. 1960-62; BS, U. Ariz., 1965, JD, 1969. Bar: Ariz. 1969. Sr. trial atty. criminal div. Maricopa County Atty.'s Office, Phoenix, 1969-71; ptnr. Carmichael, McClue and Stephens, P.C., Phoenix, 1972-74; sr. ptnr. O'Connor, Cavanagh, 1992-94, Phoenix; pvt. practice, Phoenix, 1994—; ct. commr., judge pro tem Maricopa County super. ct., Phoenix, 1974-78, spl. commr., 1979-82; legal csl. to speaker of Ariz. Ho. of Reps., Phoenix, 1975-86; mem. John K. Mangum and Assocs., P.C., Phoenix, 1974-92; sr. mem. O'Connor & Cavanaugh, 1992-94; pvt. practice, 1994—. Mem. Maricopa County Bd. Health, 1974-79, Ariz. State Commn. on Elected Ofcls. Salaries, 1987-93; chmn. curriculum com., mem. legal asst. adv. com. Phoenix Coll., 1973-75; legal counsel Maricopa County Rep. Com., 1986-90; mem. task force com. on career edn. Phoenix Mayor's Youth Commn., 1972-73; v.p. The Samaritans, 1984-87. Mem. State Bar Ariz. (exec. bd. young lawyers sect. 1974-76), Maricopa County Bar Assn. (pres. young lawyers sect. 1974-75, dir. 1973-75), Ariz. C. of C. (dir. 1974-79), Phoenix Country Club, Ariz. Club, Rotary. Republican. General corporate, Probate, Real property. Office: 340 E Palm Ln Ste 100 Phoenix AZ 85004-4529

**MANGUM, RONALD SCOTT,** lawyer; b. Chgo., Nov. 14, 1944; s. Roy Oliver and Marjorie Wilma (Etchason) M.; m. Kay Lynn Booton, July 14, 1973 (div. July 1983); children: Scott Arthur, Katherine Marie; m. Anna Maria Moser, Feb. 14, 1999. BA, Northwestern U., 1965, JD, 1968. Bar: Ill. 1968, Wis. 1986; lic. nursing home adminstr., Ill. Asst. atty. Northwestern U., 1968-73; assoc. Lord, Bissell & Brook, Chgo., 1974-76; ptnr. Liss,

Mangum & Beeler, Chgo., 1976-80, Mangum, Beeler, Schad & Diamond, Chgo., 1980-82, Azar, Mangum & Jacobs, Chgo., 1982-84, Mangum, Smietanka & Johnson, Chgo., 1984—; adj. instr. Mallinkroft Coll. North Shore, Wilmette, Ill.; lectr. Northwestern U., 1972-74, NYU Inst. Fed. Taxation, 1980, Loyola U. Med. Sch., Chgo., 1994-96; lectr. health care topics; faculty Healthcare Fin. Mgmt. Assn. Ann. Nat. Inst., Boulder; pres. Creative-Health Mgmt., Inc., 1978—, 1426 Chgo. Ave. Bldg. Corp., 1975-76, Parkinson Rsch. Corp., 1970-74. Author: (with R.M. Hendrickson) Governing Board and Administrator Liability, 1977, Tax Aspects of Charitable Giving, 1976, Designing Your Compliance Plan, 1997; contbr. articles to profl. jours. Commr. Evanston Preservation Commn., 1981-83; chmn. Am. Hearing Rsch. Found., 1977-79, v.p., 1972-77; bd. dirs. Episcopal Charities, 1978-80, U. Hosp. Chgo., 1989-97, sec. 1991-97; trustee Evanston Art Ctr., 1977-78; healthcare subcom. Nat. Fire Protection Assn., 1980-82; bd. dirs. Am. Schs. Profl. Psychology, Chgo., 1991-97; bd. trustees U. Sarasota, Fla., 1992-97. Col. USAR. Decorated knight Order of Jerusalem, officer Order of St. Lazarus of Jerusalem; recipient Appreciation cert. Ill. Inst. Continuing Legal Edn., 1972. Mem. ABA, NRA (life) Chgo. Bar Assn., Ill. Bar Assn., Art Inst. Chgo. (life), Civil Affairs Assn. (life), Res. Officers Assn. (life), Assn. U.S. Army, Army Res. Assn. (sec., gen. counsel, bd. dirs. 1993—), Alumni Assn. U.S. Army War Coll. (life), John Evans Club (bd. dirs.), Order Temple Jerusalem (grand croix), Order St. Lazarus Jerusalem (comdr.), Psi Upsilon. Health, General corporate, Administrative and regulatory. Home: 15106 Pleasant Valley Rd Woodstock IL 60098-8942 Office: 35 E Wacker Dr Chicago IL 60601-2103

**MANIAS, GILES PETER**, lawyer, construction executive; b. Buffalo, Apr. 2, 1943; s. Egidio G. and Beatrice A. (Amigone) M.; m. Rosemary, Jan. 15, 1969 (div. 1977); m. Jill Elizabeth Sdao, Oct. 17, 1945; children: Paul, Giles, Alexandra. AB, Canisius Coll., Buffalo; JD, SUNY, Buffalo; postgrad., U. Brussels, Belgium, 1968-71. Bar: N.Y. Assoc. Hall & McMahon, Buffalo, 1971-73; ptnr. Gorski & Manias, Buffalo, 1973-84; sole practitioner Law Offices of Giles Manias, Buffalo, 1984-99; pres. Terrastar Homes, Inc., Orlando, Fla., 1993-95; trustee Buffalo Sem. Sch., 1986-89; coun. mem. Niagara U., Lewiston, N.Y., 1990-95; mem. adv. bd. workers compensation com. N.Y. State, 1987-98. Active various pol. coms., N.Y., 1973-94; counsel labor com. N.Y. State Assembly, Albany, N.Y., 1977-81. Mem. ABA, Erie County Bar assn. (chair various coms.). Avocations: oil painting, architecture, golf. Office: Law Offices 160 North St Buffalo NY 14201-1525

**MANIBUSAN, JOAQUIN V.E., JR.**, territory supreme court justice; b. Sinajana, Guam, Dec. 10, 1949; s. Joaquin and Alejandrina M.; m. Eileen Bordallo; children: Joaquin III, Erwin, Michael, Maria. BA in Polit. Sci., U. Calif., Berkeley, 1971, JD, 1974. Asst. atty. gen. Govt. of Guam, 1975-77; pvt. practice Guam, 1977-95; justice Superior Ct. of Guam, Agana, 1995—. Vice-chmn., mem. Chalan Pago (Guam)-Ordot Mcpl. Planning Coun.; mem. Ret. Srs. Vol. Program; chmn., mem. Guam chpt. ARC; mem. Chalan Pago Parish Coun. Mem. Jr. Holy Name Soc. (pres.), Knights of Alter (v.p.). Office: Superior Ct Judiciary Ctr 120 W O'Brien Dr Agana GU 96910-5174*

**MANICO, WILLIAM M.**, prosecutor. JD, Cath. U., 1983. Homicide unit chief State Attys. Office, Upper Marlboro, Md. Office: State Attys Office Hamilton 4th fl Rm 352M Upper Marlboro MD 20772

**MANION, DANIEL ANTHONY**, federal judge; b. South Bend, Ind., Feb. 1, 1942; s. Clarence E. and Virginia (O'Brien) M.; m. Ann Murphy, June 29, 1984. BA, U. Notre Dame, 1964; JD, Ind. U., 1973. Bar: Ind., U.S. Dist. Ct. (no. dist.) Ind., U.S. Dist. Ct. (so. dist.) Ind. Dep. atty. gen. State of Ind., 1973-74; from assoc. to ptnr. Doran, Manion, Boynton, Kamm & Esmont, South Bend, 1974-86; judge U.S. Ct. Appeals (7th cir.), South Bend, 1986—. Mem. Ind. State Senate, Indpls., 1978-82. Office: US Ct Appeals US Courthouse & Federal Bldg 204 S Main St Rm 301 South Bend IN 46601-2122 Home: 20725 Riverlan Rd South Bend IN 46637-1029*

**MANION, PAUL THOMAS**, lawyer; b. Decatur, Ill., Apr. 7, 1940; s. Charles F. and Jeannette (Kaufman) M.; m. Bonnie J. Rivard, Aug. 12, 1961; children: Christine, Sheila, Tessy, Michael, Brian, Daniel. BBA in Fin., Notre Dame U., 1961; JD, DePaul U., 1964. Bar: Ill 1964, U.S. Ct. Appeals (7th cir.) 1975. Ins. investigator Hooper Holmes Bur., South Bend, Ind., 1958-61; supr. U.S. Dist. Ct., Chgo., 1961-64; asst. states atty. Iroquois County, Watseka, Ill., 1964-67; sr. ptnr. Manion, Devens & McFetridge, Ltd., Hoopeston, Ill., 1967—. Author: With Friends Like These, 1985. Mem. exec. com. Vermilion County Dem. Party, Danville, Ill., 1974—, county chmn. 1983-87; pres. Vermilion Mental Health Ctr., Danville, 1975-78. Mem. ATLA (bd. mgrs.), Ill. Bar Assn., Ill. Trial Lawyers Assn. (bd. mgrs. 1997—). Democrat. Roman Catholic. Personal injury, Workers' compensation, General practice. Home: RR 2 Box 80 Hoopeston IL 60942-9706 Office: Manion Devens & McFetridge 216 S Market St Hoopeston IL 60942-1508

**MANIRE, JAMES MCDONNELL**, lawyer; b. Memphis, Feb. 22, 1918; s. Clarence Herbert and Elizabeth (McDonnell) M.; m. Nathalie Davant Latham, Nov. 21, 1951 (div. 1979); children: James McDonnell, Michael Latham, Nathalie Manire Willard; m. Nancy Whitman Colbert, Dec. 30, 1995. LL.B., U. Va., 1948. Bar: Tenn. 1948, U.S. Supreme Ct. 1957. Pvt. practice Memphis, 1948—, city atty., 1968-71; of counsel Waring Cox, Memphis, 1986—. Editor in chief Va. Law Rev., 1947-48. Served to lt. comdr. USNR, 1941-46. Fellow Am. Coll. Trial Lawyers, Am. Bar Found. (life); mem. ABA, Tenn. Bar Assn. (pres. 1966-67), Memphis and Shelby County Bar Assn. (pres. 1963-64, Lawyer's Lawyer award 1995), Tenn. Bar Found. (charter), 6th Circuit Jud. Conf. (life), Raven Soc. Clubs: Memphis Country, Memphis Hunt and Polo. General practice. Home: 2927 Frances Pl Memphis TN 38111-2401 Office: Waring Cox PLC 1300 Morgan Keegan Twr 50 N Front St Memphis TN 38103-2126

**MANLEY, DAVID BOTT, III**, lawyer; b. Jacksonville, Fla., June 19, 1953; s. David Bott and Bernadette Claire Manley; m. Gayle Aileen Whitney, Nov. 1, 1978; children: David Jeremiah, Alexandra Ina Claire. BA with honors magna cum laude, U. Ga., 1975, JD, 1982. Bar: Ga. 1983, U.S. Dist. Ct. (no. dist.) Ga. 1983, U.S. Ct. Appeals (11th cir.) 1986. Auditor So. Hostess Sys., Inc., Augusta, Ga., 1975-76; prosecutorial asst. fraud investigator State Ga., Atlanta, 1976-79; assoc. Gadrix & Green, P.C., Atlanta, 1982-83, Lowe, Barham, Eubanks & Lowe, Atlanta, 1983-85; mem. Barham & Manley, Atlanta, 1985-89; dir., ptnr. Campbell Martin & Manley, LLP, Atlanta, 1989—; corp. counsel Highland Homes, Inc., Dallas, 1990—, Mast Advt. and Pub. Inc., Nashville, 1991—; corp. sec., counsel Agrisel USA, Inc., Atlanta and Hong Kong, 1998—. Pres. U.S. Jaycees, Mt. Park/Lilburn, 1985; cert. coach Lucky Shoals Youth Athletic Assn., Norcross, Ga., 1992-98; bd. dirs Fulton County, Ga. Dept. Family and Children's Svcs. (commendation, bd. resolution for bravery, 1978). Named Jaycee of Yr., U.S. Jaycees-Mt. Park/Lilburn, Ga., 1984. Mem. ABA, State Bar Ga. (legis. com. corp. and banking law sect. 1987-88, mem. corp. and banking law sect. 1987—, adv. mem. law revision com. 1989-90, mem. real property sect. 1996—, advocate for spl. needs children 1996—), Sandy Springs Bar Assn. (treas. 1987-88, pres. 1988-89, dir. 1989-90), Omicron Delta Kappa. Avocations: coaching youth sports, model railroading, photography, collecting, travel. General civil litigation, Real property, General corporate. Home: 4390 Flippen Trl Norcross GA 30092-3902 Office: Campbell Martin & Manley LLP 990 Hammond Dr NE Atlanta GA 30328-5529

**MANLEY, WALTER WILSON, II**, lawyer; b. Gainesville, Fla., Mar. 16, 1947; s. Walter Wilson and Marjorie Iley (Watkins) M.; children: Marjorie, Benjamin. BA, Fla. So. Coll., 1969; JD, Duke U., 1972; MBA, Harvard U., 1975. Atty. Blackwell, Walker & Gray, Miami, Fla., 1972-75; pvt. practice law Lakeland, Fla., 1975-84; prof. bus. adminstrn. Fla. State U., Tallahassee, 1985—; ptnr. MacFarlane, Ferguson, Allison & Kelly, Tallahassee, 1991-94; vis. prof. bus. adminstrn. Ridley Hall Coll. and Cambridge Fedn. Theol. Colls., Eng., 1988-90, Cambridge U. Faculties of Mgmt. Studies, Philosophy, Law, Social and Polit. Scis. and Divinity, 1989-90; pres. Exeter Leadership Cos. Inst., Inc., Tallahassee, 1989-94, Fla. North Shore Tech. Ctrs., Inc., 1995-97. Author: Critical Issues in Business Conduct, 1990, Executive's Handbook of Model Business Conduct Codes, 1991, Handbook of Good Business Practice, 1992, What Florida Thinks, 1997, The History of the Supreme Court of Florida and Its Predecessor Courts, 1821-1917, 1997 (nominated Littleton Griswold prize in Am. Law & Soc. 1998). Chmn. Fla. Endowment Found. for Vocat. Rehab., 1991-93; bd. dirs. Fla. Real Property and Casualty Joint Underwriters Assn., 1987-91, Consumer Coun. Fla., 1992—; bd. visitors Duke U. Sch. Law, 1991—; trustee The Webb Sch., BellBuckle, Tenn., 1983-92, nat. fund chmn., 1982; pres. Polk County Legal Aid Soc. Recipient Outstanding Alumnus award Fla. So. Coll., 1999. Mem. ABA, Fla. Bar Assn. (Pres.' Pro Bono Svc. award 1985), Lakeland Bar Assn. (pres.), Capital Duke Club (founder, past pres.), Tallahassee Quarterback Club Found. (past chmn., Biletnikoff award), Psi Chi, Omicron Delta Kappa, Sigma Alpha Epsilon (Nations Outstanding Educator award 1998), Phi Delta Phi. Episcopalian. Avocations: hot air balloons, gliders, fly fishing, wing shooting. Home: 2804 Rabbit Hills Rd Tallahassee FL 32312-3137

**MANLY, SAMUEL**, lawyer; b. Louisville, Aug. 8, 1945; s. Samuel III and Nell Thornton (Montgomery) M.; m. Tacie Jarrett Bond, Aug. 8, 1970 (div. 1978); children: Julie Elder, Elizabeth Meriwether. BA cum laude, Yale U., 1967; JD, U. Va., 1970. Bar: Ky. 1971, U.S. Dist. Ct. (we. and ea. dists.) Ky. 1972, U.S. Dist. Ct. (so. dist.) Ind. 1972, U.S. Dist. Ct. (we. dist.) Mich. 1995, U.S. Ct. Appeals (6th cir.) 1972, U.S. Ct. Appeals (10th cir.) 1997, U.S. Ct. Appeals (11th cir.) 1999, U.S. Ct. Appeals (7th cir., D.C. cir.) 1999, U.S. Supreme Ct. 1997. Pres. Madison House, U. Va., Charlottesville, 1968-70; assoc. Greenebaum Doll & McDonald, Louisville, 1970-76; ptnr. Reisz Blackburn Manly & Treitz, Louisville, 1976-78; sr. ptnr. Manly & Sears, Louisville, 1978-81, Manly & Heleringer, Louisville, 1981-84; pvt. practice Law Offices of Samuel Manly, Louisville, 1984—; sec., gen. counsel Gibbs-Inman Co., Louisville, 1972-78; contract atty. FDIC, Washington, 1976-84; counsel Winston Products Co., 1988—; dir. defender svcs. U.S. Dist. Ct. (we. dist.) Ky., 1992-94; mem. drug policy com. Ky. Criminal Justice Coun., 1998—. Contract atty. Jefferson County, 1977-78, City of Louisville, 1978-83. Capt. USAR, 1967-86. Fellow Ky. Bar Found. (life); mem. ABA (com. on products liability, subcom uninsured mfrs. sect. ligitation, com. on self-insurers and risk mgrs. sect. tort and ins. law practice), ATLA, Ky. Bar Assn. (com. on legal ethics 1978-84, 96—), Louisville Bar Assn., Ky. Assn. Criminal Def. Lawyers (v.p., bd. dirs., exec. com.), NACDL (v.p. 1998-99), Ky. Acad. Trial Lawyers, Fed. Bar Assn., Comml. Law League of Am., Am. Judicature Soc., Louisville Boat Club. Republican. Avocations: classical music, fishing, golf. General civil litigation, Criminal, Constitutional. Home: 407 S Sherrin Ave Louisville KY 40207-3817 Office: Law Offices of Samuel Manly 239 S 5th St Ste 1606 Louisville KY 40202-3208

**MANN, BRUCE ALAN**, lawyer; b. Chgo., Nov. 28, 1934; s. David I. and Lillian (Segal) M.; m. Naomi Cooks, Aug. 31, 1980; children: Sally Mann Stull, Jonathan Hugh, Andrew Ross. BBA, U. Wis., 1955, SJD, 1957. Bar: Wis. 1957, N.Y. 1958, Calif. 1961. Assoc. Davis, Polk & Wardwell, N.Y.C., 1957-60; assoc. Pillsbury, Madison & Sutro, San Francisco, 1960-66, ptnr., 1967-83; adminstrv. mng. dir. L.F. Rothschild Unterberg Towbin, San Francisco, 1983-87; ptnr. Morrison & Foerster, San Francisco, 1987—; cons. SEC, 1978; vis. prof. law Georgetown U., 1978; lectr. in field; mem. adv. bd. San Diego Securities Regulation Inst., 1973—. Contbr. articles to profl. jours. Served with USAR, 1957. Mem. Am. Law Inst., Am. Bar Assn. (chmn. fed. regulation of securities com. 1981-83, mem. bus. law sect. coun. 1996—, standing com. on ethics and profl. responsibility), State Bar Calif., Bar Assn. San Francisco (bd. dirs. 1974-75), Nat. Assn. Securities Dealers (gov. at large 1981-83). Club: The Family. General corporate, Mergers and acquisitions, Securities. Office: Morrison & Foerster 425 Market St Ste 3100 San Francisco CA 94105-2482

**MANN, DONEGAN**, lawyer; b. Birmingham, Ala., Mar. 6, 1922; s. Ephriam DeValse and Edna Atkins (Donegan) M.; m. Frances Virginia Hindman, Apr. 6, 1957 (dec. May 1993); m. Frances M. Jenkins, Jan. 7, 1995 (dec. Dec. 1997). Student, Birmingham-So., 1940-41; AB, George Washington U., 1947, JD, 1950. Bar: U.S. Dist. Ct. D.C. 1950, U.S. Ct. Appeals (D.C. cir.) 1950, U.S. Ct. Claims 1957, U.S. Supreme Ct. 1961, U.S. Ct. Appeals (fed. cir.) 1982. Acting bur. counsel Civil Aeronautics Bd., Washington, 1953-55; gen. rates atty. GAO, Washington, 1955-57; spl. rate counsel Gen. Svcs. Adminstrn., Washington, 1957-60; assoc. Wolf & Case, Washington, 1960-66; sr. atty., office gen. counsel. U.S. Dept. Treasury, Washington, 1966-79; of counsel Shands & Stupar, Washington, 1979-82; pvt. practice Washington, 1984—. Pres. Friends of Historic Great Falls Tavern, Inc., Potomac, Md., 1977-80, bd. dirs., 1980-83. With USN, 1943-46, PTO. Mem. ABA (treas. pub. contracts sect. 1965-66, chmn. awards com. 1975-76, svc. award sr. lawyers' divsn. 1991, counsel sr. lawyers divsn., 1995-97, chmn. guardianship and conservatorship com. 1989-95, sr. lawyers' divsn. task force to reform guardianship laws 1992-94, vice chmn., wills probate and trust com., 1995—, chmn. citizenship com. 1996-97, vice chmn. Law Day and citizenship com. 1997—), FBA, Fed. Energy Bar Assn., D.C. Bar Assn., Montgomery County Hist. Soc. (exec. v.p. 1980-83, bd. dirs. 1984-86). Democrat. Episcopalian. Avocations: fishing, hunting, golf, tennis, gardening. Administrative and regulatory, FERC practice, Taxation, general. Office: 1000 Connecticut Ave NW Ste 204 Washington DC 20036-5337

**MANN, J. KEITH**, arbitrator, law educator, lawyer; b. May 28, 1924; s. William Young and Lillian Myrle (Bailey) M.; m. Virginia McKinnon, July 7, 1950; children: William Christopher, Marilyn Keith, John Kevin, Susan Bailey, Andrew Curry. BS, Ind. U., 1948, LLB, 1949; LLD, Monmouth Coll., 1989. Bar: Ind. 1949, D.C. 1951. Law clk. Justice Wiley Rutledge and Justice Sherman Minton, 1949-50; practice, Washington, 1950; with Wage Stblzn. Bd., 1951; asst. prof. U. Wis., 1952; asst. prof. Stanford U. Law Sch., 1952-54, assoc. prof., 1954-58, prof., 1958-88, prof. emeritus 1988—, assoc. dean, 1961-85, acting dean, 1976, 81-82, cons. to provost, 1986-87; vis. prof. U. Chgo., 1953; mem. Sec. of Labor's Adv. Com., 1955-57; mem. Pres.'s Commn. Airlines Controversy, 1961; mem. COLC Aerospace Spl. Panel, 1973-74; chmn., mem. Presdl. Emergency Bds. or Bds. of Inquiry, 1962-63, 67, 71-72; spl. master U.S. vs. Alaska, U.S. Supreme Ct., 1980-97. Ensign USNR, 1944-46. Sunderland fellow U. Mich., 1959-60; scholar in residence Duke U., 1972. Mem. ABA, AAUP, Nat. Acad. Arbitrators, Indsl. Rels. Rsch. Assn., Acad. Law Alumni Fellows Ind. U., Order of Coif, Tau Kappa Epsilon, Phi Delta Phi. Editor book rev. and articles Ind. U. Law Jour., 1948-49. Democrat. Presbyterian. Home: 872 Lathrop Dr Stanford CA 94305-1053 Office: Stanford U Sch Law Stanford CA 94305-8610

**MANN, JAMES CHARLES**, lawyer; b. Oakland, Calif., Feb. 27, 1960; s. James Nelson and Patricia Ann (Hassett) M.; m. Francesca Marie Bianco, Sept. 13, 1986; 2 children. BS in Crim. Justice Adminstrn., Calif. State U., Hayward, 1982; JD, Golden Gate U., San Francisco, 1987. Bar: Calif. 1987. Legal rsch. asst. Alameda County Pub. Defender's Office, Oakland, 1984-88, dep. pub. defender, 1988—. Recipient Eagle Scout award Boy Scouts of America, 1975. Avocations: travel, sports. Office: Alameda County Pub Defenders Office 1225 Fallon St Oakland CA 94612-4278

**MANN, LAWRENCE MOSES**, lawyer; b. Wilmington, N.C., Jan. 30, 1940; s. Irving Murray and Ada (Frohm) M.; m. Susan Beth Bernstein, Dec. 1, 1961 (div. Nov. 1994); children: Rachel (dec.), Michael, Debra; m. Pat Rosenthal, Mar. 3, 1996. BA, U. N.C., 1962; LLB, Georgetown U., 1966. Bar: D.C. 1967, U.S. Dist. Ct. D.C. 1967, U.S. Ct. Appeals (D.C. and 7th cirs.), 1967, U.S. Ct. Claims, 1970, U.S. Tax Ct. 1970, U.S. Supreme Ct. 1972, U.S. Ct. Appeals (9th, 8th and 4th cirs.) 1975, U.S. Ct. Appeals (10th cir.) 1978, U.S. Ct. Appeals (11th and 5th cirs.) 1981, U.S. Dist. (ea. dist.) Ky. 1983, U.S. Ct. Appeals (3d cir.) 1987, U.S. Ct. Appeals (2d cir.) 1988, U.S. Ct. Appeals (6th cir.) 1990. Spl. asst. to Sen. Vance Hartke, U.S. Senate, Washington, 1964-65; legal asst. post office and civil svc. com. U.S. Ho. of Reps., Washington, 1965-66; counsel Commn. on Polit. Activity of Govt. Pers., Washington, 1967; ptnr. Alper, Mann & Wrisbaum and predecessors, Washington, 1968—. Author: What Every Railroad Worker Should Know About Federal Railroad Safety Laws, 1988. former mem. bd. dirs. Washington Hebrew Congregation. Mem. ABA, ATLA, Acad. Rail Labor Attys., D.C. Bar Assn. Avocations: art, collecting shells. Transportation, Personal injury, General practice. Office: Alper Mann & Weisbaum 1730 K St NW Ste 1107 Washington DC 20006-3808

**MANN, MICHAEL B.**, lawyer, educator; b. Dec. 12, 1946; s. Maurice F. and Beth B. Mann; m. Rita L. Mann; children: Beth, Kathy. BA, Loyola U., 1968; MA, U. Chgo., 1969; LLB, Loyola U., 1972. Bar: Ill., U.S. Dist. Ct. (no. dist.) Ill., U.S. Supreme Ct. Atty. Giachini & Mann, Maywood, Ill., 1974-82, Zavislak & Mann, Oak Brook, Ill., 1982—; appealate law clk. Ill. Cts., 5th Dist., 1971-72; arbitrator Ill. Ct. Sys., Cook and DuPage counties, 1988-98. Commr. Bd. of Police and Fire, Maywood, 1972-82. Mem. Ill. State Bar Assn., West Suburban Bar Assn. Avocations: sports, stamp collecting. Criminal, Federal civil litigation, Personal injury.

**MANN, PAMELA A.**, lawyer; b. Chgo., Sept. 30, 1948; d. Fred and Sada Lea (Rudin) Mann; m. Walter M. Meginniss, Jr., July 25, 1982; 1 child, Emma E. Mann-Meginniss. BA in History, Oberlin Coll., 1970; JD, U. Pitts., 1973. Bar: Pa. 1974, N.Y. 1977, U.S. Supreme Ct. 1987. Jud. law clk. Judge Marion K. Finkelhor, Pitts., 1973-74; staff atty. Susquehanna Legal Svcs., Sunburg, Pa., 1974-76; sr. staff atty. Nat. Employment Law Project, N.Y.C., 1976-82; clin. prof. Law Sch. Constnl. Litigation Clinic Rutgers U., Newark, 1982-84; dep. chief charities bur. N.Y. State Atty. Gen., N.Y.C., 1984-85, chief charities bur., 1985-95; prin. Law Offices of Pamela A. Mann, N.Y.C., 1995—; lectr. in field. Co-author: Advising Non-Profits, 1988, 2d edit. 1995; contbr. articles to profl. jours. Mem. govt. rels. com. Non-Profit Coording Com., 1996. Mem. Nat. Assn. State Charities Ofcls. (pres. 1994-95), N.Y. State Bar Assn. (charitable orgns. com. 1996—), Assn. Bar City N.Y. (com. on non-profit orgns. 1984-94, chmn. 1998—). Non-profit and tax-exempt organizations. Office: 225 Broadway Rm 2501 New York NY 10007-3001

**MANN, PHILIP ROY**, lawyer; b. N.Y.C., Jan. 31, 1948; s. Elias and Gertrude Esther (Levbarg) M. AB, Cornell U., 1968; JD, NYU, 1971, LLM, 1975. Bar: N.Y. 1972, U.S. Dist. Ct. (so. and ea. dists.) N.Y. 1973, U.S. Ct. Appeals (2nd cir.) 1973, U.S. Dist. Ct. (no. dist.) N.Y. 1974, U.S. Ct. Mil. Appeals 1974, U.S. Supreme Ct. 1975, D.C. 1976, U.S. Dist. Ct. (we. dist.) N.Y. 1976, U.S. Tax Ct. 1976, U.S. Ct. Appeals (D.C. cir.) 1978, Conn. 1983, U.S. Dist. Ct. D.C. 1983, U.S. Ct. Claims 1983, U.S. Ct. Appeals (3rd and fed. cirs.) 1983. Assoc. Levin & Weintraub, N.Y.C., 1971-74; assoc. Shea & Gould, N.Y.C., 1974-79, ptnr., 1979-84; sole practice N.Y.C., 1984—. Lt. col. J.A., USAR, 1969—. Mem. ABA, Fed. Bar Assn. Democrat. Jewish. Bankruptcy, Contracts commercial. Home and Office: 250 E 87th St Apt 26H New York NY 10128-3117

**MANN, RICHARD EVANS**, lawyer, arbitrator; b. Jacksonville, Ill., Jan. 9, 1922; s. Roberts John and Lecie Evans M.; m. Theodosia Ross, June 17, 1943; children: Theodosia Evans, Kristin, Richard R., Kathryn Herring, William P. AB, U. Ill., 1946, JD, 1947. State's atty. Scott County, Winchester, Ill., 1948-60; ptnr. Hutchens & Mann, Winchester, Ill., 1948-80; cir. judge 7th Jud. Cir., Winchester, Ill., 1980-88; ptnr. Bell & Mann, Winchester, Ill., 1988—. 1st lt. U.S. Army AC, 1942-45. Republican. Episcopalian. Probate, Real property, Alternative dispute resolution. Home: RR 2 Box 108 Winchester IL 62694-9534 Office: Bell & Mann PO Box 109 Winchester IL 62694-0109

**MANN, RICHARD LYNN**, lawyer; b. Columbus, Ohio, June 22, 1946; s. Clyde Earl and Kathryn Ann (Mock) M.; children: Richard Sean, Shannon Michele. BA, Ohio State U., 1968, JD, 1971. Bar: Ohio 1972, U.S. Dist. Ct. (so. dist.) Ohio 1979. Ptnr. Bolla, Mann & Caulfield, Columbus, 1973-76, Caulfield & Mann, Columbus, 1976-78, Mann & Stuhr, Columbus, 1978-81, White, Rankin, Co., L.P.A., Columbus, 1981-88, Shrim and Henry, 1988-89; atty., pvt. practice, 1989—; state counsel Ohio Assn. Secondary Adminstrs., Columbus, 1976—; lawyer; b. Columbus, Ohio, June 22, 1946; s. Clyde Earl and Kathryn Ann (Mock) M.; children: Richard Sean, Shannon Michele. BS, Ohio State U., 1968, JD, 1971. Bar: Ohio 1972, U.S. Dist. Ct. (so. dist.) Ohio 1979. Ptnr. Bolla, Mann & Caulfield, Columbus, 1973-76, Caulfield & Mann, Columbus, 1976-78, Mann & Stuhr, Columbus, 1978-81; ptnr. White, Rankin, Co., L.P.A., Columbus, 1981-88, Shrim and Henry, 1988-89; atty., pvt. practice, 1989—; state counsel Ohio Assn. Secondary Adminstrs., Columbus, 1976-86. Author article series Legal Notes, 1976-86; co-author pamphlet Due Process in Schools, 1977, Ohio Title Insurance PSI, 1990, OKID Title Insurance Ipdate PSI, 1994. Served to 1st lt. U.S. Army, 1971-73. Decorated Army Commendation medal. Mem. Edn. & Law Assn. Republican. Club: Little Turtle Country (Westerville, Ohio). Author article series Legal Notes, 1976—; co-author pamphlet Due Process in Schools, 1977, Ohio Title Insurance PSI, 1990, OKID Title Insurance Ipdate PSI, 1994. Served to 1st lt. U.S. Army, 1971-73. Decorated Army Commendation medal. Mem. Edn. & Law Assn. Republican. Club: Little Turtle Country (Westerville, Ohio). Real property, Administrative and regulatory, Education and schools.

**MANN, ROBERT DAVID**, lawyer; b. Chgo., May 27, 1941; s. Robert Lewis and Leona M. (Merillat) M. BA, DePauw U., 1963; JD, Ind. U., 1966. Bar: Ind. 1966, U.S. Dist. Ct. (so. dist.) Ind. 1966. Ptnr. Baker, Andrews Barnhart, et al., Bloomington, Ind., 1966-74, Andrews, Harrell, Mann, et al., P.C., Bloomington, 1974—; bd. dirs. Citizens Bank Ctrl. Ind., Bloomington Community Found. Chmn., mem. Bd. Pub. Safety City of Bloomington, 1969-72; chmn., bd. dirs. South Cen. Community Mental Health Ctrs., Inc., Bloomington, 1968-74; pres., bd. dirs. Mental Health Assn. of Monroe County, Bloomington, 1972; bd. dirs. WonderLab Mus., 1997—, Bloomington Area Arts Coun., 1997—. Fellow Ind. Bar Found.; mem. ABA (constrn. forum), Am. Assn. Arbitrators (former constrn. arbitrator), Ind. State Bar Assn., Monroe County Bar Assn. (pres. 1988-89), Assn. Trial Lawyers Am., Ind. Trial Lawyers Assn., Ind. Assn. Mediators (cert. mediator), Greater Bloomington C. of C. (bd. dirs., sec. 1969). Fax: 812-331-4511. E-mail: bobmann@ahmcc.com. Construction, General corporate, Insurance. Office: Andres Harrell Mann et al PC PO Box 2639 1720 N Kinser Pike Bloomington IN 47402

**MANN, ROBERT PAUL**, lawyer; b. Pitts., July 24, 1929; s. O. Paul and Floy Melinda (Foster) M.; m. Dorothy Neeld, Sept. 4, 1953; children: Robin Duvall Francik, Stewart Neeld Mann. BS, U. Md., College Park, 1951; JD, U. Md., Balt., 1953. Bar: Md. 1954, U.S. Dist. Md. 1965, U.S. Tax Ct. 1976. Pvt. practice Ruxton, Md. Probate.

**MANN, ROBERT TRASK**, lawyer, educator; b. Tarpon Springs, Fla., June 5, 1924; s. William Edgar and Lenora Eunice (Trask) M.; m. Elizabeth Brown, Dec. 27, 1947; children: Robert Trask, Margaret Elizabeth. BSBA, U. Fla., 1946, JD, 1951; MA in Govt., George Washington U., 1948; LLM, Harvard U., 1953, Yale U., 1968; LLD (hon.), Stetson U., 1979. Bar: Fla. 1951, Mass. 1952, U.S. Supreme Ct. 1960. Asst. prof. law Northeastern U., 1951-53; sole practice Tampa, Fla., 1953-68; judge 2d dist. Fla. Ct. Appeal, 1968-74, chief judge, 1973-74; prof. law U. Fla., Gainesville, 1974-86, prof. emeritus, 1986—; vis. prof. Herbert Herff chair excellence in law Memphis State U., spring 1987, 88. Editor-in-Chief U. Fla. Law Rev., 1951; contbr. articles to profl. jours. Mem. Fla. Pub. Service Commn., Tallahassee, 1978-81, chmn. 1979-81, Fla. Ho. of Reps., 1956-68; mem. Gen. Bd. Christian Social Concerns, 1960-70, treas., 1960-64; mem. Commn. on Status and Role of Women, United Meth. Ch., 1972-76, S.E. jurisdictional council, 1960-68; del. gen. conf., 1960, 64, 68, 72, lay leader Tampa dist., 1956-66; trustee Lake Junaluska Assembly, 1972-80. Recipient Most Outstanding Rep. award St. Petersburg (Fla.) Times, 1967, Disting. Service award Tampa Jaycees, 1958. Fellow Am. Bar Found. (life); mem. ABA, Am. Law Inst., Am. Judicature Soc. Democrat. Club: Rotary. Home: 1326 Riverside Ave Tarpon Springs FL 34689-6613

**MANN, SAM HENRY, JR.**, lawyer; b. St. Petersburg, Fla., Aug. 2, 1925; s. Sam Henry and Vivian (Moore) M.; m. Mary Joan Bishop, Sept. 7, 1948; children: Vivian Louise, Sam Henry III, Wallace Bishop. BA, Yale U., 1948; LLB, Fla. U., 1951, JD, 1967. Bar: Fla. 1951, U.S. Dist. Ct. (mid. and so. dists.) Fla. 1951, U.S. Ct. Appeals (5th cir.) 1955, U.S. Ct. Appeals (11th cir.) 1996, U.S. Supreme Ct. 1971. Ptnr. Greene, Mann, Rowe, Stanton, Mastry & Burton, St. Petersburg, 1951-84, Harris, Barrett, Mann & Dew, St. Petersburg, 1984—. Trustee, v.p. Mus. Fine Arts, St. Petersburg, 1980-94, Eckerd Coll., St. Petersburg, 1976-79, Webb Sch., Bell Buckle, Tenn., 1966-75; bd. dirs. Regional Community Blood Ctr., St. Petersburg, 1966—, Fla. Blood Svcs., 1993-94, mem. emeritus 1996—; mem. Disting. Alumni Soc. Webb Sch.; mem., chmn. H. Milton Rogers Heart Found.; bd. dirs., pres. Family and Children's Svc., Inc., 1956-61. Lt. (j.g.) USNR, 1943-48. Fellow Am. Coll. Trial Lawyers, Am. Bar Found., Fla. Bar Found.; mem. ABA, Fla. Bar Assn., Fla. Supreme Ct. Hist. Soc., Am. Counsel Assn., Def. Rsch. Inst., Internat. Assn. Def. Counsel, Pinellas County Trial Lawyers Assn., Nat. Assn. Railroad Trial Counsel, Fla. Def. Lawyers Assn., Assn. Hospt. Attys., Bay Area Vanderbilt, St. Petersburg Bar Assn., Yale and U. Fla. Alumni Assns., Phi Alpha Delta. Republican. Presbyterian. Avocations: RV travel, boating, gardening, workshop. General civil litigation,

Personal injury, Probate. Home: 531 Brightwaters Blvd NE Saint Petersburg FL 33704-3713 Office: Harris Barrett Mann & Dew Ste 1500 Southtrust Bank Bldg Saint Petersburg FL 33731-1441

**MANN, STUART D.,** lawyer; b. Chgo., Mar. 24, 1960; s. Robert E. and Sylvia A. Mann; m. Sara Margaret Williams, May 27, 1990; children: Siena, Kaia. BS, U. Colo., 1983; JD, U. Denver, 1986. Ptnr. Beem & Mann, Denver, 1987—; assoc. prof. Denver Paraletal Inst., 1988-90. Contbr. articles to profl. jours. Mem. Colo. Trial Lawyers Assn., Colo. Bar Assn., Denver Kickers Sports Club. General civil litigation, Real property, Personal injury. Home: 2880 21st St Boulder CO 80304-2708 Office: Beem & Mann PC 1700 Lincoln St Ste 3901 Denver CO 80203-4539

**MANN, WILLIAM CRAIG,** lawyer; b. Norwalk, Ohio, Nov. 17, 1953; s. Abraham and Shirley (Smith) M. BA, Case Western Res. U., 1976; JD, U. Dayton, 1979. Bar: Ohio 1979, U.S. Dist. Ct. (no. dist.) Ohio 1979, U.S. Supreme Ct. 1986, U.S. Dist. Ct. (so. dist.) Ohio 1988. Law clk. Ohio Supreme Ct., 1985-86; pvt. practice Cleve., 1986-87; assoc. Wolske & Blue, Columbus, Ohio, 1987-97; ptnr. Sunbury, Mann & Young, Columbus, 1997—, Mitchell, Allen, Catalano & Boda, Columbus, 1999—; spkr. various orgns. in field, including Ohio Legal Ctr. Inst., Ohio Acad. of Trial Lawyers; mem. Ohio Supreme Ct. commn. on professionalism; trustee Franklin County Trial Lawyers Assn., 1995—. Contbr. articles to profl. jours. Bd. dirs. United Way, Huron County, Ohio, 1983; mem. exec. and cen. coms. Huron County Dem. Com., 1976-79. Mem. Ohio State Bar Assn. (ethics com. 1987—), Columbus Bar Assn., Ohio Acad. Trial Lawyers. Avocations: football, jogging. Personal injury, Insurance, Product liability. Home: 2041 Ramblewood Ave Columbus OH 43235-7340 Office: Mitchell Allen Catalano & Boda 490 S High St Columbus OH 43215-5603

**MANNE, HENRY GIRARD,** lawyer, educator; b. New Orleans, May 10, 1928; s. Geoffrey and Eva (Shainberg) M.; m. Bobbette Lee Taxer, Aug. 19, 1968; children: Emily Kay, Geoffrey Adam. B.A., Vanderbilt U., 1950; J.D., U. Chgo., 1952; LL.M., Yale U., 1953, J.S.D., 1966; LLD, U. Puget Sound, 1987, U. Francisco Marroquin, Guatemala, 1987. Bar: Ill. 1952, N.Y. 1969. Practice in Chgo., 1953-54; assoc. prof. Law Sch., St. Louis U., 1956-57, 59-62; prof. Law Sch., George Washington U., 1962-68; Kenan prof. law and polit. sci. U. Rochester, 1968-74; Disting. prof. law, dir. Law and Econs. Center, U. Miami Law Sch., 1974-80; prof. law Law and Econs. Center, Emory U., Atlanta, 1980-86; dean Law Sch., chmn. Law and Econs. Ctr. George Mason U., 1986-96, univ. prof., 1986-99; vis. prof. law U. Wis., Madison, 1957-59, Stanford (Calif.) Law Sch., 1971-72; dir. Econs. Insts. Fed. Judges, 1976-89. Author: Insider Trading and the Stock Market, 1966, (with H. Wallich) The Modern Corporation and Social Responsibility, 1973, (with E. Solomon) Wall Street in Transition, 1974, Med. Malpractice Guidebook: Law and Economics, 1985; editor: (with Roger LeRoy Miller) Gold, Money and the Law, 1975; editor: (with Roger LeRoy Miller) Auto Safety Regulation: The Cure or the Problem, 1976, Economic Policy and the Regulation of Corporate Securities, 1968, The Economics of Legal Relationships, 1975; editor: (with James Dorn) Econ. Liberties and the Judiciary, 1987. Served to 1st lt. USAF, 1954-56. Recipient Salvatori award Excellence in Acad. Leadership, 1994; named Cultural Laureate of Va., 1992. Fellow Am. Bar Found.; mem. Am. Law Inst., Am. Econs. Assn., Am. Law and Econs. Assn. (hon. life), Mont Pelerin Soc., Order of Coif, Phi Beta Kappa.

**MANNHEIMER, MICHAEL JAY,** lawyer; b. Bklyn., Jan. 12, 1969; s. Ralph and Roberta Helene (Shulman) M. BA, SUNY, Binghamton, 1991; JD, Columbia U., 1994. Bar: N.Y. 1995, U.S. Dist. Ct. (so. dist.) N.Y. 1996, U.S. Dist. Ct. (ea. dist.) N.Y. 1997, U.S. Ct. Appeals (3d cir.) 1997. Staff atty. Legal Aid Soc., N.Y.C., 1994-95; law clk. to Hon. Sidney H. Stein U.S. Dist. Ct. (so. dist.) N.Y., N.Y.C., 1995-96; law clk. to Hon. Robert E. Cowen U.S. Ct. Appeals (3d cir.) N.J., Trenton, 1996-97; assoc. Paul, Weiss, Rifkind, Wharton & Garrison, N.Y.C., 1997—. Contbr. articles to profl. jours. Recipient Pro Bono award Legal Aid Soc., 1998. Mem. Bar Assn. City N.Y. Avocations: writing, golf, travel, film, bicycling. General civil litigation, Product liability. Home: 9 Barrow St Apt 4C New York NY 10014-3863 Office: Paul Weiss Rifkind Wharton & Garrison Rm 200 1285 Avenue Of The Americas New York NY 10019-6065

**MANNINA, GEORGE JOHN, JR.,** lawyer; b. Washington, Oct. 14, 1949; s. George J. Sr. and Mary Lee (Shupe) M.; m. Susan Marie Mannina, Mar. 15, 1975; 1 child, Christopher. BS, Cornell U., 1971; JD, Am. U., 1979. Bar: U.S. Dist. Ct. D.C. 1985, U.S. Ct. Appeals (D.C. cir.) 1985, U.S. Claims Ct. 1987, U.S. Ct. Appeals (7th cir.) 1995, U.S. Ct. Appeals (fed. cir.) 1988, U.S. Supreme Ct. 1996. Adminstrv. aide Congressman Gude, Washington, 1971-73; legis. dir. Congressman Forsythe, Washington, 1973-75; consel subcom. Fisheries, Wildlife Conservation and Environment, Washington, 1975-82; chief minority counsel, staff dir. House Merchant Marine and Fisheries Com., Washington, 1982-85; partner O'Connor & Hannan, LLP, Washington, 1985—. Recipient Emily Dworkin award Montgomery County (Md.) Commn. Children and Youth, 1996. Mem. ABA, D.C. Bar Assn., Lutheran Ch. St. Andrew (chairman youth bd., 1980—). Republican. Avocations: gardening, photography. Environmental, Administrative and regulatory, Legislative. Office: O'Connor & Hannan LLP 1919 Pennsylvania Ave NW Washington DC 20006-3404

**MANNING, CAROL A.,** editor. Editor Okla. Bar Jour., Oklahoma City. Office: Okla Bar Assn Dir Pub Info PO Box 53036 Oklahoma City OK 73152-3036

**MANNING, G(ERALD) STEPHEN,** lawyer; b. Maysville, Ky., Oct. 14, 1948; s. Walter Lee Manning and Loretta (Simms) McDowell; m. Amy Sue VanderHorst, Feb. 4, 1978; children: Joshua Stephen, Mary Catlin. Student, Ea. Ky. U., 1966-68; BA, U. Ky., 1971, JD, 1974. Bar: Ky. 1974, U.S. Dist. Ct. (ea. dist.) Ky. 1974, U.S. Supreme Ct. 1987, Fla. 1989, U.S. Dist. Ct. (mid. dist.) Fla. 1989. Ptnr. Oliver & Manning, Berea, Ky., 1974-77; pub. defender Office of Pub. Advocacy, Maysville, 1977-80; mng. ptnr. Manning, Bogucki & Ross, Maysville, 1980-84; sr. trial atty. environ. enforcement sect. U.S. Dept. Justice, Washington, 1984-88; assoc. Rogers, Towers, Bailey, Jones & Gay, Jacksonville, Fla., 1988-89; sr. assoc. Mahoney, Adams & Criser, Jacksonville, 1989-91; gen. counsel Environ. Capital Holdings, Inc., Jacksonville, 1991-92; shareholder Cowles & Manning, P.A., Jacksonville, 1992—. Mem. Fla. Assn. Environ. Profls. (dir. N.E. chpt. 1990-91), Nat. Assn. Environ. Profls. Democrat. Methodist. Avocation: golf. Environmental, General corporate, Land use and zoning (including planning). Home: 12163 Twain Oaks Ln Jacksonville FL 32223-3251 Office: Cowles & Manning 7077 Bonneval Rd Jacksonville FL 32216-6010

**MANNING, KENNETH ALAN,** lawyer; b. Buffalo, July 22, 1951; Jack Edwin and Dorothea Ann (Ruhland) M.; m. Diane Louise Garrold, Aug. 11, 1973; children: Michael John, Kathryn Ann. BS in Engring. Sci., SUNY, Buffalo, 1974, JD, 1977. Bar: N.Y. 1978, U.S. Dist. Ct. (we. dist.) N.Y. 1978, U.S. Dist. Ct. (no. dist.) N.Y. 1980, U.S. Ct. Appeals (2d cir.) 1983, U.S. Ct. Appeals (3d cir.) 1988. Confidential law asst. to assoc. justice Appellate Div. 4th Dept., Buffalo, 1977-79; assoc. Phillips, Lytle, Hitchcock, Blaine & Huber, Buffalo, 1979-84, ptnr., 1985—. Vol. Lawyers Project, Erie County, 1985—, Criminal Appeals Program, Erie County, 1988-89; mem. coun. Western N.Y. region NCCJ. Woodburn fellow SUNY, Buffalo, 1973-76. Mem. ABA (TIP sect.), N.Y. State Bar Assn. (ins. negligence sect.), Erie County Bar Assn., Gyro Club (pres. 1988), Park Club. Avocations: sports, hunting. Federal civil litigation, General civil litigation. Office: Phillips Lytle Hitchcock Blaine & Huber 3400 Marine Midland Ctr Buffalo NY 14203-2887

**MANNING, STEVEN DONALD,** lawyer; b. Glendale, Calif., Oct. 21, 1953; s. Donald Owen and Rose Margaret Manning; children: Christie Manning, Michelle Manning. BS, Calif. State U., L.A., 1976; JD, Whittier Coll., 1979. Bar: Calif. 1979, U.S. Dist. Ct. 1980, U.S. Ct. Appeals (9th cir.) 1980. Atty. Ray, rolston & Ress, L.A., 1979-80; ptnr., atty. Morris, Polich & Pardy, L.A., 1980-94; founding and mng. ptnr. Manning, Marder & Wolfe, L.A., 1994—. Avocations: karate, skiing, water skiing, dirt bikes, scuba diving. Federal civil litigation, State civil litigation, Civil rights. Office: Manning Marder & Wolfe 707 Wilshire Blvd Fl 45 Los Angeles CA 90017-3501

**MANNING, VICTORIA ANNE,** lawyer; b. Passaic, N.J., Aug. 28, 1961; d. Thomas Foxhall Schaffran; m. William J. Manning Jr., Jan. 17, 1988; 1 child, William Foxhall. BA, Montclair State Coll., 1987; JD, Seton Hall U., 1990. Bar: N.H. 1990, Maine 1990, N.J. 1991, D.C. 1992. Assoc. Morgan Melhuish Monaghan Arvidson Abrytyn & Lisowski, Livingston, N.J., 1991-93, Epstein, Brown, Markowitz & Gioia, Chatham Township, N.J., 1993—. Mem. N.J. Assn. Women Bus. Owners. General civil litigation, Environmental. Office: Epstein Brown Markowitz & Gioia 245 Green Village Rd Chatham Township NJ 07928

**MANNING, WILLIAM HENRY,** lawyer; b. Dallas, Feb. 5, 1951. BA, Creighton U., 1973; JD, Hamline U., 1978. Bar: Minn. 1978, U.S. Dist. Ct. Minn. 1978, U.S. Ct. Appeals (8th cir.) 1979; cert. civil trial specialist. Spl. asst. atty. gen. Minn. Atty. Gen.'s Office, St. Paul, 1980-83, dir. tort litigation div., 1984-86; ptnr. Robins, Kaplan, Miller & Ciresi, Mpls., 1986—. General civil litigation, Personal injury, Product liability. Office: Robins Kaplan Miller & Ciresi 800 Lasalle Ave Ste 2800 Minneapolis MN 55402-2015

**MANNINO, EDWARD FRANCIS,** lawyer; b. Abington, Pa., Dec. 5, 1941; s. Sante Francis and Martha Anne (Hines) M.; m. Mary Ann Vigilante, July 17, 1965 (div. 1990); m. Antoinette K. O'Connell, June 25, 1993; children: Robert John, Jennifer Elaine. BA with distinction, U. Pa., 1963, LLB magna cum laude, 1966. Bar: Pa. 1967. Law clk. 3d cir. U.S. Ct. Appeals, 1966-67; assoc. Dilworth, Paxson, Kalish & Kauffman, Phila., 1967-71, ptnr., 1972-86, co-chmn. litigation dept., 1980-86, sr. ptnr., 1982-86; sr. prin. Elliott, Mannino & Flaherty, PC, Phila., 1986-90; chmn. Mannino Griffith PC, Phila., 1990-95; sr. ptnr. Wolf, Block, Schorr & Solis-Cohen, Phila., 1995-98; ptnr. Akin, Gump, Strauss, Hauer & Feld LLP, Phila., 1998—; hearing examiner disciplinary bd. Supreme Ct. Pa., 1986-89; lectr. Temple U. Law Sch., 1968-69, 71-72; mem. Phila. Mayor's Sci. and Tech. Adv. Com., 1976-79; mem. adv. com. on appellate ct. rules Supreme Ct. Pa., 1989-95; project mgr. Pa. Environ. Master Plan, 1973; chmn. Pa. Land Use Policy Study Adv. Com., 1973-75; chmn. adv. com., hon. faculty history dept. U. Pa., 1980-85. Author: Lender Liability and Banking Litigation, 1989, Business and Commercial Litigation: A Trial Lawyer's Handbook, 1995, The Civil RICO Primer, 1996; mem. editl. bd. Litigation mag., 1985-87, Comm. Lending Litigation News, 1988—, Bank Bailout Litigation News, 1989-93, Bus. Torts Reporter, 1988—, Practical Litigator, 1989—, Civil RICO Report, 1991—; contbr. articles to profl. jours. Pres. parish coun. Our Mother of Consolation Ch., 1977-79; bd. overseers U. Pa. Sch. Arts and Scis., 1985-89, chmn. recruitment and retention of faculty com.; commonwealth trustee Temple U., 1987-90, mem. audit, bus. and fin. coms. Named one of Nation's Top Litigators Nat. Law Jour., 1990. Fellow Am. Bar Found., ABA (chmn. various coms.), Am. Law Inst., Hist. Soc. U.S. Dist. Ct. Ea. Dist. Pa. (bd. dirs.), Pa. Bar Assn., Phila. Bar Assn. (gov. 1975), Order of Coif, Phi Beta Kappa, Phi Beta Kappa Assocs. Democrat. Antitrust, General civil litigation, Professional liability. Office: Akin Gump Strauss Hauer & Feld LLP One Commerce Sq 2005 Market St Ste 2110 Philadelphia PA 19103-7073

**MANNINO, ROBERT JOHN,** lawyer; b. Phila., July 20, 1968; s. Edward Francis and Mary Ann Mannino. BA, U. Pa., 1991; JD cum laude, Am. U., 1995. Bar: Pa. 1995, N.J. 1995, U.S. Dist. Ct. N.J. 1995, U.S. Dist. Ct. (ea. dist.) Pa. 1996. Intern U.S. Dept. Justice, Washington, summers 1993-94, U.S. Senate Com. on the Judiciary, Washington, 1994; student atty. D.C. Law Students in Ct., Washington, 1994-95; assoc. Lavin, Coleman, et al, Phila., 1995-97, Gollatz, Griffin & Ewing, Phila., 1997—. Com. person Rep. Party, Phila., 1989-91; rsch. asst. Ref. Manual Chpts., U.S. Tax Manual Criminal Tax Sects., summer 1993. Mem. Penn Club N.Y.C. Roman Catholic. General civil litigation, Product liability, Labor. Office: Gollatz Griffin & Ewing 16th Fl Two Penn Center Philadelphia PA 19102

**MANNIS, ESTELLE CLAIRE,** lawyer; b. Chgo., Jan. 23, 1936; d. Carl L. and Sara (Landman) Kaplan; divorced; children: Kent L. Mannis, Kim I. Mannis. AA, L.A. City Coll., 1955; BA, Calif. State U., Hayward, 1965, MA, 1975; JD, Lincoln U., San Francisco, 1979. Bar: Calif. 1979, U.S. Ct. Appeals (9th cir.) 1979, U.S. Dist. Ct. (no. dist.) Calif. 1980, U.S. Dist. Ct. (cen. and ea. dists.) Calif. 1981, U.S. Dist. Ct. (so. dist.) Calif. 1982. Corp. counsel Bill Henson Co., Inc., Hayward, Calif., 1981-84; pvt. practice Oakland, Calif., 1984—. Editor Rhetorical Criticism Jour., 1975; editor: Law Review, Lincoln University, 1976-77. Active Landmarks Preservation Adv. Bd., Oakland, 1989-95, chair 1990-92. Mem. Alameda County Bar Assn., L.A. County Bar Assn. Avocation: skiing. Bankruptcy, Real property, General civil litigation. Office: 460 Mandana Blvd Oakland CA 94610-2005

**MANNIS, VALERIE SKLAR,** lawyer; b. Green Bay, Wis., May 26, 1939; d. Phillip and Rose (Aaron) Sklar; m. Kent Simon Mannis, Dec. 28, 1958; children: Andrea, Marci. BS, U. Wis., 1970, JD, 1975, PhD, 1997. Bar: Wis. 1974. Staff atty. Legis. Coun., Madison, Wis., 1974-75; sole practice Madison, 1975-84; asst. to pres. Bank of Shorewood Hills, Wis., 1984-86; trust officer, sr. account exec. First Wis. Nat. Bank, Madison, 1986-90; devel. dir. YWCA-Madison, 1990-92; assoc. lectr. U. Wis., Madison, 1997—. Pres. Nat. Women's Polit. Caucus Dane County, Madison, 1984; bd. dirs. Madison Estate Planning Coun., 1980-84, Madison Jewish Cmty. Coun., 1975-79, 82-84. Mem. State Bar Wis. (gov. 1980-86), Dane County Bar Assn. (chmn. property com. 1978-84), Legal Assn. for Women (founding), Bus. Forum Bd. (bd. dirs. 1988-91, 98—), Rotary (pres. 1992-93). Estate planning, Family and matrimonial. Office: Univ Wis Child Family Studies Bldg 1430 Linden Dr Madison WI 53706-1537

**MANOS, JOHN M.,** federal judge; b. Cleve., Dec. 8, 1922; m. Viola Manos; 4 children. BS, Case Inst. Tech., 1944; JD, Cleve.-Marshall Coll. Law, 1950. Bar: Ohio 1950. Asst. plant mgr. Lake City Malleable Iron Co., Cleve., 1946-50; atty. Manos & Manos, 1950-63; law dir. City of Bay Village, 1954-56; industries rep. Cleve. Regional Bd. of Rev., 1957-59; judge Ohio Ct. Common Pleas, Cuyahoga County, 1963-69, Ohio Ct. Appeals, Cuyahoga County, 1969-76; sr. judge U.S. Dist. Ct. (no. dist.) Ohio, Cleve., 1976—. With USN, 1942-45. Named Phi Alpha Delta Man of Yr., 1972, Outstanding Alumnus Cleve.- Marshall Law Alumni Assn., 1976. Mem. ABA, Fed. Bar Assn., Ohio State Bar Assn., Nat. Lawyers Club (hon.), Bar Assn. Greater Cleve., Cuyahoga County Bar Assn., Delta Theta Phi (Man of Yr. 1970). Office: US Dist Ct Key Tower 201 Superior Ave E Cleveland OH 44114-1201

**MANSFIELD, CHRISTOPHER CHARLES,** insurance company legal executive; b. 1950; married. BA, Boston Coll., 1972, JD, 1975. With Liberty Mut. Ins. Co., Boston, 1975—, v.p., 1983, sr. v.p., gen. counsel, 1983—; underwriter Liberty Lloyds of Tex. Ins. Co., 1984-94; v.p., dir. Liberty Ins. Corp., 1985—; v.p. Liberty Mut. Fire Ins. Co., 1985—, Stein Roe Svcs. Co., 1986-95; v.p., gen. counsel LEXCO Ltd., 1986—; sr. v.p., gen. counsel Liberty Mut. Capital Corp., 1986—; bd. dirs. Liberty Fin. Cos., Liberty Mut. Bermuda, Liberty Internat., Employers Ins. Wausau, Golden Eagle Ins. Corp., Wausau Gen. Ins. Co. Office: Liberty Mut Ins Co PO Box 140 175 Berkeley St Boston MA 02116-5066

**MANSFIELD, JAMES NORMAN, III,** lawyer; b. Chattanooga, Feb. 15, 1951; s. James Norman and Doris June (Hilliard) M.; m. Terry Ann Thomas, Dec. 28, 1975; children: Seth Thomas, James Norman, Scott Michael. BA, U. Tenn., Chattanooga, 1973; MA, La. State U., 1976, JD, 1979. Bar: La. 1979, U.S. Dist. Ct. (we. dist.) La. 1979. Shareholder Liskow and Lewis, Lafayette and New Orleans, La., 1979—. Pres. Raven Soc., Chattanooga, 1973. Mem. ABA, La. Bar Assn., La. Min. Law Inst. (adv. coun. mem.), Am. Assn. Profl. Landmen, Lafayette Assn. Petroleum Landmen, Order of Coif. Roman Catholic. Avocations: photography, jogging, fishing. Oil, gas, and mineral, Probate, Real property. Home: 103 Asbury Cir Lafayette LA 70503-3632 Office: Liskow & Lewis PO Box 52008 Lafayette LA 70505-2008

**MANSFIELD, KAREN LEE,** lawyer; b. Chgo., Mar. 17, 1942; d. Ralph and Hilda (Blum) Mansfield; children: Nicole Rafaela, Lori Michele. BA in Polit. Sci., Roosevelt U., 1963; JD, DePaul U., 1971; student U. Chgo., 1959-60. Bar: Ill. 1972, U.S. Dist. Ct. (no. dist.) Ill. 1972. Legis. intern Ill. State Senate, Springfield, 1966-67; tchr. Chgo. Pub. Schs., 1967-70; atty. CNA Ins., Chgo., 1971-73; law clk. Ill. Appellate Ct., Chgo., 1973-75; sr. trial atty. U.S. Dept. Labor, Chgo., 1975—, mentor Adopt-a-Sch. Program, 1992-95. Contbr. articles to profl. jours. Vol. Big Sister, 1975-81; bd. dirs. Altgeld Nursery Sch., 1963-66, Ill. div. UN Assn., 1966-72, Hull House Jane Addams Ctr., 1977-82, Broadway Children's Ctr., 1986-90, Acorn Family Entertainment, 1993-95; mem. Oak Park Farmers' Market Commn., 1996—; rsch. asst. Citizens for Gov. Otto Kerner, Chgo., 1964; com. mem. Ill. Commn. on Status of Women, Chgo., 1964-70; del. Nat. Conf. on Status of Women, 1968; candidate for del. Ill. Constl. Conv., 1969. Mem. Chgo. Council Lawyers, Women's Bar Assn. Ill., Lawyer Pilots Bar Assn., Fed. Bar Assn. Unitarian. Clubs: Friends of Gamelan (performer), 99's Internat. Orgn. Women Pilots (legis. chmn. Chgo. area chpt. 1983-86, legis. chmn. North Cen. sect. 1986-88, legis. award 1983, 85). Home: 204 S Taylor Ave Oak Park IL 60302-3307 Office: US Dept Labor Office Solicitor 230 S Dearborn St Fl 8 Chicago IL 60604-1505

**MANSFIELD, SEYMOUR J.,** lawyer; b. Chgo., Mar. 30, 1945; s. Albert H. and Anne I. (Mittleman) M.; m. Susan Ann Bronner, Jan. 21, 1968; children: Justin, Alexis. B.S. in Sociology, U. Ill., 1966; J.D. with honors, DePaul U., 1969. Bar: Minn. 1978, Ill. 1969, U.S. Dist. Ct. (no. dist.) Ill. 1969, U.S. Dist. Ct. Minn. 1978, U.S. Ct. Appeals (7th cir.) 1971, U.S. Supreme Ct. 1976. Exec. dir. Central Minn. Legal Services/Legal Aid Soc. Mpls., Inc., 1978-81; exec. dir., pres. Fund For Legal Aid Soc., 1981-82; adj. prof. civil practice skills William Mitchell Coll. Law, St. Paul, Minn., 1982—; owner, pres. Seymour J. Mansfield & Assocs., Mpls., 1981-89; ptnr., shareholder Mansfield, Tanick & Cohen, P.A., 1989—; lectr. in field; speaker, Panelist on various TV Stas. Editor-in-Chief: LAW Connections, DePaul Law Review; contbr. articles to profl jours. founder, bd. mem. Fund for Legal Aid Soc., 1982—; exec. com. Am. Jewish Com., 1998—. Recipient Pro Bono Disting. Svc. award, 1994. Mem. ABA (ho. of dels. 1994—), Minn. State Bar Assn. (bd. govs. 1988-94), Hennepin County Bar Assn. (1988-94, 96—), Hennepin County Bar Found. (bd. mem. 1994—, pres. 1997-98), Nat. Employment Lawyers Assn. (dir. 1985—, chair exec. com. 1998—). General civil litigation, Federal civil litigation, Labor. Office: Mansfield Tanick & Cohen PA 1560 Internat Ctr 900 2nd Ave S Minneapolis MN 55402

**MANSFIELD, STEPHEN W.,** state supreme court justice; b. Brookline, Mass., Aug. 21, 1952; s. Clarence E. and Mary Ann (Zeyer) M.; divorced; children: Eric, Mark, Greg. BA cum laude, Tufts U., 1974; JD, Boston U., 1977. Bar: Tex., Mass. Assoc. gen. counsel Corbel & Co., Jacksonville, Fla., 1984-86; sr. counsel VALIC, Houston, 1986-94; pvt. practice Houston, 1994; judge Tex. Ct. of Criminal Appeals, Austin, 1995—. Republican. Avocations: numismatics, rugby, running. Office: Ct Criminal Appeals PO Box 12308 Austin TX 78711-2308 also: Ct Criminal Appeals Supreme Court Bldg 201 W 14th St Austin TX 78701-1614

**MANSFIELD, WILLIAM AMOS,** lawyer; b. Redmond, Oreg., Oct. 23, 1929; s. Ellithorpe Garrett and Constance G. (Loney) M.; children—Johathan E., Frederick W., Paul F. B.S., U. Oreg., 1951, J.D., 1953. Bar: Oreg. 1953, U.S. Supreme Ct. 1960, U.S. Dist. Ct. Oreg. 1966, U.S. Ct. Appeals (9th cir.) 1982. Asst. atty. gen. State of Oreg., Salem, 1955-60; staff atty., gen. counsel U.S. Bur. Pub. Roads, Washington, 1961; city atty. City of Medford (Oreg.), 1962-64; sole practice, Medford, 1965—. Bd. dirs. Peter Britt Festival, 1963-65, Planned Parenthood, Jackson County, Oreg., 1978; bd. dirs. Rogue Valley Transp. Dist., 1976-81, chmn., 1977-78; trustee Children's Farm Home, 1970-76; bd. dirs. ACLU, 1971-77, Jackson-Josephone County Headstart, 1989-91, chmn., 1991, Rogue Valley Symphony, 1992—; mem. city council, City of Medford, 1985-96. Served as 1st lt. USAF, 1953-55. Democrat. Congregationalist. Personal injury, State civil litigation, General practice. Office: 313 S Ivy St PO Box 1721 Medford OR 97501-0134

**MANSMANN, CAROL LOS,** federal judge, law educator; b. Pittsburgh, Pa., Aug. 7, 1942; d. Walter Joseph and Regina Mary (Pilarski) Los; m. J. Jerome Mansmann, June 17, 1970; children: Casey, Megan, Patrick. B.A., J.D., Duquesne U., 1964, 67; LL.D., Seton Hill Coll., Greensburg, Pa., 1985; PhD (hon.), La Roche Coll., 1990; LLD (hon.), Widener U., 1994. Asst. dist. atty. Allegheny County, Pitts., 1968-72; assoc. McVerry Baxter & Mansmann, Pitts., 1973-79; assoc. prof. law Duquesne U., Pitts., 1973-82; judge west dist. U.S. Dist. Ct. Pa., Pitts., 1982-85; judge U.S. Ct. Appeals (3rd cir.), Phila., 1985—; Mem. Pa. Criminal Procedural Rules Com., Pitts., 1972-77; spl. asst. atty. gen. Commonwealth of Pa., 1974-79; co-adminstr. Local Criminal Rules Reorg. Project, 1978-79; chair 2 Bar Assn. CLE programs, 1982; bd. govs. Pa. Bar Inst., Harrisburg, 1984-90; mem. 3d Cir. jud. coun., 1985—; adj. prof. law U. Pitts., 1987-96; mem. U.S. Jud. Conf. on adminstrn. of magistrate-judge sys., 1990-96. Mem. bd. consultors Villanova U. Law Sch., 1985-91; trustee Duquesne U., 1987—, Sewickley Acad., 1988-91. Recipient St. Thomas More award, Pitts., 1983, Phila., 1986, Ann. Dinner award Duquesne U. Law Alumni Assn., 1986, Faculty Alumni award Duquesne U., 1987. Mem. ABA, Nat. Assn. Women Judges, Pa. Bar Assn., Fed. Judges Assn., Am. Judicature Soc., Allegheny County Bar Assn. (gov., bd. govs. 1982-85), Phi Alpha Delta. Republican. Roman Catholic. Office: US Ct Appeals 7th and Grant Sts # 712 Pittsburgh PA 15219-2403

**MANSON, GARY LYLE,** lawyer; b. Reno, Nev., Dec. 28, 1951; s. Gerald Lee and Betty Helen (Ferrari) M.; m. Carla Lynette Coleman, Mar. 23, 1985; children: Morgan Leigh, Coleman Jordan. BA magna cum laude, U. Nev., 1974; JD, U. San Francisco, 1977. Bar: Nev. 1977. Law clerk Hon. William N. Forman Washoe County Dist. Ct. 2nd Judicial Dist., Reno, 1977-78; assoc. Bissett & Logar, Reno, 1978-83; assoc./ptnr. Law Offices of Ronald J. Logar, Reno, 1983-92; pvt. practice Law Offices of Gary L. Manson, Reno, 1992—; lectr. Bar Review, Reno, 1986-91; lectr. for various cos. on law subjects. Contbr. articles to profl. jours. Coach Pop Warner Football, Reno; legis. intern State Senator Thomas "Spike" Wilson, 1973; pro tem judge Reno Mcpl. Ct., 1988—. Mem. Washoe County Bar Assn., Nev. State Bar Assn. (family law section 1985—), ABA, Phi Kappa Phi, Phi Alpha Theta, Sigma Nu, Blue Key Svc. Club, Phi Delta Phi. Republican. Avocations: sports. Family and matrimonial, Probate, Personal injury. Home: 3075 W Plumb Ln Reno NV 89509-3032 Office: 575 Forest St Ste 205 Reno NV 89509-1689

**MANSON, KEITH ALAN MICHAEL,** lawyer; b. Warwick, RI, Oct. 26, 1962; s. Ronald Frederick and Joan Patricia (Reardon) M.; m. Jennifer Annette Stearns; children: Kristin Elizabeth, Michelle Nicole. BA, R.I. Coll., 1985; cert. computer info. systems, Bryant Coll., 1988; cert. law, U. Notre Dame, London, 1990; JD, Thomas M. Cooley Law Sch., 1991. Bar: Ind. 1991, U.S. Dist. Ct. (no. dist.) Ind. 1991, U.S. Dist. Ct. (so. dist.) Ind. 1991, U.S. Dist. Ct. (so. dist.) Ga. 1992, U.S. Dist. Ct. Mil. Appeals 1991. Spl. asst. U.S. atty. U.S. Dist. Ct. Ga., Brunswick, 1992-93; pvt. practice Fernandina Beach, Fla., 1994—; atty., securities compliance divsn. Prudential Ins. Co., 1997-98; counsel Stonier Transportation Group, Jacksonville Beach, Fla., 1998-99; cons. The Law Store Ltd. Paralegal Svcs., Fernandina Beach., 1994—, Barnett Bank, Nations Bank, 1998. Contbr. articles to profl. jours. Dist. fin. and mem. chmn. North Fla. coun. Boy Scouts Am., Jacksonville, 1993—; com. mem. sea scout ship 660 St. Peter's Ch., Fernandina Beach, 1994-96; chmn. Scouting for Food Dr., Nassau County, Fla., 1994—. Lt. USN, 1985-86, 90-96. F.C. Tanner Trust, Fed. Products Inc. scholar, Providence, 1981-85, Esterline Corp. scholar, Providence, 1986. Mem. ABA, Ind. Bar Assn., Judge Advocate Assn., Jacksonville Bar Assn., Navy League U.S., Rotary (project mgr. Webster-Dudley Mass. chpt. 1986-88), Am. Legion, Phi Alpha Delta. Avocations: gardening, rugby, sports history, military history, collecting historical items. Military, Consumer commercial, Criminal. Home and Office: 1908 Reatta Ln Fernandina Beach FL 32034-8937

**MANTAGNA, MICHAEL,** lawyer; b. Newark, Aug. 9, 1942; m. Sarah Mantagna; 1 child, Bonnie; children from previous marriage: Michael Brian, Lara Kathleen. BA in Sociology, Rutgers U.; JD, Detroit Coll. Law, 1970. Sole practice Atlanta, 1970—. With U.S. Army, 1965-69, Vietnam. Recipient Bronze Star medal. State civil litigation, Criminal, Family and matrimonial. Home: 5465 Young Deer Dr Cumming GA 30041-8970

**MANTEL, ALLAN DAVID,** lawyer; b. N.Y.C., June 27, 1951; s. Bernard and Ruth (Weichman) M.; m. Janet Mantel, June 17, 1985; children: Bernard, Elizabeth. BA, NYU, 1973; JD, SUNY, Buffalo, 1976. Bar: N.Y. 1977, U.S. Dist. Ct. (so. and ea. dists.) N.Y. 1977. Assoc. Rosenthal & Herman P.C., N.Y.C., 1977-82; ptnr. Rosenthal, Herman & Mantel, N.Y.C., 1983-94, Hofheimer, Gartlir & Gross, LLP, N.Y.C., 1995-98, Stein Riso & Mantel LLP, N.Y.C., 1999—. Mem. adv. bd. Divorce Mag. Fellow: Am.

Acad. Matrimonial Lawyers (bd. mgrs. N.Y. chpt.); mem. ABA (family law sect.), N.Y. State Bar Assn. (equitable distbn. com.), Assn. of Bar of City of N.Y. (matrimonial law com. 1985-88), N.Y. County Lawyers Assn. (matrimonial law and bus. com.). Jewish. Family and matrimonial, State civil litigation. Office: Stein Riso & Mantel LLP 405 Lexington Ave New York NY 10174-0002

**MANTLE, RAYMOND ALLAN,** lawyer; b. Painesville, Ohio, Oct. 15, 1937; s. Junius Dow and Ada Louise (Stinchcomb) M.; m. Judith Ann LaGrange, Nov. 26, 1967; children: Amanda Lee, Rachel Ann, Leah Amy. BSBA summa cum laude, BA summa cum laude, Kent State U., 1961; LLB cum laude, NYU, 1964. Bar: N.Y. 1964, N.J. 1976, U.S. Supreme Ct. Asst. counsel Gov. Nelson A. Rockefeller, N.Y., 1964-65; assoc. Paul Weiss Rifkind Wharton & Garrison, 1967-69; mem. Varet & Fink P.C. (formerly Milgrim Thomajan & Lee, P.C.), N.Y.C., 1969-95; ptnr. Piper & Marbury L.L.P., N.Y.C., 1995-98, Brock Silverstein, LLC, 1998—; lectr. in computer law field. Contbr. author: Doing Business in China and Intellectual Property China, 1990—. Capt. U.S. Army, 1965-67. Mem. N.Y. State Bar Assn., N.J. Bar Assn. Republican. Methodist. Contracts commercial, General corporate, Intellectual property. Office: Brock Silverstein LLC 800 3rd Ave Fl 21 New York NY 10022-7604

**MANZO, EDWARD DAVID,** patent lawyer; b. N.Y.C., Nov. 23, 1950; s. Edward Joseph and Elvira Helen (Melone) M.; m. Fern Rita Siegel, Oct. 30, 1978 (div. 1984); 1 child, Justin Edward; m. Margaret Ruth Johnson, Oct. 11, 1985; children: Hunter Roy, Kira Nicole. BS, Polytech. Inst. Bklyn., 1972; JD cum laude, SUNY, Buffalo, 1975. Bar: N.Y. 1976, Ill. 1979, U.S. Patent and Trademark Office 1976, U.S. Ct. Appeals (fed. cir.) 1982, U.S. Supreme Ct. 1982. Assoc. Darby & Darby, P.C., N.Y.C., 1975-77; group patent counsel Schlumberger Ltd., N.Y.C., 1977-79; ptnr. Cook, Wetzel & Egan, Chgo., 1979-85, Jenner & Block, 1985-88, Cook, Alex, McFarron, Manzo, Cummings & Mehler, Ltd., Chgo., 1988—; instr. DePaul U., Chgo., 1989-91. Author (with others): Intellectual Property Law in Illinois, 1988; contbr. articles to profl. jours. Bd. dirs. Concertante di Chgo., 1997—. Jaeckle Fleishman grantee, 1973. Mem. Am. Intellectual Property Law Assn., Intellectual Property Law Assn. Chgo., Stradivari Soc., Sicilian Am. Cultural Assn. (v.p. 1999—). Avocations: classical piano and guitar, tennis, bridge. Patent, Federal civil litigation, Intellectual property. Home: Lake Forest IL 60045 Office: Cook Alex McFarron Manzo Cummings & Mehler Ltd 200 W Adams St Ste 2850 Chicago IL 60606-5206

**MANZONI, CHARLES R., JR.,** lawyer; b. San Francisco, CA, Jan. 23, 1947; s. Charles R. and Vivian M.; m. Deborah Ann Manzoni, May 27, 1989; children: Charles III, Nicholas. BA in History, U. Santa Clara, Calif., 1969, JD, 1972. Bar: Calif. 1973, Ill. 1975. Staff atty., market regulation SEC, Washington, 1972-73, legal asst. to chmn., 1973-75; asst. v.p., atty. A.G. Becker & Co., Chgo., 1975-77; assoc. Gardner Carton & Douglas, Chgo., 1977-80, ptnr., 1980-96, 98—; exec. v.p., gen. counsel Zurich Kemper Investments, Chgo., 1996-98; adj. prof. IIT-Kent Sch. Law, 1993-95. 1st lt. U.S. Army Res. Mem. ABA. Avocations: skiing, running. Securities, General corporate. Office: Gardner Carton & Douglas 321 N Clark St Chicago IL 60610-4714

**MAPES, WILLIAM RODGERS, JR.,** lawyer; b. Cleve., Nov. 29, 1952; s. William R. and Marian (Atkins) M.; m. Patricia Soochan, Sept. 3, 1984. BS in Bus. Adminstrn., Miami U., Oxford, Ohio, 1974; JD, Am. U., 1977. Bar: D.C. 1978, U.S. Ct. Appeals (D.C. cir.) 1979, U.S. Ct. Appeals (fed. cir.) 1980, U.S. Ct. Appeals (5th cir.) 1981, U.S. Supreme Ct. 1982, U.S. Ct. Appeals (3d cir.) 1985, U.S. Ct. Appeals (4th cir.) 1987, U.S. Ct. Appeals (6th cir.) 1988. Ptnr. Ross, Marsh & Foster, Washington, 1978—. Mem. ABA (editor nat. resources sect. newsletter 1984-89), Fed. Energy Bar Assn. Avocations: boating, tennis, cycling. FERC practice, Administrative and regulatory. Home: 6916 Greenvale St NW Washington DC 20015-1437 Office: Ross Marsh & Foster 2001 L St NW Ste 400 Washington DC 20036-4946

**MARA, TIMOTHY GERALD,** lawyer; b. Cin., July 30, 1949; s. Thomas James and Rose Marie (Sansone) M. B in Community Planning, U. Cin., 1972; JD, No. Ky. U., 1978. Bar: Ohio 1978, U.S. Dist. Ct. Cin. 1979, U.S. Ct. Appeals (6th cir.) 1983. Regional planner Ohio-Ky.-Ind. Regional Coun. of Govts., Cin., 1972-77; spl. asst. U.S. Rep. Thomas A. Luken, Cin., 1977-78; assoc. Metzger, Phillipps & Nichols, Cin., 1979-83; pvt. practice Cin., 1984—. Trustee Green Twp., Hamilton County, Ohio, 1982-86. Mem. Ohio State Bar Assn., Cin. Bar Assn., Hamilton County Dem. Steering Com. Roman Catholic. Avocations: nature walks, biking. Land use and zoning (including planning), Probate, Personal injury. Office: 1500 Chiquita Ctr 250 E 5th St Cincinnati OH 45202-4119

**MARABLE, SIDNEY THOMAS,** lawyer; b. Henderson, N.C., Dec. 4, 1954; s. Nathaniel and Julia M. (Vann) M.; m. Frances J. Marable; 1 child, Marcus Latham. BA in Polit. Sci., N.C. Agrl. & Tech. State U., 1976; JD, U. N.C., 1979. Bar: N.C. 1979, Ariz. 1983, U.S. Supreme Ct. 1979. Assoc. Castro, Zipf & Rogers, Phoenix, 1983-87, ptnr., 1987-92; pvt. practice Phoenix, 1992—; mem. Civil Practice Procedure Com., Phoenix, 1994-97, Maricopa County Bench/Bar Com., Phoenix, 1994-96, Fed. Dist. Ct. Local Rules Com., Phoenix, 1995—. Bd. dirs. Ctrl. Ariz. Arthritis Found., Phoenix, 1987-88; mem. Mayor's Profl. Sports Adv. Com., Phoenix, 1988-91, Bus. Ptnrs. of Phoenix Symphony, 1993-95. Capt. JAG, USAF, 1979-83. Master Sandra Day O'Connor Inn of Ct.; mem. ABA, ATLA, Nat. Bar Assn., Ariz. Trial Lawyers Assn., Ariz. State Bar Assn., N.C. State Bar Assn., Fed. Bar Assn., Maricopa County Bar Assn. (mem. pub. rels. com. 1993-95, chair 1995-96), Continuing Legal Edn. Committee, Cmty. Legal Svcs. (chair bd. dirs. 1997-98), Alpha Edn. Found. of Phoenix, Inc. (chair, bd. dirs. 1996-98). Avocations: flying, camping, skiing, sailing, hiking. General civil litigation, Personal injury, General corporate. Office: Law Offices 3030 N Central Ave Ste 1000 Phoenix AZ 85012-2717

**MARAMAN, KATHERINE ANN,** judge; b. Los Alamos, N.Mex., Aug. 13, 1951; d. William Joseph and Katherine Ann (Thorpe) M. BA, Colorado Coll., 1973; JD, U. N.Mex., 1976. Bar: N.Mex. 1976, Guam 1978, Trust Territory Pacific Islands, Commonwealth of No. Mariana Islands, U.S. Ct. Appeals (9th cir.), U.S. Supreme Ct. Draftsperson N.Mex. Legis. Coun. Svc., Santa Fe, 1976-77; atty. Brooks & Klitzkie, P.C., Agana, Guam, 1977-84; pvt. practice Agana, 1985-88; counsel Office of Gov., Agana, 1988-94; judge Superior Ct., Agana, 1994—; mem. asst. legis. counsel Guam Legis., Agana, 1977-80, mem. minority counsel, 1981-87; bd. dirs. Pub. Defender Svc. Corp., Agana, 1988-94. Trustee Guam Terr. Law Libr., 1994—. Mem. Guam Bar Assn. Counsel Rep. Party, Agana, 1981-94; bd. dirs. Guam Rehab. and Workshop, Inc., Tumon, Guam, 1983-95; deacon First Presbyn. Reformed Ch., Agana. Office: Superior Ct Guam 120 W Obrien Dr Hagatna GU 96910-5174*

**MARANO, RICHARD MICHAEL,** lawyer; b. Waterbury, Conn., June 22, 1960; s. Albert Nicholas and Angeline Domenica (Viotti) M.; m. Eileen N. Barry. BA, Fairfield U., 1982; JD, Seton Hall U., 1985. Bar: Conn. 1985, U.S. Dist. Ct. Conn. 1985, U.S. Tax Ct. 1986, U.S. Supreme Ct. 1990, U.S. Ct. Appeals (2d cir.) 1991; cert. criminal trial advocate. Assoc. Moynahan, Ruskin, Mascolo & Mariani, Waterbury, 1985-87; ptnr. Marano & Diamond, Waterbury, 1987—; alderman City of Waterbury 1988-90. Author: History of the Order Sons of Italy of Waterbury, Connecticut, 1995, Connecticut Criminal Legal Forms, 1999; co-author: Growing Up Italian and American in Waterbury, 1997; co-editor: Counsel for the Defense, 1991-93, editor, 1993-98; contbr. law articles to Conn. Bar Jour. Bd. dirs. Italian-Am. Dem. Club, Waterbury, 1988—, Ctrl. Naugatuck Valley HELP, 1992—, Anderson Boys Club, 1989— (pres. 1996-98), Waterbury Housing Police Fund, 1992-94, Waterbury Crime Stoppers Inc., 1994-97; pres. Conn. Young Dems., 1981-82; state coord. McGovern for U.S. Presdl. campaign, 1983-84; campaign mgr. Orman for Congress, 1984; commr. Waterbury Pub. Assistance, 1986-88; justice of the peace, Waterbury, 1989—; gen. counsel Waterbury Dem. Town Com., 1990-96; commr. Waterbury Fire Bd., 1996-98; trustee Our Lady of Lourdes Ch., 1993—. Mem. ABA, ATLA, KC, Conn. Bar assn., Nat. Assn. Criminal Def. Lawyers (life), Conn. Criminal Def. Lawyers Assn. (pres.-elect 1997-98, pres. 1998—), Conn. Italian-Am. Bar Assn. (pres. 1993-95), Conn. Trial Lawyers Assn., Waterbury Bar Assn. (bd. dirs. 1993—, pres. 1996-98), New Haven County Bar Assn., Nat. Italian-Am. Bar Assn., Sons of Italy (pres. lodge # 66 1994-96), Unico Club (pres. Waterbury chpt. 1997—), Elks, Alpha Mu Gamma, Pi Sigma Alpha. Roman Catholic. Criminal, Personal injury, General practice. Home: 24 Lake Dr Oxford CT 06478-1172 Office: Marano & Diamond 61 Field St Waterbury CT 06702-1907

**MARANTZ, NEIL G.,** lawyer; b. Bkyn., Apr. 9, 1957. BA, NYU, 1980; JD, Fordham U., 1985. Bar: N.Y. 1986, U.S. Dist. Ct. (so. and ea. dists.) N.Y. 1987. Ptnr. Law Offices of Neil G. Marantz, N.Y.C., 1993-97, Atlas & Marantz, N.Y.C., 1997—. Mem. Bar Assn. of the City of N.Y. (constn. law com. 1997—). Construction, General civil litigation, Real property. Office: Atlas & Marantz 400 Madison Ave New York NY 10017-1909

**MARBER, PAUL ANDREW,** lawyer; b. Glen Cove, N.Y., Jan. 19, 1960; s. Philip Marber and Ruth Brown; m. Randy Sue Kornfeld, Aug. 18, 1985; children: Elana Susan, Matthew William. BA, U. Rochester, 1982; JD, Boston U., 1985. Bar: N.Y. 1986, N.J. 1986, U.S. Dist. Ct. (ea. and so. dists.) N.Y. 1986, U.S. Dist. Ct. N.J. 1986. Asst. corp. counsel N.Y.C. Law Dept., Office of Corp. Counsel, 1985-88; assoc. Budd Larner Gross et al, N.Y.C., 1988-97, Schneider Kleinick Weitz Damashek & Shoot, N.Y.C., 1997—. Active West Birchwood Civic Assn., Jericho, 1990—; committeeman Nassau County (N.Y.) Dem. Com., 1994—; dist. ct. judge candidate 4th Dist. Ct. Nassau County, Oyster Bay, 1995, 96. Mem. N.Y. State Bar Assn., N.Y. State Trial Lawyers Assn., Nassau County Bar Assn. Personal injury, Product liability. Office: Schneider Kleinick Weitz Damashek & Shoot 233 Broadway Fl 5 New York NY 10279-0599

**MARBURG-GOODMAN, JEFFREY EMIL,** lawyer; b. Taipei, Taiwan, Feb. 20, 1957; s. Samuel and Lisl (Marburg) G. BA, Amherst Coll., 1979; JD, Harvard U., 1983; postgrad., U. Aix-Marseille, France, 1983-84. Bar: N.Y. 1986, U.S. Dist. Ct. (so. and ea. dists.) N.Y. 1988. Assoc. Shearman & Sterling, Paris, 1984, N.Y.C., 1985-89; assoc. Patton & Boggs, Washington, 1989-91; regional legal adviser US AID, U.S. State Dept., Washington, 1991—. Fundraiser, outside cons. Dukakis for Pres., Boston and N.Y.C., 1988, dep. counsel N.Y. State, 1988; in-charge credentials Dem. Nat. Conv., 1988; mem. nat. steering com. Clinton-Gore '96, Gore 2000, Washington; cons. Gore 2000, Washington. John Woodruff Simpson fellow Amherst Coll., 1980-81, Rotary fellow, 1984. Mem. ABA, N.Y. State Bar Assn., Harvard Club, Phi Beta Kappa. Avocations: running, weight tng., music, theatre, travel. Home: 1401 17th St NW Ph Apt1008 Washington DC 20036-6400 Office: US AID Office Gen Counsel Ronald Reagan Bldg & Interna C Washington DC 20523-0001

**MARCHANT, BRISTOW,** lawyer; b. Columbia, S.C., June 13, 1955; s. T. Eston and Caroline (Bristow) M.; m. Elizabeth Gilmore, May 30, 1980; children: Bristow Jr., Madison Eston, Sallie Gilmore. Student, U. S.C., 1973-74, JD, 1980; BA with honors, Coll. of Charleston, 1977. Bar: S.C. 1980, U.S. Dist. Ct. S.C. 1983, U.S. Ct. Appeals (4th cir.) 1983, U.S. Supreme Ct. 1987. Staff counsel U.S. Senate Judiciary Com., Washington, 1980-82; atty. Office Atty. Gen., State of S.C., Columbia, 1982-83; asst. chief counsel Dept. Hwys. and Pub. Transp., Columbia, 1983; ptnr. Adams, Quackenbush, Herring & Stuart, P.A., Columbia, 1983-92; apptd. U.S. magistrate judge Dist. S.C., Columbia, 1992—. Trustee Koger Ctr. for Performing Arts, Columbia, 1987-92; mem. Richland County Coun., Columbia, 1987-91, chmn., 1988; state treas. U.S. Senator Strom Thurmond Reelection Com., 1984; bd. vis. Coll. Chalreston. Mem. S.C. Bar Assn., Richland County Bar Assn. (sec., treas. 1983-90, editor newsletter 1983-90, pres. 1992). Presbyterian. Avocations: reading, boating. Real property, General corporate. Office: Strom Thurmond fed Courthouse 1845 Assembly St Columbia SC 29201-2455

**MARCHESE, MATTHEW,** lawyer; b. Bklyn., June 7, 1961; s. Mario M. and Providence Geraldi; 1 child, Adraian Rodriguez. BA in Psychology, SUNY, 1983; JD, St. John's U., 1987. Bar: N.J. 1987, N.Y. 1988, U.S. Dist. Ct. (so. and ea. dists.) N.J. 1988, U.S. Supreme Ct. 1998. Atty. Gannella & Rao, N.Y.C., 1987-89, Oliver Schavitz, Jamaica, N.Y., 1989-90, pvt. practice, Bronx, 1990—. Avocations: guitar, martial arts, fencing. Personal injury, Insurance, Real property. Office: 2403 E Tremont Ave Bronx NY 10461-2801

**MARCHETTI, MARILYN H.,** lawyer; b. Whiting, Ind., Mar. 10, 1947; d. Stephen D. and Helen F. (Ajdinovich) Hrpka; m. George Arthur Marchetti, Aug. 21, 1976; 1 child, Christine Stephanie. BA in English, Ind. U., 1969; JD, IIT, 1979. Bar: Ill. 1980. Tchr. jr. high school North Easton (Mass.) schs., 1969-70; social worker Ind. Dept. Pub. Welfare, Gary, 1970-74; medicaid specialist U.S. Dept. Health, Edn., Welfare, Chgo., 1974-78; law clk. to Justice Thomas Moran Ill. Supreme Ct., Waukegan, 1979-81; assoc. Mayer, Brown & Platt, Chgo., 1982-84; ptnr. Keck, Mahin & Cate, Chgo., 1984-94, Oppenheimer, Wolff & Donnelly, Chgo., 1994-97, Sanforth, Shaw, Fairweather & Geraldson, Chgo., 1997-99, Great Banc Trust Co., Aurora, Ill., 1999—; guest lectr. Harvard U.; cons. USSR marine industry privatization, 1990-91; speaker The Employee Stock Ownership Plan Assn. Paris Internat., London, 1991, 92; mem. U.S. del. promoting concept of employee ownership, to China, 1994, to Zimbabwe, 1995. Contbr. articles to profl. jours., chpts. to books. Asst. troop leader Girl Scouts U.S., Western Springs, Ill., 1990—; mem. parish coun. St. John of the Cross Ch., Western Springs, 1991-92; fundraiser Carol Mosely Braun Campaign, Chgo., 1992; founder Girls' Cir., 1994—; mem. bd. edn. Lyons Twp. H.S. Dist. 107, 1997—; bd. dirs., sec. Dist. 106 Ednl. found., 1995-97. Mem. Employee Stock Ownership Plan Assn. (bd. dirs., adminstrv. com. 1989—, legis. com. 1990—, founder, sec., treas. Ill. chpt.), Nat. Assn. of Women Bus. Owners, Nat. Ctr. Employee Ownership, Women in Employee Benefits (steering com. 1987). Avocations: golf, bridge, writing. Pension, profit-sharing, and employee benefits, Private international, Mergers and acquisitions. Office: Great Banc Trust Co 105 E Galena Blvd Aurora IL 60505-3338

**MARCUS, CRAIG BRIAN,** lawyer; b. Boise, Idaho, May 30, 1939; s. Claude Virgil and Marie Louise M.; m. Lynne Merryweather, Sept. 3, 1960; children: Shawn, Brian, Trent. Student, Boise Jr. Coll., 1958, U. Pa., 1958-59, Mexico City Coll., 1959-60; JD, U. Idaho, 1963. Bar: Idaho 1963, U.S. Dist. Ct. Idaho 1963. Ptnr. Marcus, Merrick & Montgomery, predecessors, Boise, 1963—. Ada County dir. Rep. Congl. Campaigns, Boise, 1964-66; Ada County coord. Rep. Senatorial Campaigns, 1969; chmn. jud. campaign Idaho Ct. of Appeals, 1984, 90. Mem. ABA, Idaho Bar Assn. (peer rev. com. 1971-73), 4th Dist. Bar Assn. (treas. 1967-68, ct. trial porcedural rules com. 1973-74), Lincoln Day Banquet Assn. (pres. 1975), Elks. Avocations: fishing, hunting, golf, skiing, trap shooting. Personal injury, Probate, General corporate. Home: 7711 Apache Way Boise ID 83703-1903 Office: Marcus Merrick & Montgomery 737 N 7th St Boise ID 83702-5595

**MARCUS, LEE WARREN,** lawyer; b. Great Neck, N.Y., May 10, 1967; s. Michael Henry and Roberta Ellen (Erlichman) M.; m. Kimberly Denise Hoff, Nov. 19, 1994; 1 child, Jason Patrick. BS, SUNY, Albany, 1989; JD, U. Fla., 1992. Bar: Fla. 1992, U.S. Dist. Ct. (mid. dist.) Fla. 1993, U.S. Dist. Ct. (so. dist.) Fla. 1995, U.S. Dist. Ct. (no. dist.) Fla. 1997, U.S. Ct. Appeals (11th cir.) 1996. Assoc. Taraska, Grower, Unger & Ketcham, P.A., Orlando, Fla., 1992-94, David H. Popper & Assocs., Orlando, Fla., 1994-96, Unger, Swartwood, Latham & Indest, P.A., Orlando, Fla., 1996—; lectr. CLE Nat. Bus. Inst., 1997—. Sr. exec. editor Fla. Law Rev., 1991. Mem. Fla. Adv. Com. on Arson Prevention, 1994—; v.p., bd. dirs. Anthony House for the Homeless, Zellwood, 1996—. Mem. Fla. Bar Assn., Orange County Bar Assn. Avocations: diving, team athletics. Insurance, General civil litigation, Personal injury. Office: Unger Swartwood Latham & Indest PA 701 Peachtree Rd Orlando FL 32804-6847

**MARCUS, MARIA LENHOFF,** lawyer, law educator; b. Vienna, Austria, June 23, 1933; came to U.S., 1938, naturalized, 1944; d. Arthur and Clara (Gruber) Lenhoff; m. Norman Marcus, Dec. 23, 1956; children: Valerie, Nicole, Eric. BA, Oberlin Coll., 1954; JD, Yale Law Sch., 1957. Bar: N.Y. 1961, U.S. Dist. Ct. (so. and ea. dists.) N.Y. 1962, U.S. Ct. Appeals (2d cir.) 1962, U.S. Supreme Ct. 1964. Assoc. counsel NAACP, N.Y.C., 1961-67; asst. atty. gen. N.Y. State, N.Y.C., 1967-78; chief litigation bur. Atty. Gen. N.Y. State, 1976-78; adj. assoc. prof., Law Sch. NYU, 1976-78; assoc. prof. law Fordham U. Law Sch., N.Y.C., 1978-86, prof. law, 1986—, Joseph M. McLaughlin prof. law, 1997—; arbitrator Nat. Assn. Securities Dealers; chair subcom. interrogatories U.S. Dist. Ct. (so. dist.) N.Y., 1983-85. Contbr. articles to profl. jours. Fellow N.Y. Bar Found.; mem. Assn. Bar City of N.Y. (v.p. 1995-96, long range planning com. 1996—, exec. com. 1976-80, com. audit 1988-95, labor com. 1981-84, judiciary com. 1975-76, chmn. civil rights com. 1972-75), N.Y. State Bar Assn. (exec. com. 1979-81, ho. dels. 1978-81, com. constitution and by-laws 1984-93), N.Y. Women's Bar Assn. (Pres.'s award 1999). Office: Fordham U Law Sch 140 W 62nd St New York NY 10023-7485

**MARCUS, MICHELLE S.,** lawyer; b. Staten Island, N.Y., Mar. 21, 1961; d. Harold and Elise Marcus. BA, Binghamton U., 1983; JD, Union U., Albany, N.Y., 1987. Bar: N.Y. 1988, U.S. Dist. Ct. (so. dist.) N.Y. 1998. Assoc. Mudge Rose Guthrie Alexander & Ferdon, N.Y.C., 1987-90, Baer Marks & Upham, N.Y.C., 1990-91, Irwin M. Portnoy & Assocs., Newburgh, N.Y., 1991-99; prin., owner Portnoy and Marcus, Newburgh, N.Y., 1999—; bd. dirs. Legal Aid Soc. Rockland County, Inc., New City, N.Y., 1994—, sec., 1998—. Mem. Rockland County Women's Bar Assn. (sec. 1994-96, v.p. 1996-98, pres. 1998—), Women's Bar Assn. Sate N.Y. (co-chair Internet com. 1997—). Administrative and regulatory. Office: Portnoy and Marcus 254 Route 17K Newburgh NY 12550-8343

**MARCUS, NORMAN,** lawyer; b. N.Y.C., Aug. 31, 1932; s. David and Evelyn (Freed) M.; m. Maria Eleanor Lenhoff, Dec. 23, 1956; children: Valerie, Nicole, Eric. BA, Columbia U., 1953; LLB, Yale U., 1957. Bar: N.Y. 1958, U.S. Dist. Ct. (so. dist.) 1960, U.S. Supreme Ct. 1964. Assoc. LaPorte & Meyers, N.Y.C., 1957-61; assoc. counsel Stanley Warner Corp., N.Y.C., 1961-63; gen. counsel N.Y.C. Planning Commn. and Dept. of City Planning, 1963-85; ptnr. Finley, Kumble, Wagner, Heine, Underberg, Manley, Myerson & Casey, N.Y.C., 1985-87; counsel Bachner, Tally, Polevoy & Misher, N.Y.C., 1987—; adj. prof. Pratt Inst., Bklyn., 1965-85, NYU Law Sch., 1977-98, Benjamin N. Cardozo Sch. Law, N.Y.C., 1983-85, NYU Wagner Sch. Pub. Svc., 1986—, Princeton (N.J.) U. Sch. Architecture, 1990-91. Contbr. articles to profl. jours. Recipient Meritorious Achievement award Am. Planning Assn., 1986. Mem. N.Y. State Bar Assn., Assn. of Bar of City of N.Y. (com. on land use planning and zoning), N.Y. County Lawyers Assn. (bd. dirs., chmn. com. on urban devel. and land use), Am. Coll. Real Estate Lawyers, The Fine Arts Fedn. N.Y. (v.p.), Century Club. Avocations: antique books, swimming, drama criticism. Real property, Land use and zoning (including planning), Environmental. Home: 91 Central Park W New York NY 10023-4600 Office: Bachner Tally Polevoy & Misher 380 Madison Ave New York NY 10017-2513 *Solve problems and you leave the world a better place.*

**MARCUS, PAUL,** law educator; b. N.Y.C., Dec. 8, 1946; s. Edward and Lillian (Rubin) M.; m. Rebecca Nimmer, Dec. 22, 1968; children: Emily, Beth, Daniel. AB, UCLA, 1968, JD, 1971. Bar: Calif. 1971, U.S. Dist. Ct. (cen. dist.) Calif. 1972, U.S. Ct. Appeals (D.C. cir.) 1972, U.S. Ct. Appeals (7th cir.) 1976. Law clk. U.S. Ct. Appeals (D.C. cir.), 1971-72; assoc. Loeb & Loeb, L.A., 1972-74; prof. law U. Ill., Urbana, 1974-83; dean Coll. Law U. Ariz., Tucson, 1983-88, prof., 1988-92; Haynes prof. law Coll. William and Mary, Williamsburg, Va., 1992—, interim dean, 1993-94, 97-98; reporter, cons. Fed. Jud. Ctr. Commn. Author: The Entrapment Defense, 1989, 2d edit., 1995, The Prosecution and Defense of Criminal Conspiracy, 1978, 4th edit., 1997, Gilbert Law Summary, 1982, 5th edit., 1995, Criminal Law: Cases and Materials, 1982, 4th edit., 1998; nat. reporter on criminal law Internat. of Comparative Law, 1978—. Nat. reporter on criminal law Internat. of Comparative Law, 1978—. Office: Coll William & Mary Sch Law Williamsburg VA 23185

**MARCUS, RICHARD STEVEN,** lawyer; b. Cin., May 26, 1950; s. Bernard Benjamin and Norma (Ginsberg) M.; m. Jane Iris Schreiber, Sept. 12, 1971; children: Rebecca, Sarah. BA in English, U. Wis., 1972; JD, Harvard U., 1975. Bar: Wis. 1975, U.S. Tax Ct. 1976, U.S. Ct. Appeals (7th cir.) 1977, U.S. Dist. Ct. (ea. dist.) Wis. 1979, U.S. Ct. Claims 1979. Assoc. Godfrey & Kahn, S.C., Milw., 1975—. Pres., Milw. Assn. for Jewish Edn., 1992; bd. dirs. Milw. Jewish Fedn., 1992, Milw. chpt. Jewish Nat. Fund, 1992. Computer, Franchising, General corporate. Office: Godfrey & Kahn SC 780 N Water St Ste 1500 Milwaukee WI 53202-3590

**MARCUS, ROBERT BRUCE,** lawyer; b. N.Y.C., June 19, 1942; s. Henry Edward and Fannie S. (Siegler) M.; children: Peter J., Gabrielle Beth; m. Jeanie Elizabeth Neyer, Dec. 14, 1984. Bar: N.Y. 1967, N.Y. Dist. Ct. (so., ea. and no. dists.) N.Y. 1968, U.S. Supreme Ct. 1980. Assoc. Shatzkin & Cooper, P.C., N.Y.C., 1967-69, Jay Wallman, P.C., N.Y.C., 1969-72, Klotz & Gould, P.C., N.Y.C., 1972-75; sr. assoc. Weiss, Molod, Berkowitz & Godosky, P.C., N.Y.C., 1975-79, Richard Frank, P.C., N.Y.C., 1979-82; ptnr. Wallman & Wechsler, P.C., N.Y.C., 1982-84, Metnick & Bernstein, P.C., N.Y.C., 1984-88, Metnick, Marcus & Schuchman, P.C., N.Y.C., 1988-89; pres. Robert B. Marcus, P.C., N.Y.C., 1989-97; counsel to Kelner and Kelner Esq., N.Y.C., 1989-97; ptnr. Marcus and Yodowitz, LLP, New City, N.Y., 1998—. Bd. advisors Art Hazzards Inst., N.Y.C., 1981—; chmn., founder Willow Tree Civic Assn., Ramapo, N.Y., 1977-81. Mem. ABA, Assn. Trial Lawyers Am., N.Y. State Trial Lawyers Assn., Assn. Trial Lawyers of City of N.Y. Fax: (914) 634-5760. Personal injury, Insurance, Federal civil litigation. Home: 203 Strawtown Rd New City NY 10956-6815

**MARCUS, STANLEY,** federal judge; b. 1946. BA, CUNY, 1967; JD, Harvard U., 1971. Assoc. Botein, Hays, Sklar & Herzberg, N.Y.C., 1974-75; asst. atty. U.S. Dist. Ct. (ea. dist.) N.Y., 1975-78; spl. atty., dep. chief U.S. organized crime sect. Detroit Strike Force, 1978-79, chief U.S. organized crime sect., 1980-82; U.S. atty. So. Dist. of Fla., Miami, 1982-85; judge U.S. Dist. Ct. (so. dist.) Fla., Miami, 1985—, U.S. Ct. Appeals (11th cir.). Office: US Dist Ct of Appeals 11th Cir 99 NE 4th St Rm 1262 Miami FL 33132-2185

**MARCUS, STEPHEN HOWARD,** lawyer; b. N.Y.C., June 30, 1945; s. Jacob and Mildren (Cohen) M.; m. Carol Sylvia Beatrice, June 11, 1967; children: Joshua David, Rebecca Lynn, Daniel Benjamin. BME, MIT, 1967; JD, Harvard U., 1970. Bar: Calif. 1971, U.S. Dist. Ct. (so. dist.) Calif. 1971, U.S. Dist. Ct. (so. dist.) Calif. 1974, U.S. Dist. Ct. (cen. dist.) Calif. 1975, U.S. Ct. Appeals (9th cir.) 1980. Assoc. Mitchell, Silberberg & Knupp, L.A., 1971-72, Greenberg, Bernhard, Weis & Karma, L.A., 1972-76; ptnr. Greenberg, Bernhard, Weiss & Rosin, L.A., 1976-85; assoc. Frandzel & Share, L.A., 1985-87, ptnr., 1987-97; ptnr. Gittler & Bradford, L.A., 1997—; judge pro tem L.A. Mcpl. Ct., 1976-83. Editor Harvard Law Rev., 1970. Mem. Los Angeles County Bar Assn. (client rels. com. arbitrator 1982—, vice chair, 1996—), Century City Bar Assn. (bd. govs. 1984-90), MIT Club So. Calif. (pres. 1978-79, bd. govs. 1979—), Sigma Xi, Tau Beta Pi. Democrat. Jewish. Avocations: senior soccer, skiing, square dancing. Banking, General civil litigation, Consumer commercial. Office: Gittler & Bradford 11620 Wilshire Blvd Ste 800 Los Angeles CA 90025-1793

**MARCUS, TODD BARRY,** lawyer; b. Newark, May 22, 1964; s. Michael Joseph and Arlene Judith Marcus; m. Caryn Lee Gelbman, Mar. 20, 1993; children: Zachary, Jenna. BS in Elec. Engring., Lafayette Coll., Easton, Pa., 1986; JD, George Washington U., 1989. Bar: N.Y. 1989. Lawyer Rosenman & Colin, N.Y.C., 1989-92, Herrick, Feinstein, N.Y.C., 1992-94, Bachner, Tally, & Polevay LLP, N.Y.C., 1995—. General civil litigation, Securities, Contracts commercial. Office: Bachner Tally & Polevay LLP 380 Madison Ave New York NY 10017-2513

**MARCUS, WALTER F., JR.,** state supreme court justice; b. New Orleans, July 26, 1927; married; children: Walter III, Adam, Barbara Ann. B.A., Yale U.; J.D., Tulane U. Bar: La. 1955. Mem. New Orleans City Council, 1962-66; judge Civil Dist. Ct., 1966-73; assoc. justice Supreme Ct. La., 1973—. Mem. ABA. Office: Supreme Ct La Supreme Court Bldg 301 Loyola Ave New Orleans LA 70112-1814*

**MARCUSS, STANLEY JOSEPH,** lawyer; b. Hartford, Conn., Jan. 24, 1942; s. Stanley Joseph and Anne Sutton (Leone) M.; m. Rosemary Daly, July 6, 1968; children: Elena Daly, Aidan Stanley. BA, Trinity Coll., 1963, Cambridge U., 1965; MA, Cambridge U., 1968; JD, Harvard U., 1968. Bar: D.C., N.Y., Conn., U.S. Supreme Ct. Staff atty. office of gen. counsel HUD, Washington, 1968; atty. firm Hogan and Hartson, Washington, 1968-73; counsel to internat. fin. subcom. U.S. Senate Com. on Banking, Housing and Urban Affairs, 1973-77; dep. asst. sec. for trade regulation Dept. Commerce, Washington, 1977-78; sr. dep. asst. sec. for industry and trade Dept. Commerce, 1978-79, acting asst. sec. for industry and trade, 1979-80, acting asst. sec. for trade regulation, 1980; mem. firm Milbank, Tweed, Hadley & McCloy, Washington, 1980-93, Bryan Cave, 1993—; former adj. prof. Am. U. Law Sch. Author: Effective Washington Representation, 1983; mem. bd. overseers U. Calif. Berkeley Law Jour.; contbr. articles to profl. jours. Former trustee Trinity Coll., Hartford. Marshall scholar. Mem. ABA, D.C. Bar (former chmn., steering com. internat. law div.), Phi Beta Kappa. Home: 4616 29th Pl NW Washington DC 20008-2105

**MARCY, ERIC JOHN,** lawyer; b. Glen Ridge, N.J., Sept. 9, 1955; s. Leonard Frederick and Lorraine Marcy; m. Karen Anne Murray, May 28, 1993; 1 child, Eric John. BA, Boston Coll., 1977; JD, Seton Hall U., 1982. Legal analyst Bell Labs., Whippany, N.J., 1980-81; law clk. Morris County Prosecutor's Office, Morristown, N.J., 1981-82; dep. atty. gen. Divson. of Criminal Justice, Trenton, N.J., 1982-85; shareholder Wilentz, Goldman & Spitzer, Woodbridge, N.J., 1985—. Mem. Middlesex County Mental Health Bd., New Brunswick, N.J., 1989-93; mem. Morris County Mental Health Bd., Morristown, 1994-97, chmn., 1996-97. Mem. N.J. Assn. Criminal Def. Attys. (co-chair legis. com. 1998—). Avocations: skiing, canoeing, sailboating, swimming. Civil rights, Criminal, Administrative and regulatory. Office: Wilentz Goldman & Spitzer PO Box 10 90 Woodbridge Ctr Dr Ste 901 Woodbridge NJ 07095-1146

**MARDINLY, PETER ALAN,** lawyer, educator; b. Phila., Apr. 30, 1952; s. Ashe John and Jane Elizabeth (Fish) M.; m. Susan D. Pulver, Sept. 6, 1981; children: Alan Robert, Shaina Beth. BA, Yale U., 1974; JD, Boston U., 1977; LLM in Taxation, Temple U., 1981. Bar: Pa. 1977, Mass. 1977, U.S. Dist. Ct. (ea. dist.) Pa. 1977, U.S. Tax Ct. 1978, U.S. Ct. Appeals (3rd cir.) 1991, U.S. Supreme Ct. 1995. Shareholder Paul, Mardinly, Durham, James, Flandreau & Rodger, P.C., Media, Pa., 1977—; adj. asst. prof. Widener U., Chester, Pa., 1981-87. Bd. dirs. Darlington Fine Arts Ctr., Wawa, Pa., 1978-83, Rotary Found., Media, 1983-87. Mem. ABA, Pa. State Bar Assn., Delaware County Bar Assn., Rotary Club of Media (bd. dirs. 1992—, pres. 1997-98), Rocky Run YMCA (bd. mgrs.). Republican. Avocations: sailing, classical piano, flying. Real property, Probate, General corporate. Home: 146 Willits Way Glen Mills PA 19342-1431 Office: Paul Mardinly Durham James Flandreau & Rodger PC PO Box D 320 W Front St Media PA 19063-2632

**MAREADY, WILLIAM FRANK,** lawyer; b. Mullins, S.C., Sept. 13, 1932; s. Jesse Frank and Vera (Sellers) M.; m. Brenda McCanless, Nov. 3, 1979. AB, U. N.C., 1955, JD with honors, 1958. Bar: N.C. 1958, U.S. Dist. Ct. N.C. 1960, U.S. Ct. Appeals (4th cir.) 1962, U.S. Supreme Ct. 1968. Assoc. Mudge, Stern, Baldwin & Todd, N.Y.C., 1958-60, Hudson, Ferrell, Carter, Petree & Stockton, Winston-Salem, N.C., 1960-65; ptnr. Petree, Stockton & Robinson, Winston-Salem, 1965-92, Robinson, Maready, Lawing & Comerford, 1992-97, Maready, Comerford & Britt, 1997-99; sole practice Law Offices of William F. Maready, 1999—. N.C. chmn. Winston-Salem/Forsyth County Bd. Edn., 1968-70, chmn., bd. dirs. and mem. exec. com., N.C. State Port Authority, 1984-97. Served with Green Berets, U.S. Army, 1952-54. Recipient Disting. Svc. award N.C. Sch. Bds. Assn. Fellow Am. Coll. Trial Lawyers, Am. Bar Found.; mem. ABA (chmn. standing com. on aero. law 1979-82, chmn. forum com. on air and space law 1982-86), N.C. Bar Assn. (chmn. litigation sect. 1981-82, adminstrn. of justice com. 1981-82), Nat. Parent Tchr. Assn. (life), Forsyth Country Club, Rotary (Winston-Salem), Order of Coif, Phi Delta Phi, Phi Beta Kappa. Republican. Methodist. Product liability, Professional liability, Toxic tort. Office: Maready Comerford & Britt LLP 250 W 1st St Ste 300 Winston Salem NC 27101-4010

**MAREK, JAMES DENNIS,** lawyer; b. Chgo., Feb. 19, 1943; s. James John and Ardis McBroom Marek; m. Shelley R. Forbess (div. May 1993); children: James J., Elizabeth A., Jordan A., Lacey A. Student, Durham (Eng.) U., 1962-63; BA, DePauw U., 1964; JD, Northwestern U., Chgo., 1967. Bar: Ill. 1967, U.S. Dist. Ct. (no. dist.) Ill. 1974, U.S. Tax Ct. 1977. With CIA, Washington, 1967-70; ptnr. Ackman, Marek & Boyd Ltd., Kankakee, Ill., 1970—. Trustee Kankakee C.C., 1992—. 1st lt. USAF, 1967-70. Fellow Am. Coll. Trial Attys., Am. Bd. Trial Advs.; mem. Ill. Def. Trial Counsel (bd. dirs. 1991—). Avocations: skiing, golf, raising llamas. General civil litigation, Personal injury, Real property. Office: Ackman Marek & Boyd Ltd One Dearborn Sq Kankakee IL 60901

**MAREK, THOMAS R.,** lawyer; b. Bayonne, N.J., Sept. 20, 1958; s. Stanley S. and Constance M. M.; m. Lezlie Ott. BA, Dartmouth Coll., 1980; JD, Notre Dame. Bar: Colo., N.J., Minn. Atty. Oppenheimer Wolff & Donnelly LLP, Mpls. Office: Oppenheimer Wolff & Donnelly LLP 45 S 7th St 3400 Plz Vii Minneapolis MN 55402

**MARGER, EDWIN,** lawyer; b. N.Y.C., Mar. 18, 1928; s. William and Fannie (Cohen) M.; m. Kaye Sanderson, Oct. 1, 1951; children: Shari Ann, Diane Elaine, Sandy Ben; m. L. Suzanne Smyth, July 5, 1968; 1 child, George Phinney; m. Mary Susan Hamel, May 6, 1987; 1 child, Charleston Faye. BA, U. Miami, 1951, JD, 1953. Bar: Fla. 1953, Ga. 1971, D.C. 1978. Sole practice Miami Beach, Fla., 1953-67, Atlanta, 1971—; gen. counsel Physicians Nat. Risk Retention Group, 1988-91, Physicians Reliance Assn., 1988-91, Physicians Nat. Legal Def. Corp., 1988-91; spl. asst. atty. gen. Fla., 1960-61; of counsel Richard Burns, Miami, 1967—. Contbr. articles to legal jours. Tchr. Nat. Inst. Trial Advocacy; mem. Miami Beach Social Svc. Commn., 1957; chmn. Fulton County Aviation Adv. Com., 1980—; trustee Forensic Scis. Found., 1984-88; v.p., 1986-88; lt. col., a.d.c. Gov. Ga., 1971-74, 80-84; col., a.d.c. Gov. La., 1977-87; Khan Bahador and mem. exiled King of Afghanistan Privy Council, 1980—. With USAAF, 1946-47. Fellow Am. Acad. Forensic Scis. (chmn. jurisprudence sect. 1977-78, sec. 1976-77, exec. com. 1983-86); mem. ABA, Fla. Bar Assn. (aerospace com. 1971-83, bd. govs. 1983-87, 90-94, exec. com. 1993-94), State Bar Ga. (chmn. sect. environ. law 1974-75, aviation law sect. 1978, bd. govs. 1999—), Ga. Trial Lawyers Assn. (bd. govs. 1999—), Nat. Assn. Criminal Def. Lawyers, Ga. Assn. Criminal Def. Lawyers, Assn. Trial Lawyers Am., Am. Judicature Soc., Am. Arbitration Assn. (commn. panel 1978), Inter-Am. Bar Assn. (sr.), World Assn. Lawyers (founding), Lawyer-Pilots Bar Assn. (founding, v.p. 1959-62), VFW, Rotary, Advocates Club. Criminal, Public international, Family and matrimonial. Office: 44 N Main St Jasper GA 30143-1501

**MARGID, LEONARD,** lawyer; b. N.Y.C., May 13, 1927; s. Irving Bert and Jean (Davis) M.; m. Loretta B. Berman, Aug. 23, 1958; 1 child, Elizabeth S. BA, U. Iowa, 1949; JD, NYU, 1951. Bar: N.Y. 1952, U.S. Dist. Ct. (ea. and so. dists.) N.Y. 1954. Assoc. Proskauer, Rose, Goetz & Mendelson, N.Y.C., 1951-58; ptnr. Otterbourg, Steindler, Houston & Rosen, N.Y.C., 1958-90; pvt. practice N.Y.C., 1991—. Sgt. U.S. Army, 1945-46, ETO. Mem. Assn. of Bar of City of N.Y. Avocations: travel, tennis, hiking, theater, investments. General corporate, Real property. Home and Office: 4455 Douglas Ave Bronx NY 10471-3519

**MARGO, ROBERT CRAVENS,** lawyer; b. Indpls., Mar. 1, 1949; s. Marvin Kenneth and Bobbie (Cravens) M.; m. Martha L. Johnson, June 12, 1971; children: Amy E., Bradley J. BA, So. Meth. U., 1971; JD, Oklahoma City U., 1974. Bar: Okla. 1974, U.S. Dist. Ct. (we. dist.) Okla. 1974, U.S. Ct. Appeals (10th cir.) 1974, U.S. Supreme Ct. 1989. Assoc. Pierce Couch et al, Oklahoma City, 1974-77; ptnr. Short Wiggins Margo & Adler, Oklahoma City, 1977—; bd. dirs. Okla. Attys. Mut. Ins. Co., Oklahoma City. Fellow Am. Coll. Trial Lawyers; mem. Okla. Bar Assn., Oklahoma County Bar Assn. (bd. dirs. 1993-95), Fedn. Ins. and Corp. Counsel, Am. Bd. Trial Advocates (pres. Okla. chpt. 1994-95). General civil litigation, Personal injury, Insurance. Home: 1615 Dorchester Dr Oklahoma City OK 73120-1204 Office: Short Wiggins Margo & Adler 3100 Oklahoma Tower 210 Park Ave Oklahoma City OK 73102-5605

**MARGOLES, ALAN D.,** lawyer; b. St. Paul, Apr. 1, 1950; s. Simon and Muriel June Margoles; m. Cheryl Speeter, Aug. 13, 1974; children: Sarah, Michael, Daniel. BA summa cum laude, U. Minn., 1976, JD cum laude, 1977. Bar: Minn. 1977, U.S. Dist. Ct. Minn. 1978, U.S. Ct. Appeals (8th cir.) 1987, U.S. Supreme Ct. 1990. Ptnr. Margoles & Gedman, St. Paul, 1978-80, Margoles & Margoles, St. Paul, 1980—. Mem. NACDL, Phi Beta Kappa. General corporate. Home: 2570 Glenhurst Ave Saint Louis Park MN 55416 Office: Margoles & Margoles 790 Cleveland Ave S Ste 223 Saint Paul MN 55116-1902

**MARGOLIN, ABRAHAM EUGENE,** lawyer; b. St. Joseph, Mo., Oct. 16, 1907; s. Jacob and Rebecca (Cohn) M.; m. Florence Solow, Feb. 1, 1931 (dec. Feb. 1998); children: Robert J., Judith (Mrs. Goodman), James S. LLB, JD, Washington U., St. Louis, 1929. Pvt. practice, Kansas City. Bd. mem. Tension Envelope Corp., UMB Mortgage Co. Pres. ctrl. governing bd. Children's Mercy Hosp., 1972-76, life mem.; dir. life Truman Med. Ctr., Menorah Med. Ctr.; mem. bd. govs. City Trust Kansas City, Rsch. Mental Health Found.; dir., v.p. Jewish Fedn. Greater Kansas City; bd. govs. Hebrew Acad. Kansas City; gov. Am. Royal Assn.; pres. coun., fellow Brandeis U.; trusteee B'nai B'rith Found.; mem. adv. bd. Anti-Defamation League; mem. nat. exec. coun. Am. Jewish Com., Am. Joint Distbn. Com. Named Disting. Law Alumnus, Washington U.; recipient Man of Yr. award Congregations Beth Shalom. Mem. ABA, ATLA, Am. Judicature Soc., Fed. Bar Assn., Mo. Bar Assn., Met. Kansas City Bar Assn., U.S. Supreme Ct. Hist. Soc., Heritage Found., Cato Inst., World Jewish Congress, Am. Jewish Congress, Kansas City Club, Oakwood Golf and Country Club, Nat. Lawyers Club, Order of Coif, Delta Sigma Rho. Construction, General corporate, Estate planning. Home: 221 W 48th St Apt 606 Kansas City MO 64112-3139 Office: 2345 Grand Blvd Ste 2500 Kansas City MO 64108-2603

**MARGOLIN, FREDERICK A.,** lawyer; b. Bklyn., June 5, 1945; s. Leo H. and Ann Margolin. BA, Am. U., Washington, 1966; JD, NYU, 1969. Bar: N.Y. 1971. Asst. counsel, pub. adminstr. Kings County, Bklyn., 1971-81. Mem. Bklyn. Bar Assn. Office: 189 Montague St Brooklyn NY 11201-3610

**MARGOLIN, JESSE,** lawyer; b. N.Y.C., Nov. 19, 1928; s. Edward I. and Henrietta (Markowitz) M.; m. Barbara Toni, Dec. 22, 1952; chidlren: Michael, David, Susan. BA, NYU, 1950; JD, Yale U. Law Sch., 1953. Bar: N.Y. 1954, U.S. Dist. Ct. (so. and ea. dists.) N.Y. 1954. Assoc. Becker, Ross & Stone, N.Y.C., 1953-64; ptnr. Becker, Ross & Stone, 1964—. General corporate, Corporate taxation, Non-profit and tax-exempt organizations. Office: Becker Ross & Stone 317 Madison Ave New York NY 10017-5201

**MARGOLIN, ROBERT JEREMY,** lawyer; b. Kansas City, Mo., Mar. 21, 1935; s. Abraham Eugene and Florence Margolin; m. Dorothy Ann Macy, Sept. 20, 1959; children: Kathryn R. Margolin Richter, Charles D. AB, Dartmouth Coll., 1957; JD, LLB, U. Mich., 1960. Ptnr. Margolin and Kirwan, Kansas City, 1960—; bd. dirs. Kansas City Kings, Field Leasing. Asst. editor Mich. Law Rev. Bd. dirs. Menorah Med. Ctr., Kansas City, Kansas City Philharm. Assn.; mem. exec. com. Jewish Vocat. Svc., Kansas City. Mem. ABA, Nat. Basketball Assn. (bd. govs.), Mo. Bar Assn., Kansas City Bar Assn. Avocations: golf, skiing. Home: 37 Sheephill Rd Apt 13 Riverside CT 06878-1425 Office: 4505 Madison Ave Kansas City MO 64111-3509

**MARGOLIS, ANITA JOY,** lawyer; b. Mpls., May 29, 1959; d. Herbert A. and Ursula (Ries) M. BA, U. Wis., 1981; JD, Calif. Western Sch. of Law, 1985. Bar: Calif. 1985, U.S. Dist. Ct. (so. dist.) Calif. 1985, U.S. Dist. Ct. (ctrl. dist.) Calif. 1993. Assoc. Phillips, Campbell, Haskett, Noone & Ingwalson, San Diego, 1986-93; pvt. practice The Law Offices of Anita J. Margolis, San Diego, 1993—. Mem. task force Women's Resource Fair San Diego Vol. Lawyers Program, 1989—, vol. lawyer, 1993—; mem. gender equity adv. bd. San Diego C.C. Dist., 1990—, chair, 1994—; mem. single parent/displaced homemakers adv. bd. San Diego C.C. Dist., 1990—; judge mock trial Calif. Sch. Law, 1991-95. Mem. San Diego County Bar Assn., Consumer Attys. San Diego, Lawyers Club of San Diego (bd. dirs. 1989-93, sec. 1991-92, asst. sec. 1992-93, chmn. cmty. rels. com. 1989-91, chmn. continuing edn. com. 1992-93). Avocations: soccer, golf, tennis, skiing. General civil litigation, Family and matrimonial, Personal injury. Office: Law Office Anita J Margolis 185 W F St Fl 7 San Diego CA 92101-6029

**MARGOLIS, BENJAMIN ROBERT,** lawyer, pharmacist; b. Phila., Jan. 15, 1945; s. Daniel and Sylvia (Rubin) M.; m. Lia Ordaz, Dec. 27, 1971; 1 child, Jonathan Daniel. BSc, Phila. Coll. Pharmacy and Sci., 1967; PharmD, U. So. Calif., 1969; JD, Southwestern U. Sch. Law, 1984. Bar: Calif. 1986, D.C. 1987, U.S. Dist. Ct. (cen. dist.) Calif. 1986, U.S. Tax Ct. 1986, U.S. Ct. Appeals (9th cir.) 1987, U.S. Supreme Ct. 1989. Dir. pharmacy Rancho Los Amigos Med. Ctr., Downey, Calif., 1993—; pvt. practice law Pacific Palisades, Calif., 1986—; expert witness pharmacy and med. malpractice. Mem. ABA, L.A. County Bar Assn., Assn. Trial Lawyers Am., L.A. Trial Lawyers Assn. General practice. Office: 1387 Monument St Pacific Palisades CA 90272-2544

**MARGOLIS, EMANUEL,** lawyer, educator; b. Bklyn., Mar. 18, 1926; s. Abraham and Esther (Levin) M.; m. Edith Cushing; m. Estelle Thompson, Mar. 1, 1959; children: Elizabeth Margolis-Pineo, Catherine, Abby Margolis Newman, Joshua, Sarah. BA, U. N.C., 1947; MA, Harvard U., 1948, PhD, 1951; JD, Yale U., 1956. Bar: Conn. 1957, U.S. Dist. Ct. Conn. 1958, U.S. Supreme Ct. 1969. Instr. dept. govt. U. Conn., 1951-53; assoc. Silberberg & Silverstein, Ansonia, Conn., 1956-60; assoc. Wofsey Rosen Kweskin & Kuriansky, Stamford, Conn., 1960-66, ptnr., 1966-96, of counsel, 1996—; arbitrator State of Conn., 1984-85, Am. Arbitration Assn., 1998—; trial referee, 1985—; adj. prof. Quinnipiac Coll. Sch. Law, 1986—. Sr. editor Conn. Bar Jour., 1971-80, 83—, editor-in-chief, 1980-83; contbr. to legal jours. Mem. nat. bd. ACLU, 1975-79; mem. Westport (Conn.) Planning and Zoning Commn., 1971-75; chmn. Conn. CLU, 1988-95, legal advisor, 1995—. Served with U.S. Army, 1944-46. Decorated Purple Heart; recipient First Award for Disting. Svc. to Conn. Bar, Conn. Law Tribune, 1987. Fellow Conn. Bar Found. (James W. Cooper fellow 1996); mem. ABA, Conn. Bar Assn. (chmn. human rights sect. 1970-73), Nat. Assn. Criminal Def. Lawyers, Am. Arbitration Assn. (arbitrator 1998—). Federal civil litigation, Civil rights, Criminal. Office: 600 Summer St Stamford CT 06901-4404 Home: 72 Myrtle Ave Westport CT 06880-3512

**MARGOLIS, EUGENE,** lawyer, government official; b. Bronx, N.Y., Dec. 19, 1935; s. Louis and Minnie (Kaplan) M.; m. Sally Fay Gellman, Sept. 22, 1962; children—Judith Miriam, Linda Aileen, Aaron Keith, Pamela June. BME, Rensselaer Poly. Inst., 1957; JD, Georgetown U., 1960, M in Patent Law, 1962. Bar: N.Y. 1961, U.S. Supreme Ct. 1969; cert. exec. U.S. Office Personnel Mgmt., 1983. Patent examiner U.S. Patent Office, Washington, 1957-60; trial atty. antitrust div. U.S. Dept. Justice, Washington, 1960-66, N.Y.C., 1966-67; chief consumer protection div. N.Y.C. Dept. Law, 1967-71; gen. counsel Mayor's Interdeptl. Com. on Pub. Utilities, N.Y.C., 1972-73; spl. counsel to commr. N.Y.C. Dept. Gen. Services, 1974-79; dir. N.Y.C. Office of Energy Conservation, 1975-79; sr. legal adviser U.S. Dept. Energy, Washington, 1979-95, dep. asst. gen. counsel, 1995—; adj. prof. Cooper Union, 1978-79; adj. assoc. prof. Grad. Sch., CUNY, 1974-80. Mem. editorial bd. Georgetown Law Jour., 1958-60. Chmn. govtl. relations and grants com. Village of Larchmont, N.Y., 1977-79, mem. cable TV com., 1977-79, mem. tax base com., 1974-79; chmn. Larchmont Democratic Com., 1976-77; vice chmn. Mamaroneck Dem. Com., 1979; mem. Westchester County Dem. Com., 1975-77, 79; bd. dirs. Jewish Community Coun. Greater Washington, 1986-94; mem. adv. bd. Dept. Volunteerism, Commonwealth Va., 1987-91; mem. pub. social policy com. United Jewish Appeal-Fedn. Greater Washington, 1988—,mem. No. Va. leadership coun. 1990—; sr. v.p. B'nai Brith Internat., 1996-98, bd. govs., 1992—, Hillel com., 1991-94, com. on community vol. svcs., 1985-89, pres. dist. 5, 1993-94, pres. Va. State Assn., 1986-87, pres. Va. Hillel Found., 1985-86. Recipient Cert. of Appreciation U.S. Dept. Energy, 1984, Sec. of Energy's Award, Outstanding Community Svc. Vol., 1990, Gov. Va.'s Cmty. Svc. and Volunteerism award, 1995. Mem. N.Y. State Bar Assn., ASME, Phi Delta Phi, Pi Delta Epsilon, Tau Epsilon Phi. Jewish. Clubs: Rensselaer Alumni (sec. chpt. 1976-77), U. Va. Fund Parents, Town and Village Synagogue Men's (pres. 1970-71). Lodge: B'nai Brith (pres. Mcpl. lodge 1976-78, Larchmont-Mamaroneck lodge 1978-80, Masada lodge 1984-85, Internat. Lodge Col. Elliot A. Niles Community Svc. award 1984, Dist. 5 Outstanding Ben Brith award 1988, Outstanding State Pres. award 1987, Hillel award 1986, Community Vol. Svc. award 1984, Va. State Assn. Herman G. Koplen Meml. award 1987, Sherry B. Rose Leadership award 1984). Home: 6504 Sparrow Point Ct Mc Lean VA 22101-1638 Office: US Dept Energy Forrestal Bldg 1000 Independence Ave SE Washington DC 20585-0001

**MARGOLIS, LAWRENCE STANLEY,** federal judge; b. Phila., Mar. 13, 1935; s. Reuben and Mollie (Manus) M.; m. Doris May Rosenberg, Jan. 30, 1960; children: Mary Aleta, Paul Oliver. BSME, Drexel U., 1957; JD, George Washington U., 1961. Bar: D.C. 1963. Patent examiner U. S. Patent Office, Washington, 1957-62; patent counsel Naval Ordnance Lab., White Oak, Md., 1962-63; asst. corp. counsel D.C., 1963-66; atty. criminal div., spl. asst. U.S. atty. Dept. of Justice, Washington, 1966-68; asst. U.S. atty. for D.C., 1968-71; U.S. magistrate judge U.S. Dist. Ct., Washington, 1971-82; judge U.S. Ct. Fed. Claims, Washington, 1982—; chmn. task force on discovery reform U.S. Claims Ct., Washington, chmn. alt. dispute resolution; mem. faculty Fed. Jud. Ctr. Editor-in-chief The Young Lawyer, 1965-66, D.C. Bar Jour., 1967-73; bd. editors The Dist. Lawyer, 1978-82. Trustee Drexel U., 1983-89; bd. govs. George Washington U. Alumni Assn., 1978-85, 93-96;. Recipient Contbn. award D.C. Jaycees, 1966, Svc. award Boy Scouts Am., 1970, Alumni Svc. award George Washington U., 1976, Disting. Alumni Achievement award George Washington U., 1985, Disting. Alumni Achievement award Drexel U., 1988, Drexel 100 award, 1992, Alternative Dispute Resolution award Ctr. for Pub. Resources, 1988, Alternative Dispute Resolution Svc. award Ct. of Fed. Claims, 1996, Alumni Recognition award George Washington U., 1996. Fellow Inst. Jud. Adminstrn., Am. Bar Found.; mem. ABA (chmn. jud. adminstrn. divsn., Disting. Svc. award 1981), ABA Nat. Conf. Spl. Ct. Judges (chmn., Disting. Svc. award 1978), D.C. Jud. Conf., Bar Assn. D.C. (bd. dirs. 1970-72, jour. editor-in-chief, Contbn. award young lawyers sect. 1983), Fed. Bar Assn., George Washington U. Nat. Law Assn. (pres. D.C. chpt. 1974-76, pres. 1983-84), Univ. Club., Rotary (bd. dirs. Washington 1984-90, pres. 1988-89, dist. gov. 1991-92, Rotarian of Yr. 1984), Charles Fahy Am. Inn of Ct. (Nat. Program award, 1997). Office: US Ct Fed Claims 717 Madison Pl NW Ste 703 Washington DC 20439-0002

**MARGOLIS, MARVIN ALLEN,** lawyer; b. Milw., Sept. 30, 1934; s. Ben William and Jen (Dekelboum) M.; m. Ann Lubell, Dec. 3, 1961; children: David, Michael, Jeffrey. BS, U. Wis., 1956, JJD, 1958. Bar: Wis. 1958, U.S. Dist. Ct. (ea. dist.) Wis. 1960. Ptnr. Margolis & Cassidy, Milw.; Ct. Commr. City of Milw., 1975—; lectr. in field. Contbr. numerous articles to profl. jours. Fellow Am. Acad. Matrimonial Lawyers (Wis. chpt. treas. 1978, v.p. 1979, pres. 1980-81), Wis. Acad. Trial Lawyers; mem. ABA, Assn. Trial Lawyers Am., Wis. Bar Assn. (bd. attys. profl. responsibility 1975—, dir. family law sect. 1982—), Milw. Bar Assn. (jud. selection com.), Jr. Milw. Bar Assn., Am. Inns of Ct. (Leander J. Foley, Jr. matrimonial chpt.). Avocation: tennis. General civil litigation, Probate, Family and matrimonial. Office: Margolis & Cassidy 324 E Wisconsin Ave # 700 Milwaukee WI 53202

**MARGULIES, BETH ZELDES,** assistant attorney general; b. Hartford, Conn., Apr. 24, 1954; d. Benjamin and Edith Rose (Herrmann) Zeldes; m. Martin B. Margulies, July 26, 1981; children: Max, Adam. BA in Anthropology, McGill U., Montreal, 1976; JD summa cum laude, U. Bridgeport, 1983; LLM, Yale U., 1985. Bar: Conn. 1983, U.S. Dist. Ct. Conn. 1983, U.S. Ct. Appeals (D.C. cir.) 1988, U.S. Supreme Ct., 1989, U.S. Ct. Appeals (2d cir.) 1992. Asst. atty. gen. Atty. Gen.'s Office State of Conn., Hartford, 1985—. Contbr. articles to profl. jours. Home: 79 High Rock Rd Sandy Hook CT 06482-1623 Office: Atty Gen Office State of Conn 55 Elm St Hartford CT 06106-1797

**MARGULIES, LAURA JACOBS,** lawyer; b. Bklyn., Feb. 5, 1956; d. David and Marcia (Reichman) Jacobs; children: Moshe, Yaakov, Miriam, Yehuda, Shira. BS in Edn., HTD, Yeshiva U., 1977; JD, U. Balt., 1988. Bar: Md. 1988, D.C. 1990. Jud. intern to Hon. James F. Schneider U.S. Bankruptcy Ct., Balt., 1986; law clk. Shawe & Rosenthal, Balt., 1987-88; law clk. to Hon. Paul E. Alpert Md. Ct. Spl. Appeals, Towson, 1988-89; assoc. Semmes, Bowen & Semmes, Balt., 1989-92, Shaw, Pittman, Potts & Trowbridge, Washington, 1992-93; pvt. practice Rockville, Md., 1993—; adj. prof. U. Md. U. Coll., College Park, 1993-96; civil mediator Cir. Ct. of Balt. City, 1991-93. Editor U. Balt. Law Review, 1986-88. Recipient David Gann scholarship U. Balt. Sch. Law, 1987. Mem. Bankruptcy Bar Assn. for Dist. of Md. (so. div. co-chmn. 1994-95, chmn. 1995-96), Md. State Bar Assn., D.C. Bar Assn. Avocations: walking, reading, swimming. Bankruptcy, Consumer commercial. Office: 5870 Hubbard Dr Rockville MD 20852-4818

**MARGULIES, MARTIN B.,** lawyer, educator; b. N.Y.C., Oct. 6, 1940; s. Max N. and Mae (Cohen) M.; m. Beth Ellen Zeldes, July 26, 1981; children: Max Zeldes, Adam Zeldes. AB, Columbia Coll., 1961; LLB, Harvard U., 1964; LLM, NYU, 1966. Bar: N.D. 1968, N.Y. 1974, Mass. 1977, U.S. Dist. Ct. Mass. 1977, U.S. Ct. Appeals (2d cir.) 1984, Conn. 1988, U.S. Supreme Ct. 1995. Asst. prof. law U. N.D., Grand Forks, 1966-69; editor-in-chief Columbia Coll. Today, Columbia U., N.Y.C., 1969-71; assoc. editor Parade Mag., N.Y.C., 1971-72; assoc. prof. law Western New Eng. Law Sch., Springfield, Mass., 1973-76; Bernard Hersher prof. law U. Bridgeport, Conn., 1977-92; prof. law Quinnipiac Coll., 1992—, Neil H. Cogan Pub. Svc. prof. law, 1997—. Author: The Early Life of Sean O'Casey, 1970. Contbr. articles to profl. jours. Cooperating atty. Conn. Civil Liberties Union, Hartford, 1979—, bd. dirs., 1982-94; bd. dirs. Conn. Attys. for Progressive Legislature, New Haven, 1982—; bd. dirs. ACLU, 1987-94, mem. free speech-assn. and poverty constitutional rights com. 1988-94; chmn. bd. dirs. Fairfield County Civil Liberties Union, 1982-87, Hampden County Civil Liberties Union, 1976-78; bd. dirs. Civil Liberties Union Mass., Boston, 1975-78, Greater Springfield Urban League, 1976-78, Conn. Civil Liberties Union, 1982-94, ACLU, 1987-94. Ctr. for First Amendment Rights, Inc., 1993—. Recipient Media award N.Y. State Bar Assn., 1972, Gavel award ABA, 1973, Outstanding Tchr. award U. Bridgeport Law Sch., 1986, 87. Mem. Mass. Bar Assn., N.Y. State Bar Assn. Jewish. Home: 79 High Rock Rd Sandy Hook CT 06482-1623 Office: Quinnipiac Coll Sch Law 275 Mt Carmel Ave Hamden CT 06518-1961

**MARGULIS, HOWARD LEE,** lawyer; b. St. Louis, Oct. 7, 1961; s. Lawrence and Rosalyn Rae (Chait) M.; m. Sharlene R. Harris, Aug. 12, 1984; children: Jennifer Lynne, Michelle Lisa, David Jonathan. BA in History, Northwestern U., 1984; JD summa cum laude, IIT, 1987. Bar: Ill. 1987, N.J. 1990, N.Y., 1999, U.S. Dist. Ct. (no. dist.) Ill. 1987, U.S. Dist. Ct. N.J. 1990, U.S. Ct. Appeals (7th and D.C. cirs.) 1988, U.S. Ct. Appeals (9th and 3d cirs.) 1989, U.S. Dist. Ct. (ea. and so. dists.) N.Y. 1998, U.S. Dist. Ct. (ea. dist.) Mich. 1998, U.S. Ct. Appeals (2d cir.) 1998; registered lobbyist, N.J. Assoc. Seyfarth, Shaw, Fairweather & Geraldson, Chgo., 1987-89, Saiber Schlesinger Satz & Goldstein, Newark, 1989-90; spl. counsel Guardian Life Ins. Co., Iselin, N.J., 1990-91; gen. counsel Energy Consortium, Inc., Iselin, N.J., 1991-95, Skadden Arps Slate Meagher & Flom, Newark, 1995-99; ptnr. Baker & McKenzie, N.Y.C., 1999—. Mem. Middlesex County Human Rels. Commn., 1997—. IIT Acad. scholar, 1984-87, others. Mem. ABA, N.Y. State Bar Assn., N.J. Assn. Energy Engrs. (dir.). Democrat. Jewish. Avocation: tennis, golf. FERC practice, Administrative and regulatory, General civil litigation. Home: 7 Pilgrim Run East Brunswick NJ 08816-3237 Office: 805 3d Ave New York NY 10022

**MARGULIS, MICHAEL HENRY,** lawyer; b. N.Y.C., Oct. 30, 1959; s. David H. and Eleanor Weinberg Margulis; m. Amy M. Sturmer, Mar. 19, 1989; children: Rebekah Geri, Daniel Aaron. AB, Princeton (N.J.) U., 1981; JD, Stanford U., 1984. Bar: N.Y. 1985. Assoc. Shea & Gould, N.Y.C., 1984-93, ptnr., 1993-94; ptnr. Duane, Morris & Heckscher LLP, N.Y.C., 1994—. Securities, Mergers and acquisitions, General corporate. Office: Duane Morris & Heckscher LLP 380 Lexington Ave New York NY 10168-0002

**MARHOFFER, DAVID,** lawyer; b. Chgo., Aug. 4, 1966; s. Dov and Marilyn L. (Edelman) M.; m. Jessica A. Segal, May 29, 1994. BSBA, U. Ariz., 1989; JD, U. Calif., San Francisco, 1994. Bar: Ariz. 1994. Law clk. to hon. judge Edward C. Rapp Maricopa County Superior Ct., Phoenix, 1993; ptnr. Marhoffer Don & Segal PLLC, Scottsdale, Ariz., 1994—. Mem. Am. Jewish Com., Phoenix, 1997—. Hastings coll. grant U. Calif. 1992, 93, 94, Legal Equal Opportunity grant, 1992, 93, 94. mem. Horace Rumpole Am. Inn of Ct., Scottsdale Bar Assn., Phi Alpha Delta, Sigma Alpha Mu (alumni adv. bd. 1996—). Jewish. Avocations: sports, creative writing, history, literature, philosophy. Real property, Contracts commercial, Landlord-tenant. Office: Marhoffer Don Segal PLLC 7373 N Scottsdale Rd Ste D222 Scottsdale AZ 85253-3506

**MARICK, MICHAEL MIRON,** lawyer; b. Chgo., Nov. 20, 1957; s. Miron Michael and Geraldyne Marilyn (Lid) M.; m. LIsa Amy Gelman, May 17, 1986. BA, Denison U., 1979; JD, Ill. Inst. Tech., 1982. Bar: Ill. 1982, U.S.

Dist. Ct. (no. dist.) Ill. 1982, Fla. 1983, U.S. Ct. Appeals (3rd cir.) 1988, U.S. Ct. Appeals (6th cir.) 1992, U.S. Supreme Ct. 1992. Assoc. Hinshaw, Culbertson, Moelmann, Hoban & Fuller, Chgo., 1982-85, Phelan, Pope & John, Chgo., 1985-90; ptnr. Pope & John, Chgo., 1990-94, Bates, Meckler, Bulger & Tilson, Chgo., 1994—; adj. prof. Ill. Inst. Tech./Chgo.-Kent Coll. Law, 1983-84, 87—; comml. arbitrator Am. Arbitration Assn., Chgo., 1983—. Mem. Ill. Inst. Tech./Chgo.-Kent Law Rev., 1980-82; contbr. articles on ins. law and litigation to profl. jours. Treas., mem. exec. com. 42d Ward Rep. Orgn., 1987-87. Denison U. Econs. fellow, 1978, State of Ill. Gov.'s fellow, 1978; recipient Disting. Svc. award Ill. Inst. Tech./Chgo. Kent Coll. Law, 1996. Mem. ABA (mem. exec. com., com. on legis. action young lawyers divsn. 1983-84, vice chmn. TIPS excess surplus lines and reins. com. 1990-92), Ill. Bar Assn. (ins. law sect. coun. 1991-96, chair 1994-95, assembly rep. 1993-96), Fla. Bar Assn., Chgo. Bar Assn., Def. Rsch. Inst., Internat. Assn. Def. Counsel, Ill. Inst. Tech./Chgo.-Kent Coll. Law Alumni Assn. (v.p. 1990-94, pres. 1994-95), Trial Lawyers Club, Omicron Delta Upsilon, Pi Sigma Alpha, Alpha Tau Omega. Presbyterian. Federal civil litigation, State civil litigation, Insurance. Home: 3605 Pebble Beach Rd Northbrook IL 60062-3109 Office: Bates Meckler Bulger & Tilson 8300 Sears Tower 233 S Wacker Dr Ste 8300 Chicago IL 60606-6339

**MARIER, RAYMOND CONRAD,** lawyer; b. Ottawa, Ont., Can., Jan. 4, 1945; s. Conrad Lucien and Mildred Ann (Patton) M.; m. Cheryl Lynn Rutherford, July 18, 1970; children: Megan Leigh, Leslie Lucienne, Elizabeth Ann. BChE, Manhattan Coll., Riverdale, N.Y., 1966; JD, Cornell U., 1969. Bar: N.Y. 1969. Law clk. N.Y. Superior Ct., Appellate divsn. 3d Dept., Albany, 1969-70; assoc. Fish & Neave, N.Y.C., 1970-73; assoc. counsel Corning Inc., Corning, N.Y., 1973-90; sr. v.p., gen. counsel Corning Life Scis., Inc., N.Y.C., 1990-96, Metpath, Inc., Tetersboro, N.J., 1992-96; v.p., gen. counsel Quest Diagnostics Inc., Tetersboro, 1997—; instr. Cornell Law Sch., Ithaca, 1976-78; pres., dir. South Tier Legal Svcs., Bath, N.Y., 1976-88. Mng. editor Cornell Law Rev., 1968-69. Vice pres., dir. Chemung County Hist. Soc., Elmira, N.Y., 1990-92; dir. Monroe County Legal Assist Corp., Rochester, N.Y., 1976-80. Republican. Roman Catholic. General corporate, Health. Home: 37 Howell Rd Mountain Lakes NJ 07046-1350 Office: Quest Diagnostics Inc One Malcolm Ave Tetersboro NJ 07608

**MARINELLO, SALVATORE JOHN,** lawyer; b. Bklyn., Oct. 10, 1946; s. John Salvatore and Virginia (Arbia) M.; m. Mary Mallia, Sept. 3, 1972 (div. 1987); m. Patricia Ann Stone, Aug. 2, 1992; children: Michelle, John. BA, CUNY, 1968; JD, N.Y. Law Sch., 1974. Bar: N.Y. 1974, U.S. Dist. Ct. (ea. dist.) N.Y. 1974, U.S. Supreme Ct. 1980. Asst. dist. atty., chief homicide investigation Queens County Dist. Atty., Queens, N.Y., 1974-78; asst. dist. atty., dep. chief rackets and comml. frauds bur. Nassau County Dist. Atty., Nassau, N.Y., 1978-83; pvt. practice law Nassau, N.Y., 1983—. Recipient Merit award Am. Acad. for Profl. Law Enforcement, 1991. Mem. Nassau Bar Assn. (criminal law com. mem. 1989-91), Columbia Lawyers Assn. (Recognition award 1991), N.Y. State Bar Assn., Nat. Assn. Criminal Def. Lawyers. Avocations: golf, basketball, boating. Criminal. Home: 14 Bondsburry Ln Melville NY 11747-3902 Address: 55 Mineola Blvd Mineola NY 11501-4220

**MARING, MARY MUEHLEN,** state supreme court justice; b. Devils Lake, N.D., July 27, 1951; d. Joseph Edward and Charlotte Rose (Schorr) Muehlen; m. David Scott Maring, Aug. 30, 1975; children: Christopher David, Andrew Joseph. BA in Polit. Sci. summa cum laude, Moorhead State U., 1972; JD, U. N.D., 1975. Bar: Minn., N.D. Law clk. Hon. Bruce Stone, Mpls, 1975-76; assoc. Stefanson, Landberg & Alm, Ltd., Moorhead, Minn., 1976-82, Ohnstad, Twichell, Breitling, Rosenvold, Wanner, Nelson, Neugebauer & Maring, P.C., West Fargo, N.D., 1982-88, Lee Hagan Law Office, Fargo, 1988-91; pvt. practice Maring Law Office, Fargo, 1991-96; assoc. justice N.D. State Supreme Ct., Bismarck, N.D., 1996—; women's bd. mem. 1st Nat. Bank, Fargo, 1977-82; career day speaker Moorhead Rotarians, 1980-83. Contbr. note to legal rev.; note editor N.D. Law Rev., 1975. Mem. ABA (del. ann. conv. young lawyers sect. 1981-82, bd. govs. 1982-83), Minn. Women Lawyers, N.D. State Bar Assn. (bd. govs. 1991-93), Minn. Trial Lawyers Assn., Clay County Bar Assn. (v.p. 1983-84), N.D. Trial Lawyers Assn. (pres. 1992-93),. Roman Catholic. Office: ND Supreme Ct State Capitol Jud Wing 1st Fl 600 E Bird Ave Bismarck ND 58505-0530

**MARINIS, THOMAS PAUL, JR.,** lawyer; b. Jacksonville, Tex., May 31, 1943; s. Thomas Paul and Betty Sue (Garner) M.; m. Lucinda Cruse, June 25, 1969; children—Courtney, Kathryn, Megan. B.A., Yale U., 1965; LL.B., U. Tex., 1968. Bar: Tex. Assoc. Vinson & Elkins, Houston, 1969-76, ptnr., 1977—. Served with USAR, 1968-74. Fellow Tex. Bar Found; mem. ABA (sec. taxation sect. 1984-85), Tex. Bar Assn. (chmn. taxation sect. 1986-87). Clubs: Houston Country, Houston Ctr., Coronado. Corporate taxation, Personal income taxation.

**MARINO, JOSEPH ANTHONY, III,** lawyer; b. New Orleans, Nov. 12, 1966; s. Joseph A. Jr. and Kathleen M. Marino; m. Micaela Carney, May 18, 1990; children: Carney, Ella. BA, La. State U., 1988; JD, U. S.C., 1992. Bar: La. 1992. Pub. defender 24th J.D. Indigent Defender, Gretna, La., 1993; pvt. practice law Gretna, 1993—. Bd. dirs. Woodland Oaks Civic Assn., Harvey, La., 1996. Mem. Nat. Assn. Criminal Def. Lawyers, La. Assn. Criminal Def. Lawyers, Jefferson Bar Assn. Republican. Criminal. Office: 501 Derbigny St Gretna LA 70053-6017

**MARINO, NINA,** lawyer; b. Hillside, N.Y., Aug. 13, 1963; d. Julio John and Vera Gretchen Marino m. Richard Kaplan, May 8, 1993; children: Carina, Cayla. Student, U. London, 1984, 86; BA, U. Miami, 1985; postgrad., Southwestern U., 1985; JD, San Fernando Valley Sch. Law, 1989. Bar: U.S. Dist. Ct. (all dists.) Calif., Calif. 1989, U.S. Supreme Ct. 1996. Sole practice L.A., 1993-98; ptnr. Kaplan Marino, APC, Beverly Hills, 1998—; lectr. Pierce Coll., 1996; spkr. to profl. and pub. orgns. Mem. ABA (criminal justice sect.), Nat. Assn. Women Lawyers, Nat. Assn. Criminal Def. Lawyers, Calif. Atty.'s for Criminal Justice, Calif. Women Lawyers (bd. govs. 1998-99), Los Angeles County Bar Assn., No. Calif. Women Defenders (bd. govs. 1999—), Women's Lawyer's Assn. L.A. (chmn. criminal justice law sect. 1996-99, bd. govs. 1996-99), Beverly Hills Bar Assn. Fax: 310-557-0008. Criminal. Office: Kaplan Marino 9454 Wilshire Blvd Ste 500 Beverly Hills CA 90212-2908

**MARINSTEIN, ELLIOTT F.,** lawyer; b. N.Y.C., June 15, 1928; s. Joseph and Rose (Zessman) M.; m. Leita A. Adeson, Dec. 1, 1957; children: Edward Ross, Jay Drew. BA, Bklyn. Coll., 1950; JD, NYU, 1953. Bar: N.Y. 1955, U.S. Dist. Ct. (no. dist.) N.Y. 1956, U.S. Supreme Ct. 1970, U.S. Dist. Ct. (so. and ea. dists.) N.Y. 1986. Sole practice Troy, N.Y., 1956-86; asst. dist. atty. County of Rensselaer, Troy, 1965-67; ptnr. Marinstein & Marinstein, Troy, 1986—; counsel charter rev. com. City of Troy, 1972-73; mem. com. on profl. standards Third Jud. Dept., 1988-94. Committeeman Rensselaer County Dem. Com., Troy, 1960-65; del. jud. convention Dem. State Com., Troy, 1978-88; chmn. housing bd. rev. City of Troy, 1979-90. Served to cpl. U.S. Army, 1953-55. Mem. ABA (corp., banking and bus. law sect.), N.Y. State Bar Assn. (count county courts com., lectr. 1978-83), Rensselaer County Bar Assn. (chmn. grievance com. 1972-75, pres. 1979-80), N.Y. State Dist. Attys. Assn., Comml. Law League Am. (practice com.). Club: Tri City Raquet (Latham, N.Y.). Lodges: Knights of Pythias (past chancellor), Masons. Avocation: tennis. Fax: (518) 274-5039. E-mail: mmlaw@capital.net. Consumer commercial, Bankruptcy, Probate. Home: 2354 Burdett Ave Troy NY 12180-2409 Office: Marinstein & Marinstein 200 Broadway Troy NY 12180-3289

**MARJERISON, THOMAS SYDNEY,** lawyer; b. Brunswick, Maine, May 20, 1967; s. Thomas Sydney and Jerilyn Faye Majerison; m. Kirsten Schultz, Sept. 7, 1996. BA, Conn. Coll., 1989; JD, U. Maine, 1993. Bar: Maine 1993. Asst. atty. gen. Dept. of Atty. Gen., Portland, Maine, 1993-96; atty. Norman, Hanson & DeTroy, Portland, 1996—; legal specialist Internat. Criminal Tribunal for Former Yugoslavia, The Hague, The Netherlands, 1998; instr. Maine Criminal Justice Acad., Waterville, 1993-96. Author: (manual) Drafting Effective Search Warrants, 1996. Recipient Cert. of Achievement, U.S. Drug Enforcement Adminstrn., 1996, Citation of Merit, City of Portland, 1996. Mem. Maine Assn. Criminal Def. Attys., Maine State Bar Assn. Federal civil litigation, State civil litigation, Criminal. Office: Norman Hanson & DeTroy 415 Congress St Ste 500 Portland ME 04101-3530

**MARK, DANIEL LEE,** lawyer; b. Big Spring, Tex., Nov. 27, 1954. BA, Baylor U., 1977; JD with honors, U. Tex., 1982, MBA, 1983. Bar: Tex. 1982, U.S. Dist. Ct. (so. dist.) Tex. 1987, U.S. Tax Ct. 1984. Assoc. Reynolds, Allen & Cook, Houston, 1982-85; mng. ptnr. Looper, Reed, Mark & McGraw, Houston, 1985-96. Mem. ABA, Tex. Bar Assn., Omicron Delta Kappa. Securities, Mergers and acquisitions, Banking. Office: Looper Reed Mark & McGraw 1300 Post Oak Blvd Ste 2000 Houston TX 77056-8000

**MARK, HENRY ALLEN,** lawyer; b. Bklyn., May 16, 1909; s. Henry Adam and Mary Clyde (McCarroll) M.; m. Isobel Ross Arnold, June 26, 1940; BA, Williams Coll., 1932; JD, Cornell U., 1935. Bars: N.Y. 1936, Conn. 1981, U.S. Dist. Ct. (so. dist.) N.Y. 1943. Assoc. firm Allin & Tucker, N.Y.C., 1935-40; mng. atty. Indemnity Ins. Co. of N.Am., N.Y.C., 1940-43; assoc. firm Mudge, Stern, Williams & Tucker, N.Y.C., 1943-50, Cadwalder, Wickersham & Taft, N.Y.C., 1950-53; ptnr. Cadwalader, Wickersham & Taft, 1953-74; lectr. Practicing Law Inst., N.Y.C., 1955-68. Mem. adv. com. zoning Village of Garden City (N.Y.), 1952-54, planning commn., 1957-59, zoning bd. appeals, 1959-61, trustee, 1961-65, mayor, 1965-67; chmn. planning commn. Town of Washington (Conn.), 1980-84; trustee The Gunnery Sch., Washington, Conn., 1980-86; mem. adv. com. on continuing care State of Conn., 1996—. Recipient Disting. Alumnus award Cornell U., 1983. Mem. ABA, N.Y. Bar Assn., Assn. Bar City of N.Y., Conn. Bar Assn., Hartford County Bar Assn., Cornell Law Assn. (pres. 1971-73), Bar Assn. Nassau County (grievance com. 1974-77), St. Andrew's Soc., Phi Beta Kappa, Sigma Phi, Phi Delta Phi. Republican. Congregationalist. Lodge: Masons. Landlord-tenant, Real property. Address: 80 Loeffler Rd Apt G405 Bloomfield CT 06002-2291

**MARK, MICHAEL DAVID,** lawyer; b. Bklyn., Sept. 16, 1944; s. Irving and Mildred Mark; m. Susan Kay Merrifield, Apr. 12, 1970; children: Dana Lynne, Stephanie Lauren. BA, Rutgers U., 1966; JD, U. Tenn., 1969. Bar: Tenn. 1969, N.J. 1970, U.S. Dist. Ct. N.J. 1970, U.S. Supreme Ct. 1973; cert. civil trial atty., N.J. Supreme Ct. 1992. House counsel Liberty Mut. Ins. Co., East Orange, N.J., 1969-71; assoc. Skoloff & Wolfe, Newark, 1971-73; pvt. practice, Union, N.J., 1973—; past assoc. bd. dirs. United Jersey Bank, Union; Police Benevolent Assn. lawyer City of Linden, N.J., 1980—, Clark Twp., Clark, N.J., 1986; mem. Union-Essex County Early Settlement Panels, Elizabeth and Newark. Mem. Am. Acad. Matrimonial Lawyers (bd. mgrs. 1982—), N.J. Bar Assn., Union County Bar Assn., Union Lawyers Club (past pub. defender). Republican. Avocation: private pilot. General civil litigation, Family and matrimonial, Real property. Office: 2444 Morris Ave Union NJ 07083-5711

**MARK, TIMOTHY IVAN,** lawyer; b. Hershey, Pa., Oct. 8, 1951; s. Howard Behm and Ethel Mae Beam Mark; m. Janice Leigh Evans, Jan. 5, 1974; children: Andrew James, Amy Elizabeth. BA cum laude, East Stroudsburg U., 1977; JD cum laude, Temple U., 1978. Bar: Pa. 1978, U.S. Dist. Ct. (mid. dist.) Pa. 1978, U.S. Supreme Ct. 1983, U.S. Ct. Appeals (3d cir.) 1983. Law clk. intern U.S. Dist. Ct. (ea. dist.) Pa., Phila., 1978; asst. atty. gen. Com. of Pa., Harrisburg, 1978-79; shareholder Goldberg, Evans and Katzman, Harrisburg, 1979-85; ptnr. Evans, Stone and Mark, Harrisburg, 1985-87; shareholder Mette, Evans and Woodside, Harrisburg, 1987-92, Caldwell & Kearns, Harrisburg, 1992-97; of counsel Thomas Thomas and Hafer, Harrisburg, 1997—; lectr. Pa. Bar Assn., Harrisburg, 1992—. Mem. Pa. Def. Inst. (bd. dirs. 1990-96), Def. Rsch. Inst., Pa. Trial Lawyers Assn., Pa. Bar Assn. Avocations: golfing, reading, computer research. Insurance, General civil litigation, Personal injury. Home: 811 Providence Cir Hummelstown PA 17036-9753 Office: Thomas Thomas and Hafer LLP 305 N Front St Fl 6 Harrisburg PA 17101-1216

**MARKE, JULIUS JAY,** law librarian, educator; b. N.Y.C., Jan. 12, 1913; s. Isidore and Anna (Taylor) M.; m. Sylvia Bolotin, Dec. 15, 1946; 1 child, Elisa Hope. BS, CCNY, 1934; LLB, NYU, 1937; BS in Lib. Sci., Columbia U., 1942. Bar: N.Y. 1938. Reference asst. N.Y. Pub. Libr., 1937-42; pvt. practice law N.Y.C., 1939-41; prof. law, law libr. NYU, 1949-83, prof. law emeritus, 1983—, interim dean of librs., 1975-77; Disting. Prof., dir. Law Libr. St. John's U. Sch. Law, 1983-95; disting. rsch. prof. law St. John's U. Sch. Law, Jamaica, N.Y., 1995—; lectr. Columbia Sch. Library Service, 1962-78, adj. prof., 1978-85; cons. Orientation Program Am. Law, 1965-68, Found. Overseas Law Libraries Am. Law, 1968-79, copyright Ford Found., law libraries, Coun. Fgn. Rels., 1990—, Shubert Archives, 1991, others. Author: Vignettes of Legal History, 1965, 2d series, 1977, rev. edit., 1999, Copyright and Intellectual Property, 1967 (with R. Sloane) Legal Research and Law Library Management, rev. edit., 1990, 99; editor: Modern Legal Forms, 1953, The Holmes Reader, 1955, The Docket Series, 1955—, Bender's Legal Business Forms, 4 vols., 1962; compiler, editor: A Catalogue of the Law Collection at NYU with Selected Annotations, 1953, Dean's List of Recommended Reading for Pre-Law and Law Students, 1958, 84, and others; chmn. editl. bd. Oceana Group, 1977—, Index to Legal Periodicals, 1978—; columnist N.Y. Law Jour., 1970—; contbr. articles to profl. jours. Mem. publs. coun. N.Y.U., 1964-80. Sgt. AUS, 1943-45. Decorated Bronze Star. Mem. ABA, Am. Assn. Law Librs. (pres. 1962-63, Disting. Svc. award 1986), Assn. Am. Law Schs., Coun. of Nat. Libr. Assns. (exec. bd., v.p. 1959, 60), Law Libr. Assn. Greater N.Y. (pres. 1949, 50, chmn. joint com. on libr. edn. 1950-52, 60-61), NYU Law Alumni Assn. (Judge Edward Weinfeld award 1987, mem. exec. bd. 1988—), Columbia Sch. Libr. Svc. Alumni Assn. (pres. 1973-75), Order of Coif (pres. NYU Law Sch. br. 1970-83), NYU Faculty Club (pres. 1966-68), Field Inn, Phi Delta Phi. Home: 4 Peter Cooper Rd Apt 8F New York NY 10010-6746

**MARKEL, GREGORY ARTHUR,** lawyer; b. N.Y.C., Aug. 6, 1945; s. Edward and Ann (Larkin) M.; m. Dorothy Flanagan (div. 1979); 1 child, Kimberly; m. Belinda Elizabeth Heym, May 3, 1981; children: Alexis, Amy, William. BA, Columbia U., 1967; MBA, U. Mich., 1968; JD, Yale U., 1972. Bar: N.Y. 1972, U.S. Dist. Ct. (so. and ea. dists.) N.Y. 1974, U.S. Ct. Appeals (2d cir.) 1975, U.S. Ct. Appeals (3rd cir.) 1978, U.S Dist. Ct. (no. dist.) Calif. 1984, U.S. Ct. Appeals (9th cirs.) 1984, U.S. Ct. Appeals (11th cir) 1987. Assoc. Cravath, Swaine & Moore, N.Y.C., 1972-80; ptnr. Davis, Markel & Edwards, 1980-93, Orrick, Herrington & Sutcliffe, N.Y.C., 1993—. Mem. ABA (litigationco-chair subcom. on fed. rules rev. of the pretrial practices and discovery com.), Fed. Bar Coun., Yale Club (N.Y.C.), Mahopac Golf Club (N.Y.). Federal civil litigation, Banking, Insurance. Home: 50 Sutton Pl S New York NY 10022-4167 Office: Orrick Herrington & Sutcliffe 599 Lexington Ave New York NY 10022-6030

**MARKELLO, JEFFREY PHILIP,** lawyer; b. Buffalo, Dec. 14, 1964; s. Anthony Philip and Nancy Hammond M. BA, U. Rochester, 1987; JD, SUNY, Buffalo, 1987. Bar: N.Y. 1991, Mass. 1991. Atty. pvt. practice, Elma, N.Y., 1991-97; ptnr. Sakowski & Markello, Elma, N.Y., 1998—. Trustee East Aurora (N.Y.) Bd. Edn., 1993—. Personal injury, General practice, Family and matrimonial. Office: Sakowski & Markello PO Box 200 Elma NY 14059-0200

**MARKER, MARC LINTHACUM,** lawyer, investor; b. Los Angeles, July 19, 1941; s. Clifford Harry and Voris (Linthacum) M.; m. Sandra Vocom. Aug. 29, 1965; children: Victor, Gwendolyn. BA in Econs. and Geography, U. Calif.-Riverside, 1964; JD, U. So. Calif., 1967. Asst. v.p., asst. sec. Security Pacific Nat. Bank, L.A., 1970-73; sr. v.p., chief counsel, sec. Security Pacific Leasing Corp., San Francisco, 1973-92; pres. Security Pacific Leasing Svcs. Corp., San Francisco, 1977-85, dir., 1977-92; bd. dirs., sec. Voris, Inc., 1973-86; bd. dirs. Refiners Petroleum Corp., 1977-81, Security Pacific Leasing Singapore Ltd., 1983-85, Security Pacific Leasing Can. Ltd., 1989-92; lectr. in field. Served to comdr., USCGR. Mem. ABA, Calif. Bar Assn., D.C. Bar Assn. Republican. Lutheran. Club: Army and Navy. Contracts commercial, Banking.

**MARKESBERG, MARIA SABA,** lawyer; b. Cin., June 2, 1961; d. Khamis Alexander and Judith Diehl Saba; m. Glenn Alan Marlesberg, Aug. 26, 1987; children: Michael, Katherine, Emily. BS, Xavier U., 1983; JD, U. Cin., 1986. Bar: Ohio. Dir. risk mgmt., legal svcs. Franciscan Health System, Cin., 1988-98, gen. counsel, 1998—. Mem. Cin. Bar Assn. Health. Office: Franciscan Health Systems 2270 Banning Rd Cincinnati OH 45239-6621

**MARKEY, BRIAN MICHAEL,** lawyer; b. Teaneck, N.J., Feb. 10, 1956; s. Raymond Joseph and Sheila (Barry) M.; m. Virginia M. Lincoln, Oct. 26, 1986. BA cum laude, Rider Coll., 1978; JD, Suffolk U., 1985. Bar: N.J. 1985, U.S. Dist. Ct. N.J. 1985, N.Y. 1988. Assoc. Kohler & Clinch, Hackensack, N.J., 1985-90, Law Office J. Dennis Kohler, Hackensack, N.J., 1990-91; pvt. practice law Glen Rock, N.J., 1991-94; ptnr. Lincoln & Markey, Glen Rock, 1995—; dir. Glen Rock Savs. Bank. Chmn. Glen Rock Planning Bd. Mem. ABA, N.J. Bar Assn., Jaycees, Glen Rock Rep. Club, Glen Rock Independence Day Assn. Roman Catholic. General practice, Real property, General civil litigation. Office: 126 Valley Rd Glen Rock NJ 07452-1796

**MARKEY, JAMES KEVIN,** lawyer; b. Springfield, Ill., July 15, 1956; s. James Owen and Marjorie Jean (Diesness) M.; m. Allison Markey; children: Lauren, Katherine. BBA with highest honors, U. Notre Dame, 1977; JD cum laude, U. Mich., 1980; MBA, U. Chgo., 1987; LLM in Taxation, DePaul U., 1993. Bar: Ill. 1980; CPA, Ill. Assoc. Chapman & Cutler, Chgo., 1980-81; atty. Quaker Oats Co., Chgo., 1981-84; corp. counsel Baxter Healthcare Corp., Deerfield, Ill., 1984-90; v.p. law and other positions Motorola, Inc., Schaumburg, Ill., 1990—. Mem. ABA, Beta Alpha Psi, Beta Gamma Sigma. Avocations: racquetball, running, bridge. General corporate, Contracts commercial, Mergers and acquisitions. Home: 14646 S 7th Pl Phoenix AZ 85048-6364 Office: Motorola Inc 2501 S Price Rd Chandler AZ 85248-2899

**MARKEY, PATRICK JOSEPH,** lawyer; b. Kittery, Maine, Feb. 1, 1964; s. Martin James and Sally Marie M.; m. Jennifer Maloney, Aug. 17, 1996; children: Brendan Martin. BA in Govt. and Internat. Rels., U. Notre Dame, 1986; JD, Georgetown U., 1992. Bar: Mass., N.Y. Vol. U.S. Peace Corps., Caaguazu, Paraguay, 1987-89; law clk. to Hon. Edward F. Harrington U.S. Dist. Ct. Mass., Boston, 1992-93; trial atty. Civil Rights Div. U.S. Dept. Justice, Washington, 1993-97; assoc. Robinson, Donovan, Madden & Barry, Springfield, Mass., 1997—. Treas. Friends Springfield Libr., 1998; parish councilor Holy Name Parish, Springfield, 1998. Mem. Fed. Bar Assn., Mass. Bar Assn., Hampden County Bar Assn., Notre Dame Club We. Mass., Rotary (mem. membership com. 1997—). Roman Catholic. Avocation: running. General civil litigation, Civil rights, Insurance. Office: Robinson Donovan Madden & Barry PC 1500 Main St Ste 1600 Springfield MA 01115-0001

**MARKHAM, CHARLES BUCHANAN,** lawyer; b. Durham, N.C., Sept. 15, 1926; s. Charles Blackwell and Sadie Helen (Hackney) M. A.B., Duke U., Durham, N.C., 1945; postgrad., U. N.C. Law Sch., Chapel Hill, 1945-46; LL.B., George Washington U., Washington, 1951. Bar: D.C. 1951, N.Y. 1961, N.C. 1980, U.S. Ct. Appeals (2d cir.) 1962, U.S. Ct. Appeals (D.C. cir.) 1955, U.S. Supreme Ct. 1964. Reporter Durham Sun, N.C., 1945; asst. state editor, editorial writer Charlotte News, N.C., 1947-48; dir. publicity and research Young Democratic Clubs Am., Washington, 1948-49, exec. sec., 1949-50; polit. analyst Dem. Senatorial Campaign Com., Washington, 1950-51; spl. atty. IRS, Washington and N.Y.C., 1952-60; assoc. Battle, Fowler, Stokes and Kheel, N.Y.C., 1960-65; dir. research U.S. Equal Employment Opportunity Commn., Washington, 1965-68; dep. asst. sec. U.S. Dept. Housing and Urban Devel., Washington, 1969-72; asst. dean Rutgers U. Law Sch., Newark, 1974-76; assoc. prof. law N.C. Central U., Durham, 1976-81, prof. law, 1981-83; mayor City of Durham, N.C., 1981-85; ptnr. Markham and Wickham, Durham, 1984-86; Trustee Hist. Preservation Soc. Durham, 1982-86; bd. dirs. Stagville Ctr., 1984-86; mem. Gov.'s Crime Commn., Raleigh, 1985; dep. commr. N.C. Indsl. Commn., Raleigh, 1986-93. Editor: Jobs, Men and Machines: The Problems of Automation, 1964. Mem. Carolina Club, Phi Beta Kappa, Omicron Delta Kappa, Phi Delta Phi, Phi Delta Theta. Republican. Episcopalian. Administrative and regulatory, Personal injury, Workers' compensation. Home: 204 N Dillard St Durham NC 27701-3404

**MARKLE, ROBERT,** lawyer; b. New Haven, July 31, 1951; s. William and Harriet (Ranger) M. BA, U. Conn., Storrs, 1976; JD, U. Conn., Hartford, 1986. Bar: Conn. 1986, U.S. Dist. Ct. Conn. 1987, U.S. Ct. Appeals (D.C. cir.) 1988, U.S. Ct. Appeals (5th cir.) 1988, D.C. 1989, La. 1993, U.S. Ct. Appeals (11th cir.) 1998, U.S. Supreme Ct. 1998. Broadcast journalist Sta. WPKN-FM, Bridgeport, Conn., 1976-83; assoc. Pullman, Comley, Bradley & Reeves, Bridgeport, 1986-87; self employed in corp. rsch. New Haven, 1987-88; staff atty. U.S. Ct. Appeals (5th cir.), New Orleans, 1988-90; law clk. to Hon. Luther Cole Supreme Ct. La., New Orleans, 1990-92, dep. jud. adminstr., 1992-93; ptnr. Appellate Resource Svc., Metairie, La., 1993-96; assoc. Adams and Reese, New Orleans, 1997—. Contbr. articles to profl. jours. Campaign worker Reagan-Bush Com., New Haven, 1980, 84, Bush-Quayle Com., New Orleans, 1988, 92. Republican. Avocations: music, travel, sports, politics. Appellate, Product liability, Constitutional.

**MARKOFF, BRAD STEVEN,** lawyer; b. N.Y.C., July 29, 1957; s. Daniel and Geri (Skitol) M.; m. Danna Kay Schmidt, May 17, 1980; children: Andrew David, Paul Steven. AB, Duke U., 1979; JD, Washington U., St. Louis, 1982. Bar: Mo. 1982, U.S. Tax Ct. 1984, N.C. 1985. Assoc. Stolar Partnership, St. Louis, 1982-84; assoc., ptnr. Moore & Van Allen, Raleigh, N.C., 1984-92; ptnr. Smith Helms Mulliss & Moore, Raleigh, N.C., 1992-97, Alston & Bird, Raleigh, N.C., 1997—; bd. dirs. Coun. for Entrepreneurial Devel., Research Triangle Park, N.C.; spl. coun. apptd. by N.C. Gov. N.C. R.R. Study Group, 1992-93; practice group head Alston & Bird's N.C. Bus. Practice, 1997—. Contbr. articles to profl. jours. Mem. ABA, Nat. Assn. Bond Lawyers, Nat. Assn. Real Estate Investment Trusts, Mo. Bar Assn., N.C. Bar Assn. Avocations: golf, astronomy. Securities, Finance, General corporate. Office: Alston and Bird 3605 Glenwood Ave Ste 310 Raleigh NC 27612-4957

**MARKOWITZ, LEWIS HARRISON,** lawyer; b. York, Pa., Aug. 28, 1933; s. Arthur and Clarisse (Harrison) M.; m. Harlene R. Freedman, June 24, 1956 (div. June 1983); children: Lawrence S., Andrew F.; m. Tobye R. Bindes, Oct. 10, 1983; 1 child, Adam D. BA in Govt., Wesleyan U., Middletown, Conn., 1955; JD, U. Mich., 1958. Bar: Pa. 1959; cert. civil trial adv. Nat. Bd. Trial Advocacy; diplomate Am. Bd. Profl. Liability Attys. Ptnr. Markowitz, Kagen & Griffith, York, 1959-80; pres. Markowitz & Seidensticker P.C., York, 1980-83, Markowitz & Markowitz, P.C., York, 1983—; asst. dist. atty. Office Dist. Atty., York, 1962-66. Contbg. author: Pleading in Pennsylvania, 1984, Evidentiary Privileges, 1985, Punitive Damages in Pennsylvania, 1987. Mem. Pa. Bar. Assn., York County Bar Assn. (pres. 1978), Assn. Trial Lawyers Am. (outstanding state committeman award 1980, Presdl. award of merit 1984), Pa. Trial Lawyers Assn. (bd. dirs. 1972-84), B'nai B'rith (Man of Yr. award 1964). Republican. Jewish. Avocations: fishing, reading, wine, travel. Antitrust, General civil litigation, Personal injury. Office: 2 W Market St York PA 17401-1208

**MARKOWITZ, LINDA WISHNICK,** lawyer; b. New Rochelle, N.Y., Sept. 25, 1945; d. John Harrison and Phyllis (Price) Wishnick; m. M. Robert Markowitz, Aug. 22, 1965 (div. Apr. 1990); Lisa Lynne, Benjamin Robert. BA, NYU, 1967; MAT, Manhattanville U., 1969; JD magna cum laude, Pace U., 1989. Bar: N.Y. 1989, Conn. 1989, Fla. 1990. Social caseworker County of Westchester, Mt. Veron and Peekskill, N.Y., 1968-69; owner, mgr. Gardner (Maine) Richmond Kampground, 1972-82; mgr. Diet Ctr., White Plains, N.Y., 1984-86; assoc. Hyman & Gilbert, Larchmont, N.Y., 1989-93; pvt. practice White Plains, N.Y., 1993—. V.p. Pace U. Sch. of Law. Mem. ABA, N.Y. State Bar Assn., Women's Bar Assn. (Westchester chpt., pres. 1999-00). Westchester County Bar Assn. Family and matrimonial, Estate planning, Probate. Home: 1503 Fairway Grn Mamaroneck NY 10543-4342 Office: 399 Knollwood Rd Ste 112 White Plains NY 10603-1937

**MARKS, ANDREW H.,** lawyer; b. N.Y.C., May 5, 1951; s. Theodore and Rosalie Ruth (Goldman) M.; m. Susan G. Esserman, Aug. 3, 1975; children: Stephen Matthew, Clifford Michael, Michael David. AB, Harvard U., 1973; JD, U. Mich., 1976. Bar: Fla. 1976, D.C., 1977, Md. 1984. Law clerk for Hon. Charles R. Richey U.S. Dist. Ct. D.C., Washington, 1976-78; exec. asst. to personal rep. of Pres. to Middle East Peace negotiations, Washington, 1979-81; assoc. Shea & Gardner, Washington, 1978-79, 81-84, ptnr., 1984-86; ptnr. Crowell & Moring L.L.P., Washington, 1986—. Mem. D.C. Bar (gen. counsel 1987-89, bd. govs. 1989-95, chmn. task force civility in the profession 1993—, pres. 1999), Harvard Club Washington (pres. 1994—).

Professional liability, Insurance. Office: Crowell & Moring LLP 1001 Pennsylvania Ave NW Fl 10 Washington DC 20004-2505

**MARKS, BRYANT MAYES, JR.,** lawyer; b. Hopewell, Va., Jan. 23, 1959; s. Bryant Mayes Sr. and Frances (Evans) M.; m. Susan Ellen Atwater, Nov. 13, 1993; children: Bryant Mayes III, Neil Atwater. BA, Coll. of William and Mary, 1981, JD, 1985. Bar: Va. 1986. Atty. Marks & Harrison, Hopewell, 1985-94; pvt. practice Hopewell, 1994—. Contbr. chpts. to seminar books. Bd. dirs. Hopewell Humane Soc., Inc., 1988—, United Way of Hopewell, 1992—. Mem. Va. Trial Lawyers Assn. (bd. govs. 1996-98). Methodist. Avocation: sports. Workers' compensation, Personal injury. Office: PO Box 27 901 W Broadway Ave Hopewell VA 23860-2536

**MARKS, LEE ROBERT,** lawyer; b. N.Y.C., Oct. 22, 1935; s. George L. and Shirley (Chassy) M.; children: Jan Philip, Benjamin Eli. BA with honors, U. Mich., 1957; LLB cum laude, Harvard U., 1960. Bar: N.Y. 1960, D.C. 1964, U.S. Supreme Ct. 1980. Lectr. law George Washington U., Washington, 1961-68; atty. Office Legal Adviser, Dept. State, Washington, 1961-65, sr. dep. legal advisor, 1977-79, mem. adv. com. on internat. investment, tech. and devel., 1983; ptnr. Ginsburg, Feldman & Bress, Washington, 1965-77, 79-98, Greenberg, Traurig, McLean, Va., 1998—. Past mem. bd. dirs. Washington Opera. Mem. ABA (chmn. com. on fgn. claims 1983). Office: Greenberg Traurig 1750 Tysons Blvd Ste 1200 Mc Lean VA 22102-4211

**MARKS, MERTON ELEAZER,** lawyer; b. Chgo., Oct. 16, 1932; s. Alfred Tobias and Helene Fannie (Rosner) M.; m. Radee Maiden Feiler, May 20, 1966; children: Sheldon, Elise Marks Vazelakis, Alan, Elaine Marks Ianchiou. BS, Northwestern U., 1954, JD, 1956. Bar: Ill. 1956, U.S. Ct. Mil. Appeals 1957, Ariz. 1958, U.S. Dist. Ct. Ariz. 1960, U.S. Ct. Appeals (9th cir.) 1962, U.S. Supreme Ct. 1970. Assoc. Moser, Compere & Emerson, Chgo., 1956-57; ptnr. Morgan, Marks & Rogers, Tucson, 1960-62; asst. atty. gen. State of Ariz., Phoenix, 1962-64, counsel indsl. commn., 1964-65; assoc., then ptnr. Shimmel, Hill, Bishop & Greunder, Phoenix, 1965-74; ptnr. Lewis & Roca, Phoenix, 1974—; lectr. on pharm., health care, product liability and ins. subjects; Judge Pro Tempore Ariz. Ct. Appeals, 1994. Contbr. articles to profl. jours. Capt. JAGC, USAR, 1957-64. Mem. ABA (tort and ins. practice sect., chmn. spl. com. on fed. asbestos legis. 1987-89, chmn. workers compensation and employers liability law com. 1983-84), Am. Bd. Trial Advocates, Acad. Hosp. Industry Attys., Am. Coll. Legal Medicine, Internat. Bar Assn. (sect. on bus. law, product liability, advt., unfair competition and consumer affairs com.), Drug Info. Assn., Am. Soc. Pharmacy Law, State Bar Ariz. (chmn. workers compensation sect. 1969-73), Nat. Coun. Self Insurers, Ariz. Self Insurers Assn., Fedn. Ins. and Corp. Counsel (chmn. pharm. litig. sect. 1989-91, chmn. workers compensation sect. 1977-79, v.p. 1978-79, 81, bd. dirs. 1981-89), Internat. Assn. Def. Counsel, Ariz. Assn. Def. Counsel (pres. 1976-77), Maricopa County Bar Assn., Def. Rsch. Inst. (drug and device com., chmn. workers compensation com. 1977-78), Assn. Internat. Droit Assurances, Union Internat. des Avocats. General civil litigation, Product liability. Office: Lewis & Roca 40 N Central Ave Ste 1900 Phoenix AZ 85004-4429

**MARKS, MURRY AARON,** lawyer; b. Carbondale, Ill., July 14, 1933. Student, Northwestern U., 1951-52; BA, Washington U., 1954; attended, U. So. Calif., 1956; JD, Washington U., 1963. Bar: Mo. 1963, U.S. Dist. Ct. (ea. and we. dists.) Mo. 1969, U.S. Ct. Appeals (8th cir.) 1969, U.S. Supreme Ct. 1972, U.S. Tax Ct. 1984. Asst. county counsellor County of St. Louis, 1963-67; ptnr. Elliott, Marks & Freeman, St. Louis, 1967-1971; pvt. practice St. Louis, 1971—. With U.S. Army, 1954-56. Fellow St. Louis Bar Found.; mem. ABA, ATLA, Am. Bd. Forensic Examiners, Nat. Assn. Criminal Def. Lawyers, St. Louis County Bar Assn., Mo. Bar Assn., Am. Coll. Legal Medicine, Mo. Assn. Trial Attys., Mo. Assn. Criminal Def. Attys. (bd. dirs. 1986-90), First Amendment Lawyers Assn., Met. Bar Assn. St. Louis (chmn. internet com. 1995—), Lawyers Assn. St. Louis, Trial Lawyers for Pub. Justice. Appellate, Criminal, Pension, profit-sharing, and employee benefits. Office: PO Box 170019 7700 Clayton Rd Ste 307 Saint Louis MO 63117-1347 also: 594 Country Club Dr Lake Ozark MO 65049-8939

**MARKS, RAMON PAUL,** lawyer; b. Washington, Dec. 9, 1948; s. Matthew J. and Simone V. (Van de Meulebroeke) M.; m. Susan Eleanor MacCarthy; children—Robert Justin, Timothy Matthews, Fletcher MacCarthy. AB magna cum laude, Dartmouth Coll., 1971; MA, Johns Hopkins U., 1973; JD, U. Va., 1976. Bar: N.Y. 1977, Tex. 1983, U.S. Dist. Ct. (so. dist.) Tex. 1984, U.S. Ct. Appeals (5th cir.) 1984, U.S. Ct. Internat. Trade 1988, U.S. Dist. Ct. (so. dist.) N.Y. 1989, U.S. Ct Appeals (fed. cir.) 1989. Assoc., Alexander & Green, N.Y.C., 1976-77; corporate atty. Schlumberger Ltd., N.Y.C., 1978; asst. legal counsel services, techniques Schlumberger Paris, 1978-80; gen. counsel Schlumberger Well Services, Houston, 1980-84; sec., gen. counsel Dowell Schlumberger, Inc., Houston, 1984-85; asst. gen. counsel Schlumberger Ltd., Houston, 1986-87; ptnr. Marks & Murase, N.Y.C., 1987—. Mem. ABA, Assn. Bar City N.Y., Tex. Bar Assn., Maritime Law Assn. U.S. (assoc.), Petroleum Equipment Suppliers Assn. (chmn. legal affairs steering com. 1984-85), Bus. Execs. Nat. Security (policy com.), Phi Beta Kappa. General corporate, Private international. Office: Marks & Murase 399 Park Ave Fl 20 New York NY 10022-4689

**MARKS, RICHARD DANIEL,** lawyer; b. N.Y.C., June 21, 1944; s. Morris Andrew and Dorothy (Schill) M.; m. Cheryl L. Hoffman, Nov. 13, 1971. BA, U. Va., 1966; JD, Yale U., 1969. Bar: D.C., U.S. Ct. Appeals (3rd, 4th, 8th, 11th and D.C. cir.), U.S. Supreme Ct. Assoc. Dow, Lohnes & Albertson, Washington, 1972-78, ptnr., 1978-97; ptnr. Vinson & Elkins, Washington, 1997—. Co-author: Legal Problems in Broadcasting, 1974. Capt. U.S. Army, 1970-72. Mem. ABA (chmn. contracting for computer com., sect. for sci. and tech., computer law div., chmn. computer law div. 1994—), Fed. Comms. Bar Assn., Am. Law Inst., Computer Law Assn., Lawyer's Roundtable on Info. Security (co-chair 1998—), Capital Area Assn. Flight Instrs. (pres. 1989-90), UVA Club of Washington (pres. 1991-92). Avocations: aviation, skiing. Computer, Communications, Trademark and copyright. Office: Vinson & Elkins 1455 Pennsylvania Ave NW Fl 7 Washington DC 20004-1013

**MARKS, RUSSELL ROBERT,** lawyer; b. Berwyn, Ill., July 22, 1946; s. Robert David and Helen Marie M.; m. Kathryn Williams, June 14, 1969; children: Brandon, Erin. BA, MacMurray Coll., 1968; PhD, Ohio U., 1972; JD, U. Md., 1977. Bar: Md., W.Va., U.S. Dist. Ct. (fed. dist.) Md., U.S. Dist. Ct. (fed. dist.) W.Va. Ptnr. Gilbert, Marks & DiGirolomo, Hagerstown, Md. Personal injury, Family and matrimonial, Construction. Home: 1024 The Ter Hagerstown MD 21742-3228 Office: Gilbert Marks & DiGirolono 35 E Washington St Hagerstown MD 21740-5605

**MARKS, SANFORD HARVEY,** jury and trial consultant; b. N.Y.C., Apr. 7, 1947; s. Howard I. and Corinne (Jaffee) M.; m. Barbara Carter, Apr. 30, 1989; 1 child, Demi R. BBA, U. Miami, 1970. Pres. Sanford Ltd., N.Y.C., 1972-76; v.p. Rafaella Sportswear, N.Y.C., 1976-87; pres. Babs & Assocs., Miami, Fla., 1988-91, Trial Technologies, Inc., Miami, 1991—. Mem. ATLA, Nat. Assn. Criminal Def. Lawyers, Fla. Assn. Criminal Def. Lawyers. Democrat. Jewish. Avocations: boating, sports, skiing, family. Home: 3201 SW 131st Ter Davie FL 33330-4608 Office: Trial Techs Inc Ste 1300 100 N Biscayne Blvd Miami FL 33132-2309

**MARKS, SCOTT CHARLES,** lawyer; b. Gloucester, MA, Nov. 19, 1956; s. Wilfred Elliot and Marjorie (Bloom) M.; m. Rhonda Ann Levine, Aug. 22, 1982; children: Eric Ian, Jesse Robert. BS, Boston U., 1978; JD, New Eng. Sch. Law, 1982. Bar: Mass. 1982, U.S. Dist. Ct. Mass. 1983. Assoc. Kline & Gardner, PC, Gloucester, Mass., 1982-87; ptnr. Channell & Marks, Beverly, Mass., 1987-90; assoc. Peter C. DiGangi, Salem, Mass., 1990-97, DiGangi & Legasey P.C., Salem, Mass., 1997—. Mem. ABA, Mass. Bar Assn., Salem Bar Assn., Essex County Bar Assn. Democrat. Jewish. General practice, Family and matrimonial, Personal injury. Office: DiGangi & Legasey PC 100 Museum Pl Salem MA 01970-3733

**MARKS, STEPHEN PAUL,** law and international affairs educator, international official; b. San Francisco, June 13, 1943; s. Marion Harris and Ruth Wise (Rosenblum) M.; m. Kathleen A. Modrowski, Feb. 28, 1978; children: Joshua, Emmanuel. BA, Stanford U., 1964; diploma, Inst. Advanced Internat. Studies, Paris, 1972; D in Law, U. Nice, 1979; advanced degree, U. Strasbourg, France, U. Besançon, France, U. Damascus, Syria. Sr. staff Internat. Inst. Human Rights, Strasbourg, 1969-73; sr. program specialist UNESCO, Paris, 1973-83; program officer Ford Found., N.Y.C., 1983-88; lectr. Law Sch. Columbia U., 1985—, adj. prof. polit. sci., 1989, adj. prof. Sch. of Internat. and Pub. Affairs, 1989-95, sr. lectr., 1995—, dir. UN studies program, 1996—; vis. prof. law Cardozo Sch. Law, Yeshiva U., N.Y.C., 1989-92, dir. program in internat. law and human rights, 1989-92; asst. to ind. jurst UN Mission for Referendum in Western Sahara, 1991-92; chief sect. UN Transitional Authority, Phnom Penh, Cambodia, 1992-93; François-Xavier Bagnoud prof. health and human rights Sch. Pub. Health, Harvard U., 1999—, dir. Françis-Xavier Bagnoud Ctr. Health & Human Rights; univ. fellow New Sch. for Social Rsch., N.Y.C., 1989-92; mem. consultative coun. Lawyers Com. for Nuclear Policy, N.Y.C., 1985—; rep. to UN Internat. Svc. for Human Rights, Geneva, 1989—; cons. MacArthur Found., 1992, UN Devel. Program, 1998, Parliamentarians for Global Action, 1999; human rights advisor Asia Found., Cambodia, 1998; vis. fellow Ctr. Internat. Studies, Woodrow Wilson Sch., Princeton U., 1993-95, lectr., 1995; pres., chmn. of bd. U.S. Com. for Internat. Svc. for Human Rights, 1995—. Mem. adv. com. Human Rights Watch/Mid. East, 1991—; bd. dirs. Cambodian Inst. Human Rights, 1993—, Albert Einstein Inst., 1994—; mem. editl. bd. Health and Human Rights, Boston; mem. nat. adv. com. human rights, UN Assn. of the U.S., 1996; mem. rev. panel U.S. Inst. of Peace, Washington, 1998. Hague Acad. Internat. Law fellow, 1967, 73, Peaslee fellow Columbia U., 1985, MacArthur Found. fellow, 1994-95. Mem. Acad. Coun. on UN Sys., Am. Soc. Internat. Law, Am. Polit. Sci. Assn., Internat. Law Assn., Assn. of Bar of City of N.Y., Ind. Commn. on Human Rights Edn., Société Française pour le Droit Internat., Acad. Polit. Sci., Internat. Studies Assn. Fax: (617) 432-4310. E-mail: smarks@hsph.harvard.edu. Home: 27 Middle Line Hwy Southampton NY 11968-1647 Office: Harvard Sch Pub Health 651 Huntington Ave # Rom705 Boston MA 02115-6009

**MARKS, STEVEN CRAIG,** lawyer; b. Miami, Sept. 22, 1960; s. Lawrence Martin and Roberta Barbara (Dilner) M. BA cum laude, U. Fla., 1982; JD cum laude, U. Miami, 1985. Bar: Fla. 1985, U.S. Dist. Ct. (so. dist.) Fla. 1985. Ptnr. Podhurst Orseck, Miami, 1985—. Editor-in-chief U. Miami Law Rev., 1985. Mem. ABA (mem. program planning com. for Nat. Inst. on Aviation Litigation 1991—, torts and ins. practice section, mem. editl. bd. The Brief), ATLA (treas. aviation law sect. 1996-97, vice chair aviation and space law com. 1996-97, chair 1998—), Dade County Trial Lawyers, Lawyer-Pilots Bar Assn., Am. Bd. Trial Advocates, The Fla. Bar, Acad. Fla. Trial Lawyers, Dade County Bar Assn., Inns. of Court, Order of the Coif, Bar Gravel Law Soc. E-mail: info@podhurst.com. Aviation, Personal injury, Product liability. Office: Podhurst Orseck & Josefsberg 25 W Flagler St Ste 800 Miami FL 33130-1720

**MARKS, STEVEN MITCHELL,** lawyer; b. North Miami, Fla., May 8, 1967; s. Ellis M. and Florine B. Marks; m. Jennifer Claire Lewis, July 31, 1969. AB, Duke U., 1988, JD, 1992. Bar: Fla. 1993, D.C. 1995. Law clk. hon. Mary M. Schroeder U.S. Ct. Appeals Ninth Cir., Phoenix, 1992-93; assoc. Steel Hector & Davis, Miami, 1993-95, Arnold & Porter, Washington, 1995-97; sr. v.p., dir. bus. affairs Rec. Industry Assn. Am., Washington, 1997—. Office: Rec Industry Assn Am 1330 Connecticut Ave NW Ste 300 Washington DC 20036-1725

**MARKS, THEODORE LEE,** lawyer; b. N.Y.C., Oct. 18, 1935; s. Irving Edward and Isabel (Goodman) M.; m. Benita Cooper, July 13, 1958; children: Eric, Robert, Jennifer. B.S., NYU, 1956, LL.B., 1958. Bar: N.Y. 1959, U.S. Dist. Ct. (so. dist.) N.Y. 1963, U.S. Supreme Ct. 1964, U.S. Ct. Appeals (2d cir.) 1975, U.S. Dist. Ct. (ea. dist.) N.Y. 1978. Assoc. Silver, Bernstein, Seawell & Kaplan, N.Y.C., 1959-65; sole practice N.Y.C., 1965-70; ptnr. Lee, Cash & Marks, N.Y.C., 1970-76, Vogel, Marks & Rosenberg, N.Y.C., 1976-79, Bromberg, Gloger, Lifschultz & Marks, N.Y.C., 1979-85, Epstein Becker Borsody & Green, P.C., N.Y.C., 1985-86, Gelberg & Abrams, 1986-87, Morrison Cohen Singer & Weinstein, 1987—; speaker at meetings of profl. assns. Contbr. articles to profl. jours. Served with Army N.G., 1958-61. Mem. N.Y. State Bar Assn. (mem. real property, banking, corp. and bus. law sects.), N.Y. County Lawyers Assn., Fed. Bar Coun., T&M. Real property, General practice, General corporate. Office: Morrison Cohen Singer & Weinstein LLP 750 Lexington Ave New York NY 10022-1200

**MARKUS, STEPHEN ALLAN,** lawyer; b. Harvey, Ill., Mar. 14, 1954; s. Fred Herman and Ruth (Kahn) M.; m. Nancy Lynn Adams, July 29, 1978; children: Andrew, Peter. BA, Case Western Res. U., 1976, JD, 1979. Bar: Ohio 1979, U.S. Dist. Ct. (no. dist.) Ohio 1979, U.S. Ct. Appeals (6th cir.) 1984, U.S. Supreme Ct. 1990. Ptnr. dept. labor and employment Ulmer & Berne, Cleve., 1979—. Trustee Cleve. Internat. Film Festival, 1977—. Jewish. Labor, General civil litigation, General corporate. Home: 2611 Ashton Rd Cleveland Heights OH 44118 Office: Ulmer & Berne 1300 E 9th St Ste 900 Cleveland OH 44114-1583

**MARKWARDT, JOHN JAMES,** lawyer; b. Phila., Jan. 12, 1950; s. John Frederick and Rita Mary (Lafferty) M.; m. Joann Marie Olivo, Aug. 16, 1969; 1 child, Kelly Ann. Student, Rutgers U., 1968-71; JD cum laude, Albany Law Sch., 1974. Bar: N.Y. 1975, U.S. Dist. Ct. (no. dist.) N.Y. 1975, N.J. 1976, U.S. Dist. Ct. N.J. 1976, Pa. 1977, U.S. Supreme Ct. 1978, U.S. Dist. Ct. (ea. dist.) Pa. 1978, U.S. Ct. Appeals (3d cir.) 1981, Fla. 1984. Staff atty. N.Y. State Law Revision Commn., Albany, 1974-75; assoc. Richard M. Meyers, Albany, 1975-76; sole practice Blackwood, N.J., 1976-82; ptnr. Horn, Kaplan, Goldberg, Gorny & Daniels, Atlantic City, 1982—; legis. aide N.J. State Senate, Trenton, 1976. Mem. Gloucester Twp. Council, Camden County, N.J., 1979-81; mem. Gloucester Twp. Rent Control Bd., 1979-81, solicitor, 1977; mem. Gloucester Twp. Planning Bd., 1980. Recipient Forneron Career award Highland Regional High Sch., 1981. Mem. N.J. State Bar Assn., Atlantic County Bar Assn. Roman Catholic. Avocations: reading, writing, golf. State civil litigation, Real property, Contracts commercial. Office: Horn Kaplan Goldberg Gorny & Daniels 1300 Atlantic Ave Ste 500 Atlantic City NJ 08401-7278

**MARLAND, MELISSA KAYE,** judge; b. Beckley, W.Va., Feb. 16, 1955; d. James Robert and Fannie Evelyn (Cook) M. BA in Polit. Sci., W.Va U., 1976, JD, 1979. Bar: W.Va. 1979, U.S. Dist. Ct. (so. dist.) W.Va. 1979, U.S. Supreme Ct. 1983. Law clk. Pub. Svc. Commn. W.Va., Charleston, 1979-82, hearing examiner, 1982-87, dep. chief adminstrv. law judge, 1987-89, chief adminstrv. law judge, 1989—; faculty mem. ann. regulatory studies program Nat. Assn. Regulatory Commrs./Inst. Pub. Utilities, Mich. State U., 1994—. Assoc. editor: West Virginia Digest of Public Utility Decisions, vols. 1-7, 1986-91; contbr. articles to profl. jours. Mem. ABA, NAFE, W.Va. State Bar (com. on corp., banking and bus. law 1987—), Nat. Assn. Regulatory Commrs. (chmn. subcom. on adminstrv. law judges 1991-95), Phi Beta Kappa, Phi Alpha Delta, Pi Sigma Alpha. Democrat. Avocations: music, reading. Office: Pub Svc Commn WVa 201 Brooks St Charleston WV 25301-1803

**MARLAR, DONALD FLOYD,** lawyer; b. Little Rock, Jan. 15, 1944; s. Floyd Howard and Ruth May (Lawson) M.; m. Janet Jeanne Clark, Mar. 29, 1963; children: Jennifer Clark, Christopher Decker. BA, Ark. State U., 1966; JD, U. Tulsa, 1969; Masters in Taxation, George Washington U., 1972. Bar: Okla. 1969. Ptnr. Pray, Walker, Jackman, Williamson & Marlar, Tulsa, Okla., 1973-96; pres. Pray, Walker, Jackman, Williamson & Marlar, 1996—; chmn. Okla. Bar Tax Section, 1979-80. Dir. Tulsa Ballet Theatre, 1987—, pres., 1991-92; gen. coun., v.p. Gilcrease Mus., Tulsa, 1989—;trustee Grace and Franklin Bernsen Found., Tulsa, 1992—.; Capt. U.S. Army, 1969-73. Mem. Am. Bar Assn., Tulsa Bar Assn., The Summit Club (bd. govs. 1986-92, pres. 1992). Contracts commercial, General corporate, Estate planning. Home: 3517 E 70th Pl Tulsa OK 74136-2647 Office: Pray Walker Jackman Williamson & Marlar 900 Oneok Plz 100 W 5th St Tulsa OK 74103

**MARLEN, MATTHEW JAMES,** lawyer; b. Belleville, Ill., Jan. 12, 1967; s. James and JoAnn M. BA in Fin., U. Ill., 1989, JD, 1992. Bar: Ill. 1992, U.S. Dist. Ct. (so. dist.) Ill. 1992, Mo. 1993, U.S. Dist. Ct. (ea. dist.) Mo. 1995. Pvt. practice Law Office of Matthew J. Marlen, Belleville, Ill., 1997—, 1997—. Mem. ABA, ATLA, Ill. Trial Lawyers Assn. (rules com., civil practice com.), Ill. State Bar Assn. (vol. flood assistance group, 1993). Federal civil litigation, Personal injury, Product liability. Office: 7012 W Main St Belleville IL 62223-3031

**MARLES, BLAKE CURTIS,** lawyer; b. Carlisle, Pa., Aug. 18, 1952; s. Frederick Arthur and Shirley Allenbach M.; m. Madalyn Louise Macknik, June 4, 1978; children: Adam Frederick, Lindsey Susannah. BA, Muhlenbert Coll., 1974; JD, Temple U., 1978. Bar: Pa. 1978, U.S. Ct. Appeals (3d cir.) 1979, U.S. Dist. Ct. (ea. dist.) Pa. 1979, U.S. Dist. Ct. (mid. dist.) Pa. 1980. Assoc. Butz, Hudders & Tallman, Allentown, Pa., 1978-83; founding shareholder Weaver, Mosebath, Piosa, Hixson & Marles, Allentown, Pa., 1984-97; ptnr. Stevens & Lee, Lehigh Valley, Pa., 1997—; lectr. in field. Contbr. articles to profl. jours. Mem. Pa. Soc. (life), Lehigh County C. of C. Republican. Lutheran. Education and schools, Real property, Municipal (including bonds). Office: 190 Brodhead Rd PO Box 20830 Lehigh Valley PA 18002-0830

**MARLING, LYNWOOD BRADLEY,** lawyer; b. Cin., Apr. 17, 1944; s. John Bertron Marling and Florence Mary (Kelly) Lyman;m. Patricia Lynne Coté, June 13, 1981; children: Burke, Brady, Dustin. B Ceramic Engring., Ga. Inst. Tech., 1967; MBA, Stanford U., 1969; JD, Tex. Tech U., 1976. Bar: Tex. 1976, U.S. Dist. Ct. (no. dist.) Tex. 1977; cert. in family law Tex. Bd. Legal Specialization. Distbn. cons. Jos. Schlitz Brewing Co., Milw., 1969-71; pres., owner Marling Industries, Lubbock, Tex., 1971-74; pvt. practice, Hurst, 1981-88; ptnr. Caston and Marling, Hurst, Tex., 1976-81, 88—; legal cons. St. John the Apostle Sch., Ft. Worth, 1982-91. Contbr. articles to legal jours. Mem. St. John the Apostle Sch. Bd., 1982-84; campaign mgr. Robert Caston for State Rep., Tarrant County, Tex., 1980, Rick Barton for Mayor, Bedford, Tex., 1992. Recipient svc. award St. John the Apostle Sch., 1988. Mem. ABA, State Bar Tex. (coll. 1987—), Tarrant County Bar Assn., N.E. Tarrant County Bar Assn. (pres. 1990-92), Soto Grande Tennis Club (Outstanding Mem. award 1980). Avocations: snow skiing, tennis, officiating high school football, public speaking. Family and matrimonial, Juvenile. Office: 1500A Norwood Dr Ste 100 Hurst TX 76054-3632

**MARLOW, JAMES ALLEN,** lawyer; b. Crossville, Tenn., May 23, 1955; s. Dewey Harold and Anna Marie (Hinch) M.; m. Sabine Klein, June 9, 1987; children: Lucas Allen, Eric Justin. BA, U. Tenn., 1976, JD, 1979; postgrad., Air War Coll., Maxwell AFB, Ala., 1990-91, Internat. Studienzentrum, Heidelberg, Germany, 1985-86. Bar: Ga. 1979, D.C. 1980, Tenn. 1980, U.S. Dist. Ct. (mid. dist.) Tenn. 1984, U.S. Ct. Fed. Claims 1987, U.S. Ct. Internat. Trade 1988, U.S. Tax Ct. 1987, U.S. Ct. Mil. Appeals 1980, U.S. Ct. Appeals (fed. cir.) 1987, U.S. Supreme Ct. 1987. Assoc. Carter & Assocs., Frankfurt, Fed. Republic Germany, 1984-85; chief internat. law USAF, Sembach AFB, Germany, 1986-96; pvt. practice Crossville, 1997—; instr. Ctrl. Tex. Coll., 1997-98; asst. prof. Embry-Riddle Aero. U., Kaiserslautern, Fed. Republic Germany, 1985—. Capt. USAF, 1980-84, Lt. Col. USAFR. Mem. Phi Beta Kappa. Avocations: genealogy, basketball, chess, German and Spanish languages. Home and Office: 5746 Highway 127 S Crossville TN 38555-1137

**MARLOW, ORVAL LEE, II,** lawyer; b. Denver, May 1, 1956; s. Jack Conger and Barbara A. (Stolzenburg) M.; m. Paige Wood, June 8, 1985; children: Lorri Wood, Orval Lee III. BA, U. Nebr., 1978, JD, 1981. Bar: Tex. 1981, U.S. Dist. Ct. (so. dist.) Tex. 1984, U.S. Ct. Appeals (5th cir.) 1984. Assoc. Krist & Scott, Houston, 1981-82; prin. Marlow & Assocs., Houston, 1982-83; ptnr. Lendais & Assocs., Houston, 1983-91; dir. Morris, Lendais, Hollrah & Snowden, 1992—. Mem. ABA, Internat. Bar Assn., Tex. Bar Assn., Houston Bar Assn., Phi Delta Phi. Lutheran. Avocations: golf, snow skiing, chess. Private international, Real property, General corporate. Office: Morris Lendais Hollrah & Snowden 1980 Post Oak Blvd Ste 700 Houston TX 77056-3881

**MARLOWE, MARY LOUISE,** lawyer; b. Pasadena, Calif., Sept. 3, 1957; d. Robert Emmet and Mary Louise (Gelera) Coughlan); m. Daniel Robert Marlowe, Aug. 16, 1986; children: Benjamin, Marisa. BS, James Madison U., 1979; JD, George Mason U., 1983. Bar: N.Mex. 1984. Law clerk tax div. Dept. Justice, Washington, 1979-81, Nat. Assn. Mfrs., Washington, 1982-83; assoc. producer The McLaughlin Group, Washington, 1983-84; asst. atty. gen. N.Mex. Atty. Gen's Office, Santa Fe, 1984-87; ptnr. Marlowe & Marlowe, Taos, N.Mex., 1987-90; gen. counsel Securities Div. State of N.Mex., Santa Fe, 1990; ptnr. The Marlowe Law Firm, Santa Fe, 1990—. Mem. ABA, N.Mex. State Bar Assn. Democrat. Roman Catholic. Avocations: spinning, soccer mom. Criminal, Personal injury. Office: Marlowe Law Firm 200 W Marcy St Ste 216 Santa Fe NM 87501-2036

**MARMAN, JOSEPH H.,** lawyer; b. Glendive, Mont., Dec. 15, 1955; s. Raymond and Mary Ann Marman; m. Denise Vomacka, Oct. 1, 1991; children: Elliott, Alexis. BA in Econs. and Polit. Sci., U. Mont., 1980; JD, U. No. Calif., Sacramento, 1985. Bar: Calif. 1987. Prin., owner Law Office of Joseph Marman, Westminster, Citrus Hts., Calif., 1990—; judge pro tem Placer County. Vol. Voluntary Legal Svcs. No. Calif., Sacramento, 1996-98; mem. Placer County Search and Rescue Com. Mem. Sacramento County Bar Assn., Placer County Bar Assn., Consumer Attys. of Calif., Sacramento Consumer Attys., Sierra Club, Common Cause, Earth Justice Watch. Democrat. Avocations: sports cars, bicycling. General civil litigation, Personal injury, Product liability. Office: Law Office Joseph Marman 6060 Sunrise Vista Dr Ste 1825 Citrus Heights CA 95610-7062

**MARMERO, FRANC J(OSEPH) H(ENRY),** lawyer, arbitrator; b. Phila., July 31, 1948; s. Albert L. and Rita (Diantonio) M.; m. Sandra L. Twin, June 27, 1971; children: Franc J., Michael D., Danielle J. BA, LaSalle U., Phila., 1970; Jd, Villanova (Pa.) U., 1973. Bar: N.J. 1973, U.S. Dist. Ct. (fed. dist.) 1973, U.S. Ct. Appeals (3rd cir.) 1978, U.S. Supreme Ct. 1978. Commr. Superior Ct. Condemnation, N.J., 1976—; prosecutor Berlin Boro, N.J., 1979-81; arbitrator N.J. Superior Ct., N.J., 1985—; arbitrator Am. Arbitration Assn., N.J., 1976—; mem. N.J. Med. Malpractice Rev. Bd., N.J., 1978-85. Avocations: baseball memorabilia, hockey, music, cars. Office: 1040 S Route 73 Berlin NJ 08009-2603

**MARMET, GOTTLIEB JOHN,** lawyer; b. Chgo., Mar. 24, 1946; s. Gottlieb John and Margaret Ann (Saylor) M.; m. Jane Marie Borkowski, Sept. 12, 1970; children: Gottlieb John, Philip Stanley, Thomas Jacob. BS with distinction in Acctg., San Diego State U., 1967; JD, Northwestern U., 1970. Bar: Ill. 1970, U.S. Dist. Ct. (no. dist.) Ill. 1970, U.S. Tax Ct. 1981; CPA, Calif., Ill., Minn. Tax acct. Touche Ross & Co., Chgo., 1970-75; assoc. atty. Howington, Elworth, Osswald & Hough, Chgo., 1975-79; tax mgr. Peat, Marwick, Mitchell & Co., Mpls., 1979-81; assoc. Shefsky, Saitlin & Froelich, Ltd., Chgo., 1981-83; prin. G. John Marmet, Glenview, Ill., 1983—; lectr. corp. law William Rainey Harper Coll., Arlington Heights, Ill., 1984; instr. Ill. Soc. CPAs, 1976, 77, Minn. Soc. CPAs, 1980. Author: Farm Corporations and Their Income Tax Treatment, 1970, 74; contbr. articles to jours., pubs. Active Northeast Ill. Coun. Boy Scouts Am., 1984—, dist. chmn. Skokie Valley, 1988, mem. exec. bd., 1989-91, 99—; bd. dirs. North Shore Sr. Ctr., 1995-99. Recipient Hon. Mention Chgo. Bar Assn. Art Show, 1972, Boy Scouts Am. Dist. award of merit, 1990, Silver Beaver award, 1997. Mem. AICPA, ABA (fed. tax com.), Ill. Bar Assn., Chgo. Bar Assn., Rotary (Service Above Self award 1986, 96, bd. dirs. 1988-90, v.p. 1990-91, pres. 1991-92), Beta Gamma Sigma, Beta Alpha Psi, Phi Alpha Delta. Probate, Corporate taxation, Personal income taxation. Office: 950 Milwaukee Ave Ste 318 Glenview IL 60025-3779

**MARNEY, RONALD DEAN, II,** lawyer; b. Houston, June 29, 1967; s. Ronald Dean and Billie C. Marney; m. Whitney Lee Withers, May 16, 1993. BA, U. Tex., 1991; JD, Tex. A&M U., 1995. Bar: Mo. 1996, Kans. 1996. Assoc. Blackwell Sanders, Kansas City, Mo., 1995—. Office: Blackwell Sanders 2300 Main St # 1100 Kansas City MO 64108-2416

**MARON, DAVID F.,** lawyer; b. Bristol, Conn., Jan. 23, 1970; s. Adolph and Maureen Plimpton Maron. BS, Miss. Coll., 1992; JD cum laude, U. Miss., 1995. Bar: Miss., U.S. Dist. Ct. (no. and so. dists.) Miss., U.S. Ct. Appeals (5th cir.), U.S. Tax Ct. Atty. Heidelberg & Woodliff, Jackson, Miss., 1995—. Assoc. editor Miss. Law Jour.; contbr. articles to profl. jours. Bd. govs. Encore!, Jackson, 1997—; trustee Metro Crime Commn., Jackson,

1998, Leukemia Soc. Miss. Chpt., Jackson, 1998. Recipient Cert. of Appreciation, Crime Victims Rights Com., 1998. Mem. FBA, Miss. Bar Assn., Hinds County Bar Assn., Jackson Young Lawyers Assn. (com. chmn. 1995—, bd. dirs. 1998-99, Outstanding Svc. award 1997). Avocations: triathlons, tennis, road races. Environmental, Constitutional, Taxation, general. Office: Heidelberg & Woodliff PA 17th Fl Capital Towers 125 S Congress St Ste 105 Jackson MS 39201-3395

**MARONEY, THOMAS J.,** prosecutor; m. Mary Katharine Maroney; children: Eileen, Michael, Ann. BS magna cum laude, Syracuse U., 1961, JD, 1963. Bar: N.Y. Assoc. White and Case, N.Y.C., 1965-67; asst. state atty. gen. Syracuse region, 1979-81; prof. law Syracuse U. Coll. Law, 1981-94; with U.S. Atty. No. Dist. N.Y., 1994-99; vis. scholar Cornell Law Sch., 1974, vis. prof., 1975; labor arbitrator for fed. and state agys.; hearing examiner in disciplinary cases for various law enforcement agys. Mem. exec. bd. Syracuse-Onondaga County Drug and Alcohol Abuse Commn.; mem., past comdr. USCG Aux. *

**MAROVICH, GEORGE M.,** federal judge; b. 1931. AA, Thornton Community Coll., 1950; BS, U. Ill., 1952, JD, 1954. Atty. Chgo. Title & Trust Co., 1954-59; mem. firm Jacobs & Marovich, South Holland, Ill., 1959-66; v.p., trust officer South Holland Trust & Savs. Bank, 1966-76; judge Cir. Ct. Cook County, Ill., 1976-88; dist. judge U.S. Dist. Ct. (no. dist.) Ill., Chgo., 1988—; adj. instr. Thornton Community Coll., 1977-88. Mem. Ill. Judges Assn., Ill. Jud. Conf., Chgo. Bar Assn., South Suburban Bar Assn. Office: US Dist Ct Chambers 1956 219 S Dearborn St Chicago IL 60604-1702

**MARQUAND, BRENT RICHARD,** lawyer; b. Tulsa, Jan. 1, 1951; s. Harold D. and Adelaide A. Marquand; m. Karen S. Lester, Mar. 30, 1979; children: Zachary B., Chelsea L., Trevor H. BA magna cum laude, Drury Coll., 1973; JD summa cum laude, Washington U., St. Louis, 1976. Bar: Tenn. 1976, U.S. Dist. Ct. (ea. dist.) Tenn. 1979, U.S. Ct. Appeals (5th and 11th cirs.) 1981, U.S. Ct. Appeals (10th and 6th cirs.) 1982, U.S. Supreme Ct. 1987, U.s. Dist. Ct. (we. dist.) Tenn. 1996. Staff atty. TVA, Knoxville, 1976-86, sr. litigation atty., 1986—. Erna Arndt scholar Washington U., 1976. Mem. ABA, Knoxville Bar Assn., Order of Coif. Office: TVA Office Gen Counsel 400 W Summit Hill Dr Knoxville TN 37999-0002

**MARQUARDT, CHRISTEL ELISABETH,** judge; b. Chgo., Aug. 26, 1935; d. Herman Albert and Christine Marie (Geringer) Trolenberg; children: Eric, Philip, Andrew, Joel. BS in Edn., Mo. Western Coll., 1970; JD with honors, Washburn U., 1974. Bar: Kans. 1974, Mo. 1992, U.S. Dist. Ct. Kans. 1974, U.S. Dist. Ct. (we. dist.) Mo. 1992. Tchr. St. John's Ch., Tigerton, Wis., 1955-56; pers. asst. Columbia Records, L.A., 1958-59; ptnr. Cosgrove, Webb & Oman, Topeka, 1974-86, Palmer & Marquardt, Topeka, 1986-91, Levy and Craig P.C., Overland Park, Kans., 1991-94; sr. ptnr. Marquardt and Assocs., L.L.C., Fairway, Kans., 1994-95; judge Kans. Ct. Appeals, 1995—; mem. atty. bd. discipline Kans. Supreme Ct., 1984-86. Mem. editorial adv. bd. Kans. Lawyers Weekly, 1992-96; contbr. articles to legal jours. Bd. dirs. Topeka Symphony, 1983-92, 95—, Arts and Humanities Assn. Johnson County, 1992-95, Brown Found., 1988-90; hearing examiner Human Rels. Com., Topeka, 1974-76; local advisor Boy Scouts Am., 1973-74; bd. dirs., mem. nominating com. YWCA, Topeka, 1979-81; bd. govs. Washburn U. Law Sch., 1987—, v.p., 1994-96, pres., 1998—; mem. dist. bd. adjudication Mo. Synod Luth. Ch., Kans., 1982-88. Named Woman of Yr., Mayor, City of Topeka, 1982; Obee scholar Washburn U., 1972-74. Fellow Am. Bar Found., Kans. Bar Found. (trustee 1987-89); mem. ABA (labor law, family and litigation sects., mem. ho. dels. 1988—, state del. 1995-99, bd. govs. 1999—, specilization com. 1987-93, chmn. 1989-93, lawyer referral com. 1993-95, bar svcs. and activities, 1995—. standing com. on comms. 1996—, bd. govs., 1999—), Kans. Bar Assn. (sec., treas. 1981-82, 83-85, v.p. 1985-86, pres. 1987-88, bd. dirs.), Kans. Trial Lawyers Assn. (bd. govs. 1982-86, lectr.), Topeka Bar Assn., Am. Bus. Women's Assn. (lectr., corr. sec. 1983-84, pres. career chpt. 1986-87, named one of Top 10 Bus. Women of Yr., 1985). Home: 3408 SW Alameda Dr Topeka KS 66614-5108 Office: 301 SW 10th Ave Topeka KS 66612-1502

**MARQUARDT, ROBERT RICHARD,** lawyer; b. Columbus, Ohio, Aug. 22, 1943; s. Robert Gustave and Ethel M. (Augur) M.; m. Alice Grant, Sept. 9, 1966 (div. 1985); children: Theresa, Robert, Christopher; m. Patricia Moore Peek, Sept. 3, 1989; children: Susan, Katherine. BS in Commerce, Rider Coll., 1965; MBA, Fairleigh Dickinson, 1966; JD, U. Ark., 1973; LLM, Temple U., 1977. Bar: Iowa 1973, Ark. 1973, U.S. Dist. Ct. (ea. dist.) Ark. 1973, N.J. 1975, U.S. Supreme Ct. 1979. Counsel RCA Corp., Camden, N.J., 1973-77; assoc. counsel Occidental Chem. Corp., Niagara Falls, N.Y., 1977-79, div. counsel, 1979-80, counsel, 1980-81, assoc. gen. counsel, 1981-87, v.p., gen. counsel electrochems. and specialty products grp., 1987-91, assoc. gen. counsel, mng. atty., 1991—; instr. bus. law Niagara U., 1978-82. Contbr. legal essays to profl. publs. Chmn. Youngstown (N.Y.) Environ. Com., 1980-84; mil. chmn. UN Operation Horseshoe, Niagara Falls, 1981; staff judge adv. USAFR, 1974-89. Served to lt. col. USAFR, 1967-89. Recipient United Way awards, 1968-76, Corp. award Am. Jurisprudence, 1972; named Judge Adv. of Yr., USAFR, 1980. Antitrust, Contracts commercial, General corporate. Office: 5005 Lbj Fwy Dallas TX 75244-6100

**MARQUESS, LAWRENCE WADE,** lawyer; b. Bloomington, Ind., Mar. 2, 1950; s. Earl Lawrence and Mary Louise (Coberly) M.; m. Barbara Ann Bailey, June 17, 1978; children: Alexander Lawrence, Michael Wade. BSEE, Purdue U., 1973; JD, W.Va. U., 1977. Bar: W.Va. 1977, Tex. 1977, U.S. Dist. Ct. (so. dist.) Tex. 1977, Colo. 1980, U.S. Dist. Ct. Colo. 1980, U.S. Ct. Appeals (10th cir.) 1980, U.S. Supreme Ct. 1984, U.S. Dist. Ct. (no. dist.) Ohio 1988, U.S. Ct. Appeals (DC cir.) 1997. Assoc. Johnson, Bromberg, Leeds & Riggs, Dallas, 1977-79, Bradley, Campbell & Carney, Golden, Colo., 1979-82; ptnr. Bradley, Campbell & Carney, Golden, 1983-84; assoc. Stettner, Miller & Cohn P.C., Denver, 1984-85; ptnr. Stettner, Miller & Cohn P.C., 1985-87, Nelson & Harding, Denver, 1987-88, Heron, Burchette, Ruckert & Rothwell, 1989-90, Harding & Ogborn, 1990-94, Otten, Johnson, Robinson, Neff & Ragonetti, Denver, 1994—; mem. faculty Am. Law Inst. - ABA Advanced Labor and Employment Law Course, 1986, 87. Mem. ABA (labor, antitrust and litigation sects.), ACLU, Colo. Bar Assn. (co-chmn. labor law com. 1989-92), Denver Bar Assn., 1st Jud. Dist. Bar Assn., Sierra Club, Nat. Ry. Hist. Soc. Democrat. Methodist. Labor, Pension, profit-sharing, and employee benefits, Federal civil litigation. Home: 11883 W 27th Dr Lakewood CO 80215-7000 Office: Otten Johnson Robinson Neff & Raginetti 950 17th St Ste 1600 Denver CO 80202-2828

**MARQUETTE, I. EDWARD,** lawyer; b. Hannibal, Mo., Oct. 15, 1950; s. Clifford M. and Doris Elizabeth (McLane) M.; m. Ansie S. Goodrich, May 20, 1972; children: Brandeis, Brooks. BA in Econs., U. Mo., 1973; JD, Harvard U., 1976. Bar: Mo. 1976. Ptnr. Spencer, Fane, Britt & Browne LLP, Kansas City, Mo., 1976—. Contbr. articles to profl. jours., chpts. to books. Bd. dirs. Midwest Christian Counseling Combined Health Appeal, Kansas City, 1988-95. Mem. ABA (new info. tech. com.), Mo. Bar Assn. (tech. com.), Kansas City Bar Assn. (chmn. antitrust study group 1984, chmn. computer law com. 1989, 90, 95, 99), Silicon Prairie Tech. Assn. Democrat. Baptist. Avocation: computer programming. Computer, Antitrust, Trademark and copyright. Office: Spencer Fane Britt & Browne LLP 1000 Walnut St Ste 1400 Kansas City MO 64106-2140

**MARQUEZ, ALFREDO C.,** federal judge; b. 1922; m. Linda Nowobilsky. B.S., U. Ariz., 1948, J.D., 1950. Bar: Ariz. Practice law Mesch Marquez & Rothschild, 1957-80; asst. atty. gen. State of Ariz., 1951-52; asst. county atty. Pima County, Ariz., 1953-54; adminstrv. asst. to Congressman Stewart Udall, 1955; judge U.S. Dist. Ct. Ariz., Tucson, 1980-91, sr. judge, 1991—. Served with USN, 1942-45. Office: US Dist Ct US Courthouse Rm 327 55 E Broadway Blvd Tucson AZ 85701-1719

**MARQUIS, WILLIAM OSCAR,** lawyer; b. Fort Wayne, Ind., Feb. 26, 1944; s. William Oscar and Lenor Mae (Gaffney) M.; m. Mary Frances Funderburk, May 11, 1976; children: Lenor, Kathryn, Timothy Patrick, Daniel, Ann. BS, U. Wis., Madison, 1973; JD, South Tex. Coll. Law, 1977. Bar: Wis. 1979, U.S. Dist. Ct. (ea. dist.) Wis. 1982, U.S. Tax Ct. 1983, U.S. Ct. Appeals (7th cir. 1985). With Wis. Dept. Vet. Affairs, Madison, 1977-79; corp. counsel Barron County, Wis., 1979-80; assoc. Riley, Bruns & Riley, Madison, 1980-81, Jastroch & LaBarge, S.C., Waukesha, Wis., 1981-84; ptnr. Groh, Hackbart & Marquis, 1984-93, Assoc. Neubecker & Marquis, 1993-95. Mem. ATLA, Nat. Assn. Criminal Def. Attys., Wis. Trial Lawyers Assn., Waukesha Bar, Milw. Bar, Wis. Assn. Criminal Def. Attys. Criminal, Personal injury, General civil litigation. Office: 230 W Wells St Ste 224 Milwaukee WI 53203-1866

**MARR, CARMEL CARRINGTON,** retired lawyer, retired state official; b. Bklyn., June 23, 1921; d. William Preston and Gertrude Clementine (Lewis) Carrington; m. Warren Marr II, Apr. 11, 1948; children: Charles Carrington, Warren Quincy III. BA, Hunter Coll., 1945; JD, Columbia U., 1948. Bar: N.Y. 1948, U.S. Dist. Ct. (ea. dist.) N.Y. 1950, U.S. Dist. Ct. (so. dist.) N.Y. 1951. Clk. Dyer & Stevens, N.Y.C., 1948-49; pvt. practice N.Y.C., 1949-53; adviser legal affairs U.S. mission to UN, N.Y.C., 1953-67; sr. legal officer Office Legal Affairs UN Secretariat, 1967-68; mem. N.Y. State Human Rights Appeal Bd., 1968-71, N.Y. State Pub. Svc. Commn., 1971-86; cons. Gas. Rsch. Inst., 1987-91; lectr. N.Y. Police Acad., 1963-67. Contbr. articles to profl. jours. Mem. N.Y. Gov.'s Com. Edn. and Employment of Women, 1963-64; mem. Nat. Gen. Svcs. Pub. Adv. Council, 1969-71; mem., former chmn. adv. coun. Gas. Rsch. Inst.; mem. chmn. tech. pipeline safety standards com. Dept. Transp., 1979-85; former mem. task force Fed. Energy Regulatory Commn. and EPA to examine PCBs in gas supply system; past chmn. gas com. Nat. Assn. Regulatory Utility Commrs.; past pres. Great Lakes Conf. Pub. Utilities Commrs., mem. exec. com.; mem. UN Devel. Corp., 1969-72; bd. dirs. Amistad Rsch. Ctr., New Orleans, 1970—, chmn. bd. dirs., 1981-94; bd. dirs. Bklyn. Soc. Prevention Cruelty to Children, Nat. Arts Stblzn. Fund, 1984-93, hon. bd. mem., 1998, Prospect Park Alliance, 1987-98; bd. visitors N.Y. State Sch. Girls, Hudson, 1964-71; mem. exec. bd. Plays for Living, N.Y.C., 1968-75; pres. bd. dirs. Billie Holiday Theatre, 1972-80; mem. nat. adv. coun. Hampshire Coll.; pres.'s coun. Tulane U., 1988-95. Mem. Phi Beta Kappa, Alpha Chi Alpha, Alpha Kappa Alpha. Republican. Episcopalian.

**MARR, DAVID E,** lawyer; b. Quincy, Mass. B.A., Colby Coll., 1961; M.A., Wesleyan U.; J.D. with honors, U. Conn. Bar: Conn. 1970, Mass. 1974, U.S. Dist. Ct. Conn. 1971, U.S. Dist. Ct. Mass. 1975, U.S. Ct. Appeals (2d cir.) 1971, U.S. Supreme Ct. 1974, U.S. Tax Ct. 1992. Assoc. Day, Berry & Howard, Hartford, Conn., 1970-73; counsel Honeywell Info. Systems, Inc., Waltham, Mass., 1973-75; pvt. practice, Boston, 1975-78, Natick, Mass., 1978—. Author: Employment Law in Connecticut; opinion editor Mass. Lawyers Weekly, 1976-86. Rep., Regional Vocat. Sch.; chmn. Hist. Dist. Com.; bd. dirs. Hist. Soc. and Mus. Mem. ABA, ATLA, Mass. Bar Assn. General civil litigation, Family and matrimonial, Land use and zoning (including planning). Office: 10 Union St Natick MA 01760-4759

**MARR, JACK WAYNE,** lawyer; b. Ft. Worth, Aug. 19, 1949; s. Norman L. and Florence (Mohn) M.; m. Sharon Lee Hutto, Jan. 2, 1971; children: Justin, Dallas. BBA, Tex. Tech. U., 1971, JD, 1974. Bar: Tex. 1994. Briefing counsel 13th Ct. Civil Appeals, Corpus Christi, Tex., 1974-75; assoc. Guittard & Henderson, Victoria, Tex., 1975-79; ptnr. Lewis & Kelly, Victoria, 1979-81, Kelly, Stephenson & Marr, Victoria, 1981-91, Kelly, Marr, Meier & Hartman, Victoria, 1991-93, Marr, Meier & Hartman, Victoria, 1993—. Contbr. articles to profl. jours. Pres. Southwest Little League, Victoria, 1991-92. Mem. State Bar Tex. (family law coun., legis. com., practice manual com.), Tex. Acad. Family Law Specialists (pres. 1994-95). Family and matrimonial.

**MARRA, RALPH PETER,** lawyer; b. S.I., N.Y., Jan. 31, 1957; s. Silvio P. and Irene E. Marraccini; m. Diane E. LaRocca, Sept. 8, 1985; children: Angeline E., Anthony J. BA, St. John's U., 1979; JD, Nova Southeastern Law Sch., 1982. Assoc. ct. atty. N.Y. State Unified Ct. System, S.I., 1983-95, prin. law clk., 1996—; mem. SMA II Claims Arbitrator, S.I., 1988—. Mem. Meals on Wheels, S.I., 1996—; dist. capt. Dem. Party of Richmond, S.I., 1996—. With USMCR, 1976-78. Mem. NAACP, Cath. Ct. Attaché Assn., Amicus Curine Columbia Assn., Assn. of Arbitrators, Nova Southeastern U. Law Alumni Assn., Phi Delta Phi. Home: 195 Hunter Ave Staten Island NY 10306-3445

**MARRAN, JOSEPH EDWARD, JR.,** lawyer; b. Pawtucket, R.I., Sept. 9, 1923; s. Joseph E. Sr. and Martha I. (Corbett) M.; m. Angelina M. Coletti, Sept. 19, 1953; children: Marty, Joseph E. III, Lynne, Colleen. BS in History, Boston Coll., 1953; LLM, Georgetown U., 1955. Bar: R.I. 1956, U.S. Supreme Ct. Dick & Carty, 1956-68; Sole practice Pawtucket, 1968—. Mem. Pawtucket Bar Assn. (pres. 1987). Family and matrimonial, Probate, Personal injury. Office: PO Box 1456 255 Main St Pawtucket RI 02862

**MARRIS, JOAN BANAN,** lawyer; b. Bklyn., May 23, 1960; d. John Francis and Barbara Jane B.; m. August Lorio, Aug. 17, 1990 (div. Dec. 1996); children: John, Kaitlin; m. Michael Frank Harris, Mar. 15, 1997; 1 child, Samantha. BA in Econs., Seton Hall U., 1982, JD, 1985. Bar: N.J. 1985, U.S. Dist. Ct. N.J. 1985. Atty. Francis & Berry, Morristown, N.J., 1986-98, Tafaro & Flynn, New Providence, N.J., 1998—. Mem. N.J. State Bar Assn., Trial Attys. N.J. Professional liability, Personal injury, General civil litigation. Home: 3 Mcbride Way Bridgewater NJ 08807-2688 Office: Tafaro & Flynn 571 Central Ave Ste 108 New Providence NJ 07974-1547

**MARROQUIN-MERINO, VICTOR MIGUEL,** lawyer; b. Lima, Peru, Feb. 10, 1962; s. Victor S. and Maria Isabel (Merino) M.; m. Marisa Jenny Torres, May 2, 1987; 1 child, Victor Andres. AB, Univ. Miami, 1989, JD, 1992; LLM, Harvard Law Sch., 1993. Staff mem. legal dept. Internat. Monetary Fund, Washington, 1993-94; sr. assoc. Baker & McKenzie, Chgo., 1994—. Contbr. articles to profl. jours. Recipient Disting. Svc. award Chgo. Vol. Legal Svcs. Found., 1994, Merit award Legal Clinic for the Disabled, 1996; named Internat. Lawyer of Yr. Univ. Miami, 1994. Avocations: writing, reading, foreign travel, tennis. Private international, Mergers and acquisitions, Oil, gas, and mineral. Office: Baker & McKenzie One Prudential Plaza Chicago IL 60601

**MARS, BURTON H.,** lawyer, title company executive; b. N.Y.C., July 4, 1933; s. Morris and Bessie Mars; m. Dorothy O'Connor, Mar. 30, 1974; children: Janice, Bruce, Kelly Powley, Melissa Koblitz. AB, Hobart Coll., Geneva, N.Y., 1954; LLB, Columbia U., 1956. Bar: N.Y. 1957, Fla. 1988, U.S. Dist. Ct. (so. and ea. dists.) N.Y. 1962, U.S. Dist. Ct. (so. dist.) Fla. 1989, U.S. Supreme Ct. 1963. Town atty. Town of Islip, N.Y., 1970-72. Family and matrimonial, Real property. Home: 2356 NE 8th St Fort Lauderdale FL 33304-3573 Office: 1 E Broward Blvd Ste 1500 Fort Lauderdale FL 33301-1845

**MARS, JOAN ROSEMARY,** law educator; b. Linden, Guyana, Feb. 11, 1954; came to U.S., 1991; d. William Fitzgerald and Marjorie Ethel (Brooms) Ward; m. Pairadeau Aldolphus Mars, Feb. 8, 1978; children: Pairdeau Jr., Jason. LLB, U. W.I., Barbados, 1978; legal edn. cert., Sir Hugh Wood Law Sch., St. Augustine, Trinidad and Tobago, 1981; PhD, Wayne State U., 1996. Bar: Guyana 1981. State counsel Atty. Gen.'s Chambers, Georgetown, Guyana, 1981-84, sr. legal advisor, 1984-86, prin. legal advisor, 1986-89; pvt. practice Georgetown, 1989-91; grad. tchr./rsch. asst. Wayne State U., Detroit, 1993-96; asst. prof. criminal justice law U. Wis., Oshkosh, 1996—; cons. atty. Guyana Human Rights Assn., Georgetown, 1989-91. Recipient gold medal U. Guyana, 1976; Sir Gaston Johnston Meml. prize U. W. Indies, 1978, Faculty Law Book prize, 1978; Dir.'s prize Sir Hugh Wooding Law Sch., 1980. Mem. NAACP, Am. Soc. Crimology, Am. Sociol. Assn., Amnesty Internat., Acad. Criminal Justice Scis. Avocations: travel, reading, human rights work. Office: U Wis Dept Pub Affairs 800 Algoma Blvd Oshkosh WI 54901-3551

**MARS, RICHARD DONALD,** lawyer; b. Stratford, N.J., July 29, 1939; m. Mary G. Mars, Nov. 10, 1972; 1 child, Susan L. Gravely. BS, Fla. State Univ., 1969, JD, 1972. Bar: Fla., U.S. Dist. Ct. (mid. dist.) Fla., U.S. Ct. Appeals. Asst. state atty. 10th Judicial Cir., Bartow, Fla., 1973-75; lawyer Bartow, Fla., 1979—. Decorated Good Conduct medal U.S. Marine Corps., Nat. Def. medal. Mem. Am. Trial Lawyers Assn., Criminal Law Fla. Bar., Am. Inns of Ct. (master). Avocations: salt water fishing, woodworking. Office: Richard D Mars 343 W Davidson St Ste 103 Bartow FL 33830-3765

**MARSEL, ROBERT STEVEN,** law educator, mediator, arbitrator; b. N.Y.C., July 23, 1947; s. Bernard and Vivian (Gilbert) M. JD, U. Calif., 1971. Bar: N.Y., D.C., U.S. Supreme Ct. Mem. Worcester Coll., Oxford, Eng.; vis. lectr. Faculty Law, U. Auckland N.Z.; spl. asst. U.S. atty., San Francisco; legal counsel U.S. Supreme Ct., Washington; vis. asst. prof. law U. Miami, 1983-84; prof. South Tex. Coll. Law, Houston, 1984-97, prof., dean Inst. for Advanced Studies, 1995—, v.p., gen. counsel Houston Mediation Project, 1995—; chmn. com. on privacy and confidentiality U.S. Dept. Commerce; trainer, lectr. on mediation and arbitration; mediator pro bono Houston Dispute Resolution Ctr.; faculty mem. Ctr. for Legal Responsibility. U. Calif. hon. traveling fellow. Fellow Houston Bar Found.; mem. Am. Arbitration Assn., Tex. Assn. Mediators, Accts. and Lawyers for the Arts (bd. dirs. mediation com.), Soc. Profls. in Dispute Resolution. Office: 4715 Ingersoll St Houston TX 77027-6601

**MARSH, LEONARD ROY,** lawyer; b. Watertown, N.Y., May 21, 1928; s. Roy Leonard and Ruby May Marsh; married; children: Jeffrey, Peter, Melissa. BS in Bus., U. Buffalo, 1953; JD, Syracuse U., 1956. Bar: N.Y. 1957. lectr., instr. numerous magistrate and police schs. and orgns.; former asst. dist. atty. Jefferson County, N.Y.; former adminstr. Indigent Defendant Program, Jefferson County. Former dir. March of Dimes, Watertown, Family Counseling Svc., Watertown, United Fund, Watertown. Sgt. USAF, 1946-49. Mem. ABA, N.Y. State Bar Assn., Jefferson County Bar Assn. Nazarene. Family and matrimonial, Criminal, General practice. Home: 1325 Holcomb St Watertown NY 13601-4419 Office: Renee Renzi Law Office 1201 Washington St Watertown NY 13601-4339

**MARSH, MALCOLM F.,** federal judge; b. Portland, Oreg., Sept. 24, 1928; m. Shari Marsh. BS, U. Oreg., 1952, LLB, 1954, JD, 1971. Bar: Oreg. 1954, U.S. Dist. Ct. Oreg. 1955, U.S. Ct. Appeals (9th cir.) 1968. Ptnr. Clark & Marsh, Lindauer & McClinton (and predecessors), Salem, Oreg., 1954-87; judge U.S. Dist. Ct. Oreg., Portland, 1987—. With U.S. Army, 1946-47. Fellow Am. Coll. Trial Lawyers; mem. ABA, Oreg. Bar Assn. Office: US Dist Ct 1507 US Courthouse 1000 SW 3d Ave Portland OR 97204

**MARSH, WESTON W.,** lawyer; b. Evergreen Park, Ill., June 7, 1950; s. Robert Edward and Julie Marie (Walter) M.; m. Nora Hurley, Nov. 28, 1976; children: Kimberly, James, Daniel. BA, Yale U., 1972; MBA, U. Chgo., 1984; JD, U. Ill., Chgo., 1976. Bar: Ill. 1976, U.S. Dist. Ct. (no. dist.) Ill. 1976, U.S. Supreme Ct. 1976. Assoc. atty. Rooks, Pitts, Fullugar & Poust, Chgo., 1976-79; trial atty., gen. counsel Atchison, Topeka & Santa Fe R.R., 1979-90; ptnr. Freeborn & Peters, Chgo., 1990—. Mem. Fed. Bar Assn. (bd. dirs. 1996-97). General civil litigation, Personal injury. Office: Freeborn & Peters 311 S Wacker Dr Ste 3000 Chicago IL 60606-6679

**MARSH, WILLIAM DOUGLAS,** lawyer; b. Sikeston, Mo., Feb. 22, 1947; s. Ray Carl and Mary Louis (Buchanan) M.; m. Georgia Kay Trigg, June 3, 1967; children: Kristin Elizabeth, Kelly Anne. BSBA, S.E. Mo. State U., 1971; JD, U. Mo., Kansas City, 1973. Bar: Fla. 1974, U.S. Dist. Ct. (no., mid. and so. dists.) Fla. 1974, U.S. Ct. Appeals (5th and 11th cir.) 1974. Shareholder Emmanuel, Sheppard & Condon, Pensacola, Fla., 1973—. Contbr. articles to profl. jours.; reviewer Fla. Torts, 1990. Active numerous polit. campaigns/polit. action groups. 1st lt. U.S. N.G., 1967-73. Mem. ABA (litigation sect., torts and ins. practice sect., com. on auto. law), Assn. Trial Lawyers Am. (diplomate), Acad. Fla. Trial Lawyers (sustaining), Am. Bd. Trial Advocacy (cert. trail lawyer), Fla. Bar Assn. (rules of civil procedure com. 1991—, trial lawyers sect. exec. coun. 1979-88, sec. 1984-85, editor trial sect. newsletter 1982-83, chmn. 1986-87). Democrat. Methodist. Avocation: sailing. Personal injury, Admiralty, Product liability. Office: Emmanuel Sheppard & Condon 30 S Spring St Pensacola FL 32501-5612

**MARSHALL, ARTHUR K.,** lawyer, judge, arbitrator, educator, writer; b. N.Y.C., Oct. 7, 1911. BS, CUNY, 1933; LLB, St. John's U., N.Y.C., 1936; LL.M., U. So. Calif., 1952. Bar: N.Y. State 1937, Calif. 1947. Practice law N.Y.C., 1937-43, Los Angeles, 1947-50; atty. VA, Los Angeles, 1947-50; tax counsel Calif. Bd. Equalization, Sacramento, 1950-51; inheritance tax atty. State Controller, Los Angeles, 1951-53; commr. Superior Ct. Los Angeles County, 1953-62; judge Municipal Ct., Los Angeles jud. dist., 1962-63, Superior Ct., Los Angeles, 1963-81; supervising judge probate dept. Superior Ct., 1968-69, appellate dept., 1973-77; presiding judge Appellate Dept., 1976-77; pvt. practice arbitrator, mediator, judge pro tem, 1981—; acting asst. prof. law UCLA, 1954-59; grad. faculty U. So. Calif., 1955-75; lectr. Continuing Edn. of the Bar; mem. Calif. Law Revision Commn., 1984—, chmn., 1986-87, 92-93, 98-99, vice chmn., 1983, 85, 98; chmn. com. on efficiency and econs. Conf. Calif. Judges, past chmn. spl. action com. on ct. improvement; past chmn. probate law cons. group Calif. Bd. Legal Specialization. Author: Joint Tenancy Taxwise and Otherwise, 1953, Branch Courts, 1959, California State and Local Taxation Text, 2 vols., 1962, rev. edit., 1969, supplement, 1979, 2d edito., 1981, Triple Choice Method, 1964, California State and Local Taxation Forms, 2 vols., 1961-75, rev. edit., 1996, California Probate Procedure, 1961, 5th rev. edit., 1994, Guide to Procedure Before Trial, 1975; contbr. articles to profl. jours. Mem. Town Hall. With AUS, 1943-46; lt. col. JAGC, USAR ret. Named Judge of Yr. Lawyers Club L.A. County, 1975; first recipient Arthur K. Marshall award established by estate planning, trust and probate sect. L.A. Bar Assn., 1981, Disting. Jud. Career award L.A. Lawyers Club, award L.A. County Bd. Suprs., 1981. Fellow Am. Bar Found.; mem. ABA (probate litigation com. real property, probate and trust sect.), Am. Arbitration Assn. (mem. nat. panel of arbitrators), Internat. Acad. Estate and Trust Law (academician, founder, 1st pres., now chancellor), Calif. State Bar (advisor to exec. com. real property, probate and trust sect. 1970-83), Santa Monica Bar Assn. (pres. 1960), Westwood Bar Assn. (pres. 1959), L.A. Bar Assn., Am. Legion (comdr. 1971-72), U. So. Calif. Law Alumni Assn. (pres. 1969-70), Phi Alpha Delta (1st justice alumni chpt.). Probate, Contracts commercial. Office: 300 S Grand Ave Fl 28 Los Angeles CA 90071-3109

**MARSHALL, CONSUELO BLAND,** federal judge; b. Knoxville, Tenn., Sept. 28, 1936; d. Clyde Theodore and Annie (Brown) Arnold; m. George Edward Marshall, Aug. 30, 1959; children: Michael Edward, Laurie Ann. AA, L.A. City Coll., 1956; BA, Howard U., 1958, LLB, 1961. Bar: Calif. 1962. Dep. atty. City of L.A., 1962-67; assoc. Cochran & Atkins, L.A., 1968-70; commr. L.A. Superior Ct., 1971-76; judge Inglewood Mcpl. Ct., 1976-77, L.A. Superior Ct., 1977-80, U.S. Dist. Ct. Central Dist. Calif., L.A., 1980—; lectr. U.S. Information Agy. in Yugoslavia, Greece and Italy, 1984, in Nigera and Ghana, 1991, in Ghana, 1992. Contbr. articles to profl. jours.; notes editor Law Jour. Howard U. Mem. adv. bd. Richstone Child Abuse Center. Recipient Judicial Excellence award Criminal Cts. Bar Assn., 1992, Ernestine Stalhut award; named Criminal Ct. Judge of Yr., U.S. Dist. Ct., 1997; rsch. fellow Howard U. Law Sch., 1959-60. Mem. State Bar Calif., Century City Bar Assn., Calif. Women Lawyers Assn., Calif. Assn. Black Lawyers, Calif. Judges Assn., Black Women Lawyers Assn., Los Angeles County Bar Assn., Nat. Assn. Women Judges, NAACP, Urban League, Beta Phi Sigma. Office: US Dist Ct 312 N Spring St Los Angeles CA 90012-4701

**MARSHALL, DAVID STANLEY,** lawyer; b. Seneca Falls, N.Y., Aug. 23, 1950; s. James Stanley and Ruth Catherine (Cratty) M.; m. Jo Ann Breuninger, Mar. 20, 1993; children: Matthew Stanley, Peter David. BA, Cornell U., 1970; JD, U. Calif., Berkeley, 1974. Bar: Wash. 1981, Calif. 1975. Dep. pros. atty. Pierce County, Tacoma, Wash., 1981-84; assoc. atty. Williams Kastner & Gibbs, Seattle, 1984-85; shareholder Prince, Kelley, Marshall & Coombs, Seattle, 1985-96; pvt. practice, Seattle, 1997—. Chmn. fellowship bd. Univ. Congl. Ch., 1985-85; chmn. citizens' adv. com. Metro Transp., Seattle, 1988-90; vol. Big Brothers King County, Seattle, 1992—; bd. dirs. Transit Discussion Group, 1995-96. Democrat. United Church of Christ. Avocations: squash, cycle touring, alpine skiing, Romance languages. Criminal, Juvenile, General civil litigation. Home: 153 Hayes St Seattle WA 98109-2811 Office: 900 4th Ave Ste 3250 Seattle WA 98164-1072

**MARSHALL, JOHN PATRICK,** lawyer; b. Bklyn., July 3, 1950; s. Harry W. and Mary Margaret (Kelly) M.; m. Cheryl J. Garvey, Aug. 10, 1975; children: Kelly Blake, Logan Brooke. BA, Rutgers U., 1972; JD cum laude, N.Y. Law Sch., 1976. Bar: N.Y. 1977, N.J. 1977, U.S. Dist. Ct. N.J. 1977, U.S. Dist. Ct. (so. and ea. dists.) N.Y. 1978, U.S. Ct. Appeals (3rd cir.) 1982, U.S. Dist Ct. (no. dist.) N.Y. 1991. Assoc. Kelley Drye & Warren, N.Y.C., 1976-84, ptnr., 1985-98. Editorial bd. N.Y. Law Sch. Law Rev., 1975-76, staff mem., 1974-75; contbr. articles to profl. jours. Mem. jud. screening com. N.Y. Dem. Com., N.Y. New Dem. Coalition, 1988; exec. v.p. Humanitarian Found. for Nicaragua, 1991; mem., sec. Respect for Law Found., 1996; mem. Southern Dist. N.Y. Mediation Panel, 1994—; mem. Coun. on Jud. Adminstrn., 1996-98. Fellow Am. Bar Found.; mem. ABA, N.Y. County Lawyers' Assn. (sec. 1984-87, mem. com. on Supreme Ct. 1984-94, mem. legal edn., admission to bar and lawyer placement com. 1983-93), Am. Arbitration Assn. (mem. nat. panel arbitrators N.Y. and N.J. regions 1991—, mem. corp. counsel com. 1993-98), Assn. of Bar of City of N.Y. (sec. judiciary com. 1989-92, mem. com. on arbitration 1994-96, sec. coun. on judicial adminstrn. 1996-98). Federal civil litigation, State civil litigation, Private international. Office: 50 Highland Ave Short Hills NJ 07078-2812

**MARSHALL, LINDA KAYE,** judge; b. Batesville, Ark.; d. Lucy Ellen (Westerfield) McDoniel. BS in Bus., U. Ark., Little Rock, 1977; MS in Ops. Mgmt., U. Ark., 1982; JD, U. Ark., Little Rock, 1987. Bar: Ark. 1987. EEO officer Ark. Power & Light Co., Little Rock, 1978-88; dep. prosecuting atty. Pulaski County Prosecuting Atty., Little Rock, 1988-90; atty. Gail Laster Law Firm, Little Rock, 1990-91; legal advisor Ark. Workers' Compensation Com., Little Rock, 1991-93, chief legal advisor, 1993-95, adminstrv. law judge, 1995—; state grievance appeal panel mem. State of Ark., Little Rock, 1993-95. Bd. dirs. Super Speech, Little Rock, 1984-88; active Big Bros./Big Sisters, Little Rock, 1988-90; vol., selection com. mem. Habitat for Humanity, Little Rock, 1994—, Carti Auxiliary, 1995. Mem. Ark. Bar Assn., Pulaski County Bar Assn. Home: 1301 Hunters Cove Dr Little Rock AR 72211-2242 Office: Ark Workers Compensation PO Box 950 Little Rock AR 72203-0950

**MARSHALL, MARGARET HILARY,** state supreme court justice; b. Newcastle, Natal, South Africa, Sept. 1, 1944; came to U.S., 1968; d. Bernard Charles and Hilary A.D. (Anderton) M; m. Samuel Shapiro, Dec. 14, 1968 (div. Apr. 1982); m. Anthony Lewis, Sept. 23, 1984. BA, Witwatersrand U., Johannesburg, 1966; MEd, Harvard U., 1969; JD, Yale U., 1976; LHD (hon.), Regis Coll., 1993. Bar: Mass. 1977, U.S. Dist. Ct. Mass., U.S. Dist. Ct. N.H., U.S. Dist. Ct. D.C., U.S. Dist. Ct. (ea. dist.) Mich., U.S. Tax Ct., U.S. Ct. Appeals (1st, 11th and D.C. cirs.), U.S. Supreme Ct. Assoc. Csaplar & Bok, Boston, 1976-83, ptnr., 1983-89; ptnr. Choate, Hall & Stewart, Boston, 1989-92; v.p., gen. counsel Harvard U., Cambridge, Mass., 1992-96; justice Supreme Jud. Ct. Commonwealth Mass., 1996—; mem. jud. nominating coun., 1987-90, 92; chairperson ct. rules subcom. Alternative Dispute Resolution Working Group, 1985-87; mem. fed. appts. commn., 1993; mem. adv. com. Supreme Judicial Ct., 1989-92, mem. gender equality com., 1989-94; mem. civil justice adv. group U.S. Dist. Ct. Mass., 1991-93; spl. counsel Jud. Conduct Commn., 1988-92; trustee Mass. Continuing Legal Edn., Inc., 1990-92. Trustee Regis Coll., 1993-95; bd. dirs. Internat. Design Conf., Aspen, 1986-92, Boston Mcpl. Res. Bur., 1990-94, Supreme Judicial Ct. Hist. Soc., 1990-94, sec., 1990-94. Fellow Am. Bar Found. (Mass. state chair); mem. Boston Bar Assn. (treas. 1988-89, v.p. 1989-90, pres.-elect 1990-91, pres. 1991-92), Internat. Women's Forum, Mass. Women's Forum, Boston Club, Phi Beta Kappa (hon.). Home: 1010 Memorial Dr Apt 7E Cambridge MA 02138-4854 Office: Supreme Jud Ct 1300 Court House Boston MA 02108*

**MARSHALL, MARILYN JOSEPHINE,** lawyer; b. Dayton, Ohio, May 31, 1945; d. Foy Wylie and Inez Virginia (Smith) Gard; m. Alan George Marshall, June 13, 1965; children: Gwendolyn Scott, Brian George. Student, Northwestern U., 1963-65; BA, Stanford U., 1967; cert. in teaching, U. B.C., Vancouver, 1977; JD, Capital Law Sch., Columbus, Ohio, 1985. Bar: Ohio 1985, Fla. 1993, U.S Dist. Ct. (so. dist.) Ohio 1986, U.S. Dist. Ct. (no. dist., mid. dist. and so. dist.) Fla. 1994, U.S. Ct. Appeals (6th cir.) 1986, U.S. Ct. Appeals (11th cir.) 1994. Tchr. Sutherland Secondary Sch., North Vancouver, B.C., 1977-79; instr. Brit. Coll. Inst. Tech., Burnaby, B.C., 1979-80; assoc. Crabbe, Brown, Jones, Potts & Schmidt, Columbus, Ohio, 1985-86; clk. to judge U.S. Dist. Ct. (so. dist.) Ohio, Columbus, 1986-88; clk. to justice Ohio Supreme Ct., 1988-89; assoc. Squire, Sanders & Dempsey, 1989-92; with Columbus City Atty.'s Office, Columbus, Ohio, 1992-93; asst. atty. gen. civil divsn. State of Fla., Tallahassee, 1994-96; pvt. practice Tallahassee, 1996—. Mem. ABA, Ohio Bar Assn., Fla. Bar Assn., Tallahassee Bar Assn., Tallahassee Women Lawyers Assn., Capitol U. Law Sch. Alumni Assn. Republican. Avocations: tennis, gardening, music. Office: 254 E 6th Ave Tallahassee FL 32303-6208

**MARSHALL, RAYMOND CHARLES,** lawyer; b. Aquadilia, Puerto Rico, July 23, 1952; m. Piper Kent-Marshall; 1 child, Kyle. BA summa cum laude, Coll. Idaho, 1975; JD, Harvard U., 1978. Bar: Calif. 1978, D.C. 1989. Ptnr. McCutchen Doyle Brown & Enersen, San Francisco. Co-author: Environmental Crimes, 1992; contbr. chpt. to manual; contbr. articles to profl. jours. Bd. dirs. Nat. Multiple Sclerosis Soc. Northern Calif. chpt., 1992—; adv. bd. United Negro Coll. Fund Northern Bay Area Chpt., 1992—; bd. trustees Alta Bates Found., 1994—; mem. San Francisco leadership bd. Am. Red Cross Bay Area; adv. coun. mem. San Francisco Sports Coun. Recipient San Francisco Neighborhood Legal Assistance Found. award, 1989, Earl Warren Legal Svcs. award NAACP Legal Def. & Ednl. Found., 1990, Unity award Minority Bar Coalition, 1992, Cmty. Svc. award Wiley Manuel Law Found., 1994. Mem. ABA (met. bar caucus exec. com. 1992-94, vice-chmn. natural resources & energy litigation com. 1989-93, environmental crimes com. 1990-92, nominating com. conf. of minority ptnrs. in maj. corp. law firms 1991, commn. on women in the profession 1994-95, co-chmn. environmental crimes subcom. of white collar crime com. 1994-95), Nat. Bar Assn., Calif. State Bar (bd. govs. 1995—, pres. 1998—), Charles Houston Bar Assn. Avocations: travel, recreational sports. Office: McCutchen Doyle Brown & Enersen Three Embarcadero Ctr San Francisco CA 94111*

**MARSHALL, RICHARD TREEGER,** lawyer; b. N.Y.C., May 17, 1925; s. Edward and Sydney (Treeger) M.; m. Dorothy M. Goodman, June 4, 1950; children: Abigail Ruth Marshall Bergerson, Daniel Brooks; m. 2d Sylvia J. Kelley, June 10, 1979. BS, Cornell U., 1948; JD, Yale U., 1951. Bar: Tex. 1952, U.S. Ct.. Appeals (5th cir.) 1966, U.S. Ct. Appeals (10th cir.) 1980, U.S. Supreme Ct. 1959; lic. Tex. Dept. Ins. Sole practice El Paso, Tex., 1952-59, 61-79; assoc. Fryer & Milstead, El Paso, 1952; sr. ptnr. Marshall & Wendorf, El Paso, 1959-61, Marshall & Volk, El Paso, 1979-81; sr. atty. Richard T. Marshall & Assocs., P.C., El Paso, 1981-85; sr. ptnr. Marshall, Thomas & Winters, El Paso, 1985-87; sr. atty. Marshall & Winters, 1987-88, Marshall, Sherrod & Winters, 1988-90; pvt. practice El Paso, 1990—; instr. polit. sci. U. Tex., El Paso, 1961-62; instr. ins. law C.L.U. tng. course Am. Coll.; officer, dir. Advance Funding, Inc., El Paso. Editor El Paso Trial Lawyers Rev., 1973-80; contbr. articles to legal jours. Mem. ATLA (sec. personal injury law sect. 1967-68, nat. sec. 1969-70, sec.-treas. environ. law sect. 1970-71, vice chmn. family law litigation sec. 1971-72), El Paso Bar Assn., El Paso Trial Lawyers Assn. (pres. 1965-66), Tex. Trial Lawyers Assn.,, Roscoe Pound-Am. Trial Lawyers Found. (commn. on profl. responsibility 1979-82), Nat. Acad. Elder Law Attys., Soc. Cert. Sr. Advisors, Nat. Assn. Charitable Estate Counselors. Email: RTMElPaso.aol.com; website: www.texseniorlaw.com. Estate planning, Personal injury, Probate. Office: 5959 Gateway Blvd W El Paso TX 79925-3331

**MARSHALL, ROBERT WILLIAM,** lawyer, rancher; b. L.A., Apr. 12, 1933; s. Kenneth I. and Helen (Putnam) M.; m. Nanette Hollenbeck, June 10, 1965; children: Thomas, Victoria, Rebecca, Kathleen. AB in Pre Law, Stanford U., 1955, JD, 1957. Bar: Calif. 1958, Nev. 1958, U.S. Dist. Ct. (so. dist.) Calif. 1958, U.S. Dist. Ct. Nev. 1958. Assoc. Vargas & Bartlett, Reno, Nev., 1958-64; ptnr. Vargas & Bartlett, Reno, 1964-85, sr. ptnr., 1985-94; chmn. of bd. Marshall, Hill, Cassas & de Lipkau, 1994—. Advisor Explorer Boy Scouts Am., Reno, 1971-76, 87-89, scoutmaster Troop 444 Boy Scouts Am., Reno, 1981-85; state chmn. Nev. Young Reps., 1962-64. Mem. ABA, Nat. Cattlemen's Assn., Calif. Bar Assn., Nev. Bar Assn., Washoe County Bar Assn., Rocky Mountain Mineral Law Inst., No. Nev. Indsl. Gas Users (organizer), No. Nev. Large Power Users (organizer), So. Nev. Large Power Users (organizer), Nev. Cattlemen's Assn., Reno Stanford Club (pres. Reno chpt. 1974). Republican. Mormon. Real property, Public utilities. Office: Marshall Hill Cassas & deLipkau 333 Holcomb Ave Ste 300 Reno NV 89502-1648

**MARSHALL, SIRI SWENSON,** corporate lawyer. BA, Harvard U., 1970; JD, Yale U., 1974. Bar: N.Y. 1975. Assoc. Debevoise & Plimpton, 1974-79; atty., sr. atty., asst. gen. counsel Avon Products, Inc., N.Y.C., 1979-85, v.p. legal affairs, 1985-89, sr. v.p., gen. counsel, 1990-94; sr. v.p., gen. counsel Gen. Mills, Inc., Mpls., 1994—; bd.dirs. NovaCare, Inc., Am. Arbitration Assn.; mem. exec. com. Ctr. Pub. resources; bd. trustees Mpls. Inst. Arts. General corporate, Administrative and regulatory. Office: Gen Mills Inc Number One Gen Mills Blvd Minneapolis MN 55426

**MARSHALL, SUSAN,** lawyer; b. Ellsworth, Kans., July 8, 1950; d. Daniel Benjamin and Elizabeth Jean (Bailey) M. BA, U. Kans., 1972; JD with honors, Washburn U., 1976. Bar: Kans. 1976. Summer legal intern, Campbell, Erickson, Cottingham, Morgan & Gibson, Kansas City, Mo., 1975; research asst., lobbyist Kans. County and Dist. Attys. Assn., Topeka, 1975-76; assoc. Metz & Metz, Lincoln, Kans., 1977-83; county atty. Lincoln County, Kans., Lincoln, 1980-85, 89-97; sole practice, Lincoln, 1983—; atty. position Kans. Commn. on Civil Rights, Topeka, 1978-86. Pres. Lincoln Carnegie Library, 1982-88. Mem. ABA, Kans. Bar Assn., Kans. County and Dist. Attys. Assn., Nat. Dist. Attys. Assn., Kans. Assn. County Commrs. (bd. dirs. 1995-97), Nat. History Soc. Republican. General practice, Probate, Taxation, general. Office: PO Box 389 117 S 4th St Lincoln KS 67455-2325

**MARSHALL, WILLIAM TAYLOR,** lawyer; b. Dallas; s. Willis A. and Jane T. Marshall; m. Peggy Taylor, May 18, 1973; 1 child, Taylor. BSPA with honors, U. Ark., 1973, MBA, 1975; JD with honors, U. Ark., Little Rock, 1981. Bar: Ark. 1981, U.S. Dist. Ct. (fed. dist.) 1982, U.S. Ct. Appeals (8th cir.) 1982, U.S. Supreme Ct. 1984; CPA, Ark. Fin. analyst Hosp. Affiliates Internat., Nashville, 1975-76, sr. fin. analyst, 1976-78; CFO Hosp. Affiliates Internat./Doctor's Hosp., Little Rock, 1978-81; assoc. House Holmes & Jewell, Little Rock, 1981-83, ptnr., 1983-85; ptnr. Robinson, Staley, Marshall & Duke, Little Rock, 1985—; lectr. in field. Contbr. articles to profl. jours. Mem. ABA, AICPAs, Ark. Bar Assn. (cert. tax specialist, health law sect. 1985—), Am. Health Lawyers Assn. Health, Corporate taxation, General corporate. Home: 1900 Beechwood St Little Rock AR 72207-2004 Office: Robinson Staley Marshall & Duke PA 400 W Capitol Ave Ste 2891 Little Rock AR 72201-3463

**MARSTILLER, PHILIP S.,** lawyer; b. Clarksburg, W.Va., Sept. 4, 1944; s. James Augustus and Marjorie Annon M.; m. Judy Rothwell Philpott, June 1, 1966 (div. Sept. 1983); children: Philip S. Jr., Spencer P.; m. Catherine Profitt Hayden, June 17, 1994. BA, Coll. William & Mary, 1966; LLB, U. Richmond, 1969. Bar: Va. 1969, U.S. Dist. Ct. (ea. and we. dists.) Va. 1969, U.S. Ct. Appeals (4th cir.) 1975, U.S. Supreme Ct. 1980. Asst. commonwealth atty. Henry County Commonwealth Attys. Office, Martinsville, Va., 1969-71; assoc. Mays & Valentine, Richmond, Va., 1972-76; ptnr. Hazel, Thomas, Fiske, Beckhorn & Hanes, Richmond, 1976-88, Parker, Pollard & Brown, Richmond, 1988-91, Cawthorn, Picard, Rowe & Marstiller, Richmond, 1991-93; pres. Philip S. Marstiller, P.C., Richmond, 1994—; adj. prof. law U. Richmond Sch. Law, 1985-89; mem. pres. coun. Coll. William & Mary, Williamsburg, Va., 1994-99; mem. alumni coun. Mercersburg (Pa.) Acad., 1999. Author: The Virginia Alcoholic Beverage Control Board Compliance Manual, 1991. Mem. 2d Presbyn. Ch., Richmond; lobbyist Va. Gen. Assembly, Richmond, 1972-92. Capt. JAGC, 1970-73. Mem. ATLA, ABA (mem. negligence-products liability litig. com. 1975-78), Am. Trial Lawyers Assn., Nat. Assn. Employment Lawyers, Nat. Health Lawyers Assn., Bar Register Preeminent Lawyers Am., Va. Bar Assn., (mem. constrn. litig. com. 1980-82), Va. State Bar (mem. com. legis. 1980, bd. govs. health law section 1984-88), Va. Trial Lawyers Assn. (mem. com. legis. 1975-78, mem. com. employment law 1996), Richmond Bar Assn. (mem. legis. liaison com. 1975-78), 4th Century Club, Deep Run Hunt Club, Farmington Country Club. Democrat. Avocations: Upland bird hunting, duck and goose hunting, fly fishing, long distance running. Labor, Product liability. Office: 16 S 2nd St Richmond VA 23219-3723

**MARSZALEK, JOHN EDWARD,** lawyer; b. Chgo., Oct. 24, 1951; s. Edward J. and Virginia F. (Yaks) M.; m. Therese E. Finn, Jan. 26, 1985. BA, Rollins Coll., Winter Park, Fla., 1972; JD, John Marshall Law Sch., Chgo., 1976. Bar: Ill. 1976, U.S. Dist. Ct. (no. dist.) Ill. 1977, Fla. 1979, U.S. Supreme Ct. 1986, U.S. Ct. Appeals (7th cir.) 1986. Assoc. Goldstein, Goldberg & Fishman, Chgo., 1976-79, John G. Phillips & Assocs., Chgo., 1979-83; proprietor Law Office of John E. Marszalek, Chgo., 1983-84; owner Marszalek & Marszalek, Chgo., 1984—. Personal injury, State civil litigation, Product liability. Home: 910 N Lake Shore Dr Apt 517 Chicago IL 60611-1585 Office: Marszalek & Marszalek 29 S La Salle St Ste 830 Chicago IL 60603-1505

**MARTELL, SAUNDRA ADKINS,** lawyer; b. Huntington, W.Va., June 26, 1946; d. Edgar and Mildred Faye (Harless) Adkins; m. Ronald E. Martell, Aug. 1, 1982; children: Thomas, Laura. BA, Vanderbilt U., 1968; JD, U. Va., 1971. Bar: Va. 1972, Minn. 1982. Trial atty. USN Dept., Washington, 1972-77; spl. U.S. atty. Dept. Justice, Washington, 1977-79; judge GSA Bd. Contract Appeals, Washington, 1979-81; prin. John Murray & Assocs., St. Paul, 1982-84; asst. gen. counsel S.J. Groves & Sons Co., Mpls., 1984-87, gen. counsel, 1987-91; pres. The MARC Group, Inc., Mpls., 1991—. Mem. ABA. Methodist. Construction, Government contracts and claims, General civil litigation. Home: 13816 Spring Lake Rd Minnetonka MN 55345-2332

**MARTENS, DAN E.,** lawyer; b. Oklahoma City, Mar. 27, 1945; s. Frank M. and Estele Alice Martens; m. Susan Jo Farmer, Apr. 3, 1976; children: Kathryn T., Daniel C. BA in Social Sci., So. Meth. U., 1967, JD, 1974. Bar: Tex. 1974, U.S. Dist. Ct. (no. dist.) Tex. 1974, U.S. Dist. Ct. (ea. dist.) Tex. 1991, U.S. Dist. Ct. (we. dist.) Okla. 1983, U.S. Ct. Appeals (5th cir.) 1984, U.S. Ct. Appeals (10th cir.) 1995, U.S. Tax Ct. 1988, U.S. Supreme Ct. 1993. Assoc. atty. Golden Potts Boeckman & Wilson, Dallas, 1974-77; ptnr. Hiersche Martens Hayward Drakeley & Urbach, Dallas, 1977—. Bd. dirs., pres. Ronald McDonald House of Dallas, 1996-98; pres. Journey of Hope Grief Support Ctr., Plano, Tex., 1998—. Lt. USNR, 1967-70, Viet Nam. Methodist. Avocations: flying, hunting, golf. General civil litigation, General practice, Probate. Home: 5810 Knightsbridge Dr Dallas TX 75252-5011 Office: Hiersche Martens Hayward Drakeley & Urbach 15303 Dallas Pkwy Ste 700 Addison TX 75001

**MARTENS, DON WALTER,** lawyer; b. Darlington, Wis., Mar. 25, 1934; s. Walter W. and Geraldine A. (McWilliams) M.; children: Kim Martens Cooper, Diane Martens Reed. BS in Engring., U. Wis., 1957; JD with honors, George Washington U., 1963. Bar: Supreme Ct. Calif. 1964, U.S. Ct. Appeals (9th cir.) 1964, U.S. Dist. Ct. (no. and cen. dists.) Calif. 1964, U.S. Supreme Ct. 1973, U.S. Dist. Ct. (so. dist.) Calif. 1977, U.S. Ct. Appeals (fed. cir.) 1982, U.S. Dist. Ct. (ea. dist.) Calif. 1984. Examiner U.S. Patent and Trademark Office, Washington, 1960-63; patent lawyer Standard Oil of Calif., San Francisco, 1963-65; ptnr. Knobbe, Martens, Olson & Bear, Newport Beach, Calif., 1965—; mem. adv. comm. Fed. Cir. Ct. Appeals, 1991-96. Lt. USN, 1957-60. Mem. Orange County Bar Assn. (pres. 1975), Orange County Legal Aid Soc. (pres. 1969), Orange County Patent Law Assn. (pres. 1984), L.A. Patent Law Assn. (pres. 1989), State Bar Calif. (bd. govs. 1984-87, v.p. 1986-87), Am. Intellectual Property Law Assn. (pres. 1995-96), State Bar Intellectual Property Assn. (chmn. 1977), 9th Cir. Jud. Conf. (del. 1985-88, 1995-98), Nat. Inventors Hall of Fame Found. (pres. 1998-99), Nat. Coun. Intellectual Property Law Assn. (chmn. 1998-99), Big Canyon Country Club. Republican. Roman Catholic. Federal civil litigation, Patent, Trademark and copyright. Office: 620 Newport Center Dr Fl 16 Newport Beach CA 92660-6420

**MARTILLOTTI, GERARD JACOB,** lawyer; b. Scranton, Pa., Feb. 15, 1966; s. Jacob and Marie Martillotti; m. Maryann McGrane, Aug. 21, 1993; children: Jacob, Matthew. BS, U. Scranton, 1988; JD, Dickinson Sch. Law, 1991. Bar: Pa. 1991, U.S. Dist. Ct. (mid. dist.) Pa. 1991, Md. 1992, D.C. 1992, U.S. Dist. Ct. D.C. 1992, U.S. Dist. Ct. Md. 1992, N.J. 1994, U.S. Dist. Ct. (ea. dist.) Pa. 1994, U.S. Dist. Ct. N.J. 1994. Lawyer Paulson, Nace, Norwind & Sellinger, Washington, 1991-94; lawyer Davis & Myers, Phila., 1994—, Northfield, N.J., 1994—. Mem. ATLA, N.J. Trial Lawyers, Pa. Trial Lawyers. General civil litigation, Personal injury, Product liability. Office: Davis & Myers 1601 Market St Ste 2330 Philadelphia PA 19103-2306

**MARTIN, ANDREW AYERS,** lawyer, physician, educator; b. Toccoa, Ga., Aug. 18, 1958; s. Wallace Ford and Dorothy LaTranquil (Ayers) M.; children: William Ayers, Malorie Ayers. BA, Emory U., Atlanta, 1980, MD, 1984; JD, Duke U., 1988. Bar: Calif. 1989, La. 1990, D.C. 1991; diplomate Am. Bd. Pathology, Nat. Bd. Med. Examiners; lic. physician, La., Miss., Ark. Intern in pediatrics Emory U./Grady Meml. Hosp., Atlanta, 1984; intern Tulane U./Charity Hosp., New Orleans, 1989-90, resident in anatomic and clin. pathology, 1990-94; surg. pathology fellow Baylor Coll. Medicine, Houston, 1994-95; law clk. Ogletree, Deakins, Smoak, Stewart, Greenville, S.C., summer 1986, Thelen Marrin Johnson Bridges, L.A., summer 1987, Duke Hosp. Risk Mgmt., 1987-88; assoc. Haight Brown Bonesteel, Santa Monica, Calif., 1988; pvt. practice L.A., 1989; physician/atty. Tulane Med. Ctr./Charity Hosp., New Orleans, 1989-94, Baylor Coll. Medicine/Tex. Med. Ctr., Houston, 1994-95; lab. dir. King's Daus. Hosp., Greenville, Miss., 1995—; asst. clin. prof. pathology Tulane U.; lab. dir., owner Vicksburg Pathology Lab., Bolivar Med. Ctr., Cleveland, Miss.; staff pathologist Delta Regional Ctr., Greenville, Miss., N.W. Miss. Regional Medical Ctr., Clarksdale, Miss., No. Sunflower County Hosp., Ruteville, Miss., Tallahatchie County Hosp., Charleston, Miss.; sr. ptnr. Mid-South Pathology Assocs.; med. dir. of labs. Vicksburg Pathology Lab., N.W. Miss. Regional Med. Ctr., Bolivar Med. Ctr., Delta Regional Med. Ctr., North Sunflower County Hosp., 1997—, Tallahatchie (Miss.) County Hosp., N.W. Miss. Regional Med. Ctr., Clarksdale, Tallahatchie County Hosp.; adj. faculty Moorhead U.; bd. dirs. Martin Bldrs., Inc., Toccoa; mem. AIDS Legis. Task Force for La.; case cons. Office of Tech. Assessment, Washington; tech. cons. and autopsy extra Oliver Stone's "JFK"; adj. clin. faculty Moorhead Coll. *Founder and senior partner of Mid-South Pathology Associates and Vicksburg Pathology Laboratory, serving six hospitals in Mississippi and clinics in Mississippi, Arkansas and Louisiana. At Mid-South Pathology, "we're not alien to new ideas", not the least of which is to provide new standards of diagnostic excellence to the citizens of the Mississippi Delta a traditionally underserved area.* Contbr. articles to profl. jours.; author: Reflections on Rusted Chrome (book of poetry). Fellow Coll. Am. Pathologists, Coll. Legal Medicine, La. State Med. Soc. (del. meeting 1992-93). Health. Home: 935 Lakehall Rd Lake Village AR 71653-6096 also: 4104 Alabama Ave Kenner LA 70065-5603 also: 3850 Old Highway 27 Vicksburg MS 39180-8829 Office: Mid-South Pathology Assocs PO Box 5880 Greenville MS 38704-5880

**MARTIN, ARTHUR JOSEPH,** lawyer; b. St. Louis, Sept. 19, 1947; s. Everett Louis and Mary Helen (Halenkamp) M.; m. Rebecca Sue Vance, Apr. 26, 1975 (div. June 1988); children: Alexia Claire, Ariel Marion; m. Janine M. Martin, June 3, 1995; children: Joseph Xavier, Francis Jude. BA, Quincy (Ill.) Coll., 1969; JD cum laude, St. Louis U., 1984. Bar: Mo. 1984, Ill. 1985, U.S. Dist. Ct. (ea. dist.) Mo. 1985, U.S. Ct. Appeals (8th cir.) 1985, U.S. Ct. Appeals (7th cir.) 1992. Organizer, vol. VISTA, Lincoln, Nebr., 1070-72; builder's laborer Crampton Constrn., Dublin, Ireland, 1972; mem. so. Ill. campaign staff McGovern for Pres., 1972; organizer cen. states region Internat. Ladies Garment Workers' Union, AFL-CIO, St. Louis, 1972-73; organizer, bus. agt., dist. mgr. so. Mo.-Ark. dist. coun. Internat. Ladies Garment Workers' Union, AFL-CIO, Little Rock, 1973-78; state dir., dist. mgr. for N.C. and S.C. Internat. Ladies Garment Workers' Union, AFL-CIO, Charlotte, N.C., 1978-81; law clk. to Hon. T. McMillian U.S. Ct. Appeals for 8th Cir., St. Louis, 1982; law clk. to Hon. W. M. Hungate U.S. Dist. Ct. for Ea. Dist. Mo., St. Louis, 1984-85; ptnr. Schuchat, Cook & Werner, St. Louis, 1985—. Editor-in-chief Pub. Law Jour., 1983-84. Mem. Christ the King Parish Sch. Bd., St. Louis, 1986-89; vol. lawyer Assn. for Community Orgn. for Reform Now, St. Louis, 1985—; active Vol. Lawyers Assn., St. Louis, 1989—. White Family Pub. Law fellow St. Louis U., 1982-84. Mem. ABA, Mo. Bar Assn., Ill. Bar Assn., St. Louis Met. Bar Assn. Roman Catholic. Civil rights, Labor. Home: 7441 Kingsbury Blvd Saint Louis MO 63130-4014 Office: Schuchat Cook & Werner 1221 Locust St Fl 2D Saint Louis MO 63103-2364

**MARTIN, ARTHUR LEE, JR.,** lawyer; b. Montgomery, Ala., Jan. 13, 1949; s. Arthur Lee and Blanche (Bush) M.; children by previous marriage: Elizabeth Leah, Rachel Blanche; m. Diane S. Lamon, Mar. 23, 1993. B.A. cum laude, Vanderbilt U., 1971; J.D. U. Chgo., 1974. Bar: U.S. Dist. Ct. (no. dist.) Ill. 1972, U.S. Ct. Appeals (7th cir.) 1972, Ill. 1975, Ala. 1979, U.S. Dist. Ct. (no. dist.) Ala. 1979, U.S. Ct. Appeals (5th cir.) 1979. Law clk. to Sr. judge U.S. Ct. Appeals (5th cir.), Montgomery, 1974-75; assoc. D'Ancona & Pflaum, Chgo., 1975-78; ptnr. Haskell, Slaughter & Young, Birmingham, Ala., 1978-89, Dominick, Fletcher & Yeilding, Birmingham, 1989-95; ptnr. Berkowitz, Lefkovitz, Isom & Kushner, 1995-98, Johnston & Conwell, 1998—. Gov. Ala. ctrl. dist. Civitan Internat., internat. judge adv. Mem. ABA, Nat. Assn. Bond Lawyers, Ala. State Bar, Birmingham Bar Assn., Am. Acad. Hosp. Lawyers, Downtown Dem. Club, Phi Delta Phi. Democrat. Methodist. Finance, Health. Home: 2463 Chuchura Rd Birmingham AL 35244-3254 Office: Johnston and Conwall 800 Shades Creek Pkwy Ste 325 Birmingham AL 35209-4534

**MARTIN, BEVERLY,** prosecutor. U.S. atty. mid. dist. Ga. U.S. Dept. Justice, 1998—. Office: 433 Cherry St Macon GA 31201*

**MARTIN, BOYCE FICKLEN, JR.,** federal judge; b. Boston, Oct. 23, 1935; s. Boyce Ficklen and Helen Artt M.; m. Mavin Hamilton Brown, July 8, 1961; children: Mary V. H., Julia H.C., Boyce Ficklen III, Robert C. G. II. AB, Davidson Coll., 1957; JD, U. Va., 1963. Bar: Ky. 1963. Law clk. to Shackelford Miller, Jr., chief judge U.S. Ct. Appeals for 6th Circuit, Cin., 1963-64; asst. U.S. atty. Western Dist. Ky., Louisville, 1964; U.S. atty. Western Dist. Ky., 1965; pvt. practice law Louisville, 1966-74; judge Jefferson Circuit Ct., Louisville, 1974-76; chief judge Ct. Appeals Ky., Louisville, 1976-79; judge U.S. Ct. Appeals (6th cir.), Cin. and Louisville, 1979-96, chief judge, 1996—; mem. jud. coun. U.S. Ct. Appeals (6th cir.), 1979-96, chmn., 1996—; mem. Jud. Conf. of U.S., 1996—, exec. com., 1998—. Mem. vestry St. Francis in the Fields Episcopal Ch., Harrods Creek, Ky., 1979-83; bd. visitors Davidson (N.C.) Coll., 1980-86, trustee, 1994-98; trustee Isaac W. Bernheim Found., Louisville, 1981-97, chmn., 1982-95; trustee Blackacre Found., Inc., Louisville, 1983-94, chmn., 1986-94; trustee Hanover (Ind.) Coll., 1982—, vice chmn., 1992-97, chmn., 1998—; mem. exec. bd. Old Ky. Home coun. Boy Scouts of Am., 1968-72; pres. Louisville Zool. Commn., 1971-74. Capt. JAGC U.S. Army, 1958-66. Fellow Am. Bar Found.; mem. Inst. Jud. Adminstrn., Am. Judicature Soc., Fed Bar Assn., ABA (com. effective appellate advocacy Conf. Appellate Judges), Ky. Bar Assn., Louisville Bar Assn. Fax: 502-625-3829. Office: US Ct Appeals 209 US Courthouse 601 W Broadway Louisville KY 40202-2238

**MARTIN, BURCHARD V.,** lawyer; b. Millville, N.J., May 9, 1933; s. William J. and Helen (Mullane) M.; m. Elizabeth Del Rossi, June 11, 1955; children: Doris, Burchard S., William J., Thomas O. BS in Econs., Villanova (Pa.) U., 1954, LLB, 1958. Bar: N.J. 1960, U.S. Dist. Ct. N.J. 1960, U.S. Ct. Appeals (3d cir.), U.S. Supreme Ct. 1976. Assoc. Carroll, Taylor & Bischoff, Camden, N.J., 1960-63; ptnr. Taylor, Bischoff, Neutze & Williams, Camden, 1963-70, Taylor, Bischoff, Williams & Martin, Camden, 1970-72, Martin, Crawshaw & Mayfield, Haddonfield-Westmont, N.J., 1972-91, Martin, Gunn & Martin, Westmont, 1991—. Bd. cons. Villanova Law Sch., 1983—. Recipient Trial Bar award, Trial Attys. of N.J., 1987. Fellow Am. Coll. Trial Lawyers (state chmn. 1982-83); mem. ABA, N.J. Bar Assn., Camden County Bar Assn. (bd. dirs., Peter J. Devine award 1981). Avocation: golf. Product liability, General civil litigation, Insurance. Office: Martin Gunn & Martin PA 216 Haddon Ave Apt 420 Collingswood NJ 08108-2812

**MARTIN, C. D.,** lawyer; b. Seminole, Okla., Mar. 24, 1943. BS, U. North Tex., 1964; LLB, U. Tex., 1967. Bar: Tex. 1967, N.Mex. 1967, U.S. Dist. Ct. N.Mex., U.S. Dist. Ct. (we. and no. dists.) Tex. Mem., mng. ptnr. Hinkle, Cox, Eaton, Coffield & Hensley, P.L.L.C., Midland, Tex., 1986—; mem. adv. bd. dirs. Norwest Bank Tex., Midland. Mem. Midland Planning and Zoning Commn., 1979-82, chmn., 1982; mem. adv. coun. Sch. Arts & Scis., U. Tex. at Permian Basin; bd. trustees Permian Basin Petroleum Mus.; past dir. U. Tex. Law Sch. Found. Fellow Tex. Bar Found. (life), N.Mex. Bar Found.; mem. ABA, State Bar Tex., State Bar N.Mex., Midland County Bar Assn. (pres. 1984-85), Phi Delta Phi. Natural resources, Oil, gas, and mineral, Contracts commercial. Office: Hinkle Cox Eaton Coffield & Hens PLLC PO Box 3580 Midland TX 79702-3580

**MARTIN, CATHLEEN A.,** lawyer; b. St. Charles, Mo., Apr. 26, 1971; d. David and Bonnie Arnold; m. Jeffrey S. Martin, June 4, 1994. BA in Bus. Adminstrn., BA in Journalism, Truman State U., 1993; JD, U. Mo., 1996.

Bar: Mo. 1996, U.S. Dist. Ct. (we. dist.) Mo. 1996, U.S. Ct. Appeals (8th cir.) 1996. Asst. atty. gen. Mo. Atty. Gen.'s Office, Jefferson City, 1996-97; assoc. Newman, Comley & Ruth P.C., Jefferson City, 1997—. Com. mem., student leader Jefferson City Young Life, 1996—; mem., children's leader Grace Evang. Free Ch., Jefferson City, 1996—; bd. dirs. Jefferson City Rape and Abuse Crisis Svc., 1999—. Mem. ATLA, ABA, Mo. Bar Assn. (labor and employment law com. 1997—), Cole County Bar Assn., Jefferson City C. of C., Jefferson City Breakfast Rotary (club svc. chair 1997-98), Order Barristers. Avocations: gardening, running, church activities. Labor, General civil litigation, Administrative and regulatory. Office: Newman Comley & Ruth PC PO Box 537 Jefferson City MO 65102-0537

**MARTIN, CHRISTOPHER W.,** lawyer, law educator; b. Plainview, Tex., Dec. 20, 1965; s. Dwight L. and Vena L. (McEachern) M.; m. Diane R. Lovell, May 22, 1988; 1 child, Joshua C. BA, Baylor U., 1987, JD, 1990. Bar: U.S. Dist. Ct. (so., ea., no. and we. dists.) Tex. 1991, U.S. Ct. Appeals (5th cir.) 1992. Atty. Butler & Binion, Houston, 1990-94; ptnr. Bracewell & Patterson, Houston, 1994—; adj. prof. law U. Houston, 1995—. Author: Lawyers Guide to the Texas Insurance Code, 1995, 3d edit., 1998. Insurance, State civil litigation, Federal civil litigation. Office: Bracewell & Patterson S Tower Pennzoil Pl 711 Louisiana St Ste 2900 Houston TX 77002-2781

**MARTIN, CLARENCE EUGENE, III,** lawyer; b. Martinsburg, W.Va., Mar. 24, 1946; s. Clarence Eugene Jr. and Catherine Dubois (Silver) M.; m. Judith Anne Gray; 2 children: McKenna Gray Martin, Morgan Elizabeth Martin. AB in English, U. Ariz., 1968; JD, Cath. U., Washington, 1974. Bar: W. Va. 1974, D.C. 1974, Md. 1987, Pa., 1992, U.S. Dist. Ct. D.C. 1975, U.S. Ct. Appeals (D.C. cir.) 1975, U.S. Dist. Ct. (no. dist.) W.Va. 1976, U.S. Dist. Ct. (so. dist.) W.Va., U.S. Dist. Ct. Md. 1986, U.S. Ct. Appeals (4th cir.) 1976, U.S. Supreme Ct. 1979, U.S. Dist. Ct. (no. and ea. dists.) Pa. 1984, U.S. Ct. Appeals (3d cir.) 1984. Asst. couonsel U.S. Ho. Reps., Washington, 1974-75; trial atty. U.S. Dept. Justice, 1975-76; assoc. Martin & Seibert, Martinsburg, 1976-79, ptnr., 1979—; bd. dirs. Mchts. & Farmers Bank, Martinsburg, W.Va. Legal Svcs. Plan. Author: (seminar) Impeachment of Witnesses, 1984; co-author ABA publ. Emerging Problems Under the Federal Rules of Evidence, 2d edit., Bad Faith Litigation, The Ethics of Surveillance. Mem. W.Va. Ho. Dels., Charleston, 1976-82; trustee Nat. parks and Conservation, Washington, 1980-85; bd. govs. Def. Trial Counsel W.Va., 1984-92; commr. Interstate Commn. Potomac River Basin, 1980-86, U.S. Commn. on Agrl. Workers, 1988-94; bd. advs. Shepherd Coll., 1989-93, 95-99, chmn. 1990-93, 95—; mem. W.Va. Coun. Cmty. and Econ. Devel.; chmn. W.Va. Devel. Found., W.Va. Devel. Corp.; pres. Discover the Real W.Va. Found.; mem. Greater Ea. Panhandle C. of C. Com., 1988—, chmn. 1988—. Recipient Am. Jurisprudence Scholastic Achievement award, 1972, Assn. Govt. Employees award, 1980. Mem. ABA, W.Va. Bar Assn. (pres. 1990-91), W.Va. State Bar, D.C. Bar Assn., Berkeley County Bar Assn. (pres. 1984), Nat. Assn. R.R. Trial Counsel, Am. Legis. Exch. Coun., Am. Judicature Soc., Def. Rsch. Inst., D.C. Bar Assn., Md. Bar Assn., Pa. Bar Assn., Am. Bd. Trial Advocates (bd. dirs. 1986-94), Internat. Assn. Def. Counsel, Def. Trial Counsel of W.Va. (founding mem., bd. dirs. 1984-92), Md. Def. Trial Counsel, W.Va. Law Inst., City Tavern Club, Antietam Hunt Club, Rotary, KC, Elks. Contracts commercial, General corporate, Personal injury. Home: Pendleton House 2550 Nollville Rd Martinsburg WV 25401-8866 Office: Martin & Seibert LC PO Box 1286 Martinsburg WV 25402-1286

**MARTIN, CONNIE RUTH,** lawyer; b. Clovis, N.Mex., Sept. 9, 1955; d. Lynn Latimer and Marian Ruth (Pierce) M.; m. Daniel A. Patterson, Nov. 21, 1987; step-children: David Patterson, Dana Patterson. B in Univ. Studies, Ea. N.Mex. U., 1976, MEd, 1977; JD, U. Mo., Kansas City, 1981. Bar: N.Mex. 1981, U.S. Dist. Ct. N.Mex. 1981. Asst. dist. atty. State of N.Mex., Farmington, 1981-84; ptnr. Tansey, Rosebrough, Gerding & Strother, PC, Farmington, 1984-93; pvt. practice Connie R. Martin, P.C., Farmington, 1993-94; domestic violence commr. 11th Judicial Dist. Ct., State of N.Mex., 1993-94; with Jeffrey B. Diamond Law Firm, Carlsbad, N. Mex., 1994-96; assoc. Sager, Curran, Sturges and Tepper PC, Las Cruces, N. Mex., 1996-97, Holt & Babington PC, Las Cruces, 1997—; dep. med. investigator State of N.Mex., Farmington, 1981-84; instr. San Juan Coll., 1987, N.Mex. State U., 1995; spkr. N.Mex. Jud. Edn. Ctr., 1993-94; chair paralegal program adv. com., 1988, Adv Com., St Francis Clin., Presbyterian Med. Svs., 1994-96; bd. Bar Examiners State of N.Mex., 1989—, vice-chair, 1995-97, chair, 1997—; asst. bar counsel Disciplinary Bd.; mem. profl. adv. com. Meml. Med. Ctr. Found., 1997—; mem. So. N.Mex. Estate Planning Coun., 1997—. Bd. dirs., exec. com. San Juan County Econ. Opportunity Coun., Farmington, 1982-83; bd. dirs. Four Corners Substance Abuse Coun., Farmington, 1984, N.Mex. Newspapers, Inc.; chmn. Cmty. Corrections-Intensive Supervision Panel, Farmington, 1987-88; jud. selection com. mem. San Juan County, 1991, Chavez County, 1995; nominating com. Supreme Ct./Ct of Appeals, 1991-96. Recipient Distinguished Svcs. award for Outstanding Young Woman San Juan County Jaycees, 1984. Mem. N.Mex. Bar. Assn. (bd. dirs. elder law sect. 1993-96, peer rev. task force 1994-95, asst. to new lawyers com. 1986-87, local bar com. 1988, bd. dirs. young lawyers divsn. 1989-91, bd. dirs. real property probate and trust sect. 1994-97), San Juan County Bar Assn. (treas. 1985-87, v.p. 1987, pres. 1988), Farmington C. of C. (bd. dirs. 1991-93). Republican. Baptist. Avocations: health, fitness, reading. Real property, Education and schools, Probate. Office: PO Box 2699 Las Cruces NM 88004-2699

**MARTIN, DAVID ALAN,** law educator; b. Indpls., July 23, 1948; s. C. Wendell and Elizabeth Bowman (Meeker) M.; m. Cynthia Jo Lorman, June 13, 1970; children: Amy Lynn, Jeffrey David. BA, DePauw U., 1970; JD, Yale U., 1975. Bar: D.C. Law clk. Hon. J. Skelly Wright U.S. Ct. Appeals (D.C. cir.), 1975-76; law clk. Hon. Lewis F. Powell U.S. Supreme Ct., Washington, 1976-77; assoc. Rogovin, Stern & Huge, Washington, 1977-78; spl. asst. bur. human rights and humanitarian affairs U.S. State Dept., Washington, 1978-80; from asst. prof. to assoc. prof. U. Va. Sch. Law, Charlottesville, 1980-86, prof., 1986-91, Henry L. & Grace Doherty prof. law, 1991—, F. Palmer Weber Rsch. prof. civil liberties and human rights, 1992-95; cons. Adminstrv. Conf. U.S., Washington, 1988-89, 91-92, U.S. Dept. Justice, 1993-95; gen. counsel U.S. Immigration and Naturalization Svc., 1995-98. Author: Immigration: Process and Policy, 1985, 4th edit., 1998, Asylum Case Law Sourcebook, 1994, 2d edit., 1998, The Endless Quest: Helping America's Farm Workers, 1994; editor: The New Asylum Seekers, 1988, Immigration Admissions, 1998, Immigration Controls, 1998; contbr. numerous articles to profl. jours. Mem. nat. governing bd. Common Cause, Washington, 1972-75; elder Westminster Presbyn. Ch., Charlottesville, 1982-84, 89-92. German Marshall Fund Rsch. Fellow, Geneva, 1984-85. Mem. ABA, Am. Soc. Internat. Law (ann. book award 1986), Internat. Law Assn. Democrat. Office: U Va Sch Law 580 Massie Rd Charlottesville VA 22903-1738

**MARTIN, DAVID MACCOY,** lawyer; b. Springfield, Ohio, Feb. 23, 1944; s. Oscar Thaddeus II and Dorothy (Traquair) M.; m. Judith Reed, Aug. 2, 1975; 1 child, Scott David. AB cum laude, Princeton U., 1971; JD, U. Denver, 1974. Bar: Ohio 1975, U.S. Supreme Ct. 1978, U.S. Tax Ct. 1976. Pvt. practice Springfield, 1975—. Served USAF, 1964-68. Mem. ABA, Ohio State Bar Assn. (mem. banking, comml. and bankruptcy law com. 1982—), Clark County Bar Assn., Am. Judicature Soc., Phi Alpha Delta. General practice, Probate, Real property. Home: 1776 Appian Way Springfield OH 45503-2773 Office: David M Martin Co LPA 4 W Main St Ste 707 Springfield OH 45502-1319

**MARTIN, ELAINE M.,** lawyer; b. Smithland, Iowa, Feb. 16, 1942; d. Walter J. and Arley (Heider) Westendorf; m. Dennis E. Martin, Aug. 14, 1965; children: Denise M., Michael W. BA cum laude, Duchesne Coll., Omaha, 1964; MA, Creighton U., 1965, JD cum laude, 1978. Bar: Nebr. 1978, U.S. Dist. Ct. Nebr. 1978. Tchr. St. Louis Pub. Schs., 1965-66; prof. U. Nebr., Omaha, 1968-69; tchr. Omaha Pub. Schs., 1967-73; assoc. McGrath, North et al, 1977-78, Peter Kiewit & Sons, 1978-79; law clk. U.S. Ct. Appeals, 8th Cir., 1979-80; assoc. Kutak, Rock & Huie, Omaha, 1980-81; atty./prin. Martin & Martin, P.C., Omaha, 1982—; ptnr. Martin Realty, Omaha, 1980—; with Westendorf Mfg. Co., Inc. and Westendorf Partnership. Asst. editor-in-chief Creighton Law Rev., 1977. Trustee Duchesne Acad., Omaha, 1991—, devel. com. head, 1991—; pres. parents bd. Creighton Prep Sch., Omaha, 1991—, ad hoc com. on discipline, 1991-92. Mem. ABA, Omaha Bar Assn., Omaha Law League, Assn. Trial Lawyers Am., Hist. Soc. of U.S. Cts., 8th Cir. General corporate, General civil litigation. Office: Martin & Martin PC 10040 Regency Cir Ste 320 Omaha NE 68114-3734

**MARTIN, FAYE SANDERS,** judge; b. Brooklet, Ga., Feb. 6, 1934; d. Carroll Eugene and Addie L. (Prosser) Sanders; m. J. Hollis Martin, Feb. 26, 1961 (dec. Dec. 1991); children: Janna, Jenny Lynn. Student, Ga. So. Coll., 1952-54; J.D., Woodrow Wilson Coll. Law, Atlanta, 1956. Bar: Ga. 1956, U.S. Dist. Ct. (so. dist.) Ga. 1971, U.S. Supreme Ct. 1978. Ptnr., Anderson & Sanders, Statesboro, Ga., 1956-78; judge Superior Ct. Ga., Statesboro, 1978—. Recipient Disting. Alumni award Ga. So. Coll. Alumni Assn., 1984. Home: 229 Magnolia Pl Statesboro GA 30461-4250 Office: PO Box 803 Statesboro GA 30459-0803

**MARTIN, GARY WAYNE,** lawyer; b. Cin., Feb. 14, 1946; s. Elmer DeForrest and Nellie May (Hughes) M.; m. Debra Lynn Goldsmith, June 25, 1982; children: Christopher, Jeremy, Joie, Casey. BA, Wilmington Coll., 1967; JD, U. Cin., 1974. Bar: Fla. 1974. Head casualty dept. Fowler White Gillen Boggs Villareal & Banker, Tampa, Fla., 1974—, also bd. dirs. Lt. USNR, 1967-71. Mem. Harbour Island Athletic Club. Republican. Presbyterian. Avocation: tennis. Office: Fowler White Gillen Boggs Villareal & Banker 501 E Kennedy Blvd Ste 1600 Tampa FL 33602-5240

**MARTIN, HARRY CORPENING,** lawyer, retired state supreme court justice; b. Lenoir, N.C., Jan. 13, 1920; s. Hal C. and Johnsie Harshaw (Nelson) M.; m. Nancy Robiou Dallam, Apr. 16, 1955; children: John, Matthew, Mary. AB, U. N.C., 1942; LLB, Harvard U., 1948; LLM, U. Va., 1982. Bar: N.C. 1948. Pvt. practice Asheville, N.C., 1948-62; judge N.C. Superior Ct., Asheville, 1962-78, N.C. Ct. Appeals, Raleigh, 1978-82; justice N.C. Supreme Ct., 1982-92; ptnr. Martin & Martin, Attys., Hillsborough, N.C., 1992—; adj. prof. U. N.C. Law Sch., 1983-92, Dan K. Moore disting. vis. prof., 1992-94; sr. conf. atty. U.S. Ct. Appeals for 4th Cir., 1994—; adj. prof. Duke U., 1990-91. With U.S. Army, 1942-45, South Pacific. Mem. U.S. Supreme Ct. Hist. Soc., N.C. Supreme Ct. Hist. Soc. (pres.). Democrat. Episcopalian. Education and schools. Home: 1 Hilltop Rd Asheville NC 28803-3017 Office: Martin & Martin PA 133 E King St Hillsborough NC 27278-2570

**MARTIN, HENRY ALAN,** public defender; b. Nashville, Sept. 5, 1949; s. James Alvin and Mary Elizabeth (Long) M.; m. Gloria B. Ballard, May 9, 1975; children: Nathan Daniel, Anna Elizabeth. BA, Vanderbilt U., 1971, JD, 1974. Bar: Tenn. 1975, U.S. Dist. Ct. (mid. dist.) Tenn. 1975, U.S. Ct. Appeals (6th cir.) 1976, U.S. Supreme Ct. 1979. Pvt. practice Nashville, 1975-76; ptnr. Haile & Martin, P.A., Nashville, 1976-82; assoc. firm Barrett & Ray, P.C., Nashville, 1982-85; fed. pub. defender U.S. Dist. Ct. (mid. dist.) Tenn., Nashville, 1985—; mem. adv. com. on rules criminal procedure U.S. Judicial Conf., 1994—. CO-author, co-editor trial manual, Tools for the Ultimate Trial, 1985, 2d edit., 1988; contbr. articles to profl. jours. Del., Witness for Peace, Managua, Nicaragua, 1987. Mem. ABA (coun. criminal justice sect. 1993-96), NACDL, Nat. Lawyers Guild, Assn. Fed. Defenders (pres. 1995-98), Nashville Bar Assn., Napier Looby Bar Assn., Nat. Legal Aid and Def. Assn., Tenn. Assn. Criminal Def. Lawyers (bd. dirs. 1978-94, pres. 1984-85, Pres.'s award 1984). Democrat. Avocations: jogging, swimming. Home: 3802 Whitland Ave Nashville TN 37205-2432 Office: Fed Pub Defender 810 Broadway Ste 200 Nashville TN 37203-3861

**MARTIN, JACK,** lawyer; b. Bklyn., Jan. 19, 1929; s. Alfred and Ioa Martin; m. Edith Martin, Dec. 11, 1948 (div. Aug. 1961); children: Steven Lawrence, Glenn David. LLB, Bklyn. Law Sch., 1953. Bar: N.Y. 1954, U.S. Dist. Ct. (ea. and no. dists.) N.Y. 1956. Mem. ATLA, N.Y. State Trial Lawyers Assn. Democrat. Jewish. Personal injury, Product liability. Home and Office: 900 Avenue H Apt 2G Brooklyn NY 11230-2834

**MARTIN, JAMES CHANDLER,** lawyer; b. Newport News, Va., Mar. 14, 1956; s. Francis Chandler and Glenna Faye (Dunkum) M. MusB, U. Md., 1978; JD, George Mason U., 1987. Bar: Va. 1987, D.C. 1989, N.C. 1991. Asst. commonwealth's atty. City of Danville, Va., 1987-90, 92—; pvt. practice law Danville, 1990-92. Prin. trombonist Philharm. Greensboro, N.C. 1988—, bd. dirs., 1991-93; prin. trombonist Danville Symphony Orch., 1992—, bd. dirs., 1992-94, 97-98. Mem. Nat. Dist. Attys. Assn., K.C. (4th degree navigator 1997-98). Roman Catholic. Avocations: musician (trombonist, vocalist, composer), writer. Home: 258 Manor Pl Danville VA 24541-2633 Office: Commonwealths Attys Office 115 S Union St Danville VA 24541-1105

**MARTIN, JAMES FRANCIS,** state legislator, lawyer; b. Atlanta, Aug. 22, 1945; s. Joseph Grant and Helen (Hester) M.; m. Joan Vohryzek, Jan. 30, 1970; children: Morgan, Rebecca, James, Frank. AB, U. Ga., 1967, JD, 1969, LLM, 1972; MBA, Ga. State U., 1980. Bar: Ga. 1972. Asst. legis. counsel Ga. Gen. Assembly, Atlanta, 1972-77; staff atty. Atlanta Legal Aid and Ga. Legal Svc. Programs, 1977-80; ptnr. Martin and McDuffie, 1980-86; of counsel Martin and Wilkes, 1986—, Martin Bros. P.C., 1986—; mem. Ga. Ho. of Reps., 1983—. Chmn. Judiciary Com., 1997—. 1st lt. U.S. Army, 1969-71, Vietnam. Democrat. Presbyterian. Office: State Capitol House Jud Com 132 State Capitol SW Atlanta GA 30334-1600

**MARTIN, JAMES HANLEY,** deputy state attorney general; b. N.Y.C., Dec. 22, 1960; s. James Patrick and Josephine Anne (Hanley) M. AB, Georgetown U., 1983; JD, Fordham U., 1986. Bar: N.J. 1986, U.S. Dist. Ct. N.J. 1986, N.Y. 1987, D.C. 1988, U.S. Dist. Ct. (so. and ea. dists.) N.Y. 1991, U.S. Ct. Appeals (D.C. and 3d cirs.) 1991, U.S. Supreme Ct. 1991. Dep. atty. gen. State of N.J., Newark, 1987—. Mem. ABA, Am. Judicature Soc., Bergen County Bar Assn., N.J. State Bar Assn., D.C. Bar, Assn. Bar of City of N.Y. Roman Catholic. Office: State of NJ Divsn Law PO Box 45029 124 Halsey St Newark NJ 07101

**MARTIN, JAMES NEAL,** lawyer; b. Glasgow, Ky., Jan. 11, 1950; s. J. Jack and Olive Katherine (Conover) M.; 1 child, Amelia Anne. BA, U. Louisville, 1972, JD, 1980. Bar: Ky. 1980, U.S. Dist. Ct. (ea. dist.) Ky. 1987. Pvt. practice Tompkinsville, Ky., 1980-82; spl. commr. Cumberland Cir. Ct. for 29th Jud. Cir. Ky., Burkesville, 1982-84; ptnr. Martin & Martin, Richmond, Ky., 1984-89; pvt. practice, Richmond, 1989—; asst. county atty., prosecutor, criminal div. Office Madison County Atty., Richmond, 1986. Bd. dirs. Richmond Little League, Inc., 1987—, chmn. exec. bd., 1988-89. Mem. ABA, Ky. Bar Assn., Ky. Assn. Hosp. Attys., Ky. Acad. Trial Attys., Ky. Assn. Criminal Def. Lawyers, Madison County Bar Assn., Richmond C. of C. (legis. affairs com. 1986-88), Rotary (bd. dirs. Richmond 1986, v.p., pres. 1991-92). Avocations: water sports, landscape gardening. E-mail: jnmatty@ibm.net. Fax: 606-623-9096. Criminal, General civil litigation, General practice. Office: 144 E Main St PO Box 828 Richmond KY 40476-0828

**MARTIN, JAMES WILLIAM,** lawyer; b. Turlock, Calif., Dec. 20, 1949. Student, Ga. Inst. Tech., 1967-69; BS, Stetson U., 1971, JD, 1974. Bar: Fla. 1974, U.S. Dist. Ct. (mid. dist.) Fla. 1974, U.S. Ct. Appeals (5th cir.) 1974, U.S. Ct. Appeals (11th cir.) 1987, U.S. Supreme Ct. 1978. Ptnr. Brickley & Martin, St. Petersburg, Fla., 1974-79; pres. James W. Martin, P.A., St. Petersburg, 1979—; presenter in field. Author: West's Florida Corporation System, 1984, West's Legal Forms, 3d edit., Non-Profit Corporations, 1991, 92, 93, 94, 96, 97, 98, 99, West's Florida Legal Forms, Business Organizations, Real Estate, Specialized Forms, 1990, 91, 92, 93, 94, 95; supplement editor Fla. Jour. Forms, Legal and Bus., 1998, 99; contbr. articles to profl. jours. including Word Perfect mag. City councilman, St. Petersburg, 1982-83; active Leadership St. Petersburg; active charter class Leadership Tampa Bay; founding trustee, sec., counsel Salvador Dali Mus., 1980—; founding dir., sec., counsel Fla. Internat. Mus., 1992-94. Recipient Outstanding Young Man award Jaycees, 1982, Outstanding Contbn. to City award St. Petersburg C. of C., 1980. Mem. Fla. Bar (chmn. coordinating com. tech. 1992-93, probate rules com. 1994—), St. Petersburg Bar Assn. (chair probate sect. 1999—), St. Petersburg C. of C. (gen. counsel 1991-92, arts task force 1987, chmn. parking com., chmn. Urban Solutions coun. 1992-93, chmn. downtown coun. 1993-94), Pres. Club (founder, hon. bd. dirs. 1985-91), Pinellas County Arts Coun. (councilman). Fax: 727-823-3479. E-mail: jamesmartinpa@msn.com. General corporate, Probate, Real property.

**MARTIN, JAY GRIFFITH,** lawyer; b. Washington, Oct. 13, 1951; s. Drexel Reese and Joyce (Towne) M.; 1 child, Trevor; m. Susan Collins, Aug. 19, 1989; stepchildren: Philip, Katherine. BBA, So. Meth. U., 1973, MPA, 1976, JD, 1976. Bar: Tex., D.C., U.S. Ct. Appeals (5th cir.), U.S. Dist. Ct. (so. dist.) Tex., U.S. Dist. Ct. D.C., U.S. Supreme Ct. Counsel Pennzoil Co., Houston, 1976-78, sr. counsel, 1978-81; divsn. counsel The Superior Oil Co., Houston, 1981-85; sr. counsel Mobil Natural Gas, Houston, 1985-87, gen. counsel, 1987-91; asst. gen. counsel Mobil Oil Corp., Fairfax, Va., 1991-96; ptnr. Andrews & Kurth LLP, Washington, 1996—; mem. adv. bd. Natural Gas Contracts Publs., Thomas Pub. Group, Washington, 1991—, Bus. Laws Inc., Chesterland, Ohio, 1997—; mem. adv. bd. Inst. Transnat. Arbitration Southwestern Legal Found., 1996—. Author: International Arbitration, 1998; contbr. articles to profl. law jours. Mem. adminstrv. counsel Trinity United Meth. Ch., Alexandria, Va., 1995-97, pastor parish rels. com., 1997-98; chair fundraising com. So. Meth. U., Washington, 1996-97. Named one of World's Leading Energy and Natural Resources Lawyers, Euromoney, 1997, 98-99. Fellow Tex. Bar Found.; mem. Tex. Bar Assn., D.C. Bar Assn., Internat. Bar Assn. (com. energy and natural resources 1994—), Fed. Energy Bar Assn. (chmn. antitrust sect. 1986-87, chmn. internat. energy com. 1998-99), ABA (exec. coun., chmn. natural resources, energy and environ. law internat. energy com. 1996-97, sr. liaison oversight responsibility for all energy and resource coms. 1998-99, liaison to Federal Energy Bar Assn. 1997-98), Houston Bar Assn., FBA (bd. dirs. 1990-91), Assn. Internat. Petroleum Negotiators, Am. Soc. Internat. Law, Delta Theta Phi. Avocations: reading history, current events, tennis, golf, jogging. FERC practice, Environmental, Oil, gas, and mineral. Home: 8329 Chapel Lake Ct Annandale VA 22003-4401 Office: Andrews & Kurth 1701 Pennsylvania Ave NW Washington DC 20006-5805

**MARTIN, JAY R.,** lawyer; b. Birmingham, Ala., Aug. 12, 1930; s. Emile Fredrick and Felicia R. M.; divorced; children: Blair, Kelly. BS, U. Calif., Berkeley, 1949, JD, 1952. Bar: Calif. Dist. atty.'s office Alameda County, Oakland, Calif., 1953-60; assoc. atty. Shirley, Saroyan et al, San Francisco, 1960-67; ptnr. Cartwright, Saroyan, Martin et al, San Francisco, 1967-77, Crosby, Hearky, Roach, & May, Oakland, 1997—. Mem. Calif. State Bar Assn. Securities, General civil litigation, State and local taxation. Home: 8 Russian Hill Pl San Francisco CA 94133-3637 Office: Crosby Hearky Roach & May 4 Embarcadero Ctr Lbby 19 San Francisco CA 94111-4106

**MARTIN, JOHN CHARLES,** judge; b. Durham, N.C., Nov. 9, 1943; s. Chester Barton and Mary Blackwell (Pridgen) M.; m. Margaret Rand; children: Lauren Blackwell, Sarah Conant, Mary Susan. BA, Wake Forest U., 1965, JD, 1967; postgrad., Nat. Judicial Coll., Reno, 1979. Bar: N.C. 1967, U.S. Dist. Ct. (mid. dist.) N.C. 1967, U.S. Dist. Ct. (ea. dist.) N.C. 1972, U.S. Dist. Ct. (we. dist.) N.C. 1975, U.S. Ct. Appeals (4th cir.) 1976. Assoc. Haywood, Denny & Miller, Durham, N.C., 1970-72, ptnr., 1973-77; resident judge Superior Ct. 14th Jud. Dist. N.C., Durham, 1977-84; judge N.C. Ct. Appeals, Raleigh, 1985-88, 93—; ptrn. Maxwell & Hutson, P.A., Durham, 1988-92; mem. study com. rules of evidence and comparative negligence N.C. Legis. Research Commn., 1980; mem. N.C. Pattern Jury Instrn. drafting com., 1978-84, N.C. Trial Judge's Bench Book Drafting Com., 1984-87; mem. bd. visitors Wake Forest U. Sch. Law, 1985—; mem. alumni coun. Wake Forest U., 1993-96; mem. state/fed. Jud. Coun. N.C., 1985-87, chmn. 1987. Mem. Durham City Coun., 1975-77. With U.S. Army, 1967-69. Recipient Disting. Svc. award Durham Jaycees, 1976. Mem. ABA, N.C. Bar Assn. (chmn. adminstrn. of justice study com. 1990-92, bench, bar and law sch. com. 1987-91, adminstrn. justice task force 1996—, conv. planning com. 1995—, appellate rules study com. 1999—, v.p. 1997-98), Durham County Bar Assn. (bd. dirs. 1991-92), Wake County Bar Assn., 10th Jud. Dist. Bar Assn., Appellate Judges Conf., N.C. Jud. Conf., Hope Valley Country Club, Appalachian State U. Parents Assn. (bd. dirs. 1997—), Phi Delta Phi. Democrat. Methodist. Office: PO Box 888 Raleigh NC 27602-0888

**MARTIN, JOHN RANDOLPH,** judge; b. Lexington, Ky., May 26, 1948; s. Harry and Geraldine (Gray) M.; m. Jacqueline Lauren Snyder, Apr. 24, 1976; 1 child, Lauren Elizabeth. BA, U. Okla., 1973, MA, 1976, JD, 1980. Bar: Okla. 1981, U.S. Ct. Mil. Appeals 1981, U.S. Dist. Ct. (we. dist.) Okla. 1982, S.C. 1983, U.S. Ct. Appeals (10th cir.) 1983, U.S. Dist. Ct. S.C. 1984, U.S. Ct. Appeals (4th cir.) 1984, U.S. Supreme Ct. 1995. Assoc. Finkel, Georgaklis et al, Columbia, S.C., 1984-86; ptnr. Mumford, Wishart & Martin, North Myrtle Beach, S.C., 1986-87, Gertz, Kastanes, Moore & Martin, North Myrtle Beach, 1987-91; with Office of Hearings and Appeals, Social Security Adminstrn., Houston, 1991—. Served to lt. col. U.S. Army, 1967-70, Vietnam, with Res. 1975-78, 84-96, Desert Storm, JAGC, 1981-84. Mem. Phi Delta Phi, Pi Kappa Alpha, Nat. Rifle Assn. Republican. Episcopalian. Lodge: Masons, Shriners, Elks. Avocations: singing, shooting. Office: Office of Hearing and Appeals 6800 West Loop S Ste 300 Bellaire TX 77401-4522

**MARTIN, JOHN SHERWOOD, JR.,** federal judge; b. Bklyn., May 31, 1935. BA, Manhattan Coll., 1957; LLB, Columbia U., 1961. Bar: N.Y. 1961, U.S. Dist. Ct. (so. dist.) N.Y. 1963, U.S. Supreme Ct. 1966, U.S. Ct. Appeals (2d cir.) 1983. Law clk. to Hon. Leonard P. Moore U.S. Ct. Appeals (2d cir.), 1961-62; asst. U.S. atty. U.S. Dist. Ct. (so. dist.) N.Y., 1962-66; ptnr. Johnson, Hekker & Martin, Nyack, N.Y., 1966-67; asst. to solicitor gen., 1967-69, sole practitioner, 1969-72; ptnr. Martin, Obermaier & Morvillo, 1972-79, Schulte, Roth & Zabel, 1979-80; U.S. atty. U.S. Dist. Ct. for So. Dist. N.Y., N.Y.C., 1980-83; ptnr. Schulte, Roth & Zabel, 1983-90; judge U.S. Dist. Ct. for So. Dist. N.Y., N.Y.C., 1990—; cons. Nat. Commn. Law Enforcement and the Adminstrn. of Criminal Justice, 1966-67; counsel to commn. to investigate disturbances Columbia U., 1968. Fellow Am. Coll. Trial Lawyers; mem. Assn. Bar City N.Y. Office: US Dist Ct So Dist NY 500 Pearl St New York NY 10007-1316

**MARTIN, JOHN WILLIAM, JR.,** retired lawyer, automotive industry executive; b. Evergreen Park, Ill., Sept. 1, 1936; s. John William and Frances (Hayes) M.; m. Joanne Cross, July 2, 1966; children: Amanda Hayes, Bartholomew McGuire. AB in History, DePaul U., 1958, JD, 1961. Bar: Ill. 1961, D.C. 1962, N.Y. 1964, Mich. 1970. Antitrust trial atty. Dept. Justice, Washington, 1961-62; assoc. Donovan, Leisure, Newton & Irvine, N.Y.C., 1962-70; sr. atty. Ford Motor Co., Dearborn, Mich., 1970-72, assoc. counsel, 1972-74, counsel, 1974-76, asst. gen. counsel, 1976-77, assoc. gen. counsel, 1977-89, v.p., gen. counsel, 1989-99; ret., 1999; trustee DePaul U., 1998—; bd. dirs. Ctr. Social Gerontology, Inc., Nat. Women's Law Ctr. Contbr. articles to profl. jours. Mem. Assn. Gen. Counsel, Am. Law Inst. Coun., Little Traverse Yacht Club. Republican. Roman Catholic.

**MARTIN, JOSEPH, JR.,** retired lawyer, former ambassador; b. San Francisco, May 21, 1915; m. Ellen Chamberlain Martin, July 5, 1946; children: Luther Greene, Ellen Myers. AB, Yale U., 1936, LLB, 1939. Assoc. Cadwalader, Wickersham & Taft, N.Y.C., 1939-41; ptnr. Wallace, Garrison, Norton & Ray, San Francisco, 1946-55, Pettit & Martin, San Francisco, 1955-70, 73-95; gen. counsel FTC, Washington, 1970-71; ambassador, U.S. rep. Disarmament Conf., Geneva, 1971-76; ret.; mem. Pres.'s Adv. Com. for Arms Control and Disarmament, 1974-78. Pres. Pub. Utilities Commn., San Francisco, 1956-60; Rep. nat. committeeman for Calif., 1960-64; treas. Rep. Party Calif., 1956-58; bd. dirs. Patrons of Art and Music, Calif. Palace of Legion of Honor, 1958-70, pres., 1963-68; bd. dirs. Arms Control Assn., 1977-84; pres. Friends of Legal Assistance to Elderly, 1983-87. Lt. comdr. USNR, 1941-46. Recipient Ofcl. commendation for Outstanding Service as Gen. Counsel FTC, 1973, Distinguished Honor award U.S. ACDA, 1973, Lifetime Achievement award Legal Assistance to the Elderly, 1981. Fellow Am. Bar Found. Clubs: Burlingame Country, Pacific Union. Antitrust, General corporate. Home: 331 Greer Rd Woodside CA 94062-4207

**MARTIN, MALCOLM ELLIOT,** lawyer; b. Buffalo, Dec. 11, 1935; s. Carl Edward and Pearl Maude (Elliot) M.; m. Judith Hill Harley, June 27, 1964; children: Jennifer, Elizabeth, Christina, Katherine. AB, U. Mich., Ann Arbor, 1958, JD, 1962. Bar: N.Y. 1963, U.S. Ct. Appeals (2d cir.) 1966, U.S. Supreme Ct. 1967. Assoc., Chadbourne, Parke, Whiteside & Wolff, N.Y.C., 1962-73, ptnr., 1974—, now Chadbourne & Parke LLP, 1986; dir., sec. Carl and Dorothy Bennett Found., Inc.; sec., counsel Copper Devel. Assn., Inc. With U.S. Army, 1958-60. Mem. ABA, N.Y. State Bar Assn., Assn. Bar City

N.Y., St. Andrew's Soc. of State of N.Y., Met. Opera Guild. Clubs: Oratamin (Blauvelt, N.Y.), Nyack Boat, Rockefeller Center, Copper (N.Y.C.). Estate planning, Probate, Estate taxation. Home: 74 S Highland Ave Nyack NY 10960-3609 Office: Chadbourne & Parke LLP 30 Rockefeller Plz New York NY 10112-0002

**MARTIN, MARK D.,** state supreme court justice; b. Apr. 29, 1963; s. M. Dean and Ann M. BSBA summa cum laude, Western Carolina U., 1985; JD with honors, U. N.C., 1988; grad., Nat. Jud. Coll., 1993; LLM, U. Va., 1998. Bar: N.C., S.C., U.S. Dist. Ct. (ea. and mid. dists.) N.C., U.S. Ct. Appeals (4th crct.). Law clk. to Hon. Clyde H. Hamilton U.S. Dist. Ct., Columbia, S.C., 1988-90; pvt. practice McNair Law Firm, Raleigh, N.C., 1990-91; legal counsel to gov. Office of Gov., Raleigh, 1991-92; superior ct. judge Jud. Dist. 3A, Greenville, N.C., 1992-94; judge N.C. Ct. Appeals, 1994-99; assoc. justice N.C. Supreme Ct., 1999—; participant Holderness Moot Ct., 1986; mem. N.C. Dept. Correction Master Plan Adv. Com., 1992; designated hearing officer Commutation Revocation Hearing of Zedie T. Smith, 1992; mem. N.C. Coun. for Women, 1992; legis. and law reform com. Conf. Superior Ct. Judges, 1993-94; co-chair legis liason com. N.C. Jud. Conf., 1995-97; mem. computer com. N.C. Appellate Cts., 1995—; sec. N.C. Jud. Conf., 1997-99. Office coord. United Way Ann. Combined Campaign, 1991, 92. Recipient Book award, 1987, Order of Long Leaf Pine, 1992, Disting. Alumnus award We. Carolina U., 1995; Lloyd C. Balfour fellow, 1987, N.C. Inst. Polit. Leadership, 1992. Mem. ABA (jud. adminstrv. divsn.), N.C. Bar Assn. (minorities in profession com. 1995—, medioco-legal liason com. 1997-99, multidisciplinary practice task force 1999—), N.C. Assn. Black Lawyers, Wake County Bar Assn., Mortar Bd. Sr. Hon. Soc., Internat. Hon. Soc., Alpha Lambda Delta, Phi Kappa Phi (v.p. for econs.), Pi Gamma Mu, Omicron Delta Epsilon (pres.), Phi Alpha Delta, Delta Sigma Phi (scholar 1986), Beta Gamma Sigma (hon.). Office: North Carolina Supreme Court PO Box 1841 Raleigh NC 27602-1841*

**MARTIN, MICHAEL DAVID,** lawyer; b. Lakeland, Fla., Jan. 4, 1944; s. E. Snow and Mary Y. (Yelvington) M.; m. Joy Lynn Jackson; children: Michael David, Mallory Thomas, Katherine Cecelia, Rachel Lynn. BA, U. of South, 1964; JD, U. Fla., 1967. Bar: Fla. 1968, U.S. Dist. Ct. Fla. 1968, U.S. Ct. Appeals (5th cir.) 1975, U.S. Supreme Ct. 1974, U.S. Ct. Appeals (11th cir.) 1982. Mem. Martin & Martin, Lakeland, Fla., 1968—; lectr. on estate planning and trial practice, pub. seminars, 1974-83. Bd. dirs. Boys Clubs of Lakeland, 1972-73; mem. Tampa Bay area Com. on Fgn. Relations; pres. Lakeland Spl. Events Inc., 1982-85; trustee John Marshall House. Named Outstanding Young Man of Yr., Lakeland Jaycees, 1969. Mem. ABA, Fla. Bar, Acad. Fla. Trial Lawyers, Assn. Trial Lawyers Am., Am. Judicature Soc., Polk County Trial Lawyers Assn. (pres. 1976-77), Lakeland C. of C. (v.p. 1980, pres. 1982, chmn. bd. 1983—), Polk County Am. Inns of Ct. (master). Clubs: Rotary (dir. club 1972-73), Lakeland Yacht and Country (pres. 1978-79). State civil litigation, Environmental, Estate planning. Office: 200 Lake Morton Dr Ste 300 Lakeland FL 33801-5305

**MARTIN, MICHAEL KEITH,** lawyer; b. Portland, Maine, Nov. 6, 1957; s. Rupert Keith and Beverly Jo Martin; m. Celeste J. Dougherty, Feb. 4, 1995; children: Mikayla Jean, Cole Dougherty. BA magna cum laude, U. So. Maine, 1985; JD cum laude, U. Maine, 1989. Bar: Maine 1989, U.S. Dist. Ct. Maine 1989. Asst. mgr. A&M Inc., Portland, Maine, 1976-79, gen. mgr., 1980-86; dist. atty. intern State of Maine, Biddeford, 1988; assoc. Petruccelli & Martin, Portland, 1989-95, ptnr., 1995—. Aid to Congressman David Emery, Washington, 1979-80. MEm. ABA, ATLA, Maine State Bar Assn. General civil litigation, Contracts commercial, Personal injury. Home: 232 Foreside Rd Cumb Foreside ME 04110-1117 Office: Petruccelli & Martin LLP 50 Monument Sq Portland ME 04101-4039

**MARTIN, MICHAEL REX,** lawyer; b. Lawton, Okla., Feb. 16, 1952; s. Rex R. and Mary L. (Smith) M.; m. Janet E. Becker, Aug. 25, 1979; children: Katy, Donnie, Melissa. BS in Bus. Adminstrn., Tulsa U., 1974, JD, 1979. Bar: Okla. 1979, U.S. Dist Ct. (we. dist.) Okla. 1984. Ptnr. Musser, Musser & Martin, Enid, Okla., 1981-85, Crowley, Pickens & Martin, Enid, Okla., 1985—. Republican. Methodist. General practice. Office: PO Box 3487 Enid OK 73702-3487

**MARTIN, PAIGE ARLENE,** lawyer; b. Pitts., Nov. 27, 1951; d. James William and Mildred Jean (Toplis) M.; m. Barry Rosenbaum, June 15, 1974 (div. 1977); m. David Kern, Feb. 21, 1988 (div. July 1996). AB, Wellesley (Mass.) Coll., 1973; JD, Case Western Res. U., Cleve., 1978. Bar: Ohio 1978, U.S. Dist. Ct. (no. dist.) Ohio 1978. Assoc. Sindell, Sindell & Rubenstein, Cleve., 1978-83, Spangenberg, Shibley, Traci & Lancione, Cleve., 1983-89; pvt. practice Cleve., 1989—; instr. Cuyahoga Community Coll., Cleve., 1979-80; adj. faculty Case Western Res. U., Cleve., 1984-85; lectr. Assn. Trial Lawyers Assn., Dallas, 1986, Ohio Acad. Trial Attys., Cin., Columbus, 1984, Ohio Legal Ctr. Inst., Sandusky, Ohio, 1985, Cleve. Acad. Trial Attys., 1987. Contbr. chpt. to book. Child advocate CASA program Franklin County. Recipient award of merit Ohio Legal Ctr. Inst., 1985; named to Outstanding Young Women of Am., 1987. Mem. Cleve. Bar Assn. (chair hospice com. 1982-83, Merit Svc. award), Greater Cleve. Bar Assn. (joint med.-legal com. 1983-90, chair 1986-87), Cleve. Acad. Trial Lawyers (dir. 1984-87), Assn. Trial Attys. Am. (diptheria, pertussis, tetnus litigation sect. 1985-87), Ohio State Bar Assn., Ohio Acad. Trial Attys. (constnl. law com. 1989-90). Personal injury, Constitutional, Estate planning. Office: 77 Outerbelt St Columbus OH 43213-1548

**MARTIN, PAUL JEFFREY,** lawyer; b. McArthur, Ohio, Nov. 29, 1951; s. Earl Raymond and Jean Smith M.; m. Alice Jane, May 8, 1970 (div. Apr. 1979); 1 child, Paul Jr.; m. Mary Young, Feb. 25, 1984. BA, Fla. State U., 1973, JD, 1975. Bar: Fla. 1976, U.S. Dist. Ct. (mid. dist.) Fla. 1976, U.S. Dist. Ct. (so. dist.) Fla. 1978, U.S. Ct. Appeals ( 11th cir.) 1981, U.S. Dist. Ct. (no. dist.) Fla. 1991. Ast. pub. defender 10th Jud. Cir. Ct., Bartow, Fla., 1975-78; atty. Boardman & Martin, Immokalee, Fla., 1978-85; asst. gen. counsel State of Fla., Dept. Transp., Tallahassee, 1985-91; asst. atty. gen. Fla. Atty. Gens. Office, Tallahassee, 1991-97; gen. counsel State of Fla., Agy. for Health Care Adminstrn., Tallahassee, 1997—. Episcopalian. Office: Agy for Health Care Adminstrn 2727 Mahan Dr Tallahassee FL 32308-5407

**MARTIN, QUINN WILLIAM,** lawyer; b. Fond du Lac, Wis., Mar. 12, 1948; s. Quinn W. and Marcia E. Martin; m. Jane E. Nehmer; children: Quinn W., William J. BSME, Purdue U., 1969; postgrad., U. Santa Clara, 1969-70; JD, U. Mich., 1973. Bar: Wis. 1973, U.S. Dist. Ct. (ea. dist.) Wis. 1973, U.S. Ct. Appeals (7th cir.) 1973. Sales support mgr. Hewlett-Packard, Palo Alto, Calif., 1969-70; assoc. Quarles & Brady, Milw., 1973-80, ptnr., 1980—; bd. dirs. Associated Bank Milw., U-Line Corp., Gen. Timber and Land, Inc., Fond du Lac. Active McCallum for Lt. Gov., Wis., U. Mich. Law Sch. Fund; bd. dirs. Milw. Zool. Soc., Found. for Wildlife Conservation. Mem. ABA, Wis. Bar Assn., Milw. Bar Assn., Milw. Club, Ozaukee Country Club, Chaine des Rottiseurs, Delta Upsilon (sec.), Milw. Alumni Club. Contracts commercial, General corporate, Antitrust. Office: Quarles & Brady 411 E Wisconsin Ave Ste 2550 Milwaukee WI 53202-4497

**MARTIN, RALPH DRURY,** lawyer, columnist; b. Pittsburg, Kans., Mar. 4, 1947; s. Kent Wills and Kathleen (Drury) M.; m. Ruchirawan Meemeskul, Oct. 28, 1982; 1 child, Chanida Kathleen. BA, Tulane U., 1969; JD, Washington U., 1972. Bar: La. 1972, D.C. 1981, Calif. 1992, U.S. Dist. Ct. (mid. dist.) La. 1985, U.S. Dist. Ct. D.C. 1991, U.S. Ct. Appeals (9th cir.) 1979, U.S. Ct. Appeals (D.C. cir.) 1991, U.S. Supreme Ct. 1976. Law clk. to Hon. Frederick J.R. Heebe U.S. Dist. Ct., Ea. Dist. La., New Orleans, 1972-74; spl. asst. to U.S. atty. U.S. Dept. Justice, Washington, 1974-75, trial atty. civil rights div., 1975-80; dep. asst. legal advisor U.S. Dept. State, Washington, 1980-82; sr. prosecutor pub. integrity sect. U.S. Dept. Justice, Washington, 1982-90; spl. counsel U.S. Dept. State, Washington, 1990-91; ptnr. Storch & Brenner, Washington, 1991—; adj. prof. Washington Coll. Law, The Am. Univ., 1991-92; chmn. Lawyers Com. Effective Assistance of Counsel, 1995—. Comments editor Washington U. Law Quarterly, 1971-72 (honors scholar award 1971). Bd. dirs. Thomas and Bertie T. Smith Arts Found., 1996—. Mem. ABA, Am. Soc. Internat. Law, Nat. Assn. Criminal Def. Lawyers, Univ. Club, D.C. Assn. Criminal Def. Lawyers (v.p. 1995-97), Order of Coif, Stan Musical Soc. Criminal, General civil litigation, Personal injury. Office: Storch & Brenner LLP 1001 Connecticut Ave NW Washington DC 20036-5504

**MARTIN, RAYMOND WALTER,** lawyer; b. Riverside, Calif., Jan. 1, 1952; s. Wilfred W. and Betty Ray (Uhrie) M.; m. Denise A. Mowry, Mar. 22, 1986; children: Justin M., Timothy K., Jeremy T., Sean W. BA, Morningside Coll., Sioux City, Iowa, 1974; JD, U. Denver, 1977. Bar: Colo. 1977, U.S. Dist. Ct. Colo. 1977, U.S. Ct. Appeals (10th cir.) 1978. Assoc. Rovira DeMuth & Eiberger, Denver, 1977-79; mng. ptnr. Eiberger, Stacy, Smith & Martin, Denver, 1979-96; dir. Parcel, Mauro, Hultin & Spaanstra, Denver, 1996-98, Freeborn & Peters, Denver, 1998—. Contbr. articles to profl. jours. Trustee, Wheat Ridge United Meth. Ch., 1983. Recipient Jaffa award for highest scholastic average, U. Denver Alumni Assn., 1976, Harold H. Widney Meml. scholar, 1976. Mem. ABA, Colo. Bar Assn., Order of St. Ives. Republican. Methodist. Avocations: golf, skiing. Labor, General civil litigation, Civil rights. Office: Freeborn & Peters 950 17th St Ste 2600 Denver CO 80202-2826

**MARTIN, ROBERT DALE,** lawyer; b. Canton, Ohio, Oct. 1, 1937; s. Charles Leroy and Edith Ruby (Turnbull) M.; m. Carla Jean Kibler, Dec. 27, 1966; 1 child, Kendall Dalene. BA, Ohio U., 1960; JD, U. Akron, 1969, M of Taxation, 1989; MBA, Ashland U., 1995; postgrad., Kent State U., 1998. Bar: Ohio 1969, U.S. Dist. Ct. (no. dist.) 1984, U.S. Ct. Appeals (6th cir.) 1984. Personnel adminstr. Hoover Co., North Canton, Ohio, 1966-67; atty. Allmon and Benson, Carrollton, Ohio, 1967-69; legal staff asst. Republic Steel Corp., Canton, Ohio, 1969-71, indsl. rels. counsel, 1971-73, supr. labor rels., 1973-78, asst. supt. indsl. rels., 1978-85; mgr. human resources Republic Engineered Steel Corp., Canton, 1985-91; gen. counsel, dir. adminstrn. Office of Summit County Engr., Akron, Ohio, 1991-95; adminstr. bus. and human svcs. Ohio Dept. Transp., New Philadelphia, Ohio, 1995—; adj. prof. bus. law Ashland (Ohio) U., 1988; gen. counsel mgmt. consulting Labor Rels. Assocs., Dayton, Ohio, 1991-93; gen. counsel human resource consulting Human Resources Assocs., Dayton, 1993-95. Sgt. U.S. Army, 1960. Mem. Ohio State Bar Assn. (gen. sect. 1970-97, labor/employment law sect. 1995-99, probate/trust sect. 1996-99, corp. law 1996-99), Nat. Assn. Cert. Govt. Fin. Mgmt. Avocations: walking, fishing, reading, fitness. Fax: (330) 868-6161. Home and Office: 850 Mcdaniel Ave Minerva OH 44657-1240

**MARTIN, ROBERT DAVID,** judge, educator; b. Iowa City, Oct. 7, 1944; s. Murray and G'Ann (Holmgren) M.; m. ruth A. Haberman, Aug. 21, 1966; children: Jacob, Matthew, David. AB, Cornell Coll., Mt. Vernon, Iowa, 1966; JD, U. Chgo., 1969. Bar: Wis. 1969, U.S. Dist. Ct. (we. dist.) Wis. 1969, U.S. Dist. Ct. (ea. dist.) Wis. 1974, U.S. Supreme Ct. 1973. Assoc. Ross & Stevens, S.C., Madison, Wis., 1969-72; ptnr. Ross & Stevens, S.C., Madison, 1973-78; chief judge U.S. Bankruptcy Ct. We. Dist. Wis., 1978—; instr. gen. practice course U. Wis. Law Sch., 1974, 76, 77, 80, lectr. debtor/creditor course, 1981-82, 83, 85, 87, farm credit seminar, 1985, advanced bankruptcy problems, 1989, 91, 96; co-chmn. faculty Am. Law Inst.-ABA Fin. and Bus. Planning for Agr., Stanford U., 1979; faculty mem. Fed. Jud. Ctr. Schs. for New Bankruptcy Judges, 1985-96; chmn. Ann. Continuing Legal Edn. Wis. Debtor Creditor Conf., 1981—. Author: Bankruptcy: Annotated Forms, 1989; co-author: Secured Transactions Handbook for Wisconsin Lawyers and Lenders, Bankruptcy-Text Statutes Rules and Forms, 1992, Ginsberg and Martin on Bankruptcy, 4th edit., 1996. Chmn., bd. dirs., exec. com. Luth. Social Svcs. for Wis. and Upper Mich., Turnaround Mgmt. Assn., 1997—. Mem. Wis. State Bar, Am. Coll. Bankruptcy, Am. Judicature Soc., Nat. Conf. Bankruptcy Judges (bd. govs. 1989-91, sec. 1993-94, v.p. 1994-95, pres. 1995-96), Nat. Bankruptcy Conf. Office: 120 N Henry Rm 340 PO Box 548 Madison WI 53701-0548

**MARTIN, ROBERT JAMES,** lawyer; b. York, Pa., July 20, 1953; s. Jane Ann (Denham) Cornish; 1 child, Danny Robert. BS in Health Care Services, So. Ill. U., 1979; JD, Western State U., 1984. Bar: Calif. 1985, U.S. Dist. Ct. (so., cen. no. and ea. dists.) Calif. 1985, U.S. Dist. Ct. Hawaii 1985, U.S. Ct. Appeals (9th cir.) 1985, U.S. Ct. Claims 1985, U.S. Tax Ct. 1985, U.S. Ct. Mil. Appeals 1985, U.S. Ct. Internat. Trade 1985. Mgr. Nat. TV Rentals, Washington, 1980; regional mgr. Nat. TV Rentals, Washington, Va. and Md. area, 1981; maintenance engr., housekeeping supr. Rockville (Md.) Nursing Home, 1980-81; assoc. Cornish & Cornish, Hemet, Calif., 1986-87; sole practice Hemet, 1987—. With U.S. Army, 1977-80. Mem. Hemet-San Jacinto (Calif.) Bar Assn., Exchange Club, Lions. Lodge: Lions. Avocations: gardening, fishing, motorcycling, swimming, softball. State civil litigation, Consumer commercial, Family and matrimonial.

**MARTIN, SHANNON E.,** law educator; b. Mansfield, Ohio, Apr. 3, 1952; d. Robert J. And Mary K. Rossi; m. Edwin A. Martin, Jr. PhD, U. N.C., 1993. Prof. Rutgers U., New Brunswick, N.J., 1993—. Author: Newspapers of Record in a Digital Age, 1998. Office: Rutgers U 4 Huntington St New Brunswick NJ 08901-1071

**MARTIN, SIVA,** lawyer; b. Chgo., Oct. 26, 1925; s. Leon and Goldie (Baronian) M.; m. Mary Kaprelian, Aug. 12, 1952; children: Robert, Jack. BS, Loyola U., 1950; MA, Northwestern U., 1951; JD, DePaul U., 1953. Bar: Ill. 1953. Loan officer Nat. Blvd. Bank, Chgo., 1955-62; v.p. Ill. State Bank, Chgo., 1962-73; sole practice Chgo., 1973—. Dist. chmn. Boy Scouts Am., Chgo., 1957; pres. Chgo. Chpt. Armenian Gen. Benevolent Union, 1978-80. Mem. ABA, Ill. State Bar Assn., Chgo. Bar Assn., Chgo. Mortgage Attys., Northwest Real Estate Bd. Democrat. Mem. Apostolic Ch. Club: Lions. Real property, Probate. Home: 6550 N Kenton Ave Chicago IL 60646-3433 Office: 5860 W Higgins Ave Chicago IL 60630-2036

**MARTIN, STEPHEN RUSSELL, II,** prosecutor; b. Richmond, Va., Oct. 19, 1968; s. Stephen Russell and Suzanne (Gallup) M. Student, U. London, 1990; BA in Polit. Sci., BA in Pub. Affairs, U. Denver, 1991; JD, Creighton U., 1994; LLM with honors, Georgetown U., 1998. Bar: Mo. 1994, Kans. 1995, D.C. 1995, U.S. Dist. Ct. (we. dist.) Mo. 1994. Asst. atty. gen. Mo. Atty. Gen.'s Office, Jefferson City, 1994-96; spl. asst. U.S. atty. U.S. Atty.'s Office D.C., Washington, 1996-98, asst. U.S. atty., 1998—. Mem. editl. staff Creighton Law Rev., 1993-94. Fraser Stryker scholar, scholar Creighton U. Law Sch. Mem. Golden Key, Phi Delta Phi, Beta Theta Pi. Democrat. Avocations: mountain biking, soccer, scuba diving, reading. Home: 3430 N Dickerson St Arlington VA 22207-2963 Office: US Atty's Office DC 555 4th St NW Washington DC 20001-2733

**MARTIN, TERRENCE KEECH,** lawyer, city councilor; b. Lynchburg, Va., Apr. 21, 1939; s. Walter Worth and Frances Louise (Keech) M.; m. Cecilia Rudy, Nov. 5, 1983 (div. 1999); children: Theodore Worth, Timothy Francis. BA, U. Notre Dame, 1961; JD, U. Va., 1964. Bar: Va. 1964. Asst. city atty. City of Newport News, Va., 1967-69; assoc. Bert A. Nachman, Atty., Newport News, 1969-70; solo practitioner Newport News, 1970-72; ptnr. Martin & Rilee, Newport News, 1972-74, Martin & Bensten, Newport News, 1974-78; atty. Terrence K. Martin & Assocs., Newport News, 1978-83; ptnr. Mason, Gibson, Cowardin & martin, Newport News, 1983-88, Overman, Cowardin & Martin, PLC, Newport News, 1988-98; atty. pvt. practice, Newport News, 1998—. Mem. coun. City of Newport News, 1990—; bd. dirs. Va. Peninsula Econ. Devel. Coun., 1996—, Youth Svcs. Commn., 1993—, Transp. Safety Commn., 1990—; mem. edn. com. Va. Mcpl. League, 1994-95; mem. task force City's Role in Edn., Nat. League of Cities, mem. comty. and econ. devel. steering com., 1999—. Capt., Mil. Police Corps, U.S. Army, 1965-67, France. Republican. Roman Catholic. E-mail: terry@visi.net. Fax: 757-873-0889. General practice, General civil litigation, Personal injury. Home: 17349 Warwick Blvd Newport News VA 23603-1331 Office: 751 Thimble Blvd Ste L Newport News VA 23606-4217

**MARTIN, THOMAS MACDONALD,** lawyer; b. Huntington, N.Y., Dec. 17, 1947; s. Raleigh Lloyd and Elizebeth Battle (Gutwein) M.; m. Sheila Lynn Wilkens, July 13, 1968. AAS in Bus. Adminstrn., SUNY, Selden, 1967; BS in Criminal Justice, SUNY, Westbury, 1976; JD, Touro Coll., 1986. Bar: Va. 1988, U.S. Ct. Appeals (4th cir.) 1988, U.S. Supreme Ct. 1993, U.S. Ct. Fed. Claims 1993, U.S. Ct. Appeals (fed. cir.) 1993, U.S. Ct. Mil. Appeals 1993; cert. fraud examiner. Customs officer, sky marshall U.S. Customs Agy. Svc., N.Y.C., 1971-75; spl. agt. U.S. Dept. Agr., N.Y.C., 1975-78; supervisory spl. agt. Office of Insp. Gen., N.Y.C., 1978-81, asst. regional insp. gen. then regional insp. gen., 1981-86; dep. div. dir. Office of Insp. Gen., Washington, 1986-88, chief internal affairs, 1988-91, sr. spl. agt. gen. investigations divsn., 1991-93, sr. spl. agt. program investigation divsn., 1993-98; ret. Fairfax, Va., 1998; pvt. practice law, 1998—; magistrate 19th Jud. Dist., Fairfax County, Va., 1999—. With USN, 1967-71. Mem. ABA (litigation/criminal justice com. 1989—), ATLA, Fairfax Bar Assn., N.Y. Bar Assn. (criminal justice sect.), Va. Trial Lawyers Assn., Nat. Geog. Soc., Fed. Law Enforcement Officers Assn., Nat. Assn. Fraud Examiners. Methodist. Avocations: karate, marksmanship, golf, fishing, reading. Criminal, General practice, General civil litigation.

**MARTIN, WALTER,** retired lawyer; b. Crookston, Minn., Nov. 7, 1912; s. Frederick and Rosalie (Mertz) M.; m. Catherine Mary Severin, May 1, 1942 (dec. May 1979); children: Frederick H., Jacqueline K., Patricia, Priscilla, Walter Jr., John E. BA, Albion Coll., 1937; JD, U. Mich., 1939. Bar: Mich. 1939, U.S. Dist. Ct. (fed. dist.) 1939, U.S. Ct. Appeals (6th cir.) 1947, U.S. Supreme Ct. 1958. Ptnr. Martin & Martin, Saginaw, Mich., 1952-94; ret., 1994. Fellow Mich. Bar Assn., Saginaw County Bar Assn. (pres. 1958). Lutheran. Avocations: hunting, fishing. Personal injury, Probate, Condemnation. Office: 803 Court St Saginaw MI 48602-4223

**MARTIN, WILLARD GORDON, JR.,** lawyer; b. Boston, Dec. 12, 1937; children: Yves, Sylvie, Melissa, Helen, Galya. AB, Bates Coll., 1959; LLB, Harvard U., 1962; LLM, Boston U., 1984. Bar: N.H. 1962, U.S. Dist. Ct. N.H. 1962. Ptnr. Martin, Lord & Osman, P.A., Laconia, N.H., 1962—; city solicitor, Laconia, 1963-66; Belknap County atty., N.H., 1967-68; rep. to gen. ct., N.H., 1969-70; mem. N.H. Jud. Coun., 1971-75; N.H. bar examiner, 1972—; Spl. justice Laconia Dist. Ct., 1973—; mem. judge family divsn. N.H. Com. Character and Fitness, 1998—. Mem. Am. Judicature Soc. (bd. dirs. 1980-84), N.H. Bar Assn. (bd. govs. 1980-82), Belknap County Bar Assn., Phi Beta Kappa. General corporate, Probate, Personal income taxation. Office: 1 Mill Plz Laconia NH 03246-3438

**MARTIN, WILLIAM CHARLES,** retired lawyer, law educator; b. Shenandoah, Iowa, May 25, 1923; s. J. Stuart and Chloe Irene (Anderson) M.; m. Marilyn Forbes, Oct. 18, 1947 (div. 1979); children: Ann, James; m. Kathryn Ann Fehr, Sept. 17, 1979. BA, U. Iowa, 1946, JD, 1947. Bar: Iowa 1947, Oreg. 1948. Sr. ptnr. Martin, Bischoff, Templeton, Biggs & Ericsson, Portland, Oreg., 1951-86; mem. Oreg. Bd. Bar Examiners, 1966-69; instr. Lewis and Clark Coll. Law, 1973-75, U. Hawaii-Hilo, West Hawaii, 1989-97. Bd. dirs. Eastmoreland Gen. Hosp., Portland, 1960-84, chmn., 1978-81; mem. Lawyers Com. for Civil Rights Under Law, Jackson, Miss., 1965; bd. dirs. Lake Oswego (Oreg.) Pub. Libr., 1981-84, chmn., 1982-84; mem. Kona bd. Am. Cancer Soc. 1st lt. USAAF, WWII. Mem. ABA, Oreg. State Bar, Kona Heavens Assn. (pres. 1994-95), Univ. Club, Kona Outdoor Cir. (Kailua Kona), Keauhou Yacht Club (bd. dirs. 1996—), Phi Delta Phi, Sigma Nu. Democrat. Roman Catholic. Probate, Insurance, General practice. Home: 73-4825 Anini St Kailua Kona HI 96740-9202

**MARTIN, WILLIAM CLIFFORD, III,** judge; b. Longview, Tex., July 15, 1938; s. William Clifford Jr. and Frankie Judith (Farmer) M.; m. Janet Marie Geist, June 3, 1961; children Melissa Marie, Charles William. AB cum laude with honors, Davidson Coll., 1961; JD, U. Tex. Sch. Law, 1963. Bar: Tex. 1966. Pvt. practice Longview, Tex., 1966; ptnr. DeWitt & Martin, Longview, 1966-67, Adams, Sheppard & Martin, Longview, 1968-70; judge, ct. domestic rels. Gregg County, Longview, 1971-77; judge, 307th jud. dist. Family Dist. Ct., Longview, 1977-90; sr. dist. judge, family law 1st Admin. Jud. Region of Tex., Dallas, 1991—; formerly mem. Juvenile Probation Commn. Tex., Govs. Juvenile Justice and Delinquency Prevention Adv. Com. Contbr. articles to profl. jours. Lt. U.S. Army, 1964-66. Mem. ABA, Tex. Bar Assn. (coun. family law sec.). Republican. Presbyterian. Avocations: history, genealogy, bladesmithing. Office: PO Box 8 Longview TX 75606-0008

**MARTIN, WILLIAM CLINTON,** lawyer; b. Sutton, W. Va., Apr. 24, 1952; s. Gilbert Clinton and Reva Clarice (Karickhoff) M.; m. Margaret Grace O'Connor, Feb. 7, 1975; Michelle Renee, Melanie Grace, William Christopher, Meghan Belen. BS, W. Va. U., 1975, JD, 1978. Bar: W. Va. 1978, U.S. Dist. Ct. (so. dist.) W. Va. 1978, U.S. Tax Ct. 1988, U. S. Dist. Ct. (no. dist.) W. Va. 1997. Ptnr. Cline & Martin, Sutton, W. Va., 1978-80, Martin & Mauser, Sutton, 1980-84; lawyer pvt. practice, Sutton, 1985-91; prosecuting atty Braxton County, Sutton, W. Va., 1993-96; owner Cooper & Martin, Sutton, 1997—; adj. asst. prosecutor Braxton County, 1979-80, adj. prosecutor 1980-84, 88-92. Pres. Sutton Lions Club 1979-88. Mem. ATLA, W. Va. State Bar Assn. (dist. 12 character com. 1984—). Democrat. Home: 475 1/2 Old Turnpike Rd Sutton WV 26601-1637 Office: 211 Main St Sutton WV 26601-1326

**MARTIN, WILLIAM JOSEPH, III,** lawyer; b. New Brunswick, N.J., Nov. 30, 1953; s. William Joseph, Jr. and Martha Jane (Clay) M.; m. Ann Blom, Aug. 21, 1977; children: William Clay, David John. BA with high honors, U. Del., 1975; JD with honors, Rutgers U., 1978; ML in Taxation, Georgetown U., 1987. Bar: Del. 1978, U.S. Tax Ct. 1979, Pa. 1996. Assoc. David Nicol Williams, PA, Wilmington, Del., 1978-81; ptnr. Williams, Gordon & Martin, PA, Wilmington, 1981-94, William J. Martin, P.A., Wilmington, 1994-96; ptnr. Prickett, Jones, Elliott & Kristol, P.A., Wilmington and Dover, Del., 1996—, Kennett Square, Pa., 1996—; spkr. Del. Tax Inst., Wilmington, 1987, 89, 91, 94. Trustee, pres. Concord Presbyn. Ch., Wilmington, 1987-90; mem. staff Del. section Am. Radio Relay League, Wilmington, 1987-88. Mem. ABA (health law sect.), Del. State Bar Assn. (tax sect. and estates and trusts sect.). Avocation: amateur radio. Pension, profit-sharing, and employee benefits, Taxation, general, Health. Home: 719 Burnley Rd Wilmington DE 19803-1730 Office: Prickett Jones Elliott & Kristol 1310 King St Wilmington DE 19801-3220

**MARTINA, CARLO JACK,** lawyer; b. Wyandotte, Mich., Jan. 1, 1954; s. Carlo and Matilda M.; divorced; children: Raphael, Ariel. BS with high distinction, U. Mich., 1976; JD, Wayne State U., 1979. Bar: Mich. 1979, U.S. Dist. Ct. (ea. dist.) Mich. 1980. Assoc. Provisor, Eisenberg et al, Southfield, Mich., 1979-81, Auslander, Babcock & Weiss, Southfield, Mich., 1981-83; atty. pvt. practice, Southfield, Mich., 1983—; mem. adv. bd. Legal Alternatives for Women, Southfield, 1985-87; co-founder Mich. br. Justice for Children, 1995-97; co-founder, co-publisher, co-owner MetroParent Mag., Southfield, 1987-95. Legal expert (video) Latchkey Kids: Home Alone & Safe, 1994. Mem. adv. bd. Gov.'s Internat. Yr. of Family Coun., Lansing, Mich., 1994-95, Roundtable of Christians, Muslims & Jews, Detroit, 1989-91, Anti-Defamation League, Southfield, 1988-90; scoutmaster Cub Scout Pack 1016, Birmingham, Mich., 1993-97. James P. Angel scholar U. Mich., 1977-79. Mem. Mich. Trial Lawyers Assn., Oakland County Bar Assn. (co-chair family court com., friend of ct. subcom.), Wayne County Bar Assn. (family law divsn.). Avocations: reading, fishing, furniture refinishing & home remodeling, model building. Family and matrimonial, Personal injury. Office: 19111 W 10 Mile Rd Ste 104 Southfield MI 48075-2449

**MARTIN-BOYAN, ANNEMARIE,** lawyer; b. Meadowbrook, Pa., July 30, 1967; d. Joseph Francis and Elizabeth Mary Martin; m. Michale Jay Boyan, June 13, 1998. BA in Polit Sci., Temple U., 1989, JD, 1992. Bar: Pa. 1992, N.J. 1992, U.S. Dist. Ct. N.J. 1992, U.S. Dist. Ct. (ea. dist.) Pa. 1994, U.S. Dist. Ct. (no. dist.) Ohio 1995, U.S. Dist. Ct. Md. 1996. Assoc. Levy, Angstreich, Finney, et al., Phila., 1992-95, Ominsky & Messa, Phila., 1995-99. Mem. Phila. Bar Assn., Phila. Trial Lawyers Assn., Camden County Bar Assn. Avocations: travel, reading, basketball. Product liability, Personal injury, Federal civil litigation. Home: 40 Whyte Dr Voorhees NJ 08043 Office: Temple Univ Health System Office of Counsel Jones Hall 1316 W Ontario St Philadelphia PA 19140-5297

**MARTINDALE, DANIEL S.,** lawyer; b. Glens Falls, N.Y., June 8, 1971; s. Ernest W. and Bonnie L. Martindale. BA in Polit. Sci., Syracuse U., 1992; JD, U. Dayton, 1995. Bar: N.J. 1996, U.S. Dist. Ct. N.J. 1996, N.Y. 1997, U.S. Dist. Ct. (no. dist.) N.Y. 1997. Law clk. Timothy J. Alden, Esq., Glens Falls, 1994-95, Delwyn J. Mulder, Esq., Glens Falls, 1995-96, Newell & Toomey, Glens Falls, 1995-96; pvt. practice Hudson Falls, N.Y., 1997—. Chmn. Glens Falls Dem. Com., 1995—, conv. del., Queensbury, 1997, 98; candidate councilman-at-large 4th Jud. Dist., Glens Falls, 1997. Recipient Cert. Meritorious Svc., Serlin Family Found., Lake George, N.Y., 1995. Mem. Warren County Bar Assn. (co-chmn. law day com. 1998), Warren County Bar Found. (dir. 1998—), Washington County Bar Assn., Theta Chi Alumni Assn. (corp. counsel, dir. Alpha Chi chpt. 1996—). Methodist. Criminal, Family and matrimonial, Real property. Office: 253 Main St Hudson Falls NY 12839-1711

**MARTINDALE, PEGGY LUTTRELL,** law librarian; b. Ft. Worth, Sept. 26, 1954; d. John Andrew Jr. and Fay Elizabeth (Renshaw) Luttrell; m. Paul Lynn Martindale, Apr. 4, 1982; children: Mendy Mendoza Knight, Eric Keith Martindale. BS magna cum laude, Tex. Woman's U., 1986, MLS, 1988. Asst. libr. for pub. svcs. Tarrant County Law Libr., Ft. Worth, 1986-90; asst. dir. Tarrant County Law Libr., 1990—. Mem. Am. Assn. Law Libr., Southwestern Assn. Law Librs., Tarrant County Assn. Law Librs. (treas. 1990-96, pres. 1996-97). Office: Tarrant County Law Libr 100 W Weatherford St Rm 420 Fort Worth TX 76102-2115

**MARTINES, SUE B.,** mediator; b. Carlisle, Pa., Sept. 28, 1962; d. Thomas Edward and Antoinette Felicia Boettger; m. Joseph Martines, May 3, 1997; 1 child, Hope Antoinette. BA, Colo. Coll., 1984; cert. in non-profit mgmt., Met. State Coll., 1985; JD, U. N.Mex., 1992. Bar: N.Mex. 1993, U.S. Ct. Appeals (10th cir.) 1995. Dep. city atty. City of Alamogordo, N.Mex., 1992-94; staff atty. Protection and Advocacy, Albuqueque, 1994-96; atty. State Pub. Defender, Alamogordo, 1996-97; owner Mediation Assocs. So. N.Mex., Ruidoso, 1997—; mem. State Bar Adr Com., Albuquerque, 1996—; trainer N.Mex. Ctr. for Dispute Resolution, Albuquerque, 1997—; instr., faculty Ea. N.Mex. U., Ruidoso, 1998—. Mem. Soc. for Profls. in Dispute Resolution. Avocations: parenting, music. Office: Mediation Assn So NMex PO Box 2716 Ruidoso NM 88355-2716

**MARTINETTI, RONALD ANTHONY,** lawyer; b. N.Y.C., Aug. 13, 1945; s. Alfred Joseph and Frances Ann (Battipaglia) M. Student, U. Chgo., 1981-82; JD, U. So. Calif., 1982. Bar: Calif. 1982; U.S. Dist. Ct. (cen. and no. dists.) Calif. 1982, U.S. Dist. Ct. Ariz., 1992; U.S. Ct. Appeals (9th cir.) 1982. Ptnr. Kazanjian & Martinetti, Glendale, Calif., 1986—; co-founder Am. Legends Website, 1996, Am. Legends Pub., 1996. Author: James Dean Story, 1995; co-author: Rights of Owners of Lost, Stolen or Destroyed Instruments Under UCC Section3-804: Can They Be Holders in Due Course, 1993; contbr. to Wall St. Jour., Washington Post, Newsday, Balt. Sun, The New Leader, 1968-76. Vol. trial lawyer Bet Tzedek Legal Svcs., 1987—; judge pro tem L.A. Superior Ct., 1994—. Mem. Calif. Bar Assn. Roman Catholic. E-mail: amlegends@AOL.com. Website: www.americanlegends.com. State civil litigation, Personal injury, Labor. Office: Kazanjian & Martinetti 520 E Wilson Ave Glendale CA 91206-4374

**MARTINEZ, ALEX,** state supreme court justice; b. Denver, CO, Apr. 1, 1951; m. Kathy Carter; children: Julia, Maggie. Diploma, Phillips Exeter Acad., N.H., 1969; student, Reed Coll., 1969-72; BA, U. Colo., 1973, JD, 1976. Bar: Colo. 1976. Dep. state pub. defender Pueblo and Denver, 1976-83; county ct. judge Pueblo, 1983-88, dist. ct. judge, 1988-97; justice Colo. Supreme Ct., Denver, 1997—; Supreme Ct. liaison Colo. Criminal Rules Com., Colo. Criminal Jury Instrns.; chmn. Child Welfare Appeals Workgroup, 1997; mem. standing com. Integrated Info. Svcs. Chmn. Pueblo adv. bd. Packard Found., 1993-96; chmn. site-based governing coun. Pueblo Sch. Arts and Scis., 1994-95; mem. site-based governing coun. Roncalli Mid. Sch., 1993-94; bd. dirs. Colo. U. Law Alumni. Mem. Colo. Bar Assn. (regional v.p. 1995-96), Colo. Hispanic Bar Assn., Pueblo Bar Assn. (mem. exec. coun. 1994-96), Pueblo Hispanic Bar Assn. E-mail: AJMarti@aol.com. Office: Colo Supreme Ct 2 E 14th Ave Rm 430 Denver CO 80203-2115

**MARTINEZ, ANDREW TREDWAY,** lawyer; b. New Orleans, Oct. 24, 1930; s. Andrew Richmond and Mary Leslie (Tredway) M.; m. Margaret Leslie Buchan, June 7, 1952; children: Andrew, Leslie, Margaret. BA, Tulane U., 1952, LLB, 1956. Bar: La. 1956, U.S. Dist. Ct. (ea. dist.) La. 1956, U.S. Ct. Appeals (5th cir.) 1962, U.S. Supreme Ct. 1971. Ptnr. Terriberry, Carroll and Yancey, New Orleans, 1956—. Assoc. editor Am. Maritime Cases, 1989—; adv. editor Tulane Maritime Jour., 1976—. Lt. (j.g.) USN, 1952-54. Mem. ABA, Maritime Law Assn. U.S., Assn. Average Adjusters U.S., La. Bar Assn., New Orleans Bar Assn. Admiralty, General corporate, Pension, profit-sharing, and employee benefits. Home: 1500 Jefferson Ave New Orleans LA 70115-4121 Office: Terriberry Carroll Yancey 3100 Energy Ctr New Orleans LA 70163

**MARTINEZ, DAVID,** lawyer; b. Slaton, Tex., July 6, 1954; s. Joe A. and Rigo (Hernandez) M.; m. Celia Diaz, July 14, 1979; children: Justin, Hilary, Zach. BBA, U. Nebr., 1976; JD, Thurgood Marshall Sch. of Law, 1979. Bar: Tex. 1979, U.S. Dist. Ct. (no. dist.) Tex., U.S. Ct. Appeals (5th cir.). Asst. dist. atty. Deaf Smith County, Hereford, Tex., 1980-82; pres. Hispanic C. of C., Lubbock, 1988, 89, Mex.-Am. Bar Assn., Lubbock, 1997. Recipient Pres.' award League of United Latin Am. Citizens, Lubbock, 1990. Home: 3414 94th St Lubbock TX 79423-3624 Office: 1663 Broadway St Lubbock TX 79401-3120

**MARTINEZ, DAVID BRIAN,** lawyer; b. Albuquerque, Aug. 9, 1956; s. Joe R. and Henrietta A. Martinez; m. Kimberley J. Gilbert, Aug. 17, 1984; children: Kellen, Madelaine. BBA, U. Notre Dame, 1978; JD, U. N.Mex., 1982. Bar: N.Mex., U.S. Dist. Ct. N.Mex. Assoc. Gilman & Maguire, Albuquerque, 1982-85; ptnr. Gilman, Maguire & Martinez, Albuquerque, 1985-90, Maguire & Martinez, Albuquerque, 1990-92; mng. ptnr., v.p. Eaton, Martinez & Hart P.C., Albuquerque, 1993—. Bd. dirs. Albuquerque Acad., 1987-95, Manzano Day Sch., Albuquerque, 1996—. Mem. ATLA, N.Mex. Trial Lawyers Assn., Albuquerque Bar Assn., U. N.Mex. Alumni Assn. (bd. dirs. 1986—). Personal injury, Professional liability, General civil litigation. Office: Eaton Martinez & Hart PC 3800 Osuna Rd NE Ste 2 Albuquerque NM 87109-4458

**MARTINEZ, DIANA MARIE,** lawyer; b. San Antonio, Mar. 5, 1967; d. Louis Lane and Gloria M. BBA, U. Tex., 1990, JD, 1993. Bar: Tex. 1994, U.S. Dist. Ct. (so. dist.) Tex. 1995. Assoc. Law Offices Allison & Huert, Corpus Christi, Tex., 1993-96, Edwards, Terry & Edwards, Corpus Christi, 1996-97, Law Offices Rene Rodriguez, Corpus Christi, 1997—. Del. State Dem. Convention, San Antonio, 1998, Nueces County Dem. Convention, Corpus Christi, 1998; bd. mem. Nueces County Juvenile Citizens Adv. Bd. Mem. Tex. Trial Lawyer Assn., Corpus Christi Young Lawyer Assn. (bd. dirs. 1996-98, v.p. 1998—), Civil Svc. Commn. (vice-chair 1997-98), Civil Svc. Bd. (bd. dirs. 1997-98). Product liability, Personal injury, General civil litigation. Office: Law Offices Rene Rodriguez 433 S Tancahua St Corpus Christi TX 78401-3422

**MARTINEZ, EDUARDO VIDAL,** lawyer; b. Travis AFB, Calif., Sept. 27, 1955; s. Vidal and Isidora (Lee) M.; m. Mary Kim Sullivan, Apr. 7, 1984. BA, U. Tex., 1978; MA, Antioch Ctr. for Legal Studies, Washington, 1983; JD, Miss. Coll., 1990. Bar: Miss. 1991, U.S. Dist. Ct. (no. and so. dist.) Miss. 1991, U.S. Ct. Mil. Appeals 1991, U.S. Ct. Appeals (5th cir.) 1991, U.S. Supreme Ct. 1994. Gen. counsel Home-Land Title & Abstract Co. Inc., Jackson, Miss., 1991; pvt. practice Jackson, 1991-92; spl. asst. atty. gen. Office of the Atty. Gen., Jackson, 1992-97; legal counsel, site adminstr. Skytel Corp., 1997—. Editor Legal Eye, 1990. Comdr. USNR, 1994. Scholar Miss. Bar Found., 1988, scholar in environ. law Am. Law Inst., 1990. Mem. ABA, Miss. Bar Assn., Naval Res. Assn. (chpt. pres.), Am. Legion, Res. Officer Assn. (chpt. pres.), Nat. Jr. Officer (co-chairperson), Sea Svcs. (nat. jr. v.p.). Roman Catholic. Administrative and regulatory, General corporate, Communications. Office: 200 S Lamar St Jackson MS 39201-4013

**MARTINEZ, JOSE, JR.,** lawyer; b. L.A., Mar. 18, 1967; s. Jose Luis Martinez and Guadalupe Figueroa-Martinez. BA, UCLA, 1990; JD, U. Calif., San Francisco, 1994. Bar: N.Y. 1995. Assoc. Weitz & Luxenberg, P.C., N.Y.C., 1994-95, Marc Israel & Assocs., N.Y.C., 1995-97; ptnr., v.p. Arthouse Inc., N.Y.C., 1996—; ptnr. Jose Martinez, Jr., Esq., N.Y.C., 1997—. Mem. adv. bd. Film Culture, N.Y.C., 1996—, Harry Smith Archives, NFC, N.Y.C., 1997—. Mem. City Bar Assn. City N.Y., Hispanic Bar Assn. Avocations: writing, cooking, movies. General corporate, Entertainment, Intellectual property. Office: Arthouse Inc One Aster Pl Ste 90 New York NY 10003

**MARTINEZ-CID, RICARDO,** lawyer; b. Havana, Cuba, May 9, 1950; came to U.S., 1962; s. Ricardo Martinez Balado and Pastora Cid Gonzalez; m. Rita Marin Pose; children from previous marriage: Maricer, Ricardo, Maite, Jordi. BA, U. Fla., 1970, JD, 1972. Bar: Fla. 1973. Assoc. Steel, Hector & Davis, Miami, Fla., 1972-76; ptnr. Martinez-Cid, Suarez & Amador, Miami, 1976-80; sole practice Miami, 1980—; bd. dirs. Belen Jesuit Prep. Sch., Miami, Casino Espanol de la Habana, Miami. Republican. Roman Catholic. Contracts commercial, General corporate, Real property. Office: 4000 SE Financial Ctr Miami FL 33131

**MARTINI, ALYSSA ANN,** lawyer; b. Greenwich, Conn., Dec. 12, 1969; d. Victor John and Cookie Ann M. BS, Gettysburg Coll., 1991; JD, Widener U., 1995. Bar: Nev. 1995, U.S. Dist. Ct. Nev. 1995, U.S. Dist. Ct. D.C. 1996. Assoc. Pantaleo, Lipkin & Moss, Washington, 1995-97; assoc. Thorndal, Armstrong, Delk, Balkenbush & Eisinger, Las Vegas, Nev., 1997—. ESL tutor Read Learning Ctr., Las Vegas, 1996-97; youth leader St. Thomas More Ch., Henderson, Nev., 1998—; mem. Las Vegas C. of C., 1998—. Mem. Nev. State Bar Assn., Clark City Bar Assn. Roman Catholic. Avocations: tennis, yoga, volleyball, travel, movies. General civil litigation, Insurance, Labor. Office: Thorndal Armstrong Delk Balkenbush & Eisinger 1100 Bridger Ave Las Vegas NV 89101-5315

**MARTINO, GARY JAMES,** lawyer; b. Clarksburg, W.Va., Dec. 9, 1956; s. David Victor and Margaret Ann (Fragmin) M. BSBA, Fairmont State Coll., 1980; JD, Thomas Cooley Law Sch., 1985. Bar: W.Va. 1985, U.S. Dist. Ct. (so. dist.) W.Va. 1985, U.S. Ct. Appeals (4th cir.) 1992, U.S. Supreme Ct. 1992. Assoc. Clagett and Gorey, Fairmont, W.Va., 1986-88; pvt. practice Fairmont, 1988--; cons. law Marion County Citizens for Better Govt., Inc., Fairmont, 1987--. Mem. Marion County Dem. Mens' Club, Fairmont, 1987--; Marion County Mental Hygiene commr., 1997—. Mem. ABA, Am. Judicature Soc., W.Va. State Bar Assn., W.Va. Trial Lawyers Assn., Marion County Bar Assn. (pres. 1997—). Roman Catholic. Avocations: softball, racquetball, golf. General practice, Personal injury, Criminal. Home: 2600 Cedar Ln Fairmont WV 26554-8971 Office: 211 Adams St Fairmont WV 26554-2834

**MARTINSON, BRADLEY JAMES,** lawyer; b. Ortonville, Minn., Oct. 16, 1945; s. Edwin James and Helen Eleanor (Christenson) M.; m. Beth Louise Nelson, June 24, 1967; children: Sara, Timothy. BA, Concordia Coll., Moorhead, Minn., 1967; JD, U. Minn., 1973. Assoc. Robert Hillstrom & Assocs., Mpls., 1973-80; shareholder Hillstrom, Bale & Martinson, Mpls., 1980-85, Martinson, Schwartz & Corey, Mpls., 1985-87, Salmen, Brinkman & Martinson, St. Paul, 1987-90; shareholder, mng. ptnr. Tews, Squires, Martin & Martinson, Mpls., 1990-97; shareholder Law Offices of Bradley J. Martinson, Mpls., 1998—. 1st lt. U.S. Army, 1968-71. Mem. Midland Hills Country Club (pres. 1997-98). General civil litigation, Alternative dispute resolution, General practice. Home: 1928 29th Ave NW New Brighton MN 55112-1737 Office: 701 4th Ave S Ste 300 Minneapolis MN 55415-1809

**MARTOCCHIO, LOUIS JOSEPH,** lawyer, educator; b. Hartford, Conn., May 12, 1966; s. Louis Joseph and Mary Noel (Higgins) M.; m. Jodie Meheran, Jan. 4, 1992. BS in Bus. Econs., So. Conn. State U., 1988; JD, U. Bridgeport, 1991. Bar: Conn. 1991. Atty. Carswell Law Offices, Bridgeport, Conn., 1991-92, Moynahan, Ruskin, Mascolo & Minnella, Waterbury, Conn., 1993—; prof. Morse Sch. Bus., Hartford, Conn., 1992-96; bd. dirs. Camelot Property, South Windsor; legal cons. Lobo Enterprises, Southington, Conn., 1994—. Recipient Univ. award U. Bridgeport, 1991. Mem. ABA, Conn. Bar Assn., Conn. Trial Lawyers Assn., Hartford Bar Assn., Waterbury Bar Assn. Personal injury, Family and matrimonial, General corporate. Office: Capitol Pl 21 Oak St Ste 604 Hartford CT 06106-8002

**MARTOCHE, SALVATORE RICHARD,** lawyer; b. Buffalo, Oct. 12, 1940; s. Charles L. and Grace (Pignone) M.; m. Mary Dee Benesh, Oct. 17, 1945; children: Amy Catherine, Claire Elizabeth, Christopher Charles. B.S., Canisius Coll., 1962; J.D., U. N.D., 1967. Bar: N.Y. 1969; U.S. Dist. Ct. (we. dist.) N.Y.; U.S. Ct. Appeals (2d cir.); U.S. Supreme Ct. Washington, D.C. Atty. Legal Aid Bur., Buffalo, 1968-72; pvt. practice Buffalo, 1969-82; asst. counsel to the majority N.Y. State Senate, Albany, 1974-82; U.S. atty. U.S. Dept. Justice (we. dist.), Buffalo, N.Y., 1982-86; asst. sec. labor mgmt. standards U.S. Dept. Labor, Washington, DC, 1986-88; asst. sec. enforcement U.S. Dept. Treasury, Washington, 1988-90; acting dir. U.S. Office of Thrift Supervision, Washington, 1990; ptnr. Hiscock & Barclay LLP, Buffalo, N.Y., 1990—. Author: (with B. Grahl) Guilty of Poverty: A Study of Bail and Pretrial Detention in Buffalo, N.Y., 1977; contbr. articles to profl. jours. Recipient Citizen of Yr. award Buffalo News, Brotherhood award NCCJ, 1981; recipient Man of Yr. award William Paca Anti-Defamation Soc., 1980; recipient LaSalle Medal Canisus Coll., 1979, Disting. Alumnus, Canisius Coll., 1986, Friend of Law Enforcement award N.Y. State Sheriff's Assn., 1978, Man of Yr. award Dwight D. Eisenhower Club, 1973, Vol. of Yr. award Addicts in Distress, 1974. Mem. State N.Y. Bar Assn., ABA, Erie County Bar Assn. Republican. Roman Catholic. Office: Hiscock & Barclay LLP 50 Fountain Plz Ste 301 Buffalo NY 14202-2291

**MARTONE, FREDERICK J.,** state supreme court justice; b. Fall River, Mass., Nov. 8, 1943. BS, Coll. Holy Cross, 1965; JD, U. Notre Dame, 1972; LLM, Harvard U., 1975. Bar: Mass. 1972, Ariz. 1974, U.S. Dist. Ct. Mass. 1973, U.S. Dist. Ct. Ariz. 1974, U.S. Ct. Appeals (1st cir.) 1973, U.S. Ct. Appeals (9th cir.) 1974, U.S. Supreme Ct. 1977. Law clk. to Hon. Edward F. Hennessey Mass. Supreme Judicial Ct., 1972-73; pvt. practice Phoenix, 1973-85; assoc. presiding judge Superior Ct. Ariz., Maricopa County; judge Superior Ct. Ariz., Maricopa County, Phoenix, 1985-92; justice Supreme Ct. Ariz., Phoenix, 1992—. Editor notes and comments Notre Dame Law Rev., 1970-72; contbr. articles to profl. jours. Capt. USAF, 1965-69. Mem. ABA, Ariz. Judges Assn., Maricopa County Bar Assn., Am. Judicature Soc., State Bar Ariz., Horace Rumpole Inn of Ct. Office: Supreme Ct Arizona 1501 W Washington St Phoenix AZ 85007-3231

**MARTONE, PATRICIA ANN,** lawyer; b. Bklyn., Apr. 28, 1947; d. David Andrew and Rita Mary (Dullmeyer) M. BA in Chemistry, NYU, 1968, JD, 1973; MA in Phys. Chemistry, Johns Hopkins U., 1969. Bar: N.Y. 1974, U.S. Dist. Ct. (so. and ea. dists.) N.Y. 1975, U.S. Ct. Appeals (2d cir.) 1975, U.S. Ct. Appeals (1st cir.) 1981, U.S. Ct. Appeals (fed. cir.) 1984, U.S. Patent and Trademark Office 1983, U.S. Supreme Ct. 1984, U.S. Dist. Ct. (ea. dist.) Mich. 1985, U.S. Dist. Ct. (no. dist.) Calif. 1995. Tech. rep. computer timesharing On-Line Systems, Inc., N.Y.C., 1969-70; assoc. Kelley Drye & Warren, N.Y.C., 1973-77; assoc. Fish & Neave, N.Y.C., 1977-82, ptnr., 1983—; adj. prof. NYU Sch. Law, 1990—, mem. adv. coun. Engelberg Ctr. Innovation Law & Policy, 1996—; participating atty. Cmty. Law Offices, N.Y.C., 1974-78; atty. Pro Bono Panel U.S. Dist. Ct. (so. dist.) N.Y., 1982-84; lectr. Practising Law Inst., N.Y.C., 1995—, Aspen Law & Bus., 1990-95, Franklin Pierce Law Sch., 1992—, Lic. Exec. Soc., 1995; chmn. bd. dirs. N.Y. Lawyers for the Pub. Interest, 1996-98, vice chair, 1998—; dir. Legal Svcs. N.Y.C., 1991-95; Mng. editor NYU Law Sch. Rev. Law and Social Change, 1972-73. Contbr. articles to profl. jours. Recipient Founder's Day award NYU Sch. Law, 1973; NSF grad. trainee John Hopkins U., 1968-69; NYU scholar, 1964-68. Mem. ABA, Assn. Bar City N.Y. (mem. environ. law com. 1978-83, trademarks, unfair competition com. 1983-86), Fed. Bar Council, Fed. Cir. Bar Assn., copyright Soc., Am. Chem. Soc., Licensing Execs. Soc., N.Y. Intellectual Property Law Assn., Univ. Club. Federal civil litigation, Patent, Trademark and copyright. Office: Fish & Neave 1251 Avenue Of The Americas New York NY 10020-1104

**MARTORANO, REBEKKA RUTH,** lawyer; b. Geneva, Sept. 13, 1967; d. Wolfgang Johannes Mittermaier and Marilyn Powers; m. Nick Martorano, Sept. 7, 1996. BA with honors, Stanford U., 1991; JD, U. Calif., Berkeley, 1994. Bar: Calif. 1994, U.S. Dist. Ct. (ea., ctrl. and no. dists.) Calif. 1995. Lawyer The Mounier Law Group, Sacramento, 1994-95, Mackenroth, Ryan & Fong, Sacramento, 1995—. Mem. ABA, Calif. State Bar Assn., Phi Beta Kappa. General civil litigation, Labor, Civil rights. Office: Mackenroth Ryan & Fong 1331 Garden Hwy Ste 300 Sacramento CA 95833-9773

**MARTORI, JOSEPH PETER,** lawyer; b. N.Y.C., Aug. 19, 1941; s. Joseph and Teresa Susan (Fezza) M. BS summa cum laude, NYU, 1964, MBA, 1968; JD cum laude, U. Notre Dame, 1967. Bar: D.C. 1968, U.S. Dist. Ct. D.C. 1968, U.S. Dist. Ct. Ariz. 1968, U.S. Ct. Appeals (9th cir.) 1969, U.S. Supreme Ct. 1977. Assoc. Sullivan & Cromwell, N.Y.C., 1967-68, Snell & Wilmer, Phienix, 1968-69; pres. Goldmar Inc., Phienix, 1969-71; ptnr. Martori, Meyer, Hendricks & Victor, P.A., Phienix, 1971-85; ptnr. Brown & Bain, P.A., Phienix, 1985-94, chmn. corp. banking & real estate dept., 1994—; chmn. bd. ILX Resorts, Inc., Phienix; bd. dirs. Firstar, Met. Bank, Phoenix, Sedona Worldwide Inc., Phoenix; chmn. ILX Inc., Varsity Clubs Am. Inc. Author: Street Fights, 1987; also articles, 1966-70. Bd. dirs. Men's Arts Coun., Phoenix, 1972—; trustee Boys' Clubs Met. Phoenix, 1974—; consul for Govt. of Italy, State of Ariz., 1987-97. Mem. ABA, State Bar Ariz., Maricopa County Bar Assn., Lawyers Com.for Civil Rights Under Law (trustee 1976—), Phoenix Country Club, Plaza Club (founding bd. govs. 1979-90). Republican. Roman Catholic. General corporate, Probate, Corporate taxation. Office: ILX Inc 2111 E Highland Ave Ste 210 Phoenix AZ 85016-4786

**MARTSON, WILLIAM FREDERICK, JR.,** lawyer; b. Carlisle, Pa., May 31, 1947; m. Deborah S. Smith, June 4, 1969; children: Alexander Fenton, Bradford Walter. Student, U. Edinburgh, Scotland, 1967-68; BA in Polit. Sci. magna cum laude, Washington & Jefferson, 1969; JD magna cum laude, U. Mich., 1972. Bar: Oreg. 1972, U.S. Dist. Ct. Oreg. 1972, U.S. Ct. Appeals (9th cir.) 1974, U.S. Ct. Claims 1973, U.S. Supreme Ct. 1979. Assoc. Davies Biggs Strayer Stoel & Boley, Portland, Oreg., 1972-74, Tonkon Torp & Galen, Portland, Oreg., 1974-78; ptnr. Tonkon Torp LLP (and predecessor firm), Portland, Oreg., 1978—; chmn. indigent representation com. U.S. Dist. Ct. Oreg. Bd. dirs., treas. Albertina Kerr Ctr., Portland, 1985-90; bd. dirs. Oreg. Hist. Soc., Portland, 1990—, treas., 1994-98, pres., 1998-99; bd. dirs., chmn. Molalla (Oreg.) Elem. Sch. Dist. # 35, 1989—; dir. Oreg. Trail Found. Fellow Internat. Soc. Barristers (bd. mem. 1999—); mem. ABA, FBA, Oreg. State Bar Assn. (chmn. com. on detention correction), Prisoners Legal Svc. of Oreg., Inc. (chmn. of the bd.), Arlington Club, Order of Coif, Phi Beta Kappa. Avocations: skiing, horseback riding. Federal civil litigation, General civil litigation, State civil litigation. Office: Tonkon Torp LLP 1600 Pioneer Tower 888 SW 5th Ave Portland OR 97204-2012

**MARTUCCI, WILLIAM CHRISTOPHER,** lawyer; b. Asbury Park, N.J., Mar. 10, 1952; s. Frank and Evelyn (Gerrity) M.; m. Julie Sessions, Aug. 2, 1980; children: Daniel Robert, William Sessions, John Andrew, James Christopher, Andrew Michael. AB magna cum laude, Rutgers U., 1974; JD with honors, U. Ark., 1977; LLM, Georgetown U., 1981. Bar: Mo. 1977. Law clk. to presiding justice Mo. Ct. Appeals, Kansas City, 1977-78; assoc. Spencer, Fane, Britt & Browne, Kansas City, 1981-86, ptnr., 1987—; mem. practice and procedure com. Nat. Labor Relations Act; adj. prof. employment law U. Mo. Law Sch., Kansas City, 1988—, chair minority affairs com. 1992—. Editor-in-chief Ark. Law Rev., 1976-77; contbr. articles to profl. jours. Chmn. adv. coun. Urban League Greater Kansas City Tng. Ctr., chmn. mentor program, 1988—; mem. Kansas City Civic Coun.; mem. Kansas City Tomorrow Leadership Program, 1992-93; adv. bd. Boys and Girls Club Kansas City. Served to lt. JAGC, USN, 1978-81. Mem. ABA, Mo. Bar Assn. (exec. com. continuing legal edn. 1987—, chair 1993—), Kansas City Bar Assn. (chmn. continuing legal edn. 1984-86, mem. exec. com. 1985-87, leadership award 1985, chmn. labor and employment law com. 1988-90, Pres. award 1992), Lawyers Assn. Kansas City (mem. exec. com. young lawyers sect. 1981-82), Nat. Inst. Mcpl. Law Officers (vice-chmn. labor rels. and pers. law com. 1988-90), Kansas City Club, Homestead Country Club, Rotary. Republican. Roman Catholic. Club: Kansas City. Labor, Federal civil litigation, General civil litigation. Home: 1251 W 59th St Kansas City MO 64113-1148 Office: Spencer Fane Britt & Browne 1400 Commerce Bank Bldg 1000 Walnut St Ste 1400 Kansas City MO 64106-2140

**MARTZ, CLYDE OLLEN,** lawyer, educator; b. Lincoln, Nebr., Aug. 14, 1920; s. Clyde O. and Elizabeth Mary (Anderson) M.; m. Ann Spieker, May 29, 1947; children: Robert Graham, Nancy. AB, U. Nebr., 1941; LLB, Harvard U., 1947. Bar: Colo. 1948, U.S. Ct. Appeals (D.C. cir.) 1968, U.S. Supreme Ct. 1969. Prof. U. Colo., Boulder, 1947-58, 60-62; jud. adminstr. State of Colo., Denver, 1959-60; ptnr. Davis, Graham & Stubbs, Denver, 1962-67, 69-80, 81-87, of counsel, 1988—; asst. atty. gen. U.S. Dept. Justice, Washington, 1967-69; solicitor U.S Dept. Interior, Washington, 1980-81; exec. dir. dept. natural resources State of Colo., 1987; adj. prof. U. Denver, 1961-79, U. Colo., Boulder, 1988-96; cons. Pres. Materials Policy Commn., 1951; mem. Colo. Adv. Bd. Bur. Land Mgmt., 1967-69; bd. dirs. Natural Resources Law Ctr. Author: Cases and Materials on Natural Resources Law, 1951, Water for Mushrooming Populations, 1954; co-author: American Law of Property, 1953, Water and Water Rights, 1963; editor, co-author: American Law of Mining, 1960. Co-chmn. Jud. Reorganization Commn., 1961-63; elder Presbyn. Ch., Boulder; pres. Rocky Mountain Mineral Law Found., 1961-62, others. Comdr. USN, 1942-58, PTO, with Res. Decorated Silver Star, Bronze Star, Letter of Commendation. Mem. ABA (chmn. natural resources sect. 1985-86), Fed. Bar Assn., Am. Health Lawyers Assn., Colo. Bar Assn. (chmn. water sect. 1957, chmn. mineral sect. 1961, award of merit 1962), Nat. Mining Assn. (Disting. Svc. award 1997), Order of Coif, Phi Beta Kappa. Democrat. Avocations: horticulture, woodworking, mountaineering, skiing. Oil, gas, and mineral, Environmental, Real property. Home: 755 6th St Boulder CO 80302-7416 Office: Davis Graham & Stubbs PO Box 185 Denver CO 80201-0185

**MARVAR, RAYMOND JAMES,** lawyer; b. Cleve., June 7, 1954; s. John K. and Helen (Hricisin) M.; m. Diana Lynn Goebel, Sept. 12, 1987; children: John G. Marvar, Kerry Ciaccia, Lindsey Ciaccia, Abbey Ciaccia. BS, Bowling Green (Ohio) State U., 1976; JD, Notre Dame (Ind) U., 1979. Bar: Ohio 1979, U.S. Dist. Ct. (no. dist.) Ohio 1980, U.S. Ct. Appeals (D.C. cir.) 1980, U.S. Ct. Appeals (6th cir.) 1984. Atty. advisor U.S. Dept. of Labor, Washington, 1980-82; assoc. Arter & Hadden, Cleve., 1982-89, ptnr., 1990-93; gen. counsel Fairview Health Sys., 1993—; acting assoc. gen. counsel U. Hosps. of Cleve., 1987. Speaker in field. Mem. Citizens League of Cleve., 1982—, Greater Cleve. Growth Assn., 1982—, Chesapeake Bay Found., Annapolis, Md., 1985—, Ohio Boys Town, 1996—; tchr. St. Christopher's Parish Sch. of Religion, Rocky River, Ohio, 1987-94. Frohman scholar Bowling Green (Ohio) State U., 1976. Mem. ABA, Ohio Bar Assn., Nat. Health Lawyers Assn., Am. Hosp. Assn., Cleve. Assn. Civil Trial Attys., Ohio Assn. Civil Trial Attys., Def. Rsch. Inst., U. Notre Dame Alumni Assn. Avocations: boating, fishing, tennis. Personal injury, Product liability, Admiralty. Office: Fairview Health Sys 18101 Lorain Ave Cleveland OH 44111-5612

**MARVEL, KENNETH ROBERT,** lawyer, corporate executive; b. July 5, 1952; s. Robert and Kay Marvel. AB, Dickinson Coll., 1974; JD, Harvard U., 1977. Bar: Tex. 1977. Ptnr. Jenkens & Gilchrist, Dallas, 1977-85; chmn., CEO Fitz & Floyd Silvestri Inc., Dallas, Tex., 1985-96; mng. dir., COO Dallas Inst. Humanities and Culture, 1996-98; mng. dir. Law Offices Kenneth R. Marvel, Dallas, 1996—; chmn., CEO Petites Choses, Ltd., Chgo., 1998—; hon. consul Republic of Korea, 1994—. Bd. dirs. USA Film Festival, Dallas, 1984-85; bd. advisers Dickinson Coll., Carlisle, Pa., 1989-94, trustee, 1994—; bd. dirs., past pres. Nat. Tabletop Assn., 1990-96; trustee Dallas Inst. Humanities and Culture, 1990-99; bd. dirs. Dallas Citizens Coun., 1995-96; bd. dirs. So. Dallas Devel. Corp., 1993-98. Mem. Tex. Bar Assn., Dallas Bar Assn., Dallas Arboretum, Kimball Mus. Avocations: constitutional law, art, wine, literature, philosophy. General corporate, Securities, Entertainment. Home: 7220 Tokalon Dr Dallas TX 75214-3560 Office: Petites Choses Ltd 1528 W Adams St Chicago IL 60607-2410

**MARVEL, L. PAIGE,** judge; b. Easton, Md., Dec. 6, 1949; d. E. Warner Marvel and Louise Harrington Harrison; m. Robert H. Dyer, Jr., Aug. 9, 1975; children: Alex W. Dyer, Kelly E. Dyer. BA magna cum laude, Notre Dame Coll., 1971; JD with honors, U. Md., 1974. Bar: Md. 1974, U.S. Dist. Ct. Md. 1974, U.S. Tax Ct. 1975, U.S. Ct. Appeals (4th cir.) 1977, U.S. Supreme Ct. 1980, U.S. Ct. Claims 1981, D.C. 1985. Assoc. Garbis & Schwait, P.A., Balt., 1974-76, shareholder, 1976-85; shareholder Garbis, Marvel & Junghans, P.A., Balt., 1985-86, Melnicove, Kaufman, Weiner, Smouse & Garbis, P.A., Balt., 1986-88; ptnr. Venable, Baetjer and Howard LLP, Balt., 1988-98; judge U.S. Tax Ct., Washington, 1998—; bd. dirs. Loyola/Notre Dame Libr., Inc.; mem. U. Md. Law Sch. Bd. Vis., 1995—; mem. adv. com. U.S. Dist. Ct. Md., 1991-93. Co-editor procedure dept. Jour. Taxation, 1989-98; contbr. chpts. to books, articles to profl. jours. Active Women's Law Ctr., 1974-85, Md. Dept. Econ. and Community Devel. Adv. Comm., 1978-80. Recipient recognition award Balt. Is Best Program, 1981; named One of Md.'s Top 100 Women, The Daily Record, 1998. Fellow Am. Bar Found., Am. Coll. Tax Counsel (regent 1995-98); mem. ABA (sect. taxation coun. dir. 1989-92, vice-chair com. ops. 1993-95, Disting. Svc. award), Am. Law Inst. (advisor Ali restatement of law third, law governing lawyers), Md. Bar Assn. (chmn. taxation sect. 1982-83, bd. dirs. 1988-90, 96-98, Disting. Svc. award), Md. Bar Found., Balt. Bar Assn. (at-large exec. coun.), Am. Tax Policy Inst. (trustee 1997-98), Serjeant's Inn,

Rule Day Club. Avocations: golf, music, travel. Home: 7109 Sheffield Rd Baltimore MD 21212-1628 Office: US Tax Ct 400 2D St NW Washington DC 20217-0001

**MARVIN, CHARLES ARTHUR,** law educator; b. July 14, 1942; s. Burton Wright and Margaret Fiske (Medlar) M.; m. Elizabeth Maureen Woodrow, July 4, 1970 (div. July 1987); m. Elizabeth Dale Wilson, Mar. 20, 1999; children: Colin, Kristin. BA, U. Kans., 1964; postgrad., U. Toulouse, France, 1964-65; JD, U. Chgo., 1968, M of Comparative Law, 1970. Bar: Ill. 1969. Legal intern EEC, Brussels, 1970; lectr. law U. Kent, Canterbury, Eng., 1970-71; asst. prof. law Laval U., Quebec City, Que., Can., 1971-73; legal adv. constnl., internat. and adminstrv. law sect. Can. Dept. Justice, Ottawa, Ont., 1973-76; assoc. prof. law U. Man., Winnipeg, Can., 1976-77; dir. adminstrv. law project Law Reform Commn., Ottawa, 1977-80; prof. law Villanova (Pa.) U., 1980-83; dir. Adminstrv. Law Reform Project Can. Dept. Justice, 1983-85; prof. law Ga. State U., 1985—, assoc. dean, 1987-89; legal advisor on administrv. code revision to Govt. of Kazakhstan, 1993; law faculty devel. adviser to Bulgaria, 1993; dir. internat. human rights law summer program Regent U. Sch. Law, 1998; vis. lectr., Ivory Coast, 1998—. Chair coun. on ministries Glenn Meml. United Meth. Ch.; acad. mem. Southwestern Legal Found. Fulbright scholar U. Toulouse, 1964-65, Summerfield scholar, 1961-64, U. Chgo. scholar, 1965-68; Ford Found. Comparative Law fellow, 1968-70. Mem. ABA, Ill. Bar Assn., Chgo. Bar Assn., Am. Soc. Internat. Law, Am. Fgn. Law Assn., Internat. Bar Assn., Internat. Law assn., Can. Bar Assn., Can. Coun. on Internat. Law, Phi Beta Kappa, Omicron Delta Kappa, Phi Beta Delta, Phi Delta Phi. Office: Ga State U Coll Law PO Box 4037 Atlanta GA 30302-4037

**MARVIN, CHARLES RODNEY, JR.,** lawyer; b. Elizabeth, N.J., Feb. 26, 1953; s. Charles Rodney Sr. and Doris Marie (Richards) M.; m. Carol Ann Welteroth, Aug. 30, 1975; children: Kathryn, Kristin, Cynthia, Gregory. BA in Econs., Mich. State U., 1975; JD, Boston U., 1978; LLM in Mil. Law, Judge Advocate Gen. Sch., 1987; LLM in Govt. Contracts, George Washington U., 1995. Bar: N.J. 1982, U.S. Dist. Ct. N.J. 1982, U.S. Ct. Mil. Appeals 1982, U.S. Ct. Appeals (fed. cir.) 1994, D.C. 1996, U.S. Ct. Claims (fed. cir.) 1996. Commd. 2nd lt. U.S. Army, 1975, advanced through grades to lt. comdr., 1993; nuclear missile officer U.S. Army, Schwaebisch Gmund, Germany, 1979-82; mil. prosecutor U.S. Army, Fort Sill, Okla., 1983-86; sr. def. counsel U.S. Army Trial Def. Svc., Ft. Polk, La., 1987-89; trial counsel, chief protest br. U.S. Army Contract Appeals Divsn., Arlington, Va., 1990-94; ptnr. Venable, Baetjer, Howard & Civiletti, Washington, 1994—. Mem. ABA (vice-chair, bid protest com., pub. contract law sect. 1992-93), FBA, Bd. Contract Appeals Bar Assn. (bd. govs. 1993-96), Fed. Cir. Bar Assn., John Carroll Soc., Nat. Contract Mgmt. Assn. Roman Catholic. Avocations: musical composing, adult education, golf. General civil litigation, Government contracts and claims, Computer. Office: Venable Baetjer et al 1201 New York Ave NW Ste 1000 Washington DC 20005-6197

**MARVIN, DAVID EDWARD SHREVE,** lawyer; b. Jan. 6, 1950; s. George Charles Marvin and Shirley Mae (Martin) Schaible; m. Mary Anne Kennedy, Sept. 16, 1972; 1 child, John. BS cum laude, Mich. State U., 1972; JD cum laude, Wayne State U., 1976. Bar: Mich. 1976, U.S. Dist. Ct. (ea. dist.) Mich. 1976, U.S. Dist. Ct. (we. dist.) Mich. 1978, U.S. Ct. Appeals (7th cir.) 1977, U.S. Ct. Appeals (6th cir.) 1979, U.S. Supreme Ct. 1979, U.S. Ct. Appeals (D.C. cir.) 1982, D.C. 1982. Asst. mgr. Alta Supply Co., Lansing, 1972-73; rsch. asst. Wayne State U., Detroit, fall 1975; jud. intern U.S. Dist. Ct., Detroit, summer 1975; shareholder Fraser Trebilcock Davis & Foster, P.C., Lansing, 1976—, chair Govt. Law dept., 1992—, v.p., 1997—, also bd. dirs.; pres. Red Rock Prodns., Inc., 1990-94; lectr. Inst. CLE, 1989. Exec. editor Wayne Law Rev., 1975-76; contbr. articles to law jours. Commr. Mich. Solar Resource Adv. Panel, Lansing, 1978-81, Mich. Commn. Profl. and Occupl. Licensure, 1981-83; chmn. Ingham County Energy Commn., Mason, Mich., 1978-80 (state bar rep. assembly 1985-88); dir., corp. sec. Friends Mich. Hist. Ctr., Inc., 1988-92; treas. Lansing Lawyer Referral Svc., 1981; state del. Nat. Solar Congress, Washington, 1978; hearing officer City of East Lansing, 1985; Tri-County Coun. of Bar Leaders (chmn. 1986); bd. dirs. East Lansing Edn. Found., 1990-92, Impression Five Sci. Mus., 1991-97; regional fin. chmn. Abraham for U.S. Senate, 1993-94, Abraham Senate 2000, 1995—; exec. bd. chief Okemos coun. Boy Scouts Am., 1996—. Recipient Disting. Vol. award Tri-County Voluntary Action Ctr., 1990, Gov.'s Minuteman award, 1990, John W. Cummiskey award State Bar Mich., 1990, George Washington Honor medal Freedoms Found., 1990; named Outstandin Young Man Am., 1984, The Outstanding Young Lawyer in Mich., 1985-86, Small Bus. Adv. Yr., C. of C., 1991; Wm. D. Traitel scholar, 1975. Fellow ABA, Am. Bar Found., Mich. State Bar Found. (life); mem. ABA, State Bar Mich. (com. chmn., sect. coun. 1982—, state chmn. 1988-89), Mich. Soc. Assoc. Execs., Ingham County Bar Assn. (pres. 1985-86), Pro Bono Lawyers Svc. (pres. 1982-83), Lansing Regional C. of C. (v.p. 1987), Mich. Audubon Soc. (bd. dirs. 1991-93), Mich. State Univ. Alumni Assn. (nat. bd. dirs. 1992—), State Capital Law Firm Group (nat. bd. dirs. 1989—, chmn. com. Can. 1990-93, chair pub. utility, energy and comm. sect. 1994—, nat. sec. 1996-97, vice-chmn. 1997-98, chmn. 1998—), Downtown Coaches Club (bd. dirs., pres. 1987), Nat. Resource Ctr. on State Laws and Regulations (nat. bd. dirs. 1993—, chmn. 1998-99), Mich. State U. Pres.'s Club, Rotary (bd. dirs. 1995-97, Paul Harris fellow), Phi Alpha Delta, Phi Eta Sigma, Theta Delta Chi (pres. 1972). Republican. Administrative and regulatory, Communications, Public utilities. Home: 1959 Groton Way East Lansing MI 48823-1347 Office: Fraser Trebilcock Davis & Foster PC Michigan Nat Towers Fl 10 Lansing MI 48933

**MARVIN, JANET L.,** lawyer; b. Falmouth, Mass., Aug. 24, 1951; d. Jack Gibson and Marilyn L. Samz; m. Max J. Marvin Sr., Oct. 6, 1969; children: Max J. Jr., Samuel A., Jason J. BS, Mt. Senario Coll., 1982; JD, U. Wis., 1982. Bar: Wis. 1986, U.S. Dist. Ct. (we. dist.) Wis. 1986—. Dist. atty. Forest County, Crandon, Wis., 1987-90; family ct. commr. Forest County, Crandon, 1990; assoc. De Bardelgben & Assocs., Park Falls, Wis., 1990-93; pvt. practice Park Falls, 1993—. Bd. dirs. Price Co. Achievement Ctr., Phillips, Wis., 1991-93, City Park Falls Task Force, 1997-98, Sr. Ctr. Task Force, Park Falls, 1998—. Roman Catholic. General practice, Family and matrimonial, General corporate. Home: 349 3rd Ave S Park Falls WI 54552-1229 Office: 177 Division St Ste 100 Park Falls WI 54552-1268

**MARVIN, MONICA LOUISE WOLF,** lawyer; b. San Francisco, Feb. 3, 1947; d. Andrew John and Hazel Louise (Bohannon) Wolf; m. Gregory Lewis Marvin, Aug. 17, 1969; children: Brett Lewis, Elizabeth Louise. Student, Pacific U., Forest Grove, Oreg., 1964-66, Sonoma State U., Rohnert Park, Calif., 1966-67; BA in Psychology, Chico (Calif.) State U., 1969; JD, Empire Coll., Santa Rosa, Calif., 1982. Bar: Calif. 1982, U.S. Dist. Ct. Calif. 1982. Assoc. Fitzgerald Fitzgerald and Gowen, Santa Rosa, Calif., 1982-83, Gowen and Marvin, Santa Rosa, 1983-85, Rodeno Robertson & Assocs., Napa, Calif., 1985-86; pvt. practice St Helena, Calif., 1986—; judge pro tempore Napa County Consol. Cts., Small Claims Divsn., 1991—. Bd. dirs., v.p. Cmty. Resources for Children, Napa, 1991-94; mem. Napa County Commn. on Children, Youth and Family, 1994-97; sec. St. Helena (Calif.) Rotary Found., 1994-96; mem. Napa County Dem. Ctrl. Com., 1994-98; mem. adv. bd. Napa County Vol. Ctr. Ombudsman Program, 1994-95; founder, chair St. Helena C. of C. Jumelage Com., Sister Chamber affiliation with Libourne C. of C. and Industry, France. Mem. State Bar Calif., Napa County Bar Assn. (bd. dirs. 1994), Napa Women Lawyers (past pres., sec. 1987-92), St. Helena C. of C. (bd. dirs. 1992-94), St. Helena Rotary Club (pres. 1998-99). General corporate, General practice, Estate planning. Office: PO Box 271 Saint Helena CA 94574-0271

**MARVIN, WENDY BYERS,** lawyer; b. Chgo., Aug. 26, 1957; d. Donald F. and Dorothy M. (Calahan) Byers; m. John F. Marvin, July 7, 1938; children: Rebecca C., John F. Jr. BA magna cum laude, Stephens Coll., 1978; JD, U. Mo., Columbia, 1981. Bar: Mo. 1981. Assoc. Watson, Ess, Marshall & Enggas, Kansas City, Mo., 1981-87; ptnr. Watson & Marshall, L.C., Kansas City, 1988-96; of counsel Sonnenschein Nath & Rosenthal, Kansas City, 1997—. Bd. dirs. Kansas City Symphony, 1995—, Jr. Achievement of Mid. Am., Kansas City, 1995-97, Steve Palermo Found. for Spinal Injuries, Kansas City, 1995-96. Mem. Order of Coif. Estate planning, Probate, Estate taxation. Office: Sonnenshein Nath & Rosenthal 4520 Main St Ste 1100 Kansas City MO 64111-7700

**MARX, GREGORY PAUL,** public defender, lawyer; b. Crowley, La., May 25, 1952; s. Elmo S. and Enez M. Marx; m. Paula Corley, May 2, 1980; children: Sarah, Lauren, Rebecca. BA, U. S.W. La., 1977; JD, La. State U., 1980. Bar: La., U.S. Dist. Ct. (ea. and we. dist.) La. 1980, U.S. Supreme Ct. 1997. Pres. La. Pub. Defenders Assn., Lafayette, 1994-96; chief pub. defender 15th Jud. Dist., Lafayette, 1984—; barrister Duhe Inn of Ct., Lafayette, 1995—; pvt. practice Lafayette, LA. Fellow La. Bar Assn. Office: 2014 W Pinhook Rd # S404 Lafayette LA 70508-8504

**MARX, PETER A.,** lawyer; b. N.Y.C., June 14, 1942; s. Robert L. and Helen (Sohn) M.; m. Barbara K. Marx, Dec. 21, 1974; children: Laura, Lisa. BA, Cornell U., 1965, MBA, JD, 1968. Bar: N.Y. 1969, D.C. 1970, Mass. 1980. Atty., advisor U.S. Securites & Exch. Commn., Washington, 1968-71; assoc. Shaw, Pittman, Potts & Trowbridge, Washington, 1971-74; v.p., gen. counsel Chase Econometrics and Interactive Data Corp., Waltham, Mass., 1975-85; ptnr. Goulston & Storrs, Boston, 1985-87; prin. The Marx Group, Wellesley, Mass., 1987—; dir. Info. Industry Assn., Washington, 1980-84, hon. counsel to bd., 1993—; chmn. N.E. Computer Law Forum, 1982-89; adv. bd. CNC Interactive, 1998, LifetecNet.com, 1999—, Forecasting Power, Inc., 1999—, Eye on Interactive, 1999—; bd. dirs. Equitrac Corp., Internet Alliance; host Venture Capital Quest, 1998—. Editor: Contracts in the Information Industry, 1988, II, 1990, III, 1995; mem. bd. advisors Computer Law Strategist, 1987—; info. law editor Info. Mgmt. Rev., 1987-90; host program N.E. Bus. Forum, Sta. WCAB-TV, 1991—; coord. editor The Info. Industry Deal Making Directory, 1994. Mem. ALI-ABA Computer Law Inst. (chmn. 1980-88), New Eng. Corp. Counsel Assn. (chmn. 1981-82). Computer, General corporate, Contracts commercial. Office: The Marx Group 60 Valley Rd Wellesley MA 02481-1448

**MASER, DOUGLAS JAMES,** lawyer, state official; b. Canton, Ohio, Nov. 21, 1951; s. David James and Mardell Margaret (Getz) M.; m. Gloria A. Bishop, Oct. 19, 1996; 1 child, Courtney Leigh. BA, Ohio State U.; JD, Capital U., Columbus, Ohio. Bar: Ohio 1976, U.S. Dist. Ct. (so. dist.) Ohio 1977. Asst. pros. atty. Franklin County Pros. Attys. Office, Columbus, 1975-80; assoc. Janes and Jack Law Offices, Columbus, 1980-85; pvt. practice, Columbus, 1985-88; ptnr. Day, Ketterer, Raley, Wright & Rybolt, Columbus, 1988-95; dep. adminstr. med. mgmt. and cost containment Ohio Bur. Worker's Compensation, Columbus, 1995—; legis. cons. Ohio Assn. Chiefs Police, Columbus, 1983-886, Franklin County Bd. Mental Health, Columbus, 1988-90, Ohio Fire Chiefs Assn., Columbus, 1985-90. 1st lt. U.S. Army, 1977; col. USAR. Mem. ABA, Ohio State Bar Assn., Columbus Bar Assn., Athletic Club Columbus. Republican. Avocations: computer simulations, war gaming, bicycling, hiking, swimming. Office: Ohio Bur Workers Comp 30 W Spring St Columbus OH 43215-2241

**MASERITZ, GUY B.,** lawyer; b. Balt., June 5, 1937; s. Isadore H. and Gertrude (Miller) M.; m. Sally Jane Sugar, Mar. 30, 1961; children—Marjorie Ellen, Michael Louis. BA Johns Hopkins U., 1959, M.A. in Econs., 1961; LL.B., U. Md., 1966. Bar: Md. 1966, D.C. 1968, U.S. Sup. Ct. 1975, U.S. Dist. Ct. Md. 1979. Atty., SEC, Washington, 1966-70; asst. gen. counsel securities Am. Life Ins. Assn., Washington, 1971-74; atty. eval. sect., chief legis. unit Antitrust div. U.S. Dept. Justice, Washington, 1974-78; spl. asst. U.S. atty. Alexandria, Va., 1978; sole practice, Columbia, Md., 1978—. Mem. Howard County (Md.) Charter Revision Commn., 1979. Served with USAR, 1960-66. Mem. Md. Bar Assn., D.C. Bar Assn., Howard County Bar Assn., Greater Howard County C. of C. (dir., gen. counsel 1981-84). Democrat. Author: U.S. Department of Justice Antitrust Report on Property-Liability Insurance Industry, 1977; contbr. articles to profl. jours. General corporate, Estate planning, Securities. Office: Hobbits Glen 5040 Rushlight Path Columbia MD 21044-1295

**MASI, JOHN ROGER,** lawyer; b. Bklyn., Jan. 18, 1954; s. John Roger and Evelyn (Teagno) M.; m. Sherrill Alaine Schlett, June 29, 1985; children: Roger C., Christopher J., Nicholas J. BA, Franklin & Marshall Coll., 1976; JD, Temple U., 1980. Bar: N.J. 1981, Pa. 1981, U.S. Dist. Ct. N.J. 1981. Assoc. Klinger, Nicolette, Mavroudis & Honig, Oradell, N.J., 1982-86, Gern, Dunetz, Roseland, N.J., 1986-87; ptnr. J. Roger Masi, Esq., Hackensack, N.J., 1987—. Committeeman County Rep., Ridgewood, N.J., 1982-84; mem. Ridgewood Zoning Bd. Adjustment, 1990-94; mem. Commerce and Industry Assn. N.J. Mem. ABA, N.J. State Bar Assn., Bergen County Bar Assn., Rotary. Roman Catholic. General corporate, State civil litigation, Personal injury. Office: 55 State St Hackensack NJ 07601-5426

**MASINTER, PAUL JAMES,** lawyer; b. New Orleans, June 28, 1961; s. Milton Paul Masinter and Shirley Mae (Rabé) Bradley; m. Audrey Renee Williams, Oct. 10, 1992. BA in Polit. Sci., La. State U., 1984, JD, 1987. Bar: La. 1987, U.S. Dist. Ct. (ea., mid. and we. dists.) La. 1987, U.S. Ct. Appeals (5th cir.) 1990, U.S. Supreme Ct. 1994. Law clk. to assoc. justice Hon. James L. Dennis La. Supreme Ct., New Orleans, 1987-88; assoc. McGlinchey, Stafford, New Orleans, 1988-90, Stone, Pigman, Walther, Wittmann & Hutchinson, New Orleans, 1990-95; ptnr. Stone, Pigman, Walter, Wittmann & Hutchinson, L.L.P., New Orleans, 1996—. Assoc. editor La. Law Rev., 1986-87. Bd. dirs. Save Our Cemeteries, New Orleans, 1993—, treas., 1998, pres., 1999. Mem. ABA, La. State Bar Assn. Democrat. Roman Catholic. Antitrust, General civil litigation, Product liability. Home: 1820 Octavia St New Orleans LA 70115-5660 Office: Stone Pigman Walther Wittmann & Hutchinson 546 Carondelet St Ste 100 New Orleans LA 70130-3588

**MASLEN, DAVID PETER,** lawyer; b. Quincy, Mass., Apr. 22, 1948; s. Frederick George and Catherine Elizabeth (Kelly) M.; m. Patricia Ann Ryan, June 17, 1972; children: Pamela Ryan, Julia Kelly. AB, Coll. of Holy Cross, Worcester, Mass., 1972; JD, New Eng. Sch. Law, Boston, 1976; LLM in Taxation, Boston U., 1985. Bar: Mass. 1977, U.S. Dist. Ct. Mass. 1977. Compliance officer U.S. Dept. Labor, Boston, 1975-85; atty. New Eng. Mutual Life Ins. Co., Boston, Burlington, Mass., 1985-87; sr. v.p. Aon Cons., Newburyport, Mass., 1987—. Pension, profit-sharing, and employee benefits, Taxation, general. Office: Aon Cons PO Box 926 Newburyport MA 01950-5626

**MASON, DONALD F., JR.,** lawyer; b. Florence, Ala., Feb. 26, 1954; s. Donald F. Sr. and Betty (Hill) M.; m. Cynthia Roberson, Oct. 6, 1990. BSBA with honors, U. Tenn., 1976, MBA, JD, 1979. Bar: Tenn. 1980, U.S. Dist. Ct. (ea. dist.) Tenn. 1980, U.S. Ct. Appeals (6th cir.) 1986, U.S. Tax Ct. 1986, U.S. Supreme Ct. 1991. Sole practice Kingsport, Tenn., 1980-85; ptnr. Shine & Mason, Kingsport, 1985—; prof. fin., econs., mktg., organizational behavior and bus. law East Tenn. State U., Johnson City, 1980, Va. Intermont Coll., Bristol, 1981; chmn. Kingsport Young Lawyers Conf., 1986-87; dist. 1 rep. Tenn. Young Lawyers Conf., 1987-88. Contbr. articles to profl. jours. Chmn. Sullivan County, Tenn. March of Dimes, Johnson City, 1983. Mem. ABA ( exec. com. labor law com. young lawyers div. 1987-88, exec. com. law student outreach com. 1988—), Kingsport Bar Assn., Tenn. Bar Assn. Avocations: snow skiing, water skiing, scuba diving. Labor, Federal civil litigation, General practice. Office: Shine & Mason 433 E Center St Ste 201 Kingsport TN 37660-4803

**MASON, HENRY LOWELL, III,** lawyer; b. Boston, Feb. 10, 1941; s. Henry Lowell and Fanny Crowninshield (Homans) M.; m. Elaine Bobrowicz, June 7, 1969. AB, Harvard U., 1963, LLB, 1967. Bar: Ill. 1967. Assoc. Leibman, Williams, Bennett, Baird & Minow, Chgo., 1967-72; assoc. Sidley & Austin, 1972-73, ptnr., 1973—. Republican. Federal civil litigation, State civil litigation, Trademark and copyright. Office: Sidley & Austin 1 First Natl Plz Chicago IL 60603-2003

**MASON, J. WILLIAM L.,** lawyer; b. Kittery, Maine, Apr. 14, 1940; s. Murray Lawrence and Dolores Elizabeth (Laird) M.; m. Mary Elizabeth Jordan; children: Joseph Patrick, Catherine Shannon, Brendan Michael. BA, U. N.H., 1973, MBA, 1979; JD, New Eng. Sch. Law, 1987. Molder Portsmouth (N.H.) Naval Shipyard, 1958-71, with labor rels., 1973-91; rehab. technician State of N.H., Concord, 1971-73; pvt. practice Portsmouth, 1991—. Staff sgt. N.H. Air Nat. Guard, 1974-81. Mem. ABA, Am. Trial Lawyers Assn., N.H. Bar Assn. Congregationalist. Avocation: coins. Personal injury, Criminal, Workers' compensation. Home: 27 Old Concord Tpke Lee NH 03824-6729 Office: 5 Greenleaf Woods Dr Ste 301 Portsmouth NH 03801-5442

**MASON, KIRBY GOULD,** lawyer; b. Bozeman, Mont., Feb. 21, 1964; m. Frank Mason. BS in English, BS in French, Whitman Coll., 1985; JD, U. Ga., 1989. Bar: Ga. 1989, U.S. Dist. Ct. (so. and no. dists.) Ga. Atty. Hunter Maclean Exley & Dunn, Savannah, Ga., 1989—. Ch. vol., Savannah, Ga., 1989—; pers. com. chair Rape Crisis Ctr., Savannah, 1996—. Labor, General civil litigation, Workers' compensation. Office: Hunter Maclean Exley & Dunn PC 200 E Saint Julian St Savannah GA 31401-2700

**MASON, ROBERT (BURT MASON),** lawyer; b. Ft. Worth, Aug. 17, 1948; s. Joe Lennard and Eugenia (Moss) M. BS, Tex. A&M U., 1970; MS, U. Ark., 1976; JD, St. Mary's U., San Antonio, 1979. Bar: Tex. 1979, Alaska 1979. Lawyer Pletcher, Slaybaugh, Anchorage, 1979-81, lawyer, prin., 1981-83; sole practitioner Anchorage, 1983-87; ptnr. Mason & Griffin, Anchorage, 1987—; legal advisor Dist 49A Lions Dist. and Found., Anchorage, 1990—. Capt. USAF, 1970-76, S.E. Asia. Mem. VFW, Lions (bd. dirs. 1990-93, chmn. 1984-94, v.p. 1994-95, pres. 1995-96, drug awareness chmn. 1990-95, Dist. Lion of Yr. 1990-91), Elks, Am. Legion. Insurance, Personal injury. Home: 20726 Jayhawk Dr Chugiak AK 99567-5880 Office: Mason & Griffin 1600 A St Ste 101 Anchorage AK 99501-5196

**MASON, STEVEN GERALD,** lawyer; b. Dayton, Ohio, Oct. 24, 1963; s. Robert G. and Pauline (Wise) M. BA in Polit. Sci. and History, U. Cen. Fla., 1985; JD, Nova U., 1989. Bar: Fla. 1990, U.S. Dist. Ct. (mid. dist.) Fla. 1990, U.S. Ct. Appeals (11th cir. 1992). Law clk. to Hon. G. Kendall Sharp, U.S. Dist. Ct. for Mid. Dist. Fla., Orlando, 1988; felony div. atty. Office Pub. Defender, Orlando, 1989-91; pvt. practice, Orlando, 1992—. Contbr. to profl. jours. Bd. dirs., Seminole County Humane Soc., Sanford, Fla., 1991—. Recipient Franklin Graham Pub. Defender award, 1990. Mem. ABA, NACDL, Fla. Bar (cert. criminal trial and criminal appellate specialist), Fla. Assn. Criminal Def. Lawyers, Orange County Bar Assn., Ctrl. Fla. Criminal Def. Attys. Assn. (sec. 1992-93, amicus com.). Democrat. Avocation: reading. Criminal, Constitutional. Office: 1643 Hillcrest St Orlando FL 32803-4809

**MASON, THEODORE W.,** lawyer; b. June 17, 1943. AB, Yale U., 1965; JD, U. Pa., 1972. Bar: Pa. 1972, Fla. 1987. Shareholder Greenberg Traurig, Phila. Treas., bd. dirs. Nat. Adoption Ctr., Adoption Ctr. Del. Valley, The Hill Top Preparatory Sch. Mem. Nat. Assn. Bond Lawyers (steering com. workshop, enforcement com.). Finance, Public international, Municipal (including bonds). Office: Greenberg Traurig One Commerce Sq 2005 Market St Ste 2050 Philadelphia PA 19103-7065

**MASON, THOMAS OWEN,** lawyer; b. Hudson, Mich., Oct. 31, 1951; s. Wendell Earl and Joan Margaret Mason; m. Georgia Land Wessel, June 28, 1975; children: Christine Margaret, Benjamin Thomas. BS, U.S. Mil. Acad., 1973; JD, U. Detroit, 1980. Bar: Mich. 1980, S.C. 1983, U.S. Ct. Appeals (fed. cir.) 1998, U.S. Ct. Fed. Claims 1995, U.S. Supreme Ct. 1985, D.C. Bar 1999. Commd. 2d lt. U.S. Army, 1973, advanced through grades to lt. col.; prosecutor, chief mil. justice U.S. Army Tng. Ctr., Ft. Jackson, S.C., 1980-84; asst. prof. JAG Sch., Charlottesville, Va., 1984-88; exec. sec. Joint Svc. Com. on Mil. Justice, Washington, 1989-91; sr. trial atty. Army Office of Chief Trial Atty., Arlington, Va., 1991-95; ret. U.S. Army, 1995; trial atty. civil divsn. Dept. of Justice, Washington, 1995-98; of counsel, head of litigation McAleese & Assocs., McLean, Va., 1998—. Bd. dirs., elder Grace Reformed Presbyn. Ch., Woodbridge, Va., 1990—. Decorated Legion of Merit; recipient Younger Lawyer award Fed. Bar Assn., 1987. Avocations: golf, jogging, reading, team sports, swimming. Federal civil litigation, Environmental, Government contracts and claims. Office: McAleese & Assocs 8201 Greensboro Dr Mc Lean VA 22102-3810

**MASSARE, EDWARD JOHN,** lawyer; b. Rochester, N.Y., Apr. 15, 1941; s. Edward Joseph and Viola (Cerulli) M.; m. Jean Sellitto, Mar. 11, 1972; children: Patrick, Danielle. BA, Cornell U., 1963, LLD, 1966. Bar: N.Y. Sole practitioner Rochester, 1969-72; atty. Monroe County Pub. Defenders, Rochester, 1972-75; ptnr. Cerulli & Massare, Rochester, 1975-95, sole proprietor, 1995—; panel atty. United Food & Comml. Workers Local 1, Utica, N.Y., 1977-99; arbitrator, Am. Arbitration Assn., Syracuse, N.Y., 1980-97. Bd. mem., pres. Genessee Valley Veteran's Housing Coalition, Rochester, 1990-99; mem. adv. com. Monroe County Veterans, 1991-95. Capt. U.S. Army, 1967-69, Vietnam. Decorated Bronze Star, Purple Heart. Mem. ATLA, N.Y. State Bar Assn., N.Y. State Trial Lawyers Assn., Monroe County Bar Assn. (com. chmn. 1975-80). Avocations: golf, skiing, hiking. General practice, General civil litigation, Personal injury. Office: Cerulli & Massare 134 S Fitzhugh St Rochester NY 14608-2268

**MASSARO, TONI MARIE,** dean, law educator. BS, Northwestern U., 1977; JD, Coll. William and Mary, 1980. With Vedder, Price, Kaufman and Kammholz; tchr. law Washington and Lee U., U. Fla.; prof. law U. Ariz., Tucson, 1989—; vis. prof. law Stanford U., U. N.C., Johann Goethe U., Frankfurt, West Germany. Author: Constitutional Literacy: A Core Curriculum for a Multi-Cultural Nation; contbr. numerous articles to law revs. Fax: 520-621-9140. E-mail: massaro@law.arizona.edu. Office: U of Ariz James E Rogers Coll Law PO Box 210176 Tucson AZ 85721-0176*

**MASSEL, ELIHU SAUL,** lawyer; b. Bklyn., May 3, 1940; s. Ezekiel and Sadie (Sutta) M.; m. Matilda Montefiore, May 15, 1968; children: Morris, Richard, Tracy. BA, Alfred U., 1962; JD, NYU, 1965. Bar: N.Y. 1966, U.S. Dist. Ct. (ea. dist.) N.Y. 1967, (so. dist.) N.Y. 1967, (no. dist.) N.Y. 1970, (we. dist.) N.Y. 1970, U.S. Ct. Appeals (2d cir.), 1967, U.S. Supreme Ct. 1970. Law guardian Legal Aid Soc., Bklyn., 1966-67; assoc. Law Offices of Henry Abrams, N.Y.C., 1967-69; asst. atty. gen. N.Y. State Dept. Law, N.Y.C., 1969-72; pvt. practice, N.Y.C., 1972—; lectr. N.Y. County Lawyers Assn., N.Y.C., 1982-96. Vice-pres. Am. Youth Hostels, Inc., Washington, 1970-79; bd. dirs., past pres. Met. N.Y. Coun. Am. Youth Hostels, Inc., 1969-90; trustee N.Y.C. chpt. Leukemia Soc. Am., 1976-96. Recipient Pro Bono award U.S. Dept. Justice, 1997, 98, Pro Bono award Am. Immigration Lawyers Assn., 1998. Mem. ABA, N.Y. State Bar Assn. (Pro Bono award 1996), Assn. Bar City N.Y., Queens County Bar Assn., Am. Immigration Lawyers Assn. (chmn. N.Y.C. chpt. 1976-77, N.Y.C. chpt. Pro Bono award 1996). Jewish. Avocations: hosteling, bicycling, photography, numismatics. Immigration, naturalization, and customs. Office: 122 E 42nd St New York NY 10168-0002

**MASSENGALE, ROGER LEE,** lawyer; b. Somerset, Ky., Mar. 23, 1953; s. Wendell Howard and Norma Jean (Neely) M.; m. Debra Kaye Marcum, Mar. 19, 1978; children: Sarah Anne, Jessica Claire. BA, U. Ky., 1975; JD, Capitol U., 1979. Bar: Ky. 1979, U.S. Dist. Ct. (ea. dist.) Ky. 1980, U.S. Ct. Appeals (6th cir.) 1986. Assoc. Lovelace, Carroll & Peck, Monticello, Ky., 1979-80; asst. county atty. Wayne County, Monticello, 1979-80; region counsel Ashland (Ky.) Exploration, Inc., 1980-83; atty. Ashland Oil, Inc., 1983-85; assoc. Wells, Porter & Schmitt, Paintsville, Ky., 1985-88, ptnr., 1988-94; pvt. practice Law Offices Roger L. Massengale, Paintsville, 1994—. Bd. dirs. Parents Anonymous Ea. Ky., Ashland, 1984, Tri-State Fair and Regatta, Ashland, 1983-85; past chmn. adminstrv. bd. First United Meth. Ch., Paintsville, lay del. to Ky. Ann. Conf. Mem. ABA, Ky. Bar Assn. (mem. ho. dels. 1991-98), Ky. Acad. Trial Attys., Johnson County Bar Assn., Def. Rsch. Inst. Avocations: fly fishing, backpacking, wood working. General civil litigation, Personal injury, Insurance. Home: 208 4th St Paintsville KY 41240-1150

**MASSENGILL, ALAN DURWOOD,** lawyer; b. Four Oaks, N.C., Feb. 16, 1937; s. Percy Bryant and Bettie Pearl (Parker) M.; children: Skip, Alan, Brian, Craig; m. Barbara Ann Berdner, Dec. 20, 1974. BS in Econs., U. Md., 1964, JD, 1966. Bar: Md. 1966, U.S. Ct. Appeals (4th cir.) 1968, U.S. Supreme Ct. 1972, U.S. Dist. Ct. D.C. 1979. Law clk. 6th Jud. Ct., Rockville, Md., 1966-67; pvt. practice Gaithersburg, Md., 1967—. Contbr. articles to profl. jours. Mem. ABA (mediation arbitration com. 1981-95), Md. Bar Assn. (spl. com. on alternative dispute resolution 1993-95), Md. Trial Lawyers Assn., Montgomery County Bar Assn. (mediation subcom. 1980-83, coms.), Frederick County Bar Assn. Avocations: writing, carving, guitar, birding, hiking. Family and matrimonial, Personal injury, Alternative dispute resolution. Office: 2 Professional Dr Ste 239 Gaithersburg MD 20879-3422

**MASSENGILL, MYERS NEWTON,** lawyer; b. Blountville, Tenn., July 12, 1941; s. Raymond McClellan and Mary Louise (Myers) M.; m. Janet Chase Tallman, June 11, 1967; children: Myers Newton II, Lee Carter, John David. BA, East Tenn. State U., 1963; JD, U. Tenn., 1964. Bar: Tenn. 1965, U.S. Dist. Ct. (ea. dist.) Tenn. 1965, U.S. Ct. Appeals (6th cir.) 1981, U.S. Tax Ct. 1981, U.S. Supreme Ct. 1986. Pres. Massengill, Caldwell & Hyder, P.C., Bristol, Tenn., 1965—; emeritus mem. bd. dirs. Legal Svcs. Upper East Tenn., Johnson City. Mem. Sullivan County Dem. Party, 1964—, chmn., 1996; adv. bd. mem. Salvation Army, Bristol, 1970-98; trustee Rocky Mount Mus., Piney Flats, Tenn., 1992-98; bd. dirs. Girls, Inc., Bristol, 1993-98. Cpl. USAR, 1964-70. Mem. ABA, ATLA, Tenn. Bar Assn., Tenn. Trial Lawyers Assn., Bristol Tenn. Bar Assn. (pres. 1983), Bristol Host Lions Club (pres. 1994-95), Phi Alpha Delta. Methodist. Avocations: tennis, golf, skiing. General practice, Personal injury, Probate. Home: 117 Westover Dr Bristol TN 37620-2947 Office: Massengill Caldwell & Hyder PC 777 Anderson St Bristol TN 37620-2276

**MASSEY, HENRY NELSON,** lawyer; b. Plainfield, N.J., Apr. 25, 1954; m. Heidi Ruth Rosenberg; children: Marshall, Haley. AB, Princeton (N.J.) U., 1976; JD, Columbia U., 1979. Bar: N.J. 1979, N.Y. 1980. Assoc. Dewey Ballantine, N.Y.C., 1979-83; ptnr. Pitney, Hardin, Kipp & Szuch, Morristown, N.J., 1983—. Sec. Adath Shalom, Dover, N.J., 1989—. General corporate, Contracts commercial, Mergers and acquisitions. Office: Pitney Hardin Kipp & Szuch PO Box 1945 Morristown NJ 07962-1945

**MASSEY, KATHLEEN MARIE OATES,** lawyer; b. Chgo., Dec. 2, 1955; d. William Robert Jr. and Ethelyn Rose (Calhoun) Oates. Student, U. Claremont-Ferrand, France, 1976-77; BA cum laude, Kalamazoo Coll., 1978; JD, U. Wis., 1981. Bar: Wis. 1981, Minn. 1981, U.S. Dist. Ct. Minn. 1981, U.S. Dist. Ct. (ea. dist.) Wis. 1983. With Larkin, Hoffman, Daily & Lindgren Ltd., Mpls., 1981-87; ptnr. Habush, Habush & Davis, Milw., 1987-90; asst. gen. counsel A.O. Smith Corp., Milw., 1992-97; sr. litigation counsel Motorola Inc., Schaumburg, Ill., 1997—. Mem. ABA, Minn. Bar Assn., Wis. Bar Assn., Phi Beta Kappa, Alpha Lambda Delta, Phi Eta Sigma. Personal injury, Insurance.

**MASSEY, RAYMOND LEE,** lawyer; b. Macon, Ga., Sept. 25, 1948; s. Ford B. and Juanita (Sapp) M.; m. Lynn Ann Thielmeier, Aug. 23, 1967; children: Daniel, Caroline. BA, U. Mo., St. Louis, 1971; JD, U. Louisville, 1974. Bar: Mo. 1974, Ill. 1976, U.S. Dist. Ct. (ea. and we. dists.) Mo. 1974, U.S. Dist. Ct. (so. dist.) Ill. 1976. Assoc. Thompson & Mitchell, St. Louis, 1974-79; ptnr. Thompson & Mitchell (now Thompson & Coburn), St. Louis, 1979—. Mem. Maritime Law Assn. of U.S. (bd. dirs., chmn. ocean and river towing). Admiralty, General civil litigation, Environmental. Home: 3 Wild Rose Dr Saint Louis MO 63124-1465 Office: Thompson & Coburn 1 Mercantile Ctr Ste 3400 Saint Louis MO 63101-1623

**MASSEY, TOM C.,** lawyer, real estate investor; b. San Angelo, Tex., Mar. 5, 1931; s. Guildord M. Cade and Villa (Ault) M.; m. Mary Anna Byrom, Dec. 22, 1957; children: Julie Halfmann, Alyson Stone, Byrom Cade, Will Truett. BA, U. Tex., 1959, JD, 1960. Bar: Tex. 1960. City atty. City of Graham, Tex., 1961-63; mem. Tex. State Legislature, 1973-81; mem. firm Massey, Balentine, Edwards & Psencik, P.C., San Angelo, 1983—; county judge Tom Green County, San Angelo, 1987-88. Adv. dir. Colorado river Mcpl. Water Dist., 1998—. Sgt. U.S. Army, 1951-53. Mem. State Bar Tex. (bd. dirs. 1992-95, real estate, probate and trust coun. 1996—), San Angelo Country Club, River Club, San Angelo Rotary club (past pres.). Methodist. Avocations: playing piano, welding, stock farming. Office: Massey Balentine et al 202 W Twohig Ave San Angelo TX 76903-6439

**MASSIE, MICHAEL EARL,** lawyer; b. Stambaugh, Mich., Aug. 12, 1947; s. Glen E. and Bernice L. (Lambert) M.; m. Vicki L. Colmark, June 11, 1977; children: Christopher, Adam. BA, U. Ill., 1969, JD, 1972. Bar: Ill. 1972, U.S. Dist. Ct. (cen. dist.) Ill. 1989, U.S. Ct. Appeals (7th cir.) 1989. Pvt. practice Galva, Ill., 1972—; dir., sec. Community State Bank Galva, 1980—. Fellow Am. Bar Found., Ill. Bar Found.; mem. ABA (chair, coun. mem. gen. practice sect. 1989—), Ill. State Bar Assn. (chmn. gen. practice sect. 1980, chmn. agrl. law com. 1980), Ill. Farm Legal Assistance Found. (chmn. bd. 1985-98). Republican. Avocations: tennis, handball. General practice, Agriculture. Office: 115 NW 3rd Ave Galva IL 61434-1325

**MASSLER, HOWARD ARNOLD,** lawyer, corporate executive; b. Newark, July 22, 1946; s. Abraham I. and Sylvia (Botwin) M.; children: Justin Scott, Jeremy Ross. BA, U. Pa., 1969; JD, Rutgers U., 1973; LLM in Taxation, NYU, 1977. Bar: N.J. 1974, U.S. Dist. Ct. N.J. 1974, D.C. 1975, U.S. Ct. Appeals (D.C. cir.) 1975, N.Y. 1977, U.S. Dist. Ct. (we. dist.) N.Y. 1977, U.S. Tax Ct. 1977. Counsel house banking, currency and housing com., chmn. sub-com. U.S. Ho. Reps., Washington, 1974-76; tax atty. Lipsitz, Green, Fahringer, Roll, Schuller & James, N.Y.C. and Buffalo, 1977-79; pvt. practice Mountainside, N.J., 1979-89; pres. Bestway Products Inc., A.A. Records Inc., Servor Corp., 1979-85; pres., chief exec. officer, chmn. bd. Bestway Group Inc., Dover, Del., 1985-91; gen. ptnr. 26/27 Law Drive Assocs., 1988—; ptnr. Shonageri, Pearce & Massler, Hackensack, N.J., 1989-90, Mott, Pearce, Williams & Lee, Hackensack and Washington, 1990-91, Pearce & Massler, Hackensack, N.J., 1991-97; prodn. staff asst. DECCA House Ltd., London, 1968; chief exec. officer Basura Pub., Inc. (affiliated with BMI), 1974-80; arbitrator U.S. Dist. Ct. N.J., 1985—; adj. prof. law Seton Hall U., Newark, N.J., 1988-89, N.J. Inst. for Continuing Legal Edn., 1986; lectr. N.J. Inst. for Continuing Legal Edn., 1986—; assoc. dir. United Jersey Bank/Franklin State Bank, 1987—; del. adv. com. on indsl. trade and econ. devel. U.S./China Joint Sessions, Beijing, People's Republic of China, 1988. Author: QDROs (Tax and Drafting Considerations), 1986, 2nd. ed., 1987; contbr. West's Legal Forms, Vol. 7., 2d edit., 1987, 3d edit., Domestic Relations with Tax Analysis, Contemporary Matrimonial Law Issues: A Guide to Divorce Economics and Practice; tax author: Matthew Bender, NYCP-Matrimonial Actions and Equitable Distribution Actions, 1988; tax author, tax editor: Matthew Bender, Alimony, Child Support & Counsel Fees-Award, Modification and Enforcement, 1988, 2d edit., 1989, 3d edit., 1991, Matthew Bender, Valuation & Distribution of Marital Property, 1988, 89, 91, 92, 94, 95; contbg. author: How to Make Legal Fees Tax Deductible, 1988, Closely Held Corporations, Forms and Checklists, Buy-Sell Agreement Forms with Tax Analysis, 1988, The Encyclopedia of Matrimonial Practice, 1991, 4th edit., 1995; author: New York Practice Guide: Negligence, Tax Law of Compensation for Sickness and Injury, 2d edit., 1992; contbg. editor Pensions and Ins. Problems, 1984—, Taxation, 1984—, Fair$hare, 1984—, Law & Bus., Inc., 1984—; staff contbr., N.J. Law Jour., 1986—; contbr. articles to law revs. and profl. jours. Bd. dirs., legal counsel western N.Y. chpt. Nat. Handicapped Sports and Recreation Assn., 1977-79; counsel Union County, N.J., 1984-85; candidate Springfield (N.J.) Twp. Commn., 1986. Mem. ABA, N.J. Bar Assn. (vice chmn. taxation comm. family law section 1987—), N.Y. Bar Assn. (taxation com., subcom. on criminal and civil penalties), D.C. Bar Assn., Erie County Bar Assn. (sec. taxation com. 1977-79, continuing edn. lectr. taxation 1977—), Essex County Bar Assn. (tax com. 1981—), Union County Bar Assn. (chmn. tax com. 1984—). Republican. Avocation: Sports Car Club Am. formula Ford racing. Corporate taxation, Estate taxation, Personal income taxation. Home: 508 Main St PO Box 399 Boonton NJ 07005-0399 Office: 508 Main St Boonton NJ 07005-1716

**MASSUCCI, RAYMOND R.,** lawyer; b. Chgo., Sept. 20, 1943; s. Romolo A. and Dolores F. (Gasparo) M.; m. Brenda Ann Best, Aug. 6, 1966; children: Amanda Rae, Matthew Robert. BSBA, Drake U., 1966; JD, John Marshall Law Sch., Chgo., 1969. Bar: Ill. 1970, U.S. Dist. Ct. (no. dist.) Ill., U.S. Ct. Mil. Appeals 1970, U.S. Supreme Ct. 1975. Atty. USAF/U.S. Dept. Justice, Omaha, 1970-74, Smith & Carponelli, Chgo., 1974-75, Carponelli, Massucci, Krug & Blomquist, Arlington Heights, Ill., 1975-81, Massucci, Blomquist, Brown & Sherwell, Arlington Heights, 1981—. Mem. Zoning Bd. of Appeals, Village of Kildeer, Ill., 1985-86; village prosecutor Village of Lisle, Ill., 1975-84. Capt. USAF, 1970-74. Fellow Am. Acad. Matrimonial Lawyers, N.W. Suburban Bar Assn. (chmn. matrimonial law com. 1991-92), Wynstone Golf Club (bd. dirs. 1991-95, pres. 1995). Family and matrimonial. Office: Massucci Blomquist Brown & Sherwell 750 W Northwest Hwy Arlington Heights IL 60004-5343

**MASTAGLIO, PETER JAMES,** lawyer; b. Flushing, N.Y., Sept. 21, 1941; s. George Washington and Katherine (Clancy) M.; m. Deidre Mary Twomey, Apr. 3, 1971; children: James Peter, Elizabeth Clare. BA, Manhattan Coll., 1963; JD, NYU, 1968. Bar: N.Y., Mass., U.S. Dist. Ct. (ea. and so. dists.) N.Y. 1971, U.S. Ct. Appeals (2d cir.) 1975, U.S. Supreme Ct. 1977. Assoc. Cullen and Dykman, Garden City, N.Y., 1969-77, ptnr., 1977—. Chmn. bd. dirs., trustee YMCA of L.I., Huntington, N.Y., 1981—; mem. com. on character and fitness 2d, 10th and 11th Jud. Dists., Bklyn., 1986—. Capt. USMC, 1966-69. Mem. N.Y. State Bar Assn., Nassau County Bar Assn. Avocations: history, basketball. Contracts commercial. Home: 25 Kensington Rd Garden City NY 11530-4240 Office: Cullen and Dykman Ste 102 100 Quentin Roosevelt Blvd Garden City NY 11530-4850

**MASTANDREA, LINDA LEE,** lawyer; b. Chgo., June 10, 1964; d. Robert Anthony and Dorothy Jean (Kilpatrick) M. BA in Speech Comm., U. Ill., 1986; JD, IIT, 1994. Bar: Ill. 1995. Account rep. Health Chgo. HMO, Lisle, Ill., 1986-87; peer counselor Peninsula Ctr. Ind. Living, Newport News, Va., 1988-89; program mgr. Progress Ctr. Ind. Living, Oak Park, Ill., 1990-91; atty. pvt. practice, Ill., 1995—; pub. spkr., Ill., 1991—; sec. assoc. bd. Rehab. Inst. of Chgo. Athlete rep. Atlanta Paralympics, 1993-96; v.p. athlete's adv. com., assoc. bd. Rehab. Inst. Chgo., 1992—, sec., assoc. bd., 1997—; athlete rep. on exec. com. Cerebral Plasy Internat. Sport and Recreation Assn. Named Athlete of Yr. Colo. Sports Coun., Denver, 1994, Outstanding Woman in Sports YWCA DuPage Dist., DuPage County, Ill., 1995, Outstanding Chgo. Women in Sports Crohn's and Colitis Found., 1997; recipient IOC Pres. Disabled Athlete award U.S. Sports Acad., Mobile, Ala., 1995, USCPAA Female Athlete of Yr., 1995. Mem. U.S. Cerebral Palsy Athletic Assn. (v.p. 1994—), Nat. Italian Bar Assn., Justinian Soc. Lawyers, Chgo. Bar Assn., ISBA. Avocations: wheelchair track world-record holder 100, 200, 400, 800 and 1500 meters; Paralympics gold medalist 200M, 1996. Labor, Civil rights, Education and schools. Address: 3660 N Lake Shore Dr Apt 3710 Chicago IL 60613-5316

**MASTERS, BARBARA J.,** lawyer; b. Denver, July 17, 1933; d. Richard P. and Ruth Ann (Savage) Johnson; children: Eliot, Joan. BA, Middlebury Coll., 1955; JD, U. Conn., 1976. Bar: Conn. 1976, U.S. Dist. Ct. Conn. 1976. Assoc. Maruzo & Lucas, Norwich, Conn., 1976-80; pvt. practice Norwich, 1980—; prin. Masters and Benson, 1994—; mem. Conn. Coun. for Divorce Mediation. Bd. dirs. United Cmty. Svcs., Norwich, 1980-87, Women's Ctr. Southeastern Conn., New London, 1983-89, Madonna Pl., Norwich, 1989-93; vice-chmn. Lebanon (Conn.) Bd. Fin., 1984-88; mem. People to People del. women lawyers to China, 1986, Norwich Arts Coun., 1989-93; alt. Old Lyme Zoning Bd. Appeals, 1993-97, Old Lyme Dem. Town Com., 1994—. Mem. Conn. Bar Assn., New London County Bar Assn. (pres. 1998-99). Unitarian. Avocations: sailing, walking, third world travel. State civil litigation, Family and matrimonial, Real property. Home: 9 Stonewood Rd Old Lyme CT 06371-1846 Office: 199 W Town St Norwich CT 06360-2106 *Notable cases include: Mallory v. Mallory, 207 Conn. 48, 539 A 2d 995, 1988, in which the normal civil standard of proof is applicable to the issue of restricted visitation with a child whom the parent has been accused of sexually abusing, where that parent retains some visitation rights.*

**MASTERS, JOHN ELLERY,** lawyer; b. Torrington, Wyo., Mar. 29, 1953; s. William Dale Jr. and Emma Rose Masters; children: Mark Mitchell, Charles Stephen. BS in Acctg. with honors, U. Wyo., 1975, JD with honors, 1979. Bar: Wyo. Staff acct. McGladrey, Hanson & Dunn, Casper, Wyo., 1975-76; atty. Dray, Madison & Thomson, Cheyenne, Wyo., 1979-89; v.p., gen. counsel High Plains Capital Corp., Laramie, Wyo., 1990-95; pvt. practice law Cheyenne, 1996—. Vice-chancellor Episcopal Diocese Wyo., Laramie, mem. diocesan coun.; founding dir. Wyo. Com. for Prevention Child Abuse, Cheyenne, 1982-85; dir. Goodwill Industries Wyo., Cheyenne, 1984-87, Rotary Club, Cheyenne, 1989, Enterprise Ctr. Laramie County, Cheyenne, 1997—; dir., mem., v.p. St. Mark's Centennial Found., 1996—; dir., fin. com. mem. Found. for the Episcopal Diocese Wyo., 1998—. Thurman Arnold scholar U. Wyo., Laramie, 1978-79. Mem. S.E. Wyo. Estate Planning Coun. (past pres., dir. 1987-88), Greater Cheyenne C. of C. (past com. chmn.). Avocations: tennis, gardening, pets. E-mail: John@Johnmasters.law.com. Fax: 307-638-1975. Office: 211 W 19th St Ste 326 Cheyenne WY 82001-4433

**MASTERSON, KENNETH RHODES,** lawyer; b. Memphis, Feb. 22, 1944; s. H. Byron and Mary (Rhodes) M.; children—Michael K., Elizabeth Megel, Grace Megel. BA, Westminster Coll., 1966; JD, Vanderbilt U., 1970. Bar: Mo. 1970, Tenn. 1976. Ptnr. Thomason, Crawford & Hendrix, Memphis, 1976-79; v.p. legal Fed. Express Corp., Memphis, 1980-81, sr. v.p., gen. counsel, 1981-93, sr. v.p., gen. counsel and sec., 1993-96, exec. v.p., gen. counsel and sec., 1996-98; exec. v.p., gen. counsel and sec. FDX Corp., Memphis, 1998—. Mem. ABA, Mo. Bar Assn., Am. Corp. Counsel Assn. General corporate. Home: 8679 Classic Dr Memphis TN 38125-8824 Office: FDX Corp 6075 Poplar Ave Ste 300 Memphis TN 38119-0113

**MASTERSON, WILLIAM A.,** judge; b. N.Y.C., June 25, 1931; s. John Patrick and Helen Audrey (O'Hara) M.; m. Julie Dohrmann Cosgrove; children: Mark, Mary, Timothy, Barbara. BA, UCLA, 1953, JD, 1958. Bar: Calif., U.S. Supreme Ct. Assoc. Sheppard, Mullin, Richter & Hampton, L.A., 1958-62; ptnr., 1962-79; ptnr. Rogers & Wells, 1979-83, Skadden, Arps, Slate, Meagher & Flom, 1983-87; judge L.A. Superior Ct., 1987-92, justice Ct. Appeal, 1993—. Author, editor: Civil Trial Practice: Strategies and Techniques, 1986. With inf. U.S. Army, 1953-55. Fellow Am. Coll. Trial Lawyers; mem. Order of Coif. Office: Ct Appeal 300 S Spring St Los Angeles CA 90013-1230

**MASTERTON, LUCINDA CRONIN,** lawyer; b. Proctor, Vt., May 18, 1950; d. John Donald and Elsie Lipstein M.; m. Lindsay Morris, Mar. 16, 1998; 1 child: Rachael Leigh. BA, Northwestern U., 1972; JD, W. Va. U., 1981. Bar: Ky. 1982. Law clerk to Hon. K.K. Hall Charleston, W. Va., 1981-82, law clerk to Hon. Edwin Flowers, 1982; assoc. Goodwin & Goodwin, Charleston, W. Va., 1982-83, Lexington, Ky., 1989-93; ptnr., assoc. Vimont & Wills, Lexington, Ky., 1983-89; pvt. practice Lexington, Ky., 1993—; trustee Chpt. 7 Bankruptcy, Ea. Dist. Ky., Lexington, 1989—. Mem. Jr. League, Parkersburg, Charleston, W. Va., Lexington, Ky., 1978-90. Mem. Fayette County Bar Assn. Avocations: horseback riding, gardening. Bankruptcy, Toxic tort, Personal injury. Office: 4857 Paynes Mill Rd Lexington KY 40510-9641

**MASTIN, SCOTT JOSEPH,** lawyer; b. Cleve., Feb. 9, 1948; s. Donald Walter and Maxine Mastin. BA in Bus., Ohio U., 1974, JD, 1977. Bar: Ohio 1977. Ptnr. Bowers & Mastin, New Philadelphia; pros. atty. Tuscaramas Pros. Office, New Philadelphia, 1977—. Capt. U.S. Army, 1967-75. Mem. ABA, Ohio State Bar Assn., Tuscaramas County Bar Assn. Criminal, Family and matrimonial, Personal injury. Home: 1420 N Cross St Dover OH 44622-1150 Office: Bowers & Mastin Law Firm 108 E High Ave New Philadelphia OH 44663-2544

**MASTROMARCO, DAN RALPH,** lawyer; b. Saginaw, Mich., Jan. 18, 1958; s. Victor and Helen (Finkbeiner) M. Student, London Sch. of Econs., Eng., 1982; JD, U. Toledo, 1983; LLM, Georgetown U., 1985. Bar: Mich. 1983, D.C. 1984. Counsel U.S. Senate, Permanent Subcom. on Investigations, Washington, 1983-85; trial atty. Tax div. U.S. Dept. of Justice, Washington, 1985-86; asst. chief counsel for tax policy U.S. SBA, Washington, 1986-92; dir. tax and fiscal policy Jefferson Group, Washington, 1992-94; pres., CEO The Argus Group, Washington, 1994—; coord. Nat. Adv. Coun. for Small Bus., Tax Com., 1986-88; hon. mem. tax com. Small Bus. Legis. Coun., 1986-90; adj. prof. internat. mgmt. program U. Md.; exec. dir. Travel Coun. for Fair Competition; chmn. The Prosperity Inst. Author: The Art of Lobbying in Poland, 1995, Out by Its Roots, 1999; contbr. author, editor profl. jours., reports. Mem. ABA, Am. Judicature Soc., Nat. Italian Am. Bar Assn. (trustee scholarship fund, counsel, v.p.), U.S. C. of C. (tax policy com.). Roman Catholic. Office: TAG 317 Mass Ave NE Washington DC 20002-5701

**MASTROMARCO, VICTOR JOSEPH, JR.,** lawyer; b. Saginaw, Mich., Oct. 29, 1956; s. Victor Joseph Sr. and Helen (Finkbeiner) M.; m. Jill Ann Schmidt, Sept. 12, 1990; 1 child, Victor Joseph III. BA, Albion Coll., 1979; JD, Drake U., 1982. Bar: Mich., Iowa. Trial lawyer Cady, Mastromarco & Jahn, Saginaw. Mem. Mich. Bar Assn., Iowa Bar Assn. Office: Cady Mastromarco & Jahn 1 Tuscola Ave Saginaw MI 48605

**MASTRONARDI, CORINNE MARIE,** lawyer; b. Binghamton, N.Y.; d. Joseph Daniel and Frances Marie (Romano) M. BS, Liberty U., 1990; JD, Regent U., 1993. Bar: Fla. 1994, D.C. 1996. V.p. corp. affairs Va. Metro Protective Svcs., Inc., Virginia Beach; atty., pres. corp. affairs Pro Rep., Inc., Ft. Lauderdale; pvt. practice Ft. Lauderdale. Treas. Christian Legal Soc. Republican. Family and matrimonial, General corporate, Sports. Office: 912 E Broward Blvd Fort Lauderdale FL 33301-2067

**MASUD, ROBERT,** lawyer; b. Havana, Cuba, Jan. 2, 1960; came to U.S., 1963; s. Roberto and Olga (Sanchez) M. B in Bus. Adminstrn., U. Miami, 1982, MBA, 1987; JD, Boston U., 1987; postgrad., Harvard Law Sch., 1991-94. Bar: Fla. 1989, Mass. 1989, U.S. Dist. Ct. Mass 1989, U.S. Ct. Appeals (1st cir.) 1989, U.S. Dist. Ct. (so. dist.) Fla. 1991, U.S. Ct. Appeals (11th cir.) 1992, U.S. Supreme Ct. 1993, U.S. Ct. Appeals (D.C. cir.) 1994. Assoc. Kelley, Drye & Warren, Miami, Fla., 1987-88; founder, operating mgr. Masud & Co., LLC (formerly Masud & Assoc.), Boston, 1989—, Miami, 1992—; founder, prin. Masud & Co., London, 1999—; dir. New England Latin Am. Bus. Coun., Boston, 1999—; spkr. in field. Contbr. to profl. jours. Dep. gen. counsel Mass. Rep. Party, Boston, 1993-94; co-chmn. exploratory com. Dole for Pres., 1995-96; bd. dirs. Assn. Kepha, The Vatican, Rome, 1998—. U. Miami scholar, 1977-82. Mem. ABA (vice chmn. arts entertainment sports law com. 1992-95), Inter-Am. Bar Assn., Fla. Bar Assn., Mass. Bar Assn., Boston Bar Assn., Dade County Bar Assn., Alpha Lambda Delta, Phi Eta Sigma. Avocations: skiing, golfing, traveling, racquetball, magic. Private international, Finance, Securities. Office: Masud & Co LLC 60 State St Boston MA 02109-1800

**MATAN, EUGENE LOUIS,** lawyer; b. Chgo., May 29, 1931; s. Louis and Pauline (Mullen) M.; divorced; children: Douglas, Kim Matan Arnett, Marcie. BA, Ohio State U., 1953, JD summa cum laude, 1958. Bar: Ohio 1958, Fla. 1988, U.S. Tax Ct. 1959, U.S. Dist. Ohio 1959, U.S. Ct. Appeals (6th cir.) 1962, U.S. Supreme Ct. 1980; cert. civil trial lawyer. Atty. pvt. practice, Columbus, Ohio, 1958-76; ptnr. Matan, Rinehart & Smith, Columbus, 1975-84; sr. ptnr. Matan & Smith, Columbus, 1984-93, Matan, Geer &Wright, Columbus, 1993—; lectr. Ohio State U. Med. Sch., Capital U., Columbus Bar Assn., Ohio Acad. Trial Lawyers. Assoc. editor and contbr. to Ohio State Law Jour. Served as lst lt. U.S. Army, 1953-55. Fellow Ohio State, Columbus Bar Found. Fellow Am. Coll. Forensic Examiners; mem. ABA, Fla. Bar Assn., Assn. Trial Lawyers Am., Ohio Acad. Trial Lawyers, Franklin County Trial Lawyers, Am. Soc. Law and Medicine, Wedgewood Golf and Country Club. Republican. Clubs: Mannechor (Columbus). General civil litigation, General practice. Office: Matan Geer & Wright 261 S Front St Columbus OH 43215-5089

**MATARESE, LAUREN A.,** police officer, lawyer; b. Framingham, Mass., Dec. 15, 1960. BS summa cum laude, Roger Williams Coll., 1991; JD cum laude, New England Sch. Law, 1995. Bar: RI. 1996, U.S. Dist. Ct. R.I. 1997, Conn. 1997. Police officer Westerly (R.I.) Police Dept. Mem. Internat. Brotherhood Police Officers (v.p.), R.I. Bar Assn., Conn. Bar Assn., Delta Theta Phi. Avocations: softball, bicycling. Office: Westerly Police Dept 5 Union St Westerly RI 02891-2158

**MATASAR, RICHARD ALLAN,** dean, law educator; b. Chgo., June 4, 1952; s. Nathan and Evelyn (Berkowitz) M.; m. Sharon Thal, June 22, 1975; children: Miriam-Jennifer, Adam. BA, U. Pa., 1974, JD, 1977. Bar: Pa. 1977, D.C. 1978, U.S. Ct. Appeals (3d cir.) 1978. Law clk. U.S. Ct. Appeals (3d cir.), Wilkes-Barre, Pa., 1977-78; assoc. firm Arnold & Porter, Washington, 1977-80; assoc. prof. law U. Iowa, Iowa City, 1980-84, prof., 1984-91, assoc. dean for acad. affairs, 1989-91; dean Chgo.-Kent Coll. Law, Chgo., 1991-96; Levin, Mabie and Levin prof. law, dean U. Fla., Gainesville, 1996—; mem. Fla. Supreme Ct. Commn. on Professionalism, 1996—; mem. AALS Task Force on Pro Bono and Pub. Svc. Opportunities, 1997—. Contbr. to law revs. Recipient M.H. Goldstein prize U. Pa., 1977. Mem. ABA, Order of Coif, Phi Beta Kappa, Pi Gamma Mu. Home: 3901 SW 98th Ter Gainesville FL 32608-4663 Office: U Fla Coll Law PO Box 117620 Gainesville FL 32611-7620

**MATAYOSHI, CORALIE CHUN,** lawyer, bar association executive; b. Honolulu, June 2, 1956; d. Peter J. and Daisy (Look) Chun; m. Ronald F. Matayoshi, Aug. 8, 1981; children: Scot, Kelly, Alana. BA, U. Calif., Berkeley, 1978; JD, U. Calif., San Francisco, 1981. Bar: Hawaii 1981, U.S. Dist. Ct. Hawaii 1981. Trial atty. U.S. Dept. Justice Antitrust, Washington, 1981-84; assoc. Chun, Kerr, & Dodd, Honolulu, 1984-86; exec. dir. Hawaii Inst. of CLE, Honolulu, 1987-90, Hawaii State Bar Assn., Honolulu, 1990—; arbitrator Ct. Annexed Arbitration Program, Honolulu, 1992—; adv. bd. Channel 2 TV Action Line, Honolulu, 1993—. Contbr. chapters to books. Bd. dirs. Neighborhood Justice Ctr., 1994-97, mediator, 1997—. Office: Hawaii State Bar Assn 1136 Union Mall Ph 1 Honolulu HI 96813-2720

**MATEAS, KENNETH EDWARD,** lawyer; b. Aurora, Ill., May 7, 1949; s. Victor Joseph and Lois Rose (Carder) M. BA, U. Ill., 1971; JD, John Marshall Sch. of Law, 1982. Bar: Ill. 1982, D.C. 1982. Assoc. Law Offices of J. Timothy Loats, Aurora, 1982-83, Law Offices of Michael Marsh, Aurora, 1983-84; atty. Kane County States Atty.'s Office, Geneva, Ill., 1985; assoc. Law Offices of Gerard Kepple, St. Charles, Ill., 1985-89; pvt. practice, Aurora, 1989—. Mem. ABA, Ill. Bar Assn., Nat. Assn. Criminal Def. Lawyers. Republican. Roman Catholic. Lodge: KC. Criminal, Family and matrimonial, Bankruptcy. Office: 408 N Lake St Aurora IL 60506-4106

**MATEER, DON METZ,** lawyer; b. Evanston, Ill., July 29, 1945; s. Bruce DeLoss and Ann (Timson) M.; m. Dawn Rebecca Hallsten, Oct. 4, 1981 children—Andrew, Alexandra; m. Jacquelyn Susan Henkin, June 7, 1969 (div. Apr. 1981); children—Kristin, Julie. B.A., U. Mich., 1967; J.D., U. Ill., 1971. Bar: Ill. 1971, U.S. Dist. Ct. (no. dist.) Ill. 1972, U.S. Ct. Appeals (7th cir.) 1974, U.S. Supreme Ct. 1981. Assoc., Gilbert & Powers, Rockford, Ill., 1971-74; ptnr. Gilbert, Powers & Mateer, Rockford, 1975, Gilbert, Powers, Mateer & Erickson, 1976, Mateer & Erickson, 1978-90, Mateer & Assocs., 1990—; arbitrator 17th Jud. Cir. State of Ill., 1988—, mediator, 1992—. Precinct and ward coord. mayoral campaign, Rockford, 1980-84; campaign chmn. Rockford Park Dist. Commr., 1989; bd. dirs. Covenant Children's Home, 1987-93, v.p. 1990-91, pres., 1991-93, chair 100 Hole Golf Marathon fundraiser, 1994-98, mem. fund devel. com. 1994-99, mem. investment adv. com., 1996—; mem. Protestant Community Svcs, 1986-92, chmn. pers. com. 1987-89, v.p. 1989-90, pres., 1990-92; mem. Bethesda Covenant Ch., chmn. bd. Christian edn., 1986-88, v.p., 1997-99, pres., 1999—. Mem. ABA (vice chair trial techniques com. tort and ins. practice sect., judge for final rounds of the nat. appellate adv. competition 1991), Am. Arbitration Assn. (arbitrator), Winnebago County Bar Assn. (chmn. jud. liaison com. 1986-87), Ill. Bar Assn. (assembly mem. 1988-94), Assn. Trial Lawyers Am., Def. Rsch. Inst., Ill. Def. Counsel, Am. Judicature Soc., Forest Hills Country Club, U. Mich. Club (bd. dirs. 1986-92, 98—, v.p. 1989-90, 99—, pres. 1990-91 ). Democrat. Federal civil litigation, State civil litigation, Personal injury. Home: 2006 Oxford St Rockford IL 61103-4833 Office: Mateer & Assocs Enterprise Bldg 401 W State St Ste 400 Rockford IL 61101

**MATER, MAUD,** lawyer. BA in English, Case Western Reserve U., 1969, JD, 1972. Asst. gen. counsel Freddie Mac, McLean, Va., 1976-78, assoc. gen. counsel, 1978-79, v.p., dep. gen. counsel, 1979-82, v.p., gen. counsel, 1982-84, sr. v.p., gen. counsel, sec., 1984-98, exec. v.p., gen. counsel, sec., 1998—. Mem. ABA (com. corp. gen. counsel), FBA, Am. Corp. Counsel Assn. (dir.), Am. Arbitration Assn. (dir.), Ohio Bar, D.C. Bar, Conf. Bd. Coun. of Chief Legal Officers, Washington Met. Corp. Counsel Assn. Office: Freddie Mac 8200 Jones Branch Dr # Ms200 Mc Lean VA 22102-3110

**MATERNA, JOSEPH ANTHONY,** lawyer; b. Passaic, N.J., June 13, 1947; s. Anthony E. and Peggy Ann Materna; m. Dolores Corio, Dec. 14, 1975; children: Jodi, Jennifer, Janine. BA, Columbia U., 1969, JD, 1973. Bar: N.Y. 1975, Fla. 1977, U.S. Dist. Ct. (ea. and so. dists.) N.Y. 1977, U.S. Supreme Ct. 1977, U.S. Tax Ct. 1978, U.S. Ct. of Claims 1978. Trusts and estates atty. Chadbourne Parke Whiteside & Wolff, N.Y.C., 1973-76, Dreyer & Traub, N.Y.C., 1976-80, Finley Kumble Wagner Heine Underberg & Casey, N.Y.C., 1980-85; ptnr., head trusts and estates dept. Newman Tannenbaum Helpern Syracuse & Hirschtritt, N.Y.C., 1985-90, Shapiro Beilly Rosenberg Aronowitz Levy & Fox LLP, N.Y.C., 1990—; lectr. in field; expert witness in trusts and estate field ct. litigations, N.Y., 1999—. Contbr. articles to profl. jours. Chmn. planned giving com., mem. bd. govs. Arthritis

Found. N.Y. Chpt., N.Y.C., 1980—; mem. bd. trustees, corp. treas. Cath. Interracial Coun., N.Y.C., 1992—; mem. bequests and planned gifts com. Cath. Archdiocese of N.Y., N.Y.C., 1988—; corp. sec. Arthritis Found. N.Y. chpt., N.Y.C., 1997—; mem. Meml. Sloan-Kettering Nat. Trusts and Estates Assocs. Recipient Planned Giving award Arthritis Found.-N.Y. Chpt., N.Y.C., 1994, Discovery Alliance award Arthritis Found.-N.Y. Chpt., N.Y.C., 1995; named Accredited Estate Planner, Nat. Assn. Estate Planners, Marietta, Ga., 1995. Mem. ABA, Fla. Bar (trusts and estate com.), N.Y. State Bar Assn. (com. on estates and trusts), Bar Assn. of the City of N.Y. (com. on surrogate's ct.), N.Y.C. Estate Planning Coun. (lectr., author), N.Y. County Lawyers Assn. (mem. com. on trusts and estates 1979—), Queen County Bar Assn. (mem. com. trusts and estates 1990—), Am. Judges Assn. (civil ct. arbitrator N.Y.C.), Am. Arbitration Assn. (panel of arbitrators), N.Y. State Trial Lawyers Assn., Richmond County Bar Assn. (com. on surrogate's ct.), Columbia Coll. Alumni Assn. of Columbia U. (class pres. 1969—). Republican. Roman Catholic. Probate, Estate planning, Estate taxation. Home: 155 Johanna Ln Staten Island NY 10309-3604 Office: Shapiro Beilly Rosenberg Aronowitz Levy & Fox LLP 225 Broadway New York NY 10007-3001

**MATERRE, GLORIA LEANN,** lawyer, media agent; b. Chgo., June 7, 1966; d. Louis F. and Jeanne Materre. BA in Journalism, U. Wis., 1988; JD, U. Ill., 1993. Bar: Ill. 1993, U.S. Dist. Ct. (no. dist.) Ill. 1993. Account exec. Golin Harris Comm., Chgo., 1988-89, Edelman Pub. Rels., Chgo., 1989-90; law clk. Lake County (Ill.) Prosecutors Office, 1991; assoc. Landau Omahana & Kopka, Chgo., 1993-94, Berger Newmark & Fencher, Chgo., 1994; instr. legal writing John Marshall Law Sch., Chgo., 1995; pvt. practice, Chgo., 1995—. Mem. Cook County Bar Assn., Cmty. Media Work S. (bd. dirs.). Real property, Entertainment. Office: 11 E Adams St Ste 1600 Chicago IL 60603-6304

**MATES, CAROL MAXINE,** lawyer; b. N.Y.C., June 6, 1948. AB, Columbia U., 1969, JD, 1972. Bar: N.Y. 1973, Mass. 1979. Assoc. Dewey, Ballantine, Bushby, Palmer & Wood, N.Y.C., 1972-75, Trubin, Sillcocks, Edelman & Knapp, N.Y.C., 1975-77; assoc. counsel, asst. v.p. Bank of Boston, 1977-81; prin. counsel Internat. Fin. Corp., Washington, 1981—; adj. prof. law Georgetown U., Washington, 1993—; lectr. Boston U. Sch. Law - Morin Ctr. for Banking and Fin. Law, Boston, 1992—. Mem. ABA (internat. law and practice sect., coun. mem. 1999—, co-chmn. internat. investment and devel. com. 1996-98, various past offices), Washington Fgn. Law Soc. (bd. govs. 1993-95), Columbia Law Sch. Alumni Assn. of Washington (v.p. 1992-95). Avocations: travel, hiking, swimming, languages. Office: Internat Fin Corp 2121 Pennsylvania Ave Washington DC 20433-0001

**MATHENY, MARY JANE,** lawyer; b. Wauchula, Fla., May 29, 1953; d. George W. and Anna Lee (Scarborough) Marsh; m. Charles W. Matheny III, Mar. 30, 1974. BA, Fla. State U., 1974, JD with honors, 1978. Cert. travel counselor, 1990, master cruise counselor, 1992. Personnel aide Office of Gov. State of Fla., Tallahassee, 1974-75; sole practice Sebring, Fla., 1978—; travel agt. Ridge Travel Agy., Sebring, 1985-94, Paradise Travel, Sebring, Fla., 1994—; operator Bed and Breakfast, 1989-97. Bd. dirs. Staywell Clinic, 1996—. Named Outstanding Young Woman of Am., 1980-81. Mem. Fla. Bar Assn. (vice chmn. travel com. 1986-87), Highlands County Bar Assn. (pres. 1983-84, treas. 1985—), Fla. Fedn. Bus. and Profl. Women (dist. dir. 1985-86, state resolutions chmn. 1986-87), Young Career Woman, Am. Retail Travel Assn., Phi Delta Phi. Republican. Baptist. Estate planning, Family and matrimonial, Probate.

**MATHENY, TOM HARRELL,** lawyer; b. Houston; s. Whitman and Lorene (Harrell) M. BA, Southeastern La. U., 1954; JD, Tulane U., 1957; LLD (hon.), Centenary Coll., 1979, DePauw U.; LHD (hon.), Oklahoma City U., Southeastern La. U., 1998. Bar: La. 1957. Ptnr. Matheny & Pierson, Hammond, La., 1957—; gen. counsel First Guaranty Bank, 1960-83; trust counsel, chmn. bd. 1st Guaranty Bank, Hammond; v.p. Edwards & Assocs., So. Brick Supply, Inc.; faculty Southeastern La. U., Holy Cross Coll., New Orleans; lectr. Union Theol. Sem., Law Sci. Acad.; mem. com. on conciliation and mediation of disputes World Peace through Law Ctr.; Matheny lectr. in humanities series Southwestern U., Hammond, La. Contbr. numerous religious and legal articles to profl. jours. Chmn. advancement com. Boy Scouts Am., Hammond, 1960-64, mem. dist. coun., 1957-66, mem. exec. bd. Istrouma coun., 1966—, adv. com. to dist. area coun.; past pres. Tangipahoa Parish Mental Health Assn.; pres. La. Mental Health Assn., 1989—; mem. La. Mental Health Advocacy Svc.; co-chmn. La. Mental Health Advocacy Bd.; sec. Chep Morrison Scholarship Found.; mem. men's com. Japan Internat. Christian U. Found; chmn. speakers com., mem. com. on community action and crime prevention, La. Commn. on Law Enforcement and Adminstrn. Criminal Justice; campaign mgr. for Dem. gov. La., 1959-60, 63-64; bd. dirs. La. Moral and Civic Found., Tangipahoa Parish ARC, 1957-67, Hammond United Givers Fund, 1957-68, La. Coun. Chs., Southeastern Devel. Found., La. Mental Health Assn.; bd. dirs. Wesley Found., La. State U., 1965-68, 70—, chmn. bd.; trustee Centenary Coll., 1964-70, Scarritt Coll., 1975-81; pres., bd. trustees Lallie Kemp Hosp. Found., 1994—; hon. trustee John F. Kennedy Coll.; del. world conf. Nat. Assn. Conf. Lay Leaders, London, 1966, Denver, 1971, Dublin, 1976, Hawaii, 1981, del. to gen. confs., 1968, 70, 72; mem. Common Cause. Recipient Man of Yr. award Hammond, 1961, 64, also La. Jaycees, 1964, Layman of Yr. award La. Ann. Conf. United Meth. Ch., 1966, 73, Disting. Alumnus award Southeastern La. U., 1981, W.L. "Bill" May Outstanding Christian Bus. award La. Moral and Civic Found., 1996; established lectureship Matheny Lectureship in the Humanities, Southeastern La. U., 1996; scholarship named in his honor United Meth. Found. for Christian Higher Edn., Centenary Coll. and Dillard U., 1997. Fellow Harry S. Truman Libr. Inst (hon.); mem. ABA (com. on probate), La. Bar Assn. (past gen. chmn. com. on legal aid, com. prison reform), 21st Jud. Dist. Bar Assn. (past sec.-treas., v.p. 1967-68, 71), Comml. Law League Am. (past mem. com. on ethics), La. Alumni Coun. (pres. 1963-65), Acad. Religion and Mental Health, La. Assn. Claimant Compensation Attys., Southeastern La. U. Alumni Assn. (dir., pres. 1961-62, dir. spl. fund 1959-62, dir. Tongipahoa chpt.), Tulane Sch. Law Alumni Assn., Am. Assn. for Family and Marriage Therapy, Internat. Soc. Barristers, Internat. Soc. Valuers, Assn. Trial Lawyers Am., Am. Judicature Soc., Law-Sci. Inst., World Peace Through Law Acad. (com. on conciliation), Acad. Polit. Sci., Am. Acad. Polit. and Social Sci., Internat. Acad. Law and Sci., Internat. Platform Assn., UN Assn. Am. Trial Lawyers Assn., La. Hist. Assn., Friends of Cabildo, Gideons Internat., Hammond Assn. Commerce (dir. 1960-65), Intern Soc. Barristers, Intern Assn. Valuers, La. Mental Health Assn. (pres.-elect), Masons (33 degree), La. Lawyers' Club, Demolay (dist. dep. to supreme coun. 1964—, Legion of Honor), Kiwanis (v.p., dir., Layman of Yr. award 1972), Rotary, Phi Delta Phi, Phi Alpha Delta. Democrat. Methodist. Lodges: Masons, Scottish Rite (33 degree), Demolay (dist. dep. to supreme council 1964—, Legion of Honor), Kiwanis (v.p., dir., Layman of Yr. award for La., Miss. and West Tenn. 1972), Rotary. Health. Home: PO Box 221 Hammond LA 70404-0221 Office: PO Box 1598 401 E Thomas St Hammond LA 70404

**MATHES, STEPHEN JON,** lawyer; b. N.Y.C., Mar. 18, 1945; s. Joseph and Beatrice M.; m. Michele Marshall, Oct. 22, 1972 (div. 1992); children: Aaron, Benjamin; m. Maria McGarry, Dec. 19, 1992; 1 child, Sara. BA, U. Pa., 1967, JD, 1970. Bar: N.Y. 1971, Pa. 1972, U.S. Dist. Ct. (ea. dist.) Pa. 1971. U.S. Ct. Appeals (3d cir.) 1972, U.S. Ct. Appeals (5th cir.) 1985, U.S. Ct. Appeals (4th cir.) 1985, U.S. Supreme Ct. 1978. Law clk. U.S. Ct. Appeals (3d cir.), Phila., 1970-71; asst. dist. atty. major felony unit, spl. investigation unit Office of Phil. Dist. Atty., Phila., 1975; assoc. Dilworth, Paxson, Kalish & Kauffman, Phila., 1971-74, 76-77, sr. ptnr., 1977-91, mem. exec. com., 1987-90, co-chmn. litigation dept., 1987-91; ptnr. Hoyle, Morris & Kerr, Phila., 1992—; bd. dirs. The Levitt Found., 1990—, sec., 1991—. Bd. dirs., exec. com. Acad. Vocal Arts, 1993—, mem. exec. com., chmn. student aid com.; mem. legal and compliance divsn. Securities Industry Assn., 1998—. Mem. ABA, Securities Industries Assn., Pa. Bar Assn., Phila. Bar Assn. (mem. compliance divsn.), Thanatopsis Soc., Racquet Club, Germantown Cricket Club. Federal civil litigation, State civil litigation. Home: 199 Lynnebrook Ln Philadelphia PA 19118-2706 Office: Holye Morris & Kerr One Liberty Pl Ste 4900 Philadelphia PA 19103

**MATHESON, ALAN ADAMS,** law educator; b. Cedar City, Utah, Feb. 2, 1932; s. Scott Milne and Adele (Adams) M.; m. Milicent Holbrook, Aug. 15, 1960; children—Alan, David Scott, John Robert. B.A., U. Utah, 1953, M.S., 1957, J.D., 1959; postgrad. asso. in law, Columbia U. Bar: Utah 1960, Ariz. 1975. Asst. to pres. Utah State U., 1961-67; mem. faculty Ariz. State U., Tempe, 1967—; prof. law Ariz. State U., 1970—, dean, 1978-84; bd. dirs. Ariz. Center Law in Public Interest, 1979-81; bd. dirs. DNA Navajo Legal Services, 1984-97. Pres. Tri-City Mental Health Citizens Bd., 1973-74. Served with AUS, 1953-55. Mem. Utah Bar Assn., Ariz. Bar Assn., Maricopa County Bar Assn., Phi Beta Kappa, Order of Coif. Democrat. Mormon. Home: 720 E Geneva Dr Tempe AZ 85282-3737 Office: Coll Law Ariz State U Tempe AZ 85287

**MATHESON, ALAN ADAMS, JR.,** lawyer; b. Logan, Utah, Jan. 24, 1962; s. Alan Adams and Milicent Joanne (Holbrook) M. AB in Internat. Rels., Stanford U., 1985; JD, UCLA, L.A., 1989. Bar: Ariz. 1990. Spl. projects dir. Dem. Policy Commn., Washington, 1985-86; judicial clk. Hon Wm. C. Canby, U.S. Ct. Appeals (9th cir.), Phoenix, 1989-90; assoc. Brown & Bain P.A., Phoenix, 1990-93; sr. atty., environ. policy advisor Ariz. Pub. Svc. Co., Phoenix, 1993-99; atty. Ryley, Carlock & Applewhite, P.A., Phoenix, 1999—; mem. Maricopa County Permits Working Group, Phoenix, 1995-96. Editor UCLA Law Rev., 1989; contbg. author: Arizona Environmental Law Handbook, 1993. Chmn. Tempe Planning and Zoning Commn., 1993—; scoutmaster Boy Scouts Am., Tempe, 1994-96, 98-99; mem. Tempe Leadership, 1995-96; bd. dirs. Tempe Comty. Action Agy., 1995—, chmn., 1999—. Avocations: fly fishing, back packing, guitar. Environmental, Real property, Natural resources. Office: Ryley Carlock & Applewhite PA PO Box 634 Phoenix AZ 85001-0634

**MATHESON, SCOTT MILNE, JR.,** dean, law educator; b. Salt Lake City, July 18, 1953; s. Scott Milne and Norma (Warenski) M.; m. Robyn Kuida, Aug. 12, 1978; children: Heather Blair, Briggs James. AB, Stanford U., 1975; MA, Oxford U., Eng.; JD, Yale U., 1980. Bar: D.C., 1981, Utah 1986. Assoc. Williams & Connolly, Washington, 1981-85; assoc. prof. law U. Utah, 1985-91; dep. atty. Salt Lake County Attys. Office, 1988-89; vis. assoc. prof. JFK Sch. Govt. Harvard U., Cambridge, Mass., 1989-90; assoc. dean law U. Utah, 1990-93, prof. law, 1991—, dean, 1998—; U.S. atty. Dist. Utah, 1993-97; mem. adv. com. on rules of evidence Utah Supreme Ct., 1987-93, Utah Constitutional Revision Commn., 1987-93, adv. com. on the local rules of practice, U.S. Dist. Ct. Utah, 1993-97; bd. dirs. Scott M. Matheson Leadership Forum, 1990-93. Contbr. articles to profl. jours. Chair U.N. Day for State of Utah, 1991; mem. Univ. Com. on Tanner Lectures on Human Values U. Utah, 1993—, Honors Program Adv. Com. U. Utah, 1986-87, 1987-88, Adv. Bd. Hinckley Inst. Politics U. Utah, 1990-93; trustee Legal Aid Soc. of Salt Lake, 1986-93, pres., 1987; trustee TreeUtah, 1992-93; campaign mgr. Matheson for Gov., 1976, 1980; vol. state dir. Clinton/Gore '92. Recipient Up'n Comers award Zions Bank, 1991, Faculty Achievement award Burlington Resources Found., 1993, Disting. Svc. to Fed. Bar award Fed. Bar Assn., Utah chpt., 1998; named one of Outstanding Young Men of Am., 1987, 1988; Rhodes scholar. Mem. ABA, Assn. Am. Law Schs. (chair sect. on mass com. law 1993), Utah State Bar, Salt Lake County Bar Assn. (exec. com. 1986-92), Golden Key Nat. Honor Soc. (hon. 1990), Phi Beta Kappa.

**MATHEWS, DANIEL FRANCIS, III,** lawyer; b. Syracuse, N.Y., July 17, 1967; s. Daniel Francis Jr. and Marcia Ann Mathews; m. Jessica Dale, Aug. 20, 1994. BS, Lynn U., Boca Raton, Fla., 1990; JD, Syracuse U., 1993. Bar: N.Y. 1994. Atty. Mathews & Hall Law Offices, Syracuse, 1994—. Firefighter, mem. rapid intervention team Solvay (N.Y.) Fire Dept., Inc., 1996—, bd. dirs., 1997—. Mem. ABA, ATLA, N.Y. State Bar Assn., Onandaga County Bar Assn., N.Y. State Trial Lawyers Assn., Lynn U. Alumni Assn. (bd. dirs. 1994—), Ducks Unltd. (mem. com. 1996—). Avocations: hunting, fishing, outdoor activities, reading. Criminal, Personal injury, General civil litigation. Home: 817 Salisbury Rd Syracuse NY 13219-2413 Office: Mathews & Hall Law Offices 913 University Bldg Syracuse NY 13202

**MATHEWS, STANTON TERRY,** lawyer; b. May 28, 1952; m. Lisa Diane Earls, Jan. 15, 1977; children: Amy Marie, Adriane Rene, Britton Lafe, Garret Tyler. BA, Brigham Young U., 1976; JD, Western State U. Coll. Law, 1981; cert. in aviation litig., Nat. Jud. Coll., Reno, Nev. Pvt. practice law Laguna Hills, Calif., 1981—; judge pro tem Orange County Superior Ct. Mem. ATLA, Orange County Bar Assn. (lectr. 1990—), Calif. Trial Lawyers Assn., Consumer Attys. of Calif., Diplomate Million Dollar Advocates Forum, Western Trial Lawyers Assn., Orange County Trial Lawyers, Orange County Coll. Trial Advocacy. Appellate, Aviation. Office: 24012 Calle De La Plata Ste 320 Laguna Hills CA 92653-7624

**MATHEWSON, GEORGE ATTERBURY,** lawyer; b. Paterson, N.J., Mar. 31, 1935; s. Joseph B. and Christina A. (Atterbury) M.; m. Ann Elizabeth, July 31, 1975; 1 child, James Lemuel. AB cum laude, Amherst Coll., 1957; LLB, Cornell U., 1960; LLM, U. Mich., 1961. Bar: N.Y. 1963. Atty. office spl. legal assts., trial atty. FTC, Washington, 1963-65; regional atty. N.Y. State Dept. Environ. Conservation, Liverpool, 1972-73; pvt. practice, Syracuse, N.Y., 1967-72, 73—; adj. instr. bus. law Onondaga Community Coll., Syracuse, 1979-84. Bd. dirs. South Side Businessmen, 1971-72, 88-91, v.p., 1992, pres., 1993; elder Onondaga Hill Presbn. Ch., 1979, 82-85; dir. Manlius C. of C., 1995, v.p. 1997. Mem. ABA, ATLA, Fed. Bar Assn., N.Y. State Bar Assn. (state and county bar assn. coms.), Kiwanis (bd. dirs. Onondaga club 1988-89, v.p. 1989, pres. 1989-91). Patentee safety device for disabled airplanes. General practice, Real property, General civil litigation. Office: 4302 S Salina St Syracuse NY 13205-2065 also: 224 Fayette St Manlius NY 13104-1804

**MATHEWSON, MARK STUART,** lawyer, editor; b. Pana, Ill., Mar. 6, 1950; s. Raymond Glenn and Frances (King) M.; m. Barbara Jean Siegert, Oct. 30, 1980; children: Margie, Molly. BA, U. Wis., Madison, 1978; JD, U. Ill., 1984; MA, U. Iowa, 1985. Bar: Ill. 1985. Reporter Ill. Times, Springfield, 1985; asst. prof. Culver Stockton Coll., Canton, Mo., 1986-87; pvt. practice Pana, Ill., 1987-88; mng. editor Ill. State Bar Assn., Springfield, 1988—; mem. adv. bd. West Pub. Editors Exchange, Eagan, Minn., 1993-95. Home: RR 1 Box 2 Athens IL 62613-9787 Office: Ill State Bar Assn Ill Bar Journal Ill Bar Ctr Springfield IL 62701

**MATHIAS, CHARLES MCCURDY,** lawyer, former senator; b. Frederick, Md., July 24, 1922; s. Charles McCurdy and Theresa McElfresh (Trail) M.; m. Ann Hickling Bradford, Nov. 8, 1958; children: Charles Bradford, Robert Fiske. B.A., Haverford Coll., 1944; student, Yale U., 1943-44; LL.B., U. Md., 1949. Bar: Md. 1949, U.S. Supreme Ct. 1954. Asst. atty. gen. of Md., 1953-54; city atty. City of Frederick, 1954-59; mem. Md. Ho. of Dels., 1958, 87th-90th Congresses from 6th Dist. Md., U.S. Senate from Md., 1969-87; ptnr. Jones Day Reavis and Pogue, Washington, 1987-93; chmn. bd. First Am. Bankshares, 1993—; Milton Eisenhower vis. prof. Johns Hopkins U., 1987—. Served from seaman to capt. USNR. Decorated Order of Merit (Federal Republic of Germany), Legion of Honor (France), Order of Orange Nassau (The Netherlands), Order of Brit. Empire (Eng.). Republican. Episcopalian. Constitutional, Private international, Trademark and copyright. Office: 51 Louisiana Ave NW Washington DC 20001-2105

**MATHIAS, JOSEPH MARSHALL,** lawyer, judge; b. Frankfort, Ky., Jan. 23, 1914; s. Harry L. and Catherine Snead (Marshall) M.; children: Mark Wellington, Marcia Ann Mathias Wilson, Marilyn Roberta. AB, U. Md., 1935; JD, Southeastern U., 1942. Bar: Md. 1942, U.S. Supreme Ct. 1949, U.S. Dist. Ct. Md. 1963. Ptnr. Moorman and Mathias, 1946-50, Jones, Mathias and O'Brien and predecessor firms, 1950-65; judge Md. Tax Ct., 1959-65; assoc. judge Circuit Ct. of Montgomery County (Md.), 1965-80; chief judge 6th Jud. Circuit of Md., 1980-81; spl. assignments, 1981-83; spl. counsel Beckett, Cromwell & Myers, P.A., 1983-88; of counsel Frank, Bernstein, Conaway and Goldman, 1988-92; past dir. Nat. Bank Md., Bank So. Md.; former mem. adv. bd. Citizens Bank and Trust Co. Chmn. Bd. Property Rev., Montgomery, Md., 1992—. Served with USN, 1942-46. Recipient cert. of disting. citizenship Gov. of Md., 1981. Mem. ABA, Md. State Bar Assn., Md. Bar Found., Montgomery County Bar Assn., Am. Judicature Soc. Democrat. Roman Catholic. Real property, Banking, General practice. Home: 10011 Summit Ave Kensington MD 20895-3835

**MATHIEU, MICHELLE ELISE,** lawyer; b. Detroit, Aug. 14, 1956; d. Kenneth G. and Geraldine M. (O'Rourke) M. BA, U. Mich., 1978; JD, Detroit Coll. Law, 1982. Bar: Mich. 1982, U.S. Dist. Ct. (ea. dist.) Mich. 1982, U.S. Ct. Appeals (6th cir.) 1991, U.S. Fed. Ct. (ea. dist.) Mich. Law clk. Joselyn, Rowe, Grinnan, Hayes & Callahan, Detroit, 1980-81; assoc. Joselyn, Rowe, Grinnan & Feldman, Detroit, 1982-88; ptnr. Joselyn & Keelean, P.C., Detroit, 1988-91; assoc., head appeal dept. Still, Nemier, Tolari & Landry, P.C., Farmington Hills, Mich., 1991—. Mem. Fed. Bar Assn. General civil litigation, Insurance, Product liability.

**MATHIEU, RICHARD LOUIS,** lawyer; b. Hanover, N.H., May 22, 1950; s. Thomas Joseph and Colomba Rachel (Simeone) M.; m. Debra Cameron, Mar. 31, 1979; children: Jessica, Alexandra. BA, Syracuse U., 1972; cert. teaching, Cen. Wash. U., 1974; JD, Willamette U., 1982. Bar: Wash. 1982. Tchr. Yakima (Wash.) Sch. Dist., 1974-79; assoc. Weeks, Dietzen & Skala, Yakima, 1982-86; sole practice Yakima, 1986—. Mem. Wash. State Bar Assn., Yakima County Bar Assn., Rotary. Avocation: bicycling. Insurance, Family and matrimonial, Bankruptcy. Home: 205 S 35th Ave Yakima WA 98902-3642 Office: 117 N 3rd St # 102 Yakima WA 98901-2766

**MATHIEU, THOMAS JOSEPH,** lawyer; b. New Bedford, Mass., June 2, 1961; s. Paul Joseph and Janet Rollande (Magnant) M.; m. Kerri Ann Haughey, Sept. 25, 1988. BA, Assumption Coll., Worcester, Mass., 1983; JD, New Eng. Sch. Law, 1987. Bar: Mass 1987, U.S. Dist. Ct. Mass. 1987. Ptnr. Law Offices Mathieu and Mathieu, New Bedford, 1983—. Bd. dirs. Jr. Achievement Greater New Bedford, 1988-89, St. Anne Credit Union, 1993-96. Mem. Mass. Bar Assn., Bristol County Bar Assn., New Bedford Bar Assn. Roman Catholic. Avocations: skiing, sailing, fishing, water skiing, surfing. Fax: 508-994-0155. General practice, Probate, Real property. Office: Mathieu & Mathieu 168 8th St New Bedford MA 02740-6003

**MATHIS, BENTON J., JR.,** lawyer; b. Atlanta, May 16, 1959; s. Benton J. and Vivian (Daniel) M.; m. Angeline Fleeman, Aug. 17, 1985. BS with honors, Ga. Inst. Tech., 1981; JD cum laude, Washington and Lee U., 1984. Bar: Ga. 1984, D.C. 1989, U.S. Dist. Ct. (no. & mid. dists.) Ga., U.S. Ct. Appeals (11th cir.). Assoc. Smith Currie & Hancock, Atlanta, 1984-89, ptnr., 1990-91; ptnr. Drew, Eckl & Farnham, Atlanta, 1991-97, Greeman Mathis & Gary LLP, Atlanta, 1997—. Editor: Employment Law for Georgia Employers, 1991, Labor Law for Georgia Employers, 1991, Personnal Law Desk Manual, 1993; contbr. articles to profl. jours. Mem. Ga. C. of C., Cobb C. of C., Leadership Cobb. Episcopalian. General civil litigation, Labor. Office: Freeman Mathis & Gary LLP 100 Galleria Pkwy SE Fl 16 Atlanta GA 30339-3179

**MATHIS, JOHN PRENTISS,** lawyer; b. New Orleans, Feb. 10, 1944; s. Robert Prentess and Lena (Horton) M.; m. Karen Elizabeth McHugh, May 31, 1966; children: Lisa Lynne Mathis Kirkpatrick, Andrew P. BA magna cum laude, So. Meth. U., Dallas, 1966; JD cum laude, Harvard U., 1969. Bar: Calif. 1970, D.C. 1975, U.S. Ct. Appeals (D.C. cir.) 1972, U.S. Ct. Appeals (5th cir.) 1975, U.S. Ct. Appeals (3rd cir.) 1980, U.S. Supreme Ct. 1982. Assoc. Latham & Watkins, Los Angeles, 1969-71; spl. asst. to gen. counsel, FPC, Washington, 1971-72; gen. counsel Calif. Pub. Utilities Commn., San Francisco, 1972-74; assoc. Baker & Botts, Washington, 1974-76, ptnr., 1976-92; ptnr. Hogan & Hartson, Washington, 1992—. Mem. ABA (litigation sect., chmn. energy litigation com. 1985-89, div. dir. 1989-90, chmn. legis. com. 1990-94, rep. to coord. group energy law 1992-97), Fed. Energy Bar Assn., Harvard U. Law Sch. Assn. D.C. (past pres.). Republican. Methodist. Clubs: Harvard U., Congl. Country, Met. (Washington). FERC practice, Nuclear power, Public utilities. Home: 9400 Turnberry Dr Potomac MD 20854-5447 Office: Hogan & Hartson 555 13th St NW Ste 1200W Washington DC 20004-1109

**MATHIS, PATRICK BISCHOF,** lawyer; b. Pinckneyville, Ill., Feb. 1, 1952; s. John Archibald and Theresa Ann (Bischof) M.; m. Rosanne Azar; children: Daniel P., Adrienne C. B.A. in Chemistry, St. Louis U., 1973; M.B.A., Washington U., St. Louis, 1978, J.D., 1978, LL.M. in Taxation, 1979. Bar: Mo. 1978, Ill. 1979, U.S. Tax Ct. 1979, U.S. Dist. Ct. (so. dist.) Ill. 1980, U.S. Ct. Appeals (7th cir.) 1980, U.S. Ct. Claims 1980, U.S. Supreme Ct. 1982. Assoc. John J. Vassen, P.C., Belleville, Ill., 1979-84; ptnr. Mathis, Marifian, Richter & Grandy, Ltd., Belleville, 1984—; spkr. in field. Contbr. articles to profl. jours. Mem. fin. com. Special Children, Inc. Mamie O. Stookey Sch., 1987-90; parish coun. Blessed Sacrament Parish, 1992-98, pres., 1993-98; chmn. annual fund drive Big Brothers/Big Sisters, St. Clair County, 1994; bd. dirs. Signal Hill Neighborhood Assn., 1989-92, St. Clair County Greenspace Found., 1990-95, Signal Hill Sch. Edn. Found., 1997-99; mem. Signal Hill Sch. Dist. Bd. Edn., 1999—. Mem. ABA (tax sect. civil and criminal penalties com., domestic rels. tax problems com., vice chmn. subcom. alimony issues, gen. practice sect. chmn. taxation com.), Ill. Bar Assn. (fed. taxation sect. council 1984-85, 89-93, chmn. 1992-93), St. Clair County Bar Assn., Bar Assn. Met. St. Louis, Ill. Inst. Continuing Legal Edn. (chmn. 1996-97, bd. dirs. 1990-98), Am. Coll. Trust and Estate Counsel. Roman Catholic. Mo. Athletic Club, Alpha Sigma Nu, Eta Sigma Phi. E-mail: pmathis@mmrg.com. Fax: 618-234-9786. General corporate, Estate planning, Taxation, general. Home: 33 Oak Knoll Pl Belleville IL 62223-1313 Office: Mathis Marifian Richter & Grundy Ltd 720 W Main St Ste 100 Belleville IL 62220-1541

**MATHUS, DAVID L.,** lawyer, business executive; b. N.Y.C., Nov. 16, 1958; s. John Folsom and Nina (Damerel) M. BA in Econs., Coll. of William and Mary, 1981; postgrad., U. Exeter, Eng., 1982; JD, Wake Forest U., 1984. Bar: Ohio 1984, N.Y. 1987. Corp. atty. Thompson, Hine & Flory, Cleve., 1984-86, Chadbourne & Parke, N.Y.C., 1986-89; pres. Am. Events Corp., N.Y.C., 1989-93; ptnr. Baer, Marks & Upham LLP, N.Y.C., 1993—. Mem. Assn. Bar City N.Y., Union League. General corporate, Computer, Communications. Home: 23 E 37th St New York NY 10016-3053 Office: Baer Marks & Upham LLP 805 3rd Ave Fl 19 New York NY 10022-7598

**MATIA, PAUL RAMON,** federal judge; b. Cleve., Oct. 2, 1937; s. Leo Clemens and Irene Elizabeth (Linkert) M.; m. Nancy Arch Van Meter, Jan. 2, 1993. BA, Case Western Res. U., 1959; JD, Harvard U., 1962. Bar: Ohio 1962, U.S. Dist. Ct. (no. dist.) Ohio 1969. Law clk. Common Pleas Ct. of Cuyahoga County, Cleve., 1963-66, judge, 1985-91; asst. atty. gen. State of Ohio, Cleve., 1966-69; adminstrv. asst. to atty. gen. State of Ohio, Columbus, 1969-70; senator Ohio State Senate, Columbus, 1971-75, 79-83; ptnr. Hadley, Matia, Mills & MacLean Co., L.P.A., Cleve., 1975-84; judge U.S. Dist. Ct. (no. dist.) Ohio, 1991-99, chief dist. judge, 1999—. Candidate Lt. Gov. Rep. Primary, 1982, Ohio Supreme Ct., 1988; vice chmn. exec. com. Cuyahoga County Rep. Orgn., Cleve., 1971-84. Named Outstanding Legislator, Ohio Assn. for Retarded Citizens, 1974, Watchdog of Ohio Treasury, United Conservatives of Ohio, 1979; recipient Heritage award Polonia Found., 1988. Mem. FBA, Am. Judicature Soc., Ohio Bar Assn., Cleve. Bar Assn. (President's award 1988), Cuyahoga County Bar Assn., Club at Society Ctr. Avocations: skiing, gardening, travel. Office: US Dist Ct 201 Superior Ave E Cleveland OH 44114-1201

**MATL, LOIS TUDOR,** lawyer; b. Madison County, Ky., Feb. 19, 1939; d. Humphrey Hill Jr. and Mary Elizabeth (Noland) Tudor; m. Gerry L. Calvert Sr., Sept. 25, 1960 (div. Apr. 1981); children: Catherine Deloach, Gerry L. II, Stephanie Hallock. Grad., Good Samaritan Hosp., 1960; BSN, U. Ky., 1966, JD, 1980. Bar: Ky. 1981. Assoc. Greenbaum Doll & McDonald, Lexington, Ky., 1981-85; atty. pvt. practice, Lexington, Ky., 1985—. Bd. trustees Lexington United Meth. Ch., 1982-84, adminstrv. bd., 1991-93; pres. PTA Beaumont Jr. High Sch., Lexington, 1982-83. Methodist. Family and matrimonial, Workers' compensation, General civil litigation. Office: 125 Church St Lexington KY 40507-1102

**MATOS, JOSE RICARDO,** patent agent, consultant; b. Arecibo, Puerto Rico, Dec. 20, 1960. BS in Chemistry, Tex. Tech. U., 1983; PhD in Chemistry, Tex. A&M U., 1988. Patent agent DuPont Merck Pharm., Wilmington, Del., 1988-95, Akin, Gump, Strauss, Hauer, Dallas, 1995—. Contbr. articles to profl. jours.; patentee in field. Recipient post-doctoral fellowship, NSF, 1984-87. Mem. Intellectual Property Owners, Intellectual Property Law Assn., Dallas Ft. Worth Intellectual Property Assn. Office: Akin Gump Strauss Hauer & Feld 1700 Pacific Ave Ste 4100 Dallas TX 75201-4675

**MATSCH, RICHARD P.,** judge; b. Burlington, Iowa, June 8, 1930. A.B., U. Mich., 1951, J.D., 1953. Bar: Colo. Asst. U.S. atty. Colo., 1959-61; dep. city atty. City and County of Denver, 1961-63; judge U.S. Bankruptcy Ct., Colo., 1965-74; judge U.S. Dist. Ct. for Colo., 1974-94, chief judge, 1994—; mem. Judicial Conf. of the U.S., 1991-94, mem. com. on criminal law, 1988-94; mem. bd. dirs. Fed. Judicial Ctr., 1995-99. Served with U.S. Army, 1953-55. Mem. ABA, Am. Judicature Soc. Office: US Court House 1929 Stout St Denver CO 80294-1929

**MATTAR, LAWRENCE JOSEPH,** lawyer; b. Buffalo, Apr. 17, 1934; s. Joseph and Anne (Abraham) M.; m. Elaine Emma Kolbe, Aug. 1, 1959; children: Lorraine, Brenda, Anne, Deborah. Grad., Canisius Coll., 1956; J.D., SUNY-Buffalo, 1959. Bar: N.Y. 1959, Fla. 1977, U.S. Supreme Ct. 1972. Sole practice, Buffalo, 1959-62; sr. ptnr. Mattar & D'Agostino and predecessors, Buffalo, 1962—; asst. to county ct. judge, 1961-66; counsel N.Y. State Senate Pub. Utilties Com., 1969-71. Bd. dirs. Better Bus. Bur. Western N.Y.; mem. exec. com. pres.'s council Canisius Coll.; mem. ho. of dels. United Way of Buffalo and Erie County; mem. Nat. Maronite Bishops' Adv. Council, U.S. Congl. Adv. Bd., Selective Service Bd. Western N.Y., Rep. Presdl. Task Force; del. Rep. Jud. Conv. 8th Dist., 1985. Decorated Knight of St. Charbiel, highest honor available to a Maronite Catholic; recipient award for outstanding service Buffalo Eye Bank, 1962, Leadership award Lions Club Buffalo, 1963, Citizen's award Erie Community Coll., 1982, Nat. Tree of Life award Bd. dirs. Jewish Nat. Fund Am., 1987. Mem. Erie County Bar Assn., Erie County Trial Lawyers Assn., N.Y. State Bar Assn., Fla. Bar Assn., N.Y. State Trial Lawyers Assn., Buffalo C. of C., NFL Players Alumni Assn. (assoc.), Di Gamma (life). Roman Catholic. Clubs: Rotary (sec. 1978-79, dir. 1978-80, trustee, sec., mem. exec. com. Buffalo Rotary Found.), Buffalo (Buffalo); Transit Valley Country (East Amherst, N.Y.). Avocations: golf, skiing. Federal civil litigation, State civil litigation, General corporate. Home: 386 Woodbridge Ave Buffalo NY 14214-1530 Office: 17 Court St Ste 600 Buffalo NY 14202-3205

**MATTES, BARRY A.,** lawyer; b. Chgo., Oct. 23, 1953; s. Jerome P. and Shirley (Cooper) M. BA in Econs., U. Rochester, 1975; JD, Chgo.-Kent Coll. Law, 1980. Bar: Ill. 1981, U.S. Dist. Ct. (no. dist.) Ill. 1981. Pvt. practice Chgo. Democrat. Avocations: musician, tropical fish breeder, record producing. Personal injury, Workers' compensation, Entertainment. Office: 3320 N Central Ave Chicago IL 60634-4324

**MATTESON, WILLIAM BLEECKER,** lawyer; b. N.Y.C., Oct. 20, 1928; s. Leonard Jerome and Mary Jo (Harwell) M.; m. Marilee Brill, Aug. 26, 1950; children: Lynn, Sandra, Holly. BA, Yale U., 1950; JD, Harvard U., 1953. Bar: N.Y. 1954. Clk. to judge Augustus N. Hand U.S. Ct. Appeals, 1953-54; clk. to U.S. Supreme Ct. Justice Harold H. Burton, 1954-55; assoc. firm Debevoise & Plimpton (and predecessors), N.Y.C., 1955-61; ptnr. Debevoise & Plimpton (and predecessors), 1961—, Debevoise & Plimpton (European office), Paris, 1973-78; presiding ptnr. Debevoise & Plimpton (European office), 1988-93, of counsel, 1997—; lectr. Columbia U. Law Sch., 1972-73, 78-80. Trustee Peddie Sch., Hightstown, N.J., 1968-73, Kalamazoo Coll., 1972-77, Miss Porter's Sch., Farmington, Conn., 1977-83, N.Y. Inst. Spl. Edn., 1981—, Salk Inst., La Jolla, Calif., 1994-96, vice-chair, 1994-96, Statue of Liberty Ellis Island Found., 1996—, Hartford Found., 1996—, Indian River Hosp. Found., 1999—; active USA Bus. and Industry Adv. Com. to the Orgn. for Econ. Coop. and Devel., Paris, 1986—; chmn. Worldwide Bus. and Industry Adv. Com., 1994-96; vice chmn. U.S. Coun. for Internat. Bus., 1990—. Mem. ABA, FBA, Internat. Bar Assn., N.Y. State Bar Assn., Assn. of Bar of City of N.Y. (chmn. securities regulation com. 1968-71), Harvard U. Law Sch. Assn. N.Y.C. (trustee 1968-73), Coun. Fgn. Rels., Union Club, Sky Club, Sankaty Head Club, John's Island and Winsdor Clubs, N.Y. Yacht Club. General corporate, Private international. Home: 291 Llwyds Ln Vero Beach FL 32963-3252 Office: Debevoise & Plimpton 875 3rd Ave Fl 23 New York NY 10022-6256

**MATTESSICH, RICHARD STEPHEN,** lawyer. BSBA, Georgetown U., 1987; MBA, NYU, 1990; JD, U. Tex., 1995. Bar: N.J. 1995, U.S. Dist. Ct. N.J. 1996; CPA. Assoc. Buchanan Ingersoll, Princeton, N.J., 1995—. Securities, General corporate. Office: Buchanan Ingersoll 500 College Rd E Princeton NJ 08540-6635

**MATTEUCCI, SHERRY SCHEEL,** prosecutor; b. Columbus, Mont., Aug. 17, 1947; d. Gerald F. and Shirley Scheel; m. William L. Matteucci, Dec. 26, 1969 (div. June 1976); children: Cory, Cody. Student, Kinman Bus. U., 1965-66, Mont. State U., 1967-69, Gonzaga U., 1971-72; BS, Eastern Wash. State U., 1973; JD, U. Mont., 1979. Bar: Mont., U.S. Dist. Ct. Mont., U.S. Ct. Appeals (9th cir.), U.S. Supreme Ct. Mont. Spl. asst. Commr. Higher Edn., 1974-76; assoc. Crowley, Haughey, Hanson, Toole & Dietrich, Billings, Mont., 1979-83, ptnr., 1984-93; U.S. atty. Dist. of Mont., Billings, 1993—; bd. visitors U. Mont. Law Sch., 1988—. Mem. editorial bd. U. Mont. Law Rev., 1977-78, contbg. editor, 1978-79. Bd. dirs. Big Bros. & Sisters, Billings, 1982-85, City/County Library Bd., Billings, 1983-93, Billings Community Cable Corp., 1986, chmn., 1987; vice chmn., bd. dirs. Parmley Billings Library Found. Named one of Outstanding Young Women in Am., 1983. Mem. ABA, State Bar Mont. (chmn. jud. polling com. 1985-87, chmn. women's law sect. 1985-86, trustee, sec., treas. 1988—), Yellowstone County Bar Assn. (dir. 1984-87, pres.-elect 1986-87, pres. 1987-88), Billings C. of C. (leadership com. 1986, legis. affairs com. 1984). Democrat. Mem. Unitarian Ch. Home: 1804 Virginia Ln Billings MT 59102-3626 Office: US Attorney Western Federal Savings & Loan Bldg 2929 3rd Ave N Billings MT 59101-1944*

**MATTHEWS, CHARLES W.,** lawyer. Grad., U. Tex., 1967, U. Houston, 1970. Trial atty. law dept. Exxon Corp., 1971-78, region atty. southeastern and southern region mktg. offices, 1978-81, assoc. gen. atty. litigation sect., gen. counsel & dir. Petroleum Casualty Co. and Exxon Risk Mgmt. Svcs., 1981-92; from assoc. gen. counsel law dept. to gen. counsel law dept. Exxon U.S.A., 1992; v.p., gen. counsel Exxon Corp., 1995—; adv. dir. U. Houston Law Found. Nat. trustee Southwest Region Boys & Girls Clubs of Am.; trustee Nat. Jud. Coll.; trustee Am. Inns Ct. Found. Fellow Am. Bar Found., Tex. Bar Found., Houston Bar Found.; mem. ABA (mem. com. of corp. gen. counsel), Houston Bar Assn., Dallas Bar Assn., Dallas Bar Found., Assn. Gen. Counsel, Internat. Assn. of Def. Counsel Found. (bd. dirs.), Southwestern Legal Found. (trustee). Office: Exxon Corp 5959 Las Colinas Blvd Irving TX 75039-2298*

**MATTHEWS, DOUGLAS EUGENE,** lawyer, educator, consultant; b. Highland Park, Mich., July 28, 1953; s. Max and Mary Elizabeth (Crane) M. BA with high distinction, Judson Coll., Elgin, Ill., 1982; JD cum laude, U. Wis., 1985, MS in Legal Instns., 1988; LLM, Harvard U., 1991. Bar: Fla. 1986, Ill. 1987, D.C. 1989. Assoc. Gunster, Yoakley, Criser & Stewart, West Palm Beach, Fla., 1986, Zukowski, Rogers, Flood & McArdle, Crystal Lake, Fla., 1987; asst. pub. defender McHenry County, Woodstock, Ill., 1988-89; law lectr. No. Ill. U., De Kalb, 1990; asst. prof. St. Thomas U. Sch. Law, Miami, Fla., 1991-94, assoc. prof., 1994-96; adj. prof. law, 1996—; co-founder, v.p. The Grifo Group, Inc., Miami, Fla., 1997—. Past v.p., bd. dirs. Youth Svc. Bur., Woodstock. Mem. ABA, Fla. Bar (sec./treas. practice mgmt. devel. sect.) , Ill. Bar Assn., D.C. Bar Assn., Ind. Computer Cons. Assn. Democrat. Unitarian. Avocations: gardening, historic preservation. Office: 686 NE 74th St Miami FL 33138-5114

**MATTHEWS, ELIZABETH WOODFIN,** law librarian, law educator; b. Ashland, Va., July 30, 1927; d. Edwin Clifton and Elizabeth Frances (Luck) Woodfin; m. Sidney E. Matthews, Dec. 20, 1947; 1 child, Sarah Elizabeth Matthews Wiley. BA, Randolph-Macon Coll., 1948, LLD (hon.), 1989; MS in Libr. Sci., U. Ill., 1952; PhD, So. Ill. U., 1972; LLD, Randolph-Macon Coll., 1989. Cert. law libr., med. libr., med. libr. III. Libr. Ohio State U., Columbus, 1952-59; libr., instr. U. Ill., Urbana, 1962-63; lectr. U. Ill. Grad. Sch. Libr. Sci., Urbana, 1964; libr., instr. Morris Libr. So. Ill. U., Carbondale, 1964-67; classroom instr. So. Ill. U. Coll Edn., Carbondale, 1967-70; med. libr., asst. prof. Morris Libr. So. Ill. U., Carbondale, 1972-74, law libr., asst. prof., 1974-79, law libr., assoc. prof., 1979-85, law libr., prof., 1985-92, prof. emerita, 1993—. Author: Access Points to Law Libraries, 1984, 17th Century English Law Reports, 1986, Law Library Reference Shelf, 1988, 2d edit., 1992, 3d edit., 1996, Pages and Missing Pages, 1983, 2d edit., 1989, Lincoln as a Lawyer: An Annotated Bibliography, 1991. Mem. AAUW (pres. 1976-78, corp. rep. 1978-88), Am. Assn. Law Librs., Beta Phi Mu, Phi Kappa Phi. Methodist. Home: 811 S Skyline Dr Carbondale IL 62901-2405 Office: So Ill U Law Libr Carbondale IL 62901

**MATTHEWS, FRANK EDWARD,** lawyer; b. Troy, N.Y., Jan. 5, 1956; s. Kyran Francis and Margaret (Gilboe) M.; m. Anne Killeen, July 21, 1978; children: Ryan Edward, Jamine Killeen. BA, U. Rochester, 1978; JD, U. Miami, 1981. Bar: Fla., N.Y., U.S. Dist. Ct. (no., mid. and so. dists.) Fla. Shareholder Hopping Green Sams & Smith, Tallahassee, Fla., 1981—. Contbr. articles to profl. jours. pres. Vineyards Homeowners Assn., Tallahassee, 1992-94. Roman Catholic. Avocations: coach youth baseball, softball. Environmental, Legislative, Administrative and regulatory. Office: Hopping Green Sams & Smith 123 Calhoun St Tallahassee FL 32301

**MATTHEWS, JAMES B., III,** lawyer; b. Cordele, Ga., Aug. 31, 1957; s. James B. and Ruth (Mixon) M.; m. Lynn Bridges, June 18, 1983; children: Walker, Charles, Mary. BS in Econs., Ga. So. U., 1980; JD, U. Ga., 1983. Bar: Ga. 1983, U.S. Dist. Ct. (so. and no. dist.) Ga. 1983, U.S. Supreme Ct. 1993, U.S. Dist. Ct. (mid. dist.) Ga. 1984, U.S. Ct. Appeals (11th cir.) 1985, Ct. Appeals Ga. 1983; registered athlete agt., Ga. Assoc. Bouhan, Williams and Levy, Savannah, Ga., 1983-86; shareholder Blasingame, Burch, Garrard & Bryant, P.C., Athens, Ga., 1986-91; ptnr. Blackwood & Matthews, Atlanta, 1991-95, Blackwood, Matthews & Steel, Atlanta, 1995—. Recipient Award of Honor, Am. Baseball Coaches Assn., 1993. Mem. Assn. Trial Lawyers Am., Ga. Trial Lawyers Assn., Def. Rsch. Inst., Am. Judicature Soc. General civil litigation, Personal injury, Professional liability. Office: 462 E Paces Ferry Rd NE Atlanta GA 30305-3301

**MATTHEWS, JOSEPH MICHAEL,** lawyer; b. Grand Rapids, Mich., Apr. 28, 1952; s. Jordan Emmanuel and Anna Mae (Moose) M.; m. JoAnne Hatch, June 29, 1974; children: Megan, Kyle. BA, The Defiance Coll., 1974; JD, U. Miami, 1977. Bar: Fla. 1977, U.S. Dist. Ct. (so. dist.) Fla. 1978, D.C. 1979. Assoc. Paul, Landy & Beiley, Miami, 1977-79; spl. counsel State of Fla. Land Sales, Tallahassee, 1979-80; adj. faculty U. Miami, Coral Gables, Fla., 1981-85; ptnr. Murai, Wald, Biondo, Matthews & Moreno, P.A., Miami, 1980-89, Colson Hicks Eidson Colson Matthews Martinez & Mendoza, P.A., Miami, 1989—; spl. counsel U.S. Senator Bob Graham, 1989. Contbr. articles to profl. jours. Commr. 3rd Dist. Jud. Nominating Com., Miami, 1983-87; mem. Fla. Bd. Bar Examiners, Tallahassee, 1987-90. Mem. ATLA (chmn. comml. litig. sect. 1994), ABA, Fla. Bar Assn., Acad. Fla. Trial Lawyers (chmn. comml. litigation sect. 1992), Dade County Bar Assn., Dade County Trial Lawyers Assn. (pres. 1996). General civil litigation, Construction. Home: 2200 Segovia Cir Miami FL 33134-4834 Office: Colson Hicks Eidson Colson Matthews Martinez & Mendoza PA 200 S Biscayne Blvd Ste 4700 Miami FL 33131-2351

**MATTHEWS, PAUL AARON,** lawyer; b. Memphis, May 7, 1952; s. Joseph Curtis and Sarah Rebecca (Barret) M.; m. Roberta Bartow, July 29, 1978; children: Sarah Pierrepont, Elizabeth Barret. AB, Duke U., 1974; JD, Vanderbilt U., 1977. Bar: Tenn. 1977, U.S. Dist. Ct. (we. dist.) Tenn. 1977, U.S. Dist. Ct. (ea. dist.) Mich. 1987, U.S. Dist. Ct. (ea. dist.) Tenn. 1991, U.S. Ct. Appeals (6th cir.) 1991, U.S. Dist. Ct. (ea. dist.) Ark. 1995, U.S. Dist. Ct. (mid. dist.) Tenn. 1998, U.S. Supreme Ct. 1998. Assoc. Armstrong, Allen, Prewitt, Gentry, Johnston & Holmes, PLLC, Memphis, 1977-82, ptnr., mem., 1982—; chief justice Vanderbilt Law Sch. Moot Ct. Bd., Nashville, 1976-77. Contbr. articles to profl. publs. Mem. com. chmn. Memphis-in-May Internat. Festival, 1977-79, Tenn. Hist. Commn., 1987-97; bd. dirs. Davies Manor Assn., Brunswick, Tenn., 1994—, pres. 1996-97; mem. Leadership Memphis Class of 1987; trustee Tenn. Hist. Commn. Found., 1998—, Shelby County Hist. Commn., 1997—, vice chmn. 1999; commr. Tenn. Wars Commn., 1994-97; vestry Ch. of the Holy Communion, 1995-98. Recipient Newman award Memphis Heritage, Inc., 1992. Mem. ABA, SAR (Shelby chpt.), Memphis Bar Assn., Memphis and Shelby County Mental Health Assn. (pres. 1984-85), Tenn. Bar Assn., Am. Bankruptcy Inst., Duke U. Alumni Assn. (pres. Memphis chpt. 1986-88), Descendants of Early Settlers of Shelby County, Sigma Alpha Epsilon. Episcopalian. Contracts commercial, General civil litigation, Bankruptcy. Home: 4271 Heatherwood Ln Memphis TN 38117-2302

**MATTHEWS, WARREN WAYNE,** state supreme court justice; b. Santa Cruz, Calif., Apr. 5, 1939; s. Warren Wayne and Ruth Ann (Maginnis) M.; m. Donna Stearns, Aug. 17, 1963; children: Holly Maginnis, Meredith Sample. A.B., Stanford U., 1961; LL.B., Harvard U., 1964. Bar: Alaska 1965. Assoc. firm Burr, Boney & Pease, Anchorage, 1964-69, Matthews & Dunn, Matthews, Dunn and Baily, Anchorage, 1969-77; assoc. justice Alaska Supreme Ct., Anchorage, 1977—, justice, chief justice. Bd. dirs. Alaska Legal Services Corp., 1969-70. Mem. Alaska Bar Assn. (bd. govs. 1974-77), ABA, Anchorage Bar Assn.

**MATTHIES, MARY CONSTANCE T.,** lawyer; b. Baton Rouge, Mar. 22, 1948; d. Allen Douglas and Mazie (Poche) Tillman. B.S., Okla. State U., 1969; J.D., U. Tulsa, 1972. Bar: Okla. 1973, U.S. Ct. Appeals (10th cir.) 1974, U.S. Ct. Appeals (8th and D.C. cirs.) 1975, U.S. Supreme Ct. 1976. Assoc., ptnr. Kothe, Nichols & Wolfe, Inc., Tulsa, 1972-78; pres. sr. prin. Matthies Law Firm, P.C., Tulsa, 1978—; guest lectr. U. Tulsa Coll. Law, U. Okla. Sch. Law, Oral Roberts U. Sch. Contbr. articles to profl. jours; mem. staff Tulsa Law Jour., 1971-72. Fellow Am. Coll. of Labor and Employment Lawyers; mem. ABA (mem. spl. subcom. for liaison with EEOC, 1974—, spl. subcom. for liaison with OFCCP, 1979—, mgmt. co-chmn. equal employment law subcoms. on nat. origin discrimination 1974-75, class actions and remedies 1975-80), Okla. Bar Assn. (coun. mem. labor law sect. 1974-80, chmn. 1978-79), Women's Law Caucus, Phi Delta Phi. Presbyterian. Labor, Civil rights, Federal civil litigation. Office: Thompson Bldg 20 E 5th St Ste 310 Tulsa OK 74103-4435

**MATTINGLY, CATHERINE A.,** electronic citations service publisher; b. Somerset, Ky., Jan. 29, 1966; d. George Francis Mattingly and Hazel Bernice Flanagan. BA, Centre Coll., 1988; JD, U. Louisville, 1995. Bar: Ky. Editl. specialist Ky. Housing Corp., Frankfort; from acct. exec. to mgr. design & usability Lexis-Nexis, Louisville, Dayton, Ohio. Mem. ABA, Ky. Bar Assn. Democrat. Office: Lexis Nexis 9443 Springboro Pike Miamisburg OH 45342-4425

**MATTSON, JAMES STEWART,** lawyer, environmental scientist, educator; b. Providence, July 22, 1945; s. Irving Carl and Virginia (Lutey) M.; m. Carol Sandry, Aug. 15, 1964 (div. 1979); children: James, Birgitta; m. Rana A. Fine, Jan. 5, 1983. BS in Chemistry, U. Mich., 1966, MS, 1969, PhD, 1970; JD, George Washington U., 1979. Bar: D.C. 1979, Fla. 1983, U.S. Dist. Ct. D.C. 1979, U.S. Dist. Ct. (so. dist.) Fla. 1984, U.S. Ct. Appeals (D.C. cir.) 1979, U.S. Ct. Claims 1985, U.S. Supreme Ct. 1985, U.S. Ct. Appeals (11th cir.) 1985, U.S. Ct. Appeals (5th cir.) 1987, U.S. Ct. Appeals (fed. cir.) 1990. Staff scientist Gulf Gen. Atomic Co., San Diego, 1970-71; dir. R & D Ouachita Industries, Inc., Monroe, La., 1971-72; asst. prof. chem. oceanography Rosenstiel Sch. Marine & Atmospheric Sci., U. Miami (Fla.), 1972-76; phys. scientist NOAA, Washington, 1976-78; mem. profl. staff & congl. liaison Nat. Adv. Commn. on Oceans and Atmosphere, 1978-80; ptnr. Mattson & Pave, Washington, Miami and Key Largo, Fla., 1980-86, Mattson & Tobin, Key Largo, 1987—; pres./CEO The Great House of Wine, Inc., Islamorada, Fla., 1997—; adj. prof. law U. Miami, 1983-93; cons. Alaska Dept. Environ. Conservation, 1981-91. Author: (with H.B. Mark) Activated Carbon: Surface Chemistry and Adsorption from Solution, 1971; editor (with others): Computers in Chemistry and Instrumentation, 8 vols., 1972-76; The Argo Merchant Oil Spill: A Preliminary Scientific Report, 1977, (with H.B. Mark) Water Quality Measurement: Modern Analytical Techniques, 1981; contbr. articles to profl. jours. Candidate dist. 120 Fla. Ho. of Reps., 1994. Fellow Fed. Water Pollution Control Adminstrn., 1967-68; recipient Spl. Achievement award U.S. Dept. Commerce, 1976-77; Regents Alumni scholar U. Mich., 1963. Mem. ABA, Am. Chem. Soc. (chmn. Symposium on Oil Spill Indentification 1971), Order of Coif. Environmental, Administrative and regulatory, Land use and zoning (including planning). Address: 88101 Overseas Hwy # 7 Islamorada FL 33036-3063

**MATTSON, LEROY HARRY,** lawyer; b. Absecon, N.J., Aug. 14, 1925; s. Leroy and Beulah May (Lawson) M.; m. Ina Ruth Anderson, Aug. 21, 1946; children: Katherine, Sherman. Student, U. Pa., 1943-45, Pa. State U., 1945, Northwestern U., 1945; JD, Dickinson Sch. Law, 1950. Bar: N.J. 1950, U.S. Dist. Ct. (Fed. dist.) 1950, U.S. Ct. Appeals (3d cir.) 1954, U.S. Supreme Ct. 1953. Assoc. Lloyd & Horn, Atlantic City, 1950-51, McCarter & English, Newark, 1954-61; ptnr. Mattson, Madden & Polito, Newark, 1961—; mcpl. judge Passaic Twp., N.J., 1961-62, mcpl. atty., 1958-61, 62-85. Capt. USNR, 1943-45, 51-54, 54—. Republican. Insurance, General civil litigation, Workers' compensation. Home: 231 Mendham Rd Bernardsville NJ 07924-1204 Office: Mattson Madden & Polito 1 Gateway Ctr Newark NJ 07102-5311

**MATTSON, LYNN PAUL,** lawyer; b. Rochester, Minn., July 19, 1947; s. L.S. (Bud) and Mavis D. (Cunningham) M.; m. Pamela Ann, Aug. 31, 1976; children: Paul Steven, Elizabeth Ann, Ryan Scott. BA, U. Minn., 1969; JD, So. Meth. U., 1973. Bar: Tex. 1973, Okla. 1973, U.S. Dist. Ct. (no., ea. and we. dists.) Okla., U.S. Ct. Appeals (3rd cir.) 1978, U.S. Ct. Appeals (10th cir.) 1974, U.S. Ct. Appeals (6th cir.) 1975, U.S. Ct. Appeals (5th cir.) 1977. Assoc. Kothe & Engleton, Tulsa, 1973-75; ptnr. Nichols & Wolfe, Inc., Tulsa, 1976-83, Doerner, Stuart, Saunders, Daniel & Anderson, Tulsa, 1983—. Mem. State Bar Tex. Avocations: walking, woodworking. Labor. Office: Doerner Stuart Saunders Daniel & Anderson 320 S Boston Ave Tulsa OK 74103-3706

**MATUG, ALEXANDER PETER,** lawyer; b. Chgo., May 25, 1946; s. Alexander J. and Marianne (Paszek) M.; m. Jeanne Marie Buker, Aug. 16, 1969; children: Alexander W., Krista E., Thomas E. BA, St. Mary's Coll., Minn., 1968; JD, Loyola U., Chgo., 1972. Bar: Ill. 1972, U.S. Dist. Ct. (no. dist.) Ill. 1972. Pvt. practice, Palos Heights, Ill., 1972—. Bd. dirs. Am. Heritage, Sertoma, Palos Heights, 1991—; profl. adv. bd. Sertoma Speech and Hearing Ctr., Palos Hills, Ill., 1991—. Mem. Ill. Bar Assn., S.W. Suburban Bar Assn. Roman Catholic. Probate, Real property, General practice. Office: 7110 W 127th St Ste 250 Palos Heights IL 60463-1571

**MATUGA, EDWARD ANTHONY,** lawyer; b. Chgo., Sept. 3, 1921; s. Joseph John and Michalene Helen (Labiak) M.; m. Pearl Elizabeth Krysiak; children: Edward, Janice, Rita, Michael. BS, Loyola U., Chgo., 1943; JD, DePaul U., 1948. Bar: Ill. 1953, U.S. Dist. Ct. (no. dist.) 1948, U.S. Ct. Appeals (4th cir.) 1975. Prosecutor Westchester, Ill., 1960—, Bellwood, Ill., 1961—, Broadview, Ill., 1965—; atty. Westchester Park Dist., 1967—; gen. counsel First Fed. Westchester, 1963—, Proviso Mental Health Commn., Melrose Park, Ill., 1970—. Capt. USAF, 1960-70. Mem. Chgo. Bar Assn., Ill. State Bar Assn., Advocates Soc., West Suburban Bar Assn. (pres. 1982-83), Butterfield Country Club. Republican. Roman Catholic. Home: 1651 Westchester Blvd Westchester IL 60154-4331 Office: 10150 W Roosevelt Rd Westchester IL 60154-2644

**MATUNE, FRANK JOSEPH,** lawyer; b. Youngstown, Ohio, Jan. 11, 1948; s. Walter John and Eve (Skiljo) M.; m. Doreen Mary Dolan, June 1, 1974; children: Molly Catherine, John Walter, Kelly Dolan. BA, Ill. Benedictine Coll., 1970; JD, Thomas M. Cooley Law Sch., Lansing, Mich., 1979; LLM, Georgetown U., 1980. Bar: Pa. 1979, Ohio, 1998, U.S. Dist. Ct. (western dist.) Pa. 1982, U.S. Tax Ct. 1980. Tax clk. Bd. Tax Appeals State Mich. Dept. Revenue, Lansing, 1978-79; ptnr. Routman, Moore, Goldstone & Valentino, Sharon, Pa., 1981-98, Nadler, Nadler & Burdman Co., LPA, Youngstown, 1998—. Author: Pennsylvania Tax Service, 1987, Federal Tax Service, 1988. Mem. ABA, Ohio Ba Assn., Pa. Bar Assn., Mercer County Bar Assn. (treas. 1983-86). Republican. Roman Catholic. Avocations: sports, classical music. Corporate taxation, Taxation, general, State and local taxation. Home: 798 Lillian Dr Hermitage PA 16148-1571 Office: Nadler Nadler & Burdman Co 20 Federal Plz W Ste 600 Youngstown OH 44503-1424

**MATUS, WAYNE CHARLES,** lawyer; b. N.Y.C., Mar. 10, 1950; s. Eli and Alma (Platt) M.; m. Marsha Rothblum, Jan. 16, 1982; children: Marshall Scott, Scott Adam. BA, Johns Hopkins U., 1972; JD, NYU, 1975. Law clk. Superior Ct. D.C., 1975-76; assoc. Marshall, Bratter, Greene, Allison and Tucker, N.Y.C., 1976-79; assoc. Christy & Viener, N.Y.C., 1979-83, ptnr., 1984-98; ptnr. Salans, Hertzfeld, Heilbronn, Christy & Viener, 1999—; faculty ABA-Am. Law Inst., 1988; neutral mediator Supreme Ct. comml. divsn. 1st jud. dist. State of N.Y. Unified Ct. Sys., 1997—. Mem. Assn. Bar City of N.Y. (com. on computer law 1985-88, chmn. com. on state cts., subcom. on motion practice 1982-84, com. product liability 1994-97), N.Y. State Bar Assn. (com. on class actions and complex civil litigation comml. and fed. litigation sect. 1990—), N.Y. Litigators Club (steering com. 1985—), Johns Hopkins U. Alumni Assn. (bd. dirs. met. N.Y. chpt. 1987—, v.p. 1988—, nat. alumni counsel 1996—). General civil litigation, Computer, Alternative dispute resolution. Office: Christy & Viener 620 Fifth Ave New York NY 10020-2402

**MATYAS, DAVID JOHN,** lawyer, judge; b. Milw., Sept. 5, 1951; s. John P. and Mary A. M.; m. Susan Kay Klein, Aug. 9, 1975; children: Molly, Elizabeth, Mark, Ellen. BA, St. Norbert Coll., 1973; JD, Marquette Law Sch., 1976. Bar: Wis. 1976, U.S. Dist. Ct. (ea. and we. dists.) Wis. 1976. Pvt. practice DePere, Wis., 1976—; bankruptcy trustee U.S. Dist. Ct. (ea. dist.) Wis., Milw., 1985-96; guardian ad Li tem panel family matters Brown County, Green Bay, Wis., 1995—; instr. Northeast Wis. Tech. Inst., Green Bay, 1980-85; mcpl. judge City of DePere, 1994—. Mem. Marquette Law Rev., 1975-76. Youth soccer coach DePere Youth Soccer, 1985-94; instr. DePere Police Citizens Acad., 1996-98. Mem. Brown County Bar Assn. Roman Catholic. Avocations: reading, sports. Home: 1614 Rusk St De Pere WI 54115-3639 Office: 366 Main Ave De Pere WI 54115-2203

**MATZKA, MICHAEL ALAN,** lawyer; b. Newark, Oct. 30, 1954; s. John and Liselotte (Heim) M. BS, MIT, 1976; JD, Boston Coll., 1984. Bar: Mass. 1985, U.S. Dist. Ct. Mass. 1985. Assoc. computer systems Index Systems, Inc., Cambridge, Mass., 1976-81; assoc. Sullivan & Worcester, Boston, 1984-92; ptnr. Sullivan & Worcester LLP, Boston, 1992—. Mem. ABA. General corporate, Intellectual property, Securities. Office: Sullivan & Worcester LLP 1 Post Office Sq Ste 2300 Boston MA 02109-2129

**MATZUS, JASON ERIC,** lawyer; b. Pitts., Jan. 11, 1968. BA in Econs. magna cum laude, Gettysburg Coll., 1990, BA in Psychology magna cum laude, 1990; JD cum laude, U. Pitts., 1995. Bar: Pa. 1995, U.S. Dist. Ct. Pa., U.S. Ct. Appeals (3rd cir.). Lawyer Gismondi & Margolis, Pitts., 1995—. Contbr. articles to profl. jours. Vol. Spl. Olympics, Uniontown, Pa. Mem. Am. Trial Lawyers Assn., Pa. Bar Assn., Pa. Trial Lawyers Assn., Western Pa. Trial Lawyers Assn. (pub. rels. com.), Alleghany County Bar Assn. Avocations: marathons, mountain biking, basketball. Personal injury, Product liability, General civil litigation. Office: Gismondi & Margolis 310 Grant St Ste 606 Pittsburgh PA 15219-2201

**MAUL, DONNA L.,** lawyer; b. Bklyn., Mar. 23, 1956; d. Charles C. M. and Ethyl Julia (McNiece. BA, Seton Hall U., 1978, JD, 1981. Bar: N.J. 1984. Assoc. James A. Polon, Howell, N.J., 1984-86, Bennett, Davison, Munoz, Freehold, N.J., 1986-88; ptnr. Bennett, Hayser, Maul, Freehold, N.J., 1988-89; assoc. Ansell, Zaro, Bennett, Eatontown, N.J., 1989-94; ptnr. Ansell, Zaro, Grimm, Ocean, N.J., 1985—. Mem. N.J. State Bar Assn., Monmouth County Bar Assn. (family law com. 1996—). Episcopalian. Avocations: travel, reading, movies, cooking, trivia. Family and matrimonial, State civil litigation. Office: Ansell Zaro Grimm & Aaron 1500 Lawrence Ave Ocean NJ 07712-3410

**MAULDIN, JOHN INGLIS,** public defender; b. Atlanta, Nov. 6, 1947; s. Earle and Isabel (Inglis) M.; m. Cynthia Ann Balchin, Apr. 15, 1967 (div. Dec. 1985); children: Tracy Rutherford, Abigail Inglis; m. Linda W. Farmer, Nov. 7, 1998. BA, Wofford Coll., 1970; JD, Emory U., 1973. Bar: S.C. 1974, U.S. Ct. Appeals (4th cir.) 1974, U.S. Dist. Ct. S.C. 1975, U.S. Supreme Ct. 1978. Asst. pub. def. Defender Corp. Greenville County, S.C., 1974-76; ptnr. Mauldin & Allison, Greenville, 1977-92; pub. defender Greenville County, S.C., 1992—; chair S.C. Commn. on Indigent Def., 1993-96; adj. prof. Greenville Tech. Coll., 1975-80; sec., treas. Def. Corp. Greenville County, 1979-92, bd. dirs. Bd. dirs. Speech Hearing & Learning Ctr., Greenville, 1977-90, pres., 1982; bd. dirs. Save Our Sons, 1995—. Named S.C. Atty. Yr. ACLU, S.C., 1986. Mem. Nat. Assn. Criminal Def. Attorneys, S.C. Trial Lawyers Assn., S.C. Assn. Criminal Def. Lawyers (bd. dirs. 1997—), S.C. Pub. Defender Assn. (bd. dirs. 1992—), Rotary, Sigma

Delta Phi. Democrat. Methodist. Office: PO Box 10264fs Greenville SC 29603

**MAUPIN, BILL,** state supreme court justice; children: Allison, Michael. BA, U. Nev., 1968; JD, U. Ariz., 1971. Atty., ptnr. Thorndal, Backus, Maupin and Armstrong, Las Vegas, 1976-93; judge 8th Jud. Dist. Clark County, 1993-97; assoc. justice Supreme Ct. Nev., 1997—; bd. govs. Nev. State Bar, 1991-95. Recipient highest rating for Retention as Dist. Ct. Judge, 1994, 96, Highest Qualitative Ratings, 1996, Las Vegas Review Jour., Clark County Bar Assn.; highest rating as Supreme Ct. Justice Clark County Bar Assn. and Las Vegas Rev. Jour. judicial poll, 1998. Mem. Nev. Supreme Ct. (study com. to review jud. elections, chmn. 1995, alternate dispute resolution implementation com. chmn. 1992-96). Office: Supreme Ct Bldg Carson City NV 89710-0001

**MAURO, RICHARD FRANK,** lawyer, investment manager; b. Hawthorne, Nev., July 21, 1945; s. Frank Joseph and Dolores D. (Kreimeyer) M.; m. LaVonne M. Madden, Aug. 28, 1965; 1 child, Lindsay Anne. AB, Brown U., 1967; JD summa cum laude, U. Denver, 1970. Bar: Colo. 1970. Assoc. Dawson, Nagel, Sherman & Howard, Denver, 1970-72; assoc. Van Cise, Freeman, Tooley & McClearn, Denver, 1972-73, ptnr., 1973-74; ptnr. Hall & Evans, Denver, 1974-81, Morrison & Forester, Denver, 1981-84; of counsel Parcel & Mauro, P.C., Denver, 1984—; pres. Parcel, Mauro & Hultin, P.C., Denver, 1988-90; of counsel Parcel, Mauro P.C., Denver, 1992-99; pres. Richard F. Mauro, P.C., Denver, 1999—, Sundance Oil Exploration Co., 1985-88; exec. v.p. Castle Group, Inc., 1992-97; prs. Richard F. Mauro, P.C., 1999—; adj. prof. U. Denver Coll. Law, 1981-84. Symposium editor: Denver Law Jour., 1969-70; editor: Colorado Corporation Manual; contbr. articles to legal jours. Pres. Colo. Open Space Coun., 1974; mem. law alumni coun. U. Denver Coll. Law, 1988-91. Francis Wayland scholar, 1967; recipient various Am. jurisprudence awards. Mem. ABA, Colo. Bar Assn., Denver Bar Assn., Colo. Assn. Corp. Counsel. (pres. 1974-75), Am. Arbitration Assn. (comml. arbitrator), Order St. Ives, Denver Athletic Club (bd. dirs. 1986-89). General corporate, Contracts commercial, Securities. Home: 2552 E Alameda Ave Unit 128 Denver CO 80209-3330 Office: 1225 17th St Fl 29 Denver CO 80202-5534

**MAURRASSE, MARIA VIDALINA FELIU,** lawyer; b. Mayari, Oriente, Cuba, Dec. 23, 1963; came to U.S., 1968; s. Carlos Manuel and Elvia Luz (Torres) Feliu; children: Flomar, Vidal. BA, Fla. Internat. U., 1987, MusB, 1988; JD, U. Miami, 1991. Bar: Fla. 1991. Atty. Texaco Group Inc., Coral Gables, Fla., 1991-97, sr. atty., 1997—. Office: Texaco 150 Alhambra Cir Coral Gables FL 33134-4527

**MAUZY, OSCAR HOLCOMBE,** lawyer, retired state supreme court justice; b. Houston, Nov. 9, 1926; s. Harry Lincoln and Mildred Eva (Kincaid) M.; m. Anne Rogers; children: Catherine Anne, Charles Fred, James Stephen. BBA, U. Tex., 1950, JD, 1952. Bar: Tex. 1951. Practiced in Dallas, 1952-87; pres. Mullinax, Wells, Mauzy & Baab, Inc. (P.C.), 1970-78; mem. Tex. Senate from 23d Dist., 1967-87, chmn. edn. com., 1971-81, chmn. jurisprudence com., 1981-87, pres. pro tempore, 1973; justice Tex. Supreme Ct., 1987-93; pvt. practice Austin, 1993—; Mem. Tex. Adv. Commn. Intergovtl. Relations, Nat. Conf. State Legislators, Edn. Commn. of the States, Am. Edn. Finance Assn., 1971-87. Vice chmn. judiciary com. Tex. Constl. Conv., 1974; nat. committeeman Young Democrats, 1954. Served with USNR, 1944-46. Home: 5000 Crestway Dr Austin TX 78731-5404

**MAVRIDES, MICHAEL FOTIOS,** lawyer; b. N.Y.C., Jan. 19, 1968; s. Fotios and Elizabeth Mavrides. BA, Columbia U., 1989; JD, U. Pa., 1992. BAr: N.Y. 1993. Atty. Emmet, Marvin & Martin, LLP, N.Y.C., 1992—. Mem. ABA, N.Y. State Bar Assn. Banking. Home: 245 E 87th St Apt 17D New York NY 10128-3242 Office: Emmet Marvin & Martin LLP 120 Broadway Fl 32D New York NY 10271-0002

**MAWHINNEY, KENT D.,** lawyer; b. Manchester, Conn., July 12, 1965; s. Walter D. and Marilyn A. Mawhinney. BS in Fin. and Entrepreneurial Studies, Babson Coll., 1987; JD cum laude, 1990. Bar: Conn., U.S. Dist. Ct. Conn., U.S. Ct. Appeals (2d cir.), U.S. Tax Ct. Ptnr. Clayman, Markowitz, Pinney & Baram, L.L.C., Bloomfield, Conn., 1990—. Contbr. articles to profl. jours. Mem. Trial Lawyers Assn., Conn. Bar Assn., Am. Builders and Contractors Assn., Jaycees. Federal civil litigation, State civil litigation. Office: Clayman Markowitz Pinney & Baram LLC Three Regency Dr Bloomfield CT 06002

**MAX, RODNEY ANDREW,** lawyer, mediator; b. Cin., Jan. 28, 1947; s. Howard Nelson and Ruth Max; m. Laurie Gilbert; children: Adam Keith, Jeffery Aaron. Student, Am. U.; BA, U. Fla., 1970; JD cum laude, Cumberland Sch., 1975; grad., Harvard Sch. Negotiation, 1997. Bar: Ala. 1975, Fla. 1975, U.S. Ct. Appeals (5th and 11th cirs.) 1975, U.S. Supreme Ct. 1982. From assoc. to ptnr. Najjar Denaburg PC, Birmingham, Ala., 1975-94; ptnr. Sirote & Permutt, P.C., Birmingham, 1994—; with Ala. State Adv. Com., U.S. Civil Rights Commn., 1985—; lectr. in field. Officer, bd. dirs. Jewish Cmty. Ctr., Birmingham, 1980—, Family and Child Svcs., Birmingham, 1984—; trustee Temple Emanu-El, sec. 1990-93, v.p., 1992—, 1st v.p., 1997-99, pres., 1999—; active Summer Youth Task Force; mem. Camp Birmingham adv. com. Leadership Birmingham, 1989-90, mem. alumni bd., 1990-93; mem. Leadership Ala., 1997-98; bd. dirs., mem. exec. com. NCCJ, 1989—; co-chmn. cmty. affairs com. Operation New Birmingham, pres. exec. com.; bd. dirs. PATH; founder A-Plus; co-chmn. Coalition Against Hate Crimes, 1992—; v.p., mem. exec. com. Mountain Brook City Sch. Found., 1992—. Nominated Citizen of Yr. award Young Bus. Club, 1989; recipient Peggy Spain McDonald award Birmingham Bd. of Edn., 1993, Operation New Birmingham Achievement award, 1996, Better Bus. Bur. Achievement award, 1996, Urban League award, 1998, Brotherhood award NCCJ, 1998, I Have A Dream award of Southern Christian Leadership Conf., 1999. Fellow Coll. Atty. Mediators; mem. ABA, ATLA, Ala. Bar Assn. (chmn. task force for alternatives to dispute resolution, co-chmn. increased minority participation, chmn. fee dispute resolution task force), Ala. Trial Lawyers Assn., Ala. Def. Lawyers Assn., Am. Arbitration Assn. (arbitrator, mediator, chmn. Ala. adv. coun.), Birmingham Bar Assn. (trustee legal aid 1985-88, mem. exec. bd. 1989-92, sec.-treas. 1993), Am. Acad. Atty. Mediators, Newcomen Soc. U.S., Kiwanis, B'nai B'rith (pres., bd. govs. 1978-85). Democrat. Avocations: sports, politics, children's athletics, religion, internat. relations, interfaith dialogue. Federal civil litigation, State civil litigation. Office: Sirote & Permutt 2222 Arlington Ave S Birmingham AL 35205-4070

**MAXEY, DAVID WALKER,** lawyer; b. Scranton, Pa., May 17, 1934; s. Paul Harold and Margaret (Walker) M.; m. Catharine Eglin, June 6, 1968; children: Paul Eglin, Margaret Wilson. AB, Harvard U., 1956, LLB cum laude, 1960. Bar: Pa. 1961, U. S. Dist. Ct. (ea. dist.) Pa. 1961, U.S. Ct. Appeals (3d cir.) 1963. Assoc. Drinker Biddle and Reath LLP, Phila., 1960-66, ptnr., 1967—, chmn. real estate dept., 1970-88, mng. ptnr., 1977-91, co-chmn., 1988-91; vis. faculty Villanova (Pa.) U. Law Sch., 1987-95. Contbr. articles to profl. jours. Sec., bd. dirs. Greater Phila. Internat. Network, 1981-94; bd. dirs. Young Audiences Ea. Pa., Phila., 1985-95, Libr. Co., Phila., 1993—, sec., 1997—; chmn. bd. dirs. Hist. Soc. Pa., Phila., 1991-93; chmn. internat. adv. com. Greater Phila. First, 1994-98; bd. dirs. Gladwyne (Pa.) Libr., 1991-98, pres., 1996-98. Recipient Hughes-Gossett award U.S. Supreme Ct. Hist. Soc., Washington, 1991. Mem. ABA, Pa. Bar Assn., Phila. Bar Assn., Am. Coll. Real Estate Lawyers, Harvard Club Phila. (pres. 1970-72), Merion Cricket Club, Sunday Breakfast Club. Avocation: historical research and publication. Real property, Banking, Environmental. Home: 829 Black Road Rd Gladwyne PA 19035 Office: One Logan Sq 18th and Cherry Streets Philadelphia PA 19103-6996

**MAXWELL, JOHN EDWARD,** lawyer; b. Waterloo, Iowa, Dec. 31, 1939; s. Nicol Eugene and Elma Lucille (Carr) M.; m. Peggy A. Maxwell, Feb. 14, 1997; children: Julie, Ryan. BA, Wash. State U., 1963, MBA, 1966; JD, Pepperdine U., 1975. Bar: Wash. 1975, Calif. 1975, U.S. Claims Ct. 1990. Sales rep. Exxon Corp., Seattle, 1966-69; analyst Exxon Corp., L.A., 1969-75; ptnr. Blechschmidt, Bingman & Maxwell, Grandview, Wash., 1975-85; pvt. practice Grandview, 1985—; bd. dirs. Grandview Devel. Corp. Pres. Men's Rep. Club, Grandview, 1977, Campfire Girls Am., Grandview, 1978. Mem. Wash. State Bar Assn. (spl. dist. counsel 1988—), Calif. Bar Assn. (inactive), Yakima County Bar Assn., Ea. Wash. Fed. Bar Assn., Grandview C. of C. (pres. 1977), Rotary (pres. Grandview chpt. 1984-85), Elks. Presbyterian. Avocations: skiing, reading. General civil litigation, Bankruptcy, Family and matrimonial. Home: 117 Ash St Grandview WA 98930-1316 Office: 201 E 2nd St Grandview WA 98930-1347

**MAXWELL, LEROY STEVENSON,** lawyer; b. Chambersburg, Pa., Jan. 12, 1915; s. Levi Houser and Maye (Stevenson) M.; m. Pauline Kauffman, Dec. 28, 1939; children: LeRoy S. Jr., Ann K. AB, Juniata Coll., 1936; JD, U. Pa., 1939. Bar: Pa. 1940, U.S. Supreme Ct. 1953, U.S. Dist. Ct. (mid. dist.) Pa. 1948. Ptnr. Minick & Maxwell, Waynesboro, Pa., 1940-46; pvt. practice law Waynesboro, Pa., 1947-52, 57-61; ptnr. Maxwell & Good, Waynesboro, Pa., 1952-57, Maxwell & Bridgers, Waynesboro, Pa., 1962-76, Maxwell & Maxwell, Waynesboro, Pa., 1977-78, Maxwell, Maxwell & Dick, Waynesboro, Pa., 1978-84, Maxwell, Maxwell, Dick & Walsh, Waynesboro, Pa., 1985-90, Maxwell, Maxwell, Dick, Walsh & Lisko, Waynesboro, Pa., 1990-94, Maxwell Maxwell Walsh & Lisko, Waynesboro, 1995-97, Maxwell, Maxwell & Walsh, Waynesboro, 1997-98; ptnr Maxwell Law Offices, Waynesboro, 1998—; dir. emeritus First Nat. Bank and Trust Co., Waynesboro, 1990-92, Waynesboro Hosp., 1990-92; dist. atty. Franklin County, Pa., Chambersburg, 1944-48. Trustee Juniata Coll., Huntingdon, 1961-64, 70-81, emeritus, 1981—. ABA, Pa. Bar Assn., Franklin County Bar Assn., Masons. Republican. Ch. of the Brethren. Avocations: golf, gardening. General practice, Probate, Real property. Office: 92 W Main St Waynesboro PA 17268-1563

**MAXWELL, ROBERT EARL,** federal judge; b. Elkins, W.Va., Mar. 15, 1924; s. Earl L. and Nellie E. (Rexstrew) M.; m. Ann Marie Grabowski, Mar. 29, 1948; children—Mary Ann, Carol Lynn, Ellen Lindsay, Earl Wilson. Student, Davis and Elkins Coll., LLD (hon.), 1984; LLB, W.Va. U., 1949; LLD (hon.), Davis and Elkins Coll., 1984. Bar: W.Va. 1949. Practiced in Randolph County, 1949, pros. atty., 1952-61; U.S. atty. for No. Dist. W.Va., 1961-64; judge, then sr. judge U.S. Dist. Ct. (no. dist.) W.Va., Elkins, 1965—; judge Temp. Emergency Ct. of Appeals, 1980-89; past chmn. budget com. Jud. Conf. U.S.; former mem. exec. com. Nat. Conf. Fed. Trial Judges; former mem. adv. bd. W.Va. U. Mem. bd. advisors W.Va. U., past chmn.; bd. advisors Mary Babb Randolph Cancer Ctr. Recipient Alumni Disting. Svc. award Davis and Elkins Coll., 1969, Religious Heritage Am. award, 1979, Outstanding Trial Judge award W.Va. Trial Lawyers Assn., 1988, Order of Vandalia award W.Va. U., Outstanding Alumnus award, 1992, Tenured Faculty Mem. Recognition award Bd. Govs., Def. Trial Coun., W.Va., 1992, Cert. of Merit, W.Va. State Bar, 1994, Justitia Officium award Coll. of Law, W.Va. U., 1994; fellow W.Va. Bar Found., 1999. Mem. Nat. Conf. Federal Trial Judges, Dist. Judges Assn. 4th Cir. (past pres.), Moose (life), Lions (life), Beta Alpha Beta (merit award), Elkins-Randolph County C. of C. (citizen of yr. 1994). Office: US Dist Ct No Dist PO Box 1275 Elkins WV 26241-1275

**MAY, ALAN ALFRED,** lawyer; b. Detroit, Apr. 7, 1942; s. Alfred Albert and Sylvia (Sheer) M.; m. Elizabeth Miller; children: Stacy Ann, Julie Beth. BA, U. Mich., 1963, JD, 1966. Bar: Mich. 1967, D.C. 1976; former registered nursing home adminstr., Mich. Ptnr. May and May, Detroit, 1967-79, pres. May & May, P.C., 1979—; spl. asst. atty. gen. State of Mich., 1970—; pres., instr. Med-Leg Seminars, Inc., 1978; lectr. Wayne State U., 1974; instr. Oakland U., 1969. Chmn. Rep. 18th Congl. Dist. Com., 1983-87, now chmn. emeritus; chmn. 19th Congl. Dist. Com., 1981-83; mem. Mich. Rep. Com., 1976-84; del. Rep. Nat. Conv., 1984, mem. rules com., 1984; del. Rep. Nat. Conv., 1988, mem. platform com., 1988; former chmn. Mich. Civil Rights Commn.; mem. Mich. Civil Svc. Commn., 1984-88; trustee NCCJ (exec. bd., vic-chmn. nat. conf. for cmty. and justice), Temple Beth El Birmingham, Mich., v.p., exec. bd.; mem. Electoral Coll.; bd. dirs. ADL, Mich.; bd. dirs., exec. bd., co-chmn. Detroit Round Table/Nat. Conf. for Cmty. and Justice, Charfoos Charitable Found. Mem. The Nat. Conf. for Comty. and Justice (exec. bd., vice-chmn.), Detroit Bar Assn., Oakland County Bar Assn., Victors Club, Franklin Hills Country Club (past pres., bd. dirs.), Presidents Club (trustee). Contbr. article to profl. jours. Probate, State civil litigation, Workers' compensation. Home: 4140 Echo Rd Bloomfield Hills MI 48302-1941 Office: May & May PC 3000 Town Ctr Ste 2600 Southfield MI 48075-1273

**MAY, BRUCE BARNETT,** lawyer; b. Portland, Oreg., Apr. 16, 1948; s. Ralph Barnett May and Barbara (Newton) Evans; m. Deborah Sue Wright, Jan. 22, 1972; children: Alexander, Christopher, Elizabeth, Andrew. BA, Princeton U., 1971; JD, U. Oreg., 1978. Bar: Ariz. 1978. Ptnr. Streich Lang, Phoenix, 1978—; lectr. various bar and trade assns. Contbr. articles to profl. jours. Dir. Phoenix Mountain Preservation Coun., 1985-89; mem. Paradise Valley Urban Village Planning Com., Phoenix, 1985-87, mem. Men's Art Coun., 1987-91; mem. adv. bd. Corp. Supportive Housing. Lt. (j.g.) USN, 1972-75. Mem. ABA (chmn. land sales regulation com., vice chair divsn. CLE, task force future of CLE, co-chmn. brokers and brokerage com.), Am. Coll. Real Estate Lawyers, Order of Coif. Republican. Episcopalian. Avocations: book collecting, running, boxing. Real property. Home: 4616 E Shadow Rock Rd Phoenix AZ 85028-6106

**MAY, CHRISTOPHER,** lawyer; b. Rochester, N.Y., Oct. 22, 1929; s. Arthur James and Hilda Jones May; m. Elisabeth Mary Hawkins, Nov. 13, 1954 (div. July 1972); children: Andrew, Corinna, Brian, Laurence; m. Carolyn M. Stearns, May 23, 1987. AB, Harvard U., 1951; JD, Georgetown U., 1978. Bar: D.C. 1979. Staff officer CIA, Washington, 1951-52, 55-77; v.p. Mortgage Data Svc., Washington, 1979—; pvt. practice law Washington, 1990—. Founding pres. McLean Gardens Residents Assn., Washington, 1971-73. Lt. USNR, 1952-55. Mem.Soc. for the Preservation and Encouragement of Barber Shop Quartet Singing in Am. Democrat. Avocations: singing, skiing, swimming, men's work. Family and matrimonial. Home: 6039 Melbourne Ave Deale MD 20751-9719 Office: 1301 20th St NW Apt 108 Washington DC 20036-6003

**MAY, DAVID STERLING,** lawyer; b. New Orleans, Nov. 14, 1943; s. James Sidney and Sophia Belle May; m. Ann Katherine Bacon, Aug. 30, 1964; children: Diane, Steven. BA, Grinnell Coll., 1965; PhD, U. Tex., 1969; JD, U. Denver, 1981. Asst. prof. biology Utica (N.Y.) Coll. Syracuse U., 1969-72; assoc. prof. biol. scis. U. Denver, 1972-82; v.p., regional counsel URS Corp., Denver, 1983-88; counsel Manville Corp., Denver, 1988-91; mng. counsel environ., health and safety Panhandle Easter Corp., Houston, 1991-98; sr. atty. safety and environ. Sonat Exploration Co., Houston, 1999—. Issue editor, author Natural Resources and Environment, 1998; contbr. articles to profl. jours. Mem. ABA (asst. editor Natural Resources and Environment mag. 1994—), AAAS, State Bar Tex., State Bar Colo. Unitarian-Universalist. Fax: 713-850-3764. E-mail: dsmay@flash.net. Office: Sonat Exploration Co Four Greenway Plz Houston TX 77046

**MAY, FRANK BRENDAN, JR.,** lawyer; b. Bronx, N.Y., Oct. 17, 1945; s. Frank Brendan and Margaret (Borza) M.; m. Mary Frances Fitzsimmons, June 19, 1976; children: David Brendan, Brian Christopher. BA in Econs., NYU, 1973, postgrad., 1973-75; JD, John Marshall Law Sch., Chgo., 1978. Bar: Ill. 1979, U.S. Dist. Ct. (no. dist.) Ill. 1979, U.S. Ct. Appeals (7th cir.), 1979, U.S. Supreme Ct. 1995, lic. Ill. real estate broker 1994. Legal intern criminal div. Cook County State's Atty.'s Office, Chgo., 1977-78; legal intern juvenile div. DuPage County State's Atty.'s Office, Wheaton, Ill., 1978; sr. assoc. atty. Lillig, Kemp & Thorness, Ltd., Oak Brook, Ill., 1978-81; v.p., gen. counsel Coldwell Banker, Oak Brook, 1981-90, Prudential Preferred Properties, Des Plaines, Ill., 1991-98, Walker & May Inc., Wheaton, Ill., 1999—; arbitrator 18th Jud. Cir. Ct., Dupage County, Ill., 1993—; legal counsel Realtor Assn. for the Western Suburbs, 1999—. Sgt. USAF, 1963-67. NYU Coun. scholar, 1971-73; David Davis Meml. scholar, 1970-71. Mem. ABA (real estate sect.), Ill. State Bar assn. (real estate sect.), DuPage county Bar Assn. (real estate law com.), Medinah Country Club (mem. legal/bylaws com. 1998—, membership com. 1997—, chmn. PGA credentials com. 1999), Ill. Assn. Realtors (mem. large brokers coun. 1998—, exec. com. 1998—, lic. law rewrite task force, nominating com. 1999—), Realtor Assn. Western Suburbs. Avocations: golf, music, gourmet cooking, wine collector. Fax: 630-462-5686. General civil litigation, General corporate, Real property. Home: 2064 Stonebridge Ct Wheaton IL 60187-7177 Office: Walker & May Inc Ste #202 1776 S Naperville Rd Bldg A Wheaton IL 60187-8133

**MAY, JOSEPH LESERMAN (JACK MAY),** lawyer; b. Nashville, May 27, 1929; s. Daniel and Dorothy (Fishel) M.; m. Natalie McCuaig, Apr. 12, 1957 (dec. May 1990); children: Benjamin, Andrew, Joshua, Maria; m. Lynn Hewes Lance, June 10, 1994. BA, Yale U., 1951; JD, NYU, 1958; postgrad., Harvard Bus. Sch., 1969. Bar: Tenn. 1959. Prodr. Candied Yam Jackson Show, 1947-51; with CIA, 1951-55; pres. Nuweave Socks, Inc., N.Y.C., 1955-59, May Hosiery Mills, Nashville, 1960-83, Athens Hosiery Mills, Tenn., 1966-83; v.p. Wayne-Gossard Corp., Chattanooga, 1972-83; pvt. practice law Nashville, 1984—; bd. dirs. Convertible Fund, Princeton, N.J., World Income Fund, Princeton, Merrill Lynch Growth Fund; dir. Signal Apparel, 1984-89; mem. adv. group Civil Justice Reform Act U.S. Dist. Ct., 1991; mem. adv. bd. Asian Strategies Group, 1994. Bd. dirs. Vanderbilt Cancer Ctr., 1994—; pres. Jewish Cmty. Ctr., 1969; chmn. Guardianship and Trust Corp., 1994-96. With USN, 1947-53, U.S. Army, 1954. Mem. Tenn. Bar Assn., Nashville Bar Assn., Tenn. Hist. Soc. (trustee, v.p. 1996), Eagle Scout Assn., Belle Meade Country Club, Shamus Club, Old Oak Club, Yale Club N.Y., Rotary (pres. Nashville 1971). Home: 133 Abbottsford Nashville TN 37215-2442 Office: PO Box 190628 424 Church St Ste 2000 Nashville TN 37219-3304

**MAY, LAWRENCE EDWARD,** lawyer; b. N.Y.C., Aug. 7, 1947; s. Jack and Ann Marie (Schnell) M.; m. Rosalind Marsha Israel, Feb. 3, 1979; children: Jeremy, Lindsey. BA, UCLA, 1969, JD, 1972. Bar: Calif. 1972, N.Y. 1973. Assoc. Paul, Weiss, Rifkind, Wharton & Garrison, N.Y.C., 1972-76, Levine, Krom & Unger, Beverly Hills, Calif., 1976-79, Weissburg & Aronson, L.A., 1979-81, Valensi & Rose, L.A., 1981-83; prin. Lawrence E. May, P. C., L.A., 1983—, 1984—; bd. dirs. Pub. Counsel, 1989-97; pres., 1995-96. Mem. editorial adv. bd. L.A. Jewish Jour., 1985-91, adv. bd. L.A. Area Coun. Boy Scouts Am., 1985—, exec. com. Pacific S.W. Region Anti-Defamation League, 1985—; bd. dirs. L.A. Youth, 1997—. Mem. State Bar Calif., Los Angeles County Bar Assn. (trustee 1987-88, pro bono coun. 1995-98), Beverly Hills Bar Assn. (bd. govs. 1981-90, pres. 1988-89, chmn. bus. law sect. 1984-85). Democrat. Avocations: current events, golf, family activities. General corporate, Real property, Estate planning. Office: 10100 Santa Monica Blvd Ste 800 Los Angeles CA 90067-4100

**MAY, MICHELLE APRIL,** lawyer; b. Ft. Worth, June 27, 1968; d. Charles Richard and Sandra (Crouch) M. BBA, Baylor U., 1989, JD, 1991. Bar: Tex 1992, bd. cert. family law, Tex., 1997. Pvt. practice Belton, Tex., 1992-97; assoc. Erwin A. Cain, P.C., Dallas, 1997-98, McCurley, Kinser, McCurley & Nelson, LLP, Dallas, 1998—. Mem. ABA, Tex. Bar Assn., Dallas Bar Assn., Bell County Bar Assn. (dir.), Bell County Young Lawyers Assn. (pres.). Avocations: geneology, reading. Family and matrimonial, Appellate, State civil litigation. Office: PO Box 800353 Dallas TX 75380-0353

**MAYBERRY, HERBERT SYLVESTER,** lawyer; b. Enid, Okla., Jan. 20, 1927; s. Herbert Sylvester and Pearl Wilma (Bridal) M.; m. Gladys Anne Cody, Nov. 21, 1951 (div. Feb. 1974); children: Martha Rebecca, Molly Nanette; m. Joan Wilma Burnette, Dec. 28, 1974. BS in Geology, U. Okla., 1949; JD, U. Denver, 1959. Bar: Colo. 1959, Tex. 1979. Geologist Shell Oil Co., Denver, 1949-58; mgr. Ball Assocs. Ltd., Denver, 1958-65; exec. asst. Western Geophys. Co., Shreveport, La., 1965-66; v.p., gen. counsel, sec. McAlester (Okla.) Fuel Co., 1966-81; assoc. gen. counsel Enstar Corp., Houston, 1977-84; v.p., gen. counsel, sec. Ultramar Oil and Gas Co., Houston, 1985-89; pvt. practice Grand Junction, Colo., 1989—. With USNR, 1945-46. Mem. ABA, Am. Assn. Petroleum Geologists, Am. Inst. Profl. Geologists. Contracts commercial, General corporate. Home: 1701 Cortland Ct Grand Junction CO 81506-5247

**MAYDEN, BARBARA MENDEL,** lawyer; b. Chattanooga, Sept. 18, 1951; d. Eugene Lester Mendel and Blanche (Krugman) Rosenberg; m. Martin Ted Mayden, Sept. 14, 1986. AB, Ind. U., 1973; JD, U. Ga., 1976. Bar: Ga. 1976, N.Y. 1980. Assoc. King & Spalding, Atlanta, 1976-79, Willkie Farr & Gallagher, N.Y.C., 1980, Morgan Lewis & Bockius, N.Y.C., 1980-82, White & Case, N.Y.C., 1982-89; spl. counsel Skadden, Arps, Slate, Meagher & Flom, N.Y.C., 1989-95; of counsel Bass, Berry & Sims PLC, Nashville, 1996—; lectr. Vanderbilt U. Sch. Law, Nashville, 1995-97. Mem. bd. visitors U. Ga., Athens, 1986-89; mem. Leadership Nashville, 1999—. Fellow Am. Bar Found. (life); mem. ABA (chair young lawyers div. 1985-86, house of dels. 1986—, commr. commn. on women 1987-91, commr. commn. opportunities for minorities in profession 1986-87, chmn. assembly resolutions com. 1990-91, select com. of the house 1989-91, membership com. of the house 1991-92, chair com. on rules and calendar 1996-98, bd. govs. 1991-94, chair bd. govs. ops. com., exec. com. 1993-94, mem. task force long range fin. planning 1993-94, com. scope correlation of work 1998—), Nat. Assn. Bond Lawyers (bd. dirs. 1985-86), Bond Attys.' Workshop (chmn. 1986), N.Y. State Bar Assn. (mem. ho. of dels. 1993-95), Assn. of Bar of City of N.Y. (internat. human rights com. 1986-89, 2d century com. 1986-90, com. women in the profession, 1989-92), N.Y. County Lawyers Assn. (com. spl. projects, chair com. rels with other bars). Democrat. Jewish. Securities, Mergers and acquisitions, General corporate. Home: 4414 Herbert Pl Nashville TN 37215-4544 Office: Bass Berry & Sims PLC 2700 First Am Ctr Nashville TN 37238-2700

**MAYER, CARL JOSEPH,** prosecutor, lawyer; b. Boston, Apr. 23, 1959; s. Arno Joseph and Nancy Sue (Grant) M. AB magna cum laude, Princeton U., 1981; JD, U. of Chgo., 1986; LLM, Harvard U., 1988. Bar: N.J. 1986, Mass. 1988, N.Y. 1989, D.C. 1989. Writer for Ralph Nader Washington, 1981-83; law clk. to presiding justice U.S. Dist. Ct., Wilmington, Del., 1986-87; law assoc., prof. Hofstra Law Sch., Hempstead, N.Y., 1989-94; atty. Milberg, Weiss, Bershad, Hynes and Lerach, N.Y.C., 1995-96; spl. counsel N.Y. State Atty. Gen.'s Office, N.Y.C., 1999—; cons. U.S. Senate Com., Washington, 1988-89. Author: Shakedown, 1998; co-author: Public Domain, Private Dominion, 1985; contbr. articles to profl. jours. Town committeeman, Princeton, N.J., 1995-98. NYU fellow, 1988-89. Mem. ABA, N.Y. Bar Assn., N.J. Bar Assn., Mass. Bar Assn. Avocations: marathon running, squash, tennis. E-mail: carl.mayer@oag.state.ny.us. Home: 58 Battle Rd Princeton NJ 08540-4902 Office: NY State Atty Gen Office 120 Broadway New York NY 10271

**MAYER, DAVID MATHEW,** lawyer; b. Kansas City, Mo., Feb. 13, 1967; s. Michael Francis and Jackie Ann Mayer; m. Karen Louise Redmond, June 23, 1990; children: Caitlin, Jonathan. BS, Boston Coll., 1989; JD, U. Mo., Kansas City, 1992. Assoc. Myerson & Morrow, Kansas City, 1991-96; ptnr. Monsees Miller & DeFeo, Kansas City, 1996—. Bd. dirs. Heads and Hearts for Children's Mercy Hosp. Victor Wilson scholar, 1991-92. Mem. Mo. Assn. Trial Attys., Mo. Bar Assn. Avocations: soccer, barbecue. General civil litigation, Product liability, Personal injury. Office: Monses Miller & DeFeo 9229 Ward Pkwy Ste 107 Kansas City MO 64114-3311

**MAYER, HALDANE ROBERT,** federal chief judge; b. Buffalo, N.Y., Feb. 21, 1941; s. Haldane Rupert and Myrtle Kathleen (Gaude) M.; m. Mary Anne McCurdy, Aug. 13, 1966; children: Anne Christian, Rebecca Paige. BS, U.S. Mil. Acad., 1963; JD, Coll. William and Mary, 1971. Bar: Va. 1971, U.S. Ct. Appeals (4th cir.) 1972, U.S. Dist. Ct. (ea. dist.) Va. 1972, U.S. Ct. Mil. Appeals, U.S. Army Ct. Mil. Rev. 1973, D.C. 1980, U.S. Supreme Ct. 1977, U.S. Ct. Claims 1984. Law clk. U.S. Ct. Appeals (4th cir.), Richmond, Va., 1971-72; atty. McGuire Woods & Battle, Charlottesville, Va., 1975-77; spl. asst. to chief justice U.S. Supreme Ct., Washington, 1977-80; atty. Baker & McKenzie, Washington, 1980-81; acting spl. counsel U.S. Merit Systems Protection Bd., Washington, 1981-82; judge U.S. Claims Ct., Washington, 1982-87; judge U.S. Ct. Appeals (Fed. cir.), Washington, 1987-97, chief judge, 1997—; adj. prof. U. Va. Sch. Law, 1975-77, 92-94, George Washington U. Law Sch., 1992—. Bd. dirs. William and Mary Law Sch. Assn., 1979-85. Served to maj. AUS, 1963-75, lt. col. res. ret. Decorated Bronze Star, two Army Commendation medals, Meritorious Service medal. Mem. West Point Assn. Grads., Army Athletic Assn., West Point Soc. D.C., Omicron Delta Kappa. Office: US Ct Appeals for Fed Cir 717 Madison Pl NW Washington DC 20439-0002

**MAYER, JAMES HOCK,** mediator, lawyer; b. Neptune City, N.J., Nov. 1, 1935; s. J. Kenneth and Marie Ruth (Hock) M.; m. Carol I. Keating, Sept. 20, 1958 (div. Feb. 1981); children: Craig, Jeffrey; m. Patrisha Renk, Mar. 28, 1981. AB with distinction, Dartmouth Coll., 1957; JD, Harvard U., 1964. Bar: Calif. 1965, U.S. Dist. Ct (no. dist., so. dist.) Calif. 1965, U.S. Ct.

Appeals (9th cir.) 1965, U.S. Supreme Ct. 1974. Assoc. Pillsbury, Madison & Sutro, San Francisco, 1964-72, ptnr., 1973—; ind. mediator, 1992—. Rear adm. USNR, 1957-93. Rufus Choate scholar Dartmouth Coll., 1956-57. Mem. Newcomen Soc., Navy League, Naval Order of U.S., Harvard Club. E-mail: just-results@msn.com. Alternative dispute resolution, Contracts commercial, General corporate. Office: 12707 High Bluff Dr Ste 200 San Diego CA 92130-2037

**MAYER, JAMES JOSEPH,** retired corporate lawyer; b. Cin., Nov. 27, 1938; s. Cletus Joseph and Berna Mae (Schroeder) M.; m. Margaret Ann Hobbs, Oct. 24, 1964; children: Kimberly, Susanne, Terri. BEE, U. Cin., 1961; JD, No. Ky. U., 1969. Registered profl. engr., Ohio. Bar: Ohio 1969, Ky. 1975. Engr. Cin. Gas & Electric Co., 1961-69, atty., 1969-85, gen. counsel, 1986-91, v.p., gen. counsel, 1991-95, ret., 1995; of counsel Taft, Stetinius & Hollister, Cin., 1995—. Served with USAFR, 1961-64. Mem. Ohio Bar Assn., Ky. Bar Assn., Cin. Bar Assn. Republican. Roman Catholic. Club: Bankers. Avocations: home remodeling, sports, golf. Public utilities, Administrative and regulatory, General corporate.

**MAYER, MICHAEL A.,** lawyer, educator; b. Bellvue, Nebr., Dec. 3, 1965; s. L.A. and Elizabeth S. Mayer. BS, Miami U., Oxford, Ohio, 1988; JD, U. Toledo, 1994. Bar: Ohio 1994. Judicial clk. Toledo (Ohio) Mcpl. Ct., 1993-95; asst. city prosecutor City of Fairborn, Ohio, 1995-98; law dir. City of Fairborn, 1999—; ptnr. Schlafman and Mayer, Fairborn, Ohio. Office: Schlafman and Mayer 224 E Main St Fairborn OH 45324-4706

**MAYER, NEAL MICHAEL,** lawyer; b. N.Y.C., Dec. 4, 1941; s. Joseph Henry and Cele (Brodsky) M.; m. Jane Ellen Greenberg, Aug. 24, 1963; children: Andrew Warren, Amy Lynn, Rebecca Ann, Jenny Leigh. BA in History with honors, Kenyon Coll., 1963; JD, Georgetown U., 1966. Bar: D.C. 1967, U.S. Dist. Ct. D.C. 1967, U.S. Ct. Appeals (D.C. cir.) 1967, U.S. Customs Ct. 1967, U.S. Supreme Ct. 1970, U.S. Ct. Appeals (5th cir.) 1975. Assoc. Coles & Goertner, Washington, 1966-71; ptnr., 1971-82; sr. ptnr. Hoppel, Mayer & Coleman, Washington, 1982—. Trustee Kenyon Coll., 1995—. Mem. ABA, D.C. Bar Assn., Maritime Adminstrv. Bar Assn. (pres. 1979), Assn. for Transp. Law, Logistics and Policy, Propeller Club of U.S. (Washington), Kenyon Coll. Alumni Assn. (pres. 1993-94). Administrative and regulatory, Admiralty, Transportation. Office: Hoppel Mayer Coleman 1000 Connecticut Ave NW Washington DC 20036-5302

**MAYER, RENEE G.,** lawyer; b. Elizabeth, N.J., Apr. 17, 1933; d. Harry and Bertha Sheinblatt Miller; m. Joseph C. Mayer, June 19, 1955; children: Douglas, Julia, Amy, Andrew. BS, Cornell U., 1955; JD, Hofstra U., 1978. Bar: N.Y. 1979, U.S. Dist. Ct. (ea. dist.) N.Y. 1979, U.S. Ct. Appeals (2d cir.) 1983, U.S. Supreme Ct. 1982. Assoc. atty. Meyer, English & Cianciulli, Mineola, N.Y., 1978-79; pvt. practice Mineola, N.Y., 1979-89; ptnr. Riebesehl, Mayer, Keegan & Horowitz, Garden City, N.Y., 1989-97; pvt. practice law Mineola, N.Y., 1997—. Mem. N.Y. State Bar Assn., Nassau Lawyers Assn. Long Island, Inc. (pres. 1996-97), Nassau County Women's Bar Assn. (pres. 1985-86), Nassau County Bar Assn. (dir. 1984-87, asst. dean acad. law 1987-91), Cornell Club (bd. govs. 1980-90), Democratic Com. (zone leader, Port. Washington, N.Y., 1980-93). Avocations: reading, theatre, travel. Family and matrimonial. Home: 7 Leeds Dr Port Washington NY 11050-4116 Office: 200 Old Country Rd Mineola NY 11501-4235

**MAYERSOHN, ARNOLD LINN, JR.,** lawyer; b. Little Rock, Mar. 26, 1955; s. Arnold Linn and Janet (Grundfest) Mayersohn; m. Elizabeth Hardin Rudel, May 31, 1981; children: Sarah K., Veronica R. BS in Bus., U. Colo., 1977; JD, U. Ark., 1981. Bar: Ark. 1981, Mo. 1991. House counsel Sterling Stores Co., Inc., Little Rock, 1981-83; assoc. Prince & Ivester, Little Rock, 1984-86; v.p., sec., counsel Worthen Banking Corp., Little Rock, 1986-90; counsel CenterMark Properties, Inc., St. Louis, 1990-95, Westfield Corp., Inc., St. Louis, 1995—. Bd. dirs. Ark. Epilepsy Soc., Little Rock, 1982-83, Ark. Assn. for Hearing Impaired Children, 1988-9o. Mem. Ark. Bar Assn., Mo. Bar, Bar Assn. Met. St. Louis. Real property, Landlord-tenant, General corporate.

**MAYERSON, HY,** lawyer; b. Phila., June 29, 1937; s. Henry and Gertrude Mayerson; m. June 13, 1964 (div. 1973); children: Merrie Joy, Benjamin, Erin Megan, Stephnie Dawn; m. Colleen Koos. BS, Temple U., 1958, JD, 1961. Bar: Pa. 1961, Phila. Ct. Common Pleas 1962, Pa. Supreme Ct. 1968, U.S. Ct. Appeals (3d cir.) 1980, U.S. Ct. Appeals (4th cir.) 1986, U.S. Dist. Ct. (ea. dist.) Pa. Pvt. practice Phila., 1961-65; sr. ptnr. Hy Mayerson Law Offices, 1965-81, Mayerson, Schniper & Gerasimowicz, Spring City, Pa., 1981-87, Mayerson, Gerasimowicz & Munsing, Spring City, 1987-91, Mayerson, Munsing, Corchin & Rosato, P.C., Spring City, 1991-95; pvt. practice The Mayerson Law Offices, P.C., Spring City, 1995—; coord. Nat. Forklift Litigation, 1978-91; lead counsel Agent Orange Product Liability Litigation. Contbr. articles to profl. jours. Mem. ATLA (emeritus chair sect. on Indsl. & Agrl. Eqipment, Product Liability adv.bd.), Pa. Trial Lawyers Assn. E-mail: hy@mayerson.com. Personal injury, Product liability. Home: Sky Farm Birchrunville PA 19421 Office: Rt 724 Spring City PA 19475

**MAYERSON CANNELLA, RENEE,** lawyer; b. N.Y.C., June 3, 1965; d. Seymour Sheldon and Edi (Wellner) Mayerson; m. Anthony Joseph Cannella, Oct. 1, 1994. BA in Polit. Sci./Legal Studies, SUNY, Purchase, 1987; JD with honors, U. Conn., 1991. Bar: Conn. 1991, U.S. Dist. Ct. Conn. 1992, U.S. Dist. Ct. (so. dist.) N.Y. 1993. Atty. Casper & de Toledo, Stamford, Conn., 1991—; advocate Rape and Sexual Abuse Crisis Ctr., Stamford, 1993—. Contbr. article to profl. jour. Mem. ATLA, Conn. Bar Assn., Stamford/Norwalk Regional Bar Assn., Conn. Trial Lawyers Assn. Personal injury, General civil litigation. Office: Casper & de Toledo 1111 Summer St Stamford CT 06905-5511

**MAYES, JAMES PAUL,** lawyer, government official; b. Mar. 10, 1952; s. James and Hattie May (Parks) M.; m. Sharon Payne, June 23, 1973 (div. Nov. 1992); children: Khadejah, Zain, Rashid, Shehu; m. Minnie Battle, Feb. 21, 1993; 1 child, Maisa Hannah. BA, Princeton U., 1974; MA, Ohio State U., 1977; JD, U. Balt., 1991. Bar: Md. 1992, U.S. Dist. Ct. Md. 1992. Escort interpreter U.S. Dept. State, Washington, 1986—; budget analyst D.C. Dept. Corrections, Washington, 1986-87; staff atty. Md. Legal Aid Bur., Balt., 1991-93; pvt. practice, Md., 1993—; exec. dir. Kuumba Na Nia Dance and Theatre Troup, 1980. Bd. dirs. Nat. Assn. Neighborhoods, Washington, 1986-94, Rehab. Coun. Balt., 1991-93. Mem. ABA. Avocations: theatre, dance. Home: 5132 Autumncrest Dr Greensboro NC 27407-5852

**MAYESH, JAY PHILIP,** lawyer; b. Davenport, Iowa, July 22, 1947; s. Samuel and Dorothy (Katz) M.; m. Leslie Helene Haupt, June 1969; children: Stacey Janet, Beth Valerie. BA, U. Wis., 1969; JD, Columbia U., 1972. Bar: N.Y. 1973, U.S. Dist. Ct. (so. dist.) N.Y. 1973, U.S. Ct. Appeals (2d cir.) 1974. Assoc. Stroock & Stroock & Lavan, N.Y.C., 1972-80, ptnr., 1981—, mem. exec. com., 1990—; instr. Cardozo Trial Advocacy program, 1988—, N.Y. State Trial Lawyers Assn. Trial Advocacy Program, 1996—. Editor Product Liability Law and Strategy, 1984. Harlan Fiske Stone scholar Columbia U., 1971. Mem. ABA, N.Y. State Bar Assn., Phi Beta Kappa. Federal civil litigation, State civil litigation, Product liability. Office: Stroock & Stroock & Lavan 180 Maiden Ln New York NY 10038-4925

**MAYFIELD, WILLIAM SCOTT,** lawyer; b. Columbia, S.C., Nov. 6, 1961; s. W.C. and Joyce B. Mayfield; m. Martha E. Mayfield, Sept. 3, 1995; children: McRae Elizabeth, Annie Beauchamp. BA, Princeton (N.J.) U., 1985; JD, U. Ga., 1989. Bar: Ga., U.S. Dist. Ct. (no., mid. and so. dist.) Ga. Assoc. Alston & Bird, Atlanta, 1989-95, Peytan & Haines, Atlanta, 1995-96; ptnr. Mayfield & Milling, L.L.C., Atlanta, 1996—. Personal injury, General civil litigation, Real property. Office: Mayfield & Milling LLC 127 Peachtree St SW Ste 720 Atlanta GA 30303-3403

**MAYKA, STEPHEN PAUL,** lawyer; b. Rochester, N.Y., Sept. 18, 1946; s. Stephen and Mary Jane M.; m. Judith Holley Aitkin, July 26, 1981; children: Stephen I., Megan J., Judith Hope, Eric A. BA, U. Mich., 1968; JD, Union U., 1973. Bar: N.Y. 1973, N.J. 1996, Pa. 1996, U.S. Dist. Ct. (we. dist.) N.Y. 1973, U.S. Supreme Ct. 1982, U.S. Dist. Ct. (ea. and so. dists.) N.Y. 1984, U.S. Ct. Appeals (2d cir.) 1984, U.S. Dist. Ct. (no. dist.) N.Y. 1985, U.S. Dist. Ct. (we. dist.) N.C. 1987, U.S. Dist. Ct. N.J. 1996, U.S. Dist. Ct. (ea. and we. dists.) Pa. 1996. Assoc. Nixon & Hargrave, Rochester, 1973-75; gen. counsel Cen. Trust Co., Rochester, 1975-78; ops. counsel GE Capital, Stamford, Conn., 1978-80; ptnr. Lacy, Katzen, Ryen & Mittleman, Rochester, 1980-97; nat. practice in creditor's rights and bankruptcy, 1985—. Mem. N.Y. State Bar Assn., N.J. State Bar Assn., N.Y. Trial Lawyers Assn. Bankruptcy, Contracts commercial, General civil litigation. Office: 111 Knollwood Dr Rochester NY 14618-3514

**MAYNARD, DANIEL DWIGHT,** lawyer; b. Ft. Belvoir, Va., July 22, 1951; s. Luther Dwight and Dorothy Louise (Hester) M.; m. Susan Patricia Holm, Aug. 19, 1972; children: Katherine Phyllis, Jill Erin, Adam Daniel, Andrew Patrick. BA, U. Ala., Tuscaloosa, 1973, MA, 1975; JD, John Marshall Law Sch., Chgo., 1979. Bar: Ill. 1979, U.S. Dist. Ct. (no. dist.) Ill. 1980, U.S. Ct. Appeals (7th cir.) 1980, Ariz. 1983, U.S. Dist. Ct. Ariz. 1983, U.S. Ct. Appeals (4th cir.) 1984, U.S. Supreme Ct. 1985. Law clk. Supreme Ct. Ill., Springfield, 1979-80; assoc., then ptnr. Winston & Strawn, Chgo. and Phoenix, 1980-89; ptnr. Johnston Maynard Grant & Parker, Phoenix, 1989—. Editor John Marshall Law Jour., 1978-79. Bd. dirs. Am. Cancer Soc., Phoenix, 1987-94, Recreation Assn. Madison Meadows, Phoenix, 1987-94; chmn. Center Dance Emsemble, Phoenix, 1990-92. Named Vol. of Yr., Am. Cancer Soc., 1987. Mem. ABA, Ariz. Bar Assn. (Vol. of Month award 1992), Lukes Men (exec. bd., chmn. spl. events 1994-95). General civil litigation, Criminal, Intellectual property. Home: 6233 N 4th Dr Phoenix AZ 85013-1369 Office: Johnston & Maynard et al 3200 N Central Ave Ste 2300 Phoenix AZ 85012-2443

**MAYNARD, ELLIOTT,** state supreme court justice; b. Williamson, W.Va.. BS in Psychology, Fla. So. Coll., 1967; JD, W.Va. U., 1974. Judge W.Va. Cir. Ct. 30th Jud. Cir., 1982-97; justice W.Va. Supreme Ct. Appeals, Charleston, 1997—; prosecuting atty., Mingo County, 1976, 80. Mng. dir. Tug Valley C. of C., 1968-70; active Boy Scouts Am.; dist. chmn. Mingo-Pike Dist., Chief Cornstalk Dist.; bd. dirs. Buckskin Coun. With USAF, 1961-66. Recipient Silver Beaver award Boy Scouts Am. Office: Bldg 1 Rm E306 Capitol Complex Charleston WV 25305*

**MAYNARD, GEORGE FLEMING,** lawyer; b. Mar. 10, 1931; s. George Fleming and Lucie Lee (Jenkins) M.; m. Isabel Barksdale, Aug. 8, 1953; children: Isabel Mims Maynard Zabriskie, George F., William Barksdale. BA, Washington and Lee U., 1953; postgrad., Harvard U., 1953-54; LLB, U. Va., 1956. Bar: Ala. 1957. Assoc. Cabaniss & Johnston, Birmingham, Ala., 1957-62; ptnr. Cabaniss, Johnston, Gardner, Dumas & O'Neal, Birmingham, Ala., 1963-84; shareholder Maynard, Cooper & Gale, P.C., Birmingham, Ala., 1984—; trustee, Episcopal Found. of Jefferson County, 1976-85, pres., 1979-81; commr. Nat. Conf. of Commrs. on Uniform State Laws, 1988-92. Chancellor Episc. Diocese of Ala., 1983-87. Mem. ABA, Am. Bar Found., Ala. State Bar, Am. Law Inst., Ala. Law Inst. (exec. com. 1984—). Club: Mountain Brook (Birmingham). Banking, General corporate, Real property. Home: 21 Woodhill Rd Birmingham AL 35213-3933 Office: Maynard Cooper & Gale PC 1901 6th Ave N Ste 2400 Birmingham AL 35203-4604

**MAYNARD, NATASHA C.,** lawyer; b. Dec. 2, 1969. AB, Harvard U., 1991, JD, 1994. Bar: N.Y. 1995. Assoc. Cravath Swaine & Moore, N.Y.C., 1994-96; corp. atty. WESTVACO, N.Y.C., 1996—. Vol. St. Luke's Hosp., N.Y.C. Mem. Am. Soc. Corp. Secs., Bar Assn. City N.Y. Avocation: volunteering. Securities. Office: WESTVACO 299 Park Ave Fl 12 New York NY 10171-0009

**MAYNARD, ROBERT HOWELL,** lawyer; b. San Antonio, Feb. 15, 1938; s. William Simpson Sr. and Lillian Isabel (Tappan) M.; m. Joan Marie Pearson, Jan. 6, 1962; children: Gregory Scott, Patricia Kathryn, Alicia Joan, Elizabeth Simms. BA, Baylor U., 1959, LLB, 1961; LLM, Georgetown U., 1965. Bar: Tex. 1961, D.C. 1969, Ohio 1973. Trial atty. gen. litigation sect. lands div. U.S. Dept. Justice, Washington, 1964-65; spl. asst. to solicitor U.S. Dept. Interior, Washington, 1965-69; legis. asst. U.S. Senate, Washington, 1969-73; ptnr., dept. head Smith & Schnacke, Dayton, Ohio, 1973-83; dir. Ohio EPA, Columbus, Ohio, 1983-85; ptnr., environ. policy and strategy devel., tech. law Vorys, Sater, Seymour and Pease, Columbus, 1985—. Trustee Ohio Found. for Entrepren. Edn., Business Technology Ctr., Episcopal Cmty. Svcs. Found., 1990-96, Industry Tech. Coun. Ctrl. Ohio, Johnson's Island Preservation Soc. USNR, 1962-65. Episcopalian. Environmental, Natural resources, Administrative and regulatory. Office: Vorys Sater Seymour & Pease PO Box 1008 52 E Gay St Columbus OH 43215-3161

**MAYNE, WILEY EDWARD,** lawyer; b. Sanborn, Iowa, Jan. 19, 1917; s. Earl W. and Gladys (Wiley) M.; m. Elizabeth Dodson, Jan. 5, 1942; children—Martha (Mrs. F.K. Smith), Wiley Edward, John. S.B. cum laude, Harvard, 1938; student, Law Sch., 1938-39; J.D., State U. Iowa, 1939-41. Bar: Iowa bar 1941, U.S. Supreme Ct. 1950. Practiced in Sioux City, 1946-66, 75—; mem. Shull, Marshall, Mayne, Marks & Vizintos, 1946-66, Mayne and Berenstein, 1975-87, Mayne & Mayne, 1988—; spl. agt. FBI, 1941-43; Mem. 90th-93d Congresses, 6th Dist. Iowa; mem. judiciary com., agr. com. Commr. from Iowa Nat. Conf. Commrs. Uniform State Laws, 1956-60; chmn. grievance commn. Iowa Supreme Ct., 1964-66; del. FAO, 1973; chmn. Woodbury County Compensation Bd., 1975-80. Chmn. Midwest Rhodes Scholar Selection Com., 1964-66; pres. Sioux City Symphony Orch. Assn., 1947-54, Sioux City Concert Course, 1982-85; vice chmn. Young Republican Nat. Fedn., 1948-50; bd. dirs. Iowa Bar Found., 1962-68. Served to lt. (j.g.) USNR, 1943-46. Fellow Am. Coll. Trial Lawyers; mem. ABA (ho. of dels. 1966-68), Iowa Bar Assn. (pres. 1963-64), Sioux City Bar Assn., Internat. Assn. Def. Counsel (exec. com. 1961-64), Harvard Club (N.Y.C.), Sioux City Country Club, Masons (Scottish Rite/33 deg.). Fax: 712 252-1535. Federal civil litigation, State civil litigation, Insurance. Home: 2728 Jackson St Sioux City IA 51104-3623 Office: Pioneer Bank Bldg 701 Pierce St Ste 400 Sioux City IA 51101-1036

**MAYORA-ALVARADO, EDUARDO RENE,** lawyer, law educator; b. Guatemala, Guatemala, Apr. 20, 1957; s. Eduardo Alfredo Mayora-Dawe and Adelaida (Alvarado) De Mayora; m. Alicia Bascunana, June 18, 1983; children: Javier Eduardo, Santiago, Jose Andres, Sebastian. JD, U. Rafael Landivar, Guatemala, 1980; LLM, Georgetown U., U.S.A., 1982; Diploma (2) in Principles Econ. Sci., U. Francisco Marroquin, Guatemala, 1991, LLD, 1997. Bar: Guatemala, 1980; cert. notary. Assoc. Mayora & Mayora, Guatemala, 1980-81, ptnr., 1982—, mem. tax adminstrn. bd., 1998—; prof. bus. law and principles of law U. Francisco Marroquin, Guatemala, 1984-87, prof. bus. law and principles of law Sch. of Econs., 1986-88, prof. constitutional law, dean Sch. of Law, 1989—, prof. principles of pvt. and pub. law, 1993; bd. dirs. Financiera de Inversión, S.A., Guatemala, 1988-96; alt. dir. Seguros Alianza S.A., Guatemala, 1988-94; trustee U. Francisco Marroquin, 1989—; vis. prof. Pontificia U. Catolica, Porto Alegre, Brazil, 1994, Montpellier U. Sch. Law, France, 1995. Co-author: El Desafio Neoliberal, 1992; author; (essay) El Drama De La Arena Movedisa, 1993 (Charles Stillman award 1993); contbr. to profl. jours. Mem. Guatemala Bar Assn. (author articles Bar Law Jour. 1990—m v.p. ethics bd. 1985-86), Assn. De Amigos Del Pais, Fundacion Para La Cultura (v.p. 1994), Inst. Guatemalteco De Derecho Notarial, Phi Delta Phi, Guatemala Country Club. Roman Catholic. Avocations: reading, sailing, golf. Office: Mayora & Mayora15 Calle 1-04, Plz Centrica 3er Nivel #301, Zona 10 Guatemala City Guatemala also: PO Box 661447 Miami FL 33266-1447

**MAYORKAS, ALEJANDRO,** prosecutor. With Patterson, Belknap, Webb & Tyler, L.A., 1986-89; aide to Nora Manella, chief office's gen. crimes sect., 1996—; U.S. atty. cen. dist. Calif. U.S. Dept. Justice, 1999—; tchr. trial advocacy Loyala Law Sch. Office: US Courthouse 312 N Spring St Los Angeles CA 90012*

**MAYS, JANICE ANN,** lawyer; b. Waycross, Ga., Nov. 21, 1951; d. William H. and Jean (Bagley) M. AB (hon.), Wesleyan Coll., Macon, Ga., 1973; JD, U. Ga., 1975; LLM in Taxation, U. Georgetown, 1980. Bar: Ga. 1976. Tax counsel com. on ways and means U.S. Ho. Reps., Washington, 1975-88, chief tax counsel com. on ways and means, staff dir. subcom. select revenue measures, 1988-93, chief counsel, staff dir. com. on ways and means, 1993-95, minority chief counsel, staff dir. com. on ways and means, 1995—. Recipient Disting. Achievement in Profession Alumnae award Wesleyan Coll., 1998. Mem. Tax Coalition (past chair). Office: Ways & Means Com 1106 Longworth Office Bldg Washington DC 20515-0001

**MAYS, WILLIAM GAY, II,** lawyer, real estate developer; b. Washington, Mo., Apr. 8, 1947; s. Frank G. and Geneva Pauline (Brookhart) M.; m. Judith Ann Kriete, Oct. 5, 1974; 1 son, Daniel Brookhart. AB, U. Mo., 1969, JD, 1972. Bar: Mo. 1972, U.S. Dist. Ct. (we. dist.) Mo. 1972. Legis. rschr. State of Mo., 1972; pub. defender 13th Jud. Cir. Mo., 1973-77; ptnr. Holt, Mays & Brady, Columbia, Mo., 1977-98; ptnr. and gen. counsel comml. real devel. firm. Mem. Jud. Planning Commn., Mo., 1977. Served to capt. USAFR, 1969-82. Named Outstanding Young Man of Am., 1974. Mem. Mo. Bar Assn., Boone and Callaway County Bar Assn., Mo. Trial Lawyers Assn., Mo. Pub. Defender Assn. (pres. 1976-77), Assisted Living Fedn. Am., Beta Theta Pi. Republican. Club: Masons. Real property, Contracts commercial, Criminal. Office: The Mays Bldg 200 E Walnut St Columbia MO 65203-4193

**MAYSEL, KYLE WAYNE,** lawyer; b. Austin, Tex., July 2, 1958; widower, Nov. 1997. Sole practice atty. San Marcos, Tex., 1984—. mem. Buda (Tex.) City Coun., 1994-99, mayor pro tem, 1997-99; bd. dirs. Old Town Buda Assn., 1995—. Mem. Hays County Bar Assn. (pres. 1995—). Avocations: gardening, outdoors. Criminal, Family and matrimonial, Juvenile. Office: 130 E San Antonio St San Marcos TX 78666-5509

**MAZAHERI, TINA,** lawyer; b. Doylestown, Pa., July 3, 1968; d. Ahmed and Mehran (Kharrazi) M. BA, George Washington U., 1990; JD, Temple U., 1993, LLM, 1997. Bar: Pa., N.J. Law clk. to Hon. Isaac S. Garb, Doylestown, 1993-94; assoc. Harris and Harris, Warrington, Pa., 1994-97; pvt. practice Doylestown, 1997—. Mem. Doylestown Hist. Soc., Bucks County Rep. Party. Mem. Bucks County Bar Assn. (bd. dirs. 1996—, chair young lawyers sect. 1997—), Bucks County C. of C. Avocations: travel, reading, sports. Office: 18 East Court St PO Box 670 Doylestown PA 18901 also: 45 N Union St Lambertville NJ 08530-1703

**MAZEY, LARRY WILLIAM,** lawyer; b. Detroit, Dec. 23, 1939; s. Emil and Charlotte M.; m. Sharon E. Levette, July 17, 1965; children: Scott L., Mark W. BA with distinction, U. Mich., 1962, JD, 1965. Bar: U.S. Dist. Ct. (ea. dist.) Mich. 1965, Mich. 1966, U.S. Supreme Ct. 1971. Atty. Rothe, Marston, Mazey, Detroit, 1965-72; pvt. practice Redford, Mich., 1972-73; atty. Rothe, Mazey, Mazey, Southfield, Mich., 1973—, pres., CEO, 1996—; arbitrator Am. Arbitration Assn., Detroit, 1970; mediator Wayne County Cir. Ct., Detroit, 1970. Pres. Ind. Hills Subdiv., Farmington Hills, Mich., 1978-81; mgr. South Farmington Baseball Championship Team, 1986. Mem. Pi Sigma Alpha. Avocations: tennis, golf. General civil litigation, Personal injury, Workers' compensation. Office: Rothe Mazey & Mazey 26645 W 12 Mile Rd Ste 212 Southfield MI 48034-7812

**MAZHARI, NILOUFAR,** lawyer; b. Tehran, Iran, Apr. 10, 1966; came to U.S., 1979; s. Ashraf and Azar Yousefi (Tehrani) M. BS in Econs., U. Western Australa, Perth, 1986; JD, Golden Gate U., 1991. Bar: Calir. 1991. Atty. Baker & Klien, San Ramon, Calif., 1991-92; sole practitioner San Francisco, 1993—. Mem. ABA, Iranian Lawyers Assn., Soc. Iranian Profls. Workers' compensation, General civil litigation, Labor. Office: 1 Sansome St Ste 2100 San Francisco CA 94104-4432

**MAZO, MARK ELLIOTT,** lawyer; b. Phila., Jan. 12, 1950; s. Earl and Rita (Vane) M.; m. Fern Rosalyn Litman, Aug. 19, 1973; children: Samantha Lauren, Dana Suzanne, Ross Elliott, Courtney Litman. AB, Princeton U., 1971; JD, Harvard U., 1974. Bar: D.C. 1975, U.S. Dist. Ct. D.C. 1975, U.S. Claims Ct. 1975, U.S. Ct. Appeals (D.C. cir.) 1976, U.S. Supreme Ct. 1979. Ptnr. Hogan & Hartson, L.L.P., Washington and Paris, 1990—. Contbr. articles to profl. jours. White House intern Exec. Office of Pres., Washington, 1972. Capt. USAR, 1971-79. Mem. ABA, Harvard Law Sch. Assn., D.C. Bar Assn., Columbia Country Club, Princeton Club (N.Y.C.), Colonial Club, City Club, Phi Beta Kappa. Republican. Private international, Mergers and acquisitions, Contracts commercial. Home: 3719 Cardiff Rd Chevy Chase MD 20815-5943 Office: Hogan & Hartson LLP 555 13th St NW Washington DC 20004-1161 Office: Hogan & Hartson Cariddi Mee Rue, 12 rue de la Paix, 75002 Paris France

**MAZOR, LESTER JAY,** law educator; b. Chgo., Dec. 12, 1936; s. Bert William and Mildred (Mazur) M.; m. Sondra R. Bernstein, Sept. 2, 1957 (div. July 1981); children: David, Shari Lynn, Marya; m. Anne Spier, Apr. 26, 1993. AB, Stanford (Calif.) U., 1957, JD, 1960. Bar: Utah 1963. Law clk. Hon. Warren E. Burger, U.S. Ct. Appeals, Washington, 1960-61; instr. U. Va. Law Sch., Charlottesville, 1961-62; asst. prof. U. Utah, Salt Lake City, 1962-66, assoc. prof., 1966-69; vis. assoc. prof. Stanford U., 1968-69; prof. law U. Utah, Salt Lake City, 1969-72; Henry Luce prof. law Hampshire Coll., Amherst, Mass., 1970-75, prof. law, 1975—; reporter ABA Com. on Prosecution and Def. Functions, 1965-69; project dir. ABF study of law tchg. materials, 1975-80; vis. rsch. scholar Macquarie U., Sydney, Australia, 1997. Co-author: Introduction to Law Study, 1965. Fulbright scholar, Germany and U.K., 1983. Mem. Internat. Soc. Assn. (rsch. com. on sociology of law), Internat. Assn. Legal and Social Philosophy, Am. Legal Studies Assn., Phi Beta Kappa, Order of Coif. Home: 52 Elizabeth St Northampton MA 01060-2320 Office: Hampshire Coll Sch Social Sci Amherst MA 01002

**MAZUREK, JOSEPH P.,** state attorney general, former state legislator; b. San Diego, July 27, 1948; B.A., U. Mont., 1970, J.D., 1975; m. Patty Mazurek; 3 children. Bar: Mont. 1975; atty. Gough, Shanahan, Johnson, and Waterman, Helena, Mont.; mem. Mont. Senate from 23d Dist., 1981-92; Senate pres., 1991-92; atty. gen., State of Mont., 1993—; mem. Revenue Oversight Com., 1983-92; chmn. Senate Judiciary Com.; assoc. editor Mont. Law Rev., 1974-75. Served with U.S. Army, 1970-72. Mem. ABA, Beta Gamma Sigma, Phi Delta Phi, Phi Delta Theta. Office: Justice Bldg PO Box 201401 215 N Sanders St Helena MT 59601-4522*

**MAZUREK, MIKE E.,** lawyer; b. Chgo., June 20, 1947; s. Edmund and Dana Mazurek; m. Jo Ellen Holm, Dec. 15, 1972 (div. June 1979); m. Patricia Mazurek, Dec. 13, 1983; children: Madalyne, April, Trish. BA, U. Ill., 1972; JD, U. Notre Dame, 1979. Bar: Calif. Dep. dist. atty. Orange County Dist. Atty.'s Office, Santa Ana, Calif., 1983-85; assoc. Sacks Rivera, Culver City, Calif., 1991-95, Borton, Petrini, San Bernardino, Calif., 1995, O'Flaherty Cross Martinez Ovando & Hatton, Anaheim, Calif., 1996—. Avocation: ballroom dancing. Workers' compensation, Professional liability. Home: 11679 Chadwick Rd Corona CA 92880-9450 Office: O'Flaherty Cross Martinez Ovando & Hatton 222 S Harbor Blvd Ste 600 Anaheim CA 92805-3701

**MAZZA, MARIE GRIMALDI,** court clerk; b. Springfield, Mass., Oct. 6, 1936; d. James L. and Lillian G. (Voyik) Grimaldi; m. Joseph S. Mazza, June 14, 1958; children: Rosemarie, James, Joanne, Thomas, Mario, Christine. JD, WNEC Law Sch., 1971. Bar: Mass., 1972. Pvt. practice Superior Ct. Hampden County, Springfield, Mass., 1972-73, asst. city solicitor, 1973-74, asst. clerk, 1974-94, clk. of ct., 1995—. Office: Superior Ct 50 State St Springfield MA 01103-2027

**MAZZAFERRI, KATHERINE AQUINO,** lawyer, bar association executive; b. Phila., May 14, 1947; d. Joseph William and Rose (Aquino) M.; m. William Fox Bryan, May 5, 1984 (div.); 1 child, Josefa Mazzaferri Bryan; 1 stepchild, Patricia M. Bryan. BA, NYU, 1969, JD, George Washington U., 1972. Bar: D.C., 1972. Trial atty. EEOC, Washington, 1972-75; dir. litigation LWV Edn. Fund, Washington, 1975-78; dep. asst. dir. for advt. practices FTC, Washington, 1978-80, asst. dir. for product liability, 1980-82, asst. dir. for advt. practices, 1982; exec. dir., v.p. pub. svcs. activities corp. D.C. Bar, Washington, 1982—; bd. dir. regulatory analysis project U.S. Regulatory Coun.; mediator D.C. Mediation Svc., 1982; vis. instr. Antioch Law Sch., Washington, 1985; mem. Bd. of Women's Bar Assn. Found., 1990-93; mem. FBA Meml. Found., 1991-96. Recipient Superior Service award FTC, 1979. Mem. ABA (rep. of the homeless project steering com. 1988-90), D.C. Bar , Womens Legal Def. (pres. 1972-73, bd. dirs. 1971-75, 76-79), FBA Meml. Found. Home: 5832 Lenox Rd Bethesda MD 20817-6070 Office: DC Bar 1250 H St NW Fl 6 Washington DC 20005-5937

**MAZZONE, A. DAVID,** federal judge; b. Everett, Mass., June 3, 1928; s. A. Marino and Philomena M.; m. Eleanor G. Stewart, May 10, 1951; children: Margaret Clark, Andrew David, John Stewart, Jan Eleanor, Martha Ann, Robert Joseph, Carolyn Cook. B.A., Harvard U., 1950; J.D., DePaul U., 1957. Bar: Ill. 1957, Mass. 1959, U.S. Supreme Ct. 1964. Asst. dist. atty. Middlesex County, Mass., 1961; asst. U.S. atty. Mass., 1961-65; partner firm Moulton, Looney & Mazzone, Boston, 1965-75; asso. justice Superior Ct., Boston, 1975-78; now sr. judge U.S. Dist. Ct., Boston, 1978—. Served with U.S. Army, 1951-52. Mem. ABA, Mass. Trial Lawyers Assn., Am. Law Inst., Mass. Bar Assn., Boston Bar Assn., Middlesex Bar Assn., Fed. Bar Assn. Democrat. Roman Catholic. Office: US Dist Ct 1 Courthouse Way Boston MA 02210-3002

**MC ADAM, PATRICK MICHAEL,** lawyer. BBA, Loyola U., 1967, JD, 1970. Bar: Calif. 1971, 9th Cir. Ct. Appeals 1971, U.S. Supreme Ct 1979, U.S. Tax Ct. 1983. Assoc. Trippet & Yoakum, L.A., 1971-72; assoc. Iverson & Yoakum, L.A., 1972-77, ptnr., 1978—. General corporate, General civil litigation, Appellate. Office: Iverson & Yoakum 624 S Grand Ave Fl 27 Los Angeles CA 90017-3335

**MCADAM, THOMAS ANTHONY, III,** lawyer; b. Louisville, July 17, 1943; s. Thomas A. and Rita (Bowman) M.; m. Margaret Ann Logsdon, June 21, 1969; 1 child, Thomas A. IV. AB in Philosophy, Bellarmine Coll., 1966; JD, U. Louisville, 1976. Bar: Ky. 1976, U.S. Dist. Ct. (we. dist.) Ky. 1976, U.S. Ct. Appeals (6th cir.) 1978, U.S. Supreme Ct. 1984. Pvt. practice Louisville, 1976—; counsel Louisville Police Dept., 1983-91, Louisville and Jefferson County Human Rels. Com., 1991; spl. counsel Louisville Bd. Aldermen, 1993—. Bd. dirs. State Libr. Adv. Coun., Frankfort, Ky., 1991-95, Jefferson County Law Libr., Louisville, 1989—, Louisville Legal Aid Soc., 1983-91. Sgt. U.S. Army, 1968-70. Named Outstanding Vol. Lawyer Louisville Legal Aid Soc., 1990. Mem. Ky. Acad. Justice (pres. 1985). Democrat. Roman Catholic. General civil litigation, Family and matrimonial, Municipal (including bonds). Home: 3031 Wickland Rd Louisville KY 40205-2769 Office: 235 S 5th St Louisville KY 40202-3232

**MCADAMS, JOHN P.,** lawyer; b. Phila., June 5, 1949; s. Eugene P. and Mary (Miller) McA.; m. Anne Christina Connelly, Sept. 5, 1970; children: Emily Lane, Anne Connelly. BA, U. N.C., 1971; JD, Wake Forest U., 1976. Bar: Fla. 1976, N.C. 1976, U.S. Dist. Ct. (mid. dist.) Fla. 1977. Assoc. Carlton, Fields, Ward, Emmanuel, Smith & Cutler, Tampa, Fla., 1976-82, ptnr., 1982—. Contbg. editor: The Developing Labor Law, 1983, Employee Duty of Loyalty, 1995; contbr. articles to profl. jours. Pres. Hillsborough Cmty. Mental Health Ctr., Tampa, 1983; trustee City of Temple Terrace (Fla.) Pension Plan, 1985-89; pres. Hyde Park Preservation, Inc., Tampa, 1993; bd. dirs. Tampa Lighthouse for the Blind, 1997, Child Abuse Coun., Inc., 1998, Alpha House, Inc., 1998. Mem. ABA, ABA Equal Rights & Responsibilities Com., Fla. Bar Assn. (exec. coun. labor sect. 1987-89). Republican. Episcopalian. Labor. Home: 820 S Delaware Ave Tampa FL 33606-2915 Office: Carlton Fields PO Box 3239 Tampa FL 33601-3239

**MCAFEE, WILLIAM JAMES,** lawyer; b. Bronx, N.Y., June 18, 1962; s. James J. and Marie A. (Theyson) McA.; m. Helen W. Wagner, Oct. 12, 1962; children: Rebecca A., Ryan P. BA, AA, U.C.F., 1984; JD, Stetson U., St. Petersburg, Fla., 1987. Bar: Fla. 1987, U.S. Dist. Ct. (so. dist.) Fla. 1988, U.S. Dist. Ct. (mid. dist.) Fla. 1989. Asst. states atty. County of Palm Beach, West Palm Beach, Fla., 1987-88; assoc. Schuler & Wilkerson, West Palm Beach, 1988-89, Slawson & Burman, West Palm Beach, 1989-90; ptnr. Wagner, Johnson & McAfee, West Palm Beach, 1990—. Contbr. articles to profl. jours. Mem. Fla. Acad. Trial Lawyers (pres. young lawyers sect. 1989-92, frequent lectr.). Avocations: family, fishing, exercise, yard work, karate. Personal injury, Insurance. Office: Wagner Johnson McAfee Bodik 1818 S Australian Ave West Palm Beach FL 33409-6452

**MCALEVY, VINCENT WILLIAM,** lawyer; b. Chgo., Sept. 19, 1938; s. George A. and Barbara M. (Dejon) McA.; m. Annette Vera Schiffgens, Aug. 13, 1960; children: Timothy, Kevin, Brian. BA, St. Ambrose Coll., Davenport, Iowa, 1962; JD, Georgetown U., 1965. Bar: Va. 1966, D.C. 1967. Assoc. corp. counsel Washington, 1966-69; assoc. commonwealth atty. Arlington County, Va., 1969-72; judge Gen. Dist. Ct., Arlington County, 1978-88; pvt. practice, Arlington, Va., 1969—. Commr. in Chancery, Arlington Cir. Ct., 1980—. Mem. Va. State Bar Assn. (chmn. dist. 10 grievance com. 1982-85). Personal injury, Bankruptcy, Family and matrimonial. Office: 2009 14th St N Ste 302 Arlington VA 22201-2522

**MCALHANY, TONI ANNE,** lawyer; b. Decatur, Ind., May 1, 1951; d. Robert Keith and Evelyn L. (Fisher) McA. BA, Ind. U., 1973; JD, Valparaiso U., 1976. Bar: Mich. 1976, Ind. 1982, Ill. 1986, U.S. Dist. Ct. (no. dist.) Ind. 1989. Asst. prosecutor Ottawa County Prosecutor's Office, Grand Haven, Mich., 1976-81; assoc. Hann, Doss & Persinger, Holland, Mich., 1981-82, Romero & Thonert, Auburn, Ind., 1982-85; ptnr. Dahlgren & McAlhany, Berwyn, Ill., 1985-88, Colbeck, McAlhany & Stewart, Angola, Ind. & Coldwater, Mich., 1988—; atty. Angola Housing Authority, 1989—. Bd. dirs. Child and Family Svcs., Ft. Wayne, Ind., 1983, Fillmore Ctr., Berwyn, 1986-88, Altrusa, Coldwater, 1989-92. Mem. ATLA, State Bar Mich., State Bar Ind., State Bar Ill., Branch County Bar Assn., Steuben County Bar Assn. Avocations: traveling, horseback riding. Family and matrimonial, General practice, Personal injury.

**MCALLISTER, KENNETH WAYNE,** lawyer; b. High Point, N.C., Jan. 3, 1949; s. John Calhoun and Ruth Welch (Buie) McA.; m. Susan Lee Haralson, May 22, 1992; children: Katherine Owen, Kenneth Grey. B.A., U. N.C., 1971; J.D., Duke U., 1974. Bar: N.C. 1974, U.S. Dist. Ct. for Middle dist. N.C. 1974, U.S. Ct. Appeals for 4th circuit 1980, U.S. Supreme Ct. 1980. Ptnr. firm Fisher, Fisher & McAllister, High Point, 1974-81; former U.S. atty. for middle dist. N.C. U.S. Dept. Justice, Greensboro, from 1981; sr. exec. v.p., gen. counsel Wachovia Corp., Winston-Salem, N.C.; bd. of visitors Wake Forest U. Sch. of Law, 1988-96, U. N.C. at Chapel Hill, 1989-93, Duke U. Law Sch., 1996—. Pres. High Point Drug Action Coun., 1977-78; chmn. High Point Rep.Com., 1976-78, 88-89; mem. adv. bd. Salvation Army, High Point, 197-79; bd. dirs. Sch. of Nursing Found., U. N.C., Chapel Hill, 1993—; vice chair Attys. Gen. Adv. Com. U.S. Atty., 1985-86; govs. commn. Bus. Laws and the Economy, 1994—; bd. govs. Presbyn. Homes, 1997—; permanent mem. Fourth Cir. Jud. Conf. John Motley Morehead scholar Morehead Found., 1967; Arthur Priest scholar Phi Delta Theta, 1971. Fellow Am. Bar Found.; mem. High Point Country Club, Phi Beta Kappa. Republican. Presbyterian. Home: 1902 La Vista Dr High Point NC 27265-9685 Office: Wachovia Corp 100 N Main St Winston Salem NC 27101-4047

**MCALPIN, KIRK MARTIN,** lawyer; b. Newark, Sept. 14, 1923; s. Aaron Champion and Margaret (Martin) McA.; m. Sarah Frances Morgan, Dec. 14, 1951; children: Kirk Martin Jr., Philip Morgan, Margaret Champion Margeson. LLB, U. Ga., 1948; postgrad., Columbia U., 1949. Bar: Ga. 1949. Asst. solicitor gen. Ea. Jud. Cir. Ct. Ga., 1951; assoc. Bouhan, Lawrence, Williams, Levy & McAlpin, Savannah, Ga., 1952-53; ptnr. Bouhan, Lawrence, Williams, Levy & McAlpin, Savannah, 1954-63; sr. ptnr. King & Spalding, Atlanta, 1963-86; pvt. practice Savannah, 1987-97, Atlanta, 1998—; chmn. Inst. Continuing Legal Edn., 1980-81, Inst. Continuing Jud. Edn. in Ga., 1981-84, Jud. Council Ga., 1979-82. Pres. Atlanta Legal Aid Soc., 1971. Fellow Am. Bar Found., Am. Law Inst., Am. Coll. Trial Lawyers, Internat. Acad. Trial Lawyers, Internat. Soc. Barristers; mem. ABA (Jr. Bar Conf. chmn. 1958-59, chmn. gen. practice sect. 1972-73, chmn. sr. lawyers div. 1986-87, ho. of dels. 1960-90, state del. 1970-90, bd. govs. 1973-76), State Bar Ga. Assn. (chmn. Young Lawyers 1953-54, bd. govs. 1953-63, pres. 1979-80), Atlanta Bar Assn., Savannah Bar Assn. (v.p. 1960-61), Nat. Conf. Bar Pres. (exec. com. 1981-83), Ga. Def. Lawyers Assn., Ga. Trial Lawyers Assn., Am. Trial Lawyers Assn., Fed. Bar Assn., Am. Judicature Soc., Assn. R.R. Trial Counsel, Soc. of Cin., Sons Colonial Wars, St. Andrews Soc., Capital City Club, Piedmont Driving Club, Oglethorpe Club, Phi Delta Phi, Sigma Alpha Epsilon. Episcopalian. Personal injury, Administrative and regulatory, General civil litigation. Office: 77 E Andrews Dr NW Apt 352 Atlanta GA 30305-1392

**MCAMIS, EDWIN EARL,** lawyer; b. Cape Girardeau, Mo., Aug. 8, 1934; s. Zenas Earl and Anna Louise (Miller) McA.; m. Malin Eklof, May 31, 1959 (div. 1979); 1 child, Andrew Bruce. AB magna cum laude, Harvard U., 1956, LLB, 1959. Bar: N.Y. 1960, U.S. Dist. Ct. (so. dist.) N.Y. 1962, U.S. Supreme Ct. 1965, U.S. Ct. Appeals (2d and 3d cirs.) 1964, U.S. Ct. Appeals (D.C. cir.) 1981. Assoc. law firm Webster, Sheffield & Chrystie, N.Y.C., 1959-61, Regan Goldfarb Powell & Quinn, N.Y.C., 1962-65; assoc. law firm Lovejoy, Wasson, Lundgren & Ashton, N.Y.C., 1965-69, ptnr., 1969-77; ptnr. Skadden, Arps, Slate, Meagher & Flom, N.Y.C., 1977-90, spl. ptnr., pro bono, 1990-93; adj. prof. law Fordham U., 1984-85, Benjamin N. Cardozo Sch. Law, N.Y.C., 1985-90. Bd. dirs. Aston Magna Found. for Music, Inc., 1982-93, Cmty. Rsch. Initiative N.Y., 1988-89; mem. Lambda Legal and Edn. Fund, 1991-95. With U.S. Army, 1961-62. Mem. ABA, Selden Soc. Federal civil litigation, State civil litigation. Home: 4110 Kiaora St Coconut Grove FL 33133-6350

**MCANANEY, KEVIN GEORGE,** lawyer; b. Yonkers, N.Y., Mar. 22, 1949; s. Francis A. and Katherine A. (McClatchy) McA.; m. Catherine R. McCabe, Sept. 9, 1978; children: Sheila, Cara, Patrick. BA, U. N.C., 1971; JD, Columbia U., 1977. Bar: N.Y. 1979, U.S. Dist. Ct. (so. dist.) N.Y. 1979, DC 1990. Assoc. Kelley Drye & Warren, N.Y.C., 1977-80; asst. counsel to Gov. Hugh Carey State of N.Y., Albany, N.Y., 1980-83; assoc. Dewey Ballantine, Washington, 1983-86, ptnr., 1986-97; chief industry guidance br., Office of Counsel to Insp. Gen. U.S. Dept. Health and Human Svcs., Washington, 1997—; Bd. dirs. Hosp. Sick Children, Washington, 1992-96. Mem. Am. Health Lawyers Assn., Peter and Adeline Ruffin Found. (trustee 1980—), Phi Beta Kappa. Health. Office: Office Counsel to Insp Gen Cohen Bldg Rm 5527 330 Independence Ave SW Washington DC 20201-0001

**MCANDREW, THOMAS J.,** lawyer; b. Providence, Oct. 19, 1945; s. Joseph E. and Amelia L. (Bonhotel) McA.; m. Mary Luise Fogarty, June 13, 1970; children: John Maxwell, Mercedes, Hope, Marya, Cornelia. BA, Providence Coll., 1968; JD, Georgetown U.-Am. U., 1971; LLM, George Washington U., Georgetown U., 1973. Bar: R.I., U.S. Dist. Ct. R.I., U.S. Ct. Claims, U.S. Tax Ct., U.S. Custom and Patent Ct., U.S. Ctp. Mil. Appeals, U.S. Ct. Appeals (1st cir.), U.S. Ct. Appeals (D.C.), U.S. Supreme Ct. Trial atty. Civil Aeros. Bd., Washington, 1971-72; legal asst. to John H. Fanning NLRB, Washington, 1972-73; labor rels. officer dept. edn. Sate of R.I., Providence, 1973-74, dep. asst. commr. edn., 1974-79, adminstr. labor rels., 1979-80; ptnr., owner Powers & McAndrew, Inc., Providence, 1980-87; pvt. practice, Providence, 1987—; adj. prof. law U. R.I., Kingston; lectr. various profl. meetings. Contbr. articles to various publs. Treas., trustee John E. Fogarty Found., Providence, 1974—; mem. adv. bd. Fogarty Internat. Ctr., Bethesda, Md., 1998—; mem. Providence Com. on Fgn. Rels., Providence; mem. beach com. and pub. safety com. Weekapaug (R.I.) Fire Dist. Mem. ABA (com. on labor law) FBA, ATLA, Am. Arbitration Assn. (adv. coun.). Avocations: golf, tennis, walking. Home: 6 Wingate Rd Providence RI 02906-4910 Office: 1800 BankBoston Tower Providence RI 02903

**MCARTHUR, JOHN WILLIAM, JR.,** lawyer, educator; b. Lyons, Ga., May 28, 1955. BBA in Acctg., Emory U., 1976; JD, U. Ga., 1979; LLM in Taxation, Georgetown U., 1985. Bar: Ga. 1979. Tax specialist Coopers & Lybrand, Atlanta, 1979-81; tax supr. Nat. Office Tax Svcs.-Tax, Washington, 1981-84; state and local tax counsel Coca-Cola Co., Atlanta, 1984—; adj. prof. M. in Taxation program Ga. State U., Atlanta, 1986—, Emory U. Sch. Law, Atlanta, 1989—; advisor to editor Multistate Tax Analyst; mem. adv. coun. Nat. Inst. on State and Local Taxation; mem. state and local taxation adv. bd. NYU Sch. Continuing Edn. State tax columnist Corp. Taxation; mem. editorial adv. bd. Jour. State Taxation, Corp. Taxation, Jour. Calif. Taxation, Jour. N.Y. Taxation; contbr. articles to legal jours. Active Com. on State Taxation. Mem. State Bar Ga. (co-chmn. state and local taxation com.), Atlanta Bar Assn., Atlanta C. of C. (chmn. task force on taxation and pub. fin.). Avocations: broadcasting, hunting, whitewater rafting, tennis. State and local taxation. Office: The Coca-Cola Co PO Box 1734 Atlanta GA 30301-1734

**MCATEE, DAVID RAY,** lawyer; b. Rosebud, Tex., Nov. 20, 1941; s. Lee Ray and Florine (Davis) McA.; m. Carole Kay Pendergraft, Jan. 28, 1967; children—David Ray, Kristin Carole. B.B.A. with honors, Baylor U., 1964; LL.B., U. Tex., 1967. Bar: Tex. 1967; U.S. Dist. Ct. (no. dist.) Tex. 1968, (so. dist.) Tex., 1994; U.S. Ct. Appeals (5th cir.) 1969, (11th cir.) 1981; U.S. Tax Ct., 1993. Briefing atty. Supreme Ct. Tex., Austin, 1967-68; ptnr. Thompson & Knight, Dallas, 1968-90; ptnr. Gibson Dunn & Crutcher, Dallas, 1990-95; with Akin, Gump, Strauss, Hauer & Feld, L.L.P., Dallas, 1995—. Founder, bd. dirs. No. Hills Neighborhood Assocs., Inc., 1974-76; pres., bd. dirs. Montessori Sch. of Park Cities, 1975-78; mem. Goals for Dallas Com., City of Dallas Citizens Safety Adv. Com., 1975-77; chmn. City of Dallas Thoroughfare Com., 1979-81; mem. City of Dallas Plan Commn., 1979-83, vice-chmn., 1981-83. Mem. Dallas Bar Assn. (legal ethics com. 1979-81), Tex. Bar Assn. (legal ethics com. 1975-81), ABA (antitrust sect.). Democrat. Methodist. Antitrust, Federal civil litigation, State civil litigation. Office: Akin Gump Strauss Hauer & Feld 1700 Pacific Ave Ste 4100 Dallas TX 75201-4675

**MCATEE, JAMES STUART,** lawyer; b. Deland, Fla., Dec. 10, 1965; s. James Ray McAtee and Barbara (Jones) Dye; m. Betsy Underwood, June 12, 1992; 1 child, Ella Stuart. BA in Econs., U. West Fla., 1987, MBA, 1991; JD, Birmingham Sch. Law, 1995. Bar: Ala. 1995, U.S. Dist. Ct. (no., mid., and so. dists.) Ala. Jud. law clk. U.S. Ct. Appeals 10th cir., Birmingham, Ala., 1995-96; assoc. Lamar Miller & Norris, Birmingham, 1996—. Mem. ABA, Birmingham Bar Assn. Republican. Episcopalian. Insurance, Workers' compensation, Personal injury. Home: 3801 Spring Valley Cir Birmingham AL 35223-1405 Office: Lamar Miller & Norris 1600 Fin Ctr 505 20th St N Birmingham AL 35203-2605

**MCATEER, MELANIE,** lawyer; b. Chester, Pa., Dec. 6, 1956; d. Francis Leo and Lorraine Edna McAteer. BA in Polit. Sci., Widener Coll., 1978; JD, Del. Law Sch., 1982. Bar: Pa. 1982, U.S. Supreme Ct. 1986. Staff atty. Hyatt Legal Svcs., Drexel Hill, Pa., 1982-83; sole practice Folsom, Pa., 1984; family ct. adminstr. Chester County Cts., West Chester, Pa., 1984—. Organizer ann. Christmas toy collection Chester County Ct., 1990—. Mem. Chester County Bar Assn. (chair social com. 1992—, bd. dirs. 1994-96). Office: Chester County Family Ct Ste 310 2 N High St PO Box 2748 West Chester PA 19380-0991

**MCAULIFFE, J. GERARD,** lawyer; b. Amsterdam, N.Y., Aug. 27, 1964; s. James Gerard and Marguerite Mary McA.; m. Maureen Evelyn Gallagher, June 10, 1994; children: Gregory, Augustus, Matthew. BA cum laude, Siena Coll., 1985; JD, Union U., 1988. Bar: N.Y. Assoc. Amdursky Law Office, Oswego, N.Y., 1988-92; ptnr. Schur & McAuliffe, Mayfield, N.Y., 1995—; pub. defender Fulton County, Johnstown, N.Y., 1996—; bd. dirs. Ctrl. N.Y. Legal Aid Soc., Utica, 1996—. Bd. dirs. Charities of Fulton County, Johnstown, 1995—, Citizens in Cmty. Svc., Johnstown, 1996—. Republican. Mem. N.Y. State Bar Assn., Fulton County Bar Assn. Avocations: religious education instructor, softball, fishing, canoeing. Criminal, Personal injury, Family and matrimonial. Home: 1173 County Highway 107 Fort Johnson NY 12070-1214 Office: Schur & McAuliffe 2431 S Hwy 30 Mayfield NY 12117

**MCAULIFFE, JOHN F.,** retired judge; b. Washington, Nov. 4, 1932; m. Barbara McAuliffe, Nov. 4, 1955; children: John M., Mary K. JD, Am. U., 1955. Assoc. judge Cir. Ct. for Montgomery County, Md., 1972-85; judge Md. Ct. Appeals, Annapolis, 1985-92. Office: MD Ct of Appeals Rm 301 50 Maryland Ave Rockville MD 20850-2320

**MCAULIFFE, ROSEMARY,** lawyer; b. New Rochelle, N.Y., May 24, 1927; d. William J. and Rose B. (Payne) McA. BA, Regis Coll., 1949; JD, New Eng. Sch. Law, 1954; MEd, Boston State Coll., 1971, Cert. advanced grad studies, 1981. Bar: Mass. 1956, U.S. Dist. Ct. Mass. 1957, U.S. Supreme Ct. 1961. Pvt. practice law Boston, 1956—; tchr. City of Boston, 1965-93. Active World Affairs Coun., Boston, 1980-95; sec. Italian Hist. Assn. Mass., 1988—. Mem. Mass. Bar Assn., Am. Acad. Trial Lawyers, Mass. Assn. Women Lawyers (bd. dirs. 1989—). Avocation: conducting walking tours of Boston. General practice. Home and Office: 61 Prince St Boston MA 02113-1829

**MCAULIFFE, STEVEN JAMES,** federal judge; b. 1948. BA, Va. Mil. Inst., 1970; JD, Georgetown U., 1973. Capt. appellate coun. U.S. Army Judge Advocate Gens. Corps, 1973-77; asst. atty. gen. Office N.H. Atty. Gen., 1977-80; ptnr. Gallagher, Callahan, Gartrell, P.A., Concord, N.H., 1980-92; fed. judge U.S. Dist. Ct. (N.H. dist.), Concord, 1992—. Trustee Univ. System of N.H., 1986-94; bd. dirs. N.H. Med. Malpractice Stabilication Res. Fund Trust, 1987-92, Office Pub. Guardian, 1980-92, Challenger Ctr. for Space Sci. Edn.; active N.H. Dem. Leadership Coun., 1988-92. Capt. U.S. Army, 1970-77, USAR, 1977-80, N.H. Army NG, 1980-88. Fellow N.H. Bar Found.; mem. ABA, N.H. Bar Assn. (pres. 1991-92, pres.-elect 1990-91, v.p. 1989-90, mem. ex-officio N.H. Supreme Ct. com. profl. conduct 1989-90, mem. ethics com. 1984-86), Nat. Conf. Bar Pres., Merrimack County Bar Assn., D.C. Bar Assn., U.S. Supreme Ct. Hist. Soc., N.H. Jud. Coun. (vice-chmn. 1991-92), Aircraft Owners and Pilots Assn., N.H. Hist. Soc., Concord Country Club. Office: US Dist Ct 55 Pleasant St Concord NH 03301-3954

**MCAVOY, THOMAS JAMES,** federal judge; b. 1934. AB, Villanova U., 1960; JD, Union U., 1964. Bar: N.Y. 1964, U.S. Dist. Ct. (no. dist.) N.Y. 1964. Assoc. Hinman, Howard & Kattell, Binghamton, N.Y., 1964-69, Kramer, Wales, & McAvoy, Binghamton, 1969-84, McAvoy & Hickey, P.C., Binghamton, 1984-85; from judge to chief judge U.S. Dist. Ct. (no. dist.) N.Y., Binghamton, 1986—. With USMC, 1958. Office: US Dist Ct/No Dist NY Fed Bldg & US Courthouse Rm 225 15 Henry St Binghamton NY 13901-2723

**MCBARNETTE, BRUCE OLVIN,** lawyer, corporate executive; b. N.Y.C., Oct. 7, 1957; s. Olvin R. and Yvette Fay (Francis) McB. BA, Princeton U., 1980; JD, NYU, 1983. Bar: N.Y. 1985, Hawaii 1987, D.C. 1989. Atty. Natural Resources Def. Coun., N.Y.C., 1984; atty. U.S. Judge Adv.Gen.'s Corp., Aberdeen Proving Grand, Md., 1988-89, Schofield, Hawaii, 1985-88; legis. asst. U.S. Ho. of Reps., Washington, 1989; counsel impeachment trial com. U.S. Senate, Washington, 1989-90; sr. counsel Fed. Nat. Mortgage Assn., Washington, 1990-93; pres. Summit Connections, Inc., Washington, 1993—; faculty mem. George Washington U. Coord. Achieve Speakers Bur., Washington, 1990. Capt. U.S. Army, 1985-88. Mem. ABA (contbg. author newsletter for mil. pers.), D.C. Bar Assn., N.Y. Bar Assn., Hawaii Bar Assn., Screen Actors Guild. Democrat. Episcopalian. Avocation: track and field. Military, Securities, Banking. Home: 248 Willow Ter Sterling VA 20164-1628 Office: Summit Connections Inc 248 Willow Ter Sterling VA 20164-1628

**MCBIRNEY, BRUCE HENRY,** lawyer; b. L.A., June 16, 1954; s. Bruce H. and Gretta (Doyle) McB.; m. Joanne Stillman McBirney, May 31, 1980; children: James Stillman, Esther Kathleen. BA summa cum laude, Loyola Marymount U., L.A., 1976; JD, U. Calif., Berkeley, 1979. Bar: Calif. 1979, U.S. Dist. Ct. (ctrl. dist.) 1979. Mem. Thorpe & Thorpe, L.A., 1979-95, mng. ptnr., 1991, pres., 1992-94, dir., 1992-95, v.p., 1994-95; shareholder, dir., v.p. McBirney & Chuck, L.A., 1995—. Named Scholar of Yr. Loyola Marymount U., L.A., 1976, assoc. editor Calif. Law Review, Berkeley, 1977-79, Eagle Scout Boy Scouts Am., 1968. Mem. Bldg. Owners and Mgrs. Assn., L.A. Serra Club, L.A. County Bar Assn., State Bar Calif. Real property, Landlord-tenant. Office: McBirney & Chuck 611 W 6th St Ste 2500 Los Angeles CA 90017-3102

**MCBRIDE, DAVID CLINTON,** lawyer; b. Columbus, Ohio, June 10, 1949; s. Clinton Conrad and Inez Angelina (Valenti) McB.; m. Sally Fisher, Aug. 23, 1973; children: Sean, Daniel, Timothy. BSFS, Georgetown U., 1971; JD, Emory U., 1975. Bar: Del. 1975, U.S. Dist. Ct. Del. 1976, U.S. Ct. Appeals (3d cir.) 1984, U.S. Ct. Appeals (D.C. cir.) 1992. Assoc. Bayard, Brill & Handeman, Wilmington, Del., 1975-78; assoc. Young Conaway Stargatt & Taylor, LLP, Wilmington, 1978-81, ptnr., 1981—; presenter in field. Editor The Del. Lawyer, 1982—; mem. bd. editors Emory Law Jour., 1974-75; contbr. articles to profl. publs. Bd. dirs. Del. Tech. Park, Newark, 1992—, Inst. for Applied Composites, Newark, 1992—; deacon Westminster Presbyn. Ch., Wilmington, 1996—. Mem. Am. Law Inst., Hist. Soc. Ct. Chancery State of Del. (bd. dirs. 1990—), Ct. of Chancery (rules com. 1994—). Avocations: golf, tennis, squash, racquetball, hiking. Home: 2316 W 17th St Wilmington DE 19806-1331 Office: Young Conaway Stargatt & Taylor LLP 11th and Market Sts Wilmington DE 19801

**MCBRIDE, EILEEN LOUISE,** lawyer; b. West Palm Beach, Fla., Aug. 18, 1956; d. Donald William and Theresa Ann (Thiele) McB.; m. Joseph S. Ramirez, June 5, 1982; children: Eric M., Michael A., Daniel J., Gregory S. BS, U. Nebr., Lincoln, 1978, JD, 1981. Bar: Nebr. 1981. Dep. county atty. Lincoln County Atty.'s Office, North Platte, Nebr., 1981-83; assoc. Ruff & Florom, North Platte, 1983-84, Jewell, Gatz & Collins, Norfolk, Nebr., 1985-86; assoc. gen. counsel Farm Credit Svcs. of the Midlands, Omaha, 1986—; bd. dirs. FCE Credit Union, Omaha, 1990—. Officer Madison County Dems., Norfolk, 1991-93; mem. Douglas County Dem. party, Omaha, 1996—. Mem. Nebr. State Bar Assn. (mem. com.), Omaha Bar Assn. (pub. svc. com.), Rotary (bd. dirs., pres.-elect 1991-93). Roman Catholic. Avocation: family. Office: Farm Credit Svcs Legal Dept 206 S 19th St Omaha NE 68102-1759

**MCBRIDE, GORDON SCOTT,** lawyer; b. Cleve., Sept. 22, 1961; s. Gordon Charles and Patricia Jo (McCormick) McB.; m. Joyce Marie Gordon, June 20, 1987; children: Alyse Marie, Christine Ann. BA cum laude, Ohio U., 1983; JD, Ohio No. U., 1986. Assoc. Spurlock, Sears, Pry & Griebling, Bucyrus, Ohio, 1986-93; ptnr. Spurlock, Sears, Pry, Griebling & McBride, Bucyrus, 1994—. Assoc. editor Ohio No. U. Law Rev. Bd. dirs., cons. Turning Point, Buryrus, Marion, Upper Sandbury, Ohio, 1994-99, Waycraft, Bucyrus, 1993—, Crawford County Park Dist., Bucyrus, 1995—, Crawford County Law Libr., Buryrus, 1987-96. Mem. Ohio State Bar Assn., Crawford County Bar Assn., Ohio Acad. Trial Lawyers, Moose Lodge. Republican. Lutheran. Avocations: tennis, racquetball, golf. Family and matrimonial, Personal injury, General civil litigation. Office: Spurlock Sears Pry Griebling & McBride 120 N Lane St Bucyrus OH 44820-2338

**MCBRIDE, JAMES FRANCIS,** lawyer; b. N.Y.C., Aug. 7, 1946; s. Francis Patrick and Ruth Ann (Flynn) McB.; m. Catherine Lucille Schlick, Mar. 17, 1978; children: Brian, Mary Catherine, Elizabeth, Ann Marie. BS, Villanova U., 1968, JD, 1974. Bar: Pa. 1974, U.S. Dist. Ct. (ea. dist.) Pa. 1974, U.S. Ct. Appeals (3d cir.) 1976, U.S. Dist. Ct. (mid. dist.) Pa. 1980. Assoc. Nino V. Tinari, P.C., Phila., 1974-79, Donald J. Farage, Phila., 1979-82; ptnr. Farage and McBride, Phila., 1982—. Served with U.S. Army, 1968-71, Vietnam. Mem. ABA, Pa. Bar Assn. (co-author publs. on tort law in Pa. 1983—), Phila. Bar Assn., Assn. Trial Lawyers Am., Pa. Trial Lawyers Asssn., Phila. Trial Lawyers Assn., Brehon Law Soc., Phila. Lawyers Club, VFW. Democrat. Roman Catholic. Personal injury, Federal civil litigation, State civil litigation. Home: 13491 Trevose Rd Philadelphia PA 19116-1706 Office: Farage & McBride 836 Suburban Sta Bldg Philadelphia PA 19103

**MCBRIDE, JUDITH BLISS,** lawyer, educator; b. East Cleveland, Ohio, Nov. 11, 1959; d. Jack Clarence and Gene Marie (Dowd) Bliss; m. James Dominick McBride; children: Jean Marie, Madelyn Ann. BA cum laude, John Carroll U., 1982; JD, Case Western U., 1985. Bar: Ohio 1986, U.S. Dist. Ct. (no. dist.) Ohio 1988. Sole practice, Cleve., 1986—; staff instr. Mead Data Cen., Inc., Cleve., 1986-88, account rep., 1988, sr. account rep., 1989-91; atty. editor product devel. Banks-Baldwin Law Pub. Co., Cleve., 1991-93; product mgr. electronic svcs. Banks-Baldwin Law Pub. Co., 1992-93; rep. Primerica Fin. Svcs., Cleve., 1991-95; freelance atty.-editor, 1993—. Deacon Lyndhurst (Ohio) Bapt. Ch., 1986-88, bd. stewardship and missions, 1989-91, moderator, 1991-92, vice moderator, 1993-94; bd. christian edn. Brecksville United Ch. of Christ, Christian Edn. Ctr, 1997—, chair 1999; Christian Edn. Sch. Tchr., 1999—; bldg. land task force, 1997—. Mem. Ohio Bar Assn., Alpha Sigma Nu, Lambda Iota Tau (v.p. 1981-82). Republican. General practice. Home: 7886 Cambridge Dr Brecksville OH 44141-1063

**MCBRIDE, KENNETH EUGENE,** lawyer, title company executive; b. Abilene, Tex., June 8, 1948; s. W. Eugene and I. Jean (Wright) McB.; m. Peggy Ann Waller, Aug. 7, 1969 (div. 1980); m. Katrina Lynne Small, June 1, 1985; children: Katherine Jean, Kellie Elizabeth. BA, Central State U., 1971; JD, Oklahoma City U., 1974. Bar: Okla. 1974. Assoc. Linn, Helms & Kirk, Oklahoma City, 1974-76; city atty. City of Edmond (Okla.), 1976-77;

v.p., gen. counsel Am. First Land Title Ins., Oklahoma City, 1977-81; pres. Am. First Abstract Co., Norman, Okla., 1981-90, Lawyers Title of Oklahoma City, Inc., 1990—; CEO Am. Eagle Title Ins. Co., 1994—; pres. Okla. Land Title Assn., 1987-88, LT Exch. Corp., 1996—. Bd. dirs. Norman Bd. Adjustment, 1982-85, Leadership Okla., Inc., 1986-94, pres., 1989-90, 93-94. Fellow Okla. Bar Found.; mem. ABA, Okla. Bar Assn. (bd. dirs. Real Property Sect. 1992-94), Oklahoma County Bar Assn., Oklahoma City Met. Assn. Realtors (bd. dirs. 1995-96), Oklahoma City Real Property Lawyers Assn., Leadership Norman Alumni. Democrat. Presbyterian. Avocation: sailing. Real property, General corporate. Office: Lawyers Title Oklahoma City Inc 1141 N Robinson Ave Oklahoma City OK 73103-4929

**MCBRIDE, MILFORD LAWRENCE, JR.,** lawyer; b. Grove City, Pa., July 16, 1923; s. Milford Lawrence and Elizabeth B. (Douthett) McB.; m. Madeleine Coulter, Aug. 6, 1947; children: Marta, Brenda, Trip, Randy, Barry. AB, Grove City Coll., 1944; BS, N.Y.U., 1944; JD, U. Pa., 1949. Bar: Pa. 1949, U.S. Dist. Ct. (we. dist.) Pa. U.S. Supreme Ct. Ptnr., McBride & McBride, Grove City, 1949-77, sr. ptnr., 1992—; ptnr. McBride and McNickle, Grove City, 1977-92; dir. Integra Fin. Corp., 1988-93; trustee Grove City Coll., 1995—. Served to 1st lt. USAAF, 1943-46. Mem. Mercer County Bar Assn. (state treas. 1970-77), ABA, Am. Bar Found. Republican. Clubs: Oakmont Country, University (Pitts.). Probate, Real property, General corporate. Office: 211 S Center St Grove City PA 16127-1508

**MCBRIDE, TED,** prosecutor. With state Game, Fish and Pks. Dept.; clk. Chief Judge Fred J. Nichol S.D. Supreme Ct.; fed. prosecutor Rapid City (S.D.) Office, 1994—; asst. U.S. atty. S.D.; U.S. atty. S.D. dist. U.S. Dept. Justice. Office: Ste 600 230 Phillips Ave Sioux Falls SD 57104*

**MCBRIDE, THOMAS JOHN,** lawyer; b. Chgo., July 1, 1940; s. John Michael and Agnes Lorraine (Abbot) McB.; m. Catherine Louise Wentz, Aug. 23, 1969 (div. 1978); 1 child, John. BA, St. Mary's U., Winona, Minn., 1962; JD, Cath. U. Am., 1972. Bar: N. Mex. 1972, U.S. Dist. Ct. N. Mex. 1974, U.S. Supreme Ct. 1980. Law clk. N. Mex. Ct. Appeals, Santa Fe, 1972-73; asst. dist. atty. Office of Dist. Atty., Albuquerque, N. Mex., 1973; assoc. Johnson Paulantis & Lanphere, Albuquerque, 1973-79; shareholder Johnson & Lanphere, Albuquerque, 1979-87, Lanphere, McBride & Gross, Albuquerque, 1987-89; ptnr. Hinkle, Cox, Eaton, Coffield & Hensley, LLP, Albuquerque, 19896. Sgt. U.S. Army, 1965-69, Vietnam. Federal civil litigation, State civil litigation, Professional liability. Home: 12117 Palm Springs Rd Albuquerque NM 87111 Office: Hinkle Cox Eaton Coffield & Hensley LLP 500 Marquette Ave NW Ste 800 Albuquerque NM 87102-5305

**MCBRIDE, WILLIAM HOWARD, JR.,** lawyer; b. Belleville, Ill., May 10, 1945; s. William Howard McBride and Patricia (Sullivan) Sweat; m. Adelaide Alexander Sink, July 10, 1986; children: William Albert, Cheryle Alexander. BA, U. Fla., 1967, JD, 1975. Bar: Fla. 1976, D.C. 1978. With Holland & Knight, Tampa, Fla., 1975—, mng. ptnr., 1992—; bd. dirs. Lawyers Com. for Civil Rights Under Law. Chmn. United Way Campaign, Tampa, 1991, Community Needs Assessment, Tampa, 1990; pres. Hillsborough County Bar Assn., Tampa, 1983-84. Capt. USMC, 1968-71, Vietnam. Fellow Am. Bar Found.; mem. ABA, Am. Law Inst. Democrat. Avocations: fishing, history, science fiction. General corporate, Banking, Contracts commercial. Home: PO Box 219 Thonotosassa FL 33592-0219 Office: Holland & Knight PO Box 1288 Tampa FL 33601-1288

**MCBRYDE, JOHN HENRY,** federal judge; b. Jackson, Oct. 9, 1931; m. Betty Vinson; children: Rebecca McBryde Dippold, Jennifer, John Blake. BS in Commerce, Tex. Christian U., 1953; LLB, U. Tex., 1956. Bar: Tex. 1956, U.S. Ct. Appeals (5th cir.) 1958, U.S. Dist. Ct. (no. dist.) 1958, U.S. Dist. Ct. (ea. dist.) 1989, U.S. Supreme Ct. 1972. Assoc. Cantey, Hanger, Johnson, Scarborough & Gooch, Ft. Worth, 1956-62; ptnr. Cantey & Hanger and predecessor firm, Ft. Worth, 1962-69, McBryde, Bennett and predecessor firms, Ft. Worth, 1969-90; judge U.S. Dist. Ct. (no. dist.) Tex., Ft. Worth, 1990—. Fellow Am. Bar Found. (life), Tex. Bar Found. (life), Am. Coll. Trial Lawyers. Office: US Dist Ct US Courthouse 501 W 10th St Ste 202 Fort Worth TX 76102-3640

**MCBRYDE, NEILL GREGORY,** lawyer; b. Durham, N.C., Jan. 11, 1944; s. Angus M. and Priscilla (Gregory) McB., m. Margaret McPherson, Aug. 1, 1970; children: Margaret Courtauld, Neill Gregory Jr. AB cum laude, Davidson Coll., 1966; JD with high honors, U. N.C., 1969. Bar: N.C. 1969, Ga. 1972. Assoc. King & Spalding, Atlanta, 1971-76; ptnr. Fleming, Robinson, Bradshaw & Hinson, Charlotte, N.C., 1977-81, Helms, Mulliss & Johnston, Charlotte, 1981-86, Smith Helms Mulliss & Moore, Charlotte, 1986-90, Moore & Van Allen PLLC, Charlotte, 1990—; lectr. in field, conducter workshops in field. Author, editor: First Union National Bank of North Carolina Will Book, 1986; contbr. to profl. jours. Elder and Deacon Myers Park Presbyn. Ch., Charlotte, 1980-86, 92-95; dir. sec. Presbyn. Home for Aged, Charlotte, 1978-82; trustee Charlotte Latins Schs., Inc., 1980-86, 87-93. Fellow Am. Coll. Trust and Estate Counsel (mem. bd. regents, pres.-elect), Am. Coll. Tax Counsel; mem. ABA, Ga. Bar Assn., N.C. Bar Assn. (probate and fiduciary law sect.), Order of Coif, Phi Beta Kappa, Omicron Delta Kappa. Republican. Avocations: tennis, golf, fishing. Estate planning, General corporate, Mergers and acquisitions. Office: Moore & Van Allen PLLC Nations Bank Corp Ctr 100 N Tryon St Fl 47 Charlotte NC 28202-4000

**MCBURNEY, CHARLES WALKER, JR.,** lawyer; b. Orlando, Fla., June 6, 1957; s. Charles Walker McBurney and Jeane (Brown) Chappell. BA, U. Fla., 1979, JD, 1982. Bar: Fla. 1982, U.S. Dist. Ct. (mid. dist.) Fla. 1983, U.S. Ct. Appeals (11th cir.) 1984. Assoc. Mathews, Osborne, McNatt, Gobelman & Cobb, Jacksonville, Fla., 1982-84; asst. state's atty. State's Atty.'s Office, Jacksonville, 1984-90, civil atty., 1987-88, sr. trial atty., 1988-90; ptnr. Fischette, Owen, Held & McBurney, Jacksonville, 1990—; dir. Serious or Habitual Juvenile Offender Program, 1986. Bd. dirs. Civic Round Table, 1988-92, treas., 1988-89, pres. 1989-90; chmn. com. congl. campaigns, Jacksonville, 1982, 84, 88; mem. Mayor's Bicentennial Constnl. Commn., 1989-91; dir. Internat. Rels. and Mktg. Devel. Commn. for Jacksonville, 1993—, treas., 1995-97; bd. dirs. Am. Heart Assn. N.E. Fla., 1990-92. Mem. ABA, Jacksonville Bar Assn. (chmn. bankruptcy sect. 1998—, dir. 1999—), Jacksonville Bankruptcy Bar Assn. (bd. dirs. 1999—), Nat. Dist. Attys. Assn., Comml. Law League (So. region exec. coun. 1998—), Fla. Jaycees (legal counsel 1987-88, most outstanding local pres. award 1987), Jacksonville Jaycees (pres. 1986, Jaycee of yr. 1984), Jacksonville C. of C. (bd. govs. 1987), Summit Civitan (judge adv. 1991-93, ctrl. civitan 1991—, bd. dirs.), Masons, Bull Snort Club (pres. 1995-96, 99—, chmn. bd. 1996-97, 1998—), C. of C. (trustee 1996-98, govtl. affairs com. 1998—), N.E. Fla. Alumni Assn. (v.p. 1998—), James Madison Inst., Jacksonville Hist. Soc., Phi Beta Kappa. Republican. Presbyterian. Juvenile, Criminal. Home: 6326 Christopher Creek Rd E Jacksonville FL 32217-2485 Office: Fishette Owen Held & McBurney Riverplace Tower Ste 1916 Jacksonville FL 32207

**MCCAA, JAMES CURETON, III,** lawyer; b. Memphis, Jan. 31, 1949; s. James Cureton McCaa Jr. and Madeline Perkins Jehl; m. Betty Driver, Aug. 23, 1969; children: Hunter D., Margaret C. BSBA, U. Ark., 1971; JD, U. Memphis, 1974. Bar: Ark. 1974, Tenn. 1974, Va. 1985. Assoc. Skillman & Durrett, West Memphis, Ark., 1974-76; ptnr. Hightower & McCaa, West Memphis, 1977-85; asst. city atty. City of West Memphis, 1978-85; instr. East Ark. C.C., West Memphis, 1983-85; assoc. Preston Wilson & Crandley, Virginia Beach, Va., 1985-89, Vandeventer Black Meredith & Marlin, Norfolk, Va., 1989-90; ptnr. Taylor & Walker, Norfolk, 1990—. Mem. Va. Assn. Def. Attys. Episcopalian. Avocations: golf, home. General civil litigation, Insurance, Personal injury. Office: Taylor & Walker PC 555 E Main St Ste 1300 Norfolk VA 23510-2235

**MCCABE, CHARLES KEVIN,** lawyer, author; b. Springfield, Ill., Nov. 2, 1952; s. Charles Kenneth and Betty Lou (Williams) McC. BS in Aero. and Astronautical Engring. magna cum laude, U. Ill., 1975; JD, U. Mich., 1978. Bar: Ill. 1978, U.S. Dist. Ct. (no. dist.) Ill. 1978, U.S. Ct. Appeals (7th cir.) 1980. Engring. co-op. student McDonnell Aircraft, St. Louis, 1972-74; chief aerodynamicist Vetter Fairing Co., Rantoul, Ill., 1974-75; with Lord, Bissell, & Brook, Chgo., 1978—. Author: Qwiktran: Quick FORTRAN, 1979; FORTH Fundamentals, 1983, Steam Locomotive Fundamentals, 1999; co-author: 32 BASIC Programs, 1981. Contbr. articles on aviation, computers to various mags., 1974—. pres., dir. Ill. Railway Mus., 1992-98. Nat. Merit scholar U. Ill., Urbana, 1970. Mem. Chgo. Bar Assn. Aviation, Insurance, Personal injury. Office: Lord Bissell & Brook 115 S La Salle St Ste 3200 Chicago IL 60603-3972

**MCCABE, LAWRENCE JAMES,** lawyer, food products company executive; b. Uniontown, Pa., July 19, 1935; s. Patrick J. and Beatrice A. (Kane) McC.; m. Gretchen Ann Rittmeyer, Apr. 20, 1963; children—Susan M., Megan P., Kevin J., Heather K., Erin K. B.A., Pa. State U.-State College, 1957; J.D., U. Pitts., 1960. Bar: Pa. 1961, U.S. Dist. Ct. (we. dist.) Pa. 1961. Atty. Duquesne Light Co., Pitts., 1961-66; atty. H.J. Heinz Co., Pitts., 1966-72, asst. gen. counsel, 1972-75, dir. legal affairs, 1975-82, v.p., assoc. gen. counsel, 1982-89, v.p., gen. counsel, 1990-91, sr. v.p., gen. counsel, sec., 1991—; lectr. Conf. Am. Legal Execs., San Francisco, 1981, ABA, Boston, 1982. Bd. dirs. Pitts. Coun. for Internat. Visitors, 1980-86, North Hills Passavant Hosp., Pitts., 1980-89. With U.S. Army, 1960-61. Mem. ABA, Pa. Bar Assn., Allegheny County Bar Assn., Wildwood Golf Club, Duquesne Club. Republican. Roman Catholic. General corporate, Securities, Private international. Home: 400 Gass Rd Wexford PA 15090-9430 Office: H J Heinz Co PO Box 57 Pittsburgh PA 15230-0057

**MCCABE, MATTHEW CLARK,** lawyer, forensic economist; b. New Hartford, N.Y., Nov. 22, 1958; s. Kenneth Ethan and Caroline Ruth McC.; m. Gayle Marie Grimaldi, June 6, 1981; childre: Catherine, Alexander, Jonathan, Matthew. BA in Econs., SUNY, 1983; MBA, Syracuse U., 1986, JD, 1986. Bar: N.Y. 1988. Economist, assoc. atty., investment advisor Blitman & King, Syracuse, N.Y., 1986-88; forensic economist, investment advisor J.P. Jeannret Assocs., Syracuse, N.Y., 1988-94; forensic economist North Main Cons., Jordan, N.Y., 1994—; presenter in field. Chmn. Village Jordan Planning Bd., 1989—. Mem. Nat. Assn. Forensic Econs., Onondaga County Bar Assn. State civil litigation, Federal civil litigation, Family and matrimonial. Home: 20 N Main St PO Box 298 Jordan NY 13080-0298 Office: North Main Cons 20 N Main St PO Box 921 Jordan NY 13080-0921

**MCCABE, MICHAEL J.,** insurance executive; b. Denver, June 19, 1945; s. Joseph J. and Mary J. (Kane) McC.; m. Catherine Corrine Marquette, July 21, 1978; children: Brian Michael, Shannon Marquette. BS, U. No. Colo., 1967; JD, Cath. U. Am., 1971. Bar: D.C. Air transport econ. analyst U.S. Civil Aeronautics Bd., Washington, 1967-71; Washington counsel Allstate Ins. Co., 1971-74; of counsel Allstate Ins. Co., Northbrook, Ill., 1974-82, asst. v.p. bus. planning, 1982-84, v.p. corp. planning, 1984-89, group v.p., gen. atty., 1989-95; v.p., gen. counsel Allstate Corp.; sr. v.p., gen. counsel Allstate Ins. Co., 1999—; bd. advisors No. Ill. U. Sch. Bus., DeKalb, 1986—. Chmn. Gateway Found. Mem. ABA, Fed. Bar Assn., D.C. Bar Assn., Planning Forum, Sigma Chi, Pi Alpha Delta. Democrat. Roman Catholic. Office: Allstate Ins Co Allstate Pla Northbrook IL 60062*

**MCCABE, MONICA PETRAGLIA,** lawyer; b. Bronx, N.Y., Jan. 11, 1959; d. John Francis and Eleanor Angela (Gengaro) Petraglia; m. Edward D. McCabe, May 27, 1984; 1 child, Eleanor Angela. BA summa cum laude, Fordham U., 1981; MA in Polit. Sci., U. of Chgo., 1984; JD cum laude, Georgetown U., 1985. Bar: N.Y. 1986, D.C. 1987, U.S. Dist. Ct. (so. dist.) N.Y. 1987, U.S. Dist. Ct. (ea. dist.) N.Y. 1988, U.S. Supreme Ct. 1991, 2d Cir. Ct. of Appeals. Law clk. U.S. Dept. of State, Washington, 1984-85; jud. clk. to judge U.S. Dist. Ct. U.S. Dist. Ct., Washington, 1985-86; assoc. Simpson, Thacher & Bartlett, N.Y.C., 1986-89; assoc. Reid & Priest, N.Y.C., 1989-95, ptnr., 1995-98; of counsel Piper & Marbury LLP, 1998—; assoc. counsel gov.'s jud. screening com. 1st Jud. Dept., 1991-96. Exec. editor Internat. Law Rev., 1988-91, editor-in-chief, 1991-94, mem. adv. bd., 1994—; editor Law Policy in Internat. Bus., 1985. Bd. dirs. Bay Street Landing Homeowners Corp; Rush Arts Philanthropic Found. Mem. ABA, N.Y. State Bar Assn., Assn. Bar City of N.Y. (fgn. and comparative law com. 1990-93, internat. human rights com. 1993-96), Women in Music, Women's Innter Cir. of Achievement (N.Am.), Phi Beta Kappa. General civil litigation, Entertainment, Trademark and copyright. Home: 20 Bay Street Lndg # Bij Staten Island NY 10301-2534 Office: Piper & Marbury LLP 1251 Avenue Of The Americas New York NY 10020-1104

**MCCABE, THOMAS EDWARD,** lawyer; b. Washington, Jan. 22, 1955; s. Edward Aeneas and Janet Isabel McCabe; m. Kelly Marie McCarthy; children: Edward Charles, Benjamin Patrick, Adrienne Marie, Therese Eileen, Luke Stevens, Nicholas Joseph. AB, Georgetown U., 1977; MBA, U. Notre Dame, 1981, JD, 1981. Bar: D.C. 1982, U.S. Dist. Ct. D.C. 1983, U.S. Ct. Appeals (D.C. cir.) 1983, Va. 1989, U.S. Supreme Ct. 1990. Law clk. U.S. Dist. Ct. Judge Hon. Charles R. Richey, Washington, 1981-82; assoc. Reavis & McGrath, Washington, 1982-84, Venable Baetjer Howard & Civiletti, Washington, 1984-85, McCarthy & Durrette, Washington, 1985-88; ptnr. McCarthy & Burke, Washington, 1988-91; sr. v.p., dir. corp. devel., gen. counsel, sec. GRC Internat., Inc., Vienna, Va., 1992—. Republican. Roman Catholic. General corporate, Securities, Government contracts and claims. Office: GRC Internat Inc 1900 Gallows Rd Vienna VA 22182-3865

**MCCAFFREY, CARLYN SUNDBERG,** lawyer; b. N.Y.C., Jan. 7, 1942; d. Carl Andrew Lawrence and Evelyn (Back) Sundberg; m. John P. McCaffrey, May 24, 1967; children: John C., Patrick, Jennifer, Kathleen. Student, Barnard Coll., 1963; AB in Econs., George Washington U., 1963; LLB cum laude, NYU, 1967, LLM in Taxation, 1970. Bar: N.Y. 1974. Law clk. to presiding justice Calif. Supreme Ct., 1967-68; teaching fellow law NYU, N.Y.C., 1968-70, asst. prof. law, 1970-74; assoc. Weil, Gotshal & Manges, N.Y.C., 1974-80, ptnr., 1980—; prof. in residence Rubin Hall NYU, 1971-75; adj. prof. law NYU, 1975—, U. Miami, 1979-81; lectr. in field. Contbr. articles to profl. jours. Mem. ABA (chmn. generation-skipping transfer tax 1979-81, 93—, real property probate and trust law sect.), N.Y. State Bar Assn. (exec. com. tax sect. 1979-80, chmn. estate and gift tax com. 1976-78, 95—, life ins. com. 1983-85, trusts and estates sect.), Assn. of Bar of City of N.Y. (matrimonial law com., chmn. tax subcom. 1984-86, ACTEC (bd. regents 1992—, mem. exec. com. 1995—). Probate, Family and matrimonial. Home: PO Box 232 Waccabuc NY 10597-0232 Office: Weil Gotshal & Manges 767 5th Ave Fl Concl New York NY 10153-0119*

**MCCALEB, JOE WALLACE,** lawyer; b. Nashville, Dec. 9, 1941; s. J.W. McCaleb and Majorie June (Hudson) DePriest; m. Glenda Jean Queen, June 26, 1965. BA, Union U., 1964; JD, Memphis State U., 1970; MSEL cum laude, Vt. Law Sch., 1995. Bar: Tenn. 1971, U.S. Dist. Ct. (mid. dist.) Tenn. 1977, U.S. Ct. Appeals (6th cir.) 1984, U.S. Supreme Ct. 1978. Law clk. to presiding justice Tenn. Supreme Ct., Memphis, 1970-71; staff atty. Tenn. Dept. of Pub. Health Bur. Environ. Svcs., Nashville, 1971-77; pvt. practice Hendersonville, Tenn., 1977-94, 96—. Chmn. Hendersonville Recycling Com., 1990-91. Mem. ATLA, Tenn. Bar Assn., Sierra Club (chmn. local chpt. 1980-81, chmn. mid.-Tenn. group 1989-90, 93-94, chmn. water quality com., co-chmn. forestry com.), Tenn. Environ. Coun. (v.p. 1987-88, conservation adv. 1991-92), Defenders of Wildlife, Tenn. Forest Def. Coun. Democrat. Avocations: wilderness backpacking, photography, forestry, environmental protection. Administrative and regulatory, Federal civil litigation, Environmental. Home and Office: 100 Colonial Dr Hendersonville TN 37075-3205

**MCCALL, DANIEL THOMPSON, JR.,** retired judge; b. Butler, Ala., Mar. 12, 1909; s. Daniel Thompson and Caroline Winston (Bush) McC.; m. Mary Edna Montgomery, Apr. 3, 1937; children: Mary Winston McCall Laseter, Daniel Thompson III, Nancy McCall Poynor. A.B., U. Ala., 1931, LL.B., 1933, LL.D. (hon.), 1981. Bar: Ala. 1933, U.S. Supreme Ct. 1960. Practice law Mobile, 1933-60; ptnr. Johnston, McCall & Johnston, 1943-60; cir. judge Mobile County, 1960-69; assoc. justice Supreme Ct. Ala., 1969-75; dir. Title Ins. Co., 1959-69; pres. Jr. Bar Ala., 1937. Author McCall Reprot on U. Ala. Hosps. Elected to Mobile County Bd. Sch. commrs., 1950-56, 58-60; co-founder, trustee Julius T. Wright Sch. Girls, 1953-63; dir. U. Ala. Law Sch. Found., Ala. Bar. Commrs., 1957-60; trustee U. Ala., 1965-79, nat. alumni pres., 1963, pres. Mobile chpt., 1961, Disting. Alumnus award, 1995. Lt. USNR, World War II. Named to Ala. Acad. of Hon.; recipient Dean's award, U. Ala. Law Sch., 1974, Julius T. Wright Sch. Disting. Svc. award, 1979, M.O. Beale Scroll Merit, 1979, U.M.S. Preparator Sch. Outstanding Alumnus award, 1980. Mem. ABA, Ala. Bar Assn. (grievance com. 1954-57), Mobile Bar Assn. (pres. 1953), Am. Judicature Soc., Farrah Law Soc. (charter), Cumberland Law Sch. Order Jurisprudence, Inst. Jud. Adminstrn., Nat. Trust Hist. Preservation, Hist. Mobile Preservation Soc., Navy League U.S. (co-founder, pres. Mobile chpt. 1963-65), Am. Legion, Ala. Hist. Soc., Res. Officer's Assn. U.S., 40 and 8, U. Tuscaloosa Club, Omicron Delta Kappa, Phi Delta Phi, Sigma Nu. Democrat. Episcopalian. Home: 2253 Ashland Place Ave Mobile AL 36607-3242

**MCCALL, JACK HUMPHREYS, JR.,** lawyer; b. Nashville, Jan. 10, 1961; s. Jack Humphreys Sr. and Patricia Jean (Holmes) McC.; m. Jennifer Lynn Ashley, Oct. 4, 1992; 1 child, Margaret Ashley. BA, Vanderbilt U., 1983; JD, U. Tenn., 1991. Bar: Tenn. 1992, U.S. Ct. Appeals (10th cir.) 1993. Clk. Hon. Gilbert S. Morritt, Chief Judge U.S. Ct. Appeals 6th Cir., Nashville, 1991-92; assoc. Farris, Warfield & Kanaday, Nashville, 1992-94, Hunton & Williams, Knoxville, Tenn., 1994—; adj. prof. U. Tenn. Coll. Law, Knoxville, 1997—. Contbr. chpt. to book and articles to profl. jours. Mem. alumni adv. coun. U. Tenn. Coll. Law, Knoxville, 1992-95. Capt. U.S. Army, 1983-88. Recipient Loevinger prize ABA Sect. of Sci. and Tech., 1992, Bruno Bittker award ABA Standing Com. World Order Law, 1993. Mem. Nashville Bar Assn. (elder law com. chair young lawyers divsn. 1993-94), Knoxville Bar Assn. Barristers (com. chair young lawyers sect. 1995-97), Nat. Assn. Real Estate Investment Trusts, U. Club (Knoxville). Lutheran. Avocations: history, writing, genealogy, languages, travel. General corporate, Finance, Securities. Office: Hunton & Williams 900 S Gay St Ste 2000 Knoxville TN 37902-1861

**MCCALL, WAYNE CHARLES,** lawyer; b. Ocala, Fla., Dec. 26, 1946; s. Wayne Cassius and Catherine (Hilly) M. m. Beth Wasson, 1975; children: Diana, Melody, Matthew. BA in English, U. Fla., 1968, JD with honors, 1972. Bar: Fla. 1973. Commd. 2d. lt. U.S. Army, 1968, advanced through grads to 1st. lt., 1970; assoc. Ayres, Cluster, Curry, McCall & Briggs P.C., Ocala, Fla., 1973—; mem. 5th Dist. Ct. Appeal Jud. Nominating Commn., 1986-87 (chmn. 1987); chmn. 5th Jud. Cir. Jud. Nominating Commn. Former mem., pres. U. Fla. Nat. Alumni Assn.; mem. U. Fla. Pres's. Coun.; former pres. Marion County Gator Club; mem. bd. dirs. Gator Boosters, Inc.; mem. bd. dirs. U. Fla. Athletic Assn.; former mem. Marion County Dem. Com.; former St. Paul United Meth. Ch. Sunday Sch. tchr. (also former mem. bd. trustees.). Named to U. Fla. Athletic Hall of Fame, Fla. Blue Key. Mem. ABA, ATLA, Acad. Fla. Trial Lawyers, Marion County Bar Assn. Democrat. Methodist. General civil litigation, Personal injury. Home: 7073 SE 12th Cir Ocala FL 34480-6656 Office: Ayres Cluster Curry McCall & Briggs PA PO Box 1148 Ocala FL 34478-1148

**MCCALLA, JON P.,** federal judge; b. Memphis, Feb. 16, 1947; m. Mary R. McCalla; children: Marjorie Katherine, Elisabeth Clair. BS in Agrl. Econs., U. Tenn., 1969; JD, Vanderbilt U., 1974. Law clk. to Hon. Bailey Brown U.S. Dist. Ct. (we. dist.) Tenn., 1974-75; fed. judge U.S. Dist. Ct. (we. dist.) Tenn., Memphis, 1992—; assoc. Armstrong, Allen, Braden, Goodman, McBride & Prewitt, 1975-80; ptnr. Armstrong, Allen, Prewitt, Gentry, Johnson & Holmes, 1980-87, Heiskell, Donelson, Bearman, Adams, Williams & Kirsch, 1987-92. Active Ctrl. Gardens Area Neighborhood Assn., 1979-84; church deacon pers. com., Sunday Sch. tchr., 1987-90; bd. dirs. Idlewild Friends of Music. 2nd lt., then 1st lt. U.S. Army, 1969-71. Decorated Bronze Star. Mem. Fed. Bar Assn., Tenn. Bar Assn., Memphis Bar Assn., 6th Cir. Jud. Conf. Presbyterian. Office: US Dist Ct 167 N Main St Ste 907 Memphis TN 38103-1873

**MCCALLISTER, JOHN WILSON,** lawyer; b. Panacea, Fla., Sept. 24, 1942; s. Walker W. and Eliza I. McCallister; m. Molly J. McCallister, June 8, 1968 (dec. 1996); children: Ian W., Andrew J.; m. Theresa M. McCallister, May 16, 1998. BA, Fla. State U., 1964; JD, U. Iowa, 1969. Bar: Iowa 1969, Fla. 1970, Ill. 1981, U.S. Dist. Ct. (no. dist.) Iowa 1971, U.S. Dist. Ct. (ctrl. dist.) Ill. 1986, U.S. Ct. Appeals (8th cir.) 1973. Asst. Dubuque County Atty. Dubuque, Iowa, 1969-70; assoc. M.M. Cooney Law Offices, Dubuque, 1971-76; ptnr. Cooney, McCallister & Zwack, Dubuque, 1976-81; sr. atty. Deere & Co., Moline, Ill., 1981-87, asst. gen. counsel, 1987-92, assoc. gen. counsel, 1992—; presenter product safety and liability videos, 1991-95. Mem. Product Liability Adv. Coun., 1995—; dist. commr. Babe Ruth Baseball, Rock Island, Ill., 1987; pres. Islander Little League, Rock Island, 1982. Mem. ACMIE (co-chair specialized litigation group), Def. Rsch. Inst., Worthington Country Club, Rock Island Arsenal Country Club. Republican. Avocations: golf, running. Product liability, Personal injury.

**MC CALLUM, CHARLES EDWARD,** lawyer; b. Memphis, Mar. 13, 1939; s. Edward Payson and India Raimelle (Musick) McC.; m. Lois Ann Gowell Temple, Nov. 30, 1985; children: Florence Andrea, Printha Kyle, Chandler Ward, Sabra Nicole Temple. BS, MIT, 1960; JD, Vanderbilt U., 1964. Bar: Mich., Tenn. 1964. Assoc. Warner Norcross & Judd LLP, Grand Rapids, Mich., 1964-69, ptnr., 1969—, mng. ptnr., 1992-97; rep. assemblyman State Bar Mich., 1973-78; dir. Rsch. and Tech. Inst. West Mich., 1986-96, chmn., 1989-91; lectr. continuing legal edn. programs; chmn., bd. dirs. Butterworth Ventures, 1987-96; mem. West Mich. World Trade Week Com., 1988—, chmn., 1990-91; mem. Mich. Dist. Export Coun., 1990-99, chmn., 1992-97. Chmn. Grand Rapids Area Transit Authority, 1976-79, mem., 1972-79; regional v.p. Nat. Mcpl. League, 1978-86, mem. coun., 1971-78; pres. Grand Rapids Art Mus., 1979-81, 96-98, trustee, 1976-83, 94-99; chmn. Butterworth Hosp., 1979-87, trustee, 1977-87; chmn. Butterworth Health Corp., 1982-89, dir., 1982-97, vice chmn., 1989-91, sec., 1991-97; vice chmn. Citizens Com. for Consolidation of Govt. Svcs., 1981-82; mem. nat. alumni bd. Vanderbilt U. Sch. Law, 1998—; chmn. Priority Health, 1995—, bd. dirs., 1995—. Woodrow Wilson fellow, 1960-61; Fulbright scholar U. Manchester, Eng., 1960-61. Fellow Coll. Law Practice Mgmt.; mem. ABA (com. on law firms bus. law sect. 1982-94, chmn. com. on law firms 1994-98, coun. mem. bus. law sect. 1998—, mem. fed. regulation of securities com., mem. internat. bus. law com.), Am. Bar Found., Am. Law Inst., Tenn. Bar Assn., Mich. Bar Assn. (mem. coun. bus. law sect. 1983-89, sect. chmn. 1988-89, ex-officio coun. bus. law sect. 1989—, chmn. takeover laws subcom. 1986-88, co-chmn. internat. bus. law com., internat. law sect. 1988-89), Grand Rapids Bar Assn., Internat. Bar Assn., Grand Rapids C. of C. (pres. 1975, bd. dirs. 1970-76), Univ. Club, Peninsular Club, Order of Coif, Sigma Xi. General corporate, Mergers and acquisitions, Private international. Home: 110 Bittersweet Ln NE Ada MI 49301-9552

**MCCANN, BERNARD THOMAS,** lawyer; b. Lackawannna, N.Y., June 28, 1943; s. Francis Daniel Sr. and Catherine Louise (Moran); children: Kelly, Casey, Brigid. BA cum laude, Niagara U., 1965; JD, Union U., 1968. Bar: N.Y., U.S. Dist. Ct. (no. dist.) N.Y. Assoc. McPhillips, Fitzgerald & Meyer, Glens Falls, N.Y., 1970-72; city atty. City of Glen Falls, 1973-77; sole practice Glens Falls, 1973-81, Lake George, N.Y., 1982—; assoc. dir. legis. program rep. N.Y. State Nurses Assn., Guilderland, 1982—; atty. Minerva Cen. Sch., Olmstedville, N.Y. 1974—. Bd. dirs. Glens Falls Housing Authority, 1972; exec. sec. Glens Falls Indsl. Devel. Agy., 1975-77; bd. dirs. Adirondack chpt. ARC, Glens Falls, 1974—; active Warren County Dem. Com., Glens Falls, 1974-79. Served as capt. U.S. Army, 1968-70. Mem. ABA, Indsl. Labor Relations Research Assn. Roman Catholic. Club: Glens Falls Figure Skating (bd. dirs. 1985—). Avocations: golf, reading, travel, coaching basketball and softball. Labor, Legislative. Home: 89 Gurney Ln Queensbury NY 12804-8249 Office: NY State Nurses Assn 89 Gurney Ln Queensbury NY 12804-8249

**MCCANN, JAMES PATRICK,** lawyer, educator; b. Augusta, Ga., Oct. 8, 1951; s. Thomas Murray and Ella (Bridge) McC.; m. Rebecca S. Myers, Sept. 6, 1975 (div. Jan. 1986); 1 child, Sean Patrick; m. Angelyn Leigh Dale, Aug. 8, 1987; children: Larkin Patrick, Molleigh Aidan. BA, U. San Francisco, 1973, JD, 1975. Bar: Iowa 1975, Calif. 1976, U.S. Ct. Mil. Appeals 1975, Okla. 1981, U.S. Ct. Appeals (10th cir.) 1981, U.S. Supreme Ct. 1995. Atty., ptnr. Doerner, Saunders, Daniel & Anderson, Tulsa, 1981—; adj. faculty U. Tulsa Coll. Law, 1989—; sr. adj. settlement judge U.S. Dist. Ct. (no. dist.) Okla., Tulsa, 1990—. Bd. dirs. Theatre Tulsa, 1986-90, Summerstage, Tulsa, 1989-93, Sinfonia, Tulsa, 1996—. Capt. U.S. Army, 1973-81. Democrat. Methodist. Avocations: travel, reading, theatre. Alternative dispute resolution, General civil litigation. Office: Doerner Saunders et al 320 S Boston Ave Ste 500 Tulsa OK 74103-3725

**MCCANN, JOHN JOSEPH,** lawyer; b. N.Y.C., Feb. 4, 1937; s. John and Katherine (McKeon) Mc C.; m. June M. Evangelist, Oct. 16, 1965; children: Catherine Anne, John Bernard, Robert Joseph, James Patrick. AB, Fordham U., 1958; LLB, Columbia U., 1961. Bar: N.Y. 1962, N.J. 1974, Fla. 1994. Exec. v.p., chief legal officer Orion Capital Corp., Farmington,

Conn.; mem. legal adv. com. N.Y. Stock Exch., 1989-92. Mem. ABA (chair bus. law sect. 1992-93), Am. Law Inst., Am. Coll. Investment Counsel (pres. 1984-85), Am. Arbitration Assn. (bd. govs. 1985-96), Tiro A Segno Club, Canoe Brook Golf and Country Club. Roman Catholic. General corporate, Mergers and acquisitions, Insurance. Office: Orion Capital Corp 9 Farm Springs Rd Farmington CT 06032-2526

**MCCANN, JOSEPH LEO,** lawyer, government official; b. Phila., Aug. 27, 1948; s. Joseph John and Christina Mary (Kirwan) McC.; m. Aida Laico Kabigting, Dec. 6, 1986; 1 child, Angela Kathleen. BA, St. Charles Sem., Phila., 1970, postgrad. in theology, 1970-71; MA, Temple U., 1975, JD, 1977. Bar: Pa. 1977, U.S. Dist. Ct. (ea. dist.) Pa. 1977, U.S. Dist. Ct. (mid. dist.) Pa. 1978, U.S. Ct. Appeals (3d cir.) 1978, D.C. 1986, U.S. Supreme Ct. 1986, Md. 1987, U.S. Ct. Appeals (Fed. cir.) 1988, U.S. Ct. Internat. Trade 1988. Law clk. to chief justice Pa. Supreme Ct., Phila., 1977-78; dep. atty. gen. Pa. Dept. Justice, Harrisburg, 1978-80; sr. atty. U.S. GAO, Washington, 1980-96; sr. asst. gen. counsel GSA, Washington, 1996-99; pres., counsel, headmaster The Kabigting-Kirwan Meml. Nonprofit Corp., 1999—. Mem. ABA, Pa. Bar Assn., Phila. Bar Assn., D.C. Bar Assn., Md. State Bar Assn. Roman Catholic. Home: 204 Bookham Ln Gaithersburg MD 20877-3789 Office: Gen Counsel US GSA Rm 4133 204 Bookham Ln Gaithersburg MD 20877-3789

**MCCANN, LOUISE MARY,** paralegal; b. Bklyn., Apr. 12, 1949; d. James Joseph and Edith Dorothea (Wubbe) McC. AAS, Elizabeth Seton Coll., 1967; BS, N.Y. Inst. Tech., 1981; paralegal cert., Adelphi U., 1987. Cert. ind. adjustor, motor vehicle and casualty, N.Y. Adminstrv. asst. J.P. Stevens & Co., Inc., N.Y.C., 1969-86; para-legal asst. Congdon, Flaherty, O'Callaghan, Reid, Donlon, Travis & Fishlinger, Garden City, N.Y., 1986—. Capt. tng. divsn. Aux. Police Force, N.Y.C. Police Dept., 1975-92; trooper Boots & Saddles Civil War Re-enactment Unit, 10th N.Y. Cavalry Co. C; contbg. sponsor U.S. Equestrian Team, Gladstone, N.J., 1980; trustee Inc. Village of Roslyn. Master sgt. USAR, 1979—. Decorated Meritorious Svc. medal, Nat. Def. Svc. medal, Army Achievement medal, Army Commendation medal, Armed Forces Res. medal. Mem. Nassau Suffolk (L.I.) Horseman's Assn. Republican. Roman Catholic. Avocations: horseback riding, swimming, needlepoint, crocheting, golf. Home: 305 Main St Roslyn NY 11576-2114 Office: 377 Oak St Garden City NY 11530-6553

**MCCANN, MAURICE JOSEPH,** lawyer; b. St. Louis, July 26, 1950; s. James M. and Marie V. (Del Commune) M.; m. Suzanne Marie Grob, Dec. 29, 1990; 1 child, Mathew Maurice. BS, So. Ill. U., 1972, MA, 1974, PhD, 1976, JD, 1986. Bar: Ill. 1986, Mo. 1987, U.S. Dist. Ct. (ea. dist.) Mo. 1987, U.S. Dist. Ct. (so. dist.) Ill. 1988, U.S. Ct. Appeals (7th cir.) 1998. Teaching asst. So. Ill. U., Carbondale, 1972-76; asst. dir. Vermillion County Comprehensive Employment and Tng. Act, Danville, Ill., 1976; prof. John A. Logan Coll., Carterville, Ill., 1977; adj. prof. St. Louis U., 1977-78; exec. dir. Jackson County Comprehensive Employment and Tng. Act, Murphysboro, Ill., 1978-81, Jackson County YMCA, Carbondale, 1982-83; ptnr. McCann & Foley, Murphysboro, 1986-88; pvt. practice law Murphysboro, 1988—; atty. Murphysboro Fire Protection Dist., Jackson County, 1988—; instr. dept. fin. So. Ill. U., 1988—, instr. dept. higher edn., 1994-96. Author: A Prelude to McCarthyism, 1974, Truman Administration and Federal Aid to Education, 1976, The Black Sox Scandal, 1986. Mem. Found. for Restoration of Ste. Genevieve, Mo., 1984; bd. dirs. So. Ill. Spl. Olympics, Carbondale, 1983-86; commr. Murphysboro Pk. Dist., 1990-92. Harry S. Truman scholar Truman Libr., Independence, Mo., 1975. Mem. ABA, Ill. Bar Assn., St. Louis Bar Assn., Mo. Bar Assn., Jackson County Bar Assn. Roman Catholic. Probate. Home: 42 Brian Ave Murphysboro IL 62966-6171 Office: 1331 Walnut St Murphysboro IL 62966-2026

**MCCANN, RICHARD STEPHEN,** lawyer; b. Wilmington, Del., Dec. 26, 1938; s. Francis E.B. and Naomi H. (Riley) McC.; m. Gloria M. Baum (div. 1973); 1 child, Heather Marie; m. Sharon R. Cannon. BA, Georgetown U., 1960, JD, 1963; M in City Planning, U. Pa., 1965. Bar: Del. 1964. Pvt. practice law Newark, 1964-66, 70—; alderman City of Newark, 1964-66; city planner Dover, Del., 1966-70; atty. Del. Police Chief's Coun., Dover, 1971—, Del. Police Chief's Found., Dover, 1983—. Atty. Aetna Hose, Hook & Ladder Co., Newark, 1975—. Mem. ABA, Del. Bar Assn. Avocations: Skiing, gardening, cannons. Real property, Probate, Family and matrimonial. Home: 19 Carriage Ln Newark DE 19711-2023 Office: 94 E Main St Newark DE 19711-4644

**MCCARRON, ANDREW,** lawyer, educator; b. Jacksonville, Fla., June 28, 1960; s. Frank Raymond and E. Elaine (Biondi) McC.; m. Stephanie Ann Johnson; children: Brandon Andrew, Blake Andrew. BA in Polit. Sci., Calif. State U., Long Beach, 1985; JD, Western State U., 1987. Bar: Calif. 1988, U.S. Dist. Ct. (ctrl., so., no. and ea. dists.) 1988, U.S. Ct. Appeals (9th cir.) 1988. Real estate/bus. litigation atty. Pothier & Hinrichs, Santa Ana, Calif., 1988-92, Harbin & Frost, Santa Ana, 1992—; adj. prof. U. Phoenix, 1993—, Simon Greenleaf Sch. Law, 1992-97, Trinity Law Sch., 1997—; vis. lectr. in field. Contbg. writer Orange County Lawyer; contbr. articles to profl. jours. Mem. Orange County Bar Assn. (bus. and corp. law sect., real estate sect., bus. litigation sect.), State Bar Calif. (litigation sect., real property sect., bus. law sect.), Orange County Escrow Assn. Republican. Real property, General corporate, General civil litigation. Office: Harbin & Frost 2122 N Broadway Ste N1 Santa Ana CA 92706-2614

**MCCARRON, JEFFREY BALDWIN,** lawyer; b. Bryn Mawr, Pa., Mar. 7, 1961; s. John R. and Bette R. McC.; m. Kathryn Gilmour, Oct. 18, 1982; children: Sarah Jane, Jacqueline Lillian. BA, Hampshire Coll., 1983; JD, Temple U., 1987. Bar: Pa. 1987, N.J. 1987, U.S. Dist. Ct. N.J. 1987, U.S. Dist. Ct. (ea. dist.) Pa. 1989, U.S. Ct. Appeals (3d cir.) 1990; diplomate Am. Bd. Profl. Liability Attys. Atty. maj. trial divsn. Defender Assn. Phila., 1987-90; ptnr. Swartz, Campbell & Detweiler, Phila., 1990—. Contbr. articles to law jours. Mem. ABA, Pa. Bar Assn. (vice chmn. profl. liability com. 1997-98), Phila. Bar Assn. Professional liability. Office: Swartz Campbell & Detweiler 1601 Market St Fl 34 Philadelphia PA 19103-2397

**MC CARTAN, PATRICK FRANCIS,** lawyer; b. Cleve., Aug. 3, 1934; s. Patrick Francis and Stella Mercedes (Ashton) McC.; m. Lois Ann Buchman, Aug. 30, 1958; children: M. Karen, Patrick Francis, III. AB magna cum laude, U. Notre Dame, 1956, JD, 1959. Bar: Ohio 1960, U.S. Ct. Appeals (6th cir.) 1961, U.S. Ct. Appeals (3rd cir.) 1965, U.S. Ct. Appeals (D.C. cir.) 1980, U.S. Ct. Appeals (5th cir.) 1981, U.S. Ct. Appeals (4th cir.) 1989, U.S. Ct. Appeals (7th cir.) 1992, U.S. Supreme Ct. 1970. Law clk. to Hon. Charles Evans Whittaker, U.S. Supreme Ct., 1959; asso. Jones, Day, Reavis & Pogue, Cleve., 1961-65, ptnr., 1966-93, mng. ptnr., 1993—; trustee Nat. Inst. for Trial Adv., Boulder, Colo., 1987-92, U. Notre Dame, Cleve. Clinic Found., Greater Cleve. Roundtable. Fellow Am. Coll. Trial Lawyers, Internat. Acad. Trial Lawyers; mem. ABA, 6th Cir. Jud. Conf. (life), Coun. on Fgn. Rels., U.S.-Japan Bus. Coun., Ohio Bar Assn., Bar Assn. Greater Cleve. (pres. 1977-78), Musical Arts Assn. (trustee), Greater Cleve. Growth Assn. (chmn. 1997—). Roman Catholic. Federal civil litigation, State civil litigation, General corporate. Home: 7570 Thistle Ln Novelty OH 44072-9500 Office: Jones Day Reavis & Pogue North Point 901 Lakeside Ave E Cleveland OH 44114-1116

**MCCARTER, W. DUDLEY,** lawyer; b. St. Louis, Dec. 20, 1950; s. Willard Dudley and Vera Katherine (Schneider) McC.; m. Elizabeth Dunlop, June 14, 1986; children: Katherine, Elizabeth, Emily. BA, Knox Coll., 1972; JD, U. Mo., 1975. Bar: Mo. 1975, U.S. Dist. Ct. (ea. dist.) Mo. 1976, U.S. Ct. Appeals (8th cir.) Mo. 1977. Assoc. Mann & Poger, St. Louis, 1975-76, Suelthaus & Krueger, St. Louis, 1976-80; ptnr. Suelthaus & Kaplan, P.C., St. Louis, 1980-92, Behr, Mantovani, McCarter & Potter P.C., St. Louis, 1992—; atty. for the City of Creve Coeur, Mo., 1992—. Author editor: Missouri Civil Litigation Handbook, 1992; author Jour. of the Mo. Bar, St. Louis Bar Jour. and Mo. Law Rev. Recipient W. Oliver Rasch award, 1985, 1989, Outstanding Young Lawyer award St. Louis County Bar Assn. 1983. Fellow ABA; mem. The Missouri Bar (pres. 1993-94). General civil litigation, Construction. Office: Behr Mantovani McCarter & Potter 7777 Bonhomme Ave Ste 1810 Saint Louis MO 63105-1911

**MCCARTHY, ANN PRICE,** lawyer; b. L.A., Jan. 30, 1947; d. Frank Judson and Marianna (Chase) Price; 1 child, Sundae Jan Cloe; m. Joseph Stephen McCarthy, Dec. 15, 1974; 1 child, Caitlin Price. BA, Old Coll., Reno, 1983; JD, Nev. Sch. Law, 1987. Bar: Nev. 1987, Calif. 1988, U.S. Dist. Ct. (no. dist.) Calif. 1988, U.S. Ct. Appeals (9th cir.) 1989. Legal asst. Aebi, FitzSimmons & Lambrose, Carson City, Nev., 1981-84; ind. legal researcher Reno, 1985; law clk. Martin H. Wiener, Esquire, Reno, 1985-87, Hon. Robin C. Wright, Reno, 1987-88, Hon. John C. Mowbray, Carson City, 1988; ptnr. Eck & McCarthy, Carson City, 1988-90; pvt. practice Ann Price McCarthy, Ltd., Carson City, 1990-91; ptnr. Aebi & McCarthy, Carson City, 1991—; lectr. Nat. Bus. Inst., Reno, 1992, 93; instr. Juvenile Drug and Alcohol Edn. Program, Carson City, 1992. Bd. dirs., sec. Brewery Arts Ctr., Carson City, 1992, bd. dirs., pres., 1993-95. Mem. Am. Trial Lawyers Assn., Nev. Trial Lawyers Assn., Washoe County Bar Assn., First Jud. Dist. Bar Assn. (pres. 1991-92, 92-93). Family and matrimonial, Bankruptcy, Personal injury. Office: Aebi and McCarthy 204 N Minnesota St Carson City NV 89703-4151 Address: Ann Price McCarthy & Assoc 77 E William St Ste 201 Carson City NV 89701

**MCCARTHY, BERNARD FRANCIS,** lawyer; b. Butte, Mont., Aug. 20, 1955; s. John Joseph and Helen Patricia (Ryan) McC.; m. Helen Jean Waldbillig, Sept. 1, 1990; children: Sean Michael, Patrick Nicholas. BA, Carroll Coll., 1977; JD, U. Mont., 1983. Bar: Mont. 1983, U.S. Dist. Ct. Mont. 1983. Mgmt. analyst Mont. Supreme Ct., Helena, 1978-79; ptnr. O'Leary & McCarthy, Helena, 1983-85; Justice of the Peace Lewis & Clark County, Helena, 1984-89; clk. U.S. Bankruptcy Ct., Butte, Mont., 1990—; chair edn. com. Fed. Jud. Ctr., Washington, 1994—; mem. law practice com. State Bar Mont., Helena, 1994—; v.p., pres.-elect, pres. Nat. Conf. Bankruptcy Clks., Dayton, Ohio, 1996—; mem. Nat. Integrated Bankruptcy System user group Adminstr. Office U.S. Cts., Washington, 1996—. Pres. bd. Big Bros. and Sisters, Helena, 1985-86. Mem. KC, Lions (pres./sec. 1992—). Democrat. Roman Catholic. Avocations: horse riding, fishing, reading, traveling, ranching. Home: PO Box 523 176 Paul Gulch Rd Whitehall MT 59759 Office: US Bankruptcy Ct PO Box 689 Butte MT 59703-0689

**MCCARTHY, CHARLES FRANCIS, JR.,** lawyer; b. Springfield, Mass., Dec. 9, 1926; s. Charles Francis and Maude Veronica (Clayton) McC.; m. Dorothy Bray, June 14, 1952 (dec. June 1987); children: Richard J., Linda A. Moylan, Robert P. AB, St. Michael's Coll., 1949; JD, Boston Coll., 1951. Bar: Mass. 1952, U.S. Dist. Ct. Mass. 1953. Assoc. Ganley, Crook & Smith, Springfield, Mass., 1954-67, Laming, Smith & Auchter, Springfield, 1967-80; of counsel Bacon & Wilson, P.C. and predecessor firms, Springfield, 1980-94; ret., 1994; clk. Ellis Title Co., Inc., Springfield, 1988-94. Democrat. Roman Catholic. Real property, Probate. Home: 48 Palmyra St Springfield MA 01118-2027

**MCCARTHY, GAIL KATHLEEN,** lawyer; b. Chgo., Oct. 20, 1952; d. Daniel Patrick and Joanne Marie (Sullivan) McC.; m. Francisco A. Urbina, Sept. 25, 1985; children: Daniel P., Mary K. BA, U. Ill., 1974; JD, U. Mich., 1977. Bar: Mich., 1977, Wis. 1980, U.S. Dist. Ct. (ea. dist.) Wis. 1981, U.S. Dist. Ct. (we. dist.) Wis. 1993. Staff atty. Mich. Migrant Legal Assistance Project, Berrien Springs, Mich., 1977-80; staff atty. Legal Action Wis., Madison, 1980-83, dir. migrant project, 1983-85, staff atty., 1985-88; assoc. Law Office Thomas C. Hochstatter, Milw., 1988-90; ptnr. Hochstatter, McCarthy & Rivas, S.C., Milw., 1991—; bd. dirs. Migrant Legal Action Program, Inc., Washington, 1985-90, chmn. bd. dirs., 1988-90. Parent vol. Milw. Pub. Schs., 1993-97. Mem. Am. Immigration Lawyers Assn. (sec. Wis. chpt. 1993, vice chmn. 1996-97, chair 1998—, coord. essay contest 1997—). Immigration, naturalization, and customs. Home: 3143 S Superior St Milwaukee WI 53207-3074 Office: Hochstatter McCarthy Rivas Ste 302 5555 N Port Washington Rd Milwaukee WI 53217-4928

**MCCARTHY, GEORGE P.,** prosecutor, educator. BA, U. N.H., 1987; JD, Ohio Northern U., 1990. Bar: Ohio 1990, U.S. Dist. Ct. (so. dist.) Ohio 1992, U.S. Supreme Ct. 1997. Hearing officer mcpl. divsn. Lima (Ohio) Prosecutor's Office, 1988-90; prosecutor Allen County Prosecutor's Office, Lima, 1989-90; asst. prosecutor Meigs County Prosecutor's Office, Pomeray, Ohio, 1991-93; city prosecutor City of Athens (Ohio), 1993—; instr. Adult Career Ctr., Athens, 1998—. Contbr. articles newsletter. Mem. Athens County Domestic Violence Task Force, Athens, 1994—; mem. Children's Sexual Assault Treatment Program Com., Athens,1993—; sec. Richland Fire Dept., Athens, 1995—. Mem. Nat. Dist. Atty.'s Assn., Ohio Mcpl. Atty.'s Assn. (co-founder 1996—), Kiwanis Internat. Office: Athens City Prosecutor's Office 8 E Washington St Athens OH 45701-2444

**MCCARTHY, J. THOMAS,** lawyer, educator; b. Detroit, July 2, 1937; s. John E. and Virginia M. (Hanlon) McC.; m. Nancy Irene Orrell, July 10, 1976. BS, U. Detroit, 1960; JD, U. Mich., 1963. Bar: Calif. 1964. Assoc. Julian Caplan, San Francisco, 1963-66; prof. law U. San Francisco, 1966—; vis. prof. law U. Calif., Berkeley, 1976-77, Davis, 1979-80; cons. in field; mem. Trademark Rev. Commn., 1986-88. Author: McCarthy on Trademarks and Unfair Competition, 6 vols., 4th edit., 1996, McCarthy on Rights of Publicity and Privacy, 1987, McCarthy's Desk Encyclopedia of Intellectual Property, 2d edit., 1995; mem. editl. bd. Trademark Reporter. Recipient Jefferson medal N.J. Intellectual Property Assn., 1994, Ladas award Brand Names Ednl. Found., 1997. Mem. Am. Intellectual Property Law Assn. (Watson award 1965, Centennial award in Trademark law 1997), Internat. Assn. for Advancement of Teaching and Rsch. in Intellectual Property, Am. Law Inst. (adv. com. on restatement of law of unfair competition), IEEE.

**MCCARTHY, KEVIN BART,** lawyer; b. Washington, May 7, 1948; s. Frank Jeremiah and Frances Patricia (Bilderback) McC.; m. Patrice Borders, Apr. 3, 1971; children: Kevin Patrick, Charles Ryan, Molly Virginia, Bridget Louise, Moira Patrice. BBA, U. Notre Dame, 1970; JD, Ind. U., Indpls., 1973. Bar: Ind. 1973, U.S. Dist. Ct. (so. dist.) Ind. 1973, U.S. Ct. Appeals (7th cir.) 1974, Ill 1976, U.S. Dist. Ct. (cen. dist.) Ill. 1985, U.S. Ct. Appeals (6th cir.) 1985. Bail commr. Mcpl. Ct. Marion County, Indpls., 1972-73; asst. regional counsel Fed. Hwy. Adminstrn., Homewood, Ill., 1973-75; 1st asst., chief counsel Ill. Dept. Transp., Springfield, 1975-77; counsel com. on interstate and fgn. commerce, subcom. on transp. and commerce Ho. Reps., Washington, 1977-79, asst. counsel com. on pub. works and transp., 1979-82, counsel com. on pub. works and transp., 1982; pvt. practice law Springfield, 1982-87; acting U.S. trustee Dept. Justice, Springfield, 1987-88; U.S. trustee Dept. Justice, Indpls., 1988—; pvt. practice Indpls. and Springfield. Mem. Ill. State Bd. Agrl. Advisors, 1987-88. Home: 5619 Surrey Hill Rd Indianapolis IN 46226-1561

**MCCARTHY, KEVIN JOHN,** lawyer; b. N.Y.C., Apr. 8, 1941; s. Vincent Patrick and Mary (H.) McC.; m. Marianne Pitts, Nov. 5, 1966; children: Mary Rita, Kevin, Colin. BS, U. Md., 1963; JD, U. Md., Balt., 1966. Bar: Md. 1966, U.S. Dist. Ct. Md. 1966, U.S. Ct. Appeals (4th cir.) 1966, U.S. Supreme Ct. 1972, D.C. 1976, U.S. Dist. Ct. D.C. 1976, U.S. Ct. Appeals (D.C. cir.) 1976, Fla. 1998. Law clk. Cir. Ct. for P.G. County, Upper Marlboro, Md., 1964-66; assoc., ptnr. Sasscer, Clagett & Channing, Upper Marlboro, Md., 1966-76; ptnr. O'Malley, Miles & McCarthy, Upper Marlboro, Md., 1976-86, McCarthy, Bacon & Costello, Landover, Md., 1986—; arbitrator Am. Arbitration Assn., Washington, 1972—. Contbg. author: Maryland Civil Patter Jury Instructions, 1975, 2d edit., 1984, 3d edit., 1993. Named The Best Lawyers in Am., Woodward/White. Fellow Am. Bar Found., Md. Bar Found.; mem. Internat. Assn. Ins. Counsel, Fedn. Ins. and Corp. Counsel, Def. Rsch. Inst., Am. Trial Lawyers Assn., Md. Trial Lawyers Assn., Assn. Def. Trial Attys., Million Dollar Advocates Forum, Trial Lawyers for Pub. Justice. Avocations: golf, racquetball, coaching soccer and lacrosse. General civil litigation, Personal injury, Product liability. Office: McCarthy Bacon & Costello 4640 Forbes Blvd Lanham Seabrook MD 20706-4323

**MCCARTHY, ROBERT EMMETT,** lawyer; b. Bklyn., May 26, 1951; s. John Joseph and Leona Mary (Hart) McC.; m. Elizabeth Anne Naumoff, May 20, 1978; children: John Philip, Emily Jane. BS in Fgn. Studies, Georgetown U., 1973, MS in Fgn. Studies, JD, 1978. Bar: N.J. 1978, U.S. Dist. Ct. (ea. and so. dists.) N.Y. 1979. Assoc. Patterson, Belknap et al, N.Y.C., 1978-84; gen. counsel MTV Networks Inc., N.Y.C., 1984-86; v.p., counsel/communications Viacom Internat., N.Y.C., 1986-87; exec. v.p. Nelson Vending Tech., Ltd., N.Y.C., 1987-89; exec. v.p., gen. counsel Cateret Savs. Bank FA, Morristown, N.J., 1989-91; cons. McCarthy Comms., Elizabeth, N.J., 1991-95; sr. v.p., gen. counsel Time, Inc., N.Y.C., 1996—; cons. UN Ctr. on Transnat. Corps., N.Y.C., 1979; exec. dir. Spl. Master Reapportionment of N.Y., 1982; term mem. Council Fgn. Relations, N.Y.C., 1980-84. Founder, pres. Elizabeth (N.J.) Dem. Assn., 1980; coordinator Florio for Gov., Union County, N.J., 1981. Mem. ABA, N.Y. State Bar Assn., N.J. State Bar Assn., N.Y. County Lawyers Assn., Assn. Bar City N.Y. Roman Catholic. Communications, Entertainment, General corporate. Home: 3 Woods Ln Chatham NJ 07928-1760 Office: Time Inc 33rd Fl 1271 Avenue Of The Americas New York NY 10020-1300

**MCCARTHY, STEVEN MICHAEL,** lawyer; b. Morristown, N.J., May 2, 1949; s. George Doane and Frances (Jones) McC. BA in Philosophy, U. Va., 1971; MA in Philosophy, Calif. State U., San Francisco, 1975; JD, Golden Gate U., 1978. Diplomate Nat. Inst. for Trial Advocacy; bar: Calif. 1979, U.S. Dist. Ct. (no. dist.) Calif. 1979; cert. tchr. secondary school law, philosophy, religion, Calif.; cert. diver rescue specialist, instr. Law clk. United Farm Workers Union, 1973, San Francisco Lawyers' Com. on Urban Affairs, 1975, San Francisco Pub. Defender, 1975, Bayview Hunters' Point Cmty. Defender, 1976-77; pvt. practice, 1979-98; ptnr. McCarthy & Wakeley, Oakland, Calif., 1988-91; judge pro tempore Contra Costa Superior Ct. Judge Pro Tem Panel and EASE program evaluator, 1993—; domestic violence emergency protective order judge Solano County Superior Ct., 1994—; arbitrator Solano County Mcpl. Ct., 1994—, Alameda County Bar Assn. Fee Arbitration Panel, 1989—; judge pro tem small claims and traffic, Alameda County Mcpl. Ct., 1981—, others. Bd. dirs. Mental Health Assn. of Alameda County, 1994-97; pres. bd. dirs. Elms Homeowners Assn., 1992-94; treas. bd. dirs. Oaks Homeowners Assn., 1989-90; lectr. Alameda H.S. Spkrs. Program; vol. mounted patrol East Bay Regional Parks Dist., 1999—. Mem. NRA, Calif. State Bar Assn. (spl. master), Alameda County Bar Assn., Solano County Bar Assn., Back Country Horsemen of Calif., Calif. Rifle and Pistol Assn., Tri Valley Trailblazers, Alameda Divers, Ctrl. Calif. Coun. Dive Clubs, Chabot Gun Club. Avocations: scuba diving, horseback riding, bicycling, sailing, spearfishing. Personal injury, State civil litigation, Professional liability. Office: 2100 Embarcadero Ste 100 Oakland CA 94606-5309

**MCCARTHY, THOMAS JAMES, JR.,** lawyer; b. Pulaski, Va., Nov. 24, 1943; s. Thomas James and Jane (Osborne) McC.; m. Sally Stockdale, July 25, 1987. BA in Econs., Washington and Lee U., 1967; JD, U. Va., 1970. Bar: Va. 1970, U.S. Dist. Ct. (we. dist.) Va. 1974. Asoc. Gilmer, Sadler, Ingram Sutherland & Hutton, Pulaski, 1970-75, ptnr., 1975—; county atty. Pulaski County, Pulaski, 1983—; adminstrv. hearings officer Commonwealth of Va., 1983—; commr. of accts. Pulaski County, 1989—. Bd. dirs. New River C.C., 1980-88, 96—, vice chair, 1981-88, mem. found. bd., 1989-91. Col. JAGC, U.S. Army Res., 1970. Decorated Legion of Merit, Meritorious Svc. medal, Army Commendation medal. Mem. Va. Bar Assn., 27th Jud. Cir. Bar Assn. (pres. 1978-81), Pulaski County Bar Assn., Sigma Chi, Phi Alpha Delta. Democrat. Episcopalian. Home: PO Box 818 Pulaski VA 24301-0818 Office: Gilmer Sadler et al 65 E Main St Pulaski VA 24301-5013

**MCCARTHY, THOMAS O.,** lawyer; b. Denver, Aug. 3, 1947; s. Thomas E. and Edna D. (Davis) McC.; m. Sharon K., June 22, 1974; children: Jennifer, Julianne. BSEE cum laude, U. Mo., 1970, JD, 1972. Bar: Mo. 1973, U.S. Supreme Ct. 1994, U.S. Ct. Appeals (8th cir.) 1974, U.S. Dist. Ct. (ea. dist.) Mo. 1974. Mng. ptnr. McMahon, Berger, Hanna, Linihan, Cody & McCarthy, St. Louis. Bd. dirs. BJC Healthsys., St. Louis, 1997—, Mo. Bapt. Med. Ctr., St. Louis, 1996—, Humane Soc. Mo. Mem. St. Louis Bar Assn. (chmn. labor law com. 1985-86, labor and employment sect., litigation sect.). Avocations: hunting, skiing. Home: 13522 Weston Park Dr Saint Louis MO 63131-1044 Office: McMahon Berger Hanna Linihan Cody & McCarthy 2730 N Ballas Rd Ste 200 Saint Louis MO 63131-3039

**MCCARTNEY, BRIAN PALMER,** lawyer; b. Northampton, Mass., July 6, 1956; s. Kenneth Hall and June Palmer McC.; m. Deborah Gair, Oct. 14, 1978 (div. Mar. 1998); children: Allison, Kevin. BA, Colby Coll., 1978; JD, Union U., 1985. Bar: N.Y. 1986, N.C. 1996, U.S. Dist. Ct. (no. dist.) N.Y. 1986. Atty. Bouck, Holloway, Kiernan & Casey, Albany, 1985-86, DeLorenzo Pasquariello, Schenectady, N.Y., 1986—. Atty. Town of Rotterdam (N.Y.), 1998; dir., 1st v.p. Bridge Ctr. Schenectady, 1992-98; dir. sec. Bridge Ctr. Facilities Corp., Schenectady, 1992—; mem. Town Niskayuna Multiple Residence Bd., 1994. Mem. N.Y. State Bar Assn., Schenectady County Bar Assn., Estate Planning Coun. Ea. N.Y. Avocations: tennis, mountain biking. Estate planning, Real property, Land use and zoning (including planning). Home: 13 Sunrise Ter Clifton Park NY 12065-2306 Office: DeLorenzo Pasquariello Weiskopf & Gorman 201 Nott Terr Schenectady NY 12307-1025

**MCCARTY, WILLIAM EDWARD,** lawyer; b. Milw., Jan. 30, 1937; s. James Edward and Josephine Mary McCarty; m. Donna Kott, Aug. 26, 1961 (div. Dec. 1990); children: James, Mary Eileen, Kathleen, William. BS, Marquette U., 1959, LLB, 1962. Bar: Wis. 1962, U.S. Dist. Ct. (ea. dist.) Wis. 1962. Law clk. Wis. Supreme Ct., Madison, 1962-63; assoc. Charne & Tehan, Milw., 1963-68; ptnr. Charne, Glassner, Tehan, Clancy & Taitelman, S.C., Milw., 1968-91, McCarty, Lenz & Doyle, Milw., 1991-96, McCarty, Lenz & Tolkan, Milw., 1996—; bd. dirs. Cath. Knights Ins. Co., Milw. Sec., pres. Mequon (Wis.) Police and Fire Commn., 1978-88; bd. dirs., sec. Legal Action of Wis., Milw., 1968-95, Milw. Women's Ctr., 1989-96. Named One of Top Lawyers in Milw., Milw. Mag., 1990, 95. Mem. ABA, State Bar Wis., Milw. Bar Asn. Democrat. Roman Catholic. Family and matrimonial, Personal injury, General civil litigation. Office: McCarty Lenz & Tolkan SC 735 N Water St Milwaukee WI 53202-4100

**MCCASLIN, LEON,** lawyer; b. Royal, Ark., Oct. 3, 1931; s. Robert O. and Gladys M. (Williamson) McC.; widowed; children: Robyn, Marcus, Jennifer, David, Ted. BS in Sci., U. Oreg., 1956; LLB, LaSalle Extension U., 1968. Bar: U.S. Dist. Ct. (no. dist.) Calif. 1968, U.S. Dist. Ct. (ea. dist.) Calif. 1969, U.S. Ct. Appeals (9th cir.) 1973, U.S. Tax Ct. 1974, U.S. Dist. Ct. (cen. dist.) Calif. 1980. Police officer Marysville Police Dept., Calif., 1956-59; adjuster CalFarm Ins. Co., Yuba City, Calif., 1959-68; sole practice Yuba City, 1968—; ptnrshp. McCaslin & McCaslin LLP, 1999—; dist. claims mgr. CalFarm Ins. Co., 1968-69; dep. dist. atty. Yuba City, 1970-74. Past pres., bd. dirs. Sutter Buttes Regional Theatre; treas. Sutter County Dem. Cen. Com., Buttes Area Counsel. Mem. ABA, Calif. Bar Assn., Assn. Trial Lawyers Am., Calif. Trial Lawyers Assn. Am. Arbitration Assn., Am. Judicature Soc., Ducks Unltd., Lambda Chi Alpha. Club: Toastmasters. Lodges: Masons, Shriners, Elks. Avocations: travel, marathon running, tennis, reading. Criminal, Personal injury, Workers' compensation. Office: 1408 Live Oak Blvd # A Yuba City CA 95991-2970

**MCCAULEY, BRIAN CHARLES,** lawyer; b. Augsburg, Germany, May 31, 1959; (parents Am. citizens); BA in Econs., U. Pa., 1981; JD, Boston U., 1984. Bar: N.J. 1985, Pa. 1985. Assoc. Bash, Rosati, Donini & Ramsey, Ewing, N.J., 1985-87; asst. prosecutor Office Mercer County Prosecutor, Trenton, N.J., 1987-97, chief trial sect., 1998—. Mem. Mercer County Bar Assn. Office: Office Mercer Co Prosecutor PO Box 8068 209 S Broad St Trenton NJ 08650

**MCCAULEY, CLEYBURN LYCURGUS,** lawyer; b. Houston, Feb. 8, 1929; s. Reese Stephens and Elizabeth Ann (Burleson) McC.; m. Elizabeth Kelton McKoy, June 7, 1950; children: Stephens Francis, Lillian Elizabeth, Cleyburn, Lucy Annette. BS, U.S. Mil. Acad., 1950; MS in Engring. Econ., Statistical Quality Control and Indsl. Engring., Stanford U., 1959; JD, Coll. William and Mary, 1970. Bar: D.C. 1971, Va. 1970, Tex. 1970, U.S. Ct. Claims 1971, U.S. Tax Ct. 1971, U.S. Supreme Ct. 1973. Commd. 2d lt. U.S. Air Force, 1950, advanced through grades to lt. col., 1971, ret., 1971; pvt. practice law, Washington, 1975—. Mem. Fed. Bar Assn., Va. Bar Assn., Tex. Bar Assn., D.C. Bar Assn., IEEE, AIAA, Am. Soc. Quality Control, Phi Alpha Delta. Corporate taxation, Banking, General corporate. Home: 402 S 3rd St Wilmington NC 28401-5102

**MCCAULEY, DAVID W.,** lawyer, educator; b. Wheeling, W.Va., June 29, 1958; s. David A. and Patricia S. (Clark) McC.; children from previous marriages: Ashley Lynn, Connor Bryan. BA, U. W.Va., 1980, JD, 1983. Bar: W.Va. 1983, U.S. Dist. Ct. (no. and so. dists.) W.Va. 1983. Assoc. Coleman & Wallace, Buckhannon, W.Va., 1983-86; guardian ad litem child abuse, neglect 26th Judicial Dist., Buckhannon, W.Va., 1983—; ptnr. Coleman & Wallace, Buckhannon, W.Va., 1986-94; city atty. City of

Buckhannon, 1983—; instr. bus. law W.Va. Wesleyan Coll., Buckhannon, 1983-94, asst. prof., 1994—, dir. MBA program, 1994—, gen. legal counsel, 1993—; spkr. W.Va. Mcpl. League Conv., 1989; presenter sexual harrassment workshops. Sec. Upshur-Buckhannon Main St. Project, 1987-89, pres., 1989-90; bd. dirs., legal counsel W.Va. Strawberry Festival, 1986—; Upshur County United Way, Buckhannon, 1986-89, v.p., 1987; v.p. Buckhannon-Upshur Work Adjustment Ctr., 1990—. Mem. ABA, Internat. Municipal Lawyers Assn., W.Va. Bar Assn., W.Va. State Bar Assn., Upshur County Bar Assn. (pres. 1990-93), W.Va. Trial Lawyers Assn., W.Va. U. Alumni Assn., Mountaineer Athletic Club (Upshur County chpt.), Lions (pres. Buckhannon club 1988), Nat. Assn. of Bus. Schs. and Programs. Avocation: sports. General civil litigation, Construction. Home: 10 Meade St Buckhannon WV 26201-2630 Office: WVa Wesleyan Coll PO Box 121 Buckhannon WV 26201-0121

**MCCAULEY, MICHAEL BARRY,** lawyer; b. Phila., Sept. 23, 1951. BS, U.S. Merchant Marine Acad., 1973; JD, U. Miami, 1978. Assoc. Palmer, Biezup & Hend, Phila., 1979-86, ptnr., 1987-93, mng. ptnr., 1993—. Author: Deep Ocean Mining in Legal Perspective, 1973, Recreational Boating Law, 1992, Admiralty Desk Reference, 1996. Lt. comdr. USNR, 1973-83. Mem. Meritime Law Assn. U.S. (chmn. com. recreational boating 1993-97). Admiralty, Insurance, Private international. Office: Palmer Biezup & Henderson 1223 Foulk Rd Wilmington DE 19803-2723

**MCCLAIN, RICHARD DOUGLAS,** lawyer; b. Lincoln, Nebr., June 28, 1927; s. Leo LeRoy and Laura Thelma (Strong) McC.; s. Donna J. Burbach, July 25, 1949; children: Daniel Douglas, Laurie Lynn. BA, U. Nebr., 1951; JD, U. So. Calif., 1959. Bar: Calif. 1960, Nebr. 1970, Oreg. 1991, U.S. Dist. Ct. Nebr. 1970, U.S. Supreme Ct. 1978. Atty. Union Pacific R.R., L.A., 1960-64, Hindin, Sterling, McKittrick & Powsner, Beverly Hills, Calif., 1964-67, Carnation Co., L.A., 1967-68, Atlantic Richfield Co., L.A., 1968-69; dep. county atty. County Atty., Lincoln, 1970-74; pvt. practice Lincoln, 1974—. Pres. Exec. Toastmasters 412, L.A., 1967, Res. Officers Assn., Lincoln, 1990—, pres. Nebr. dept. 1993—; counsellor Footprinters, Lincoln, 1990—. Lt. USNR, 1951-55. Republican. Avocations: sailing, skating, shooting. General practice, Real property, Probate. Home: 3235 W Pershing Rd Lincoln NE 68502-4844 Office: 1919 S 40th St Ste 111 Lincoln NE 68506-5247

**MCCLAIN, WILLIAM ANDREW,** lawyer; b. Sanford, N.C., Jan. 11, 1913; s. Frank and Blanche (Leslie) McC.; m. Roberta White, Nov. 11, 1944. AB, Wittenberg U., 1934; JD, U. Mich., 1937; LLD (hon.), Wilberforce U., 1963, U. Cin., 1971; LHD, Wittenberg U., 1972. Bar: Ohio 1938, U.S. Dist. Ct. (so. dist.) Ohio 1940, U.S. Ct. Appeals (6th cir.) 1946, U.S. Supreme Ct. 1946. Mem. Berry, McClain & White, 1937-58; dep. solicitor, City of Cin., 1957-63, city solicitor, 1963-72; mem. Keating, Muething & Klekamp, Cin., 1972-73; gen. counsel Cin. br. SBA, 1973-75; judge Hamilton County Common Pleas Ct., 1975-76; judge Mcpl. Ct., 1976-80; of counsel Manley, Burke, Lipton & Cook, Cin., 1980—; adj. prof. U. Cin., 1963-72, Salmon P. Chase Law Sch., 1965-72. Mem. exec. com. ARC, Cin., 1978—; bd. dirs. NCCJ, 1975—. Served to 1st lt. JAGC, U.S. Army, 1943-46. Decorated Army Commendation award; recipient Nat. Layman award, A.M.E. Ch., 1963; Alumni award Wittenberg U., 1966; Nat. Inst. Mcpl. Law Officers award, 1971, Ellis Island Medal of Honor, 1997. Fellow Am. Bar Found.; mem. ABA, FBA, Am. Judicature Soc., Cin. Bar Assn., Ohio Bar Assn., Nat. Bar Assn., Friendly Sons St. Patrick, Bankers Club, Masons (33d degree), Alpha Phi Alpha, Sigma Pi Phi. Republican. Methodist. Federal civil litigation, Administrative and regulatory. Home: 2101 Grandin Rd Apt 904 Cincinnati OH 45208-3346

**MCCLAUGHERTY, JOE L.,** lawyer, educator; b. June 1, 1951; s. Frank Lee and Elease (Terrell) McC. BBA with honors, U. Tex., 1973, JD with honors, 1976. Bar: Tex. 1976, N.Mex. 1976, U.S. Dist. Ct. N.Mex. 1976, U.S. Ct. Appeals (10th cir.) 1976, U.S. Supreme Ct. 1979, Colo. 1988. Assoc. Rodey, Dickason, Sloan, Akin & Robb, P.A., Albuquerque, 1976-81, ptnr., dir., 1981-87; resident ptnr. Rodey, Dickason, Sloan, Akin & Robb, P.A., Santa Fe, N.Mex., 1983-87, mng. ptnr., 1985-87; ptnr. Kemp, Smith, Duncan & Hammond, P.C., 1987-92, mng. ptnr., 1987-92; ptnr. McClaugherty & Silver, P.C., Santa Fe, 1992—; adj. prof. law U. N.Mex., Albuquerque, 1983—; faculty Nat. Inst. Trial Advocacy, so. regional, So. Meth. U. Law Sch., 1983—, Rocky Mt. regional, U. Denver Law Sch., 1986—, nat. session U. Colo. Law Sch., 1987; faculty Hastings Ctr. for Trial and Appellate Advocacy, 1985—; bd. dirs. MCM Corp., Raleigh, N.C., Brit.-Am. Ins. Co., Ltd., Nassau, The Bahamas, 1985-91. Mem. N.Mex. Bar Assn. (bd. dirs. trial practice sect. 1976-85, chairperson 1983-84, dir. young lawyers divsn. 1978-80), N.Mex. Assn. Def. Lawyers (pres. 1982-83, bd. dirs. 1982-85). Federal civil litigation, State civil litigation, Personal injury. Office: McClaugherty Silver & Downes PC PO Box 8680 Santa Fe NM 87504-8680

**MCCLAVE, WILKES, III,** business executive; b. N.J., Apr. 22, 1947. BA cum laude, Yale U., 1969; JD, U. Denver, 1976. Bar: Colo. 1977, Calif. 1983. Atty. U.S. EPA, 1979-81; asst. gen. counsel, v.p. Tosco Corp., Stamford, Conn., 1981-91, sr. v.p., gen. counsel, 1991—. Mem. ABA, Conn. Bar Assn., Colo. Bar Assn., State Bar Calif., Los Angeles County Bar Assn. Office: Tosco Corp 72 Cummings Point Rd Ste 1 Stamford CT 06902-7922

**MCCLEAN, JAMES ALLEN, JR.,** lawyer, consultant; b. Phila., Apr. 15, 1953; s. James Allen Sr. and Elizabeth Anne (Swingler) McC. BA, Pa. State U., 1971; JD, Rutgers U., 1987. Bar: Pa. 1987, N.J. 1989, U.S. Dist. Ct. Pa. 1987, U.S. Dist. Ct. N.J. 1989. Cons. Garofolo and Curtiss, Ardmore, Pa., 1981-84; assoc. Cy Goldberg and Assocs., Phila., 1987-91; ptnr. Mayerson Munsing Corchin Rosato and Ostroff, Spring City, Pa., 1991—. Mem. Green Valley Assn., Birchrunville, Pa., 1981, Brandywine Battlefield Assn., Chad's Ford, Pa., Pickering Trust, St. Peters, Pa. Mem. Assn. Trial Lawyers Am., Pa. Trial Lawyers Assn., Phila. Trial Lawyers Assn., Pa. Bar Assn., Phila. Bar Assn., Chester County Bar Assn. Avocation: equestrian sports. Criminal, Personal injury. Home: PO Box 79 Birchrunville PA 19421-0079

**MCCLEARY, SCOTT FITZGERALD,** lawyer; b. Oak Park, Ill., Nov. 19, 1962; s. John Mark and Beverly Jane (Stange) McC.; m. Kelly Elizabeth Shaff, Sept. 5, 1987; children: Ian Fitzgerald, Kara Hope. BA in Polit. Sci. and History, North Ctrl. Coll., 1984; JD, Northwestern U., 1987. Bar: Ill. 1987. Assoc. Moses and Heimsoth, Aurora, Ill., 1988-89; asst. city atty. City of Aurora, 1989-92, exec. asst. to mayor, 1992-97, asst. corp. counsel, 1997, 1999—, budget analyst, 1997-99. Mem. Villa Park (Ill.) Pub. Libr. Bd., 1983-89, pres., 1985-88, v.p., 1988-89, sec., 1989; mem. Villa Park Hist. Preservation Commn., 1985-89, vice chmn., 1985-87, chmn., 1987-89; mem. Aurora Pub. Libr. Bd., 1991-98, DuPage Libr. Sys. Bd., Geneva, Ill., 1992-98, pres., 1996-98; sec., mem. Cmtys. in Schs. Bd., Aurora, 19 96—; mem. Big Bros./Big Sisters Resource Bd., Aurora, 1997-98, Family Counseling Svcs. Bd., Aurora, 1997—, treas., 1999—. Mem. Ill. State Bar Assn., Kane County Bar Assn. Avocations: reading, walking, traveling, stamps. Municipal (including bonds). Home: 206 S Gladstone Ave Aurora IL 60506-4838 Office: City of Aurora 44 E Downer Pl Aurora IL 60505-3302

**MCCLELLAN, CRAIG RENE,** lawyer; b. Portland, Oreg., June 28, 1947; s. Charles Russell and Annette Irene (Benedict) McC.; m. Susan Armistead Nash, June 7, 1975; children: Ryan Alexander, Shannon Lea. BS in Econs., U. Oreg., 1969; JD magna cum laude, Calif. We. U., 1976. Bar: Calif. 1976, U.S. Dist. Ct. (so. dist.) Calif. 1976, U.S. Dist. Ct. (ea., ctrl., no. dists.) Calif. 1991, U.S. Supreme Ct. 1991. Compliance specialist Cost of Living Coun. and Price Commn., Washington, 1972-73, dir. Oil Policy subcom., 1973; ptnr. Luce, Forward, Hamilton & Scripps, San Diego, 1976-87; owner McClellan & Brown, San Diego, 1987—. Chmn. annual fundraising auction KPBS, 1984. Capt. USMC, 1969-72. Mem. Assn. Trial Lawyers Am., Am. Bd. Trial Advocates, Am. Inns of Ct. (master), Calif. State Bar Assn., San Diego County Bar Assn., Calif. Trial Lawyers Assn. (bd. govs. 1985-87), San Diego Trial Lawyers Assn. (bd. dirs. 1983-90), Nat. Forensics League, Phi Gamma Delta, Phi Alpha Delta. Presbyterian. Avocations: reading, running, tennis, chess, civic activities. Personal injury, Product liability. Office: McClellan & Brown 1144 State St San Diego CA 92101-3529

**MCCLELLAN, DONALD WILLIAM, JR.,** lawyer; b. Salem, Ohio, Nov. 5, 1960; s. Donald William and Doris Louis (McGhee) McC.; m. Bonnie Lynn Bailey, Aug. 9, 1986. BA, Kent State U., 1983; JD, Catholic U. Am., 1986. Bar: Ohio 1986, D.C. 1988, U.S. Ct. Appeals (D.C. cir.) 1988, U.S. Dist. Ct., D.C., 1989, U.S. Supreme Ct. 1989. With FCC, Washington, 1986-89; spl. asst. office of Chief Mass Media Bur. FCC, 1986-87, legal asst. to commr., 1987, spl. asst. office div. chief, policy div. Mass Media Bur., 1987-89; legis. counsel Office of U.S. Senator Conrad Burns, 1989-93; telecom. lawyer, policy mgr. Intel Corp., 1993-94; sr. comm. counsel U.S. Senate Com. on Commerce, Sci., and Transp., 1994-97; sr. fellow comm. legal and policy issues The Progress & Freedom Found., 1997-98; dir. govt. rels. Gateway Inc., Washington, 1998—. Mem. Fed. Communications Bar Assn., ABA (forum com. communications law), Ohio Bar Assn., Fed. Bar Assn., D.C. Bar Assn., Young Republicans Fedn. (pres. coll. republicans), Phi Alpha Delta, Omicron Delta Kappa, Alpha Lambda Delta, Blue Key, Alpha Kappa Mu, Alpha Epsilon Rho, Pi Sigma Alpha. Avocations: music, movies, golf, politics, television. Fax: 202-737-2688. E-mail: donald.mcclellan@gateway.com. Home: 5984 Wescott Hills Way Alexandria VA 22315-4746 Office: Gateway Inc 707 D St NW Washington DC 20004-2810

**MCCLELLAND, DENISE H.,** lawyer; b. Lebanon, Mo., June 12, 1952; d. Thomas L. and Anna J. Hough; m. Robert L. McClelland, Oct. 13, 1986; children: Ethan L., Luke E. BS in Edn., S.W. Mo. State U., 1974; MLS, Vanderbilt U., 1978; JD, No. Ky. U., 1983. Bar: Mo. 1983, Ky. 1985, Ohio 1986. Tchr., libr. Ozark (Mo.) Pub. Schs., 1974-77; edn. analyst Tenn. Higher Edn. Commn., Nashville, 1977-79; asst. dir. rsch. and grants No. Ky. U., Highland Heights, 1979-83; atty. in pvt. practice, Springfield, Mo., 1983-84; law clk. U.S. Dist. Ct., Covington, Ky., 1984-86; atty. Frost & Jacobs, Cin., also Lexington, Ky., 1986—. Mem. No. Ky. Law Rev., 1983. Trustee Coll. Law., No. Ky. U., 1990-94; bd. dirs. Ctr. for Women, Diversity and Leadership, Midway Coll., 1998; active in Rep. politics. Mem. Ky. Bar Assn. (pres. civil litigation sect. 1994-96). Baptist. Avocations: reading, gardening. Contracts commercial, Banking, Securities. Office: Frost & Jacobs 1100 Vine Ctr Lexington KY 40507

**MCCLENAHAN, GREGORY ALAN,** lawyer; b. Belmond, Iowa, July 14, 1951; s. Guy Edwin and Betty Jane (Frye) M. B.S. in Psychology, U. Iowa, 1974, M.B.A., J.D., 1979. Bar: Iowa 1979, Minn. 1982, U.S. Dist. Ct. (no. dist.) Iowa 1979, U.S. Ct. Appeals (8th cir.) 1979, U.S. Dist. Ct. Minn. 1983. Staff atty., corp. counsel Iowa Elec. Light & Power Co., Cedar Rapids, Iowa, 1979-83; sole practice, Mpls., 1983-96; assoc. Chadwick, Johnson & Gordon, 1986-89, ptnr., 1990—; prin. Evergreen Real Estate Devel. Corp., 1996—. Contbr. articles to profl. jours. Mem. ABA, Iowa Bar Assn., Minn. State Bar Assn., Hennepin County Bar Assn., Assn. Trial Lawyers Am., Minn. Mcpl. Utilities Assn. Home: 5212 Hope St SE Prior Lake MN 55372-1820 Office: 7235 Ohms Ln Minneapolis MN 55439-2148

**MCCLOSKEY, JAY P.,** prosecutor. Asst. U.S. atty. Dept. Justice, Bangor, Maine; U.S. atty. Dept. Justice, Portland, Maine, 1993—. Office: US Attys Office East Tower 6th Fl PO Box 9718 Portland ME 04104-5018

**MCCLOSKEY, MICHAEL PATRICK,** lawyer; b. Inglewood, Calif., Oct. 30, 1955; s. James Francis and Myrtle Helena (Hill) McC.; m. Diane Eleanore Bregand, June 12, 1976; children: Michael Patrick Jr., Jason Andrew, Megan Alise. BS, U. So. Calif., 1976. Bar: Calif. 1982, U.S. Dist. Ct. (so. dist.) Calif. 1982, U.S. Ct. Appeals (9th cir.) 1998, U.S. Dist. Ct. (cen. dist.) Calif. 1999. Of trial counsel Office of Staff Judge Adv., Camp Pendleton, Calif., 1982-85; litigation atty. Office of Judge Adv. Gen., Alexandria, Va., 1985-88; assoc. Solomon Ward Seidenwurn & Smith, 1988-93; ptnr. Baker & McKenzie, 1993—. Editor Pacific Law Jour., 1981-82. Served to col. USMC, 1976—. Mem. ABA, Am. Trial Lawyers Assn., Assn. Bus. Trial Lawyers, Phi Delta Phi. Democrat. Avocations: running, weight lifting. Office: Baker & McKenzie 101 W Broadway Fl 12 San Diego CA 92101-8201

**MCCLOUD, ROBERT OLMSTED, JR.,** lawyer; b. Chgo., Dec. 7, 1951; s. Robert Olmsted and Suzanne (Eyerly) McC.; m. Kathryn Bartholomees, June 3, 1978; children: Lyle Olmsted, Stewart Wilcox, Kathryn Suzanne. Student, U. Ga., 1970-72; AB, Duke U., 1974; JD, U. Ga., 1977. Bar: Ga. 1977, U.S. Dist. Ct. (no. dist.) Ga. 1977, U.S. Ct. Appeals (5th and 11th cirs.) 1977. Assoc. Webb, Young, Daniel & Murphy, Atlanta, 1977-80, Jones & Van Gerpen, Atlanta, 1980-82, Carter & Ansley, Smith & McLendon, Atlanta, 1982-84; ptnr. Carter & Ansley, Atlanta, 1985—, mng. ptnr., 1991-94. Bd. dirs. Wildwood Civic Assn., Atlanta, 1984-86. Mem. ABA, Atlanta Bar Assn., Lawyers Club Atlanta (treas. 1988-89, exec. com. 1988-90), Cherokee Town and Country Club. Republican. Presbyterian. General corporate, Bankruptcy, Communications. Home: 3137 Rockingham Dr NW Atlanta GA 30327-1234 Office: Carter & Ansley Peachtree Tower 191 Peachtree St NE Ste 1000 Atlanta GA 30303-1741

**MCCLOW, ROGER JAMES,** labor lawyer; b. St. Johns, Mich., July 23, 1947; s. Jack Gordon and Madalene V. (Mahaffy) McC.; m. Suzanne Terese Posler, July 13, 1978. BA in Polit. Sci. with distinction, U. Mich., 1969; JD magna cum laude, Wayne State U., 1976. Bar: Mich. 1977, U.S. Dist. Ct. (ea. dist.) Mich. 1977, U.S. Ct. Appeals (6th cir.) 1985, U.S. Ct. Appeals (8th cir.) 1987, U.S. Supreme Ct. 1988. Assoc. Miller, Cohen, Martens & Sugerman, Detroit, 1977-81, Klimist, McKnight & Sale, P.C., Southfield, Mich., 1981-83; ptnr. Klimist, McKnight, Sale, McClow & Canzano, P.C., Southfield, 1983—. Bd. dirs. Hemid (Sr. Citizen's Agy.), Detroit, 1982—; tutor Children's Ctr., Detroit, 1990-93; vol. Hospice Legal Aid, Detroit, 1991—; mem. gun safety com. Alliance for Greater, Safer Detroit, 1993-95. Recipient Outstanding Vol. Svc. award Children's Ctr. Detroit, 1993. Mem. State Bar Mich. (coun. mem., labor law and employment sect. 1992-96), Detroit Bar Assn., Oakland County Bar Assn., Assn. Trial Lawyers Am., Mich. Trial Lawyers Assn., Indsl. Rels. Rsch. Assn., Phi Sigma Alpha. Democrat. Avocations: antiques, tennis, historic home restoration, landscaping. Labor, Pension, profit-sharing, and employee benefits, Personal injury. Office: Klimist McKnight Sale McClow & Cazano 400 Galleria Officentre Ste 117 Southfield MI 48034-2161

**MCCLUNG, MERLE STEVEN,** lawyer; b. Montevideo, Minn., June 30, 1943. BA, Harvard U., 1965, JD, 1972; AB, MA, Oxford U., Eng., 1967. Bar: Mass. 1973. Instr. Miles Coll., Birmingham, Ala., 1969-70; staff atty. Harvard Ctr. Law & Edn., Cambridge, Mass., 1972-79; dir. law and edn. ctr. Edn. Commn. States, Denver, 1979-81; gen. counsel Pendleton Land & Exploration, Inc., Denver, 1981-94, Accelerated Cos., Englewood, Colo., 1994—; legal cons. Conn. Dept. Edn., Hartford, 1974-77, Calif. Dept. Edn., Sacramento, 1978-81. Contbr. articles to profl. jours. Rhodes scholar Oxford U., Eng., 1965. Mem. ABA, Mass. Bar Assn., Phi Beta Kappa. Avocations: biking, books. General corporate, Consumer commercial, Civil rights. Home: 6048 S Locust Cir Englewood CO 80111-4465 Office: Accelerated Companies 5295 Dtc Pkwy Englewood CO 80111-2752

**MCCLURE, ANN CRAWFORD,** lawyer, judge; b. Cin., Sept. 5, 1953; d. William Edward and Patricia Ann (Jewett) Crawford; m. David R. McClure, Nov. 12, 1983; children: Kinsey Tristen, Scott Crawford. BFA magna cum laude, Tex. Christian U., 1974; JD, U. Houston, 1979. Bd. cert. in family law and civil appellate law Tex. Bd. Legal Specialization. Assoc. Piro and Lilly, Houston, 1979-83; pvt. practice, El Paso, Tex., 1983-92; ptnr. McClure and McClure, El Paso, 1992-94; justice 8th Ct. of Appeals, El Paso, 1995—; former mem. Tex. Bd. Law Examiners, Bd. Disciplinary Appeals; mem. Family Law Specialization Exam Com., 1989-93. Contbr. articles to profl. jours.; past editor The Family Law Forum; contbg. editor: Texas Family Law Service; mem. editl. bd. Tex. Family Law Practice Manual, 1982-93. Mem. State Bar Tex. (dir. family law sect. 1987-91, treas. 1993-94, vice chmn. 1995-96, chmn.-elect 1996-97, chmn. 1997-98), dir. appellate and advocacy sect. 1991-95, treas. 1996-97, sec. 1997-98, vice chmn. 1998-99, chmn.-elect 1999—), Tex. Acad. Family Law Specialists (past dir.). Democrat. Presbyterian.

**MCCLURE, GEORGE MORRIS, III,** lawyer; b. Danville, Ky., Nov. 12, 1934; s. George Morris Jr. and Helen Louise (McCormack) McC.; m. Judith DeGolier Selee, July 6, 1957 (div. Jan. 1969); 1 child, George Morris IV; m. Patricia Moberly, Dec. 11, 1971; children: Joseph Scott Kirk, Patrick Spencer McClure. AB, Princeton U., 1956; JD, Denver U., 1963. Bar: Colo. 1963, Ky. 1970, U.S. Dist. Ct. (ea. dist.) Ky. 1970. Assoc. Yegge, Hall, Schulenberg, Denver, 1963-65; sole practitioner Denver, 1965-67; assoc. Zarlengo, Mott & Carlin, Denver, 1967-69, James G. Sheehan, Danville, Ky., 1970-71; sole practitioner Danville, 1971-72, 72—; county atty. Boyle County, Danville, 1972—. Adv. div. Comty. Theatre, Danville, 1984—. 1st lt. USMC, 1956-59. Mem. ABA, Ky. Bar Assn. Democrat. Avocations: golf, fishing, amateur radio, flying, gardening. Office: Boyle County Court House 321 W Main St Danville KY 40422-1848

**MCCLURE, JAMES FOCHT, JR.,** federal judge; b. Danville, Pa., Apr. 6, 1931; s. James Focht and Florence Kathryn (Fowler) McC.; m. Elizabeth Louise Barber, June 14, 1952; children: Holly McClure Kerwin, Kimberly Ann Pacala, Jamee McClure Sealy, Mary Elizabeth Hudec, Margaret McClure Persing. AB, Amherst Coll., 1952; JD, U. Pa., 1957. Bar: D.C. 1957, Pa. 1958, U.S. Dist. Ct. D.C. 1957, U.S. Dist. Ct. (ea. and mid. dist.) Pa. 1958, U.S. Ct. Appeals (3d cir.) 1959. Atty., advisor Dept. State, Washington, 1957-58; assoc. Morgan, Lewis & Bockius, Phila., 1958-61; atty. Merck & Co., Inc., N.Y.C., 1961-65; ptnr. McClure & McClure, Lewisburg, Pa., 1965-77, McClure & Light, Lewisburg, 1978-84; pres. judge Ct. Common Pleas, 17th Jud. Dist. Pa., Lewisburg, 1984-90; dist. judge U.S. Dist. Ct. (mid. dist.) Pa., Williamsport, Pa., 1990—; dist. atty. Union County, Lewisburg, 1974-75. Pres. bd. sch. dirs. Lewisburg Area Sch. Dist., 1969-74. Cpl. U.S. Army, 1952-54. Mem. Pa. Bar Assn., Union County Bar Assn., Bucknell U. Golf Club, Susquehanna Valley Chorale, Order of Coif, Phi Beta Kappa. Republican. Presbyterian. Office: US Dist Ct Federal Bldg PO Box 1448 240 W 3rd St Williamsport PA 17701-6438

**MCCLURE, PEGGY ALLISON,** corporate lawyer; b. Lexington, Ky., Feb. 10, 1942; d. Richard Floyd and Clara Elizabeth (Hunley) Allison; m. Maurice Scott McClure, Nov. 18, 1995 (dec. Aug. 1997); children: Steven Werdehoff, Kevin Werdehoff (dec.). BA in Polit. Sci. with honors, U. Ala., 1964, MA in Secondary Edn. with honors, 1966; JD Cum Laude, Cumberland Sch. Law Samford U., 1979; postgrad., Columbia Theol. Sem., 1998—. Bar: Ala. 1979. Tchr. Vance Elem. Sch., Bessemer, Ala., 1965-67; English tchr. Dupont Jr. H.S., Tacoma, 1968; History tchr. Heidelberg (Germany) H.S., 1970-71; tchr. Huntsville (Ala.) H.S., 1973-76; law clerk, atty. South Ctrl. Bell Tel. Co., 1979-80, atty., 1981; fed. law clerk Judge J. Foy Guin Jr., Ala., 1980-81; adj. prof. Cumberland Sch. Law, 1993; atty. USX Corp., Birmingham, Ala., 1981-89; asst. sec. USX Corp., 1983-98, gen. atty., 1989-98, part-time atty., 1998—; mem. Birmingham Bar Assn. Law Week Com., 1982-83, chmn. Law Day Banquet, 1983, Scholarship Com., 1985-86 (co-chair 1986), Grievence Com., 1990, Ea. Mineral Law Found., 1986—, Nat. Assn. Sch. Bds., 1987-92, Ala. Assn. Sch. Bds., 1987-92, Bus. Coun. Ala., 1985-98, Birmingham C. of C., 1988-98, Ala. Task Force Workmen's Compensation, 1982-89, Third Citizen's Conf. Ala. State Cts., 1995, State Bar Com. Correctional Instns. Procedures, 1994-96. Ala. Symphony bd. dirs. 1983-93, chmn. Artistic Adv. Com. 1985-93, search com. 1984-85, corp. sec. 1986-93, chmn. search com. 1987-88, mgmt. coun. 1987-89, bd. pers. com. 1987, 91, capt. annual fund dr. 1988-89, bd. exec. com. 1986-93, bd. nominating com. 1990-92, bd. negotiating com. 1991; Vestavia Hills bd. zoning adjustment 1983-87, 40th Anniversary Com. 1990, C. of C. 1990-92; Downtown Birmingham Rotary Club 1989—, world cmty. svc. com. 1991-97 (chmn. 1991-92), Paul Harris Fellow 1991, chmn. subcommittee world monetary grants 1995-96, program com. 1996-97; Jr. Achievement bd. dirs. 1994—, exec. com. 1995-96, vice chmn. elem. program 1995-96; Ala. symphonic Assn bd. dirs. 1995—; United Way bd. dirs. 1997-98, planning com. 1997-98; Vestavia Hills bd. edn. 1987-92 (pres. 1990-91); Sta. WBHM-FM Friends bd. trustees 1994-98, v.p. 1994-96, pres. 1996-97, fundraiser on-the-air 1991-96; Vestavia Hills United Methodist Ch. sanctuary choir 1981-95, bd. trustees 1985-87, adminstrv. bd. 1985-94, occasional soloist 1985-95, AIDS care team 1994-95, cert. lay leader 1994-95, fin. com. 1988-92, Stephen Min. 1989-93; Springville Presbyterian Ch. choir 1995—, elder, 1998—; Springville Presbyterian Ch. Found., Inc. bd. dirs. 1997—, corp. sec. 1997—; Bus. Sci. Roundtable 1991; Young Men's Bus. Club 1991. Recipient Most Wanted Female Exec. award, March of Dimes, 1991. Republican. Presbyterian. Avocations: playing tennis, snow skiing, bicycling, hiking, singing. Office: USX Corp Law Dept 6200 Ej Oliver Blvd Ste 44 Fairfield AL 35064-1218

**MCCLURE, ROGER JOHN,** lawyer; b. Cleve., Nov. 22, 1943; s. Theron R. and Colene (Irwin) McC. BA, Ohio State U., 1965, JD cum laude, 1972; MA, Northwestern U., 1966. Bar: U.S. Ct. Appeals (D.C. cir.) 1974, U.S. Supreme Ct. 1978, Va. 1973, Md. 1973, Ohio, U.S. Ct. Appeals (4th, 5th & 10th cirs.). Asst. atty. gen. State of Ohio, Columbus, 1972; trial atty. FTC, Washington, 1972-76; sr. assoc. Law Offices of A.D. Berkeley, Washington, 1976-81; pvt. practice, Alexandria, Va., 1981—; pres. Roger J. McClure, P.C., Alexandria, 1987—; del. Va. Gen. Assembly, 1992—, co-chmn. militia & police com., 1998—; adj. prof. Antioch Sch. Law, Washington, 1982-84; host talk show Sta. WRC Radio, 1987-93, Sta. WPGC, 1993-94. Co-author: Winning the Syndication Game, 1988, Advanced Estate Planning in Virginia, 1997, Virginia Elder Law, 1998, Family Limited Partnerships and LLCS, 1999; bd. editors Ohio State U. Law Rev., 1970-72; contbr. numerous articles to profl. jours.; contbg. reviewer and author: Conspectus, Estate and Wealth Strategies Planning. Bd. dirs. No. Va. Cmty. Found., 1995—. Served with U.S. Army, 1967-69. Decorated Bronze Star; Masters Fellow Esperti Peterson Inst., 1996—. Mem. D.C. Bar Assn. (real estate steering com. 1982-84, chmn. antitrust divsn. 1975-76), No. Va. Apt. Assn. (bd. dirs. 1988-92, 1st v.p. 1987-88, pres. 1988-89), Nat. Network Estate Planning Attys., Dulles Area Transp. Assn. (bd. dirs.), Wolf Trap Found. (adv. coun.), Washington Nat. Cathedral. Avocation: sailing. Real property, Estate taxation, Estate planning. Office: 500 N Washington St Alexandria VA 22314-2314

**MCCLURE, THOMAS JAMES,** lawyer; b. Chgo., Feb. 19, 1955. BA in Humanities cum laude, St. Norbert Coll., 1977; JD, Marquette U., 1980. Bar: Wis. 1980, U.S. Dist. Ct. (we. dist.) Wis. 1980, U.S. Dist. Ct. (ea. dist.) Wis. 1981, U.S. Ct. Appeals (7th cir.) 1984. Asst. dist. atty. Washington County, West Bend, Wis., 1980-81, Milwaukee (Wis.) County, 1982, Rock County, Janesville and Beloit, Wis., 1982-85; assoc. deVries, Vlasak & Schallert, Milw., 1985-88, McLario Law Offices S.C., Menomonee Falls, Wis., 1988-92; ptnr. Osinga & McClure, Milw., 1992—; instr. Am. jurisprudence Am. Inst. Paralegal Studies Alverno Coll., Milw., 1986. Elder, bd. dirs. Kettle Moraine Evang. Free Ch., Delafield, Wis., 1987—; mem. police fire commn. City of Delafield, 1988, planning commn., 1988-90; alderman city coun. City of Delafield, 1988-90, pres. city coun., 1989-90. Named One of Outstanding Young Men in Am. U.S. Jaycees, 1984. Mem. Milw. County Bar Assn., Assn. Trial Lawyers Am., Wis. Acad. Trial Lawyers, Wis. State Bar (young lawyers div. subcom. mem. and presenter, Law Day for Clergy 1991), The Rutherford Inst.(Wis. state coord., 1993—). General civil litigation, General practice, Criminal. Home: W318n737 Partridge Run Delafield WI 53018-2820 Office: Osinga & McClure Ste 901 11801 W Silver Spring Dr Milwaukee WI 53225-3092

**MCCLURG, DOUGLAS P.,** lawyer; b. Cleve., Feb. 17, 1949; s. Donald Wayne and Helen Mildred (Tulin) McC.; m. Christie Jene Cobourn, Aug., 1976; children: Kelly Cobourn, Douglas Paul, Jr., Lauren Christie. BA, U. Fla., 1973, JD, 1976. Bar: Fla. 1976, U.S. Ct. Appeals (11th cir.) 1981, U.S. Dist. Ct. (mid. dist.) Fla. 1976. Assoc., shareholder Mahoney, Hadlow & Adams, Jacksonville, Fla., 1976-81; shareholder Smith & Hulsey, Jacksonville, Fla., 1981-84; ptnr. Holland & Knight, Tampa, 1984-92; shareholder Hill, Ward & Henderson, Tampa, 1992—; chmn. Bankruptcy/UCC com. of Bus. Law Section of The Fla. Bar, 1984-85, chmn. Legislation Com. Bus. Law Sect., 1986-87, pres., chmn. Tampa Bay Bankruptcy Bar Assoc., 1989-91. Trustee The Tampa Mus. of Art, 1991-92, pres. The Tampa Club, 1992, Exec. Com. mem. Young Life of Tampa, 1994-85; trustee U. Fla. Law Ctr. Assn., 1996—, Gulf Ridge coun. Boy Scouts Am., 1996—. Decorated Bronze Star (with Vdevice), Purple Heart (with Oak Leaf Cluster). Mem. Ye Mystic Krewe of Gasparilla, The Tampa Yacht and Country Club. Republican, Episcopalian. Avocation: competitive shooting, gun collecting, hunting, camping. Bankruptcy, General civil litigation. Office: Hill Ward & Henderson 101 E Kennedy Blvd Ste 3700 Tampa FL 33602-5156 Home: 2721 W Terrace Dr Tampa FL 33609-4025

**MCCLURG, E. VANE,** lawyer. Bar: Fla. 1969. Gen. counsel Publix Super Markets, Inc., Lakeland, Fla., 1990-96; ptnr. Hahn, McClurg, Watson, Griffith and Bush, Lakeland, 1996—. Real property. Address: PO Box 38 Lakeland FL 33802-0038

**MCCOBB, JOHN BRADFORD, JR.,** lawyer; b. Orange, N.J., Oct. 14, 1939; s. John Bradford and Dorothea Joyce (Hoffman) M.; m. Maureen

Kelly, Oct. 6, 1973; 1 dau., Carrie Elizabeth. A.B., Princeton U. cum laude, 1961; J.D., Stanford U., 1966; LL.M., NYU, 1973. Bar: Calif. 1967. Assoc., IBM, Armonk, N.Y., 1966-1974, gen. counsel, Tokyo, 1974-77, lab. counsel, Endicott, N.Y., 1977-79, sr. atty., White Plains, N.Y., 1979-81, regional counsel, Dallas, 1981-83; counsel, sec. IBM Instruments, Inc., Danbury, Conn., 1983-87; area counsel European Labs, Hursley, England, 1987-90; counsel govtl. programs IBM, Washington, 1990-97. Trustee Princeton-in-Asia, Inc., 1970-86 . Princeton-in-Asia-teaching fellow at Chinese Univ. of Hong Kong, 1963-65. Mem. ABA, State Bar of Calif., Phi Beta Kappa. Contbr. articles to profl. jours. Private international, Computer, Antitrust.

**MCCOID, NANCY KATHERINE,** lawyer; b. Tacoma, July 30, 1953; d. Francis Patnck and Kathleen Grace McCoid; m. Tom Mash, Aug. 25, 1989; 1 child, Kelly Elizabeth. BS in Psychology summa cum laude, U. Wash., 1976; MA in Psychology summa cum laude, Western Wash. U., 1979; JD with high honors, U. Wash., 1980. Bar: Wash., U.S. Dist. Ct. (we. dist.) Wash., U.S. Ct. Appeals (9th cir.), U.S. Supreme Ct. Law clk. divsn. I Ct. Appeals, Seattle, 1983-85; assoc. Merrick, Hofstedt & Lindsey, Seattle, 1985-90, shareholder, 1991—; mentor to 1st-yr. law students U. Wash., Seattle, 1990—; arbitrator King County Superior Ct., Seattle, 1991—; mem. health-care panel counsel Tenet, 1996—; spkr. in field. Vol. atty. Bar Assn. Pro Bono Program, Seattle, 1991—, Fed. Pro Bono Program, Seattle, 1992; mem. Gov. Gary Locke's Transition Team. Mem. Am. Law Firm Assn. (health practices com., employment law com.), Wash. State Bar Assn. (com. on profl. liability 1995—, vol. spkr. 1998), Wash. Def. Trial Lawyers (com. on profl. liability 1995—), Def. Rsch. Inst. (com. on profl. liability 1990—), King County Bar Assn. (com. on professionalism 1995, gender bias com., com. on jud. evaluation 1998, pres.'s coun. mem.), Order of Coif. Avocations: jazz, theater, gardening, traveling. General civil litigation, Personal injury, Professional liability. Office: Merrick Hofstedt & Lindsey 710 9th Ave Seattle WA 98104-2099

**MCCOLLUM, JAMES FOUNTAIN,** lawyer; b. Reidsville, N.C., Mar. 24, 1946; s. James F. and Dell (Frazier) McC.; m. Susan Shasek, Apr. 26, 1969; children: Audra Lynne, Amy Elizabeth. BS, Fla. Atlantic U., 1968; JD, Fla. State U., 1972. Bar: U.S. Ct. Appeals (5th cir.) 1973, Fla. 1972, U.S. Ct. Appeals (11th cir.) 1982. Assoc. Kennedy & McCollum, 1972-73; prin. James F. McCollum, P.A., 1973-77, McCollum & Oberhausen, P.A., 1977-80, McCollum, Oberhausen & Tuck, L.L.P. (and predecessor firm), Sebring, Fla., 1977—; bd. dirs. Comml. Bancorp, Inc., Comml. Bank Highlands County; pres. Highlands Devel. Concepts, Inc., Sebring, 1982—; sec. Focus Broadcast Comm., Inc., Sebring, 1982-87; mng. ptnr. Highlands Investment Service. Treas. Highlands County chpt. ARC, 1973-76; vestryman St. Agnes Episcopal Ch., 1973—, chancellor, 1978—; mem. Fla. Sch. Bd. Atty.'s Assn., 1974—, bd. dirs., 1989-97, pres., 1995-96; mem. Com. 100 of Highlands County, 1975-83, bd. dirs., 1985-87, chmn., 1991-92; chmn. Highlands County High Speed Rail Task Force; chmn. bd., treas. Ctrl. Fla. Racing Assn., 1976-78; chmn. Leadership Sebring: life mem., past pres. Highlands Little Theatre, Inc.; bd. dirs. Palms of Sebring Nursing Home, 1988-90, Palms Estate Mobile Home Park, Sebring Airport Authority, 1988-90, treas., 1988, chmn. indsl. com., 1988, vice-chmn., 1989-90, chmn., 1990-91, Highlands County High Speed Rail Task Force, 1986-89; bd. dirs. Highlands County Family YMCA, 1985-93, pres. Sebring br., 1992-93, chmn. bldg. com., 1992-94. Recipient ARC citation, 1974, Presdl. award of appreciation Fla. Jaycees, 1980-81, 82, 85, Outstanding Svc. award Highlands Coun. of 100, 1988, Most Valuable Player award Highlands Little Theatre, Inc., 1986, Zenon Significant Achievement award, 1991; named Jaycee of Year, Sebring Jaycees, 1981, Outstanding Local Chpt. Pres., U.S. Jaycees, 1977. Outstanding Service award Highlands Council of 100, 1988. Mem. ABA, ATLA, Comml. Law League Am., Am. Arbitration Assn. (comml. arbitration panel), Nat. Assn. Retail Credit Attys., Fla. Bar (jour. com.), Highlands County Bar Assn. (past chmn. legal aid com.), Fla. Sch. Bd. Attys. Assn. (dir. 1989—, v.p. 1993-94, pres. 1994-95), Greater Sebring C. of C. (dir. 1982-89, pres. 1986-87, chmn. transp. com. 1986—, Most Valuable Dir. award 1986, 87), Fla. Jaycees (life mem. internat. senate 1977—), Lions (bd. dirs. 1972-73, v.p. 1994-95, Disting. award 1984). Republican. Episcopalian. Probate, Real property. Office: 129 S Commerce Ave Sebring FL 33870-3602

**MCCONAUGHY, BENNET ALAN,** lawyer; b. Des Moines, Mar. 5, 1954; s. Willis D. McConaughy and Joan M. Whitney; m. Dawn M. Thiry, July 1, 1988; children: Kate, Joe. BS, U. Wasington, 1976, JD, 1979. Bar: Wash. 1979, Alaska 1980. Judicial law clk. U.S. Dist. Ct. Wash., Seattle, 1979-81; assoc. Roberts & Shefelman, Seattle, 1981-85, ptnr., 1985-87; ptnr. Foster, Pepper & Shefelman, P.L.L.C., 1987-97; mng. mem. Sandler Ahern & McConaughy PLLC, Seattle, 1997—. Contbr. articles to profl. jours. Trustee Fed. Bar Assn., 1997—. Federal civil litigation, General civil litigation, Pension, profit-sharing, and employee benefits. Office: Sandler Ahern & McConaughy PLLC 1200 5th Ave Ste 1900 Seattle WA 98101-3135

**MCCONKIE, OSCAR WALTER,** lawyer; b. Moad, Utah, May 26, 1926; s. Oscar Walter and Margaret Vivian (Redd) M.; m. Judith Stoddard, Mar. 17, 1951; children: Oscar III, Ann, Daniel, Gail, Clair, Pace Jefferson, Roger James, Edward. BS in Polit. Sci., U. Utah, 1949, JD, 1952. Bar: Utah 1952, U.S. Ct. Appeals (10th cir.) 1952, U.S. Supreme Ct. 1981, U.S. Ct. Appeals (8th cir.) 1994. County atty. Summit County (Utah), 1959-63; instr. bus. law Stevens Henager Coll., Salt Lake City, 1952-67; ptnr. Kirton & McConkie, Salt Lake City, 1967—. Served with USN, 1944-46. Mem. Utah House of Reps., 1955-57; pres. Utah State Senate, 1965-66; chmn. Utah Bd. Edn., 1983-85. Mem. Utah Bar Assn., Salt Lake County Bar Assn. Democrat. Mormon. Author: The Kingdom of God, 1962; God and Man, 1963; The Priest in the Aaronic Priesthood, 1964; Angels, 1975; Aaronic Priesthood, 1977; She Shall Be Called Woman, 1979. Legislative, General practice. Home: 1954 Laird Dr Salt Lake City UT 84108-1823 Office: 1800 Eagle Gate Tower 60 E South Temple Salt Lake City UT 84111-1004

**MCCONNAUGHEY, GEORGE CARLTON, JR.,** lawyer; b. Hillsboro, Ohio, Aug. 9, 1925; s. George Carlton and Nelle (Morse) McC.; m. Carolyn Schlieper, June 16, 1951; children: Elizabeth, Susan, Nancy. *Daughter Elizabeth McConnaughey Owen and her husband Mark M. Owen have two children: Katherine, born in 1979, and Lisa, born in 1981. Daughter Susan McConnaughey McCamy and her husband Samuel C. McCamy III have two children: George (Spike), born in 1985, and Callie, born in 1988. Daughter Nancy McConnaughey Leggett and her husband David G. Leggett have three children: Christine, born in 1984, Laura, born in 1986, and Daniel, born in 1989.* B.A., Denison U., 1949; LL.B., Ohio State U., 1951, J.D., 1967. Bar: Ohio 1951. Sole practice Columbus; ptnr. McConnaughey & McConnaughey, 1954-57, McConnaughey, McConnaughey & Stradley, 1957-62, Laylin, McConnaughey & Stradley, 1962-67, George, Greek, King, McMahon & McConnaughey, 1967-79, McConnaughey, Stradley, Mone & Moul, 1979-81, Thompson, Hine & Flory (merger McConnaughey, Stradley, Mone & Moul with Thompson, Hine & Flory), Cleve., Columbus, Cin., Dayton and Washington, 1981-93; ret. ptnr. Thompson, Hine & Flory, Columbus, 1993—; bd. dirs. N.Am. Broadcasting Co. (Sta. WMNI and WBZX Radio); asst. atty. gen. State of Ohio, 1951-54. Pres. Upper Arlington (Ohio) Bd. Edn., 1967-69, Columbus Town Meeting Assn., 1974-76; chmn. Ohio Young Reps., 1956; U.S. presdl. elector, 1956; trustee Buckeye Boys Ranch, Columbus, 1967-73, 75-81, Upper Arlington Edn. Found., 1987-93; elder Covenant Presbyn. Ch., Columbus. With U.S. Army, 1943-45, ETO. Fellow Am. Bar Found., Ohio Bar Found., Columbus Bar Found.; mem. ABA, Ohio Bar Assn., Columbus Bar Assn., Am. Judicature Soc., Scioto Country Club, Athletic Club, Rotary, Masons. Public utilities, General corporate. Home: 1993 Collingswood Rd Columbus OH 43221-3741 Office: Thompson Hine & Flory One Columbus 10 W Broad St Ste 700 Columbus OH 43215-3435

**MCCONNELL, DAVID KELSO,** lawyer; b. N.Y.C., July 12, 1932; s. David and Caroline Hanna (Kelso) McC.; m. Alice Schmitt, Dec. 26, 1963; children: Elissa Anne, Kathleen Anne, David Willet. BCE, CCNY, 1954; LLB, Yale U., 1962. Bar: Conn. 1962, U.S. Dist. Ct. Conn. 1963, U.S. Ct. Appeals (2d cir.) 1964, U.S. Ct. Appeals (3d cir.) 1966, U.S. Sip. Ct. 1970, U.S. Dist. Ct. (ea. dist.) Pa. 1971, Pa. 1975, N.Y. 1986. Asst. counsel N.Y.N.H. & H. R.R., New Haven, 1962-65; counsel N.Y.N.H. & H. R.R., 1966-68; asst. atty. gen. U.S. V.I., 1965-66; asst. gen. atty. Pa. Cen. Transp. Co., New Haven, 1969-70; asst. gen. counsel Pa. Cen. Transp. Co., Phila., 1970-71; sr. reorganization atty. Pa. Cen. Transp. Co., 1971, adminstrv. officer, spl. counsel to trustees, 1971-76, gen. atty., 1977-78; asst. to chmn., CEO The Penn Cen. Corp., N.Y.C., 1979-80; corp. sec. The Penn Cen. Corp., 1980-82; v.p., gen. counsel Gen. Cable Co., Greenwich, Conn., 1982-85; pvt. practice law Stamford, Conn., 1985-86, Pelham, N.Y., 1989-91, Greenwich, Conn., 1991—; of counsel McCarthy, Fingar, Donovan, Drazen & Smith, White Plains, N.Y., 1986-89. Dep. supr., councilman Town of Pelham, N.Y., 1986-90; dep. mayor, trustee Village of Pelham, 1992-95, village atty., 1995-96, budget officer, 1996; clk. of session, elder, trustee, deacon Huguenot Meml. Ch., Pelham N.Y. With U.S. Navy, 1954-59, USNR, 1959-79. Mem. Conn. Bar Assn., Assn. of Bar of City of N.Y., Yale U. Law Sch. Assn. (exec. com. 1988-91), N.Y. State Bar Assn., The Corinthians (mem. afterguard, dir, The Corinthians Assn., Trustee, Pres. The Corinthians Endowment Fund), St. Andrews Soc. N.Y. (bd. mgrs. 1986-89, 96-99, chmn. bd. mgrs. 1988-89), Rotary Club (pres. 1993-94). General corporate, General practice, Municipal (including bonds). Home: 68 1/2 Roseneath Ave Newport RI 02840-3849

**MCCONNELL, EDWARD BOSWORTH,** legal organization administrator, lawyer; b. Greenwich, Conn., Apr. 3, 1920; s. Raymond Arnott and Anna Bell (Lee) McC.; m. Jeanne M. Rotton (dec. 1984); children: Annalee, Marilyn, Edward, Barbara, William; m. Florence M. Leonard, (dec. 1991); stepchildren: Susan L. Little, William R. Leonard, Molly M. Leonard. AB, U. Nebr., 1941, LLB, 1947; MBA with distinction, Harvard U., 1943. Bar: Nebr. 1947, N.J. 1950. Mem. faculty Rutgers U. Sch. Bus. Adminstrn., Newark, 1947-53; assoc. firm Toner, Speakman and Crowley, Newark, N.J., 1949-50; adminstrv. asst. and law sec. to Chief Justice of N.J., 1950-53; adminstrv. dir. Cts. of N.J., Trenton, 1953-73; also standing master Supreme Ct., 1953-73; pres. Nat. Center for State Cts., Williamsburg, 1973-90, bd. dirs., 1980-90, pres. emeritus, 1990—, cons. on ct. mgmt., 1990—; mem. U.S. Dept. Justice Coun. on Role of Cts. in Am. Soc., 1978-83; mem. adv. com. Dispute Resolution Policy Study, Social Sci. Rsch. Inst., U. So. Calif., 1975-79, Civil Litigation Rsch. Project, U. Wis. and U. So. Calif., 1979-83, nat. judg. edn. program to promote equality for men and women in the cts., 1980—; mem. Nat. Inst. Criminal Justice Task Force, Urban Consortium, 1979-83; participant Access To Justice Colloquium, European Univ. Inst., Florence, Italy, 1979; nat. adv. coun. Ctr. Adminstrn. Justice, Wayne Stae U., 1973-77; nat. project com. State Jud. Info. Sys. Project SEARCH Group, 1973-76; lectr. Inst. of Local and State Govt. Wharton Sch. U. Pa., 1955-65, Appellate Judges Seminar, Inst. Jud. Adminstrn., NYU, 1962-75; vis. expert UN Asia and Far East Inst., Tokyo, 1971; mem. Cts. Task Force Nat. Adv. Commn. Criminal Justice Standards and Goals, 1971-73; nat. adv. com. D.C. Ct. Mgmt. Project, 1966-70; trustee Inst. Ct. Mgmt., 1969-73, 84-86; chmn. Nat. Conf. Ct. Adminstrv. Officers, 1956; mem. nat. task force on gender bias in cts. Nat. Assn. Women Judge's 1985-90; mem. adv. bd. Nat. Ctr. for Citizen Participation in Admisntrn. of Justice, 1984-90; mem. Nat. Commn. Trial Ct. Performance Standards, 1991-95. Mem. adv. com. on article III Commn. on the Bicentennial of the Constitution, 1989-91; adv. com. Judicary Leadership Coun., 1990-95. Maj. C.E., AUS, 1943-46. Decorated Bronze Star medal; recipient Warren E. Burger award for greatest contbn. to improvement of ct. adminstrn. Inst. for Ct. Mgmt.., 1975, Herbert Lincoln Harley award for efficient adminstrn. justice Am. Judicature Soc., 1973, Glenn R. Winters award for outstanding service in jud. adminstrn. Am. Judges Assn., 1974, Tom C. Clark award for outstanding contbns. to field of ct. adminstrn. Nat. Conf. Met. Cts., 1983, Award of Merit Nat. Assn. Ct. Mgmt., 1987, Spl. award, Nat. Assn. Women Judges, 1989, Paul C. Reardon award for disting. svc. Nat. Ctr. for State Cts., 1991, Alumni Achievement award U. Nebr., 1991, Robert B. Yegge award ABA Jud. Divsn. Lawyers Conf., 1997. Fellow Nat. Acad. Pub. Adminstrn. (mem. panel on evaluation budget decentralization project of fed. cts. 1989-91, chmn. panel long range planning in fed. cts. 1991-92, mem. panel for study of fed. trial ct. adminstrv. structure 1995-96—); mem. ABA (fellow-at-large, coun. mem. 1960-66, 71-80, house of dels., 1977-80, chmn. com. on oversight and goals 1975-76, chmn. com. on jud. compensation jud. adminstrn. div. 1984-89, chmn. jud. adminstrn. div. 1976-77, sect. of litigation task force on excess litigiousness in Am. 1986-88, task force on reduction of litigation cost and delay, jud. adminstrn. dir. 1984-94, chmn. 1991-94, mem. long range planning com. 1989-94), N.J. Bar Assn., Nebr. Bar Assn., Warren E. Burger Soc., Kingsmill (Va.) Golf, Tennis and Yacht Clubs, Order of Coif (hon.), Delta Upsilon, Sigma Delta Phi, Phi Delta Phi.

**MCCONNELL, JAMES GUY,** lawyer; b. Hinsdale, Ill., Sept. 24, 1947; s. William F. and Virginia (Brown) McC.; m. Linda McConnell; children: Colin, Nicholas, Joanna, Cameron, Gabriel. BS in Journalism, Iowa State U., 1969; JD, Northwestern U., 1973. Bar: Ill. 1973, U.S. Dist. Ct. (no. dist.) Ill. 1973, U.S. Ct. Appeals (7th cir.) 1973, U.S. Supreme Ct. 1977. Assoc. Rooks, Pitts & Poust, Chgo., 1973-80, ptnr., 1980-85; ptnr. Bell, Boyd & Lloyd, Chgo., 1985-88, Freeborn & Peters, Chgo., 1990-96, Goldstein, Fluxgold & McConnell, Chgo., 1996—; adj. prof. Kent Coll. Law Ill. Inst. Tech., Chgo., 1978-83. Author: Comparative Negligence Defense Tactics, 1985; contbg. editor jour. Hazardous Waste & Toxic Torts Law & Strategy. Mem. Dist. 102 Sch. Bd., LaGrange Park, Ill., 1975-76; mem. Dist. 106 Sch. Bd., Bannockburn, Ill., 1989-92. Mem. ABA, Ill. Bar Assn., Chgo. Bar Assn., Soc. Trial Lawyers. Clubs: Legal of Chgo., Law of Chgo. Federal civil litigation, State civil litigation, Personal injury. Office: Susan E Loggans & Assocs 200 W Madison St Ste 2850 Chicago IL 60606-3498

**MCCONNELL, MARIANNE,** lawyer. BSN, Rutgers U., 1982; JD, Seton Hall U., 1986. Bar: N.J., 1986; RN, Ohio, N.J. Pub. health nurse Morris County Vis. Nurse Assn., 1982-86; law clk. Scerbo, Kobin, Litwin and Wolffe, Morristown, N.J., 1983-85; legal intern N.J. Dept. Pub. Advocate-Legis. Unit, 1984-85; law clk. Judge Herbert S. Friend/Superior Ct., Morris, N.J., 1986-87; assoc. counsel Forster, Pompello and Arbore, Ledgewood, N.J., 1987-89; asst. v.p., counsel to govt. rels. dept. Beneficial Mgmt. Corp., Peapack, N.J., 1989—; bd. dirs. Child and Family Resources. Producer/host: (cable TV program) As We See It, 1992—; contbr. articles to profl. jours. Apptd. by gov. to N.J. Med. Practitioner Rev. Panel, 1992—; pres. Morris County Women's Polit. Caucus, 1994—; treas. Frank Herbert for Congress, 1994; trustee Morris County Legal Aid Soc., 1993—; vice-chair Morris County Dem. Com., 1987-92; bd. dirs. N.J. Women's Polit. Caucus, 1994—; chair sponsor adv. com. Women Execs. in State Govt., 1997; mem. Morris 2000 Cmty. Coun., 1997—, others. Mem. ABA, N.J. Bar Assn., Morris County Bar Assn., Am. Assn. Nurse Attys., others. Roman Catholic. Avocations: golf, skiing, running, reading, gardening. Office: Beneficial Mgmt Corp 200 Beneficial Ctr Peapack NJ 07977

**MCCONNELL, MARY ANN,** lawyer; b. Greenville, Pa., June 16, 1951; d. Robert Addison and Lucille Elizabeth (Baer)Kelso; m. Findley L. McConnell, Feb. 10, 1973; children: Katherine, Nicholas. BA, Dickinson Coll., 1973; JD, U. Pitts., 1976. Bar: Pa. 1976, U.S. Dist. Ct. (we. dist.) Pa. 1989. Pvt. practice Mercer, Pa., 1976-79; ptnr. Jones-McConnell, P.C., Mercer, Pa., 1979—; dir. Legal Svcs. N.W. Pa., 1983-92. Bd. dirs. Mercer County Assn. Retarded Citizens, Hermitage, Pa., 1988-94, Pa. Coun. Rep. Women, Harrisburg, 1994—; Rep. candidate for U.S. Ho. of Reps. from Pa. 21st dist.; mem. adminsrv. bd. Mercer United Meth. Ch., 1990—; membership chmn. Mercer Area Coun. Rep. Women, 1994—. Mem. Pa. Bar Assn. (com. exceptional children 1989-91, spl. achievement award 1990), Mercer County Bar Assn., Mercer Area C. of C. (pres. 1988-89). Avocations: speaking, reading, cooking. Real property, Family and matrimonial, Probate. Home: 720 Clarksville Rd Mercer PA 16137-5002 Office: Jones-McConnell PC PO Box 579 Mercer PA 16137-0579

**MCCONOMY, JAMES HERBERT,** lawyer; b. Pitts., Mar. 24, 1937; s. Murray Michael and Catherine Elizabeth (Herbert) McC.; m. Jeanne Margaret Cronin, Sept. 3, 1960 (div. Apr. 1989); children: Margaret Jeanne, Michael Murray; m. Roberta L. Cavanaugh, June 30, 1989. AB cum laude, Harvard U., 1959, LLB, 1962. Bar: Pa. 1963, U.S. Ct. Appeals (3d cir.) 1972, U.S. Supreme Ct. 1977. Ptnr. Reed, Smith, Shaw & McClay, Pitts., 1962-92; mng. ptnr. Titus & McConomy, Pitts., 1992—. Fellow Am. Coll. Trial Lawyers; mem. ABA, Pa. Bar Assn. Allegheny County Acad. Trial Lawyers. Roman Catholic. Clubs: Duquesne, Harvard-Yale-Princeton (Pitts.). Avocations: photography, travel. Federal civil litigation, State civil litigation, Contracts commercial. Home: 1117 Harvard Rd Pittsburgh PA 15205-1726 Office: Titus & McConomy Four Gateway Ctr 20th Fl Pittsburgh PA 15222

**MC CORD, JOHN HARRISON,** lawyer, educator; b. Oceanside, N.Y., Dec. 22, 1934; s. John Francis and Elsie (Powers) McC.; m. Maureen Ursula Maclean, Dec. 30, 1961; children: John F.X., Paul V., David G., Maureen E. AB, Fordham Coll., 1957; JD magna cum laude, St. John's U., 1960; LLM, U. Ill., 1965. Bar: N.Y. 1960, Ill. 1964. Atty. U.S. Dept. Justice, Washington, 1960-61; mem. faculty U. Ill. Coll. Law, Champaign, 1964—; prof. law U. Ill. Coll. Law, 1965—, assoc. dean for acad. affairs., 1990-92; of counsel Meyer Capel Hirschfeld Muncy Jahn & Aldeen, 1998—; acad. cons. Ill. Inst. Continuing Legal Edn., 1968-72; vis. prof. law U. N.C., 1975, U. Hawaii, 1976. Author: (with Keeton and O'Connell) Crisis in Car Insurance, 1967, Buying and Selling Small Businesses, 1969, (with O'Byrne) Deskbook for Illinois Estate Planners, 1969, Closely Held Corporations, 1971, (with O'Neill, Pearlman and Stroud) Buying, Selling and Merging Businesses, 1975, (with Lowndes and Kramer) Estate and Gift Taxes, 3d edit, 1974, (with McKee) Federal Income Taxation-A Summary Analysis, 1975, (with Kramer) Problems for Federal Estate and Gift Taxes, 1976, Estate and Gift Tax Reform, 1977, Estate and Gift Tax Summary, 15th edit. 1993, Estate, Gift and Generation-Skipping Taxes, 1999; editor: Dimensions and Academic Freedom, 1969, With All Deliberate Speed: Civil Rights Theory and Reality, 1969, Ill. Law Forum, 1965-69; contbr. articles to profl. jours.; author computer programs for estate planning, 1984—. Served to capt. JAGC, USAF, 1961-64. St. Thomas More fellow St. John's U., 1960. Fellow Am. Coll. Trust and Estate Counsel; mem. ABA (com. CLE and chief reporter for study outline on buying, selling and merging businesses sect. fed. tax 1969-73, com. estate and gift taxes 1973-84, chmn. subcom. gross estate issues 1976-78, subcom. tax reform 1978-84), Ill. Bar Assn. (exec. coun. fed. tax sect. 1966-73, chmn. sect. 1971-72, exec. coun. bus. planning sect. 86-91), Champaign County Bar Assn., Am. Arbitration Assn. (nat. panel arbitrators 1969-90), Eastern Ill. Estate Planning Coun. (pres. 1970-71), U. Miami Inst. Estate Planning (adv. coun. 1979-87), Assn. Am. Law Schs. (fed. taxation roundtable coun. 1969-72), Ill. Inst. CLE (bd. dirs. 1991—), U.S. Navy League, Order of Coif. Home: 104 E Sherwin Dr Urbana IL 61802-7133 Office: U Ill Coll Law Champaign IL 61820

**MCCORD, ROBERT BRYAN,** judge; b. Atlanta, Apr. 28, 1917; s. Robert B. McCord Sr. and Clara Brown; m. Virginia Crane, June 12, 1942 (dec.); children: Nancy M. Storey, Kathy M. Bradley, Elaine M. DeLong, Charles E. AB, Ga. State U.; LLB, Woodrow Wilson Coll. of Law. Ptnr. McCord and Cooper, Hapeville, Ga.; mcpl. judge City of Hapeville, 1996—. City atty. Hapeville, Ga., 1950-58. Capt. U.S. Air Corps, 1940-45. Mem. Atlanta Lawyers Club, Atlanta Bar Assn. (com. mem. 1951-52), Tri-City Bar Assn. (bd. dirs. 1994-98), Hapeville Exch. Club (pres. 1949). Republican. Methodist. Avocations: travel, Sunday sch. teaching, service club activities. Home: 347 Northwoods Pl Hapeville GA 30354-1514

**MCCORD, WILLIAM KIRK,** lawyer; b. New Orleans, Jan. 29, 1950; s. William Palmer and Martha (Helm) McC.; m. Beverly Elizabeth Bonner, Mar. 12, 1978; children: Michael W., Matthew K., Kelly B., Mark H. BS cum laude, Tulane U., 1970; MS, Naval Postgrad. Sch., 1971; JD magna cum laude, U. San Diego, 1978. Bar: Calif. 1978, Tex. 1979, U.S. Patent Office 1978. Atty. Tex. Instruments, Inc., Dallas, 1978-81, Hubbard, Thurman, Turner & Tucker, Dallas, 1981-85; pvt. practice Dallas, 1985-89; with Glaser, Griggs & Schwartz, Dallas, 1989-92; asst. gen. counsel Lennox Internat. Inc., Richardson, Tex., 1992—; adj. instr. Law Sch. Southern Methodist U., Dallas, 1982-83, 84-85. Author: (booklet) Home Education: Is It Working?, 1986-87; co-author: (booklet) Handbook for Texas Homes Schoolers, 1983-88. Campaign treas. Tex. Home Sch. Coalition PAC, Richardson, 1986—; bd. dirs. Tex. Home Sch. Coalition, Lubbock, 1986—; trustee Town North Presbyn. Ch., Richardson, 1998—. Lt. USN, 1970-77. Recipient Founder's award Tex. Home Sch. Coalition, 1996. Mem. Dallas Bar Assn., North Dallas Bar Assn. (pres. 1993-94), Christian Legal Soc. Avocations: fishing, hunting. Intellectual property. Home: 3308 Canyon Creek Dr Richardson TX 75080-1511

**MCCORKINDALE, DOUGLAS HAMILTON,** lawyer, publishing company executive; b. N.Y.C., June 14, 1939; s. William Douglas and Kathleen (Miles) McC.; m. Nancy Walsh, Dec. 24, 1991; children by previous marriage: Laura Ann, Heather Jean. BA, Columbia U., 1961, LLB cum laude (Harlan Fiske Stone scholar), 1964. Bar: N.Y. 1964. Assoc. Thacher Proffitt & Wood, N.Y.C., 1964-70, ptnr., 1970-71; gen. counsel, sec. Gannett Co., Inc., 1971-72, v.p., gen. counsel, sec., 1972-77, sr. v.p. fin. and law, 1977-79, sr. v.p., chief fin. officer, 1979-83, pres. diversified media div., 1980-83, exec. v.p., 1983; vice chmn., CFO Gannett Co., Inc., Arlington, Va., 1984—, chief adminstrv. officer, 1986—; vice chmn., pres., 1997—; dir. all subsidiaries and joint ventures Gannett Co., Inc., Arlington, Va.; bd. dirs. Continental Airlines Inc., Frontier Corp., The Global Govt. Plus Fund Inc., Prudential Global Genesis Fund Inc., Prudentual Natural Resources Fund Inc., Prudential Multi-Sector Fund Inc.; trustee Prudential Equity Income Fund, Prudential Allocation Fund, Prudential Mcpl. Bond Fund, Mut. Ins. Co. Ltd. Mem. ABA (chmn. com. Exch. Art of 1934 1971-73), Newspaper Assn. Am., Oak Hill Country Club, Pine Valley Golf Club, Mid Ocean Club, Burning Tree Club. General corporate, Securities, Mergers and acquisitions. Office: Gannett Co Inc 31st Fl 1100 Wilson Blvd Ste 2100 Arlington VA 22209-2299

**MCCORMACK, DAVID RICHARD,** lawyer; b. Macon, Ga., Apr. 19, 1945; s. Richard and Margaret Helen (Pivarnik) McC. BA, Yale U., 1967; MA, Northwestern U., 1969; JD, So. Meth. U., 1976. Bar: Tex. 1977, Ariz. 1977, U.S. Dist. Ct. Ariz. 1977, U.S. Dist. Ct. (no. dist.) Tex. 1977, U.S. Dist. Ct. (so. dist.) Tex. 1987, U.S. Ct. Appeals (5th cir.) 1989; diplomate Am. Bd. Forensic Examiners. Outreach dir. Planned Parenthood, Benton Harbor, Mich., 1971-72; exec. dir. Am. Cancer soc., St. Joseph, Mich., 1973-74; asst. atty. gen. Ariz. Atty. Gen., Phoenix, 1979-84; trial atty. U.S. Dept. Justice, Dallas, 1984-85; assoc. Bruner, McColl, McCulloch & McCurley, Dallas, 1985-86; pvt. practice Houston, 1986—; registered arbitrator Am. Registry of Arbitrators, 1994—; lectr. Tex. Assn. Lic. Investigators; cons. and expert witness. Author: RICO, 2 vols., 1988, Extraneous Offenses, 1986; contbr. articles to profl. publs. Vol. VISTA, Crawfordville, Ga., 1969; Dem. candidate from 4th dist. Mich. for U.S. Ho. of Reps., 1970, from 44th dist. for Mich. State Ho. of Reps., 1972; Dem. del. from Mich. to Nat. Convention, 1972; party chmn. Mich. Dem. Party, 1971-73. Mem. Am. Coll. Forensic Examiners, Assn. Cert. Fraud Examiners (cert., lectr.), Cajun French Music Assn., Northwestern U. Wildcat Fund., Titanic Historical Soc., Titanic Internat. Nat. Assn. Investigative Specialist, Napoleonic Alliance, Napoleonic Soc. Am. Criminal. Office: 3935 Westheimer Rd Ste 204 Houston TX 77027-5011

**MC CORMACK, FRANCIS XAVIER,** lawyer, former oil company executive; b. Bklyn., July 9, 1929; s. Joseph and Blanche V. (Dengel) Mc C.; m. Margaret V. Hynes, Apr. 24, 1954; children: Marguerite, Francis Xavier, Sean Michael, Keith John, Cecelia Blanche, Christopher Thomas. AB cum laude, St. Francis Coll., Bklyn., 1951; LLB, Columbia U., 1954. Bar: N.Y. 1955, Mich. 1963, Calif. 1974, Pa. 1975. Assoc. Cravath, Swaine & Moore, N.Y.C., 1956-62; sr. atty. Ford Motor Co., 1962-64, asst. gen. counsel, 1970-72; v.p., gen. counsel, sec. Philco-Ford Corp., 1964-72; v.p., gen. counsel Atlantic Richfield Co., 1972-73, sr. v.p., gen. counsel, 1973-94. Editor Columbia U. Law Rev., 1954. Decorated commendatore Ordine al Merito (Italy); Stone scholar Columbia U., 1954. Mem. Calif. Club, Chancery Club, Annandale Golf Club. Home and Office: 975 Singingwood Dr Arcadia CA 91006-1924

**MCCORMACK, HOWARD MICHAEL,** lawyer; b. Bklyn., Aug. 26, 1932; s. Michael Francis and Sarah Catherine (Russell) McC.; m. Patricia Anne Riley, Aug. 24, 1957; children: Sean M., Maureen A. MacDougall. AB cum laude, Coll. Holy Cross, Worcester, Mass., 1954; LLB, Fordham U., N.Y.C., 1961; LLM in Internat. Law, NYU, 1965. Bar: N.Y. 1962, U.S. Dist. Ct. (so. and ea. dists.) N.Y. 1963, U.S. Ct. Appeals (2d cir.) 1964, U.S. Ct. Appeals (4th cir.) 1977, U.S. Supreme Ct. 1966, U.S. Dist. Ct. Md. 1975, U.S. Dist. Ct. (so. dist) Tex. 1983, U.S. Dist. Ct. (5th cir.) 1984, U.S. Ct. Mil. Appeals 1994. Acct. exec. C.R. Black Jr. Corp., N.Y.C., 1958-61; ptnr. Zock, Petrie, et al., N.Y.C., 1961-71; maritime counsel Bethlehem Steel Corp., N.Y.C., 1972-79; ptnr. Healy & Baillie LLP, N.Y.C., 1979—. Contbr. articles to profl. publs. Lt. (j.g.) USN, 1954-57; comdr. JAGC, USNR, ret. Mem. Maritime Law Assn. U.S. (pres. 1998—). Avocations: tennis, golf, wine studies. Admiralty, Federal civil litigation, Insurance. Office: Healy & Baillie LLP New York NY 10006

**MCCORMACK, JOANNE MARIE,** lawyer; b. Evanston, Ill., Apr. 11, 1967; d. Joseph Robert and Audrey Helene (Gineman) Taylor; m. Colin Patrick McCormack, Jan. 2, 1993. BA, Loyola U., 1989, JD, 1994. Bar: Ill., 1994, Wis., 1995. Atty. Godfrey, Neshek, Worth, Elkhorn, Wis., 1994-95, Oliver, Close, Worden, Lake Geneva, Wis., 1995-97, 99—, Hinshaw & Culbertson, Lake Geneva, Wis., 1997-99. Real property, General corporate, Estate planning. Office: Oliver Close Worden 252 Center St Lake Geneva WI 53147-1902

**MCCORMACK, JOHN LEO,** law educator; b. Milw., Dec. 10, 1942; s. Joseph James and Mariah (Schroeder) McC. BS, U. Wis., Milw., 1964; JD, U. Wis., 1968. Bar: Ill. 1970. Law clk. judge Thomas E. Fairchild U.S. Ct. Appeals 7th Cir., Milw., 1968-69; assoc. Sidley & Austin, Chgo., 1969-71; prof. Loyola U. Sch. Law, Chgo., 1971—. With U.S. Army, 1965-71. Mem. ABA. Home: 151 N Kenilworth Ave Oak Park IL 60301-1271 Office: Loyola U Sch Law Ste 530 One E Pearson St Chicago IL 60611-2055

**MCCORMACK, JOHN ROBERT,** lawyer; b. Middletown, Conn., Mar. 30, 1962; s. John Francis and Ann Jane (Monarca) McC.; m. Cristina Dorthea Dwyer, Sept. 27, 1986; children: Kevin, Cara. BS, Univ. Conn., 1984; JD, Stetson Univ., 1990. Assoc. Kelly & McKee, P.A., Tampa, Fla., 1990-92; ptnr. Wiggins & McCormack, Clearwater, Fla., 1992-94; sole practitioner J. Robert McCormack, P.A., Clearwater, Fla., 1994—. Editor: Labor and Employment in Florida, 1990, Critical Issues in Labor and Employment Labor, 1990. Mem. ABA (labor and employment law sect.), Fla. Bar Labor and Employment Law Sect., Barney Masterson Inn of Ct. (treas. 1998-99), Clearwater Bar Employment Law Com. (co-chair 1997-99). Labor, Administrative and regulatory. Office: J Robert McCormack P A 2723 Belle Haven Dr Clearwater FL 33763-1002

**MCCORMACK, MICHAEL,** state supreme court justice; b. Omaha, July 20, 1939. JD, Creighton U., 1963. Asst. pub. defender Douglas County, Nebr., 1963-66; pvt. practice Omaha, 1966-97; justice Nebr. Supreme Ct., 1997—. Office: State Capitol Bldg Rm 2218 Lincoln NE 68509*

**MCCORMICK, DAVID ARTHUR,** lawyer; b. McKeesport, Pa., Oct. 26, 1946; s. Arthur Paul and Eleanor Irene (Gibson) McC. BA, Westminster Coll., 1967; JD, Duquesne U., 1973; MBA, U. Pa., 1975. Bar: Pa. 1973, D.C. 1978, U.S. Ct. Appeals (3d cir.) 1977, U.S. Ct. Appeals (4th and D.C. cirs.) 1980, U.S. Supreme Ct. 1980. Asst. commerce counsel Penn Cen. R.R., Phila., 1973-76; assoc. labor counsel Consol. Rail Corp., Phila., 1976-78; atty. Dept. Army, Washington, 1978—. Author various geneal. and hist. works; contbr. articles to profl. jours. Mem. ATLA, Pa. Bar Assn., Phila. Bar Assn., D.C. Bar Assn., Assn. Transp. Practitioners, Soc. Cin. (Del. chpt.), SAR (Pitts. chpt.), Am. Legion, Res. Officers Assn., Masons, Phi Alpha Delta, Theta Chi. Presbyterian.

**MCCORMICK, DAVID JOSEPH,** lawyer; b. Milw., 1962; s. David Richard and Jean Ellen McC.; m. Tammy L., May 28, 1995. BBA cum laude, U. Wis., 1985; JD, Marquette U. Law Sch., 1989. Bar: Wis. 1989, U.S. Dist. Ct. (ea. dist.) Wis. 1989. Pvt. practice, 1989-90; law clk. Milw. County Civil Jud. Divsn., 1990-94; assoc. Techmeier & Van Grunsven, Milw., 1994—. Mem. ATLA, State Bar Wis. (litigation sect.), Milw. Bar Assn., Wis. Acad. Trial Lawyers. Roman Catholic. State civil litigation, Personal injury, Product liability. Office: Techmeier & Van Grunsven 411 E Wisconsin Ave Ste 1100 Milwaukee WI 53202-4464

**MCCORMICK, HOMER L., JR.,** lawyer; b. Frederick, Md., Nov. 11, 1928; s. Homer Lee McCormick and Rosebelle Irene Biser; m. Jacquelyn R.; children: Deidre Ann and Thomas Lee. Student, George Washington U., 1946-48; AB, San Jose State U., 1951; JD, U. Calif., San Francisco, 1961. Bar: Calif. 1961, U.S. Dist. Ct. Ctrl. Dist. Calif. 1972, U.S. Dist. No. Calif. 1961, U.S. Dist. Ct., So. Dist. Calif. 1976, U.S. Dist. Ct. of Appeals (9th cir. 1961), U.S. Tax Ct. 1977, U.S. Ct. Claims 1977, U.S. Supreme Ct. 1977. Atty. Holiway Jones State of Calif., 1961-63; atty. assoc. Rutan & Tucker, Santa Ana, Calif., 1963-66, atty. ptnr., 1966-70; atty., sr. ptnr. Rutan & Tucker, Costa Mesa, Calif., 1970-88, dept. head pub. law, 1974-88, mng. ptnr., 1984-88; founding ptnr., sr. ptnr. McCormick, Kidman & Behrens, Costa Mesa, 1988—; Arbitrator Am. Arbitration Assn., 1966-88; judge pro tem Orange County Superior Ct., 1975, 81, 84; spkr., lectr. Cal. Continuing Edn. of the Bar, 1976-88; profl. designation Internat. Right of Way Assn.; elected mem. Cal. Condemnation Lawyers, 1994—. Contbg. author: Real Property Remedies, 1982; contbr. articles to profl. jours. Mem. bd. govs. Bus. Com. Arts, Orange County Philharm. Soc. Lt. USMCR, 1951-56; pilot, Korea. Named Alumnus of Year Hastings Law Sch., 1992. Mem. ABA (com. chair 1991), Am. Bd. Trial Adv. (pres. O.C. chpt. 1973), Orange City Atty. Assn. (pres. 1972), Fed. Bar Assoc., Consumer Attys. Calif., Am. Judicature Soc., Orange County Bar Assn. (com. chair 1991-92), Orange County Bus. Trial Lawyers, Order Coif, Thurston Soc., Hastings Alumni Assn. (pres. 1973), Springs Country Club, Delta Theta Pi. Republican. Episcopalian. Avocations: boating, fishing, flying, golf, foreign travel. General civil litigation, Condemnation, Real property.

**MCCORMICK, HUGH THOMAS,** lawyer; b. McAlester, Okla., Nov. 24, 1944; s. Hugh O. and Lois (McGucken) McC.; m. Suzanna G. Weingarten, Dec. 5, 1975; 1 child, John B. BA, U. Mich., 1968; JD, Rutgers U., 1977; LLM in Taxation, Georgetown U., 1980. Bar: N.Y. 1977, D.C. 1979, Maine 1981. Atty. office chief counsel interpretative divsn. IRS, Washington, 1977-81; assoc. Perkins, Thompson, Hinkley & Keddy, Portland, Maine, 1981-83; assoc. LeBoeuf, Lamb, Leiby & MacRae, N.Y.C., 1983-88, counsel, 1989-91; ptnr. LeBoeuf, Lamb, Greene & MacRae, L.L.P., N.Y.C., 1992—; dir. Ins. Tax. Conf., 1993—, v.p., sec., 1996—. Mem. bd. contbrs. and advisors Jour. of Taxation of Investments; contbr. articles to profl. jours. Trustee U.S. Team Handball Found., N.J., 1985-95. Fellow Am. Bar Found.; mem. ABA (chmn. com. on taxation of ins. cos. 1989, chmn. subcom. sect. of taxation 1989-96, mem. torts and ins. practice sect., sect. on taxation), D.C. Bar Assn., Assn. of Bar of City of N.Y. Democrat. Corporate taxation, Insurance. Home: 555 Pelham Manor Rd Pelham Manor NY 10803-2525 Office: LeBoeuf Lamb Greene MacRae LLP 125 W 55th St New York NY 10019-5369

**MCCORMICK, JOHN HOYLE,** lawyer; b. Pensacola, Fla., July 30, 1933; s. Clyde Hoyle and Orrie Brooks (Frink) McC.; m. Patricia McCall, Dec. 27, 1974. BS, U. Fla., 1955; JD, Stetson U., 1958. Bar: Fla. 1958. Ptnr. McCormick, Drury & Scaff, Jasper, Fla., 1958-74; county atty., 1973—; sr. ptnr. McCormick, Drury & Scaff, Jasper, 1974-91; pvt. practice Jasper, 1991—; county judge, Hamilton County, Fla., 1960-72; local counsel So. Ry. System, 1968—, CSX, Ry., 1972—; atty. Hamilton County Devel. Authority, 1970-91; bd. dirs. 1st Fed. Savs. Bank Fla.; bd. dirs., v.p., atty. Hamilton County Bank. Mayor City of White Springs, Fla., 1959; pres. Hamilton County C. of C., Jasper, 1961. Mem. Phi Delta Phi. Democrat. Methodist. Lodges: Masons. Avocations: gardening, motorhome camping, college football. Banking, Probate, Government contracts and claims. Home: 403 SE 2nd Ave Jasper FL 32052-3242 Office: 215 2nd St NE Jasper FL 32052-6616 Address: PO Drawer O Jasper FL 32052-0695

**MCCORMICK, KAREN ELIZABETH,** lawyer; b. Charleston, S.C., Apr. 10, 1959; d. Harvey Wilson and Barbara L. (Lofton) McC. BS cum laude, Clemson U., 1980; JD, U. S.C., 1988. Bar: S.C. 1988, U.S. Dist. Ct. 1988, U.S. Ct. Claims 1991. Clk. Belser, Baker, Barwick, Ravenel, Toal & Bender, Columbia, S.C., 1986-88; assoc. Rosen, Rosen & Hagood, Charleston, 1988-92; pvt. practice Karen E. McCormick, P.A., Charleston, 1992-96; ptnr. litigation firm McCormick and O'Dell, Charleston, 1996—. Mem. ABA (family law sect. 1991—), S.C. Bar Assn. (family law sect.), DAR. Republican. Episcopalian. Avocations: water skiing, gardening, running. Family and matrimonial, Civil rights. Office: 215 E Bay St Ste 500 Charleston SC 29401-2638

**MCCORMICK, MICHAEL JERRY,** judge; b. Fort Lewis, Wash., Oct. 17, 1945; s. Thaddeus Charles and Geraldine (Fogle) McC.; m. Katleen Karen Kelley, Sept. 2, 1967; children: Patrick Kelley, Karen Michelle. BA, U. Tex.-Austin, 1967; JD, St. Mary's U., 1970. Bar: Tex. 1970. Briefing atty. Tex. Ct. Criminal Appeals, 1970-71; asst. dist. atty. Travis County, Tex., 1971-72; exec. dir. Tex. Dist. and County Attys. Assn., Austin, 1972-80; judge Tex. Ct. Criminal Appeals, Austin, 1981—, chief presiding judge, 1988—; dir. Tex. Ctr. for Judiciary, 1983; vice-chmn. Tex. Commn. on Sentencing, 1984; mem. Tex. Jud. Budget Bd., 1983; co-chair Tex. Jud. Coun., 1997—. Author: Branch's Annotated Penal Code, 3d edit., Criminal Forms and Trial Manual, 10th edit., Tex. Justice Court Deskbook, Tex. Constables Civil Process Handbook. Pres. Joslin (Tex.) P.T.A., 1981-82. Served with U.S. Army, 1966-72. Named Rosewood Gavel Outstanding Jurist, St. Mary's U. Sch. Law, 1984, Disting. Law Grad., 1992. Mem. State Bar Tex., Tex. Dist. and County Attys. Assn. Office: Tex Ct Criminal Appeals Supreme Ct Bldg PO Box 12308 Austin TX 78711-2308

**MCCORMICK, TIMOTHY BRIAN BEER,** lawyer; b. Northampton, Mass., May 16, 1959; s. Brian Beer and Margaret Ann McCormick; m. Lee Hillary Kadis, Sept. 2, 1979 (div. June 1991); m. Virginia Lee Kostner, June 30, 1991 (div. May 1995); 1 child, Cameron A.; m. Jill Ann Knowland, Apr. 23, 1997; 1 child, Britton K. BA, U. Calif., Berkeley, 1984; JD, Am. U., 1987. Bar: Calif. 1987, U.S. Dist. Ct. (no. dist.) Calif. 1987, U.S. Ct. Appeals (9th cir.) 1987, U.S. Dist. Ct. (ea. dist.) Calif., 1991, U.S. Dist. Ct. (ctrl. dist.) Calif. 1994. Staff asst. Office of Lt. Gov., Sacramento, 1982-83; cons. Calif. Rep. Party, Sacramento, 1984; rsch. asst. Nat. Right to Work Found., Springfield, Va., 1985-86; assoc. Graham & James, San Francisco, 1987-93, McPharlin & Mahl, San Jose, Calif., 1993-94; ptnr. McPharlin & Sprinkles, San Jose, 1994-95; v.p., assoc. coun. Fidelity Nat. Title Ins. Co., Walnut Creek, Calif., 1995—; prin. McCormick Dispute Resolution Svcs., Piedmont, Calif., 1996—; judge pro tem Santa Clara County Superior Ct., 1993—. Comments editor Adminstrv. Law Jour., 1986-87. Treas., Hom for Mayor, San Francisco, 1995; mem. Rep. State Cen. Com. of Calif., 1983-85, assoc. mem., 1985—, mem. exec. com., 1983-84; gen. coun. Asian Am. Polit. Edn. Found., 1992—. Mem. ABA (litigation sect.), Santa Clara County Bar Assn., Bar Assn. San Francisco, Engring. and Utility Contractors Assn. (legis. com. 1991-95, co-chair, 1994-95). Avocations: skiing, bicycling, cooking, scuba diving. General civil litigation, Insurance, Real property. Home: 235 Park View Ave Piedmont CA 94610-1041

**MCCORMICK, WALTER BERNARD, JR.,** lawyer; b. Kansas City, Mo., Feb. 8, 1954; s. Walter Bernard and Dorothy Ann (Power) M.; m. Mary Lou Edlefsen, Jan. 3, 1987; children: Walter Patrick, Megan Boutin. Student, Georgetown U., 1975; BJ, U. Mo., 1976, JD, 1979. Bar: Mo. 1979, D.C. 1980. Assoc. Leighton, Conklin, Lemov & Jacobs, Washington, 1980-81, Pepper, Hamilton & Scheetz, Washington, 1981-82; legis. asst. U.S. Senate, Washington, 1982-84; gen. counsel U.S. Senate Com. Commerce, Sci. and Transp., Washington, 1985-87, minority chief counsel, staff dir., 1988-92; gen. counsel U.S. Dept. Transp., Washington, 1992-93; partner Bryan Cave LLP, Washington, 1993—. Mem. City Club, Washington, 1993—. Republican. Roman Catholic. Avocation: skiing. Administrative and regulatory, Legislative, Transportation. Office: Bryan Cave LLP 700 13th St NW Fl 7 Washington DC 20005-5921

**MCCORVEY, JOHN HARVARD, JR.,** lawyer; b. Jacksonville, Fla., Feb. 10, 1962; s. John Harvard McCorvey and Janice (Phillips) Buck. BBA, Stetson U., 1984, JD with honors, 1989. Bar: Fla. 1990, U.S. Dist. Ct. (mid. dist.) Fla. 1990. Assoc. Rogers, Towers, Bailey, Jones & Gay, Jacksonville, Fla., 1990-93, Gabel, Hair, Jacksonville, 1993-94, Gobelman and Love, Jacksonville, 1994-96; pvt. practice Jacksonville, 1996—. Bd. dirs., pres. Webb Ctr. for Ind. Living, Jacksonville, 1999—; bd. dirs. Willing Hands, Jacksonville, 1994. Cecil and Augusta Baily scholar Stetson Coll. Law, 1989. Mem. Fla. Bar, Jacksonville Bar Assn. (pres. young lawyers sect. 1997). Democrat. Methodist. General civil litigation, Personal injury, Workers' compensation. Office: 200 W Forsyth St Ste 800 Jacksonville FL 32202-4321

**MCCOURT, JOYCE ELISE,** lawyer; b. Framingham, Mass., Jan. 31, 1949; d. Paul Joseph and Joyce Loraine McCourt; m. Ronald Richard Perry, June 29, 1980 (dec. July 1997). BA in Psychology, U. Mass., 1971; JD, Boston Coll., 1976. Bar: Mass. 1977 (1st and 2d cirs.). Asst. regional counsel Dept. HHS, Boston, 1976—. Home: 291 Lions Mouth Rd Amesbury MA 01913-5426 Office: Dept HHS Rm 2250 JFK Bldg Boston MA 02203

**MCCOY, D. CHAD,** lawyer; b. Lexington, Ky., Oct. 5, 1970; s. Dustan E. and Becky McCoy; married, Aug. 7, 1993. BS in Fin., Va. Inst. Tech., 1992; JD magna cum laude, U. Ky., 1995. Rafting guide N.Am. River Runners, Hico, W.Va., 1992; assoc. Stites & Harbison, Lexington, Ky. Mem. ABA, Ky. Bar Assn., Fayette County Bar Assn., Trout Unltd. Republican. Roman Catholic. Avocations: fly fishing, fly tying, skiing, camping, reading. Labor, Computer. Office: Stites & Harbison 250 W Main St Ste 2300 Lexington KY 40507-1758

**MCCOY, JAMES M.,** lawyer; b. Misawa, Japan, Feb. 22, 1963; parents U.S. citizens; s. Warren W. and Mary K. McCoy; m. Susan Elora LePage, May 28, 1993; 1 child, Michael Thomas. BA in History, U. Mo., Kansas City, 1985; JD, U. Mo., 1996. Bar: Mo., U.S. Dist. Ct. (we., ea. and so. dists.) Mo., U.S. Ct. Appeals. Law clk. Dept. Social Svcs./Divsn. Legal Svcs., Jefferson City, Mo., 1996-97; legal asst. Dept. Social Svcs./Divsn. Legal Svcs., Jefferson City, 1997, staff atty., 1997-98, mng. atty. pers., 1998—. Office: Divsn Legal Svcs 221 W High St Jefferson City MO 65101-1516

**MCCOY, JERRY JACK,** lawyer; b. Pitts., Aug. 4, 1941; s. Norris and Martha (Jack) McC.; m. Alexandra Armstrong; children: MadeleineRena, Allison Norah, Jonathan Howard. BS, W.Va. U., 1963; LLB, Duke U., 1966; LLM in Taxation, N.Y.U., 1967. Bar: D.C. 1968, N.Y. 1967. Assoc. Silverstein & Mullens, Washington, 1968-72, ptnr., 1973-92; of counsel Reid and Priest, N.Y.C., Washington, 1992-94; sole practitioner Washington, 1994—; adj. law faculty George Washington U., Washington, 1977-87, U. Miami, Fla., 1983—, Law Ctr. Georgetown U., 1996—. Exec. editor Tax Mgmt., Estates Gifts and Trusts series, Washington, 1972-92; co-editor Charitable Gift Planning News, Dallas, 1983—; contbr. articles to profl. jours. Mem. ABA, Am. Law Inst., Am. Coll. Trust and Estate Counsel (chair com. on charitable planning and exempt orgns.), Am. Coll. Tax Counsel. Democrat. Jewish. Non-profit and tax-exempt organizations, Estate taxation, Estate planning. Home: 3560 Winfield Ln NW Washington DC 20007-2368 Office: PO Box 66491 Washington DC 20035-6491

**MCCOY, REAGAN SCOTT,** oil company executive, lawyer; b. Port Arthur, Tex., Nov. 25, 1945; s. William Murray and Elizabeth (Gilbert) McC.; m. Pat Kowalski, June 21, 1969; 1 child, Traci. BCE, Ga. Inst. Tech., 1968; JD, Loyola U., 1972. Bar: Tex. 1972, La. 1978; registered profl. engr., Tex., La. Structural engr. McDermott Inc., New Orleans, 1966-72; data processing mgr. McDermott Inc., London, 1972-76; cons. engr. McDermott Inc., New Orleans, 1976-79; adminstrv. mgr. Concord Oil Co., San Antonio, 1979-81, v.p., 1981—; mem. World Affairs Coun., Tex. Luth. Coll. Bus. Sch. Adv. Com. Treas. Countryside San Pedro Recreation Club, 1981-82; bd. dirs. Countryside San Pedro Homeowners Assn., 1984-86; v.p. Bluffview Homeowners Assn., 1998-99; pres. San Antonio Baylor U. Parents League, 1995-96; mem. Tex. State Bd. Pub. Accountancy, 1997—. Fellow Tau Beta Pi; mem. ABA, NSPE, ASCE, Am. Assn. Profl. Landmen (San Antonio chpt. treas. 1990-91, v.p. 1991-93, pres. 1993-94), La. State Bar Assn., Tex. State Bar, San Antonio Bar Assn. (natural resources com. treas. 1986-87, vice chmn. 1987-88, chmn. 1988-89), Tex. Soc. Profl. Engrs., La. Soc. Profl. Engrs., So. Tex. Assn. Divsn. Order Analysts (v.p. 1993, pres. 1994, 98, bd. dirs. 1999—), Fin Execs. Inst. (treas. 1991-92, sec. 1992-93, v.p. 1993-94, pres. 1994-95, bd. dirs. 1995-97), Soc. Mining Engrs., Real Estate Fin. Soc. (bd. dirs. 1986-89, v.p. 1987-88, pres. 1988-89, 98-99, pres. coun.), Adminstrv. Mgmt. Soc. (pres. 1985-86, 89-90), Plz. Club, Sonterra Club, Tex. Ind. Producers and Royalty Owners Assn., Am. Petroleum Inst. (South Tex. chpt. pres. 1997-99). Presbyterian. Avocations: water sports, reading, woodworking. Home: 14103 Bluff Manor Dr San Antonio TX 78216-7976 Office: Concord Oil Co 105 S Saint Marys St Ste 1500 San Antonio TX 78205-2898

**MCCRACKEN, ELLIS W., JR.,** lawyer, corporation executive; B.A., Lebanon Valley Coll., 1963; LL.B., St. John's U., 1967. Bar: N.Y. 1967, N.J. 1969, Ohio 1972, Mo. 1993. Primary contract atty. foods div. Borden, Inc., 1970-74; assoc. Milbank, Tweed, Hadley & McCloy, 1967-70; v.p., gen. counsel Campbell Taggart, Inc., Dallas, 1980-92, v.p. gen. coun. Anheuser-Busch Co., Saint Louis, 1992—. General corporate. Office: Anheuser-Busch Co One Busch Pl Saint Louis MO 63118

**MCCRACKEN, STEVEN CARL,** lawyer; b. Artesia, Calif., Oct. 29, 1950; s. Glenn A. and Helen V. (Fears) McCracken; m. Susan Lee Waggener, July 29, 1979; children: Casey James, Scott Kevin. BA magna cum laude, U. Calif., Irvine, 1972; JD, U. Va., 1975. Bar: Calif. 1975, U.S. Dist. Ct. (cen. dist.) Calif. 1975, U.S. Ct. Appeals (9th cir.) 1976, U.S. Dist. Ct. (no. dist.) Calif. 1977, D.C. 1979, U.S. Supreme Ct. 1985, U.S. Dist. Ct. (so. dist.) Calif. 1990. Assoc. Gibson, Dunn & Crutcher, L.A., 1975-82; ptnr. Gibson, Dunn & Crutcher, Irvine, Calif., 1983-94; v.p., sec. and gen. counsel Callaway Golf Co., Carlsbad, Calif., 1994-96; exec. v.p., gen. counsel and sec. Callaway Golf Co., Carlsbad, 1996-97, exec. v.p. licensing, chief legal officer, sec., 1997—; lawyer rep. Ninth Cir. Jud. Conf., 1989-91. Editor Va. Law Rev., 1973-75, mng. bd. 1974-75, bd. editors The Computer Lawyer, 1984-96. Mem. ABA (antitrust sect.), Orange County Bar Assn. (bd. dirs. 1988-90, chmn. fed. ct. com. 1988-89, chmn. bus. litigation sect. 1990, sec. 1991, treas. 1992, pres.-elect 1993, pres. 1994). Democrat. Antitrust, General civil litigation, Federal civil litigation. Office: Callaway Golf Co 2285 Rutherford Rd Carlsbad CA 92008-8815

**MCCRAY, DOUGLAS GERALD,** lawyer; b. Royal Oak, Mich., Sept. 17, 1962; s. W. Gerald and Charlotte McC.; m. Jennine Elizabeth McCray, Sept. 20, 1992; 1 child, Charlotte Elizabeth. BS, Ctrl. Mich. U., 1985; MS, Oakland U., 1989; JD, Wayne State U., 1996. Bar: Mich. 1996, U.S. Dist. Ct. (ea. dist.) Mich. 1996. Rsch. asst. Wayne State U., Detroit, 1989-91; rsch. assoc. William Beaumont Hosp., Royal Oak, Mich., 1991-94; law clk. Ferriby S. Houston, Detroit, 1995-96; atty. Goodman, Eden, Millender and Bedrosian, Detroit, 1996-98, Koory & Fakhoury, PLC, Royal Oak, 1998—. Asst. editor Wayne Law Rev., Detroit, 1994-95, note and comment editor, 1995-96; contbr. articles to Wayne Law Rev. Personal injury, General civil litigation, Civil rights.

**MCCREADY, GUY MICHAEL,** lawyer, foundation administrator; b. Tulsa, Mar. 21, 1960; s. John McCready and Patsy Ann (Xander) Ryman; m. Ida Maxwell, June 29, 1985; children: Sean, Loren. BA, Ft. Hays State U., 1984; JD, Washburn Law Sch., 1987; diploma, Nat. Inst. for Trial Advocacy, 1992. Bar: Colo. 1987, U.S. Dist. Ct. Colo. 1989, U.S. Ct. Appeals (10th cir.) 1990. Ptnr. Tremaroli & McCready, P.C., Colorado Springs, Colo., 1987-89; pvt. practice Colorado Springs, 1989—; founder, exec. dir. Access to Justice Found., Colorado Springs, 1992—; prof. ethics U. So. Colo., Colorado Springs, 1991. Asst. author: Yearbook of School Law, 1987; contbr. articles to profl. jours. Vol. Pikes Peak Legal Svcs., Colorado Springs, 1987—. Mem. Assn. Trial Lawyers Am., Colo. Trial Lawyers Assn., Colo. Bar Assn., El Paso County Bar Assn., Order of Barristers. Avocations: skiing, hiking, jogging. General civil litigation, Constitutional, Personal injury. Office: 102 S Tejon St Ste 1100 Colorado Springs CO 80903-2253

**MCCREARY, DAVID SEAN,** lawyer; b. Euclid, Ohio, June 10, 1968. BA in Econs. cum laude, So. Meth. U., 1990; JD, U. Tex., 1993. Bar: Tex. 1994, U.S. Dist. Ct. (no. dist.) Tex. 1996, U.S. Ct. Appeals (5th cir.) 1998. Atty. McCreary & Assocs., Dallas, 1994—. City councilman City of The Colony, Tex., 1996; mem. Pro Bono Coll. State Bar Tex., Austin, 1997. Mem. ATLA, Tex. Trial Lawyers Assn., Coll. State Bar Tex. General civil litigation, Criminal, Personal injury. Office: McCreary & Assocs 5050 Quorum Dr Ste 320 Dallas TX 75240-7070

**MCCREARY, LYNN S.,** lawyer; b. Mineola, N.Y., Oct. 22, 1959; d. Edward K. and Joan (Salerno) Schneider; m. Richard A. Cundall, June 26, 1982 (div. sept. 1985); m. Terry L. McCreary, Oct. 2, 1986; 1 child, Morgan T. BA, Western New Eng. Coll., Springfield, Mass., 1981; JD, Washburn U., 1994. Bar: Kans. 1994. Mktg. dir. First Nat. Bank, Overland Park, Kans., 1985-86; v.p. Metmor Fin., Inc., Overland Park, 1986-91; law clk. Shawnee County Dist. Ct., Topeka, 1992-94; lawyer, assoc. Frieden, Haynes & Forbes, Topeka, 1994-96, Bryan Cave LLP, Overland Park, 1996—. Mem. com. Child Abuse Prevention Coalition, Overland Park, 1996-98; mem. Stop Violence Coalition Com., Kansas City, Mo., 1983-85; vol. various charities. Mem. ABA, Kans. Bar Assn., Alpha Xi Delta (bd. dirs. 1996-97). Democrat. Roman Catholic. Federal civil litigation. Home: 14027 W 113th St Lenexa KS 66215-4834

**MCCREEDY, EDWIN JAMES,** lawyer; b. Atlanta, Dec. 29, 1939; s. Harold D. McCreedy and Annette Raymond (Denton) Chapman; m. Linda Jandora, Mar. 20, 1965; children: James M., Matthew B. BA, Columbia U., 1961; JD, Fordham U., 1968. Bar: N.J. 1968, U.S. Dist. Ct. N.J. 1968, U.S. Supreme Ct. 1982, cert. civil trial atty. N.J. Supreme Ct. 1982. Assoc. Conant & McGuire, Elizabeth, N.J., 1968-69, Conant, Haberstadter & McGuire, Elizabeth, 1969-72; ptnr. Conant & McCreedy, Elizabeth, 1972-82; pvt. practice Elizabeth, 1982-84; ptnr. McCreedy & Fox, Cranford, N.J., 1984—; pres. Richard J. Hughes Inn of Court, Elizabeth, 1991-92; mem. civil practice com. Supreme Ct. N.J., 1985-96. Fellow ABA, Internat. Soc. Barristers, Am. Coll. Trial Lawyers (chair state com, 1995-97); mem. N.J. State Bar Assn. (trustee 1997—, chmn. jud. adminstrn. com. 1994-96), Trial Attys. N.J. (trustee), Union County Bar Assn. (pres. 1987). Avocations: golf, travel. State civil litigation, Personal injury, Professional liability. Office: McCreedy & Cox 6 Commerce Dr Ste 13 Cranford NJ 07016-3551

**MCCRERY, DAVID NEIL, III,** lawyer; b. Ames, Iowa, Mar. 7, 1957; s. David Neil Jr. and Judith Ann (Purlee) McC.; m. Katherine Marie Meridith, June 9, 1979; children: Evelyn Judith, David Neil IV. BS in Agrl., U. Ill., 1979; JD, So. Ill. U., Carbondale, 1993. Bar: Ill. 1993, U.S. Dist. (ctrl. dist.) Ill. 1993. Dist. mgr. Ralston Purina Co., St. Louis, 1979-83; farmer, businessman McCrery Farms, Monmouth, Ill., 1984-90; grad. rsch. asst. So. Ill. U. Sch. Law, 1991-93; pvt. practice Law Offices David N. McCrery, III, Galesburg, Ill., 1993—; judge Knox County Teen Ct., 1997-99. Assoc. del. U.S.-Can. Gt. Lakes Conf., 1984; assoc. bd. dirs. Warren County Soil and Water Dist., Monmouth, 1986; bd. dirs., v.p. West Ctrl. Ill. Legal Assistance, 1996-98; bd. dirs. Head Start Ops. for Presch. Edn.-HOPE, 1996-98, Galesburg Youth Athletic Club, 1994-98; mem. Ill. Agr. Leadership Program, 1986-87. Recipient Outstanding State Dir. award Monmouth Jaycees, 1988. Mem. Knox County Bar Assn. Presbyterian. Avocations: hunting, fishing, collecting antiques, travel, mission work. Criminal, Family and matrimonial, Personal injury. Home: 105 N Carlysle Ave Abingdon IL 61410-1403 Office: 311 E Main St Ste 511 Galesburg IL 61401-4834

**MCCROHON, CRAIG,** lawyer; b. Harvey, Ill., Oct. 17, 1961; s. Maxwell and Nancy McCrohon. BA, Harvard U., 1984; postgrad., London Sch. Econs., 1988; JD, U. Pa., 1989, MBA, 1989. Bar: Ill. 1989, U.S. Dist. Ct. (no. dist.) Ill. 1989. With Winston & Strawn, Chgo., 1989-91; ptnr. Freeborn & Peters, Chgo., 1991—. *Craig McCrohon, partner at the law firm of Freeborn & Peters, specializing in technology, corporate and banking law. Prior to Freeborn & Peters, with Winston & Strawn, worked with the legal staff of United States Senate Committee on Banking, Housing and Urban Affairs. Served on Strategic Planning Committee of Economic Development Commission for City of Chicago. Member, Chicago Bar Association, past chair Committee on Consumer Financial Services. President, Technology Executives Roundtable, Evanston/Northwestern University Research Park, on Board of Directors of Midwest Entrepreneurs' Forum. Mr. McCrohon has spoken and written extensively on topics concerning the ownership and management of technology and other rapidly growing companies.* Editor: Let's Go: USA, 1983. Mem. strategic planning com. Econ. Devel. Commn. City of Chgo., 1991; mem. Cook County Transition Team-Econ. Devel., 1995. Mem. Ill. C. of C. (working group econ. devel. com.), Chgo. Bar Assn. (chmn. com. consumer fin. svcs. 1991-92), Bus. Execs. for Econs. Justice (exec. com.), Midwest Bus. Brokers and Intermediaries (mem. bd. dirs.), Tech. Execs. Roundtable Northwestern/Evanston Rsch. Park (chmn. bd. dirs.), Com. to Lower Utility Bills (chmn. 1984), Dem. Leadership for the Twenty-First Century (mem. bd. dirs.), Midwest Entrepreneurs' Forum (mem. bd. dirs.), Phi Alpha Delta. Banking, General corporate, Computer. Home: 2 E 8th St Apt 2708 Chicago IL 60605-2134 Office: Freeborn & Peters 311 S Wacker Dr Ste 3000 Chicago IL 60606-6679

**MCCRORY, ANNE O.,** lawyer; b. Bridgeport, Conn., Aug. 8, 1962; d. John R. and Barbara W. O'Connor; m. Hugh G. McCrory Jr., Aug. 13, 1988; children: Alice T., Luke H., Robert G. BA, Boston Coll., 1984, JD, 1989. Assoc. Conn. Energy Corp., Bridgeport. Bd. dirs. Cardinal Shehan Ctr., Bridgeport, Conn., 1996—. Mem. ABA, Conn. Bar Assn. (exec. com. pub.

utilities sect. 1998—). Public utilities, Securities. Office: Conn Energy Corp 855 Main St Bridgeport CT 06604-4915

**MCCRORY, TOM M., III,** lawyer, real estate broker; b. Dallas, Sept. 2, 1945; s. Thomas Milton and Rene (Jarrett) McC.; m. Susan Blanche McCrory, Nov. 29, 1966; 1 child, Thomas Milton IV. BBA, Baylor U., 1967, JD, 1970. Bar: Tex. 1970, U.S. Dist. Ct. (no. dist.) Tex. Gen. counsel Preston State Bank, Dallas, 1970-80; sole practitioner Dallas, 1980—. Mem. Dallas BarAssn., Dallas Trial Lawyers Assn. Family and matrimonial, Personal injury. Office: 8117 Preston Rd Ste 490 Dallas TX 75225-6336

**MCCRUM, ROBERT TIMOTHY,** lawyer; b. Pitts., Nov. 4, 1958; s. Robert Terrence and Gertrude Callanan McCrum; m. Andrea Nourie, Mar. 16, 1960; children: Megan, Kelsey, Brian, Colleen, Shane. BA in Geology, Franklin & Marshall Coll., 1980; JD, Lewis & Clark Coll., 1983. Atty. U.S. Dept. Interior, Washington, 1984-86; ptnr. Crowell & Moring LLP, Washington, 1986—. Co-author: (books) RCRA Hazardous Waste Handbook, 1996, Superfund Manual, 1997, (book chpt.) Natural Resources Law Manual, 1995. Mem. ABA (chair mining com. sect. environment, energy and resources 1997-98), Rocky Mt. Mineral Law Found. Republican. Roman Catholic. Avocation: prestidigitation. Environmental, Natural resources. Office: Crowell & Moring LLP 1001 Pennsylvania Ave NW Washington DC 20004-2505

**MCCUE, STEPHEN PATRICK,** public defender; b. Montclair, N.J., June 12, 1956; s. Francis James and Mary Theresa (Carroll) McC.; m. Wendy Ellen York, May 2, 1987; 1 child, Alexander York. BA cum laude, Harvard U., 1978; JD, U. Colo., 1983. Bar: N.Mex. 1983, U.S. Dist. Ct. N.Mex. 1983, Colo. 1985, U.S. Ct. Appeals (10th cir.) 1986), U.S. Supreme Ct. 1986. Assoc. Poole, Tinnin & Martin, Albuquerque, 1983-84; asst. pub. defender N.Mex. Pub. Defender Dept., 1984-86; asst. fed. pub. defender Fed. Pub. Defender-N.Mex., Albuquerque, 1986-93, supervisory asst. fed. pub. defender, 1993-95; sr. litigator, 1995-98, asst. fed. pub. defender, 1998-99, fed. pub. defender, 1999—. Mem. ABA, Nat. Assn. Criminal Def. Lawyers, N.Mex. State Bar (bd. dirs. criminal law sect. 1991—, chair 1993-94), N.Mex. Assn. Criminal Def. Lawyers (bd. dirs. 1996—). Avocations: t'ai chi, jogging. Office: Fed Pub Defender 111 Lomas Blvd NW Ste 501 Albuquerque NM 87102-2373

**MCCULLOUGH, EDWARD EUGENE,** patent agent, inventor; b. Baldwin, N.D., June 4, 1923; s. Elmer Ellsworth and Emma Izelda (Nixon) McC. BA, U. Minn., 1957; postgrad., Utah State U., 1965. Machine designer Sperry Rand Corp., Mpls., 1952-58; patent adminstr. Thiokol Corp., Brigham City, Utah, 1958-86; patent cons. Thiokol Corp., Brigham City, 1986; pvt. practice, 1986—. Patentee 34 U.S. patents including instruments for making perspective drawings, apparatus for forming ignition surfaces in solid propellant motors, passive communications satellite or similar article, flexible bearings and process for their manufacture, rocket nozzel support and pivoting system, cavity-shaping machine, others. Pianist Aldersgate Meth. Ch., Brigham City, 1959—. Staff Sgt. U.S. Army, 1949-52. Decorated two battle stars. Avocations: philosophy, music composition, hiking in the mountains. Home: PO Box 46 Brigham City UT 84302-0046

**MCCULLOUGH, FRANK WITCHER, III,** lawyer; b. New Orleans, Dec. 13, 1945; s. Frank Witcher Jr. and Kathleen Elizabeth (Van Pelt) McC.; m. Barry Jean Bock, Mar. 7, 1981; children: William David Oat, Frank Witcher IV, Elizabeth Layton. BA, Stetson U., 1967; JD, W.Va. U., 1970. Bar: W.Va. 1970, Tex. 1970, U.S. Dist. Ct. (so. dist.) W.Va. 1970, U.S. Dist. Ct. (so. dist.) Tex. 1972, U.S. Ct. Appeals (5th cir.) 1972, U.S. Supreme Ct. 1980, U.S. Dist. Ct. (no. dist.) Calif. 1983, U.S. Dist. Ct. (we. dist.) Tex. 1987, U.S. Dist. Ct. (ea. dist.) Tex. 1993. Indsl. rels. specialist Continental Oil Co., Houston, 1970-72; asst. U.S. atty. U.S. Atty.'s Office, Houston, 1972-75; assoc. Baker & Botts, Houston, 1975-76, Austin, Tex., 1985-89; ptnr. Weiner Strother & Lamkin, Houston, 1983-85; regional counsel GATX Leasing Corp., Houston, 1976-78; ptnr. Walsh Squires Tompkins & McCullough, Houston, 1978-82; shareholder Sheinfeld, Maley & Kay, Austin, 1989—. Spl. commr. Harris County, Houston, 1982; mem. Bellaire (Tex.) Bd. Adjustment, 1982; bd. dirs. Big Bros. and Big Sisters of Austin, 1991-94. Mem. State Bar Tex. (grievance com. 1979-87, 95—), chmn. unauthorized practice law com. 1984-87), Austin Country Club, SAR. Republican. Episcopalian. General civil litigation, Consumer commercial. Home: 6707 Bridge Hill Cv Austin TX 78746-1338 Office: Sheinfeld Maley & Kay 301 Congress Ave Austin TX 78701-4026 *Notable cases include: Univ. Savs. Assn. vs. Springwoods Shopping Ctr., 1982, in which the Tex. Supreme Ct. created significant exception to the rule of law that the terms and provisions of deed of trust must be strictly followed in foreclosure proceeding.*

**MCCULLOUGH, JAMES ALTUS, II,** lawyer; b. Jackson, Miss., Aug. 6, 1968; s. James Altus McCullough and Mary Katherine Walley; m. Tammie Miles. BBA in Mktg., U. Miss., 1992, JD, 1995. Bar: Miss. 1995, U.S. Dist. Ct. Miss., U.S. Ct. Appeals (5th cir.) 1995. Assoc. Brunini Grantham Grower & Hewes PLLC, Jackson, Miss., 1995—. Mem. ABA, Miss. Bar Assn., Miss. Bankruptcy Conf., Am. Bankruptcy Inst. General civil litigation, Bankruptcy, Consumer commercial. Office: Brunini Grantham Grower & Hewes PLLC 248 E Capitol St Ste 1400 Jackson MS 39201-2503

**MCCULLOUGH, MARSHALL WILLIAM,** lawyer; b. Bottineau, N.D., June 26, 1962; s. William F. and Carol E. McCullough; m. Mari O. O'Neil, July 21, 1984; children: Connor, William, Shane. BBA in Acctg., U. N.D., 1984; JD, U. Denver, 1987. Bar: Colo. 1987, Calif. 1994, N.D. 1995. Tax mgr. Price Waterhouse, San Francisco, 1987-94; lawyer Ohnstad Twichell P.C., Fargo, N.D., 1994—. Mem. Red River Zool. Soc. (v.p. 1996-98), Fargo Optimist Club (dir. 1998—). Office: Ohnstad Twichell PC 901 13th Ave E West Fargo ND 58078-3306

**MCCULLOUGH, RALPH CLAYTON, II,** lawyer, educator; b. Daytona Beach, Fla., Mar. 28, 1941; s. Ralph C. and Doris (Johnson) McC.; m. Elizabeth Grier Henderson, Apr. 5, 1986; children from previous marriage: Melissa Wells, Clayton Baldwin. B.A., Erskine Coll., 1962; J.D., Tulane U., 1965. Bar: La. 1965, S.C. 1974. Assoc. Baldwin, Haspel, Maloney, Rainold and Meyer, New Orleans, 1965-68; asst. prof. law U. S.C., 1968-71, asso. prof., 1971-75; prof. U. S.C., 2, 1975—; chair prof. of advocacy U. S.C., 1982—, asst. dean Sch. Law, 1970-75, instr. Med. Sch., 1970-79, adj. prof. law and medicine Med. Sch., 1979—; adj. prof. medicine Med. U. S.C., 1984—; of counsel Finkel & Altman, 1978—; adj. prof. pathology Med. U. S.C., 1985—; asst. dean U. S.C. Sch. Law 1970-75. Author: (with J.L. Underwood) The Civil Trial Manual, 1974, 7th supplement, 1987, The Civil Trial Manual II, 1984, 87, (with Myers and Felix) New Directions in Legal Education, 1970, (with Finkel) S.C. Torts II, 1986, III, 1990, IV, 1995; co-reporter S.C. Criminal Code, 1977, S.C. Study Sentencing, 1977. Trustee S.C. dist. U.S. Bankruptcy Ct., 1979—; exec. dir. S.C. Continuing Legal Edn. Program.; bd. visitors Erskine Coll.; reporter S.C. Jury Charge Commn., 1991-95. Mem. ABA, La. Bar Assn., S.C. Bar (sec. 1975-76, exec. dir. 1972-76, award of service 1978), New Orleans Bar Assn., Am. Trial Lawyers Assn., Am. Law Inst., Southeastern Assn. Am. Law Schs. (pres.), S.C. Trial Lawyers Assn. (bd. govs. 1984-88), Phi Alpha Delta. Republican. Episcopalian. Club: Forest Lake. Home: PO Box 1799 Columbia SC 29202-1799 Office: U SC Sch Law Columbia SC 29208-0001

**MC CUNE, BARRON PATTERSON,** retired federal judge; b. West Newton, Pa., Feb. 19, 1915; s. James Patterson and Lyda Barron (Hammond) McC.; m. Edna Flannery Markey, Dec. 23, 1943; children: Edward M., James H., Barron Patterson. AB, Washington and Jefferson Coll., 1935; LLB, U. Pa., 1938. Bar: Pa. bar 1939. Practiced in Washington, Pa., 1939-64; judge 27th Jud. Dist. Ct. Common Pleas, Washington, Pa., 1964-71; judge U.S. Dist. Ct., Western Dist. Pa., Pitts., 1971-95, sr. fed. judge; ret., 1995. Trustee emeritus Washington and Jefferson Coll.; bd. dirs. emeritus Washington (Pa.) Hosp. Served with USNR, 1942-45. Home: 144 Lemoyne Ave Washington PA 15301-3636

**MCCUNE, GEORGE MOODY,** international lawyer, international business consultant; b. Salt Lake City, Aug. 31, 1943; s. James Paxman and Elizabeth Irene (Moody) McC.; m. Eiko Nakama, Apr. 30, 1970; children: Chiemi, Dean Nakama, Ted Carrington. BA, Brigham Young U., 1968; grad. cert., U.S. Army Intelligence Sch., Ft. Holabird, Md., 1968; JD, U. Utah, 1973. Bar: Utah, 1973, U.S. Dist. Ct. Utah 1973. Ptnr. McCune & McCune, Provo, Utah, 1973-83; sole propr. McCune, McCune & Suzuki, Salt Lake City, 1983—; pres., CEO, Asia Mktg. & Cons. Corp., Salt Lake City, 1983—, ind. dir. Rexall Showcase Internat., 1998—. Author: Testimony, 1968, Practical Legal Aspects of U.S. Commodity Export to Japan, 1972, The Blessings of Temple Marriage in the Church of Jesus Christ of Latter-day Saints, 1973, Personalities in the Doctrine and Covenants and Joseph Smith-History, 1989, Gordon B. Hinckley—Shoulder for the Lord, 1996; editor: Matthew McCume Family History, Vol. 1AB, 1986, Vol. 2AB, 1993, Far East Law Newsletter, Sec.Inter-Law, ABA 1973-78. With U.S. Army, 1968-70. Mem. Sertoma (life, club pres. 1977-78, 1 of 14 Disting. Club Pres. of 1300 Clubs 1978). Mem. LDS Ch. Avocations: writing, history, genealogy, horsemanship, Japanese language. Fax: 801-964-0551. E-mail: asiamarketing@worldnet.att.net. Private international, Immigration, naturalization, and customs, Trademark and copyright. Home and Office: McCune McCune & Suzuki Asia Mktg & Consulting Corp PO Box 18044 Salt Lake City UT 84118-0044

**MCCUNE, PHILIP SPEAR,** lawyer; b. Spokane, Wash., Sept. 14, 1965; s. Calmar A. McCune and Katrina Y. Spear; m. Joey Leigh Hankins, Jan. 15, 1993; children: Emma Sophia, Jackson Spear. BA magna cum laude, Dartmouth Coll., 1987; JD cum laude, U. Mich., 1991. Bar: Wash. 1991, U.S. Dist. Ct. (we. dist.) Wash. 1991, U.S. Ct. Appeals (9th cir.) 1992, U.S. Dist. Ct. (ea. dist.) Wash. 1993, U.S. Dist. Ct. Utah 1998. Law clk. hon. John C. Coughenour chief judge U.S. Dist. Ct. (we. dist.) Wash., Seattle, 1991-93; assoc. Heller, Ehrman, White and Maculliffe, Seattle, 1993-97; ptnr., founding mem. Summit Law Group, Seattle, 1997—. Author: The Forest Practices Act, Washington Environmental Law and Practice, 1997; sr. editor U. Mich. Jour. Law Reform, 1989-91; contbr. articles to profl. jours. Young leaders bd. mem. Seattle Art Mus., 1996-98; bd. mem. Cmty. Svc. for the Blind, Seattle, 1997—; jr. bd. Seattle Repatory Theater, 1999—. Mem. ABA (bd. dirs. young lawyers divsn. 1996), Washington State Bar Assn., King County Bar Assn., Wash. Athletic Club, U. Mich. Law Sch. Barristers. Avocations: hiking, running. General civil litigation, Environmental, Land use and zoning (including planning). Office: Summit Law Group 1505 Westlake Ave N Ste 300 Seattle WA 98109-6211

**MCCURDY, GARY DEAN,** assistant district attorney, educator; b. Tulsa, Sept. 22, 1952; s. Carl Leon and Helen (Manthus) McC.; m. Janie Marie Fischer, May 31, 1975; children: Christopher John, Elizabeth Kay. BA in Polit. Sci., Okla. State U., 1974; JD, U. Tulsa, 1980. Bar: Okla. 1980, U.S. Dist. Ct. (no. dist.) Okla. 1980. Asst. dist. atty. Tulsa County (Okla.) Dist. Atty.'s Office, Tulsa, 1980-84; pvt. practice Tulsa, 1984-86; asst. dist. atty. Kingfisher County (Okla.) Dist. Atty.'s Office, Kingfisher, 1986-88, Canadian County (Okla.) Dist. Atty.'s Office, El Reno, 1988—; adj. faculty criminal justice Redlands C.C., El Reno, 1988—; speaker in field. Mem. Okla. Bar Assn. (chmn. criminal law com. 1997—), Kingfisher county Bar Assn. (pres. 1987), Okla. Dist. Attys. Assn. Democrat. Office: Canadian County Dist Atty Office 303 N Choctaw Ave Ofc El Reno OK 73036-2468

**MCCURLEY, MARY JOHANNA,** lawyer; b. Baton Rouge, La., Oct. 3, 1953; d. William Edward and Leora Elizabeth (Block) Trice; m. Carl Michael McCurley, June 6, 1983; 1 stepchild, Melissa Reneé McCurley. BA, Centenary Coll., 1975; JD, St. Mary's U., 1979. Bar: Tex. 1979; cert. family law 1984. Assoc. Martin, Withers & Box, Dallas, 1979-82, Raggio & Raggio, Inc., Dallas, 1982-83; ptnr. Bruner, McColl, McColloch & McCurley, Dallas, 1983-87; assoc., ptnr. Selligson & Douglass, Dallas, 1987-90; jr. ptnr. Koons, Fuller, McCurley & VanderEykel, Dallas, 1990-92; ptnr. McCurley, Kinser, McCurley & Nelson, Dallas, 1992—; Contbr. numerous articles to profl. jours. Adv. Women's Service League, Dallas, 1993—. Mem. Am. Acad. Matrimonial Lawyers (treas. Tex. chpt. 1995, sec. 1996, pres. 1997, pres.-elect 1998, nat. bd. dirs., bd. govs., pres. Tex. chpt. 1997-98), Dallas Bar Assn. (chairperson family law sect. 1985), Tex. State Bar Assn. (mem. family law coun.), Tex. Acad. Family Law Specialist, Dallas Bar Assn. Methodist. Avocations: golf, travel, jogging, horseback riding. Family and matrimonial. Home: 4076 Hanover Ave Dallas TX 75225-7009 Office: McCurley Kinser McCurley & Nelson LLP 1201 Elm St Dallas TX 75270-2102

**MCCURN, NEAL PETERS,** federal judge; b. Syracuse, N.Y., Apr. 6, 1926. LL.B., Syracuse U., 1952, J.D., 1960. Bar: N.Y. 1952. Ptnr. Mackenzie Smith Lewis Mitchell & Hughes, Syracuse, 1957-79; judge U.S. Dist. Ct. (no. dist.) N.Y., 1979-88; chief judge U.S. Dist. Ct. (no. dist.), N.Y., 1988-93; sr. judge, 1993—; del. N.Y. State Constl. Conv., 1976; mem. 2d Cir. Jud. Council. Pres. Syracuse Common Coun., 1970-78. Mem. ABA, N.Y. State Bar Assn. (chmn. state constn. com.), Onondaga County Bar Assn. (past pres.), Am. Coll. Trial Lawyers, Am. Judicature Soc. (bd. dirs. 1980-84). Office: US Dist Ct 100 S Clinton St Rm 33 Syracuse NY 13261-6100

**MCCURRACH, DUNCAN C.,** lawyer; b. Rochester, N.Y., 1959; Bar: N.Y. 1985.; AB, Cornell U., 1981; JD, U. Chgo., 1984. Ptnr. Sullivan & Cromwell, N.Y.C. General corporate, Mergers and acquisitions, Securities. Office: Sullivan & Cromwell 125 Broad St Fl 28 New York NY 10004-2489

**MCCUSKER, WILLIAM LAVALLE,** lawyer; b. Mpls., July 27, 1918; s. John Thomas and Emma Ernestine (Helfmann) McC.; m. Phyllis E. Kischel, June 19, 1943; children: Patricia, Barbara, Marcia (dec.), William James, Nancy. BS, U. Wis.-Superior, 1941; postgrad. U. Minn. Law Sch., 1943-44; JD, U. Wis., 1946. Bar: Wis. 1946, U.S. Dist. Ct. (ea and we. dists.) Wis. 1946, U.S. Ct. Appeals (7th cir.) 1970, U.S. Supreme Ct. 1974. Assoc. Hill, Beckwith & Harrington, Madison, Wis., 1945-48; dep. dist. atty. Dane County, Wis., 1948-50; ptnr. Wilkie, McCusker and Wilkie, Madison, 1950-53; ptnr., pres., sr. mem. McCusker and Robertson, SC., Madison, 1953-94; prin. William L. McCusker Law Offices, Madison, 1994—; spl. asst. atty. gen., Wis., 1955; instr. seminars. Kellogg scholar, 1943-44. Recipient jud. achievement award Wis. Acad. Trial Lawyers. Fellow Internat. Soc. Barristers; mem. ATLA, State Bar of Wis., Dane County Bar Assn., Wis. Acad. Trial Lawyers (pres. 1977-78), Elks Club. Personal injury, Workers' compensation, Product liability. Home: 3018 Pelham Rd Madison WI 53713-3468 Office: 2800 Royal Ave Ste 304B Madison WI 53713-1518

**MCCUTCHAN, B. EDWARD, JR.,** lawyer; b. Santa Rosa, Calif., Oct. 20, 1960; s. Ben E. McCutchan and Barbara L. Smith; m. Suzanne T. Volski, Sept. 24, 1994; 1 child, Tristan C. AB, U. Calif., Davis, 1982; JD, Golden Gate U., 1985; LLM, U. of the Pacific, 1986. Atty. Sonoma County Dist. Atty., Santa Rosa, 1985-86, Wagner-Kirkin, Sacramento, 1986-89, Rifkind & Fuerch, Hayward, Calif., 1989-96, DeMeo & DeMeo, Santa Rosa, 1996—. Avocations: fly fishing, ranching, gardening, hiking. General civil litigation, Contracts commercial, Real property. Office: DeMeo & DeMeo 565 W College Ave Santa Rosa CA 95401-5064

**MCCUTCHAN, GORDON EUGENE,** lawyer, insurance company executive; b. Buffalo, Sept. 30, 1935; s. George Lawrence and Mary Esther (De Puy) McC.; m. Linda Brown; children: Lindsey, Elizabeth. BA, Cornell U., 1956, MBA, 1958, LLB, 1959. Bar: N.Y. 1959, Ohio 1964. Pvt. practice Rome, N.Y., 1959-61; atty., advisor SEC, Washington, 1961-64; ptnr. McCutchan, Druen, Maynard, Rath & Dietrich, 1964-94; mem. office of gen. counsel Nationwide Mut. Ins. Co., Columbus, Ohio, 1964-94, sr. v.p., gen. counsel, 1982-89; exec. v.p., gen. counsel Nationwide Mut. Ins. Co., 1989-94; exec. v.p. Law and Corp. Svcs., Nationwide Ins. Enterprise, 1994-98. Trustee, bd. govs. Franklin U., 1992-97; trustee Ohio Tuition Trust Authority, 1992-97. Mem. Columbus Bar Assn., Ohio Bar Assn., Am. Corp. Counsel Assn., Assn. Life Inst. Counsel (bd. govs. 1990-94), Fedn. Ins. and Corp. Counsel, Am. Coun. Life Ins. (chair legal sect. 1992-93). Home: 2376 Oxford Rd Columbus OH 43221-4011 Office: Nationwide Mut Ins Co 1 Nationwide Plz Columbus OH 43215-2239 also: Employers Ins Wausau 2000 Westwood Dr Wausau WI 54401-7802

**MCCUTCHEON, JAMES EDWARD, III,** lawyer; b. San Antonio, Aug. 7, 1968; s. James Edward McCutcheon Jr. and Barbara Letitia Rogers; m. Elizabeth Jean Cooper, Aug. 21, 1992; children: Davis, Ashley Grace. BA in Econs., Dartmouth Coll., 1990; JD, U. Tex., 1994. Bar: Tex. 1994, U.S. Tax Ct. 1995, Wash. 1998, U.S. Ct. Appeals (5th cir.) 1999. Assoc. Gresham, Davis Gregory, Worthy & Moore, San Antonio, 1994-97, of counsel, 1997—; of counsel Vander Wel, Jacobson, Bishop & Magnusson PLLC, Bellevue, Wash., 1998—. Mem. ABA, San Antonio Bar Assn., Tex. Bar Assn., Wash. Bar Assn., Phi Beta Kappa, Order of Coif, Chancellors. E-mail: james@mccutcheon-law.com. Estate planning, Taxation, general, Probate. Office: 10500 NE 8th St Ste 1900 Bellevue WA 98004-4358

**MCDADE, JOE BILLY,** federal judge; b. 1937. BS, Bradley U., 1959, MA, 1960; JD, U. Mich., 1963. Staff atty. antitrust divsn. U.S. Dept. Justice, 1963-65; exec. trainee First Fed. Savs. and Loan Assn., 1965; exec. dir. Greater Peoria (Ill.) Legal Aid Soc., 1965-69; ptnr. Hafele & McDade, Peoria, Ill., 1968-77; pvt. practice Peoria, 1977-82; assoc. cir. judge State of Ill., 1982-88; cir. judge Cir. Ct. Ill., 1988-91; fed. judge U.S. Dist. Ct. (ctrl. dist.) Ill., 1991—. Bd. dirs. Peoria (Ill.) Pub. Libr., 1965-77, Peoria YMCA, ARC, Peoria Tri-Centennial; fin. chmn. St. Peters Cath. Ch.; active Peoria Civic Ctr. Authority, 1976-82; pres. Ill. Health Systems Agy., 1978-80, bd. dirs., 1975-82. Mem. Ill. State Bar Assn., Peoria County Bar Assn. (bd. dirs. 1980-82). Office: US Dist Ct 100 NE Monroe St Peoria IL 61602-1003

**MCDANIEL, DONALD HAMILTON,** lawyer; b. Washington, Apr. 26, 1948; s. Roy Hamilton and Mildred Dean (Borden) McD.; m. Eva Styron, Dec. 29, 1973; children: Sharon, Michelle. BS, La. State U., 1970; JD, U. Miss., 1973. Bar: Miss. 1973; bd. cert. tax atty., 1987—; bd. cert. estate planning & adminstrn. atty. Atty. IRS, Washington, 1974-77; tax law specialist Bourgeois Bennett Thokey, New Orleans, 1977-81; ptnr. McCloskey Dennery Page, New Orleans, 1981-85, Lemle & Kelleher, New Orleans, 1985—. Author: Estate Planning in Louisiana, 1991. Trustee St. Martins Episcopal Sch., New Orleans, 1993, East Jefferson Hosp. Found., New Orleans, 1995, United Meth. Found., New Orleans, 1995. Mem. ABA, La. State Bar Assn. (chmn. com. on trusts, estates and immovable property 1997—), Miss. State Bar Assn., New Orleans Estate Planning Coun. Avocations: golf, fishing. Estate planning, Estate taxation, Taxation, general. Office: Lemle & Kelleher LLP 601 Poydras St Ste 2100 New Orleans LA 70130-6021

**MCDANIEL, JAMES ALAN,** lawyer; b. St. Joseph, Mo., June 10, 1953; s. John Redmond and Mary Jane (Chiles) McD.; m. Margaret L. Randle, Sept. 20, 1990; children: Susan, John. AB with distinction, Stanford U., 1975; JD, Harvard U., 1978. Bar: Mass. 1978, U.S. Dist. Ct. Mass. 1979, U.S. Ct. Appeals (1st cir.) 1979. Assoc. Choate, Hall & Stewart, Boston, 1978-85, ptnr., 1986—, chmn. bus. dept., 1993-96, mem. firm mgmt. com., 1998—. Co-founder, editor-in-chief Harvard Environ. Law Rev., 1976-77. Bd. dirs. DARE Family Svcs., Inc. Fellow Am. Coll. Investment Counsel; mem. ABA, Mass. Bar Assn., Boston Bar Assn. (chmn. banking law com. 1996-98, bus. law sect. 1999—), Am. Soc. Corp. Secs., Boston Athenaeum, Phi Beta Kappa. Democrat. Episcopalian. Securities, Public utilities, Health. Home: 326 Highland St Weston MA 02493-2626

**MCDANIEL, JAMES EDWIN,** lawyer; b. Dexter, Mo., Nov. 22, 1931; s. William H. and Gertie M. (Woods) McD.; m. Mary Jane Crawford, Jan. 22, 1955; children: John William, Barbara Anne. AB, Washington U., St. Louis, 1957, JD, 1959. Bar: Mo. 1959. Assoc. firm Walther, Barnard, Cloyd & Timm, 1959-60; assoc. firm McDonald, Barnard, Wright & Timm, 1960-63, ptnr., 1963-65; ptnr. firm Barnard, Timm & McDaniel St. Louis, 1965-73; ptnr. firm Barnard & Baer, St. Louis, 1973-82; ptnr. Lashly & Baer, St. Louis, 1982—, prosecuting atty., 1968—; city atty. City of Glendale, Mo., 1996—; bd. dirs. Eden. Theol. Sem., Airtherm Mfg. Co.; lectr. Latvian U., Riga, Inst. Fgn. Rels., Banking in Am., 1992-93. Leader legal del. Chinese-Am. Comparative Law Study, People's Republic China, 1988, Russian-Am. Comparative Law Study, USSR, 1990; trustee, past chmn., past treas. 1st Congl. Ch. St. Louis. With USAF, 1951-55. Fellow Am. Bar Found. (life), St. Louis Bar Found. (life); mem. ABA (bd. govs. 1997—, ho. of dels. 1976-80, 84-92, 97—, state del. 1986-92, chmn. lawyers conf., jud. adminstrn. divsn. 1992-95, 8th cir. rep. standing com. on fed. jud. 1995-98, mem. standing com. on jud. qualification, tenure and compensation 1996-97), The Mo. Bar (pres. 1981-82, bd. govs. 1974-83), Mo. Assn. Def. Counsel, Bar Assn. Met. St. Louis (pres. 1972), Internat. Assn. Ins. Counsel, Assn. Def. Counsel St. Louis (past pres.), Phi Delta Phi. General civil litigation, Labor, Insurance. Home: 767 Elmwood Ave Saint Louis MO 63122-3216 Office: Lashly & Baer 714 Locust St Saint Louis MO 63101-1699

**MCDANIEL, JARREL DAVE,** lawyer; b. Clovis, N. Mex., Oct. 17, 1930; s. Raymond Lee and Blanch (Booth) McD.; m. Anne Louise McAllister; children: Jarrel Dave Jr., Julia Anne. A.A., Riverside Coll., 1951; B.A., U. Tex., 1956, LL.B., 1957. Bar: Tex. 1957. Assoc. Vinson & Elkins, Houston, 1957-69, ptnr., 1969-96; of counsel Sheinfeld, Maley & Kay, Houston, 1997—; author, lectr. in field. Served with USAF, 1950-54. Mem. ABA, Am. Coll. Bankruptcy, State Bar Tex., Am. Bankruptcy Inst., Tex. Bd. Legal Specialization in Bankruptcy (mem. adv. com. 1976—). Roman Catholic. Clubs: Houston, Houston Ctr. Bankruptcy, General civil litigation, Contracts commercial. Home: 1217 Potomac Dr Houston TX 77057-1919 Office: Sheinfeld Maley & Kay PC 1001 Fannin St Houston TX 77002-6706

**MCDANIEL, MARK STEVEN,** lawyer; b. Murfreesboro, Tenn., Sept. 5, 1958; s. Donald Rhea and Barbara Ann (Wood) McD.; m. Kimberley Carol Carter, Nov. 28, 1987; children: Sara Elizabeth, Mark Steven Jr., John Cameron, Alexandra Gabrielle. BS, Mid. Tenn. State U., 1980; JD, Memphis State U., 1983. Assoc. Jay Fred Friedman, Atty., Memphis, 1983-85; ptnr. Friedman & McDaniel, Attys., Memphis, 1985-86; pvt. practice Memphis, 1986—; prosecutor Town of Collierville (Tenn.) Mcpl. Ct., 1992—. Del. Memphis Shelby County Rep. Conv., 1986. Mem. Memphis Bar Assn. (chmn. criminal law sect.), Memphis Trial Lawyers Assn., Phi Delta Phi. Republican. Baptist. Avocations: golf, hunting, fishing, skiing. Criminal, Personal injury, General practice. Office: 243 Exchange Ave Memphis TN 38105-3503 also: Town of Collierville Mpcl Ct 156 N Rowlett St Collierville TN 38017-2678

**MCDANIEL, MYRA ATWELL,** lawyer, former state official; b. Phila., Dec. 13, 1932; d. Eva Lucinda (Yores) Atwell; m. Reuben Roosevelt McDaniel Jr., Feb. 20, 1955; children: Diane Lorraine, Reuben Roosevelt III. BA, U. Pa., 1954; JD, U. Tex., 1975; LLD, Huston-Tillotson Coll., 1984, Jarvis Christian Coll., 1986. Bar: Tex. 1975, U.S. Dist. Ct. (we. dist.) Tex. 1977, U.S. Dist. Ct. (so. and no. dists.) Tex. 1978, U.S. Ct. Appeals (5th cir.) 1978, U.S. Supreme Ct. 1978, U.S. Dist. Ct. (ea. dist.) Tex. 1979. Asst atty. gen. State of Tex., Austin, 1975-81, chief taxation div., 1979-81, gen. counsel to gov., 1983-84, sec. of state, 1984-87; asst. gen. counsel Tex. R.R. Commn., Austin, 1981-82; gen. counsel Wilson Cos., San Antonio and Midland, Tex., 1982; assoc. Bickerstaff, Heath & Smiley, Austin, 1984, ptnr., 1987-96; mng. ptnr. Bickerstaff, Heath, Smiley, Pollan, Kener & McDaniel, Austin, 1996—; mem. asset. mgmt. adv. com. State Treasury, Austin, 1984-86; mem. legal affairs com. Criminal Justice Policy Coun., Austin, 1984-8, Inter-State Oil Compact, Oklahoma City, 1984-86; bd. dirs. Austin Cons. Group, 1983-86; mem. Jud. Efficiency Coun., Austin, 1995-96; lectr. in field. Contbr. articles to profl. jours., chpts. to books. Del. Tex. Conf. on Librs. and Info. Sci., Austin, 1978, White House Conf. on Librs. and Info. Scis., Washington, 1979; mem. Libr. Svcs. and Constrn. Act Adv. Coun., 1980-84, chmn., 1983-84; mem. long range plan task force Brackenridge Hosp., Austin, 1981; clk. vestry bd. St. James Episcopal Ch., Austin, 1981-83, 89-90; bd. visitors U. Tex. Law Sch., 1983-87, vice chmn., 1983-85; bd. dirs. Friends of Ronald McDonald House Ctrl. Tex., Women's Advocacy, Inc., Capital Area Rehab. Ctr.; trustee Episcopal Found. Tex., 1986-89, St. Edward's U., Austin, 1986—, chmn. acad. com., 1988—; chmn. divsn. capital area campaign United Way, 1986; active nat. adv. bd. Leadership Am.; trustee Episcopal Sem. S.W., 1990-96, Assn. Governing Bds. Univs. and Colls., Leadership Edn. Arts Program, 1995—; adv. bd. mem. Women Basketball Coaches Assn., 1996—; bd. dirs. U.Tex. Law Sch. Found., 1997—; trustee Episcopal Health Charities, 1997—. Recipient Tribute to 28 Black Women award Concepts Unltd., 1983; Focus on women honoree Serwa Yetu chpt. Mt. Olive grand chpt. Order of Eastern Star, 1979, Woman of Yr. Longview Metro C. of C., 1985, Woman of Yr. Austin chpt. Internat. Tng. in Communication, 1985, Citizen of Yr. Epsilon Iona chpt. Omega Psi Phi, Lone Star Girl Scout Coun. Women of Distinction, 1997. Master Inns of Ct.; mem. ABA, Am. Bar Found., Tex. Bar Found. (trustee 1986-89), Travis County Bar Assn., Travis County Women Lawyers' Assn., Austin Black Lawyers Assn., State Bar Tex. (chmn. Profl. Efficiency & Econ. Rsch. subcom. 1976-84), Golden Key Nat. Honor Soc., Longhorn Assocs. for Excellence in Women's Athletes (adv. coun. 1988—), Order of Coif (hon. mem.), Omicron Delta Kappa, Delta Phi Alpha. Democrat. Administrative and regulatory, State civil litigation, State and local taxation. Home: 3910 Knollwood Dr Austin TX 78731-2915 Office: Bickerstaff Heath & Smiley 1700 First Bank Plz 816 Congress Ave Austin TX 78701-2442

**MCDANIEL, TIMOTHY ELLIS,** lawyer; b. Detroit, Oct. 4, 1951; s. Jeremiah and Jerutha McD.; m. Verna Barden, Dec. 17, 1983; children: Stacy, Samantha. BA, Mich. State U., 1973, JD, 1984; MA, U. Mich., 1979. Bar: Mich. 1984, U.S. Dist. Ct. (ea. dist.) Mich. 1984, U.S. Supreme Ct. 1990. Planner Wayne County Manpower Dept., Detroit, 1974-76; dep. dir., dir. dept. employment and tng. City of Ann Arbor, Mich., 1976-84; ptnr. McCoy and McDaniel Law Firm, Ann Arbor, 1984-98, McDaniel, Cotton & Eason Attys.-at-Law, Ann Arbor, 1998—. Co-author: Game Plan, 1994. Mem. SPECTRUM, Ann Arbor, 1998. Named to Million Dollar Advs. Forum, 1996; recipient Commendation, City of Ann Arbor, 1984. Mem. Vanzetti Hamilton Bar Assn. (bd. dirs. 1992—, pres. 1995-96), Nat. Football League Players Assn. Avocations: reading, attending major sports events. General civil litigation, Insurance, General practice. Home: 2850 Atterberry Dr Ann Arbor MI 48103-2083 Office: 325 E Eisenhower Pkwy Ste 300 Ann Arbor MI 48108-3307

**MCDANIELS, WILLIAM E.,** lawyer; b. Needham, Mass., July 1, 1941. BA, Williams Coll., 1963; JD, Georgetown U., 1966. Bar: D.C. 1967, Md. 1983. Grad. fellow criminal law, litigation U. Pa., Phila., 1966-68; pub. defender Phila. Pub. Defender's Office, 1966-68; adj. prof. evidence, criminal law, advanced criminal procedure Georgetown U. Law Ctr., Washington, 1970-87; mem. Williams & Connolly, Washington, 1968—; instr. Nat. Inst. Trial Advocacy, 1975—. Fellow Am. Coll. Trial Lawyers; mem. ABA, Md. State Bar Assn, D.C. Bar. General civil litigation, Criminal, Intellectual property. Office: Williams & Connolly 725 12th St NW Washington DC 20005-5901

**MCDAVID, JANET LOUISE,** lawyer; b. Mpls., Jan. 24, 1950; d. Robert Matthew and Lois May (Bratt) Kurzeka; m. John Gary McDavid, June 9, 1973; 1 child, Matthew Collins McDavid. BA, Northwestern U., 1971; JD, Georgetown U., 1974. Bar D.C. 1975, U.S. Ct. Appeals (fed. cir.) 1975 (D.C. cir. 1976), U.S. Supreme Ct. 1980, U.S. Ct. Appeals (5th cir.) 1983, (9th cir.) 1986. Assoc. Hogan & Harston, Washington, 1974-83, ptnr., 1984—; gen. counsel ERAmerica, 1977-83; mem. antitrust task force Dept. Defense, 1993-94, 96-97; mem. antitrust coun. U.S. C. of C., 1994—. Contbr. articles to profl. jours. Participant Clinton adminstrn. transition team FTC. Mem. ABA (antitrust sect., vice chmn. civil practice com. 1986-89, sect. 2 com. 1989-90, chmn. franchising com. 1990-91, coun. mem. 1991-94, program officer 1994-97, vice chair 1997-98, chair-elect 1998-99, chair 1999-2000, governing com. of forum on franchising 1991-97), ACLU, U.S. C. of C. (antitrust coun. 1995—), Washington Coun. Lawyers, D.C. Bar Assn., Fed. Bar Assn., Womens Legal Def. fund. Democrat. Antitrust, Federal civil litigation, Franchising. Office: Hogan & Hartson 555 13th St NW Ste 800E Washington DC 20004-1161

**MCDAVID, WILLIAM HENRY,** lawyer; b. N.Y.C., May 10, 1946; s. William H. and Margaret B. (Carmody) McD.; m. Sylvia Noin, Dec. 21, 1984; children: Andrew, Madeline, William, Flora. AB, Columbia Coll., N.Y.C., 1968; JD, Yale U., 1972. Assoc. Debevoise & Plimpton, N.Y.C., 1972-81; asst. gen. counsel Bankers Trust Co., N.Y.C., 1981-83, assoc. gen. counsel, 1983-84, v.p., 1984-85, v.p., counsel, 1986-88; gen. counsel Chase Manhattan Corp., N.Y.C., 1988—. Banking, General corporate, Finance. Office: The Chase Manhattan Corp Office Gen Coun 270 Park Ave Fl 8 New York NY 10017-2014

**MCDERMITT, EDWARD VINCENT,** lawyer, educator; b. Hagerstown, Md., Nov. 29, 1953; s. Edward Bernard and Genevieve Natalie (Gallo) McD.; m. Jane Langmead Springmann, June 28, 1986; children: Edward S., Maureen K. BA, Georgetown U., 1975, MA, 1978; JD, U. Santa Clara, 1980; LLM, U. Pa., 1984. Bar: D.C. 1981, U.S. Dist. Ct. D.C. 1981. Rsch. asst. U. Santa Clara, Calif., 1980; pvt. practice law Washington, 1981-82; assoc. Law Offices of Miller & Loewinger, Washington, 1982; pvt. practice law Washington, 1983; rsch. asst. U. Pa., Phila., 1983-84; pvt. practice law Washington, 1984—; adj. asst. prof. Yale Gordon Coll. Liberal Arts, U. Balt., 1991—, vis. asst. prof., 1996, adj. assoc. prof. U. Md. Univ. Coll., 1998—, lectr. law Columbus Sch. Law, Cath. U. Am., 1999—; mng. ptnr. J-L-S Svcs., Washington, 1985—, Early and Valuable Memorabilia, Md., 1985—; congl. intern to rep. Pat Schroeder, Washington, 1975; vol. atty. ACLU Nat. Capital area, Washington, 1982—; lectr. writing The Writer's Ctr., 1987—; participant program instrn. lawyers Harvard Law Sch., 1989—. Author: Overruled, Mr./Ms. Writer: An Argument in Favor of Accuracy in Depiction, How to Write an Uncommonly Good Novel, 1990, Pemberton's Mademoiselle/Chasing Mlle./They're Back!, 1996. Vol. McGovern for Pres. campaign, Washington and Md., 1972, United Farmworkers Union, Washington, 1973-77, Urban Coalition Basketball League, Washington, 1977-78, Sarbanes re-election campaign, Md., 1982. Mem. D.C. Bar (cons., mem. lawyer/tchr. partnership program 1987—), Superior Ct. Trial Lawyers Assn., Washington Writers Group, Internat. Platform Assn., Pi Sigma Alpha. Roman Catholic. Avocations: photography, poetry, fiction writing, military history, bridge. Constitutional, Civil rights, Criminal. Home and Office: 8000 Wildwood Dr Silver Spring MD 20912-7425

**MCDERMOTT, CHRISTOPHER MANNING,** lawyer; b. New Haven, Conn., Sept. 1, 1960; s. Thomas Manning and Gloria Florence McD.; m. Lucy Yun Shen, Apr.30, 1983; children: Amanda, Sarah. BA, Williams Coll., 1982; JD, Duke U., 1986. Bar: N.Y. 1987. Assoc. Simpson, Thacher & Bartlett, N.Y.C., 1986-95; assoc. Cadwalader, Wickersham & Taft, N.Y.C., 1995-97, ptnr., 1998—. Mem. N.Y. State Bar Assn., Assn. Bar of City of N.Y. Banking, Contracts commercial, General corporate. Office: Cadwalader Wickersham & Taft 227 W Trade St Ste 2400 Charlotte NC 28202-1689

**MCDERMOTT, FRANCIS OWEN,** lawyer; b. Denver, Feb. 25, 1933; s. Paul Harkins and Agnes (Clark) McD.; divorced; children: Diana, Daniel, Christopher, Anthony, Justine; m. Estella Marina Idiaquez, June 6, 1986. JD, Am. U., 1960. Bar: D.C. 1960, U.S. Dist. Ct. D.C., 1960, U.S. Ct. Appeals (D.C. cir.) 1960, u.S. Tax Ct. 1961, U.S. Supreme Ct. 1964. Trial atty. office regional counsel IRS, Washington, 1961-65; mem. profl. staff com. on fin. U.S. Senate, Washington, 1965-68; tax counsel Assn. Am. R.R.s, Washington, 1968-73; assoc. Hopkins & Sutter, Washington, 1973-76, ptnr., 1976-98, of counsel, 1999; gen. counsel Inst. Ill., Washington, 1987-96. Mem. ABA, Fed. Bar Assn., Nat. Def. Transp. Assn. (v.p., gen. counsel 1974—). Roman Catholic. Avocation: tennis. Legislative, Corporate taxation, Taxation, general. Home: 1 S Montague St Arlington VA 22204-1007

**MCDERMOTT, FRANK CLARK,** lawyer; b. Bklyn., Sept. 1, 1926; s. Charles Paul and Florence (Ferris) McD.; m. Margot Schinzel, Aug. 27, 1955; children: Charles, Michele, Stacie, Steven. LLB, Bklyn. Law Sch, 1951. Bar: N.Y. 1952, U.S. Dist. Ct. N.Y. 1953, U.S. Supreme Ct. 1957. Pvt. practice law Bklyn., 1952-55, 56-60; assoc. Copans & Kanon, N.Y.C., 1955-56; adj. prof. N.Y. City Tech. Coll., 1962-92. Pres. Madison Marine Civic Assn., Bklyn., 1990-96; mem. Community Bd. #15, Bklyn., 1975—, Bishop's Lay Com. of Cath. Charities, Bklyn., 1978—. With U.S. Army, 1944-46. Mem. Bklyn. Bar Assn. (trustee 1984-90), Cath. Lawyers Guild (bd. dirs. 1981-82, pres. 1979-80), Lawyers Club Bklyn., Friendly Sons of St. Patrick in City of N.Y., Bklyn. Club, St. Patricks Soc. Bklyn., Ancient Order Hibernians. Democrat. Roman Catholic. Avocations: golf, antiques. Office: 26 Court St Brooklyn NY 11242-0103

**MCDERMOTT, FRANK XAVIER,** lawyer, lobbyist; b. N.Y.C., Oct. 15, 1924; s. Peter Joseph and Helen (Gildea) McD.; m. Patricia Mary Keogh, Sept. 11, 1954; children: Gregory Sean, Colleen Maura, Marita Patricia, Matthew Peter, Brendan Xavier. BA, Columbia Coll., 1948, JD, 1949; MPA, NYU, 1953, LLM in Trade Regulation, 1962. Bar: N.Y. 1949, N.J. 1962, D.C. 1981, U.S. Supreme Ct. 1969. Claims adjuster Aetna Casualty & Surety, N.Y.C., 1949-52; asst. dir., indsl. rels. N.J. Mfg. Assn., Trenton, 1952-57; labor rels. Am. Bakeries Co., N.Y.C., 1957-59; exec. dir. N.J. Orgn. for a Better State, Trenton, 1959-73; atty. Seifert, Frisch & McDermott, New Brunswick, N.J., 1963-64; sr. ptnr., of counsel Apruzzese, McDermott, Mastro & Murphy, Liberty Corner, N.J., 1964—; bd. dirs. Peerless Tube Co., Bloomfield, N.J.1970—, Suburban Trust Co., Westfield, N.J., 1967-72, Nat. Bank N.J., New Brunswick, 1972-78 co-adj. staff Inst. Mgmt. and Labor Rels. Rutgers U., 1956-68. Author: New Jersey Labor Laws-Synopsis of Then-Current Laws, 1954. Assemblymen N.J. Gen. Assembly, 1964-67, 76-78; senator N.J. Senate, 1968-74, pres. senate, 1969; acting gov. State of N.J., 1969; del. White House Conf. Edn., 1955; chmn. Union County Rep. Com., 1989—, N.J. Turnpike Authority, 1994—. With USAF, 1943-46. Recipient Outstanding Young Legislator award Carnegie Found., 1965. Mem. County Chmns. Assn. N.J. (chmn.), Army and Navy Club, Baltusrol Golf Club. Roman Catholic. Avocations: golf, politics. Legislative, Labor. Home: 940 Wyandotte Trl Westfield NJ 07090-3733 Office: Apruzzese McDermott Mastro Murphy PO Box 112 Liberty Corner NJ 07938-0112

**MCDERMOTT, JOHN ARTHUR,** lawyer; b. Rochester, N.Y., Nov. 23, 1944; s. David E. and Doris L. McDermott; m. Gail Ann Van Putte, Sept. 24, 1965; children: Shawn, Ashley, Wendy. BA, U. Fla., 1966, JD with honors, 1968. Bar: Fla. 1969, U.S. Ct. Mil. Appeals 1969, Colo. 1973, U.S. Dist. Ct. Colo. 1973, U.S. Ct. Appeals (10th cir.) 1981. Rsch. asst. to chief judge Fla. Ct. Appeals, Lakeland, 1969; pvt. practice, Canon City, Colo., 1973—; county atty. Fremont County, Canon City, 1987-89; city atty. Canon City, Colo., 1989-90. pres. Fremont Rel Sch. Bd., 1977-81, mem. 1975-81; bd. dirs. West Cen. Mental Health Clinic, Canon City, 1973-75. Capt. U.S. Army, 1969-73. Mem. Colo. Bar Assn. (v.p. 1984-85), Colo. Trial Lawyers Assn. (bd. dirs. 1987-89, 91-97, exec. com. 1988-89), Colo. Bar Found., 11th Jud. Dist. Bar Assn. (pres. 1980-82, mem. jud. nominating com. 1980-81), Assn. Trial Lawyers Am., Lions (prs. 1985-86), Elks. Democrat. Avocations: skiing, motorcycling, amateur radio. Personal injury, Labor, General civil litigation. Home: 715 Pisgah St Canon City CO 81212-4340 Office: PO Box 1040 Canon City CO 81215-1040

**MCDERMOTT, KEVIN R.,** lawyer; b. Youngstown, Ohio, Jan. 26, 1952; s. Robert J. and Marion D. (McKeown) McD.; m. Cindy J. Darling, Dec. 11, 1976; children: Ciara, Kelly. AB, Miami U., Oxford, Ohio, 1974; JD, Ohio State U., 1977. Bar: Ohio 1977, U.S. Dist. Ct. (so. dist.) Ohio 1978, U.S. Dist. Ct. (no. dist.) Ohio 1988, U.S. Dist. Ct. (we. dist.) Mich. 1993, U.S. Supreme Ct. 1990, U.S. Ct. Appeals (3rd cir.) 1996, U.S. Ct. Appeals (6th cir.) 1988. Assoc. ptnr. Murphey Young & Smith, Columbus, Ohio, 1977-88; ptnr. Squire Sanders & Dempsey, Columbus, Ohio, 1988-90, Schottenstein Zox & Dunn, Columbus, Ohio, 1990—; adv. bd. mem. Capital U. Legal Asst. Program, Columbus, Ohio, 1988—. Bd. pres. Easter Seal Soc. Ctrl. Ohio, Columbus, 1992-94, bd. mem. 1988-92; pres. Upper Arlington Civic Svc. Commn., Columbus, Ohio, 1988-93. Securities, General civil litigation, Constitutional. Office: Schottenstein Zox & Dunn 41 S High St Ste 2600 Columbus OH 43215-6109

**MCDERMOTT, THOMAS JOHN, JR.,** lawyer; b. Santa Monica, Calif., Mar. 23, 1931; s. Thomas J. Sr. and Etha Irene (Cook) McD.; m. Yolanda; children: Jodi Friedman, Kimberly E., Kish S. BA, UCLA, 1953, JD, 1958. Bar: Calif. 1959. Ptnr., Gray, Binkley and Pfaelzer, Los Angeles, 1964-67, Kadison, Pfaelzer, Woodward, Quinn and Rossi, Los Angeles, 1967-87, Rogers & Wells, 1987-93, Bryan Cave, 1993-95, Manatt, Phelps & Phillips, LLP, 1995—. Served with U.S. Army, 1953-56, Korea. Fellow Am. Coll. Trial Lawyers; mem. ABA, UCLA Law Alumni Assn. (pres. 1961-62), Assn. of Bus. Trial Lawyers (pres. 1980-81, mem. exec. com. 9th cir. jud. conf. 1993—, chair 1997), State Bar Calif. (chair litigation sect. 1993-94), Order of Coif. Federal civil litigation, General civil litigation, State civil litigation. Office: Manatt Phelps & Phillips LLP 11355 W Olympic Blvd Los Angeles CA 90064-1614

**MCDEVITT, CHARLES FRANCIS,** state supreme court justice; b. Pocatello, Idaho, Jan. 5, 1932; s. Bernard A. and Margaret (Hermann) McD.; m. Virginia L. Heller, Aug. 14, 1954; children: Eileen A., Kathryn A., Brian A., Sheila A., Terrence A., Neil A., Kendal A. LLB, U. Idaho, 1956. Bar: Idaho 1956. Ptnr. Richards, Haga & Eberle, Boise, 1956-62; gen. counsel, asst. sec. Boise Cascade Corp., 1962-65; mem. Idaho State Legislature, 1963-66; sec., gen. counsel Boise Cascade Corp., 1965-67, v.p. sec., 1967-68; pres. Beck Industries, 1968-70; group v.p. Singer Co., N.Y.C., 1970-72, exec. v.p., 1973-76; pub. defender Ada County, Boise, 1976-78; co-founder Givens, McDevitt, Pursley & Webb, Boise, 1978-89; justice Idaho Supreme Ct., Boise, 1989-97, chief justice, 1993-97; ptnr., founder McDevitt & Miller, LLP, Boise, 1997—; served on Gov.'s Select Com. on Taxation, Boise, 1988-89; mem. State Select Com. on Campaign Ethics and Campaign Finances, State Select Com. on Legis. Compensation. Chair Idaho Jud. Coun., 1993-97, Cts. Advisors Coun., 1994-98. Home: 4940 Boise River Ln Boise ID 83706-5706 Office: McDevitt & Miller LLP 537 W Bannock St Ste 215 Boise ID 83702-5759

**MCDIARMID, ROBERT CAMPBELL,** lawyer; b. N.Y.C., July 13, 1937; s. Norman Hugh and Dorothy (Shoemaker) McD.; m. Ruth Sussman, 1963 (div. 1996); children—Jennifer, Alexander Samuel; m. Frances Enseki Francis, 1996. B.S. in Mech. Engring., Swarthmore Coll., 1958; M.S. in Engring. Physics, Cornell U., 1960; LL.B., Harvard U., 1963. Bar: D.C. 1964, Va. 1964, U.S. Supreme Ct. 1967, U.S. Ct. Appeals (1st, 2d, 3d, 4th, 5th, 6th, 7th, 8th, 9th, 10th, 11th, fed. cirs.). Assoc. Weaver & Glassie, Washington, 1963-64; trial atty. Civil Div., Appellate Sect., Dept. Justice, Washington, 1964-68; asst. to gen. counsel Fed. Power Commn., Washington, 1968-70; assoc. Law Office of George Spiegel, Washington, 1970-73; ptnr. Spiegel & McDiarmid, Washington, 1973—. Mem. alumni coun. Swarthmore Coll., 1986-89. Mem. ABA, Va. State Bar, Bar Assn. D.C., D.C. Bar, Fed. Energy Bar Assn. (exec. com. 1982-83, bd. dirs. 1997—). Democrat. Mem. Soc. of Friends. FERC practice, Antitrust, Federal civil litigation. Home: 3625 Fulton St NW Washington DC 20007-1452 Office: Spiegel & McDiarmid 1350 New York Ave NW Ste 1100 Washington DC 20005-4798

**MCDONALD, ALAN ANGUS,** federal judge; b. Harrah, Wash., Dec. 13, 1927; s. Angus and Nell (Britt) McD.; m. Ruby K., Aug. 22, 1949; children: Janelle Jo, Saralee Sue, Stacy. BS, U. Wash., 1950, LLB, 1952. Dep. pros. atty. Yakima County, Wash., 1952-54; assoc. Halverson & Applegate, Yakima, 1954-56; ptnr. Halverson, Applegate & McDonald, Yakima, 1956-85; judge U.S. Dist. Ct. (ea. dist.) Wash., Yakima, 1985-95, sr. judge, 1995—. Fellow Am. Coll. Trial Lawyers; Yakima C. of C. (bd. dirs.). Clubs: Yakima Country, Royal Duck (Yakima). Office: US Dist Ct PO Box 2706 Yakima WA 98907-2706

**MCDONALD, ALAN JAMES,** lawyer; b. Lowville, N.Y., Dec. 31, 1946; s. Gordon and Martha (Repak) McD.; m. Wendy Scott, Apr. 16, 1983; children: Molly Nora, Betsy Martha, Timothy Gordon. BA, LeMoyne Coll., 1968; JD, Boston Coll., 1973. Bar: Mass. 1973, U.S. Dist. Ct. Mass. 1974, U.S. Ct. Appeals (1st cir.) 1974. Assoc. Grady & Kaplan, Boston, 1973-75; ptnr. Grady & McDonald, Boston, 1975-81, McDonald, Noonan & Lamond (and predecessors), Newton, Mass., 1982-94, McDonald & Assocs., Newton, Mass., 1994—; adj. faulty New Eng. Sch. Law, Boston, 1980-86. Author: Annual Survey of Massachusetts Law, Labor and Employment Law, 1986, 87; author: (with others) Judicial Employment Law Reference Guide, 1989. With USAR, 1969-75. Recipient Outstanding Legal Svc. award Mass. Nurses Assn., Boston, 1983. Mem. ABA, Mass. Bar Assn. (chmn. dispute resolutions com. 1982-84), Boston Bar Assn. (labor law sect. 1973—). Labor. Home: 59 Main St Southborough MA 01772-1508 *Notable cases include: Sch. Com. of Newton vs. Labor Rels. Commn., et al, 338 Mass. 557, 1983; which established the obligation of a mcpl. employer to bargain in good faith over the means employed to reduce the work force in the pub. sector; Blue Hills Regional Sch. Dist. Com. vs. Flight 1981 Mass. Adv. Bd. 1240, 421 N.E. 2d 755, 1981, which established an exception to the gen. non-arbitrability of sch. com. managerial appointments, where such appointments were grounded upon discriminatory investigation.*

**MCDONALD, ANDREW M.,** lawyer; b. Kingston, Pa., Feb. 22, 1958; s. Keith D. and Sarah Ann McD. BA, Yale U., 1979; JD, U. Va., 1985. Assoc. Whiteford, Taylor & Preston, Balt., 1985-90; asst. atty. gen. Office of Atty. Gen. Md., Balt., 1990-96; atty. Zurich-am. Ins. Group, Balt., 1996-97, Zurich Comml./Zurich Sm. Bus., Balt., 1997—. Mem. ABA, Md. State Bar Assn. Office: Zurich Comml/Zurich Sm Bus 3910 Keswick Rd Baltimore MD 21211-2226

**MCDONALD, BRADLEY G.,** lawyer; m. Ann Gilbert, Sept. 2, 1964; 1 child, Perry. BA, U. Okla.; JD, Georgetown U., 1961. Bar: D.C. 1961, U.S. Ct. Appeals (D.C., 11th and 4th cirs.), U.S. Supreme Ct. With McDonald & Karl, Washington; lawyer; b. Okla.; m. Ann Gilbert, Sept. 3, 1964; 1 child, Perry. BA, U. Okla.; JD, Georgetown U., 1961. Bar: D.C. 1961, U.S. Ct. Appeals (D.C. cir.), U.S. Ct. Appeals (11th cir., 4th cir.) U.S. Supreme Ct. Nat. Alumni Adv. Coun. U. Okla.; mem. Arlington Com. of 100; bd. dirs. McLean Montessori, , Sigma Nu Ednl. Found.; trustee, treas. Randolph-Macon Acad. Served to 1st lt. USMC, 1956-58. Named to Legion of Honor, Delta Epsilon, Sigma Nu; recipient 1st Regent's Alumni award U. Okla. Mem. nat. alumni adv. coun. U. Okla; mem. Arlington Com. of 100; bd. dirs. McLen Montessori; trustee, treas. Randolph-Macon Acad. 1st lt. USMC, 1956-58. Recipient 1st Regent's Alumni award U. Okla. Mem. Sigma Nu (mem. Ednl. Found.), Delta Epsilon. General practice.

**MCDONALD, BRIAN MARTIN,** prosecutor; b. N.Y.C., May 5, 1962; s. Robert Leo and Jeanne A. McDonald; m. Rose Y. Cheu, May 21, 1988; 1 child, May. BA, Stanford U., 1984; JD, U. Mich., 1988. Bar: Calif. 1988, Wash. 1990, U.S. Supreme Ct. 1997. Assoc. Thelen, Marrin, Johnson & Bridges, San Francisco, 1988-90, Cairncross & Hempelmann, Seattle, 1990-93; dep. pros. atty. King County Pros. Atty., Seattle, 1993-97, sr. dep. pros. atty., 1998—; chaiperson hiring com. King County Pros. Attys. Office, Seattle, 1998—. Dir. Chinese Info. and Svc. Ctr., Seattle, 1992-94. Mem. Wash. State Bar Assn. (ct. rules com. 1998—). Office: King County Pros Atty 1850 Key Tower 700 5th Ave Seattle WA 98104-5058

**MCDONALD, CHARLES EDWARD,** lawyer; b. El Paso, Tex., Nov. 13, 1957; s. Carlos and Armida (Adauto) McD.; 1 child, Miranda Lee. BA in Philosophy, U. St. Thomas, Houston, 1980; JD, South Tex. Coll. Law, 1985. Bar: Tex. 1985, U.S. Ct. Appeals. (5th cir.) 1991, U.S. Supreme Ct. 1992. Prin. Law Office Charles E. McDonald, El Paso, 1985—. Comms. liaison Coleman Re-election Congl. Campaign, El Paso, 1984, 86. Mem. ATLA, Tex. Trial Lawyers Assn., State Bar Tex., El Paso County Bar Assn. (ethics com. 1997-98, rules com. 1997-98, clin. law coun. 1997-98), Nat. Assn. Cave Divers. Roman Catholic. Avocations: cave diving, chess, traveling, foreign language (Spanish). General civil litigation, Civil rights, Professional liability. Office: 4150 Rio Bravo St Ste 136 El Paso TX 79902-1013

**MCDONALD, DANIEL WILLIAM,** lawyer; b. Omaha, Mar. 18, 1961; s. John Albert and Jeannine Mary (Van Horn) McD.; m. Wendy Marie Marti, Dec. 30, 1983. BSEE, U. Minn., 1982, JD, 1985. Bar: Minn. 1985, U.S. Dist. Ct. Minn. 1985, U.S. Ct. Appeals (8th, 9th, 10th and fed. cirs.), U.S. Supreme Ct. 1991. Assoc. Merchant & Gould, Mpls., 1985-90, officer, 1991—. Deacon, Roseville (Minn.) Covenant Ch., 1989-96. Mem. ABA, Minn. State Bar Assn. (chair computer law sect.), Minn. Intellectual Property Assn. (chair litigation com.), Tau Beta Pi. Mem. Evangelical Covenant Ch. Avocations: tennis, outdoor sports, astronomy. Patent, Trademark and copyright, Computer. Office: Merchant & Gould 3100 Norwest Ctr Minneapolis MN 55402

**MCDONALD, FRANCIS MICHAEL,** state supreme court justice; b. Waterbury, Conn., Jan. 22, 1931; s. M. Francis and Margaret (Kelly) McD.; m. Mary Kelly, Jan. 28, 1956; children: Michael, Mary Ann, John K. AB, Holy Cross Coll., 1953; LLB, Yale U., 1956. Bar: Conn. 1956. Spl. agt. FBI, Washington, 1956-57; asst. U.S. atty. Dist. of Conn., New Haven, 1958-60; asst. prosecutor Cir. Ct., Waterbury, 1961-68; state's atty. Waterbury, 1968-84; judge Superior Ct., Waterbury, 1984-96; assoc. justice Conn. Supreme Ct., Hartford, 1996-99, chief justice, 1999—. Avocations: fishing, skiing, fly tying. Home: 257 Christian Rd Middlebury CT 06762-2908

**MCDONALD, JOHN BARRY, JR.,** lawyer; b. Fall River, Mass., Aug. 22, 1970; s. John Barry Sr. and Gabrielle Marie (Pires) McD. BA summa cum laude, Boston Coll., 1992; JD, U. Chgo., 1995. Assoc. Goodwin, Procter & Hoar LLP, Boston, 1995—. Campaign coord. Citizens for Silber, Fall River, 1990. Mem. Phi Beta Kappa, Alpha Sigma Nu. Banking, General corporate, Finance. Home: 2022 Highland Ave Fall River MA 02720-4311 Office: Goodwin Procter & Hoar Exchange Pl Boston MA 02109-2803

**MCDONALD, JOSEPH F., III,** lawyer; b. Rockville Centre, N.Y., Feb. 6, 1956; s. Joseph F. Jr. and Rita M. McD.; m. Laurie Hurd, Nov. 24, 1978; children: Geoffrey, Ryan, Molly. BA, St. Anselm's Coll., 1978; JD, Suffolk U., 1983; LLM, Boston U., 1987. Bar: N.H., U.S. Dist. Ct., U.S. Tax Ct. Dir., shareholder Cleveland, Waters & Bass, Concord, N.H., 1988-92, 94-98; v.p. trust New London (N.H.) Trust Co., 1992-94; ptnr. McDonald & Kanyuk, PLLC, Concord, 1998—. Dir. AAA No. New England, Portland, Maine, 1997—. Fellow Am. Coll. Trust and Estate Counsel. Estate planning, Probate, Estate taxation. Office: McDonald & Kanyuk PLLC 9 Hills Ave Ste B Concord NH 03301-4804

**MCDONALD, MARY M.,** lawyer; b. 1944. BA, D'Youville Coll., 1966; JD, Fordham U., 1969. Bar: N.Y. 1969. Staff Merck & Co., 1974-91, asst. gen. counsel, internat., 1990-91, v.p., gen. counsel, 1991-93, sr. v.p., gen counsel, 1993—. General corporate. Office: Merck & Co One Merck Dr PO Box 100 Whitehouse Station NJ 08889-0100

**MCDONALD, MICHAEL EUGENE,** lawyer, educator, clergyman; b. Buffalo, N.Y., Aug. 13, 1956; s. Ned and Margaret (Hereford) McD.; m. Darlene Carver, July 1, 1989; 1 child, Miranda Danielle. AA, BS, Middle Tenn. State U., 1979; MPA, So. Ill. U., 1984; JD, John Marshall Sch. Law, 1987; MDiv, Vanderbilt U., 1993. Bar: Ill. 1986, Tenn. 1990; cert. adminstr. elections, Tenn., 1994; ordained to ministry United Meth. Ch., 1996. Legis. intern Office of the Speaker, Ill. Ho. of Reps., Springfield, 1982-83; fellow Exec. Office of the Gov., State of Ill., Springfield, 1983-84; law clk. intern U.S. Dist. Ct. No. Dist. Ill., Chgo., 1984-85; adminstrv. asst. to dir. Ill. Dept. State Police, Chgo., 1984-87; asst. atty. gen. Ill. Atty. Gen.'s Office, Chgo., 1986-87; spl. asst. to mayor Exec. Office of the Mayor, Nashville, 1987-90; assoc. King & Ballow, Nashville, 1991-93; election adminstr. Davidson County Election Commn., Nashville, 1993-97; adj. prof. polit. sci., bus. law and paralegal studies program Middle Tenn. State U., Murfreesboro, 1987—; gen. counsel Gov.'s Alliance for a Drug Free Tenn., Davidson County, 1987—; mem. Leadership Nashville, Class 1991; asst. prof. The Hons. Program, Tenn. State U., 1996—; instr. U. tenn. Ctr. for Govt. Tng., 1995—. Vol. Buddies of Nashville, 1988—; loaned exec. United Way Mid. Tenn., 1990; mem. Leadership Nashville Class of 1990-91. Recipient Disting. Young Alumni Achievement award Middle Tenn. State U., 1987. Mem. ABA (del. ho. of dels.), Nat. Bar Assn., Ill. State Bar, Alpha Phi Alpha, Phi Alpha Delta. Avocations: basketball, running, karate, sport card collecting. Home: 1603 Benjamin St Nashville TN 37206-2511 Office: Election Commn Met Govt of Nashville Howard Sch Bldg Rm 153 2d Ave S Nashville TN 37210-0650

**MCDONALD, MICHAEL SCOTT,** lawyer; b. Ft. Stockton, Tex., Feb. 6, 1962; s. Roland R. and Harriett L. McD.; m. Sara; children: Matthew, Michael. BA, U. Tex., El Paso, 1984; JD, U. Tex., Austin, 1987. Bar: Tex. 1987, U.S. Ct. Appeals (5th and 10th cirs.), U.S. Dist. Ct. (all dists.) Tex. With Littler Mendelson, Dallas; shareholder Littler, Mendelson, Dallas. Co-author, editor: Chapter 9, The 1999 National Employer; The Texas Employer; contbg. editor, Covenents Not to Compete-A State by State Survey, 1995-98, Employee Duty of Loyalty, 1995-98, Trade Secrets — A State by State Survey, 1998; contbr. articles to profl. jours. Mem. ABA (litigation sect., labor and employment law sect.), Tex. Bar Assn. (labor and employment law sect.), Tex. Assn. Bus. (employee rels. chair Dallas chpt.), Dallas Bar Assn. (employment law sect., mem. exec.com. 1994—, vice chair 1999). Labor, General civil litigation. Office: Littler Mendelson 2001 Ross Ave Ste 2600 Dallas TX 75201-2931

**MCDONALD, PATRICK K.,** lawyer, shareholder; b. Dodgeville, Wis., June 5, 1948; s. Francis L. and Agnes J. McD.; m. Kathryn F. McDonald, June 10, 1978; children: David, Thomas, Bridget, Andrew, Matthew. BA, Loras Coll., 1970; STB, Catholic U. Am., 1972, JCB, 1973; JD, St. Louis U., 1976. Bar: Wis. 1976, U.S. Dist. Ct. (we. dist.) Wis. 1976, U.S. Ct. Appeals (7th cir.) 1983. Assoc. Gilbert D. Sedor, S.C., Janesville, Wis., 1976-78; v.p., stockholder Sedor, McDonald & Hoag, S.C., Janesville, Wis., 1978-84; pres., stockholder McDonald & Gustafson, S.C., Janesville, Wis., 1985—; mem., chmn. legal sec. program com. Blackhawk Tech. Coll., Janesville, 1979—. speaker, presenter Wis. Acad. Trial Lawyers, 1991, Wis. Bar Assn., 1992. Chmn. attys. sect. United Way of Rock County, Janesville; chmn. fundraising Echo, Janesville, 1998. Mem. Nat. Bd. Trial Advocacy (cert. civil trial advocate). Personal injury. Office: McDonald & Gustafson SC 200 S Main St Janesville WI 53545-3927

**MCDONALD, PAUL KIMBALL,** lawyer, investment executive; b. Worcester, Mass., June 8, 1932; s. Irving Thomas McDonald and Marie Agnes Haggerty; m. Sally Lou Kirkendall, Oct. 26, 1957; children: Katrina Louise Greenly, Linda Marie Bennett, Heidi Ann Bishop. AB, Harvard U., 1953, LLB, 1956, JD, 1957. Asst. to pres. W.R. Grace & Co., N.Y.C., 1956-65; pres. Paul McDonald & Co., N.Y.C., 1965-89; bd. dirs. several corps. Trustee St. Vincent's Hosp., N.Y.C., 1967-74, N.Y. Foundling Hosp., 1967-74, others. Home: 128 Cutler Rd Greenwich CT 06831-2511

**MCDONALD, SANDRA K.,** lawyer; b. Moscow, Idaho, Dec. 25, 1951; d. Ira Thomas and Betty Harrod (LaFaver) Myers; m. Gary L. McDonald, May 23, 1972 (div. May 1982); children: George R., Peter L., D. Alyssa, Seth R. BA in English, Brigham Young U., 1972; JD, U. Utah, 1995. Bar: Utah 1995; CPCU. With claims dept., claims dept. mgr. Preferred risk, Salt Lake City, 1981-96; sole practitioner Sandy, Utah, 1996—. General civil litigation, Insurance, Personal injury.

**MCDONALD, SCOTT K.,** lawyer; b. Dallas, Aug. 2, 1952; s. Charles G. and Jacqueline K. McDonald; m. Donna P. McDonald, Aug. 27, 1983; 1 child, L. Sedona. BA, So. Meth. U., 1973; JD, U. Tex., 1977. Bar: Tex., U.S. Dist. Ct. (no. dist.) Tex. Atty. Law Offices of F. Ward Steinbach, Dallas, 1977-79, Brice & Barron, Dallas, 1979-83, Denton & Guinan, Dallas, 1983-90, Bonnet Resources Corp., Dallas, 1990-92, Mankoff Hill Held Metzger, Dallas, 1992-97, Prager, Metzger & Kroemer, Dallas, 1998—. Real property. Home: 1535 Jewett Ln De Soto TX 75115-2755 Office: Prager Metzger & Kroemer PLLC 2626 Cole Ave Ste 900 Dallas TX 75204-4033

**MCDONALD, WILLIAM HENRY,** lawyer; b. Niangua, Mo., Feb. 27, 1946; s. Milburn and Fannie M. McDonald; m. Janice E. Robinson, July 13, 1968; children: Melissa L., Meghan M. BS in Pub. Adminstrn., Southwest Mo. State U., 1968; JD, U. Mo., 1971. Bar: Mo. 1971, U.S. Dist. Ct. (we. dist.) Mo. 1973, U.S. Supreme Ct. 1978, U.S. Ct. Appeals (8th cir.) 1982. Ptnr., pres. Woolsey, Fisher, Whiteaker & McDonald, PC, 1973-95; pres. William H. McDonald & Assocs., PC, Springfield, Mo., 1995—. Chmn. blue ribbon task force on Delivery of Mental Health Services to Southwest Mo., Mo. Commn. Continuing Legal Edn.; pres. Tan Oaks Homeowners Assn.; mem. fin. com. Child Adv. Council, Rep. Nat. Com., Mo. Rep. Com., Greene County Nat. Com.; active various Southwest Mo. State U. Clubs; bd. dirs. Greene County div. Am. Heart Assn., Ozarks regional Am. Athletic Union Jr. Olympics; pres., bd. dirs. Springfield Little Theatre; v.p. pub. affairs Springfield Area C. of C., bd. dirs., 1995-98. Capt. U.S. Army, 1971-73. Named one of Outstanding Young Men Am., 1978, 81, Outstanding Young Men Springfield, 1980. Fellow ABA (life, antitrust and litigation and torts and ins. sects.); mem. ATLA, Fed. Bar Assn., Mo. Bar Assn. (chmn. spol. com. on mandatory continuing edn., various coms., Pres.'s award 1986), Mo. Assn. Trial Attys. (bd. govs. 1998—), Springfield Met. Bar Assn. (bd. dirs., chmn. pub. edn. speakers bur.), Met. Bar Assn. St. Louis, Def. Rsch. Inst., Am. Judicature Soc., Am. Bd. Trial Advs. (state coord.), Nat. Bd. Trial Advs., 31st Jud. Cir. Bar Com. (chmn.), Supreme Ct. Hist. Soc., U. Mo.-Kansas City Sch. Law Found., Springfield Claims Assn. (pres.), Beta Omega Tau, Kappa Epsilon. Presbyterian. Federal civil litigation, State civil litigation, Personal injury. Home: 4857 E Royal Dr Springfield MO 65809-2425

**MCDONELL, NEIL EDWIN,** lawyer; b. Johnson City, N.Y., May 30, 1952; s. Alexander Edwin McDonell and Loretta Arlene Terry; m. Margaret Lynn Moline, June 18, 1978; children: Adam, Aaron. AB in Philosophy and English Lit., U. Mich., 1974; PhD in Philosphy, Harvard U., 1979; JD, Columbia U., 1983. Bar: N.Y. 1984. Asst. prof. philosophy Middlebury (Vt.) Coll., 1979-80; assoc. Battle Fowler, N.Y.C., 1983-89; assoc. Marks & Murase, N.Y.C., 1989-92, ptnr., 1992-96; ptnr. Dorsey & Whitney LLP, N.Y.C., 1996—. Editor-in-chief Columbia Jour. Tranational Law, 1982-83, bd. dirs., 1989—; contbr. articles to profl. jours. Mem. ABA (internat. and antitrust sects.), N.Y. State Bar Assn., Internat. Trade Commn. Trial Lawyers Assn., Harvard Club, Phi Beta Kappa. Avocations: genealogy, history. Private international, General civil litigation, Alternative dispute resolution. Office: Dorsey & Whitney LLP 250 Park Ave New York NY 10177-0001

**MCDONOUGH, JOSEPH RICHARD,** lawyer; b. Newark, July 7, 1950. BA, Middlebury Coll., 1972; JD, Rutgers U., 1978. Bar: N.J. 1978, U.S. Ct. Appeals (3d cir.) 1983, U.S. Supreme Ct. 1985. Law sec. appellate div. N.J. Superior Ct., 1978-79; assoc. Carpenter, Bennett & Morrissey, Newark; now ptnr. Graham, Curtin & Sheridan, Morristown. Pres. Delbarton Sch. Alumni Assn., Morristown, N.J., 1986-89. Recipient Outstanding Achievement in Oral Advocacy award Internat. Acad. Trial Lawyers, 1978. Fellow Am. Bar Found.; mem. ABA, N.J. State Bar Assn., Morris County Bar Assn. Federal civil litigation, State civil litigation. Office: Graham Curtin & Sheridan Four Headquarters Plz Morristown NJ 07960

**MCDONOUGH, PATRICK JOSEPH,** lawyer; b. Los Angeles, Oct. 11, 1943; s. Thomas John and Cecilia Veronica (Roach) McD.; m. Susan Ann Singletary, Dec. 30, 1967; 1 child, Colleen Marie. BA, Calif. State U., Northridge, 1967; JD, Loyola U., Los Angeles, 1971. Bar: Calif. 1971, U.S. Dist. Ct. (cen. dist.) Calif. 1971. Assoc. counsel. Auto Club So. Calif., Los Angeles, 1971-77, sec., assoc. counsel, 1977-86; sr. v.p., gen. counsel, prin. Johnson & Higgens Calif., Los Angeles, 1986-96; sr. v.p., Pacific region legal dept. mgr. J & H Marsh & McLennan, 1996-99; dir. Stirling Cook Brown Holdings, Ltd., Encino, Calif., 1999—. Active United Way Koko Challenge, 1993—; bd. visitors Loyola Law Sch., 1994—; mem. adv. bd. Georgetown U. Law Ctr. Corp. Counsel Inst., 1999—. Mem. ABA, Calif. State Bar Assn. (ins. law com. 1993-95, 97), L.A. Bar Assn. (chmn. corp. law sect. 1987-88, Outstanding Corp. Coun. 1992), Univ. of Calif. Law Ctr., Inst. of Corp Counsel (chmn. 1986-87, bd. govs. 1982—), Am. Corp. Counsel Assn. So. Calif. (bd. dirs. 1985-87), Assn. Calif. Tort Reform (bd. dirs. 1986—), L.A. Bar Found. (bd. dirs. 1993-94), Town Hall Calif. Roman Catholic. Avocations: boating, sailing, fishing. Fax #: (818) 342-9438. E-mail: pjmcdonough@earthlonk.net. Insurance, General corporate, Legislative. Office: 3906 Lake Vista Ct Encino CA 91316-4440

**MCDONOUGH, RUSSELL CHARLES,** retired state supreme court justice; b. Glendive, Mont., Dec. 7, 1924; s. Roy James and Elsie Marie (Johnson) McD.; m. Dora Jean Bidwell, Mar. 17, 1946; children: Ann Remmich, Michael, Kay Jensen, Kevin, Daniel, Mary Garfield. JD, George Washington U., 1949. Bar: Mont. 1950. Pvt. practice Glendive, Mont., 1950-83; judge Gen. Jurisdiction State of Montana, Glendive, 1983-87; justice Mont. Supreme Ct., Helena, 1987-93, ret., 1993. City atty. City of Glendive, 1953-57; county atty. Dawson County, Mon., 1957-63; del. Mont. Constl. Conv., Helena, 1972. 1st lt. AC, U.S. Army, 1943-45, ETO. Decorated DFC. Mem. Mont. Bar Assn. Roman Catholic. Home: PO Box 60 Circle MT 59215

**MCDONOUGH, SANDRA MARTIN,** lawyer, administrator; b. Albany, N.Y., Feb. 5, 1939; d. Stevens John and Louise Jane (Minshall) Martin; 1 child, Lora Elizabeth Couture. BA, U. State N.Y.-Regents Coll., Albany, 1979; JD, U. Bridgeport, 1982. Bar: Conn. 1982, U.S. Dist. Ct. 1983; lic. airline transport pilot, flight inst. Rsch. assoc. Yale U., New Haven, 1958-61; svc. rep. Conn. Blue Cross, New Haven, 1962-67; project dir. Bridgeport Hosp. (Conn.), 1967-68; dir. patient accounts Park City Hosp., Bridgeport, 1968-74; adminstr., pres. Med. Personnel Pool, Fairfield, Conn., 1975-90; sole practice, Fairfield and Stratford, 1982—. Adult advisor Safe Rides of Fairfield, 1984-86; N.E. region legal officer Civil Air Patrol, 1988-98. Mem. NTSB (founding mem., v.p. 1990—), Lawyer-Pilots Bar Assn., Conn. Trial Lawyers Assn. (exec. com. family law sect.), Regents Coll. Alumni Assn. (trustee Regents Coll. 1983-87), Mensa. Republican. Episcopalian. Aviation, Family and matrimonial, Real property. Office: 3333 Main St Stratford CT 06614-4820

**MCDOUGALL, GERALD DUANE,** lawyer; b. Hammond, Ind., Sept. 18, 1931; s. John and Carol Maxine (Lind) McD.; m. Ingrid Rosina Kempf, Jan. 26, 1960; children: Manfred, James. JD, Mercer U., 1971. Bar: U.S.V.I. 1972, Colo. 1973, Germany 1973, Tex. 1985. Atty. USVI Dept. Labor, St. Thomas, 1971-72; pvt. practice Denver, 1972-74, 76-84, Heilbronn, Neckar, Germany, 1974-76, Amarillo, Tex., 1985—. Precinct committeeman Rep. Ctrl. Com., Denver, 1978-84. Sgt. U.S. Army, 1951-54, ETO, 61-67, Vietnam. Mem. Nat. Assn. Criminal Defense Lawyers, Tex. Bar Assn., Tex. Criminal Defense Lawyers Assn., Amarillo Bar Assn., State Bar Coll. Criminal, State civil litigation, Government contracts and claims. Home: 7910 Merchant Dr Amarillo TX 79121-1028 Office: PO Box 50898 Amarillo TX 79159-0898

**MCDOUGALL, JOHN OLIN,** lawyer; b. Charleston, S.C., Apr. 8, 1944; s. Robert Franklin and Allene Virginia (Rodgers) McD.; m. Jodie Ann Parnell, May 1, 1992; children: Joseph Reilley, Johnston Calhoun; child from a previous marriage: John Olin II. B.A., Wofford Coll., 1967; J.D., U.S.C., 1971. Bar: S.C. 1971, U.S. dist. ct. S.C. 1973. Legal advisor S.C. Dept. Corrections, Columbia, 1971-72; pub. defender Richland County, Columbia, 1972-73; dir. pretrial intervention program, 1973; assoc. Walter W. Brooks, Columbia, 1973-74; assoc. Weinberg, Bryan, Warner & Brown, Sumter, S.C., 1974; ptnr. Weinberg, Bryan, Warner, Brown & McDougall, 1975-95, McDougall & SCIF, 1995—. Bd. dirs. Sumter County Housing Authority, 1981-85. Served with Army N.G., 1973-77. Fellow Am. Acad. Matrimonial Lawywrs (pres. S.C. chpt. 1991-93); mem. ABA, S.C. Bar Assn. (pres.), Am. Trial Lawyers Assn., S.C. Trial Lawyers Assn. (pres. 1993-94), Sumter County Bar Assn., Am. Coll. Family Trial Lawyers, S.C. Law Inst. Democrat. Baptist, Presbyterian. Club: Rotary, Elks. Family and matrimonial. Home: 6107 Marthas Glen Rd Columbia SC 29209-1312 Office: McDougall & SCIF PO Box 2197 Sumter SC 29151-2197

**MCDOWELL, DONNA SCHULTZ,** lawyer; b. Cin., Apr. 23, 1946; d. Robert Joseph and Harriet (Parronchi) Schultz; m. Dennis Lon McDowell, June 20, 1970; children: Dawn Megan, Donnelly Lon. BA in English with honors, Brandeis U., 1968; MEd, Am. U., 1972; CASE with honors, Johns Hopkins U., 1979; JD with honors, U. Md., 1982, MS, Hood Coll., 1995. Bar: Md. 1982. Instr., Anne Arundel & Prince George's C.C., Severna Park and Largo, Md., 1977-78; coll. adminstr. Bowie State Coll. (Md.), 1978-79; assoc. Miller & Bortner, Lanham, Md., 1982-83; sole practice, Lanham, 1983-87; Gaithersburg, Md. 1987—; ednl. cons. Chmn. Housing Hearing Com., Bowie, 1981-83; trustee Unitarian-Universalitst Ch., Silver Spring, Md., 1979-83; bd. dirs. New Ventures, Bowie, 1983, Second Mile (Runaway House), Hyattsville, Md., 1983; officer Greater Laytonsville Civic Assn., 1989—; founding mem. People to Preserve, Laytonsville; mem. Solid Waste Adv. Com., Montgomery County, Md.; election judge. Recipient Am. Jurisprudence award U. Md., 1981. Mem. Montgomery County Bar Assn., Prince George's Bar Assn., Phi Kappa Phi. Democrat. Avocations: gardening, reading, bluebirds, movies. General practice, Personal injury, State civil litigation. Home: 24308 Hipsley Mill Rd Gaithersburg MD 20882-3132 Office: PO Box 5205 Laytonsville MD 20882-0205

**MCDOWELL, KAREN ANN,** lawyer; b. Ruston, La., Oct. 4, 1945; d. Paul and Opal Elizabeth (Davis) Bauer; m. Gary Lee McDowell, Dec. 22, 1979. BA, N.E. La. U., 1967; JD, U. Mich., 1971; diploma, John Robert Powers Sch., Chgo., 1976, Nat. Inst. Trial Advocacy, 1990. Bar: Ill. 1973, Colo. 1977, U.S. Dist. Ct. (so. dist.) Ill. 1973, U.S. Dist. Ct. Colo. 1977. Reference libr. assoc. Ill. State Library, Springfield, 1972-73; asst. atty. gen. State of Ill., Springfield, 1973-75; pvt. practice Boulder, Colo., 1978-79, Denver, 1979—. Mem. So. Poverty Law Ctr. Mem. ABA, DAR, Am. Assn. Retired Persons, Amnesty Internat., Colo. Bar Assn. (com. alcohol and related problems), Denver Bar Assn., Colo. Women's Bar Assn. (editor newsletter 1982-84), Denver Zool. Found., Survivors United Network (legal c oord. 1992-93), Survivors United Network Profls. (exec. com. 1992), Mensa (local sect. Ann Arbor, Mich. 1968), Colonial Dames, Nat. Soc. Magna Carta Dames, Am. Inns of Ct., Minora Yasui Inn, Toastmasters Internat. (Able Toastmaster 1992), Toastmasters (Cherry Creek), Col. Order of Crown, Ams. Royal Descent, Sovereign Col. Soc., Phi Alpha Theta, Sigma Tau Delta, Alpha Lambda Delta. Avocations: philately, chess, needlework, dinosaurs, Horatio Alger stories. Family and matrimonial. Office: 1660 Lincoln St Ste 1550 Denver CO 80264-1502

**MCDOWELL, MARGARET HOLMES,** lawyer; b. Great Falls, Mont., Aug. 4, 1916; d. John J. and Kathryn (Gillespie) H.; children: Catherine Brooks, Maura Kealeg, John, Ann. JD, U. Mont., 1938, LLD (hon.), 1996. Atty. Nat. Labor Rels. Bd., Washington, 1938-43, War Labor Bd., Denver, 1943-45, Legal Aid Soc., N.Y.C., 1967-96, Family Law Ctr., N.Y.C., 1996-97. Recipient Disting. Alumni award U. Mont., 1994. Mem. Mont. Bar Assn., N.Y. State Bar Assn. (Dennison Ray award 1995), Assn. of Bar of City of N.Y. (Legal Svc. award 1990), N.Y. County Lawyers Assn. (Oliver Nelson Cromwell award 1991, Leonard Lerner Pro-Bono award 1997). Democrat. Avocation: oil painting.

**MCDOWELL, MICHAEL DAVID,** lawyer, utility executive; b. Lewisburg, Pa., May 10, 1948; s. David Leonard and Mary Ellen (Scallan) McD.; m. Martha LaMantia, Aug. 4, 1973; 1 child, Daniel Joseph. B.S. in Bus. Mgmt., U. Dayton, 1970; J.D., U. Pitts., 1973. Bar: Pa. 1973, U.S. Ct. Appeals (3d cir.) 1974, U.S. Dist. Ct. (we. dist.) Pa. 1975, U.S. Supreme Ct. 1977. Asst. U.S. atty. Dept. Justice, Lewisburg, Pa., 1973-75; assoc. Hirsch, Weise & Tillman, Pitts., 1975-76, Plowman & Spiegel, Pitts., 1976-80; counsel Dravo Corp., Pitts., 1980-86, sr. counsel, 1987; sr. atty. Allegheny Power Svc. Corp. (formerly West Penn Power Co.), Greensburg, Pa., 1987—; mem. panel of arbitrators Am. Arbitration Assn., 1978-94, Pa. Bur. Mediation, 1983—, Pa. Labor Relations Bd., 1985—. Contbr. articles to profl. jours. Mem. nat. panel consumer arbitrators Better Bus. Bur., 1986—; sr. arbitrator, 1989—. Recipient Dravo Corp. Editorial Achievement awards, 1982, 83, 85, 86; nominated as one of Outstanding Young Men Am., 1983, 84. Mem. ABA (Ho. of Dels. 1985-91, exec. coun. sect. labor and employment law 1983-85, exec. council young lawyers div. 1982-84, chmn. YLD Labor Law Com. 1981-83, fellow, 1985—), Pa. Bar Assn. (Ho. of Dels. 1980-94, chmn. special rules subcom. Disciplinary Bd. Study Com. 1983-93, com. on legal ethics and profl. responsibility, 1983—, arbitrator lawyer dispute resolution program 1987—, house com. on rules and calendar 1991-94, Outstanding Young Lawyer award 1984, Spl. Achievement award 1986, ), Allegheny County Bar Assn. (profl. ethics com. 1980-94, bd. govs. 1979, 85-91, asst. sec.-treas. 1979, chmn. young lawyers sect. 1978, council professionalism 1988-90, bylaws com. 1990—, award for outstanding leadership and valuable contbns. to bar 1979), Am. Corp. Counsel Assn., Phi Alpha Delta (justice 1972-73, cert. Outstanding Service 1973). Republican. Roman Catholic. Labor, General civil litigation, Public utilities. Office: Allegheny Power Svc Corp 800 Cabin Hill Dr Greensburg PA 15601-1689

**MCELDREW, JAMES JOSEPH, III,** lawyer; b. Phila., Sept. 14, 1957; s. James J. and Helen (Haberle) McE.; m. Deborah Anne McCullough, Mar. 23, 1985; children: Caitlin, Theresa Kelly, James, Michael. BS, Georgetown U., 1979; JD, Del. Law Sch., 1982. Bar: Pa., N.Y., U.S. Dist. Ct. (ea. dist.) Pa., U.S. Ct. of Appeals (3rd cir.), U.S. Supreme Ct., U.S. Dist. Ct. (so. dist.) N.Y., U.S. Ct. of Appeals (2d cir.). Assoc. McEldrew, Hanamirian et al, Phila., 1982-88; ptnr. Smith, McEldrew & Levenberg, Phila., 1988-95, McEldrew & Fullam, P.C., N.Y.C., 1996—; legal counsel Transport Worker's Union, Phila., 1983—, Local 2013, 2001, Phila., 1993—; settlement master Common Ct. of Pleas, Phila., 1994—; dir. Fed. Employers' Liability Act program Transport Workers Union RR Divsn., N.Y.C., 1994—; mem. hearing com. Pa. disciplinary Bd., 1995. Mem. ATLA, Phila. Trial Lawyers (bd. govs. 1995—), Pa. Trial Lawyers, Phila. Bar Assn. (fee dispute com. 1987—, edn. com. 1993—, VIP 1988—, bd. dirs. 1995-97, treas. 1997—). Roman Catholic. Avocations: tennis, golf, martial arts. Labor, Personal injury, Transportation. Office: McEldrew & Fullam PC 1650 Market St Fl 31A Philadelphia PA 19103-7325

**MC ELHANEY, JOHN HESS,** lawyer; b. Milw., Apr. 16, 1934; s. Lewis Keck and Sara Jane (Hess) McE.; m. Jacquelyn Masur, Aug. 4, 1962; children—Scott, Victoria. B.B.A., So. Meth. U., 1956, J.D., 1958. Bar: Tex. bar 1958. Pvt. practice law Dallas, 1958—; shareholder Locke Purnell Rain Harrell, 1976—; lectr. law So. Meth. U., 1967-76. Contbr. articles to legal jours. Trustee St. Mark's Sch. Tex., 1980-86. Fellow Am. Coll. Trial Lawyers; mem. Am. Bd. Trial Advs., ABA, Tex. Bar Assn., So. Meth. U. Law Alumni Assn. (pres. 1972-73, dir. 1970-73), Town and Gown Club (pres. 1981-82). Presbyterian. Federal civil litigation, General civil litigation, Libel. Home: 5340 Tanbark Dr Dallas TX 75229-5555 Office: Locke Liddell & Sapp 2200 Ross Ave Ste 2200 Dallas TX 75201-2748

**MCELLIGOTT, JAMES PATRICK, JR.,** lawyer; b. Chgo., Jan. 11, 1948; s. James Patrick and Helen Cecelia (Hogan) McE.; children: Michael Sean, Andrew David; m. Trina Reff, Aug. 25, 1985. BA, U. Ill., Urbana, 1970; JD, Harvard U., 1973. Bar: Va. 1974, U.S. Dist. Ct. (ea. and we. dists.) Va. 1974, U.S. Ct. Appeals (4th cir.) 1974, U.S. Supreme Ct. 1979. Research asst. U. Ill., 1970; assoc. McGuire, Woods & Battle, Richmond, 1973-79; ptnr. McGuire, Woods, Battle & Boothe, Richmond, 1979—. Mem. exec. com. Va. Home for Boys, Richmond, 1976—, pres. bd. govs., 1981-83; mem. Leadership Metro Richmond-Met. C. of C., 1984-85; bd. dirs. ARC Greater Richmond Chpt., 1990—, chmn., 1994-95. Mem. ABA, Va. Bar Assn. (exec. com., chmn. pub. rels. com. 1978-82, producer pub. svc. message 1973, Hot Spot award 1973), Richmond Bar Assn., Fed. Bar Assn. (pres. Richmond chpt. 1986), Nat. Sch. Bds. Assn., Coun. of Sch. Attys., Phi Beta Kappa, Phi Kappa Phi, Omicron Delta Epsilon. Federal civil litigation, Labor, Pension, profit-sharing, and employee benefits. Home: 203 Cyril Ln Richmond VA 23229-7740 Office: McGuire Woods Battle & Boothe One James Ctr Richmond VA 23219-3229

**MCELROY, DAVID CARLETON,** retired lawyer; b. Balt., Feb. 6, 1931; s. James Ramsey and Flora Lee (Monette) McE.; m. Dorothy Ellen Siegrist, Dec. 24, 1954. Student, Brown U., 1948-52; JD, U. Balt., 1960. Bar: Md. 1961. Br. mgr., asst. sec. Baltimore Fed. Savs. and Loan, Columbia, Md., 1968-73, asst. v.p., 1974-76, v.p., atty., 1976-86; atty. First Nat. Bank Md., Glenburnie, Md., 1986-95, ret., 1995; mem. legis. ref. com. Savings and Loan, Balt., 1968-86, former chmn. Chmn. bd. trustees First Christian Ch., Balt. Lt. j.g. USNR, 1953-57, Korea. Mem Kiwanis Club (Kiwanian of Yr. 1977-78, Outstanding Svc. award 1977-78; fiscal officer 1977-81, treas. 1981-85). Republican. Avocations: drawing, painting, traveling. Banking, Real property. Home: 10049 Carrigan Dr Ellicott City MD 21042-3619

**MCELROY, HOWARD CHOWNING,** lawyer; b. Shreveport, La., Mar. 26, 1946; s. Charles Imogene and Verna Mae (Snow) McE.; m. Heidi Margot Hansen, June 17, 1970; children: Andrew, Christopher, Karen. BS, U.S. Mil. Acad., 1968; JD, Georgetown U., 1977. Bar: Va. 1977, U.S. Dist. Ct. (we. dist. eas. dist.) Va. 1977, U.S. Ct. Appeals (4th cir.) 1977. Ptnr. White, Bundy, McElroy, Hodges & Sargent, Abingdon, Va., 1995—; mem. mandatory continuing legal edn. bd. Va. State Bar 1986-89, professionalism course faculty, 1991-94. Capt. M.I. U.S. Army, 1968-73, Vietnam. Mem. ABA, Am. Bd. Trial Advocates (Va. chpt.), Def. Rsch. Inst., Va. Bar Assn. (exec. com. 1991-95, sec. 1993-95), Va. Assn. Def. Attys. (pres. 1995-96), Internat. Assn. Def. Counsel, Assn. Def. Trial Attys., Rotary (pres. local club 1983-84). Episcopalian. Federal civil litigation, State civil litigation, Insurance. Home: 160 Crestview Dr NE Abingdon VA 24210-2010 Office: White Bundy McElroy & Hodges 330 Cummings St Abingdon VA 24210-3208

**MCELROY, MICHAEL ROBERT,** lawyer; b. Providence, Feb. 7, 1951; s. Gerald Robert and Jeannette (Belanger) McE.; m. Christine Anne O'Donnell, June 5, 1976; children: Brian Robert, Dianne Elizabeth, Erin Christine. BA with highest distinction, U. R.I., 1973; JD cum laude, Boston U., 1976; MS in Taxation cum laude, Bryant Coll., 1987. Bar: Tenn. 1976, U.S. Dist. Ct. (ea. dist.) Tenn. 1977, U.S. Ct. Appeals (5th cir.) 1977, U.S. Supreme Ct. 1979, U.S. Ct. Appeals (6th cir.) 1980, R.I. 1981, U.S. Dist. Ct. R.I. 1981, U.S. Ct. Appeals (1st cir.) 1981, Mass. 1985. Trial atty. TVA, Knoxville, 1976-81; counsel R.I. Pub. Utilities Commn., Providence, 1982-83; spl. asst. atty. gen. Office Atty. Gen., Providence, 1982-83; ptnr. O'Leary & McElroy, Providence, 1981-85; sole practice Providence, 1985-87; ptnr. Schacht & McElroy, Providence, 1987—; pres. Utility Cons., Inc., Providence, 1983; ptnr. McElroy, Lawrence, Edge & Assocs., Providence, 1983-85. Legal counsel for candidate Congl. campaign, Providence, 1982; legal counsel Pawtuxet Valley Preservation and Hist. Soc., West Warwick, R.I., 1983—; chief speech writer for candidate gubernatorial campaign, R.I., 1984; chief legal counsel for candidate gubernatorial campaign, R.I., 1988, Gov. Bruce Sundlun's successful gubernatorial campaign, 1990; legal counsel to R.I. Pers. Appeal Bd., 1991—; arbitrator Superior Ct. R.I., 1992—; spl. master/commr., 1993—; mediator Superior Ct., 1999—. Danforth Found. hon. fellow, 1973; Rhodes scholar nominee, 1973; honoree for life-saving CPR, TVA, 1980; nominated for judgeship Jud. Nom. Commn. Superior Ct., 1994. Mem. ATLA, Assn. Trial Lawyers R.I., R.I. Bar Assn., R.I. Fed. Ct. and Superior Ct. Bench/Bar Coms., Million Dollar Advs. Forum. Democrat. Roman Catholic. General civil litigation, Personal injury, General practice. Home: 345 Sharon St Providence RI 02908-2220 Office: PO Box 6721 Providence RI 02940-6721

**MCELVEIN, THOMAS IRVING, JR.,** lawyer; b. Buffalo, N.Y., Apr. 19, 1936; s. Thomas I. and Edith Marian (Bowen) McE.; m. Ernesta F. McElvein, June 26, 1965; children: Christopher, Andrew, Kathryn. BA, Antioch Coll., 1959; JD, Yale U., 1962. Bar: N.Y. 1962, U.S. Dist. Ct. (we. dist.) N.Y. 1969. Atty. Village Akron, N.Y., 1993—. Mem. N.Y. State Bar Assn., Erie County Bar Assn. General corporate, Estate planning, Municipal (including bonds). Home: 295 Nottingham Ter Buffalo NY 14216-3125 Office: 1500 Liberty Bldg Buffalo NY 14202-3612

**MC ELWAIN, LESTER STAFFORD,** lawyer; b. San Mateo, Calif., Jan. 1, 1910; s. George Walter and Ethel (Dickson) McE.; m. Loretta F. Barksdale, July 12, 1977; children from previous marriage: Roderick, Malcolm, Douglas. BA, Stanford U., 1931, JD, 1934. Bar: Calif. 1934, U.S. Supreme Ct. 1955. Assoc. Donahue, Richards & Hamlin, Oakland, Calif., 1934-41; pvt. practice, Oakland, 1946—. Past pres. Alameda County Rep. Assembly. With USN, 1941-46, to comdr. USNR. Mem. ABA, Calif. Bar Assn., Alameda County Bar Assn., Assn. Trial Lawyers Am., Am. Arbitration Assn., Ret. Officers Assn. (past pres.), Phi Alpha Delta, Phi Sigma Kappa, Jr. C. of C. (state v.p. 1940). Clubs: Athenian-Nile. Lodges: Kiwanis (past lt. gov.), Masons (33d degree, past grand master), Elks. Family and matrimonial, Personal injury, Probate. Home: 14333 Saratoga Ave Apt 2 Saratoga CA 95070-5939 Office: 436 14th St Oakland CA 94612-2703

**MCELWEE, DENNIS JOHN,** lawyer, former pharmaceutical company executive; b. New Orleans, July 30, 1947; s. John Joseph and Audrey (Nunez) McE. BS, Tulane U., 1970; JD, U. Denver, 1992. Clean room and quality control analyst Sci. Enterprises Inc., Broomfield, Colo., 1975-76; analytical chemist in toxicology Poisonlab. Inc., Denver, 1977; analytical chemist, then dir. quality control program Colo. Sch. Mines Rsch. Inst., 1977-79; dir. quality control, then dir. compliance Benedict Nuclear Pharms. Co., Golden, Colo., 1979-84; pres. MC Projections Inc., Morrison, Colo., 1985-86; dir. regulatoroy affairs Electromedics Inc., Englewood, Colo., 1986-89; pvt. practice, 1992—. Author: Mineral Research Chemicals, Toxic Properties and Proper Handling, 2d edit., 1979; mem. editl. bd. CF Network Mag.; contbr. articles to profl. jours. Bd. dirs. Denver chpt. Cystic Fibrosis Found., 1996, Assn. of Vols. for Children's Hosp., Denver, 1999. Recipient Sutton prize in internat. law U. Denver Sch. Law, 1991. Mem. Colo. Bar Assn., Colo. Criminal Def. Bar, Denver Bar Assn., 1st Jud. Dist. Bar Assn. Office: 2009 Wadsworth Blvd Ste 200 Lakewood CO 80215-2031

**MCELYEA, MONICA SERGENT,** lawyer; b. Pennington Gap, Va., Jan. 15, 1967; d. Birg Eugene and Lana Kay (Turner) Sergent; m. Jeffrey Earl McElyea, Dec. 16, 1994. BA, Randolph-Macon Woman's Coll., Lynchburg, Va., 1988; JD, Mercer U., 1991. Bar: Ga. and Va. 1991, Tenn. 1993, U.S. Dist. Ct. (no. dist.) Ga. 1991, U.S. Dist. Ct. (we. dist.) Va. 1992, U.S. Dist. Ct. (ea. dist.) Va. 1995, U.S. Ct. Appeals (4th cir.) 1992, U.S. Supreme Ct. 1995, Colo. 1997. Law clerk U.S. Magistrate Judge Cynthia D. Kinser, Abingdon, Va., 1991-92; assoc. atty. Birg & Sergent Atty. at Law, Pennington Gap, Va., 1992-93; asst. Commonwealth's atty. Lee County, Jonesville, Va., 1993-94; pvt. practice Pennington Gap, Va., 1993-94; asst. atty. gen. Office of Atty. Gen., Richmond, Va., 1994-97; assoc. Law Offices David A. Helmer, Frisco, Colo., 1997—. Methodist. Criminal, General civil litigation, Personal injury. Office: Law Offices David A Helmer PO Box 868 611 Main St Frisco CO 80443

**MCEVERS, DUFF STEVEN,** lawyer; b. L.A., Apr. 21, 1954; s. Milton Stoddard and Virginia Mary (Tongue) McE.; m. Jeannine Marie Matthews, July 14, 1984; children: Tay Colleen, Reily Maureen. BA, U. So. Calif., 1976; JD, Western State U., 1980. Bar: Calif. 1981, U.S. Dist. Ct. (so. dist.)

Calif. 1993, U.S. Dist. Ct. (ctrl. dist.) Calif. 1982, U.S. Ct. Appeals (9th cir.) 1988. Assoc. Donald B. Black Inc., Laguna Beach, Calif., 1981-85; pvt. practice Laguna Beach and Newport Beach, Calif., 1985-88, Assoc. Law Office of Terry J. Coniglio, Inc., Long Beach, Calif., 1988-89; with Barclay Law Corp., 1989-91; pvt. practice Newport Beach and Sonoma, Calif., 1992—; of counsel Walker Law Firm, P.C., Newport Beach, Calif., 1992—. Editor: Law Review, 1979. Mem. Calif. Bar Assn., Assn. Bus. Trial Lawyers, St. Timothy's Men's Club. State civil litigation, Real property, Private international. Office: 1301 Dove St Ste 450 Newport Beach CA 92660-2474

**MCEVILLY, JAMES PATRICK, JR.,** lawyer; b. Phila., July 30, 1943; s. James P. and Virginia Frances (Madden) McE.; m. Joan Elizabeth O'Connor; children: James III, Christopher (dec.), Sara, Michael. BS, St. Joseph's U., 1965; JD, Temple U., 1971. Bar: Pa. 1971, U.S. Dist. Ct. (ea. dist.) Pa. 1972, U.S. Ct. Appeals (3d cir.) 1975, U.S. Supreme Ct. 1982. Law clk to president judge Phila. Mcpl. Ct., 1971-73; assoc. Galfand, Berger, Lurie & March, Phila., 1973-76; asst. dist. atty. Phila. Dist. Atty., 1976-79; prin. McEvilly & Assocs., Feasterville, Pa., 1979—. Editor Temple U. Law Rev., 1971. Mem. Pa. Trial Lawyers Assn., Phila. Bar Assn., Trial Lawyers Am. Personal injury, Criminal, General practice. Home: 1401 Silo Rd Yardley PA 19067-4240 Office: McEvilly & Assocs 1200 Bustleton Pike Ste 1B Trevose PA 19053-4108

**MCEVILY, DANIEL VINCENT SEAN,** lawyer, author; b. N.Y.C., June 25, 1944; s. Patrick Vincent and Margaret Dolores (Hawley) McE.; m. Adele Carroll Daly, Sept. 1, 1973 (div. Nov. 1986); 1 child, Kathleen Kerry. BS in Fgn. Svc., Georgetown U., 1966; JD, Cath. U., 1972. Bar: D.C. 1973, Tex. 1994, U.S. Supreme Ct. 1976. Assoc., ptnr. Hamilton and Hamilton, Washington, 1973-81; ptnr. Foley & McEvily, Washington, 1981-89, Alexander & McEvily, Houston, 1991—. Author: Anthem for No Nation, 1989, A Tangled Woven Web, 1990. Capt. USMC, 1966-69, Viet Nam. Decorated 13 personal and unit decorations USMC, 1967. Mem. Am. Legion (post #1 Paris, counsel 1990—). Roman Catholic. Avocations: sculling, rugby, fox hunting. Antitrust, General civil litigation, Education and schools. Address: Alexander & Associates 700 Louisiana St Fl 37 Houston TX 77002-2700

**MCEVOY, SHARLENE ANN,** law educator; b. Derby, Conn., July 6, 1950; d. Peter Henry Jr. and Madaline Elizabeth (McCabe) McE. BA magna cum laude, Albertus Magnus Coll., 1972; JD, U. Conn., West Hartford, 1975; MA, Trinity Coll., Hartford, 1980, UCLA, 1982; PhD, UCLA, 1985. Bar: Conn., 1975. Pvt. practice Derby, 1984—; asst. prof. bus. law Fairfield (Conn.) U. Sch. Bus., 1986—; adj. prof. bus. law, polit. sci. Albertus Magnus Coll., New Haven, Conn., 1978-80, U. Conn., Stamford, 1984-86; acting chmn. polit. sci. dept. Albertus Magnus Coll., 1980; assoc. prof. law Fairfield U., 1992-98, prof. bus. law, 1998—; Chmn. Women's Resource Ctr., Fairfield U., 1989-91. Staff editor Jour. Legal Studies Edn., 1989-94; reviewer Am. Bus. Law Assn. jour., 1988—, staff editor, 1995—; sr. articles editor N.E. Jour. of Legal Studies in Bus., 1995-96. Mem. Derby Tercentennial Commn., 1973-74; bd. dirs. Valley Transit Dist., Derby, 1975-77, Justice of Peace, City of Derby, 1975-83; alt. mem. Parks and Recreation Commn., Woodbury, 1995-99; mem., treas. Woodbury Dem. Town Com., 1995-96, corr. sec. 1996-98. Recipient Best Paper award N.E. Regional Bus. Law Assn., 1990, Best Paper award Tri-State Regional Bus. Law Assn., 1991; Fairfield U. Sch. Bus. rsch. grantee 1989, 91, 92, Fairfield U. rsch. grantee, 1994. Mem. ABA, Conn. Bar Assn., Acad. Legal Studies in Bus., Mensa (coord. SINISTRAL spl. interest group 1977—). Democrat. Roman Catholic. Avocations: running, chess, tennis, swimming. Office: 198 Emmett Ave Derby CT 06418-1258

**MCFADDEN, FRANK HAMPTON,** lawyer, business executive, former judge; b. Oxford, Miss., Nov. 20, 1925; s. John Angus and Ruby (Roy) McF.; m. Jane Porter Nabers, Sept. 30, 1960; children—Frank Hampton, Angus Nabers, Jane Porter. B.A., U. Miss., 1950; LL.B., Yale U., 1955. Bar: N.Y. 1956, Ala. 1959. Assoc. firm Lord, Day & Lord, N.Y.C., 1955-58; assoc. firm Bradley, Arant, Rose & White, Birmingham, Ala., 1958-63, partner, 1963-69; judge U.S. Dist. Ct. No. Dist. Ala., Birmingham, 1969-73; chief judge U.S. Dist. Ct. No. Dist. Ala., 1973-81; sr. v.p., gen. counsel Blount, Inc., Montgomery, Ala., 1982-91, exec. v.p. adminstrn. and govt. affairs, 1991, exec. v.p. legal affairs, 1991-93, exec. v.p., gen. counsel, 1993-95; mem. Capell & Howard, P.C., Montgomery, 1995—; chmn. Blount Energy Resource Corp., Montgomery, 1983-88. Mem. jud. panel CPR Inst. for Dispute Resolution, 1985—. Served from ensign to lt. USNR, 1944-49, 51-53. Fellow Am. Coll. Constrn. Lawyers; mem. Am. Corp. Counsel Assn. (bd. dirs. 1984-93, chmn. 1989). General civil litigation, Construction, Alternative dispute resolution. Office: Capell & Howard PC 57 Adams Ave Montgomery AL 36104-4001

**MCFADDEN, HELEN TYLER,** lawyer; b. Kingstree, S.C., Oct. 7, 1950; d. Jackson E. and Marianna Tyler McFadden. BA, Agnes Scott Coll., 1971; MEd, U. S.C., 1974, JD, 1982. Bar: S.C., U.S. Dist. Ct. S.C., U.S. Ct. Appeals (4th cir.), U.S. Supreme Ct. Tchr. Williamsburg County, Kingstree, S.C., 1971-74, Berkeley County, Moncks Corner, S.C., 1974-79; atty. S.C. Senate, Columbia, 1982-84, 1982-85; with S.C. Procurement Rev., Columbia, 1984-87; atty. House Judiciary, Columbia, 1985-86, Bridges & Orr, Florence, S.C., 1986-90, Jenkinson & Jenkinson, Kingstree, S.C., 1990-95, Jebaily & Glass, Kingstree, 1995-96; pvt. practice Kingstree, S.C., 1996—. Parliamentarian S.C. Edn. Assn., Columbia, 1979—, S.C. Dem. Party, 1986—, S.C. Credit Union League, 1986-98, Nat. Dem. Party, Washington, 1996—; dir. Pee Dee Edn. Fedn., Florence, 1988—. Personal injury, Workers' compensation, General practice. Office: 411 Martin Luther King Ave Kingstree SC 29556-4016

**MCFADDEN, MONICA ELIZABETH,** lawyer. BS, Cornell U., 1973; MA, Mich. State U., 1976; JD, U. Chgo., 1993. Bar: Ill. 1993, U.S. Dist. Ct. (no. dist.) Ill. 1993. Campaign mgr. Iowa ERA, Des Moines, 1979-80; dep. campaign mgr. Conlin for Gov., Des Moines, 1980-82; message coord. Cranston for Pres., Washington, 1982-84; dir. polit. programs Nat. Women's Polit. Caucus, Washington, 1984-86; dir. govt. rels. Bus. and Profl. Women USA, Washington, 1987-89; sr. staff U.S. Bipartisan Com. on Health Care, Washington, 1989-90; clk. Hofeld & Schaffner, Chgo., 1990-93, assoc., 1993-96; prin. McFadden Law Offices, Chgo., 1996—; prin. McFadden Consulting, Washington and Chgo., 1984—. Contbr. articles to profl. jours. Fellow AAUW, Washington, 1992; named Outstanding Young Woman of Am. Mem. ATLA (com. chair 1993—, sect. officer employment sect. 1997—), Ill. Trial Lawyers Assn., Ill. State Bar Assn. (sect. rep. 1996—), Women's Bar Assn. Personal injury, Civil rights, General civil litigation. Office: McFadden Law Offices 140 S Dearborn St Ste 815 Chicago IL 60603-5202

**MCFADDEN, NANCY ELIZABETH,** lawyer; b. Wilmington, Del., Oct. 20, 1958; d. William P. and Mary Elizabeth (Adams) McF. BA, San Jose State U., 1984; JD, U. Va., 1987. Judicial clk. Hon. John P. Wiese U.S. Claims Ct., Washington, 1987-88; atty. O'Melveny & Myers, Washington, 1988-91; deputy communications dir. Office of Pres.-Elect, Washington, 1992-93; asst. ti atty. gen. U.S. Dept. Justice, Washington, 1993, prin. deputy assoc. atty. gen., 1993-95; gen. counsel Dept. Transp., Washington, 1996—. Nat. deputy polit. dir. Clinton for Pres. Campaign, 1992, nat. surrogate dir. Clinton-Gore for Fres. Campaign, 1992.

**MCFALL, JAMES ALAN,** lawyer; b. Washington, Sept. 3, 1958; s. Eugene Harrison and Elizabeth Ann (Green) McF.; m. Karen Lynn Chance, Dec. 9, 1988; children: Kyle, Caitlin, Guy. BA, U. Calif., San Diego, 1981; JD, U. Calif., Hastings, 1985. Bar: Calif. 1985, U.S. Ct. Appeals (9th cir.), U.S. Dist. Ct. (so. and ea. dists.) Calif. Shareholder Neil, Dymott, Perkins Brown & Frank, San Diego, 1986—. Mem. Assn. So. Calif. Defense Counsel, San Diego Defense Lawyers, San Diego County Bar Assn., Def. Rsch. Inst. Republican. Roman Catholic. Appellate, Insurance, Toxic tort. Office: Neil Dymott Perkins Brown & Frank 1010 2nd Ave Ste 2500 San Diego CA 92101-4906

**MCFALL, SARA WEER,** lawyer; b. Balt., Oct. 17, 1953; d. James Edward and Anna Mary (Gumpert) Weer. BFA, U. Hawaii, 1989; JD, U. Okla., 1992. Bar: Okla. 1992, U.S. Dist. Ct. (we. dist.) Okla. 1992. Legal intern Okla. County Pub. Defender, Oklahoma City, 1990-92; assoc. Talley & Perrine, Norman, Okla., 1993-95, Rodney D. Watson & Assoc., Norman, 1995-97; pvt. practice Norman, 1997—. Mem. Okla. Bar, Cleve. County Bar, Okla. Criminal Def. Lawyers Assn., Order of Barristers. Criminal, Family and matrimonial, Personal injury. Office: 216 E Eufaula St Norman OK 73069-6019

**MCFARLAND, CAROL ANNE,** lawyer; b. Eugene, Oreg., Aug. 25, 1951; d. Harvey John and Muriel Anne (Walker) McF.; children: Annette Catherine, Miles Patrick. BS, Oreg. State U., 1973; JD, Western State U., 1977. Bar: Calif. 1977, U.S. Dist. Ct. (so. dist.) Calif. 1977. Assoc. Sankary & Sankary, San Diego, 1977-81; pvt. practice San Diego, 1981-88; dep. dist. atty. Family Support divsn., Clackamas County, Oreg., 1990—. Vol. atty. Supervision Ctr. Women's Studies-Clinic Domestic Violence Restraining Orders, 1983—, San Diego Vol. Lawyers Assn., 1986—. Mem. ABA, Calif. Bar Assn., Oreg. State Bar Assn., Clackamas County Bar Assn., Rotary, Delta Theta Phi. Family and matrimonial, General practice, Probate. Office: 812 7th St Oregon City OR 97045-2324

**MCFARLAND, KAY ELEANOR,** state supreme court chief justice; b. Coffeyville, Kans., July 20, 1935; d. Kenneth W. and Margaret E. (Thrall) McF. BA magna cum laude, Washburn U., Topeka, 1957, JD, 1964. Bar: Kans. 1964. Sole practice Topeka, 1964-71; probate and juvenile judge Shawnee County, Topeka, 1971-73; dist. judge Topeka, 1973-77; assoc. justice Kans. Supreme Ct., 1977-95, chief justice, 1995—. Mem. Kans. Bar Assn., Women Attys. Assn. Topeka. Office: Kans Supreme Ct Kans Jud Ctr 301 W 10th St Topeka KS 66612

**MCFARLAND, MATTHEW GABRIEL,** lawyer; b. Sturgis, Mich., Oct. 31, 1969; s. Thomas Dalton and Beverly Ann McFarland; m. Catherine Marie Osbaugh, Aug. 12, 1995; children: Tyler Christian, Jackson Ryan. BA, U. Colo., 1992; JD, U. Denver, 1995. Bar: Colo. 1995, U.S. Dist. Ct. Colo. 1995, U.S. Ct. Appeals (10th cir.) 1995, U.S. Dist. Ct. Ariz. 1997. Assoc. Hopper and Kanouff, P.C., Denver, 1995-96, McKenna & Cuneo, LLP, Denver, 1996—. Mem. ABA, Colo. State Bar Assn., Denver Bar Assn. Federal civil litigation, State civil litigation, Construction. Office: McKenna and Cuneo LLP 370 17th St Ste 4800 Denver CO 80202-5648

**MCFARLAND, ROBERT EDWIN,** lawyer; b. St. Louis, July 25, 1946; s. Francis Taylor and Kathryne (Stephens) McF.; m. Jeannine M. Ghekiere, Feb. 26, 1982. BA, U. Mich., 1968, JD, 1971. Bar: Mich. 1971, U.S. Dist. Ct. (ea. dist.) Mich. 1971, U.S. Ct. Appeals (6th cir.) 1974, U.S. Supreme Ct. 1975, U.S. Ct. Appeals (D.C. cir.) 1978. Law clk. to chief judge Mich. Ct. Appeals, 1971-72; assoc. William B. Elmer, St. Clair Shores, Mich., 1972-74, James Elsman, Birmingham, Mich., 1974-75; ptnr. McFarland, Schmier, Stoneman & Singer, Troy, Mich., 1975-77; sr. ptnr. McFarland & Bullard, Bloomfield Hills, Mich., 1977-90, McFarland & Niemer, Farmington Hills, Mich., 1990-91; shareholder Foster, Swift, Collins & Smith, P.C., Farmington Hills, 1992—, mem. exec. com., 1995—. Chmn. bd. govs. Transp. Law Jour., U. Denver Coll. Law, 1981-83. Mem. bd. control Intercollegiate Athletics, U. Mich., 1966-68; mem. rulemaking study com. Mich. Pub. Svc. Commn., 1983-84, Motor Carrier Adv. Bd., 1984-88. Capt. USAR, 1971-80. Mem. ABA, Transp. Lawyers Assn. (officer 1998—, Disting. Svc. awad 1997), Assn. Transp. Law, Logistics and Policy, State Bar Mich. (vice-chmn. transp. law com. adminstrn. law sect. 1990—, sect. coun. adminstrv. law sect. 1994—), Am. Judicature Soc. Administrative and regulatory, Labor, Transportation.

**MCFARLANE, WALTER ALEXANDER,** lawyer, educator; b. Richlands, Va., May 4, 1940; s. James Albert and Frances Mae (Padbury) McF.; m. Judith Louise Copenhaver, Aug. 31, 1962. BA, Emory and Henry Coll., 1962; JD, U. Richmond, 1966. Bar: Va. 1966, U.S. Supreme Ct. 1970, U.S. Ct. Appeals (4th cir.) 1973, U.S. Ct. Appeals (D.C. cir.) 1977, U.S. Dist. Ct. (ea. dist.) Va. 1973. Asst. atty. gen. Office Va. Atty. Gen., Richmond, 1969-73, dep. atty. gen., 1973-90; exec. asst., chief counsel, dir. policy Gov.'s Office Commonwealth of Va., 1990-94, supt. Dept. Correctional Edn., 1994—; acting dir. Dept. Juvenile Justice, 1997; prof. adj. staff U. Richmond, 1978—; chmn. transp. law com. Transp. Rsch. Bd., Nat. Rsch. Bd. Nat. Acads. Sci. and Engring., Washington, 1977-85, 88-94, chmn. legal affairs com., 1978-85, chmn. environ., archeological and hist. com., 1985-90; mem. State Water Commn., 1994-96, mem., State Counc. of Govts. Henry Toll Fell., 1988; Legal Task Force, 1988—. Contbr. articles to profl. jours. Mem. exec. com., bd. govs. Emory and Henry Coll., 1985-98; pres. Windsor Forest Civic Assn., Midlothian, Va., 1975-76; bd. dirs. Greater Midlothian Civic League, 1981-86, v.p., 1980; instr. water safety ARC, 1962-87; chmn. bldg. com. Mt. Pisgah United Meth. Ch., 1980-85, pres. men's club, 1980-81; bd. dirs. cen. Va. chpt. Epilepsy Assn. Va., 1988-91, Woodland Pond Civic Assn., 1988-89; mem. State Criminal Justice Svcs. Bd., 1994—. Capt. JAGC, USAF, 1966-69. Recipient J.D. Buscher Disting. Atty. award Am. Assn. State Hwy. and Transp. Ofcls., 1983, John C. Vance legal writing award Nat. Acads. Sci. and Engring., 4th ann. outstanding evening lectr. award Student Body U., Richmond, 1980; Henry Toll fellowship State Coun. of Govts., 1988. Mem. Chesterfield Bar Assn., Richmond Bar Assn. (bd. dirs. 1989-93), Richmond Scottish Soc. (bd. dirs. 1980-82), Emory and Henry Coll. Alumni Assn. (chpt. pres. 1971-73, regional v.p. 1974-77, pres. 1981-83), Meadowbrook Country Club. Home: 9001 Widgeon Way Chesterfield VA 23838-5274 Office: 101 N 14th St Richmond VA 23219-3684

**MCFARLEN, GERALD DALE,** lawyer; b. Corpus Christi, Tex., Aug. 15, 1951; s. Julian Detroy and Dorothy (Fuller) McF.; ;m. Jane Ann Wrede, July 4, 1976; children: Christopher Joel, Sarah Catherine. BA in Govt., U. Tex., 1975; JD, U. Houston, 1981. Bar: Tex. 1981, U.S. Dist Ct. (so. dist.) Tex. 1982, U.S. Dist. Ct. (we. dist.) Tex. 1990, U.S. Dist. Ct. (no. dist.) Tex. 1992, U.S. Ct. Appeals (5th cir.) 1993. Briefing atty. 13th Ct. Appeals, Corpus Christi, Tex., 1981-83; assoc. Porter, Rogers, Dahlman & Gordon, Corpus Christi, 1983-84, Law Offices Robert Patterson, Corpus Christi, 1984=86, Brin & Brin P.C., San Antonio, Tex., 1986-90; shareholder Brin & Brin P.C., San Antonio, 1990—. Episcopalian. Avocations: sailing, golf. General civil litigation, Insurance, Personal injury. Office: Brin & Brin 8200 W Ih 10 Ste 610 San Antonio TX 78230-3848 Address: 28 Fabra Oaks Rd Boerne TX 78006-7901

**MCFERRIN, JAMES HAMIL,** lawyer; b. Mobile, Ala., July 26, 1960. BS in Criminal Justice, U. Ala., 1982; JD, Cumberland Sch. of Law, 1987. Bar: Ala. 1987, U.S. Dist. Ct. (no. dist.) Ala. 1987. Pvt. practice, Birmingham, Ala., 1987—; legal dir. Behavioral Health Systems, Birmingham, 1991—, Risk Reduction, Inc., Birmingham, 1991—; mem. task force Birmingham Area C. of C., 1992; mem. task force on utilization rev. State of Ala.; cons., com. chair Ala. Supreme Ct. Author: Informed Consent: A New Standard For Proximate Cause, 1987; rsch. editor Cumberland Law Rev. Recipient Dean's scholarschip Cumberland Law Sch., 1984-87, Book awards Am. Jurisprudence, 1984-87. Mem. Am. Trial Lawyers Assn. (state capt. worker's compensation), Nat. Employment Assn., Ala. Bar Assn., Ala. Trial Lawyers Assn., Birmingham C. of C. Health, General civil litigation, Workers' compensation.

**MCFETRIDGE, JOHN DAVID,** lawyer; b. Regina, Saskatch., Can., Oct. 1, 1950; came to U.S., 1952; s. James Gordon and Mary Joan (Newton) McF.; m. Bernadette Catherine Bahen, June 5, 1976; children: Katherine Marie, Michael James. AA, Black Hawk Jr. Coll., Moline, Ill., 1973; BA, Augustana Coll., 1975; JD, U. Ill., 1978. Bar: Ill 1978, U.S. Dist. Ct. (ctrl. dist.) Ill. 1979, U.S. Ct. Appeals (7th cir.) 1991. Assoc. Lawrence Johnson and Assocs., Champaign, Ill., 1978-83; 1st asst. Vermilion County Pub. Defender, Danville, Ill., 1983-88; assoc. Manion, Janov & Devens, Danville, 1988-90; ptnr. Manion, Devens & McFetridge, Ltd., Danville, 1990—; instr. Roosevelt U., Danville, 1992-93. Bd. dirs. Vermilion County Mental Health Bd., Danville, 1994—. With U.S. Army, 1968-71. General practice, Criminal, Personal injury. Office: Manion Devens & McFetridge Ltd 24 E North St Danville IL 61832-5804

**MCGAFFEY, JERE D.,** lawyer; b. Lincoln, Nebr., Oct. 6, 1935; s. Don Larsen and Doris (Lanning) McG.; m. Ruth S. Michelsen, Aug. 19, 1956; children: Beth, Karen. BA, BSc with high distinction, U. Nebr., 1957; LLB magna cum laude, Harvard U., 1961. Bar: Wis. 1961. Mem. firm Foley & Lardner, Milw., 1961—, ptnr., 1968—; dir. Wis. Gas Co., Smith Investment Co., WICOR. Author works in field. Chmn. bd. dirs. Helen Bader Found.; former chmn. bd. dirs. Aurora Health Care; vice chmn. legis. Milw. Met. Assn. Commerce; former chmn. Wis. Taxpayers Alliance, sec., treas., 1994—; mem. bd. visitors U. Wis. Med. Sch., Madison; chmn. bd. advisors U. Wis. Nursing Sch., Milw. Mem. ABA (chmn. tax sect. 1990-91, ho. dels. 1995—), AICPA, Wis. Bar Assn., Wis. Inst. CPA's, Am. Coll. Tax Counsel (chmn. 1996-98, regent), Am. Coll. Trust and Estate Counsel (chmn. bus. planning com. 1994-97), Am. Law Inst., Univ. Club, Milw. Club, Milw. Country Club, Harvard Club N.Y.C., Univ. Club Washington, Phi Beta Kappa, Beta Gamma Sigma, Delta Sigma Rho. Corporate taxation, Estate taxation, General corporate. Home: 12852 NW Shoreland Dr Thiensville WI 53097-2304 Office: Foley & Lardner 777 E Wisconsin Ave Ste 3600 Milwaukee WI 53202-5302

**MCGAHREN, RICHARD GEORGE,** lawyer; b. Bayonne, N.J., June 18, 1928; s. Eugene Dewey and Cecelia (Paulsen) McG.; m. Marjorie J. Waterhouse, Jan. 29, 1994; stepchildren: Lawrence Waterhouse III, Kevin Waterhouse, Patrick Waterhouse, Christine Waterhouse Krizman, Jennifer Waterhouse Pacchiana. AB, Columbia U., 1952, LLB, 1959. Bar: N.Y. 1960, U.S. Dist. Ct. (so. and ea. dists.) N.Y. 1961, U.S. Ct. Appeals (2nd cir.) 1962. Assoc. LeBoeuf Lamb Leiby & MacRae, N.Y.C., 1960-71; ptnr. D'Amato Costello & Shea, N.Y.C., 1971-78; founding ptnr. D'Amato & Lynch, N.Y.C., 1978-94, counsel, 1994—. With U.S. Army, 1946-47. Mem. ABA. Avocations: skiing, sailing. Federal civil litigation, General civil litigation, State civil litigation. Office: D'Amato & Lynch 70 Pine St Fl 41 New York NY 10270-0110

**MCGAIR, JOSEPH J.,** lawyer; b. Panama City, Fla., Mar. 25, 1945; s. William J. McGair and Rita M. Kenney; m. Mary Jane McGair, June 6, 1970; children: Charles J., Melanie J. BA, Providence Coll., 1967; JD, Suffolk U., 1970. Bar: R.I., U.S. Dist. Ct. R.I., U.S. Ct. Appeals (1st cir.), U.S. Supreme Ct., U.S. Bankruptcy Ct. City prosecutor City of Warwick; pres. Petrarca and McGair Inc., Warwick, 1972—. Mem. Warwick City Coun., 1977-84, pres. pro tem, vice chair fin. com., chair spl. legislation com., chair properties com.; mem. R.I. State Senate, 1991-95, first dep. majority leader, chair senate informational caucus, vice chair, jud. reform com., state investment commn.; baseball coach Warwick Police Athletic League, Am. Little League; coach, sponsor Warwick Fire Fighters Soccer Assn.; sec., legal advisor Warwick Housing Devel. Corp.; bd. dirs. Prevent Blindness, Foster Grandparents, Ken County Vis. Nurses, Warwick Ctrl. Geriatric Assn., Warwick Arts Found., Conimicut Village Assn.; vice chair Channel One; chmn. bd. Justice Assistance; bd. incorporators Warwick Boys and Girls Club, Kent County Meml. Hosp.; adv. bd. Ctrl. Adult Day Care and Cornerstone; founder, legal advisor Ctrl. R.I. Devel. Corp.; legal advisor Warwick Civic Chorale; advisor Forever Friends. Mem. Rotary Club, Conimicut Village Assn., Warwick Arts Found., Warwick Elks Club, Warwick Coun. K.C., R.I. State Coun. K.C. (asst. advocate, legal advisor). General civil litigation, General practice. Office: Petrarca and McGair Inc 797 Bald Hill Rd Warwick RI 02886-0714

**MCGARRY, CHARLES WILLIAM,** lawyer; b. Mt. Kisco, N.Y., June 23, 1957; m. Lori J. Voss. BA in Philosophy, SUNY, Binghamton, 1979; JD, U. Tex., 1982. Bar: Tex. 1983. Law clk. Atty. Gen. of Tex., Austin, 1980-82; briefing atty. Tex. Ct. of Appeals, Dallas, 1982-83; pvt. practice Dallas, 1984-93, 95—; chief justice Tex. Ct. Appeals, Dallas, 1993-94; mediator Dallas County Juvenile Dept., 1984-93; arbitrator Better Bus. Bur., Dallas, 1985-93. Editor: Aviation Litigation, 1986. Chmn. Irving (Tex.) Dems., 1987-91; pres. Dallas Jazz Orch., 1990-92. Mem. Tex. Bar Assn., Dallas Bar Assn., Irving Bar Assn. Democrat. Roman Catholic. Federal civil litigation, Entertainment. Home: 612 Brookhaven Dr Irving TX 75061-7949 Office: 900 Jackson St Ste 600 Dallas TX 75202-4425

**MCGARRY, RICHARD LAWRENCE,** lawyer; b. Flushing, N.Y., Jan. 12, 1960; s. Richard J. and Loretta (McCarthy) McG.; m. Lynda R. Jones, Dec. 21, 1987; children: Abraham A. Eichelberger, Chelsea M. Eichelberger, David B. Eichelberger. BS, Hampden Sydney Coll., 1982; JD, Washington and Lee U., 1989. Bar: Va. 1989, U.S. Dist. Ct. (we. dist.) Va., U.S. Supreme Ct., 1993. Assoc. Jeffrey H. Krasnow and Assocs., Roanoke, Va., 1989-93; ptnr. Johnson & McGarry, P.C., Charlottesville, Va., 1993-94; pvt. practice Roanoke, 1994—; bd. dirs. Roanoke Valley SPCA. Mem. Va. Trial Lawyers Assn., Assn. Trial Lawyers Am., Roanoke Bar Assn., Va. Bar Assn. Personal injury, Product liability, General civil litigation. Office: 302 Washington Ave SW Roanoke VA 24016-4312

**MCGARVEY, JACK F(RANCIS),** lawyer; b. Balt., Sept. 20, 1940; s. Francis James and Catherine Elizabeth (Doyle) McG.; m. April Russell, Feb. 9, 1993; children: Michelle, Patrick. JD, U. Balt., 1967. Bar: Md. 1974, U.S. Dist. Ct. Md. 1975, U.S. Ct. Appeals (4th cir.) 1983. mem. atty. grievance commn. inquiry panel, State of Md., 1994—. Bd. dirs. Richcroft, Inc., Hunt Valley, Md., 1986—. Mem. Baltimore County Bar Assn. (alt. dispute resolution com. 1994-97), Trial Table Law Club, Elks (presiding justice 1985-96). Republican. Roman Catholic. Avocation: golf. Health, General civil litigation, Administrative and regulatory. Office: Blue Cross/Blue Shield of Md Tower II Suite 700 100 S Charles St Baltimore MD 21201-2725

**MCGAUKIAN, RACHEL THEORA,** lawyer; b. Silver Spring, Md., Mar. 28, 1968; d. Paul Ambrose and Eileen Sarah McG.; m. David Joseph Brendel, Nov. 11, 1995. BA, Johns Hopkins U., 1990; JD, U. Balt., 1993. Bar: Md., U.S. Dist. Ct. Md., U.S. Dist. Ct. D.C., U.S. Ct. Appeals (5th cir.), U.S. Supreme Ct. Law clk. U.S. Dist. Ct. Md., Balt., 1993-94; assoc. Ecclestan & Wolf, Balt., 1994-96, Miles & Stockbridge, Rockville, Md., 1996—. Mem. Md. State Bar Assn. (sect. coun.). Democrat. Avocations: field hockey, skiing, travel. General civil litigation, Insurance. Office: Miles & Stockbridge 22 W Jefferson St Rockville MD 20850-4215

**MCGEADY, PAUL JOSEPH,** lawyer; b. Jersey City, Nov. 12, 1920. BS, St. Peters Coll., 1942; LLD, Fordham U., 1948. Bar: N.Y. 1949, U.S. Supreme Ct. 1988, D.C. Circuit Ct. 1989. Asst. v.p., counsel Continental Corp., N.Y.C., 1950-78; gen. counsel Morality in Media, N.Y.C., 1978—; dir. Nat. Obscenity Law Ctr., N.Y.C., 1978—. Author: Rise and Fall of the ACA, 1972, ABC Statutes and Regulations, 1977; editor (book) Obscenity Law Reporter, 1986. Bd. dirs. Morality in Media, Inc., 1987—. Served to 1st lt. USAAF, 1943-45, MTO. Decorated Air medal, Knight of Holy Sepulchre. Republican. Roman Catholic. Lodge: KC. Criminal, Legislative. Office: Morality in Media Inc 475 Riverside Dr Ste 239 New York NY 10115-0056

**MCGEE, JAMES FRANCIS,** lawyer; b. N.Y.C., Sept. 19, 1950; s. James F. and Elizabeth J. (Mooney) M.; m. Annamarie Saunders, Feb. 13, 1988; children: James, Brooke Nicole. BS, U. Penn., 1972; JD, Western State U., Fullerton, Calif., 1980. Bar: Calif. 1980. Founder McGee & Assocs., Newport Beach, Calif., 1980—. Chmn. Laguna Beach Bd. Adjustment, 1985-87, Laguna Beach Architecture Review Bd., 1985-87; pres. Junior All Am. Football, 1997; pres. Pelican Hill Cmty. Assn., 1995-97; pres. Newport Coast Cmty. Assn., 1997; chief Indian Guides Chumash Tribe, 1996-97; chief Newport Beach-Costa Mesa YMCA Indian Guides Dolphin Nation, 1997. Recipient 20-30 Internat. So. Calif. Man of Yr., 1985. Mem. ABA, ATLA, Calif. Bar Assn., Orange County Bar Assn., Calif. Trial Lawyers Assn., Orange County Trial Lawyers Assn. Avocations: sports, flying, public speaking. Real property, Construction, Environmental. Office: 23 Corp Plaza Ste 230 Newport Beach CA 92660

**MCGEE, JOHN PAUL, JR.,** lawyer; b. Portsmouth, N.H., Feb. 21, 1950; s. John P. and Louise (Flynn) McG.; m. Diane O'Leary, Aug. 19, 1972. BA, Yale U., 1972; JD, William and Mary Coll., 1975. Bar: N.H. 1975, U.S. Dist. Ct. N.H. 1975. Assoc. Flynn, McGuirk & Blanchard, Portsmouth, N.H., 1975-83; ptnr. Flynn & McGee, Portsmouth, 1984-85, Flynn, McGee & Sanderson, Portsmouth, 1986-91; pvt. practice Flynn & McGee, P.A., Portsmouth, 1991—; proprietor, sec. Portsmouth Athenaeum, 1985-92, v.p., 1992—. Ward moderator, Portsmouth, 1985-89; chmn. Portsmouth Rep. City Com., 1985-87; chmn. N.H. Labor Bd. Appeal, 1978-79; instr. St. Catherine's Religious Edn. Program, 1977-93. Mem. Elks (presiding justice 1982-86). Republican. Roman Catholic. Avocations: reading, archaeology, history. General practice. Office: Flynn & McGee PA 222 Court St Portsmouth NH 03801-4416

**MCGEE, P. SCOTT,** lawyer; b. Bayreuth, Germany, Nov. 16, 1947; s. Palmer Scott and Elizabeth (Replogle) McG.; m. Catherine Conner, June 8,

1969; children: Conner, Ross. BA, Amherst Coll., 1970; JD, Cath. U., Washington, 1975. Bar: Vt. 1975, U.S. Dist. Ct. Vt. 1975, U.S. Ct. Appeals (2d cir.) 1981. Atty. Lamoille County State's Atty., Hyde Park, Vt., 1976-80; asst. U.S. atty. U.S. Attys. Office, Burlington, Vt., 1980-84; ptnr. Hershenson Carter Scott & McGee, Norwich, Vt., 1984—; mem. adv. com. criminal rules Supreme Ct. Vt., 1977-80, 90-94, chair, 1994—. Mem. ABA, Vt. Bar Assn. (vice-chair profl. responsibility com. 1981—), Windsor County Bar Assn., Vt. Trial Lawyers Assn. General civil litigation, Family and matrimonial, Criminal. Office: Hershenson Carter Scott & McGee PO Box 909 Norwich VT 05055-0909

**MCGEOUGH, ROBERT SAUNDERS,** lawyer; b. Aug. 30, 1930; s. Edward James and Florence Isabelle (Saunders) McG.; m. Janet James, Nov. 24, 1961; children: Maureen, Michael, Molly. AB, Duke U., 1952; JD, U. Mich., 1959. Assoc. Hoppe, Frey, Hewitt & Milligan, Warren, Ohio, 1965-70, ptnr., 1970-98; of counsel Harrington, Hoppe & Mitchell, Warren, Ohio, 1999—; dir. First Fed. Savs. and Loan Assn., Warren; state trustee Jaycees, Warren, 1963; pres. Warren Exchange Club, 1965; pres. Children's Rehab. Ctr. Found., Warren, 1979, trustee, 1983—. Editor Lawyer's Desk Book, 1978, 98. Recipient award of merit Ohio Legal Ctr. Inst., 1978. Mem. Ohio State Bar Assn., Trumbull County Bar Assn. Republican. Avocation: golf. Banking, Contracts commercial, General corporate. Home: 3264 Crescent Dr NE Warren OH 44483-6306 Office: Harrington Hoppe & Mitchel Ltd 108 Main Ave SW Ste 500 Warren OH 44481-1010

**MC GIFFERT, DAVID ELIOT,** lawyer, former government official; b. Boston, June 27, 1926; s. Arthur Cushman and Elizabeth (Eliot) McG.; m. Enud De Kibedi-Varga, Jan. 21, 1966; children: Laura, Carola.; m. Nelse Greenway, Apr. 9, 1983. Student, U. Calif.-Berkeley, 1944; B.A., Harvard U., 1949, LL.B., 1953; postgrad., Cambridge (Eng.) U., 1950. Bar: D.C. 1954. With firm Covington & Burling, Washington, 1953-55, 57-61; ptnr. Covington & Burling, 1969-77, 81—; lectr. law U. Wis., 1956; asst. to sec. def. for legis. affairs Dept. Def., 1962-65, undersec. army, 1965-69, asst. sec. for internat. security affairs, 1977-81. Served with USNR, 1944-46. Mem. Am. Bar Assn., Council Fgn. Relations, Alpha Delta Phi. Club: Metropolitan (Washington). Home: 3819 Veazey St NW Washington DC 20016-2230 Office: Covington & Burling PO Box 7566 1201 Pensylvania Ave NW Washington DC 20044-7566

**MCGILL, GILBERT WILLIAM,** lawyer; b. Glen Cove, N.Y., Mar. 28, 1947. BS, L.I. U., 1972; JD, Hofstra U., 1975. Bar: N.Y. 1975, U.S. Dist. Ct. 1976, U.S. Supreme Ct. 1979. Sole practice Huntington, N.Y., 1975-76; ptnr. Dunne & McGill, Huntington and Sea Cliff, N.Y., 1976-81; sole practice, 1981—. Mem. citizens adv. com. North Shore Schs., Glen Head, N.Y., 1977-79, mem. local waterfront revitalization com. Town of Oyster Bay, 1988—; chmn. legal adv. com. Sea Cliff Civic Assn., 1978-79; adv. com. North Shore Republican Club, Glen Head, 1979-81; trsutee Sea Cliff Village Libr., 1980-86; trustee Angelo J. Melillo Ctr. for Mental Health, 1986—, pres., 1986—. Mem. ABA, N.Y. State Bar Assn., Nassau County Bar Assn., Nassau County Lawyers Assn., North Shore Lawyers Assn. (chmn. 1977-78), Sea Cliff Bus. Assn. (pres. 1979-85), Rotary (pres. Glen Head 1983-84, 97—). General practice. Office: 203 Glen Cove Ave Sea Cliff NY 11579-1437

**MCGILL-MEMBRINO, DEBORAH LYNN,** lawyer; b. Waterbury, Conn., May 23, 1955; d. Hugh John and Helen (Alishauskas) McGill; 1 child, Hugh John. BA in Econs./Sociology summa cum laude, Marymount Coll., 1977; JD, Western New Eng. Sch. of Law, 1980. Bar: Conn. 1981, D.C. 1983. Pvt. practice Waterbury, Conn., 1982—. Mem. Wolcott (Conn.) Town Coun., 1980-82; magistrate Waterbury Ct. System, 1994; mem. alumni bd. Cheshire (Conn.) Acad., 1993. Waterbury Bar scholar, 1979. Mem. ABA, ATLA, Waterbury Bar Assn. (med.-legal com. 1993, 94, co-chair women in law sect. 1993-98, scholarship com. 1996-98, com. mem. 1996—, personal injury law com. 1997), Conn. Trial Lawyers. Avocations: gardening, swimming, skiing, softball, writing. Office: 571 Wolcott St Waterbury CT 06705-1310

**MCGINLEY, JAMES DUFF,** lawyer; b. Pasadena, Calif., Apr. 8, 1959; m. Maribeth Walton McGinley, Apr. 28, 1984. BA, Calif. State U., Long Beach, 1981; JD, Pepperdine U., 1991. Bar: Calif. 1992, U.S. Dist. Ct. (ctrl. and ea. dists.) Calif. 1992. Assoc. Sedgwick, Detert, Moran & Arnold, L.A., 1990-94; ptnr. Hiepler & Hiepler, Oxnard, Calif., 1994—; chmn. Mealey's Publ. HMO Liability Conf. Contbr. articles to Pepperdine Law Rev. Civil Justice Program leader Leadership Glendale, Calif., 1997. Lt. col. USMCR, 1981—. Decorated USN and USMC Commendation medal, 1998. Mem. Ventura County Bar Assn., Pepperdine U. Alumni Assn. (pres. 1997-99), Million Dollar Advocates Forum (Achievements award). General civil litigation, Health, Product liability. Office: Hiepler & Hiepler 500 Esplanade Dr Ste 1550 Oxnard CA 93030-0576

**MCGINLEY, JOHN REGIS, JR.,** lawyer; b. Pitts., Nov. 26, 1943; s. John R. and Marie E. (Rooney) McG.; m. Nancy Carey, Aug. 15, 1968; children: John, Cathleen, Mary. BS, St. Bonaventure U., 1965; JD, Duquesne U., 1968. Bar: Pa. 1968, U.S. Dist. Ct. (we. dist.) Pa. 1968, U.S. Ct. Appeals (3d cir.) 1973, U.S. Supreme Ct. 1983. Asst. dist. atty. Allegheny County, Pa., 1968-70; assoc. Duff Grogan & Doyle and Duff, Grogan Graffam, Pitts., 1970-71; chmn. Grogan, Graffam, McGinley & Lucchino, Pitts., 1971—; mem. disciplinary bd. Pa. Supreme Ct.; mem., chmn. Pa. Ind. Regulatory Rev. Commn. Contbr. articles to legal jours.; contbr. to Duquesne U. Law Rev., 1968. Trustee, chmn. Mercy Hosp. Found.; trustee St. Bonaventure U., mem. exec. com.; bd. dirs. Easter Seals Soc. of Allegheny County, 1981-88. Fellow Am. Coll. Trial Lawyers; mem. ABA, Pa. Bar Assn., Allegheny County Bar Assn., Acad. Trial Lawyers, Duquesne U. Law Alumni (pres. 1998). Democrat. Roman Catholic. Federal civil litigation, State civil litigation. Office: 22nd Flr Three Gateway Center Pittsburgh PA 15222

**MCGINLEY, NANCY ELIZABETH,** lawyer; b. Columbia, Mo., Feb. 29, 1952; d. Robert Joseph and Ruth Evangeline (Garnett) McG. BA with high honors, U. Tex., 1974, JD, 1977. Bar: Tex. 1977, U.S. Dist. Ct. (no. dist.) Tex. 1979. Law clk. U.S. Dist. Ct. (no. dist.) Tex., Fort Worth, 1977-79; assoc. Crumley, Murphy and Shrull, Fort Worth, 1979-81; staff atty. SEC, Fort Worth, 1981-87, br. chief, Houston, 1990-92, sr. counsel, Washington, 1992—. Mem. editorial staff Urban Law Rev. Mem. Mortar Bd., Phi Beta Kappa, Phi Kappa Phi, Alpha Lambda Delta. Methodist. Home: 1505 Crystal Dr Apt 908 Arlington VA 22202-4171

**MCGINLEY, PAUL ANTHONY, JR.,** lawyer; b. Allentown, Pa., Apr. 24, 1948; s. Paul A. Sr. and Mary (McGurl) McG.; m. Deborah C. Reinhart; children: Paige, Laura, Paul Anthony III, Jonathan. AB, Princeton U., 1970; JD, Georgetown U., 1974. Bar: Pa. 1974, U.S. Dist. Ct. (ea. dist.) Pa. 1974, U.S. Supreme Ct. 1987. Assoc. Gross & Brown, Allentown, 1974-76; asst. pub. defender Lehigh County, Allentown, 1976-77, asst. county solicitor, 1977-78; ptnr. Gross, McGinley & McGinley, Allentown, 1976-83, Gross, McGinley, McGinley & LaBarre, Allentown, 1983-86, Gross, McGinley & LaBarre, Allentown, 1986-87, Gross, McGinley, LaBarre & Eaton, Allentown, 1987—; mem. legal affairs com. Mag. Pubs. Am., 1994—; chmn. hearing com. disciplinary bd. Supreme Ct. of Pa., 1986-90, 97—. Bd. dirs. Swain Sch., Allentown, 1984-89, Cedar Crest Coll. Bd. Assocs., Allentown, 1986-88; trustee Allentown YWCA, 1985-88. Mem. ABA, Pa. Bar Assn., Lehigh County Bar Assn. (bd. dirs. 1978-84, pres. 1987), Pa. Trial Lawyers Assn., Allentown-Lehigh County C. of C., Princeton Quadrangle Club (bd. dirs.), Velodrome Fund (dir., sec. 1995—), Rodale Inst. (dir. 1998—), Rodale Inc. (asst. sec. 1999—). Democrat. Roman Catholic. Avocations: skiing, tennis. Federal civil litigation, General corporate, Real property. Office: Gross McGinley LaBarre & Eaton 33 S 7th St Allentown PA 18101-2436

**MCGINN, BARBARA ANN,** lawyer; b. Phila., June 17, 1962; d. Joseph F. and Helen E. McGinn; m. Alan D. Haight, Aug. 13, 1988; children: Lillian M., Russ M. Haight. BA summa cum laude, Pa. State U., 1984; MS, U. Wis., 1988; JD, Cornell U., 1996. Bar: Ohio 1997. Assoc. Eastman & Smith Ltd., Toledo, 1996—. Contbr. chpts. to book. Mem. ABA, Ohio State Bar Assn., Wood County Bar Assn., Toledo Bar Assn., Cornell Law Assn., Phi Beta Kappa. Environmental, Administrative and regulatory, Land use and zoning (including planning). Office: Eastman & Smith Ltd One Seagate 24th Fl PO Box 10032 Toledo OH 43699-0032

**MCGINN, MAX DANIEL,** lawyer; b. Lexington, N.C., July 30, 1942; s. Max Terry and Ethel Mae (Peck) McG.; m. Judith Eaton McBee, June3, 1965; children: Brian, Tracie. BA magna cum laude, Wake Forest U., 1964, JD cum laude, 1967. Bar: U.S. Dist. Ct. (mid. dist.) N.C. 1971, U.S. Supreme Ct. 1977, U.S. Ct. Appeals (4th cir.) 1976, U.S. Dist. Ct. (we. and ea dists.) N.C. 1979. Atty. NLRB, Winston-Salem, N.C., 1967, 1970; ptnr. Brooks, Pierce, McLendon, Humphrey & Leonard, Greensboro, N.C., 1971—. Lt., atty. Judge Adv. Gen.'s Corps, USN, 1967-70. Fellow Am. Coll. of Trial Lawyers; mem. ABA, N.C. Bar Assn. (chmn. Labor and Employment Law sect. 1989). Presbyterian. Avocations: tennis, sports, reading. Labor, Federal civil litigation, Civil rights. Home: 3008 Redford Dr Greensboro NC 27408-3116 Office: Brooks Pierce McLendon Humphrey & Leonard 230 N Elm St Greensboro NC 27401-2436

**MCGINNIS, THOMAS MICHAEL,** lawyer; b. Royal Oak, Mich., July 13, 1954; s. Donald Edward Sr. and Maryjane Carney (Jex) McG.; m. Tracy Chris, Mar. 4, 1993. BA, Regis U., 1976; JD, Thomas M. Cooley Sch. Law, 1980. Bar: Mich. 1981, U.S. Dist. Ct. (ea. dist.) Mich. 1981, U.S. Ct. Appeals 1984. Assoc. Wilson, Portnoy & Leader, 1980-83; pvt. practice Troy, Mich., 1983—; chairperson Lawyer Referral Svc., Pontiac, Mich., 1985-86. Mem. Soc. Irish/Am. Lawyers. Avocations: water skiing, snow skiing, guitar. Criminal, Family and matrimonial, Probate. Office: 802 E Big Beaver Rd Troy MI 48083-1404

**MCGINTY, BRIAN DONALD,** lawyer, author; b. June 22, 1937; s. Donald Bruce and Natalia Vellejo (Haraszthy) M. AB, U. Calif., Berkeley, 1959, JD, 1962. Bar: Calif. 1963. Assoc. Twohig, Weingarten & Haas, Seaside, Calif., 1962-63; ptnr. Weingarten & McGinty, Seaside, Calif., 1963-70; sole practice Monterey, Calif., 1970-73, San Francisco, 1973-83; writer, editor Matthew Bender & Co., San Francisco, Oakland, Calif., 1984-93. Author: Haraszthy at the Mint (Famous Calif. Trials Series), 1975, The Palace Inns, 1978, We the People, 1987, Strong Wine: The Life and Legend of Agoston Haraszthy, 1998; contbg. author: The Craft of the Essay, Historical Times Illustrated Encyclopedia of the Civil War, Portrait of America, 5th edit., 1990, California Real Estate Law and Practice, California Forms of Pleading and Practice, California Legal Forms, California Insurance Law, California Probate Law and Practice, California Public Agency Law and Practice, California Wills and Trusts; editor: Napa Wine (Rounce and Coffin Club award 1975), 1974; contbr. numerous articles to profl. jours. Recipient Excellence in Writing award Nat. Hist. Soc., 1976, Editor's award for Hist. Scholarship, Sonoma County Hist. Soc., 1999. Mem. Calif. Hist. Soc. Real property, Estate planning.

**MCGINTY, ELIZABETH CARYL,** lawyer; b. Brooklyn, N.Y., Dec. 13, 1941; d. Matthew Brennan and Caryl Elizabeth Cleary; m. James Patrick McGinty, Mar. 6, 1965; children: Caryl Elizabth, Allison Sara (dec.). BA, Notre Dame of Md., 1963; JD, St. John's U., 1968. Assoc. Davoli, McMahon & Kublick, Syracuse, N.Y., 1983-90; ptnr. McMahon, Kublick, McGinty & Smith, PC, Syracuse, N.Y., 1990—. Mem. jud. screening com. U.S. Senator Charles Schumer, N.Y.C., 1999—. Mem. N.Y. State Bar Assn., N.Y. State Trial Lawyers Assn., Onondaga County Bar Assn., Central N.Y. Women's Bar Assn. Democrat. Roman Catholic. Avocations: reading, gourmet cooking, painting. General civil litigation, Personal injury, Land use and zoning (including planning). Office: McMahon Kublick McGinty Smith PC 500 S Salina St Syracuse NY 13202-3311

**MCGIVERIN, ARTHUR A.,** state supreme court chief justice; b. Iowa City, Iowa, Nov. 10, 1928; s. Joseph J. and Mary B. McG.; m. Mary Joan McGiverin, Apr. 20, 1951; children: Teresa, Thomas, Bruce, Nancy. BSC with high honors, U. Iowa, 1951, JD, 1956. Bar: Iowa 1956. Pvt. practice law Ottumwa, Iowa, 1956; alt. mcpl. judge Ottumwa, 1960-65; judge Iowa Dist. Ct. 8th Jud. Dist., 1965-78; assoc. justice Iowa Supreme Ct., Des Moines, 1978-87, chief justice, 1987—. Mem. Iowa Supreme Ct. Commn. on Continuing Legal Edn., 1975. Served to 1st lt. U.S. Army, 1946-48, 51-53. Mem. Iowa State Bar Assn., Am. Law Inst. Roman Catholic. Avocation: golf. Office: Iowa Supreme Ct State Capital Bldg Des Moines IA 50319-0001*

**MCGLAMRY, MAX REGINALD,** lawyer; b. Wilcox County, Ga., Sept. 12, 1928; s. Edgar Lee and Allie Bea (Faircloth) McG.; m. Jean Louise Hilyer, Dec. 28, 1950; children: Sharon Kay McGlamry Hendrix, Michael Lee. BS, Auburn U., 1948; LLB cum laude, Mercer U., 1952, JD cum laude, 1970. Bar: Ga. 1953, U.S. Dist. Ct. (mid. dist.) Ga. 1954, U.S. Ct. Appeals (5th cir.) 1964, U.S. Supreme Ct. 1972, U.S. Ct. Appeals (11th cir.) 1981, U.S. Ct. Appeals (4th cir.) 1985, U.S. Dist. Ct. (no. dist.) Calif. 1988, U.S. Dist. Ct. (no. dist.) Ga. 1989. Pvt. practice Columbus, Ga., 1953-64; from ptnr. to officer Swift, Pease, Davidson & Chapman (name changed to Page, Scrantom, Harris, McGlamry, & Chapman, P.C.), Columbus, 1964-85; ptnr. Pope, Kellogg, McGlamry, Kilpatrick & Morrison, Columbus, 1985-90, Pope, McGlamry, Kilpatrick & Morrison, LLP, Columbus, 1990—. Mem. exec. com. Muscogee County Dem. Orgn., Columbus, 1956-60; bd. dirs. Columbus Jr. C. of C. Ens. USN, 1948-49. Am. Coll. Trust & Estate Counsel fellow, 1973, Lawyers Found. Ga. fellow, 1983. Mem. ABA, ATLA, State Bar Ga., Ga. Trial Lawyers Assn., Assn. U.S. Army, Ga. Golfers Sr. Assn., Metro Columbus Urban League, Inc., Columbus Lawyers Club (pres. 1964-65), Lions (Columbus chpt. pres. 1967-68), Chattahoochee River Club, Green Island Country Club, Phi Kappa Phi, Alpha Epsilon Delta, Phi Alpha Delta, Pi Kappa Alpha. Democrat. Methodist. Avocations: golf, fishing. General civil litigation, Personal injury, Product liability. Home: 6941 Wethersfield Rd Columbus GA 31904-3317 Office: Pope McGlamry Kilpatrick & Morrison LLP PO Box 2128 2d Fl 318 11th St Columbus GA 31902-2128

**MCGLONE, MICHAEL ANTHONY,** lawyer; b. New Orleans, Jan. 6, 1951; s. James Godfrey and Dorothy (Barta) McG.; m. Suzanne Blanchard, Nov. 27, 1976; children: Kevin, Kathleen, Meghan. BBA cum laude, Loyola U., New Orleans, 1972, JD, 1975. Bar: La. 1975, U.S. Dist. Ct. (ea. dist.) La. 1975, U.S. Ct. Appeals (5th and 11 cirs.) 1975, U.S. Dist. Ct. (we. dist.) La. 1978, U.S. Dist. Ct. (mid. dist.) La. 1979, U.S. Supreme Ct. 1981. Law clk. to Hon. Herbert W. Christenberry U.S. Dist. Ct., New Orleans, 1975-76; ptnr. Lemle and Kelleher, New Orleans, 1976—. Mem. ABA, ALA, FBA (bd. dirs. New Orleans chpt. 1986—, pres. 1995-96), La. Bar Assn., Southeastern Admiralty Law Inst., New Orleans Bar Assn., Maritime Law Assn., St. Thomas More Inn of Ct. (master barrister), Alpha Sigma Nu, Beta Gamma Sigma. Democrat. Roman Catholic. Admiralty, Federal civil litigation, Personal injury. Home: 4708 N Turnbull Dr Metairie LA 70002-1447 Office: Lemle and Kelleher 601 Poydras St New Orleans LA 70130-6029

**MCGLYNN, JOSEPH LEO, JR.,** federal judge; b. Phila., Feb. 13, 1925; s. Joseph Leo and Margaret Loretta (Ryan) McG.; m. Jocelyn M. Gates, Aug. 26, 1950; children: Jocelyn, Leo, Timothy, Suzanne, Alisa, Deirdre, Caroline, Elizabeth, Meghan, Brendan. B.S., Mt. St. Mary's Coll., 1948; LL.B., U. Pa., 1951. Bar: Pa. 1952. Asst. U.S. atty. Phila., 1953-60, 1st asst., 1957-60; assoc., then ptnr. Blank Rudenko Klaus & Rome, Phila., 1960-65; judge County Ct. of Phila., 1965-68, Ct. of Common Pleas, 1st Jud. Dist. of Pa., 1968-74; judge U.S. Dist. Ct. (ea. dist.) Pa., Phila., 1974-90, sr. judge, 1990—; mem. County Bd. Law Examiners, 1961-65, adv. com. bankurptcy rules U.S. Judicial Conf., 1987-93. Mem. bd. mgrs. Phila. Youth Study Ctr., 1961-65. Served with USN, 1943-46, PTO. Mem. Phila. Bar Assn. Office: US Dist Ct 16614 US Courthouse 501 Market St Philadelphia PA 19106

**MCGOLDRICK, JOHN LEWIS,** lawyer; b. Plainfield, N.J., Mar. 2, 1941; s. John Leslie and Sarah (Walker) McG.; m. Ann Chapman Puffer, Oct. 1, 1966; children: Scott Runyon, Jennifer Winslow. BA cum laude, Harvard U., 1963, LLB, 1966. Bar: N.J. 1966, N.Y. 1985. Assoc. McCarter & English, Newark, 1966-73, ptnr., 1974-95; pres. Med. Devices Group, sr. v.p., gen. counsel Bristol-Myers Squibb Co., N.Y.C., 1995—; vice-chmn., bd. dirs. N.J. Transit Corp., Newark; dir. Bristol-Myers Squibb Found., Health Industry Mfrs. Assn. Chmn. zoning bd. Borough of Princeton, N.J.; trustee Essex-Newark Found. Legal Svcs. N.J., Newark YMCA-YWCA; adv. bd. United Negro Coll. Fund. Fellow Am. Coll. Trial Lawyers, Am. Bar Found., Am. Acad. Appellate Advocacy; mem. ABA, Health Industry Mfrs. Assn. (bd. dirs.), N.J. Bar Assn., N.Y. Bar Assn., Essex County Bar Assn., Mercer County Bar Assn., Internat. Bar Assn., Assn. Bar City of N.Y., Assn. Fed. Bar N.J. (former pres., mem. adv. bd.), Am. Law Inst., Assn. Gen. Counsel, Chief Legal Officers Roundtable, Coun. of Chief Legal Officers (The Conf. Bd. Inc.), CPR Inst. for Dispute Resolution (mem. exec. com.), Am. Arbitration Assn. (nat. panel), Regional Plan Assn. (dir.), Harvard Clubs (N.Y.C. and N.J.), Harvard Law Sch. Assn. N.J. (former pres.). Home: 25 Vandeventer Ave Princeton NJ 08542-6937 Office: Bristol-Myers Squibb Co 345 Park Ave New York NY 10022-6000

**MCGOLRICK, J. EDWARD, JR.,** lawyer; b. N.Y.C., June 23, 1932; s. James Edward and Emily May (Venezia) McG.; m. Jean Marie MacInnis, Nov. 10, 1956; children: Elizabeth Anne McGowan, Ellen Marie Rowan, James Edward III, William John. BA, Coll. of Holy Cross, Worcester, Mass., 1954; JD, Georgetown Law Ctr., Washington, 1961. Bar: Va. 1961, U.S. Dist. Ct. D.C. 1961, U.S. Ct. Appeals (D.C. cir.) 1961, U.s. Dist. Ct. (ea. dist.) Va. 1961, U.S. Supreme Ct. 1971, Fla. 1973; diplomate Nat. Bd. Trial Advocacy. Pvt. practice, Manassas, Va., 1961—. Served as capt. USMCR, 1954-58. Mem. ABA, Fla. Bar Assn., Prince William County Bar Assn. (past pres.), Va. State Bar Assn., Assn. Trial Lawyers Am., Congl. Country Club (Bethesda, Md.), Wild Dunes Club (Isle of Palms, S.C.). Roman Catholic. General civil litigation. Home: 9502 Nelson Ln Manassas VA 20110-4310 Office: 9257 Lee Ave Manassas VA 20110-5514

**MCGONIGLE, RICHARD THOMAS,** lawyer; b. Columbus, Ohio, Jan. 29, 1951; s. Francis Phillip and Mary Lou (Daughtery) McG.; m. Janet Christine Bowser, Aug. 17, 1974; children: Richard K., Michael P., Robin C. BA, St. Leo Coll., 1978; JD, Duquesne U., 1981. Bar: Pa. 1981, Okla. 1986, U.S. Supreme Ct. 1994, U.S. Dist. Ct. (we. dist.) Pa. 1981, U.S. Dist. Cts. (ea., we., and no. dists.) Okla. 1985, U.S. Ct. Appeals (5th and 10th cirs.) 1985. Police officer City of Hilliard, Ohio, 1973-74, City of Virginia Beach, Va., 1974-78; atty. Eckert Seamans Cherin & Mellot, Pitts., 1981-85, Hall, Estill, Tulsa, Okla., 1985-95; of counsel Ronald D. Wood & Assocs., Tulsa, 1995-96; ptnr. Wood & McGonigle, Tulsa, 1997—; faculty mem., co-author seminar materials Nat. Bus. Inst., 1992. Author: (case notes) Duquesne Law Rev., 1979. Pres. Eastwood Lake Homeowners Assn., Owasso, Okla., 1993-96; mem. Associated Builders & Contractors, Inc., Tulsa, 1994. Recipient Acad. Achievement award Franklin County Sheriff's Acad., Columbus, 1973, Honor Grad. award Fraternal Order of Police Assn., Norfolk, Va., 1975, Best Oralist award Mugel Nat. Tax Moot Ct., Buffalo, N.Y., 1980. Mem. ABA, Okla. Bar Assn., Pa. Bar Assn., Tulsa County Bar Assn., Muscogee (Creek) Nation Bar Assn. Republican. Roman Catholic. Avocations: motorcycling, hunting, fishing, camping, reading. General civil litigation, Condemnation, Workers' compensation. Home: 18432 E 90th St N Owasso OK 74055-8019 Office: Ronald D Wood & Assocs 2727 E 21st St Ste 500 Tulsa OK 74114-3536

**MCGOUGH, JAMES KINGSLEY,** lawyer; b. Binghamton, N.Y., Jan. 8, 1971; s. James Ivvin and Sharon Ann McGough. BA in English, U. St. Thomas, 1993; JD, Creighton U., 1996. Bar: Ga. 1996, Nebr. 1997, U.S. Dist. Ct. Nebr. 1997, U.S. Ct. Appeals (8th cir.) 1997. Lawyer Copple & Rockey, P.C., Norfolk, Nebr. Assoc. editor Creighton Law Rev., 1994-96. Mem. ABA, ATLA, Nat. Criminal Def., Nebr. Criminal Def., Nebr. Trial Lawyers Assn., Madison County Bar Assn., Phi Delta Phi. Republican. Roman Catholic. General civil litigation, Criminal, Personal injury. Office: Copple & Rockey PC 2425 Taylor Ave Norfolk NE 68701-4511

**MCGOUGH, PHILLIP ALLAN,** lawyer; b. Lake Village, Ark., Nov. 12, 1951; s. Phillip Alexander McGough and Edith Morene Turner. BS in History and English, Southern Ark. U., 1979; JD, U. Ark., 1983. Bar: Ark. 1983, U.S. Dist. Ct. Ark. 1983, U.S. Ct. Appeals (8th cir.) 1984. Radio announcer Sta. WGVM, WBAQ, Greenville, Miss., 1970-72; pvt. practice Little Rock, Ark., 1983-87, 92—; atty. Herrod, McGough, Herrod, North Little Rock, 1988-92. With USAF, 1972-76. Mem. Masons. Buddhist. Avocations: music, hunting and fishing, canoeing, reading. General civil litigation, Criminal, Probate. Office: 220 Willow St North Little Rock AR 72114-5520

**MCGOVERN, DAVID CARR,** lawyer; b. Taunton, Mass., Sept. 3, 1946; s. James Edward and Dorothea Elizabeth (Carr) McG.; m. Pamela Lee Compton, Mar. 22, 1975; 1 child, William David. AB, Coll. of Holy Cross, 1968; JD, U. Va., 1979. Bar: Calif. 1980, U.S. Dist. Ct. (ctrl. dist.) Calif. 1980, U.S. Dist. Ct. (so. dist.) Calif. 1981. Assoc. Rosenfeld, Meyer and Susman, Beverly Hills, Calif., 1979-81; ptnr. Engstrom, Lipscomb and Lack, L.A., 1981-90, Haight, Brown and Bonesteel LLP, Santa Monica, Calif., 1990—. Bd. dirs. United Cerebral Palsy/Spastic Children's Found., L.A., 1985-94; men's com. John Tracy Clinic Women's Aux., L.A., 1988-94; founding mem. Friends of John Tracy Clinic, L.A., 1996—; benefit com. Boys and Girls Club Venice, Calif., 1994—. Mem. ABA, State Bar Calif., Aviation Ins. Assn. Avocations: running, reading, coaching youth basketball, travel. Fax: (310) 829-5117. E-mail: mcgoverd@hbblaw.com. Aviation, Product liability, General civil litigation. Home: 7812 W 80th St Playa del Rey CA 90293-7905 Office: Haight Brown and Bonesteel LLP 1620 26th St Ste 4000N Santa Monica CA 90404-4013

**MC GOVERN, WALTER T.,** federal judge; b. Seattle, May 24, 1922; s. C. Arthur and Anne Marie (Thies) McG.; m. Rita Marie Olsen, June 29, 1946; children: Katrina M., Shawn E., A. Renee. B.A., U. Wash., 1949, LL.B., 1950. Bar: Wash. 1950. Practiced law in Seattle, 1950-59; mem. firm Kerr, McCord, Greenleaf & Moen; judge Municipal Ct., Seattle, 1959-65, Superior Ct., Wash., 1965-68, Wash. Supreme Ct., 1968-71; judge U.S. Dist. Ct. (we. dist.) Wash., 1971-87, chief judge, 1975-87, sr. judge, 1987—; mem. subcom. on supporting personnel Jud. Conf. U.S., 1981-87, chmn. subcom., 1983, mem. adminstrn. com., 1983-87, chmn. jud. resources com., 1987-91. Mem. Am. Judicature Soc., Wash. State Superior Ct. Judges Assn., Seattle King County Bar Assn. (treas.), Phi Delta Phi. Club: Seattle Tennis (pres. 1968). Office: US Dist Ct US Courthouse 5th Fl 1010 5th Ave Ste 215 Seattle WA 98104-1189

**MCGOWAN, JAMES FRANCIS, III,** lawyer; b. Bklyn, Nov. 30, 1955; s. James F. Jr. and Anne Smith McGowan; m. Terry Johnson, July 1, 1978; children: Catherine, James IV, Clare. BA in Polit. Sci., Tulane U., 1977, BBS in Bus., 1977; JD, St. John's U., 1982; LLM in Labor Law, Georgetown U., 1991. Bar: Va. 1983, N.Y. 1983, U.S. Dist. Ct. (ea. and so. dists.) N.Y. 1983. Comd. 2nd lt. USMC, 1977, advanced through grades to lt. col., ret., 1997; assoc. Ritzert & Leyton, PC, Fairfax, Va., 1997—. Bd. dirs. Fairfax Little League. Mem. Fairfax Bar Assn. Roman Catholic. Avocations: coaching youth sports, Little League baseball. Labor, Criminal, Military. Office: Ritzert & Leyton PC 10387 Main St Ste 200 Fairfax VA 22030-2413

**MCGOWAN, MATTHEW J.,** lawyer; b. Boston, Nov. 25, 1955; s. James R. and Mary Louise McGowan; m. Ann Marie Russo, May 20, 1982; children: Ryan, Nicholas, Daniel, Thomas, Kayla, Alexandra. BS, U. R.I., 1978; JD, Cath. U. Am., 1982. Bar: R.I. 1982, U.S. Dist. Ct. R.I., U.S. Dist. Ct. Mass., U.S. Dist. Ct. Conn., U.S. Ct. Appeals (1st, 2d and 11th cirs.), U.S. Supreme Ct.; bd. cert. in bus. and consumer bankruptcy law. Atty., U.S. Trustee's Office, U.S. Dept. Justice, Boston, 1982-95; ptnr. Salter McGowan Swartz & Sylvia, Inc., Providence, 1985—; adj. prof. bankruptcy law Roger Williams U. Law Sch., Bristol, R.I., 1996—; mem. panel of pvt. bankruptcy trustees U.S. Bankruptcy Ct., Providence, 1986—. Contbr. articles to profl. jours.; presenter in field. Mem. Am. Bankruptcy Inst., Nat. Assn. Bankruptcy Trustees. Avocations: skiing, woodworking. Bankruptcy, Banking, Consumer commercial. Office: Salter McGowan Swartz & Sylvia 321 S Main St Providence RI 02903-7108

**MCGOWAN, PATRICK FRANCIS,** lawyer; b. N.Y.C., July 23, 1940; s. Francis Patrick and Sonia Veronica (Koslow) M.; m. Patricia Neil, June 6, 1964; children: Susan Claire, Kathleen Anne. BA, Rice U., 1962; JD, U. Tex., Austin, 1965. Bar: Tex. 1965, U.S. Tax Ct. 1972, U.S. Ct. Appeals (5th cir.) 1993, U.S. Supreme Ct. 1970. Briefing atty. Tex. Supreme Ct., Austin, 1965-66; ptnr. Strasburger & Price, Dallas, 1966-98, Akin, Gump, Strauss, Hauer & Feld, Dallas, 1998—; pres., chmn. bd. Tex Lex, Inc., 1991-98. Contbr. numerous articles on trademark, copyright and franchise law. Bd. advisors Dallas Ft. Worth Sch. Law. Fellow Coll. State Bar Tex. (faculty Franchising Inst. 1987, Intellectual Property Inst. 1992, S.W. Legal Found. Patent Law Inst. 1992, Practising Law Inst. 1996); mem. ABA (forum com. on franchising, trademark and unfair competition com., patent, trademark and copyright law sect.), State Bar Tex. (intellectual property sect., com.

continuing legal edn.), Dallas Bar Assn. (dir. intellectual property law sect. 1994—, chmn. I.P. Basics seminar 1999), ALFA Internat. Tel. Symposium, Internat. Anti-Counterfeiting Assn., Tex. Law Rev. Editors Assn., Phi Delta Phi. Antitrust, Federal civil litigation, Trademark and copyright. Office: Akin Gump 1700 Pacific Ave Ste 4100 Dallas TX 75201-4675

**MCGOWIN, WILLIAM CLAUDE,** lawyer; b. Montgomery, Ala., Aug. 17, 1964; s. Claude Mastin and Josephine (Screws) McG.; m. Anne Elizabeth Dooley, Oct. 26, 1991; children: Elizabeth Drake, Margaret Preston. BS in Finance, U. Ala., 1986; JD, Cumberland Sch. Law, Birmingham, 1991. Bar: Ala. 1991. Golf profl. PGA of Am., Orlando, Fla., 1986-88; atty. Hill, Hill, Carter, Franco, Cole & Black, Montgomery, 1991—. Mem. Ala. Def. Lawyers Assn. (pres. 1998), Kiwanis. Episcopalian. Insurance, Transportation, Product liability. Office: Hill Hill Carter Franco Cole & Black 425 S Perry St Montgomery AL 36104-4235

**MCGRADY, JONATHAN L.,** lawyer; b. Knoxville, Tenn., Oct. 29, 1969; s. Joseph Harry and Ann Abate McG.; m. Jennifer Blackmon, Aug. 5, 1995. BA, Hampden-Sydney Coll., 1991; JD, Coll. William & Mary, 1995. Bar: Va. 1995, U.S. Dist. Ct. (we. dist.) Va. 1995, U.S. Ct. Appeals (4th cir.) 1995. Ptnr. McGrady & McGrady, LLP, Hillsville, Va., 1996—. Chmn. Carroll County Dem. Party, 1996—; deacon Hillsville Christian Ch. Mem. Va. Trial Lawyers Assn., Va. Bar Assn., Carroll Bar Assn., Hillsville Masonic Lodge. Criminal, Family and matrimonial, Personal injury. Home: 414 Chinquapin Trl Hillsville VA 24343-1676 Office: McGrady & McGrady LLP 127 Mill St Hillsville VA 24343-1314

**MCGRAIL-SZABO, SHARON JOAN,** lawyer; b. Scranton, Pa., Feb. 20, 1965; d. Thomas J. and Joan Mildred Kennedy McGrail; m. Scott A Szabo, Oct. 22, 1988; 1 child, Brett Thomas. AB, Lafayette Coll., 1987; JD, Widener U., 1994. Bar: Pa. 1994. Account claims rep. PMA Ins., Allentown, Pa., 1987-90; paralegal Cohen, Knaf Feeley & Ortwein, Easton, Pa., 1990; law clk. Brown, Brown, Solt & Ferretti, Allentown, 1991-93, Law Offices of Erv McLain, Bethlehem, Pa., 1993-94; assoc. atty. Post and Schell, P.C., Allentown, 1994-97; mng. assoc. Swartz, Campbell Detweiler, Allentown, 1997—; faculty Lorman Bus. Svcs. Seminar, Fogelsville, Pa., 1998. Mem. Lehigh Valley and Reading Claims Assn. Workers' compensation, Consumer commercial, Insurance. Office: Swartz Campbell & Detweiler 5100 W Tilghman St Ste 230 Allentown PA 18104-9144

**MCGRANE, VIRGINIA LAURA,** lawyer; b. Mineola, N.Y., May 16, 1959; d. Thomas Francis and Anna Marie McGrane; m. L. Scott Williford, Oct. 5, 1996; 1 child, Caroline Lee. BS, Georgetown U., 1981; JD, Fordham U., 1987. Bar: N.Y. 1988, N.J. 1994, U.S. Dist. Ct. (so. and ea. dists.) N.Y., U.S. Dist. Ct. N.J. Nurse N.Y. Hosp., N.Y.C., 1981-83; RN N.Y.C. Fire Dept., 1983-84; lawyer Martin Clearwater & Bell, N.Y.C., 1987-91, Keck Mahin & Kate, N.Y.C., 1991-93, White Fleischner & Fino, N.Y.C., 1993—. Mem. ABA, N.Y. Bar Assn., N.Y. County Lawyers Assn. Avocations: skiing, tennis, singing, shopping, child rearing. Personal injury. Home: 599 Midland Ave # 1-2 Rye NY 10580-3900 Office: White Fleischner & Fino 140 Broadway New York NY 10005

**MCGRATH, CHRISTOPHER THOMAS,** lawyer; b. Inwood, N.Y., Nov. 25, 1958; s. John J. and Dolores Marie McG.; m. Monica Jean DiPalma, Sept. 15, 1984; children: Kristin Marie, Kelli Anne, Katelynn. BS cum laude, St. John's U., Jamaica, N.Y., 1980; JD, U. Dayton, 1983. Bar: N.Y. 1984, U.S. Dist. Ct. (so. and ea. dists.) N.Y. 1984, U.S. Supreme Ct. 1987; bd. cert. civil trial advocacy Nat. Bd. Trial Advocacy. Assoc. Sullivan & Liapakis, N.Y.C., 1983-89, ptnr., 1989-99; ptnr. Sullivan, Papain, Block, McGrath & Cannavo P.C., N.Y.C., 1999—; lectr. N.Y. State Bar Assn., N.Y. State Trial Lawyers Assn., Assn. Trial Lawyers Am. Chmn. humanitarian award Nassau County 4th Precinct Police, 1985—. Mem. Assn. Trial Lawyers Am., N.Y. State Trail Lawyers Assn., Nassau County Bar Assn. (bd. dirs., chair med. legal com. 1997-98, chair jud. com. 1999—), N.Y. State Bar Assn., Kiwanis (pres.-elect Hewlet, N.Y., disting. past pres. Peninsula chpt. 1988-89). Republican. General civil litigation, Personal injury, State civil litigation. Home: 1348 Hewlett Ln Hewlett NY 11557-2208 Office: Sullivan Papain Block McGrath Cannavo PC 120 Broadway New York NY 10271-0002 also: 55 Mineola Blvd Mineola NY 11501-4220

**MCGRATH, DANIEL SCOTT,** lawyer; b. Mpls., July 7, 1962; s. Dennis Britton and Susan Jane (Flapler) McG. BA, U. Minn., 1984; JD, William Coll. Law, 1988. Assoc. Flakne Law Offices, Bloomington, Minn., 1986-92; pvt. practice Bloomington, Burnsville, Minn., 1992—. Mem. Minn. State Bar Assn., Minn. Trial Lawyers Assn., Mpls. Athletic Club. Avocations: golf, squash, running, opera. Personal injury, General civil litigation, Family and matrimonial. Office: 501 Highway 13 E Ste 114 Burnsville MN 55337-2877

**MCGRATH, J. NICHOLAS,** lawyer; b. Hollywood, Calif., Feb. 12, 1940; m. Margaret Crowley, Oct. 4, 1980; children: Nicholas Gerald, Molly Inez. BA with honors, Lehigh U., 1962; LLB magna cum laude, Columbia U., 1965. Bar: D.C. 1966, Calif. 1969, U.S. Supreme Ct. 1970, Colo. 1971. Law clk. to presiding justice U.S. Ct. Appeals (D.C. cir.), 1965-66; law clk. to assoc. justice Thurgood Marshall U.S. Supreme Ct., Washington, 1967-68; assoc. Pillsbury, Madison & Sutro, San Francisco, 1968-70; from assoc. to ptnr. Oates, Austin, McGrath, Aspen, Colo., 1970-80; ptnr. Austin, McGrath & Jordan, Aspen, 1980-82; sole practice Aspen, 1982—; chmn. grievance com. Colo. Supreme Ct., 1989, mem. 1984-89. Mem. bd. editors Columbia Law Review, 1964-65. Vice chair Pitkin Co. Home Rule Charter Com., 1976-78; mem. Planning Commn., Town of Basalt, Colo., 1992-93, town trustee, 1993-94; bd. dirs. CLE in Colo., Inc., 1995-96, lectr. nat. and state CLE programs on ethics, litigation and land use subjects; pres. Basalt Children's Recreation Fund, Inc., 1994—; chair Basalt Hwy. 82 Citizens Task Force, 1996-97; mem. Aspen-Pitkin Co. Alt. H Hwy 82 Task Force, 1996-97, cmty. forum task force on Pitkin Co. charter, 1997-98; bd. dirs. Club 20, 1997-98; pres. Basalt Soccer Club, 1997-99; sec.-treas. Western Slope State Youth Soccer League, 1996—. Mem. Colo. Bar Assn. (v.p. 1991-92), Pitkin County Bar Assn. (pres. 1977). Democrat. Avocations: skiing, tennis, computers. E-mail: jnm@jnmpc.com, www.jnmpc.com. State civil litigation, Real property, Land use and zoning (including planning). Home: 415 Elk Cir Basalt CO 81621-8202 Office: 600 E Hopkins Ave Ste 203 Aspen CO 81611-2933

**MCGRATH, PATRICK EDWARD,** lawyer; b. Kansas City, Mo., Dec. 27, 1963; m. Adele R. McGrath, June 5, 1993. BA, U. Kans., 1986, JD, 1989. Atty. Wallace Saunders, Overland Park, Kans., 1989—. Mem. ABA, Kans. Bar Assn., Mo. Bar Assn., Johnson County Bar Assn., Kansas City Metro. Bar Assn. Workers' compensation. Home: 6700 W 66th Ter Overland Park KS 66202-4145 Office: Wallace Saunders 10111 Santa Fe Dr Overland Park KS 66212-4673

**MCGRATH, THOMAS J.,** lawyer, writer, film producer; b. N.Y.C., Oct. 8, 1932; m. Mary Lee McGrath, Aug. 4, 1956 (dec.); children: Maura Lee, J. Connell; m. Diahn Williams, Sept. 28, 1974; 1 child, Courtney C. B.A., NYU, 1956, J.D., 1960. Bar: N.Y. 1960. Assoc. Milbank, Tweed, Hadley & McCloy, N.Y.C., 1960-69; ptnr. Simpson, Thacher & Bartlett, N.Y.C., 1970-95; retired, 1995; lectr., writer Practicing Law Inst., 1976—, Am. Law Inst. ABA, 1976-81; bd. dirs. Fast Food Devel. Corp. Author: Carryover Basis Under Tax Reform Act, 1977; contbg. author: Estate and Gift Tax After ERTA, 1982; producer: feature film Deadly Hero, 1977. Bd. dirs. N.Y. Philharm.; pres. Am. Austrian Found., Tanzania Wildlife Fund. With U.S. Army, 1953-54. Fellow Am. Coll. Trust and Estate Coun.; mem. ABA, N.Y. State Bar Assn., Assn. Bar City N.Y. Estate planning, Probate, Estate taxation. Home: 988 5th Ave New York NY 10021-0143 Office: Simpson Thacher & Bartlett 425 Lexington Ave New York NY 10017-3954

**MC GRAW, DARRELL VIVIAN, JR.,** state attorney general; b. Mullens, W.Va., Nov. 8, 1936; s. Darrell Vivian and Julia (ZeKany) McG.; m. Jorea Marple; children: Elizabeth, Sarah, Darrell, Elliott. AB, W.Va. U., 1961, JD, 1964, MA, 1977. Bar: W.Va. 1964. Gen. atty. Fgn. Claims Settlement Commn., U.S. Dept. State, 1964; counsel to gov. State of W.Va., 1965-68; pvt. practice Charleston, Shepherdstown and Morgantown, 1968-76; judge W.Va. Supreme Ct. Appeals, Charleston, 1977-88, chief justice, 1982, 83; atty. gen. State of W.Va., Charleston, 1993—. Served with U.S. Army, 1954-57. Fellow W.Va. U., Nat. Ctr. Edn. in Politics/Ford Found. Fellow Am. Polit. Sci. Assn., Rotary. Democrat. Office: Office of Atty Gen 1900 Kanawha Blvd E Rm E-26 Charleston WV 25305-0009

**MCGRAW, FRANK WILLIAM, JR.,** lawyer; b. Newport News, Va., Aug. 21, 1944; s. Frank William and Mary Jean (Head) McG.; 1 child, Virginia LaVaughan. AA, U. Fla., 1965, BS in Journalism, 1967; BA in Polit. Sci., U. N.C., 1974; MS in Criminal Justice, Nova U., 1980; MPA in Justice Adminstrn., Golden Gate U., 1981; JD, U. Houston, 1973. Bar: Va. 1975, U.S. Dist. Ct. (ea. dist.) Va. 1978, U.S. Claims Ct., U.S. Mil. Appeals, U.S. Dist. Ct. (we. dist.) Va. 1979, D.C. 1979, U.S. Supreme Ct. 1979, U.S. Ct. Appeals (D.C. cir.) 1980. Asst. commonwealth atty. City of Va. Beach, Virginia Beach, 1976-79, 85-87, dep. commonwealth atty., 1987-89; pvt. practice Virginia Beach, 1975-76, 79-85, 89—; bd. dirs. Ea. Va. Health Sys. Agy., Inc., 1982-86; faculty advisor Nat. Coll. Dist. Attys., Houston, 1978; faculty advisor Nat. Coll. Dist. Attys., 1978; adj. prof. Nova U., 1982; adj. faculty mem. Tidewater C.C., 1980-85. 1st lt. U.S. Army, 1967-70, Vietnam. Recipient bronze star with oak leaf cluster U.S. Army, 1969. Mem. ATLA (mem. criminal and family law sects.), ABA (criminal justice and family law sects.), Nat. Assn. Criminal Def. Lawyers, Va. State Bar (criminal and family law sects.), Va. Bar Assn. (criminal law sect. coun., domestic rels. sect.), D.C. Bar Assn. (criminal law and individual rights divsn.), Virginia Beach Bar Assn., Va. Trial Lawyers Assn. (mem. criminal and family law sects.). Criminal, Family and matrimonial, Juvenile. Office: 1200 First Colonial Rd Ste 204G Virginia Beach VA 23454-2207 Address: 3712 Jefferson Blvd # B Virginia Beach VA 23455-1638

**MCGRAW, PATRICK JOHN,** lawyer; b. Detroit, Feb. 3, 1956; s. John William and Elizabeth Kay (Foley) McG.; m. Susan Elaine Borowiak, Jan. 14, 1978; children: Kelly Elizabeth, Ryan Patrick, Brandon David, Kyle Elaine. BS, Cen. Mich. U., 1979; JD, Cooley Law Sch., 1982. Bar: Mich. 1982. Ptnr. McGraw, Martin & Heyn, P.C., Saginaw, Mich., 1982—; lectr. ACLS Legal Implications, Saginaw, 1985; instr. Ctrl. Mich. U., Mt. Pleasant, Mich., 1986-90; spkr. Sponsor of Malpractice Issues Delta Coll. and Saginaw Valley State Coll., 1986—. Atty. Sch. Program, Saginaw, 1986—; mem. YMCA; bd. trustees Saginaw Twp., 1988—; sch. coun. mem. Saginaw Nouvel Cath. Cen. High Sch., 1988—; apptd. Mich. Bd. of Counseling, 1994—. Mem. ABA, ATLA, Mich. Bar Assn., Saginaw County Bar Assn., Mich. Soc. Hosp. Attys., Mich. Def. Trial Counsel, Phi Alpha Delta. Avocations: black belt karate, hunting, fishing, racquetball. State civil litigation, Insurance, Personal injury. Home: 5220 Overhill Dr Saginaw MI 48603-1727 Office: McGraw Martin & Heyn PC PO Box 6490 Saginaw MI 48608-6490

**MCGRAW, WARREN RANDOLPH,** state supreme court justice; b. Wyoming County, W.Va., May 10, 1939; m. Peggy Shufflebarger; children: W. Randolph, H. Suzanne, Rebecca L. AB, U. Charleston, 1960; postgrad., W.Va. U.; JD, Wake Forest U., 1963. Bar: W.Va. 1963. Trial atty. U.S. Dept. Justice, Washington; legal svc. atty.; elected W.Va. Ho. of Dels., 1968, 70, W.Va. Senate, 1972, 76, 80; elected prosecuting atty. Wyoming County, 1996; justice W.Va. Supreme Ct. Appeals, 1998—; instr. W.Va. U. Ext. Agy.; W.Va. del. Dem. Nat. Conv., 1972, 74; mem. Del. and Senatorial Dist. Exec. Coms.; del. State Dem. Jud. Conv. and State Dem. Conv.; elected pres. W.Va. Senate, 1980, 82; co-chmn. Crime Commn.; mem. Nat. Conf. Lt. Govs. Featured on Nat. Pub. TV series Bill Moyers Journal. Trustee 1st United Meth. Ch., Pineville; participant Marshall U.'s Taft Lectr. Series; elected W.Va. del. Dem. Nat. Conv., 1972, 74, Wyo. County Bd. Edn., 1986, 44th pres. W.Va. Sen., 1980, 82; del. State Dem. Jud. Conv., State Dem. Conv.; past pres. Jaycees; mem. Nat. Conf. Lt. Govs., Heart Fund, Wyoming County Cancer Fund, Del. and Sen. Dist. Exec. Coms.; past chmn. Wyoming County Dem. Exec. Com.; co-chmn. Crime Commn. Named one of nation's Outstanding Legislators, Rutgers U.; recipient Friend of Edn., Margaret Baldwin award W.Va. Edn. Assn. Mem. Wyo. Bar Assn., Raleigh County Bar Assn., Rotary Internat. Office: Bldg 1 Rm E-302 Capitol Complex Charleston WV 25305*

**MCGRAW, WARREN RANDOLPH, II,** state legislator; b. Pineville, W.Va., June 13, 1963; s. Warren R. and Peggy (Shufflebarger) McG. BS in Edn., East Tenn. State U., 1985; JD, John Marshall Law Sch., 1988. Asst. atty. gen., 1988-89; mem. W.Va. Ho. of Dels., 1992—. Vol. Boys Club of Am., Spl. Olympics; mem. Raleigh County YMCA; bd. dirs. Tri-County Baseball Assn.; chmn. bd. dirs. Beckley Tri-County Baseball Assn.; past mem. 9th Senatorial Dist. Dem. Exec. Com., 4th Congl. Dist.; active NAACP. Mem. NFL Players Assn., W.Va. State Bar Assn., Ga. State Bar Assn., Raleigh Bar Assn., Wyo. Bar Assn., AFL-CIO, Beckley Rotary Club. Democrat. Methodist. Avocation: former professional football player.

**MCGREGOR, JOHN JOSEPH,** lawyer; b. Fort Knox, Ky., Nov. 18, 1946; s. Arden Durham and Ruth Marguerite (Funkner) McG.; m. Rebecca Lounsbury, 1989. AB, U. San Francisco, 1968; JD, U. Calif. Hastings Coll. Law, 1971; LLM, NYU, 1974. Bar: Calif. 1972, U.S. Dist. Ct. (no. dist.) Calif. 1972, U.S. Ct. Appeals (9th cir.) 1979, U.S. Dist. Ct. (ea. dist.) Calif. 1988; cert. specialist in taxation law. Sports info. dir. U. San Francisco, 1966-68; staff atty. Community Legal Svcs., San Jose, Calif., 1972-73; cons. IRS Project, Washington, 1974-75; assoc. Thomas, Snell, Jamison, Russell, Williamson & Asperger, Fresno, Calif., 1975-78; shareholder Thomas, Snell, Jamison, Russell & Asperger, Fresno, 1978-91, McGregor, Dahl, Sullivan & Klug, Fresno, 1991—; asst. sec., gen. counsel The Vendo Co., Fresno, 1985-88; mem. Fresno County Assessment Appeals Bd., 1993-98. Author: Taxation of Real Property Transfers, 1981. Bd. dirs. Fresno (Calif.) Storyland, 1976-81; mem. Fresno Ski Patrol, 1976-93, Sierra Summit Ski Patrol, Lakeshore, Calif., 1985-93, The Acad., Fresno, 1981—. Named Vol. Atty. of the Year Fresno County Bar Assn., 1983. Mem. Am. Law Inst., Calif. State Bar Assn. (dir. taxation sect., exec. com. 1983-86, chair standards of tax practice com. 1995, 98), Fresno County Bar Assn. (dir. 1982-86). Roman Catholic. Avocations: skiing, golf, reading. E-mail: jmcgregor@mdsklaw.com. Home: 4774 N Wishon Ave Fresno CA 93704-3144 Office: McGregor Dahl Sullivan & Klug 7080 N Whitney Ave Fresno CA 93720-0154

**MCGREGOR, MARTIN LUTHER, JR.,** lawyer; b. Rossville, Ga., Mar. 25, 1940; s. Martin Luther and Ora Louise (Stanley) McG.; m. Linda Joyce Buehler, June 31, 1978; children: Martin Luther III, James Franklin. BS in Chemistry, U. Ga., 1962; PhD, U. S.C., 1969; JD, Okla. U., 1978. Bar: Tex. 1979, U.S. Patent Office 1978, U.S. Supreme Ct. 1985. Various teaching positions Ga. and S.C., 1966-70; rsch. assoc. Okla. State U., Stillwater, 1971-76; rsch. chemist FMC Corp., Middleport, N.Y., 1976-77; assoc. atty. Baker & Botts, Houston, 1978-85; atty. Norvell & Assocs., Houston, 1985-86; mng. ptnr. Jamison McGregor & Harris, Houston, 1986-89; sr. biotech. specialist Baker & Botts, Houston, 1989-94; head biotech. Gardere & Wynne, LLP, Dallas, 1994-95; ptnr. McGregor & Adler LLP, Houston, 1996—; sec., gen. counsel Sapient Catalytechs, Inc., Houston, 1997-98; exec. v.p. Gemini Health Technologies, Inc., Houston, 1998—; adj. prof. chemistry U. Tex., Arlington, 1995; biotech. adv. bd. Tex. Healthcare and Biosci. Inst., 1997—. Mem. editorial bd. Biotech. Law Reports; contbr. articles to profl. jours. Mem. steering com. Bio '97, BioInternat. '93 Found. for the Future, Houston, 1992—, Andrews Campaign, Houston, 1992, Biotech. Industry Orgonizatio, 1997; bd. dirs. Mangum Manor Civic Assn., Houston, 1986; mem. biotech. adv. com. Tex. Healthcare & Bioscience Inst., 1997—. Named to Order of the Coif, Okla. U., 1978. Mem. AAAS, Houston Intellectual Property Law Assn., Am. Chem. Soc., Am. Arbitration Assn. (panel of patent arbitrators), Biotech. Ind. Orgn. (co-chmn. law 1993—), Assn. Biotech. Cos. (chmn. tech. transfer 1992-93, co-chmn. regulatory and patents 1991-92, gen. counsel S.W. chpt.). Unitarian Universalist. Avocations: camping, soccer coaching, chess. Patent, Federal civil litigation. Office: McGregor & Adler LLP 26415 Oak Ridge Dr Spring TX 77380-1964

**MCGREGOR, RUTH VAN ROEKEL,** state supreme court justice; b. Le Mars, Iowa, Apr. 4, 1943; d. Bernard and Marie Frances (Janssen) Van Roekel; m. Robert James McGregor, Aug. 15, 1965. BA summa cum laude, U. Iowa, 1964, MA, 1965; JD summa cum laude, Ariz. State U., 1974. Bar: Ariz. 1974, U.S. Dist. Ct. Ariz. 1974, U.S. Ct. Appeals (9th cir.), U.S. Supreme Ct. 1982. Assoc. Fennemore, Craig, von Ammon, Udall & Powers, Phoenix, 1974-79, ptnr., 1980-81, 82-89; law clk. to justice Sandra Day O'Connor U.S. Supreme Ct., Washington, 1981-82; judge Ariz Ct. Appeals, 1989-98, vice chief judge, 1993-95, chief judge, 1995-98; justice Ariz. Supreme Ct., 1998—; mem. disciplinary commn. Ariz. Supreme Ct., 1984-89, City of Mesa jud. adv. bd., 1997—. Mem., newsletter editor Charter 100, Phoenix, 1981—; bd. dirs., mem. Ctr. for Law in Pub. Interest, Phoenix, 1977-80. Mem. ABA (chmn. state memberships 1985—), Ariz. Bar Assn. (disciplinary com. 1984—), Ariz. Judges Assn. (exec. com. 1990—, sec. 1991-92, v.p. 1992-93, pres. 1993-94), Nat. Assn. Women Judges (chair first time attendees com. 1990-91, 1994 conv. com.; exec. com. 1995—). Democrat. Lutheran. Lodge: Soroptomists. Office: Arizona Supreme Court 1501 W Washington St Phoenix AZ 85007-3231*

**MCGREW, ANNE ELIZABETH,** lawyer; b. Cleve., Jan. 26, 1970; d. Frank Augustus III and Sharrel (Brown) M. BA, U. Va., 1992; JD, So. Meth. U., 1995. Bar: Tenn. 1995, U.S. Dist. Ct. (we. dist.) Tenn. Atty. Sofamor Danek Group, Inc., Memphis, 1995-96; sr. labor atty. Young & Perl PLC, Memphis, 1996—. Bd. dirs. Memphis Arts Coun. Urban Art, 1998—; mem. Memphis Bot. Gardens, Jr. League of Memphis; active Young Reps., Memphis, 1995—. Mem. Assn. Women Attys., Memphis Bar Assn., Kiwanis of Memphis. Presbyterian. Avocation: antiques. Labor. Office: Young and Perl PLC One Commerce Sq Ste 2380 Memphis TN 38103

**MCGUANE, FRANK L., JR.,** lawyer; b. White Plains, N.Y., July 10, 1939; s. Frank L. and Dorothy P. (McGrath) McG.; m. Carla L. Miller, June 26, 1993; children: Lauri Elizabeth, Molly Elizabeth. BA, U. Notre Dame, 1961; JD, U. Cin., 1968. Bar: Colo. 1968, U.S. Dist. Ct. Colo. 1968, U.S. Ct. Appeals (10th cir.) 1970, U.S. Supreme Ct. 1971. Shareholder McGuane and Malone, P.C., Denver, 1981-95; pres. Frank McGuane & Assocs., P.C., Denver, 1995-97; ptnr. McGuane & Hogan, LLP, Denver, 1997—; lectr. in field. Author: Domestic Relations-Colorado Methods of Practice, 1983; co-author: Colorado Family Law and Practice, 1999; contbr. articles to profl. jours. Chmn. Denver award chpt. Nat. Eagle Scout Assn. Boy Scouts Am,. 1980-82. With USMC, 1961-63. Fellow Am. Acad. Matrimonial Lawyers (jour. editor 1990-95, bd. govs. 1988-95, pres. Colo. chpt. 1988-89), Internat. Acad. Matrimonial Lawyers (founding fellow); mem. ABA, Colo. Bar Assn. (chmn. family law sect. 1977-78), Denver Bar Assn., Arapahoe County Bar Assn., Douglas-Elbert County Bar Assn., Pitkin County Bar Assn., Am. Coll. Family Trial Lawyers (diplomate), Cath. Lawyers Guild. Family and matrimonial. Office: The Galleria 720 S Colorado Blvd Ste 910N Denver CO 80246-1935

**MCGUCKIN, JOHN HUGH, JR.,** lawyer; b. Bryn Mawr, Pa., Nov. 8, 1946. AB magna cum laude, Harvard Coll., 1968, JD, 1971. Bar: Mass. 1971, Calif. 1973. Assoc. Orrick, Herrington, Rowley & Sutcliffe, 1972-79; sr. counsel legal divsn. Bank Am., 1979-81; exec. v.p., gen. counsel Union BanCal Corp./Union Bank Calif., N.A., San Francisco, 1981—, UnionBanCal Corp., 1998—; adj. instr. Hastings Coll. Law U. Calif., 1980-82; judge pro tem San Francisco Superior Ct. Contbr. articles to profl. jours. Mem. ABA, State Bar Calif. (v.p., treas., bd. govs., chmn. subcom. duties and liabilities trustees probate and trust law sect. 1985-86, legal svcs. trust fund commn. 1989-90, minimum CLE com.), Calif. Bankers Assn. (legal affairs com. 1988-90), Bar Assn. San Francisco (chmn. probate and trust law sect. 1985, exec. com., vice chmn. corp. law dept. sect. 1985-87), Phi Beta Kappa. General corporate. Office: Union Bank of Calif NA 400 California St Ste 1200 San Francisco CA 94104-1320

**MCGUCKIN, RONALD V.,** lawyer; b. Bristol, Pa., Nov. 26, 1955; s. Harry F. and Cecelia H. McGuckin. BS, U. Scranton, 1977; JD, Duquesne U., 1980. Bar: Pa. Assoc. Wood & Floge, Langhorne, Pa., 1980-82; sr. ptnr. Ronald V. McGuckin, Lumberville, Pa., 1982—; CEO Support Svcs. for Childcare Profls., Lumberville, 1987—. Author: (books) Current Issues in Child Care, 1993, Model Personnel Policy, 1997, (TV show) Legal Issues in Head Start, 1998. Bd. dirs., pres. Bucks City Head Start, Pa., 1983-87. Named Humanitarian of Yr., United Way, 1996, Vol. of Yr., Head Start, 1996. General practice, Education and schools, Family and matrimonial. Office: 3613 River Rd Lumberville PA 18933

**MCGUIGAN, PHILIP PALMER,** lawyer; b. N.Y.C., Aug. 28, 1944; s. E. Gayle and Alice Montant McG. AB, Brown U., 1966; JD, U. Minn., 1969. Bar: N.Y. 1969, Utah 1981, Ill. 1998, U.S. Supreme Ct. Assoc. LeBoeuf, Lamb, Leiby & MacRae, N.Y.C. and Salt Lake City, 1969-76, ptnr., 1977-85; founder, CEO, Cellular Sys. Corp., Salt Lake City, 1983; pres., CEO, Intermountain Premium Bakeries, Inc., Salt Lake City, 1985-90; ptnr. Snell & Wilmer, Salt Lake City, 1991-96, Gordon & Glickson, Chgo., 1996—; mem. Atty. Gen.'s Consumer Adv. Coun., 1982; mem. adv. com. Utah Securities Commn., 1982-83. Mergers and acquisitions, Finance, Computer. Office: Gordon & Glickson LLC 444 N Michigan Ave Ste 3600 Chicago IL 60611-3901

**MCGUIGAN, THOMAS RICHARD,** lawyer; b. Ardmore, Pa., Nov. 28, 1947; s. Paul J. and Claire T. (Piersol) McG.; m. Nancy Crofoot, Aug. 21, 1971; children: Brendan T., Erin K. BA, La Salle U., 1969; JD, U. Miami, 1974. Bar: Fla. 1974, U.S. Dist. Ct. (so. dist.) Fla. 1974. Assoc. Steel, Hector & Davis, LLP, Miami, Fla., 1974-78; ptnr. Steel, Hector & Davis, LLP, Miami, 1978—. Mem. bd. govs. Dade Comty. Found., Miami, 1996—. Mem. ABA (com. on negotiated acquisitions, bus. law sect. 1991-98), Fla. Bar Assn. (chmn. corp. law revision com., bus. law sect., 1986-90, mem corp. laws subcom. 1994—) Carribean Law Inst. (co. law adv. com. 1989-90), Fla. Exec. Forum, Miami (sponsor 1998—). E-mail: TRU@steelhector.com. Mergers and acquisitions, Securities, General corporate. Office: Steel Hector & Davis LLP 200 S Biscayne Blvd Ste 4000 Miami FL 33131-2310

**MCGUINN, MARTIN GREGORY,** banker, lawyer; b. Phila., Sept. 9, 1942; s. Martin G. and Rita (Horgan) McG.; m. Ann M. Muldoon, Sept. 17, 1977; children: Patrick J., Christopher M. AB, Villanova U., 1964, JD, 1967. Bar: Pa. 1967, N.Y. 1970. Assoc. Sullivan & Cromwell, N.Y.C., 1970-77; mng. counsel The Singer Co., Stamford, Conn., 1977-80; chmn., CEO Mellon Bank, Pitts., 1998; bd. consultors Villanova Law Sch., 1972—, chmn. 1985-87; bd. dirs. U.S.-Japan Bus. Coun., Inc., Allegheny Conf. on Cmty. Devel. Editor in chief Villanova Law Rev., Vol. 12, 1966-67. Bd. dirs. UPMC Health Sys.; trustee Carnegie Mus. of Pitts.; chmn. Hist. Soc. Western Pa. Mem. ABA, N.Y. State Bar Assn., Pa. Bar Assn., Allegheny County Bar Assn., Am. Law Inst., The Fin. Svcs. Roundtable, Am. Soc. Corp. Secs. (chmn. 1990-91). Home: 714 Amberson Ave Pittsburgh PA 15232-1446 Office: Mellon Bank Corp 1 Mellon Bank Ctr Pittsburgh PA 15258-0001

**MCGUIRE, ANDREW PHILIP,** lawyer; b. Albuquerque, Jan. 3, 1967; s. Eugene Joseph and Coralie Audrey McGuire. BA, U. Calif., Berkeley, 1989; JD, U. N.Mex., 1993. Bar: N.Mex. 1993, D.C. 1994, U.S. Dist. Ct. D.C. 1996, U.S. Ct. Fed. Claims 1997, U.S. Supreme Ct. 1997, U.S. Ct. Appeals (D.C. cir.) 1998. Lawyer Law Office of Andrew McGuire, Washington, 1994—. Contbr. articles to profl. jours. Mem. ABA, ATLA, Nat. Assn. Criminal Def. Lawyers. General civil litigation, Criminal, Appellate. Office: 601 Pennsylvania Ave NW Ste 900 Washington DC 20004-2601

**MCGUIRE, EDWARD DAVID, JR.,** lawyer; b. Waynesboro, Va., Apr. 11, 1948; s. Edward David and Mary Estelle (Angus) McG.; m. Georgia Ann Charuhas, Aug. 15, 1971; children: Matthew Edward, Kathryn Ann. BS in Commerce, U. Va., 1970; JD, Coll. William and Mary, 1973. Bar: Va. 1973, D.C. 1974, Md. 1990, Pa. 1995, U.S. Dist. Ct. (ea. dist.) Va. 1974, U.S. Dist. Ct. D.C. 1974, U.S. Dist. Ct. Md. 1990, Ct. Appeals (4th cir.) 1974, U.S. Ct. Appeals (D.C. cir.) 1974, U.S. Supreme Ct. 1993. Assoc. Wilkes and Artis, Washington, 1973-78; gen. corp counsel Mark Winkler Mgmt., Alexandria, Va., 1978-80; sr. contracts officer Amtrak, Washington, 1980-81; sr. real estate atty., asst. corp. sec. Peoples Drug Stores, Inc., Alexandria, 1981-88; of counsel Cowles, Rinaldi & Arnold, Ltd., Fairfax, Va., 1989-91; sr. assoc. Radigan, Rosenberg & Holmes, Arlington, Va., 1991; pvt. practice, Annandale, Va., 1992-97; sr. assoc. Stein, Sperling, Bennett, DeJong, Driscoll, Greenfeig Metro, Rockville, Md., 1997—. Co-author: Legacy: Plan, Protect and Preserve Your Estate, 1995, Generations: Planning Your Legacy, 1998. Bd. dirs. Dist. XVI Va. Student Aid Found., 1978-85, George Washington dist. Boy Scouts Am., 1986; active William and Mary Law Sch. Assn., bd. dirs., 1983-96, pres., 1987-88, treas., 1990-91. Capt. JAGC, USANG, 1973-79. Mem. ABA, Va. Bar Assn., Va. State Bar, D.C. Bar, Md. State Bar Assn., Fairfax Bar Assn., Am. Trial Lawyers Am., Arlington County Bar Assn., Va. Trial Lawyers Assn., Nat. Network Estate Planning Attys., William and Mary Alumni Soc. (bd. dirs. D.C. chpt. treas. 1990-92), U. Va. Club of Washington (schs. com. chmn. 1995—, v.p. outreach 1997-99, pres.-

elect 1998-99, bd. dirs. 1996—), Rotary (treas. Springfield chpt. 1985-86, sec. 1986-87, pres.-elect 1987, chmn. World Affairs Conf. 1985-88, bd. dirs. 1984-88, 96-97, Dist. 7610 youth leadership awards chmn. 1994-97, Outstanding Rotarian award 1985). Greek Orthodox. Avocations: racquetball, coaching youth sports. Estate planning, Real property, General civil litigation. Home: 31 W Myrtle St Alexandria VA 22301-2422 Office: 25 W Middle Ln Rockville MD 20850-2214

**MCGUIRE, EUGENE GUENARD,** lawyer; b. Apr. 1, 1945; s. Edward Joseph and Carmen Isabel (Guenard) McG.; m. Pamela Jean Cottam, Sept. 14, 1969; children: Lauren Lambert, Christopher Cottam. BArch, Cornell U., 1967; JD, Columbia U., 1970. Bar: N.Y. 1971, U.S. Dist. Ct. (so. dist.) N.Y. 1972, U.S. Dist. Ct. (ea. dist.) N.Y. 1972, U.S. Ct. Appeals (2d cir.) 1974, Conn. 1988. Assoc. Winthrop, Stimson, Putnam & Roberts, N.Y.C., 1970-79; counsel Texasgulf, Inc., N.Y.C., 1979-81, sr. counsel, asst. sec., 1981-90, sec., asst. gen. counsel, 1990-94; sr. counsel, asst. sec. Elf Aquitaine Inc., N.Y.C., 1983-90, sec., asst. gen. counsel, 1990-94, sec., gen. counsel, 1995-97, v.p., sec., gen. counsel, 1998—; v.p.-law Elf Techs., Inc., N.Y.C., 1987-94, 96-98. Mem. Am. Corp. Counsel Assn., Assn. Bar of City of N.Y., Corp. Bar Assn. of Westchester and Fairfield, Am. Yacht Club (Rye, N.Y.), Cornell Club. Quaker. Antitrust, General corporate, Securities. Office: Elf Aquitaine Inc 444 Madison Ave Fl 20 New York NY 10022-6903

**MCGUIRE, J(AMES) GRANT,** lawyer; b. Ashland, Ky., Nov. 9, 1955; s. E.E. and Martha (Spillman) McG.; m. Kheng Yap, Dec. 31, 1984. AB, Duke U., 1980; JD, Washington & Lee U., 1984. Bar: W.Va. 1984, D.C. 1984, Ky. 1985, Va. 1997. Assoc. Campbell, Woods, Bagley, Huntington, W.Va., 1984-88, ptnr., 1988—; adminstr. UN High Commn. on Refugees, Kuala Lumpur, Malaysia, 1980-81; bd. dirs. Guaranty Bank & Trust Co. Trustee Huntington Mus. of Art, 1991-97, pres. bd. dirs., 1994-97, Teubert Found. for Blind, 1991—, chmn. bd. dirs., 1994—; elder Enslow Park Presbyn. Ch., 1998—. With U.S. Army, 1975-78. Henry Luce Found. fellow, 1980-81. Mem. ABA, W.Va. State Bar (bd. govs. 1998—, bd. dirs.), W.Va. Bar Assn., City Club Huntington (nominating com. 1990), Guyan Country Club, W.Va. C. of C. (bd. mem. 1997—). Republican. Avocations: golf, tennis. Banking, General corporate, General civil litigation. Home: 123 Ridgewood Rd Huntington WV 25701-4857

**MCGUIRE, JEFFREY THOMAS,** lawyer; b. Phila., Aug. 16, 1966; s. Edward F. and Ruth E. M.; m. Michelle L. Barlow, June 20, 1992; children: Luke P., Kelly M., Sean P. BS in Math., Pa. State U., 1988; JD, Temple U., 1994. Bar: Pa. 1994, N.J. 1994, U.S. Dist. Ct. (mid. dist.) Pa. 1998, U.S. Dist. Ct. (ea. dist.) Pa. 1999. Acturial assoc. Pridential Ins. Co., Roseland, N.J., 1988-90; acturial analyst Union Fidelity Life Ins. Co., Trevose, Pa., 1990-91; assoc. Roberts, Miceli & Boileau, Lock Haven, Pa., 1995-98, Caldwell & Kearns, Harrisburg, Pa., 1998—. Bd. dirs. Clinton County United Way, Lock Haven, 1997-98. Mem. Pa. Trial Lawyers Assn., Pa. Defense Inst., Kiwanis (bd. dirs. Lock Haven chpt. 1997-98). Roman Catholic. General civil litigation, Personal injury, Professional liability. Office: Caldwell & Kearns 3631 N Front St Harrisburg PA 17110-1500

**MCGUIRE, J(OSEPH) MICHAEL,** lawyer; b. Riverdale, Md., Feb. 26, 1953. BA, U. Md., 1975, JD with honors, 1978. Bar: Md. 1978. Ptnr. Shawe & Rosenthal, Balt., 1978—. Contbr. articles to profl. jours. Mem. ABA (labor and employment law sec., com. on equal employment opportunity), Md. Assn. Def. Trial Counsel (chmn. employment and labor com. 1993, 94, 96), Bar Assn. of Balt. City, Md. State Bar Assn. (exec. coun., labor law sect. 1986). E-mail: mcguire@shawe.com. Labor. Office: Shawe & Rosenthal 20 S Charles St Fl 11 Baltimore MD 21201-3220

**MCGUIRE, KENDRA DIANE,** lawyer; b. Chambersburg, Pa., Mar. 29, 1962. BA, Franklin and Marshall Coll., 1984; JD, U. Pitts., 1987. Bar: Pa. 1987, U.S. Dist. Ct. (ea. and mid. dists.) Pa. Law clk. to Hon. Michael A. Georgelis, Ct. Common Pleas, Lancaster, Pa., 1987-88; assoc. Barley, Snyder, Senft & Cohen, Lancaster, 1988-94, ptnr., 1994—. Sec. Vist. Nurse Assn., Lancaster; bd. dirs. Lancaster Symphony Assn., United Way, Lancaster. Mem. Pa. Bar Assn., Lancaster Bar Assn. Republican. General civil litigation, Health, Probate. Office: Barley Snyder Senft & Cohen 126 E King St Lancaster PA 17602-2832

**MCGUIRE, MATTHEW FRANCIS,** lawyer; b. Pitts., Mar. 19, 1960; s. Francis Edward and Jean Anne (Blatt) McG. BS, Carnegie Mellon U., 1982; MBA, U. Pitts., 1987; JD, Duquesne U., 1992. Bar: Pa., U.S. Dist. (we. dist.) Pa.; cert. mgmt. acct. Engr. Jones and Laughlin Steel Corp., Aliquippa, Pa., 1980-82; nuclear ops. engr. Duquesne Light Co., Shippingport, Pa., 1982-85, budget and cost contr., 1985-87, mgmt. svcs. engr., 1987-89; acctg. coord. Duquesne Light Co., Pitts., 1989-93; assoc. Hull McGuire, P.C., Pitts., 1993—. Mem. NSPE, ASME, ABA, Inst. Mgmt. Accts. Avocations: golf, skiing, other sports. Construction, General corporate, Probate. Home: 215 Shafer Rd Moon Township PA 15108-1058 Office: Hull McGuire PC Usx Tower 600 Grant St Ste 3280 Pittsburgh PA 15219-2713

**MCGUIRE, WILLIAM B(ENEDICT),** lawyer; b. Newark, Feb. 14, 1929; m. Joan Glinane, June 3, 1968 (dec. Mar. 1996); children: Joan Ellen, Ralph R., James C., Keith P., Grant W. BS, Fordham U., 1950; JD, Seton Hall U., 1958; LLM in Taxation, NYU, 1963. Bar: N.J. 1958, U.S. Dist. Ct. N.J. 1958, U.S. Supreme Ct. 1971, U.S. Ct. Appeals (3rd cir.) 1980, N.Y. 1982. Chief acct. Hanover Fire Ins. Co., N.Y.C., 1950-58; sr. ptnr. Lum, Biunno & Tompkins, Newark, 1958-83, Tompkins, Mc Guire & Wachenfeld, 1984—, mng. ptnr.; asst. prosecutor Essex County, N.J., 1964-65; bd. dirs. Ind. Coll. Fund of N.J., St. Peter's Coll., Delbarton Sch.; trustee St. Barnabas Corp., St. Barnabas Med. Ctr. and Irvington Gen. Hosp.; mem. Essex County Ethics Com., 1974-77; mem. com. to review State Commn. of Investigation, 1982. Fellow Am. Coll. Trial Lawyers, Am. Bar Found. (state chmn.), Am. Bd. Trial Advocates, Internat. Acad. Trial Lawyers, Internat. Soc. Barristers; mem. ABA, N.J. State Bar Assn. (trustee 1982-89, sec. 1989-90, treas. 1990-91, 2d v.p. 1991-92, 1st v.p. 1992-93, pres. elect 1993-94, pres. 1994-95), N.J. State Bar Found. (pres. 1988-89), Essex County Bar Assn. (pres. 1975-76), Internat. Assn. Ins. Counsel, Fedn. Ins. Counsel, Def. Research Inst., Maritime Law Assn. U.S., Am. Arbitration Assn., Trial Attys. N.J., Assn. Fed. Bar N.J. (pres. 1985-88). Roman Catholic. Club: Essex County Country (pres. 1983), Newark. Federal civil litigation, Insurance, State civil litigation. Office: Tompkins McGuire & Wachenfeld 4 Gateway Ctr 100 Mulberry St Newark NJ 07102-4070

**MCGUIRL, MARLENE DANA CALLIS,** law librarian, educator; b. Hammond, Ind., Mar. 22, 1938; d. Daniel David and Helen Elizabeth (Baludis) Callis; m. James Franklin McGuirl, Apr. 24, 1965. AB, Ind. U., 1959; JD, DePaul U., 1963; MALS, Rosary Coll., 1965; LL.M., George Washington U., 1978, postgrad. Harvard U., 1985. Bar: Ill. 1963, Ind. 1964, D.C. 1972. Asst., DePaul Coll. of Law Libr., 1961-62, asst. law libr., 1962-65; ref. law librarian Boston Coll. Sch. Law, 1965-66; libr. dir. D.C. Bar Library, 1966-70; asst. chief Am.-Brit. Law Div. Libr. of Congress, Washington, 1970, chief, 1970-90, environ. cons., 1990—; counsel Cooter & Gell, 1992-93; adminstr. Washington Met. Transit Authority, 1994—; libr. cons. s. Nat. Clearinghouse on Poverty Law, OEO, Washington, 1967-69, Northwestern U. Nat. Inst. Edn. in Law and Poverty, 1969, D.C. Office of Corp. Counsel, 1969-70; instr. law librarianship Grad. Sch. of U.S. Dept. of Agr., 1968-72; lectr. legal lit. Cath. U., 1972; adj. asst. prof., 1973-91; lectr. environ. law George Washington U., 1979—; judge Nat. and Internat. Law Moot Ct. Competition, 1976-78, 90—; pres. Hamburger Heaven, Inc., Palm Beach, Fla., 1981-91, L'Image de Marlene Ltd., 1986-92, Clinique de Beauté Inc., 1987-92, Heads & Hands Inc., 1987-92, Horizon Design & Mfg. Co., Inc., 1987—; dir. Stoneridge Farm Inc., Gt. Falls, Va., 1984—. Contbr. articles to profl. jours. Mem. Georgetown Citizens Assn.; trustee D.C. Law Students in Ct.; del. Ind. Democratic Conv., 1964. Recipient Meritorious Svc. award Libr. of Congress, 1974, letter of commendation Dir. of Pers., 1976, cert. of appreciation, 1981-84. Mem. ABA (facilities law libr. Congress com. 1976-89), Fed. Bar Assn. (chpt. council 1972-76), Ill. Bar Assn., Women's Bar Assn. (pres. 1972-73, exec. bd. 1973-77, Outstanding Contbn. to Human Rights award 1975), D.C. Bar Assn., Am. Bar Found., Nat. Assn. Women Lawyers, Am. Assn. Law Libraries, (exec. bd. 1973-77), Law Librarians Soc. of Washington (pres. 1971-73), Exec. Women in Govt. Home: 3416 P St NW Washington DC 20007-2705

**MCGUIRL, ROBERT JOSEPH,** lawyer; b. Jersey City, June 16, 1952; s. Joseph Francis and Edna Louise (Davis) McG.; m. Gloria Pauline Clemente, Oct. 10, 1981; children: Brian, Jennifer. BA cum laude, Coll. Holy Cross, Worcester, Mass., 1974; JD, Georgetown U., 1977. Bar: N.Y. 1978, U.S. dist. Ct. (so. and ea. dists.) N.Y. 1979, N.J. 1981, U.S. Dist. Ct. N.J. 1981, U.S. Supreme Ct. 1987, U.S. Ct. Appeals (3d cir.) 1988. Asst. dist. atty. Office of Dist. Atty. New York County, N.Y.C., 1977-81; ptnr. Priestley, McGuirl & Wachenfeld, Westwood, N.J., 1981-92; pvt. practice law Westwood, N.J., 1992—. Mem. ABA (vice-chmn., com. profl. officers' and dir.'s liability 1987-89, contbg. editor self-insurers, risk mgrs. com. newsletter 1990), N.J. State Bar Assn. (chair products liability and toxic tort com. 1992—), Trial Attys. N.J., Essex County Bar Assn. (vice-chmn. med. legal com. 1986-87), Def. Rsch. Inst. Roman Catholic. General civil litigation, Personal injury, Product liability. Office: 345 Kinderkamack Rd Ste B Westwood NJ 07675-1600

**MCGUNNIGLE, GEORGE FRANCIS,** lawyer; b. Rochester, N.Y., Feb. 22, 1942; s. George Francis and Mary Elizabeth (Curran) McG.; m. Priscilla Ann Lappin, July 13, 1968; children: Cynthia A., Brian P. AB, Boston Coll., 1963; LLB, Georgetown U., 1966; LLM, George Wash. U., 1967. Bar: Conn. 1971, Minn. 1972, U.S. Dist. Ct. D.C. 1967, U.S. Dist. Ct. Conn. 1971, U.S. Dist. Ct. Minn. 1972, U.S. Ct. Appeals (2d cir.) 1971, U.S. Ct. Appeals (8th cir.) 1977. Asst. U.S. atty. Office of U.S. Atty., Bridgeport, Conn., 1971-72; assoc. Leonard, Street & Deinard, Mpls., 1972-73, ptnr., 1974—; mem. adv. bd. Minn. Inst. Legal Edn., Mpls., 1986—; mem. bd. editors Bus. Torts Reporter, N.Y.C., 1988—; panelist Minn. Inst. Legal Edn., 1991, moderator, 1989; panelist Leadership Mpls. Pvt. Sector Day Greater Mpls. C. of C., 1987; co-chmn. Minn. Inst. Legal Edn., 1987. Author: (with others) 50-State Survey, 1982-92. Bd. dirs. Minn. chpt. Arthritis Found.,Mpls., 1986-92, 94—, mem. exec. com., 1988-92, 95—; mem. planned giving com. Nat. Arthritis Found., Atlanta, 1992—. Lt. USN, 1967-71. Recipient Nat. Vol. Svc. citation Arthritis Found., 1992. Mem. ABA (chmn. bus. torts litigation com. 1988-91, divsn. dir. sect. litigation 1991-92, coun. 1992—, co-moderator tng. video 1992, 93, panelist trial evidence com. and bus. torts litigation com. sect. litigation 1988, co-chmn. Satellite Seminar 1988, editor Bus. Torts Litigation 1992), Minn. State Bar Assn. (lectr. Minn. Continuing Legal Edn. 1987, panelist civil litigation sect. 1992), Minn. Trial Lawyers Assn. (panelist 1992). Avocations: reading, boating. Federal civil litigation, General civil litigation, State civil litigation. Office: Leonard Street & Deinard 150 S 5th St Ste 2300 Minneapolis MN 55402-4238

**MCHALE, MICHAEL JOHN,** lawyer; b. N.Y.C., Apr. 14, 1960; s. Michael Joseph and Mary Beatrice (Graddy) McH. BA, U. of the South, 1982; JD, Samford U., 1985. Bar: Ala. 1986, U.S. Dist. Ct. (no., mid. and so. dists.) Ala. 1986, U.S. Ct. Appeals (11th cir.) 1986, Fla. (cert. admiralty and maritime law) 1991, U.S. Dist. Ct. (mid. and so. dists.) Fla. 1991, U.S. Dist. Ct. (no. dist.) Fla. 1997, U.S. Supreme Ct. 1991; cert. admiralty and maritime lawyer Fla. Bar Bd. of Legal Specialization, mediator, arbitrator Fla. Supreme Ct. Assoc. Wagner, Nugent, Johnson, Roth, Romano, Eriksen & Kupfer, West Palm Beach, Fla., 1989-92; ptnr. Whalen & McHale, West Palm Beach, Fla., 1992-95, Daves, Whalen, McHale & Considine, West Palm Beach, Fla., 1995-98; sole practitioner Jensen Beach, Fla., 1998—; of counsel Deorchis, Corsa & Hillenbrand LLP, Miami, Fla., 1998—. Author: Strategic Use of Circumstantial Evidence, 2nd edit., 1991, Evaluating and Settling Personal Injury Claims, 1992, supplement through present, Making Trial Objections, 1993, supplement through present, Expert Witnesses: Direct and Cross Examination, 1993, supplement through present; editor, author: Litigating TMJ Cases, 1993 and yearly supplements. Named one of Outstanding Young Men of Am., 1988. Mem. ABA (mem. admiralty com.), ATLA, Am. Acad. Fla. Trial Lawyers, Maritime Law Assn. U.S. (procter), Southeastern Admiralty Law Inst., Fla. Bar (admiralty law com. editl. bd., admiralty and maritime cert. com.), Palm. Beach Bar Assn., Martin County Bar Assn., Sigma Nu Phi. Avocation: vessel building. Fax: 305-571-9250. Admiralty, Contracts commercial, Federal civil litigation. Home: 1905 NE River Ct Jensen Beach FL 34957-6423 Office: Deorchis Corsa & Hillenbrand LLP 2650 Biscayne Blvd Miami FL 33137-4531

**MCHALE, ROBERT MICHAEL,** lawyer; b. Youngstown, Ohio, Oct. 14, 1932; s. John F. and Elizabeth (Prendergast) M.; children: John F. II, Rachel Anne, Robert M. Jr. Student, St. Mary's Coll., Moraga, Calif., 1950-53; JD, Tulane U., 1956. Bar: La. 1956, U.S. Dist. Ct. (we. dist.) La. 1958, U.S. Ct. Mil. Appeals 1959, U.S. Supreme Ct. 1959, U.S. Ct. Appeals (5th cir.) 1960, U.S. Dist. Ct. (ea. dist.) La. 1963. Ptnr. Rogers, McHale & St. Romain, Lake Charles, La., 1960-70; prin. McHale, Bufkin & Dees, Lake Charles, 1970-94, McHale Schwartzberg, Lake Charles, 1995-98, McHale Law Firm, Lake Charles, 1998—; bd. dirs. Cameron (La.) State Bank; chair mineral bd. State of La., 1992-94, 96, chair legal and title controversy commn., 1994-96. Democrat. Roman Catholic. Avocations: horse racing, railroads. Personal injury, General practice, Municipal (including bonds). Office: 1901 Oak Park Blvd Lake Charles LA 70601-8915

**MCHOLD, SHARON LAWRENCE,** lawyer, mediator; b. Albion, Mich., Mar. 26, 1941; d. Ted E. and Ruth M. (Whelan) McH.; m. Frank H. Lawrence, Apr. 4, 1964 (div. July 1987); children: Christopher, Brian, Kimberly. BS, U. Del., 1963; MS, Tufts U., 1965; JD, U. Maine, 1983. Researcher U. Ind. Med. Sch., Indpls., 1966-67; instr. Marian Coll., Indpls., 1967-70, Westbrook Coll., Portland, Maine, 1973-79; assoc. Curtis Thaxter, Portland, 1985-91; pvt. practice Yarmouth, Maine, 1991-93; mediator Conflict Solutions, Portland, 1993—. Trustee Maine Audubon Soc., Falmouth, Maine, 1975-79; clk. Island Inst., Rockland, Maine, 1985-92; trustee Maine Island Trail Assn., Portland, 1993-94. Nat. Def. fellow, 1963-65. Mem. Maine Bar Assn., Mass. Bar Assn., SPIDR. Alternative dispute resolution. Home: 127 Spruce Point Rd Yarmouth ME 04096-5337 Office: Conflict Solutions 75 Pearl St Portland ME 04101-1102

**MCHUGH, JAMES JOSEPH,** lawyer; b. Phila., Sept. 15, 1961; s. James Joseph and Helene Anne (Kiernan) McH.; m. Colette Marie Taylor, May 20, 1989; children: Albert Taylor, James Joseph III. BSME, Drexel U., 1985; JD magna cum laude, Villanova (Pa.) Law Sch., 1992. Bar: Pa. 1992, N.J. 1992, U.S. Dist. Ct. (ea. dist.) Pa., U.S. Dist. Ct. N.J. Ptnr. McHugh Plumbing & Heating, Phila., 1984-89; project mgr. Fluidics Mech Contractors, Phila., 1989-92; assoc. Pepper, Hamilton & Scheetz, Phila., 1992-94, Beasley, Casey & Erbstein, Phila., 1994—. Author, editor case notes. Mem. adv. com. Penn Pub. Svc. Program, Sch. Law, U. Pa. Named to Order of the Coif, Villanova Law Sch., 1992. Mem. ATLA, Pa. Bar Assn., Phila. Bar Assn. Civil rights, Libel, Personal injury. Home: 65 Brooks Rd Moorestown NJ 08057-3855 Office: Beasley Casey & Erbstein 1125 Walnut St Philadelphia PA 19107-4918

**MCHUGH, RICHARD PATRICK,** lawyer; b. Wilmington, Del., Oct. 22, 1955; s. Thomas Francis Sr. and Roberta Jean McHugh; m. Sallie A. Spillman, Jan. 5, 1980; children: Margaret A., Emily J. AB in Econ. cum laude, Georgetown U., 1977, JD, 1980. Bar: Ohio 1980, U.S. Tax Ct. 1982, D.C. 1984. Assoc. Emens Hurd Kegler & Ritter, Columbus, Ohio, 1980-83, Dow Lohnes & Albertson, Washington, 1983-88; ptnr. Dow Lohnes & Albertson PLLC, Washington, 1989—; chair legis. com. So. Employee Benefits Conf., Atlanta, 1993-95, treas., 1998—, mem. steering com., 1998—. Pres. St. James Sch. PTO, Falls Church, Va.; league commr. Arlington Girls Softball Assn., 1998—. Mem. ABA (taxation sect. employee benefit com.), Assn. Pvt. Pension and Welfare Plans, Washington Golf & Country Club, Georgetown U. Hoop Club, Alpha Sigma Nu. Democrat. Roman Catholic. Avocations: golf, collecting sports memorabilia, reading, politics. Pension, profit-sharing, and employee benefits, Corporate taxation, Mergers and acquisitions. Office: Dow Lohnes & Albertson PLLC Ste 800 1200 New Hampshire Ave NW Washington DC 20036-6800

**MCHUGH, RICHARD WALKER,** lawyer; b. Sullivan, Ind., Dec. 9, 1952; s. Richard Harrison and Virginia Ann (Robinson) McH.; m. Marsha J. Marshall, May 24, 1975; children: Walker, Cora. BA, Wabash Coll., 1975; JD, U. Mich., 1978. Bar: Mich. 1984, Ky. 1979, U.S. Supreme Ct. 1987. Assoc. Youngdahl Law Firm, Little Rock, 1978-79; staff atty. Legal Aid Soc., Louisville, 1979-84; assoc. gen. counsel Internat. Union UAW, Detroit, 1984-95; pvt. practice, Ann Arbor, Mich., 1995-98; staff atty. Mich. Poverty Law Prgm., 1998—; dir. Mich. Legal Svcs., Detroit, 1986-91. Mem. Nat. Acad. Social Ins. Democrat. Avocations: fishing, backpacking. Labor, Civil rights, Constitutional. Office: Mich Poverty Law Prgm 611 Church St Ste 4D Ann Arbor MI 48104-3000

**MCHUGH, THOMAS EDWARD,** state supreme court justice; b. Charleston, W.Va., Mar. 26, 1936; s. Paul and Melba McHugh; m. Judith McHugh, Mar. 14, 1959; children: Karen, Cindy, James, John. AB, W.Va. U., 1958, LLB, 1964. Bar: W.Va. 1964. Pvt. practice law Charleston, 1964-66, 69-74; law clk. to presiding judge Harlan Calhoun W.Va. Supreme Ct. of Appeals, 1966-68; chief judge Cir. Ct. (13th cir.) W.Va., Charleston, 1974-80; assoc. justice W.Va. Supreme Ct., Charleston, 1980-97; chief justice W. Va Supreme Ct, Charleston, 1984, 88, 92; pvt. practice King, Allen, Guthrie, & McHugh, Charleston, 1997—, Allen, Guthrie & McHugh, Charleston, 1999—. Served to 1st lt. U.S. Army, 1958-61. Mem. W.Va. Jud. Assn., W.Va. Bar Assn., Order of the Coif. Democrat. Roman Catholic. Office: Allen Guthrie & McHugh 1300 Bank One Ctr PO Box 3394 Charleston WV 25333-3394

**MCILLWAIN, WILLIAM JOHN,** lawyer; b. Indpls., Sept. 9, 1953; s. Ernest A. and Mary Jane (McGaughey) McI.; m. Sara J. Mattocks, June 12, 1981; 1 child, Mary Jayne. BA, Ind. U., 1974; JD, Valparaiso U., 1977. Bar: Ind. 1977, Colo. 1979. Assoc. Chudom & Meyer, Schererville, Ind., 1977-78, Golden Law Group, Denver, 1979, O'Donnell & Ripple, Denver, 1979-80, Jeffrey I. Tompkins, P.C., Colorado Springs., Colo., 1983-84, Bennett, Hinds & Reiner, Colorado Springs., 1984-87; pvt. practice Carmel, Ind., 1980-83, Colorado Springs, 1987—. Office: 5265 N Academy Blvd Ste 3200 Colorado Springs CO 80918-4083

**MCILWRATH, MICHAEL J.,** lawyer; b. Columbia, Mo., Aug. 26, 1962; s. James J. and Rolleen K. McIlwrath; m. Mariane A. Grin, Feb. 18, 1997; 1 child, Samuel. AB, U. Calif., Berkeley, 1985; JD, Cornell U., 1994. Assoc. Willkie Farr and Gallagher, N.Y.C., 1994—; dir. Nat. Ctr. for Sci. Edn., Berkeley, 1998—; sec. com. on product liability City Bar of N.Y., N.Y.C., 1996—. Office: Willkie Farr & Gallagher 787 7th Ave Rm 203 New York NY 10019-6099

**MCINNIS, TERRENCE REILLY,** lawyer; b. Seattle, July 19, 1966. BA, Whitman Coll., 1988; JD, Columbia U., 1991. Bar: Calif. 1991, D.C. 1992, U.S. Dist. Ct. (no., ctrl., ea. and so. dists.) Calif. 1994, U.S. Dist. Ct. (D.C. cir.) 1996, U.S. Ct. Appeals (D.C. and 9th cirs.) 1996. Law clk. Hon. John Nixon U.S. Dist. Ct. (mid. dist.) Tenn., Nashville, 1991-92; mem. Ross, Dixon & Bell, LLP, Washington, 1992-98, Irvine, Calif., 1998—. Named Harlan Fiske Stone scholar Columbia U., N.Y.C., 1988-91. Mem. ABA. Insurance, General civil litigation, Federal civil litigation. Office: Ross Dixon & Bell LLP 5 Park Plz Ste 1200 Irvine CA 92614-8592

**MCINTOSH, JAMES ALBERT,** lawyer; b. Long Beach, Calif., Nov. 2, 1933; s. James H. and Grace I. (Greenwell) McI.; m. Earlene Rae Bagley, June 22, 1956; children: Richard, Robert, Debra, Bruce, Linda, Sheri, Diane. BS, U.S. Mil. Acad., 1955; JD, U. Utah Law Sch., 1961. Bar: Utah 1961. Law clk. to justice Utah Supreme Ct., 1960-61; dep. county atty. Salt Lake County, 1962-66; legal adv. flood control and storm drainage matters Bd. Salt Lake County Commrs., 1967-73; prin. James A. McIntosh & Assocs., Salt Lake City, 1974-77; pvt. practice, Salt Lake City, 1961-74, 1984-85; v.p., ptnr. McMurray & McIntosh, 1977-84; officer, pres. James A. McIntosh & Assocs. P.C., 1985—. Trustee, U.S. Bankruptcy Ct. Utah, 1962-69. 1st lt. airborne artillery U.S. Army, 1955-58. Recipient Am. Jurisprudence award, 1961, Jumpmaster Badge, U.S. Army Ranger Tab. Mem. Utah State Bar, Utah Trial Lawyers Assn., Salt Lake County Bar Assn., Phi Delta Phi, Exchange Club (dist. pres. 1980-81). LDS. General civil litigation, Personal injury, Real property. Office: James A McIntosh & Assocs PC 2038 Royal Cir Salt Lake City UT 84108-2231

**MCINTOSH, RHODINA COVINGTON,** lawyer; b. Chicago Heights, Ill., May 26, 1947; d. William George and Cora Jean (Cain) Covington; m. Gerald Alfred McIntosh, Dec. 14, 1970; children: Gary Allen, Garvey Anthony, Ayana Kai. BA cum laude, Mich. State U., 1969; JD, U. Detroit, 1978. Asst. to dir. equal opportunity program Mich. State U., East Lansing, 1969-70; law clk. Bell & Hudson, P.C., Detroit, 1977-79; main rapporteur 1st All-Africa Law Conf., U. Swaziland and Botswana, 1981, lectr., 1981-83; chief info. and tech. assistance Office Pvt. and Vol. Cooperation, U.S. AID, Washington, 1983-87, chief info. and program support, 1987-88; corp. counsel Automation Rsch. Systems, Ltd., Alexandria, Va., 1988—; ptnr. Covington & McIntosh, Alexandria, 1992—; founding bd. mem. Women's Justice Ctr., Detroit, 1975-77; coord. women's leadership conf. Wayne State U., Detroit, 1979, participant confs. and workshops. Contbr. articles and documents to profl. publs. Rep. coord. urban program, Lansing, Mich., 1979-81; chair fgn. rels. subcom. Nat. Black Women's Polit. Caucus, Washington, 1984; bd. dirs. Mayor's Com. to Keep Detroit Beautiful, 1980, Detroit Urban League, 1981, Am. Opportunity Found., Washington, 1984—; mem. Woman Within, 1993, Suburban Treatment and Outpatient Programs, 1993; mem. adv. coun. Ctr. for Biog. Rsch., 1989—, Internat. Biog. Ctr., 1990—. Nat. Achievement scholar Ednl. Testing Svc., Princeton, N.J., 1965, Martin Luther King Jr. Ctr. for Social Change scholar, Atlanta, 1976; recipient Detroit Edison award, 1980, New Repubs. award, Mich., 1981, Disting. Leadership award ABI, 1987. Mem. ABA (vice chair small bus.com. pub. contracts law sect. 1991), Nat. Bar Assn., NAFE, GOP Women's Network, U. Detroit Law Sch. Alumni Assn., Phi Alpha Delta, Delta Sigma Theta. Roman Catholic. General corporate, Government contracts and claims, Real property.

**MCINTYRE, ANITA GRACE JORDAN,** lawyer; b. Louisville, Ky., Jan. 29, 1947; d. Blakely Gordan and Shirley Evans (Grubbs) Jordan; m. Kenneth James McIntyre, Oct. 11, 1969; children: Abigail, Jordan Kenneth. BA, Smith Coll., 1969; JD, U. Detroit, 1975. Bar: Mich. 1975, U.S. Dist. Ct. (ea. dist.) Mich. 1975, U.S. Dist. Ct. (we. dist.) Mich. 1979, U.S. Ct. Appeals (6th cir.) 1979. Ptnr. Rollins White & Rollins, Detroit, 1975-79; vis. assoc. prof. Detroit Coll. Law, 1979-81; assoc. Tyler & Canham, Detroit, 1981-82; prin. Anita G. McIntyre, P.C., Grosse Pointe, Mich., 1982-87, 91—; of counsel Nederlander Dodge & Rollins, Detroit, 1987-90; assoc. Damm & Smith, P.C., Detroit, 1990-91; hearing panel chmn. Atty. Discipline Bd., 1985—. Editor, author (case notes) U. Detroit Jour. Urban Law, 1975; contrbr. articles to profl. jours. Sec. Berry Subdivsn. Assn., Detroit, 1975-77; pres. Smith Coll. Club Detroit, 1982-86; mem. parents bd. U. Liggett Sch., Grosse Pointe, Mich., 1991-95; chmn. polit. action com. Jr. League Detroit, 1998-99. Mem. State Bar Mich., Wayne County (Mich.) Probate Bar Assn., Wayne County Juvenile Trial Lawyers Assn., Edgmont Park Assn. (sec.), Jr. League Detroit (chair pub. affairs com. 1998—, vice chair Mich. state pub. affairs com. 1999). Episcopalian. Avocations: skiing, swimming, needle point. Real property, Family and matrimonial, General civil litigation. Office: 15324 Mack Ave Ste 201 Grosse Pointe MI 48224-3397

**MCINTYRE, CARL HENRY, JR.,** lawyer; b. Washington, May 9, 1958; s. Carl Henry and Joyce Lee (Booker) McI. BA cum laude, Am. U., 1980; JD, Howard U., 1984. Bar: Pa. 1985, U.S. Ct. Appeals (D.C. cir.) 1986, U.S. Ct. Appeals (9th cir.) 1987, U.S. Ct. Appeals (5th cir.) 1988, U.S. Ct. Appeals (10th cir.) 1989, U.S. Ct. Appeals (7th, 1st, 3d and 4th cirs.) 1991, U.S. Supreme Ct. 1990, D.C. 1991. Motions atty. Ct. Appeals (D.C.), 1984-85; atty., advisor U.S. Labor Dept., Washington, 1985-86; clk. to presiding justice Ct. Appeals (D.C.), 1986-87; trial atty. civil div. U.S. Dept. Justice, Washington, 1987-95, sr. litigation counsel, 1995—; voting del. Jud. Conf. D.C., 1988-98; profl. musician trumpet, flugelhorn; toured with Gladys Knight and the Pips; performed with Temptations, Four Tops, Dells, Manhattans, O'Jays, Thad Jones and Mel Lewis Big Band, Melba Moore, Dave Brubeck, Jerry Butler; prin. trumpet Internat. Festival Orch., Internat. Festival of Youth Orch., Aberdeen, Scotland, 1974. Assoc. editor Howard Law Jour., 1983-84. Active Friends of the Kennedy Ctr., Washington, 1988-92, Washington Area Tennis Patrons Found., 1988-90; bd. dirs. Takoma Park Symphony Orch., 1990—. D.C. Youth Orch. Trumpet scholar, 1974; recipient Civil Divsn. Quality Step Increase U.S. Dept. Justice, 1989, 93, 95, 97, Spl. Achievement award, 1990, 91, 92, 94, 96, 98. Mem. ABA, Nat. Bar Assn., Internat. Platform Assn. Democrat. Roman Catholic. Home: 3900 16th St NW Apt 631 Washington DC 20011-8326

**MCINTYRE, DOUGLAS CARMICHAEL, II,** congressman; b. Lumberton, N.C., Aug. 6, 1956; s. Douglas Carmichael and Thelma Riley

(Hedgpeth) McI.; m. Lola Denise Strickland, June 26, 1982; children: Joshua Carmichael, Stephen Christopher. BA, U. N.C., 1978, JD, 1981. Bar: N.C. 1981, U.S. Dist. Ct. (ea. dist.) N.C. 1984, U.S. Dist. Ct. (mid. dist.) N.C. 1985., U.S. Ct. Appeals (4th cir.) 1987, U.S. Supreme Ct., 1987. Assoc. Law Office Bruce Huggins, Lumberton, 1981-82, McLean, Stacy, Henry & McLean, Lumberton, 1982-86; ptnr. Price & McIntyre P.A., Lumberton, 1987-89; prin. McIntyre Law Firm, P.A., Lumberton, 1989-96; congressman U.S. Ho. of Reps., 1997—; mem. law-focused edn. adv. com. N.C. Dept. Pub. Instrn., 1986-87; mem. U.S. Ho. Com. on Agr., 1997—, Nat. Security Com., 1997—; co-chmn. Coalition Task Force on Edn., 1997-98, Congrl. Task Force on Promotion of Fatherhood; mem. President's Summit on Am.'s Future, 1997. Del. Dem. Nat. Conv., N.Y.C., 1980, N.C. Dems., Raleigh, 1974—; pres. Robeson County Young Dems., Lumberton, 1982; sec.-treas. 7th Congl. Dist. Young Dems., N.C., 1983, chmn., 1984; 2d vice chmn. 7th Congl. Dist. Dems. So. N.C., 1986-89, 1st vice chmn., 1989; mem. state adv. bd. North Carolinians Against Drug and Alcohol Abuse, Raleigh, 1984-85; chmn. Morehead Scholarship Selection Com., Robeson County, 1985-94; deacon, elder, clk. of session Presbyn. Ch.; active Boy Scouts Am., Lumberton, 1983; mem. N.C. Commn. on Children and Youth, 1987-89, N.C. Commn. on the Family, 1989-91; mem. Young Life Lumberton com., 1987-89; chmn. Robeson County U.S. Constn. Bicentennial com., 1986-87; mem. lawyers' adv. com. to N.C. Commn. on Bicentennial of U.S. Constn., 1986-89; bd. dirs. Robeson County Group Home, Lumberton, 1984-87, Lumberton Econ. Advancement for Downtown, Inc., 1987-90, pres., 1988-89, 89-90; chmn. legis. affairs com. C. of C., 1991, 92, 93, bd. dirs., 1992-94; mem. N.C. Mus. of History Assocs., 1987-89; mem. regional selection com. Gov.'s Award for Excellence in Teaching Social Studies, 1991. Morehead Found. scholar, 1974-78; named one of Outstanding Young Men in Am., 1981, 84, 85, 88; Outstanding Young Dem. Robeson County Young Dems., 1984-85; one of State's Outstanding Young Dems. Young Dems. N.C., 1984, 85; recipient Algernon Sydney Sullivan award U. N.C., 1978, Outstanding Young North Carolinian award N.C. Jaycees, 1988, Outstanding Young North Carolinians, Heart Robeson Jaycees, 1988, Nat. Bicentennial Leadership award for Individual Achievement Coun. for Advancement of Citizenship and Ctr. for Civic Edn., Washington, 1987, Gov.'s Outstanding Vol. Svc. award, 1989, Thomas Jefferson award Food Distbrs. Internat., 1998. Mem. ABA (exec. com. citizenship edn. com. 1985-87, nat. cmty. law week com. 1982-83), Internat. Platform Assn., N.C. Bar Assn. (chmn. youth edn. and constn. bicentennial com. 1986-87, youth edn. com., exec. coun. young lawyers divsn. 1986-87), Robeson County Bar Assn. (founder, chmn. citizenship edn. com. 1982-94, law day com.), 16th Jud. Dist. Bar Assn., N.C. Acad. Trial Lawyers, N.C. Coll. Advocacy, Christian Legal Soc. (state adv. bd. 1986-90, state pres. 1987), Lumberton C. of C. (bd. dirs. 1992-94), Order of Old Well, Lumberton Rotary Club (bd. dirs. 1995-96), Phi Beta Kappa, Phi Eta Sigma. Avocations: tennis, snow skiing, softball, dancing, Bible study. Consumer commercial, Personal injury, Real property. Home: 1701 N Chestnut St Lumberton NC 28358-3839 Office: 1405 Longworth Washington DC 20515-0001

**MCIVOR, MARCIA LYNN,** law educator, program director, editor; b. Ann Arbor, Mich., Nov. 8, 1937; d. Edgar William and Roberta (Evans) McI.; m. Morton Gitelman, May 15, 1977; children: Neil Gitelman, Lynn Wood Ohl, Eliot Gitelman, Bruce Wood, Ronald Gitelman. BA, Mich. State U., 1958; JD, U. Ark., 1977. Staff atty. Ozark Legal Svcs., Fayetteville, Ark., 1977-85, dir. of litigation, 1985-90, dep. dir., 1990-92; supr. atty. Sch. of Law, U. Ark., Fayetteville, 1992-93, assoc. prof., acting dir. local clinic, 1993, dir. clin. edn., 1993—; editor M&M Press., Fayetteville, 1988—; spl. assoc. justice U.S. Supreme Ct.; del. Ark. Constitutional Conv. Co-author: (books) Arkansas Rules of Evidence, 1988; contbr. chpts. to books in field. Mem. exec. com. Ark. Juvenile Justice Commn., Little Rock, 1989; chair Washington County Juvenile Justice Adv. Bd., 1992-94. Recipient Clin. Legal Edn. award U.S. Dept. Edn., 1993, 94, 95, Law Sch. Legal Edn. award Legal Svcs. Corp., 1994. Mem. ABA, Am. Judicature Soc., Ark. Bar Assn., Ark. Bar Found. Democrat. Unitarian. Avocations: gardening, photography. Family and matrimonial, General civil litigation, Juvenile. Office: Sch of Law U Ark Fayetteville AR 72701

**MCKAY, DAN BOIES, JR.,** lawyer; b. Monroe, La., Aug. 31, 1948; s. Dan Boies and Joanna Irwin (McCoy) McK.; m. Adrienne Lee, Aug. 20, 1977; children: Holly, Managan, Dan B. III. BA, N.E. La. U., 1970; BS, U. Tex., 1975; JD, La. State U., 1980. Bar: La. 1980, U.S. Dist. Ct. (mid. dist.) La. 1981, U.S. Dist. Ct. (we. and ea. dists.) La. 1982, U.S. Ct. Appeals (5th cir.) 1982, U.S. Supreme Ct. 1993. Assoc. N.M. Lee & Assocs., Bunkie, La., 1980-83; sole practice Bunkie, 1984—; atty. City of Bunkie, 1982-90; magistrate, atty. Village of Hessmer, La., 1984—. Defender indigents Avoyelles Parish, Marksville, La., 1984-88, chief indigent defender, 1991—. Mem. ABA, La. State Bar Assn. (ho. of dels. 1984-87, 92—), La. Pub. DefendersAssn., Rotary (pres. Bunkie chpt. 1984-85), La. City Attys. Assn. (pres. 1988-89). Democrat. Southern Baptist. Avocation: martial arts. General civil litigation, Criminal. Home: 701 Lake St Bunkie LA 71322-1734 Office: 1019 Shirley Rd PO Box 720 Bunkie LA 71322-0720

**MCKAY, GORDON ANDREW,** lawyer; b. Detroit, Sept. 1, 1947; s. Gordon Charles McKay and Evelyn Jane Gray; m. Susan Gavin McElligott, Oct. 19, 1991; children: Elizabeth J., Ellen K. BA, Oakland U., 1968; postgrad., Princeton Theol. Sem., 1968-71; JD, Am. U., 1976. Bar: D.C. 1977, U.S. Dist. Ct. D.C. 1977, U.S. Ct. Appeals (D.C. cir.) 1977, U.S. Supreme Ct. 1985, Va. 1988. Chief clks. office of records and registration U.S. Ho. of Reps., Washington, 1971-75; asst. staff div. Fed. Election Commn., Washington, 1975-78; staff dir., gen. counsel U.S. Congress Joint Com. Printing, Washington, 1978-82; v.p. Indian Head's Info. Tech. Group, Arlington, Va., 1982; asst. U.S. atty. U.S. Dept. Justice, Washington, 1983-86; exec. v.p., gen. counsel, sec. Fairfax Group, Falls Church, Va., 1986-97; exec. v.p., COO, dep. gen. counsel DSFX, Falls Church, 1997—. Mem. Am. Corp. Counsel Assn. (vice chmn./chmn. nat. litigation com. 1996, Am. Corp. Counsel Found. (bd. dirs. 1998), Washington Chpt. Am. Corp. Counsel Assn. (v.p., pres. 1991-96, bd. dirs. 1993-99). Episcopalian. Avocation: sailing. Office: DSFX 3141 Fairview Park Dr Ste 850 Falls Church VA 22042-4507

**MCKAY, JOHN,** lawyer; b. Seattle, June 19, 1956; s. John Larkin and Kathleen (Tierney) M. BA, U. Wash., 1978; JD, Creighton U., 1982. Bar: Wash. 1982, U.S. Dist. Ct. (we. dist.) Wash. 1982, U.S. Supreme Ct. 1990, U.S. Ct. Appeals (9th cir.) 1990. Ptnr. Lane Powell Spears Lubersky, Seattle, 1982-92, Cairncross & Hempelmann, Seattle, 1992-97; pres. Legal Svcs. Corp., Washington, 1997—. White House fellow, Washington, 1989-90. Mem. ABA (bd. govs. 1991-94), Wash. State Bar Assn. (pres. young lawyers divsn. 1988-89). Republican. Roman Catholic. Avocations: soccer, golf. General civil litigation.

**MCKAY, JOHN DOUGLAS,** lawyer; b. Wheeling, W.Va., Feb. 27, 1960; s. Douglas and Margaret Ann McK.; m. Jennifer Hall, June 13, 1987; children: John Wallace, Megan Diane, Hannah Nadine. BA with distinction, U. Va., 1982; JD, U. Maine, 1985. Bar: W.Va. 1985, Maine 1985, U.S. Dist. Ct. (so. dist.) W.Va. 1985, U.S. Dist. Ct. Maine 1985, U.S. Ct. Appeals (1st cir.) 1986, Va. 1988, U.S. Ct. Appeals (4th cir.) 1988, U.S. Dist. Ct. (we. dist.) Va. 1988, Colo. 1997. Assoc. Petruccelli, Cohen, Erler & Cox, Portland, Maine, 1985-88, Taylor & Zunka, Ltd., Charlottesville, Va., 1988-91; ptnr. McKay & Cattano PLC, Charlottesville, 1991-97; prin. McKay Law Offices, Charlottesville, 1997—. Founder, editor (legal newsletter) Equine Law & Bus. Letter, 1990-95; contbr. articles to profl. jours. Elder Presbyn. Ch. Recipient Best Adv. award U. Maine Sch. of Law, 1988. Mem. Va. State Bar (7th dist. disciplinary com.), W.Va. State Bar, Charlottesville-Albemarle Bar Assn. (bd. dirs. 1994-96), Thomas Jefferson Inn of Ct. (past pres). General civil litigation, Contracts commercial, Communications. Office: McKay Law Offices 205 E High St PO Box 2018 Charlottesville VA 22902-2018

**MCKAY, JOHN JUDSON, JR.,** lawyer; b. Anderson, S.C., Aug. 13, 1939; s. John Judson and Polly (Plowden) McK.; m. Jill Hall Ryon, Aug. 3, 1961 (div. Dec. 1980); children: Julia Plowden, Katherine Henry, William Ryon, Elizabeth Hall; m. Jane Leahey, Feb. 18, 1982; children: Andrew Leahey, Jennifer McFaddin. AB in History, U. S.C., 1960, JD cum laude, 1966. Bar: S.C. 1966, U.S. Dist. Ct. S.C. 1966, U.S. Ct. Appeals (4th cir.) 1974, U.S. Supreme Ct. 1981, U.S. Dist. Ct. (so. dist.) Ga. 1988, U.S. Ct. Appeals (11th cir.), 1990. Assoc. Haynsworth, Perry, Bryant, Marion & Johnstone, Greenville, S.C., 1966-70; ptnr. Rainey, McKay, Britton, Gibbes & Clarkson, P.A., and predecessor, Greenville, 1970-78; sole practice, Hilton Head Island, S.C., 1978-80; ptnr. McKay & Gertz, P.A., Hilton Head Island, 1980-81, McKay & Mullen, P.A., Hilton Head Island, 1981-88, McKay & Taylor, Hilton Head, 1988-91; pvt. practice, 1991—. Served to lt. (j.g.) USNR, 1961-64; lt. comdr. Res. (ret.). Mem. ABA, S.C. Bar Assn. (pres. young lawyers sect. 1970, exec. com. 1971-72, assoc. mem. grievance and disciplinary com. 1983-87), S.C. Bar, Beaufort County Bar Assn., Hilton Head Bar Assn., Assn. Trial Lawyers Am., S.C. Trial Lawyers Assn., S.C. Bar Found. (pres. 1977), Blue Key, Wig and Robe, Phi Delta Phi. Episcopalian. Clubs: Poinsett (Greenville). Editor-in-chief U. S.C. Law Rev., 1966; contbr. articles to legal jours. Federal civil litigation, State civil litigation, Personal injury. Home: 17 Foxbriar Ln Hilton Head Island SC 29926 Office: 203 Watersedge Hilton Head Island SC 29928-3541

**MCKAY, M. DALE,** lawyer; b. Menominee, Mich., May 23, 1938; s. Milton David and Elizabeth Jane McK.; m. Ellen Cecella Doyle, June 16, 1962; children: Michael, James, Terrie, David, Susan. BBA, GM Inst., 1961; MBA, Mich. State U., 1962; JD, Wayne State U., 1966. Bar: Mich., U.S. Dist. Ct. (ea. and we. dists.) Mich., U.S. Tax Ct., U.S. Supreme Ct. Atty. pvt. practice, Madison Heights, Mich., 1966-68, Lansing, Mich., 1968—. Mem. Ingham County Bar Assn. (sec., bd. dirs. 1991-94, chair mediation facilities 1994), Olds Forge Flyers, Inc. Roman Catholic. Avocations: flying, skiing, biking. Aviation, Personal injury, Workers' compensation. Office: 1592 Charlotte Landing Rd Springport MI 49284-9418

**MCKAY, MICHAEL DENNIS,** lawyer; b. Omaha, May 12, 1951; s. John Larkin and Kathleen (Tierney) McK.; m. Christy Ann Cordwin, Apr. 22, 1978; children: Kevin Tierney, Kathleen Lindsay, John Larkin. BA in Polit. Sci. with distinction, U. Wash., 1973; JD, Creighton U., 1976. Bar: Wash. 1976, U.S. Dist. Ct. (we. dist.) Wash. 1978, U.S. Dist. Ct. (ea. dist.) Wash. 1982, U.S. Ct. Appeals (9th cir.) 1982, U.S. Supreme Ct. 1993. Sr. dep. pros. atty. King County, Seattle, 1976-81; ptnr. McKay & Gaitan, Seattle, 1981-89; U.S. atty. we. dist. Wash. Seattle, 1989-93; ptnr. Lane Powell Spears Lubersky, Seattle, 1993-95, McKay Chadwell PLLC, Seattle, 1995—. Bd. dirs. Mental Health North, Seattle, 1982-85, St. Joseph Sch. Bd., 1984-87, Our Lady of Fatima Sch. Commn., 1994-97, Creighton U., 1988-90; mem. stadium adv. bd. Seattle Kingdome, 1987-89; mem. U.S. Atty. Gen. Adv. Com., 1991-93, vice chmn., 1992; mem. Washington Citizens' Commn. on Salaries for Elected Officials, 1997—; vice chmn., 1999—; vice chmn. Seattle Panel Citizen Experts, 1999—. Mem. Creighton U. Alumni Assn. (pres. 1988-90, nat. alumni bd. 1988-92), Wash. Athletic Club, Columbia Tower Club. Republican. Roman Catholic. Avocations: tennis, swimming, golf. Federal civil litigation, State civil litigation, Criminal. Office: McKay Chadwell PLLC 701 5th Ave Seattle WA 98104-7097

**MCKAY, MONROE GUNN,** federal judge; b. Huntsville, Utah, May 30, 1928; s. James Gunn and Elizabeth (Peterson) McK.; m. Lucile A. Kinnison, Aug. 6, 1954; children: Michele, Valanne, Margaret, James, Melanie, Nathan, Bruce, Lisa, Monroe. B.S., Brigham Young U., 1957; J.D., U. Chgo., 1960. Bar: Ariz. 1961. Law clk. Ariz. Supreme Ct., 1960-61; assoc. firm Lewis & Roca, Phoenix, 1961-66; ptnr. Lewis & Roca, 1968-74; assoc. prof. Brigham Young U., 1974-76, prof., 1976-77; judge U.S. Ct. Appeals for 10th Cir., Denver, 1977-91, chief judge, 1991-94, sr. judge, 1994—. Mem. Phoenix Community Council Juvenile Problems, 1968-74; pres. Ariz. Assn. for Health and Welfare, 1970-72; dir. Peace Corps, Malawi, Africa, 1966-68; bd. dirs., pres. Maricopa county Legal Aid Soc., 1972-74. Served with USMCR, 1946-48. Mem. ABA, Ariz. Bar Assn., Maricopa County Bar Assn., Am. Law Inst., Am. Judicature Soc., Order of Coif, Blue Key, Phi Kappa Phi. Mem. LDS Ch. Office: US Ct Appeals for 10th Cir Fed Bldg 125 S State St Ste 6012 Salt Lake City UT 84138-1181

**MCKEAGUE, DAVID WILLIAM,** judge; b. Pitts., Nov. 5, 1946; s. Herbert William and Phyllis (Forsyth) McK.; m. Nancy L. Palmer, May 20, 1989; children: Mike, Melissa, Sarah, Laura, Elizabeth, Adam. BBA, U. Mich., 1968, JD, 1971. Bar: Mich. 1971, U.S. Dist. Ct. (we. dist.) Mich. 1972, U.S. Dist. Ct. (ea. dist.) 1978, U.S. Ct. Appeals (6th cir.) 1988. Assoc. Foster, Swift, Collins & Smith, Lansing, Mich., 1971-76, ptnr., 1976-92; sec.-treas. Foster, Swift, Collins & Smith, 1990-92; judge U.S. Dist. Ct., Western Dist. Mich., Lansing, 1992—; adj. prof. Thomas M. Cooley Law Sch., Detroit Coll. Law, Mich. State U. Nat. com. U. Mich. Law Sch. Fund, 1980-92; gen. counsel Mich. Rep. Com., 1989-92; adv. coun. Wharton Ctr., Mich. State U., 1996—. Mem. FBA (bd. dirs. Western Mich. chpt. 1991—), Mich. Bar Assn., Am. Inns of Ct. (pres. Detroit Coll. of Law at Mich. State U. chpt. 1999—), Country Club Lansing (bd. govs. 1988-92, 96—), The Federalist Soc. for Law and Pub. Studies (lawyers divsn. Mich. chpt. 1996—). Roman Catholic. Office: US Dist Ct 315 W Allegan St Lansing MI 48933-1500

**MCKEARIN, ROBERT R.,** lawyer, director; b. Bennington, Vt., June 1, 1948; m. Mary Kathryn McKearin, June 6, 1971; children: Christopher, Laura. BA, Gettysburg Coll., 1970; JD, So. Meth. U., 1974. Bar: Tex. 1974, Vt. 1978. Asst. regional counsel U.S. EPA Region VI, Dallas, 1974-77; law clk. U.S. Dist. Ct. Vt., Rutland, 1977-78; ptnr./dir. Dinse, Knapp & McAndrew, Burlington, Vt., 1978—; editor Vt. Employment Law Letter, 1997—;. Bd. dirs. Lake Champlain Com., Burlington, 1988—, King St. Neighborhood Corp., 1990—, South End Cmty. Housing Corp., 1998—. Mem. Internat. Assn. Def. Counsel, Def. Rsch. Inst. Avocations: biking, skiing. Education and schools, Constitutional, Labor. Office: Dinse Knapp & McAndrew 209 Battery St Burlington VT 05401-5261

**MCKEE, CATHERINE LYNCH,** law educator, lawyer; b. Boston, June 7, 1962; d. Robert Emmett and Anne Gayle (Tanner) Lynch; m. Bert K. McKee Jr., Dec. 25, 1990; children: Timothy Kingston, Shannon Lancaster. BA in Biol. Sci., U. Calif. Berkeley, 1984; JD, U. San Diego, 1988. Bar: Calif. 1988, U.S. Dist. Ct. (cen., so. and ea. dists.) Calif. 1989, U.S. Ct. Appeals (9th cir.) 1989. Assoc. Parkinson, Wolf, Lazar & Leo, L.A., 1988-89, McCormick & Mitchell, San Diego, 1989-91; prof., mock trial coach Mt. San Antonio Coll., Walnut, Calif., 1994—; certification review hearing officer, Orange County, 1994—; legal counsel Imperial Valley Lumber Co., Valley Lumber and Truss Co., 1998—. Contbr. weekly newspaper column, 1993—; prodr., star videos An Attorney's Guide to Legal Research on the Internet, 1999; co-author: Jeff and Catherine's World's Best List of Legal (and Law-related) Internet Sites. Chair scholarship com. U. Calif. Alumni Assn., Diamond Bar, 1995—. Named Cmty. Person of Yr. Diamond Bar C. of C., 1995. Mem. ABA, State Bar Calif. (probation monitor 1993—), Ea. Bar Assn. L.A., Am. Inns of Ct., Calif. Assn. Lanterman-Petris-Short Hearing Officers. Avocations: weight lifting, photography, reading. Office: Mount San Antonio Coll 1100 N Grand Ave Walnut CA 91789-1341

**MCKEE, FRANCIS JOHN,** medical association executive, lawyer; b. Bklyn., Aug. 31, 1943; s. Francis Joseph and Catherine (Giles) McK.; m. Antoinette Mary Sancis; children: Lisa Ann, Francis Dominic, Michael Christopher, Thomas Joseph. AB, Stonehill Coll., 1965; JD, St. John's U., 1970. Bar: N.Y. 1971. Assoc. Samuel Weinberg, Esquire, Bklyn., 1970-71, Finch & Finch, Esquire, Long Island City, N.Y., 1971-72; staff atty. Med. Soc. of State of N.Y., Lake Success, N.Y., 1972-77; prin. Francis J. McKee Assocs., Clinton, N.Y., 1984—; exec. dir. Suffolk Physicians Rev. Orgn., East Islip, N.Y., 1977-81, N.Y. State Soc. Surgeons, Inc., Clinton, N.Y., 1981—, N.Y. State Soc. Orthopaedic Surgeons, Inc., Clinton, 1981—, Upstate N.Y. chpt. ACS, Inc., Clinton, 1981—, N.Y. State Ophthalmol. Soc., 1984-92, N.Y. State Soc. Obstetricians and Gynecologists, 1985—, Orthopac of N.Y., 1986—, Nat. Com. for the Preservation Orthopaedic Practice, Clinton, 1989—; L.I. Ophthalmological Soc., 1994—. With U.S. Army, 1966-68. Mem. N.Y. State Bar Assn., Oneida County Bar Assn., Am. Soc. Assn. Execs., Am. Assn. Med. Soc. Execs., Nat. Health Lawyers Assn., Skenandoa Club, Am. Legion. Republican. Roman Catholic. Home: 19 Mulberry St Clinton NY 13323-1532 Office: PO Box 308 40 Chenango Ave Clinton NY 13323-1341

**MCKEE, RALPH DYER, JR.,** lawyer; b. Pitts., Jan. 1, 1925; s. Ralph Dyer and Ruth Mason (Chapman) M.; m. Doris Ann Reimers, June 4, 1949; children: Scott Dyer, Elizabeth M. Beswick, Jane M. Hardman. AB, Princeton U., 1948; JD, U. Pitts., 1951. Bar: Pa. 1952, U.S. Dist. Ct. (we. dist.) Pa. 1952, U.S. Supreme Ct. 1956, U.S. Ct. Mil. Appeals 1956. Ptnr. Alter, Wright & Barron, Pitts., 1951-90; of counsel Sherrard, German & Kelly, Pitts., 1990—. Past pres. mgmt. North Boroughs YMCA Bellevue, Pa., 1952-57; bd. dirs., past pres. Avonworth Sch., Ben Avon, Pa., 1957-73, Allegheny County (Pa.) Schs., 1962-72. Served to maj. USAF, 1943-45, ETO. Fellow Am. Coll. Trust and Estate Counsel; mem. ABA, Pa. Bar Assn. (Ho. of Dels. 1983-89), Allegheny County Bar Assn. (probate and trust law sect., chmn. profl. ethics com. 1980-82), Edgeworth Club, Masons, Moose. Republican. Presbyterian. Avocations: tennis, golf, fishing, gardening, hiking. Probate, General corporate, General practice. Home: 6903 Merton Rd Pittsburgh PA 15202-1822 Office: Sherrard German & Kelly 1 Oliver Plz Fl 35 Pittsburgh PA 15222-2600

**MCKEE, ROGER CURTIS,** retired federal judge; b. Waterloo, Iowa, Feb. 11, 1931; s. James A. and Leonace (Burrell) McK.; m. Roberta Jeanne Orvis, Sept. 3, 1954; children: Andrea Jane, Brian Curtis, Paul Robert. BA, State Coll. of Iowa, 1955; MA, U. Ill., 1960; JD, U. San Diego, 1968. Bar: Calif. 1970, U.S. Dist. Ct. (so. dist.) Calif. 1969, U.S. Ct. Appeals (9th cir.) 1971. Telegrapher, agt. Ill. Cen. R.R., 1950-55; tng. asst. No. Ill. Gas Co., Aurora, 1959-60; with indsl. rels. dept. Convair div. Gen. Dynamics Corp., San Diego, 1960-68; contract adminstr. and supr. Datagraphix div. Gen. Dynamics Corp., San Diego, 1968-69, asst. counsel, 1969-70; ptnr. Powell & McKee, San Diego, 1970-75, Millsberg, Dickstein & McKee, San Diego, 1975-83; magistrate judge U.S. Dist. Ct. for So. Dist. Calif., San Diego, 1983-97; presiding magistrate judge, 1993-97. Bd. trustees So. Calif. Presbyn. Homes, L.A., 1979-81; moderator Presbytery of San Diego, 1980. Capt. USNR, 1949-85. Mem. Calif. Bar Assn., Fed. Magistrate Judges Assn., Navy League U.S., Naval Res. Officers Assn., Res. Officers Assn., Dixieland Jazz Soc. (bd. dirs. San Diego chpt. 1984—). Republican.

**MCKEE, THEODORE A.,** federal judge; b. 1947. B.A., SUNY, Cortland, 1969; J.D. magna cum laude, Syracuse U. Coll. of Law, 1975. Dir. of minority recruitment & admissions SUNY, Binghamton, 1969-72; atty. Wolf, Block, Schorr & Solis-Cohen, Phila., 1975-77; asst. U.S. atty., Eastern Dist. PA, 1977-80, asst. U.S. atty., Eastern Dist. Gen. Crimes Unit, Narcotics and Firearms Unit, then Polit. Corruption Unit; lecturer Rutgers U. Coll. of Law, 1980-91; dep. city solicitor Law Dept., Phila., 1980-83; gen. counsel Phila. Parking Auth., 1983; judge Ct. of Common Pleas, 1st Jud. Dist, PA, 1984-94, judge major felony program, 1986, judge orphans' ct. divsn., 1992; judge U.S. Ct. Appeals (3d cir.), Phila., 1994—; bd. dirs. Diagnostic and Rehab. Ctr. of Phila. Mem. World Affairs Coun., New Directions for Women, Inc.; trustee Edna McConnell Clark Found. Mem. ABA, Nat. Bar Assn., Am. Law Inst., Barristers' Assn. Phila., Temple Inn of Ct., Crime Prevention Assn. (bd. dirs.). Office: 601 Market St Rm 20614 Philadelphia PA 19106-1715*

**MCKEE, THOMAS FREDERICK,** lawyer; b. Cleve., Oct. 27, 1948; s. Harry Wilbert and Virginia (Light) McK. BA with high distinction, U. Mich., 1970; JD, Case Western Rs. U., 1975. Bar: Ohio 1975, U.S. Dist. Ct. (no. dist.) Ohio 1975, U.S. Supreme Ct. 1979. Assoc. firm Calfee, Halter & Griswold, Cleve., 1975-81, ptnr., 1982—, also mem. exec. com., chmn. operating com.; sec. McDonald & Co. Investments, Inc., Chart Industries, Inc., Heathometer Products, Inc., Collaborative Clin. Rsch., Inc.; bd. dirs. Mr. Coffee, Inc. Contbg. editor Going Public, 1985. Mem. ABA (com. fed. regulation securities law sect.), Bar Assn. Greater Cleve., Order of Coif., Union Club, Tavern Club, Country Club, Hillbrook Club. General corporate, Securities. Home: 210 Pheasant Run Dr Chagrin Falls OH 44022-2968 Office: Calfee Halter & Griswold 800 Superior Ave E Ste 1400 Cleveland OH 44114-2688

**MCKEE, WALTER FREDERIC,** lawyer; b. Easley, S.C., Oct. 26, 1967; s. Robert Steel and Linda Rogers McKee; m. Kristin Lee Aiello, Sept. 10, 1994; 1 child, Anne Aiello McKee. BA, U. Maine, 1989, JD, 1993. Bar: S.C. 1993, Maine 1994, U.S. Dist. Ct. Maine 1994, U.S. Ct. Appeals (1st cir.) 1994. Pvt. practice Portland, Maine, 1993-95; assoc. Lipman & Katz, PA, Augusta, Maine, 1995-97, ptnr., 1998—. Capt. U.S. Army/Maine N.G., 1996—. Mem. ATLA, Nat. Assn. Criminal Def. Lawyers, Maine Trial Lawyers Assn., Maine Assn. Criminal Def. Lawyers (bd. dirs. 1995-98). Criminal, Personal injury, General civil litigation. Office: Lipman & Katz PA PO Box 1051 Augusta ME 04332-1051

**MCKELVEY, JUDITH GRANT,** lawyer, educator, university dean; b. Milw., July 19, 1935; d. Lionel Alexander and Bernadine R. (Verdun) Grant. B.S. in Philosophy, U. Wis., 1957, J.D., 1959. Bar: Wis. 1959, Calif. 1968. Atty. FCC, Washington, 1959-62; adj. prof. U. Md., Europe, 1965; prof. law Golden Gate U. Sch. Law, San Francisco, 1968-99, dean, 1974-81; mem. State Jud. Nominees Evaluation Commn., 1981-82. Contbr. to: Damages Book, 1975, 76. Bd. dirs. San Francisco Neighborhood Legal Assistance Found. Fellow Am. Bar Found.; mem. ABA, Wis. Bar Assn., Calif. Bar Assn., San Francisco Bar Assn. (dir. 1975-77, chmn. legis. com., sec.-treas., pres.-elect 1980-83, pres. 1984), Calif. Women Lawyers (1st pres.), Law in a Free Soc. (exec. com.), Continuing Edn. of Bar (chmn. real estate subcom., mem. joint adv. com.), Legal Svcs. to Children Inc. (pres. 1987-89), San Francisco Neighborhood Legal Assistance Found. (dir. and exec. com. 1985-87), Lawyers Com. for Urban Affairs (dir. and exec. com. 1985-87, co-chairperson 1988-90). Office: Golden Gate U Sch Law 536 Mission St San Francisco CA 94105-2921

**MCKELVIE, RODERICK R.,** federal judge; b. 1946. BA, Harvard U., 1968; ME, Roosevelt U., 1970; JD, U. Pa., 1973. Law clk. to Hon. Caleb Layton U.S. Dist. Ct., Wilmington, Del., 1973-74; assoc. Richards, Layton & Finger, Wilmington, 1974-79; ptnr. Ashby, McKelvie & Geddes, Wilmington, 1979-92; fed. judge U.S. Dist. Ct. (Del. dist.), Wilmington, 1992—. Active World Affairs Coun., 1988—, United Way Govt. Rels. Commn. Mem. ABA, Del. State Bar, Richard S. Rodney Inn of Ct. (mem. exec. com., pres. 1992-93). Office: US Dist Ct Lock Box 10 844 N King St Ste 18 Wilmington DE 19801-3570

**MCKENDRY, JOHN H., JR.,** lawyer, educator; b. Grand Rapids, Mich., Mar. 24, 1950; s. John H. and Lois R. (Brandel) McK.; m. Linda A. Schmalzer, Aug. 11, 1973; children: Heather Lynn, Shannon Dawn, Sean William. BA cum laude, Albion Coll., 1972; JD cum laude, U. Mich., 1975. Bar: Mich. 1975. Assoc., then ptnr. Landman, Latimer, Clink & Robb, Muskegon, Mich., 1976-85; ptnr. Warner, Norcross & Judd, Muskegon, 1985—; dir. debate Mona Shores High Sch., Muskegon, 1979-90; adj. prof. of taxation (employee benefits), Grand Valley State U., 1988—; debate instr. Muskegon C.C., 1999—. Pres. local chpt. Am. Cancer Soc., 1979; bd. dirs. West Shore Symphony, 1993—, v.p. 1995-97, pres., 1997-99; bd. dirs. Cath. Social Svcs., 1998—; chair profl. divsn. United Way, 1994, 98. Recipient Disting. Service award Muskegon Jaycees, 1981; named 1 of 5 Outstanding Young Men in Mich., Mich. Jaycees. 1982; named to Hall of Fame, Mich. Speech Coaches, 1986, Diamond Key Coach Nat. Forensic League, 1987. Mem. ABA, Mich. Bar Assn., Muskegon County Bar Assn. (dir. 1992-98, pres. 1996-97), Muskegon C. of C. (bd. dirs. 1982-88), Mich. Interscholastic Forensic Assn. (treas. 1979-86), Optimists (pres. 1992). Republican. Roman Catholic. Pension, profit-sharing, and employee benefits. Home: 1575 Brookwood Dr Muskegon MI 49441-5276 Office: Warner Norcross & Judd LLP PO Box 900 400 Terrace Pla Muskegon MI 49443-0900

**MCKENNA, FREDERICK GREGORY,** lawyer, consultant; b. Chgo., Oct. 4, 1952; s. Frederick Hilary and Jean Elizabeth (Henneberry) McK.; m. Cornelia Ann Burns, Nov. 17, 1984; children: Kieran Padraig, Conor Burns. BA with honors, Coll. Holy Cross, 1974; JD, Georgetown U., 1978; postgrad., U. Nev., Las Vegas, U. Denver. Bar: D.C. 1978, Md. 1981, Nev. 1986, U.S. Supreme Ct. 1987, Colo. 1993. Assoc. Joseph, McDermott et al, Washington, 1979-82, Hudson & Creyke, Washington, 1982-85; sr. counsel Reynolds Elec. & Engring. Co., Inc., Las Vegas, 1985-90; dep. gen. counsel EG&G Rocky Flats, Golden, Colo., 1990-92, v.p., gen. counsel, 1992-96; ptnr. Hall & Evans, Denver, 1996—. Mem. Community Svc. Commn., Md., 1984-85. Mem. ABA, D.C. Bar Assn. (D.C. procurement com.), Mensa. Republican. Roman Catholic. Avocations: weightlifting, science history. Government contracts and claims, Environmental. Home: 5954 Wood Sorrel Way Littleton CO 80123-6758 Office: Hall & Evans 1200 17th St Ste 1700 Denver CO 80202-5817

**MCKENNA, J. FRANK, III,** lawyer; b. Pitts., Nov. 9, 1948; s. J. Frank Jr. and Antoinette (Schlafly) McK.; m. Colleen Shaughnessy, Mar. 25, 1972; children: Collette M., J. Frank IV, Laura J., Stephen J. BA, Williams Coll.,

1970; JD, U. Pitts., 1973. Bar: Pa. 1973. Assoc. Thorp, Reed & Armstrong, Pitts., 1973-82, ptnr., 1982-88; ptnr. Babst, Calland, Clements & Zomnir, Pitts., 1988—. Served to lt. USAFR, 1973-74. Named one of Outstanding Young Men In Am., 1982. Mem. ABA, Pa. Bar Assn., Allegheny County Bar Assn. (chmn. young lawyers sect. 1980, v.p. 1987, bd. govs. 1988-90, pres.-elect 1991, pres. 1992), Am. Law Inst., Acad. Trial Lawyers Allegheny County, Am. Judicature Soc., Allegheny County Bar Found. (pres. 1996—),. Construction, Contracts commercial, Federal civil litigation. Home: 101 Fox Ridge Farms Dr Pittsburgh PA 15215-1142 Office: Babst Calland Clements & Zonmir 2 Gateway Ctr Pittsburgh PA 15222-1425

**MCKENNA, PETER J.,** lawyer; b. Glen Cove, N.Y., 1946. BA cum laude, Fordham U., 1968; JD, Georgetown U., 1974. Bar: N.Y. 1975. Mem. Skadden, Arps, Slate, Meagher & Flom, N.Y.C. Assoc. editor Am. Criminal Law Review, 1971-72; editor Georgetown Law Jour., 1973-74. Office: Skadden Arps Slate Meagher & Flom 919 3rd Ave New York NY 10022-3902

**MCKENNAN, JOHN T.,** lawyer; b. New Hartford, N.Y., Nov. 25, 1918; s. John Patrick and Rena C. (Dowd) McK.; m. Marguerite Gallagher, May 7, 1955; children: John, Timothy. BS, Utica Acad., 1938, Scarborough Sch., 1939; postgrad., Syracuse U., 1939-41; LLB, Union U., 1945. Bar: N.Y. 1945. Assoc. Hawkins, Delafield & Longfellow, N.Y.C., 1945; pvt. practice Utica, N.Y., 1946—; judge N.Y. State Supreme Ct. for 5th Jud. Dist., 1982. Mem. N.Y. State Senate, 1949-51; mayor City of Utica, 1956-60; sec. N.Y. State Constl. Conv., Albany, 1967. Mem. Yahnundasis Golf Club. Democrat. Roman Catholic. Avocation: golf. Personal injury, Probate, General practice. Home: 15 Foxcroft Rd New Hartford NY 13413-2734

**MC KENNEY, WALTER GIBBS, JR.,** lawyer, publishing company executive; b. Jacobsville, Md., Apr. 22, 1913; s. Walter Gibbs and Mary (Starkey) McK.; m. Florence Roberta Rea, July 17, 1939. Student, Dickinson Sem., 1935-37; Ph.B. Dickinson Coll., 1939; J.D., U. Va., 1942; LL.D., Dickinson Sch. Law, 1964; LHD, Lycoming Coll., 1984. Bar: Md. 1942. Practiced in Balt., 1942—; partner McKenney, Thomsen & Burke; partner, gen. mgr., editor Taxes & Estates Pub. Co., Balt., 1946—; chmn. trust com. Equitable Bank, N.A., Balt., 1970-84; dir. Equitable Bancorp., 1960-84; lectr. Southwestern Grad. Sch. Banking, 1966-76. Editor Taxes and Estates, 1946—, Minimizing Taxes, 1964-84, The Educator, 1965—, The Patron, 1968-84. Pres. Kelso Home for Girls; mem. bd. child care Balt. Conf. Meth. Ch., pres., 1961-64; pres. Balt. Estate Planning Council, 1963-64; trustee Goucher Coll., 1968-84, Dickinson Coll., Lycoming Coll., Wesley Theol. Sem., Loyola Coll. at Balt., 1975-83, Franklin Sq. Hosp., Franklin Square Found., Franklin Square Health System, Helix Health System. Served to lt. USNR, 1942-45. Mem. ABA, Md., Balt. bar assns. Republican. Methodist. Estate planning, Probate, Taxation, general. Home: 105 Brightwood Club Dr Lutherville MD 21093-3628

**MCKENNON, RICHARD OTEY,** lawyer; b. Wichita Falls, Tex., Apr. 30, 1964; s. Richard Ernest and Linda Sue (Wallace) McK.; m. Kayla L. McKennon; children: Matthew Richard, Meagan Kelley. BA, North Tex. State U., 1985; JD, Tex. Tech U., 1987. Bar: Tex. 1988, U.S. Dist. Ct. (no. dist.) Tex. 1988, U.S. Dist. Ct. (ea. dist.) Tex. 1990, U.S. Supreme Ct. 1994; cert. in personal injury trial law Tex. Bd. Legal Specialization. Assoc. McGuire & Levy, Irving, Tex., 1987-89, Stradley, Schmidt & Wright, Dallas, 1989-92; ptnr. Royse & McKennon, Dallas, 1992-95, Richard O. McKennon, P.C., Dallas, 1995—; instr. civil litigation paralegal program Tex. Wesleyan U. Sch. Law, 1993; presenter in field. Mem. ATLA, Tex. Trial Lawyers Assn., Dallas Bar Assn. Avocations: martial arts, writing fiction and nonfiction. Personal injury, Civil rights, General civil litigation. Office: Ste 1030 Abrams Ctr 9330 LBJ Fwy Dallas TX 75243

**MCKENZIE, CURTIS DAVID,** lawyer; b. Corvallis, Oreg., Feb. 9, 1969; s. Ray and Symone McK.; m. Renee S., Aug. 7, 1993; 1 child, Jackson. BA, Northwest Nazarene Coll., 1992; JD, Georgetown U., 1995. Bar: Md. 1995, D.C. 1996, U.S. Dist. Ct. Md. 1996, Idaho 1997. Assoc. Arter & Hadden, Washington, 1995-97; deputy prosecutor Ada County Prosecutor, Boise, 1997-98; assoc. Stoel Rives, Boise, 1998—. Mem. Order of Coif. Republican. General civil litigation.

**MCKENZIE, JAMES FRANKLIN,** lawyer; b. Mobile, Ala., May 3, 1948; s. Frank L. McKenzie and Mary K. (Crow) McKenzie O'Neal; m. Randy Jo Jones, June 25, 1977; children: Katherine J., J. Alistair. BA magna cum laude, U. W. Fla., 1970; JD with honors, U. Fla., 1973. Bar: Fla. 1973, U.S. Dist. Ct. (no. dist.) Fla. 1973, U.S. Ct. Appeals (5th cir.) 1975, U.S. Ct. Appeals (11th cir.) 1982, U.S. Supreme Ct. 1988. Lectr. bus. law U. Fla., Gainesville, 1972-73; assoc. Levin, Warfield et al, Pensacola, Fla., 1973-76; ptnr. Myrick & McKenzie, PA, Pensacola, Fla., 1976-82, McKenzie & Taylor, PA, Pensacola, Fla., 1982—. Contbr. chpts. to books, articles to profl. jours. Pres. N.W. Fla. Easter Seal Soc., Pensacola, 1975; bd. dirs. Five Flags Sertoma Club, 1977; trustee Fla. Lawyers Action Group, Tallahassee, 1996—; adv. bd. Lupus Soc., N.W. Fla., 1992. Mem. ABA, ATLA (sustaining), Acad. Fla. Trial Lawyers (bd. dirs. 1986-93, exec. com., coll. diplomates, Silver Eagle award 1989, ABCD award 1991), 1st Cir. Acad. Trial Lawyers (founding mem., pres. 1984), Fla. Bar Assn. (cert. in civil trial law), Escambia-Santa Rosa Bar Assn., Nat. Bd. Trial Advocacy (cert. civil trial advocacy), Civil Justice Found. (founding sponsor), Million Dollar Advocates Forum, Order of Coif, Pensacola Country Club, Exec. Club, Phi Kappa Phi, Omicron Delta Kappa, Phi Delta Phi, Omicron Delta Kappa, Phi Delta Phi. Republican. Methodist. Personal injury, Insurance, General civil litigation. Home: 12 Tristan Way Pensacola Beach FL 32561 Office: McKenzie & Taylor PA 905 E Hatton St Pensacola FL 32503-3931

**MCKENZIE, JAMES W.,** lawyer; b. Oct. 3, 1959. AB, Dartmouth Coll., 1982; MBA, U. Pa., 1987, JD, 1987. Bar: Pa. 1987. Assoc. Morgan, Lewis & Bockius LLP, Phila. Office: Morgan Lewis & Bockius LLP 1701 Market St Philadelphia PA 19103-2903

**MCKENZIE, ROBERT ERNEST,** lawyer; b. Cheboygan, Mich., Dec. 7, 1947; s. Alexander Orlando and Edna Jean (Burt) McK.; m. Theresia Wolf, Apr. 26, 1975; 1 child, Robert A. BA in Personnel Adminstrn., Mich. State U., 1970; JD with high honors, Ill. Inst. Tech., 1979. Bar: Ill. 1979, U.S. Dist. Ct. (no. dist.) Ill. 1979, U.S. Tax Ct. 1979, U.S. Ct. Appeals (7th cir.) 1979, U.S. Supreme Ct. 1984; lic. pvt. pilot. Revenue officer IRS, Chgo., 1972-78; ptnr. McKenzie & McKenzie, Chgo., 1979—; lectr. Tax Seminars Inst., Chgo., 1984—. Author: Representation Before the Collection Divison of the IRS, 1989; co-author: Representing the Audited Taxpayer Before the IRS, 1990; contbr. articles to profl. jours. Mem. tax adv. com. Nat. Bankruptcy Rev. Commn., 1997; del. Rep. Nat. Conv., Detroit, 1980, Ill. State Rep. Conv., Peoria, 1980. Served with U.S. Army, 1970. Recipient scholarship Mich. State U., 1966-70, State of Mich., 1966-70, Silas Strawn scholarship ITT, 1977. Mem. ABA (chmn. employment tax com. tax sect. 1992-94, co-chmn. bankruptcy task force 1997-98, coun. tax sect. 1998—), Chgo. Bar Assn. (chmn. com. devel. tax com. 1996-97), N.W. Suburban Bar Assn. (chmn. econs. of law com. 1986-87), Fed. Bar Assn. (tax com.), Rotary (pres. Norridge club 1985-86). Avocation: flying, genealogy. Personal income taxation, Corporate taxation. Office: 5450 N Cumberland Ave Chicago IL 60656-1484

**MCKENZIE, THOMAS JAMES,** lawyer, insurance consultant; b. Hastings, Nebr., May 7, 1930; s. Martin O. and Mary Ella (Graves) McK.; m. Harriet J. Beck, Nov. 10, 1951; children: Bruce, Craig, Scot, Mark. BA, State U. Iowa, 1955, JD, 1958. Bar: Iowa 1958, Ind. 1967, Pa. 1972, U.S. Dist. Ct. (we. dist.) Pa. 1993; CPCU. Atty. Benke & McKenzie, Parkersburg, Iowa, 1958; adjuster State Farm Ins., Dubuque, Iowa, 1958-64; claim and litig. mgr. State Auto Ins., Indpls., 1964-71; ins., claim and litig. mgr. Motor Freight Express, York, Pa., 1971-83; v.p. claims-litig. Mut. Benefit Ins., Huntingdon, Pa., 1983-92; ins. litigator Murphy, Taylor, P.C., Pitts., 1992—; seminar speaker in field. Served to staff sgt. USAF, 1951-53. Mem. ABA, Pa. Bar Assn., Masons, Shriners, Phi Alpha Delta. Insurance, Personal injury, Workers' compensation. Home: 137 Lakeshore Dr Kimberling City MO 65686-9694 Office: Murphy Taylor PC 326 3rd Ave Pittsburgh PA 15222-1911

**MCKEON, GEORGE A.,** lawyer; b. Orangeburg, N.Y., Jan. 22, 1937; s. Thomas Patrick and Elizabeth Anna McKeon; m. Eileen Ann Connors, June 27, 1959 (dec. Aug. 1977); children: John, Alice, Thomas; m. Fay L. Akins, Aug. 28, 1981. BA, Fairleigh Dickinson U., 1959; LLB, Fordham U., 1963. Bar: N.Y., 1964, Conn., 1967, U.S. Dist. Ct., Conn., 1971. With contracts negotiation Bendix Corp., Teterboro, N.J., 1958-65; div. asst. counsel United Technologies, Windsor Locks, Conn., 1965-69; asst. counsel Travelers Ins. Co., Hartford, Conn., 1969-73, assoc. counsel, 1973-76, counsel, 1976-81; assoc. gen. counsel Travelers Ins. Co., Hartford, 1981-84; gen. counsel Travelers Ins. Co., Hartford, Conn., 1984-94; with Hebb & Gitlin PC, Hartford, 1994—; mem. faculty U. Conn. Referee Vol. Pub. Defender Program, Conn. Mem. ABA (chmn. corp. counsel com. tort and ins. practice sect. 1985-87, mem. commn. on Mass. torts 1987-88), N.Y. Bar Assn., Conn. Bar Assn., Hartford County Bar Assn. Roman Catholic. Home: 36 Bradley Brook Dr North Granby CT 06060-1521 Office: Hebb & Gitlin PC 1 State St Ste 26 Hartford CT 06103-3178

**MCKEON, JAMI WINTZ,** lawyer; b. Mar. 13, 1957. BA, Pa. State U., 1978; JD, Villanova U., 1981. Bar: Pa. 1981, U.S. Supreme Ct. 1984. Ptnr. Morgan, Lewis & Bockius LLP, Phila. Intellectual property, Federal civil litigation, Bankruptcy. Office: Morgan Lewis & Bockius LLP 1701 Market St Philadelphia PA 19103-2903

**MCKEONE, MARK R.,** lawyer; b. Cozad, Nebr., Oct. 13, 1960; s. Joe J. and Betty L. McK.; m. Julie M. Rolands, Aug. 13, 1983 (div. June 1997); children: Alexandra C., Austin T.; m. Cindy K. McKeone, Dec. 14, 1997; 1 child, Julie R. JD, Creighton U., 1987; BSBA, Kearney State Coll., 1983. Sole practice Omaha, 1988-91; atty. Hart Law Office PC, Cozad, 1991—; pres. Cozad Devel. Corp., 1995-97; chmn. bd. dirs. Dawson County Area Econ. Devel., Cozad, 1997. State civil litigation, Contracts commercial, Personal injury. Office: Hart Law Office PC PO Box 229 Cozad NE 69130-0229

**MCKEOWN, H. MARY,** lawyer, educator; b. West Palm Beach, Fla., Sept. 17, 1952; d. Honore Stephen McKeown and Margaret Berg McKeown Growney; m. Jon Henry Barber, Sept. 18, 1981; children: Sean Patrick, Mary Kathleen. AA, St. Petersburg Jr. Coll., Fla., 1970; BA in Polit. Sci. and Sociology, U. South Fla., 1972; JD cum laude, Samford U., 1976. Bar: Fla. 1976, U.S. Dist. Ct. (mid. dist.) Fla. 1977, U.S. Ct. Appeals (5th and 11th cirs.) 1981, U.S. Supreme Ct. 1992. Asst. state atty. 6th Jud. Ct., Clearwater, Fla., 1976-90; ptnr. Growney, McKeown & Barber, St. Petersburg, 1976—; adj. prof. Stetson Coll. of Law, St. Petersburg, 1990—. Chairperson Child Welfare Std. and Tng. Coun., 1995-98; mem. Health and Human Svcs. Bd., nominee qualifications review com. Dist. 5, 1992—; mem. Study Commn. Child Welfare, 1990-91; Suncoast Girl Scout leader, 1991—. Recipient Victim Advocacy award Pinellas County Victims Rights Coalition, 1984, Law and Order award Elks, Pinellas County, 1991. Mem. ABA, ATLA, Acad. Fla. Trial Lawyers, Fla. Bar Assn., St. Petersburg Bar Assn., Phi Alpha Delta. Personal injury. Office: 7455 38th Ave N Saint Petersburg FL 33710-1228

**MCKEOWN, MARY MARGARET,** judge; b. Casper, Wyo., May 11, 1951; d. Robert Mark and Evelyn Margaret (Lipsack) McK.; m. Peter Francis Cowhey, June 29, 1985; 1 child, Megan Margaret. BA in Internat. Affairs and Spanish, U. Wyo., 1972; JD, Georgetown U., 1975. Bar: Wash. 1975, D.C. 1982. Assoc. Perkins Coie, Seattle, 1975-79, Washington, 1979-80; White House fellow U.S. Dept. Interior and White House, Washington, 1980-81; ptnr., mem. exec. com. Perkins Coie, Seattle, 1981-98, mng. dir. strategic planning and client rels., 1990-95; judge U.S. Ct. Appeals (9th cir.) Wash., 1998—; trustee The Pub. Defender, Seattle, 1982-85; rep. 9th Cir. Judicial Conf., San Francisco, 1985-89, mem. gender bias task force, 1992-93. Author: Girl Scout's Guide to New York, 1990; contbr. chpt. to book and articles to profl. jours. Nat. bd. dirs. Girl Scouts U.S., N.Y.C., 1976-87; bd. dirs. Family Svcs., Seattle, 1982-84; mem. exec. com. Corp. Coun. for the Arts, Seattle, 1988-98; bd. gen. counsel Downtown Seattle Assn., 1986-89; mem. exec. com. Wash. Coun. Internat. Trade, 1994—; bd. mem. YMCA Greater Seattle, 1998—. Recipient Rising Stars of the 80's award Legal Times Washington, 1983, 100 Young Women of Promise, Good Housekeeping, 1985; named Washington's Winningest Trial Lawyers Washington Journal, 1992; Japan leadership fellow, 1992-93, Top 50 Women Lawyers, Nat. Law Jour., 1998. Fellow ABA (ho. of dels. 1990—); Fed. Bar Assn. (trustee western dist. Wash. 1980-90), Wash. Bar Assn. (chmn. jud. recommendations 1989-90), Seattle-King County Bar Assn. (trustee, sec. 1984-85, Outstanding Lawyer award 1992), Legal Found. Wash. (trustee, pres. 1989-90), Washington Women Lawyers (bd. dirs., pres. 1978-79), Nat. Assn. Iolta Programs (bd. dirs. 1989-91), White House Fellows Found. (bd. dirs. 1998—). Avocations: travel, classical piano, hiking, gourmet cooking, tennis. Office: US Ct Appeals 1200 6th Ave Fl 21 Seattle WA 98101-3123

**MCKEY, ARTHUR DUNCAN,** lawyer; b. Washington; s. Richard Kendall and Mary Deru McKey; m. Virginia Ruth Hubbell, Mar. 19, 1983; 1 child, Richard. BA, Boston Coll., 1970, MA, 1973; MA, U. Md., 1975; JD, U. Idaho, 1978. Bar: Idaho 1978, D.C. 1979; U.S. Dist. Ct. Idaho 1978, U.S. Dist. Ct. (D.C.) 1979, U.S. Supreme Ct. 1983, U.S. Dist. Ct. (we. dist.) Mich. 1985, U.S. Ct. Appeals (D.C. cir.), U.S. Ct. Appeals (6th cir.) Mich. 1985, U.S. Dist. Ct. (no. dist.) Tex. 1992, U.S. Dist. Ct. (no. dist.) Calif. 1992. Assoc., ptnr. Hanson O'Brien Birney & Butler, Washington, 1978-90; sr. atty. Whitman & Ransom, N.Y.C., 1991-93; spl. appointment Antitrust divsn. U.S. Dept. Justice, Washington, 1993-95; ptnr. Hanson & Molloy, Washington, 1995—; adj. faculty Dept. of Mass Comm. Washington State U., Pullman, 1978; adv. bd., mMedia law reporter Bur. of Nat. Affairs, Washington, 1989—. Contbr. articles to profl. jours.; patentee in field. Gen. counsel The Children's Inn at NIH, Bethesda, 1989—, Creative Internet Applications Inc., Washington. Mem. The Barristers, Gibson Island Club and Yacht Squadron, Army and Navy Club, U.S. Sailing Assn. (Rescue medal 1992—). E-mail: amckey@hanson-molloy.com. Computer, Communications, Environmental. Office: Hanson & Malloy 1250 I St NW Ste 701 Washington DC 20005-5980

**MCKIBBEN, HOWARD D.,** federal judge; b. Apr. 1, 1940; s. James D. and Bernice McKibben; m. Mary Ann McKibben, July 2, 1966; children: Mark, Susan. BS, Bradley U., 1962; MPA, U. Pitts., 1964; JD, U. Mich., 1967. Assoc. George W. Abbott Law Office, 1967-71; dep. dist. atty. Douglas County, Nev., 1969-71, dist. atty., 1971-77; dist. ct. judge State of Nev., 1977-84; judge U.S. Dist. Ct. Nev., Reno, 1984—. Mem. Nev. Bar Assn., Am. Inns of Ct. (pres. Nev. chpt. 1986-88). Methodist. Avocations: tennis, golf, racquetball. Home: PO Box 588 Verdi NV 89439-0588 Office: US Dist Ct 400 S Virginia St Ste 804 Reno NV 89501-2197

**MCKIM, SAMUEL JOHN, III,** lawyer; b. Pitts., Dec. 31, 1938; s. Samuel John and Harriet Frieda (Roehl) McK.; children: David Hunt, Andrew John; m. Eugenia A. Leverich. AA cum laude, Port Huron Jr. Coll., 1959; BA cum laude, U. Mich., 1961, JD cum laude, U. Mich., 1964. Bar: Mich. 1965, U.S. Dist. Ct. (so. dist.) Mich. 1965, U.S. Ct. Appeals (6th cir.) 1969, U.S. Supreme Ct., 1994. Assoc. Miller, Canfield, Paddock and Stone, P.L.C., Detroit, Bloomfield Hills, Kalamazoo, Lansing, Monroe and Grand Rapids, Mich., Washington, N.Y.C., Pensacola, St. Petersburg, Fla., Gdansk, Warsaw, Katowice, Poland, 1964-71, sr. mem., 1971—, head state and local tax sect., 1985—, chmn. tax dept., 1989-94, mng. ptnr., 1979-85, chmn., mng. ptnr., 1984-85; mem. tax coun. State Bar Mich., 1981-94, chmn. state and local tax com. real property sect., 1982-90; adj. prof. law sch. Wayne State U., 1993—. Bd. dirs., past chmn. Goodwill Industries of Greater Detroit, 1970—; dir. Goodwill Industries Found., 1982-95; elder Presbyn. ch., Stevens min.; coun. mem. at large Detroit area coun. Boy Scouts Am., 1987—. Fellow Am. Coll. Tax Counselors; mem. ABA, Mich. Bar Assn., Detroit Bar Assn., Barrister's Soc., Ostego Ski Club, Port Huron Golf Club, Order of Coif, Phi Delta Phi. Assoc. editor Mich. Law Rev. State and local taxation, General corporate. Home: 32778 Friar Tuck Ln Beverly Hills MI 48025-2500 Office: Miller Canfield Paddock & Stone 150 W Jefferson Ave Ste 2500 Detroit MI 48226-4416

**MCKINLEY, JOHN CLARK,** lawyer; b. Lima, Peru, Nov. 5, 1960; came to U.S., 1961; s. Stuart M. and Barbara C. (Clark) McK.; m. Kathleen F. Jolovich, Nov. 2, 1985; children: Jesse F., Elizabeth C., Laura K. BS in Agrl. Bus., U. Wyo., 1983, MBA, 1984, JD, 1989. Bar: Utah 1989, Wyo. 1989; U.S. Dist. Ct. Utah 1989, U.S. Dist. Ct. Wyo. 1989. Gen. ptnr. J.M. Constrn., Torrington, Wyo., 1984-85; contract landman Marathon Oil Co., Casper, Wyo., 1985-86; assoc. Richards, Brandt, Miller & Nelson, Salt Lake City, 1989-94; ptnr. Davis & Cannon, Cheyenne, Wyo., 1994—. Mng. editor Land and Water Law Rev., U. Wyo. 1989. Recipient Am. Jurisprudence award 1987. Mem. Utah Bar Assn., Wyo. Bar Assn., Order of the Coif, Phi Kappa Phi. Republican. Avocations: skiing, fly fishing. General corporate, Insurance, Oil, gas, and mineral. Office: Davis & Cannon 2710 Thomes Ave Cheyenne WY 82001-3029

**MCKINNEY, CAROLYN JEAN,** lawyer; b. Holly Springs, Miss., Sept. 28, 1956; d. Walter H. and Elizabeth (Lawrence) McK. BA in History and Polit. Sci., Rust Coll., Holly Springs, 1977; JD, Harvard U., 1980. Bar: Tex. 1980, U.S. Dist. Ct. (no., ea., so. and we. dists.) Tex. 1980, Ill. 1995, U.S. Supreme Ct. 1997. Atty. Gulf Oil Corp., Houston, 1980-84; sr. atty. ARCO, Dallas, 1984-90; atty. Amoco Corp., Houston, 1990-94, 1996—, Chgo., 1994-96; vis. prof., mentor black exec. exch. program Nat. Urban League, 1985—; mem. adv. bd. Nat. Soc. Black Engrs., 1987—. Vol. Meals on Wheels program Vis. Nurse's Assn., 1985, Kid Care, 1992; participant Miss. Gov.'s Leadership Conf. on Youth, 1988; mentor gifted and talented program Fort Bend (Tex.) Ind. Sch. Dist., 1997—; exec. bd. mem. Teen Incentive Program, Cystic Fibrosis Found. Tex. Gulf Coast Chpt. Recipient Outstanding Alumni award Nat. Assn. for Equal Opportunity in Higher Edn., 1989. Mem. ABA. Labor, Federal civil litigation. Office: BP Amoco PLC 501 Westlake Park Blvd Houston TX 77079-2607

**MCKINNEY, DAN GEORGE,** lawyer; b. San Jose, Calif., June 21, 1956; s. George William McKinney and Joanne Marie Hatfield; m. Tina Jane Peacock, Nov. 27, 1982; children: Jennifer, Penny, Martin, Shannon. BA, George Mason U., 1978; JD with distinction, McGeorge Sch. of Law, 1981. Bar: Calif. 1981, Oreg. 1986. Assoc. Reid & Hellyer, Riverside, Calif., 1981-87, sr. atty., 1987—; pres. Riverside County Pub. Svc. Law Corp., 1997—. Bd. dirs. Riverside Youth Mus., 1996—. Mem. ABA, State Bar Calif. (pres. award for legal svc. 1994), State Bar Oreg., Riverside County Bar Assn. (pres. 1993), Riverside County Barristers (pres. 1985). Avocations: scouts, gardening. State civil litigation, Real property. Office: Reid & Hellyer 3880 Laman St 5th Fl Riverside CA 92501

**MCKINNEY, JAMES DEVAINE, JR.,** lawyer; b. Muscatine, Iowa, Dec. 13, 1931; s. James D. and Jeffie Lillian (Eblen) McK.; m. Betty A. Guy, June 10, 1966; children: James D. III, Cynthia Dee, Jennifer Jean. BA, U. Iowa, 1956, LLB, 1958. Bar: Iowa 1958, D.C. 1960, U.S. Ct. Appeals (D.C. cir.) 1961, U.S. Supreme Ct. 1962. Trial atty. FPC, Washington, 1958-60; assoc. Law Offices Charles E. McGee, Washington, 1960-65; assoc. Ross, Marsh & Foster, Washington, 1965-68, ptnr., 1968—. Mem. ABA, D.C. Bar Assn., Fed. Energy Bar Assn. (exec. com. 1979-82), Met. Club, Washington Golf and Country Club. FERC practice, Appellate, Administrative and regulatory. Home: 6105 Lee Hwy Arlington VA 22205-2110 Office: Ross Marsh & Foster 2001 L St NW Washington DC 20036-4910

**MCKINNEY, JANET KAY,** law librarian; b. Kansas City, Mo., Feb. 15, 1959; d. Charles Durward and Helen Jean (Bost) Freeman; m. Larry Emmett McKinney, July 11, 1981. BA, Avila Coll., 1981; MA in Libr. Sci., U. Mo., 1989; MA in Religious Studies, Ctrl. Bapt. Theol. Sem., 1997. Circulation libr. Midwestern Bapt. Theol. Sem., Kansas City, 1981-84, acquisitions libr., 1984-85, reference libr., 1985-90; environ. divsn. libr. Black & Veatch, Kansas City, 1990-91; dir. collection resources U. Mo. Leon E. Bloch Law Libr., Kansas City, 1991—. Mem. ALA, Am. Assn. Law Librs. (com. on rels. with info. vendors 1994-96, editl bd. Tech. Svcs. Law Libr. 1994-96, tech. svcs. spl. interest sect. vice chair/c hair elect, 1998-99), Mid-Am. Assn. Law Librs. (newsletter adv. mgr. 1993-94, treas. 1997-99), Mo. Libr. Assn. (Spl. Librs. Coun. chmn. 1997-98),Southwestern Assn. Law Librs., N.Am. Serials Interest Group, Spl. Librs. Assn. (chpt. employment com. chmn. 1990-91, chpt. treas. 1991-94, chpt. pres.-elect 1994-95, chpt. pres. 1995-96). Kansas City Assn. Law Libraries (v.p., pres-elect 1999). Office: U Mo Kansas City Leon E Bloch Law Libr 5100 Rockhill Rd Kansas City MO 64110-2446

**MCKINNEY, LARRY J.,** federal judge; b. South Bend, Ind., July 4, 1944; s. Lawrence E. and Helen (Byers) McK.; m. Carole Jean Marie Lyon, Aug. 19, 1966; children: Joshua E., Andrew G. BA, MacMurray Coll., Jacksonville, Ill., 1966; JD, Ind. U., 1969. Bar: Ind. 1970, U.S. Dist. Ct. (so. dist.) Ind. 1970. Law clk. to atty. gen. State of Ind., Indpls., 1969-70, dep. atty. gen., 1970-71; ptnr. Rodgers and McKinney, Edinburgh, Ind., 1971-75, James F.T. Sargent, Greenwood, Ind., 1975-79; judge Johnson County Cir. Ct., Franklin, Ind., 1979-87, U.S. Dist. Ct. (so. dist.) Ind., Indpls., 1987—. Presbyterian. Avocations: reading, jogging. Office: US Dist Ct 204 US Courthouse 46 E Ohio St Indianapolis IN 46204-1903

**MCKINNEY, LINDA OTANI,** prosecutor; b. Manhattan, N.Y., July 29, 1959; d. Raymond Yoshiteru and Michi Otani; m. Jim McKinney, Apr. 15, 1988; children: Jimmy, Mark. BA, Brigham Young U., 1981; JD, Georgetown U., 1987. Bar: D.C., D.C. Superior Ct., Pa., U.S. Dist. Ct. D.C., U.S. Ct. Appeals (D.C. cir.). Law clk. D.C. Superior Courthouse, Washington, 1987-90; asst. U.S. atty. U.S. Attys. Office for D.C., Washington, 1990—. Office: US Attys Office for DC 555 4th St NW Washington DC 20001-2733

**MCKINNEY, RONALD W.,** lawyer; b. Greenville, S.C., Mar. 23, 1948; s. William R. and Doris (Chadwick) McK.; m. Kathleen Crum, Jan. 13, 1979; children: William, Kathleen. BA, Furman U., 1970; MA, U. N.C., 1973; JD, U. S.C., 1978. Bar: S.C. 1978. Atty. S.C. Consumer Advocate's Office, Columbia, 1978-81; ptnr. Duggan, Reese & McKinney, Greer, S.C., 1981-95; city atty. City of Greenville, S.C., 1995—. Chair Greenville County Transportation Com., 1994-95. Mem. ABA, S.C. Bar Assn., Internat. Mcpl. Lawyers Assn., S.C. Mcpl. Attys. Assn. (pres. 1997). Methodist. Avocations: travel, reading. Office: City of Greenville PO Box 2207 Greenville SC 29602-2207

**MCKINNEY, ROZANNE MOORE,** lawyer; b. Kansas City, Mo., Jan. 23, 1953; d. Raymond Ernest and Maxine Williams Moore; m. Samuel McKinney, III, Nov. 14, 1978. BA in Govt., LaVerne U., 1975; JD, U. Houston, 1980. Bar: Tex.; U.S. Dist. Ct. (5th and 7th cirs.), Tex. Assoc. Brown, Sims, Wise & White, Houston, 1981-86; co-owner McKinney & McKinney, PC, Houston and Fairfield, Tex., 1986—. Co-author: (book) Big Debt Survival Guide, 1986, 91. Mem. Profl. Women of Freestone County, 1996—. Recipient Pub. Svc. award Common Cause Tex., Austin, 1992. Mem. Common Cause (nat. governing bd. 1988-91), Lions Club, Tex. Employment Lawyers Assn. (founding bd. dirs. 1998), Nat. Employment Lawyers Assn. Democrat. Presbyterian. Avocations: playing piano, internat. travel, reading. Labor. Office: McKinney & McKinney PO Box 947 Fairfield TX 75840-0947

**MCKINNEY, RUSSELL RAYMOND,** lawyer; b. Visalia, Calif., Sept. 26, 1942; s. Russell R. and Alice (McKerral) McK.; m. Sharon K. McKinney, Aug. 22, 1964; children: Kristin, Russell L. BA, Stanford U., 1964; JD, U. Calif., 1967; postgrad., U.S. Naval War Coll., 1995. Pvt. practice Visalia, Calif., 1968—. Comdr. JAGC, USNR, 1981—. Paul Harris fellow Rotary Internat. State civil litigation, Construction, Personal injury. Office: 220 S Mooney Blvd Visalia CA 93291-4512

**MCKINSTRY, RONALD EUGENE,** lawyer; b. Bakersfield, Calif., Aug. 11, 1926; s. Melville Jack and Lillian Agatha (Saner) McK.; m. Shirley Danner, June 19, 1948; children: Michael R., Jill I. McKinstry Epperson, Jeffrey A., Carol A. McKinstry Sundquist. BS, U. Wash., 1950, JD, 1951. Bar: Wash. 1951, U.S. Ct. Claims 1970, U.S. Ct. Appeals (D.C. cir.) 1981, U.S. Supreme Ct. 1982. Assoc. Evans, McLaren, Lane, Powell & Beeks, Seattle, 1951-55, Bogle, Bogle & Gates, Seattle, 1955-61; ptnr. Bogle & Gates, Seattle, 1962-91, chmn. litigation dept., 1970-91; sr. trial ptnr. Ellis Li & McKinstry, Seattle, 1992—; apptd. spl. master by U.S. Dist. Ct. (we. dist.) Wash., 1976-81, apptd. settlement mediator, 1980—. Editor-in-chief Washington Civil Procedure Before Trial Deskbook, 1981, Supplement to Deskbook, 1986; contbr. articles to profl. jours. Attends Christ Meml. Ch., Poulsbo, Wash. With USN, 1944-46, PTO. Recipient Svc. award Western Ctr. for Law and Religious Freedom, 1990. Fellow Am. Coll. Trial Lawyers (regent 1978-82); mem. ABA, Internat. Assn. Def. Counsel (mem. exec. com. 1974-78, voted

Best Lawyers in Am., 1983—), CPR Panels of Disting. Legal Neutrals, AAA Club Wash. (mem. exec. com. 1983-98), Seattle Tennis Club. Republican. Christ Meml. Ch. Avocations: golf, traveling. Federal civil litigation, General civil litigation, Environmental. Office: Ellis Li & McKinstry Two Union Square 601 Union St Ste 4900 Seattle WA 98101-3906

**MCKITTRICK, NEIL VINCENT,** lawyer; b. Framingham, Mass., June 21, 1961; s. Harold Vincent and Dorothy Frances (Alexander) McK.; m. Karen Beth Hoffman, May 30, 1987; children: Kerry Alexandra, Brian Hoffman, Robert Hoffman. AB magna cum laude, Brown U., 1983; JD, U. Va., 1987. Bar: Mass. 1988, U.S. Dist. Ct. Mass. 1989, U.S. Ct. Appeals (1st cir.) 1989, U.S. Supreme Ct. 1999. Law clk. to Hon. Frank M. Johnson Jr. U.S. Ct. Appeals (11th cir.), Montgomery, Ala., 1987-88; assoc. Hill & Barlow, Boston, 1988-95, mem., 1995—; pub. defender Suffolk County (Mass.) Bar Advocate, 1990-91; asst. dir. White House sec. rev. U.S. Dept. Treasury, 1994-95; case conf./mediator Boston Mcpl. Ct. Alternative Dispute Resolution Program, 1997—; mem. steering com. Lawyers' Com. Civil Rights Under Law, 1998—. Editor U. Va. Law Rev., 1985-87. Dillard fellow U. Va., 1985-86; recipient Arc Mass. Disting. Citizens award, 1996. Mem. ABA, Mass. Bar Assn., Fed. Bar Assn. (exec. com. 1997—), Boston Bar Assn. (lawyers' com. civil rights, steering com., 1998—), Order of the Coif, Phi Beta Kappa, Theta Delta Chi. General civil litigation, Criminal, Personal injury. Office: Hill & Barlow One International Pl Boston MA 02110

**MCKITTRICK, WILLIAM DAVID PARRISH,** lawyer; b. Phila., June 10, 1942; s. Robert William and Marianna Virginia (Jones) McK.; m. Maureen Elaine Kerr, Jan. 20, 1964 (div. June 1980); children: Terrance, Allison; m. Teresa Jane Hopkins, Mar. 20, 1982; children: Parrish, Tyler. BA, Marshall U., Huntington, W.Va., 1965; JD, W.Va. U., 1968. Bar: W.Va. 1968, U.S. Dist. Ct. (so. dist.) W.Va. 1968. Asst. prosecutor Kanawha County, Charleston, W.Va., 1968-70; ptnr. McKittrick & Vaughn, St. Albans, W.Va., 1970-85, McKittrick & Murray, St. Albans, 1968-89, McKittrick & Assocs., St. Albans, 1990-93, McKittrick & Tantlinger, St. Albans, 1993—; lectr. numerous seminars. Mem. Am. Trial Lawyers Assn., W.Va. Trial Lawyers Assn. Personal injury, Product liability, Criminal. Office: 450 2nd St Saint Albans WV 25177-2857

**MCKNIGHT, CHARLES NOEL,** lawyer; b. Darby, Pa., Dec. 25, 1944; s. John Agustine and Mildred (Collins) McK.; div.; children: Charles Sean, Carolyn Noel, Jennifer Lauren. BSc, Spring Hill Coll., 1971; JD, U. Ala., 1974. Bar: U.S. Dist. Ct. (so. dist.) Ala. 1976, U.S. Ct. Appeals (5th cir.) 1976, U.S. Ct. Appeals (11th cir.) 1981. Law clk. to judge U.S. Dist. Ct. (so. dist.) Ala., Mobile, 1974-76; pvt. practice Mobile, 1976-81, 88—; ptnr. Bryant and McKnight, Mobile, 1981-85, McKnight and Seidel, Mobile, 1986-88; bd. dirs. Ala. Aviation Hall of Fame, Birmingham, 1990-91; judge Town of Dauphin Island, Ala., 1989—; dep. judge City of Mobile, 1990—; spl. probate judte, spl. dist. judge County of Mobile, 1992—. STaff sgt. USAF, 1964-68. Mem. Assn. Trial Lawyers Am., Ala. Trial Lawyers Assn., Mobile Bar Assn., Ala. Bar Assn. Democrat. Roman Catholic. Avocations: boating, fishing, flying. Insurance, Probate, Family and matrimonial. Home: 11301 Getchell Dr Theodore AL 36582-8472 Office: 250 Congress St Mobile AL 36603-6481

**MCKONE, THOMAS CHRISTOPHER,** lawyer; b. Hartford, Conn., Oct. 31, 1917; s. Thomas C. and Elizabeth (Lally) McK.; m. Mary W. Sullivan, Dec. 27, 1945; children: Mary K., Thomas C. III, Ellen M. Stafford. BA cum laude, Coll. of Holy Cross, 1940; LLB, U. Conn., 1949. Bar: Conn. 1949, U.S. Dist. Ct. Conn. 1949, U.S. Ct. Appeals (2d cir.) 1949, U.S. Tax Ct. 1949, U.S. Ct. Claims 1949. Asst. clk. Hartford Probate Ct., 1949-53, clk., 1953-58; ptnr. Reid & Riege, P.C., Hartford, 1958—. Co-author: Conn. General Statues Probate Courts and Procedure, 1948. Corporator St. Francis Hosp., Hartford, 1963—; trustee U. Conn. Law Sch. Found., Hartford, 1972—. Capt. U.S. Army, 1941-46, ETO. Recipient Citizen of the Year award Conn. Probate Cts., 1992. Fellow Am. Coll. Trust and Estate Counsel, Internat. Soc. Barristers; mem. Hartford County Bar Assn. (bd. dirs. 1962-92). Democrat. Roman Catholic. Avocation: golf. Estate planning, Pension, profit-sharing, and employee benefits. Home: 5 Drury Ln West Hartford CT 06117-1611 Office: Reid & Riege PC 1 State St Ste 16 Hartford CT 06103-3185

**MCKOWEN, LAURIE GARRIGAN,** lawyer; b. Washington, June 29, 1956; d. Daniel P. and Catherine M. (Carroll) Garrigan; m. James Anthony McKowen, Aug. 30, 1986 (div. Dec. 1993); children: James Andrew, Ryan D., Patrick S. BA, Radford Coll., 1978; JD, W.Va. U., 1981. Bar: W.Va. 1981, U.S. Dist. Ct. (so. and no. dists.) W.Va. 1981, U.S. Ct. Appeals (4th cir.) 1988. Asst. atty. gen. W.Va. Office Atty. Gen., Charleston, 1981-82; law clk. U.S. Dist. Ct. (so. dist.) W.Va., Charleston, 1982-83; assoc. Preiser & Wilson, Charleston, 1983-87; ptnr. Hunt & Wilson, Charleston, 1987-90; mem. Masters & Taylor, Charleston, 1990—. Vice pres., treas. W.Va. Heady Injury Found. Inst., W.Va., 1984-91. Mem. W.Va. Trial Lawyers Assn. (med. negligence com. 1983—), Assn. Trial Lawyers of Am., Kanawha County Bar Assn., W.Va. Bar Assn., Phi Kappa Phi, Omicron Delta Kappa, Pi Gamma Mu, Alpha Lamda Delta. Personal injury. Office: Masters & Taylor LC 4th Flr/Peoples Bldg 181 Summers St Charleston WV 25301-2134

**MCKUSICK, VINCENT LEE,** former state supreme court justice, lawyer, arbitrator, mediator; b. Parkman, Maine, Oct. 21, 1921; s. Carroll Lee and Ethel (Buzzell) McK.; m. Nancy Elizabeth Green, June 23, 1951; children: Barbara Jane McKusick Liscord, James Emory, Katherine McKusick Ralston, Anne Elizabeth. AB, Bates Coll., 1943; SB, SM, MIT, 1947; LLB, Harvard U., 1950; LLD, Colby Coll., 1976, Nasson Coll., 1978, Bates Coll., 1979, Bowdoin Coll., 1979, Suffolk U., 1983; LHD, U. So. Maine, 1978, Thomas Coll., 1981. Bar: Maine 1952. Law clk. to Chief Judge Learned Hand, 1950-51; to Justice Felix Frankfurter, 1951-52; partner Pierce, Atwood, Scribnér, Allen & McKusick and predecessors, Portland, Maine, 1953-77; chief justice Maine Supreme Jud. Ct., 1977-92; of counsel to Pierce Atwood (formerly Pierce, Atwood, Scribner, Allen, Smith, & Lancaster), Portland, Maine, 1992—; mem. adv. com. rules civil procedure Maine Supreme Jud. Ct., 1957-59, chmn., 1966-75, commr. uniform state laws, 1968-76, sec. nat. conf., 1975-77; mem. Conf. Chief Justices, 1977-92, bd. dirs., 1980-82, 91-92, pres.-elect, 1989-90, pres., 1990-91; dir. Nat. Ctr. for State Ctrs., 1988-89, chmn.-elect, 1989-90, chmn., 1990-91; spl. master U.S. Supreme Ct. Conn. v. N.H., 1992-93, La. v. Miss., 1994-96; master Mass. S.J.C. Liquidation Am. Mutual Liability Ins. Co., 1995-96; leader Am. Judges Del. to China, 1983, USSR, 1988, U.S. State Dept. Rule of Law Del. to Republic of Ga., 1992; mem. permanent com. Oliver Wendell Holmes Devise, 1993—. Author: Patent Policy of Educational Institutions, 1947, (with Richard H. Field) Maine Civil Practice, 1959, supplements, 1962, 67, (with Richard H. Field and L. Kinvin Wroth) 2d edit., 1970, supplements, 1972, 74, 77; also articles in legal publs. Trustee emeritus Bates Coll.; mem. adv. com. on pvt. internat. law U.S. State Dept., 1980-85, Fed.-State Jurisdiction com., Jud. Conf. of U.S., 1987-89. With AUS, 1943-46. Recipient The Maine prize U. Maine Sys., 1993, Benjamin E. Mays award Bates Coll., 1994, Big M award Maine State Soc. Washington, 1995, Paul C. Reardon award Nat. Ctr. for State Ctrs., 1999. Fellow Am. Bar Found. (bd. dirs. 1977-87), Am. Philos. Soc. (coun. 1990-96, 97—); mem. ABA (chmn. fed. rules com. 1966-71, bd. editors jour. 1971-80, chmn. 1976-77, mem. study group to China 1978, ho. dels. 1983-87, coun. sr. lawyers divsn. 1997—), Maine Bar Assn., Cumberland County Bar Assn., Am. Arbitration Assn. (bd. dirs. 1994—), Am. Judicature Soc. (dir. 1976-78, 92-98), Am. Law Inst. (coun. 1968—), Maine Jud. Coun. (chmn. 1977-92), Inst. Jud. Adminstrn., Supreme Ct. Hist. Soc. (trustee 1994—), Rotary Club (hon., past pres.), Portland Yacht Club, Phi Beta Kappa, Sigma Xi, Tau Beta Pi. Republican. Unitarian. Home: 1152 Shore Rd Cape Elizabeth ME 04107-2115 Office: 1 Monument Sq Portland ME 04101-4033

**MCLAIN, CHRISTOPHER M.,** lawyer; b. San Luis Obispo, Calif., July 21, 1943; s. James Latane and Marjorie Patricia (McNalley) McL.; m. Barbara McFarland, Nov. 23, 1968; children—Beth, Brian, Amy. BS in Bus. Adminstrn., U. Calif.-Berkeley, 1965, JD, 1968. Assoc. Knox, Goforth & Ricksen, Oakland, Calif., 1968-69; assoc. Donahue, Gallagher, Thomas & Woods, Oakland, 1969-73, ptnr., 1973-83; sec., counsel Lucky Stores, Inc., Dublin, Calif., 1984-89, v.p., 1985-89; ptnr. Sonnenschein, Nath & Rosenthal, San Francisco, 1989-90; sr. v.p., gen. counsel, sec. Transam. Corp., San Francisco, 1990-94; of counsel Sonnenschein Nath & Rosenthal, San Francisco, 1994-95; sr. v.p., gen. counsel, sec. Crown Vantage Inc., Oakland, Calif., 1995-99; ptnr., gen. counsel Sequoia Assocs., LLC, Menlo Park, Calif., 1999—. Mem. ABA, State Bar Calif., Alameda County Bar Assn., San Francisco Bar Assn., Am. Soc. Corps. Secs. Avocation: skiing. General corporate. Office: Sequoia Assocs LLC Menlo Park CA 94025

**MCLAIN, WILLIAM ALLEN,** lawyer; b. Chgo., Oct. 19, 1942; s. William Rex and Wilma L. (Raschka) McL.; divorced; children: William A., David M., Heather A.; m. Kristine R. Zierk. BS, So. Ill. U., 1966; JD, Loyola U., Chgo., 1971. Bar: Ill. 1971, U.S. Dist. Ct. (no. dist.) Ill. 1971, U.S. Ct. Appeals (7th cir.) 1971, Colo. 1975, U.S. Dist. Ct. Colo. 1975, U.S. Ct. Appeals (10th cir.) 1975. Law clk. U.S. Dist. Ct. (no. dist.) Ill., Chgo., 1971-72; assoc. Sidley & Austin, Chgo., 1972-75; ptnr. Welborn, Dufford, Brown & Tooley, Denver, 1975-86; pres. William A. McLain PC, 1986—; ptnr. McLain & Singer, 1990—. Mem. Dist. 10 Legis. Vacancy Commn., Denver, 1984-86. Served with U.S. Army, 1966-68. Recipient Leadership and Scholastic Achievement award Loyola U. Alumni Assn., 1971. Mem. ABA, Colo. Bar Assn. (lobbyist 1983-85), Denver Bar Assn., Colo. Assn. Commerce and Industry (legis. policy coun. 1983-88), Colo. Mining Assn. (state and local affairs com. 1978-88), Inst. Property Taxation. Republican. Clubs: Mount Vernon Country Club, Roundup Riders of the Rockies. Lodges: Masons, Shriners, Scottish Rite, York Rite. Legislative, State and local taxation. Home and Office: 3962 S Olive St Denver CO 80237-2038

**MCLATCHEY, RUSSELL FRANCIS,** lawyer; b. Boston, Sept. 12, 1959; s. Clifford J. and Margaret E. McL.; m. Shannon C. Skinner, Dec. 19, 1997. BA, Rollins Coll., 1981; degree in paralegal tng., Nat. Ctr. Paralegal Tng., Atlanta, 1981; JD, Miss. Coll., 1985. Bar: Fla. 1986, U.S. Dist. Ct. Fla. 1988, U.S. Ct. Appeals (11th cir.) 1989, U.S. Supreme Ct. 1992. Adminstr. asst. Miss. Workers Compensation Commn., Jackson, 1985; asst. pub. defender Seminole County Pub. Defender's Office, Sanford, Fla., 1987-89; pvt. practice Longwood, Fla., 1989—; instr. So. Coll. Paralegal Program, Orlando, 1994—; mem. faculty adv. bd. So. Coll., Orlando, 1994—; mem. Criminal Law Advocacy Inst. U. Fla. Law Sch., Gainesville. Vol., participant Sentinel Santa Program, Orlando Sentinel, Fla., 1998. Mem. ABA, Fla. Bar Assn., Ctrl. Fla. Criminal Def. Atty's Assn., Fla. Assn. of Criminal Def. Lawyers. Avocations: golf, music, watersports. Criminal, Juvenile, Personal injury. Home: 2136 Eagles Rest Dr Apopka FL 32712-2039 Office: 531 Dog Track Rd Longwood FL 32750-6547

**MCLAUGHLIN, EDWARD FRANCIS, JR.,** lawyer; b. Boston, Aug. 18, 1920; s. Edward Francis and Helen Celia McLaughlin; m. Elizabeth Drake, Apr. 14, 1945; children: Edward F., Patricia A. (deceased), Paul R. (deceased), Robert D., Richard J., Elizabeth A. AB in Bus., Dartmouth Coll., 1942; LLB, Northeastern U., 1949. Bar: Mass. 1949, U.S. Dist. Ct. Mass. 1950, U.S. Ct. Appeals (1st cir.) 1950, U.S. Supreme Ct. 1963. Asst. U.S. atty. U.S. Dept. Justice, Boston, 1950-53; assoc. Sullivan & Worcester, Boston, 1953-61; lt. gov. Commonwealth of Mass., Boston, 1961-63; gen. counsel Metropolitan Transit Authority, Mass. Bay Transportation Authority, Boston, 1962-70; assoc. Herrick & Smith, Boston, 1970; ptnr. Herrick & Smith, Boston, 1971-86; ptnr. Nutter, McClennen & Fish, LLP, Boston, 1986-90, of counsel, 1990—; dir. nat. coun. Northeastern U., Boston, 1979—. Councillor Boston City Coun., 1954-61; del. Dem. Nat. Conv., L.A., 1960. Lt. USN, 1942-45. Named Outstanding Alumnus Northeastern U., 1974. Fellow Mass. Bar Assn. Roman Catholic. Avocations: sports, political activities, reading. Fax: 508-771-8079. General civil litigation, Condemnation, Criminal. Office: Nutter McClennen & Fish LLP Rte 132 1513 Iyannough Rd Hyannis MA 02601-1862

**MCLAUGHLIN, JEFFREY REX,** lawyer; b. Decatur, Ala., May 2, 1960; s. Francis Joseph and Pat Fitzpatrick McLaughlin; m. Stacy Deason, June 3, 1995; 1 child, John Francis Lynne. BA, Birmingham-So. Coll., 1982; postgrad., Trinity Coll., Dublin, Ireland, 1985-86; JD, Harvard U., 1990. Bar: Ala. 1991, U.S. Dist. Ct. (no. dist.) Ala. 1991, U.S. Ct. Appeals (11th cir.) 1998. History and civics tchr. John Carroll H.S., Birmingham, Ala., 1982-87; law clk. to presiding judge Seybourn Lynne U.S. Dist. Ct. (no. dist.) Ala., 1990-91, U.S. Ct. Appeals (11th cir.), 1998; assoc. Maynard Cooper & Gale, P.C., Birmingham, 1991-94; ptnr. McLaughlin & Marshall, LLC, Guntersville, Ala., 1995—. Mem. Marshall County chpg. ARC, Guntersville, 1995-97. Rotary Found. scholar, 1985-86. Mem. Marshall County Bar Assn. (pres. 1998—), Civitan, Phi Beta Kappa. Roman Catholic. Avocations: home restoration, woodworking, bicycling, hiking, fishing. General civil litigation, Probate, General corporate. Office: McLaughlin & Marshall LLC 321 Blount Ave PO Box 1037 Guntersville AL 35976-7037

**MCLAUGHLIN, JOHN SHERMAN,** lawyer; b. Pitts., Apr. 1, 1932; s. John H. and Dorothy I. (Schrecongost) McL.; m. Suzanne Shaver, June 5, 1971; children—Dorothy, Sarah, Martha. A.B., Harvard U., 1954, LL.B., 1957. Bar: Pa. 1958, U.S. Supreme Ct. 1967. Assoc. Reed, Smith, Shaw & McClay, Pitts., 1957-71; ptnr. Reed, Smith, Shaw & McClay, 1971—. Trustee Harmarville Rehab. Ctr., Inc., 1980-87; pres., trustee Western Pa. Sch. for the Deaf, 1985—; pres. Pa. NG Assn., 1976-78; justice of peace Borough of Edgewood, 1963-73; trustee Winchester Thurston Sch., 1987-94, emeritus trustee, 1994—; life trustee Carnegie Libr. of Pitts., Carnegie Inst., 1994—, Carnegie Mus. Art, 1997—; dir. Pitts. Symphony, 1985-95, adv. 1996—. Lt. col. Air NG, 1957-79. Mem. Am. Law Inst., Am. Coll. Trust and Estate Counsel, Allegheny County Bar Assn., Duquesne Club, Rolling Rock Club (Ligonier, Pa.). Probate, General practice. Office: Reed Smith Shaw & McClay 435 6th Ave Ste 2 Pittsburgh PA 15219-1886

**MCLAUGHLIN, JOSEPH MICHAEL,** federal judge, law educator; b. Brooklyn, N.Y., Mar. 20, 1933; s. Joseph Michael and Mary Catherine (Flanagan) McL.; m. Frances Elizabeth Lynch, Oct. 10, 1959; children: Joseph, Mary Jo, Matthew, Andrew. A.B., Fordham Coll., 1954, LL.B., 1959; LL.M., NYU, 1964; LL.D., Mercy Coll., White Plains, N.Y., 1981. Bar: N.Y. 1959. Assoc. Cahill, Gordon, N.Y.C., 1959-61; prof. law Fordham U., N.Y.C., 1961-71, dean Sch. of Law, 1971-81, adj. prof., 1981—; judge U.S. Dist. Ct. Eastern Dist. N.Y., Bklyn., 1981-90; judge to sr. judge U.S. Ct. Appeals (2nd Cir.), N.Y.C., 1990—; adj. prof. St. John's Law Sch., N.Y.C., 1982—; chmn. N.Y. Law Revision Commn., Albany, 1975-82. Author: (with Peterfreund) New York Practice, 1964, Evidence, 1979; also articles. Served to capt. U.S. Army, 1955-57, Korea. Mem. ABA, Assn. of Bar of City of N.Y., N.Y. State Bar Assn. Roman Catholic. Club: Lotos. Office: US Courthouse US Ct Appeals 40 Foley Sq Rm 2402 New York NY 10007-1502*

**MCLAUGHLIN, KEVIN THOMAS,** lawyer; b. St. Louis, Aug. 4, 1970; s. James W. and Jane E. McL.; m. Laura A. McLaughlin, Aug. 24, 1996. BA in English, Boston Coll., 1992; JD, U. Mo., 1995. Assoc. McCarthy, Leonard, Kaemmerer, Owen, Lamkin & McGovern, LC, St. Louis, 1995—. Editor: Mo. Law Rev., Note and Comment, 1994-95. Mem. U. Mo. Sch. Law Student Bar Assn. (pres. 1994-95). Labor, General civil litigation, Civil rights. Office: McCarthy Leonard Kaemmerer Owen Lamkin & McGovern LC 16141 Swingley Ridge Rd Ste 300 Chesterfield MO 63017-1781

**MCLAUGHLIN, MICHAEL JOHN,** insurance company executive; b. Cambridge, Mass., Feb. 14, 1944; s. Michael John and Evelyn Katherine (Quinn) McL. A.B., Boston Coll., 1965; J.D., N.Y. U., 1968. Bar: N.Y., Mass. With N.Y. Life Ins. Co., 1968—, sr. v.p. info. systems and services dept., 1982-88, sr. v.p., 1988-91, sr. v.p., dep. gen. counsel, 1991-95, sr. v.p., gen. counsel, 1995—. Mem. ABA, N.Y. State Bar Assn. Office: NY Life Ins Co 51 Madison Ave New York NY 10010-1603

**MCLAUGHLIN, MICHAEL V.,** lawyer; b. Buffalo, May 9, 1967; s. William F. Sr. and Arlene McLaughlin; m. Alison J. Taylor, Aug. 15, 1995; children: Declan, Riley. BA, Williams Coll., 1989; JD, U. Buffalo, 1994. Assoc. atty. Hodgson, Russ, Andrews, Woods & Goodyear, LLP, Buffalo, 1994—. Home: 33 Regalwood Dr Orchard Park NY 14127-2955 Office: Hodgson Russ et al 1800 One M & T Plz Buffalo NY 14203-2931

**MCLAUGHLIN, PHILIP T.,** state attorney general; b. Nashua, N.H., Jan. 23, 1945; s. Philip J. and Pauline (Reilly) McL.; m. Janice Livingston, 1968; children: Matthew, Timothy, Emily, Katherine, Philip. AB in History, Holy Cross coll., 1967; MPA, U. R.I., 1971; JD, Boston Coll., 1974. Bar: N.H. 1974. Atty. Belknap County, N.H., 1979-81; ptnr. McLaughlin, Hemeon & Lahey, P.A., Laconia, N.H., 1981-97; atty. gen. State of N.H., 1997—. Past pres. Lakes Region Mental Health Ctr., Laconia; mem. Laconia City Coun., 1976-80; del. N.H. Constl. Conv., 1984; mem. Laconia Sch. Bd., 1985-94, also chair; mem. prof. conduct com. N.H. Suprmee Ct., 1983-92, 94-97. Lt. USN, 1969-71. Office: Atty Gen Office 33 Capitol St Concord NH 03301-6397

**MCLAUGHLIN, SEAN J.,** judge; b. 1955. AB, Georgetown U., 1977, JD, 1980. Law clerk Hon. William W. Knox, 1980-81, Hon. Gerald J. Weber; ptnr. Knox, McLaughlin, Gornall & Sennett, Erie, Penn, 1981-94; dist. judge U.S. Dist. Ct. (we. dist.) Pa., 1994—. Mem. ABA, Pa. Bar Assn., Erie County Bar Assn. Office: Federal Bldg & US Courthouse Rm 240 617 State St Erie PA 16501-1143

**MCLEAISH, ROBERT BURNS,** lawyer; b. Houston, Jan. 20, 1923; s. Robert Burns and Janet Mabel (Nonus) McL.; m. Ellen Francis Rinehart, 1945 (div. 1953); 1 dau., Janet Nancy McLeaish Robinson; m. 2d Penelope Ann Payte, Dec. 21, 1954; children—Laurel Theresa, Heather Elizabeth, Jeremy Glen. B.A., Tex. A&M U., 1947; J.D., Tex. U., 1953. Bar: Tex. 1953, U.S. Dist. Ct. (so. dist.) Tex. 1954, U.S. Ct. Appeals (5th cir.) 1994, U.S. Supreme Ct. 1997. Sole practice, McAllen, Tex., 1953—; pres. Tandem Enterprises, Inc., McAllen, 1976-96. County auditor Hidalgo County (Tex.), 1956-76. Served with USMCR, World War II. Decorated D.F.C. Mem. ABA, Tex. Bar Assn., Comml. Law League Am., Am. Assn. Atty.-C.P.A.s. Democrat. Roman Catholic. Clubs: Lions, McAllen Country, Elks, McAllen Tower. Consumer commercial, State civil litigation, Bankruptcy. Home: 100 E Hibiscus Ave Mcallen TX 78501-9445 Office: 809 Quince Ave Mcallen TX 78501-2445

**MCLEAN, GARY P.,** lawyer; b. Oceanport, N.J., Sept. 9, 1961. BA in History, Moravian Coll., 1983; JD, Villanova U., 1992. Bar: N.J. 1992. Asst. prosecutor Monmouth County, Freehold, N.J., 1993-96; assoc. Lomurro, Davison, Eastman and Munoz, Freehold, 1996—. Mediator Mcpl. Ct., Spring Lakes Heights, N.J., 1997-98. Mem. Monmouth County Bar Assn. (juvenile law com. 1999). General civil litigation, Criminal, General corporate. Office: Lomurro Davison Eastman and Munoz Willowbrook Rd Freehold NJ 07728

**MCLEAN, PATRICIA JO,** prosecutor; b. Cannonsburg, Pa., May 4, 1961. BA, Dayton U., 1983; JD, Ind. U., 1986. Bar: Pa. 1986, Washington 1988. Pvt. practice Ferry & McLean, Butler, Pa., 1987-92; conflicts counsel Butler (Pa.) County, 1988-91; asst. pub. defender Lawrence County, Pa., 1991; asst. dist. atty. Butler (Pa.) County, 1992—. Office: Govt Jud Ctr PO Box 1208 Butler PA 16003-1208

**MCLEAN, ROBERT ALEXANDER,** lawyer; b. Memphis, Oct. 24, 1943; s. Albert A. and Harriet Spencer (Pond) McL.; m. Sydney Ross, July 16, 1977; children: Robert Alexander, Ross Andrew. BA with honors, Rhodes Coll., 1965; MA, Princeton U., 1968, PhD, 1974; JD, U. Memphis, 1978. Bar: Tenn. 1979, U.S. Dist. Ct. (we. dist.) Tenn. 1979, U.S. Dist. Ct. (ea. dist.) Wis. 1985, U.S. Ct. Appeals (5th cir.) 1986, U.S. Dist. Ct. (ea. and we. dists.) Ark. 1990, U.S. Ct. Appeals (8th cir.) 1990, U.S. Ct. Appeals (10th cir.) 1991, U.S. Ct. Appeals (6th cir.) 1998, U.S. Supreme Ct. 1998. Asst. prof. Russian lit. U. Calif., Santa Cruz, 1971-76; staff atty. FCA, Washington, 1979-81; assoc. Wildman, Harrold, Allen, Dixon & McDonnell, Memphis, 1981-88, ptnr., 1988-89; ptnr. McDonnell Boyd, Memphis, 1989-94; mem. McDonnell Dyer, PLC, Memphis, 1994-95; spl. counsel Wolff Ardis, P.C., Memphis, 1995-96, shareholder, 1997; mem. Farris Mathews Branan & Hellen, PLC, 1997—; asst. city atty. Germantown, Tenn., 1981—; adj. asst. prof. Russian lang. Rhodes Coll., Memphis, 1982-86. Translator: Mozart and Salieri, 1973; mem. U. Memphis Law Rev., 1977-78. Mem. session Germantown (Tenn.) Presbyn. Ch., 1988—, chmn. fin. com., 1989-94, also trustee. Charlotte Elizabeth Procter fellow Princeton U., 1968, Fulbright fellow U.S.S.R., 1969, Regents fellow U. Calif., Santa Cruz, 1975. Mem. ABA, Tenn. Bar Assn., Memphis Bar Assn. Republican. Avocations: golf, quail hunting, tennis. General civil litigation, Environmental, Private international. Home: 8820 Somerset Ln Germantown TN 38138-7375 Office: Farris Matthews et al Ste 2000 One Commerce Sq Memphis TN 38103

**MCLEAN, STEPHEN M.,** lawyer; b. Minot, N.D., May 19, 1948; s. Robert M. and Louise M. McLean; m. Susan J. Sheldon, May 29, 1971; 3 children. BA, N.D. State U., 1970; JD, U. N.D., 1973. Bar: N.D. Pvt. practice law Oakes, N.D., 1974—; city atty. City of Oakes, 1974—; Dickey County State's atty., Oakes-Ellendale, 1998—; indigent def. atty. barnes, Dickey and LaMoure Counties, N.C., 1989—. Adv. bd. Oakes Good Samaritan Ctr., 1976-94; pres. ch. coun. Grace Luth. Ch., 1997-98. Capt. USAF, 1973. Mem. S.E. N.D. Bar Assn. (sec.-treas. 1998—), N.D. Mcpl. Attys. Assn. (pres. bd. dirs. 1995-97), N.D. State Bar Assn., Oakes C. of C. (sec.-treas. 1974-86), Lions (pres. 1992), Oakes Country Club (pres. 1975). Republican. Office: 606 Main Ave Oakes ND 58474-1639

**MCLEAN, SUSAN RALSTON,** lawyer; b. Fayetteville, Tenn., Feb. 28, 1948; d. Joseph Frederick and Clara (Robertson) Ralston; m. Arthur Edward McLean, Apr. 16, 1983. AB, Randolph-Macon Woman's Coll., 1970; MAT in English, Vanderbilt U., 1971; JD, U. Tenn., 1979; LLM in Taxation, So. Meth. U., 1984. Bar: Tenn. 1979, Tex. 1981, Ark. 1984. Assoc. Rose Law Firm, Little Rock, 1984-85, Brice & Mankoff, Dallas, 1986-87; counsel tax divsn. Dept. Justice, Dallas, 1987-96. Contbr. articles to profl. jours. Advocate for treatment of reactive attachment disorder. Mem. ABA (tax, litigation, bus. law sects.), Tex. Bar Assn. (tax and litigation sects.), Randolph-Macon Woman's Coll. Alumnae (pres. 1992-94). Presbyterian. Avocations: swimming, golf, art, music, hiking. Corporate taxation, Estate taxation, Taxation, general. Home: 4025 McFarlin Blvd Dallas TX 75205-1723

**MCLEES, JOHN ALAN,** lawyer; b. Mpls., Jan. 19, 1948; s. Alan L. and Marian G. (Melby) McL.; m. Bozena Nowicka, June 25, 1993; children: Alexandra, Thomas. BA, U. Chgo., 1970, MBA, 1973, JD, 1974; MS in Econs., London Sch. Econs., 1971. Bar: D.C., 1974, Ill., 1975. Assoc. Keck Mahin & Cate, Chgo., 1975-79; atty. advisor office of sec. U.S. Dept. Energy, Washington, 1979-81; mng. atty. Sidley & Austin, Muscat, Oman, 1981-83; assoc. Sidley & Austin, Chgo., 1983-88, Morgan Lewis & Bockius, Washington, 1988-91; dir. Latin Am. tax svc. Coopers & Lybrand, Chgo., 1991-97; ptnr. Baker & McKenzie, Chgo., 1997—; organizer, chmn. confs. on Mex. and Latin Am. tax laws, 1992—. Editor (loose leaf treatise) CCH Latin Am. Tax Guide, 1999; contbr. articles to profl. jours. Adv. bd. Com. for Pub. Autonomous Schs., Washington, 1989—; chmn. of bd. dirs. Mid Am. Chpt., U.S. Mex. C. of C., 1993-97. Named Leading Tax Advisor, Euromoney Guide to Leading U.S. Tax Lawyers, 1997, Euromoney Guide to the World's Leading Tax Advisors, 1999, Leading Advisor on Latin Am. Tax, Internat. Tax. Review, 1996-98. Mem. ACLU, ABA, Internat. Fiscal Assn. Episcopalian. E-mail: John.A.McLees@Bakernet.com. Corporate taxation, Private international, Mergers and acquisitions. Home: 1434 S Plymouth Ct Chicago IL 60605-2005 Office: Baker & McKenzie 130 E Randolph Dr Ste 3700 Chicago IL 60601-6342

**MCLELLAN, DALE J.,** lawyer; b. Detroit, June 6, 1949; s. Allan Daniel and Mary Alice (MacDonald) McL.; m. Mary Jo Schneider, Feb. 26, 1971; children: Jessica, Daniel. BA, Wayne State U., 1971, JD, 1976. Bar: U.S. Dist. Ct. (ea. dist.) Mich. 1976, U.S. Ct. Appeals (6th cir.) 1981, U.S. Dist. Ct. (we. dist.) Mich. 1989. Sr. ptnr., v.p. Collins, Einhorn, Farrell & Ulanoff, P.C., Southfield, Mich., 1976—. Contbr. articles to profl. jours. Recipient Am. Jurisprudence Book award Martindale Hubble. Mem. ABA, Detroit Bar Assn., Assn. of Def. Trial Counsel, Def. Rsch. Inst., Mich. Def. Trial Counsel, Oakland County Bar Assn. (chmn. environ. law com. 1991-92), Southfield Bar Assn., St. Valentine's Men's Club (pres.). Avocations: hockey, golf, rollerblading. Construction, Insurance, Toxic tort. Office: Collins Einhorn Farrel & Ulanoff 4000 Town Ctr Ste 909 Southfield MI 48075-1473

**MCLELLAN, JOHN SIDNEY, III,** judge; b. Kingsport, Tenn., Jan. 16, 1946; s. John Sidney Jr. and Opal Lee (Poe) McL.; m. Wanda Ruth (Gulley), June 5, 1966; children: John Richardson, Jason Ray. BS, U. Tenn., 1968, JD, 1970. Bar: Tenn. 1971, U.S. Dist. Ct. Tenn. 1971, U.S. Ct. Appeals (6th cir.) 1972. Atty. McLellan Law Offices, Kingsport, 1971-94; cir. judge

County of Sullivan, 1994—; county atty. Sullivan County, Blountville, Tenn., 1978-1994; pres. Wishing Well Found. Inc., Tenn. 1996-97. Recipient Honor for Support award Tenn. Paralegal Assn. (Tri-cities chpt.), 1994. Mem. Am. Trial Lawyers Assn., Am. Judges Assn., Tenn. Jud. Conf. (exec. com. 1997—, sec. 1995-96), Tenn. Trial Judges Assn. (v.p. 1996-97), Kingsport Bar Assn. Democratic. Episcopal. Office: City Hall 225 W Center St Kingsport TN 37660-4238

**MCLEMORE, MICHAEL KERR,** lawyer, minister; b. Atlanta, May 19, 1949; s. Gilbert Carmichael Sr. and Jeannie (Gulley) M.; m. Colleen Owen, Aug. 19, 1972; children: Megan, Shannon. BA, Haverford Coll., 1971; JD, U. Ga., 1974; MDiv, Candler Sch. Theology, 1997. Bar: Fla. 1974, U.S. Dist. Ct. (mid. and so. dists.) Fla. 1974, U.S. Ct. Appeals (5th cir.) 1974, U.S. Ct. Appeals (11th cir.) 1981, U.S. Supreme Ct. 1984. Shareholder Kimbrell & Hamann P.A., Miami, Fla., 1974-91. Pres. Haverford Soc. South Fla., Miami, 1978-91; Fla. Alumni admissions rep. coord. Haverford Coll., 1978-91, alumni coun., 1980-91; lay leader 1st United Meth. Ch., South Miami, 1986-90; lay del. Fla. Ann. Conf., 1986-90, chmn. adminstrv. bd., 1991—, property and compensation com., 1988-90; co-chmn. Miami dist. Work Area on Stewardship, 1987—; chair deferred gifts Epworth Village, 1990-91; pastor Bishop Circuit United Meth. Ch., 1995-97, New Pentecost United Meth. Ch., 1997—. 1st lt. USAR, 1976-78. Mem. ABA, Fla. Bar Assn. (aviation sect.), Dade County Def. Bar Assn. (bd. dirs. 1989—, treas. 1990—), Nat. Transp. Safety Bd. Assn., Lawyer-Pilot Bar Assn. Democrat. Methodist. Federal civil litigation, State civil litigation. Home: 268 Moss Side Dr Athens GA 30607-2109 Office: New Pentecost United Meth Ch 385 Pleasant Hill Church Rd Winder GA 30680

**MCLENDON, MELBURNE DEKALB,** lawyer, arbitrator; b. Atlanta, Apr. 21, 1921; s. Jesse Martin and Elizabeth Lee (Sartain) McL.; m. Loyce Jacqueline Kirkland, Dec. 31, 1949; children: James Kirkland, Loyce Eloise McLendon Snyder. LLB, U. Ga., 1948. Bar: Ga. 1949, U.S. Dist. Ct. (no. dist.) Ga. 1949, U.S. Ct. Appeals (5th cir.) 1965, U.S. Supreme Ct. 1973, U.S. Dist. Ct. (mid. dist.) Ga. 1985. Law clk. Fulton County Superior Ct., Atlanta, 1949-50; ptnr. Carter Ansley Smith & McLendon, Atlanta, 1950-86; dir. Amica Mutual Ins. Co., 1976-96; cons. U.S. VA Hosp., Decatur, Ga., 1996—; arbitrator N.Y. Stock Exch., 1980-88, U.S. Dist. Ct. (mid. dist.) Ga., Macon, 1988—. Scout master Boy Scouts Am., Atlanta, 1959-70. Staff sgt. USAAF, 1942-45. Recipient Disting. Svc. award U. Ga., 1996, Exceptional Performance citation def. Rsch. Inst., 1985. Mem. Ga. Def. Lawyers Assn. (pres. 1984), Atlanta Bar Assn., Lawyer's Club of Atlanta, Univ. Yacht Club, Buckhead Men's Garden Club, Masons (32 deg.). Republican. Methodist. Avocations: gardening, woodwork, travel, fishing, spectator sports.

**MCLENDON, SUSAN MICHELLE,** lawyer, nurse; b. N.Y.C., Mar. 5, 1964; d. James U. McLendon, Sr. BSN, Binghamton U., 1986; JD, Hofstra U., 1990. Bar: N.J. 1991, Washington 1998; RN, N.Y., 1986. Asst. regional counsel Social Security Adminstrn., Office Gen. Counsel, N.Y.C., 1990-98; RN Access Nursing Corp., N.Y.C., 1998—; mentor Practicing Attys. for Law Students, N.Y.C., 1992—. Health, Entertainment, General corporate.

**MCLEOD, CHRISTINE QUILLIAN,** lawyer; b. Coral Gables, Fla., Sept. 3, 1965. BS in Computer Sci., Fla. Internat. U., Miami, 1989, BS in Elec. Engring., 1989; JD, U. Miami, 1991. Bar: Fla. 1992, D.C. 1992, U.S. Dist. Ct. (so. dist.) 1992, U.S. Patent Office 1992, U.S. Dist. Ct. (mid. dist.) Fla. 1993, U.S. Ct. Appeals (11th and D.C. cirs.) 1998, U.S. Dist. Ct. (no. dist.) Fla. 1997. Lawyer Lott & Friedland, Miami, Fla., 1992-95, Ruden, McClosky et al, Ft. lauderdale, Fla., 1995-97, Saliwanchik, Lloyd & Saliwanchik, Gainesville, Fla., 1997—. Mem. Am. Intellectual Property Assn., Patent Law Assn. S. Fla., Soc. Women Engrs., Assn. U. Tech. Mgrs. Intellectual property, Patent, Trademark and copyright. Office: Saliwanchik Lloyd & Saliwanchik 2421 NW 41st St Gainesville FL 32606-6669

**MCLEOD, GIA NICOLE,** lawyer; b. Forest, Miss., Sept. 20, 1967; d. Wayne Edwin and Patricia V. Eubanks; m. Mark Edward McLeod, Apr. 26, 1997. BA, Miss. State U., 1989; JD, Miss. Coll., 1992. Bar: Miss. 1993, U.S. Dist. Ct. (so. dist.) Miss. 1994. Pvt. practice Jackson, Miss., 1993-94; dep. pub. defender City Pub. Defender, Jackson, 1994-95; assoc. Stewart & Assocs., Brandon, Miss., 1995-97; pvt. practice Madison, Miss., 1997—; statewide dir. inmate legal assistance program Miss. Dept. Corrections, 1999—. Mem. Miss. Trial Lawyers Assn. Republican. Baptist. Avocations: scuba diving, backpacking. Family and matrimonial, General civil litigation, Criminal. Office: McLeod & McLeod PO Box 13765 Jackson MS 39236-3765

**MCLEOD, WALTON JAMES,** lawyer, state legislator; b. Walterboro, S.C., June 30, 1937; s. Walton James Jr. and Rhoda Lane (Brown) M.; m. Julie Edwina Hamiter, Feb. 15, 1969; 1 child, Walton James IV. BA, Yale U., 1959; LLB, U. S.C., 1964. Bar: S.C. 1964, U.S. Supreme Ct. 1974. Law clk. to Chief Judge Clement Haynsworth U.S. Ct. Appeals (4th cir.), Richmond, Va., 1964-65; assoc. Pope and Schumpert, Newberry, S.C., 1965-67; asst. U.S. Atty. Columbia, S.C., 1967-68; gen. counsel S.C. Dept. Health & Environ. Ctrl., Columbia, 1968-94, spl. counsel, 1994-96; dep. S.C. atty. gen. Columbia, 1987-88; magistrate Newberry County, Little Mountain, S.C., 1973-81; mcpl. judge Town of Little Mountain, 1981-83, mayor, 1983-89, 93-96; mem. S.C. Ho. of Reps., Columbia, 1996—. Author: Legal Perspectives of Environmental Health, 1973; co-author: Environmental Quality Law, 1975, Hospital Franchising Law and Regulation, 1979. Pres. Newberry (S.C.) Jaycees, 1967; bd. dirs. S.C. Housing Fin. & Devel. Authority, Columbia, 1977-96; chair Ctrl. Midlands Coun. Govts., Columbia, 1981-82; trustee S.C. State Mus., Columbia, 1981-85. Lt. (j.g.) USN, 1959-61, Capt. USNR, 1961-92. Recipient Outstanding Jaycee award Newberry Jaycees, 1967, Howell Excellence award Naval Res. Law Program, Washington, 1991; named Outstanding Freshman Rep. of Yr. Carolina Hist. Found. Soc., Inc., 1997. Fellow S.C. Bar Found.; mem. S.C. Magistrates Assn. (pres. 1976-77, Disting. Jud. Svc. award 1975, 77), Judge Advs. Assn. (nat. pres. 1991-92), S.C. Res. Officers Assn. (state pres. 1981-82, Res. Officer of Yr. 1998), S.C. Soc. (pres. 1990-93). Democrat. Luth. Avocations: jogging, reading. Fax: 803-345-0770. Home: 308 Pomaria St Little Mountain SC 29075-9003 Office: SC House of Reps PO Box 11867 Columbia SC 29211-1867

**MCLURKIN, THOMAS CORNELIUS, JR.,** lawyer; b. L.A., July 28, 1954; s. Thomas Cornelius and Willie Mae (O'Connor) McL.; m. Charmaine Bobo. BA, U. So. Calif., 1976, MPA, 1980, PhD in Pub. Adminstrn., 1998; JD, U. LaVerne, 1982. Bar: Calif. 1984, U.S. Dist. Ct. (ctrl. dist.) Calif. 1984, U.S. Dist. Ct. Hawaii 1984, U.S. Ct. Appeals (9th cir.) 1984, U.S. Dist. Ct. (ea., no. and so. dists.) Calif. 1985, U.S. Tax Ct. 1988, U.S. Ct. Mil. Appeals 1989, U.S. Army Ct. Mil. Rev. 1993, U.S. Supreme Ct., 1995. Law clk. dept. water and power City of L.A., 1979-82; jud. clk. cen. dist. U.S. Dist. Ct., L.A., 1983-84; law clk. Office City Atty., L.A., 1983-84, dep. city atty., 1984—. Author (with others): Facts in American History, 1968, 2nd edit. 1989, Eagle Scout, 1970. Mem. L.A. World Affairs Coun., 1980—, Smithsonian Assocs.; bd. dirs. L.A. Area coun. Boy Scouts Am., Hillsides Homes for Children; provisional patron Tournament of Roses Assn., Pasadena, 1994—; mem. Verdugo Hills Area coun. Boy Scouts Am. Mem. ABA, ALA, ASPA, Los Angeles County Bar Assn., Assn. Trial Lawyers Am., Langston Law Assn. L.A., U. So. Calif. Gen. Alumni Assn. (bd. govs. exec. bd. 1986-90), U. So. Calif. Black Alumni Assn.-Ebonics (pres. 1988-89), U. So. Calif. Pres.'s Cir., Elks, Am. Legion, Phi Alpha Delta, Kappa Alpha Psi. Republican. United Methodist. Avocations: sailing, tennis, volunteer work, American and world history. Office: LA City Atty Office 200 N Main St Ste 1700 Los Angeles CA 90012-4110

**MCMAHON, COLLEEN,** judge; b. Columbus, Ohio, July 18, 1951; d. John Patrick and Patricia Paterson (McDanel) McM.; m. Frank V. Sica, May 16, 1981; children: Moira Catherine, Patrick McMahon, Brian Vincent. BA summa cum laude, Ohio State U., 1973; JD cum laude, Harvard U., 1976. Bar: N.Y. 1977, U.S. Dist. Ct. (so. and ea. dists.) N.Y. 1977, U.S. Ct. Appeals (2d cir.) 1978, U.S. Supreme Ct. 1980, U.S. Ct. Appeals (5th cir.) 1985, D.C. 1985. Spl. asst. U.S. mission to the UN, N.Y.C., 1979-80; assoc. Paul, Weiss, Rifkind, Wharton & Garrison, N.Y.C., 1976-79, 80-84, ptnr., 1984-95; judge N.Y. Ct. Claims, N.Y.C., 1995-98; acting justice N.Y. Supreme Ct., 1995-98; judge U.S. Dist. Ct. (so. dist.) N.Y., White Plains, 1998—; chair The Jury Project, N.Y. Office Ct. Adminstrn., 1993-94; mem. 1st jud. dist. com. Litigation Delay Reduction, 1997. Bd. dirs. Vol. Lawyers for the Arts, N.Y.C., 1979-83, Dance Theater Workshop, 1978-83; vice chancellor Episcopal Diocese of N.Y., 1992-95. Mem. ABA, Assn. of Bar of City of N.Y. (mem. coun. on jud. adminstrn. 1983-87, chmn. com. on state cts. of superior jurisdiction 1984-87, com. on women profession 1989-95, chmn. 1992-95, chmn. nominating com. 1996, mem. ad hoc com. jud. conduct 1996—), Am. Law Inst., Am. Judicature Soc., Westchester County Bar Assn., N.Y. State Bar Assn. (mem. ho. of dels. 1986-89), Fed. Bar Coun., N.Y. County Lawyers Assn. (chmn. com. changing trends in the profession 1998). Republican. Episcopalian. Office: United States Courthouse 300 Quarropas St White Plains NY 10601-4140

**MCMAHON, CRAIG ROGER,** lawyer; b. Meriden, Conn., July 5, 1950; s. Roger and Marie (Couch) McM. BA, George Washington U., 1972; JD, New Eng. Sch. Law, 1976. Bar: Conn. 1976. Magistrate Alaska Ct. Sys., Aniak, 1977-84, Bethel, 1984—. Mem. Bethel Actor's Guild (v.p. 1991—), Bethel Coun. on Arts (treas. 1988—). Avocations: genealogy, photography, travel. Home: PO Box 1346 Bethel AK 99559-1346 Office: Alaska Court Sys PO Box 130 Bethel AK 99559-0130

**MCMAHON, DENNIS C.,** lawyer, writer; b. Bklyn., Aug. 4, 1950; s. John Thomas and Ruth Mildred McMahon. BA summa cum laude, Fordham U., 1972; JD, Bklyn. Law Sch., 1977. Bar: N.Y. 1978, U.S. Dist. Ct. (so. and ea. dists.) N.Y. 1978, U.s. Dist. Ct. (no. dist.) N.Y. 1984, U.S. Ct. Appeals (3d cir.) 1992. Reporter, editor News Home Reporter, Bklyn., 1972-77; weekly press coord. Speakers' Office, N.Y. State Assembly, N.Y.C., 1977; atty. Hugh & Conor, N.Y.C., 1978-87, Peter F. Broderick, N.Y.C., 1987-93; sole practitioner N.Y.C., 1993—; arbitrator N.Y.C. Small Claims Ct., Bklyn., 1985—; cons. various law firms in Republic of Ireland. Author column Bklyn. Spectator, 1983—. Bd. dirs. N.Y.c. Econ. Devel. Corp., 1987-97; mem. Sch. Bd. Dist. 20, Bklyn., 1977-93. Recipient numerous local civic awards. Mem. Am. Arbitration Assn. (arbitrator), KC, Commodore Barry Club, Ancient Order of Hibernians, Downtown Athletic Club (bd. dirs.). Democrat. Roman Catholic. Avocations: philately, Irish events, music, travel, politics. Personal injury, General civil litigation, Contracts commercial. Home: 7032 4th Ave Brooklyn NY 11209-1666 Office: 17 Battery Pl New York NY 10004-1207

**MCMAHON, EDWARD RICHARD,** lawyer; b. Jersey City, June 7, 1949; s. Edward Barnawall and Jean (Sullivan) McM.; m. Ellen Mary Bosek; children: Meghan Jean, Kerry Eileen, Ryan Edward. AB, Colgate U., 1972; JD, Seton Hall U., 1975. Bar: N.J. 1975, U.S. Dist. Ct. N.J. 1975, U.S. Ct. of Appeals (3rd circ.) 1980. Law clk. to judge U.S. Dist. Ct., Newark, 1975-77; assoc. Lum, Biunno & Tompkins, Newark, 1977-83; ptnr. Lum, Danzis, Drasco, Positan & Kleinberg, Roseland, 1983—. Mem. Morris County Rep. Com., N.J., 1982-94; mem. Chatham (N.J.) Boro Rep. com., 1982-94, chmn., 1986-94; bd. dirs. Madison area YMCA, 1989-95; mem. N.J. State Rep. Com., 1994—. Mem. ABA (litigation and banking sects.), N.J. Bar Assn., Assn. Fed. Bar N.J., Am. Judicature Soc., Morris County Bar Assn., Essex County Bar Assn., Delbarton Sch. Alumni Assn. (class rep. 1984—), 200 Club Morris County, Delta Upsilon, Phi Alpha Delta . Republican. Roman Catholic. Club: Colgate (No. N.J.). Banking, Federal civil litigation, State civil litigation. Home: 150 Van Houton Ave Chatham NJ 07928-1239 Office: Lum Danzis Drasco Positan & Kleinberg LLC 103 Eisenhower Pkwy Roseland NJ 07068-1029

**MCMAHON, JAMES CHARLES,** lawyer; b. Bklyn., Dec. 4, 1951; s. James Charles and Rosemary Margaret (Gilroy) McM.; m. Nancy M. Neble, Oct. 30, 1984; children: Deirdre Kathleen Wright, Laura Elizabeth, Elizabeth Jane. BA, Boston Coll., 1973; JD, Fordham U., 1977. Bar: N.Y. 1978, Mass. 1996, U.S. Supreme Ct. 1996. Assoc. Winthrop Stimson Putnam & Roberts, N.Y.C., 1977-78, Brodsky, Linett, Altman, Schechter & Reicher, N.Y.C., 1978-82; ptnr. Brodsky, Altman & McMahon, N.Y.C., 1982—, mng. ptnr., 1988—; exec. sec., counsel N.Y. Movers Tariff Bur., Inc., N.Y.C., 1984—; gen. counsel Mass. Movers Assn., Woburn, 1986—, Commonwealth Transp. Compensation Corp., Andover, Mass., 1992—, Transport Health Plan, Woburn, 1994—, N.Y. State Movers and Warehousemen's Assn., N.Y.C., 1984—, Nat. Moving and Storage Assn., Fairfax, Va., 1988-98. Mem. editl. bd. Fordham Urban Law Jour., 1976. Recipient Disting. Svc. award Mass. Movers Assn., 1992. Mem. N.Y. State Bar Assn. (labor and employment law sect.), Assn. Bar City N.Y. (transp. com. 1997—), Assn. Comml. Fin. Attys., Transp. Lawyers Assn., Assn. for Transp. Law, Logistics and Policy, N.Y. Athletic Club. Democrat. Roman Catholic. Antitrust, Labor, Transportation. Home: 196 Pinesbridge Rd Ossining NY 10562-1428 Office: Brodsky Altman & McMahon 475 Park Ave S Fl 7 New York NY 10016-6901 also: 10 State St Woburn MA 01801-6820

**MCMAHON, MARK PRESTON,** lawyer; b. Evansville, Ind., Mar. 7, 1952; m. Patti Schrank; 5 children. BBA, U. Tex., Austin, 1974; JD, St. Mary's U., San Antonio, 1976. Bar: Tex. 1977, U.S. Dist. Ct. (ea. dist.) Tex. 1979, U.S. Ct. Appeals (5th cir.) 1980, U.S. Dist. Ct. (we. dist.) Tex., 1984, U.S. Supreme Ct. 1984. Asst. counsel House Judiciary Com. Tex. Legis., Austin, 1977; briefing atty. Ct. of Civil Appeals 6th Jud. Dist. Tex., Texarkana, 1977-78; assoc. Kenley, Boyland, Coghlan & Erskine, Longview, Tex., 1978-80; ptnr. Erskine, Dunn & McMahon, Longview, 1980-83, Erskine, Smith & McMahon, Longview, 1983-87, Erskine & MacMahon, Longview, 1987-88, Erskine, McMahon & Stroup, Longview, 1989—. Mem. ABA, State Bar Tex., Gregg County Bar Assn., Assn Trial Lawyers Am., Tex. Trial Lawyers Assn., Bar Assn. 5th Fed. Cir., East Tex. Trial Lawyers Assn. Personal injury, Workers' compensation. Home: 15 Oak Forest Dr Longview TX 75605-1713

**MCMAHON, RAYMOND JOHN,** lawyer; b. Pawtucket, R.I., Dec. 23, 1921; s. Raymond John and Irene Mary (Smith) McM.; m. Mary Elise Russell, Sept. 16, 1961 (div. Mar. 1998); children: Raymond J., Brian R., Patrick J., Kevin J. AB, Dartmouth Coll., 1943; LLB, Harvard U., 1945. Bar: Mass. 1946, R.I. 1946, U.S. Ct. Appeals (1st cir.) 1947, U.S. Dist. Ct. R.I. 1947. Mem. newsroom NBC, N.Y.C., 1946; trial atty. Office Chief Counsel, War Dept., Nuremberg, Germany, 1946-47; ptnr. McMahon & McMahon, Providence, 1947—; bd. dirs. Magnetic Seal Corp, Warren, R.I., Patco Corp., Bristol, R.I., Sargeant & Wilbur Inc., Pawtucket. Mem. ABA, Am. Coll. Trust and Estate Counsel, R.I. Bar Assn., Wannamoisett Country Club (sec., bd. govs. 1989-90). Avocations: golf, reading, travel. General corporate, Probate, Pension, profit-sharing, and employee benefits. Home: 104 Glenwood Ave Pawtucket RI 02860-6118 Office: McMahon & McMahon 15 Westminster St Providence RI 02903-2424

**MCMAHON, RICHARD H.,** lawyer; b. Rome, N.Y., July 3, 1930; s. Johnson D. and Helen C. McMahon; m. Rugh M. McLaughlin, Sept. 12, 1953 (dec. Aug. 1998); children: patricia A., Richard H. Jr., Timothy S., Mary Ellen, Johnson J., Joseph P., Christopher M. AB, Dartmouth Coll., 1952, MS in Civil Engring., 1953; LLB, Cornell U., 1960. Bar: N.Y. 1960. Assoc. Office of Johnson D. McMahon, Rome, 1960-64; ptnr. McMahon, Grow & Getty and predecessor firms, Rome, 1964—. Bd. dirs., past pres. Rome United Way; bd. dirs. Cerebral Palsy Handicapped Persons Assn., Utica, 1986—; bd. dirs., chmn. loan com. Rome Indsl. Devel. Corp., 1990—. Fellow Elks; mem. Rome Bar Assn. (treas. 1966—). Roman Catholic. Avocations: reading, tennis, refinishing furniture. Probate, Real property, Estate planning. Office: McMahon Grow & Gerry 301 N Washington St Rome NY 13440-5105

**MCMAHON, RICHARD MICHAEL, SR.,** lawyer; b. Ridgway, Pa., Dec. 9, 1938; s. Edward L. and Catherine (Stangel) McM.; m. Angela Scally, Aug. 3, 1963; children: Kimberly, R. Michael Jr., Karen, Edward. BS in Engring., Pa. State U., 1960; JD, U. Ala., Tuscaloosa, 1969. Bar. Ala., U.S. Patent Office, Md., U.S. Ct. Appeals (4th and 5th cirs.), U.S. Dist. Ct. Md. Ptnr. Scally, Scally & McMahon, P.A., Upperco, Md. Mem. Fed. Bar Assn., Md. Patent Law Assn., Md. State Bar Assn., Balt. County Bar Assn., Knights of Columbus. Fax: 410-374-6972. E-mail: mcmahon@mcpat.com. Intellectual property, General corporate, Sports. Office: 3 Hunter Lake Ct Upperco MD 21155-9404

**MCMAHON, ROBERT ALBERT, JR.,** lawyer; b. New Orleans, July 23, 1950; s. Robert Albert and Marie Rose (Kennedy) McM.; m. Cynthia Ann Steffan, June 29, 1979; children: Angela, Jennifer, Robyn. BA cum laude, U. Southwestern La., 1972; JD, Loyola U., 1975. Bar: La. 1975, U.S. Dist. Ct. (ea. dist.) La. 1977, U.S. Ct. Appeals (5th cir.) 1978, U.S. Dist. Ct. (mid. dist.) La. 1985, U.S. Supreme Ct. 1989, U.S. Dist. Ct. (we. dist.) La. 1991. Atty. Brown & Hull, Metairie, La., 1975-76, Stewart Title La., New Orleans, 1976, Duplechin & Assocs., Gretna, La., 1977-80, Zelden & Zelden, New Orleans, 1980-81; ptnr. Bernard, Cassisa, Elliott & Davis, Metairie, La., 1982—; vol. New Orleans Pro Bono Project, 1991—. Mem. New Orleans Pachyderm Club, 1992—, NRA-Inst. for Legis. Action, Washington, 1991—; chief YMCA Indian Guide/Princess Program, Metairie, 1988-89. Recipient scholarship U. New Orleans, 1968, U. Southwestern La., 1968. Mem. Def. Rsch. Inst., La. Assn. Def. Counsel, Maritime Law Assn. U.S., Jefferson Bar Assn., La. State Bar Assn.(ho. dels. 1993—), Hibernians, Phi Kappa Theta. Republican. Roman Catholic. Avocations: military history, hunting, tennis, golf. Product liability, Admiralty, Insurance. Office: Bernard Cassisa Elliott & Davis 1615 Metairie Rd Metairie LA 70005-3926

**MCMAHON, THOMAS MICHAEL,** lawyer; b. Evanston, Ill., May 11, 1941; s. Robert C. and Kathryn D. (Dwyer) McM.; m. M. Ann Kaufman, July 11, 1964; children—Michael, Patrick. Student, U. Notre Dame, 1959-61; BA, Marquette U., 1963; JD magna cum laude, Northwestern U., 1970. Bar: Ill. 1970. Mgr. legal adv. sect. Ill. EPA, Springfield, 1970-72; assoc. Sidley & Austin, Chgo., 1972-75, ptnr., founder nat. environ. group, 1975—; lectr. in field; mem. City of Evanston Environ. Control Bd., 1981-83. Author: The Superfund Handbook, 1989, International Environmental Law and Regulation, 1992, Legal Guide to Working with Environmental Consultants, 1992, The Environmental Manual, 1992. Lt. USN, 1963-67. Decorated Republic of Vietnam Campaign medal. Mem. ABA (past vice-chmn. environ. quality com., environ. aspects of bus. trans. com., internat. environ. law com., lectr. confs., teleconfs. and satellite seminars), Order of Coif. Environmental, General corporate, Alternative dispute resolution. Office: Sidley & Austin 1 First Natl Plz Chicago IL 60603-2003

**MCMANAMAN, KENNETH CHARLES,** lawyer; b. Fairfield, Calif., Jan. 25, 1950; s. Charles James and Frances J. (Holys) McM.; m. Carol Ann Wilson, Apr. 15, 1972; children: Evan John, Kinsey Bridget, Klerin Rose. BA cum laude, S.E. Mo. State U., 1972; JD, U. Mo., Kansas City, 1974; grad., Naval Justice Sch., Newport, R.I., 1975; MS in Bus. Mgmt. summa cum laude, Troy State U., Montgomery, Ala., 1978. Bar: Mo. 1975, U.S. Dist. Ct. (we. dist.) Mo. 1975, Fla. 1976, U.S. Dist. Ct. (No. and mid. dists.) Fla. 1976, U.S. Dist. Ct. Mil. Appeals 1977, U.S. Ct. Appeals (5th and 8th cirs.) 1977, U.S. Dist. Ct. (ea. dist.) Mo. 1978, U.S. Supreme Ct. 1978, D.C. 1991; cert. mil. judge; diplomate Am. Bd. Forensic Examiners. Ptnr. O'Loughlin, O'Loughlin & McManaman, Cape Girardeau, Mo., 1978—; prof. bus. law Troy (Ala.) State U., 1976-78; prof. bus. law S.E. Mo. State U., Cape Girardeau, 1978-84, prof. criminal justice, 1998; prof. bus. mgmt. William Woods U., 1998—; prof. bus. mgmt., Cert. to Teach Trial Advocacy Nat. Inst. Trial Advocacy; prof. bus. law Troy State U., Ala., 1976-78, S.E. Mo. State U., Cape Girardeau, 978-84; prof. criminal justice, bus. mgmt. Wm. Woods U., 1998—; instr. Mo. Dept. pub. Safety, S.E. Mo. Regional Law Enforcement Tng. Acad., 1979—, Cape Girardeau Police Res., 1983-93, Naval Justice Sch., 1996; mcpl. judge City of Jackson, Mo., 1980-89, 94—; spl. mcpl. judge City of Cape Girardeau, 1981-89; atty. Ct. Appts. Spl. Advs./Guardians in Ct. for Children, 1994—; spl. mcpl. judge city of Frederickson, Mo., 1995. Mem. Cape Cirardeau County Coun. on Child Abuse, 1980-89; membership dir. S.E. Mo. Scouting coun. Boy Scouts Am., 1980-82; mem. Cape Girardeau County Mental Health Assn., 1982-92; active local and state Dem. Party, del. Nat. Dem. Conv., San Francisco, 1984, chmn. County Dem. Com., 1984-96; mem. 8th Congl. Dist. Dem. Com., 1984-86, 27th State Dem. Senatorial Com., 1984-86, ward committeeman, 1984-94; bd. dirs. Area wide Task Force on Drug and Alcohol Abuse, 1984-87; sponsor drug edn./prevention program in schs.; bd. dirs. Cape County chpt. Nat. Kidney Found., 1988-93; pres. Jackson Area Soccer Assn., 1987-93. Capt. HAGC, USNR, 1994—. Recipient Robert Chilton award City of Jackson for Leadership, Integrity and Responsibility, 1995-97; named One of Outstanding Young Men Am., 1981, 82, 84, 85, Outstanding Pub. Svc. award Cape Girardeau Police Dept. Mem. ABA (Mo. del. young lawyers divsn. 1982-83), Mo. Bar Assn. (chmn. trial advicacy task force 1983), Mo. Bar (young lawyers sect. coun. rep. dist. 13 1980-85), Fla. Bar Assn., Kansas City Bar Assn., Assn. Trial Lawyers Am., Fed. Bar Assn., Nat. Coll. Dist. Attys., Cape Girardeau County Bar Assn. (founder, pres. young lawyers sect. 1981-82), Naval Res. Assn. (v.p. Southeast Mo/So. Ill. chpt. 1980-85), S.E. Mo. State Alumni Coun., Sigma Chi (numerous awards), Sigma Tau Delta, Pi Delta Epsilon. Roman Catholic. General practice, Workers' compensation. Home: 1162 Trailridge Dr Jackson MO 63755-3507 Office: O'Loughlin O'Loughlin McManaman 1736 N Kingshighway St Cape Girardeau MO 63701-2190

**MCMANIS, JAMES,** lawyer; b. Haverhill, Mass., May 28, 1943; s. Charles and Yvonne (Zinn) McM.; m. Sara Wigh, Mar. 30, 1968. BA, Stanford U., Palo Alto, Calif., 1964; JD, U. Calif., Berkeley, 1967. Bar: Calif. 1967, U.S. Dist. Ct. (no. dist.) Calif. 1967, U.S. Ct. Appeals (9th cir.) 1967, U.S. Supreme Ct. 1971. Dep. dist. atty. Santa Clara County Dist. Atty., 1968-71; mem. McManis, Faulkner & Morgan, San Jose, Calif., 1971—; spl. master tech. equities litigation, 1987—; spl. examiner State Bar Calif., 1995-98; prof. law Lincoln U. Law Sch., San Jose, 1972-82; lectr. Calif. Continuing Edn. of Bar, 1989-90; instr. U. Calif. Law Sch., 1992-96, Stanford U. Sch. Law, 1994-99. Pres. Santa Clara County Bar Assn. Law Found., 1996, dir., 1987—. Fellow Am. Coll. Trial Lawyers; mem. ABA, State Bar Calif., Calif. Trial Lawyers Assn., Santa Clara County Bar Assn., Boalt Hall Alumni Assn. Avocations: history, books, travel, running. Fax: 408-279-3244. E-mail: jmcmanis@mfmlaw.com. General civil litigation, Criminal, Intellectual property. Office: McManis Faulkner & Morgan Inc 160 W Santa Clara St Fl 10 San Jose CA 95113-1701

**MCMANUS, CLARENCE ELBURN,** judge; b. New Orleans, June 3, 1934; s. Otis Clarence and Odell (Hawsey) McM.; m. Barbara Isabella Edmundson, Apr. 3, 1976; children—Elizabeth Ann, Bryan Stephen. B.B.A., Tulane U., 1958; J.D., 1961. Bar: La. 1961, U.S. Ct. Appeals (5th cir.) 1961, U.S. Dist. Ct. (ea. dist.) La. 1961, U.S. Supreme Ct. 1987. Sole practice, Metairie, La., 1961-69; asst. dist. atty. Jefferson Parish, La., 1969-82; state dist. judge 24th Jud. Dist. Ct., Gretna, La., 1982—. Republican. Home: 824 Bonnabel Blvd Metairie LA 70005-2059 Office: Gretna Courthouse Annex Gretna LA 70053

**MCMANUS, CONSTANCE,** lawyer; b. Savannah, Ga., Sept. 16, 1951; d. Joseph John McManus and Lucy McIntosh (Bowyer) Youngquist; (div.); 1 child, Kristen Marie. BS in Edn., U. Ga., 1972; postgrad., Coll. of William & Mary, 1972; JD, Woodrow Wilson Coll. Law, 1980. Bar: Ga. 1980, U.S. Dist. Ct. (no. dist.) Ga. 1981, U.S. Supreme Ct. 1985. Tchr. West Point, Va., 1973; claims supr. Home Ins. Co., Atlanta, 1974-77; pvt. practice Marietta, Ga., 1980—. Editor Law Rev., Woodrow Wilson Coll. of Law, 1979-80. Former mem. bd. dirs., officer Horseshoe Bend Civic Club, Marietta; bd. dirs., officer Anna L. Haas Humane Soc., Marietta, 1985-92; bd. dirs. Stingrays, Inc.,1989-93; chmn. Ga. AAU, 1991-93. Mem. ATLA, Ga. Bar Assn. (juvenile com. Marietta chpt., Law Day com. 1993-94, cir. defender panel 1993-96), Atlanta Bar Assn., Ga. Criminal Def. Lawyers, Atlanta Track Club, Chattahoochee Road Runners Club (v.p. 1992-94, pres. 1994-95). Baptist. Avocations: running, tennis, aerobics. Office: 540 Powder Springs St SE Marietta GA 30064-3549

**MC MANUS, EDWARD JOSEPH,** federal judge; b. Keokuk, Iowa, Feb. 9, 1920; s. Edward W. and Kathleen (O'Connor) McM.; m. Sally A. Hassett, June 30, 1948 (dec.); children: David P., Edward W., John N., Thomas J., Dennis Q.; m. Esther Y. Kanealy, Sept. 15, 1987. Student, St. Ambrose Coll., 1936-38; B.A., U. Iowa, 1940, J.D., 1942. Bar: Iowa 1942. Gen. practice of law Keokuk, 1946-62, city atty., 1946-55; mem. Iowa Senate, 1955-59; lt. gov. Iowa, 1959-61; chief U.S. judge No. Dist. Iowa, 1962-85, sr. U.S. judge, 1985—. Del Democratic Nat. Conv., 1956, 60. Served as lt. AC USNR, 1942-46. Office: US Dist Ct 329 US Courthouse 101 1st St SE Cedar Rapids IA 52401-1202

**MCMANUS, FRANK SHIELDS,** lawyer; b. Phila., July 28, 1947; s. Frank A. and Sara (Shields) McM.; m. Bertha Marie Harrison, Sept. 21, 1968; children: Barry Shields, Justin Harrison. AA, St. John Vianney Coll., 1967; BA, Fla. State U., 1969, JD cum laude, 1972. Bar: Fla. 1972, U.S. Dist. Ct. (so. dist.) Fla. 1972, U.S. Ct. Appeals (5th cir.) 1972. U.S. Supreme Ct. 1978, U.S. Ct. Appeals (11th cir.) 1984, U.S. Dist. Ct. (mid. dist.) Fla. 1993. Assoc. Beasley & Geiger, Stuart, Fla., 1972-73; ptnr. Beasley & McManus,

Stuart, 1973-74, McManus, Stewart, Ferraro, Stuart, 1974-89, Kohl, Bobko, McKey, McManus, Higgins, Stuart, 1990-93, Gary, Williams, Parenti, Finney, Lewis, McManus, Watson, Stuart, 1993—; mem. com. on Stds. of Conduct of Governing Judges Fla. Supreme Ct., 1987; mem. grievance com. 19th Cir. Ct., 1983-85, chmn. nominating commn., 1982-84; instr. legal rsch. Indian River C.C., Stuart, 1989. Contbr. articles to profl. publs. Mem. adv. bd. Cath. Charities, Martin/St. Lucie Counties, 1988—; bd. dirs. St. Lucia Island Found., Fla., 1989—; v.p. Alliance for a Balanced Cmty., 1991-94; legal advisor Holy Redeemer Cath. Ch., Palm City, Fla., 1983—; bd. dirs. Chapman Sch. of Seamanship, 1984—, chmn., 1995—; mem. Marin County Planning and Zoning Bd./Local Planning Agy., 1992-94, chmn., 1993-94; vol. Marin County United Way Campaign. Capt. USAR, 1971-81. Mem. Fla. Bar (bd. govs. young lawyers sect. 1977-81, chmn. legal forms com. 1980-81, chmn. jud. nominating procedures com. 1984-85, joint commn. on delivery of legal svcs. to the poor 1990-92, civil procedure rules com. 1993-97), Fla. Bar Found. (bd. dirs. 1989-92, legal aid com. 1988-93), Martin County Bar Assn. (pres. 1982-83), 19th Cir. Civil Trial Bar Assn. (v.p. 1988-92), Martin Downs Country Club. Personal injury, General civil litigation. Home: 5910 SE Forest Glade Trl Hobe Sound FL 33455-7899 Office: Gary Williams Parenti et al Waterside Profl Bldg 221 SE Osceola St Ste 300 Stuart FL 34994-2289

**MCMANUS, JAMES WILLIAM,** lawyer; b. Kansas City, Mo., Aug. 1, 1945; s. Gerald B. and Mary M. (Hagan) McM.; m. Julie C. Waters, Feb. 17, 1973. BA, Rockhurst Coll., 1967; JD, St. Louis U., 1971. Bar: Mo. 1971, U.S. Dist. Ct. (we. dist.) Mo. 1972, U.S. Ct. Appeals (8th cir.) 1974, U.S. Supreme Ct. 1979, U.S. Ct. Appeals (10th cir.) 1984. Law clk. to presiding justice U.S. Dist. Ct. (we. dist.) Mo., 1971-73; assoc. Shughart, Thomson & Kilroy, P.C., Kansas City, 1973-76, dir., 1977-94; counsel Dysart, Taylor, Lay, Cotter & McMonigle, P.C., Kansas City, 1994—; course lectr. med. jurisprudence U. Health Scis., Coll. Osteo. Medicine, Kansas City, 1994. Mem. adv. coun. St. Joseph Health Ctr., 1989—. Mem. ABA, Mo. Bar Assn., Kansas City Lawyers Assn., Kansas City Met. Bar Assn. (chmn. alternate dispute resolution com. 1996-97, vice chmn. 1994-95, chmn. med. malpractice com. 1989), Mo. Orgn. Def. Lawyers, St. Louis Alumni Assn. (pres. 1984-92), St. Louis U. Law Sch. Alumni Assn. General civil litigation, Personal injury, Federal civil litigation. Home: 6824 Valley Rd Kansas City MO 64113-1929 Office: Dysart Taylor Lay Cotter & McMonigle PC 4420 Madison Ave Kansas City MO 64111-3407

**MCMANUS, MARTIN JOSEPH,** lawyer, priest; b. Toledo, Mar. 24, 1919; s. Martin Joseph and Elizabeth Marie (McDermott) McM. AB, John Carroll U., 1939; LLB, Georgetown U., 1942; LLM, U. So. Calif., 1946; D in Juridical Sci., NYU, 1961; B in Canon Law, Cath. U. Am., 1964; Licentiate in Canon Law, D in Canon Law, The Pontifical Univ. Lateran, 1965; Licentiate in Sacred Theology, The Pontifical Univ. Urbanianum, 1966; DST, The Pontifical Univ. Angelicum, 1967. Bar: Calif. 1947, U.S. Supreme Ct. 1960; ordained priest Roman Cath. Ch., 1959. Pvt. practice L.A., 1947-54; prof. law Southwestern U., L.A., 1947-57; prof. law U. San Diego, 1959-63, dean Law Sch., 1960-63; atty.-advisor U.S. Govt., Washington, 1977-82; counsel to bishop 2d Vatican Coun., Rome, 1962-65; advisor, cons. Republican Nat. Com., Washington, 1968-73; adminstrv. law judge HHS, Southfield, Mich., 1982—.

**MCMANUS, RICHARD GRISWOLD, JR.,** lawyer; b. Rockville Centre, N.Y., May 12, 1943; s. Richard Griswold and Ruth Mary (Frost) McM. BBA, U. Notre Dame, 1965; JD, U. Denver, 1970. Bar: Colo. 1970, U.S. Dist. Ct. Colo. 1970, U.S. Ct. Appeals (10th cir.) 1971, U.S. Supreme Ct. 1974. Law clk. Office Atty. Gen., State of Colo., Denver, 1969-70, asst. atty. gen., 1970-78; pvt. practice Denver, 1978-80, 88—; ptnr. Miles & McManus, Denver, 1980-86, Miles, McManus & Epstein, Denver, 1986-88; mcpl. judge Aurora, Colo., 1993—, Federal Heights, Colo., 1996—. Rep. candidate for Colo. Atty. Gen., 1990. 1st lt. U.S. Army, 1965-67. Fellow Colo. Bar Found.; mem. Colo. Bar Assn. (conv. com. 1977-89, 97—, co-chmn. 1982-85, bar press com. 1980-88, vice chmn. 1982-83, chmn. 1983-84, adminstrv. law com. 1984—, awards com. 1988—, bd. govs. 1984-86, v.p. 1986-87, labor law com. 1988—, membership svcs. com. 1988-90, chmn. 1989-90, health law forum com. 1988—, polit. edn. com. 1994—), Denver Bar Assn. (jud. adminstrn. com. 1983-89, awards 1987—), Catholic Lawyers Guild. Administrative and regulatory, Health, Labor. Home: 1521 Central St Unit 3F Denver CO 80211-3945 Office: Ste 1100 1801 Broadway Denver CO 80202-3839

**MCMEEN, ELMER ELLSWORTH, III,** lawyer, guitarist; b. Lewistown, Pa., June 3, 1947; s. Elmer Ellsworth II and Frances Josephine McM.; m. Sheila Ann Taenzler, July 31, 1971; children: Jonathan Ellsworth, Daniel Biddle, James Cunningham and Mary Josephine (twins). AB cum laude, Harvard U., 1969; JD cum laude, U. Pa., 1972. Bar: 1973, U.S. Ct. Appeals (2d cir.) 1973, U.S. Dist. Ct. (so. and ea. dists.) N.Y. 1975. Assoc. Cravath, Swaine & Moore, N.Y.C., 1972-75; assoc. LeBoeuf, Lamb, Greene & MacRae L.L.P., N.Y.C., 1975-78, ptnr., 1979—; lectr. Editor U. Pa. Law Rev., 1970-72. Author numerous guitar books Mel Bay Pub.; contbr. articles to profl. jours; solo guitar recs. Of Soul and Spirit, Irish Guitar Encores by Shanachie Records, Solo Guitar Serenade, Playing Favorites and Acoustic Guitar Treasures by Piney Ridge Music, solo guitar instructional audio and video lessons and performance videos for Stefan Grossman's Guitar Workshop and Rounder Records. Chmn. N.Y.C. regional com. for U. Pa. Law Sch., 1984-86; class sec. Mt. Hermon Sch. Class of 1965, Mass., 1984-91. Fellow Am. Coll. Investment Counsel; mem. ABA, N.Y. State Bar Assn. (mem. corp. law com.), Rockaway River Country Club, Harvard Club. General corporate, Securities, Public utilities. Office: LeBoeuf Lamb Greene & MacRae LLP 125 W 55th St New York NY 10019-5369

**MCMICHAEL, DONALD EARL,** lawyer; b. Denver, Aug. 8, 1931; s. Earl L. and Charlotte F. McM.; m. Zeta Hammond, July 6, 1955; children: Lauren A. McMichael Burnett, Thomas D., Susan E. McMichael Markle. AB, Dartmouth Coll., 1953; LLB, U. Colo., 1956. Bar: Colo. 1956, U.S. Dist. Ct. Colo. 1956, U.S. Ct. Appeals (10th cir.) 1956. Assoc. Holme Roberts & Owen, 1956-58; pres. Corp. Ins. Assocs., 1958-70; dir. trust devel. Ctrl. Bank Denver, 1970-72; ptnr. Brenman, Sobol & Baum, Denver, 1972-74, McMichael, Sell & Agresti (formerly McMichael, Multz & Lipton), Denver, 1974-99; sole practitioner, 1999—. Chmn. Denver Ctrl. YMCA, 1971-83. Capt. USAR, 1956-64. Named Layman of Yr. Denver Ctrl. YMCA, 1973, named to Denver Metro YMCA Hall of Fame, 1989. Mem. Colo. Bar Assn., Denver Bar Assn., Denver Estate Planning Coun. (sec. 1971-73). Republican. Methodist. Estate planning, Probate, General corporate. Office: 6325 W Mansfield Ave Unit 234 Denver CO 80235-3015

**MCMILLAN, JAMES GARDNER,** lawyer; b. Montreal, Sept. 2, 1959; came to U.S., 1968; s. Gardner Craddock and Lois Ellen McMillan; m. Ann D. Catron, Oct. 25, 1991; children: Chelsea Ann, Aislinn Katherine. BA, U. Va., 1981; JD, Harvard U., 1984. Bar: D.C. 1985, Md. 1985. Assoc. Skadden, Arps, Slate, Meagher & Flom, Washington, 1985-87, Hogan & Hartson, Washington, 1987-90; counsel to Senate Minority Leader, Robert J. Dole U.S. Senate, Washington, 1990-93; ptnr. Hogan & Hartson LLP, Washington, 1993—. Mem. Raven Soc., Phi Beta Kappa. Securities, General corporate, Legislative. Office: Hogan & Hartson LLP 555 13th St NW Ste 800E Washington DC 20004-1161

**MCMILLAN, LEE RICHARDS, II,** lawyer; b. New Orleans, Aug. 26, 1947; s. John H. and Phoebe (Skillman) McM.; m. Lynne Clark Pottharst, June 27, 1970; children: Leslie Clark, Hillary Anne, Lee Richards III. BS in Commerce, Washington and Lee U., 1969; JD, Tulane U., 1972; LLM in Taxation, NYU, 1976. Bar: La. 1972. Assoc. Jones, Walker, Waechter, Poitevent, Carrere & Denegre, New Orleans, 1976-79, ptnr., 1979—, sect. head, corp. and securities sect., 1987-90, 94—, exec. com., 1990-94, 96—, chmn. exec. com., 1991-94, 96-98; vice-chmn. Mech. Equipment Co., Inc., New Orleans, 1980-86, chmn. bd., 1986—, pres. 1989—; mem. The Bus. Coun. Greater New Orleans, 1998—, exec. com., 1999—; bd. dirs. The Chamber/New Orleans and the River Region, 1996-98; bd. tr ustees Alton Ochsner Med. Found., 1995—. Trustee New Orleans Mus. Art., 1989-95; bd. dirs. bur. Govt. Rsch. New Orleans, 1987-93, Louise S. McGehee Sch., New Orleans, 1982-88, co-chmn. capital fund dr., 1984-86, pres. bd. dirs., 1986-88; bd. govs. Isidore Newman Sch., New Orleans, 1991-95. Lt. JACG USNR, 1972-75. Mem. ABA (com. on negotiated acquisitions 1986-94), La. State Bar Assn. (chmn. corp. and bus. law sect. 1985-86, mem. com. on bar admissions 1986-87), Young Pres. Orgn., Washington and Lee U. Alumni Assn. (bd. dirs. 1995—). Republican. Episcopalian. Avocation: sailing. Securities, Mergers and acquisitions, Banking. Office: Jones Walker Waechter Poitevent Carrere & Denegre 201 Saint Charles Ave Ste 5200 New Orleans LA 70170-5100

**MCMILLEN, JAMES THOMAS,** lawyer; b. Murfreesboro, Tenn., Mar. 4, 1942; s. James Clyde and Mable Bell (Waldron) McM.; m. Janice Elaine Ligon, June 29, 1974; children: Rachel Leeanne, Shayne Brandon. BS in Math., Middle Tenn. State U., 1968; JD, Nashville Sch. Law, 1975. Bar: Tenn. 1975, Tex. 1985, U.S. Dist. Ct. (mid. dist.) Tenn. 1976, U.S. Dist. Ct. (so. dist.) Tex. 1985, U.S. Dist. Ct. (we. and no. dists.) Tex. 1989, U.S. Ct. Appeals (6th cir.) 1977, U.S. Ct. Appeals (5th cir.) 1985, U.S. Supreme Ct. 1978; cert. bus. and consumer bankruptcy law Tex. Bd. Legal Specialization, Am. Bankruptcy Inst. Programmer Baird-Ward Printing Co., Nashville, 1968-69; project mgr. Norvel Systems, Inc., Memphis, 1969-70; computer technician Concept Data Svc., Memphis, 1970; programmer, analyst Baird-Ward Printing Co., Nashville, 1970-75; atty., pvt. practice Nashville, 1975-78, Murfreesboro, 1978-83; atty. disaster loan program SBA, Nashville, 1983-84; br. counsel atty. SBA, Corpus Christi, Tex., 1984-85; sr. assoc. atty. Kleberg, Dyer, Redford & Weil, Corpus Christi, Tex., 1985-87; atty., pvt. practice Corpus Christi, Tex., 1987—; speaker at ann. conv. Nat. Assn. Consumer Bankruptcy Attys., 1994-99. Com. chmn. Troop 220 Gulf Coast Coun. Boy Scouts Am., 1993. Recipient Cert. of Appreciation, State of Tenn., 1972; named Boss of Yr., Murfreesboro Legal Secs. Assn., 1981. Mem. ABA, Am. Bankruptcy Inst. (cert. bus. and consumer bankruptcy law), Nat. Assn. Consumer Bankruptcy Attys. (bd. dirs.), Nat. Assn. Consumer Attys., Tex. Bar Assn., Coastal Bend Bankruptcy Assn. (pres. 1991-92, bd. dirs. 191—), Am. Arbitration Assn., Coll. of State Bar, Cooper's Inn Honor Soc., Alpha Psi Omega. Democrat. Episcopalian. Avocations: travel, RVing. Bankruptcy, Consumer commercial. Office: 801 Ayers St Corpus Christi TX 78404-1914

**MCMILLEN, ROBERT STEWART,** lawyer; b. Yonkers, N.Y., Feb. 25, 1943; s. David Harry and Blodwyn Elizabeth (Evans) McM; m. Dorothea Anne Murray, July 2, 1966; children: Elissa London, Tara Evans. BS, U. Rochester, 1964; JD cum laude, Albany Law Sch. Union U., 1969. Bar: N.Y. 1969, U.S. Dist. Ct. (no. dist.) N.Y. 1969. Assoc. Clark, Bartlett & Caffry, Glens Falls, N.Y., 1969-73; ptnr. Caffry, Pontiff, Stewart, Rhodes & Judge, Glens Falls, 1974-80; prin. Bartlett, Pontiff, Stewart & Rhodes, P.C., Glens Falls, 1981—; sr. law examiner N.Y. State Bd. Law Examiners, Albany, 1986—; pres., bd. dirs. Community Title Agy., Inc., Glens Falls, 1984—. Editor-in-chief Albany Law Rev., 1968-69. Bd. dirs., officer Voluntary Action Ctr. of Glens Falls Area, Inc., 1970-97; bd. dirs., treas. Arts and Crafts Ctr. of Warren County, Inc., Glens Falls, 1984-94; mem. Warren County Rep. Com., Queensbury, N.Y., 1979—; alt. or del. Rep. Jud. Nomination Com. 4th Jud. Dist. N.Y., 1977—. Recipient Disting. Svc. award Voluntary Action Ctr. of Glens Falls Area, Inc., 1990. Mem. ABA, N.Y. State Bar Assn. (mem. com. profl. ethics 1990-99), Warren County Bar Assn. (bd. dirs. 1979-82), Adirondack Regional C. of C. (bd. dirs. 1997—, vice chmn. 1999—). Avocations: family activities, downhill skiing, boating, hockey. Real property, Pension, profit-sharing, and employee benefits, General corporate. Home: 27 Moorwood Dr Queensbury NY 12804-1010 Office: 1 Washington St Glens Falls NY 12801-2963

**MCMILLIAN, THEODORE,** federal judge; b. St. Louis, Jan. 28, 1919; m. Minnie E. Foster, Dec. 8, 1941. BS, Lincoln U., 1941, HHD (hon.), 1981; LLD, St. Louis U., 1949; HHD (hon.), U. Mo., St. Louis, 1978. Mem. firm Lynch & McMillian, St. Louis, 1949-53; asst. circuit atty. City of St. Louis, 1953-56; judge U.S. Ct. Appeals (8th cir.), 1978—; judge Circuit Ct. for City St. Louis, 1956-72, Mo. Ct. Appeals eastern div., 1972-78; asso. prof. adminstrn. justice U. Mo., St. Louis, 1970—; asso. prof. Webster Coll. Grad. Program, 1977; mem. faculty Nat. Coll. Juvenile Justice, U. Nev., 1972—. Served to 1st lt. Signal Corps U.S. Army, 1942-46. Recipient Alumni Merit award St. Louis U., 1965, ACLU Civil Liberties award, 1995, Disting. Lawyer award Bar Assn. Met. St. Louis, 1996, Salute to Excellence Civil Rights award St. Louis Am., 1997. Mem. Am. Judicature Soc., Am. Bd. Trial Advs. (hon. diplomate), Lawyers Assn. Mo., Mound City Bar Assn., Phi Beta Kappa, Alpha Sigma Nu. Office: US Ct Appeals 8th Circuit 526 US Ct & Custom House 1114 Market St Saint Louis MO 63101-2043

**MCMORROW, MARY ANN G.,** state supreme court justice; b. Chgo., Jan. 16, 1930; m. Emmett J. McMorrow, May 5, 1962; 1 dau., Mary Ann. Student, Rosary Coll., 1948-50; JD, Loyola U., 1953. Bar: Ill. 1953, U.S. Dist. Ct. (no. dist.) Ill. 1960, U.S. Supreme Ct. 1976. Atty. Riordan & Linklater Law Offices, Chgo., 1954-56; asst. state's atty. Cook County, Chgo., 1956-63; sole practice Chgo., 1963-76; judge Cir. Ct. Cook County, 1976-85, Ill. Appellate Ct., 1985-92, Supreme Ct. Ill., 1992—; faculty adv. Nat. Jud. Coll., U. Nev., 1984. Contbr. articles to profl. jours. Mem. Chgo. Bar Assn., Ill. State Bar Assn., Women's Bar Assn. of Ill. (pres. 1975-76, bd. dirs. 1970-78), Am. Judicature Soc., Northwestern U. Assocs., Ill. Judges Assn., Nat. Assn. Women Judges, Advocates Soc., Northwest Suburban Bar Assn., West Suburban Bar Assn., Loyola Law Alumni Assn. (bd. govs. 1985—), Ill. Judges Assn. (bd. dirs.), Cath. Lawyers Guild (v.p.), The Law Club of the City of Chgo., Inns of Ct. Office: Supreme Ct of Ill 160 N La Salle St Chicago IL 60601-3103

**MCNALLY, GERALD, JR.,** lawyer; b. Kalamazoo, Dec. 28, 1947; s. Gerald and Elizabeth Louise (Lake) McN.; m. Barbara Frances Robinson, Mar. 17, 1979 (div.); children: Charles Patrick Ritchie, Fiona Kathleen. Student, Mich. State U., 1965-67; JD, Whittier Coll., 1984. Bar: Calif., 1984. Treas. Ch. of Scientology, San Diego, 1971-74; customer svc. rep. Xerox Corp., L.A., 1974-78; acct., enrolled agt. L.A., 1978-84; pvt. practice Glendale, Calif., 1984—. Served with USN, 1967-71. Mem. ABA, Assn. for Childbirth at Home Internat. (bd. dirs. 1980). Republican. Avocations: computers, golf, swing dancing. E-mail address: mcnallylaw@relaypoint.net. Taxation, general, Bankruptcy, General corporate. Home: 3800 La Crescenta Ave Ste 200 La Crescenta CA 91214-3957

**MCNALLY, JOHN BERNARD,** lawyer; b. Phila., Mar. 17, 1943; s. John Bernard and Elizabeth Marie McNally; m. Gail Frances Miller, Jan. 5, 1991; 1 child, Amelia Mairead. BA in Econs., LaSalle U., 1968; JD, Widener U., 1975. Bar: Pa. 1976, Fla. 1979, U.S. Dist. Ct. (ea. dist.) Pa. 1976, U.S. Supreme Ct. 1982. Trial lawyer in pvt. practice, Jenkintown, Pa., 1976—. Mem. Jenkintown Boro Zoning Bd., 1979-85, 97—; mem. Jenkintown Planning Commn., 1985-97. Served with U.S. Army, 1965-71. Mem. Pa. Bar Assn., Montgomery County Bar Assn., Fla. Bar. Avocations: history, birding, travel, art, antiques, antique autos. General civil litigation, Criminal, Personal injury. Office: 216 Summit Ave Jenkintown PA 19046-3111

**MCNALLY, PATRICK T.,** lawyer; b. Augsburg, Germany, Aug. 7, 1955; s. Henry J. and Hareth V. McNally; m. Carla C. McNally, Oct. 31, 1981; children: Morgan Chandler, Collin Patrick,. BA, Wake Forest U., 1977; JD, U. Tenn., 1982. Bar: Tenn. 1982, Ky. 1984, U.S. Dist. Ct. (mid. dist.) Tenn. 1991, U.S. Ct. Appeals (6th cir.) 1994. Asst. pub. adv. Ky. Pub. Defender, Hazard, 1982-86; sr. asst. pub. adv. Nashville Pub. Defender, 1986-91; assoc. Hollins, Wagster & Yarbrough, P.C., Nashville, 1991—. Criminal. Office: Hollins Wagster & Yarbrough Suntrust Ctr 424 Church St Fl 22 Nashville TN 37219-2301

**MCNALLY, SEAN PATRICK,** prosecutor; b. Scranton, Pa., Aug. 5, 1953; s. John Patrick and Elizabeth Jane McNally; m. Diane Maureen Campanaro, June 29, 1985; 1 child, Brigid S. AA, Citrus Coll., 1973; BA, UCLA, 1975; JD, Western State U., 1979; postgrad. cert., U. So. Calif., 1981, 82. Bar: U.S. Tax Ct. 1980, U.S. Dist. Ct. (ctrl. dist.) Calif. 1980, U.S. Dist. Ct. (so. dist.) Calif. 1981, U.S. Ct. Appeals (8th cir.) 1981. Law libr. Orange County Law Libr., Santa Ana, Calif., 1975-80; intern Orange County Dist. Atty., Santa Ana, 1978; assoc. Law Offices of Leon Najman, Costa Mesa, Calif., 1980-81; dep. dist. atty. San Bernardino County, Calif., 1981—. Mem. ABA, San Bernardino County Bar Assn., Calif. Trial Lawyers Assn., Assn. of Trial Lawyers of Am., Calif. Dist. Atty. Assn., Emerald Soc., L.A. Trial Lawyers Assn., Riverside County Bar Assn., Orange County Bar Assn., Elks. Republican. Roman Catholic. Avocations: boating, running, collegiate sporting events. Home: 6007 E Brighton Ln Anaheim CA 92807-4702 Office: San Bernardino County Dist Atty 316 N Mountain View Ave San Bernardino CA 92401-1610

**MCNAMARA, A. J.,** federal judge; b. 1936. BS, La. State U., 1959; JD, Loyola U., New Orleans, 1968. Bailiff, law clk. U.S. Dist. Ct., New Orleans, 1966-68, sole practice, 1968-72; ptnr. Monton, Roy, Carmouche, Hailey, Bivens & McNamara, New Orleans, 1972-78, Hailey, McNamara, McNamara & Hall, 1978-82; judge U.S. Dist. Ct. (ea. dist.) La., New Orleans, 1982—. Mem. La. Ho. of Reps., 1976-80. Office: US Dist Ct C-367 US Courthouse 500 Camp St New Orleans LA 70130-3313

**MCNAMARA, ANNE H.,** lawyer, corporate executive; b. Shanghai, Republic of China, Oct. 18, 1947; came to U.S. 1949; d. John M. and Marion P. (Murphy) H.; m. Martin B. McNamara, Jan. 15, 1977. AB, Vassar Coll., 1969; JD, Cornell U., 1973. Bar: N.Y. 1973, Tex. 1981. Assoc. Shea, Gould, Climenko & Casey, N.Y.C., 1972-76; from asst. corp. sec. to corp. sec. Am. Airlines, Inc., Dallas, 1976-88, v.p. pers. resources, 1988; sr. v.p., gen. counsel Am. Airlines (AMR Corp.), Dallas, 1988—; bd. dirs. Louisville Gas & Electric Co., LG&E Energy Corp., Sabre Group Holdings, Inc. General corporate, Securities, Antitrust. Office: Am Airlines Inc Dallas/ Fort Worth Airport PO Box 619616 Dallas TX 75261-9616*

**MCNAMARA, EILEEN,** lawyer; b. San Diego, Sept. 13, 1953; children: Teresa, Mitchell. JD. Bar: Calif. 1987. Pvt. practice Orange, Calif. Family and matrimonial. Office: Law Office Eileen McNamara 595 The City Dr S Ste 203 Orange CA 92868-3313

**MCNAMARA, JOHN C.,** lawyer; b. Pittston, Pa., Aug. 24, 1947; m. Sharon T. McNamara, Apr. 28, 1979; children: Kathleen, Molly. BS in Bus. Adminstrn., Georgetown U., 1969, JD, 1973. Bar: Pa. 1973, U.S. Dist. Ct. (ea. and mid. dists.) Pa., U.S. Ct. Appeals (3rd cir.), U.S. Tax Ct., U.S. Supreme Ct. Assoc. Fox Rothschild O'Brien & Frankel, Phila., 1973-79; ptnr. LaBrum & Doak, Phila., 1979-80, German Gallagher & Murtagh, Phila., 1980-91, Butler & McNamara PC, Phila., 1992—. Capt. Pa. Army Nat. Guard, 1970-80. Mem. Phila. Assn. Def. Coun. (exec. com. 1998—), Georgetown U. Alumni Assn. (b.p. sch. bus. 1982-90, alumni senate 1990—, bd. govs.). General civil litigation, Insurance, Product liability. Home: 27 Golfview Rd Ardmore PA 19003-1625 Office: Butler & McNamara PC 1700 Market St Ste 2630 Philadelphia PA 19103-3903

**MCNAMARA, JOSEPH BURK,** lawyer, corporate executive; b. Williamsport, Pa., Dec. 25, 1930; s. Joseph C. and Anna F. (Burk) McN.; Wayne M., Paul D., Janet L. BS in ChemE, Lehigh U., 1952; MBA, Rutgers U., 1959; cert. advanced study in English Lit., No. Ill. U., 1981; JD, Loyola U., Chgo., 1987. Bar: Ill. 1987, D.C. 1988, U.S. Dist. Ct. (no. dist.) Ill. 1987, U.S. Ct. of Appeals (7th cir.) 1987, U.S. Tax Ct.1987. Dir. indsl. relations, mgr. planning Union Carbide Corp., Bound Brook, N.J., 1952-63; tech. dir. Borg-Warner, Inc., Chgo., 1963-71; pres. Freundorfer, Inc., Elgin, Ill., 1971-86, also bd. dirs., 1971-88, v.p., 1986—; dist. counsel IRS, Chgo., 1987-88; assoc. Franks & Filler, Marengo, Ill., 1988—; cons. Venture Mgmt. Services, Crystal Lake, Ill., 1984-86; adj. faculty McHenry County Coll., 1993—. Contbr. numerous articles to profl. jours., 1964—. Bd. dirs. United Way, Elgin and McHenry County, Ill., 1979—, Hospice Northeastern Ill. (v.p., bd dirs., pres.), McHenry County Coll. Found. With U.S. Army, 1955-56. Mem. ABA, Ill. State Bar Assn., McHenry County Bar Assn., Phi Beta Kappa, Tau Beta Pi. Avocations: running, writing, classical music, theater. General corporate, Taxation, general, General practice. Home: PO Box 1280 Crystal Lake IL 60039-1280 Office: PO Box 4 Wonder Lake IL 60097-0004

**MCNAMARA, MICHAEL JOHN,** lawyer; b. Hutchinson, Minn., July 1, 1948; s. John Oliver and Lucille Violet (Wedell) M.; m. Kathleen Elizabeth Dahl; children: Jennifer, Kelly. BA, U. Utah, 1976; JD, U. Minn., 1980. Bar: Minn. 1981, U.S. Dist. Ct. Minn. 1981, U.S. Ct. Appeals (8th cir.) 1982, U.S. Supreme Ct. 1988, Wis. 1992. Pvt. practice Mpls., 1981—; panel arbitrator Am. Arbitration Assn., Hennepin County Dist. Ct.; panelist No-Fault Arbitrators Minn. Supreme Ct. Contbr. articles to profl. jours. Sgt. U.S. Army, 1968-71, Vietnam. Nat. Merit scholar. Mem. FBA, ATLA, The Federalist Soc., Internat. Platform Assn., Minn. State Bar Assn., Minn. Trial Lawyers Assn., Hennepin County Bar Assn. (mem. spkrs. bur.). Avocations: jogging, biking, hiking. General civil litigation, General corporate, Criminal. Office: Henderson Howard et al 6200 Shingle Creek Pkwy Ste 385 Minneapolis MN 55430-2176

**MCNAMARA, PATRICK JAMES,** lawyer; b. Bethpage, N.Y., Mar. 27, 1959; s. James Francis and Kathleen (Marrinan) McN.; m. Kimberly McNamara, Dec. 7, 1991; 1 child, James Patrick. BA in History, Rutgers U., New Brunswick, N.J., 1981, MA in Polit. Sci., 1985; JD, Rutgers U., Camden, N.J., 1987. Bar: N.J. 1987, U.S. Dist. Ct. N.J. 1987, Pa. 1987. Legal sec. to Hon. Neil F. Deighan Jr., Appellate Divsn. N.J. Superior Ct., 1987-88; with Giordano, Halleran & Ciesla, Middletown, N.J., 1988-91; assoc. Carpenter, Bennett and Morrissey, Newark, 1991-94, Scarinci & Hollenbeck, Secaucus, N.J., 1994—; gen. counsel Nat. Assn. Fruits, Flavors & Syrups, Inc., 1995—, Chem. Sources Assn., 1998—. Assoc. editor Food Exec. mag., 1997, Food Product Design mag., 1999—; contbr. author to profl. jours. Mcpl. atty. Township of Aberdeen, 1992-95; spl. counsel Twp. of Aberdeen, 1996-97. Rutgers U. Grad. fellow Eagleton Inst. Politics, 1984-85. Mem. N.J. State Bar Assn., N.J. Inst. Mcpl. Attys., Environ. Law Inst., N.J. Group Small Chem. Businesses, Rutgers Alumni Assn. (bd. dirs.), Irish Bus. Orgn. Avocations: sports, travel, golf, politics. Fax: 201-348-3877. E-mail: patrick@njlegalink.com. Environmental, Real property, Administrative and regulatory. Office: Scarinci & Hollenbeck 500 Plaza Dr PO Box 3189 Secaucus NJ 07096-3189

**MCNAMARA, PATRICK ROBERT,** lawyer; b. Conneaut, Ohio, Dec. 16, 1950; s. Robert John and Retagene (Bailey) McN.; m. Sue Brozina, July 12, 1975; children: Brian, Meghan, Erin, Robert. BS, Northwestern U., 1973; JD, U. Ariz., 1976. Bar: Ariz. 1976, U.S. Dist. Ct. Ariz. 1976, U.S. Ct. Appeals (9th cir.) 1981; cert. specialist workers' compensation law Ariz. Bd. Legal Specialization. Assoc. Davis, Eppstein & Tretschok, Tucson, 1976-79; adminstrv. law judge Indsl. Commn. Ariz., Tucson, 1979-81; ptnr. Tretschok, McNamara & Patten, P.C., Tucson, 1981—. Mem. Pima County Bar Assn., Assn. Trial Lawyers Am., Ariz. Trial Lawyers Assn., Ariz. State Bar (past pres. worker's compensation law sect.), So. Ariz. Workers Compensation Claims Assn., Nat. Orgn. Social Security Claimants Reps. Democrat. Roman Catholic. Fax: 520 792 2417. E-mail: mcnamara@tmpllaw.com. Workers' compensation. Office: Tretschok McNamara & Patten PC PO Box 42887 Tucson AZ 85733-2887

**MCNAMARA, ROBERT M., JR.,** lawyer; m. Patti Devenney; children: Brendan, Caitlin. BA, Mt. Carmel Coll., 1967; AB, John Carroll U., 1968; JD, Georgetown U., 1973. Law clk. to Hon. George C. Edwards, Jr. U.S. Ct. Appeals (6th cir.), Cin.; dep. dir. enforcement Commodity Futures Trading Commn.; gen. counsel Peace Corps.; legis. counsel U.S. Senate Judiciary com.; asst. U.S. atty. U.S. Senate Watergate Com., asst. majority counsel; asst. gen. counsel enforcement Dept. Treasury; gen. counsel CIA, 1997—; adj. prof. law Georgetown U. Law Ctr. Symposium editor: Am. Criminal Law Rev. Office: CIA Office of Gen Counsel Washington DC 20505-0001*

**MCNAMEE, STEPHEN M.,** federal judge; b. 1942. B.A., U. Cinn., 1964; M.A., J.D., U. Ariz., 1969. U.S. atty. Dist. of Ariz., Phoenix, 1985-90; judge U.S. Dist. Ct. Ariz., Phoenix, 1990—. Office: City of Phoenix US Court Ho & Fed Bldg 230 N 1st Ave Phoenix AZ 85025-0230

**MCNAUGHTON, ALEXANDER BRYANT,** lawyer; b. Atlanta, Apr. 2, 1948; s. William James and June Florence (Gibson) McN.; m. Susan Mary Knox, Mar. 7, 1981; children: Alexis Loren, Elizabeth Adelyn. BS, Ga. State U., 1974; postgrad., Oxford (England) U., 1980; JD, U. Okla., 1981. Bar: Okla. 1981, U.S. Dist. Ct. (we. dist.) Okla. 1981, U.S. Ct. Appeals (10th cir.) 1982, U.S. Ct. Mil. Appeals 1984, U.S. Supreme Ct. 1985. Social worker State of Ga. Dept. Human Svcs., Bainbridge, 1974-75; farmer MC Farms, Cole, Okla., 1975-81; trial lawyer Mattoon Law Offices, Norman, Okla., 1981-82, Jones, Gungoll, Jackson et al, Enid, Okla., 1982-83, Jones, McNaughton & Blakley, Enid, 1983-85, McNaughton & McNaughton, Enid, 1985-94; ptnr. Norman, Edem, McNaughton & Wallace, Enid, 1994—;

expert cons. in field. Contbr. to book chpt. Scoutmaster Boy Scouts Am., Norman. With U.S. Army, 1966-68. Mem. ABA (litigation med. negligence, tort and ins. sects.), ATLA (sustaining), Okla. Trial Lawyers Assn. (bd. dirs. 1993—), Okla. Bar Assn. (rules of profl. conduct com., 1997—, chnmn. medical-legal code subcom., 1997—). Avocations: camping, bicycling, sports car racing, swimming. Personal injury, Federal civil litigation, State civil litigation. Home: 2567 Homestead Rd Enid OK 73703-1647 Office: Norman Edem McNaughton & Wallace 110 N Independence St Enid OK 73701-4001

**MCNEARNEY, JOHN PATRICK,** lawyer; b. St. Louis, Oct. 25, 1956; s. Robert O. and Rosalie M. McNearney; m. Lynne M. Hays, Sept. 6, 1985; children: Patrick, Taylor, Douglas, Colin. BA in Econs. and History, U. Va., 1979; JD, Northwestern U., Chgo., 1983. Bar: Mo. 1983, Ill. 1984. Assoc. Thompson & Mitchell, St. Louis, 1983-85; asst. counsel Gen. Am. Life Ins. Co., St. Louis, 1985-87; counsel, 1st v.p. 1st Nationwide Bank, St. Louis, 1987-92; ptnr. Peper, Martin, Jensen, Maichel & Hetlage, St. Louis, 1992—. Contbg. author: Banking and Lending Institution Forms, 1993, Foreclosure Law and Related Remedies, 1995. Mem. ABA, Mo. Bar, Ill. Bar Assn., Bar Assn. Met. St. Louis. Republican. Roman Catholic. Avocations: tennis, golf. Bankruptcy, Real property, Banking. Home: 1212 Somerset Field Dr Chesterfield MO 63005-1339 Office: Blackwell Sanders Peper Martin LLP 720 Olive St Fl 24 Saint Louis MO 63101-2338

**MCNEELY, JAMES LEE,** lawyer; b. Shelbyville, Ind., May 4, 1940; s. Carl R. and Elizabeth J. (Orebaugh) McN.; m. Rose M. Wisker, Sept. 5, 1977; children: Angela, Susan, Meg, Matt. AB, Wabash Coll., 1962; JD, Ind. U., 1965. Bar: Ind. 1965, U.S. Dist. Ct. (so. dist.) Ind. 1965, U.S. Ct. Appeals (7th cir.) 1970. Assoc. Pell & Matchett, Shelbyville, 1965-70; ptnr. Matchett & McNeely, Shelbyville, 1970-74; sole practice Shelbyville, 1974-76; sr. ptnr. McNeely & Sanders, Shelbyville, 1976-86, McNeely, Sanders & Stephenson, Shelbyville, 1986-89, McNeely, Sanders, Stephenson & Thopy, Shelbyville, 1989-96, McNeely, Stephenson, Thopy & Harrold, Shelbyville, 1997—; guest lectr. Franklin Coll., Ind., 1965-72; judge Shelbyville City Ct., 1967-71. Chmn. Shelbyville County Rep. Cen. Com., 1968-88; bd. dirs. Ind. Lung Assn., 1972-75, Crossroads Council Boy Scouts Am., 1982; bd. dirs., pres. Shelbyville Girls Club. Named Sagamore of the Wabash, gov. Otis Bowen, 1977, gov. Robert Orr, 1986, 88, gov. Evan Bayh, 1996. Fellow Ind. Bar Found. (patron); mem. ABA, Ind. Bar Assn. (sec. 1985-87, bd. dirs. 1976-78, chair-elect Ho. Dels. 1994-95, chair 1995-96, v.p. 1996-97, pres.-elect 1997-98, pres. 1998-99), Shelby County Bar Assn. (pres. 1975), Ind. Lawyers Commn. (pres., dir.), Fed. Merit Selection Commn., Shelbyville Jaycees (Distinguished Service award 1969, Good Govt. award 1970), Wabash Coll. Nat. Assn. Wabash Men (dir. 1983-89, sec. 1989-91, v.p. 1991-93, pres. 1993-95, Man of Yr. 1995), Kappa Sigma Alpha Pi chpt. (Hall of Fame 1995). Methodist. Lodges: Lions, Elks, Eagles. Avocations: golf, travel. Labor, Insurance, State civil litigation. Home: 1902 E Old Rushville Rd Shelbyville IN 46176-9569*

**MCNEELY, ROBERT A.,** lawyer; b. Dallas, Apr. 24, 1959; s. W. Eugene McNeely and Joan M. (McCampbell) Schmedemann; m. Cynthia A. Myers, May 26, 1990; children: R. Andrew II, John R., Jade E., Jazlyn A. BS in Journalism, U. Kans., 1981; JD, Fla. State U., 1993. Morning news anchor, editor Kans. Info. Network, Wichita, 1982-83; statehouse bur. chief Kans. Info. Network, Topeka, 1983-84; spl. assignment reporter Sta. KANU-FM, Lawrence, Kans., 1984-85; news dir. Sta. WFSU-FM, Tallahassee, Fla., 1985-88; statehouse bur. chief Kans. Pub. Radio, Topeka, 1989-90; rsch. analyst Fla. Taxwatch, Tallahassee, Fla., 1990-91; law clerk Steel, Hector & Davis, Tallahassee, 1991-93; assoc. Steel, Hector & Davis, Miami, Fla., 1993-95, McFarlain, Wiley, Cassedy & Jones, Tallahassee, 1995—; pres. Nat. Congress for Fathers and Children (Fla. Chpt.), Tallahassee, 1995—. Mem. Fla. Commn. on Responsible Fatherhood, 1996—. Recipient 1st place award Kans. Assn. Broadcasters, 1981-83, UPI, 1982-88, Assn. of News Broadcasters of Kans., 1986, Fla. Tchg. Profession-NEA, 1988. Mem. ABA (family law sect., litig. sect.), Fla. Bar (family law sect., trial lawyers sect.). Dem. Presbyn. E-mail: rmcneely@mcfarlain.com. Family and matrimonial, Appellate, Entertainment. Office: McFarlain Wiley Cassedy & Jones PA 215 S Monroe St Ste 600 Tallahassee FL 32301-1804

**MCNEIL, ANDREW M.,** lawyer; b. Piqua, Ohio, Mar. 23, 1969; s. William B. and Karen A. McNeil; m. Laurie A. Randall, Aug. 15, 1992; children: Ethan J., Jack M. BA summa cum laude, Taylor U., 1992; JD cum laude, U. Mich., 1995. Bar: Ind., 1996, U.S. Dist. Ct. (so. and no. dists.) Ind., 1996, U.S. Ct. Appeals (7th cir.), 1998. Assoc. Bose McKinney & Evans, Indpls., 1996—. Founder (jour.) Mich. Law Policy Rev., 1994-95. Mem. ABA, Ind. State Bar Assn., Indpls. Bar Assn. Republican. Avocations: running, historical nonfiction, constitutional law. Labor, Federal civil litigation. Office: Bose McKinney & Evans 135 N Pennsylvania St Ste 2700 Indianapolis IN 46204-4407

**MCNEIL, LEESA A.,** court administrator; b. Aberdeen, S.D., July 14, 1958; d. Earl Richard and Beverly Ann (Dunker) McN.; m. Jon C. Nylen, Dec. 17, 1988; children: Kimberly J. Nylen, Jeffrey A. Nylen. BS, U. S.D., Vermillion, 1979; MS in Jud. Adminstrn., U. Denver, 1981. Dep. ct. adminstr. 70th Dist. Ct. of Mich., Saginaw, 1981-82; asst. dist. ct. adminstr. Third Jud. Dist. Ct., LeMars, Iowa, 1983-84; dist. ct. adminstr. Third Jud. Dist. Ct., Sioux City, Iowa, 1984—; mem. Iowa Supreme Ct. Improvement Project for Children in Need of Assistance Cases, 1996-97; chmn. Iowa Supreme Ct. Com. on Mgmt. Info., 1997—; mem. planning implementation com. for report of Commn. on Planning for the 21st Century, 1997. MSJA Alumni fellow, 1980. Mem. Nat. Assn. Ct. Mgmt., Am. Judicature Soc. Avocations: photography, golden retrievers. Office: Dist Ct Adminstrn Woodbury County Courthouse 620 Douglas St Ste 210 Sioux City IA 51101-1249

**MCNEIL, MALCOLM STEPHEN,** lawyer; b. San Francisco, Jan. 7, 1956; s. Stephen Henry and Adeline Elizabeth (LaVoie) McN.; m. Gloria Ellen Margolis, Apr. 6, 1974 (div. 1986); children: Jennifer Rose, Geoffrey Stephen; m. Shahrezad Mabourakh, July 6, 1991; 1 stepchild, Vanessa Mabourakh. Student, L.A. City Coll., 1974-76; AA, UCLA, 1977; BA, Antioch U., L.A., 1979; JD, Loyola U., L.A., 1983. Bar: Calif. 1983, U.S. Dist. Ct. (cen. dist.) Calif. 1984, U.S. Ct. Appeals (9th cir.) 1989, U.S. Dist. Ct. (no. dist.) 1991. Sales mgr. Met. Life Ins. Co., L.A., 1977-83; assoc. Briedenbach, Swainston and Crispo, L.A., 1983-84, Law Office of Brian Zimmerman, L.A., 1984; pvt. practice L.A., 1984—; instr. Northrop U., L.A., 1987—. Pres. Repub. Law Forum, L.A., 1981-83. Mem. ABA, Marina de Rey C. of C., Assn. Internat. Jeunes Avocats, Westchester C. of C., Phi Alpha Delta, Sigma Tau Sigma. Roman Catholic. Avocations: book collecting, judo, skiing. General corporate, Insurance, Personal injury. Office: 5777 W Century Blvd Ste 1475 Los Angeles CA 90045-7408

**MCNEIL, MARK SANFORD,** lawyer; b. Shawnee, Okla., Feb. 4, 1950; s. Irving Jr. and Sylvia Louise (Sanford) McN.; m. Cathy Marleen Yandell, Sept. 7, 1974; children: Elizabeth, Laura. Assoc. Lillick McHose & Charles, San Francisco, 1974-76; rsch. asst. Kyoto (Japan) U., 1976-77; internat. law cons. Amita & Hirokawa, Osaka, Japan, 1976-77, Ono Law Office, Osaka, 1976-77; internat. counsel Medtronic, Inc., Mpls., 1978-84; mgr. contract adminstrn. Cray Rsch., Inc., Mpls., 1985, internat. counsel, 1986-88, dir. internat. contracts, 1988-91, dir. corp. contacts, 1991; assoc. Briggs and Morgan, P.A., Mpls., 1995-97; adj. prof. William Mitchell Coll. Law, St. Paul, 1989-91. Bd. dirs. Midwest China Ctr. Mem. ABA, Minn. Bar Assn. (chmn. internat. bus. law sect. 1986-87), Hennepin County Bar Assn., Corp. Counsel Assn., Minn. World Trade Assn. (bd. dirs. 1996—, pres. 1998-99). Avocations: photography, music, fiction writing, rafting. Private international, Computer, General corporate. Home: 514 5th St E Northfield MN 55057-2220 Office: Lindquist and Vennum PLLP 4200 IDS Ctr Minneapolis MN 55402

**MCNEILL, FREDERICK WALLACE,** lawyer, educator, writer, government consultant, former military and commercial pilot; b. Chgo., Jan. 4, 1932; s. James Joseph and Irene Gertrude (Stevenson) McN.; m. Judith Carol Austin, Feb. 9, 1957; children: Marjorie, Tamelyn, Kenneth, Patricia, Darcy, Sean, Meghan. BBA, U. Ariz., 1974, JD, 1977. Bar: Ariz. 1977, U.S. Dist. Ct. Ariz. 1977. Served to maj. USAF, 1949-73, ret., 1973; bus. mgr. Engring. & Research Assocs., Inc., Tucson, 1973-74; mng. ptnr. ERA Shopping Ctr., Tucson, 1973-75; chief pilot, spl. agt. Narcotics Strike Force, Ariz., 1975-77; dep. county atty. Pima County, Ariz., 1977-79; atty. Ariz. Drug Control Dist., 1977-79; ptnr. Rees & McNeill, Tucson, 1979-84; writer, 1984—; coord. legal asst. studies program and adj. prof. Nova U.-Panama Ctr., Republic of Panama, 1987-90; adj. prof. Ctrl. Tex. Coll., Germany, 1990-92, Univ. Phoenix and Pima County Coll., Tucson, 1992—; pvt. practice U.S. law U.S. mil. and PCC installations, 1987-90; of counsel Carreira-Pitti P.C., Abogados, Panama, 1989-90; pvt. practice Wurzburg, Fed. Republic of Germany, 1990-92, Tucson, 1992—; adj. prof. Ctrl. Tex. Coll., Germany, 1990-92, U. Phoenix, Pima C.C., Tuscon, 1992—; ret., 1999; lectr. air smuggling seminars, organized crime seminars, Ariz., 1977-79. V.p. Indian Ridge Homeowners Assn., 1980-82; bd. dirs. Tucson Boys Chorus Bldg. Fund Com., 1972-74; lt. Ariz. Rangers. Decorated DFC, Air medal (5), Air Force Commendation medal (2). Mem. ABA, ATLA, Ariz. Bar Assn., Pima County Bar Assn., Ariz. Trial Lawyers Assn., Lawyer Pilots Bar Assn., Internat. Platform Assn., Ret. Officers Assn., Air Force Assn., DAV, Vietnam Vets. Am., Order of Daedelians, Quiet Birdmen. Criminal, General practice, Aviation. Home: 9957 E Stella Rd Tucson AZ 85730-3160

**MCNEILL, THOMAS RAY,** lawyer; b. Pitts., June 2, 1952; s. Thomas William McNeill and Mary (Shiveley) Hiss; m. Patsy Lynch, June 25, 1977; children: Elizabeth, Kathleen, Thomas. BSBA, U. Fla., 1974; JD, Emory U., 1977. Bar: Ga. 1977, U.S. Dist. Ct. (no. dist.) Ga. 1977. Assoc. Powell, Goldstein, Frazer & Murphy, LLP, Atlanta, 1977-84, ptnr., 1984—, mgr. corp. dept., 1993-95, bd. ptnrs., 1998—. Mem. Ga. Bar Assn., Emory U. Alumni Assn. (pres. exec. com. Atlanta chpt. 1988-89, Law Sch. coun. 1990—), Soc. of Internat. Bus. Fellows, Beta Gamma Sigma. Finance, Franchising, Mergers and acquisitions. Office: Powell Goldstein Frazer & Murphy 191 Peachtree St NE Ste 1600 Atlanta GA 30303-1736

**MCNEIL STAUDENMAIER, HEIDI LORETTA,** lawyer; b. Preston, Iowa, Apr. 7, 1959; d. Archie Hugo and Heidi (Waltert) McN.; m. L. William Staudenmaier III; 1 child Kathleen Louise McNeil Staudenmaier. BA in Journalism and Broadcasting with distinction, U. Iowa, 1981; JD with distinction, 1985. Bar: Ariz. 1985, U.S. Dist. Ct. Ariz. 1985, U.S. Ct. Appeals (9th cir.) 1985, U.S. Ct. Appeals (10th cir.) 1990. Sports journalist The Daily Iowan, Iowa City, 1977-81, Quad City Times, Davenport, Iowa, 1981-82; ptnr. Snell & Wilmer, Phoenix, 1985—; judge pro tem, Maricopa County, Phoenix, 1992—, Ariz. Ct. Appeals, 1998—. Mem. ABA (mem. domestic violence commn. 1995-98, Ho. of Dels. 1995-98, chair young lawyers career issues com. 1992-93, mem. affiliate assistance program com. 1992-93, dir. 1993-94, spl. projects coord. 1994-95, bus. law sect., mem. editl. bd. bus. Law Today), Internat. Assn. Gaming Attys., Ariz. Bar Assn. (Indian law sect. exec. coun. and chair, 1995-99, young lawyers exec. coun. 1991-94), Maricopa County Bar Assn. (bd. dirs. 1991—, young lawyers divsn. 1987-93, pres. 1991-92, 99—), Ariz. Women Lawyers, Phoenix Assn. Def. Counsel, Native Am. Bar Assocs., Phi Beta Kappa, Phi Eta Sigma. Lutheran. Avocations: running, golf, skiing, hiking, bicycling. General civil litigation, Native American.

**MCNERNEY, JOSEPH JAMES,** trial lawyer; b. Oak Park, Ill., July 20, 1954; s. Joseph James and Loretta Isabel (Wray) McN.; m. Mary Katherine Palutsis, May 1, 1980; children: Joseph, Michael, Daniel, Scott. BS in Biology, Loyola U., Chgo., 1976; JD, John Marshall Law Sch., 1980. Bar: Ill. 1980, U.S. Dist. Ct. (no. dist.) Ill. 1980. Asst. state's atty. Cook County State's Atty.'s office, Chgo., 1980-94, supr. homicide/sex divsn., 1988-89, supr. felony trial divsn., 1989-94; ptnr. Johnson & Bell, Ltd., Chgo., 1994—; adj. prof. law Chgo.-Kent Coll. Law, 1990—; chief adminstr. tng. State's Atty.'s Office, Chgo., 1991-93; mem. faculty Nat. Inst. for Trial Advocacy, South Bend, Ind.; former contbg. mem. Ill. Pattern Jury Instr. com. Head coach nat. champions trial competition ABA, Chgo., 1991; chmn. Criminal Justice Com., Chgo., 1994. Recipient V.P.'s award for excellence in trial of capital cases Assn. of Govt. Attys. in Capital Litigation, 1993-94, Excellence in Crime Prevention Pub. Sector award Chicagoland C. of C., 1995. General civil litigation, Professional liability, Criminal. Office: Johnson & Bell Ltd 222 N Lasalle St Chicago IL 60601-1003

**MCNIDER, JAMES SMALL, III,** lawyer; b. Richmond, Va., Aug. 23, 1956; s. James Small Jr. and Phoebe Warwick (Johnston) McN.; m. Anna Mary Van Buren, Apr. 30, 1983; children: Anna Lee, Mary Tyler, James S. IV, Elle Page. BS, Washington & Lee U., 1978, JD, 1981. Bar: Va. 1981, U.S. Tax Ct. 1981, U.S. Dist. Ct. (ea. dist.) Va. 1986. Assoc. Kaufman & Canoles, Norfolk, Va., 1981-85; assoc. Willcox & Savage, Norfolk, 1985-87, ptnr., 1987-95; ptnr. James S. McNider, III P.L.C., Hampton, Va., 1995—. Author: (with others) ABA Sales and Use Tax Handbook, 1988. Mem. ABA, Va. Bar Assn. (chmn. tax sect. 1993-94), Princess Anne Country Club, Omicron Delta Kappa. Episcopalian. Avocations: pvt. pilot, tennis, golf. Corporate taxation, State and local taxation, General corporate. Home: 808 Park Pl Hampton VA 23669-4152 Office: PO Box I Hampton VA 23669-0256

**MCNISH, DOUGLAS SCOTT,** judge; b. Portland, Oreg., Feb. 11, 1944; s. Vance Alvin and Arlene (Dunning) McN.; m. Gale Elizabeth Pierson, Oct. 6, 1973; children: Zachary, Tyler. BA in Polit. Sci./Econs., Willamette U., 1966, JD, 1969. Bar: Hawaii 1973, U.S. Dist. Ct. Hawaii 1973. Law clk. Hawaii State Jud. 2d Cir., Wailuku, Hawaii, 1973-74; family ct. judge Hawaii State Jud. 2d Cir., Wailuku, 1984—; assoc. Ueoka, Vail & Luna, Wailuku, 1974-77; ptnr. Romanchak & McNish, Kahului, 1977-82, McNish Brumbaugh & Honda, Kahului, 1982-84. Author: A Guide to Maui Family Court for Separating Parents, 1997. Vol. Peace Corps, Peru, 1970-72; mem. Maui County Domestic Violence Task Force, Wailuku, 1992—; mem. Child Advocacy Ctr., Wailuku, 1989—. Recipient Disting. Svc. award Family Law Sect. Hawaii State Bar Assn., 1996. Mem. ABA (family law sect., co-chair joint task force on parent edn. programs 1995-97), Assn. of Family and Conciliation Cts. (pres. 1994-95, dir. 1989-96, exec. com. 1993-96, editl. bd. rev. 1997—). Avocations: travel, hiking, golf, U.S. History. Fax: 808-244-2704. E-mail: mcnish@maui.net. Office: 2145 Main St Wailuku HI 96793-1679

**MCNULTY, MICHELLE ALLAIRE,** lawyer; b. Brockton, Mass., Apr. 3, 1963; d. Roger Louis Allaire and Lucille Yenovkian Gregory. BA, Boston U., 1985; JD, Boston Coll. Law, 1988. Bar: Mass. 1988, U.S. Dist. Ct. Mass. 1992, U.S. Supreme Ct. 1996. Ptnr. Murphy, Lamere & Murphy, P.C., Braintree, Mass., 1988—. Mem. Mass. Bar Assn., Norfolk Bar Assn., Quincy Bar Assn., Mass. City Solicitors and Town Counsel Assn. Education and schools, Labor, Municipal (including bonds). Office: Murphy Lamere & Murphy Ten Forbes Rd W PO Box 859003 Braintree MA 02185-9003

**MCPHERON, ALAN BEAUMONT,** lawyer; b. McAlester, Okla., July 6, 1914; s. Robert Lee and Jeannette (Kridler) McP.; m. Mary Jane Bass, Apr. 8, 1938; 1 dau., Jill McPheron Wigington. LL.B., U. Okla., 1937. Bar: Okla. 1937, U.S. Dist. Ct. (no., ea. and we. dists.) Okla., U.S. Dist. Ct. (no. dist.) Tex. Asst. county atty., Durant, Okla., 1939-42, county atty., 1942-43; sole practice, Durant, 1946-65, 75—; dist. judge Bryan County, Okla., 1965-75; tchr. bus. law So. Okla. State U., 1970-73. Mem. War Vets Commn. Okla., 1949-51; mem. bd. rev. Okla. Employment Security Commn., 1951-59; mem. Okla. Jud. Nominating Commn., 1983-89, 95—, Ct. on Judiciary Appeal Divsn., 1993-94. Served to m/sgt. U.S. Army, 1943-46; ETO. Decorated Bronze Star; Croix de Guerre (France). Mem. ABA, Okla. Bar Assn. (bd. govs. 1990-92), Okla. Trial Lawyers Assn., Am. Judicature Soc., Okla. Criminal Def. Lawyers Assn. (charter mem.). Am. Legion, VFW. Democrat. Presbyterian. Club: Elks. Probate, State civil litigation, Family and matrimonial. Office: 1919 W University Blvd # 106 Durant OK 74701-3076

**MCPHERSON, GARY LEE,** lawyer, state representative; b. Auburn, Wash., Dec. 4, 1962; s. Percy Ivan and Vicki Mae (Voyles) McP.; children: Christina, Elizabeth, Ashley. BS in Bus. Adminstrn., Union Coll., 1985; JD, U. Nebr., 1988. Bar: Colo. 1989, Nebr. 1989, U.S. Dist. Ct. Colo. 1989, U.S. Ct. Appeals (10th cir.) 1989. Legal/legis. aide Knudsen, Berkheimer & Richardson, Lincoln, Nebr., 1981-85; law clk. Crosby, Guenzel & Davis, Lincoln, 1986; law clk. ethics com. Nebr. State Bar Assn., Lincoln, 1987; assoc. Hall & Evans, Denver, 1987-89, Elrod, Katz, Preeo & Look, P.C., Denver, 1989-90, Fortune & Lawritson, P.C., Denver, 1990-93; ptnr. McPherson & Hull, P.C., Aurora, Colo., 1993-98, Kissinger & Fellman, P.C., Denver, Colo., 1998—; state rep. State of Colo., Denver, 1994—. Author: Handbook on Professional Malpractice, 1987, rev. edit., 1988; contbr. articles to profl. jours. Bd. dirs. Arapahoe Park and Recreation Bd., Aurora, 1991-95; dist. capt. Arapahoe County Rep. Dist. 8, Aurora, 1992-95; vice chmn. Ho. Dist. 40, Aurora, 1993-95, state rep.; chmn. Senate Dist. 28, Aurora, 1993-95. Recipient Internat. Acad. Trial Lawyers award, 1987, 88, Aurora Pub. Schs. Supts. award, 1992. Mem. ABA (bd. dirs., litigations com. 1992-93, chmn. young lawyers divsn. prelaw counseling com. 1992-94), Colo. Bar Assn. (sec., treas. young lawyers divsn. 1991-93, chair-elect 1993-94, chmn. 1994-95), Arapahoe County Bar Assn., Aurora Rep. Forum, Arapahoe County Rep. Mens Club. Avocations: aviation, scuba, politics, backpacking, snow skiing. Contracts commercial, General civil litigation, General corporate. Office: 3773 Cherry Creek North Dr Denver CO 80209-3804

**MCQUAID, JOHN GAFFNEY,** lawyer; b. N.Y.C., Jan. 4, 1918; s. Paul Augustine and Louise (Gaffney) McQ.; m. Betty Frances Seay, May 27, 1989; children from previous marriage: John G. Jr., Catherine M., Elizabeth L. BA, Yale Coll., 1940, LLB, 1947. Bar: N.Y. 1948, U.S. Supreme Ct. 1954. Assoc. Townley Updike Carter & Rodgers, N.Y.C., 1947-52; with Nat. Prodn. Auth., Washington, 1952-54; pvt. practice White Plains, N.Y., 1954-60; ptnr. Fingar & McQuaid, White Plains, 1960-65; ptnr. McCarthy, Fingar, Donovan, Drazen & Smith, White Plains, 1965-94, counsel, 1995—; dir., asst. sec. Dewey Electronics Corp., Oakland, N.J., 1955—. Co-author, editor: New York Wills and Trusts, 2d edit., 1961, 3d edit., 1990; nat., N.Y. co-editor: Will Manual Svc. Bd. dirs. Westchester Cmty. Found.; bd. advisors Westchester Cmty. 2d lt. U.S. Army, 1942-46. Fellow Am. Coll. Trust and Estate Counsel, Am. Bar Found., N.Y. Bar Found.; mem. N.Y. State Bar Assn. (chmn. trusts and estates law sect. 1981), White Plains Bar Assn. (pres. 1961), Westchester County Bar Assn., Ardsley Country Club. Estate planning, Probate. Home: Hudson House PO Box 11 Ardsley on Hudson NY 10503-0011 Office: McCarthy Fingar Donovan Drazen & Smith 11 Martine Ave White Plains NY 10606-1934

**MCQUIGG, JOHN DOLPH,** lawyer; b. Abilene, Tex., Oct. 19, 1931; s. John Lyman and Dorothy Elinor (King) McQ.; m. Sandra Elaine Duke, Oct. 18, 1969 (div. 1989); 1 child, John Revel. BA, Denison U., 1953; LLB, U. Tex., 1962. Bar: Fla. 1962, U.S. Supreme Ct. 1971. Account exec. San Antonio Light, 1957-59; assoc. Shackleford, Farrior, Stallings & Evans, 1962-66; ptnr. Shackleford, Farrior, Stallings & Evans, Tampa, Fla., 1966-73; pres. John McQuigg, P.A., Tampa, 1973-80; shareholder Fowler, White, Gillen, Boggs, Villareal & Banker, P.A., Tampa, 1980-92; of counsel Stephen Rosen, P.A., Tampa, 1993; pvt. practice Tampa, 1994—. Judge Compensation Claims pro hac vice, 1993; bd. dirs. Fla. Gulf Coast R.R. Mus., Inc., Am. Assn. Pvt. Railroad Car Owners; pres. Fla. Coalition R.R. Passengers, 1990-99. 1st lt. USAF, 1953-57. Mem. ABA, Fla. Bar, Tampa Club. Episcopalian. Workers' compensation, General civil litigation. Home: 11509 Areca Rd Tampa FL 33618-3609 Office: PO Box 2480 Tampa FL 33601-2480

**MCQUILLAN, BARBARA GLATZ,** paralegal; b. Buffalo, June 11, 1945; d. Edward D. and Lauretta (May) Glatz; m. David C. McQuillan, Nov. 10, 1979. BA, SUNY, Buffalo, 1967. Asst. concert mgr. SUNY, 1963-67; editl. asst., proofreader Christian Sci. Monitor, Boston, 1967-74; proofreader Christian Sci. Pub. Soc., Boston, 1974-79; paralegal McNair Law Firm, Columbia, S.C., 1979—. Pres. Elmwood Pk. Neighborhood Assn., Columbia, 1990; mem. Columbia Coun. of Neighborhoods, 1990; dir. Sterling Chamber Players, Columbia, 1997—; chmn. exec. bd. 1st Ch. of Christ Scientist, Columbia, 1992-93, treas., 1995-99, organist, 1995-99. Mem. Palmetto Paralegal Assn. (2nd v.p., treas., pres., bd. dirs.). Home: 32 Gibbes Ct Columbia SC 29201-3924 Office: McNair Law Firm 1301 Gervais St Ste 17 Columbia SC 29201-3326

**MCRAE, CHARLES R.,** state supreme court justice. Assoc. justice MS Supreme Ct, Jackson, MS, 1992—. Office: Supreme Court Carroll Gartin Bldg Jackson MS 39205*

**MCRAE, DONALD JAMES,** lawyer; b. Kewanee, Ill., May 5, 1926; s. Ross J. and Wilna Louise (Warner) McR. B.S., Northwestern U., 1948, J.D., 1951. Bar: Ill. 1951, U.S. Dist. Ct. (cen. dist.) Ill. 1954. Prin. Don McRae & Assocs., Kewanee, Ill., 1951—; dir. Peoples Nat. Bank, Kewanee. Served with USN, 1944-46; to lt. comdr. USNR ret. Mem. Ill. Trial Lawyers Assn., Ill. State Bar Assn., Henry County Bar Assn., Kewanee C. of C. Republican. Presbyterian. Club: Midland Country (pres. 1974-93), Rotary (pres. 1968-69), Elks, Masons (Kewanee, Ill.). State civil litigation, Probate, Federal civil litigation. Home: RR 2 Kewanee IL 61443-9802 Office: 217 W 2nd St Kewanee IL 61443-2105

**MCRAE, HAMILTON EUGENE, III,** lawyer; b. Midland, Tex., Oct. 29, 1937; s. Hamilton Eugene and Adrian (Hagaman) McR.; m. Betty Hawkins, Aug. 27, 1960; children: Elizabeth Ann, Stephanie Adrian, Scott Hawkins. BSEE, U. Ariz., 1961; student, USAF Electronics Sch., 1961-62; postgrad., U. Redlands, Calif., 1962-63; JD with honors and distinction, U. Ariz., 1967; LHD (hon.), Sterling Coll., 1992; vis. fellow, Darwin Coll. and Martin Ctr., Cambridge (Eng.) U., 1996-97. Bar: Ariz. 1967, U.S. Supreme Ct. 1979; cert. real estate specialist, Ariz. Elec. engr. Salt River Project, Phoenix, 1961; assoc. Jennings, Strouss & Salmon, Phoenix, 1967-71, ptnr., 1971-85, chmn. real estate dept., 1980-85, mem. policy com., 1982-85, mem. fin. com., 1981-85, chmn. bus. devel. com., 1982-85; ptnr. and co-founder Stuckey & McRae, Phoenix, 1985—; co-founder, chmn. bd. Republic Cos., Phoenix, 1985—; magistrate Paradise Valley, Ariz., 1983-85; juvenile referee Superior Ct., 1983-85; pres., dir. Phoenix Realty & Trust Co., 1970—; officer Indsl. Devel. Corp. Maricopa County, 1972-86; instr. and lectr. in real estate; officer, bd. dirs. other corps.; adj. prof. Frank Lloyd Wright Sch. Architecture, Scottsdale, Ariz., 1989—; instr. Ariz. State U. Coll. Architecture and Environ. Design; lead instr. ten-state-bar seminar on Advanced Real Estate Transactions, 1992; evaluation com. for cert. real estate specialist Ariz. Bar, 1994-96; mem. real estate adv. commn. Ariz. Bar, 1996—. Exec. prodr. film documentary on relief and devel. in Africa, 1990; contbr. articles to profl. jours. Elder Valley Presbyn. Ch., Scottsdale, Ariz., 1973-75, 82-85, 96-98, chair evangelism com. 1973-74, corp. pres., 1974-75, 84-85, trustee, 1973-75, 82-85, chmn. exec. com., 1984, mem. mission com. 1993—, chmn. 1998; trustee Upward Found., Phoenix, 1977-80, Valley Presbyn. Found., 1982-83, Ariz. Acad., 1971—; trustee, mem. exec. com. Phi Gamma Delta Ednl. Found., Washington, 1974-84; trustee Phi Gamma Delta Internat., 1984-86; bd. dirs. Archon, 1986-87; founder, trustee, pres. McRae Found., 1980—; bd. dirs. Food for Hungry Inc. (Internat. Relief), 1985-95, exec. com., 1986-95, chmn. bd. dirs., 1987-92; chmn. bd. dirs. Food for Hungry Internat., 1993-95, pres. adv. coun., 1995—; trustee, mem. exec. com. Ariz. Mus. Sci. and Tech., 1984—, 1st v.p., 1985-86, pres., 1986-88, chmn. bd. dirs., 1988-90, exec. com. 1984-90, exhibits com. 1990—; Lambda Alpha Internat. Hon. Land Econs. Soc, 1988-98; sec.-treas. Ariz. State U. Coun. for Design Excellence, 1989-90, bd. dirs. 1988—, pres. 1990-91; mem. Crisis Nursery Office of the Chair, 1988-89, Maricopa Community Colls. Found., 1988—, sec. 1990-91, 2d v.p. 1993-94, 1st v.p. and pres. elect 1994-95, pres. 1995-96, capital campaign cabinet, 1995-96, mem. nominating com., 1997, Phoenix Cmty. Alliance, 1988-90, Interchurch Ctr. Corp., 1987-90, Western Art Assocs., bd. dirs., 1989-91, Phoenix Com. on Fgn. Rels., 1988-99, U. Ariz. Pres.'s Club, 1984—, chmn., 1991-92; bd. dirs. Econ. Club of Phoenix, 1987—, sec.-treas., 1991-92, v.p., 1992-93, pres. 1993-94; bd. dirs. Ctrl. Ariz. Shelter Svcs., 1995—, Ariz. Community Found., 1996—, invest. com., 1996, exec. com. 1997—, treas. 1997—, chair nominating com. 1997-98, vice chair bd. dirs., 1999—, chair devel. com., 1999—, mem. Elsner scholarship com., 1999—; founding mem. Alliance linking poverty and homelessness, 1996-98, bd. dirs., 1996—, mem. exec. com., 1996—, co-chair long range planning com., 1997-98; mem. adv. bd. Help Wanted USA, 1990-92; vol. fund raiser YMCA, Salvation Army, others; bd. dirs. Frank Lloyd Wright Found., 1992—, chair fin. com. 1997-98, chmn. bd. dirs., 1998—; mem. Taliesin Coun., 1985—; bd. dirs. Taliesin Arch., 1992-98, Taliesin Conservation Com. (Wis.), 1992; founding mem. Frank Lloyd Wright Soc., 1993—; mem. fin. com. Kyl for Congress, 1985-92, bd. dir. campaign bd. Kyl for U.S. Senate, 1993-94, 99—; Senator Kyl Council, 1995—; campaign com. Symington for Gov. '90, 1989-90, mem. gubernatorial adv. bd., 1; mem. Gov.'s Selection Com. for State Revenue Dir., 1993; mem. bond com. City of Phoenix, 1987-88; mem. Ariz. State U. Coun. of 100, 1985-89, investment com., 1985-89; bd. govs. Twelve Who Care Hon Kachina, 1991; mem. adv. coun. Maricopa County Sports Authority, 1989-93; mem. Ariz. Coalition for Tomorrow, 1990-92; founding mem., bd. dirs. Waste Not Inc., 1990-94, pres., 1990-92, chmn., 1992-94, adv. bd. 1996—; bd. dirs. Garden Homes at Teton Pines Home Owners Assn., 1996—; selected as bearer for the Olympic Torch Relay Team, 1996; adv. bd. KAET TV PBS (Channel 8); mem. Elsner Scholarship Com.,

1999—. 1st lt. USAF, 1961-64,. Recipient various mil. award; 1st place award Ariz. Bar exam, 1967. Mem. ABA, AIEE, AIME, Ariz. Bar Assn., Maricopa County Bar Assn., U. Ariz. Alumni Assn., Nat. Soc. Fund Raising Execs. (Philanthropy award Ariz. chpt. 1991, 97), Clan McRae Soc. N.Am. Phoenix Exec. Club, Internat. Platform Assn., Am. Friends of the U. Cambridge (Eng.), Jackson Hole Racquet Club, Teton Pines Country Club, Tau Beta Pi. Republican. Home: 8101 N 47th St Paradise Valley AZ 85253 Address: Republic Companies 11811 N Tatum Blvd Ste 1005 Phoenix AZ 85028

**MCRAE, ROBERT MALCOLM, JR.,** federal judge; b. Memphis, Dec. 31, 1921; s. Robert Malcolm and Irene (Pontius) McR.; m. Louise Howry, July 31, 1943; children: Susan Campbell, Robert Malcolm III, Duncan Farquhar, Thomas Alexander Todd. BA, Vanderbilt U., 1943; LLB, U. Va., 1948. Bar: Tenn. 1948. Practice in Memphis, 1948-64; judge Tenn. Circuit Ct., 1964-66; judge U.S. Dist. Ct. (we. dist.) Tenn., Memphis, 1966-94, chief judge, 1979-86, sr. judge, 1987-94, inactive sr. judge, 1995—; mem. Jud. Council 6th Cir., 1982-85, Jud. Conf. Commn. Adminstrn. Criminal Law, 1979-86, Jud. Conf. U.S., 1984-87. Pub.: Oral History of the Desegregation of the Memphis City Schools (1954-74), 1997. Pres. Episcopal Ch. men of Tenn., 1964-65. Mem. Dist. Judges Assn. 6th Circuit (pres.). Home: 220 Baronne Pl Memphis TN 38117-2906

**MCREYNOLDS, GREGG CLYDE,** lawyer; b. Omaha, July 19, 1954; s. Zach A. and Mary M. (McCulloh) McR.; m. Dianne Worth McReynolds; children: Elizabeth, Heather, Kevin. BA, St. Johns Coll., Santa Fe, N.Mex., 1976; JD, U. N.Mex., 1979. Bar: N/Mex. 1979, Colo. 1982. Atty. Menig & Sager, Albuquerque, Anderson & Campbell, Denver, pvt. practice; instr. advocacy U. Colo. Law Sch., Boulder, 1992—. Author: Primer on Employment Law, 1990; contbr. articles to profl. jours. Commr. Parks, Trails Commn., Greenwood Village, 1994-97; mem. Sundance Hills Metro Dist. Bd., 1997—. Recipient Nat. Hon. Soc. award, 1972. Mem. ABA, Colo. Bar Assn., Denver Bar Assn. Labor, Workers' compensation, Insurance. Office: 7720 E Belleview Ave Ste 200 Englewood CO 80111-2614

**MCREYNOLDS, MARY ARMILDA,** lawyer; b. Carthage, Mo., Sept. 2, 1946; d. Allen and Virginia Madeliene (Hensley) McR. BA, Mt. Holyoke Coll., 1968; JD, Georgetown U., 1971; LLM, Harvard U., 1973. Bar: D.C. 1971, U.S. Ct. Appeals (D.C. cir.) 1971, U.S. Ct. Appeals (2d cir.) 1975, U.S. Ct. Appeals (4th cir.) 1979, U.S. Ct. Appeals (1st, 5th, 6th, 9th 10th cirs.) 1980, U.S. Supreme Ct. 1980, U.S. Ct. Appeals (11th cir.) 1981, U.S. Ct. Appeals (3rd, 7th, 8th cirs.) 1983, U.S. Ct. Appeals (fed. cir.) 1988. Law clk. U.S. Ct. Appeals for D.C. cir., 1971-72; assoc. Wilmer, Cutler & Pickering, Washington, 1973-77; sr. trial atty. civil divsn. fed. program br. U.S. Dept. Justice, 1977-79, mem. appellate staff, 1979-81; ptnr. McReynolds & Mutterperl, Washington, 1981-83, Wilner & Scheiner, Washington, 1983-89, Haley, Bader & Potts, 1989-92; prin. Law Offices of Mary A. McReynolds, P.C., 1992—; bd. dirs., gen. counsel Washington Bach Consort, 1977-81, 1985-92, pres. 1981-82, 89-90; pres. Calla, 1993—. Contbr. articles to profl. jours. Bd. dirs., gen. counsel Washington Bach Consort, 1977-81, 85-92, pres. 1981-82, 89-90; pres. Calla, 1993—. Mem. ABA, Fed. Comms. Bar Assn., Kenwood Club, City Tavern Club. Episcopalian. Administrative and regulatory, Federal civil litigation, Communications. Home: 2101 Connecticut Ave NW Apt 26 Washington DC 20008-1754 Office: 888 16th St NW Ste 400 Washington DC 20006-4103

**MCREYNOLDS, STEPHEN PAUL,** lawyer; b. Sacramento, Oct. 16, 1938; s. Leslie N. and Mary C. McR.; m. Chodi D. Greeno, Sept. 29, 1970. A.B., U. Calif., Davis, 1969; J.D., U. Calif., 1972. Bar: Calif. 1972. Sole practice Sunnyvale, Calif., 1972—. Served with U.S. Navy, 1956-62. Mem. Mensa Internat. General practice. Office: 1111 W El Camino Real # 329 Sunnyvale CA 94087-1056

**MCSLOY, STEVEN PAUL,** lawyer; b. Syosset, N.Y., June 12, 1964; s. Paul Thomas and Emilie Helen (Winter) McS.; m. Alison Jane Rooney, Oct. 26, 1991. BA magna cum laude, NYU, 1985; JD cum laude, Harvard U., 1988. Bar: N.Y. 1989. Atty. Cravath, Swaine & Moore, N.Y.C., 1988-91, 98—; prof. St. John's Law Sch., Queens, N.Y., 1991-95; gen. counsel Oneida Indian Nation, Oneida, N.Y., 1995-98; lectr. BAR/BRI Bar Rev., N.Y.C., 1991—; adj. prof. law Syracuse (N.Y.) Law Sch., 1995-98, NYU Law Sch., 1993-95, Cardozo Law Sch., N.Y.C., 1990, 93-95. Contbr. articles to law revs. General corporate, Native American. Office: Cravath Swaine & Moore Worldwide Plz 825 8th Ave Fl 38 New York NY 10019-7475

**MCSOLEY, PATRICK SHANNON,** lawyer; b. Bedford, Ind., Sept. 19, 1954; s. Vollie and Darlene Kay (Steele) McS.; m. Marguerite Ruth Donohoue, Aug. 29, 1981; 1 child, Connor Shane. BA, Ind. U., 1977, JD, 1980. Bar: Ind. 1980, U.S. Dist. Ct. (so. dist.) Ind. 1980. Assoc., then ptnr. Steele, Steele, McSoley & McSoley and predecessor firms, Bedford, 1980—. Mem. Bedford C. of C. (pres. 1995). Avocation: golf. Personal injury, General civil litigation. Home: 1506 13th St Bedford IN 47421-3112 Office: Bank Ste 1 Bedford IN 47421

**MCSWINEY, CHARLES RONALD,** lawyer; b. Nashville, Apr. 23, 1943; s. James W. and Jewell (Bellar) Mc.; m. Jane Detrick McSwiney, Jan. 2, 1970. BA, Kenyon Coll., Gambier, Ohio, 1965; JD, U. Cin., 1968. Assoc. Smith & Schnacke, Dayton, Ohio, 1968-72, ptnr., 1972-89, pres. and mng. ptnr., 1984-89; sr. v.p., gen. counsel The Danis Cos., Dayton, 1989-92; vice chmn. Carillon Capital, Inc., Dayton, 1992—; chmn., CEO Crysteco, Inc., Wilmington, Ohio, 1995—; pres. interchange exec. Presdl. Commn. on Personnel Interchange, Washington, 1972-73. Chmn., pres. bd. trustees Dayton Ballet Assn., 1985-88; trustee Columbus (Ohio) Symphony Orch., 1981-84; chmn. Dayton Performing Arts Fund, 1989-92, Dayton Devel. Coun., 1987-90, Wright State U. Found., Dayton, 1988-94, Miami Valley Sch., Dayton, 1988-94, Arts Ctr. Found., 1986—; mem. bd. advisors Wright State U. Coll. Bus. Adminstrn., 1988—; bd. vis. U. Cin. Coll. Law, 1987-89. Recipient Bronze Medal for Performance U.S. EPA, 1973. Mem. ABA, Ohio Bar Assn., Dayton Bar Assn., Dayton Area C. of C. (trustee 1987-90). Republican. Presbyterian. General corporate, Banking, Finance. Home: 448 Stonehaven Rd Dayton OH 45429-1646 Office: Carillon Capital Inc Kettering Tower Ste 1480 Dayton OH 45423-1000

**MCTURNAN, LEE BOWES,** lawyer; b. N.Y.C., Sept. 13, 1937; s. Lee M. and Alice (Light) McT.; m. Susan Cassady, Aug. 2, 1969; children: John M., Sarah D. AB magna cum laude, Harvard U., 1959; Diploma in Law, Oxford (Eng.) U., 1961; JD, U. Chgo., 1963. Bar: Ill. 1965, U.S. Dist. Ct. (no. dist.) Ill. 1965, U.S. Ct. Appeals (7th cir.) 1966, U.S. Supreme Ct. 1969, Ind. 1978, U.S. Dist. Ct. (so. dist.) Ind. 1978, U.S. Dist. Ct. (no. dist.) Ind. 1987. Law clk. to hon. justice U.S. Supreme Ct., Washington, 1963-64; assoc. Sidley & Austin, Chgo., 1964-69, ptnr., 1970-78; ptnr. Hackman, McClarnon & McTurnan, Indpls., 1978-88, McTurnan & Turner, Indpls., 1989—; assoc. spl. counsel procs. on chief justice R.I. Commn. Jud. Tenure and Discipline, Providence, 1985; mem. Local Rules Com. for So. Dist. Ind. Adminstrv. bd. Meridian St. United Meth. Ch., 1987-90. Mem. ABA, Ind. Bar Assn., Ill. Bar Assn., Indpls. Bar Assn., 7th Cir. Bar Assn., Law Club of Indpls. (pres. 1988-90), Legal Club of Chgo., Columbia Club, Woodstock Club, Lit. Club, Rotary. Republican. Avocations: running, reading, gardening. Federal civil litigation, General civil litigation, Antitrust. Home: 115 Bennington Dr Zionsville IN 46077-1134 Office: McTurnan & Turner 2400 Market Tower 10 W Market St Indianapolis IN 46204-2954

**MCWHORTER, ROBERT TWEEDY, JR.,** lawyer; b. Sheffield, Ala., Sept. 28, 1943; s. Robert Tweedy and Martha Jane (Hotchkiss) McW.; m. Kathleen Marie Morrison, Oct. 27, 1967; 1 dau., Cary Garth Bankhead. BS, U. Ala., Tuscaloosa, 1965; JD, Samford U., 1969. Bar: Ala. 1969, U.S. Dist. Ct. (no. dist.) Ala. 1970. Trust officer First Nat. Bank, Decatur, Ala., 1969-70; sole practice, Decatur, 1971—; judge Decatur City Ct., 1971-73, Morgan County Justice Ct., Decatur, 1973-77; tchr. real estate law Savs. and Loan Real Estate Law Sch., Decatur, 1981-83; lect. continuing legal edn. program of Ala., 1986. Lord mayor Albany Hist. Soc., Decatur, 1982-83; bd. zoning adjustment City of Decatur, 1986—, chmn., 1992—. Served with USCGR, 1966-70. Recipient Outstanding Service award Savs. and Loan Real Estate Law Sch., 1983; lectr. continuing legal edn. program of Ala. State Bar., 1986—. Mem. Morgan County Bar Assn. (sec. 1972-73, v.p. 1987-88, pres. 1988-89). Presbyterian. Lodge: Lions. (legislation com. Decatur club). Avocations: history, sailing. State civil litigation, Real property, Probate. Home: 652 Sherman St SE Decatur AL 35601-3142 Office: 303 Cain St NE Decatur AL 35601-1983

**MCWILLIAMS, JOHN MICHAEL,** lawyer; b. Annapolis, Md., Aug. 17, 1939; s. William J. and Helen (Disharon) McW.; m. Frances Edelen McCabe, May 30, 1970; children: M. Edelen, J. Michael Jr., James McC. B.S., Georgetown U., 1964; LL.B., U. Md., 1967; LLD (hon.), U. Balt., 1993. Bar: Md. 1967, U.S. Supreme Ct. 1970, U.S. Ct. Internat. Trade 1991, U.S. Ct. Mil. Appeals 1992; cert. mediator NASD. Law clk. Chief Judge Roszel C. Thomsen, U.S. Dist. Ct. Md., 1967-68; assoc. Piper and Marbury, Balt., 1968-69; asst. atty. gen. State of Md., 1969-76; gen. counsel Md. Dept. Transp., 1971-76; sr. ptnr. Tydings and Rosenberg, Balt., 1977-97; pres. McWilliams Dispute Resolution, Balt., 1997—; permanent mem. 4th Cir. Jud. Conf.; mem. panel of disting. neutrals CPR Inst. for Dispute Resolution, 1994—; mem. Md. Alt. Dispute Resolution Commn. Asst. editor Law Rev., U. Md., 1967; mem. nat. bd. advisors Ohio State Jour. Dispute Resolution; mem. editl. adv. bd. The Daily Record. Chmn. Md. adv. coun. to Nat. Legal Svcs. Corp., 1975-78; mem. Gov.'s Commn. to Revise Annotated Code of Md., 1973-78; transition dir. Md. Gov.-Elect Harry Hughes, 1978-79; mem. Md. Indsl. Devel. Financing Authority, 1980; mem. Greater Balt. Com., 1979-94; mem. exec. com. Econ. Devel. Coun. Greater Balt., 1979-83; vice chmn. bd. Washington/Balt. Regional Assn., 1980-83; mem. Md. Econ. and Cmty. Devel. Adv. Commn., 1983-87; chmn. bd. Md. Econ. Devel. Corp., 1984-89. Served to 1st lt. U.S. Army, 1958-60. Fellow Am. Bar Found. (bd. dirs. 1986-88, 91-93), Internat. Acad. Mediators (v.p. 1998—), Md. Bar Found. (dir. 1980-82); mem. ABA (pres. 1992-93, mem. ho. of dels. 1976—, chmn. 1986-88, chmn. Md. del. 1976-86, bd. editors jour. 1986-88, 91-93) Md. Bar Assn. (pres. 1981-82), Nat. Conf. Bar Pres. (exec. council 1982-85), Bar Assn. Balt. City, Am. Law Inst., Am. Judicature Soc. (dir. 1974-81, exec. com. 1975-77), Am. Acad. Judicature Edn. (dir. 1977), Md. Law Rev. (trustee 1980-83), Md. Inst. Continuing Edn. Lawyers (trustee 1980-83), Inst. Internat. Bus. Law and Practice (corr.), Md. Club, Rule Day Club. Democrat. Roman Catholic. Alternative dispute resolution. Home: 3 Merryman Ct Baltimore MD 21210-2815 Office: 26 South St Baltimore MD 21202-3215

**MCWILLIAMS, ROBERT HUGH,** federal judge; b. Salina, Kans., Apr. 27, 1916; s. Robert Hugh and Laura (Nicholson) McW.; m. Catherine Ann Cooper, Nov. 4, 1942 (dec.); 1 son, Edward Cooper; m. Joan Harcourt, Mar. 8, 1986. A.B., U. Denver, 1938, LL.B., 1941. Bar: Colo. bar 1941. Colo. dist. judge Denver, 1952-60; justice Colo. Supreme Ct., 1961-68, chief justice, 1969-70; judge U.S. Ct. Appeals (10th cir.), Denver, 1970—, now sr. judge. Served with AUS, World War II. Mem. Phi Beta Kappa, Omicron Delta Kappa, Phi Delta Phi, Kappa Sigma. Republican. Episcopalian. Home: 137 Jersey St Denver CO 80220-5918 Office: Byron White US Courthouse 1823 Stout St Rm 216 Denver CO 80257-1823

**MEADE, COLLEEN A.,** lawyer; b. N.Y.C., Dec. 15, 1969; d. Garrett Francis and Brenda Bernadette (Delargy) M. BA, St. Francis Coll., Bklyn., 1991; JD, Bklyn. Law Sch., 1995. Bar: N.Y. 1995, N.J. Atty. Gas Energy Inc., Bklyn., 1995-97, Keyspan Energy, Bklyn., 1998—. Mem. ABA, N.Y. State Bar Assn., Womens Bar Assn. N.Y., Assn. Bar City N.Y. Home: 26 45th Ave Apt 200 Bayside NY 11361 Office: Keyspan Energy 1 Metrotech Ctr Brooklyn NY 11201-3831

**MEADE, EVAN MCDANIEL,** trial lawyer; b. Kingsport, Tenn., July 5, 1949; s. Henry Earl and Emma Lou M.; m. Paula Lucille Jenkins, July 1979 (dec. Mar. 1984); 1 child, Mac; m. Kathy Ann Malone, June 11, 1988. BA, U. Tenn., 1972; JD, U. Memphis, 1977. Bar: Tenn. 1977, U.S. Dist. Ct. (ea. dist.) Tenn. 1977. Atty. Legal Svcs. Johnson City, Tenn., 1977-78; asst. dist. atty. Tenn. Dist. Attys. Office, Johnson City, 1978-79; trial lawyer Evan Meade & Assoc., Johnson City, 1979—. Election com. Washington County, Tenn., 1982-84; bd. dirs. Boys & Girls Club, Johnson City, 1989-98. Mem. ATLA, Tenn. Bar Assn., Tenn. Trial Lawyers Assn. (bd. govs. 1989-98). Avocation: boating. Personal injury, Professional liability, Workers' compensation. Office: 215 N Boone St Johnson City TN 37604-5603

**MEADE, STEVEN A.,** lawyer, educator; b. Lebanon, Va., Sept. 21, 1966; s. Farrell and Sadie Irene Meade; m. Angela Kaye Smith, June 1, 1991; 1 child, Alexander Jefferson. BA, U. Va., 1991; JD, Coll. William and Mary, 1994. Bar: Va. 1994, U.S. Dist. Ct. (ea. dist.) Va. 1994, U.S. Ct. Appeals (4th cir.) 1994. Assoc. Patten, Wornom & Watkins, L.C., Newport News, Va., 1994—; adj. law faculty Coll. William and Mary, Williamsburg, Va., 1997—. Mem. Newport News Wetlands Bd., 1997—, Bd. of Zoning Appeals, Williamsburg, 1995-96. Mem. ABA, Va. Trial Lawyers Assn., Va. Bar Assn. (com. liaison constrn. law 1998—), Newport News Bar Assn. Avocation: karate. Construction, General civil litigation, Contracts commercial. Office: Patten Wornom & Watkins LC 12350 Jefferson Ave Ste 360 Newport News VA 23602-6951

**MEADER, JOHN DANIEL,** judge; b. Ballston Spa, N.Y., Oct. 22, 1931; s. Jerome Clement and Doris Luella (Conner) M.; m. Joyce Margaret Cowin, Mar. 2, 1963; children: John Daniel Jr., Julia Rae, Keith Alan. BA, Yale U., 1954; JD, Cornell U., 1962. Bar: N.Y. 1963, U.S. Dist. Ct. (no. dist.) N.Y. 1963, U.S. Ct. Appeals (2d cir.) 1966, U.S. Supreme Ct. 1967, U.S. Ct. Mil. Appeals 1973, Ohio 1978, U.S. Dist. Ct. (no. dist.) Ohio 1979, Fla. 1983, U.S. Ct. Appeals (4th cir.) 1992, U.S. Ct. Appeals (fed. cir.) 1993. Sales engr. Albany (N.Y.) Internat. Corp., 1954-59; asst. track coach Cornell U., 1959-62; asst. sec., asst. to pres. Albany Internat. Corp., 1962-65; asst. atty. gen. State of N.Y., Albany, 1965-68; ops. counsel, attesting sec. GE, Schenectady, 1968-77; gen. counsel, asst. sec. Glidden div. SCM Corp., Cleve., 1977-81; chmn. bd., pres. Applied Power Tech. Co., Fernandina Beach, Fla., 1981-84; pres. Applied Energy, Inc., Ballston Spa, 1984-88; judge N.Y. State Workers Compensation Bd., Albany, 1988—; dir. Saratoga Mut. Fire Ins. Co. Author: Labor Law Manual, 1972, Contract Law Manual, 1974, Patent Law Manual, 1978. Candidate U.S. Ho. of Reps., 29th Dist. N.Y., 1964, N.Y. Supreme Ct., 1975, 87, 93. Col. JAGC, USAR, 1968—, dep. staff judge adv. 3d U.S. Army & Cen. Command, 1984. Nat. AAU High Sch. 1000 Yard Indoor Track Champion, 1949, Nat. AAU Prep. Sch. 440 and 880 Yard Indoor Track Champion, 1950, Nat. AAU Outstanding Performer award, Melrose Games Assn., 1950, Heptagonal Track 880-Yard Champion 1954. Mem. ABA, N.Y. State Bar Assn., Fla. Bar, Amelia Island Plantation Club, Cyprus Temple Club, Yale Club Jacksonville (pres.), Masons. Republican. Presbyterian. Home: 271 Round Lake Rd Ballston Lake NY 12019-1714 Office: NY State Workers Compensation Bd 100 Broadway Albany NY 12204-2797

**MEADOR, DANIEL JOHN,** law educator; b. Selma, Ala., Dec. 7, 1926; s. Daniel John and Mabel (Kirkpatrick) M.; m. Janet Caroline Heilmann, Nov. 19, 1955; children: Janet Barrie, Anna Kirkpatrick, Daniel John. BS, Auburn U., 1949; JD, U. Ala., 1951; LLM, Harvard U., 1954; LLD (hon.), U. S.C., 1998. Bar: Ala. 1951, Va. 1961. Law clk. to Justice Hugo L. Black U.S. Supreme Ct., 1954-55; assoc. firm Lange, Simpson, Robinson & Somerville, Birmingham, Ala., 1955-57; faculty U. Va. Law Sch., Charlottesville, 1957-66, prof. law, 1961-66; prof., dean U. Ala. Law Sch., 1966-70; James Monroe prof. law U. Va., Charlottesville, 1970-94, prof. emeritus, 1994—; asst. atty. gen. U.S., 1977-79, dir. grad. program for judges, 1979-95; Fulbright lectr., U.K., 1965-66; vis. prof. U.S. Mil. Acad., 1984; chmn. Southeastern Conf. Assn. Am. Law Schs., 1964-65; chmn. Cts. Task Force Nat. Adv. Commn. on Criminal Justice, 1971-72; dir. appellate justice project Nat. Ctr. for State Cts., 1972-74; mem. Adv. Coun. on Appellate Justice, 1971-75, Coun. on Role of Cts., 1978-84; bd. dirs. State Justice Inst., 1986-92; exec. dir. commn. on structural alternatives Fed. Ct. Appeals, 1998-99. Author: Preludes to Gideon, 1967, Criminal Appeals-English Practices and American Reforms, 1973, Mr. Justice Black and His Books, 1974, Appellate Courts: Staff and Process in the Crisis of Volume, 1974, (with Carrington and Rosenberg) Justice on Appeal, 1976, Impressions of Law in East Germany, 1986, American Courts, 1991, (with J. Bernstein) Appellate Courts in the United States, 1994, His Father's House, 1994, Unforgotten, 1999, (with Rosenberg and Carrington) Appellate Courts: Structures, Functions, Processes, and Personnel, 1994; editor: Hardy Cross Dillard: Writings and Speeches, 1995; editor Va. Bar News, 1962-65; contbr. articles to profl. jours. 1st lt. U.S. Army, 1951-53; col. JAGC, USAR ret. Decorated Bronze Star.; IREX fellow German Dem. Republic, 1983. Mem. ABA (chmn. standing com. on fed. jud. improvements 1987-90), Ala. Bar Assn., Va. Bar Assn. (exec. com. 1983-86), Am. Law Inst., Am. Judicature Soc. (bd. dirs. 1975-77, 80-83), Soc. Pub. Tchrs. Law, Am. Soc. Legal History (bd. dirs. 1968-71), Order of Coif, Raven Soc., Phi Delta Phi, Omicron Delta Kappa, Kappa Alpha. Presbyn. Office: U Va Sch Law 580 Massie Rd Charlottesville VA 22903-1738

**MEADOR, ROSS DESHONG,** lawyer; b. Mexico City, Aug. 23, 1954; s. Bruce Staffel and Betty Lee M.; m. Carol Corrine Davis, June 12, 1986 (div. Aug. 1991); m. Michelle Hyunae Chang, Mar. 14, 1997; 1 child, Amy Chang. BA in Comm. and Visual Arts, U. Calif., San Diego, 1980; JD, U. Calif., Berkeley, 1986. Bar: Calif. Atty. Morrison & Foerster, San Francisco, 1986-89; fgn. legal advisor Kim & Chang, Seoul, 1989-95, Soewito, Suhardiman, Eddymurthy & Kardono, Jakarta, Indonesia, 1996-97; of counsel Morrison & Foerster, 1997—. Exec. editor Internat. Tax & Bus. Lawyer, 1985-86. Bd. dirs. Theatre Bay Area, San Francisco, 1988-89. Mem. ABA, Calif. Bar Assn., Internat. Assn. Korean Lawyers, Pan Am. Soc. No. Calif., Am. C. of C. in Korea (chmn. legal svcs. com.), Korean Am. C. of C. of Northern Calif. (v.p. 1998—). Avocation: travel. Contracts commercial, Intellectual property, Private international. Home: 1533 Hearst Ave Berkeley CA 94703-1218 Office: Morrison & Foerster 425 Market St San Francisco CA 94105-2482

**MEADOWS, JOHN FREDERICK,** lawyer; b. Manila, Mar. 7, 1926; s. Grover Cleveland and Millie M.; m. Karen Lee Morris, Nov. 17, 1962; children: Ian Joseph, Marie Irene. AA, U. Mich., 1944; BA (Freshman Alumni Scholar, 1943), U. Calif., Berkeley, 1948; LLB, Boalt Hall, 1951. Bar: Calif 1952, U.S. Dist. Ct. (no. dist.) Calif. 1952, U.S. Ct. Apls. (9th cir.) 1952, U.S. Sup. Ct. 1958. Assoc. Wallace, Garrison, Norton & Ray, San Francisco, 1952-56; atty. advisor Maritime Adminstrn, U.S. Dept. Commerce, Washington, 1956; trial atty., Admiralty and Shipping Sect. U.S. Dept Justice, West Coast Office, San Francisco, 1956-64, atty. in charge, 1964-72; sr. resident ptnr. Acret & Perrochet, San Francisco, 1972-76; sr. ptnr. Meadows, Smith, Lenker, Sterling & Davis, San Francisco, 1976-93, Long Beach, Calif., 1976-93, Seattle, 1976-93; mng. ptnr. west coast Kirlin, Campbell, Meadows & Keating, N.Y.C., 1993; ptnr. Jedeikin Meadows & Schneider, San Francisco, 1994; cons. maritime law, UN; lectr. seminar Taipei, Taiwan, 1968. Author: Preparing a Ship Collision Case for Trial, 1970, Ship Collision Cases: Technical and Legal Aspects; Investigation and Preparation for Suit, 1997, contbr. articles to legal publs.; assoc. editor: Am. Maritime Cases. Lt. M.I. AUS, 1944-46. Mem. ABA, Maritime Law Assn., San Francisco Bar Assn. Republican. Roman Catholic. E-mail: jmands@aol.com. Fax 415-421-5658. Admiralty, Insurance, Federal civil litigation. Home: 205 The Uplands Berkeley CA 94705-2818 Office: 300 Montgomery St Ste 450 San Francisco CA 94104-1906

**MEADOWS, ROD G.,** lawyer; b. Manchester, Ga., Aug. 2, 1949; s. Earl F. and Sara R. (Moncus) M.; m. Betty Foster, Jan. 29, 1972; children: Mandy J., Monica E. BS Edn cum laude, Ga. So. U., Statesboro, 1971; JD, U. Ga., 1976. Bar: Ga. 1976, U.S. Dist. Ct. (no. and mid. dists.) Ga. 1977, U.S. Ct. Appeals (5th cir.) 1977, U.S. Ct. Appeals (11th cir.) 1981. Ptnr. Smith, Welch & Meadows, McDonough, Ga., 1976-85; ptnr., pres. Meadows & Futch P.C., McDonough, 1985—; founder, chair Long-Term Health Care Law in Ga. conf., Athens, 1992—; counsel Hosp. Authority of Henry Country and Henry County Devel. Authority, 1985—. Bd. mem. Ga. So. U. Found., Statesboro, 1995—; past-pres., bd. mem. Henry Med. Ctr. Found., Stockbridge, Ga., 1984—; elder, deacon, fin chair McDonough Presbyn. Ch. Lt. USCG, 1971-74. Mem. Ga. Acad. Hosp. Attys. (bd. mem. 1985—, pres. 1992-93), Am. Health Lawyers Assn., Am. Counsel Assn., Ga. Hosp. Assn. (coun. on trustee devel. 1985—), McDonough Kiwanis Club (pres., bd. mem. 1978—). Avocations: travel, musical theater, music, church activities. Health, General civil litigation, General corporate. Home: PO Box 734 Mcdonough GA 30253-0734

**MEANS, ELIZABETH ROSE THAYER,** financial consultant, lawyer; b. N.Y.C., Aug. 29, 1960; d. Cyril Chesnut and Rosaline (Limtiuco y Sy) M. Student, Sch. of Am. Ballet, N.Y.C., 1970-75, Harvard Coll., 1980, Tufts U., 1981, Fletcher Sch. Law/Diplomacy, 1983-84; BS, Chatham Coll., 1983; cert. in comparative law, Heidelberg U., 1988; JD, Samford U., 1989; LLM in Internat. Banking Law, Boston U., 1990. Bar: Mass. 1991, Pa. 1991; cert. for piloting, seamanship and small boat handling USCG Aux. Dancer The N.Y.C. Ballet Co., 1971, Balanchine Cast for PBS The Nutcracker Suite, N.Y.C., 1971; docent The Hammond Castle Mus., Gloucester, Mass., 1982-85; asst. mgr. The Gallery, Rockport, Mass., 1977-83; cons. The Galleries, Ltd., Wellesley, Mass., 1988; legal intern U. Ala. Health Svcs. Found., Birmingham, 1988-89; loan officer UN/UNFCU, N.Y.C., 1984-86; contracts mgr. for Eastern Region Unisys Corp., Berkeley Heights, N.J., 1990-92; fin. cons. Innovatech, Lexington, Mass., 1992-93, 94-95; contract analyst Guy Carpenter & Co., Inc., N.Y.C., 1994; gen. counsel Mojo Working Prodns., N.Y.C., 1996; chair Cordell Hull Speakers' Forum, Birmingham, 1988-89; alumnae class sec. Chatham Coll. Class of 1980s, Pitts., 1983-87, 97—. Clk. of vestry The Ch. of the Resurrection, N.Y.C., 1993-95, mem. vestry, 1995-97; overnight counselor The Germaine Lawrence Sch., Arlington, Mass., 1989-90. Recipient Cert. of Appreciation 1990 Alumni award Cumberland Sch. Law, 1990; named to Nat. Dean's List, 1989-90. Mem. DAR (Cape Ann chpt. const. week chair 1993-94, Mass. const. week chair 1995-97, N.Y.C. chpt. jr. com. mem. Sons and Daus. Gala Ball 1996), The Federalist Soc. (Cumberland chpt. treas. 1988-89, adv. bd. 1983, sec. 1987-88), Clan Menzies Soc. N.Am., Clan Menzies Soc. Scotland, Princeton Club, Thayer Families Assn., Daus. Union Vets. of Civil War 1861-65, Mass. Soc. Mayflower Descs., Baronial Order Magna Charta, Dames of Ct. of Honor, Nat. Soc. Magna Charta Dames and Barons, Nat. Soc. First Families of Minn., Soc. the Friends of St. George's, Knights of the Garter, Hugenot Soc. Am., Order of Wash., N.Y. State Continental Soc. Daus. of Indian Wars 1607-1900, St. Georges Soc. N.Y., First Families Ohio, Colonial Order the Crown, The Sovereign Colonial Soc. Ams. of Royal Descent, The Plantagenet Soc. Republican. Episcopalian. Avocations: lobstering, sailing, fishing, swimming, bicycling. Address: 13 Salt Island Rd Gloucester MA 01930-1972

**MEANS, TERRY ROBERT,** federal judge; b. Roswell, N.Mex., July 3, 1948; s. Lewis Prude and Doris Emaree (Hightower) M.; m. JoAnn Huffman Harris, June 2, 1973; children: Robert, MaryAnn, Emily. BA, So. Meth. U., 1971, JD, 1974. Bar: Tex. 1974, U.S. Dist. Ct. (no. dist.) Tex. 1976, U.S. Ct. Appeals (5th cir.) 1978, U.S. Dist. Ct. (we. dist., ea. dist.) Tex. 1991. Ptnr. Means & Means, Corsicana, Tex., 1974-88; Presdl. elector, 1980; justice 10th Ct. Appeals, Waco, Tex., 1989-90; judge U.S. Dist. Ct. for No. Dist. Tex., Ft. Worth, 1991—. Chmn. Navarro County Rep. Party, Corsicana, 1976-88; pres. YMCA, Corsicana, 1984, Ft. Worth Youth Soccer Assn., 1996-97. Mem. State Bar Tex., Tarrant County Bar Assn., McLennan County Bar Assn. Baptist. Avocations: coaching soccer, racquetball. Office: 201 US Courthouse 501 W 10th St Fort Worth TX 76102-3637

**MEARS, MICHAEL,** lawyer; b. Tupelo, Miss., Aug. 14, 1943; s. James Nash and Victoria (Taylor) M.; m. Sue Ellen Owens, May 25, 1973; 1 child, Alexander Taylor. B.S., Miss. State U., 1968, M.A., 1969; J.D., U. Ga., 1977. Bar: Ga. 1977, U.S. Dist. Ct. (no. dist.) Ga. 1977, U.S. Ct. Appeals (5th cir.) 1977, U.S. Ct. Appeals (11th cir.) 1981, U.S. Supreme Ct. 1980. Tchr., asst. prin. Decatur (Ga.) City Schs., 1969-74; assoc. firm McCurdy & Candler, Attys., Decatur, 1977-81, ptnr., 1981—. Author: Teaching Russian History, 1971; contbr. articles to profl. jours. Mem. bd. appeals City of Decatur, 1977-83; bd. dirs. Decatur-DeKalb YMCA, 1982—; commr. City of Decatur, 1983-84, mayor, 1984—. Served with USN, 1961-67. Fellow U.S. Coll. Mortgage Attys.; mem. Atlanta Lawyers Club, DeKalb C. of C. (dir. 1982—), Phi Kappa Phi, Kappa Delta Pi. Democrat. Episcopalian. State civil litigation, State and local taxation. Home: 303 Adams St Decatur GA 30030-5205 Office: McCurdy & Candler PO Box 57 Decatur GA 30031-0057

**MEARS, PATRICK EDWARD,** lawyer; b. Oct. 3, 1951; s. Edward Patrick and Estelle Veronica (Mislik) M.; m. Geraldine O'Connor, July 18, 1981. BA, U. Mich., 1973, JD, 1976. Bar: N.Y. 1977, Ill. 1996, Ind. 1997, U.S. Dist Ct. (so. and ea. dists) N.Y. 1977, Mich. 1980, U.S. Dist. Ct. (we. and ea. dists.) Mich. 1980, U.S. Ct. Appeals (6th cir.) 1983, Ill. 1996, Ind. 1997, U.S. Dist. Ct. (no. dist.) Ill. 1998, U.S. Dist. Ct. (no. dist.) Ind. 1998. Assoc. Milbank, Tweed, Hadley & McCloy, N.Y.C., 1976-79; ptnr. Warner, Norcross & Judd, Grand Rapids, Mich., 1980-91; sr. mem. Dykema Gossett PLLC, memnd Rapids, Mich., 1991—; adj. prof. Grand Valley State U., Allendale, Mich., 1981-84; dir. Children's Law Ctr., 1994, Grand Rapids

Ballet, 1994-99, East Grand Rapids Pub. Sch. Found., 1994-98. Author: Michigan Collection Law, 1981, 2d edit., 1983, Basic Bankruptcy Law, 1986, Bankruptcy Law and Practice in Michigan, 1987; contbg. author Collier Bankruptcy Practice Guide; contbr. articles to profl. jours. Chmn. legis. com. East Grand Rapids PTA, 1992-94. Fellow Am. Coll. Bankruptcy; mem. ABA (vice chmn. loan practices and lender liability com. ABA real property sect. 1997—), Mich. State Bar Assn. (mem., sec. coun. real property sect. 1993-97), Am. Bankruptcy Inst., Fed. Bar Assn. (chmn. bankruptcy sect. We. Mich. chpt. 1992-94, v.p. ops. 1998—), Grand Rapids Rotary, Peninsular Club (Grand Rapids), East Hills Athletic Club, Urban Inst. Contemporary Art (bd. dirs.). Bankruptcy, Consumer commercial. Office: Dykema Gossett PLLC 300 Ottawa Ave NW Ste 700 Grand Rapids MI 49503-2308

**MEARS, RONA ROBBINS,** lawyer; b. Stillwater, Minn., Oct. 3, 1938; d. Glaydon Donaldson and Lois Lorane (Hoehne) Robbins; m. John Ashley Mears, Aug. 20, 1960; children: John LaMonte, Matthew Von. BS, U. Minn., 1960; MBA, JD, So. Meth. U., 1982. Bar: Tex. 1992. Bus. adminstr. 1st Unitarian Ch., Dallas, 1973-77; assoc. atty. Haynes and Boone, Dallas, 1982-89, ptnr., internat. sect., 1989—. Co-editor: International Loan Workouts and Bankruptcies, 1989; contbr. articles to profl. jours. Mem. U.S. Delegation, NAFTA Adv. Com. on Pvt. Comml. Disputes, 1994—. Rsch. fellow Southwestern Legal Found., Dallas, 1986—; recipient 1st prize INSOL Internat. Article Competition, 1989. Mem. ABA (sec. internat. sect. 1994-96), State Bar Tex. (chmn. internat. sect. 1993-94, divorce chmn. 1996—), Tex. -Mex. Bar Assn. (co-chair 1994-95, co-chair 1995—), Dallas Bar Assn. (chmn. internat. sect. 1984-86), Internat. Bar Assn. (mem. com. on creditors rights, coord. internat. insolvency coop. project 1988-91), U.S. - Mex. C. of C. (bd. dirs. S.W. chpt. 1987—). Democrat. Private international, General corporate. Office: Haynes and Boone LLP 3100 Nations Bank Plz 901 Main St Ste 3100 Dallas TX 75202-3789

**MEATH, GREGORY THOMAS,** lawyer; b. Lodi, Calif., Sept. 23, 1967; s. Thomas Wayne and Beverly Ann Meath; m. Fernanda Manuela Pereira, Jan. 8, 1998. BS in Bus., U. of the Pacific, Stockton, Calif., 1990; JD, U. of the Pacific, Sacramento, 1995, LLM, 1996. Bar: Calif. 1995, U.S. Dist. Ct. (no. dist.) Calif. 1995. Assoc. atty. Neumiller & Beardslee, Inc., Stockton, 1997—. Mem. Internat. Bar Assn., San Joaquin County Bar Assn. (profl. liaison com. 1997, cmty. outreach com. 1997). Roman Catholic. Private international, Transportation. Office: Neumiller & Beardslee 509 W Weber Ave Stockton CA 95203-3167

**MEBUS, ROBERT GWYNNE,** lawyer; b. Ft. Worth, Aug. 28, 1940; s. Robert Lee and Lucille (Cooke) M.; children: Elizabeth, Mary Ellen. BBA, So. Meth. U., 1962, LLB, 1965. Bar: Tex. 1965, U.S. Dist. Ct. (no. and ea. dists.) 1966, U.S. Ct. Appeals (5th cir.) 1965, U.S. Supreme Ct. 1969. Assoc. Malone, Seay & Gwinn, Dallas, 1965-67; ptnr. Seay, Gwinn, Crawford, Dallas, 1967-69, Seay, Gwinn, Crawford, Mebus, Dallas, 1969-82, Haynes and Boone, Dallas, 1982—; mem. Tex. Bd. Legal Specialization; adj. prof. Sch. Law So. Meth. U. Contbg. editor: (book) Developing Labor Law, 1967, 2d edit., 1987. Mem. ABA (labor law sect.), Tex. Bar Found., Tex. State Bar (chmn. labor law sect. 1982-83, chmn. labor law adv. commn. 1982-83). Avocations: tennis, photography, gardening. Labor. Office: Haynes and Boone 3100 Nations Bank Plz 901 Main St Ste 3100 Dallas TX 75202-3789

**MECHAM, GLENN JEFFERSON,** lawyer, mayor; b. Logan, Utah, Dec. 11, 1935; s. Everett H. and Lillie (Dunford) M.; m. Mae Parson, June 5, 1957; children: Jeff B., Scott R., Marcia, Suzanne. BS, Utah State U., 1957; JD, U. Utah, 1961; grad., Air Command and Staff Coll., 1984, Air War Coll., 1984. Bar: Utah 1961, Supreme Ct. U.S., U.S. Ct. Appeals (10th cir.), U.S. Dist. Ct. Utah, U.S. Ct. Claims. Gen. practice law, 1961-65; atty. Duchesne County, Utah, 1962, City of Duchesne, 1962; city judge Roy City, Utah, 1963-66; judge City of Ogden, Utah, 1966-69; mayor City of Ogden, 1992—; lectr. law and govt. Stevens-Henager Coll., Ogden, 1963-75; asst. U.S. atty., 1969-72; ptnr. Mecham & Richards, Ogden, Utah, 1972-82; pres. Penn Mountain Mining Co., South Pacific Internat. Bank, Ltd.; mem. Bur. Justice Stats. Adv. Bd., U.S. Dept. Justice, U.S. Conf. Mayors. Chmn. Ogden City Housing Authority; chmn. bd. trustees Utah State U., Space Dynamics Lab.; mem. adv. coun. Fed. Home Loan Bank; pres. Utah League Cities and Towns, 1981-82; vice chmn. Wasatch Front Reg. Coun. Col. USAF, 1957. Mem ABA, Weber County Bar Assn. (pres. 1966-68), Utah Bar Assn., Am. Judicature Soc., Weber County Bar Legal Svcs. (chmn. bd. trustees 1966-69), Utah Assn. Mcpl. Judges (sec.), Sigma Chi, Phi Alpha Delta. General corporate, Real property, Education and schools. Home: 1715 Darling St Ogden UT 84403-0556 Office: City of Ogden 2484 Washington Blvd Ste 300 Ogden UT 84401-2342

**MECHEM, EDWIN LEARD,** judge; b. Alamogordo, N.Mex., July 2, 1912; s. Edwin and Eunice (Leard) M.; Dorothy Heller, Dec. 30, 1932 (dec. 1972); children: Martha M. Vigil, John H., Jesse (dec. 1968), Walter M.; m. Josephine Donavan, May 28, 1976. L.L.B., U. Ark., 1939; L.L.D. (hon.), N.Mex. State U., 1975. Bar: N.Mex. 1939, U.S. Dist. Ct. N.Mex. 1939. Lawyer Las Cruces and Albuquerque, 1939-70; judge U.S. Dist. Ct. N.Mex., Albuquerque, 1970-82, sr. judge, 1982—; spl. agt. FBI Dept. Justice, various locations, 1942-45; mem. legislature State of N.Mex., 1947-48, gov., 1951-54, 57-58, 61-62; senator U.S. Govt., Washington, 1963-64. Mem. ABA, N.Mex. Bar Assn., Am. Law Inst. Republican. Methodist. Avocation: travel. Office: US Dist Ct PO Box 97 Albuquerque NM 87103-0097*

**MECOLI KAMP, CARLA MARIE,** lawyer; b. Detroit, Nov. 24, 1962; d. Pasquale Rocco and Agnes Eunice Mecoli; m. James Frederick Kamp, Sept. 25, 1987; 1 child, Nicholas William. BS, Oakland U., 1985; JD, Wayne State U., 1994. Bar: Mich. 1994. Med. technologist William Beaumont Hosp., Royal Oak, Mich., 1986-91; assoc. Jaffe Raitt Heuer & Weiss, Detroit, 1994—. Mem. ABA, State Bar of Mich. Estate planning, Probate, Real property. Office: Jaffe Raitt Heuer & Weiss PC One Woodward Ave Ste 2400 Detroit MI 48226

**MEDAGLIA, MARY-ELIZABETH,** lawyer; b. Suffern, N.Y., Oct. 13, 1947; d. Joseph Mario and Edith Elizabeth (Price) M. BA, Sweet Briar Coll., 1969; JD, U. Va., 1972. Bar: Va. 1972, D.C. 1974, U.S. Ct. Appeals (D.C. cir.) 1974, U.S. Supreme Ct. 1980, U.S. Ct. Appeals (4th, 5th, 9th and 11th cirs.) 1981, U.S. Ct. Appeals (10th cir.) 1982, Md. 1990, U.S. Ct. Appeals (2d cir.) 1998. Law clk. to judge D.C. Ct. Appeals, Washington, 1972-74; asst. atty. U.S. Atty.'s Office, Washington, 1974-79; deputy solicitor Fed. Labor Relations Authority, Washington, 1979-82, acting solicitor, 1982; assoc. Jackson & Campbell P.C., Washington, 1982-84, ptnr., 1984—; sec. D.C. Bar, 1983-84, bd. govs. 1984-87. Fellow Am. Bar Found.; mem. ABA (chmn. TIPS com. on ins. coverage litigation 1989-91, ho. of dels. 1981-83), D.C. Bar Assn. (bd. dirs. 1980-83, chmn. young lawyers sect. 1980-81), Women's Bar Assn. D.C. (pres. 1982-83), Charles Fahy Am. Inn of Ct. (pres. 1990-92), Fedn. of Ins. and Corp. Counsel, Am. Soc. of Writers on Legal Subjects, Phi Beta Kappa. State civil litigation, Insurance, Federal civil litigation. Office: Jackson & Campbell PC South Tower 1120 20th St NW Ste 300S Washington DC 20036-3437

**MEDAK, WALTER HANS,** lawyer; b. Vienna, Austria, May 10, 1915; came to U.S., 1938; s. Hugo and Grete (Figdor) M.; m. Edith Rhodes, 1944 (div. 1957); 1 child, Ronald Harvard; m. Renée Rasens, 1996. Grad., Acad. of Commerce, Vienna, 1934, U. Vienna, 1938; postgrad., U. Ga., 1939-40; MA in Econs., U. Calif., Berkeley, 1949; JD, Harvard U., 1948. Prodn. mgr. Mabs, Inc., L.A., 1942-43; prodn. engr. Kaiser Co., Richmond, Calif., 1943-45; atty. Belli & Medak, Walnut Creek, Calif., 1957-59; pvt. practice law Walnut Creek and Moraga, Calif., 1950—; bd. dirs. Snyder/Newell, Inc., San Francisco; bd. dirs. Carnelian Woods, Carnelian Bay, Calif., pres., 1974-80. Mem. ABA, Calif. County Bar Assn., Assn. Trial Lawyers Am., Calif. Trial Lawyers Assn., Harvard Club (chmn. admissions and scholarship com. San Francisco chpt. 1973-74). Avocations: skiing, swimming, music, travel. Personal injury, State civil litigation, Insurance. Home: 2833 Ptarmigan Dr Apt 3 Walnut Creek CA 94595-3135

**MEDALIE, SUSAN DIANE,** lawyer, management consultant; b. Boston, Oct. 7, 1941; d. Samuel and Matilda (Bortman) Abrams; m. Richard James Medalie, June 5, 1960; children: Samuel David, Daniel Alexander. BA, Sarah Lawrence Coll., 1960; MA, George Washington U., 1962, Cert. Pubs. Spec., 1977; JD, Am. U., 1986. Bar: Pa., 1987, D.C., 1987. Pres. Medalie Cons., Washington, 1980—; dep. dir. U.S. Holocaust Meml. Coun., Washington, 1980-82; assoc. pub. Campaigns & Elections, Washington, 1983-84; legis. analyst Subcom./House Energy and Commerce, Washington, 1985; ea. regional dir. Josephson Found. for Adv. Ethics, L.A., 1986-88; asst. dean for external affairs George Washington U. Nat. Law Ctr., Washington, 1988-90; exec. dir. Internat. Soc. Global Health Policy, Washington and Paris, 1990-93; pvt. practice law Washington, 1993—; corp. liaison First Hosp. Corp., Norfolk, Va., 1986-88; assoc. producer and cons. Prof. Arthur Miller's "Headlines on Trial" (NBC), N.Y.C., 1987-91. Editor/pub.: Getting There mag., 1977-80; sr. editor: Am. Univ. Law Rev., Washington, 1984-86. Nat. dep. fin. dir. Edward M. Kennedy for Pres. Com., Washington, 1979-80; del. D.C. Ward 3 Dem. Ctrl. Com.; mem. exec. bd., D.C. Bar rep. D.C. Coalition Against Drugs and Violence, 1997—. Mem. ABA, D.C. Bar. Education and schools, Non-profit and tax-exempt organizations. Office: Medalie Cons 1750 K St NW Ste 1200 Washington DC 20006-2303

**MEDEIROS, MATTHEW FRANCIS,** lawyer; b. Little Compton, R.I., Apr. 30, 1945; s. Manuel S. and Marie F. (Goulart) M.; m. Sarah Judith Medjuck, July 26, 1970. AB, Brown U., 1967; JD, NYU, 1970. Bar: R.I. 1970, Mass. 1985, U.S. Dist. Ct. R.I. 1971, D.C. 1971, U.S. Dist. Ct. D.C. 1971, U.S. Ct. Appeals (1st cir.) 1972, U.S. Ct. Appeals (D.C. cir.) 1972, U.S. Supreme Ct. 1974. Summer assoc. Lewis & Roca, Phoenix, 1969; law clk. to chief judge U.S. Dist. Ct. R.I., 1970-71; assoc. Covington & Burling, Washington, 1971-76, on leave with Neighborhood Legal Services Program, Washington, 1973; ptnr. Edwards & Angell, Providence, 1977-87, Flanders & Medeiros Inc., Providence, 1987—. Chmn. planning com. 1st Cir. Jud. Conf., 1980-81; mem. jud. screening coms. U.S. Bankruptcy Judge and U.S. Magistrate, 1981-82; mem. adv. com. for U.S. Ct. Appeals (1st cir.), 1983-88; adj. prof. fed. trial practice So. New Eng. Sch. Law, 1986-88. Editor: NYU Law Rev., 1969-70. Bd. dirs. Associated Alumni Brown U., 1969-71; bd. dirs. R.I. br. ACLU, 1977-79. Mem. ABA, Fed. Bar Assn. (pres. R.I. chpt. 1978-80), R.I. Bar Assn. Antitrust, General civil litigation, Federal civil litigation. Office: Medeiros & Sanford Inc One Turks Head Pl Ste 700 Providence RI 02903

**MEDFORD, LEANE CAPPS,** lawyer; b. Kansas City, Kans., Jan. 14, 1969; d. Norman Edward and Shirley (Lee) Capps; m. William Lawrence Medford, Jr., Jan. 10, 1998. BS, Tex. Christian U., 1990; JD cum laude, Baylor U., 1996. Bar: Tex. 1996, U.S. Dist. Ct. (no. dist.) Tex. 1996, U.S. Dist. Ct. (so. dist.) Tex. 1997, U.S. Dist. Ct. (ea. dist.) Tex. 1998, U.S. Dist. Ct. (we. dist.) Tex. 1999. Assoc. atty. Vial, Hamilton, Koch & Knox LLP, Dallas, 1996-98, Calhoun & Stacy PLLC, Dallas, 1998—. Mem. ABA (litigation sect.), Dallas Bar Assn. (bus. litigation sect.), Phi Delta Phi. Avocations: gourmet cooking, reading, travel. E-mail: medford@calhounstacy.com. Federal civil litigation, State civil litigation. Office: Calhoun & Stacy PLLC 901 Main St Ste 5700 Dallas TX 75202-3726

**MEDINA, LUIS ANIBAL,** lawyer; b. San Juan, P.R., Aug. 19, 1951; s. Perfecto and Genoveva Medina. BS, Pace U., 1980, JD, 1985. Bar: N.Y. 1987, Conn. 1987, U.S. Dist. Ct. N.Y. 1990, U.S. Dist. Ct. Conn. 1998. Dir. mechanization N.Y. Telephone, 1967-87; sr. ptnr. Medina & O'Brien, P.C., Hawthorne, N.Y., 1987—. Bd. dirs. West C.O.D.A. Cmty. Rels. Adv. Bd., White Plains, N.Y., 1995—. Mem. Westchester County Bar Assn. Republican. Criminal, Bankruptcy, General practice. Office: Medina & O'Brien PC 151 Broadway Hawthorne NY 10532-1103

**MEDINA, OMAR F.,** lawyer; b. Santa Clara, Cuba, Oct. 7, 1959; came to U.S., 1961; s. Omar Pedro and Zulima Carmen M.; m. Deborah Eileen Ticknor, Aug. 7, 1981; children: Dominic, Justine, Xavier. BA in English, Ea. Ky. U., 1981; JD, U. Fla., 1985. Bar: Fla. 1988, U.S. Dist. Ct. (mid. dist.) Fla., U.S. Ct. Appeals (11th cir.), U.S. Dist. Ct. (so. dist.) Tex., U.S. Dist. Ct. (ea. dist.) Ohio. Pvt. practice Law Offices Omar F. Medina, Tampa, Fla., 1988-92, sr. atty., 1997—; ptnr. Medina, Pihsei & Dowell, Tampa, 1992-96; vice chmn. jud. nominating com. 13th Jud. Cir. State of Fla., Tampa, 1995—. Mem. NACDL, Acad. Fla. Trial Lawyers. Avocations: private pilot, tae kwon do. Personal injury, Criminal, Workers' compensation. Office: 705 E Kennedy Blvd Tampa FL 33602-5011

**MEDLIN, CHARLES MCCALL,** lawyer; b. Florence, S.C., Dec. 29, 1960. BA magna cum laude, Duke U., 1982; JD with honors, U. N.C., 1990. Bar: Ga. 1990, U.D. Dist. Ct. (no. dist.) Ga. 1990, U.S. Ct. Appeals (11th cir.) 1990. Teaching asst., property contracts U. N.C. Sch. Law, Chapel Hill, 1988-90; ptnr. Bovis Kyle & Burch, LLC, Atlanta, 1990—; coach Mock Trial Team, Holderness Moot Ct., 1991—. Van Hecke scholar, 1987-90; recipient Am. Jurisprudence award civil procedure. Mem. Ga. Bar Assn., Toastmasters Internat., Lawyers Club of Am. Insurance, General civil litigation, Environmental. Home: 8975 Martin Rd Roswell GA 30076-3260 Office: Bovis Kyle & Burch 53 Perimeter Ctr E Fl 3 Atlanta GA 30346-2294

**MEDONIS, ROBERT XAVIER,** lawyer; b. Pitts., May 31, 1931; s. Vincent X. and Anastasia T. (Puida) M.; m. M. Kathleen Castor, Dec. 29, 1962; children: Meg Toomey, Robert Xavier, Mark D. BEd, Duquesne U., 1953, MA, 1985; JD, U. Pitts., 1958. Bar: Pa. 1959, U.S. Supreme Ct. 1966, U.S. Ct. Appeals (3d cir.) 1976. Trial atty. criminal div. Legal Aid Soc., Pitts., 1960-61; trial atty. Allegheny County Dist. Atty.'s Office, Pitts., 1964-71; assoc. Cleland, Hurt & Bowman, Pitts., 1961-63; pvt. practice, 1958-60, 63-64, 71-93; assoc. Karlowitz and Cromer, Pitts., 1993-95; v.p., gen. counsel Marquee Group, 1995-96, Internat. Investment Group, Pitts., 1996-97, I. Gravy's Internat. Bd. dirs. World Trade Ctr., Pitts. Capt. U.S. Army, 1953-55. Mem. ABA, Pa. Bar Assn., Allegheny County Bar Assn., Internat. Bar Assn., Pa. Trial Lawyers Assn., We. Pa. Trial Lawyers Assn., Lithuanian Am. Bar Assn., Am. Ins. of Ct., China-Am. Trade Soc. (founder, pres.), Rotary (Oakmont, Pa., pres.). General civil litigation, General corporate, Private international. Home: 737 Shady Ln Pittsburgh PA 15228-2450 Office: 204 Tower Suites 531 5th St Oakmont PA 15139-1626

**MEDVECKY, THOMAS EDWARD,** lawyer; b. Bridgeport, Conn., Apr. 22, 1937; s. Stephen and Elizabeth P. Medvecky; m. Patricia Conneally, Aug. 25, 1967; 1 son, Thomas Edward, II. A.B., Bowdoin Coll., 1959; LL.B., St. John's U., 1962. Bar: Conn. 1962. Assoc., Louis Katz, Danbury, Conn., 1963-68; sole practice, Bethel, Conn., 1968—; asst. town counsel Town of Bethel, 1963-67; assoc. dir. State Nat. Bank Conn. Mem. budget com. Danbury (Conn.) Community Chest, 1966-68. Served with USAR, 1962-68. Recipient Am. Jurisprudence award 1962. Mem. ABA, Conn. Bar Assn., Danbury Bar Assn. Democrat. Lutheran. Probate, Real property, General practice. Office: 99 Greenwood Ave PO Box 272 Bethel CT 06801-0272

**MEDVED, ROBERT ALLEN,** lawyer; b. Cleve., July 22, 1945; s. Joseph Jack and Mary (Blasko) M. BBA, Kent State U., 1968; JD cum laude, U. Puget Sound, 1975. Bar: Wash. 1976, U.S. Ct. Appeals (9th cir.) 1976, U.S. Dist. Ct. (we. dist.) Wash. 1976, U.S. Dist. Ct. (ea. dist.) Wash. 1979, U.S. Supreme Ct. 1981, U.S. Ct. Appeals (D.C. cir.) 1989. Fin. analyst Ford Motor Co., Sandusky, Ohio, 1972; rsch. asst. U. Puget Sound, 1973; arbitration asst. to labor arbitrator, Tacoma, 1975; law clk. to judge U.S. Ct. Appeals (9th cir.), Seattle, 1974, to judge U.S. Dist. Ct. Cen. Dist. Calif., L.A., 1976; assoc. Graham & Dunn, Seattle, 1976-82, ptnr., 1982-83; ptnr. Drake and Whiteley, Bellevue, Wash., 1983-86, Foster Pepper & Shefelman, Seattle, 1986-97; Bellevue, Wash., 1997—; spl. dist. counsel 8th Congl. Dist. Wash., 1983-96. Editor-in-chief U. Puget Sound Law Rev. Bd. dirs. Bellevue C.C. Found., 1986—. Lt. USN, 1968-71. U. Puget Sound scholar, 1974. Mem. ABA, Wash. State Bar Assn., Seattle C. of C., Bellevue C. of C. Roman Catholic. Corporate taxation, General corporate, Environmental. Office: 212 108th Ave SE Bellevue WA 98004-6209

**MEECHAN, RICK JAMES,** lawyer; b. Rochester, July 17, 1955; s. James A. and Kathryn (Devereaux) M.; m. Susan Marie Fisher, Aug. 16, 1982; children: Alexandria, Jacob. BA in Mgmt., Sonoma State U., 1979; JD, Empire Coll., 1987. Bar: Calif. 1987. Asst. mgr. Chgo. Pizza, Petaluma, Calif., 1980-81; solar energy salesman Native Sun, Petaluma, Calif., 1982; new accts. rep. Northbay Savings & Loan, Rohnert Park, Calif., 1983-85; assoc. Richens L. Wootton, Santa Rosa, Calif., 1985-90; pvt. practice Santa Rosa, Calif., 1990—; Mem. adv. bd. Compensation Alert, Santa Rosa, 1992-96. Editor: Basic Stuff, 1991, (newsletter) Donkey Tail, 1986. Bd. dirs. Ctrl. Soccer, Santa Rosa, 1993-96, Sant Rosa Youth Soccer League, 1996, Christ Meth. Ch., 1991-93. With USN, 1973-79; Capt. USNG, 1982-89. Mem. Northbay Applicants Attorneys, Empire Soccer Club. Democrat. Avocations: stream restoration, fly fishing, politics. Workers' compensation. Office: 50 Santa Rosa Ave Fl 4 Santa Rosa CA 95404-4901

**MEEHAN, JOHN JUSTIN,** lawyer; b. N.Y.C., Feb. 14, 1947; m. Daizy Rice; children: John, Jason. Student, Javeriana U., Colombia, 1967; BA cum laude, St. Louis U., 1969, JD, 1975. Bar: Mo. 1976, U.S. Dist. Ct. (we. dist.) Mo. 1976, U.S. Dist. Ct. (ea. dist.) Mo. 1977, U.S. Ct. Appeals (8th cir.) 1978. Tchr. St. Francis Xavier Grad Sch., St. Louis, 1970-72; assoc. Howard, Richardson & Singer, St. Louis, 1976-78; pvt. practice, St. Louis, 1978—; tchr. tai chi and qigong St. Louis U., Mo. Bot. Gardens; tchr. tai chi I and II, St. Louis C.C.-Meramec, 1994-98; lectr. in field. Mo. bd. dirs. Chinese Cultural Assn., 1976-80; pres. Chinese Internal Arts Ctr., 1991—; v.p. Lafayette Towne Neighborhood Assn., 1994; bd. dirs. Better Family Life, 1995—, Nigerian Cultural Assn., 1994—, Laclede Towne Cmty., 1976-80; active Big Bro. program Pruitt Igoe, 1965-69; mem. Forsyth Diversity Com., 1998; pro bono legal counsel Eiretrean Assn., Brazilian Assn., Vietnamese Buddhist Assn. Recipient Human Rights award St. Louis Coalition for Human Rights, 1997. Mem. Mo. Bar Assn., Met. Bar Assn. St. Louis, Mound City Bar Assn. (mem.-at-large 1991-92, 98-99, Legal Svc. award 1998), NAACP (life). Roman Cath. Avocation: foreign travel. Fax: 314-772-3604. Civil rights, Criminal, Personal injury. Office: Lafayette Towne Profl Bldg 2734 Lafayette Ave Ste 1 Saint Louis MO 63104-2040

**MEEHAN, MICHAEL JOSEPH,** lawyer; b. St. Louis, Aug. 28, 1942; s. Joseph Michael and Frances (Taylor) M.; m. Sharon Kay McHenry (div. 1988); m. Patricia Ann Shive, July 8, 1989. BS in Engring., U.S. Coast Guard Acad., 1964; JD with high distinction, U. Ariz., 1971. Bar: Ariz. 1971, U.S. Ct. Appeals (6th, 8th, 9th and 10th cirs.), U.S. Supreme Ct. 1975. Law clk. Assoc. Justice William H. Rehnquist, U.S. Supreme Ct., 1972; assoc. Molloy, Jones & Donahue, P.C., Tucson, 1971-75, shareholder, 1975-93; chmn. exec. com., head trial dept., 1986-93; founder Meehan & Assocs., Tucson, 1993—; mem. fed. appellate rules adv. com. Jud. Conf. U.S., 1994—. Author chpt. on appellate advocacy: State Bar of Arizona Appellate Practice Handbook. Fellow Am. Acad. Appellate Lawyers; mem. ABA (sect. on litig., sect. on intellectual property), Ariz. Bar Assn. (exec. coun., chair appellate practice sect. 1995—). Republican. Lutheran. Avocation: golf. Federal civil litigation, Communications, Securities. Office: Meehan & Assocs PO Box 1671 Tucson AZ 85702-1671

**MEEHAN, RICHARD THOMAS, JR.,** lawyer; b. Bridgeport, Conn., Jan. 11, 1949; s. Richard Thomas and Elvira (Avola) M.; m. Kathy Lynn Mucci, Aug. 23, 1969; children—Michael, Brian, Daniel, Timothy, Richard. B.A., U. Notre Dame, 1970; J.D. with honors, U. Conn., 1974. Bar: Conn. 1974, U.S. Dist. Ct. Conn. 1975, U.S. Ct. Appeals (2d cir.) 1975, U.S. Supreme Ct. 1980. Clk., Conn. Supreme Ct., Hartford, 1974-75; ptnr. Meehan and Meehan, Bridgeport, Conn., 1975—; adj. assoc. prof. paralegal program Sacred Heart U., Fairfield, Conn., 1976-79; lectr. Fairfield U., 1988—, Coun. Trial Lawyer's Assn. The People's Law sch., 1990—, Fairfield County Detective Sch., 1988—; adj. prof. Quinnipiac Coll. Law Sch., 1997—; Fairfield. Bd. editors U. Conn. Law Rev., 1972-73, research and spl. projects editor, 1973-74. Alderman, City of Bridgeport, 1975-79; commr. Airport Commn., Bridgeport, 1977-79; pres. Common Council, Bridgeport, 1977-79; mem. exec. bd. North End Little League, Bridgeport, 1983; mgr. Shelton Am. Little League, 1985-92; v.p. Flag Football League, Shelton, Conn., 1991—; varsity basketball coach Shelton Cath. Regional Jr. High Sch., 1991-95; pres., adv. bd. Cath. Family Svcs. Fairfield County, 1997—. Recipient Am. Jurisprudence award for torts Lawyers Coop, 1972; Am. Jurisprudence award advance criminal procedure Lawyers Coop, 1972; Am. Jurisprudence award contracts Lawyers Coop, 1972. Mem. Assn. Trial Lawyers Am., Conn. Bar Assn. (exec. com. criminal law 1981-83), Conn. Trial Lawyers Assn., Bridgeport Bar Assn. (exec. com. 1982-85, chmn. criminal law sect. 1981-82, 84-85, pres.-elect 1985-86, pres. 1986-87), Nat. Council Bar Pres., Conn. Council Bar Pres's. Democrat. Roman Catholic. E-mail: thefirm@meehanlaw.com. Criminal, State civil litigation, Family and matrimonial. Home: 28 Elderberry Ln Shelton CT 06484-3757 Office: Meehan and Meehan 76 Lyon Ter Bridgeport CT 06604-4022

**MEER, CARY JESSE,** lawyer; b. N.Y.C., Mar. 8, 1957; d. George and Gladys (Dallal) Meer; m. Charles Phipps Thomas, Sept. 23, 1984; 1 child, Daniel Phipps Thomas. BS in Econs. summa cum laude, U. Pa., 1979; JD cum laude, Harvard U., 1982. Bar: N.Y. 1983, D.C. 1986. Assoc. Stroock & Stroock & Lavan, N.Y.C., 1982-86; assoc. Kirkpatrick & Lockhart LLP, Washington, 1986-91, ptnr., 1992—; counselor Am. Woman's Econ. Devel. Corp., Washington, 1993-96. Contbr. articles to profl. jours.; co-author chpt. in Money Manager's Compliance Guide, 1994. Democrat. General corporate, Securities, Commodities. Home: 5417 Nevada Ave NW Washington DC 20015-1727 Office: Kirkpatrick & Lockhart LLP 1800 Massachusetts Ave NW Fl 2 Washington DC 20036-1800

**MEER, JESSE ROSS,** lawyer; b. N.Y.C., Nov. 18, 1931; s. Alan J. and Belle T. M.; m. Joan Backer, Apr. 18, 1959; children: Jeffrey Adam, Jonathan David, Julie Beth. AB, Bklyn. Coll., 1953; LLB, Harvard U., 1958. Bar: N.Y. 1958, U.S. Dist. Ct. (so. and ea. dists.) N.Y. 1977, U.S. Ct. Appeals (2d cir.) 1977. Assoc. Berlack Israels & Liberman, N.Y.C., 1958-64, ptnr., 1964—; lectr. in field. Pres. Advance the Dance, Bklyn., 1962—; trustee, treas. Bklyn. Coll. Found., 1996—, Cmty. Temple Beth Ohr, Bklyn., 1973—; dir. Continental Stock Transfer, N.Y.C., 1975-99. With U.S. Army, 1954-56. Mem. Assn. of Bar of City of N.Y. Avocations: tennis, counselling cancer patients. General corporate. Home: 789 E 18th St Brooklyn NY 11230-1804 Office: Berlack Israels & Liberman LLP 120 W 45th St New York NY 10036-4041

**MEFFORD, R. DOUGLAS,** lawyer; b. Harrisonburg, Va., Oct. 12, 1963; s. David H. and Mae S. Mefford. BS, Western Ky. U., 1985; JD, U. Ky., 1991. Bar: Tenn. 1991, U.S. Dist. Ct. (mid. dist.) tenn. 1991, Ky. 1992. Acctg. officer Trans Fin. Inc., Bowling Green, Ky., 1985-88; assoc. Bass, Berry & Sims, Nashville, 1991-96; v.p., assoc. gen. counsel PhyCor Inc., Nashville, 1996—. Securities, General corporate, Health. Office: PhyCor Inc 30 Burton Hills Blvd Ste 400 Nashville TN 37215-6140

**MEHLE, ROGER W.,** federal agency administrator; b. Long Beach, Calif., Dec. 28, 1941. BS, U.S. Naval Acad., 1963; MBA, NYU, 1972; JD, Fordham U., 1976. Mng. dir. The First Boston Corp., N.Y.C., 1969-79; sr. v.p., dir. Dean Witter Reynolds, Inc., N.Y.C., 1979-81; asst. sec. for domestic fin. Dept. Treasury, Washington, 1981-83; exec. v.p., mng. dir. PaineWebber, Inc., N.Y.C., 1983-84; banking and securities atty. Washington, 1985-94; chmn. Fed. Ret. Thrift Investment Bd., Washington, 1985-94; exec. dir. Fed. Retirement Thrift Investment Bd., Washington, 1994—. Office: Fed Ret Thrift Investment Bd 1250 H St NW Washington DC 20005-3952

**MEHLMAN, MARK FRANKLIN,** lawyer; b. L.A., Dec. 18, 1947; s. Jack and Elaine Pearl (Lopater) M.; m. Barbara Ann Novak, Aug. 20, 1972; children: David, Jennifer, Ilyse. BA, U. Ill., 1969; LLB, U. Mich., 1973. Bar: Ill. 1973; U.S. Dist. Ct. (no. dist.) Ill. 1973. Assoc. Sonnenschein, Nath & Rosenthal, Chgo., 1973-80, mem. policy and planning com., 1989—. Trustee Groveland Health Svcs., Highland Park (Ill.) Hosp., 1991—; trustee, treas., mem. exec. com. Spertus Inst. Jewish Studies, Chgo., 1992—; vice chmn. regional bd. Anti-Defamation League, 1987-89, hon. life mem. nat. commn., 1993—. Mem. ABA (chmn. mortgages and other debt financing subcom. 1991-95, group chmn. Group I subcom. 1995-97—, supervisory coun. mem. 1997—, mem. com. on coms. 1997—, mem. nominations com. 1997—, mem. goal IX com. 1997—), Am. Coll. Real Estate Lawyers (vice chair membership selection com. 1998—), Legal Club of Chgo., Lake Shore Country Club, Standard Club. Real property, Contracts commercial, Finance. Office: Sonnenschein Nath & Rosenthal 233 S Wacker Dr Ste 8000 Chicago IL 60606-6342

**MEHTA, EILEEN ROSE,** lawyer; b. Colver, Pa., Apr. 1, 1953; d. Richard Glenn and Helen (Wahna) Ball; m. Abdul Rashid Mehta, Aug. 31, 1973. Student, Miami U., 1971-73; BA with distinction, Fla. Internat. U., 1974; JD cum laude, U. Miami, 1977. Bar: Fla. 1977, U.S. Dist. Ct. (so. dist.) Fla. 1977, U.S. Ct. Appeals (11th cir.) 1981. Law clk. to presiding judge U.S. Dist. Ct. (so. dist.) Fla., Miami, 1977-79; asst. atty. County of Dade, Miami, 1979-89; shareholder Fine Jacobson Schwartz Nash Block &

England, Miami, Fla., 1989-94; ptnr. Eckert Seamans Cherin & Mellott, Miami, 1994-98, Bilzin Sumberg Dunn Price & Axelrod, Miami, 1998—; lectr. in field; v.p., bd. dirs. Mehtatron Enterprises, Inc., Miami, Shalimar Homes Inc., Anderson, S.C. Miami U. scholar, 1971-73. Mem. Fla. Bar Assn., Dade County Bar Assn. Land use and zoning (including planning), Appellate, Government contracts and claims. Office: Bilzin Sumberg Dunn Price and Axelrod 2500 First Union Fin Ctr Miami FL 33131

**MEIBEYER, CHARLES WILLIAM, JR.,** lawyer; b. Saginaw, Mich., Nov. 12, 1951; s. Charles William Sr. and Shirley Ann (Coty) M.; children: Coty Walker, Leland Mathew, Melissa Campbell. BA (with distinction), U. Mich., 1975; JD, U. Calif., Berkeley, 1982; postgrad., U. Calif., San Francisco, 1979-80. Bar: Calif. 1982. Assoc. Morrison & Foerster, San Francisco, 1982-83, Dickenson, Peatman & Fogarty, Napa, Calif., 1983-88; ptnr. Dickenson, Peatman & Fogarty, Napa, 1988-89; pvt. practice Napa, 1989—. Assoc. editor Indsl. Rels. Law Jour., 1980-81. Pres. Mental Health Assn., Napa, 1987-89; bd. dirs. Calif. Mental Health Assn., 1987-89, Napa Valley Unified Edn. Found., 1989-93, pres., 1992-93; trustee Napa Valley Unified Sch. Dist., 1992-96, pres., 1996. Milton D. Green scholar, 1979-80. Mem. ABA (bus. law, law practice mgmt., real property, probate and trust law sects.), Solono County Bar Assn., Napa County Bar Assn., State Bar Calif. (real property and bus. sects.). Alternative dispute resolution, Real property, Contracts commercial. Office: 1001 2nd St Ste 333 Napa CA 94559-3030

**MEIER, MATTHEW HAMILTON,** lawyer; b. Stoneham, Mass., Feb. 10, 1965; s. Joseph and Mary (Hamilton) M. BA in Polit. Sci., Reed Coll., 1987; JD, Northeastern U., 1992; LLM in Tax Law, Boston U., 1998. Bar: Mass. 1996, Hawaii 1993, U.S. Dist. Ct. Hawaii 1994, U.S. Ct. Appeals (9th cir.) 1994. Jud. clk. Alaska Ct. Appeals, Anchorage, 1992-93; assoc. Alston, Hunt, Floyd & Ing, Honolulu, 1993-95, Ross & Hardies, N.Y.C., 1996; sole practitioner Stoughton, Mass., 1996-98; alternative dispute resolution atty. John Hancock Mut. Life Ins. Co., Boston, 1998—; internat. tax atty. Pricewaterhouse Coopers, 1999—; tax advisor VISTA, Boston, 1997-98. Author: Seagulls, A Collection of Short Stories, 1994. Democrat. Avocations: community theater, fiction writing, illustration. Taxation, general, Probate, Corporate taxation.

**MEIKLEJOHN, DONALD STUART,** lawyer; b. Chgo., Oct. 27, 1950; s. Donald and Elizabeth (Moore) M.; m. Rebecca Schneider, Aug. 9, 1975; children: David Alexander, Sarah. AB, Harvard U., 1971, JD, 1975. Bar: N.Y. 1976, U.S. Dist. Ct. (so. and ea. dists.) N.Y. 1976, U.S. Ct. Appeals (2d cir.) 1981, U.S. Ct. Appeals (5th cir.) 1982, U.S. Supreme Ct. 1986, U.S. Ct. Appeals (1st and 8th cirs.) 1990, U.S. Ct. Appeals (3d cir.) 1996, U.S. Ct. Appeals (9th cir.) 1997, U.S. Ct. Appeals (D.C. and 11th cirs.) 1998. Assoc. Sullivan & Cromwell, N.Y.C., 1975-83, ptnr., 1983—. Bd. dirs. Union Settlement, N.Y.C., Lawyer's Com. Civil Rights Under Law, Legal Aid Soc. Mem. ABA, N.Y. State Bar Assn., Assn. of Bar of City of N.Y. Antitrust, Securities, General civil litigation. Office: Sullivan & Cromwell 125 Broad St Fl 28 New York NY 10004-2489

**MEINDERS, HILDRED MCCANTS,** lawyer; b. Guthrie, Okla., Jan. 27, 1908; d. James Franklin and Maude Alberta (Putman) McCants; m. Wesley H.meinders,May 22, 1937 (dec.); children: Janet Ruth Charalampous, Don Wesley, Ann Hildred Heaton, Mary Joan Johnson. BS, U. Okla., 1932; JD, John B. Ogden Law Sch., Ardmore, Okla., 1941. Bar: Okla. 1942. Tchr. Carter County (Okla.) Schs., 1927-32; sec. County Agt./Carter County, 1932-36, U.S. Govt., 1936-60; pvt. law practice Garvin County, Okla., 1960—; county atty. Garvin County. Mem. AAUW, Order Eastern Star. Democrat. Methodist. Home: 405 N Chickasaw St Pauls Valley OK 73075-2405

**MEISELMAN, ALYSON,** lawyer, mediator/arbitrator; b. Washington, Jan. 24, 1951. BA, U. Md., 1973; JD, Potomac Sch. Law, Washington, 1979. Bar: U.S. Dist. Ct. Md. 1981, Md. 1981, U.S. Supreme Ct. 1993, U.S. Ct. Appeals (4th cir.) 1994. Pvt. practice Frederick, Md., 1981-84, Rockville, Md., 1986-87, 92—; assoc. Alan D. Massengill, PA, Gaithersburg, Md., 1984-86; prin. Haspel & Meiselman, Chartered, Rockville, 1987-92. Mem. ABA, ATLA, Assn. Family and Conciliation Cts., Md. Bar Assn., Bar Assn. Montgomery County, Nat. Lesbian and Gay Law Assn., Women's Bar Assn. Family and matrimonial, Alternative dispute resolution. Office: 14400 Lake Winds Way North Potomac MD 20878-4309

**MEISER, KENNETH EDWARD,** lawyer; b. Cin., Apr. 21, 1945; s. Edward M. and Margaret (Lowe) M.; m. Mirelynne Gisser, Sept. 2, 1979; children—Rebecca Anne, Michelle Jo. A.B. summa cum laude, Xavier U., 1967; J.D. cum laude, Harvard U., 1973. Bar: N.J. 1973, U.S. Dist. Ct. N.J. 1973, U.S. Ct. Appeals (3d cir.) 1974. Staff atty. Camden Regional Legal Services, N.J., 1973-74; asst. dep. pub. advocate N.J. Dept. Pub. Advocate, Trenton, 1974-80; dep. dir., Trenton, 1980-85; ptnr. Frizell, Pozycki & Meiser, Metuchen, N.J., 1985-92 sr. trial atty. Office of Thrift Supervision, 1992-94; of counsel Szaferman, Lakind, Blumstein, Watter & Blader, 1994-97; ptnr. Hill Wallack, 1997—; lectr. N.J. Inst. Continuing Legal Edn., Newark, 1979—; adj. prof. Rutgers Law Sch., 1992. Author: Tenant-Landlord Law in N.J., 1979, 85. Vol. VISTA, Camden, N.J., 1970-72; mem. mobile home adv. com. HUD, Washington, 1976-77. Mem. Accts. for Pub. Interest (bd. dirs. 1975-76), N.J. Bar Assn., N.J. Tenant Orgn. (bd. dirs. 1972-74, v.p. 1973-74, pres. Alliance for Affordable Housing 1986-91, bd. dirs. land use sect. 1994—, bd. dirs. mcpl. law sect. 1995-96), Alpha Sigma Nu. Roman Catholic. Home: 8 Frost Ave East Brunswick NJ 08816-4502 Office: Hill Wallach 202 Carnegie Ctr Princeton NJ 08540-6239

**MEISTER, ROBERT ALLEN,** lawyer; b. N.Y.C., July 17, 1936; s. Milton and Sheba M.; m. Margaret A. Lewiston Goodman, July 15, 1962 (div. Oct. 15, 1969); 1 child, Deborah A.; m. Jeanne C. Cioffi, June 15, 1986; 1 child, Danielle M. AB, N.Y.U., 1959; LLB, Columbia U., 1962. Bar: N.Y. 1963, U.S. Dist. Ct. (so. dist.) N.Y., U.S. Dist. Ct. (no. dist.) N.Y., U.S. Dist. Ct. (ea. dist.) N.Y., U.S. Dist. Ct. (we. dist.) N.Y., U.S. Ct. Appeals (2d, 3rd, 5th, 9th, 11th, D.C. and fed. cirs.), U.S. Ct. Claims, U.S. Supreme Ct. Assoc. Dewey, Ballantine, Bushby, Palmer & Wood, N.Y.C., 1962-72; mem. Varet & Fink, P.C., A/K/A/ Milgrim, Thomajan & Lee, P.C., N.Y.C., 1972-95; ptnr. Piper & Marbury, L.L.P., N.Y.C., 1995—; adj. prof. law Cardozo Sch. Law, N.Y.C., 1999—; arbitrator civil ct. City of N.Y., 1971—. Inspector Office of Equal Opportunity, Washington, 1966; coord. rules and credentials McCarthy for Pres., 1968; coord. Kennedy for Pres. com., N.Y.C., 1972. Joseph P. Chamberlain fellow Columbia U. Sch. Law, 1961-62. Mem. ABA, N.Y. State Bar Assn., Assn. of the Bar of the City of N.Y. (mem. fed. cts. com. 1970-73). Democrat. Avocations: classical music, skiing, tennis. General civil litigation, Securities, Intellectual property. Office: Piper & Marbury LLP 1251 Avenue Of The Americas New York NY 10020-1104

**MEKEEL, ROBERT K.,** lawyer; b. Ossining, N.Y., Mar. 21, 1950; s. Ira III and Carmen E. (Munson) M.; m. Martha J. Keller, Sept. 29, 1979; 1 child, Meryl Fox. BA, Wesleyan U., Middletown, Conn., 1972; JD, U. Puget Sound, 1978. Bar: N.H. 1978, N.Y. 1979, U.S. Dist. Ct. (so. dist.) N.Y. 1980, U.S. Ct. Appeals (2d cir.) 1981, U.S. Dist. Ct. N.H. 1983, U.S. Ct. Appeals (1st cir.) 1983. Asst. dist. atty. Westchester County N.Y. Dist. Atty., White Plains, N.Y., 1979-82; assoc. Craig Wenners & McDowell, Manchester, N.H., 1983-84; clk. ct. Coos County Superior Ct., Lancaster, N.H., 1985; ptnr. McKible & Mekeel, P.A., Concord, N.H., 1986-89, Cullity Kelley & McDowell, Manchester, 1989-93, McDowell & Mekeel P.A., Manchester, 1994-96; prin. Robert K. Mekeel, P.A., Concord, 1996—; mem. mentor program Franklin Pierce Law Sch., Concord, 1992; lectr. Nat. Bus. Inst., Eau Claire, Wis., 1993-95; mem. Million Dollar Advocates forum; mediator N.H. Superior Cts.; pvt. mediator, arbitrator disputes involving personal injury claims. Fellow N.H. Bar Found.; mem. ATLA (N.H. rep.), N.H. Trial Lawyers Assn. (amicus com. 1994-96), N.H. Bar Assn. (com. on cooperation with cts., lectr. evidence seminar 1994). Democrat. Avocations: running, biking, swimming, drawing, wood working. Product liability, Personal injury, Workers' compensation. Home: 73 Main St Hopkinton NH 03229-2628 Office: Century Bldg 185 N Main St Concord NH 03301-5039

**MEKEEL, STEVEN LEYON,** lawyer; b. Davenport, Iowa, Aug. 15, 1945; s. Herman Temple and Maxine Elizabeth (Hughett) M.; m. Susan J. Crume, June 22, 1967 (div. Sept. 1981); children: Kristin L., David S.; m. Diane L. Mathieus, June 15, 1982. BA, Knox Coll., Galesburg, Ill., 1967; JD, Washington U., St. Louis, 1970; postgrad., Johnson Mgmt. Inst., Racine, Wis., 1981. Bar: Wis., Ind. Atty. Barnes, Hickam, Pantzer & Boyd, Indpls., 1970-72; with S.C. Johnson & Son, Inc., Racine, 1972—, now corp. counsel; bd. dirs. Racine Comml. Airport Corp., 1996—; officer, bd. dirs. numerous subs. of S.C. Johnson & Son, Inc., 1972—. Mem. bd. editors Washington U. Law Rev., 1967-70,. Bd.dirs., chmn. Racine Redevel. Authority, 1976-80; bd. dirs., officer Racine Montessori Sch., Coop. Nursery Sch., Ch. of the Covenant, Racine Area Soccer Assn., others. Mem. ABA, Wis. Bar Assn., Racine County Bar Assn., Friar's Honor Frat. of Knox Cl., Order of Coif. Avocations: reading, cooking, boating, gardening. Home: 4527 Bluebird Ln Racine WI 53406 Office: SC Johnson & Son Inc 1525 Howe St Racine WI 53403-2237

**MELAMED, ARTHUR DOUGLAS,** lawyer; b. Mpls., Dec. 3, 1945; s. Arthur Charles and Helen Beatrix (Rosenberg) M.; m. Carol Drescher Weisman, May 26, 1983; children: Kathryn Henrie, Elizabeth Allyn. B.A., Yale U., 1967; J.D., Harvard U., 1970. Bar: D.C. 1970, U.S. Ct. Internat. Trade 1985, U.S. Ct. Appeals (9th cir.) 1971, U.S. Ct. Appeals (2d cir.) 1975, U.S. Ct. Appeals (D.C. cir.) 1978, U.S. Ct. Appeals (8th cir.) 1981, U.S. Ct. Appeals (fed. cir.) 1985, U.S. Ct. Appeals (4th cir.) 1989, U.S. Ct. Appeals (10th cir.) 1993, U.S. Supreme Ct. 1981. Law clk. U.S. Ct. Appeals for 9th Circuit, 1970-71; assoc. Wilmer, Cutler & Pickering, Washington, 1971-77, ptnr., 1978-96; prin. dep. asst. atty. gen. antitrust divsn. U.S. Dept. Justice, 1996—; vis. prof. Georgetown U. Law Ctr., 1992-93, adj. prof., 1993-94. Contbr. articles to profl. jours. Class agt. Alumni Fund Yale U.; D.C. area chair Yale campaign, 1993—; mem. social scis. coun. com. Yale U., 1989-94; trustee Nat. Child Rsch. Ctr., 1990-93. Mem. ABA, D.C. Bar Assn., Am. Law Inst., Yale Club (N.Y.C.), Kenwood Country Club. Antitrust, Federal civil litigation. Office: 950 Pennsylvania Rm 3208 Washington DC 20037-1435

**MELAMED, RICHARD,** lawyer; b. Houston, Dec. 22, 1952; s. Gerald Sylvan and Elaine (Rubenstein) M.; m. Ann Roosth, Sept. 17, 1978; children: Faith Elizabeth, Tina Cecile, Tanya Grace. BA, U. Tex., 1975; JD, S. Tex. U., 1978. Bar: Tex. 1978, U.S. Dist. Ct. (so. dist.) Tex. 1979, U.S. Ct. Claims 1981, U.S. Tax Ct. 1981, U.S. Ct. customs and Patent Appeals 1981, U.S. Ct. Appeals (5th cir.) 1981, U.S. Supreme Ct. 1981. Assoc. Evans & Birnberg, Houston, 1978-80; counsel Stewart Title Co., Houston, 1980-83; sole practice Houston, 1984-85; ptnr. Jacobus & Melamed, Houston, 1986-97; pvt. practice Houston, 1997—; assoc. prof. Houston Community Coll., continuing edn. U. Houston. Mem. ATLA, ABA, Fed. Bar Assn., State Bar Tex. (broker-lawyer joint com.). E-mail: melamed@swbell.net. Real property, Contracts commercial, Banking. Home: 5109 Mimosa Dr Bellaire TX 77401-4937 Office: 2500 Tanglewilde St Ste 267 Houston TX 77063-2124

**MELANCON, SYBIL O.,** legal secretary; b. Dierks, Ark., Mar. 2, 1942; d. Harmon and Dessie (Shelton) McAnelly; m. Paul Edward Melancon, Dec. 6, 1964 (dec. 1986); children: Leslie, Jamie. Legal sec. Bryone Goodson, De Queen, Ark., 1960-71; abstractor De Queen Abstract Office, 1971-83; legal sec. Henry C. Morris & William Hodge, De Queen, 1983-94, Jim Bob Steel, Nashville, Ark., 1995—. Mem. Dem. Women Sevier County. Mem. Assembly of God Ch. Avocations: gardening, shopping. Home: PO Box 91 De Queen AR 71832-0091

**MELANÇON, TUCKER LEE,** judge; b. 1946. BS, La. State U., 1968; JD, Tulane U., 1973. Atty. Knoll & Knoll, 1973-75; pvt. practice Marksville, La., 1975-83; prin. Melancon & Rabalais, Marksville, 1984-94; judge U.S. Dist. Ct. (we. dist.) La., Lafayette, 1994—; Mem. adv. bd. Catalyst Old River Hydroelectric Partnership, Vidalia, La., 1989-92, La. Workers Compensation, 1990-91; mem. com. Study Backlog in Cts. of Appeal, 1st and 3d Cirs., 1991; bd. dirs. Catalyst Vidalia Corp., N.Y.C., 1993-94. Mem. Am. Judicature Soc., Am. Inns of Ct., La. State Bar Assn., Bar Assn. 5th Fed. Cir. Office: US Dist Ct 705 Jefferson St Ste 303 Lafayette LA 70501-6936

**MELBARDIS, WOLFGANG ALEXANDER,** lawyer; b. Bayreuth, Ger., June 21, 1946. BA, Hartwick Coll., 1968; JD, St. John's U., 1971; MBA, L.I. U., 1977. Bar: N.Y. 1972, U.S. Dist. Ct. (ea., no. and so. dists.) N.Y. 1979, U.S. Ct. Mil. Appeals 1972, U.S. Supreme Ct. 1977. Asst. prof. law U.S. Mil. Acad., 1974-77; asst. atty. gen. Appeals and Opinions Bur. State of N.Y., Albany 1977-79; ptnr. Gramer & Melbardis, Coram, N.Y., 1979-96; served as arbitrator of personal injury cases for Am. Arbitration Assn., 1991-94. Author: Legal Rights When Hospital Appointment Denied, The Suffolk County Med. Soc. Bull., vol. 61, 1983. Capt. U.S. Army, 1972-77. N.Y. State Regents scholar, 1964. Mem. ABA, Am. Arbitration Assn., N.Y. State Bar Assn., Suffolk County Bar Assn., Hartwick Coll. Alumni Assn. (bd. dirs.). State civil litigation, Estate planning, Personal injury. Office: 2780 Middle Country Rd Lake Grove NY 11755-2124 also: 194 Main St Setauket NY 11733-2945

**MELDMAN, CLIFFORD KAY,** lawyer; b. Milw., July 27, 1931; s. Edward H. and Rose (Bortin) M.; children: Mindy, David, Linda, James, Noah. JD, Marquette U., 1956. Bar: Wis. 1956. Ptnr. Meldman & Meldman, Milw., 1956-73; pres. Meldman & Meldman S.C., Milw., 1973-98; pvt. practice Milw., 1956—. Contbr. articles to profl. jours., also editor. Fellow Am. Acad. Matrimonial Lawyers (pres. 1982); mem. Milw. Bar Assn. (bd. dirs. 1984-86, pres. 1986-87, chmn. family law sect.), Wis. Bar Assn. (chmn. family law sect.). Family and matrimonial. Home: 170 W Cherokee Cir Milwaukee WI 53217-2716 Office: PO Box 17397 Milwaukee WI 53217-0397

**MELDMAN, ROBERT EDWARD,** lawyer; b. Milw., Aug. 5; s. Louis Leo and Lillian (Gollusch) M.; m. Sandra Jane Setlick, July 24, 1960; children—Saree Beth, Richard Samuel. B.S., U. Wis., 1959; LL.B., Marquette U., 1962; LL.M. in Taxation, NYU, 1963. Bar: Wis. 1962, fla. 1987, colo. 1990, U.S. Ct. Fed. Claims, U.S. Tax Ct. 1963, U.S. Supreme Ct. 1970. Practice tax law Milw., 1963—; pres. Meldman, Case & Weine, Ltd., Milw., 1975-85; dir. tax div. Mulcahy & Wherry, S.C., Milw., 1985-90; shareholder Reinhart, Boerner, Van Deuren, Norris & Rieselbach, S.C., 1991—; adj. prof. taxation U. Wis., Milw., 1970—, mem. tax adv. coun., 1978—; sec. Profl. Inst. Tax Study, Inc., 1978—; bd. dirs. Wis. Bar Found., 1988-94; exec. in residence Deloitte & Touche Ctr. for Multistate Taxation, U. Wis., Milw., 1996—. Co-author: Federal Taxation Practice and Procedure, 1983, 86, 88, 92, 98, Practical Tactics for Dealing with the IRS, 1994, A Practical Guide to U.S. Taxation of International Transactions, 1996, 97, Federal Taxation Practice and Procedure Study Guide/Quizzes, 1998, A Quizzer Study Guide for Federal Taxation Practice and Procedure, 1998; editor Jour. Property Taxation; mem. editorial bd. Tax Litigation Alert, 1995—; contbr. articles to legal jours. Recipient Adj. Taxation Faculty award UWM Tax Assn., 1987; named Outstanding Tax Profl. 1992 Corp. Reports Wis. Mag. and UWM Tax Assn. Fellow Am. Coll. Tax Coun.; mem. ABA, Fed. Bar Assn. (pres. Milw. chpt. 1966-67), Milw. Bar Assn. (chmn. tax sect. 1970-71), Wis. Bar Assn. (bd. dirs. tax sect. 1964-78, chmn. 1973-74), Internat. Bar Assn., The Law Assn. for Asia and the Pacific (dep. chair tax sect. 1999—), Marquette U. Law Alumni Assn. (bd. dirs. 1972-77), Milw. Athletic Club, Wis. Club, Country Club of Wis., B'nai B'rith (trustee, Ralph Harris Meml. award Century Lodge 1969-70), Phi Delta Phi, Tau Epsilon Rho (chancellor Milw. chpt. 1969-71, supreme nat. chancellor 1975-76, v.p. Wis. chpt., tech. 1992—). Jewish (trustee congregation 1972-77). Corporate taxation, Private international, Personal income taxation. Home: 7455 N Skyline Ln Milwaukee WI 53217-3327 Office: 1000 N Water St Ste 2100 Milwaukee WI 53202-3197

**MELI, SALVATORE ANDREW,** lawyer; b. N.Y.C., Sept. 18, 1947; s. Andrew and Marie (Ruggiero) M.; m. Barbara Ann Chiesa, Aug. 16, 1970. BA, St. John's U., Jamaica, N.Y., 1969, JD, 1975. Bar: N.Y. 1976, Fla. 1976, U.S. Dist. Ct. (ea. and so. dist.) N.Y. 1976. Sole practice Flushing, N.Y., 1976-78; ptnr. Muratori & Meli, Flushing and Lake Worth, Fla., 1978-97; sole practice Flushing and Lake Worth, Fla., 1997—; lectr. Lawyers in the Classroom program, N.Y.C., 1977-81; mem. adv. bd. Title Ins. Co., Queens, N.Y., 1985—. Recipient Regents Scholarship, N.Y. State Bd. Regents, 1965. Mem. ABA, N.Y. State Bar Assn., Fla. Bar Assn., Queens County Bar Assn. Real property, Probate.

**MELILLO, JOSEPH MICHAEL,** lawyer; b. N.Y.C., Aug. 31, 1951; s. Joseph Michael Sr. and Yvonne (Marguerite) M.; m. Kandace Foust, Oct. 15, 1977; children: Daniel, Amy. BA, SUNY, Stony Brook, 1973; JD, SUNY, Buffalo, 1977. Bar: Pa. 1977. Law clk. to Hon. Ann Mikol Supreme Ct. N.Y., Buffalo, 1977; law clk. to William Magavern Erie County Atty., Buffalo, 1976-77; law clk. to Hon. Gene Creany Edensburg, Pa., 1978-80; assoc. Angino & Rovner, Harrisburg, Pa., 1980—. Contbr. articles to profl. jours. Bd. trustees Unitarian Ch., Harrisburg, 1984-86, pres., 1997-99. Mem. Am. Assn. Trial Lawyers, Pa. Trial Lawyers (amicus com.), Torch Club (pres. 1996-97), Forest Hills Assn. Neighbors (pres. 1996-98), Million Dollar Advs. Forum. Avocations: chess, computer. Personal injury, Product liability. Office: Angino & Rovner PC 4503 N Front St Harrisburg PA 17110-1799

**MELIN, ROBERT ARTHUR,** lawyer; b. Milw., Sept. 13, 1940; s. Arthur John and Frances Magdalena (Lanser) M.; m. Mary Magdalen Melin, July 8, 1967; children: Arthur Walden, Robert Dismas, Nicholas O'Brien, Madalyn Mary. B.A. summa cum laude, Marquette U., 1962, J.D., 1967. Bar: Wis. 1966, U.S. Dist. Ct. (ea. dist.) Wis. 1966, U.S. Ct. Appeals (7th cir.) 1966, U.S. Ct. Mil. Appeals 1967, U.S. Supreme Ct. 1975. Law clk. U.S. Dist. Ct. Eastern Dist. Wis., 1966; instr. bus. law U. Ga., Hinesville, 1968, also lectr. bus. law U. Md., Asmara, 1970; lectr. law Haile Selassie I U. Law Faculty, Addis Ababa, Ethiopia, 1971-72; mem. firm Walther & Halling, Milw., 1973-74, Schroeder, Gedlen, Riester & Moerke, Milw., 1974-82; ptnr. Schroeder, Gedlen, Riester & Melin, Milw., 1982-84, Schroeder, Riester, Melin & Smith, 1984—; rep. Class of 2000, West Point Parent Assn. of Wis., 1996-97, 97-98, 99—. Lectr. charitable solicitations and contracts Philanthropy Monthly 9th Ann. Policy Conf., N.Y.C., 1985. Chmn. Milw. Young Democrats, 1963-64; Class of 2000 rep. West Point Parent Assn. of Wis., 1996-98, 98—, exec. bd., 1997-98, 98—. Served to capt. JAGC, AUS, 1967-70. Mem. Wis. Acad. Trial Lawyers, ABA, Wis. Bar Assn., Milw. Bar Assn., Am. Legion, Friends of Ethiopia, Delta Theta Phi, Phi Alpha Theta, Pi Gamma Mu. Roman Catholic. Author: Evidence in Ethiopia, 1972; contbg. author to Annual Survey of African Law, 1974; contbr. numerous articles to legal jours. State civil litigation, Federal civil litigation, Non-profit and tax-exempt organizations. Home: 8108 N Whitney Rd Milwaukee WI 53217-2752 Office: 135 W Wells St Milwaukee WI 53203-1807 *Notable cases include: Anderson vs. Continental Ins. Co. 85 Wis. 2d 675, 271 NW 2d 368, 1978, new tort cause of action for insurer's bad-faith refusal to honor claim of 1st party insured; Allstate Ins. Co. vs. Met. Sewerage Commn. 80 wis. 2d 10, 258 N.W. 2d 148, 1977, broad application of remaining vestiges of mcpl. immunity doctrine in Wis. applied in favor of mcpl. client; Met. Sewerage Commn. vs. R.W. Constrn., Inc. 78 Wis 2d 451, 255 NW 2d 293, 1977, breach of sewer constrn. contract case.*

**MELLEN, FRANCIS JOSEPH, JR.,** lawyer; b. Williamsport, Pa., Dec. 19, 1945; s. Francis Joseph and Mary Emma (Oberst) M.; m. Mary Wilder Davison, Aug. 2, 1975 (div. 1987); children: Elizabeth, Catherine, Robert, Christine. BA, U. Ky., 1967, MA, 1971; JD, Harvard U., 1973. Bar: N.Y. 1974, Ky. 1975, U.S. Dist. Ct. (so. dist.) N.Y. 1974, U.S. Dist. Ct. (ea. dist.) Ky. 1977, U.S. Dist. Ct. (we. dist.) Ky. 1978, U.S. Ct. Appeals (2d cir.) 1975, U.S. Ct. Appeals (6th cir.) 1982. Assoc. atty. Rogers & Wells, N.Y.C., 1973-75, Wyatt, Grafton & Sloss, Louisville, 1975-80; ptnr. Wyatt, Tarrant & Combs, Louisville, 1980—. Co-author: Kentucky Mineral Law, 1986, Kentucky Forms and Transactions, 1991. Contbr. articles to profl. jours. Mem. spl. study com. for Uniform Commercial Code, Ky. Legis. Rsch. Comsn., Frankfort, 1984-91; bd. dirs. Leadership Louisville Found., counsel, 1996-98; bd. dirs. Stage One: The Louisville Children's Theatre, v.p., 1997-98, pres., 1998—; bd. dirs. Louisville-Jefferson County A.W.A.R.E. Coalition, 1994-98. Mem. ABA, Am. Arbitration Assn. (panel), Ky. Bar Assn. (ho. dels. 1986-92), Louisville Bar Assn. (chmn. com. profl. responsibility 1992-94), Jefferson Club, Filson Club, Am. Mensa. Republican. General corporate, Mergers and acquisitions. Home: 429 Trinity Hills Ln Louisville KY 40207-2132 Office: Wyatt Tarrant & Combs 2800 Citizens Plz Louisville KY 40202

**MELLER, ROBERT LOUIS, JR.,** lawyer; b. Mpls., Apr. 24, 1950; s. Robert Louis and June Louise (Grenacher) M. B.A., Carleton Coll., 1972; J.D., Cornell U., 1975. Atty., Best & Flanagan, Mpls., 1977—, ptnr., 1982—. Bar: Minn., 1975, U.S. Dist. Ct. (no dist.) 1975. Mem. ABA, Minn. State Bar Assn., Phi Beta Kappa, Sigma Xi. Republican. Episcopan Club: Mpls. Federal civil litigation, State civil litigation. Home: 1800 Major Dr N Minneapolis MN 55422-4153 Office: Best and Flanagan 4000 US Bank Pl 601 2nd Ave S # D Minneapolis MN 55402-4303

**MELLEY, STEVEN MICHAEL,** lawyer; b. Rhinebeck, N.Y., Jan. 3, 1950; s. James Christopher and Virginia (Madonna) M.; children: Aliza, Jonathan, Olivia, Bennett; m. Phoebe Kirkwood. BA in Russian Studies with honors, Colgate U., 1972; JD, Tulane U., 1975. Bar: N.Y. 1976, U.S. Dist. Ct. 1976, U.S. Supreme Ct. 1980. Law clk. to hon. Matthew Braniff Criminal Dist. Judge, Orleans Parish, New Orleans; assoc. Woody N. Klose Law Offices, Red Hook, N.Y., 1975-78; ptnr. Klose & Melley, Rhinebeck, 1978-83; pvt. practice Rhinebeck, 1983—; atty. Village of Tivoli, N.Y., 1977-78. Assoc. editor Tulane Forum, 1974-75. Mem. ABA, ATLA (sustaining), N.Y. State Bar Assn. (former mem. com. on specialization, Dutchess County Bar Assn. (sustaining mem.), N.Y. State Trial Lawyers Assn., Million Dollar Advocates Forum, Phi Alpha Delta, Kappa Delta Rho. Fax: (914) 876-5745. E-mail: maizefield@aol.com. Fax: 914-876-5745. Personal injury. Office: 22 E Market St Rhinebeck NY 12572-1646

**MELLINGER, ROBERT LOUIS,** lawyer; b. McKeesport, Pa., June 25, 1956; s. Robert Louis and Ines Dina (Agostini) M.; m. Doris Ann Padron, Nov. 17, 1984. BA, Washington & Jefferson Coll., 1978; JD, Southwestern U., Los Angeles, 1981. Bar: Calif. 1983, U.S. Dist. Ct. (cen. dist.) Calif. 1983, U.S. Ct. Appeals (9th cir.) 1983, Pa. 1986, U.S. Dist. Ct. (we. dist.) Pa. 1986, U.S. Ct. Appeals (3d cir.) 1986, U.S. Supreme Ct. 1987, Fla. 1989, U.S. Dist. Ct. (so. dist.) Fla. 1989, U.S. Ct. Appeals (11th cir.) 1989. Assoc. E.L. Sanabria & Assocs., Los Angeles, 1981-83, PL Lago, Law Corp., Downey, Calif., 1984-86, Cauley, Conflenti & Latella, Pitts., 1986-88; ptnr. Aguilera & Mellinger, Coral Gables, Fla., 1989—, Routman, Mellinger & Aguilera-Rodriguez, Miami, Fla., 1993—. Editor-in-chief law sch. newspaper The Commentator, Southwestern U., 1979-81 (#1 award ABA, Assoc. Collegiate Press); writer legal newspaper Metropolitan News, Los Angeles, 1980. Vol. law clk. East Los Angeles Immigration Clinic, 1980, Mental Health Advocacy Service, Los Angeles, 1980; charter mem. Olympic Alumni Orgn., Los Angeles, 1984. Named one of Outstanding Young Men Am. U.S. Jaycees, 1980. Mem. ABA, Internat. Bar Assn., Am. Arbitration Assn. (panel mem.), Pa. Trial Lawyers Assn., Pa. Bar Assn., Calif. Bar Assn., Orange County Bar Assn., Allegheny County Bar Assn., Los Angeles Bar Assn., Assn. Trial Lawyers Am., Italian Am. Lawyers Assn., Fla. Bar Assn., The Acad. Fla. Trial Lawyers, Amateur Athletic Union, Phi Alpha Delta (merit cert. 1981). Lodge: Order Sons of Italy in Am. Avocation: writing. Personal injury, General civil litigation, General practice. Office: Aguilera & Mellinger 815 Ponce De Leon Blvd Ste 200 Coral Gables FL 33134-3007 also: Routman Mellinger & Aquilera-Rodriguez 700 NE 90th St Miami FL 33138-3206

**MELLON, THOMAS S.,** lawyer; b. Phila., Nov. 18, 1956. BA, Ohio Wesleyan U., 1978; JD cum laude, Vt. Law Sch., 1989. Bar: Pa. 1989, N.J. 1991, U.S. Dist. Ct. N.J., U.S. Dist. Ct. Pa. (ea. and mid. dists.), U.S. Ct. Appeals (3d Cir.). Atty. DeSantis DeSantis & Essig, Reading, Pa., 1989-90, Krusen Evans and Byrne, Phila., 1990-94, Murphy & O'Connor, Phila., 1994-99; alumni dir. William Penn Charter Sch.; Donna Adelsberger & Assocs., Glenside, Pa., 1999—. Avocations: golf, squash, racketball, softball. General civil litigation, Insurance, Personal injury. Office: Murphy & O'Connor PO Box 530 115 E Glenside Ave Ste 14 Glenside PA 19038-4618 also: 1 Greentree Ctr Ste 201 Marlton NJ 08053-3105

**MELLOY, MICHAEL J.,** federal judge; b. 1948; m. Jane Anne Melloy; children: Jennifer, Katherine, Bridget. BA, Loras Coll., 1970; JD, U. Iowa, 1974. With O'Conner & Thomas P.C. (formerly O'Conner, Thomas, Wright, Hammer, Bertsch & Norby, Dubuque, Iowa, 1974-86; judge U.S. Bankruptcy Ct. (no. dist.) Iowa, 1986-92; chief judge U.S. Dist. Ct. (no. dist.) Iowa, Cedar Rapids, 1992—. With U.S. Army, 1970-72, USAR, 1972-76. Mem. ABA, Comml. Law League Am., Nat. Conf. Bankruptcy Judges, Eighth Cir. Judicial Coun. (bankruptcy judge rep., bankruptcy com.), Iowa State Bar Assn. (coun. mem. bankruptcy and comml. law sect.), Ill. State Bar Assn., Dubuque County Bar Assn., Linn County Bar Assn., Mason L. Ladd

Inn of Ct., Rotary. Office: US Dist Ct 101 1st St SE Ste 304 Cedar Rapids IA 52401-1202

**MELLUM, GALE ROBERT,** lawyer; b. Duluth, Minn., July 5, 1942; s. Lester Andrew and Doris Esther (Smith) M.; m. Julie Murdoch Swanstrom, July 23, 1966; children: Eric Scott, Wendy Jane. BA summa cum laude, U. Minn., 1964, JD magna cum laude, 1968. Bar: Minn. 1968. Assoc. Faegre & Benson, Mpls., 1968-75, ptnr., 1976—, mem. mgmt. com., 1986-98; planning com. Garret Corp. and Securities Law Inst., Northwestern U. Law Sch., 1984—; adv. bd. Quali Tech Inc., Chaska, Minn., 1985-98, bd. dirs.; bd. dirs. The Tesseract Group, Inc., Mpls.; corp. sec. Excelsior-Henderson Motorcycle Mfg. Co., Belle Plaine, Minn., 1997—. Hockey chmn. LARC Bd., Mpls., 1980-85. Mem. ABA (fed. securities regulation com.), Minn. Bar Assn., Hennepin County Bar Assn. (securities regulation com.). Republican. Lutheran. Avocations: tennis, golf, snow and water skiing, handball, boating. General corporate, Mergers and acquisitions, Securities. Home: 4889 E Lake Harriet Pky Minneapolis MN 55409-2222 Office: Faegre & Benson 2200 Norwest Ctr 90 S 7th St Ste 2200 Minneapolis MN 55402-3901

**MELNICK, ROBERT RUSSELL,** lawyer; b. Youngstown, Ohio, May 15, 1956; s. Arseny Anthony and Gladys Marie (Peppel) M.; m. Diana May Baum, May 5, 1984; children: Joshua Robert, Joel Russell, Isaac James, Melissa Marie. BA in Polit. Philosophy magna cum laude, Hiram Coll., 1978; JD, Ohio No. U., 1981. Bar: Ohio 1983, U.S. Dist. Ct. (no. dist.) Ohio 1984, U.s. Ct. Appeals (6th cir.) 1986, U.S. Ct. Appeals (3d cir.) 1998, U.S. Supreme Ct. 1991, U.S. Army Ct. Mil. Appeals 1993. Legal intern atty. gen.'s office State of Ohio, Columbus, 1979-80, Creation-Sci. Legal Def. Fund, San Diego, 1982-83; ptnr. Melnick & Melnick, Youngstown, 1983—; asst. pros. atty. Mahoning County, Sebring, Ohio, 1986-88. Host weekly radio show, 1988-89; contbr. articles to Ohio No. U. Law Rev., 1981, Internat. Conf. Creationism, 1986, 90; contbr. articles to profl. jours. Mem. ministry outreach to teenagers, Youngstown, 1984-86; trustee Cre-Sci. Fellowship, Pitts., 1986—; pres. Rutherford Inst. Ohio, 1986—; mem. adv. bd. on home edn. State of Ohio Dept. Edn., 1988-89. Capt. JAG Corps, USAR, 1990—. Partial voice scholar Hiram Coll., 1977-78, Arthur Benedict award in polit. sci., 1978. Mem. Ohio Bar Assn., Mahoning County Bar Assn. (legis. coms., med./legal and public rels.), Phi Beta Kappa. Avocations: reading, skiing, singing at churches and public events. Constitutional, General civil litigation, Insurance. Home: 9711 W Calla Rd Salem OH 44460-9631 Office: 18 N Phelps St Ste 300 Youngstown OH 44503-1132

**MELNICOFF, JOEL NIESEN,** lawyer, sports agent; b. Syracuse, N.Y., Mar. 30, 1939; s. Morris Gerson and Anne (Weiner) M.; m. Judith Ellen Lebwohl, July 6, 1969; children: Marlena Carol, Matthew Ryan. BA in Polit. Sci., Syracuse U., 1961, LLB (now JD), 1964. Bar: N.Y., 1965. Assoc. Eric S. Rose, Atty., Syracuse, 1965-66; sole practitioner Syracuse, 1966—; spkr. on collection law to trade law, 1985—. Exec. vice chmn., then chmn. N.Y. State Conservative Party, Onandaga County, Syracuse, 1975-76. Staff sgt. U.S. Army and USAR, 1964-70. Mem. Nat. Assn. Retail Collection Attys. (v.p. 1996, candidate for nat. treas. 1997), Comml. Law League of Am. Republican. Jewish. Avocations: sports, spectator sports, travel. Consumer commercial, Personal injury, Real property. Home: 4756 Edgeworth Dr Manlius NY 13104-2106 Office: 622 University Bldg Syracuse NY 13202

**MELNIK, SELINDA A.,** lawyer; b. Ft. Worth, Aug. 22, 1951; d. Mitchell Mandel Melnik and Sylvia (Hoffman) Goldberg. BA, Temple U., 1972; M of City and Regional Planning, Rutgers U., 1974; JD summa cum laude, N.Y. Law Sch., 1984. Bar: N.Y. 1985, U.S. Dist. Ct. (so. and ea. dists.) N.Y. 1985, U.S. Ct. Appeals (D.C. cir.) 1993, Ct. Internat. Trade 1993. Program assoc. to John D. Rockefeller III, 1974-78; cons. to various orgns. U.S., internat., 1975—; sr. policy analyst Planned Parenthood, 1978-79; dir. Ms. and Free to Be Founds., 1979-81; assoc. Milbank, Tweed, Hadley & McCloy, N.Y.C., 1984-87, LeBoeuf, Lamb, Leiby, MacRae, N.Y.C., 1987-90; ptnr. Dechert, Price & Rhoads, N.Y.C., 1991-93; internat. counsel Rogers & Wells, N.Y.C., 1993-96; pres. Internat. Counsel, NYC, 1996—; founder, 1st pres. Internat. Women's Insolvency and Restructring Confederation, cons. internat. law, trade Cross Border Insolvency and Bankruptcy Prevention Planning, 1987—; cons. fgn. govts. internat. trade and insolvency law; writer, lectr. internat. trade and insolvency law. Mem. ABA, Internat. Bar Assn. (chair membership, chair com. on creditor's rights & insolvency, rep. to UN Commn. on Status of Women), Internat. Lawyers Club, N.Y. State Bar Assn., Internat. Women's Insolvency and Restructuring Confedn. (chair), Order of Coif. Bankruptcy, Contracts commercial, Private international. Office: International Counsel 1349 Lexington Ave New York NY 10128-1511

**MELONI, KATHRYN ANN,** lawyer; b. Wilmington, Del., July 22, 1965; d. Art and Sylvia Marie (Serafini) M. BS, West Chester U., 1987; JD, Widener U., 1990. Bar: Pa. 1990, N.J. 1990. Jud. law clk. Phila. Ct. Common Pleas, 1990-91; assoc. Michael A. Paul and Assocs., Media, Pa., 1991-96; pvt. practice law Media, 1996—; adj. prof. Villanova (Pa.) U., 1996—. Judge of elections Chadds Ford Twp., 1998—. Mem. Pa. Bar Assn., Delaware County Bar Assn. (Nicholas Vadino award). Family and matrimonial, Personal injury, Workers' compensation. Home: 1615 Painters Xing Chadds Ford PA 19317-9659 Office: 2 S Orange St Ste 205 Media PA 19063-2619

**MELOWSKI, DENNIS MICHAEL,** lawyer; b. Ft. Lauderdale, Fla., Nov. 13, 1968; s. Richard L. and Shirley W. M.; m. Margaret A., July 13, 1996. BA in Polit. Sci., U. Denver, 1990; JD, Marquette U., 1993. Bar: Wis. 1993, U.S. Dist. Ct. (ea. dist.) Wis. 1993. Atty. Barry S. Cohen Law Offices, Elkhart Lake, Wis., 1995—. Mem. NAt. Assn. Criminal Defense Lawyers (life, legis. com.). Roman Catholic. Criminal. Office: Barry S Cohen Law Offices N9661 Willow Rd Elkhart Lake WI 53020-1640

**MELTON, BARRY,** lawyer, musician; b. N.Y.C., June 14, 1947; s. James Gerald and Terry Melton; m. Barbara Joy Langer; children: Kingsley, Kyle. Bar: Calif. 1982, U.S. Dist. Ct. (no. dist.) Calif. 1982, U.S. Dist. Ct. (cen. dist.) Calif. 1983, U.S. Ct. Appeals (9th cir.) 1983, U.S. Dist. Ct. (ea. dist.) Calif. 1985, U.S. Supreme Ct. 1988. Pvt. practice law San Francisco, 1982-94; chief asst. pub. defender Yolo County, Woodland, CA; musician, pub. Seafood Music, San Francisco, 1965—; pro-tem judge San Francisco Mcpl. Ct., 1987-94. Musician, composer various phonograph records, 1965—. Mem. State Bar Calif. (cert. criminal law specialist 1993—, vol. legal svc. awards 1983-87), San Francisco Bar Assn. (vol. legal svc. award 1985), Calif. Attys. Criminal Justice, Calif. Pub. Defenders Assn. (bd. dirs. 1999). Criminal, Juvenile. Office: Yolo County Pub Defender 814 North St Woodland CA 95695-3538

**MELTON, HOWELL WEBSTER, SR.,** federal judge; b. Atlanta, Dec. 15, 1923; s. Holmes and Alma (Combee) M.; m. Margaret Catherine Wolfe, Mar. 4, 1950; children—Howell Webster, Carol Anne. JD, U. Fla., 1948. Bar: Fla. 1948. With Upchurch, Melton & Upchurch, St. Augustine, 1948-61; judge 7th Jud. Circuit of Fla., St. Augustine, 1961-77; judge U.S. Dist. Ct. (mid. dist.) Fla., Jacksonville, 1977-91, sr. judge, 1991—; past chmn. Fla. Conf. Cir. Judges, 1974; past chmn. coun. bar pres.'s Fla. Bar. Trustee Flagler Coll., St. Augustine. Served with U.S. Army, 1943-46. Recipient Disting. Service award St. Augustine Jaycees, 1953. Mem. ABA, St. Johns County Bar Assn., Jacksonville Bar Assn., Fed. Bar Assn., Fla. Blue Key, Ponce de Leon Country Club, Marsh Creek Country Club, St. Augustine Fla. Officers Club, Masons, Phi Delta Theta, Phi Delta Phi. Methodist. Office: US Dist Ct PO Box 52957 Jacksonville FL 32201-2957

**MELTON, MICHAEL ERIC,** lawyer, engineer; b. Dallas, Sept. 14, 1958. BSEE, U. Mo., 1981, JD, 1984. Bar: Mo. 1984, Tex. 1992, U.S. Dist Ct. (ea. dist.) Mo. 1984, U.S. Ct. Appeals (fed. and 8th cirs.) 1984, U.S. Dist. Ct. (no. dist.) Tex. 1991, U.S. Patent and Trademark Office 1986. Patent advisor Office of Naval Rsch. U.S. Dept. Navy, Washington, 1984-86; assoc. Haverstock, Garrett and Roberts, St. Louis, 1986-87, Spensley, Horn, Jubas and Lubitz, Washington, 1987-88; license counsel Tex. Instruments, Inc., Dallas, 1988-92; European counsel Tex. Instruments, Inc., Nice, France, 1993-95; corp. sec. Texas Instruments Info. Engring. Internat., Inc., 1993-96; corp. patent counsel mgr. legis. affairs intellectual property, 1995-96; assoc. tech. counsel, chief patent counsel MCI Comms. Corp., Washington, 1996-99; ptnr. Hickman Stephens and Coleman, Washington, 1999—; mem. U.S. Naval Rsch. Lab., EEOC, 1985-86; lectr. continuing legal edn. Mound City Bar Assn., St. Louis, 1986-87. Editl. assoc. Insight into Cts. newsletter, 1989-92, Jour. Cts., Health Sci. and the Law, 1989-92. Statewide officer Mo. Young Dems., 1986-87; vol. lectr. Mo. and Tex. Pub. Sch. Dists., 1986-96, others; bd. govs. Dallas Symphony Assn., 1991-94, mem. mktg. com., 1992, cmty. affairs com., 1992. Fellow Dallas Bar Found.; mem. ABA, Am. Intellectual Property Lawyers Assn. (vice chmn. minority issues com. 1997-98, vice-chair licensing com. 1998—), Nat. Bar Assn., J.L. Turner Legal Assn. (v.p. 1991, bd. dirs. 1992, co-chair polit. action com. 1996), Dallas Bar Assn., Fed. Bar Assn., Nat. Soc. Black Engrs. (Region V adv. bd. 1991-92), Am. Inn of Ct., Coll. State Bar of Tex. Roman Catholic. Legislative, Mergers and acquisitions, Patent. Home: PO Box 320 Dunn Loring VA 22027

**MELTZ, JONATHAN SCOTT,** defender; b. Boston, June 30, 1969; s. Howard and Ellen Meltz. BS in Comm., U. Miami, 1991; JD, CUNY, Flushing, 1996. Bar: Fla. 1996. Legal intern The Legal Aid Soc., Queens, N.Y., summer 1994; cert. legal intern The Legal Aid Soc., Queens, 1995-96; law clk. Fed. Defenders San Diego, summer 1995; asst. pub. defender Law Offices Bennett Brummer, Miami, Fla., 1996—. Mem. Fla. Assn. Criminal Def. Lawyers, Fla. Bar Assn. (consumer protection law com.), Dade County Bar Assn. (criminal ct. com.). Office: Law Offices Bennett Brummer 1320 NW 14th St Miami FL 33125-1609

**MELTZER, BERNARD DAVID,** law educator; b. Phila., Nov. 21, 1914; s. Julius and Rose (Welkov) M.; m. Jean Sulzberger, Jan. 17, 1947; children: Joan, Daniel, Susan. A.B., U. Chgo., 1935, J.D., 1937; LL.M., Harvard U., 1938. Bar: Ill. 1938. Atty., spl. asst. to chmn. SEC, 1938-40; assoc. firm Mayer, Meyer, Austrian & Platt, Chgo., 1940; spl. asst. to asst. sec. state, also acting chief fgn. funds control div. div. State 1941-43; asst. trial counsel U.S. stafff Internat. Nuremberg War Trials, 1945-46; from professorial lectr. to disting. svc. prof. law emeritus U. Chgo. Law Sch., 1946—; counsel Vedder, Price, Kaufman & Kamnholz, Chgo., 1954-55, Sidley and Austin, Chgo., 1987-89; hearing commr. NPA, 1952-53; labor arbitrator; spl. master U.S. Ct. Appeals for D.C., 1963-64; bd. publs. U. Chgo., 1965-67, chmn., 1967-68; mem. Gov. Ill. Adv. Commn. Labor-Mgmt. Policy for Pub. Employees in Ill., 1966-67, Ill. Civil Service Commn., 1968-69; cons. U.S. Dept. Labor, 1969-70. Author: Supplementary Materials on International Organizations, 1948, (with W.G. Katz) Cases and Materials on Business Corporations, 1949, Labor Law Cases, Materials and Problems, 1970, supplement, 1972, 75, 2d edit., 1977, supplements, 1980, 82 (with S. Henderson), 3d edit. (with S. Henderson), 1985, supplement, 1988; also articles. Bd. dirs. Hyde Park Community Conf., 1954-56, S.E. Chgo. Commn., 1956-57. Served to lt. (j.g.) USNR, 1943-46. Mem. ABA (co-chmn. com. devel. law under NLRA 1959-60, mem. spl. com. transp. strikes), Ill. Bar Assn., Chgo. Bar Assn. (bd. mgrs. 1972-73), Am. Law Inst., Coll. Labor and Employment Lawyers, Am. Acad. Arts and Scis., Order of Coif, Phi Beta Kappa. Home: 1219 E 50th St Chicago IL 60615-2908 Office: U Chgo Law Sch 1111 E 60th St Chicago IL 60637-2776

**MELTZER, JAY H.,** lawyer, retail company executive; b. Bklyn., Mar. 30, 1944; s. Solomon G. and Ethel L. (Kraft) M.; m. Bonnie R. Rosenberg, June 27, 1965; children: Wendy, Elizabeth, Jonathan. A.B., Dartmouth Coll., 1964; JD, Harvard U., 1967. Bar: N.Y. 1968, Mass. 1978, U.S. Dist. Ct. Mass. 1979. Law clk. to U.S. dist. judge, 1967-68; assoc. firm Shearman & Sterling, N.Y.C., 1968-72; with Damon Corp., Needham Heights, Mass., 1972-84; gen. counsel, sec. Damon Corp., 1973-84, v.p., 1979-84; v.p., corp. counsel The TJX Cos., Inc., Framingham, Mass., 1984-87, v.p., gen. counsel, sec., 1987-89, sr. v.p., gen. counsel, sec., 1989—. Dir. coun. Better Bus. Bur., 1990-93. Mem. ABA, Am. Soc. Corp. Secs., Am. Corp. Counsel Assn. (bd. dirs. N.E. chpt.), Retailers Assn. Mass. (bd. dirs., exec. com., sec.), New Eng. Corp. Counsel Assn. (bd. dirs.). Contracts commercial, General corporate, Securities. Office: TJX Cos Inc 770 Cochituate Rd Framingham MA 01701-4672

**MELTZER, ROBERT CRAIG,** lawyer, educator; b. Chgo., July 31, 1958; s. Franklyn Richard and Zelma (Cohen) M. BA, U. Colo., 1980; cert., Inst. de Internat., Strasbourg, France, 1984; JD, No. Ill. U., DeKalb, 1985; postgrad., U. Salzburg, Austria, 1985. Bar: Ill. 1985, U.S. Dist. Ct. (no. dist.) Ill. 1985, U.S. Ct. Appeals (7th cir.) 1988, U.S. Supreme Ct. 1989. Law clk. Hurwitz & Abramson, Washington, 1980, Mayer, Brown & Platt, Chgo., 1983; lawyer UN WHO, Geneva, Switzerland, 1985, Robert C. Meltzer & Assocs., Chgo., 1985-91, Katz, Randall & Weinberg, Chgo., 1991-93, Arnstein & Lehr, Chgo., 1993-98, Grotefeld & Denenberg, Chgo., 1998—. Contbr. articles to profl. jours.; editor The Globe, Springfield, Ill., 1984—. Pro bono lawyer Fed. Bar Assn., Chgo., 1985—. Recipient Medal of Appreciation, Ministry of Justice, Beijing, 1996. Mem. Ill. State Bar Assn. (internat. and immigration law sect. 1985—, pres. internat. law sect. 1990-91, Editor's award 1989, 94), Am. Immigration Law Assn. Avocations: history, racquet sports, golf, arts, music. Private international, Immigration, naturalization, and customs. Home: 1250 N Lasalle St Chicago IL 60610-1949 Office: Grotefeld & Denenberg 100 W Monroe St Ste 1800 Chicago IL 60603-1907

**MELVILLE, CHARLES HARTLEY,** lawyer, educator; b. Cin., Jan. 18, 1937; s. John W. and Jane (Akin) M.; m. Linda Smith Melville, Aug. 29, 1959; children: Jeffrey W., Frances C., Thomas A. AB, Princeton U., 1959; JD, U. Cin., 1962; postgrad., Harvard U., 1981-82. Bar: Ohio 1962. Assoc. Melville, Strasser, Foster & Hoffman, Cin., 1962-72; gen. counsel Senco Products, Cin., 1972-75, v.p. mktg., 1975-80, sr. v.p., gen. mgr. internat. divsn., 1980-85; pres., COO Pryde, Inc., Cin., 1986-89; chmn., CEO Advanced Data & Title Sys., Cin., 1989-92; of counsel Strauss & Troy, Cin., 1992—; bd. dirs. Terronics Devel. Corp., Elwood, Ind. Author: (with others) Legal Environment of Business, 1994, 2d edit., 1997; contbr. articles to profl. jours. Mem. Cin. Bar Assn., Cincinnatus Assn. (pres. 1974-75). Republican. Presbyterian. Intellectual property, General civil litigation, Contracts commercial. Office: Strauss & Troy The Fed Reserve Bldg 150 E 4th St Cincinnati OH 45202-4018

**MEMEL, SHERWIN LEONARD,** lawyer; b. Buffalo, Mar. 28, 1930; s. Maurice and Nellie (Munshen) M.; m. Iris C. Gittleman, Aug. 17, 1952; children: Jana Sue, Steven Keith, David Scott, Mara Jean. BA, UCLA, 1951, JD with honors, 1954. Bar: Calif. 1955, U.S. Ct. Appeals (9th cir.) 1955, U.S. Dist. Ct. (cen. dist.) Calif. 1959, U.S. Supreme Ct. 1963, D.C. 1979. Ptnr., chmn. health law dept. Manatt, Phelps & Phillips, LA, 1987—; chmn. bd. Pac. Pub. Radio Sta. KLON; past instr. health law USC Sch. Pub. Adminstrn.; past instr. health UCLA; cons. and lectr. in field. Co-author: (with R. Barak) Real Estate Issues in the Health Care Industry, 1996; contbr. articles to profl. jours. Chmn. LA Arts Council, 1986-87; vice-chmn. Dem. Bus. Council, Washington, 1985-86; past pres. Calif. Bd. Med. Quality Assurance. Recipient Disting. Service award Fedn. Am. Hosps., 1970. Mem. ABA (com. health law), Am. Hosp. Assn. (life, Award of Honor 1971), Am. Soc. Law and Medicine, Am. Health Lawyers Assn., Calif. Soc. for Healthcare Attys. (life, pres. 1983), Calif. Bar Assn., D.C. Bar Assn., L.A. County Bar Assn. Health, Legislative, Administrative and regulatory. Office: Manatt Phelps & Phillips 11355 W Olympic Blvd Los Angeles CA 90064-1614

**MENACK, STEVEN BOYD,** lawyer, mediator; b. Phoenix, Ariz., Nov. 13, 1959; s. Max Joseph and Clara (Fischer) M.; m. Stefanie Menack; 1 child, Daniel Alexander. BA in Psychology, U. Ariz., 1982; MPA, Harvard U., 1984; JD, Columbia U., 1987; postgrad., Seton Hall U., 1991-92. Bar: N.J. 1987, U.S. Dist. Ct. N.J. 1987, N.Y. 1988, U.S. Dist. Ct. (so. dist.) N.Y. 1989, U.S. Dist. Ct. (ea. dist.) N.Y. 1989. Assoc. Phillips, Nizer, Benjamin, Krim & Ballon, N.Y.C., 1987-90, Herrick, Feinstein, N.Y.C., 1990-91; atty., mediator Porzio, Bromberg & Newman, P.C., Morristown, N.J., 1991-93; pres., CEO A Better Solution-Quality Mediation and Arbitration Svcs., locations throughout U.S., 1993—; CEO Law Offices of Steven Boyd Menack, Esquire, N.Y.C., Mountain Lakes, N.J., 1993—; intern to Gov. Bruce Babbit, Tucson, Ariz., 1979-82, Senator Dennis DeConcini, U.S. Senate, Washington, 1980, 1983; fair housing tech. cons. Town of Arlington, Mass., 1984; divorce mediator Inst. Dispute Resolution Seton Hall U., Montclair, N.J., 1991-92; civil comml. mediator N.J. Superior Ct. Morris County, Morristown, N.J., 1992; contract and comml. mediator, gen. equity chancery mediator N.J. Superior Ct. Bergen County, Hackensack, N.J., 1992—; mediator and arbitrator Am. Arbitration Assn., 1993—, panelist Panel of Arbitrators, 1993—; arbitration cons.; lectr., spkr. in field. Contbr. articles to profl. jours. Precinct comitteeman Pima County, Ariz., Tucson, 1981. Mem. ABA (cert. civil litigation, alternative dispute resolution com. family law sect., divorce laws and procedural com., pretrial practice and discovery com.), N.J. Bar Assn. (dispute resoltion com., mediation subcom.), N.J. Assn. Profl. Mediators (founder and cert. divorce mediator, 1991, pres. elect 1992-93, cert. bus. and commercial mediator 1992, cert. advanced divorce and bus. mediator 1992, statewide pres. 1993-94), Nat. Assn. of Profl. Mediators (founder, pres. 1997). Avocations: travel. Family and matrimonial, Contracts commercial, Alternative dispute resolution. Address: 280 Park Ave S Ste 8M New York NY 10010-6129

**MENAKER, FRANK H., JR.,** lawyer; b. Harrisburg, Pa., Aug. 23, 1940; s. Frank H. and Romaine (Sadler) M.; m. Sharon Ann Lynch, Feb. 21, 1981; children: Denise L., Jamie E.; children by previous marriage: David C., Michelle R. BA, Wilkes Coll., 1962; JD, Am. U., 1965. Bar: D.C. 1966, Md. 1975, U.S. Supreme Ct. 1975. Formerly staff counsel Office Gen. Counsel, GAO, Washington; v.p., gen. counsel Martin Marietta Corp., 1981-95; v.p., gen. counsel Lockheed Martin, 1995-96, sr. v.p., gen. counsel, 1996—; spl. counsel U.S. Commn. on Govt. Procurement, 1971. Mem. ABA (mem. sect. pub. contract law, chair-elect), Md. Bar Assn., Wash. Met. Corp. Counsel Assn. (bd. dirs. 1988—). General corporate, Government contracts and claims, Mergers and acquisitions. Office: Lockheed Martin 6801 Rockledge Dr Bethesda MD 20817-1836*

**MENCER, GLENN EVERELL,** federal judge; b. Smethport, Pa., May 18, 1925; s. Glenn Hezekiah and Ruth Leona (Rice) M.; m. Hannah Jane Freyer, June 24, 1950; children—Ruth Ann, Cora Jane, Glenn John. B.B.A., U. Mich., 1949, J.D., 1952. Bar: Pa. 1953, U.S. Dist. Ct. (we. dist.) Pa. 1953, U.S. Supreme Ct. 1958. Sole practice Eldred, Pa., 1953-64; dist. atty. McKean County, Pa., 1956-64; judge 48th Jud. Dist. Ct., Smethport, 1964-70, Commonwealth Ct. of Pa., Harrisburg, 1970-82, U.S. Dist. Ct., Erie, Pa., 1982—. Served with U.S. Army, 1943-45, ETO. Mem. Fed. Judges Assn., Pa. Bar Assn., McKean County Bar Assn. Republican. Methodist. Lodge: Masons (33 degree). Home: 30 W Willow St Smethport PA 16749-1524 Office: US Dist Ct Fed Courthouse PO Box 1820 Erie PA 16507-0820

**MENCHETTI, DAVID BARRY,** lawyer; b. Chgo., Dec. 13, 1959; s. Leo and Diane M.; m. Lorraine C. Dorff, June 2, 1984; children, Cecilia, Quinn. BA, Stanford U., 1981; JD, Loyola U., Chgo., 1984. Bar: Ill. 1984. Staff atty. Ill. State Senate, Sprinfield, 1984-86; ptnr. Cullen, Haskins, Nicholson & Manchetti P.C., Chgo., 1986—. Author: (notebook) Penalties in Workers' Compensation Illinois Trial Lawyers WC Notebook, 1990—. Mem. Ill. State Bar Assn. (chair workers compensation com. 1996-97), Chgo. Bar Assn. (chair workers' compensation com., 1993-94), Workers Compensation Lawyers Assn. (pres. Chgo. 1999). Democrat. Roman Catholic. Workers' compensation. Office: Cullen Haskins Nicholson & Menchetti 35 E Wacker Dr Ste 1760 Chicago IL 60601-2271

**MENDEL, DAVID PHILLIP,** lawyer; b. Columbus, Ohio, June 11, 1956; s. Leon Earl and Barbara (Kollus) K.; m. Frances Elissa Hess, May 25, 1980 (div. Nov. 1996); children: Jeremy Isaac, Hilary Myra, Risa Brianne. BSc in Orgnl. Comm. cum laude, Ohio U., 1979; JD, Capital U., 1982. Bar: Ohio 1982, U.S. Dist. Ct. (so. dist.) Ohio 1984. From law clk. to assoc. Leon E. Mendel Co., LPA, Columbus, Ohio, 1980-86; ptnr. Mendel & Weiss, Columbus, 1986-90; sole practice law Columbus, 1990—. Treas. Maccabee Lodge B'nai B'rith, Athens, Ohio, Columbus, 1985; publicity com. Reynoldsburg (Ohio) Sch. Levy Campaign, 1986; bd. dirs. Jewish Nat. Fund, Columbus, 1995—. Mem. ATLA, Columbus Bar Assn., Ohio State Bar Assn., Franklin County Trial Lawyers Assn., Mensa, Delta Theta Phi. Democrat. Avocations: singing, acting, sailing, skiing. DavidMendel@aol.com. Personal injury, Alternative dispute resolution, Entertainment. Office: 118 E Main St Columbus OH 43215-5208

**MENDELSOHN, ALLAN IRVING,** lawyer; b. Chgo., May 15, 1932; s. Herman Martin and Rosamond (Kanter) M.; m. Rona Hirsch, Oct. 16, 1964; children: Herman Martin, Bruce Robert, Aaron Hirsch. BS, U. Ill., 1954, LLB, 1955; LLM, Harvard U., 1956; diplome, Sorbonne, France, 1962. Bar: Ill. 1955, U.S. Supreme Ct. 1961, D.C. 1966. Atty. office of gen. counsel NLRB, Washington, 1959-62; atty. office of legal advisor U.S. Dept. State, Washington, 1963-68; ptnr. Glassie, Pewett, Beebe & Shanks, Washington, 1968-80, Ward & Mendelsohn, P.C., Washington, 1980-90, Mendelsohn & Szymkowicz, Washington, 1990—; cons. UN, Washington, 1971-72, com. pub. works U.S. Senate, Washington, 1971-77, U.S. Dept. Interior, Washington, 1972-74; adj. prof. law ctr. Georgetown U., Washington, 1980—. Bd. editors Jour. Maritime Law & Commerce, 1969-97, Jour. Air Law & Commerce, 1984—; contbr. articles to profl. jours. With JAGC, U.S. Army, 1956-59. Recipient Goldenes Ehrenzeichen award Govt. of Austria, 1985. Mem. ABA (chmn. subcom. on pvt. internat. transp. law), D.C. Bar Assn., Walter Reed Soc. Democrat. Jewish. Avocations: skiing, bicycling, parenting. Aviation, Private international, General civil litigation. Home: 3310 Cathedral Ave NW Washington DC 20008-3411 Office: Mendelsohn & Szymkowicz 1233 20th St NW Fl 8 Washington DC 20036-2304

**MENDELSOHN, MARTIN,** lawyer; b. Bklyn., Sept. 6, 1942; s. Hyman and Gertrude M.; m. Syma Barbara Rossman, Aug. 15, 1964; children: Alice S., James D. BA, Bklyn. Coll., 1963; LLB, George Washington U., 1966. Bar: D.C. 1967, U.S. Ct. Appeals (D.C. cir.) 1967, U.S. Ct. Appeals (3d cir.) 1971, U.S. Ct. Appeals (7th cir.) 1973, Ill. 1973 U.S. Ct. Appeals (9th cir.) 1987, U.S. Tax Ct. 1988, U.S. Ct. Appeals (2d cir.) 1988, U.S. Supreme Ct. 1970. With Gen. Counsel's Office, HEW, Washington, 1966-67; legal svcs., Washington, 1967-70, Pa., 1971-72, Ill., 1973-75; counsel Legal Svcs. Corp., Washington, 1976; adminstrv. asst. U.S. Congress, Washington, 1977; chief spl. litigation U.S. Dept. Justice, Washington, 1977-79, dep. dir. office spl. investigations, 1979-80; counsel House Judiciary Com., 1980; pvt. practice law, Washington, 1980-88; ptnr. Dilworth, Paxon, Kalish & Kauffman, 1989-91, Verner, Liipfert, Bernhard, McPherson and Hand, 1991—. Author: (with Aaron Freiwald) The Last Nazi, 1994. Mem. ABA, D.C. Bar Assn. Jewish. Private international, Public international, Legislative. Home: 5705 Mckinley St Bethesda MD 20817-3638 Office: 901 15th St NW Ste 700 Washington DC 20005-2327

**MENDELSON, ALAN CONRAD,** lawyer; b. Chgo., Jan. 26, 1942; s. Richard and Viola Henryetta (Nelson) M.; m. Lisa Victoria Sigg, Aug. 13, 1983; children: Edward Alan, Carl Richard, Paul Douglas. BA, U. Ill., 1963, JD, 1966. Bar: Ill. 1966, U.S. Dist. Ct (no. dist.) Ill., U.S. Dist. Ct. (no. dist.) Ind. Assoc. Law Office of Edward R. Vrdolyak, Chgo., 1966-77; pvt. practice Chgo., 1978—. Mem. ABA, Ill. Bar Assn., Chgo. Bar Assn., Assn. Trial Lawyers Am., Ill. Trial Lawyers Assn. Personal injury, Federal civil litigation, State civil litigation. Office: 77 W Washington St Ste 1019 Chicago IL 60602-2805

**MENDELSON, STEVEN EARLE,** lawyer; b. Los Angeles, Mar. 24, 1948; s. Robert Alexander and Nell Earle (Jacobs) M.; children: Carolyn, Laurel. BA, U. Calif., Santa Cruz, 1971; JD, Golden Gate U., 1975. Bar: Calif. 1975, U.S. Dist. Ct. (no. dist.) Calif. 1975. Assoc. Law Offices Robert A. Mendelson, Los Angeles, 1975-76, Law Offices Paul A. Eisler, San Francisco, 1976-77; sole practice Oakland, Calif., 1977-84; ptnr. Mendelson & Mendelson, Oakland, 1985—. Founding sponsor Civil Justice Found., 1986. Mem. Assn. Trial Lawyers Am., Calif. Trial Lawyers Assn. (speaker), Alameda Contra Costa Trial Lawyers Assn., Calif. Applicant Atty's Assn., Am. Back Soc. (workshop dir., speaker, bd. dirs. com. on programs and interprofl. relations, incorporator, legal counsel 1981—). Personal injury, General civil litigation. Office: Mendelson & Mendelson 120 11th St Oakland CA 94607-4806

**MENDELSON, VICTOR HOWARD,** lawyer; b. N.Y.C., Dec. 11, 1967; s. Laurans Adam and Arlene Hope Mendelson; m. Lisa Michelle Mendelson, Apr. 12, 1968; children: Lindsey Sue, Nicole Erin. AB, Columbia U., 1989; JD, U. Miami, 1992. Bar: Fla. 1992. Assoc. gen. counsel Heico Corp., Hollywood, Fla., 1992-93; exec. v.p., chief ops. officer Meditek Health Corp., Miami, Fla., 1994-96; pres. Heico Aviation Products Corp., Miami, Fla., 1996—; v.p., gen. counsel Heico Corp., Hollywood, Fla., 1993—, also bd. dirs. Trustee St. Thomas U., Miami, 1997—; mem. fin. com. Fla. Grand Opera, Miami, 1995—. Avocations: travel, swimming, art collecting. Contracts commercial, Securities, General corporate. Office: Heico Corp Ste 1644 825 Brickell Bay St Miami FL 33131

**MENDENHALL, HARRY BARTON,** lawyer; b. Oct. 31, 1946. BA, Colo. Coll., 1968; JD, U. Colo., 1971. Bar: Colo. 1971. Ptnr. Mendenhall & Malouff, R.L.L.P., Rocky Ford, Colo., 1971—; mem. nominating com. Colo. Supreme Ct., Denver, 1986-91; pres. Colo. Lawyer Trust Account Found., Denver, 1995-97. Mem. Colo. Bar Assn. (pres. 1999—). E-mail: bmendenhall@rmi.net. Real property, Estate planning, Probate. Office: Mendenhall & Malouff 805 Chestnut Ave Rocky Ford CO 81067-1224

**MENDOZA, JOANNA R.,** lawyer; b. Sacramento, Dec. 23, 1963; d. Roy J. Delk and Beth-Marie Shilkett; m. Joseph A. Mendoza, Aug. 15, 1992; children: Joseph, Joshua. BA, U. Calif. San Diego, La Jolla, 1987; JD, U. Calif. San Diego, Berkeley, 1990. Bar: Calif. 1990, U.S. Dist. Ct. (no. and ea. dists.) Calif. 1990, U.S. Ct. Appeals (9th cir.) 1990. Atty. Carroll Burdick & McDonough, Sacramento, 1990-96, Graham & James LLP, Sacramento, 1996—; officer, bd. dirs. Floors Factory Outlet Inc., Rocklin, Calif., 1992—; mem. tech. transfer com. Access Capitol, Sacramento, 1998. Mem. ABA, Sacramento County Bar Assn. (bd. dirs. 1998—, program chair intellectual property sect. 1998—), Davis Area Tech. Assn. Intellectual property, General civil litigation, Product liability. Office: Graham & James LLP 400 Capitol Mall Ste 2400 Sacramento CA 95814-4421

**MENEFEE, SAMUEL PYEATT,** lawyer, anthropologist; b. Denver, June 8, 1950; s. George Hardiman and Martha Elizabeth (Pyeatt) M. BA in Anthropology and Scholar of Ho. summa cum laude, Yale U., 1972; diploma in Social Anthropology, Oxford (Eng.) U., 1973, BLitt, 1975; JD, Harvard U., 1981; LLM in Oceans, U. Va., 1982, SJD, 1993; MPhil in Internat. Rels., U. Cambridge, Eng., 1995. Bar: Ga. 1981, U.S. Ct. Appeals (11th cir.) 1982, Va. 1983, La. 1983, U.S. Ct. Mil. Appeals 1983, U.S. Ct. Internat. Trade 1983, U.S. Ct. Claims 1983, U.S. Ct. Appeals (10th cir.) 1983, U.S. Ct. Appeals (fed., 1st, 3d, 4th, 5th, 6th, 7th, 8th and 9th cirs.) 1984, D.C. 1985, Nebr. 1985, Fla. 1985, U.S. Supreme Ct. 1985, U.S. Ct. Appeals (D.C. cir.) 1986, Maine 1986, Pa. 1986. Assoc. Phelps, Dunbar, Marks, Claverie & Sims, New Orleans, 1983-85; of counsel Barham & Churchill PC, New Orleans, 1985-88; sr. assoc. Ctr. for Nat. Security Law U. Va. Sch. Law, 1985—, fellow Ctr. for Oceans Law and Policy, 1982-83, sr. fellow, 1985-89, Maury fellow, 1989—, adv. bd., 1997—; vis. lectr. U. Cape Town, 1987; vis. asst. prof. U. Mo.-Kansas City, 1990; law clk. Hon. Pasco M. Bowman, U.S. Ct. Appeals (8th cir.), 1994-95; vis. prof. Regent U., 1996-97, scholar-at-large, 1997—, prof., 1998—; adv. The Am. Maritime Forum/The Mariners' Mus., 1997-98; lectr. various nat. and internat. orgns.; mem. ICC Consultative Task Force on Comml. Crime, 1996—. Author: Wives for Sale: An Ethnographic Study of British Popular Divorce, 1981, Contemporary Piracy and International Law, 1995, Trends in Maritime Violence, 1996; co-editor: Materials on Ocean Law, 1982; contbr. numerous articles to profl. jours. recipient Katharine Briggs prize Folklore Soc., 1992; Bates traveling fellow Yale U., 1971, Rhodes scholar, 1972; Cosmos fellow Sch. Scottish Studies U. Edinburgh, 1991-92, IMB fellow, ICC Internat. Maritime Bur., 1991—, Piracy Reporting Ctr. fellow, Kuala Lampur, 1993—, Huntington fellow The Mariners Mus., 1997. Fellow Royal Anthrop. Inst., Am. Anthrop. Assn., Royal Asiatic Soc., Royal Soc. Antiquaries of Ireland, Soc. Antiquaries (Scotland), Royal Geog. Soc., Soc. Antiquaries; mem. ABA (vice-chmn. marine resources com. 1987-90, chmn. law of the sea com. subcom. naval warfare, maritime terrorism and piracy 1989—, mem. law of the sea com. steering com. 1996—, mem. working group on terrorism), Southeastern Admiralty Law Inst. (com. mem.), Maritime Law Assn. (proctor, com. mem., chmn. subcom. law of the sea 1988-91, vice chmn. com. internat. law of the sea 1991— , chair working group piracy 1992—, UNESCO study group, 1998—), Marine Tech. Soc. (co-chmn. marine security com. 1991—), Selden Soc., Am. Soc. Internat. Law, Internat. Law Assn. (com. mem., rapporteur Am. br. com. EEZ 1988-90, rapporteur Am. br. com. Maritime Neutrality 1992, observer UN conv. on Law of the Sea meeting of States Parties 1996, chmn. Am. br. com. on Law of the Sea 1996—), rapporteur joint internat. working group on uniformity of the law of piracy 1998—, (Com. Maritime Internat.), Am. Soc. Indsl. Security (com. mem.), U.S. Naval Inst., USN League, Folklore Soc., Royal Celtic Soc., Internat. Studies Assn., Royal Scottish Geog. Soc., Royal African Soc., Egypt Exploration Soc., Arctic Inst. N.Am., Internat. Studies Assn., Am. Hist. Soc., Internat. Assn. Rsch. on Peasant Diaries (nat. editor 1996—), Nat. Eagle Scout Assn., Raven Soc., Jefferson Soc., Fence Club, Mory's Assn., Elizabethan Club, Yale Polit. Union, Leander Club, Cambridge Union, United Oxford and Cambridge Univ. Club, Yale Club (N.Y.C.), Paul Morphy Chess Club, Pendennis Club, Round Table Club (New Orleans), Phi Beta Kappa, Omicron Delta Kappa. Republican. Episcopalian. Avocations: anthropology, archaeology, social history, crew, hill walking. Office: U Va Ctr Nat Sec Law 580 Massie Rd Charlottesville VA 22903-1738

**MENENDEZ, MANUEL, JR.,** judge; b. Tampa, Fla., Aug. 2, 1947; s. Manuel and Clara (Marin) M.; m. Linda Lee Stewart, Aug. 31, 1969; children: Jennifer Kay, Christine Marie. AA, U. Fla., 1967, BA, 1969, JD with Honors, 1972. Bar: Fla. 1972, U.S. Dist. Ct. (mid. dist.) Fla. 1973, U.S. Ct. Appeals (5th cir.) 1973, U.S. Ct. Claims 1974, U.S. Tax Ct. 1974, U.S. Ct. Customs and Patent Appeals 1974, U.S. Supreme Ct. 1976, U.S. Ct. Appeals (11th cir.) 1983, U.S. Ct. Appeals (D.C. cir.) 1984. Asst. U.S. atty. Dept. Justice, Jacksonville, Fla., 1973-77; chief asst. U.S. atty. Dept. Justice, Tampa, 1978-83; assoc. Law Office Jack Culp, Jacksonville, 1977-78; ptnr. Culp & Menendez, P.A., Jacksonville, 1978; county judge jud. br. State of Fla., Tampa, 1983-84, cir. judge jud. br., 1984—; dept. head, faculty mem. Fla. Coll. of Advanced Jud. Studies; faculty mem. pre-bench program Fla. New Judges Coll., 1993; faculty mem. Fla. Bar Prosecutor-Pub. Defender Advocacy Tng. Program, 1989-91, 94—; mentor judge coord. 13th Cir. Ct., 1995—; co-chair edn. steering com. Fla. Cir. Judge's Conf., 1996. Exec. editor U. Fla. Law Rev., 1971-72. Mem. adv. bd. Salvation Army, 1988-91. Recipient Pub. Service Meritorious Achievement award West Tampa Civic Clubs Assn., 1983. Mem. ABA, Fla. Bar Assn. (mem. criminal procedure rules com. 1988-94, chmn. 1991-92, chmn. rules and jud. adminstrn. com. 1995-96), Fed. Bar Assn. (v.p. Jacksonville chpt. 1974-75, pres. Tampa Bay chpt. 1980-85), Hillsborough County Bar Assn. (media law com. 1984—, trial lawyers sect. 1985—, Liberty Bell award selection com. 1991-93, jud. evaluation com. 1993, Outstanding Jurist award 1998-99), Am. Judicature Soc., Am. Judges Assn., Am. Inns of Ct. (master of bench, pres. 1991—), U. Fla. Alumni Assn., U. Fla. Law Ctr. Assn., First U.S. Calvary Regiment Rough Riders Inc., Propellor Club, Tampa Gator Club. Avocations: fishing, golf, Univ. Fla. athletics, coaching little league sr. girls softball. Office: Hillsborough County Courthouse 419 N Pierce St Ste 375 Tampa FL 33602-4025

**MENGEL, CHRISTOPHER EMILE,** lawyer, educator; b. Holyoke, Mass., Sept. 11, 1952; s. Emile Oscar and Rose Ann (O'Donnell) M.; m. Ellen Christine Creager, Dec. 6, 1991; children: Meredith Anne, Celia Claire; stepchildren: Cara Elizabeth Creager, Kristen Michele Creager. Student, U. Notre Dame, 1970-71; BA, Holy Cross Coll., 1974; JD, Detroit Coll. Law, 1979. Bar: Mich. 1979, U.S. Dist. Ct. (ea. dist.) Mich. 1989, U.S. Ct. Appeals (6th cir.) 1990. Tchr. Holyoke Pub. Schs., 1974-76; assoc. Fried & Sniokaitis P.C., Detroit, 1980-82; prof. Detroit Coll. Law, 1982-85; pvt. practice Detroit, 1982-91; mng. ptnr. Berkley, Mengel & Vining, PC, 1992—. Mem. coun. St. Ambrose Parish, Grosse Pointe Park, Mich., 1985-88, pres. 1986-87. Matthew J. Ryan scholar, 1970; recipient Disting. Brief award Thomas M. Cooley Law Rev., 1996. Mem. ABA, Mich. Bar Assn., Detroit Bar Assn. Democrat. Roman Catholic. Avocations: baseball, sailing, photography. General practice, Appellate, State civil litigation. Home: 1281 N Oxford Rd Grosse Pointe MI 48236-1857 Office: Berkley Mengel & Vining PC 3100 Penobscot Bldg Detroit MI 48226

**MENGES, CHARLES L.,** lawyer; b. Newport News, Va., Dec. 16, 1950; s. Martin John and Margaret Post (Smith) M.; m. Penelope Ward Kyle, Oct. 10, 1981; children: Kyle Ward, Penelope Whitley, Patricia Lee. BA, Coll. William and Mary, 1974; JD, U. Va., 1977. Bar: Va. 1977. Assoc. McGuire, Woods & Battle, Richmond, Va., 1977-85; ptnr. McGuire, Woods, Battle & Boothe, Richmond, 1985—; gen. counsel RF&P Corp., Richmond, 1996-97. Pres. Jackson-Feild Homes, Jarratt, Va., 1997-99; allocations com. United Way, Richmond, 1983-90. Mem. ABA, Va. Bar Assn. (chmn. real estate sect. coun. 1993-95), Richmond Bar Assn., Country Club of Va., Commonwealth Club, Order of Coif. Episcopalian. Office: McGuire Woods Battle & Boothe 901 E Cary St Richmond VA 23219-4057

**MENGES, EUGENE CLIFFORD,** lawyer; b. East St. Louis, Ill., Feb. 3, 1952; s. Eugene Varley and Carol Lee (Kane) M.; m. Joan Carol Westrich, July 22, 1980; children: Carson Clifford, Sarah Elizabeth, Grant Tyler. BS in Econs., Boston Coll., 1974; JD, St. Louis U., 1977, MBA, 1979. Bar: Ill. 1977, U.S. dist. ct. (so. dist.) Ill. 1977, U.S. Ct. Appeals (7th cir.) 1981. Ptnr. Wagner, Bertrand, Bauman & Schmieder, 1977-86, Hinshaw, Culbertson, Moelman, Hoban & Fuller, 1986-92; pvt. practice, 1992—; assoc. prof. Belleville Area Coll., 1977-80; sec.-treas. Goehner & Eaves, Inc.; invited atty; appted. asst. pub. defender, St. Clair County, Ill., 1995. Mem. dist. com. Okaw Valley coun. Boy Scouts Am., 1981—. Fellow St. Louis U., 1975-76, 76-77. Mem. ABA, AIA, East St. Louis Bar Assn. (sec./treas.), St. Clair County Bar Assn. (chmn.), Ill. Bar Assn., Phi Delta Phi. Roman Catholic. Federal civil litigation, State civil litigation, Personal injury. Home: 105 Lamoine Ln Belleville IL 62223-1102 Office: 2027 W Main St Belleville IL 62226-7458

**MENGES, JOHN KENNETH, JR.,** lawyer; b. Louisville, Sept. 23, 1957; s. John Kenneth and Barbara Jean (Vick) M. BSBA, Boston U., 1979; JD, Harvard U., 1982. Bar: Tex. 1982. Assoc. Akin, Gump, Strauss, Hauer & Feld, Dallas, 1982-89, ptnr., 1989—. Pres. Dallas County Young Dems., 1985-88, Dallas Dem. Forum, 1990-91, bd. dirs., 1986-89; pres. sch. mgmt. Boston U., 1987—, bd. trustees, 1995—; bd. dirs. Friends of Fair Park; bd. trustees Boston U.; Dallas County chair North Tex. Clean Air Coalition. Mem. ABA, Tex. State Bar Assn., Dallas Bus. League (pres. 1989), Dallas Coun. on World Affairs, Dallas Assn. Young Lawyers, Harvard U. Law Sch. Assn. Tex. (bd. dirs. 1984-87, 90-91, pres. 1993), Boston U. Nat. Alumni Coun. (Young Alumni award 1987). Democrat. Methodist. Avocation: basketball. General corporate, Securities, Mergers and acquisitions. Office: Akin Gump Strauss Hauer & Feld 1700 Pacific Ave Ste 4100 Dallas TX 75201-4675

**MENGHINI, HENRY DAVE,** lawyer; b. St. Louis, Dec. 24, 1934; s. Costante and Oliva (Rauzi) M.; m. Nancy A. Scott, Sept. 8, 1958; children: Matthew, Karen, Michael, Mark. BA, Washington U., 1956, JD, 1959. Bar: Mo. 1959, U.S. Dist. Ct. (ea. dist.) Mo. 1959, U.S. Ct. Appeals (8th cir.). Assoc. Murray Steinberg Law Office, St. Louis, 1959; assoc. Evans & Dixon Attys. at Law, St. Louis, 1960-66, ptnr., 1967-96; ptnr. Husch & Eppenberger, Attys. and Counselors at Law, St. Louis, 1997—; bd. dirs. Mega Bank Holding Co., St. Louis. Capt. USAR, 1958-64. Recipient Lon O. Hocker Meml. Trial Lawyer award, 1967. Fellow Am. Coll. Trial Lawyers; mem. Mo. Athletic Club. Roman Catholic. Avocations: handball, racquetball, tennis, hunting, fishing. General civil litigation. Home: 9038 Whitehaven Dr Saint Louis MO 63123-2042 Office: Husch & Eppenberger 100 N Broadway Ste 1300 Saint Louis MO 63102-2789

**MENGLER, THOMAS M.,** dean; b. May 18, 1953. BA in Philosophy magna cum laude, Carleton Coll., 1975; MA in Philosophy, U. Tex., 1977, JD, 1981. Bar: Ill., Tex., D.C., U.S. Ct. Appeals (5th, 7th and 10th cirs.), U.S. Dist. Ct. (we. dist.) Tex. Law clk. to Hon. James K. Logan U.S. Ct. Appeals for 10thCir., Olathe, Kans., 1980-81; assoc. atty. Arnold & Porter, Washington, 1982-83; asst. atty. gen. Office of Atty. Gen. of Tex., Austin, 1983-85; asst. prof. law U. Ill. Coll. Law, Champaign, 1985-89, assoc. prof., 1989-91, prof. law, 1991—, assoc. dean for acad. affairs, 1992-93, dean, 1993—. Contbr. numerous articles to profl. jours. Mem. ABA, Ill. State Bar Assn., Order of Coif, Phi Beta Kappa. Office: U Ill Coll Law 202 Law Bldg 504 E Pennsylvania Ave Champaign IL 61820-6909*

**MENOYO, ERIC FELIX,** lawyer; b. N.Y.C., May 9, 1944; s. Enrique and Frances (Villela) M.; m. Deirdre Caitlin Ryan, Aug. 12, 1967; children: Eric Edward, Sarah Micela. AB in English, Georgetown U., 1966, JD, 1969; LLM in Taxation, NYU, 1975. Bar: N.Y. 1969, Mass. 1976, U.S. Dist. Ct. (ea. dist.) Mass. 1976, U.S. Ct. Appeals (1st cir.) 1976. Assoc. Barrett Smith Schapiro & Simon, N.Y.C., 1969-76; assoc. Palmer & Dodge, Boston, 1976-77, ptnr., 1978—; lectr. law Northeastern U., 1986-87, Mass. Continuing Legal Edn., Boston, 1978—. Trustee Nashoba-Brooks Sch. Concord (Mass.), Inc., 1984-90, 1st Parish Sudbury, 1979-82, Sudbury Valley Trustees, Inc., 1991—, pres., 1994-96; mem. Pool Adv. Coun., Sudbury, Mass., 1987-89. Fellow Am. Coll. Trust and Estate Counsel; mem. ABA, Boston Bar Assn., Am. Law Inst., Larchmont Yacht Club. Unitarian. Avocations: sailing, hiking. Probate, Private international, Estate taxation. Home: 388 Willis Rd Sudbury MA 01776-1332 Office: Palmer & Dodge LLP 1 Beacon St Boston MA 02108-3190

**MENSER, MARK CHRISTOPHER,** lawyer; b. Middletown, Conn., July 4, 1950; s. Lawrence Joseph and Mary Madelain Menser; m. Martha Elaine Walters, May 20, 1972; children: Joseph Patrick, James Lawrence. BA in Polit. Sci., Fla. Atlantic U., 1972; JD, Nova Southeastern U., 1977. Bar: Fla. 1977, U.S. Dist. Ct. (so. dist.) Fla. 1978, U.S. Dist. Ct. (mid. dist.) Fla. 1979, U.S. Dist. Ct. (no. dist.) Fla. 1986, U.S. Ct. Appeals (5th cir.) 1978, U.S. Ct. Appeals (11th cir.) 1981, U.S. Supreme Ct. 1983. Sole practitioner Ft. Lauderdale, Fla., 1978-81; asst. atty. gen. Fla. Atty. Gen. Office, Daytona Beach, 1981-84; sr. asst. atty. gen. Fla. Atty. Gen. Office, Tallahassee, 1984—. Coach, bd. dirs. Capital Soccer Assn., Tallahassee, 1985-94; pres., dist. chmn. Broward Young Reps., 1977. Mem. Assn. Govt. Attys. in Capital Litigation (bd. dirs. 1988, regional v.p. 1989), Tallahassee Chess Club (pres. 1997—). Lutheran. Avocations: chess, soccer coaching, photography. Office: Fla Atty Gen's Office PL-01 The Capitol Tallahassee FL 32311

**MENSON, RICHARD L.,** lawyer; b. Chgo., Nov. 10, 1943; s. John Lewis and Elizabeth Eileen (Carroll) M.; m. Lynne Patricia Lemke, Apr. 24, 1971; children: Melissa Lynne, Kristin Anne. BA, Ripon Coll., 1965; JD, Northwestern U., 1968; LLM in Taxation, George Washington U., 1973. Bar: Ill. 1968, U.S. Dist. Ct. (no. dist.) Ill. 1973, U.S. Ct. Mil. Appeals 1968, U.S. Ct. Claims 1973, U.S. Tax Ct. 1975. Commd. lt. U.S. Army, 1965, advanced through grades to capt., with JAG office, 1965-73, resigned, 1973; assoc. Gardner, Carton & Douglas, Chgo., 1973-77, ptnr., 1977-98; ptnr. McGuire, Woods, Battle & Boothe, LLP, Chgo., 1998—. Mem. bd. edn. Oak Grove Sch. Dist. #68, Libertyville, Ill., 1983-87; elder First Presbyn. Ch., Libertyville, 1979-83, mem. bd. deacons, 1975-79. Mem. ABA, Ill. State Bar Assn., Chgo. Bar Assn., Lake County Bar Assn., Legal Club Chgo., Conway Farms Golf Club, Army Navy Country Club, Profit Sharing Coun. Am. (legal and legis. com.), Internat. Pension and Employee Benefits Lawyer Assn. (steering com.). Presbyterian. Pension, profit-sharing, and employee benefits, Taxation, general. Home: 1000 Ashley Ln Libertyville IL 60048-3813 Office: McGuire Woods Battle & Boothe LLP 77 W Wacker Dr Ste 4500 Chicago IL 60601-1635

**MENTEL, MICHAEL CHRISTOPHER,** lawyer; b. Columbus, Ohio, Nov. 27, 1961; s. James Michael and Victoria K. (Haslett) M.; m. Marisa Ann Rotolo, Oct. 7, 1989; children: Angela, Connor. BA, Capital U., 1984, JD, 1987. Bar: Ohio 1988, U.S. Supreme Ct. 1992, U.S. Ct. Appeals (6th cir.) Ohio 1994, U.S. Dist. Ct. (so. and no. dists.) Ohio 1995. Intern U.S. Sen. John Glenn/Washington Workshops, Washington, summer 1980; account clk. Ohio Atty. Gen., Columbus, 1981-82; intern Columbus City Atty., 1983-84; legal intern Franklin County Pub. Defender, Columbus, 1987-88, staff atty., 1988-89; atty. Ohio EPA, Columbus, 1990-93, supr. atty., 1993-94; atty. Crabbe, Brown, Jones, Potts & Schmidt, 1994—; bd. dirs. Hilliard Edn. Found.; vice chair Franklin County Jud. Salute Com., 1997. Mem. Ohio Dems for 90's, 1990—; vol. Operation Feed Columbus, 1990. Mem. ABA, Ohio State Bar Assn., Columbus Bar Assn. (environ. law coms.), Ancient Order of Hibernians, Shamrock Club. Democrat. Roman Cathlic. Avocations: golf, Irish culture. Home: 3152 Rockfence Dr Columbus OH 43221-4726

**MENTER, MARTIN,** retired lawyer; b. Syracuse, N.Y., July 1, 1915; s. Benjamin and Sarah (Kasmovitch) M.; m. Irene Rothschild, Nov. 10, 1940; children: Toby M. Berger, Joshua Lewis Menter. AB, Syracuse U., 1937, JD, 1939; LLM, George Wash. U., 1949. Bar: N.Y. 1939, U.S. Supreme Ct. 1948, U.S. Dist. Ct. (we. dist.) N.Y. 1939, U.S. Ct. Appeals D.C. 1962, Supreme Ct. Japan 1953. Pvt. practice Rochester, N.Y., 1939-40, Washington, 1971-88; commd. 2d lt. U.S. Army, 1940-48; commd. 2d lt. USAF, 1948-70, advanced through grades to brig. gen., ret., 1970; writer, speaker, 1950—; atty., assoc. gen. counsel FAA, Washington, 1959-65; staff judge advocate USAF Far East Air Forces and UN Air Command, Tokyo, 1951-53, USAF Aerospace Def. Command and N.Am. Def. Command, Colorado Springs, 1965-70; speaker in field. Author: Astronautical Law, 1959; contbr. numerous articles to profl. jours., 1955-85. Bd. govs. World Hdqrs. USO, Washington, 1976-88, chair pers. com., mem. exec. com., 1974-78, chair bylaws com., 1983-86; life mem. bd. visitors Coll. of Law, Syracuse U., 1967—; bd. dirs. Nat. Jewish Welfare Bd., N.Y.C., 1970-78; v.p. Internat. Inst. Space Law, 1979-85, hon. dir., 1985—. Decorated D.S.M., Legion of Merit with Oak Leaf Cluster, Bronze Star; recipient Recognition Cert., Air Force Assn., 1969; Disting. Contbn. Internat. Inst. of Space Law, 1990, Lawyers Lawyer award N.Y.C. Assn. of USAFR Judge Advocates, 1964, Inter-Am. Bar Found. Space Law award, 1990. Mem. ABA, Am. Soc. Internat. Law, Am. Astronautical Soc., Fed. Bar Assn., Internat. Acad. Astronautics. Avocations: swimming, walking, reading, writing. Home: 4701 Willard Ave Apt 1726 Chevy Chase MD 20815-4632

**MENTZ, BARBARA ANTONELLO,** lawyer; b. Kansas City, Mo., July 4, 1944; d. John Francis and Eleanor Barbara (Vagnino) Antonella; m. Lawrence Mentz, Nov. 10, 1973; children: Kathleen Elizabeth, Lawrence Goodwin. BA in Econs., U. Kans., 1965; JD magna cum laude, U. Notre Dame, 1973. Bar: N.Y. 1974, U.S. Dist. Ct. (so. and ea. dists.) N.Y. 1974, U.S. Ct. Appeals (2d cir.) 1974, U.S. Supreme Ct. 1977, U.S. Ct. Appeals (9th cir.) 1981, U.S. Ct. Appeals (3d cir.) 1983, N.J. 1985, U.S. Dist. Ct. N.J. 1986. Various positions with ins. cos. Chgo., 1965-68, Kansas City, Mo., 1968-70; assoc. Sullivan & Cromwell, N.Y.C., 1973-77, Forsyth, Decker, Murray and Hubbard, N.Y.C., 1977-79; ptnr. Hall, McNicol, Hamilton & Clark, N.Y.C., 1979-86; assoc. gen. counsel, prin. Deloitte & Touche USA LLP, N.Y.C., 1988—. Contbr. articles to profl. jours., chpt. to supplements, publs. Mem. ABA (antitrust sect. 1979-90), Nat. Futures Assn. (panel of arbitrators 1985—), Assn. Bar City of N.Y. (prof. discipline com. 1983-86, antitrust and trade regulation com. 1983-86). Antitrust, Federal civil litigation, Securities. Home: 140 W 86th St Apt 2B New York NY 10024-4067 Office: Deloitte & Touche USA LLP 1633 Broadway New York NY 10019-6708

**MENTZ, HENRY ALVAN, JR.,** federal judge; b. New Orleans, Nov. 10, 1920; s. Henry Alvan and Lulla (Bridewell) M.; m. Ann Lamantia, June 23, 1956; children: Ann, Carli, Hal, Frederick, George. BA, Tulane U., 1941; JD, La. State U., 1943. Bar: La. 1943, U.S. Dist. Ct. (ea. dist.) La. 1944. With legal dept. Shell Oil, New Orleans, 1947-48; pvt. practice Hammond, 1948-82; judge U.S. Dist. Ct. (ea. dist.) La., New Orleans, 1982—, sr. judge, 1992—. Editor: Combined Gospels, 1976. Pres. La. Soc. Music and Performing Arts, 1994-97, L.A. Civil Svc. League, 1979-81; bd. dirs. Southea. La. U. Found., Salvation Army; chmn. Tulane U. 50th Anniversary Reunion for 1991. Decorated 2 Battle Stars, Bronze Star; recipient Disting. Svc. award AMVETS, 1950. Mem. SAR, Royal Soc. St. George (pres.), Boston Club New Orleans, Delta Tau Delta. Republican. Episcopalian. Home: 2105 State St New Orleans LA 70118-6255 Office: US Dist Ct C-114 US Courthouse 500 Camp St New Orleans LA 70130-3313

**MENTZ, LAWRENCE,** lawyer; b. N.Y.C., Nov. 5, 1946; s. Joseph Walter and Audrey Cecilia (Armstrong) M.; m. Barbara Antonello, Nov. 10, 1973; children: Kathleen Elizabeth, Lawrence Goodwin. BS in Physics, Rensselaer Poly. Inst., 1968; JD, U. Notre Dame, 1973. Bar: N.Y. 1973; Washington 1974. Assoc. Condon & Forsyth, N.Y.C., 1973-80, ptnr., 1981-89; ptnr. Biedermann, Hoenig, Massamillo & Ruff, N.Y.C., 1990—; counsellor at law; speaker Worldwide Airlines Customer Rels. Assn. Conf., Singapore, 1983, 2d Cir. Speakers Bur., Com. on BiCentennial of U.S. Constn., 1987; arbitrator U.S. Dist. Ct. (ea. dist.) Bklyn., 1986—. With USNR, 1969-70. Mem. ABA, Fed. Bar Coun., N.Y. State Bar Assn. (exec. com. sect. on comml. and fed. litigation, fed. judiciary com., 1993, com. Supreme Cts.), Assn. of Bar of City of N.Y. (com. on aeronautics law, task force on N.Y. Constl. Conv., com. on state legis.), Wings Club. Roman Catholic. Avocations: swimming, running, philately. Aviation, Insurance, Federal civil litigation. Office: Biedermann Hoenig Massamillo & Ruff 90 Park Ave New York NY 10016-1301

**MERCADANTE, STEPHEN G.,** lawyer, educator; b. Mount Vernon, N.Y., Aug. 20, 1954; s. Gerard and Grace (Scarola) M.; m. Lynne P. Sims, June 25, 1978; children: Joseph S., Michael D. BS, U. Fla., 1977; JD, Stetson U., 1980. Bar: U.S. Dist. Ct. (mid., so. and no. dists.) Fla. Ptnr. Schackow & Mercadante, Gainesville, Fla., 1980—; prof. Santa Fe Jr. Coll., Gainesville, 1993—. Vol. Gainesville Recreation Dept., 1986-93, Boys Club, 1987-92. Avocations: jogging, weight training, baseball, community volunteer. Personal injury, General civil litigation. Home: 3602 SW 84th St Gainesville FL 32608-3614 Office: Schackow & Mercadante 112 NW 33rd Ct Gainesville FL 32607-2560

**MERCANT, JON JEFFRY,** lawyer, educator, musician; b. San Jose, Calif., Dec. 17, 1950; s. Anthony J. and Margie Vivian (Diaz) M. BA, U. Calif., Berkeley, 1972; JD, U. Calif., L.A., 1975. Bar: Calif. 1975. Atty. Redondo Beach, Calif., 1975—; prof. El Camino Coll., Torrance, Calif. Mem. exec. bd. Calif. Dem. Party, 1986—; mem. exec. bd., COPE chmn. El Camino Coll. Fedn. Tchrs., Torrance, 1991—; Dem. nominee for State Assembly, 1986, Los Angeles County Ctrl. Co., 1986-90; dir. Peninsula Symphony Assn., Consumer Coalition Calif., Enrichment Through Employment; dir., founder South Bay Concern, Coastal Environ. Coalition; vice chmn., legal counsel Ret. Sr. Vol. Program. Named one of Outstanding Young Men of Am., 1984. Mem. Rotary (bd. dirs., pres. North Redondo, Calif.), Redondo Beach C. of C. (pres., bd. dirs. 1990—), Phi Beta Kappa. Avocations: music performance, theatre, wine collecting, jogging, travel. Probate, Estate planning, General corporate. Office: 707 Torrance Blvd Ste 220 Redondo Beach CA 90277-3492

**MERCER, EDWIN WAYNE,** lawyer; b. Kingsport, Tenn., July 19, 1940; s. Ernest LaFayette and Geneva (Frye) M. BBA, Tex. Tech U., 1963; JD, S. Tex. Coll. Law, 1971. Bar: Tex. 1971, U.S. Dist. Ct. (no. dist.) Tex 1975, U.S. Supreme Ct. 1976, U.S. Ct. Appeals (5th Cir.) 1979. Pvt. practice law Houston, 1971-73; gen. counsel, corp. sec. Alcon Labs., Inc., Ft. Worth, 1973-81; ptnr. Gandy Michener Swindle Whitaker Pratt & Mercer, Ft. Worth, 1981-84; v.p., gen. counsel, corp. sec. Pengo Industries, Inc., Ft. Worth, 1984-90, also bd. dirs. Bd. dirs. Soc. for Prevention Blindness, 1979—. Mem. ABA, State Bar Tex., Houston Bar Assn., Ft. Worth-Tarrant County Bar Assn., Coll. State Bar Tex., South Tex. Coll. Law Alumni Assn., Tex. Tech U. Ex-Assn., Ft. Worth Club, Delta Theta Phi, Phi Delta Theta. Methodist. General corporate, Public international.

**MERCURIO, JEAN WILLIAMS,** lawyer; b. Mannassett, N.Y., July 17, 1965; d. George Edward Williams and Rosemary Elizabeth Lorenz; m. Richard R. Mercurio, Dec. 4, 1993; children: Marissa Jean, Teressa Lee. BS, U. Scranton, 1987; JD, Cath. U. Am., 1990. Bar: Pa. 1990, N.Y. 1995, U.S. Dist. Ct. (so. and ea. dists.) N.Y. 1997. Assoc. Firestone & Firestone, Hauppauge, N.Y., 1992-96, Cartier, Hogan, Sullivan, Bernstein & Auerbach, Patchogue, N.Y., 1996—; coach Pt. Jeff (N.Y.) H.S. Mock Trial Team, 1990; judge Pace Law Sch. Moot Ct., Westchester, N.Y., 1996. Com. mem. Conservative Party, Smithtown, N.Y., 1998. Mem. ABA, N.Y. Bar Assn., Suffolk County Women's Bar Assn., Suffolk County Bar Assn. Roman Catholic. Family and matrimonial. Office: Cartier Hogan Sullivan Bernstein & Auerbach PC 77 Medford Ave Patchogue NY 11772-1230

**MERHIGE, ROBERT REYNOLD, JR.,** lawyer; b. N.Y.C., Feb. 5, 1919; s. Robert Reynold and Eleanor (Donovan) M.; m. Shirley Galleher, Apr. 24, 1957; children: Robert Reynold III, Mark Reynold. *Judge Robert Reynold Merhige has been selected by the Valentine Museum and StyleMagazine as one of the 100 most influential Richmonders of the century. Son Robert, III, an attorney, has two children, Robert IV and Christopher A. Son Mark, a real estate developer, has two daughters, Sayre Donovan and Mariah Rowe and two sons, Mark R. Jr., and Alexander Kent. Grandson Robert IV has one son, Robert V.* LLB, U. Richmond, 1942, LLD (hon.), 1976; LLM, U. Va., 1982; LLD (hon.), Washington and Lee U., 1990, Wake Forest U., 1994. Bar: Va. 1942. Ptnr. Bremner Merhige Montgomery & Baber, Richmond, 1945-67; judge U.S. Dist. Ct., Richmond, 1967—; resigned, 1998; assoc. Hunton & Williams, Richmond, 1998—; guest lectr. trial tactics Law Sch. U. Va., Ewald disting. prof. law, 1987-88; adj. prof. Law Sch. U. Richmond, 1973-87; appeal agt. Henrico County Draft Bd., 1954-67; mem. NCAA spl. com. on discipline rules; profl.-in-residence, Zambia, Africa, 1994. Co-author: Virginia Jury Instructions. Mem. Richmond Citizens Assn. Served with USAAF, World War II. Decorated Air medal with four oak leaf clusters; recipient Amara Civic Club award, 1968, Spl. award City of

Richmond, 1967; named Citizen of the Yr., 3d Dist. Omega Psi Phi, 1972, Citizen of the Yr., Richmond Urban League, 1977, Richmonder of Yr. Style mag., 1984, 87, Citizen of Yr., 1986; recipient Disting. Alumni award U. Richmond, 1979, Disting. Svc. award Nat. Alumni Coun., U. Richmond, 1979, Herbert T. Harley award Am. Judicature Soc., 1982, Athenian Ciitizen medal, 1979, Torch of Liberty award Anti-Defamation League of B'nai Brith, 1982, T.C. Williams Sch. of Law Disting. Svc. award, 1983, Pres.'s award Old Dominion Bar Assn., 1986, William J. Brennan award, 1986, Merit Citation award NCCJ, 1987, William B. Green award for professionalism U. Richmond, 1989, Marshall-Wythe medallion (William & Mary Faculty award), 1989. Fellow Va. Law Found.; mem. Va. Bar Assn., Richmond Bar Assn. (pres. 1963-64, multi-dist. litigation panel 1990—, Hill-Tucker award 1991), Am. Law Inst. (faculty), Va. Trial Lawyers Assn. (chmn. membership com. 1964-65, Disting. Svc. award 1977), Jud. Conf. U.S., John Marshall Inns of Ct. (founding mem.), Omicron Delta Kappa (Hunter W. Martin profl. award 1998). Alternative dispute resolution, General civil litigation, Intellectual property. Office: Hunton & Williams Riverfront Plz East Tower 951 E Byrd St Richmond VA 23219-4074

**MERKEL, CHARLES MICHAEL,** lawyer; b. Nashville, Nov. 2, 1941; s. Charles M. and Lila K. Merkel; m. Donna White, Jan. 7, 1967; children: Kimberly Dale, Charles M. III. BA, U. Miss., 1964, JD, 1966; LLM in Taxation, Georgetown U., 1969. Bar: Miss. Trial atty. U.S. Dept. Justice, Washington, 1966-70; ptnr. Dunbar & Merkel, Clarksdale, Miss., 1970-73, Holcomb Dunbar Connell & Merkel, Clarksdale, 1973-82, Merkel & Cocke, Clarksdale, 1982—; pres. Miss. chpt. Am. Bd. Trial Advs., 1989. Bd. dirs. Lula Rich Edn. Found., Clarksdale, 1983-89. Carrier scholar U. Miss. 1959-63. Fellow Miss. State Bar Found.; mem. ATLA, Am. Bd. Trial Advocates, Am. Coll. Trial Lawyers, Miss. Trial Lawyers Assn. (sec. 1985-87). Episcopalian. Avocations: hunting, tennis, skiing. Personal injury, Product liability, Federal civil litigation. Home: 101 Cypress Ave Clarksdale MS 38614-2603 Office: PO Box 1388 30 Delta Ave Clarksdale MS 38614

**MERKIN, DAVID,** reference librarian; b. Bklyn., Sept. 16, 1958; s. William and Doris (Beart) M.; m. Martine Merkin, Aug. 28, 1983; 1 child, Jennifer. BA, Bklyn. Coll., 1980; cert. in paralegal studies, L.I. U., 1982; MLS, Pratt U., 1997. Clk. Bklyn. Pub. Libr., 1975-77; clk. Shearman & Sterling, N.Y.C., 1981-83, libr. asst., 1983-85, asst. reference libr., 1985-93, reference libr., 1993—. Mem. Am. Assn. Law Librs., Law Libr. Assn. of Greater N.Y.C. (co-chmn. pro bono com. 1996—). Jewish. Avocations: swimming, bicycle riding, kite flying, bowling, baseball. Office: Shearman & Sterling 599 Lexington Ave Fl C2 New York NY 10022-6069

**MERKLE, ALAN RAY,** lawyer; b. Boise, Idaho, Oct. 14, 1947; s. John William and Arlene June (Hawkins) M.; m. Diane M. Martin, June 15, 1973 (div. 1978); m. Linda Jo Todd, Mar. 15, 1980; children: Amanda, Lindsay. AS, Boise State U., 1967; BSME, U. Idaho, 1970, MBA, 1971; JD, Lewis & Clark Coll., 1982. Bar: Oreg. 1983, Wash. 1983, U.S. Dist. Ct. (Oreg.) 1983, U.S. Dist. Ct. (we. dist.) Wash. 1984; registered profl. engr. Wash., Oreg., Idaho. Field engr. GE, N.Y., Oreg., Wash., other location, 1971-74; svc. specialist GE, Seattle, 1974-77; svc. mgr. steam turbines GE, Portland, Oreg., 1977-80; mgr. hydro ops. GE, 1980-82; assoc. Stoel, Rives LLP, Seattle, 1982-86, ptnr., 1987—. Author: Construction Law, Licensing and Registration, 1988, Damages, Liability of Architects and Engineers, 1989, 93, Public Contracting in Washington, 1992, 93, 94, Washington Lien Law, 1992, Defending Claims Against the Owner, 1994, 96, Construction Law, 1996, 97, Advanced Construction Law in Washington, 1997. Apptd. Mercer Is. City Coun., 1996, elected 4 yr. term, 1997, dep. mayor, 1999. Recipient Cornelius honor award. Mem. ABA, Oreg. State Bar Assn., Wash. State Bar Assn., Fed. Energy Bar Assn. (past chair pub. procuement, pvt. law sect., associated gen. contractors, legal affairs com.). Democrat. Avocations: skiing, sailing, fishing. Construction, Government contracts and claims, State civil litigation. Office: Stoel Rives L L P 3600 One Union Sq 600 University St Seattle WA 98101-1176

**MERLO, PERRY DAVID,** lawyer; b. Newark, Ohio, June 11, 1965; s. David A. and Sylvania (Knackstedt) M.; m. Andrea Lynn Mitchell, Sept. 16, 1995. BA, Elizabethtown Coll., 1987; JD, Dickinson Coll., 1990. Bar: U.S. Dist. Ct. (cen. dist.) Pa. 1991. Assoc. Post & Schell, Camp Hill, Pa. Mem. Pa. Bar Assn., Dauphin County Bar Assn. Workers' compensation. Office: Post & Schell 240 Grandview Ave Camp Hill PA 17011-1706

**MERMELSTEIN, EDWARD A.,** lawyer; b. Mogileu, Ukraine, Oct. 22, 1967; came to U.S., 1976; s. Alexander and Fay M.; m. Rose Caiola, Oct. 14, 1995. BA, NYU, 1991; JD, Thomas M. Cooley Sch. of Law, Lansing, Mich., 1995. Assoc. Hayt & Percy, N.Y.C., 1995-96; ptnr. Hayt, Percy & Mermelstein, N.Y.C., 1996—. Bd. dirs. 68th St. Assn., 1995—. With U.S. Army, 1987-91. Mem. ATLA, N.Y. State Trial Lawyers Assn., N.Y. State Bar Assn. General civil litigation, Personal injury. Office: Hayt Percy & Mermelstein 299 Broadway Rm 1010 New York NY 10007-1901

**MERMELSTEIN, JULES JOSHUA,** lawyer, township official; b. Phila., Apr. 25, 1955; s. Harry and Ellen Jane (Greenberg) M.; m. Ruth Susan Applebaum, Aug. 18, 1974; children: Hannah Leona, Benjamin Isaac. BA, Temple U., 1977; JD, Am. U., 1979; MEd Beaver Coll., 1994. Bar: Pa. 1980, U.S. Dist. Ct. (ea. dist.) Pa. 1980, U.S. Ct. Appeals (3d cir.) 1982, U.S. Supreme Ct. 1983. Ptnr. Mermelstein & Light, Norristown and Hatboro, Pa., 1980-83; v.p., gen. counsel Am. Ins. Cons., Feasterville, Pa., 1983; vol. atty. ACLU, Phila., 1980-93; staff atty. Hyatt Legal Svcs., Phila., 1983-84, mng. atty., 1984-85; pvt. practice, Phila. and Montgomery County, 1985-93; tchr., social studies coord. The Bridge, 1997—; ednl. cons. Interim House, 1998—; prof. law, St. Matthew Sch. Law, Phila., 1985-87; adj. prof. criminal justice Glassboro State U., N.J., 1988; faculty polit. sci. dept. Temple U., 1989; atty. Levin & Baltz, Wyncote, Pa., 1998—. Editor The Montco Democrat, 1990-92. Chmn. Tikkun Olam (Repair the World) Com., 1989-92, 98—; area rep. Montgomery County Dem. Exec. Com., 1982-85, 88-94, treas., 1994-98, candidate coord., 1982, nominee for dist. atty., 1983, committeeman, 1973-77, 82-85, 88-92, campaign mgr. Talbot for state legis., 1988; Upper Dublin chmn. Dukakis-Bentsen, 1988, chair Upper Dublin Dem. Com., 1990-91, commr. Upper Dublin Twp., 1992—; bd. dirs. Reconstructionist Congregation Or Hadash, Ft. Washington, Pa., 1988-92, 96—, confirmation tchr. 1994—. Jewish. Constitutional, State civil litigation, Appellate. Home: 18 Northview Dr Glenside PA 19038-1318

**MEROLA, FRANK A.,** lawyer; b. Syracuse, N.Y., June 17, 1963; s. Francis Anthony and Marian Nancy M.; m. Marta Elena Mascaro, Sept. 7, 1986; children: Francesco Antonio, Giancarlo Yarini, Marcello Alberto. BSBA cum laude, Georgetown U., 1985; JD, UCLA, 1988. Bar: Calif. 1988, U.S. Dist. Ct. (ctrl. and ea. dists.) Calif. 1988. Atty. Stutman, Treister & Glatt, L.A., 1988-94, shareholder, 1994—. Mem. State Bar Calif. (com. debtor/creditor rels. 1997—), Turnaround Mgrs. Assn. (dir. 1998—). Democrat. Roman Catholic. Bankruptcy. Office: Stutman Treister & Glatt 3699 Wilshire Blvd Ste 900 Los Angeles CA 90010-2766

**MERRAN, HAROLD,** lawyer; b. N.Y.C., July 5, 1931; s. Jacob and Eva (Cohen) M.; m. Bernice Taub Merran, Oct. 30, 1968 (widowed July 1980); 1 child, Marjorie. BA, CCNY, 1953; LLB, N.Y.U., 1958. Bar: N.Y. 1959, U.S. Dist. Ct. (so. and ea. dist.) N.Y. 1962, U.S. Ct. Appeals (2nd cir.) 1962, U.S. Supreme Ct. 1964. Staff atty. Cosmo Casualty Ins. Co., N.Y.C., 1959-64; assoc. atty. pvt. practice, N.Y.C., 1964-69; asst. corp. counsel Law Dept. City of N.Y., N.Y.C., 1969-73; assoc. atty. Nayor & Edmiston, Yonkers, N.Y., 1973-77; atty. pvt. practice, White Plains, N.Y., 1977—. Author: Conflict Rules for Contracts, 1958. Cpl. U.S. Army, 1953-55, Korea. Mem. Kiwanis. General civil litigation, Insurance. Office: 199 Main St White Plains NY 10601-3200

**MERRIAM, DWIGHT HAINES,** lawyer, land use planner; b. Norwood, Mass., Apr. 20, 1946; s. Austin Luther and Lillian Diana (Olsen) M.; m. Cynthia Ann Hayes, May 21, 1966 (div. June 1992); children: Sarah Ann Leilani, Jonathan Hayes; m. Susan Manning Standish, May 6, 1995; children: Alexander Harlan, Lucy Caroline. BA cum laude, U. Mass., 1968; M in Regional Planning, U. N.C., 1974; JD, Yale U., 1978. Bar: Conn. 1978, Mass. 1980, U.S. Dist. Ct. Conn. 1981, U.S. Dist. Ct. Hawaii 1984, U.S. Supreme Ct. 1990, U.S. Ct. Appeals (4th cir.) 1993. Land use planner Charles E. Downe, Newton, Mass., 1968; assoc. Byrne, Buck & Steiner, Farmington, Conn., 1978, Robinson, Robinson & Cole, Hartford, Conn., 1979-83; ptnr. Robinson & Cole, Hartford, 1984—; adj. prof. law Western New Eng. Coll., 1978-86, U. Conn., 1982, 84-87, Vt. Law Sch., 1994—; instr. planning U. Bridgeport, 1981-83, U. Conn., 1986-92; mem. faculty Nat. Coll. Dist. Attys., 1983-87, Nat. Jud. Coll., 1994; mem. faculty Am. Law Inst.-ABA Land Use Inst., 1988—; instr. city and regional planning Memphis State U., 1989, 94; speaker in field. Co-author: The Takings Issue, 1999; co-editor: Inclusionary Zoning Moves Downtown, 1985; contbr. more than 60 articles and book revs. to profl. jours. Bd. dirs. Conn. chpt. Appleseed Found., 1997—, Am. Boat Builders and Repairers Assn., 1995—, Growth Mgmt. Inst., Washington, 1992—, Housing Edn. Resource Ctr., 1984-88, Housing Coalition for Capitol Region, Inc., 1984-86; bd. dirs. Conn. Fund for Environment, 1981-85, legal adv. com., 1985-88, legal adv. bd., 1978-81; mem. Environment 2000 environ. plan adv. bd. Conn. Dept. Environ. Protection, 1987-91; assoc. Environ. Law Inst., 1987—; mem. housing task force Conn. Dept. on Aging, 1981; mem. Gov.'s Housing Task Force, Conn., 1980-81. With USN, 1968-75, Vietnam; capt. USNR, 1975-99. Mem. ABA, Conn. Bar Assn. (exec. com. zoning & planning sect. 1985-87, 91—), Am. Planning Assn. (bd. dirs. 1988-90, chmn. planning & law divsn. 1984-86, exec. com. planning & law divsn. 1978-88, chmn. legis. com. Conn. chpt. 1978-80, editorial adv. bd. 1984-92), Internat. Mcpl. Law Assn. (chmn. sect. on zoning, planning & land devel. 1988-89, sect. vice-chmn. 1987), Assn. State Floodplain Mgrs., Am. Inst. Cert. Planners (pres. 1988-90), Am. Coll. Real Estate Lawyers. Democrat. Unitarian. Avocations: sailing, skiing. Land use and zoning (including planning), Real property, Environmental. Home: 1 Linden Pl Apt 410 Hartford CT 06106-1745 Office: Robinson & Cole LLP 280 Trumbull St Ste 31 Hartford CT 06103-3597

**MERRIFIELD, LEROY SORENSON,** law educator; b. Mpls., Nov. 18, 1917; s. Edgar Eugene and Alice Sorenson M.; m. Marian Grace Hansen, Apr. 25, 1943; children: Lois, Eric, Randall, Karen. BA, U. Minn., 1938, JD, 1941; MBA, Harvard U., 1943, SJD, 1956. Bar: Minn. 1941, D.C. 1979, U.S. Supreme Ct. 1957. Atty. U.S. Office Price Adminstrn., Boston, 1942, U.S. Dept. Justice, Washington, 1946; prof. law George Washington U., Washington, 1947-87; prof. emeritus, 1987—. Lt. USN, 1943-45. Mem. ABA, Am. Arbitration Assn., Internat. Indsl. Rels. Assn., Order of Coif, Phi Beta Kappa. Democrat. Unitarian. Avocations: singing, tennis, golf.

**MERRILL, ABEL JAY,** lawyer; b. Balt., Mar. 25, 1938; s. Yale and Evelyn (Cordish) M.; m. Susan Stein, June 15, 1963; children: Adam L., Julie F. BA, Colgate U., 1959; LLB, U. Md., 1964. Bar: Md. 1964. Law clk. U.S. Ct. Appeals, Balt., 1964-65; assoc. Gordon, Feinblatt & Rothman, Balt., 1965-70; atty. pvt. practice, Annapolis, Md., 1970-78, 83—; prin. Blumenthal, May, Downs & Merrill, Annapolis, Md., 1979-83; mem. inquiry com. Atty. frievance Commn. Md., 1975-85, character com. Ct. of Appeals, 1987-88; mem. pension oversight bd. Anne Arundel County, Md. Fellow Am. Coll. Probate Counsel; mem. ABA, Md. Bar Assn., Anne Arundel County Bar Assn. Probate, Estate planning, Estate taxation.

**MERRILL, GEORGE VANDERNETH,** lawyer, investment executive; b. N.Y.C., July 2, 1947; s. James Edward and Claire (Leness) M.; m. Janice Anne Humes, May 11, 1985; children: Claire Georgina, Anne Stewart. Student, Phillips Exeter Acad., 1960-64; AB magna cum laude, Harvard U., 1968, JD, 1972; MBA, Columbia U., 1973. Bar: N.Y. 1973, U.S. Dist. Ct. (so. and ea. dists.) N.Y. 1974, U.S. Ct. Appeals (2d cir.) 1974. Assoc. Cleary, Gottlieb, Steen & Hamilton, N.Y.C., 1974-77, Hawkins, Delafield & Wood, N.Y.C., 1977-79; v.p. Irving Trust Co., N.Y.C., 1980-82; v.p., gen. counsel Listowel, Inc., N.Y.C., 1982-84; bd. dirs., exec. v.p., gen. counsel Listowel, Inc., 1984-93; also bd. dirs. Pres. Arell Found., N.Y.C., 1985-93, also bd. dirs., pres. Northfield Charitable Corp., N.Y.C., 1986-93; v.p., sec. Brougham Prodn. Co., N.Y.C., 1986-89, bd. dirs., sr. v.p., sec., 1990-93; v.p., sec. Marinetics Inc., N.Y.C., 1988-90, sr. v.p., sec., 1991-93, also bd. dirs., 1989-93; v.p. Sci. Design and Engring. Co., Inc., N.Y.C., 1987-88, bd. dirs., exec. v.p., 1989-93; v.p. Instl. Portfolio Mgmt., Shawmut Investment Advisors, 1993-95; co-mgr. Shawmut Growth & Income Equity Mut. Fund; v.p. Instl. Portfolio Mgmt., Fleet Investment Advisors, 1995-96; co-mgr. Galaxy Growth & Income Equity Mutual Fund; v.p. Trust and Instl. Portfolio Mgmt., No. Trust Corp., Chgo., 1996—. John Harvard scholar; recipient Detur award Harvard U., 1968. Mem. ABA, Am. Mgmt. Assn., Assn. Bar City N.Y., Nat. Cum Laude Soc., The Brook, Union Club (N.Y.C.), Down Town Assn., Racquet and Tennis Club, Somerset Club (Boston), Signet Soc. (Cambridge), Pilgrims of U.S., Riviera Country Club (Coral Gables, Fla.). General corporate, Finance, Estate planning. Home: 4011 Granada Blvd Coral Gables FL 33146-1235 Office: Northern Trust Bank 700 Brickell Ave Miami FL 33131-2802

**MERRILL, MICHAEL GORDON,** lawyer; b. Seattle, Jan. 4, 1961; s. John Moore and Elizabeth May (Jensen) M.; m. Amy Dewing, June 29, 1991; children: Jensen Michael, James Rolland. BA in English, U. Wash., 1983, BA in Comms., 1984; JD cum laude, U. Puget Sound, 1987. Bar: Wash. 1987, U.S. Dist. Ct. (we. dist.) Wash. 1988. Atty. Hawkins, Ingalls & West, Auburn, Wash., 1987-88; labor rels. rep. Allied Employers, Inc., Redmond, Wash., 1988—; trustee Taft Hartley Benefit Trust, 1989—. Mem. Internat. Found. Employee Benefit Plans, Indsl. Rels. Rsch. Assn. Avocations: fishing, hiking, scuba, reading, competitive sports. Labor, Contracts commercial. Office: Allied Employers Inc 2425 152nd Ave NE Redmond WA 98052-5573

**MERRIMAN, KEVIN THOMAS,** lawyer; b. Rochester, N.Y., Sept. 17, 1966; s. William Emmett and Anne Flaherty Merriman; m. Joy Alexandria Mautner, May 23, 1992; children: Samuel, Alexander. BS, Cornell U., 1989; JD, SUNY, Buffalo, 1992. Bar: N.Y. 1993. Assoc. Allen, Lippes & Shonn, Buffalo, 1993-98, Hurwitz & Fine, P.C., Buffalo, 1998—. Mem. Erie County Bar Assn. Democrat. Toxic tort, General civil litigation, Insurance. Home: 516 North St East Aurora NY 14052-1446 Office: Hurwitz & Fine PC 1300 Liberty Bldg Buffalo NY 14202

**MERRING, ROBERT ALAN,** lawyer; b. Middletown, N.Y., Oct. 5, 1951; s. Merton Joseph and Mabel Ruth M.; m. Lynn S. Connor, Mar. 16, 1996. Student, Ohio Wesleyan U., 1969-70; A.B. with distinction and dept. honors, Stanford U., 1973; JD in Internat. and Fgn. Law with honors, Columbia U., 1977; cert. Pepperdine Sch. Law, Inst. for Dispute Resolution, 1996. Bar: Calif. 1977, U.S. Dist. Ct. (cen. dist.) Calif. 1978, U.S. Dist. Ct. (so. and ea. dists.) Calif. 1980, U.S. Ct. Appeals (9th cir.) 1980, U.S. Dist. Ct. (no. dist.) Calif. 1983, U.S. Supreme Ct. 1987, Colo. 1989. Assoc. Pacht, Ross, Warne, Bernhard & Sears, Inc., L.A., 1977-79, Donovan Leisure Newton & Irvine, L.A., 1979-81, Cutler and Cutler, L.A., 1983-88, Friedemann & Hart, Irvine, 1988-89; pvt. practice Newport Beach and Irvine, Calif., 1989-99, Richard Hamlin Attys., Marina del Rey, Calif., 1999—; mem. San Diego-Orange County Am. Arbitration Assn. panel comml. arbitrators, 1993—; civil arbitrator, judge pro tem Orange County Superior Ct., 1993—; mediator U.S. Bankruptcy Ct. (ctrl. dist.) Calif., 1996—; mediator Orange County Superior Ct., 1998—; clin. prof. Loyola U. Law Sch., Los Angeles, 1981-82. Editor Columbia Jour. Transnat. Law, 1976-77. Columbia U. Internat. fellow, 1975-76. Mem. ABA, Orange County Bar Assn., Assn. Bus. Trial Lawyers, Internat. Trademark Assn., Am. Arbitration Assn., State Bar of Calif. (del. 1998—). General civil litigation, Intellectual property, Alternative dispute resolution. Home: 1300 Park Newport Apt 217 Newport Beach CA 92660-5031

**MERRIS, DONNA ROSE,** lawyer; b. Bluffs, Ill., Nov. 25, 1939; d. Donald Doyle and Helen Louise (Frohwitter) M.; children: Laura Katherine Merris Huffman, Kristen Rose Merris Huffman. BS in Edn., Ill. State U., 1961; MMus, Northwestern U., 1965; JD, Bklyn. Law Sch., 1987. Bar: N.Y. 1989, N.J. 1989. Dir. instrumental music Lanark (Ill.) Pub. Schs., 1961-64, Winchester (Ill.) H.S., 1965-66; dir. music edn. Malden (Mass.) Pub. Schs., 1966-74; instr. music Mannes Coll. Music, N.Y.C., 1974-80; exec. dir. Bklyn. Music Sch., 1977-85; spl. asst. U.S. Atty. U.S. Dist. Ct. (so. dist.) N.Y., N.Y.C., 1988-90; asst. gen. counsel Office of the Comptroller, N.Y.C., 1990-94; gen. counsel Mayor's Office of Contracts, N.Y.C., 1994-99; adminstrv. law judge Office of Adminstrv. Trials and Hearings, N.Y.C., 1999—; adv. bd. Bklyn. Music Sch., 1986—; trustee Nat. Guild Cmty. Schs. of the Arts, N.Y.C., 1993-99. Mem. Assn. Bar City of N.Y. Home: 255 W End Ave Apt 13A New York NY 10023-3607 Office: 40 Rector St Fl 6 New York NY 10006-1705

**MERRITT, GILBERT STROUD,** federal judge; b. Nashville, Tenn., Jan. 17, 1936; s. Gilbert Stroud and Angie Fields (Cantrell) M.; m. Louise Clark Fort, July 10, 1964 (dec.); children: Stroud, Louise Clark, Eli. BA, Yale U., 1957; LLB, Vanderbilt U., 1960; LLM, Harvard U., 1962. Bar: Tenn. 1960. Asst. dean Vanderbilt U. Law Sch., 1960-61, lectr., 1963-69, 71-75, assoc. prof. law, 1969-70; assoc. Boult Hunt Cummings & Conners, Nashville, 1962-63; city atty. City of Nashville, 1963-66; U.S. Dist. atty. for (mid. dist.) Tenn., 1966-69; ptnr. Gullett, Steele, Sanford, Robinson & Merritt, Nashville, 1970-77; judge U.S. Ct. Appeals (6th cir.), Nashville, 1977-89, 1998-; chief judge U.S. Ct. Appeals (6th cir.), 1989-98; exec. sec. Tenn. Code Commn., 1977. Mng. editor: Vanderbilt Law Rev, 1959-60; contbr. articles to law jours. Del. Tenn. Constl. Conv., 1965; chmn. bd. trustees Vanderbilt Inst. Pub. Policy Studies. Mem. ABA, Fed. Bar Assn., Tenn. Bar Assn., Nashville Bar Assn., Vanderbilt Law Alumni Assn. (pres. 1979-80), Am. Law Inst., Order of Coif. Episcopalian. Office: US Ct Appeals Customs Ho 701 Broadway Rm 303 Nashville TN 37203-3944*

**MERRITT, LARAMIE DEE,** lawyer; b. Montpelier, Idaho, June 5, 1967; s. Leon T. and Laurel Merritt; m. Gretchen Merritt; children: Tyler, Caleb. BA, Brigham Young U., 1992, JD, 1995. Bar: Utah 1995, U.S. Dist. Ct. Utah 1996. Law clk. to hon. Steven L. Hansen, Utah 4th Dist. Ct., Provo, 1995-96; assoc. Duval Hansen Witt & Morley, Pleasant Grove, Utah, 1996—; part-time faculty J. Reuben Clark Law Sch., Provo, 1997-98. Editor Brigham Young U. Jour. Pub. Law, 1994-95, note and comment editor, 1995. Mem. Mendelssohn Men's Chorus. Republican. Mem. LDS Ch. Avocations: vocal performance, hiking, writing, accordian. Real property, Municipal (including bonds), Contracts commercial. Office: Duval Hansen Witt & Morley PC 110 S Main St Pleasant Grove UT 84062-2631

**MERRITT, THOMAS BUTLER,** lawyer; b. Toledo, Apr. 3, 1939; s. George Robert and Bernice (Gerwin) M.; m. Mary Jane Bothfeld, July 23, 1966; children—Thomas Butler, Haidee Soule, Theodore Bothfeld. AB magna cum laude, Harvard U., 1961, LLB cum laude, 1966. Bar: Mass. 1966, U.S. Supreme Ct. 1974, N.H. 1994. Intern Office of Legal Advsier U.S. Dept. of State, 1965; law clk. to assoc. justice Arthur E. Whittemore Supreme Jud. Ct. Mass., Boston, 1966-67; assoc. Nutter, McClennen & Fish, Boston, 1967-69, Palmer & Dodge, Boston, 1969-73; asst. counsel to Gov. Mass., 1973; reporter of decisions Supreme Jud. Ct. Mass., Boston, 1974-94; pvt. practice Hollis, N.H., 1994—. Contbr. articles to profl. jours. Mem. Conservation Commn. Town of Sherborn, Mass., 1969-74, chmn., 1972-74; mem. corp. Tenacre Country Day Sch., Wellesley, Mass., 1972-84, trustee, 1973-78; planning bd. Town of Hollis, N.H., 1995-98. 1st lt. U.S. Army, 1962-63, capt. USAR, 1963-69. Mem. Mass. Bar Assn., N.H. Bar Assn., Fed. Bar Assn., Am. Law Inst., Am. Soc. Internat. Law, Internat. Law Assn. (Am. br.), Nat. Assn. Reporters of Jud. Decisions (pres. 1983-84). Episcopalian. Clubs: Union, Harvard (Boston). Public international. Office: PO Box 1646 Hollis NH 03049-1646

**MERRITTS, JACK MICHAEL,** lawyer; b. Denver, Oct. 1, 1948; s. William Maxwell Merritts and Anne Eva Yonko; m. Victoria Ann Neils, Aug. 24, 1974; children: Karl, Daniel, Andrew. BS in Mining Engring., Pa. State U., 1970; JD, Harvard U., 1973. Bar: Colo., U.S. Dist. Ct. Colo. 1973, U.S. Ct. Appeals (10th cir.) 1989. Assoc. Sherman & Howard, Denver, 1973-78; assoc., ptnr. Hall and Evans, Denver, 1978-81; ptnr. Montgomery, Little and McGrew, Englewood, Colo., 1981-92, McKenna & Cuneo, Denver, 1992-94; spl. counsel Burns, Wall, Smith & Mueller, Denver, 1994—. Contbr. articles to profl. jours. Trustee Rocky Mountain Mineral Law Found., Denver, 1990-95; boy scout leader Boy Scouts Am., Lakewood, 1984-96. Mem. Soc. of Mining Engring., Denver Coal Club, Ind. Petroleum Assn. of Mountain States (exec. com., bd. dirs. 1986-95), Phi Kappa Phi, Tau Beta Pi, Sigma Tau, Phi Delta Kappa. Avocations: hunting, fishing, trap shooting. Oil, gas, and mineral, General civil litigation, Environmental. Home: 470 Cody Dr Lakewood CO 80226-1146 Office: Burns Wall Smith & Mueller 303 E 17th Ave Ste 800 Denver CO 80203-1299

**MERRYDAY, STEVEN D.,** federal judge; b. 1950. BA, U. Fla., 1972, JD, 1975. With Holland & Knight, Tampa, 1975-83; ptnr. Glenn, Rasmussen, Fogarty, Merryday & Russo, Tampa, 1983-91; federal judge U.S. Dist. Ct. (mid. dist.), Fla., 1992—. Mem. Fed. Bar Assn., The Fla. Bar, Hillsborough County Bar Assn. Office: US Courthouse 801 N Florida Ave Tampa FL 33602-3849*

**MERSMAN, RICHARD KENDRICK, III,** lawyer; b. Des Moines, Sept. 14, 1949; s. Richard K. Jr. and Mary Jane Mersman; children: Richard K. IV, Thomas R. BA, Tulane U., 1971, JD, 1975. Bar: Mo. 1976. Atty. Boyce & Mersman, St. Louis, 1976-81; gen. counsel Mason Group, Inc., St. Louis, 1981-90; CFO The Forsythe Group, St. Louis, 1990-92; atty. The Stolar Partnership, St. Louis, 1992—. Roman Catholic. Avocations: golf, soccer coaching. Finance, Real property, Land use and zoning (including planning). Office: The Stolar Partnership 911 Washington Ave Ste 700 Saint Louis MO 63101-1290

**MERTES, ARTHUR EDWARD,** lawyer; b. Addison, Ill., June 7, 1966; s. Arthur Christian and Kathleen Celia (England) M. BSME, U. Ill., 1988, JD magna cum laude, 1994, MBA, 1994. Application engr. Ingersoll-Rand, Elmhurst, Ill., 1988-89, systems engr. tech. sales, 1989-90; assoc. Altheimer & Gray, Chgo., 1994-96, Burke, Warren, Mackey, Serritella, PC, Chgo., 1996—. Avocations: fitness, travel, sailing. General corporate, Contracts commercial, Mergers and acquisitions. Office: Burke Warren MacKay & Serritella 330 N Wabash Ave Fl 22 Chicago IL 60611-3603

**MERZ, MICHAEL,** federal judge; b. Dayton, Ohio, Mar. 29, 1945; s. Robert Louis and Hazel (Appleton) M.; m. Marguerite Logan LeBreton, Sept. 7, 1968; children: Peter Henry, Nicholas George. AB cum laude, Harvard U., 1967, JD, 1970. Bar: Ohio 1970, U.S. Dist. Ct. (so. dist.) Ohio 1971, U.S Supreme Ct. 1974, U.S. Ct. Appeals (6th cir.) 1975. Assoc. Smith & Schnacke, Dayton, Ohio, 1970-75, ptnr., 1976-77; judge Dayton Mcpl. Ct., 1977-84; magistrate U.S. Dist. Ct. (so. dist.) Ohio, 1984—; adj. prof. U. Dayton Law Sch., 1979—; mem. rules adv. com. Ohio Supreme Ct., 1989-96. Bd. dirs. United Way, Dayton, 1981-95; trustee Dayton and Montgomery County Pub. Libr., 1991—, Montgomery County Hist. Soc., 1995—, Ohio Libr. Coun., 1997—. Mem. ABA, Fed. Bar Assn., Am. Judicature Soc., Fed. Magistrate Judges Assn., Ohio State Bar Assn., Dayton Bar Assn. Republican. Roman Catholic. Office: US Dist Ct 902 Federal Bldg 200 W 2nd St Dayton OH 45402-1430

**MESCHKE, HERBERT LEONARD,** retired state supreme court justice; b. Belfield, N.D., Mar. 18, 1928; s. G.E. and Dorothy E. Meschke; m. Shirley Ruth McNeil; children: Marie, Jean, Michael, Jill. BA, Jamestown Coll., 1950; JD, U. Mich., 1953. Bar: N.D. Law clk. U.S. Dist. Ct. N.D., 1953-54; practice law Minot, N.D., 1954-85; mem. N.D. Ho. of Reps., 1965-66, N.D. Senate, 1967-70; justice N.D. State Supreme Ct., 1985-98; of counsel Pringle & Herigstad Law Firm, Minot, 1999—. Mem. ABA, Am. Law Inst., Am. Judicature Soc., N.D. Bar Assn.

**MESCHKOW, JORDAN M.,** patent lawyer; b. Bklyn., Mar. 25, 1957; s. Gerald Meschkow and Florence Y. (Katz) Silverman; m. Susan G. Scher, Aug. 10, 1980; children: Sasha Hayley, Alisha Sadie. BS in Biology, SUNY, Stony Brook, 1979; JD, Chgo. Kent Coll. Law, 1982. Bar: Ariz. 1982, Fla. 1983; registered U.S. Patent and Trademark Office 1983. Assoc. James F. Duffy, Patent Atty., Phoenix, Ariz., 1982; ptnr. Duffy & Meschkow, Phoenix, 1983-84; sole practice Phoenix, 1984-92; sr. ptnr. Meschkow & Gresham, P.L.C., Phoenix, 1992—; frequent talk radio guest and spkr. at seminars on patent, trademark and copyright law. Contbr. article series to profl. jours.; patentee in field. Exec. bd. City of Phoenix Fire Pub. Awareness League, 1996—. Mem. Am. Intellectual Property Law Assn., State Bar Ariz. (intellectual property sect. 1982—), State Bar Fla. Avocations: gardening, motorcycling, bicycling, skating, swimming. E-mail: M&GPatent@mcimail.com. Patent, Intellectual property, Trademark and copyright. Office: 5727 N 7th St Ste 409 Phoenix AZ 85014-5818

**MESHBESHER, RONALD I.,** lawyer; b. Mpls., May 18, 1933; s. Nathan J. and Esther J. (Balman) M.; m. Sandra F. Siegel, June 17, 1956 (div. 1978); children: Betsy F., Wendy S., Stacy J.; m. Kimberly L. Garnaas, May 23, 1988; 1 child, Jolie M. BS in Law, U. Minn., 1955, JD, 1957. Bar: Minn.

1957, U.S. Supreme Ct. 1966. Prosecuting atty. Hennepin County, Mpls., 1958-61; pres. Meshbesher and Spence Ltd., Mpls., 1961—; lectr. numerous legal and profl. orgns.; mem. adv. com. on rules of criminal procedure Minn. Supreme Ct., 1971-91; cons. on recodification of criminal procedure code Czech Republic Ministry of Justice, 1994. Author: Trial Handbook for Minnesota Lawyers, 1992; mem. bd. editors Criminal Law Advocacy Reporter; mem. adv. bd. Bur. Nat. Affairs Criminal Practice Manual; contbr. numerous articles to profl. jours. Mem. ATLA (bd. govs. 1968-71), ABA, Minn. Bar Assn., Internat. Acad. Trial Lawyers, Am. Coll. Trial Lawyers, Am. Bd. Trial Advs., Am. Bd. Criminal Lawyers (v.p. 1983), Am. Acad. Forensic Scis., Nat. Assn. Criminal Def. Lawyers (pres. 1984-85), Minn. Trial Lawyers Assn. (pres. 1973-74), Minn. Assn. Criminal Def. Lawyers (pres. 1991-92), Trial Lawyers for Pub. Justice, Calif. Attys. for Criminal Justice. Avocations: biking, photography, travel, flying. General civil litigation, Criminal, Personal injury. Home: 2010 Sugarwood Dr Orono MN 55356-9339 Office: Meshbesher & Spence 1616 Park Ave Minneapolis MN 55404-1695

**MESKILL, THOMAS J.,** federal judge; b. New Britain, Conn., Jan. 30, 1928; s. Thomas J. M.; m. Mary T. Grady; children—Maureen Meskill Heneghan, John, Peter, Eileen, Thomas. B.S., Trinity Coll., Hartford, Conn., 1950, LL.D., 1972; J.D., U. Conn., 1956; postgrad., Sch. Law, NYU; LL.D., U. Bridgeport, 1971, U. New Haven, 1974. Bar: Conn. 1956, Fla. 1957, D.C. 1957, U.S. Ct. Appeals (2d cir.) 1975, U.S. Supreme Ct. 1971. Former mem. firm Meskill, Dorsey, Sledzik and Walsh, New Britain; mem. 90th-91st Congresses 6th Conn. Dist.; gov. Conn., 1971-75; judge U.S. Ct. Appeals (2d cir.), New Britain, Conn., 1975—, chief judge, 1992-93, now sr. judge. Pres. New Britain Council Social Agys.; Asst. corp. council City of New Britain, 1960-62, mayor, 1962-64, corp. counsel, 1965-67; mem. Constl. Conv., Hartford, 1965. Served to 1st lt. USAF, 1950-53. Recipient Disting. Svc. award Jr. C. of C., 1964, Jud. Achievement award ATLA, 1983, Learned Hand medal for Excellence in Fed. Juridprudence, Fed. Bar Coun., 1994. Mem. Fla. Bar Assn., Con. Bar Assn. (Henry J. Naruk Jud. award 1994), Hartford County Bar Assn., New Britain Bar Assn., KC. Republican. Office: US Ct Appeals 114 W Main St New Britain CT 06051-4223

**MESSA, JOSEPH LOUIS, JR.,** lawyer; b. Phila., Mar. 24, 1962; s. Joseph Louis and Virginia (Ciaffoni) M. BS, Tulane U., 1984; JD, Temple U., 1988. Bar: Pa. 1988, N.J. 1988, U.S. Dist. Ct. N.J. 1988, U.S. Dist. Ct. (eastern dist.) Pa. 1998, U.S. Ct. Appeals (3d cir.) 1996. Assoc. Duane Morris & Heckscher, Phila., 1988-90; ptnr. Ominsky & Messa, Phila., 1990—. Ward leader Rep. Party, Phila. 1985—, city com., 1985—, exec. com., 1985—. Mem. ATLA, ABA, Pa. Trial Lawyers (cons., seminar presenter, liability com.), Phila. Trial Lawyers. Roman Catholic. Avocations: physical fitness, bodybuilding, waterskiing, boating, traveling. Personal injury, Product liability, Professional liability. Office: Ominsky & Messa 1760 Market St Fl 10 Philadelphia PA 19103-4104

**MESSENGER, JAMES LOUIS,** lawyer; b. Youngstown, Ohio, Oct. 18, 1942; s. William Robert and Georgette Elizabeth (Capehart) M.; m. Barbara Ann Vasslides, June 21, 1969; children: William, John. BBA, Ohio U., 1964; LLB, Syracuse U., 1967. Bar: Ohio 1967, U.S. Dist. Ct. (no. dist.) Ohio 1968, U.S. Ct. Appeals (6th cir.) 1976, U.S. Supreme Ct. 1982, U.S. Ct. Appeals (3d cir.) 1989. Assoc. Henderson, Covington, Stein & Donchess, Youngstown, 1967-74; ptnr./ Henderson, Covington, Stein, Donchess & Messenger, Youngstown, 1974-94, Henderson, Covington, Messenger, Newman & Thomas, Co., L.P.A., Youngstown, 1995—; bd. dirs. YSD Industries, Inc., Youngstown. Chmn., bd. dirs., founding mem. Ohio Coun. Sch. Bd. Attys., Columbus, Ohio, 1975—; active Civil Svc. Commn., Youngstown, 1991—. Mem. ABA, Ohio State Bar Assn., Mahoning County Bar Assn. (pres., award 1983). Republican. Episcopal. Avocations: thoroughbred horse racing, golf, handball. Education and schools, General civil litigation, General corporate. Home: 1811 Bears Den Rd Youngstown OH 44511-1361 Office: 600 Wick Ave Youngstown OH 44502-1215

**MESSER, SUSAN J.,** lawyer; b. Mt. Pleasant, Pa., Nov. 17, 1967; d. Angelo M. and Doris J. Rizza; m. Timothy M. Messer, Nov. 11, 1995; 1 cild, Matthew Ryan. BSBA, Duquesne U., 1989; JD, U. Pitts., 1992. Bar: Pa. 1992, U.S. Dist. Ct. (we. dist.) Pa. 1992. Atty. Bart Tyson, P.C., Pitts., 1992-93, McClune & Watkins P.C., Pitts., 1993-98, Titus & McConomy LLP, Pitts., 1998—. Mem. ABA, Pa. Bar Assn., Allegheny County Bar Assn. General corporate, Mergers and acquisitions, Real property. Office: Titus & McConomy LLP 4 Gateway Ctr 20th Fl Pittsburgh PA 15222

**MESSERLY, CHRIS ALAN,** lawyer; b. Ft. Dodge, Iowa, Oct. 8, 1958; s. Don Howard and Janice Lee (Hovey) M.; m. Joanne Esther Lerner, June 20, 1981. BA, Bowdoin Coll., Brunswick, Maine, 1981; JD cum laude, Hamline U., St. Paul, 1986. Bar: Minn. 1986, U.S. Dist. Ct. Minn., U.S. Ct. Appeals (8th cir.) 1986, Wis. 1992, U.S. Dist. Ct. Wis. 1992. Spl. asst. city atty. City of St. Paul, 1986-87; ptnr. Robins, Kaplan, Miller & Ciresi, Mpls., 1986—; adj. law prof. Hamline U., 1992—. Mem. ABA, Assn. Trial Lawyers Am., Minn. Trial Lawyers Assn., Wis. Acad. Trial Lawyers, Hennepin County Bar Assn., Ramsey County Bar Assn. Personal injury, Professional liability, General civil litigation. Office: Robins Kaplan Miller Ciresi 800 Lasalle Ave Ste 2800 Minneapolis MN 55402-2015

**MESSERSMITH, LANNY DEE,** lawyer; b. Laverne, Okla., Oct. 3, 1942; s. Harry D. and Vivian D. (Bowers) M.; m. Christine Diane Smith, Sept. 28, 1974; 1 child, Nicholas Ryan. BA, U. N.Mex., 1966, JD, 1969; DCL (hon.), Holy Cath. Apostolic Ch., 1975. Bar: N.Mex. 1969, U.S. Ct. Claims 1978, U.S. Supreme Ct. 1981. Asst. dist. atty. 1st Dist. State of N.Mex., Santa Fe, 1969-70, asst. atty. gen., 1974-76; assoc. Rhodes & McCallister, Albuquerque, 1970-72; ptnr. McCallister, Messersmith & Wiseman, Albuquerque, 1972-74, Lanny D. Messersmith, PA, Albuquerque, 1974-85, Messersmith, Eaton & Keenan, Albuquerque, 1985-89, Schuler, Messersmith, McNeill & Daly, Albuquerque, 1989—; cons., hon. consul Govt. of Fed. Republic of Germany, 1981—. Mem. Albuquerque Com. on Fgn. Rels., 1988—, Sister Cities, 1988—. Mem. N.Mex. Bar Assn. (bd. dirs. internat. com.), Albuquerque Bar Assn., N.Mex. Retail Assn. (pres. 1987), Albuquerque UN Assn. (bd. dirs. 1985), Albuquerque Country Club, Masons (scholarship chmn. Albuquerque chpt. 1984-87), Shriners, Rotary Internat. Avocations: sailing, reading. Federal civil litigation, Private international, Probate. Home: 7904 Woodridge Dr NE Albuquerque NM 87109-5258 Office: Schuler Messersmith McNeill & Daley 4300 San Mateo Blvd NE Ste B380 Albuquerque NM 87110-8401

**MESSICK, DAPHNE JEANNE,** lawyer; b. Middletown, Conn., Oct. 22, 1953; d. Edgar Neil and Marilyn Beth (Smith) M.; m. Gary Charles Nixon, July 6, 1989. BA in Hispanic Studies and Anthropology, Conn. Coll., 1975; JD, U. Conn., 1981. Assoc. Brenner, Saltzman & Wallman, New Haven, 1981-83, Dzialo, Pickett & Allen, Middletown & Old Saybrook, Conn., 1983-89; prin. Dzialo, Pickett & Allen, Middletown & Old Saybrook, 1989—; dir. Ctrl. Conn. Bus. and Estate Planning Coun., Hartford, Conn., 1988-91, pres., 1990-91. Pres. Mercy Alumnae Assn., Middletown, 1988; mem. prin.'s coun. Mercy H.S., Middletown, 1993—. Recipient German Consulate Book prize German Consular, Conn. Coll., New London, 1973, 75. Mem. Conn. Bar Assn. (real property, probate and trust sect., elder law sect.), Middlesex County Bar Assn. (chair Law Day 1984, sec. 1985-87), Phi Beta Kappa. Office: Dzialo Pickett & Allen PC 15 Elm St Old Saybrook CT 06475-1101

**MESSINA, BONNIE LYNN,** lawyer; b. Lima, Ohio, Mar. 17, 1961; m. Dominick Messina. BA, We. Md. Coll., 1983; JD magna cum laude, U. Balt., 1991. Bar: Md. 1991. Claim adjuster The Hartford, Hunt Valley, Md., 1983-86; claim supr. The Hartford, Hunt Valley, 1986-88; assoc. Venable, Baetjer & Howard, Balt., 1991-94; sr. counsel U.S. Fidelity & Guaranty Co., Balt., 1994-98; sr. counsel St. Paul Fire & Marine Ins. Co., Balt., 1999—, group claims counsel, 1999—. Assoc. editor U. Balt. Law Rev., 1990-91. Mem. jud. selection com. Women's Law Ctr., Balt., 1993—; mentor U. Balt. Sch. of law, Balt., 1993-97. Recipient Am. Jurisprudence award Balt., 1989, 90 (2). Mem. ABA (vice chair fidelity and surety sect.), Md. State Bar Assn., Balt. County Bar Assn., Md. Assn. Def. Trial Counsel, Def. Rsch. Inst., Inc., Psi Chi. General civil litigation, Insurance. Office: St Paul Fire & Marine Ins Co Ins Co 6225 Smith Ave Baltimore MD 21209-3652

**MESSINGER, J. HENRY,** lawyer; b. N.Y.C., Sept. 7, 1944; s. Benjamin and Edna (Balser) M.; m. Karen Gilbert D'Abo, Feb. 5, 1977 (div.); 1 child, Alan Toby. BA, Union Coll., 1965; JD, NYU, 1968, MA in Edn., 1969, MA in Polit. Sci., U. N.Mex. 1996. Bar: N.Y. 1968, N.Mex. 1973, U.S. Tax Ct. 1973. Pvt. practice, Woodstock, N.Y., 1970-72; assoc. Stephen Natelson, Esq., Taos, 1972-73; ptnr. Natelson & Messinger, Taos, 1974-75; pvt. practice, Taos, 1976-94, Albuquerque, 1994—. Bd. dirs. Taos Sch. Music, 1982-97, R.C. Gorman Found., 1986—; bd. dirs. Taos Valley Sch., 1979-82, pres. 1980-81. Mem. ABA, Am. Polit. Sci. Assn., Law and Soc. Assn. Personal income taxation, Estate planning. Office: 809 Branding Iron St SE Albuquerque NM 87123-4207

**MESSINGER, SHELDON L(EOPOLD),** law educator; b. Chgo., Aug. 26, 1925; s. Leopold J. and Cornelia (Eichel) M.; m. Mildred Handler, June 30, 1947; children—Adam J., Eli B. Ph.D. in Sociology, UCLA, 1969. Assoc. rsch. sociologist Ctr. Study Law and Soc. U. Calif., Berkeley, 1961-69, rsch. sociologist, 1969-70, prof. criminology, 1970-77, prof. law jurisprudence and social policy program, 1977-88, Elizabeth J. Boalt prof. law, 1988-91, prof. law emeritus, 1991—, prof. grad. sch., 1995-97, vice chmn., 1961-69, acting dean criminology, 1970-71, dean criminology, 1971-75, chmn. program, 1983-87. Author, co-author numerous books, articles. Mem. Coun. U. Calif. Emeriti Assns. (pres.-elect 1999—). Home: 860 Indian Rock Ave Berkeley CA 94707-2051 Office: U Calif Sch Law Boalt Hall Berkeley CA 94720

**MESSITTE, PETER JO,** judge; b. Washington, July 17, 1941; s. Jesse B. and Edith (Wechsler) M.; m. Susan P. Messitte, Sept. 5, 1965: children: Zachariah, Abigail. BA cum laude, Amherst Coll., 1963; JD, U. Chgo., 1966. Bar: Md. 1969, D.C. 1969, U.S. Ct. Appeals (4th cir.) 1977, U.S. Supreme Ct. 1973, U.S. Ct. Appeals (DC cir.) 1982, U.S. Ct. Appeals (5th cir.) 1983. Assoc. Zuckert, Scoutt & Rasenberger, Washington, 1968-71; solo practice Chevy Chase, Md., 1971-75; mem. Messitte & Rosenberg, P.A., Chevy Chase, 1975-81; prin. Peter J. Messitte, P.A., Chevy Chase, 1981-85; assoc. judge Cir. Ct. for Montgomery County Rockville, Md., 1985-93; judge U.S. Dist. Ct. Md., Greenbelt, 1993—; mem. internat. jud. rels. com. Jud. Conf. U.S. Bd. dirs. Cmty. Psychiat. Clinic, Montgomery County, Md., 1974-85, v.p. 1980-85; Peace Corps vol. , Sao Paulo, Brazil, 1966-68; Md. del. Dem. Nat. Conv., N.Y.C., 1980. Recipient teaching citations Fed. Deposit Ins. Corp. Bank Exam. Sch., 1975, 79, Am. Inst. Banking, 1978, Elizabeth Scull award for Outstanding Svc. to Montgomery County, Md., 1993, Spl. citation Divsn. Roundtable Montgomery County, 1993, Contbr. Mental Health Cmty. Psychiat. Clinic, 1986. Mem. ABA, FBA, Inter-Am. Bar Assn., D.C. Bar Assn., Md. Bar Assn., Montgomery County Bar Assn. (Century of Svc. award 1999), Am. Law Inst., Fed. Judges Assn. (4th jud. cir.), Charles Fahy Inn of Ct. (master 1987-88), Montgomery County Inn of Ct. (pres. 1988-90), Jud. Inst. Md. (bd. dirs. 1989-93). Jewish. Office: US Courthouse 6500 Cherrywood Ln Greenbelt MD 20770-1249

**MESSNER, ROBERT THOMAS,** lawyer, banking executive; b. McKeesport, Pa., Mar. 27, 1938; s. Thomas M. and Cecilia Mary (McElhinny) M.; m. Anne Margaret Lux, Dec. 3, 1966; children: Megan Anne, Michael Thomas. A.B., Dartmouth Coll., 1960; LL.B., U. Pa., 1963. Bar: Pa. 1965. With firm Rose, Schmidt & Dixon, Pitts., 1965-68; with G.C. Murphy Co., McKeesport, 1968-86; corp. sec. G.C. Murphy Co., 1974—, gen. counsel, 1975-86, v.p., 1976-86; v.p., gen. counsel, corp. sec. Dollar Bank, Pitts., 1986—; dir. G.C. Murphy Found. Bd. dirs. McKeesport YMCA, Downtown Pitts. YMCA, Mon-Yough Heritage Found., 1981-83, Braddock's Field Hist. Soc., 1994—; mem. adv. bd. Pa. Human Rels. Commn., 1968, 69; Rep. candidate for Pa. Legis., 1986, fin. adv. bd. Wilkinsburg, Pa., 1988—. 1st lt. U.S. Army, 1963-65. Decorated Commendation medal. Mem. ABA, Pa. Bar Assn. (chmn. corp. law dept. com.), Allegheny County Bar Assn. (coun. on corp., banking and bus. law), Am. Soc. Corp. Secs. (pres. Pitts. regional group, dir.), Am. Mgmt. Assn., Pa. Assn. Savs. Instns. (chmn. legal com. 1989—), Am. Corp. Counsel Assn., Theta Delta Chi. Clubs: Dartmouth Western Pa., Rivers. Consumer commercial, Banking, General corporate. Home: 1061 Blackridge Rd Pittsburgh PA 15235-2719 Office: Dollar Bank Three Gateway Ctr Pittsburgh PA 15222

**MESSURI, NICHOLAS JOSEPH,** prosecutor; b. Somerville, Mass., Aug. 24, 1960; s. Nicholas Anthony and Anne Marie (Salerno) M.; m. Ernestine R. Pacheco; children: Matthew, Brittany, Nathan. BS, Northeastern U., 1982; JD, New Eng. Sch. Law, Boston, 1985. Bar: Mass. 1985. Asst. dist. atty. Middlesex County Dist. Atty., Cambridge, Mass., 1986-92; asst. atty. gen. Office Atty. Gen., Boston, 1992—; dir. med. fraud control unit, Atty. Gen., Boston, 1995—. Office: Office of Atty Gen 200 Portland St Boston MA 02114-1722

**MESTEL, MARK DAVID,** lawyer; b. Bklyn., May 15, 1951; s. Oscar L. and Katherine (Waldner) M.; m. Linda Antonik, Jan. 6, 1984; children: Brenton V., Spenser Andrew. BA, Northwestern U., 1973; JD, U. Mich., 1976. Bar: Mich. 1976, D.C. 1977, Wash. 1978, U.S. Dist. Ct. (we. dist.) Wash. 1979, U.S. Ct. Appeals (9th cir.) 1984, U.S. Dist. Ct. (ea. dist.) Wash. 1986, U.S. Supreme Ct., 1991; cert. criminal trial specialist Nat. Bd. Trial Advocacy, 1982, 86, 91. Atty., EPA, Washington, 1976-77; sole practice, Washington, 1977-78, Everett, 1981-84; staff atty. Snohomish County Pub. Defender, Everett, Wash., 1978-80, dir., atty., 1980-81; ptnr. Mestel & Muenster, Everett, 1984-94; sole practitioner Law Office of Mark D. Mestel Inc., P.S., 1994—. Mem. ATLA, Nat. Assn. Criminal Def. Lawyers, Wash. Trial Lawyers Assn., Wash. Assn. Criminal Def. Lawyers. Criminal, Civil rights, Personal injury. Office: Mark D Mestel Inc PS 3221 Oakes Ave Everett WA 98201-4407

**MESTRES, RICARDO ANGELO, JR.,** lawyer; b. N.Y.C., Aug. 12, 1933; s. Ricardo Angelo and Anita (Gwynne) M.; m. Ann Farnsworth, June 18, 1955; children: Laura, Ricardo III, Lynn, Anthony. AB, Princeton U., 1955; LLB, Harvard U., 1961. Bar: N.Y. 1962, U.S. Supreme Ct. 1970. Assoc. Sullivan & Cromwell, N.Y.C., 1961-67, ptnr., 1968—, chmn., sr. ptnr., 1995—. Trustee Unitarian Ch. All Souls, N.Y.C., 1973-79, 84-87; trustee Phillips Exeter Acad., 1989-99, pres. bd. trustees, 1993-99. Served to lt. USN, 1955-58. Mem. ABA, N.Y. State Bar Assn., Assn. Bar City N.Y. (corp. law, securities regulation law and state legis. coms.), Am. Law Inst., Phi Beta Kappa. Clubs: Downtown Assn., Links (N.Y.C.); Mill Reef (Antigua). General corporate, Mergers and acquisitions, Securities. Office: Sullivan & Cromwell 125 Broad St Fl 28 New York NY 10004-2489

**METCALFE, JAMES ASHFORD,** lawyer; b. Washington, Nov. 8, 1940; s. Edward Conrad and Agnes Malcolm (Ashford) M.; m. Claire Elizabeth Madison, Dec. 23, 1963; children: Luta Marguerite, James Madison. BS, U.S. Naval Acad., 1963; JD, Coll. William and Mary, 1975. Bar: Va. 1975, U.S. Dist. Ct. (ea. dist.) Va. 1975, U.S. Ct. Appeals (4th cir.) 1975, U.S. Ct. Claims 1979, U.S. Supreme Ct. 1979, U.S. Ct. Appeals (5th cir.) 1983. Commd. ensign USN, 1963; advanced through grades to capt. USNR, 1986; resigned USN, 1972; law clk. to presiding judge U.S. Dist. Ct. (ea. dist.) Va., Norfolk, 1975-76; assoc. Seawell, McCoy et al, Norfolk, 1976-80; asst. U.S. atty. Dept. Justice, Norfolk, 1980—, sr. litigation counsel, 1991-99. Mng. editor William and Mary Law Rev., Williamsburg, Va., 1974-75. Bd. dirs. Thalia Civic League, Virginia Beach, Va., 1973-78, Friends Sch., Virginia Beach, 1977-90. Commd. lt. USNR, 1972, advanced to capt. 1986, ret. 1993. Mem. Fed. Bar Assn. (v.p. Tidewater chpt. 1989-90, pres. 1990-91), U.S. Naval Inst., Aircraft Owners and Pilots Assn., Norfolk-Portsmouth Bar Assn., Virginia Beach Bar Assn. Club: YMCA. Office: US Atty 8000 World Trade Ctr 101 W Main St Norfolk VA 23510-1651

**METCALFE, OLGA,** lawyer, educator; b. Hialeah, Fla., Dec. 21, 1969; d. Aniceto A. and Otilia A. Ruiz; m. George Lambeth Metcalfe, July 27, 1998; stepchildren: George, Justin, Gabriella, Andrew. BA in Polit. Sci., Fla. Internat. U., 1989; JD, U. Miami, 1992. Bar: Fla. 1992, U.S. Dist. Ct. (so. and mid. dists.) Fla. 1993, U.S. Ct. Appeals (11th cir.) 1996. Assoc. Blaxberg, Grayson & Singer P.A., Miami, Fla., 1993; atty., law clk. U.S. Magistrate Linnea R. Johnson, Miami, 1993, 95; pvt. practice law Miami, 1993-98; assoc. Law Offices of Stephen A. Papy, Miami, 1995-96; asst. dist. legal counsel Fla. Dept. Children and Families, Miami, 1997-98; ptnr. Metcalfe & Metcalfe, Miami, 1998—; prof. debtor-creditor law Rollins Coll., Tampa, Fla., 1994, 95. Vol. teen ct. judge Teen Ct., Tampa, 1994-95; vol. lawyer Put Something Back Pro Bono Project Dade Bar, Miami, 1996—; bd. dirs. Am. Cancer Soc. New Directions, Miami, 1996-97; guardian ad litem Dade County, Miami, 1996-97. Mem. ABA, Concerned Matrimonial Lawyers, Juvenile Justice Attys. Assn. Republican. Avocations: reading, crocheting, aerobics with weights, cooking, role-playing games. Family and matrimonial, Juvenile, Appellate. Office: Metcalfe & Metcalfe 1313 Ponce De Leon Blvd Ste 301 Coral Gables FL 33134-3343

**METCALFE, ROBERT DAVIS, III,** lawyer; b. Bridgeport, Conn., July 2, 1956; s. Robert Davis Jr. and Barbara Ann (Peaslee) M. BA summa cum laude, U. Conn., 1978, JD, 1981; MA, Trinity Coll., 1982, Am. Mil. U., 1997. Bar: Conn. 1981, U.S. Supreme Ct. 1986, D.C. 1990, Md. 1991. Judge adv. USN, Norfolk, Va., 1982-85; spl. asst. U.S. atty. U.S. Dept. Justice, Norfolk, 1985; trial atty. U.S. Dept. Justice, Washington, 1985—. Instr. ARC, Hartford, Conn., 1976-80; legis. asst. Conn. Gen. Assembly, Hartford, 1977. Served to lt. USN, 1982-85. Mem. Fed. Bar Assn., Conn. Bar Assn., Judge Adv. Assn., Mensa, Phi Beta Kappa. Republican. Roman Catholic. Avocations: martial arts, reading, sailing, trap and skeet shooting, philately.

**METCALFE, WALTER LEE, JR.,** lawyer; b. St. Louis, Dec. 19, 1938; s. Walter Lee and Carol (Crowe) M.; m. Cynthia Williamson, Aug. 26, 1965; children—Carol, Edward. AB, Washington U., St. Louis, 1960; JD, U. Va., 1964. Bar: Mo. 1964. Ptnr. Armstrong, Teasdale, Kramer & Vaughan, St. Louis, 1964-81; sr. ptnr. Bryan Cave LLP, St. Louis, 1982—, now chmn. Bd. dirs. Grand Ctr., Inc. chmn., 1994—, St. Louis Regional Health Care Corp. Mem. ABA, Mo. Bar Assn., St. Louis Bar Assn., Bogey Club, Noonday Club. Episcopalian. General corporate. Home: 26 Upper Ladue Rd Saint Louis MO 63124-1675 Office: Bryan Cave 211 N Broadway 1 Metropolitan Sq Ste 3600 Saint Louis MO 63102-2750

**METH-FARRINGTON, TINA MARIE,** lawyer; b. Washington, Iowa, Dec. 12, 1962; d. Raymond Charles and Ruth Marie (Crom) Meth; m. Rusty James Farrington, Aug. 20, 1983; children: Wesley, Brady, Lucas. BA, U. Iowa, 1985; JD, Drake Law Sch., 1988. Bar: Iowa 1988. Atty. Child Support Recovery Unit, Fort Dodge, Iowa, 1988-98; asst. Sac and Calhoun County Atty., Sac City/Rockwell City, Iowa, 1998—. Contbr. articles to profl. jours. V.p. Calhoun County Rep. Women, 1996-99; Sunday sch. tchr. St. Paul's Luth. Ch., Rockwell City, Iowa, 1993—. Mem. Iowa State Bar Assn. (family law sect. 1990—, coun. 1994-96, chairperson support com. 1990-95), Calhoun County Bar Assn., CSRU (com. pit crew 1996—, team leader 1996). Republican. Lutheran. Avocations: bowling, baseball, gardening, reading, travel. Office: Calhoun County Atty 418 Main St Rockwell City IA 50579-1419 Office: Sac County Atty 100 W State St Sac City IA 50583

**METROPULOS, MITCHELL JAMES,** lawyer; b. Crystal Lake, Ill., Aug. 5, 1960; s. James Peter and Phyllis Ann M.; m. Teri Gail Dahlby, Oct. 29, 1994; children: Sarah, Nicholas. BSc, Bradley U., 1982; JD, U. Wis., 1986, MA in Pub. Policy and Adminstrn., 1986. Bar: Wis. 1987, U.S. Dist. Ct. (western dist.) Wis. 1987. Asst. dist. attorney Chippiwa County, Chippawa Falls, Wis., 1987-88, Outagamie County, Appleton, Wis., 1988—. Big Brother Pals Program Appleton, Wis., 1988-97; mem. Domestic Intervention Program Appleton, 1998. Avocations: golf, softball, volleyball. Office: District Attorneys Office 320 S Walnut St Appleton WI 54911-5918

**METTER, RONALD ELLIOT,** lawyer; b. Phila., June 27, 1945; s. Harry H. and Ann (Shapiro) M.; m. Helene Rochelle Gross, June 22, 1968 (div. June 1974); children: Jodi, Jamie; m. Angela Marie Carricato, Sept. 26, 1981; children: Jonathan, David. BS, Temple U., 1968, JD, 1971. Bar: Pa. 1971, U.S. Dist. Ct. (ea. dist.) Pa. 1971. Assoc. Samuel C. Katz Ltd., Phila., 1971-74; ptnr. Metter & Simon, Phila., 1974-85; prt. practive Phila., 1985-88; counsel Semanoff & Hendler, Phila., 1988-92; ptnr. Metter & Gusoff, Phila., 1992—; panelist Law Jour. WXYZ TV; bd. dirs. Awbury Sch., Phila. (adv. bd.); judge pro tem Phila. Ct. Comm. Pleas. Editor Temple Law Quarterly. Commnr. Pa. Valley Sports Assn., Narberth, 1980-84. Recipient Jacob Kossman award, Hon. Chas. Weiner award. Mem. ATLA (judge student trial advocacy competition), Pa. Bar Assn., Pa. Trial Lawyers Assn., Phila. Bar Assn. (legal rights persons with disabilities com., spkrs. bur., medico-legal com., bar news media com.), Phila. Trial Lawyers Assn. Avocations: sports, antique automobiles, travel, tropical fish, music. Personal injury, Product liability. Home: 1333 Bobarn Dr Narberth PA 19072-1135

**METZ, CRAIG HUSEMAN,** legislative administrator; b. Columbia, S.C., Aug. 26, 1955; s. Leonard Huseman and Annette (Worthington) M.; m. Karen Angela McCleary, Aug. 11, 1984; 1 child, Preston Worthington. BA, U. Tenn., 1977; JD, U. Memphis, 1986; cert., U.S. Ho. of Reps. Rep. Leadership Parlimentary Law Sch., 1987. Bar: S.C., D.C., U.S. Ct. Claims, U.S. Supreme Ct., U.S. Ct. Appeals (4th cir.). Canvass coord., liaison Campaign to Re-elect Congressman Floyd Spence, 1978; del., chmn. Shelby County Del. to 1983 Tenn. Young Rep. Fedn. Conv.; vice chmn. Shelby County Young Reps., 1983-84, chmn., 1984-85; Shelby County adminstr., asst. to Tenn. state exec. dir. Reagan-Bush Campaign, 1984; field rep. Campaign to Re-elect Congressman Floyd Spence, 1986; spl. asst. to Congressman Floyd Spence, 1986-88; counsel com. on labor and human resources U.S. Senate, 1988-90; commr.'s counsel U.S. Occupational Safety and Health Rev. Commn., Washington, 1990-91; spl. asst. to asst. sec. for legis. and congl. affairs; dep. asst. sec. for congl. liaison U.S. Dept. Edn., Washington, 1991-93; asst. dir. Divsn. Congl. Affairs AMA, Washington, 1993; chief of staff Congressman Floyd Spence, Washington, 1993—. Judge nat. writing competition U.S. Constn. Bicentennial, S.C. 1987-88; mem. Ch. of the Ascension and Saint Agnes, Washington. Recipient award of merit Rep. Party of Shelby County, 1985, Outstanding Leadership award Shelby County Young Reps., 1985. Mem. Rep. Nat. Lawyers Assn. (state chmn. S.C. chpt. 1987-90), Freedoms Found. Valley Forge, Va. Hist. Soc., Assn. for Preservation Va. Antiquities, Va. Geneal. Soc., U. South Caroliniana Soc., Palmetto Trust for Historic Preservation, Lowcountry Heritage Soc., Orangeburg County Hist. Soc., Nat. Trust for Hist. Preservation (assoc. Capital region), SAR, St. David's Soc., St. Andrew's Soc. Washington, Mil. Soc. War of 1812, Vet. Corps Arty. State of N.Y., Gen. Soc. War of 1812, Mil. Order Loyal Legion of U.S., Order of St. John (Hospitaller), SCV, Mil. Order Stars and Bars, Nat. Cathedral Assn., U. Tenn. Nat. Alumni Assn., Sigma Alpha Epsilon, Phi Alpha Delta (v.p. McKellar chpt., Outstanding Svc. award 1983). Republican. Episcopalian. Home: 8505 Westown Way Vienna VA 22182-2513 Office: 2405 Rayburn Bldg Washington DC 20515-4002

**METZ, LARRY EDWARD,** lawyer; b. Phila., Mar. 20, 1955; s. Harry Franz and Joan (Nye) M.; m. Mariko Tomisato, Mar. 26, 1980; children: Marla Jo, Christina Jill. BA, U. Fla., 1976; JD with high honors, Fla. State U., 1983. Bar: Fla. 1983, U.S. Dist. Ct. (so., mid. and no. dists.) Fla. 1984, U.S. Ct. Appeals (11th cir.) 1984, U.S. Supreme Ct. 1987. Assoc. Fleming, O'Bryan & Fleming, Ft. Lauderdale, Fla., 1983-86; atty. Westinghouse Electric Corp., Coral Springs, Fla., 1986-88; pvt. practice Ft. Lauderdale, 1988-91, Coral Springs, 1991-93; assoc. Herzfeld & Rubin, Miami, 1993-96; ptnr. Herzfeld & Rubin, Ft. Lauderdale, 1996-99; assoc. Unger, Swartwood, Indest & Acree, Orlando, Fla., 1999—. Area leader, sign co-chmn., spkr. George Bush for Pres. Broward County (Fla.) Victory Com., 1988; pres. Broward County Regional Rep. Club, 1991, 95; mem. exec. com. Broward County Reps., 1988-91, 93-96; Rep. nominee U.S. Ho. Reps. 19th dist., Fla., 1992. Capt. USMC, 1976-82. Mem. ABA, Broward Lawyers Care (pro bono project, Outstanding Mem. award 1989, 90), Order of the Coif. General civil litigation, Insurance, Product liability. Office: Unger Swartwood Indest & Acree 701 Peachtree Rd Orlando FL 32804-6847

**METZER, PATRICIA ANN,** lawyer; b. Phila., Mar. 10, 1941; d. Freeman Weeks and Evelyn (Heap) M.; m. Karl Hormann, June 30, 1980. BA with distinction, U. Pa., 1963, LLB cum laude, 1966. Bar: Mass. 1966, D.C. 1972, U.S. Tax Ct. 1988. Assoc., then ptnr. Mintz, Levin, Cohn, Glovsky and Popeo, Boston, 1966-75; assoc. tax legis. counsel U.S. Treasury Dept., Washington, 1975-78; shareholder, dir. Goulston & Storrs, P.C., Boston, 1978-98; stockholder Hutchins, Wheeler & Dittmar, P.C., Boston, 1998—; lectr. program continuing legal edn. Boston Coll. Law Sch., Chestnut Hill, Mass., spring 1974; mem. adv. com. NYU Inst. Fed. Taxation, N.Y.C., 1981-87; mem. practitioner liaison com. Mass. Dept. Revenue, 1985-90; spkr. in field. Author: Federal Income Taxation of Individuals, 1984; mem. adv. bd. Corp. Tax and Bus. Planning Review, 1996—; mem. editl. bd. Am. Jour. Tax Policy, 1995-98; contbr. articles to profl. jours., chpts. to books. Bd. mgrs. Barrington Ct. Condominium, Cambridge, Mass., 1985-86; bd. dirs.

University Road Parking Assn., Cambridge, 1988—; trustee Social Law Libr., Boston, 1989-93. Mem. ABA (tax sect., mem. coun. 1996-99, chmn. subcom. allocations and distbns. partnership com. 1978-82, vice chmn. legis. 1991-93, chmn. 1993-95, com. govt. submissions, vice liaison 1993-94, liaison 1994-95, North Atlantic region, co-liaison 1995-96, N.E. region, regional liaison meetings com.), FBA (coun. on taxation, chmn. corp. taxation com. 1977-81, chmn. com. partnership taxation 1981-87), Mass. Bar Assn., Boston Bar Assn. (coun. 1987-89, chmn. tax sect. 1989-91), Am. Coll. Tax Counsel (bd. regents 1999—), Boston Estate Planning Coun. (exec. com. 1975, 79-82). Avocation: vocal performances (as soloist and with choral groups). Taxation, general, Corporate taxation, Estate taxation. Office: Hutchins Wheeler & Dittmar PC 101 Federal St Boston MA 02110-1817

**METZGER, JEFFREY PAUL,** lawyer; b. St. Louis, Oct. 13, 1950; s. John E. and Ellen J. M.; m. Stephanie Ann Stahr, Dec. 27, 1977. BA magna cum laude, Amherst Coll., 1973; JD, Georgetown U., 1976. Bar: D.C., 1977. Legis. asst. to U.S. Senator Joseph Biden, Jr. of Del., 1973; assoc. Collier, Shannon, Rill and Scott, Washington, 1976-79, Cole and Groner, P.C., Washington, 1979-82; trial atty. comml. litigation br. civil div. U.S. Dept. Justice, Washington, 1982-85; mem. profl. staff Pres.'s Blue Ribbon Commn. on Def. Mgmt., 1985-86; asst. gen. counsel Unisys Corp., McLean, Va., 1986-88, v.p., assoc. gen. counsel, 1989—. Mem. ABA.

**METZGER, JOHN MACKAY,** lawyer; b. Princeton, N.J., Mar. 8, 1948; s. Bruce Manning and Isobel Elizabeth (Mackay) M.; m. Sandra Kay Wellington, May 8, 1999. BA cum laude, Harvard U., 1970; JD, NYU, 1973; postgrad., London Sch. Econs., 1973-74. Bar: Pa. 1976, N.J. 1976, U.S. Dist. Ct. N.J. 1976, U.S. Tax Ct. 1977, D.C. 1978, U.S. Ct. Appeals (fed. cir.) 1982. Tax adminstr. N.J. Div. Taxation, Trenton, 1976-86, 88—; atty. McCarthy & Schatzman PA, Princeton, 1986-88; mem. N.J. Econ. Devel. Coun., 1987-90. Contbr. articles to profl. jours. Mem. ABA, Am. Soc. Internat. Law, Mercer County Bar Assn., Harvard Club of N.Y.C., N.J. Hist. Soc. Republican. Home: 52 Coriander Dr Princeton NJ 08540-9434 Office: 50 Barrack St Trenton NJ 08646-0001

**METZINGER, TIMOTHY EDWARD,** lawyer; b. L.A., Aug. 21, 1961; s. Robert Cole and Mary Jean (Cusick) M.; m. Cynthia Lee Stanworth, Nov. 16, 1991. BA, UCLA, 1986; JD, U. San Francisco, 1989. Bar: Calif. 1989, U.S. Dist. Ct. (ctrl., so., ea. and no. dists.) Calif. 1989, U.S. Ct. Appeals (9th cir.) 1989, U.S. Supreme Ct. 1994. Assoc. Bronson, Bronson & McKinnon, L.A., 1989-93, Price, Postel & Parma, Santa Barbara, Calif., 1993—. Bd. dirs. Santa Barbara County Bar Assn. Mem. Santa Barbara Mus. Natural History (bd. advisors), Santa Barbara Barristers Club (pres.), Order of Barristers, Am. Inns. Ct. Avocations: diving, moutaineering, sailing. General civil litigation, Environmental, Contracts commercial. Office: Price Postel & Parma 200 E Carrillo St Ste 400 Santa Barbara CA 93101-2190

**METZNER, CHARLES MILLER,** federal judge; b. N.Y.C., Mar. 13, 1912; s. Emanuel and Gertrude (Miller) M.; m. Jeanne Gottlieb, Oct. 6, 1966. A.B., Columbia U., 1931, LL.B., 1933. Bar: N.Y. 1933. Pvt. practice, 1934; mem. Jud. Council State N.Y., 1935-41; law clk. to N.Y. supreme ct. justice, 1942-52; exec. asst. to U.S. atty. Gen. Herbert Brownell, Jr., 1953-54; mem. firm Chapman, Walsh & O'Connell, 1954-59; judge U.S. Dist Ct. (so. dist.) N.Y., 1959—; Mem. Law Revision Commn. N.Y. State, 1959; chmn. com. adminstrn. magistrates system U.S. Jud. Conf., 1970-81; chmn. Columbia Coll. Coun., 1965-66. Pres. N.Y. Young Republican Club, 1941; Trustee Columbia U., 1972-84, trustee emeritus, 1984—; bd. dirs. N.Y.C. Ctr. Music and Drama, 1969-74. Recipient Lawyer Div. of Joint Def. Appeal award, 1961, Columbia U. Alumni medal, 1966, Founders award Nat. Coun. U.S. Magistrates, 1989. Mem. ABA, Am. Law Inst., Fed. Bar Coun. (cert. Disting. Jud. Svc. 1989).

**MEVEC, EDWARD ROBERT,** lawyer, funeral director; b. Binghamton, N.Y., Aug. 27, 1958; s. Edward John and Margaret B. (Puskar) M.; m. Barbara Ann Vines, May 14, 1988; children: Benjamin A. Vines-Mevec, Daniel L. Vines-Mevec. BS summa cum laude, St. Thomas Aquinas Coll., Sparkill, N.Y., 1985; JD, U. Bridgeport, Conn., 1988. Bar: N.Y. 1990, U.S. Dist. Ct. (so. dist.) N.Y. 1992, U.S. Dist. Ct. (ea. dist.) N.Y. 1994, U.S. Ct. Appeals for the Armed forces 1995, U.S. Ct. Appeals (2d cir.) 1996, U.S. Supreme Ct. 1996. Atty. The Legal Aid Soc., Bronx, N.Y., 1988-89; assoc. Bruce W. Braswell, Esq., Peekskill, N.Y., 1989-91, Michael T. Ridge, Esq., Bronx, N.Y., 1991-92; trial atty. Gerlad G. Cowen, Esq., Elmsford, N.Y., 1992; arbitrator small claims N.Y.C. Civil Ct., Bronx, 1996—; hearing officer N.Y. State Supreme Ct., White Plains, 1996—; panel mem. Surrogate Decision Making Com., New City, N.Y., 1996—; arbitrator Lemon Law-AAA. Mem. Zoning Bd. Appeals, Peekskill, 1997; adv. legal affairs com. Youth Bd., Peekskill, 1997. Mem. Am. Judges Assn., Def. Assn. N.Y., N.Y. State Dispute Resolution Assn., N.Y. State Bar Assn., Westchester County Bar Assn. (grievance com. 1997), N.Y. State Trial Lawyers Assn., Assn. Small Claims Arbitrators, Alpha Sigma Lambda. Republican. Roman Catholic. State civil litigation, Personal injury, Product liability. Office: Gerald G Cowen Esq 570 Taxter Rd Elmsford NY 10523-2311

**MEWHINNEY, LEN EVERETTE,** lawyer; b. Temple, Tex., Sept. 16, 1958; s. Cindy Mayfield Mewhinney, May 28, 1983; children: Lauren Lynn, Jacob Cole. BBA in Acctg., Tex. Tech. U., 1981, JD cum laude, 1984. Bar: Tex. 1984. Assoc. Daugherty Kuperman Golden & Morehead, Austin, 1984-87, Johnson & Wortley f/k/a Johnson & Gibbs, Austin, 1987-95; shareholder Kuperman Orr Moyer & Albers, Austin, 1995-96; v.p., legal sec., gen. counsel McLane Co. Inc., Temple, Tex., 1996—. Mem. ABA, Am. Corp. Counsel Assn., Tex. Soc. CPA's, State Bar Tex. Contracts commercial, Mergers and acquisitions, General corporate.

**MEYER, ANDREW C., JR.,** lawyer; b. N.Y.C., June 28, 1949; s. Andrew and Myra Meyer; m. Kathleen A. Sullivan, May 7, 1982; children—Joshua Andrew, Daniel Gregory, Jessica Kathleen. B.S., C.W. Post Coll., 1971; J.D., Suffolk U., 1974. Bar: Mass. 1974, U.S. Dist. Ct. Mass. 1974, U.S. Ct. Appeals (1st cir.) 1974. Ptnr. Lubin & Meyer, P.C., Boston, 1974—. Contbr. articles to law jours. Mem. Mass. Bar Assn. (chmn. trial practice com. 1983-84, award 1984, seminar speaker, 21st Century Club award 1984, Continuing Legal Edn. Faculty award 1984), Mass. Acad. Trial Attys. (gov. to bd. govs. appointed), Boston Bar Assn. Federal civil litigation, State civil litigation, Personal injury. Office: Lubin & Meyer PC 141 Tremont St Boston MA 02111-1209

**MEYER, CHRISTOPHER RICHARD,** lawyer; b. Springfield, Ohio, June 18, 1952; s. Eugene Francis and Marilyn Crawford (Hopping) M.; m. Sharman Elizabeth, Sept. 8, 1973; children: Elizabeth Ann, Emily McClead, Timothy Joseph. BA summa cum laude, Ohio State U., 1974, JD, 1977. Bar: Ohio, U.S. Dist. Ct. (so. and no. dists.) Ohio. Ptnr. Reese, Pyle, Drake & Meyer, NEwark, Ohio, 1977—; legal counsel Licking Meml. Hosp., Newarkl Ohio, 1983—, State Farm Ins. Co., Bloomington, Ill., 1977—, St. Paul Ins. Co., Columbus, Ohio, 1977—, Buckeye Egg Farm, Croton, Ohio, 1994—. Mem. Am. Acad. Hosp. Attys., Ohio State Bar Assn. (negligence com., litigation sect.), Ohio Assn. Civil Trial Attys., Soc. Ohio Hosp. Attys., Phi Beta Kappa. Personal injury, Product liability. Home: 976 Briarhill Dr Newark OH 43055-2249 Office: Reese Pyle Drake & Meyer 36 N 2d St PO Box 919 Newark OH 43058-0919

**MEYER, DAVID DOUGLAS,** lawyer, educator; b. Grinnell, Iowa, Nov. 4, 1961; s. Richard DeWitt and Nancy Meyer; m. Amy Gajda, Aug. 29, 1986; children: Michael, Matthew. BA, U. Mich., 1984, JD, 1990. Bar: Mich. 1992, Ill. 1995, U.S. Ct. Appeals (7th cir.) 1995. Spl. asst. U.S. Senator Chas McC. Mathias, Washington, 1984-87; judicial law clk. D.C. Cir. Ct., 1990-91, U.S. Supreme Ct., Washington, 1992-93; assoc. Sidley & Austin, Chgo., Washington, 1991-92, 94-96; legal advisor Iran-U.S. Claims Tribunal, The Hague, The Netherlands, 1993-94; asst. prof. law U. Ill., Champaign, 1996—; editor-in-chief Mich. Law Rev., Ann Arbor, 1989-90. Mem. ABA. Office: U Ill Coll Law 504 E Pennsylvania Ave Champaign IL 61820-6909

**MEYER, FERDINAND CHARLES, JR.,** lawyer; b. San Antonio, Sept. 30, 1939. Student, Tulane U.; BBA, U. Tex., 1961, LLB, 1964. Bar: Tex. 1966, U.S. Dist. Ct. (we. dist.) Tex. 1969, U.S. Ct. Appeals (5th cir.) 1971, U.S. Supreme Ct. 1975, U.S. Ct. Appeals (11th cir.) 1979, D.C. 1986. V.p., gen. counsel CSW Svcs.; ptnr. Matthews & Branscomb, San Antonio; v.p. asst. gen. counsel CSW Corp., 1986-88; v.p., gen. counsel Ctrl. & S.W. Corp., 1988-90, sr. v.p., gen. counsel, 1990-98, gen. counsel, 1990—, exec. v.p., gen. counsel, 1998—; instr. trial advocacy St. Mary's Sch. Law, 1980-86. Capt. USAR. Fellow Am. Coll. Trial Lawyers, Tex. Bar Found.; mem. ABA, Am. Bd. Trial Advs. (adv.), State Bar Tex., Dallas Bar Assn., San Antonio Bar Assn., Internat. Assn. Def. Counsel, Phi Alpha Delta. General corporate, Public utilities. Office: Ctrl & SW Corp PO Box 660164 1616 Woodall Rodgers Fwy Dallas TX 75202-1234

**MEYER, GEORGE HERBERT,** lawyer; b. Detroit, Feb. 19, 1928; s. Herbert M. and Agnes F. (Eaton) M.; m. Carol Ann Jones, 1958 (div. 1981) children: Karen Ann, George Herbert Jr.; m. Katherine Palmer White, Nov. 12, 1988. AB, U. Mich., 1949; JD, Harvard U., 1952; cert., Oxford (Eng.) U., 1955; LLM in Taxation, Wayne State U., 1962. Bar: D.C. bar 1952, Mich. bar 1953. Assoc. firm Fischer, Franklin & Ford, Detroit, 1956-63; mem. firm Fischer, Franklin & Ford, 1963-74; established firm George H. Meyer, 1974-78; sr. mem. firm Meyer and Kirk, 1978-85; sr. mem. Meyer, Kirk, Snyder & Safford PLLC, Bloomfield Hills and Detroit, Mich., 1985—; curator Step Lively exhibit Mus. Am. Folk Art, N.Y.C., 1992; lectr. Am. Folk Art. Author: Equalization in Michigan and Its Effect on Local Assessments, 1963, Folk Artists Biographical Index, 1986, American Folk Art Canes: Personal Sculpture, 1992. Chmn. Birmingham (Mich.) Bd. Housing Appeals, 1964-68; vice chmn. Birmingham Bd. Zoning Appeals, 1966-69; mem. Birmingham Planning Bd., 1968-70; trustee, Bloomfield Village, Mich., 1976-80, pres., 1979-80; trustee Mus. Am. Folk Art, N.Y.C., 1987—; mem. exec. bd. Detroit Area coun. Boy Scouts Am., 1976—, counsel, 1986-95,v.p., 1996—; mem. nat. adv. bd. Folk Art Soc. Am., 1994—; trustee Detroit Sci. Ctr., 1985—. 1st lt. JAG, USAF, 1952-55, maj. Res. ret. Recipient Silver Beaver award Detroit Area coun. Boy Scouts Am., 1989. Mem. ABA, Detroit Bar Assn., Oakland County Bar Assn., State Bar Mich., Harvard Law Sch. Assn. Mich. (dir. 1959—, pres. 1970-78), Detroit Sci. Mus. Soc. (pres. 1961-74, chmn. 1974-76), Am. Folk Art Soc., Prismatic Club, Scarab Club, Harvard Club (N.Y.C.), Detroit Athletic Club, Masons, Rotary, Phi Beta Kappa, Alpha Phi Omega, Pi Sigma Alpha. Republican. Unitarian. General corporate, Real property, Trademark and copyright. Office: Meyer Kirk Snyder & Safford PLLC 100 W Long Lake Rd Ste 100 Bloomfield Hills MI 48304-2773

**MEYER, GRACE TOMANELLI,** lawyer; b. Bklyn., Aug. 7, 1935; d. Cosmo and Grace (Giabia) Tomanelli; m. Heinz Meyer, May 26, 1956; children: Kenneth, Carolyn, Christa, Karla. BA, Ramapo Coll. of N.J., 1975; JD, Seton Hall U., 1978. Bar: N.J. 1978, U.S. Supreme Ct. 1983, N.Y. 1988. Adminstrv. sec. U.S. Atomic Energy Commn., N.Y.C., 1955-58; assoc. lawyer Beattie & Padovano, Montvale, N.J., 1978-80; counselor Grace T. Meyer Law offices, River Vale, N.J., 1980—; adj. prof. Ramapo Coll., 1980, 81, Nyack Coll., 1994, 95; facilitator Pressing Onward, Pascack Bible Ch., Hillsdale, 1991—. Contbr. various articles to profl. jours. Honored for pro bono work by Bergen County Legal Svcs., 1993. Mem. N.J. Bar Assn., Bergen County Bar Assn., Christian Legal Soc., Rutherford Inst., Concerned Women for Am., Am. Family Assn. Republican. Avocations: writing, counseling, walking, arts and crafts. Family and matrimonial, Estate planning, Real property. Office: Grace T Meyer Law Offices 669 Westwood Ave Ste H River Vale NJ 07675-6336

**MEYER, IRWIN STEPHAN,** lawyer, accountant; b. Monticello, N.Y., Nov. 14, 1941; s. Ralph and Janice (Cohen) M.; children: Kimberly B., Joshua A. BS, Rider Coll., 1963; JD, Cornell U., 1966. Bar: N.Y. 1966; CPA, N.J. Tax mgr. Lybrand Ross Bros. & Montgomery, N.Y.C., 1966-71; mem. Ehrenkranz, Ehrenkranz & Schultz, N.Y.C., 1971-74; prin. Irwin S. Meyer, 1974-77, 82-96; mem. Levine, Honig, Eisenberg & Meyer, 1977-78, Eisenberg, Honig & Meyer, 1978-81, Eisenberg, Honig, Meyer & Fogler, 1981-82, Janow & Meyer, LLC., 1997—. With U.S. Army, 1966-71. Mem. ABA, N.Y. Bar Assn., Am. Assn. Atty.-CPA, N.Y. Assn. Atty.-CPA, N.J. Soc. CPA. Taxation, general, Personal income taxation, Estate taxation. Office: 1 Blue Hill Plz Ste 1006 Pearl River NY 10965-3100

**MEYER, J. THEODORE,** lawyer; b. Chgo., Apr. 13, 1936; s. Joseph Theodore and Mary Elizabeth (McHugh) M.; m. Marilu Bartholomew, Aug. 16, 1961; children: Jean, Joseph. B.S., John Carroll U., 1958; postgrad. U. Chgo.; J.D., DePaul U., 1962. Bar: Ill. 1962, U.S. Dist. Ct. (no. dist.) Ill. 1962. Ptnr. Bartholomew & Meyer, Chgo., 1963-83; mem. Ill. Gen. Assembly, House of Rep., 28th Legis. Dist., 1966-72, 74-82, chmn. House environ. study com., 1968; chmn. energy environ. com. and natural resources com.; mem. appropriations and exec. com.; chmn. Joint House/Senate com. to review state air and water plans, 1968; mem. Fed. State Task Force on Energy; chmn., founder Midwest Legis. Coun. on Environ., 1971; mem. Ill. Pollution Control Bd., Chgo., 1983-98; with Ill. EPA, Chgo., 1998—; mem. Joint Legis. Com. on Hazardous Waste in Lake Calumet Area, 1987; lectr. in field. Recipient Appreciation award Ill. Wildlife Fedn., 1972, Environ. Quality award Region V, EPA, 1974, Pro Bono Publico award Self-Help Action Ctr., 1975, Merit award Dept. Ill. VFW, 1977, Environ. Legislator of Yr. award Ill. Environ. Coun., 1978-79; Disting. Lawyer Legislator of Yr.; commd. hon. lt. aide-de-camp Ala. State Militia; commd. Hon. Tex. Citizen. Fellow Chgo. Bar Found.; mem. ABA, Ill. Bar Assn., Chgo. Bar Assn., Nat. Rep. Legis. Assn., Nat. Trust Hist. Preservation, Nat. Wildlife Fedn., Ill. Hist. Soc. Republican. Roman Catholic. FERC practice, Administrative and regulatory, Environmental. Office: State of Ill Ctr 100 W Randolph St Ste 4-900 Chicago IL 60601-3218

**MEYER, JOHN ALBERT,** lawyer; b. Sioux Falls, S.D., Dec. 6, 1946; s. John Richard Meyer and Beryl Geneva (Birkland) Ritz; m. Donna Rae Finch, Jan. 21, 1983; 1 child, Elizabeth Ann. B.S., Iowa State U., 1969; J.D., U. Iowa, 1972. Bar: Iowa 1972, Ill. 1972, U.S. Dist. Ct. (no. dist.) Ill. 1972, U.S. Ct. Appeals (7th cir.) 1972, U.S. Supreme Ct. 1977, U.S. Tax Ct. 1981. Asst. U.S. atty. U.S. Atty.'s Office U.S. Dist. Ct. (no. dist.) Ill., Chgo., 1972-77; ptnr. Johnson & Colmar, Chgo., 1977-83, Bortman, Meyer & Barasa, Chgo., 1983—. Recipient Disting. Service award FBI, 1975. Mem. Chgo. Bar Assn., Ill. State Bar Assn., ABA. State civil litigation, Federal civil litigation, Criminal. Office: 20 S Clark St Ste 2210 Chicago IL 60603-1805

**MEYER, JOHN MICHAEL,** judge; b. San Francisco, Apr. 7, 1947; s. Julian John and Anne L. Meyer; m. Susan L. Johnson, Oct. 26, 1968; children: Jennifer, Erika. BA, U. Wash., 1968; JD, U. Calif., San Francisco, 1971. Bar: Calif. 1972, Wash. 1973, U.S. Dist. Ct. (we. dist.) Wash. 1976, U.S. Ct. Appeals (9th cir.) 1979. Staff atty. FPC, Washington, 1973-75; ptnr. Gilbert & Meyer, Mt. Vernon, Wash., 1975-94; dist. judge, 1995-97; judge Superior Ct. Skagit County, 1997—. Pres. Skagit Valley YMCA, Mt. Vernon, 1977-79, Skagit Valley Coll. Found., Mt. Vernon, 1986-88; trustee Skagit Valley Coll., 1993-97. 1st lt. Q.M.C. 1971-73. Mem. U. Wash. Alumni Assn. (past bd. dirs., past treas., pres. 1997-98), Skagit County Bar Assn. (pres. 1993-94), Rainier Club. Lutheran. Office: Superior Court 202 Courthouse 205 W Kincaid St Ste 202 Mount Vernon WA 98273-4225

**MEYER, JOHN STRAUCH, JR.,** lawyer; b. St. Louis, June 12, 1958; s. John Strauch Meyer and Margaret (Bragdon) Shepley; m. Laura Lewis, May 29, 1983; children: Emily H., Julia E. AB, Yale U., 1980; JD, Washington U., St. Louis, 1984. Bar: Mo. 1984. Legis. asst., corr. to Sen. John C. Danforth Washington, 1980-81; summer assoc. Greensfelder, Hemker, St. Louis, 1982; summer assoc. Bryan Cave LLP, St. Louis, 1983, assoc., 1984-92, ptnr., 1993—; mem. panel of arbitrators Am. Arbitration Assn., N.Y.C., 1994. Co-author: (desk book) Mechanic's Liens and Construction Bonds under Missouri Law, 1991, rev. edits. Dir., past pres., past treas. Planned Parenthood of St. Louis Region, 1989-98, 99—; dir., past v.p. of devel., pres. The Forsyth Sch., St. Louis, 1994—, pres., 1998—; mem. St. Louis 2004 Urban Devel. Taskforce, 1997-98. Mem. ABA, Bar Assn. of Met. St. Louis, Robert Burns Club of St. Louis (pres. 1994), Mo. Athletic Club. Unitarian. Avocations: outdoor activities, gourmet cooking, single malt whiskeys. E-mail: JSMeyer@Bryan.Cave.Com. Office: Bryan Cave LLP 211 N Broadway Saint Louis MO 63102-2733

**MEYER, LAWRENCE GEORGE,** lawyer; b. East Grand Rapids, Mich., Oct. 2, 1940; s. George and Evangeline (Boerma) M.; children from previous marriage: David Lawrence, Jenifer Lynne; m. Linda Elizabeth Buck, May 31, 1980; children: Elizabeth Tilden, Travis Henley. BA with honors, Mich. State U., 1961; JD with distinction, U. Mich., 1964. Bar: Wis., 1965, Ill. 1965, U.S. Supreme Ct. 1968, D.C. 1972. Assoc. Whyte, Hirschboeck, Minahan, Hardin & Harland, Milw., 1964-66; atty. antitrust div. U.S. Dept. Justice, Washington, 1966-68; legal counsel U.S. Senator Robert P. Griffin, Mich., 1968-70; dir. policy planning FTC, Mich., 1970-72; ptnr. Patton, Boggs & Blow, Washington, 1972-85, Arent, Fox, Kintner, Plotkin & Kahn, Washington, 1985-96, Gadsby & Hannah, 1996—. Contbr. articles on antitrust and trial practice to law jours.; asst. editor. U. Mich. Law Rev., 1960-61. Bd. dirs. Hockey Hall of Fame, Toronto, 1993-99, Woodrow Wilson House, 1997—. Recipient Disting. Svc. award FTC, 1972. Mem. ABA, D.C. Bar Assn., Wis. Bar Assn., Ill. Bar Assn., U.S. Senate Ex S.O.B.s Club, City Tavern Club, Congl. Country Club. Antitrust, Federal civil litigation, Administrative and regulatory. Home: 8777 Belmart Rd Potomac MD 20854-1610

**MEYER, LOUIS B.,** judge, retired state supreme court justice; b. Marion, N.C., July 15, 1933; s. Louis B. and Beulah (Smith) M.; m. Evelyn Spradlin, Dec. 29, 1956; children: Louis B. III, Patricia Shannon, Adam Burden. B.A., Wake Forest U., 1955, J.D., 1960; LLM, U. Va., 1992. Bar: N.C. 1960, U.S. Dist. Ct. (ea. dist.) N.C. 1960, U.S. Ct. Appeals (4th cir.) 1960, U.S. Supreme Ct. 1962. Law clk. Supreme Ct. N.C., Raleigh, 1960; spl. agent FBI, 1961-62; atty. Lucas, Rand, Rose, Meyer, Jones & Orcutt P.A., Wilson, N.C., 1962-81; assoc. justice Supreme Ct. N.C., Raleigh, 1981-95, ret., 1995; spl. judge Superior Ct., 1995—. Former county chmn. Wilson County Dems., N.C.; former mem. N.C. State Exec. Com. Dem. Party. Served to 1st lt. U.S. Army, 1955-57. Mem. Wilson County Bar Assn. (former pres.), 7th Jud. Dist. Bar Assn. (former pres.), N.C. Bar Assn. (former v.p.), Masons. Baptist.

**MEYER, M. HOLT,** retired judge; b. Hong Kong, Sept. 28, 1930; s. Clarence E. and Thresa (Heidecke) M.; m. Catherine Dindia, Sept. 2, 1956; children: Christopher M., Holt V. BA, Harvard U., 1952; LLB, Columbia U., 1957. Bar: N.Y. 1958, U.S. Dist. Ct. (so. and ea. dists.) N.Y. 1963. Atty. Webster & Sheffield, N.Y.C., 1959-66; asst. to mayor City of N.Y., 1966-73; judge N.Y. State Family Ct., Staten Island, 1973-95; jud. hearing officer N.Y. State Supreme Ct., Richmond County, 1996—; ret. Cpl. U.S. Army, 1952-54, Germany. Mem. N.Y. State Family Ct. Judges Assn. (pres. 1990-91), N.Y.C. Family Ct. Judges Asns. (pres. 1985-86). Office: NY State Supreme Ct County Court House Staten Island NY 10301-1954

**MEYER, MARTIN JAY,** lawyer; b. Wilkes-Barre, Pa., Aug. 1, 1932; s. Max and Rose (Wruble) M.; m. Joan Rosenthal, Aug. 24, 1954; children: Leah, Gary. B.A., Wilkes Coll., 1954; postgrad. U. Miami, 1956-57; LL.B., Temple U., 1959. Bar: Pa. 1960, U.S. Dist. Ct. (mid. dist.) Pa. 1961, U.S. Ct. Appeals (3d cir.) 1966, U.S. Supreme Ct., 1978. Assoc. Mack, Kasper & Meyer, Wilkes-Barre, 1961-66; assoc. Mack & Meyer, Wilkes-Barre, 1966-68, ptnr., 1968-80; ptnr. Meyer & Swatkoski, Kingston, Pa., 1980—, sr. ptnr., 1980—; chmn. disciplinary hearing com. Pa. Supreme Ct.; apptd. spl. trial master State Ct., 1995; Co-author weekly article You Be the Jury, Times Leader, 1984-90, What is the Verdict Sunday Ind., 1990-93. Chmn. Muscular Dystrophy Assn., 1960; co-chmn. March of Dimes, 1962; trustee Temple Israel Wilkes-Barre; bd. dirs. Jewish Home Scranton, Family Service Assn.; arbitrator U.S. Arbitration and Mediation of N.E., Inc., Am. Arbitration Assn. Served with U.S. Army, 1955-56. Fellow Pa. Bar found.; mem. DAV, ATLA, Am. Arbitration Assn., Pa. Bar Assn. (former co-chmn. adoption com. family law sect.), Nat. Conf. Bar Pres's., Pa. Trial Lawyers Assn. (lectr.), Luzerne County Bar Assn. (pres. 1984, 85), Tau Epsilon Rho. Republican. Lodges: Elks (trustee), Masons (32 deg.), B'nai B'rith (pres. 1967), The Pa. Soc. General civil litigation, General practice, Family and matrimonial. Office: 405 3rd Ave Kingston PA 18704-5802

**MEYER, MATTHEW J.,** lawyer; b. Albany, N.Y., Feb. 19, 1970; s. Alfred F. and Barbara J. Meyer. BA, Cornell U., 1992; JD, Villanova U., 1995. Bar: N.Y. 1995, D.C. 1998. Corp. atty. Pfizer Inc., N.Y.C., 1995—. Mem. N.Y. State Bar Assn., Union League of Phila., Cornell Club of N.Y., Phi Beta Kappa. Mergers and acquisitions, General corporate, Intellectual property. Home: 170 E 87th St New York NY 10128-2214

**MEYER, MAX EARL,** lawyer; b. Hampton, Va., Oct. 31, 1918; s. Earl Luther and Winifred Katherine (Spacht) M.; m. Betty Maxwell Dodds, Sept. 22, 1945; children—Scott Maxwell, Ann Culliford. AB, U. Nebr., 1940, JD, 1942. Bar: Nebr. 1942, Ill. 1946. Assoc. firm Lord, Bissell & Brook, Chgo., 1945-53; ptnr. Lord, Bissell & Brook, 1953-85; chmn. Chgo. Fed. Tax Forum, 1965, U. Chgo. Ann. Fed. Tax Conf., 1972; mem. Adv. Group to Commr. of IRS, 1967; lectr. in field. Bd. dirs. Music Acad. of the West, chmn. 1993-94. Mem. ABA (mem. council tax sec. 1969-72), Ill. Bar Assn. (mem. council tax sect. 1973-76), Nebr. Bar Assn., Chgo. Bar Assn. (chmn. taxation com. 1959-61), Am. Coll. Tax Counsel. Republican. Presbyterian. Clubs: Legal, Law (Chgo.); Valley Club of Montecito, Birnam Wood Golf. Lodge: Masons. General corporate, Mergers and acquisitions, Taxation, general.

**MEYER, PATRICIA R.,** lawyer; b. Des Moines, July 12, 1950; d. Myron C. and Ruth L. Meyer. AS, Emory U., 1971; BS, U. Ga., 1975, MS, 1979; JD, U. S.C., 1995. Bar: S.C. 1995. Human svcs. specialist EOA, Atlanta, 1975-76; animal health specialist USDA, Miami, 1976-78; consumer svcs. specialist AAMMC, City of Industry, Calif., 1979-81; nutrition program specialist Richmond County (Ga.) Health Dept., 1988-91; dir. dietetics Ga. Reg. Hosp., Augusta, 1991-92; assoc. atty. Hastell & Clark, Sumter, S.C., 1997-98; assoc. Bell & Moore, Sumter, 1998—. Bd. dirs. Golden Harvest Food Bank, Augusta, N.Am. Riding for the Handicapped. Mem. ATLA, ABA, S.C. Trial Lawyers Assn., Mensa, Internat. Arabian Horse Assn., Palmetto Shag Club, Phi Alpha Delta. General civil litigation, Personal injury, Workers' compensation. Home: 126 Thornhill Rd Columbia SC 29212-1838

**MEYER, PAUL RICHARD,** lawyer; b. St. Louis, Apr. 12, 1925; s. Abraham Paul and Adele (Rosenfeld) M.; m. Alice Turtledove., Mar. 16, 1958; David Paul, Sarah Elizabeth, Andrea Ruth. BA, Columbia U., 1949; JD, Yale U., 1952. Bar: Oreg. 1953, Calif. 1953, N.Y. 1953, U.S. Dist.Ct. Oreg. 1953, U.S. Dist. Ct. (no. dist.) Calif. 1953, U.S. Ct. Appeals (9th cir.) 1953, U.S. Supreme Ct. 1958, U.S. Ct. Claims 1958, U.S. Tax Ct. 1958, U.S. Ct. Appeals (fed. cir.) 1958. Assoc. law sch. U. Calif., Berkeley, 1952-53; assoc. King, Miller et al, Portland, Oreg., 1953-60; ptnr. Kobin & Meyer, Portland, 1960-85; pvt. practice law Portland, 1985—; mem. Bd. of Mediators and Arbitrators, Am. Arbitration Assn., U.S. Mediation and Arbitration, Oreg., NASD;. Mem. nat. bd., exec. com. ACLU, N.Y.C., 1971-93, ACLU nat. adv. coun., 1993—. With U.S. Army, 1943-46, ETO. Decorated Purple Heart. Construction, General civil litigation, General corporate. Home and Office: 1325 SW Myrtle Dr Portland OR 97201-2274

**MEYER, PAUL SETH,** lawyer; b. N.Y.C., June 19, 1947. BA, UCLA, 1968, JD, 1971. Pros. atty. Orange County Dist. Atty., Santa Ana, Calif., 1972-81; pvt. practice law Costa Mesa, Calif., 1981—. Named Atty. of the Yr., Orange County Trial Lawyers Assn., 1995-96. Fellow Am. Coll. Trial Lawyers. Criminal. Office: 695 Town Center Dr Ste 1450 Costa Mesa CA 92626-7190

**MEYER, PAUL T.,** lawyer, civil engineer; b. Mpls., Mar. 27, 1952; s. Thore P. and Joyce I. (Vergin) M.; m. Laurie Stedje, Sept. 1, 1979; children: Rachel, Erik. BSCE, U. Minn., 1974, MSCE, 1977; JD, William Mitchell Coll. Law, St. Paul, 1986. Bar: Minn. 1986, U.S. Dist. Ct. Minn. 1986. Engr. Meyer-Rohlin, Inc., Buffalo, Minn., 1975-86; atty. Hart, Bruner & O'Brien, Mpls., 1986-90, Fabyanske, Svoboda et al, Mpls., 1990-92; atty., shareholder Johnson, Larson, Peterson & Meyer, Buffalo, 1992-96, Hammargren & Meyer, P.A., Mpls., 1996—. Mem. NSPE, Minn. Bar Assn., Hennepin County Bar Assn. Construction, State civil litigation. Office: One Corporate Ctr IV 7301 Ohms Ln Ste 360 Minneapolis MN 55439-2336

**MEYER, PHILIP GILBERT,** lawyer; b. Louisville, June 26, 1945; s. Henry Gilbert and Adele (Gutermuth) M.; m. Jackie Darlene Watson, Jan. 30, 1971 (div. Apr. 1976); m. Sylvia Saunders, Oct. 9, 1976. BBA, U. Mich., 1967; JD, U. Tex. 1970. Bar: Tex. 1970, Mich. 1971, U.S. Tax Ct. 1972, U.S. Dist. Ct. (ea. dist.) Mich. 1971, U.S. Ct. Appeals (6th cir.) 1972, U.S. Dist. Ct. (no. dist.) Ohio 1976, U.S. Dist. Ct. (we. dist.) Mich. 1993, U.S. Dist. Ct. (no. dist.) Ill. 1998. Law clk., Wayne County Cir. Ct., Detroit, 1970-72; atty. Leonard C. Jaques, Detroit, 1972; assoc. Christy & Robbins, Dearborn, Mich., 1972-73; ptnr. Foster, Meadows & Ballard, Detroit, 1973-79; of counsel Christy, Rogers & Gantz, Dearborn, 1979-81, Rogers & Gantz, Dearborn, 1981-86, prin. Philip G. Meyer and Assocs., 1986—; adj. prof. U. Detroit Sch. Law, 1979. Mem. ABA (com. vice chmn. rules and procedure 1982-88), Maritime Law Assn. U.S., Mich. Bar Assn. (vice chmn. admiralty sect. 1978), Tex. Bar Assn., Detroit Bar Assn. (vice chmn. admiralty com. 1991-93, chmn. admiralty sect. 1993-95). Republican. Club: Propeller-Port of Detroit (pres. 1984-85). Personal injury, Insurance, Admiralty. Home: 5905 Independence Ln West Bloomfield MI 48322-1854 Office: 5767 W Maple Rd Ste 100 West Bloomfield MI 48322-4445

**MEYERING, CHRISTOPHER P.,** lawyer; b. Syracuse, N.Y., Oct. 12, 1958; s. John R. and Gloria J. Meyering; m. Patricia Elizabeth Jackman, May 6, 1986; children: Kara, Kelly, Kristin. AB, Georgetown U., 1980, JD, 1983. Bar: Conn. 1983, U.S. Dist. Ct. Conn. 1983, U.S. Dist. Ct. (ea. dist.) N.Y. 1985. Assoc. Whitman & Ransom, Greenwich, Conn., 1983-87, Day, Barry & Howard, Stamford, Conn., 1987-89; asst. gen. counsel, dir. govtl. affairs Pittston Co., Richmond, Va., 1989-98; v.p., sec., gen. counsel Pure Energy Corp., N.Y.C., 1998—. Mem. ABA, Conn. Bar Assn. General corporate, FERC practice, Oil, gas, and mineral. Office: Pure Energy Corp 1 World Trade Ctr Ste 5301 New York NY 10048-5399

**MEYERS, DAVID W.,** lawyer, writer, educator; b. Hobart, Tasmania, Australia, July 19, 1942; came to U.S., 1946; s. Philip T. and Margaret M. Meyers; m. Jane Arthur Meyers, Dec. 27, 1969; children: Duncan, Vanessa. BA magna cum laude, U. Redlands, 1964; JD, U. Calif., Berkeley, 1967; LLM, U. Edinburgh, Scotland, 1968. Bar: Calif. 1968, U.S. Dist. Ct. (no. dist.) Calif. 1971, U.S. Ct. Appeals (10th cir.) 1994, U.S. Supreme Ct. 1976. Tutor dept. comparative law U. Edinburgh, Scotland, 1967-68; assoc. Rutan & Tucker, Santa Ana, Calif., 1968-71; ptnr. Dickenson, Peatman, Fogarty, Napa, Calif., 1972—; adj. lectr. U. Calif. Med. Sch., San Francisco, 1985-87; vis. fellow U. Edinburgh, Scotland, 1999. Author: Human Body and the Law, 1972, rev. edit., 1990, Medical-Legal Implications of Death & Dying, 1981; contbr. chpts. to books, articles to profl. jours. Pres. Napa Valley Coll. Found., 1997—; trustee Queen of the Valley Hosp., 1987-93 (pres. 1990-93). Mem. State Bar Calif., Napa County Bar Assn. (pres. 1986), Am. Inns of Ct., Rotary. Democrat. Avocations: writing, bicycling, skiing, sailing, travel. General civil litigation, Real property, Municipal (including bonds). Office: Dickenson Peatman & Fogarty 809 Coombs St Napa CA 94559-2994

**MEYERS, GREGORY WILLIAM,** lawyer; b. Lakewood, Ohio, July 27, 1954; s. Robert William and Charmane Virginia (Bailey) M.; m. Leslie Armstrong, May 30, 1991. BA with honors, Oberlin Coll., 1980; JD, Ohio State U., 1983. Bar: Ohio 1983, U.S. Dist. Ct. (so. dist.) Ohio 1983, U.S. Dist. Ct. (no. dist.) Ohio 1984. Staff atty. Ohio Legal Rights Svc., Columbus, 1983-84, Franklin County Pub. Defender, Columbus, 1984-89; ptnr. Owen & Meyers, Columbus, 1989-90, Weiner, Shartzer & Meyers, Columbus, 1990-92, Meyers & Armstrong, Columbus, 1992—; trustee Ohio Mock Trial Program, Columbus, 1989-91. Chmn. Cen. Ohio ACLU, Columbus, 1987-89; trustee Van Pelt Dance Ensemble, Columbus, 1989-90. Recipient Harry S. Lett Meml. for Civil Rights Dedication Ohio State U. Coll. of Law, 1983. Mem. Ohio Assn. Criminal Def. Lawyers, Nat. Assn. Criminal Def. Lawyers, Am. Inns of Ct. Avocations: motorcycling, camping, gardening. Criminal. Home: 476 Tibet Rd Columbus OH 43202-2232 Office: Meyers & Armstrong 8 E Long St Ste 900 Columbus OH 43215-2914

**MEYERS, HOWARD L.,** lawyer; b. Dec. 22, 1948. BS, U. Del., 1970; JD, U. Va., 1973. Bar: Pa. 1973. Sr. ptnr. in bus. and fin. sect., mem. firm governing bd. Morgan, Lewis & Bockius, Phila. Mem. ABA, Pa. Bar Assn., Phila. Bar Assn., Greater Phila. C. of C. (mem. exec. com., bd. dirs., gen. counsel). Office: Morgan Lewis & Bockius 1701 Market St Philadelphia PA 19103-2903

**MEYERS, JEFFREY T.,** lawyer; b. Detroit, Jan. 30, 1956; s. Carl and Nancy M.; m. Jody Ann Kommel; children: Scott, David, Will. BS, Mich. State U., 1979; JD, Wayne State U., 1982. Bar: Mich. Ptnr. Chambers Steiner, Detroit, 1982—. Pres.'s Coun. Mich. Dem. Party. Mem. Mich. Trial Lawyers Assn. (exec. bd. 1992—). Office: Chambers Steiner 149 1st Nat Bldg Detroit MI 48226

**MEYERS, JERRY IVAN,** lawyer; b. McKeesport, Pa., Mar. 26, 1946; s. Eugene J. and Gladys Claire (Rubenstein) M.; m. Judith Drake Aughenbaugh, June 26, 1971; 1 child, Lindsey Drake. BA in Philosophy and Rhetoric, U. Pitts., 1972; JD cum laude, U. Miami, 1975. Bar: Pa. 1975, U.S. Dist. Ct. (we. dist.) Pa. 1975. Assoc. Berger & Kapetan, Pitts., 1975-78; ptnr. Kapetan Meyers Rosen & Louik P.C., Pitts., 1978—. Mem. Assn. Trial Lawyers Am., Pa. Trial Lawyers Assn. (past pres. western Pa. chpt., bd. govs. legis. policy com., med.-legis. com.), Acad. Trial Lawyers Allegheny County. E-mail: Meyers@meyersmedmal.com. Personal injury. Office: Kapetan Meyers Rosen & Louik PC The Frick Building Ste 200 Pittsburgh PA 15219-6002

**MEYERS, JOEL G.,** lawyer; b. Skokie, Ill., Aug. 8, 1967. BS cum laude, U. Ill., 1989, JD, 1992. Bar: Ill. 1992, U.S. Dist. Ct. (no. dist.) Ill. 1992. With Horwood, Marcus & Berk, Chgo. Harno fellow U. Ill. Coll. Law, 1992. Mem. Ill. State Bar Assn., Chgo. Bar Assn. Real property, Landlord-tenant, General corporate. Office: Horwood Marcus & Berk 333 W Wacker Dr Ste 2800 Chicago IL 60606-1227

**MEYERS, LAWRENCE EDWARD,** state judge; m. Barbara; children: Kelli, Clay. BA in History and Chemistry, So. Meth. U., 1970; JD, U. Kans., 1973; postgrad., U. Tex., Arlington, Tex. Wesleyan U. Asst. dist. atty. Montgomery County, Kans., 1973-75; pvt. practice Ft. Worth, 1975-88; assoc. justice U.S. Ct. Appeals (2nd cir.), Ft. Worth, 1988-92; judge Ct. Criminal Appeals, Ft. Worth, 1992—; instr. Tex. Christian U., Ft. Worth. Mem. parish coun. St. Mary's of Assumption, Ft. Worth. Mem. State Bar Tex., State Bar Kans., Tarrant County Bar Assn. Republican. Office: Court of Criminal Appeals PO Box 12308 Supreme Court Bldg 201 West 14th St Austin TX 78701

**MEYERS, PAMELA SUE,** lawyer; b. Lakewood, N.J., June 13, 1951; d. Morris Leon and Isabel (Leibowitz) M.; m. Gerald Stephen Greenberg, Aug. 24, 1975; children: David Stuart Greenberg, Allison Brooke Greenberg. AB with distinction, Cornell U., 1973; JD cum laude, Harvard U., 1976. Bar: N.Y. 1977, Ohio 1990. Assoc. Stroock & Stroock & Lavan, N.Y.C., 1976-80; staff v.p., asst. gen. counsel Am. Premier Underwriters, Inc., Cin., 1980-96; legal counsel Citizens Fed. Bank, Dayton, Ohio, 1997-98; gen. counsel, sec. Mosler Inc., Hamilton, Ohio, 1998—. Bd. dirs. Hamilton County Alcohol and Drug Addiction Svc. Bd., 1996—. Mem. Cin. Bar Assn., Greater Cin. Women Lawyers Assn., Harvard Club of Cin. (pres. 1998-99, bd. dirs. 1993—), Phi Beta Kappa. Jewish. Avocations: piano, reading, golf. General corporate, Contracts commercial, Banking. Home: 3633 Carpenters Creek Dr Cincinnati OH 45241-3824 Office: Mosler Inc 8509 Berk Blvd Hamilton OH 45015-2213

**MEYERSON, AMY LIN,** lawyer; b. New Orleans, May 26, 1967; m. Brandon Aaron Meyerson, Mar. 25, 1995. AB, Duke U., 1989; JD, U. Conn., 1994. Bar: Ga. 1994, D.C. 1997, U.S. Dist. Ct. (no. dist.) Ga. 1995. Atty. Appelbaum & LaRoss, Atlanta, 1994-95, Gerry, Friend & Sapronor LLP, Atlanta, 1995—; spkr. in field. Mem. ABA (vice chair public utility, transp. and telecomm. sect. 1998-99), Nat. Asian Pacific Am. Bar Assn. (Ga. chpt. dir. 1996-97), State Bar of Ga. (elections com. 1997—), Phi Delta Phi. General corporate, Communications, Computer. Office: Gerry Friend & Sapronov LLP 3 Ravinia Dr Ste 1450 Atlanta GA 30346-2117

**MEYERSON, CHRISTOPHER CORTLANDT,** law scholar; b. Princeton, N.J., July 7, 1962; s. Dean and Beatrice Meyerson; m. Megumi Kawaguchi; 1 child, Kenneth. BA in Govt. magna cum laude, Harvard U., 1985, cert. in L.Am. studies, 1985, MA in History, 1985; MPhil in Polit. Sci., Columbia U., 1993; LLM, Kyoto (Japan) U., 1994. Intern Bur. Inter-Am. Affairs, Office Policy Planning/Coord. U.S. State Dept., Washington, summer 1982; rsch. asst. Harvard U., 1982-83; intern, rschr. macro econ. rsch. dept. Banco Itau, São Paulo, 1983-84; human rights intern Coalition for Homeless, N.Y.C., summer 1988; legal intern gen. counsel Mus. Modern Art, N.Y.C., summer 1989; law clk. Office of Chief Counsel for Internat. Commerce U.S. Commerce Dept., Washington, summer 1991; editl. asst. Kyoto Comparative Law Ctr., summer 1994, 95; vis. scholar Associated Kyoto Program, 1996; summer assoc. Venable, Baetjer, Howard & Civiletti, Washington, 1998; law clk. Office of Chief Counsel for Import Adminstrn., U.S. Commerce Dept., Washington, 1999. Contbr. articles to bus. jours., Columbia Internat. Affairs Online. Mem. Am. Soc. Internat. Law, Soc. Legislation Comparee, Am. Polit. Sci. Assn. (presenter papers ann. meetings), Internat. Studies Assn. (presenter papers ann. meetings), Assn. for Asian Studies (presenter papers ann. meetings), Assn. Japanese Bus. Studies (Young Scholar 1996), Internat. House of Japan. Episcopalian. Home: 4381 Embassy Park Dr NW Washington DC 20016-3625

**MEYERSON, IVAN D.,** corporate lawyer, holding company executive. AB, U. Calif., Berkeley, 1966; JD, Stanford U., 1969. Bar: Calif. 1970. Assoc. Herzstein & Maier, San Francisco, 1970-75, ptnr., 1976-78; atty. SEC, 1975-76; assoc. gen. counsel McKesson Corp, San Francisco, 1984-87; v.p., gen. counsel McKesson Corp., San Francisco, 1987-98; sr. v.p., gen. counsel McKesson - HBOC Inc., San Francisco, 1998—. General corporate. Office: McKesson Corp 1 Post St Ste 3275 San Francisco CA 94104-5292*

**MEYERSON, STANLEY PHILLIP,** lawyer; b. Spartanburg, S.C., Apr. 13, 1916; s. Louis A. and Ella Meyerson; m. Sherry Maxwell, Nov. 30, 1996; children: Marianne Martin, Camilla Meyerson, Margot Ellis, Stanley P. A.B., Duke U., 1937, J.D., 1939. Bar: S.C. 1939, N.Y. 1940, Ga. 1945, U.S. Supreme Ct. Ptnr. Johnson Hatcher & Meyerson, Atlanta, 1945-55, Hatcher, Meyerson, Oxford & Irvin, Atlanta, 1955-78, Westmoreland, Hall, McGee, Oxford & Meyerson, Atlanta, 1978—; former adj. prof. Ga. State U.; dir., officer various corps. Co-founder West Paces Ferry Hosp., Atlanta, Annandale at Suwanee for the handicapped; trustee Hudson Libr., Inc., Highlands, N.C.; del. Moscow Conf. Law and Bilateral Econ. Rels., 1990. Contbr. articles to legal jours. Served to lt. comdr. USNR, 1943-45. Mem. ABA (professionalism com.), Duke U. Alumni Assn. (former pres. Atlanta chpt.), Ga. Bar Assn. (former chmn. tax com.), Atlanta Bar Assn. (former sec.). General corporate, Entertainment, Estate planning.

**MEYRICH, STEVEN,** arbitrator, mediator; b. Woodmere, N.Y., Oct. 31, 1951; s. Fred and Geraldine (Ehrman) M.; m. Mary Ann Shea, Dec. 24, 1984. BA, Univ. Rochester, 1973; JD, U. Colo., 1976. Bar: Colo. 1976, U.S. Ct. Appeals (10th cir.) 1976. Dep. dist. atty. Boulder, Colo., 1977-79; assoc. Snyder Neuman Enwall, Boulder, 1979-80; pvt. practice Boulder, 1981-85; assoc. Lamm and Young, Boulder, 1985-86; ptnr. Lirtzman, Nehls and Meyrich, Boulder, 1986-89; sr. program mgr. CDR Assocs., Boulder, 1988-90; pvt. practice mediator, arbitrator Boulder, 19990—. Counsel Coloradans for David Staggs, Boulder Cunty, 1987-89. Mem. Boulder County Bar Assn. (trustee 1987-90, chmn. ethics com. 1984-87), Colo. Bar Assn. (bd. govs. 1990-94), Acad. Family Mediators, Am. Arbitration Assn., Soc. Profls. in Dispute Resolution, Nat. Assn. Securities Dealers. Jewish. Avocations: horse-back riding, cross-country skiing. Office: 100 Arapahoe Ave Ste 14 Boulder CO 80302-5862

**MEZA-MORENO, BEATRIZ ELIZABETH,** lawyer; b. Guayaquil, Ecuador, Jan. 14, 1967; came to U.S., 1970; d. Marcelo and Isabel Maria (Ruiz) M.; m. Enrique Marco Moreno, Oct. 22, 1995. BA, Rutgers U., 1989; JD, Seton Hall U., 1993. Bar: N.J. 1993. Law clk. Caridad F. Rigo, Passaic, N.J., 1985-90; assoc. Cristina R. Byrne, 1991-92; intern Hon. Daniel J. Moore, 1993; assoc. Essex County Ctr. Social Justice, 1993-94, Gelman & Gelman, Elmwood Park, N.J., 1992-96; atty. pvt. practice, Clifton, N.J., 1996—; of counsel Eva's Village, Paterson, N.J., 1997, Essencia Dominicana, Paterson, 1996-97. Mem. Nat. Hispanic Bar Assn., Passaic County Bar Assn. Avocations: cooking, painting. Home: 58 N 14th St Hawthorne NJ 07506-3761 Office: 246 Clifton Ave Clifton NJ 07011-1900

**MEZVINSKY, EDWARD M.,** lawyer; b. Ames, Iowa, Jan. 17, 1937; m. Marjorie Margolies; 11 children. BA, U. Iowa, 1960; MA in Polit. Sci., U. Calif., Berkeley, 1963, JD, 1965. State rep. Iowa State Legislature, 1969-70; U.S. congressman 1st Dist., Iowa, 1973-77; U.S. rep. UN Commn. on Human Rights, 1977-79; chmn. Pa. Dem. State Com., 1981-86. Author: A Term to Remember; contbr. articles to law jours. Mem. Pa. Bar Assn., Bar of the Supreme Ct. of U.S., Omicron Delta Kappa. General practice, Private international, Public international. Office: 815 N Woodbine Ave Narberth PA 19072-1430

**MEZZULLO, LOUIS ALBERT,** lawyer; b. Balt., Sept. 20, 1944; m. Judith Scales, Jan. 2, 1970. BA, U. Md., 1967, MA, 1976; JD, T.C. Williams Law Sch., 1976. Bar: Va. 1976. Sales rep. Humble Oil (name now Exxon), Richmond, Va., 1970-72; acctg. Marcoin, Inc., Richmond, 1972-73; pvt. practice bookkeeping, tax preparation Richmond, 1973-76; assoc. McGuire, Woods, Battle and Boothe, Richmond, 1976-79; dir. Mezzullo & McCandlish, Richmond, 1979—. Contbr. articles to profl. jours. Bd. dirs. Richmond Symphony; former pres. Southampton Citizens Assn., Richmond, 1986. Served with USAR, 1969-75. Mem. ABA (tax sect.), Internat. Acad. Estate and Trust Law, Am. Coll. Trust and Estate Counsel, Am. Coll. Tax Counsel, Va. State Bar (tax sect.), Va. Bar Assn., Am. Bar Found., Va. Law Found., Estate Planning Coun. Richmond, Trust Adminstrs. Coun., Willow Oaks Country Club. General corporate, Estate planning, Corporate taxation. Home: 2961 Westchester Rd Richmond VA 23225-1842 Office: Mezzullo & McCandlish PO Box 796 Richmond VA 23218-0796

**MICALE, FRANK JUDE,** lawyer; b. Pitts., Jan. 10, 1949; s. Frank Jacob and Catherine Anna (Wagner) M. BA, Duquesne U., 1971, J.D., 1977. Bar: Pa. 1977, U.S. Dist. Ct. (we. dist.) Pa. 1977, U.S. Ct. Appeals (3d cir.) 1978; U.S. Supreme Ct., 1986. Law clk. to judge U.S. Ct. Appeals (3d cir.), 1977-78, U.S. Dist. Ct. (we. dist. Pa.), 1978-79; assoc. Egler & Reinstadtler, Pitts., 1979-80; dep. atty. gen., sr. dep. atty. gen. in charge torts litigation sect. western region Office of Atty. Gen. Commonwealth of Pa., 1980-92; pvt. practice, 1992—. Mem. ABA, Pa. Bar Assn., Allegheny County Bar Assn. General civil litigation, Personal injury, Product liability. Home: 555 S Negley Ave Apt 9 Pittsburgh PA 15232-1634 Office: 200 One Williamsburg Pl Warrendale PA 15086

**MICALE, FREDERICK J.,** law educator; b. Syracuse, N.Y., Oct. 17, 1947; s. Frank Joseph and Genevieve Dolores M.; m. Cathy Ann, June 10, 1995; children; Jonathan, Gregory, Emily. AB cum laude, Assumption Coll., 1969; JD, Syracuse U., 1972. Bar: N.Y. 1973, U.S. Dist. Ct. (no. dist.) N.Y. 1974, U.S. Supreme Ct. 1978, U.S. Dist. Ct. (so. dist.) N.Y. 1985. Atty. MacKenzie Smith Lewis Michell & Hughes, Syracuse, N.Y.; adj. prof. Syracuse U. Mem. ABA (bus. law sect.), N.Y. State Bar Assn. (corp., banking & bus. law sect.), Onondaga County Bar Assn. (corp. coun. sect.). Office: MacKenzie Smith Lewish Michell & Hughes 101 S Salina St Ste 600 Syracuse NY 13202-4304 also: PO Box 4967 Syracuse NY 13221-4967

**MICCA, LOUIS JOSEPH,** lawyer; b. Rochester, N.Y., Jan. 28, 1963; s. Louis Joseph and Phyllis Micca; m. Jacquelyn Marie Kraus, Sept. 10, 1988; children: Elizabeth, Emily, Hannah. BS in Acctg., SUNY, Binghamton, 1985; JD cum laude, Albany U., 1988. Bar: N.Y. 1989, U.S. Dist. Ct. (no. dist.) N.Y. 1989, U.S. Dist. Ct. (we. dist.) N.Y. 1989. Assoc. Harris, Maloney et al, Rochester, 1988-94; from assoc. to ptnr. Hodgson, Russ et al, Rochester, 1994-98; with Boylan Brown et al, Rochester, 1999—. Adv. bd. Ret. Sr. Vol. Program, Rochester, 1991-95. Mem. N.Y. State Bar Assn., Monroe County Bar Assn. Avocations: hiking, antique automobiles, hunting. General civil litigation, Contracts commercial, Personal injury. Home: PO Box 77333 Rochester NY 14617-8333 Office: Boylan Brown et al 2400 Chase Sq Rochester NY 14604-1915

**MICCIO, G. KRISTIAN,** law educator; b. N.Y.C., Dec. 14, 1951; d. Guy Joseph and Lucille (D'Andrea) M.; m. Peri L. Rainbow, June 18, 1993. BA, Marymount Coll., Tarrytown, N.Y., 1973; MA, SUNY, Albany, 1975; JD, Antioch U., Washington, 1985; postgrad., Columbia U. Bar: N.Y. 1986, U.S. Dist. Ct. (so. and ea. dists.) N.Y., 1986, U.S. Ct. Appeals (2d cir.) 1986, U.S. Supreme Ct. 1989. Asst. dist. atty. Bronx (N.Y.) Dist. Atty.'s, 1985-87; prof. law CUNY, Queens, 1987-91; adj. prof. law CUNY, N.Y.C., 1990-92; adj. prof. N.Y. Law Sch., 1990-93; clin. prof. Albany (N.Y.) Law Sch., Albany, N.Y., 1993-96; sr. rsch. assoc., dir. project for domestic violence studies Ctr. for Women in Govt., Rockefeller Inst., U. N.Y., Albany, 1996—; prof. law and pub. policy U. N.Y., Albany, 1996—; lectr. in field. Contbr. articles to profl. and law jours. Founding dir., atty.-in-charge Ctr. for Battered Women's Legal Svcs., N.Y.C., 1988-93; pres. bd. Coalition of Battered Women's Advs., N.Y.C., 1989—; bd. dirs. Prisoners Legal Svcs., N.Y.C., 1990-93, N.Y.C. Adv. Bd. for N.Y. Police Dept. on Gay and Lesbian Affairs, 1991-93; chair domestic violence com. N.Y.C. Commn. on Status of Women, 1992-93, mayoral appointee, 1992-93; faculty mem. N.Y. State Jud. Inst. Recipient Susan B. Anthony award NOW, 1991, Atty. of Yr. award Kings County D.A.'s Office, 1993, Making Waves award NOW Albany Chpt., 1996; named Outstanding Lawyer of the Yr. on Behalf of Women and Children of the City of New York, CUNY Law Sch. at Queens Coll., 1991. Mem. N.Y. Bar Assn. (task force on family law 1993—), N.Y. County Lawyers Assn (Outstanding Pub. Svc. award 1991, Pro-Bono award 1992), Assn. of Bar of City of N.Y. (Pub. Interest Lawyer award 1993). Office: Albany Law Sch 80 New Scotland Ave Albany NY 12208-3494

**MICELI, FRANK S.,** lawyer; b. N.Y.C., Dec. 26, 1958; s. Santo P. and Josephine R. Miceli; m. Colleen M. Curtin, May 21, 1983; children: Margaret, Stephen. BA, Pa. State U., 1980; JD, Villanova U., 1983. Law clk. Hon. William W. Vogel, Mongomery County Ct., Norristown, Pa., 1983-86; lawyer Roberts Miceli & Boileau. Mem. Spring Twp. Planning Commn., Bellefonte, Pa., 1998—. Personal injury, Workers' compensation, Real property. Home: 106 Squirrel Ridge Rd Bellefonte PA 16823-6807 Office: Roberts Miceli & Boileau 146 E Water St Lock Haven PA 17745-1355

**MICHAEL, CHARLES JOSEPH,** lawyer; b. Natchitoches, La., July 31, 1939; s. Faris Edgar and Mamie (Solomon) M.; m. Margo Farrer, Aug. 25, 1965; children: Charles J. II, Jonathan Laird. BA, Northwestern State U., 1961; JD, U. Houston, 1965. Bar: Tex. 1965. Pvt. practice Houston. Family and matrimonial, Personal injury, Workers' compensation. Office: 16874 Royal Crest Dr Houston TX 77058-2529

**MICHAEL, DOUGLAS CHARLES,** law educator; b. Omaha, Dec. 8, 1957; s. B.B. and Arleen M. (Heinz) M.; m. Susan Lindsey, Jan. 11, 1986; children: Stuart Douglas, Amanda Lindsey. AB, Stanford U., 1979; MBA, U. Calif., Berkeley, 1982, JD, 1983. Bar: Calif. 1984, D.C. 1988. Staff atty. SEC, Washington, 1983-85, commr.'s counsel, 1985-87; assoc. Arnold and Porter, Washington, 1987-89; asst. prof. U. Ky. Coll. Law, Lexington, 1989-93, assoc. prof., 1993-97, prof., 1997—. Contbr. articles to legal jours.; author: Legal Accounting: Principles and Applications, 1997. Mem. ABA, Am. Bankruptcy Inst., Order of Coif. Home: 4625 Hickory Creek Dr Lexington KY 40515-1509 Office: U Ky Coll Law Lexington KY 40506-0001

**MICHAEL, GEOFFREY PALMER,** lawyer, financial manager; b. Concord, N.H.. BS in Mgmt. with honors, U.S. Air Force Acad., Colorado Springs, 1973; JD, Northop U., 1982. Bar: Calif., 1995, U.S. Dist. Ct. (cen. dist.) Calif., 1995, N.H., 1996, U.S. Dist. Ct. N.H., 1996; cert. contracts mgr. Pvt. practice fin. mgr. Redondo Beach, Calif., 1973-95; pvt. practice atty. Redondo Beach, 1995—. Capt. USAF, 1969-79. Avocations: music, skiing, swimming, hiking, investments. Finance, Contracts commercial, Taxation, general. Office: PO Box 582 Redondo Beach CA 90277-0582

**MICHAEL, HELEN KATHERINE,** lawyer; b. Atlanta, Aug. 14, 1959; d. William Shaw Michael and Patricia Ann (Dillon) Carmichael. BA in Philosophy, Hampshire Coll., Amherst, Mass., 1981; JD with honors, U. N.C., 1986; LLM with highest honors, George Washington U., 1990; student, Sussex U., Brighton, England, 1979-80. Bar: Md. 1988, D.C. 1990. Teaching fellow law George Washington U., Washington, 1986-88; ptnr. Howrey and Simon, Washington, 1988—. Mem. ABA, D.C. Bar, Md. Bar. Democrat. Avocations: downhill skiing, jogging, gourmet cooking. Antitrust, General civil litigation, Product liability. Office: Howery & Simon 1299 Pennsylvania Ave NW Washington DC 20004-2400

**MICHAEL, JAMES HARRY, JR.,** federal judge; b. Charlottesville, Va., Oct. 17, 1918; s. James Harry and Reuben (Shelton) m. Barbara E. Puryear, Dec. 18, 1946; children: Jarrett Michael Stephens, Victoria von der Au. BS, U. Va., 1940, LLB, 1942. Bar: Va. 1942. Sole practice Charlottesville; ptnr. Michael & Musselman, 1946-54, J.H. Michael, Jr., 1954-59, Michael & Dent, 1959-72, Michael, Dent & Brooks Ltd., 1972-74, Michael & Dent, Ltd., 1974-80; assoc. judge Juvenile and Domestic Rels. Ct., Charlottesville, 1954-68; judge U.S. Dist. Ct., Charlottesville, 1980-95, sr. judge, 1996—; mem. Va. Senate, 1968-80; exec. dir. Inst. Pub. Affairs, U. Va., 1952; chmn. Council State Govts., 1975-76, also mem. exec. com.; chmn. So. Legis. Conf., 1974-75. Mem. Charlottesville Sch. Bd., 1951-62; bd. govs. St. Anne-Belfield Sch., 1952-76. Served with USNR, 1942-46; comdr. Res. ret. Wilton Park fellow Wilton Park Conf., Sussex, Eng., 1971. Fellow Am. Bar Found.; mem. ABA, Va. Bar Assn. (v.p. 1956-57), Charlottesville-Albermarle Bar Assn. (pres. 1966-67), Am. Judicature Soc., 4th Jud. Conf., Va. Trial Lawyers Assn. (Va. disting. svc. award 1993), Assn. Trial Lawyers Am., Raven Soc., Sigma Nu Phi, Omicron Delta Kappa. Episcopalian (lay reader). Office: US Dist Ct 255 W Main St Rm 320 Charlottesville VA 22902-5058

**MICHAEL, M. BLANE,** federal judge; b. Charleston, S.C., Feb. 17, 1943. AB, W.Va. U., 1965; JD, NYU, 1968. Bar: N.Y. 1968, U.S. Dist. Ct. (so. and ea. dists.) N.Y. 1968, W.Va. 1973, U.S. Ct. Appeals (4th cir.) 1974, U.S. Dist. Ct. (no. dist.) W.Va. 1975, U.S. Dist. Ct. (so. dist.) W.Va. 1981. Counsel to Gov. W.Va. John D. Rockefeller IV, 1977-80; atty. Jackson & Kelly, Charleston, W.Va., 1981-93; fed. judge U.S. Ct. Appeals (4th cir.), Charleston, W.Va., 1993—; active 4th Cir. Jud. Conf. Mem. ABA, W.Va. Bar Assn., Kanawha County Bar Assn., Phi Beta Kappa. Office: US Circuit Judge Robert C Byrd US Courthouse 300 Virginia St E Rm 7404 Charleston WV 25301-2504

**MICHAEL, ROBERT ROY,** lawyer; b. Washington, Dec. 28, 1946; s. Colin Lamar and Mary Elva (Wilson) M.; m. Carolyn Ann Sandberg, Dec. 20, 1975; children: Shawn Robert, Erika Rae, Andrew Jon. BA, George Washington U., 1968, JD, 1971. Bar: Md. 1972, D.C. 1972, U.S. Dist. Ct. Md. 1972, U.S. Dist. Ct. D.C. 1972, U.S. Ct. Appeals (4th cir.) 1972, U.S. Supreme Ct. 1973. Assoc A.D. Massengill, Esq., Gaithersburg, Md., 1972-73, Massengill & Jersin, Gaithersburg, 1973-74; ptnr. Massengill, Jersin & Michael, Gaithersburg, 1974-77; pres. Robert R. Michael, Chartered, Bethesda, Md., 1977-84; ptnr. Shadoan & Michael L.L.P., Rockville, Md., 1984—; lectr. continued profl. edn. of lawyers Md. Inst., Balt., 1984—, continuing legal edn., Rockville, 1984—, continuing legal edn. of Montgomery and Prince George's Counties; lectr. various schs. and bar assns., 1983—. Author: Videotape Depositions, 1987, Comparative Liability; co-author: Automobile Accident Deskbook; co-editor: The Annual Review of Maryland Case Law, 1983; contbr. Product Liability in Maryland, articles to profl. jours. Mem. legis. taskforce product liability, Annapolis, 1980; trustee Redland Bapt. Ch.; founder Trial Lawyers for Pub. Justice, 1982. Named Sect. Chmn. of Yr., Montgomery County, 1986-87. Mem. ABA, ATLA (gov. 1984-86, del. 1982-83), Md. Trial Lawyers Assn. (pres. 1982-83, lectr.), Montgomery County Bar Assn. (jud. selections com. chmn. 1990-91, exec. com. 1991-93, trial cts. jud. nominating commn., 1992-94, adminstrn. of Justice Comm., 1993-94, pres. 1995), Montgomery County Bar Assn. Found. (pres. bar leaders 1996-97), Am. Bar Assn. Found., Assn. Plaintiffs Trial Lawyers Met. Washington, Civil Justice Found. (trustee 1987-89), Md. State Bar (jud. selections com. 1988-94, litigation sect. coun. 1989—, chair 1997—), Am. Inns Ct. (exec. com. 1988—, chpt. LXI program chmn. 1988-89, organizer, pres. 1990, bd. govs., founder Montgomery chpt. program chair 1989-90, pres. 1990-91), Nat. Inst. Advocacy (lectr.), Am. Bd. Trial Advocates, Am. Coll. Trial Lawyers. Democrat. Baptist. Personal injury, Product liability, Professional liability. Home: 8921 Brink Rd Gaithersburg MD 20882-1013 Office: Shadoan & Michael LLP 108 Park Ave Rockville MD 20850-2694

**MICHAELIS, KAREN LAUREE,** law educator; b. Milw., Mar. 30, 1950; d. Donald Lee and Ethel Catherine (Stevens) M.; m. Larry Severtson, Aug. 2, 1980 (div. Aug. 1982); 1 child, Quinn Alexandra Michaelis. BA, U. Wis., 1972, BS, 1974; MA, Calif. State U., L.A., 1979; MS, U. Wis., 1985, PhD, 1988, JD, 1989. Bar: Wis., U.S. Dist. Ct. (we. dist.) Wis. Asst. prof. law Hofstra U., Hempstead, N.Y., 1990-93; assoc. prof. law Ill. State U., Normal, 1993-95; asst. prof. law Wash. State U., Pullman, 1995—. Author: Reporting Child Abuse: A Guide to Mandatory Requirements for School Personnel, 1993, Theories of Liability for Teacher Sexual Misconduct, 1996, Postmodern Perspectives and Shifting Legal Paradigms: Searching For A

Critical Theory of Juvenile Justice, 1998; Student As Enemy: A Legal Construct of the Other, 1999; editor Ill. Sch. Law Quarterly, 1993-95; mem. editl. bd. Nat. Assn. Profs. of Ednl. Adminstrn., 1994-95, Planning and Changing, 1993-95, Jour. Sch. Leadership, 1991—, People & Education: The Human Side of Edn., 1991-96. Mem. ABA, State Bar of Wis., Nat. Coun. Profs. Ednl. Adminstrn. (program com. 1994-95, morphet fund com. 1993—), Nat. Orgn. Legal Problems in Edn. (publs. com. 1993—, program com. 1995, exec. bd.), Edn. Law Assn. (bd. dirs. 1998, co-chair publs. com.). Office: Wash State U Dept Ed Leadership & Co Psy Pullman WA 99164-0001

**MICHAELS, GARY DAVID,** lawyer; b. Pitts., Apr. 27, 1955; s. Edgar Wolfe and Norma Flora (Barker) M.; m. Joan Marie Kelly, June 9, 1984; children: Jeffrey Thomas, Abbey Rose. BA, U. Pa., 1977; JD, George Washington U., 1980. Bar: D.C. 1980, U.S. Dist. Ct. D.C. 1981, U.S. Ct. Appeals (D.C. cir.) 1981, U.S. Ct. Appeals (4th cir.) 1985, U.S. Supreme Ct. 1985, U.S. Ct. Appeals (1st cir.) 1987. Assoc. Troy, Malin & Pottinger, Washington, 1981-82, Ballard, Spahr, Andrews & Ingersoll, Washington, 1982-84, Krivit & Krivit P.C., Washington, 1984-98, Fed. Comm. Commn., Washington, 1998—; bd. dirs. Hinkel-Hofmann Supply Co. Inc., Pitts., 1976—. Mem. The George Washington Law Rev., 1978-80. Vol. legal staff Gary Hart Presdl. Campaign, Washington, 1983, field coord. N.H. and Pa., 1984; bd. dirs. Van Ness South Tenants Assn., Inc., 1986-88, v.p., 1987, pres., 1988, of counsel, 1989-90. Mem. ABA, D.C. Bar Assn. Democrat. Jewish. Administrative and regulatory, Federal civil litigation, Communications. Home: 11922 Coldstream Dr Potomac MD 20854-3602 Office: Fed Comm Commn 445 12th St SW Washington DC 20554-0001

**MICHAELS, JENNIFER ALMAN,** lawyer; b. N.Y.C., Mar. 1, 1948; d. David I. and Emily (Arnow) Alman; 1 child, Abigail Elizabeth. BA, Douglas Coll., 1969; JD, Cardozo Sch. of Law, 1990. Ptnr. Alman & Michaels, Highland Park, N.J., 1990—. Author, composer: (record) Music for 2's and 3's, 1981; producer, writer: (film) Critical Decisions in Medicine, 1983. Mem. ABA, Middlesex County Bar Assn., N.J. State Bar Assn., Am. Trial Lawyers Assn., Phi Kappa Phi. Avocations: aviculture, sailing. General civil litigation, Family and matrimonial, General practice. Office: Alman and Michaels 611 S Park Ave Highland Park NJ 08904-2928

**MICHAELS, KEVIN RICHARD,** lawyer; b. Buffalo, Feb. 9, 1960; s. Richard Ronald and Marlene Constance (Mnich) M.; m. Beatrice Mary Szeliga, Jan. 15, 1983; 1 child, Jaena René. BS in Govt., U. Houston, 1987; JD, South Tex. Coll. Law, 1992. Bar: Tex. 1992, U.S. Dist. Ct. (so. dist.) Tex. 1996. Ct. coord. Harris County Dist. Clk., Houston, 1985-88; paralegal O'Quinn, Kerensky, McAninch & Laminack, Houston, 1988-92, atty., 1992-97; atty. Davis & Shank, P.C., Houston, 1997—. Recipient Commendation medal U.S. Army, 1984, Oak Leaf Cluster, 1985, Good Conduct medal, 1985. Mem. ABA, ATLA (Tex. gov. New Lawyers div. 1994-97), Houston Bar Assn., Def. Rsch. Inst., Tex. Assn. Def. Counsel. Avocations: golf, camping. State civil litigation, Federal civil litigation. Office: Davis & Shank PC 1415 Louisiana St Ste 4200 Houston TX 77002-7355

**MICHAELS, MARTHA A.,** lawyer; b. St. Louis, Oct. 28, 1930; d. Harold Udell and Martha Ann (Reed) M. Student, Mount Holyoke Coll., 1948-49; BA, Rockford Coll., 1952; JD, Ind. U., 1973. Bar: Ind. 1973, Ill. 1979, N.J. 1988, Pa. 1988, Mo. 1990, U.S. Ct. Appeals (7th cir.) 1973, U.S. Ct. Appeals (fed. cir.) 1982, U.S. Patent Office 1961. Analytical chemist G.D. Searle and Co., Skokie, Ill., 1952-56; patent asst. Internat. Minerals and Chemicals, Inc., Skokie, 1956-61; patent agent Corn Products Co., Chgo., 1961-71; patent agent/atty. Eli Lilly and Co., Indpls., 1971-76; pvt. practice Indpls., 1976-78; patent atty. Johnson and Johnson, New Brunswick, N.J., 1978-86; ptnr. Hale and Michaels, Highstown, N.J., 1986-89; sr. patent atty. Fisher Controls, St. Louis, 1989-91; pvt. practice St. Louis, 1991-94; of counsel Polster, Lieder, Woodruff & Lucchesi, LC, 1994—. Mem. Am. Intellectual Property Law Assn., Mo. Bar Assn., Bar Assn. Met. St. Louis. Presbyterian. Intellectual property, Patent, Trademark and copyright. Home: 14636 Chesterfield Trails Dr Chesterfield MO 63017-5631

**MICHAELS, RICHARD EDWARD,** lawyer; b. Chgo., June 10, 1952; s. Benjamin and Lillian (Borawski) Mikolajczewski; m. Karen Lynn Belau Michaels, May 17, 1980; children: Jonathan R., Timothy R., Matthew R. BS in Commerce summa cum laude, DePaul U., 1973; JD, Northwestern U., 1977. Bar: Ill. 1977, U.S. Dist. Ct. (no. dist.) Ill. 1977, U.S. Ct. Appeals (7th cir.) 1977; CPA, Ill. Acct. Touche Ross & Co., Chgo., 1973-74; assoc. Schuyler, Roche & Zwirner and predecessor firm Hubachek & Kelly Ltd., Chgo., 1977-83; ptnr. Schuyler, Roche & Zwirner, Chgo., 1983—, pres., 1994—. Mem. Northwestern U. Law Rev., 1976-77. Mem. mission bd. St. Andrew's Luth. Ch., Park Ridge, Ill., 1983-87, chmn. visitation com., 1989, vice chmn. congregation, 1990-92, chmn. congregation, 1992-94. Mem. ABA, Internat. Bar Assn., Ill. Bar Assn., Chgo. Bar Assn., DePaul U. Alumni Assn., DePaul U. Boosters, Chgo. Athletic Assn., Northwestern Club, C.A.A. Club, Beta Gamma Sigma, Pi Gamma Mu, Beta Alpha Psi. Lutheran. Avocations: photography, golf. General corporate, Private international, Antitrust. Home: 808 Elm St Park Ridge IL 60068-3312 Office: Schuyler Roche & Zwirner 130 E Randolph St Chicago IL 60601-6207

**MICHAELSEN, HOWARD KENNETH,** lawyer; b. Odessa, Wash., May 1, 1927; s. Henry Emil and Anna Marie (Ropte) M.; m. Fayetta Mable Moulton, May 27, 1929; children: Barbara Ann, Howard David, Steven Hardy, Angelia Jean. BA in Social Studies, Wash. State U., 1952; JD, Gonzaga U., 1958. Bar: Wash. 1959, U.S. Dist. Ct. (ea. dist.) Wash. 1959. Tchr. Spokane (Wash.) Sch. Dist. 81, 1954-60; pvt. practice law Spokane, 1960—. Dir. Spokane Lilac Festival Assn., 1974. With U.S. Army, 1945-47, 1950-52. Mem. Wash. Bar Assn. (arbitrator), Wash. Trial Lawyers Assn., Lions, Masons, Shriner. Democrat. United Ch. of Christ. Avocations: fishing, hiking, swimming. Real property, Consumer commercial, Estate planning. Home: 8004 N Fox Point Dr Spokane WA 99208-6430 Office: 320 W Spofford Ave Spokane WA 99205-4750

**MICHAELSON, BENJAMIN, JR.,** lawyer; b. Annapolis, Md., May 30, 1936; s. Benjamin and Naomi Madora (Dill) M.; m. Frances Means Blackwell, Apr. 12, 1986; children: Benjamin, Robert Wendell. BA, U. Va., 1957; JD, U. Md., 1962. Bar: Md. 1962, U.S. Dist. Ct. Md. 1976. Assoc. Goodman, Bloom & Michaelson, Annapolis, Md., 1962-63; atty. pvt. practice, Annapolis, Md., 1963-73, 77-81; sr. ptnr. Michaelson & Christhilf, Annapolis, Md., 1973-77; ptnr. Michaelson & Simmons, Annapolis, Md., 1982-86, Michaelson & Newell, Annapolis, Md., 1987-88, Michaelson, Krause & Ferris, Annapolis, Md., 1988-91; atty. pvt. practice, Annapolis, Md., 1991—; pres. Michaelson Title & Escrow Co., 1993—; gen. counsel, dir. Annapolis Fed. Savs., 1965-94. Counsel Anne Arundel County (Md.) Bd. Edn., 1966-76; mem. vestry St. Anne's Episcopal Ch., Annapolis, 1997—, sr. warden, 1999—. Lt. U.S. Army, 1957-59. Fellow Am. Coll. Mortgage Attys.; mem. Md. Bar Assn. (chmn. real property, planning and zoning sect. coun. 1982-84, grievance commn. inquiry panel 1976-85, vice chmn. 1983-85, grievance commn. rev. bd. 1985-88), Anne Arundel County Bar Assn., Jaycees (Md. state legal counsel 1964-65, nat. dir. 1965-66, Outstanding Young Men Am. 1995), Sailing Club Chesapeake (commodore 1982), Rotary (pres. 1975-76, Paul Harris fellow), Delta Theta Phi Republican. Episcopalian. Real property, Probate, Banking. Home: 3 Southgate Ave Annapolis MD 21401-2709 Office: 275 West St Ste 216 Annapolis MD 21401-3463

**MICHALIK, JOHN JAMES,** legal educational association executive; b. Bemidji, Minn., Aug. 1, 1945; s. John and Margaret Helen (Pafko) M.; m. Diane Marie Olson, Dec. 21, 1968; children: Matthew John, Nicole, Shane. BA, U. Minn., 1967, JD, 1970. Legal editor Lawyers Coop. Pub. Co., Rochester, N.Y., 1970-75; dir. continuing legal edn. Wash. State Bar Assn., Seattle, 1975-81, exec. dir., 1981-91; asst. dean devel. and cmty. rels. Sch. of Law U. Wash., 1991-95; exec. dir., CEO Assn. Legal Adminstrs., Vernon Hills, Ill., 1995—. Fellow Coll. Law Practice Mgmt.; mem. Am. Soc. Assn. Execs., Am. Mgmt. Assn., Nat. Trust Hist. Preservation, Coll. Club Seattle. Lutheran. Office: Assn Legal Adminstrs #325 175 E Hawthorn Pkwy Vernon Hills IL 60061-1463

**MICHEL, C. RANDALL,** judge, lawyer; b. Meridian, Miss., May 21, 1949; s. Arnaud Simon and Maureen Mabel (White) M.; m. Shelley Elaine Cooper, Jan. 4, 1971; children: Mark Michael, Natalie Marie. BA, Baylor U., 1971; MS, U. Okla., 1972; JD, U. Ky., 1979. Bar: Ky. 1980, U.S. Ct. Appeals (6th cir.) 1982, Tex. 1983, U.S. Dist. Ct. (we. dist.) Ky. 1988, U.S. Dist. Ct. (we., ea. and so. dists.) Tex. 1988, U.S. Ct. Appeals (5th cir.) 1993; bd. cert. Tex. Bd. Legal Specialization, Nat. Bd. Trial Advocacy. Assoc. E.R. Gregory & Assocs., Bowling Green, Ky., 1980-81; ptnr. Gregory & Michel, Bowling Green, 1981-83; assoc. D. Brooks Cofer Jr. Inc., Bryan, Tex., 1983-84; assoc. Vance, Bruchez & Goss, Bryan, 1984-86, ptnr., 1987-90; ptnr., shareholder Bruchez, Goss, Thornton Meronoff, Michel & Hawthorne, P.C., Bryan, 1990-98; judge County Ct. at Law #1, Brazos County, 1999—; mediator Nat. Mediation Arbitration Svcs., Inc., Dallas, 1993-96; bd. dirs. Brazos County Legal Aid, Bryan, 1990-95; judge Mcpl. Ct., City of College Station, Tex., 1992-98; mediator Am. Arbitration Assn., 1990-95. Commn. Planning and Zoning Commn., City of College Station, 1988-92; dir. Brazos Food Bank, Bryan-College Station, 1990-95, Am. Diabetes Assn., Bryan-College Station, 1984-85. Capt. USAF, 1973-77. Decorated Commendation medal, 1st oak leaf cluster; recipient Pro Bono award Brazos County Bar Assn., Bryan, 1990. Fellow Tex. Bar Found.; mem. ABA, ATLA, Def. Rsch. Inst., Am. Judicature Soc., State Bar Tex., Ky. Bar Assn., Brazos County Bar Assn. (pres.-elect 1995-96, pres. 1996-97), Omicron Delta Kappa. Avocations: computers, golf, reading, political cartooning, refinishing antiques. General civil litigation, Consumer commercial, Insurance. Office: County Ct at Law #1 300 E 26th St Ste 210 Bryan TX 77803-5360

**MICHEL, CLIFFORD LLOYD,** lawyer, investment executive; b. N.Y.C., Aug. 9, 1939; s. Clifford William and Barbara Lloyd (Richards) M.; m. Betsy Shirley, June 6, 1964; children: Clifford Fredrick, Jason Lloyd, Katherine Beinecke. AB cum laude, Princeton U., 1961; JD, Yale U., 1964. Bar: N.Y. 1964, U.S. Dist. Ct. (so. dist.) N.Y. 1968, U.S. Ct. Appeals (2d cir.) 1967, U.S. Supreme Ct. 1972. Assoc. Cahill Gordon & Reindel, N.Y.C., 1964-67, Paris, 1967-69, N.Y.C., 1969-71; ptnr. Cahill Gordon & Reindel, Paris, 1972-76, N.Y.C., 1976—; bd. dirs. Alliance Capital Mgmt. Mut. Funds, Placer Dome Inc. Bd. dirs. Jockey Hollow Found., Michel Found., St. Mark's Sch., Morristown Meml. Hosp., Meml. Health Found., Atlantic Health Sys. Mem. ABA, FBA, N.Y. State Bar Assn., New York County Lawyers Assn., Am. Soc. Internat. Law, Racquet and Tennis Club, River Club, The Links, Shinnecock Hills Golf Club, Somerset Hills Country Club, Essex Hunt Club, Sankaty Head Golf Club (Mass.), Golf de Morfontaine (France), Travellers Club (Paris), Loch Lomond Club (Scotland), Nantucket Golf Club. Republican. General corporate, Private international, Securities. Office: Cahill Gordon & Reindel 80 Pine St Fl 17 New York NY 10005-1790

**MICHEL, PAUL REDMOND,** federal judge; b. Philadelphia, Pa., Feb. 3, 1941; s. Lincoln M. and Dorothy (Kelley) M.; m. Sally Ann Clark, 1965 (div. 1987); children: Sarah Elizabeth, Margaret Kelley; m. Elizabeth Morgan, 1989. BA, Williams Coll., 1963; JD, U. Va., 1966. Bar: Pa. 1967, U.S. Supreme Ct., 1970. Asst. dist. atty. Dist. Atty's Office, Phila., 1967-71, dep. dist. atty. for investigations, 1972-74; asst. spl. prosecutor Watergate investigation Dept. Justice, Washington, 1974-75, dep. chief pub. integrity sect., Criminal div. and prosecutor "Koreagate" investigation, 1976-78, assoc. dep. atty. gen., 1978-81, acting dep. atty. gen., 1979-80; asst. counsel intelligence com. U.S. Senate, 1975-76, counsel and adminstrv. asst. to Sen. Arlen Specter, 1981-88; judge U.S. Ct. Appeals (Fed. cir.), Washington, 1988—; instr. appellate practice and procedure George Wash. U. Nat. Law Ctr., 1991—, appellate advocacy John Marshall Law Sch., Chgo. 2d lt. USAR, 1966-72. Office: US Ct Appeals Fed Cir 717 Madison Pl NW Ste 808 Washington DC 20439-0002*

**MICHELEN, OSCAR,** lawyer; b. Santo Domingo, Dominican Republic, May 1, 1960; came to U.S., 1962; s. Nasry and Marie (Armaly) M.; m. Christine Nicolaou, June 14, 1987; children: Steven, Marcus, Peter. BA, SUNY, 1982; JD, NYU, 1985. Bar: N.Y. 1986, N.J. 1986, U.S. Dist. Ct. (so. and ea. dists.) N.Y. 1986, U.S. Dist. Ct. N.J. 1986. Trial atty. Corp. Counsel of N.Y.C. Torts, 1985-86, sr. trial atty. tort divsn., 1986-87, sr. trial specialist spl. litigation unit, 1987-89; assoc. Sandback & Birnbaum, Mineola, N.Y., 1989-95; ptnr. Sandback, Birnbaum & Michelen, Mineola, N.Y., 1995—. Contbr. articles to profl. jours.; rsch. editor N.Y. Law Sch. Law Rev., 1984-85. Mem. parish coun. Archangel Michael Greek Orthodox Ch., Roslyn, N.Y., 1996. Criminal, Personal injury. Office: Sandback Birnbaum & Michelen 200 Old Country Rd Mineola NY 11501-4235

**MICHELI, CHRISTOPHER MICHAEL,** lawyer; b. Sacramento, Mar. 14, 1967; s. Paul Lothar and Vima Nina (de Marchi) M.; m. Liza Marie Hernandez, Sept. 4, 1994; 2 children: Morgan, Francesca. Attended, George Washington U., 1985-86; BA in Polit. Sci. and Pub. Svc., U. Calif., Davis, 1989; JD, McGeorge Sch. Law, 1992. Bar: Calif. 1992, U.S. Dist. Ct. (no. and cen. dists.) 1993, (ea. dist.) 1992, U.S. Ct. Appeals (D.C. and 9th cirs.) 1993. Assoc. Bell & Hiltachk, Sacramento, 1992-93; gen. counsel Calif. Mfrs. Assn., Sacramento, 1993-94; atty., legis. advocate Carpenter, Snodgrass & Assocs., Sacramento, 1994—; mem. editl. adv. bd. State Income Tax Alert, Ga., 1997—, Interstate Tax Report, 1997—, Sacramento Lawyer, 1995—; mem. legis. com. Inst. Govtl. Advocates, Sacramento, 1994-95; mem. adv. bd. Franchise Tax Bd., Sacramento, 1996—. Columnist The Daily Recorder, 1994—; contbr. articles to newspapers and profl. jours. Bd. dirs. Jesuit H.S. Alumni Assn., Sacramento, 1992—; soccer referee and coach Del Dayo Sch., Carmichael, Calif., 1994—. Scholar William D. James Found., 1989. Mem. ABA, State Bar Calif., Sacramento County Bar Assn., Phi Delta Phi. Democrat. Roman Catholic. Avocations: politics, martial arts, travel, soccer. Legislative, Administrative and regulatory, State and local taxation. Home: 5511 Ivanhoe Way Carmichael CA 95608-5913 Office: Carpenter Snodgrass Assocs 1121 L St Ste 210 Sacramento CA 95814-3926

**MICHELS, DIRK,** lawyer; b. Wupperful, Germany, Mar. 10, 1962; s. Wolfgang and Ingrid Michels; m. Claudia I. Olson, Aug. 2, 1995. Grad., U. Hamburg Sch. Law, Germany, 1988; LLM, U. San Diego, 1996. Bar: Hamburg 1992, Calif. 1996. Law clk. Hamburg Ct. Appeals, 1989-92; assoc. Huth Dietrich Hahn, Hamburg, 1992-95, Hillyer & Irwin, San Diego, 1996—; bd. dirs. UN Trade Point, San Diego. Mem. German-Am. Lawyers Assn., German-Am. Cultural Soc., Am. Coun. on Germany. Private international, Mergers and acquisitions, Intellectual property. Office: Hillyer & Irwin 550 W C St Fl 16 San Diego CA 92101-3540

**MICHELS, KEVIN HOWARD,** lawyer; b. Newark, Dec. 30, 1960; s. Herbert Phillip and Alice Barbara Michels; m. Kathryn Ann Hockenjos, Oct. 6, 1990. BA with honors, Rutgers U., 1983, JD, 1986. Bar: N.J. 1986, U.S. Dist. Ct. N.J. 1986, U.S. Tax Ct. 1990. Law clk. N.J. Supreme Ct., Morristown, 1986-87; assoc. Pitney, Hardin, Kipp & Szuch, Morristown, 1987-88, Herold and Haines, Liberty Corner, N.J., 1988-90; pvt. practice Stirling, N.J., 1990—; ptnr. Michels & Hockenjos, P.C., Stirling. Author: New Jersey Attorney Ethics, 1997; rsch. editor Rutgers Law Rev., 1985-86. Mem. ABA, N.J. Bar Assn., Phi Beta Kappa. General corporate, General civil litigation, Intellectual property. Home: 28 Rittenhouse Cir Flemington NJ 08822-3129 Office: 1390 Valley Rd Stirling NJ 07980-1346

**MICHELSEN, DIANE,** lawyer; b. Jersey City, N.J.. BA in Social Sci., U. Calif., Berkeley, 1968; MSW, San Francisco State U., 1974; JD, Golden Gate U., 1979. Bar: Calif. 1980. Therapist, adoption and surrogacy related issues Family Systems; cons. adoption and foster care State of Calif. Dept. Social Svcs.; social worker, adoption worker internat. and ind. adoptions State of Calif.; adoption worker L.A. County; lawyer, practice limited to family formation matters Lafayette, Calif., 1986—. Contbr. various mags., including Barrister Mag., Fair, Conceive Mag., ADOPT Net, Resolve, Parent's Monthly. Mem. Am. Acad. Adoption Attys. (v.p. 1995, pres. 1997, bd. dirs. 1990-95), Acad. Calif. Adoption Attys. (pres. 1987-93). Family and matrimonial. Office: Law Office Diane Michelsen 3190 Old Tunnel Rd Lafayette CA 94549-4198

**MICHELSON, GAIL IDA,** lawyer; b. N.Y.C., Sept. 19, 1952; d. Max and Virginia (Seames) M. BA, Columbia U., 1984; JD, W.Va. U., 1993. Bar: W.Va. 1993, U.S. Dist. Ct. (so. dist.) W.Va. Assoc. Kopelman & Assocs., Charleston, W.Va., 1994; asst. atty. gen. consumer protection, profl. licensing bd. Atty. Gen. State of W.Va., Charleston, 1995—; counsel to state licensing boards; defender state agencies in workers compensation litigation. contbg writer W.Va. Quar. Dir./staff Am. Theatre of Actors, N.Y.C., 1985-90; mem. policy bd. Mental Health Assn. Mem. ABA, ACLU, W.Va. Bar Assn., W.Va. Trial Lawyers Assn., Mental Health Assn. (policy making com.). Consumer commercial, Criminal, General civil litigation. Home: 300 Park Ave Charleston WV 25302-1510 Office: Atty Gen State of W Va Capitol Complex Charleston WV 25305-0009

**MICHELSTETTER, STANLEY HUBERT,** lawyer; b. Milw., July 8, 1946; s. Donald Lee and Gloria (Menke) M.; m. Joyce Bladow, Apr. 29, 1972; children: Chad S., Chris E. BA in Math., U. Wis., 1968, JD, 1972. Bar: Wis. 1972, U.S. Dist. Ct. (we. dist.) Wis. 1972. Staff atty. Wis. Employment Rels. Commn., Milw., 1972-80; pvt. practice, Milw., 1980—; adminstrv. law judge, equal rights div. adminstrat. Wis. Dept Industry, Labor & Human Rels., Milw., 1992-93. Chmn. North Shore Rep. Club, Milw., 1984-86. Served to 2d lt. Wis. N.G., 1968-74. Mem. Wis. Bar Assn. (chmn. 1993), Milw. Bar Assn., Nat. Acad. Arbitrators, Indsl. Rels. Rsch. Assn. (bd. dirs. 1987—), Rotary. Republican. Jewish. Labor, Alternative dispute resolution, General practice. Home: 1500 W Green Brook Rd Milwaukee WI 53217-1515 Office: 1568 N Farwell Ave Milwaukee WI 53202-2366 also: 601 S Lasalle St Ste M786 Chicago IL 60605-1700

**MICHENFELDER, ALBERT A.,** lawyer; b. St. Louis, July 21, 1926; s. Albert A. and Ruth Josephine (Donahue) M.; m. Lois Barbara Sullivan, Sept. 30, 1949 (div. May 2, 1967); children: Michael J., Ann C. Michenfelder Yancey, Elizabeth D. Michenfelder Brown; m. Ramona Jo Dysart, July 12, 1968 (dec. Jan. 2, 1998); 1 child, Julie D. Michenfelder Wolf. B of Naval Sci., Marquette U., 1946; LLB, St. Louis U., 1950. Bar: Mo. 1950, U.S. Dist. Ct. (ea. dist.) Mo. 1950, U.S. Supreme Ct. 1975. Assoc. Flynn & Challis, St. Louis, 1950-54; pvt. practice St. Louis, 1954-55; prin., chmn. Ziercher & Hocker, P.C., St. Louis, 1955—; mem. 21st Cir. Jud. Commn., St. Louis, 1981-87. Contbr. articles to profl. jours. City atty. City of Webster Groves, Mo., 1966-79; mem. John Marshall Club, St. Louis. Lt. (j.g.) USNR, 1944-47. Mem. Mo. Bar Assn., Bar. Assn. Met. St. Louis, St. Louis County Bar Assn. (pres. 1966), Westborough Country Club. Republican. Avocations: golf, tennis. Land use and zoning (including planning), General civil litigation, Appellate. Office: Ziercher and Hocker PC 231 S Bemiston Ave Saint Louis MO 63105-1914

**MICHIE, DANIEL BOORSE, JR.,** lawyer; b. Phila., July 28, 1922; s. Daniel Boorse and Mae (Mueller) M.; m. Barbara F. Maddox, Aug. 29, 1970. BS, Harvard U., 1943; LLB, U. Va., 1948. Bar: Pa. 1949. Lawyer Phila., 1949-94; assoc. Harry J. Alker (Esq.), 1949, Kephart & Kephart, 1950-51; assoc. Fell & Spalding, 1952-53, ptnr., 1954-68; ptnr. Fell, Spalding, Goff & Rubin, 1969-82, Fell & Spalding, 1982-94; of counsel Richard W. Stevens, Esq., Jenkintown, Pa., 1994—; spl. master U.S. Ct. Appeals (3d cir.), 1970—; solicitor Twp. Abington, Pa., 1958-78; Pres. Phila. Council Internat. Visitors, 1957-60, chmn., 1979-81; pres. Phila. Crime Commn., 1960-63, Phila. Fellowship Commn., 1970-71; chmn. Pa. Adv. Com. on Probation, 1966-92, Bd. Phila. Prisons, 1968-71. Pres. Nat. Assn. Citizens Crime Commns., 1961-62, Unitarian Universalist Svc. Com., 1969-72; regional co-chmn. NCCJ, 1967-71, nat. bd. govs., 1971-80, nat. trustee, 1968-98, nat. exec. bd., 1981-88, nat. advisor, 1998—; vice chmn. Southeastern Pa. chpt. ARC, 1978-82; bd. dirs. Urban League Phila., 1981-83; bd. dirs. Valley Forge coun. Boy Scouts Am., 1955-84, mem. adv. bd., 1984-96, mem. adv. coun. Cradle of Liberty coun., 1996—; mem. St. Andrew's Soc., counselor, 1989-95; mem. Friendly Sons of St. Patrick, counselor, 1989-98. Lt. USNR, 1943-46. Mem. ABA (chmn. organized crime com. 1964-65), Phila. Bar Assn. (gov. 1970-72), Pa. Bar Assn. (ho. of dels. 1971—), Am. Coll. Real Estate Lawyers, Fed. Bar Assn., Am. Judicature Soc., Navy League (dir. Phila. 1967-73, v.p. 1973-76, pres. 1976-78, nat. dir. 1977-83). Republican. Unitarian Universalist (ch. pres. 1961-62, dist. pres. 1966-69). Clubs: Union League (Phila.); Marathon Yacht (Fla.). General corporate, Probate, Real property. Home: PO Box 522722 Marathon Shores FL 33052-2722 Office: Ste 108 115 West Ave Jenkintown PA 19046-2031 *The most important standard of conduct I have attempted to follow is to respect the individuality and dignity of every person—including myself. Early in the practice of law I learned I could best represent my client in a business matter by gaining an understanding of the motivations and needs of the persons on the other side. Only then could I determine whether an agreement or settlement was feasible—as it almost always was. I found this same approach invariably helpful in other human endeavors.*

**MICHIGAN, ALAN,** lawyer; b. N.Y.C., May 26, 1945; s. Norman and Miriam (Cooper) M.; m. Teri Ruth Samach, June 29, 1980; 1 child, Edward. BA, Hobart Coll., 1966; JD, Fordham U., 1974. Bar: N.Y. 1975, U.S. Dist. Ct. (so. and ea. dists.) N.Y. 1975. Atty. Met. Life Ins. Co., N.Y.C., 1974-76; assoc. Dreyer and Traub, N.Y.C., 1976-77, Trubin, Sillcocks, Edelman & Knapp, N.Y.C., 1977-79, Gordon, Hurwitz, Butowsky, Baker, Weitzner & Shalov, N.Y.C., 1979-81; ptnr. Brauner, Baron, Rosenzweig & Klein, LLP, N.Y.C., 1981—. Mem. N.Y.C. Mayor's Commn. for Vietnam Vets. Meml., 1984; founder, bd. dirs. N.Y. Vietnam Vets. Leadership Program, N.Y.C., 1982-97. Lt. USN, 1968-71, USNR, 1971-79. Mem. N.Y. State Bar Assn. Democrat. Jewish. Avocations: military history, old house restoration, antique autos. Real property, Contracts commercial, Construction. Home: 626 James St Pelham Manor New York NY 10803 Office: Brauner Baron Rosenzweig & Klein LLP 61 Broadway New York NY 10006-2701

**MICHOD, CHARLES LOUIS, JR.,** lawyer; b. Champaign, Ill., July 19, 1943; s. Charles Louis Sr. and Florence Wise Michod; m. Susan Alexander, Aug. 16, 1969; children: Alexander, Richard, Michael. AB, Princeton U., 1995; JD, U. Mich., 1968. Bar: N.Y. 1968, Ill. 1969. Assoc. Shearman & Sterling, N.Y.C., 1968-69, Hopkins & Sutter, Chgo., 1969-72; ptnr. Martin, Craig, Chester & Sonnenschein, Chgo., 1972-94, Kelly, Olson, Michod & Siepker, Chgo., 1995—; ptnr. DePaul Devels., Chgo., 1986—, Carpenter Ventures, Chgo., 1989—; bd. dirs. Bouquet Assocs., Chgo. and St. Gallen, Switzerland. Mem. exec. com. Sch. Art Inst., Chgo., 1990—, bd. govs., 1990—; chmn. Oxbow, Inc., Saugatuck, Mich., 1995—. Recipient Cert. of Appreciation, Law Club of the City of Chgo., 1997. Mem. ABA, Chgo. Bar Assn., Univ. Club Chgo., Law Club (pres. 1996-97), Legal Club, Saddle & Cycle Club, Point O'Woods Country Club. Avocations: golf, squash, art, jazz. General corporate, Real property, State and local taxation. Office: Kelly Olson Michod & Siepker 181 W Madison St Ste 4800 Chicago IL 60602-4583

**MICKEL, JOSEPH THOMAS,** lawyer; b. Monroe, La., Nov. 12, 1951; s. Toufick and Ruth Ella (Phelps) M.; m. Carlene Elise Nickens, Dec. 10, 1981 (div.); children: Thomas, Matthew. BA, La. State U., 1975; postgrad., Tulane U., 1977-78; JD, So. U., 1979. Bar: La. 1979, U.S. Dist. Ct. (mid. dist.) La. 1981, U.S. Ct. Appeals (5th cir.) 1981, U.S. Dist. Ct. (we. dist.) La. 1983, U.S. Ct. Mil. Appeals 1985, U.S. Supreme Ct. 1985. Staff atty. Pub. Defenders Office, Baton Rouge, La., 1979-80; assoc. Law Offices of Michael Fugler, Baton Rouge, 1981; asst. dist. atty. La. 4th Jud. Dist. Atty.'s Office, Monroe, 1982-89; ptnr. Bruscato, Loomis & Street, Monroe, 1984-85; Asst. U.S. Atty. Western Dist., U.S. Atty.'s Office, Lafayette, 1989—; adj. prof. Northeast La. U., Monroe, 1988; mem. U.S. Dept. Justice Organized Crime Drug Task Force, 1992-93; instr. Acadiana Law Enforcement Tng. Acad., U. Southwestern La., Lafayette, 1995—; asst. bar examienr, com. on bar admissions Supreme Ct. State of La. Elder Presbyn. Ch., 1995—. Mem. ABA. Republican. Avocations: trapshooting, skeetshooting, bird hunting, fishing. Home: PO Box 91961 Lafayette LA 70509-1961 Office: US Atty Office 800 Lafayette St Ste 2200 Lafayette LA 70501-6955

**MICKELSEN, EINER BJEGAARD,** judge; b. Elba, Nebr., Aug. 19, 1922; s. Marius K. and Marie (Pedersen) M.; m. Geraldine Marie Finney, Nov. 4, 1949; children: Michael E., Karen M. Bennett, Richard Einer, Rick Eric. Grad. high sch., Cushing, Nebr. Sheriff County of Platte, Wheatland, Wyo., 1967-87, coroner, 1992—; mcpl. judge Town of Wheatland, 1987—. Sec. Platte County Peace Officers, Wheatland, 1989-90; mem., rider Nat. Pony Express. Mem. Wyo. Sheriff's Assn. (pres. 1976), Masons (sec. 1987-91, past master). Republican. Home: 1104 Front St Wheatland WY 82201-9109 Office: Wheatland Mcpl Ct 609 9th St Wheatland WY 82201-2913

**MIDDENDORF, HENRY STUMP, JR.,** lawyer; b. Balt., Feb. 23, 1923; s. Henry Stump and Sarah Kennedy (Boone) M. Student, McDonogh (Md.) Sch., 1934-35, Groton (Mass.) Sch., 1935-41; AB, Harvard U., 1945, JD cum laude, 1952; LLM, NYU, 1957. Bar: N.Y. 1953. Assoc. Milbank, Tweed, Hope & Hadley, N.Y.C., 1952-56, Gilbert & Segall, N.Y.C., 1956-59; pvt. practice N.Y.C., 1959—; sec., dir. The Van Waveren Corp., N.Y.C., 1959-61, M. Van Waveren & Sons, Inc., Holland, 1961-71. Editor: Law Today, 1963-

69. Bd. dirs. Youth Found., 1970—, sec., 1980—; mem. N.Y. County Rep. Com., 1955-61, exec. com. 9th assembly dist., 1956-61; gen. counsel Goldwater for Pres. com., 1964; former mem., chmn. N.Y. County com. Conservative Party; former mem. State com. N.Y. Conservative Party, former mem. exec. com. 1st Lt. inf. AUS, 1945-46. Mem. ATLA, ABA, Assn. Bar City N.Y., N.Y. Bar Assn., Bronx Bar Assn., Independent Bar Assn. (pres. 1962-64, chmn. bd. govs. 1964-69), Am. Bar Found., N.Y. County Lawyers Assn., N.Y. Geneal. and Biog. Soc. (mem. heraldry com., pres. 1989-98), SR (N.Y., pres. 1996—), Soc. Colonial Wars, Pilgrims of U.S., Union Club. Episcopalian. General practice. Address: 175 W 12th St # 15 New York NY 10011-8275

**MIDDLEBROOK, STEPHEN BEACH,** lawyer; b. Hartford, Conn., 1937. BA, Yale U., 1958, LLB, 1961. Bar: Conn. 1961. Counsel Aetna Life and Casualty Co., Hartford, Conn., 1969-71, asst. gen. counsel, 1971-78, corp. sec., 1973-83, v.p., gen. counsel, 1981-88, sr. v.p., gen. counsel, 1988-90, sr. v.p., exec. counsel, 1990-94; spl. counsel Day, Berry & Howard, Hartford, 1995—; vis. fellow Rand, Santa Monica, Calif., 1994. Insurance, General corporate. Office: Day Berry & Howard City Place I Hartford CT 06103-3499

**MIDDLEDITCH, LEIGH BENJAMIN, JR.,** lawyer, educator; b. Detroit, Sept. 30, 1929; s. Leigh Benjamin and Hope Tiffin (Noble) M.; m. Betty Lou Givens, June 27, 1953; children: Leigh III, Katherine Middleditch McDonald, Andrew B. BA, U. Va., 1951, LLB, 1957. Bar: Va. 1957. Assoc. James H. Michael, Jr., Charlottesville, Va., 1957-59; ptnr. Battle, Neal, Harris, Minor & Williams, Charlottesville, 1959-68; legal adviser U. Va., Charlottesville, 1968-72; ptnr. McGuire, Woods, Battle & Boothe, Charlottesville, 1972—; lectr. Grad. Bus. Sch., U. Va., Charlottesville, 1958-94, lectr. Law Sch., 1970-90. Co-author: Virginia Civil Procedure, 1978, 2d edition, 1992; contbr. articles to profl. jours. Chmn. U. Va. Health Svcs. Found., 1988-97; bd. mgrs. U. Va. Alumni, 1994—, v.p., 1999—; bd. dirs., chmn. Va. Health Care Found., 1997-98; trustee Claude Moore Found., 1991—; mem. Va. Health Planning Bd., 1989—; bd. visitors U. Va., 1990-91; trustee Thomas Jefferson Meml. Found., Monticello, 1994—. Fellow Am. Bar Found., Va. Bar Found., Am. Coll. Tax Counsel; mem. ABA (bd. govs. 1999—), Va. State Bar (coun., chmn. bd. govs. various sects.), Charlottesville-Albemarle Bar Assn. (pres. 1979-80), U. Va. Law Sch. Alumni Assn. (pres. 1979-81), U.S. C. of C. (bd. dirs. 1998—), Va. C. of C., Omicron Delta Kappa. Episcopalian. Probate, Estate planning, Non-profit and tax-exempt organizations. Office: McGuire Woods Battle & Boothe LLP PO Box 1288 Charlottesville VA 22902-1288

**MIDDLETON, JACK BAER,** lawyer; b. Phila., Jan. 13, 1929; s. Harry C. and Mildred Cornell (Baer) M.; m. Ann Dodge, Aug. 22, 1953; children: Susan D., Jack B. Jr., Peter C. AB, Lafayette Coll., 1950; JD cum laude, Boston U., 1956. Bar: N.H. 1956, U.S. Dist. Ct. Vt. 1988, U.S. Ct. Appeals (1st cir.) 1957, U.S. Supreme Ct. 1972. Assoc. McLane, Graf, Raulerson & Middleton, Manchester, N.H., 1956-62; ptnr., dir. McLane, Graf, Raulerson & Middleton, Manchester, 1962—; spl. justice Merrimack (N.H.) Dist. Ct., 1964-87; bd. dirs. Greater Manchester Devel. Corp., 1983-95; commr. Uniform State Laws, 1971-74; trustee New Eng. Law Inst., 1977-80. Author: (with others) Summary of New Hampshire Law, 1964, Compendium of New Hampshire Law, 1969, Trial of a Wrongful Death Action in New Hampshire, 1977; editor Boston U. Law Rev., 1954-56; contbr. articles to legal jours. Mem. Mt. Washington Commn., 1969—, Bedford (N.H.) Sch. Bd., 1960-66; mem. adv. bd. Merrimack Valley Coll.; trustee, sec. Mt. Washington Obs., 1957—; chmn. bd. trustees White Mountain Sch., 1976-79; campaign chmn. United Way Greater Manchester, 1987, bd. dirs., 1986-92, chmn., 1990-91; bd. dirs. N.H. Pub. Radio, 1988-91; bd. govs. N.H. Pub. TV, 1994—, chmn., 1997—. Sgt. USMCR, 1950-52. Fellow Am. Coll. Trial Lawyers (chmn. N.H. sect. 1988-90), Am. Bar Found. (life); mem. ABA (ho. dels. 1984—, bd. govs. 1996—, sec.-elect 1998-99), New Eng. Bar Assn. (bd. dirs. 1977-88, pres. 1982-83), N.H. Bar Assn. (pres. 1979-80), N.H. Bar Found. (bd. dirs. 1979-92, chair 1983-90), Nat. Conf. Bar Found. (trustee 1985-92, pres. 1989-90), Nat. Conf. Bar Pres. (exec. coun. 1987-95, pres. 1993-94), N.H. Bus. and Industry Assn. (bd. dirs. 1988—, sec. 1990—), Manchester C. of C. (bd. dirs. 1967-89, chmn. 1984-85), New Eng. Coun. (bd. dirs. 1991—). General civil litigation, Appellate, Personal injury. Office: McLane Graf Raulerson & Middleton 900 Elm St Ste 1001 Manchester NH 03101-2029

**MIDDLETON, JAMES BOLAND,** lawyer; b. Columbus, Ga., Aug. 19, 1934; s. Riley Kimbrough and Annie Ruth (Boland) M.; 1 child, Cynthia. BA in Psychology, Ga. State U., 1964; JD, Woodrow Wilson Coll. Art, 1972. Bar: Ga. 1972, U.S. Patent Office. Draftsman, paralegal and office mgr. to patent atty. Atlanta, 1955-68; draftsman, paralegal and office mgr. Jones & Thomas, Atlanta, 1968-72, assoc., 1972-76; pvt. practice intellectual property Decatur, Ga., 1976-98; ret., 1998. Mem. editl. bd. Atlanta Lawyer, 1973-82, assoc. editor, 1978-81, editor-in-chief, 1981-82. Dir. arts coun. Unitarian-Universalist Congregation Atlanta, 1989-91; bd.d irs. Unitarian-Universalist Endowment Fund, 1993-96, vice chair, 1994-95, sec., 1995-96; bd. dirs., sec. Decatur Arts Alliance, 1990-94. With U.S. Army, 1957-59. Mem. ABA, Am. Intellectual Property Law Assn., Am. Arbitration Assn. (comml. panel 1983-94), DeKalb Bar Assn., State Bar Ga. (editl. bd. jour. 1985-92, patent trademark and copyright sect. 1972—, chmn. 1982-83, pub. rels. com. 1982-88), Fed. Cir. Bar Assn. Intellectual property. Office: PO Box 1968 Decatur GA 30031-1968

**MIDGETT, JAMES CLAYTON, JR.,** lawyer; b. Nashville, June 19, 1950; s. James Clayton Sr. and Helen Marie (Baxter) M. BS with high honors, U. Tenn., 1972; JD, Emory U., 1975. Bar: Tenn. 1975, U.S. Ct. Mil. Appeals 1976, U.S. Dist. Ct. (mid. dist.) Tenn. 1983, U.S. Supreme Ct. 1986. Assoc. Finch & McBroom, Nashville, 1983-86, Miles, Dozier, Spann, Midgett & Bates, Nashville, 1986—; instr. bus. law U. Tampa, 1977-78, Tenn. State U., Nashville, 1984. Pres. Joelton Neighborhood Assn.; mem. exec. bd. Nashville Neighborhood Alliance. Capt. with JAGC, USAF, 1976-80. Recipient Torchbearer award U. Tenn., 1972. Mem. ABA, Tenn. Bar Assn., Nashville Bar Assn., Arnold Air Soc., Scabbard and Blade, Phi Beta Kappa, Phi Delta Phi, Pi Sigma Alpha, Omicron Delta Kappa, Phi Kappa Phi. Lodge: Elks. Avocations: traveling, flying. Personal injury, State civil litigation, Insurance. Office: Miles Dozier Spann Midgett & Bates 315 Deaderick St Ste 1445 Nashville TN 37238-0002

**MIDKIFF, KIMBERLY ANN,** paralegal; b. Kingsport, Tenn., Nov. 27, 1958; d. Harold Douglas and Mary Lou (Carden) M. Student, U. Tenn., 1976-80, 94—. Cert. legal asst. Nat. Assn. Legal Assts. Legal sec. Gilreath & Rowland, Knoxville, Tenn., 1981-83, Tenn. State Atty. Gen.'s Office, Knoxville, 1983-84, Bond, Carpenter & O'Connor, Knoxville, 1984; paralegal Gilreath & Assocs., Knoxville, 1984-89, Lewis, King, Krieg, Waldrop & Catron, P.C., Knoxville, 1989—. Active Westminster Presbyn. Ch., Knoxville. Mem. Nat. Assn. Legal Assts., Tenn. Paralegal Assn., Knoxville Paralegal Assn., Irish Water Spaniel Club of Am., Delta Gamma Alumnae Assn., Golden Key Phi Kappa Phi, Phi Alpha Theta. Democrat. Presbyterian. Avocations: vocal and piano music, horseback riding, reading, theater, hiking. Office: Lewis King Krieg Waldrop & Catron PC One Centre Square 5th Fl 620 Market St Knoxville TN 37902-2231

**MIELKE, DONALD EARL,** lawyer, lobbyist; b. Chgo., Oct. 5, 1944; s. Martin Edward and Mildred Hedwig (Bieresdorf) M.; m. Mary Ellen Thompson, Apr. 27, 1968 (div. 1977); m. Susan Joyce Hobbs, Aug. 12, 1978. BS in Aerospace and Sci. Engring., U. Mich., 1967; JD, U. Denver, 1973; MEngring., Pa. State U., King of Prussia, 1974. Bar: Colo. 1973, U.S. Dist. Ct. Colo. 1973, U.S. Ct. Appeals (10th cir.) 1973, U.S. Supreme Ct. 1989. Sys. engr. GE Missile & Space Co., King of Prussia, 1967-69, Martin Marietta Aerospace, Denver, 1969-73; assoc. Holley, Boatright & Villano, Wheat Ridge, Colo., 1973-75; ptnr. Mielke & Mielke, Lakewood, Colo., 1975-77; pvt. practice, Lakewood, 1977-80, 93-98; of counsel Leabrand & Scheffel, Lakewood, 1981-86, Watrous & Ehlers, Lakewood, 1993-98; dist. atty. 1st Jud. Dist., Golden, Colo., 1986-93; ptnr. Watrous, Ehlers, Mielke & Goodwin, Lakewood, 1998—; mem. Nat. Conf. Commn. on Uniform State Laws, Chgo., 1982-92; instr. real estate law Red Rocks C.C., Golden, 1976-79, Araraphoe C.C., Littleton, Colo., 1976-79; instr. bus. law Regis Coll., Denver, 1979-82; mem. Commn. on Jud. Performance for 1st Jud. Dist., 1993—. Mem. Colo. Ho. of Reps., Denver, 1981-86, mem. judiciary com., 1995-86; mem. Nat. Environ. Enforcement Coun., Washington, 1988-92, chmn., 1992; mem. Colo. Tourism Bd., Denver, 1983-86; pres., treas., chmn. bldg. coms. Bethlehem Luth. Ch., Lakewood, 1969-95; mem. bd. Colo. Luth. H.S., Denver, 1973-80; dist. capt. Jefferson County Rep. Com., Golden, 1993—. Named Legislator of Yr., 1981-86; recipient certs. of merit, 1986-93, innovative mgmt. awards Nat. Assn. Counties, 1986-93. Mem. ABA (vice chmn. environ. crimes and nat. resoruce sect. 1988-90), Am. Acad. Forensic Sci., Nat. Dist. Attys. Assn. (bd. dirs. 1988-93). Avocations: travel, antiques, grandchildren. General practice, Legislative, Real property. Home: 7037 S Miller Ct Littleton CO 80127-2950 Office: Watrous Ehlers Mielke Et Al 3333 S Wadsworth Blvd Ste 207 Lakewood CO 80227-5122

**MIERS, HARRIET E.,** lawyer; b. Dallas, Aug. 10, 1945. BS, So. Meth. U., 1967, JD, 1970. Bar: Tex. 1970. Pres. Locke Purnell Rain Harrell, PC, Dallas; chair Tex. Lottery Commn.; bd. dirs. Capstead Mortgage Corp., Coamerica Bank, Tex. Comments editor Southwestern Law Jour., 1969-70. Former mem.-at-large Dallas City Coun.; trustee Southwestern Legal Found. Named 1 of 50 Top Women Lawyers Nat. Law Jour., 1998. Fellow Am. Bar Found., Tex. Bar Found. (life); mem. ABA (jour. bd. editors, ho. dels., chair credentials and admissions com., election law com., bus. and cmty. activities), Dallas Bar Found., Dallas Bar Assn. (pres. 1985, chmn. bd. dirs. 1981), State Bar Tex. (pres. 1992-93, dir. 1986-89), Attys. Liability Assurance Soc. (bd. dirs.). E-mail: hemiers@lprh.com. General civil litigation, Antitrust, Trade. Office: Locke Purnell Rain Harrell 2200 Ross Ave Ste 2200 Dallas TX 75201-6776*

**MIERZWA, JOSEPH WILLIAM,** lawyer, legal communications consultant; b. Chgo., Nov. 21, 1951; s. Joseph Valentine and Betty Ann (Ray) M.; m. Rolana Conley, May 18, 1974. BA, U. Kans., 1981, JD, 1985. Bar: Kans. 1985, U.S. Dist. Ct. Kans. 1985. Pvt. practice, Prairie Village, Kans., 1985-86; gen. counsel Hyatt Legal Svcs., Kansas City, Mo., 1986-87; corp. counsel NLS Corp., Inc., Lakewood, Colo., 1988; owner, mgr. Joseph W. Mierzwa Cons., Lakewood, 1988-92; pres. Prose Assocs., Inc., Highlands Ranch, Colo., 1991—; cons. Nat. Legal Shield, Lakewood, 1988-92, Reader's Digest Assn., Pleasantville, N.Y., 1988—, Hyatt Legal Svcs., Cleve., 1988-94, Media Resources Internat., 1992-94; editor OverDrive Sys., Inc., Cleve., 1990-95. Author: The 21st Century Family Legal Guide, 1994. Mem. ABA, Kans. Bar Assn. Avocations: cooking, travel, creative writing. General practice. Office: 9889 S Spring Hill Dr Highlands Ranch CO 80126

**MIGHELL, KENNETH JOHN,** lawyer; b. Schenectady, N.Y., Mar. 17, 1931; s. Richard Henry and Ruth Aline (Simon) M.; m. Julia Anne Carstarphen, Aug. 24, 1961; children: Thomas Lowry, Elizabeth Anne. BBA, U. Tex., 1952, JD, 1957. Bar: Tex. 1957. Assoc. Scurry, Scurry, Pace & Wood, Dallas, 1957-61; asst. U.S. Atty. Justice Dept., Dallas, 1961-77; 1st asst. No. Dist. Tex., 1972-77; U.S. Atty. No. Dist., Tex., 1977-81; ptnr. Cowles & Thompson, 1981-96, of counsel, 1996—. Chmn. bd. mgmt. Downtown Dallas YMCA, 1974-76; pres. Dallas Area Am. Lung Assn., 1985-87; bd. dirs. YMCA Met. Dallas, 1987—; chmn. adv. bd. Southwestern Law Enforcement Inst., 1994-98. With USN, 1952-54; capt. USNR, 1954-78. Mem. Fed. Bar Assn., Dallas Bar Assn. (bd. dirs. 1984-89, chmn. 1989, v.p. 1990-91, pres. 1993, trustee 1994—, vice chmn. 1999), State Bar Tex. (bd. dirs. 1994-95), Nat. Assn. Former U.S. Attys. (pres. 1995). Democrat. Methodist. Personal injury, General civil litigation, Alternative dispute resolution. Office: Cowles & Thompson 901 Main St Ste 4000 Dallas TX 75202-3793

**MIHAN, RALPH GEORGE,** lawyer; b. San Francisco, Mar. 30, 1941; s. Ralph William and Norma Rose (Holmes) M.; m. Eleanor Mae Green, Sept. 24, 1966; children: Gregory Scott, Jeffrey Matthew. BA, St. Mary's Coll., 1963; JD, U. San Francisco, 1966. Bar: Calif. 1966, U.S. Dist. Ct. (no. dist.) Calif. 1967, U.S. Ct. Appeals (9th cir.) 1967. Atty. U.S. Dept. Interior, San Francisco, 1967-74, field solicitor (area counsel) Office of the Solicitor, 1974—; lectr. Nat. Park Svc. Rangers Acad., 1976—. Dir. coach St. Raphael's Cath. Youth Orgn. Basketball Program, San Rafael, 1977-88, San Rafael Youth Soccer League, 1978-88, San Rafael Little League, 1979-89; commr. City San Rafael Pk. and Recreation Commn., 1982—. Recipient Outstanding Community Svc. award Calif. Pk. and Recreation Soc., 1983. Mem. San. Francisco Bar Assn., Fed. Bar Assn. (pres. San Francisco chpt. 1974-75, exec. com. 1976—, Outstanding Contbn. award 1977). Office: US Dept Interior Office of the Solicitor 600 Harrison St Ste 545 San Francisco CA 94107-1370

**MIHELIC, KRISTIN TAVIA,** lawyer; b. Chgo.. BA, Northwestern U., 1992; JD, Boston U., 1995. Bar: Ill. 1995, U.S. Dist. Ct. (no. dist.) Ill. 1995, U.S. Dist. Ct. (so. and ctrl. dists.) Ill. 1997. Law clk. to Justice Fred A. Geiger State of Ill. Appellate Ct. Second Dist., Libertyville, Ill., 1999—. Mem. Def. Rsch. Inst. (comml. sect. liaison 1997—), Ill. State Bar Assn. (comml., banking and bankruptcy sect. coun. 1999—). General civil litigation, Contracts commercial, Insurance. Office: Ill Appellate Ct 611 S Milwaukee Ave #12 Libertyville IL 60048

**MIHM, MICHAEL MARTIN,** federal judge; b. Amboy, Ill., May 18, 1943; s. Martin Clarence and Frances Johannah (Morrissey) M.; m. Judith Ann Zosky, May 6, 1967; children—Molly Elizabeth, Sarah Ann, Jacob Michael, Jennifer Leah. BA, Loras Coll., 1964; JD, St. Louis U., 1967. Asst. prosecuting atty. St. Louis County, Clayton, Mo., 1967-68; asst. state's atty. Peoria County, Peoria, Ill., 1968-69; asst. city atty. City of Peoria, Ill., 1969-72; state's atty. Peoria County, Peoria, Ill., 1972-80; sole practice Peoria, Ill., 1980-82; U.S. dist. judge U.S. Govt., Peoria, Ill., 1982—; chief U.S. dist. judge U.S. Dist. Ct. (ctrl. dist.) Ill., 1991-98; chmn. com. internat. jud. rels. U.S. Jud. Conf., 1994-96, mem. exec. com., 1995-97, mem. com. jud. br., 1987-93, mem. com. internat. jud. rels., 1998—; adj. prof. law John Marshall Law Sch., 1990—. Past mem. adv. bd. Big Brothers-Big Sisters, Crisis Nursery, Peoria; past bd. dirs. Salvation Army, Peoria, W.D. Boyce council Boy Scouts Am., State of Ill. Treatment Alternatives to Street Crime, Gov.'s Criminal Justice Info. Council; past vice-chmn. Ill. Dangerous Drugs Adv. Council; trustee Proctor Health Care Found., 1991—. Recipient Good Govt. award Peoria Jaycees, 1978. Mem. Peoria County Bar Assn. (former bd. dirs., past chmn. entertainment com.). Roman Catholic. Office: US Dist Ct 204 Federal Bldg 100 NE Monroe St Peoria IL 61602-1003

**MIKALS, JOHN JOSEPH,** lawyer; b. N.Y.C., Feb. 24, 1947; s. John J. Sr. and Eleanor (Kapchen) M.; children: Jonas, Marisa; m. Carolyn A. Ruff, May 30, 1987; 1 child, Kyle. BA, Iona Coll, 1969; JD, U. Va., 1972. Bar: Fla. 1972. Assoc., ptnr. Mahoney, Hadlow, Chambers and Adams, Jacksonville, Fla., 1972-79; ptnr. Gallagher, Mikals & Cannon PA, Jacksonville, 1979-89; ptnr., exec. ptnr. Holland & Knight, Jacksonville, 1989—, dir., 1992—. Mem. ABA, Fla. Bar Assn., Jacksonville Bar Assn., Jacksonville C. of C. Democrat. Roman Catholic. Avocations: golf, reading, traveling. Real property. Office: Holland & Knight Barnett Ctr Ste 3900 50 N Laura St Jacksonville FL 32202-3664

**MIKELS, RICHARD ELIOT,** lawyer; b. Cambridge, Mass., July 14, 1947; s. Albert Louis and Charlotte Betty (Shapiro) M.; m. Deborah Gwen Katz, Aug. 29, 1970; children: Allison Brooke, Robert Jarrett. BS in Bus. Adminstrn., Boston U., 1969, JD cum laude, 1972. Bar: Mass. 1972, U.S. Dist. Ct. Mass. 1974, U.S. Ct. Appeals (1st cir.) 1978. Legal examiner ICC, Washington, 1972-74; ptnr. Riemer & Braunstein, Boston, 1974-80; ptnr., chmn. comml. law sect. Peabody & Brown, Boston, 1980-88; mem., chmn. comml. law sect. Mintz, Levin, Cohn, Ferris, Glovsky and Popeo, P.C., Boston, 1988—. Contbr. articles to profl. jours. Tng. adv. com. Jewish Vocat. Svc., Boston, 1991, 95, 96, bd. dirs., 1995-99, vice chair microenterprise adv. com. 1997; vice-chair lawyers com. Combined Jewish Philanthropies, 1994, 95. Fellow Am. Coll. Bankruptcy; mem. ABA, Am. Bankruptcy Inst., Assn. Comml. Ins. Attys., Comml. Law League Am., Mass. Bar Assn., Boston Bar Assn., Boston U. Law Alumni Assn. (mem. exec. com., v.p. exec. com.). Home: 4 Barley Ln Wayland MA 01778-1600 Office: Mintz Levin Cohn Ferris Glovsky & Popeo PC Financial Center Boston MA 02111

**MIKESELL, RICHARD LYON,** lawyer, financial counselor; b. Corning, N.Y., Jan. 29, 1941; s. Walter Ray and Clara Ellen (Lyon) M.; m. Anna May Creese, Mar. 16, 1973; 1 child, Joel. BSChemE, U. Calif., Berkeley, 1962; LLB, Duke U., 1965; BA in Liberal Studies, UCLA, 1977. Bar: U.S. Supreme Ct. 1971, Ohio 1965, Calif. 1967, U.S. Ct. Appeals (9th cir.) 1982, U.S. Ct. Appeals (2d cir.) 1993, U.S. Patent Office 1967. Patent atty. Procter & Gamble, Cin., 1965-66, Rocketdyne divsn. N.Am. Aviation, L.A., 1966-69; pvt. practice law L.A., 1969-81; prin. Law Offices of R.L. Mikesell, L.A., 1981—; fin. counselor L.A. Police Dept., 1986—; arbitrator Am. Arbitration Assn., L.A., 1980—. Pres. San Fernando Valley Fair Housing Coun., L.A., 1969-72, Valley Women's Ctr., L.A., 1990; line res. officer L.A. Police Dept., 1969-72. Named Res. Officer of Yr. L.A. Police Dept., 1990, 98; recipient 1st Place award Nat. SPAM Recipe Contest, 1998. Avocation: high power rifle shooting. General civil litigation, Patent, Real property. Office: 14540 Hamlin St Ste B Van Nuys CA 91411-4147

**MIKKELSON, ERIC T.,** lawyer; b. Madison, Wis., July 27, 1967; s. Gerald E. Mikkelson and Ruth Elaine Lee. AB, Stanford U., 1990; JD, U. Kans., 1994. Bar: Kans. 1994, Mo. 1995. Pvt. practice, 1994-97; mcpl. judge Kansas City, 1996-97; assoc. Shook, Hardy & Bacon LLP, Kansas City, 1997—. Mem. ABA, Kans. Bar Assn. Avocations: sports, travel, arts. Taxation, general, General civil litigation, General corporate. Office: Shook Hardy & Bacon PO Box 15607 Kansas City MO 64106-0607

**MIKVA, ABNER JOSEPH,** lawyer, retired federal judge; b. Milw., Jan. 21, 1926; s. Henry Abraham and Ida (Fishman) M.; m. Zoe Wise, Sept. 19, 1948; children: Mary, Laurie, Rachel. JD cum laude, U. Chgo., 1951; DL (hon.), U. Ill., Am. U., Northwestern U., Tulane U.; DHL (hon.), Hebrew U.; DHL (Hon.), U. Wis.; DL (hon.), Ill. Inst. Tech. Bar: Ill. 1951, D.C. 1978. Law clk. to U.S. Supreme Ct. Justice Sherman Minton, 1951; ptnr. Devoe, Shadur, Mikva & Plotkin, Chgo., 1952-68, D'Ancona, Pflaum, Wyatt & Riskind, 1973-74; lectr. Northwestern U. Law Sch., Chgo., 1973-75, U. Pa. Law Sch., 1983-85, Georgetown Law Sch., 1986-88, Duke U. Law Sch., Durham, N.C., 1990-91, U. Chgo. Law Sch., 1992-93; mem. Ill. Gen. Assembly from 23d Dist., 1956-66, 91st-92d Congresses from 2d Dist. Ill., 94th-96th Congresses from 10th Dist. Ill., ways and means com., judiciary com.; chmn. Dem. Study Group; resigned, 1979; judge U.S. Circuit Ct. Appeals D.C., 1979-91, chief judge, 1991-94; counsel to the President The White House, Washington, 1994-96; vis. prof., Walter Schaefer chair in pub. policy U. Chgo., 1996-98; vis. prof. U. Ill. Coll. Law, 1998—. Author: The American Congress: The First Branch, 1983, The Legislative Process, 1995, An Introduction to Statutory Interpretation, 1997. With USAAF, WWII. Sr. fellow Inst. Govt. & Pub. Affairs U. Ill., 1998—; recipient Page One award Chgo. Newspaper Guild, 1964, Best Legislator award Ind. Voters Ill., 1956-66, Alumni medal U. Chgo., 1996, Paul Douglas Ethics in Govt. award, 1998; named one of ten Outstanding Young Men in Chgo., Jr. Assn. Commerce and Industry, 1961. Mem. ABA, Chgo. Bar Assn. (bd. mgrs. 1962-64), D.C. Bar Assn., Am. Law Inst., U.S. Assn. Former Mems. Congress, Order of Coif, Phi Beta Kappa. Home: 5020 S Lake Shore Dr Ph 8 Chicago IL 60615-3253

**MILAM, ROGER ARLING,** lawyer; b. Nashville, Jan. 4, 1945; s. John S. and Margaret Y. (Young) M.; m. Marguerite Ehle Milam, Dec. 29, 1965; 1 child, Erik C. BS in Commerce, Washington & Lee U., 1967; JD, Vanderbilt U., 1981. Comm. officer USN, 1969-72; sales mgr. John S. Milam Optical Co., Nashville, 1972-73; lending officer 3d Nat. Bank, Nashville, 1973-78; assoc. Manier & Herod, Nashville, 1981-84; pvt. practice Nashville, 1984-95; court clerk U.S. Dist. Ct. (mid. dist.), Nashville, 1995—. Capt. USNR, 1969-95. Fellow Nashville Bar Assn.; mem. Tenn. Bar Assn. Avocations: golf, guitar. Home: 4111 Skyline Dr Nashville TN 37215-2320 Office: US Dist Ct 801 Broadway Ste 800 Nashville TN 37203-3869

**MILAZZO, THOMAS GREGORY,** lawyer; b. New Orleans, Sept. 18, 1957; s. Anthony Joseph and Lucille Catherine (Fontana) M.; m. Robyn Denise Sanders, Jan. 31, 1987; children: Jordan Thomas, Devin Thomas. BA in Broadcast Journalism, La. State U., 1979; JD, Loyola U., 1982. Bar: La. 1982, U.S. Dist. Ct. (ea. dist.) La. 1983, U.S. Dist. Ct. (mid. and we. dists.) La. 1987, U.S. Ct. Appeals (5th cir.) 1993. Assoc. Francipane, Regan & St. Pé, Metairie, La., 1982-87; ptnr. Regan, St. Pé & Milazzo, Metairie, 1987-91, St. Pé & Milazzo, Metairie, 1991-95, LeBlanc, Miranda & deLaup, Metairie, 1995—. Mem. Def. Res. Inst., La. Assn. Def. Counsel, Jefferson Parish Bar Assn. General civil litigation, Insurance, Product liability. Office: LeBlanc Miranda & deLaup The Pelican Bldg 2121 Airline Hwy Ste 601 Metairie LA 70001-5995

**MILBERG, MELINDA SHARON,** lawyer; b. L.A., May 11, 1953; d. Albert Irving and Gloria Joy (Nathanson) M.; m. Philip B. Benjamin, Aug. 8, 1976; children: Jason G.M., Alex N.M. BA magna cum laude, Brandeis U., 1974; JD, Boston U., 1977. Bar: Mass. 1977, U.S. Dist. Ct. Mass. 1980, U.S. Ct. Appeals (1st cir.) 1985. Civil rights compliance atty. Mass. Com. Criminal Justice, Boston, 1978-80; counsel Mass. Dept. Correction, Boston, 1980-83; spl. asst. atty. gen. Exec. Office Human Svcs., Boston, 1983-85; assoc. Glovsky & Assocs., Boston, 1985-95; instr. Boston U. Sch. Law, 1983-85, Flaschner Jud. Inst., Boston, 1990-91; pub. mem. Bd. Registration in Medicine, Boston, 1985-88; mem. faculty Mass. Continuing Legal Edn., 1989-90, 95. Co-author: Chapter 93A Rights and Remedies, 1989, supplements, 1994, 95. Recipient Pub. Svc. award Am. Jewish Congress, Boston, 1988, Svc. award Bd. Registration in Medicine, Boston, 1988. Fellow Mass. Bar Found.; mem. Mass. Bar Assn. (pub. law sect. coun. 1984-87), Women's Bar Assn. Mass. (pres., v.p. 1981-82), Am. Arbitration Assn. (panel mem. 1993—). General civil litigation, Labor, Probate.

**MILBOURN, DOUGLAS RAY,** lawyer; b. Grand Island, Neb., Jan. 14, 1947; s. Ivan Keith and Valonne L. (Simms) M.; m. Susanne R. Milbourn, Nov. 22, 1969. BBA, U. Neb., 1969, JD, 1973. Bar: Nebr. 1973, U.S. Dist. Ct. (fed. dist.) Nebr. 1973, U.S. Ct. Appeals (8th cir.) 1976, U.S. Supreme Ct. 1976. Dep. county atty. Platte (Neb.) County, 1973-77, county atty., 1977-78; partner Milbourn, Fehringer, Kessler & Peetz, P.C., Columbus, Neb., 1978—. Pres. Columbus (Neb.) YMCA, 1988-89. Mem. ATLA (profl. negligence group, 1995—, traumatic brain injury group, 1993—, bd. govs., 1993—), Roscoe Pound Found., Trial Lawyers for Pub. Justice, Neb. Assn. Trial Attys. (bd. dirs., 1985—, pres., 1990-91), Platte County Bar Assn. (pres. 1985-86), Rotary Club (pres. 1995-96). Dem. Lutheran. Avocations: golf, bridge. General civil litigation, Professional liability, Personal injury. Office: Milbourn Fehringer Kessler & Peetz PC 2362 26th Ave Columbus NE 68601-2527

**MILBOURNE, WALTER ROBERTSON,** lawyer; b. Phila., Aug. 27, 1933; s. Charles Gordon and Florie Henderson (Robertson) M.; m. Georgena Sue Dyer, June 19, 1965; children: Gregory Broughton, Karen Elizabeth, Walter Robertson, Margaret Henderson. A.B., Princeton U., 1955; LL.B., Harvard U., 1958. Bar: Pa. 1959. Assoc. firm Pepper, Hamilton & Sheetz, Phila., 1959-65, Obermayer, Rebmann, Maxwell & Hippel, Phila., 1965-67; ptnr. Obermayer, Rebmann, Maxwell & Hippel, 1968-84, Saul, Ewing, Remick & Saul, 1984—; bd. dirs. Pa. Lumbermen's Mut. Ins. Co., Phila. Reins. Corp.; co-chmn. Nat. Conf. Lawyers and Collection Agys., 1979-90; chmn. bus. litigation com. Def. Rsch. Inst., 1986-89, mem. law instsn. com., 1989-95. Chmn. mental health budget sect. Phila. United Fund, 1967-70; pres. Found. Internat. Assn. Def. Counsel, 1997—. Served with Army N.G., 1958-64. Fellow Am. Coll. Trial Lawyers (mem. internat. com. 1992-96); mem. ABA, Pa. Bar Assn., Phila. Bar Assn., Internat. Assn. Def. Counsel (exec. com. 1985-88, pres. IADC Found. 1997—), Assn. Def. Counsel, Union League, Merion Cricket Club, Princeton Club, Idle Hour Tennis Club (pres. 1968-68, Phila. Lawn Tennis Assn. (pres. 1969-70). Republican. Federal civil litigation, State civil litigation, Insurance. Home: 689 Fernfield Cir Wayne PA 19087-2002 Office: Saul Ewing Remick & Saul 3800 Centre Sq W Philadelphia PA 19102

**MILDER, FORREST DAVID,** lawyer; b. Oceanside, N.Y., Sept. 28, 1953; s. Arthur Aaron and Helen Claire M.; m. Sara Packard, June 15, 1975; children: Stephen, Elinor. SB in Math., MIT, 1973, MS in Econs., 1974; JD, Harvard U., 1977; LLM in Taxation, Boston U., 1983. Bar: Mass. 1977, U.S. Dist. Ct. Mass. 1978, U.S. Supreme Ct. 1985, U.S. Ct. Appeals (1st cir.) 1978, U.S. Tax Ct. 1981, U.S. Claims Ct. 1985. Assoc. Goodwin Procter & Hoar, Boston, 1977-81; ptnr. Brown, Rudnick, Freed & Gesmer, Boston, 1981—; lectr. law Boston U., 1990-95; exec. bd. mem. MIT Enterprise Forum, Cambridge, Mass., 1998—. Author: Rehabilitation Tax Credit and Low Income Housing Tax Credit, 1996; mem. bd. editors Matrimonial Strategist. Mem. ABA, Boston Bar Assn., Phi Beta Kappa. Personal income taxation, Corporate taxation, General corporate. Home: 122 Hoover Rd Needham MA 02494-1548 Office: Brown Rudnick Freed & Gesmer 1 Fin Ctr Boston MA 02111

**MILES, DAVID R.,** lawyer; b. Richmond, Ind., Apr. 13, 1955; s. John R. and Joyce L. M.; m. Mary E. McMorrow, Apr. 17, 1982; children: Julie, Kathleen. BA in Polit. Sci., Wittenberg U., 1977; JD, U. Toledo, 1980. Bar: Ohio 1981, U.S. Dist. Ct. (so. dist.) Ohio 1981. Pvt. practice Fairburn, Ohio, 1981—. Editor Dayton Bar Assn. Mem. Southwe. Ohio Assn. Businessmen, Phi Gamma Delta. Avocation: sports. Criminal, Family and matrimonial, General civil litigation. Office: 125 W Main St Ste 201 Fairborn OH 45324-4714

**MILES, GAVIN WENTWORTH,** lawyer; b. Cambridge, Mass., Sept. 10, 1960; s. Perry Ambrose and Kathleen (McCartney) B.; m. Sarah Jane Berger, Jan. 16, 1995; 1 child: Benjamin. BA in Pol. Sci., Columbia Coll., 1982; JD, Emory U., 1989. Bar: N.Y. 1990. Asst. dist. atty. King's County (N.Y.) Dist. Atty's. Office, Bklyn., 1989-94, sr. asst. dist. atty., 1994-96, spl. counsel, rackets, 1996—. Mem. N.Y.C. Bar Assn. (criminal cts. com. 1996-98). Avocations: history, family outings. Office: Kings County DA'S Office 350 Jay St Brooklyn NY 11201-2900

**MILES, PATRICIA ANN,** lawyer; b. Harrisburg, Pa., Mar. 31, 1951; d. Clyde Leroy and Althea (Gartland) M.; m. Jonathan Barkasy Sprague, Apr. 1, 1978 (div. Dec. 1982); m. Gregory Edward Grybowski, July 9, 1988; 1 child, Anne Miles Grybowski. BS with distinction, Pa. State U., 1972; MS, Columbia U., 1977; JD, U. Pa., 1986. Bar: Pa. 1986. Caseworker, social worker Dauphin County Children & Youth, Harrisburg, 1972-75, 77-78; social work supr. Support Ctr. for Child Advocates, Phila., 1978-80; writer, ceremonies asst. Office of the Gov., Harrisburg, 1980-81; dir. Gov.'s Action Ctr., Harrisburg, 1981-83; assoc. Wolf, Block, Schorr & Solis-Cohen, Phila., 1986-88; asst. counsel Pa. Human Rels. Commn., Harrisburg, 1988-89; assoc., shareholder Howett, Kissinger, Miles, P.C., Harrisburg, 1989-93, 94—; author, spkr. on continuing legal edn. Pa. Bar Inst., 1990—. Author: (children's book) Going to Family Court, 1980. Mem., bd. mgrs. Camp Curtin YMCA, Harrisburg, 1996—; bd. dirs. Ct. Apptd. Spl. Advocates, Harrisburg, 1981-82, 97-98, Parents Anonymous Pa., 1999—; mem. adv. coun. Harrisburg Hosp. Mental Health/Mental Retardation Ctr., 1979-83. Fellow Internat. Ladies Garment Workers, 1976-77; legal writing instr. grantee U. Pa. Law Sch., 1985-86. Mem. ABA, Pa. Bar Assn. (coun. family law sect. 1996—), Dauphin County Bar Assn. (bd. dirs. 1996-99, sec. 1999—). Family and matrimonial. Office: Howett Kissinger & Miles PC PO Box 810 130 Walnut St Harrisburg PA 17108

**MILES, TERRI,** lawyer; b. Baton Rouge, Dec. 25, 1950; d. James Austin and Marjory Noble McDonough; m. David L. Miles Sr., Jan. 7, 1978; children: Danny, David Jr., Dawn, Douglas. BA, N.E. La. U., 1985; JD, Tulane U., 1992. Bar: La. 1992, U.S. Dist. Ct. (ea. and mid. dists.) La. 1993. Ptnr. Bowes & Marrero, Gretna, La., 1993-97; assoc. Halpern Danner & Winsberg, Metairie, La., 1997—. Mem. La. State Bar, Jefferson Parish Bar, Orleans Parish Bar, Christian Legal Soc. Family and matrimonial, General practice, Juvenile. Office: Halpern Danner Winsberg One Parkway Ctr Ste 605 3900 N Causeway Blvd Metairie LA 70002-1746

**MILES, WENDELL A.,** federal judge; b. Holland, Mich., Apr. 17, 1916; s. Fred T. and Dena Del (Alverson) M.; m. Mariette Bruckert, June 8, 1946; children: Lorraine Miles, Michelle Miles Kopinski, Thomas Paul. AB, Hope Coll., 1938, LLD (hon.), 1980; MA, U. Wyo., 1939; JD, U. Mich., 1942; LLD (hon.), Detroit Coll. Law, 1979. Bar: Mich. Ptnr. Miles & Miles, Holland, 1948-53, Miles, Mika, Meyers, Beckett & Jones, Grand Rapids, Mich., 1961-70; pros. atty. County of Ottawa, Mich., 1949-53; U.S. dist. atty. Western Dist. Mich., Grand Rapids, 1953-60; U.S. dist. judge Western Dist. Mich., 1974—, chief judge, 1979-86, sr. judge, 1986—; cir. judge 20th Jud. Cir. Ct. Mich., 1970-74; instr. Hope Coll., 1948-53, Am. Inst. Banking, 1953-60; adj. prof. Am. constl. history Hope Coll., Holland, Mich., 1979—; mem. Mich. Higher Edn. Commn.; apptd. Fgn. Intelligence Surveillance Count, Washington, 1989—. Pres. Holland Bd. Edn., 1952-63. Served to capt. U.S. Army, 1942-47. Recipient Liberty Bell award, 1986. Fellow Am. Bar Found.; mem. ABA, Mich. Bar Assn., Fed. Bar Assn., Ottawa County Bar Assn., Grand Rapids Bar (Inns of Ct. 1995—), Am. Judicature Soc., Torch Club, Rotary Club, Masons. Office: US Dist Ct 236 Fed Bldg 110 Michigan St NW Ste 452 Grand Rapids MI 49503-2363

**MILGRIM, ROGER MICHAEL,** lawyer; b. N.Y.C., Mar. 22, 1937; s. Isreal and Iola (Lash) M.; m. Patricia Conway, July 10, 1971; children: Justin. BA, U. Pa., 1958; LLB, NYU, 1961, LLM, 1962. Bar: N.Y., U.S. Supreme Ct. Assoc. Baker & McKenzie, Paris, 1963-65, Nixon Mudge et al, N.Y.C., 1965-68; mem. Milgrim Thomajan & Lee P.C., N.Y.C., 1968-92; ptnr. Paul, Hastings, Janofsky & Walker, N.Y.C., 1992—, chmn. litigation dept., 1999—; adj. prof. sch. law NYU, N.Y.C., 1974—; bd. dirs. Colfexip S.A. Author: Milgrim on Trade Secrets, 1968, supplement, 1998, Milgrim on Licensing, 1990, supplement, 1998. Trustee Coll. Wooster, 1994-97, Bklyn. Hosp., 1982-91; bd. dirs. Fulbright Assn., 1998—, chmn. Fulbright Prize com. Mem. Knickerbocker Club, Phila. Cricket Club. Republican. Intellectual property, General corporate, Private international. Home: 301 E 52nd St New York NY 10022-6319 Office: Paul Hastings Janofsky & Walker 399 Park Ave Fl 30 New York NY 10022-4697

**MILHAM, JULEE LYNN,** lawyer, mediator, arbitrator; b. Chapel Hill, N.C., May 24, 1963; d. Richard Joseph and Peggy Jouce Milham. BA, Stetson U., DeLand, Fla., 1983; JD, Stetson U., St. Petersburg, Fla., 1986. Bar: Fla. 1986, Calif. 1987, D.C. 1989, U.S. Dist. Ct. (mid. dist.) Fla. 1991, U.S. Ct. Appeals (11th cir.) 1994; cert. mediator, Fla. Atty. at law sole propr., St. Petersburg, 1986—; traffic ct. hearing officer Pinellas County Ct., Fla., 1994—, small claims hearing officer, 1997—; mediator/arbitrator, 1994—. Mem. Fla. Bar (sec. entertainment sect. 1998, mem. small claims rules com. 1998). Alternative dispute resolution, Appellate, Entertainment. Office: 505 76th Ave Saint Pete Beach FL 33706-1805

**MILICICH, LOUIS,** lawyer; b. Gary, Ind., Sept. 22, 1959; married Marya Savich. BA with honors in Polit. Sci., Northwestern U., Ill., 1981, BS in Comm. Rhetorical Studies, 1981, JD, 1984. Bar: Ill., 1984; U.S. Dist. Ct. (no. dist.) Ill., 1984; U.S. Ct. Appeals (7th cir.) Ill., 1991. With Hinshaw & Culbertson, Ill., 1983-85, Arnstein & Lehr., Ill., 1985-88, Keck, Mahin & Cate, Ill., 1988-89, Jenner & Block, Chgo., 1989—; mem. Chgo Coun. on Fgn. Rels., Com. on Fgn. Affairs; lectr. in field. Author: (with others) Illinois Handbook of Product Liability Law, 1990, 93, 96, 99; contbr. to profl. jours. Mem. diocesan coun. Serbian Orthodox Diocese of U.S. & Canada, Ill.; pres. bd. trustees St. Basil Serbian Orthodox Ch., Ill. Mem. ABA (litigation sect., tort and insurance practice sect., internat. sect.), Ill. State Bar Assn., Chgo. Bar Assn., Serbian Bar Assn. of Am. Fax: 312-840-7773. E-mail: Lmilicich @jenner.com. Office: Jenner & Block One IBM Plz Chicago IL 60611

**MILIO, LOUIS ROMOLO,** retired law educator, social worker; b. Balt.; s. Placido and Rose (Pirrotti) M.; m. Ellenor K. Stafford, July 8, 1978 (dec. Sept. 1990). LLB, U. Balt., 1948, LLM, 1950, JD, 1972; LLD (hon.), We. U., 1951. Cert. social worker asst., Md. Copy boy Balt. Sun, 1943; cost acct. Continental Can Co., Balt., 1945; tax bailiff City Bur. Collections, Balt., 1946-49; atty. City Bur. Recreation, Balt., 1948—, social worker/drug counselor, 1970—; staff dept. welfare City of Balt., 1964-65; case worker Hdqrs. Office, Balt., 1965-66; instr. Italian and pub. speaking YWCA, Balt., 1944; prof. law Ea. Coll. of Commerce, Balt., 1950-51; prof. philosophy Johns Hopkins Univ., Balt.; pres. Milio Cometics Co., Internat., Lady Eleanor Beauty Soap. Author: Faith, Hope & Charity, 1949; patent pending Milio Aviation Safety Sys. Co-founder, sec. Good Neighbor League, Balt., 1948; candidate U.S. Congress, 1946, 50; candidate Mayor Balt. City, 1952, 56, 59; candidate gov. Md., 1966-74. Pvt. 1st Class Md. State Guard, 1943-94. Mem. Star Spangled Banner Flag House Assn (last living resident). Dem. Roman Cath. Avocations: swimming, walking, bowling, cooking, gardening. Home and Office: Village of Cross Keys 2 Cross Keys Rd Apt C Baltimore MD 21210-1719

**MILITA, MARTIN JOSEPH,** lawyer; b. Vineland, N.J., May 14, 1953; s.Martin Joseph and Mary Elizabeth (Gavigan) M.; m. Janet D. Milita, Oct. 3, 1981; 1 child, Samantha Anne. BA, Kings Coll., 1976; JD, Temple U., 1979. Bar: Pa. 1979, N.J. 1979, U.S. Dist. Ct. N.J. 1979. Tchg. fellow Temple U., Phila., 1978; asst. dist. atty. Bucks County Dist. Atty.'s Office, Doylestown, Pa., 1979-81; asst. prosecutor Hunterdon County Prosecutor's Office, Flemington, N.J., 1981-84; dep. atty. gen. State of N.J., Trenton, 1984-90; assoc. Sills Cummis et al, Newark, 1990-94; counsel Riker, Danzig, Scherer, Hyland & Perretti, LLP, Morristown, N.J., 1994—. Contbr. articles to law jours. Mem. adv. bd. Rep. Nat. Com., Washington, 1994—. Mem. N.J. Bar Assn. Roman Catholic. Avocations: Civil War history, collecting Civil War art and artifacts. Legislative, Environmental, Administrative and regulatory. Office: A Fiore & Sons 1230 Mccarter Hwy Newark NJ 07104-3710

**MILITELLO, SAMUEL PHILIP,** lawyer; b. Buffalo, Dec. 16, 1947; s. Samuel Anthony and Katherine (Pesono) M.; m. Anne Little, May 27, 1972; children: Matthew Samuel, Rebecca Anne, Caitlin Frances. BA, Canisius Coll., 1969; JD, SUNY, Buffalo, 1972. Bar: N.Y. 1972, U.S. Ct. Mil. Appeals 1973, U.S. Army Ct. of Mil. Rev. 1976, U.S. Ct. Claims 1977, U.S. Supreme Ct. 1977, U.S. Dist. Ct. (we. dist.) N.Y. 1986, U.S. Dist. Ct. (no. dist.) N.Y. 1987, U.S. Dist. Ct. (ea. dist.) N.Y. 1994, U.S. Ct. Appeals (2d cir.), 1990. Assoc. Williams & Katzman, Watertown, N.Y., 1978-79; legal counsel, mgr. of litigation Parsons Corp., Pasadena, Calif., 1979-84; gen. counsel, sec. Envirogas, Inc., Hamburg, N.Y., 1984-86; assoc. Bond, Schoeneck & King, Watertown, 1987-88; mng. ptnr. The Militello Law Office, P.C., Watertown, 1989—; counsel Parsons Gilbane, New Orleans, 1979-81; gen. counsel The Stebbins Engring. and Mfg. Co. and subs., 1986—. Capt. JAGC, U.S. Army, 1973-78. Decorated Army Commendation medal with one oak leaf cluster, Meritorious Service medal. Mem. ABA (pub. contracts sect.), N.Y. State Bar Assn., N.Y. Criminal and Civil Cts. Bar Assn., Bar Assn. of Erie County (N.Y.), Bar Assn. of Jefferson County (N.Y.), No. N.Y. Builders Exchange, Assoc. Gen. Contractors Am., Am. Legion, K.C. (adv. 1978-79). Roman Catholic. Construction, Oil, gas, and mineral, General corporate. Office: PO Box 6800 1619 Ohio St Watertown NY 13601-3032

**MILLAR, RICHARD WILLIAM, JR.,** lawyer; b. L.A., May 11, 1938. LLB, U. San Francisco, 1966. Bar: Calif. 1967, U.S. Dist. Ct. (cen. dist.) Calif. 1967, U.S. Dist. Ct. (no. dist.) Calif. 1969, U.S. Dist. Ct. (so. dist.) Calif. 1973, U.S. Supreme Ct. Assoc. Iverson & Hogoboom, Los Angeles, 1967-72; ptnr. Eilers, Stewart, Pangman & Millar, Newport Beach, Calif., 1973-75, Millar & Heckman, Newport Beach, 1975-77, Millar, Hodges & Bemis, Newport Beach, 1979—. Fellow Am. Bar Found.; mem. ABA (litigation sect., trial practice com., ho. of dels. 1990—), Calif. Bar Assn. (lectr. CLE), Orange County Bar Assn. (sec. 1999, chmn. bus. litig. sect. 1981, chmn. judiciary com. 1988-90, sec. 1999), Balboa Bay Club, Bohemian Club (San Francisco), Pacific Club. State civil litigation, Federal civil litigation. Home: 2546 Crestview Dr Newport Beach CA 92663-5625 Office: Millar Hodges & Bemis One Newport Pl Ste # 900 Newport Beach CA 92660

**MILLARD, NEAL STEVEN,** lawyer; b. Dallas, June 6, 1947; s. Bernard and Adele (Marks) M.; m. Janet Keast, Mar. 12, 1994; 1 child, Kendall Layne. BA cum laude, UCLA, 1969; JD, U. Chgo., 1972. Bar: Calif. 1972, U.S. Dist. Ct. (cen. dist.) Calif. 1973, U.S. Tax Ct. 1973, U.S. Ct. Appeals (9th cir.) 1987, N.Y. 1990. Assoc. Willis, Butler & Schiefly, Los Angeles, 1972-75; ptnr. Morrison & Foerster, Los Angeles, 1975-84, Jones, Day, Reavis & Pogue, Los Angeles, 1984-93, White & Case, L.A., 1993—; instr. Calif. State Coll., San Bernardino, 1975-76; lectr. Practising Law Inst., N.Y.C., 1983-90, Calif. Edn. of Bar, 1987-90; adj. prof. USC Law Ctr., 1994—. Citizens adv. com. L.A. Olympics, 1982-84; trustee Altadena (Calif.) Libr. Dist., 1985-86; bd. dirs. Woodcraft Rangers, L.A., 1982-90, pres., 1986-88; bd. dirs. L.A. County Bar Found., 1990—, pres., 1997-98; mem. Energy Commn. of County and Cities of L.A., 1995-99; bd. dirs. Inner City Law Ctr., 1996-99; mem. jud. procedures commn. L.A. County, 1999—. Mem. ABA, Calif. Bar Assn., N.Y. State Bar Assn., L.A. County Bar Assn. (trustee 1985-87), Pub. Counsel (bd. dirs. 1984-87, 90-93), U. Chgo. Law Alumni Assn. (pres. 1998—), Calif. Club, Phi Beta Kappa, Pi Gamma Mu, Phi Delta Phi. Banking, Private international, Real property. Office: White and Case 633 W 5th St Ste 1900 Los Angeles CA 90071-2087

**MILLBERG, JOHN C.,** lawyer; b. New London, Conn., Jan. 4, 1956; s. Melvin Roy and Dorothy (Van Zandt) M.; m. Lori Bruce, Oct. 18, 1981; children: Kathryn Faye, Rebecca Ann, Melvin Roy III. BA, Bowling Green State U., 1977; JD, Wake Forest U., 1980. Bar: Tex. 1980, N.C. 1986, U.S. Dist. Ct. (so. dist.) Tex. 1981, U.S. Dist. Ct. (ea., mid. and we. dists.) N.C. 1986, U.S. Ct. Appeals (4th cir.) 1986, U.S. Ct. Appeals (5th and 11th cir.) 1981. Assoc. Crain Caton James & Womble, Houston, 1981-85; assoc., dir. Maupin, Taylor, Ellis & Adams, Raleigh, N.C., 1985-94; mng. ptnr. Millberg & Gordon, Raleigh, N.C., 1994—; mem. bar candidate com. N.C. Bd. Law Examiners, 1988-90. Scholar Wake Forest U. Sch. Law, 1977-80. Mem. N.C. Assn. Def. Attys. (exec. com.), Nat. Assn. R.R. Trial Counsel. General civil litigation, Insurance, Personal injury. Office: Millberg & Gordon 1030 Washington St Raleigh NC 27605-1258

**MILLER, ALLEN TERRY, JR.,** lawyer; b. Alexandria, Va., Sept. 19, 1954; s. Allen Terry and Eleanor Jane (Thompson) M.; m. Maureen Ann Callaghan, June 22, 1985; children: Brendan Allen, Patrick Joseph, Brigit Eleanor. BA, U. Va., 1977; JD, Seattle U., 1982. Bar: Wash. 1982, U.S. Dist. Ct. (we. dist.) Wash. 1982, U.S. Ct. Appeals (9th cir.) 1985, U.S. Dist. Ct. (ea. dist.) Wash. 1986, U.S. Dist. Ct. (no. dist.) N.Y. 1990, U.S. Dist. Ct. (we. dist.) Mich. 1990, U.S. Supreme Ct. 1990, U.S. Ct. Appeals (2d and 6th cirs.) 1991. Legis. asst. Congressman Paul N. McCloskey Jr., Washington, 1978-79; asst. atty. gen. State of Washington, Olympia, 1982-92; prin. Connolly, Holm, Tacon & Meserve, Olympia, 1992—; adj. prof. environ. law Seattle U., 1991—. Commr. Olympia Planning Commn., 1987-92, vice chair, 1991, chair, 1992; mem. North Capitol Campus Heritage Pk. Devel. Assn., 1989—, sec., 1989-90, pres., 1991—; pres. Olympia Chorale and Light Opera Co., 1984-85; mem. St. Michael's Sch. Bd., 1993-96, chair, 1994-96; bd. dirs. South Sound YMCA, 1996—. Recipient merit award Am. Planning Assn., 1989, 92, Citizen of Yr. award Thurston County, 1998. Mem. ABA, Wash. Bar Assn. (mem. environ. law sect. 1984—, ct. rules com. 1985-89, jud. recommendation com. 1991-94, legis. com. 1994—), Thurston County Bar Assn., Leadership Thurston County, Olympic-Thurston C. of C. (trustee 1996—, pres.-elect 1997, pres. 1998), Rotary. Democrat. Roman Catholic. Avocations: mountaineering, kayaking, tennis, piano. Environmental, Land use and zoning (including planning), Real property. Home: 1617 Sylvester St SW Olympia WA 98501-2228 Office: Heritage Bldg. 5th and Columbia Olympia WA 98501-1114

**MILLER, ARTHUR MADDEN,** lawyer, investment banker; b. Greenville, S.C., Apr. 10, 1953; s. Charles Frederick and Kathryn Irene (Madden) M.; m. Roberta Beck Connolly, Apr. 17, 1993; children: Isabella McIntyre Madden, Roberta Beck Connolly. AB in History, Princeton U., 1973; MA in History, U. N.C., 1976; JD with distinction, Duke U., 1978; LLM in Taxation, NYU, 1982. Bar: N.Y. 1979, U.S. Dist. Ct. (so. dist.) N.Y. 1979. Assoc. Mudge Rose Guthrie Alexander & Ferdon, N.Y.C., 1978-85; v.p. pub. fin. Goldman, Sachs & Co., N.Y.C., 1985—. mem. adv. bd. Mary Baldwin Coll., Staunton, Va., 1982-86; trustee Princeton U. Rowing Assn., N.J., 1980—, pres., 1986-95; trustee Rebecca Kelly Dance Co., N.Y.C., 1984-86; mem. Power Ten, N.Y., steward, 1992-95. Mem. ABA (tax sect. com. on tax exempt financing 1985—), Nat. Assn. Bond Lawyers (lectr. 1985—), Pub. Securities Assn. (cons. 1985—), Practising Law Inst. (lectr. 1980, editor/author course materials 1980), Bond Attys. Workshop (editor/author course material 1983—, lectr. 1983—), Princeton Club. Municipal (including bonds), Personal income taxation, Securities. Office: Goldman Sachs & Co 85 Broad St New York NY 10004-2456

**MILLER, ARTHUR RAPHAEL,** law educator; b. N.Y.C., June 22, 1934; s. Murray and Mary (Schapin) M.; m. Ellen Monica Joachim, June 8, 1958 (div. 1978); 1 child, Matthew Richard.; m. Marilyn Tarmy, 1982 (div. 1988.); m. Sandra L. Young, 1992. AB, U. Rochester, 1955; LLB, Harvard U., 1958; student, Bklyn. Coll., 1952, 55, CCNY, 1955. Bar: N.Y. 1959, U.S. Supreme Ct. 1959, Mass. 1983. With Cleary, Gottlieb, Steen & Hamilton, N.Y.C., 1958-61; assoc. dir. Columbia Law Sch. Project Internat. Procedure, N.Y.C., 1961-62; instr. Columbia U. Law Sch., 1961-62; asso. prof. U. Minn. Law Sch., 1962-65; prof. law U. Mich. Law Sch., 1965-72; vis. prof. Harvard U. Law Sch., 1971-72, prof., 1972-86, Bruce Bromley prof., 1986—; rsch. assoc. Mental Health Research Inst., 1966-68; dir. project computer assisted instn. Am. Assn. Law Schs., 1968-75; spl. rapporteur State Dept. concerning chpt. II of Hague Conv., 1967; del. U.S.-Italian Conf. Internat. Jud. Assistance, 1961, 62; chmn. task force external affairs Interuniv. Communications Council, 1966-70; mem. law panel, com. sci. and tech. info. Fed. Council Sci. and Tech., Pres.'s Office Sci. and Tech., 1969-72; mem. adv. group Nat. Acad. Sci. Project on Computer Data Banks, 1970-78; mem. spl. adv. group to chief justice Supreme Ct. on Fed. Civil Litigation; mem. com. on automated personal data systems HEW, 1972-73; chmn. Mass. Security and Privacy Council, Mass. Commn. on Privacy; mem. U.S. Commn. New Technol. Uses Copyrighted Works, 1975-79; reporter U.S. Supreme Ct.'s Adv. Com. on Civil Rules, 1978-86, mem. 1986-91; faculty Fed. Jud. Ctr.; reporter study on complex litigation Am. Law Inst.; bd. dirs. Research Found. on Complex Litigations, 1975-80. Author: The Assault on Privacy: Computers, Data Banks, and Dossiers, 1971, Miller's Court, 1982; (with others) New York Civil Practice, 8 vols., Civil Procedure Cases and Materials, 7th edit., 1997, Federal Practice and Procedure: Civil, 34 vols., 1969—, CPLR Manual, 1967; host syndicated TV shows in Context, Miller's Law, Miller's Court, Headlines on Trial; legal expert Good Morning America. Served with AUS, 1958-59. Recipient Nat. Emmy award for The Constitution, That Delicate Balance. Mem. Am. Law Inst. Office: Harvard U Law Sch Cambridge MA 02138 also: Good Morning Am 147 Columbus Ave New York NY 10023-5900

**MILLER, BARBARA KAYE,** lawyer; b. Omaha, Aug. 21, 1964; d. Carl Reuben and Sandra Jean (Matthews) Wright; m. Julius Anthony Miller, May 4, 1991. BA, U. Iowa, 1987, JD, 1990. Bar: Ohio 1990, U.S. Dist. Ct. (no. dist.) Ohio 1991. Assoc. Fuller & Henry, Toledo, Ohio, 1990-92; law clk. to Hon. John W. Potter U.S. Dist. Ct. (no. dist.) Ohio, Toledo, 1992-93; asst. prosecutor Lucas County Prosecutor's Office, Toledo, 1994-96; ptnr. Wise People Mgmt., Toledo, 1994—, Ryan, Wise, Miller & Dorner, Toledo, 1995—; adj. prof. Lourdes Coll., Sylvania, Ohio, 1994—. Bd. dirs. Toledo Ballet Assn., 1992-94, Hospice, Toledo, 1992-94. Martin Luther King scholar, 1987; named to Profl. Women in Christ, 1992. Mem. ABA, Lucas County Bar Assn., Toledo Bar Assn. (mem. grievance com. 1994—), Thurgood Marshall Law Assn. (v.p. 1993-94), Lawyers Roundtable of Toledo (mem. steering com., recruiting program com. 1994—). Avocations: tennis, biking, swimming. Labor, General civil litigation. Office: Wise People Mgmt 151 N Michigan St Ste 333 Toledo OH 43624-1941 also: Ryan Wise Miller & Dorner 151 N Michigan St Ste 333 Toledo OH 43624-1941

**MILLER, BENJAMIN K.,** state supreme court justice; b. Springfield, Ill., Nov. 5, 1936; s. Clifford and Mary (Luthyens) M. BA, So. Ill. U., 1958; JD, Vanderbilt U., 1961. Bar: Ill. 1961. Ptnr. Olsen, Cantrill & Miller, Springfield, 1964-70; prin. Ben Miller-Law Office, Springfield, 1970-76; judge 7th jud. cir. Ill. Cir. Ct., Springfield, 1976-82, presiding judge Criminal div., 1977-81, chief judge, 1981-82; justice Ill. Appellate Ct., 4th Jud. Dist., 1982-84, Ill. Supreme Ct., Springfield, 1984—; chief justice Ill. Supreme Ct., 1991-93; adj. prof. So. Ill. U., Springfield, 1974—; chmn. Ill. Cts. Commn., 1988-90; mem. Ill. Gov.'s Adv. Coun. on Criminal Justice Legis., 1977-84, Ad Hoc Com. on Tech. in Cts., 1985—. Mem. editorial rev. bd. Illinois Civil Practice Before Trial, Illinois Civil Trial Practice. Pres. Cen. Ill. Mental Health Assn., 1969-71; bd. govs. Aid to Retarded Citizens, 1977-80; mem. Lincoln Legals Adv. Bd., 1988—. Lt. USNR, 1964-67. Mem. ABA (bar admissions com. sect. of legal edn. and admissions to bar 1992—), Ill. State Bar Assn. (bd. govs. 1970-76, treas. 1975-76), Sangamon County Bar Assn., Women's Bar Assn. of Ill., Ctrl. Ill. Women's Bar Assn., Am. Judicature Soc. (bd. dirs. 1990-95), Abraham Lincoln Assn. (bd. dirs. 1988-98). Office: Supreme Ct Ill Nat City Ctr Ste 560 Springfield IL 62701

**MILLER, BRUCE NORMAN,** lawyer, retired podiatrist; b. N.Y.C., Dec. 18, 1944; s. Michael and Florence M.; m. Ann Pauline Hills Holton, Aug. 1982 (div. 1989); 1 child, Michael Frank; m. Nancy Denise Davis, Oct. 15, 1994; 1 child, Laura MacKenzie. AS, L.I. U., 1966; D in Podiatric Medicine, Ohio U., Cleve., 1970; JD, BS in Law, U. W. L.A., 1986. Bar: Calif. 1987, U.S. Dist. Ct. (cen. dist.) Calif. 1987. Podiatric physician, surgeon L.A. and Marina Del Ray, Calif., 1972-83; assoc. Law Offices Bruce Fagel, Beverly Hills, Calif., 1987, Law Offices Ralph S. Hemer, Glendale, Calif., 1987-94; sr. assoc. Gittler & Bradford, L.A., 1994—. Editor-in-chief U. W. L.A. Law Jour., 1985-86. Mem. ABA. Avocations: hockey, working out, reading, camping. Personal injury, Professional liability, Real property. Office: Gittler & Bradford 11620 Wilshire Blvd Ste 800 Los Angeles CA 90025-1793

**MILLER, CARLA DOROTHY,** lawyer; b. Honesdale, Pa., Jan. 15, 1951; d. Carl K. Miller and Dorothy Ruth (Schubert) Jones. BA in Criminology, Fla. State U., 1972; JD, U. Fla., 1979. Bar: Fla. 1980. Asst. atty. U.S. Justice Dept., Jacksonville, Fla., 1980-83; sole practice Jacksonville, 1983—. Mem. Leadership Jacksonville, 1985, Jr. League, 1983—; ethics officer City of Jacksonville, 1999. Mem. Jax Bar Assn. (bd. govs. 1985-92), Fed. Bar Assn., Jax Ethics Commn. (chair 1999), Human Rights Advocacy Com. (chair 1997-99). Computer, Criminal, Personal injury. Home: 1979 Brista De Mar Dr Jacksonville FL 32233-4525 Office: 221 E Church St Jacksonville FL 32202-3131

**MILLER, CARROLL GERARD, JR. (GERRY MILLER),** lawyer; b. San Antonio, Tex., Dec. 12, 1944; s. Carroll Gerard Sr. and Glyn (Roddy) M.; m. Sylvia Louise Mertins, Mar. 7 1971 (dec. 1982); children: Glyn Marie Bennett, Roddy Gerard, Gina Louise. AS, Del Mar Coll., 1965; BS, U. Houston, 1967; JD, Tex. Tech. U., 1970. Bar: Tex. 1970, Colo. 1987, D.C. 1989, U.S. Dist. Ct. (so. dist.) Tex. 1971, U.S. Ct. Appeals (5th cir.) Tex. 1973, U.S. Supreme Ct. 1974, U.S. Ct. Appeals (D.C. 1986); bd. cert. in criminal law. Assoc. Allison, Madden, White & Brin, Corpus Christi, Tex., 1970-71; asst. city atty. City of Corpus Christi, 1971; asst. dist. atty. Nueces County Dist. Attys. Office, Corpus Christi, 1971-73; asst. city atty. civil div. City of Corpus Christi, 1973-74; atty. Corpus Christi Police Dept.-City of Corpus Christi, 1974-77; pvt. practice Corpus Christi, 1973—; adj. prof. Bee County Coll., Beeville, Tex., 1973-74, Tex. A & I U., Corpus Christi, 1975-76. Past treas. and diaconate First Presbyn. Ch., Corpus Christi; bd. dirs., incorporator Iron Curtain Outreach; 20/20 coun. Open Doors. Mem. SAR, SCV, Assn. Trial Lawyers Am., Tex. Criminal Def. Lawyers Assn., Nat. Criminal Def. Lawyers Assn., Coll. State Bar Tex., Sons of Republic Tex., Crime Stoppers, Inc. (past dir.), Bay Yacht Club (dir.). Republican. Avocations: sailing, scuba diving, photography. Criminal, Personal injury. Home: 1209 Sandpiper Dr Corpus Christi TX 78412-3821 Office: 1007 Kinney St Corpus Christi TX 78401-3009

**MILLER, CHARLES MAURICE,** lawyer; b. L.A., Sept. 7, 1948. BA cum laude, UCLA, 1970; postgrad., U. So. Calif., L.A., 1970-71; JD, U. Akron, 1975. Bar: Ohio 1975, Calif. 1978, U.S. Dist. Ct. (cen. dist.) Calif. 1978, U.S. Ct. Appeals (9th cir.) 1978, U.S. Supreme Ct. 1981. Gen. atty. U.S. Immigration & Naturalization Svc., U.S. Dept. Justice, L.A., 1976-79; ptnr. Miller Law Offices, L.A., 1979—; adj. prof. law U. West L.A., 1989-90. Co-editor: The Visa Processing Guide: Process and Procedures at U.S. Consulates and Embassies, 7th edit., 1999; articles editor U. Akron Law Rev., 1974-75. Mem. Calif. Bd. Legal Specialization, San Francisco, 1988-89. Mem. Bar of Calif. (chmn. immigration splty. 1988-89, commr. immigration splty. 1987-90), Am. Immigration Law Found. (bd. trustees 1995-98), Am. Immigration Lawyers Assn. (bd. dirs. 1998—, mem. bd. govs., chair So. Calif. chpt. 1993-94, INS headquarters liaison com. 1997-98, co-chair mentor program 1990-91, co-chair visa office liaison 1991-92, vice chair 1994-95, co-chair consular rev. task force 1993-95, Jack Wasserman Meml. award for excellence in immigration litigation 1995). Immigration, naturalization, and customs. Office: Miller Law Offices 12441 Ventura Blvd Studio City CA 91604-2407

**MILLER, CHARLES WILLIAM, III,** lawyer; b. Phillipsburg, N.J., June 7, 1955; s. Charles William Jr. and Carol Beam M.; m. Carrie Lynn Makowski, Oct. 14, 1989; children: Nicole, Amanda. BA, Princeton U., 1977; JD, Washington & Lee U., 1981. Bar: N.J. 1981, U.S. Dist. Ct. N.J. 1981, U.S. Ct. Appeals (3d cir.) 1994. Assoc. Stover & Stover, Washington, N.J., 1981-82, William Albrecht, Belvidere, N.J., 1982-86; ptnr. Golden, Rothschild, Spagnola & DiFazio, Somerville, N.J., 1986-95, Norris, McLaughlin & Marcus, Somerville, N.J., 1995—. Councilman Raritan (N.J.) Borough, 1993-94; mem. adv. bd. Lifeline Counselling, Bridgewater, N.J., 1995-98. Recipient Mayor of Raritan Borough award, 1994. Mem. N.J. Def. Assn., Profl. Liability Underwriting Soc., Def. Rsch. Inst., Fedn. Ins. & Corp. Coun. Avocations: coaching youth recreational sports, reading, minor-league baseball. General civil litigation, Product liability, Computer. Office: Norris McLaughlin & Marcus 721 Rte 202-206 Somerville NJ 08876

**MILLER, CHRISTINE F.**, lawyer; b. Dec. 6, 1949; d. Robert J. and Marie C. Feloney; m. D. Ross Miller, Jr., Aug. 3, 1974 (div. June 1997); children: Sarah, Matthew. BA, Wellesley Coll., 1972; MEd, Boston U., 1978; JD with honors, U. Tex., 1983. Bar: Tex. 1983. Tchr. pub. schs., 1972-80; assoc. McGinnis, Lochridge & Kilgore, LLP, Austin, Tex., 1983-89, ptnr., 1989—; mem. legal rsch. com. U. Tex. Law Sch., Austin, 1981-82. Contbr. chpts. to textbook, articles to profl. jours. Troop leader Girl Scouts U.S., Austin, 1994—. Pension, profit-sharing, and employee benefits. Office: McGinnis Lochridge & Kilgore LLP 1300 Capitol Ctr 919 Congress Ave Ste 1300 Austin TX 78701-2499

**MILLER, CHRISTINE ODELL COOK**, judge; b. Oakland, Calif., Aug. 26, 1944; m. Dennis F. Miller. BA in Polit. Sci., Stanford U., 1966; JD, U. Utah, 1969. Bar: Calif., D.C. Law clk. to Hon. David T. Lewis U.S. Ct. Appeals (10th cir.), Salt Lake City; trial atty. Dept. Justice, U.S. Ct. Claims, 1970-72; team leader atty. FTC, 1972-74; atty. Hogan & Hartson, Washington, 1974-76; spl. counsel Pension Benefit Guaranty Corp., 1976-80; dep. gen. counsel U.S. Rlwy. Assn., 1980-82; atty. Shack & Kimball, Washington, 1980-82; judge U.S. Ct. Fed. Claims, Washington, 1982—. Comment editor Utah law Rev. Mem. D.C. Bar Assn., Calif. State Bar, Univ. Club (bd. govs.), Order of Coif. Office: US Ct Fed Claims 717 Madison Pl NW Ste # 617 Washington DC 20005-1011

**MILLER, CLAIRE CODY**, lawyer, mediator; b. Staten Island, N.Y., Feb. 17, 1961; d. William Michael Jr. and Elvira (Cavallaro) C.; m. Bradley Noah Miller, Sept. 25, 1988; children: Rachael F., Brian W. BA, SUNY, Albany, 1983; JD, N.Y. Law Sch., 1986. Assoc. Bruce G. Behrins & Assoc., Staten Island, 1987-90; pvt. practice Claire Cody Miller, Esq., Staten Island, 1990—; mediator Edgewater Mediation, Staten Island, 1995; com. mem. character and fitness com. appellate divsn. 2nd dept. Supreme Ct. N.Y., 1997. Del. to jud. nominations Richmond County Dem., Bklyn., 1992, 94, 95, 96, 97, 98. Mem. Staten Island Women's Bar (pres. 1991-93), Women's Bar Assn. N.Y. (del. 1992, 94, co-chair working mother's com. 1995—), Richmond County Bar Assn. (mem. grievance com. 1993—), Assn. Bar City of N.Y. (mem. matrimonial com.). Family and matrimonial, Real property, General practice. Office: Claire Cody Miller Esq 1 Edgewater Plz Ste 201 Staten Island NY 10305-4900

**MILLER, CLIFFORD JOEL**, lawyer; b. L.A., Oct. 31, 1947; s. Eugene and Marian (Millman) M. BA, U. Calif., Irvine, 1969; JD, Pepperdine U., 1973. Bar: Calif. 1974, Hawaii 1974, U.S. Dist. Ct. Hawaii 1974. Ptnr. Rice, Lee & Wong, Honolulu, 1974-80, Goodsill Anderson Quinn & Stifel, Honolulu, 1980-89, McCorriston, Miho, Miller & Mukai, Honolulu, 1989—. Mem. ABA, Calif. Bar Assn., Hawaii Bar Assn., Am. Coll. Real Estate Lawyers. Avocations: sailing, volleyball, swimming, history. Real property, Private international, General corporate. Office: McCorriston Miho Miller Mukai 5 Waterfront Plz 500 Ala Moana Blvd Ste 400 Honolulu HI 96813-4920

**MILLER, CLINTON J., III**, lawyer; b. Lima, Ohio, Oct. 29, 1947; s. Clinton J. II and Rosemary A. M.; m. Bettie Sue Stevinson, June 12, 1971; children: Emily Anne, Hilary Vick, Sarah Rosemary. AB in Polit. Sci., U. Mich., 1969; JD cum laude, Ohio State U., 1975. Bar: Ohio 1975, U.S. Dist. Ct. (so. dist.) Ohio 1976, U.S. Ct. Appeals (6th cir.) 1978, U.S. Supreme Ct. 1980, D.C. 1981, U.S. Ct. Appeals (7th cir.) 1981, U.S. Ct. Appeals (D.C. and 2d cirs.) 1982, U.S. Ct. Appeals (5th cir.) 1983, U.S. Ct. Appeals (4th cir.) 1984, U.S. Dist. Ct. (no. dist.) Ohio 1985, U.S. Ct. Appeals (1st cir.) 1986, U.S. Ct. Appeals (8th cir.) 1987, U.S. Ct. Appeals (3rd and 9th cirs.) 1988. Asst. atty. gen. Ohio Atty. Gen., Columbus, 1975-77; ptnr. Miller, Noga & Miller, Columbus, 1977-79; assoc. Marsh, Minzing & Metzner, Delphos, Ohio, 1979-80; assoc. Highsaw & Mahoney, Washington, 1980-83, ptnr., 1983-85; asst. gen. counsel United Transp. Union, Cleve., 1985-91, gen. counsel, 1991—. With USN, 1969-72. Democrat. Roman Catholic. Labor. Office: United Transp Union 14600 Detroit Ave Ste 200 Cleveland OH 44107-4250

**MILLER, CORINNE**, lawyer; b. Newcastle, Wyo., Jan. 8, 1958; d. Edwin Jay Prell and Kay Darlene (Bayne) Burgener; m. James Robert Miller; 1 child, Alan Vincent Burke II. AAS, Casper Coll., 1979; BS, U. Wyo., 1983, JD, 1988. Bar: Wyo. 1989, U.S. Dist. Ct. Wyo. 1989, U.S. Ct. Appeals (10th cir.) 1993. Jud. law clk. 7th Dist. Ct., Casper, Wyo., 1988-89; asst. pub. defender State of Wyo., Gillette, 1989-91; pvt. practice, Casper, 1991—. Criminal, Family and matrimonial, General practice. Office: 111 W 2d St Ste 603 Casper WY 82601-2469

**MILLER, CRAIG DANA**, lawyer; b. L.A., Dec. 9, 1968; s. Ovvie and Diane Miller; m. Jacqueline Shelton, Sept. 7, 1997. AB summa cum laude, Occidental Coll., 1990; JD magna cum laude, Loyola U., 1993. Bar: Calif. 1993, U.S. Dist. Ct. (ctrl. dist.) Calif. 1993. Assoc. Manatt, Phelps & Phillips, L.A., 1993—. Vice chmn., mem. exec. com. Jewish Fedn. ACCESS, L.A., 1998—; bd. dirs. Jewish Fedn. Met. Region, 1996—. Mem., Calif. State Bar Assn., Order of Coif, Phi Beta Kappa. Avocations: flea markets, writing poetry. Mergers and acquisitions, General corporate, Banking. Office: Manatt Phelps & Phillips 11355 W Olympic Blvd Los Angeles CA 90064-1614

**MILLER, DANIEL RAYMOND**, prosecutor; b. Evansville, Ind., Sept. 20, 1963; s. Daniel Edgar and Virginia Sue (Baumgart) M. BA magna cum laude, DePauw U., 1985; JD cum laude, Ind. U., 1989. Bar: Ind. 1989. Clk. to presiding judge William I. Garrard, Ind. Ct. of Appeals, Indpls., 1989-90; dep. pros. atty. Vanderburgh County Pros.'s Office, Evansville, 1990—. Pres. Substance Abuse Coun. Vanderburgh County, 1997-98; chmn. pastoral coun. St. John Cath. Ch., Evansville, 1995-98; mem. Diocese of Evansville Pastoral Coun., 1997—; pres. 4-H Coun., 1999. Meml. Ind. Bar Assn., Ind. Drug Enforcement Assn., Nat. Dist. Attys. Assn., 4-H Club Assn. (bd. dirs. 1995-98, leader Energetics club 1991—), St. Vincent DePaul Soc. (sec. conf. 1994, 95—). Republican. Roman Catholic. Avocations: gardening, church choir. Home: 13521 N Green River Rd Evansville IN 47725-9769 Office: Vanderburgh Co Pros Office Rm 108 City County Adm Bldg Evansville IN 47708

**MILLER, DAVID A.**, lawyer; b. Charleroi, Pa., Dec. 7, 1952; s. Francis E. and Betty L. Miller. A. in Specialized Tech., Pa. Tech. Inst., Pitts., 1975; BA, George Mason U., 1982; JD, U. Va., 1985. Bar: Va. 1985, Pa. 1987. Assoc. Roeder, Duartte & Davenport, Fairfax, Va., 1985-86; law clk. Hon. David L. Gilmore, Washington, Pa., 1986-87; assoc. Karlowitz, Hoffman, McCall & Kane, Pitts., 1987-89, Amatangelo, Baisley & Rega, Donora, 1989—. Mem. Pa. Bar Assn., Va. State Bar (assoc.), Washington County Bar Assn. Avocations: golf, skiing, computers. Bankruptcy, Family and matrimonial, Personal injury. Office: 100 4th St Donora PA 15033-1541

**MILLER, DAVID ANTHONY**, lawyer; b. Linton, Ind., Oct. 6, 1946; s. Edward I. and Jane M. (O'Hern) M.; m. Carol E. Martin, Aug. 9, 1970; 1 child, Jennifer Rose. Student, Murray State U., 1965; BS, Ind. State U., 1969; JD, Ind. U., Indpls., 1973. Bar: Ind. 1973, U.S. Dist. Ct. (so. dist.) Ind. 1973, U.S. Supreme Ct. 1981, U.S. Ct. Appeals (7th cir.) 1982. Dep. atty. gen. State of Ind., Indpls., 1973-76, dir. consumer protection divsn. office atty. gen., 1976-93, asst. atty. gen., 1977-80, chief counsel office atty. gen., 1981-93; prin. Hollingsworth, Meek, Miller and Minglin, Indpls., 1993—; bd. dirs. Greater Indianapolis Republican Fin. Com. Youth dir. Emmanuel Luth. Ch., Indpls., 1981-85, exec. dir., 1988-90; chmn. bd. Chambers Found., 1994—; pres. bd. Lutheran H.S., 1996—. Mem. ABA, Ind. State Bar. Assn., Indpls. Bar Assn., Ind. State U. Alumni Assn., Columbia Club, Lambda Chi Alpha. Republican. Avocations: numismatics, golfing. Contracts commercial, Legislative, Administrative and regulatory. Home: 6454 Forrest Commons Blvd Indianapolis IN 46227-7105 Office: 9202 N Meridian St Ste 100 Indianapolis IN 46260-1810

**MILLER, DEBORAH SLYE**, lawyer; b. Navasota, Tex., July 13, 1949; d. Bennie F. and Peggy Slye Miller; children: Brian M. Rollings, Terry Brett Rollings. BA magna cum laude, U. Tex.-Dallas, Richardson, 1990; JD, U. Houston, 1993. Bar: Tex., U.S. Dist. Ct. (no. dist.) Tex. Ptnr. Miller & Shelton, Dallas, 1993—. Bd. dirs. Dallas O.K., 1996—. Mem. Coll. of State Bar Tex. Family and matrimonial, Criminal, Personal injury. Office: Miller Shelton & Place 4514 Cole Ave Ste 525 Dallas TX 75205-4172

**MILLER, DOUGLAS ANDREW**, lawyer, educator; b. Chgo., May 10, 1959; s. Walter William and Jean (Johnson) M.; m. Birgitte Jorgensen, Aug. 4, 1984. BS, Boston Coll., 1981; JD, Ill. Inst. Tech. Chgo., 1986. Bar: Fed. Trial, Ill., U.S. Dist. Ct. (no. dist.) Ill. Assoc. Bresnahan, Garvey, O'Halloran & Colman, Chgo., 1986-90; ptnr. Williams & Montgomery, Ltd., Chgo., 1990—; adj. prof. law Loyola U., Chgo., 1997—. Contbr. articles to profl. jours. Mem. ABA, Ill. State Bar Assn. (civil practice sect., torts sect.), Chgo. Bar Assn. (vice-chmn. bench and bar com., trial techniques sect., ins. law sect.), Ill. Assn. of Def. Trial Counsel. Avocation: distance running. State civil litigation, Insurance, Personal injury. Office: Williams & Montgomery Ltd 20 N Wacker Dr Ste 2100 Chicago IL 60606

**MILLER, EDWARD C.**, lawyer; b. Morristown, Tenn., Feb. 20, 1964; s. James K. and Jean C. M.; m. Lea Anna Richardson, Aug. 12, 1983; children: Matthew, Lucas, Ali. BA, Carson Newman Coll., 1985; JD, U. Tenn., 1988. Bar: Tenn. 1988, U.S. Dist. Ct. (ea. dist.) Tenn. 1989, U.S. Supreme Ct. 1993. Assoc. Strand & Goddard, Dandridge, Tenn., 1988-89; pub. defender 4th jud. dist. State Tenn., Dandridge, 1989—; Mem. exec. com. Tenn. Pub. Defenders Conf., Nashville, 1997-98. Legal advisor County Schs. Mock Trial, Jefferson City, Tenn., 1988-90. H.C. Warner scholar U. Tenn. Sch. Law, 1985. Mem. Tenn. Bar Assn., Tenn. Assn. Criminal Def. Lawyers. Avocations: golfing, long distance running. Home: 1230 Country Club Rd Dandridge TN 37725-4344 Office: Pub Defenders Office 1232 Circle Dr Dandridge TN 37725-4749

**MILLER, EVAN**, lawyer; b. Bklyn., Sept. 18, 1956; s. Richard and Lois Pearl (Hirsch) M. BA, Columbia U., 1978; JD, Georgetown U., 1981. Bar: N.Y. 1982, D.C. 1983, U.S. Dist. Ct. D.C. 1984, U.S. Ct. Appeals (D.C. and 11th cirs.) 1985. Law clk. to presiding justice U.S. Dist. Ct. (so. dist.) Ga., Brunswick, 1981-82; assoc. Pepper, Hamilton & Scheetz, Washington, 1982-88; ptnr. Johnson & Gibbs, Washington, 1988-94, Hogan & Hartson, Washington, 1994—. Mem. ABA (task force on prohibited trans. tax sect., employee benefits com. labor sect., employee benefits com. labor sect. and corp. and bus sect., co-chmn. subcom. on fiduciary devels.). Pension, profit-sharing, and employee benefits. Office: Hogan & Hartson LLP 555 13th St NW Ste 800E Washington DC 20004-1161

**MILLER, FRANK C., III**, lawyer; b. Lake Charles, La., Nov. 25, 1963; s. Frank Chavanne Jr. and Angela Marie (Liggio) M.; m. Nathalie Therése Julie Praile, Aug. 25, 1990; children: Gavin Chavanne, Megan Ariel. BA in French and Polit. Sci. with honors, La. State U., 1985, postgrad., 1985-86, JD, 1989. Bar: La., U.S. Dist. Ct. La. 1989, U.S. Ct. Appeals (5th cir.) 1989, U.S. Dist. Ct. (ea. dist.) Tex. 1997. Clk. Carmouche, Gray & Hoffman, Lake Charles, La., 1986-89, assoc., 1989-91; assoc. Carmouche & Gray, Lake Charles, 1991-92; assoc. The Carmouche Law Firm, Lake Charles, 1992-94, ptnr., 1994-95; ptnr. Alexander, Miller & Gaharan, Lake Charles, 1995-96; pvt. practice Lake Charles, 1996—. Advisor local chpt. Am. Cancer Soc., 1990-96, local chpt. Am. Heart Assn., 1995. Mem. ABA (torts and ins. practice com. 1990—), La. Bar Assn. Fed. Bar Assn.,World Jurist Soc., Am. Inn of Ct., Phi Kappa Phi, Phi Delta Phi. Avocations: poetry, Zen, work, family. Construction, General civil litigation, Appellate. Office: One Lakeshore Dr Ste #1250 Lake Charles LA 70829

**MILLER, FRANK LEWIS**, lawyer, writer; b. Denver, Feb. 1, 1951; s. Frank Lewis III and Lucille Alice (McBride) M.; m. Janice Brenner, Nov. 26, 1987 (div. July 1996); children: Jessica Jean, Alexander Palani; m. Etsuko Tatsuta, June 21, 1997; 1 child, Kai Lewis Tatsuta. BA, U. Hawaii, Manoa, 1973; JD, U. Santa Clara, 1978. Bar: Hawaii, 1978, U.S. Dist. Ct. Hawaii, 1978. Vista atty. Life of Land, Honolulu, 1978-79; dep. pub. defender Hawaii Office Pub. Defender, Kealakekua, 1979-80, Honolulu, Capt. Cook, Hawaii, 1984-95; staff writer West Hawaii Today, Kailua-Kona, 1980-83, 84; pvt. practice Kailua-Kona, 1995—. Contbr. poems, short stories to profl. mags. Avocations: running, surfing, photography. Criminal, Family and matrimonial, Personal injury. Office: 75-5744 Alii Dr Kailua Kona HI 96740-1784

**MILLER, FRANK WILLIAM**, lawyer; b. N.Y., July 11, 1953; s. Samuel J. and Anne (Horkott) M.; m. Lisa A. Barrett; children: Shaun Patrick, Stephanie Ann, Emily Christine. BS magna cum laude, U. Scranton, 1975; JD, Albany Law Sch., 1978. Bar: N.Y. 1979, U.S. Dist. Ct. (no. dist.) N.Y. 1979, U.S. Ct. Appeals (2d cir.) 1983, U.S. Supreme Ct. 1991, U.S. Dist. Ct. (we. dist.) 1998. Assoc. Coughlin & Gerhart, Binghamton, 1978-83, ptnr., 1983-97; ptnr. Ferrara, Fiorenza, Larrison, Barrett & Reitz, P.C., Syracuse, N.Y., 1997—; bd. dirs. NYPENN Health Sys. Agy., N.Y. State Coun. Sch. Attys., 1997-98; labor counsel Binghamton City Sch. Dist.; counsel Union-Endicott Ctrl. Sch. Dist., Afton Ctrl. Sch. Dist., Whitney Point Ctrl. Sch. Dist.; lectr., spkr. Broome County C. of C.; presenter Nat. Sch. Bds. Assn., Coun. Sch. Attys., 1996; lectr. and author in fields of labor rels. and edn. law. Chief labor negotiator City of Binghamton, 1989-90; mem. N.Y. State Divsn. Youth Adv. Bd., Binghamton, 1986—; chair profl. divsn. Broome County United Way, 1994. Mem. ABA, N.Y. State Bar Assn. (labor and employment law sect. com on govt. employment rels. 1995—, young lawyer's sect., exec. com. 1981-84, lectr. standing com. pub. employment rels. 1990—), Broome County Bar Assn., Binghamton Club. Fax: 315-437-7744. General civil litigation, Labor, Education and schools.

**MILLER, GALE TIMOTHY**, lawyer; b. Kalamazoo, Sept. 15, 1946; s. Arthur H. and Eleanor (Johnson) M.; m. Janice Lindvall, June 1, 1968; children: Jeremy L., Amanda E., Timothy W. AB, Augustana Coll., 1968; JD, U. Mich., 1971. Bar: Mich. 1971, Colo. 1973, U.S. Dist. Ct. Colo. 1973, U.S. Ct. Appeals (10th cir.) 1979, U.S. Supreme Ct. 1997. Trial atty. FTC, Washington, 1971-73; assoc. Davis, Graham & Stubbs, LLP, Denver, 1973-77, ptnr., 1978—, chmn. exec. com., 1998—. Bd. dirs. Sr. Housing Options, Inc., 1980-93, Colo. Judicature Inst., 1999—; chair Colo. Lawyers Com., 1989-91, bd. dirs., 1987—, Individual Lawyer of Yr., 1994. Recipient Cmty. Svc. award Colo. Hispanic Bar Assn., 1996. Mem. ABA (antitrust sect. task force on model civil antitrust jury instrns.), Colo. Bar Assn. (chair antitrust sect. 1996-98), bd. dirs., Colo. Judicature Inst., 1998—, Denver Bar Assn. Democrat. Lutheran. Antitrust, Federal civil litigation, State civil litigation. Office: Davis Graham & Stubbs LLP PO Box 185 Denver CO 80201-0185

**MILLER, GARDNER HARTMANN**, paralegal; b. Strasbourg, France, Mar. 26, 1934; came to U.S., 1934; s. L. Gardner and Elisabeth Lydia (Fischer) M.; m. Frances Carroll Rothe, June 20, 1955 (div. July 1960); 1 child, Catherine Louise Miller Hudson; m. Marlyn Jeanette Wiggins, Dec. 31, 1967; 1 child, Andrea Marlise. BA in Polit. Sci., UCLA, 1955; B of Fgn. Trade, Thunderbird Grad. Sch., 1960; AS in Legal Asst. Studies, Albuquerque Tech. Vocat. Inst., 1989. Fgn. trade analyst U.S. Dept. of Commerce, L.A., 1960-62; market analyst Douglas Aircraft Co., Santa Monica, Calif., 1962-66; field office mgr. McDonnell Douglas Corp., San Bernardino, Calif., 1966-70; regional mktg. mgr. Tracor, Inc., San Bernardino, 1970-72; dir. mktg. Dikewood Corp., Albuquerque, 1972-84, Deuel and Assocs., Albuquerque, 1984-88; paralegal specialist Criminal divsn. U.S. Atty., Albuquerque, 1989—. Inventor, patentee TruStroke Putting Aid. Naval aviator USNR, 1955-81, capt. USNR ret. Recipient Spl. Achievement award U.S. Dept. of Justice, 1992, Meritorious award, 1996, Outstanding Performance awards, 1997, 98. Mem. State Bar of N.Mex. (legal assts. divsn.), N.Mex. Alliance of Profession Paralegals (bd. dirs. 1993-95), Legal Assts. of N.Mex. (bd. dirs. 1991-93). Avocations: golf, skiing. Office: US Attys Office 201 3d St NW Ste 900 Albuquerque NM 87102-3155

**MILLER, GARY H.**, lawyer; b. New Orleans, Mar. 11, 1957; s. Leo Jr. and Suzanne Robinowitz (Meltzer) M.; m. Ellen Baldwin Hoffman, Oct. 18, 1986; children: Matthew Hilliard, Katherine Elise. BA magna cum laude, New Eng. Coll., 1979; JD cum laude, Tulane U., 1982. Assoc. Jones Walker, New Orleans, 1982-89, ptnr., 1990—; mem. moot ct. bd. Tulane U. Sch. Law, 1980-82; lectr. in field. Bd. dirs. Golden Retriever Club Greater New Orleans, Inc., 1980, Burtheville Cmty. Assn., Inc., 1997—. Mem. La. Bar Assn. (treas. consumer protection, lender liability and bankruptcy sect. 1990-91, chmn. consumer protection, lender liability and bank sect. 1991-92), Phi Tau Beta. Democrat. Jewish. Avocations: Retriever and obedience training, fishing, hunting, guitar. Real property, Contracts commercial, Intellectual property. Office: Jones Walker 201 Saint Charles Ave Ste 5200 New Orleans LA 70170-5100

**MILLER, GAY DAVIS**, lawyer; b. Florence, Ariz., Dec. 20, 1947; d. Franklin Theodore and Mary (Belshaw) Davis; m. John Donald Miller, May 15, 1971; 1 child, Katherine Alexandra. BA, U. Colo., 1969; JD, Am. U., 1975. Bar: D.C. 1975. Atty., spl. asst. to gen. counsel, sr. counsel corp. affairs Inter Am. Devel. Bank, Washington, 1975-78, 83—; atty. Intelsat, Washington, 1978-80. Articles editor Am. U. Law Rev., 1974-75. Bd. dirs. Hist. Mt. Pleasant, Inc., Washington, 1985-86, Washington Bridle Trails Assn., 1992—. Mem. ABA, Am. Soc. Internat. Law, Inter Am. Bar Assn., Women's Bar Assn. General corporate, Public international, Labor. Office: Inter Am Devel Bank 1300 New York Ave NE Washington DC 20002-1621

**MILLER, GEORGE DEWITT, JR.**, lawyer; b. Detroit, Aug. 20, 1928; s. George DeWitt and Eleanor Mary Miller; m. Prudence Brewster Saunders, Dec. 28, 1951; children: Margaret DeWitt, Joy Saunders. BA magna cum laude, Amherst Coll., 1950; JD with distinction, U. Mich., 1953. Bar: Mich. 1953, U.S. Dist. Ct. (so. dist.) Mich. 1953, U.S. Ct. Appeals (6th cir.) 1960, U.S. Tax Ct. 1960. Assoc. Bodman, Longley & Dahling, Detroit, 1957-61, ptnr., 1962—. Trustee, mem. Matilda R. Wilson Fund, 1993—, pres., 1998—; trustee Maplegrove Ctr./Kingswood Hosp., Henry Ford Health Sys., 1995—. Capt. USAF, 1953-56. Recipient Commendation medal. Fellow Mich. State Bar Found.; mem. ABA, State Bar Mich., Detroit Bar Assn., Detroit Athletic Club, Orchard Lake Country Club, Order of Coif, Phi Beta Kappa. Episcopalian. Avocations: yacht racing, shooting, gardening. Probate, Estate planning, Estate taxation. Home: 320 Dunston Rd Bloomfield Hills MI 48304-3415 Office: Bodman Longley & Dahling 100 Renaissance Ctr Ste 34 Detroit MI 48243-1001

**MILLER, GORDON DAVID**, lawyer; b. Huntington, N.Y., May 6, 1940; s. Gordon Stanley and Marie Christine (Smith) M.; m. Leueen Mary O'Connor, Aug. 6, 1966; children—Christine Victoria, Heather Leueen, Winston Gordon Malachie. A.B. cum laude, Colgate U., 1962; LL.B., Harvard U., 1965; LL.M., NYU, 1974. Bar: N.Y. 1966, U.S. Dist. Ct. (so. and ea. dists.) N.Y. 1968. Sr. atty. N.Y. Life Ins. Co., N.Y.C., 1966-69; assoc. Winthrop Stimson Putnam & Roberts, 1969-70; atty. Pfizer Inc., 1970-73; legal officer and asst. sec., Internat. Nickel Co. Inc., 1973—; dir. numerous subs. Bd. dirs. Colgate U. Alumni Corp., 1976-80; mem. exec. com. Colgate U. Ann. Fund, 1970-84. Recipient maroon citation Colgate U. Alumni Corp., 1977. Mem. ABA. Club: Colgate (N.Y.C., bd. govs. 1970—, pres. 1972-73, 1983-85). Antitrust, Labor. Home: 360 1st Ave New York NY 10010-4912 Office: Inco Limited 1 New York Plz Fl 38 New York NY 10004-2004

**MILLER, GREGORY R.**, lawyer. Chief asst. U.S. atty. Dept. Justice, Tallahassee, Fla., U.S. atty., 1993-98; assoc. Fowler, White, Gillen, Boggs, Villareal and Banker, PA, Tallahassee, 1998—. General civil litigation, Criminal. Office: Fowler White Gillen Boggs Villareal and Banker PA 101 N Monroe St Ste 1090 Tallahassee FL 32301-1570

**MILLER, HAROLD ARTHUR**, lawyer; b. St. Marie, Ill., Aug. 18, 1922; s. Arthur E. and Luletta (Noé) M.; m. Michele H. Rogivue, Nov. 21, 1947; children: Maurice H., Jan Leland, Marc Richard. BS in Acctg., U. Ill., 1942, JD, 1950. Bar: Ill. 1950, U.S. Dist. Ct. Ill. 1950, U.S. Tax Ct. 1950. Fgn. svc. officer U.S. State Dept., Paris, France, 1945-48; ptnr. Filson, Williamson & Miller, Champaign, Ill., 1950-60, Williamson & Miller, Champaign, 1960-72, Miller & Hendren, Champaign, 1972—; atty. Christie Clinic Assn., Champaign, 1960—; atty. pub. schs. dists., Champaign & Vermilion Counties, Ill., 1960—; atty. for municipalities in Champaign County, Ill., 1970—. Author: Estate Planning for Doctors, 1961, Intervivos Trusts Alternative to Probate, 1996. Bd. dirs., officer Urbana Ill. Sch. Dist., 1957-69; chmn., trustee Parkland Coll., Champaign, 1971-91; founding bd. mem. CCDC Found., Champaign-Urbana Ednl. Found., Moore Heart Found., Christie Found.; life mem. PTA. With inf. U.S. Army, 1942-45, ETO. Mem. ABA, Am. Judicature Soc., Ill. and Local Bar Assns., Ill. Trial Lawyers Assn., Alpha Kappa Psi. Presbyterian. Education and schools, Estate planning. Office: Miller & Hendren Attys 30 E Main St #200 Champaign IL 61820-3629

**MILLER, HARRY B(ENJAMIN)**, lawyer; b. Lexington, Ky., Jan. 4, 1924; s. Harry Benjamin Miller and Ann (Walcutt) Winn; m. Patricia Griffin, Mar. 22, 1946 (dec.); children: Thomas, Robin, John, Harry Benjamin III. LLM, U. Ky., 1948. Bar: Ky. 1948, U.S. Dist. Ct. (ea. dist.) Ky. 1948, U.S. Ct. Appeals (6th cir.) 1952, U.S. Supreme Ct. 1962. Pres. Miller, Griffin & Marks, P.S.C., Lexington, 1962—. Mng. editor U. Ky. Law Rev., 1948. Treas. Ky. Dem. State Party, Frankfort, 1960-68. Mem. Order of Coif. Presbyterian. Avocation: golf. General civil litigation, Family and matrimonial, Probate. Home: 111 Woodland Ave Lexington KY 40502-6415 Office: Miller Griffin & Marks PSC Security Trust Bldg Ste 600 Lexington KY 40507-1232

**MILLER, HENRY FRANKLIN**, lawyer; b. Phila., May 19, 1938; s. Lester and Bessie (Posner) M.; m. Barbara Ann Gendel, June 20, 1964; children: Andrew, Alexa. AB, Lafayette Coll., 1959; LLB, U. Pa., 1964. Bar: Pa. 1965. Law clk. U.S. Dist. Ct. Del., Wilmington, 1964-65; assoc. Wolf, Block, Schorr & Solis-Cohen, Phila., 1965-71, ptnr., 1971—. Pres. Soc. Hill Synagogue, Phila., 1978-79, Big Brothers/Big Sisters Assn. of Phila., 1980-81, Jewish Family & Children's Agy., Phila., 1986-88. 1st lt. U.S. Army, 1959-60. Mem. Am. Coll. Real Estate Lawyers. Avocations: swimming, hiking, reading. Real property, Construction. Office: Wolf Block Schorr & Solis-Cohen 12th Fl Packard Bldg 1650 Arch St Fl 21 Philadelphia PA 19103-2097

**MILLER, HERBERT H.**, lawyer; b. Balt., May 24, 1921; s. Louis Miller and Rebecca Platt; m. Irene R. Rosen, Aug. 27, 1944; children: Rose, Marjorie, Fran. JD cum laude, U. Balt., 1942; ABA in Acctg., Balt. Coll. of Commerce, 1947. Bar: Md. 1943, U.S. Dist. Ct. Md. 1944, U.S. Supreme Ct. 1986; notary pub., Md. Law clk. Rubenstein and Rubenstein, Balt., 1939-42, Joel J. Hochman, Balt., 1939-42, Feikin & Talkin, Balt., 1939-42; atty. Sherbow, Harris & Medwedeff, Balt., 1943-45, Harris & Medwedeff, Balt., 1943-45; pvt. practice Balt. and Towson, Md., 1946—; mem. inquiry panel Atty. Grievance Com. Md., Balt. County, 1985—; panel chmn. Health Claims Arbitration, Balt., 1994—. Bd. trustees Balt. Coll. Commerce, 1948-52, Beth El Congregation, Balt. County, 1990-94; youth advisor B'nai B'rith, Balt., 1943-88, mem. B'nai B'rith Youth Orgn., pres., 1940-42. Mem. Md. State Bar Assn., Balt. City Bar Assn., Balt. County Bar Assn., Mensa Internat. (arbitrator Md.). Avocations: reading, handyman work, walking. General corporate, Probate, Real property. Office: 200 E Joppa Rd Ste 205 Towson MD 21286-3107

**MILLER, JAMES M.**, lawyer; b. Berwyn, Ill., Apr. 25, 1950; m. Luz Angela Aristizabal, July 13, 1991; children: Hillary Daniela, Maxwell James. BA magna cum laude, U. Miami, 1972; JD, U. Chgo., 1975. Bar: Fla. 1975. Shareholder Akerman, Senterfitt & Eidson P.A., Miami, Fla. Bd. dirs. Miami Mus. Sci., pres. 1989-91. Mem. ABA (litigation sect., corp., banking and bus. law sect.), Fla. Bar (vice-chmn. 11th jud. cir. grievance com. B 1982-84), Dade County Bar Assn. General civil litigation, Securities, Banking. Office: Akerman Senterfitt & Eidson SunTrust International Center One SE 3d Ave 28th Fl Miami FL 33131

**MILLER, JAMES MONROE**, lawyer; b. Owensboro, Ky., Apr. 20, 1948; s. James Rufus and Tommie (Melton) M.; m. Patricia Kirkpatrick, Nov. 28, 1975; children: Marian Elizabeth, James Graham. Student, George Washington U., 1966-67; BE, U. Ky., 1970, JD, 1973. Bar: Ky. 1973, U.S. Dist. Ct. Ky. 1973, U.S. Ct. Appeals (6th cir.) 1976, U.S. Supreme Ct. 1976. Law clk. to chief judge U.S. Dist. Ct. (we. dist.) Ky., Louisville and Owensboro, 1973-74; ptnr. Sullivan, Mountjoy, Stainback & Miller, P.S.C., Owensboro, 1974—. Mem. Leadership Ky., 1988, Leadership Owensboro, 1986; bd. dirs. Wendell Foster Ctr. Endowment Found., Inc., Owensboro; sec., trustee Owensboro-Daviess County Pub. Library, Owensboro; chmn. subcom. on sch. system merger Strategies for Tomorrow, Owensboro; v.p. legal Owensboro-Daviess County C. of C.; bd. dirs., sec. Owensboro-Daviess County Indsl. Found., Inc. Mem. ABA, Ky. Bar Assn. (chmn. Law Day/Spkrs. Bur. com. 1989-91), Daviess County Bar Assn., Ky. Coun. on Higher Edn. (chmn. programs com. 1991-93, chmn. 1993-96), Coun. Postsecondary Edn., Gov.'s Higher Edn. Rev. Commn. (chmn. 1993), Gov.'s Task Force on Tchr. Edn. Democrat. Methodist. Avocations: fishing, hunting, hiking, golf, skiing. General corporate, General practice, Public utilities. Home: 1920

Sheridan Pl Owensboro KY 42301-4525 Office: Sullivan Mountjoy Stainback & Miller PSC PO Box 727 100 Saint Ann St Owensboro KY 42303-4144

**MILLER, JAMES ROBERT,** lawyer; b. McKeesport, Pa., Aug. 2, 1947; s. Robert Charles and Ethel Margaret (Yahn) M.; m. Kathleen Ann Galka, June 6, 1975; children: Jesse J., Cassidy A. BA, NYU, 1969; JD, Duquesne U., 1972. Bar: Pa. 1972, U.S. Dist. Ct. (we. dist.) Pa. 1974, U.S. Ct. Appeals (3d cir.) 1978, U.S. Ct. Appeals (11th cir.) 1989, U.S. Supreme Ct. 1990. Law clerk to Hon. James C. Crumlish, Jr. Commonwealth Ct. of Pa., Phila., 1972-74; shareholder Dickie, McCamey & Chilcote, Pitts., 1974—. Mem. ABA, Am. Coll. Trial Lawyers, Pa. Bar Assn., Acad. Trial Lawyers. Avocation: sports. General civil litigation, Personal injury, Product liability. Office: Dickie McCamey & Chilcote Two PPG Pl Ste 400 Pittsburgh PA 15222

**MILLER, JANISE LUEVENIA MONICA,** lawyer; b. Atlanta, Dec. 25, 1956; d. James Thomas and Vera Luevenia (Brown) M.; 1 child, Brandyn Matthew Cooper. BA, Spalding U., 1976; JD, John Marshall Law Sch., 1979. Bar: Ga. 1982, U.S. Ct. Appeals (11th cir.) 1989. Mental health law specialist Ga. Legal Svcs., Atlanta, 1987-88; atty., paralegal Rogers & Sparks, Atlanta, 1980-82; staff counsel Ga. Dept. Med. Assistance, Atlanta, 1982-83; assoc. atty. Cuffie, Mitchell & Assocs., Atlanta, 1983-84, Cuffie & Assocs., Atlanta, 1984-85; pvt. practice Atlanta, 1985-86; of counsel Albert A. Mitchell & Assocs., Atlanta, 1987-92, A.A. Mitchell & Assocs., Atlanta, 1987-92; pvt. practice, 1993—; judge pro hac vice Atlanta Mcpl. Ct. 1989-91. Assoc. editor Nexus, 1980. Chairperson, pres. United Schleroderma Found., Atlanta, 1991-92. Fellow Ga. Bar Found.; mem. State Bar of Ga., Ga. Assn. of Black Women Attys. (Svc. award 1986), Atlanta Bar Assn. (chairperson, seminar com. 1987-88, sec./treas. criminal law sect. 1988-89), Nat. Bar Assn. (chairperson Gertrude Rush Dinner 1992), Gate City Bar Assn. (pres. 1987, editor newsletter 1992). Democrat. Roman Catholic. Avocations: reading, writing, swimming, cooking. Family and matrimonial, General civil litigation, Criminal. Office: PO Box 11229 Atlanta GA 30310-0229

**MILLER, JEFFREY D.,** lawyer; b. Bethlehem, Pa., Aug. 28, 1970; s. Douglas H. and Martha D. Miller. BA in Polit. Sci., Pa. State U., 1992; JD, Wake Forest U., 1996, MBA, 1996. Bar: N.C. 1996, U.S. Dist. Ct. N.C. 1996. Lawyer Smith Helms Mulliss & Moore, Charlotte, N.C., 1996, Raleigh, N.C., 1997; lawyer Alston & Bird LLP, Raleigh, 1997—. Mem. Nat. Assn. Real Estate Investment Trusts, N.C. Bar Assn. Avocation: golf. Securities, Mergers and acquisitions, Finance. Office: Alston & Bird LLP 3605 Glenwood Ave Ste 310 Raleigh NC 27612-4957

**MILLER, JERROLD DUANE,** lawyer; b. Washington, Nov. 15, 1942; s. Samuel and Rose (Lipman) M.; m. Betty J. Goldberg, July 2, 1967 (div. June 1980); children: Michele, Jason; m. Barbara Zimmet, Jan. 9, 1990. BSEE, MIT, 1963; MSEE, U. Wis., 1964; JD, Am. U., 1972. Bar: Md. 1972, D.C. 1973. Assoc. Law Offices of Samuel Miller, Washington, 1972-73; atty. FCC, Washington, 1973-78; ptnr. Miller & Miller P.C., Washington, 1978—. Mem. Fed. Comms. Bar Assn. Avocation: bridge (life master). Home: 7542 Heatherton Ln Potomac MD 20854-3221 Office: Miller & Miller PC 1990 M St NW Ste 760 Washington DC 20036-3415

**MILLER, JILL LEE,** lawyer; b. Framingham, Mass., Aug. 22, 1966; d. Robert F. and Harriet (Leventhal) M. BS, Cornell U., 1988, JD cum laude, 1991; LLM in Taxation, NYU, 1996. Bar: N.Y. 1992, Mass. 1992. Assoc. Stroock & Stroock & Lavan, N.Y.C., 1991-93; ct. intern Surrogates Ct., N.Y.C., 1993-94; assoc. Rosenman & Colin, N.Y.C., 1994-95, Riker, Danzig, Morristown, N.J., 1995-96; mgr. trusts/estates dept. Morea & Schwartz, N.Y.C., 1995—; chair, founder Trusts and Estates Discussion Group, N.Y.C., 1997—. Mem. N.Y. State Bar Assn. (chair subcom. women in the profession 1994-97), Cornell Club, Cornell Law Assn. Avocations: foreign travel, painting, photography, horticulture. Estate planning, Probate, Estate taxation. Home: 205 Hudson St Apt 401 Hoboken NJ 07030-5839 Office: Morea & Schwartz 120 Broadway Ste 1010 New York NY 10271-1099

**MILLER, JOHN EDDIE,** lawyer; b. Wayne, Mich., Nov. 14, 1945; s. George Hayden and Georgia Irene (Stevenson) M.; m. Nancy Carol Sanders, Jan. 7, 1968; children: Andrea Christine, Matthew Kit. BA, Baylor U., 1967; JD, U. Memphis, 1973; LLM, U. Mo., 1980. Bar: Mo. 1974, U.S. Dist. Ct. (we. dist.) Mo. 1974, Tex. 1982. Asst. prof. Central Mo. State U., Warrensburg, 1973-74; sole practice, Sedalia, Mo., 1974-79; sr. contract adminstr. Midwest Research Inst., Kansas City, Mo., 1979-81; sr. contract adminstr Tracor Inc., Austin, Tex., 1981-84; contract negotiator Tex. Instruments, Austin, 1984-86; sr. contract adminstr., Tracor Aerospace Inc., Austin, 1986-87, Radian Corp., Austin, 1987-96; counsel, asst. co. sec., Radian Internat. LLC, Austin 1996—, Radian Corp., Austin, 1987-96; corp. sec. Radian Southeast Asia (SEA) Ltd., Bangkok, 1995—, dir. Radian Southeast Asia (SEA) Ltd., Bangkok, 1996—; corp. sec. Radian Internat. Overseas Mgmt. Co., 1996—; instr. bus. law State Fair Community Coll., Sedalia, 1974-79, Austin Community Coll., 1983-84. Bd. dirs. Legal Aid Western Mo., 1977-79, Boy's Club, Sedalia, 1974-79, Austin Lawyers Care, 1987—. Served with U.S. Army, 1968-71. Mem. Mo. Bar Assn. (mem. internat. law com., mem. computer law com.), Tex. Bar Assn. (intellectual property law sec., internat. law sect., corp. sec.), Coll. of State Bar of Tex., Nat. Contract Mgmt. Assn., Travis County Bar Assn., U.S. Tennis Assn., U.S. Handball Assn., AM Tennis Club, Phi Alpha Delta. Baptist. Private international, Intellectual property, Computer. Office: Radian International LLC 8501 N Mopac Blvd PO Box 201088 Austin TX 78720-1088

**MILLER, J(OHN) KENT,** lawyer, educator; b. Chanute, Kans., Mar. 9, 1944; s. Ernest William and Margery (Olson) M.; m. Toni R. Taff, June 5, 1965 (div. Apr. 1975); children: Gentry, Callan; m. Leslie J. Jaffe, Sept. 14, 1979; children: Todd, Morgan. BS, U. Kans., 1966; JD, U. Denver, 1970. Bar: Colo. 1970, U.S. Dist. Ct. Colo. 1970, U.S. Supreme Ct. 1975. Mng. ptnr. Anderson, Campbell & Langesen, Denver, 1970-83; v.p. Gerash, Robinson, Miller & Miranda, Denver, 1984-87; pres. Miller & McCarren, P.C., Denver, 1988-94; of counsel Miller, McCarren & Helms, P.C., Denver, 1994—; adj. prof. U. Denver Sch. Law, 1990—. Author: (with others) Annual Survey Colorado Law, 1982—; author (2 vols.) Colorado Personal Injury Practice, 1989. Mem. ABA, ATLA, Am. Bd. Trial Advs. (adv.), Colo. Trial Lawyers Assn. (bd. dirs. 1984-87), Denver Bar Assn., Colo. Bar Assn., Def. Rsch. Inst., Colo. Def. Lawyers Assn. Avocations: squash, skiing. Personal injury, Insurance, Professional liability. Office: Miller & McCarren PC 410 17th St Ste 1200 Denver CO 80202-4425

**MILLER, JOHN LEED,** lawyer; b. Geneva, Ill., May 7, 1949; s. John Axel and Martha Mary (Masilunis) M. *John Miller's fiancee Veronica Virgita Hutabarat founded and served as chairperson of the Indonesian-American Association of the Midwest. Ms. Hutabarat has a masters of Arts with honors in International Relations with an emphasis in Peace and Conflict Studies at United States International University, San Diego, California, 1995, with additional coursework at University of California, San Diego in International Enviromental Policy, 1993. She graduated State College of Indiana, Jakarta, with a BA in Business Administration, 1976. She served as Public Relations Manager, Hotel Indonesia, Jakarta, and as Commercial Attache Assistant, Indonesian Embassy, London. She currently works as a private consultant* BA, Northwestern U., 1971; JD, U. Chgo., 1975. Bar: Ill. 1975. Assoc. counsel Profl. Ind. Mass-Mktg. Adminstrs., Chgo., 1975-76; legis. counsel to minority leader Ill. Ho. of Reps., Chgo. and Springfield (Ill.), 1977-80; chief legal counsel, 1980, chief counsel to speaker of Ho. of Reps., 1981-83; ptnr. Shaw and Miller, P.C., Chgo., 1981-84, Theodore A. Woerthwein, P.C., 1984-85, Woerthwein & Miller P.C., 1985—. Statewide chmn. Ill. Young Voters for the Pres., 1972; dir. Ill. Ho. Rep. campaign com., 1976, 78, cons., 1982; pres. Newberry Pla. Condominium Assn., 1989-91. With USNG, 1969-75. James scholar, 1970. Mem. Lawyers for the Creative Arts, Primitive Art Soc. Chgo. (treas. 1984-86, v.p. 1987, pres. 1988-89), Indonesia-Am. Assn. Ill. (bd. dirs.), Phi Eta Sigma, Phi Beta Kappa. Lutheran. Legislative, General corporate. Home: 1030 N State St Apt 9D Chicago IL 60610-5484 Office: Woerthwein & Miller PO Box A 3612 Chicago IL 60690-3612

**MILLER, JOHN SAMUEL, JR.,** lawyer; b. Eutaw, Ala., July 1, 1936; s. John S. Sr. and Anne Elizabeth (Raby) M.; m. Mary Jane Roberts, Sept. 1, 1961 (div. June 1965); 1 child, Mary Anne; m. Pamela Ailstock, Mar. 30, 1972; children: Jill A., Abigail duPree. BS, Fla. State U., 1961, JD, 1968; MSJA, U. Denver, 1983. Bar: Fla. 1969, U.S. Dist. Ct. (no. dist.) Fla. 1969, U.S. Supreme Ct. 1974. Atty. Truett and Watkins, Tallahassee, 1969-70, Roberts, Miller, Baggett, LaFace, Tallahassee, 1970-82, Asst. Atty. Gen. State Fla., Tallahassee, 1984-85; gen. counsel Fla. Dept. Health & Rehab. Svcs., Tallahassee, 1985-90, McKenzie Tank Lines, Inc., Tallahassee, 1991—; bd. dirs. Marine State Bank, Tallahassee. Bd. dirs., atty. Fla. State U. Seminole Boosters, Tallahassee, 1976-82. Pvt. 1st class U.S. Army, 1956-58. Mem. ABA, Fla. State Bar Assn., Tallahassee Bar Assn., Soc. Cincinnati. Presbyterian. Avocations: gardening, fishing. General corporate, Personal injury. Office: McKenzie Tank Lines Inc PO Box 1200 Tallahassee FL 32302-1200

**MILLER, JOHN T., JR.,** lawyer, educator; b. Waterbury, Conn., Aug. 10, 1922; s. John T. and Anna (Purdy) M.; children: Kent, Lauren, Clare, Miriam, Michael, Sheila, Lisa, Colin, Margaret. AB with high honors, Clark U., 1944; JD, Georgetown U., 1948; Docteur en Droit, U. Geneva, 1951; postgrad., U. Paris, 1951. Bar: Conn. 1949 (inactive), D.C. 1950, U.S. Ct. Appeals (2d, 3d, 5th, 10th, 11th and D.C. cirs.), U.S. Supreme Ct. 1952. With Econ. Cooperation Adminstn. Am. Embassy, London, 1950-51; assoc. Covington & Burling, 1952-53, Gallagher, Connor & Boland, 1953-62; pvt. practice Washington, 1962—; adj. prof. law Georgetown U. Law Ctr., Washington, 1959—; mem. Panel on Future of Internat. Ct. Justice. Coauthor: Regulation of Trade, 1953, Modern American Antitrust Law, 1948, Major American Antitrust Laws, 1965; author: Foreign Trade in Gas and Electricity in North America: A Legal and Historical Study, 1970, Energy Problems and the Federal Government: Cases and Material, 8th edit., 1996, Deregulating the Interstate Natural Gas and Electric Power Industries, 1998; contbr. articles, book revs. to legal publs. Trustee Clark U., 1970-76; bd. trustees De Sales Sch. of Theology, 1993-97; bd. advisors Georgetown Visitation Prep. Sch., 1978-94, bd. trustees, 1994-96, emeritus trustee, 1996—; former fin. chmn. troop 46 Nat. Capital Area coun. Boy Scouts Am.; pres. Thomas More Soc. Am., 1996-97. 1st lt. U.S. Army, 1943-46, 48-49. Recipient 10 yr. teaching award Nat. Jud. Coll., 1983. Mem. ABA (coun., chmn. adminstrv. law sect. 1972-73, ho. dels. 1991-93), AAUP, D.C. Bar Assn., Fed. Energy Bar Assn. (pres. 1990-91), Congl. Country Club, Army and Navy Club, DACOR, Prettyman-Leventhal Am. Inn of Ct. (master 1988-99, pres. 1995-96), Sovereign Mil. Order of Malta (knight). Republican. Roman Catholic. FERC practice, Administrative and regulatory, Antitrust. Home: 4721 Rodman St NW Washington DC 20016-3234 Office: 1001 Connecticut Ave NW Washington DC 20036-5504

**MILLER, J(OHN) WESLEY, III,** lawyer, author; b. Springfield, Mass., Oct. 3, 1941; s. John Wesley Jr. and Blanche Ethel (Wilson) M. AB, Colby Coll., 1963; AM, Harvard U., 1964, JD, 1981. Bar: Mass. 1984, U.S. Dist. Ct., 1984, U.S. Supreme Ct. 1993. Instr. English Heidelberg Coll., Tiffin, Ohio, 1964-69, U. Wis., 1969-77; real estate broker, 1977-84; founder Miller-Wilson Family Papers, U. Vt., Madison (Wis.) People's Poster and Propaganda Collection, St. Hist. Soc. Wis. Author: History of Buckingham Junior High School, 1956, The Millers of Roxham, 1958, Giroux Genealogy, 1958, Symphonic Heritage, 1959, Community Guide to Madison Murals, 1977, Aunt Jennie's Poems, 1986; founding editor: Hein's Poetry and the Law Series, 1985—; editor: The Curiosities and Law of Wills, 1989, The Lawyers Alcove, 1990, Famous Divorces, 1991, Legal Laughs, 1993, Coke in Verse, 1999; founding editor: Law Libr. Microform Consortium Arts Law Letters Collection, 1991—; exhibitor A Salute to Street Art, State Hist. Soc. Wis., 1974; represented in permanent collections U. Vermont, Colby Coll. Archives, State Hist. Soc. Wis., Boston Pub. Libr., Pierpont Morgan Libr.; contbr. The Poems of Ambrose Philips, 1969, Dictionary of Canadian Biography, 1980, Collection Building Reader, 1992, Oxford English Dictionary 1995—; contbr. numerous articles on Am. street lit., bibliography, ethics, history, edn., law, religion, librarianship, mgmt. of archives. Mem. MLA, Am. Philol. Assn., Milton Soc., New Eng. Historic Geneal. Soc., Vt. Hist. Soc., Wis. Acad. Scis., Arts & Letters, Social Law Library, Pilgrim Soc., Ancient and Hon. Arty. Co., Mayflower Soc., Soc. Colonial Wars, Sons and Daus. of the Victims of Colonial Witch Trials, Mensa, Springfield Renaissance Group. Recipient Cmty. Activism award Bay State Objectivist, 1993, 94, 95. Trademark and copyright, Entertainment, Art. Office: 5 Birchland Ave Springfield MA 01119-2708 *The advancement of learning is my goal. Professionalism is the standard, and nothing else will do.*

**MILLER, JONATHAN LEWIS,** lawyer, computer consultant; b. Boston, Dec. 9, 1947; s. Harold Irving and Maida (Rosenberg) M.; m. Arleen Garfinkle, Nov. 2, 1985; 1 child, Jonah Maxwell. BA in Sociology, Colby Coll., 1973; BS in Physics, U. Washington, 1980; JD, U. Denver, 1994. Bar: Colo. 1994. Proprietor, cons. J. Miller & Assoc., Colo., 1982-85; pres., atty. J. Miller & Assoc., Inc., Boulder, Colo., 1985-95; assoc. Martin & Mehaffy LLC, Boulder, 1995—. Mng. editor: Transp. Law Jour., 1992-94; author: Legal Software Reviews, Orange County Lawyer, 1998. Avocations: skiing, biking, flying, reading, horseback riding. E-mail: jonmesq@aol.com. Patent, Trademark and copyright, Intellectual property. Home: 173 Wild Tiger Rd Boulder CO 80302-9263 Office: Martin & Mehaffy 1655 Walnut St Ste 300 Boulder CO 80302-5436

**MILLER, JOSEPH AARON,** lawyer, musician; b. Bklyn., N.Y., Oct. 24, 1961; s. Bernard and Caroline (Ashe) M. BA, Emory U., Atlanta, 1984; JD, Coll. William & Mary, Williamsburg, Va., 1987. Atty. Miller & Bonourant, Portsmouth, Va., 1988—. Mem. ABA, Assn. of Trial Lawyers of Am., Va. Trial Lawyers Assn., N.C. Bar Assn., N.C. Acad. Trial Attys. Personal injury, Toxic tort, General civil litigation. Office: Miller & Bonourant Ltd 706 London Blvd Portsmouth VA 23704-2413

**MILLER, JOSEPHINE WELDER,** legal administrator; b. Beeville, Tex., Jan. 18, 1942; d. Ray and Mary (McCurdy) Welder; m. John H. Miller, Jr., 1967; children: Mary Catherine, George. BA in English, U. Tex., 1963. Cert. tchr. English, history, Spanish, libr. sci. Libr. Alamo Heights High Sch., 1965-67; libr. coord. Sinton Ind. Sch. Dist., 1982-89; county judge San Patricio County, Tex., 1991—. Active city coun. Sinton, Tex., 1980-85, 88-90; del. Dem. Nat. Convention, 1984; past mem. State Dem. Exec. Com.; mem. policy coun. Corpus Christi Nat. Estuary Program, 1997; chair Met. Planning Orgn., Corpus Christi, 1997, mem. aquarium bd., Corpus Christi, 1997; bd. dirs. Maria Stella Kenedy Found. Recipient Nat. Conf. Humanitarian award, 1996, YWCA Women in Govt. award, 1996, Road Hand award Tex. Dept. Transp., 1996. Mem. Kiwanis. Roman Catholic. Office: 400 W Sinton St Ste 109 Sinton TX 78387-2450

**MILLER, JUDITH A.,** federal official. BA summa cum laude, Beloit Coll., 1972; JD, Yale U., 1975. Bar: U.S. Supreme Ct., U.S. Ct. Appeals (D.C. cir.), U.S. Ct. Appeals (armed forces cir.). Clk. to Judge Harold Leventhal, U.S. Ct. of Appeals for D.C. cir., Washington; clk. to Assoc. Justice Potter Stewart Supreme Ct. of U.S., Washington; asst. to sec., dep. sec. of def. Office of Spl. Asst., Washington, 1977-79; assoc., ptnr. Williams & Connolly, Washington, 1979-94; adv. bd. on investigative capability Dept. Def., Washington, gen. counsel, 1994—; civil justice reform act adv. group U.S. Dist. Ct. D.C.; mem. jud. conf. D.C. Cir. Recipient Vol. Recognition award Nat. Assn. of Attys. Gens.; DOD medal for Disting. Pub. Svc., 1997, Beloit Coll. Disting. Svc. Citation, 1997. Fellow Am. Bar Found.; mem. ABA, Am. Law Inst. Office: Office of Gen Counsel 1600 Defense Pentagon Washington DC 20301-1600

**MILLER, KERRY LEE,** lawyer; b. West Palm Beach, Sept. 11, 1955; s. Clyde Howard and Alice (Hummel) M.; m. Myrna Patricia Garza, June 9, 1979; children: Alexander James, Eric Anthony. BA, George Mason U., 1977; JD, Cath. U., 1981. Bar: D.C. 1981, Va. 1982, U.S. Dist. Ct. (D.C. dist.) 1982, U.S. Ct. Appeals (D.C. and 4th cirs.) 1982, U.S. Ct. Appeals (fed. cir.) 1989, U.S. Ct. Claims 1989, U.S. Supreme Ct. 1989, U.S. Dist. Ct. (ea. and we. dists.) Va. 1993. Asst. gen. counsel Office Gen. Counsel U.S. Govt. Printing Office, Washington, 1981-87, assoc. gen. counsel contracts and procurement, 1987-99; adminstrv. law judge Bd. Contract Appeals U.S. Govt. Printing Office, Washington, 1999—. Mem. Fed. Bar Assn. (Capital Hill chpt.), Bd. Contract Appeals Judges Assn., Computer Law Assn. Office: US Govt Printing Office Office Bd Contract Appeals 732 N Capitol St NW Washington DC 20401-0001

**MILLER, KIRK EDWARD,** lawyer, health foundation executive; b. San Jose, Calif., June 9, 1951. BA in Polit. Sci., U. Calif., Riverside, 1973; JD, Syracuse U., 1976. Bar: Colo. 1976, Calif. 1980, Tex. 1993. Assoc. Hughes & Dorsey, Denver, 1977-78; v.p., assoc. gen. counsel Am. Med. Internat., Inc., Dallas, 1979-88, v.p., sec., gen. counsel, 1988-91; with McGlinchey Stafford Lang, Dallas, 1991-94; sr. v.p., sec., gen. counsel Kaiser Found. Health Plan, Inc., Kaiser Found. Hosps., Inc., Oakland, Calif., 1994—; instr. Syracuse U., 1975-76. Mem. ABA (co-vice chair com. health care fraud and abuse 1995-96). Office: Kaiser Found Health Plan 1 Kaiser Plz Oakland CA 94612-3610

**MILLER, LESLIE ANNE,** lawyer; b. Franlin, Ind., Nov. 4, 1951; d. G. Thomas and Anne (Gaines) Miller; m. Richard B. Worley, Feb. 14, 1987. AB cum laude, Mt. Holyoke Coll., South Hadley, Pa., 1973; MA in Polit. Sci., Eagle Inst. Politics Rutgers U., New Brunswick, N.J., 1974; JD, Dickinson Sch. of Law, Carlisle, Pa., 1977; LLM with honors, Temple U., 1994. Bar: Pa. 1977, U.S. Dist. Ct. (ea. dist.) Pa. 1977, U.S. Ct. Appeals (3d cir.) 1980, U.S. Dist. Ct. (ea. dist.) Pa. 1987. Assoc. LaBrum & Doak, Phila., 1977-81; ptnr. LaBrum & Doak, 1982-86, Goldfein & Joseph, Phila., 1986-95, McKissock & Hoffman, P.C., Phila., 1995—; bd. dirs. WHYY-TV, 1996—; del. Third Circuit Jud. Conf., 1981, 82, 85; mem. Jud. Inquiry and Rev. Bd., 1990-94, chair, 1993-94; mem. faculty trial advocacy program Dickinson Sch. Law, 1992, 94; mem. hearing com., disciplinary bd. Supreme Ct. Pa., 1996—; mem. faculty Acad. Advocacy Temple U., 1994—; judge pro tem Ct. of Common Pleas. mem. acad. ball com. Phila. Orch., 1986-87, 89-91, 95-96; mem. Open Space Task Force Com., Lower Merion Twp., Pa., 1990, bd. dirs., 1990-94, mem. counsel, 1990—, Lower Merion Conservancy, 1995-97, others; bd. dirs. Med. Coll. Pa., 1985-96, sec., 1987-92, chair presdl. search com., 1993, chair presdl. inauguration, 1987, chair com. on acad. affairs, 1989-95, chair dean's search com., 1994—, chair nomenclature com., 1996; bd. dirs. Allegheny Health Edn. and Rsch. Found., 1993-96, Hahnemann U. Med. Sch., 1994-96, United Hosps., 1991-94, Pa. Ballet, 1994—, St. Christopher's Hosp. for Children, 1991-94, vice chair, 1992-94; bd. dirs. Phila. Free Libr., 1997—. Recipient Mary Lyon award, Mt. Holyoke Alumni Assn., 1985, Alumnae Medal of Honor, 1988, Hon. Alumnae award, 1989, Pres.'s award Med. Coll. Pa., 1993, Sylvia Rambo award Dickinson Sch. of Law, 1997, Star award Forum of Exec. Women, 1998, Ann Alpern award PBA Women in the Profession, 1999, Sandra Day O'Connor award Phila. Bar Assn., 1999; named to Pa. Honor Roll of Women, 1996. Fellow Am. Bar Found., Pa. Bar Found.; mem. ABA, Phila. Bar Assn. (mem. exec. com. divsn. young lawyers 1982-85, mem. bicentennial com 1986-87, bd. govs. 1990-93, mem. gender bias task force 1993, chair com. on jud. selection and retention 1987-89, chair Andrew Hamilton Ball 1989, trustee Phila. Bar Found. 1990-97, co-chair century three commn. 1995-97, others), Pa. Bar Assn. (found. ho. dels. life fellow, bd. govs. 1980-83, 84-87, 91-93, chair young lawyers divsn. 1982-83, mem. long range planning com. 1985-87, mem. com. on professionalism, 1987-91, vice chmn. jud. inquiry and rev. bd. study com. 1989-91, sec. 1984-87, chair ho. dels. 1991-93, chair commn. on women in the profession 1993-95, v.p. 1996-97, pres. 1998-99, immediate past pres. 1999—), Pa. Bar Inst. (mem. faculty, course planner), Phila. Assn. Def. Counsel (mem. exec. coun. 1987-90, 94, mem. joint trial demonstration with Phila. Trial Lawyers Assn. 1993), Def. Rsch. Inst. (spkr. toxic torts seminar 1983), Phila. Bar Edn. Advocacy Women Litigators (course planner, mem. faculty), Women's Assn. Women's Alternatives (bd. dirs. 1983-94, vice chair 1985-94), Mt. Holyoke Alumnae Assn. (bd. dirs. 1986-89). Democrat. Lutheran. Avocations: collecting Am. antiques, gardening, running. General civil litigation, Personal injury. Office: McKissock & Hoffman PC 1700 Market St Ste 3000 Philadelphia PA 19103-3932

**MILLER, LOUIS H.,** lawyer; b. Lampeter, U.K., Apr. 22, 1945; m. Diane Matuszewski, Dec. 31, 1973; children: Margaret, Anthony. BA in History, Rutgers Coll., 1967; JD, Temple U., 1970. Bar: N.J. 1970, U.S. Dist. Ct. N.J. 1970, U.S. Supreme Ct. 1996. Law clk. to Judge Thomas Beetel Hunterdon County Ct., Flemington, N.J., 1970-71; law clk. to Judge Baruch Seidman Superior Ct. N.J. Chancery, Trenton, N.J., 1971-72; assoc. Jefferson, Jefferson & Vaida, Flemington, 1972-75; ptnr. Vaida & Miller, Flemington, 1975-78; pvt. practice Flemington, 1978-81, 88—; judge Superior Ct. N.J., Flemington, 1981-88; of counsel Levinson Axelrod Wheaton & Grayzel, Flemington, 1990-97; spl. dep. atty. gen. N.J. Hunterdon County Prosecutor Office, Flemington, 1972-73; condemnation commr. Appt. Superior Ct. N.J., Flemington, 1988—, assembly spkrs. commr.; commr. N.J. State Commn. Investigation, Trenton, 1993-97; arbitrator U.S. Fed. Dist. Ct. N.J., 1989—. Twp. committeeman Alexandria Twp. Com., R.D. Milford, N.J., 1978-81. Mem. Am. Judges Assn., Am. Judicature Soc., N.J. State Bar Assn. (mem. dist. ethics com. 1980-81, mem. mcpl. ct. practice com. 1996—), Hunterdon County Bar Assn., Warren County Bar Assn., Consular Law Soc., Welsh Am. Geneal. Soc., Welsh North Am. C. of C. (bd. dirs.). Republican. Avocations: paleontology, traveling, hiking. Personal injury, Family and matrimonial, Criminal. Office: PO Box 850 40 Main St Flemington NJ 08822-1411

**MILLER, LOUIS R., III,** lawyer; b. Chgo., Feb. 3, 1947; s. Louis R. Jr. and Barbara S. (Shure) M.; m. Sherry B. Miller, Dec. 27, 1969; children: Daniel S., James M. BSBA, U. Denver, 1969; JD, UCLA, 1972. Law clk. to Hon. Jesse W. Curtis U.S. Dist. Ct. (cen. dist.) Calif., L.A., 1972-73; assoc. Wyman, Bauter, L.A., 1973-78, ptnr., 1978-88; ptnr. Christensen, Miller, Fink, Jacobs, Glaser & Shapiro, L.A., 1988—. Bd. dirs. John Tracy Clinic, L.A., 1992—, D.A.R.E., L.A., 1995—. Federal civil litigation, General civil litigation, State civil litigation. Office: Christensen Miller Fink Jacobs Glaser & Shapiro 2121 Ave Of Stars Los Angeles CA 90067-5010

**MILLER, MAX DUNHAM, JR.,** lawyer; b. Des Moines, Oct. 17, 1946; s. Max Dunham and Beulah (Head) M.; m. Melissa Ann Dart, Jan. 10, 1969 (div. July 1975); 1 child, Ann Marie Victoria; m. Caroline Jean Armendt, Sept. 19, 1981; children: Alexander Bradshaw, Benjamin Everrett. BS with high honors, Mich. State U., 1968; postgrad., George Washington U., 1970-71; JD, U. Md., 1975. Bar: Md. 1976, U.S. Dist. Ct. Md. 1976, U.S. Ct. Appeals (4th cir.) 1981, U.S. Supreme Ct. 1982. Engr. U.S. Dept. of Def., Aberdeen Proving Ground, Md., 1968-72; law clk. to presiding judge Md. Cir. Ct., Higinbothom in Bel Air, Md., 1975-76; asst. county atty. Harford County, Bel Air, 1976-79; assoc. Lentz & Hooper P.A., Balt., 1979-81; ptnr. Miller, Olszewski & Moore, P.A., Bel Air, 1981-94; prin. Law Offices of Max D. Miller, P.A., 1994—; county atty. Harford County, Md., 1983-88. Mem. Md. Bar Assn., Assn. Trial Lawyers Am., Md. Trial Lawyers Assn., Harford County Bar Assn., Phi Kappa Phi, Phi Eta Sigma. Avocations: carpentry, sailing, canoeing, bicycling, ice and roller hockey. General civil litigation, General corporate, Real property. Home: 308 Whetstone Rd Forest Hill MD 21050-1332 Office: 5 S Hickory Ave Bel Air MD 21014-3732

**MILLER, MICHAEL DOUGLAS,** lawyer; b. Tucson, Dec. 25, 1948; s. Robert Friend and Mary (Fawcett) M.; m. Jennifer Louise Hunter, Dec. 23, 1960; 1 child, Hunter Douglas. BS, U. Ariz., 1973, JD, 1976. Bar: Ariz. 1977. Pvt. practice Tucson, 1977—. Mem. Ariz. Bar Assn., Ariz. Trial Lawyers Assn., Pima County Bar Assn. Avocations: fishing, camping, outdoor activities. Personal injury, Family and matrimonial, Real property. Office: 2101 N Country Club Rd Tucson AZ 85716-2845 also: 2830 N Swan Rd Ste 140 Tucson AZ 85712-6301

**MILLER, MICHAEL PATIKY,** lawyer; b. Huntington, N.Y., Apr. 16, 1944; s. George J. and Alida (Patiky) M.; m. Dorothy Denn, Dec. 25, 1966; children: Lauren M. Golubtchik, Jonathan M., Rachel B. AB, Rutgers U., 1965; JD, NYU, 1968. Bar: N.J. 1968, U.S. Dist. Ct. N.J. 1968, Calif. 1975, U.S. Dist. Ct. (no. dist.) Calif. 1975, U.S. Tax Ct. 1977, U.S. Ct. Appeals (9th cir.) 1977, U.S. Ct. Appeals (fed. cir.) 1984, U.S. Dist. Ct. (cen. dist.) Calif. 1982, U.S. Supreme Ct. 1983, U.S. Claims Ct. 1986. Atty. Electric Power Research Inst., Palo Alto, Calif., 1974-77; assoc. Weinberg, Ziff & Kaye, Palo Alto, 1977-78; ptnr. Weinberg, Ziff & Miller, Palo Alto, 1978—, mng. ptnr., 1990-98; lectr. on tax and estate planning U. Calif. Extension, 1980—. Author: Creditor Rights in Proceedings Outside Estate Adminstrn., 1995, rev., 1999; contbg. author: California Wills and Trusts, 1991, Estate Planning for Unmarried Couples, 1998, California Trust Administration, 1999; contbr. articles to profl. jours. Treas. No. Calif. region United Synagogue Am., 1985-89, pres., 1992-95. Capt. U.S. Army, 1969-74, Vietnam, Ethiopia. Recipient Lion of Judah award, 1984, Cert. Merit U. Judaism, 1992. Mem. ABA (chmn. region VI pub. contract law sect. 1975-78, commn. tax practice in small law firms, com. on taxation of trusts, estates, taxation sect. 1986—), N.J. State Bar, State Bar of Calif. (commr. tax law adv. commn. 1989-92, 93-95, chair 1994-95, mem. bd. legal specialization 1994-95), Santa Clara County Bar Assn. (chmn. estate planning, probate and trust sect. 1982, trustee 1983-84), California Trust Admin., 1999. Personal income taxation, Probate, Estate taxation. Office: Weinberg Ziff & Miller 400 Cambridge Ave Palo Alto CA 94306-1507

**MILLER, MICHAEL THOMAS,** lawyer; b. Mpls., Jan. 22, 1959. BA, U. Minn., 1981, JD, 1985. Bar: Minn. 1985, U.S. Dist. Ct. Minn. 1985, U.S. Ct. Appeals (8th cir.) 1987, U.S. Ct. Appeals (10th cir.) 1996, U.S. Supreme Ct. 1989. Law clk. Hon. Peter S. Popovich Minn. Ct. Appeals, St. Paul, 1985-87; assoc. Briggs & Morgan, P.A., Mpls., 1987-92, shareholder, 1992—. Contbr. articles to profl. jours. Labor, Appellate. Office: Briggs & Morgan 2400 IDS Ctr Minneapolis MN 55402

**MILLER, MILTON ALLEN,** lawyer; b. Los Angeles, Jan. 15, 1954; s. Samuel C. and Sylvia Mary Jane (Silver) M.; m. Mary Ann Toman, Sept. 10, 1988; 1 child, Mary Ann. AB with distinction and honors in Econs., Stanford U., 1976; JD with honors, Harvard U., 1979. Bar: Calif. 1979, U.S. Ct. Appeals (9th cir.) 1979, U.S. Dist. Ct. (cen., no. and so. dists.) Calif., U.S. Supreme Ct. 1989. Law clk. U.S. Ct. Appeals (9th cir.), Sacramento, 1979-80; assoc. Latham & Watkins, L.A., 1979-87, ptnr., 1987—; chmn. ethics com. Latham & Watkins. Author: Attorney Ethics; articles editor Harvard Law Rev., 1978-79. Mem. Am. Cancer Soc., L.A. Mem. ABA, ATLA, Calif. State Bar Assn. (mem. com. on profl. responsibility), Los Angeles County Bar Assn. (chmn. profl. responsibility and ethics com.), Phi Beta Kappa. Federal civil litigation, General civil litigation, Insurance. Office: Latham & Watkins 633 W 5th St Ste 4000 Los Angeles CA 90071-2005 *Notable cases include Raquel Welch vs. MGM Corp.; served as trial and insurance counsel in San Juan Dupont Plaza Hotel Fire litigation.*

**MILLER, MORRIS HENRY,** lawyer; b. Thomasville, Ga., June 14, 1954; s. Gibbes Ulmer and Marianne (Morris) M.; m. Anita Carol Payne, Mar. 23, 1985; children: Morris Payne, Rose Elizabeth, David Gibbes, Paul Louis Henry, John Henry. BS in Acctg. summa cum laude, Fla. State U., 1976; JD, U. Va., 1979. Bar: Fla. 1979. Assoc. Holland & Knight, Tampa, Fla., 1979-84; ptnr. Holland & Knight, Tallahassee, Fla., 1984—, chmn. health law practice, 1989—. Dist. fin. chmn. Gulf Ridge coun. Boy Scouts Am., 1988-89, mem. pack com., cubmaster Pack 23, Suwannee River Area coun., 1995-98, scoutmaster Troop 182, 1997—, dist. nominating com.; mem. Leadership Tampa, 1986, Leadership Tampa Bay, 1989; bd. dirs. John G. Riley House Mus. Ctr. for African-Am. History and Culture, 1998—, Tallahassee YMCA, 1994—, chmn. long range planning com., 1997; founder, chmn. Tampa Bus. Com. for Arts, Inc., 1988-89; elder Presbyn. Ch. Mem. ABA (health law sect.), Fla. Bar Assn. (chmn., vice chmn. computer law com. 1983-89, Fla. corp. law revision com. 1986-89, health law sect.), Tallahassee Bar Assn., Tallahassee Area C. of C. (strategic plan implementation com., Tallahassee trustees), Fla. Acad. Hosp. Attys. (chair govtl. hosp. com.). General corporate, Health, Computer. Office: Holland & Knight 315 S Calhoun St Ste 600 Tallahassee FL 32301-1897

**MILLER, NEIL SCOTT,** lawyer; b. N.Y.C., Jan. 2, 1969. BA in Polit. Sci., U. Vt., 1991; JD, Bklyn. Law Sch., 1994. Assoc. Agins, Siegel & Reiner, N.Y.C., 1995-97, Graham & James, N.Y.C., 1997—. Banking, Contracts commercial, Real property. Office: Graham & James LLP 885 3d Ave New York NY 10022

**MILLER, NODINE,** judge; b. Dayton, Ohio, Dec. 13, 1938; d. Joseph Frederick and Nellie Naomi (Balzer) Cook; 1 child, Jessica Inez; m. Donald Alan Antrim, Jan. 2, 1998. Student, U. Vienna, Austria, 1961, Georgetown U., 1959; BA, Miami U., 1960; JD, Capital U., 1976. Bar: Ohio 1976, U.S. Dist. Ct. (so. and ea. dists.) Ohio 1981. Legal asst. Mayer, Tingley, Hurd & Emens, Columbus, Ohio, 1971-72; law clk. Brownfield, Kosydar, Bowen, Bally & Sturtz, Columbus, Ohio, 1975; atty. assigned to commr. Divsn. Securities, Ohio Dept. Commerce, Columbus, 1976-79, atty. inspector securities, 1977-79, deputy commr. securities, 1978-81; atty. Luper, Wolinetz, Sheriff & Niedenthal, Columbus, 1981-92; judge Franklin County Mcpl. Ct., Columbus, 1982-92. Mem. ABA, Am. Inn of Ct., Ohio State Bar Ass., Columbus Bar Assn.,. Avocations: quilting, biking, fly fishing, skiing, reading. Office: Common Pleas Ct Hall of Justice 369 S High St Fl 6B Columbus OH 43215-4516

**MILLER, NORY,** lawyer; b. Chgo.; d. Byron S. and Jeannette R. Miller; m. Jonathan Barnett, May 19, 1983. BA, Swarthmore Coll.; JD, Columbia U., 1988. Bar: D.C. 1989, N.Y. 1989, U.S. Dist. Ct. D.C. 1992, U.S. Ct. Appeals (DC cir.) 1993, U.S. Dist. Ct. (so. dist.) N.Y. 1904, U.S. Ct. Appeals (8th cir.) 1998, U.S. Supreme Ct. 1993. Law clk. Hon. Abner Mikva U.S. Ct. Appeals (D.C. cir.), Washington, 1988-89; law clk. Hon. Justice William Brennan U.S. Supreme Ct., Washington, 1989-90; assoc. Wilmer, Cutler & Pickering, Washington, 1991-92; assoc. Jenner & Block, Washington, 1992-95, ptnr., 1996—. Mem. ABA (Pro Bono Work award 1998), D.C. Bar Assn. Constitutional, Appellate, General civil litigation. Office: Jenner & Block 601 13th St NW Ste 1200S Washington DC 20005-3823

**MILLER, PAUL J.,** lawyer; b. Boston, Mar. 27, 1929; s. Edward and Esther (Kalis) M.; children—Robin, Jonathan; m. Michal Davis, Sept. 1, 1965; children—Anthony, Douglas. B.A., Yale U., 1950; LL.B., Harvard U., 1953. Bar: Mass. 1953, Ill. 1957. Assoc. Miller & Miller, Boston, 1953-54; assoc. Sonnenschein Nath & Rosenthal, Chgo., 1957-63, ptnr., 1963—; bd. dirs. Oil-Dri Corp. Am., Chgo. Trustee Latin Sch. of Chgo., 1985-91. 1st lt. JAGC, U.S. Army, 1954-57. Fellow Am. Bar Found.; mem. Tavern Club, Saddle and Cycle Club, Law Club, Phi Beta Kappa. Avocations: jogging; sailing. General corporate, Securities, Contracts commercial. Office: Sonnenschein Nath & Rosenthal 233 S Wacker Dr Ste 8000 Chicago IL 60606-6342

**MILLER, PAUL S(AMUEL),** lawyer; b. Paterson, N.J., Apr. 8, 1939; s. Louis and Etta (Wolff) M.; m. Carol Plesser, Mar. 26, 1961; children: Nicole F., Margo H., Jason E. BA, Rutgers U., 1960, JD magna cum laude, 1962. Bar: N.Y. 1963. Assoc. Kaye, Scholer, Fierman, Hayes & Handler, N.Y.C., 1962-63, Rubin, Baum & Levin, N.Y.C., 1964; ptnr. Fishman, Miller & Zimet, N.Y.C., 1964-70; counsel Leasing Cons., Inc., Roslyn, N.Y., 1970-71; with Pfizer Inc., N.Y.C., 1971—, assoc. gen. counsel, v.p., gen. counsel, 1986-92, sr. v.p., gen. counsel, 1992—; official corr. Pharm. Mfrs. Assn., mem., chmn. exec. com. law sect., 1989-90. Mem. United Jewish Appeal Com., Essex County, 1981-83, co-chmn. Livingston sect., 1982; mem. bus. adv. coun. Touro Law Sch.; bd. dirs. Mgmt. Decision Lab. NYU Sch. Bus. Adminstrn., 1982—, Citizens Crime Commn. of N.Y.C., Inc., Jewish Conciliation Bd. Am., Inc., Nat. Com. for Futherance of Jewish Edn., Lawyers for Civil Justice; mem. exec. com. Am. Israel Pub. Affairs Com. Mem. ABA (antitrust law sect., corp. banking and bus. law sect., natural resources law sect., sci. and tech. sect., mem. health law forum com.), N.Y. State Bar Assn. (antitrust law sect., food and drug law sect., mem. internat. trade com., mem. long range policy proposals com.), Nat. Inst. Dispute Resolution (bd. dirs.), U.S. C. of C. (mem. govt. and regulatory affairs com.). Avocation: golf. General corporate, Environmental. Office: Pfizer Inc 235 E 42nd St New York NY 10017-5755

**MILLER, PHILIP CHARLES,** lawyer; b. Syracuse, N.Y., June 1, 1950; s. Hyman and Anne (Horwitz) M.; m. Barbara Tracy Hatfield, June 1, 1986; children: Sasha, Jonelle. BA, Syracuse U., 1972; JD, Hofstra U., 1976. Bar: N.Y. Dep. county atty. County of Onondaga, Syracuse, 1978-87; pvt. practice law Syracuse, 1988—; settlement agt. PHH Mortgage Svcs. Corp., Syracuse, 1997—, Parkway Mortgage, Syracuse, 1997—, Contimortgage, Syracuse, 1997—; owner Miller Title Agy., Inc., Syracuse, 1998; v.p., sec., treas. The Mortgage Orgn., Inc., Syracuse, 1994—. Town justice Onondaga, N.Y., 1988—. Mem. N.Y. State Magistrates Assn., Onondaga County Bar Assn., Onondaga County Magistrates Assn., Neighborhood Watch Ctrl. N.Y. Inc. (founding adv. bd. mem.). Office: 465 S Salina St Ste 10 Syracuse NY 13202-2409

**MILLER, RANDAL J.,** lawyer, educator; b. Joliet, Ill., Apr. 16, 1952; s. William D. Jr. and Joyce N. Miller; m. Mary Kaluzny, Oct. 4, 1980; children: Randal J. Jr., Hayley K., Hannah S. AA, Joliet Jr. Coll., 1973; BS, Lewis U., Lockport, Ill., 1975; JD, John Marshall Law Sch., Chgo., 1978. Bar: Ill. 1978, U.S. Dist. Ct. (no. dist.) Ill. 1982, U.S. Ct. Appeals (7th cir.) 1982. Real estate and trust atty. Heritage Bank, Crest Hill, Ill., 1978-79; asst. state's atty. County of Will, Joliet, 1979-86, asst. pub. defender, 1986-89; ptnr. Dunn, Martin & Miller, Ltd., Joliet, 1991—; adj. prof. Joliet Jr. Coll., 1980-84, U. St. Francis, Joliet, 1988—. cons. atty. Reflex Sympathetic Dystrophy Assn., Chgo., 1996—. Mem. exec. com. Will County Rep. Orgn., Joliet, 1985-90. Mem. Ill. State Bar Assn. (assemblyman 1991-97, standing com. supreme ct. rules 1997—), Will County Bar Assn. (bd. dirs. 1992-95, pres. 1999—), Masons. Avocations: music, collectibles, fine art. State civil litigation, Personal injury, Workers' compensation. Home: 2604 Glasgow St Joliet IL 60435-1335 Office: Dunn Martin & Miller Ltd 15 W Jefferson St Ste 300 Joliet IL 60432-4301

**MILLER, RANDY E.,** lawyer; b. Manhattan, Kans., Oct. 24, 1953; s. Darrel Earl and Ruth Cheryl (DeBey) M.; m. Julie Sauder, May 28, 1983. BA, Yale U., 1976; JD, Georgetown U., 1982. Bar: D.C. 1983. Staff asst. to Congressman Keith G. Sebelius, U.S. Ho. of Reps., Washington, 1977-79; legis. asst. to Senator Robert J. Dole, U.S. Senate, Washington, 1979-81, policy dir., 1981-83; assoc. Hogan & Hartson, Washington, 1983-89, ptnr., 1990—; treas., sec. Mainstream, Inc., Washington, 1983-98. Dep. counsel to chmn. Rep. Nat. Com., Washington, 1986-89, counsel rules com., 1986-88; nat. rules advisor Dole for Pres. Campaign, Washington, 1987-88. Mem. ABA, D.C. Bar, Internat. Trade Commn. Trial Lawyers Assn., Yale Club. Methodist. Administrative and regulatory, Private international, Public international. Home: 5210 Albemarle St Bethesda MD 20816-1829 Office: Hogan & Hartson LLP 555 13th St NW Ste 800E Washington DC 20004-1109

**MILLER, RAYMOND VINCENT, JR.,** lawyer; b. Providence, July 1, 1954; s. Raymond Vincent and Mary Eunice (Mullen) M.; m. Elizabeth Ann White, May 31, 1980; children: Travis, Charles. BA, U. R.I., 1976; JD cum laude, U. Miami, 1981. Bar: Fla. 1981, U.S. Dist. Ct. (so. dist.) Fla. 1981, U.S. Ct. Appeals (11th cir.) 1986, U.S. Dist. Ct. (mid. dist. ) Fla. 1987. Area supr. job devel. and tng. div. R.I. Dept. Econ. Devel., Providence, 1977-78; assoc. Thornton & Herndon, Miami, Fla., 1981-83, Britton, Cohen et al, Miami, 1983-85, Edward A. Kaufman, P.A., Miami, 1985-88; ptnr. Kaufman, Miller, Dickstein & Grunspan, Miami, 1988—. Mem. ABA, Fla. Bar Assn., Nat Order Barristers, Soc. Bar and Gavel, Acad. Fla. Trial Lawyers (chair comml. law sect. 1993-95). Federal civil litigation, State civil litigation, Personal injury. Office: Kaufman Miller Dickstein & Grunspan PA 200 S Biscayne Blvd Ste 4650 Miami FL 33131-2354

**MILLER, RENÉE JACQUES,** legal administrator; b. Rochester, N.Y., Jan. 12, 1963; d. Montraville Allan and Shirley May (Peterson) Jacques; m. David Keith Miller, Dec. 26, 1981; children: Kendall Peterson, Jed Baron. AA in Bus., Pensacola (Fla.) Jr. Coll., 1983; BA in Acctg. cum laude, U. West Fla., 1985, postgrad., 1990—. Accounting clk. U. West Fla., 1983-84; staff acct. Mo. Money Assn., 1984-85; acct., office mgr. Kerrigan, Estess & Rankin, Pensacola, Fla., 1985-89; acct. Wengor of Panama City (Fla.), Inc., 1989-93, Sunshine Cellular, 1990-94; legal adminstr. Kerrigan, Estess, Rankin & McLeod, Pensacola, Fla., 1989-98; career network database participant U. West Fl., Pensacola, Fla., 1993—; adminstr., pres. Christian Resource Warehouse Inc., 1999—; v.p., adminstr. Power from on High Ministries, Inc., 1999—; co-owner, adminstr. Miller & Miller Contractors, Pensacola, Fla., 1988—; tour planner Sunshine Express Tours Inc., Pensacola, 1995—. Mem. office systems tech. adv. com. Pensacola Jr. Coll., 1990—, legal secretarial tech. adv. com., 1990-91; dep. campaign treas. Fla. State Rep., Pensacola, 1986; care group leader Olive Bapt. Ch., Pensacola, 1987—. Kahn scholar U. West Fla., 1984. Mem. Inst. Mgmt. Accts., Internat. Platform Assn., Concerned Women for Am. Democrat. Baptist. Avocations: traveling, visiting with friends, sports. Office: Miller & Miller Contractors 9525 Baron Miller Rd Pensacola FL 32514-5696

**MILLER, RICHARD ALLAN,** lawyer; b. N.Y.C., Oct. 28, 1947; s. Harold B. and Helen (Schwartz) M.; m. Karen R. Mangold, July, 5, 1970; children: David, Matthew. BA, SUNY, Buffalo, 1969; MA, Ohio State U., 1970; JD, NYU, 1973. Bar: N.Y. 1974, U.S. Dist. Ct. (so. and ea. dists.) N.Y. 1974, U.S. Ct. Appeals (2d cir.) 1977, U.S. Supreme Ct. 1980. Assoc. Paul Weiss et al, N.Y.C., 1973-75; asst. dist. atty. N.Y. County, N.Y.C., 1975-77; ptnr. Newman, Tannenbaum et al, N.Y.C., 1980-91, Katten Muchin & Zavis, N.Y.C., 1992-96, White & Case, 1996—; staff counsel Presdl. Task Force on Market Mechanisms, 1987-88; speaker Internat. Conf. Futures Money Mgmt., 1990-92. Editor, pub. Futures & Derivatives L. Rpt., 1981—, Securities Arbitration Commentator, 1988—. Mem. Assn. of the Bar of the City of N.Y. (chair futures regulations com.). Jewish. Avocations: skiing, golf. Administrative and regulatory, Federal civil litigation, Securities. Home: 22 Roosevelt Rd Maplewood NJ 07040-2116 Office: White & Case 1155 Ave Americas New York NY 10036

**MILLER, RICHARD ALLEN,** lawyer; b. East Chicago, Ind., Nov. 22, 1945; s. Ernest R. and Sophie D. (Kurmis) M.; m. Patricia Annette Bratton, July 26, 1969 (div. May 1974); 1 child, Jason Todd; m. Kathleen Patrice Sills, Jan. 3, 1976; children: Andrew Christian, Caroline Grace. BS, Ind. U., 1967; JD, Valparaiso U., 1973. Bar: Ind. 1974, U.S. Dist. Ct. (no. dist.) Ind. 1974, U.S. Supreme Ct. 1985, U.S. Ct. Appeals (7th cir.) 1987, U.S. Claims Ct. 1990. Assoc. Owen W. Crumpacker & Assocs., Hammond, Ind., 1974-76, Benjamin, Greco & Gouveia, Gary, Ind., 1976-77; ptnr. Greco, Gouveia, Miller & Pera, Gary, 1978-79, Greco, Gouveia, Miller, Pera & Bishop, Merrillville, Ind., 1979-85, Gouveia & Miller, Merrillville, 1985—; spl. counsel City of Hammond, 1974-76; trial counsel Ind. Toll Rd. Com., South Bend, 1981-82, Ind. Dept. Highways Toll Rd. Div., Granger, 1982-87; spl. asst. U.S. Rep. Peter J. Visclosky, Gary and Washington, 1985-86. Author: Indiana Rules of Evidence Applying to Expert Testimony, 1991. Campaign mgr. Visclosky for U.S. Congress, 1st Congl. Dist., Ind., 1983-88; dist. coordinator Nat. Bicentennial Competition on U.S. Constitution and Bill of Rights, 1st Congl. Dist., Ind., 1987-88. Mem. Ind. Bar Assn., Assn. Trial Lawyers Am., Ind. Trial Lawyers Assn. Democrat. Lutheran. Avocations: fishing, sports (coach and spectator), reading, writing short stories. General civil litigation, Personal injury, Condemnation. Home: 10313 Marlou Dr Munster IN 46321-4339 Office: Gouveia & Miller 521 E 86th Ave Merrillville IN 46410-6173

**MILLER, RICHARD SHERWIN,** law educator; b. Boston, Dec. 11, 1930; s. Max and Mollie Miller; m. Doris Sheila Lunchick, May 24, 1956; children: Andrea Jayne Armitage, Matthew Harlan. BSBA, Boston U., 1951, JD magna cum laude, 1956; LLM, Yale U., 1959. Bar: Mass. 1956, Mich. 1961, Hawaii 1977. Pvt. practice law Boston, 1956-58; assoc. prof. law Wayne State U., Detroit, 1959-62, prof., 1962-65; prof. Ohio State U., Columbus, 1965-73, dir. clin. and interdisciplinary program, 1971-73; prof. U. Hawaii, Honolulu, 1973-95, prof. emeritus, 1995—, dean, 1981-84; vis. prof. law USIA/U. Hawaii, Hiroshima U. Affiliation Program, Japan, fall 1986, Victoria U., Wellington, N.Z., Spring 1987; del. Hawaii State Jud. Conf., 1989-92; cons. Hawaii Coalition for Health, 1997—. Author: Courts and the Law: An Introduction to our Legal System, 1980; editor: (with Roland Stanger) Essays on Expropriations, 1967; editor-in-chief: Boston U. Law Rev., 1955-56; contbr. articles to profl. jours. Mem. Hawaii Substance Abuse Task Force, 1994-95; arbitrator Hawaii Ct. Annexed Arbitration Program, 1995—; bd. dirs. Drug Policy Forum Hawaii, 1996—. 1st lt. USAF, 1951-53. Sterling-Ford fellow Yale U., 1958-59; named Lawyer of Yr. Japan-Hawaii Lawyers Assn., 1990; recipient Cmty. Svc. award Hawaii Med. Assn. Alliance, 1999, Vol. Yr., 1999. Mem. ABA, Hawaii State Bar Assn., Hawaii ACLU, Am. Inn of Ct. IV (emeritus founding mem., master of the bench), Am. Law Inst., Honolulu Cmty-Media Coun. (pres. 1994-98, v.p. 1998—). Office: U Hawaii Richardson Sch Law 2515 Dole St Honolulu HI 96822-2328

**MILLER, RICHARD WAYNE,** lawyer; b. Grosse Pointe, Mich., Nov. 3, 1964; s. Richard Henry and Jeanette Faye Miller; m. Renee Audrey Saffell, Feb. 15, 1996. BS in Biology, U. Mich., 1986; JD, Wayne State U., 1990. Bar: Calif. 1991, U.S. Dist. Ct. (ctrl. and so. dists.) Calif. 1991, U.S. Ct. Appeals (9th cir.) 1991. Atty. Even, Crandall, Wade, Lowe and Gates, Irvine, Calif., 1990—. Mem. ABA, Assn. Trial Lawyers Am., Assn. So. Calif. Def. Counsel, Def. Rsch. Inst. Product liability, Personal injury, General civil litigation. Office: Even Crandall Wade Lowe & Gates 7700 Irvine Center Dr Irvine CA 92618-2923

**MILLER, RICHARD WILLIAM,** lawyer; b. Kansas City, Mo., Oct. 15, 1932; s. Robert W. and Mary Jane (Tierney) M.; m. Bernadette Owens, June 1, 1957; children: Stephen, Mark, Paul, Anne, Susan, Julie, Jim, Rich, Michelle. BA in History and Lit., Rockhurst Coll., 1952; JD, U. Mo., Kansas City, 1955, LLM, 1956. Bar: Mo. 1955. Sr. ptnr. Miller Law Firm, P.C., Kansas City, Mo., 1991—; counsel Nat. Assn. Surety Bond Prodrs., 1984-87; lectr. Sch. Engring., U. Wis. Author: Payment and Performance Bonds, 1976, Subcontractor's Rights, 1982, Mistakes in Bids, 1983, 3d edit., 1995, Miller Act Bonds, 1992, Insurance and Bonding for Joint Ventures, Construction Projects, Chapter 5, Construction Joint Ventures: Forms and Practice Guide, 1992, Joint Ventures, 3d edit., 1993. Founder Christmas in October, Kansas City; bd. trustees Rockhurst Coll., Kansas City, 1977-99, Sch. Law Found., U. Kansas City, Mo., Cath. Charities, 1981—, Lyric Opera, 1979—; lay min. Visitation Parish. Recipient Kansas City Spirit award, 1991, Humanitarian award St. Teresa's Acad., 1991, Bishop Sullivan Svc. award 1997; named to Sovereign Mil. Order of Knights of Malta, 1984, Alumnus of the Yr. Rockhurst Coll., 1990, VFW Person of the Yr., 1992, Notre Dame Man of the Yr., 1994. Banking, General civil litigation, Communications. Office: Miller Bldg 4310 Madison Ave Kansas City MO 64111-3435

**MILLER, ROBERT ARTHUR,** state supreme court chief justice; b. Aberdeen, S.D., Aug. 28, 1939; s. Edward Louis and Bertha Leone (Hitchcox) M.; m. Shirlee Ann Schlim, Sept. 5, 1964; children: Catherine Sue, Scott Edward, David Alan, Gerri Elizabeth, Robert Charles. BSBA, U. S.D., 1961, JD, 1963. Asst. atty. gen. State of S.D., Pierre, 1963-65; pvt. practice law Philip, S.D., 1965-71; state atty. Haakon County, Philip, 1965-71; city atty. City of Philip, 1965-71; judge State of S.D. (6th cir.), Pierre, 1971-86, presiding judge, 1975-86; justice S.D. Supreme Ct., Pierre, 1986—, now chief justice; bd. dirs. Nat. Conf. of Chief Justices, 1996-97, State Justice Inst., 1998—, chair, 1998—; trustee S.D. Retirement Sys., Pierre, 1974-85, chmn., 1982-85; mem. faculty S.D. Law Enforcement Tng. Acad., 1975-85; bd. dirs. U. S.D. Law Sch. Found., 1990—. Mem. S.D. State Crime Commn., 1979-86; mem. adv. commn. S.D. Sch. for the Deaf, 1983-85, Communications Svcs. to Deaf, 1990-92; cts. counselor S.D. Boy's State, 1986—, Nat. Awards Jury Freedoms Found., 1991. Mem. State Bar of S.D., S.D. Judges' Assn. (pres. 1974-75). Roman Catholic. Lodge: Elks. Avocations: golf, hunting. Office: SD Supreme Ct State Capitol Bldg 500 E Capitol Ave Pierre SD 57501-5070*

**MILLER, ROBERT DANIEL,** lawyer; b. Houston, May 3, 1960; s. Robert Thomas and Joyce (Danielson) M.; m. Lisa Anne Davis, May 23, 1987. BA, Rice U., 1982; JD, U. Tex., Austin, 1985. Bar: Tex. 1985. Legis. aide Senator Don Henderson, Austin, Tex., 1983; assoc. Locke Liddell & Sapp LLP, Houston, 1985-91, ptnr., 1992—; ptnr. Locke Liddell & Sapp LLP and predecessor, Houston, 1999—; sec., treas. Com. for Jud. Merit Election, Tex., 1987-89. Chmn. Battleship Tex. Adv. Bd., 1988-92; mem. fin. com. Houston Conv. Fund, 1991-95, Leadership Houston Class X, 1991-92; bd. dirs. Citizens Commn. on Tex. Judiciary, 1991-95, Greater Houston Preservation Alliance, 1994-95, Tex. Lyceum, 1994-98, Vote Tex., 1995-98, Houston Internat. Festival, 1997—; chmn. Met. Transit Authority, 1998—. Named one of Five Outstanding Young Houstonians, Jaycees, 1992. Fellow Am. Leadership Forum; mem. State Bar Tex., Houston Bar Assn., Houston Club, Coronado Club, Order of Coif, Phi Delta Phi, Omicron Delta Epsilon. Republican. Real property, Banking, Legislative. Office: Locke Liddell & Sapp LLP 600 Travis St Ste 3400 Houston TX 77002-2910

**MILLER, ROBERT L., JR.,** federal judge; b. 1950; m. Jane Woodward. BA, Northwestern U., 1972; JD, Ind. U., 1975. Law clk. to presiding justice U.S. Dist. Ct. (no. dist.) Ind., 1975; judge St. Joseph Superior Ct., South Bend, Ind., 1975-86, chief judge, 1981-83; judge U.S. Dist. Ct. (no. dist.) Ind., South Bend, Ind., 1985—. Office: US Dist Ct 325 Fed Bldg 204 S Main St South Bend IN 46601-2122

**MILLER, ROGER WAYNE,** court reporter; b. Tahoka, Tex., Apr. 14, 1953; s. Wayne Howard and Wyenema Miller; m. Leah Anne Fowlkes; children: Kathryn Mackenzie, Collin Lee. Student, Stenograph Inst. Tex., Abilene, 1973; LLD (hon.), Northwood Inst., Cedar Hills, Tex., 1995. Cert. shorthand reporter, Tex., N.Mex. Freelance ct. reporter Curtis D. Ruff & Assocs., Lubbock, Tex., 1973; ct. reporter U.S. Dist. Ct., Lubbock, 1973-87; ct. reporter, officer Stanley, Harris, Rice, Dallas, 1987-92, Keith & Miller, El Paso, 1992—, Fuller & Parker, Dallas, 1996—; litigation support officer Am. LegalTech, El Paso and Dallas, 1994—; mem. adv. bd. Educorp Internat., 1987-90, Rapidtext, Inc., 1988—; mem. profl. ct. reporting adv. bd. Coll. of Richardson, Tex., 1990; mem. profl. adv. bd. ct. reporting divsn. El Paso C.C., 1991, 92; numerous presentations in field. Contbr. articles to law jours. Mem. jr. livestock com. State Fair Tex., 1988-90; asst. coach Coppell (Tex.) Little League, 1990; active Indian princess program YMCA, 1988-90, Indian guides program 1991. Scholar in his name at Stenograph Inst. Tex., 1986—; Hall of Fame fellow Acad. Profl. Reporters. Mem. U.S. Ct. Reporters Assn. (nat. bd. dirs. 1983-87), Nat. Ct. Reporters Assn. (cert. of proficiency, registeree merit, profl. and dilomate reporter, nat. bd. dirs., pres. 1987-94), Tex. Ct. Reporters Assn. (bd. dirs. 1985-86, Disting. Svc. award 1994), EPCCRA, DCRA. Avocations: hiking, travel, reading. Home: 5880 Via Cuesta Dr El Paso TX 79912-6608 Office: Keith & Miller 100 N Stanton St Ste 1320 El Paso TX 79901-1448

**MILLER, RUTH LOYD,** lawyer, author; b. Ida, La., May 29, 1922; d. Cecil A. and Gladys (Means) Loyd; m. Minos D. Miller, Jr., Dec. 22, 1942; children: Bonner M. Cutting, Minos D. III, James Valcour. BA in Speech, La. State U., 1942. Bar: La. 1957. Sole practice Jennings, La., 1957—; sec. Jennings Gas Co., 1959—. Author, editor: Shakespeare Identified, 3rd edit., 1975, Hidden Allusions in Shakespeare's Plays, 3rd edit., 1975, A Hundreth Sundrie Flowers, 2d edit., 1975. First v.p. La. Constnl. Conv., 1973; mem. La. Mineral Bd., 1972-73; mem. bd. suprs. La. State Univ. Sys., 1974-88, chmn., 1983-84; active polit. campaigns, La. Named Nat. Woman of Yr., Delta Zeta, 1983. Mem. ABA, La. State Bar Assn. Republican. Methodist. Education and schools, Intellectual property, Oil, gas, and mineral. Home: PO Box 1309 Jennings LA 70546-1309

**MILLER, RUTH RYMER,** lawyer; b. Denver, June 2, 1931; d. Charles Albert and Marion (Reinhardt) Rymer; children: Nevin Lane, Stefanie Joan. BA with honors, San Francisco State U., 1965; JD with highest honors, Golden Gate U., 1970, LLM in Taxation, 1985; PhD in Human and Orgn. Sys., The Fielding Inst., 1995. Bar: Colo. 1971, Calif. 1971. Sole practice, San Mateo, Calif.; chmn. family law adv. commn. Calif. Bd. Legal Specialization, 1977-82. Mem. Queen's Bench (pres. 1976), State Bar Calif. (chmn. exec. com. family law sect. 1978-79), San Mateo County Bar Assn. (chmn. conf. dels. 1979, dir. 1980-82, chmn. family law sect. 1978-79, chmn. women and the law com. 1975), Am. Acad. Matrimonial Lawyers (No. Calif. chpt. pres. 1987). Editor, pub.: Family Law Brief Briefs; author: California Divorce Through the Legal Maze, 1997. Family and matrimonial. Office: 177 Bovet Rd Ste 600 San Mateo CA 94402-3122

**MILLER, SAM SCOTT,** lawyer; b. Ft. Worth, July 26, 1938; s. Percy Vernon and Mildred Lois (MacDowell) M.; m. Mary Harrison FitzHugh, May 10, 1969. BA, Mich. State U., 1960; JD, Tulane U., 1964; LLM, Yale U., 1965. Bar: La. 1965, N.Y. 1966, Minn. 1969. Assoc. Simpson Thacher & Bartlett, N.Y.C., 1965-68; sr. counsel Investors Diversified Services, Mpls., 1968-73; ptnr. Ireland Gibson Reams & Miller, Memphis, 1973-74; gen. counsel Paine Webber Group, Inc., N.Y.C., 1974-87, sr. v.p., 1976-87; ptnr. Orrick, Herrington & Sutcliffe, N.Y.C., 1987—; adj. prof. NYU Law Sch., 1986-90; vis. lectr. Yale Law Sch., 1980-85, Inst. for Internat. Econs. and Trade, Wuhan, China, 1983, U. Calif., 1986; trustee Omni Mut., Inc., 1988-; ombudsman Kidder Peabody Group, 1988-, Charles Schwab & Co., 1991-, Gruntal & Co., 1995-. Contbr. articles to profl. jours.; editor-in-chief: Tulane Law Rev, 1964-65; bd. editors Securities Regulation Law Jour., 1982—. Bd. dirs. Guthrie Theatre Found., Mpls., 1971-74; bd. dirs. Minn. Opera Co., 1971-74, Yale U. Law Sch. Fund., 1981—; bd. govs. Investment Co. Inst., 1980-87. Fellow Fgn. Policy Assn.; mem. ABA (vice chmn. com. fed. regulation of sec. 1995-98, chmn. subcom. market regulation 1985-93), Assn. Bar City N.Y. (treas. and mem. exec. com. 1994-96, chmn. broker-dealer investment co. and regulations subcom. 1982-83), Internat. Bar Assn., Securities Industry Assn. (chmn. fed. regulation com. 1976-78), Down Town Assn., Knickerbocker Club, Order of Coif, Omicron Delta Kappa. Democrat. Baptist. Administrative and regulatory, General corporate,

Legislative. Office: Orrick Herrington & Sutcliffe 666 5th Ave Rm 203 New York NY 10103-1798

**MILLER, SAMUEL AARON,** lawyer; b. Providence, June 4, 1955; s. Max and Miriam (Siperstein) M.; m. Pamela Lynn Kaitin, May 26, 1980; children: Shoshana Dina, David Daniel, Michaela Aleeza. Grad., Clark U., 1977; JD, Western New Eng. Coll., 1980. Bar: R.I. 1980, Mass. 1980, U.S. Dist. Ct. R.I. 1980, U.S. Dist. Ct. Mass. 1981, U.S. Ct. Appeals (1st cir.) 1981. Assoc. Quinn, Cuzzone & Geremia, Providence, 1980—. Mem. ABA, Mass. Bar Assn., Assn. Trial Lawyers Am., R.I. Trial Lawyers Assn., Am. Judicature Soc., Def. Research Assn. Jewish. State civil litigation, Environmental, Personal injury. Home: 68 Ogden St Providence RI 02906-4904 Office: Quinn Cuzzone & Geremia 189 Canal St Providence RI 02903-1319

**MILLER, STEPHEN RALPH,** lawyer; b. Chgo., Nov. 28, 1950; s. Ralph and Karin Ann (Olson) M.; children: David Williams, Lindsay Christine. m. Sheila L. Krysiak, Feb. 2, 1998. BA cum laude, Yale U., 1972; JD, Cornell U., 1975. Bar: Ill. Assoc. McDermott, Will & Emery, Chgo., 1975-80, income ptnr., 1981-85, equity ptnr., 1986—, mgmt. com. mem., 1992-95; mem. spl. task force on post-employment benefits Fin. Acctg. Standards Bd., Norwalk, Conn., 1987-91. Contbr. articles to profl. jours. Mem. Chgo. Coun. on Fgn. Rels., 1978—, mem. devel. com., 1997—; trustee police pension bd., Wilmette, Ill., 1992-98; trustee Seabury We. Theol. Sem., Evanston, Ill., 1994—, chancellor, 1996-97. Mem. ABA, Ill. Bar Assn., Yale Club Chgo., Chgo. Athletic Assn., Hundred Club Cook County, Legal Club of Chgo. Avocations: sailing, water skiing, cross-country skiing. Pension, profit-sharing, and employee benefits. Office: McDermott Will & Emery 227 W Monroe St Ste 3100 Chicago IL 60606-5096

**MILLER, STEPHEN WILEY,** lawyer; b. Washington, Feb. 27, 1958; s. Robert Wiley and Betty Ruth (Brown) M.; m. Andrea Brill, Feb. 12, 1982; children: Ashley, Craig, Kevin. BA, Denison U., 1980; JD, U. Va., 1984. Bar: Va. 1984, U.S. Dist. Ct. (ea. dist.) Va. 1987, U.S. Ct. Appeals (4th cir.) 1984. Assoc. Hunton & Williams, Richmond, Va., 1984-87; asst. U.S. atty. U.S. Atty.'s Office, U.S. Dept. Justice, Richmond, 1987—. Contbr. articles to profl. jours. Mem. ABA, Va. State Bar, Va. Bar Assn., Phi Alpha Delta (chpt. pres. 1982-83, state coordinator 1986—, outstanding svc. award 1983). Office: US Attys Office 600 E Main St Richmond VA 23219-2441

**MILLER, STEVEN RICHARD,** lawyer; b. N.Y.C., Nov. 11, 1953; s. Arnold and Beatrice Miller. BA summa cum laude, NYU, 1974, M of Urban Planning, JD, 1977. Bar: D.C. 1978, N.Y. 1979, U.S. Supreme Ct. 1981. Intern U.S. Energy Rsch. and Devel. Adminstrn., Washington, 1977; intern U.S. Dept. Energy, Washington, 1977-78, atty.-advisor, 1978-91, dep. asst. gen. counsel for environ., 1991—. Contbr. articles to profl. jours.; assoc. editor NYU Rev. of Law and Social Change, 1977. CPR program chmn. Adas Israel Synagogue Men's Club, Washington, 1985—, mem. exec. bd., 1986-88, bd. dirs., 1985-86, 88—; rec. sec. Adas Israel Singles Aux., Washington, 1986-88; chair Adas Israel Sr. Citizens Seder, Washington, 1985. Recipient award for chairing and organizing sr. citizen Passover seder Adas Israel Synagogue, Washington, 1985, Recognition Vol. Svc. award Folger Shakespeare Theater, Washington, 1990, Yasher Koach award Adas Israel Men's Club, 1990, Pres.'s Point of Light award, 1992. Mem. ASME (mixed waste com.), Fed. Bar Assn. (chairperson energy law com. 1988-91, chair sect. on energy, environment and natural resources 1991—, award for sustained leadership 1989), Am. Nuclear Soc. (chair session orgn. 1984-88, exec. com. mem. environ. sci. div. 1984-86), Phi Beta Kappa. Jewish. Avocations: theater, photography, music, walking, eating.

**MILLER, SUZANNE MARIE,** law librarian, educator; b. Feb. 25, 1954; d. John Gordon and Dorothy Margaret (Sabatka) M.; 1 child, Altinay Marie. B.A. in English, U. S.D., 1975; M.A. in Library Sci., U. Denver, 1976, postgrad. in law, 1984. Librarian II U. S.D. Sch. of Law, Vermillion, 1977-78; law libr. U. LaVerne, Calif., 1978-85, instr. in law, 1980-85; asst. libr. tech. svcs. McGeorge Sch. Law, Calif., 1985-99, prof. advanced legal rsch., 1994-99; state librarian S.D. State Library, Pierre, S.D., 1999—. Coauthor (with Elizabeth J. Pokorny) U.S. Government Documents: A Practical Guide for Library Assistants in Academic and Public Libraries, 1988; contbr. chpt. to book, articles to profl. jours. Recipient A. Jurisprudence award Bancroft Whitney Pub. Co., 1983. Mem. Am. Assn. Law Librs., So. Calif. Assn. Law Libs. (arrangements com. 1981-82), No. Calif. Assn. Law Librs. (mem. program com., inst. 1988), Western Pacific Assn. Law Librs. (sec. 1990-94, pres. elect 1994-95, pres. 1995-96, lical arrangements chair 1997). Roman Catholic. Home: 4030 Jeffrey Ave Sacramento CA 95820-2551 Office: SD State Library 800 Governors Dr Pierre SD 57501-2235

**MILLER, THEODORE HILLIS,** retired judge; b. Des Moines; s. Ray Gilbert and Ellen Lea Hillis Miller; m. Lois Jane Mitchell, June 4, 1942; children: Theodore Hillis Jr., Linda Jane Miller Knudsen. JD, Drake U., 1947. Bar: Iowa 1947. Ptnr. Tesdell Miller Rydell & Hall, Des Moines, 1950-76; judge Dist. Ct. Iowa, Des Moines, 1976-90, sr. judge, 1990-97; mem. edn. com. Iowa Judges Assn., 1980-87. Chief atty. Legal Aid Office, Iowa, 1950-52. Civilian supr. U.S. Army Ground Sch., 1943-46, 1st lt. JAG U.S. Army, 1948-50. Fellow Iowa Acad. Trial Lawyers (bd. dirs., cofouunder); mem. Assn. Trial Lawyers Iowa (founder, bd. dirs.), Des Moines Golf and Country Club (past bd. dirs., pres.). Methodist. Home: 1119 22d St West Des Moines IA 50265

**MILLER, THOMAS EUGENE,** lawyer, writer; b. Bryan, Tex., Jan. 4, 1929; s. Eugene Adam and Ella Lucille (Schroeder) M. BA, BS, Tex. A&M U., 1950; MA, U. Tex., 1956, JD, 1966; postgrad., U. Houston, 1956-58, U. Calif., 1983. Bar: Tex. 1966. Rsch. technician M.D. Anderson Hosp., Houston, 1956-58; claims examiner trainee Social Security Adminstrn., New Orleans, 1964; trademark examiner U.S. Patent and Trademark Office, Washington, 1966; editor Bancroft-Whitney Co., San Francisco, 1966-92. Author: (under pseudonym Millard Thomas) Home From 7-North, 1984. Contbg. mem. Dem. Nat. Com., 1981-99; mem. Celebrate Bryan Com. Mem. ABA, World Lit. Assn., World Inst. Achievement, United Writers Assn. India, Nat. Trust for Hist. Preservation, Tex. Bar Assn., African Wildlife Found., World Wildlife Fund, Internat. Platform Assn., Nat. Writers Assn., Scribes, Press Club, Commonwealth Club, Rotary Club (Paul Harris fellow), Menninger Found., Tex. A&M U. Faculty Club, Phi Kappa Phi, Psi Chi, Phi Eta Sigma. Methodist. Home: 101 N Haswell Dr Bryan TX 77803-4848 *Personal philosophy: Use your experience and abilities not only to understand life and to succeed, but also to help others' journeys through life.*

**MILLER, THOMAS J.,** state attorney general; b. Dubuque, Iowa, Aug. 11, 1944; s. Elmer John and Betty Maude (Kross) M.; m. Linda Cottington, Jan. 10, 1981; 1 child, Matthew. B.A., Loras Coll., Dubuque, 1966; J.D., Harvard U., 1969. Bar: Iowa bar 1969. With VISTA, Balt., 1969-70; legis. asst. to U.S. rep.John C. Culver, 1970-71; legal edn. dir. Balt. Legal Aid Bur., also mem. part-time faculty U. Md. Sch. Law, 1971-73; pvt. practice McGregor, Iowa, 1973-78; city atty. McGregor, 1975-78, Marquette, Iowa; atty. gen. of Iowa, 1979-91, 95—; ptnr. Faegre & Benson, Des Moines, 1991-95. Pres. 2d Dist. New Democratic Club, Balt., 1972. Mem. Am. Bar Assn., Iowa Bar Assn., Common Cause. Roman Catholic. Office: Office of the Atty Gen Hoover State Office Bldg Fl 2 Des Moines IA 50319-0001*

**MILLER, TIMMIE MAINE,** lawyer; b. Worcester, Mass., June 29, 1969; d. Craigen and Billie (Weinrich) Maine; m. James Kay Miller, Sept. 14, 1996. BA, U. Mass., 1991; JD, MPA, Suffolk U., 1995. Bar: Mass. 1995, N.H. 1998. V.p. mktg. White Pond Investments, Framingham, Mass., 1987-92; dir. health policy Brandon Assocs., Boston, 1994-95, dir. policy, 1995-98; assoc. Gallagher, Callahan & Gartrell, PA, The Gout Group, Concord, N.H., 1998—. Contbr. numerous articles to various publs. Grad fellow Suffolk U., 1994-95. Mem. N.H. Bar Assn., N.H. Women's Bar Assn. Avocations: skiing, weight training, running, music, theatre. Legislative, Insurance, Administrative and regulatory. Home: 19 Kalmia Way Bedford NH 03110-5317 Office: Gallaher Callahan & Gartrell 214 N Main St Concord NH 03301-5050

**MILLER, WARREN LLOYD,** lawyer; b. Bklyn., July 18, 1944; s. Allan and Ella (Faecher) M.; m. Jana Lee Morris, May 13, 1978; children: Lindsey Beth, Alan Gregory, William Brett. BA with honors, Am. U., 1966; JD with honors, George Washington U., 1969. Bar: Va., 1969, D.C., 1969, U.S. Supreme Ct., 1981. Law clk. to Hon. Edward A. Beard Superior Ct. D.C., 1968-69; asst. U.S. atty. for D.C., 1969-74; ptnr. Stein, Miller & Brodsky, 1974-85; pres. Warren L. Miller, P.C., 1986—; of counsel Reed, Smith, Shaw & McClay, 1986-93; lectr. Georgetown U. Law Sch., 1970-71, Am. U., 1971-72; guest spkr. various TV programs and legal forums; mem. Jud. Conf. D.C. Cir., 1984—; pres. Asst. U.S. Attys. Assn. of D.C., 1983-84. contbr. articles to profl. jours. Parliamentarian credentials and rules coms. Rep. Nat. Conv., 1984, commr. D.C. Law Revision Commn., 1987-91 (apptd. by Pres. Reagan); commr. U.S. Commn. for Preservation of Am.'s Heritage Abroad, 1992— (apptd. by Pres. Bush, reapptd. by Pres. Clinton 1996); bd. dirs. Found. for Buchenwald and Mittelbau-Dora Memls., 1994—; spkr. ceremonies commemorating 50th anniversary of liberation of Buchenwald Concentration Camp, Buchenwald, Germany, 1995; spkr. U.S. Holocaust Meml. Mus., 1995; fundraiser for Rep. Nat. Com. and Pres. Bush, 1988-92; co-chmn. dinner for V.P. Bush, 1988; vice-chmn. Pres.'s Dinner, 1989; co-chmn. Pres.'s Club, Washington, 1990-92; chmn. fundraiser for U.S. Senator Christopher Bond, 1992, 97; chmn., fundraiser U.S. Senator John Warner, 1996; vice-chmn., fundraiser Senator Bob Dole, 1996; co-chmn., fundraiser Gov. George W. Bush Jr. Presdl. Exploratory Com., 1999. Mem. Congl. Country Club (Bethesda, Md.), Phi Delta Phi, Omicron Delta Kappa, Pi Gamma Mu. Office: 2300 N St NW Washington DC 20037-1122

**MILLER, WAYNE HAMILTON,** lawyer; b. Arlington, Va., Dec. 27, 1944; married Beverly Harrison, Jan. 20, 1968; children: Brooke Harrison, Noah Harrison. BSEE, Duke Univ., 1966; MBA, Univ. Conn., 1973; JD, Harvard Law Sch., 1976. Ptnr. Hill & Barlow, Boston, 1976—. Chmn., mem. Historic Dist. Commn., Concord, Mass., 1989-98. With US Navy, 1966-69. Mem. Am. Bar Assn. Democrat. Pension, profit-sharing, and employee benefits, Corporate taxation. Home: 54 Lexington Rd Concord MA 01742-2520 Office: Hill & Barlow One Internat Pl Boston MA 02110

**MILLER, WILLIAM CARL,** lawyer; b. Biloxi, Miss., Nov. 19, 1955; s. Harold Eugene and Kathryn Cordelia (McPherson) M.; m. Moira Halsey Anderson, Nov. 21, 1993; 1 child, Olivia Kathryn Miller. BA, U. So. Ala., Mobile, 1983, MA in English Lit., 1985; JD, U. Miss., Oxford, 1988. Owner Billy's Hole in the Wall, Biloxi, Miss., 1976-85; assoc. Levi & Denham, Ocean Springs, Miss., 1988-90; sole practitioner William Carl Miller Law Firm, Biloxi, Miss., 1990-94; ptnr. McDonnell & Miller, Biloxi, 1994-95; mng. ptnr. Miller & Fowlkes, PLLC, Biloxi, 1995—. Served with USN, 1972-76. Mem. ATLA, Miss. Trial Lawyers Assn., Harrison County Bar Assn., Biloxi Bar Assn., Miss. Bar Assn., Nat. Assn. Criminal Def. Lawyers. Democrat. General civil litigation, Criminal, Civil rights. Office: Miller & Fowlkes PLLC 2555 Marshall Rd Biloxi MS 39531-4705

**MILLER, WILLIAM SCOTT,** lawyer; b. Williford, Ark., Apr. 15, 1921; s. William Scott and Thelma (Camp) M.; m. Margaret Imogene Puckett, May 9, 1944; children: Gary, Alan. BS, Miss. State U., 1943; LLB, U. Ark., 1949. Assoc. Eichenbaum Law Firm, Little Rock, Ark., 1948-51, ptnr., 1951—. Chmn. bd. Bapt. Med. System, Little Rock, 1985-86; pres. Little Rock Boys Club, 1979-80. Mem. Pulaski County Bar Assn. (pres. 1964-65). Avocations: pottery, fishing. Corporate taxation, Real property, Labor. Office: Eichenbaum Law Firm 124 W Capitol Ave Little Rock AR 72201-3704

**MILLER-LERMAN, LINDSEY,** state supreme court justice; b. L.A., July 30, 1947. BA, Wellesley Coll., 1968; JD, Columbia U., 1973; LHD (hon.), Coll. of St. Mary, Omaha, 1993. Bar: N.Y. 1974, U.S. Dist. Ct. (so. dist.) N.Y. 1974, U.S. Ct. Appeals (2d cir.) 1974, Nebr. 1976, U.S. Dist. Ct. Nebr. 1976, U.S. Ct. Appeals (8th cir.) 1979, U.S. Supreme Ct. 1982, U.S. Ct. Appeals (6th cir.) 1984, U.S. Ct. Appeals (10th cir.) 1987. Law clk. U.S. Dist. Ct., N.Y.C., 1973-75; from assoc. to ptnr. Kutak Rock, Omaha, 1975-92; judge Nebr. Ct. Appeals, Lincoln, 1992-98, chief judge, 1996-98; justice Nebr. Supreme Ct., 1998—. Contbr. articles to profl. jours. Bd. dirs. Tuesday Musical, Omaha, 1985—. Office: Nebr Supreme Ct State Capitol Rm 222 Lincoln NE 68509*

**MILLHAUSER, MARGUERITE SUE,** lawyer; b. Balt., Dec. 30, 1953; d. Ernest and Gusti (Rosner) M. BS, U. Md., 1974, JD, 1977. Bar: Md. 1977, D.C. 1978. Instr. U. Md., College Park, 1975; assoc. Steptoe & Johnson, Washington, 1977-84, ptnr., 1985-87; lectr. law U. Md., 1987; founder, prin. CONFLICT Cons., Washington, 1988—. Author: The Unspoken Resistance to Alternative Dispute Resolution, In Choosing ADR, The People, As Well As the Problem, Count, Rush to Meditation, Where is the Bandwagon Going, ADR as a Process of Change, Gladiators and Conciliators-- ADR: A Law Firm Staple, Integrating ADR into Law Firm Practice, Corporate Culture and ADR Teaching by Example: Can We Do H?, ADR As a Process of Change, ADR-A Conversation; editor: Sourcebook: Federal Agency Use of Alternative Means of Dispute Resolution; creator (video) Paths to Resolution, 1990. Mem. Am. Arbitration Assn. (panel of arbitrators and mediators), Soc. Profls. in Disbute Resolution, Order of Coif. Office: 2604 Connecticut Ave NW Washington DC 20008-1547

**MILLIGAN, CYNTHIA HARDIN,** university dean, lawyer. BA, U. Kans., 1967; JD, George Washington U., 1970. Bar: D.C. 1970, Nebr. 1977. Assoc. Arent, Fox, Kintnor, Plotkin & Kahn, Washington, 1970-77; ptnr. Rembolt, Ludtke, Milligan & Berger, Lincoln, Nebr., 1977-87; dir. Nebr. Dept. Banking and Fin., Lincoln, 1987-91; pres. CMA, Lincoln, 1991-98; dean U. Nebr. Coll. Bus. Adminstrn., Lincoln, 1998—; bd. dirs. Wells Fargo & Co., San Francisco, Gallup Orgn., Princeton, N.J. Trustee W.K. Kellogg Found., Battle Creek, Mich. Fellow Nebr. Bar Found.; mem. Nebr. Bar Assn. Office: U Nebr Coll Bus Adminstrn PO Box 880405 Lincoln NE 68588-0405

**MILLIGRAM, STEVEN IRWIN,** lawyer; b. N.Y.C., July 16, 1953; s. Harry William and Judith Edith (Soffen) M.; children: David Michael, Brian Harry. BA, SUNY, Buffalo, 1976; JD, Pace U., 1981. Bar: N.Y. 1982, U.S. Dist. Ct. (ea. and so. dists.) N.Y. 1982, N.J. 1982, U.S. Dist. Ct. N.J. 1982, U.S. Dist. Ct. (no. dist.) N.Y. 1993. Asst. dist. atty. County of Bronx, N.Y., 1982-86; assoc. Meiselman, Farber, Packman & Eberz, Poughkeepsie, N.Y., 1986-91; assoc. Drake, Sommers, Loeb, Tarshis and Catania, P.C., Newburgh, N.Y., 1991-96, ptnr., 1996—; founding atty. Bedford (N.Y.) Mt. Kisco Youth Ct., 1984-85; lectr. Nat. Bus. Inst., 1991, 92, Practising Law Inst., 1993. Contbg. author: Trial Advocacy in New York, 1991, Civil Trial Procedures in New York, 1991, Winning the Slip and Fall Case, 1993. Mem. ABA, Assn. Trial Lawyers Am., N.Y. State Trial Lawyers Assn., N.Y. State Bar Assn., Fed. Bar Council, Pace U. Alumni Assn. Democrat. Jewish. E-mail: smilligram@dsltc.com. State civil litigation, Personal injury, Insurance. Home: 22 Redwood Dr Highland Mls NY 10930-2813 Office: Drake Sommers Loeb Tarshis and Catania One Corwin Ct Newburgh NY 12550

**MILLIKEN, CHARLES BUCKLAND,** lawyer; b. New Haven, June 2, 1931; s. Arthur and Susan Lord (Buckland) M.; m. Sandra Stewart, July 6, 1957; children: Susan S., Andrew S. BA, Yale U., 1952; JD, Harvard U., 1957. Bar: Conn. 1957. Assoc., Shipman & Goodwin, Hartford, Conn., 1957-60, ptnr., 1961-92, counsel, 1993—; lectr. law corp. taxation U. Conn. Trustee Westminster Sch., Simsbury, Conn., 1969—, sec., 1970-74, chmn., 1974-80; bd. dirs. Hartford Symphony, 1959-74, 1980—, sec., 1960-62, pres., 1962-64; bd. dirs. Greater Hartford Arts Council, 1971-90; trustee Hartt Sch. Music, 1980-94, 95—, chmn., 1988-90; regent U. Hartford, 1988-94. With U.S. Army, 1952-54. Fellow Am. Coll. Trust and Estate Counsel, Am. Coll. Tax Counsel; mem. ABA, Conn. Bar Assn. (chmn. tax sect. 1979-82), Hartford County Bar Assn. Contbr. articles on law to profl. jours. Taxation, general, General corporate, Probate. Home: 56 Ely Rd Farmington CT 06032-1707 Office: 1 American Row Hartford CT 06103-2833

**MILLIMET, ERWIN,** lawyer; b. N.Y.C., Oct. 7, 1925; s. Maurice and Henrietta (Cohen) M.; m. Mary Malia; children: Robert, James, Rachel, Sarah. BA magna cum laude, Amherst Coll., 1948; LLB cum laude, Harvard U., 1951. Bar: N.Y. 1952. Formerly sr. ptnr., chmn. exec. com. Stroock & Stroock & Lavan, N.Y.C., ret. 1991. Mem. bd. visitors U. San Diego Law Sch.; mem. faculty Grad. Sch. Mgmt., U. Mass.; active Nat. Support Group for Africa; founder Citizens for Am., Washington, 1984; mem. Rep. Presdl. Task Force; mem. Rep. Club, N.Y.C. and Washington. Served with inf. U.S. Army, 1943-46. Mem. N.Y. State Bar Assn., Assn. of Bar of City of N.Y., Fed. Bar Assn., Phi Beta Kappa. General corporate, Mergers and acquisitions, Securities.

**MILLMAN, BRUCE RUSSELL,** lawyer; b. Bronx, N.Y., June 4, 1948; s. Meyer and Garie (Solomon) M.; m. Lorrie Jan Liss, Aug. 12, 1973; children: Noemi, Avi. AB, Princeton U., 1970; JD, Columbia U., 1973. Bar: N.Y. 1974, U.S. Dist. Ct. (ea. and so. dists.) N.Y. 1975, U.S. Ct. Appeals (2nd cir.) 1978, U.S. Supreme Ct. 1978. Assoc. Rains & Pogrebin and predecessors Rains, Pogrebin & Scher, Mineola, N.Y., 1973-79, ptnr., 1980—; arbitrator Nassau County Dist. Ct., Mineola, 1981-83. Contbr. New York Employment Law, 1995, Labor and Employment Law for the Corporate Counselor and General Practitioner, 1994, Updating Issues in Employment Law, 1986, Public Sector Labor and Employment Law, 1988. Bd. dirs. West Side Montessori Sch., N.Y.C., 1984-90, sec. 1985-87, pres. 1987-90. Harlan Fiske Stone scholar Columbia U. Law Sch., N.Y.C., 1971, 73. Mem. ABA, N.Y. State Bar Assn. (chairperson labor and employment law sect. 1997-98), Nassau County Bar Assn., Indsl. Rels. Rsch. Assn. (bd. dirs. L.I. chpt. 1984—, pres. 95-96). Bd. dirs. West Side Montessori Sch., N.Y.C., 1984-90, sec. 1985-87, pres., 1987-90. Labor, Civil rights, Education and schools. Home: 60 Riverside Dr New York NY 10024-6108 Office: Rains & Pogrebin PC 210 Old Country Rd Ste 12 Mineola NY 11501-4288 also: 375 Park Ave New York NY 10152-0002

**MILLMAN, JODE SUSAN,** lawyer; b. Poughkeepsie, N.Y., Dec. 28, 1954; d. Samuel Keith and Ellin Sadenberg (Bainder) M.; m. Michael James Harris, June 20, 1982; children: Maxwell, Benjamin. BA, Syracuse U., 1976, JD, 1979. Bar: N.Y. 1980, U.S. Dist. Ct. (so. and ea. dists.) N.Y. 1982, U.S. Supreme Ct. 1983. Asst. corp. counsel City of Poughkeepsie, 1979-81; assoc. Law Office of Lou Lewis, Poughkeepsie, 1981-85; pvt. practice Poughkeepsie, 1985—; staff counsel City of Poughkeepsie Office of Property Devel., 1990—; gen. mgr. WCZX-Communicatons Corp. Author: (children's books) Birthday Wishes and Rock'n Roll Dreams, The Firebird Ballet, Goldie Lox and the Three Behrs; contbg. author: Kaminstein Legislative History of the Copyright Law, 1979. Pres. Dutchess County (N.Y.) Vis. Bur., 1980-82; bd. dirs. Poughkeepsie Ballet Theater, 1982, Jewish Comty. Ctr., 1988; mem. assigned counsel program Dutchess County Family Ct., 1985—; trustee Greater Poughkeepsie Libr. Dist., 1991-94, Poughkeepsie Day Sch., 1995—. Mem. N.Y. State Bar Assn., Dutchess County Bar Assn. (grievance com. 1994—), Mid-Hudson Women's Bar Assn. Democrat. Jewish. Entertainment, General corporate, Family and matrimonial. Office: 97 Cannon St Poughkeepsie NY 12601-3303

**MILLNER, ROBERT B.,** lawyer; b. N.Y.C., Apr. 20, 1950; s. Nathan and Babette E. (Leventhal) M.; m. Susan Brent, June 5, 1983; children: Jacob, Daniel, Rebecca. BA, Wesleyan U., 1971; JD, U. Chgo., 1975. Bar: Ill. 1975. Law clk. to Hon. George C. Edwards U.S. Ct. Appeals for 6th Cir., Cin., 1975-76; with Sonnenschein Nath & Rosenthal, Chgo., 1976—, ptnr., 1982—; mem. Panel of Bankruptcy Trustees, Chgo., 1992-97. Editorial bd. Jour. Corp. Disclosure and Confidentiality, 1989-92; contbr. articles to profl. jours. Trustee Anshe Emet Synagogue, Chgo., 1990-93; v.p. Am. Jewish Cong. midwest region, 1995—. Fellow Am. Bar Found.; mem. ABA (co-chair bankruptcy and insolvency com. litigation sect. 1992-95), Am. Bankruptcy Inst., Chgo. Bar Assn., Comml. Bar Assn. (hon. overseas mem.), Legal Club, Std. Club, Wesleyan Alumni Club Chgo. (pres. 1988-90), Phi Beta Kappa. Bankruptcy, Federal civil litigation, Contracts commercial. Office: Sonnenschein Nath & Rosenthal 8000 Sears Tower Chicago IL 60606

**MILLS, CHARLES GARDNER,** lawyer; b. Griffin, Ga., Feb. 29, 1940; s. Charles G. and Marguerite (Powell) M. AB, Yale U., 1962; JD, Boston Coll., 1967. Bar: N.Y. 1967, U.S. Dist. Ct. (so. and ea. dists.) 1972, U.S. Ct. Appeals (2d cir.) 1975, U.S. Supreme Ct., 1977, U.S. Ct. Claims 1991, U.S. Ct. Vets. Appeals 1996, U.S. Ct. Appeals (fed. cir.) 1997, U.S. Dist. Ct. (no. dist.) N.Y. 1999. Assoc. Smart & McKay, N.Y.C., 1967-68, Smart & Mills, N.Y.C., 1969-71, Eaton & VanWinkle, N.Y.C., 1971-82, Payne, Wood & Littlejohn, Glen Cove and Melville, N.Y., 1982-91; pvt. practice, Glen Cove, 1991—. With U.S. Army, 1962-64, ETO. Mem. N.Y. State Bar Assn., Assn. Bar City N.Y., Nassau County Bar Assn., Rotary (pres. Glen Cove Club 1989-90), Am. Legion (comdr. Locust Valley, N.Y. post 1988-90, comdr. Nassau County com. 1995-96, N.Y. Judge Advocate, 1998—), Soc. Colonial Wars, SCV, Order of the Arrow. Republican. Roman Catholic. Federal civil litigation, Libel, Civil rights. Office: 56 School St Glen Cove NY 11542-2512

**MILLS, EDWARD JAMES,** lawyer, insurance consultant; b. Pitts., Jan. 16, 1954; s. Joseph Christopher and Marie Claire (Good) M.; m. Carol Donaghy, Aug. 4, 1979; children: Kymberly Shannon, Michael Edward. BA, U. Pitts., 1976; JD cum laude, Duquesne U., 1985. Bar: Pa. 1985, U.S. Dist. Ct. (we. dist.) Pa. 1985. Claims adjuster U.S. Fidelity & Guaranty Ins. Co., Pitts, 1977-85; claims mgr. Allegheny Internat. Inc., Pitts, 1985-87; gen. counsel, ins. cons. J&H Marsh & McLennan Inc., Pitts, 1987—; mem. policy rev. com. X.L. Ins. Co., 1989-96; mem. ins. Litigation Evaluation Com., Pitts., 1988. Mem. Duquesne Law Rev., 1982-85. Recipient Am. Jurisprudence award 1982-83; Senatorial scholar, 1975. Mem. ABA (standing com. on probate and estate planning 1987-88), Pa. Bar Assn. Personal injury, Professional liability, Toxic tort. Home: 3511 Wallace Dr Pittsburgh PA 15227-4425 Office: J&H Marsh & McLennan Inc 300 6th Ave Pittsburgh PA 15222-2514

**MILLS, KEVIN PAUL,** lawyer; b. Detroit, Oct. 1, 1961; s. Raymond Eugene and Helene Audrey M.; m. Holly Beth Fechner, June 15, 1986. BA, Oberlin Coll., 1983; JD, U. Mich., 1987. Bar: Mich. 1988. High sch. tchr., asst. dir. summer environ. inst. The Storm King Sch., Cornwall-on-Hudson, N.Y., 1983-84; staff atty. E. Mich. Environ. Action Coun., Birmingham, Mich., 1987-90; assoc. Tucker & Rolf, Southfield, Mich., 1988-89; sr. atty., pollution prevention program dir. Environ. Def. Fund, Washington, 1990—; low-level radioactive waste cons. State Mich., Lansing, 1988; founder Pollution Prevention Alliance, 1991, co-founder Great Printer's Project, 1992—, staff to co-chair eco-efficiency Pres. Coun. Sustainable Devel., 1993-95, Auto Pollution Prevention adv. group, 1994-98, EPA Auto Mfr. CSI, 1994-97; mem. adv. bd. Nat. Pollution Prevention Roundtable, 1996—; mem. adv. com. Working Group on Cmty. Right-to-Know, 1997—; mem. Nat. Adv. Coun. on Environ. Policy and Tech., 1997—. Bd. dirs., v.p. Ea. Mich. Environ. Action Coun., Birmingham, 1985-87; pres. Environ. Law Soc., Ann Arbor, Mich., 1986-87. Mem. State Bar Mich. Environmental, Transportation. Office: Environ Def Fund 1875 Connecticut Ave NW Washington DC 20009-5728

**MILLS, LAWRENCE,** lawyer, business and transportation consultant; b. Salt Lake City, Aug. 15, 1932; s. Samuel L. and Beth (Neilson) M. BS, U. Utah, 1955, JD, 1956. Bar: Utah 1956, ICC 1961, U.S. Supreme Ct. 1963. With W.S. Hatch Co. Inc., Woods Cross, Utah, 1947-89, gen. mgr., 1963-89, v.p., 1970-89, also dir.; bd. dirs. Nat. Tank Truck Carriers, Inc., Washington, 1963—, pres., 1974-75, chmn. bd., 1975-76; mem. motor carrier adv. com. Utah State Dept. Transp., 1979—; keynote speaker Rocky Mountain Safety Suprs. Conf., 1976; mem. expedition to Antartica, 1996, Titanic Expedition, 1996. Contbr. articles to legal and profl. jours. and transp. publs. Del. to County and State Convs., Utah, 1970-72; v.p. Utah Safety Coun., 1979-82, bd. dirs., 1979—, pres., 1983-84; mem. Utah Gov's Adv. Com. on Small Bus.; capt. Easter Seal Telethon, 1989, 90; state vice chmn. High Frontier, 1987—; mem. adv. com. Utah State Indsl. Commn., 1988—, chmn. com. studying health care cost containment and reporting requirements 1990—; mem. expdn. to Antarctica, 1996, Titanic '96 expedition. Recipient Safety Dir. award Nat. Tank Carriers Co., 1967, Outstanding Svc. and Contbn. award, 1995, Trophy award W.S. Hatch Co., 1975, Disting. Svc. award Utah State Indsl. Commn., 1992, Outstanding Svc. award Utah Safety Coun., 1994. Mem. Salt Lake County Bar Assn., Utah Motor Transport Assn. (dir. 1967—, pres. 1974-76, Outstanding Achievement Award 1989), Utah Hwy. Users Assn. (dir. 1981—), Indsl. Rels. Coun. (dir. 1974—), Salt Lake City C. of C., U.S. Jaycees (life Senator 1969—, ambassador 1977—, pres. Utah Senate 1979-80, Henry Giessenbier fellow 1989), Nat. Petroleum Coun., Utah Associated Gen. Contractors (assoc. 1975-77, 88—), Silver Tank Club, Hillsdale Coll. President's Club, Traveler's Century Club. Administrative and regulatory, Transportation. Home and Office: 77 Edgecombe Dr Salt Lake City UT 84103-2219 *Personal philosophy: Excessive government regulation stifles individual initiative. We should learn from the downfall of communism.*

**MILLS, MICHAEL PAUL,** state supreme court justice; b. Charleston, S.C., Aug. 25, 1956; s. Paul H. and Shirley (Dulaney) M.; m. Mona Robinson, Aug. 2, 1976; children: Alysson, Chip, Rebekah, Penn. AA, Itawamba C.C., Fulton, Miss., 1976; BA, U. Miss., 1978, JD, 1980. Bar: Miss. 1980, U.S. Ct. Appeals (fed. cir.) 1986, U.S. Ct. Appeals (5th cir.) 1980, U.S. Supreme Ct. 1990. Pvt. practice, Miss., 1980-95; legis. Miss. Ho. of Reps., Jackson, 1983-95, chmn. jud. com., 1992-95; mem. Nat. Conf. Commrs. on Uniform State Laws, 1993—; justice Miss. Supreme Ct., Jackson, 1995—. Home: PO Box 38 Fulton MS 38843-0038

**MILLS, RICHARD HENRY,** federal judge; b. Beardstown, Ill., July 19, 1929; s. Myron Epler and Helen Christine (Greve) M.; m. Rachel Ann Keagle, June 16, 1962; children: Jonathan K., Daniel Cass. BA, Ill. Coll., 1951; JD, Mercer U., 1957; LLM, U. Va., 1982. Bar: Ill. 1957, U.S. Dist. Ct. Ill. 1958, U.S. Ct. Appeals 1959, U.S. Ct. Mil. Appeals 1963, U.S. Supreme Ct. 1963. Legal advisor Ill. Youth Commn., 1958-60; state's atty. Cass County, Virginia, Ill., 1960-64; judge Ill. 8th Jud. Cir., Virginia, 1966-76, Ill. 4th Dist. Appellate Ct., Springfield, Ill., 1976-85, U.S. Dist. Ct. (cen. dist.) Ill., Springfield, 1985—; adj. prof. So. Ill. U. Sch. Medicine, 1985—; mem. adv. bd. Nat. Inst. Corrections, Washington, 1984-88, Ill. Supreme Ct. Rules Com., Chgo., 1963-85. Contbr. articles to profl. jours. Pres. Abraham Lincoln coun. Boy Scouts Am., 1978-80. With U.S. Army, 1952-54, Korea, col. res.; maj. gen. Ill. Militia. Recipient George Washington Honor medal Freedoms Found., 1969, 73, 75, 82, Disting. Eagle Scout Boy Scouts Am., 1985. Fellow Am. Bar Found.; mem. ABA (joint com. profl. sanctions), Nat. Conf. Fed. Trial Judges (exec. com.), Ill. Bar Assn., Chgo. Bar Assn., Cass County Bar Assn. (pres. 1962-64, 75-76), Sangamon County Bar Assn., 7th Cir. Bar Assn., Am. Law Inst., Fed. Judges Assn., Army and Navy Club (Washington), Sangamo Club, Masons (33 degree). Republican. Office: US Dist Ct Ste 117 600 E Monroe St Springfield IL 62701-1626

**MILLSTEIN, DAVID J.,** lawyer; b. N.Y.C., Apr. 15, 1953; s. Stanley and Irma (Klein) M. AB, U. Calif., Berkeley, 1975, JD, 1979. Bar: Calif. 1979, U.S. Dist. Ct. (no. dist.) Calif. 1979, U.S. Dist. Ct. (ea. dist.) Calif. 1984. Assoc. Bostwick & Tehin, San Francisco, 1991-93; asst. dist. atty. San Francisco Dist. Atty.'s Office, 1993—; pvt. practice San Francisco, 1982-95, 97—; ptnr. Millstein & Doolittle, San Francisco, 1996-97; chief asst. dist. Atty. City and County of San Francisco, 1996; ptnr. Millstein & Assocs., San Francisco, 1997—; judge pro tem San Francisco Mcpl. Ct., 1983—; probation monitor Calif. State Bar, 1995—; panelist Calif. Psychol. Assn.; lectr. San Francisco Gen. Hosp., Stanford U., 1994, Boalt Hall Sch. of Law, U. Calif., Berkeley, 1995-96; adj. prof. Hastings Coll. Law, San Francisco, 1993-96, co-chair advocacy sect., 1994-95; legal analyst KBO-ABC News, San Francisco, 1995—, KTVV-Fox News, Oakland, Calif., 1994—; chief asst. dist. atty. City and County of San Francisco, 1996. Author supplement to How to Prepare For, Take and Use a Deposition, 1995; contbr. articles to law jours. Office: 580 California St Ste 500 San Francisco CA 94104-1000

**MILMAN, ALYSSA ANN,** lawyer, educator; b. Bklyn., Jan. 16, 1969; d. Leon Arthur and Barbara Lee (Hoops) M. Grad., U. Mass., 1989; JD, Calif. Western U., San Diego, 1992. Bar: Calif. 1992, U.S. Ct. Appeals (9th cir.) 1992. Asoc. Angelo & Assocs., Newport Beach, Calif., 1992-97; ptnr. Angelo & Milman, Newport Beach, Calif., 1999—; adj. prof. Whittier Law Sch., Costa Mesa, Calif., 1998. Editor Calif. Western Law Rev./Internat. Law Jour., 1991-92. Vol., Shortshop, Orange County, 1995—, VIP, Orange County, 1995—. Mem. ABA, Orange County Bar Assn. Avocations: running, tennis, skiing. Fax: 949-644-0803. E-mail: alyssa@milmanlaw.com. State civil litigation, Personal injury, General corporate. Office: Angelo and Milman 23 Corporate Plaza Dr Ste 135 Newport Beach CA 92660-7912

**MILMED, PAUL KUSSY,** lawyer; b. Newark, Oct. 15, 1944; s. Leon Sidney and Bella (Kussy) M.; m. Debra R. Anisman, Oct. 23, 1988; children: Laura, Julia. AB, Amherst Coll., 1966; MSc, U. London, 1968; EdM, Harvard U., 1969; JD, NYU, 1975. Bar: N.J. 1975, N.Y. 1976, U.S. Ct. Appeals (2d cir.) 1975, U.S. Dist. Ct. N.J. 1975, U.S. Dist. Ct. (so. dist.) N.Y. 1976, U.S. Dist. Ct. (ea. dist.) N.Y. 1994. Law clk. Hon. Alan B. Handler N.J. Superior Ct. Appellate Divsn., Newark, 1975-76; assoc. Weil, Gotshal & Manges, N.Y.C., 1976-83; asst. U.S. atty. U.S. Atty.'s Office, So. Dist. N.Y., N.Y.C., 1983-93, chief environ. protection unit, 1990-93; of counsel White & Case, N.Y.C., 1993—; ct.-apptd. mediator U.S. Dist. Ct., So. Dist. N.Y., 1996—. Rsch. editor NYU Rev. of Law and Social Change, 1974-75; editl. adv. bd. Fordham Environ. Law Jour., 1993—; contbr. articles to profl. jours. Mem. bd. trustees The Town Sch., N.Y.C. Mem. ABA, Assn. Bar City of N.Y. Avocation: photography. General civil litigation, Environmental, Alternative dispute resolution. Home: One Gracie Terr New York NY 10028 Office: White & Case 1155 Avenue Of The Americas New York NY 10036-2787

**MILMOE, J. GREGORY,** lawyer; b. White Plains, N.Y., 1947. AB, Cornell U., 1970; JD, Fordham U., 1975. Bar: N.Y. 1976. Mem. Skadden, Arps, Slate, Meagher & Flom, N.Y.C. Articles editor: Fordham Law Review, 1974-75. Office: Skadden Arps Slate Meagher & Flom 919 3rd Ave New York NY 10022-3902

**MILNE, GARY E.,** lawyer; b. L.A., Oct. 5, 1940; s. Edward A. and Eleonora L. Milne; children: Sean J., Ryan A. BS, U. Calif., Santa Barbara, 1964; JD, Ventura County Law Sch., 1975. Bar: Calif. 1976. Sole practitioner Ventura, Calif., 1976%. Capt. U.S. Army, 1964-72, ETO. State civil litigation. Office: Gary & Milne 2323 Portola Rd Ste 100 Ventura CA 93003-7768

**MILNER, KENNETH PAUL,** lawyer; b. Phila., June 2, 1951; s. Stanley O. and Marcia Elva Milner; m. Ruth Marie Kosonovich, June 16, 1973; children: Zachary Stanton, Adrienne Nicole. BA, U. Pa., 1973; JD, Boston U., 1976. Bar: Pa. 1976, U.S. Dist. Ct. (ea. dist.) Pa. 1976. Assoc. Law Office of Donald Joel, Phila., 1976-77; assoc. counsel, gen. counsel Cottman Transmission System, Inc., Ft. Washington, Pa., 1977-82; owner Law Office of Kenneth P. Milner, Phila., 1982-88; ptnr. Gold & Bowman, Phila., 1988-90, Starfield & Payne, P.C., Ft. Washington, 1990-94; dir., shareholder McTighe, Weiss, O'Rourke & Milner, P.C., Norristown, Pa., 1994—; Sec., vice chair Montgomery County Realtor/Atty. Joint Liaison Com., 1996—. Contbr. articles to profl. jours. Counsel, mem. exec. bd. Montgomery County Literacy Network, 1996—; co-chair diversity Upper Dublin (Pa.) Strategic Planning Com., 1993-96. Recipient Chmn.'s award Am. Heart Assn., Eastern Montgomery, Pa., 1996. Mem. ABA, Pa. Bar Assn., Montgomery Bar Assn. (chair franchise law com. 1994-98, mem. long range planning com. 1998—, bd. dirs. 1999—, mem. exec. com. 1999—), Upper Dublin Soccer club (bd. dirs., sec. 1990-96). Franchising, General corporate, Real property. Office: McTighe Weiss O'Rourke & Milner PC PO Box 510 Norristown PA 19404-0510

**MILONE, FRANCIS MICHAEL,** lawyer; b. Phila., June 18, 1947; s. Michael Nicholas and Frances Theresa (Fair) M.; m. Maida R. Crane, Nov. 25, 1991; children: Michael, Matthew. BA, LaSalle Coll., 1969; MS, Pa. State U., 1971; JD, U. Pa., 1974. Bar: Pa. 1974, U.S. Dist. Ct. (ea dist.) Pa. 1974, U.S. Dist. Ct. (mid. dist.) Pa. 1979, U.S. Dist. Ct. (ea. dist.) Mich. 1983, U.S. Ct. Appeals (3d cir.) 1978, U.S. Ct. Appeals (4th and 5th cirs.) 1979, U.S. Supreme Ct. 1979. Assoc. Montgomery, McCraken, Walker & Rhoads, Phila., 1974-77; ptnr. Morgan, Lewis & Bockius, Phila., 1977—. Mem. ABA (labor and litigation sects.), Pa. Bar Assn., Phila. Bar Assn. Labor, Federal civil litigation, State civil litigation. Home: 912 Field Ln Villanova PA 19085-2003 Office: Morgan Lewis & Bockius 1701 Market St Philadelphia PA 19103-2903

**MILSTEIN, ELLIOTT STEVEN,** legal educator, academic administrator; b. Hartford, Conn., Oct. 19, 1944; s. Samuel M. and Mildred K. Milstein; m. Bonnie Myrun, Oct. 1, 1967 (div. Oct. 1992); 1 child, Jacob. BA, U. Hartford, 1966, LLD (hon.), 1997; JD, U. Conn., 1969; LLM, Yale U., 1971. Bar: Conn. 1969, D.C. 1972, U.S. Dist. Ct. Conn. 1969, U.S. Ct. Appeals (D.C.) 1972. Lectr. in law U. Conn. Clin. Program. 1969-70; staff atty. New Haven Legal Assistance Assn., 1971-72; asst. prof. law, dir. clin. programs Washington coll. law Am. U., 1972-74, assoc. prof., dir. clin. programs, 1974-77, prof., dir. clin. programs, 1977-88, interim dean, 1988-90, dean, 1990—, assoc. dean Law Sch., 1977-78, interim pres., 1993-94; dean. Washington Coll. Law Am. Univ., 1994-95, prof. law, 1995—; co-dir. Nat. Vets. Law Ctr., 1978-84; cons. Calif. Bar Bd. of Bar Admissions, Nat. Conf. of Bar Examiners, lawyer tng. Practising Law Inst., N.Y.C.; chmn. D.C. Law Students in Ct. Program, 1982-83; mem. Law Tchrs. for Legal Svcs. Bd. dirs. Alliance for Justice, 1996-97. Ford Urban Law fellow, 1971-72. Mem. Soc. Am. Law Tchrs., Assn. Am. Law Schs. (chmn. sect. clin. edn. 1982, mem. accreditation com. 1984-86, chmn. standing com. clin. edn. 1993—, exec. com. 1996—, pres.-elect 1999), ABA (skills tng. com. 1983-85, govt. rels. com. 1992—), ACLU. Democrat. Home: 3216 Brooklawn Ct Bethesda MD 20815-3941 Office: Am U Washington Coll Law 4801 Massachusetts Ave NW Washington DC 20016-8196

**MILSTEIN, RICHARD CRAIG,** lawyer; b. N.Y.C., July 16, 1946; s. Max and Hattie (Jacobson) Worchel; children: Brian Matthew, Rachel Helanie. AA with honors, Miami-Dade Jr. Coll., 1966, AB cum laude, U. Miami, Fla., 1968, JD, 1973. Bar: Fla. 1974, U.S. Dist. Ct. Fla. 1974, U.S. Ct. Appeals (5th cir.) 1974, U.S. Supreme Ct. 1977, U.S. Ct. Appeals (11th cir.) 1982. Assoc., August, Nimkoff & Pohlig, Miami, Fla., 1974-76; mng. ptnr. Jepeway, August, Gassen & Pohlig, Miami, 1976-78, August, Gassen, Pohlig & Milstein, Miami, 1978-80, August, Pohlig & Milstein, P.A., Coral Gables, Fla., 1980-83; sr. ptnr. Milstein & Wayne, Coral Gables, 1983-85; ptnr. Tescher & Milstein, PA, Coral Gables, 1986-90, Akerman, Senterfitt & Eidson, P.A. 1990—. Co-founder Dade County Vol. Lawyers for Arts; mem. Met. Dade County Ind. Rev. Panel, 1984-86; councilor Metro Dade County Cultural Affairs Coun., 1986-91; sec./treas. Ops. SafeDrive, 1988; bd. dirs. South Fla. Mediation Ctr., 1982-89, chmn. bd. dirs., 1985-86; bd. dirs. Ptnrs. for Youth, 1981-91, Bet Shira Congregation, 1986—, pres., 1985-86, South Fla. Inter-Profl. Council Inc., 1986-87, v.p., 1985-86, sec. 1984-85, bd. dirs., 1983—; bd. dirs. Dance Umbrella Inc., 1983-87, Miami Coalition Inc., 1988-94; Fla. bar elder law sect., chair U. Miami, 1996-97; chair Dade County Cultural Alliance, 1993—. Fellow Am. Coll. Trust and Estate Counsel, Nat. Acad. Elder Law, Nat. Coun. Aging; mem. ABA, Am. Trial Lawyers Assn., Dade County Bar Assn. (dir. 1980-83, treas. 1983-84, sec. 1984-85, v.p. 1985-87, pres.-elect 1987-88, pres. 1988-89,), Coral Gables Bar Assn., Fla. Bar Assn. (professionalism com. guest lectr. real property and probate sect., Pro Bono awards 1986), Acad. Fla. Trial Lawyers (City of Miami Beach transition team), U. Miami Law Alumni (pres. 1997—), Phi Theta Kappa, Delta Theta Mu, Omicron Delta Kappa, Phi Alpha Theta, Kappa Delta Pi, Phi Kappa Phi, Alpha Kappa, Zeta Epsilon Nu. Democrat. General practice, Family and matrimonial, Probate. Home: North Bay Island 1311 Bay Ter North Bay Village FL 33141-4002 Office: Akerman Senterfitt & Eidson One SE 3rd Ave Fl 28 Miami FL 33131

**MILSTEON, RACHELLE H. (SHELLY MILSTEON),** lawyer; b. Livingston, N.J., Oct. 6, 1968; m. Jed M. Milstein, Sept. 17, 1994. AB in English with honors, U. Mich., 1990; JD, Georgetown U., 1993. Bar: N.J. 1993, U.S. Dist. Ct. N.J. 1993, U.S. Dist. Ct. N.Y. 1994, U.S. Ct. Appeals (3d cir.) 1998. Law clk. Superior Ct. N.J., Union County, Elizabeth, 1993-94; assoc. Fishman & Callahan, East Hanover, N.J., 1994-98, Shanley & Fisher, Morristown, N.J., 1998—. General civil litigation. Office: Shanley & Fisher 131 Madison Ave Morristown NJ 07960-6097

**MILTON, CHAD EARL,** lawyer; b. Brevard County, Fla., Jan. 29, 1947; s. Rex Dale and Mary Margaret (Peacock) M.; m. Ann Mitchell Bunting, Mar. 30, 1972; children: Samuel, Kathleen, Kelsey. BA, Colo. Coll., 1969; JD, U. Colo., 1974; postgrad., U. Mo., 1976-77. Bar: Colo. 1974, Mo. 1977, U.S. Dist. Ct. Colo. 1974, U.S. Dist. Ct. (we. dist.) Mo. 1977. Counsel Office of Colo. State Pub. Defender, Colo. Springs, 1974-76; pub. info. officer, counsel Mid-Am. Arts Alliance, Kansas City, Mo., 1977-78; claims counsel Employers Reinsurance Corp., Kansas City, Mo., 1978-80; sr. v.p. Media/Profl. Ins., Kansas City, Mo., 1981—; reporter, photographer, editor Golden (Colo.) Daily Transcript, 1970; investigator, law clk. Office of Colo. State Pub. Defender, Denver, Golden, 1970-74; assoc. Gage, Tucker, Hodges, Kreamer, Kelly & Varner (now Lathrop & Gage), Kansas City, 1973; participant Annenberg Project on the Reform of Libel Laws, Washington, 1987-88; adj. prof., comm. and advt. law Webster U., 1989-93; lectr. in field. Pres. bd. dirs. Folly Theater, 1992-94. Mem. ABA (chair intellectual property law com. of the torts and ins. practice sect., forum com. on comm. law), Mo. Bar Assn., Kansas City Met. Bar Assn., Libel Def. Resource Ctr. (editorial bd., exec. com.). Avocations: tennis, golf, skiing, sailing, antique maps. Libel, Trademark and copyright, Insurance. Home: 8821 Alhambra St Shawnee Mission KS 66207-2357 Office: Media and Profl Ins 2 Pershing Sq 2300 Main St Ste 800 Kansas City MO 64108-2415

**MILTON, JOSEPH PAYNE,** lawyer; b. Richmond, Va., Oct. 24, 1943; s. Hubert E. and Grace C. Milton; children: Michael Payne, Amy Barrett, David King; m. Cela Cabler Milton, Apr. 8, 1989. BS in Bus. Adminstrn., U. Fla., 1967, JD, 1969. Bar: Fla. 1969, U.S. Ct. Appeals (5th cir.) 1971, U.S. Supreme Ct. 1972, U.S. Ct. Appeals (11th cir.) 1981. Assoc. Toole, Taylor, Moseley & Gabel, Jacksonville, 1969-70; ptnr. Toole, Taylor, Moseley, Gabel & Milton, Jacksonville, 1971-78, Howell, Liles, Braddock & Milton, Jacksonville, 1978-89, Milton & Leach, Jacksonville, 1990-95, Milton, Leach & D'Andrea, Jacksonville, 1996—. Mem. Mayor's Blue Ribbon Task Force; mem. Law Ctr. Coun., U. Fla. Coll. Law, 1972-78, mem. alumni coun., 1995—; campaign chmn. N.E. Fla. chpt. March of Dimes, 1973-74, v.p., 1974-75; pres. Willing Hands, 1974-75; chmn. attys.' divsn. United Way, 1977; pres. Civic Round Table of Jacksonville, 1980-81; mem. exec. com. Jacksonville Area Legal Aid, Inc., 1982-83; chmn. pvt. bar involvement com. Legal Aid Bd. Dirs., 1982-83. Recipient Outstanding Svc. award for individual contbns. in support of legal svcs. for the poor, 1981. Fellow Am. Bar Found., Internat. Soc. Barristers, Southeastern Admiralty Law (com., dir. Port, Jacksonville 1996-99); mem. ATLA, ABA, Fla. Chpt. Am. Bd. Trial Advs. (treas. 1999, mem. exec. com. 1997—), Am. Bd. Trial Advs. (charter, pres. Jacksonville chpt. 1997, nat. bd. mem. 1999—, chpt. selected as Best in the Nation 1997), Jacksonville Bar Assn. (pres. 1980-81, pres. young lawyers sect. 1974-75, Lawyer of Yr. award 1999), Fla. Bar (bd. cert. civil trial lawyer, bd. cert. admiralty and maritime law, grievance com. 1975-77, chmn. 1976, 4th jud. cir. nominating commn. 1980-82, mem. exec. coun. for trial sect. 1982-89, voluntary bar liaison com. 1982-83, chmn.-elect 1986-87, chmn. 1987, 88, bd. govs. 1988-90, charter mem. admiralty and maritime law bd. cert. 1996—, chmn. 1997, chmn. 4th jud. cir. professionalism com. 1998—, chmn. recipient of Outstanding Professionalism Program 1999), Fla. Coun. Bar Assn. Pres. (exec. com. 1982-88, v.p. 1984, pres. 1985-86), Jacksonville Assn. Def. Counsel (pres. 1981-82, lectr. CLE programs, guest lectr. U. Fla. Nat. Assn. R.R. Trial Counsel), Nat. Assn. R.R. Trial Counsel (exec. com. 1979—, v.p. southeastern region 1984-86, pres.-elect 1989-90, pres. 1990-91), Maritime Law Assn. U.S. (mem. com. professionalism 1996—), Acad. Fla. Trial Lawyers, Am. Judicature Soc., San Jose Country Club, Univ. Club, Gulf Life Tower Club, Country Club Sapphire Valley (N.C.). Republican. Personal injury, Admiralty, General civil litigation. Home: 4655 Corrientes Cir N Jacksonville FL 32217-4329 Office: Milton Leach & D'Andrea 1660 Prudential Dr Ste 200 Jacksonville FL 32207-8181

**MIMBU, ROBERT TERUO,** lawyer; b. Seattle, July 8, 1962; s. William Y. and Toshiko M. BA, U. Washington, 1985; JD, U. Puget Sound, 1990. Bar: Wash. 1991. Assoc. Franco Asian Bensussen Coe, Seattle, 1991-92, Gaitan & Cusack, Seattle, 1993-95, Coe, Nordwall & Liebman, Seattle, 1996—. Immigration, naturalization, and customs. Office: Coe Nordwall & Liebman LLP 720 Olive Way Ste 1300 Seattle WA 98101-1855

**MIMMS, THOMAS BOWMAN, JR.,** lawyer; b. Atlanta, Oct. 11, 1944; s. Thomas Bowman and Alice Buehl Mimms; m. Alison Hayward, July 22, 1967; children: Karen Mimms Swift, Christine Mimms Couret. BA, U. N.C., 1965; JD, Columbia U., 1969. Bar: Fla. 1969, U.S. Dist. Ct. (mid. dist.) Fla. 1972, U.S. Supreme Ct. 1973, U.S. Ct. Appeals (11th cir.) 1981. Assoc. atty. Fleming O'Bryan, Fort Lauderdale, Fla., 1969-72; shareholder Macfarlane Ferguson & McMullen, Tampa, Fla., 1972-99. Fellow Am. Bar Found.; mem. Fla. Bar Assn. (exec. coun. bus. law sect. 1987-99, bus. law legislation com. 1995-99, chair bus. law bankruptcy/UCC com. 1988-89), Tampa Bay Bankruptcy Bar Assn. (pres. 1992-93), Columbia U. Alumni Club (dir. 1991-99), Tiger Bay Club, Grande Krewe de Libertalia. Democrat. Episcopalian. Bankruptcy, Real property, Contracts commercial. Office: Mimms Enterprises 85A Mill St Ste 100 Roswell GA 30075-4910

**MINARDI, RICHARD A., JR.,** lawyer; b. Mobile, Ala., Aug. 15, 1943; s. Richard A. and Martha F. (Beck) M.; m. Frances Archer Guy, Oct. 21, 1989. BA, Yale U., 1965, LLB, 1968. Bar: Va. 1969. Assoc. McGuire Woods & Battle, Richmond, Va., 1968-71; ptnr. Staples, Greenberg Minardi & Kessler, Richmond, 1971-86, Mays & Valentine, Richmond, 1986—. Mem. ABA, Va. Bar Assn., Richmond Bar Assn. General corporate, Securities, Corporate taxation. Home: 211 Santa Clara Dr Richmond VA 23229-7152 Office: Mays & Valentine PO Box 1122 Richmond VA 23218-1122

**MINCHEW, JOHN RANDALL,** lawyer; b. Washington, July 31, 1957; s. John Richard and Lucile Elizabeth (Shaw) M. AB, Duke U., 1980; JD, Washington & Lee U., 1984; Cert. in Jurisprudence, Oxford U., 1982. Bar: Va. 1984, U.S. Dist. Ct. (ea. dist.) Va. 1985, U.S. Ct. Appeals (4th cir.) 1985, U.S. Supreme Ct. 1997. Jud. clk. Supreme Ct. Va., 1984-85; mng. ptnr. Loudoun County Office, Walsh, Colucci, Stackhouse, Emrich & Lubeley, P.C., Leesburg, Va., 1998—; v.p., dir. devel. The Minchew Corp., Fairfax, Va., 1985—; chmn. Loudoun County Econ. Devel. Commn., 1996-98; pres. Va. Shelter Corp. Adminstrv. editor: Washington & Lee Law Rev., 1984. Pro bono caseworker Legal Aid Soc. Roanoke Valley, Lexington, Va., 1982-84. Mem. ABA, Va. State Bar (mem. Commn. on Unauthorized Practice of Law 1994-98), Fairfax Bar Assn., Loudoun Bar Assn. (pres. 1995-96), Phi Delta Phi. Avocations: scuba diving, aviation, rugby. Fax: 703-737-3633. Land use and zoning (including planning), Condemnation, Real property. Home: 330 W Market St Leesburg VA 20176-2601 Office: Walsh Colucci Stackhouse Emrich & Lubeley PC 1 E Market St Ste 3 Leesburg VA 20176-3014

**MINCKLEY, CARLA BETH,** lawyer; b. N.Y.C., Mar. 3, 1957; d. Jerome J. and Estelle (Franklin) Landsman; m. Steven D. Minckley, May 10, 1985; children: Taylor F., Amanda K. BA magna cum laude, U. Albany, N.Y., 1979; JD, U. Denver, 1987. Bar: Colo. 1988, U.S. Dist. Ct. Colo. 1988, U.S. Ct. Appeals (10th cir.) 1992. Asst. compliance officer Integrated Resources Equity Corp., Englewood, Colo., 1981-85; law clk. Tallmadge, Tallmadge, Wallace & Hahn, P.C., Denver, 1985-88; assoc. Law Office of Fay Matsugage, Denver, 1988-90, Brega & Winters, P.C., Denver, 1990-95; pvt. practice Englewood, Colo., 1995—. Mem. Colo. Women's Agenda, Denver, 1995, Planned Parenthood Assn., Denver, 1992—, ACLU, Denver, 1992—. Recipient Am. Jurisprudence awards in corps., legislation, trusts and estates, 1986-87. Mem. ABA, Colo. Bar Assn., Denver Bar Assn. Democrat. Avocations: aerobics instruction, skiing, boating. General civil litigation, Securities, Probate. Office: 10164 W Powers Ave Littleton CO 80127-1841

**MINER, ROGER JEFFREY,** federal judge; b. Apr. 14, 1934; s. Abram and Anne M.; m. Jacqueline Mariani; 4 children. BS, SUNY; LLB cum laude, N.Y. Law Sch., 1956; postgrad., Bklyn. Law Sch., Judge Advocate Gen.'s Sch., U. Va.; LLD (hon.), N.Y. Law Sch., 1989, Syracuse U., 1990, Albany Law Sch./Union U., 1996; attended, Emory U. Bar: N.Y. 1956, U.S. Ct. Mil. Appeals 1956, Republic of Korea 1958, U.S. Dist. Ct. (so. and ea. dists.) N.Y. 1959. Ptnr. Miner & Miner, Hudson, N.Y., 1959-75; corp. counsel City of Hudson, 1961-64; asst. dist. atty. Columbia County, 1964, dist. atty., 1968-75; justice N.Y. State Supreme Ct., 1976-81; judge U.S. Dist. Ct. (no. dist.) N.Y., 1981-85; judge U.S. Ct. Appeals (2d cir.), Albany, N.Y., 1985—, now sr. judge; adj. assoc. prof. criminal law State U. System, N.Y., 1974-79; adj. prof. law N.Y. Law Sch., 1986-96, Albany Law Sch. Union U., 1997—; lectr. state and local bar assns.; lectr. SUNY-Albany, 1985; N.Y. Law Sch. Bd. Trustees, 1991-96; mem. jud. coun. 2d Cir., 1992-96; chmn. 2d Cir. Com. on Hist. and Commemorative Events, 1989-94; Cameras in the Courtroom Com., 1993-96, No. Dist. Hist. Com., 1981-85; State, Fed. Jud. Coun. of N.Y., 1986-91, chmn., 1990-91; Jud. Conf. of U.S. com. on fed.-state jurisdiction, 1987-92; trustee Practicing Law Inst. Mng. editor N.Y. Law Sch. Law Rev.; contbr. articles to law jours. 1st lt. JAGC, U.S. Army, 1956-59, capt. USAR ret. Recipient Dean's medal for Disting. Profl. Svc., N.Y. Law Sch., Disting. Alumnus award, Charles W. Froessel award for Valuable Contbn. to Law. Albany Jewish Fedn. award, Abraham Lincoln award, Community Svc. award Kiwanis, others; named Columbia County Man. of Yr., 1984, Ellis Island medal of Honor. Mem. ABA, N.Y. State Bar Assn., Assn. of Bar of City of N.Y., Columbia County Bar Assn., Am. Law Inst., Am. Judicature Soc., Fed. Judges Assn., Fed. Bar Coun., Am. Soc. Writers on Legal Subjects, Assn. Trial Lawyers Am., Columbia County Magistrates Assn., Supreme Ct. Hist. Soc., Columbia County Hist. Soc., N.Y. Law Sch. Alumni Assn. (hon. mem., bd. dirs.), B'nai Brith, Elks (past exalted ruler). Jewish. Office: US Ct Appeals 445 Broadway Ste 414 Albany NY 12207-2926

**MINES, DENISE CAROL,** law librarian; b. Phila., June 20, 1956; d. Alexander Abraham and Shirley (Gelman) M.; m. Ivan Bell, Nov. 18, 1990. BA, George Washington U., 1978; M of Librarianship, Emory U., 1979. Asst. libr. Alston Miller & Gaines, Atlanta, 1979-81; libr. Smith Cohen Ringel Kohler & Martin, Atlanta, 1981-84; asst. libr. Schnader Harrison Segal & Lewis, Phila., 1984-87; libr. Reed Smith Shaw & McClay, Phila., 1987-90, Mesirov Gelman Jaffe Cramer & Jamieson, Phila., 1990—. Mem. Am. Assn. Law Librs., Greater Phila. Law Librs. Assn. (sec. 1986-87, v.p. 1993-94, pres. 1994-95). Office: Mesirov Gelman Jaffe Cramer & Jamieson 1735 Market St Ste 3901 Philadelphia PA 19103-7503

**MINES, MICHAEL,** lawyer; b. Seattle, May 4, 1929; s. Henry Walker and Dorothy Elizabeth (Bressler) M.; m. Phyllis Eastham, Aug. 24, 1957; children: Linda Mines Elliott, Sandra, Diane Paull, Michael Lister. Student Whitman Coll., 1947-49; BA, U. Wash., 1951, JD, 1954. Bar: Wash. 1954, U.S. Dist. Ct. (we. dist.) Wash. 1957, U.S. Dist. Ct. Mont. 1970, U.S. Ct. Appeals (9th cir.) 1961, U.S. Supreme Ct. Assoc. Skeel, McKelvy, Henke, Evenson & Uhlman, Seattle, 1956-66, ptnr., 1966-68, Hullin, Roberts, Mines, Fite & Riveland, Seattle, 1968-75, Skeel, McKelvy, Henke, Evenson & Betts, Seattle, 1975-79, Betts, Patterson & Mines, Seattle, 1978—. Moderator Wash.-No. Idaho conf. United Ch. of Christ, 1975-76; bd. trustees Plymouth Housing Group, 1991-97; chair adult edn. bd. Plymouth Congl. Ch., Seattle. With U.S. Army, 1954-56. Mem. ABA, Wash. State Bar Assn., Seattle-King Bar Assn., Am. Coll. Trial Lawyers (state chair 1982-83, Internat. Assn. Def. Counsel, Wash. Assn. Def. Counsel (pres. 1971-72), Internat. Acad. Trial Lawyers (bd. dirs. 1991-96), U. Wash. Law Sch. Alumni Assn. (trustee, pres. bd. dirs. 1995-97). Federal civil litigation, State civil litigation, Insurance. Home: 2474 Crestmont Pl W Seattle WA 98199-3714 Office: Betts Patterson Mines PS 800 Financial Ctr 1215 4th Ave Ste 700 Seattle WA 98161-1090

**MINIHAN, JOHN EDWARD,** lawyer; b. Sellersville, Pa., Apr. 8, 1956; s. William F. and Joan C. Minihan; m. Paula I. Landis, Nov. 17, 1990; children: Mercerdi, Hilary, Aubrie, Chase. BS, Pa. State U., 1984; JD, Temple U., 1990. Bar: Pa. 1991, U.S. Dist. Ct. (ea. dist.) Pa. 1998. Environ. specialist Pa. Dept. Environ. Resources, Norristown, 1985-91; assoc. Mattioni, Mattioni & Mattioni Ltd., Phila., 1991-97; corp. counsel Envirosource, Inc., Horsham, Pa., 1997—. Co-author: Pennsylvania Environmental Law Handbook, 3d. edit., 1991, 4th. edit., 1994, 5th edit., 1997. Chmn. Twp. Environ. Adv. Coun., Towamencin Township, Pa., 1995—. With USN, 1975-81. Mem. Pa. Bar Assn., Phila. Bar Assn. Avocations: golf, cross-country skiing, hiking. Environmental, Contracts commercial. Office: Envirosource Inc 1155 Business Center Dr Horsham PA 19044-3422

**MINKEL, HERBERT PHILIP, JR.,** lawyer; b. Boston, Feb. 11, 1947; s. Herbert Philip and Helen (Sullivan) M. BA, Holy Cross Coll., 1969; JD, NYU, 1972. Bar: Mass. 1973, N.Y. 1976, U.S. Dist. Ct. Mass. 1973, U.S. Dist. Ct. (so. dist.) N.Y. 1976. Law clk. U.S. Dist. Ct. Mass., Boston, 1972-73; assoc. Milbank, Tweed, Hadley & McCloy, N.Y.C., 1973-79; ptnr. Fried, Frank, Harris, Shriver & Jacobson, N.Y.C., 1979-94; mem. adv. com. on bankruptcy rules Jud. Conf. U.S., 1987-93; adj. assoc. prof. NYU Law Sch., 1987-94. Contbg. author: American Bankers Assn. Bankruptcy Manual, 1979; contbg. editor: 5 Collier on Bankruptcy, 15th edit., 1979-96; contbr. articles to profl. jours. Bd. advisors Yacht Restoration Sch., Newport, R.I., Spl. Olympics, Spl. Smiles; bd. visitors Goldman Gra. Sch. Dentistry Boston U. Root-Tilden scholar NYU, 1969-72. Mem. ABA, Nat. Bankruptcy Conf., Mass. Bar Assn., Assn. Bar City of N.Y. Bankruptcy. Home: 85 E India Row Boston MA 02110-3320 Office: Ste 3200 Exch Pl 53 State St Boston MA 02109-2804

**MINKIN, DAVID JUSTIN,** lawyer; b. N.Y.C., Aug. 12, 1953; s. Gilbert William and Rita Claire M.; m. Barbara Emiko Furugen, Sept. 5, 1988; children: Ellen, Michael, Elise. BA, SUNY, 1975; MPH, U. Hawaii, 1980, JD, 1984. Bar: Hawaii 1984, U.S. Dist. Ct. 1984, U.S. Ct. Appeals (9th cir.) 1996. Deputy prosecuting atty. Dept. of Prosecuting Atty., Honolulu, 1984-

94; counsel McCorriston Miho Miller Mukai, Honolulu, 1995-96, ptnr., 1996—; prof. Kapiolani C.C., Honolulu, 1994-97. Dir. CrimeStoppers-Honolulu, 1997—, Am. Youth Soccer Assn., Honolulu, 1998. General civil litigation, Consumer commercial, Insurance. Office: McCorriston Miho Miller Mukai 500 Ala Moana Blvd 5 Waterfront Plz 4th Fl Honolulu HI 96813

**MINKOWITZ, MARTIN,** lawyer, former state government official; b. Bklyn., 1939; s. Jacob and Marion (Kornblau) M.; m. Carol L. Ziegler; 1 son from previous marriage, Stuart Allan. AA, Bklyn. Coll., 1959, BA, 1961; JD, Bklyn. Law Sch., 1963, LLM, 1965. Bar: N.Y. 1963, U.S. Supreme Ct. 1967, U.S. Tax Ct. 1974, all four U.S. Dist. Cts. N.Y. Ptnr. Minkowitz, Hagen & Rosenbluth, N.Y.C., 1964-76; gen. counsel State of N.Y. Workers' Compensation Bd., N.Y.C., 1976-81; dep. supt. and gen. counsel State of N.Y. Ins. Dept., N.Y.C., 1981-88; instr. CUNY, 1975; ptnr. Stroock & Stroock & Lavan, N.Y.C., 1988—; mem. adv. bd. Coll. Ins., 1987-90; adj. prof. law N.Y. Law Sch., N.Y.C., 1982—; lectr. ABA, N.Y. C. of C., Practicing Law Inst., N.Y. State Bar Assn., Nat. Assn. Ins. Commrs., Nat. Conf. Ins. Legis.; hearing officer N.Y.C. Transp. Dept., 1970-75; cons. City Coun. N.Y.C. 1969. Author: (with others) Rent Stabilization and Control, 1973; (with others) Handling the Basic Workers' Compensation Law Case, 1982, 85, 87; co-author: Workers Compensation, Insurance and Law Practice-The Next Generation, 1989; commentaries to McKinney's Consol. Laws, 1982—; mem. editl. bd. Jour. Occupl. Rehab. U. Rochester, 1991—; contbr. numerous articles to profl. jours. Bd. dirs., sec. Kingsbay YM-YWHA, Bklyn., 1978-99, elected dir. emeritus, 1999—; pres. bd. dirs. Shore Terrace Co-op., Bklyn., 1982-83; co-chmn. exec. bd., met. coun., nat. v.p. Am. Jewish Congress, N.Y.C., 1983-91; bd. dirs. Met. Coord. Coun. on Jewish poverty, 1993—, Nat. Conf. for Cmty. and Justice (bd. dir. N.Y. divsn. 1994—, nat. bd. trustees 1995—, chair N.Y. divsn. 1998—). Recipient cert. meritorious svc. Bklyn. Law Sch., Outstanding Pub. Svc. award Ind. Ins. Agt. Assn., citation outstanding performance State of N.Y. Workers' Compensation Bd., Disting. Leadership award N.Y. Claims Assn., City of Peace award State of Israel Bonds, Brotherhood award NCCJ. Fellow N.Y. State Bar Found.; mem. N.Y. County Lawyers Assn. (chmn. unlawful practice of law com. 1982-86, mem. profl. ethics com. 1985-91, chair worker's compensation com. 1988-91, bd. dirs. 1997—), N.Y. State Bar Assn. (mem. ho. of dels., chmn. unlawful practice of law com. 1981-83, mem. com. on profl. ethics 1981-84, chmn. com. profl. discipline 1988-92, Sustaining Mem. of Yr. award 1995), Soc. Ins. Receivers, Bklyn. Law Sch. Alumni Assn. (v.p. bd. dirs. 1984-92, pres. elect 1993-94, pres. 1995-96). Office: Stroock Stroock & Lavan 180 Maiden Ln New York NY 10038-4925

**MINNEY, MICHAEL JAY,** lawyer; b. Lancaster, Pa., Aug. 15, 1948; s. Jay W. and Mary Jane (Erisman) M.; m. Barbara Ann Dunlap, June 28, 1975; 1 child, Michael Jayson. Student, U.S. Mil. Acad., 1967; BA, Ohio Wesleyan U., 1970; JD, Villanova U., 1973. Bar: Pa. 1973, U.S. Dist. Ct. (ea. dist.) Pa. 1974, U.S. Supreme Ct. 1977, U.S. Ct. Appeals (3d cir.) 1979. Ptnr. Minney, Mecum & Kohr, Lancaster, 1975-78, 1978-84; sole practice Lancaster, 1973-75, 84—; regional council Govs. Justice Commn., Harrisburg, Pa., 1975-78; commr. Pa. Commn. on Sentencing, Harrisburg, 1979-81. Candidate U.S. House of Reps., 16th Dist., Pa., 1974, 76; bd. dirs. United Cerebral Palsy, Lancaster, 1976-84, pres. 1983-84; treas. James Buchanan Found; mem., prin. Bring Black Baseball to Lancaster. Named one of Outstanding Young Men of Am., 1976. Mem. Lancaster County Bar Assn., Pa. Bar Assn., James Buchanan Found. for the Presvn. of Wheatland (treas, 1998-99). Republican. Lutheran. Clubs: Hamilton, Conestoga Country (Lancaster). Lodge: Elks. Avocations: running, golf, photography. Real property, Criminal. Home: 1011 Woods Ave Lancaster PA 17603-3126 Office: 145 E Chestnut St Lancaster PA 17602-2740

**MINNEY, R. BRENT,** lawyer; b. Parkersburg, W.Va., Oct. 7, 1953; s. Ronzel Dalton and Lura Maude Minney; m. Marilyn Smith, Aug. 8, 1981. BA, Ohio No. U., 1975; JD, U. Dayton, 1978. Bar: Ohio 1978, U.S. Dist. Ct. (so. dist.) Ohio 1979, U.S. Dist. Ct. (no. dist.) Ohio 1981, U.S. Ct. Appeals (6th cir.) 1985. Legal intern Muskingum County Prosecutor, Zanesville, Ohio, 1978, asst. pros. atty., 1978-81; assoc., atty. Dennis M. Whalen Co., L.P.A., Cuyahoga Falls, Ohio, 1981-86; assoc., atty. Whalen & Compton Co., L.P.A., Akron, Ohio, 1986-90, prin., atty., 1990—; atty., legal svcs. dir. Ohio Mid-Eastern Edn. Svc. Agy., Steubenville, 1979—. Contbr. articles to profl. jours. Mem. exec. com. Ohio Coun. Sch. Bd. Attys., 1991—, chmn., 1997. Mem. ABA, Ohio State Bar Assn., Akron Bar Assn. Republican. Methodist. Education and schools, Labor, General civil litigation. Office: Whalen & Compton Co LPA 565 Wolf Ledges Pkwy PO Box 2020 Akron OH 44309-2020

**MINNICH, DIANE KAY,** state bar executive; b. Iowa City, Feb. 17, 1956; d. Ralph Maynard Minnich and Kathryn Jane (Obye) Tompkins. BA in Behavioral Sci., San Jose State U., 1978. Tutorial program coord./instr. Operation SHARE/La Valley Coll., Van Nuys, Calif., 1979-81; field exec. Silver Sage Girl Scout Coun., Boise, Idaho, 1981-85; continuing legal edn. dir. Idaho State Bar/Idaho Law Found. Inc., Boise, 1985-88, dep. dir., 1988-90, exec. dir., 1990—; mem. adv. bd. legal asst. program Boise State U. Mem. Assn. CLE Adminstrs., Chgo., 1985-90; bd. dirs. Silver Sage coun. Girl Scouts, Boise, 1990-93, 99—, mem. nominating com., 1990-94, 97—, chair nominating com., 1991-92; mem. legal asst. program adv. bd. Boise State U. Named one of Outstanding Young Women in Am., 1991. Mem. Nat. Orgn. Bar Execs. (membership com. 1992-97, chair 1996-97), Zonta Club Boise (pres. 1991-92, bd. dirs. 1989-93), Rotary Club Boise (chair mem. com. 1994-97, bd. dirs. 1996-97, 99—). Avocations: softball, jogging, golf. Office: Idaho State Bar Idaho Law Found PO Box 895 525 W Jefferson St Boise ID 83702-5931

**MINNICK, BRUCE ALEXANDER,** lawyer; b. New London, Conn., Apr. 16, 1943; s. Robert Wood Minnick and Nedra Louise (Alexander) Wiesman; m. Judith Anita Saxon, Sept. 23, 1967 (div. 1981); children: Audra Anne, Lisa Michelle; m. Charlotte Ann Springfield, Apr. 10, 1983 (div. 1991); 1 child, Matthew Alexander; m. Debra C. Williams, July 3, 1997; 1 stepchild, Brandy Michelle Williams. AA, Broward Community Coll., 1970; BS with honors, Fla. State U., 1971, JD, 1977. BarL Fla. 1978, U.S. Dist. Ct. (no. dist.) Fla. 1979, U.S. Dist. Ct. (mid. and so. dists.) Fla. 1982, U.S. Supreme Ct. 1981, U.S. Ct. Appeals (11th cir.) 1982, U.S. Tax Ct. 1983, U.S. Ct. Claims 1983, U.S. Dist. Ct. (ea. dist.) Mich. 1990. Staff dir., counsel rules com. Fla. Ho. Reps., Tallahassee, 1976-78; v.p., gen. counsel Fla. Credit Union League, Tallahassee, 1978-80; asst. atty. gen. dept. legal affairs State of Fla., Tallahassee, 1981-86; ptnr. Mang, Rett & Collette, P.A., Tallahassee, 1986-93, Mang, Rett & Minnick PA, Tallahassee, 1994-95; pvt. practice Bruce A. Minnick PA, Tallahassee, 1996—; lectr. state agys., 1982—, Fla. Bar, 1986—. Mem. Leon County Dist. Adv. Com., 1980-82, 92-94; mem. exec. com. Leon County Dems., 1984—. Mem. ABA (labor sect., local govt. and law sect.), Fla. Bar Assn. (chmn. com. labor sect. 1987-91, mem. exec. coun. labor sect. 1989-93, founding chmn. Fed. Ct. practice com. 1990-92, del. to 11th Cir. Jud. Conf. 1990-92, com. chmn. govt. lawyer sect. 1991—, rep. mem. pub. rels. com. 1991-93), Tallahassee Bar Assn., Fla. Govt. Bar Assn., Fla. Women Lawyers Assn., Fed. Bar Assn. (pres.-elect Tallahassee chpt. 1995, pres. 1996), Govs. Club, Univ. Ctr. Club, Phi Alpha Delta. Christian Scientist. Avocations: golf, astronomy, writing. Fax: 850-385-8414. Civil rights, Labor, Securities. Home: 9017 Eagles Ridge Dr Tallahassee FL 32312-4046 Office: 2874 Remington Green Cir PO Box 15588 Tallahassee FL 32317-5588

**MINOR, STERLING ARTHUR,** lawyer; b. Sioux City, Iowa, July 1, 1952; s. Harold DeForrest and Mary Ruth (Thompson) M.; children: Elizabeth Anne, Lauren Camille; m. Ellen L. Luby, June 28, 1998. BS, Duke U., 1974; JD, So. Meth. U., 1977. Bar: Tenn. 1977, Tex. 1982, U.S. Ct. Appeals (6th cir.) 1978, U.S. Ct. Appeals (D.C. cir.) 1978, U.S. Ct. Appeals (5th cir.) 1982; bd. cert. bus. bankruptcy law Tex. Bd. Legal Specialization. With Martin & Cochran, Nashville, Sheinfeld, Maley & Kay, Houston, Baker, Brown, Sharman & Parker, Houston; pvt. practice Houston; spkr. in field. Reviewing editor: Guide to Asset Protection Planning, 1998; columnist Legal Minutes, West U Mag., The Mag. River Oaks, Meml./Villages Mag., Tanglewood Mag., Bellaire Mag., Downtown Voice, 1993-95. Chmn. Zoning Bd. Adjustment, City West University Place, Tex., 1987-97; adminstrv. bd. mem. West University United Meth. Ch., 1988-90, 96-98; bd. mem. West University Elem. Sch. PTA, 1989-92, Rotary Club West University, 1995-96, The Sentinel Club, Inc., 1996-97; pres. Art League Houston, 1998-99. Fellow Houston Bar Found.; mem. Coll. State Bar Tex. Fax: 713-520-8711. E-mail: sminor@minordavis.com. Estate planning, Bankruptcy, General corporate. Home: 2031 Dunstan Rd Houston TX 77005-1621 Office: 3306 Sul Ross St Houston TX 77098-1808

**MINOR, STEVEN RAY,** lawyer; b. Ashland, Ky., Oct. 6, 1964; s. Ray C. and Susie C. Minor; m. Dana Marie Hymack, Oct. 20, 1990. BA, U. Va., 1986; JD, Coll. William and Mary, 1989. Bar: Va. 1989, U.S. Dist. Ct. (we. dist.) Va. 1990, U.S. Dist. Ct. (ea. dist.) Tenn. 1991, U.S. Ct. Appeals (4th cir.) 1990, U.S. Ct. Appeals (6th cir.) 1993, U.S. Supreme Ct. 1993. Law clk. U.S. Dist. Ct., Abingdon, Va., 1989-90; assoc. White Elliott & Bundy, Bristol, Va., 1990-94; assoc., shareholder Elliott Lawson & Pomrenke, Bristol, 1994—. Labor, General civil litigation, Civil rights. Home: 169 West Valley St Abingdon VA 24210 Office: Elliott Lawson & Pomrenke 110-112 Piedmont Ave Bristol VA 24201

**MINORCHIO, JAMES W.,** lawyer; b. Tacoma, June 3, 1957; s. Armand and Marie D. Minorchio; m. Cheryl L. Bender, June 30, 1979; children: Nicholas James, John William. BA in Bus. Adminstrn., U. Wash., 1979; JD, Seattle U., 1982; LLM in Taxation, U. Fla., 1983. Bar: Wash. 1982, U.S. Dist. Ct. (we. dist.) Wash. 1983, U.S. Tax Ct. 1983. Ptnr. Williams, Kastner & Gibbs, Seattle, 1985-96; of counsel Garvey, Schubert & Baver, Seattle, 1996-97; ptnr. Graham & James, Seattle, 1997—. Mem. planned giving com. Cath. Archdiocese of Seattle, 1985—, United Cerebral Plasy Assn. of King and Snohomish Counties, 1987-93; pres. sch. bd. Cath. Archdiocese of Seattle, 1993-99. Mem. ABA, Wash. State Bar Assn., King County Bar Assn. (chmn. tax sect. 1989-90). Republican. Roman Catholic. Corporate taxation, Estate taxation. Home: 1311 NW 188th St Seattle WA 98177-3329 Office: Graham & James LLP 1001 4th Ave Ste 4500 Seattle WA 98154-1192

**MINSKY, BRUCE WILLIAM,** lawyer; b. Queens, N.Y., Sept. 28, 1963; m. Jill R. Heinter, May 1992; children: Aryeh Hanan, Elisheva Yael, Calev Betzalel. BA in Polit. Sci., Boston U., 1985; JD, Southwestern U., 1988; LLM in Am. Banking, Boston U., 1989. Bar: Calif. 1988, Conn. 1989, N.Y. 1990, U.S. Dist. Ct. (ea. and so. dist.), U.S. Ct. Appeals. Assoc. Quirk & Bakalor, N.Y.C., 1989-91; house counsel, v.p. Banco Popular N.Am., N.Y.C., 1991—, Banco Poplur N. Am., 1999. Atty. Monday Night Law Pro Bono Svcs., N.Y.C. Mem. Assn. of Bar of City of N.Y. (mem. young lawyers com. 1993-95). Avocations: music, sports, literature. Banking, General practice, General corporate. Office: 7 W 51st St New York NY 10019-6910

**MINTER, GREGORY BYRON,** lawyer, educator; b. Omaha, Dec. 6, 1940; s. Byron H. and Martha E. (Nelson) M.; m. Jane A. Baumhover, June 15, 1999; children: Deborah Anne, Brian Thomas, David Barton, Timothy J., Rhea A., Jordanna F. BSBA, Mcpl. U. Omaha, 1964; JD, Creighton U., 1965. Bar: Nebr. 1965, U.S. Supreme Ct. 1972. Assoc., Fitzgerald, Schorr, Barmettler & Brennan, P.C., Omaha, 1965-71, ptnr., 1971—; adj. prof. Creighton U. Sch. Law, 1969—, U. Nebr. Sch. Law, 1981-86; dir., 1980—, v.p.-pres. elect, 1984-86, pres., 1986-88, chmn. curriculum com., publs. com., 1988—. Nebr. Continuing Legal Edn., Inc., 1980-86; dir. Nebr. Jud. Coll., chmn. seminars com., 1985-88; cons. U.S. Dept. Justice, 1981; mem. faculty SEC, 1969—. Pres., Omaha Ballet Soc., 1982-83, bd. dirs., 1980-84 ; v.p., sec. Omaha Symphony Coun., 1980-83, pres., 1983-84; bd. dirs. Omaha Symphony Assn., 1984-93, v.p., 1985-88, sec. 1988-90, pres. 1990-92; chairperson cmty. adv. bd. Sta KVNO Pub. Radio, 1983-84; mem. Nebr. House of Dels., 1990—. Served to capt. JAGC, U.S. Army, 1967-78. Mem. Nebr. Bar Assn., Omaha Bar Assn., Nebr. State Bar Found. (Outstanding Legal Educator award 1997), Nat. Assn. Bond Lawyers, Am. Immigration Lawyers Assn., Alpha Sigma Nu. Republican. Presbyterian. Author legal publs. Securities, General corporate, Immigration, naturalization, and customs. Home: 2331 N 53rd St Omaha NE 68104-4231 Office: Fitzgerald Schorr Barmettler & Brennan PC 1100 Woodmen Tower Omaha NE 68102

**MINTON, DON WAYNE,** lawyer; b. Beaumont, Tex., Jan. 26, 1968; s. Beamont C. and Mary Ann Minton; m. Lourdes Villa, July 3, 1992; 1 child, Luke Girard. BS, U.S. Mil. Acad., Westpoint, N.Y., 1990; JD, U. Tex., 1996. Bar: Calif. 1997, Tex. 1998, U.S. Dist. Ct. (we. dist.) Tex., U.S. Dist. Ct. (so. and ctrl. dists.) Calif., U.S. Ct. Appeals (5th cir.). Stockbroker Edward D. Jones & Co., Austin, 1993-94; atty. Klinedinst Fliehman & McKillop, San Diego, 1997, James Goldman & Haugland PC, El Paso, Tex., 1997—. Capt. U.S. Army, 1990-93. Office: James Goldman & Haugland 201 E Main Dr El Paso TX 79901-1340

**MINTON, HARVEY STEIGER,** lawyer; b. Columbus, Ohio, Dec. 16, 1933; s. Harvey Alan and Elsie (Steiger) M.; m. Jane Rickey Grimm, July 21, 1956; children: Harvey Randall, Jennifer Thelma. BS, Ohio State U., 1956, JD, 1962. Bar: Ohio 1956, N.Y. 1985. Atty. Shumaker, Loop & Kendrick, Toledo, 1962-65; asst. atty. Owens Ill., Toledo, 1965-82; sec., pres. Sun Master (subs. Corning), N.Y.C., 1983-84; v.p. Leeward Capital, Columbus, Ohio, 1985-87; gen. counsel, sr. ptnr. Harvey S. Minton & Assocs., Worthington, Ohio, 1987--. Pres. bd. trustees Toledo Symphony, 1973-76; chmn. Law Week, Toledo, 1964, jail action, Toledo, 1973; mem. Worthington Zoning Bd. Appeals, 1992. Capt. USAF, 1958-59. Mem. Rotary (named Man of the yr. 1988). Republican. Presbyterian. General corporate, Bankruptcy, Estate planning. Home: 617 Hartford St Worthington OH 43085-4119 Office: 6641 N High St Worthington OH 43085-4038

**MINTON, KENT W.,** lawyer; b. Independence, Mo., May 16, 1955; s. Roy V. and Donabelle M. Minton; m. Karen S. MacDonald, Oct. 21, 1989; children: Kathy, Megan, Abby. BS, Ctrl. Mo. State U., 1976; postgrad., U. Tulsa, 1979-80; JD, U. Mo., Kansas City, 1982. Bar: Mo. 1982, U.S. Dist. Ct. (we. dist.) Mo. 1982, U.S. Ct. Claims 1986. Assoc. Paxton, Block et al, Independence, 1982-83, Holliday & Holliday, Kansas City, 1983-85; ptnr. Raymond, Raymond & Minton, Kansas City, 1985-96, Stewart, Cook, Constance, Stewart & Minton LLC, Independence, 1996—; bd. dirs. Comprehensive Mental Health Svcs. Found., Independence. Contbr. chpt. to book. Mem. Mo. Bar (trust law revision subcom.), Kansas City Metro Bar Assn. (probate com.). Estate planning, Probate, State civil litigation. Office: Stewart Cook Constance Stewart & Minton LLC 501 W Lexington Ave Independence MO 64050-3648

**MINTON, MICHAEL HARRY,** lawyer, business exec.; b. Indpls., May 14, 1946; s. Bernard Jerome and Dorothy Louise (Groene) M.; children—Melanie, Michael. B.A., U. Notre Dame, 1968; intermediate degree London Sch. Econs., 1970; J.D., Northwestern U., 1971. Bar: Ill. 1971, U.S. Dist. Ct. (no. dist.) Ill. 1971, U.S. Supreme Ct. 1980; cert. civil trial advocacy specialist Nat. Bd. Trial Advocacy. Assoc. Biestek & Facchini, Arlington Heights, Ill., 1971-74; ptnr. Facchini & Minton, Schaumburg, Ill., 1974-85; sole practice, Chgo., 1985—. Trustee Village of Mt. Prospect (Ill.), 1974-78, chmn. fire and police com. 1977-78, bldg. com. 1978. Mem. ABA, Ill. Bar Assn., Chgo. Bar Assn. (matrimonial law com. 1972—), DuPage County Bar Assn., N.W. Suburban Bar Assn. (chmn. family law sect. 1979—), Assn. Trial Lawyers Am., Ill. Trial Lawyers Assn. Roman Catholic. Clubs: Meadow (Rolling Meadows, Ill.); Union League (Chgo.). Mem. bd. editors Fair Share, Newsletter of Divorce, 1981; author: What Is a Wife Worth?, 1983; contbr. numerous articles to legal jours. Family and matrimonial. Home: 1020 Blackburn Dr Palatine IL 60067-4218 Office: 222 N La Salle St Ste 1950 Chicago IL 60601-1102

**MINTZ, CARL A.,** retired lawyer; b. Cleve., Oct. 7, 1909; s. Jacob and Mina (Arnold) M.; m. Lois Lovett, Aug. 30, 1940 (dec. June 1995); children: Carl A. Jr., Roger J. BS in Econs., U. Pa., 1931; JD, Cleve. State U., 1935. Pvt. practice Cleve., 1935—. General civil litigation, State and local taxation, Labor. Home: 23305 Chagrin Blvd Apt 301 Beachwood OH 44122-5518

**MINTZ, JEFFRY ALAN,** lawyer; b. N.Y.C., Sept. 15, 1943; s. Aaron Herbert and Lillian Betty (Greenspan) M.; m. Susan Politzer, Aug. 22, 1979; children: Jennifer, Melanie, Jonathan. AB, Tufts U., 1964; LLB, Rutgers U., 1967; postgrad., U. Pa. Law Sch., 1968-70. Bar: D.C. 1968, N.Y. 1970, U.S. Supreme Ct. 1972, N.J. 1973, Pa. 1983. Law clk. to judge U.S. Ct. Appeals, New Orleans, 1967-68; asst. defender Defender Assn. Phila., 1968-70; asst. counsel NAACP Legal Def. and Ednl. Fund, N.Y.C., 1970-74; dir. Office Inmate Advocacy, N.J. Dept. Pub. Adv., Trenton, 1974-81; pvt. practice Haddonfield and Medford, N.J, 1982; ptnr. Stein & Shapiro, Medford, 1982-83, Cherry Hill, N.J., 1983-84; ptnr. Mesirov, Gleman, jaffe, Cramer & Jamieson, Cherry Hill, Phila., 1984-90, Schlesinger, Mintz & Pilles, Mt. Holly, N.J., 1990-92; pvt. practice Mt. Holly, 1992—. Trustee Congregation M'Kor Shalom, Cherry Hill, 1990-97; mem. Burling County and Mt. Laurel Dem. Coun. Com., 1993-95; chair Moorestown Dem. Com., 1995—. Mem. ABA, ATLA, N.J. Bar Assn. (del., gen. coun. 1986-88, 89-91), D.C. Bar Assn., Camden County Bar Assn., Burlington County Bar Assn. (trustee 1989-92), Assn. Trial Lawyers N.J. (bd. govs. 1990-95), Barrister, Burlington Am. Inn. of Ct. (founder). Jewish. General civil litigation, Personal injury. Home: 224 Quakerbridge Ct Moorestown NJ 08057-2823 Office: 129 High St Mount Holly NJ 08060-1401

**MINTZ, JOEL ALAN,** law educator; b. N.Y.C., July 24, 1949; s. Samuel Isaiah and Eleanor (Streichler) M.; m. Meri-Jane Rochelson, Aug. 25, 1975; children: Daniel Rochelson, Robert Eli. BA, Columbia U., 1970, LLM, 1982, JSD, 1989; JD, NYU, 1974. Bar: N.Y. 1975, U.S. Dist. Ct. (so. and ea. dists.) N.Y. 1982, U.S. Ct. Appeals (2d cir.) 1982. Atty. enforcement div. EPA, Chgo., 1975-76, chief atty. case devel. unit, 1977-78, policy advisor to regional adminstr., 1979; sr. litigation atty. Office Enforcement, EPA, Washington, 1980-81; asst. prof. environ. law Nova U. Law Ctr., Ft. Lauderdale, Fla., 1982-85, assoc. prof., 1985-87, prof., 1987—. Author 2 books; contbr. articles to legal jours. and treatises. Mem. ABA, Environ. Law Inst. Assocs., Fla. Bar (assoc.), Internat. Coun. Environ. Law, Internat. Union for Conservation of Nature (commn. on environ. law), Assn. Am. Law Schs. (exec. com., state and local govt. law sect.), Phi Alpha Delta. Avocations: reading, fitness walking, canoeing. Home: 2060 NE 209th St Miami FL 33179-1628 Office: Nova Southeastern U Law Ctr 3305 College Ave Fort Lauderdale FL 33314-7721

**MINTZ, M. J.,** lawyer; b. Phila., Oct. 29, 1940; s. Arthur and Lillian (Altenberg) M.; children: Robert A., Christine L.; m. Judith E. Held. BS, Temple U., 1961, JD, 1968. Bar: D.C.; C.P.A., Pa., D.C. Atty. adv. to judge U.S. Tax Ct., Washington, 1968-70; asst. gen. counsel Cost of Living Coun. Exec. Office of Pres., Washington, 1971-73; ptnr. Dickstein, Shapiro & Morin, Washington, 1973—; adj. prof. George Mason U. Law Sch., Va., 1974-78; adv. to U.S. sec. of labor Employee Ret. Income Security Act of 1974, Adv. Coun., Washington, 1982-85. Contbr. articles to profl. jours. Apptd. by Pres. Ronald Reagan to advisory com. Pension Benefit Guaranty Corp., 1987; reapptd. and designated chmn. by Pres. George Bush; apptd. by Gov. George Allen of Va., Bd. of the Va. Pub. Bldg. Authority, 1996—; rep. candidate Fairfax County Bd. of Suprs., 1971. Star fellow. Fellow Nat. Assn. Watch & Clock Collectors; mem. ABA, AICPA, Antiquarian Horological Soc. (London), Cosmos Club, Belle Haven Country Club, Met. Club (Washington), Chappaquiddick Beach Club, Naval Club (London). Avocation: antiquarian horologist. Pension, profit-sharing, and employee benefits, Estate taxation, Taxation, general.

**MINTZ, RICHARD L.,** lawyer; b. South Bend, Ind., Jan. 23, 1946; s. Charles and Matilda M.; m. Linda Stern, June 24, 1975; children: Jacob, Brian, David. BA, Antioch Coll., 1969; student, Oxford U., 1996-97; JD, U. Mich., 1971. Ptnr. Ferguson & Mintz, Kalamazoo, 1972; staff atty. Consumers Power Co., Jackson, Mich., 1973-76; mng. ptnr. Roemer & Mintz, South Bend, 1977—. Chmn. endowment investment com. Jewish Fedn. St. Joseph County, South Bend, 1996—, dir., 1998—; dir. Project Future, South Bend, 1998—. Mem. ABA, Ind. Bar Assn. Avocations: golfing, skiing, photography, reading, traveling. General corporate, Real property. Office: Roemer & Mintz LLP PO Box 4757 South Bend IN 46634-4757

**MINTZ, ROBERT A.,** lawyer; b. N.Y.C., May 16, 1959; s. Ira Leonard and Nancy Rose M.; m. Janice Ellen Mitchell Mintz, Nov. 18, 1989; children: Daniel, Elizabeth. BA, Duke U., 1984; JD, Vanderbilt U., 1981. Bar: N.J. 1985, Pa. 1985, U.S. Dist. Ct. N.J. 1985. Asst. counsel Govs. Office Statehouse, Trenton, N.J., 1984-89; asst. U.S. atty. U.S. Attys. Office, Newark, 1989-98; deputy chief McCanter & English, Newark, 1998—. Criminal, Health, Government contracts and claims. Office: McCanter & English 100 Mulberry St Newark NJ 07102

**MINTZ, RONALD STEVEN,** lawyer, photojournalist; b. Bklyn., Aug. 16, 1947; s. Herbert and Phoebe (Gilman) M.; children: Raymond, Gloria. JD, Western State U., Fullerton, Calif., 1978. Bar: Calif. 1978, U.S. Dist. Ct. (no., so., ea. and cen. dists.) Calif. 1978, U.S. Ct. Appeals (9th cir.) 1979, U.S. Supreme Ct. 1982. Pvt. practice law Berkeley, Calif., 1978-80, Canyon Country, Calif., 1980-83, Chino, Calif., 1983-84, Ontario, Calif., 1984-88, Pomona, Calif., 1988-91, San Fernando, Calif., 1991-92; pvt. practice Joshua Tree, Calif., 1993-94, Hollywood, Calif., 1994—; founder legal aid orgn. to protect civil rights Tactical Law Command. Producer film on air pollution: State of Emergency, 1971, videotape documentary: America-A True Glimpse, 1987; publisher opposition newspaper: Ten Penny Press. Recipient Am. Jurisprudence awards Bancroft Whitney Law Book Pub. Co., 1977, 78. Mem. Lawyers in Mensa (charter), State Bar Calif. (criminal law sect. 1983-84, police misconduct lawyer referral service), Mensa. Fax: 213-465-4600. Avocations: photography, film, video, guns, cars. Civil rights, Criminal, Appellate. Office: 5858 Hollywood Blvd Ste 306A Los Angeles CA 90028-5654

**MINUS, JOSEPH J., JR.,** lawyer; b. Epes, Ala., Sept. 12, 1959; m. Nancy Collier; children: Joseph, Laura, Matthew, Leigh. BS, U. Ala., 1981; JD, Samford U., 1985. Bar: Ala. 1985, U.S. Dist. Ct. (no. dist.) Ala. 1992, U.S. Dist. Ct. (so. dist.) Ala. 1993, U.S. Ct. Appeals (11th cir.) 1993. City atty. City of Satsuma, Office of City Atty., Ala.; ptnr. Lyons Pipes & Cook, Mobile. Mem. ABA, Mobile Bar Assn., Ala. Def. Lawyers Assn., Southeastern Admiralty Law Inst., Nat. Inst. Trial Advocacy. General civil litigation, Insurance, Admiralty. Office: Lyons Pipes & Cook 2 N Royal St Mobile AL 36602-3896

**MINUSE, CATHERINE JEAN,** lawyer; b. Port Jefferson, N.Y., Feb. 5, 1951; d. William Brewster and Jean (Fairservis) M.; m. Henry E. Stevenson, 1988; children; James Minuse Stevenson, Robert Minuse Stevenson. BA, SUNY-Stony Brook, 1972; JD, Cornell U., 1975. Bars: N.Y. 1976, U.S. Dist. Ct. (so. and ea. dists.) 1977, U.S. Ct. Appeals (2d and 11th cirs.) 1986. Law clk. to judge So. Dist. N.Y., 1975-77; assoc. Poletti, Freidin, Prashker, Feldman & Gartner, and successor firm Poletti, Freidin, Prashker & Gartner, N.Y.C., 1977-85; mgr. labor rels. Trans World Airlines, 1985-86; assoc. O'Donnell & Schwartz, 1986-90; supervisory staff atty. U.S. Ct. Appeals (2d cir.) N.Y., 1990—; adj. instr. legal writing and rsch. Cardozo Sch. Law, 1983-94, moot ct., 1986-94. Mem. ABA, DAR. Democrat. Episcopalian. Note editor Cornell Law Rev., 1974-75. Home: Apt 5F 20 E 9th St New York NY 10003-5944

**MINZNER, PAMELA B.,** state supreme court justice; b. Meridian, Miss., Nov. 19, 1943. BA cum laude, Miami U., 1965; LLB, Harvard U., 1968. Bar: Mass. 1968, N.Mex. 1972. Pvt. practice Mass., 1968-71, Albuquerque, 1971-73; adj. prof. law U. N.Mex., Albuquerque, 1972-73, asst. prof., 1973-77, assoc. prof., 1977-80, prof. law, 1980-84; judge N.Mex. Ct. Appeals, Albuquerque, 1984-94; justice N.Mex. Supreme Ct., Santa Fe, 1994—, chief justice, 1998—; mem. faculty Inst. Preparativo Legal U., N.Mex. Sch. Law, 1975, 79; participant NEH Summer Seminar for Law Tchrs. Stanford Law Sch., 1982, U. Chgo. Law Sch., 1978. Author: (with Robert T. Laurence) A Student's Guide to Estates in Land and Future Interests: Text, Examples, Problems & Answers, 1981, 2d edit. 1993. Mem. ABA, State Bar N.Mex. (co-editor newsletter 1979-83, bd. dirs. 1978-79, 83-84, sect. on women's legal rights and obligations), Gamma Phi Beta. Democrat. Avocations: reading, bridge, movies. Office: NMex Supreme Ct PO Box 848 Santa Fe NM 87504-0848*

**MIRABEL, FARRAH,** lawyer; b. Tehran, Iran, Sept. 23, 1966; came to U.S., 1985; BSEE, Wayne State U., 1989; JD, U. Detroit, 1992. Elec. engr. Ford Motor Co., Dearborn, Mich., 1988-92; pvt. practice law Newport Beach, Calif., 1993—. State civil litigation, Intellectual property, Patent. Office: 4590 Macarthur Blvd Ste 220 Newport Beach CA 92660-2025

**MIRABELLO, FRANCIS JOSEPH,** lawyer; b. Ft. Lauderdale, Fla., Mar. 2, 1954; s. Frank Guy and Mary (Sorce) M.; m. Marianna Hay O'Neal, Aug. 5, 1978; childen: Diana H., A. Paul. BS in Civil Engring., Princeton U.,

1975; JD, Harvard U., 1978. Bar: Calif. 1978, Pa. 1981, Fla. 1983. Assoc. Irell & Manella, Los Angeles, 1978-81; ptnr. Morgan, Lewis & Bockius, Phila., 1981—; lectr. law Villanova (Pa.) U. Law Sch., adj. prof. law U. Pa., Phila. Mem. ABA, ACTEC. Club: Martins Dam, Merion Cricke. Avocation: tennis. Probate, Estate planning, Personal income taxation. Office: Morgan Lewis & Bockius 1701 Market St Philadelphia PA 19103-2903

**MIRABILE, CAROLYN ROSE,** lawyer; b. Norristown, Pa., June 12, 1966; d. Paul Joseph and Norma Jean (DiFerdinando) M.; m. Richard Lawrence Giles, Sept. 26, 1992; 1 child, Gabriella Savannah. BA in Polit. Sci., Villanova U., 1988, JD, 1991. Bar: Pa. 1991, N.J. 1991. Assoc. Gultanoff & Lynch, Norristown, 1992-93, Gultanoff Lynch & Tornetta, Norristown, 1993-94; ptnr. Lynch Tornetta & Mirabile, Norristown, 1994-96, Lynch & Mirabile, Norristown, 1996—; assoc. Montgomery County Family Law Com., 1991—, Family Law Discovery Subcom., Doris Jonas Freed Am. Inn. of Ct., 1994—; co-chair Montgomery County Law Day, Norristown, 1993, 94, 95, Family Law Practicum, 1996. Avocation: golf, volleyball. Fax: 610-277-2043. Family and matrimonial, Pension, profit-sharing, and employee benefits. Office: Lynch & Mirabile 617 Swede St Norristown PA 19401-3901

**MIRACLE, DALE NEIL,** lawyer; b. Tenino, Wash., Oct. 15, 1936; s. Gordon Tipler and Corine Adriana Miracle; children: Mark, Dawn. BBA, U. Wis., 1958, JD, 1962. Bar: Wis. 1962, U.S. Dist. Ct. (ea. dist.) Wis. 1966, U.S. Dist. Ct. (we. dist.) Wis. 1984. Assoc. Johnson & DeBauffer, Attys., Whitewater, Wis., 1962-64; atty. Travelers Ins. Co., Milw., 1964-67, Wis. Gas Co., Milw., 1967-70, Wausau Ins. Co., Milw., 1970-82, Continental Ins. Co., Milw., 1982-85; prin. Miracle Law Office, Elm Grove, Wis., 1985—. With U.S. Army Res., 1959-64. Mem. State Bar Wis., Waukesha Bar Assn. Insurance, Personal injury. Office: Miracle Law Office PO Box 5016 13435 Watertown Plank Rd Elm Grove WI 53122-2201

**MIRIKITANI, ANDREW KOTARO,** lawyer; b. N.Y.C., Aug. 25, 1955; s. Carl Mamoru and Hisa (Yoshimura) M. BA magna cum laude, U. So. Calif., 1978; JD, U. Santa Clara, 1982. Bar: Hawaii 1984, U.S. Dist. Ct. Hawaii 1984, U.S. Ct. Appeals (9th cir.) 1984. Law clk. to chief judge James S. Burns Intermediate Ct. of Appeals, State of Hawaii, Honolulu, 1985-86; atty. Case, Kay & Lynch, Honolulu, 1986-87; mem., vice-chmn. Honolulu City Coun., 1990—; atty. Char Hamilton Campbell & Thom, Honolulu, 1988-92; v.p. Am. Beltwrap Corp. Honolulu, 1986—. Editor Santa Clara Law Rev., 1982; patentee in field. Trustee Carl K. Mirikitani Meml. Scholarship Fund, Honolulu, 1984—; pres. East Diamond Head Community Assn., Honolulu, 1988-89; chmn. Waialae-Kahala Neighborhood Bd., Honolulu, 1988-89; bd. dirs. Legal Aid Soc. of Hawaii, 1988-90, Protection ad Advocacy Agy., Honolulu, 1989; del. Dem. Party of Hawaii, Honolulu, 1990-92; pres. Save Diamond Head Beach, Honolulu, 1993—; mem. Nat. Women's Polit. Caucus, Hawaii Women's Polit. Caucus. Recipient award Am. Soc. for Pub. Adminstrs., 1997, Outstanding Pub. Svc. Media Program award, Nat. Achievement award Nat. Assn. of Counties, 1997. Mem. ABA, Hawaii Bar Assn., am. Trial Lawyers Assn., Hawaii Women Lawyers Assn., Advocates for Pub. Interest Law, Alpha Mu Gamma, Phi Beta Kappa. Democrat. Legislative, General civil litigation, Insurance. Office: City Council Honolulu Hale Honolulu HI 96813

**MIRIKITANI, RICHARD KIYOSHI,** lawyer; b. N.Y.C., June 19, 1958; s. Carl Mamoru M. and Hisa Yoshimura; m. Susan Meryl Kurisaki. BA, Stanford U., 1980; JD, Harvard U., 1983. Bar: Hawaii, U.S. Dist. Ct. Hawaii. Assoc. Goodsill, Anderson, Quinn & Stifel, Honolulu, 1985-91, ptnr., 1992-96; sr. v.p., sr. corp. counsel Castle & Cooke Homes Hawaii, Honolulu, 1997—, Castle & Cooke Properties, Honolulu, 1997—; pres. Castle & Cooke Land Co., Honolulu, 1997—; d. dirs. Oceanic Ins., Inc., Honolulu, Hawaii Dental Svc., Honolulu; lectr. min ority bar program U. Hawaii Law Sch., 1992-93. Mem. Hawaii Bar Assn., Hawaii C. of C., Phi Beta Kappa. Contracts commercial, General corporate, Banking. Office: Castle & Cooke Hawaii 650 Iwilei Rd Honolulu HI 96817-5088

**MIRON, JAMES R.,** lawyer; b. Bridgeport, Conn., July 7, 1965; s. Richard A. and Ann (Gargiulo) M. AS, Housatonic C.C., 1988; BA, Ctrl. Conn. State U., 1990; JD, Western New Engl. Coll., 1994. Bar: Conn. 1994, U.S. Dist. Ct. Conn. 1995, Fla. 1995, U.S. Ct. Internat. Trade 1996, D.C. 1997. Pvt. practice Stratford, Conn., 1994—, asst. town atty., 1995—. Town Com. mem., Stratford Dem. Town Com., 1992—. With U.S. Army, 1983-86. Mem. ABA, Conn. Bar Assn., Conn. Trial Lawyers Assn. Dem. Avocations: golf, running. Office: 125 Ferry Blvd Stratford CT 06615-6007

**MIRRAS, MICHAEL JOHN,** lawyer; b. Geneva, N.Y., Mar. 8, 1969; s. John J. and Maryann V. Mirras. BA, Syracuse U., 1991; JD, Western New Eng. Coll., 1994. Bar: N.Y. 1995. Atty. in pvt. practice Geneva, 1996—. Exec. bd. dirs. Athletic Booster Club Geneva H.S. Mem. ABA, N.Y. State Defenders' Assn., N.Y. State Bar Assn., Ontario County Bar Assn., Seneca County Bar Assn. Criminal, Family and matrimonial, Sports. Office: PO Box 1069 Geneva NY 14456-8069

**MIRVAHABI, FARIN,** lawyer; b. Tehran, Iran; d. Ali and Azar Mirvahabi; children: Bobby Naemi, Jimmy Naemi. Degree in Law, Tehran U., Iran, 1968; M of Comparative Law, Georgetown U., 1972; LLM, George Washington U., 1976; JSD, NYU, 1978; diploma, The Hague Acad. Internat. Law, 1983. Bar: Va. 1989, U.S. Dist. Ct. (ea. and we. dists.) Va. 1990, D.C. 1990, U.S. Dist. Ct. D.C. 1990, U.S. Supreme Ct. 1997. With Gold & Cutner, N.Y.C., 1979-80; in-house counsel IRA Engring. and Constrn., Tehran, London, 1981-82; legal advisor Bank Markazi, Tehran, 1982; practiced law The Hague, The Netherlands, 1982-87; arbitrator Iran Air-Pan Am Arbitration Tribunal, Paris, 1984-87; legal cons. Rooney, Barry & Fogerty, Washington, 1987-88; atty. sole practice, Washington, 1989—; law prof. No. Va. Law Sch., Alexandria, 1989-90; instr. Paralegal Inst., Arlington, Va., 1988-89; prof. Tehran U., 1982; panelist Am. Arbitration Assn.; guest speaker in field; life dep. gov. Am. Biog. Inst. Rsch. Assn., 19995—. Contbr. numerous articles to profl. jours. Named Maxplank fellow Maxplank Inst. of Internat. Law, 1986; recipient Clyde Eagleton award NYU, 1977, Woman of Yr. medallion honoring Cmty. Svc. and Profl. Achievement, 1995. Mem. ABA, Internat. Bar Assn., Arbitration Forum Inc., D.C. Bar Assn. (panelist client-atty. arbitration bd. 1990—), D.C. Bar & Lawyers Assn., Trial Lawyers Assn., Va. Bar Found., Am. Soc. Internat. Law. Avocations: reading, writing, Broadway shows, picnic, swimming. Private international, Public international. Office: 1730 K St NW Ste 304 Washington DC 20006-3839

**MISCH, PAUL MICHAEL,** lawyer; b. Bloomington, Ill., Feb. 1, 1953; s. Harold E. and Helen F. (Fanghan) M. Student, Georgetown U., 1972; BS, U. Ill., 1975; JD, John Marshall Law Sch., 1978, postgrad., 1987—. Bar: Ill. 1978, U.S. Dist. Ct. (cen. dist.) Ill. 1979, U.S. Dist. Ct. (no. dist.) Ill. 1980, U.S. Tax Ct. 1980. Ptnr. Bane, Allison & Saint, Bloomington, 1978-82, Misch & Reinhart, Chartered, Tulsa, Cin., Chgo., Bloomington, N.Y.C., Mpls., San Antonio, 1982—. Author: Advising Churches for the 1980's, 1984; editor Ill. Student Lawyer, 1975-81. Mem. 43d Ward Rep. Orgn., Chgo. Mem. ABA (silver key award 1978), Ill. Bar Assn., Ill. Trial Lawyers Assn., Chgo. Bar Assn., McLean County Bar Assn., Chgo. Council Lawyers, Phi Delta Phi. Republican. Clubs: Lincoln (Bloomington) (pres. 1979-81); Racquet (Chgo.), Financial Club (Tulsa). Avocations: tennis, camping, travel. Office: 55 W Monroe St Ste 2720 Chicago IL 60603-5001

**MISCI, JOHN A., JR.,** lawyer; b. Vineland, N.J., June 9, 1964; s. John A. Sr. and Helen B. Misci; m. Karen Beilenson, July 14, 1990; children: Mikkell, Johnny. BS in Bus. Adminstrn., Thomas Edison State Coll., Trenton, N.J., 1992; JD, Widener U., 1994. Bar: N.J. 1995, Pa. 1995, U.S. Dist. Ct. N.J. 1995. Atty. Mattleman, Weinroth and Miller, Cherry Hill, N.J., 1995-97; city atty. City of Camden, N.J., 1997—. Bd. dirs. Assn. for Retarded Citizens, Gloucester County, N.J., 1996—. Avocations: scuba diving, collecting ancient weapons. Home: 48 Aldridge Way Sewell NJ 08080-3336 Office: City of Camden City Hall Camden NJ 08101

**MISHKIN, BARBARA FRIEDMAN,** lawyer; b. Phila., Feb. 19, 1936; d. Maurice Harold and Gertrude (Sanders) F.; m. Martin S. Thaler, Mar. 22, 1958 (div. 1970); children: Diane Sanders, Paul Sanders, David Emile, Amy Suzanne; m. Mortimer Mishkin, May 27, 1971. AB, Mount Holyoke Coll., 1957; MA, Yale U., 1958; JD, Am. U., 1981. Bar: D.C. 1982, U.S. Supreme Ct. 1989, U.S. Ct. Appeals (4th cir.) 1995. Research psychologist NIMH, Bethesda, Md., 1968-69; spl. asst. to chief judge U.S. Ct. Appeals (D.C. cir.), Washington, 1970-71; spl. asst. to scientific dir. Nat. Inst. Child Health, Bethesda, 1971-74; asst. staff dir. Nat. Commn. for the Protection of Human Subjects, Washington, 1974-78; staff dir. Ethics Adv. Bd. HEW, Washington, 1978-80; dep. dir. Pres.' Commn. on Ethics in Medicine and Research, Washington, 1980-83; assoc. Hogan and Hartson, Washington, 1983-89; counsel Hogan and Hartson, 1990-93; ptnr. Hogan & Hartson, 1994—; cons. Ctr. for Law and Health Scis., Boston, 1970-73; cons., lectr. Johns Hopkins U. Sch. of Medicine, Balt., 1971-73; bd. dirs. Bon Secours Health Systems, Inc., Columbia, Md., 1984-90. Contbr. numerous articles on health law, med. ethics and biomed. research to jours. in field. Mem. policy bd. Legal Counsel for the Elderly, Washington, 1984-88, vice chair, 1988-90; trustee Mt. Holyoke Coll., 1985-90; mem. Mayor's Adv. Task Force on Hospice Licensure, Washington, 1985-87; bd. dirs. Hebrew Home Greater Washington, 1987-91. Mem. ABA (chair sect. on health and environment 1988-92, chair com. on regulating rsch. 1996-98), D.C. Bar Assn. (subcom. rights of the elderly and the handicapped 1985-92, Pro Bono Atty. Yr. 1988), AAAS (com. on sci. freedom and responsibility 1986-92, AAAS/ABA Nat. Conf. Lawyers and Scientists 1992, ABA co-chair 1993-97), Am. Soc. Law, Medicine and Ethics (bd. dirs. 1995-98). Administrative and regulatory, Government contracts and claims, Health. Home: 5610 Wisconsin Ave Apt 402 Chevy Chase MD 20815-4429 Office: Hogan & Hartson Columbia Sq 555 13th St Washington DC 20004

**MISHKIN, JEREMY DAVID,** lawyer; b. Pensacola, Fla., Apr. 21, 1955; s. Mark M. and Barbara (Mintz) M.; m. Barbara Sagar, May 20, 1979; children: Benjamin Sagar, Maxwell Stuart. BA, Ind. U., 1976; JD, U. Pa., 1979. Bar: Pa. 1979, U.S. Dist. Ct. (ea. dist.) Pa. 1980, U.S. Ct. Appeals (3d cir.) 1982, U.S. Tax Ct. 1986, U.S. Supreme Ct. 1986. Assoc. Montgomery, McCracken, Walker & Rhoads, Phila., 1979-86, sr. assoc., 1986-88, mng. ptnr., 1996—. Bd. dirs. Wynnewood (Pa.) Civic Assn., 1986—, sec., 1989—, pres., 1992-94. Mem. ABA, Pa. Bar Assn., Phila. Bar Assn. (compulsory arbitration com. 1987—). Avocations: trout fishing, tennis. General civil litigation, Personal injury, Libel. Office: Montgomery McCracken Walker & Rhoads 123 S Broad St Fl 28 Philadelphia PA 19109-1029

**MISHKIN, KATHLEEN ANNE,** lawyer; b. Southington, Conn., Apr. 22, 1956; d. Joseph E. and Mary Elizabeth (Brown) Moreshead; m. Eric Marc Mishkin, Dec. 22, 1981. BS summa cum laude, U. Md., 1987; JD cum laude, Pace Law Sch., 1991. Assoc. Mudge, Rose Guthrie, Alexander & Ferdon, N.Y.C., 1991-94, O'Melveny & Meyers, N.Y.C. and N.J., 1994-96; asst. county atty. Orange County, N.Y., 1996-98; of counsel Drake, Somers, Loeb, Tarshis & Catania, Newburgh, N.Y., 1998—. Editor-in-chief: Pace Law Rev., 1990-91. Mem. Women's Assn. of Law Students (v.p. 1989-90). General civil litigation, Appellate, Federal civil litigation. Home: 893 Laroe Rd Monroe NY 10950-5025 Office: Drake Somers Loeb Tarshis & Catania PO Box 1479 Newburgh NY 12551-1479

**MISHLER, JACOB,** federal judge; b. N.Y.C., Apr. 20, 1911; s. Abraham and Rebecca M.; m. Lola Mishler, Sept. 1, 1936; m. Helen Mishler, Aug. 26, 1970; children: Alan, Susan Lubitz; stepchildren: Bruce Shillet, Gail Shillet Unger. Degree, NYU, 1931, JD, 1933. Pvt. practice L.I. City, N.Y., 1934-50; ptnr. Mishler & Wohl, 1950-59, 60; judge N.Y. State Supreme Ct., 1959; sr. judge U.S. Dist. Ct. (ea. dist.), Uniondale, N.Y., 1960—; chief judge U.S. Dist. Ct., 1969-80; mem. U.S. Jud. Conf., Dist. Judge Rep., 2nd cir., 1974-77. Office: US Dist Ct LI Courthouse Rm 311 2 Uniondale Ave Uniondale NY 11553-1258

**MISHLER, MARK SEAN,** lawyer; b. Princeton, N.J., Oct. 18, 1956. BA, Brandeis U., 1978; JD, Boston Coll., 1981. Bar: Mass. 1981, N.Y. 1982, U.S. Dist. Ct. (no. dist.) N.Y. 1982, U.S. Ct. Appeals (2nd cir.) 1997. Dir. Student Legal Svcs., Albany, N.Y., 1981-87; assoc. Walter, Thayer & Long, Albany, 1987-88; ptnr. Walter, Thayer & Mishler, Albany, 1988—; adj. instr. Cornell U. Sch. Indsl. and Labor Rels., 1997—. Exec. bd. mem. Albany Br. NAACP, 1985—, PTA, Albany, 1996—; mem. Albany Cmty./Police Rels. Bd., 1986-88. Recipient award for disting. svc. in legal redress Albany Br. NAACP, 1986, Frederick Douglas Struggle for Justice award Ctr. for Law & Justice, Albany, 1992, Progressive Leadership award Capital Dist. Citizen Action, 1998. Mem. Nat. Lawyers Guild, N.Y. State Assn. Criminal Def. Lawyers. Civil rights, Labor, Criminal. Office: Walter Thayer & Mishler PC 756 Madison Ave Ste 4 Albany NY 12208-3832

**MISKIMIN, ALICE SCHWENK,** retired lawyer; b. Newark, Feb. 20, 1932; d. Otto Gustav and Alice Moore (Coy) Schwenk; divorced; children: Sidonie Ann Miskimin Clauss, Matthew Charles. BA, Vassar Coll., 1953; MA, Yale U., 1954, PhD, 1964, JD, 1982. Bar: Conn. 1982, U.S. Dist. Ct. Conn. 1982, U.S. Ct. Appeals (2d cir.) 1983. Sr. lectr. Yale U., New Haven, 1963-79; assoc. Day, Berry & Howard, Hartford, Conn., 1982-84; ptnr. Jacobs, Grudberg, Belt & Dow, New Haven, 1984-97; ret., 1997; town counsel Town of Woodbridge, Conn., 1991—; counsel Conn. Acad. Arts and Scis., New Haven, 1988, East Rock Inst., New Haven, 1988—. Author: The Renaissance Chaucer, 1975; editor: Susannah, 1965; sr. editor Conn. Bar Jour., 1995—. Cooper fellow Ct. Bar Found., 1994—. Mem. Conn. Bar Assn. (profl. ethics com. 1990—), Conn. Bar Found. (bd. dirs., v.p. 1990—). Municipal (including bonds), Environmental, Land use and zoning (including planning).

**MISSAN, RICHARD SHERMAN,** lawyer; b. New Haven, Oct. 5, 1933; s. Albert and Hannah (Hochberg) M.; m. Aileen Louise Missan; children: Hilary, Andrew, Wendy. B.A., Yale U., 1955, J.D., 1958. Bar: N.Y. 1959, U.S. Dist. Ct. (so. and ea. dists.) N.Y. 1979, U.S. Ct. Appeals (2d cir.) N.Y. 1993. Assoc. Kaye, Scholer, Fierman, Hays & Handler, N.Y.C., 1962-67; ptnr. Schoenfeld & Jacobs, N.Y.C., 1968-78, Walsh & Frisch, N.Y.C., 1979-80, Gersten, Savage & Kaplowitz, N.Y.C., 1980-87, v.p., gen. counsel, Avis, Inc., 1987-88; pvt. practice, N.Y.C., 1988—; spl. prof. law Hofstra U., 1988—; mem. panel of mediators U.S. Dist. Ct. (ea. dist.) N.Y. Revision author: Corporations, New York Practice Guide (Business and Commercial). Mem. ABA, N.Y. State Bar Assn., Fed. Bar Council, Assn. of Bar of City of N.Y. (com. on corrections, chmn. subcom. on legis., com. on juvenile justice, chmn. subcom. on juvenile facilities, com. on atomic energy, mem. com. on mcpl. affairs, com. on housing and urban devel.), Yale Club. General corporate, General civil litigation, Real property.

**MITCHELL, ALLAN EDWIN,** lawyer; b. Okemah, Okla., May 13, 1944; m. Neva G. Ream; children: Brian, Amy. BA in Mass. Comm., Northwestern Okla. State U., Alva, 1991; JD, U. Okla., 1994. Bar: Okla. 1994, U.S. dist. ct. (we. and no. dists.) 1994. Asst. state mgr. Oklahomans for Right to Work, Oklahoma City, 1967-68; exec. dir. London Sq. Village, Oklahoma City, 1968-73; dist. mgr. Farmland Ins. Svc., Oklahoma City, 1974-80, Nat. Farmers Union, Oklahoma City, 1980-85; dist. agt. Prudential Ins., Cherokee, Okla., 1985-89; atty. Hughes & Grant, Oklahoma City, 1994-96, Collins & Mitchell, Cherokee, Okla., 1996—; asst. dist. atty Alfalfa County, Okla., 1996—. Mem. Cherokee Bd. Edn., 1985-90; mem. fin. com. Rep. Party of Okla., 1995, state com., 1997—; scoutmaster, 1981-86, bd. mem. Great Salt Plains Coun. Boy Scouts Am.; adult advisor Girl Scouts Am.; pres. United Way Cherokee, 1984; mem. Okla. Sch. Bd. Mems. Legis. Network, 1985-90, state com. Okla. Rep. Party, 1997; vol. Okla. Spl. Olympics, 1996, 97. Mem. Ch. of the Nazarene. Avocations: public speaking, politics, civic activities. Criminal, General corporate, General practice. Office: Collins & Mitchell 214 S Grand Ave Cherokee OK 73728-2030

**MITCHELL, AUSTIN L.,** lawyer; b. St. Louis, Apr. 6, 1947; s. William Melvin and Janet Elizabeth (Austin) M.; m. Rebecca A. Mitchell; children: John Adam, Anthony Lyle. BS in Bus. Adminstrn., S.E. Mo. State U., Cape Girardeau, 1968; JD, St. Louis U., 1974. Bar: Mo. 1974, U.S. Tax Ct. 1979; CPA, Mo. Staff acct. Price Waterhouse & Co., St. Louis, 1968-70; mgr. R.C. Fietsam & Co., CPA, Belleville, Ill., 1970-73; tax cons. Peat, Marwick, Mitchell & Co., St. Louis, 1974-76; owner Austin L. Mitchell, CPA, Salem, Mo., 1976-82; ptnr. Pratt, Mitchell & Co., PC, CPA, Salem, 1982—; owner Austin L. Mitchell, Atty., Salem, 1976—. Co-author: (textbook) Qualified Employee Benefit Plans, 1975. Trustee Bonebrake-McMurtrey Found., Ltd., Salem, 1989—; bd. dirs. IDA of Dent County, Salem, 1980-86. Mem. ABA, AICPA, Mo. Bar, Am. Assn. Attys.-CPAs, Mo. Soc. CPAs (chair profl. ethics com. 1991-92). Taxation, general, Administrative and regulatory, General practice. Office: 301 N Washington St Salem MO 65560-1278

**MITCHELL, BURLEY BAYARD, JR.,** state supreme court chief justice; b. Oxford, N.C., Dec. 15, 1940; s. Burley Bayard and Dorothy Ford (Champion) M.; m. Mary Lou Willett, Aug. 3, 1962; children: David Bayard, Catherine Morris. BA with honors, N.C. State U., 1966, DHL (hon.), 1995; JD, U. N.C., 1969; LLD (hon.), Campbell U., 1998. Bar: N.C. 1969, U.S. Ct. Appeals (4th cir.) 1970, U.S. Supreme Ct. 1972. Asst. atty. gen. State of N.C., Raleigh, 1969-72, dist. atty., 1973-77, judge Ct. Appeals, 1977-79, sec. crime control, 1979-82; justice Supreme Ct. N.C., Raleigh, 1982-94; chief justice Supreme Ct. of N.C., Raleigh, 1995-99; ptnr. Womble Carlyle Sandridge and Rice, Raleigh, 1999—. Served with USN, 1958-62, Asia. Recipient N.C. Nat. Guard Citizen Commendation award, 1982. Mem. ABA, VFW, N.C. Bar Assn., Mensa, Am. Legion, Phi Beta Kappa. Democrat. Methodist. Home: 4301 City of Oaks Wynd Raleigh NC 27612-5316 Office: 2100 First Union Cptl Ctr 150 Fayetteville St Mall PO Box 831 Raleigh NC 27602*

**MITCHELL, C. MACNEIL,** lawyer; b. N.Y.C., Sept. 22, 1942; s. MacNeil and Katherine Mitchell; m. Laura Ann Grossen, July 3, 1948; children: Abigail Grace, Ian MacNeil. BA, Yale U., 1964; JD, U. Calif., Berkeley, 1967. Assoc. Breed, Abbott & Morgan, N.Y.C., 1969-75, ptnr., 1975-93; ptnr. Whitman Breed Abbott & Morgan LLP, N.Y.C., 1993—; spkr./lectr. in field. Contbr. articles to profl. jours. Pres. Cannon Point North, Inc., N.Y.C., 1988; bd. dirs. 455 E 57th St., Inc., N.Y.C., 1998. Served with U.S. Army, 1967-69. Mem. Assn. Bar City N.Y., Maidstone Club, Devon Yacht Club, Yale Club of N.Y.C. Republican. Avocations: science, computer technology, skiing, golf, tennis. General civil litigation, Product liability, Insurance. Home: 455 E 57th St New York NY 10022-3065 Office: Whitman Breed Abbott & Morgan 200 Park Ave New York NY 10166-0005

**MITCHELL, CAROL ANN,** lawyer; b. New Bedford, Mass., Sept. 2, 1957; d. John E. and Edith A. (Mogensen) M. AB, Vassar Coll., 1979; JD, William and Mary Coll., 1982. Bar: D.C. 1983, U.S. Ct. Appeals (Fed. cir.) 1988, U.S. Ct. Internat. Trade 1986. Atty.-advisor Benefits Rev. Bd., Washington, 1982-83; import compliance specialist Internat. Trade Adminstrn. U.S. Dept. Commerce, Washington, 1983-85; assoc. Collier, Shannon & Scott, Washington, 1985-90, Akin, Gump, Strauss, Hauer & Feld, Washington, 1990-91, Dewey, Ballantine, Washington, 1991-94; Steptoe & Johnson, Washington, 1994—. Mem. Vassar Club. Private international, Administrative and regulatory, Immigration, naturalization, and customs. Office: 1330 Connecticut Ave NW Washington DC 20036-1704

**MITCHELL, CHARLES EDWARD,** lawyer; b. Seymour, Ind., July 7, 1925; s. Edward Charles Mitchell and Lula Belle (Thompson) Browning; m. Julia Viola Sarjeant, Sept. 15, 1951; children: Charles Leonard, Albert Bascom. Student, Morehouse Coll., Atlanta, 1943-44, 46-47, NYU, 1949; JD, Temple U., Phila., 1954. Bar: D.C. 1970, U.S. Ct. Appeals (3d cir.) 1971, Pa. 1972, U.S. Supreme Ct. 1973, U.S. Ct. Appeals (6th cir.) 1984; cert. labor arbitrator. Tchr. City of Phila. Budget Bur., 1954-55; mgmt. trainee Office of Dir. of Fin., Budget Bur., Phila., 1955-56; legal asst. Office of Phila. Dist. Atty., 1956-60; claims rep., claims authorizer U.S. HEW, Social Security Adminstrn., Phila., 1960-64; atty., examiner NLRB, Phila., 1964-72; mgmt. labor counsel E.I. duPont de Nemours & Co., Phila., 1972-92; pvt. practice Phila., 1993—. 1st class seaman USN, 1944-46. Mem. ABA (mgmt. mem. sect. labor and employment law, practice and procs. com. 1973-92), Fed. Bar Assn. (pres. Del. chpt. 1974-76, nat. chpt. del. 1973-78), Indsl. Rels. Rsch. Assn. (v.p. 1970-72), Phila. Bar Assn. Democrat. Episcopalian. Avocations: golf, tennis, chess, bridge, travel. Office: 5500 Wissahickon Ave Ste M-907A Philadelphia PA 19144-5653

**MITCHELL, CHARLES F.,** lawyer; b. Washington, Oct. 18, 1963; s. John Joseph and Duane (Schwertner) M.; m. Sherrie Ilyse Braude, June 7, 1986; children: Matthew Ryan, Sydni Paige, Jake Bradley. BA, U. Md., 1985; JD, Georgetown U., 1989. Bar: Md. 1989, D.C. 1991, U.S. Ct. Md. 1990, U.S. Ct. Appeals (4th and fed. cirs.) 1991, U.S. Ct. Fed. Claims 1991. Assoc. Holland & Knight (formerly Donnelly & Duvall), Washington, 1989-93; gen. counsel John J. Kirlin, Inc., Rockville, Md., 1993—. Contbr. articles to profl. jours. Mem. Am. Inns of Ct., ABA (vice-chmn. subcontracts com. for constrn. industry 1995, mem. public contract law/litigation sects.). Avocations: golf, tennis. Construction, Government contracts and claims. Home: 9814 Bald Cypress Dr Rockville MD 20850-3494 Office: John J Kirlin Inc 643 Lofstrand Ln Rockville MD 20850-1389

**MITCHELL, CLARK A.,** lawyer; b. Pitts., Feb. 1, 1947; s. Clark N. and Nancy K. M.; m. Mary Ellen MacKenzie, Aug. 23, 1969; children: Meredith, Kimberly, Clark. BA, Washington & Jefferson Coll.; JD, U. Akron. Bar: Pa. Bd. dirs., treas. Washington County Am. Cancer Soc. Mem. Pa. Bar Assn., Pa. Trial Lawyers Assn., Washington County Bar Assn., Reserve Officers Assn., Elks, Scottish Rite, Masons. Avocations: flying, hunting. General civil litigation, Personal injury, Workers' compensation. Office: 17 S College St Washington PA 15301-4821

**MITCHELL, DAVID BENJAMIN,** lawyer, mediator, arbitrator; b. Miami Beach, Fla., Nov. 3, 1950; s. Quintus Eugene and Gertrude (Ziegler) M.; m. Lynn Stewart, Dec. 11, 1993. BA, U. Miami, Coral Gables, Fla., 1973; JD, Stetson U., 1978. Bar: Fla. 1979, U.S. Dist. Ct. (so. dist.) Fla. 1979, U.S. Tax Ct. 1987; cert. family mediator; cert. arbitrator; cert. ins. mediator. Assoc., sr. assoc. Semet, Lickstein, Morgenstern & Berger, P.A., Coral Gables, 1987-90; pres. David B. Mitchell, P.A., Coral Gables, 1990—; pres. South Fla. Mediation Assocs., Inc., Coral Gables, 1990-92. Mem. Coral Gables Cmty. Found., 1996—; grad. Leadership Miami, 1987; bd. dirs. Ponce de Leon Devel. Assn., pres., 1992-93; bd. dirs. Internat. Zen Found. of Fla., 1997—, Coral Gables Citizens Crime Watch, 1998—. Mem. The Fla. Bar (mem. family law sect.), Dade County Bar Assn. (family law com., county cts. com., Cert. of Appreciation 1994-95), Coral Gables Bar Assn. (law day com. 1996, scholarship com. 1996, bd. dirs. 1997—), Fed. Bar Assn. (appellate arbitrator, prudential class action remediation plan 1999—), Acad. Trial Lawyers Am., Dade County Trial Lawyers Assn., Acad. Fla. Trial Lawyers, Acad. Family Mediators, U. Miami Alumni Club of Greater Miami (sec., dir. 1996-98), Coral Gables C. of C. (govt. affairs and legal com. 1995—). Democrat. Buddhist. Avocations: boating, reading, travel. E-mail: mitchelaw@aol.com. Family and matrimonial, General corporate. Office: Gables Corp Plz #920 2100 Ponce De Leon Blvd Coral Gables FL 33134-5215

**MITCHELL, GUY HAMILTON,** lawyer; b. N.Y.C., Dec. 3, 1966; s. Napoleon and Gloria M. BSc, SUNY, Brockport, 1988; JD, Ohio Northern U., 1991. Bar: Conn. 1991, N.Y. 1992, N.J. 1992, U.S. Dist. Ct. N.J. 1992, U.S. Dist. Ct. (ea. and so. dist.) N.Y. 1997. Intern Office of Town Atty., Elmsford, N.Y., 1989, Westchester Dist. Atty., White Plains, N.Y., 1989, Office of Dist. Atty., Bronx, N.Y., 1990; asst. dist. atty. Office of Dist. Atty., Bronx, 1991—; assoc. Aiello, Cannick & Esposito, Queens, N.Y., 1992; asst. atty. gen., chief of criminal divsn. Dept. Justice/Office of Atty. Gen., 1999—; rep. 46th Precinct Coun., Bronx, 1995—. Mentor Children's Aid Soc., N.Y.C., 1995—. Recipient Appreciation award Tiebout Cmty. Ctr., Bronx, 1996, Cmty. Svc. award Cmty. Affairs Unit Bronx Dist. Atty.'s Office, 1998, Appreciation award Justice Resource Ctr., N.Y.C., 1996-98. Mem. Nat. Black Prosecutors Assn., Bronx Black Bar Assn., Kappa Alpha Psi. Avocations: drawing, painting, martial arts, weight lifting, basketball. Home: 2850 Caflin Ave Bronx NY 10468 Office: Office of Dist Atty 198 E 161st St Bronx NY 10451-3506

**MITCHELL, HUGH ALLEN, JR.,** lawyer; b. Olney, Md., May 9, 1956; s. Hugh Allen and Ruth Anne (Waple) M.; m. Denise A. Eldridge, Aug. 19, 1979; children: Jason, Samuel, Timothy, Hugh, Kayla, Josiah, Eben. BA in Econs., U. Md., 1977; JD, U. Va., 1980. Bar: Md. 1980, D.C. 1982. Law clk. to Hon. Ridgely P. Melvin, Jr., Md. Ct. Spl. Appeals, Annapolis, 1980-81; assoc. Glassie, Pewett, Dudley, Beebe & Shanks, Washington, 1981-83, Law Office Ronald R. Holden, Annapolis, Md., 1983-87; dir. devel. Annapolis Area Christian Sch., 1987-91; assoc. Barr & Testa, P.A., Balt., 1991-93; ptnr. Barr & Mitchell, P.A., Balt., 1993-96, Stewart, Plant & Blumenthal, LLC, Balt., 1996—; spkr., instr. Md. Inst. for Continuing Edn. Lawyers, Balt. and Annapolis, 1992—, Md. Assn. CPAs, Balt. and Gambrills, Md., 1995—. Contbr. articles to law publs. Elder Evang. Presbyn. Ch., Annapolis, 1985-89; founder, pres. Recreational Youth Athletic League, Annapolis, 1993—; mem. Anne Arundel County Human Rights Adv. Com., Annapolis, 1994-97. Fellow Am. Coll. Trust and Estate Counsel; mem. Md. Bar Assn. (augmented estate com. 1994—, coun. elder law sect. 1994-96, coun. estates and trusts sect. 1996-98). Avocations: reading, teaching. Estate planning, Probate, Estate taxation. Office: 7 Saint Paul St Ste 910 Baltimore MD 21202-1672

**MITCHELL, LANSING LEROY,** federal judge; b. Sun, La., Jan. 17, 1914; s. Leroy A. and Eliza Jane (Richardson) M.; m. Virginia Jumonville, Apr. 18, 1938; children—Diane Mitchell (Mrs. Donald Lee Parker), Lansing Leroy. B.A., La. State U., 1934, LL.B., 1937. Bar: La. 1937. Pvt. practice Pontchatoula, 1937-38; spl. agt. FBI, 1938-41; atty. SEC, 1941-42; asst. U.S. atty. Eastern Dist. La., 1946-53; also engaged in pvt practice; ptnr. Deutsch, Kerrigan & Stiles., New Orleans, 1953-66; U.S. dist. judge Eastern Dist. La., 1966—. Chmn. nat. security com. New Orleans C. of C., 1963-66; vice chmn. New Orleans Armed Forces Day, 1964, 65, New Orleans Heart Fund campaign, 1959-60; mem. New Orleans Municipal Auditorium Adv. Com., 1957-61, New Orleans Municipal Com. Finance, 1955-67, Small Bus. Adv. Council La., 1963-66; pres. Camp Fire Girls Greater New Orleans, 1965-67; La. chmn. Lawyers for Kennedy-Johnson, 1960. Served to lt. col. AUS, 1942-46; col. Res. (ret.). Decorated Royal Order St. George Royal Order Scotland. Mem. ABA, Inter-Am. Bar Assn., La. Bar Assn., New Orleans Bar Assn., Maritime Law Assn. U.S., Judge Adv. Assn., Soc. Former Spl. Agts. FBI, Am. Legion, Mil. Order World Wars, V.F.W., Navy League, Assn. U.S. Army (pres. La. 1964-65, pres. New Orleans 1961-64, v.p. 4th Army region 1963-66), Soc. Mayflower Descendants in State of La. (assoc.), Scabbard and Blade, SAR, S.R., Soc. War 1812 La., Pi Kappa Alpha, Phi Delta Phi, Theta Nu Epsilon. Clubs: Mason (33 degree, New Orleans) (Shriner), Press (New Orleans), Southern Yacht (New Orleans), Bienville, Pendennis (New Orleans). Office: US Dist Ct C-508 US Courthouse 500 Camp St New Orleans LA 70130-3313 *To serve my country as a soldier, praying that I need never be called to arms again; to serve the people as a jurist, knowing that I too shall someday be judged; to serve my family as a shepherd, finding that my love for them begets greater loving.*

**MITCHELL, MATTHEW KYLE,** lawyer; b. Phila., Mar. 12, 1968; s. Bertram Harold and Joanne (Oritsky) M. AB in Govt. and Law, Lafayette Coll., Easton, Pa., 1990; JD cum laude, U. Miami, 1993. Bar: Fla. 1993, N.J. 1993, U.S. Dist. Ct. N.J. 1994, U.S. Dist. Ct. (so. dist.) Fla. 1994, U.S. Ct. Appeals (11th and 3d cirs.) 1994, U.S. Supreme Ct. 1998. Assoc. Angones, Hunter, McClure, Lynch & Williams, Miami, Fla., 1993-95, Green, Lundgren & Ryan, Haddonfield, N.J., 1995—. Mem. ABA, ATLA, N.J. Bar Assn., Camden County Bar Assn. Office: Green Lundgren and Ryan PC PO Box 70 Haddonfield NJ 08033-0085

**MITCHELL, MEADE WESTMORELAND,** lawyer; b. Pascagoula, Miss., Aug. 20, 1968; s. Melvin L. and Sara (Westmoreland) M.; m. Holly Henderson, Dec. 31, 1995; 1 child, William Westmoreland. B in Acctg., U. Miss., 1990, JD, 1993. Bar: Miss. 1993, U.S. Dist. Ct. (so. dist.) Miss. 1993, U.S. Ct. Appeals (5th cir.) 1993. Law clk. U.S. Dist. Ct. So. Dist. Miss., Jackson, 1993-94; assoc. Holcomb, Dunbar P.A., Jackson, 1994-97, Butler, Snow, O'Mara, Stevens & Cannada, P.L.L.C., Jackson, 1997—. Contbr. articles and comments to law jours. Mem. Jackson Exch. Club, 1994—. Mem. ABA, Am. Inns of Ct., Def. Rsch. Inst., Miss. Def. Lawyers Assn., Jackson Young Lawyers Assn. (treas. 1996-97, pres.-elect 1998—), Hinds County Bar Assn. (bd. dirs. 1998—). Avocations: basketball, golf, jogging. Bankruptcy, Insurance, State civil litigation. Office: PO Box 22567 Jackson MS 39225-2567

**MITCHELL, MICHAEL CHARLES,** lawyer; b. L.A., Feb. 13, 1947; s. Dominic Chester and Dorothy Marie (Dolmage) M.; m. Ingrid Burkard, June 21, 1969; children: Daniel, Alicia. BA, Loyola U., Los Angeles, 1969, JD, 1972. Bar: Calif. 1972, U.S. Supreme Ct. 1977. Assoc. Hanna & Morton, Los Angeles, 1972-79; ptnr. Anglea & Burford, Pasadena, Calif., 1979-82; sr. ptnr. MacFarlane, Lambert & Mitchell, Pasadena, 1982-85; sole practice Pasadena, 1985-98; dir. planned giving Loyola Marymont Univ., 1999—; lectr. various founds., chs., and service clubs. Columnist Pasadena Jour. of Bus., 1985-88; guest appearances on TV. Legal counsel Lions Eye Found. So. Calif. Inc., Meml. Trust, Dorland Mountain Colony, Tournament of Toys and Star News Charities; area chmn. San Gabriel Valley Council Boy Scouts Am., 1982-83; mem. adv. bd. Salvation Army, Pasadena Tabernacle, 1989—; bd. of govs. Arthritis Found. of So. Calif.; bd. dirs. Pasadena Dispensary of Huntington Hosp., Escalon, Altadena, Pasadena, 1985-86. Named Outstanding Vol. Advs. for the Quiet Minority, 1986. Mem. ABA, Calif. Bar Assn., Los Angeles County Bar Assn., Pasadena Bar Assn. (sec., bd. dirs. 1985-86), San Gabriel Valley Estate Planning Council, Tournament of Roses Assn., Pasadena C. of C., Phi Alpha Delta, Pasadena Jaycees (Dist. Service award 1982). Republican. Roman Catholic. Club: Univ. (bd. govs.), Quarterbacks (Pasadena). Lodge: Lions (pres. 1980-81, bd. dirs. 1985—). Avocations: philately, racquetball, photography. Estate planning, Probate, Estate taxation. Office: Loyola Marymount Univ 7900 Loyola Blvd Los Angeles CA 90045-2699

**MITCHELL, MICHAEL SHERMAN,** lawyer; b. Walla Walla, Wash., Oct. 28, 1953; s. Sherman Raley and Mary Ella (Hirsch) M.; m. Judy A. Stein, Aug. 16, 1975 (div. May 1988); children: Kelsey, Kyle, Ryan; m. Lisa Anderson, Feb. 11, 1999. AA, Walla Walla Community Coll., 1972; BA, Wash. State U., 1975; JD, Willamette U., 1978. Bar: Wash. 1978, U.S. Dist. Ct. (ea. dist.) Wash. 1981, U.S. Dist. Ct. (western dist.) Wash. 1986. Dep. pros. atty. Walla Walla County, 1978-81; assoc., ptnr. Roach, Votendahl, Monahan & Mitchell, Walla Walla, 1981-89; sole practitioner Michael S. Mitchell, Atty., Walla Walla, 1989—; instr. Walla Walla Community Coll., 1981. Bd. dirs. Planned Parenthood Bd., Walla Walla, 1981-82, Blue Mountain Cougar Club, Walla Walla, 1988—, United Way Walla Walla, 1991-94, Blue Mountain Sr. Housing Group, 1993—. Mem. Wash. State Bar Assn. (corrections com. 1981-82, fee arbitration bd. 1989-91, exec. com. gen. practice sect. 1994—, chair 1997-98), Walla Walla County Bar Assn. (sec.-treas. 1992, v.p. 1993, pres. 1994), Walla Walla Country Club. Avocation: athletics. Personal injury, General civil litigation, General practice. Office: 129 W Main St Walla Walla WA 99362-2817

**MITCHELL, ROBERT BURDETTE,** lawyer; b. Bremerton, Wash., Mar. 27, 1953; s. Ronald Burdette and Patricia Joan (Thompson) M.; m. Lois Jean Griffith, Aug. 24, 1974; children: Reese Burdette, Charles Franklin. BA, Ohio Wesleyan U., 1975; JD, Tulane U., 1978. Bar: N.Y. 1979, U.S. Dist. Ct. (so. dist.) N.Y. 1979, La. 1980, U.S. Dist. Ct. (ea. dist.) La. 1980, U.S. Ct. Appeals (5th and 11th cirs.) 1981, U.S. Dist. Ct. (we. dist.) La. 1987, Conn. 1988, U.S. Dist. Ct. Conn. 1988. Assoc. Haight, Gardner, Poor & Havens, N.Y.C., 1978-80, Kullman, Lang, Inman & Bee, New Orleans, 1980-83; ptnr. McGlinchey, Stafford, Mintz, Cellini & Lang, New Orleans, 1983-87, Durant, Sabanosh, Nichols & Houston, Bridgeport, Conn., 1987—. Editor Tulane Law Rev., 1976-78. Mem. ABA (chmn. young lawyer div. labor com. 1985-87), N.Y. Bar Assn., La. Bar Assn., Conn. Bar Assn., Bridgeport Bar Assn., Order of Coif. Republican. Presbyterian. Avocations: history, bicycling, camping, legal philosophy. Federal civil litigation, Labor, Civil rights. Home: 327 Fan Hill Rd Monroe CT 06468-1352 Office: Durant Sabanosh Nichols & Houston 855 Main St Bridgeport CT 06604-4915

**MITCHELL, ROBERT EVERITT,** lawyer; b. Port Washington, N.Y., June 14, 1929; s. Everitt and Alice (Fay) M.; m. Anne Nordquist, Nov. 2, 1957; children: Anne C. Mitchell Coneys, Maura A. Kelly, Michael E. BS, U. Mich., 1952; JD, Georgetown U., 1956. Bar: N.Y. 1957, U.S. Dist. Ct. (so. dist). N.Y. 1958, U.S. Supreme Ct. 1966. Assoc. Sullivan & Cromwell, N.Y.C., 1956-63; v.p., sec., gen. counsel Lambert & Co. Inc., N.Y.C., 1963-65; ptnr. Campbell & Mitchell, Manhasset, N.Y., 1965-80; asst. gen. counsel J.P. Stevens & Co. Inc., N.Y.C., 1980-82, gen. counsel, 1982-88; pvt. practice Peconic, N.Y., 1988—. Atty. Village Baxter Estates, Port Washington, 1967-83; Counsel Mobilized Community Resources, Roslyn, N.Y., 1969-80; asst. scout master Troop 1001 Boy Scouts Am., Port Washington, 1976-79; justice Village Sands Point, N.Y., 1966-85. Served to lt. USNR, 1952-55. Mem. ABA. Republican. Roman Catholic. Clubs: Manhasset Bay Yacht (Port Washington) (commodore 1972-73); N.Y. Yacht (N.Y.C.). Avocations: sailing, fishing, camping, platform tennis, music. General corporate, Securities, Antitrust. Home and Office: 3905 Wells Rd Peconic NY 11958-1738

**MITCHELL, RONNIE MONROE,** lawyer, educator; b. Clinton, N.C., Nov. 10, 1952; s. Ondus Corneilius and Margaret Ronie (Johnson) M.; m. Martha Cheryl Coble, May 25, 1975; children: Grant Stephen, Mitchell, Meredith Elizabeth Mitchell. BA, Wake Forest U., 1975, JD, 1978. Bar: N.C. 1978, U.S. Dist. Ct. (ea. dist.) N.C. 1978, U.S. Ct. Appeals (4th cir.) 1983, U.S. Supreme Ct. 1984. Assoc. atty. Brown, Fox & Deaver, Fayetteville, N.C., 1978-81; ptnr. Harris, Sweeny & Mitchell, Fayetteville, 1981-91, Harris, Mitchell & Hancox, 1991-96, Harris & Mitchell, 1997-98, Harris, Mitchell & Burns, 1998—; adj. prof. law Norman Adrian Wiggins Sch. of Law, Campbell U; bd. dirs. Mace, Inc. Contbr. chpts. to books. Chmn. Cumberland County Bd. Adjustment, 1985-92, Cumberland County Rescue Squad, 1986-93; bd. dirs. Cumberland County Rescue Squad, Fayetteville, 1983-91. Recipient U.S. Law Week award Bur. Nat. Affairs, 1978. Mem. ABA, ATLA, Twelfth Judicial Dist. Bar Assn. (pres. 1988-89), N.C. Bar Assn. (councillor Young Lawyers divsn. 1982-85), N.C. Legis. Rsch. Commn. (family law com. 1994), Cumberland County Bar Assn. (mem. family law com., N.C. State Bar Bd. legal specialization), N.C. Acad. Trial Lawyers, Fayetteville Ind. Light Infantry Club, Dem. Men's Club (pres. 1993-94), Moose, Masons. Home: RR 23 Box 108C Fayetteville NC 28301-9125 Office: Harris Mitchell & Burns 308 Person St Fayetteville NC 28301-5736

**MITCHELL, ROY SHAW,** lawyer; b. Sherwood, N.Y., Jan. 16, 1934; s. Malcolm Douglas and Ruth Landon (Holland) M.; m. Nancy Elizabeth Bishop, Aug. 27, 1955; children: Mark E., Jeffrey B., Jennifer R. BS, Cornell U., 1957; JD with honors, George Washington U., Washington, D.C., 1959. Bar: D.C. 1959, Ohio 1960, Va. 1967, U.S. Ct. Fed. Claims 1963, U.S. Supreme Ct. 1965. Atty. Squire, Sanders & Dempsey, Cleve., 1960-61, Hudson & Creyke, Washington, 1961-67, Lewis, Mitchell & Moore, Vienna, Va., 1967-87, Morgan, Lewis & Bockius LLP, Washington, 1987—; vice-chmn. Ameribanc Savs. Bank, Annandale, Va., 1980-95; trustee Ameribanc Investors Group, Annandale, 1980-95. Co-author: (with others) Handbook of Construction Law and Claims, 1982, 89; contbr. numerous articles to profl. jours. Fellow ABA (pub. contract law sect.), Am. Coll. Construction Lawyers, Va. Bar Assn., D.C. Bar Assn. Presbyterian. Avocation: boating. Construction, Government contracts and claims, Private international. Home: 5 Jefferson Run Rd Great Falls VA 22066-3200 Office: Morgan Lewis & Bockius 1800 M St NW Washington DC 20036-5802

**MITCHELL, SHELLEY MARIE,** lawyer; b. Norfolk, Va., Aug. 8, 1959; d. Vance Garland Mitchell and Dorothy Mitchell Robertson. BS in Comms., Nova U., Ft. Lauderdale, Fla., 1981; AA, U. Fla., 1978, JD, 1984. Bar: Fla. 1985. Assoc. Ginsburg, Byrd, Jones & Dahlgaard, P.A., Sarasota, Fla., 1985-86, Frumkes & Greene, P.A., Miami, Fla., 1986-87, Abrams & Abrams, P.A., Coconut Grove, Fla., 1987-88; sole practitioner Ft. Lauderdale, 1988—; presenter seminars in field. Contbr. articles to profl. jours. Mem. Fla. Bar Assn. (family ct. rules sect. 1993—, exec. coun. family law com. 1989-97). Avocation: creative writing. Family and matrimonial, Appellate. Office: 212 SE 8th St Ste 103 Fort Lauderdale FL 33316-1014

**MITCHELL, WILLIAM D.,** lawyer; b. Great Falls, Mont., June 15, 1947; s. William Howard and Dorothy Elizabeth (Lane) M.; m. Mary Claire McDonough, Aug. 15, 1973; children: James Edward, Andrew Elliott, Thomas Michael. BA cum laude, U. Wash., Seattle, 1969; MA in Econs., U. Calif., Berkeley, 1976, JD, 1976; MLT, Georgetown U., 1982. Bar: Calif. 1977, DC 1978, Del. 1982, Mont. 1981, Fla. 1983, U.S. Ct. Appeals (11th cir.) 1994, U.S. Dist. Ct. (no. dist.) Fla. 1992, U.S. Dist. Ct. (so. dist.) Fla. 1986, U.S. Dist. Ct. (mid. dist.) Fla. 1984, U.S. Dist. Ct. Mont. 1981, U.S. Tax Ct. 1992. Atty. Fed. Trade Commn., Washington, DC, 1976-79; assoc. Koteen & Burt, Washington, DC, 1979-80, Tipp, Hoven & Skjelset, Missoula, Mont., 1980-81, Murdoch & Walsh, Wilmington, Del., 1982-83, Carlton, Fields, Ward, Smith & Cutler, Tampa, 1983-88; of counsel Foley & Lardner, Tampa, 1988-90; ptnr. Langford, Hill, Mitchell, Trybus & Whalen, Tampa, Fla., 1991-92; pres. Mitchell Law Group, Tampa, 1992—. Co-author: (book) Employee Fringe and Welfare Benefit Plans, 1988; author: Estate and Retirement Answer Book, 1994; contbr. articles to numerous jours. Lt. U.S. Navy, 1969-72. Mem. ABA (sect. taxation, com. on employee benefits, labor and employment law sect., com. on employee benefits, MEWA subcom., mgmt. co-chair), Greater Tampa Sertoma Club (dir. 1993-96, pres. 1996—), Tampa Bay Writers Alliance, Mensa. Lutheran. Avocations: creative writing, acting, golf, weight lifting, auto sports. Labor, Estate planning.

**MITCHELL, WILLIAM GRAHAM CHAMPION,** lawyer, business executive; b. Raleigh, Dec. 24, 1946; s. Burley Bayard and Dorothy Ford (Champion) M.; children: William Graham, Margaret Scripture. AB, U. N.C., 1969, JD with highest hons., 1975. Bar: N.C. 1975, U.S. Dist. Ct. (ea., mid. and we. dists.) N.C. 1976, U.S. Ct. Appeals (4th cir.) 1978. Ptnr. Womble, Carlyle, Sandridge & Rice, Winston-Salem, 1975-87; sr. v.p. for external affairs RJR Nabisco, Atlanta, 1987-89; exec. v.p. R.J. Reynolds Tobacco Co., Winston-Salem, 1988-89; ptnr. Howrey & Simon, Washington, 1990-94; spl. counselor to chmn. bd. True North Comm., Inc., Chgo., 1996; chmn. bd., CEO Global Exch. Carrier Co., Leesburg, Va., 1997—; pres., CEO Global Comms. Techs. Inc., Reston, Va., 1999—; bd. dirs. Fed. Agrl. Mortgage Corp., Washington; chmn. bd., CEO Convergence Equipment Co., Reston, Va., 1999—. Mem. Pres.'s Adv. Com. on Trade Policy and Negotiations, Indsl. Policy Adv. Com., Washington, 1991—; exec. com. Nat. Assn. Mfrs., Washington, 1988-89, Nat. Fgn. Trade Coun., 1988-89; chmn. Tobacco Inst., Washington, 1988-89; bd. dirs. Washington Performing Arts Soc., 1988-92; bd. advisors Dem. Leadership Coun., 1988—; founding trustee Progressive Policy Inst., 1988—; vice chmn. fin. Bush Campaign. Mem. ABA (vice chmn. antitrust sect., pvt. litigation com. 1987-89, chmn. subcom. of FTC com. 1986), Georgetown Club, City Club of Washington, Forsyth Country Club, Order of the Coif. Antitrust, Mergers and acquisitions, Product liability. Office: 7740 Donegan Dr Manassas VA 20109-2868

**MITLAK, STEFANY (LYNN),** lawyer; b. N.Y.C., Oct. 1, 1958; d. Irwin and Karel Sondra (Sperling) Cooperman; m. Bruce H. Mitlak, Sept. 20, 1987. BS, U. Mich., 1980; JD, Western New Eng. Coll., 1983; LLM, Boston U., 1989. Bar: R.I. 1984, Mass. 1985, Md. 1986, Ind. 1996. Spl. asst. atty. gen. Atty. Gen.'s Office State of R.I., Providence, 1984-85; assoc. McCormack & Putziger, Boston, 1985-90, Fitch, Wiley, Richlin & Tourse, Boston, 1990-92; spl. asst. corp. counsel pub. facilities dept. City of Boston, 1992-95; assoc. Johnson, Smith, Densborn, Wright & Heath, Indpls., 1995-96; devel. atty. Simon DeBartolo Group, Indpls., 1996—. Fundraiser Women's Polit. Caucus, Providence, 1984-85; chairwoman bldg. and licensing com. Neighborhood Assn. of the Back Bay, Boston, 1992. Avocations: running, skiing. Real property.

**MITRANO, PETER PAUL,** lawyer, engineer; b. Newton, Mass., Sept. 27, 1951; s. Peter Paul and Mary Ann (Hirrel) M.; m. Virginia Lee Kelly, Oct. 6, 1984 (div.); children: Christina Lee, Peter Paul, Christopher Louis. BS in Civil Enging., Northeastern U., 1973; JD, George Mason U., 1977. Bar: Va. 1977, D.C. 1987, N.H. 1993, Mass. 1998, U.S. Dist. Ct. (ea. dist.) Va., U.S. Dist. Ct. D.C., U.S. Ct. Fed. Claims, U.S. Patent Office, U.S. Ct. Appeals (4th cir.), U.S. Ct. Appeals (fed. cir.), U.S. Ct. Appeals (11th cir.), U.S. Ct. Appeals (D.C. cir.), U.S. Supreme Ct., U.S. Dist. Ct. N.H.; registered profl. engr., Va. Sole practice Fairfax, Va., 1979-93, Etna, N.H., 1993—. Mem. ABA, D.C. Bar Assn., N.H. Bar Assn., Va. Bar Assn. Avocations: skiing, baby sitting. Government contracts and claims, Construction, Patent. Office: PO Box 12 Etna NH 03750-0012

**MITTENTHAL, PETER A.,** lawyer; b. White Plains, N.Y., June 16, 1953. BA, U. Fla., Gainesville, 1975; JD, U. LaVerne, 1978. Bar: Calif. 1979, U.S. Dist. Ct. (ctrl. dist.) Calif. 1980, 9th Cir. Ct. Appeals Calif. 1982, U.S. Dist. Ct. (no. dist.) Calif. 1998; FCC radio broadcasting lic., Fla., 1972. Assoc. Snyder, Dorenfeld and Tannenbaum, Encino, Calif., 1996—; prosecutor discipinary proceedings (pro bono) State Bar Calif., L.A., 1988; former disc jockey and comml. voiceover artist, Fla.; arbitrator L.A. Superior Ct. Former judge Pro Tem. L.A. Mcpl. Ct., 1985—. Mem. ABA, So. Calif. Fraud Investigator's Assn., Am. Horse Shows Assn. Avocation: equestrian showjumping. General civil litigation, Personal injury, Sports. Office: Snyder, Dorenfeld and Tannenbaum 16633 Ventura Blvd Ste 1401 Encino CA 91436-1880

**MIXTER, CHRISTIAN JOHN,** lawyer; b. Basel, Switzerland, Mar. 13, 1953; s. Keith Eugene and Beatrice Maria (Ruf) M.; m. Linna M. Barnes, Dec. 17, 1977; children: Sara Elizabeth Barnes Mixter, Laura Ellen Barnes Mixter. BA, Ohio State U., 1974; JD, Duke U., 1977. Bar: N.Y. 1978, D.C. 1981. Assoc. Davis Polk & Wardwell, N.Y.C. and Washington, 1977-87; assoc. counsel Office Ind. Counsel, Washington, 1987-91; asst. chief litigation counsel Enforcement divsn. SEC, Washington, 1991-97, chief litigation counsel, 1997—. Mem. ABA, Assn. Bar City N.Y., Phi Beta Kappa, Order of the Coif. Office: Securities & Exch Commn 450 5th St NW Washington DC 20001-2739

**MIYAGI, ERICK YUKIHIKO,** lawyer; b. Baton Rouge, Mar. 29, 1967; s. Masaaki and Patricia Gail Miyagi; m. Barrye Panepinto Miyagi, Jan. 7, 1995; 1 child, Matthew Masaaki. BA, La. State U., 1990, JD, 1993. Lawyer Taylor Porter Brooks and Philipps L.L.P., Baton Rouge, 1993—. Instr. Jr. Achievement, Baton Rouge, 1996-98. Mem. Baton Rouge Bar Assn., La. Assn. of Def. Counsel, Order of Coif, Phi Kappa Phi. Office: Taylor Porter Brooks and Philips LLP 451 Florida St Baton Rouge LA 70801-1700

**MIYAGI, MELVYN MING,** lawyer; b. Yokohama, Japan, Aug. 30, 1949; s. Edward Shigeo and Lola (Young) M.; m. Nadine Naoko Yabuno, Oct. 1, 1978. BA, U. Hawaii, 1971; JD, Santa Clara U., 1975. Bar: Hawaii 1975. Law clk. 1st Cir. Ct. Hawaii, Honolulu, 1975-76; dep. atty. gen. State of Hawaii, Honolulu, 1976-81; assoc. Davis & Playdon, Honolulu, 1981-86; ptnr. Reid, Richards & Miyagi, Honolulu, 1986—. Mem. Am. Bd. Trial Advs. (assoc.). Avocation: surfing. Office: Reid Richards & Miyagi 1200 Pauahi Tower 1001 Bishop St Honolulu HI 96813-3429

**MIYASAKI, SHUICHI,** lawyer; b. Paauilo, Hawaii, Aug. 6, 1928; s. Torakichi and Teyo (Kimura) M.; m. Pearl Takeko Saiki, Sept. 11, 1954; children: Joy Michiko, Miles Tadashi, Jan Keiko, Ann Yoshie. BSCE, U. Hawaii-Honolulu, 1951; JD, U. Minn., 1957; LLM in Taxation, Georgetown U., 1959; grad. Army War Coll., 1973. Bar: Minn. 1957, Hawaii 1959, U.S. Supreme Ct. 1980. Examiner, U.S. Patent Office, 1957-59; dep. atty. gen. State of Hawaii, 1960-61; mem., dir., sec./treas. Okumura Takushi Funaki & Wee, Honolulu, 1961-90; pvt. practice, Honolulu, 1991—; atty. Hawaii Senate, 1961, chief counsel ways and means com., 1962, chief counsel judiciary com., 1967-70; civil engr. Japan Constrn. Agy., Tokyo, 1953-54; staff judge adv., col. USAR, Ft. DeRussy, Hawaii, 1968-79; local legal counsel Jaycees, 1962; lectr. Nat. Assn. Pub. Accts. Hawaii Chpt. Ann. Conv., 1990, 94, Mid Pacific Inst. Found., Honolulu, 1990, Econ. Study Club of Hawaii, 1990, Meiji Life Ins. Co. Japan, 1992, Cent. YMCA, 1992, City Bank Honolulu, 1997. Legis. chmn. armed services com. C. of C. of Hawaii, 1973; instl. rep. Aloha council Boy Scouts Am., 1963-78; exec. com., sec., dir. Legal Aid Soc. Hawaii, 1970-72; state v.p. Hawaii Jaycees, 1964-65; dir., legal counsel St. Louis Heights Community Assn., 1963, 65, 73, 91—; dir., legal counsel Citizens Study Club for Naturalization of Citizens, 1963-68; advisory bd. Project Dana Honolulu, 1991—, vice chair 91, 92; life mem. Res. Officers Assn. U.S. Served to 1st lt., AUS, 1951-54. Decorated Meritorious Service medal with oak leaf cluster. Mem. ABA, Hawaii Bar Assn., U.S. Patent Office Soc., Hawaii Estate Planning Council, Rotary, Central YMCA Club, Waikiki Athletic Club, Army Golf Assn., Elks, Phi Delta Phi. Estate planning, Corporate taxation, Estate taxation. Office: 1001 Bishop St Ste 1030 Honolulu HI 96813-3408 *Personal philosophy: Study hard, work hard, play hard, love hard, have time for nonsense, help others and be fair to all concerned.*

**MIZELL, MICHAEL S.,** lawyer; b. Winter Park, Fla., Apr. 27, 1967; s. Marvin F. Mizell and Sue Butler Peart; m. JoAnn Hough, Feb. 13, 1992. BS, Nova Southeastern U., 1994; JD, Samford U., 1997. Bar: Tenn. 1997, U.S. Dist. Ct. (mid. and ea. dists.) Tenn. Ops. analyst Am. Express, Ft. Lauderdale, Fla., 1988-94; assoc. Waller Lansden Dortch & Davis, Nashville, 1997—. Bd. dirs. Music City divsn. March of Dimes, Nashville, 1997—. Mem. ABA, Am. Immigration Lawyers Assn. Fax: 615-244-6804. E-mail: mmizell@wallerlaw.com. Office: Waller Lansden Dortch & Davis 511 Union St Ste 2100 Nashville TN 37219-1760

**MLSNA, KATHRYN KIMURA,** lawyer; b. Yonkers, N.Y., Apr. 23, 1952; d. Eugene T. and Grace (Watanabe) Kimura; m. Timothy Martin Mlsna, Oct. 4, 1975; children: Lauren Marie, Matthew Christopher, Michael Timothy. BA, Northwestern U., 1974, JD, 1977. Bar: Ill. 1977, U.S. Dist. Ct. (no. dist.) Ill. 1977. Dept. dir. McDonald's Corp., Oak Brook, Ill., 1977—; speaker in field. Contbr. chpt. to book. Bd. dirs. Japanese Am. Svc. Com. Mem. ABA, Ill. Bar Assn., Chgo. Bar Assn., Asian Am. Bar Assn. (bd. dirs.), Promotion Mktg. Assn. Am. (v.p. 1988-92, chmn., pres. 1992-93, chmn. integrated mktg. com. 1993-94, chmn. assn. alliance com.), Northwestern U. Alumni Assn. (officer, bd. dirs.). Entertainment, Intellectual property. Office: McDonald's Corp 1 Mcdonalds Plz Oak Brook IL 60523-1928

**MOAK, ROGER MARTIN,** lawyer, insurance company executive; b. Bklyn., Mar. 22, 1947; s. Lester and Phoebe Elkins Moak. BS, Cornell U., 1969; JD, Georgetown U., 1972. Bar: N.Y. 1974, U.S. Tax Ct. 1974, U.S. Ct. Appeals (2d cir.) 1974, U.S. Dist. Ct. (so. and ea. dist.) N.Y. 1974, D.C. 1975, U.S. Supreme Ct. 1977, U.S. Ct. Appeals (7th and D.C. cirs.) 1980, U.S. Dist. Ct. D.C. 1980. Law, clk., assoc., then mem. Speiser & Krause, P.C., Washington and N.Y.C., 1970-80; asst. then dep. gen. counsel, sr. v.p., gen. counsel Ins. Svcs. Office, Inc., N.Y.C., 1980-91; sr. v.p., gen. counsel The Home Ins. Cos., N.Y.C., 1991—; exec. v.p., gen. counsel Risk Enterprise Mgmt. Ltd., N.Y.C., 1995—, Zurich Risk Mgmt. Svcs. (US), N.Y.C., 1999—. Charter mem. Rep. Nat. Com., 1981—. Mem. ABA, Am. Corp. Counsel Assn., New York County Lawyers Assn., Assn. Bar City N.Y. (chmn. com. on ins. law 1996-99), D.C. Bar, Ins. Fedn. N.Y. (pres. 1999), Federalist Soc., Met. Mus. Art, Police Athletic League, Central Park Conservancy, Herbert F. Johnson Mus. (Cornell U.), Handgun Control. Avocations: art, antiques. Fax: 212-530-3413; email: roger.moak@zurich.com. Insurance, General corporate, Administrative and regulatory. Home: 930 5th Ave New York NY 10021-2651 Office: Risk Enterprise Mgmt Ltd 59 Maiden Ln New York NY 10038-4502

**MOATES, G. PAUL,** lawyer; b. Los Angeles, May 26, 1947; s. Guy Hart and Virginia Rose (Mayolett) M. B.A., Amherst Coll., 1969; J.D., U. Chgo., 1975. Bar: Ill. 1975, D.C. 1976, U.S. Ct. Appeals (D.C. cir.) 1976, U.S. Supreme Ct. 1980, U.S. Ct. Appeals (6th cir.) 1984, U.S. Ct. Appeals (3d cir.) 1991, U.S. Ct. Appeals (7th cir.) 1993. Assoc. firm Sidley & Austin, Washington, 1975-82, ptnr., 1982—. Contbr. articles to profl. jours. Served with U.S. Army, 1970-73. Mem. ABA, Ill. Bar Assn., D.C. Bar Assn. Administrative and regulatory, Antitrust, Transportation. Office: Sidley & Austin 1722 I St NW Fl 9 Washington DC 20006-3705

**MOBLEY, JOHN HOMER, II,** lawyer; b. Shreveport, La., Apr. 21, 1930; s. John Hinson and Beulah (Wilson) M.; m. Sue Lawton, Aug. 9, 1958; children: John Lawton, Anne Davant. AB, U. Ga., 1951, JD, 1953. Bar: Ga. 1952, U.S. Dist. Ct. D.C. Ptnr. Kelley & Mobley, Atlanta, 1956-63, Gambrell & Mobley, 1963-83; sr. ptnr., Sutherland, Asbill & Brennan, 1983—. Chmn. Cities in Schs. of Ga.; dir. Cities in Schs. Capt. JAGC, USAF, 1953-55. Mem. ABA, D.C. Bar, State Bar Ga., Atlanta Bar Assn., Am. Judicature Soc., Atlanta Lawyers Club, Phi Delta Phi. Clubs: Atlanta Athletic, Atlanta Country, Commerce, Piedmont Driving, Georgian (Atlanta), N.Y. Athletic, Metropolitan (Washington). Municipal (including bonds). Home: 4348 Sentinel Post Rd NW Atlanta GA 30327-3910 Office: Sutherland Asbill & Brennan 999 Peachtree St NE Ste 2300 Atlanta GA 30309-3996

**MOBLEY, KATHRYN A.,** prosecutor; b. L.A., Aug. 25, 1947; d. Owen W. and Nancy L. Mobley; m. Robert Lloyd Cumpstone, Feb. 20, 1982. BA, So. Oreg. State U., 1970; JD, U. Denver, 1975. Bar: U.S. Dist. Ct. Conn. 1979, U.S. Ct. Appeals (2nd cir.) 1986. Vol. Vista, Denver, 1975-76; hearings staff atty. Social Security Adminstrn., Hartfield, Conn., 1976-79; pvt. practice Hartfield, 1979-81; asst. atty. gen. Atty. Gen. State Conn., Hartfield, 1983—; mem. environ. issues in transp. law com. NAS, NRC, Transp. Rsch. Bd., Washington, 1988-95; spkr. in field. Active Immanuel Congl. Ch., 1976—, chair bd. Christian edn., 1980—, Sunday sch. tchr., 1988, 93, deacon amaritus, 1992—, others; vol. Big Sister/Oakhill Sch. for Blind, 1977-80, Girl Scouts, 1981, 83, 85, Senator Lieberman's Campaign, 1988; mem. Adv. Com. on Handicaps, Hartford, 1979-85, chair, 1979-82; active Disability Issues,

1980; bd. dirs. Conn. Valley Girl Scout Coun., 1981; chair Sub-com. on Accessibility on Bldg. Code Compliance, Hartford, 1983-85; chair, bd. dirs. Ctr. Ind. Living, Hartford, 1986-88; supporter Hartfield Symphony Orch., others. Recipient Certs. of Svc., Conn. Prison Assn., Hartford, 1977-78, Proclamation of Outstanding Svc., City of Hartford, 1982; grantee Nat. Com. for the Handicapped, Hartford, 1982-83. Democrat. Avocations: meditation, swimming, sailing, attending classical music concerts. Office: Atty Gens Office 110 Sherman St Hartford CT 06105-2267

**MOCK, ERIC V.,** lawyer; b. N.Y.C., Apr. 24, 1942; s. Vern F. and Esther G. Mock; children: Sarah, Stephen. AB, Duke U., 1963; LLB, Harvard U., 1966. Bar: N.Y. 1967. Assoc. Dewey Ballantine, N.Y.C., 1966-76; atty. Revlon, Inc., N.Y.C., 1977-78; asst. v.p., counsel Capital Holding Corp., Louisville, 1979-87; assoc. Dornbush, Mensch, Mandelstam & Schaeffer, N.Y.C., 1987—. Avocation: bridge. General corporate, Finance, Securities. Office: Dornbush Mensch Mandelstam & Schaeffer 747 3d Ave New York NY 10017

**MOCK, RANDALL DON,** lawyer; b. Oklahoma City, Aug. 9, 1943; s. J. Haskell and M. Louise M.; m. Sally Merkle, June 4, 1966; children: Adam Peterson, Caroline Louise. BBA, U. Okla., 1965, JD, 1968; LLM in Taxation, NYU, 1970. Bar: Okla. 1968, U.S. Tax Ct. 1970, U.S. Supreme Ct. 1974; CPA. With Mock, Schwabe, Waldo, Elder, Reeves & Bryant, Oklahoma City; sec., vice chmn. Okla. Attys. Mut. Ins. Co. Editor: Oklahoma Law Review, Tax Law Review; co-author: Oklahoma Corporate Forms. Pres. Oklahoma City Estate Planning Coun., 1987-88, dir., 1980-88; pres. Oklahoma City Tax Lawyers Group, 1973; bd. dirs., mem. exec. com. Met. YMCA; trustee Westminster Sch., Okla. Med. Rsch. Found. Fellow Am. Coll. Tax Counsel; mem. Okla. Bar Assn. (sect. taxation), Beacon Club (pres., bd. dirs.), Order of Coif. Taxation, general, General corporate, Estate planning. Office: Mock Schwabe Waldo Elder Reeves & Bryant 14th Fl 2 Leadership Sq 211 N Robinson Ave Oklahoma City OK 73102-7109

**MODE, PAUL J., JR.,** lawyer; b. Columbus, Ohio, Feb. 23, 1938; s. Paul J. and Dorothy O. Mode; m. Elaine Rush, June 13, 1961; children: Rebecca D., David B. BME with distinction, Cornell U., 1961; LLB magna cum laude, Harvard U., 1967. Bar: D.C., U.S. Supreme Ct. Assoc. Wilmer, Cutler & Pickering, Washington, 1967-70, 73-74, ptnr., 1975—, mem. mgmt. com., 1983-86, chmn. mgmt. com., 1987-95; chief counsel U.S. Senate Subcom. on Constl. Amendments, Washington, 1970-73; panelist Ctr. for Pub. Resources Panel of Disting. ADR Neutrals, 1989—. Author: (with others) Litigation, vol.12, No.4, 1986; mem. editorial bd. Harvard Law Rev., 1966-67, Alternatives to the High Cost of Litigation, 1991—; contbr. articles to profl. jours. Mem. issues staff Robert F. Kennedy Presdl. campaign, 1968. Lt. (j.g.) USN, 1961-64. Avocations: tennis, collecting antique maps. Administrative and regulatory, General civil litigation. Home: 2750 Brandywine St NW Washington DC 20008-1040 Office: Wilmer Cutler & Pickering 2445 M St NW Ste 500 Washington DC 20037-1487

**MODEROW, JOSEPH ROBERT,** lawyer, package distribution company executive; b. Kenosha, Wis., 1948. Grad., Calif. State U., Fullerton, 1970; JD, Western State U., 1975. Bar: Calif. 1975, U.S. Dist. Ct. (cen. dist.) Calif. 1975, U.S. Supreme Ct. 1982. Sr. v.p. legal and pub affairs, sec., gen. counsel, dir. United Parcel Svc. Am., Inc., Atlanta, Ga., 1986—. General corporate. Office: United Parcel Svc of Am Inc 55 Glenlake Pkwy NE Atlanta GA 30328-3498

**MODIN, RICHARD F.,** lawyer; b. Kansas City, Mo., Feb. 2, 1951; s. C.F. and Helen Majorie M.; m. Jeanne A. Modin, Oct. 31, 1975; children: Rebecca, Andrew, Lindsey, Luke. BA in Polit. Sci., U. Mo., Kansas City, 1977, JD with distinction, 1979. Bars: Mo. 1979, U.S. Dist. Ct. (ea. dist) Mo. 1979, Kans. 1994, U.S. Dist. Ct. Kans. 1994. Pvt. practice Kansas City, Mo., 1983—. Mem. sch. bd. Platte County, 1991-92; pastor Ch. of Christ, Kansas City, 1995—. Lt. cmdr. USN, 1979-82. Mem. Nat. Lawyers Assn., Lawyers for Life, Mo. Bar Assn., Platte County Bar Assn. Insurance, General civil litigation, Product liability. Office: Dougherty Modin & Holloway 1600 City Ctr Sq 1100 Main St Kansas City MO 64105-2105

**MODISETT, JEFFREY A.,** state attorney general; b. Windfall, Ind., Aug. 10, 1954; s. James Richard and Diana T. (Tutewiler) M.; m. Jennifer Ashworth, June 9, 1990; 2 children: Matthew Hunter Ashworth, Haden Nicholas. BA, UCLA, 1976; MA, Oxford (Eng.) U., 1978; JD, Yale U., 1981. Bar: Ind., Calif., D.C. Clk. to Hon. R. Peckham U.S. Dist. Ct. (no. dist.) Calif., San Francisco, 1981-82; asst. U.S. atty. Office U.S. Atty. (ctrl. dist.) Calif., L.A., 1982-88; issues dir. Evan Bayh for Gov., Indpls., 1988; exec. asst. to gov. State of Ind., Indpls., 1989-90; prosecutor Marion County, Indpls., 1991-94; sr. counsel Ice Miller Donadio & Ryan, Indpls., 1995-96; attorney genl. State of Ind., 1997—; chmn. Gov. Commn. for Drug Free Ind., Indpls., 1989—, Gov. Coun. on Impaired & Dangerous Driving, Indpls., 1989—; pres. Family Advocacy Ctr., Indpls., 1991-94, Hoosier Alliance Against Drugs, Indpls., 1993-96; dir. Cmty. Couns. of Indpls., 1991-93; chmn. Ind. Criminal Justice Inst., Indpls., 1989-90, dir., 1989—; vice chmn. Juvenile Justice and Youth Gang Study Com., Indpls., 1992-94; legal analyst Sta. WTHR-TV, Indpls., 1995-96. Author: Prosecutor's Perspective, 1991-94; editor-in-chief Yale Jour. Internat. Law, 1980-81. Co-chair Ind. State Dem. Coordinated Campaign, Indpls., 1996. Recipient Spl. Enforcement award U.S. Customs, 1988, Child Safety Adv. award Automotive Safety for Children, 1997, STAR Alliance Impact award, 1998; named Top Lawyer, Indpls. Monthly mag., 1993; named to Sagamore of Wabash, State of Ind., 1995. Mem. Ind. Bar Assn., Indpls. Bar Assn. Avocation: bicycling. Office: Atty Gen 401 W Washington St Fl 5 Indianapolis IN 46204-2705

**MODLIN, HOWARD S.,** lawyer; b. N.Y.C., Apr. 10, 1931; s. Martin and Rose Modlin; m. Margot S., Oct. 18, 1956; children: James, Laura, Peter. AB, Union Coll., Schenectady, 1952; JD, Columbia U., 1955. Bar: N.Y. 1956, D.C. 1973. Assoc., Weisman, Celler, Spett & Modlin, P.C., N.Y.C., 1956-61, ptnr., 1961-76, mng. ptnr., 1976-95, pres., 1996—; sec., dir. Gen. DataComm Industries, Inc., Middlebury, Conn.; dir. Am.-Book-Stratford Press, Inc., N.Y.C., Fedders Corp., Liberty Corner, N.J., Trans-Lux Corp., Norwalk, Conn. Chmn. bd. dirs. Daus. of Jacob Geriat. Ctr., Bronx, N.Y. Mem. ABA, Assn. of Bar of City of N.Y., D.C. Bar Assn. Contracts commercial, General corporate, Securities. Office: Weisman Celler Spett & Modlin PC 445 Park Ave New York NY 10022-2606

**MODLIN, REGINALD ROY,** lawyer; b. Dearborn, Mich., June 6, 1949; s. Roy S. and Frances M.; m. Kathleen Modlin; children: Ryan N., Samual A., Devon R., Alexandra L. BS in Aerospace, U. Mich., 1971; JD, Detroit Coll. Law, 1981. Bar: Mich. 1982, U.S. Ct. of Appeals (6th cir.), 1982 U.S. Supreme Ct. 1997. Various legal positions Daimler Chrysler, Auburn Hills, Mich.; mgr. environ. affairs Daimler Chrysler, Auburn Hills, 1991—. Environmental, Transportation. Home: 797 Crestwood Ln Rochester Hls MI 48309-1063

**MODY, RENU NOOR,** lawyer; b. Boston, Aug. 6, 1964; d. Suresh Chandra and Omi Vati Gupta Mody; 1 child, Medina. Student, Franklin Coll., Lugano, Switzerland, 1981-82; AB, Georgetown U., 1985; JD, U. Miami, 1990. Bar: Fla. 1992, D.C. 1993, U.S. Dist. Ct. (so. dist.) Fla. 1993, U.S. Ct. Appeals (11th cir.) 1994, U.S. Supreme Ct. 1995; cert. pvt. investigator, 1992; pvt. investigation agy. lic. 1994. Counselor, ct. adminstr. juvenile correctional facility Goodwill Industries Boston, 1985; spl. asst. U.S. Rep. Joe Kennedy Campaign, 1986; pres. Think Video Corp., 1987-90; in house counsel Boston Investors Group, 1991—; pres., owner Miami Eyes, PI Agy., 1992—; pvt. practice law, 1992—; with Fla. Bar Young Lawyers Divsn. Summer Honors Program, 1988; dist. counsel law clk. VA Med. Ctr. Miami, 1988-89; consumer litigation intern Fla. Atty. Gen., 1988-90; tribal ct. counsel Miccosukee Indian Reservation, 1990; presenter in field. Prodr. (documentary) Georgetown: Discourses in Blue and Gray, 1987. Democrat. Avocations: kayaking, community service. General civil litigation, Federal civil litigation, Non-profit and tax-exempt organizations. Office: 1717 N Bayshore Dr Apt 2234 Miami FL 33132-1159

**MOE, THOMAS O.,** lawyer; b. Des Moines, 1938. BA, U. Minn., 1960, LLB, 1963. Bar: Minn. 1963. Ptnr. Dorsey & Whitney LLP, Mpls., 1964-89, chmn., mng. ptnr., 1989-99, chmn., 1999—. Mem. Order of Coif. Office: Dorsey & Whitney 220 S 6th St Ste 2200 Minneapolis MN 55402-1498

**MOEHLE, CARM ROBERT,** lawyer; b. Indio, Calif., June 10, 1948; s. Robert Rudolph Moehle and Catherine Marie Whitcraft. BSCE, U. Mo., Rolla, 1970; JD, U. Mo., 1974. Bar: Mo. 1974, Ariz. 1978, Colo. 1986, U.S. Dist. Ct. Ariz. 1978, U.S. Dist. Ct. (we. dist.) Mo. 1974, U.S. Supreme Ct. 1980. Law clk. Mo. Ct. Appeals (we. dist.), Kansas City, 1974-75; prosecuting atty. Greene County, Springfield, Mo., 1975-77; law clk. Ariz. Supreme Ct., Phoenix, 1977-78; staff atty. Ariz. Ct. Appeals, Phoenix, 1978-82; atty. Bosco & DiMatteo, P.C., Phoenix, 1983-91, Scult, Lazarus, French, Zwillinger and Smock, P.A., Phoenix, 1992-93; pvt. practice Phoenix, 1994—. Chmn. bd. dirs. Ariz. Coun. Trout Unlimited, Phoenix, 1989—; trustee Maricopa County Bar Found., Phoenix, 1992-95. Mem. Ariz. Trial Lawyers Assn., Maricopa County Bar Assn. (vol. lawyers program). Avocations: backpacking, hiking, flyfishing, golf, skiing. E-mail: carm.moehle@azbar.org. General civil litigation, Personal injury, Real property. Office: 77 E Columbus Ave Ste 200 Phoenix AZ 85012-2352

**MOELING, WALTER GOOS, IV,** lawyer; b. Quantico, Va., Feb. 16, 1943; s. Walter Goos III and Dorothy (Tritle) M.; m. Nell Frances Askew, Aug. 27, 1965; children: Charles H., Christine E. BA, Duke U., 1965, JD, 1968. Bar: Ga. 1968. Assoc. Powell, Goldstein, Frazer & Murphy, Atlanta, 1968-75, ptnr., 1975—. Bd. dirs. So. Banking Law and Policy Conf., 1989-96, Southeastern Conf. for Bank Dirs., 1996—, Children's Rehab. Ctr., Atlanta, 1982—, Gatchell Home, Atlanta, 1983—; bd. dirs. REACH, Inc., 1989—, chmn. bd. dirs., 1993. Mem. ABA (mem. banking com. 1986—), Ga. C. of C. (bd. dirs. 1998—), Ga. Bar Assn., Ga. Bankers Assn. (assoc., chairperson bank counsel sect. 1992-95, bd. dirs. 1998—), Cmty. Bankers Assn. (assoc.), Capital City Club, Willow Point Country Club. Democrat. Unitarian. E-mail: wmoeling@pgfm.com. Avocations: golf, fly-fishing. Banking, General corporate, Finance. Office: Powell Goldstein Frazer & Murphy 191 Peachtree St NE Ste 16 Atlanta GA 30303-1740

**MOELLER, FLOYD DOUGLAS,** lawyer; b. Safford, Ariz., Aug. 16, 1949; s. Floyd Albert and Helen Lou (Posey) M.; m. Tyra Brown, Dec. 18, 1970; children: Kristin, Sam, John, Susan. BS in Police Sci., Brigham Young U., 1972, JD, 1977; MS in Mgmt., Lesley Coll., 1985, MA in Counseling Psychology, 1987; LLM in Tax, Washington Sch. Law, 1992. Bar: N.Mex. 1978, U.S. Dist. Ct. N.Mex., 1978, U.S. Ct. Appeals (10th cir.) 1979, U.S. Tax Ct. 1981, U.S. Supreme Ct. 1981, Navajo Nation, Hopi Tribe, Jicarilla Apache Tribe, White Mountain Apache Tribe, So. Ute Tribe. Assoc. Wade Beavers & Assocs., Farmington, N.Mex., 1978-79; ptnr. Nunn & Moeller, Farmington, 1979; sole practice Farmington, 1979-80, 87—; ptnr. Moeller & Burnham, Farmington, 1980-87. Mem. exec. com. Better Bus. Bur. of 4 Corners, 1978, bd. dirs., 1978—; bd. dirs. Farmington Pub. Library Bd., 1979-86, San Juan Med. Found., San Juan Pub. Library Found., Halvorson House; mem. paralegal adv. com. San Juan Community Coll.; chmn. local troop coms. Boy Scouts Am., Farmington, 1985—. Named diplomat Nat. Bd. Trial Advocacy, 1986. Mem. ABA, J. Reuben Clark Law Soc., Nat. Panel Consumer Arbitrators, Am. Mgmt. Assn., Am. Arbitration Assn., Assn. Trial Lawyers Am., Am. Judicature Soc., Am. Assn. for Counseling and Devel., N.Mex. Trial Lawyers Assn., N.Mex. State Bar Assn. (CLE, fee arbitration coms. 1985, pres. trial practice sect. 1988), Navajo Nat. Bar Assn., San Juan County Bar Assn., 4 Corners Inn of Ct. Republican. Mormon. Avocations: reading, tennis, gardening, bicycling. General practice, General civil litigation, Personal injury. Office: PO Box 15249 Farmington NM 87401-5249

**MOELLER, GALEN ASHLEY,** lawyer; b. Ballinger, Tex., Jan. 17, 1950; s. Norbert Edward and Magdaline O. (Kocich) M.; m. Roseann Dominguez, Aug. 12, 1977; children—Tatum Cheree, Taylor Ashley. B.A. in History, St. Mary U., San Antonio, 1972, J.D., 1974. Bar. Tex. 1975, U.S. Dist. Ct. (no. dist.) Tex. 1976. Sole practice, San Angelo, 1975—. Mem. ABA, Tex. Bar Assn., Tom Green County Bar Assn., Tex. Trial Lawyers Assn., Tex. Criminal Def. Lawyers Assn., Sons of Hermann Rowena, Lambda Chi Alpha (hon.). Democrat. Roman Catholic. Lodges: Elks, K.C. General practice, Personal injury, Probate. Home: 2503 Douglas Dr San Angelo TX 76904-5446 Office: 331 W Avenue B San Angelo TX 76903-6811

**MOERBEEK, STANLEY LEONARD,** lawyer; b. Toronto, Ont., Can., Nov. 12, 1951; came to U.S., 1953; s. John Jacob and Mary Emily Moerbeek; m. Carol Annette Mordaunt, Apr. 17, 1982; children: Sarah, Noah. BA magna cum laude, Calif. State U., Fullerton, 1974; student, U. San Diego-Sorbonne, Paris, 1977; JD, Loyola U., 1979. Bar: Calif. 1980; cert. in internat. bus. transactions, bankruptcy and bus. rehab., and civil trial practice. From law clk. to assoc. McAlpin Doonan & Seese, Covina, Calif., 1977-81; assoc. Robert L. Baker, Pasadena, Calif., 1981-82, Miller Bush & Minnott, Fullerton, 1982-83; prin. Law Office of Stanley L. Moerbeek, Fullerton, 1984—; judge pro tem Orange County Superior Ct., Calif., 1984—; notary pub., lt. gov. 9th cir. law student divsn. ABA, 1979. Mem. Heritage Found., Washington, 1989—. Calif. Gov.'s Office scholar, 1970; recipient Plaque of Appreciation, Fullerton Kiwanis, 1983. Mem. Calif. Assn. Realtors (referral panel atty. 1985—), Orange County Bar Assn. (Coll. of Trial Advocacy 1985), Calif. C. of C., Phi Kappa Phi. Roman Catholic. Avocations: history, politics, sports. Real property, General civil litigation, Personal injury. Office: 1370 N Brea Blvd Ste 210 Fullerton CA 92835-4128

**MOERDLER, CHARLES GERARD,** lawyer; b. Paris, Nov. 15, 1934; came to the U.S., 1946, naturalized, 1952; s. Herman and Erna Anna (Brandwein) M.; m. Pearl G. Hecht, Dec. 26, 1955; children: Jeffrey Alan, Mark Laurence, Sharon Michele. BA, L.I.U., 1953; JD, Fordham U., 1956. Bar: N.Y. 1956, U.S. Supreme Ct. 1962. Assoc. Cravath, Swaine & Moore, N.Y.C., 1956-65; spl. counsel coms. City of N.Y. and judiciary N.Y. State Assembly, 1960-61; commr. bldgs. City of N.Y., 1966-67; sr. ptnr., chmn. litigation dept. Stroock & Stroock & Lavan, N.Y.C., 1967—; bd. dirs., gen. counsel, dir. N.Y. Post Co., Inc., 1987-92; cons. housing, urban devel. and real estate to Mayor of N.Y.C., 1967-73; mem. com. on character and fitness of applicants for admission to Bar, Appellate divsn. 1st Dept., N.Y., 1977—, vice chmn. 1998—; mem. disciplinary com. (policy com.) appellate divsn. 1st Dept., N.Y., 1998—, commr. N.Y. State Ins. Fund, 1978-97, vice chmn., 1986-94, chmn., 1995-97; mem. Mayor's Com. on Judiciary, 1994—; mem. N.Y.C. Housing Devel. Corp., 1997—; bd. dirs. N.Y.C. Residential Mortgage Ins. Corp., 1997—. Mem. editorial bd. N.Y. Law Jour., 1985—; assoc. editor Fordham Law Rev., 1956. Asst. dir. Rockefeller nat. presdl. campaign com., 1964; adv. bd. Sch. Internat. Affairs Columbia U., 1977-80; bd. govs. L.I.U., 1966, trustee, 1985-91; chmn. Cmty. Planning Bds. 8 and 14, Bronx County, 1977-78; nat. bd. govs. Am. Jewish Congress, 1966; bd. overseers Jewish Theol. Sem. Am., 1993-95; trustee St. Barnabas Hosp., Bronx, N.Y., 1985—. Recipient Walker Metcalf award L.I. U., 1966. Mem. Am. Bar Assn., N.Y. State Bar Assn., N.Y. County Lawyers Assn., Internat. Bar Assn., Assn. of Bar of City of N.Y., Free Sons of Israel, World Trade Ctr. Club, Metro. Club. Federal civil litigation, Labor, Real property. Home: 7 Rivercrest Rd Bronx NY 10471-1236 Office: Stroock Stroock & Lavan 7 Hanover Sq New York NY 10004-2616

**MOFFAT, MARIAN MACINTYRE,** lawyer; b. Coral Gables, Fla., Apr. 15, 1947; d. James and Elinore (Tomlinson) M.; m. Thomas E. Jepson, May 26, 1972. BA, U. Mo., 1970, MPA, 1975, JD, 1977. Bar: Calif. 1979, Mo. 1978, U.S. Dist. Ct. (we. dist.) Mo. 1978, U.S. Dist. Ct. (no. dist.) Calif. 1979, U.S. Ct. Appeals (8th cir.) 1985. Staff atty. Legal Aid of Western Mo., Kansas City, 1979-81; dep. dir. Office of Human Rels. and Citizen Complaints, Kansas City, 1981-82; pvt. practice Kansas City, 1982—. Pres. Coleman Highlands Neighborhood Assn., Kansas City, 1992-94; bd. dirs. Citizens Assn. Kansas City, 1995-97, 98, treas. 1999—, sec., 1996-97; sec. Westpoint Citizens Action Coalition, 1994-97, v.p. issues, 1997-99. Recipient Robert C. Welch Vol. Atty. Project award Kansas City Met. Bar Assn., 1984. Avocations: crossword puzzles, gardening. Family and matrimonial, Probate, Bankruptcy. Home: 3333 Karnes Blvd Kansas City MO 64111-3648 Office: 900 Merc Tower 1101 Walnut St Kansas City MO 64106-2134

**MOFFATT, MICHAEL ALAN,** lawyer; b. Indpls., Feb. 22, 1964; s. James L. Kelso and Peggy A. Tackett; m. Nancy Norman, Sept. 23, 1989; children: Patricia Margaret, Michael Alan, Nicole Elizabeth. BA in Polit. Sci., Depauw U., 1986; JD, Ind. U., 1989. Bar: Ind. 1989, U.S. Dist. Ct. (so. and no. dists.) Ind. 1989, U.S. Ct. Appeals (7th cir.) 1991. Law clk., assoc. White & Raub, Indpls., 1987-94; assoc. Wooden McLaughlin & Sterner, Indpls., 1994-95, Barnes & Thornburg, Indpls., 1995—; lectr. litigation, paralegal program, Ind. U./Purdue U., Ind. CLE Forum & labor/employmemt seminars. Contbr. articles to legal jours. Cons. pediatric ethics com. Meth. Hosp., Indpls., 1990-92; co-chmn. Keep Am. Beautiful, Greencastle, Ind., 1986, bd. dirs., sec., 1990-94; mem. devel. control com. Geist Harbors Property Owners' Assn., Indpls., 1993-94, cons., 1994, pres., 1997—; winners cir. mentor U.S. Auto Club. Mem. ABA (labor and employment sect.), Fed Bar Assn., Ind. Bar Assn., Indpls. Bar Assn. (exec. coun. labor law sect., vice chmn.), Exch. Club (pres.-elect 1997-98, pres. 1998—). Avocations: golf, basketball, war gaming, softball. Labor, General civil litigation. Office: Barnes & Thornburgg 1313 Merchants Bank Bldg 11 S Meridian St Indianapolis IN 46204-3506

**MOFFATT, THOMAS SWIFT,** lawyer; b. Lawrence, Mass., Jan. 26, 1964; s. Thomas F. and Jane P. Moffatt; m. Alexandra S. Swift, Aug. 22, 1992; children: Ryan, William. AB in History, Harvard U., 1987; JD, Northeastern U., 1993. Bar: Mass. 1993. Assoc. Mintz, Levin, Cohn, Ferris, Glovsky & Popeo, P.C., Boston, 1993-97; corp. legal counsel CVS Pharm., Inc., Woonsocket, R.I., 1997—. Avocations: family, sports, reading. Securities, Contracts commercial, Mergers and acquisitions. Office: CVS Pharm Inc One CVS Dr Woonsocket RI 02895

**MOFFEIT, MICHAEL PAUL,** lawyer, mediator; b. Tyler, Tex., Oct. 15, 1951; s. Thomas Lee and Gladys I. (Jackson) M.; m. Jeanne Pattee; children: Michael Paul Jr., Ariel Lindsey. BA ampla cum laude, U. Tex., Austin, 1974; JD, U. Houston, 1977. Bar: Tex., 1977, Colo., 1996. Dir. Office Students Atty., U. Tex., El Paso, 1978-80; pvt. practice, El Paso, 1980—; host, prodr. radio program Environ. Law, 1975-77, radio talk show Legal Ease, 1978-82; mediator El Paso County Dispute Resolution Ctr., 1998—. Newspaper columnist Case Notes, 1978-80. Bd. dirs. Meml. Park Improvement Assn., El Paso, 1980-85, ETCOM, El Paso, 1981-82; trustee Western Hills United Meth. Ch., El Paso, 1993-94; leader cub pack 72 Boy Scouts Am., El Paso. Mem. El Paso Bar Assn. (ethics com. 1990—), Masons (32d degree), Shriners, Alpha Kappa Delta. Avocations: skiing, backpacking, computers. Personal injury, General civil litigation, Probate. Home: 304 Sharondale Dr El Paso TX 79912-4250 Office: Chase Bank Bldg 2829 Montana Ave Ste 204 El Paso TX 79903-2421

**MOFFET, KENNETH WILLIAM,** lawyer; b. Mpls., Mar. 29, 1959; s. Donald Pratt and Sally (Hullsiek) M. BA, Denison U., 1981; JD, Am. U., 1984. Bar: Fla. 1984, U.S. Dist. Ct. (so. dist.) Fla. 1985, U.S. Ct. Appeals (11th cir.) 1987. Assoc. Fleming, O'Bryan & Fleming, Ft. Lauderdale, Fla., 1984-86; assoc. Roberts & Reynolds, P.A., West Palm Beach, Fla., 1986-89, ptnr., 1989-96; pres. Moffet & Alexander, P.A., West Palm Beach, Fla., 1997, sr. ptnr., 1997—. Bd. dirs. adv. Am. Lung Assn. S.E. Fla., 1996—. Mem. Palm Beach County Bar Assn., Fla. Def. Lawyers Assn., Phi Beta Kappa. Republican. Presbyterian. Avocations: skiing, tennis. Insurance, General civil litigation, Product liability. Office: Moffet & Alexander PA 1601 Forum Pl West Palm Beach FL 33401-8101

**MOFFETT, HOWARD MACKENZIE,** lawyer; b. New Orleans, Dec. 26, 1943; s. Howard F. and Margaret Delphia (Mackenzie) M.; m. Karin Ingrid Henrikson, July 26, 1986 (div. Dec. 1993); a child, Anna Kristin. BA in History, Yale Coll., 1966; MA in Econ., Cambridge (Eng.) U., 1969; JD, U. Calif., Berkeley, 1975. Bar: N.H. 1975, U.S. Dist. Ct. N.H. 1975, U.S. Ct. Appeals (1st cir.) 1994. Reporter Viet Nam Guardian, Saigon, 1966-67, Newsweek, Saigon, 1966-67; legis. & adminstrv. asst. U.S. Rep. John B. Anderson, Washington, 1969-72; assoc. Orr and Reno PA, Concord, N.H., 1975-82, ptnr., 1982—, also bd. dirs. Trustee Canterbury (N.H.) Shaker Village, 1985—, Lakes Region Conservation Trust, Meredith, N.H., 1994-98. Democrat. Presbyterian. Health, FERC practice, Intellectual property. Office: Orr and Reno PA One Eagle Square Concord NH 03301

**MOFFETT, J. DENNY,** lawyer; b. Atlanta, Sept. 20, 1947; s. James Denny Moffett Jr. and Dorothy (Mckenzie) McCall; m. Mary F. Ray, June 6, 1987; children: David, Jenny. BA, U. Okla., 1969; JD with honors, George Washington U., 1972, LLM in Taxation, 1974. Bar: Okla. 1972, U.S. Tax Ct. 1973. Legis. asst. U.S. Senate, Washington, 1973-74; ptnr. Conner & Winters, Tulsa, 1974-90, McKenzie, Moffett, Elias & Books, Tulsa, Oklahoma City, 1990-97, Moffett & Assocs., P.C., Tulsa, 1997—; adj. faculty U. Tulsa Law Sch., 1978; arbitrator Nat. Assn. Securities Dealers. Commr. Ark.-Okla. River Compact Commn., 1990-94; pres. Nicholas Club Tulsa, 1984; endowment com. Trinity Episcopal Ch., 1990—. 2d lt. U.S. Army, 1972-74; bd. dirs. Am. Cancer Soc., Tulsa, 1991-94. Mem. Am. Arbitration Assn., Tulsa Tax Club (pres. 1981, 94). Republican. Taxation, general, Bankruptcy, General corporate. Home: 2132 E 32nd Pl Tulsa OK 74105-2222 Office: Moffett & Assocs PC 1000 Philtower Bldg Tulsa OK 74103

**MOFFETT, MARTIN LEE,** lawyer; b. Hollywood, Fla., Dec. 30, 1962; s. Jerry L. and Barbara L. Moffett. BS, U. No. Colo., 1986; JD, DePaul U., 1993. Bar: Calif.; CPA, Calif. Ptnr. KPMG Peat Marwick, L.A., 1986-90, 93—. Mem. AICPA (tax sect.), Calif. Bar Assn., L.A. County Bar Assn. (tax sect.). Corporate taxation. Office: KPMG Peat Marwick 725 S Figueroa St Los Angeles CA 90017-5524

**MOFFETT, T(ERRILL) K(AY),** lawyer; b. Becker, Miss., July 11, 1949; s. Elmer C. and Mary Ethel (Meek) M.; m. Rita C. Millsaps, Mar. 11, 1972; 1 child, Tara Leigh. BS, U.S. Mil. Acad., 1971; MA in Polit. Sci., U. Hawaii, 1974; JD, U. Miss., 1979. Bar: Miss. 1979, Ala. 1998. Grad. tchr. Am. govt. U. Miss., Oxford, 1977-80; ptnr. Moffett and Thorne, Tupelo, Miss., 1980-88; owner Moffett Law Firm, Tupelo, Miss., 1988—; pros. atty. City of Tupelo, 1989-99. Rep. candidate for U.S. Congress 1st Miss. Dist., 1978, 80; 1st dist. coord. Reagan for Pres., 1980; co-chmn. Lee County George Bush for Pres. Com., 1988, 92; mem. Lee County Rep. Exec. Com., 1980—; chmn. Tupelo Rep. Exec. Com., 1988—; active 1st Bapt. Ch., Tupelo; bd. dirs. Sav-A-Life Tupelo, Inc. Capt. U.S. Army, 1971-76; brig. gen. Miss. Army N.G., 1996. Harvard fellow, 1995-96. Mem. ABA, Miss. State Bar Assn., Lee County Bar Assn., Ala. State Bar Assn., Civitan, Masons, Habitat for Humanity, Phi Sigma Alpha. Avocations: music, hunting, tennis, travel. General civil litigation, Family and matrimonial, General practice. Home: 5 N Parc Cir Tupelo MS 38804-9753 Office: Moffett Law Firm PO Drawer 1707 330 N Broadway St Tupelo MS 38804-3926

**MOFFITT, DAVID LOUIS,** lawyer, county and state official; b. Alexandria, Va., June 8, 1953; s. Otis Breheon and Lillian Vlasta (Svatik) M.; m. Kathleen Ann Brata, Aug. 20, 1988 (div. Nov. 1999); children: David Lachlan, Drake Lorne. BA in Philosophy, U. Mich., 1976; JD, U. Detroit, 1979. Assoc. Plunkett, Cooney, Rutt, Watters, Stanczyk and Pedersen, PC, Detroit, 1979-80, Kitch, Suhreheinrich, Smith, Saurbier and Drutchas, PC, Detroit, 1980-81, Alan R. Miller, PC, Birmingham, Mich., 1981-83; pvt. practice Bingham Farms, 1983—; lectr. real estate law U. Mich. Grad. Sch. Bus. Adminstrn./Mich. Assn. Realtors. Contbr. articles to profl. jours. Active Oakland County Bd. Commrs., 1985—, pers. com., 1985-94, 99—, vice-chmn., 1988-89, chmn. pub. svcs. com., 1998-99, vice-chmn., 1999—, vice-chmn. majority party caucus, 1987-89, 99, vice-chmn. planning and bldg. com., 1989-91, pers. appeals bd., 1992-93; chmn. Oakland County Zoning Coordinating Bd., 1991, 93, vice chmn., 1992, chmn. ct. reform study com., 1996-98, chmn. rules revision study com., 1998; exec. coun. Southeast Mich. Coun. Govts., 1993—; justice and law enforcement com. Mich. Assn. Counties, 1999—; pub. lands nat. policy steering com. Nat. Assn. Counties, 1996—, vice-chmn. Payment In Lieu of Taxation subcom., 1997; mem. Environ., Energy & Land Use Nat. Policy Steering Com., 1992-96; pub. hearing officer Oakland County Road Commn., 1983-85; adminstr. emeritus David L. Moffit Scholarships for Outstanding Legal Editl. Achievement and Outstanding Achievement in Legal Journalism, U. Detroit Mercy Sch. Law; apptd. to Mich. State Hazardous Waste Site Rev. Bd., 1995—. Named Clarence M. Burton/ Dean's scholar U. Detroit, 1979; recipient Most Disting. Brief to Mich. Supreme Ct. award Thomas M. Cooley Law Sch., 1988. Land use and zoning (including planning), Federal civil litigation, Real property. Office: 30600 Telegraph Rd Ste 3250 Bingham Farms MI 48025-5701

**MOFFITT, WILLIAM BENJAMIN,** lawyer; b. N.Y.C., Jan. 16, 1949; s. William Benjamin and Victoria Lucinda Moffitt; 1 child, Pilar. BA, U.

Okla., 1971; JD, Am. U., 1975. Bar: Va. 1976, U.S. Dist. Ct. (ea. dist.) Va. 1976, U.S. Ct. Appeals (4th cir.) 1980, U.S. Ct. Appeals (5th cir.) 1981, U.S. Ct. Appeals (11th cir.) 1982, U.S. Ct. Appeals (6th cir.) 1988, U.S. Ct. Appeals (1st cir.) 1991, U.S. Dist. Ct. Md. 1994, U.S. Ct. Appeals (3rd cir.) 1994. Ptnr. Lowe, Mark & Moffitt, Alexandria, Va., 1976-81, Mark & Moffitt, Alexandria, 1981-85, Moffitt, Keats & Jones, Alexandria, 1985-87, Moffitt & Jones, Alexandria, 1987-89, William B. Moffitt & Assocs., Alexandria, 1989-91, Moffitt, Zwerling & Kemler, Alexandria, 1991-96, Asbill, Junkin & Moffitt, Chartered, Washington, 1996—; pres. Va. Coll. Criminal Def. Lawyers, 1983. Bd. dirs. ACLU, 1981. Fellow Am. Bd. Criminal Lawyers; mem. Nat. Assn. Criminal Def. Lawyers (bd. dirs. 1988—, strike force chair 1993, nat. sec. 1994, nat. treas. 1995, second v.p. 1996, first v.p. 1997). Criminal, Appellate. Office: Asbill Junkin & Moffitt Chartered 1615 New Hampshire Ave NW Washington DC 20009-2520

**MOGLEN, LELAND LOUIS,** lawyer, educator; b. N.Y.C., Apr. 5, 1944; s. Maxwell David and Ruth Leah (Weiss) M.; m. Phyllis Jane Moglen, June 26, 1976; children: David Joseph, Kimberly Hanna, Daniel Justin, Marc Edward. BA, Columbia U., 1966; MSBA, San Francisco State U., 1981, JD, 1982. Bar: Calif. 1989. Tchr. Great Hollow Jr. High Sch., Smithtown, N.Y., 1966-68; tchr. English Ecole Nickerson, Paris, 1968-70; owner Nature's Best Health Foods, Kodiak, Alaska, 1970-72; acct. City/County of San Francisco, 1972-76, departmental mgr., 1976-86; assoc. prof. Chapman Coll., Sacramento, 1987-89; pvt. practice, Auburn, Calif., 1989—; pro bono atty. Voluntary Legal Svcs. Program, Auburn, 1990; pro tem judge Placer Mcpl. Ct., 1995. Prin. Nevada City (Calif.) Jewish Community Ctr. Sunday Sch., bd. dirs., 1988—. Avocations: tennis, racquetball, chess. Fax: 530-268-6828. E-mail: moglop@jps.net. Real property, Personal injury, General corporate. Home and Office: 23286 Lone Pine Dr Auburn CA 95602-8027

**MOGOL, ALAN JAY,** lawyer; b. Balt., July 29, 1946; s. Jesse and Kitty (Stutman) m.; m. Ellen Epstein, June 19, 1969; children: Andrew Stephen, Jonathan David. BA with distinction, U. Va., 1968, JD, 1971. Bar: Md. 1972, U.S. Dist. Ct. Md. 1972, U.S. Ct. Appeals (4th cir.) 1972, U.S. Supreme Ct. 1978. Assoc. Ober, Kaler, Grimes & Shriver, Balt., 1971-77, ptnr., 1978—; chmn. bus. dept. Ober, Kaler, Grimes & Shriver, Balt., 1980-81, 84-85, 91-97, chmn. equipment leasing practice group, 1998—; lectr. on continuing edn. Md. Inst. Continuing Profl. Edn. for Lawyers, 1988-92, trustee, 1990-93; spkr. seminars Nat. Health Lawyers Assn., Washington, 1986-87, Rocky Mountain Mgmt., Denver, 1987, Med. Imaging Expo., 1995, Washington, 1995. Co-author: In Structuring the Secured Loan Agreement, 1991, Commercial Finance Guide, 1997, Equipment Leasing; contbr. articles to profl. jours. and local newspapers. Bd. dirs. Transitional Living Coun., Balt., 1972-92; bd. trustees Md. Inst. of Continuing Profl. Edn. for Lawyers, 1990-93. Mem. ABA, Equipment Leasing Assn. Am. (lawyers com. 1986-89, program com. 1986-91, speaker seminars), Md. Bar Assn. (uniform comml. code com. 1988—, chmn. 1991-93, vice chmn. bus. sect. 1995-96, chmn. bus. sect. 1996-97). Avocation: tennis. Contracts commercial, General corporate. Office: Ober Kaler Grimes & Shriver 120 E Baltimore St Ste 800 Baltimore MD 21202-1643

**MOHAMMED, SOHAIL,** lawyer; b. Hyderabad, A. Pradesh, India, Aug. 12, 1963; came to U.S., 1980; s. Ahsanuddin and Syeda (Tahira) M.; m. Ashraf Mohammed, Nov. 20, 1994; 1 child, Omair. BS in Elec. Engring., N.J. Inst. Tech., 1988; JD, Seton Hall U., 1993. Bar: Pa. 1993, U.S. Ct. Appeals 1995, N.J. 1993, Wash. 1995. Elec. engr. GEC-Marconi Electronic Sys. Corp., Totowa, N.J., 1988-97; pvt. practice Clifton, N.J., 1993—. Mem. City Clifton (N.J.) Cultural Awareness Com., 1995—. Recipient Highest Acad. Achievement award Bur. Nat. Affairs, 1993. Mem. ABA (young lawyers divsn. scholarship, 1996), N.J. Bar Assn. (profl. achievement award, 1997), N.J. State Bar Young Lawyer Divsn. (exec. bd., 1994—). Muslim. Avocations: tennis, jogging, auto racing, reading. Immigration, naturalization, and customs, Municipal (including bonds), Real property. Office: 1030 Clifton Ave Clifton NJ 07013-3522

**MOHAN, JOHN J.,** lawyer; b. Streator, Ill., Nov. 1, 1918; s. John Jay and Lillian M. Mohan; m. Mary E. Haley, June 22, 1946; children: James, Mary Ann, Elizabeth, Nancy. BS in Commerce, U. Ill., 1940, JD, 1942. Bar: Ill. 1942. Ptnr. John & richart Mohan, Streator, 1946—. Capt. U.S. Army JAG, 1942-46. Mem. Streator C. of C., Streator C.C. (bd. dirs. 1966-69), Rotary, Elks, K.C. Roman Catholic. Avocation: golf. General practice, Probate, General civil litigation. Office: 112 S Park St Streator IL 61364-2954

**MOHLER, ROBERT E.,** lawyer; b. Akron, Ohio, Aug. 14, 1912; s. Rueben Albert and Pearl (Carter) M.; married; children: Roger A., Jocelyn Lance, Janice Grove. MA, Ohio State U.; AB with distinction, U. Akron, 1936, LLB, 1947. Bar: Ohio 1947, U.S. Dist. Ct. (no. dist.) Ohio 1958, U.S. Supreme Ct. 1971. Asst. prosecutor, then prosecutor Summit County, Ohio; past mem. Akron Child Guidance Ctr.; mem., past pres. Summit County Juvenile Ct. Adv. Com.; asst. counsel Firestone Tire & Rubber. Author publs. on history of Summit County. Active numerous civic orgns.; mem., past pres. Akron Bd. Edn., Summit County Hist. Soc.; candidate for mayor City of Akron, candidate for mcpl. judge. Democrat. Avocation: reading. Criminal, Probate, General corporate. Home and Office: 321 Mull Ave Akron OH 44313-7654

**MOHN, MAYNARD MARTIN,** lawyer; b. Storm Lake, Iowa, May 11, 1944; s. William H. and Sadie (Otto) M.; m. Roxanne Berg, June 17, 1966 (div. 1978); 1 child, Suzanne; m. Linda G. Harrison, June 16, 1978; 1 child, Jill. BS in Bus., U. S.D., 1966, JD, 1969. Bar: Iowa 1971, U.S. Dist. Ct. (no. dist.) Iowa 1972, U.S. Dist. Ct. (so. dist.) Iowa 1976, U.S. Ct. Appeals (8th cir.) 1976, U.S. Supreme Ct. 1976. Asst. atty. County of Woodbury, Iowa, 1972-74; ptnr. Rosendahl, Foryth and Mohn, Estherville, Iowa, 1974-89, Mitchell & Mohn, Estherville, 1989-96, Mohn Law Office, Estherville, 1996—. Pres. Estherville C. of C., 1981. Capt. U.S. Army, 1970-72, Vietnam. Mem. Iowa Bar Assn. (mem. comml. law and bankruptcy com. 1990-91, chmn. comml. law and bankruptcy video libr. 1990-91), Kiwanis (pres. 1980), Pi Omega Pi. Republican. Lutheran. Bankruptcy, General civil litigation, Consumer commercial. Home: 1103 N 6th St Estherville IA 51334-1337 Office: Mohn Law Office PO Box 347 Estherville IA 51334-0347

**MOHR, ANTHONY JAMES,** judge; b. L.A., May 11, 1947; s. Gerald Leonard and Rita Lenore (Goldstein) M. BA in Govt. cum laude with honors, Wesleyan U., 1969; JD, Columbia U., 1972; diploma with honors, 1975. Bar: Calif. 1972, U.S. Dist. Ct. (cen. dist.) Calif. 1973, U.S. Ct. Appeals (9th cir.) 1974, D.C. 1976, U.S. Supreme Ct. 1981. Law clk. to judge U.S. Dist. Ct. (cen. dist.) Calif., 1972-73; assoc. Alschuler Grossman, Stein & Kahan, 1973-75; pvt. practice L.A., 1976-94; judge L.A. Mcpl. Ct., 1994-97, L.A. Superior Ct., 1997—; faculty atty. asst. tng. program UCLA, 1982-97, bd. dirs. internat. student ctr., 1986—. Mem. editl. bd. Calif. Bar Jour., 1979-80, L.A. Lawyer Mag., 1989-94; contbr. articles to profl. jours. Del. White House Conf. on Youth, 1971; faculty Ctr. Jud. Edn. and Rsch, 1997—; nat. adv. coun. Ctr. for Study of Presidency, 1974—; mem. L.A. Dist. Atty.'s Adv. Coun., 1976-82; hearing officer L.A. County Employees Ret. Assn., 1986-94. Mem. ABA, Calif. Judges Assn., Beverly Hills Bar Assn. (bd. govs. 1975-80, chmn. litig. sect. 1983-85, chair resolutions com. 1991-92, ex. officio bd. dirs. 1998—, Dist. Svc. award 1992), Barristers of Beverly Hills Bar Assn. (pres. 1979-80), Am. Judicature Soc. (dir. 1982-83), L.A. County Bar Assn., Phi Beta Kappa, Phi Delta Phi. Office: LA Superior Ct 6230 Sylmar Ave Van Nuys CA 91401-2712

**MOHRMAN, HENRY J(OE), JR.,** lawyer, investment manager; b. St. Louis, Jan. 28, 1948; s. Henry Joseph and Mavis Claire (Lynch) M.; m. Mary Beth Mohrman, Aug. 26, 1969; children: Aaron Henry, Anna Rose. BA, Yale U., 1969; JD, U. Chicago, 1973. Bar: Mo. 1973, Ill. 1974, U.S. Supreme Ct. 1997. Assoc. Greenfield & Davidson, St. Louis, 1973-76; asst. gen. counsel LaBarge, Inc., St. Louis, 1976-77; tax mgr. Ernst & Young, St. Louis, 1977-81; pvt. practice St. Louis, 1982—; gen. counsel Miss. Valley Equipment Co., St. Louis, 1982—, MKT Mfg., Inc., St. Louis, 1986—. Mem. ABA, U. Chicago Law Sch. Alumni Assn. (pres. St. Louis chpt. 1986—). Republican. Jewish. Avocations: horsemanship, literature, theater, mathematics. General corporate, Taxation, general, Private international. Office: 7751 Carondelet Ave Ste 805 Clayton MO 63105-3369

**MOISE, STEVEN KAHN,** lawyer, rancher, merchant banker; b. Lubbock, Tex., July 28, 1944; s. Joseph J. and Marguerite K. M.; m. Beth Maxwell, June 2, 1968; children: Adam, Grant. BA, U. Colo., 1966, JD, 1969. Bar: Colo. 1969, N.Mex. 1971. Assoc. Rothgerber, Appel & Powers, Denver, 1969-71; assoc. Sutin, Thayer & Browne, Albuquerque, 1971-74, ptnr., 1974-94, pres., CEO, 1984-88, chmn., 1989-94, of counsel, 1995; pres. Moise & Co., Albuquerque, 1995—; bd. dirs. Wells Fargo Bank, N.Mex., N.A. Bd. dirs. U. Colo. Found., Boulder, 1969-79, 87-94; bd. dirs. U. Colo. Sch. Law Alumni, 1985-89, N.Mex. Amigos, 1987—; bd. dirs., exec. com. Albuquerque Cmty. Found., 1981—, pres. 1984-88; bd. dirs. Albuquerque Econ. Devel., 1982—, sec., 1984-86, v.p., 1986-88, pres., 1988-90, exec. com., 1984—; mem. Albuquerque Econ. Forum, 1989-98; chmn. Bingaman Circle, 1990-96. Mem. ABA, N.Mex. Bar Assn., Colo. Bar Assn. Democrat. Jewish. Real property, Oil, gas, and mineral, Finance. Home: 6611 Guadalupe Trl NW Albuquerque NM 87107 Office: Moise & Co PO Box 1705 Albuquerque NM 87103-1705

**MOIZE, JERRY DEE,** lawyer, government official; b. Greensboro, N.C., Dec. 19, 1934; s. Dwight Moody and Thelma (Ozment) M.; m. Margaret Ann Wooten, Aug. 13, 1976; 1 child, Jerry Dee Jr. AB cum laude, Elon (N.C.) Coll., 1957; JD, Tulane U., New Orleans, 1960; diploma, Army Command & Gen. Staff Sch., USAR, 1981. Bar: Colo. 1961, U.S. Dist. Ct. Colo. 1961, U.S. Ct. Mil. Appeals 1962, U.S. Supreme Ct. 1965, N.C. 1965. Legal clk. Air Def. Commd., Colorado Springs, Colo., 1960-61, assistance officer, 1962-63; chief legal assistance divsn. 2nd Army, Ft. Meade, Md., 1964-65; staff JAG, Indiantown Gap Mil. Reservation, 1965; law clk. to hon. Eugen Gordon U.S. Dist. Ct. (mid. dist.) N.C., Winston-Salem, 1965-66; dir. Legal Aid Soc. Forsyth County, Winston-Salem, 1966-69; exec. dir. Forsyth Bail Project, Winston-Salem, 1968-69, Lawyer Referral Svc. of Bar of 21st Jud. Dist., Winston-Salem, 1968-69; staff atty. office of gen. counsel FAA, Washington, 1969-70, acting chief admin. & legal resources, 1970-71; staff atty. office of gen. counsel Dept. Housing & Urban Devel., Washington, 1971; counsel Jackson (Miss.) area office Dept. Housing & Urban Devel., 1971-83, chief counsel Jackson (Miss.) field office, 1983-94; chief counsel Office Gen. Counsel Miss., Jackson, 1994—; HUD del. Miss. Fed. Exec. Assn., 1997—; lectr. U. W.Va. Conf. on Poverty Law, 1968. Editor N.C. Legal Aid Reporter, 1968-69, N.C. Legal Aid Directory, 1968, Avlex Legal Index (2nd supplement), 1971, developed Miss. low income housing financing mechanism 1975-76; contbr articles to profl. jours., articles to splty. mags. Dem. candidate N.C. Ho. of Reps., Guilford County, 1964; mem. mil. com. Forsyth County N.C. Red Cross, 1967-68; pack leader Andrew Jackson coun. Boy Scouts Am., 1986-92; active Project Adv. Group U.S. Office Econ. Opportunity Legal Svcs. Program, 1968-69, Adv. Com. on Housing & Urban Devel., Miss., Law Rsch. Inst., 1980-81, Pilot Mountain Preservation & Park Com., Winston-Salem, 1968-70; mem. Race Com. Whitworth Hunt Races, 1973-76; Am. Master of Foxhounds Assn., 1976-79; adv. Order DeMolay, 1997—. Capt. AUS, 1960-65; ret. lt. col. USAR, 1966-87. Decorated Meritorous Svc. medal, Army Commendation medal with oak leaf cluster, Army Res. Forces Achievement medal with three oak leaf clusters, Nat. Def. Svc. medal, Armed Forces Res. medal; named Rosicrucian Hon. Knight Mason, 1999. Mem. NRA, Fed. Bar Assn., N.C. State Bar, Miss. Hist. Assn., Miss. Track Club, Iron Bridge Hunt (v.p. 1964-65), Whitworth Hunt (founder, master of foxhounds 1975-76), The Austin Hunt (joint master of foxhounds 1976-79), Caledonian Soc. Miss., Sons of Confederate Vets., Mason (32 degree), KT (hon.), Order Eastern Star, Shriner, Rosicrucian, Pi Gamma Mu. Republican. Episcopal. Avocations: riding to hounds, running, book collecting. Home: Ivanhoe 935 Bellevue Pl Jackson MS 39202 Office: Miss State Dept Housing & Urban Devel Fed Bldg 100 W Capitol 9th Flr Jackson MS 39269

**MOLDOFF, WILLIAM MORRIS,** retired lawyer; b. Phila., Jan. 1, 1921; s. David and Pauline (Arcusin) Moldoff; m. Irene Morstad, June 1946 (div. 1950); m. Doris Elaine Johnson (dec.); children: Phillip Douglas, Laura Ellen, Janet Susan Sayers, Allan William. BA, U. Iowa, 1943; JD cum laude, U. Miami, 1950; LLM, U. Mich., 1955. Law editor Lawyers Coop. Pub. Co., Rochester, N.Y., 1952-54, 57-61; instr. Ohio Northern U. Coll. of Law, 1955-57; adminstrv. asst. to exec. dep. Sec. of State State of N.Y., 1961-63; pvt. practice Nassau, N.Y., 1963-66; veterans claims examiner Vets. Adminstrn. Regional, N.Y.C., 1966-85; ret., 1985. Lt. (j.g.) USNR, 1943-46. Republican. Jewish. Home: PO Box 151 Nassau NY 12123-0151

**MOLENKAMP, JACK A.,** lawyer; b. Grand Rapids, Mich., Oct. 1, 1952; s. Jacob and Henrietta Lillian (Kregel) M.; m. Sally McConnell, Aug. 24, 1974; children: Sarah, Greg. BA, Mich. State U., 1974; JD, U. Mich., 1979. Bar: Va. 1979, D.C. 1999. Sch. tchr. Portland (Mich.) Sch., 1974-76; assoc. Hunton & Williams, Richmond, Va., 1979-87, ptnr., 1987—. Author: Virginia Partnerships Under Revised Uniform Partnership Act, 1997. Pres., West Richmond Little League, 1994-98. Mem. ABA (chmn. REIT subcom. bus. law sect. 1994-98, Va. Bar Assn. (past chmn. bus. law bd. govs.), City of Richmond Bar. Presbyterian. Avocations: baseball, golf, antiques, primitive art. Finance, Securities, General corporate. Office: Hunton & Williams 1900 K St NW Washington DC 20006-1110

**MOLESKI, ANTHONY G.,** lawyer; b. Phila., Apr. 4, 1957; s. Anthony and Claire (Schoppy) M. BA, BS, U. Pa., 1979; JD, U. Iowa, 1985, MBA, 1986. Bar: Tex. 1986, Pa. 1990, N.J. 1991, D.C. 1991, Calif. 1992. Instr. U. Iowa, Iowa City, 1985-86; assoc. Bracewell & Patterson, Houston, 1986-90, Blank, Rome, Comisky & McCauley, Cherry Hill, N.J., 1990—. Mem. Calif. Bar Assn., Tex. Bar Assn., N.J. Bar Assn., Phila. Bar Assn., Mensa, Beta Gamma Sigma. Republican. Roman Catholic. Securities, General corporate, Private international. Office: Blank Rome Comisky & McCauley Woodland Falls Corp Park 210 Lake Dr E Ste 200 Cherry Hill NJ 08002-1163

**MOLINARO, THOMAS J.,** lawyer; b. Cleve., June 4, 1952; s. Albert J. and Marilyn M.; m. Betty E., Oct. 22, 1989; children: Daniel, Paul, Marisa, Anna. BS, U. Wis., 1976; JD, U. Wis. Law Sch., 1979. Bar: Wis., U.S. Dist. Ct. (we. and ea. dists.) Wis. Law clk. Wis. Ct. Appeals, Wankesha, 1979-80; assoc. Crooks, Law & Connell, Wausau, 1980-83; ptnr. Brady, Hoover & Molinaro, Wausau, 1983-85, Brady & Molinaro, Wausau, 1986-92; sole practice law Wausau, 1993—. Bd. dirs. Marathon Civic Corp., Wausau, 1988-94, Wausau Area Youth Soccer Assn., 1990-94; membership com. YMCA, Wausau, 1988-90. Mem. ATLA, Wis. Bar Assn., Marathon County Bar Assn. Avocations: antique collecting and restoration, skiing, soccer. Family and matrimonial, Personal injury, Workers' compensation. Office: 215 Grand Ave Wausau WI 54403-6220

**MOLINARO, VALERIE ANN,** lawyer; b. N.Y.C, Oct. 21, 1956; d. Albert Anthony and Rosemary Rita (Zito) M.; m. Howard Robert Birnbach; 1 child, Michelle Annalise Birnbach. BA with honors, SUNY, 1978; JD, Syracuse U., 1980, MPA, 1980. Asst. counsel. New York State Housing Finance Agy., N.Y.C., 1980-82; assoc. counsel, asst. secy. N.Y. State Urban Devel. Corp., N.Y.C., 1982-85; assoc. Mudge Rose Guthrie Alexander & Ferdon, N.Y.C., 1985-87, Bower & Gardner, N.Y.C., 1988, Hawkins, Delafield & Wood, N.Y.C., 1988-91; of counsel McKenzie McGhee, N.Y.C., 1991-98; assoc. Battle Fowler, N.Y.C., 1998—. Author: Am. Bar Assn. Jour., 1981. Mem. N.Y.C. Commn. on Status of Women, 1995—. Mem. ABA, N.Y. State Bar Assn., (tax exempt fin. com.), Assn. Bar City of N.Y., Nat. Assn. Bond Lawyers, N.Y.C. Commn. on the Status of Women (legis. chmn.). Municipal (including bonds). Office: Battle Fowler LLC Park Ave Tower 75 E 55th St New York NY 10022-3205

**MOLINARO-BLONIGAN, MARY ROBIN,** corporate lawyer. BA in Econs., U. Iowa, 1991; JD, Ohio No. U., 1995. Bar: Iowa 1995, Fla. 1996, Colo. 1997. Corp. counsel Warren Transport, Inc., Waterloo, Iowa, 1995—. Mem. ABA, ATLA, Transp. Lawyers Assn., Assn. Transp. Law, Logistics & Policy. Transportation. Office: Warren Transport Inc PO Box 420 Waterloo IA 50704-0420

**MOLITOR, KAREN ANN,** lawyer; b. Chgo., Apr. 20, 1953; d. Edward William and Elizabeth M. (Schmolke) Swanson; m. Patrick John Molitor, Apr. 26, 1971; children: Elizabeth Ann, Patrick John Jr. BS with honors, U. Ark., 1986, JD, 1990. Bar: Conn. 1990, U.S. Dist. Ct. Conn. 1990, U.S. Ct. Appeals (2d cir.) 1994. Assoc. atty. Shipman & Goodwin, Hartford, Conn., 1990-93; asst. atty. gen. Conn. Atty. Gen.'s Office, Storrs, Conn., 1993-94; gen. coun. The Meadows Music Theatre, Hartford, 1994—. Mem. ABA, Conn. Bar Assn., Nat. Assn. Coll. and Univ. Attys., Phi Beta Kappa. Roman Catholic. Avocations: bicycling, reading, physical fitness. General corporate, Federal civil litigation, Entertainment. Home: 28 Sunset Ter West Hartford CT 06107-2738 Office: Meadows Music Theatre 32 Midland St Windsor CT 06095-4334

**MOLITOR, STEVEN JOHN,** lawyer; b. May 19, 1962; Bar: N.Y. 1988.; BA, Franklin and Marshall Coll., 1984; JD, Cornell U., 1987. Bar: N.Y. 1988, Pa. 1996. Assoc. Morgan, Lewis & Bockius LLP, N.Y.C. and Phila., ptnr. Office: Morgan Lewis & Bockius LLP 101 Park Ave Fl 44 New York NY 10178-0060 also: 1701 Market St Philadelphia PA 19103-2903

**MOLLEUR, RICHARD RAYMOND,** lawyer; b. Adams, Mass., May 14, 1932; s. Raymond Emory and Germaine (Ouellette) M.; m. Rita M. Desaulniers, Sept. 5, 1955; children: Denis Richard, Michelle Annette, Suzanne Nicole, Celeste Marie. A.B., Assumption Coll., Worcester, Mass., 1954; J.D., Georgetown U., 1957. Bar: D.C. 1958. Counsel Office of Architect of the Capital, Washington, 1957-60; trial atty. U.S. Dept. Justice, Washington, 1960-65; dir. D.C. bail project Georgetown Law Center, Washington, 1965-66; dir. D.C. bail agy., 1966, asst. dean, asso. prof. law, 1967-69; v.p., gen. counsel Fairchild Industries, Inc., Germantown, Md., 1979-85; ptnr. Herron & Burchett, 1986-90, Winston & Strawn, 1990; corp. v.p., gen. counsel Northrop Corp., L.A., 1991—. Author: Bail Reform in Nation's Capital, 1966. Recipient Alumni Achievement award Georgetown Law Center, 1966. General corporate, Environmental. Office: Northrop Corp 1840 Century Park E Los Angeles CA 90067-2199

**MOLLICA, SALVATORE DENNIS,** lawyer; b. Waterbury, Conn., Nov. 27, 1948; s. Dennis Salvatore and Nellie (Albani) M. BA in History, St. Johns U., Jamaica, N.Y., 1970; JD, U. Fla., 1975. Bar: Fla. 1975, U.S. Dist. Ct. (no., mid. and so. dists.) Fla. 1975. Investigator State of Fla. Pub. Defenders Office, Gainesville, 1972-75; asst. pub. defender State of Fla., Gainesville, 1975-76; div. chief State of Fla. Pub. Defenders Office, Gainesville, 1976-80; sole practice Gainesville, 1980; ptnr. Mollica & Vipperman, Gainesville, 1981-82; sole practice Gainesville, 1982-90; asst. pub. defender, div. chief Levy/Gilchist Satellite Office, Gainesville, 1990-94, asst. pub. defender, chief felony div. II, 1994—. Democrat. Roman Catholic. Criminal, Juvenile, State civil litigation. Home: PO Box 694 Gainesville FL 32602-0694 Office: PO Box 2820 Gainesville FL 32602-2820

**MOLLING, CHARLES FRANCIS,** lawyer; b. Grafton, Wis., Jan. 5, 1940; s. Frank Joseph and Gertrude Catherine (Tillmann) M.; m. Gretchen Arlene Lundberg, Sept. 27, 1961. BA magna cum laude, U. Mo., 1973; JD, Loyola U., Chgo., 1977. Bar: Colo. 1977, Ill. 1977, U.S. Dist. Ct. Colo. 1979, U.S. Dist. Ct. (no. dist.) Ill. 1979, U.S. Ct. Appeals (7th and 10th cirs.) 1979, U.S. Ct. Claims 1979. Claims and bond underwriting positions various ins. cos., Milw. and other locations, 1961-76; assoc. state counsel Pioneer Title Ins. Co., Denver, 1976-77; assoc. Boatright & Deuben, Wheat Ridge, Colo., 1977-78, McNeela & Griffin, Chgo., 1979; ptnr. Boatright Molling & Ripp, Wheat Ridge, 1980-88; pvt. practice law Denver, 1988—. Author: Public Trustee Foreclosures in Colorado--A Systems Approach, 1983; (computer software) MicroLawyer, 1985. Cpl. USMC, 1960-61. Mem. Colo. Bar Assn., Denver Bar Assn., 1st Jud. Dist. Bar Assn., POETS. Avocations: computers, photography. Real property, Contracts commercial, General corporate. Office: 4704 Harlan St Ste 300 Denver CO 80212-7418

**MOLNAR, LAWRENCE,** lawyer; b. Czygand, Hungary, Apr. 14, 1927; came to U.S., 1954; s. Alexander and Marie (Vavra) M.; m. Karla Lehmann, Jan. 8, 1955. Juris Utriusque Candidatus, Charles U., Prague, Czechoslovakia, 1951; JD, NYU, 1962; LLM, LLD (hon.), Charles U., 1991. Bar: N.Y. 1962, U.S. Dist. Ct. (so. and ea. dists.) N.Y. 1970, Czech Republic, 1991. With U.S. Intelligence, Berlin, 1951-54, Lansen, Naeve Corp., N.Y., 1955-56; asst. mgr. export traffic Intra-Mar Shipping Corp., N.Y., 1957-58; mgr. export traffic Melchior, Armstrong, Ridgefield, N.J., 1958-59; assoc. Hamburger, Weinschenk, N.Y.C., 1963-69; ptnr. Hamburger, Weinschenk, Molnar & Fisher, N.Y.C., 1969—. Mem. ABA, Assn. of Bar of City of N.Y., Consular Law Soc. (v.p. 1980—), Fgn. Law Assn., Queens Bar Assn. Private international, Probate, Estate planning. Office: Hamburger Weinschenk Molnar & Fisher 36 W 44th St New York NY 10036-8102

**MOLO, STEVEN FRANCIS,** lawyer; b. Chgo., June 30, 1957; s. Steven and Alice (Babinski) M.; m. Mary Wood, Dec. 31, 1986; children: Alexander, Madeline, Julia, Allison. BS, U. Ill., 1979, JD, 1982. Bar: Ill. 1982. Asst. atty. gen. criminal pros. and trial divsn. Chgo., 1982-86; assoc. Winston & Strawn, Chgo., 1986-89, ptnr., 1989—; adj. prof. Loyola U. Law Sch., Chgo., 1988-93,. Northwestern U. Law Sch., Chgo., 1989—; mem. faculty Nat. Inst. Trial Advocacy, Chgo., 1989—; lectr. on trial advocacy, appellate advocacy, and evidence to various orgns. Co-author: Corporate Internal Investigations, 1993, updated annually, 1993—; bd. editors Bus. Crimes Bull: Litigation and Compliance, 1994—; contbr. articles to legal jours. Spl. counsel Ill. Jud. Inquiry Bd., 1986-90; spl. reapportionment counsel Cook County Judiciary, 1988-89, spl. reapportionment counsel to Rep. leadership Ill. Ho. of Reps. and Senate, 1991-92. Named one of World's Leading White Collar Crime Lawyers, Euromoney PLC, 1995, Leading Ill. Attys. Comml. Litigation and Criminal Law, 1996, Crain's Chicago Bus. "40 Under 40" Chicago Leaders, 1997. Mem. ABA, FBA, Ill. Bar Assn., Chgo. Bar Assn., Theodore Roosevelt Assn., Chgo. Athletic Assn., Econ. Club Chgo., Tavern Club, Chgo. Inn of Ct. (master of bench, pres. 1997-98), Saddle & Cycle Club, Gilda's club Chgo. (presdl. gov. bd. 1999—). General civil litigation, Criminal, Federal civil litigation. Office: Winston & Strawn 35 W Wacker Dr Ste 4200 Chicago IL 60601-1695

**MOLONEY, STEPHEN MICHAEL,** lawyer; b. L.A., July 1, 1949; s. Donald Joseph and Madeline Marie (Sartoris) M.; m. Nancy Paula Barile, Jan. 15, 1972; children: Michael, John, Kathleen. Student, St. John's Sem., Camarillo, Calif., 1967-69; BS, U. Santa Clara, 1971, JD, 1975. Bar: Calif. 1975, U.S. Dist. Ct. (cen. dist.) Calif. 1976, U.S. Supreme Ct. 1990. Assoc. Gilbert, Kelly, Crowley & Jennett, L.A., 1975-80, from ptnr. to sr. ptnr., 1980—; arbitrator, settlement officer Los Angeles Superior Ct., 1985—. Contbr. articles to profl. jours. Dir. Calif. Def. Polit. Action Com., Sacramento, 1991—. With USAR. Recipient Svc. award to Pres. of So. Calif. Def. Counsel, Def. Rsch. Inst., Chgo., 1992. Mem. Assn. So. Calif. Def. Counsel (pres. 1992-93), Calif. Def. Counsel (dir. 1991—), L.A. County Bar Assn. (vols. in parole, 1976-77, exec. com. alternative dispute resolution com. 1992-96), Oakmont Country Club, La Quinta Resort and Club. Democrat. Roman Catholic. Avocations: politics, golf, reading, travel. Personal injury, Construction, Labor. Office: Gilbert Kelly Crowley & Jennett 1200 Wilshire Blvd Ste 6 Los Angeles CA 90017-1908

**MOLONY, MICHAEL JANSSENS, JR.,** lawyer; b. New Orleans, Sept. 2, 1922; s. Michael Janssens and Marie (Perret)M.; m. Jane Leslie Waguespack, Oct. 21, 1951; children: Michael Janssens III (dec.), Leslie, Megan, Kevin, Sara, Brian, Ian, Duncan. JD, Tulane U., 1950. Bar: La. 1950, D.C. 1979, U.S. Dist. Ct. (ea. and mid. dists.) La. 1951, U.S. Ct. Appeals (5th cir.) 1953, U.S. Supreme Ct. 1972, U.S. Dist. Ct. (we. dist.) La. 1978, U.S. Ct. Appeals (11th and D.C. cirs.) 1981. Ptnr. Molony & Baldwin, New Orleans, 1950; assoc. Jones, Flanders, Waechter & Walker, New Orleans, 1951-56; ptnr. Jones, Walker, Waechter, Poitevent, Carrere & Denegre, New Orleans, 1956-75, Milling, Benson, Woodward, Hillyer, Pierson & Miller, New Orleans, 1975-91, Chaffe, McCall, Phillips, Toler & Sarpy, New Orleans, 1991-92, Sessions & Fishman, New Orleans, 1993—; instr., lectr. Med. Sch. and Univ. Coll. Tulane U., 1953-59; mem. Eisenhower Legal Com., 1952. Bd. commrs. Port of New Orleans, 1976-81, pres., 1978; mem. bd. rev. Associated Br. Pilots, 1990-96; bd. dirs. La. World Expn. Inc., 1974-84; bd. dirs., exec. com. New Orleans Tourist and Conv. Commn., 1971-74, 78, chmn.; family attractions com. 1973-75; chmn. La. Gov.'s Task Force on Space Industry, 1971-73; chmn. La. Gov.'s Citizens' Adv. Com. Met. New Orleans Transp. and Planning Program, 1971-77; mem. La. Gov.'s Task Force Natural Gas Requirements, 1971-72; mem. La. Gov.'s Proaction Commn. for Higher Edn., 1995; mem. Goals Found. Coun. and ex-officio mem. Goals Found., Met. New Orleans, 1969-73; vice chmn. Port of New Orleans Operation Impact, 1969-70, mem. Met. Area Com., New Orleans, 1970-84; trustee, Pub. Affairs Rsch. Coun. La., 1970-73, mem. exec. com. Bus./Higher Edn. Coun., U. New Orleans, 1980-94, bd. dirs., 1980—, v.p. 1986-88, pres., 1988-90, chmn. Task Force on Pub. Higher Edn. Funding, 1990-95, chmn. governmental affairs, 1995—, Task Force on Edn./Econ. Devel. Alliances, 1993-95; mem.

Mayor's Coun. on Internat. Trade and Econ. Devel., 1978; mem. Mayor's Transition Task Force Econ. Devel., 1994; bd. dirs. La. Partnership for Tech. and Innovation, 1989—; bd. dirs. Acad. Sacred Heart, 1975-77, Internat. House, 1985-86, adv. coun. 1985—; bd. dirs. U. New Orleans Found., 1991—; mem. vis. com. Sch. Bus. Adminstrn., Loyola U., New Orleans, 1981—, trustee Loyola U., 1985-91, vice chmn. bd. trustees, 1990-91; mem. Dean's Coun. Tulane U. Law Sch., 1988-96, vice chmn. building com., 1991-95; bd. dirs., mem. exec. com. Internat. Trade Mart, chmn. internat. bus. com., 1983-85; World Trade Ctr.-New Orleans (bd. dirs. 1983—, mem. Port Activity com. 1985-91, transp. com. 1991-95, govt. affairs com. 1996—); chmn. Task Force on Internat. Banking, 1982; mem. Mayor's Task Force on Drug Abuse, 1989-90. Capt. JAGDR, USAAF, 1942-46, PTO. Recipient Leadership award AIAA, 1971, Yenni award Loyola U., New Orleans, 1979, New Orleans Times Picayune Loving Cup, 1986, First Citizen of the Learning Soc. Dean's award UNO Met. Coll., 1992; also various civic contbn. awards; co-recipient Silver Anvil award Pub. Rels. Soc. Am., 1991. Fellow Coll. Labor and Employment Lawyers; mem. ABA (labor and employment law and litigation sects., com. equal opportunity law, chmn. regional com. liaison with equal opportunity commn., office of fed. contract compliance programs), D.C. Bar Assn., Fed. Bar Assn., La. Bar Assn. (past sec.-treas., bd. govs. 1957-60, editor jour. 1957-59, sec. spl. supreme ct. com. on drafting code jud. ethics), New Orleans Bar Assn. (dir legal aid bur. 1954, chmn. standing com. legis. 1968, vice chmn. standing com. pub. rels. 1970-71), Am. Judicature Soc., La. Law Inst. (asst. sec.-treas. 1958-70), Am. Arbitration Assn. (bd. dirs., 1995-98, chmn. reg. adv. coun., chmn. reg. adv. coun. employment law cases, mem. spl. panel large complex arbitration/mediation cases, Whitney North Seymour Sr. award 1991), So. Inst. Mgmt. (founder), AIM, U.S. C. of C. (urban and regional affairs com. 1970-73), La. C. of C. (bd. dirs. 1963-66), New Orleans and River Region C. of C. (v.p. met. devel. and urban affairs 1969, past chmn. labor rels. coun., bd. dirs. 1970-78, pres.-elect 1970, pres. 1971, dir., exec. com. 1972, ex officio mem., bd. dirs. 1979—), Bienville Club, English Turn Golf and Country Club, Pickwick Club, Plimsoll Club, Serra Club, So. Yacht Club, Sigma Chi (pres. alumni chpt. 1956). Roman Catholic. Labor, General civil litigation, Alternative dispute resolution. Home: 3039 Hudson Pl New Orleans LA 70131-5337 Office: Sessions & Fishman 201 Saint Charles Ave Ste 3500 New Orleans LA 70170-3500

**MOLOUGHNEY, KEVIN PATRICK,** lawyer; b. Southfield, Mich., Sept. 14, 1968; s. James J. and Sharon Lynn (Huxford) M.; m. Tracy Baker, Aug. 12, 1995. BA with honors, Mich. State U., 1991; JD magna cum laude, Detroit Coll. Law, 1994. Bar: Mich. 1994. Assoc. Collins, Einhorn, Farrell & Ulanoff P.C., Southfield, 1994—. Mem. Mich. Bar Assn., Oakland County Bar Assn., Golden Key. Personal injury, General civil litigation, Professional liability. Office: Collins Einhorn Farrell & Ulanoff PC 4000 Town Ctr Ste 909 Southfield MI 48075-1473

**MOLSEED, MICHAEL CLYDE,** lawyer; b. L.A., June 3, 1942; s. Joseph Kenneth and Lois Mae (Witt) M. AA, El Camino J.C., Gardena, Calif., 1971; BA, Calif. State U., Dominguez Hills, 1973; JD, Calif. Coll. of Law, 1978. Pvt. practice Newport Beach, Calif., 1989—. With USN, 1964-66. Family and matrimonial, Real property, Bankruptcy. Home and Office: 400 Colton St Newport Beach CA 92663-1812

**MOLTZ, MARSHALL JEROME,** lawyer; b. Chgo., May 22, 1930; s. Nathan and Rose (Nathanson) M.; m. Rita G., Dec. 26, 1954; m. 2d, Mary Ann, Nov. 4, 1967; children: Alan J., Michelle S. Yastrow, Marilyn F. Moltz-Hohmann, Julie A., Steven E., Rachel N. BS, Northwestern U., 1951, JD, 1954. Bar: Ill. 1954, Mo. 1954. Assoc., John B. Moser, Chgo., 1957; assoc. Goldberg, Devoe, Shadur & Mikva, Chgo., 1957-58; assoc. Lester Plotkin, Chgo., 1958-59; sole practice, Chgo., 1959-65; ptnr. Moltz & Spagat, Chgo., 1966-67; sole practice, Chgo., 1967-68; ptnr. Moltz & Wexler, Chgo., 1968-80; sole practice Chgo. 1980—; pres. Mercury Title Co.; faculty mem. profl. liab. in real estate transactions ABA Regional Inst., 1993; mem. Blue Ribbon com. Cook County Recorder of Deeds; speaker real estate law; atty. Counseling Ctr. of Lake View Mental Health Orgn., Chgo. With M.I., U.S. Army, 1955-56; ETO. Recipient Louden Wigmore prize Northwestern U. Law Sch., 1954. Mem. ABA, Ill. State Bar Assn., Chgo. Bar Assn. (mem. real property law com. 1958—, chmn. Torrens sub-com. 1968-75, vice chmn. real property law com. 1974-75, chmn. real property law com. 1975-76, speaker and faculty mem. various seminars 1993-96, faculty mem. residential real estate seminar, 1995, 96), VFW, Phi Alpha Delta (law fraternity). Author course outlines Ill. Inst. Continuing Legal Edn., 1972, 73; editorial bd. Northwestern U. Law Rev., 1953-54. Real property, Contracts commercial, Landlord-tenant. Home: 112 Harvard Ct Glenview IL 60025-5917 Office: 77 W Washington St Ste 1620 Chicago IL 60602-2903

**MOLTZ, MARTIN PAUL,** lawyer; b. Chgo., Nov. 22, 1944; s. Joseph and Celia Moltz; m. Ann Kaplan, May 26, 1974; 1 child, Benjamin Harold. BA, U. Ill., Chgo., 1966; JD, U. Okla., 1969. Bar: Ill. 1971, Fla. 1976. Asst. states atty. Cook County States Atty.'s Office, Chgo., 1970-72; staff atty. States Atty.'s Appellate Prosecutor's Office, Elgin, Ill., 1972-98, dep. dir., 1997—; instr. Roosevelt U., Chgo., 1987—. Contbr. articles to profl. jours. Mem. 49th Ward Dems., Chgo., 1970—. With U.S. Army, 1969-75. Mem. Chgo. Bar Assn. (bd. mgrs. 1997—; bd. dirs. pub. interest law initiative 1997—). Jewish. Avocations: amusement parks, roller coasters, tournament bridge. Home: 7306 N Winchester Ave Chicago IL 60626-5529 Office: States Attys Appellate Prosecutor 2032 Larkin Ave Elgin IL 60123-5845

**MOLZEN, CHRISTOPHER JOHN,** lawyer; b. Manhattan, Kans., Sept. 5, 1961; s. Gilbert John and Janice Molzen; m. Robin Larson. BA in Polit. Sci., U. Mo., 1983, JD, 1987. Bar: Mo. 1987, U.S. Dist. Ct. (we. dist.) Mo. 1987, U.S. Tax Ct. 1994, U.S. Supreme Ct. 1994. Assoc. Shughart Thomson & Kilroy, Kansas City, 1995—. Co-author, editor The Judicial Handbook of Kansas City, 1993. Pegasus scholar Inner Temple, London, 1991, William L. Bradshaw scholar, 1982. Mem. ATLA, Mo. Assn. Trial Attys., Kansas City Met. Bar Assn., Young Lawyer's (pres. 1996-97), Federalist Soc., Ross T. Roberts Inn of Ct., Order of Barristers, Phi Delta Phi. General civil litigation, Personal injury. Home: PO Box 6938 Lees Summit MO 64064-6938 Office: Shughart Thomson & Kilroy Twelve Wyandotte Plz 120 W 12th St Ste 1500 Kansas City MO 64105-1929

**MONAGHAN, MATTHEW JOHN,** lawyer; b. Portland, Maine, June 14, 1961; s. Thomas Francis and Anne Marie (Perry) M.; m. Karen Ellen Hopkins, Aug. 10, 1985; children: Erin, Casey. BA, Bowdoin Coll., 1984; JD, Lewis & Clark Coll., 1987. Bar: Maine 1987, U.S. Dist. Ct. Maine, 1987, U.S. Ct. Appeals (1st cir.) 1991, U.S. Supreme Ct., 1991. Assoc. Monaghan, Leahy, Hochadel & Libby, Portland, 1987-92, ptnr., 1992-99; litigation counsel UNUMProvident Corp., Portland, 1999—. Bd. dirs., v.p. Am. Heart Assn., Maine affil., 1993-96; deacon Woodfords Congregational Ch., Portland, 1994-97, mem. gov. bd. dirs., 1997-99; bd. dirs. Portland divsn. ARC, 1997-99, chair nominating com., 1998-99. Named Best Portland Lawyer Casco Bay Weekly, 1997. Mem. Maine State Bar Assn., (co-chmn. legal edn. and admission com. 1991-95), Maine Trial Lawyers, ABA. General civil litigation, Personal injury, Workers' compensation. Office: UNUMProvident Corp Legal Dept M194 2211 Congress St Portland ME 04122

**MONAGHAN, PETER GERARD,** lawyer; b. Belfast, Ireland, July 12, 1949; came to U.S., 1961; s. William Liam and Elizabeth (Eccles) M.; m. Barbara Marion Farrenkopf, Sept. 24, 1972; children: Brian Patrick, Kevin James, Allison Mary. BS, Fordham U., 1970; JD, St. John's U., Jamaica, N.Y., 1977. Bar: N.Y. 1978, U.S. Dist. Ct. (so. dist.) N.Y. 1978, U.S. Dist. Ct. (ea. dist.) N.Y. 1979, U.S. Supreme Ct. 1986. Claims examiner Royal Ins. Co., N.Y.C., 1970-76; assoc. Kroll, Edelman, Elser and Dicker, N.Y.C., 1976; assoc. Bower and Gardner, N.Y.C., 1977-83, ptnr., 1984-91; ptnr. Bartlett, McDonough, Bastone & Monaghan, LLP, Mineola, N.Y., 1992—. Cubmaster Boy Scouts Am., Bayside, N.Y., 1985-89. Capt. U.S. Army Res., 1970-78. Mem. ABA, Queens County Bar Assn., N.Y. State Bar Assn. (trial lawyers sect. com. on med. malpractice 1988—), Assn. of Trial Lawyers of Am., Nassau-Suffolk Trial Lawyers Assn., Nassau County Bar Assn. State civil litigation, Federal civil litigation, General practice. Office: Bartlett McDonough Bastone & Monaghan LLP 300 Old Country Rd Mineola NY 11501-4198

**MONAGHAN, THOMAS JUSTIN,** prosecutor. U.S. atty. Dept. Justice, Omaha, 1993—. Office: US Attys Office 1620 Dodge St Ste 1400 Omaha NE 68102-1594

**MONAHAN, COURTNEY WILSON,** lawyer; b. L.A., Sept. 14, 1963; d. Bruce and Joyce Wilson; m. Michael John U. Monahan, Oct. 22, 1994; 1 child, Lauren Marie. BA, U. Colo., 1985; JD, Suffolk U., 1989. Bar: N.Y. 1990, U.S. Dist. Ct. (ea. and so. dist.) N.Y. 1990. Assoc. attorney Colucci & Umans, N.Y.C., 1990-96, partner, 1997—. Intellectual property. Office: Colucci & Umans 101 E 52nd St New York NY 10022-6018

**MONAHAN, MARIE ADORNETTO,** law educator; b. Buffalo, Feb. 26, 1951; d. Samuel Adornetto and Josephine Lucci; m. Peter A. Monahan, May 23, 1981; children: Matthew, Joseph. BA, SUNY, Buffalo, 1973; MA, SUNY, 1975; JD, DePaul U., Chgo., 1981; PhD, Northwestern U., 1986. Bar: Ill., U.S. Dist. Ct. (no. dist.) Ill. Instr. Northwestern U., Evanston, Ill., 1975-81; law clk. Ill. Appellate Ct., Chgo., 1981-83; assoc. atty. Baker & McKenzie, Chgo., 1983-88; asst. prof. No. Ill. U. Sch. Law, DeKalb, 1988-89; asst. prof. law John Marshall Law Sch., Chgo., 1989—; hearing officer Atty. Registration and Disciplinary Commn., Chgo., 1998-9. Co-author casebook; author tng. manual; contbr. articles to legal cjours. Mem. ABA, Chgo. Bar Assn. (investigator, mem. hearing panel jud. evaluation com. 1993-98). Democrat. Roman Catholic. Office: John Marshall Law Sch 315 S Plymouth Ct Chicago IL 60604-3968

**MONAHAN, MARIE TERRY,** lawyer; b. Milford, Mass., June 26, 1927; d. Francis V. and Marie I. (Casey) Terry; m. John Henry Monahan, Aug. 25, 1951; children: Thomas F., Kathleen J., Patricia M., John Terry, Moira M., Deirdre M. AB, Radcliffe Coll., 1949; JD, New Eng. Sch. Law, 1975. Bar: Mass. 1977, U.S. Dist. Ct. Mass. 1978, U.S. Supreme Ct. 1982. Tchr. French and Spanish Holliston (Mass.) High Sch., 1949-52; pvt. practice Newton, Mass., 1977—. Mem. Mass. Assn. Women Lawyers (pres. 1986). Avocations: reading, travel. State civil litigation, Family and matrimonial, Probate. Home and Office: 34 Foster St Newton MA 02460-1511

**MONAHAN, RICHARD F.,** lawyer; b. Walla Walla, Wash., Feb. 20, 1940; s. Donald H. and Ina L. (Applegate) M.; m. Brenda A. Titus, May 4, 1944; children: Bridie Lynn Monahan Hood, E. Casey. BS, U. Idaho, 1962, JD, 1968. Bar: Wash. 1968, U.S. Dist. Ct. Wash. 1970, U.S. Ct. Appeals 1993. Assoc. Minnick & Hayner, Walla Walla, 1969-75, ptnr., 1975; ptnr. Roach & Monahan, Walla Walla, 1976—. Pres. Walla Walla YMCA, 1988-94, Walla Walla United Way, 1984. Mem. Walla Walla County Bar Assn. (pres. 1985), AQHA (dir. 1985—), Walla Walla C. of C. (pres. 1978). Avocations: quarter horse racing, golf. Personal injury, General civil litigation, Insurance. Home: 1015 Bryant St Walla Walla WA 99362-9328 Office: Roach and Monahan PO Box 1815 11 S Second Walla Walla WA 99362

**MONCHARSH, PHILIP ISAAC,** lawyer; b. N.Y.C., May 27, 1948; s. Bernard J. and Betty R. (Chock) M.; m. Karen L. Fellows, Nov. 1, 1981; children: Rachael, Anna. BA, Yale U., 1970; JD, Columbia U., 1973. Bar: Calif. 1973, U.S. Dist. Ct. (cen. dist.) Calif. 1979, U.S. Ct. Appeals (9th cir.) 1981. Trial dep. L.A. County Pub. Defender, L.A., 1973-78; assoc. Strote & Whitehouse, Beverly Hills, Calif., 1978-81, Ghitterman, Hourigan, et al, Ventura, Calif., 1981-86, Heily & Blase, Ventura, Calif., 1986-87; of counsel Hecht, Diamond & Greenfield, Pacific Palisades, Calif., 1988; ptnr. Benton, Orr, Duval & Buckingham, Ventura, 1988-89, Rogers & Sheffield (now Rogers Sheffield & Herman), Santa Barbara, Calif., 1989—; arbitrator, judge pro tem Superior and Mcpl. Cts., Ventura and Santa Barbara, 1986—. Pres. Ojai Valley (Calif.) Land Conservancy, 1988-94. Mem. Calif. Trial Lawyers Assn., Santa Barbara Trial Lawyers Assn., Ventura Trial Lawyers Assn., L.A. Trial Lawyers Assn., Assn. Trial Lawyers Am., Consumer Attys. of Calif., Consumer Attys. of L.A., Yale Club Santa Barbara, Ventura and San Luis Obispo Counties (pres.). Avocations: hiking, backpacking, travel. General civil litigation, Personal injury, Insurance. Office: Rogers Sheffield & Herman 427 E Carrillo St Santa Barbara CA 93101-1401

**MONDRY, PAUL MICHAEL,** lawyer; b. Ludlow, Mass., June 15, 1953. BA, Western New Eng. Coll., 1975, JD, 1980. Bar: Mass. 1980, U.S. Dist. Ct. Mass. 1981. Pvt. practice, Ludlow, 1980—; asst. treas. Hampden County, Springfield, Mass., 1982-83; legal counsel Hampden County Retirement Bd., Springfield, 1983—, City Springfield Retirement Bd., 1996—. Selectman Town of Ludlow, 1981-87, chmn. bd., 1983-84, 86-87; mem. Ludlow Dem. Com., 1978-91, vice chmn., 1981-85; v.p. Polish Am. Citizens Club, Inc., Ludlow, 1985; bd. dirs. Ludlow Boys Club and Girls Club, Inc., 1990-93, charitable trust trustee, 1994—. Mem. ABA, Mass. Bar Assn., Hampden County Bar Assn., Unity Athletic Club, Hampden County Bar Assn., Hampden County Estate Planning Coun., Mass. Acad. of Trial Attys. Avocations: golf, collecting sports memorabilia. General practice, Probate, Administrative and regulatory. Office: 154 East St Ludlow MA 01056-3409

**MONDUL, DONALD DAVID,** patent lawyer; b. Miami, Fla., Aug. 24, 1945; s. David Donald and Marian Wright (Heck) M.; children: Alison Marian, Ashley Megan; m. Anna Marie Towle, Oct. 12, 1996. BS in Physics, U.S. Naval Acad., 1967; MBA, Roosevelt U., 1976; JD, John Marshall Law Sch., 1979. Bar: Ill. 1979, Fla. 1980, Tex. 1998; U.S. Patent Office 1980; U.S. Ct. Appeals (fed. cir.) 1982; U.S. Supreme Ct. 1990. Commd. ensign USN, 1967, advanced through grades to comdr., 1977; mktg. rep. Control Data Corp., Chgo., 1977-79; patent atty. Square D Co., Palatine, Ill., 1979-81; group patent counsel Ill. Tool Works Inc., Chgo., 1981-87; assoc. Cook, Wetzel & Egan, Chgo., 1987-89; ptnr. Foley & Lardner, Chgo. and Milw., 1989-95; sr. patent atty. IBM, East Fishkill, N.Y., 1995-96; gen. patent counsel Ericsson, Inc., Richardson, Tex., 1996—. Patentee in methods and apparatus for multiplying plurality of numbers, N numbers, determining the product of two numbers, air baffle appartus, electrical encoding device. Commander, USNR, 1967-87. Patent. Office: Ericsson Inc 740 E Campbell Rd Richardson TX 75081-6718

**MONEY, KENNETH F., JR.,** lawyer; b. Dayton, Ohio, Aug. 12, 1969; s. Kenneth F. and Barbara J. Money. BA in Econs., U. N.H., 1991; JD, U. Miami, 1994. Bar: N.H. 1994, Fla. 1995, Maine 1996. Assoc. Mulhern & Scott P.A., Portsmouth, N.H., 1994-97; pvt. practice Portsmouth, 1997—. Bd. dirs. Learning Skills Acad., Rye, N.H., 1997—, Seacoast Area Widowed Persons Svc., Dover, N.H., 1997—, Greater Portsmouth C. of C. Found., 1998—. Republican. Roman Catholic. Avocations: golf, tennis, travel, sports. Estate planning, Estate taxation, Probate. Office: Money Law Officers PLLC 118 Maplewood Ave Ste B4 Portsmouth NH 03801-3787

**MONGAN, ANTHONY DAVID,** lawyer; b. Honolulu, Feb. 27, 1960; s. Gary Chandler and Patricia Ann (Einolander) M.; m. Leanna Sulak, Sept. 28, 1990; children: Mary Kate, Anthony Levin. BA, U. Calif., Berkeley, 1983; JD, U. Calif., San Francisco, 1986. Bar: Calif. 1986. Clk. Calif. Indian Legal Svcs., Oakland, 1985-86; assoc. Edwards, White & Sody, San Diego, 1986-87; sr. assoc. Haasis, Pope & Correll, San Diego, 1987-96; supervising assoc. Jaroszek, Roth & Kennedy, San Diego, 1996—; legal advisor Prayer in the Home Press, Tijuana, Mex., 1996—; coord. counsel for porcelan litig. Black & Decker, Towson, Md., 1997—. Mem. Optimist Club (pres. San Diego chpt. 1993-94). Republican. Roman Catholic. Avocations: politics, historical simulation gaming. Product liability, State civil litigation, Appellate. Office: Jaroszek Roth & Kennedy 1230 Columbia St Ste 600 San Diego CA 92101-8502

**MONHEIT, HERBERT,** lawyer; b. Atlantic City, Dec. 12, 1929; s. Philip and Yetta (Abel) M.; m. Patricia Silver, Mar. 13, 1959; children: Michael, Maryann. BA, Rutgers Coll., 1951, LLB, 1956; postgrad., Georgetown U., 1953-55. Bar: Pa. 1957, U.S. Dist. Ct. (ea. dist.) Pa. 1957, U.S. Supreme Ct. 1974. Pub. defender Phila., 1957-58, pvt. practice, 1960—; spl. asst. atty. gen., 1968-70; mem. County Bd. Law Examiners, 1961; lectr. U. Del. Law Sch., 1975. Rep. committeeman, 1964-70; active Cheltenham Twp. Sch. Authority, 1965. Mem. Philmont Country Club, Atlantic City Country Club, Linwood Country Club. Federal civil litigation, Personal injury, Product liability. Home: 112 S Oxford Ave Ventnor City NJ 08406-2845 Office: Monheit Monheit Silverman & Fodera PC 2010 Chestnut St Philadelphia PA 19103-4411

**MONHOLLON, LELAND,** lawyer; b. Corbin, Ky., Nov. 8, 1925; s. Lewis Tom and Thelma (Prewitt) M.; m. Gawinna Owens, 1946 (div. 1969); 1 child, Patricia Lynn; m. Alice Faye Burden, July 3, 1970. JD, U. Ky., 1952. Bar: Ky. 1952. Supervising adjustor Travelers Ins. Co., Louisville, 1955-69; pvt. practice law Madisonville, Ky., 1969-97, ret., 1997. With USN, 1943-46, PTO, USNR, 1963-69. Mem. Ky. Bar Assn., Hopkins County Bar Assn., Am. Legion, VFW. Republican. Methodist. Home: 185 Threadneedle Dr Madisonville KY 42431-6439 Office: 111 S Main St Madisonville KY 42431-2555

**MONK, WILLIAM BOYCE,** lawyer; b. Lake Charles, La., Dec. 28, 1957; s. Boyce Clayton and Mary Ann Maxfield M.; m. Elizabeth Aimee Judice, Sept. 21, 1985; children: Margaret Ellen, Mary Lucile, James William, Anne Aimee, John Boyce. BA, La. State U., 1978, JD, 1981. Assoc. Stockwell Law Firm, Lake Charles, La., 1981-84, ptnr., 1984—; coun. mem. La. State U. Mineral Law Inst., 1989-91. Bd. dirs. Chamber Southwest La., 1986-92; pres. Young Men's Bus. Club Lake Charles, 1986. Mem. La. State Bar Assn. (coun. chmn. mineral law sect. 1991-92, coun. chmn. young lawyers sect. 1990-91), La. State Law Inst. (coun. mem. 1990-97), Krewe Contraband, Lake Charles Country Club. Republican. Roman Catholic. Avocations: hunting, golf. Environmental, General civil litigation, Oil, gas, and mineral. Home: 918 Pujo St Lake Charles LA 70601-4452 Office: Stockwell Law Firm 1 Lakeside Plz Lake Charles LA 70602

**MONROE, CARL DEAN, III,** lawyer; b. Birmingham, Ala., Sept. 15, 1960; s. Carl D. and Martha Jo M. BA, Birmingham-So. Coll., 1982; JD, Georgetown U., 1985. Bar: Ala. 1986, U.S. Ct. Appeals (11th cir.) 1988. Scheduler Siegelman for Atty. Gen., Montgomery, 1986; legal rsch. aide Office of Sec. of State State of Ala., Montgomery, 1986; asst. atty. gen., adminstrv. asst. Office of Atty. Gen., Montgomery, 1987-89; atty.-advisor Office Gen. Counsel, U.S. Dept. Energy, Washington, 1989—; mem. panel of judges Georgetown Law Ctr. Moot Ct., 1991, 92, CIA Environ. Roundtable; lectr. waste mgmt. Johns Hopkins U. Mem. panel of judges Ala. YMCA Youth Legislature, Montgomery, 1979, 87, 88, 89; office coord. blood dr. ARC, Montgomery, 1987, 88; com. mem. Georgetown Alumni Admissions, Washington, 1986-91; mem. Nat. Trust for Hist. Preservation. Mem. ABA (author environ. law sect. newsletter Looking Ahead), Acad. Polit. Sci., Ala. Bar Assn., Birmingham-So. Alumni (alumni leader 1986—), Smithsonian Assocs., Phi Beta Kappa. Democrat. Presbyterian. Avocations: water skiing, tennis, horseback riding. Home: 1200 N Nash St Apt 264 Arlington VA 22209-3620

**MONROE, KENDYL KURTH,** retired lawyer; b. Clayton, N.Mex., Sept. 6, 1936; s. Dottis Donald and Helen (Kurth) M.; m. Barbara Sayre, Sept. 12, 1956; children: Sidney, Dean, Loren. AB, Stanford U., 1958, LLB, 1960. Bar: N.Y. 1961, Calif. 1961. Assoc. Sullivan & Cromwell, N.Y.C., 1960-67, ptnr., 1968-94; chmn. TEB Charter Svcs., Inc., Teterboro, N.J., Air/West Aviation, Santa Fe, N.Mex., El Valle Escondido Ranch Ltd. Co., Seneca, N.Mex., Highland Forests, Keeseville, N.Y., Eklund Assn. Clayton, N.Mex. ; bd. dirs. No. Minerals Co., Keeseville. Chmn. Hope Entertainment, Inc., N.Y.C.; bd. dirs. Pub. Health Rsch. Inst., N.Y.C., N.Mex. First, Albuquerque, N.Y. Chamber Soloists, N.Y.C.; mem. bd. advisors N.Mex. Pilots Assn. Mem. State Bar Calif., Assn. of Bar of City of N.Y., N.Mex. Amigos, Met. Club (N.Y.C.). Corporate taxation, Securities, Real property. Home: Kenton Rte Seneca NM 88437

**MONSANTO, RAPHAEL ANGEL,** lawyer; b. N.Y.C., Oct. 3, 1946; s. Rafael Monsanto and Margarita Velazquez. BSEE, NYU, 1969, JD, 1975. Bar: N.J. 1975, U.S. Patent Office 1976, N.Y. 1978, Mich. 1998. Atty. Bell Telephone Lab., Murray Hills, N.J., 1975-78; intellectual property counsel J.C. Penney, N.Y.C., 1978-80; atty. Kenyon & Kenyon, N.Y.C., 1980-84, Rohm & Monsanto Plc, Detroit, 1984—; instr. Practicing Law Inst., N.Y.C., 1994—; intellectual property cons. various orgns., Detroit, 1996—; presenter, author seminar course, 1996. Holder patent. Dir., counsel Boys Choir of Detroit, 1998—. Recipient Achievement award Ctr. for Hemispherical Coop., 1996. Mem. ABA, N.Y. Intellectual Property Law Assn., N.J. Trial Lawyers Assn. Avocation: musician. Federal civil litigation, Patent, Intellectual property. Office: Rohm & Monsanto PLC 660 Woodward Ave Ste 1525 Detroit MI 48226-3518

**MONSEES, TIMOTHY WILLIAM,** lawyer; b. Kansas City, Mo., May 19, 1955; s. William Eugene and Barbara Jo (Simons) M.; m. Laura Franklin, July 19, 1980; children: W. Benjamin, Samuel R., Megan E. BS, U. Mo., 1977, JD, 1981. Bar: Mo. 1981, Tex. 1986, Kans. 1994. Ptnr. Myerson, Monsees & Morrow, P.C., Kansas City, until 1995, Monsees, Miller & DeFeo, P.C., Kansas City, 1995—. Mem. ATLA (sustaining), Internat. Soc. Primerus Law Firms, Mo. Bar Assn., Tex. Bar Assn., Kans. Bar Assn., Mo. Assn. Trial Lawyers (bd. govs.), Kansas City Met. Bar Assn. (chmn. tort law com.), Hillcrest Country Club, Order of Coif, Order of Barristers, Million Dollar Advocates Forum, Leadership Club, U. Mo. Jefferson Club, Delta Upsilon. Reorganized Ch. of Jesus Christ of LDS. Avocations: snow skiing, running, youth athletics, golfing, basketball. General civil litigation, Personal injury, Product liability.

**MONSMA, ROBBIE ELIZABETH,** lawyer, mediator, arbitrator, real estate executive; b. L.A., Nov. 4, 1952; d. Robert Euart and Bessie Esadean Cook; m. Thomas H. Tyrell Jr., Jan. 11, 1970 (div. 1977); 1 child, Trace; m. Durham J. Monsma, Aug. 12, 1979; children: Ian, Mallory. BA, Calif. State U., 1976; JD, UCLA, 1979; MA in Christian Leadership, Fuller Theol. Seminary, 1997. Bar: Colo. 1994. Law clk. The Times Mirror Co., L.A., 1977-78; assoc. Cox, Castle & Nicholson, L.A., 1979-81; corp. counsel, v.p., sec. Becket Investment Corp., Santa Monica, Calif., 1981-85; corp. counsel, sr. v.p. SoPac Real Estate Group, Pasadena, Calif., 1985-94; corp. counsel, exec. v.p. PacificUS Real Estate Group, Pasadena, 1994-98; ptnr. Stott Monsma & Assoc. Conflict Mgmt Tng. and System Design, 1993-97; receiver panel mem. L.A. Superior Ct., 1992-94; mem. jud. arbitration panel, L.A. and Ventura Counties, 1992-94; vol. settlement officer, L.A. County, 1992-94; vol. judge pro-tem Pasadena Sml. Claims Ct., 1992-94; cert. vol. mediator The Mediator Ctr., Irvine, Calif., 1992, Christian Conciliation Svc., Hollywood, Calif., 1992; trainer Dispute Resolution Svcs., L.A., 1992; cert. conciliator Inst. for Christian Conciliation, 1993; mem. Industry Dispute Resolution Task Force, 1994-98. Bd. mem. Westside Legal Svcs., Santa Monica, Calif., 1983-84; pro bono advisor I Love La Cañada (Calif.) Flintridge Com., 1989-91; mem. bd. dir. Concerned Citizens of La Cañada Flintridge, 1987-91, Hill an' Dale Family Learning Ctr., Santa Monica, 1984-85, West L.A. Bapt. Sch. Parent-Tchr. Club, West Los Angeles, Calif., 1984-85, Ctr. Leadership Devel., 1996-98; mem. stewardship bd. Mission Hills Ch., 1995-98; bd. dirs. Peacemaker Ministries, 1996-98; mem., bd. dirs. Conciliation Ministries of Colo., 1997—. Mem. Soc. Profls. Dispute Resolution.

**MONSON, JOHN RUDOLPH,** lawyer; b. Chgo., Feb. 4, 1941; s. Rudolph Agaton and Ellen Louise (Loeffler) M.; m. Susan Lee Brown, May 22, 1965; children: Elizabeth Louisa, Christina Lee, Donald Rudolph. BA with honors, Northwestern U., 1963; JD with distinction, U. Mich., 1966. Bar: Ill. 1966, N.H. 1970, Mass. 1985. Atty. assoc. Chapman & Cutler, Chgo., 1966-68, Levenfeld, Kanter, Baskes & Lippitz, Chgo., 1968-70, Nighswander, Martin & Mitchell, Laconia, N.H., 1970-71; mem., ptnr. Wiggin & Nourie, P.A., Manchester, N.H., 1972-96; pres. Wiggin & Nourie, P.A., Manchester, 1991-94; sec., gen. counsel Rock of Ages Corp., 1996—. Mem. N.H. Fish and Game Commn., Concord, 1980-94, chmn., 1983-93; sr. bd. dirs. Brown-Monson Found., 1991—; incorporator Cath. Med. Ctr., 1988-95, Optima Health, 1994—; commr. N.H. Land and Cmty. Heritage Commn., 1998—. Fellow Am. Coll. Trust and Estate Counsel, Safari Club Internat. (v.p. 1999—, dir.-at-arge 1997-99). Republican. Avocations: skiing, hunting, running. General corporate, Estate planning. Home: 24 Wellesley Dr Bedford NH 03110-4531 Office: Wiggin & Nourie PA 20 Market St Manchester NH 03101-1931

**MONTAGNET, O. STEPHEN,** lawyer; b. New Orleans, Feb. 19, 1969; s. Oliver S. Jr. and Monica C. Montagnet; m. Anne McCarley Elliott, Aug. 12, 1995; 1 child, Olivia. BBA, U. Notre Dame, 1991; JD, U. Miss., 1995. Bar: Miss. 1995, U.S. Ct. Appeals (5th cir.) 1995. Assoc. Lake Tindall, LLP, Jackson, Miss., 1995—. Mem. ABA, Miss. Bar Assn., Miss. Def. Lawyers Assn., Hinds County Bar Assn. (bd. mem. 1999—), Jackson Young Lawyers Assn. (sec. 1997-98, pres.-elect 1999—). Product liability, Contracts commercial. Office: Lake Tindall LLP One Jackson Pl 118 E Capitol St Ste 450 Jackson MS 39201-2103

**MONTAGUE, ROBERT LATANE, III,** lawyer; b. Washington, Sept. 18, 1935; s. Robert Latane and Frances Breckinridge (Wilson) M.; m. Prudence Darnell, June 20, 1964; children: Anne Steele Mason Montague, Robert Latane IV. BA, U. Va., 1956, LLB, 1961. Bar: Va. 1961, D.C. 1966, U.S. Supreme Ct. 1966. Asst. atty. gen. Ky., 1961-64; pres. Historic Alexandria Found., 1968-70; chmn. Alexandria Environ. Policy Commn., 1970-74; pres. Conservation Coun. Va., 1978-80; chmn. Alexandria Commn. on Bicentennial of U.S. Constitution, 1987-91, Alexandria Historical Restoration and Preservation Commn., 1988—; trustee Assn. for Preservation of Va. Antiquities, 1990-96. chmn. Bd. of Vis. of Gunston Hall, 1987-92; del. Moscow Conf. on Law and Econ. Coop., 1990. Comdr. USNR, 1956-79. Mem. Va. Bar Assn., Va. State Bar (chmn. environ. law sect. 1973-74), Alexandria Bar Assn. Office: 1007 King St Alexandria VA 22314-2922

**MONTANO, ARTHUR,** lawyer; b. Audubon, N.J., 1923; s. Domenick and Theresa (Grasso) M.; m. Ann B. Durkin; children: Sharon Adams, Sandra Bumgardner, Cheryl Ann Hughes, Arthur Jr., Bernadette, Michael. BME, Villanova U., 1950; LLB, Rutgers U., 1954. Bar: N.J. 1955, U.S. Dist. Ct. N.J. 1955, U.S. Ct. Appeals 1967, U.S. Supreme Ct. 1969. Assoc. Orlando, Devine & Tomlin, Camden, N.J., 1955-56, Orlando, Kisselman & Devine, Camden, 1956-58, Kisselman, Devine & Deighan, Camden, 1958-60; ptnr. Kisselman, Devine, Deighan & Montano, Camden, 1960-65, Kisselman, Devine, Deighan, Montano, King & Summers, Camden, 1965-71, Kisselman, Deighan, Montano & Summers, Cherry Hill, N.J., 1971-77; sr. ptnr. Montano, Summers, Mullen & Manuel, Cherry Hill, 1977-88; of counsel Montano, Summers, Mullen, Manuel & Owens, P.A., 1988-99; pvt. practice Audubon, N.J., 1998—; lawyer; b. Audubon, N.J.; s. Domenick and Theresa (Grasso) M.; m. Ann B. Durkin; children—Sharon Adams, Sandra Bumgardner, Cheryl Ann Hughes, Arthur Jr., Bernadette, Michael. BME, Villanova U., 1950; LLB, Rutgers U., 1954. Bar: N.J. 1955, U.S. Dist. Ct. N.J. 1955, U.S. Ct. Appeals 1967, U.S. Supreme Ct. 1969. Assoc. Orlando, Devine & Tomlin, Camden, N.J., 1955-56; assoc. Orlando, Kisselman & Devine, Camden, 1956-58; assoc. Kisselman, Devine & Deighan, Camden, 1958-60; ptnr. Kisselman, Devine, Deighan & Montano, Camden, 1960-65, Kisselman, Devine, Deighan, Montano, King, & Summers, Camden, 1965-71, Kisselman, Deighan, Montano & Summers, Cherry Hill, N.J., 1971-77; sr. ptnr. Montano, Summers, Mullen & Manuel, Cherry Hill, 1977-88; of counsel Montano, Summers, Mullen, Manuel & Owens, P.A. 1988-98; pvt. practice, Audubon, N.J., 1998—; adj. prof. law Rutgers Law Sch., Camden, N.J., 1984-93; arbitrator Am. Arbitration Assn., state and fed. cts. Served as navigator AC, U.S. Army, 1943-45. Recipient award for professionalism in law, 1997. Fellow Am. Coll. Trial Lawyers, Am. Bar Found.; mem. N.J. State Bar Assn. (trustee 1977-84), Trial Attys. N.J. (trial bar 1978), Camden County Bar Assn., Tavistock Country Club (Haddonfield, N.J.). Roman Catholic. Navigator AC, U.S. Army, 1943-45. Recipient award for professionalism in law, 1997. Fellow Am. Coll. Trial Lawyers, Am. Bar Found.; mem. N.J. State Bar Assn. (trustee 1977-84), Trial Attys. N.J. (trial bar 1978), Camden County Bar Assn., Tavistock Country Club (Haddonfield, N.J.). Roman Catholic. Federal civil litigation, State civil litigation, Personal injury. Office: 201 S White Horse Pike Audubon NJ 08106-1306

**MONTEDONICO, JOSEPH,** lawyer; b. Washington, May 30, 1937; s. Joseph and Linda (Love) M.; m. Lynne Morrell, Nov. 12, 1979; 1 child, Maria. BA, U. Md., 1962, JD, 1965. Bar: Md. 1965, D.C. 1965, U.S. Dist. Ct. D.C. 1965, U.S. Dist. Ct. Md. 1965. Law clk. to justice Rockville, Md., 1965-66; assoc. Donahue, Ehrmantraut Mitchell, Rockville, 1966-78; ptnr. Donahue, Ehrmantraut, Montedonico, Washington, 1978-88, Montedonico & Mason, Rockville, 1988-91, Montedonico, Hamilton & Altman, PC, Chevy Chase, Md., 1991—; cons., lectr. in field. Author: Medical Malpractice and Health Care Care, 1987; (with others) Anesthesia Clinics, 1987, Surgical Pathology, 1989. With U.S. Army, 1956-58. Named one of Best Lawyers in Am., Washingtonian Mag., 1989-96, one of Best Lawyers in Washington. Mem. Am. Bd. Trial Lawyers (pres. D.C. chpt.), Inns of Ct., Md. Bar Assn., D.C. Bar Assn. Republican. Avocations: scuba, skiing, photography. Personal injury, General civil litigation, Health. Office: Montedonico Hamilton & Altman 5454 Wisconsin Ave Ste 1300 Chevy Chase MD 20815-6901

**MONTEIRO, RICARDO J.,** lawyer; b. Caldas Da Rainha, Portugal, Apr. 16, 1967; s. Luis S. and Maria J. (Malaquias) M. BA in Psychology, L.I. U., 1989; JD cum laude, Widener U., 1992. Bar: N.J. 1992, U.S. Dist. Ct. N.J. 1992. Office mgr. Atlas Metal Finishing, Inc., Newark, 1987-90; mgr., atty. Globe Metal Finishing, Inc., Newark, 1990-92; assoc. Fausto Simoes, Esq., Newark, 1992-94; ptnr. Simoes and Monteiro, P.C., Newark, 1994—. Counsel Portuguese Am. Police Assn., Newark, 1992, C.A.F.I.C., Newark, 1993, Portuguese Americans United, Newark, 1994. Recipient Am. Jurisprudence award Lawyers Coop. Pub., 1991. Mem. ABA, ATLA, Assn. Regional Caldense (pres. 1994), Phi Kappa Phi, Phi Delta Phi. Avocations: skiing, golf. General practice. Home: PO Box 190 541 Bethany Rd Holmdel NJ 07733-1682

**MONTGOMERY, BETTY DEE,** state attorney general, former state legislator. BA, Bowling Green State U.; JD, U. Toledo, 1976. Former criminal clk. Lucas County Common Pleas Ct.; asst. pros. atty. Wood County, Ohio, 1977-78, pros. atty., 1981-88; pros. atty. City of Perrysburg, Ohio, 1978-81; mem. Ohio Senate, 1989-94; atty. gen. State of Ohio, Columbus, 1995—. Mem. Nat. Dist. Atty. Assn., Ohio Bar Assn., Toledo Bar Assn., Wood County Bar Assn. Office: Attorney Generals Office State Office Tower 30 E Broad St Columbus OH 43215-3414*

**MONTGOMERY, CHARLES HARVEY,** lawyer; b. Spartanburg, S.C., Jan. 28, 1949; s. Dan Hugh and Ann Louise (Gasque) M.; m. Renée Jean Gubernot, Mar. 27, 1971; children: Charles Scott, Marie Renée. BA, Duke U., 1971; JD, Vanderbilt U., 1974. Bar: N.C. 1974, U.S. Dist. Ct. (ea. dist.) N.C. 1974, U.S. Supreme Ct. 1979, U.S. Dist. Ct. (mid. dist.) N.C. 1991; cert. family law specialist, N.C., 1995. Assoc. Jordan Morris & Hoke, Raleigh, N.C., 1974-75; atty. Wake County Legal Svcs., Raleigh, 1975-76; pvt. practice, Raleigh, 1977; ptnr. Montgomery & Montgomery, Cary, N.C., 1978-79, Sanford Adams McCullough & Beard, Raleigh, 1979-86, Adams McCullough & Beard, Raleigh, 1986-88, Toms Reagan & Montgomery, Cary, 1989-92, Toms & Montgomery, Cary, 1992-93; pvt. practice, Cary, 1993—; bd. dirs. Br. Bank and Trust, Cary; pres. Family Law Mediation, Inc. Councilman Town of Cary, 1977-81, 83-87; vice-chmn. Wake County Dem. party, Raleigh, 1991-92; commr. Wake County, Raleigh, 1992; bd. dirs. East Cen. Cmty. Legal Svcs., Inc., 1997—. Mem. ABA, N.C. Bar Assn. (chmn. pub. info. com. 1994-96, dir. family law coun. 1994-97), N.C. Acad. Trial Lawyers (chair family law sect. 1996-98). Methodist. Avocation: sailing. Family and matrimonial, State civil litigation, Land use and zoning (including planning). Office: PO Box 1325 1135 Kildaire Farm Rd Ste 315 Cary NC 27511-4566

**MONTGOMERY, JAMES EDWARD, JR.,** lawyer; b. Champaign, Ill., Feb. 8, 1953; s. James Edward Sr and Vivian M.; m. Linda C.; children: James III, Anne, Heather, Leslie. AB Polit. Sci., Duke U., 1975; JD, So. Meth. U., 1978. Bar: Tex., 1978, Md., 1994; U.S. Dist. Ct. (ea. dist.) Tex. 1978, U.S. Dist. Ct. (we. dist.) Tex., 1985, U.S. Dist. Ct. (so. dist.) Tex. 1986, U.S. Dist. Ct. (no. dist.) Tex. 1987, U.S. Dist. Md., 1994; U.S. Ct. Appeals (5th cir.) 1979; U.S. Supreme Ct., 1993. Assoc. Strong, Pipkin, Nelson & Parker, Beaumont, Tex., 1978-81; owner Sibley & Montgomery, Beaumont, 1981-85; assoc. Law Offices of Gilbert Adams, Beaumont, 1985; prin. James E. Montgomery, Beaumont, 1985-88; ptnr. Montgomery & Koniusczy, Beaumont, 1988-89; assoc. Sawtelle, Goode, Davidson & Troilo, San Antonio, Tex., 1989-91; shareholder Davidson & Troilo, San Antonio, 1991-94; pres. Montgomery & Assocs., San Antonio, 1994-97; ptnr. Soules & Wallace, P.C., San Antonio, 1997—. Editor: Fifth Cir. Reporter, 1983-86. Bd. dirs. Boys and Girls Clubs of San Antonio, 1995-97; dist. chmn. Boy Scouts, San Antonio, 1994. Mem. ABA, State Bar of Tex., San Antonio Bar Assn., Rotary (pres. Alamo Hts. chpt. 1997-98), 5th Cir. Bar Assn. (bd. dirs. 1983-86), Jefferson County Bar Assn. (treas. 1986). Avocations: tennis, skiing, golf, reading. General civil litigation, Contracts commercial, Product liability. Office: Soules & Wallace PC Frost Bank Tower 100 W Houston St Ste 1500 San Antonio TX 78205-1433

**MONTGOMERY, JAMES ISSAC, JR.,** lawyer; b. Louisville, Ky., Apr. 18, 1956; s. James Isaac Sr. and Marie Ann M.; children: Gwendolyn, Jennifer, James III. BA, Northwestern U.; JD, UCLA, 1981. Ptnr. Daniels, Baratta & Fine, L.A. Mem. ABA, Nat. Bar Assn., African-Am. Ins. Profls., Assn. So. Calif. Def. Coun., John M. Langston Bar Assn. (pres. 1996). General civil litigation, Insurance, Personal injury. Office: Daniels Baratta & Fine 1801 Century Park E Los Angeles CA 90067-2302

**MONTGOMERY, JOHN BISHOP,** lawyer; b. N.Y.C., Aug. 28, 1957; s. Parker Gilbert and Jan (McMillan) M.; m. Linda Patten, Sept. 5, 1987; children: Spencer, Paige. AB, Stanford U., 1980; JD, Lewis and Clark Coll., 1984. Bar: Calif. 1985. Atty. The Cooper Cos., Inc., Palo Alto, Calif., 1984-88; assoc. Wilson, Sonsini, Goodrich & Rosati, Palo Alto, 1988-90, Baker & McKenzie, Palo Alto, 1990-94; ptnr. Gen. Counsel Assocs. LLP, Mountain View, Calif., 1994—; mem. bd. advisors Peninsula Open Space Trust, Menlo Park, Calif., 1996—. Mem. Palo Alto Pub. Arts Commn., 1988-94; mem. urban design com. City of Palo Alto, 1988-94. Mem. Calif. State Bar (corps. com. 1996-97). General corporate, Securities. Office: Gen Counsel Assocs LLP 1891 Landings Dr Mountain View CA 94043-0848

**MONTGOMERY, JOHN WARWICK,** law educator, theologian; b. Warsaw, N.Y., Oct. 18, 1931; s. Maurice Warwick and Harriet (Smith) M.; m. Joyce Ann Bailer, Aug. 14, 1954; children: Elizabeth Ann, David Warwick, Catherine Ann; m. Lanalee de Kant, Aug. 26, 1988. Lord of Morris. AB in Philosophy with distinction, Cornell U., 1952; BLS, U. Calif., Berkeley, 1954, MA, 1958; BD, Wittenberg U., 1958, MST, 1960; PhD, U. Chgo., 1962; Docteur de l'Université, mention Théologie Protestante, U. Strasbourg, France, 1964; LLB, LaSalle Extension U., 1977; diplôme cum laude, Internat. Inst. Human Rights, Strasbourg, 1978; MPhil in Law, U. Essex, Eng., 1983; D in Civil and Cannon Law (hon.), Inst. Religion and Law, 1999. Bar: Va. 1978, Calif. 1979, D.C. 1985, Wash. 1990, U.S. Supreme Ct. 1981, Eng. 1984; lic. real estate broker Calif.; cert. law librarian; diplomate Med. Library Assn.; ordained to ministry Luth. Ch., 1958. Librarian, gen. reference service U. Calif. Library, Berkeley, 1954-55; instr. Bibl. Hebrew, Hellenistic Greek, Medieval Latin Wittenberg U., Springfield, Ohio, 1956-59; head librarian Swift Libr. div. and Philosophy, mem. federated theol. faculty U. Chgo., 1959-60; assoc. prof., chmn. dept. history Wilfred Laurier U. (formerly Waterloo Luth. U.), Ont., Can., 1960-64; prof., chmn. div. ch. history, history of Christian thought, dir. European Seminar program Trinity Evang. Div. Sch., Deerfield, Ill., 1964-74; prof. law and theology George Mason U. Sch. Law (formerly Internat. Sch. of Law), Arlington, Va., 1974-75; theol. cons. Christian Legal Soc., 1975-76; dir. studies Internat. Inst. Human Rights, Strasbourg, France, 1979-81; founding dean, prof. jurisprudence, dir. European program Simon Greenleaf U. Sch. Law, Anaheim, Calif., 1980-88; lic. disting. prof. theology and law, dir. European program Faith Evang. Luth. Sem., Tacoma, Wash., 1989-91; from prin. lectr. to reader in law Luton U., Eng., 1991-93, prof. law and humanities, dir. Ctr. Human Rights, 1993-97, emeritus prof., 1997—; disting. prof. apologetics and history of Christian thought, v.p. acad. affairs U.K. and Europe Trinity Coll. and Theol. Sem., Newburgh, Ind., 1997—; disting. prof. law Regent U., Va., 1997—; sr. counsel European Ctr. Law and Justice, 1997—; vis. prof. Concordia Theol. Sem., Springfield, Ill., 1964-67, DePaul U., Chgo., 1967-70; hon. fellow Revelle Coll., U. Calif., San Diego, 1970; rector Freie Fakultaten Hamburg, Fed. Republic Germany, 1981-82; lectr. Rsch. Scientists Christian Fellowship Conf. St. Catherines Coll., Oxford U., 1985, Internat. Anti-Corruption Conf., Beijing, China, 1995; Pascal lectr. on Christianity and the Univ., U. Waterloo, Ont., Can., 1987; A. Kurt Weiss lectr. biomed. ethics U. Okla., 1997; adj. prof. Puget Sound U. Sch. Law, Tacoma, 1990-91; numerous other invitational functions. Author: The Writing of Research Papers in Theology, 1959; A Union List of Serial Publications in Chicago Area Protestant Theological Libraries, 1960; A Seventeenth-Century View of European Libraries, 1962; Chytraeus on Sacrifice: A Reformation Treatise in Biblical Theology, 1962; The Shape of the Past: An Introduction to Philosophical Historiography, 1962, rev. edition, 1975; The Is God Dead Controversy, 1966; (with Thomas J.J. Altizer) The Altizer-Montgomery Dialogue, 1967; Crisis in Lutheran Theology, 2 vols., 1967, rev. edit., 1973; Es confiable el Christianismo?, 1968; Ecumenicity, Evangelicals, and Rome, 1969; Where is History Going?, 1969; History and Christianity, 1970; Damned Through the Church, 1970; The Suicide of Christian Theology, 1970; Computers, Cultural Change and the Christ, 1970; In Defense of Martin Luther, 1970; La Mort de Dieu, 1971; (with Joseph Fletcher) Situation Ethics: True or False?, 1972; The Quest for Noah's Ark, 1972, rev. edit., 1974; Verdammt durch die Kirche, 1973; Christianity for the Toughminded, 1973; Cross and Crucible, 2 vols., 1973; Principalities and Powers: The World of the Occult, 1973, rev. edit., 1975; How Do We Know There is a God?, 1973; Myth, Allegory and Gospel, 1974; God's Inerrant Word, 1974; Jurisprudence: A Book of Readings, 1974, 4th edit., 1992; The Law Above the Law, 1975; Cómo Sabemos Que Hay un Dios?, 1975; Demon Possession, 1975; The Shaping of America, 1976; Faith Founded on Fact, 1978; Law and Gospel: A Study for Integrating Faith and Practice, 1978, 3rd edit., 1994; Slaughter of the Innocents, 1981; The Marxist Approach to Human Rights: Analysis & Critique, 1984; Human Rights and Human Dignity, 1987; Wohin marschiert China?, 1991; Evidence for Faith: Deciding the God Question, 1991; Giant in Chains: China Today and Tomorrow, 1994; Law and Morality: Friends or Foes?, 1994; Jésus: La Raison Rejoint L'Histoire, 1995; (with C.E.B. Cranfield and David Kilgour) Christians in the Public Square, 1996, Conflicts of Law, 1997; The Transcendental Holmes, 1999; editor: Lippincott's Evangelical Perspectives, 7 vols., 1970-72; International Scholars Directory, 1973, Simon Greenleaf Law Rev., 7 vols., 1981-88; contbg. editor: Christianity Today, 1965-84, New Oxford Review, 1993-95; films: Is Christianity Credible?, 1968; In Search of Noah's Ark, 1977; Defending the Biblical Gospel, 1985 (11 videocassette series); (TV series) Christianity on Trial, 1987-93; contbr. articles to acad., theol., legal encys. and jours., chpts. to books. Nat. Luth. Ednl. Conf. fellow, 1959-60; Can. Council postdoctoral sr. research fellow, 1963-64; Am. Assn. Theol. Schs. faculty fellow, 1967-68; recipient Angel award Nat. Religious Broadcasters, 1989, 90, 92. Fellow Trinity Coll. (Newburgh, Ind.), Royal Soc. Arts (Eng.), Victoria Inst. (London), Acad. Internat. des Gourmets et des Traditions Gastronomiques (Paris), Am. Sci. Affiliation (nat. philosophy sci. and history sci. commn. 1966-70); mem. ALA, European Acad. Arts, Scis. and Humanities (corr. mem., Paris), Acad. Lit. France (titulary mem.), Lawyers' Christian Fellowship (hon. v.p. 1995—), Nat. Conf. U. Profs., Calif. bar Assn. (human rights commn. 1980-83), Internat. Bar Assn., World Assn. Law Profs., Mid. Temple and Lincoln's Inn (barrister mem.), Am. Soc. Internat. Law, Union Internat. des Avocats, Nat. Assn. Realtors, Tolkien Soc. Am., N.Y. C.S. Lewis Soc., Am. Hist. Assn., Soc. Reformation Rsch., Creation Rsch. Soc., Tyndale Fellowship (Eng.), Stair Soc. (Scotland), Presbyn. Hist. Soc. (North Ireland), Am. Theol. Libr. Assn., Bibliog. Soc. U. Va., Evang. Theol. Soc., Internat. Wine and Food Soc., Soc. des Amis des Arts (Strasbourg), Chaine des Rôtisseurs (commandeur), Athenaeum (London), Wig and Pen (London), Players' Theatre Club (London), Sherlock Holmes Soc. London, Soc. Sherlock Holmes de France (hon.), Club des Casseroles Lasserre (Paris), Ordre des chevaliers du Saint-Sepulcre Byzantin (commandeur), Phi Beta Kappa, Phi Kappa Phi, Beta Phi Mu. E-mail: 106612.1066@compuserve.com. Office: 4 Crane Ct # 9, Fleet St, London EC4A 2EJ, England also: 2 rue de Rome, 67000 Strasbourg France

**MONTGOMERY, JULIE-APRIL,** lawyer; b. Chgo., June 17, 1957; d. Constance Louise Montgomery. BS, U. San Francisco, 1978; MBA, Roosevelt U., 1979; JD, NYU, 1983, LLM in Taxation, 1985. Bar: Ill. 1983, U.S. Dist. Ct. (no. dist.) Ill. 1983, N.Y. 1990, U.S. Supreme Ct. 1995. Legis. advisor Ill. State Senator Charles Chew, Chgo., 1983-84; staff atty. Ill. Indsl. Comm., Chgo., 1984; sole practice Chgo., 1985-86; asst. corp. counsel City of Chgo. Office of Corp. Counsel, 1986—. Co-author Ill. Inst. Cont. Legal Edn. States and Local handbook, 1990; contbr. articles to profl. jours. Instr. Minority Legal Edn. Resources Inc., Chgo., 1983—; vol. March of Dimes Chgo., 1995—; shelter vol. children's program Chgo. Christian Indsl League, 1996—. Mem. ABA, Ill. State Bar Assn. (state local tax sect. 1996—), Ill. Cert. Pub. Accts. Soc. (state and local tax sect. 1995—), Chgo. Bar Assn. (state and local tax sect. 1986—, chmn. com. 1994-95), Phi Alpha Delta, Phi Chi Theta, Alpha Sigma Nu. Lutheran. Avocations: cross-stitching, collecting Betty Boop, puzzles, movies, history. State and local taxation, Administrative and regulatory, State civil litigation. Office: City of Chgo Corp Counsel 30 N La Salle St Ste 1040 Chicago IL 60602-2503

**MONTGOMERY, KENDALL CHARLES,** lawyer; b. Houston, Nov. 10, 1958; s. Charles Hunter and Jean (Shepherd) M.; m. Julie Elaine Jones, Aug. 13, 1983; children: Riley, Meredith. BBA in Fin. with honors, U. Houston, 1981; JD, U. Tex., 1984. Bar: Tex. 1984, Ohio 1991, U.S. Dist. Ct. (so. dist.) Tex. 1985, U.S. Ct. Appeals (5th cir.) 1986, U.S. Dist. Ct. we. dist.) Tex. 1995, U.S. Dist. Ct. (ea. dist.) Tex. 1997. Assoc. Deaton, Briggs & McCain, Houston, 1984-90, Kimble, Clay & Limestone, Dover, Ohio, 1990-91, John M. O'Quinn, P.C., Houston, 1991—. General civil litigation, Contracts commercial, Personal injury. Home: 4 Blalock Cir Houston TX 77024-6513 Office: O'Quinn & Laminack 440 Louisiana St Ste 2300 Houston TX 77002-4205

**MONTGOMERY, RICHARD C.,** lawyer; b. Pitts., June 25, 1936; s. Harry M. and Bertha W. M.; m. Elizabeth Elliott; (dec.); m. Kathleen Weber, Sept 29, 1979; 1 child, Mary. AB, Brown U., 1958; LLB, U. Pa., 1964. Bar: Pa., U.S. Dist. Ct. (we. dist) Pa., U.S. Tax Ct. Ptnr. Kirkpatrick & Lockhart LLP, Pitts., 1964—; bd. dirs. Sedloff Publs., Portage, Pa., PC Solutions, Pitts., Hook-Up, Inc., Joplin, Mo. Past pres., bd. dirs. Pitts. Dance Coun., legal counsel Trinity Cathedral, Pitts.. Lt. j.g. U.S. Navy, 1958-61. Mem. ABA (mem. real estate tax problems com.), Pa. Bar Assn. (mem. judicial reform, ethics and sr. lawyers coms.), Allegheny County Bar Assn. (coun. mem., taxation and fee dispute com.). Taxation, general. Office: Kirkpatrick & Lockhart LLP 1500 Oliver Bldg Pittburg PA 15222

**MONTGOMERY, SETH DAVID,** retired state supreme court chief justice; b. Santa Fe, Feb. 16, 1937; s. Andrew Kaye and Ruth (Champion) M.; m. Margaret Cook, Oct. 29, 1960; children: Andrew Seth, Charles Hope, David Lewis. AB, Princeton U., 1959; LLB, Stanford U., 1965. Bar: N.M. 1965. Ptnr. Montgomery & Andrews, P.A., Santa Fe, 1965-89, of counsel, 1994—; justice N.Mex. Supreme Ct., 1989-94, chief justice, 1994; adj. prof. law U. N.Mex. Sch. Law, Albuquerque, 1970-71; chmn. N.Mex. adv. coun. Legal Svcs. Corp., Santa Fe, 1976-89. Bd. visitors Stanford U. Sch. Law, 1967-70, 82-85, U. N.Mex. Sch. Law, 1982-89; pres., chmn. Santa Fe Opera, 1981-86; pres. Santa Fe Opera Found., 1986-89; chmn., vice chmn. Sch. Am. Rsch., Santa Fe, 1985-89; bd. dirs. New Vistas, Santa Fe, 1986-89, First Interstate Bank of Santa Fe, 1977-89, Old Cienega Village Mus., 1980-89. Lt. (j.g.) USN, 1959-62. Named Citizen of Yr., Santa Fe C. of C., 1986, Sunwest Bank of Santa Fe, 1994; recipient Disting. Cmty. Svc. award Anti-Defamation League, 1991, Western Area Outstanding Achievement award Nat. Multiple Sclerosis Soc., 1992, award for advancement of law N.Mex. Trial Lawyers, 1994, Award for Outstanding Judge Albuquerque Bar Assn., 1994. Fellow Am. Coll. Trial Lawyers, Am. Coll. Trust and Estate Counsel, Am. Bar Endowment, N.Mex. Bar Assn. (bd. bar commrs. 1986-89, sec., treas. 1988-89, Professionalism award 1993); mem. ABA, Am. Judicature Soc. Democrat.

**MONTGOMERY, WILLIAM ADAM,** lawyer; b. Chgo., May 22, 1933; s. John Rogerson and Helen (Fyke) M.; m. Jane Fauver, July 28, 1956 (div. Dec. 1967); children: Elizabeth, William, Virginia; m. Deborah Stephens, July 29, 1972; children: Alex, Katherine. AB, Williams Coll., 1955; LLB, Harvard U., 1958. Bar: D.C. 1958, Ill. 1959, U.S. Ct. Appeals (7th cir.) 1959, U.S. Supreme Ct. 1977. Atty. civil div., appellate sect. Dept. Justice, Washington, 1958-60; assoc. Schiff Hardin & Waite, Chgo., 1960-68, ptnr., 1968-93; v.p., gen. counsel State Farm Ins. Cos., Bloomington, Ill., 1994-97, sr. v.p., gen. counsel, 1997-99; ptnr. Schiff Hardin & Waite, Chgo., 1999—. Author: (39 corp. practice series) Tying Arrangements, 1984, also articles. Fellow Am. Coll. Trial Lawyers; mem. ABA (coun. antitrust sect. 1989-92), Chgo. Bar Assn., Seventh Cir. Bar Assn. (pres. 1988-89), Legal Club Chgo., Law Club Chgo., Econ. Club Chgo. Avocations: skiing, woodturning. Antitrust, Federal civil litigation, General civil litigation. Office: Waite Hardin & Schiff 6600 Sears Tower Chicago IL 60606

**MONTROSS, W. SCOTT,** lawyer; b. Milw., Apr. 16, 1947; s. William Phillips and Gay (Altenhofen) M.; m. Janice Townsend, May 25, 1968; children—Eric, Christine. B.B.A., U. Mich., 1969; J.D., Ind. U., 1971. Bar: Ind. 1971, U.S. Dist. Ct. (so. dist.) Ind. 1971, U.S. Ct. Appeals (7th cir.) 1973, U.S. Dist. Ct. (so. dist.) Wis. 1978, U.S. Dist. Ct. (so. dist.) Ohio 1983. Assoc., Townsend, Hovde & Townsend, Indpls., 1971-76, ptnr. Townsend, Hovde, Townsend & Montross, Indpls., 1976-84; ptnr. Townsend, Hovde and Montross, 1984-96. Contbr. articles to profl. jours. Fellow Am. Coll. Trial Lawyers, Indpls. Bar Found., Ind. Coll. Trial Lawyers; mem. Assn. Trial Lawyers Am., ABA, Am. Bd. Trial Advocates, Am. Judicature Soc., Am. Assn. Automotive Medicine, Am. Arbitration Assn., Ind. Trial Lawyers Assn. (lifetime bd. dirs., treas. 1984, sec. 1985, 1st v.p., 1986, pres.-elect 1987, pres. 1988). Clubs: Crooked Stick. State civil litigation, Federal civil litigation, Personal injury. Office: 230 E Ohio St Indianapolis IN 46204-2160

**MONYPENY, DAVID MURRAY,** lawyer; b. Jackson, Tenn., Apr. 29, 1957; s. Kent Brooks Monypeny and Kathryn (Warner) Sadowski. BBA, U. Okla., 1980; JD, U. Memphis, 1983. Bar: Tenn. 1983; CPA, Tenn. Assoc. Glankler, Brown et al, Memphis, 1983-85; acct. Frazer, Thomas & Tate, Memphis, 1985-87; ptnr. Diamond, Finklestein, Monypeny, Memphis, 1987-88, Lowrance & Monypeny, Memphis, 1988-94, Monypeny, Simpson Walker & Schatz, Memphis, 1994-97; sole practice Law Offices of David Monypeny, PLLC, 1997—; tax atty., cons. to nat. entertainers and celebrities. Author: (video) Wiping Out Tax Debt You Can't Afford To Pay, 1993. Mem. Bellevue Ch., Memphis, 1983—; campaign fin. chair Neil Small Chancellor, Memphis, 1990. Featured on TV, in mags. and newspapers for his client's tax settlements. Republican. Baptist. Avocations: music, video. Construction, Entertainment, Taxation, general. Office: Law Offices of David Monypeny M PLLC 5100 Poplar Ave Ste 2700 Memphis TN 38137-2701

**MOODY, JAMES T(YNE),** federal judge; b. LaCenter, Ky., June 16, 1938. BA, Ind. U., 1960, JD, 1963. Bar: Ind. 1963, U.S. Dist. Ct. (no. and so. dists.) Ind. 1963, U.S. Supreme Ct. 1972. Atty. Cities of Hobart and Lake Station, Ind., 1963-73; sole practice Hobart, 1963-73; judge Lake County (Ind.) Superior Ct., 1973-79; magistrate U.S. Dist. Ct. (no. dist.) Ind., Hammond, 1979-82, judge, 1982—; mem. faculty bus. law Ind. U., 1977-80. Republican. Office: US Dist Ct 128 Fed Bldg 507 State St Hammond IN 46320-1503

**MOODY, KEVIN JOSEPH,** lawyer; b. Wyandotte, Mich., May 30, 1956; s. Clarence John and Marilyn Joyce (Johnston) M.; m. Nancy Jean Nolan, Aug. 8, 1981; children: Nolan John, Maureen Joyce. BA, Kalamazoo Coll., 1978; JD, U. Detroit, 1981. Rsch. fellow Inst. for Labor and Econ. Law, Cologne, 1981-82; rsch. atty. Mich. Ct. Appeals, Lansing, 1982-84; law clk. Chief Judge Robert Danhof, Lansing, 1984-85; assoc. atty. Miller Canfield Paddock & Stone, Lansing, 1985-90, prin., 1991—. Bd. dirs. Gateway Cmty. Svcs., East Lansing, Mich., 1996. Fulbright grantee U. Cologne, Germany, 1981-82. Native American, Insurance, Contracts commercial. Office: Miller Canfield Paddock & Stone 1 Michigan Ave Ste 900 Lansing MI 48933

**MOODY, WILLARD JAMES, SR.,** lawyer; b. Franklin, Va., June 16, 1924; s. Willie James and Mary (Bryant) M.; m. Betty Glenn Covert, Aug. 21, 1948; children: Sharon Paige Moody Edwards, Willard J. Jr., Paul Glenn. AB, Old Dominion U., 1946; LLB, U. Richmond, 1952. Bar: Va. 1952. Pres. Moody, Strople & Kloeppel Ltd., Portsmouth, Va., 1952—; commr. Chancery, Portsmouth, 1960—, Accounts, 1960—. Del. Va. Ho. of Reps., Portsmouth, 1956-68; senator State of Va., 1968-83; chmn. Portsmouth Dems., 1983—. Recipient Friend of Edn. award Portsmouth Edn. Assn., 1981. Mem. ABA, Va. Bar Assn., Portsmouth Bar Assn. (pres. 1960-61, lectr. seminars), Va. Trial Lawyers Assn. (pres. 1968-69), Hampton Roads C. of C. (bd. dirs. 1983-86), Portsmouth C. of C. (bd. dirs. 1960-61), Inner Circle Advs., VFW, Cosmopolitan Club, Moose. General civil litigation, Labor, Personal injury. Home: 120 River Point Cres Portsmouth VA 23707-1028 Office: Moody Strople & Kloeppel Ltd 500 Crawford St Portsmouth VA 23704-3844

**MOOERS, DANIEL WILLIAM,** lawyer; b. Belfast, Maine, Mar. 11, 1943; s. Darrell Linwood and Dorothy (Whitcomb) M.; m. Sarah Shaw, Sept. 1, 1962 (div. Sept. 1980); 1 child, Daniel W. Jr.; m. Shirley Aldrich, Dec. 31, 1986. BS, Am. U., Washington, 1965; JD, U. Maine, 1968. Bar: Maine 1968, U.S. Dist. Ct. Maine 1968, U.S. Ct. Appeals (1st cir.) 1969, U.S. Ct. Internat. Trade 1985. Assoc. atty. Bennett, Swarz & Reef, Portland, Maine, 1968-69; legal advisor, atty. Office of Gov., Augusta, Maine, 1970; ptnr. Reef

& Mooers, Portland, 1969-86; pvt. practice Portland, 1986—. Bd. dirs. Susan B. Curtis Found., Augusta, Maine, 1970-78; trustee Samantha Smith Found., 1987—; mem. Urban Renewal Authority, South Portland, 1972-74, Civil Svc. Commn., South Portland, 1974-79. Mem. ABA, Assn. Trial Lawyers Am. (chmn. young lawyers 1970-71), Maine Bar Assn., Rotary Internat. (bd. govs. 1990-91, internat. bd. dirs. 1994-96, recipient citation for meritorious svc. 1990). Democrat. General civil litigation, Personal injury, Construction. Office: PO Box 2234 S Portland ME 04116-2234

**MOOG, MARY ANN PIMLEY,** lawyer; b. Havre, Mont., May 29, 1952; d. Orville Leonard and Della Mae (Cole) Pimley; m. Daren Russell Moog, Apr. 15, 1978; children: Eric John, Keith Cole, Trygg Orville. BS, Mont. State U., 1975; JD, U. Mont., 1981; LLM, NYU, 1983. Bar: Mont. Law clk. Mont. Supreme Ct., Helena, 1981-82; assoc., ptnr., staff atty. Bosch, Kuhr, Dugdale, Martin & Kaze, Havre, 1984—. Recipient Am. Jurisprudence Book award Lawyers Coop. Publ. Co., 1980-81, Tax award Prentice Hall, Inc., 1981, Northwestern Union Trust Co. award, 1981. Mem. ABA, Mont. Bar Assn., 12th Jud. Bar Assn. (pres. 1987-88), Phi Delta Phi. Democrat. Roman Catholic. Avocations: sports, arts and crafts, photography. Estate taxation, Personal income taxation, Estate planning. Home: 925 Wilson Ave Havre MT 59501-4331 Office: Bosch Kuhr Dugdale Martin & Kaze PO Box 7152 Havre MT 59501-7152

**MOON, DEBORAH JOAN,** paralegal; b. Pine Bluff, Ark., Apr. 20, 1956; d. Fletcher Leon and Joann Talley (Shepherd); m. David Carlton Taylor, Apr. 7, 1989. BA in Sociology, U. So. Ill., Edwardsville, 1979; BS in Paralegal Studies, U. So. Ill., Carbondale, 1984. Paralegal/intern Kionka & Assocs., Carbondale, Ill., 1984; paralegal Roath & Brega, Denver, 1985-86, Bridges, Young, Matthews & Drake, Pine Bluff, Ark., 1987—; participant paralegal com. Ark. Bar Assn., 1996-98. Pres. Jefferson County Humane Soc., 1996-97, bd. dirs., 98—, treas. 1999; mem. paralegal adv. com. S.E. Ark. Tech. Coll., 1996—. mamed Legal Asst. of Yr. Ark. Assn. Legal Assts., 1991-97. Mem. ABA (assoc.), Nat. Assn. Legal Assts. (profl. devel. com. 1993-94, 96-98, Affiliates award 1995), Ark. Assn. Legal Assts. (chmn. regional and membership coms. 1991-94, 2d v.p. 1992-94, mem. exec. bd. dirs. 1991-98, liaison to Nat. Assn. 1993-94, 1st v.p. 1994-96, dir. region 5 1996-98, chmn. edn. and seminar com. 1994-96), Ark. Assn. Bankruptcy Assts. Office: Bridges Young Matthews & Drake PLC PO Box 7808 315 E 8th St Pine Bluff AR 71611

**MOON, RONALD T. Y.,** state supreme court justice; b. Sept. 4, 1940; m. Stella H. Moon. B in Psychology and Sociology, Coe Coll., 1962; LLB, U. Iowa, 1965. Bailiff, law clk. to Chief Judge Martin Pence U.S. Dist. Ct., 1965-66; dep. prosecutor City and County of Honolulu, 1966-68; assoc. Libkuman, Ventura, Ayabe, Chong & Nishimoto (predecessor firm Libkuman, Ventura, Moon & Ayabe), Honolulu, 1968-72, ptnr., 1972-82; judge 9th div. 1st cir., Cir. Ct., State of Hawaii, Honolulu, 1982-90; assoc. justice Supreme Ct., State of Hawaii, Honolulu, 1990-93; chief justice Supreme Ct., State of Hawaii, 1993—; apptd. arbitration judge 1st cir. cir. ct.; adj. prof. law U. Hawaii, 1986, 87, 88; lectr., guest spkr. numerous events. Mem. ABA, Hawaii Bar Assn., Assn. Trial Lawyers Am., Am. Bd. Trial Advocates (pres. 1986-93, nat. sec. 1989-91), Am. Inns of Cts. IV (bencher 1983—), Am. Judicature Soc., Hawaii Trial Judges' Assn. Office: Supreme Ct Hawaii 417 S King St Honolulu HI 96813-2902

**MOONEY, DONALD B.,** lawyer; b. Inglewood, Calif., Aug. 26, 1960; m. Samantha McCarthy. BA, Pacific Luth. U., Tacoma, 1982; JD, U. Oreg., 1989. Fellow, atty. Tulane Environ. Law Clinic, New Orleans, 1989-90; atty. McDonough, Holland & Allen, Sacramento, 1990-91; atty., shareholder DeCuir & Somach, Sacramento, 1991—. Real property, Environmental, Condemnation. Office: DeCuir & Somach 400 Capitol Mall Ste 1900 Sacramento CA 95814-4436

**MOONEY, JEROME HENRI,** lawyer; b. Salt Lake City, Aug. 7, 1944; s. Jerome Henri and Bonnie (Shepherd) M.; m. Carolyn Lasrich, Aug. 10, 1965 (div. Dec. 1978); 1 child, Dierdre Nicole; m. Kaitlyn Cardon, Sept. 23, 1995. BS, U. Utah, 1966, JD, 1972. Bar: Utah 1972, Calif. 1998, U.S. Ct. Appeals (10th cir.) 1974, U.S. Supreme 1984. Sole practice Salt Lake City, 1972-75, 79-83; sr. ptnr. Mooney, Jorgenson & Nakamura, Salt Lake City, 1975-78, Mooney & Smith, Salt Lake City, 1983-87, Mooney & Assoc., Salt Lake City, 1987-94, Mooney Law Firm, Salt Lake City, 1995—; bd. dirs. Mooney Real Estate, Salt Lake City. Mem. Gov.'s Coun. on Vet. Affiars, Salt Lake City, 1982-89; trustee Project Realty, Salt Lake City, 1976—, P.E.A.C.E.; FDA sponsor Project Reality, 1994—; vice chair State Mil. Acad. Assoc., 1992-93. Mem. ABA (criminal justice sect. U.S. Sentencing Commn. com.), Utah Bar Assn. (chmn. criminal bar sect. 1987-88), Utah NG Assn. (trustee 1976), 1st Amendment Lawyers Assn. (v.p. 1986-88, pres. 1988-89), Nat. Assn. Criminal Def. Lawyers, Families Against Mandatory Minimums (adv. coun.), VFW. Democrat. Jewish. Avocations: sailing, computers. Entertainment, Criminal. Home: 128 I St Salt Lake City UT 84103-3418 Office: 50 W Broadway Ste 100 Salt Lake City UT 84101-2020

**MOONEY, MICHAEL EDWARD,** lawyer; b. Beloit, Wis., Jan. 21, 1945; s. William C. and Edith (Slothower) M. BA in Econs., St. Norbert Coll., 1966; JD, Boston Coll., 1969. Bar: Mass. 1969, Maine 1969, U.S. Tax Ct. 1975, U.S. Ct. Internat. Trade 1986. Assoc. Nutter, McClennen & Fish, LLP, Boston, 1969-77, sr. ptnr., 1978—; v.p., exec. dir. Fed. Tax Inst. New Eng.; spkr., lectr. numerous seminars. Co-editor: Considerations in Buying or Selling a Business, 1985; mem. bd. editors Accounting for Law Firms, 1988—. Bd. dirs. Lincoln and Therese Filene Found., Boston, Alliance Francaise of Boston, 1987-97, Artery Bus. Com., Internat. Bus. Ctr. New Eng., 1986-89; clk. U.S.S. Constn. Bicentennial Salute, Inc. Fellow Am. Coll. Tax Counsel; mem. Boston Bar Assn. (chmn. tax highlights com. 1986-95, mem. fin. com. 1990-92), Boston Tax Forum, Boston Ptnrs. in Edn. (lawyers fund com.). Corporate taxation, Personal income taxation, General corporate. Office: Nutter McClennen & Fish 1 International Pl Boston MA 02110-2699

**MOONEY, THOMAS ROBERT,** lawyer; b. Montclair, N.J., June 16, 1933; s. Thomas Edward and Ruth Evelyn (Meurling) M.; m. Mary Frances Davis, Aug. 23, 1958; children: Terrance Kevin, Rebecca Lee Poyner, Thomas Edward. BA in Econs., Fla. So. Coll., Lakeland, 1956; LLB, Stetson U., St. Petersburg, Fla., 1961, JD, 1961. BAr: Fla. 1961, Ga. 1962, U.S. Dist. Ct. (mid. dist.) 1964, U.S. Supreme Ct. 1965. Claims adjuster State Farm Mut. Ins. Co., Atlanta, 1961-63; atty. Maguire, Voorhis & Wells, P.A., Orlando, Fla., 1963-64, Meyers & Mooney, P.A., Orlando, 1964-94, Meyers, Mooney Meyers Stanley & Hollingsworth, Orlando, 1994—; chair Workers Compensation Ednl. Conf., Fla., 1980-81. Chmn. bd. dirs. Epilepsy Assn. Ctrl. Fla., Orlando, 1964-67; bd. dirs. Children's Home Soc., Orlando, 1970-75, chmn., 1970-72. 1st lt. U.S. Army, 1956-58, Korea. Mem. ATLA, ABA, Fla. Bar Assn., Ga. Bar Assn., Acad. Fla. Trial Lawyers (chair workers compensation sect. 1985), Fla. Workers Advocates (bd. dirs. 1992—). Democrat. Methodist. Avocations: skiing, golf, travel, hiking, rafting. Workers' compensation, Personal injury. Office: Meyers Mooney & Meyers 17 Lake Ave Orlando FL 32801-2797

**MOORE, ANDREW GIVEN TOBIAS, II,** investment banker, law educator; b. New Orleans, Nov. 25, 1935; m. Ann Elizabeth Dawson, June 5, 1965; children—Cecily Elizabeth, Marianne Dawson. B.B.A., Tulane U., 1958, J.D., 1960. Bar: La. 1960, Del. 1963. Law clk. to chief justice Del. Dover, 1963; assoc. firm Killoran & Van Brunt, Wilmington, Del., 1964-70; partner Killoran & Van Brunt, 1971-76; partner firm Connolly, Bove & Lodge, Wilmington, 1976-82; justice Del. Supreme Ct., Wilmington, 1982-94; sr. mng. dir. Wasserstein Perella & Co., Inc., N.Y.C., 1994—; mem. Del. Bar Examiners, 1975-82; mem. Del. Gen. Corp. law com., 1969-83; chmn. joint com. Del. Bar Assn.-Del. Bankers Assn., 1978-79; chmn. Del. Jud. Proprieties Com., 1983-94, Del. Bench and Bar Conf., 1988-94; trustee Del. Bar Found., 1984-94; faculty Tulane Inst. European Legal Studies, Paris Inst., 1990-96, 99; adj. prof. law Georgetown U. Law Ctr., Widener U. Sch. Law, U. Iowa Coll. Law; guest lectr. law Columbia U., Tulane U., U. Toronto, Can., U. Tex., Villanova U., Washington U., St. Louis, U. Iowa, George Mason U., DeVrije U. van Brussel, Cath. U. Louvain La Neuve; mem. pres.'s coun. Tulane U., 1990—; chmn. Tulane Corp. Law Inst., 1988-95; Lehmann disting. vis. prof. law Washington U., St. Louis, 1994, 96; Mason Ladd disting. vis. prof. U. Iowa, 1995; disting. vis. prof. law St. Louis U., 1995, 96, 99; bd. dirs. Am. Lawyer Media, Inc. Trustee Del. Home and Hosp. for Chronically Ill, Smyrna, 1966-70, chmn., 1966-69; mem. New Castle County Hist. Rev. Bd., Wilmington, 1974-82; mem. Del. Cts. Planning Com., 1982-94; dean's coun. Tulane U. Law Sch., 1988—; bd. visitors Walter F. George Sch. Law, Mercer U., 1985-91, chmn., 1988-90. With JAGC, USAF, 1960-63. Mem. ABA, La. Bar Assn., Del. Bar Assn. (v.p. 1976-77, exec. com. 1982-83), Am. Judicature Soc. (bd. dirs. 1982-86), Order Barristers, Phi Delta Phi, Delta Theta Phi (hon.), Omicron Delta Kappa. Democrat. Presbyterian. Office: Wasserstein Perella & Co 31 W 52nd St Fl 26 New York NY 10019-6118

**MOORE, BETTY JO,** legal assistant; b. Medicine Lodge, Kans., July 10; d. Joseph Christy and Helen Blanche (Hubbell) Sims; m. Harold Frank Moore, June 19, 1941; children: Terrance C., Harold Anthony, Trisha Jo. Cert., U. West L.A., 1978; student, Wichita (Kans.) U., 1940-41. Cert. legal asst./escrow officer. Sec. UCLA, 1949-59; escrow officer Security Pacific Nat. Bank, L.A., 1959-62, Empire Savs. & Loan Assn., Van Nuys, Calif., 1962-64; escrow supr. San Fernando Valley Bank, Van Nuys, 1964; escrow officer Heritage Bank, Westwood, Calif., 1964-66; escrow coord. Land Sys. Corp., Woodland Hills, Calif., 1966-67; escrow officer/asst. mgr., real estate lending officer Security Pacific Nat. Bank, L.A., 1967-80; real estate paralegal Pub. Storage, Pasadena, 1980-81; asst. mgr. escrow dept. First Beverly Bank, Century City, Calif., 1982-84; escrow trainer/officer Moore's Tng. Temps Inc., Canoga Park, Calif., 1984—; participant People to People Ambassador Program/Women in Mgmt. to USSR, 1989; observer Internat. Fedn. Bus. and Profl. Women's Congress, Washington, 1965, 81, Nassau, Bahamas, 1989, Narobi, Kenya, 1991. Adv. bd. escrow edn. Pierce Coll., Woodland Hills, Calif., 1968-80. Recipient Cert. of Appreciation, Pierce Coll., 1979, Calif. Fedn. Bus. and Profl. Women, 1989, Nat. Women's History Project, 1995. Mem. Nat. Fedn. Bus. and Prof. Women's Clubs, Calif. Fedn. Bus. and Profl. Women (pres. dist. 1987-88, Calif. Found. chmn. 1988-89, internat. concerns chmn. 1996—), Woodlands Hills Bus. and Profl. Women ((pres. 1991-92, 94-95), Tri Valley Dist. Bus. and Profl. Women (legis. chair 1992-93, exec./corr. sec. 1993-94, 94-95), Internat. Fedn. Bus. and Profl. Women, Nat. Women's Polit. Caucus (coord., sec. San Fernando Valley caucus 1986-87, legis. co-chair 1991-92, 92-93), Women's Orgn. Coalition San Fernando Valley (sec. 1992, mem. exec. com. L.A. Women's Equality Day 1995), San Fernando Valley Escrow Assn. (bd. dirs. 1962-64), Woodland Hills C. of C. (assoc.), San Fernando Valley Bd. Realtors, L.A. Women's Legis. Coalition, U. West L.A. Alumni Assn. Democrat. Methodist. Avocations: reading, musical theater.

**MOORE, BLAINE AUGUSTA,** lawyer; b. Greenwood, S.C., July 3, 1961; d. Blaine C. and Betty Springer Moore; m. Scott Kiefer, July 28, 1996. BS, Presbyn. Coll., 1983; JD, Cumberland Sch. of Law, 1987; LLM in Admiralty Law, Tulane U., 1988. Bar: La. 1987, U.S. Dist. Ct. (ea., mid. and we. dists.) La. 1987. Assoc. Ellefson, Pulver & Staines, New Orleans, 1989-94, Duncan & Courington, New Orleans, 1995—; pvt. practice New Orleans, 1994-95. Vol. Big Bros./Big Sisters Am., New Orleans, 1994—. Mem. ABA, La. Bar Assn., New Orleans Bar Assn. Republican. Baptist. Avocations: travel, reading, refinishing furniture. Toxic tort, Product liability, Admiralty. Office: Duncan & Courington 322 Lafayette St New Orleans LA 70130-3244

**MOORE, BRADFORD L.,** lawyer; b. Brownfield, Tex., Feb. 9, 1952; s. Billie Buell and Jimmy (Green) M.; m. Carmelita Chaffin, June 20, 1971; children: April V., Ashli F. BA, Tex. Tech U., 1974, JD, 1977. Bar: Tex. 1978, U.S. Dist. Ct. (no. dist.) Tex. 1978, U.S. Dist. Ct. (we. dist.) Tex. 1987, U.S. Supreme Ct. 1987. V.p. McGowan & McGowan PC, Brownfield, 1978-90; pvt. practice, Brownfield, 1990—; mayor city of Brownfield, 1998—. Pres. Brownfield Little Girls Basketball, 1987-90. Recipient award for outstanding representation of abused children Tex. Dept. Human Svcs., 1984. Mem. Brownfield Bar Assn. (social chmn. 1980—), Rotary (sgt.-at-arms Brownfield 1980-81, pres. 1997-98), Kiwanis (pres. Brownfield 1984-86). General civil litigation, General corporate, Contracts commercial. Office: PO Box 352 Brownfield TX 79316-0352

**MOORE, CHRISTOPHER MINOR,** lawyer; b. L.A., Oct. 12, 1938; s. Prentiss Elder and Josephine (French) M.; m. Gillian Reed, Sept. 29, 1965; children: Stephanie Kia Conn, Carrie Christine McKay. AB, Stanford U., 1961; JD, Harvard U., 1964. Dep. county counsel Los Angeles County Counsel, 1965-66; ptnr. Moore & Lindelof, L.A., 1966-69, Burkley & Moore, Torrance, Calif., 1969-74; pvt. practice Law Offices of Christopher Moore, Torrance, 1974-81; ptnr. Burkley, Moore, Greenberg & Lyman, Torrance, 1981-90; prin. Christopher M. Moore & Assoc., Torrance, 1990—. Mem. bd. edn. Palos Verdes (Calif.) Peninsula Unified Sch. Dist., 1972-77. Fellow Am. Coll. Trust and Estate Counsel, Am. Acad. Matrimonial Lawyers; mem. L.A. Yacht Club. Avocations: sailing, golf. Family and matrimonial, Estate planning, Probate. Office: Christopher Moore & Assoc 21515 Hawthorne Blvd Ste 490 Torrance CA 90503-6525

**MOORE, DANIEL ALTON, JR.,** retired state supreme court justice; b. 1933. BBA, U. Notre Dame, 1955; JD, U. Denver, 1961. Dist. ct. magistrate judge Alaska, 1961-62; pvt. practice law, 1962-80; judge 3d Jud. Dist. Superior Ct., 1980-83; justice Alaska Supreme Ct., Anchorage, 1983-92, chief justice, 1992-95; ret., 1995; mediator for J.A.M.S./Endispute, 1996—.

**MOORE, DAVID ROBERT,** lawyer; b. Champaign, Ill., Jan. 1, 1959; s. Robert P. and Barbara L. (James) M. BA, Butler U., 1980; JD, Ind. U., 1982. Bar: Ill. 1983, Ind. 1983, U.S. Dist. Ct. (ctrl. dist.) Ill. 1983, (so. dist.) Ind. 1988. Assoc. Moore & Assocs., Champaign, 1983-90; ptnr. David R. Moore, P.C., Urbana, Ill., 1990-93, Follmer & Moore, Urbana, 1993—. Mem. Ind. State Bar Assn., Ill. State Bar Assn., Dram Shop Def. Bar Assn. General civil litigation, Criminal, Insurance. Office: 1717 Philo Rd Urbana IL 61802-6044

**MOORE, DIANA DOWELL,** lawyer; b. Trenton, Mo., Apr. 28, 1961; d. Herbert Ray and Mary Alice Dowell. BS, Ctrl. Mo. State U., 1982; JD with honors, U. Mo., Kansas City, 1986. Bar: Kans. 1986, U.S. Dist. Ct. Kans. 1986, Mo. 1994. Ptnr. Blackwell Sanders Peper Martin, Kansas City, 1986—; mem. initiating bd. Komen Found., Kansas City, 1998—. Vol. Youth Friends, Kansas City, 1998. Mem. Kans. Bar Assn., Mo. Bar Assn., Kansas City Met. Bar Assn. Baptist. Avocations: golf, softball, reading. Professional liability, State civil litigation, Personal injury. Office: Blackwell Sanders Peper Martin 2300 Main St Ste 1100 Kansas City MO 64108-2416

**MOORE, DIANE PRESTON,** lawyer; b. Trenton, N.J., Apr. 11, 1965; d. Willard George and Dolores Ann Preston; m. Michael David Moore, Sept. 6, 1997. BS, Coll. William and Mary, 1987, JD, 1996. Bar: Va. 1996, Md. 1997, D.C. 1997, U.S. Dist. Ct. (ea. dist.) Va. 1998, U.S. Dist. Ct. (DC dist.) 1998, U.S. Ct. Appeals (DC cir.) 1998, U.S. Bankruptcy Ct. (ea. dist.) Va. 1998. Buyer table linens Hecht's Dept. Stores, Arlington, Va., 1987-93; assoc. Whiteford, Taylor & Preston LLP, Washington, 1996—. Mem. Va. Women Attys. Assn. (chair program com. 1998), Cmty. Assns. Inst. General civil litigation, Insurance, Personal injury. Office: Whiteford Taylor & Preston LLP 1025 Connecticut Ave NW Ste 400 Washington DC 20036-5410

**MOORE, DONALD FRANCIS,** lawyer; b. N.Y.C., Dec. 14, 1937; s. John F. and Helen A. (McLoughlin) M.; m. Alice L. Kalmar; children: Christina M., Marianne, Karen L., Alison A. AB, Fordham U., 1959; JD, St. John's U., Bklyn., 1962. Bar: N.Y. 1962, D.C. 1970, U.S. Supreme Ct. 1993. Assoc. Paul, Weiss, Rifkind, Wharton & Garrison, N.Y.C., 1962-70, ptnr., 1970-97, of counsel, 1998—. Editor in chief St. John's U. Law Rev., 1962. Served to 1st lt. U.S. Army, 1962-64. Mem. N.Y. State Bar Assn., Assn. of Bar of City of N.Y. Roman Catholic. Avocation: fishing. Pension, profit-sharing, and employee benefits, Probate. Home: 7 Wedgewood Ct Glen Head NY 11545-2229 Office: Paul Weiss Rifkind Wharton & Garrison Ste 4200 1285 Avenue Of The Americas Fl 21 New York NY 10019-6065

**MOORE, DWIGHT TERRY,** lawyer; b. Nashville, Apr. 22, 1948; s. George Howard and Minnie Laura (Gregory) M.; m. Barbara Franklin, May 7, 1977; 1 child, Marian. BA, Vanderbilt U., 1970; MPA, U. Memphis, 1975, JD, 1983. Bar: Tenn. 1984, U.S. Dist. Ct. (we. dist.) Tenn. 1984, U.S. Ct. Appeals (6th cir.) 1991. With State of Tenn., Nashville, 1970-73, Shelby County, Memphis, 1974-79; asst. prof. Memphis State U., 1983-88; ptnr. Gardner & Moore, Memphis, 1984-91, Olsen, Kuhn & Moore, Memphis, 1991-93, Lowrance & Monypeny, Memphis, 1993-94; pvt. practice Memphis, 1994—. Mem. ABA, Memphis Bar Assn. Libertarian. Unitarian. Avocations: tae kuk, fitness, reading. Entertainment, Trademark and copyright, General practice. Office: 5050 Poplar Ave Ste 2408 Memphis TN 38157-0101

**MOORE, ERNEST CARROLL, III,** lawyer; b. Honolulu, Oct. 24, 1944; s. Ernest Carroll Jr. and Frances (Miller) M.; children: Tiffany Meredith, Alyssa Judi. BA, Dartmouth Coll., 1967; JD, So Meth. U., 1974. Bar: Hawaii 1974, U.S. Dist. Ct. Hawaii 1974, U.S. Ct. Appeals (9th cir.) 1974. Ptnr. Torkildson, Katz, Fonseca, Jaffe, Moore & Hetherington, Honolulu, 1974—; trustee Hawaii Sch. Girls, 1998—. Bd. dirs. Hawaii chpt. ARC, Honolulu, 1979, trustee La Pietra-Hawaii Sch. for Girls, 1998—. Mem. Am. Acad. Hosp. Attys., Nat. Health Lawyers Assn., Indsl. Relations Research Assn., Soc. for Human Resources Mgmt., Order of Coif, Pacific Club, Outrigger Canoe Club. Republican. Episcopalian. Avocations: tennis, photography. Labor. Office: Torkildson Katz Fonseca Jaffe Moore & Hetherington 700 Bishop St Fl 15 Honolulu HI 96813-4187

**MOORE, EVERETT DANIEL,** lawyer; b. Warren, Ohio, Sept. 28, 1951; s. Everett William and Mary Lucile M.; m. Cheryl Ann Yelverton, Oct. 13, 1979; children: Jason, Nicole. BS in Edn., Kent State U., 1974; JD, U. Toledo, 1977. Bar: Ohio 1977, U.S. Dist. Ct. (no. dist.) 1978. Pvt. practice Toledo and Manmee, Ohio, 1977—. Probate, Real property, General practice. Office: 5714 Monclova Rd Maumee OH 43537-1838

**MOORE, GARLAND CURTIS,** lawyer, consultant; b. Ft. Riley, Kans., Sept. 5, 1954; s. Durward Elworth and Edna Blanche (Jordan) M.; m. Irene Ruth Stoddard, Aug. 30, 1981; 1 child, Carey Elizabeth. AB in Polit. Sci., U. Ga., 1985; JD, Ga. State U., 1989. Bar. Ga. 1990, U.S. Dist. Ct. (no. dist.) Ga. 1990, U.S. Ct. Appeals (11th cir.) 1990. V.p., dir. rsch. Ross, Russell, Ellis & Bailey, Atlanta, Marietta, Ga., 1987-91; pvt. practice Conyers, Ga., 1991—; cons. Fortune 500 Co. and subsidiaries, 1987-91; neutral chairperson Labor-Mgmt. Com., Atlanta, 1991; bd. dirs. Rockdale Dept. Family and Children Svcs., 1992—. Asst. scoutmaster Boy Scouts Am., Conyers, 1991—; Dem. candidate State Ho. of Reps., Conyers, 1992; treas. Rockdale County Dem. Party. With U.S. Army, 1972-74, Res., 1985—. Recipient Am. Jurisprudence award Ga. State U. and Lawyers Coop. Publ., 1988; named Outstanding Ga. Citizen, Ga. Sec. of State, 1991. Mem. State Bar Ga., Rockdale County Bar Assn., Pvt. Industry Coun. Atlanta (advisor 1991—), Nat. Eagle Scout Assn., Delta Theta Phi. Methodist. Avocations: travel, reading, politics. Legislative, General practice. Home: 2083 Beachwood Dr SE Conyers GA 30013-2325 Office: Bertollo & Moore PO Box 81367 945 Court St NE # B Conyers GA 30207-4539

**MOORE, HUGH JACOB, JR.,** lawyer; b. Norfolk, Va., June 29, 1944; s. Hugh Jacob and Ina Ruth (Hall) M.; m. Jean Garnett, June 10, 1972; children: Lela Miller, Sarah Garnett. BA, Vanderbilt U., 1966; LLB, Yale U., 1969. Bar: Tenn. 1970, U.S. Dist. Ct. (mid. dist.) Tenn. 1970, U.S. Supreme Ct. 1973, U.S. Ct. Appeals (6th cir.) 1973, U.S. Dist. Ct. (ea. dist.) Tenn. 1973, U.S. Dist. Ct. (we. dist.) Tenn. 1982, U.S. Ct. Claims 1993. Law clk. U.S. Dist. Ct. (mid. dist.) Tenn., Nashville, 1969-70; trial atty. civil rights divsn. U.S. Dept. Justice, Washington, 1970-73; asst. U.S. atty. Eastern Dist. of Tenn., Chattanooga, 1973-76; assoc. Witt, Gaither & Whitaker, P.C., Chattanooga, 1976-77, shareholder, 1977—, also bd. dirs.; mem. Commn. Women and Minorities Profession Law; mem. hearing com. Bd. Profl. Responsibility Supreme Ct. Tenn.; mem. mediation panel U.S. Dist. Ct. (ea. dist.) Tenn.; cert. arbitrator, cert. mediator Tenn. Rule 31 Nat. Assn. Securities Dealers; cert. artbitrator N.Y. Stock Exch., Nat. Arbitration Forum; mem. adv. commn. on rules of civil and appellate procedure Tenn. Supreme Ct., chmn., 1999—. Contbr. articles to profl. jours. Bd. dirs. Adult Edn. Coun., Chattanooga, 1976-81, pres., 1977-79; bd. dirs. Chattanooga Symphony and Opera Assn., 1981-87, Riverbend Fesitval, 1983-85, 91—, pres., 1995-97, Landmarks Chattanooga, 1983-84, Cornerstones, 1995-98, Orange Grove Sch., 1996—; mem. alumni coun. McCallie Sch., 1980-85; trustee St. Nicholas Sch., 1983-89, chmn., 1986-88. Fellow Am. Coll. Trial Lawyers, Tenn. State Com., Tenn. Bar Found., Chattanooga Bar Found.; mem. ABA (mem. bd. editors jour. Litigation News 1983-90), Tenn. Bar Assn., Chattanooga Bar Assn. (mem. bd. govs. 1985-87), Mountain City Club, Rotary. Methodist. General civil litigation, Federal civil litigation, Criminal. Home: 101 Ridgeside Rd Chattanooga TN 37411-1830 Office: Witt Gaither & Whitaker 1100 SunTrust Bank Bldg Chattanooga TN 37402

**MOORE, JAMES CONKLIN,** lawyer; b. Albany, N.Y., Dec. 20, 1939; s. James Alexander and Doris Virginia (Conklin) M.; m. Shirley Jean Mitchell, June 17, 1961; children: James, Jennifer, David, Eliza. BS, Cornell U., 1961, LLB, 1964. Bar: N.Y. 1964, U.S. Dist. Ct. (we. dist.) N.Y. 1966, U.S. Dist. Ct. (mid. dist.) Pa. 1981, U.S. Dist. Ct. (no. dist.) N.Y. 1980, U.S. Ct. Mil. Appeals 1965. Assoc. Wiser, Shaw, Freeman, VanGraafeiland, Harter & Secrest, Rochester, N.Y., 1966-74; ptnr. Harter, Secrest & Emery, Rochester, 1974—. Author several articles and book chpts. Trustee, pres. Friends of Rochester Pub. Libr., 1993-98. Capt. U.S. Army, 1964-66, Vietnam. Adv. Bd. Rochester Area Ednl. Television, 1981-87; elder, trustee Third Presbyn. Ch., Rochester. Fellow ABA Found., Am. Coll. Trial Lawyers, N.Y. Bar Found. (bd. dirs. 1997—); mem. ABA, Am. Law Inst. (elected), N.Y. State Bar Assn. (pres. 1998-99, mem. ho. dels. 1984-87, 89—, chmn. ins. sect. 1984-85, chmn. task force on liability ins. 1986-87, chmn. com. ins. programs 1988-94, mem. exec. com. 1992—, v.p. 1994-97), Monroe County Bar Assn. (judiciary com. chmn. 1982-85), Def. Rsch. Inst., Cornell Club of Rochester (bd. dirs. 1967-73), Genesee Valley Club, Cornell Club N.Y.C. Republican. Avocations: U.S. history, refinishing old furniture. Federal civil litigation, General civil litigation, State civil litigation. Home: 251 Windemere Rd Rochester NY 14610-1342 Office: Harter Secrest & Emery 700 Midtown Tower Rochester NY 14604-2006

**MOORE, JAMES E.,** state supreme court justice; b. Laurens, S.C., Mar. 13, 1936; s. Roy Ernest and Marie (Hill) M.; m. Mary Alicia Deadwyler, Jan. 27, 1963; children—Erin Alicia, Travis Warren. B.A., Duke U., 1958, J.D., 1961. Bar: S.C. 1961, U.S. Dist. Ct. S.C. 1961. pvt. practice, Greenwood, S.C., 1961-76; cir. judge 8th Jud. Cir. S.C., Greenwood, 1976-1991; Assoc. Justice S.C. Supreme Ct., 1992—; Mem. S.C. Ho. of Reps., Columbia, 1968-76. Mem. S.C. Bar Assn., ABA, Am. Judicature Soc. Baptist. Home: 148 Amherst Dr Greenwood SC 29649-8901 Office: PO Box 277 Greenwood SC 29648-0277

**MOORE, JOHN HENRY, II,** federal judge; b. Atlantic City, Aug. 5, 1929; s. Harry Cordery and Gertrude (Wasleski) M.; m. Joan Claire Kraft, Dec. 29, 1951; children—Deborah Joan, Katherine Louise. Student, Cornell U., 1947; BS, Syracuse U., 1952; JD, U. Fla., 1961. Bar: Fla. 1961. Assoc. Fisher & Phillips, Atlanta, 1961; ptnr. Flemming O'Bryan & Fleming, Fort Lauderdale, Fla., 1961-67, Turner, Shaw & Moore, Fort Lauderdale, Fla., 1967; judge 17th Jud. Circuit, Fort Lauderdale, Fla., 1967-77, U.S. Dist. Ct. Appeals for 4th Cir., West Palm Beach, Fla., 1977-81; judge U.S. Dist. Ct. for Mid. Dist. Fla., Jacksonville, 1981-92, chief judge, 1992-95, sr. judge, 1995—; mem. Fla. Constitution Revision Comn., 1977-78; chmn. Fla. Jud. Qualifications Commn., 1977-81. Bd. dirs. Community Service Council, Fort Lauderdale, 1970-75; pres. Broward County Assn. for Retarded Children, Fort Lauderdale, 1962; hon. bd. trustees Broward Community Coll., Fort Lauderdale, 1970. Served to comdr. USNR, 1948-71, Korea. Named hon. Alumnus Nova U., 1977; recipient cert. of good govt. Gov. of Fla., 1967. Mem. ABA, Fla. Bar Assn., Fed. Bar Assn., Jacksonville Bar Assn., Fla. Conf. Circuit Judges (chmn.-elect 1977), Fla. Blue Key (hon.), U.S. Navy League, Naval Res. Assn., Ret. Officers Assn. Republican. Presbyterian. Clubs: Timuquana Country, Jacksonville Quarterback, Seminole (Jacksonville). Lodge: Rotary. Avocations: golf, tennis, boating. Office: US Dist Ct PO Box 53137 311 W Monroe St Jacksonville FL 32201

**MOORE, JOHN LESLIE,** lawyer; b. Gainesville, Fla., July 18, 1966; s. Robert Leslie and Janice (Appleby) M.; m. Kristie Marie Roenick, July 20, 1996; 1 child, Collin Leslie. BA in History, Stetson U., Deland, Fla., 1988; JD, U. Va., 1991. Bar: Fla. 1991. Assoc. Williams, Parker, Harrison, Dietz & Getzen, Sarasota, Fla., 1991-98, shareholder, 1998—. Harry S Truman scholar Truman found., 1985, George F. Hixon fellow Kiwanis Internat., 1997. Mem. Fla. Bar (health law sect.), Am. Health Lawyers Assn., Kiwanis

Club of Progressive Sarasota (pres. 1993, 98). Health, General corporate, Mergers and acquisitions. Office: Williams Parker et al 200 S Orange Ave Sarasota FL 34236-6802

**MOORE, KAREN NELSON,** judge; b. Washington, Nov. 19, 1948; d. Roger S. and Myrtle (Gill) Nelson; m. Kenneth Cameron Moore, June 22, 1974; children—Roger C., Kenneth N., Kristin K. A.B. magna cum laude, Radcliffe Coll., 1970, J.D. magna cum laude, Harvard U., 1973. Bar: D.C. 1973, Ohio, 1976, U.S. Ct. Appeals (D.C. cir.) 1974, U.S. Supreme Ct. 1980, U.S. Ct. Appeals (6th cir.) 1984. Law clk. Judge Malcolm Wilkey, U.S. Ct. Appeals (D.C. cir.), 1973-74; law clk. Assoc. Justice Harry A. Blackmun, U.S. Supreme Ct., Washington, 1974-75; assoc. Jones, Day, Reavis & Pogue, Cleve., 1975-77; asst. prof. Case Western Res. Law Sch., Cleve., 1977-80, assoc. prof., 1980-82, prof., 1982-95; judge U.S. Ct. Appeals (6th cir.), Cleve., 1995—; vis. prof. Harvard Law Sch., 1990-91. Mem. Harvard Law Rev., 1971-73. Contbr. articles to legal publs. Trustee Lakewood Hosp., Ohio, 1978-85, Radcliffe Coll., Cambridge, 1980-84. Fellow Am. Bar Found.; mem. Am. Law Inst., Harvard Alumni Assn. (bd. dirs. 1984-87), Phi Beta Kappa. Office: US Ct Appeals 6th Cir 328 US Courthouse 201 Superior Ave E Cleveland OH 44114-1201

**MOORE, KENNETH CAMERON,** lawyer; b. Chgo., Oct. 25, 1947; s. Kenneth Edwards and Margaret Elizabeth (Cameron) M.; m. Karen M. Nelson, June 22, 1974; children: Roger Cameron, Kenneth Nelson, Kristin Karen. BA summa cum laude, Hiram Coll., 1969; JD cum laude, Harvard U., 1973. Bar: Ohio 1973, U.S. Dist. Ct. Md. 1974, U.S. Ct. Appeals (4th cir.) 1974, D.C. 1975, U.S. Dist. Ct. (no. dist.) Ohio 1976, U.S. Ct. Appeals (6th cir.) 1977, U.S. Ct. Appeals (D.C. cir.) 1979, U.S. Supreme Ct. 1980. Law clk. to judge Harrison L. Winter U.S. Ct. Appeals (4th cir.), Balt., 1973-74; assoc. Squire, Sanders & Dempsey, Washington, 1974-75; assoc. Squire, Sanders & Dempsey, Cleve., 1975-82, ptnr., 1982—, mem. fin. com., 1990—, profl. ethics ptnr., 1996—. Chmn. Ohio Fin. Com. for Jimmy Carter presdl. campaign, 1976; del. Dem. Nat. Conv., 1976; chief legal counsel Ohio Carter-Mondale Campaign, 1976; mem. Cleve. com. Cleve. Coun. World Affairs; trustee Hiram Coll., 1997—, mem. exec. com., 1999, chair audit com., 1999. With AUS, 1970-76. Mem. ABA, Fed. Bar Assn., Ohio Bar Assn., Cleve. Bar Assn., Cleve. City Club. Environmental, Federal civil litigation, State civil litigation. Home: 15602 Edgewater Dr Cleveland OH 44107-1212 Office: Squire Sanders & Dempsey 4900 Society Ctr 127 Public Sq Ste 4900 Cleveland OH 44114-1304

**MOORE, KEVIN JOHN,** lawyer; b. N.Y.C., Aug. 13, 1956; s. John Seymour and Maxine (Brown) M.; m. Mary Alice Fitzpatrick, May 18, 1985. BA, Drew U., 1978; JD, NYU, 1981. Bar: N.J. 1981, U.S. Dist. Ct. N.J. 1981. Assoc. Jamieson, Moore, Peskin & Spicer, Princeton, N.J., 1981-86, ptnr., 1986—; teaching asst. polit. sci. dept. Drew U., Madison, N.J., 1974-78; mem. NYU Rev. of Law and Social, 1979-80. Contbr. articles to profl. law revs. Participant Fenwick for Senate Campaign, Princeton, 1981; mem., sec. Delaware Valley Regional Coun. of Hyacinth AIDS Found. Trustee scholar Drew U., Madison, 1974-78. Mem. ABA, N.J. Bar Assn. (hard use, real property, trust and probate sects.), Princeton Bar Assn. (pres. 1991-92). Avocations: reading, theatre, art. Real property, Land use and zoning (including planning). Home: 8 Hillside Ct Lambertville NJ 08530-1051 Office: Jamieson Moore Peskin & Spicer 300 Alexander Park Princeton NJ 08540-6396

**MOORE, KEVIN MICHAEL,** federal judge; b. 1951. BA, Fla. State U.; JD, Fordham U. Bar: Fla. 1976. U.S. atty. no. dist. State of Fla., Tallahassee, 1987-89; dir. U.S. Marshals Svc., Arlington, Va., 1989-92; judge US. Dist. Ct. So. Dist. Fla., Miami, 1992—. Office: US Dist Ct Federal Justice Bldg 99 NE 4th St Rm 1168 Miami FL 33132-2139

**MOORE, LEE ALAN,** lawyer, accountant; b. Mattoon, Ill., Nov. 23, 1966; s. Wendell E. and Carolyn I. Moore; m. Teresa A. Wiesley, Oct. 8, 1994; children: Samuel, Anna. BSBA, Ohio State U., 1989; JD, U. Mo., Kansas City, 1992. Bar: Mo. 1992, U.S. Dist. Ct. (we. dist.) Mo. 1992, Kans. 1993, U.S. Tax Ct. 1994; CPA, Mo. Atty., CPA Raymond E. Moore P.C., Independence, Mo., 1990—. Personal income taxation, Estate taxation, Estate planning. Home: 6329 Mcgee St Kansas City MO 64113-2301 Office: Raymond E Moore PC 4401 S Noland Rd Ste C Independence MO 64055-4793

**MOORE, MARIANNA GAY,** law librarian, consultant; b. La Grange, Ga., Sept. 12, 1939; d. James Henry and Avanelle (Gay) M. AB in French, English, U. Ga., 1961; MLS, Emory U., 1964; postgrad., U. Ga., 1965-66, U. Ill., 1967-68. Asst. law libr. U. Ga., Athens, 1964-66; asst. libr. Yavapai Coll. Libr., Prescott, Ariz., 1969-72; libr. U. Ill. Law Libr., Urbana, 1966-68; law libr. Leva, Hawes, Symington, Washington, 1972-75; libr. project coord. Wash. Occupational Info. Svc., Olympia, 1976-80, Wash. State Health Facilities Assn., Olympia, 1981-82; mgr. Wash. State Ret. Tchrs. Assn., Olympia, 1982-83, exec. dir., 1984-89; exec. dir. Wash. State Retired Tchrs. Found., Olympia, 1986-89; law libr. Solano County Law Libr., Fairfield, Calif., 1989—; libr. LIBRARY/USA N.Y. World's Fair, N.Y.C., 1965; consulting law libr. Dobbins, Weir, Thompson & Stephenson, Vacaville, Calif., 1989—; law libr. cons. Coconino County Law Libr., Flagstaff, Ariz., 1968-70. Author: Guide to Fin. Aid for Wash. State Students, 1979; tng. package to introduce librs. to Wash. State Info. Svc., 1980; indexer For Your Information, 1988. Bd. dirs. Thurston County Sr. Ctr., Olympia, 1976-84, Thurston-Mason Nutrition Program, Olympia, 1977-79, Wash. Soc. Assn. Execs., Edmonds, 1987-89. Mem. Am. Assn. Law Librs., No. Calif. Assn. Law Librs., Calif. Coun. of County Law Librs. Avocations: reading, tatting, travel, music, calligraphy, cats. E-mail: mmoore@solanocounty.com. Office: Solano County Law Libr Hall of Justice 600 Union Ave Fairfield CA 94533-6324

**MOORE, MARILYN PAYNE,** lawyer; b. Summit, N.J., Sept. 2, 1970; d. Ervin Carroll and Rosemary M. BA in Polit. Sci., Spanish and Sociology, Rice U., 1992; JD, U. Houston, 1995. Bar: Tex. 1995. Assoc. corp. and securities sect. Bracewell & Patterson LLP, Houston, 1995-97; assoc. internat. and corp. and securities sects. Baker & McKenzie, Dallas, 1997—; dir. John C. Ford Program, Dallas, 1998—. Contbr. articles to profl. jours. Ct. appointed adv. abused children Child Advs., Inc., Houston, 1995-97. Mem. ABA (mem. internat. and bus. sects. 1996—), Dallas Bar Assn. (mem. internat. sect., mem. corp. sect.), Women in Internat. Trade Tex. Avocations: traveling, writing, tennis, horseback riding. Private international, General corporate, Securities. Office: Baker & McKenzie 2001 Ross Ave Ste 4500 Dallas TX 75201-2968

**MOORE, MCPHERSON DORSETT,** lawyer; b. Pine Bluff, Ark., Mar. 1, 1947; s. Arl Van and Jesse (Dorsett) M. BS, U. Miss., 1970; JD, U. Ark., 1974. Bar: Ark. 1974, Mo. 1975, U.S. Patent and Trademark Office 1977, U.S. Dist. Ct. (ea. dist.) Mo. 1977, U.S. Ct. Appeals (8th, 10th and Fed. cirs.). Design engr. Tenneco, Newport News, Va., 1970-71; assoc. Rogers, Eilers & Howell, St. Louis, 1974-80; ptnr. Rogers, Howell, Moore & Haferkamp, St. Louis, 1981-89; ptnr. Armstrong, Teasdale, Schlafly & Davis, St. Louis, 1989-95; ptnr. Polster, Lieder, Woodruff & Lucchesi, St. Louis, 1995—. Bd. dirs. Legal Services of Eastern Mo. With USAR, 1970-76. Mem. ABA, Bar Assn. Met. St. Louis (chmn. young lawyers sect. 1981-82, sec. 1984-85, v.p. 1985-86, chmn. trial sect. 1986-87, pres. 1988-89), Ark. Bar Assn., St. Louis Bar Found. (sec. 1984-85, v.p. 1988-89, pres. 1989-90), The Mo. Bar (chmn. patent, trademark and copyright law com. 1992-94, co-chmn. 1994-95), St. Louis County Bar Assn., Women Lawyers Assn., Am. Intellectual Property Law Assn., Mound City Bar Assn., Phi Delta Theta Alumni (treas. St. Louis chpt. 1987-88, sec. 1988-89, v.p. 1989-90), engr. City of Ladue, Mo., mem. Ladue Zoning and Planning Commn., 1998—. Mem. U. Club (St. Louis). Episcopalian. Patent, Trademark and copyright, Federal civil litigation. Home: 33 Deerfield Rd Saint Louis MO 63124-1412 Office: Polster Lieder Woodruff & Lucchesi 763 S New Ballas Rd Ste 160 Saint Louis MO 63141-8750

**MOORE, MICHAEL CALVIN,** lawyer; b. Royal Oak, Mich., Aug. 31, 1965; s. Calvin Silliman and Patricia Thomas M.; m. Susan Denise Sager, June 6, 1998. BA with dinstinction, Va. Mil. Inst., 1987; JD cum laude, Washington and Lee U., 1992. Bar: Va. 1992, U.S. Dist. Ct. (ea. dist.) Va. 1992, U.S. Ct. Appelas (4th cir.) 1992. Law clk. U.S. Ct., Norfolk, Va., 1992-93; asst. atty. Virginia Beach (Va.) Commonwealth Attys. Office, 1993-98; assoc. Pender & Coward, Virginia Beach, 1998—. 2d lt. U.S. Army, 1988. Mem. Virginia Beach Bar Assn. Avocations: running, backpacking. Insurance, General civil litigation, Criminal. Office: Pender & Coward 4th Fl Greenwich Ctr 192 Ballard Ct Ste 400 Virginia Beach VA 23462-6557

**MOORE, MICHAEL T.,** lawyer; b. Mullins, S.C., Feb. 21, 1948; s. Claude Richard and Melinda Doris (Stone) M.; m. Leslie Jean Lott, Nov. 12, 1978; children: Michael T. Jr., Emmett Russell Lott. BA, U. Fla., 1970, JD, 1974. Assoc. Burlingham, Underwood & Lord, N.Y.C., 1974-77, Hassan, Mahassni, Burlington, Underwood & Lord, Jeddah, Saudi Arabia, 1977-79; ptnr. Holland & Knight, Miami, Fla., 1982—; bd. dirs. Holland & Knight, Miami, 1986—, exec. ptnr. Miami office, 1993—; bd. dirs. Marine Arbitration Bd., Inc., Miami, 1985—; pres. The Marine Coun., 1989-90. Editor-in-chief Southern District Digest, 1980-82; contbr. articles to profl. jours. Mem. Orange Bowl Com.; bd. dirs. United Way Greater Miami, 1994—, U.S. Sailing Ctr., YMCA; chmn. Alexis de Tocqueville Soc.; mem. Miami River Coordinating Com.; trustee St. Stephens Sch.; mem. Coral Gables (Fla.) Youth Adv. Bd. Mem. ABA, Maritime Law Assn. U.S., Fla. Bar Assn., Dade County Bar Assn. (bd. dirs. 1981—, Outstanding Young Lawyer award 1982). Republican. Admiralty, Transportation, Personal injury. Home: 3515 Anderson Rd Miami FL 33134-7050 Office: Holland & Knight 701 Brickell Ave Flr 30 PO Box 15441 Miami FL 33131-5441

**MOORE, MIKE,** state attorney general; m. Tisha Moore; 1 child, Kyle. Grad., Jackson County Jr. Coll., 1972; BA, U. Miss., 1974, JD, 1976. Asst. dist. atty. State of Miss., 1977-78, dist. atty., 1979, atty. gen., 1988—. Office: Office of Atty Gen PO Box 220 Jackson MS 39205-0220

**MOORE, MITCHELL JAY,** lawyer, law educator; b. Lincoln, Nebr., Aug. 29, 1954; s. Earl J. and Betty Marie (Zimmerlin) M.; m. Sharon Lea Campbell, Sept. 5, 1987. BS in Edn., U. Mo., Columbia, 1977, JD, 1981. Bar: Mo. 1981, U.S. Dist. Ct. (we. dist.) Mo. 1981, Tex. 1982, U.S. Ct. Appeals (8th cir.) 1998. Sole practice Columbia, Mo., 1981—; coordinating atty. student legal svcs. ctr. U. Mo., Columbia, 1983-89. Mem. Columbia Substance Abuse Adv. Commn., 1989—; bd. dirs. Planned Parenthood of Ctrl. Mo., Columbia, 1984-86, Opportunities Unltd., Columbia, 1984-86, ACLU of Mid-Mo., 1991-98; Libertarian candidate for Atty. Gen. of Mo., 1992, for 9th congl. dist. U.S. Ho. of Reps., 1994, 96, for Mo. State Rep. 23d dist., 1998; mem. Probation and Parole Citizens Adv. Bd., 1995—. Mem. Boone County Bar Assn., Assn. Trial Lawyers Am., Mo. Assn. Trial Attys., Phi Delta Phi. Libertarian. Unitarian. Avocations: softball, camping. Family and matrimonial, Personal injury, Criminal. Office: 1210 W Broadway Columbia MO 65203-2126

**MOORE, PATRICK NEILL,** lawyer; b. Fort Smith, Ark., Apr. 4, 1946; s. George Hugh and Mildred (Troy) M.; m. Janice Beth Barker De Bauge, Aug. 21, 1967 (div. June 1990); children: Shawn Patrick, Colin Hugh. BA magna cum laude, Harding Coll., 1967; JD, So. Meth. U., 1970. Bar: Ark. 1970, Tex. 1970. Ptnr. Warner Smith & Harris, Fort Smith, 1970—; bd. dirs. We. C.C. Found., Fort Smith. Trustee Fort Smith Employees Pension Plan, 1982-88; bd. dirs. Holt Krock Clinic Instl. Rev. Bd. Fellow Am. Coll. Trust and Estate Coun.; mem. ABA, Ark. Bar Assn., State Bar Tex., Phi Alpha Theta, Alpha Chi. Mem. Disciples of Christ Ch. Estate planning, Pension, profit-sharing, and employee benefits, Estate taxation. Home: 4018 S 25th St Fort Smith AR 72901-7703 Office: Warner Smith & Harris PLC 214 N 6th St Fort Smith AR 72901-2106

**MOORE, PEGGY BRADEN,** lawyer; b. Salem, Oreg., July 18, 1944; d. Clifton Leo Cass and Geraldene Mae (Arnett) Pendleton; m. Frank Horace Moore II, Aug. 30, 1980; children: Charles Edward, Douglas Andrew. BA, U. Pacific, 1965; JD, U. Denver, 1968. Bar: Colo. 1968, N.Y. 1969, U.S. Dist. Ct. (so. & ea. dists.) N.Y. 1970, U.S. Ct. Appeals (2d cir.) 1970, U.S. Ct. Appeals (D.C. cir.) 1973, Calif. 1976, U.S. Ct. Appeals (9th cir.) 1980, U.S. Dist. Ct. (we. dist.) N.Y. 1981, U.S. Ct. Appeals (3d cir.) 1981, Conn. 1984, U.S. Dist. Ct. Conn. 1988. Atty. Travelers' Ins. Co., N.Y.C., 1969-71; ptnr. Jackson, Lewis, Schnitzler & Krupman, N.Y.C., 1971-79; sr. atty. The Singer Co., Stamford, Conn., 1979-86; pvt. practice Stamford, 1986—; magistrate Conn. Superior Ct., Stamford, 1988—. Bd. dirs. Boys and Girls Club of Stamford, 1990—; mem. Rep. Town Meeting, Greenwich, Conn., 1982—. Mem., N.Y. State Bar Assn., Corp. Bar, Stamford-Norwalk Regional Bar. Democrat. Episcopalian. Labor, Pension, profit-sharing, and employee benefits, Workers' compensation. Office: PO Box 3454 Stamford CT 06905-0454

**MOORE, RANDALL D.,** lawyer; b. Lubbock, Tex., May 13, 1960; s. Donnie Dean and Donna Biggers M.; m. Cynthia Ann Lindblad, July 11, 1981; children: Sara Allison, Jonathan Dean, David Randall. BBA, U. Tex., Arlington, 1982; JD, So. Meth. U., Dallas, 1985. Bar: Tex. 1985, U.S. Dist. Ct. (no., so., ea. and we. dists.) Tex.; cert. personal injury trial law. Asst. dist. atty. Tarrant County Dist. Atty., Ft. Worth, 1985-88; assoc. Rhone, Hoodenplye, Lobert & Myers, Arlington, Tex., 1988-89; assoc. then ptnr. Shannon, Gracey, Ratliff & Miller, Ft. Worth, 1989-91; shareholder, officer atty. Wallach & Moore PC, Ft. Worth, 1991—; spkr. in field. Mem. Tex. Assn. Def. Counsel, Def. Rsch. Inst., Tarrant County Bar Assn., N. Tex. Healthcare Risk Mgrs. Soc., Health Industry Coun. Personal injury, Product liability, Health. Office: Wallach & Moore PC 1300 Summit Ave Ste 300 Fort Worth TX 76102-4417

**MOORE, RICHARD GEORGE,** lawyer; b. Indpls., July 15, 1957; s. E. James and Joyce Judith (Dobeck) M.; m. Alison Ann Holladay, Feb. 25, 1984; children: Richard George Jr., Stephanie Ellen, Ryan James. BBA magna cum laude, Baylor U., 1979, JD, 1982. Bar: Tex. 1982. Briefing atty. U.S. Dist. Ct. (no. dist.) Tex., Dallas, 1982-84; assoc. Worsham, Forsythe, Sampels & Wooldridge, Dallas, 1984-87; supervising atty. Fed. Asset Disposition Assn., Dallas, 1987-89; asst. gen. counsel NationsBank, Dallas, 1989-95; pvt. practice Dallas, 1995—. Mng. editor, contbr. Baylor U. Law Rev., 1981-82. Mem. Tex. Bar Assn., Dallas Bar Assn., Tex. State Bd. Pub. Accountancy, Sigma Alpha Epsilon. Republican. Roman Catholic. Avocations: fishing, basketball, softball. General corporate, Real property. Home and Office: 6955 Lakeshore Dr Dallas TX 75214-3551

**MOORE, ROBERT MADISON,** food industry executive, lawyer; b. New Orleans, June 21, 1925; s. Clarence Greer and Anna Omega (Odendahl) M.; m. Evelyn Eileen Varva, Apr. 11, 1953; children: Eileen Alexandria Moore Wynne, John Greer. BBA, Tulane U., 1943; JD, U. Va., 1952; LLM (Food Law Inst. fellow), NYU, 1953. Bar: La. 1956, Calif. 1972. Asst. to pres., gen. counsel Underwear Inst., N.Y.C., 1953-55; pvt. practice law New Orleans, 1955-56; asst. gen. atty., dir. Legal services, sec. and gen. atty. Standard Fruit & Steamship Co., New Orleans, 1957-72; v.p., gen. counsel Castle & Cooke Foods, 1972-81; v.p., gen. counsel Castle & Cooke, Inc., 1973-81, sr. v.p. law and govt., 1981-82; pres. Internat. Banana Assn., 1983-98; acting exec. dir. Pan Am. Devel. Found., 1999—; dir. Ferson Optics of Del., Inc., 1958-69, Baltime Securities Corp., Pan American Devel. Found. Asst. atty. gen., La., 1958-63. Served with AUS, 1943-46. Mem. ABA, Calif. Bar Assn., La. Bar Assn., SAR (sec. 1960-61), Cosmos Club, Phi Delta Phi, Alpha Tau Omega. Democrat. Roman Catholic. Home: 3323 R St NW Washington DC 20007-2310 Office: Pan Am Devel Found 1929 39th St NW Washington DC 20007-2110

**MOORE, ROY WORSHAM, III,** lawyer; b. Atlanta, Sept. 6, 1941; s. Roy Worsham Jr. and Mary (Townsend) M.; m. Margaret Troyano, June 27, 1967; children: Angela S., Roy W., John T. BA, Harvard U., 1963; LLB, Duke U., 1966. Bar: Conn. 1966, U.S. Dist. Ct. Conn. 1969, U.S. Ct. Appeals (2d cir.) 1969. Ptnr. Marsh, Day & Calhoun, Southport, Conn., 1969-84; of counsel Brody, Wilkinson & Ober (formerly Marsh, Day & Calhoun), Southport, Conn., 1999—. Bd. dirs. Oaklawn Cemetery Assn. Lt. USNR, 1966-69. Mem. Conn. Bar Assn., Country Club Fairfield, Am. Legion. Republican. Episcopalian. Avocations: boating, golf, other sports. Real property, Probate, General corporate. Office: 2507 Post Rd Southport CT 06490-1259

**MOORE, S. CLARK,** judge; b. Norfolk, Va., Aug. 28, 1924; s. Samuel Clark and Mary Elizabeth (Pate) M. BA, San Diego State Coll., 1949; JD, U. So. Calif., L.A., 1957, LLM, 1960. Bar: Calif. 1957, U.S. Dist. Ct. (cen. dist.) Calif. 1957, U.S. Ct. Appeals (9th cir.) 1960. Dep. atty. gen. Calif. State Atty. Gen., L.A., 1957-72, asst. atty. gen., 1972-75, sr. asst. atty. gen., 1975-82, chief asst. atty. gen., 1982-83; judge Santa Anita Mcpl. Ct., 1984-94, Pomona Mcpl. Ct., Calif., 1995—; mem. Fed. cts. practice standards com., 1981-84, countywide criminal justice coord. com., 1989-90, courthouse security task force, 1989-90. With U.S. Army, 1943-46. Decorated European Theater medal, Asiatic Pacific medal, Am. Theater medal, Victory medal, Good Conduct medal, Philipine Liberation medal. Mem. L.A. Bar Assn. (former chmn. criminal justice sect., exec. com. bar delegation 1982-84), L.A. Mcpl. Cts. Judges Assn. (sec. 1989, vice chair 1988-89, chair 1989-90, exec. com. 1987-88, 90-91), Presiding Justices Assn. Republican. Office: Pomona Mcpl Ct 350 W Mission Blvd Pomona CA 91766-1607

**MOORE, STEPHANIE Y.,** lawyer. BA, Oberlin Coll.; JD, Harvard U. Bar: Pa. 1986. Gen. counsel Commn. on Civil Rights, Washington. Office: Commn on Civil Rights 62 49th St NW Washington DC 20019*

**MOORE, STEPHEN JAMES,** lawyer; b. Kansas City, Mo., Aug. 9, 1947; s. James Andrew and Frances Clare (Kennedy) M. BSBA, Rockhurst Coll., 1969, BA, 1975; JD, U. Mo., Kansas City, 1977, LLM, 1997. Bar: Mo. 1978, U.S. Dist. Ct. (we. dist.) Mo. 1978, U.S. Ct. Appeals (8th cir.) 1980, U.S. Ct. Appeals (10th cir.) 1981, U.S. Ct. Fed. Claims 1991, U.S. Ct. Appeals (6th cir.) 1997. Law intern Mo. Atty. Gen.'s Office, Kansas City, 1976-77, asst., 1978; assoc. Popham, Conway, Sweeny, Fremont & Bundschu PC, Kansas City, 1978-84, Freilich, Leitner & Carlisle, P.C., Kansas City, 1985, Herrick, Feinstein, Kansas City, 1985-86, Freilich, Leitner, Carlisle & Shortlidge, Kansas City, 1986-90; ptnr. Freilich, Leitner & Carlisle, Kansas City, Dallas, L.A., 1987—, Aspen, Colo., 1997—; adj. prof. law U. Mo., Kansas City, 1995—. Mem. Friends of Art, Nelson-Atkins Mus. Art, Kansas City, 1988—, Smithsonian Inst., Washington, 1985—, Nat. Trust for Historic Preservation, Washington, 1988—, Libr. of Congress Assocs., The Federalist Soc., Nat. Audubon Soc. Mem. ABA, Assn. Trial Lawyers Am., Kansas City Metro Bar Assn., Sports Car Club Am., Am. Mus. Nat. History, Porsche Club Am., Lake Ozarks Yacht Assn., Boat Owners Assn. U.S., Delta Theta Phi, Tau Kappa Epsilon. Roman Catholic. Avocations: vintage sportscars, boating. E-mail: flc@qni.com; smoore7488@aol.com. Land use and zoning (including planning), Real property, Municipal (including bonds). Home: 5840 McGee St Kansas City MO 64113-2132 Office: Freilich Leitner & Carlisle 4600 Madison Ave Ste 1000 Kansas City MO 64112-3041

**MOORE, STEVEN WOODROW,** lawyer; b. Norfolk, Va., Sept. 7, 1967; s. Woodrow Wilson and Helena (Sorzano) M.; m. Erin Torda, May 22, 1993; 1 child, Madeline Lois. BA in English, Old Dominion U., 1989; JD, U. Denver, 1993. Bar: Colo. 1993, Calif. 1997, U.S. Dist. Ct. Colo. 1993, U.S. Ct. Appeals (10th cir.) 1993. Assoc. atty. Nathan Davidovich and Assocs., Denver, 1993-95; ptnr. Lindquist-Kleissier, Cooper and Moore, LLC, Denver, 1995-98; sr. asst. city atty. Denver City Atty.'s Office, Denver, 1998—. Mem. ABA, Colo. Bar Assn., Denver Bar Assn., State Bar Calif., Faculty Fed. Advocates. Avocations: skiing, golf, hiking. Home: 3444 S Akron St Denver CO 80231-4639 Office: Denver City Attys Office 1445 Cleveland Pl # 303 Denver CO 80202-5392

**MOORE, TERRY MASON,** lawyer, tribal judge; b. Fairfax, Okla., May 11, 1955; d. Benjamin Joseph and Bonnie Louise (Elliott) Mason; m. Theodore Vern Moore, Jr., Aug. 3, 1984; children: Jessica, Dillon, Erica, Elizabeth. BS, Northeast Okla. State U., 1977; JD, U. N.Mex., 1983; MBA, U. Minn., 1992. Bar: Okla. Mgmt. accounting specialist Andrew Skeeter, Inc., Tulsa, 1977-79; asst. dir. S.W. Mo. State U. Ctr. Resource Mgmt., Springfield, 1979-80; lawyer Okla. Indian Legal Svcs., Oklahoma City, 1984-85, Moore Law Office, Fairfax, 1985-90, Ind. Child Welfare Law Ctr., Mpls., 1993-95, BlueDog, Olson & Small, Mpls., 1995—; judge Prairie Island Mdewakanton Dakota Cmty., 1995—, Lower Sionx Indian Cmty., 1998—. Mem. FBA, Nat. Am. Indian Ct. Judges Assn., Minn. Am. Indian Bar Assn., Minn. Tribal Judges Assn. Contracts commercial, Native American, Non-profit and tax-exempt organizations. Office: BlueDog Olson & Small 5001 W 80th St Ste 500 Minneapolis MN 55437-1116

**MOORE, THELMA WYATT,** judge; b. Amarillo, Tex., July 6, 1945; d. James Odis and Annie LaVernia (Lott) Wyatt; m. Luke C. Moore (dec. Nov. 1994); children: Khan Khari Cummings, Ayanna Cummings. BA, UCLA, 1965; JD, Emory U., 1971. Bar: Ga. 1971. Atty. Ward and Wyatt, Atlanta, 1974-77; judge Mcpl. Ct., Atlanta, 1977-80, City Ct., Atlanta, 1980-85, State Ct., Fulton County, Ga., 1985-90; judge, chief judge Superior Ct., Fulton County, 1990—; mem. exec. com. Nat. Jud. Coun., 1987—, chmn., 1986-87; spkr. in field. Assoc. editor Jour. Pub. Law, 1969-71; contbr. articles to profl. jours. Former chair adminstrv. bd. Cascade United Meth. Ch. Recipient WSB TV Living Legend award, 1991, 92, Disting. Alumni award Emory U., 1986, Essence award, 9182, numerous others; John Hay Whitney fellow; Nat. Urban League fellow; Emory Law scholar; State of Ill. fellow. Mem. ABA, Nat. Bar Assn., Ga State Bar Assn., Atlanta Bar Assn., Gate City Bar Assn. (historian 1990-93), World Peace Through Law Ctr., Am. Judges Assn., Ga. Assn. Black Women Attys., Nat. Assn. Women Judges, Mo-So Lit. Circle, The Links, Inc., Order of Coif, Bryanm Soc., Alpha Kappa Alpha, Phi Delta Phi. Office: 185 Central Ave SW Ste T4905 Atlanta GA 30303-3653

**MOORE, THOMAS KAIL,** territory chief supreme court justice; b. Idaho Falls, Idaho, Jan. 15, 1938; s. Burton L. and Clara E. (Kail) Moore; m. Judith Diane Gilman, July 30, 1966; children: David T., Jonathan G. AB in Phys. Scis., Harvard U., 1961; JD, Georgetown U., 1967. Bar: D.C., V.I., Va. Law clk. to Hon. John A. Danaher U.S. Ct. Appeals (D.C. Cir.), 1967-68; staff atty. Office Gen. Coun., Office Sec. Dept. Transp., Washington, 1968-69; assoc. Stanford, Reed & Gelenian, Washington, 1969-70; asst. U.S. Atty. U.S. Attys. Office, Washington, 1970-71; asst. U.S. Atty. U.S. Attys. Office (ea. dist.), Va., 1971-76, prin. asst. Alexandria office, 1974-76; asst. U.S. Atty. U.S. Attys. Office (V.I. dist.), 1976-78; pvt. practive St. Thomas, V.I., 1978-81; shareholder Hoffman & Moore, P.C., St. Thomas, 1981-87; ptnr. Grunert, Stout, Moore & Bruch, St. Thomas, 1987-92; chief judge U.S. Dist. Ct. (V.I. dist.), 1992—. Editor-in-chief Georgetown Law Journal, 1966-67. Scoutmaster Antilles Sch. Troop; trustee V.I. Montessori Sch. Capt. USAF, 1961-64, USAFR. Mem. ABA, V.I. Bar Assn. (judicial), V.I. C. of C., St. Thomas Yacht Club. Avocations: tennis, swimming, sailing. Office: Dist Ct of VI 5500 Veterans Dr Ste 310 Saint Thomas VI 00802-6424

**MOORE, THOMAS RONALD (LORD BRIDESTOWE),** lawyer; b. Duluth, Minn., Mar. 27, 1932; s. Ralph Henry and Estelle Marguerite (Hero) M.; m. Margaret C. King, Sept. 10, 1955; children: Willard S., Clarissa, Charles R.H. BA magna cum laude, Yale U., 1954; JD, Harvard U., 1957. Bar: N.Y. 1958, U.S. Supreme Ct. 1958. Instr. Internat. Program in Taxation Harvard Law Sch., 1956-57; assoc. Dewey Ballantine, N.Y.C.; ptnr. Breed, Abbott & Morgan, N.Y.C., Finley Kumble & Wagner, N.Y.C., Hawkins, Delafield & Wood, N.Y.C.; Law Offices of Thomas R. Moore, N.Y.C.; lectr. on law Cornell Law Sch., NYU, Practising Law Inst., N.Y.C., Las Vegas, New Orleans; lectr. N.Y.C., San Antonio, Tampa, L.A., Moscow, Charlottesville, Va., Washington, Kansas City. Author: Plantagenet Descent, 31 Generations from William the Conqueror to Today, 1995; co-author: Estate Planning and the Close Corporation; editor-in-chief Gastronome; bd. editors: The Tax Lawyer; contbr. articles to profl jours., popular press and TV commentaries. Bd. dirs. exec. com. Citymeals on Wheels; pres. bd. dirs. Nat. Soc. to Prevent Blindness, 1973-81, chmn., 1981-83, now hon. pres.; sec.-treas., trustee A.D. Henderson Found., Del.; trustee, Fla.; bd. dirs. Phoenix Theatre Inc., Inst. Aegean Prehistory, Found. Future of Man, Am. and Internat. Friends of Victoria and Albert Mus., London; conservator N.Y. Pub. Libr.; trustee Found. for Renaissance of St. Petersburg (Russia), Malcolm Wiener Found., Lawrence W. Levine Found. Recipient Coat of Arms and created Knight of St. John by Queen Elizabeth II, Order of Crown of Charlemagne, Order of Plantagenet, Order of Barons of Magna Charta; recipient Key to Kansas City by Mayor of Kansas City, Mo., 1989; Yale scholar of House, 1954; honoree Thomas R. Moore Disting. Pub. Servant award Nat. Soc. to Prevent Blindness. Mem. ABA, N.Y. State Bar Assn. (exec. com.), Assn. of Bar City of N.Y., Confrerie de la Chaine des Rotisseurs (nat. pres., dir., exec. com. world coun. Paris), Chevalier du Tastevin, Nat. Wine Coalition (bd. dirs. 1989—), The Pilgrims, St. George Soc., Downtown Assn., Univ. Club, Church Club, Delta Sigma Rho. Republican. Episcopalian. General civil litigation, Taxation, general, Estate planning. Office: 730 5th Ave Ste 900 New York NY 10019-4105

**MOORE, THOMAS SCOTT,** lawyer; b. Portland, Oreg., Nov. 17, 1937; s. Harry Alburn and Geraldine Elizabeth (Scott) M.; m. Saundra L. Wagner, Sept. 7, 1957 (div. 1974); children: Cindy, Kristin, Thomas, Victoria, Wendy; m. Alice H. Zeisz, Nov. 5, 1976; 1 child, Alice G. BA, Willamette U., 1959, JD cum laude, 1962. Bar: Oregon 1962. Pvt. practice Portland, 1962—. Contbr. articles to law jours. Republican. Avocation: tennis. Federal civil litigation, General civil litigation, State civil litigation. Office: 4425 SW Corbett Ave Portland OR 97201-4206

**MOORE, THURSTON ROACH,** lawyer; b. Memphis, Dec. 10, 1946; s. Richard Charlton Moore and Halcyon Hall (Roach) Lynn; m. Corell Luckhardt Halsey, Sept. 26, 1998. BA with distinction, U. Va., 1968, JD, 1974. Bar: Va. 1974. Rsch. analyst Scudder, Stevens & Clark, N.Y.C., 1968-71; ptnr. Hunton & Williams, Richmond, Va., 1974—; bd. dirs. Met. Advantage Corp., Richmond. Bd. dirs. Met. Bus. Found., Richmond, Mary Morton Parsons Found., Charlottesville, Va., The Nature Conservancy, Charlottesville, vice chmn. Va. chpt.; trustee Va. Aerospace Bus. Roundtable, Hampton, 1989—, Va. Ea. Shore Sustainable Devel. Corp., 1995—. Mem. ABA (bus. law sect., chmn. ptnrs. com. 1992-96, mem. fed. regulation security com.), Va. Bar Assn., Va. State Bar. Office: Hunton & Williams PO Box 1535 Richmond VA 23218-1535

**MOORE, WILLIAM THEODORE, JR.,** judge; b. Bainbridge, Ga., May 7, 1940; s. William T. and Mary (Talbert) M.; m. Jane Hodges, July 18, 1964; children: Sarah S., Mary T. William T III. AA, Ga. Military Coll., 1960; JD, U. Ga., 1964; Law (hon.), Ga. Military Coll., 1978. Bar: Ga. 1964, U.S. Dist. Ct. (so. dist.) Ga. 1964, U.S. Ct. Appeals (5th and 11th cirs.) 1979, U.S. Supreme Ct. 1980. U.S. atty. So. Dist. Ga. U.S. Dept. of Justice, Savannah, 1977-81; ptnr. Corish, Smith, Remler & Moore, Savannah, 1967-77, Sparkman, Harris & Moore, Savannah, 1981-87, Oliver Maner & Gray, Savannah, 1988-94; atty. Savannah-Chatham County Bd. Pub. Edn., 1975-77, mem. U.S. Atty. Gen's. Adv. com. D.C. 1978-81. Recipient Spl. Appreciation award Ga. Bur. of Investigation, 1980, U.S. Dept. Treasury Bur. of Alcohol, Tobacco & Firearms, D.C., 1980; Extraordinary Svc. award Savannah Chapt. Fed. Bar Assn., 1980. Fellow Am. Bd. Criminal Lawyers (pres. 1993); mem. Nat. Assn. Criminal Def. Lawyers, Nat. Assn. Former U.S. Attys. (bd. dirs. 1984—), Ga. Assn. Criminal Def. Lawyers (v.p. 1986—), Ga. Bar Assn. Democrat. Epsicopalian. Avocations: jogging, weight training. Office: US Dist Courthouse 125 Bull St PO Box 10245 Savannah GA 31412-0445

**MOORE, WILLSON CARR, JR.,** lawyer; b. Honolulu, Nov. 24, 1928; s. Willson Carr and Jenna Vee (McMillan) C.; m. Sally Churchill, Apr. 25, 1952; children: Willson C. III, Brian C., Sharon Moore Fink. BA, U. Calif., Berkeley, 1950; JD, U. Calif., San Francisco, 1953. Law clk. to Hon. Jon Wiig U.S. Dist. Ct., Honolulu, 1953-54; dep. atty. gen. State of Hawaii, 1955-59; pvt. practice Moore & Moore, Honolulu, 1959-64; with Rush, Moore, Craven, Sutton, Morry & Beh, Honolulu, 1965—; bd. dirs. Hawaii Def. Lawyers, 1990-94, Def. Rsch. Inst., 1989-93; mem. appellate mediation panel Supreme Ct. State of Hawaii, 1995—; settlement master U.S. Dist. Ct. Hawaii, 1996—. Col. USAR, 1950-81. Fellow Am. Coll. Trial Lawyers; mem. ABA, Am. Bd. Trial Lawyers (adv.), Am. Judacature Soc., Assn. Def. Trial Attys. (pres. 1989-90, mem. exec. coun. 1983-91), Phi Alpha Delta. Aviation, General civil litigation, Personal injury. Office: Rush Moore Craven Sutton Morry & Beh 745 Fort Street Mall Ste 2000 Honolulu HI 96813-3820

**MOOTS, JEFFREY ALAN,** lawyer; b. Topeka, Kans., Feb. 26, 1962; s. James Leland and Twila June (Allerheiligen) M.; m. Lisa Ann Nathonson, Sept. 20, 1992 (div. Feb. 1995). BBA, N.Mex. State U., 1984; JD, Washburn U., 1991. Bar: Kans. 1991, U.S. Dist. Ct. Kans. 1991. Atty. Shawnee County Pub. Defender's Office, Topeka, 1991-95, State of Kans. Death Penalty Def. Unit, Topeka, 1995—. 1st lt. U.S. Army, 1984-88. Mem. NACDL, Kans. Assn. Criminal Def. Lawyers (sec. 1989—), Phi Delta Phi. Democrat. Lutheran. Bankruptcy, Criminal. Office: State of Kans Death Penalty Unit 112 SW 6th Ave Ste 302 Topeka KS 66603-3810

**MORALES, JULIO K.,** lawyer; b. Havana, Cuba, Jan. 17, 1948; came to U.S., 1960; s. Julio E. and Josephine (Holsters) M.; m. Suzette M. Dussault, May 31, 1970 (div. 1978); children: Julio E., Karel A.; m. Barbara A. Miller, July 14, 1979 (div. 1988); 1 child, Nicolas W. *Father, Hon. Judge Julio E. Morales of Helena City, was born in Havana, Cuba, 1911. His parents, Colonel Julio A. Morales Brodermann and M. Mercedes Robelin Lopez De Carrizosa, died in 1997. Mother, Josephine Holsters Morales, was born in Boom, Belgium, 1912. She was a violinist and concertmistress of the Helena Symphony Orchestra in Helena, Montana. Her parents, Karel Holsters and Angelina Verbruggen, died in 1998.* BA, Carroll Coll., 1969; JD, U. Mont., 1972. Bar: Mont. 1972, U.S. Dist. Ct. Mont. 1972, U.S. Ct. Mil. Appeals 1972, U.S. Ct. Appeals (9th cir.) 1980. Law clk. to presiding justice Mont. Supreme Ct., Helena, 1972; sole practice Missoula, Mont., 1973-78, 88—; sr. ptnr. Morales & Volinkaty, Missoula, 1978-88; pvt. practice law Morales Law Office, 1988—. Author: Estate Planning for the Handicapped, 1975. Pres. Rockmont, Inc., Missoula, 1985—. Served to 2d lt. U.S. Army, 1972. Named Boss of the Yr., Missoula chpt. Mont. Assn. Legal Secs., 1988. Mem. ABA (dist. rep. 1975-79, exec. coun. young lawyer divsn. 1977-79), Mont. Bar Assn. (chmn. law day 1974, 75, 77), Am. Judicature Soc., Assn. Trial Lawyers Am., World Assn. Lawyers, Missoula Soccer Assn. (pres. 1983-85), Mont. Sailing Assn. (bd. dirs. 1994—), Nat. Exch. Club (bd. dirs. Yellowstone dist. 1987-88, pres. 1990-91), Missoula Exch. Club, Phi Delta Phi. Roman Catholic. Avocations: sports, coaching youth, boating, skiing, golf. Personal injury, Workers' compensation, Probate. Office: PO Box 9311 430 Ryman St Missoula MT 59802-4208

**MORAN, DAVID E., JR.,** lawyer; b. Milw., July 20, 1955; s. David E. and Joanne R. Moran; m. Betsy Davis, Sept. 4, 1981 (div. Apr. 1996); children: Mike, Andy, Tom, Kate; m. Molly Ann Moyna, Aug. 17, 1996; stepchildren: Tyler, Megan. BA, Gustavus Adolphus U., 1977; JD, U. Minn., 1981. Assoc. Stolpestad, Brown & Smith, St. Paul, 1981-84, Winthrop & Weinstine, Mpls., 1984—. Office: Winthrop & Weinstine 3000 Dain Rauscher Plz 60 S 6th St Minneapolis MN 55402-4400

**MORAN, EDWARD KEVIN,** lawyer, consultant; b. N.Y.C., Mar. 4, 1964; s. Edward Joseph and Margaret Anne (Hauff) M.; m. Janet Athanasidy, Dec. 9, 1990. BA, SUNY, Binghamton, 1986; JD, N.Y. Law Sch., 1989; MBA, NYU, 1999. Bar: Conn. 1989, N.Y. 1990, N.J. 1990. Summer assoc. N.Y.C. Police Dept. Legal Bur., 1987; mng. atty. Landau, Miller and Moran, N.Y.C., 1990-97; cons. Windham Digital Design, Inc., N.Y.C., 1997—; cons. Bottom Line Group, N.Y.C., 1992—. Editor-in-chief N.Y. Law Sch. Jour. Internat. and Comparative Law, 1988-89. Mem. Conn. Bar Assn., N.Y. State Bar Assn., Assn. Trial Lawyers Am., N.Y. State Trial Lawyers Assn. General civil litigation, Insurance, Personal injury. Office: Landau Miller and Moran 233 Broadway Rm 1082 New York NY 10279-0048

**MORAN, JAMES BYRON,** federal judge; b. Evanston, Ill., June 20, 1930; s. James Edward and Kathryn (Horton) M.; children: John, Jennifer, Sarah, Polly; stepchildren: Katie, Cynthia, Laura, Michael. AB, U. Mich., 1952; LLB magna cum laude, Harvard U., 1957. Bar: Ill. 1958. Law clk. to judge U.S. Ct. of Appeals (2d cir.), 1957-58; assoc. Bell, Boyd, Lloyd, Haddad & Burns, Chgo, 1958-66, ptnr., 1966-79; judge U.S. Dist. Ct. (no. dist.) Ill., Chgo., 1979—. Dir. Com. on Ill. Govt., 1960-78, chmn., 1968-70; vice chmn., sec. Ill. Dangerous Drug Adv. Coun., 1967-74; dir. Gateway Found., 1969—; mem. Ill. Ho. of Reps., 1965-67; mem. Evanston City Council, 1971-75. Served with AUS, 1952-54. Mem. Chgo. Bar Assn., Chgo. Council Lawyers, Phi Beta Kappa. Clubs: Law, Legal. Home: 117 Kedzie St Evanston IL 60202-2509 Office: US Dist Ct 219 S Dearborn St Chicago IL 60604-1702

**MORAN, JOHN THOMAS, JR.,** lawyer; b. Oak Park, Ill., Mar. 15, 1943; s. John T. and Corinne Louise (Dire) M.; m. Catherine Casey Pyne, May 16, 1981; 1 child, Sean Michael Pyne-Moran. AB cum laude, U. Notre Dame, 1965; JD, Georgetown U., 1968. Bar: Ill. 1969, Colo. 1976, U.S. Supreme Ct. 1973. Chief appeals div. Pub. Defender Cook County, Ill., 1970-82; gen. counsel Pub. Defender Cook County, Chgo., 1984-86; chief litigation atty. Frank & Flaherty, Chgo., 1982; cons. ABA, Chgo., 1982-83; sole practice Chgo., 1986-93; founder Law Offices of John Thomas Moran, 1993-97, John T. Moran & Assocs., 1993—. Editor: Gideon Revisited, 1983. Bd. dirs. Lawyers for the Creative Arts, 1973-97. Ford Found. grantee Internat. Common Law Colloquium, London, 1976, NEH grantee, Harvard Law Sch., 1977. Mem. Ill. State Bar Assn., Appellate Lawyers Assn., Nat. Legal Aid and Defenders Assn., Am. Soc. Internat. Law, Georgetown U. Law Ctr. Alumni Soc., Sorin Soc. U. Notre Dame. Avocation: sailing. General civil litigation, Libel, Criminal. Home: 930 Oakwood Ave Wilmette IL 60091-3320 Office: John T Moran & Assocs 309 W Washington St Ste 900 Chicago IL 60606-3207

**MORAN, RACHEL,** lawyer, educator; b. Kansas City, Mo., June 27, 1956; d. Thomas Albert and Josephine (Portillo) M. AB, Stanford U., 1978; JD, Yale U., 1981. Bar: Calif. 1984. Assoc Heller, Ehrman, White & McAuliffe, San Francisco, 1982-83; prof. law U. Calif., Berkeley, 1984—, Robert D. and Leslie-Kay Raven prof. law, 1998—; vis. prof. UCLA Sch. Law, 1988, Stanford (Calif.) U. Law Sch., 1989, N.Y.U. Sch. of Law, 1996, U. Miami Sch. Law, 1997; chair Chicano/Latino Policy Project, 1993-96. Contbr. numerous articles to profl. jours. Recipient Disting. Tchg. award U. Calif. Mem. ABA, Assn. of Am. Law Schs. (mem. exec. com.), Am. Law Inst., Calif. Bar Assn., Phi Beta Kappa. Democrat. Unitarian. Avocations: jogging, aerobics, reading, listening to music. Office: U Calif Sch Law Boalt Hall Berkeley CA 94720

**MORD, IRVING CONRAD, II,** lawyer; b. Kentwood, La., Mar. 22, 1950; s. Irving Conrad and Lillie Viva (Chapman) M.; m. Julia Ann Russell, Aug. 22, 1970 (div. Apr. 22, 1980); children: Russell Conrad, Emily Ann; m. Kay E. McDaniel, Aug. 31, 1985; children: Kurt August, Clayton Troy. BS, Miss. State U., 1972; JD, U. Miss., 1974. Bar: Miss. 1974, U.S. Dist. Ct. (no. dist.) Miss. 1974, U.S. Dist. Ct. (so. dist.) Miss. 1984. Counsel to bd. suprs. Noxubee County, Miss., 1976-80, Walthall County, Miss. 1980—, Bd. Educ., Walthall County, 1980—. Trustee, Walthall County Gen. Hosp., 1982—; county pros. atty. Noxubee County, Miss., Macon, 1974-80, Walthall County, Tylertown, 1982-88, 91-96. Bd. dirs. East Miss. Coun., Meridian, 1978-80, Trustmark Nat. Bank, Tylertown, 1986—; v.p. Macon counc. Boy Scouts Am., 1978, mem. coun., 1979; county crusade chmn. Am. Cancer Soc., Macon, 1976-78, county pres., 1979; chmn. fund drive fine arts complex Miss. State U., Macon, 1979. Recipient Youth Leadership award Miss. Econ. Coun., 1976; Walthall County family master, 1996—, Walthall County Youth referee, 1996—. Mem. ATLA, Miss. Prosecutors Assn., Miss. Assn. Board Attys. (v.p. 1985, pres. 1986), Miss. Assn. Sch. Bd. Attys., Miss. State Bar, Am. Judicature Soc. (Torts award 1972), Miss. Criminal Justice Planning Commn., Nat. Fed. Ind. Bus., Miss. State U. Alumni Assn., Macon-Noxubee County C. of C., Phi Kappa Tau (bd. govs. 1976-80, grad. coun., 1972—, pres. grad. coun. 1977-80, pres. house corp. 1977-80, Alumnus of Yr. Alpha Chi chpt. 1979), Phi Delta Phi. Republican. Methodist. Lodge: Rotary (sec. treas. 1977, v.p. 1978, pres. Macon 1979, pres. Tylertown club 1986—). Office: 816 Morse Ave Tylertown MS 39667-2130

**MORDY, JAMES CALVIN,** lawyer; b. Ashland, Kans., Jan. 3, 1927; s. Thomas Robson and Ruth (Floyd) M.; m. Marjory Ellen Nelson, Nov. 17, 1951; children: Jean Claire Mordy Jongeling, Rebecca Jane Mordy King, James Nelson. AB in Chemistry, U. Kans., 1947; JD, U. Mich., 1950; postgrad., George Washington U., 1950-51. Bar: Kans. 1950, Mo. 1950; cert. in bus. bankruptcy law Am. Bankruptcy Bd. Cert. Assoc. Morrison, Hecker, Buck, Cozad & Rogers, Kansas City, Mo., 1950-59; ptnr. Morrison & Hecker LLP, Kansas City, 1959-96, sr. counsel, 1996-97, of counsel, 1997—. Contbg. author: Missouri Bar Insurance Handbook, 1968, Missouri Bar Bankruptcy Handbook, 1991, also supplements; contbr. articles to profl. jours. Chmn. bd. Broadway United Meth. Ch., Kansas City, 1964-70, chmn. bd. trustees, chmn. fin. com., 1988-90, 94; bd. dirs., exec. com. Della C. Lamb Neighborhood House, Kansas City, 1973-80; coun. mem. St. Paul Sch. Theology, Kansas City, 1986-99; del. 17th World Meth. Conf., Rio de Janeiro, 1996. Comdr. USNR, ret. Summerfield scholar, 1943-47; recipient Shepherd of the Lamb award Della C. Lamb Neighborhood House, 1980. Fellow Am. Coll. Bankruptcy, Am. Bar Found. (life); mem. ABA, Am. Judicature Soc., Am. Bankruptcy Inst., Mo. Bar Assn., Kansas City Met. Bar Assn., Lawyers Assn. Kansas City, Workout Profs. Assn. Kansas City, Univ. Club (v.p., bd. dirs. 1983, 86), Barristers Soc., Phi Beta Kappa, Delta Tau Delta (pres. Kansas City alumni chpt. 1965-72, pres. U. Kans. House Corp. 1966-72), Alpha Chi Sigma, Phi Alpha Delta. Avocations: travel, geography (maps), history, music, theology. Bankruptcy, Contracts commercial, Public utilities. Home: 8741 Ensley Ln Leawood KS 66206-1615 Office: Morrison & Hecker LLP 2600 Grand Ave Kansas City MO 64108-4606

**MORE, JOHN HERRON,** lawyer, classicist; m. Livezey Hickenlooper, June 19, 1965; children: Anna Herron, Paul Livezey. BA, Yale U., 1964; PhD, Classical Philology, Harvard U., 1969, JD, 1979. Bar: D.C. 1979, U.S. Dist. Ct. D.C. 1979, U.S. Ct. Appeals (D.C. cir.) 1980, U.S. Ct. Appeals (4th cir.) 1998. Asst. prof. classics Brown U., Providence, 1967-74, 75-76, Centro Univ per i Studi Classici, Rome, 1974-75; assoc. Covington & Burling, Washington, 1979-84, Shaw, Pittman, Potts & Trowbridge, Washington, 1984-88; counsel Shaw, Pittman, Potts & Trowbridge, 1989-92, Wiley, Rein & Fielding, 1992-93, Winston & Strawn, 1993-96, Rogers & More, Washington, 1996—; lectr. classics Georgetown U., Washington, 1981-82. Contbr. to scholarly and profl. publs.; lectr. Bd. dirs. Cushings Island Conservation Corp., Portland, Maine, 1974—; co-chmn. Washington Interfaith Network, Inc. Mem. ABA, Am. Soc. Internat. Law. Episcopalian. Banking, Private international, Securities. Office: Rogers & More 1510 H St NW Ste 950 Washington DC 20005-1028

**MOREFIELD, RICHARD WATTS,** lawyer; b. St. Louis, Apr. 2, 1961; s. Richard Watts and Shirley Faye (Smith) M.; m. Judy Jane Oliver, Mar. 8, 1986; children: Stephen Richard, Michael Robert, Ashley Jane, Matthew David. BA, Rice U., 1983; JD, U. Kans., 1986. Bar: Mo. 1986, U.S. Dist. Ct. (we. dist.) Mo. 1986, Kans. 1987, U.S. Dist. Ct. Kans. 1987, U.S. Supreme Ct. 1993. Assoc. Morrison & Hecker, Kansas City, Mo., 1986-93; ptnr. Beamer, Slagg, McCormick & Thompson, Kansas City, 1993-96, Bottaro, McCormick & Morefield, L.C., Kansas City, Mo., 1996—. Mem. Am. Parkinson Disease Assn. (bd. dirs. Kansas City chpt., 1991-94). Mem. ABA (AOP Team, affiliate assistance com. 1991-92, exec. coun. rep. 1991-93, nat. confs. com. 1992-93, exec. coun. coord. 1993-94, chair midyr. meeting host com. 1994, parliamentarian 1993, 94, YLD assembly clk. 1995, 96, assembly spkr. 1996, 97, sect. officer 1995-97), Kans. Bar Assn., Mo. Bar Assn. (ABA-YLD rep.), Kansas City Met. Bar Assn., Lawyers Assn. Kansas City (pres. 1993-94, treas. 1992-93, bd. dirs. 1990—, chair membership com. 1993-94). Avocations: raquetball, music. Federal civil litigation, Personal injury, State civil litigation. Home: 11219 W 116th Ter Shawnee Mission KS 66210-3466 Office: Bottaro McCormick & Morefield LC 4700 Belleview Ave Ste 404 Kansas City MO 64112-1359

**MORELAND, JEFFREY R.,** lawyer. Sr. v.p. law, gen. counsel Burlington No., Santa Fe Corp., Ft. Worth. Office: Burlington No Santa Fe Corp PO Box 961039 2500 Lou Menk Dr Fort Worth TX 76131-2828

**MORELAND, MARY LOUISE,** lawyer; b. Houston, Dec. 27, 1968; d. Jon Marvin and Jane (Philp) M. BA, Washington & Lee U., 1991; JD, Tulane U., 1997. Bar: Tex. 1997. Average adjustor trainee Richards Hogg Internat., N.Y.C., 1991-93; intern Inst. Internat. Edn., Mexico City, 1994; summer assoc. Badiak Will & Maloof, N.Y.C., 1995, 96, Bell & Murphy, Houston, 1995; assoc. Bracewell & Patterson, Houston, 1997—. Editor Tulane Maritime Law Jour., 1996-97. Mem. ABA, Tex. Young Lawyers Assn., Houston Bar Assn., Phi Delta Phi. General civil litigation. Office: Bracewell & Patterson LLP 711 Louisiana St Ste 2900 Houston TX 77002-2781

**MORELL, PHILIP M.,** lawyer; b. Queens, N.Y., May 14, 1963; s. Perry M. and Florence R. Morell; m. Carol A. Fine, Apr. 30, 1989; 1 child, Meredith. BS, SUNY, Buffalo, 1985; JD, We. New Eng. Coll., Springfield, Mass., 1988. Bar: N.Y., N.J., U.S. Dist. Ct. (so. dist.) N.Y., U.S. Dist. Ct. (ea. dist.) N.Y., U.S. Dist. Ct. N.J. Assoc. Weiner & Catlett, Nanuet, N.Y., 1988-93, Levy, Phillips & Konigsberg, N.Y.C., 1993-97; ptnr. Jasne & Morell, LLP, White Plains, N.Y., 1997—; arbitrator Supreme Ct. Westchester County, White Plains, 1998—. Mem. ABA, Assn. Trial Lawyers Am. Avocation: kayaking. State civil litigation, Federal civil litigation, Personal injury. Office: Jasne and Morell LLP 2 William St Ste 300 White Plains NY 10601-1910

**MORELLI, CARMEN,** lawyer; b. Hartford, Conn., Oct. 30, 1922; s. Joseph and Helen (Carani) M.; m. Irene Edna Montminy, June 26, 1943; children: Richard A., Mark D., Carl J. BSBA, Boston U., 1949, JD, 1952. Bar: Conn. 1955, U.S. Dist. Ct. Conn. 1958. Mem. Conn. Ho. of Reps., 1959-61; rep. Capitol Regional Planning Agy., 1965-72; atty. Town of Windsor, 1961; asst. prosecutor Town of Windsor, 1957-58. Mem. Windsor Town Com., 1957-82, chmn. 1964-65, treas., 1960-64, mem. planning and zoning commn., 1965-74, mem. charter revision com., 1963-64, Rep. Presdl. Task Force. Served with USN, 1943-45. Mem. ABA, Conn. Bar Assn., Hartford Bar Assn., Windsor Bar Assn. (pres. 1979), Windsor C. of C. (v.p. 1978), Am. Arbitration Assn. Roman Catholic. Club: Elks, Rotary (sgt. arms, sec. 1989-90. pres. 1990-91). General practice, Personal injury, Probate. Home: 41 Farmstead Ln Windsor CT 06095-1834 Office: 66 Maple Ave Windsor CT 06095-2926

**MORENO, CHRISTINE MARGARET,** lawyer; b. Miami, Fla., Sept. 7, 1960; d. Arthur and Christine Moreno. BS magna cum laude, Barry U., 1981; JD cum laude, U. Miami, Coral Gables, Fla., 1984. Bar: Fla. 1984, D.C. 1985, U.S. Dist. Ct. (so. dist.) Fla. 1985, U.S. Dist. Ct. (mid. dist.) Fla. 1987, U.S. Tax Ct. 1987, U.S. Supreme Ct. 1988, U.S. Ct. Appeals (11th cir.) 1988; CPA, Fla. Law intern U.S. Securities Exch. Commn., Miami, Fla., 1984; assoc. atty. Ruden, Barnett, McCloskey, Ft. Lauderdale, Fla., 1984-85, Koppen, Watkins, Ptnrs. & Assocs., Miami, 1985-89; mayor City of North Miami, 1989-91; owner, atty., CPA Law Offices of Christine M. Moreno, North Miami, Stuart, Fla., 1989—; commr. Jensen Beach (Fla.) Cmty. Redevelopment Agy., 1994—; legal counsel to Ambassador Ray Cantillo, rep. to U.N. Miccosukee Nation, 1998—; bd. dirs. North Miami Energy Adv. Bd.; life time dir. Mayor's Econ. Task Force, North Miami, 1989—. Co-author: (book) Senior Citizens Handbook, 1990; mem. staff U. Miami Law Review, 1982-84. Bd. dirs. Nat. League of Cities, Washington, 1990-91; v.p. polit. action Miami Dade Cmty. Coll. Alumni, 1991—. Mem. AICPA, North Dade Bar Assn. (bd. dirs.), Fla. Inst. CPAs, North Miami Jaycees (Jaycee of yr. 1993), Rep. Party Dade County (com. woman 1990-94), Phi Alpha Delta Internat. Law Fraternity (Miami alumni chpt. justice 1985—). Avocation: public service. Real property, General corporate, Estate planning. Office: 13122 W Dixie Hwy North Miami FL 33161-4131

**MORENO, PATRICIA FRAZIER,** legal assistant; b. Lebanon, Pa.; d. Joseph James and Cariella Agnes (Rothermel) Frazier; m. Camille Quijada Moreno, Dec. 4, 1982; children: William David, Helen Grace, Camille Fitzcarraldo. Student, Millersville U., 1969-71, Cochise Coll., 1992-93; BA in Polit. Sci., U. Ariz., Sierra Vista, 1997; postgrad., U. Ariz., 1998—. Cert. profl. legal sec. Nat. Assn. Legal Secs., 1992; cert. legal asst. Nat. Assn. Legal Assts., 1994. Legal asst. Fred Talmadge, Esq., Sierra Vista, 1985-94; child support officer Office of the Cochise County Atty., Bisbee, Ariz., 1994-98; assoc. faculty Cochise Coll., Sierra Vista, 1996-97. Mem. Salvation Army Adv. Bd., Sierra Vista, 1988-92, City of Sierra Vista Human Rels. Commn., 1982-83. Named Sec. of the Yr., S.E. Ariz. Legal Secs. Assn., Cochise County, Ariz., 1993. Mem. Borderline Mensa (officer 1987-93, scholar 1992), Phi Kappa Phi. Democrat. Avocations: electronic research on the World Wide Web, family activities.

**MORENO, RICHARD DALE,** lawyer; b. Lake Charles, La., Feb. 1, 1951; s. Fred Mercica and Elsie Mae (Savant) M.; m. Mary Mellanie Denton, Aug. 11, 1972; 1 child, Victoria. BSEE, La. Tech. U., 1972; JD, La. State U., 1991. Bar: La. 1991, U.S. Dist. Ct. La. 1991, U.S. Ct. Appeals (5th cir.) 1991. Engr. Hughes Aircraft Co., Canoga Park, Calif., 1974-78, Standard Sys., Inc., Sulphur, La., 1978-88; law clk. Alvin J. Rubin, Cir. Judge U.S. Ct. Appeals, 5th Cir., Baton Rouge, 1991; law clk. Henry A. Politz, Chief Judge U.S. Ct. Appeals, 5th Cir., Shreveport, 1991-92; assoc. Kantrow, Spaht, Weaver and Blitzer, Baton Rouge, 1992—; mem. lease law rev. com. La. Law Inst., Baton Rouge, 1991—. Contbr. articles to profl. jours.; editor/revisor: Louisiana Landlord and Tenant Law, 1993-95. Mem. ABA, La. State Bar Assn. General practice, Construction, Landlord-tenant. Office: Kantrow Spaht Weaver & Blitzer PO Box 2997 (70821) 445 North Blvd Ste 300 Baton Rouge LA 70802-5747

**MORETTI, JAY DONALD,** lawyer; b. Waukesha, Wis., May 20, 1947; s. Orest and Jeanne A. (Charlevoix) M.; m. Joann Senn, Nov. 8, 1975; children: Angela, Rocco, Luciano. BA in History, U. Wis., 1969, JD, 1971. Bar: Wis. 1972, U.S. Dist. Ct. (we. dist.) Wis. 1972, U.S. Dist. Ct. (ea. dist.) Wis. 1973. Atty. Reigel Law Office, Madison, Wis., 1971-72; pvt. practice Madison, 1973-76, Cross Plains, Wis., 1975—. Supr. Dane County, Madison, 1990-96, chmn. pub.protection and judiciary com., chmn. planning structure com., vice chmn. ways and means com., mem. EXPO expansion com.; mem. Bd. Health; mem. exec. bd. Dane County Rep. Com., 1988-90; mem. Wis. Citizens com. AODA, 1987-91. Recipient William Campbell award Wis. Rep. Com., 1989, svc. award, 1991; community svc. award Cross Plains Jaycees, 1980. Mem. State Bar Wis., Dane County Bar Assn., Cross Plains Bus. Assn. (pres. 1979,99, v.p.), Am. Legion, Italian Workmen's Club (pres. 1976), Lions (pres. Cross Plains 1985, dist. parliamentarian 1986—, zone chmn. 1988-91). Roman Catholic. Avocations: canoeing, gardening. Real property, Estate planning, Family and matrimonial. Office: 2305 Main St Cross Plains WI 53528-9529

**MORGAN, CHARLES RUSSELL,** lawyer; b. New Orleans, Oct. 15, 1946; s. Charles and Marian E. (Wetzel) M.; children: Charles Bradford, William Russell, Elizabeth Anne. BA, U. N.C., 1968; JD, Columbia U., 1971. Bar: N.Y. 1973, Ill. 1981, Ohio 1994. Law clk. to cir. judge U.S. Ct. Appeals (D.C. cir.), Washington, 1971-72; atty. Davis Polk & Wardwell, N.Y.C., 1972-80; sr. staff counsel Household Internat., Inc., Prospect Heights, Ill., 1980-83; v.p., asst. gen. counsel Kraft, Inc., Glenview, Ill., 1983-85; v.p., sr. corp. counsel Kraft, Inc., Glenview, 1985-88; v.p., gen. counsel, sec. Chiquita Brands Internat., Cin., 1988-95; ptnr. Mayer Brown & Platt, Chgo., 1995-98; exec. v.p., gen. counsel BellSouth Corp., Atlanta, 1998—; v.p., sec., dir. John Morrell & Co., Inc. Contbg. editor The Corp. Counselor, 1986—, The Environmental Corporate Counsel Report. Mem. ABA (chmn. corp. counsel com. 1983-86, chmn. comm. com. 1986—), Am. Law Inst., Am. Corp. Counsel Assn. (bd. dirs.), Am. Arbitration Assn. (bd. dirs.), Legal Club Chgo., Army-Navy Club of Washington. General corporate, Securities, Mergers and acquisitions. Office: BellSouth Corp 1155 Peachtree St NE Atlanta GA 30309-3610*

**MORGAN, COLBY SHANNON, JR.,** lawyer; b. Marshalltown, Iowa, Mar. 29, 1949; s. Colby and Elizabeth Perkinson (Robertson) M.; m. Leslie Marmon, Apr. 5, 1975; children: Colby Shannon III, Jeffrey Michael, Sarah Elizabeth. AB cum laude, Dartmouth Coll., 1971; JD, Vanderbilt U., 1974. Bar: N.Y. 1975, Tenn. 1977, U.S. Dist. Ct. (so and ea. dists.) N.Y. 1976, U.S. Dist. Ct. (we. dist.) Tenn. 1978, U.S. Dist. Ct. (ea. and we. dists.) Ark. 1983, U.S. Dist. Ct. (no. dist.) Calif. 1994, (no. dist.) N.Y. 1998, U.S. Ct. Appeals (6th cir.) 1980, U.S. Ct. Appeals (8th cir.) 1987, U.S. Ct. Appeals (3d cir.) 1995, U.S. Ct. Appeals (9th cir.) 1996, U.S. Ct. Appeals (4th cir.) 1996, U.S. Supreme Ct. 1998. Assoc. Crowe, McCoy, Agoglia & Zweibel, Mineola, N.Y., 1974-78, Rosenfield, Borod & Kremer, Memphis, 1978-83, Apperson, Crump, Duzane & Maxwell, Memphis, 1983-86, Shuttleworth, Smith, Young & Webb, Memphis, 1986; sr. atty. Holiday Inns, Inc., Memphis, 1986-91; assoc. Petkoff & Lancaster, Memphis, 1991-92; sr. litig. atty. Fed. Express Corp., Memphis, 1992—. Chancellor, bd. dirs. Memphis Boys Town, 1979-86; chmn. Memphis Civil Svc. Commn., 1980-83; bd. dirs., chmn. bd. dirs. Memphis Emmaus Cmty., 1983—; bd. dirs. Christ Meth. Adminstrv. Bd., Memphis, 1984-86; former mem. Leadership Memphis, 1984—; cubmaster Pack 241 Boy Scouts Am., Memphis, 1992-93; treas., bd. dirs. Memphis Symphony Chorus, 1981-85. Mem. ABA, Dartmouth Lawyers Assn., Order of the First Families of Tenn., Gen. Soc. Colonial Wars, N.Y. Sons of the Revolution, Mil. Order of the Stars and Bars (lt. comdr. 1994—), Tenn. Geneaol. Soc., Clan Donnachaidh Soc., Mensa, SAR (chancellor, past pres. Memphis chpt. 1992—; chancellor, bd. govs. Tenn. chpt. 1994—), Scottish Rite. Republican. Methodist. Avocations: genealogy, marathon runner, tennis, golf, reading. General civil litigation, General corporate, Environmental. Home: 5521 Fiesta Dr Memphis TN 38120-2826 Office: Fed Express Corp 1980 Nonconnah Blvd Memphis TN 38132-2103

**MORGAN, DENNIS RICHARD,** lawyer; b. Lexington, Va., Jan. 3, 1942; s. Benjamin Richard and Gladys Belle (Brown) M. BA, Washington and Lee U., 1964; JD, U. Va., 1967; LLM in Labor Law, NYU, 1971. Bar: Ohio

1967, Va. 1967, U.S. Ct. Appeals (4th cir.) 1968, U.S. Ct. Appeals (6th cir.) 1971, U.S. Supreme Ct. 1972. Law clk. to chief judge U.S. Dist. Ct. Ea. Dist. Va., 1967-68; mem. Marshman, Snyder & Seeley, Cleve., 1971-72; dir. labor rels. Ohio Dept. Adminstrv. Svcs., 1972-75; asst. city atty. Columbus, Ohio, 1975-77; dir. Ohio Legis. Reference Bur., 1979-81; assoc. Clemans, Nelson & Assocs., Columbus, 1981; pvt. practice, Columbus, 1978-92; lectr. in field; guest lectr. Cen. Mich. U., 1975; judge moot ct. Ohio State U. Sch. Law, 1981, 83, grad. div., 1973, 74, 76, Baldwin-Wallace Coll., 1973; legal counsel Dist. IV Communications Workers Am., 1982-88; pers. dir. Pub. Utilities Commn. Ohio, 1989-91; asst. atty gen. State of Ohio, 1991—. Vice-chmn. Franklin County Dem. Party, 1976-82, dem. com. person Ward 58, Columbus, 1973-95; chmn. rules com. Ohio State Dem. Conv., 1974; co-founder, trustee Greater West Side Dem. Club; negotiator Franklin County United Way, 1977-81; regional chmn. ann. alumni fund-raising program U. Va. Sch. Law; commr. Greater Hilltop Area Commn., 1989—; pres. Woodbrook Village Condominium Assn., 1985—; bd. dirs. Hilltop Civic Coun., Inc., 1997-99; trustee Hilltop Civic Coun., Inc., 1997-99. Robert E. Lee Rsch. scholar, summer, 1965; recipient Am. Jurisprudence award, 1967. Capt. U.S. Army, 1968-70. Mem. Indsl. Rels. Rsch. Assn., ABA, Fed. Bar Assn., Am. Judicature Soc., Pi Sigma Alpha. Roman Catholic. Clubs: Columbus Metroplitan (charter). Labor, Administrative and regulatory, Legislative. Home: 1261 Woodbrook Ln # G Columbus OH 43223-3243

**MORGAN, DONALD CRANE,** lawyer; b. Detroit, Sept. 17, 1940; s. Donald Nye and Nancy (Crane) M.; m. Judith Munro, June 23, 1962; children: Wendy, Donald. BA, Ohio Wesleyan U., 1962; JD, U. Mich., 1965. Bar: Mich. 1966, U.S. Dist. Ct. (ea. dist.) Mich. 1966, U.S. Ct. Appeals (6th cir.) 1967, U.S. Supreme Ct. 1971. Ptnr. Kerr, Russell and Weber, Detroit, 1965-87; of counsel Draugelis & Ashton, Plymouth, Mich., 1988-93; pvt. practice Plymouth, Mich., 1993—; twp. atty. Plymouth Twp., 1970-85, Northville Twp., 1972-85; city atty. City of Plymouth, 1995-98; mediator Wayne County Mediation Tribunal, Detroit, 1981—, Oakland County Mediation Tribunal, Pontiac, Mich., 1992—; hearing panelist Mich. Atty. Discipline Bd., 1981—. Chmn. Wayne County II congl. Dist. Rep. Party, 1979-81; bd. dirs. Growth Works, Inc., treas., 1992-95, pres. 1995—; ruling elder 1st Presbyn. Ch., Plymouth, 1976-79, 90-93; local bd. 222 mem. U.S. Selective Svc. Sys.; mem. spl. grants and agy. admissions com. United Way Cmty. Svcs. Paul Harris fellow, 1980. Mem. ABA, Mich. Def. Trial Counsel, State Bar of Mich. (rep. assembly 1979-85, 89-95, chmn. medicolegal problems com. 1995-96), Detroit Assn. Def. Trial Counsel, Plymouth Rotary (pres. 1985-86), Plymouth Rotary Found., Inc. (sec. 1996-98, dir. 1995, 99—), Phi Alpha Delta, Sigma Alpha Epsilon. Republican. Presbyterian. Avocations: reading, travel, sports. General civil litigation, General corporate, Real property. Home: 1440 Woodland Pl Plymouth MI 48170-1569 Office: 134 N Main St Plymouth MI 48170-1236

**MORGAN, GLENN L.,** lawyer, photography; b. New Orleans, Dec. 1943; m. S.E. and S.T. Morgan. BA, U. Southwestern La., 1965; JD, Loyola U., 1972. Bar: La. 1972, U.S. Dist. Ct. (all dists.) La. 1972, U.S. Ct. Appeals (5th cir.) 1972, U.S. Supreme Ct. 1975, U.S. Ct. Appeals (fed. cir.) 1982, U.S. Claims Ct. 1982, U.S. Internat. Trade Ct. 1982, U.S. Mil. Appeals Ct. 1986. Mem. An Am. Inn of Ct. (charter master). Republican. Fax: 318-332-0584. E-mail: glmorgan@lawyer4u.com. Appellate, General civil litigation, Criminal. Home: PO Box 354 Breaux Bridge LA 70517-0354 Office: PO Box 5006 Lafayette LA 70502-5006

**MORGAN, HENRY COKE, JR.,** judge; b. Norfolk, Va., Feb. 8, 1935; s. Henry Coke and Dorothy Lea (Pebworth) M.; m. Margaret John McGrail, Aug. 18, 1965; 1 stepchild, A. Robertson Hanckel Jr.; children: Catherine Morgan Stockwell, Coke Morgan Stewart. BS, Washington and Lee U., 1957, JD, 1960; LLM in Jud. Process, U. Va., 1998. Bar: Va. 1960, U.S. Dist. Ct. (ea. dist.) Va. 1961, U.S. Ct. Appeals (4th cir.) 1964. Asst. city atty. City of Norfolk, 1960-63; ptnr., CEO Pender & Coward, Virginia Beach, Va., 1963-92; vice chmn., gen. counsel Princess Anne Bank, 1986-92; judge U.S. Dist. Ct. (ea. dist.) Va., 1992—. Served with U.S. Army, 1958-59. Episcopalian. Office: US Dist Ct Eastern Dist Va Walter E Hoffman US Courthouse 600 Granby St Ste 183 Norfolk VA 23510-1915

**MORGAN, JAMES EDWARD,** lawyer; b. Toledo, Ohio, July 23, 1951; s. Charles E. and Betty C. (Yonker) M.; m. Mary E. McLaughlin, Sept. 30, 1977 (div. 1991); children: Craig W., Rebecca A. BA, Univ. Toledo, 1973, JD, 1976. Bar: Ohio 1976, Fla. 1978, U.S. Dist. Ct (no. dist.) Ohio 1976. Asst. pub. defender Toledo Legal Aid Soc., Toledo, 1977-87; judge advocate Ohio Army Nat. Guard, 1979—; ptnr. Shindler, Neff, Holmes & Schlageter, Toledo, 1987—; magistrate Toledo Mcpl. Ct., Toledo, 1997; pers. fin. analyst Primerica Fin. Svcs., Holland, Ohio, 1996—; instr. PFS Univ., Holland, 1996—. Vol. atty. Lutheran Social Svcs., Toledo, 1986—. Recipient Outstanding Vol. award Luth. Social Svcs., 1992-96. Mem. Ohio Acad. of Trial Lawyers, Fla. Bar Assn., Ohio State Bar Assn., Toledo Bar Assn. (chmn. mcpl. 1998—), Masonic Lodge & Scottish Rite. Presbyterian. Probate, Criminal, State civil litigation. Office: Shindler Neff Holmes Schlageter 300 Madison Ave Ste 1200 Toledo OH 43604

**MORGAN, JAMES EVAN,** lawyer; b. Poughkeepsie, N.Y., Nov. 8, 1959; s. Evan and Johnnie Lu Morgan; m. Catherine Barr Altman, Sept. 21, 1991. BA, Lynchburg Coll., 1984; JD, N.Y. Law Sch., 1989. Bar: N.Y. 1993. Talk show host Sta. WLGM-AM Radio, Lynchburg, Va., 1982-86; legal editor Matthew Bender & Co., Inc., N.Y.C., 1989-91; ptnr. Morgan Cons., Chgo., 1992—; sr. investigator Chgo. Bd. Options Exch., 1993-97; mgr. internat. and instl. mktg. Chgo. Bd. Options Exch., 1997-98. Editor: Bender's Federal Tax Service, 1989-91, Modern Estate Planning, 1989-91; pub., editor: Minerva, 1990. Mem. ABA (bus. law sect., com. on fed. regulation of securities, market regulation subcom. 1994—), Coun. on Fgn. Rels. Avocations: playing violin and viola, composing music. Securities, Administrative and regulatory, Constitutional.

**MORGAN, JO VALENTINE, JR.,** lawyer; b. Washington, June 26, 1920; s. Jo. V. and Elizabeth Parker (Crenshaw) M.; m. Norma Jean Lawrence, May 22, 1943; children: Carol Jo, Jo Lawrence, Susan Leigh. AB magna cum laude, Princeton U., 1942; LLB, Yale U., 1947. Bar: D.C., 1948, Md., 1948. Ptnr. Whiteford, Hart, Carmody & Wilson, Washington, 1948-85, ptnr., 1953-76, sr. ptnr., 1976-85; mem., dir. Jackson & Campbell, P.C., 1985-95, ret., 1995. Chmn. Bethesda USO, 1949-52; pres. Sumner Citizens Assn., 1958-61; pres. Westmoreland Citizens Assn., 1956-57. Bd. dirs., gen. counsel Internat. Soc. Protection Animals; gen. counsel Fedn. Am. Socs. Experimental Biology; pres., bd. dirs. Montgomery County Humane Soc. 2d lt. to capt., AUS, 1942-45, ETO. Decorated D.F.C., Purple Heart, Air medals (AAC). Fellow Am. Coll. Trial Lawyers; mem. ABA, Bar Assn. D.C. (bd. dirs. 1958-60, 73-75), D.C. Lawyers Club, Order of Coif, Phi Beta Kappa, Chevy Chase Club, Met. Club, Princeton Club, The Barristers Club, Wesley Heights Community Club (pres. 1964-67). Republican. Episcopalian. General practice, Probate, Real property. Home: 5120 Westpath Way Bethesda MD 20816-2318

**MORGAN, JOHN JOSEPH, JR.,** lawyer; b. Newark, Sept. 6, 1934; s. John Joseph Sr. and Aldine (Frame) M.; children: Christopher, Mariah. BS, Villanova (Pa.) U., 1956; JD, Duquesne U., 1971. Bar: Pa. 1971, U.S. Dist. Ct. (we. dist.) Pa. 1971, U.S. Supreme Ct. 1976. Assoc. Evans, Ivory & Evans, Pitts., 1971-79; prin. John J. Morgan, Pitts., 1980—. Mem. coun. Peters Twp., McMurray, Pa.; pres. Western Pa. chpt. Leukemia Soc. of Am. Lt. col. USAF. Mem. Pa. Bar Assn., Allegheny County Bar Assn., Nat. Acad. Arbitrators. Avocations: flying, tennis, skiing, scuba diving. General practice, General civil litigation. Home: 1034 5th Ave # 300 Pittsburgh PA 15219-6202 Office: 1034 5th Ave Ste 300 Pittsburgh PA 15219-6202

**MORGAN, KERMIT JOHNSON,** lawyer; b. Henderson, Iowa, Feb. 13, 1914; s. Samuel Jr. and Jennie Amelia Morgan; m. Georgina R. Morgan, Oct. 12, 1940 (dec. 1958); children: Georgina Morgan Street, Wilson S.; m. Ortrud Impol, Dec. 9, 1960. BA, U. Iowa, 1935; JD, U. So. Calif., 1937. Bar: Calif. 1939. Pvt. practice, L.A., 1940-45, 71-80; ptnr. McBain & Morgan, L.A., 1945-65, McBain, Morgan & Roper, L.A., 1965-71, Morgan & Armbrister, L.A., 1980-91; pvt. practice, Santa Monica, Calif., 1991—. Mem. ABA, Am. Bd. Trial Advs. (diplomate, nat. pres. 1973, pres. L.A. 1972, 77), Assn. Def. Trial Attys. (bd. dirs. 1982-85), Internat. Assn. Ins. Counsel, Calif. State Bar, Assn. So.Calif. Def. Counsel (bd. dirs. 1966-67), L.A. Bar Assn., Wilshire Bar Assn. Republican. Congregationalist. Avocation: golf. Insurance, Personal injury. Home: 2108 Stradella Rd Los Angeles CA 90077-2325 Office: 2850 Ocean Park Bld Santa Monica CA 90405

**MORGAN, MARY ANN,** lawyer; b. Orlando, Fla., Mar. 12, 1955; d. Charles Clayburn and Eileen Louise (Mutzbauer) M.; m. Patrick Thomas Burke, Dec. 12, 1992. BS in Criminology, Fla. State U., 1978, JD, 1986. Bar: Fla. 1986, U.S. Dist. Ct. (mid. dist.) Fla. 1986. Investigator Auditor Gen.'s Office State of Fla., Orlando, 1979-83; staff analyst criminal justice com. Fla. Ho. of Reps., Tallahassee, 1985-86; ptnr. Billings, Cunningham, Morgan & Boatwright, Orlando, 1986—. Chmn. renovation com. Orange County Hist. Mus., Orlando, 1995—; spkr. Physician/Lawyer Drug Awareness Program, Orange County Schs., Orlando, 1997. Mem. ABA, ATLA, Fla. Bar Assn. (speaker's bur. 1997, chairperson grievance com. 1993-96), Orange County Bar Assn. (exec. coun. 1991—, chmn. renovation com. 1995—, del. ABA 1989, 90, pres. young lawyers sect. 1990-91), Acad. Fla. Trial Lawyers, Ctrl. Fla. Assn. for Women Lawyers (bd. dirs. 1990-92), Fla. State U. Alumni Assn. (bd. dirs. 1996—), Orange County Legal Aid Soc. (bd. dirs. 1997—, pres.-elect 1998-99, pres. 1999—), Nat. Assn. Women Lawyers, Am. Inns of Ct., Tiger Bay Club. Avocations: waterskiing, golf, boating. General civil litigation, Personal injury. Office: Billings Cunningham Morgan & Boatwright 330 E Central Blvd Orlando FL 32801-1921

**MORGAN, MICHAEL VINCENT,** lawyer; b. Detroit, July 31, 1947; s. Stanley William and Alice (Michalski) M.; m. Susan Wanda Staub, Aug. 21, 1970; children—Jason, Allison. B.A., U. Detroit, 1969, J.D., 1972. Bar: Mich. 1972, U.S. Dist. Ct. (ea. dist.) Mich., 1972. Chmn. Lic. Appeal Bd. Mich. Dept. State, Detroit, 1972-73; sole practice, Detroit, 1973-75, Troy, Mich., 1975—; lectr. in field. Editor: Michigan Drunk Driving Law & Practice, 1986; contbr. articles to profl. publs. Bd. dirs. U. Detroit Nat. Alumni Bd., 1974-77. Recipient Athletic Dirs. award U. Detroit, 1983. Mem. Mich. Bar Assn., U. Detroit Law Alumni Assn. (bd. dirs. 1996—), Titan Club (bd. dirs. 1982-86), Advocates Club (Detroit). Roman Catholic. Criminal. Office: 3155 W Big Beaver Rd Ste 100 Troy MI 48084-3006

**MORGAN, RICHARD GEORGE,** lawyer; b. Suffern, N.Y., Oct. 23, 1958; s. George H. and Margaret W. Morgan; m. Stacy V. Orr, Aug. 9, 1980; children: Nicholas, Philip, Gregory. BA, Cornell U., 1980; MA, U. Minn., 1984, JD, 1984. Bar: Minn. 1984, U.S. Dist. Ct. Minn. 1984, U.S. Ct. Appeals (8th cir.) 1989. Assoc. Fredrikson & Byron, P.A., Mpls., 1988-90; asst. U.S. atty. U.S. Attys. Office, Mpls., 1990-95; ptnr. Bowman and Brooke, LLP, Mpls., 1995—; adj. prof. U. Minn. Law Sch., Mpls., 1991-95. Bd. mem. Humphrey Inst. Adv. Bd., Mpls., 1995—. Capt. U.S. Army, 1984-88. Product liability, General civil litigation, Environmental. Office: Bowman and Brooke LLP 150 S 5th St Ste 2600 Minneapolis MN 55402-4244

**MORGAN, RICHARD GREER,** lawyer; b. Houston, Dec. 23, 1943; s. John Benjamin (stepfather) and Audrey Valley (Brickwede) Haus; children: Richard Greer, Jonathan Roberts. AB in History, Princeton U., 1966; JD, U. Tex., 1969. Bar: Tex. 1969, D.C. 1970, Minn. 1976, U.S. Ct. Appeals (D.C. cir.) 1970, U.S. Ct. Appeals (5th and 9th cirs., temporary emergency ct. appeals) 1976. Atty., advisor to commr. Lawrence J. O'Connor, Jr. Fed. Power Commn., Washington, 1969-71; assoc. Morgan, Lewis & Bockius, Washington, 1971-75; ptnr. O'Connor & Hannan, Washington, 1975-89, Lane & Mittendorf, Washington, 1989-97; mng. ptnr. Shook, Hardy & Bacon, L.L.P., Houston, 1997—; bd. dirs. Hexagon, Inc.; instr. law seminars; lectr. in field. Author: Gas Lease and Royalty Issues, Natural Gas Yearbook, 1989, 90, 91, 92; contbr. articles on energy law to profl. jours. Bd. dirs. Mighty Spl. Music Makers, U. Tex. Law Sch. Found. Mem. ABA, Fed. Bar Assn., Fed. Energy Bar Assn. (bd. dirs.), D.C. Bar Assn., Princeton Alumni Coun., Princeton Club Washington (exec. com., pres.), Energy Law Found. (bd. dirs.). FERC practice, Oil, gas, and mineral, Public utilities. Office: Shook Hardy and Bacon LLP 600 Travis St Houston TX 77002-3002

**MORGAN, RICHARD J.,** dean, educator. JD, UCLA, 1971. Bar: Calif. Assoc., ptnr. Krueger & Marsh, L.A., 1972-80; dean, prof. U. Wyo. Coll. Law, 1987-89; assoc. dean Ariz. State U. Coll. Law, Tempe, 1983-87, dean, prof., 1990-97; dean, prof. William S. Boyd Sch. Law U. Nev., Las Vegas, 1997—. Office: U Nev-Las Vegas William S Boyd Sch Law 4505 Maryland Pkwy Las Vegas NV 89154-1004*

**MORGAN, TIMI SUE,** lawyer; b. Parsons, Kans., June 16, 1953; d. James Daniel and Iris Mae (Wilson) Baumgardner; m. Rex Michael Morgan, Oct. 28, 1983; children: Tessa Anne, Camma Elizabeth. BS, U. Kans., 1974; JD, So. Meth. U., 1977. Bar: Tex. 1977, U.S. Dist. Ct. (no. dist.) Tex. 1978, U.S. Ct. Appeals (5th cir.) 1979, U.S. Tax Ct. 1980; cert. tax law specialist. Assoc. Gardere & Wynne, Dallas, 1977-79; assoc. Akin, Gump, Strauss, Hauer & Feld, Dallas, 1979-83, ptnr., 1984-86; of counsel Stinson, Mag & Fizzell, Dallas, 1986-88; sole practice Dallas, 1988—; adj. lectr. law So. Meth. U., 1989-90, 92-98. Bd. dirs. Dallas Urban League Inc., 1987-91. Mem. State Bar Tex. (mem. taxation sect.), Dallas Bar Assn., So. Meth. U. Law Alumni Coun. (sec. 1985-86), Order of Coif, Beta Gamma Sigma. Republican. Episcopalian. Taxation, general, Personal income taxation, State and local taxation.

**MORGANROTH, FRED,** lawyer; b. Detroit, Mar. 26, 1938; s. Ben and Grace (Greenfield) M.; m. Janice Marilyn Cohn, June 23, 1963; children: Greg, Candi, Erik. BA, Wayne State U., 1959, JD with distinction, 1961. Bar: Mich. 1961, U.S. Dist. Ct. (ea. dist.) Mich. 1961, U.S. Ct. Claims 1967, U.S. Supreme Ct. 1966; trained matrimonial arbitrator. Ptnr. Greenbaum, Greenbaum & Morganroth, Detroit, 1963-68, Lebenbom, Handler, Brody & Morganroth, Detroit, 1968-70, Lebenbom, Morganroth & Stern, Southfield, Mich., 1971-78; pvt. practice, Southfield, 1979-83; ptnr. Morganroth & Morganroth P.C., Southfield, 1983-94, Morganroth, Morganroth, Alexander & Nye, P.C., Birmingham, Mich., 1994-98, Morganroth, Morganroth, Jackman & Kasody, PC, Birmingham, 1999—. Mem. ABA (family law sect. 1987—), Mich. Bar Assn. (hearing panelist grievance bd. 1975—, Oakland County family law com. 1988—, vice chmn. 1992-93, chair 1993—), State Bar Mich. (mem. family law coun. of family law sect. 1990—, treas. 1993-94, chmn.-elect 1994-95, chmn. 1995-96), Detroit Bar Assn., Oakland Bar Assn. (cir. ct. mediator 1984—), Am. Arbitration Assn. (Oakland County family law com. 1985—, vice chmn. 1992-93, chmn. 1993-94, trained matrimonial arbitrator), Detroit Tennis Club (Farmington, Mich., pres. 1978-82), Charlevoix Country Club. Jewish. Avocations: comml. pilot, golfing. Alternative dispute resolution, Family and matrimonial. Home: 30920 Woodcrest Ct Franklin MI 48025-1435 Office: 300 Park St Ste 410 Birmingham MI 48009-3482

**MORGANROTH, MAYER,** lawyer; b. Detroit, Mar. 20, 1931; s. Maurice Jack Morganroth and Sophie (Reisman) Blum; m. Sheila Rubinstein, Aug. 16, 1958; children: Lauri, Jeffrey, Cherie. JD, Detroit Coll. Law, 1954. Bar: Mich. 1955, U.S. Dist. Ct. Mich. 1955, Ohio 1958, U.S. Dist. Ct. (no. dist.) Ohio 1958, U.S. Ct. Appeals (6th cir.) 1968, U.S. Supreme Ct. 1971, N.Y. 1983, U.S. Dist. Ct. N.Y. 1985, U.S. Tax Ct. 1985, U.S. Ct. Appeals (4th cir.) 1985, U.S. Ct. Claims 1986, U.S. Ct. Appeals (2d cir.) 1986, U.S. Ct. Appeals (fed. cir.), U.S. Ct. Appeals (8th cir.) 1994. Sole practice Detroit, 1955—, N.Y.C., 1983—; ptnr. Morganroth & Morganroth, 1989—; cons. to lending instns.; lectr. on real estate NYU, 1980—, bus. entities and structures Wayne State U., 1981—; trial atty. in fed. and state jurisdictions, nationwide. Served with USN, 1948-50. Mem. ABA, FBA, N.Y. State Bar Assn., Southfield Bar Assn., Oakland Bar Assn., Assn. Trial Lawyers Am., Assn. Trial Lawyers Mich., Am. Judicature Soc., U.S. Supreme Ct. Hist. Soc., Nat. Criminal Def. Assn., West Bloomfield (Mich.) Club, Fairlane Club (Dearborn, Mich.), Knollwood Country Club, Edgewood Athletic Club (pres. 1963-65). Democrat. Jewish. Federal civil litigation, General civil litigation, Criminal. Office: 3000 Town Ctr Ste 1500 Southfield MI 48075-1186 also: 156 W 56th St Ste 1101 New York NY 10019-3800

**MORGANSTERN, GERALD H.,** lawyer, mayor; b. N.Y.C., Dec. 19, 1942; s. Jack and Mildred M.; m. Karen Gibbs, Apr. 28, 1968; children: Jeffrey, Bradley. BS in Econs., U. Pa., 1963; LLB, Columbia U., 1966. Bar: N.Y. 1967, U.S. Dist. Ct. (ea. dist.) N.Y. 1967. Atty. Hofheimer Gartlin & Gross LLP, N.Y.C., 1967—. Mayor Village Hewlett Harbor (N.Y.), 1990—, trustee, 1982-90. General practice, Real property, Non-profit and tax-exempt organizations. Home: 207 Richards Ln Hewlett Harbor NY 11557-2629 Office: Hofheimer Gartlir & Gross LLP 530 5th Ave New York NY 10036-5101

**MORGANSTERN, MYRNA DOROTHY,** lawyer; b. Chgo., June 12, 1946; d. Harry and Sarah (Fisher) Selwyn; m. Russell Jay Frackman, Aug. 3, 1980; children: Steven, Abigail. BA in English, U. Nev., 1967; MA in English, U. Calif., 1969; JD, U. Minn., 1975. Bar: Calif. 1976, U. S. Dist. Ct. (cen. dist.) Calif. 1977. Writer, researcher Calif. Cancer Control Project, L.A., 1975-77; deputy atty. gen. Atty. Gen. Calif., L.A., 1977-80; assoc. Gang, Tyre & Brown, L.A., 1980-81, Finley, Kumble, Wagner, Heine, Underberg & Manley, L.A., 1981-82; atty. U.S. Securities & Exch. Commn., L.A., 1984-88; atty., aide Mayor Larry Agran, Irvine, Calif., 1989-90; counsel George McGovern Exploratory Com., Irvine, Calif., 1991; chief counsel Agran for Pres. '92, Irvine, Calif., 1991-92; trial atty. U.S. Commodity Futures Trading Commn., 1996—; commr. L.A. County Rent Adjustment Commn., 1984-85; com. mem. Sci. Adv. Com., Irvine, 1989-91. Co-author: Cancer Control in the United States, 1977. Mem. ACLU, NAACP, Amnesty Internat. Avocations: travel, book collecting, piano, theatre, movies. Securities, Federal civil litigation, Election. Office: US Commodity Futures Trading Commn 10900 Wilshire Blvd Ste 400 Los Angeles CA 90024-6525

**MORGAN-WHITE, STEPHANIE LYNN,** lawyer; b. Elizabethtown, Ky., Sept. 3, 1970; d. James Carroll and Evelyn Jeanette Morgan. BA cum laude, Wittenberg U., 1992; JD, Samford U., 1995. Bar: Ky. 1995, Ala. 1996, U.S. Dist. Ct. (mid. dist.) Ala. 1996, U.S. Dist. Ct. (we. dist.) Ky. 1997, U.S. Dist. Ct. (ea. dist.) Ky. 1998, U.S. Ct. Appeals (6th cir.) 1998. Staff atty. Ky. Ct. Appeals, Bowling Green, 1995-97; assoc. Goldberg & Simpson, Louisville, 1997—. Mem. Jr. League Louisville, Alpha Delta Pi. Avocation: scuba diving. Family and matrimonial, Appellate. Office: Goldberg & Simpson 3000 National City Tower Louisville KY 40202

**MORGENS, WARREN KENDALL,** lawyer; b. Oklahoma City, May 25, 1940; s. Alvin Gustav and Helen Alene (McFarland) M. Student, Westminster Coll., Fulton, Mo., 1958-60; BSBA, Washington U., St. Louis, 1962, JD, 1964. Bar: Mo., 1964, U.S. Supreme Ct. 1968, D.C., 1981. Atty. gen. counsel's office SEC, Washington, 1968-69; asst. atty. gen. State of Mo., St. Louis, 1969-72; ptnr. Park, Craft & Morgens, Kansas City, Mo., 1973-76; pvt. practice law Kansas City, 1976-81; mng. atty. Hoskins. King, McGannon & Hahn, Washington, 1981-85; spl. ptnr. Barnett & Alagia, Washington, 1985-89; of counsel Anderson, Hibey, Nauheim & Blair, Washington, 1989-93; pvt. practice Washington, 1993—; bd. dirs. George Washington Nat. Bank, Alexandria, Va., Cmty. Nat. Bank & Trust, Staten Island, N.Y., 1986-87, George Washington Banking Corp., George Washington Fin. Corp., Washington and France. Patron Nat. Symphony, Washington, 1966-68, 81-85, Washington Performing Arts Soc., 1989—, Kansas City Philharmonic, 1974-80, Supreme Ct. Hist. Soc., Washington, 1982—, The Williamsburg (Va.) Found., 1982—. Named one of Outstanding Young Men Am., 1977. Mem. Mo. Bar Assn., D.C. Bar Assn., Univ. Club (St. Louis). Republican. Presbyterian. Avocations: hiking, sailing, fishing, golf. General corporate, Private international, Securities. Office: 1805 Crystal Dr Apt 201 Arlington VA 22202-4402

**MORGENSTERN, DENNIS MICHAEL,** lawyer; b. Sharon, Pa., Nov. 5, 1951; s. Albert Willard and Margaret Agnes Morgenstern. BS, U.S. Mil. Acad., 1973; JD, U. Pitts., 1982. Bar: Pa. 1982, Fla. 1993. Assoc. Rose, Schmidt, Dixon & Hasley, Pitts., 1982-84; litigation counsel Joy Mfg. Co., Pitts., 1984-87; assoc. Evans, Ivory P.C., Pitts., 1987-91, shareholder, 1991-98, of counsel, 1998—; trial atty. Law Offices of Peter J. Brudny, P.A., Tampa, Fla., 1998—; mem. adv. bd. Indsl. Automation & Control, Inc., Freeport, Pa., 1997—. Maj. U.S. Army and USAR, 1973-95. Decorated Meritorious Svc. medal. Republican. Lutheran. Avocations: scuba, travel. Personal injury, Product liability, Professional liability. Office: Law Offices of Peter J Brudny 813 W Kennedy Blvd Tampa FL 33606-1418

**MORGENTHALER, ALISA MARIE,** lawyer; b. St. Louis, June 3, 1960; d. Gerald Thomas and Mary Louise (Neece) M. BA, S.W. Mo. State U., 1982; JD, Cornell U., 1985. Bar: N.Y. 1986, D.C. 1988, Calif. 1990. Law clk. City of Springfield, Mo., 1981; bd. govs. FRS, Washington, 1984; staff atty. Fed. Res. System, Washington, 1985-86; assoc. Kirkpatrick & Lockhart, Washington, 1986-88, Stroock & Stroock & Lavan, Washington, 1988-89, Christensen, Miller, Fink, Jacobs, Glaser, Weil & Shapiro, L.A., 1989—. Mem. ABA, Calif. Bar Assn. (del. to com. on adminstrn. justice), D.C. Bar Assn., N.Y. Bar Assn., L.A. County Bar Assn., Beverly Hills Bar Assn., Century City Bar Assn., Women Lawyers Assn. of L.A. (bd. dirs.), 3019 Third St. Owners Assn. (bd. dirs.), Alpha Iota House Corp. (bd. dirs.), Order of Omega, Phi Alpha Delta, Rho Lambda, Phi Kappa Phi, Pi Sigma Alpha, Gamma Phi Beta. Banking, General civil litigation. Office: Christensen Miller Fink Jacobs Glaser Weil & Shapiro 2121 Ave Of Stars Fl 18 Los Angeles CA 90067-5010

**MORGENTHAU, ROBERT MORRIS,** prosecutor; b. N.Y.C., July 31, 1919; s. Henry Jr. and Elinor (Fatman) M.; m. Martha Pattridge (dec.); children: Joan, Anne, Elinor, Robert P., Barbara; m. Lucinda Franks, Nov. 19, 1977; children: Joshua, Amy. Grad., Deerfield (Mass.) Acad., 1937; BA, Amherst Coll., 1941, LLD (hon.), 1966; LLB, Yale U., 1948; LLD (hon.), N.Y. Law Sch., 1968, Syracuse Law Sch., 1976, Albany Law Sch., 1982, Colgate U., 1988. Bar: N.Y. 1949. Assoc. firm Patterson Belknap & Webb, N.Y.C., 1948-53; ptnr. Patterson Belknap & Webb, 1954-61; U.S. atty. So. Dist. N.Y., 1961-62, 62-70; dist. atty. New York County, 1975—; former pres. N.Y. State Dist. Attys. Assn.; lectr. London Sch. Econs., 1993. Chmn. Police Athletic League; Dem. candidate for Gov. of N.Y., 1962; bd. dirs. P.R. Legal Def. and Edn. Fund; trustee Baron de Hirsch Fund, Federated Jewish Philanthropies, Temple Emanu-El, N.Y.C.; chmn. Gov.'s Adv. Com. on Sentencing, 1979; counsel N.Y. State Law Enforcement Coun.; mem. N.Y. exec. com. State of Israel Bonds; chmn. A Living Meml. to the Holocaust-Mus. of Jewish Heritage. Lt. comdr. USNR, 1941-45. Recipient Emory Buckner award Fed. Bar Coun., 1983, Yale Citation of Merit, 1982, Fordham-Stein prize, 1988, Thomas Jefferson award in law U. Va., 1991, Brandeis medal U. Louisville, 1995, Omanut award Yeshiva U., 1995, Trumpeter award Nat. Consumers League, 1995, Matheson-Morgenthau Disting. Professorship in Law named in his honor, Va. Law Sch. Fellow Am. Bar Found.; mem. ABA, N.Y. State Bar Assn., Assn. of the Bar of the City of N.Y., N.Y. County Lawyers Assn. (Disting. Pub. Svc. award 1993), Phi Beta Kappa. Office: Office Dist Atty 1 Hogan Pl New York NY 10013-4311

**MORGERA, VINCENT D.,** lawyer; b. Providence, R.I., Aug. 7, 1935; s. Frank and Elena (Andreoli) M. BA, U. R.I., 1960; JD, St. John's U., 1963. Bar: N.Y. 1963, U.S. Dist. Ct. (so. dist.) N.Y. 1965, R.I. 1977, U.S. Ct. Appeals (1st cir.) 1979, U.S. Supreme Ct., Mass. 1996. Ptnr. Kourakos & Morgera, N.Y.C., 1964-69; mgr. Legal Svc. Clinic, Bronx, N.Y., 1969; ptnr. Ruderman & Morgera, N.Y.C., 1970-73, Kuzmier & Morgera, N.Y.C., 1973-76; assoc. Kirshenbaum & Kirshenbaum, Providence, 1977-81; ptnr. Lovett & Morgera, Providence, 1981-82; pvt. practice Providence, 1982-97; ptnr. Lang & Morgera, LLP, Boston, 1997—. With USAF, 1954-58. Mem. ABA, Am. Trial Lawyers Assn. (bd. govs. 1985-87), R.I. Bar Assn. (spkr., chmn. Bench Bar 1981-85), R.I. Trial Lawyers Assn. (spkr.). Avocation: race car driver. Personal injury, Admiralty, General civil litigation. Office: 9 Park St Boston MA 02108-4807

**MORIARTY, GEORGE MARSHALL,** lawyer; b. Youngstown, Ohio, Sept. 16, 1942; s. George Albert Moriarty and Caroline (Jones) Bass; m. Elizabeth Bradley Moore, Sept. 11, 1965 (div. 1986); children: Bradley Marshall, Caroline Walden, Sarah Cameron. BA magna cum laude, Harvard U., 1964, LLB magna cum laude, 1968. Bar: Mass. 1969, U.S. Dist. Ct. Mass. 1973, U.S. Ct. Appeals (1st cir.) 1976, U.S. Ct. Appeals (D.C. cir.) 1984, U.S. Claims Ct. 1983, U.S. Supreme Ct. 1976, U.S. Ct. Appeals (2d cir.) 1997. Law clk. to Hon. Bailey Aldrich U.S. Ct. Appeals (1st cir.), Boston, 1968-69; law clk. to Hon. Warren Burger, Hon. Hugo Black, Hon. Potter Stewart, Hon. Byron White U.S. Supreme Ct., Washington, 1969-70; spl. asst. to Hon. Elliot L. Richardson, Dept. Health, Edn. & Welfare, Washington, 1970-71, exec. asst., 1971-72; assoc. Ropes & Gray, Boston, 1972-77, ptnr., 1977—. Trustee Boston Athenaeum, Brigham & Women's Hosp., Ptnrs. Health Care Sys. Inc., Ptnrs. Cmty. HealthCare, Inc.; warden Trinity Ch. in City of Boston, vestryman. Mem. ABA, Am. Law Inst., Boston Bar Assn., Somerset Club, Tavern Club, Met. Club. Federal civil litigation, General civil litigation, State civil litigation. Office: Ropes & Gray 1 Internat Pl Boston MA 02110

**MORIARTY, RICHARD BRILES,** lawyer; b. Detroit, Aug. 23, 1949; s. William Joseph and Jeanne Kathleen (Ackerman) M.; m. Sara Jean Briles, Oct. 7, 1978; 1 child, Dustin Lincoln. BA in History, Loyola U., 1971; JD, DePaul U., 1974. Bar: Ill. 1975, U.S. Dist. Ct. (no. dist.) Ill. 1975, U.S. Ct. Appeals (7th cir.) 1978, U.S. Dist. Ct. (mid. dist.) Ala. 1981, U.S. Dist. Ct. (so. dist.) Ill. 1982, U.S. Dist. Ct. (mid. dist.) Ill. 1985, Wis. 1985, U.S. Supreme Ct. 1985, U.S. Dist. Ct. (we. and ea dists.) Wis. 1990. Law clk. to Justice Robert J. Downing Ill. Appellate Ct., Chgo., 1975-76; asst. state's atty. State's Atty.'s Office, Galena, Ill., 1976-77; law clk. to Justice William G. Clark Ill. Supreme Ct., Chgo., 1977; staff atty., sr. staff atty. Prairie State Legal Svcs., Rockford, Ill., 1977-80; sr. staff atty. Legal Svcs. Corp. of Ala., Opelika, 1980-82; dir. Bur. Legal Svcs. Wis. Equal Rights Divsn., Milw., 1988-90; asst. atty. gen. Wis. Dept. Justice, Madison, 1990—; presenter in field. Contbr. articles, rev. to profl. publs. Home: 4109 Odana Rd Madison WI 53711-1650 Office: Wis Dept Justice 123 W Washington Ave Madison WI 53702-0009

**MORIE, G. GLEN,** lawyer, manufacturing company executive. BA, Bowdoin Coll., 1964; LLB, U. Pa., 1967. Bar: Wash. 1968. Pvt. practice law Wash., 1970-73; asst. counsel PACCAR, Inc., Bellevue, Wash., 1973-79, asst. gen. counsel, 1979-82, gen. counsel, 1983-85, v.p., gen. counsel, 1985—. General corporate, Securities. Office: PACCAR Inc PO Box 1518 Bellevue WA 98009-1518

**MORITZ, JOHN REID,** lawyer; b. Hamilton, Ohio, Nov. 30, 1951; s. Edward and Betty (Reid) M.; m. Darla F. Winter, July 26, 1986; children: Alexander R., Andrew F., Kathryn Ann. BA, Alma Coll., 1978; JD, Thomas M. Cooley Sch. Law, 1982. Bar: Mich. 1982. Law clk. Mich. 30th Jud. Cir., Lansing, 1981, Mich. 20th Jud. Cir., Grand Haven, 1982-83; legis. aide to rep. Mich. Ho. of Reps., Lansing, 1981-82; ptnr. Swaney, Thomas & Moritz P.C., Holland, Mich., 1983-99, Moritz & Verde, Holland, 1999—. With U.S. Army, 1973-76. Mem. ABA, Mich. Bar Assn., Ottawa County Bar Assn., Mich. Trial Lawyers Assn. Avocations: stamp collecting, antiques, tennis. Personal injury, General civil litigation, Family and matrimonial. Home: 4345 Lakeshore Dr N Holland MI 49424-5650 Office: Swaney Thomas & Moritz PC 30 E 9th St Holland MI 49423-3508

**MORLEY, PATRICK ROBERT,** lawyer; b. Wausau, Wis., Dec. 28, 1950; s. William Charles II and Elizabeth Sarah (Johnston) M.; m. Candace Elizabeth Luger, Oct. 5, 1985; children: Jessica, Bridget, Troy, Greg, Erin, Sarah. BSBA, U. N.D., 1972, JD, 1976. Bar: N.D. 1976, U.S. Dist. Ct. N.D. 1976, Minn. 1977, U.S. Ct. Appeals (8th cir.) 1981. Staff atty. Burleigh County (N.D.), Bismarck, 1976-77; assoc. O'Grady & Morley, Grand Forks, N.D., 1977-82; pntr. Morley, Morley & Light, Grand Forks, 1982—; arbitrator N.D. Worker's Compensation, Bismarck, 1991—; mem. N.D. Fed. Practice Com., 1984—, N.D. Pattern Jury Instrn. Commn., 1990—. Mem. Grand Forks County Bar Assn. (pres. 1992). Republican. Roman Catholic. Avocation: powerlifting. General civil litigation, Personal injury, Contracts commercial. Home: 901 University Ave Apt 504 Grand Forks ND 58203-3611

**MORLEY, RANDAL DEAN,** lawyer; b. Parsons, Kans., May 15, 1954; s. Mahlon Charles and Vera Lee M.; m. Donna J. Priore. BS magna cum laude, Wichita State U., 1976; JD, U. Tulsa, 1979. Bar: Okla. 1979, U.S. Dist. Ct. (no. dist.) Okla. 1980, U.S. Ct. Appeals (10th cir.) 1988, U.S. Supreme Ct. 1991. Atty. Sandlin & Payne, Muskogee, Okla., 1980; pvt. practice Tulsa, 1980-84, 87-92; appellate law clk. Okla. Ct. Appeals, Tulsa, 1985-86; atty. Birmingham, Morley, Weatherford & Priore, P.A., Tulsa, 1992—; bd. dirs., v.p. Valley State Bank, Belle Plaine, Kans., 1987—; bd. dirs. Morley Bancshares Corp., Belle Plaine, 1987—, Morley Ins., Inc., Belle Plaine, 1987—;. Mem. NACDL, Fed. Bar Assn. (treas. Tulsa chpt. 1985-96), Okla. Bar Assn. (applellate sect.). Democrat. Appellate, Criminal, General practice. Office: Birmingham Morley Weatherford & Priore PA 1141 E 37th St Tulsa OK 74105-3103

**MORNING, LEIGH SUZANNE,** lawyer; b. Indpls., Aug. 10, 1971; d. Donald Ray and Judy Gay Morning. BA, Ind. U., 1992, JD, 1996. Bar: Ind. 1996, U.S. Dist. Ct. (no. and so. dists.) Ind. 1996. Assoc. Earnest Foster Eder & Levi, Rushville, Ind., 1996—; atty. Rush County, Rushville, 1997—, Rush Meml. Hosp., 1997—. Recipient Joe Washington award Indpls. Metro Amateur Softball Assn. Am. Mem. Rush County Bar Assn. (pres. 1998). Avocation: softball umpire and coach. General practice, Government contracts and claims, Family and matrimonial. Office: Earnest Foster Eder & Levi 114 W 3rd St Rushville IN 46173-1846

**MOROCHNIK, PAUL J.,** lawyer; b. New Britain, Conn., Dec. 19, 1967; s. Sidney A. and Phyllis P. Morochnik; m. Halley Steele, Aug. 14, 1993; children: Rachel, Ilana. BA in Econs., Hofstra U., 1990; JD, Emory U., 1993. Bar: Ga. 1993, U.S. Dist. Ct. (no. dist.) Ga. 1993, U.S. Ct. Appeals (11th cir. 1993), U.S. Dist. Ct. (mid. dist.) Ga. 1998, U.S. Supreme Ct. 1998. Assoc. Alexander and Oliver, Atlanta, 1993, Alexander & Assocs., Atlanta, 1993-95, Thompson, O'Brien, Kemp & Nasuti, P.C., Norcross, Ga., 1995—. Banking, State civil litigation, Labor. Office: Thompson O'Brien Kemp & Nasuti PC 4845 Jimmy Carter Blvd Norcross GA 30093-3614

**MORODOMI, MARK TAKESHI,** lawyer; b. Berkeley, Calif., June 26, 1960. BA, Stanford U., 1982; JD, NYU, 1985. Bar: Calif. 1985, U.S. Dist. Ct. (no. dist.) Calif. 1985, U.S. Dist. Ct. (ea. dist.) Calif. 1990, U.S. Ct. Appeals (9th cir.) 1990. Assoc. McCutchen, Doyle, Brown & Enersen, San Francisco, 1985-88, Teraoka and Assocs., San Francisco, 1989-90; sr. counsel Fair Polit. Practices Commn., Sacramento, Calif., 1990—; cons. Bolivian Nat. Electoral Ct., La Paz, Bolivia, 1997. Pres. Japanese Am. Citizens League, Florin, 1994. Named one of 21 Leaders Leading Us Into the 21st Century Barrister Mag., ABA, 1995. Mem. Asian Bar Assn. Sacramento (v.p. 1995-97, pres. 1998), Nat. Asian Pacific ABA (gov. 1991-92), Sacramento County Bar Assn. Office: Calif Fair Polit Practices Commn 428 J St Ste 450 Sacramento CA 95814-2328

**MORONEY, LINDA L. S.,** lawyer, educator; b. Washington, May 27, 1943; d. Robert Emmet and Jessie (Robinson) M.; m. Clarence Renshaw II, Mar. 28, 1967 (div. 1977); children: Robert Milnor, Justin W.R. BA, Randolph-Macon Woman's Coll., 1965; JD cum laude, U. Houston, 1982. Bar: Tex. 1982, U.S. Ct. Appeals (5th cir.) 1982, U.S. Dist. Ct. (so. dist.) Tex. 1982, U.S. Supreme Ct. 1988. Law clk. to assoc. justice 14th Ct. Appeals, Houston, 1982-83; assoc. Pannill and Reynolds, Houston, 1983-85, Gilpin, Pohl & Bennett, Houston, 1985-89, Vinson & Elkins, Houston, 1989-92; adj. prof. law U. Houston, 1986-91, dir. legal rsch. and writing, 1992-96, civil trial and appellate litigation and mediation, 1996—. Fellow Houston Bar Found.; mem. ABA, State Bar Tex., Houston Bar Assn., Assn. of Women Attys., Tex. Women Lawyers, Order of the Barons, Phi Delta Phi. Episcopalian. General civil litigation, Education and schools, Alternative dispute resolution. Home and Office: 3730 Overbrook Ln Houston TX 77027-4036

**MORONEY, MICHAEL JOHN,** lawyer; b. Jamaica, N.Y., Nov. 8, 1940; s. Everard Vincent and Margaret Olga (Olson) M.; children: Sean, Megan, Matthew. BS in Polit. Sci., Villanova U., 1962; JD, Fordham U., 1965; Police Sci. (hon.), U. Guam, 1976. Bar: Hawaii 1974, U.S. Dist. Ct. Hawaii 1974, U.S. Ct. Appeals (9th cir.) 1974, Guam 1976, U.S. Dist. Ct. (Guam dist.) 1976, U.S. Ct. Claims 1976, U.S. Tax Ct. 1976, U.S. Ct. Mil. Appeals 1977, U.S. Supreme Ct. 1977, High Ct. Trust Ters. 1977, U.S. Dist. Ct. (No. Mariana Islands) 1983. Spl. agt. FBI, Memphis and Nashville, 1965-67, Cleve. and Elyria, Ohio, 1967-71; spl. agt., prin. legal advisor FBI, U.S. Dept. Justice, Honolulu, 1971-97; v.p. Merrill Corp., Honolulu, 1997—; bar examiner and applications rev. com. Supreme Ct. Hawaii, 1980—; pres. Hawaii State Law Enforcement Assn., 1985-86; mem. and del. to congress Gov.'s Task Force on Hawaii's Internat. Role, 1988; commr. Charter Commn., City and County of Honolulu, 1998—; mem. Consular Corps of Hawaii, 1997—. Mem. gov.'s task force, del. gov.'s congress on Hawaii's Internat. Role, 1988—; apptd. hon. consul gen. Republic of Palau, Pres. Kunio Nakamura, 1999. Recipient Govs. Award for Outstanding Contbns. to Law Enforcement, Gov. of Guam, 1974, 76, cert. of appreciation Supreme Ct. Hawaii, 1981, cert. of appreciation Honolulu Police Commn., 1984, 86; named Fed. Law Enforcement Officer of Yr., State of Hawaii, 1992. Mem. ABA, Hawaii Bar Assn., Guam Bar Assn., Assn. Trial Lawyers Am., Inst. Jud. Adminstrn., Hawaii State Law Enforcement Ofcls. Assn., Hilo Yacht Club, Oahu Country Club, Plaza Club. E-mail: mmoro007@aol.com. FAX: 808-531-5354. Address: 7858 Makaaoa Pl Honolulu HI 96825-2848 Office: Merrill Corp 1154 Fort Street Mall Ste 300 Honolulu HI 96813-2712

**MORPHONIOS, DEAN B.,** lawyer; b. Miami, Fla., Apr. 27, 1956; s. Alexander George and Ellen (James) M.; m. Joan Julien, Aug 7, 1982; children: Kimberly Anne, Matthew James. BA, Fla. Internat. U., Miami, 1979; JD, Fla. State U., 1983. Bar: Fla. 1983, U.S. Dist. Ct. (so. dist.) Fla. 1985, U.S. Dist. Ct. (mid. and no. dists.) 1988, U.S. Ct. Appeals, U.S. Supreme Ct. 1989. Assoc. gen. counsel Fla. Police Benevolent Assn., Tallahassee, 1983-84; sole practitioner Miami, 1984-86; asst. state atty. State Attys. Office/2d Jud. Cir., Tallahassee, 1986-88; assoc. Kitchen Judkins Simpson & High, Tallahassee, 1988-97; sole practitioner Tallahassee, 1997—; mem. Bench Bar Com., Tallahassee, 1996—, Conflict Rev. Com., Tallahassee, 1996—. Mem. Fla. Assn. Criminal Defendant Attys. (pres. Tallahassee chpt. 1994-95). Democrat. Christian. Criminal, Family and matrimonial. Office: 610 N Duval St Tallahassee FL 32301-1135

**MORPHY, JAMES CALVIN,** lawyer; b. Pitts., Jan. 16, 1954; s. Robert Samson and Autumn (Phillips) M.; m. Priscilla Winslow Plimpton, July 11, 1981; children: Calvin, Katherine, Victoria. BA, Harvard U., 1976, JD, 1979. Bar: N.Y. 1980. Assoc. Sullivan & Cromwell, N.Y.C., 1979-86, ptnr., 1986—, mng. ptnr. com., 1992—, mng. ptnr. M&A group, 1995—. Contbg. author New York and Delaware Business Entities: Choice Formation, Operation, Financing and Acquisitions. Trustee Greenwich Acad. Mem. ABA (com. on fed. securities law 1992—), Assn. Bar of City of N.Y., Wianno Club (bd. govs.), Greenwich Country Club, Harvard Club N.Y., Wianno Yacht Club, Phi Beta Kappa. Mergers and acquisitions, Securities. Office: Sullivan & Cromwell 125 Broad St Fl 28 New York NY 10004-2489

**MORREAU, JAMES EARL, JR.,** lawyer, entrepreneur; b. Richmond, Ky., Mar. 23, 1955; s. James E. and Betty Ann (Willoughby) M.; m. Jane Cecil, Apr. 11, 1981; children: Jacqueline Mary, Gregory James. BA, U. Louisville, 1977, JD, 1980. Bar: Ky. 1980, U.S. Dist. Ct. (we. dist.) Ky. 1984, U.S. Dist. Ct. (we. dist.) Tenn. 1985, U.S. Ct. Appeals (6th cir.) 1987, U.S. Supreme Ct. 1988, U.S. Ct. Appeals (9th cir.) 1995. Assoc. Taustine, Post et al, Louisville, 1980-87; co-owner, v.p., gen. counsel Investment Properties Assocs., Louisville, 1987—; pres., chief counsel Morreau Law Offices, P.S.C., Louisville, 1991; chief litigation ptnr. Kruger, Schwartz & Morreau, 1992—; gen. counsel MKS Enterprises, Memphis, 1987-93; owner, operator Mother & Child, Louisville, 1988-91. Mem. ABA, ATLA, Ky. Assn. Trial Lawyers, Ky. Bar Assn., Louisville Bar Assn., Louisville Entrepreneur Soc. Republican. Roman Catholic. Avocations: business start-ups, computers. Fax: (502) 485-9220. E-mail: jemjr@concentric.net. General civil litigation, Personal injury, General corporate. Home: 8108 Limehouse Ln Louisville KY 40220-3831 Office: 2 Paragon Ctr Ste 220 Louisville KY 40205

**MORRELL, DIANE MARIE,** lawyer; b. Savannah, Ga., Jan. 26, 1966; d. Alice (Keyes) Morrell. BS in Criminal Justice, Armstrong State U., 1988; JD, Ga. State U., 1991. Bar: Ga. 1992, Ga. Ct. Appeals 1992, U.S. Dist. Ct. (so. dist.) Ga. 1992, U.S. Ct. Appeals (11th cir.) 1992. Assoc. Allen and Assocs., Savannah, Ga., 1991-92; ptnr. Allen & Morrell, Savannah, 1992-94; pvt. practice law, 1994—; judge protem Chatham County Recorder's Ct.; atty., coach mock trial competition Ga. State Bar. Bd. dirs. Hope House of Savannah, King Tisdell Cottage Found., Frank Callen Boys Club; vol. Big Bros./Sisters, Davenport House. Mem. ABA, Assn. Trial Lawyers Am., Ga. Trial Lawyers Assn., Ga. Assn. Women Lawyers, State Bar Ga., Port City Bar Assn. Personal injury, General practice, Criminal. Office: PO Box 9434 Savannah GA 31412-9434

**MORRIONE, MELCHIOR S.,** management consultant, accountant; b. Bklyn., Dec. 31, 1937; s. Charles and Dionisia (Eletto) M.; m. Joan Finnerty, June 22, 1968; children: Karyn Morrione Frick, Nicole. BBA magna cum laude, St. John's U., 1959. CPA, N.J., N.Y. Tax ptnr. Arthur Andersen & Co., N.Y.C., 1959-91; mng. dir. MSM Consulting LLC, Woodcliff Lake, N.J., 1992—; lectr. in field. Contbr. articles to profl. jours. With U.S. Army, 1960-61. Mem. CPAs, N.Y. State Soc. CPAs, N.J. Soc. CPAs, Internat. Fiscal Assn., Internat. Tax Assn., Ridgewood Country Club. Republican. Roman Catholic. Avocations: golf, tennis. E-mail: morricone@idt.net. Office: MSM Consulting LLC 11 Ginny Dr Woodcliff Lake NJ 07675-8115

**MORRIS, AUDREY M.,** lawyer; b. Annapolis, Md., Dec. 6, 1963; d. Thomas M. and Audrey M. (Kunzinger) Burton; m. Michael S. Morris, Apr. 20, 1985; children: Matthew L., Andrew S. AA in Bus., Manatee Jr. Coll., Bradenton, Fla., 1983; BA in Acctg., U. West Fla., 1984; JD, U. Miami, Fla., 1990. Bar: Tex. 1991, U.S. Tax Ct. 1991, U.S. Dist. Ct. (no. dist.) Tex. 1992, U.S. Supreme Ct. 1998. Revenue agt. IRS, Miami, 1986-88; revenue agt. IRS, Dallas, 1988-91, tax atty., 1991—. Mem. ABA. Roman Catholic. Office: IRS District Counsel 4050 Alpha Rd 13th Fl MC 2000 NWSAT Dallas TX 75244

**MORRIS, BENJAMIN HUME,** lawyer; b. Louisville, Ky., Sept. 25, 1917; s. Benjamin Franklin and Mary (Hume) M.; m. Lacy Hibbs Abell, July 7, 1942; children: Benjamin Hume, Lacy Wayne; m. Mary Fraces Fowler Gatlin, Nov. 9, 1968. JD, U. Louisville, 1941. Bar: Ky. 1940, U.S. Supreme Ct. 1966. Assoc. Doolan, Helm, Stites & Wood, Louisville, 1941-50; atty. Brown-Forman Distillers Corp., Louisville, 1950-56; resident counsel Brown-Forman Distillers Corp., 1956-64; v.p. resident counsel, 1964-73, v.p., gen. counsel, 1973-81, corp. sec., 1981; pres., dir. Can. Mist Distillers, Ltd., Collingwood, Ont., Can., 1971-81; of counsel Morris, Nicolas, Welsh & Vandeventer, Louisville, 1982-86, Ray & Morris, 1986-89, Morris, Hawkins and Dutton, 1990-94, Morris & Dutton, 1995—. Reviser corp. sect. Banks-Baldwin's Ky. Legal Forms Book, 1982. Trustee W.L. Lyons Brown Found., 1964—, City of Riverwood, Ky., 1977-81; chmn. Jefferson County Social Svc. Adv. Com., 1959-62; bd. govs. Jefferson Alcohol and Drug Abuse Ctr., 1983-90; past bd. dirs. Ky. C. of C., Better Bus. Bur. Louisville. Capt. USAF, 1941-45; col. Res., ret. Decorated Air medal with oak leaf cluster; recipient Disting. Alumni award U. Louisville, 1981, medal of honor Na.t Soc., DAR, 1990. Fellow Am. Coll. Genealogists; mem. Ky. Bar Assn., Ky. Soc. SAR (pres. 1978), Nat. Soc. SAR (v.p. 1980, chancelor gen. 1982-83, sec. gen. 1984, pres. gen. 1985, Minuteman award 1984, Gold Good Citizenship medal 1986), Ky. Distillers Assn. (chmn. 1969), Distilled Spirits Coun. U.S. (pres. 1973, chmn. 1973-74, chmn. emeritus 1982—), Assn. Can. Distillers (bd. dirs. 1971-81), Soc. Colonial Wars, soc. War 1812 (v.p. gen. 1987-89, 92-96, judge advocate gen. 1996—, pres. Ky. soc. 1990-92), Soc. Sons and Daus. Pilgrims, Mil. Order of World Wars, Sons of the Revolution, Flagon and Trencher Soc., Sons Am. Colonists, Continental Soc., Sons of Indian Wars, Ams. of Royal Descent, Order of the Crown of Charlemagne in the U.S., Louisville Boat Club, Filson. Republican. Presbyterian. General corporate. Home: 2005 High Ridge Rd Louisville KY 40207-1125

**MORRIS, BRUCE H.,** lawyer; b. Atlanta, Jan. 10, 1949; s. Perry B. and Anita M. M.; m. Jaclynn Harrison, May 6, 1978; children: Peter I., Emily R. AB in Polit. Sci., U. N.C., 1971; JD, Emory U., 1974. Assoc. Fierer & Devine, Atlanta, 1974-77; ptnr. Devine & Morris, Atlanta, 1977-89, Finestone & Morris, Atlanta, 1989—; adj. prof. Ga. State U. Sch. Law, Atlanta, 1991—. Mem. ABA, ATLA, ACLU (pres. Ga. chpt. 1985-87). Jewish. Criminal, Personal injury. Home: 915 Curlew Ct NW Atlanta GA 30327-4761 Office: Finestone & Morris 3340 Peachtree Rd NE Ste 2540 Atlanta GA 30326-1038

**MORRIS, CECELIA G.,** lawyer; b. Quanah, Tex., May 26, 1946; d. Harpie Eugene and Oleta Belle (Green) Morris; children: Carmen Cecelia Oviedo, Marcia Mari Oviedo. BS, West Tex. State U., Canyon, 1968; JD, John Marshall Law Sch., Atlanta, 1977. Bar: Ga. 1977, U.S. Dist. Ct. (no. dist.) Ga. 1978, U.S. Dist. Ct. (mid. dist.) Ga. 1987, D.C. 1999. Pvt. practice Griffin, Ga., 1977-79; adminstr. civil divsn., child support recovery unit Asst. Dist. Atty., Griffin, Ga., 1979-81; atty. in pvt. pratice Macon, Ga., 1981-86; clk. U.S. Bankruptcy Ct., Mid. Dist. Ga., 1986-88, U.S. Bankruptcy Ct., So. Dist. N.Y., 1988—; arbitrator Nat. Assn. Securities Dealers, N.Y.C., 1996; mediator U.S. Dist. Ct. So. Dist. N.Y., 1994; bd. dirs. Nat. Conf. Bankruptcy Clks, Macon, 1988; mem. Ct. Registry Investment System, 1991—. Editor newsletter Nat. Conf. Bankruptcy Clks., 1987; author articles and reports. Fellow Am. Coll. Bankruptcy; mem. Assn. Bar City N.Y. (ex-officio mem. bankruptcy and reorgn. com. 1997—), State Bar N.Y. Office: US Bankruptcy Ct So Dist NY One Bowling Green New York NY 10004

**MORRIS, DEE DODSON,** lawyer, physical scientist; b. Austin, Tex., Feb. 3, 1954; d. Richard Stanton and Charlotte (Spence) Dodson; m. Robert Wesley Morris, Apr. 26, 1980 (div. 1995); 1 child, Seth Richard. BS in Textile Chemistry, Va. Tech., 1976; JD, U. Detroit, 1989. Bar: Tex. 1990, D.C. 1991. Commd. 2d lt. U.S. Army, 1976, advanced through grades to lt. col., 1993; adjutant, platoon leader U.S. Army Tech. Excort Unit, Aberdeen, Md., 1976-78; chem. stff officer 6th Calvary Brigade, Ft. Hood, Tex., 1978-80; comdr. 181st Chemical Co., Ft. Hood, Tex., 1980-81; chemical staff officer 3d Infantry Divsn., Wurzburg, Germany, 1982-85; chemical adv. Readiness Group, Selfridge ANG Base, Mich., 1985-88; chief, vehicle NBC def. Tank-Automotive Command, Warren, Mich., 1988-90; surety officer Army Chemical Activity, Pacific, Johnston Atoll, 1991; mission comdr. On-Site Inspection Agency, Washington, 1992-94; exec. officer Chemical Activity, Pacific, Johnston Atoll, 1995; chief, combat support evaluation Operational Evaluation Command, Alexandria, Va., 1996; dep. dir. investigation and analysis Spl. Asst. Gulf War Illnesses, Falls Church, Va., 1996-98, dir. lessons learned implementation, 1998—. Mem. Am. Assn. Textile Chemists & Colorists. Avocations: fiber arts. Office: Spl Asst Gulf War Illnesses 5113 Leesburg Pike Ste 901 Falls Church VA 22041-3226

**MORRIS, EDITH HENDERSON,** lawyer; b. Birmingham, Ala., Mar. 25, 1944; d. William and Roberta (Sterrett) H.; m. Joseph M. Morris Jr., Nov. 29, 1963; children: Robert Joseph, Edith L. BA, Our Lady of Holy Cross Coll., New Orleans, 1974; JD, Loyola U., New Orleans, 1985. Bar: La. 1985, U.S. Dist. Ct. (ea. dist.) La. 1985. Assoc. Sessions & Fishman, New Orleans, 1985-87, Lowe, Stein, Hoffman & Allweis, New Orleans, 1987-89; pvt. practice New Orleans, 1989—; instr. family skills course Law Sch. Loyola U., 1989—; spkr. on divorce, mediation and adoption. Bd. dirs. La. Mediation Coun., 1991-94. Fellow Am. Acad. Matrimonial Lawyers; mem. ABA, Am. Acad. Adoption Attys. (trustee 1999), Assn. Women Attys., Acad. Family Mediators (practitioner), La. State Bar Assn. Avocation: walking. Family and matrimonial. Home: 241 Rosa Ave Metairie LA 70005-3415 Office: 1515 Poydras St Ste 1870 New Orleans LA 70112-3770

**MORRIS, EDWARD WILLIAM, JR.,** lawyer; b. Medford, Oreg., Apr. 12, 1943; s. Edward William and Julia Loretta (Sullivan) M.; m. Margaret Ellen McKenna, 1976; children—John McKenna, Elizabeth Anne. B.S., Fordham Coll., 1965, J.D., 1971. Bar: N.Y. 1973. Dir. Drug Products Co., Inc., Union City, N.J., 1968-71; asst. arbitration dir. N.Y. Stock Exchange, N.Y.C., 1971-73, arbitration dir., 1973-74, asst. sec., arbitration dir., 1974-89, v.p. arbitration, 1989-91, chief hearing officer, 1991—; dir. Stock Clearing Corp., N.Y.C.; mem. Securities Industry Conf. on Arbitration, N.Y.C., 1977—; lectr. in field. Served to sgt. U.S. Army, 1965-68, Vietnam. Mem. ABA, Am. Arbitration Assn. (comml. law com. 1983—), Assn. of the Bar of City of N.Y. (retail fin. svcs. com. 1989—), N.Y. County Lawyers Assn. (sec. com. on arbitration 1983—), High Mountain Golf Club, N.Y. Roadrunners Club. Securities. Home: 67 Arlton Ave Allendale NJ 07401-1331 Office: NY Stock Exch Inc 11 Wall St Fl 7 New York NY 10005-1974

**MORRIS, GARY WAYNE,** lawyer; b. El Paso, Tex., Jan. 14, 1945; s. Harold W. and Ruth (Ingram) M.; m. Janet S. Young; children: Patricia Woodbury, Jennifer, Michael, John. BA, Point Loma Nazarene U., Pasadena; JD, U. Loyola. Assoc. Hart & Mieras, L.A., 1971-74, ptnr., 1974-96; ptnr. Hart, Mieras, Morris & Peale, Pasadena, Calif., 1996—. Presenter (audio cassette) Living Trust, 1992. Sec. L.A. Dist. Adv. Bd., Pasadena, 1976—; trustee Point Loma Nazarene U., San Diego, 1994—. Recipient Pres.'s award Optimist Club, 1975, Alumnus award Point Loma Nazarene U. Pasadena, 1980. Mem. State Bar Calif., Christian Legal Soc., L.A. County Bar Assn. Republican. Avocations: sandrail, fishing, tennis. Estate planning, General corporate, Real property. Office: Hart Mieras Morris & Peale 135 N Los Robles Ave Ste 850 Pasadena CA 91101-4526

**MORRIS, GRETCHEN REYNOLDS,** lawyer; b. Miami, Jan. 26, 1938; d. Lincoln C. and Damaris (Peck) Reynolds; m. John E. Morris, Mar. 23, 1958; children: KImberly P., Courtney J. BA, Stanford U., 1959; JD, U. Oreg., 1973; LLM in Taxation, Georgetown U., 1984. Bar: Oreg. 1973, U.S. Dist. Ct. Oreg. 1976, U.S. Supreme Ct. 1984, U.S. Tax Ct. 1984, U.S. Claims Ct. 1984. Law clk. to justice Oreg. Supreme Ct., Salem, 1973-74; instr. U. Chgo. Law Sch., 1974-75; assoc. Fenner & Barnhisel, Corvallis, 1975-76; ptnr. Fenner, Barnhisel, Morris & Willis, Corvallis, 1977-83; pvt. practice Corvallis, Oreg., 1984-90, 1998—; ptnr. Marek & Morris, Corvallis, 1990-98; pres. Oreg. Law Inst., Portland, 1988-89, Bus. Enterprise Ctr., Corvallis, 1987-94. Bd. dirs. Corvallis Arts Ctr., 1977-80; chair Corvallis Pub. Schs. Found., 1995—. Mem. ABA, Oreg. State Bar Assn., Benton County Bar Assn. (pres. 1987-88), Nat. Network of Estate Planning Attys., Corvallis Area C. of C. (bd. dirs. 1976-79). Estate taxation, Probate, Estate planning. Home and Office: 810 SW Madison Ave Corvallis OR 97333-4513

**MORRIS, JAMES EDGAR,** lawyer; b. Berlin, N.H., Apr. 19, 1948; s. Robert Joseph Morris and Lillian Louise Luby; m. Deborah de Peyster, June 19, 1982; children: Allison de Peyster Morris, Benjamin de Peyster Morris. AB, Harvard Coll., 1970; JD, Boston U., 1974. Bar: N.H. 1974, U.S. Dist. Ct. N.H. 1974, Calif. 1979, U.S. Dist. Ct. (no. dist.) Calif. 1979, U.S. Ct. Appeals (1st cir.) 1979, U.S. Supreme Ct. 1979. Jud. law clk. N.H. Supreme Ct., Concord, 1974-75; asst. atty. gen. N.H. Atty. Gen., Concord, 1975-80; asst. corp. counsel Allianz Ins. Co., L.A., 1980-81; ptnr. Orr & Reno, P.A., Concord, 1981—; chief counsel N.H. Dept. Transp., Concord, 1978-80; seminar instr. Nat. Bus. Inst., Eau Claire, Wis. Bd. editors N.H. Bar Jour., 1983-87. Avocations: running, hiking, restoring antique cars, restoring antique wooden boats. Real property, Condemnation, Land use and zoning (including planning). Office: Orr & Reno PA One Eagle Sq PO Box 3550 Concord NH 03302-3550

**MORRIS, JAMES MALACHY,** lawyer; b. Champaign, Ill., June 5, 1952; s. Walter Michael and Ellen Frances (Solon) M.; m. Mary Delilah Baker, Oct. 17, 1987; children: James Malachy Jr., Elliot Rice Baker, Walter Michael. Student, Oxford U. (Eng.), 1972; BA, Brown U., 1974; JD, U. Pa., 1977. Bar: N.Y. 1978, U.S. Dist. Ct. (so. and ea. dists.) N.Y. 1978, Ill. 1980, U.S. Tax Ct. 1982, U.S. Supreme Ct. 1983; admitted to Barristers Chambers, Manchester, Eng., 1987. Assoc. Reid & Priest, N.Y.C., 1977-80; sr. law clk. Supreme Ct. Ill., Springfield, 1980-81; assoc. Carter, Ledyard & Milburn, N.Y.C., 1981-83; sole practice N.Y.C., 1983-87; counsel FCA, Washington, 1987—; acting sec., gen. counsel FCS Ins. Corp., McLean, Va., 1990-98; cons. Internat. Awards Found., Zurich, 1981—, Pritzker Architecture Prize Found., N.Y.C., 1981—, Herbert Oppenheimer, Nathan & VanDyck, London, 1985—. Contbr. articles to profl. jours. Mem. ABA, Ill. Bar Assn., N.Y. State Bar Assn., N.Y. County Lawyers Assn., Assn. Bar City N.Y., Brit. Inst. Internat. and Comparative Law, Lansdowne Club (London), Casanova (Va.) Hunt Club. General practice, General corporate, Probate. Office: PO Box 1407 Mc Lean VA 22101-1407

**MORRIS, JOHN E.,** lawyer; b. N.Y.C., Sept. 30, 1916; s. John and Honora C. (Long) M.; m. Patricia E. Grojean. A.B., CCNY; A.M., Columbia U.; J.D., Harvard U. Bar: N.Y. 1942, U.S. Dist. Ct. (so. and ea. dists.) N.Y. Trial lawyer Clarke & Reilly, 1946-50; ptnr. Morris & Duffy, N.Y.C., 1950-98. Served to lt. USCG, 1942-46; ETO. Mem. ABA, N.Y. State Bar Assn., N.Y. County Lawyers Assn. (mem. judiciary com.), Harvard Law Sch. Assn., Airplane Owners & Pilots Assn., Internat. Assn. Ins. Counsel, USCG Combat Vets. Assn., Harvard Club, N.Y. Athletic Club (N.Y.C.), Great Dane Club Am. (bd. dirs.). Roman Catholic. Deceased. Personal injury, Insurance, Federal civil litigation. Office: 170 Broadway Fl 7 New York NY 10038-4154

**MORRIS, JOHN WHELCHEL,** lawyer, educator; b. Gainesville, Ga.; s. Jean Morton and Mary (Whelchel) M.; m. Virginia Fraser Morris, June 14, 1969; 1 child, John Whelchel Morris Jr. BA, Yale U., 1967; JD, U. Pa., 1970. Assoc. Clark, Ladner, Fortenbaugh & Young, Phila., 1970-73; first asst. dist. atty. Phila. Dist. Atty. Office, 1973-78; ptnr. Pierson, Jones & Morris, Phila., 1978-82; pvt. practice Phila., 1982—; sr. counsel Reading Co., Phila. 1982—, New Piper Aircraft, Vero, 1995—; instr. Temple U. La Sch.; mem. Disciplinary Bd. Pa. Mem. Pa. Assn. Criminal Defense Lawyers (dir.

1994-96), Nat. Assn. Criminal Defense Lawyers, Phila. Bar Assn. Product liability, Criminal, Consumer commercial. Home: 257 S 25th St Philadelphia PA 19103-5551 Office: 30 S 15th St Philadelphia PA 19102-4826

**MORRIS, JOSEPH ANTHONY,** lawyer; b. Dothan, Ala., Oct. 12, 1968; m. Louise Jensen, Aug. 20, 1994; children: Andrew Jensen, Walter Patrick. BS in Fin., U. Ala., 1991; JD, Samford U., 1994. Bar: Ala. 1994, U.S. Dist. Ct. (no. dist.) Ala. 1994, U.S. Dist. Ct. (mid. dist.) Ala. 1995, U.S. Ct. Appeals (11th cir.) 1995, U.S. Dist. Ct. (so. dist.) Ala. 1998. Law clk. Baxley, Dillard & Dauphin, Birmingham, Ala., 1992-93, Gorham & Waldrep, Birmingham, Ala., 1993; assoc. Simmons, Brunson, Sasser & Callis Attys., P.A., Gadsden, Ala., 1994-95, Cobb & Shealy, P.A., Dothan, Ala., 1995-99, Morris, Cary & Fischer, LLC, Dothan, Ala., 1999—; adj. prof. Troy State U., Dothan, 1996, 98. Bd. dirs. Boys and Girls Club. Mem. ABA, Houston County Bar Assn., Houston County Young Lawyers Assn. (pres.) Ala. State Bar Assn., Kiwanis (Dothan and Gadsden chpts.). General civil litigation, Personal injury, Workers' compensation. Office: Morris Cary & Fischer LLC 170 E Main St Dothan AL 36301

**MORRIS, JULES JAY,** lawyer, mechanical engineer; b. N.Y.C., Dec. 3, 1953; s. Samuel and Lilian Oberman Morris; m. Leticia Helena d'Aquino, June 26, 1979. BA in History, CUNY, Queens, 1974; BS in Mech. Engring., MIT, 1976; JD, Suffolk U., 1981. Bar: Mass. 1981, U.S. Patent and Trademark Office 1982, U.S. Ct. Appeals (fed. cir.) 1984. Engr. GE Aircraft Engine Group, Lynn, Mass., 1976-81; assoc. patent atty. Hamilton, Brook, Smith & Reynolds, Lexington, Mass., 1981-84; chief physics sect. USAF Patent Office, Waltham, Mass., 1985-88; chief patent counsel The Foxboro (Mass.) Co., 1988-96, Siebe plc, Foxboro, 1996—. Mem. Boston Patent Law Assn., Bay State Soc. Model Engrs., MIT Club Boston. Democrat. Avocations: model railroading, swimming. E-mail: jmorris@foxboro.com. Fax: 508-549-6295. Office: Siebe Intellectual Property Dept 33 Commercial St Foxboro MA 02035-2530

**MORRIS, KENNETH DONALD,** lawyer; b. Montclair, N.J., Apr. 5, 1946; s. Thomas Almerin and Katherine Louise (Jacobs) M.; m. Susan Sauer, May 1, 1976; children: Ian, Jennifer. BA, Ohio Wesleyan U., 1968; MBA, George Washington U., 1971, JD, 1972. Bar: Pa. 1973, N.J. 1975, D.C. 1989. Atty. Westinghouse Electric, Pitts., 1972-74, Tenneco Chems., Inc., N.J., 1974-76; asst. corp. counsel Ronson Corp., Bound Brook, N.J., 1976-78; assoc. Walder, Sondak, Berkley & Brogan, Newark, 1978-81; sec., gen. counsel, mem. mgmt. com. NOR-AM Chem. Co. subs. Schering AG, Wilmington, Del., 1981-94, environ. com. 1987—, fiduciary com., 1988—; sec., gen. counsel AgrEvo USA Co., Wilmington, 1994—. Incorporator, pres. Charter Oaks Assn. Wolcott Found. scholar, 1969. Mem. Internat. Assn. Def. Counsel, Am. Arbitration Assn. (panel arbitrators), Am. Corp. Counsel Assn., Def. Rsch. Inst. (corp. counsel com.), George Washington U. Sch. Govt. and Bus. Adminstrn. Alumni Assn. (Phila. chpt.), George Washington U. Nat. Law Ctr. Alumni Assn., European-Am. Gen. Counsel Assn., Fed. Bar Assn. Republican. Presbyterian. Avocations: classical music, running, sailing, tennis. General corporate, Personal injury, Contracts commercial. Office: AgrEvo USA Co 2711 Centerville Rd Wilmington DE 19808-1643

**MORRIS, LEAH CURTIS,** lawyer; b. Greenville, Tex., Nov. 21, 1961; d. Harold F. Jr. and Carol (Fischer) Curtis; m. Allen McCullouch, Nov. 6, 1993. BA in Art History, Newcomb Coll., 1984; JD, St. Mary's U., 1987. Bar: Tex. 1987. Asst. criminal dist. atty. Bexar County Criminal Dist. Atty.'s Office, San Antonio, 1988-95; ptnr. Curtis, Alexander, McCampbell & Morris, Greenville, Tex., 1995—. Mem. adminstrv. bd. Kavanaugh Meth. Ch., 1997—; pres. Boys and Girls Club of Hunt County, 1997-98. Named one of Outstanding Young Women of Am., YMCA, 1997, Hidalgo de San Antonio de Bexar, Bexar County Commr.'s Ct., 1995. Mem. Hunt County Bar Assn., Rotary (pres.-elect Greenville chpt. 1998-99, pres. 1999—, Rotarian of Yr. 1998). General practice, Health. Office: PO Box 1256 2708 Washington Greenville TX 75403-1256

**MORRIS, LEAH MCGARRY,** lawyer; b. Boston, Mar. 27, 1951; d. A. Louis and Shirley L. (Pustilnick) McGarry; m. Justin T. Loughry, May 19, 1990; children: Benjamin, Lindsay, Nora. AB, Bryn Mawr Coll., 1972; JD, Temple U., 1975. Bar: Pa. 1975, N.J. 1976. Staff atty. Camden (N.J.) County Pub. Defender's Office, 1976-96, first asst. dep., 1996—; Bd. trustees Camden Regional Legal Svcs., 1996—. Mem. Camden County Youth Svcs. Commn., 1984—, Camden County Vicinage Com. Minority Concerns, Camden County Human Rels. Commn., 1997—; vice chair Haddonfield (N.J.) Human Rels. Commn., 1994—; chair Haddonfield Neighborhood Disputes Mediation Commn., 1997—; mem. Camden County Citizens Adv. Bd. Named one of the Women Who Have Made a Difference Camden County Bd. Freeholders and Camden County Commn. Women, 1996; fellow Leadership N.J. (Partnership for N.J., 1998). Mem. Assn. Criminal Def. Lawyers N.J. (bd. trustees 1994—), N.J. Network Drug Ct. Profls., Camden County Bar Assn. (co-chair criminal practice com. 1997—, bd. trustees 1998—). Democrat. Avocations: mediation, advocacy for youth, writing. Home: 106 Prospect Rd Haddonfield NJ 08033-1314 Office: Camden County Pub Defenders 101 Haddon Ave Camden NJ 08103-1468

**MORRIS, LYNN KEITH,** lawyer; b. Temple, Tex., Oct. 24, 1944. AS, Tyler Jr. Coll., 1966; BA, North Tex. State U., 1966; JD, So. Meth. U., 1971. Bar: Tex. 1972, U.S. Dist. Ct. (no. dist.) Tex. 1976, U.S. Ct. Appeals (5th cir.). Assoc. Fanning & Harper, Dallas, 1972-75; assoc. counsel J.C. Penny Life Ins. Co., Plano, Tex., 1979-83; assoc. coun., asst. sec. J.C. Penney Life Ins. Co., Plano, Tex., 1983-95, v.p. regulatory rels., asst. sec., 1995-96, v.p., asst. sec., 1996—. Mem. ABA, Am. Coun. Life Ins. (mem. legal sect.), Assn. Life Ins. Counsel, State Bar Tex., Phi Alpha Delta. Office: JC Penny Life Ins Co 2700 W Plano Pkwy Plano TX 75075*

**MORRIS, NORVAL,** criminologist, educator; b. Auckland, New Zealand, Oct. 1, 1923; s. Louis and Vera (Burke) M.; m. Elaine Richardson, Mar. 18, 1947; children: Gareth, Malcolm, Christoper. LLB, U. Melbourne, Australia, 1946, LLM, 1947; PhD in Criminology (Hutchinson Silver medal 1950), London Sch. Econs., 1949. Bar: called to Australian bar 1953. Asst. lectr. London Sch. Econs., 1949-50; sr. lectr. law U. Melbourne, 1950-58, prof. criminology, 1955-58; Ezra Ripley Thayer teaching fellow Harvard Law Sch., 1955-56, vis. prof., 1961-62; Boynthon prof., dean faculty law U. Adelaide, Australia, 1958-62; dir. UN Inst. Prevention Crime and Treatment of Offenders, Tokyo, Japan, 1962-64; Julius Kreeger prof. law and criminology U. Chgo., 1964—, dean Law Sch., 1975-79; chmn. Commn. Inquiry Capital Punishment in Ceylon, 1958-59; mem. Social Sci. Rsch. Coun. Australia, 1958-59; Australian del. confs. div. human rights and sect. social def. UN, 1955-66; mem. standing adv. com. experts prevention crime and treatment offenders. Author: The Habitual Criminal, 1951, Report of the Commission of Inquiry on Capital Punishment, 1959, (with W. Morison and R. Sharwood) Cases in Torts, 1962, (with Colon Howard) Studies in Criminal Law, 1964, (with G. Hawkins) The Honest Politicians Guide to Crime Control, 1970, The Future of Imprisonment, 1974, Letter to the President on Crime Control, 1977, Madness and the Criminal Law, 1983, Between Prison and Probation, 1990, The Brothel Boy and Other Parables of the Law, 1992, The Oxford History of the Prison, 1995. Served with Australian Army, World War II, PTO. Decorated Japanese Order Sacred Treasure 3d Class. Fellow Am. Acad. Arts and Scis. Home: 1207 E 50th St Chicago IL 60615-2908 Office: U Chgo Law Sch 1111 E 60th St Chicago IL 60637-2776

**MORRIS, ROY LESLIE,** lawyer, electrical engineer, venture capitalist; b. N.Y.C., BE, SUNY, Stony Brook, 1975; EE, MIT, 1978, SM, 1978; JD, George Washington U., 1984; MBA, Wharton U., 1995. Bar: D.C. 1984, U.S. Patent Office. Mem. tech. staff Bell Telephone Labs., Holmdel, N.J., 1978-80; sr. staff engr. FCC, Washington, 1981-83; assoc. regulatory counsel MCI Communications, Washington, 1983-87; dep. gen. counsel Allnet Comms., Washington, 1988-95; dir. pub. policy and regulatory affairs Allnet/Frontier Comms., Washington, 1989-96; mng. ptnr. RoyLyn L.L.C., Arlington, Va., 1996—; v.p. govt. affairs and revenue devel. US ONE Comms., McLean, Va., 1996-97; mng. ptnr. Strategic Tech. Investors LLC, Arlington, Va., 1998—; pres. MIT Enterprise Forum, Washington/Balt., 1998—; ednl. counselor MIT; adj. prof. Capitol Coll., Laurel, Md., 1998—; CFO, gen. counsel WebPerfect Solutions, Inc., 1999—. Contbr. numerous articles to profl. publs. Mem. ABA, IEEE, MIT Enterprise Forum, Sigma Xi, Tau Beta Pi. Administrative and regulatory, Communications, Finance. Address: Strategic Tech Investors LLC 4001 9th St N Apt 306 Arlington VA 22203-1957

**MORRIS, SANDRA JOAN,** lawyer; b. Chgo., Oct. 13, 1944; d. Bernard and Helene (Davies) Aronson; m. Richard William Morris, May 30, 1965 (div. Jan. 1974); children: Tracy Michelle, Bretton Todd; m. William Mark Bandt, July 12, 1981; 1 child, Victoria Elizabeth. BA, U. Ariz., 1965; JD, Calif. Western U., 1969. Bar: Calif. 1970, U.S. Dist. Ct. (so. dist.) Calif. 1970; diplomate Am. Coll. Family Trial Lawyers. Ptnr. Morris & Morris, APC, San Diego, 1970-74; sole practice San Diego, 1974—; mem. Adv. Commn. on Family Law, Calif. Senate, 1978-79. Contbr. articles to profl. jours. Pres. San Diego Community Child Abuse Coordinating Coun., 1977; mem. human rsch. rev. bd. Children's Hosp., San Diego, 1977-92. Fellow Am. Acad. Matrimonial Lawyers (chpt. pres. 1987-88, nat. bd. govs. 1987-89, 93-94, parliamentarian 1989-91, treas. 1994-97, v.p. 1997—), Internat. Acad. Matrimonial Lawyers (joint editl. bd./family law, Nat. Conf. of Commrs. on Uniform State Laws 1999—); mem. ABA (family law sect exec. com. marital property 1982-83, 87-94), State Bar Calif. (cert. family law specialist 1980—), Lawyers Club San Diego (bd. dirs. 1973), San Diego Cert. Family Law Specialists (chair 1995-96). Republican. Jewish. Avocations: skiing, travel. Family and matrimonial. Office: 3200 4th Ave Ste 101 San Diego CA 92103-5716

**MORRIS, THOMAS BATEMAN, JR.,** lawyer; b. Columbus, Ohio, Aug. 11, 1936; s. Thomas Bateman and Margaret (O'Shaughnessy) M.; m. Ann Peirce, Feb. 23, 1963; children: Lauren, Thomas III, Richard. AB, Princeton U., 1958; JD, Harvard U., 1962. Bar: Pa. 1962. Sr. ptnr. Dechert Price & Rhoads, Phila., 1962—, chmn., 1990-96; bd. dirs. PNC Bank N.A., Phila., Berwind Corp., Phila., Asten, Inc., Charleston, S.C., Envirite Corp., Plymouth Meeting, Pa., Peirce-Phelps, Inc., Phila., Harmac Med. Products, Inc., Buffalo. Co-chmn. Greater Phila. First, 1996—; trustee Princeton U., 1975-80; bd. trustees Thomas Jefferson U., 1989—. Hon. Consul King of Belgium, Phila., 1974-89. Mem. ABA, Pa. Bar Assn., Phila. Bar Assn. (chmn. city tax policy com.), Internat. Bar Assn. (chmn. com. on structure and ethics of law practice), Phila. Club, Phila. Cricket Club, Princeton Club, Sunnybrook Golf Club, Pine Valley Golf Club. Home: 8320 Seminole St Philadelphia PA 19118-3932 Office: Dechert Price & Rhoads 4000 Bell Atlantic Tower Philadelphia PA 19103-2793

**MORRISON, DAVID EUGENE,** lawyer; b. York, Nebr., May 6, 1952; s. Louis Eugene and Eleanor (Curry) M. BA, U. Nebr., 1974; JD, Duke U., 1977. Bar: Tex. 1977. Sr. ptnr. Thompson & Knight LLP, Dallas, civ, 1977—. Mem. bd. govs. Dallas Symphony Assn., Inc., 1990—, mem. exec. bd., 1993—, sec., 1993-98; trustee Tex. Internat. Festivals, Inc., Dallas, 1997-98, mem. exec. com., 1997-98, sec., 1997-98; mem. bd. mgmt. Town North Family YMCA, Dallas, 1997—. Methodist. Avocations: spectator sports, gardening, woodworking. Securities, Mergers and acquisitions, General corporate. Home: 4738 San Gabriel Dr Dallas TX 75229-4233 Office: Thompson & Knight LLP 1700 Pacific Ave Ste 3300 Dallas TX 75201-4693

**MORRISON, JOHN MARTIN,** lawyer; b. McCook, Nebr., June 18, 1961; s. Frank Brennor and Sharon Romain (McDonald) M.; m. Catherine Helen Wright, Aug. 17, 1991; children: Allison Kay, Amanda Grace. BA, Whitman Coll., 1983; JD, U. Denver, 1986. Bar: Mont. 1987, U.S. Dist. Ct. Mont. 1988, U.S. Ct. Appeals (9th cir.) 1989, U.S. Supreme Ct., 1996. Legis. asst., legal counsel U.S. Senate, Washington, 1987-88; ptnr. Morrison Law Offices, Helena, Mont., 1988-93, Meloy & Morrison, Helena, 1994—. Author: Mavericks: The Lives and Battles of Montana's Political Legends, 1997; contbr. articles to profl. jours. Alt. del. Dem. Nat. Conv., N.Y.C., 1980; del. Dem. Nat. Platform Com., 1992. Recipient Lewis F. Powell/ACTL/Bur. of Nat. Affairs Advocacy awards, 1986. Mem. ATLA, Mont. Bar Assn., Mont. Trial Lawyers Assn. (past pres., bd. dirs. 1991—), Western Trial Lawyers Assn. (bd. govs. 1990-95), Trial Lawyers Pub. Justice (chair 1989-90). Avocations: skiing, fly fishing, mountain climbing, river rafting, running. General civil litigation, Personal injury, Insurance. Office: Meloy & Morrison 80 S Warren St Helena MT 59601-5700

**MORRISON, MICHAEL DEAN,** lawyer, law educator. BA with high honors, Okla. U., 1971, JD, 1974. Bar: Okla. 1975, Kans. 1975, Tex. 1981, U.S. Ct. Appeals (5th cir.) 1980, U.S. Dist. Ct. (ea., no. and so. dists.) Tex. 1983, U.S. Dist. Ct. (we. dist.) Tex. 1980, U.S. Dist. Ct. (we. dist.) Okla. 1975, U.S. Supreme Ct. 1979. Pvt. practice Wichita, Kans., 1974-75; asst. dir. Law Ctr. Okla. U., 1975-77, asst. prof., 1977-80, assoc. prof., 1980-82, prof. law, 1982-90, William J. Boswell chair of law, 1990—; mediator Atty.-Mediators Inst., Inc., 1993; trainer Am. Arbitration Assn., 1992; presenter Tex. A&M U., 1990, Tex. Apellate Cts. Chief Justices Meeting, 1990, Baylor U., 1990, 92, Nat. League of Cities Congress of Cities and Exposition, San Antonio, 1996, Assn. Mayors, Waco, 1997, among others. Contbr. articles to profl. publs. Mem. 1st Presbyn. Ch. Waco, ordained elder, stated clk. of session, 1996—; chair Waco/McLennan County Met. Planning Orgn., 1997—; elder, mem. session, 1995—; mayor City of Waco, 1996—; mem. Waco City Coun. for Dist. III, 1994-96; chmn. Cmty. of Cities, 1996—; chair Waco/McLennan County Met. Planning Orgn., 1996—; mem. Tex. Atty. Gen.'s Mcpl. Adv. Com., 1996-97; bd. dirs. Econ. Opportunities Advancement Corp., Planning Region XI, 1994-95, Waco Symphony Assn., 1988-91, exec. com., 1989-90; bd. dirs. Waco Montessori Sch., 1993-94, Cmtys. in Schs., McClennan County Youth Collaboration Inc., 1997—, Heart of Tex. Coun. Govts., 1995—; mem. adv. coun. Local Leaders of Tex. State Tech. Coll., Waco, 1995—, Salvation Army, 1997—; chair Waco Charter Commn., 1986; mem. Waco-McLenna County Task Force on AIDS, 1988-89; vol. Toys for Tots, 1990—. Recipient Cmty. Builder award Masonic Grand Lodge of Tex., Disting. Achievement award VFW Post 2983, 1998. Mem. Rotary (Waco Downtown club 1984-96), Order of Coif, Phi Beta Kappa. Office: PO Box 97288 Waco TX 76798-7288

**MORRISON, STEPHEN GEORGE,** lawyer; b. Pasadena, Calif., Aug. 10, 1949; s. Ira George and Virginia Lee (Zimmer) M.; m. Gail Louise Moore, June 10, 1972; 1 child, Gregory Stephen. BBA, U. Mich., 1971; JD, U. S.C., 1975. Ptnr. Nelson, Mullins, Riley & Scarborough, Columbia, S.C., 1975—; adj. prof. U. S.C., Columbia, 1973-75, 82—; pres. Defense Rsch. Inst., 1995-96; exec. v.p., gen. counsel, sec., chief adminstrv. officer Policy Mgmt. Sys. Corp.; presenter in field. Author/editor: Products Liability Pretrial Notebook, 1989, South Carolina Appellate Practice Handbook, 1986. Bd. dirs. S.C. Com. Humanities, Columbia, 1986—, S.C. Gov. Sch. Arts, Columbia, 1988-95; pres., bd. dirs. Richland County Pub. Defender Assn., Columbia, 1991-95. Fellow S.C. Bar Found.; mem. Internat. Assn. Defense Coun., Lawyers for Civil. Justice (bd. dirs. 1995—, pres. elect 1997—). Democrat. Episcopalian. Avocations: fishing, country music, chamber music, physics, history. General civil litigation, Product liability, Computer. Home: 2626 Stratford Rd Columbia SC 29204-2342 Office: Nelson Mullins Riley & Morrison 1330 Lady St Fl 3 Columbia SC 29201-3300

**MORRISROE, DONALD PATRICK,** lawyer; b. Youngstown, Ohio, Mar. 10, 1954; s. Donald Joseph Morrisroe (dec.) and Margie Louise Seidner; m. Barbara Lorene McMahon, Mar. 18, 1989; children: Erin M., Kyle P. BS, Miami U., 1976; JD, U. Cin., 1979. Bar: Ohio 1979, U.S. Dist. Ct. (so. dist.) Ohio 1979, U.S. Ct. Appeals (6th cir.) 1979, Ky. 1991, U.S. Dist. Ct. (ea. dist.) Ky. 1992. Atty. Goodman & Goodman, Cin., 1979—; chmn. Hamilton County Common Pleas Ct. Arbitration Office, 1986—; barrister Am. Inns. Ct., 1992-94. Mem. Nat. Bd. Trial Advocacy (bd. cert. civil trial atty. 1994), Ohio Trial Lawyers Assn., Ohio State Bar Assn., Cin. Bar Assn. Roman Catholic. Avocations: racquetball, cycling, in-line skating, golfing, water skiing. Personal injury, State civil litigation, Labor. Office: Goodman & Goodman 123 E 4th St Flr 5 Cincinnati OH 45202-4000

**MORRISSEY, ELLEN C.,** lawyer; b. Iowa City, Feb. 2, 1946; d. Hugh and Ellen M. (McColl) Clark. BA, U. N.H., 1968; JD, Thomas M. Cooley Law Sch., 1981. Flight attendant Trans World Airlines, N.Y.C., 1968-72; pvt. practice Lansing, Mich., 1982-94, West Hartford, Conn., 1994—. Mem. Leadership Greater Hartford, 1996; vol. Police Athletic League, Hartford, 1995—. Mem. Conn. Bar Assn., Mich. State Bar Found., Mich. Bar Assn., Hartford County Bar Assn. General practice, Family and matrimonial, Criminal. Office: 65 LaSalle Rd West Hartford CT 06107-2374

**MORRISSEY, GEORGE MICHAEL,** judge; b. Chgo., Aug. 12, 1941; s. Joseph Edward and Mary Bernice (Shields) M.; m. Mary Kay McCarthy, Jan. 3, 1976; children: Meghan Catherine, Colleen Mary. BS, Ill. Inst. Tech., 1963; JD, De Paul U., 1971. Bar: Ill. 1972, U.S. Dist. Ct. (no. dist.) Ill. 1978, U.S. Supreme Ct. 1981. Auditor Touche Ross & Co., Chgo., 1963-68; pvt. practice Evergreen Park and Worth, Ill., 1972-77; chief 5th Mcpl. Dist. Cook County Pub. Defender, Chgo., 1978-90; assoc. judge Cook County Cir. Ct., Chgo., 1991—; mem. spl. commn. on adminstrn. of justice in Cook County, Chgo., 1984-91. Mem. commn. on future of Ill. Inst. Tech., Chgo., 1976-77; bd. trustees Oak Lawn (Ill.) Library, 1979-85; bd. dirs. Crisis Ctr. for South Suburbia, Worth, 1979—. Served with U.S. Army, 1963-69. Mem. Chgo. Bar Assn. (jud. retention com., bar pres. com.), S.W. Bar Assn. (past pres.), Coalition of Suburban Bar Assn. (past pres.), Alpha Sigma Phi. Roman Catholic. Clubs: Columbia Yacht (commodore 1976-78) (Chgo.), Chgo. Yachting (commodore 1982). Lodge: Elks. Office: Cir Ct of Cook County 2600 Richard J Daley Ctr Chicago IL 60602

**MORRISSY, MARY JULE,** court reporter; b. Chgo., June 15, 1952; d. Eugene Vincent Morrissy and Margaret Mary (Lucitt) Leonard; m. Jeffrey Byron, July 23, 1978 (div. June 1988); children: Matthew Jason, Daniel Scott. Student MacCormac Jr. Coll., 1973, Chgo. Coll. Commerce, 1974, Daley Jr. Coll., 1972, Southwest Sch. Bus., 1971. Cert. shorthand reporter; registered profl. reporter. Court reporter Cen. Reporters, Chgo., 1973-74; co-owner Morrissy & McGuire, Chgo., 1974-78, v.p., 1990—; owner Morrissy & Others, Chgo., 1978-82; pres. Morrissy & Others, Ltd., Chgo., 1983-90; v.p. Morrissy & McGuire Ltd., Chgo. Sec., Del Mar Woods Improvement Assn., Deerfield, Ill., 1980-82. Mem. Nat. Shorthand Reporters Assn., Ill. Shorthand Reporters Assn., Assn. for Info. and Image Mgmt. Home: 2620 Wildwood Ln Deerfield IL 60015-1260

**MORSE, JAMES L.,** state supreme court justice; b. N.Y.C., Sept. 11, 1940; m. Gretchen B, June 19, 1965; children: Rebecca Penfield, Rachel Lasell. AB, Dartmouth Coll., 1962; JD magna cum laude, Boston U., 1969. Bar: Vt. 1970, U.S. Dist Ct. Vt. 1970, U.S. Ct. Appeals (2d cir.) 1970, U.S. Supreme Ct. 1973. Law clk. to Judge Sterry R. Waterman U.S. Ct. Appeals (2nd cir.), 1969-70; pvt. practice Burlington, Vt., 1970-73, 75-76; asst. atty. gen. State of Vt., Montpelier, 1973-75, defender gen., 1976-81; judge Vt. Superior Ct., Montpelier, 1981-88; assoc. justice Vt. Supreme Ct., Montpelier, 1988—. Editor in chief Boston U. Law Rev., 1967-69. Lt. USNR, 1963-66. Mem. Vt. Bar Assn. Office: Vt Supreme Ct 109 State St Montpelier VT 05609-0001*

**MORSE, M. HOWARD,** lawyer; b. Louisville, Ky., May 30, 1959; s. Marvin Henry and Betty Anne (Hess) M.; m. Laura E. Loeb, Apr. 17, 1988; children: Elizabeth Loeb, Marni Loeb. AB summa cum laude, Dartmouth Coll., 1981; JD cum laude, Harvard U., 1984. Bar: D.C. 1984, U.S. Ct. of Internat. Trade 1985, U.S. Ct. Appeals (fed. cir.) 1985, U.S. Dist. Ct. D.C. 1986, U.S. Ct. Appeals (D.C. cir.) 1986, U.S. Ct. Appeals (4th cir.) 1987. Assoc. Arnold & Porter, Washington, 1984-88; atty. FTC Bur. Competition, Washington, 1988-91; dep. asst. dir. for policy FTC Bur. Competition, 1991-93, asst. dir. for merger litigation, 1993-97; ptnr. Drinker, Biddle & Reath, Washington, 1998—; adj. prof. law Georgetown Law Ctr., Washington, 1995—. Mem. ABA (mem. antitrust sect., chair computer industry com. 1996-99, chair antitrust issues in high-tech industries program 1999, chair intellectual property com. 1999—), FBA, D.C. Bar Assn., Phi Beta Kappa. E-mail: morsemh@dbr.com. Office: Drinker Biddle & Reath 1500 K St NW Ste 1100 Washington DC 20005-1209

**MORSE, SAUL JULIAN,** lawyer; b. Jan. 17, 1948; s. Leon William and Goldie (Kohn) M.; m. Anne Bruce Morgan, Aug. 21, 1982; children: John Samuel, Elizabeth Miriam. BA, U. Ill., 1969, JD, 1972. Bar: Ill. 1973, U.S. Dist. Ct. (so. dist.) Ill. 1976, U.S. Ct. Appeals (7th cir.) 1983, U.S. Supreme Ct. 1979, U.S. Tax Ct. 1982. Law clk. State of Ill. EPA, 1971-72; law clk. Ill. Commerce Commn., 1972, hearing examiner, 1972-73; trial atty. ICC, 1973-75; asst. minority legal counsel Ill. Senate, 1975, minority legal counsel, 1975-77; mem. Ill. Human Rights Commn., 1985-91; dir., treas., chair grievance com. Ill. Comprehensive Health Ins. Plan; gen. counsel Ill. Legis. Space Needs Commn., 1978-92; pvt. practice Springfield, Ill., 1977-79; ptnr. Gramlich & Morse, Springfield, 1980-85; prin. Saul J. Morse and Assocs., 1985-87; ptnr. Morse, Giganti and Appleton, 1987-92; v.p., gen. counsel Ill. State Med. Soc., 1992—; lectr. in continuing med. edn., 1986-90; counsel symposia; adj. asst. prof. med. humanities So. Ill. Sch. Medicine; pres. Springfield Profl. Baseball, LLC. Bd. dirs. Springfield Ctr. for Ind. Living, 1984-89, Ill. Comprehensive Health Ins. Plan Bd., United Cerebral Palsy Land of Lincoln, United Way Cen. Ill., Inc., 1991-97; treas. City of Leland Grove, Ill., 1999; dir. Hope Sch., mem., bd. dirs. Springfield Jewish Fedn., 1992-95, mem. bd. dirs. Hope Sch., Springfield; mem. task force on transp. Rep. Nat. Com., 1979-80, Springfield Jewish Comty. Rels. Coun., 1976-79, 82; mem. spl. com. on zoning and land use planning Sangamon County Bd., 1978. Named Disabled Adv. of Yr., Ill. Dept. Rehab. Svcs., 1985; recipient Chmn.'s Spl. award Ill. State Med. Soc., 1987, Susan S. Suter award as outstanding disabled citizen of Ill., 1990. Mem. ABA (vice-chmn. medicine and law com. 1988-90, tort and ins. practice sect., forum com. on health law), Am. Assn. Health Lawyers, Am. Soc. Law and Medicine, Ill. State Bar Assn. (spl. com. on reform of legis. process 1976-82, spl. com. on the disabled lawyer 1978-82, young lawyers sect. com. on role of govt. atty. 1977-80, chmn. 1982, sect. coun. adminstrv. law, vice-chmn. 1981-82), Sangamon County Bar Assn., Am. Soc. Med. Assn. Counsel, Phi Delta Phi. Insurance, Health, Legislative. Home: 1701 S Illini Rd Springfield IL 62704-3301 Office: Ill State Med Soc 600 S 2nd St Ste 200 Springfield IL 62704-2542

**MORTENSON, R. STAN,** lawyer; b. Columbia, S.C., Feb. 14, 1945; s. Edwin M. and Marie E. M.; m. (div. 1988); 1 child, J. Charisse. BA, Ohio U., 1967; JD, U. Mich., 1970. Bar: U.S. Dist. Ct. D.C. 1972, U.S. Dist. Ct. (ea. dist.) Mich. 1987, U.S. Ct. Appeals (D.C. cir.), 1972, U.S. Supreme Ct. 1975. Law clk. U.S. Ct. Appeals (9th cir.), La., 1970-71; assoc. Paul, Weiss, Rifkind, Wharton & Garrison, Washington, 1971-75; ptnr. Miller, Cassidy, Larroca & Lewin, Washington, 1975—. Fellow Am. Coll. Trial Lawyers (Fed. Criminal Procedures com.); mem. Edward Bennett Williams Am. Inn Ct., NACDL, D.C. Assn. Criminal Def. Lawyers (R. Kenneth Mundy Lawyer Yr. award 1995). Criminal, Federal civil litigation, Professional liability. Office: Miller Cassidy Larroca & Lewin 2555 M St NW Ste 500 Washington DC 20037-1353

**MORTHORST, MICHAEL EDWARD,** prosecutor; b. Cin., Aug. 8, 1950; s. Arthur Francis and Mary Jean Morthorst. BA, Xavier U., 1972; JD, No. Ky. U., 1977. Bar: Ohio 1977, Ky. 1978, U.S. Dist. Ct. (ea. dist.) Ky. 1977, U.S. Dist. Ct. (ea. dist.) Ky. 1978, U.S. Tax Ct. 1982, U.S. Ct. Appeals (6th cir.) 1977. Staff editor Anderson Law Pubs., Cin., 1975-78; editor-in-chief No. Ky. Law Rev., Highland Heights, 1976-77; pvt. practice law Cin., 1978-86; staff atty. Hamilton County Dept. Human Svcs., Cin., 1986-92; asst. pros. atty. Hamilton County Prosecutors Office, Cin., 1992—. Author: Miami & Erie Canal in Miami and Shelby Counties Ohio, 1997; contbr. articles in field of bankruptcy to profl. jours. Pres., past sec. Silverton (Ohio) Rep. Club, 1996-98; chair law com. Silverton City Coun., 1997—; ctrl. com. mem. Hamilton County Rep. Party, Cin., 1998. Capt. USAR, 1972-80, ret. Mem. Cin. Bar Assn. (chair juvenile com. 1992-93), Canal Soc. Ohio (v.p. 1996—), Canal Soc. Ind. (trustee 1997—). Roman Catholic. Avocations: amateur historian, industrial and commercial archaeology, historical canals. Home: 6914 Ohio Ave Cincinnati OH 45236-3506 Office: Hamilton County Prosecutors Office 230 E 9th St Ste 4000 Cincinnati OH 45202-2174

**MORTIER, JEFFREY JAMES,** lawyer; b. Ottawa, Ill., May 15, 1965; s. James G. and K. Ann M.; m. Lisa A., Mar. 9, 1991; children: Logan A., Graham E. BA, Northwestern U., 1987; JD, Valparaiso U., 1991. Bar: Ind. 1991, U.S. Dist. Ct. (no. and so. dists.) Ind. 1991, U.S. Ct. Appeals (7th cir.) 1991. Assoc. Locke Reynolds, Indpls., 1991-98, ptnr., 1999—. Mem. ABA, Defense Trial Counsel Ind., Ind. State Bar Assn., Indpls. Bar Assn., Defense Rsch. Inst. Democrat. Avocations: tennis, gardening, wine, travel. Product liability, Personal injury, General civil litigation. Office: Locke Reynolds 1000 Capital Ctr S 201 N Illinois St Ste 1000 Indianapolis IN 46204-4210

**MORTIER, RAYMOND DAVID,** lawyer; b. L.A., July 8, 1966; s. Ray C. and Aline M.; m. Andrea R. Mortier, June 30, 1995; 1 child, Madeline. BS, U. Calif. (San Diego), 1988; JD, Calif. Western Sch. Law, 1992. Atty. Mortier & Assocs., San Diego, 1992—. General civil litigation. Office: Mortier & Associates 401 W A St Fl 12 San Diego CA 92101-7901

**MORTIMER, ANITA LOUISE,** lawyer, consultant, educator; b. Jefferson City, Mo., July 2, 1950; d. Ross Maitland Snell and Viola Alice (Leigh) M.; 1 child, Caleb Ross. BA, Graceland Coll., 1973; JD, Washburn U., 1976; MA in Religion with honors, Park Coll., 1992. Bar: Kans. 1976, U.S. Dist. Ct. Kans. 1976, Mo. 1980, U.S. Dist. Ct. (we. dist.) Mo. 1980, U.S. Ct. Appeals (8th cir.) 1980, U.S. Supreme Ct. 1980. Tng. cons. Orgn. to Counter Sexual Assault, Mo., Iowa, Kans., Ill., 1979-80; asst. dist. atty. Wyandotte County, Kansas City, Kans., 1976-80; asst. U.S. atty. U.S. Dept. Justice, Kansas City, Mo., 1980—; appointee Organized Crime and Drug Enforcement Task Force, 1988; cons. Govs. Task Force on Rape Prevention, Mo., 1979-80; instr. Nat. Coll. Dist. Attys., 1980, various camps and retreats, family-related topics, various seminars for fed. agts.; bd. dirs. SHARE, Inc. Contbr. articles to profl. jours. Bd. dirs. Met. Orgn. to Counter Sexual Assault, Kansas City, 1976-80; apptd. to Presdl. Com. on Status of Women, 1979-80; trustee Independence (Mo.) Regional Health Ctr., 1990-94; mem. Ctr. Stake Strategic Planning Commn. RLDS, 1989-90; apptd. chair World Ch. Task Force on Singles' Ministry RLDS, 1990—; chair del. caucus RLDS World Conf., 1992, 94. Named to Honorable Order of Ky. Cols., Gov., 1980. Mem. ABA, Mo. Bar Assn., Assn. Women Lawyers, Kansas City Met. Bar Assn.; Alumni Assn. Graceland Coll. (bd. dirs. 1987, pres. 1988), John Whitmer Hist. Soc. Mem. Reorganized Ch. of Jesus Christ of Latter Day Saints. Clubs: MOCSA (Kansas City), Friends of Art. Office: US Dept Justice 1201 Walnut St Ste 2300 Kansas City MO 64106-2189

**MORTIMER, RORY DIXON,** lawyer; b. Flint, Mich., Jan. 6, 1950; s. Kenneth N. and Phyllis (Rouleau) M.; m. Patricia Ann Amstadt, Sept. 18, 1971; children: Melissa Marie, Ryan Douglas. BA, Mich. State U., 1972, JD, 1978. Bar: S.C. 1978, Mich. 1979, U.S. Ct. Appeals (4th cir.) U.S. Tax Ct., U.S. Supreme Ct. 1979. Trust officer C&S Nat. Bank, Charleston, S.C., 1978-79; pvt. practice law Summerville, S.C., 1979-80; ptnr. Chellis & Mortimer, Summerville, 1980-85, Chellis, Mortimer & Frampton, Summerville, 1985-95; sr. ptnr. Mortimer & Rose, Summerville, 1995-99, Mortimer Law Firm, 1999—. Atty. Dorchester County Human Devel. Bd., 1987—. Mem. ATLA, S.C. Bar Assn., S.C. Trial Lawyers Assn., Mich. Bar Assn., Am. Soc. CLUs and ChFC (pres. 1989). Republican. Roman Catholic. Avocations: golf, tennis. General civil litigation, State civil litigation, General corporate. Home: 105 Old Postern Rd Summerville SC 29483-3770 Office: Mortimer Law Firm 1810 Trolley Rd Summerville SC 29485-8224

**MORTIMER, WENDELL REED, JR.,** judge; b. Alhambra, Calif., Apr. 7, 1937; s. Wendell Reed and Blanche (Wilson) M.; m. Cecilia Vick, Aug. 11, 1962; children: Michelle Dawn, Kimberly Grace. AB, Occidental Coll., 1958; JD, U. So. Calif., L.A., 1965. Bar: Calif. 1966. Trial atty. Legal div. State of Calif., L.A., 1965-73; assoc. Thelen, Marrin, Johnson & Bridges, L.A., 1973-76, ptnr., 1976-93; pvt. practice San Marino, Calif., 1994-95; judge L.A. Superior Ct., 1995—; mem. exec. com. L.A. Superior Ct. With U.S. Army, 1960-62. Mem. ABA, Los Angeles County Bar Assn., Calif. Judges Assn., Am. Judicature Soc., Am. Judges Assn., Legion Lex., ABOTA. Home: 1420 San Marino Ave San Marino CA 91108-2042

**MORTON, DEBORAH BURWELL,** lawyer; b. Midwest City, Okla., June 15, 1953; d. Thornton Allen and Dona (Morine) Burwell; 1 child, Stephen Chase. BS in Edn., Tex. Christian U., 1973; JD, So. Meth. U., 1978. Bar: Md. 1979, Tex. 1984, U.S. Dist. Ct. (no. dist.) Tex. 1985. Ptnr. Neubauer & DeLuca, Balt., 1979-84; assoc. Simon, Anisman, Doby, Wilson & Skillern, Ft. Worth, 1985-88; prin. Law Offices Deborah B. Morton, Ft. Worth, 1988-98; assoc. Law, Snakard & Gambill, Ft. Worth, 1998—. Mem. Tarrant County Bar Assn. Bankruptcy. Office: Law Snakard & Gambill 500 Throckmorton St Ste 3200 Fort Worth TX 76102-3859

**MORTON, DONNA THERESA,** lawyer; b. Louisville, Apr. 20, 1946; d. robert McCreary and Virginia Hurle (Ehrhardt) M.; children: Sophie, Richard, Jonathan. BA, U. Louisville, 1967, JD, 1971; MDiv, Louisville Presbyn. Seminary, 1975, D of Ministry, 1982. Bar: Ky. 1971, U.S. Dist. Ct. (we. dist.) Ky. 1972, U.S. Ct. Appeals (6th cir.) 1972. Atty. in pvt. practice Louisville, 1971—; juvenile defender Jefferson Fiscal Ct., Louisville, 1972-75; exec. dir. Planned Parenthood, Louisville, 1991—; adj. prof. law. U. Louisville, 1980-86, 92, 98, Louisville Presbyn. Seminary, 1994, 1998; pastor United Meth. congregations, Louisville, Ft. Washington, Md., 1975-77, 90-91; assoc. gen. sec. United Meth. Bd. Ch. and Soc. on Capital Hill, Washington, 1986-90; v.p. bd. dirs. Youthworks, Louisville, 1991-96, Nat. Coalition to End Gun Violence, Washington, 1987-90; mem. Planned Parenthood Clergy Adv. Bd., 1996—. Contbr. numerous articles to profl. jours. Commr. Interfaith Commn. on Civil Rights, Chgo., 1987-90; chair bd. dirs. Interfaith Action Econ. Justice, Washington, 1989-90; bd. dirs. The Advocado Press, Louisville, 1993-97. Mem. Ky. Bar Assn. Civil rights, Family and matrimonial, Health. Office: Planned Parenthood 1025 S 2nd St Louisville KY 40203-5442

**MORTON, JAMES RUSSELL,** lawyer; b. Chgo., June 19, 1950; s. Herbert and Marilyn Miller Morton; m. Marlene Cahill, Aug. 23, 1974; children: Cory, Tracy, Jennifer. BS, Tulane U., 1973; JD, Loyola U., 1981. Bar: U.S. Dist. Ct. (ea. and mid. dists.) La. 1981, U.S. Ct. Appeals (5th cir.) 1981. Engr. Dresser Atlas, Belle Chasse, La., 1973-75; ind. oil operator Sidney Lazard, New Orleans, 1975-76; petroleum landman Shell Oil Co., New Orleans, 1977-81; atty. Monroe & Lemann, New Orleans, 1981-97, Taggart & Morton, New Orleans, 1997—. Bd. dirs. New Orleans Legal Assistance Corp., 1996—. Mem. New Orleans Bar Assn. (bd. dirs. 1995—, 3d v.p. 1998). Avocations: golf, bridge, tennis, basketball, orchid growing. Real property, Oil, gas, and mineral, Land use and zoning (including planning). Office: Taggart Morton Ste 2100 1100 Poydras St New Orleans LA 70163-2100

**MORTON, KATHRYN R.,** lawyer; b. Santa Paula, Calif., Dec. 9, 1966; d. Lee Bruce Larrimore and Lynda Carroll Grimes Wales; m. Nason N. Morton, July 29, 1989; 1 child, Nicholas N. BA, Northeastern State U., Tahlequah, Okla., 1989; JD, U. Okla., 1993. Bar: Okla. 1993, Cherokee Nation 1997. Atty. Birdwell & Assocs., Oklahoma City, 1993, Legal Svcs. of Eastern Okla., Stilwell, 1993—; advisor Stilwell H.S. Mock Trial, 1997—, Street Law, Inc., Stilwell, 1997—, Indian Capital Vo-Tech. Cmty. Adv. Bd., Stilwell, 1996—. Recipient Cmty. Svc. award Help-in-Crisis, Inc., Tahlequah, 1998, Indian Capitol Vo-Tech, 1997. Mem. Adair County Bar Assn., Cherokee County Bar Assn., Provider Agy. Locating Svcs., Kiwanis. Democrat. Family and matrimonial, Consumer commercial, General civil litigation. Home: 315 W Poplar St Stilwell OK 74960-2645 Office: Legal Svcs Eastern Okla 219 W Division St Stilwell OK 74960-3011

**MORTON, RICHARD,** lawyer, financial consultant; b. Jamaica, N.Y., Sept. 25, 1925; s. Lawrence and Irma (Gross) M.; student Union Coll., 1946-47; B.S. in Bus. Adminstrn., U. Denver, 1949; postgrad. Stetson Coll. of Law, 1961; J.D., U. Miss., 1963; LL.M. (grad. fellow 1964), Yale U., 1964; m. Helen Malone, June 9, 1965; children—Bruce , Greg, Terri L. Sloan. Vice pres. Gross-Morton Co., Glen Oaks, N.Y., 1950-51; builder, developer, N.Y., Fla., 1952-60; prof. law U. Ga., Athens, 1965-68; admitted to Fla. bar, 1971; pvt. practice law, Miami, Fla., 1971—; pres., dir. S. Fla. Savs. & Loan, Miami, 1980-84; dir. Bank of Fla., Founders Nat. Mortgage Corp, of counsel Katz, Barron, Squitero, Faust & Berman, 1998—. Mem. adv. com. Apt. Investment & Mgmt. Co., Denver. Served to 1st lt., U.S. Army, 1943-57. Decorated Bronze Star. Contbr. articles to profl. jours. Home: 180 Solano Prado Coral Gables FL 33156-2350 Office: 2699 S Bayshore Dr Fl 7 Miami FL 33133-5408

**MORYTKO, JEREMIAH JOSEPH,** lawyer; b. Willimantic, Conn., June 24, 1955; s. John Andrew and Jean Ann Morytko; m. Joanne P. Morytko, Aug. 16, 1980; children: Jason Jeremiah, Timothy Joseph. BA, U. Conn., 1977; JD, New Eng. Sch. Law, Boston, 1981. Bar: Conn. 1981. Assoc. Canozzella & Richardson, Wallingford, Conn., 1981-94; ptnr. Giulietti and Morytko LLC, North Haven, Conn., 1994—. Pres. bd. dirs. Child Guidance Clinic, Meriden, 1992—; mem. golf commn. City of Meriden, 1992-96. Mem. Conn. Bar Assn., New Haven Bar Assn., Meriden-Wallingford Bar Assn., Conn. Trial Lawyers Assn., Hunter Golf Club (pres. 1988-89). Democrat. Roman Catholic. Avocations: golf, coaching youth baseball, soccer and basketball. Personal injury, Family and matrimonial, Bankruptcy. Office: Giulietti and Morytko LLC 22 Broadway North Haven CT 06473-2303

**MOSBACKER, MERVYN,** prosecutor; b. Cuidad Victoria, Mex.. JD, U. Tex., 1982. Prosecutor Cameron County Dist. Atty.'s Office; asst. U.S. atty. Brownsville; U.S. atty. so. dist. Tex. U.S. Dept. Justice, 1999—. Office: US Courthouse 515 Rusk Houston TX 77002*

**MOSCHOS, DEMITRIOS MINA,** lawyer; b. Jan. 8, 1941; s. Constantine Mina and Vasiliky (Strates) M.; m. Celeste Thomaris, Sept. 28, 1975; children: Kristin M., Thomas W. BA magna cum laude, U. Mass., 1962; JD magna cum alude, Boston U., 1965; grad. basic courses, U.S. Army JAG Sch., Charlottesville, va., 1966. Bar: Mass. 1965, U.S. Dist. Ct. Mass. 1975, U.S. Ct. Mil. Appeals 1966. Exec. asst. to city mgr., spl. legal counsel City of Worcester, 1968-75, asst. city mgr., spl. legal counsel, 1975-80; assoc. Mirick, O'Connell, Worcester, 1980-81, ptnr., 1982—; lectr. labor rels. Worcester State Coll., 1975-88, Clark U., 1978—; chmn. Worcester Housing Com., 1968-78, Worcester Energy Com., 1978-80; mem. Mass. Joint Labor Mgmt. Com., 1978-80. Drafter adminstrv. codes; contbr. articles to profl. jours. Trustee United Way, Hellenic Coll., Brookline, Mass.; past pres. archdiocesan coun. Greek Orthodox Archdiocese of Am.; bd. dirs. Worcester Mcpl. Rsch. Bur. Capt. JAGC, U.S. Army, 1966-68. Decorated Army Commendation medal; recipient Alumni Acad. Achievement award Boston U. Law Sch., 1965; named Outstanding Young Man of Worcester County, Worcester County Jaycees, 1969, named in resolution of commendation Worcester City Coun., 1980. Mem. ABA, Mass. Bar Assn. (Comty. Svc. award 1987), Worcester Bar Assn. (chmn. labor sect.), Tatnuck Country Club. Greek Orthodox. Labor, Administrative and regulatory, Municipal (including bonds). Office: Mirick O'Connell 100 Front St Ste 1700 Worcester MA 01608-1402

**MOSCHOS, MICHAEL CHRISTOS,** lawyer; b. Worcester, Mass., Jan. 8, 1941; s. Constantine Mina and Vassiliky (Strates) M.; m. Mary Patricia Dermody, Feb. 20, 1977 (div. Dec. 1991); children: Charles, Michael Patrick; m. Susan Smith Harrington, June 6, 1998; 1 stepchild, Katherine L. BBA cum laude, U. Mass., 1962; JD, Boston U., 1965. Bar: Mass. 1965, N.Y. 1970, U.S. Dist. Ct. Mass. 1981, U.S. Supreme Ct. 1982. Lawyer Investors Group, N.Y.C., 1968-72; assoc., spl. counsel Cabot, Cabot, Forbes, Boston, 1972; pvt. practice Boston, 1973, Worcester, 1979—; spl. counsel Esso-Pappas, S.A., Athens, Greece, 1969-70; investment banker, counsel Worcester Bancorp., 1974-79; cons. atty. Baskins-Sears Esq., N.Y.C., 1979; counsel Downtown Worcester Bus. Devel. Corp., 1974-76. Legal officer Worcester Heritage Soc., 1975-82; mems. coun. Worcester Art Mus., 1975-83; incorporator Worcester Natural History Soc., 1977-98; spl. counsel, acting mng. dir. Hellenic Bottling Co., S.A., Hellenic Canning Industries, S.A., Internat. Canning Industry, S.A., Athens, Greece, 1973. Capt. U.S. Army, 1965-67. Mem. Worcester County Bar Assn. Greek Orthodox. Family and matrimonial, Construction, Real property. Home: 4004 Brompton Cir Worcester MA 01609-1160 Office: 446 Main St Ste 1900 Worcester MA 01608-2359

**MOSELEY, CARY POWELL,** lawyer, entrepreneur; b. Lynchburg, Va., Feb. 18, 1967. BA, U. Va., 1988; JD, Washington and Lee U., 1991. Jud. law clk. Va. Ct. Appeals, 1991-92; assoc. atty. James McElroy & Diehl, Charlotee, N.C., 1992-94; atty. Davidson, Sakolosky & Moseley, P.C., Lynchburg, 1994-97, ptnr., 1997—. Vol. Big Bros., Lynchburg, 1991—, United Way, Lynchburg, 1995—; coach Lynchburg Parks and Recreation, 1997—. Echols scholar U. Va., 1984-88, Washington scholar George Washington H.S., 1984. E-mail: dsmpc@aol.com. Office: Davidson Sakolosky & Moseley PC 916 Main St Ste 200 Lynchburg VA 24504-1608

**MOSELEY, JAMES FRANCIS,** lawyer; b. Charleston, S.C., Dec. 6, 1936; s. John Olin and Kathryn (Moran) M.; m. Anne McGehee, June 10, 1961; children: James Francis Jr., John McGehee. AB, The Citadel, 1958; JD, U. Fla., 1961. Bar: Fla. 1961, U.S. Supreme Ct. 1970. Pres. Moseley, Warren, Prichard & Parrish, Jacksonville, Fla., 1963—; chmn. jud. nominating com. 4th Jud. Cir., 1978-80. Assoc. editor: American Maritime Cases; contbr. articles on admiralty, transp. and ins. law to legal jours. Pres. Jacksonville United Way, 1979; chmn. bd. dirs. United Way Fla., 1992-93, S.E. regional coun. United Way, 1992-96; trustee Jacksonville Cmty. Found.; chmn. bd. trustees Jacksonville Pub. Libr.; trustee Libr. Found., sec., 1987-91; trustee CMI Am. Found.; chmn. Jacksonville Human Svcs. Coun., 1989-91; chmn. bd. trustees United Way N.E. Fla., 1995-97; bd. govs. United Way Am., 1996—. Recipient Meritorious Pub. Svc. award/medal U.S. Dept. Transp./ USCG, 1998. Fellow Am. Coll. Trial Lawyers, Am. Bar Found.; mem. Jacksonville Bar Assn. (pres. 1975), Fla. Coun. Bar Pres. (chmn. 1979), Maritime Law Assn. U.S. (exec. com. 1978-81, chmn. navigation com. 1981-88, v.p. 1992-96, pres. 1996-98), Comm. Maritime Internat. (titulary), Com. on Collision (Lisbon Rules), Fed. Ins. Corp. Counsel (chmn. maritime law sect.), Internat. Assn. Def. Counsel (chmn. maritime com. 1989-91), Am. Inns of Ct. (master of bench), Assn. of Citadel Men (bd. mem. 1989-93, exec. com. 1994, Man Yr. award 1992), Citadel Inn of Ct. (sr. bencher), Deerwood Club, River Club, India House (N.Y.C.), Army Navy Club (Washington), St. John's Dinner Club (pres. 1988). Admiralty, Federal civil litigation, Insurance. Home: 7780 Hollyridge Rd Jacksonville FL 32256-7134 Office: Moseley Warren Prichard & Parrish 1887 West Rd Bay St Jacksonville FL 32216-4542

**MOSENSON, STEVEN HARRIS,** lawyer; b. Phila., Dec. 3, 1956. BS, NYU, 1978, M of Pub. Adminstrn., 1979; JD, Yeshiva U., 1982. Bar: N.Y. 1983, U.S. Ct. Appeals (2d cir.) 1983, U.S. Dist. Ct. (so. and ea. dists.) N.Y. 1983, U.S. Ct. Internat. Trade 1985, U.S. Supreme Ct. 1986. Assoc. Baden Kramer Huffman & Brodsky, N.Y.C., 1982-85; asst. corp. counsel N.Y.C. Law Dept., 1985-89; gen. counsel United Cerebral Palsy Assns. of N.Y. State, Inc., N.Y.C., 1989—. Pres. bd. dirs. Bklyn. Heights Ctr. for Counseling, Inc., 1992—; bd. dirs. Walden, N.Y. Local Devel. Corp., 1998—; mem. Walden Cmty. Coun., 1998—. Mem. N.Y. State Bar Assn. (chmn. com. on issues affecting people 1997—), Guardianship Assn. of N.Y. State, Inc. (v.p. 1995—). Fax: 212-356-0746. E-mail: mosenson@aol.com. Office: United Cerebral Palsy Assns of NY 330 W 34th St Fl 13 New York NY 10001-2488

**MOSER, C. THOMAS,** lawyer; b. Seattle, Aug. 10, 1947; s. Carl Thomas and Helen Louise (Felton) M.; m. Deborah J. St. Clair, Sept. 25, 1976; children: Nicole, Lauren. BA, Cen. Wash. U., 1972; M in Pub. Adminstrn., George Washington U., 1974; JD, Gonzaga U., 1976. Bar: Wash. 1977; U.S. Dist. Ct. (we. dist.) Wash. 1977, U.S. Dist. Ct. (ea. dist.) Wash. 1980, U.S. Ct. Appeals (9th cir.) 1980, U. S. Supreme Ct. 1981. Dep. pros. atty. Skagit County Pros. Atty., Mount Vernon, Wash., 1976-77, chief civil dep., 1979-80, pros. atty., 1980-86; pros. atty. San Juan County Pros. Atty., Friday Harbor, Wash., 1977-79; pvt. practice Mount Vernon, 1987—; hearing examiner pro tem Skagit County, 1992—. Author: Gonzaga Law Review, 1975. Bd. dirs. Wash. Environ. Coun., Seattle, 1971-72, Padilla Bay Found., Skagit County, Wash., 1988; bd. trustees Wash. Assn. County Officials, Olympia, 1983; exec. bd. North Pacific Conf. Evang. Covenant Ch., vice sec. 1991-96. Sgt. U.S. Army, 1967-69, Korea. Recipient Silver Key award ABA Student Law Div., 1976, Legion of Honor award Internat. Order DeMolay, Kansas City, Mo., 1982, Chevalier award 1982. Mem. ATLA, Nat. Coll. Advocacy (advocate), Wash. State Trial Lawyers Assn. (bd. govs. 1990-92, 96-97), Wash. Assn. Pros. Attys. (bd. dirs. 1983-85), Skagit County Bar Assn. (pres. 1995-96), Kiwanis Club Mt. Vernon, Affiliated Health Svc. (ethics com.), Christian Legal Soc. Democrat. Evangelical. Avocations: skiing, golf, jogging, woodworking. Criminal, Personal injury, Land use and zoning (including planning). Office: 411 Main St Mount Vernon WA 98273-3837

**MOSER, DAVID E.,** lawyer; b. San Diego, Feb. 18, 1960; s. John Livingston and Elizabeth C. Moser; m. Barbara G. Walsh, May 30, 1958; children: Joshua, Jeremy. BS, U. Calif., Berkeley, 1981; JD, U. Oreg., 1985. BAr: Wash. 1985, Calif. 1988, U.S. Dist. Ct. (no. dist.) Calif. 1988. Assoc. Hillis, Clark, Martin & Peterson, Seattle, 1985-87; assoc. McCutchen, Doyle, Brown & Enersen, San Francisco, 1987-93, ptnr., 1993—. Mem. ABA (sect. natural resources, energy and environ. law 1985—), Internat. Bar Assn. (environ. law com. 1990—), Calif. Mining Assn. (environment com. 1993—). Avocations: fly fishing, hiking, travel. Environmental, Natural resources. Office: McCutchen Doyle Brown & Enersen 3 Embarcadero Ctr Ste 1800 San Francisco CA 94111-4003

**MOSER, M(ARTIN) PETER,** lawyer; b. Balt., Jan. 16, 1928; s. Herman and Henrietta (Lehmayer) M.; m. Elizabeth Kohn, June 14, 1949; children—Mike, Moriah, Jeremy. AB, The Citadel, Charleston, S.C., 1947; LLB, Harvard U., 1950. Bar: Md. 1950, U.S. Supreme Ct., U.S. Ct. Appeals (4th cir.), U.S. Dist. Ct. Md. Asst. states atty. City of Balt., 1951, 53-54; assoc. Blades Rosenfeld, Balt., 1950, 53-54; ptnr. Frank, Bernstein, Conaway & Goldman and predecessor firms, Balt., 1955-90, co-chmn. firm, 1983-86; counsel, 1991-92; of counsel Piper & Marbury, 1992—; instr. U. Balt. Law Sch., 1954-56, 86, U. Md. Law Sch., 1986-87. Contbr. articles to profl. jours. Del., chmn. local govt. com. Md. Constl. Conv., 1967-68; mem. Balt. City Planning Commn., 1961-66, Balt. Regional Planning Council, 1963-66, Md. Commn. to Study Narcotics Laws, 1965-67, Mayor's Task Force on EEO, 1966-67, Met. Transit Authority Adv. Council, 1962, Com. to Revise Balt. City Planning Laws, 1962, Com. to Revise Balt. City Charter Provision on Conflicts of Interest, 1969-70; mem. Citizens Adv. Com. on Dist. Ct., chmn., 1971, Dist. Adv. Bd. for Pub. Defender System for Dist. 1, 1973-85; mem. Atty. Grievance Commn. of Md., 1975-78, chmn. 82-86; chmn. Md. State Ethics Commn., 1987-89; bd. dirs. Sinai Hosp., 1983—, Lifebridge Health Sys., 1998—, Ct. of Appeals Comm. to Study the Model Rules, 1983-86. Served with JAGC, U.S. Army, 1951-53. Fellow Am. Bar Found., Md. Bar Found. (treas.); mem. ABA (ho. of dels. 1978—, treas. 1993-96, bd. govs. 1984-87, 92-96, ethics com. 1981-84, 87-90, 96—, chmn. 1981-82, 87-90, 98-99, scope and cor. com. 1987-92, chmn. 1990-91), Md. State Bar Assn. (pres. 1979-80), Balt. Bar Assn. (pres. 1971-72), Fed. Bar Assn., Am. Law Inst., Wednesday Law Club, Lawyers' Round Table Club, Hamilton St. Club. Democrat. Jewish. General corporate, Health, Estate planning. Office: Piper & Marbury Fl 13 36 S Charles St Baltimore MD 21201-3020

**MOSES, ALFRED HENRY,** lawyer, former ambassador; b. Balt., July 24, 1929; s. Leslie William and Helene Amelia (Lobe) M.; m. Carol Whitehill, Nov. 24, 1955; Barbara, Jennifer, David, Amalie. BA, Dartmouth, 1951; postgrad., Woodrow Wilson Sch., Princeton U., 1951-52; JD, Georgetown U., 1956. Bar: D.C. 1956. Assoc. Covington & Burling, Washington, 1956-65, ptnr., 1965-94, 97—; spl. advisor, spl. counsel Pres. Jimmy Carter, Washington, 1980-81; amb. to Romania, Am. Embassy, Bucharest, 1994-97; legal advisor minority rights Dem. Nat. Com., Washington, DC Commn. on Urban Renewal; lectr. Am. Law Inst., ABA , New Orleans, Am. Inst. CPAs, ABA, Washington, Georgetown U. Law Ctr., Tax Exec. Inst., Washington, Tulane Tax Inst., New Orleans; guest lectr. on non-legal subjects at Coun. of Europe, Yale U., Princeton U., Dartmouth Coll.; commr. Pub. Housing, Fairfax County, Va., 1971-72. Contbr. articles, commentaries to internat. jours. and press. Co-chmn. legal div. United Givers Fund, Washington, 1975-76; mem. Coun. Fgn. Rels., N.Y.C., 1977—; bd. dirs. Paralysis Cure Rsch. Found., 1978-81; trustee Phelps Stokes Fund, N.Y.C., 1978-84; pres. Nat. Children's Island, Washington, 1975-76; pres. Golda Meir Assn., 1986-88, nat. chmn., 1988-93; trustee Jewish Publ. Soc., 1989-94, Haifa U., 1988-90; pres. Am. Jewish Com., 1991-94; mem. bd. regents Georgetown U., 1986-92. Mem. ABA, D.C. Bar Assn., Met. Club. Democrat. Jewish. General civil litigation, General corporate, Real property. Home: 7710 Georgetown Pike Mc Lean VA 22102-1431 Office: PO Box 7566 Washington DC 20044-7566

**MOSES, SHAYNE DANIEL,** lawyer; b. Ft. Worth, Oct. 12, 1961; s. R.D. and Beverley R. Moses; m. Lisa G.; children: Madison, Meagan A. Bar: Tex., U.S. Dist. Ct. (no. and so. dist.) Tex. Ptnr. Cantey & Hanger, Ft. Worth, 1986—; adj. prof. Tex. U., Ft. Worth, 1987-91. V.p. Big Bros. & Sisters, Tarrant County, Tex.; bd. dirs. Jewish Fedn., Tarrant County, Congregation Ahavath Sholom, Tarrant County. General civil litigation, Oil, gas, and mineral, Contracts commercial. Office: Cantey & Hanger LLP 801 Cherry St Ste 200 Fort Worth TX 76102-6842

**MOSIER, DAVID MICHAEL,** lawyer; b. Erie, Pa., Dec. 18, 1955; s. Daniel Jacob and Cecelia (Holtzhauser) M. BS, John Carroll U., 1978; JD, Cleve. State, 1981. Bar: Pa. 1981. Assoc. Knox, McLaughlin, Gornall & Sennett P.C., Erie, Pa., 1981—. Contbr. articles to profl. jours. Mem. Community House, Inc. (officer, dir.), 1991-98, United Way, Erie (fund distbn. com.), 1989-93. Mem. ABA (mem. bus. section, banking section), Erie County Bar Assn., Presque Isle Rotary (officer, dir., Club Rotarian of Yr., 1995-96). Avocations: racquetball, bicycling, rotary. Taxation, general, Pension, profit-sharing, and employee benefits, Banking. Home: 4622 Colonial Ave Erie PA 16506-4083 Office: Knox McLaughlin Gornall & Sennett PC 120 W 10th St Erie PA 16501-1410

**MOSK, RICHARD MITCHELL,** lawyer; b. L.A., May 18, 1939; s. Stanley and Edna M.; m. Sandra Lee Budnitz, Mar. 21, 1964; children: Julie, Matthew. AB with great distinction, Stanford U., 1960; JD cum laude, Harvard U., 1963. Bar: Calif. 1964, U.S. Supreme Ct. 1970, U.S. Ct. Mil. Appeals 1970, U.S. Dist. Ct. (no., so., ea., and cen. dists.) Calif 1964, U.S. Ct. Appeals (9th dist.) 1964. Mem. staff Pres.'s Commn. on Assassination Pres. Kennedy, 1964; research clk. Calif. Supreme Ct., 1964-65; ptnr. Mitchell, Silberberg & Knupp, L.A., 1965-87; prin. Sanders, Barnet, Goldman, Simons & Mosk, P.C., L.A., 1987—; spl. dep. Fed. Pub. Defender, L.A., 1975-76; instr. U. So. Calif. Law Sch., 1978; judge Iran-U.S. Claims Tribunal, 1981-84, 97—, substitute arbitrator, 1984-97; mem. L.A. County Jud. Procedures Commn., 1973-82, chmn., 1978; co-chmn. Motion Picture Assn. Classification and Rating Adminstrn., 1994—. Contbr. articles to profl. jours. Mem. L.A. City-County Inquiry on Brush Fires, 1970; bd. dirs. Calif. Mus. Sci. and Industry, 1979-82, Vista Del Mar Child Ctr., 1979-82; trustee L.A. County Law Libr., 1985-86; bd. govs. Town Hall Calif., 1986-91; mem. Christopher Commn. on L.A. Police Dept., 1991; mem. Stanford U. Athletic Bd., 1991-95. With USNR, 1964-75. Hon. Woodrow Wilson fellow, 1960; recipient Roscoe Pound prize, 1961. Fellow Am. Bar Found.; mem. ABA (coun. internat. law sect. 1986-90), FBA (pres. L.A. chpt. 1972), L.A. County Bar Assn., Beverly Hills Bar Assn., Internat. Bar Assn., Am. Arbitration Assn. (comml. panel, large complex case panel, Asia/Pacific panel), Hong Kong Internat. Arbitration Ctr. (mem. panel 1986—), Am. Film Mktg. Assn. (arbitration panel), B.C. Internat. Arbitration Ctr. (mem. panel), World Intellectual Property Orgn. (mem. arbitration panel), Ctr. Pub. Resources (mem. arbitration panel), Phi Beta Kappa. State civil litigation, Federal civil litigation, Public international. Office: Sanders Barnet Goldman Simons & Mosk PC 1901 Avenue Of The Stars Los Angeles CA 90067-6078

**MOSK, STANLEY,** state supreme court justice; b. San Antonio, TX, Sept. 4, 1912; s. Paul and Minna (Perl) M.; m. Edna Mitchell, Sept. 27, 1937 (dec.); 1 child, Richard Mitchell; m. Susan Hines, Aug. 27, 1982 (div.); m. Kaygey Kash, Jan. 15, 1995. Student, U. Tex., 1931; PhB, U. Chgo., 1933; postgrad., U. Chgo. Law Sch., 1934; JD, Southwestern U., 1935; postgrad., The Hague Acad. Internat. Law, 1970, U. Pacific, 1970; LLD, U. San Diego, 1971, U. Santa Clara, 1976, Calif. Western U., 1984, Whittier Coll. Law, 1993, Pepperdine U., 1995, Western State U., San Diego, 1995. Bar: Calif. 1935, U.S. Supreme Ct. 1956. Practiced in Los Angeles, until 1939; exec. sec. to gov. Calif., 1939-42; judge Superior Ct. Los Angeles County, 1943-58; pro tem justice Dist. Ct. Appeal, Calif., 1954; atty. gen. Calif., also head state dept., justice, 1959-64; justice Supreme Ct. Calif., 1964—; mem. Jud. Coun. Calif., 1973-75, Internat. Commn. Jurists. Author: Democracy in America-Day by Day, 1995. Chmn. San Francisco Internat. Film Festival, 1967; mem. Dem. Nat. Com, Calif., 1960-64; mem. bd. regents U. Calif., 1940; pres. Vista Del Mar Child Care Svc., 1954-58; bd. dirs. San Francisco Law Sch., 1971-73, San Francisco Regional Cancer Found., 1980-83. With AUS, WWII. Recipient Disting. Alumnus award U. Chgo., 1958, 93. Mem. ABA, Nat. Assn. Attys. Gen. (exec. bd. 1964), Western Assn. Attys. Gen. (pres. 1963), L.A. Bar Assn., San Francisco Bar Assn., Am. Legion, Manuscript Soc., Calif. Hist. Soc., Am. Judicature Soc., Inst. Jud. Adminstrn., U. Chgo. Alumni Assn. No. Calif. (pres. 1957-58, 67), Order of Coif (hon.), B'nai B'rith, Hillcrest Country Club (L.A.), Commonwealth Club, Beverly Hills Tennis Club. Office: Supreme Ct Calif 350 Mcallister St San Francisco CA 94102-4712

**MOSK, SUSAN HINES,** lawyer; b. Pitts., Dec. 14, 1946; d. William James and Catherine Elizabeth (Cook) Hines; m. Stanley Mosk, Aug. 27, 1982 (div. Jan. 1995). B in Music Edn., Fla. State U., 1968, M in Music Edn., 1970; JD, U. Calif., San Francisco, 1990. Bar: Calif. 1990, U.S. Dist. Ct. (no. dist.) Calif. 1990, U.S. Ct. Appeals (9th cir.) 1990. Assoc. Payne, Thompson & Walker, San Francisco, 1990-94; of counsel Knecht, Haley, Lawrence & Smith, San Francisco, 1994-95; prin. Law Offices of Susan H. Mosk, San Francisco, 1995—; commr. Jud. Nominees Evaluation Commn., 1992-96.

Author/editor: Rainmaking Guide to Corporate Counsel, 1993. Mem. steering com. Women's Leadership Coun. for U.S. Senator Diane Feinstein, 1992—; chair No. Calif. Women's Cabinet for Kathleen Brown Gubernatorial Campaign, San Francisco, 1994; co-chair fin. Willie L. Brown Mayoral Campaign, 1995. Mem. State Bar of Calif., Calif. Women Lawyers (bd. govs. 1992-94, 1st v.p. 1993-94), Queen's Bench. Democrat. Avocations: music, skiing, traveling, reading. Family and matrimonial, Real property, Labor. Office: 57 Post St Ste 604 San Francisco CA 94104-5023

**MOSKOVITZ, STUART JEFFREY,** lawyer; b. Phila., Jan. 21, 1949; s. Martin and Jean (Sandler) M.; m. Toni Cheryl Gans, June 1, 1980; children: Lauren Michelle, Leanne Meredith, Lisa Morgan. BA, Hofstra U., 1970; JD, Boston U., 1973. Bar: Pa. 1973, U.S. Dist. Ct. (mid. dist.) Pa. 1974, U.S. Claims Ct. 1975, U.S. Supreme Ct. 1979, N.Y. 1981, U.S. Dist. Ct. (so. dist.) N.Y. 1982, U.S. Ct. Appeals (2d cir.) 1983, N.J. 1993, U.S. Dist. Ct. N.J. 1993. Asst. atty. gen. Pa. Dept. Transp., Harrisburg, 1973-79; atty. Westinghouse Electric Corp., Pitts., 1980-81; ptnr. Berman, Paley, Goldstein & Berman, N.Y.C., 1981-90, Tanner, Propp & Farber, N.Y.C., 1991-94, Stadtmauer Bailkin, L.L.P., N.Y.C., 1995-98, McGowan & Moskovitz, L.L.P., N.Y.C. & South Amboy, N.J., 1999—. Pres. Ivanhoe Village Homeowner's Assn., 1984; mem. Coun. Excellence in Govt., Washington, 1991-93, N.Y. Bldg. Congress, 1991-94; elected Manalapan Twp. Com., 1999. Mem. ABA (forum com. on constrn. indusltry), N.Y. State Bar Assn. (comml. fed. litigation sect. com. on constrn.), Assn. of Bar of City of N.Y., Pa. Bar Assn., N.J. State Bar Assn. General civil litigation, Construction, Contracts commercial. Office: McGowan & Moskovitz LLP 207 S Stevens Ave South Amboy NJ 08879-1821

**MOSKOWITZ, JAMES HOWARD,** lawyer; b. Cin., Apr. 26, 1969; s. Joel S. and Susan R. Moskowitz; m. Sara Felter, May 28; 1 child, Hannah F. BA, Ohio State U., 1991; JD, Salmon P. Chase Sch. Law, 1994. Ptnr. Moskowitz & Moskowitz, Cin., 1995—. Mem. ABA, Ohio State Bar Assn., Cin. Bar Assn. Family and matrimonial, Probate. Office: Moskowitz & Moskowitz 4300 Carew Tower 441 Vine St Ste 441 Cincinnati OH 45202-2813

**MOSKOWITZ, STUART STANLEY,** lawyer; b. N.Y.C., Aug. 27, 1955; s. Arthur Appel and Rebecca (Gordon) M. BS magna cum laude, SUNY, Albany, 1977; JD with honors, Union U., Albany, 1981; LLM, NYU, 1990. Bar: N.Y. 1982, U.S. Tax Ct. 1983, U.S. Dist. Ct. (so. dist.) N.Y. 1985. Law clk. to presiding judge U.S. Tax Ct., Washington, 1981-83, U.S. Ct. Appeals for 2d cir., N.Y.C., 1983-84; sr. counsel IBM, Armonk, N.Y., 1984—; research asst. fin. SUNY Sch. of Bus., Albany, 1976-77, corp. law Albany Law Sch., 1980-81; instr. acctg. Ednl. Opportunities Program SUNY, Albany, 1977-78. Tax counselor for elderly Am. Assn. Ret. Persons, Westchester County, N.Y., Corp. Lawyers of Svc. to the Elderly, Westchester County Legal Svcs., N.Y. Mem. ABA, Order of Justinian. Contracts commercial, General corporate, Securities. Home: 153 Princeton Dr Hartsdale NY 10530-2010 Office: IBM New Orchard Rd Armonk NY 10504

**MOSLEY, DEANNE MARIE,** lawyer; b. Meridian, Miss., Oct. 24, 1969; d. James Alton and Betty Anne (Rutledge) Mosley. B in Pub. Adminstrn., U. Miss., 1991, JD, 1994. Bar: Miss. 1994, U.S. Dist. Ct. Miss. 1994, U.S. Supreme Ct. 1997. Assoc. Hamilton & Linder, Meridian, Miss., 1994-95, Langston Frazer Sweet & Freese, Jackson, Miss., 1995-98; spl. asst. atty. gen. State of Miss., Jackson, 1999—; instr. Ctr. for Legal Studies, Golden, Colo., 1998—. Editor: A Guide to Women's Legal Rights in Mississippi, 1998. Mem. Miss. Supreme Cts. Gender Fairness Task Force, Jackson, 1998—. Mem. Miss. Bar Assn. (mem. disciplinary rules and procedures adv. com. 1998—, bd. dirs. young lawyers divsn. 1998—), Miss. Women Lawyers Assn. (treas., bd. dirs.), Jackson Young Lawyers Assn. (publ. editor 1997-98), Ctrl. Miss. Ole Miss Alumni Assn. (bd. dirs. 1998—). Government contracts and claims, Administrative and regulatory. Office: Contract Rev Bd 301 N Lamar St Jackson MS 39201-1404

**MOSLEY, JERALD LEE,** lawyer; b. Mexico City, July 16, 1949; s. Ramon Thomas and Frances (Smith) M. BA in Religion, Loma Linda U., 1971; BA in Philosophy, Western Ill. U., 1972; MA in Philosophy, U. of Calif., Davis, 1976, PHD in Philosophy, 1979; JD, UCLA, 1982. Bar: Calif. 1982. Atty./assoc. Carter & Mosley, Pasadena, Calif., 1983-87, atty./ptnr., 1987—. Contbr. articles to profl.jours. Mem. Am. Philos. Assn., ABA, Calif. State Bar Assn., Los Angeles County Bar Assn., Pasadena Bar Assn. Avocation: philosophical writing.

**MOSS, BILL RALPH,** lawyer; b. Amarillo, Tex., Sept. 27, 1950; s. Ralph Vonlver and Virginia May (Atkins) M.; 1 child, Brandon Price. BS with spl. honors, West Tex. State U., 1972, MA, 1974; JD, Baylor U., 1976; cert. regulatory studies program, Mich. State U., 1981. Bar: Tex. 1976, U.S. Dist. Ct. (no. dist.) 1976, U.S. Tax Ct. 1979, U.S. Ct. Appeals (5th cir.) 1983. Briefing atty. Ct. Appeals 7th Supreme Jud. Dist. Tex., Amarillo, 1976-77; assoc. Culton, Morgan, Britain & White, Amarillo, 1977-80; hearings examiner Pub. Utility Commn. Tex., Austin, 1981-83; asst. gen. counsel State Bar Tex., Austin, 1983-87; founder, owner Price & Co. Publs., Austin, 1987-97; asst. gen. counsel Tex. Ethics Commn., Austin, 1997—; election inspector State of Tex., 1998—; instr., lectr. West Tex. State U., Canyon, Ea. N.Mex. U., Portales, 1977-80; election inspector State of Tex., 1998—. Active St. Matthew's Episcopal Ch.; election inspector State of Tex., 1998—. Mem. ABA, Tex. Bar Assn. (speaker profl. devel. programs 1983—), Nat. Orgn. Bar Counsel, Internat. Platform Assn., Alpha Chi, Lambda Chi Alpha, Omicron Delta Epsilon, Phi Alpha Delta, Sigma Tau Delta, Pi Gamma Mu. Administrative and regulatory, Professional liability, Ethics. Home: 506 Explorer St Lakeway TX 78734-3447 Office: Sam Houston Bldg 201 E 14th St Fl 10 Austin TX 78701

**MOSS, FRANCINE HOPE,** lawyer; b. Bklyn., Nov. 9, 1951; d. Simon and Anne (Cohen) Itzkowitz; m. Steven H. Moss, Aug. 20, 1978; children: Ian H., Hillary C. BA, Bklyn. Coll., 1973; JD, NYU, 1978. Bar: N.Y. 1979, U.S. Dist. Ct. (ea. and so. dists.) N.Y. 1979, U.S. Ct. Appeals (fed. cir.) 1991, U.S. Ct. Mil. Appeals 1991, U.S. Claims Ct. 1991, U.S. Supreme Ct. 1991. Law clk. Dept. of Housing and Urban Devel., N.Y.C., 1976-77; assoc. Flower & Plotka, Bayshore, N.Y., 1978-80; mng. lawyer Jacoby & Meyers, Bohemia, N.Y., 1980-86, ptnr., 1986-94; ptnr. Judd & Moss, P.C., Ronkonkoma, N.Y., 1994—. Mem. ABA, N.Y. Bar Assn., Suffolk County Bar Assn. Democrat. Jewish. Family and matrimonial, General practice. Office: Judd & Moss PC 3505 Veterans Memorial Hwy Ronkonkoma NY 11779-7613

**MOSS, JACK GIBSON,** lawyer; b. Jackson, Miss., Sept. 1, 1956; s. Joe G. and Permelia (Williams) M. AA, Hinds Jr. Coll., Raymond, Miss., 1975; BS, Miss. State U., 1977; JD, U. Miss., 1980. Bar: Miss. 1980, U.S. Dist. Ct. (no. and so. dists.) Miss. 1980. Assoc. Keyes, Moss & Piazza, Jackson, 1980-82; pvt. practice Raymond, 1982—. Mem. ABA, Miss. Bar Assn., Hinds County Bar Assn., Hinds Community Coll. Alumni Assn. (pres. Hinds chpt. 1987-88), Ducks Unltd. (regional v.p.). Baptist. Avocation: sports. Real property, Probate, General practice. Office: PO Box 49 Raymond MS 39154-0049

**MOSS, LOGAN VANSEN,** lawyer; b. Atlanta, Apr. 17, 1957; s. Joseph Henry Moss and Elsie Louise (McCown) Daniels. BA, Bates Coll., 1979; JD, U. Tulsa, 1982. Bar: Okla. 1982, U.S. Dist. Ct. Okla. 1982, Maine 1984, U.S. Dist. Ct. Maine 1984, U.S. Supreme Ct. 1986. Law clk. to presiding justice Okla. Ct. Appeals, Tulsa, 1982-84; assoc. Strout, Payson et al, Rockland, Maine, 1984-87, Joseph M. Cloutier & Assocs., Camden, Maine, 1987-88, Armstrong & Assoc., Tulsa, Okla., 1988-91; with Temple-Island Forest Products Corp., Diboll, Tex., 1991—. Mem. Assn. Trial Lawyers Am. Republican. Roman Catholic. Avocation: sports. Personal injury, Federal civil litigation, State civil litigation. Office: Temple Inland Forest Products Corp 303 S Temple Dr Diboll TX 75941-2419

**MOSS, RAYMOND LLOYD,** lawyer; b. N.Y.C., Apr. 9, 1959. BA in Polit. Sci. cum laude, Bucknell U., 1981; JD, Hofstra U., 1984. Bar: Conn., N.Y., N.J., Ga., U.S. Supreme Ct. Atty. Dreyfus Corp., N.Y.C., 1984-85; corp. atty. Kramer, Levin, Nessen, Kamin & Frankel, N.Y.C., 1985-88; ptnr. Glass, McCullough, Sherill & Harold, Atlanta, 1988-92, Holland & Knight (and predecessor firms), Atlanta, 1993-97; arbitrator Nat. Assn. Securities Dealers. Author column Conscience, 1983-84. Mem. ABA, N.Y. State Bar Assn., Assn. of Bar of City of N.Y., Ga. State Bar Assn., Phi Eta Sigma. Avocations: tai chi chuan, tennis, golf. Securities, General corporate, Mergers and acquisitions. Office: Sims Moss Kline & Davis LLP 400 Northpark Town Ctr 1000 Abernathy Rd NE Atlanta GA 30328-5606

**MOSS, STEPHEN B.,** lawyer; b. Jacksonville, Fla., July 14, 1943; s. Rudy and Betty (Sobel) M.; m. Rhoda Goodman, Nov. 24, 1984; children: Kurt, Shannon. BA, Tulane U., 1964; JD, Samford U., 1968. Bar: Fla. 1968, U.S. Dist. Ct. (so. dist.) Fla., U.S. Tax Ct. From assoc. to ptnr. Heiman & Crary, Miami, Fla., 1971-74; pvt. practice law So. Miami, Fla., 1974-75; ptnr. Glass, Schultz, Weinstein & Moss P.A., Coral Gables, Fla., 1975-78, Ft. Lauderdale, Fla., 1978-80; ptnr. Holland & Knight, Ft. Lauderdale, 1980—. Active mem. pro bono com. 17th Jud. Cir., 1999; chair steering com. Broward County Child Welfare Initiative, 1999, hon. chair Broward Edn. Found. BRACE awards, 1999. Capt. U.S. Army, 1968-70, Vietnam. Named Outstanding Kiwanian, Miami, 1974; Olympic torchbearer, 1996. Fellow ABA, Fla. Bar Found.; mem. Fla. Bar Assn., Legal Aid Svc. of Broward County (bd. dirs.), Greater Ft. Lauderdale C. of C. (gen. counsel 1991-92, chmn. bd. dirs., bd. govs. 1995, 99—, Chmn.'s award 1991), Tower Club, Tower Forum (pres. 1993-94, bd. dirs. 1999—). Democrat. Jewish. Avocations: running, softball, hiking. Real property, Land use and zoning (including planning), Probate. Office: Holland & Knight LLP Fl 13 1 E Broward Blvd Fort Lauderdale FL 33301-1804

**MOSS, STEPHEN EDWARD,** lawyer; b. Washington, Nov. 22, 1940; s. Morris and Jean (Sober); children: Aubrey, Hilary. BBA, Baldwin-Wallace Coll., 1962; JD with honors, George Washington U., 1965, LLM, 1968. Bar: D.C. 1966, Md. 1971. Assoc. Cole & Groner, Washington, 1965-70; pvt. practice law Bethesda, Md., 1971-80; pres. Stephen E. Moss, P.A., Bethesda, 1981-89, Moss, Strickler & Weaver, Bethesda, 1990-94, Moss, Strickler & Sachitano, P.A., Bethesda, 1995—; lectr. in family law and trial practice. Fellow Am. Acad. Matrimonial Lawyers (cert.), Internat. Acad. Matrimonial Lawyers; mem. Montgomery County Bar Assn. Inc. (chmn. family law sect. 1980), Md. Bar Found., Inc. (cert. mediator). Family and matrimonial, General civil litigation, General practice. Office: Moss Strickler & Sachitano PA 4550 Montgomery Ave Ste 700 Bethesda MD 20814-3304

**MOSSINGHOFF, GERALD JOSEPH,** lawyer, educator; b. St. Louis, Sept. 30, 1935; m. Jeanne Carole Jack, Dec. 29, 1958; children: Pamela Ann Jennings, Gregory Joseph, Melissa M. Ronayne. BSEE, St. Louis U., 1957; JD with honors, George Washington U., 1961. Bar: Mo. 1961, D.C. 1965, Va. 1981. Project engr. Sachs Electric Corp., 1954-57; dir. congl. liaison NASA, Washington, 1967-73, dep. gen. counsel, 1976-81; asst. Sec. Commerce, commr. patents and trademarks U.S. Patent Office, 1981-85; pres. Pharm. Rsch. and Mfrs. Am., Washington, 1985-96; Cifelli prof. intellectual property law George Washington U., Washington, 1996—; sr. counsel Oblon, Spivak, McClelland, Maier & Neustadt, Arlington, Va., 1997—; amb. Paris Conv. Diplomatic Conf.; adj. prof. George Mason U. Law Sch. Recipient Exceptional Svc. medal NASA, 1971, Disting. Svc. medal, 1980, Outstanding Leadership medal, 1981, Disting. Alumnus George Washington U., 1996; granted presdl. rank of meritorious exec., 1980; Disting. Pub. Svc. award Sec. of Commerce, 1983. Fellow Am. Acad. Pub. Adminstrn.; mem. Reagan Alumni Assn. (bd. dirs.), Cosmos Club, Knights of Malta, Order of Coif, Eta Kappa Nu, Pi Mu Epsilon. Patent, Health. Home: 1530 Key Blvd Penthouse 28 Arlington VA 22209-1532 Office: Oblon Spivak McClelland Maier & Neustadt 1755 Jefferson Davis Hwy 4th Flr Arlington VA 22202-3509

**MOSSMAN, MARK E.,** lawyer; b. Vinton, Iowa, Mar. 26, 1950; s. Keith D. and Rebecca Mossman; m. Kathryn R. Donnelly, Aug. 18, 1972; children: John, Burns. BA in Fin. with honors, U. Iowa, 1972; JD with distinction, Drake U., 1975. Atty. Benton County, Vinton, 1979-83; ptnr. Mossman & Mossman, LLP, Vinton, 1975—. Bd. dirs. Virginia Gay Hosp., Vinton, 1995—, Vinton Park and Recreation Com., 1988-95. Mem. ABA, Iowa State Bar Assn. (bd. govs. 1996—). Avocations: golf, biking, racquetball, photography. General civil litigation, General practice, Probate. Office: Mossman & Mossman LLP PO Box 390 Vinton IA 52349-0390

**MOST, JACK LAWRENCE,** lawyer, consultant; b. N.Y.C., Sept. 24, 1935; s. Meyer Milton and Henrietta (Meyer) M.; children: Jeffrey, Peter; m. Irma Freedman Robbins, Aug. 8, 1968; children: Ann, Jane. BA cum laude, Syracuse U., 1956; JD, Columbia U., 1960. Bar: N.Y. 1960, U.S. Dist. Ct. (so. and ea. dists.) N.Y. 1963. Assoc. Hale, Grant, Meyerson and O'Brien, N.Y.C., 1960-66; dep. assoc. dir. OEO, Exec. Office of The Pres., Washington, 1965-67; asst. to gen. counsel C.I.T. Fin. Corp., N.Y.C., 1968-70; corp. counsel PepsiCo, Inc., Purchase, N.Y., 1970-71; v.p. legal affairs Revlon, Inc., N.Y.C., 1971-76; asst. gen. counsel Norton Simon, Inc., N.Y.C., 1976-79; ptnr. Rogers Hoge and Hills, N.Y.C., 1979-86; ptnr. Finkelstein Bruckman Wohl Most & Rothman LLP, N.Y.C., 1986-97, mng. ptnr., 1990-93; mng. ptnr. Ferster Bruckman Wohl Most & Rothman LLP, 1997-99; ptnr. Goetz, Fitzpatrick, Most & Bruckman LLP, 1999—; corp. sec. Requa, Inc., Flowery Beauty Products, Inc., 1987—. Contbr. articles to profl. jour. and mags. Bd. dirs. Haym Salomon Home for the Aged, 1978-91, pres., 1981-91; bd. dirs. The Jaffa Inst. for Advancement Edn., 1994-95; bd. dirs. Jewish Fellowship of Hemlock Farms, 1995—, treas., 1996-98, sec. 1998-99; bd. dirs., pres. Haym Salomon Found., 1992-99; mem. bd. advisors Touro Coll. Health Scis., 1989-90. Mem. ABA (food, drug and cosmetic law com., trademark and unfair competition com.), N.Y. State Bar Assn. (food, drug and cosmetics sect.), YRH Owners Corp. (bd. dirs., pres. 1989-92), Lords Valley Country Club (bd. govs. 1984-90, 1st v.p. 1987-88, 2d v.p. 1989-90), Zeta Beta Tau, Omicron (trustee Syracuse chpt. 1988-91). Jewish. General corporate, Administrative and regulatory, Trademark and copyright. Home: 429 E 52nd St New York NY 10022-6430 Office: Goetz Fitzpatrick Most & Bruckman LLP One Penn Plz New York NY 10119

**MOTEJUNAS, GERALD WILLIAM,** lawyer; b. Boston, Jan. 18, 1950; s. Peter and Eva C. (Jankus) M.; m. Patricia A. McKeon, June 23, 1984; children: Scott Peterson, Mark Whitney. BA, Northeastern U., 1972; JD, Suffolk U., 1976. Bar: Mass. 1976, U.S. Dist. Ct. Mass., 1977, U.S. Supreme Ct. 1983. Assoc. Lecomte, Emanuelson, Motejunas & Doyle, Boston, 1976-85, ptnr., 1985—. Author: Suffolk U. Law Rev., 1975; editor, 1976. Mem. ABA (chmn., editor, vice chmn. property ins. law com.), ATLA, Def. Rsch. Inst., Mass. Bar Assn., Boston Bar Assn., Loss Execs. Assn., Boston Athenaeum, Appalachian Mountain Club (exec. com. 1980-81). Avocations: skiing, golf. Insurance, General civil litigation, General practice. Office: Lecomte Emanuelson Motejunas & Doyle 1250 Hancock St Quincy MA 02169-4339

**MOTES, CARL DALTON,** lawyer; b. May 31, 1949; s. Carl Thomas and Orpha Jeanette (McGauley) M.; m. Maria Eugenia Aguirre, Apr. 19, 1975. AA with honors, St. Johns River Jr. Coll., 1969; BA, Fla. State U., 1971, JD with honors, 1974. Bar: Fla. 1974, U.S. Dist. Ct. (cen., no. and so. dists.) Fla. 1975, U.S. Ct. Appeals (11th cir.) 1980. Assoc. Maguire, Voorhis & Wells P.A., Orlando, Fla., 1975-79, ptnr., 1979-97; ptnr. Motes & Sears P.A., Winter Park, Fla., 1998-99, Motes & Carr, P.A., Orlando, 1999—; asst. to pres. Fla. Bar, Tallahassee, 1974-75; dir. Legal Aid Soc., Orlando, 1979-83, pres., 1983-84; lectr. at various Bar Assns. and ednl. insts. Mem. editl. bd. Jour. Trial Advocate Quar., 1981-91, 95—, chmn., 1989-91; contbr. articles to profl. jours. Active in Planning & Zoning Bd., Altamonte Springs, Fla., 1977-79, Capital Funds Project Rev. Com., Cen. Fla., 1983; bd. dirs. Cen. Fla. coun. Boy Scouts Am., mem. exec. bd., v.p. adminstrn. 1993-94. Mem. ABA, Internat. Assn. Def. Counsel, Fla. Def. Lawyer's Assn. (bd. dirs. 1989-94, sec., treas. 1991-92, pres.-elect 1992-93, pres. 1993-94), Fed. of Ins. and Corp. Coun., Orange County Bar Assn. (sec. 1979-80, exec. coun. 1980-83, named Outstanding Mem. 1981-82, Outstanding Com. Chmn. 1977), Fla. State U. Alumni Assn. (bd. dirs. 1975-78, pres. 1979), Def. Rsch. Inst. (state chair 1994), Phi Delta Phi. Republican. E-mail: carl@moteslaw.com. Fax: (407) 897-6949. State civil litigation, Federal civil litigation, Professional liability. Office: Motes & Carr PO Box 3426 Orlando FL 32802-3426

**MOTLEY, CONSTANCE BAKER (MRS. JOEL WILSON MOTLEY),** federal judge, former city official; b. New Haven, Sept. 14, 1921; d. Willoughby Alva and Rachel (Huggins) Baker; m. Joel Wilson Motley, Aug. 18, 1946; 1 son, Joel Wilson, III. AB, NYU, 1943; LLB, Columbia U., 1946. Bar: N.Y. bar 1948. Mem. Legal Def. and Ednl. Fund, NAACP, 1945-65; mem. N.Y. State Senate, 1964-65; pres. Manhattan Borough, 1965-66; U.S. dist. judge So. Dist. N.Y., 1966-82, chief judge, 1982-86, sr. judge, 1986—. Author: Equal Justice Under Law, 1998. Mem. N.Y. State Adv. Council Employment and Unemployment Ins., 1958-64. Mem. Assn. Bar City N.Y. Office: US Dist Ct US Courthouse 500 Pearl St New York NY 10007-1316

**MOTOLA, DAVID HENRY,** lawyer; b. N.Y.C., Sept. 23, 1961; s. Gabriel and Francine Ruth Motola; m. Melissa Motola, Oct. 28, 1989; children: Alexandra, Kyra, Jack. BA cum laude, U. Albany, 1983; JD, Fordham U., 1986. Bar: N.Y. 1987, U.S. Dist. Ct. (so., ea. and we. dists.) N.Y. 1987, N.J. 1990, U.S. Dist. Ct. N.J. 1990. Assoc. Mendes and Mount, N.Y.C., 1986-88, Kurzman Karlson & Frank, N.Y.C., 1988-89, Lester Schwab Katz & Pager, N.Y.C., 1989-93; mng. ptnr., founding mem. Motola Klar & Dinowitz, LLP, N.Y.C., 1993—; coun. mem. Albany (N.Y.) U. Coun. for Inter-Collegiate Athletics, 1998—. Mem. ABA, N.Y. State Bar Assn. General civil litigation, Personal injury, Contracts commercial. Office: Motola Klar & Dinowitz LLP 185 Madison Ave New York NY 10016-4325

**MOTSINGER, JOHN KINGS,** lawyer, mediator, arbitrator; b. Winston-Salem, N.C., Aug. 13, 1947; s. Madison Eugene and Margaret Mary (Kings) M.; m. Elisabeth Sykes, June 18, 1989; children: Christian Sykes, Lissa Sykes, John, Jr. BA, Washington & Lee U., 1970; MS, Georgetown U., 1972; JD, Wake Forest U., 1983. Bar: N.C. 1983, U.S. Dist. Ct. (mid. dist.) N.C. 1984. Consumer affairs assoc. U.S Postal Svc., Washington, 1972-73; pres., gen. mgr. Sta. WIPS-Radio, Ticonderoga, N.Y., 1973-79; staff atty. United Guaranty Corp., Greensboro, N.C., 1983-86, Republic Mortgage Ins. Co., Winston-Salem, 1986-91; v.p. law RMIC Corp., Winston-Salem, 1988-91; exec. dir. Carolina Concilation Svcs. Corp., 1992—. Past pres. Unitarian-Universalist Fellowship of Winston-Salem, 1993-94. Mem. ABA, N.C. Bar Assn. (corp. counsel sect. councilor 1989-93), N.C. State Bar, Acad. of Family Mediators (practitioner mem., approved cons.), Am. Arbitration Assn. Democrat. Unitarian-Universalist. Avocations: jogging, music, reading. General corporate, Family and matrimonial, Alternative dispute resolution. Home: 204 Cascade Ave Winston Salem NC 27127-2029 Office: Carolina Conciliation Svcs Corp 204 Cascade Ave Winston Salem NC 27127-2029

**MOTT, H. CHRISTOPHER,** lawyer; b. Bethesda, Md., May 12, 1958; s. Walter Neal and Helen Kay (Davis) M.; m. Cindy Charisse Beck, Dec. 21, 1982; children: Ryan Christopher, Rebecka Charisse. BBA, Tex. Tech U., 1980, JD, 1983. Bar: Tex. 1983. Ptnr. Ginnings Birkelbach & Keith, PC, El Paso, Tex., 1983-93, Kemp, Smith, Duncan & Hammond, El Paso, 1993-94, Krafsur Gordon Mott P.C., El Paso, 1994—. Mem. Sun Bowl Com., El Paso, 1993-97. Mem. Tex. State Bar (cert. in bus. bankruptcy). Avocations: running, swimming, fly fishing, scuba diving, golf. Bankruptcy, Corporate taxation, Federal civil litigation. Office: Krafsur Gordon Mott PC PO Box 1322 El Paso TX 79947-1322

**MOTTA, ROBERT MICHAEL,** lawyer; b. Chgo., May 11, 1945; s. Michael Joseph and Josephine M. (Mondelli) M.; 1 child, Robert Michael II. Student, DePaul U., 1966-69; JD, Ill. Inst. Tech., 1972. Bar: Ill. 1972, U.S. Dist. Trial Bar, 1988, U.S. Ct. Appeals (7th cir.) 1995. Supr. felony trial divsn. Cook County Pub. Defender, Chgo., 1972-77; pvt. practice Chgo. and Oak Park, Ill., 1977—; ptnr. Lavelle, Motta Klopfenstein & Saletta, Ltd., Franklin Park, Ill.; legal cons. TV prodn. Am. Justice, 1996; lectr. defense of insanity, defense of the serial killer. Contbg. author: Ilinois Institute for Continuing Lega; Education, Trial Issues. Mem. Delta Theta Phi. General civil litigation, Criminal, Personal injury. Office: Lavelle Motta Klopfenstein & Saletta Ltd Eversharp Bldg 9240 Belmont Ave Franklin Park IL 60131-2808

**MOTZ, DIANA GRIBBON,** federal judge; b. Washington, July 15, 1943; d. Daniel McNamara and Jane (Retzler) Gribbon; m. John Frederick Motz, Sept. 20, 1968; children: Catherine Jane, Daniel Gribbon. BA, Vassar Coll., 1965; LLB, U. Va., 1968. Bar: U.S. Dist. Ct. Md. 1969, U.S. Ct. Appeals (4th cir.) 1969, U.S. Supreme Ct. 1980. Assoc. Piper & Marbury, Balt., 1968-71; asst. atty. gen. State of Md., Balt., 1972-81, chief of litigation, 1981-86; ptnr. Frank, Bernstein, Conaway & Goldman, Balt., 1986-91; judge Md. Ct. of Special Appeals, Md., 1991-94, U.S. Ct. Appeals (4th Cir.), 1994—. Mem. ABA, Md. Bar Assn., Balt. City Bar Assn. (exec. com. 1988), Am. Law Inst., Am. Bar Found., Md. Bar Found., Lawyers Round Table, Fed. Cts. Study Com., Wranglers Law Club. Roman Catholic. Office: 101 W Lombard St Ste 920 Baltimore MD 21201-2611

**MOTZ, JOHN FREDERICK,** federal judge; b. Balt., Dec. 30, 1942; s. John Eldered and Catherine (Grauel) M.; m. Diana Jane Gribbon, Sept. 20, 1968; children: Catherine Jane, Daniel Gribbon. AB, Wesleyan U., Conn., 1964; LLB, U. Va., 1967. Bar: Md. 1967, U.S. Ct. Appeals (4th cir.) 1968, U.S. Dist. Ct. Md. 1968. Law clk. to Hon. Harrison L. Winter U.S. Ct. Appeals (4th cir.), 1967-68; assoc. Venable, Baetjer & Howard, Balt., 1968-69; asst. U.S. atty. U.S. Atty.'s Office, Balt., 1969-71; assoc. Venable, Baetjer & Howard, Balt., 1971-75, ptnr., 1976-81; U.S. atty. U.S. Atty.'s Office, Balt., 1981-85; judge U.S. Dist. Ct. Md., Balt., 1985-94, chief judge, 1994—. Trustees Friends Sch., Balt., 1970-77, 1981-88, Sheppard Pratt Hosp., 1987-97, 99—. Mem. ABA, Md. State Bar Assn., Am. Bar Found., Am. Law Inst., Am. Coll. Trial Lawyers. Republican. Mem. Soc. of Friends. Office: US Dist Ct 101 W Lombard St Rm 510 Baltimore MD 21201-2607

**MOUGHAN, PETER RICHARD, JR.,** lawyer; b. Phila., July 29, 1951; s. Peter R. Sr. and Catherine L. (Gavin) M.; m. Janice Billick, Aug. 3, 1974, (dec. Dec. 1995); children—Peter R. III, Gavin Patrick, Jacob Daniel. B.A., Wheeling Coll., 1973; M.S., Gonzaga U., 1975, M.B.A., 1977, J.D., 1977. Bar: Pa. 1977, N.Mex. 1980. Legal researcher Am. Law Inst.-ABA, Phila., 1977-78; claim rep. Allstate Ins., Phila., 1978-79; assoc. Larry D. Beall, P.A., Albuquerque, 1979-81; pvt. practice law, Albuquerque, 1981—. Pres. Ancient Order of Hibernians, Albuquerque, 1984-85, 1992—. Mem. Assn. Trial Lawyers Am., N.Mex. Trial Lawyers Assn., Albuquerque Bar Assn., Albuquerque Lawyers Club, Phi Alpha Delta, Albuquerque Aardvarks Rugby Football Club (chmn. 1980-84), K.C. Democrat. Roman Catholic. Personal injury, Contracts commercial, Probate. Office: PO Box 715 Albuquerque NM 87103-0715

**MOUL, ROBERT GEMMILL, II,** lawyer; b. Washington, July 7, 1961; s. Robert Gemmill and Mary Ann (Sargent) M.; m. Susan Marie Beck, Apr. 30, 1994. BA in History, George Washington U., 1983; JD, George Mason U., 1987. Bar: Va. 1988, U.S. Ct. Appeals (4th cir.) 1993, U.S. Dist. Ct. (ea. dist.) Va. 1994. Intern D.C. Corp. Counsel, Washington, 1982; law clk. Dunaway, McCarthy & Dye, Washington, 1983-85, Holland & Knight, Washington, 1985-86; gen. counsel Piedmont Photo Svcs., Charlotte, N.C., 1988-93; pvt. practice Vienna, Va., 1988-93; assoc. Lotfi & Assocs., P.C., Washington, 1993—; legal corr. NBC News, 1994. Spokesman Arlington (Va.) St. People Assistance Network, 1994. Pro Bono Publico, Alexandria and Arlington Bar Assns., 1993. Mem. ABA, Assn. Trial Lawyers Am., Va. Trial Lawyers Assn. Avocations: tennis, running, chess. State civil litigation, Criminal, Immigration, naturalization, and customs. Office: Lotfi & Assocs PC 11921 Rockville Pike # 3 Rockville MD 20852-2737

**MOULDS, JOHN F.,** federal judge; m. Elizabeth Fry, Aug. 29, 1964; children: Donald B., Gerald B. Student, Stanford U., 1955-58; BA with honors, Calif. State U., Sacramento, 1960; JD, U. Calif, Berkeley, 1963. Bar: U.S. Supreme Ct., U.S. Dist. Ct. (no. dist.) Calif., U.S. Dist. Ct. (ea. dist.) Calif. 1968, U.S. Ct. Claims 1982, U.S. Ct. Appeals (9th cir.) 1967, Calif. Rsch. analyst Calif. State Senate Fact-Finding Com. on Edn., 1960-61; adminstrv. asst. Senator Albert S. Rodda, Calif., 1961-63; staff atty. Calif. Rural Legal Assistance, Marysville, 1966-68; dir. atty. Marysville field office and Sacramento legis. adv. office Calif. Rural Legal Assistance, 1968-69; staff atty. Sacramento Legal Aid, 1968-69; ptnr. Blackmon, Isenberg & Moulds, 1969-85, Isenberg, Moulds & Hemmer, 1985; magistrate judge U.S. Dist. Ct. (ea. dist.) Calif., 1985—, chief magistrate jdudge, 1988-97; moot ct. and trial practice judge U. Calif. Davis Law Sch., 1975—, U. of Pacific McGeorge Coll. Law, 1985—; part-time U.S. magistrate judge U.S. Dist. Ct. (ea. dist.) Calif., 1983-85; mem. 9th Cir. Capital Case Com., 1992—, U.S. Jud. Conf. Com. on the Magistrate Judge Sys., 1992—, Adv. Com. to the Magistrate Judges' Divsn. Adminstv. Office of U.S. Jud. Conf., 1989—. Author: (with others) Review of California Code Legislation, 1965, Welfare Recipients'

Handbook, 1967; editor: Ninth Circuit Capital Punishment Handbook, 1991. Atty. Sacramento Singlemen's Self-Help Ctr., 1969-74; active Sacramento Human Relations Commn., 1969-75, chair, 1974-75; active community support orgn. U. Calif. at Davis Law Sch., 1971—; mem., atty. Sacramento Community Coalition for Media Change, 1972-75; bd. dirs. Sacramento Country Day Sch., 1982-90, Sacramento Pub. Libr. Found., 1985-87; active various polit. orgns. and campaigns, 1960-82. Mem. ABA, Fed. Bar Assn., Nat. Coun. Magistrates (cir. dir. 1986-88, treas. 1988-89, 2d v.p. 1989-90, 1st v.p. 1990-91), Fed. Magistrate Judges Assn. (pres.-elect 1991, pres. 1992-93), Calif. State-Fed. Jud. Coun. Conf. (panelist capital habeas corpus litigation 1992), Fed. Jud. Ctr. Training Conf. for U.S. Magistrate Judges (panel leader 1993), Milton L. Schwartz Inns of Ct. Office: 8240 US Courthouse 501 I St Ste 8-240 Sacramento CA 95814-7300

**MOULTHROP, ROSCOE EMMETT,** lawyer; b. Kansas City, Mo., Apr. 8, 1913; s. Roscoe Emmett and Jennie Jerome (Sullivan) M.; m. Esther Myrtle Burton, Nov. 27, 1937; Esther Joan Muench, Roscoe Emmett III, Jean Kathryn, Wolff, Jeanette Marie Babyok. LLB, Kansas City Sch. Law, 1936. Bar: Mo. 1936. Pvt. practice Kansas City, 1936-41, Bethany, Mo., 1941-99; prosecuting atty. Harrison County, Bethany, Mo., 1999—; pros. atty. Harrison County, Bethany, 1943-44, 47-48, 51-54, 77-80. Scout leader Pony Express Coun. Boy Scouts Am., Bethany. Lt. USN, 1944-46, WWII. Mem. ABA, Mo. Bar Assn. (bd. govs. 1964-68). Avocation: farm operation. General practice. Office: PO Box 271 Bethany MO 64424-0271

**MOULTON, HUGH GEOFFREY,** lawyer, business executive; b. Boston, Sept. 18, 1933; s. Robert Selden and Florence (Bracq) M.; m. Catherine Anne Clark, Mar. 24, 1956; children: H. Geoffrey, Cynthia C. Moulton Bassett. B.A., Amherst Coll., 1955; LL.B., Yale U., 1958; postgrad. Advanced Mgmt. Program, Harvard U., 1984. Bar: Pa. 1959. Assoc. Montgomery, McCracken, Walker-Rhoads, Phila., 1958-66, ptnr., 1967-69; v.p., counsel Dolly Madison Industries, Inc., Phila., 1969-70; sec. Alco Std. Corp., Valley Forge, Pa., 1970-72, v.p. law, 1973-79, v.p., sec., gen. counsel, 1979-83, sr. v.p., gen. counsel, 1983-92, exec. v.p., chief adminstrv. officer, gen. counsel, 1992-94; exec. v.p. Alco Std. Corp. now IKON Office Solutions Inc., Valley Forge, Pa., 1994—. Pres. Wissahickon Valley Watershed Assn., Ambler, Pa., 1975-78, treas., 1978—; mem. Pa. Coun. for Econ. Edn., bd. dirs., 1985-95; trustee Beaver Coll., 1991—. Mem. ABA, Pa. Bar Assn., Phila. Bar Assn., Am. Corp. Counsel Assn. (bd. dirs. Delaware Valley chpt. 1984-88, pres. 1986-87), Nature Conservancy (trustee Pa. chpt. 1991—, chmn. 1993—), Sunnybrook Golf Club (Plymouth Meeting, Pa.). Home: 300 Williams Rd Fort Washington PA 19034-2015 Address: IKDN Office Solutions Inc 70 Valley Stream Pkwy Malvern PA 19355-1453

**MOUNT, JOE HORN,** lawyer; b. Tampa, Dec. 18, 1935; s. Joe Horn Mount and Marjorie Louise Day; m. Jan McDonald, June 9, 1956; children: Melinda, Jeffrey, Bonnie Jo, Michael, Sarah. JD, Vanderbilt U., 1961; BS, SUNY, N.Y.C., 1987. Bar: Fla. 1961, Vt. 1997. With U.S. Dept Justice, Dept. Immigration and Naturalization, Napanoch, N.Y. With U.S. Army, 1954-57. Episcopalian. Home: PO Box 782 23 Stones Throw Ln Manchester VT 05254

**MOURSUND, ALBERT WADEL, III,** lawyer, rancher; b. Johnson City, Tex., May 23, 1919; s. Albert Wadel and Mary Frances (Stribling) M., Jr.; m. Mary Allen Moore, May 8, 1941; children: Will Stribling, Mary Moore Moursund. LLB, U. Tex., 1941. Bar: Tex. 1941, U.S. Ct. Appeals (5th cir.) 1964, U.S. Dist. Ct. (so. dist.) Tex. 1964, U.S. Dist. Ct. (we. dist.) Tex. 1964, U.S. Tax Ct. 1972. Pvt. practice law, Johnson City, 1946-63; mem. Moursund & Moursund Johnson City, Round Mountain and Llano, Tex., 1963-80; ptnr. Moursund, Moursund, Moursund & Moursund, 1980—, county judge Blanco County, Tex., 1953-59; chmn. bd. Arrowhead Bank, 1963—, Cattleman's Nat. Bank, Round Mountain; bd. dirs., pres. Arrowhead Co., Arrowhead West, Inc., Tex. Am. Moursund Corp., S.W. Moursund Corp., Ranchlander Corp. Mem. Parks and Wildlife Commn., 1963-67, Tex. Ho. reps., 1948-52. With USAAF, 1942-46. Mem. ABA, Tex. Bar Assn., Hill County Bar Assn. (past pres.), Blanco County Hist. Soc. (charter), Masons, Woodmen of World. General practice. Office: Moursund Moursund Moursund & Moursund PO Box 1 Round Mountain TX 78663-0001

**MOUSEL, CRAIG LAWRENCE,** lawyer; b. St. Louis, July 22, 1947; s. George William and Charlotte (Howard) M.; m. Polly Deane Burkett, Dec. 21, 1974; children: Donna, Dennis, D'Arcy. AB, U. So. Calif., 1969; JD, Ariz. State U., 1972. Bar: Ariz. 1973, U.S. Dist. Ct. Ariz. 1973, U.S. Ct. Appeals (9th cir.) 1973, U.S. Dist. Ct. (cen. dist.) Calif. 1984, Colo. 1993. Adminstrv. asst. to Hon. Sandra O'Connor Ariz. State Senate, Phoenix, 1971-72; asst. atty. gen. Ariz. Atty. Gen.'s Office, Phoenix, 1973-75; ptnr. Sundberg & Mousel, Phoenix, 1975—; spl. counsel City of Chandler, 1991; varsity baseball coach Valley Luth. H.S., 1995-97; varsity asst. baseball coach St. Mary's H.S., 1997—; lectr. Ariz. State U. Coll. Bus., 1993—. Hearing officer Ariz. State Personnel Bd., 1976-80, spl. appeals counsel, 1978—; hearing officer Ariz. Outdoor Recreation Coordinating Commn., 1975; dep. state land commr. Ariz. State Land Dept., 1978; precinct capt. Rep. Com.; mem. Ariz. Kidney Found., Orpheum Theatre Found., Phoenix Zoo Curators Club. Fellow Ariz. Bar Found.; mem. ABA, ATLA, Ariz. Bar Assn., Maricopa County Bar Assn., Sports Lawyers Assn., Internat. Platform Assn., Ariz. Club, Am. Baseball Coaches Assn., Nat. High Sch. Baseball Coaches Assn., Ariz. Baseball Coaches Assn., USC Ptnrs. Alumni Group. General corporate, Entertainment, Administrative and regulatory. Office: Sundberg & Mousel 934 W Mcdowell Rd Phoenix AZ 85007-1730

**MOW, ROBERT HENRY, JR.,** lawyer; b. Cape Girardeau, Mo., Dec. 10, 1938; s. Robert H., Sr. and Ann Elise (Beck) M.; m. Jody K. Boggs, Aug. 29, 1987; children: Robert M., Brynn A., W.Brett, Rebecca M., W. Kirk, Allison M. Student, Westminster Coll., 1956-57; AB with distinction, U. of Mo., 1960; LLB magna cum laude, So. Meth. U., 1963. Bar: Tex. 1963, U.S. Dist. Ct. (no. dist.) Tex. 1965, U.S. Dist. Ct. (so. dist.) Tex. 1969, U.S. Dist Ct. (ea. dist.) Tex. 1976, U.S. Dist. Ct. (we. dist.) Tex. 1976, U.S. Ct. Claims 1973, U.S. Ct. Appeals (5th cir. 1972, U.S. Ct. Appeals (11th cir.) 1981, U.S. Ct. Appeals (Fed. cir.), 1994, U.S. Supreme Ct. 1978. Assoc., Carrington, Johnson & Stephens, Dallas, 1963-69; ptnr. Carrington, Coleman, Sloman, & Blumenthal, Dallas, 1970-85; Hughes & Luce, L.L.P., Dallas, 1985—. Editor-in-chief Southwestern Law Jour., 1962-63. Served to 1st lt. U.S. Army, 1963-65. Fellow Am. Coll. of Trial Lawyers, mem. Dallas Jr. Bar Assn. (pres. 1968), Dallas Assn. of Def. Counsel (chmn. 1976-77), Tex. Assn. of Def. Counsel (v.p. 1981-82), Am. Bd. of Trial Advocates (pres. Dallas chpt. 1983-84). Republican. Baptist. Federal civil litigation, State civil litigation, Professional liability. Office: Hughes & Luce LLP 1717 Main St Ste 2800 Dallas TX 75201-4685

**MOWELL, GEORGE MITCHELL,** lawyer; b. Balt., July 31, 1951; s. George Robert and Polly (Sattler) M.; m. Patricia Edith Forbes, Sept. 23, 1978; children: Rachel Elizabeth, George Robert. BA, Washington Coll., Chestertown, Md., 1973; JD, U. Balt., 1977. Bar: Md. 1978, U.S. Dist. Ct. Md. 1981, U.S. Bankruptcy Ct. 1982. Claims authorizer Social Security Adminstrn., Balt., 1973-79; law clk. to presiding justice Kent County Cir. Ct., Chestertown, 1979-81; ptnr. Boyer & Mowell, Chestertown, 1981-87, Mowell, Nunn & Wadkorsky, Chestertown, 1987—; atty. Kent County Planning Commn., Chestertown, 1982—, Betterton Planning Commn., 1987—, Town of Rock Hall, 1987—; panel atty Public Defenders Office, 1981—, Md. Vol. Lawyers, 1981—; mem. adv. bd. Farmers Bank of Md., 1994—. Bd. dirs. Kent County Heart Assn., Chestertown, 1983-84; mem. Galena Planning Commn., 1997—. Mem. ABA, Md. Bar Assn. (com. on laws 1984-87), Kent County Bar Assn. (sec. 1985-86, treas. 1987-88, v.p. 1988-89, pres. 1990-93), Balt. Bar Assn., Md. Trial Lawyers Assn., Elks. Democrat. Episcopalian. Fax: 410-778-9325. General practice, Land use and zoning (including planning), Family and matrimonial. Home: 140 Deer Field Dr Chestertown MD 21620-2482 Office: Mowell Nunn & Wadkorsky 107 Court St Chestertown MD 21620-1507

**MOY, MARY ANASTASIA,** lawyer; b. Melrose Park, Ill., Aug. 13, 1964; d. Kenneth Kwok and Chuk Ying (Tsang) M. BA cum laude, Wellesley Coll., 1986; JD, U. Pa., 1989. Bar: N.Y. 1991, D.C. 1993, U.S. Dist. Ct. (so. and ea. dists.) N.Y. 1992. Law clk. to Hon. Glenn E. Mencer U.S. Dist. Ct. (we. dist.), Pitts., 1989-90; assoc. Thelen, Reid & Priest, N.Y.C., 1990-93; assoc. Ladas & Parry, N.Y.C., 1993-98, ptnr., 1999—; asst. counsel N.Y. State Gov.'s Jud. Screening Com. for 1st Jud. Dept., 1991-92. Articles editor U. Pa. Jour. of Internat. Bus. Law, 1988-89. Mem. Asian Am. Bar Assn. of N.Y., Internat. Trademark Assn., Internat. Anticounterfeiting Coalition. Republican. Avocations: opera, music, dance, travel. Federal civil litigation, Trademark and copyright. Office: Ladas & Parry 26 W 61st St New York NY 10023-7604

**MOYA, OLGA LYDIA,** law educator; b. Weslaco, Tex., Dec. 27, 1959; d. Leonel V. and Genoveva (Tamez) M.; m. James Troutman Byrd, Aug. 24, 1985; children: Leanessa Geneva Byrd, Taylor Moya Byrd. BA, U. Tex., 1981, JD, 1984. Bar: Tex. 1984. Legis. atty. Tex. Ho. of Reps., Austin, 1985; atty. Tex. Dept. Agr., Austin, 1985-90; asst. regional counsel U.S. EPA, Dallas, 1990-91; from asst. prof. to assoc. prof. South Tex. Coll. of Law Tex A&M Univ., Houston, 1992-97, prof. South Tex. Coll. of Law, 1997—. Author: (with Andrew L. Fono) Federal Environmental Law: The User's Guide, 1997. Bd. dirs. Hermann Children's Hosp., Houston, 1993-97; mem. Leadership Tex., Austin, 1991—; bd. trustees Meml. Hermann Healthcare Sys. Found., 1997—; bd. dirs. Tex. Clean Water Coun., Austin, 1992, Met. Transit Authority of Harris County, 1999—; U.S. del. to UN Conf. on the Environ. for Latin Am. and the Caribbean, San Juan, P.R., 1995. Recipient Nat. Top 12 Hispanics in Law, Miller Brewing Co., 1996; Vol. of Yr. award George H. Hermann Soc., 1995, Hispanic Law Prof. of Yr. Hispanic Nat. Bar Assn., 1995. Mem. ABA (environ. law sect.), Hispanic Bar Assn. (bd. dirs. 1992—, Excellence award 1995, 96), Mex.-Am. Bar Assn. Office: South Tex Coll of Law 1303 San Jacinto St Houston TX 77002-7013

**MOYA, PATRICK ROBERT,** lawyer; b. Belen, N.Mex., Nov. 7, 1944; s. Adelicio E. and Eva (Sanchez) M.; m. Sara Dreier, May 30, 1966; children: Jeremy Brill, Joshua Dreier. AB, Princeton U., 1966; JD, Stanford U., 1969. Bar: Calif. 1970, Ariz. 1970, D.C. 1970, U.S. Dist. Ct. (no. dist.) Calif. 1970, U.S. Ct. Claims 1970, U.S. Tax Ct. 1970, U.S. Ct. Appeals (D.C. cir.) 1970, U.S. Supreme Ct. 1973. Assoc. Lewis and Roca, Phoenix, 1969-73, ptnr., 1973-83; sr. ptnr. Moya, Bailey, Bowers & Jones, P.C., Phoenix, 1983-84; ptnr., mem. nat. exec. com. Gaston & Snow, Phoenix, 1985-91; ptnr., Ariz. legal practice coord. Quarles & Brady, Phoenix, 1991—; instr. sch. of law Ariz. State U., 1972; bd. dirs. homebid.com, inc. Mem. Paradise Valley Bd. Adjustment, 1976-80, chmn., 1978-80; mem. Paradise Valley Town Coun., 1980-82; bd. dirs. Phoenix Men's Arts Coun., 1973-81, pres., 1979-80; bd. dirs. The Silent Witness, Inc., 1979-84, pres., 1981-83; bd. dirs. Enterprise Network, Inc., 1989-94, pres., 1991-92; bd. dirs. Phoenix Little Theatre, 1973-75, Interfaith Counseling Svc., 1973-75; precinct committeeman Phoenix Rep. Com., 1975-77; dep. voter registrar Maricopa County, 1975-76; mem. exec. bd. dirs. Gov.'s Strategic Partnership for Econ. Devel.; pres. GSPED, Inc.; mem. of Steering Com. for Sonora-Ariz. Joint Econ. Plan; mem. Gov.'s Adv. Com., Ariz. and Mex., Ariz. Corp. Commn. Stock Exch. Adv. Coun., Ariz. Town Hall. Mem. ABA, Nat. Hispanic Bar Assn., Los Abogados Hispanic Lawyers Assn., Nat. Assn. Bond Lawyers, Ariz. Bar Assn., Maricopa County Bar Assn., Paradise Valley Country Club, Univ. Club. General corporate, Mergers and acquisitions, Securities. Office: Quarles & Brady 1 E Camelback Rd Ste 400 Phoenix AZ 85012-1668

**MOYÉ, ERIC VAUGHN,** judge; b. N.Y.C., Aug. 22, 1954; s. Lemuel Alexander and Florence (Miller) M.; 1 child, Amy Michelle. BA in Polit. Sci. with distinction, So. Meth. U., 1976; JD, Harvard U., 1979. Bar: Tex. 1979, U.S. Dist. Ct. (no. dist.) Tex. 1980, U.S. Ct. Appeals (5th cir.) 1980, N.Y. 1985, U.S. Supreme Ct. 1985, U.S. Dist. Ct. (no. dist.) Calif. 1986, U.S. Ct. Claims 1986. With Office Gen. Counsel CIA, McLean, Va., 1978; assoc. Akin, Gump, Strauss, Hauer & Feld, Dallas, 1979-83; prin. Law Office of Eric V. Moyé & Assocs., Dallas, 1983-89; ptnr. Lannen & Moyé, Dallas, 1990-92; judge 101st Jud. Dist. Ct. of Tex., Dallas, 1992—; adj. prof. history So. Meth. U. Mem. Permit and License Appeals Bd., 1984-88, Dallas Bail Bond Bd., 1988—; chmn. Mayor's Task Force on Housing and Econ. Devel., Dallas, 1983-85; bd. dirs. Dispute Mediation Service, Dallas, 1980-89, Dallas Urban League, 1980-84, Pub. Utility Counsel Adv. Bd., 1984-85; barrister, Dallas Inn of Ct., 1988; gov. Dallas Symphony Assn. Named one of Outstanding Young Men in Am., 1982, 83. Fellow Tex. Bar Found.; mem. Assn. of Bar of City of N.Y., Nat. Bar Assn., Dallas Bar Assn. (chmn. membership com. 1990), State Bar Tex. (com. on admissions dist. 6, liaison with fed. judiciary com. 1990—), Tex. Assn. Young Lawyers, Am. Arbitration Assn. (arbitrator), Mayor's Commn. on Race Rels. (Dallas Together), Dallas Assembly, Dallas Alliance. Democrat. Methodist. Avocations: aikido, motorcycling, chess. Home: 4656 Christopher Pl Dallas TX 75204-1611

**MOYE, JOHN EDWARD,** lawyer; b. Deadwood, S.D., Aug. 15, 1944; s. Francis Joseph and Margaret C. (Roberts) M.; children: Kelly M., Mary S., Megan J. BBA, U. Notre Dame, 1965; JD with distinction, Cornell U., 1968. Bar: N.Y. 1968, Colo. 1971. Prof. law U. Denver, 1972-78, assoc. dean Coll. Law, 1974-78; prof. law So. Meth. U., Dallas, 1973; ptnr. Moye, Giles, O'Keefe, Vermeire & Gorrell, Denver, 1976—; lectr. Harcourt Brace Jovanovich, Chgo., 1972-95, Profl. Edn. Group, Minnetonka, Minn., 1982-95, West Profl. Tng. Program, 1995-98; chmn. Bd. Law Examiners, Denver, 1988-92. Chmn. Denver Urban Renewal Authority, 1988-93, Colo. Hist. Found., Denver, 1987—; pres. Downtown Denver, Inc., 1986-88; mem. Consumer Credit Commn., 1985-99; chmn. Stapleton Devel. Corp., 1995—; bd. dirs. Denver Bot. Gardens, 1996—, Colo. Pub. Radio, 1998—. Named Prof. of Yr., U. Denver, 1972-74, 76-78, Outstanding Faculty Mem., 1997. Fellow Am. Bar Found.; mem. ABA, Colo. Bar Assn. (chmn. corp., banking and bus. sect. 1982-84, Young Lawyer of Yr. award 1980), N.Y. State Bar Assn., Denver Bar Assn. (Young Lawyer of Yr. award 1980), Law Club (pres. 1982-84). Republican. Roman Catholic. Contracts commercial, General corporate, Banking. Office: 1225 17th St Denver CO 80202-5534

**MOYER, CARL FREDERICK,** lawyer; b. Houston, July 2, 1954; s. John Henry and Mary (Hughes) M.; m. Alice E., Dec. 27, 1984. BBA, U. Pitts., 1980; JD, Okla. City U., 1983. Bar: Ark. 1990, U.S. Dist. Ct. Ark. 1990. Dep. prosecuting atty. Benton County, Bentonville, Ark., 1984-85; retail mgmt. cons. Nat. Convenience Stores, San Antonio, 1985-87; mgmt. cons. United Photo Industry, Fayetteville, Ark., 1989-90; atty. The Moyer Law Firm, Eureka Springs, Ark., 1990-91; atty. for state Ark. Dept. of Human Svcs., Office of Chief Counsel, Fayetteville, 1991—; v.p. Carroll County Bar Assn., Berryville, Ark., 1991—. Mem. Kiwanis Club, Eureka Springs, 1990. Mem. ABA, Ark. Trial Lawyer Assn., Ark. Bar Assn. Assn. Trial Lawyers of Am., Phi Delta Phi. Avocations: flying, skydiving, horseback riding, canoeing. Home: 404 S Arch St Green Forest AR 72638-3200 Office: Dept of Human Svcs Office of Chief Counsel 4044 Frontage Rd Fayetteville AR 72703-5134

**MOYER, CRAIG ALAN,** lawyer; b. Bethlehem, Pa., Oct. 17, 1955; s. Charles Alvin and Doris Mae (Schantz) M.; m. Candace Darrow Brigham, May 3, 1986; 1 stepchild, Jason; 1 child, Chelsea A. BA, U. So. Calif., 1977; JD, U. Calif., L.A., 1980. Bar: Calif. 1980, U.S. Dist. Ct. (cen. dist.) Calif. 1980. Assoc. Nossaman, Krueger et al, L.A., 1980-83, Finley, Kumble et al, Beverly Hills, Calif., 1983-85; ptnr. Demetriou, Del Guercio, Springer & Moyer, L.A., 1985—; instr. Air Resources Bd. Symposium, Sacramento, 1985—, U. Calif., Santa Barbara, 1989—; lectr. Hazmat Conf., Long Beach, Calif., 1986—, Pacific Automotive Show, Reno, Nev., 1989—; lectr. hazardous materials, environ. law UCLA; lectr. environ. law U. Calif., Santa Barbara; lectr. hazardous materials regulatory framework U. Calif., Santa Barbara. Co-author: Hazard Communication Handbook: A Right to Know Compliance Guide, 1990, Clean Air Act Handbook, 1991, Brownfields: A Practical Guide to the Cleanup, Transfer and Redevelopment of Contaminated Property, 1997; contbr. articles to profl. jours. Pres. Calif. Pub. Interest Rsch. Group, L.A., 1978-80. Mem. ABA (natural resources sect.), Calif. Bar Assn., L.A. County Bar Assn. (environ. law sect., chmn. legis. rev. com., mem. exec. com.), Tau Kappa Epsilon (pres. L.A. chpt. 1975-76, Outstanding Alumnus 1983). Republican. Avocation: bicycling. Environmental, Oil, gas, and mineral. Office: Demetriou Del Guercio Springer & Moyer Chase Plz 801 S Grand Ave Fl 10 Los Angeles CA 90017-4613

**MOYER, JAY EDWARD,** lawyer, professional sports league executive; b. Sellersville, Pa., July 28, 1940; s. J. Edward and Frances (Apple) M.; m. Ellen W. Boldt, Sept. 20, 1960 (div. Sept. 1979); children—Sherrill Ann, Jennifer Lee, James Edward, Judith A.; m. Terry Jane Brown, Sept. 27, 1980. A.B. magna cum laude, Dartmouth Coll., 1962; J.D., Duke U., 1965. Bar: Ohio 1965, U.S. Dist. Ct. (no. dist.) Ohio 1967, U.S. Supreme Ct. 1972. Assoc. Squire, Sanders & Dempsey, Cleve., 1965-72; gen. counsel NFL, N.Y.C., 1972—, exec. v.p., 1985—; speaker numerous ednl. seminars, 1971—; witness various congl. and state legis. coms., 1980—. Contbr. articles to profl. jours. Bd. dirs. Wesley Seminary Found. Mem. ABA, Sports Lawyers Assn. (bd. dirs.), Am. Arbitration Assn. (regional adv. council 1970-72), Order of Coif. Phi Beta Kappa. Republican. Methodist. Antitrust, General civil litigation, Sports. Office: National Football League 280 Park Ave # 12 New York NY 10017-1216

**MOYER, THOMAS J.,** state supreme court chief justice; b. Sandusky, Ohio, Apr. 18, 1939; s. Clarence and Idamae (Hessler) M.; m. Mary Francis Moyer, Dec. 15, 1984; 1 child, Drew; stepchildren: Anne, Jack, Alaine, Elizabeth. BA, Ohio State U., 1961, JD, 1964. Asst. atty. gen. State of Ohio, Columbus, 1964-66; pvt. practice law Columbus, 1966-69; dep. asst. Office Gov. State of Ohio, Columbus, 1969-71, exec. asst., 1975-79; assoc. Crabbe, Brown, Jones, Potts & Schmidt, Columbus, 1972-75; judge U.S. Ct. Appeals (10th cir.), Columbus, 1979-86; chief justice Ohio Supreme Ct., Columbus, 1987—. Sec. bd. trustees Franklin U., Columbus, 1986-87; trustee Univ. Club, Columbus, 1986; mem. nat. council adv. com. Ohio State U. Coll. Law, Columbus. Recipient Award of Merit, Ohio Legal Ctr. Inst.; named Outstanding Young Man of Columbus, Columbus Jaycees, 1969. Mem. Ohio State Bar Assn. (exec. com., council dels.), Columbus Bar Assn. (pres. 1980-81), Critchon Club, Columbus Maennerchor Club. Republican. Avocations: sailing, tennis. Office: Ohio Supreme Ct 30 E Broad St Fl 3 Columbus OH 43266-0001*

**MOYLAN, DANA,** lawyer; b. Balt., June 26, 1966; d. Daniel Wheeler and Ann (Eckhardt) M.; m. Brett Robert Wilson, Dec. 19, 1992. BS, Johns Hopkins U., 1988; JD, U. Balt., 1992. Bar: Md. 1992, U.S. Dist. Ct. Md. 1993. Staff atty. People's Counsel Md., Balt., 1993-94; assoc. atty. Miller Oliver Beachley & Stone, Hagerstown, Md., 1994-97; ptnr. Miller Oliver Baker Moylan & Stone, Hagerstown, 1998—. Bd. dirs. Washington County SPCA, Hagerstown, 1997—, Parent Child Ctr., Hagerstown, 1998—. Insurance, General civil litigation, Family and matrimonial. Office: Miller Oliver Baker Moylan & Stone 29 W Washington St Hagerstown MD 21740-4833

**MOYLAN, JAMES HAROLD,** lawyer; b. Omaha, Oct. 17, 1930; s. Harold Thomas and Margaret Ellen (Emery) M.; m. Lila Marie Fitzgerald, July 9, 1960; children: James P., Michael T., Patrick W., Jean M., Mary M., Molly C. BS, Creighton U., 1952, JD, 1957. Bar: Nebr. 1957, Iowa 1957, U.S. Dist. Ct. Nebr. 1957, U.S. Dist. Ct. (so. dist.) Iowa 1957. Assoc. Richling, Shrout & Brown, Omaha, 1957-60; dep. atty. Douglas County, Omaha, 1960-67; ptnr. Garvey, Nye, Crawford, Kirchner & Moylan, Omaha, 1967-87, Nye, Fellman, Moylan & Brown, Omaha, 1987-99, Fellman, Moyland Natvig & Kelly, Omaha, 1999—. Chmn. Douglas County Dem. Com., 1966-68; mem. Christ and King Sch. Bd., Omaha, 1967-71, Archbishop's Com. on Ednl. Devel., Omaha, 1975—; assoc. bd. regents St. Mary's Coll., Omaha, 1968-72; bd. regents U. Nebr., 1971-89. Mem. Nebr. Bar Assn. (exec. coun. 1975-81), Am. Bar Assn., Iowa Bar Assn., Sokol Club, Regency Lake and Tennis Club, Westroads Racquet Club, Eagles, Elks, Am. Legion. Avocation: politics. Legislative, Probate, General corporate. Home: 2245 S 86th St Omaha NE 68124-2131 Office: Fellman Moylan Natvig & Kelly 100 Continental Bldg Omaha NE 68046

**MOYLAN, JAMES JOSEPH,** lawyer; b. Forest Hills, N.Y., Feb. 3, 1948; s. James Gerard and Jessie Cora (Geary) M.; m. Barbara Chesrow, Aug. 29, 1970; children: James C., Joseph O., Alicia G. B.S.B.A., U. Denver, 1969, J.D., 1971. Bar: Colo. 1972, D.C. 1972, Ill. 1975, U.S. Dist. Ct. Colo. 1972, U.S. Supreme Ct. 1975. Trial atty. SEC, Washington, 1972-75; assoc. gen. counsel Chgo. Bd. Options Exch., Ill., 1975-77; assoc. Abramson & Fox, Chgo., 1977-80; ptnr. Bowen, Knepper & Moylan Ltd., Chgo., 1980-82; ptnr. Moylan & Early, Ltd., Chgo., 1983-84; prin. James J. Moylan and Assocs., Ltd., Chgo., 1984-95; ptnr. Arnstein & Lehr, 1995—; adj. prof. law IIT Chgo. Kent Coll. Law, 1976—; former pub. dir. MidAm. Commodity Exch. div. Chgo. Bd. Trade, Chgo. Contbr. articles to profl. jours. Mem. Ill. State Bar Assn. (sect. council mem.), Chgo. Bar Assn., D.C. Bar Assn., ABA (sect. corp., banking and bus. law, sect. litigation), Theta Chi (grand chpt, 1993—). Republican. Roman Catholic. Club: Chgo. Athletic Assn. Securities, Commodities, General corporate.

**MOYNIHAN, JOHN BIGNELL,** lawyer; b. N.Y.C., July 25, 1933; s. Jerome J. and Stephanie (Bignell) M.; m. Odilia Marie Jacques, Nov. 13, 1965; children—Blair, Dana. B.S., Fordham U., 1955; J.D., St. John's U., N.Y.C., 1958. Bar: Tex. 1961, U.S. Supreme Ct. 1965, U.S. Dist. Ct. (we. dist.) Tex. 1968, U.S. Ct. Apls. (5th cir.) 1973. Sole practice Brownsville, Tex., 1961-62; asst. city atty. City of San Antonio, 1962-63; sole practice, San Antonio, 1963-65; estate tax atty. IRS, San Antonio, 1965-73; dist. counsel EEOC, San Antonio, 1973-79; asst. U.S. atty. Office U.S. Atty., San Antonio, 1980-87, sr. litigation counsel, 1987-94; sole practice, San Antonio, 1995-98. Served with U.S. Army, 1958-60; lt. col. USAFR (ret.), 1986. Mem. San Antonio Bar Assn. (chmn. state and nat. legis. com. 1972-73, Meritorious Service award 1968), Fed. Bar Assn. (bd. dirs. San Antonio chpt. 1983—, pres. elect 1986, pres. 1987). Chmn. reform and renewal com. San Antonio Roman Catholic Archdiocese, 1968. Lodge: K.C. (pres. 1967). Labor, Civil rights, Federal civil litigation. Home and Office: 11011 Whispering Wind St San Antonio TX 78230-3746

**MRACHEK, LORIN LOUIS,** lawyer; b. Fairmont, Minn., Jan. 5, 1946; s. Louis L. and Kathleen (Loring) M.; m. Elizabeth Moss, Aug. 31, 1968; children: Kathleen Elizabeth, Louis Moss. BA with honors, Fla. State U., 1968; MBA, Columbia U., 1974, JD, 1974. Bar: Fla. 1974, Va. 1977, U.S. Ct. Mil. Appeals 1977, U.S. Supreme Ct. 1978; cert. in civil trial law and bus. litigation Fla. Bar Bd. Certification; cert. in bus. bankruptcy law Am. Bd. Bankruptcy Certification; cert. in civil trial advocacy Nat. Bd. Trial Advocacy. Commd. 2d lt. USMC, 1969, advanced through grades to capt., 1974; chief def. counsel Marine Corps. Recruit Depoit, USMC, Paris Island, 1975-77; resigned USMC, 1977; spl. asst. to gen. counsel U.S. Ry. Assn., Washington, 1977-78; shareholder Gunster, Yoakley, Valdes-Fauli & Stewart, P.A., West Palm Beach, Fla., 1978—. Editor-in-chief Columbia Jour. Law and Social Problems, 1973-74; contbr. articles to profl. jours. Fellow Am. Coll. Trial Attys.; mem. ABA, Am. Bankruptcy Inst., Fla. Acad. Trial Lawyers, So. Fla. Bankruptcy Bar Assn. Avocations: running, tennis, golf. General civil litigation, Bankruptcy. Office: 777 S Flagler Dr Ste 500E West Palm Beach FL 33401-6121

**MROZ, RICHARD S.,** lawyer; b. Camden, N.J., June 16, 1961; s. Stanley and Jeanette Mroz; m. Lynne Mroz, Sept. 9, 1995; 1 child, Julia Jeanette. BA, U. Del., 1983; JD, Villanova U., 1986. Bar: N.J., Pa., D.C., U.S. Ct. Appeals (3d cir.), U.S. Supreme Ct. Law sec. Judge I.V. DiMentino, Camden, N.J., 1986-87; assoc. Cahill, Wilinski & Cahill, Haddonfield, N.J., 1987-91; asst. county counsel County of Camden, N.J., 1991, county counsel, 1991-94; dir. state authorities Office of Gov., Trenton, N.J., 1994-98, spl. counsel, 1998—, chief counsel, 1999—. Campaign atty. County Rep. Comm., Camden County, 1990-91, Rep. committeeman, 1989-91. Mem. N.J. Bar Assn., Camden County Bar Assn., Copernicus Soc. So. N.J. (sec., treas., pres.). Roman Catholic. Avocations: sport, running, skiing, golf, wine tasting. Home: 331 Knolltop Ln Haddonfield NJ 08033-3718 Office: Office of Gov PO Box 1-stateh Trenton NJ 08625-0001

**MUCCI, GARY LOUIS,** lawyer; b. Buffalo, Nov. 12, 1946; s. Guy Charles and Sally Rose (Battaglia) M.; m. Carolyn Belle Taylor, May 4, 1991. BA cum laude, St. John Fisher Coll., 1968; JD, Cath. U., 1972. Bar: N.Y. 1972. Law clk. to Hon. John T. Curtin U.S. Dist. Ct., Buffalo, 1972-74; assoc. atty. Donovan Leisure Newton & Irvine, N.Y.C., 1974-75; assoc. atty. Saperston & Day P.C., Buffalo, 1975-80, sr. ptnr., 1980—. Chmn. bd. Buffalo Philharm. Orch., 1985-86; pres. Hospice Buffalo, 1986-87; mem. N.Y. State Coun. on the Arts, 1987; chmn. Citizens Com. on Cultural Aid, Buffalo, 1992—; trustee St. John Fisher Coll. Recipient Brotherhood award NCCJ, Buffalo, 1983; named Man of Yr. William Paca Soc., 1984. Mem. Erie County Bar Assn., N.Y. State Bar Assn. Antitrust, Real property, General corporate. Home: 27 Tudor Pl Buffalo NY 14222-1615 Office: Saperston & Day PC 3 Fountain Plz Ste 1100 Buffalo NY 14203-1486

**MUCCIA, JOSEPH WILLIAM,** lawyer; b. N.Y.C., May 31, 1948; s. Joseph Anthony and Charlotte (Mohring) M.; m. Margaret M. Reynolds,

June 29, 1985. BA magna cum laude, Fordham U., 1970, JD, 1973. Bar: N.Y. 1974, U.S. Dist. Ct. (so. dist.) N.Y. 1974, U.S. Dist. Ct. (ea. dist.) N.Y. 1980, U.S. Ct. Appeals (2d cir.) 1974, U.S. Ct. Appeals (D.C. cir.) 1980, U.S. Supreme Ct. 1980. Assoc. Cahill Gordon & Reindel, N.Y.C., 1973-82; ptnr. Corbin Silverman & Sanseverino, N.Y.C., 1983—. Assoc. editor Fordham Law Rev., 1972-73. Mem. ABA (litigation sect.), N.Y. County Lawyers Assn., Fed. Bar Coun., N.Y. State Bar Assn. (com. litigation sect.), Phi Beta Kappa, Pi Sigma Alpha. Federal civil litigation, State civil litigation, Securities. Office: Corbin Silverman & Sanseverino 805 3rd Ave New York NY 10022-7513

**MUCHA, JOHN, III,** lawyer; b. Flint, Mich., Jan. 28, 1955; s. John Jr. and Mary M.; m. Patricia Brautigan, Sept. 25, 1981; 1 child, Thomas. AB cum laude, U. Mich., 1977, M in Pub. Policy, 1979, JD, 1987. Bar: Mich. 1987 (coun. litigation sect. 1995-99, chair 1998-99), U.S. Dist. Ct. (ea. dist.) Mich. 1987, U.S. Ct. Appeals (6th cir.) 1990. Assoc. Cord Bissell & Brook, Chgo., 1986, Pepper, Hamilton & Scheetz, Detroit, 1987-95; ptnr. Dawda, Mann, Mulcahy & Sadler, Bloomfield Hills, Mich., 1995—. Contbg. author: Business Opportunities in the United States, 1992. Bd. dirs. Families for Adoption, Canton, Mich., 1994-96. Recipient Disting. Vol. Legal Svcs. award Detroit Bar Assn., 1994. Federal civil litigation, General civil litigation, State civil litigation. Home: 4446 Apple Valley Ln West Bloomfield MI 48323-2804 Office: Dawda Mann Mulcahy & Sadler 1533 N Woodward Ave Ste 200 Bloomfield Hills MI 48304-2815

**MUCHIN, ALLAN B.,** lawyer; b. Manitowoc, Wis., Jan. 10, 1936; s. Jacob and Dorothy (Biberfeld) M.; m. Elaine Cort, Jan. 28, 1960; children: Andrea Muchin Leon, Karen, Margery Muchin Goldblatt. BBA, U. Wis., Manitowoc, 1958, JD, 1961. Gen. counsel IRS, Chgo., 1961-65; assoc. Altman, Kurlander & Weiss, Chgo., 1965-68, ptnr., 1968-74; co-mng. ptnr. Katten Muchin & Zavis, Chgo., 1974-95, chmn. bd., 1995—; bd. dirs. Chgo. Bulls, Chgo. White Sox, Alberto-Culver Co., Acorn Investment Trust; bd. visitors U. Wis. Law Sch.; trustee Noble St. Charter Sch. Trustee Ravinia Music Festival, Highland Park, Ill., 1992—, Lyric Opera Chgo., 1993—; mem. adv. com. Loyola Family Bus. Ctr., Chgo., 1991—; co-com. chmn. Am. Com. for Weizmann Inst. of Sci., Chgo., 1991—. Mem. Econ. Club Chgo., Econ. Devel. Commn. (com. mem.), Comml. Club Chgo. Avocations: travel, tennis, reading. Office: Katten Muchin & Zavis 525 W Monroe St Ste 1600 Chicago IL 60661-3693

**MUCHIN, ARDEN ARCHIE,** lawyer, director; b. Manitowoc, Wis., Dec. 9, 1920; s. Alfred and Ida (Golden) M.; m. Bettie Lou Barenbaum, Dec. 19, 1948; children: Ann L., Efrem B., Jay Z. BA, U. Wis., 1942, JD, 1947; IA, Harvard U. Grad. Sch. Bus. Adminstrn., 1943. Bar: Wis. 1947, U.S. Dist. Ct. (ea. dist.) Wis. 1948, U.S. Tax Ct. 1965. Pres. Muchin, Muchin & Bruce, S.C. and predecessors, Manitowoc, 1947-92; ptnr. Nash, Spindler, Dean & Grimstad, 1993—; sec. and/or dir. Foster Needle Co., Inc., Manitowoc, Foster Needle Ltd. (Eng.), Sorenson Industries, Inc., Manitowoc; sec., dir. WaterCare Corp., Kaysun Plastics Inc., Water Svcs. Corp.; sec. Schwartz Mfg. Co., Heresite Protective Coatings, Inc.; sec., v.p. CUB Radio, Inc., Manitowoc; gov. State Bar Wis., 1976-80. Bd. dirs. Manitowoc United Way Inc., 1968-92; mem. Wis. adv. com. U.S. Commn. Civil Rights, 1985-89. Mem. ABA, Manitowoc County Bar Assn. (pres. 1972-73), B'nai Brith (nat. commn. anti-defamation league). General corporate, Probate, Labor. Home: 1426 Arden Ln Manitowoc WI 54220-2517 Office: Nash Spindler Dean & Grimstad 201 E Waldo Blvd Ste 101 Manitowoc WI 54220-2992

**MUCK, STACEY LYNN,** lawyer; b. Toledo, Feb. 25, 1966; d. Thomas Jude and Rebecca Jean (Heilman) M. BA, Fla. So. Coll., 1988; JD, Thomas M. Cooley Law Sch., Lansing, Mich., 1992. Bar: Fla. 1992, U.S. Dist. Ct. (mid. dist.) Fla. 1993, U.S. Ct. Appeals (11th cir.) 1993. Asst. state atty. 6th Jud. Cir. Office of State Atty., Clearwater, Fla., 1992—. Avocations: golf, tennis, snow skiing. Home: PO Box 144 San Antonio FL 33576-0144 Office: Office State Atty 6th Jud Cir 7530 Little Rd Rm 210 New Port Richey FL 34654-5598

**MUCKLESTONE, PETER JOHN,** lawyer; b. Seattle, Aug. 21, 1955; s. Robert Stanley and Susan (Quilliam) M. BA in History, U. Wash., 1977; JD, Columbia U., 1981. Bar: Wash. 1981, U.S. Dist. Ct. (we. and ea. dist.) Wash. Assoc. Bogle & Gates, Seattle, 1981-83; counsel Rainier Nat. Bank, Seattle, 1983-89, Security Pacific Bank, Seattle, 1989-92; sr. counsel Seattle First Nat. Bank, 1992; counsel West One Bank, Seattle, 1992-95, U.S. Bancorp, Seattle, 1995-97; of counsel Davis Wright Tremaine LLP, Seattle, 1997—. Banking, Consumer commercial, Contracts commercial. Office: Davis Wright Tremaine LLP 1501 4th Ave Seattle WA 98101-1688

**MUDD, JOHN O.,** lawyer; b. 1943. BA, Cath. U., 1965, MA, 1966; JD, U. Mont., 1973; LLM, Columbia U., 1986; JSD of Law, 1994. Bar: Mont. 1973. Pntr. Mulroney, Delaney, Dalby & Mudd, Missoula, Mont., 1973-79; lectr. U. Mont., Missoula, 1973-74, 75-76; prof. law, dean U. Mont., 1979-88; ptnr. Garlington, Lohn & Robinson, Missoula, 1988—; pres. Mid-Continent Assn. Law Schs., 1982-83. Editor: Mont. Law Rev., 1972-73. Bd. dirs. St. Patrick Hosp., 1985-90, Providence Svcs. Corp., 1992-97; elected Dem. candidate U.S. Senate, 1994; chmn. Mont. Commn. Future of Higher Edn., 1980-90. With U.S. Army, 1967-73. Mem. ABA, Am. Judicature Soc. (bd. dirs. 1985-89), State Bar Mont. General civil litigation, Legislative, Labor. Office: Garlington Lohn & Robinson PO Box 7909 Missoula MT 59807-7909

**MUDD, JOHN PHILIP,** lawyer; b. Washington, Aug. 22, 1932; s. Thomas Paul and Frances Mary (Finotti) M.; m. Barbara Eve Sweeney, Aug. 10, 1957; children: Laura, Ellen, Philip, Clare, David. BSS, Georgetown U., 1954; JD, Georgetown Law Center, 1956. Bar: Md. 1956, D.C. 1963, Fla. 1964, Calif. 1973. Pvt. practice Upper Marlboro, Md., 1956-66; v.p., sec., gen. counsel Deltona Corp., Miami, Fla., 1966-72; sec., gen. counsel Nat. Community Builders, San Diego, 1972-73; gen. counsel Continental Advisers (adviser to Continental Mortgage Investors), 1973-75, sr. v.p., gen. counsel, 1975-80; sr. v.p., gen. counsel Am. Hosp. Mgmt. Corp., Miami, 1980-89; legal coord. Amerifirst Bank, Miami, 1989-92; v.p., legal counsel Cartaret Savs. Bank, Morristown, N.J., 1991-93, cons., 1991-92; gen. counsel Golden Glades Hosp., Miami, 1992-93, Bank of N.Am., Miami, 1994—; gen. counsel Golden Glades Hosp., Miami, 1992-93; cons. FSLIC, 1988-89, J.E. Robert Cos., Alexandria, Va., 1988-89, Real Estate Recovery, Inc., Boca Raton, Fla., 1991-92, Bank N.Am., Ft. Lauderdale, Fla., 1992; dir. Unitower Mortgage Corp., Miami, Fla.; dir. Unitower Mortgage Corp., Miami; pres. Marquette Realty Corp., Miami. Former mem. Land Devel. Adv. Com. N.Y. State; chmn. student interview com. Georgetown U.; bd. dirs. Lasalle High Sch., Miami; corp. counsel Com. of Dade County, Fla.; trustee Golden Glades Gen. Hosp., Miami, Fla., 1992—, gen. counsel, 1991—, Bank of North Am., Miami, 1992—. Mem. Fla. Bar Assn., Calif. Bar Assn., Md. Bar Assn., D.C. Bar Assn., Fla. State Bar (exec. com. on corp. counsel com.). Democrat. Roman Catholic. Real property, Health, General corporate. Home: 607 Velarde Ave Coral Gables FL 33134-7044 Office: Bank of North Am Golden Glades Med Plz 8701 SW 137th Ave Ste 301 Miami FL 33183-4498

**MUDIE, F. PATRICIA,** lawyer; b. Greenville, S.C., July 31, 1940; d. Joe Thomgs and P.C. Hodgens; m. Samuel Mudie, June 16, 1962 (div. 1977); children: Heather, Jason; m. Robert G. Linde, Sept. 20, 1997. BA, U. Pa., 1962; JD, U. So. Calif., 1977. Bar: Calif. Assoc. Greenberg, Glusker, L.A., 1977-86, Jeffer, Mangels, L.A., 1986-89; ptnr. Nachshin & Mudie, L.A., 1989-90; pvt. practice F. Patrician Mudie, P.C., L.A., 1990—; judge pro tem program for family law L.A. County Superior Ct., L.A., 1995-96. Mentor, mem. Harriet Buhai Ctr., L.A., 1994-98. Mem. L.A. County Bar Assn., Beverly Hills (Calif.) Bar Assn. (chmn. family law 1995-96). Family and matrimonial. Office: 12100 Wilshire Blvd Ste 1650 Los Angeles CA 90025-7107

**MUECKE, CHARLES ANDREW (CARL MUECKE),** federal judge; b. N.Y.C., Feb. 20, 1918; s. Charles and Wally (Roeder) M.; m. Claire E. Vasse; children by previous marriage: Carl Marshall, Alfred Jackson, Catherine Calvert. B.A., Coll. William and Mary, 1941; LL.B., U. Ariz., 1953. Bar: Ariz. 1953. Rep. AFL, 1947-50; reporter Ariz. Times, Phoenix, 1947-48; since practiced in Phoenix; with firm Parker & Muecke, 1953-59, Muecke, Dushoff & Sacks, 1960-61; U.S. atty. Dist. Ariz., 1961-64, U.S. dist. judge, 1964—, now sr. judge. Mem. Phoenix Planning Commn., 1955-61, chmn., 1960; chmn. Maricopa County Dem. Party, 1961-62. Maj. USMC, 1942-45, USMCR, 1945-60. Mem. Fed. Bar Assn., Ariz. Bar Assn., Maricopa Bar Assn., Dist. Judges Assn. Ninth Circuit, Phi Beta Kappa, Phi Alpha Delta, Omicron Delta Kappa.

**MUELLER, DANIEL EDWARD,** lawyer; b. Boothwyn, Pa., June 14, 1962; s. Walter Edward and Elizabeth (Billingsly) M. BA, Furman U., 1986; postgrad., U. S.C., 1990; JD, U. S.C. Sch. Law, 1993. Bar: Wash. Bus. owner Columbia, S.C., 1989-90; law clk. Suggs & Kelly, P.A., Columbia, 1991-93, atty., head spl. and mass litigation, 1993-95; pvt. practice Seattle, 1996—. Assoc. editor, editor S.C. Environ. Law Jour., 1991-93; case law update editor, writer S.C. Lawyer, 1994-96; editor, writer Complex Litigation Reporter, 1994-95. Mem. ATLA, Wash. State Trial Lawyers Assn., Wash. Bar Assn. Avocation: guitar. E-mail: daniel.mueller@usa.net. Bankruptcy, Consumer commercial, General practice. Office: 600 1st Ave Ste 300 Seattle WA 98104-2239

**MUELLER, DIANE MAYNE,** lawyer; b. Milw., Aug. 8, 1934; d. George and Ann (Matuszewski) Markussen; widowed; 1 child, Paul Wilhite; m. Milton W. Mueller, Jan. 1, 1990. AB, Valparaiso U., 1956; MSW, Fla. State U., 1963; JD summa cum laude, DePaul U., 1974. Bar: Ill. 1974, U.S. Dist. Ct. (no. dist.) Ill. 1974, U.S. Dist. Ct. (ea. dist.) Wis. 1977, N. Mex., 1996. Assoc. Seyfarth, Shaw, Fairweather & Geraldson, Chgo., 1974-82, ptnr., 1982-86; asst. group counsel LTV Steel Co., Cleve., 1986-93, sr. atty., 1993-95; adj. prof. Northwestern U. Sch. Law, 1984-86. Mem. Chgo. Club, Chgo. Yacht Club, Univ. Club, Exec. Club of Chgo. (chmn. bd. 1984-85, mem. adv. bd. 1986-96), Econ. Club Chgo. General corporate. Home: 1216 Rock Rose Rd Albuquerque NM 87122-1115

**MUELLER, MARK CHRISTOPHER,** lawyer; b. Dallas, June 19, 1945; s. Herman August and Hazel Deane (Hatzenbuehler) M.; m. Linda Jane Reed. BA in Econs., So. Meth. U., 1967; MBA in Acctg., 1969, JD, 1971. Bar: Tex. 1971, U.S. Dist. Ct. (no. dist.) Tex. 1974, U.S. Tax Ct. 1974; CPA, Tex. Acct. Arthur Young & Co., Dallas, 1967-68, A.E. Krutilek, Dallas, 1968-71; pvt. practice law Dallas, 1971—; assoc. L. Vance Stanton, Dallas, 1971-72; instr. legal writing and rsch. So. Meth. U., Dallas, 1970-71, instr. legal acctg., 1975; mem. unauthorized practice of law com. Supreme Ct. Tex. Leading articles editor Southwestern Law Jour., 1970-71. Mem. NRA, Tex. Bar Assn., Tex. State Rifle Assn., Tex. Soc. CPA's, Dallas Bar Assn., SAR, Sons Republic Tex., Sons of Union Vets. of Civil War, Sons Confederate Vets., Mil. Orer Stars and Bars, Order of Coif, Dallas Hist. Soc., Dallas County Pioneer Assn., Rock Creek Barbeque Club, Masons, Shriners, York Rite, Grotto, Scottish Rite (32 degree KCCH), Beta Alpha Psi, Phi Delta Phi, Sigma Chi. General practice, Real property, State civil litigation. Home: 7310 Brennans Dr Dallas TX 75214-2804 Office: 6510 Abrams Rd Ste 565 Dallas TX 75231-7292

**MUELLER, PHILIP WINFIELD,** lawyer; b. Little Falls, N.Y., Oct. 8, 1953; s. Allen William and Phyllis Jane (Whitaker) M. BA, Union Coll., Schenectady, N.Y., 1975; JD, Cornell U., 1979. Bar: Oreg. 1980, Mass. 1981, D.C. 1991, N.Y. 1991. Law clk. U.S. Dist. Ct., Portland, Oreg., 1979-80; atty. Foley Hoag and Eliot, Boston, 1981-83, 85-89; dep. chief asst. dist. atty. Schenectady County, N.Y., 1990—. Editor-in-chief Cornell Law Rev., 1978-79. Named Lawyer of Yr. Schenectady County Bar Assn., 1998. Avocations: athletics, reading. Criminal. Office: 612 State St Schenectady NY 12305-2112

**MUELLER, RENEE ANN,** lawyer; b. Brenham, Tex., May 18, 1962; d. Johnnie Dewayne and Shirley Fuchs Mueller. AA, Blinn Jr. Coll., 1981; BA, Tex. Luth. Coll., 1983; JD, South Tex. Coll. Law, 1986. Bar: Tex. 1986. Asst. dist. atty. 21st Jud. Dist. Attys. Office, Brenham, 1987-96; county atty. Washington County, Brenham, 1997—; chmn. legal assts. adv. com. Blinn Coll., Brenham, 1995-98; panel chair Dist. 8A Grievance Com., Brenham, 1994-97; part-time criminal justice instr., Blinn Coll., 1998—. Mem. ethics com. Trinity Hosp., Brenham, 1990—. Mem. Washington County Bar Assn. (pres. 1990-92), Tex. Dist. and County Attys. Assn., Nat. Dist. Attys. Assn., Rotary, Washington County C. of C. (bd. dirs. 1995-97). Democrat. Lutheran. Avocations: tennis, beadwork. Office: Washington County Atty 100 E Main St Ste 103 Brenham TX 77833-3701

**MUELLER, ROBERT SWAN, III,** lawyer, former federal official; b. N.Y.C., Aug. 7, 1944; s. Robert Swan Jr. and Alice (Truesdale) M.; m. Ann Standish, Sept. 3, 1966; children: Cynthia, Melissa. BA, Princeton U., 1966; MA, NYU, 1967; JD, U. Va., 1973. Bar: Mass., U.S. Dist. Ct. Mass., U.S. Ct. Appeals (1st cir.), Calif., U.S. Dist. Ct. (no. dist.) Calif., U.S. Ct Appeals (9th cir.). Assoc. Pillsbury, Madison & Sutro, San Francisco, 1973-76; asst. U.S. atty. U.S. Atty.'s Office, No. Dist. Calif., San Francisco, 1976-80; chief unit spl. prosecutions, Calif. no. dist. U.S. Atty.'s Office, San Francisco, 1980-81, chief criminal div., 1981-82; chief criminal div. Mass. dist. U.S. Atty.'s Office, Boston, 1982-85, 1st asst. U.S. atty. in Boston, 1985, U.S. atty. for Mass. dist., 1986-87, dep. U.S. atty. for Mass. dist., 1987-88; ptnr. Hill and Barlow, Boston, 1988-89; asst. to atty. gen. for criminal matters U.S. Dept. Justice, Washington, 1989-90, asst. atty. gen. for criminal div., 1990-93; lawyer Hale & Dorr, Washington, 1993—; interim U.S. arry. no. dist. Calif. U.S. Dept. Justice, 1998—. Capt. USMC, 1967-70; Vietnam. Decorated Bronze Star, Purple Heart, Vietnamese Cross of Gallantry. Office: US Atty Box 36055 450 Golden Gate Ave San Francisco CA 94102*

**MUELLER, VIRGINIA SCHWARTZ,** lawyer; b. Palo Alto, Calif., Apr. 27, 1924; d. William Leonard and Anstrice (Bryant) S.; m. Paul F.C. Mueller, Sept. 24, 1945; children: Christian William, Lisa Turcotte. AB in Polit. Sci. and Law, Stanford U., 1944; JD, Cornell U., 1946; LLD, U. Paris, 1950. Bar: Calif. 1946, Wash. 1952, U.S. Supreme Ct. 1966. Research atty. Calif. Dist. Ct. Appeals, San Francisco, 1946-49; atty.-at-law Karr and Combelic, Seattle, 1952-53; dep. pros. atty. King County Pros. Atty., Seattle, 1953-56; dep. supr. Inheritance Tax div. Wash. State Tax Commn., Olympia, 1956-58; asst. atty. counsel Calif. Bd. of Equalization, Sacramento, 1959; dep. dist. atty. Sacramento County Dist. Atty., 1959-66; legal counsel Legal Aid Soc. of Sacramento, 1966-71; pvt. practice Sacramento, 1971—; chmn. Port of Sacramento, 1988-90, commr., 1983-91; mem. adv. bd. Alternative Sentencing Program, Sacramento, 1976—. Contbr. articles to profl. jours. Pres. No. Calif. chpt. Sister Cities Internat., 1990-93, state rep., Alexandria, Va., 1987-89, coord. for No. Calif., 1993—; counselor Soc. Mayflower Descs. in Calif., 1981—; chmn. bd. visitors spl. com. on status of women in law Stanford U., 1973-75; pres. World Affairs Coun. Sacramento, 1971-72, chmn. by-laws com., 1976-77; No. Calif. rep. nat. com. UNICEF, 1972-75. Named Outstanding Woman YMCA Sacramento, 1985, Disting. Businesswoman Sacramento C. of C., 1980; named Lawyer of Yr., Sacramento County Bar Assn., 1995. Mem. ABA (mem. standing com. World Order under Law 1979-86, council mem. sect. of internat. law 1976-80), Nat. Assn. Women Lawyers (pres. 1985-86), Fedn. Internat. des Femmes des Carrieres Juridiques (bd. 1972-88, 97—), State Bar Calif. (sec. exec. com. sr. lawyer sect. 1998—), Union Internat. des Avocats, Women Lawyers of Sacramento (pres. 1964, 65, Frances Newell Carr Achievement award 1995), AAUW (pres. 1978-79, Centennial award 1981), Soroptimist (pres. 1975-76). Avocation: internat. travel. Estate planning, Family and matrimonial, Probate. Home: 4310 Moss Dr Sacramento CA 95822-1662 Office: 106 L St Sacramento CA 95814-3227

**MUES, ROBERT LEIGHTON,** lawyer; b. Summit, N.J., Apr. 14, 1954; s. Edward Frederick Jr. and Evelyn (Moulton) M.; m. Elizabeth Ann Beard, Aug. 26, 1978; children: Jeffrey Scott, Robert Colin. BA, Wittenberg U., Springfield, Ohio, 1975; JD, U. Dayton, 1978. Bar: Ohio 1978, U.S. Dist. Ct. (so. dist.) Ohio 1978, U.S. Ct. Appeals (6th cir.) 1995. With firm Meily & Mues Attys., Dayton, Ohio, 1981-91, Holzfaster, Cecil, McKnight & Mues, Dayton, 1991—; impartial due process hearing officer Ohio Dept. Edn., 1981-96, State of Ohio hearing rev. officer, 1997. Author brochure: Divorce in Ohio, 1994. Bd. dirs. For Love of Children, Inc., Dayton, 1983-91, Montgomery County Children Svcs. Bd., Dayton, 1988-91. Mem. ABA, Assn. Trial Lawyers Am., Ohio State Bar Assn., Ohio Acad. Trial Lawyers, Dayton Bar Assn. (com. on profl. ethics 1982—), Miami Valley Trial Lawyers Assn. Family and matrimonial, Personal injury, General practice. Office: Holzfaster Cecil McKnight & Mues 1105 Wilmington Ave Ste 1 Dayton OH 45420-4108

**MUGRIDGE, DAVID RAYMOND,** lawyer; b. Detroit, Aug. 6, 1949; s. Harry Raymond and Elizabeth Lou (Aldrich) M.; m. Sandra Lee Jackson, June 25, 1988; children: James Raymond, Sarah Lorraine. BA, U. of Ams., Puebla, Mex., 1970; MA, Santa Clara U., 1973; JD, San Joaquin Coll. of Law, 1985. Bar: Calif. 1986, U.S. Dist. Ct. (ea. dist.) Calif. 1986, U.S. Ct. Appeals (9th cir.) 1987, U.S. Supreme Ct. 1996; cert. specialist in criminal law. Staff atty. to presiding justice 5th Dist. Ct. Appeals, Fresno, Calif., 1985-87; assoc. Law Office of Nuttall, Berman, Magill, Fresno, 1987-88; pvt. practice Fresno, 1988—; tchr. Fresno City Coll., 1988-96; tchr. Spanish for legal profession, Fresno, 1994; tchr. Fresno Pacific U., 1997-99; arbitrator Fresno County Bar Assn., 1988—; judge pro-tem juvenile, traffic and small claims Fresno County Superior Ct., 1988—. Contbg. author: Practical Real Estate Law, 1995. Mem. ABA, NACDL, Calif. Attys. for Criminal Justice, Calif. Trial Lawyers Assn. (cert. specialist in criminal law). Republican. Roman Catholic. Avocations: fishing, travel, photography, hiking. Criminal, Personal injury, Appellate.

**MUHLBACH, ROBERT ARTHUR,** lawyer; b. Los Angeles, Apr. 13, 1946; s. Richard and Jeanette (Marcus) M.; m. Kerry Eldene Mahoney, July 26, 1986. BSME, U. Calif., Berkeley, 1967; JD, U. Calif., San Francisco, 1976; MME, Calif. State U., 1969; M in Pub. Adminstrn., U. So. Calif., 1976. Bar: Calif. 1976. Pub. defender County of Los Angeles, 1977-79; assoc. Kirtland & Packard, Los Angeles, 1979-85, ptnr., 1986—. Chmn. Santa Monica Airport Commn., Calif., 1984-87, chmn., bd. dirs. Hawthorne Airport Cmty. Assn. Inc. Served to capt. USAF, 1969-73. Mem. ABA, AIAA, Internat. Assn. Def. Counsel, Am. Bd. Trial Advs. Federal civil litigation, Personal injury, Insurance. Office: Kirtland & Packard Ste 2600 1900 Avenue Of The Stars Los Angeles CA 90067-4507

**MUHLSTOCK, ARTHUR C.,** lawyer; b. N.Y.C., Aug. 13, 1935; s. Rudolph A. Muhlstock and Freda Kaplan; m. Jacqueline Mernit, June 8, 1958; children: Gary, Jeffrey, Richard. BA, NYU, 1956, JD, 1959. Bar: N.Y., U.S. Dist. Ct. (so. dist.) N.Y., U.S. Dist. Ct. (ea. dist.) N.Y., U.S. Ct. Appeals (2d cir.). Asst. dist. atty. N.Y. County Office of Dist. Atty., N.Y.C., 1959-63; assoc. Brower, Brill & Gangel, N.Y.C., 1963-65; pvt. practice N.Y.C., 1965—. Probate, Estate planning, Estate taxation. Office: 305 Madison Ave Ste 5118 New York NY 10165-0006

**MUIR, J. DAPRAY,** lawyer; b. Washington, Nov. 9, 1936; s. Brockett and Helen Cassin (Dapray) M.; m. Louise Rutherfurd Pierrepont, July 16, 1966. A.B., Williams Coll., 1958; J.D., U. Va., 1964. Bar: Md., Va., D.C. 1964, U.S. Supreme Ct. 1967. Asst. legal advisor for econ. and bus. affairs U.S. Dept. State, 1971-73; ptnr. Ruddy & Muir, LLP, Washington; mem. U.S. del. to Joint U.S./USSR Comml. Commn., 1972; chmn. D.C. Securities Adv. Com., 1981-84, mem. 1985-88. Bd. editors Va. Law Rev, 1963-64; contbr. articles to profl. jours. Mem. bd. adv. G.W. Jour. Internat. Law & Econs.; bd. dirs. Trust Mus. Exhbns. Lt. (j.g.) USNR, 1958-61. Mem. D.C. Bar (chmn. internat. law div. 1977-78, chmn. environ., energy and natural resources div. 1982-83, Met. Club (Washington), Chevy Chase (Md.) Club, Am. Arbitration Assn. (panel of comml. arbitrators 1997—). General corporate, Securities. Home: 3104 Q St NW Washington DC 20007-3027 Office: 1825 I St NW Ste 400 Washington DC 20006-5415

**MUIR, MALCOLM,** federal judge; b. Englewood, N.J., Oct. 20, 1914; s. John Merton and Sarah Elizabeth Muir; m. Alma M. Brohard, Sept. 6, 1940 (dec. 1985); children: Malcolm, Thomas, Ann Muir Weinberg, Barbara (dec.), David Clay. B.A., Lehigh U., 1935; LL.B., Harvard U., 1938. Sole practice Williamsport, Pa., 1938-42, 45-49, 68-70; mem. firm Williamsport, 1949-68; judge U.S. Dist. Ct. (mid. dist.) Pa., 1970—. Active charitable orgns., Williamsport, 1939-70. Mem. ABA, Pa. Bar Assn. (pres.-elect 1970). Avocation: reading. Office: US Dist Ct PO Box 608 Williamsport PA 17703-0608

**MUIRHEAD, DOUGLAS JAMES,** lawyer; b. Mpls., Feb. 6, 1951; s. John Allen and Eunice Myrtle (Mattson) M.; m. Faye Knowles, May 21, 1977; children: Elisabeth Knowles, Emily Faye. BA in History, U. Minn., 1973, JD, 1978. Bar: Minn. 1979, U.S. Ct. Appeals 1984, U.S. Supreme Ct. 1987. Assoc., then ptnr. Meagher & Geer, Mpls., 1979—. Mem. ABA. Avocations: reading, fishing, boating, woodworking. Federal civil litigation, Insurance, Personal injury. Office: Meagher & Geer 4200 Multifoods Twr 33 S 6th St Ste 4200 Minneapolis MN 55402-3788

**MUKAMAL, STEVEN SASOON,** lawyer; b. Bagdad, Iraq, Aug. 5, 1940; s. Abraham and Mary (Murad) M.; m. Nancy Barst, Aug. 3, 1963 (div. Mar. 1983); children: Wendy, Betsy, Thomas; m. Kathleen Nanowsky, Nov. 25, 1983; children: Theodore Douglas, Andrew John. BA, Mich. State U., 1962; JD, Bklyn. Law Sch., 1965. Bar: N.Y. 1966, U.S. Dist. Ct. (so. dist.) N.Y. 1967, (ea. dist.) N.Y., U.S. Ct. Appeals (1st, 2nd and 3rd cirs.) 1968, U.S. Supreme Ct. 1975. Sr. ptnr. Barst & Mukamal, N.Y.C., 1965—; pres. Immigration Info. Sys., Hong Kong, L.I.C. Mortgage Corp., Around the Clock Realty Corp., 33-00 No. L.I.C. Assocs., The Factory L.P.; bd. dirs. The A Cons. Team Inc. Author: U.S. Immigration Laws: Working, Living, and Staying in America, 1993, translated into Chinese and Japanese, 1993; mem. editorial bd. Transnational Immigration Lawyer Reporter, 1978—; contbr. articles to profl. jours. Exec. dir., spl. immigration counsel Nat. Com. for Furtherance of Jewish Edn., 1980—, v.p., 1996—; mayor Village of Woodsburg, N.Y., 1975-78. Recipient Internat. Humanitarian award Nat. Com. for Furtherance of Jewish Edn., 1981. Mem. Am. Immigration Lawyers Assn. (chair com. cert. 1991, life mem. bd. dirs., lectr. 1970—, chmn. ann. conf. 1967-81, treas. 1974-75, 1st v.p. 1975-76, 2d v.p. 1976-77, pres. 1977-78), Coun. on Fgn. Rels. Avocations: tennis, art, thoroughbred horse racing and breeding, human motivation. Immigration, naturalization, and customs. Office: Barst & Mukamal 2 Park Ave Rm 1902 New York NY 10016-9396

**MUKASEY, MICHAEL B.,** federal judge; b. 1941. AB, Columbia U., 1963; LLB, Yale U., 1967. Assoc. Webster Sheffield Fleischmann Hitchcock & Brookfield, 1967-72, Patterson, Belknap, Webb & Tyler, 1976-88; asst. U.S. atty. U.S. Dist. Ct. (so. dist.) N.Y., 1972-76, dist. judge, 1988—; lectr. in law Columbia Law Sch. Contbr. articles to profl. jours. Office: US Dist Ct US Courthouse Foley Sq New York NY 10007-1316

**MULCAHEY, GARIE JEAN,** lawyer; b. Stamford, Conn., Dec. 7, 1943; d. Gary John and Shirley Ruth Wozniak; divorced; 1 child, Sean Patrick. BA, U. Conn., 1978; JD, Pace U., 1981. Bar: Conn. 1981, N.Y. 1982, U.S. Dist. Ct. Conn. 1982, U.S. Dist. Ct. (so. dist.) N.Y. 1997. Atty. Bai, Pollock & Coyne, Bridgeport, Conn., 1981—. Mem. Am. Bd. Trial Advs. (assoc.), Conn. Med. Def. Lawyers Assn. Avocations: golfing, reading. Personal injury, Professional liability. Home: 1112 Foxboro Dr Norwalk CT 06851-1151 Office: Bai Pollock & Coyne 10 Middle St Bridgeport CT 06604-4257

**MULCAHY, CHARLES CHAMBERS,** lawyer, educator; b. Milw., Oct. 5, 1937; s. Thomas Lawrence and Mary (Chambers) M.; m. Judith Ann Schweiger, June 29, 1963; children: Mary Mulcahy Muth, Meg Mulcahy Ekmark, Beth. BS, Marquette U., 1959, JD, 1962. Bar: Wis. 1962, Fla. 1987. Atty., pres. Mulcahy & Wherry, Milw., 1966-91; atty. Whyte Hirschboeck Dudek S.C., Milw., 1991—; adj. prof. Marquette U. Law Sch., Milw., 1975-90; hon. consul Belgium, Milw., 1985—; pres. Pub. Policy Forum, 1992-94; bd. dirs. Wis. Mfrs. and Commerce, 1988-95; mem. Wis. Coun. on Mcpl. Collective Bargaining, 1993—; bd. dirs. Med. Coll. Wis., 1980—, Greater Milw. Com., 1976—. Author: Public Employer Managers Manual, 1968; co-editor: Public Employment Law , 1974, 2nd edit., 1979, 3rd. edit., 1988. County supr. Milw. County, 1964-76; pres. Milw. Tennis Classic, 1975—; chmn. War Meml. Corp., 1976-84; pres. Wis. World Trade Ctr., 1987-91 (Meritorious Svc. award 1991). With USAF, 1962-68. Recipient County Achievement award Nat. Assn. Counties, 1976, Human Rels. award Nat. Conf. on Cmty. and Justice, 1998, Annual Svc. award Nat. Sports Law Inst., 1998, Bill Letwin Tennis award, 1998, O' Neill award Nat. Sports Law Inst., 1998. Mem. Milw. County Hist. Soc. (pres. 1980-81), Marquette Law Alumni Assn. (pres. 1971-72). Republican. Roman Catholic. Avocations: tennis, history, reading, travel. General corporate, Labor. Home: 1820 E Fox Ln Fox Point WI 53217-2858 Office: Whyte Hirschboeck Dudek SC 111 E Wisconsin Ave Ste 2100 Milwaukee WI 53202-4861

**MULCAHY, ROBERT JOSEPH,** lawyer; b. Evergreen Park, Ill., Jan. 22, 1942; s. Robert J. and Mary J. Mulcahy. BS, U. Ill., 1964; JD, Calif. Western Law Sch., 1972. Bar: Calif. 1973, Ill. 1973; cert. legal specialist in work compensation, Calif. Pvt. practice, Chgo., 1973-81, San Diego, 1981-85; dep. city atty. criminal divsn. City of San Diego, 1986-91, dep. city atty. work compensation divsn., 1991—. Capt. USMC, 1964-67, Vietnam. Decorated Purple Heart. Office: City of San Diego 1200 3d Ave Ste 1200 San Diego CA 92101

**MULCHINOCK, DAVID STEWARD,** lawyer; b. Allentown, Pa., Feb. 10, 1945; s. Daniel F. and May E. (Heffner) M. BA, Georgetown U., 1967; JD, Cornell U., 1970. Bar: N.Y. 1971, N.J. 1974, U.S. Supreme Ct. 1978, Pa. 1994. Assoc. Hale, Grant, Meyerson, O'Brien & McCormick, N.Y.C., 1970-72, ptnr., 1972-77; pvt. practice law Princeton, N.J., 1977—. Probate, Taxation, general, General corporate. Home: 107 Windy Bush Rd New Hope PA 18938 Office: One Palmer Sq Princeton NJ 08542

**MULDOON, FRANCIS CREIGHTON,** Canadian federal judge; b. Winnipeg, Manitoba, Canada, Aug. 3, 1930; s. William John and Laura Grace (Meredith) M.; m. M. Lucille Shirtliff, Aug. 6, 1955; 2 children. BA, U. Manitoba, 1952, LLB, 1956. Cert. barrister, solicitor, notary pub. Lawyer Monnin, Grafton, Deniset & Co., Winnipeg, Man., 1956-70; chmn. Manitoba Law Reform Commn., Winnipeg, 1970-77; v.p. Law Reform Commn. Can., Ottawa, 1977-78, pres., 1978-83; judge Fed. Ct. Can., Ottawa, 1983—, Ct. Martial Appeal Ct., Ottawa, 1983—; Bencher Law Soc. Manitoba, Winnipeg, 1986-71. Contbr. articles to profl. jours. President Children Aid Soc. Winnipeg, 1969-70, Manitoba Medico-Legal Soc., Winnipeg, 1973-77. Lt. Can. Army, 1952-60. Disting. Svc. Manitoba Bar Assn., 1987; hon. mem. Bar U.S. Ct. Milit. Appeals, 1991. Mem. Med. Legal Soc. Ottawa-Carleton (co-founder), St. Paul's Coll. (hon.). Roman Catholic. Avocations: reading, bicycling, public speaking. Office: Fed Ct Can, Kent & Wellington Sts, Ottawa, ON Canada K1A 0H9

**MULDOON, JAMES RAYMOND,** lawyer; b. St. Joseph, Mich., Dec. 29, 1960; s. Raymond Albert and Pauline Anne Muldoon; m. Mary Kathleen Muldoon, Dec. 28, 1983; children: Conor P., Megan K., Emily C. SBCE, MIT, 1983; JD, U. Chgo., 1990; postgrad., Northwestern U., 1991-92. Bar: Ill. 1990, N.Y. 1990, U.S. Dist. Ct. (no. and so. dists.) Ill., U.S. Dist. Ct. (no. dist.) N.Y. 1993, U.S. Dist. Ct. (so. dist.) N.Y. 1997, U.S. Ct. Appeals (2d cir.) 1995, U.S. Ct. Appeals (fed. cir.) 1998, U.S. Ct. Mil. Appeals 1990, U.S. Patent and Trademark Office 1994. Atty. Bond, Schoeneck & King, LLP, Syracuse, N.Y., 1992-97, Hancock & Estabrook, LLP, Syracuse, 1997—. Bd. dirs., pres. Exceptional Family Resources, Syracuse, 1994—. Lt. comdr. USN, 1983-92. Mem. N.Y. State Bar Assn., Am. Intellectual Property Law Assn., Licensing Exec. Soc., Ctrl. N.Y. Patent Law Assn. Intellectual property, Patent, Federal civil litigation. Office: Hancock & Estabrook LLP 1500 MONY Tower I PO Box 4976 Syracuse NY 13221-4976

**MULE, JOSEPH,** legal administrator; b. Trenton, N.J., Oct. 13, 1953; s. John and Pauline M.; children: Maria Alene, John Raymond, Chelsea Rose. BS in Psychology, St. Joseph's Coll., 1975; MSW, U. Mich., 1976. Program analyst Hennepin County Dept. Econ. Assistance, Mpls., 1979-81; sr. adminstrv. asst. Hennepin County Atty.'s Office, Mpls., 1981-85; adminstr. Petersen, Tews & Squires, St. Paul, 1985-87, Hansen, Dordell, Bradt, Odlaug & Bradt, St. Paul, 1987-89; exec. dir. Felhaber, Larson, Fenlon & Vogt, Mpls., 1989-97, Mackall, Crounse & Moore, Mpls., 1997—. Bd. dirs. Sight & Hearing Assn., St. Paul; commr. City of Oakdale (Minn.) Planning & Parks Commn., 1993-94. Mem. ABA, Acad. Mgmt., Assn. Legal Adminstrs., Minn. Legal Adminstrs. Assn. (treas. 1990-91). Office: Mackall Crounse & Moore 901 Marquette Ave Ste 1400 Minneapolis MN 55402-2859

**MULHEARN, CHRISTOPHER MICHAEL,** lawyer; b. Providence, R.I., June 14, 1969; s. Michael R. and Judith A. Mulhearn. BA in Polit. Sci., Marquette U., 1991; JD, Cleveland-Marshall Coll. Law, 1994. Bar: R.I. 1994, U.S. Dist. Ct. R.I. 1995, Mass. 1995, U.S. Dist. Ct. Mass. 1996. Assoc. Rodio & Brown, Ltd., Providence, 1994-96, Tate & Elias, Providence, 1996-99, Carroll, Kelly & Murphy, Providence, 1999; prin. Christopher M. Mulhearn, Esq., Counselor at Law, P.C., Providence, 1999—. Pres. bd. dirs. Children's Shelter of Blackstone Valley, Inc., Pawtucket, R.I., 1996—; mem. alumni bd. dirs. Bishop Hendricken H.S., Warwick, R.I., 1996—. Mem. ABA, Am. Health Lawyers Assn., Mass. Bar Assn., R.I. Bar Assn. Avocations: golf, music. FAX: 401-351-7778. Health, Probate, General civil litigation. Home: 167 Blanchard Ave Warwick RI 02888-4002 Office: Christopher M Mulhearn Esq Counselor at Law PC 312 S Main St Ste 4 Providence RI 02903-2911

**MULHERN, EDWIN JOSEPH,** lawyer; b. Bklyn., Mar. 8, 1927; s. Edward Thomas and Jennie (Keenan) M.; m. Maureen P. Purcell, Oct. 2, 1964; children: Edwin T., Deborah J., Kevin T. BBA, St. John's U., 1950, LLB, 1954. Bar: N.Y. 1954, U.S. Dist. Ct. (ea. and so. dists.) N.Y. 1954, U.S. Supreme Ct. 1960. Sr. acct. Susquehanna Mills Inc., N.Y.C., 1947-53; chief acct. Rockwood Chocolate Co., Bklyn., 1953-54; trial atty. Allstate Ins. Co., Freeport, N.Y., 1954-57; claims rep. State Farm Ins. Co., Hempstead, N.Y., 1957-58; sole practice, Bellmore, N.Y., 1958-70, Mineola, N.Y., Carle Place, N.Y., 1970—; mem. joint grievance com. for 10th jud. dist. (N.Y.), 1981-89. Pres. Christian Bros. Boys' Assn., 1975-82; bd. dirs. Legal Aid Soc. of Nassau County, 1980—. Served with USAAF, 1945-46. Mem. ABA, N.Y. State Bar Assn., Nassau Bar Assn. (bd. dirs. 1981-83, chmn. admissions com. 1979, chmn. grievance com. 1980-82), Suffolk County Bar Assn., Nassau Lawyers Assn. (pres. 1975, exec. dir. 1993—, Man of Yr. 1981), Criminal Cts. Bar Assn. of Nassau County (pres. 1976), Criminal Cts. Bar Assn. of Suffolk County, Am. Assn. Trial Lawyers. Clubs: University of L.I. (Hempstead), K.C. (new Hyde Park, N.Y.). Criminal, Family and matrimonial, Personal injury. Office: 1 Old Country Rd Ste 145 Carle Place NY 11514-1801

**MULL, GALE W.,** lawyer; b. Hillsdale, Mich., Sept. 8, 1945; s. Wayne E. and Vivian M. (Bavin) M.; m. Holly Ann Allen, Aug. 2, 1969 (div. Nov. 1983); 1 child, Carter B.; m. Jeanne Anne Haughey, Aug. 18, 1985. BA, Mich. State U., 1967; MA in Sociology, Ind. U., 1969; JD, Emory U., 1972. Bar: Ga. 1972, U.S. Dist. Ct. (no. dist.) Ga. 1972, U.S. Ct. Appeals (5th cir.) 1973, U.S. Ct. Appeals (11th cir.) 1981. Instr. sociology Clemson (S.C.) U., 1968-69, Spelman Coll., Atlanta, 1969-70; pvt. practice, Atlanta, 1972-75; ptnr. Mull & Sweet, Atlanta, 1975-81; pres. Gale W. Mull, P.C., Atlanta, 1981—; bd. dirs. BOND Community Fed. Credit Union, Atlanta, 1975-81; directing atty. Emory Student Legal Services, Atlanta, 1975-91; Sociology instr. Clemson U., Clemson, S.C., 1968-69, Spelman Coll., Atlanta, Ga., 1969-70. Pres. Inman Park Restoration, Inc., Atlanta, 1972-74, BASS Orgn. for Neighborhood Devel., Inc., 1974-78; mem. Housing Appeals Bd., Atlanta, 1982-88; mem. Mayor's Task Force on Prostitution, 1984-86; bd. dirs. ACLU Ga., 1981-92, sec. bd. dirs., 1983-85, cooperating atty., 1972—; vestry St. John's Episcopal Ch., 1992-99, sr. warden, 1998-99; bd. dirs. St. John's Episcopal Day Sch., 1992-97, Bethlehem Ministries, 1997—, Trinity Towers, Inc., 1999—. Mem. ABA, Ga. Bar Assn., Atlanta Bar Assn., Lawyers Club Atlanta. Club: Quail Unltd. (bd. dirs., sec. 1984-86). General practice, Family and matrimonial, Criminal. Office: 990 Edgewood Ave NE Atlanta GA 30307-2581

**MULLADY, RAYMOND GEORGE, JR.,** lawyer; b. Elizabeth, N.J., Mar. 20, 1957; s. Raymond George and Dorothy M. Mullady; m. Melissa Johnson, Sept. 7, 1985; children: Kelsey L., Raymond George III, Jamie L. BS in Journalism, U. Md., 1979; JD, U. Md., Balt., 1983. BAr: Md. 1983. Assoc. Smith, Somerville & Case, Balt., 1983-89; assoc. Piper & Marbury, L.L.P., Balt., 1989-92, ptnr., 1993—. Mem. ABA (co-chair toxic and environ., law com. 1991—), Md. Def. Lawyers Assn. (chair products liability com. 1990-91). Product liability, Toxic tort, Libel. Office: Piper & Marbury LLp 36 S Charles St Baltimore MD 21201-3020

**MULLALLY, DAVID SMART,** lawyer; b. Oakland, Calif., Jan. 30, 1948; s. Walter E. and Jeanne S. Mullally; m. Linda B. Baxendale, Oct. 9, 1983; 1 child, Christopher D. BA, UCLA, 1974; JD, Western State U., Fullerton, Calif., 1976; MA, John F. Kennedy U., Orinda, Calif., 1984. Bar: Calif. 1976, Hawaii 1988, D.C. 1988. Assoc. Law Office Robert Kaiser, Oakland, 1976-78; ptnr. Mullally, Cederborg & Mullally, Oakland, 1978-79; pvt. practice, Walnut Creek, Calif., 1980-84, Monterey, Calif., 1984—; prof. law Monterey Coll. Law, 1984-85. Vol. firefighter Carmel Valley (Calif.) Fire Dept., 1992-96; dir. fundraising Carmel chpt. ARC, 1995. Avocations: jogging, scuba diving, travel, photography, painting. General practice. Office: PO Box 369 Carmel Valley CA 93924-0369

**MULLANAX, MILTON GREG,** lawyer; b. Galveston, Tex., Mar. 16, 1962; s. Milton Gayle and Sharon Kay (Sanders) M.; m. Susan Lynn Griebe, Apr. 19, 1986; children: Adrienne Irene, Mason Glenn. BA in History, U. Tex., Arlington, 1987; JD, U. Pacific, 1991. Bar: Calif., 1991, Nev., 1992, Tex., 1993, Colo., 1993, Minn., 1994, D.C., 1993; U.S. Dist. Ct. (ea. dist.) Calif. 1991, U.S. Dist. Ct. Nev., 1993, U.S. Dist. Ct. (no. dist.) Tex. 1996. Congrl. intern U.S. Rep. Richard K. Armey, Arlington, Tex., 1985; senate aide U.S. Sen. Phil Gramm, Dallas, 1985-86; legis. aide State Rep. Kent Grusendorf, Austin, Tex., 1987; law clk. Criminal Divsn. U.S. Atty., Sacramento, 1989-90; legal researcher Nev. Atty. Gen., Carson City, 1991-92, dep. atty. gen., 1992-94; pvt. practice Fort Worth, Tex., 1995—. Vol. Reagan/Bush 1984, Dallas/Ft. Worth, 1984, Rep. Nat. Conv., Dallas, 1984, Armey for Congress, Arlington, 1984, Vol. Lawyers of Washoe County, Reno, Nev., 1993-94. Mem. ABA, ATLA, Tarrant County Bar Assn., State Bar of Tex. Avocations: sports, politics, reading, shortwave radio. General civil litigation, Estate planning, General practice. Office: 500 W 7th St Ste 1212 Fort Worth TX 76102-4734

**MULLANEY, JOSEPH E.,** retired lawyer; b. Fall River, Mass., Mar. 22, 1933; s. Joseph E. and Beatrice (Hancock) M.; m. Rosemary Woodman, June 22, 1957; children: Joseph E. III, Brian, Sean, Evan. AB magna cum laude, Coll. Holy Cross, Worcester, Mass., 1955; LLB magna cum laude, Harvard U., 1958. Bar: Ohio bar, D.C. bar, Mass. bar. Ptnr. Jones, Day, Cockley & Reavis, Cleve., 1960-70; gen. counsel Office Spl. Rep. Trade Negotiations, Exec. Office Pres., Washington, 1970-71, Cost of Living Council, 1971-72; assoc. gen. counsel Gillette Co., Boston, 1972-77, sr. v.p., gen. counsel, 1977-90, vice-chmn. bd., 1990-98; ret., 1998; dir. Park St. Corp., Greater Boston Legal Services Corp.; mem., dir. Boston Mcpl. Research Bur. Bd. dirs. New Eng. Legal Found.; trustee Boston Pub. Libr.

**MULLANEY, PATRICK JOSEPH,** lawyer; b. Erie, Pa., Mar. 22, 1961; s. James Rembert Mullaney and Julia Alice Kosco; m. Kari Shannon Kelly, Aug. 28, 1988 (div. 1995); 1 child: James Edward. BS, Penn State, State College, PA, 1984; JD, Seattle U., Tacoma, Wash., 1992. Bar: Wash., U.S. Dist Ct. (we. dist.) Wash. Assoc. Danielson, Harrigan & Tollefson, Seattle, 1992-97; of council Foster, Pepper & Shefelman, PLLC, Seattle, 1997—. Com. mem. Seattle Mountaineers, Seattle, 1997—. Mem. King County Bar Assn. Democrat. Catholic. Avocations: mountaineering, travel, rock climbing, reading. Land use and zoning (including planning), Environmental. Home: 9025 Dayton Ave N Seattle WA 98103-3716 Office: Foster Pepper & Shefelman 1111 3rd Ave Ste 3400 Seattle WA 98101-3299

**MULLANEY, THOMAS JOSEPH,** lawyer; b. N.Y.C., Feb. 9, 1946; s. James Joseph and Dorothy Mary (Fulling) M.; m. Christine E. Hampton, Aug. 16, 1969; children: Richard, Jennette. BA, Fordham U., 1967; JD, U. Va., 1970; LLM, NYU, 1977. Bar: Va. 1970, N.Y. 1971, U.S. Dist. Ct. (so. and ea. dists.) N.Y. 1972, U.S. Ct. Appeals (2d cir.) 1972, U.S. Supreme Ct. 1975. Assoc. Brown, Wood, Ivey, Mitchell & Petty, N.Y.C., 1970-79, Law Offices of John M. Kenney, Garden City, N.Y., 1979-84; ptnr. Abrams, Thaw & Mullaney, N.Y.C., Farmingdale, N.Y., 1985-91; dir., sr. counsel law dept. Merrill Lynch & Co., Inc., N.Y.C., 1991—. Capt. JAGC, U.S. Army, 1971-74. Mem. Va. State Bar Assn., N.Y. State Bar Assn. Republican. Roman Catholic. Federal civil litigation, State civil litigation, Securities. Home: 104 Huntington Rd Garden City NY 11530-3122 Office: 222 Broadway Fl 14 New York NY 10038-2510

**MULLARE, T(HOMAS) KENWOOD, JR.,** lawyer; b. Milton, Mass., Jan. 19, 1939; s. Thomas Kenwood and Catherine Marie (Leonard) M.; m. Joan Marie O'Donnell, May 27, 1967; children: Jennifer M. Cedrone, Tracy K., Jill M., Joyce M. AB, Holy Cross Coll., 1961; LLB, Boston Coll., 1964. Bar: Mass. 1964. Atty. New Eng. Electric System, 1964-70; v.p., gen. counsel, sec. AVX Corp., N.Y.C., 1970-73; v.p., gen. counsel, clk. Tyco Labs., Inc., Exeter, N.H., 1973-78; v.p., gen. counsel, sec. SCA Svcs., Inc., Boston, 1978-84; spl. counsel Houghton, Mifflin Co., Boston, 1984-85, v.p., dir. bus. software divsn., 1985-90; pres. North River Capital Co., Inc., Norwell, Mass., 1990—; atty. Daly, Kehoe & Crosson, L.L.P., Boston, 1999—; bd. dirs. North River Capital Co., Inc., PartnerSoft Co. Mem. regional adv. bd. Commonwealth of Mass. Dept. Mental Retardation, 1994-97; bd. dirs. Barque Hill Assn., Norwell, 1980-84, pres., 1981-83; pres. Ch. Hillers, Norwell, 1983-84; bd. dirs. South Shore Assn. for Retarded Citizens, Weymouth, Mass., 1993-98, chmn., 1995-97. Mem. Mass. Bar Assn., Boston Bar Assn. Computer, Intellectual property, Mergers and acquisitions. Home: 31 Barque Hill Dr Norwell MA 02061-2815 Office: Daly Kehoe & Crosson 285 Summer St Boston MA 02210-1503

**MULLARKEY, MARY J.,** state supreme court justice; b. New London, Wis., Sept. 28, 1943; d. John Clifford and Isabelle A. (Steffes) M.; m. Thomas E. Korson, July 24, 1971; 1 child, Andrew Steffes Korson. BA, St. Norbert Coll., 1965; LLB, Harvard U., 1968; LLD (hon.), St. Norbert Coll., 1989. Bar: Wis. 1968, Colo. 1974. Atty.-advisor U.S. Dept. Interior, Washington, 1968-73; asst. regional atty. EEOC, Denver, 1973-75; 1st atty. gen. Colo. Dept. Law, Denver, 1975-79, solicitor gen., 1979-82; legal advisor to Gov. Lamm State of Colo., Denver, 1982-85; ptnr. Mullarkey & Seymour, Denver, 1985-87; justice Colo. Supreme Ct., Denver, 1987—, chief justice, 1998—. Recipient Alumni award St. Norbert Coll., De Pere, Wis., 1980, Alma Mater award, 1993. Fellow ABA Found., Colo. Bar Found.; mem. ABA, Colo. Bar Assn., Colo. Women's Bar Assn. (recognition award 1986), Denver Bar Assn., Thompson G. Marsh Inn of Ct. (pres. 1993-94). Office: Supreme Ct Colo Judicial Bldg 435 2 E 14th Ave Denver CO 80203-2115*

**MULLEN, GRAHAM C.,** federal judge; b. 1940. BA, Duke U., 1962, JD, 1969. Bar: N.C. 1969. Ptnr. Mullen, Holland, Cooper, Morrow, Wilder & Sumner, 1969-90; judge U.S. Dist. Ct. (we. dist.) N.C., Charlotte, 1990—. Lt. USN, 1962-66. Mem. N.C. Bar Assn. (bd. govs. 1983-88), Mecklenburg County Bar Assn. Office: US Courthouse 401 W Trade St Rm 230 Charlotte NC 28202-1619

**MULLEN, MICHAEL T.,** lawyer; b. Evanston, Ill., Apr. 15, 1956; s. George Martin and Marguerite (Tully) M.; m. Patricia Reilley, Apr. 24, 1987; children: Claire, Catharine, Michael. BA, Marquette U., 1978; JD, Loyola U., 1981. Bar: Ill. 1981, U.S. Dist. Ct. (no. dist.) Ill. 1981, U.S. Ct. Appeals (7th cir.) 1981. Asst. atty. gen. Ill. Atty. Gen., Chgo., 1981-85; asst. U.S. atty. U.S. Atty., Chgo., 1985-90, 90-92, dep. chief, 1990-92; ptnr. Mullen & Minella, Chgo., 1992-98, Paul B. Episcope, Ltd., Chgo., 1998—. Contbr. articles to profl. jours. Trustee Village of Western Springs (Ill.), 1995—. Recipient Spl. Achievement award for sustained superior U.S. Dept. Justice, 1988, performance award 1990. Mem. Ill. State Bar Assn., Ill. Trial Lawyers Assn. Personal injury, Transportation. Office: Paul B Episcope Ltd 77 W Washington St Ste 300 Chicago IL 60602-2896

**MULLEN, PETER P.,** lawyer; b. N.Y.C., Apr. 8, 1928; m. Cecilia Kirby; 5 children. AB cum laude, Georgetown U., 1948; LLB, Columbia U., 1951. Bar: N.Y. 1951. Ptnr. Skadden, Arps, Slate, Meagher & Flom LLP, N.Y.C., 1961-98, exec. ptnr., 1981-94, of counsel, 1998—; co-chmn. Cardinal's Com. Laity Archdiocese N.Y., 1992—; bd. dirs., sec., treas., Eye Surgery, Inc.; bd. dirs. 1st Unum Life Ins. Co. Formerly mem., pres. Bd. Edn. Pub. Schs., Bronxville, N.Y., 1979-81; chmn. Skadden Fellowship Found., 1988—; bd. dirs., vice-chmn. Lawrence Hosp., Bronxville, 1984-89; bd. dirs. Project Orbis, Georgetown U., Washington, 1982-99, chmn., 1985-92; bd. dirs. Legal Aid Soc., 1987-93, Vols. Legal Svcs., Inc., 1988-99, United Way Bronxville, 1985-93, Practicing Attys. Law Students; trustee Lawyer's Commn. Civil Rights Under Law, 1984—; chmn. Gregorian U. Found., 1989—; bd. dirs., mem. exec. com. Vatican Obs. Found., 1993. Named Man of Yr. Cath. Big Bros., 1987; recipient John Carroll award Georgetown U., 1984, John Carroll Medal Merit, 1988, Thomas More award Lawyers Com. Cardinal's Com. of the Laity, 1996, Elizabeth Ann Seton award Nat. Cath. Edn. Assn., 1998. Mem. Am. Bar Assn., N.Y. State Bar Assn. (com. securities regulation 1980-83), Assn. Bar City N.Y. (com. corp. law 1964-67, com. admissions 1965-68, com. securities regulation 1970-73), Soc. Friendly Sons St. Patrick (N.Y., pres. 1989-90), Knight Malta. Office: Skadden Arps Slate et al LLP 919 3rd Ave New York NY 10022-3902

**MULLEN, THOMAS TERRY,** lawyer; b. Ashtabula, Ohio, Nov. 19, 1951; s. Gordon L. and Dorothy M. (Terry) M.; m. Barbara Devereaux, June 2, 1984 (div. July 1991); m. Vera Patera, Aug. 25, 1995. BA in Psychology/Sociology, Kent State U., 1975; MSSA, Case Western Res. U., 1979; JD, U. Akron, 1986. Bar: Ohio 1987, U.S. Dist. Ct. (no. dist.) Ohio 1989, U.S. Ct. Appeals (6th cir.) 1990. Social worker Summit County Children's Svcs., Akron, 1975-78; family therapist Akron Child Guidance, 1979-84; trauma counselor Akron Gen. Med. Ctr., 1986-90; asst. pros. Boston Heights, Ohio, 1989-91; pvt. practice law Akron, 1996—; assoc. Blakemore Meeker & Bowler, Akron, 1998—. Trustee Western Res. Legal Svcs., Akron, 1980-93, Summit County Mental Health Assn., Akron, 1998; mem. Zoning Bd. Appeals, Sagamore Hills, Ohio, 1998—; bd. dirs. Soap Box Derby Support Group, Akron, 1996—; mem. Mothers Against Drunk Driving, Akron, 1996—; sponsor Battered Women's Shelter, Akron, 1995—. Recipient Harmon DeGraff scholarship award Akron YMCA/U. Akron, 1977-79, Summit County Children's Svcs. Bd. scholar, 1977-79. Fellow Akron Bar Assn. (mentor U. Akron 1997—, co-chair reg. Ohio mock trial com. 1997—), Summit County Trial Lawyers Assn., Ohio Bar Assn. Avocations: quarter horses, gardening. Insurance, Family and matrimonial, Criminal. Office: Blakemore Meeker & Bowler 19 N High St Akron OH 44308-1912

**MULLEN, WILLIAM DAVID,** lawyer; b. Walnut Ridge, Ark., Jan. 15, 1949; s. William Lemoyne and Margaret V. (Finley) M.; m. Judy C. McNamee, Jan. 24, 1970 (div. Aug. 1977); children: Gwen, Mary. Student, Harding U., 1967-68; BS, Ark. State U., 1970; JD, U. Ark., Little Rock, 1976. Bar: Ark. 1976, U.S. Dist. Ct. (Ark.) 1976; lic. abstracter, real estate broker. Owner, operator Mullen Real Estate, Walnut Ridge, 1977—, Area Health Club, 1990—; abstracter Little Rock Abstract Co., 1972-76; sole practice Walnut Ridge, 1976—; agt. Chgo. Title Ins. Co., 1977-90, So. Title Ins. Co., Knoxville, Tenn., 1982-90, First American Title Ins. Co., Walnut Ridge, 1990—; county atty., dep. prosecutor Lawrence County, Walnut Ridge, 1979; atty. City of Ravenden, Ark., 1980—; lectr. So. Bapt. Coll., Walnut Ridge, 1980-90; cons. Lawrence County Bank, Portia, Ark., 1984—; sec. Northeast Ark. Legal Services, Newport, 1986-89, bd. dirs. 1978-81, 86-89. Coach Walnut Ridge Little League, 1979-84; dir. Walnut Ridge Christmas Parade, 1981—. Mem. ABA, Ark. Bar Assn. (named Outstanding Citizen 1982), Lawrence-Randolph County Bar Assn. (pres. 1983-85), Walnut Ridge Jaycees (pres. 1982, bd. dirs. 1981-87, named Key Man 1981, named Outstanding Local Pres. Ark. Jaycees 1982, recipient BUBBA award 1983). Democrat. Mem. Christian Ch. Avocations: boating, duck hunting. Fax: 870-886-5929. General practice, State civil litigation, Criminal. Home: PO Box 567 Walnut Ridge AR 72476-0567 Office: 119 SW 2d St PO Box 567 Walnut Ridge AR 72476-0567

**MULLENBACH, LINDA HERMAN,** lawyer; b. Sioux City, Iowa, Dec. 25, 1948; d. Verner Wilhelm and Margaretta Victoria (Grant) Herman; m. Hugh James Mullenbach, Aug. 22, 1970; children: Erika Lynn, Linnea Britt. BS in Speech, Northwestern U., 1971, MS in Speech, 1972, JD, 1979. Bar: Ill. 1979, U.S. Dist. Ct. (no. dist.) Ill. 1979, D.C. 1983, U.S. Dist. Ct. D.C. 1983, U.S. Ct. Appeals (7th, D.C. and fed. cirs.), 1983, U.S. Supreme Ct. 1984. Assoc. Jenner & Block, Chgo., 1979-83; assoc. Dickstein, Shapiro & Morin, Washington, 1983-85, prin., 1985-87, ptnr., 1988-93; v.p., assoc. gen. counsel Zurich Small Bus. and Zurich Comml. Legal Divsn., Balt., 1994-99; asst. gen. counsel, v.p. Corp. Law Divsn. Zurich U.S., Balt., 1999—. Mem. ABA (litigation sect.), D.C. Bar Assn., Women's Bar Assn. D.C., Women's Legal Def. Fund, Assn. Trial Lawyer Am., Mortar Bd., Zeta Phi Eta. Federal civil litigation, Criminal, Labor. Home: 8201 Killean Way Potomac MD 20854-2728

**MULLER, EDWARD ROBERT,** lawyer; b. Phila., Mar. 26, 1952; s. Rudolph E. and Elizabeth (Steiner) M.; m. Patricia Eileen Bauer, Sept. 27, 1980; children: Margaret Anne, John Frederick. AB summa cum laude, Dartmouth Coll., 1973; JD, Yale U., 1976. Assoc. Leva, Hawes, Symington, Martin & Oppenheimer, Washington, 1977-83; dir. legal affairs Life Scis. group Whittaker Corp., Arlington, Va., 1983-84; v.p. Whittaker Health Svcs., Arlington, Va., 1984-85; v.p., gen. counsel, sec. Whittaker Corp., L.A., 1985-93, chief adminstrv. officer, 1988-92, CFO, 1992-93, bd. dirs., 1993-99; v.p., gen. counsel, sec. BioWhittaker, Inc., Walkersville, Md., 1991-93; pres., CEO, bd. dirs. Edison Mission Energy, Irvine, Calif., 1993—; mem. Brookings Task Force on Civil Justice Reform, 1988-89; chmn. U.S.-Philippines Bus. Com., 1998—; bd. dirs. Global Marine, Inc.; mem. adv. bd. Tennenbaum & Co., 1997—; mem. Coun. on Fgn. Rels., 1998—; dep. chmn. Contact Energy Ltd., 1999—. Trustee Exceptional Children's Found., L.A., 1988-94, treas., 1988-93; bd. dirs. Oasis Resdl., Inc., 1995-98; co-chair Internat. Energy Devel. Coun., Washington, 1993—; bd. govs. Jr. Achievement of Orange County and the Inland Empire, 1995-96. General corporate, Federal civil litigation. Office: Edison Mission Energy 18101 Von Karman Ave Ste 1700 Irvine CA 92612-0178

**MULLER, KURT ALEXANDER,** lawyer; b. Chgo., June 21, 1955; s. Jack and Janet (Kasten) M.; m. Sylvia Saltoon, Apr. 6, 1986; 1 child, Marissa Grace. BS, U. Wis., Parkside, 1977; JD, John Marshall Law Sch., 1986. Bar: Ill. 1986, U.S. Dist. Ct. (no. dist.) Ill. 1986, Ariz. 1987, U.S. Dist. Ct. (ea. dist.) Wis. 1989. Creative dir. Brand Advt., Chgo., 1977-80; dep. sheriff Cook County, Chgo., 1978-86; broker Gerstenberg Commodities, Chgo., 1980-83; assoc. Gordon & Glickson, P.C., Chgo., 1986-87, Michael Harry Minton, P.C., Chgo., 1987-90; pvt. practice Chgo., 1990-92; ptnr. Law Offices of Richter-Muller, P.C., Chgo., 1992-95; lawyer, CEO The Muller Firm, Ltd., Chgo., 1995—. Author: In Consideration of Divorce: Giving Credit (and Debits) to Dissolution, 1991, 3d edit., 1998; contbr. The Jewish American Prince Handbook, 1986; contbr. articles to profl. jours. and newspapers; host (radio show) Kurt Muller's Uncommon Law. Mem. ABA, ACLU, Nat. Smoker's Alliance, Chgo. Bar Assn., Masons. Avocations: interior design, films, theater, writing. Fax: 312-855-9362. E-mail: www. mullaw.com. Family and matrimonial, Alternative dispute resolution, Juvenile. Office: 200 N Dearborn St Apt 4602 Chicago IL 60601-1628

**MULLER, PETER DEPPISH,** lawyer; b. Savannah, Ga., July 16, 1962; s. Joseph Charles and Margaret Robinson M.; m. Elizabeth Massey, Aug. 11, 1984; children: Mary Elizabeth, Peter Robinson. BA in Journalism, U. Ga., 1984, JD, 1987. Bar: Ga. 1987. Assoc. Bouhan, Williams & Levy, Savannah, Ga., 1987-93, ptnr., 1994—. Mem. State Bar Ga. (younger lawyers sect. exec. coun. 1988-99, bd. dirs. 1993-98). General civil litigation. Office: Bouhan Williams & Levy 447 Bull St Savannah GA 31401-4960

**MULLER, WILLIAM MANNING,** corporate lawyer; b. N.Y.C., Mar. 20, 1959; s. Eugene Lee and Patricia Anne (Manning) M. AB, Brown U., 1981; JD, Northwestern U., 1987. Bar: N.Y. 1989, Conn. 1989, Ga. 1996. Assoc. Milbank, Tweed, Hadley & McCloy, N.Y.C., 1987-90; legal counsel Rockefeller & Co., Inc., N.Y.C., 1991-93; assoc. Reid & Priest, N.Y.C., 1993-95; counsel Turner Broadcasting Sys., Inc., Atlanta, 1995-96, sr. counsel, 1996—. Mem. ABA, Conn. Bar Assn., State Bar Ga., Assn. Bar City of New York, TV Assn. Programmers (chmn. govt. and legal affairs com.), Univ. Club New York. Communications, Entertainment, Private international. Office: Turner Broadcasting Sys Inc One CNN Ctr Atlanta GA 30303

**MULLIGAN, ELINOR PATTERSON,** lawyer; b. Bay City, Mich., Apr. 20, 1929; d. Frank Clark and Agnes (Murphy) P.; m. John C. O'Connor, Oct. 28, 1950; children: Christine Fulena, Valerie Clark, Amy O'Connor, Christopher Criffan O'Connor; m. William G. Mulligan, Dec. 6, 1975. BA, U. Mich., 1950; JD, Seton Hall U., 1970. Bar: N.J. 1970. Assoc. Springfield and Newark, 1970-72; pvt. practice, Hackettstown, N.J., 1972; ptnr. Mulligan & Jacobson, N.Y.C., 1973-91, Mulligan & Mulligan, Hackettstown, 1976—; atty. Hackettstown Planning Bd., 1973-86, Blairstown Bd. Adjustment, 1973-95; sec. Warren County Ethics Com., 1976-78, sec. Dist. X and XIII Fee Arbitration Com., 1979-87, mem. and chair, 1987-91, mem. dist. ethics com. XIII, 1992—; mem. spl. com. on atty. disciplinary structure N.J. Supreme Ct., 1981—; lectr. Nat. Assn. Women Judges, 1979, N.J. Inst. Continuing Legal Edn., 1988—. Contbr. articles to profl. jours. Named Vol. of Yr., Attys. Vols. in Parole Program, 1978. Fellow Am. Acad. Matrimonial Lawyers (pres. N.J. chpt. 1995-96); mem. ABA, Warren County Bar Assn. (pres. 1987-88), N.J. State Bar ASsn., N.J. Women Lawyers Assn. (v.p. 1985—), Am. Mensa Soc., Union League Club (N.Y.C.), Baltusrol Golf Club (Springfield, N.J.), Panther Valley Golf and Country Club (Allamuchy, N.J.), Kappa Alpha Theta. Republican. Family and matrimonial, State civil litigation, Probate. Home: 12 Goldfinch Way Hackettstown NJ 07840-3007 Office: 933 County Road 517 Hackettstown NJ 07840-4654

**MULLIKIN, ANU RADHA,** lawyer; b. Ft. Worth, Dec. 23, 1966; d. Suresh Chandra and Padma Ramaswamy Mathur; m. John Francis Mullikin, Aug. 15, 1993; 1 child, Katelyn Radha Mullikin. BS in Acctg., U. Lowell, 1988; JD, Boston U., 1991, LLM, 1996. Bar: N.H. 1991. Atty. Devine Millimet & Branch, Manchester, N.H., 1991—; mem. N.H. Estate Planning Coun., 1992—, sec., 1995-97, v.p., 1997-98, pres., 1998—. Bd. dirs. Daniel Webster coun. Boy Scouts Am., 1996—. Estate planning, Probate, Estate taxation. Office: Devine Millimet & Branch PO Box 719 Manchester NH 03105-0719

**MULLIN, PATRICK ALLEN,** lawyer; b. Newark, N.J., Jan. 13, 1950; s. Gerard Vincent and Frances Regina (Magnanti) M. BA, William Paterson U., 1972, MEd, 1974; JD, NYU, 1979, LLM in Taxation, 1990; postgrad., Harvard U., 1979; Gerry Spense's Trial Lawyers Coll., Duboise, Wyo., 1997. Bar: N.J. 1979, D.C. 1980, N.Y. 1990; cert. criminal trial atty. N.J. Supreme Ct. Law clk. to Hon. Dickinson R. DeBevoise, U.S. Dist. Ct. N.J., Trenton, 1979-80; assoc. Charles Morgan Assocs., Washington, 1980-81, Michael A Querques, Orange, N.J., 1985-88; pvt. practice, Hackensack, N.J., 1988—; mem. practitioners adv. com. U.S. Sentencing Commn. Mem. ABA. Roman Catholic. Avocations: jogging, martial artist. Fax: 201-487-2840. E-mail: pmullin@bellatlantic.net. Criminal, Taxation, general. Address: 25 Main St # 200 Hackensack NJ 07601-7015

**MULLINIX, EDWARD WINGATE,** lawyer; b. Balt., Feb. 25, 1924; s. Howard Earl and Elsie (Wingate) M.; m. Virginia Lee McGinnes, July 28, 1944; children: Marcia Lee Ladd, Edward Wingate. Student, St. John's Coll., 1941-43; JD summa cum laude, U. Pa., 1949. Bar: Pa. 1950, U.S. Supreme Ct. 1955. Assoc. Schnader Harrison Segal & Lewis LLP, Phila., 1950-55, ptnr., 1956-92, now sr. coun.; mem. adv. bds. Antitrust Bull., 1970-81, BNA Antitrust and Trade Regulation Report, 1981-94; mem. Civil Justice adv. group U.S. Dist. Ct. (ea. dist.) Pa., 1998—; mem. Civil Justice Reform Act of 1990 adv. group U.S. Dist. Ct. (ea. dist.) Pa., 1991-98; co-chmn. Joint U.S. Dist. Ct./Phila. Bar Assn. Alternative Dispute Resolution Com., 1990—; cons. on revision of local civil rules U.S. Dist. Ct. (ea. dist.) Pa., 1995—; mem. adv. com. U. Pa. Law Sch. Ctr. on Professionalism, 1988-92; judge pro tem Ct. Common Pleas of Phila. County Day Forward program; faculty participant Pa. Bar Inst., Phila. Bar Edn. Ctr., others. Trustee Sta. KYW-TV Project Homeless Fund, 1985-86. Served with USMCR, 1943-44; to lt. (j.g.) USNR, 1944-46. Fellow Am. Bar Found. (life), Am. Coll. Trial Lawyers (emeritus, mem. complex litig. com. 1980-91, vice-chmn. com. 1981-83); mem. ABA (spl. com. complex and multidist. litig. 1969-73, co-chmn. com. 1971-73, coun. litig. sect. 1976-80), Pa. Bar Assn., Phila. Bar Assn., Hist. Soc. U.S. Dist. Ct. (ea. dist.) Pa. (bd. dirs. 1984—, pres. 1991-94), Juristic Soc., Order of Coif, Union League (Phila.), Socialegal Club (Phila.), Aronimink Golf Club (Newtown Sq., Pa.). Republican. Presbyterian. Alternative dispute resolution, Federal civil litigation, Professional liability. Home: 251 Chamounix Rd Saint Davids PA 19087-3605 Office: 1600 Market St Ste 3600 Philadelphia PA 19103-7240

**MULLINS, MARGARET ANN FRANCES,** lawyer, educator; b. Jersey City, Feb. 3, 1953; d. William Francis Sr. and Ada Louise (Pellizzari) M.; m. Robert Laurence Tortoriello, Sept. 29, 1979; children: Lauren, Christopher, Kenneth. AB, Coll. of St. Elizabeth, 1975; JD, Seton Hall U., 1978. Bar: N.J. 1978, U.S. Dist. Ct. N.J. 1978, U.S. Ct. Appeals (3d cir.) 1982, U.S. Supreme Ct. 1982, N.Y. 1984, D.C. 1985, U.S. Ct. Appeals (D.C. cir.) 1986. Assoc. Edwin C. Eastwood Jr., North Bergen, N.J., 1978-79; asst. prosecutor Essex County Prosecutor's Office, Newark, 1980-82, Passaic County County Prosecutor's Office, Paterson, N.J., 1982-86; mem. faculty Seton Hall U. Sch. Law, Newark, 1987—. Mem. ABA, N.J. Bar Assn., N.Y. State Bar Assn. Republican. Roman Catholic. Home: 112 Heller Way Montclair NJ 07043-2512

**MULLKOFF, DOUGLAS RYAN,** lawyer; b. Detroit, June 20, 1955. BA, U. Mich., 1977; JD, Detroit Coll. Law, 1981. Bar: Mich. 1981, U.S. Dist. Ct. (ea. dist.) Mich. 1982, U.S. Dist. Ct. (we. dist. Mich. 1984, U.S. Ct. Appeals (6th cir.) 1986, U.S. Supreme Ct. 1988, U.S. Ct. Appeals (7th cir.) 1995. Rsch. attorney State Appellate Defender, Detroit, 1981-82; assoc. Hugh M. Davis, P.C., Ann Arbor, Mich., 1982-83; pvt. practice Ann Arbor, Mich., 1983-90; partner Kessler, Mullkoff & Hooberman, Ann Arbor, Mich., 1990—. Recipient Civility in Practice of Law award Washtenaw County Bar Assn., Ann Arbor, 1996. Mem. Nat. Assn. Criminal Def. Attys., Criminal Def. Attys. Mich. (pres. 1998). Criminal, Civil rights. Office: Kessler Mullkoff Hooberman 402 W Liberty St Ann Arbor MI 48103-4343

**MULLMAN, MICHAEL S.,** lawyer; b. N.Y.C., Sept. 17, 1946; s. Herbert and Harriet (Weissman) M.; m. Ellen Mullman, 1975; children: Jeremy, Cassie. BA in Polit. Sci. cum laude, Union Coll., Schenectady, N.Y., 1968; JD, Columbia U., 1971. Bar: N.Y. 1972, U.S. Ct. Appeals (2d cir.), U.S. Dist. Ct., 1975. Atty. Paskus, Gordon & Hyman, N.Y.C., 1976-80; ptnr. Schonwald, Schaffzin & Mullman, N.Y.C., 1980-89, Tenzer Greenblatt LLP, N.Y.C., 1989—. Bd. editors Columbia Jour. Law and Soc. Problems, articles edition, 1970-71. Nott scholar Union Coll., 1967, Harlan Fiske Stone scholar Sch. Law Columbia U., 1971. Mem. Bar Assn. N.Y.C., Phi Beta Kappa. Avocations: tennis, skiing, reading, gardening. General corporate, Real property, Mergers and acquisitions. Office: Tenzer Greenblatt LLP The Chrysler Bldg 405 Lexington Ave New York NY 10174-0002

**MULROY, THOMAS ROBERT, JR.,** lawyer; b. Evanston, Ill., June 26, 1946; s. Thomas Robert and Dorothy (Reiner) M.; m. Elaine Mazzone, Aug. 16, 1969. Student, Loyola U., Rome, 1966; BA, U. Santa Clara, Calif., 1968; JD, Loyola U., Chgo., 1972. Bar: Ill. 1973, U.S. Dist. Ct. (no. dist.) Ill. 1973, U.S. Ct. Appeals (7th cir.) 1973. Asst. U.S. atty. No. Dist. Ill., Chgo., 1972-76; ptnr. Jenner & Block, Chgo. 1976—, chmn. products liability group; adj. prof. Northwestern U. Sch. Law, Chgo., 1978-85, Loyola U. Sch. Law, 1983—, DePaul U. Sch. Law, Chgo., Nova U. Ctr. for Study of Law. Editor: Annotated Guide to Illinois Rules of Professional Conduct; contbr. articles to profl. jours.; bd. dirs. Loyola U. Trial Advocacy Workshop, 1982—, Legal Assistance Found., Ill. Inst. for Continued Legal Edn.; chmn. inquiry panel Ill. Atty. Registration and Disciplinary Commn., spl. counsel, 1989—. Mem. Chgo. Crime Commn., 1978—. Mem. ABA, (torts and ins. pratcie, chmn. rules and evidence com.), Am. Judicature Soc., Fed. Trial Bar, Legal Club Chgo., Law Club, 7th Fed. Cir. Bar Assn., Chgo. Bar Assn., Ill. Assn. Def. Trial Counsel, Ill. Bar Assn. Clubs: Univ., Execs. of Chgo., Union League. Federal civil litigation, State civil litigation, Product liability. Office: Jenner & Block 1 E Ibm Plz Fl 42 Chicago IL 60611-7693

**MULVANEY, JAMES E.,** lawyer; b. N.Y.C., Apr. 17, 1930; s. Thomas A. and Ann G. (Gillespie) M.; divorced; children: James Jr., Patrick J. AB, St. Peter's Coll., 1951; LLB, Cornell U., 1954; LLM, Georgetown U., 1955. Atty. V.M. McInerney, Hollis, N.Y., 1955-63; asst. dist. atty. Queens Dist. Atty., Kow Gardens, N.Y., 1963-65; ptnr. McInerney & Mulvaney, New Hyde Park, N.Y., 1966-83; pvt. practice Rockaway, N.Y., 1983—. Contbr. Notre Dame Law Rev., 1955. Democrat. Roman Catholic. Avocations: writing, theater. Criminal. Home and Office: 10710 Shore Front Pkwy Rockaway Park NY 11694-2637

**MULVANIA, WALTER LOWELL,** lawyer; b. Rock Port, Mo., Sept. 20, 1905; s. Jesse L. and Eva Viola (Stewart) M.; m. Eunice Mary Umbarger, Jan. 31, 1945; 1 child, Eva Jo Mulvania Van Meter. BA, William Jewell Coll., Liberty, Mo., 1927; JD, U. Mo., 1931. Pvt. practice law Rock Port, 1931—. Fellow Am. Coll. of Trust and Estate Counsel; mem. ABA, Mo. Bar Assn. (bd. govs. 1965-71), Rotary (pres. 1951-52). Democrat. Baptist. Estate planning, Probate, Real property. Office: 213 S Main St Rock Port MO 64482-1531

**MULVEY, RICHARD IGNATIUS,** lawyer; b. Geneva, N.Y., Mar. 2, 1929; s. Leo J. and Edith (Connell) M.; m. Ann Marshall, Apr. 3, 1982. Student, Niagara U., 1954-56; BA, U. Buffalo, 1959; JD, Albany Law Sch., 1960. Bar: N.Y. 1961, U.S. Dist. Ct. (no. and we. dists.) N.Y. 1970. 1st lt. U.S. Army, 1950-53. Mem. N.Y. Bar Assn., N.Y. Trial Lawyers Assn., Rotary. Republican. Roman Catholic. Avocation: sailing. General civil litigation, General practice, Personal injury. Office: PO Box 837 Ithaca NY 14851-0837

**MULVIHILL, DAVID BRIAN,** lawyer; b. Pitts., Jan. 21, 1956; s. Mead J. Jr. and Margaret (O'Brien) M.; m. Elizabeth Miles, May 21, 1988; stepchildren: Jennifer A. Miles, Heath A. Miles. BA, U. Pitts., 1977; JD, Duquesne U., 1981. Bar: U.S. Dist. Ct. (we. dist.) Pa. 1981, U.S. Ct. Appeals (3d cir.) 1985. Assoc. Mansmann, Cindrich & Titus, Pitts., 1981-86; ptnr. Cindrich & Titus, Pitts., 1986-94, Titus & McConomy, Pitts., 1994-98; v.p. adminstrv. svcs., gen. counsel Make-A-Wish Found. Am., Phoenix, 1998—. Bd. dirs. Make-A-Wish Found. Am., 1992-98; bd. dirs. Make-A-Wish Found. Western Pa., 1986-93, v.p., 1989-90, pres. 1990-92. Recipient Jefferson medal Am. Inst. for Pub. Svc., 1991, Outstanding Citizen award Pitts. Post-Gazette, 1991. Mem. ABA, Pa. Bar Assn., Allegheny County Bar Assn., Acad. Trial Lawyers of Allegheny County, Nat. Order of Barristers. Avocations: reading, kayaking, classic cars. Office: Make-A-Wish Found Am 100 W Clarendon Ave Ste 2200 Phoenix AZ 85013-3596

**MULVIHILL, JOSEPH JAMES,** lawyer, police commissioner; b. Kansas City, Mo., Aug. 3, 1944; s. John Thomas and Mary Margaret Mulvihill. BS in Bus. Adminstrn., Rockhurst Coll., Kansas City, Mo., 1966; JD, U. Mo., Kansas City, 1969. Bar: Mo. 1969. Asst. prosecutor Kansas City, Mo., 1969-72; atty. for county assessor Jackson County, Kansas City, 1969-73; delinquent tax atty. Jackson County Collector, Kansas City, 1973-74; sole practitioner Kansas City, 1969-90; ptnr. Mulvihill & Hunter, Kansas City, 1990—; chmn. Jackson County Assessors Adv. Commn., Kansas City, 1972-73, Kansas City Bd. Zoning Adjustment, 1980-85. Mem. Bd. Police Commrs., Kansas City, Mo., 1997—; committeeman Jackson County Dem. Party, Kansas City, 1976. Roman Catholic. Avocations: golf, politics. Real property. Office: Mulvihill & Hunter 417 E 13th St Kansas City MO 64106-2802

**MULVIHILL, KEITHLEY D.,** lawyer; b. Pitts., Oct. 16, 1956; s. Bernard H. and Doris L. M.; m. Donna Colella, 1980; children; Michael, Mary Katherine. BA in History, Ind. U. Pa., 1978; JD, U. Pitts., 1981. Bar: Pa. 1981, U.S. Dist. Ct. (we. dist.) Pa. 1981, U.S. Ct. Appeals (3d cir.) 1982. Assoc. Rose, Schmidt, Hasley & DiSalle, Pitts., 1981-88, shareholder, 1988—. Mem. ABA, Pa. Bar Assn., Pa. Def. Inst. (treas. 1998—), Allegheny County Bar Assn., Assn. Def. Trial Attys., Def. Rsch. Inst. General civil litigation, Insurance, Professional liability. Office: Rose Schmidt Hasley & DiSalle 900 Oliver Bldg Pittsburgh PA 15222

**MUMAUGH, BRIAN MICHAEL,** lawyer; b. Cheyenne, Wyo., July 19, 1957; s. John Robert and Viola Joan (Butera) M.; m. Jody Lynn Niemann, July 10, 1981; children: Andrew Michael, Ashley Katherine, Lauren Elizabeth, Daniel John. BS, U. Nebr., 1979; JD, Creighton U., Omaha, 1982. Bar: Nebr. 1983, U.S. Dist. Ct. Nebr. 1983, Colo. 1989, U.S. Dist. Ct. Colo. 1989, U.S. Ct. Appeals (10th cir.) 1989, U.S. Ct. Appeals (D.C. cir.) 1998. Assoc. Hotz, Kitler & Jahn, Omaha, 1982-84, Buenzle & Hill, Washington, 1984; labor atty. United Airlines, Chgo., 1984-89; ptnr. Holland & Hart, Denver, 1989—; speaker Ill. Youth Leadership Conf., Chgo., 1986-88; speaker on race, sex and age discrimination and other topics. Author, editor: UAL Employment Manual, 1988, Holland and Hart Colorado Employment Law Letter, 1991; author: Arbitration of Employment Disputes After Gilmer, Colorado Lawyer, 1991. Vol. Mobile Meals, Omaha, 1982-84, Denver Pub. Schs. Tutoring Program, 1990—. Mem. ABA, Nebr. Bar Assn., Colo. Bar Assn., Colo. Def. Lawyers Assn., Denver Bar Assn. Avocations: writing, running, fishing, travel, reading. Labor, General civil litigation. Office: Holland & Hart 555 17th St Ste 2900 Denver CO 80202-3979

**MUMM, CHRISTOPHER ERIC,** lawyer, county government official; b. Reno, Dec. 9, 1950; s. Hans Heinrich and Yolanda Victoria (Erickson) M.; m. Stephanie Wasile, Nov. 27, 1984; children: Melody Anishka, Alexander Matthew. AAS in Real Estate, Truckee Meadows Community Coll, 1976; JD, U. Nev., 1985. Bar: Nev. 1987, Calif. 1987; lic. real estate broker, Nev. Dep. appraiser Washoe County, Reno, 1976-80; dep. tax assessor Washoe County, 1980-89; ind. real estate broker Reno, 1979—, pvt. practice law, 1987—; chief tribal ct. judge Pyramid Lake Indian Reservation, 1994-98. With U.S. Army, 1970-72. Mem. Calif. Bar Assn., Nev. Bar Assn., Soc. Real Estate Appraisers (v.p. edn. Reno chpt. 1984-86), Internat. Assn. Assessing Ofcls., Nev. Jr. C. of C. (pres. 1986), U.S. Jaycees (exec. bd. dirs. 1986), Acquarian Toastmasters (pres. 1988), Sertoma. Democrat. Roman Catholic. Home: 1100 Gault Way Sparks NV 89431-1812

**MUND, GERALDINE,** judge; b. L.A., July 7, 1943; d. Charles J. and Pearl (London) M. BA, Brandeis U., 1965; MS, Smith Coll., 1967; JD, Loyola U., 1977. Bar: Calif. 1977. Bankruptcy judge U.S. Ctrl. Dist. Calif., 1984—, bankruptcy chief judge, 1997—. Past pres. Temple Israel, Hollywood, Calif.; mem. Bd. Jewish Fedn. Coun. of Greater L.A. Mem. ABA, L.A. County Bar Assn. Office: 21041 Burbank Blvd Woodland Hills CA 91367-6606

**MUNDHEIM, ROBERT HARRY,** law educator; b. Hamburg, Germany, Feb. 24, 1933; m. Guna Smitchens; children: Susan, Peter. BA, Harvard U., 1954, LLB, 1957; MA (hon.), U. Pa., 1971. Bar: N.Y. 1958, Pa. 1979. Assoc. Shearman & Sterling, N.Y.C., 1958-61; spl. counsel to SEC Washington, 1962-63; vis. prof. Duke Law Sch., Durham, N.C., 1964; prof. law U. Pa., Phila., 1965—; univ. prof. law and fin., 1980-93, dean, 1982-89, Bernard G. Segal prof. law, 1987-89; co-chmn. Fried, Frank, Harris, Shriver & Jacobson, N.Y.C., 1990-92; exec. v.p., gen. counsel Salomon Inc., 1992-97; sr. exec. v.p ., gen. counsel Salomon Smith Barney Holdings, Inc., 1997-98; of counsel Shearman & Sterling, 1999—; gen. counsel U.S. Dept. Treasury, Washington, 1977-80; dir. Ctr. for Study of Fin. Instns., U. Pa.; pres. Appleseed Found.; bd. dirs. Salzburg Seminars, The Kitchen, Benjamin Moore & Co.; gen. counsel Chrysler Loan Guarantee Bd., 1980; mng. dir., mem. mgmt. bd. Salomon Bros. Inc., N.Y.C., 1992—. Author: Outside Director of the Publicity Held Corporation, 1976; American Attitudes Toward Foreign Direct Investment in the United States, 1979; Conflict of Interest and the Former Government Employee: Re-thinking the Revolving Door, 1981; chmn. adv. bd. Jour. Internat. Econ. Law, 1996—. With USAF, 1961-62. Recipient Alexander Hamilton award U.S. Dept. Treasury, 1980, Harold P. Seligson award Practicing Law Inst., 1988, Francis J. Rawle award, ABA-ALI, 1992, Anti-Defamation League Human Rels. award, 1999. Mem. Am. Law Inst. (mem. coun., mem. exec. com.), Nat. Assn. Securities Dealers (gov.-at-large, vice-chmn.), San Diego Securities Regulation Inst. (chmn.). Office: Shearman & Sterling 599 Lexington Ave New York NY 10022

**MUNDIS, DARYL ALAN,** lawyer, naval officer; b. Parsons, Kans., Dec. 16, 1963; s. Carl Frederick Mundis and Marilyn Kay Lett Beal; m. Deborah T. Leipziger, June 23, 1991. BA, Manhattanville Coll., Purchase, N.Y., 1988; M. Internat. Affairs, Columbia U., 1993, JD, 1992. Bar: N.Y. 1993, N.J. 1993, U.S. Dist. Ct. N.J. 1993, U.S. Ct. Appeals for Armed Forces 1994. Commd. lt. USNR, 1992—; claims atty., trial counsel Naval Legal Svc. Office, Phila., 1993-94, sr. trial counsel, 1994—; spl. asst. U.S. Atty. (ea. dist.) Pa., 1993—; lectr. Manhattanville Coll., 1991. Co-editor Internat. Security Reader, 1990-92; mem. editorial bd. Am. Rev. of Internat. Arbitration, 1991-92. Tony Patino fellow Columbia Law Sch., 1988-92; Harry S. Truman Scholarship Found. scholar, 1986-90, Manhattanville Coll. Presdl. scholar, 1984-88. Mem. ABA, Judge Advocates Assn., Arms Control Assn. Democrat. Jewish. Avocations: photography, railfanning, travel, reading history. Home: 423 Spruce St Philadelphia PA 19106-3706

**MUNDY, GARDNER MARSHALL,** lawyer; b. Roanoke, Va., July 19, 1934; s. Gardner Adams and Betty (Marshall) M.; m. Jean Stephens, Nov. 13, 1956 (div. 1979); children: Stephens M., Liza I.; m. Jenice Hamrick, June 21, 1980 (div. 1998); children: G. Marshall Jr., Natalie J.; m. Monika Ferguson, Aug. 28, 1999. BA, Va. Mil. Inst., 1956; LLB, U. Va., 1962. Bar: Va. 1962, U.S. Dist. Ct. (we. dist.) Va. 1962, U.S. Ct. Appeals (4th cir.) 1962. Ptnr. Woods, Rogers & Hazlegrove, Roanoke, 1962-71, Mundy & Garrison, Roanoke, 1973-76, Mundy & Strickland, Roanoke, 1976-82; pvt. practice Roanoke, 1982-86; ptnr. Mundy, Rogers & Frith, Roanoke, 1986—. 1st lt. U.S. Army, 1957-59. Fellow Am. Coll. Trial Lawyers, Am. Bd. Trial Advocates (pres. Western Va. chpt. 1990-91), Am. Bar Found., Va. Bar Found.; mem. ABA, Va. State Bar Assn. (chmn. bd. govs. litig. sect. 1985-86), Roanoke Bar Assn. (bd. dirs. 1986-90, pres. 1990-91), Shenandoah Club, Roanoke Country Club, Coral Beach and Tennis Club (Bermuda). Presbyterian. Avocations: tennis, skiing, cooking, growing roses. Fax #: 540-982-1362. General civil litigation, Family and matrimonial, Personal injury. Home: 1542 Electric Rd Roanoke VA 24018-1106 Office: Mundy Rogers & Frith 1328 3rd St SW Roanoke VA 24016-5219

**MUNDY, JAMES FRANCIS,** lawyer; b. Wilkes Barre, Pa., Jan. 22, 1943; s. James F. and Mary Elizabeth (Lenahan) M.; m. Rose Ellen Zelonis, Mar. 15, 1969 (div. Jan. 1990); children: Leo, Timothy, Krystn. BS in Acctg., Kings Coll., 1965; JD, Cath. U., 1968. Bar: Pa., U.S. Dist. Ct. (ea. and mid. dists.) Pa. 1970, U.S. Ct. Appeals (3d. cir.), U.S. Supreme Ct. 1982; diplomate Am. Bd. Trial Advocates 1991. Assoc. Richter, Syken, Ross, Binder and O'Neill, Phila., 1970-72, Raynes, McCarty and Binder, Phila., 1972-76; ptnr. Raynes, McCarty, Binder and Mundy, Phila., 1976—; apptd. chair Atty. Disciplinary Bd., Pa., 1984-90; apptd. chair Pa. Appellate Ct. Nominating Commn., 1987-94; apptd. Trial Ct. Nominating Commn., Phila. County, 1987-94; apptd. Mandatory Legal Edn. Bd., 1992—. Co-author: The New Financial Responsibility Law, 1986. Mem. com. to benefit the children St. Christopher's Hosp. for Children, Phila., 1982-92; finance chair bd. trustees Coll. Misericordia, Dallas, 1983-90; co-chair statewide med. malpractice com. Pa. Senate, 1984-87; bd. trustees Kings Coll., Wilkes Barre, 1990—. Recipient Equal Justice award Cmty. Legal Svcs., 1990. Fellow Am. Coll. Trial Lawyers; mem. Pa. Bar Assn. (v.p. 1994-95, pres.-elect 1995—), Pa. Trial Lawyers Assn. (past pres. 1983-84, Milton Rasenberg Meml. award 1982), Phila. Trial Lawyers Assn. (past pres. 1979-80, Justice Michail Mussmano Meml. award 1987). General civil litigation, Personal injury, Product liability. Home: 174 Damview Rd Media PA 19063-1832 Office: Raynes McCarty Binder Ross & Mundy 20th Flr 1845 Walnut St Ste 20 Philadelphia PA 19103-4708

**MUNGER, THOMAS JOGUES,** lawyer; b. Detroit, Jan. 26, 1960; s. James Elliot and Patricia Ann M.; m. Virginia Gayle Morrow, July 5, 1986; children: Alexander James, Patrick Thomas. BA, Mich. State U., 1982; JD, U. N.C., 1985. Bar: Ga. 1985. Assoc. Kilpatrick & Stockton, Atlanta, 1985-89; atty. Delta Air Lines, Inc., Atlanta, 1989-92, sr. atty., 1992-94, gen. atty., 1995-98, asst. gen. counsel, 1998—; spkr. in field. Democrat. Presbyterian. Avocations: traveling, public speaking. Labor. Home: 819 Wildwood Rd NE Atlanta GA 30324-4911 Office: Delta Air Lines Inc Dept Law 1030 Delta Blvd Atlanta GA 30320

**MUNGIA, SALVADOR ALEJO, JR.,** lawyer; b. Tacoma, Feb. 19, 1959; s. Salvador Alejo Sr. and Susie (Tamaki) M. BA, Pacific Luth. U., 1981; JD, Georgetown U., 1984. Bar: Wash. 1984, U.S. Dist. Ct. (we. dist.) Wash. 1985, U.S. Ct. Appeals (9th cir.) 1986, U.S. Supreme Ct. 1992. Law clk. to Justice Fred Dore Wash. State Supreme Ct., Olympia, 1984-85; law clerk to Hon. Carolyn R. Dimmick U.S. Dist. Ct. (we. dist.) Wash., Seattle, 1985-86; assoc. Gordon, Thomas, Honeywell, Malanca, Peterson & Daheim, Tacoma, 1986-91, ptnr., 1991—; adj. prof. Pacific Luth. U., 1993-94. Vol. atty. ACLU, Tacoma, 1986—, bd. dirs., 1987-92; commr. Tacoma Human Rights Commn., 1990-96; bd. dirs. Legal Aid for Washington, 1992-96, life bd. dirs., 1997—. Mem. ABA, Wash. State Bar Assn., Fed. Bar Assn. Western Wash., Tacoma-Pierce County Bar Assn. (pres. 1999), Pierce County Young Lawyers Assn. (trustee 1988-90), Wash. Alpine Club, Tacoma Lawn Tennis Club, Tacoma Club. Avocations: mountain climbing, skiing, tennis, running. Federal civil litigation, State civil litigation. Home: 615 N C St Tacoma WA 98403-2810 Office: Gordon Thomas Honeywell Malance Peterson & Daheim PO Box 1157 Tacoma WA 98401-1157

**MUNI, STEVEN DONALD,** lawyer, columnist; b. Manila, The Philippines, Dec. 26, 1951; came to U.S., 1966; s. Donald Stuart and Noreen (Angell) M. BA, Yale U., 1973; JD cum laude, Calif. Western U., 1976; LLM, U. London, Eng., 1977. Bar: Calif. 1977, U.S. Dist. Ct. (no. dist.) Calif. 1985. Asst. dist. atty. County of Santa Cruz, Calif., 1977-87; sr. trial counsel Law Firm of Alexander Anolik, APL, San Francisco, 1987-90; pvt. practice Santa Cruz, Calif., 1990-96; dep. dist. atty. County of Amador, Jackson, Calif., 1996—; alt. traffic referee Santa Cruz Mcpl. Ct., 1992-96; contract juvenile ct. judge pro tem Superior Ct., Santa Cruz, 1994-96; judge pro tempore Santa Cruz Mcpl. Ct., 1990-96, Alameda Mcpl. Ct., Hayward, Calif., 1994-96. Columnist (newspaper) Amador Ledger-Dispatch, 1996-98. Commr. Juvenile Justice Commn., Santa Cruz, 1981-87, Downtown Commn., Santa Cruz, 1993-96; vice pres., bd. dirs. Ct. Apptd. Spl. Advocates, Santa Cruz, 1993-96. Named Outstanding Citizen of Yr. Santa Cruz Police Officers Assn., 1994. Mem. County Bar of Amador, Yale U. Alumni Assn. (schs. com. 1980—), Calif. Dist. Atty.s Assn., Lions (Jackson club). Avocations: polo, cooking, singing, showing dogs, gardening. Home: PO Box 1542 Jackson CA 95642-1542 Office: Amador Dist Atty 702 Court St Jackson CA 95642-2130

**MUNIC, MARTIN DANIEL,** lawyer; b. Duluth, Minn., Feb. 16, 1959; s. Robert Solomon and Pearl (Daniels) M.; m. Barbara Stimson, May 30, 1993; 1 child, Sophia Miriam. BA, Drake U., 1981; JD, U. Minn., 1984. Bar: Minn. 1984, U.S. Dist. Ct. Minn. 1986, U.S. Ct. Appeals (8th cir.) 1989. Law clk. to Hon. Harry H. MacLaughlin U.S. Dist. Ct., Mpls., 1984-86; assoc. Tanick & Heins, Mpls., 1986-89, Opperman Heins & Paquin, Mpls., 1989-92; asst. county atty. Hennepin County Atty.'s Office, Mpls., 1993—; bd. dirs. Loan Assistance Repayment Program Minn., 1991-96, pres., 1991-94; arbitrator Nat. Futures Assn. Contbr. articles to profl. jours. Alt. Dem.-Farmer-Labor State Conv., Mpls., 1990, del., 1994; vol. atty. Minn. Civil Liberties Union, Mpls., 1988-92; bd. dirs. Minn. NARAL, 1996—. Recipient William O. Douglas award U. Minn., 1984, Edward J. Devitt award, 1983. Mem. Nat. Assn. Securities Dealers, Minn. Justice Found. (bd. dirs. 1983-84, 88-92, pres. bd. dirs. 1989-91), Minn. Assn. Parliamentarians, Nat. Assn. Parliamentarians, Hennepin County Bar Assn., Order of Coif, Phi Beta Kappa. Jewish. Avocations: baseball, cross-country skiing. Office: Hennepin County Atty Office A2000 Government Ctr Minneapolis MN 55487-0001

**MUÑIZ, NICOLAS JOSE,** lawyer; b. Madrid, Spain, Oct. 22, 1962; came to U.S., 1977; s. Nicolas and Olga (Arias) M. BS, Tulane U., 1984; MBA, Fla. Internat. U., 1986; JD, U. Fla., 1989; postgrad., Rijksuniversiteit te Leiden, The Netherlands, 1989. Bar: Fla. 1989, N.Y. 1990. Savs. counselor Citicorp Savs., Miami, Fla., 1984-86; compliance asst. Consolidated Bank, Hialeah, Fla., 1987, 88; tax specialist KPMG Peat Marwick, N.Y.C., 1989-91, sr. tax specialist, 1991-92; supervising sr. tax specialist KPMG Peat Marwick, N.Y.C. and Miami, Fla., 1992—. Exec. mgmt. editor Fla. Internat. Law Jour., 1988. Mem. ABA, French Inst. Roman Catholic. Avocations: soccer, history, reading. Corporate taxation, Banking, Private international. Office: KPMG Peat Marwick 2 S Biscayne Blvd Miami FL 33131-1806

**MUNOZ, LILIA ANA,** lawyer; b. Bayamo, Cuba, Apr. 16, 1959; came to the U.S., 1967; d. Jose Ernesto and Lidia Rosa (Ros) M.; m. Roberto Muniz, Oct. 11, 1986; children: Lilia Cristina, Roberto Jose. BA in Polit. Sci., Seton Hall U., 1981; JD, Rutgers U., 1984. Assoc. Robert Menendez, P.A., Union City, N.J., 1984-88; ptnr. Menendez & Munoz, P.A., Union City, 1988-90; pvt. practice West N.Y., N.J., 1990—; presenter West N.Y. Alcoholic Beverage Control Bd., 1996—; trustee Legal Svcs. Hudson County, Jersey City, N.J., 1994—. Active Bergen County Rep. Club, Hackensack, N.J., 1995—, Bergen County Hispanic Rep. Orgn., 1997—, Bergen County Women's Rep. Club, 1997—. Mem. N.J. Hispanic Bar Assn. (Hudson County regional trustee 1995—), Hudson County Bar Assn. (membership sec. 1997-98), Rotary. Roman Catholic. Avocations: tennis, swimming, travel. Office: 5202 Bergenline Ave West New York NJ 07093-5524

**MUNOZ, SHANE THOMAS,** lawyer; b. New Orleans, Oct. 12, 1955; s. Scott Muni and Frances Isabelle Davis; m. Elizabeth Joan DeDeyn, Aug. 16, 1986; m. Margaret Anne, Sarah Catherine. Student, Northwe. U., 1973-74; BS in Plant Sci., U. N.H., 1977; JD, U. Conn., 1989. Bar: Conn. 1989, U.S. Dist. Ct. Conn. 1990, U.S. Dist. Ct. (no., mid. and so. dists.) Fla. 1995, U.S. Ct. Appeals (11th cir.). Mgr. Tuttle Market Gardens, Inc., Dover, N.H., 1977-86; lawyer Day, Berry & Howard, Hartford, Conn., 1989-95, Brown, Clark & Walters, Sarasota, Fla., 1995-97, Zinober & McCrea, P.A., Tampa, Fla., 1997—; mem. standing com. on advt. Fla. Bar, 1999; bd. dirs. W. Ctrl. Fla., Indsl. Rels., Rsch. Assn. Recipient Book award Am. Jurisprudence, 1987, 88. Labor, Federal civil litigation, Civil rights. Office: Zinober & McCrea PA 201 E Kennedy Blvd Ste 800 Tampa FL 33602-5825

**MUNSCH, RICHARD JOHN,** lawyer; b. Pitts., Dec. 14, 1946. BA in History, U. Notre Dame, 1968; JD, U. Mich., 1973. Bar: Pa. 1973, U.S. Dist. Ct. (we. dist.) Pa. 1973, U.S. Ct. Appeals (3d cir.) 1979, U.S. Ct. Appeals (8th cir.) 1980, U.S. Ct. Appeals (6th cir.) 1982, U.S. Supreme Ct. 1983. Law clk. to Hon. Harry A. Kramer Commonwealth Ct. Pa., Pitts.,

1974-76; atty. USX (formerly U.S. Steel Corp.), Pitts., 1976—. Mem. Pa. Bar Assn., Allegheny County Bar Assn., Fed. Energy Bar Assn., Am. Corp. Counsel Assn. Contracts commercial, Public utilities, Transportation. Office: 600 Grant St Ste 1569 Pittsburgh PA 15219-2702

**MUNSELL, JAMES FREDERICK,** lawyer; b. N.Y.C., Dec. 12, 1941; s. Stephen Francis and Alice (King) M.; m. Judith Shaw, May 28, 1968 (dec. June 1990); children: James C., Gregory S., Alison E. B in Engring. Physics, Cornell U., 1964; LLB, Harvard U., 1967. Bar: N.Y. 1969. Assoc. Cleary, Gottlieb, Steen & Hamilton, N.Y.C., London, 1969-75; ptnr. Cleary, Gottlieb, Steen & Hamilton, N.Y.C., Hong Kong, 1976—. Sgt. USMCR, 1967-68. General corporate, Securities. Office: Cleary Gottlieb Steen & Hamilton 1 Liberty Plz Fl 38 New York NY 10006-1470

**MUNSINGER, HARRY L.,** lawyer, educator; b. Spaulding, Nebr., Jan. 16, 1935; s. John David and Elsie Dora M.; m. Helen Beattie, July 8, 1959 (div. June 1966); children: Douglas Spence, David Blake, Dennis John; m. Kim MacInnis, Feb. 9, 1970; children: Brita Ann, Inga Lee. BA, U. Calif., Berkeley, 1957; PhD, U. Oreg., 1961; JD, Duke U., 1985. Bar: Tex., U.S. Dist. Ct. (so. dist.) Tex. Assoc. U. Ill., Urbana, 1963-65, U. Calif. San Diego, La Jolla, 1965-80; clin. psychologist San Diego; lawyer Heard Linebarger Graham Goggan Blair Peña & Sampson LLP, San Antonio; adj. prof. U. Tex. Austin Law Sch. Author: Child Development, 1977, Clinical Psychology, 1984. Republican. Avocations: sailing, running, music, reading. General civil litigation, Contracts commercial, Personal injury. Office: Heard Linebarger Graham Goggan Blair Peña & Sampson LLP 310 South St Plz San Antonio TX 78205

**MUNSON, ALEX ROBERT,** judge; b. L.A., Sept. 25, 1941; s. Robert Alexander and Lillian Agnus (Hamel) M.; m. Kathleen Rae Abernathey, June 29, 1968. BA, Long Beach (Calif.) State Coll., 1964, MA, 1965; EdD, U. So. Calif., L.A., 1970; JD, Loyola U., L.A., 1975. Atty. Kirtland and Packard, L.A., 1978-82; chief justice High Ct. of The Trust Terr. of The Pacific Islands, Saipan, Commonwealth of the No. Mariana Islands, 1982-88; chief judge U.S. Dist. Ct. of No. Mariana Islands, Saipan, Commonwealth of the No. Mariana Islands, 1988—. Mem. ABA, Calif. Bar Assn. Republican. Home: PO Box 5356 CHRB Saipan MP 96950-5356 Office: US Dist Ct PO Box 687 Saipan MP 96950-0687

**MUNSON, HOWARD G.,** federal judge; b. Claremont, N.H., July 26, 1924; s. Walter N. and Helena (O'Halloran) M.; m. Ruth Jaynes, Sept. 17, 1949; children: Walter N., Richard J., Pamela A. B.S. in Economics, U. Pa., 1948; LL.B., Syracuse U., 1952. Bar: N.Y. With Employers' Assurance Corp., Ltd., White Plains, N.Y., 1949-50; mem. firm Hiscock, Lee, Rogers, Henley & Barclay, Syracuse, N.Y., 1952-76; judge U.S. Dist. Ct. No. Dist. N.Y., Syracuse, 1976—. Mem., pres. Syracuse Bd. Edn.; bd. dirs. Sta. WCNY-TV; chmn. ethics com. Onondaga County Legislature. Served with U.S. Army, 1943-45, ETO. Decorated Bronze Star, Purple Heart. Mem. Am. Coll. Trial Lawyers, Nat. Assn. R.R. Trial Counsel, Am. Arbitration Assn., Justinian Soc., Alpha Tau Omega, Phi Delta Phi. Office: US Dist Ct US Courthouse P O Box 7376 Syracuse NY 13261-7376

**MUNSON, NANCY KAY,** lawyer; b. Huntington, N.Y., June 22, 1936; d. Howard H. and Edna M. (Keenan) Munson. Student, Hofstra U., 1959-62; JD, Bklyn. Law Sch., 1965. Bar: N.Y. 1966, U.S. Supreme Ct. 1970, U.S. Ct. Appeals (2d cir.) 1971, U.S. Dist. Ct. (ea. and so. dists.) N.Y. 1968. Law clk. to E. Merritt Weidner Huntington, 1959-66, sole practice, 1966—; mem. legal adv. bd. Chgo. Title Ins. Co., Riverhead, N.Y., 1981—; bd. dirs., legal officer Thomas Munson Found. Trustee Huntington Fire Dept. Death Benefit Fund; pres., trustee, chmn. bd. Bklyn. Home Aged Men Found.; bd. dirs. Elderly Day Svcs. on the Sound. Mem. ABA, N.Y. State Bar Assn., Suffolk County Bar Assn., Bklyn. Bar Assn., NRA, DAR, Soroptimists (past pres.). Republican. Christian Scientist. General practice, Probate, Real property. Office: 197 New York Ave Huntington NY 11743-2711

**MUNTEANU, VICTOR JOHN,** lawyer; b. Ft. Devens, Mass., Jan. 11, 1958; s. Virgil Peter and Ligita (Gutmanis) M.; m. Kathleen Galman, Oct. 10, 1987; children: Sydney Rose, Peter John. BA in Polit. Sci., Lebanon Valley Coll., Annville, Pa., 1979; JD, U. Tenn., 1981. Bar: Colo. 1981, U.S. Dist. Ct. Colo. 1981, U.S. Ct. Appeals (10th cir.) 1981. Assoc. Caskins & Chanzit, Denver, 1981-90; pvt. practice law Denver, 1990—. General civil litigation, General corporate, Real property. Office: Ste 575 3773 Cherry Creek North Dr Denver CO 80209-3825

**MUNYON, WENDY NELSON,** lawyer; b. Montclair, N.J., Jan. 13, 1949; d. George Peter and Mary Louise (Dodd) Nelson; m. Paul G. Munyon, June 12, 1971; children: Charles, Peter. BA, Wellesley Coll., 1970; JD, Emory U., 1975, LLM, 1976. Bar: Ga. 1976, D.C. 1978, Iowa 1983. Law clk. to Hon. C.A. Moye, U.S. Dist. Ct., Atlanta, 1976-78; assoc. Jones, Day, Reavis & Pogue, Washington, 1978-79, Crowell & Moring, Washington, 1979-82; counsel Grinnell (Iowa) Mut. Reins. Co., 1983-88, asst. gen. counsel, 1988—. Bd. dirs. Grinnell LWV, 1982-85; mem. Grinnell-Newburg Bd. Edn., 1985-92, 98-99; mem. Grinnell Cmty. Chorus. Mem. ABA, Iowa Bar Assn., Iowa Def. Counsel Assn. (bd. dirs. 1994—), Iowa Ins. Guaranty Assn. (chmn. 1993—), Iowa Claims Execs. Assn. (pres. 1999). Avocations: singing, tennis, bicycling. Insurance, General corporate. Office: Grinnell Mut Reins Co 4215 Highway 146 Grinnell IA 50112-8110

**MUNZER, CYNDE HIRSCHTICK,** lawyer; b. Chgo.; d. Nathaniel and Joyce Hirschtick; m. Patrick S. Munzer, Nov. 10,1 985; children: David, Lena. BA in Journalism, U. Ill., 1979; JD with high honors, Chgo.-Kent Coll. Law, 1983. Bar: Ill. 1983, U.S. Dist. Ct. (no. dist.) Ill. 1983. Jud. law clk. Ill. Appellate Ct., Chgo., 1983-86; assoc. Arnstein & Lehr, Chgo., 1986-90, ptnr., 1990—; news writer/prodr. Sta. WCFL, Chgo., 1982-84; presenter seminars in field. Mem. ABA, Assn. for Corp. Growth, Nat. Assn. Women Bus. Owners (Chgo. chpt. past bd. dirs.), Phi Kappa Phi. General corporate. Office: Arnstein & Lehr 120 S Riverside Plz Chicago IL 60606-3913

**MUNZER, STEPHEN IRA,** lawyer; b. N.Y.C., Mar. 15, 1939; s. Harry and Edith (Isacowitz) M.; m. Patricia Eve Munzer, Aug. 10, 1965; children: John, Margaret. AB, Brown U., 1960; JD, Cornell U., 1963. Bar: N.Y. 1964, U.S. Supreme Ct. 1974, U.S. Dist. Ct. (so. and ea. dists.) N.Y., U.S. Ct. Appeals (3rd cir.). Formerly ptnr. Pincus Munzer Bizar & D'Alessandro, 1978-83; atty. and real estate investor Munzer & Saunders, LLP, 1984—; pres. Simcor Mgmt. Corp., N.Y.C., 1984—. Served to lt., USNR, 1965-75. Mem. Assn. of Bar of City of N.Y., N.Y. State Bar Assn., City Athletic Club, Washington Club. Jewish. Avocations: golf, skiing. Real property, General civil litigation, Federal civil litigation. Home: 429 Greenwich St New York NY 10013-2051 also: 170 Shearer Rd Washington CT 06793-1013 Office: 609 5th Ave New York NY 10017-1021

**MUNZING, RICHARD HARRY,** lawyer; b. N.Y.C., July 8, 1949; s. Harry E. Munzing and Ruth E. Schonberg; m. Orly Enzer, Aug. 6, 1977; children: Michael, Daniel. AB, Muhlenberg Coll., 1971; JD, Boston U., 1976. Bar: Vt. 1976, U.S. Dist. Ct. Vt. 1976, U.S. Ct. Appeals (2d cir.) 1983, U.S. Supreme Ct. 1984. Staff atty. Vt. Sr. Citizens Law Project, Springfield, 1976-79, Vt. Legal Aid Inc., Springfield, 1979-84; assoc. Weber Perra & Wilson, Brattleboro, Vt., 1984-87; ptnr., prin. Weber Perra & Munzing P.C., Brattleboro, 1987—. Bd. dirs. Morningside Emergency Shelter, 1981-82; active Cmty. Action, Brattleboro area, 1982-84; sec. Brattleboro Music Ctr., 1992-95. With U.S. Army, 1971-73, Germany. Mem. Vt. Bar Assn., Vt. Trial Lawyers Assn., Windham County Bar Assn. Personal injury, Workers' compensation, General civil litigation. Office: Weber Perra & Munzing PC PO Box 558 Brattleboro VT 05302-0558

**MUONEKE, ANTHONY,** lawyer; b. Enugu, Nigeria, Sept. 10, 1965; came to U.S., 1987; s. Vincent and Emmie M.; m. Cristal Lynch, Nov. 9, 1991; 1 child, Awari Kenneth. LLB, U. Nigeria, 1984; BL, Nigerian Law Sch., 1985; LLM, U. San Diego, 1989. Counsel Nigeria Stock Exchange, Lagos, Nigeria, 1985-87; attorney Onteabo Obi & Co., Lagos, Nigeria, 1987-88, Akubilo & Muoneke, L.A., 1990-92, Muoneke & Ogan, L.A., 1992—. Civil rights, Insurance, Product liability. Office: Muoneke & Ogan APC 3701 Wilshire Blvd Ste 504 Los Angeles CA 90010-2812

**MURAI, RENE VICENTE,** lawyer; b. Havana, Cuba, Mar. 11, 1945; came to the U.S., 1960; s. Andres and Silvia (Muñiz) M.; m. Luisa Botifoll, June 12, 1970; 1 child, Elisa. BA, Brown U., 1966; JD cum laude, Columbia U., 1969. Bar: Fla. 1970, N.Y. 1972, U.S. Supreme Ct. 1977. Atty. Reginald Heber Smith Fellow Legal Svcs. Greater Miami, Fla., 1969-71; assoc. Willkie, Farr & Gallagher, N.Y.C., 1971-73; ptnr. Paul, Landy & Beiley, Miami, 1973-79; shareholder Murai, Wald, Biondo & Moreno, Miami, 1979—; acting chmn. bd. dirs. PanAm. Bank, Miami; dir. Cuban Am. Bar Assn., 1982-96, pres., 1985; vice chmn., lectr. Internat. Conf. for Lawyers of the Ams., 1982, chmn. and lectr., 1984; mem. panel grievance com. Fla. Bar, 1983-86. Mng. editor Columbia Law Rev., 1967-69. Bd. dirs., sec. Archtl. Club of Miami, 1978-86; bd. dirs. Dade Heritage Trust, 1979-82, Facts About Cuban Exiles, Inc., 1982—, pres., 1989, Legal Svcs. of Greater Miami, Inc., 1980-90, pres. 1986-88, ARC, 1984-90, exec. com., 1988-90, Mercy Hosp. Found., 1985-91, United Way, 1989-95, dir. Dade Cmty. Found., 1988-93, chair grants com., 1991-93; chmn. adminstrn. of justice com. Fla. Bar Found., 1996-98, bd. dirs., 1991—, chmn. audit and fin. com., 1993-98, sec., 1997-98, pres. elect 1998-99; mem. task force leadership Dade County Ptnrs. for Safe Neighborhoods, 1994-95, Code Enforcement Bd. City of Coral Gables, 1982-86, Bd. Adjustment, 1987-89, city mgr. selection com., 1987, charter rev. commn., 1980; trustee U. Miami, 1994-96. Mem. ABA, Cuban-Am. Bar Assn., Dade County Bar Assn. (dir. 1987-88), Greater Miami C. of C., Spain-U.S.C. of C. Democrat. Roman Catholic. Avocation: sports. Banking, Contracts commercial, General corporate. Home: 3833 Alhambra Ct Coral Gables FL 33134-6229 Office: Murai Wald Biondo & Moreno PA 25 SE 2nd Ave Ste 900 Miami FL 33131-1600

**MURAKAMI, STEVEN KIYOSHI,** lawyer; b. St. Paul, July 8, 1967; s. George Kiyoshi and Judith Emi Murakami. BA in Journalism, U. Minn., 1990, JD, 1997. Bar: Minn. 1994, U.S. Dist. Ct. Minn. 1996. Law clk. 3d Jud. Dist. Ct. Minn., Rochester, 1994-95; assoc. Ryan & Grinde, Ltd., Rochester, 1995-96; ptnr., shareholder Gagniefski & Murakami, P.L.L.P., Rochester, 1996—. Treas. Rochester Better Chance, 1995-97; mentor Cmty. Youth Mentorship Program, Rochester, 1995—. Mem. ABA, Minn. Bar Assn. General practice, Personal injury. Office: Bagniefski & Murakami PLLP 9 1st St NW Rochester MN 55901-3027

**MURANTE, DAVID ALAN,** lawyer; b. Rochester, N.Y., May 21, 1946; s. Anthony Michael and Angelina Marie (Franjose) M.; m. Debra Jean Rankin, Jan. 2, 1981; children: Kris, Beth, Kate, Alec, Tessa, Abram, Aaron. BA, U. Rochester, 1968; JD cum laude, Union U., 1973. Bar: N.Y. 1974, U.S. Dist. Ct. (we. dist.) N.Y. 1974, U.S. Supreme Ct. 1979. Asst. pub. defender Monroe County, Rochester, 1974-77; pvt. practice Rochester, 1977—; vis. instr. SUNY, Brockport, 1977-78, 88. Trustee Delphi House, Rochester, 1976-77; bd. dirs. Pre-Trial Svcs. Corp., Rochester, 1984-88, Love The Children, Rochester, 1990-91, Legal Aid Soc. Rochester, 1990-92; mem. Pax Humana Award Com., Rochester, 1990—; mem. select com. to study impact of drugs on jud. system Monroe County, 1992. Sgt. U.S. Army, 1968-70. Recipient Disting. Svc. award Urban League Rochester, 1977. Fellow Am. Coll. Trial Lawyers; mem. N.Y. Bar Assn., Monroe County Bar Assn. (criminal com. 1990, Adolph J. Rodenbech award 1991), Greater Rochester Assn. Women Attys., Criminal Def. League Rochester (Robert J. Napier award 1991). Criminal. Home: 659 Hubbell Rd Churchville NY 14428-9357 Office: 8 Exchange Blvd Rochester NY 14614-1841

**MURASKI, ANTHONY AUGUSTUS,** lawyer; b. Cohoes, N.Y., July 28, 1946; s. Adam Joseph and Angeline Mary (Vozzy) M.; m. Janice Kay Selberg, Nov. 25, 1978; children: Adam Peter, Emily Jo. BA, MA in Speech/Hearing, Sacramento State Coll., 1970; PhD in Audiology/ Hearing Sci., U. Mich., 1977; JD, Detroit Coll. Law, 1979. Bar: Mich. 1980, U.S. Dist. Ct. (ea. dist.) Mich. 1981, U.S. Ct. Appeals (6th cir.) 1982, U.S. Claims Ct. 1989, U.S. Supreme Ct. 1990, Pa. 1990. Asst. Kresge Hearing Research Inst. U. Mich., Ann Arbor, 1971-77; asst. prof. Wayne State U. Med. Sch., Detroit, 1979-82; assoc. Kitch, Suhrheinrich, Saurbier & Drutchas, Detroit, 1982-83; assoc. prof. Detroit Coll. Law, 1983-85; mng. ptnr. Muraski & Sikorski, Ann Arbor, 1985—; cons. audiology Ministry of Environment, Ont., Can., 1980-81; trustee Deaf, Speech and Hearing Ctr., Detroit, 1981—; legal adv. on air WWJ Radio, Detroit, 1984—; mem. mental health adv. bd. on deafness Dept. Mental Health, 1984, vis. com. U. Mich. Sch. Edn., 1986—. Author: Legal Aspects of Audiological Practice, 1982, Hearing Conservation in Industry: Licensure, Liability and Forensics, 1985. Mem. ABA, Mich. Bar Assn., Washtenaw County Bar Assn., Am. Speech-Lang.-Hearing Assn. (sci. merit award, 1981), Ann Arbor C. of C. Avocations: photography, running. Health, Private international, Labor. Home: 1603 Westminster Pl Ann Arbor MI 48104-4358

**MURCHISON, BRADLEY DUNCAN,** lawyer; b. Washington, Jan. 5, 1957; s. David Claudius and June Margaret (Guilfoyle) M.; m. Anita Lynne Cadieu, Oct. 14, 1957; children: Grace Guilfoyle, Meredith Lynne, Duncan Michael. AB in Polit. Sci., U. N.C., 1979; JD, George Washington U., 1982. Bar: N.C. 1983, U.S. Dist. Ct. (we. dist.) N.C. 1983, U.S. Tax Ct. 1983. Assoc. Thigpen and Hines, P.A., Charlotte, N.C., 1982-85; assoc. Moore & Van Allen, Charlotte, 1985-87, ptnr., 1988; assoc. gen. counsel Collins & Aikman Corp., Charlotte, 1988-89; asst. gen. counsel Collins & Aikman Products Co., Charlotte, 1989—. Active Lincoln Forum, N.C., 1995. Mem. N.C. Bar Assn., Am. Corp. Counsel Assn., Mecklenburg County Bar Assn. Republican. Roman Catholic. Avocations: saltwater, fishing. General corporate, Contracts commercial, Antitrust. Office: Collins & Aikman Products 701 Mccullough Dr Charlotte NC 28262-3318

**MURCHISON, DAVID CLAUDIUS,** lawyer; b. N.Y.C., Aug. 19, 1923; s. Claudius Temple and Constance (Waterman) M.; m. June Margaret Guilfoyle, Dec. 19, 1946; children: David Roderick, Brian, Courtney, Bradley, Stacy. A.A., George Washington U., 1947, J.D. with honors, 1949. Bar: D.C. 1949, Supreme Ct. 1955. Assoc. Dorr, Hand & Dawson, N.Y.C., 1949-50; founding ptnr. Howrey & Simon, Washington, 1956-90; of counsel Howrey & Simon, 1990—; legal asst. under sec. army, 1949-51; counsel motor vehicle, textile, aircraft, ordinance and shipbldg. divsns. Nat. Prodn. Authority, 1951-52; assoc. gen. counsel Small Def. Plants Adminstrn., 1952-53; legal adv. and asst. to chmn. FTC, 1953-55. Chmn. So. Africa Wildlife Trust. With AUS, 1943-45, ETO. Mem. ABA (chmn. com. internat. restrictive bus. practices sect. antitrust law 1954-55, sect. adminstrv. law, sect. litigation), FBA, D.C. Bar Assn., N.Y. State Bar Assn., Order of Coif, Met. Club, Chevy Chase Club, Talbot Country Club. Republican. Private international, Antitrust, Federal civil litigation.

**MURCHISON, DAVID RODERICK,** lawyer; b. Washington, May 28, 1948; s. David Claudius and June Margaret (Guilfoyle) M.; m. Kathy Ann Kohn, Mar. 15, 1981; children: David Christopher, Benjamin Michael. BA cum laude, Princeton U., 1970; JD, Georgetown U., 1975. Bar: D.C. 1975, Fla. 1993. Legal asst. to vice chmn. CAB, Washington, 1975-76, enforcement atty., 1976-77; sr. atty. Air Transport Assn., Washington, 1977-80, asst. v.p., sec., 1981-85; sr. assoc. Zuckert, Scoutt and Rasenberger, Washington, 1980-81; v.p., asst. gen. counsel Piedmont Aviation, Inc., Winston-Salem, N.C., 1985-88; v.p., gen. counsel, sec. Braniff, Inc., Dallas, 1988-89; chief exec. officer Braniff, Inc., Orlando, 1990-94; fed. adminstrv. law judge Office of Hearings and Appeals, Charleston, W.Va., 1994-96; chief adminstrv. law judge Office of Hearings and Appeals, Mobile, Ala., 1996—; lectr. continuing legal edn. program Wake Forest U., Winston-Salem, 1988. Contbr. articles to legal jours. Lt. USNR, 1970-72. Mem. ABA, Met. Club Washington. Republican. Roman Catholic. Administrative and regulatory, General corporate, Legislative. Office: Office Hearings and Appeals 3605 Springhill Bus Park Mobile AL 36608-1239

**MURDOCH, DAVID ARMOR,** lawyer; b. Pitts., May 30, 1942; s. Armor M. and N. Edna (Jones) M.; m. Joan Wilkie, Mar. 9, 1974; children: Christina, Timothy, Deborah. AB magna cum laude, Harvard U., 1964, LLB, 1967. Bar: Pa. 1967, U.S. Dist. Ct. (we. dist.) Pa. 1967, U.S. Ct. Mil. Appeals 1968, U.S. Supreme Ct. 1990, U.S. Ct. Appeals (3d cir.) 1991. Assoc. Kirkpatrick & Lockhart, LLP, Pitts., 1971-78, ptnr., 1978—; mem. adv. bd. Ctr. for Internat. Legal Edn., U. Pitt., 1997—. Co-author: Business Workouts Manual. V.p., bd. dirs. Avonworth Sch. Dist., 1977-83; mem. bd. dirs. Pitts. Expt., 1988-93, chmn., 1989-90; mem. Pa. Housing Fin. Agy., 1981-88, vice chmn., 1983-87; alt. del. Rep. Nat. Conv., 1980; elder The Presbyn. Ch. of Sewickley, 1986-92; past pres. Harvard Law Sch. Assn. W. Pa.; bd. advisors Geneva Coll., 1993-94, trustee, 1994-97; trustee Sewickley Pub. Libr., 1994—, World Learning, Inc., 1995—, vice-chmn., 1998—; dir. Allegheny County Libr. Assn., 1994-96; chair Czech Working Group, Presbyn. Ch. USA, 1995—; bd. visitors U. Ctr. Internat. Studies, U. Pitts., 1996—; bd. advisors The Ctr. for Bus., Religion, and Professions, Pitts. Theol. Sem., 1997—; bd. dirs. World Affairs Coun. Pitts., 1998—, Am. Coun. Germany, 1998—. Capt. U.S. Army, 1968-71. Fellow Am. Coll. Bankruptcy, Am. Bar Found.; mem. ABA (mem. bus. bankruptcy com., chmn. subcom. on bankruptcy coms., trust indentures and claims trading 1991-97). Bankruptcy, Contracts commercial, General corporate. Office: Kirkpatrick & Lockhart LLP 1500 Oliver Building Pittsburgh PA 15222-2312

**MURDOCK, CHARLES WILLIAM,** lawyer, educator; b. Chgo., Feb. 10, 1935; s. Charles C. and Lucille Marie (Tracy) M.; m. Mary Margaret Hennessy, May 25, 1963; children: Kathleen, Michael, Kevin, Sean. BSChemE, Ill. Inst. Tech., 1956; JD cum laude, Loyola U., Chgo., 1963. Bar: Ill. 1963, Ind. 1971. Asst. prof. law DePaul U., 1968-69; assoc. prof. law U. Notre Dame, 1969-75; prof., dean Law Sch. Loyola U., Chgo., 1975-83, 86—; dep. atty. gen. State of Ill., Chgo., 1983-86; of counsel Chadwell & Kayser, Ltd., 1986-89; vis. prof. U. Calif., 1974; cons. Pay Bd., summer 1972, SEC, summer 1973; co-founder Loyola U. Family Bus. Program; arbitrator Chgo. Bd. Options Exch., Nat. Assn. Securities Dealers, N.Y. Stock Exch., Am. Arbitration Assn.; co-founder, mem. exec. com. Loyola Family Bus. Ctr., 1990—; bd. dirs. Plymouth Tube Co., 1993—. Author: Business Organizations, 2 vols., 1996; editor: Illinois Business Corporation Act Annotated, 2 vols., 1975; tech. editor The Business Lawyer, 1989-90. Chmn. St. Joseph County (Ind.) Air Pollution Control Bd., 1971; bd. dirs. Nat. Center for Law and the Handicapped, 1973-75, Minority Venture Capital Inc., 1973-75. Capt. USMCR. Mem. ABA, Ill. Bar Assn. (cert. of award for continuing legal edn.), Chgo. Bar Assn. (cert. of award for continuing legal edn., bd. mgrs. 1976-78), Ill. Inst. Continuing Legal Edn. (adv. com). Roman Catholic. General corporate, Securities. Home: 2126 Thornwood Ave Wilmette IL 60091-1452 Office: Loyola U Sch Law 1 E Pearson St Chicago IL 60611-2055

**MURDOCK, DOUGLAS WILLIAM,** law librarian; b. Akron, Ohio, Dec. 22, 1950; s. William Atkinson and Martha (Jenkins) M.; m. Rebecca Therese Bruckner, Sept. 19, 1987. BA in Anthropology, Kent State U., 1974, MA in Anthropology, 1977; MLS, Case Western Reserve U., 1983. Shelver Sears Library Case Western Reserve U., Cleve., 1978-79, stack supr. law sch. library, 1979-83; catalog and reference librarian Ahmanson Law Sch. Creighton U., Omaha, 1983-90; head of reference svcs. Sioux Falls (S.D.) Pub. Libr., 1990—. Mem. Am. Assn. Law Libraries. Roman Catholic. Avocations: reading, music, antiques, art collecting. Home: 2600 S West Ave Sioux Falls SD 57105-4518 Office: Sioux Falls Pub Libr 201 N Main Ave Sioux Falls SD 57104-6002

**MURGUIA, RAMON,** lawyer; b. Kansas City, Kans., Mar. 13, 1959; s. Alfredo Olivarez and Amalia Fernandez M.; m. Sally Atha, Jan. 20, 1996; children: R. Miguel, Amalia A. BS, U. Kans., 1981; JD, Harvard U., 1984; postgrad., Mex. and Am. Solidarity Found., Mexico City, 1994, Inst. de Estudios Superiores, Mexico City, 1996. Bar: Mo. 1985, U.S. Dist. Ct. (we. dist.) Mo. 1987. Assoc. Armstrong, Teasdale, Schafly, Davis & Dicus and predecessor, Kansas City, Mo., 1984-91; prin., owner Murguia Law Offices, Kansas City, Mo., 1991—; of counsel Watson & Dameron, LLP, Kansas City, Mo., 1991—; ptnr., cons. Access Internat., Kansas City, Kans., 1996—. commr. Kans. Citizens Justice Initiative, 1997—; del. Pres.'s Summit for Am.'s Future, Phila., 1997; mem. adv. bd. Initiative for Competitive Inner City, Kansas City, Mo., 1998—; mem. Kansas City Tomorrow, Kansas City, Kans. Planning Commn., 1987-90, Kansas City, Kans. Bd. of Edn., 1990-91; chmn. Greater Kansas City Hispanic Devel. Fund, 1987—, Greater Kansas City Empowerment Zone Steering Com., 1994-98, Greater Kansas City Enhanced Enterprise Community Exec. Com.; bd. dirs. KCPT-TV, 1987-91, Hispanics in Philanthropy, San Francisco, 1990-95, Youth Opportunities Unltd., Kansas City, Kans., 1994-98, Learning Exch., Kansas City, Mo., 1994—, Greater Kansas City C. of C., 1995—, Francis Families Found., Kansas City, Mo., 1997—, Wyandotte Health Found., Kansas City, Kans., 1998—; bd. dirs., Nat. Coun. of La Raza, Washington, 1992—, chmn. 1998—; bd. dirs. Greater Kansas City Community Found. and Affiliated Trusts, 1990-96, 98—, sec., 1995-96. Recipient Outstanding Svc. to Kansas City Met. Community award, Mid-Am. Regional Coun., 1994, Community Svc. award Greater Kansas City Hispanic Heritage Month Com. Inc., 1995, Piñata Buster award Greater Kansas City Hispanic Scholarship Fund, 1997, Kans. City Spirit award, 1999, Delta award Donnelly Coll., Kans. City, 1999. Mem. Hispanic Nat. Bar Assn. Democrat. Roman Catholic. Avocation: basketball. General corporate, Probate, Personal injury. Home: 2500 Strong Ave Kansas City KS 66106-2138 Office: 2500 Holmes St Kansas City MO 64108-2743

**MURNAGHAN, FRANCIS DOMINIC, JR.,** federal judge; b. Baltimore, Md., June 20, 1920; m. Diana Edwards; children: Sheila H., George A., Janet E. B.A., Johns Hopkins U., 1941; LL.B., Harvard U., 1948. Bar: Md. 1949. Asso. firm Barnes Dechert Price Smith & Clark, Phila., 1948-50; staff atty. Office of Gen. Counsel, U.S. High Commr. for Ger., 1950-52; asst. atty. gen. State of Md., 1952-54; asso. firm Venable Baetjer & Howard, Balt., 1952-57; partner Venable Baetjer & Howard, 1957-79; judge U.S. Ct. Appeals for 4th Circuit Balt., 1979—. Chmn. Balt. Charter Rev. Commn., 1963-64; trustee Walters Art Gallery, 1961, v.p. 1961-63, pres. 1963-80, chmn. 1980-85, chmn. emeritus, 1985—; pres. Balt. Sch. Bd., 1967-70; trustee Johns Hopkins U., 1976—. Lt. USNR, 1942-46. Mem. ABA, Am. Coll. Trial Lawyers. Office: US Ct Appeals 4th Cir 101 W Lombard St Baltimore MD 21201-2626

**MUROFF, ELENA MARIE,** lawyer; b. Waterbury, Conn., Mar. 14, 1957; d. John Andrew Muroff. AS in Bus. Adminstrn. summa cum laude, Teikyo Post Coll., Waterbury, 1979, BS in Mktg. in summa cum laude, 1981; JD, U. Bridgeport, 1986; postgrad., U. Conn. Bar: Conn., U.S. Dist. Ct. Conn. Legal intern Fl. Woodward Lewis, Yalesville, Conn., 1986-87; clk. New Haven Superior Ct., 1987-88; asst. appellate clk. Supreme and Appellate Ct., Hartford, Conn., 1988-89; asst. atty. gen. Office Atty. Gen., Hartford, 1990-91; pvt. practice, pro bono Waterbury, 1989-90, 91—; legal instr. Nat. Acad. Paralegal Studies, West Hartford, Conn., 1991; instr. living sckills Greenshire Sch., Cheshire, Conn., 1988; care provider to mentally challenged Respite Resources, Wallingford, Conn., 1994—; co-facilitator group therapy Mental Health Assn., Wethersfield, Conn., 1995—; spkr. Rose Traurig scholars program Teikyo Post U., 1992, also for legal asst. program. Mem. Dem. Nat. Com.; U.S. del. Moscow Conf. Law and Bilateral Econ. Rels., 1990. Recipient letter of commendation Conn. Valley Hosp., 1990; scholar Teikyo Post Coll., 1980-81, Max Traurig scholar, 1981; Bank of Boston Marguerite McGraw scholar U. Bridgeport, 1983, Conn. grad. scholar, 1983, Sch. Law scholar, 1983-86. Mem. ATLA, ACLU, NOW, Conn. Bar Assn., Conn. Edn. and Legal Fund, Conn. Mental Health Assn., Conn. Assn. for Human Svcs., Campaign for Children, So. Poverty Law Ctr. Roman Catholic. Avocations: writing poetry, music and arts, avidly following politics. Government contracts and claims, Health, Landlord-tenant. Home and Office: 959 Meriden Rd Apt 4 Waterbury CT 06705-3143

**MURPHREE, SHARON ANN,** lawyer, mediator; b. Maryville, Tenn., June 14, 1949; d. R.L. and Alice (Pierick) M. BS, U. Tenn., 1970; JD, South Tex. Coll. Law, 1987. Bar: Tex. 1988. Pvt. practice, Houston, 1988—; negotiations trainee Harvard Negotiation Project, 1900. advanced negotiator, 1991; founding chair Cmty. Mediation Ctr., 1994-95, v.p., 1998, chmn., 1999; tchr. mediation clinic U. Tenn. Coll. Law, 1993-95; gen. sessions mediator, trainer and mentor; mediator Dept. Justice Americans with Disabilities Act; adj. prof. criminal justice dept. Walters State C.C., 1999. Conbtr. articles to profl. jours. Bd. dirs. Disability Resource Ctr., 1996-99, sec. bd., 1999—; mem. Coalition on Domestic Violence, 1995-96; chair social justice com. Knoxville Project Change, 1997-99; mem. adv. bd. Southeastern Cmty. Oriented Policing Edn., 1998-99; mem. edn. com. Knoxville Hate/Bias Crimes Working Group, 1997-99. Sem. Knoxville Bar Assn., Mediation Assn. Tenn. (sec. 1994-96, v.p. Knoxville chpt. 1994), Soc. Profls. in Disbute Resolution, Citizens' Police Acad. Alumni Assn. Knoxville Police Dept. (v.p. 1996-97, pres. 1997-99), Knoxville Writer's Guild, Torch Club Internat. (v.p. Knoxville chpt. 1995-97, pres. 1997-98), Phi Delta Phi. Democrat. Roman Catholic. Avocations: photography, writing, flying, tennis, sailing. General civil litigation, Alternative dispute resolution. Office: 1074 Scenic Dr Knoxville TN 37919-7640

**MURPHY, C. WESTBROOK,** lawyer; b. 1940. AB, Duke U.; LLB, Yale U. Bar: 1966. Gen. counsel Harry S. Truman Scholarship Found., Washington. Mem. ABA. Office: Harry S Truman Scholarship Found 712 Jackson Pl NW Washington DC 20006-4901 also: Price Waterhouse 1301 K St NW Washington DC 20005-3317*

**MURPHY, DANIEL IGNATIUS,** lawyer; b. Phila., Mar. 14, 1927; s. John Anthony Murphy and Irene Cooper Thorn; m. Jeanne B. Genetti, July 28, 1956 (div. Aug. 1978); children: Jewel A., Daniel I. Jr.; m. Barbara Ann Uncles, Jan. 1, 1979. BS in Econs., U. Pa., 1950; LLB, Yale U., 1953. Bar: Pa. 1954, U.S. Dist Ct. (ea. dist.) Pa. 1954, U.S. Ct. Appeals (3d cir.) 1954, U.S. Tax Ct. 1956, U.S. Supreme Ct. 1959. Assoc. Evans, Bayard & Frick, Phila., 1953-55; asst. city solicitor City of Phila., Pa., 1956-59; ptnr. Cavanaugh, Murphy & Kalodner, Phila., 1958-64, Shapiro, Stalberg, Cook, Murphy & Kalodner, Phila., 1964-66, Takiff, Bolger & Murphy, Phila., 1966-72, Waters, Gallagher, Collins & Masterson, Phila., 1972-80; ptnr. Stradley, Ronon, Stevens & Young, Phila., 1980-92, ret., of counsel, 1993; tchr. Am. Soc. CLUs, Villanova, Pa., 1956-57; mem. exec. com. Phila. Estate Planning Coun., 1958-60; lectr. Pa. Bar Inst., Harrisburg, 1974-92, Pa. Coll. Orphans Ct. Judges, Harrisburg, 1978, Pitts., 1991; apptd. spl. master for trial mgmt. of complex litigation Phila. County Ct. Common Pleas, 1994—. Editor: Phila. Bar Assn. Mag. The Shingle, 1958-67; contbr. chpts. to manuals and articles to profl. jours. Chmn. Phila. Chpt. Am. Cancer Soc., 1956-63; mem. Com. of 70, Phila., 1968—, chmn., 1972-74; dir. Inst. for Cancer & Blood Diseases, Phila., 1975-97; trustee Hahnemann U., Phila., 1983-86. With USN, 1945-46. Fellow Pa. Bar Found. (life); mem. ABA, Pa. Bar Assn., Phila. Bar Assn. (vice-chmn. com. censors 1971), Union League Phila., Soc. Colonial Wars, Phila. Country Club, Pa. Soc. S.R. Democrat. Roman Catholic. Avocation: U.S. Civil War history. General civil litigation, Probate. Office: 2600 One Commerce Sq Philadelphia PA 19103

**MURPHY, DENNIS PATRICK,** lawyer; b. Evanston, Ill., May 25, 1948; s. William F. and Virginia L. M.; m. Victoria T. Halford, Jan. 27, 1979; children: Benjamin P., Carl R., Katherine Monica. BA, U. N. Mex., 1970; JD, U. Denver, 1975. Bar: N. Mex. 1975, U.S. Dist. Ct. N. Mex. 1975. Asst. dist. atty. Office of Dist. Atty., Santa Fe, N. Mex., 1975-76; asst. atty. gen. N. Mex. Atty. Gen."s Office, Santa Fe, 1976-78; ptnr. Montoya, Murphy, Garcia, Santa Fe, 1978—. Bd. dirs., fund raiser Equal Access to Justice, Albuquerque, N. Mex., 1996. Mem. ATLA (N.Mex. state del. 1997-98), N. Mex. Trial Lawyers Assn. (bd. dirs. 1990—, vol. legis. lobbyist 1990—), N. Mex. State Bar Assn. (lawyers assistance com. 1993—). Democrat. Roman Catholic. Avocation: skiing. Personal injury, Product liability. Home: 1803 Arroyo Chamiso Santa Fe NM 87505-5734 Office: Montoya Murphy & Garcia 303 Paseo De Peralta Santa Fe NM 87501-1860

**MURPHY, DIANA E.,** federal judge; b. Faribault, Minn., Jan. 4, 1934; d. Albert W. and Adleyne (Heiker) Kuske; m. Joseph Murphy, July 24, 1958; children: Michael, John E. BA magna cum laude, U. Minn., 1954, JD magna cum laude, 1974; postgrad., Johannes Gutenberg U., Mainz, Germany, 1954-55, U. Minn., 1955-58. Bar: Minn. 1974, U.S. Supreme Ct. 1980. Assoc. Lindquist & Vennum, 1974-76; mcpl. judge Hennepin County, 1976-78, Minn. State dist. judge, 1978-80; judge U.S. Dist. Ct. for Minn., Mpls., 1980-94, chief judge, 1992-94; judge U.S. Ct. of Appeals (8th cir.), Minneapolis, 1994—. Bd. editors: Minn. Law Rev., Georgetown U. Jour. on Cts., Health Scis. and the Law, 1989-92. Bd. dirs. Spring Hill conf. Ctr., 1978-84, Mpls. United Way, 1985—, treas., 1990-94, vice chair, 1996-97, chmn. bd. dirs., 1997-98; bd. dirs. Bush Found., 1982—, chmn. bd. dirs., 1986-91; bd. dirs. Amicus, 1976-80, also organizer, 1st chmn. adv. coun.; mem. Mpls. Charter Commn., 1973-76, chmn., 1974-76; bd. dirs. Ops. De Novo, 1971-76, chmn. bd. dirs., 1974-75; mem. Minn. Constl. Study Commn., chmn. bill of rights com., 1971-73; regent St. Johns U., 1978-87, 88-98, vice chmn. bd., 1985-87, chmn. bd. 1995-98, bd. overseers sch. theology, 1998—; mem. Minn. Bicentennial Commn., 1987-88; trustee Twin Cities Pub. TV, 1985-94, chmn. bd., 1990-92; trustee U. Minn. Found., 1990—, treas., 1992-98; bd. dirs. Sci. Mus. Minn., 1988-94, vice chmn., 1991-94; trustee U. St. Thomas, 1991—; dir. Nat. Assn. Pub. Interest Law Fellowships for Equal Justice, 1992-95; bd. dirs. Minn. Opera, 1998—. Fulbright scholar; recipient Amicus Founders' award, 1980, Outstanding Achievement award U. Minn., 1983, Outstanding Achievement award YWCA, 1981, Disting. Citizen award Alpha Gamma Delta, 1985. Fellow Am. Bar Found.; mem. ABA (mem. ethics and profl. responsibility judges adv. com. 1981-88, chmn. ethics and profl. responsibility judges adv. com. 1997—, standing com. on jud. selection, tenure and compensation 1991-94, mem. standing com. on fed. jud. improvements, 1994-97, Appelate Judges conf. exec. com. 1996—), Minn. Bar Assn. (bd. govs. 1977-81), Hennepin County Bar Assn. (gov. coun. 1976-81), Am. Law Inst., Am. Judicature Soc. (bd. dirs. 1982-93, v.p. 1985-88, treas. 1988-89, chmn. bd. 1989-91), Nat. Assn. Governing Bds. Univs. Colls. (dir. 1998—), Nat. Assn. Women Judges (Leadership Judges Jud. Adminstrn. award 1998), Minn. Women Lawyers (Myra Bradwell award 1996), U. Minn. Alumni Assn. (bd. dirs. 1975-83, nat. pres. 1981-82), Fed. Judges Assn. (bd. dirs. 1982—, v.p. 1984-89, pres. 1989-91), Hist. Soc. for 8th Cir. (bd. dirs. 1988-91), Fed. Jud. Ctr. (bd. dirs. 1990-94, 8th cir. jud. coun. 1992-94, 97—, mem. U.S. jud. conf. com. on ct. adminstrn. and case mgmt. 1994—, chair gender fairness implementation com. 1997-98, convener task force 1993), Order of Coif, Phi Beta Kappa. Office: 11 E US Courthouse 300 S 4th St Minneapolis MN 55415-1320

**MURPHY, DONALD JAMES,** lawyer; b. Milw., July 7, 1958. BBA, U. Wis., Whitewater, 1981; JD, Pepperdine U., 1984. Bar: Calif. 1984, Wis. 1985, U.S. Dist. Ct. (we. dist.) Wis. 1986, U.S. Ct. Appeals (7th cir.) 1989. Assoc. McLean & Irvin, L.A., 1985; ptnr. Pressentin & Murphy, Monona, Wis., 1985-92; sr. ptnr. Pressentin, Murphy & Roberts, Monona, Wis., 1992—; owner, broker Murphy Assocs., Madison, Wis., 1993—. Bd. dirs. East YMCA, Madison, 1990-94. Mem. ATLA, Wis. Trial Lawyers Assn., Wis. Bar Assn., Calif. Bar Assn., Wis. Realtors Assn., Optomists Club. Personal injury, Product liability. Office: Pressentin Murphy & Roberts 100 River Pl Ste 240 Monona WI 53716-4027

**MURPHY, EDWARD J.,** lawyer; b. Chgo., Mar. 18, 1947; s. Maurice W. Murphy and Joan L. Fitzgerald; m. Pamela Neely, Aug. 25, 1973 (div. July 1989); children: Katherine, Karen, Mary, Sarah; m. Carol P. Woosley, Jan. 8, 1994. BSME, Ill. Inst. Tech., 1969; JD, DePaul U., 1980. Bar: Ill. 1980, U.S. Dist. Ct. (no. dist.) Ill. 1980, U.S. Dist. Ct. (so. dist.) Ill. 1994. Engr. Continental Can Co., Chgo., 1969-70; police officer Chgo. Police Dept., 1970-80; atty. Williams & Montgomery Ltd., Chgo., 1980—. Mem. Ill. State Bar Assn., Chgo. Bar Assn., Univ. Club Chgo., East Bank Club, Def. Rsch. Inst. Roman Catholic. General civil litigation, Product liability. Office: Williams & Montgomery Ltd 20 N Wacker Dr 2100 Chicago IL 60606

**MURPHY, EDWARD J., III,** lawyer; b. Quantico, Va., Feb. 11, 1956; s. Edward J. Jr. and Jacqueline (Smith) M.; m. Gayle Towne, Oct. 2, 1987; children: Kyle Marie, Tara Lynn. BA, Hamilton Coll., Clinton, N.Y., 1978; JD, SUNY, Buffalo, 1984. Bar: N.Y. 1985, U.S. Dist. Ct. (we. dist.) N.Y. 1985, U.S. Dist. Ct. (no. dist.) N.Y. 1995, U.S. Bankruptcy Ct. 1985. Title examiner Ticor Title Guarantee, Rochester, N.Y., 1978-79; tchr. Wilbraham & Monson Acad., Wilbraham, Mass., 1979-81; assoc. atty. Cox, Barrel et al, Buffalo, 1985-86; atty., assoc., ptnr. Smith, Murphy & Schoepperle, Buffalo, 1986-95; atty. Jeffrey Freedman Attys., Buffalo, 1995—. Mem. ATLA, N.Y. State Bar Assn., N.Y. Trial Lawyers Assn. Republican. Roman Catholic. Avocations: home improvement, running, sports in general. General civil litigation, Personal injury, Real property. Office: Jeffrey Freedman Attys 424 Main St Rm 622 Buffalo NY 14202-3506

**MURPHY, EMALEE GODSEY,** lawyer; b. Bristol, Va., Jan. 1, 1945; d. John Drew and Emalee (Caldwell) G.; m. Aug. 28, 1971; children: Jessie Lynn, Thomas Henry. AB in Polit. Sci., Oberlin Coll., 1968; JD cum laude, Am. U., 1980. Regulatory/sci. affairs liaison Animal Health Inst., Alexandria, Va., 1970-74; editl. and conf. dir. Food and Drug Law Inst., Washington, 1974-80; asst. gen. counsel, staff atty. Cosmetic, Toiletry & Fragrance Assn., Washington, 1980-83, dir. internat. affairs, asst. gen. counsel, 1983-85, v.p. internat. affairs, 1985-87; ptnr. Graham & James, Washington, 1988-93; of counsel Bryan Cave LLP, Washington, 1993-96, McKenna & Cuneo, LLP, Washington, 1996—; mem. Internat. Soc. Regulatory Toxicology and Pharmacology, Washington, 1987-90; mem., subcom. chmn. ASTM Com. on Rsch. and Tech. Planning, Washington, 1987-91. Mem. editl. bd. Regulatory Affairs, 1991-95; contbr. chpts. to books. Mem. Industry Functional Adv. Com. on Stds. Administrative and regulatory. Office: McKenna & Cuneo LLP 815 Connecticut Ave NW Washington DC 20006-4004

**MURPHY, EWELL EDWARD, JR.,** lawyer; b. Washington, Feb. 21, 1928; s. Ewell Edward and Lou (Phillips) M.; m. Patricia Bredell Purnell, June 26, 1954 (dec. 1964); children: Michaela, Megan Patricia, Harlan Ewell. BA, U. Tex., 1946, LLB, 1948; DPhil, Oxford U., Eng., 1951. Bar: Tex. 1948. Assoc. Baker & Botts, Houston, 1954-63, ptnr., 1964-93, head internat. dept., 1972-89; pres. Houston World Trade Assn., 1972-74; trustee Southwestern Legal Found., 1978—; chmn. Houston Com. on Fgn. Rels., 1984-85, Inst. Transnat. Arbitration, 1985-89, Internat. and Comparative Law Ctr., 1986-87; mem. J. William Fulbright Fgn. Scholarship Bd., 1991-96, vice chmn., 1992-93, chmn., 1993-95; vis. prof. U. Tex. Law Sch., 1993-97; Disting. lectr., U. Houston Law Ctr., 1996—; bd. dirs. Fulbright Assn. Contbr. articles to profl. jours. Served to lt. USAF, 1952-54. Recipient Carl H. Fulda award U. Tex. Internat. Law Jour., 1980; Rhodes scholar, 1948-51. Mem. ABA (chmn. sect. internat. law 1970-71), Houston Bar Assn. (chmn. internat. law com. 1963-64, 70-71), Houston C. of C. (chmn. internat. bus. com. 1964, 65), Philos. Soc. Tex., Internat. Law Inst. (bd. dirs. 1994—), Fulbright Assn. (bd. dirs. 1999—). Private international, General corporate. Home: 17 W Oak Dr Houston TX 77056-2117 Office: Baker & Botts 3000 One Shell Plz Houston TX 77002-4995

**MURPHY, HAROLD LOYD,** federal judge; b. Haralson County, Ga., Mar. 31, 1927; s. James Loyd and Georgia Gladys (McBrayer) M.; m. Jacqueline Marie Ferri, Dec. 20, 1958; children: Mark Harold, Paul Bailey. Student, West Ga. Coll., 1944-45, U. Miss., 1945-46; LL.B., U. Ga., 1949. Bar: Ga. 1949. Pvt. practice Buchanan, Ga., from 1949; ptnr. Howe & Murphy, Buchanan and Tallapoosa, Ga., 1958-71; judge Superior Cts., Tallapoosa Circuit, 1971-77; U.S. dist. judge No. Dist. of Ga., Rome, 1977—; rep. Gen. Assembly of Ga., 1951-61; asst. solicitor gen. Tallapoosa Jud. Circuit, 1956; mem. Jud. Qualifications Commn., State of Ga., 1977. With USNR, 1945-46. Fellow Am. Bar Found.; mem. ABA, Ga. Bar Assn., Dist. Judges Assn. for 11th Cir. Bar Assn., Am. Judicature Soc., Tallapoosa Cir. Bar Assn., Old War Horse Lawyers Club, Am. Inns Ct. (past pres. Joseph Henry Lumpkin sect.), Fed. Judges Assn. Methodist. Home: 321 Georgia Highway 120 Tallapoosa GA 30176-3114 Office: US Dist Ct PO Box 53 Rome GA 30162-0053

**MURPHY, JAMES GILMARTIN,** lawyer; b. N.Y.C., June 13, 1959; s. Maurice Joseph and Irene Abigail (Fay) M.; m. Patricia Ann O'Malley, Jan. 26, 1991. BBA, U. Notre Dame, 1981; JD, Wake Forest U., 1984. Bar: Ga. 1984, N.C. 1986, N.Y. 1989. Law clk. to Hon. Daniel A. Manion U.S. Ct. Appeals 7th Cir., South Bend, Ind., 1986-88; of counsel Epstein, Becker & Green, P.C., 1998—. Mem. editorial staff Wake Forest U. Law Review, 1982-84. Republican. Roman Catholic. Avocations: golf, reading. Labor. Office: 250 Park Ave New York NY 10177-0001

**MURPHY, JO ANNE,** lawyer; b. Binghamton, N.Y., Oct. 23, 1957; d. William T. and Shirley Anne (Merriam) M.; m. Noureddine M. Dourafei, Jan. 2, 1986; children: Zachary Dourafei, Adam Dourafei. BA summa cum laude, SUNY, Albany, 1978; JD magna cum laude, Cornell U., 1981. Bar: N.Y. 1982, Tex. 1991, U.S. Dist. Ct. (so. dist.) N.Y. 1982. Assoc. Cleary, Gottlieb, Steen & Hamilton, N.Y.C., 1981-85, 86-90, London, 1985-86; counsel Exxon Corp., Irving, Tex., 1990—. Mem. ABA, State Bar Tex., Dallas Bar Assn., Order of Coif. Securities, Finance, General corporate.

**MURPHY, LAWRENCE JOHN,** lawyer; b. Winthrop, Mass., Nov. 8, 1948; s. Lawrence John and Edna Louise (Lavery) M.; m. Sharon C. Ginchereau, June 29, 1974; children: Leah M., John L., Matthew J. BA in English cum laude, U. Mass., 1976; JD, Suffolk U., 1979. Bar: Mass. 1979, U.S. Dist. Ct. Mass. 1979, N.H. 1989, U.S. Dist. Ct. N.H. 1990. Asst. dist. atty. Essex County (Mass.) Dist. Atty., 1979-82; ptnr. McKay, Murphy & Graham, Anesbury, Mass., 1983-88, Murphy & Graham, Newburyport, Mass., 1988-90, Murphy, Graham & Gardner, Newburyport, Mass., 1990-93; sole practice Newburyport, 1993—. With USN, 1968-72, Vietnam. General practice, Criminal, General civil litigation. Home and Office: 182 State St Newburyport MA 01950-6637

**MURPHY, LAWRENCE JOHN,** lawyer; b. Brynn Mahr, Pa., May 3, 1954; s. Lawrence Edward and Wanda Kathryn Murphy; m. Catherine Welton, Feb. 27, 1982; children: John, Lauren. Student, Ctrl. Mich. U., 1972-74; B of Gen. Studies, U. Mich., 1976; JD, Wayne State U., 1979. Bar: Mich. 1979, Ind. 1988, Ill. 1990, Wis. 1999. Assoc., shareholder Howard & Howard, Kalamazoo, 1979-98; ptnr. Varnum Riddering Schmidt & Howlett, Kalamazoo, 1998—; editor Mich. Labor Letter, 1996—. Mem. ABA, Mich. Bar Assn., Ind. Bar Assn., Ill. Bar Assn., Kalamazoo C. of C. (subcom. chair 1991). Republican. Roman Catholic. Avocations: travel, golf, snow skiing, sailing. Labor. Office: Varnum Riddering Schmidt & Howlett 350 E Michigan Ave Ste 500 Kalamazoo MI 49007-3880

**MURPHY, LEWIS CURTIS,** lawyer, former mayor; b. N.Y.C., Nov. 2, 1933; s. Henry Waldo and Elizabeth Wilcox (Curtis) M.; m. Carol Carney, Mar. 10, 1957; children—Grey, Timothy, Elizabeth. B.S. in Bus. Adminstrn, U. Ariz., 1955, LL.B., 1961. Bar: Ariz. bar 1961. Individual practice law Tucson, 1961-66; trust officer So. Ariz. Bank & Trust Co., 1966-70; atty. City of Tucson, 1970-71; mayor, 1971-87, ret.; mem. law firm Schroeder & Murphy, Tucson, 1978-88; trustee U.S. Conf. Mayors, 1978-87, chmn. transp. com., 1984-87; mem. pub. safety steering com. Nat. League Cities, 1973-87, mem. transp. steering com., 1973-87; v.p. Ctrl. Ariz. Project Assn., 1978-87; bd. dirs. Community Food Bank; mem. adv. bd. Ariz. Bank, Tucson. Bd. dirs. United Way Greater Tucson, 1988-92. Served with USAF, 1955-58. Mem. Ariz. Bar Assn., Pima County Bar Assn., Ariz. Acad. Republican. Presbyterian.

**MURPHY, MARGARET HACKETT,** federal judge; b. Salisbury, N.C., 1948. BA, Queens Coll., Charlotte, N.C., 1970; JD, U. N.C., Chapel Hill, 1973. Bar: Ga. 1973, U. S. Dist. Ct. (no. dist.) Ga. 1973, U.S. Ct. Appeals (5th cir.) 1974, U.S. Ct. Appeals (11th cir.) 1982. Assoc. Smith, Cohen, Ringel, Kohler and Martin, Atlanta, 1973-79; ptnr. Smith, Gambrell & Russell (formerly Smith, Cohen, Ringel, Kohler and Martin), Atlanta, 1980-87; U.S. bankruptcy judge U.S. Dist. Ct. (no. dist.) Ga., Atlanta, 1987—. Office: 1290 US Courthouse 75 Spring St SW Atlanta GA 30303-3309

**MURPHY, MAX RAY,** lawyer; b. Goshen, Ind., July 18, 1934; s. Loren A. and Lois (Mink) M.; m. Ruth Leslie Henricson, June 10, 1978; children: Michael Lee, Chad Woodrow. BA, DePauw U., 1956; JD, Yale U., 1959; postgrad., Mich. State U., 1960. Bar: Mich. 1960. Assoc. Glassen, Parr, Rhead & McLean, Lansing, Mich., 1960-67, Lokker, Boter & Dalman, Holland, Mich., 1967-69; ptnr. Dalman, Murphy, Bidol, & Bouwens, P.C., Holland, 1969-91; ptnr. Cunningham Dalman, P.C., Holland, 1991—; instr. Lansing Bus. U., 1963-67; asst. pros. atty. Ottawa County, Mich., 1967-69. Democratic candidate for Ingham County (Mich.) Pros. Atty., 1962, 1964. Mem. ABA, Ottawa County Bar Assn. (sec. 1970-71), Mich. Bar Assn. (mem. family law sect.), Ingham County Bar Assn. Family and matrimonial, General practice. Home: 363 Oak Harbor Ct Holland MI 49424-6632 Office: 321 Settlers Rd Holland MI 49423-3706

**MURPHY, MICHAEL R.,** federal judge; b. Denver, Aug. 6, 1947; s. Roland and Mary Cecilia (Maloney) M.; m. Maureen Elizabeth Donnelly, Aug. 22, 1970; children: Amy Christina, Michael Donnelly. BA in History, Creighton U., 1969; JD, U. Wyo., 1972. Bar: Wyo. 1972, U.S. Ct. Appeals (10th cir.) 1972, Utah 1973, U.S. Dist. Ct. Utah 1974, U.S. Dist. Ct. Wyo. 1976, U.S. Ct. Appeals (5th cir.) 1976, U.S. Tax Ct. 1980, U.S. Ct. Appeals (9th cir.) 1981, U.S. Ct. Appeals (fed. cir.) 1984. Law clk. to chief judge U.S. Ct. Appeals (10th cir.), Salt Lake City, 1972-73; with Jones, Waldo, Holbrook & McDonough, Salt Lake City, 1973-86; judge 3d Dist. Ct., Salt Lake City, 1986-95, pres. judge, 1990-95; judge U.S. Ct. Appeals (10th cir.), Salt Lake City, 1995—; mem. adv. com. on rules of civil procedure Utah Supreme Ct., 1985-95, mem. bd. dist. ct. judges, 1989-90; mem. Utah State Sentencing commn., 1993-95, Utah Adv. Com. on child Support Guidelines, 1989-95, chair 1993-95; mem. Utah Child Sexual Abuse Task Force, 1989-93. Recipient Freedom of Info. award, Soc. Profl. Journalists, 1989, Utah Minority Bar Assn. award, 1995, alumni Achievement citation, Creighton U., 1997; named Judge of Yr., Utah State Bar, 1992. Fellow Am. Bar Found.; mem. ABA (editl. bd. Judges' Jour. 1997—), Utah Bar Assn. (chmn. alternative dispute resolution com. 1985-88), Sutherland Inn of Ct. II (past pres.). Roman Catholic. Office: 5438 Federal Bldg 125 S State St Salt Lake City UT 84138-1102

**MURPHY, PATRICK DAVID,** lawyer; b. South Bend, Ind., Dec. 24, 1962; s. Edward Joseph and Mary Ann (Hanson) M.; m. Tonia Ann Hap, Aug. 18, 1990; children: Eileen Taylor, Maria Clare, Emily Ann, Margaret Ann. BBA, U. Notre Dame, 1985; JD, Ind. U., Indianapolis, 1988; LLM, U. Ill., 1995. Bar: Ind. 1988, U.S. Dist. Ct. (no. and so. dists.) Ind. 1988; U.S. Ct. Appeals (7th cir.) 1989. Law clerk Hon. James E. Noland U.S. Dist. Ct. (so. dist.) Ind., Indpls., 1988-90; visiting instr. U. Ill. Coll. Law, Urbana-Champaign, 1990-91; atty. Jones, Obenchain, Ford, Pankow & Lewis, South Bend, Ind., 1991-95, Barnes & Thornburg, South Bend, Ind., 1995—; adj. prof. Valparaiso U. Sch. Law, 1999—. 1st Lt. JAGC, USAR, 1985-94. Mem. Coun. Oak Inn of Ct. Roman Catholic. General civil litigation. Office: Barnes & Thornburg 600 1st Source Bank Ctr 100 N Michigan St Ste 600 South Bend IN 46601-1632

**MURPHY, PETER MICHAEL,** lawyer; b. Yonkers, N.Y., Jan. 31, 1945; s. Henry Michael and Mary Agnes (McGloine) M.; m. Kathryn Mary Alexa, Sept. 13, 1980; 1 child, Michaela Alexa. BA, L.I. U., 1972; JD, St. John's U., Queens, N.Y., 1974. Bar: N.Y. 1975, D.C. 1989. Asst. counsel Navy Ships Parts Control Command, Mechanicsburg, Pa., 1974-76; asst. counsel Naval Supply Sys. Command, Washington, 1976-78, dep. counsel, 1980-84; asst. to gen. counsel Office of Gen. Counsel, Dept. Navy, Washington, 1978-80; counsel for the commandant USMC, Washington, 1984—. Recipient Presdl. Rank award-Meritorious Exec. award Pres. of U.S., 1993, Presdl. Rank award-Disting. Exec. award, Washington, 1996, Disting. Civilian Svc. award Dept. of Def., Washington, 1997. Mem. Sr. Exec. Assn. (bd. dirs. 1997—), St. John's Law Sch. Alumni Assn. (Washington) (v.p. 1995—), St. John's U. Alumni Assn. (Washington) (v.p. 1990—). Roman Catholic.

**MURPHY, RICHARD PATRICK,** lawyer; b. Elizabeth, N.J., Dec. 13, 1954. AB with distinction, Cornell U., 1976; JD cum laude, AM, U. Mich., 1980. Bar: D.C. 1980, U.S. Dist. Ct. (D.C.) 1981, U.S. Ct. Appeals (D.C. cir.) 1981, U.S. Supreme Ct. 1984, Calif. 1987, U.S. Dist. Ct. (so. dist.) Calif. 1987, U.S. Dist. Ct. (cen. dist.) Calif. 1992, Ga. 1993, U.S. Dist. Ct. (no. dist.) Ga. 1993, U.S. Ct. Appeals (11th cir.) 1993. Assoc. Bergson, Borkland, Margolis & Adler, Washington, 1980-82; atty. enforcement div. SEC, Washington, 1982-84, br. chief enforcement div., 1984-87; assoc. Gray, Cary, Ames & Frye, San Diego, 1987-92; sr. trial counsel SEC, Atlanta, 1993-99, asst. dist. adminstr., 1999—. Mem. ABA, D.C. Bar Assn., Calif. Bar Assn., Ga. Bar Assn. Office: SEC 3475 Lenox Rd NE Ste 1000 Atlanta GA 30326-1239

**MURPHY, RICHARD VANDERBURGH,** lawyer; b. Syracuse, N.Y., May 9, 1951; s. Robert Drown and Reta (Vanderburgh) M.; m. Patricia Lynn Eades, May 18, 1973; children: Alan Christopher, Ryan Patrick. AB, Dartmouth Coll., 1973; JD, U. Ky., 1976. Bar: Ky. 1976, U.S. Dist. Ct. (ea. dist.) Ky. 1977, U.S. Supreme Ct. 1980. Corp. counsel Lexington-Fayette Urban County Govt., Lexington, 1976-82; asst. county atty. Fayette County, Lexington, 1982-84; assoc. H. Foster Pettit, Lexington, 1982-83; ptnr. Pettit & Murphy, Lexington, 1983-84; sr. atty., prin. Wyatt, Tarrant & Combs, Lexington, 1984-88; pvt. practice, 1988—; cons. zoning ordinance update Lexington-Fayette Urban County Govt., Lexington, 1982-83. Author: Kentucky Land Use and Zoning Law, 1991. Elder, chmn. bd. South Elkhorn Christian Ch., Lexington, 1982—. Mem. Am. Planning Assn., ABA, Ky. Bar Assn., Order of Coif, Phi Beta Kappa. Democrat. Land use and zoning (including planning), Real property, Administrative and regulatory. Home: 3278 Pepperhill Rd Lexington KY 40502-3545 Office: 175 E Main St Ste 300 Lexington KY 40507-1368

**MURPHY, ROBERT EUGENE,** lawyer; b. Chgo., May 18, 1951; s. Eugene Francis and Roberta Ann M.; m. Susan Marie Fix, Aug. 19, 1978 (div. Jan. 1990); children: Kelli, Ryan. BA, St. Lawrence U., 1973; JD, SUNY, Buffalo, 1976. Bar: N.Y. 1977, U.S. Dist. Ct. (ctrl. dist.) N.Y. 1977, Calif. 1982, U.S. Dist. Ct. (ctrl. dist.) Calif. 1983. Atty. mayor's task force City of Buffalo, 1977-78; assoc. Dixon & DeMarie, Buffalo, 1978-82; dir., prin. Evan, Crandall, Wade, Lowe & Gates, Woodland Hills, Calif., 1982—. Mem. So. Calif. Def. Counsel Assn., So. Calif. Fraud Investigation Assn., Woodland Hills C. of C. Insurance, General civil litigation, Construction. Office: Even Crandall Wade Lowe & Gates 2103 Ventura Blvd Woodland Hills CA 91364

**MURPHY, SEAN,** lawyer; b. Poughkeepsie, N.Y., June 12, 1959; s. Matthew Patrick and Elizabeth (Moore) M. BA in Econs., SUNY, Albany, 1981; JD, Union U., Albany, 1991. Bar: N.Y. 1992, U.S. Dist. Ct. (no. and so. dists.) N.Y. 1993. Mgr. The Hudges Restaurant, West Park, N.Y., 1981-83; waiter, bartender Marcel's Restaurant, West Park, 1983-89; assoc. Di Stasi and Moriello, PC, Highland, N.Y., 1992-96; ptnr. Di Stasi, Moriello & Murphy, PC, Highland, 1996—. Mem. Ulster County Bar Assn. (treas. 1995-97, 2d v.p. 1997-98, 1st v.p. 1998-99, pres. 1999—, jud. evaluation com. 1995-96, 98), So. Ulster County C. of C., N.Y. State Bar Assn. Avocations: reading, tennis, golf, hiking, skiing. General practice, General civil litigation, Family and matrimonial. Home: PO Box 105 Old Post Rd West Park NY 12493 Office: Di Stasi Moriello & Murphy PO Box 915 Highland NY 12528-0915

**MURPHY, SEAN PATRICK,** lawyer; b. Rochester, N.Y., Aug. 22, 1963; s. Thomas Edward and Mary Patricia (Brasted) M.; m. Susan Marie Barnes, June 10, 1989; children, Katherine Anne, Caroline Grace. BS of Fgn. Svc., Georgetown U., 1985, JD, 1989. Bar: N.Y. 1989, D.C. 1991, Fla. 1995, Maryland, 1998, U.S. Ct. Fed. Claims 1991, U.S. Ct. Appeals (fed. cir.) 1991, U.S. Supreme Ct. 1995, U.S. Ct. Appeals (9th cir.) 1994, U.S. Ct. Appeals (11th cir.) 1995, U.S. Dist. Ct. (so., mid., no. dists.) Fla. 1995, U.S. Dist. (so. dist.) N.Y. 1991, U.S. Dist. Ct. (D.C. dist.) 1997, U.S. Ct. Appeals (D.C. cir.) 1997. Assoc. Dewey Ballantine, N.Y.C., 1989-91; fed. trial atty. U.S. Dept. Justice, Washington, 1991-95; sr. assoc. Annis Mitchell, Tampa, Fla., 1995-97; of counsel Muldoon, Murphy & Faucette LLP, Washington, 1997—; instr. trial preparedness courses Fla. Bar, Miami, Ft. Lauderdale and Tampa, 1995-97. Bd. dirs., dir. athletic adv. bd. Georgetown U., Washington, 1989-99; mem. bd. trustees, v.p. Serra Club of Washington, 1991-99, John Carroll Soc., Washington, 1991-99; vol. trial atty. Archdiocesan Pro Bono Legal Network, 1992-99 (recipient Cardinal's medal, 1998). Mem. Am. Inns of Ct. (barrister William Glen Terrell 1995-97), Univ. Club Washington, Potomac Boat Club. Democrat. Roman Catholic. General civil litigation, Securities, Banking. Office: Muldoon Murphy & Faucette LLP 5101 Wisconsin Ave NW Ste 508 Washington DC 20016-4156

**MURPHY, TAMELA JAYNE,** lawyer; b. Parkersburg, W.Va., Apr. 18, 1960; d. Robert Gene and Lena Virginia Vaughn Murphy. BBA, Ohio U., 1982; JD, Capital U., 1991; cert. entertainment law, UCLA, 1998. Bar: Ohio 1992, U.S. Dist. Ct. (so. and ea. dist.) Ohio 1993, Calif. 1997, U.S. Dist. Ct. (ctrl. dist.) Calif. 1997, U.S. Ct. Appeals (6th and 9th cir.) 1998. Pvt. practice Marina del Rey, Calif., 1992—. Co-chair Ripe Celebration and Benefit to Fight AIDS, 1993, Brazilian Land and Sea Music Coffee Festival, 1998; coord. Columbus Bar Assn. Sports Law Seminar, 1990; screening com. Hermosa Beach Film Festival, 1998; bd. trustees City of Hope, Marina del Rey chpt., 1997—; trustee bd. dirs. ACME Art Co., 1992-95; program chair Am. Inns of Ct., Franklin Inn, 1992-93, membership chair 1993-94. Recipient Outstanding Svc. award City of Hope, 1997. Mem. ABA (sports and entertainment forum 1990—), Santa Monica Bar Assn., Beverly Hills Bar Assn., L.A. County Bar Assn. Democrat. Avocations: collecting art, listening to music, attending cultural events. Entertainment, Sports, Criminal. Home: 415 Washington Blvd Marina Del Rey CA 90292 Office: 415 Washington Blvd Marina Del Rey CA 90292

**MURPHY, TIMOTHY JAMES,** lawyer; b. Topeka, Sept. 30, 1946; s. Miles J. and Norine D. Murphy; m. Patricia MacKinnon, Apr. 7, 1990. BA, U. Ga., 1968; JD, Washington & Lee U., 1970; LLM, Harvard U., 1976. Bar: Va. 1970, Fla. 1972. Atty. Shutts & Bowen, Miami, Fla., 1976—. Col. JAG Corps USAFR, 1970-95. Democrat. Roman Catholic. General corporate,

Private international, Immigration, naturalization, and customs. Office: Shutts & Bowen 201 S Biscayne Blvd Ste 1500 Miami FL 33131-4308

**MURPHY, WILLIAM ROBERT,** lawyer; b. New Haven, Oct. 6, 1927; s. Michael David and Loretta Dorothy (Murphy) M.; m. Virginia Anne Selfors, July 23, 1960; children: David M., Christopher W. B.A., Yale U., 1950, LL.B., 1953. Bar: Conn. 1953, U.S. Dist. Ct. Conn. 1957, U.S. Ct. Appeals (2d cir.) 1966, U.S Supreme Ct. 1956, U.S. Ct. Appeals (Fed. cir.) 1986. Assoc. Tyler Cooper & Alcorn, New Haven, 1957-60, ptnr., 1960—. Exec. editor: Yale Law Jour., 1952-53. Sec. John Brown Cook Found., 1971—; mem. Woodbridge Bd. Edn., Conn., 1969-75, Woodbridge Planning and Zoning Commn., 1967-69.Served to lt (j.g.) USNR, 1945-46, 53-56. James Cooper fellow Conn. Bar Found. Fellow Am. Coll. Trial Lawyers, Am. Bar Found.; mem. ABA, Conn. Bar Assn., New Haven County Bar Assn., Quinnipiack Club, Mory's Assn. Federal civil litigation, State civil litigation, Antitrust. Home: 15 Ledge Rd Woodbridge CT 06525-1801 Office: Tyler Cooper & Alcorn 205 Church St New Haven CT 06510-1805

**MURPHY-PETROS, MELISSA ANIELA,** lawyer; b. Bloomington, Ind., Oct. 30, 1965; d. John Anthony Murphy and Aniela Klekowski Berreth; m. Anthony George Petros, Sept. 17, 1994. BA, Ind. U., 1987; MA, U. Notre Dame, 1989; JD, Loyola U., 1995. Bar: Ill. 1995, U.S. Dist. Ct. (no. dist.) Ill. 1995, N.Y. 1996, U.S. Ct. Appeals (6th and 7th cirs.) 1996, U.S. Ct. Appeals (2d cir.) 1998. Atty. Clausen Miller P.C., Chgo., 1995—. Mem. music dept. Immaculate Conception Roman Cath. Ch., Elmhurst, Ill., 1998—. Mem. N.Y. State Bar Assn., Appellate Lawyers Assn., Chgo. Bar Assn. Avocations: reading, music, travel. Appellate. Office: Clausen Miller PC 10 S Lasalle St Ste 1600 Chicago IL 60603-1098

**MURR, GEORGE BASHIER,** lawyer; b. Houston, Jan. 1, 1970; s. Abe George Murr and Betty Jean Barrow. BA, U. Tex., 1992, JD, 1995. Legal clk. Tex. Ct. Criminal Appeals, Austin, 1993, Hoffman, Sutterfield, Austin, 1995; assoc. Brill & Byrom, PLLC, Houston, 1995-97, Ware, Snow, Fogel, Jackson & Greene, P.C., Houston, 1997—. Eagle Boy Scouts Am., Houston, 1981-88; steward St. Luke's United Meth. Ch., Houston, 1997—. Mem. Houston Young Lawyers Assn. (arts and entertainment com. 1998—), Phi Beta Kappa. Avocations: jogging, music, public speaking, marathons. E-mail: georgemurr@wsfjg.com. Fax: 713-659-6400. Office: Ware Snow Fogel Jackson & Greene PC 1111 Bagby St Fl 49 Houston TX 77002-2551

**MURRAY, ANTHONY,** lawyer; b. Los Angeles, Apr. 25, 1937; s. Bernard Anthony and Frances Louise (Simpson) M.; children—Matthew Anthony, Thomas Andrew. J.D., Loyola U., Los Angeles, 1964. Bar: Calif. 1965. Assoc. firm Ball, Hunt & Hart, Long Beach, Calif., 1964-68; ptnr. Hitt & Murray, 1968-79, Ball, Hunt, Hart, Brown & Baerwitz, Los Angeles, 1979-95, Loeb & Loeb LLP, 1995—; instr. Calif. State U., 1966; adj. prof. Loyola U., Los Angeles, 1975-85; active various profl. cons.; guest lectr. and panelist various legal subjects before numerous groups. Contbr. articles to legal jours. Trustee, mem. fin. com. St. Mary Med. Center Found., Long Beach. Served with U.S. Army, 1956. Fellow Am. Coll. Trial Lawyers (bd. regents 1995-99, mem. Calif. jud. coun. 1983-85); mem. ABA, Chancery Club, Los Angeles County Bar Assn.; mem. Long Beach Bar Assn.; Mem. State Bar Calif. (mem. disciplinary bd. 1975-78, chmn. exec. com. criminal law sect. 1978-79, mem. commn. on jud. nominees evaluation 1978-79, bd. govs. 1980-83, pres. 1982-83), Am. Judicature Soc. Democrat. State civil litigation, Criminal, Personal injury. Home: 1061 E Tehachapi Dr Long Beach CA 90807-2451 Office: Loeb & Loeb LLP 10000 Wilshire Blvd Los Angeles CA 90024-4702

**MURRAY, ARCHIBALD R.,** lawyer; b. Barbados, Aug. 25, 1933; came to U.S., 1950; m. Kay Crawford, July 29, 1961. BA, Howard U., 1954; LLB, Fordham U., 1960; LittD (hon.), Coll. New Rochelle, 1983; LLD (hon.), N.Y. Law Sch., 1988, John Jay Coll. CUNY, 1990, Fordham U., 1992. Bar: N.Y. 1960, U.S. Dist. Ct. (so. dist.) N.Y. 1967, U.S. Ct. Appeals (2d cir.) 1982, U.S. Supreme Ct. 1984. Asst. dist. atty. N.Y. County Dist. Atty., N.Y.C., 1960-62; asst. counsel Gov., Albany, N.Y., 1962-65; pvt. practice N.Y.C., 1965-68; counsel Crime Control Coun. N.Y.S., N.Y.C., 1968-71, adminstr. div. Criminal Justice, 1971-72, commr. div. Criminal Justice Svcs., 1972-74; atty. in chief, exec. dir. Legal Aid Soc., N.Y.C., 1975-94, chair of the bd., 1994-98; trustee Columbia U., N.Y.C., 1981-92, Fordham U., N.Y.C., 1992-98. Vestry mem. St. Philip's Ch., N.Y.C., 1970-93; mem. City Charter Revision Commn., N.Y.C., 1982-83, 86-89, mem. City/State Commn. on Integrity in Govt., N.Y.C., 1986. Recipient Cromwell award N.Y. County Lawyers Assn., 1977, Ruth Whitehead Whaley award Fordham U., Black Am. Law Students Assn., 1982, Alumni award Fordham Law Alumni Assn., 1985, Leadership award Associated Black Charities, 1987, Emory Buckner award Fed. Bar Coun., 1989, Sp. Merit award Metro. Black Bar Assn., 1991. Mem. ABA (ho. of dels. 1985-98), N.Y. State Bar Assn. (pres. 1993, Defender award 1986), Assn. Bar of City of N.Y. (chmn. exec. com. 1981-82). Episcopalian.

**MURRAY, BRIAN WILLIAM,** lawyer; b. Newton, Mass., Jan. 20, 1960; s. William Andrew and Arleen Veronica (Dagnese) M.; m. Emily Gottschling, Aug. 22, 1987; children: Alexandra Leland, John William, Leah Jane. BA, Stonehill Coll., Newton, Mass., 1981; JD, New Eng. Sch. Law, Boston, 1984. Bar: Mass. 1985, R.I. 1985, U.S. Dist. Ct. Mass. 1985. Assoc. William A. Murray Law Office, Milford, Mass., 1985—; conveyancing atty. Milford Fed. Savs. & Loan, 1992—; mem. hearing com. Bd. Bar Overseers, Boston, 1993—. Mem., chmn. War Meml. Com., Milford, 1986-93, Milford Sch. Com., 1989—; mem. Milford Sch. Bldg. Com., 1991—; pres. Friends Milford Sr. Ctr., 1990—; pro bono atty. Vol. Lawyers Svc., Worcester, Mass., 1993—. Recipient Fenn award for leadership John F. Kennedy Libr., Boston, 1992, citation Milford Bd. Selectmen, 1993, citations State Senate and Ho. of Reps., 1993. Mem. Mass. Bar Assn., R.I. Bar Assn., Worcester County Bar Assn., Mass. Acad. Trial Lawyers. Democrat. Avocations: bicycling, skiing, home. Personal injury, General practice. Home: 23 Congress Ter Milford MA 01757-4021 Office: 260 Main St Milford MA 01757-2504

**MURRAY, DANIEL CHARLES,** trial lawyer; b. Evanston, Ill., Jan. 21, 1949; s. John Joseph and Marjorie Ellen (Pequignot) M.; m. Martha Jane Gerity, Dec. 18, 1971; children: Michaela, Tyler, Brian. BA in Econs., Marquette U., 1971; JD, Loyola U., Chgo., 1976. Bar: Ill. 1976, U.S. Ct. Appeals (7th cir.) 1979, U.S. Dist. Ct. (no. dist.) Ill. 1980, U.S. Dist Ct. (ea. dist.) Mich. 1992, U.S. Dist. Ct. (ea. dist.) Wis. 1994, U.S. Tax Ct. 1997. Staff atty. U.S. Ct. Appeals for 7th Cir., Chgo., 1976-78; asst. U.S. atty. Office U.S. Atty. U.S. Dept. Justice No. Dist., Chgo., 1978-91; shareholder, chmn. pro bono program Johnson & Bell, Ltd., Chgo., 1991—; trial instr. U.S. Atty. Gen.'s Advocacy Inst., Washington, 1989; mem. Environ. Crimes Task Force, 1991. Active Chgo. Vol. Legal Svcs. Found., 1977—, Chgo. Legal Aid to Incarcerated Mothers, 1995—; participant Chgo. North-of-Howard Task Force. Recipient Disting. Svc. award Chgo. Vol. Legal Svcs. Found., 1983, 87, award for significant contbns. in drug law enforcement U.S. Drug Enforcement Adminstrn., 1988, Insp. Gen.'s nat. award GSA, 1989, Spl. Achievement award U.S. Dept. Justice, 1990. Mem. Fed. Bar Assn. (bd. dirs. Chgo. chpt.), 7th Fed. Cir. Bar Assn. Federal civil litigation, Criminal, Environmental. Office: Johnson & Bell Ltd 222 N Lasalle St Ste 2200 Chicago IL 60601-1106

**MURRAY, DANIEL RICHARD,** lawyer; b. Mar. 23, 1946; s. Alfred W. and Gloria D. Murray. AB, U. Notre Dame, 1967; JD, Harvard U., 1970. Bar: Ill. 1970, U.S. Dist. Ct. (no. dist.) Ill. 1970, U.S. Ct. Appeals (7th cir.) 1971, U.S. Supreme Ct. 1974. Ptnr. Jenner & Block, Chgo., 1970—; trustee Chgo. Mo. and Western Rlwy. Co., 1988-97; adj. prof. U. Notre Dame, 1997—. Co-author: Secured Transactions, 1978, Illinois Practice: Uniform Commercial Code with Illinois Code Comments, 1997. Bd. regents Big Shoulders Fund, Archdiocese of Chgo., Bernadin Ctr., Cath. Theol. Union. Mem. Am. Bankruptcy Inst., Am. Law Inst., Am. Coll. Comml. Fin. Lawyers (bd. regents), Transp. Lawyers Assn., Assn. Transp. Practitioners, Cath. Lawyers Guild (bd. dirs.), Law Club, Legal Club. Roman Catholic. Bankruptcy, Contracts commercial, Transportation. Home: 1307 N Sutton Pl Chicago IL 60610-2007 Office: Jenner & Block One IBM Plz Chicago IL 60611-3605

**MURRAY, FLORENCE KERINS,** retired state supreme court justice; b. Newport, R.I., Oct. 21, 1916; d. John X. and Florence (MacDonald) Kerins; m. Paul F. Murray, Oct. 21, 1943 (dec. June 2, 1995); 1 child, Paul F. AB, Syracuse U., 1938; LLB, Boston U., 1942; EdD, R.I. Coll. Edn., 1956; grad., Nat. Coll. State Trial Judges, 1966; LLD (hon.), Bryant Coll., 1956, U. R.I., 1963, Mt. St. Joseph Coll., 1972, Providence Coll., 1974, Roger Williams Coll., 1976, Salve Regina Coll., 1977, Johnson and Wales Coll., 1977, Suffolk U., 1981, So. New Eng. Law Sch., 1995; D (hon.), New England Inst. Tech., 1998. Bar: Mass. 1942, R.I. 1947, U.S. Dist. Ct. 1948, U.S. Tax Ct. 1948, U.S. Supreme Ct. 1948. Sole practice Newport, 1947-52; mem. firm Murray & Murray, Newport, 1952-56; assoc. judge R.I. Superior Ct., 1956-78; presiding justice Superior Ct. R.I., 1978-79; assoc. justice (ret.-active) R.I. Supreme Ct., 1979—; staff, faculty adv. Nat. Jud. Coll., Reno, Nev., 1971-72, dir., 1975-77, chmn., 1979-87, chair emeritus, 1990—; mem. com. Legal Edn. and Practice and Economy of New Eng., 1975—; former instr. Prudence Island Sch.; legal adv. R.I. Girl Scouts; sec. Commn. Jud. Tenure and Discipline, 1975-79; apptd. by Pres. Clinton to bd. dirs. State Justice Inst., 1994-99; participant, leader various legal seminars; presdl. appointment R.I. State Justice Inst. Mem. R.I. Senate, 1948-56; chmn. spl. legis. com.; mem. Newport Sch. Com., 1948-57, chmn., 1951-57; mem. Gov.'s Jud. Coun., 1950-60, White House Conf. Youth and Children, 1950, Ann. Essay Commn., 1952, Nat. Def. Adv. Com. on Women in Service, 1952-58, Gov.'s Adv. Com. Mental Health, 1954, R.I. Alcoholic Adv. Com., 1955-58, R.I. Com. Youth and Children, Gov.'s Adv. Com. on Revision Election Laws, Gov.'s Adv. Com. Social Welfare, Army Adv. Com. for 1st Army Area; mem. civil and polit. rights com. Pres.'s Commn. on Status of Women, 1960-63; mem. R.I. Com. Humanities, 1972—, chmn., 1972-77; mem. Family Ct. Study Com., R.I. com. Nat. Endowment Humanities; bd. dirs. Newport YMCA; sec. Bd. Physicians Service; bd. visitors Law Sch., Boston U.; bd. dirs. NCCJ; mem. edn. policy and devel. com. Roger Williams Jr. Coll.; trustee Syracuse U.; pres. Newport Girls Club, 1974-75, R.I. Supreme Ct. Hist. Soc., 1988—; chair Supreme Ct. Mandatory Continuing Legal Edn. Com., 1993—; apptd. bd. dirs. Touro Synagogue; apptd. R.I. Found. Served to lt. col. WAC, World War II. Decorated Legion of Merit; recipient Arents Alumni award Syracuse U., 1956, Carroll award R.I. Inst. Instn., 1956, Brotherhood award NCCJ, 1983, Herbert Harley award Am. Judicature Soc., 1988, Melvin Eggers Sr. Alumni award Syracuse U., 1992, Merit award R.I. Bar Assn., 1994, John Manson/Carl Robinson award, 1996, Longfellow Humanitarian award ARC, 1997; named Judge of Yr. Nat. Assn. Women Judges, 1984, Outstanding Woman, Bus. and Profl. Women, 1972, Citizen of Yr. R.I. Trial Lawyers Assn.; Newport courthouse renamed in her honor, 1990. Mem. ABA (chmn. credentials com. nat. conf. state trial judges 1971-73, chair judges adv. com. on standing com. on ethics and profl. responsibility 1991—, joint com. on jud. discipline of standing com. on profl. discipline 1991-94), R.I. Found. (bd. dirs. 1998—), AAUW (chmn. state edn. com. 1954-56), Am. Arbitration Assn., Nat. Trial Judges Conf. (state chmn. membership com., sec. exec. com.), New Eng. Trial Judges Conf. (com. chmn. 1967), Boston U. Alumni Coun., Am. Legion (judge adv. post 7, mem. nat. exec. com.), Bus. and Profl. Women's Club (past state v.p., past pres. Newport chpt., past pres. Nat. legis. com.), Auota Club (past gov. internat., past pres. Newport chpt.), Alpha Omega, Kappa Beta Pi.

**MURRAY, FRED F.,** lawyer; b. Corpus Christi, Tex., Aug. 1, 1950; s. Marvin Frank and Suzanne Louise Murray. BA, Rice U., 1972; JD, U. Tex., 1974. Bar: Tex. 1975, U.S. Dist. Ct. (so. dist.) Tex. 1976, U.S. Ct. Claims 1976, U.S. Tax Ct. 1976, U.S. Ct. Appeals (5th, D.C. and fed. cirs.) 1976, U.S. Supreme Ct. 1978, U.S. Ct. Internat. Trade 1985, N.Y. 1987, D.C. 1987, U.S. Dist. Ct. (ea. dist.) Tex. 1987; CPA, Tex. Ptnr. Chamberlain, Hrdlicka, White, Williams & Martin, P.C., Houston, 1985-92; spl. counsel (legislation) U.S. Dept. Treasury, IRS, Washington, 1992-96; v.p. tax policy Nat. Fgn. Trade Coun., 1996—; mem. Tax Law Adv. Commn., Tex. Bd. Legal Specialization, 1984—, vice chmn., 1987-92; mem. Commn. Tax Law Examiners, 1984—, vice chmn., 1987-92; adj. prof. U. Houston Law Ctr., 1984-92, U. Tex. Sch. Law, 1987; faculty lectr. Rice U. Jones Grad. Sch. Adminstrn., 1987-92; spkr. various assns. and univs.; mem. bd. advisors Houston Jour. Internat. Law, 1986-92, chmn., 1987-91. Author various publs. Del. Bishop's Diocesan Pastoral Com., 1979-80; chmn. parish coun. Sacred Heart Cathedral, Cath. Diocese Galveston-Houston, 1979-81, 89, mem. Red Mass steering com., 1986-92; mem. exec. com., bd. dirs., 1987-91, chmn. deferred giving com. Houston Symphony Soc., 1987-88, chmn. govt. and pub. affairs com., 1988-91; co-trustee Houston Symphony Soc. Endowment Fund, 1987-91; mem. fund coun. Rice U., 1987—, exec. com. 1988-92, chmn. Major Gifts Com., 1988-92; gen. counsel, bd. dirs., com. on fin. and adminstrn. S.E. Tex. chpt. Nat. Multiple Sclerosis Soc.; mem. Red Mass com. Archdiocese Washington, 1993—; bd. dirs. John Carroll Soc., Archdiocese of Washington, 1996—, chmn. pilgrimage com. Knighted equestrian order Holy Sepulchre Jerusalem, 1998—. Fellow Am. Coll. Tax Counsel; mem. ABA (officer various coms.), FBA (mem. steering com. tax sect. 1995—, chmn. tax sect. 1998—), AICPA, Am. Arbitration Assn. (panels comml. and internat. arbitrators 1980—), Internat. Bar Assn., Houston Bar Assn., State Bar of Tex. (various coms.), N.Y. State Bar Assn., D.C. Bar Assn., Tex. Soc. CPAs, Internat. Tax Forum of Houston (sec. 1981-84, pres. 1984-92), Internat. Fiscal Assn., Am. Soc. Internat. Law, Am. Fgn. Law Assn., Am. Law Inst. (tax adv. group 1990—).

**MURRAY, GLENN EDWARD,** lawyer; b. Niskayuna, N.Y., Dec. 11, 1955. BA cum laude, Siena Coll., 1977; JD, Union U., Albany, N.Y., 1980. Bar: N.Y. 1981, U.S. Dist. Ct. (no. dist.) N.Y. 1981, U.S. Ct. Mil. Appeals 1981, U.S. Dist. Ct. (we. dist.) N.Y. 1985, U.S. Supreme Ct. 1987, U.S. Bankruptcy Ct. 1989, U.S. Ct. Appeals (2d cir.) 1992. Pvt. practice Buffalo, 1990—; prosecutor Village of Williamsville, 1992—; adj. prof. Am. constl. law Canisius Coll., 1993-94. Author: Collateral Consequences of Criminal Conduct, 1989, Civil Consequences of Criminal Conduct, 51 Am. Jr. Trials 337, 1994; contbr. articles to profl. jours. Mem. social action com. Temple Beth Am, Amherst, N.Y., 1987—; instr. Jewish Community Ctr. Greater Buffalo, 1988—; instr. police legal survival Operation Tri-Star (SWAT team conf.), Ft. Drum, N.Y., 1989-91. Capt. U.s. Army, 1981-84, mem. N.Y. Army N.G. ret. Decorated Bronze Star. Mem. ABA, N.Y. State Bar Assn. (chmn. spl. com. on mil. and vet. affairs 1991-94), Erie County Bar Assn. (instr., panelist), N.Y. Defenders Assn., N.Y. State Assn. Criminal Def. Lawyers, N.Y. Civil Liberties Union. Criminal, General civil litigation, Family and matrimonial. Home: 84 Highland Dr Buffalo NY 14221-6802 Office: The Cornell Mansion 484 Delaware Ave Buffalo NY 14202-1304

**MURRAY, GWEN E.,** lawyer; d. Adelaide W. Murray. BBA cum laude, Western Conn. State U., 1988; JD cum laude, Quinipiac Coll., 1996. Bar: Conn. 1996, U.S. Dist. Ct. Conn. 1997. Data processing and acctg. coord. Union Savs. Bank of Danbury, Conn., 1985-88; mgr. data processing Southington (Conn.) Bd. Edn., 1988-91; programmer, analyst H. Muehlstein & Co. Inc., Norwalk, Conn., 1991-92; cons., prin. GEM Cons., Danbury, 1992-95; intern Pub. Defender Svcs., Danbury, 1995-96; assoc., rsch. asst. Portanova & Rutigliano, Bridgeport, 1995-97; pvt. practice Bethel, Conn., 1997—. Casenotes editor Quinnipiac Law Rev., 1995-96. Mem. Conn. Bar Assn., Bethel C. of C. General practice, Personal injury, Real property. Office: 153 Greenwood Ave Bethel CT 06801-2527

**MURRAY, JAMES MICHAEL,** librarian, law librarian, legal educator, lawyer; b. Seattle, Nov. 8, 1944; s. Clarence Nicholas and Della May (Snyder) M.; m. Linda Monthy Murray. MLaw Librarianship, U. Wash., 1978; JD, Gonzaga U., 1971. Bar: Wash. 1974, U.S. Dist. Ct. (we. dist.) Wash. 1975, U.S. Dist. Ct. (ea. dist.) Wash. 1985. Reference/reserve libr. U. Tex. Law Libr., Austin, 1978-81; assoc. law libr. Washington U. Law Libr., St. Louis, 1981-84; law libr., asst. prof. Gonzaga U. Sch. Law, Spokane, 1984-91; libr. East Bonner County Libr., 1991-97, U.S. Cts. Libr., Spokane, 1997—; mem. state adv. bd. Nat. Reporter on Legal Ethics and Profl. Responsibility, 1982-91; cons. in field. Author: (with Reams and McDermott) American Legal Literature: Bibliography of Selected Legal Resources, 1985, (with Gasaway and Johnson) Law Library Administration During Fiscal Austerity, 1992; editor Tex. Bar Jour. (Books Appraisals Column), 1979-82; contbr. numerous articles and revs. to profl. jours., acknowledgements and bibliographies in field. Bd. dirs. ACLU, Spokane chpt., 1987-91, Wash. Vol. Lawyers for the Arts, 1976-78. Mem. ABA, Idaho Libr. Assn., Wash. State Bar Assn. (law sch. liaison com. 1986-88, civil rights com. 1996-97). Home: 921 W 29th Ave Spokane WA 99203-1318 Office: US Cts Libr 920 W Riverside Ave Ste 650 Spokane WA 99201-1008

**MURRAY, JOHN DANIEL,** lawyer; b. Cleve., Feb. 13, 1944; s. Clarence Daniel and Mary Anne (Bormann) M.; m. Pamela Mary Seese, Aug. 20, 1966 (div. Sept. 1978); children: Laura Jane, Joshua Daniel, Katherine Anne; m. Marilyn Nohren, June 15, 1979. BA, Marquette U., 1965, JD, 1968. Bar: Wis. 1968, Ill. 1968, U.S. Dist. Ct. (ea. and we. dist.) Wis. 1968, U.S. Supreme Ct. 1971, U.S. Ct. Appeals (7th cir.) 1979. Assoc. Law Offices of Elmo Koos, Peoria, Ill., 1968-70; ptnr. Coffey, Lerner & Murray, Milw., 1970-72, Coffey, Murray & Coffey, Milw., 1972-76, Murray & Burke, S.C., Milw., 1976-83; pvt. practice Milw., 1983-85; shareholder Habush, Habush, Davis & Rottier, S.C., Appleton, Wis., 1985—; adj. prof. law Marquette U., Milw., 1993—; lectr. Law Sch. U. Wis., Madison, 1976-80. Contbg. author to Wis. Civil Procedure During Trial Pub. state Par Wis., 1999. Mem. ABA, ATLA, Nat. Bd. Trial Advocacy (cert.), Am. Soc. Law and Medicine, Wis. State Bar (chmn. criminal law sect. 1977-78, tort law com. 1990-94, bd. dirs. litigation sect. 1995—, chmn. 1997-98), Wis. Acad. Trial Lawyers (bd. dirs. 1990—), Woolsack Soc. Roman Catholic. Avocations: golf, travel. State civil litigation, Personal injury, Product liability. Home: 1867 E Shady Ln Neenah WI 54956-1177 Office: Habush Habush Davis Rottier PO Box 1915 Appleton WI 54912-1915

**MURRAY, MICHAEL KENT,** lawyer; b. Missoula, Mont., Feb. 14, 1948; s. Paul R. and Virginia F. Murray; children: Britton M., Spencer J. BA, U. Calif., Santa Barbara, 1970; JD, U. Santa Clara, 1974. Bar: Wash. 1974, U.S. Ct. Claims 1975, U.S. Tax Ct. 1976, U.S. Dist. Ct. Wash. 1977, U.S. Ct. Appeals (fed. cir.) 1982. Trial atty. honor law grad. program U.S. Dept. Justice, Washington, 1974-76; atty. Foster Pepper & Riviera, Seattle, 1976-79; ptnr. Foster Pepper & Riviera, Seattle and Bellevue, 1980-86; ptnr.-in-charge Foster Pepper & Riviera, Bellevue, 1983-86; atty., pres. Michael K. Murray, P.S., Seattle, 1986—; pres. N.W. Properties Devel. Corp., Seattle, 1986-92; of counsel Lasher Holzapfel Sperry & Ebberson, Seattle, 1992—. Articles editor Santa Clara Lawyer, U. Santa Clara Sch. Law, 1973-74. Trustee Pacific Northwest Ballet, Seattle, 1979-81; dir. Bellevue Downtown Assn., 1984-87. Mem. Wash. State Bar Assn., King County Bar Assn., Seattle Yacht Club, Seattle Tennis Club. Avocations: sailing, fly fishing, biking, computing. Real property, Construction, Land use and zoning (including planning). Home: 1570 9th Ave N Edmonds WA 98020-2627 Office: Lasher Holzapfel Sperry & Ebberson 601 Union St Ste 2600 Seattle WA 98101-2302

**MURRAY, MICHAEL PATRICK,** lawyer; b. Milw., Jan. 31, 1930; s. Michael James and Florence Mary M.; m. Allene Vereen, May 8, 1976; children: Bryan Patrick, Laura Renee. BA, Milton (Wis.) Coll., 1953; JD, Marquette U., 1958; LLM, John Marshall Law Sch., 1960; D of Juridicial Sci., George Washington U., Washington, D.C., 1973; M of Liberal Arts, Johns Hopkins U., 1996. Bar: Wis. 1958, Calif. 1966, U.S. Supreme Ct. 1967, U.S. Ct. Appeals (9th cir.) 1982, D.C. 1989, Va. 1989, U.S. Ct. Appeals (D.C. cir.) 1989, U.S. Ct. Appeals (4th cir.) 1990. Commd. 2d lt. USMC, 1953, advanced through grades to col., 1975, prosecutor and def. counsel, 1960-66, trial judge and SJA, 1966-69; dir. policy and research USMC, Washington, 1969-72; dir. Law Ctr. USMC, Iwakuni, Japan, 1973-74; ret. USMC, 1978; trail atty. Anderson & Murphy, Milw., 1958-60; counsel to the chmn. Joint Chiefs of Staff, Washington, 1974-75; apellate judge USN Ct. of Rev., Washington, 1975-78; pvt. practice, San Diego, 1982-89; atty., counsel Clary, Lawrence, Lickstein & Moore, Falls Church, Va., 1989-91; ptnr. Michael Patrick Murray & Assocs., Fairfax, Va., 1991—; asst. gen. counsel NRA, Washington, 1992-95; assoc. prof. law Pepperdine U., Malibu, Calif., 1978-80, Marquette U., Milw., 1980-81; adj. prof. law Western State U., San Diego, 1983-88, Nat. U. Coll. Law, 1988-89; pro bono vol. atty. for indigents, San Diego, 1982-89. Author: Quarter: the Warrior's Dilemma, 1967, (law study) Eichman and Major German War Criminal Trials, 1973, O'Ryans Law, 1992, Murder By Class, 1997. Mem. Calif. Bar Assn., Wis. Bar Assn., D.C. Bar Assn., Va. Bar Assn., Am. Legion, First and Third Marine Div. Assn., Marine Corps Assn., Phi Delta Phi. Roman Catholic. Avocations: poetry, creative writing. General civil litigation, Constitutional, General corporate. Office: Michael Patrick Murray & Assocs 4124 Meadow Field Ct Fairfax VA 22033-2830

**MURRAY, PHILIP EDMUND, JR.,** lawyer; b. Floral Park, N.Y., Mar. 4, 1950; s. Philip Edmund and Anne Marie (Mackin) M.; m. Karen Anne McLeavey, Aug. 14, 1976; children: Erin Anne, Philip E. III. BS cum laude, Boston Coll., 1972, JD, 1975. Bar: Mass. 1975, U.S. Dist. Ct. Mass. 1976, U.S. Supreme Ct. 1992. Law clk. to presiding justices Mass. Superior Ct., Boston, 1975-76; sr. ptnr. Martin Magnuson McCarthy & Kenney, Boston, 1976—; hearing officer Bd. of Bar Overseers of the Supreme Judicial Ct., Boston, 1990-96. Editor: Boston Coll. Law Rev., 1973-75; contbr. articles to profl. jours. Mem. Mass. Bar Assn., Mass. Bar Found.; mem. Am. Soc. Law and Medicine, Am. Coll. Legal Medicine. General civil litigation, Health, Personal injury. Office: Martin Magnuson McCarthy & Kenney 101 Merrimac St Ste 700 Boston MA 02114-4716

**MURRAY, PHILIP JOSEPH, III,** lawyer; b. Pitts., Sept. 20, 1961; s. Philip Joseph Jr. and Dorothy Cecelia (Hollinger) M.; m. Carol Jean Gibson, July 7, 1990; children: Vanessa Lee, Keenan Patrick. BS in Psychology, U. Pitt., 1985; JD, Duquesne U., 1988. Bar: Pa. 1988, U.S. Dist. Ct. (we. dist.) Pa. 1988, U.S. Ct. Appeals (3d cir.) 1992, U.S. Ct. Appeals (8th cir.) 1995. Law clk. to Hon. Barron P. McCune U.S. Dist. Ct. We. Dist., Pitts., 1988-90; assoc. Thorp, Reed & Armstrong, Pitts., 1990—. Exec. dir. William P. Fralic Found., Pitts., 1992—. Mem. Allegheney County Bar Assn. Republican. Roman Catholic. Avocations: golf, athletics. Labor, Federal civil litigation. Office: Thorp Reed and Armstrong One Riverfront Ctr Pittsburgh PA 15222

**MURRAY, REBECCA BRAKE,** lawyer; b. Kingsport, Tenn., Jan. 31, 1949; d. Joseph Albert and Marie (Stinnett) Brake; m. David W. Murray III, Sept. 18, 1971; children: Allison Marie, David W. IV. BS, cert. in phys. therapy, U. Mich., 1971; MS in Health Scis., Case Western Res. U., 1978; postgrad., Cleve. State Law Sch., 1981-83; JD, U. Tenn., 1985. Bar: Tenn. 1985, U.S. Dist. Ct. (ea. dist.) Tenn. 1986, U.S. Ct. Appeals (6th cir.) 1988. Assoc. Kennerly Montgomery & Finley, P.C., Knoxville, 1985-90, shareholder, 1991—. Editor: (law rev.) Cleve. State Law Sch., 1983. Mem. ABA, Tenn. Bar Assn., Knoxville Bar Assn., Def. Rsch. Inst., Tenn. Def. Lawyers Assn. General civil litigation, Product liability, Workers' compensation. Office: Kennerly Montgomery & Finley PC 550 W Main St Knoxville TN 37902-2515

**MURRAY, ROBERT ARTHUR,** lawyer; b. St. Louis, Apr. 25, 1957; s. Joseph A. and Jacquelin G. (Green) M.; m. Wendy Ellen Lutz, Dec. 27, 1992; children: Benjamin, Sophia, Elliott, Jacob. BA in Polit. Sci., U. Mo., 1981, JD, 1985. Bar: Mo. 1985, U.S. Dist. Ct. (we. dist.) Mo. 1985. Asst. pub. defender Pub. Defender's Office, Columbia, Mo., 1985-89; pvt. practice Columbia, 1989—. Coach Columbia Soccer Club, 1995—; cub scout leader Columbia coun. Boy Scouts Am., 1996-97. Mem. NACDL, Mo. Assn. Criminal Defense Lawyers, Mo. Bar Assn., Boone County Bar Assn. Roman Catholic. Avocations: camping, snorkeling. Fax: 573-442-1566. Criminal, Juvenile. Office: Law Offices Robert A Murray PO Box 7066 Columbia MO 65205-7066

**MURRAY, ROBERT FOX,** lawyer; b. Burlington, Vt., Feb. 28, 1952; s. Robert and Mary (Fox) M.; m. Ann Marie Bevilacqua, Aug. 20, 1988. BA, Colgate U., 1974; JD, Boston U., 1978. Bar: Mass. 1978, U.S. Dist. Ct. Mass. 1979. Assoc. Law Offices of George Howard, Dedham, Mass., 1978-80, from assoc. to ptnr. Fairbanks & Silvia Koczera, Fountain, Murray, New Bedford, Mass., 1980-84; pvt. practice, New Bedford, 1984—. Bd. dirs., clk. Downtown New Bedford, Inc. Mem. New Bedford C. of C., Waterfront Hist. Area League, Assn. Trial Lawyers Am., Mass. Acad. Trial Attys., Mass. Bar Assn., New Bedford Bar Assn., Bristol County Bar Assn. Democrat. State civil litigation, Environmental, Personal injury. Office: 201 Middle St New Bedford MA 02740-6015

**MURRAY, STEPHEN JAMES,** lawyer; b. Phila., Jan. 27, 1943; s. Paul Martin and Hannah (Smith) M.; m. Linda Sanders, June 20, 1970; children: Gordon Joshua, Cara Sanders. AB cum laude, Brown U., 1963; LLB, Harvard U., 1966; LLM, George Washington U., 1967. Bar: N.Y. 1968, U.S. Ct. Appeals (2nd cir.) 1971, U.S. Ct. Appeals (fed. cir.) 1998, U.S. Dist. Ct. (so. and ea. dists.) N.Y. 1972, U.S. Ct. Claims 1974, U.S. Supreme Ct. 1975, Conn. 1988, U.S. Dist. Ct. Conn. 1988, U.S. Ct. Internat. Trade 1998. Spl. asst. SEC, Washington, 1966-67, Maritime Adminstrn., Washington, 1967-68; assoc. Hill, Betts & Nash, N.Y.C., 1970-76; transp. atty. Union Carbide Corp., N.Y.C., 1976-78, sr. transp. atty., 1978-85; chief transp.

counsel Union Carbide Corp., Danbury, Conn., 1985—, group counsel, 1986—, real estate counsel, 1992—, comml. counsel, 1993—, customs and internat. trade counsel, 1997—; spkr. in field. Contbr. articles to profl. jours. Lt. JAGC, USN, 1968-70. Mem. ABA, Conn. State Bar, U.S. Naval Inst., Navy League of U.S., Maritime Law Assn., U.S. Transp. Lawyers Assn., N.Y. State Bar Assn., Am. Corp. Counsel Assn., Conn. Maritime Assn., Harvard Club, Brown Club (co-pres.), Brown Faculty Club, Brown Alumni Schs. Commn. (chmn. Fairfield County), Brown Alumni Assn. (bd. govs.). Admiralty, Real property, Private international. Home: 14 Pilgrim Ln Weston CT 06883-2412 Office: Union Carbide Corp Law Dept 39 Old Ridgebury Rd Danbury CT 06817-0001

**MURRAY, WILLIAM MICHAEL,** lawyer; b. Buffalo, Dec. 21, 1953; s. William Joseph and Mary Ann (Lichtenthal) M.; m. Suzanne M. Raynor; children: Colleen Elizabeth, William Michael Jr., Caitlin Anne, Matthew Francis Johnson. BA, U. Notre Dame, 1975; JD, U. Detroit, 1978. Bar: N.Y. 1978, U.S. Dist. Ct. (we. dist.) N.Y. 1980. Asst. county atty. Erie County, Buffalo, 1978-79; ptnr. Stamm & Murray, Williamsville, N.Y., 1979-96, Renaldo Myers & Palumbo, Williamsville, N.Y., 1996-98; dep. atty. Town of Amherst, N.Y., 1993-96; gen. counsel Town of Amherst Indsl. Devel. Agy., 1996—. Mem. Amherst (N.Y.) Rep. Com., 1980-98; chmn. Amherst Zoning Bd. Appeals, 1986-93. Mem. N.Y. State Bar Assn., Erie County Bar Assn., Williamsville Bus. Assn. (bd. dirs., v.p. 1985-96), Rotary (pres. Williamsville 1989). Roman Catholic. General practice, Municipal (including bonds), Land use and zoning (including planning). Office: 130 John Muir Dr Amherst NY 14228-1148

**MURRAY, WILLIAM MICHAEL (MIKE MURRAY),** lawyer; b. Ottumwa, Iowa, Dec. 28, 1947; s. William Bernard and Thelma Jean (Hart) M.; m. Ann Elizabeth Wawzonek, Oct. 11, 1973; children: Kathleen Elizabeth, Daniel Webster. BA, U. Iowa, 1970; JD, 1973. Bar: Iowa 1973, U.S. Dist. Ct. (so. dist.) Iowa 1976, U.S. Dist. Ct. (no. dist.) Iowa 1978, U.S. Ct. Appeals (8th cir.) 1978. Staff counsel Iowa Civil Rights Commn., Des Moines, 1973-76; assoc. Bertroche & Hagen, Des Moines, 1976-78; ptnr. Murray, Jankins & Noble, Des Moines, 1978—. Bd. dirs. Iowa Civil Liberties Union, Des Moines, 1978-83, pres., 1982-83; bd. dirs. Polk County Legal Aide Soc., Des Moines, 1984-88. Mem. ABA, Asn. Trial Lawyers Am., Assn. Trial Lawyers Iowa, Iow Assn. Workers' Compensation Lawyers, Iowa State Bar Assn., Polk County Bar Assn., Des Moines Jaycees Club (bd. dirs. legal counsel 1980-81). Democrat. E-mail attorney@lawyer.com. State civil litigation, Personal injury, Workers' compensation. Home: 600 SW 42nd St Des Moines IA 50312-4605 Office: Murray Jankins & Noble 2903 Ingersoll Ave Des Moines IA 50312-4014

**MURRIAN, ROBERT PHILLIP,** judge, educator; b. Knoxville, Tenn., Apr. 1, 1945; s. Albert Kinzel and Mary Gilbert (Eppes) M.; m. Jerrilyn Sue Boone, Oct. 29, 1983; children—Kimberley Ann, Jennifer Rebecca, Albert Boone, Samuel Robert. B.S., U.S. Naval Acad., 1967; J.D., U. Tenn., 1974. Bar: Tenn. 1974, U.S. Dist. Ct. (ea. dist.) Tenn. 1975, U.S. Ct. Appeals (6th cir.) 1982. Law clk. to judge U.S. Dist. Ct. (ea. dist.) Tenn., 1974-76; assoc. Butler, Vines, Babb & Threadgill, Knoxville, 1976-78; magistrate, judge U.S. Dist. (ea. dist.) Tenn., Knoxville, 1978—; adj. prof. U. Tenn. Coll. Law, 1990-93, 95-96. Lt. USN, 1967-71. Green Scholar, 1973-74; Nat. Moot Ct. scholar, 1974. Fellow Tenn. Bar Found.; mem. ABA, Knoxville Bar Assn. (bd. govs. 1994), Tenn. Bar Assn., Order of Coif, Am. Inn of Ct. (master of the bench, pres. 1997-98). Presbyterian. Office: US Dist Ct 800 Market St ste 144 Knoxville TN 37902-2303

**MURRY, HAROLD DAVID, JR.,** lawyer; b. Holdenville, Okla., June 30, 1943; s. Harold David Sr. and Willie Elizabeth (Dees) M.; m. Ann Moore Earnhardt, Nov. 1, 1975; children: Elizabeth Ann, Sarah Bryant. BA, Okla. U., 1965, JD, 1968. Bar: Okla. 1968, D.C. 1974. Asst. to v.p. U. Okla., Norman, 1968-71, legal counsel Research Inst., 1969-71; atty. U.S. Dept. Justice, Washington, 1971-74; spl. asst. U.S. Atty., Washington, 1972; assoc. Clifford & Warnke, Washington, 1974-78, ptnr., 1978-91; ptnr. Howrey & Simon, Washington, 1991-98, Baker & Botts, LLP, Washington, 1998—. Mem. ABA, Okla. Bar Assn., D.C. Bar Assn., Fed. Bar Assn., Met. Club (Washington), Chevy Chase Club (Md.), Phi Alpha Delta. Democrat. General practice, Federal civil litigation, Administrative and regulatory. Home: 8931 Bel Air Pl Potomac MD 20854-1606 Office: Baker & Botts LLP Ste 1200 1299 Pennsylvania Ave NW Washington DC 20004-2408

**MURTHA, J. GARVAN,** federal judge; b. Hartford, Conn., Mar. 3, 1941; s. John Stephen and Emily Winifred (Garvan) M.; m. Margaret Munro McDonald, May 24, 1969; 3 children. BA, Yale U., 1963; LLB, U. Conn., 1968; LLM, Georgetown U., 1972. Bar: Conn. 1968, D.C. 1968, Vt. 1970. Vol., coord. Peace Corps, Colombia, 1963-65; pub. defender Washington, 1968-70; dep. state's atty. for Windham County Dept. Justice, Vt., 1970-73; ptnr. Kristensen, Cummings and Murtha, 1973-95; judge U.S. Dist. Ct. Vt., Brattleboro, 1995—, now chief judge; mem. Second Cir. Task Force on Gender, Racial and Ethnic Fairness, Second Cir. Com. on Fed. Rules, Vt. Jud. Nominating Bd., 1980-86, Vt. Profl. Conduct Bd., 1993-95; chair Vt. Commn. on Low-Level Nuc. Waste, 1987-90. Mem. ABA, Vt. Bar Assn., Windham County Bar Assn., Am. Bd. Trial Advocates, Am. Inns of Ct. (so. Vt. chpt., bencher), Jud. Coun. 2nd Cir. Roman Catholic. Office: US Dist Ct Vt US Post Office & Courthouse PO Box 760 Brattleboro VT 05302-0760

**MUSCATO, ANDREW,** lawyer; b. Newark, Aug. 28, 1953; s. Salvatore and Bertha (Kubilus) M.; m. Ann Marie Hughes, Aug. 19, 1978; children: Amy, Andrew Joseph, Amanda. AB magna cum laude, Brown U., 1975; JD, Seton Hall U., 1978. Bar: N.J. 1978, U.S. Dist. Ct. N.J. 1978, U.S. Ct. Appeals (3d cir.) 1981, N.Y. 1984, U.S. Dist. Ct. (so. and ea. dists.) N.Y. 1984, U.S. Dist. Ct. (no. dist.) N.Y. 1998. Law clk. to presiding judge, appellate div. N.J. Superior Ct., Somerville, 1978-79; staff atty. Adminstrv. Office of Cts., Trenton, N.J., 1979-80; assoc. Simon & Allen, Newark, 1980-86; ptnr. Kirsten & Simon, Newark, 1987-89, Whitman & Ransom, Newark, 1989-93, Whitman Breed Abbott & Morgan, LLP, Newark, 1993-99; counsel Skadden, Arps, Slate, Meaghen & Flom LLP, 1999—; commr. N.J. Pub. Employee Rels. Commn., 1999—; atty. Irvington (N.J.) Rent Leveling Bd., 1980—. Author: Executing on a Debtor's Interest in a Tenancy by the Entirety, 1986. Mem. ABA, Essex County Bar Assn., Trial Attys. N.J., N.J. Inst. Mcpl. Attys., Def. Rsch. Inst. Republican. Roman Catholic. State civil litigation, Federal civil litigation, Contracts commercial. Home: 66 Addison Dr Basking Ridge NJ 07920-2202 Office: Skadden Arps Slate Meaghen & Flom LLP One Newark Ctr Newark NJ 07102-5297

**MUSGRAVE, R. KENTON,** federal judge; b. 1927. Student, Ga. Inst. Tech., 1945-46, U. Fla., 1946-47; BA, U. Wash., 1948; JD with distinction, Emory U., 1953. Asst. gen. counsel Lockheed Internat., 1953-62; v.p., gen. counsel Mattel, Inc., 1963-71; mem. firm Musgrave, Welbourn and Fertman, 1972-75; asst. gen. counsel Pacific Enterprises, 1975-81; v.p., gen. counsel Vivitar Corp, 1981-85; v.p., dir. Santa Barbara Applied Rsch., 1982-87; judge U.S. Ct. Internat. Trade, N.Y.C., 1987—. Trustee Morris Animal Found., The Dian Fossey Gorilla Fund, Dolphins of Sharks Bay (Australia); hon. trustee Pet Protection Soc.; mem. United Way, South Bay-Centinela Svc. Orgn., Save the Redwoods League; active LWV, Legal Aid, Palos Verdes Community Assn. Mem. ABA, Internat. Bar Assn., Pan Am. Bar Assn., State Bar Calif. (chmn. corp. law sect. 1965-66, del. 1966-67), L.A. County Bar Assn., State Bar Ga., Fng. Trade Assn. So. Calif. (bd. dirs.), Sierra Club. Office: US Ct Internat Trade 1 Federal Plz New York NY 10278-0001

**MUSICK, ROBERT LAWRENCE, JR.,** lawyer; b. Richlands, Va., Oct. 3, 1947; s. Robert Lawrence and Virginia (Brooks) M.; m. Beth Pambianchi, 1996; children: Elizabeth, Robert. BA in History with honors, U. Richmond, 1969; JD, U. Va., 1972, MA in Legal History, 1972; LLM, Coll. William and Mary, 1986. Bar: Va. 1972, U.S. Ct. Appeals (4th cir.) 1974. Law clk. Supreme Ct. Va., Richmond, 1972-73; assoc. Williams, Mullen & Christian, Richmond, 1973-78; ptnr. Williams, Mullen, Christian & Dobbins, Richmond, 1978—; bd. govs. estates and property sect. Va. State Bar, 1977-80, chmn., 1980. Author: RIA Non Qualified Deferred Compensation, 1997, (with others) CCH Federal Tax Service, 1989; contbr. articles to profl. jours. Trustee U. Richmond, 1991-94; mem. Estate Planning Coun. Richmond, 1981—, U. Richmond Estate Planning Coun., 1984—; bd. dirs. Barksdale Theatre, 1994—, Va. Bapt. Homes, Inc., 1994—. Lt. col. USAR. Mem. ABA, Va. Bar Assn., Richmond Bar Assn., So. Pension Conf., Va. Assn. Professions (pres. 1980-81), Commonwealth Club, Willow Oaks Country Club. Baptist. Avocations: tennis, golf, scuba. Pension, profit-sharing, and employee benefits, Estate planning, General corporate. Office: Williams Mullen Christian & Dobbins 2 James Center PO Box 1320 Richmond VA 23218-1320

**MUSKIN, VICTOR PHILIP,** lawyer; b. N.Y.C., Mar. 1, 1942; s. Jacob Cecil and Fanya (Solomonoff) M.; m. Odette Cheryl Spreier, June 10, 1979; children: Adam James, Liana Jeanne. BA, Oberlin Coll., 1963; JD, NYU, 1966. Bar: N.Y. 1969, U.S. Dist. Ct. (so. and ea. dists.) N.Y. 1972, U.S. Ct. Appeals (2d cir.) 1974, U.S. Supreme Ct. 1974, U.S. Ct. Appeals (9th and 10th cirs.) 1978, U.S. Ct. Appeals (3d cir.) 1987. Asst. corp. counsel divsn. gen. litigation City of N.Y., 1969-73; assoc. Wolf, Popper, Ross, Wolf & Jones, N.Y.C., 1973-74, Reavis and McGrath, N.Y.C., 1974-78; pvt. practice N.Y.C., 1979; ptnr. Gruen & Muskin, N.Y.C., 1980-81, Gruen, Muskin & Thau, N.Y.C., 1981-89, Munves, Tanenhaus & Storch, N.Y.C., 1989-90, Solin & Brandiel, N.Y.C., 1991-92; pvt. practice N.Y.C., 1992—. Served with Peace Corps, 1966-68. Mem. N.Y.C. Bar Assn. (com. computer law 1982-84, com. internat. law 1996—). Federal civil litigation, State civil litigation, Private international. Home: 529 E 84th St New York NY 10028-7330 Office: 445 Park Ave Fl 14 New York NY 10022-2606

**MUSLEH, VICTOR JOSEPH, JR.,** lawyer; b. Ocala, Fla., May 2, 1968; s. Victor Joseph and Barbara Goolsby M.; m. Kelly Bowen Harkness, March 25, 1995; 1 child, Victor J. Musleh III. BA, U. Fla., 1990; JD, Stetson U., 1993. Bar: Fla. 1994, U.S. Dist. Ct. (mid. dist.) Fla. 1995. Lawyer Piccin & Musleh, Ocala, Fla., 1994—. Vol. Teen Court, Ocala, 1998, 99; lector Blessed Trinity Ch., Ocala, 1998, 99, parish coun., 1990-01. Mem. Am. Inns of Ct., Ocala Quarterback Club, Phi Kappa Phi. Avocations: hunting, fishing, running, kayaking. Personal injury, Workers' compensation, Insurance. Office: Piccin & Musleh PO Box 159 Ocala FL 34478-0159

**MUSSER, SANDRA G.,** retired lawyer; b. Hollywood, Calif., July 23, 1944; d. Donald Godfrey Gumpertz and Gloria G. (Rosenblatt) King; m. Michael R.V. Whitman, Feb. 19, 1980. BA, UCLA, 1965; JD, Hastings Coll. of Law, 1970. Bar: Calif. 1971, U.S. Dist. Ct. (no. dist.) Calif. 1971, U.S. Ct. Appeals (9th cir.) 1971. Clk. 9th Cir. Ct. of Appeals, 1971-72; lawyer pvt. practice of family law, 1972-86; ptnr. Musser & Ryan, San Francisco, 1986-97; pvt. practice San Francisco, 1997-98; ret., 1998; judge pro tem San Francisco County Superior Ct., 1988-98; dealer antique Chinese rugs and textiles, 1996—. Contbr. articles to profl. jours. Mem. adv. coun. Textile Mus., Washington, 1996—. Fellow Acad. Matrimonial Lawyers; mem. ABA (chair litig. sect. domestic rels. and family law com. 1993-94), State Bar Calif. (state bar family law sect. 1977—, chair 1982-83, advisor 1983-84), Bar Assn. San Francisco. Family and matrimonial. Office: 361 Oak St San Francisco CA 94102-5615

**MUSSER, WILLIAM WESLEY, JR.,** lawyer; b. Enid, Okla., July 17, 1918; s. William Wesley Sr. and Ethel Rice (McElroy) M.; m. Estelle Bee Wiedeman, Jan. 19, 1947; children: James William, Mary Bee Clark. BA, U. Okla., 1939, LLB, 1941. Bar: Okla. 1941. Ptnr. Elam, Crowley & Musser, Enid, 1946-47; probate judge Garfield County, Okla., 1949-51; ptnr. Otjen, Carter & Musser, Enid, 1952-54; asst. county atty. Garfield County, 1955-56; sole practice Enid, 1957—; chmn. bd. dirs. Tax Roll Corrections, Garfield County, 1950-51; 6th congrl. dist. rep. Okla. Jud. Nominating Com., Enid, 1967-74; judge Okla. Ct. Appeals, Enid, 1982. Pres. Great Salt Plains council Boy Scouts Am., 1955; gen. chmn. St. Mary's Hosp. Bldg. Fund, 1949; bd. dirs. Enid Community Chest, 1950-51, N.W. Okla. Pastoral Care Assn., 1978; v.p. Phillips U., Enid, 1955-74, mem. exec. com., 1955-78, trustee, 1978-82; bd. dirs. Enid Estate Planning Council, 1971-74, sec., 1972, pres., 1973-74. Served to maj. AUS, 1941-45, ETO. Decorated Bronze Star. Fellow Okla. Bar Found.; mem. ABA, Okla. Bar Assn. (v.p. bd. govs. 1957), Garfield County Bar Assn. (pres. 1962), Am. Judicature Soc., U. Okla. Alumni Assn. (exec. bd. 1959-61), Sons and Daus. of Cherokee Strip Pioneers Assn. (exec. bd. dirs. 1967-70), Greater Enid C. of C. (bd. dirs. 1969-71), VFW, Am. Legion, Phi Delta Phi, Alpha Tau Omega. Republican. Mem. Christian Ch. (Disciples of Christ). Clubs: Am. Bus. (pres. 1947), Oakwood Country (Enid). Probate, Real property, Estate taxation. Home: 1301 Indian Dr Enid OK 73703-7012 Office: Broadway Tower 3d Fl 114 E Broadway Ave Enid OK 73701-4126

**MUSSMAN, DAVID C.,** lawyer; b. Ohiowa, Nebr., Dec. 20, 1960; s. Kenneth L. and Nadine R. Mussman; m. Laura L. Burklund, Aug. 25, 1990; children: Ian Andrew, Ruby Olivia, Grace Emma. BA, U. Nebr., 1983, JD, 1990. Bar: Nebr., U.S. Dist. Ct. Nebr. Paramedic Ea. Ambulance, Lincoln, Nebr., 1980-83; sales mgr. Prudential Ins. Co., Omaha, 1984-87; lawyer Erickson & Sederstrom, P.C., Lincoln, 1990—; moot ct. judge U. Nebr. Coll. Law, Lincoln, 1990—. Mem. Nebr. State Bar Assn., Lincoln Bar Assn. Republican. Lutheran. Avocations: fly fishing, duck hunting. General civil litigation, Personal injury. Home: 1910 Devonshire Dr Lincoln NE 68506-1610 Office: Erickson & Sederstrom PC 301 S 13th St Ste 400 Lincoln NE 68508-2571

**MUSSMAN, WILLIAM EDWARD,** lawyer, oil company executive; b. Mpls., Feb. 10, 1919; s. William Edward and Vera Marie (Chamberlain) M.; m. Janet Jonn Skittone, Dec. 19, 1948; children: William Edward III, Ann C. BS in Law, U. Minn., 1941, JD, 1946. Bar: Minn. 1946, Calif. 1950, U.S. Supreme Ct. 1960. Asst. prof. law U. Minn., 1946-49; vis. prof. U. Calif., Berkeley, 1949; assoc. firm Pillsbury, Madison & Sutro, San Francisco, 1949-56; partner Pillsbury, Madison & Sutro, 1956-74; v.p., legal, dir. Standard Oil Co. of Calif., San Francisco, 1974-84; ptnr. Carr, Mussman & Harvey, San Francisco, 1984—. Served with USMCR, 1942-45. Decorated D.F.C. Fellow Southwestern Legal Found.; mem. ABA, Am. Arbitration Assn., Chevron Retirees Assn. (nat. pres. 1995-97). Antitrust, Federal civil litigation, State civil litigation. Office: Mussman and Mussman 1101 Sylvan Ave Modesto CA 95350-1607

**MUSSMAN, WILLIAM EDWARD, III,** lawyer; b. San Francisco, Jan. 31, 1951; s. William Edward and Janet Jonn (Skittone) M.; m. Carol Lynne Johnson, Jan. 9, 1988; children: Katherine Ann, Laura Lynne, Elizabeth Ashley; BS cum laude, Stanford U., 1973; JD, U. Calif.-San Francisco, 1976. Bar: Calif. 1976, U.S. Dist. Ct. (no. dist.) Calif. 1976, U.S. Dist. Ct. (cen. dist.) Calif. 1982, U.S. Dist. Ct. (ea. dist.) Calif. 1998, U.S. Supreme Ct., 1986, U.S. Ct. Appeals (9th cir.) 1987. Assoc. Lasky, Haas, Cohler & Munter, San Francisco, 1980-82, Pillsbury, Madison & Sutro, San Francisco, 1982-84; assoc. Carr & Mussman, San Francisco, 1984-91, ptnr., 1991-95; ptnr. Carr, Mussman & Harvey, LLP, San Francisco, 1996—. Missionary Ch. Jesus Christ Latter Day Sts., Tokyo, 1977-78. Contbr. articles to profl. jours. Mem. Calif. State Bar Assn. (litigation sect., law practice mgmt. sect.), San Francisco Bar Assn., Stanford Alumni Assn. (life), Tau Beta Pi. Antitrust, Alternative dispute resolution, General civil litigation. Office: Carr Mussman & Harvey 3 Embarcadero Ctr Ste 1060 San Francisco CA 94111-4056

**MUSTO, JOSEPH JOHN,** lawyer; b. Pittston, Pa., Nov. 22, 1943; s. James and Rose (Frushon) M.; m. Fortunata Giudice, July 5, 1969; children: Laura, Joseph Robert. BA, King's Coll., Wilkes-Barre, Pa., 1965; JD, Dickinson Sch. Law, Carlisle, Pa., 1968. Bar: Pa. 1968, U.S. Ct. Appeals (3d cir.) 1968, U.S. Dist. Ct. (mid. dist.) Pa. 1971. Asst. dist. atty. City of Phila., 1968-69; assoc. Bedford, Waller, Griffith, Darling & Mitchell, Wilkes-Barre, 1969-73; ptnr. Griffith, Darling, Mitchell, Aponick & Musto, Wilkes-Barre, 1973-75; prin. Griffith, Aponick & Musto, Wilkes-Barre, 1975-90; ptnr. Rosenn, Jenkins & Greenwald, Wilkes-Barre, 1990-93; judge Ct. Common Pleas of Luzerne County, 1993-94; mem. Hourigan, Kluger, Spohrer & Quinn, Wilkes-Barre, Pa., 1994-97; prin. Musto & Saunders, PC, Plymouth, Pa., 1997—; solicitor Yatesville (Pa.) Borough, 1973-80, Duryea (Pa.) Borough, 1975-80, Pittston Area Sch. Dist., 1973-93. Mem. Luzerne County Gov. Study Com., Wilkes-Barre, 1973-74; mem., chmn. No. Luzerne Health Adv. Coun., Wilkes-Barre, 1976-80; pres., mem. Health Sys. Agy. of N.E. Pa., Avoca, 1980-86; pres. Pa. Health Planning Assn., Harrisburg, 1985-86; mem. civil justice reform act adv. com. Fed. Dist. Ct. Pa. Ct., 1991-95. Mem. Fed. Bar Assn. (past pres. Ctrl. Pa. chpt.), Pa. Bar Assn., Wilkes-Barre Law and Libr. Assn. Democrat. Roman Catholic. Health, Alternative dispute resolution. Home: 7 Prospect Pl Pittston PA 18640-2627 Office: Musto & Saunders 117 W Main St Plymouth PA 18651-2926

**MUTTERPERL, WILLIAM CHARLES,** lawyer; b. N.Y.C., July 15, 1946; s. Martin and Muriel (Wurtzel) M.; m. Nancy Fay Borson, July 2, 1968; children: Matthew, Adam. BA, Dartmouth Coll., 1968; JD, Columbia U., N.Y.C., 1971. Bar: N.Y. 1972, R.I. 1978, U.S. Dist. Ct. (so. and ea. dists.) N.Y. 1973, U.S. Dist. Ct. R.I. 1979. Assoc. atty. Cleary, Gottleib, Steen and Hamilton, N.Y.C., 1971-77; asst. gen. counsel Fleet Nat. Bank, Providence, 1977-79, gen. counsel, 1979-85; v.p., gen. counsel, sec. Fleet Fin. Group, Inc. (now Fleet/Norstar Fin. Group, Inc.), Providence, 1985-89, sr. v.p., gen. counsel, sec., 1989—. Mem. Phi Beta Kappa. Democrat. Jewish. Office: Fleet/Norstar Fin Group Inc 1 Federal St Boston MA 02110-2012

**MYERS, ALAN C.,** lawyer; b. Bklyn., 1951. BA magna cum laude, Dickinson Coll., 1972; JD cum laude, U. Pa., 1975. From assoc. to ptnr. Skadden, Arps, Slate, Meagher & Flom LLP, N.Y.C. Mem. Phi Beta Kappa. Office: Skadden, Arps, Slate, Meagher & Flom LLP 919 3rd Ave New York NY 10022-3902

**MYERS, ANDREW S.,** lawyer; b. N.Y.C., Oct. 13, 1952; m. Robin S. Merrill, June 27, 1978; 1 child, Alan Stewart Harry. BA in Polit. Sci., San Diego State U., 1976; MPH, UCLA, 1978; JD, Washburn U., 1988. Bar: Nev. 1988, Colo. 1989, Kans. 1989, U.S. Dist. Ct. Kans. 1989, U.S. Dist. Ct. Nev. 1989, U.S. Supreme Ct. 1995. Hosp. adminstr. various hosps., Calif., 1978-85; jud. clk. Hon. Michael Wendell, Las Vegas, Nev., 1988-89, Hon. Joseph Pavlikowski, Las Vegas, 1989-90; dep. pub. defender Clark County Pub. Defender, Las Vegas, 1991; law ptnr. Bell, Davidson & Myers, Las Vegas, 1992-94, Davidson & Myers, Las Vegas, 1994—; mem. State Bar So. Nev. Disciplinary Com., 1993—, State Bar Fee Dispute Com., 1994—; hearing master for civil commitments 8th Jud. Dist. Ct., 1993-95, URESA hearing master, 1994—. Fund raiser Stewart Bell for Dist. Atty., Las Vegas, 1994. Mem. ABA, ATLA, Nat. Assn. Criminal Def. Lawyers, Clark County Bar Assn., Am. Coll. Legal Medicine, Nat. Health Lawyers Assn. Avocation: travel. Criminal, Family and matrimonial, Health. Office: Davidson & Myers 601 Bridger Ave Las Vegas NV 89101-5805

**MYERS, DANE JACOB,** lawyer, podiatrist; b. Murray, Utah, June 20, 1948; s. Lorin LaVar Myers and Irma Lee (Bell) Willette; m. Mary Jo Jackson, June 22, 1970; children: Troy, Chad, Melissa, Apryll, Tristan, Remington. DPM, Pa. Coll. Podiatric Medicine, 1977; BA, U. Utah, 1983; JD, U. Ark., 1986. Bar: Ark. 1986. Pres. Tooele (Utah) Foot Clinic, 1977-83; owner N.W. Ark. Foot Clinic, Rogers, Ark., 1983—; pvt. practice law Fayetteville, 1986-97. Mem. ABA, APHA, Am. Coll. Foot and Ankle Surgeons (assoc.), Am. Diabetes Assn., Ark. Bar Assn., Am. Soc. Law and Medicine, Am. Podiatric Med. Assn., Ark. Podiatric Med. Assn., Delta Theta Phi. Republican. Mormon. Avocations: golf, computers, history. Health. Home: 106 Woodcliff Rd Springdale AR 72764-3691 Office: NW Ark Foot Clinic 700 N 13th St Rogers AR 72756-3436

**MYERS, FRANKLIN,** lawyer, oil service company executive; b. Pensacola, Fla., Nov. 2, 1952; s. T.F. Sr. and D. Bernice (Brewer) M.; children: Amanda C., Adam F., Anne Marie M. BS, Miss. State U., 1974; JD, U. Miss., 1977. Bar: Miss. 1977, Tex. 1978. Ptnr. Fulbright and Jaworski, Houston, 1978-88; sr. v.p., gen. counsel Baker Hughes Inc., Houston, 1988-95; sr. v.p., gen. counsel, corp. sec. Cooper Cameron Corp., Houston, 1995-99; sr. v.p., divsn. pres. Cooper Cameron Corp. (now Cooper Energy Svcs.), Houston, 1998—; adj. prof. U. Tex. Sch. Law, 1990—; bd. dirs. Reunion Industries, Inc., Metals, Inc.; bd. dirs., sec. Tex. Bus. Law Found. Bd. dirs., sec. Tex. Bus. Law Found. Fellow Houston Bar Found., Tex. Bar Assn., Miss. Bar Assn., Houston Bar Assn. Baptist. Securities, Mergers and acquisitions, General corporate. Office: Cooper Cameron Corp 13013 Northwest Fwy PO Box 1212 Houston TX 77251-1212

**MYERS, HARDY,** state attorney general, lawyer; b. Electric Mills, Miss., Oct. 25, 1939; m. Mary Ann Thalhofer, 1962; children: Hardy III, Christopher, Jonathan. AB with distinction, U. Miss., 1961; LLB, U. Oreg., 1964. Bar: Oreg., U.S. Ct. of Appeals (9th cir.), U.S. Dist. Ct. Law clerk U.S. Dist. Judge William G. East, 1964-65; pvt. practice Stoel Rives LLP, 1965-96; atty. gen. State of Oregon, 1997—; mem. Oreg. Ho. of Reps., 1975-85, speaker of the ho., 1979-83. Pres. Portland City Planning Commn., 1973-74; chair Oreg. Jail Project, 1984-86, Citizens' Task Force on Mass Transit Policy, 1985-86, Oreg. Criminal Justice Coun., 1987-91, Portland Future Focus, 1990-91, Metro Charter com., 1991-92, task force on state employee benefits, 1994; co-chair gov. task force on state employee compensation, 1995. Office: Oreg Atty Gen Justice Dept 1162 Court St NE Salem OR 97310-1320

**MYERS, JAMES R.,** lawyer; b. Valdosta, Ga., Aug. 29, 1952; s. J. Walter Jr. and Mary (Gallion) M.; m. Monica Faeth Myers, Sept. 19, 1992. BA cum laude, Harvard U., 1972, JD, 1975. Bar: Mass. 1975, U.S. Dist. Ct. (D.C. dist.) 1976, D.C. 1977, U.S. Ct. Appeals (D.C. cir.) 1977, U.S. Supreme Ct. 1983, U.S. Ct. Appeals (fed. cir.) 1991, Va. 1992, U.S. Ct. Appeals (4th cir.) 1992. Assoc. Wald, Harkrader & Ross, Washington, 1976-77; assoc. solicitor U.S. Dept. Energy, Washington, 1977-79; assoc. Andrews & Kurth, Washington, 1980-85; ptnr. Steele, Simmons & Fornaciari, Washington, 1985-86, Robbins & Laramie, Washington, 1986-89, Venable, Baetjer, Howard & Civiletti, Washington, 1990-97, Kilpatrick Stockton LLP, 1997—. Author Jour. Space Law, 1984, Space Mfg., 1983. Federal civil litigation, Patent, Trademark and copyright. Office: Kilpatrick Stockton LLP 700 13th St NW Ste 800 Washington DC 20005-3960

**MYERS, JAMES WOODROW, III,** lawyer; b. Gary, Ind., Aug. 3, 1954; s. James Woodrow Jr. and Martha G. (Ladd) M.; m. Barbara Anne Johnson, Aug. 15, 1980; 1 child, James Woodrow IV. BA, Valparaiso U., 1976, JD, 1979. Bar: U.S. Dist. Ct. (so. and no. dists.) Ind. 1979, Ind. 1980, Ill. 1983, U.S. Dist. Ct. (no. dist.) Ill., U.S. Ct. Appeals (7th cir.) Ill. 1988. Assoc. Law Offices of J. Diaz P.C., Portage, Ind., 1979-83, Leonard M. Ring & Assocs., Chgo., 1983-87; sole practice Crown Point, Ind., 1987-90; assoc. Sweeney, Pfeifer and Blackburn, South Bend, Ind., 1990—. Mem. ABA, Ind. Bar Assn., Ill. Bar Assn., Mich. Bar Assn., Chgo. Bar Assn., Assn. Trial Lawyers Am., Ill. Trial Lawyers Assn., Ind. Trial Lawyers Assn., Mich. Trial Lawyers Assn., Lake County Bar Assn. Federal civil litigation, State civil litigation, Personal injury. Home: 4004 Oak Grove Dr Valparaiso IN 46383-2095 Office: Sweeney Pfeifer & Blackburn 53600 Ironwood Rd South Bend IN 46635-1503

**MYERS, KENNETH RAYMOND,** lawyer; b. N.Y.C., Apr. 14, 1939; s. Cyril Burleigh and Dorothy (Podolyn) M.; m. Susan Kay Plotnick, Sept. 9, 1962; children: Lisa R., Jonathan S., Andrew C. SB, MIT, 1960; JD, Harvard U., 1963. Bar: Ill. 1963, Pa. 1968. Assoc. Ross, Hardies & O'Keefe, Chgo., 1963-68; assoc. Morgan, Lewis & Bockius, Phila., 1968-71, ptnr., 1972—; mem. rules com. Environ. Hearing Bd., Harrisburg, Pa., 1984-89. Editor: Environmental Spill Reporting Handbook, 1992—; contbg. author: Environmental Law Practice Guide, 1992—; contbr. articles to profl. jours. Dir. Water Resources Assn. Del. River Basin, Valley Forge, Pa., 1975—, Albert Einstein Healthcare Network, 1997—, Germantown Hosp., 1998—; pres. Am. Jewish Congress, Phila., 1996—, mem. nat. commn., N.Y.C., 1984—. Mem. ABA (rep. to U.S. Office Personnel Mgmt. 1975—), Pa. Bar Assn., Phila. Bar Assn., Eta Kappa Nu. Environmental, Public utilities, Administrative and regulatory. Office: Morgan Lewis & Bockius 2000 One Logan Sq Philadelphia PA 19103-6993

**MYERS, PHILIP HAROLD,** lawyer, petroleum exploration company executive; b. Norfolk, Va., Mar. 28, 1942; s. Joseph Issac and Lee (Adler) M.; children: Laura Beth Kanter, Joseph William. BBA, Old Dominion U., 1964; JD, U. Richmond, Va., 1967. Bar: Va. 1967, U.S. Ct. Appeals Va., U.S. Dist.Ct. (ea. dist.) Va. Atty. Philip H. Myers Atty., Norfolk, Va., 1967—; sr. mng. mem. Myers, Myers, Attys., Norfolk, 1997—. Mem. Va. State Bar, Norfolk Portsmouth Bar Assn., Virginia Beach Bar Assn., Phi Alpha Delta. Avocations: skiing, big game fishing, golf. Office: Myers Myers and Myers 2476 E Little Creek Rd Norfolk VA 23518-3231

**MYERS, RICHARD P.,** state legislator. Ill. state rep. Dist. 95, 1995—. Office: PO Box 170 Macomb IL 61455-0170

**MYERS, RODMAN NATHANIEL,** lawyer; b. Detroit, Oct. 27, 1920; s. Isaac Rodman and Fredericka (Hirschman) M.; m. Jeanette Polisei, Mar. 19,

1957 (dec. 1996); children: Jennifer Sue, Rodman Jay. BA, Wayne State U., 1941; LLB, U. Mich., 1943. Bar: Mich. 1943, U.s. Supreme Ct. 1962. Agt. IRS, Detroit, 1943; from assoc. to ptnr. Butzel, Keidan, Simon, Myers & Graham, Detroit, 1943-90; of counsel Honigman Miller Schwartz and Cohn, Detroit, 1991—. Bd. dirs. United Cmty. Svcs. of Met. Detroit, 1978-85, v.p., 1981-85, chmn. social svcs. divsn., 1982-85; bd. dirs. Children's Ctr. of Wayne County (Mich.), 1963—, pres., 1969-72; mem. blue ribbon task force Mich. Dept. Edn., 1988-89; founding mem., trustee Detroit Sci. Ctr.; trustee Mich. chpt. Leukemia Soc. Am., founding pres., 1984-86, nat. trustee, 1984—; commr. Detroit Mcpl. Parking Authority, 1963-71; trustee Temple Beth El, Bloomfield Hills, Mich., Bloomfield Twp. Pub. Libr. Mem. ABA, State Bar Mich. (chmn. atty. discipline panel, past vice chmn. unauthorized practice of law com., past mem. character and fitness com.), Detroit Bar Assn. General corporate. Home: 3833 Lakeland Ln Bloomfield Hills MI 48302-1328 Office: 2290 1st National Bldg Detroit MI 48226

**MYERS, RONALD LYNN,** lawyer; b. Houston, Jan. 18, 1949; s. E. Carlton and Elizabeth Anne (Boyette) M.; m. Nancy G. Finney, May 20, 1972. B.S. in History, Kans. State U., 1971; J.D., U. Kans., 1974. Bar: Mo. 1974, U.S. Dist. Ct. (we. dist.) Mo. 1974, U.S. Ct. Appeals (8th cir.) 1977, U.S. Supreme Ct. 1978. Assoc. Strop, Watkins et al, St. Joseph, Mo., 1974-76; ptnr. Daniel, Clampett et al, Springfield, Mo., 1976-84; sole practice, Springfield, 1984—. Author: Exemplifying Punitive Damages, 1976. Mem. com. counsel Springfest '84, Springfield, 1984; dir., counsel Agape House Springfield, 1984. Mem. ABA, Mo. Bar Assn., Greene County Bar Assn., Springfield Claims Assn. (pres. 1984-85, bd. dirs. 1980-85), Assn. Trial Lawyers Am. Republican. Methodist. Personal injury, Insurance, Federal civil litigation. Home: 920 E Northfield Rd Springfield MO 65803-9229 Office: 1909 E Bennett St Springfield MO 65804-1419

**MYERS, ROSS S,** lawyer; b. Dubuque, Iowa, 1954; s. Waldo and Elizabeth M.; m. Honour Myers, 1993. BA, William Jewell Coll, 1976; JD, U Mo., 1984. Bar: Mo. 1984, Kans. 1988; cert. charter and property casualty Am. Inst. CPCU, 1998, assoc. risk mgmt. Ins. Inst. Am., 1998. Asst. prosecutor Kansas City, Mo., 1984-87; asst. county counselor Jackson County, Mo., 1984-87; trial atty. Am. Family Ins., St. Louis, 1987-90; shareholder Blevins Pietz & Myers, Independence, Md., 1990-94; claims atty. Federated RE Ins., Lenexa, Kans., 1994—. Contbr. articles to profl. jours. Lt.-sr. grade U.S. Navy, 1976-81. Mem. Mo. Bar (ins. law com. 1988), Kans. Bar, CPCU Soc., Md. Org. Def. Lawyers. Insurance, General civil litigation. Office: 11875 W 85th St Lenexa KS 66214-1519

**MYERS, STEPHEN HAWLEY,** lawyer; b. Washington, Mar. 28, 1953; s. Robert Holt and Antoinette (Hawley) M.; children: Stephen, Hampton, Brielle; m. Laura Lee Fuller, Dec. 1, 1989. BA in Polit. Sci. with honors, Union Coll., 1976; JD, Loyola U., 1979. Bar: D.C. 1979, La. 1979, U.S. Dist. Ct. D.C. 1980, U.S. Tax Ct. 1980, U.S. Ct. Claims 1980, U.S. Ct. Appeals (fed. and D.C. cirs.) 1980, U.S. Ct. Appeals (5th cir.) 1985, U.S. Dist. Ct. (we., mid. and ea. dists.) La. 1985, U.S. Supreme Ct. 1989. Atty. advisor to hon. judge Edward S. Smith U.S. Ct. Appeals (Fed. cir.), Washington, 1979-80; assoc. Duncan Allen & Mitchell, Washington, 1980-82; atty. advisor to Judge Jules G. Körner U.S. Tax Ct., Washington, 1982-84; assoc. Davidson Meaux Sonnier & McElligott, Lafayette, La., 1984-85; ptnr. Roy Forrest, Lopresto, DeCourt & Myers and predecessor firms, Lafayette, 1985-97; pvt. practice Stephen Hawley Myers, LLC, Lafayette, La., 1997—; lectr. for continuing legal edn. seminars on corp., sales tax and personal injury litigation. Vice chmn., bd. dirs. La. Coun. for Fiscal Reform, New Orleans, 1986-96; bd. dirs., treas. Acadiana Youth, Inc., Lafayette, 1986-94. Mem. ABA, Am. Platform Assn., Lafayette Bar Assn., La. Counsel Def. Attys., La. Trial Lawyer's Assn., Phi Delta Phi. Avocations: writing, photography, skeet shooting, sports clay shooting, hunting. General civil litigation, Contracts commercial, Taxation, general. Home: 100 Old Settlement Rd Lafayette LA 70508-7030 Office: 600 Jefferson St Ste 401 Lafayette LA 70501-8919 also: 15 W Lenox St Chevy Chase MD 20815-4208

**MYERSON, TOBY SALTER,** lawyer; b. Chgo., July 20, 1949; s. Raymond King and Natalie Anita (Salter) M. BA, Yale U., 1971; JD, Harvard U., 1975. Bar: N.Y. 1977, Calif. 1977. Assoc. Coudert Bros., N.Y.C., 1975-77, 81, San Francisco, 1977-81; assoc. Paul, Weiss, Rifkind, Wharton & Garrison, N.Y.C., 1981-83, ptnr., 1983-89; mng. dir. Wasserstein Perella & Co., Inc., N.Y.C., 1989-90; ptnr. Paul, Weiss, Rifkind, Wharton & Garrison, N.Y.C., 1990—; lectr. U. Calif. Berkeley, 1979-81, Harvard U., Cambridge, Mass., 1982-83; visiting lectr. Yale U., New Haven, 1983-84; bd. dirs. Myerson, Van Den Berg & Co., Santa Barbara, Calif. Contbg. editor: Doing Business in Japan, 1983, Council on Foreign Rels., 1993—, Foreign Policy Assn., 1995—. Sec. Japan Soc., Inc., N.Y.C., 1985-89; bd. dirs. 1056 Fifth Ave. Corp., N.Y.C., 1985-88; mem. univ. resources com. Harvard U., 1997—. Mem. ABA (subcom. internat. banking, corp. and bus. law sect.), Internat. Bar Assn., N.Y. State Bar Assn., Assn. Bar City N.Y. (com. on fgn. and comparative law, chmn. 1988-89), Calif. Bar Assn. Avocations: art, music, literature, tennis, golf. General corporate, Mergers and acquisitions, Banking. Home: 1056 5th Ave New York NY 10028-0112 Office: Paul Weiss Rifkind Wharton & Garrison 1285 Ave of the Americas New York NY 10019-6065

**MYERS-WILKINS, CRYSTAL ANN,** lawyer; b. Nov. 14, 1960; d. George Myers and Helen Zachery; m. Riley Wilkins, Aug. 29, 1987; children: Natasha, Brianna. JD, Ind. U., Indpls., 1992. Asst. counsel Ill. EPA, Springfield, 1997—. Mem. ABA, Chgo. Bar Assn. Avocations: bowling, jogging. Home: 2312 Lombard Ave Springfield IL 62704-4253 Office: Ill EPA 1021 N Grand Ave E Springfield IL 62702-4059

**MYHAND, WANDA RESHEL,** paralegal, legal assistant; b. Detroit, Aug. 15, 1963; d. Ralph and Geraldine (Leavell) M. Office mgr./adminstrv. asst. Gregory Terrell & Co., CPA, Detroit, 1987-90; legal sec. Ford Motor Co., Detroit, 1990-91; office mgr. M.G. Christian Builders, Inc., Detroit, 1991; paralegal, legal asst. Law Office of Karri Mitchell, Detroit, 1991-98; legal sec., paralegal KPM Group, Southfield, Mich., 1998—. Vol. UNCF Telethon Detroit, 1988. Mem. NAFE. Avocations: crossword puzzles, travel, theatre/concerts.

**MYHRE, DEANNA SHIRLEY,** lawyer, litigator, mediator; b. Atascadero, Calif., Oct. 11, 1938; d. William George and Shirley Corinne Moore; m. Ronald William Myhre, July 13, 1957; children: Janell, Cari Myhre Moyles, Cathi. Grad., Heald Bus. Coll., San Francisco, 1957; JD, Lincoln U., Sacramento, 1982. Cert. family law specialist. Lawyer, owner Law Offices of Deanna S. Myhre, Vacaville, Calif., 1983—; judge pro tem Solano County Superior Ct., Fairfield, Calif., 1989—. Trustee Vacaville Mus., Vacaville Community Found., 1990—; co-founder pro tem duty judge Program for Emergency Protection Orders. Recipient Outstanding Bar Pres. award Solano County Superior Ct. Judges, 1989, Solano County Legal Assistance Pro Bono Svcs. award, 1990. Mem. ABA, Calif. State Bar Assn., Solano County Bar Assn. (past pres.), Lawyer-Pilots Bar Assn., Calif. Women Lawyers Inc. (past gov.), Solano County Women Lawyers Inc. (past pres.), Vacaville C. of C. (bd. dirs. 1986-92), Vacaville Rotary (dir., 1988), Internat. Fellowship of Flying Rotarians. Republican. Family and matrimonial, Juvenile. Office: 600 E Main St Ste F Vacaville CA 95688-3933

**MYRE, DONALD PAUL,** lawyer; b. Grand Rapids, Mich., Feb. 29, 1960; s. Donald Francis and Dorothy Pearl Myre; m. Cathy Ann Johnson, Aug. 4, 1984 (dec. Oct. 1995); children: Allison E., Zachary B. Student, St. Peters Coll., Oxford, Eng., 1981; BA in Bus. and History, William Jewell Coll., 1982; JD, U. Mo., Kansas City, 1985. Bar: Mo. 1985, U.S. Dist. Ct. (ea. dist.) Mo. 1986. Assoc. Anderson & Gilbert, St. Louis, 1985-93, ptnr., 1994—. Trustee Manchester (Mo.) Bapt. Ch., 1986-91; basketball coach Rockwood Sch. Dist., Chesterfield, Mo., 1997-98. Mem. Mo. Bar Assn., Mo. Orgn. Def. Lawyers, Lawyer's Assn. St. Louis. Baptist. Avocations: softball, volleyball, Tae Kwon Do, Bible study leader, Awana Kids Club director. Personal injury, Insurance, General civil litigation. Office: Anderson & Gilbert 200 S Hanley Rd Ste 710 Saint Louis MO 63105-3415

**MYTELKA, ARNOLD KRIEGER,** lawyer; b. Jersey City, July 24, 1937; s. Herman Donald and Jeannette (Krieger) M.; m. Rosalind Marcia Kaplan, Dec. 17, 1961; children: Andrew Charles, Daniel Sommer. AB, Princeton U., 1958; LLB cum laude, Harvard U., 1961; postgrad., London Sch. Econs., 1961-62. Bar: N.J. 1961, U.S. Dist. Ct. N.J. 1963, U.S. Supreme Ct. 1970, U.S. Ct. Appeals (3d cir.) 1978, U.S. Dist. Ct. (so. and ea. dist.) N.Y. 1983. Law sec. Chief Justice N.J. Supreme Ct., Newark, 1962-63; assoc. Clapp & Eisenberg, Newark, 1963-68, ptnr., 1968-94; prin. Kraemer, Burns, Mytelka, Lovell & Kulka, Springfield, N.J., 1994—; lectr. Rutgers Law Sch., Newark, 1973; mem. Am. Law Inst., Phila., 1989—; mem. cons. group The Law Governing Lawyers, 1990—; founding trustee Newark Legal Svcs. Project, 1965-68; trustee Edn. Law Ctr., 1974-75; chmn. dist. V ethics com. Supreme Ct. N.J., 1981-84, mem. 1981-84; trustee Legal Svcs. Found. Essex County, 1982—, pres., 1990-92. Mem. editorial bd. N.J. Law Jour., 1991—; contbr. legal articles to profl. jours. Chmn. bd. trustees Ramapo Coll. N.J., 1979-80, mem. 1975-80; mediator chancery divsn. The N.J. Superior Ct., 1990—. Frank Knox Meml. fellow Harvard U., London Sch. Econs. and Polit. Sci., 1961-62. Mem. ABA (mem. litigation sect.), N.J. State Bar Assn. (chmn. appellate practices study com. 1977-79, chmn. land use sect. 1984-85). General civil litigation, Land use and zoning (including planning), Administrative and regulatory. Home: 56 Hall Rd Chatham NJ 07928-1723 Office: Kraemer Burns Mytelka Lovell & Kulka 675 Morris Ave Springfield NJ 07081-1523

**NACE, BARRY JOHN,** lawyer; b. York, Pa., Nov. 28, 1944; s. John Harrison and Mildred Louise (Orwig) N.; m. Andrea Marcia Giardini. Apr. 28, 1973; children: Christopher Thomas, Jonathan Barry, Matthew Andrew. BS, Dickinson Coll., 1965, JD, 1969, DL, 1994. Bar: Md. 1970, D.C. 1971, Pa. 1972, W.Va. 1997, U.S. Ct. Appeals (3d, 4th and D.C. cirs.), U.S. Supreme Ct. Ptnr. Davis & Nace, Washington, 1972-78, Paulson & Nace, Bethesda, Md., 1978-85, 98—; sr. ptnr. Paulson, Nace & Norwind, Washington, 1986-97. Fellow Roscoe Pound Found. (trustee); mem. Nat. Bd. Trial Advocacy in Civil Litigation, D.C. Bar Assn., Montgomery County Bar Assn., Assn. Trial Lawyers Am. (gov. 1976-87, pres. 1993-94), Met. D.C. Trial Attys. (pres. 1977-78, 87-88, Atty. of Yr. 1976), Trial Lawyers for Pub. Justice, Internat. Acad. Trial Lawyers, Lambert Soc., Am. Inns of Ct., Am. Law Inst. Am. Bd. of Profl. Liability Attorneys. Avocations: golf, tennis, reading, racquetball. E-mail: BJN@LAWTORT.COM. Personal injury, State civil litigation, Federal civil litigation. Home: 6208 Garnett Dr Bethesda MD 20815-6618 Office: Paulson & Nace 1814 N St NW Washington DC 20036-2404

**NACHMAN, ERWIN B(EHR),** lawyer; b. Newport News, Va., Nov. 22, 1934; s. Max E. and Sadye (Bodner) N.; 1 child, Elizabeth S. BS in Commerce, U. Va., 1956, LLB, 1960. Bar: Va. 1960, U.S. Dist. Ct. (ea. dist.) Va. 1961, U.S. Ct. Appeals (4th cir.) 1966, U.S. Supreme Ct. 1966, U.S. Claims Ct. 1966, U.S. Ct. Mil. Appeals 1966. Assoc. Fine, Fine, Legum & Fine, Norfolk, Va., 1961-67; atty. sole practice Erwin B. Nachman, Newport News, 1967-75, 88—; ptnr. Frank, Nachman & Frank, Newport News, 1975-79, Frank, Poinsett, Nachman & Frank, Newport News, 1979-88; trustee in bankruptcy U.S. Bankruptcy Ct., Newport News, 1974—; commr. in chancery Newport News Cir. Ct., 1989-98, asst. commr. accounts, 1993-98, chief commr. accounts, 1998—. Chmn. Newport News Cable TV Adv. Com., 1990-92. 1st lt. U.S. Army Res., 1964-67. Mem. Nat. Assn. Bankruptcy Trustees, Va. Bar Assn., Newport News Bar Assn., Tidewater Bankruptcy Bar Assn. (treas. 1998-99, sec. 1999—), Phi Delta Phi (treas. 1959-60). Fax: 757-873-3028. E-mail: erwin.nachman@gte.net. Bankruptcy, Family and matrimonial, Probate. Office: Erwin B Nachman Atty 708 Thimble Shoals Blvd Ste C Newport News VA 23606-4547

**NACHMAN, NORMAN HARRY,** lawyer; b. Chgo.; s. Harry and Mary (Leibowitz) N.; m. Anne Lev, June 19, 1932; children: Nancy Nachman Laskow, James Lev, Susan Lev. PhB, U. Chgo., 1930, JD, 1932. Bar: Ill. 1932, U.S. Dist. Ct. (no. dist.) Ill. 1932, U.S. Dist. Ct. (we. dist.) Tex. 1978, U.S. Ct. Appeals (7th cir.) 1942, U.S. Ct. Appeals (4th cir.) 1978, U.S. Ct. Appeals (8th cir.) 1994, U.S. Supreme Ct. 1942. Assoc. Michael Gesas, Chgo., 1932-35; assoc. Schwartz & Cooper, Chgo., 1936-40, ptnr., 1940-46; pvt. practice, Chgo., 1947-67; founder, sr. ptnr. Nachman, Munitz & Sweig, Ltd., Chgo., 1967-87; ptnr. Winston & Strawn, 1987-94; counsel McDermott, Will & Emery, 1994—; mem. adv. com. bankruptcy rules Jud. Conf. U.S., 1960-76, 78-88; mem. Nat. Bankruptcy Conf., 1952—, mem. com. bankruptcy reorganization plans and securities problems, 1977-85; mem. faculty numerous bankruptcy seminars throughout U.S. Contbg. editor: Collier on Bankruptcy, 1981, 84. Chmn. appeals bd. Chgo. Dept. Environ. Control, 1960-80. Served to lt. USN, 1943-46. Mem. ABA (past chmn. comml. bankruptcy com.), Chgo. Bar Assn. (pres. 1963-64), Ill. Bar Assn., Standard Club, Law Club. Jewish. Bankruptcy, Contracts commercial, General corporate. Office: McDermott Will & Emery 227 W Monroe St Ste 3100 Chicago IL 60606-5096

**NACHTIGAL, PATRICIA,** lawyer, equipment manufacturing company executive; b. 1946. BA, Montclair State U.; JD, Rutgers U.; LLM, NYU. Tax atty. Ingersoll-Rand Co., Woodcliff Lake, N.J., 1979-83, dir. taxes and legal, 1983-88, sec., mng. atty., 1988-91, v.p., gen. counsel, 1991—. General corporate. Office: Ingersoll-Rand Co 200 Chestnut Ridge Rd Woodcliff Lake NJ 07675-7700

**NACHWALTER, MICHAEL,** lawyer; b. N.Y.C., Aug. 31, 1940; s. Samuel J. Nachwalter; m. Irene, Aug. 15, 1965; children: Helynn, Robert. BS, Bucknell U., 1962; MS, L.I. U., 1967; JD cum laude, U. Miami, 1967; LLM, Yale U., 1968. Bar: Fla. 1967, D.C. 1979, U.S. Dist. Ct. (so. dist.) Fla. 1967, U.S. Dist. Ct. (mid. dist.) Fla. 1982, U.S. Ct. Appeals (5th and 11th cirs.) 1967, U.S. Supreme Ct. 1975. Law clk. to judge U.S. Dist. Ct. (so. dist.) Fla.; shareholder Kelly, Black, Black & Kenny; now shareholder Kenny Nachwalter Seymour Arnold Critchlow & Spector, P.A., Miami; lectr. Law Sch. U. Miami. Fellow Am. Coll. Trial Lawyers (vice-chair); vice-chair. Jud. Qualifica tions Commn.; mem. ABA, FBA, Am. Bd. Trial Advs., Fla. Bar Assn. (bd. govs. 1982-90), dir. Internat. Soc. Barristers, Dade County Bar Assn., Iron Arrow, Soc. Wig and Robe, Omicron Delta Kappa, Phi Kappa Phi, Phi Delta Phi. Editor-in-chief U. Miami Law Rev., 1966-67. Antitrust, Federal civil litigation, State civil litigation. Office: Kenny Nachwalter Seymour Arnold Critchlow & Spector PA 201 S Biscayne Blvd Ste 1100 Miami FL 33131-4327

**NACLERIO, GREGORY J.,** lawyer; b. Bronx; s. Joseph Salvatore and Gloria Theressa N.; m. Charleen, Dec. 21, 1968; 1 child, Barbara. BS in Mgmt., St. John's U., 1968, JD, 1971. Bar: U.S. Dist. Ct. (so. and ea. dists.) N.Y. 1972. Bur. chief Nassau Legal Aide Soc., Mineola, N.Y., 1971-76; regional dir. N.Y. State Atty. Gen. for Medicaid Fraud, Hauppauge, 1976-88; of counsel Ruskin, Moscou, Evans & Faltischek, P.C., Mineola, 1988-91, ptnr., 1991—; chair lectures Cert. Fraud Examiners, 1998—. Contbr. articles to profl. jours. Bd. govs. St. Charles Hosp., 1996—. Mem. N.Y. State Bar Assn., Health Care Fin. Mgmt. Assn. Avocation: golf. Health, Criminal. Office: Ruskin Moscow Evans & Faltischek PC 170 Old Country Rd Mineola NY 11501-4307

**NACOL, MAE,** lawyer; b. Beaumont, Tex., June 15, 1944; d. William Samuel and Ethel (Bowman) N.; children: Shawn Alexander Nacol, Catherine Regina Nacol. BA, Rice U., 1965; postgrad., South Tex. Coll. Law, 1966-68. Bar: Tex. 1969, U.S. Dist. Ct. (so. dist.) Tex. 1969. Diamond buyer/appraiser Nacol's Jewelry, Houston, 1961—; pvt. practice law Houston, 1969—. Author, editor ednl. materials on multiple sclerosis, 1981-85. Nat. dir. A.R.M.S. of Am. Ltd., Houston, 1984-85. Recipient Mayor's Recognition award City of Houston, 1972; Ford Found. fellow So. Tex. Coll. Law, Houston, 1964. Mem. Houston Bar Assn. (chmn. candidate com. 1970, chmn. membership com. 1971, chmn. lawyers referral com. 1972), Assn. Trial Lawyers Am., Tex. Trial Lawyers Assn., Am. Judicature Soc. (sustaining), Houston Fin. Coun. Women, Houston Trial Lawyers Assn. Presbyterian. Personal injury, General corporate, Admiralty. Office: 600 Jefferson St Ste 750 Houston TX 77002-7326

**NADEAU, ROBERT BERTRAND, JR.,** lawyer; b. Miami Beach, Fla., July 15, 1950; s. Robert B. and Ernestine Inez (Nicholson) N. BBA, U. Notre Dame, 1972; JD, U. Fla., 1975. Bar: Fla. 1975, U.S. Dist. Ct. (mid. dist.) Fla. 1976, U.S. Dist. Ct. (so. dist.) Fla. 1982, U.S. Ct. Appeals (11th cir.) 1982. Asst. to pres. The Fla. Bar, Tampa, Fla., 1975-76; ptnr. Akerman, Senterfitt & Eidson, P.A., Orlando, Fla., 1976—; arbitrator Am. Arbitration Assn., Orlando, 1987—. Mem. ABA, The Fla. Bar (chmn. student edn. and admission to bar com., vice chmn. 9th cir. grievance com.), Notre Dame Club Greater Orlando (pres. 1979-80). Avocations: golf, running. Construction, Securities, General civil litigation. Office: Akerman Senterfitt & Eidson PA 255 S Orange Ave Orlando FL 32801-3445

**NADEAU, ROBERT MAURICE AUCLAIR,** lawyer; b. Sanford, Maine, Feb. 8, 1955; s. Roland Maurice Nadeau and Nancy Lee (Leighton) Auclair; m. Kimberly J. Brennan, Oct. 11, 1982; children: Matteson Leigh, Ian Robert, Erin Roland. BA, Johns Hopkins U., 1977; JD, Widener U., 1980. Bar: Mass. 1981, U.S. Ct. Appeals (1st cir.) 1982, U.S. Ct. Mil. Appeals 1982, U.S. Dist. Ct. Mass. 1986, Maine 1992, N.H. 1994, U.S. Dist. Ct. Maine 1994, U.S. Dist. Ct. N.H. 1994. Asst. probation officer Mcpl. Ct., Wilmington, Del., 1978-80; with U.S. Army Judge Advocate Gen.'s Corps, 1981-85; spl. asst. U.S. atty. (Kans.), 1982-83; asst. town prosecutor Hampden, Mass., 1985-87, Wilbraham, Mass., 1985-87; city prosecutor Law Dept., Chicopee, Mass., 1988-90; pvt. practice Springfield, Mass., 1985-93; sr. assoc. Smith Elliott Smith and Garmey, P.A., Kennebunk, Maine, 1993-95; sr. ptnr. Nadeau & Penney P.A., 1995—; judge York County Probate, 1997—; dir. Kennebunk Health and Home Care Svcs., 1994. Trustee Seashore Trolley Mus., 1994-97; dir. York County chpt. ARC, 1998—. Capt. U.S. Army, 1980-85. Mem. Sanford Kiwanis Club, Wells Rotary Club. Democrat. Roman Catholic. Avocations: sports, running, music collecting, travel. General civil litigation, Personal injury, General practice. Office: Nadeau & Penney P A 199 Main St Sanford ME 04073-3517 also: Nadeau & Penney PA 1332 Post Rd Wells ME 04090-4561

**NADELSON, EILEEN NORA,** lawyer; b. N.Y.C., Sept. 10, 1938; d. Morton and Sally (Malkin) N. BA in Econ./Polit. Sci., Ariz. State U., 1960; postgrad., CUNY, 1964-69, New Sch., N.Y.C., 1979-81; JD, Touro Coll., 1984. Bar: N.Y. 1985, U.S. Dist. Ct. (so. and ea. dists.) N.Y. 1987, U.S. Supreme Ct. 1990. Tchr. Massapequa (N.Y.) Sch. Dist., 1962-67, N.Y.C. Bd. Edn., 1967-68, 71-73; adminstrv. asst. Cox & Co. Inc., N.Y.C., 1968-71; mng. editor, reporter Our Town Newspaper, N.Y.C., 1972-75; bus. mgr. Eng-Hill Drug Plan, Inc., Plainview, N.Y., 1973-78; legal asst. Traub & Lesser, N.Y.C., 1978-79, 81-85, assoc., 1987-89; community dist. rep. N.Y. State Senator Goodman, N.Y.C., 1979-81; asst. dir. law and taxation NYU, N.Y.C., 1986-87; pvt. practice N.Y.C., 1989—; arbitrator Am. Arbitration Assn., N.Y.C., 1986—, Better Bus. Bur., N.Y.C., 1987—; adj. instr. law and taxation div. NYU, N.Y.C., 1987—; reporter CBS Network Election Svc., Massapequa, 1964; tutor, supr. Vol. Svcs. for Children, N.Y.C., 1971-73; moderator civic program WNYC Radio, N.Y.C., 1973; tutor Jewish Child Care, N.Y.C., 1979-80, Fortune Soc., N.Y.C., 1981; legal counsel Rep. Vols., 1987-89, Fed. Rep. Club, 1987—; lectr. Nat. C. of C. Women, 1994—, N.Y.C. Dept. Bus. Svcs., 1994—; mem. N.Y. Ednl. Priorities Panel, 1997—. Contbr. articles to profl. jours. Vol. advisor Consumer Affairs Bur., Mineola, N.Y., 1975; researchist, editor Common Cause, N.Y.C., 1976; researchist transp. Community Bd. #8, N.Y.C., 1978-79; alt. del. Jud. Conv., N.Y.C., 1979, 80, 86; researchist, writer LWV, N.Y.C., 1980-82, 87, chair alt. to incarceration, 1992; campaign mgr. N.Y. State Assembly Candidate, N.Y.C., 1988; mem. Regional Plan Assn.; candidate N.Y.C. Coun., 1993; chair Com. for Campaign Reform, 1993; mem. exec. bd. League of Women Voters, N.Y.C., 1993—; del., chair com. on taxation White House conf. on Small Bus., 1994-95. Mem. ABA, N.Y. State Bar Assn., N.Y. Women's Bar Assn., Assn. of Bar of N.Y., Touro Coll. Law Alumni Assn. Jewish. Avocations: tennis, poetry, philos. and polit. analysis. General civil litigation, Contracts commercial, General corporate.

**NAFFAH, ELI A.,** law school dean; b. Youngstown, Ohio, Dec. 9, 1950; s. Assad Farris and Odette Amin Naffah; m. Cynthia Marie Hunter, May 26, 1985. BA, John Carroll U., 1973; JD, Southland U., Pasadena, Calif., 1983. Grad. Realtors Inst. Dean Law Sch., N.Am. Coll., Anaheim, Calif., 1983-87, Newport U., Newport Beach, Calif., 1987—. Pres. Windrift Homeowners Assn., Laguna Niguel, Calif., 1986-88, Fieldstone Homeowners Assn., Laguna Niguel, 1991-93; mem. Laguna Niguel Community Coun., 1988-89. Mem. Am. Soc. for Pub. Adminstrn., Calif. Law Sch. Assembly, Laguna Niguel C. of C. Roman Catholic. Avocations: photography, golf, bicycling. Office: Newport U 2220 University Dr Newport Beach CA 92660-3319

**NAFTALIS, GARY PHILIP,** lawyer, educator; b. Newark, Nov. 23, 1941; s. Gilbert and Bertha Beatrice Naftalis; m. Donna Arditi, June 30, 1974; children: Benjamin, Joshua, Daniel, Sarah. AB, Rutgers U., 1963; AM, Brown U., 1965; LLB, Columbia U., 1967. Bar: N.Y. 1967, U.S. Dist. Ct. (so. dist.) N.Y. 1969, U.S. Ct. Appeals (2d cir.) 1968, U.S. Ct. Appeals (3d cir.) 1973, U.S. Ct. Appeals (D.C. cir.) 1993, U.S. Supreme Ct. 1974. Law clk. to judge U.S. Dist. Ct. So. Dist. N.Y., 1967-68; asst. U.S. atty. So. Dist. N.Y., 1968-74, asst. chief criminal divsn., 1972-74; spl. asst. U.S. atty. for V.I., 1972-73; spl. counsel U.S. Senate Subcom. on Long Term Care, 1975, N.Y. State Temp. Commn. on Living Costs and the Economy, 1975; ptnr. Orans, Elsen, Polstein & Naftalis, N.Y.C., 1974-81, Kramer, Levin, Naftalis & Frankel, N.Y.C., 1981—; lectr. Law Sch. Columbia U., 1976-88; vis. lectr. Law Sch. Harvard U., 1979; mem. deptl. disciplinary com. Appellate div. 1st Dept., 1980-86. Author: (with Marvin E. Frankel) The Grand Jury: An Institution on Trial, 1977, Considerations in Representing Attorneys in Civil and Criminal Enforcement Proceedings, 1981, Sentencing: Helping Judges Do Their Jobs, 1986, SEC Actions Seeking to Bar Securities Professionals, 1995, SEC Cease and Desist Powers Limited, 1997, The Foreign Corrupt Practices Act, 1997, Prosecuting Lawyers Who Defend Clients in SEC Actions, 1998, Obtaining Reports from a Credit Bureau for Litigation May be a Crime, 1999; editor: White Collar Crimes, 1980. Trustee Boys Brotherhood Rep., 1978—, Blueberry Treatment Ctr., 1981-91, Joseph Haggerty Children's Fund, 1991—. Fellow Am. Coll. Trial Lawyers; mem. ABA (white collar crime com. criminal justice sect. 1985—), Assn. of Bar of City of N.Y. (com. criminal cts. 1980-83, com. judiciary 1984-87, com. on criminal law 1987-90, 97—, coun. criminal justice 1985-88), Fed. Bar Coun. (com. cts. 2d cir. 1974-77), N.Y. Bar Assn. (com. state legis. 1974-76, exec. com. comml. and fed. litigation sect.), Internat. Bar Assn. (bus. crimes com. 1988—). Criminal, Federal civil litigation, Administrative and regulatory. Home: 1125 Park Ave Apt 7B New York NY 10128-1243 Office: Kramer Levin Naftalis & Frankel 919 3rd Ave New York NY 10022-3902

**NAFZIGER, JAMES ALBERT RICHMOND,** lawyer, educator; b. Mpls., Sept. 24, 1940; s. Ralph Otto and Charlotte Monona (Hamilton) N. BA, U. Wis., 1962, MA, 1969; JD, Harvard U., 1967. Bar: Wis. 1967. Law clk. to chief judge U.S. Dist. Ct. (ea. dist.) Wis., 1967-69; fellow Am. Soc. Internat. Law, Washington, 1969-70, adminstrv. dir., 1970-74; exec. sec. Assn. Student Internat. Law Socs., 1969-70; lectr. Sch. Law Cath. U. Am., Washington, 1970-74; assoc. prof. law Coll. Law Willamette U., Salem, Oreg., 1977-80; prof. Willamette U., Salem, 1980-95, Thomas B. Stoel prof., 1995—, assoc. dean, 1985-86, dir. internat. programs, 1984—; scholar-in-residence Rockefeller Found. Ctr., Bellagio, Italy, 1985; vis. assoc. prof. Sch. Law, U. Oreg. 1974-77; vis. prof. Nat. Autonomous U. Mex., 1978; hon. prof. East China U. of Politics and Law, 1999—; lectr. tutor Inst. Pub. Internat. Law and Internat. Rels., Thessaloniki, Greece, 1982; cons. Adminstrv. Conf. U.S., 1988-90, Internat. Com. Migration, 1997—; mem. bd. advisors Denver Jour. Internat. Law and Policy, Am. Jour. Comparative Law (bd. dirs. 1985—). Editor Procs. of Am. Soc. Internat. Law 1977; Am. author: Conflict of Laws: A Northwest Perspective, 1985, International Sports Law, 1988; contbr. articles to profl. jours. Bd. dirs. N.W. Regional China Coun., 1987-89. 1st lt. U.S. Army, 1962-64. Recipient Burlington No. Faculty Achievement award, 1988. Mem. ABA (legal specialist ctrl. and east European law initiative 1992—), Am. Soc. Internat. Law (exec. coun. 1983-86, 92-95, exec. com. 1994-95, chmn. ann. meeting 1988, chmn. nominating com. 1989), Am. Soc. Comparative Law (bd. dirs. 1985—, treas. 1997—), Internat. Law Assn. (rapporteur cultural heritage law com. 1990—, Am. br. exec. com. 1986—, v.p. 1994—, co-dir. studies 1991-95, chmn. human rights com. 1983-88), UNA-USA (pres. Oreg. divsn. 1987-90, bd. dirs. 1990—, exec. com. coun. chpt. and divsn. prof., v.p. 1990-94), Washington Fgn. Law Soc. (v.p. 1973-74), Internat. Studies Assn. (exec. bd. 1974-77, internat. law sect.), ACLU (pres. chpt. 1980-81, mem. state bd. 1982-88, sec. 1983-87), Assn. Am. Law Schs. (chmn. law and arts sect. 1981-83, 89-91, chmn. immigration law sect. 1990-91, chmn. internat. law sect. 1984-85, com. on sects. and ann. meeting 1995-98, chmn. internat. law workshop, 1995), Am. Law Inst., Oreg. Internat. Coun. (pres. 1990-92), Internat. Sports Law Assn. (v.p. 1992—), Phi Beta Kappa, Phi Kappa Phi. Home: 3775 Saxon Dr S Salem OR 97302-6041 Office: Willamette U Coll Law Salem OR 97301

**NAGEL, BRUCE H.,** lawyer; b. Paterson, N.J., Aug. 28, 1952; s. David A. and Norma N.; m. Marla Nagel, July 15, 1978; children: Arielle, Emma, Molly. BS in Indsl. and Labor Rels., Cornell U., 1974; JD, NYU, 1977. Bar: N.J. 1977, U.S. Dist. Ct. N.J. 1977, U.S. Ct. Appeals (3rd cir.) 1977, U.S. Ct. Appeals (4th cir.) 1995; cert. civil trial atty. Sr. ptnr. Nagel, Rice & Dreifuss, Livingston, N.J., 1983—; lectr. Inst. Continuing Legal Edn.; chmn. bd. trustees Kairos Inst., Madison, N.J., 1998—; bd. dirs. Teardrop Golf Co., Morton Grove, Ill.; moderator and lectr. in field. Contbr. articles to profl. jours. Mem. ATLA, N.J. Bar Assn., Essex County Bar Assn., Million Dollar Advocate Forum. Personal injury, Product liability, General civil litigation. Office: Nagel Rice & Dreifuss 301 S Livingston Ave Ste 201 Livingston NJ 07039-3991

**NAGEL, STUART,** lawyer; b. Bklyn., Nov. 17, 1953; s. Paul and Sara (Abadinsky) N.; m. Ashley Nagel, Aug. 6, 1954; children: Michael Joseph, Sommer Nicole, Kanan Peri, River Ian. BA, Bklyn. Coll., 1975; JD, San Fernando Valley Coll., 1979. Bar: Calif. 1979, U.S. Dist. Ct. (cen. dist.) Calif. 1980. Atty. Sydney Gordon, Tarzana, Calif., 1980-81; atty. Garabedian & Ayres, Canoga Park, Calif., 1981-84, Lautman, Nagel & Pearl, L.A., 1984-87; pvt. practice L.A., 1987—. Workers' compensation. Office: 433 N Camden Dr Ste 400 Beverly Hills CA 90210-4408

**NAGIN, STEPHEN E.,** lawyer, educator; b. Phila., Nov. 7, 1946; s. Harry S. and Dorothy R. (Pearlman) N.; m. Marjorie Riley. BBA, U. Miami, 1969, JD, 1974. Bar: Fla. 1974, D.C. 1976, U.S. Supreme Ct. 1978. Asst. atty. gen. State of Fla., Miami, 1974-75; atty., FTC, 1975-80; spl. asst. U.S. atty. D.C., 1980-81; ptnr. Nagin, Gallop & Figueredo, P.A.; adj. prof. St. Thomas U. Sch. Law, 1984-94; instr. Nat. Inst. Trial Advocacy, 1992—. Mem. Fla. Correctional Med. Authority, 1990-91. Mem. ABA (antitrust and litigation coms.), Fed. Bar Assn., D.C. Bar Asn., Fla. Bar Assn. (editor, trial lawyers sect. 1983-84; mem. spl. antitrust task force 1983—, chmn. editorial bd., 1982-83, chmn. antitrust com. 1996-98, vice chmn. intellectual property com. 1998—), Coral Gables Bar Assn. (bd. dirs. 1983-87), Assn. Trial Lawyers Am., Am. Arbitration Assn., Nat. Health Lawyers Assn. Antitrust, Federal civil litigation, Intellectual property. Office: Nagin Gallop & Figueredo PA 3225 Aviation Ave Fl 3D Miami FL 33133-4741

**NAGLE, CLAIRE WALLER,** lawyer; b. New Brunswick, N.J., July 13, 1925; d. Clifford Albert and Eunice (Waller) N. AB, Rutgers U., 1946, LLD (hon.), 1978; JD, NYU, 1949. Bar: N.J. 1950. Assoc. Hicks, Kuhlthau, Thompson & Molineux, New Brunswick, 1950-57; ptnr. Kuhlthau, Nagle, Hamilton & Conroy and predecessor firms, New Brunswick, 1957-77; pvt. practice New Brunswick, 1977—. Mem. bd. govs. Rutgers U., New Brunswick, 1967-76, chair, 1973-76, bd. trustees, 1964—; overseer Rutgers U. Found., 1974-79; trustee Middlesex Gen. Hosp., 1964-70; mem. State Bd. of Higher Edn., 1973-76. Republican. Estate planning, Probate, Estate taxation. Home and Office: 33 Oak Hills Rd Edison NJ 08820-3611

**NAGLE, DAVID EDWARD,** lawyer, columnist; b. Natick, Mass., May 31, 1954; s. Edward G. and Eleanor (Fitz) N.; m. Sue Ellen Southard, Oct. 1, 1988. BS in Govt. and Philosophy, Coll. William and Mary, 1976; JD, U. Richmond, 1981; LLM in Labor Law, Georgetown U., 1983. Bar: Va. 1981. Police officer City of Richmond (Va.), 1976-79; atty. Williams, Mullen & Christian, Richmond, Va., 1981-86; sole practice Richmond, Va., 1986-89; ptnr. Hazel & Thomas, Richmond, Va., 1989-93; columnist Richmond News-Leader, Va., 1986-90; ptnr. LeClair Ryan, Richmond, Va., 1993—; lectr. U. Richmond Sch. Law and Sch. Bus., Med. Coll. Va. Sch. Hosp. Adminstrn. Contbr. articles to law revs. Mem. Va. Polygraph Bd., 1985-89, Richmond Corrections Bd., 1988-92; dir. Fan Dist. Assn., 1995-97, Monument Ave. Preservation Soc., 1994-97, Richmond Area Assn. Retarded Citizens, 1993-99. Mem. ABA, Va. Bar Assn., Bar Assn. City of Richmond, Am. Arbitration Assn. (arbitrator 1982-85). Labor, Civil rights, Appellate. Office: LeClair Ryan 707 E Main St Richmond VA 23219-2814

**NAGLE, ROBERT E.,** lawyer; b. Chgo., Nov. 2, 1948; s. Milton and Lillian Nagle; m. Lynne Salomone, Apr. 5, 1975; children: David, Katherine. BS, Pepperdine U., 1979; JD, Southwestern U., 19893. Bar: Calif. 1984. Ops. mgr. Mid-West Veal Distbrs., L.A., 1975-80; contract adminstr. Northrop Corp., El Segundo, Calif., 1980-83; litigation atty. Bakst & Garber, L.A., 1983-86; sr. corp. counsel Farmers Group, Inc., L.A., 1986-96; gen. counsel, sr. v.p., sec. Superior Nat. Ins. Group, Inc., Calabasas, Calif., 1996—; exec. com. USC Inst. for Corp. Counsel, L.A., 1997, 98. Mem. Am. Soc. Corp. Secs. (L.A. chpt.), Am. Corp. Counsel Assn. (L.A. chpt.), L.A. County Bar (exec. com. corp. counsel sect. 1996—). General corporate, Insurance, General civil litigation. Office: Superior Nat Ins Group Inc 26601 Agoura Rd Calabasas CA 91302-1959

**NAHITCHEVANSKY, GEORGES,** lawyer, educator; b. N.Y.C., Dec. 7, 1958. BS in Fgn. Svc., Georgetown U., 1979; MA, Northwestern U., 1981; JD magna cum laude, Bklyn. Law Sch., 1991. Bar: N.Y. 1992, U.S. Dist. Ct. (so. dist.) N.Y. 1993, U.S. Dist. Ct. (ea. dist.) N.Y. 1997, U.S. Ct. Appeals (2d cir.) 1998. Atty. Kramer Levin Naftalis Kamin & Frankel, N.Y.C., 1991-94, Fross Zelnick Lehrman & Zissu, PC, N.Y.C., 1994—; adj. prof. Bklyn. Law Sch., 1992—. Prodr., dir.: (film) Refugees in Our Backyard, 1991. Bd. dirs. Russian Children's Welfare Soc., Inc., N.Y.C., 1995—. Mem. ABA, Assn. of Bar of City of N.Y. Intellectual property. Office: Fross Zelnick Lehrman & Zissu PC 866 United Nations Plz New York NY 10017-1822

**NAHM, NATHAN IHRU,** lawyer; b. Seoul, Korea, Sept. 30, 1939; came to U.S., 1965; s. Sang Mann and Chan Oak Lee N.; m. Hangja H., June 23, 1965; 1 child, Nara K. LLB, Seoul Nat. U., 1961, BA, 1963; AM in Philosophy, Brown U., 1967; PhD in Philosophy, Princeton U., 1976; LLM, NYU, 1986; JD, Harvard U., 1982. Bar: N.Y. 1983, U.S. dist. Ct. N.Y. (so. and ea. dists.) 1983, U.S. Tax Ct. 1983. Assoc. Debevoise & Plimpton, N.Y.C., 1982-84; sr. assoc. Skadden Arps, N.Y.C., 1984-87, Willkie Farr & Gallagher, N.Y.C., 1987-91; internat. counsel Debevoise & Plimpton, N.Y.C., 1991-95; of counsel Gibson, Dunn & Crutcher, N.Y.C., 1995-97; ptnr. Hughes, Hubbard & Reed, N.Y.C., 1997—. Trustee Presbyn. Ch., Mt. Kisco, N.Y., 1993-96. 2d lt. Korean Army Corps Engrs., 1963-65. Brown U. fellow, 1965-67, Princeton U. Nat. fellow, 1967-71. Mem. ABA, N.Y. State Bar Assn., N.Y.C. Bar Assn. (tax & internat. coms. 1982—), Internat. Bar Assn. Avocations: golf, music, reading, hiking, swimming. Private international, Mergers and acquisitions, Finance. Home: 42 Kerry Ln Chappaqua NY 10514-1626 Office: Hughes Hubbard & Reed 1 Battery Park Plz Fl 12 New York NY 10004-1482

**NAKATA, GARY KENJI,** lawyer; b. Okinawa, Japan, Nov. 13, 1964; came to the U.S., 1971; s. Hiroshi Nakata and Miwako Kin; m. Jo Ann Akiko Tengan, Aug. 22, 1998. BBA in Fin., U. Hawaii, 1988; JD with distinction, U. of the Pacific, 1995. Bar: Hawaii 1996, Calif. 1996, U.S. Dist. Ct. Hawaii, 1996; cert. mgmt. acct.; cert. fin. mgr.; cert. grad. Am. Banker's Assn. Nat. Sch. Regulatory Compliance. Credit analyst Bank of Hawaii, Honolulu, 1988-90, sr. credit analyst, 1990-92; law clk. Hawaii Atty. Gen. Tax Divsn., Honolulu, 1994; sr. assoc. Kobayashi, Sugita & Goda, Honolulu, 1995—; mem. new product devel. adv. bd. Warren Gorham & Lamont, N.Y.C., 1997-98. Editor-in-chief: The Transnational Lawyer, 1994, 95. pres., enlisted adv. coun. Hawaii Air Nat. Guard, Honolulu, 1986-92; mem. ex officio alumni coun., mem. membership com., mem. membership benefits subcom. U. Hawaii Alumni Assn., Honolulu, 1990-91; mem. fin. com. and bylaws subcom. Soc. Coll. Bus. Alumni and Friends, U. Hawaii Coll. Bus. Adminstrn. Alumni Affairs, Honolulu, 1990-91, founding mem., treas., 1990-91, mem. steering com. to form alumni orgn., 1997—, pres., 1998—; at-large rep., treas., legis. liaison Neighborhood Bd., Kaneohe, Hawaii, 1991-92. Mem. ABA (bus. law sect., comml. fin. svcs. com., electronic commerce com., consumer fin. svcs. com., comml. loan documentation sub-com., comml. loan workout subcom. 1997—), Hawaii State Bar Assn. (mem. real property and fin. svcs. sect. 1997—), Calif. State Bar Assn., Inst. Cert. Mgmt. Accts. (bd. dirs. 1998—, dir. mem. acquistion 1998—), Hawaii Fin. Regulatory Compliance Assn. (bd. dirs. 1997—, chairperson fair credit reporting act regulatory update com. 1998—), Hawaii Bus. Jaycees (charter mem. 1991—, charter pres. 1991-92, chmn. bd. 1992-93, R. Allen Watkins Outstanding Chpt. Pres. award 1992, Hampton Whetsell award 1992, Clarence Howard award 1992). General corporate, Real property, Banking. Office: Kobayashi Sugita & Goda 999 Bishop St Ste 2600 Honolulu HI 96813-4430

**NAKAYAMA, PAULA AIKO,** state supreme court justice; b. Honolulu, Oct. 19, 1953; m. Charles W. Totto; children: Elizabeth Murakami, Alexander Totto. BS, U. Calif., Davis, 1975; JD, U. Calif., 1979. Bar: Hawaii 1979. Dep. pros. atty. City and County of Honolulu, 1979-82; ptnr. Shim, Tam & Kirimitsu, Honolulu, 1982-92; judge 1st Cir. Ct. State of Hawaii, Oahu, 1992-93; justice State of Hawaii Supreme Ct., Honolulu, 1993—. Mem. Am. Judicature Soc., Hawaii Bar Assn., Sons and Daughters of 442. Office: Ali'iolani Hale Hawaii Supreme Ct 417 S King St Honolulu HI 96813-2902*

**NALITZ, WILLIAM ROBERT,** judge; b. Pitts., Oct. 16, 1944; s. Stanley Robert and Clare P. Nalitz; m. Linda Ann White, June 29, 1968; children: Jennifer (dec.), Thaddeus, Carolyn. BA, Georgetown U., 1966; JD, Duquesne U., 1973. Claims adjuster Travelers Ins., Pitts., 1968-70; field agt. Pa. Bd. Probation/Parole, Pitts., 1970-73; assoc. Sayers, King & Keener, Waynesburg, Pa., 1973-75; ptnr. King and Nalitz, Waynesburg, 1975-97; judge Greene County Ct. Common Pleas, Waynesburg, 1998—. 1st lt. U.S. Army, 1966-68, Vietnam. Home: Cabin Rd Waynesburg PA 15370 Office: Greene County Courthouse High St Waynesburg PA 15370

**NANCE, ALLAN TAYLOR,** retired lawyer; b. Dallas, Jan. 31, 1933; s. A.Q. and Lois Rebecca (Taylor) N. BA, So. Meth. U., 1954, LLB, 1957; LLM, NYU, 1978. Bar: Tex. 1957, N.Y. 1961. With Simpson Thacher & Bartlett, N.Y.C., 1960-65; asst. counsel J.P. Stevens & Co., Inc., N.Y.C., 1965-70, sec., 1970-78, asst. gen. counsel, 1970-89; asst. counsel J.P. Stevens & Co. Inc. and WestPoint-Pepperell Inc., 1989-93; asst. gen. counsel WestPoint Stevens Inc., N.Y.C., 1993-98, ret., 1998. With USNR, 1957-59. Woodrow Wilson fellow Columbia U., 1959-60. Mem. Phi Beta Kappa. General corporate, Mergers and acquisitions, Real property. Home: 201 E 66th St New York NY 10021-6451

**NANCE, JOHN JOSEPH,** lawyer, writer, air safety analyst, broadcaster, consultant; b. Dallas, July 5, 1946; s. Joseph Turner and Margrette (Grubbs) N.; m. Benita Ann Priest, July 26, 1968; children: Dawn Michelle, Bridgitte Cathleen, Christopher Sean. BA, So. Meth. U., 1968, JD, 1969; grad., USAF Undergrad. Pilot Tng., Williams AFB, Ariz., 1971. Bar: Tex. 1970, U.S. Ct. Appeals (fed. cir.), 1994. News reporter, broadcaster, newsman various papers and stas. Honolulu and Dallas, 1957-66; radio news anchorman Sta. WFAA-AM, Dallas, 1966-70; newsman including on camera Sta. WFAA-TV, Dallas; pvt. practice law Dallas, 1970—; news dir. Newscom Network, Dallas, 1970; airline pilot Braniff Internat. Airways, Dallas, 1975-82, Alaska Airlines, Inc., Seattle, 1985—; chmn., pres. Exec. Transport, Inc., Tacoma, 1979-85; chmn., chief exec. officer EMEX Corp., Kent, Wash., 1987—; mng. ptnr. Phoenix Ptnrs., Ltd., Tacoma, Wash., 1995—; project devel. assoc. Columbia Tristar TV, 1997—; sr. ptnr. Nance & Carmichael, PLLC, Austin, Tex., 1997—; project devel. assoc. Columbia TriStar TV, 1997—; profl. speaker Human Mgmt., 1984—, Teamwork and Comms. in the Med. Profession; airline safety, advocate Ind. Cons., earthquake preparedness spokesman Ind. Cons.; dir. steering com. Found. for Issues Resolution in Sci. Tech., Seattle, 1987-89; speaker Northwestern Transp. Ctr. Deregulation and Safety Conf., 1987; cons. NOVA Why Planes Crash, PBS, 1987, ABC World News Tonight Crash of US AIR 427, 1994; aviation analyst ABC-TV and radio, 1995—; aviation editor: ABC Good Morning Am., 1995—; broadcast analyst, 1986—; spkr. in field. Author: Splash of Colors, 1984, Blind Trust, 1986 (Wash. Gov.'s award 1987), On Shaky Ground, 1988, Final Approach, 1990, What Goes Up, 1991, Scorpion Strike, 1982, Operating Handbook USAF Air Carrier Safety and Inspection Office, 1991, Phoenix Rising, 1994, Pandora's Clock, 1995, Medusa's Child, 1997, The Last Hostage, 1998; contbr. to Transportation Deregulation in the U.S., 1988; aviation editor: ABC Good Morning Am., 1995—; appeared in Sheep on the Runway Tacoma Little Theater, 1975; tech. advisor, actor Pandora's Clock NBC mini-series, 1996; appeared in Medusa's Child, ABC Mini-series, 1997; prodr., writer, dir. USAF Video Prodns.: ANG Introduction to CRM, 1992, USAF SOC CRM Program, 1992, Test and Evaluation CRM, 1993, The Teamwork Connection, 1996. Prs. Fox Glen Homeowners Assn., Tacoma, 1974-77; cons. Congl. Office Tech. Assessment, Tacoma, 1987; witness numerous air safety hearings U.S. Congress, Washington, 1986-88; bd. dirs. St. Charles Borromeo Sch., Tacoma, 1975-78, Nat. Patient Safety Found. of AMA, 1997—; mem. Mayor's Vets. Task Force, Tacoma, 1991; bd. advisors Jour. Air Law and Commerce So. Meth. Sch. Law, 1995—, exec. bd. Sch. of Law, 1998—; bd. advisors Pacific Northwest Writer's Conf., 1994—; mem. adv. bd. supply and logistics mgmt. program Portland State U., 1997—; exec. bd. mem. SMU Sch. Law, 1998—. Capt. USAFR, 1975-94; lt. col. Persian Gulf. Decorated Merit Svc. medal; named Airline Safety Man of Year Wash. State Div. of Aeronautics, 1987. Fellow Chartered Inst. Transport (Canberra, Australia); mem. ABA, SAG, Tex. Bar Assn., Author's Guild Am., Res. Officers Assn. (life), Aircraft Owners' and Pilots' Assn., Phi Alpha Delta, Delta Chi. Home and Office: John Nance Prodns 4512 87th Ave W Tacoma WA 98466-1920 Office: Phoenix Ptnrs Ltd PO Box 24465 Federal Way WA 98093-1465

**NANDA, VED PRAKASH,** law educator, university official; b. Gujranwala, India, Nov. 20, 1934; came to U.S., 1960; s. Jagan Nath and Attar (Kaur) N.; m. Katharine Kunz, Dec. 18, 1982; 1 child, Anjali. MA, Punjab U., 1952; LLB, U. Delhi, 1955, LLM, 1958; LLM, Northwestern U., 1962; postgrad., Yale U., 1962-65; LLD (hon.), Soka U., Tokyo, 1997. Asst. prof. law U. Denver, 1965-68, assoc. prof., 1968-70, prof. law, dir. Internat. Legal Studies Program, 1970—, Thompson G. Marsh prof. law, 1987—, Evans Univ. prof., 1992—, asst. provost, 1993-94, vice provost, 1994—; vis. prof. Coll. Law, U. Iowa, Iowa City, 1974-75, Fla. State U., 1973, U. San Diego, 1979, U. Colo., 1992; disting. vis. prof. internat. law Chgo. Kent Coll. Law, 1981, Calif. We. Sch. Law, San Diego, 1983-84; disting. vis. scholar Sch. Law, U. Hawaii, Honolulu, 1986-87; cons. Solar Energy Rsch. Inst., 1978-81, Dept. Energy, 1980-81. Author: (with David Pansius) Litigation of International Disputes in U.S. Courts, 1987; editor: (with M. Cherif Bassiouni) A Treatise on International Criminal Law, 2 vols., 1973, Water Needs for the Future, 1977; (with George Shepherd) Human Rights and Third World Development, 1985; (with others) Global Human Rights, 1981, The Law of Transnational Business Transactions, 1981, World Climate Change, 1983, Breach and Adaption of International Contracts, 1992, World Debt and Human Conditions, 1993, Europe Community Law After 1992, 1993, International Environmental Law and Policy, 1995; (with William M. Evan) Nuclear Proliferation and the Legality of Nuclear Weapons, 1995, (with others) European Union Law After Maastricht, 1996, (with S.P. Sinha) Hindu Law and Legal Theory, 1996, (with D. Krieger) Nuclear Weapons and the World Court, 1998; editor, contbr.: Refugee Law and Policy, 1989; editl. bd. Jour. Am. Comparative Law, Indian Jour. Internat. Law, Transnational Pubs. Co-chmn. Colo. Pub. Broadcasting Fedn., 1977-78; mem. Gov.'s Commn. on Pub. Telecommunications, 1980-82. Mem. World Jurist Assn. (v.p. 1991—, pres. 1997—), World Assn. Law Profs. (pres. 1987-93), UN Assn. (v.p. Colo. divsn. 1973-76, pres. 1986-88, 93-96, nat. coun. UNA-USA 1990—, mem. governing bd. UNA-USA 1995—), World Fedn. UN Assns. (vice-chmn. 1995—), Am. Assn. Comparative Study Law (bd. dirs. 1980—), Am. Soc. Internat. Law (v.p. 1987-88, exec. coun. 1969-72, 81-84, bd. rev. and devel. 1988-91, hon. v.p. 1995—), Assn. Am. Law Schs., U.S. Inst. Human Rights, Internat. Law Assn. (mem. exec. com. 1986—), Colo. Coun. Internat. Orgns. (pres. 1988-90), Assn. U.S. Mems. Internat. Inst. Space Law (bd. dirs., mem. exec. com. 1980-88), Internat. Acad. Comparative Law (assoc.), Order St. Ives (pres.), Rotary, Cactus. Office: U Denver Coll Law 1900 Olive St Denver CO 80220-1857

**NANGLE, JOHN FRANCIS,** federal judge; b. St. Louis, June 8, 1922; s. Sylvester Austin and Thelma (Bank) N.; m. Jane Adams, June 7, 1986; 1 child, John Francis Jr. AA, Harris Tchrs. Coll., 1941; BS, U. Mo., 1943; JD, Washington U., St. Louis, 1948. Bar: Mo. 1948. Pvt. practice law Clayton, 1948-73; judge U.S. Dist. Ct., St. Louis, 1973—, chief judge, 1983-90, sr. judge, 1990—; sr. judge Ga., 1991—; mem. 8th Cir. Jud. Coun.; mem. exec. com. Jud. Conf. U.S.; chmn. Jud. Panel on Multidist. Litigation, mem. working group on mass torts, mem. jud. resources working group. Mem. Mo. Rep. Com., 1958-73; mem. St. Louis County Rep. Cen. Com., 1958-73, chmn., 1960-61; pres. Mo. Assn. Reps., 1961, Reps. Vets. League, 1960; mem. Rep. Nat. Com., 1972-73; bd. dirs. Masonic Home Mo. With AUS, 1943-46. Named Mo. Republican of Year John Marshall Club, 1970, Mo. Republican of Year Mo. Assn. Reps., 1971; recipient Most Disting. Alumnus award Harris-Stowe Coll., Most Disting. Alumnus award Washington U. Sch. Law, 1986. Mem. ABA, Am. Judicature Soc., Legion of Honor DeMolay, Mo. Bar Assn., St. Louis Bar Assn., St. Louis County Bar Assn. Address: Washington DC Fed Judicial Bldg Washington DC 20002

**NANTS, BRUCE ARLINGTON,** lawyer; b. Orlando, Fla., Oct. 26, 1953; s. Jack Arlington and Louise (Hulme) N. BA, U. Fla., 1974, JD, 1977. Bar: Fla. 1977. Asst. state's atty. State Atty.'s Office, Orlando, 1977-78; pvt. practice, Orlando, 1979—. Columnist The Law and You, 1979-80. Auctioneer pub. TV sta., 1979; campaign coord. cen. Fla. steering com. Bob Dole for Pres., 1988; bd. dirs. Cystic Fibrosis Found. Mem. Acad. Fla. Trial Lawyers, Am. Arbitration Assn., Fellowship Christian Athletes (past bd. dirs. Cen. Fla.), Tiger Bay Club Cen. Fla., Orlando Touchdown Club, Fla. Blue Key, Omicron Delta Kappa, Phi Beta Kappa, Phi Delta Theta. Democrat. Baptist. Avocations: tennis, golf, swimming, scuba diving. Home: 1112 Country Ln Orlando FL 32804-6934 Office: PO Box 547871 Orlando FL 32854-7871

**NAPIER, RONALD LEWIS,** lawyer; b. Alexandria, Va., Oct. 12, 1954; s. William Wilson and Lee Elizabeth (Moore) N.; m. Katherine Winston Pritchard, May 27, 1979; children: Andrew Lewis, William Hamilton, Mary Katherine. BS in Math., Mary Washington Coll., Fredericksburg, Va., 1977; JD, U. Va., 1981. Bar: Va. 1981, U.S. Dist. Ct. (we. dist.) Va. 1981. Ptnr. Napier & Napier, P.C., Front Royal, Va., 1981-98; pres. Napier, Pond, Athey & Athey, P.C., 1998—. Mem. Warren County Bar Assn. (pres. 1994-96), Rotary (bd. dirs. Front Royal Club 1987-94, pres. 1993-94, asst. gov. Internat. Dist. 7570 1996-98, Paul Harris Fellowship award Rotary Found. 1993). Baptist. General civil litigation, Criminal, Family and matrimonial. Home: 545 Locust Dale Rd Front Royal VA 22630-4531 Office: Napier Pond Athey & Athey PC 35 N Royal Ave Front Royal VA 22630-2662

**NAPIERSKI, EUGENE EDWARD,** lawyer; b. Albany, N.Y., Jan. 9, 1944; s. Eugene J. and Elizabeth (Doran) N.; children: Christine, Eugene, Michelle, Daniel. BA, Siena Coll., 1965; JD, Union U., 1968. Bar: N.Y. 1968, U.S. Dist. Ct. (fed. dist.) N.Y. 1968, U.S. Supreme Ct. 1975. Atty. Forsyth, Howe & O'Dwyer, Rochester, N.Y., 1968-69; staff atty. Rsch. Found. SUNY, Albany, N.Y., 1969-70; assoc. Carter & Conboy, Albany, 1970-76; ptnr. Carter, Conboy, Case, Blackmore, Napierski & Maloney, Albany, 1976—. Mem. Am. Bd. Trial Advocates (pres. upstate N.Y.), N.Y. State Bar Assn., Capitol Dist. Trial Lawyers Assn. (past pres.), Ft. Orange Club, Wolferts Roost Country Club. Avocations: reading, golf, travel. Personal injury, Product liability. Home: 7 Woodridge St Albany NY 12203-5362 Office: Carter Conboy Case Blackmore Napierski & Maloney PC 20 Corporate Woods Blvd Ste 8 Albany NY 12211-2362

**NAPLETON, ROBERT JOSEPH,** lawyer; b. Evergreen Park, Ill., Jan. 13, 1963; s. Francis Edward and Elizabeth (Raynor) N.; m. Clare Therese McEnery, June 6, 1992; children: Martin Joseph, Nora Elizabeth, Patricia Clare. BBA, Loyola U., Chgo., 1985, JD, 1988. Bar: Ill. 1988, U.S. Dist. Ct. (no. dist.) Ill. 1989, U.S. Dist. Ct. (cen. dist.) Ill. 1995, U.S. Dist. Ct. (we. dist.) Wis. 1998, U.S. Supreme Ct. 1999. Law clk. to Chief Judge James E. Murphy Circuit Ct. of Cook County, Chgo., 1985-87; mem. staff State's Atty. Office of Cook County, Markham, Ill., 1987-88; assoc. Motherway & Glenn, Chgo., 1988-98; ptnr. Motherway, Glenn & Napleton, Chgo., 1999—; spkr., presenter in field. Treas. campaign Citizens to Elect James Brosnahan State Rep. for 36th Dist., Ill., 1996. Fellow Roscoe Pound Found.; mem. ATLA (aviation law com.), Ill. Trial Lawyers Assn. (bd. advocates 1993-97, bd. mgrs. 1997—, med. negligence and product liability coms. 1994—, civil practice com. 1995—), Ill. State Bar Assn. (bd. govs. 1994—, tort law sect. coun. 1992-95), Southwest Bar Assn., Chgo. Bar Assn. (trial techniques com. 1991-92), Catholic Lawyers Guild, Brother Rice H.S. St. Thomas More Soc. Democrat. Roman Catholic. Avocations: golf, skiing, ice hockey, reading. Personal injury, Product liability, Professional liability. Home: 400 Sunset Ave La Grange IL 60525-6115 Office: Motherway Glenn & Napleton 100 W Monroe St Ste 200 Chicago IL 60603-1902

**NAPOLITANO, JANET ANN,** state attorney general; b. N.Y.C., Nov. 29, 1957; d. Leonard Michael and Jane Marie (Winer) N. BS, U. Santa Clara, Calif., 1979; JD, U. Va., 1983. Bar: Ariz. 1984, U.S. Dist. Ct. Ariz. 1984, Ct. Appeals (9th cir.) 1984, U.S. Ct. Appeals (10th cir.) 1988. Law clk. to hon. Mary Schroeder U.S Ct. Appeals (9th Cir.), 1983-84; assoc. Lewis & Roca, Phoenix, 1984-89, ptnr., 1989-93; U.S. Atty. Dist. Ariz., Phoenix, 1993-97; atty. Lewis and Roca, Phoenix, 1997-98; atty. gen. State of Ariz., Phoenix, 1998—; mem. Atty. Gen.'s Adv. Com., 1993—, chair, 1995-96. Vice-chair Ariz. Dem. Party, 1991-92; mem. Dem. Nat. Com., 1991-92; State Bd. Tech. Registration, 1989-92; Phoenix Design Standards Rev. Com., 1989-91; bd. dirs. Ariz. Cmty. Legal Svcs. Corp., 1987-92; bd. regents Santa Clara U., 1992—. Truman Scholarship Found. scholar, 1977. Mem. ABA, Am. Law Inst., Ariz. Bar Assn., Maricopa County Bar Assn., Am. Judicature Soc., Ariz. State Bar (chmn. civil practice and procedure com. 1991-92), Phi Beta Kappa, Alpha Sigma Nu. Avocations: hiking, trekking, travel, reading, film. Office: 1275 W Washington St Phoenix AZ 85007-2926

**NARAIN, CAMY TRIBENI,** lawyer; b. New Amsterdam, Guyana, June 8, 1971; d. Moonesar and Juliana N. BA, SUNY, Binghamton,, 1994; JD, New Eng. Sch. of Law, Boston, 1997. Bar: N.J. 1997, U.S. Dist. Ct. N.J. 1997, N.Y. 1998, U.S. Dist. Ct. (so. and ea. dists.) N.Y. 1998. Legal intern Embassy Republic of Guyana, N.Y.C., 1995, Mass. Trial Ct., Roxbury, 1996; law clk. Law Firm of Kuldip Kusuri, Jackson Hghts., N.Y., 1996; desk asst. New Eng. Sch. of Law, Boston, 1995-97; law clk. Law Office of Clement Forteau, Bklyn., 1997-98, assoc., 1998; ptnr. Forteau & Narain, S. Ozone Park, N.Y., 1998—; ct. evaluator Office of Ct. Adminstrn., N.Y.C., 1998—. Editor-in-chief New Eng. Internat. and Comparative Law Annual, 1997. Recipient Outstanding Scholastic Achievement award West Publishing Co., Boston, 1997. Mem. N.Y. State Bar Assn., N.Y. County Lawyers' Assn. General practice, General civil litigation, Immigration, naturalization, and customs. Office: Forteau & Narain 11023 Rockaway Blvd South Ozone Park NY 11420

**NARANJO, CAROLYN R.,** lawyer; b. Far Rockaway, N.Y., Nov. 28, 1954; d. Anthony J. and Mary (Lautazi) Spina; m. James Naranjo, Apr. 28, 1989. BA summa cum laude in Spl. & Elem. Edn., Bklyn. Coll., CUNY, 1976; JD, Temple U., 1981; student, Fordham U., 1980-81. Asst. counsel to head regional counsel First Am. Title Insurance, N.Y.C., 1981-82; legal counsel Creative Abstract Corp., N.Y.C., 1982-84; assoc. firm Friedman & Kornheiser, N.Y.C., 1982-84; assoc. Quinn, Cohen, Shields & Bock, N.Y.C., 1984-86; mng. ptnr. Collier, Cohen, Crystal & Bock, N.Y.C., 1986-94; pvt. practice Baldwin, N.Y., 1994—. Mem. ABA, Columbian Lawyers Assn. of Nassau County, Nassau Bar Assn., N.Y. State Bar Assn. Consumer commercial, Finance, Estate planning. Office: Ralph M Verni Bldg 746 Merrick Rd Baldwin NY 11510-3517

**NARAYAN, BEVERLY ELAINE,** lawyer; b. Berkeley, Calif., June 19, 1961; d. Jagjiwan and Alexandra (Mataras) N.; m. James Dean Schmidt, Jan. 7, 1989; children: Sasha Karan, Kaiya Maria. Student, San Francisco State U., 1979-80; BA, U. Calif., Berkeley, 1983; JD, U. Calif., San Francisco, 1987. Bar: Calif. 1987, U.S. Dist. Ct. (no. dist.) Calif. 1987, U.S. Dist. Ct. (ctrl. dist.) 1988. Atty. Daniels Barratta & Fine, L.A., 1988-89, Kornblum Ferry & Frye, L.A., 1990-91, Clapp Moroney Bellagamba Davis & Vucinich, Menlo Park, Calif., 1991-93, pvt. practice, Burlingame, Calif., 1993—; arbitrator Nat. Assn. Securities Dealers, San Francisco, 1987—, Pacific Stock Exch., San Francisco, 1994—; mediator Peninsula Conflict Resolution Ctr., San Mateo, Calif., 1995—; judge pro tem San Mateo Superior Ct., Redwood City, Calif., 1994—. Candidate Sch. Bd. San Mateo (Calif.) Unified Sch. Dist., 1993; mem. San Mateo County Task Force Violence Against Women. Recipient U. Calif. Hastings Coll. Law Achievement award, 1986; named Barrister of Yr., San Mateo County, 1996. Mem. ABA, San Mateo County Bar Assn. (co-chair women lawyers 1995, bd. dirs. 1994-96), Nat. Women's Polit. Caucus (bd. dirs., diversity chair 1993-96), San Mateo County Barristers Club (bd. dirs. 1993—, child watch chair 1995—), No. Calif. Indo-Am. Bar Assn. Avocations: baking, cooking, reading, travel, motorcycles, family. Securities, Alternative dispute resolution, General civil litigation. Office: 1508 Howard Ave Burlingame CA 94010-5216

**NARBER, GREGG ROSS,** lawyer; b. Iowa City, Sept. 4, 1946; s. James R. and Marguerite Maxine (Lasher) N.; m. Kathleen Joyce Andriano; children: Joshua Ross, Zachary Edward. BA, Grinnell Coll., 1968; MA, JD, Washington U., St. Louis, 1971. Bar: Iowa 1971, U.S. Ct. Mil. Appeals 1974, U.S. Supreme Ct. 1974. Atty. The Principal Fin. Group, Des Moines, 1975-76, asst. counsel, 1976-80, assoc. counsel, 1980-85, counsel, 1985-89, v.p., gen. counsel, 1989-92, sr. v.p., gen. counsel, 1993—; bd. dirs. Sargasso Mut. Ins. Co., Bermuda, Ban Renta Co. Seguros de Vida, Chile; prin. Life Compania de Seguros S.A., Argentina, Internat. Argentina S.A., Compania de Seguros de Retiro S.A., Argentina; lectr. Iowa Humanities Bd., 1981-82, Arts Midwest, 1987. Co-author: New Deal Mural Projects in Iowa, 1982; also articles; artist various works. Pres. intercultural program Am. Field Svc. Internat., West Des Moines, 1990-94; mem. acquisitions com., bd. trustees Edmundson Art Found./Des Moines Art Ctr., 1989—, pres. 1998-99; bd. dirs. Des Moines Symphony, 1989-94, Metro Arts Coun. Greater Des Moines, 1990-94, Edmundson Art Found., 1992—, pres. 1998—. Mem. ABA (ho. of dels. 1995-98), Iowa Bar Assn., Polk County Bar Assn., Prairie Club (sec. 1982-84, 86-87, pres. 1991-92), West Des Moines Soccer Club (coach 1982-89, referee 1984-89). Democrat. Mem. Congregational Ch. Avocations: art history and collecting, soccer. Pension, profit-sharing, and employee benefits, Corporate taxation, Insurance. Home: 1701 Casady Dr Des Moines IA 50315-1831 Office: The Prin Fin Group 711 High St Des Moines IA 50392-0002

**NARDI, RICHARD ANTHONY,** lawyer; b. N.Y.C., June 16, 1954; s. Richard Joseph and Carmela (Petitto) N.; m. Joan Rose Di Martino, July 15, 1978; children: Jenna, Richard. BA, Fordham Coll., Bronx, N.Y., 1976; JD, Fordham U., N.Y.C., 1979. Bar: N.Y. 1980, U.S. Dist. Ct. (so. and ea. dists.) N.Y. 1980. Assoc. Kelley Drye & Warren, N.Y.C., 1979-83; assoc. Corbin Silverman & Sanseverino, N.Y.C., 1983-86, ptnr., 1987—; bd. mem. Stewart Title Ins. Co. N.Y., N.Y.C. Pres. Bryan Hills Edn. Found., N.Y.; bd. mem., sec. Cardinal Spellman H.S. Found., Bronx. Mem. Mortgage Bankers Asns. N.Y. (pres. 1996, bd. govs. 1997), Assn. Bar of City N.Y. (com. chair condo and coops. 1995-98). Office: Corbin Silverman & Sanseverino 805 3rd Ave New York NY 10022-7513

**NARDI, STEPHEN J.,** lawyer; b. Kalispell, Mont., Feb. 11, 1951; s. Micheal Stephen and Grace Elaine N.; m. Darlene R. Nardi, May 26, 1979. BA in History, U. Mont., 1974, BA in Polit. Sci., JD, 1977. Bar: Mont. 1977, U.S. Dist. Ct. Mont. 1977, U.S. Ct. Appeals (9th cir.) 1977. Ptnr. Sherlock & Nardi, Kalispell, 1977—; instr. Flathead Valley C.C., Kalispell, 1979-84. Mem. Assn. Criminal Def. Attys., Mont. State Bar Assn., Exch. Club. Avocations: boating, golf, skiing, scuba diving. Criminal. Office: Sherlock & Nardi 30 5th St E Ste 101 Kalispell MT 59901-4999

**NARDI RIDDLE, CLARINE,** association administrator, judge; b. Clinton, Ind., Apr. 23, 1949; d. Frank Jr. and Alice (Mattioda) Nardi; m. Mark Alan Riddle, Aug. 15, 1971; children: Carl Nardi, Julia Nardi. AB in Math with honors, Ind. U., 1971, JD, 1974; LHD (hon.), St. Joseph Coll., 1991. Bar: Ind. 1974, U.S. Dist. Ct. (so. dist.) Ind. 1974, Conn. 1979, Fed. Dist. Ct. Conn. 1980, U.S. Supreme Ct. 1980, U.S. Ct. Appeals (2d cir.) 1986, U.S. Ct. Appeals (D.C. cir.) 1994. Staff atty. Ind. Legis. Svc. Agy., Indpls., 1974-78, legal counsel, 1978-79; dep. corp. counsel City of New Haven, 1980-83; counsel to atty. gen. State of Conn., Hartford, 1983-86, dep. atty. gen., 1986-89, acting atty. gen., 1989, atty. gen., 1989-91; judge Superior Ct. State of Conn., 1991-93; sr. v.p. for govtl. affairs, gen. counsel Nat. Multi-Housing Coun., Nat. Apartment Assn., 1995—; asst. counsel state majority Conn. Gen. Assembly, Hartford, 1979, legal rsch. asst. to prof. Yale U., New Haven, 1979; legal counsel com. on law revision Indpls. State Bar Assn., 1979; mem. Chief Justice's Task Force on Gender Bias, Hartford, 1988-90; mem. ethics and values com. Ind. Sector, Washington, 1988-90; co-organizer Ind. Continuing Legal Edn. Forum Inst. Legal Drafting Legislature and Pvt. Practice; Internat. Women's Yr. panelist Credit Laws and Their Enforcement; mem. Atty. Gen.'s Blue Ribbon Commn., Chief Justice's Com. Study Publs. Policy Conn. Law. Jour., Law Revision Commn. Adminstrv. Law Study, Chief Justice's Task Force Gender, Justice and Cts., Gov.'s Task Force Fed. Revenue Enhancements; mem. exec. com. Jud. Dept.; mem. panel arbitrators Am. Arbitration Assn., 1994; gen. counsel Nat. Multi Housing Coun.; lectr in field. Author: (with F.R. Rembusch) Drafting Manual for the Indiana General Assembly, 1976; sr. editor Ind. U. Law Sch. Interdisciplinary Law Jour.; contbr. articles to profl. jours. Bd. visitors Ind. U., Bloomington, 1974-92; mem. Gov.'s Missing Children Com., Hartford, Conn. Child Support Guidelines Com., Gov.'s Task Force on Justice for Abused Children, Hartford, 1988-90; mem. Mayor's City of New Haven Task Force Reorganization Corp. Counsel's Office, Gov.'s Child Support Commn., Mayor of New Haven's Blue Ribbon Commn.; former bd. dirs. New Haven Neighborhood Music Sch.; bd. dirs., mem. youth adv. com. Gov.'s Partnership Prevent Substance Abuse Workforce-Drugs Don't Work. Recipient Women in Leadership Recognition award Hartford Region YWCA, 1986, Award of Merit, Women & Law Sect. Conn. Bar Assn., 1989, Fellowship award South End Ladies Dem. Club, 1989, Woman of Yr. award Greater Hartford Fedn. of Bus. & Profl. Women's Clubs, 1990, Conn. Original award Somers-Mabelle B. Avery Sch., 1990, Cert. of Recognition, Consortium Law-Related Edn., 1990, Citizen award Conn. Task Force Children's Constl. Rights, 1991, Ann. award Hartford Assn. Women Attys., 1993; named Conn. History Maker, U.S. Dept. Labor, Women's Bur. & Permanent Commn. Status Women, 1989, Impact Player, The Conn. Law Tribune, 1992. Mem. ABA, Conn. Bar Assn. (chair com. on gender bias, Citation of Merit women and law sect. 1989), Nat. Assn. Attys. Gen. (chair charitable trusts and solicitation 1988-90), New Haven Neighborhood Music Sch. (bd. dirs.), Am. Arbitration Assn. (arbitration panel 1994), Ind. Bar Assn., Conn. Bar Assn. (chair com. gender bias legal profession), Indpls. Bar Assn., Ind. Civil Liberties Union (bd. dirs., mem. exec. com., chair long range planning com., mem. women's rights project, membership v.p., Disting. Svc. award), Conn. Consortium Law and Citizenship Edn., Inc. (bd. dirs.), Conn. Judges Assn. (mem. legislation com.), Ind. U. Law Sch. Alumni Assn. (bd. dirs.), Enomene Hon. Soc., Pleiades Hon. Soc., Mortar Bd. (nat. fellow), Alpha Lambda Delta. Democrat. Presbyterian. Office: Nat Multi Housing Coun 1850 M St NW Ste 450 Washington DC 20036-5816

**NARDONE, GLENN A.,** lawyer; b. Newton, Mass., Aug. 2, 1955. BA, Oberlin Coll., 1977; JD, New Eng. Sch. Law, Boston, 1981. Bar: Mass. 1981. Sole practitioner Boston, 1981—. General practice. Office: 60 Commercial Wharf Boston MA 02110-3801

**NARDONE, RICHARD,** lawyer, consultant; b. Poughkeepsie, N.Y., Dec. 29, 1945; s. Michael and Rosemary (Murden) N.; children: Richard David, Jorinda Suzanne. BA, Syracuse U., 1970; JD, Albany Law Sch., 1973. Bar: N.Y. 1974, U.S. Dist. Ct. (no. dist.) N.Y 1974, U.S. Dist. Ct. (so. dist.) N.Y. 1977. Ptnr. Nardone & Nardone, Highland, N.Y., 1977-79; sole practice Highland, 1979—. Fellow mem. ABA, N.Y. State Bar Assn., N.Y. State Trial Lawyers Assn., Ulster County Bar Assn., Dutchess County Bar Assn. Avocations: fishing, hunting, boating, auto racing. Personal injury, State civil litigation, Family and matrimonial. Office: N Roberts Rd Highland NY 12528-2003

**NARDONE, WILLIAM ANDREW,** lawyer; b. Groton, Conn., June 16, 1954; s. Henry Joseph and Mary Frances (Herley) N.; m. Diane Ruth Hall, July 1, 1988; children: Madison Catherine, William Chase. BA, U. R.I., 1976; JD, Suffolk U., 1980. Bar: R.I. 1981, U.S. Dist. Ct. R.I. 1981, U.S. Supreme Ct. 1991. Assoc. Law Office of M.L. Lewiss, Westerly, R. I., 1980-83; ptnr. Orsinger & Nardone Law Offices, Westerly, 1983—; solicitor Westerly Sch. Dept., 1984-90, 94-96, 98—. Mem. com. Westerly YMCA, 1980, bd. dirs., 1991—, exec. com., 1994—; bd. dirs., pres. Westerly Adult Day Care Ctr., 1985-93; trustee Westerly Hosp., 1993—, SNEPHO, 1994—. Mem. Nat. Coun. Sch. Attys., R.I. Bar Assn. (rep. Ho. of Dels. 1984-90), Nat. Assn. Legal Problems in Edn. Republican. Roman Catholic. Contracts commercial, Real property, Land use and zoning (including planning). Home: 38 Wicklow Rd Westerly RI 02891-3644 Office: Orsinger & Nardone 53 High St Westerly RI 02891-6001

**NARMONT, JOHN STEPHEN,** lawyer; b. Auburn, Ill., June 24, 1942; s. Stephen and Luriel (Welle) N.; m. Sondra J. Nicholls, Feb. 12, 1978. BBA magna cum laude, U. Notre Dame, 1964; JD, U. Ill., Champaign, 1967. ar: Ill. 1967, U.S. Dist. Ct. (so. dist.) Ill. 1967, U.S. Ct. Appeals (7th cir.) 1967, U.S. Tax Ct. 1978, U.S. Supreme Ct. 1973. Pvt. practice Springfield, Ill.; founder, pres., owner Richland Ranch, Inc., Auburn; originator, pres. The Solid Gold Futurity, Ltd. em. ABA, Sangamon County Bar Assn., Ill. State Bar Assn., Assn. Trial Lawyer Am., Am. Agrl. Law Assn., Ill. Inst. for Continuing Legal Edn., Internat. Livestock Exposition (pres., founder). Family and matrimonial, General civil litigation, Bankruptcy. Office: 209 N Bruns Ln Springfield IL 62702-4612

**NASH, BRIAN JOSEPH,** lawyer; b. Orange, N.J., Aug. 27, 1946; s. Harry Thomas and Ethel (Doherty) N.; m. Charree Kristine Hungate, Sept. 7, 1968 (div. May 1995); children: Kristine, Terence, Sean, Daniel; m. Marian L. Hogan, Sept. 16, 1995. BA in English, Cath. U. Am., 1969, JD, 1974. Bar: Md. 1974, U.S. Ct. Appeals (4th cir.) 1974, U.S. Dist. Ct. Md. 1974, U.S. Ct. Appeals (D.C. cir.) 1976, D.C. 1976. Law clk. to Hon. Herbert Murray U.S. Dist. Ct. Md., Balt., 1974-75; assoc. Donahue & Ehrmantraut, Rockville, Md., 1975-79; ptnr. Donovan & Nash, Silver Spring, Md., 1979-87, Montedonico, Hamilton, Altman & Nash, Washington, 1987-92, Wharton, Levin, Ehrmantraut, Klein & Nash, Bethesda, Md., 1992—; guest lectr. Medlantic Health Care Sys., Washington, 1988-94, Sch. of Law Am. U., Washington, 1990. Casenotes editor Cath. U. of Am. Law Rev., 1974. Mem. ABA, D.C. Bar, D.C. Def. Lawyers' Assn. Avocations: golf, gardening. Personal injury, General civil litigation, Health. Home: 6004 Charlesmead Rd Baltimore MD 21212-2213 Office: Wharton Levin Ehrmantraut Klein & Nash PO Box 551 Annapolis MD 21404-0551

**NASH, GORDON BERNARD, JR.,** lawyer; b. Evergreen, Ill., Feb. 24, 1944; s. Gordon Bernard and Lilyan (Grafft) N.; m. Roseanne Joan Burke, Aug. 24, 1968; children: Caroline, Brian, Terry, Maureen. BA, Notre Dame U., 1966; JD, Loyola U., Chgo., 1969. Bar: Ill., U.S. Dist. (no. dist.) Ill. Atty. Office U.S. Atty. No. Dist. Ill., Chgo., 1971-78; ptnr. Gardner, Carton & Douglas, Chgo., 1978—. Chmn. Ill. Bd. Ethics, Springfield, 1980-85. Served to capt. U.S. Army, 1969-71. Recipient John Marshall award U.S. Dept. Justice, 1978, Spl. Commendation award, 1975, Disting. Achievement award Internat. Acad. Trial Lawyers, 1969. Mem. ABA, Ill. Bar Assn., Chgo. Bar Found. (bd. dirs. 1983-85, 87-89), Fed. Bar Assn. (bd. govs. 1986-91), Chgo. Bar Assn. (bd. mgrs. 1983-85, pres. 1990-91), Constl. Rights Found. Com. (bd. dirs. 1993—, vice chmn. 1998—), Am. Coll. Trial Lawyers, Ctr. For Conflict Resolution (bd. 1992—, v.p. 1995—), Chgo. Inn of Ct. (pres. 1996-97), Olympia Fields Country Club. Democrat. Roman Catholic. Criminal, Federal civil litigation, State civil litigation. Home: 5101 Harvey Ave Western Springs IL 60558-2042 Office: Gardner Carton & Douglas Quaker Tower 321 N Clark St Ste 3400 Chicago IL 60610-4717

**NASH, MELVIN SAMUEL,** lawyer; b. Atlanta, Aug. 26, 1949; s. Ralph Samuel and Mary Pauline (Quarles) N.; m. Cynthia Joanna Hamrick, Aug. 21, 1980 (div.); m. Kristine Marie Clark, Nov. 22, 1997. A.B., Ga. State U., 1974; J.D., U. Fla., 1976. Bar: Ga. 1978, U.S. Ct. Claims 1983, U.S. Ct. Internat. Trade 1983, U.S. Tax Ct. 1982, U.S. Ct. Appeals (5th cir.) 1978, U.S. Ct. Appeals (11th cir.) 1981, U.S. Supreme Ct. 1985. Asst. solicitor State Ct., Cobb County, Marietta, Ga., 1977-78; assoc. Milam & Smith, Austell, Ga., 1978; ptnr. Milam, Smith & Nash, Austell, 1978-79; sole practice, Marietta, 1979—; spl. master Cobb Superior Ct., 1982—; dir. Nash Trucking Co., Inc., Marietta, Security Fiedelity Mortgage, Marietta, Nash Properties, Marietta. Magistrate Prohac Vice State Ct. Cobb County, Marietta, 1980-82; candidate state rep. State of Ga. Dist. 21, Marietta, 1982. Served with USAF, 1967-71. Mem. ABA, Acad. Fla. Trial Lawyers, Assn. Trial Lawyers Am., Nat. Assn. Criminal Def. Lawyers, Ga. Assn. Criminal Def. Lawyers, Cobb County Bar Assn. (com. 1983-84), Cobb Criminal Def. Bar Assn. (sec., Seminar award 1984), State Bar Ga. (fee arbitrator 1982—). Democrat. Presbyterian. Clubs: Atlanta Ski, Atlanta Track (Marathon finisher). Criminal, Personal injury.

**NASH, PAUL LENOIR,** lawyer; b. Poughkeepsie, N.Y., Jan. 29, 1931; s. George Matthew and Winifred (LeNoir) N.; m. Nancy Allyn Thouron, Dec. 30, 1961; children—Andrew Gray, Laurie LeNoir, Daphne Thouron. B.A., Yale U., 1953; LL.B., Harvard U., 1958. Bar: N.Y. 1959. Assoc., Dewey, Ballantine, Bushby, Palmer & Wood, N.Y.C., 1958-66, ptnr., 1966—. Pres. bd. trustees Peck Sch., Morristown, N.J., 1978-82. Served to capt. USMC, 1953-55; Japan. Mem. ABA, N.Y. State Bar Assn., Assn. Bar City of N.Y. Republican. Mergers and acquisitions, General corporate, Securities. Home: 4 Westminster Pl Morristown NJ 07960-5810 Office: Dewey Ballantine LLP 1301 Avenue Of The Americas New York NY 10019-6022

**NASON, JUDITH A.,** lawyer; b. Bennington, Vt., Apr. 29, 1959; d. Howard A. and Elsie J. N. BA, SUNY, Albany, 1981; MM, SUNY, Stony Brook, 1984; JD, Rutgers U., 1988. Bar: N.J. 1988, N.Y. 1989. Law clk. to Hon. Robert N. Wilentz N.J. Supreme Ct., 1988-89; atty. Kaye, Scholer, Fierman, Hays & Handler, N.Y.C., 1989-91, LeBoeuf, Lamb, Leiby & MacCrae, Newark, 1991-92; dep. atty. gen. N.J. Atty. Gens. Office, Trenton, 1993—. Avocations: scuba diving, animal rights, origami, tropical aquariums. Office: Div Law Hughes Justice Complex PO Box 112 Trenton NJ 08625-0112

**NASON, LEONARD YOSHIMOTO,** lawyer, writer, publisher; b. N.Y.C., Feb. 17, 1954; s. Leonard Hastings and Mary Yukiko (Yoshimoto) N.; m. Linda Thayer, Sept. 26, 1981; children: Victoria, Kelsey, Jennifer. BA, Tufts U., 1975; JD, Northeastern U., Boston, 1979. Bar: Mass. 1979, U.S. Dist. Ct. 1979, U.S. Ct. Appeals (1st cir.) 1985. Assoc. Ricklefs & Uehlein, Natick, Mass., 1979-84; ptnr. Uehlein, Nason & Wall, Natick, 1985-95, Nason, Wall & Wall, P.C., Lexington, Mass., 1995—; pres. Legal Info. Svcs., Inc., Lexington, 1986—. Author: (handbook) Mass. Workers' Compensation, 1986, (statute book) Mass. Workers' Compensation, 1987; co-author: Massachusetts Practice Series, Vol. 29, 1989, 95; contbg. author: A Judicial Guide to Labor and Employment Law, 1990. Bd. dirs. Newton Community Service Ctr., 1981. Mem. ABA, Mass. Bar Assn., Boston Bar Assn., Assn. Trial Lawyers Am. Avocations: tennis, sailing, softball, music. Workers' compensation, Personal injury. Office: Nason Wall & Wall PC 430 Bedford St Ste 250 Lexington MA 02420-1528

**NASSAR, WILLIAM MICHAEL,** lawyer; b. Methuen, Mass., June 5, 1958; s. William M. and Catherine M. Nassar; m. Ermelinda Amezcua, June 26, 1982; children: Brandon Michael, Elyse Renae. AAS, R.I. C.C., 1978; BSBA, U. Redlands, 1980; JD, Western State Coll. of Law, 1986. Legal adminstr. Bourns Inc., Riverside, Calif., 1988-90, dir. worldwide contracts adminstr., 1990-94, dir. worldwide contracts/legal counsel, 1994-97, sr. legal counsel, 1997—; v.p., gen. counsel, 1999—; bd. dirs. Advanced Med. Inc., Riverside, Calif., Global Pathways Inc., Riverside; v.p. Bourns Employees Fed. Credit Union, bd. dirs. Adv. bd. Ronald McDonald House, Loma Linda, Calif., 1994-98. Roman Catholic. Avocations: sailing, boating, skiing, reading. General corporate, Contracts commercial, Intellectual property. Home: 13015 Burns Ln Redlands CA 92373-7415 Office: Bourns Inc 1200 Columbia Ave Riverside CA 92507-2114

**NASSAU, MICHAEL JAY,** lawyer; b. N.Y.C., June 3, 1935; s. Benjamin and Belle (Nassau) N.; m. Roberta Bluma Herzlich, June 26, 1971; children: Stephanie Ellen, William Michael. BA summa cum laude, Yale U., 1956, LLB cum laude, 1960. Bar: N.Y. 1960, U.S. Ct. Appeals (2d cir.) 1963, U.S. Tax Ct. 1963, U.S. Supreme Ct. 1965, U.S. Dist. Ct. (so. dist.) N.Y. 1978, D.C. 1992. Asst. instr. in constl. law Yale U., 1959-60; law clk. to judge U.S. Ct. Appeals 2d Cir., 1960-61; assoc. tax dept. Paul, Weiss, Rifkind, Wharton & Garrison, N.Y.C., 1961-73; ptnr. Kramer Levin Naftalis & Frankel LLP, and predecessor, N.Y.C., 1974—; mem. adv. bd. Matthew Bender Fed. Pension Law Service, 1975-76; mem. adv. com. NYU Ann. Inst. Employee Plans and Exec. Compensation, 1976-79; mem. steering com. Am. Pension Conf., 1981-83; lectr. in field; panelist various seminars on employee benefits; panelist Pension Video Seminar, 1983. Mem. editl. bd. Bank and Corp. Governance Law Reporter, 1989—; contbr. chpts. to books and articles to profl. jours. Mem. ABA (sect. taxation, employee benefits com. 1993—), N.Y. State Bar Assn. (co-chmn. employee benefits sect. taxation 1976-78, mem. exec. com. sect. taxation 1976-79), Assn. of Bar of City of N.Y. (chmn. subcom. pension legis. of com. taxation 1975-76, employee benefits com. 1987-92), WEB (N.Y. chpt. bd. dirs. 1990—, pres. 1993-94), Phi Beta Kappa. Pension, profit-sharing, and employee benefits. Office: Kramer Levin Naftalis & Frankel LLP 919 3rd Ave New York NY 10022-3902

**NAST, DIANNE MARTHA,** lawyer; b. Mount Holly, N.J., Jan. 30, 1948; d. Henry Daniel and Anastasia (Lovenduski) N.; m. Joseph Francis Roda, Aug. 23, 1980; children: Michael, Daniel, Joseph, Joshua, Anastasia. BA, Pa. State U., 1965; JD, Rutgers U., 1976. Bar: Pa. 1976, U.S. Dist. Ct. Pa. 1976, N.J. 1976, U.S. Dist. Ct. N.J. 1976, U.S. Ct. Appeals (3d, 5th, 6th, 7th, 8th and 11th cirs.) 1976, U.S. Supreme Ct. 1982, U.S. Dist. Ct. Ariz. 1985. Dir., v.p. Kohn, Nast & Graf, P.C., Phila., 1976-95, Roda & Nast, P.C., Lancaster, Pa., 1995—; mem. lawyers adv. com. U.S. Ct. Appeals (3d cir.), 1982-84, chmn., 1983-84, mem. com. on revision jud. conf. conduct rules, 1982-84; mem. U.S. Ct. Appeals for the 3d Cir. Jud. Conf. Permanent Planning Com., 1983-90; bd. dirs. 3d Cir. Hist. Soc., 1993—; bd. dirs. Phila. Pub. Def., 1980-89; dir. U.S. Fed. Judicial Ctr. Found., 1991—, chair, 1996—; chmn. lawyers adv. com. U.S. Dist. Ct. (ea. dist.) Pa., 1982-90. Pres. Hist. Soc., 1988-91. Fellow ABA (coun. litigation sect. 1986-89, co-chmn. anti-trust com. litigation sect. 1984-86, div. dir. 1990-91, practical litigation editl. bd. 1989—, ho. of dels. 1992-94, mem. task force state justice initiatives, mem. task force state of justice system, 1993, mem. task force long range planning com. 1994), Am. Law Inst. (chair internat. professionalism com. 1991-94, civil justice task force 1993-95), Am. Arbitration Assn. (bd. dirs., mem. alt. dispute resolution and mass torts task force), Am. Judicature Soc., Pa. Bar Assn. (bd. of dels. 1983-95), N.J. Bar Assn., Pa. Trial Lawyers Assn., Phila. Bar Assn. (bd. govs. 1985-87, chmn., bicentennial com. 1986-87, chmn. bench bar conf. 1988-89), Lancaster Bar Assn. (co-chair civil litigation and rules com. trial law sect.), Rutgers Law Sch. Alumni Assn. Antitrust, Product liability, Federal civil litigation. Home: 1059 Sylvan Rd Lancaster PA 17601-1923 Office: Roda & Nast PC 801 Estelle Dr Lancaster PA 17601-2130

**NATALE, FRANK ANTHONY, II,** lawyer; b. New Castle, Pa., Dec. 21, 1968; s. Frank Anthony Sr. and Delores Ann Natale; m. Regina Ann Johnson, Aug. 17, 1996. BA, U. Pitts., 1990; JD, U. Dayton, 1993. Bar: Pa. 1993, Ohio, U.S. Dist. Ct. (we. dist.) Pa., U.S. Dist. Ct. (so. and we. dists. Ohio. Assoc. Dallas W. Hartman P.C., New Castle, 1993-96, Cusick & Leymarie, New Castle, 1996—. Vol., Salute to Courage, St. Francis Hosp., New Castle, 1997, 98, vol. Festival of Trees, 1997. Avocations: skiing, golf, cooking. Labor, Personal injury, General civil litigation. Home: 2410 Highland Ave New Castle PA 16105-2182

**NATCHER, STEPHEN DARLINGTON,** lawyer, business executive; b. San Francisco, Nov. 19, 1940; s. Stanlus Zoch and Robena Lenore Collie (Goldring) N.; m. Carolyn Anne Bowman, Aug. 23, 1969; children: Tanya Michelle, Stephanie Elizabeth. A.B. in Polit. Sci., Stanford U., 1962; J.D., U. Calif., San Francisco, 1965. Bar: Calif. 1966. Assoc. firm Pillsbury, Madison & Sutro, San Francisco, 1966-68; counsel Douglas Aircraft div. McDonnell Douglas Corp., Long Beach, Calif., 1968-70; v.p., sec. Security Pacific Nat. Bank, 1971-79; asst. gen. counsel Security Pacific Corp., 1979-80; v.p., sec., gen. counsel Lear Siegler, Inc., Santa Monica, Calif., 1980-87; v.p., gen. counsel Computer Scis. Corp., El Segundo, Calif., 1987-88; exec. v.p., gen. counsel, sec. CalFed Inc., 1989-90; sr. v.p. adminstrn., gen. counsel, sec. Wyle Electronics, Irvine, Calif., 1991-98; gen. counsel VEBA Electronics Inc., Santa Clara, Calif., 1998—. With USCG, 1965-71. Mem. St. Francis Yacht Club (San Francisco), The Pacific Club (Newport Beach). Republican. General practice, General corporate, Securities.

**NATES, JEROME HARVEY,** publisher, lawyer; b. N.Y.C., Sept. 19, 1945; s. Louis and Lillian (Berger) N.; m. Marilyn Arlene Weiss, June 6, 1971; children: Lori Jennifer, Scott Eric. BA, Hunter Coll., 1968; JD, Bklyn. Law Sch., 1972. Bar: N.Y. 1973. Assoc. atty. Natiss & Rogers, Long Island, N.Y., 1972-73; editorial dir. Matthew Bender & Co., N.Y.C., 1973-84; editor-in-chief Kluwer Law Book Pub., N.Y.C., 1984-88; legal pub. cons., 1988-98; mng. editor Aspen Law & Bus., N.Y.C., 1998—. Co-author: Damages in Tort Actions, 1982; editor: Personal Injury Deskbook-1983, Personal Injury Deskbook-1984. Avocations: tennis, golf. Home: 19 Hummingbird Ct Marlboro NJ 07746-2510

**NATHAN, ANDREW JONATHAN,** lawyer, real estate developer; b. Honolulu, Mar. 20, 1957; s. Joel Joseph and Wendy Barbra (Bernstein) N.; m. Bonnie Lynn Raymond, Aug. 16, 1981 (div. Sept. 1987); m. Holly Lorraine Marshall, Feb. 17, 1990; children: Jake, Tyler. BA cum laude, Brandeis U., 1978; JD with distinction, Hofstra U., 1981. Assoc. Schulte Roth & Zabel, N.Y.C., 1981-87; counsel Tishman Speyer Properties, N.Y.C., 1987, gen. counsel, 1990, gen. counsel, mng. dir., 1993-97, sr. mng. dir., co-head domestic acquisitions and devel., 1997—. Articles editor Hofstra Law Rev., 1981. Mem. ABA, N.Y. State Bar Assn. Real property, Private international, General corporate. Office: Tishman Speyer Properties 520 Madison Ave New York NY 10022-4213

**NATHAN, EDWARD SINGER,** lawyer; b. Newark, Aug. 14, 1954; s. Emanuel and Evelyn (Lachter) N.; m. Merridith Elaine Cramer, Feb. 23, 1995. BA, U. Rochester, 1976; JD, Rutgers U., 1986. Bar: N.J. 1986. Ptnr. Stern & Greenberg, Roseland, N.J., 1998—. V.p. The Children's Inst., Livingston, N.J., 1993-96, pres., 1996—; life mem. South Orange (N.J.) Rescue Squad, 1976-86. Mem. N.J. Bar Assn., Essex County Bar Assn. Avocations: bicycling, fitness. General civil litigation, Contracts commercial, Consumer commercial. Home: 768 Springfield Ave Apt B-8 Summit NJ 07901-2331 Office: 75 Livingston Ave Roseland NJ 07068-3701

**NATHAN, J(AY) ANDREW,** lawyer; b. St. Louis, Aug. 25, 1947; s. Ira L. Nathan and Babette Gross Simon; m. Linda L. Berenbeim, July 27, 1969; children: Joshua, Marni. BA, U. Mo., 1969; JD, U. Colo., 1972. Bar: Colo. 1972, U.S. Dist. Ct. Colo. 1972, U. S. Ct. Appeals (10th cir.) 1972. Assoc. atty. Burnette, Watson, Horan & Hilgers, Denver, 1972-73; shareholder, pres. Watson, Nathan & Bremer, P.C., Denver, 1973-97, Nathan, Bremer, Dumm & Myers, P.C., Denver, 1997—. Mem Colo. Def. Lawyers Assn., Def. Rsch. Inst., Am. Bd. Trial Advs. (pres. Colo. chpt. 1990, nat. bd. dirs. 1990-96). Avocations: scuba diving, golf, oenology. Personal injury, Insurance, Civil rights. Office: Nathan Bremer Dumm & Myers PC 3900 E Mexico Ave Ste 1000 Denver CO 80210-3945

**NATHANSON, DAVID J.,** lawyer, prosecutor; b. Passaic, N.J., Jan. 15, 1963; s. Bernard and Elaine Nathanson. BA, Rutgers U., 1985; JD, Vt. U., 1988. Bar: N.J. Chief spl. investigations, chief confidential investigations Bergen County Pros. Office, Hackensack, N.J.; instr. N.J. Dept. Law and Pub. Safety, Trenton. Mem. Bergen County Bar Assn. Avocations: flag football, coach.

**NATIONS, HOWARD LYNN,** lawyer; b. Dalton, Ga., Jan. 9, 1938; s. Howard Lynn and Eva Earline (Armstrong) Lamb; m. Ella Lois Johnson, June 4, 1960 (div. Nov. 1976); children: Cynthia Lynn Nations Garcia, Angela Jean Gordon. BA, Florida State U., 1963; JD, Fla. State U., 1966. Bar: Tex. 1966. Assoc. Butler, Rice Cook & Knapp, Houston, 1966-71; pres. Nations & Cross, Houston, 1971—; v.p., dir., co-founder Ins. Corp. Am., Houston, 1972—; pres. Caplinger & Nations Galleries, Houston, 1973—, Nations Investment Corp., Houston, 1975—, NCM Trade Corp., Houston, 1975; v.p. Delher Am. Inc., Houston, 1975—; pres. Howard L. Nations, PC, Houston, 1971—; adj. prof. So. Tex. Coll. Law, Houston, 1967—; speaker in field. Author: Structuring Settlements, 1987; co-author: Texas Workers' Compensation, 1988, (with others) The Anatomy of a Personal Injury Lawsuit, 3rd rev. edit. 1991; editor: Maximizing Damages in Wrongful Death and Personal Injury Litigation, 1985; contbr. articles to profl. jours. Chmn., trustee Nat. Coll. Advocacy, Washington, 1985-92. With M.I. Corps, U.S. Army, 1957-60. Fellow Tex. Bar Found., Houston Bar Found. (life); mem. ATLA (exec. com. 1991-95), Nat. Bd. Trial Advocacy (diplomate civil trial advocacy), So. Trial Lawyers Assn. (pres. 1994-95), Tex. Trial Lawyers Assn. (pres. 1992-93), Tex. Assn. Cert. Trial Lawyers (past pres.). Personal injury, Product liability, General civil litigation. Office: The Sterling Mansion 4515 Yoakum Blvd Houston TX 77006-5821

**NAUGHTON, EDWARD JOSEPH,** lawyer; b. Syosset, N.Y., June 19, 1968; m. Jennifer E. Pawloski, Aug. 14, 1993. AB in Chemistry and Philosophy, Amherst (Mass.) Coll., 1989; JD magna cum laude, Georgetown U., 1993. Bar: Md. 1993, Mass. 1995, D.C. 1995. Assoc. Shea and Gardner, Washington, 1993-95, Sherburne, Powers & Needham, Washington, 1995—. Mem. ABA, Md. State Bar Assn., Boston Bar Assn., Order of the Coif. Federal civil litigation, Trademark and copyright, Intellectual property. Office: Sherburne Powers & Needham One Beacon St Boston MA 02108

**NAUGHTON, JOHN ALEXANDER,** lawyer; b. Chgo., Jan. 26, 1947; s. Hugh and Margaret (Durkin) N.; m. Raydeen E. Banfi, Dec. 27, 1969; children: Teryn Alisa, Tysen Anne, Ryan Eric, Justen Aran. BS in Commerce, De Paul U., 1970; JD, John Marshall Law Sch., Chgo., 1977. Bar: Ill. 1977, U.S. Dist. Ct. (no. dist.) Ill. 1978. Assoc. Kusper & Raucci, Chartered, Chgo., 1978-81; city atty. Berwyn, 1981-82; pvt. practice Berwyn, Ill., 1981—; twp. atty. Berwyn Health Dept., 1982-85. Bd. dirs. Altenheim, Forest Park, Ill., 1977-88; alderman Berwyn City Council, 1977-80, mayor, 1980-81. Mem. Ill. Bar Assn., W. Suburban Bar Assn. Family and matrimonial, Criminal, Real property.

**NAUHEIM, STEPHEN ALAN,** lawyer; b. Washington, Nov. 17, 1942; s. Ferdinand Alan and Beatrice Lillian (Strasburger) N.; children: Terry Beth, David Alan. BS in Acctg., U. N.C., 1964; JD, Georgetown U., 1967; LLM, George Washington U., 1970. Bar: D.C. 1968, U.S. Ct. Claims 1968, U.S. Tax Ct. 1971. Atty. adviser office chief counsel IRS, Washington, 1967-71, asst. br. chief, 1970-71; assoc. Surrey & Morse, Washington, 1971-75, ptnr., 1975-81; prin. Anderson, Hibey, Nauheim & Blair, Washington, 1981-91, Schall, Boudreau & Gore, Washington, 1991-93; pres., gen. counsel CMW Group, Ltd., Washington, 1994-96; dir. Pricewaterhouse Coopers LLP, 1996—; mem. adv. bd. World Trade Inst., N.Y.C., 1978—, Tax Mgmt. Adv. Bd., Washington, 1980—. Mem. editl. bd. Internat. Tax Jour., N.Y.C., 1982—; contbr. to profl. publs. Mem. ABA (former com. chmn. taxation sect.), Internat. Fiscal Assn., D.C. Bar Assn. (mem. steering com. tax sect. 1987-92, chmn. tax sect. 1990-92), Am. Coll. of Tax Counsel. Avocations: travelling, sailing. Corporate taxation, General corporate, Real property. Office: Pricewaterhouse Coopers 1301 K St NW Ste 800W Washington DC 20005-3317

**NAVARRETE, YOLANDA,** lawyer; b. Havana, Cuba, May 12, 1960; came to U.S., 1962; d. Concepcion (Bernardez) N.; children: Kristopher Suris, Adam Suris, Jonah Mendez. BA in Bilingual/Bicultural Edn., Kean Coll., 1983; JD, Rutgers U., 1991. Bar: N.J. 1991. Tchr. Eliz (N.J.) Bd. Edn., 1983-85, Dover (N.J.) Bd. Edn., 1990-91; atty. Jose Navarette, Union City, N.J., 1991—; linguistic cons. Aguirre Internat., Calif., 1985-87. Bd. mem. Cesarean Prevention Movement, N.J., 1985. Mem. ABA, North Hudson Lawyers. Personal injury, Family and matrimonial, Criminal. Office: Navarrete & Navarrete 3916 Bergenline Ave Union City NJ 07087-4820

**NAVARRO, BRUCE CHARLES,** lawyer; b. West Lafayette, Ind., Oct. 30, 1954; s. Joseph Anthony and Dorothy Gloria (Gnazzo) N.; children: Philip Joseph, Joanna Christina. BA, Duke U., 1976; JD, Ind. U., 1980. Bar: D.C. 1980. Asst. counsel U.S. Senate Labor Subcom., Washington, 1981-84; acting dep. undersec. for legis. affairs Dept. Labor, Washington, 1984-85; atty. advisor EEOC, Washington, 1985-86; dir. Office of Congl. Rels. Office of Pers. Mgmt., Washington, 1986-89; prin. dep. asst. atty. gen. for legis. U.S. Dept. of Justice, Washington, 1989-91; spl. asst. to gen. counsel U.S. Dept. HHS, Washington, 1991; expert cons. U.S. Dept. Def., Washington, 1992; counsel to the vice chmn. U.S. Consumer Product Safety Commn., Bethesda, Md., 1992-95; prin. Navarro Regulatory and Legis. Affairs, Washington, 1995—. Mem. Arlington County Republican Com. (Va.), 1983; bd. dirs. Prince William Cmty. Safe Kids Coalition, 1997-99. Mem. D.C. Bar Assn. Roman Catholic. Avocation: music, golf. Administrative and regulatory, Legislative, Health. Home: 6305 Lone Oak Dr Bethesda MD 20817-1745 Office: 1742 N St NW Washington DC 20036-2907

**NAVATTA, ANNA PAULA,** lawyer; b. Hackensack, N.J., Jan. 7, 1956; d. Jack Anthony and Natalie (Pretto) N. BA, Rutgers U., 1978, MA, 1979; JD, Seton Hall U., 1982. Bar: N.J. 1983, U.S. Dist. Ct. N.J. 1983, U.S. Ct. Appeals (3d cir.) 1986. Law clk. to presiding justice Superior Ct. N.J., Hackensack, 1982-83; staff atty. Bergen County Legal Svcs., Hackensack, 1983—; instr. Am. Inst. Paralegal Studies, Mahwah, N.J., 1986—; atty. Lyndhurst (N.J.) Planning Bd., 1987-89. Mem. ABA, Fed. Bar Assn., N.J. State Bar Assn., Bergen County Bar Assn., Emblem Club. Democrat. Roman Catholic. Administrative and regulatory, Landlord-tenant, Land use and zoning (including planning). Office: Bergen County Legal Svcs 47 Essex St Hackensack NJ 07601-5418

**NAYLOR, BRIAN THOMAS,** lawyer; b. North Salem, N.Y., Dec. 7, 1949; s. Edward Charles and Ann Marie (Gargan) N.; m. Maureen Catherine Murphy, Aug. 7, 1971; children: Katie, Cory, Colin. AB, Fordham U., 1971; JD, Columbia U., 1974. Bar: N.Y. 1975, U.S. Dist. Ct. (so. and ea. dists.) N.Y. 1975, U.S. Ct. Appeals (2d cir.) 1975, N.J. 1978, U.S. Dist. Ct N.J. 1978. Assoc. Simpson, Thacher & Bartlett, N.Y.C., 1974-79; assoc. counsel Beneficial Mgmt. Corp., Morristown, N.J., 1979-81; v.p., gen. counsel Avon Capital Corp., N.Y.C., 1981-84; asst. gen. counsel, chief counsel NCR Corp., Dayton, Ohio, 1984-88; v.p., gen. counsel Qantel Corp., Hayward, Calif., 1988-91, Candle Corp., Santa Monica, Calif., 1991-94; v.p. bus. devel. Interlink Electronics, Camarillo, Calif., 1994-96; CEO, pres. Object Tech. Licensing Corp., Cupertino, Calif., 1996—. Mem. ABA, N.Y. State Bar Assn. (corp. counsel sect.), Am. Corp. Counsel Assn., Silicon Valley Intellectual Property Law Assn., Santa Clara County Bar Assn. (mem. exec. com., high tech. law sect.). Fax: 408-974-0190. Intellectual property, Computer, General corporate. Office: Object Technology Licensing Corp 1 Infinite Loop MS 38-OTL Cupertino CA 95014

**NAYLOR, PAUL DONALD,** lawyer; b. St. Bernard, Ohio, May 28, 1925; s. David Frederick and Erna Helen (Miller) N.; m. Geraldine L. Lacy, Jan. 20, 1945; children: Linda S., Paul Scott, Todd L. JD, U. Cin., 1948. Bar: Ohio 1948. Ptnr. Pulse & Naylor, Cin., 1949-65; pvt. practice Cin., 1965—. Mem. Nat. Rep. Com. Lt. (j.g.) USN, 1943-46. Recipient Svc. to Mankind award Sertoma Internat. Mem. Cin. Bar Assn. (real property com. 1966-86), Ohio Bar Assn., Cin. Lawyers Club (pres. 1955), Order of the Coif. Real property. Office: 30 E Central Pky Ste 210 Cincinnati OH 45202-1118

**NAYOR, CHARLES FRANCIS,** lawyer; b. Boston, Dec. 28, 1913; s. Harry H. and Rose (Rofelsohn) N.; m. Phyllis Joyce Ponn, June 28, 1959; 1 child, Nancy. AB, Dartmouth Coll., 1935; LLB, Harvard Law Sch., 1938, JD, 1964. Bar: Mass. 1938. counsel Mass. Speech & Hearing Found., Boston, 1960-92; atty. Les Dames d'Escoffier, Boston, 1970-91. Chmn. Mass. Outdoor Advt. Authority, Boston, 1975. Lt. (j.g.) USCG, 1942-46. Republican. Jewish. Personal injury. Home: 205 Gardner Rd Brookline MA 02445-4562

**NAZARIAN, DOUGLAS RICHARD MILLER,** lawyer; b. New Haven, Oct. 30, 1966; s. Lawrence F. and Sharon L. (Carlson) N.; m. Jeanette Tucker Miller, Aug. 10, 1991. BA, Yale U., 1988; JD, Duke U., 1991. Bar: D.C. 1992, Md. 1993, N.Y. 1995; U.S. Dist. Ct. D.C. 1994, U.S. Dist. Ct. Md. 1995, U.S. Dist. Ct. (ea. dist.) Mich. 1997, U.S. Ct. Appeals (4th cir.) 1997. Law clerk, Hon. James B. Loken U.S. Ct. Appeals, 8th Cir., St. Paul, 1991-92; assoc. Ross, Dixon & Masback, LLP, Washington, 1992-95, Hogan & Hartson LLP, Balt., 1995—; adj. prof. U. Md. Sch. Law, Balt., 1997—. Federal civil litigation, General civil litigation, Criminal. Office: Hogan & Hartson LLP 111 S Calvert St Ste 1600 Baltimore MD 21202-6106

**NAZARYK, PAUL ALAN,** lawyer, environmental consultant; b. Denver; s. Milton Paul and Margaret Ann Nazaryk; m. Jennifer Phillips, June 16, 1990; children: Krista Brooke, Carly Rebekah. BA, U. No. Colo., 1976; MA, Colo. State U., 1979; JD, U. Denver, 1986. Bar: Colo. 1987. Legis. intern Rep. James P. Johnson Ho. Reps., Washington, 1976; policy analyst U.S. Water Resources Coun., Washington, 1979, water policy specialist, 1979-81; environ. policy specialist, atty. Colo. Dept. Pub. Health and Environment, Denver, 1981-90; regulatory specialist ERM-Rocky Mountain Inc., Englewood, Colo., 1990-96; regulatory specialist, in-house atty. Harding Lawson Assocs., Denver, 1996—; adj. faculty, U. Denver. Contbr. articles to profl. jours. Advisor Sanders-Vanderbeck Ctr., Virginia City, 1998. Mem. Colo. Bar Assn. (environ. law sect. 1987—), Denver C. of C. (environ. com. 1997-98). Democrat. Episcopalian. Avocations: western history, camping, cycling, skiing. Environmental, Natural resources, Administrative and regulatory. Office: Harding Lawson Assocs 1610 B St Helena MT 59601-6417

**NEAL, A. CURTIS,** retired lawyer; b. Nacogdoches, Tex., Nov. 25, 1922; s. Berry W. and Mattie E. (Shepherd) N.; m. Martha E. Bishop, Apr. 16, 1942; children: Curtis Jr., Patricia Ann, Dick (dec. 1968). BBA, U. Tex. 1948, LLB 1952. Bar: Tex. 1951; CPA., Tex.; soc. lic., Tex.; lic. E.M.T., Tex., 1983. With Office of Tex. Sec. of State 1948-52; pvt. practice, Amarillo, Tex., 1952-90; ret., 1990. Counsel, exec. com., advancement chmn. Boy Scouts Am., 1957-67; mem. Kids, Inc. (bd. dirs. 1954-68, pres. 1960), Western Merchandisers (bd. dirs. 1970-90), Hastings Books, Music, Video (bd. dirs.1971-93); mem. Key Presdl. Legion of Merit (Rep. Presdl. award 1994); formerly active Amarillo Jaycees, Amarillo C. of C., Amarillo Symphony, United Fund, Nat. Com. Rep. Presdl. Task Force, Barber Shop Quartett Singing in Am., Inc.; deacon, bd. mem. and vol. First Christian Ch. and Paramount Ter. Christian Ch.; vol. High Plains Bapt. Hosp., Amarillo Garden Club, Hospice and ch. work. With USN, 1942-45. Decorated with 12 Combat Stars USN, South Pacific. Fellow Tex. Bar Found. (life); mem. ABA, Am. Inst. Accts., State Bar Tex. Assn. (com. assistance to local bar assns. 1979-84, chmn. 1982-83, com. on coordination with accts. 1977-79, spl. services to membership div. 1982, state bar coll. law 1981-90), Tex. Soc. CPAs, Amarillo Bar Assn. (pres. 1981-82), Amarillo Jaycees, Amarillo C. of C., Disabled Am. Vets., Masons, York Rite (comdr. 1961) Scottish Rite Masons, Amarillo Club, Starlighters Dance Club, Amarillo Knife & Fork Club (dir. 1995-97), Tex. Shrine Assn. (all-state dir. gen. 1962, Khiva Temple potentate 1970), Cabiri (pres. 1974), Khiva Stage Band (pres. 1978), Downtown Lions Club, Delta Theta Phi, Beta Alpha Psi. Republican. Banking, Estate planning, General corporate. Home: HC 2 Box 36-344 Panhandle TX 79068-9605

**NEAL, AUSTIN BAYLOR,** lawyer; b. Long Beach, Calif., Apr. 20, 1965; s. Marion Joseph Neal and Joan Carole Böhn; m. Brenda Gale Griffin, Mar. 23, 1991; 1 child, Elizabeth Baylor Neal. BS, Fla. State U., 1991, JD, 1994. Atty. McConnaughgay Roland Maida & Cherr PA, Tallahassee, Fla., 1994-97, Maida Galloway & Neal PA, Tallahassee, 1997-98, Foley & Lardner PA, Tallahassee, 1998—. Mem. ABA, Phi Delta Phi. Avocation: golf. Administrative and regulatory, General corporate, Insurance. Office: Foley & Larner PA 300 E Park Ave Tallahassee FL 32301-1514

**NEAL, EDWARD GARRISON,** lawyer; b. Abingdon, Va., Mar. 20, 1940; s. James Wiley Neal and Edna Mae (Felty) Millsap; m. Carole Elkins, June 20, 1964; children: Jay Garrison, Heather Leigh. BA, Fla. State U., 1962; JD, U. Balt., 1966; LLM, George Washington U., D.C., 1969. Bar: Md. 1966, U.S. Dist. Ct. Ct. Md. 1968, U.S. Supreme Ct. 1972. Asst. trust officer Md. Nat. Bank, Balt., 1964-66; gen. counsel Hatch Act Study Commn., Washington, 1967; exec. asst. U.S. Sen. Daniel Brewster, Washington, 1966-68; asst. states atty. Office of States Atty., Balt., 1968-71; chief criminal div. States Atty. Prince George's County, Upper Marlboro, Md., 1971-76; assoc. county atty. Prince George's County Office of Law, Upper Marlboro, 1976-79; pvt. practice College Park, Md., 1979—; law lectr. Prince Georges County and Md. State Police Acads., 1971-76. Dem. precinct chmn., Univ. Pk. Md., 1972-80; vice chmn. Women's Sexual Assault Commn., Upper Marlboro, Md., 1974-75; pres. PTA Concordia Luth. Sch., Hyattsville, Md., 1976-77; pres. bd. trustees, Md. Summer Inst. for Performing Arts, College Park, Md. , 1986-89. Recipient Cert. of Appreciation Prince George's County Coun., Upper Marlboro, Md., 1975. Mem. Md. State Bar Assn., (various coms.), Md. State's Attys. Assn. (legislative liason Md. Gen. Assembly 1972-76), Nat. Dist. Attys. Assn. (scholarship award 1968, '70, '75. '76), Kiwanis Internat., George Washington U. Alumni Assn. (bd. dirs. 1980—), Phi Alpha Delta (dist. v.p. 1962—, pres. 1963). Episcopalian. Avocations: music, reading, tennis, basketball, bridge. General civil litigation, Criminal, Personal injury. Home: Ste 916 6100 Westchester Park Dr College Park MD 20740-2847 Office: 7309 Baltimore Ave Ste 117 College Park MD 20740-3200

**NEALON, WILLIAM JOSEPH, JR.,** federal judge; b. Scranton, Pa., July 31, 1923; s. William Joseph and Ann Cannon (McNally) N.; m. Jean Sullivan, Nov. 15, 1947; children: Ann, Robert, William, John, Jean, Patricia, Kathleen, Terrence, Thomas, Timothy. Student, U. Miami, Fla., 1942-43; B.S. in Econs, Villanova U., 1947; LL.B., Cath. U. Am., 1950; LL.D. (hon.), U. Scranton, 1975. Bar: Pa. 1951. With firm Kennedy, O'Brien & O'Brien (and predecessor), Scranton, 1951-60; mem. Lackawanna County Ct. Common Pleas, 1960-62; U.S. dist. judge Middle Dist. Pa., 1962—, chief judge, 1976-88, sr. judge, 1989—; mem. com. on adminstrn. of criminal law Jud. Conf. U.S., 1979—; lectr. bus. law and labor law U. Scranton, 1951-59; mem. jud. council 3d Cir. Ct. Appeals, 1984—; dist. judge rep. from 3d Cir. Jud. Conf. of U.S., 1987—. Mem. Scranton Registration Commn., 1953-55; hearing examiner Pa. Liquor Control Bd., 1955-59; campaign dir. Lackawanna County chpt. Nat. Found., 1961-63; mem. Scranton-Lackawanna Health and Welfare Authority, 1963—; assoc. bd. Marywood Coll., Scranton; pres. bd. dirs. Cath. Youth Center; pres. Father's Club Scranton Prep. Sch., 1966; chmn. bd. dirs. Mercy Hosp., 1991-95; chmn. bd. trustees U. Scranton; vice chmn. bd. trustees Lackawanna Jr. Coll., Scranton; bd. dirs. St. Joseph's Children's and Maternity Hosp., 1963-66, Lackawanna County unit Am. Cancer Soc., Lackawanna County Heart Assn., Lackawanna County chpt. Pa. Assn. Retarded Children, Scranton chpt. ARC, Lackawanna United Fund, Mercy Hosp., Scranton, 1975—; trustee St. Michael's Sch. Boys, Hoban Heights; adv. com. Hosp. Service Assn. Northeastern Pa. Served to 1st lt. USMCR, 1942-45. Recipient Americanism award Amos Lodge B'nai B'rith, 1975; Cyrano award U. Scranton Grad. Sch., 1977; Disting. Service award Pa. Trial Lawyers Assn., 1979; named one of 50 Disting. Pennsylvanians Greater Phila. C. of C., 1980, Outstanding Fed. Trial Judge Assn. Trial Lawyers Am., 1983. Mem. Pa. Bar Assn., Lackawanna County Bar Assn. (Chief Justice Michael J. Eagen award 1987), Friendly Sons St. Patrick (pres. Lackawanna County 1963-64), Pi Sigma Alpha. Club: Scranton Country (Clarks Summit, Pa.) (bd. dirs.). Lodge: K.C. Office: US Courthouse PO Box 1146 Scranton PA 18501-1146

**NEARY, BRIAN JOSEPH,** lawyer; b. Jersey City, Feb. 14, 1951; s. Bernard and Betty (Kenny) N.; children: Aedan, Liam. AB with high honors, U. Notre Dame, 1973; JD, NYU, 1976. Bar: N.J. 1976, U.S. Dist. Ct. N.J. 1976, Mass. 1980, N.Y. 1983, U.S. Dist. Ct. (so. and ea. dists.) N.Y. 1983, U.S. Supreme Ct. 1983; cert. criminal trial atty. N.J. Supreme Ct.; cert. in criminal trial advocacy Nat. Bd. Trial Advocacy. Asst. prosecutor Hudson County Prosecutor's Office, Jersey City, 1976-77, Bergen County Prosecutor's Office, Hackensack, N.J., 1977-81; assoc. counsel N.Y. State Adv. Commn. on the Adminstrn. of Justice (Liman Commn.), N.Y. and N.J., 1981-82; pvt. practice Hackensack, 1982—; mem. N.J. Supreme Ct. com. on criminal practice, 1988—; adj. prof. law Rutgers Sch. Law, Newark, 1983—; instr. Nat. Inst. Trial Advocacy, Hempstead, N.Y., 1984—; mem. ethics com. N.J. Supreme Ct. Dist. II-B, 1990—, vice chmn., 1992-93, chmn., 1993—. Active county com. Dem. Party, Ridgewood, Bergen County, Hackensack, 1983—. Mem. Assn. Criminal Def. Lawyers N.J. (trustee 1987-92, sec.-treas. 1992-93, v.p. 1993-96, pres.-elect 1996-97, pres. 1997—), Bergen County Bar Assn. (chmn. criminal practice com. 1987-90), Nat. Assn. Criminal Def. Lawyers. Roman Catholic. Criminal. Office: 190 Moore St Hackensack NJ 07601-7418

**NEAVES, NANCY J.,** lawyer; b. Elmhurst, Ill., May 18, 1966. BA, U. So. Fla., 1987; JD, Stetson U., St. Petersburg, Fla., 1992. Bar: Fla. Law clk., program atty. Guardian Ad Litem, Tampa, Fla., 1990-93; juvenile/misdemeaner atty. Pub. defenders Office, Tampa, 1993-94; assoc. Hendrix Law Firm, Tampa, 1994—. Mem. Hillbrook Bar Assn. Avocations: skiing, boating, scuba. Criminal. Office: Hendrix Tampa Theatre Bldg 707 N Franklin St Ste 750 Tampa FL 33602-4423

**NEBEKER, FRANK QUILL,** federal judge; b. Salt Lake City, Apr. 23, 1930; s. J. Quill and Minnie (Holmgren) N.; m. Louana M. Visintainer, July 11, 1953; children: Caramaria, Melia, William Mark. Student, Weber Coll., 1948-50; B.S. in Polit. Sci, U. Utah, 1953; J.D., Am. U., 1955. Bar: D.C. 1956. Corr. sec. The White House, 1953-56; trial atty. Internal Security div. Justice Dept., Washington, 1956-58; asst. U.S. atty., 1958-69; assoc. judge D.C. Ct. Appeals, 1969-87; dir. Office Govt. Ethics, Washington, 1987-89; chief judge U.S. Ct. of Vets. Appeals, Washington, 1989—; cons. Nat. Commn. on Reform of Fed. Criminal Laws, 1967-68; adj. prof. Am. U. Washington Coll. Law, 1967-85. Mem. Am., D.C. Bar Assn., Am. Law Inst. Office: US Court of Veterans Appeals 625 Indiana Ave NW Ste 900 Washington DC 20004-2950

**NEBEKER, STEPHEN BENNION,** lawyer; b. Salt Lake City, Feb. 21, 1929; s. Acel Hulme and Lora (Bennion) N.; m. June Wilkins, June 18, 1951; children: Jeanne N. Jardine, Mary N. Larson, Stephen W., Ann. JD, U. Utah, 1954. Bar: Utah 1957, U.S. Dist. Ct. Utah 1957, U.S. Ct. Appeals (10th cir.) 1957. Assoc. Ray Quinney & Nebeker, Salt Lake City, 1957-63, ptnr., 1963—, mem. exec. com., 1972—, pres., 1992—. Bd. editors Utah Law Rev., 1953-54. Mem. S.J. and Jessie Quinney Found., Salt Lake City, 1982—; chmn. nat. adv. coun. U. Utah; trustee Ray Quinney & Nebeker Found., Salt Lake City, 1982—. 1st lt. U.S. Army, 1954-57. Recipient Disting. Alumnus award U. Utah, 1992, named Lawyer of Yr. by Law Sch., 1988. Fellow Am. Coll. Trial Lawyers (bd. regents 1984-87), Am. Bd. Trial Advocates, Internat. Assn. Ins. Counsel, Fedn. Ins. Counsel, Am. Bar Found., Utah Bar Found. (trustee 1988-95), Utah State Bar (outstanding lawyer of yr. 1986, trial lawyer of yr. 1994), Legal Aid Soc., Am. Inn of Ct. II (pres. 1982-83), Alta Club, Rotary, Salt Lake City Area C. of C. (bd. govs. 1986-89, U. Utah Law Sch. Alumni Assn. (pres. 1985-86). Republican. Mormon. Avocations: skiing, golf, fly fishing, tennis, hunting. Product liability, Insurance, Personal injury. Home: 746 16th Ave Salt Lake City UT 84103-3705 Office: Ray Quinney & Nebeker 400 Deseret Bldg Salt Lake City UT 84111

**NECCO, ALEXANDER DAVID,** lawyer, educator; b. Gary, Ind., Jan. 31, 1936; s. Alesandro Necco and Mary Millonovich; m. Caroline Chappel, Apr. 20, 1958 (dec. Mar. 1978); 1 child, Laurie Ann Necco Stansbury; m. Edna Joanne Painter, July 1, 1989. BA in Philosophy, U. Nev., 1958; JD, Oklahoma City U., 1965. Bar: Okla. 1965, U.S. Dist. Ct. (we. dist.) Okla. 1965, U.S. Ct. Appeals (10th cir.) 1987), U.S. Ct. Claims 1989, U.S. Ct. Vets. Appeals 1994. Assoc. Robert Jordan, Oklahoma City, 1965-66, Stuckey & Witcher, Oklahoma City, 1968-69; atty. Okla. Hwy. Dept., Oklahoma City, 1966, Oklahoma City Urban Renewal, 1966-67; ptnr. Stuckey & Necco, Oklahoma City, 1969-71, Necco & Dyer, Oklahoma City, 1978-82, Dyer, Necco & Byrd, Oklahoma City, 1982-88; pvt. practice Oklahoma City, 1965—; ptnr. Necco & Byrd, Oklahoma City, 1988—; adj. prof. Oklahoma City U. Sch. Bus., 1965—, Webster U., 1995—. Cubmaster Boy Scouts Am., Oklahoma City. With USMC, 1953-82, lt. col. Res. ret. Named Pro-bono Atty. of Month Okla. County. Mem. Assn. Trial Lawyers Assn., Okla. Trial Lawyers Assn., Marine Corps Res. Officers Assn. (pres. Oklahoma City 1984-85), Phi Delta Phi, Sigma Nu. Republican. Roman Catholic. Avocations: golf, swimming, tennis. General civil litigation, Family and matrimonial, Probate. Office: Necco & Byrd PC 5700 N Portland Ave Ste 121 Oklahoma City OK 73112-1662

**NECHELES, SUSAN R.,** lawyer; b. Chgo., Feb. 14, 1959; d. Robert Thomas and Carmen (Castaneda) N. BA, U. Rochester, 1980; JD, Yale U., 1983. Bar: N.Y. 1985, U.S. Dist. Ct. (so. and ea. dists.) N.Y. 1985, U.S. Ct. Appeals (2d cir.) 1987. Asst. dist. atty. Kings County Dist. Atty.'s Office, Bklyn., 1983-84; assoc. Rosenman & Colin, N.Y.C., 1984-87; ptnr. Goldman & Hafetz, N.Y.C., 1987—. Editor Yale Law Jour., 1983. Mem. N.Y.C. Bar Assn. (criminal procedure com. 1985-87), Nat. Assn. Criminal Def. Attys. Criminal. Office: Goldman & Hafetz 500 5th Ave Fl 29 New York NY 10110-2900

**NEEDHAM, CAROL ANN,** lawyer, educator; b. Chgo., Nov. 1, 1957; d. Robert Michael and Loretta Ann (Grabowy) Needham; m. Thomas Joseph Timmermann, July 23, 1994. BA in English, Northwestern U., 1979, JD, 1985; MA in English, U. Va., 1982. Bar: Calif. 1987, D.C. 1989, Ill. 1985. Jud. law clk. U.S. Dist. Ct., Honolulu, 1985-86; assoc. Gibson, Dunn & Crutcher, L.A., 1986-90, Chadbourne & Parke, L.A., 1990-91; prof. law St. Louis U. Sch. Law, 1992—; mem. corp. ethics com. St. Mary's Health Sys. Bd. Contbr. articles to profl. jours. Chair scholarship com. Verbum Dei H.S., L.A., 1987-95. Mem. ABA, Ctrl. States Law Assn. (treas. 1995-96, v.p. 1996-98, pres. 1998-99), Mo. Bar (vice chmn. com. on lawyers' advt. 1995—), Am. Assn. Law Schs. (profl. responsibility exec. com. 1995-98). Office: St Louis U Sch Law 3700 Lindell Blvd Saint Louis MO 63108-3412

**NEEDLE, JEFFREY LOWELL,** lawyer; b. Gt. Neck, N.Y., Feb. 21, 1947. BSBA, Boston U., 1969; JD, Am. U., 1972. Bar: Wash. 1975, U.S. Dist. Ct. (we. dist.) Wash. 1978, U.S. Ct. Appeals (9th cir.) 1984, U.S. Supreme Ct. 1991. VISTA atty. Pierce County Legal Svcs., Tacoma, 1972-73; pvt. practice, Seattle, 1977—; adj. instr. law and justice dept. Cen. Wash. U., Seattle, 1989-92; commentator on Constn., Sta. KIRO, 1990—. Civil rights columnist Trial News, 1986-92. Bd. dirs. Country Doctor Health Clinic, Seattle, 1981-85; mem. legal com. ACLU-Wash., Seattle, 1984—. Mem. Wash. State Bar Assn., Assn. Trial Lawyers Am. (chmn. civil rights com. 1991-92, civil rights sect. 1992-93, bd. govs. 1993-96, chair employment rights sect. 1999—), Wash. State Trial Lawyers Assn. (chmn. civil rights sect. 1986-92), Trial Lawyers for Pub. Justice, Nat. Employment Lawyers Assn., Washington Employees Lawyers Assn. (chair amicus com. 1997—). Avocations: music, reading, camping, sailing. Civil rights, Personal injury, Labor. Office: 119 1st Ave S Ste 200 Seattle WA 98104-3416

**NEELY, RICHARD,** lawyer; b. Aug. 2, 1941; s. John Champ and Elinore (Forlani) N.; m. Carolyn Elaine Elmore, 1979; children: John Champ, Charles Whittaker. AB, Dartmouth Coll., 1964; LLB, Yale U., 1967. Bar: W.Va. 1967. Practiced in Fairmont, W.Va., 1969-73; chmn. Marion County Bd. Pub. Health, 1971-72; mem. W.Va. Ho. of Dels., 1971-73; justice, chief justice W.Va. Supreme Ct. of Appeals, Charleston, 1973-95; ptnr. Neely & Hunter, Charleston, 1995—; chmn. bd. Kane & Keyser Co., Belington, W.Va., 1970-88. Author: How Courts Govern America, 1980, Why Courts Don't Work, 1983, The Divorce Decision, 1984, Judicial Jeopardy: When Business Collides with the Courts, 1986, The Product Liability Mess: How Business Can Be Rescued from State Court Politics, 1988, Take Back Your Neighborhood: A Case for Modern-Day Vigilantism, 1990, Tragedies of our Own Making: How Private Choices have Created Public Bankruptcy, 1994; contbr. articles to nat. mags. Capt. U.S. Army, 1967-69. Decorated Bronze Star, Vietnam Honor medal 1st Class. Mem. Am. Econ. Assn., W.Va. Bar Assn., Fourth Cir. Jud. Conf. (life), Internat. Brotherhood Elec. Workers, VFW, Am. Legion, Moose, Phi Delta Phi, Phi Sigma Kappa. Episcopalian. Federal civil litigation, General civil litigation, State civil litigation. Office: Neely & Hunter 159 Summers St Charleston WV 25301-2134

**NEELY, WILLIAM F.,** lawyer; b. Abingdon, Va., Dec. 3, 1951; s. John D. and Ann F. Neely; m. Vickie M. Neely, July 27, 1974; 1 child, Sarah. BA, Emory and Henry Coll., 1974; JD, U. Richmond, 1981. Assoc. Martin, Corboy Hartley, Pearisburg, Va., 1981-82; asst. commonwealth's atty. Spotsylvania (Va.) County C.A., 1982-88; commonwealth atty. Sportsylvania (Va.) County C.A., 1988—. Mem. Spotsylvania County Dem. Com., 1988—; charter mem., elder Spotsylvania Presbyn. Ch., 1984—; legal advisor Spotsylvania Vol. Rescue Squad, 1986-97. Mem. Lions Club. Democrat. Presbyterian. Office: PO Box 2629 Spotsylvania VA 22553-6816

**NEESE, MARTHA L.,** lawyer, nurse; b. Storm Lake, Iowa; d. William D. and Donna J. McCuen; m. Eugene F. Neese, Nov. 9, 1974; children: Brion D., Colan M., Malesha C. Degree in nursing, Des Moines Area C.C., Ankeny, Iowa, 1974; BS in Gen. Studies, Drake U., 1980, JD, 1984. Bar: Minn. 1984, Iowa 1984, Ariz. 1986, U.S. Dist. Ct. Minn. 1986, U.S. Ct. Appeals (8th cir.) 1987, U.S. Dist. Ct. Ariz. 1990, U.S. Dist. Ct. (we. dist.) Tex. 1990, U.S. Dist. Ct. (we. dist.) N.Y. 1991, U.S. Dist. Ct. (ea. dist.) Wis. 1992, U.S. Dist. Ct. (ctrl. dist.) Ill. 1992, U.S. Ct. Claims 1992, U.S. Ct. Appeals (9th cir.) 1993, U.S. Ct. Appeals (5th cir.) 1994, U.S. Supreme Ct. 1996, U.S. Ct. Appeals (6th cir.) 1999; RN, Minn.; cert. nat. bd. trial advocacy. Psychiat., surg. and open-heart surg. nurse; shareholder Sawicki, Neese & Phelps P.A., Woodbury, Minn.; mem. bd. Trial Cert. Coun., 1996-97, Creative Dispute Resolution, 1997-99; condr. seminars on personal injury and med. malpractice. Contbr. articles to profl. jours., including Hawkeye Osteo. Jour., Minn. Trial Lawyer, Am. Jour. Trial Advocacy. Coach mock trial team Eastview H.S., 1998-99. Mem. ATLA (chmn. mil. law sect. 1992-93, 97-98, 98-99, vice chmn. fed. tort liability and mil. law sect. 1997-98), Minn. Bar Assn. (cert. trial specialist), Iowa Bar Assn., Ariz. Bar Assn., Minn. Trial Lawyers Assn. (bd. govs. 1996-99), Million Dollar Advs. Forum, Am. Arbitration Assn. (arbitrator 1991—). Fax: 612-730-8110. Office: Sawicki Neese & Phelps 1811 Weir Dr Ste 275 Woodbury MN 55125-2201

**NEFF, A. GUY,** lawyer; b. Calcutta, India, Mar. 24, 1951. BA, Vanderbilt U., 1972; JD, U. Fla., 1975. Bar: Fla. 1975. Lawyer Holland & Knight, LLP, Orlando, Fla. Mem. ABA, Inter-Am. Bar Assn., Am. Immigration Lawyers Assn. (dir. ctrl. Fla. chpt. 1984-85, 86-87, 90-91), Fla. Bar (internat. law sect.), Orange County Bar Assn., Phi Delta Phi (magister 1975). Immigration, naturalization, and customs, Private international, Real property.

Office: Holland & Knight LLP 200 S Orange Ave Ste 2600 Orlando FL 32801-3449

**NEFF, FRED LEONARD,** lawyer; b. St. Paul, Nov. 1, 1948; s. Elliott Ira and Mollie (Poboisk) N.; m. Christa Ruth Powell, Sept. 10, 1989. BS with high distinction, U. Minn., 1970; JD, William Mitchell Coll. Law, 1976. Bar: Minn. 1976, N.D. 1994, U.S. Dist. Ct. Minn. 1977, U.S. Ct. Appeals (8th cir.) 1985, U.S. Supreme Ct. 1985, Wis. 1986, U.S. Dist. Ct. (ea. and we. dists.) Wis. 1992. Tchr. Hopkins (Minn.) Pub. Schs., 1970-72; instr. U. Minn., Mpls., 1974-76; pvt. practice Mpls., 1976-79; asst. county atty. Sibley County, Gaylord, Minn., 1979-80; mng. atty. Hyatt Legal Svcs., St. Paul, 1981-83, regional ptnr., 1983-85, profl. devel. ptnr., 1985-86; pres. Neff Law Firm, PA, Mpls., 1986—; CEO Profl. Devel. Inst. Inc., Edina, Minn., 1994—, also bd. dirs.; instr. Inver Hills Coll., 1973-77; counsel Am. Tool Supply Co., St. Paul, 1976-78; cons. Nat. Detective Agy., Inc., St. Paul, 1980-83; CEO A Basic Legal Svc., Bloomington, 1990—; CEO, bd. dirs. Profl. Devel. Inst., Inc., Edina, Minn., 1994—; lectr., guest instr. U. Wis., River Falls, 1976-77; spl. instr. Hamline U., St. Paul, 1977; vis. lectr. Coll. St. Scholastica, Duluth, Minn., 1977; program. faculty, cons. Employment Law Seminar for Colo., Fla., La., Oreg., Employment and Labor Law Seminar for Ala., Alaska, Calif., Conn., Ind., N.C., Ohio, Va., N.C. Safety and Health at the Workplace, S.C. Labor Law, Ohio Safety at the Workplace; bd. dirs. Acceptance Ins. Holdings, Inc., Omaha; active Internat. Confederation Jurists, 1993; mem. faculty sem. Ariz. Safety at Workplace, Hawaii Employment & Labor, Miss. Employment & Labor Law, Del. Employment & Labor, Alaska Employment and Labor Law, Ga. Employment & Labor Law, N.J. Employment & Labor, Wash. Employment Law, Mass. Employment & Labor Law, 1995—, Ark. Employment and Labor Law, Mo. Employment and Labor Law, Iowa Employment and Labor Law, Utah Employment and Labor Law; pres. Martial Arts Bookstore Internat., Inc., 1998; pres. Endless Fist Soc., Inc., 1998. Author: Fred Neff's Self-Defense Library, 1976, Everybody's Self-Defense Book, 1978, Karate Is for Me, 1980, Running Is for Me, 1980, Lessons from the Samurai, 1986, Lessons from the Art of Kempo, 1986, Lessons from the Western Warriors, 1986, Lessons from the Fighting Commandos, 1990, Lessons from the Ancient Japanese Masters of Self-Defense, 1990, Lessons from the Eastern Warrors, 1990, Mysterious Persons of the Past, 1991, Great Mysteries of Crime, 1991; host TV series Great Puzzles In History; co-host TV series Great Unsolved Crimes, Minn.; asst. editor: Hennepic County Lawyer, 1992—. Advisor to bd. Sibley County Commrs., 1979-80; speaker civic groups, 1976-82; mem. Hennepin County Juvenile Justice Panel, 1980-82, Hennepin County (Minn.) Pub. Def. Conflict Panel, 1980-82, 86—, Hennepin County Bar Assn. Advice Panel Law Day, 1987, mem. dist. ethics com., 1990—; mem. Panel Union Privilege Legal Svcs. div. AFL-CIO, 1986—, Montgomery Wards Legal Svcs. Panel, 1986—, Edina Hist. Soc., Decathlon Athletic Club; charter mem. Commn. for the Battle of Normandy Mus.; founding sponsor Civil Justice Found., 1986—; mem. com. for publ. Hennepin County Lawyer, 1992; pres. Endless Fist Soc., Inc., 1998. Recipient Outstanding Tchr. award Inver Hills Coll. Student Body, 1973, St. Paul Citizen of Month award Citizens Group, 1975, Kempo Club award U. Minn., 1975, U. Minn. Student Appreciation award Kempo Club, 1978, Sibley County Atty. Commendation award, 1980, Good Neighbor award WCCO Radio, 1985, Lamp of Knowledge award Twin Cities Lawyers Guild, 1986, N.W. Cmty. TV Commendation award, 1989-91, Presdl. Merit medal Pres. George Bush, 1990, N.W. Cmty. TV award, 1991, HLS Leadership award, 1984, Mng. Attys. Guidance award, 1985, Creative Thinker award Regional Staff, 1986, HLS Justice award, 1986, Honors cert. for Authors, Childrens Reading Round Table of Chgo., 1988, Wisdom Soc. Wisdom award, 1998. Fellow Roscoe Pound Found., Nat. Dist. Attys. Assn.; mem. ABA, ATLA, Minn. Bar Assn. (com. on ethics 1994—, com. on alternative dispute resolution 1994—), Minn. Trial Lawyers Assn., Hennepin County Bar Assn. (dist. ethics com. 1990—), Wis. Bar Assn., Ramsey County Bar Assn., Am. Judicature Soc., Internat. Platform Assn., Am. Arbitration Assn. (panel of arbitrators 1992), Minn. Martial Arts Assn. (pres. 1974-78, Outstanding Instr. award 1973), Nippon Kobudo Rengokai (bd. dirs. North Ctrl. States 1972-76, regional dir. 1972-76), Endless Fist Soc. (pres. 1998), Internat. Confedn. Jurists, Edina C. of C., Southview Country Club, Masons, Kiwanis, Scottish Rite, Sigma Alpha Mu. Avocations: reading, Far Eastern and Oriental studies, civic activities, physical conditioning, gardening. Criminal, Labor, General civil litigation. Home: 4515 Andover Rd Minneapolis MN 55435-4031 Office: 5930 Brooklyn Blvd Ste 206 Brooklyn Center MN 55429-2518 also: 1711 County Road B W Ste 340N Roseville MN 55113-4077 also: Minn Ctr 7760 France Ave S Ste 720 Bloomington MN 55435-5921

**NEFF, MICHAEL ALAN,** lawyer; b. Springfield, Ill., Sept. 4, 1940; s. Benjamin Ezra and Ann (Alpert) N.; m. Lin Laghi, Mar. 26, 1977; 1 son, Aaron Benjamin. Student U. Ill., 1958-61; B.A., U. Calif.-Berkeley, 1963, postgrad. 1963-64; J.D., Columbia U., 1967. Bar: N.Y. 1967, U.S. Dist. Ct. (so. and ea. dists.) N.Y. 1969, U.S. Ct. Appeals (2nd cir.) 1988, U.S. Supreme Ct. 1988. Assoc., Sage Gray Todd & Sims, N.Y.C., 1967-74, Fellner & Rovins, N.Y.C., 1974-75; ptnr. Polier Tulin Clark & Neff, N.Y.C., 1976-77; sole practice, N.Y.C., 1977—; counsel St. Dominic's Home, 1971-74, Louise Wise Services, 1976-77, Edwin Gould Service for Children, 1969-74, 76—, Family Services of Westchester, Inc., 1977-95, The Children's Village, 1977-84, Puerto Rican Assn. for Community Affairs, Inc., 1979-92, Brookwood Child Care, 1980—, Forestdale, 1988—, Cen. Bklyn. Coord. Counsel, 1989-95, Miracle Makers, 1989—, Fam. Support Systems Unlimited, 1990—, Soc. Children and Families, 1996—; teaching asst. U. Calif., 1963-64; congl. intern U.S. Ho. of Reps., summer 1965; instr. Marymount Manhattan Coll., 1973; mem. Indigent Defendant's Legal Panel, Appellate Div., First Dept., 1974-84; participant N.Y. State Conf. on Children's Rights, 1974; asst. sec. Edwin Gould Services for Children, 1977—; cons. N.Y. Task Force on Permanency Planning For Children in Foster Care, 1985-90, N.Y. State Foster and Adoptive Parent Assn., Inc., 1988—, N.Y. Spaulding for Children, 1988-90, Ct. Appointed Spl. Advocates, 1988-91. Mem. ABA, Assn. Bar City of N.Y. Contbr. articles to profl. jours. Family and matrimonial, State civil litigation, General practice. Home: 5 W 86th St Apt 6B New York NY 10024-3664 Office: 36 W 44th St Ste 1212 New York NY 10036-8102

**NEFF, ROBERT CAREY,** lawyer; b. Orange, N.J., Nov. 9, 1935; s. Walter Holt and Nan Carey Neff; m. Shirley Ruth Fitzeram, May 6, 1961; children: Robert C. Jr., Sandra Wilichowski, Carl J., Thomas H. BA, Yale U., 1957; LLB, Georgetown U., 1964. Cert. N.J. 1965, U.S. Dist. Ct. N.J. 1965, U.S. Supreme Ct. 1965. Assoc. Carey & Jardine, Newark, 1965-67; ptnr. Meth, Wood Neff & Cooper, Newark, 1967-76, Shanley & Fisher, Newark, 1976-82, Kraft & Hughes, Newark, 1982-87, Pitney, Hardin, Kipp & Szuch, Morristown, N.J., 1987—. Trustee N.J. Cmty. Found., Morristown, 1990-97; commr. N.J. State Racing Commn., 1986-90; mem. Rumson Fair Haven Regional Bd. Edn., 1985-86; councilman Borrough of Shrewsbury, N.J., 1969-71. Capt. USMCR, 1957-61. Fellow Am. Coll. of Trust and Estate Counsel; mem. ABA (chmn. com. legal svcs. for elderly 1989-91), N.J. Bar Assn. Republican. Roman Catholic. Probate, Estate planning, Estate taxation. Home: 85 Grange Ave Fair Haven NJ 07704-3039 Office: Pitney Hardin Kipp & Szuch PO Box 1945 Morristown NJ 07962-1945

**NEFF, ROBERT CLARK, SR.,** lawyer; b. St. Marys, Ohio, Feb. 11, 1921; s. Homer Armstrong and Irene (McCulloch) N.; m. Betty Baker, July 3, 1954 (dec.); children: Cynthia Lee Neff Schifer, Robert Clark Jr., Abigail Lynn (dec.); m. Helen Picking, July 24, 1975. BA, Coll. Wooster, 1943; postgrad., U. Mich., 1946-47; LLB, Ohio No. U., 1950. Bar: Ohio 1950, U.S. Dist. Ct. (no. dist.) Ohio, 1978. Pvt. practice Bucyrus, Ohio, 1950—; ptnr. Neff Law Firm Ltd.; law dir. City of Bucyrus, 1962-95. Chmn. blood program Crawford County (Ohio) unit ARC, 1955-89; life mem. adv. bd. Salvation Army, 1962—; clk. of session 1st Presbyn. Ch., Bucyrus, 1958-96; bd. dirs. Bucyrus Area Cmty. Found., Crawford County Bd. Mental Retardation and Devel. Disabilities, 1977-82. With USNR, WWII; comdr. Res. ret. Recipient "Others" plaque for 30 yrs. adv. bd. svc. Salvation Army, Ohio No. U. Coll. Law Alumni award for cmty. svc., 1996; inducted Ohio Vets. Hall Fame, Columbus, 1996. Mem. Ohio Bar Assn., Crawford County Bar Assn., Naval Res. Assn., Ret. Officers Assn., Am. Legion, Bucyrus Area C. of C. (past bd. dirs., Outstanding Citizen award, 1973, Bucyrus Citizen of Yr. 1981), Kiwanis (life mem., past pres.), Masons. Republican. Fax: 419-562-1660. General practice, Probate, Estate planning. Home: 1085 Mary Ann Ln Bucyrus OH 44820-3145 Office: 840 S Sandusky Ave PO Box 406 Bucyrus OH 44820-0406

**NEGRON-GARCIA, ANTONIO S.,** territory supreme court justice; b. Rio Piedras, P.R., Dec. 31, 1940; s. Luis Negron-Fernandez and Rosa M. Garcia-Saldana; m. Gloria Villardefrancos-Vergara, May 26, 1962; 1 son, Antonio Rogelio. B.A., U. P.R., 1962, LL.B., 1964. Bar: P.R. bar 1964. Law aide and lawyer legal div. Water Resources Authority, 1962-64; judge Dist. Ct., 1964-69, Superior Ct., 1969-74; justice P.R. Supreme Ct., San Juan, 1974—; administrating judge, 1969-71; exec. officer Constl. Bd. for Revision Senatorial and Rep. Dists., 1971-72; mem. Jud. Conf., 1974; first exec. sec. Council for Reform of System of Justice in P.R., 1973-74; chmn. Gov.'s Advisory Com. for Jud. Appointments, 1973-74; lectr. U. P.R. Law Sch., 1973-74. Mem. P.R. Bar Assn., Am. Judicature Soc. Roman Catholic. Office: Supreme Ct PR PO Box 2392 San Juan PR 00902-2392*

**NEHRA, GERALD PETER,** lawyer; b. Detroit, Mar. 25, 1940; s. Joseph P. and Jeanette M. (Bauer) N.; children: Teresa, Patricia; m. Peggy Jensen, Sept. 12, 1987. B.I.E., Gen. Motors Inst., Flint, Mich., 1962; J.D., Detroit Coll. Law, 1970. Bar: Mich. 1970, U.S. Dist. Ct. (ea. dist.) Mich. 1970, N.Y. 1972, U.S. Dist. Ct. (so. dist.) N.Y. 1972, U.S. Dist. Ct. (no. dist.) N.Y. 1976, U.S. Ct. Appeals (6th cir.) 1978, Colo. 1992. Successively engr., supr., gen. supr. Gen. Motors Corp., 1958-67; mktg. rep., to regional counsel IBM Corp., 1967-79; v.p., gen. counsel Church & Dwight Co., Inc. 1979-82; dep. chief atty-Amway Corp., 1982-83, dep. gen. counsel, 1983-92; dir. legal div., 1989-91, sec. and dir. corp. law, 1991-92; v.p. gen. counsel Fuller Brush, Bolder, Colo., 1991-92; pvt. practice, 1992—; adj. instr. Dale Carnegie Courses, 1983-91. Recipient Outstanding Contbn. award Am. Cancer Soc., 1976. Mem. Mich. Bar Assn., Colo. Bar Assn., N.Y. State Bar Assn., ABA. Contbr. chpt. to book. Antitrust, Contracts commercial, General corporate. Home and Office: 1710 Beach St Muskegon MI 49441-1008

**NEHRBASS, JENNIFER STULLER,** lawyer; b. Lafayette, La., Mar. 22, 1955; d. Gilbert Fitch and Alma Branner (Bowen) Stuller; m. Douglas J. Nehrbass Jr., Oct. 6, 1979; children: Derek Bowen, Amanda Elizabeth. BA, La. State U., 1977, JD, 1980. Bar: La. 1981, U.S. Dist. Ct. (we dist.) La. 1987. Clk. to Judge Douglas J. Nehrbass 15th Judicial Dist. Ct., Lafayette Parish, La., 1979-80; pvt. practice Lafayette, 1981—; asst. dist. atty. Office of Dist. Atty., Lafayette Parish, 1983-84. General civil litigation, Criminal, Family and matrimonial. Office: 119 E Main PO Drawer 4624 Lafayette LA 70502-4624

**NEHRBASS, SCOTT C.,** lawyer; b. Topeka, Kans., Nov. 23, 1966; s. Carl Herbert and Connie Kay Nehrbass; m. Jennifer Ann Nehrbass, Aug. 17, 1991; 1 child, John Carl. BA in Econs./Polit. Sci., Kans. U., 1989, JD, 1993. Law clk. to U.S. Dist. judge U.S. Dist. Ct. Kans., Wichita, 1993-95; assoc. Shook, Hardy & Bacon LLP, Overland Park, Kans., 1995—. Coauthor: Kansas Federal Practice Handbook; contbr. articles to profl. jours. Precinct committeeman Rep. Party, Johnson County, 1998—; bd. dirs. Children's Benefits Senders for Families, Kansas City, 1998—. Mem. Johnson County Bar Assn., Kans. Bar Assn., Christian Legal Soc., Kans. Assn. of Def. Counsel. Office: Shook Handy and Bacon LLP 84 Mastin Rd Overland Park KS 66225

**NEILL, JOSEPH VINCENT,** lawyer; b. St. Louis, Mar. 19, 1953; s. Thomas Patrick and Agnes J. Neill; m. Elizabeth Gidionsen, Dec. 27, 1986; children: John Francis, Joseph Holland, Thomas Patrick. Bar: Mo. 1977, U.S. Dist. Ct. (ea. dist.) Mo. 1977, U.S. Ct. Appeals (8th cir.) 1988. Sole proprietor St. Louis, 1978—; mem. jud. commn. St. Louis Cir. Ct., 1986-91. Mem. bd. election commrs. City of St. Louis, 1994—. Democrat. Roman Catholic. General practice, Personal injury, Workers' compensation. Office: 5201 Hampton Ave Saint Louis MO 63109-3102

**NEILSON, BENJAMIN REATH,** lawyer; b. Phila., July 11, 1938; s. Harry Rosengarten and Alberta (Reath) N.; m. Judith Rawle, June 20, 1959 (div. May 1983); children: Benjamin R. Jr., Theodora C., Johanna K., Alberta R., Marshall R.; m. Meta B. Grace, Dec. 26, 1983. AB magna cum laude, Harvard U., 1960, LLB, 1963. Bar: Pa. 1964. Law clk. to chief justice Pa. Supreme Ct., Phila., 1963-64; assoc. Ballard, Spahr, Andrews & Ingersoll, Phila., 1964-71, ptnr., 1971—. Sec.-treas. The Chanticleer Found., Wayne, Pa.; pres. bd. trustees St. Paul's Sch., Concord, N.H. Mem. ABA, Pa. Bar Assn., Phila. Bar Assn., Am. Coll. Estate & Trust Counsel,Phi Beta Kappa. Episcopalian. Estate planning, Probate.

**NEIMAN, TANYA MARIE,** legal association administrator; b. Pitts., June 28, 1949; d. Max and Helen (Lamaga) N. AB, Mills Coll., 1970; JD, U. Calif. Hastings Coll. of Law, San Francisco, 1974. Bar: Calif. 1975. Law assoc. Boalt Hall U. Calif., Berkeley, 1974-76; pub. defender State of Calif., San Francisco, 1976-81; assoc. gen. counsel, dir. vol. legal services Bar Assn. San Francisco, 1982—; bd. dirs. Jack Berman Advocacy Ctr. Tanya Neiman Day proclaimed in her honor by Mayor of San Francisco, 1991; recipient Disting. Citizen award Harvard Club San Francisco, 1995, Kutka-Dodds prize Nat. Legal Aid and Defender Assn., 1996. Mem. ABA (mem. ABA Commn. on Homelessness 1993-96, speaker 1985—, Harrison Tweed award 1985), Calif. Bar Assn. (exec. com. 1984—, legal svcs. sect., chair steering com. State Bar Legal Corps), Golden Gate Bus. Assn. Found. (v.p. grant making 1985—), Nat. Conf. Women and Law (speaker 1975—), Nat. Lawyers Guild. Office: The Bar Assn San Francisco 465 California St Ste 1100 San Francisco CA 94104-1804

**NEITZKE, ERIC KARL,** lawyer; b. Mobile, Ala., Dec. 10, 1955; s. Howard and Otti S. Neitzke; m. Kathryn Sloan; children: Kyle, Blake, Blaire. BA, U. Fla., 1979, JD, 1982. Bar: Fla. 1982, U.S. Dist. Ct. (mid. dist.) Fla. 1987. Asst. state atty. 7th Jud. Cir., State Atty., Daytona Beach, Fla., 1982; atty. Dunn, Smith & Withers, Daytona Beach, 1982-88, Monaco, Smith, Hood and Perkins, Daytona Beach, 1988—; adj. faculty family law and criminal law Daytona C.C.; chmn. adv. com. Juvenile Detention Ctr. Contbr. articles to profl. jours. Mem. Fla. Acad. Trial Lawyers, Assn. Trial Lawyers Am., Volusia Bar Assn., Fla. Assn. Criminal Def. Lawyers, Phi Beta Kappa. Avocations: water sports, shooting, travel. Criminal, Family and matrimonial, Personal injury. Home: 19 Lost Creek Ln Ormond Beach FL 32174-4840 Office: Eric K Neitzke PA 444 Seabreeze Blvd Ste 900 Daytona Beach FL 32118-3953

**NELLIGAN, KENNETH EGAN,** lawyer; b. Revere, Mass., Mar. 21, 1952; s. Kenneth P. and Lillian M. N.; m. S.C. Nelligan. BS in Math., U. N.H., 1974; JD cum laude, Suffolk U., 1977. Bar: Mass. 1977, D.C. 1979, U.S. Claims Ct. 1981, U.S. Supreme Ct. 1983. Asst. counsel Naval Electronic Sys. Command, Arlington, Va., 1977-81; counsel Naval Rsch. Lab., Washington, 1981-85, Naval Underwater Sys. Ctr., Newport, R.I., 1985-92, Naval Undersea Warfare Ctr. Divsn., Newport, 1992—. Assoc. editor Law Rev., 1977. Recipient Am. Jurisprudence awards The Lawyer's Co-op Pub. Co., 1975. Mem. Mass. Bar Assn., D.C. Bar Assn. Avocations: basketball, tennis. Administrative and regulatory, Government contracts and claims. Office: Office of Counsel Code OOOC Bldg 11 Naval Undersea Warfare Ctr Newport RI 02840

**NELMS, K. ANDERSON,** lawyer; b. Atlanta, Aug. 18, 1965; s. Claude Anderson and Virginia N. BA, Mercer U., 1987; JD, Faulkner U., 1995. Bar: U.S. Dist. Ct. Ala., U.S. Ct. Fed. Claims, U.S. Ct. Appeals (11th cir.). General civil litigation, Family and matrimonial, Administrative and regulatory. Home: PO Box 70508 Montgomery AL 36107-0508 Office: 5755 Carmichael Rd Montgomery AL 36117-2328

**NELSON, DAVID ALDRICH,** federal judge; b. Watertown, N.Y., Aug. 14, 1932; s. Carlton Low and Irene Demetria (Aldrich) N.; m. Mary Dickson, Aug. 25, 1956; 3 children. AB, Hamilton Coll., 1954; postgrad., Cambridge U., Eng., 1954-55; LLB, Harvard U., 1958. Bar: Ohio 1958, N.Y. 1982. Atty.-advisor Office of the Gen. Counsel, Dept. of the Air Force, 1959-62; assoc. Squire, Sanders & Dempsey, Cleve., 1958-67, ptnr., 1967-69, 72-85; cir. judge U.S. Ct. Appeals (6th cir.), Cin., 1985—; gen. counsel U.S. Post Office Dept., Washington, 1969-71; sr. asst. postmaster gen., gen. counsel U.S. Postal Svc., Washington, 1971; mem. nat. coun. Coll. Law, Ohio State U., 1988-98. Trustee Hamilton Coll., 1984-88. Served to maj. USAFR, 1959-69. Fulbright scholar, 1954-55; recipient Benjamin Franklin award U.S. Post Office Dept., 1969. Fellow Am. Coll. Trial Lawyers; mem. Fed. Bar Assn., Ohio Bar Assn., Cleve. Bar Assn., Cin. Bar Assn., Emerson Lit. Soc., Ct. of Nisi Prius (sgt. emeritus), Phi Beta Kappa. Office: US Ct Appeals 6th Cir Potter Stewart US Ct House 5th and Walnut St Cincinnati OH 45202-3988

**NELSON, DAVID EUGENE,** lawyer; b. Waterloo, Iowa, Dec. 1, 1946; s. Woodrow Irving and Irene Ella (Marsau) N.; m. Phyllia Ann Webb, Mar. 26, 1974 (div. Oct. 1987); children: Jessica, Julia; m. Judith Fuente, May 5, 1990. BA, Stanford U., 1968; JD, Yale U., 1971. Dep. pub. def. Contra costa County, Martinez, Calif., 1971-73; ptnr. Nelson & Riemenschneider, Ukiah, Calif., 1974—; dist. dir. Congressman Dan Hamburg, Washington, 1992-94; dir. Redwood Legal assistance, Ukiah, 1976-82, North Coast R.R. Authority, Eureka, Calif., 1996—; bd. dirs. 1st Dist. Appellate Project, San Francisco, 1993—. Chmn., treas. Mendocino Dem. Ctrl. Com., Ukiah, 1978—. Inductee Rochester (Minn.) Sports Hall of Fame, 1996. Mem. Mendocino County Bar Assn. (pres. 1995), Mendocino County Criminal Def. Bar Assn. (pres. 1990, 93). Criminal. Home: 544 Hazel Ave Ukiah CA 95482-3715 Office: Nelson & Riemenschneider 106 N School St Ukiah CA 95482-4809

**NELSON, DAVID K.,** lawyer; b. Baton Rouge, Sept. 9, 1959; s. Robert E. Jr. and Helen C. Nelson; m. Desiree Vila, May 16, 1981; children: David K. Jr., Danny, McKenzie. BS, La. State U., 1982, JD, 1985. Bar: La. 1985. Ptnr. Kean, Miller, Hawthorne, D'Armond, McCowan & Jarman, Baton Rouge, 1989—; bd. dirs., atty. La. Coun. on Child Abuse, Baton Rouge, 1993-94; instr. Nat. Inst. Trial Advocacy for Gulf Coast Regional Program, Loyola, New Orleans, 1993-95, La. State U. Trial Advocacy Program, Baton Rouge, 1993—; tech. presenter for Internat. Tech. Corp., Ann. Indsl. Hygiene Conf., 1993. Pres. Round Oak Homeowners Assn., Baton Rouge, 1989-90; legal coord. Baton Rouge H.S. and Baker High Mock Trial, 1989-90; mock trial coord. Cath. H.S., 1999; lectr. La. Assn. Educators, Baton Rouge, 1990—. Mem. ABA, La. Bar Assn., La. Assn. Def. Counsel, Baton Rouge Bar Assn. Toxic tort, Education and schools, Labor. Office: Kean Miller Hawthorne D Armond McCowan & Jarman LLP One American Pl 22nd Fl Baton Rouge LA 70825

**NELSON, DAVID S.,** federal judge; b. Boston, Mass., Dec. 2, 1933; s. Maston A. and Enid M.N. BS, Boston Coll., 1957, JD, 1960. Ptnr. Crane, Inker & Oteri, Boston, 1960-73; U.S. commr., 1968-69; asst. atty. gen. State of Mass., 1971-73; justice Superior Ct. Mass., Boston, 1973-79; judge U.S. Dist. Ct. Mass., Boston, 1979-91, sr. judge, 1991—. Fellow Am. Bar Found.; mem. Am. Law Inst. Office: US Dist Ct 1 Courthouse Way Boston MA 02210-3002

**NELSON, DEBRA STEINBERG,** lawyer; b. Miamia Beach, Fla., Dec. 2, 1953; d. Irvin and Cecelia Steinberg; m. Michael Robert Nelson, July 30, 1989; 1 child, Tracy. BA in Psychology, U. South Fla., 1975; JD, Southern Tex. Coll. Law, 1979. Bar: Fla., Tex., U.S. Ct. Appeals (11th cir.), U.S. Dist. Ct. Fla. Asst. state atty. Broward County State's Office, Ft. Lauderdale, Fla., 1980-83; staff counsel Fla. Dept. Agriculture, Tallahassee, 1983-86; atty., ptnr. Borough Grimm & Bennet, Orlando, Fla., 1986-92; ptnr. Debra Steinberg Nelson P.A., Orlando, Fla., 1992—; bd. dirs. Fla. Lawyers Legal Ins. Corp.; chmn. Orange County State and Fed. Practice, Orlando. Mem. Jewish War Vet. Ladies Aux. Mem. Ctrl. Fla. Assn. Women Lawyers, Orange County Bar Assn. Avocations: photography, reading. Office: 105 E Robinson St Ste 301 Orlando FL 32801-1622

**NELSON, DOROTHY WRIGHT (MRS. JAMES F. NELSON),** federal judge; b. San Pedro, Calif., Sept. 30, 1928; d. Harry Earl and Lorna Amy Wright; m. James Frank Nelson, Dec. 27, 1950; children: Franklin Wright, Lorna Jean. B.A., UCLA, 1950, J.D., 1953; LL.M., U. So. Calif., 1956; LLD honoris causa, U. San Diego, 1997, U. So. Calif., 1983, Georgetown U., 1988, Whittier U., 1989, U. Santa Clara, 1990; LLD (honoris causa), Whittier U., 1989. Bar: Calif. 1954. Research assoc. fellow U. So. Calif., 1953-56; instr., 1957, asst. prof., 1958-61, assoc. prof., 1961-67, prof., 1967, assoc. dean., 1965-67, dean., 1967-80; judge U.S. Ct. Appeals (9th cir.), 1979-95, sr. judge, 1995—; cons. Project STAR, Law Enforcement Assistance Adminstrn.; mem. select com. on internal procedures of Calif. Supreme Ct., 1987—; co-chair Sino-Am. Seminar on Mediation and Arbitration, Beijing, 1992; dir. Dialogue on Transition to a Global Soc., Weinacht, Switzerland, 1992. Author: Judicial Adminstration and The Administration of Justice, 1973, (with Christopher Goelz and Meredith Watts) Federal Ninth Circuit Civil Appellate Practice, 1995; Contbr. articles to profl. jours. Co-chmn. Confronting Myths in Edn. for Pres. Nixon's White House Conf. on Children, Pres. Carter's Commn. for Pension Policy, 1974-80, Pres. Reagon's Madison Trust; bd. visitors U.S. Air Force Acad., 1978; bd. dirs. Council on Legal Edn. for Profl. Responsibility, 1971-80, Constnl. Right Found., Am. Nat. Inst. for Social Advancement, Pacific Oaks Coll., Childrens Sch. & Rsch. Ctr., 1996-98; adv. bd. Nat. Center for State Cts., 1971-73; adv. bd. World Law Inst., 1997—; chmn. bd. Western Justice Ctr., 1986—; mem. adv. com. Nat. Jud. Edn. Program to promote equality for woman and men in cts.; bd. advisors Tahirih Justice Inst., Washington, 1998—; chair 9th Cir. Standing Com. on ADR, 1998—. Named Law Alumnus of Yr. UCLA, 1967, Disting. Jurist, Ind. U. Law, 1994; recipient Profl. Achievement award, 1969; named Times Woman of Yr., 1968; recipient U. Judaism Humanitarian award, 1973; AWARE Internat. award, 1970; Ernestine Stalhut Outstanding Woman Lawyer award, 1972; Pub. Svc. award Coro Found., 1978, Pax Orbis ex Jure medallion World Peace thru Law Ctr., 1975, Hollzer Human Rights award Jewish Fedn. Coun., L.A., 1988, Medal of Honor UCLA, 1993, Emil Gumpert Jud. ADR Recognition award L.A. County Bar Assn., 1996, Julia Morgan award YWCA Pasadena, 1997, Samuel E. Gates Litigation award Am. Coll. Trial Lawyers, 1999; Lustman fellow Yale U. 1977. Fellow Am. Bar Found., Davenport Coll., Yale U.; mem. Bar Calif. (bd. dirs. continuing edn. bar commn. 1967-74), Am. Judicature Soc. (dir., Justice award 1985), Assn. Am. Law Schs. (chmn. com. edn. in jud. adminstrn.), Am. Bar Assn. (sect. on jud. adminstrn., chmn. com. on edn. in jud. adminstrn. 1973-89), Phi Beta Kappa, Order of Coif (nat. v.p. 1974-76), Jud. Conf. U.S. (com. to consider standards for admission to practice in fed. cts. 1976-79). Office: US Ct Appeals Cir 125 S Grand Ave Ste 303 Pasadena CA 91105-1621

**NELSON, DOUGLAS CLARENCE,** lawyer, consultant; b. Norfolk, Nebr., May 30, 1946; s. Clarence Nels Peter and DeLoris Ella (Kleveland) N. BS, U. Nebr., 1968, JD, 1971, MS, 1973, PhD in Resource Econs., 1981. Bar: Nebr. 1971, Ariz. 1976, U.S. Dist. Ct. Nebr., U.S. Dist. Ct. Ariz. Lectr. U. Nebr., Lincoln, 1971-73; property mgr. Northwestern Mut. Life Ins. Co., Milw., 1973-78; assoc. Rawlins, Ellis, Burris & Kiewit, Phoenix, 1978-81; pres. Douglas C. Nelson PC, Phoenix, 1981—. Mem. Maricopa County Flood Control Adv. bd., Phoenis, 1988-92; mem. adv. bd. Ariz. Water Resources Rsch. Ctr., 1987—; active Valley Leadership Assn., PHoenix; chmn. Ariz. Water Quality Appeals Bd., Phoenix, 1998. Recipient cert. of appreciation Am. Right of Way Assn., 1978, Hohakam Resource Conservation and Defel. Area, 1988, Prescott C. of C., 1990, Ariz. Planning Assn., 1991. Mem. FBA (pres. Ariz. chpt. 1983-84), Am. Water Resources Assn. (chmn. water law sect. 1983-87), Ariz. Agrl. Law Assn. (founder, chmn. 1982-86), Ariz. Rural Water Assn. (exec. v.p. 1984—). Natural resources, FERC practice, Environmental. Home: 7525 N 21st Pl Phoenix AZ 85020-4751 Office: 7000 N 16th St Phoenix AZ 85020-5547

**NELSON, EDWARD REESE, III,** lawyer; b. Ft. Worth, Mar. 8, 1971; s. Edward Reese Jr. and Judy Hill Nelson; m. Laura Alene Nelson, Sept. 6, 1997. BA in Econs., Tex. Christian U., 1993; JD, U. Tex., 1996. Bar: Tex. 1996, U.S. Dist. Ct. (no. dist.) Tex. 1997, U.S. Ct. Appeals (5th cir.) 1999. Law clk. Justice James Baker Tex. Supreme Ct., Austin, 1996; assoc. Brown, Herman, Dean, Wiseman, Liser & Hart, LLP, Ft. Worth, 1996—. Mem. Tarrant County Bar Assn., Tarrant County Young Lawyers Assn., Steeplechase, Phi Beta Kappa. Republican. Methodist. Avocations: basketball, coaching, snow skiing, water sports, golf. General civil litigation, Sports, Appellate. Home: 5608 El Campo Ave Fort Worth TX 76107-4706 Office: Brown Herman Dean Wiseman Liser & Hart LLP 306 W 7th St Ste 200 Fort Worth TX 76102-4905

**NELSON, EDWARD SHEFFIELD,** lawyer, former utility company executive; b. Keevil, Ark., Feb. 23, 1941; s. Robert Ford and Thelma Jo (Mayberry) N.; m. Mary Lynn McCastlain, Oct. 12, 1962; children: Cynthia, Lynn (dec.), Laura. BS, U. Cen. Ark., 1963; LLB, Ark. Law Sch., 1968; JD, U. Ark., 1969. Mgmt. trainee Ark. La. Gas Co., Little Rock, 1963-64; sales engr. Ark. La. Gas Co., 1964-67, sales coordinator, 1967-69, gen. sales mgr., 1969-71, v.p., gen. sales mgr., 1971-73, pres., dir., 1973-79, pres., chmn., chief exec. officer, 1979-85; ptnr., chmn. bd., chief exec. officer House, Wallace, Nelson & Jewel, Little Rock, 1985-86; pvt. practice law Little Rock, 1986—; of counsel Jack, Lyon & Jones, P.A., 1991—; bd. dirs. Fed. Res. Mem. N.G., 1957-63, Fellowship Bible Ch.; bd. dirs. U. Ark., Little Rock, vice chmn. bd. visitors, 1981; bd. dirs. Philander Smith Coll., 1981; chmn. Ark. Indsl. Devel. Commn., 1987, 88; past chmn. Little Rock br. Fed. Res. Bd. St. Louis; chmn. Econ. Expansion Study Commn., 1987—; bd. dirs. Ark. Ednl. TV Found., Ark. Game and Fish Commn. Found.; founder, 1st pres. Jr. Achievement Ark., 1987-88; Rep. nominee for Gov. of Ark., 1990, 94; co-state chmn. Ark. Reps., 1991-92, nat. committeeman Ark. GOP, 1993—. Named Ark.'s Outstanding Young Man Ark. J. C. of C., 1973; One of Am.'s Ten Outstanding Young Men U.S. Jr. C. of C., 1974; Citizen of Yr. Ark. chpt. March of Dimes, 1983; Humanitarian of Yr. NCCJ, 1983; Best Chief Exec. Officer in Natural Gas Industry Wall Street Transcript, 1983; recipient 1st Disting. Alumnus award U. Cen. Ark., 1987. Mem. Am., Ark., Pulaski County bar assns., Ark. C. of C. (dir.), Little Rock C. of C. (dir., pres. 1981), Sales and Mktg. Execs. Assn. (pres. 1975, Top Mgmt. award 1977), U. Ark. Law Sch. Alumni Assn. (pres. 1980). Fellowship Bible Ch. General corporate, Finance. Office: 6th and Broadway 3400 Tcby Bldg Little Rock AR 72201

**NELSON, EDWIN L.,** federal judge; b. 1940. Student, U. Ala., 1962-63, Samford U., 1965-66; LLB, Samford U., 1969. Mem. firm French & Nelson, Ft. Payne, Ala., 1969-73; pvt. practice Ft. Payne, Ala., 1974—; magistrate U.S. Dist. Ct. (no. dist.) Ala., Birmingham, 1974-90, judge, 1990—. With USN, 1958-62. Mem. Ala. Bar Assn., Birmingham Bar Assn., 11th Cir. Assn. U.S. Magistrates, Nat. Coun. Magistrates, Phi Alpha Delta. Office: US Dist Ct Hugo L Black Courthouse Rm 786 1729 5th Ave N Fl 7 Birmingham AL 35203-2000

**NELSON, FREDERICK HERBERT,** lawyer; b. Ft. Bragg, N.C., Sept. 19, 1960; s. Grant H. II Nelson and Sandra J. (Dexter) Bergen. BA magna cum laude, Toccoa Falls (Ga.) Coll., 1989; JD, Stetson U., 1993. Bar: Fla. 1993, U.S. Dist. Ct. (ea. dist.) Wis. 1993, U.S. Ct. Appeals (11th cir.) 1993, U.S. Dist. Ct. (mid. dist.) Fla. 1994, U.S. Ct. Appeals (D.C., 6th, 7th, 9th, 10th cirs.) 1994, U.S. Dist. Ct. (no. and so. dists.) Fla. 1995, U.S. Ct. Appeals (2d, 3d, 4th, 5th, 8th cirs.) 1995. Rsch. asst. Stetson U. Coll. Law, St. Petersburg, Fla., 1992-93; exec. counsel Liberty Counsel, Orlando, Fla., 1993—; pres., gen. counsel Am. Liberties Inst., Orlando, 1994—. Contbg. editor: The International Sale of Goods, 1994; contbr. articles to profl. jours. Bd. dirs. Cmty. Issues Forum, Orlando, 1994—, Ctrl. Fla. CLS, Orlando, 1994—. Mem. ABA (mem. bd. dirs.), ATLA (Fla. bar appellate practice & advocacy sect., Fla. bar fed. appellate practice com.), Phi Delta Phi. Avocations: scuba diving, snow skiing, sky diving. Civil rights, Constitutional, General civil litigation. Home: 528 Terraceview Cv Altamonte Springs FL 32714-1700 Office: Liberty Counsel 1900 Summit Tower Blvd Ste 540 Orlando FL 32810-5912

**NELSON, GARY MICHAEL,** lawyer; b. Mpls., July 12, 1951; s. Emery Marshal and Henrietta Margaret (Flategraff) N.; divorced; children: Rachel Mary, Amy Margaret. BA, Gustavus Adolphus Coll., St. Peter, Minn., 1973; JD, Harvard U., 1976. Bar: Minn. 1976, U.S. Dist. Ct. Minn. 1976. Ptnr., CEO Oppenheimer Wolff & Donnelly, Mpls., 1976-97; v.p., gen. counsel Ceridian Corp., Mpls., 1997—; chair corp. practice inst. Minn. Inst. Legal Edn., Mpls., 1978-93. Sec., v.p. Mpls. Girls' Club, 1978-83. Recipient Significant Contbns. award Am. Girls' Clubs Am., 1982. Mem. ABA. Lutheran. Avocations: fishing, hunting, hiking, reading. Securities, General corporate, Mergers and acquisitions. Home: 2685 Maplewood Rd Wayzata MN 55391 Office: Ceridian Corp 3400 Plaza VII 8100 34th Ave S Minneapolis MN 55425-1640

**NELSON, JAMES C,** state supreme court justice; m. Chari Werner; 2 children. BBA, U. Idaho, 1966; JD cum laude, George Washington U., 1974. Fin. analyst SEC, Washington; pvt. practice Cut Bank; county atty. Glacier County; justice Mont. Supreme Ct., 1993—; former mem. State Bd. Oil and Gas Conservation, also chmn.; former mem. State Gaming Adv. Counsel, Gov. Adv. Coun. on Corrections and Criminal Justice Policy; liaison to Commn. of Cts. of Ltd. Jurisdiction, mem. adv. com. Ct. Assessment Program. Served U.S. Army. Office: Justice Bldg Supreme Ct of Mont 215 N Sanders St Rm 315 Helena MT 59601-4522*

**NELSON, KEITHE EUGENE,** state court administrator, lawyer; b. Grand Forks, N.D.; m. Shirley Jeanne Jordahl, June 10, 1955; children: Kirsti Lynn Nelson Hoerauf, Scott David, Kenen Edward, Karen Lee Nelson Strandquist. PhB, U. N.D., 1958, JD, 1959. Bar: N.D. 1959, U.S. Ct. Mil. Appeals 1967., U.S. Supreme Ct. 1967. With Armour & Co., Grand Forks, 1958-59; commd. 2d lt. USAF, 1958, advanced through grades to maj. gen., 1985; judge advocate USAF, N.D. and, Fed. Republic Germany and Eng., 1959-73; chief career mgmt. USAF, Washington, 1973-77; comdt. USAF JAG Sch., Montgomery, Ala., 1977-81; staff judge adv. Tactical Air Command USAF, Hampton, VA., 1981-82, SAC, Omaha, 1984-85; dir. USAF Judiciary, Washington, 1982-84; dep. JAG USAF, Washington, 1985, JAG,, 1988-91, JAG, 1988, ret. JAG, 1991; dir. jud. planning Supreme Ct. N.D.; state ct. administr., 1992—. Chmn. editorial bd. USAF Law Rev., 1977-81. Decorated D.S.M., Legion of Merit with two oak leaf clusters. Mem. ABA. Lutheran. Avocations: skeet shooting, hunting, tennis, theater. Home: 800 Munich Dr Bismarck ND 58504-7050

**NELSON, L. BRUCE,** lawyer; b. Mpls., Aug. 6, 1946; s. Leo W. and Sylvia E. Nelson; m. Nancy E. Cook, Aug. 23, 1969; 1 child, Andrew C. AB, Hamilton Coll., 1968; JD, U. Colo., 1971. Bar: Colo., D.C., U.S. Ct. Appeals (10th cir.). Assoc./ptnr. Sherman & Howard, Denver, 1972-83; dir., shareholder Isaacson, et al, Denver, 1983-91; counsel Inverness Properties, Denver, 1991-94; dir., shareholder Ducker, Montgomery, et al, Denver, 1994—; clk. Judge Jean Breitenstein, 10th Cir. Ct. Appeals, Denver, 1971. Mem. ABA, Colo. Bar Assn., Colo. Corp. Counsel. Office: Ducker Montgomery 1560 Broadway Ste 1500 Denver CO 80202-5151

**NELSON, RANDY SCOTT,** lawyer; b. Milw., Dec. 4, 1952; s. Seymour and Mildred (Rosen) N.; m. Judy Ann, Jan. 4, 1975; children: Stefanie, Jeffrey. BBA, U. Wis. at Milw., 1974; JD (cum laude), Marquette U., 1977. Bar: Wis., U.S. Dist. Ct. (ea. dist., we. dist.) Wis. 1977, U.S. Tax Ct. 1984. Tax acct. Arthur Andersen & Co., Milw., 1977-80; lawyer Weiss, Berzowski, Brady & Donahue LLP, Milw., 1980—; adj. asst. prof. Marquette U. Law Sch., 1985—; continuing edn. instr. State Bar Wis., Wis. Inst. CPAs, 1982—. Co-author: Workbook for Wisconsin Estate Planners, 1990. Mem. ABA, State Bar Wis. (chairperson real property, probate and trust law sect. 1998-99), Milw. Bar Assn., Am. Coll. Trust and Estate Counsel, AICPA, WICPA (Outstanding Instr. 1987-94). Estate planning, Probate, Estate taxation. Office: Weiss Berzowski Brady & Donahue LLP 700 N Water St Ste 1500 Milwaukee WI 53202-4206

**NELSON, RICHARD ARTHUR,** lawyer; b. Fosston, Minn., Apr. 8, 1947; s. Arthur Joseph and Thelma Lillian Nelson; m. Kathryn Louise Sims, Sept. 25, 1976; children: Jennifer Kathryn, Kristen Elizabeth. BS in Math., U. Minn., 1969, JD, 1974. Bar: Minn. 1974, U.S. Ct. Appeals (D.C. cir.) 1975, U.S. Dist. Ct. Minn. 1975. Law clk. U.S. Ct. Appeals (D.C. cir.), Washington, 1974-75; ptnr. Faegre and Benson, Mpls., 1975—; seminar lectr. in employee benefits and labor laws, 1983—. Note and articles editor Minn. Law Rev., 1973-74. Active Dem.-Farmer-Labor State Cen. Com., Minn., 1976—, del. dist. and local coms. and convs., 1970—, state exec. com., 1990—; student rep. bd. regents U. Minn., Mpls., 1973-74; adv. coun. IRS Mid-states Key Dist. EP/EO, 1996—; v.p. Minn. Student Assn., 1968-69. Served with U.S. Army, 1970-72. Mem. ABA, Minn. Bar Assn. (chair employee benefits sect. 1997-98), Order of Coif, Tau Beta Pi. Lutheran. Pension, profit-sharing, and employee benefits, Labor, Immigration, naturalization, and customs. Office: Faegre and Benson 2200 Norwest Ctr 90 S 7th St Ste 2200 Minneapolis MN 55402-3901

**NELSON, RICHARD M.,** lawyer; b. Newark, N.J., July 19, 1961; m. Jackie Orth, Feb. 28, 1996; children: J.C., Erika, Michael, Daniel, Sean. BA, U. Fla., 1983; JD, Nova Law Sch., 1986. Bar: Fla. 1986, U.S. Dist. Ct. (so. dist.) Fla. 1987. Assoc. Bunnel & Woulfe, Fort Lauderdale, Fla., 1986-88, Barnett & Clark, Miami, Fla., 1988-92; ptnr. Clark, Sparkman, Robb, Nelson and Mason, Miami, Fla., 1992-95, mng. ptnr., 1995—. Review editor: Nova Law Review, 1984, editor, 1985, 86. Recipient Goodwin Rsch. fellow Nova Law, 1984, 85, 86. Avocations: roller hockey, fishing, reading, volunteer work, boxing. State civil litigation, Insurance, Labor. Office: Sparkman Robb & Nelson 19 W Flagler St Ste 1003 Miami FL 33130-4410

**NELSON, ROBERT LOUIS,** lawyer; b. Dover, N.H., Aug. 10, 1931; s. Albert Louis and Alice (Rogers) N.; m. Rita Jean Hutchins, June 11, 1955; children: Karen, Robin Andrea. BA, Bates Coll., Lewiston, Maine, 1956; LLB, Georgetown U., 1959. Bar: D.C. 1960. With U.S. Commn. Civil Rights, 1958-63, AID, 1963-66; program sec. U.S. Mission to Brazil, 1965-66; exec. dir. Lawyers Com. Civil Rights Under Law, 1966-70; dep. campaign mgr. Muskie for Pres., 1970-72; v.p. Perpetual Corp., Houston, 1972-74; sr. v.p., gen. counsel Washington Star, 1974-76; pres. broadcast div. Washington Star Communications, Inc., 1976-77; asst. sec. of army U.S. Dept. Def., 1977-79; spl. advisor to chief N.G. Bur., Dept. Def., 1980-85; pres., dir. Mid-Md. Communications Corp., 1981-85; ptnr. Verner, Liipfert, Bernhard, McPherson and Hand,, 1979-87; gen. counsel Paralyzed Vets. Am., 1988—. Vice chmn. D.C. Redevel. Land Agy., 1976-77; bd. dirs. Community Found. Greater Washington, 1977-78 ; bd. dirs. Friends of Nat. Zoo, 1975—, pres., 1982-84; bd. dirs. Downtown Progress, 1976-77, Fed. City Council, 1976-77, 83-87, Pennsylvania Ave. Devel. Corp., 1976-77. Served with AUS, 1953-54. Mem. ABA, D.C. Bar Assn., Army Navy Club (Washington). Democrat. Episcopalian. General corporate, Non-profit and tax-exempt organizations. Home: Robins Nest PO Box 52 Orrs Island ME 04066-0052 Office: 801 18th St NW Washington DC 20006-3517

**NELSON, ROBERT R.,** lawyer, investor; b. Yankton, S.D., Sept. 24, 1961; s. Lawrence N. and Nancy L. Nelson; m. Kellee L. Haub, Sept. 5, 1987; children: Alyssa L., Andrew R., Amanda M. BS in Bus. Adminstrn., U. S.D., 1983, MBA, 1987, JD, 1987. Bar: S.D. 1988, U.S. Dist. Ct. S.D. 1992. Dir. risk mgmt. Presentation Health Sys., Yankton, 1987-92; assoc. Bierle Porter & Nelson, Yankton, 1987-89,, 1989-92; patient accounts atty. Avera Health (formerly Presentation Health Sys.), Sioux Falls, S.D., 1992—. Contbr. articles to law revs.; assoc. editor Law Rev. Mem. ch. coun. Vangen Luth. Ch., Yankton, 1990-92; den leader Boy Scouts Am., Brandon, 1996-97; youth softball coach/umpire YMCA/YWCA, Brandon and Sioux Falls, 1995—; trustee Queen of Peace Hosp., Mitchell, 1990—. Mem. ABA (dir. Young Lawyers divsn. 1996-97, mem. health law sect. coun. 1998—), ATLA, S.D. State Bar (pres. Young Lawyer sect. 1996-97), Am. Health Lawyers Assn., S.D. Trial Lawyers Assn., Am. Judicature Soc., Ducks Unltd., Nat. Wild Turkey Fedn., Mortar Board, Phi Eta Sigma, Omicron Delta Epsilon, Delta Sigma Pi. Republican. Lutheran. Avocations: upland bird and big game hunting, stock market, skiing, fly fishing, coaching children's softball. Consumer commercial, General civil litigation, Health. Home: 312 Kirkwood Blvd Brandon SD 57005-1628 Office: Avera Health 3007 E 10th St # 1843 Sioux Falls SD 57103-2101

**NELSON, ROY HUGH, JR.,** lawyer, mediator, arbitrator; b. St. Paul, May 13, 1955; s. Roy H. and Helen S. Nelson; m. MaryJean G. Froehlich, Aug. 13, 1994; children: Benjamin, Calla. BS, U. Wis., Milw., 1979, MS, 1985; JD, U. Wis., 1988. Bar: Wis. 1988, U.S. Dist. Ct. (ea. and we. dists.) Wis. 1988, U.S. Dist. Ct. (ea. dist.) Mich. 1991, U.S. Ct. Appeals (7th cir.) 1988, U.S. Ct. Appeals (fed. cir.) 1996. Police officer City of Brookfield, Wis., 1978-88; assoc. Borgelt, Powell, Peterson & Frauen, Milw., 1988-92; shareholder, dir. Petrie & Stocking SC, Milw., 1992—; mediator, arbitrator, dir. Conflict Resolution Svcs., Milw., 1997—; exec. dir. Conflict Mgmt. Edn. Project, 1999; chair adv. bd. Mediation Ministries, Sun Prairie, Wis., 1998—. Mem. ABA, Wis. Bar Assn., Milw. Bar Assn., Christian Legal Soc., Acad. Family Mediators, Alliance Advancement Profl. Mediation, Bus. Network Internat., Am. Arbitration Assn., Am. Intellectual Property Law Assn., Wis. Intellectual Property Law Assn., Wis. Assn. Mediators. Lutheran. Alternative dispute resolution, General civil litigation, Intellectual property. Office: Petrie & Stocking SC 111 E Wisconsin Ave Ste 1500 Milwaukee WI 53202-4808 also: Conflict Resolution Svcs Ste 310 756 N Milwaukee St Milwaukee WI 53202

**NELSON, SONJA BEA,** paralegal; b. Calif., Jan. 20, 1961; d. John Bruce and Anita Pauline (Dean) Nelson. BA in Spanish with honors, U. Calif., Santa Barbara, 1983. Cert. paralegal, corp. specialist, 1984, litigation specialist, 1988. Paralegal Lawler, Felix & Hall, L.A., 1985-88, Adams, Duque & Hazeltine, L.A., 1988-89, Schramm & Raddue, Santa Barbara, 1989-92, Seed, Mackall & Cole LLP, Santa Barbara, 1992—; instr. and mem. adv. bd. Paralegal program U. Calif., Santa Barbara, 1993—. Com. mem. Semana Nautica Masters Volleyball, Santa Barbara, 1995—. Recipient Affiliates award Nat. Assn. Legal Assts., 1997. Mem. Legal Assts. Assn. Santa Barbara (pres. 1993-95, 1st v.p. 1992-93, treas., seminar chair, membership sec. 1989-92, budget 1992—). Democrat. Avocation: volleyball. Office: Seed Mackall & Cole LLP 1332 Anacapa St Ste 200 Santa Barbara CA 93101-6077

**NELSON, STEVEN DWAYNE,** lawyer; b. Austin, Minn., Jan. 30, 1950; s. Dwayne Ronald and Verna Nathelle (Larick) N.; m. Vicky L. Staab, July 6, 1990. BA in English, SUNY, Buffalo, 1972; JD, U. Mont., 1978. Bar: Mont. 1978, U.S. Dist. Ct. Mont. 1978. Sole practice Bozeman, Mont., 1978—; city prosecutor City of Bozeman, 1979-82; city atty. City of Ennis (Mont.), 1980-82; prof. U. Great Falls, Mont., 1990—, mediator, 1998—. Mem. ABA, Mont. State Bar Assn., Phi Delta Phi. Avocations: fishing, skiing, hiking. General practice, Criminal, General civil litigation. Home and Office: PO Box 1962 Bozeman MT 59771-1962

**NELSON, THOMAS G.,** federal judge; b. 1936. Student, Univ. Idaho, 1955-59, LLB, 1962. Ptnr. Parry, Robertson, and Daly, Twin Falls, Idaho, 1965-79, Nelson, Rosholt, Robertson, Tolman and Tucker, Twin Falls, from 1979; judge U.S. Cir. of Appeals (9th cir.), Boise, Idaho, 1990—. With Idaho Air N.G., 1962-65, USAR, 1965-68. Mem. ABA (ho. of dels. 1974, 87-89), Am. Bar Found., Am. Coll. Trial Lawyers, Idaho State Bar (pres., bd. commrs.), Idaho Assn. Def. Counsel, Am. Bd. Trial Advocates (pres. Idaho chpt.), Phi Alpha Delta, Idaho Law Found. Office: US Ct Appeals 9th Circuit 304 N Eighth St PO Box 1339 Boise ID 83701-1339

**NELSON, TIMOTHY ANDREW,** lawyer; b. Brookings, S.D., Sept. 26, 1963; s. Barry James and Jane Elizabeth (Ardich) N. BA with highest honors, U. N.C., 1985; JD with honors, George Washington U., 1988. Bar: Ill. 1988, D.C. 1989, U.S. Dist. Ct. D.C. 1990, U.S. Ct. Appeals (D.C. cir.) 1993, Ariz. 1995, U.S. Dist. Ct. Ariz. 1995, U.S. Ct. Appeals (9th cir.) 1995. Assoc. Vinson & Elkins, Washington, 1988-94, Lowe & Berman P.A., 1994-96; ptnr. Brown & Bain P.A., Phoenix, Ariz., 1997—. Legal intern U.S. Senate Jud. Com., Washington, 1987-88; bd. dirs. Genesis Program, Inc., 1995—; mem. Ariz Town Hall, 1995—. Mem. ABA (litigation sect.), Phi Delta Phi. Democrat. Avocation: marathon running. General civil litigation. Office: Brown & Bain PA 2901 N Central Ave Ste 2000 Phoenix AZ 85012-2788

**NELSON, WALTER GERALD,** retired insurance company executive; b. Peoria, Ill., Jan. 2, 1930; s. Walter Dennis and Hazel Marie (Tucker) N.; m. Mary Ann Olberding, Jan. 28, 1952 (dec. Nov. 1989); children—Ann (Mrs. Michael Larkin), Michael, Susan (Mrs. Jay Boor), Patrick, Thomas, Timothy, Molly (Mrs. David Edwards); m. Mary Jo Sunderland, Apr. 6, 1991. Student, St. Benedict's Coll., Atchison, Kans., 1947-49, Bradley U., Peoria, Ill., 1949; JD, Creighton U., Omaha, 1952. Bar: Nebr. 1952, Ill. 1955; CLU. Practice in Peoria, 1955-56; with State Farm Life Ins. Co., Bloomington, Ill., 1956—; counsel State Farm Life Ins. Co., 1968—, v.p., 1970-96; adj. prof. Ill. State U., Bloomington, 1996—; past dir. Ill. Life Ins. Coun.; past chmn. legal sect. Am. Coun. Life Ins.; spkr. in field. Contbr. articles to profl. jours. Community bd. dirs. St. Joseph Med. Ctr., Bloomington, Ill., 1994. Mem. ABA, Ill. Bar Assn., Nebr. Bar Assn., Assn. Life Ins. Counsel (bd. govs., past pres.), Nat. Orgn. Life and Health Ins. Guaranty Assns. (past chmn., bd. dirs.), Bloomington Country Club, KC. Republican. Roman Catholic.

**NELSON, WILLIAM EUGENE,** lawyer; b. Roland, Iowa, Sept. 23, 1927; s. Sam J. and Katherine A. (Coffey) N.; m. Sherlee M. Stanford, July 11, 1959; children: Anne, Kristin, William. BA, U. Iowa, 1950; JD, Drake U., 1957. Bar: Iowa 1957, D.C. 1965, Md. 1976. Trial atty. civil divsn. U.S. Dept. Justice, 1957-65, asst. chief tort sect., 1966-70, chief r.r. reorgn. unit, 1970-71; gen. counsel Cost of Living Coun. Phase I, 1971, chief econ. stblzn. sect., 1971-74; ptnr. Nelson and Nelson, LLP, Washington, Bethesda, Md., 1975—; gen. counsel the Communicators, Inc., Jefferson, Md. Assoc. editor Drake Law Rev., 1955-57. With USN, 1945-46. Recipient Atty. Gen.'s Disting. Svc. award, 1972. Mem. Order of Coif, Omicron Delta Kappa. Estate planning, General civil litigation, General practice. Home: RR 5 Box 48A Hedgesville WV 25427-9201 Office: Nelson & Nelson LLP 3 Bethesda Metro Ctr Ste 700 Bethesda MD 20814-6300

**NELTNER, MICHAEL MARTIN,** lawyer; b. Cin., July 31, 1959; s. Harold John and Joyce Ann Neltner; m. Barbara Ann Phair, July 9, 1988; children: Brandon August, Alexandra Nicole. BA, Mercy Coll., 1981; MA, Athenaeum of Ohio, 1987; JD, U. Cin., 1994. Bar: Ohio 1994, U.S. Dist. Ct. (so. dist.) Ohio 1995. Tchr. Elder H.S., Cin., 1985-91; ins. agt. Ky. Ctrl., Cin., 1987-91; mediator City of Cin., 1992-94; tchg. asst. Ohio Gov.'s Inst., Cin., 1992; legal extern to Chief Justice Thomas Moyer Ohio Supreme Ct., 1993; assoc. Eagen, Wykoff & Healy, LPA, Cin., 1994-99, Thompson Hine & Flory, Cin., 1999—. Editor-in-chief Mercy Coll. Lit. Mag., 1980-81, U. Cin. Law Rev., 1993-94. Campaign coord. Rep. Orgn. Detroit, 1980. Recipient Merit scholarship Cin. Enquirer, 1977-81, Sage scholarship Mercy Coll., 1980, Am. Jurisprudence award Lawyers Coop. Publishing, 1994. Mem ABA, Ohio Bar Assn., Cin. Bar Assn. (mem. acad. medicine com. 1995—, chair Ct. Appeals com. 1998—). Estate planning, Insurance, Personal injury. Home: 3344 Milverton Ct Cincinnati OH 45248-2865 Office: Thompson Hine & Flory LLP 312 Walnut St Cincinnati OH 45202-4089

**NEMEROFF, ROBERT HOWARD,** lawyer; b. Phila., Apr. 5, 1956; s. Milton Arthur and Shirley Nemeroff; m. Robyn Dana Stiller, June 7, 1980; children: Julie R., Michelle C. BA, Drew U., 1978; JD, Del. Law Sch., 1981. Bar: Pa. 1981, U.S. Dist. Ct. (ea. dist.) Pa. 1981, U.S. Ct. Appeals (3d cir.). Assoc. Nemeroff & Roberts, P.C., Phila., 1981-86; shareholder Nemeroff, Roberts, Jaffe & Nemeroff, Elkins Park, Pa., 1986-88, Jaffe & Nemeroff, P.C., Elkins Park, 1988-90, Jaffe, Friedman, Nemeroff & Applebaum, Elkins Park, 1990-92, Jaffe, Friedman, Schuman, Nemeroff & Applebaum, Elkins Park, 1992-95, Jaffe, Friedman, Schuman, Sciolla, Nemeroff & Applebaum, Elkins Park, 1995—; solicitor Warminster (Pa.) Mcpl. Authority, 1987—. Mem. ABA, ATLA, Pa. Trial Lawyers Assn., Shir Ami Men's Club (pres. 1997—), Pa. Mcpl. Authoriries Assn. (assoc.). Democrat. Jewish. Avocations: astronomy, reading, sports, music, golf. General civil litigation, Personal injury, Municipal (including bonds). Office: Jaffe Friedman 7848 Old York Rd Ste 200 Elkins Park PA 19027-2541

**NEMEROV, JEFFREY ARNOLD,** lawyer; b. Bklyn., Sept. 2, 1942; s. David and Florence Nemerov; m. Susan Ellen Florentino, Sept. 8, 1968; 1 child, Jennifer Courtney Nemerov Cahill. BS, Bucknell U., 1964; LLB, JD, Bklyn. Law Sch., 1967. Bar: U.S. Dist. Ct. (so. and ea. dists.) N.Y. 1967, U.S. Supreme Ct. Mng. atty. Segan Nemerov and Singer P.C., N.Y.C., 1968—. Mem. Assn. Trial Lawyers Am., N.Y. County Lawyers Assn. Avocations: tennis (ranked), golf, biking. Personal injury, Libel, Product liability. Office: Segan Nemerov & Singer 112 Madison Ave New York NY 10016-7416

**NEMETH, CHARLES PAUL,** lawyer, educator, writer, consultant; b. Pitts., July 30, 1951; s. Stephen J. and Rosemary M. (Mille) N.; m. Jean Marie Murray, May 14, 1971; children: Eleanor, Stephen, Anne Marie, John, Joseph, Mary Claire. BA, U. Del., 1972; JD, U. Balt.; MS, Niagara U., 1982; LLM, George Washington U., 1987; postgrad., Duquesne U., 1990—. Bar: Pa. 1980, N.C. 1989. Prof. of criminal justice Niagara U., 1977-80; prof. law, justice U. Balt., 1979-80, Glassboro (N.J.) State Coll., 1980-86; sole practice Chadds Ford, Pa., 1980-86; prof., dir. pub. svc. adminstrn. Waynesburg (Pa.) Coll., 1988—; writer, educator Higher Edn. Svcs., Carnegie, 1985—; mem. grad. faculty St. Joseph's U., 1985-88. Author: Directory of Criminal Justice Education, 1986, 90, The Paralegal Handbook, 1986, Legal Research, 1986, Private Security and the Law, 1989, Status Report in Criminal Justice Education, 1989, The Paralegal Resource Mnaual, 1990, Litigation, Pleadings and Arbitration, 1990, The Paralegal Workbook vol. 1, 1989, vol. 2, 1990, Private Security and the Investigative Process, 1992, Evidence for the Paralegal, 1993, Estates and Trusts for the Paralegal, 1993, Legal Research Excercises for Paralegals, 1993, A Canonical Inquiry into the Case of Archbishop Marcel LeFebvre, 1994, Corporate Law for the Pennsylvania Paralegal, 1994. Mem. Northeastern Assn. Criminal Justice (bd. dirs. 1985), Acad. Criminal Justice and Scis., Assn. Trial Lawyers Am., Scribes, Pa. Bar Assn., N.C. Bar Assn. Roman Catholic. Home and Office: Rosslyn Farms 415 Kings Hwy Carnegie PA 15106-1016

**NEMETH, JOHN CHARLES,** lawyer; b. Cleve., June 24, 1945; s. John and Dorothy Ann Nemeth; m. Martha Beard Junk, Nov. 24, 1973 (div. Aug. 1984); children: John Christian, Megan Jeannette, Ashley Jane. BA, Kent State U., 1967; JD, Ohio State U., 1970. Diplomate Nat. Bd. Civil Trial Advocacy. Atty. Franklin Co. Pub. Defender, Columbus, Ohio, 1971-73, Graham & Nemeth, Columbus, 1973-75, John C. Nemeth Law Office, Columbus, 1975-76, Nemeth & Gantz, Columbus, 1976-79, Graham Dutro & Nemeth, Columbus, 1979-86, Nemeth & Assocs., Columbus, 1986-96, Nemeth Caborn & Butanski, Columbus, 1997—; arbitrator, mediator Am. Arbitration Assn., Columbus, 1973—; faculty/spkr. Ohio Jud. Coll., Columbus, 1985-90; spkr., author Ohio CLE Inst., Columbus, 1985—. Parish mem. St. Andrews Ch., Columbus, 1980—; vol., contbr. Salvation Army, Columbus, 1985—; del. Ohio State Bar Assn., Columbus, 1990-96. With USAR, 1972-78. Recipient Spl. Recognition, Ohio Ho. of Reps., Columbus, 1994, Cert. Appreciation, U.S. Dist. Ct. (so. dist.) Ohio, 1996. Mem. Am. Profl. Liability Attys. Assn. (bd. cert.), Am. Bd. Civil Trial Attys., Million Dollar Advs. Forum. Republican. Roman Catholic. Avocations: running, golf, traveling, snorkling, skiing. Professional liability, Personal injury, Product liability. Home: 4260 Greensview Dr Columbus OH 43220-3928 Office: Nemeth Caborn & Butauski 21 E. Frankfort St Columbus OH 43206-1009

**NEMETH, PATRICIA MARIE,** lawyer; b. Flint, Mich., Sept. 18, 1959; d. Gyula Nemeth and Marie (Glaska) Adkins. BA, U. Mich., 1981; JD, Wayne State U., 1984, LLM, 1990. Bar: Ill. 1987, Mich. 1984, U.S. Ct. Appeals (6th cir.), U.S. Dist. Ct. (ea. dist.) Mich., U.S. Dist. Ct. (we. dist.) Mich. Teaching asst. Wayne State U., Detroit, 1982; intern. U.S. Dist. Ct. (ea. dist.) Mich., Detroit, 1983; assoc. Bloom & Bloom, Birmingham, Mich., 1984-85, Stringari, Fritz, Kreger, Ahearn, Bennett & Hunsinger, Detroit, 1985-92; prin. Law Offices of Patricia Nemeth, P.C., Detroit, 1992-97, Nemeth Burwell, P.C., Detroit, 1998—; lectr. labor law seminar Inst. Continuing Legal Edn., 1990, Mich. Mcpl. Risk Mgmt. Assn., 1995; adj. prof. Walsh Coll., 1992-94. Guest appearance (TV) Straight Talk, 1994, 95; contbr. articles to profl. jours. Mem. ABA (labor sect.), Mich. Bar Assn. (labor sect.), Ill. Bar Assn., Nat. Order Barristers, Nat. Assn. Women Bus. Owners, Women Lawyer's Assn. Mich., Detroit Bar Assn., Health Care Assn. of Mich., Small Bus. Assn. Mich. Roman Catholic. Avocations: sailing, golf, tennis, rollerblade. E-mail: nemethburwell@michbar.org. Labor, Civil rights. Office: 243 W Congress St Ste 1060 Detroit MI 48226-3214

**NEMETH, VALERIE ANN,** lawyer; b. Sutton Surrey, Eng., Mar. 23, 1954; d. Gerald Arnold and Louise Marian (Ross) N.; m. Larry Nagelberg, Dec. 28, 1978 (div. Nov. 1979); m. Hyman Joseph Zacks, Oct. 28, 1984 (div. 1997). BA, UCLA, 1976; JD, Whittier Coll., 1979. Assoc. Grayson, Gross, Friedman, L.A., 1979-80; gen. counsel Red Wind Prodns., L.A., 1979-80; sole practice L.A., San Diego, 1980—; gen. counsel, ptnr. MarValUs Entertainment Co., L.A., 1984—; arbitrator Los Angeles County Superior Ct., 1985—, San Diego Superior Ct., 1985—; legal cons. Centre Devel., San Diego, 1985-87; adj. prof. mgmt. and bus. U. Redlands, 1994—. Mem. legal com. Fairbanks Ranch Assn., Rancho Santa Fe, Calif., 1987—; adminstrv. dir. community svcs. dist. Fairbanks Ranch, 1988-92. Mem. Am. Film Inst., State Bar Calif. (mem. intellectual property sect.), Variety Clubs Internat., Hadassah (life), Zool. Soc. San Diego. Republican. Jewish. Avocations: films, art, outdoors, travel. Fax: 760-942-6043. E-mail: vanemeth@cs.com. Entertainment, Trademark and copyright, Intellectual property. Office: 619 S Vulcan Ave Ste 215 Encinitas CA 92024-3654

**NEMIR, DONALD PHILIP,** lawyer; b. Oakland, Calif., Oct. 31, 1931; s. Philip F. and Mary (Shavor) N. AB, U. Calif., Berkeley, 1957, JD, 1960. Bar: Calif. 1961, U.S. Dist. Ct. (no. dist.) Calif. 1961, U.S. Ct. Appeals (9th cir.) 1961, U.S. Dist. Ct. (ctrl. dist.) Calif. 1975, U.S. Supreme Ct. 1980. Pvt. practice, San Francisco, 1961—; pres. Law Offices of Donald Nemir, A

Profl. Corp. Mem. Calif. State Bar Assn. General civil litigation, General corporate, Real property. Home: PO Box 1089 Mill Valley CA 94942-1089

**NEMIRON, RONALD H.,** lawyer; b. Denver, July 4, 1957; s. Nathan and Eleanor Nemiron; m. Erin Shay, Feb. 12, 1959; children: Flannery Shay-Nemiron, Asher Shay-Nemiron. BA, Brown U., 1979; JD, Harvard U., 1985. Bar: Colo. 1985, U.S. Dist. Ct. Colo. 1985, U.S. Ct. Appeals (10th cir.) 1985. Assoc. Morrison & Foerster, Denver, 1985-87; assoc., shareholder Cooper & Kelley, P.C., Denver, 1987—; shareholder Kennedy & Christopher, P.C., Denver. Professional liability, Insurance, Appellate. Home: 4230 King St Denver CO 80211-1614 Office: Kennedy & Christopher PC 1660 Wynkoop St Ste 900 Denver CO 80202-1197

**NEMO, ANTHONY JAMES,** lawyer; b. St. Paul, May 18, 1963; s. Joseph Marino Jr. and Dianne Marie (Wegner) N.; m. Mary Rose Mazzitello, July 17, 1987; children: Anne Marie, Katherine Mary, Anthony James Jr. BA in English Lit., U. St. Thomas, 1986; JD, William Mitchell Coll. Law, 1991. Bar: Minn. 1991, U.S. Dist. Ct. Minn., U.S. Dist. Ct. Ariz., U.S. Ct. Appeals (4th cir.), U.S. Supreme Ct. Account exec. div. info. svcs. TRW, Mpls., 1986-90; ptnr. Meshbesher & Spence, Ltd., St. Paul, 1990—. Assoc. editor William Mitchell Law Rev., 1988-90; author law rev. note. Recipient R. Ross Quaintance award, Douglas K. Amdahl-Mary O'Malley Lyons Trial Advocacy award. Mem. ABA, Minn. Trial Lawyers Assn., Assn. Trial Lawyers Am., Minn. State Bar Assn., Hennepin County Bar Assn., John P. Sheehy Legal History Soc. Roman Catholic. Personal injury, Product liability, Criminal. Home: 2125 Heath Ave N Oakdale MN 55128-5207 Office: Meshbesher & Spence Ltd 2603 White Bear Ave N Maplewood MN 55109-5110

**NEMOYER, PATRICK H.,** prosecutor; b. Sept. 18, 1952; s. Edgar and Mary (Carroll) N.; m. Elyse S. Hurwitz, Aug. 6, 1977; children: Erin Michelle, Caitlin Carroll, Amanda Nicole, Rachel Elizabeth. BS, SUNY, Binghamton, 1974; JD, SUNY, Buffalo, 1977, MA, 1984. Bar: N.Y. 1978, U.S. Dist. Ct. (we. dist.) N.Y. 1978, U.S. Tax Ct. 1979, U.S. Supreme Ct. 1981, U.S. Dist. Ct. (ea. dist.) N.Y., U.S. Dist Ct. (so. dist.) N.Y. 1992. Prin. law clerk to Hon. James B. Kane N.Y. State Supreme Ct., 1977-87; atty. Erie County, N.Y., 1988-93, U.S. Dept. Justice, Buffalo, 1993—; justice U.S. Supreme Ct. Mem. ABA, Assn. Trial Lawyers of Am., N.Y. State Bar Assn., Erie County Bar Assn., Defense Rsch. Inst., Omicron Delta Epsilon. Democrat. Roman Catholic. Office: New York State Supreme Court US Attorney 50 Delaware Ave Buffalo NY 14202-3803

**NEPPLE, JAMES ANTHONY,** lawyer; b. Carroll, Iowa, Jan. 5, 1945; s. Herbert J. and Cecilia T. (Irlmeier) N.; m. Jeannine Ann Jennings, Sept. 9, 1967; children: Jeffrey B., Scott G., Carin J., Andrew J. BA, Creighton U., 1967; JD, U. Iowa, 1970; postgrad. in bus., Tex. Christian U., 1971; LLM in Taxation, NYU, 1982. Bar: Iowa 1970, Ill. 1973, U.S. Dist. Ct. (so. dist.) Iowa 1972, U.S. Dist. Ct. (no. dist.) Iowa 1975, U.S. Ct. Claims 1976, U.S. Dist. Ct. (cen. dist.) Ill. 1973, U.S. Tax Ct. 1976, U.S. Ct. Appeals (7th and 8th cirs.) 1975, U.S. Supreme Ct. 1975. Tax acct. Arthur Young & Co., Chgo., 1970; v.p., treas., bd. dirs. Stanley, Rehling, Lande & VanDerKamp, Muscatine, Iowa, 1972-92; pres. Nepple, VanDerKamp & Flynn, P.C., Rock Island, Ill., 1992-98; prin. Nepple Law Offices, P.L.C., 1999—. Scoutmaster Boy Scouts Am., Muscatine, 1982-85; trustee State Hist. Soc. Iowa, 1986-92, vice-chmn., 1991-92; bd. dirs. Iowa Hist. Found., 1988-95, pres., 1991-93. Capt. U.S. Army, 1971-72. Recipient Gov.'s Vol. award State of Iowa, 1988, 90. Fellow Am. Coll. Trust and Estate Counsel; mem. ABA (tax sect. 1972—), IA (tax com. 1979-91, chmn. 1988-91), Fed. Bar Assn., Ill. Bar Assn. (mem. fed. tax sect. coun. 1993—, chair 1997-98), Muscatine and Scott County (Iowa) and Rock Island County (Ill.) Bar Assn. (pres. 1982-83), Iowa Assn. Bus. and Industry (chmn. tax com. 1986-88, leadership Iowa award 1985), Quad City Estate Planning Coun. (pres. 1987), Muscatine C. of C. (pres. 1985), Geneva Golf and Coutry Club (pres. 1990-91), Kiwanis (pres. Muscatine chpt. 1978), Elks. Republican. Roman Catholic. Taxation, general, Estate planning, Pension, profit-sharing, and employee benefits. Home: 2704 Mulberry Ave Muscatine IA 52761-2746

**NEREBERG, ELIOT JOEL,** lawyer; b. N.Y.C., May 15, 1949; s. Harry and Muriel (Gravitz) N.; m. Amy V. Jaffe, June 1, 1973; children: Rebecca, Kate. BS, CCNY, 1970; JD, NYU, 1973. Bar: Conn. 1973, U.S. Dist. Ct. Conn. 1973, U.S. Ct. Appeals (2d cir.) 1975. Clin. supr. sch. law. U. Conn., West Hartford, 1973-75; pvt. practice West Hartford, 1975—; spl. masters Hartford County Family Ct., 1985—. Mem. ABA (bd. dirs. publ. bd. family law sect.), Conn. Bar Assn. (chair family law sect.), Hartford County Bar Assn. (co-chmn. family law sect. 1990-92). Democrat. Jewish. Family and matrimonial, Real property, General corporate. Home: 62 Walbridge Rd West Hartford CT 06119-1343 Office: 10 N Main St West Hartford CT 06107-1903

**NERONE, MICHAEL F.,** lawyer; b. Pitts., Mar. 28, 1966; s. F. Regan and Margaret Nerone; m. Amy R. Thomas, June 24, 1989; children: Katherine R., Amanda, Sean. BS, BA, Duquesne U., 1988, JD, 1991. Bar: Pa. Assoc. Dickie McCamey & Chilcote PC, Pitts., 1991—. Mem. ABA, Allegheny County Bar Assn., Pitts. Claims Assn., Pa. Def. Inst. Product liability, Insurance, General civil litigation. Office: Dickie McCamey & Chilcote 2 Pittsburgh Pl Ste 400 Pittsburgh PA 15222

**NESBIT, PHYLLIS SCHNEIDER,** judge; b. Newkirk, Okla., Sept. 21, 1919; d. Vernon Lee and Irma Mae (Biddle) Schneider; m. Peter Nicholas Nesbit, Sept. 14, 1939. BS in Chemistry, U. Ala., 1948, BS in Law, 1958, JD, 1969. Bar: Ala. 1958. Ptnr. Wilters, Brantley and Nesbit, Robertsdale, Ala., 1958-74; pvt. practice, Robertsdale, 1974-76; dist. judge Baldwin County Juvenile Ct., 1977-88; supernumerary dist. judge and juvenile ct. judge Baldwin County, 1989—. Bd. dirs. Baldwin Youth Services; bd. dirs., v.p. women's activities So. Ala. chpt. Nat. Safety Council, 1978-83; chmn. quality assurance com. The Homestead Retirement Vill., 1992-95. Mem. Nat. Assn. Women Lawyers, Nat. Assn. Women Judges, N.Am. Judges Assn., Ala. Dist. Judges Assn., Ala. Council Juvenile Judges, Am. Judicature Soc., Baldwin County Bar Assn., Baldwin Sr. Travelers (sec. 1994-98), Spanish Fort, Fairhope Bus. and Profl. Women's, Phi Alpha Delta. Democrat. Methodist.

**NESBITT, CHARLES RUDOLPH,** lawyer, energy consultant; b. Miami, Okla., Aug. 30, 1921; s. Charles Rudolph and Irma Louise (Wilhelmi) N.; m. Margot Dorothy Lord, June 6, 1948; children: Nancy Margot Nesbitt Nagle, Douglas Charles, Carolyn Jane Nesbitt Gresham. BA, U. Okla., 1942; JD, Yale U., 1947. Bar: Okla. 1947, U.S. Supreme Ct. 1957. Pvt. practice, Oklahoma City, 1948-62, 67-69, 75-91, 95—; atty. gen. Okla., 1963-67; mem. Okla. Corp. Commn., 1968-75, chmn., 1969-75; sec. of energy State of Okla., Oklahoma City, 1991-95; pvt. practice Oklahoma City, 1995—; Okla. rep., v.p. Interstate Oil and Gas Compact. Bd. dirs., trustee endowment fund St. Gregory's Coll.; trustee Oklahoma City U.; pres. Hist. Preservation, Inc.; pres. bd. trustees Okla. Mus. Art; v.p., bd. dirs. Western History Collections Assocs., U. Okla. Librs.; mem. panel arbitrators Am. Arbitration Assn., NASD, NYSE; mem. Ecclesiastical Ct., Diocese Okla. With AUS, 1942-46. Mem. Am., Okla. bar assns., Oklahoma City C. of C., Phi Beta Kappa, Phi Delta Phi. Episcopalian. Oil, gas, and mineral, General civil litigation, General practice. Home: 1703 N Hudson Ave Oklahoma City OK 73103-3428 Office: 125 NW 6th St Oklahoma City OK 73102-6014

**NESBITT, LENORE CARRERO,** federal judge; m. Joseph Nesbitt; 2 children: Sarah, Thomas. A.A., Stephens Coll., 1952; BS, Northwestern U., 1954; student U. Fla. Law Sch., 1954-55; LLB, U. Miami, 1957. Rsch. asst. Dist. Ct. Appeal, 1957-59, Dade County Cir. Ct., 1963-65; pvt. practice Nesbitt & Nesbitt, 1960-63; spl. asst. attorney gen., 1961-63; with Law Offices of John Robert Terry, 1969-73; counsel, Fla. State Bd. Med. Examiners, 1970-71; with Petersen, McGowan & Feder, 1973-75; judge Fla. Cir. Ct., 1975-82, U.S. Dist. Ct. (so. dist.) Fla., Miami, 1983—. Mem. exec. com. U.S. Dist. Ct. (so. dist.) Fla. Bd. trustees U. Miami; bd. dirs. Miami Children's Hosp. Mem. FBA, Fla. Bar Assn., Internat. Women's Forum. Office: US Dist Ct 301 N Miami Ave Miami FL 33128-7702

**NESCI, VINCENT PETER,** lawyer; b. New Rochelle, N.Y., Feb. 27, 1947; s. Vincent S. and Carmela (DeMasi) N.; m. Donna M. Dahlgren, July 21, 1968; children: Vincent P. Jr., Joseph E., Patricia A. BA, Sacred Heart U., 1969; JD, St. John's U., 1971. Bar: N.Y. 1972, U.S. Dist. Ct. (ea. dist.) N.Y. 1973, U.S. Dist. Ct. (so. dist.) N.Y. 1978), N.Y. Supreme Ct. 1976. Assoc. Campbell, Hyman & Lang, New Rochelle, 1972-76; ptnr. Lang & Nesci, P.C., New Rochelle, 1976-79; pvt. practice Yonkers, N.Y., 1980-93; gen. counsel Liberty Lines, Yonkers, 1979-93; CEO Specialized Risk Mgmt., White Plaine, N.Y., 1993—; mgr. ptnr. Nesci Keane Piekarski Keogh & Corrigan, White Plains, 1993—; cons. Summit Investment, Queensland, Australia, 1992—. Avocation: auto racing. State civil litigation, Transportation, Personal injury. Home: RR 2 Bedford NY 10506-9802 Office: 305 Old Tarrytown Rd White Plains NY 10603-2825

**NESLAND, JAMES EDWARD,** lawyer; b. Mobridge, S.D., Aug. 13, 1944; s. Virgil Robert and Thelma Loretta Nesland; m. Carol Ann Ide, Nov. 9, 1946; children: Matthew James, John Edward. BA, U. Denver, 1966; JD, George Washington U., 1970. Bar: N.Y. 1971, U.S. Dist. Ct. (so. dist.) N.Y. 1971, U.S. Ct. Appeals (2nd cir.) 1971, U.S. D.C. Colo. 1976, U.S. Ct. Appeals (10th cir.) 1976, Colo. 1977, U.S. Supreme Ct. 1988. Assoc. Donovan Leisure Newton & Irvine, N.Y.C., 1970-73; asst. U.S. atty. U.S. Atty.'s Office, N.Y.C., 1973-76, Denver, 1977-78; assoc., ptnr. Ireland, Stapleton LLC, Denver, 1978-94; ptnr. Cooley Godward LLP, Denver, 1994—. Author: Federal Criminal Law, 1988. Mem. ABA, Colo. Bar Assn., Denver Bar Assn. General civil litigation, Criminal. Home: 14252 E Caley Ave Aurora CO 80016-1090 Office: Cooley Godward LLP 1200 17th St Ste 2100 Denver CO 80202-5821

**NESS, ANDREW DAVID,** lawyer; b. San Francisco, Oct. 29, 1952; s. Orville Arne and Muriel Ruth (Trendt) N.; m. Rita M. Kobylenski, May 25, 1980; children: Katherine, Austin, Emily. BS, Stanford U., 1974; JD, Harvard U., 1977. Bar: Calif. 1977, D.C. 1979, Va. 1986, U.S. Dist. Ct. (no. dist.) Calif. 1977, U.S. Dist. Ct. D.C. 1983, U.S. Dist. Ct. (ea. dist.) Va. 1988, U.S. Ct. Appeals (4th cir.) 1989. Law clk. U.S. Dist. Ct., San Francisco, 1977-78; assoc. Lewis, Mitchell & Moore, Vienna, Va., 1979-82, ptnr., 1982-87; ptnr. Morgan, Lewis & Bockius LLP, Washington, 1987—; instr. U. Md., College Park, 1987-90; mem. faculty constrn. exec. program Stanford (Calif.) U., 1984-87. Contbr. chpt. to book, 1990, also articles to profl. jours. Mem. ABA (chair divsn. 10, forum on constrn. industry, pub. contract law sect.). Avocations: hiking, bicycling. Construction, Government contracts and claims. Office: Morgan Lewis & Bockius LLP 1800 M St NW Washington DC 20036-5802

**NESSER, JOSEPH GEORGE,** lawyer; b. Rochester, N.Y., Mar. 13, 1957; s. Joseph and Celig Nesser; m. Helen M. Ferris, Feb. 19, 1997. BS, St. John Fisher Coll., 1979; JD, Ohio No. U., 1985. Sole practice Rochester, N.Y., 1986—. Mem. Monroe County Bar Assn. (criminal law sect., family law sect.). Republican. Roman Catholic. Avocations: golf, kung fu. Personal injury, Family and matrimonial, Criminal. Office: 144 Exchange Blvd Rochester NY 14614-2117

**NETTLES, BERT SHEFFIELD,** lawyer; b. Monroeville, Ala., May 6, 1936; s. George Lee and Blanche (Sheffield) N.; m. Elizabeth Duquet, Sept. 16, 1967; children: Jane, Mary Katherine, Susan, Anne. BS, U. Ala., Tuscaloosa, 1958, JD, 1960. Bar: Ala. 1960. Asst. atty. gen. State of Ala., Montgomery, 1961-62; ptnr. Johnston, Johnston & Nettles, Mobile, Ala., 1962-69, Nettles & Cox, Mobile, 1969-81, Nettles, Barker, Janecky & Copeland, Mobile, 1981-89, Spain, Gillon, Grooms, Blan & Nettles, Birmingham, Ala., 1989-94, London & Yancey, Birmingham, 1995—. Contbr. articles to profl. jours. Mem. Ala. Ho. of Reps., 1969-74; bd. dirs. U. South Ala. Med. Sci. Found., Mobile, 1982-89, U. So. Ala. Health Svcs. Found., 1985-89; chancellor Episcopal Diocese of Cen. Gulf Coast, Mobile, 1983-88. 2d lt. inf. U.S. Army, 1960-61. Recipient Exceptional Performance citation Def. Rsch. Inst. and ATLA, 1987. Mem. ABA (chmn. standing com. on legis. 1978), Ala. Bar Assn. (chmn. young lawyers divsn. 1966-67, chair task force on appellate restructuring 1988-91), Am. Right of Way Assn. (sr.), Ala. Def. Lawyers Assn. (pres. 1986-87). Republican. Avocations: reading, children. General civil litigation, Insurance, Professional liability. Home: 1416 Windsor Cir Birmingham AL 35213-3434 Office: London & Yancey 2001 Park Pl Birmingham AL 35203-2735

**NETTLES, GAYLON JAMES,** lawyer, social work consultant; b. Detroit, Jan. 16, 1947; s. Lemuel James and Florence Junell Nettles; m. Bungon Sookka, May 18, 1970; children: Linda, Catherine. BS, Campbell Coll., 1974; MS in Counseling, Am. Tech. U., Killeen, Tex., 1978; MSW, Our Lady of Lake Coll., San Antonio, 1981; JD, Ind. U., Indpls., 1997. Bar: Ind. 1991, U.S. Dist. Ct. (no. and so. dists.) Ind. 1998; lic. clin. social worker, Ind. Enlisted man US. Army, 1967, advanced through grades to capt.; assignments included Thailand, Korea, Germany; ret., 1989; social work cons. Ind. Dept. Edn., Indpls., 1989—, state attendance officer; pvt. practice, Indpls., 1997—. Capt. USAR, 1981. Mem. NASW, Ind. State Bar Assn. (com. on civil rights of children 1998), Indpls. Bar Assn., Assn. Trial Lawyers of Am. Avocations: music, collecting art. Education and schools, Civil rights, General corporate. Office: 101 W Ohio St Ste 2000 Indianapolis IN 46204-4204

**NETZLY, DWIGHT H.,** lawyer; b. Navarre, Ohio, May 7, 1919; s. Harry E. Netzly and Lillian N. Ramsey; m. Martha L. Emerick, Jan. 29, 1949; children: Duane, Dwight K., Doyle, Derek. BSBA, Kent State U., 1948; LLB, William McKinley Law Sch., 1952. Bar: Ohio 1952. Acct. H.C. Schwitzgebul, Canton, Ohio, 1948-52; pvt. practice law and acctg. Massillon, Ohio, 1952—. Sgt. U.S. Army, 1941-45. Mem. Am. Assn. Atty. CPAs, Ohio State Bar Assn., Ohio Soc. CPAs, Am. Legion (state treas. 1993-94). Republican. Probate, Taxation, general, General corporate. Home: 6179 Pigeon Run Rd SW Navarre OH 44662-8738 Office: 1237 Lincoln Way E Massillon OH 44646-6954

**NEUER, PHILIP DAVID,** lawyer, real estate consultant; b. Bklyn., May 31, 1946; s. Murray and Adele (Jacobs) N.; m. Rena Donna Levine, July 30, 1972 (div. 1987); children: Jeremy Evan, Linzy Michelle, Sari Faith. BBA, CCNY, 1968; postgrad., Boston U., 1968-69; JD, Seton Hall U., 1976. Bar: N.J. 1976, U.S. Dist. Ct. N.J. 1977, U.S. Supreme Ct. 1980. Asst. town atty. Town of West Orange (N.J.), 1976-77; assoc. Margolis and Bergstein, Verona, N.J., 1979-80; ptnr. Slavitt and Slavitt, West Orange, 1980-81; assoc. Mandelbaum and Targan, West Orange, 1981-83; ptnr. Margolis Neuer, Verona, 1984-91; of counsel Slavitt Simon & Neuer, Parsippany, 1991—; exec. v.p., gen. counsel Safer Prints Inc., Safer Devel. and Mgmt. Co., Newark, 1993—. Mem. editl. bd. Internat. Jour. for Corp. Real Estate, 1998—. With USN, 1969-73. Mem. ABA, N.J. State Bar Assn., Essex County Bar Assn., Internat. Assn. Corp. Real Estate Execs. (pres., bd. dirs., gen. counsel N.J. chpt., designated internat. assoc., Mem. of Yr. 1993, N.J. Corp. Real Exec. of Yr. 1993, internat. bd. dirs.), Inst. Corporate Real Estate (bd. dirs., pres. 1998—), Internat. Real Estate Inst. (registered internat. mem.), Urban Land Inst., Mensa. Real property, Land use and zoning (including planning), Contracts commercial. Office: 1875 McCarter Hwy Newark NJ 07104-4211

**NEUHAUS, JOSEPH EMANUEL,** lawyer; b. Glen Ridge, N.J., Aug. 17, 1957; s. Gottfried and Helen (Bull) N.; m. Cynthia Ann Loomis. BA, Dartmouth Coll., 1979; JD, Columbia U., 1982. Bar: N.Y. 1986, D.C. 1986, U.S. Dist. Ct. (so. and ea. dists.) N.Y. 1987. Law clk. to sr. judge U.S. Ct. Appeals, Washington, 1982-83; law clk. to Hon. Lewis F. Powell, Jr. U.S. Supreme Ct., Washington, 1983-84; legal asst. Iran-U.S. Claims Tribunal, The Hague, Netherlands, 1984-85; assoc. Covington & Burling, Washington, 1986-87; assoc. Sullivan & Cromwell, N.Y.C., 1987-91, ptnr., 1992—. Co-author: Guide to the UNCITRAL Model Law on International Commercial Arbitration, 1989. Mem. Assn. Bar City N.Y. (com. sec. 1989-92). General civil litigation, Private international.

**NEUKOM, WILLIAM H.,** corporate lawyer; b. Chgo., Nov. 7, 1941; s. John Goudey and Ruth (Horlick) N.; m. Diane McMakin, Dec. 28, 1963 (div. Jun. 1977); children: Josselyn, Samantha, Gillian, John. BA, Dartmouth Coll., 1964; LLB, Stanford U., 1967. Bar: Calif., Wash., U.S. Dist. Ct. (we. dist.) Wash., U.S. Dist. Ct. (no. dist.) Calif., U.S. Ct. Appeals (9th cir.) 1968, U.S. Supreme Court 1974. Atty. MacDonald, Hoague & Bayless, Seattle, 1968-77; ptnr. Shidler, McBroom, Gates & Lucas, Seattle, 1978-85; v.p., law, corp. affairs Microsoft Corp., Redmond, Wash., 1985-93, sr. v.p. law & corp. affairs, sec., 1994—; bd. visitors U. Puget Sound, 1985-90, U. Wash., 1993—; speaker in field. Mem. dean's coun. Dartmouth Coll., 1993—; candidate Wash. Atty. Gen., 1980; trustee Planned Parenthood Seattle-King County, 1986-93, Seattle Art Mus., 1993—; mem. Assn. Gen. Counsel, 1994—; bd. dirs. Greater Seattle C. of C., 1987—, exec. com. 1988—, Washington Roundtable (dep.), 1994—, Assn. Wash. Bus., 1990—, YMCA Greater Seattle, 1988—, Corporate Coun. Arts, 1988—, exec. com. 1993—, Nature Conservance (Wash. chpt.), 1991—, U. Wash. Found., 1993—, Oreg. Shakespeare Festival, 1993—. Fellow ABA (ho. dels. 1978-80, 83—, assn. comm. com. 1991—, bd. editors ABA Jour. 1987-93, alternate dispute resolution com. 1987-91, exec. coun. sect. individual rights and responsibilities 1972-75, 87-92, sec. 1983-87, asst. sec. 1979-83, chmn. young lawyers divsn. 1977-78); mem. Seattle-King County Bar Assn. (long range planning com. 1972-75, 88-91, mgmt., orgn. and planning com. 1986-87, indigent defense svcs. task force 1981-83, trustee legal aid bur. 1974-77, chmn. young lawyers sect. 1972-73), Wash. State Bar Assn., (sec. 1983, pres., chmn., 1977-78, task force professionalism 1986-89, judicial recommendation com. 1985-88, planning com., faculty mem. Pacific Rim Computer Law Inst. 1984-91, orgn. and govt. of bar com. 1973-75, trustee young lawyers sect. 1973-76), Wash. State Trial Lawyers Assn. Avocations: fly-fishing, skiing, running, golf, jazz. Office: Microsoft Corp 1 Microsoft Way Redmond WA 98052-8300

**NEUMAIER, MARK ADAM,** lawyer; b. Johnson AFB, Japan, Apr. 2, 1958; (parents Am. citizens); s. Richard Eugene and Alice Jane (Allen) N.; m. June B. Bouchillon, Apr. 12, 1986 (div.). BA in Psychology, U. Fla., 1979, JD with honors, 1984. Bar: Fla. 1984, U.S. Dist. Ct. (mid. dist.) Fla. 1984, U.S. Ct. Appeals (11th cir.) 1988. Assoc. E.F. Gerace, P.A., Tampa, Fla., 1984-85, Muga & Real, P.A., Tampa, 1985-88; pvt. practice Tampa, 1988—. General civil litigation, Family and matrimonial. Home: PO Box 8623 Tampa FL 33674-8623 Office: 5118 N 56th St Ste 100 Tampa FL 33610-5481

**NEUMAN, LINDA KINNEY,** state supreme court justice; b. Chgo., June 18, 1948; d. Harold S. and Mary E. Kinney; m. Henry G. Neuman; children: Emily, Lindsey. BA, U. Colo., 1970, JD, 1973. Lawyer Betty, Neuman, McMahon, Hellstrom & Bittner, 1973-79; v.p., trust officer Bettendorf Bank & Trust Co., 1979-80; dist. ct. judge, 1982-86; supreme ct. justice State of Iowa, 1986—; mem. adj. faculty U. Iowa Grad. Sch. of Social Work, 1981; part-time jud. magistrate Scott County, 1980-82; mem. Supreme Ct. continuing legal edn. commn.; chair Iowa Supreme Ct. commn. planning 21st Century; mem. bd. counselors Drake Law Sch., time on appeal adv. com. Nat. Ctr. State Cts. Dir. Nat. Assn. Women Judges. Recipient Regents scholarship. Fellow ABA (chair appellate judges conf., mem. appellate standards com., JAD exec. coun.); mem. Am. Judicature Soc., Iowa Bar Assn., Iowa Judges Assn., Scott County Bar Assn. Office: Iowa Supreme Ct State Capitol Bldg/Courthse Davenport IA 52801-1104*

**NEUMAN, TODD HOWARD,** lawyer; b. Buffalo, Dec. 1, 1967; s. Melvin M. and Elaine Neuman; m. Lee Anne Stepanick, Aug. 23, 1997. BS in Fin., Ohio State U., 1989; JD, W.Va. U., 1992. Bar: Ohio 1992, Fla. 1993, U.S. Dist. Ct. (so. dist.) Ohio 1993. Assoc. Thompson, Hine Y Flory, Columbus, Ohio, 1992-95, Swedlow, Butler, Levine, Lewis & Dye Co., LPA, Columbus, 1995—. Gen. counsel, mem. exec. bd. Columbus U.S.A. Orgn., 1993-95; active Jr. Achievement-Young Profls., Columbus, 1998—. Mem. ABA, Ohio Bar Assn., Columbus Bar Assn. (various coms., bd. dirs. barrister leadership program 1996-97), Inns of Ct. Avocations: sports, outdoor activities, family. General civil litigation, Land use and zoning (including planning), Securities. Office: Swedlow Butler Levine Et Al 10 W Broad St Ste 2400 Columbus OH 43215-3469

**NEUMANN, GORDON RICHARD, JR.,** lawyer, shareholder; b. Des Moines, Sept. 30, 1950; s. Gordon R. Neumann and Mary Jane Gray; m. Elizabeth Montgomery, July 25, 1949; children: Jeannette, Eleanore, Neil. BA in Econs., U. Colo., 1972; JD, Drake U., 1976. Bar: Iowa 1976. Nyemaster, Goode, Voigts, West, Hansell & O'Brien, P.C., Des Moines, 1976-80, Shareholder, 1980—; lectr. securities law, Drake U. Law Sch., Des Moines, 1981; spkr., presenter, and panelist in field of bus. law, various orgns. Contbr. articles to profl. jours. Head United Way campaign for law firms, Des Moines, 198; dir. Waldinger Corp., 1997—; chair Pub. Libr. of Des Moines 21st Century com., 1994; dir. Iowa Luth. Hosp. Found., 1991-94, sec., 1992-94; treas., dir., Civic Music Assn., 1989-94; dir. Friends of Iowa Pub. TV, 1990-93, treas., 1991-92, v.p., 1993; organizer Friends of Pub. Libr. of Des Moines, 1990, dir. and treas., 1991. Mem. Greater Des Moines C. of C. Fedn. (chair chamber edn. task force 1997-98, bd. dirs. 1995—, 1992-93, exec. com. 1996—, chair govt. policy com. 1995—, mem. chamber met. major project impact com. 1990-93, chmn. 1992, mem. Ames-Des Moines alliance com. 1991—, other com. and Leadership Inst. work; Vol. of Yr. 1997), Des Moines Pioneer Club (pres. 1998, v.p. 1996-97), Des Moines Club (pres. 1988-89, trustee 1982-90). Fax: 515-283-3108. Mergers and acquisitions, Securities, General corporate. Home: 3950 John Lynde Rd Des Moines IA 50312-3036 Office: 700 Walnut St Ste 1600 Des Moines IA 50309-3800

**NEUMANN, RITA,** lawyer; b. New Brunswick, N.J., Apr. 23, 1944; d. Arno Otto and Florence (Alligier) N. BA in Math., Trenton State Coll., 1965; MS in Math., Stevens Inst. Tech., 1970; JD, Seton Hall U., 1976; LLM in Tax Law, U. San Diego, 1983. Bar: D.C. 1984, U.S. Tax Ct. 1984, N.Y. 1985, N.J. 1986, U.S. Supreme Ct. 1989, Mont. 1990, U.S. Ct. Appeals (9th cir.) 1991. Instr. math. Middlesex County Coll., Edison, N.J., 1971-74; tax cons. Evan Morris Esq. Offices, Woodland Hills, Calif., 1975-85; asst. to editor Jour. Taxation, N.Y.C., 1985-86; pvt. practice law New Brunswick, 1986-94, Las Cruces, N.Mex., 1994—; mcpl. prosecutor Manville, N.J., 1987; adj. instr. bus. law and fin. L.A. C.C. Dist., 1976-82; adj. instr. law and bus. calculus Ventura (Calif.) C.C. Dist., 1977-82; adj. prof. bus. calculus Calif. State U., Northridge, 1981-83; adj. instr. internat. law Laverne U. and San Fernando Valley Coll. Law, 1983-85; disting. lectr. in law and mgmt. Troy State U., Holloman AFB/White Sands Missile Range. Author: Doing Business in North America, 1994, 95, 96; contbr. articles to profl. publs. Vol. to farm workers ctr., Moorpark, Calif., 1979; instr. community extension ctr. for women, Calif., 1980; vol. atty. for N.J. Vietnam Vets., 1986; organizer 10-kilometer run to benefit ill children, Manville, N.J., 1986; guest lectr. taxes Second Ann. Bus. Seminar for Vets. and Non-Vet. Am. Indians of N.W. U.S., Billings, Mont., 1988; candidate for freeholder, Middlesex County, 1988; active with numerous Am. Indian tribes thoughout the U.S. in bus. devel. and Indian rights. Fellow Nat. Sci. Found., 1968-71. Mem. Kappa Delta Phi. Avocation: 10-kilometer runs (recipient several medals). Labor. Office: 1850 N Solano Dr Las Cruces NM 88001-1851

**NEUMANN, WILLIAM ALLEN,** state supreme court justice; b. Minot, N.D., Feb. 11, 1944; s. Albert W. and Opal Olive (Whitlock) N.; m. Jaqueline Denise Buechler, Aug. 9, 1980; children: Andrew, Emily. BSBA, U. N.D., 1965; JD, Stanford U., 1968. Bar: N.D. 1969, U.S. Dist. Ct. N.D. 1969. Pvt. practice law Williston, N.D., 1969-70, Bottineau, N.D., 1970-79; former judge N.D. Judicial Dist. Ct., N.E. Judicial Dist., Rugby and Bottineau, 1979-92; justice N.D. Supreme Ct., Bismarck, 1993—; chmn. elect N.D. Jud. Conf., 1985-87, chmn. 1987-89. Mem. ABA, State Bar Assn. N.D., Am. Judicature Soc. (bd. dirs. 1998—). Lutheran. Office: ND Supreme Ct Jud Wing 1st Fl Dept 180 600 E Boulevard Ave Bismarck ND 58505-0660

**NEUMARK, MICHAEL HARRY,** lawyer; b. Cin., Oct. 28, 1945; s. Jacob H. and Bertha (Zubor) N.; m. Sue Daly, June 5, 1971; children: Julie Rebecca, John Adam. BS in Bus., Ind. U., 1967; JD, U. Cin., 1970. Bar: Ohio 1970, D.C. 1972. Atty. chief counsel's office IRS, Washington, 1970-74; acting br. chief IRS, 1974-75; sr. atty. regional counsel's office IRS, Cin., 1975-77; assoc. Paxton & Seasongood Legal Profl. Assn., Cin., 1977-80; ptnr. Thompson, Hine & Flory, 1980—, mem. mgmt. com., 1993—; chmn. So. Ohio Tax Inst., 1987; mem. IRS and Bar Liaison Com., 1991-93; spkr. at profl. confs. Contbr. articles to profl. jours. Bd. dirs. 1987 World Figure Skating Chamionship, Cin., 1986-89; precinct exec. Hamilton County Rep. Orgn., 1980-86; vol. referee Hamilton County Juvenile Ct., 1980-86; trustee Cin. Contemporary Arts Ctr., St. Rita Sch. for Deaf, 1991-97, Legal Aid Soc. Cin., 1997—. Recipient Commendation Resolution Sycamore Twp., 1987. Mem. ABA (del. 1999—), Ohio State Bar Assn., Cin. Bar Assn. (pres. 1996-97, recognition award 1985, treas., bd. trustees 1988-91, trustee 1992—, chair tax sect., 1990-91), Leadership Cin., Ohio Met. Bar Assn. (pres. 1996-97), Kenwood Country Club, Indian Hill Club, Ohio Met. Bar (pres. 1996-

97), Cin. Acad. of Leadership for Lawyers (founder, chair). Republican. Avocations: golf, travel. General corporate, Taxation, general. Office: Thompson Hine & Flory 312 Walnut St Ste 1400 Cincinnati OH 45202-4089

**NEUMEIER, MATTHEW MICHAEL,** lawyer; b. Racine, Wis., Sept. 13, 1954; s. Frank Edward and Ruth Irene (Effenberger) N.; m. Annmarie Prine, Jan. 31, 1987; children: Ruthann Marie, Emilie Irene, Matthew Charles. B in Gen. Studies with distinction, U. Mich., 1981; JD magna cum laude, Harvard U., 1984. Bar: N.Y. 1987, Mich. 1988, Ill. 1991, U.S. Dist. Ct. (ea. dist.) Mich. 1988, U.S. Dist. Ct. (ea., no. dists. and trial bar) Ill. 1991, U.S. Ct. Appeals (7th cir.) 1992, U.S. Ct. Appeals (fed. cir.) 1998, U.S. Supreme Ct. 1991. Sec.-treas. Ind. Roofing & Siding Co., Escanaba, Mich., 1973-78; mng. ptnr. Ind. Roofing Co., Menominee, Mich., 1977-78; law clk. to presiding justice U.S. Ct. Appeals (9th cir.), San Diego, 1984-85; law clk. to chief justice Warren E. Burger U.S. Supreme Ct., Washington, 1985-86; spl. asst. to chmn. U.S. Constn. Bicentennial Commn., Washington, 1986; assoc. Cravath, Swaine & Moore, N.Y.C., 1986-88; spl. counsel Burnham & Ritchie, Ann Arbor, Mich., 1988; assoc. Schlussel, Lifton, Simon, Rands, Galvin & Jackier, P.C., Ann Arbor, 1988-90, Skadden, Arps, Slate, Meagher & Flom, Chgo., 1990-96; ptnr. Jenner & Block, Chgo., 1996—. Editor Harvard Law Rev., 1982-84. Pres., bd. dirs. Univ. Cellar Inc., Ann Arbor, 1979-81; bd. dirs. Econ. Devel. Corp., Menominee, 1978-79, Midwestern divsn. Am. Suicide Found., sec., 1992-97; mem. vestry Ch. of Our Savior, 1997—; bd. dirs. Chgo. Children's Mus., 1999—; chair Harvard Law Sch. 15 Yr. Reunion Gift Fund, 1999. Mem. ABA, State Bar Mich., Assn. of Bar of City of N.Y., Chgo. Bar Assn., Def. Rsch. Inst., The 410 Club. Republican. Avocations: classic automobiles, piano, choir. Product liability, General civil litigation, Consumer commercial. Office: Jenner & Block Ste 4200 One IBM Plz Chicago IL 60611

**NEUMEIER, RICHARD L.,** lawyer; b. Boston, Nov. 22, 1946; s. Victor L. and Crystal Gladys (Mueller) N.; m. Mary Edna Malcolm, Mar. 15, 1975; children: Hannah Catherine, Edmund Malcolm, Thomas Richard. AB, U. Chgo., 1968, AM, 1968; JD, Columbia U., 1971. Bar: N.Y. 1972, U.S. Dist. Ct. (so. dist.) N.Y. 1972, Mass. 1973, U.S. Dist. Ct. Mass. 1973, U.S. Ct. Appeals (1st cir.) 1974, R.I. 1979, U.S. Supreme Ct. 1985. Assoc. Hart & Hume, N.Y.C., 1971-73; from assoc. to ptnr. Parker, Coulter, Daley & White, Boston, 1973-95; ptnr. McDonough, Hacking & Neumeier, Boston, 1995—. Mem. editl. bd. Def. Counsel Jour., 1989-92, editor, chmn. bd. editors, 1992—; mem. editl. bd. Boston Bar Jour., 1988-94; contbr. articles to profl. jours. Bd. dirs. Common Cause/Mass., Boston, 1980-91, 94-96, chmn., 1990-91; active Town Meeting, Lexington, Mass., 1989—. Fellow Am. Bar Found.; mem. ABA, Fed. Bar Assn. (pres. Mass. chpt. 1989-90), Am. Law Inst., Mass. Bar Assn., Boston Bar Assn. (chmn. ethics com. 1991-94, chmn. torts com. 1994-96), Internat. Assn. Def. Counsel (exec. com. 1992-97). Democrat. Personal injury, Civil rights, Insurance. Home: 2 Pitcairn Pl Lexington MA 02421-7134 Office: McDonough Hacking & Neumeier 11 Beacon St Ste 1000 Boston MA 02108-3013

**NEUMEYER, SUSAN LEE,** lawyer; b. Wolf Point, Mont., Dec. 27, 1945. BA magna cum laude, St. Olaf Coll., Northfield, Minn., 1967; JD with honors, U. Ariz., 1975. Tchr. H.S. West Branch, Iowa, 1968-71; assoc. Curtin, Emerich & Mahoney, Mpls., 1975-91; ptnr. Hanbery, Neumeyer & Carney, Mpls., 1991—. Author: Minnesota Wills and Estate Planning, 1993. Bd. dirs. Greater Mpls. Girl Scout Coun., Brooklyn Center, Minn., 1979-84. Mem. Minn. State Bar Assn. (chair bus. and profl. corps. com. 1997—), Hennepin County Bar Assn. (sects. corp., banking and bus., employee benefit, probate and trust, co-chair gen. practice, solo and small firm com. 1991-93). General corporate, Estate planning, Contracts commercial. Office: Hanbery Neumeyer & Carney PA 3725 Multifoods Tower Minneapolis MN 55402

**NEUNER, GEORGE WILLIAM,** lawyer; b. Buffalo, Oct. 3, 1943; s. George J. and Geraldine M. (O'Connor) N.; m. Kathleen M. Stoeckl, Aug. 28, 1965; children: George W., Kathleen E. BSChemE, SUNY, Buffalo, 1965; SM, MIT, 1966; JD, George Washington U., 1975. Bar: Va. 1975, N.Y. 1976, D.C. 1976, Mass. 1978, U.S. Dist. Ct. Mass. 1978, U.S. Ct. Appeals (Fed. cir.) 1982. From engr. to patent atty. Eastman Kodak Co., Rochester, N.Y., 1966-77; assoc. Dike Bronstein Roberts & Cushman, LLP, Boston, 1977-80, ptnr., 1980—, mng. ptnr., 1988—; arbitration panelist 4th Judicial Dept., Rochester, 1976-77. Grantee Sun Oil Co. MIT, 1966. Mem. ABA, Mass. Bar Assn., Am. Intellectual Property Lawyers Assn., Boston Patent Law Assn. (treas. 1985-86, v.p. 1986-87, pres. elect 1987-88, pres. 1988-89, U.S. Bar/Japanese Patent Office liason coun. 1990—, vice chair 1999), Assn. Patent Law Firms (sec. 1999), Fed. Cir. Bar Assn., Tau Beta Pi, MIT Club (Rochester) (bd. dirs. 1976-77). Patent, Trademark and copyright, Federal civil litigation. Home: 8 Ravenscroft Rd Winchester MA 01890-3807 Office: Dike Bronstein Roberts & Cushman LLP 130 Water St Boston MA 02109-4280

**NEUROCK, MITCHEL,** lawyer; b. Kindley AFB, Bermuda, Mar. 31, 1966; s. Isadore and Frances Neurock; m. Kara Elizabeth Koller, May 26, 1990; children: Aryn Grace, Bennett Edwards. Student, Hebrew U., 1987-88; BA, Rice U., 1989; JD, Washington & Lee U., 1992. Bar: Tex., 1992, U.S. Ct. Appeals Armed Forces, 1993, Colo., 1994, U.S. Supreme Ct., 1997. Claims officer USAF, Whiteman AFB, Mo., 1992-94; dep. staff judge adv. USAF, Izmir Air Sta., Turkey, 1994-96; appellate govt. counsel Air Force Legal Svcs. Agy., Washington, 1996-98; counsel adminstrv. affairs Overseas Pvt. Investment Corp., Washington, 1998-99; assoc. Howrey & Simon, Washington, 1999—; appellate govt. counsel USAFR, 1998—. Capt. USAF, 1992-98. Mem. Fed. Bar Assn. (bd. dirs. young lawyers divsn. 1997—, sec. Pentagon chpt. 1998-99). Republican. Jewish. Government contracts and claims, Appellate, Military. Office: Howrey & Simon 1299 Pennsylvania Ave NW Ste 1 Washington DC 20004-2420

**NEUWIRTH, GLORIA S.,** lawyer; b. N.Y.C., Aug. 16, 1934; d. Nathan and Jennie (Leff) Salob; m. Robert S. Neuwirth, June 9, 1957; children: Susan Madeleine Guerra, Jessica Anne, Laura Helaine, Michael Jonathan. BA, Hunter Coll., 1955; JD, Yale U., 1958. Bar: N.Y. 1959, Fla. 1979, U.S. Supreme Ct. 1976, U.S. Dist. Ct. (so. and ea. dists.) N.Y. 1976. Assoc. dir. Joint Rsch. Project on Ct. Calendar Congestion, Columbia U., N.Y.C., 1958-61; assoc. Kridel and Friou, N.Y.C., 1974-76; ptnr. Kridel, Slater and Neuwirth, N.Y.C., 1976-82; assoc. Kaye, Scholer, Fierman, Hays and Handler, N.Y.C., 1982-84; assoc. Graubard Moskovitz McGoldrick Dannett & Horowitz, N.Y.C., 1984-86; ptnr. Kridel & Neuwirth, N.Y.C., 1986-94, ptnr. Davidson, Dawson & Clark, 1995—; vol. arbitrator Better Bus. Bur. Author: (with R.B. Hunting) Who Sues in New York City: A Study of Automobile Accident Claims, 1962; contbr. articles to law jours. Trustee Blueberry Inc., 1962-70, Riverdale Country Sch., 1981-86; trustee, v.p., sec. Nat. Kidney Found. Inc., N.Y./N.J., 1980—, trustee nat. office, 1980—; dir. State Planning Coun. N.Y.C., Riverdale Mental Health Assn., Bronx Opera Co., The Ruth Turner Fund. Recipient C. LaRue Munson prize Yale Law Sch., 1958. Fellow Am. Coll. Trust & Estate Counsel; mem. ABA, N.Y. State Bar Assn. (chmn. com. on law of the elderly charitable planning), Assn. Bar City N.Y. (bd. dirs.), Estate Planning Coun. of N.Y., Nat. Health Lawyers Assn., Sierra Club, Appalacian Mountain Club. Probate, Estate taxation, Non-profit and tax-exempt organizations. Office: Davidson Dawson & Clark 330 Madison Ave Fl 35 New York NY 10017-5094

**NEVELOFF, JAY A.,** lawyer; b. Bklyn., Oct. 11, 1950; s. Cydelle (Weber) Elrich; m. Arlene Sillman, Aug. 26, 1972; children: David, Kevin. BA, Bklyn. Coll., 1971; JD, NYU, 1974. Bar: N.Y. 1975, D.C. 1992, U.S. Dist. Ct. (so. and ea. dists.) N.Y. 1975, U.S. Ct. Appeals (2d cir.) 1975, U.S. Supreme Ct. 1982. Assoc. Marshall, Bratter, Greene, Allison & Tucker, N.Y.C., 1974-82; assoc. Rosenman, Colin, Freund, Lewis & Cohen, N.Y.C., 1982-83, ptnr., 1983-88; ptnr. Kramer, Levin, Naftalis, Nessen, Kamin & Frankel, N.Y.C., 1988—. Editor N.Y. Real Property Service. Mem. planning bd. Briarcliff Manor, 1995—. Mem. ABA (vice chmn. com. partnerships, joint ventures and other investment vehicles 1988-95), Am. Law Inst., Am. Coll. Real Estate Attys., N.Y. State Bar Assn. (financing com.), Practising Law Inst. (lectr. 1988—, mem. adv. bd. 1991—), N.Y. County Lawyers Assn. (lectr. 1984—), Assn. of Bar of City of N.Y. (real property law com., chmn. condominium resale contract com., lectr. 1984-88), Cmty. Assns. Inst. (lectr. 1986), Law Jours. Seminars (lectr. 1987—), Strategic Resources Inst. (lectr. 1994—), Internat. Health Network Soc. (vice chmn. 1995—), Inst. Internat. Rsch. (lectr. 1994—). Real property. Home: 134 Alder Dr Briarcliff Manor NY 10510-2218 Office: Kramer Levin Naftalis & Frankel 919 3rd Ave New York NY 10022-3902

**NEVES, KERRY LANE,** lawyer; b. San Angelo, Tex., Dec. 19, 1950; s. Herman Walter and Geraldine (Ball) N.; m. Sharon Lynn Briggs, July 28, 1973; 1 child, Erin Lesli. BBA, U. Tex., 1975, JD, 1978. Bar: Tex. 1978, U.S. Dist. Ct. (so. and ea. dists.) Tex. 1979, U.S. Ct. Appeals (5th cir.) 1979, U.S. Dist. Ct. (we. dist.) 1980; cert. personal injury trial law, Tex. Bd. Legal Specialization, 1994. Ptnr. Mills, Shirley, Eckel & Bassett, Galveston, Tex., 1978-93, Neves & Crowther, Galveston, Tex., 1993—. Vice-chmn. Bldg. Stnds. Commn., Dickinson, Tex., 1991-98; mem. City Coun. Dickinson, Tex., 1998—. Sgt. USMC, 1969-72. Fellow Tex. Bar Found. (life); mem. ABA, State Bar Tex. (grievance com. 1989-92, disciplinary rules profl. conduct com. 1990-92, dir. dist. 5 1997—), Galveston County Bar Assn. (pres. 1989-90), U. Tex. Law Alumni Assn. (pres. 1991-92). Avocations: gardening, bicycling, wine, books. Personal injury, Product liability, General civil litigation. Home: RR 2 Box 95 Dickinson TX 77539-9204 Office: Neves & Crowther 1802 Broadway St Ste 206 Galveston TX 77550-4953

**NEVILLE, JAMES EDWARD,** lawyer; b. East St. Louis, Ill., Jan. 1, 1955; s. Hugh Edward and Eugenia Catherine Neville; m. Carol Sullivan; children: Jared, Suzanne, Patrick, Evan. BSBA, St. Louis U., 1977, JD, 1980. Bar: Ill. 1980, U.S. Dist. Ct. (so. and ctrl. dists.) Ill. 1980, U.S. Dist. Ct. (ea. dist.) Mo. 1991, U.S. Ct. Appeals (7th cir.) 1991, Mo. 1992. Atty. Gundlach Lee Eggmann Boyle & Roessler, Belleville, Ill., 1980-94, Neville Richards DeFranco & Wuller, Belleville, 1994—; spkr. in field. Contbr. articles to profl. jours. Coach Belle Clair Soccer League, Belleville, Ill., 1984—, West End Khoury League, Belleville, 1984—. Roman Catholic. Avocations: sports, coach, reading. Professional liability, Personal injury, General civil litigation. Home: 501 Oak Hill Dr Belleville IL 62223-2258 Office: Neville Richards DeFranco & Wuller #5 Park Pl Profl Ctr Belleville IL 62226

**NEVILLE, JAMES MORTON,** lawyer, consumer products executive; b. Mpls., May 28, 1939; s. Philip and Maurene (Morton) N.; m. Judie Martha Proctor, Sept. 9, 1961; children: Stephen Warren, Martha Maurene Hereford. BA, U. Minn., JD magna cum laude, 1964. Bar: Minn. 1964, Mo. 1984. Assoc. firm Neville, Johnson & Thompson, Mpls., 1964-69, ptnr., 1969-70; assoc. counsel Gen. Mills, Inc., Mpls., 1970-77, sr. assoc. counsel, 1977-83, corp. sec., 1976-83; v.p., sec., asst. gen. counsel Ralston Purina Co., St. Louis, 1983-84, v.p., gen. counsel, sec., 1984-96, v.p., gen. counsel, 1996—; lectr. bus. law. U. Minn., 1967-71. Named Man of Yr. Edina Jaycees, 1967. Mem. ABA, Minn., Mo. Bar Assns., U.S. Supreme Ct. Bar Assn., Hennepin County Bar Assn., St. Louis Bar Assn., U. Minn. Law Sch. Alumni Assn., Am. Soc. Corp. Secs., Am. Corp. Counsel Assn., Old Warson Country Club, Ladue Racquet Club, Noonday Club, Order of Coif, Phi Delta Phi, Psi Upsilon. Episcopalian. General corporate. Home: 9810 Log Cabin Ct Saint Louis MO 63124-1133 Office: Ralston Purina Co Checkerboard Sq Saint Louis MO 63164-0001

**NEVIN, HUGH WILLIAMSON, JR.,** lawyer; b. Sewickley, Pa., Dec. 9, 1946; s. Hugh Williamson and Eleanore (George) N.; m. Eliza Scott Nevin, June 16, 1972; 1 child, John Irwin. BA, Harvard, 1968, JD, 1974. Bar: Pa. 1975, U.S. Dist. Ct. (we. dist.) Pa. 1975. Pres./CEO, chmn. internat. bus. group Cohen & Grigsby, Pitts., 1986—. With U.S. Army, 1968-70. Mem. Phi Beta Kappa. Presbyterian. Taxation, general, Private international, General corporate. Office: Cohen & Grigsby 11 Stanwix St Ste 15 Pittsburgh PA 15222-1312

**NEVIN, RONALD KENT,** lawyer; b. Vicksburg, Miss., Oct. 31, 1947; s. Louis S. and Lois Regina (Kaufman) N.; m. Brenda L. Howell, Sept. 2, 1972; children: Ashley, Andrew, Ryan, Caroline. BS, U. Tenn., 1969, JD, 1972. Bar: Tenn. 1973. Pvt. practice Nashville, 1973—; pub. guardian Davidson County, Nashville, 1975—. Contbr. chpt. to book. Chmn. Multiple Sclerosis Soc., Nashville, 1979-81; bd. dirs. Davidson County chpt. U. Tenn. Alumnae, 1985-88. Mem. Tenn. Bar Assn., Nashville Bar Assn. (chmn. admission to practice com. 1987-88, probate com. 1989—, chmn. probate ct. com. 1998), Nashville C. of C. (chmn. legis. network 1993, chmn. met. coun. rels. com. 1984), Nashville City Club. Probate, Family and matrimonial, Bankruptcy. Office: Ste 1850 404 James Robertson Pkwy Nashville TN 37219-1596

**NEVINS, ARTHUR GERARD, JR.,** lawyer; b. Bklyn., Dec. 23, 1948; s. Arthur Gerard Sr. and Gertrude Anna May (Schlueter) N.; m. Reine T. Hughes, June 26, 1982; m. Amanda Mitchell, May 16, 1989. BS, Cornell U., 1971; JD, Fordham U., 1974. Bar: N.Y. 1975, N.J. 1976. Assoc. Lester, Schwab, Katz & Dwer, N.Y.C., 1975-77, Law Offices of Peter De Blasio, N.Y.C., 1977-80, Law Offices of Robert Ginsberg, N.Y.C., 1980-82; pvt. practice N.Y.C., 1982—. Mem. ABA, N.Y. State Bar Assn., N.J. Bar Assn., N.Y. County Bar Assn., Hudson County Bar Assn., Phi Gamma Delta. Roman Catholic. Club: Downtown Athletic (N.Y.C.). Personal injury, Professional liability, Workers' compensation. Home: 138 Central Ave Jersey City NJ 07306-2119 Office: 225 Broadway Ste 3111 New York NY 10007-3001

**NEVOLA, ROGER PAUL,** lawyer; b. N.Y.C., Apr. 30, 1947; s. Frank S. and Kathryn N.; m. Molly Cagle; children: Adrienne L., Jake F. Student, U. Notre Dame, 1964-66; BSME, Stanford U., 1968; JD, U. Tex., 1974. Bar: Tex. 1974. Assoc. Vinson & Elkins, Houston, 1974-79; assoc. Vinson & Elkins, Austin, 1979-81, ptnr., 1981-95; pvt. practice Austin, 1995—; Tex. reporter Mineral Law Newsletter/Rocky Mountain Mineral Law Found., 1984—. Fellow Tex. Bar Found. (life); mem. Tex. Water Conservation Assn. (dir. 1978—). Avocations: golf, hiking, travel. Administrative and regulatory, Environmental, Real property. Home: 4304 Bennedict Ln Austin TX 78746-1940 Office: PO Box 2103 Austin TX 78768-2103

**NEWACHECK, DAVID JOHN,** lawyer; b. San Francisco, Dec. 8, 1953; s. John Elmer and Estere Ruth Sybil (Nelson) N.; m. Dorothea Quandt, June 2, 1990. AB in English, U. Calif., Berkeley, 1976; JD, Pepperdine U., 1979; MBA, Calif. State U., Hayward, 1982; LLM in Tax, Golden Gate U., 1987. Bar: Calif. 1979, D.C. 1985, N.Y. 1987, U.S. Dist. Ct. (no. dist.) Calif. 1979, U.S. Ct. Appeals (9th cir.) 1979, U.S. Supreme Ct. 1984. Tax cons. Pannell, Kerr and Forster, San Francisco, 1982-83; lawyer, writer, editor Matthew Bender and Co., San Francisco, 1983—; instr. taxation Oakland (Calif.) Coll. of Law, 1993—; lawyer, tax cons., fin. planner San Leandro, Calif., 1983—; bd. dirs. Aztec Custom Co., Orinda, Calif., 1983—; cons. software Collier Bankruptcy Filing Sys., 1984. Author/editor: (treatises) Ill. Tax Service, 1985, Ohio State Taxation, 1985, N.J. Tax Service, 1986, Pa. Tax Service, 1986, Calif. Closely Held Corps., 1987, Texas Tax Service, 1988; author: (software) Tax Source 1040 Tax Preparation, 1987, Texas Tax Service 1988, California Taxation, 1989, 2d edit., 1990, Bender's Federal Tax Service, 1989, Texas Litigation Guide, 1993, Family Law: Texas Practice & Procedure, 1993, Texas Transaction Guide, 1994, Ohio Corporation Law, 1994, Michigan Corporation Law, 1994, Massachusetts Corporation Law, 1994. Mem. youth com. Shepherd of the Valley Luth. Ch., Orinda, 1980-85, ch. coun., 1980-82; bd. dirs. Oakland Coll. Law, treas., CFO, 1997—. Mem. ABA, Internat. Platform Assn., State Bar Assn. Calif., Alameda County Bar Assn., U. Calif. Alumni Assn., U. Calif. Band Alumni Assn., Kiwanis Club San Leandro (bd. dirs. 1998—), Commonwealth Club (San Francisco chpt.), Mensa. Republican. Avocations: music, competitive running, sports. Personal income taxation, Estate planning, State and local taxation. Home: 5141 Vannoy Ave Castro Valley CA 94546-2558 Office: 438 Estudillo Ave San Leandro CA 94577-4908

**NEWBERN, WILLIAM DAVID,** retired state supreme court justice; b. Oklahoma City, May 28, 1937; s. Charles Banks and Mary Frances (Harding) N.; m. Barbara Lee Rigsby, Aug. 19, 1961 (div. 1968); 1 child, Laura Harding; m. Carolyn Lewis, July 30, 1970; 1 child, Alistair Elizabeth. B.A., U. Ark., 1959, J.D., 1961; LL.M., George Washington U., 1963; M.A., Tufts U., 1967. Bar: Ark. 1961, U.S. Dist. Ct. (we. dist.) Ark. 1961, U.S. Supreme Ct. 1968, U.S. Ct. Appeals (8th cir.) 1983. Commd. 1st lt. advanced to maj. U.S. Army JAGC, 1961-70; Prof. law U. Ark., Fayetteville, 1970-84; adminstr. Ozark Folk Ctr., Mountain View, Ark., 1973; judge Ark. Ct. Appeals, Little Rock, 1979-80; assoc. justice Ark. Supreme Ct., Little Rock, 1985-99; mem. faculty sr. appellate judges seminar NYU, 1987-91. Editor Ark. Law Rev., 1961; author: Arkansas Civil Practice and Procedure, 1985, 2d edit., 1993. Mem. Fayetteville Bd. Adjustment, 1972-79; bd. dirs. Decision Point, Inc., Springdale, Ark., 1980-85; bd. dirs. Little Rock Wind Symphony, 1993—, pres. 1993-95. Fellow Ark. Bar Found.; mem. Ark. Bar Assn., Am. Judicature Soc. (bd. dirs. 1985-89), Washington County Bar Assn., Inst. Jud. Adminstrn., Ark. IOLTA Found. (bd. dirs. 1985-87). Democrat. Avocation: string band-guitar, mandolin, banjo and brass quintet-tuba.

**NEWBLATT, STEWART ALBERT,** federal judge; b. Detroit, Dec. 23, 1927; s. Robert Abraham and Fanny Ida (Grinberg) N.; m. Flora Irene Sandweiss, Mar. 5, 1965; children: David Jacob, Robert Abraham, Joshua Isaac. BA with distinction, U. Mich., 1950, JD with distinction, 1952. Bar: Mich. 1953. Ptnr. White & Newblatt, Flint, Mich., 1953-62; judge 7th Jud. Cir. Mich., 1962-70; ptnr. Newblatt & Grossman (and predecessor), Flint, 1970-79; judge U.S. Dist. Ct. (ea. dist.) Mich., Flint, 1979-93, sr. judge, 1993—; adj. instr. U. Mich.-Flint, 1977-78, 86. Mem. Internat. Bridge Authority Mich., 1960-62. Served with AUS, 1946-47. Mem. Fed. Bar Assn., State Bar Mich., Dist. Judges Assn. 6th Circuit. Jewish. Office: PO Box 522 Glen Arbor MI 49636-0522

**NEWCOM, JENNINGS JAY,** lawyer; b. St. Joseph, Mo., Oct. 18, 1941; s. Arden Henderson and Loyal Beatrice (Winans) N.; m. Cherry Ann Phelps, Apr. 4, 1964; children: Shandra Karine, J. Derek Arden. BA, Graceland Coll., Lamoni, Iowa, 1964; JD, Harvard U., 1968. Bar: Ill. 1968, Calif. 1973, Mo. 1979, Kans. 1981. Atty. McDermott, Will & Emery, Chgo., 1968-73; ptnr. Rifkind, Sterling & Lockwood, Beverly Hills, Calif., 1973-79, Shook, Hardy & Bacon L.L.P., Kansas City, Mo., 1979—; chmn. bd. Graceland Coll. Trustee Hubbard Found., Linde Found. Mem. Kansas City Bar Assn., State Bar Assn. Calif., Lawyers Assn. Kansas City, Greater Kansas City Cmty. Found. Mergers and acquisitions, Securities, General corporate. Office: Shook Hardy & Bacon 1 Kansas City Plz 1200 Main St Ste 3100 Kansas City MO 64105-2139 Office: Davis Graham & Stubbs LLP 370 17th St Ste 4700 Denver CO 80202-5682

**NEWCOMER, CLARENCE CHARLES,** federal judge; b. Mount Joy, Pa., Jan. 18, 1923; s. Clarence S. and Marion Clara (Charles) N.; m. Jane Moyer Martin, Oct. 2, 1948; children: Judy (Mrs. Kenneth N. Birkett Jr.), Nancy Jane Newcomer (Mrs. Edward H. Vick), Peggy Jo Pollack (dec.). A.B., Franklin and Marshall Coll., 1944; LL.B., Dickinson Sch. Law, 1948. Bar: Pa. 1950, U.S. Dist. Ct. Pa., U.S. Ct. Appeals (3rd cir.), U.S. Supreme Ct. Pvt. practice Lancaster, 1950-52; spl. dep. atty. gen. Dept. Justice, Commonwealth of Pa., 1952-54; partner firm Rohrer, Honaman, Newcomer & Musser, Lancaster, 1957-60; with Office of Dist. Atty., Lancaster, 1960-64; 1st asst. dist. atty. Office of Dist. Atty., 1964-68, dist. atty., 1968-72; partner Newcomer, Roda & Morgan, 1968-72; fed. dist. judge Eastern Dist. Pa., Phila., 1972-88, sr. judge, 1988—. Served to lt. (j.g.) USNR, 1943-46, PTO. Office: US Dist Ct 13614 US Courthouse 601 Market St Philadelphia PA 19106-1713

**NEWELL, KEITH DOUGLAS,** paralegal; b. Kingston, Pa., Aug. 3, 1968; m. Mary Kay D. Riscavage, July 23, 1989; 1 child, Alexzander H. Assoc. in Bus. Adminstrn., St Petersburg Jr. Coll., 1990; paralegal cert., Blackston Sch. Law, Tex., 1995. Internal auditing and compliance mgr. Zwicker & Assocs, P.C., Andover, Mass., 1996—. Mem. Nat. Capital Area Assn. Paralegals. Avocation: British car restorations. Home: 116 N Shore Rd Derry NH 03038-5819 Office: Zwicker & Assocs PC 3 Riverside Dr Andover MA 01810-1141

**NEWELL, ROBERT MELVIN,** lawyer; b. Anacortes, Wash., Oct. 29, 1918; s. Seymour Melvin and Hildur (Apenese) N.; m. Gertrude A. Brawner, Oct. 31, 1942 (div. Oct. 1954); children: Robert M. Jr., Christine N. Jones, William C.; m. Mary Will, Apr. 2, 1955. AB, Stanford U., 1941, JD, 1946. Bar: Calif., 1946, U.S. Dist. Ct. (cen. dist.) Calif., U.S. Ct. Appeals (9th cir.), U.S. Supreme Ct. Ptnr. Newell & Chester, Los Angeles, 1947-88. Served to lt. USN, 1942-46, PTO. Mem. ABA, Calif. Bar Assn., Los Angeles County Bar Assn. Democrat. Federal civil litigation, State civil litigation, Family and matrimonial. Office: 600 Wilshire Blvd Fl 17 Los Angeles CA 90017-3212

**NEWENDORP, PAUL WILLIAM,** lawyer; b. Escanaba, Mich., Dec. 24, 1957; s. Leonard Beach and Carolyn Leah Newendorp; m. Janet Patrice Hurley, Dec. 15, 1997 (div. July 1998). BA, Mich. State U., 1979; postgrad., Creighton U., 1979-80; JD, Case Western Res U., 1982. Bar: Ohio 1982, U.S. Dist. Ct. (no. dist.) Ohio 1983. Asoc. atty. Pomerantz & Pomerantz Co., CPAs, Cleve., 1982-94; assoc. atty. Weiner, Suit & Coury, Warren, Ohio, 1994—. Mem. Trumbull County Bar Assn. (unauthorized practice com.), Cleve. Bar Assn. (law sch. liaison com.), Ohio Acad. Trial Attys. Avocations: skiing, outdoor activities. Workers' compensation, Personal injury, Product liability. Office: Weiner Suit & Coury 552 N Park Ave Warren OH 44481-1117

**NEWHOUSE, JAMES HOWARD,** lawyer; b. N.Y.C., Nov. 22, 1938; s. Sidney Duval and Eleanor (Bauman) N.; m. Karen Ross, Dec. 27, 1978; children: Adam, Zachary. BA, U. Calif., Santa Barbara, 1961; JD, U. Calif., Berkeley, 1965. Bar: Calif. 1965, U.S. Dist. Ct. (no. dist.) Calif. 1969, U.S. Dist. Ct. (ctrl. and so. dists.) Calif. 1970, U.S. Ct. Appeals (9th cir.) 1972; cert. criminal law specialist, Calif. Atty. Alameda County Pub. Defender, Oakland, Calif., 1966-69, Cooper & Newhouse, Berkeley, 1969-79; atty., sole practitioner Monterey, Calif., 1980—; founding mem., bd. dirs. Calif. Attys. for Criminal Justice, L.A., 1974-79. Contbr. articles to profl. jours. With U.S. Army, 1961-63. Avocations: golf, tennis. Criminal. Office: 460 Alma St Ste 100 Monterey CA 93940-3247

**NEWITT, JOHN GARWOOD, JR.,** lawyer; b. Charlotte, N.C., Apr. 9, 1941; s. John Garwood and Sarah Elizabeth (Stratford) N.; m. Catherine Elizabeth Hubbard, Aug. 28, 1965; children: Catherine Stratford, Elizabeth Blake. BA, Wake Forest U., 1963, JD, 1965; postgrad., U. Va., 1966-68. Bar: N.C. 1965, U.S. Ct. Mil. Appeals 1965, U.S. Dist. Ct. (we. dist.) N.C. 1968, U.S. Ct. Claims 1968, U.S. Tax. Ct. 1968, U.S. Ct. Appeals (4th cir.) 1984. Ptnr. Newitt & Newitt, Charlotte, 1968-73; sr. ptnr. Newitt & Bruny, Charlotte, 1973—; lectr. The Judge Advocate Gen.'s Sch., 1965-68, United Way Vol. Leadership Devel. Program, 1986-93. Contbr. articles to law revs. Chmn. Bd. Zoning Adjustment, 1971-77; bd. dirs. Carolina Group Homes, 1992-95. Recipient awards ASCAP. Mem. N.C. Bar Assn., Mecklenburg County Bar Assn., N.C. Coll. Advocacy (cert. competency), Myers Park Country Club (past pres., bd. dirs.), Selwyn Men's Fellowship (past pres.), Good Fellows, Phi Delta Phi (past sec.). Republican. Presbyterian. Avocations: jogging, golf. General civil litigation, Mergers and acquisitions, General corporate. Home: 3216 Ferncliff Rd Charlotte NC 28211-3259 Office: Newitt & Bruny 417 East Blvd Ste 104 Charlotte NC 28203-5163

**NEWKIRK, THOMAS CHARLES,** lawyer; b. N.Y.C., June 6, 1942; s. Rudolph H. and Ruth H. (Wilson) N.; m. Nancy W., Dec. 23, 1965; children: Jennifer L., Christopher T. BA, Cornell U., 1964, LLB with distinction, 1966. Bar: N.Y. 1966, D.C. 1976, U.S. Ct. Appeals (2d cir.) 1968, U.S. Ct. Appeals (D.C. cir.) 1974. Assoc. Donovan Leisure Newton & Irvine, N.Y., 1966-72; asst. chief counsel Securities Industry Study, U.S. Senate, Washington, 1972; assoc. Donovan Leisure Newton & Irvine, Washington, 1973-75; sr. atty. Office of Legal Counsel, Dept. Justice, Washington, 1975-78; asst. gen. counsel Dept. Energy, Washington, 1978-79, dep. gen. counsel, 1979-85, chief counsel for jud. litigation, 1985; chief litigation counsel SEC, Washington, 1986-93, assoc. dir. div. of enforcement, 1993—; lectr. in field. Contbr. articles to profl. jours. Recipient Presdl. Meritorious Exec. award Pres. of U.S., 1980, 92, Disting. Svc. award SEC, 1992, Exceptional Svc. award Sec. of Energy, 1985, Outstanding Svc. medal Sec. of Energy, 1981. Mem. ABA, Assn. Bar City of N.Y. Office: SEC 450 5th St NW Ste 81 Washington DC 20001-2739

**NEWLIN, WILLIAM RANKIN,** lawyer; b. Pitts., Dec. 1, 1940; s. Theodore F. Newlin and Elizabeth Crooks; m. Ann Kleinschmidt, Aug. 25, 1962; children: Steffler Ann, Shelley Kay, William Rankin II. AB, Princeton U., 1962; JD, U. Pitts., 1965; DBA (hon.), Robert Morris Coll., 1997. Bar: Pa. 1965. Assoc. Buchanan Ingersoll, Pitts., 1965-71, ptnr., 1971—, mng. dir., 1980—; mng. gen. ptnr. CEO Venture Fund, Pitts., 1985—; chmn. bd. Kennametal Inc., Latrobe, Pa., 1996—, JLK Direct Distbn. Inc., 1997—;

bd. dirs. bd. Nat. City Bank Pa., Pitts., Parker/Hunter, Pitts., Black Box Corp., Pitts., Pitts. Regional Alliance. Editor in chief U. Pitts. Law Rev., 1963; contbr. articles to profl. jours. Chmn., Gov. Thornburgh's Corp. Adv. Com., 1980-82; bd. dirs. Mfr. Studies Bd. nat. Rsch. Coun., Washington, 1988-89, Pitts. High Tech. Coun., 1982—, Pa. Tech. Coun. Recipient Entrepreneur of Yr. award Ernst & Young, Inc. Mag./ Merrill Lynch, 1991. Fellow Am. Bar Found., Pa. Bar Found.; mem. ABA (corp. banking, bus. law sect.), Pa. Bar Assn. (mem. coun. corp. banking and bus. law sect. 1973-82, chmn. sect. 1979-81, Spl. Achievement award 1982), Allegheny County Bar Assn., Assn. of Bar of City of N.Y., Am. Law Inst., Pa. S.W. Assn. (trustee), Greater Pitts. C. of C. (bd. dirs.), Duquesne Club (dir. 1982-85), Rivers Club (bd. dirs. 1983—), Laurel Valley Golf Club, Allegheny Country Club (bd. dirs. 1988—). General corporate, Finance, Mergers and acquisitions. Office: Buchanan Ingersoll One Oxford Centre 301 Grant St Fl 20 Pittsburgh PA 15219-1410

**NEWMAN, BOBBY KING,** lawyer; b. Houston, Dec. 4, 1968; s. Bobby Lynn and Olivia Anne N.; m. Michele Newman, Jan. 18, 1997. BBA in Fin., U. Tex., 1991; JD, South Tex. Coll. Bus., 1994. Assoc. Nass & Brown, P.C., Houston, 1993-96; ptnr. Grady, Schneider & Newman, L.L.P., Houston, 1996—. Mem. The Burta Rhoads Raborn, Family Law Inns of Ct., Houston Bar Assn. (bd. mem.). Family and matrimonial, Personal injury. Office: Grady Schneider & Newman LLP 1301 Mckinney St Ste 3636 Houston TX 77010-3034

**NEWMAN, CAROL L.,** lawyer; b. Yonkers, N.Y., Aug. 7, 1949; d. Richard J. and Pauline Frances (Stoll) N. AB/MA summa cum laude, Brown U., 1971; postgrad., Harvard U. Law Sch., 1972-73; JD cum laude, George Washington U., 1977. Bar: D.C. 1977, Calif. 1979. With antitrust divsn. U.S. Dept. Justice, Washington and L.A., 1977-80; assoc. Alschuler, Grossman & Pines, L.A., 1980-82, Costello & Walcher, L.A., 1982-85; assoc. Rosen, Wachtell & Gilbert, L.A., 1985-88, ptnr., 1988-90; ptnr. Keck, Mahin & Cate, L.A., 1990-94; pvt. practice L.A., 1994—; adj. prof. Sch. Bus., Golden Gate U., spring 1982. Candidate for State Atty. Gen., 1986; L.A. city commr. L.A. Bd. Transp. Commrs., 1993-98, v.p., 1995-96; pres. Bd. Taxicab Commrs., 1999—; bd. dirs. Women's Progress Alliance, 1996-98. Mem. ABA, State Bar Calif., L.A. County Bar Assn., L.A. Lawyers for Human Rights (co. pres. 1991-92), Log Cabin (bd. dirs. 1992-97, pres. 1996-97), Calif. Women Lawyers (bd. dirs., bd. govs. 1991-94), Order of Coif, Phi Beta Kappa. Appellate, General civil litigation, Antitrust.

**NEWMAN, CHARLES A.,** lawyer; b. L.A., Mar. 18, 1949; s. Arthur and Gladys (Barnett) N.; children: Anne R., Elyse S. BA magna cum laude, U. Calif., 1970; JD, Washington U., 1973. Bar: Mo. 1973, D.C. 1981, U.S. Dist. Ct. (ea. dist.) Mo. 1973, U.S. Dist. Ct. (ctrl. dist.) Ill., 1996, U.S. Ct. Appeals (3d, 5th, 7th and 10th cirs.) 1996, (8th cir.) 1975, (9th cir.) 1995, (11th cir.) 1994, U.S. Tax Ct. 1981, U.S. Claims Ct. 1981, U.S. Supreme Ct. 1976. From assoc. to ptnr. Thompson & Mitchell, St. Louis, 1973-96; ptnr. Thompson Coburn, St. Louis, 1996-97, Bryan Cave LLP, St. Louis, 1997—; lectr. law Washington U., St. Louis, 1976-78. Bd. dirs. Hawthorn Found., 1997—; trustee Mo. Bar Found., 1990-96, mem. Mo. Bar Bd. Govs, 1980-84; bd. dirs. United Israel Appeal, N.Y.C., 1990-93, Coun. Jewish Fedns., N.Y.C., 1992-95, United Jewish Appeal Young Leadership Cabinet, N.Y.C., 1985-88, Ctr. for Study of Dispute Resolution, 1985-88, Legal Svcs. Ea. Mo., 1985-94, St. Louis Community Found., 1992—, vice-chmn. 1997-99, St. Louis chpt. Young Audiences 1993-95, Planned Parenthood St. Louis, 1986-89, Jewish Fedn., St. Louis, 1986-98, asst. treas., 1989-90, v.p. fin. planning, 1990-93, asst. sec., 1994—; v.p. Repertory Theatre, St. Louis, 1986-89, sr. v.p., 1990-91; pres. St. Louis Opportunity Clearinghouse, 1974-78. Recipient Lon O. Hocker Meml. Trial award Mo. Bar Found., 1984. Mem. Bar Assn. Met. St. Louis (Merit award 1976). Democrat. Avocations: golf, reading, music. General civil litigation, Appellate, Transportation. Office: Bryan Cave LLP One Metropolitan Square Saint Louis MO 63102-2750

**NEWMAN, EDWARD HENRY,** judge, lawyer; b. Providence, Nov. 21, 1947; m. Dinae J. Newman. BA, Providence Coll., 1969; JD, Suffolk Coll., Boston, 1972. Vis. lectr. Providence Coll., 1975-85; probate judge Richmond, R.I., 1988—; town solicitor, Richmond, 1975-81; mem. ethics adv. panel, Supreme Ct., 1996—. Chmn. Richmond Dem. Town Com., 1984-86; bd. dirs. Olean Ctr., Westerly, R.I., 1983-87; treas. Woodriver Health Ctr., Hopkinton, R.I., 1984-93. Mem. R.I. Trial Lawyers (v.p. 1980-84), Washington County Bar (pres. 1991—). Office: 42 Granite St Westerly RI 02891-2250

**NEWMAN, ELIZABETH L.,** lawyer; b. N.Y.C., Apr. 19, 1948; d. Ellis Newman and Ruth Weiss; m. John C.F. Tillson, May 11, 1975; 1 child, Susannah. BA, Skidmore Coll., 1970; JD, Georgetown U., 1973. Bar: U.S. Ct. Appeals (D.C. cir.) 1973, U.S. Dist. Ct. D.C. 1974, U.S. Supreme Ct. 1977, U.S. Ct. Appeals (fed. cir.) 1983, U.S. Dist. Ct. Md. 1987, U.S. Ct. Appeals (4th cir.) 1992, U.S. Claims Ct. 1992. Trial atty. U.S. Office of Pers. Mgmt., Washington, 1973-79; ptnr. Ambler & Newman, Washington, 1980-83; pvt. practice law Washington, 1983-85; of counsel Dobrovir & Gebhardt, Washington, 1985-90; ptnr. Kalijarvi, Chuzi & Newman, Washington, 1990—. Author: Security Clearance Law and Procedure, 1998. Mem. ABA (vice chair sect. on def. and nat. security 1998—). Labor, Federal civil litigation, Civil rights. Home: 1605 35th St NW Washington DC 20007-2316 Office: Kalijarvi Chuzi & Newman 1730 K St NW Washington DC 20006-3868

**NEWMAN, FREDRIC SAMUEL,** lawyer, business executive; b. York, Pa., June 22, 1945; s. Nat. Howard and Josephine (Farkas) N.; m. Mary E. Kiley, May 19, 1973; children: Lydia Ann, Anne Marie, Pauline. AB cum laude, Harvard U., 1967; JD, Columbia U., 1970; cert. the exec. program, U. Va., 1984. Bar: N.Y. 1971, U.S. Dist. Ct. (so. and ea. dists.) N.Y. 1972, U.S. Ct. Appeals (2d cir.) 1974, U.S. Ct. Claims 1993. Assoc. White & Case, N.Y.C., 1970-80; asst. gen. counsel Philip Morris Cos., N.Y.C., 1981-87; gen. counsel, v.p., sec. Philip Morris, Inc., N.Y.C., 1987-90; chief exec. officer TeamTennis, Inc., 1991; prin. Law Office of Fredric S. Newman, N.Y.C., 1992-95; founding ptnr. Hoguet Newman & Regal, LLP, 1996—; pres., CEO, Pathe Comm. Corp., N.Y.C., 1993-97; bd. dirs. Exel Ins. Co., Bermuda. Trustee Calhoun Sch., N.Y.C., 1985-88; bd. dirs. N.Y. Fire Safety Found., N.Y.C., 1985-88. Fellow Am. Bar Found. General corporate, General civil litigation, Product liability. Office: 10 E 40th St New York NY 10016-0200

**NEWMAN, GARY,** lawyer; b. Paterson, N.J., June 13, 1948; s. Arthur Oscar and Helen (Bloom) N.; m. Gara, Dec. 6, 1986; 1 child, Griffin Hayes. BA in Polit. Sci., Syracuse U., 1969; JD, Am. U., 1972. Bar: N.J. 1972, Fla. 1975, N.Y. 1980. Law sec. Judge Edward F. Broderick, Morristown, N.J., 1972-73; asst. prosecutor Hudson County Prosecutors Office, Jersey City, N.J., 1973-76; assoc. Skoloff & Wolfe, Livingston, N.J., 1976-78; ptnr. Newman & Carey, East Orange, N.J., 1978-85, La Bue Farber Newman, West Orange, N.J., 1985-87; atty. pvt. practice, Roseland, N.J., 1987—; dir. N.Y. Susquehanna & W. Rlwy., Ridgefield Park, N.J., 1980—. Mem. exec. com. Martini for Congress, Cedar Grove, N.J., 1994. Fellow Am. Acad. Matrimonial Lawyers; mem. Nat. Assn. R.R. Trial Counsel, N.J. State Bar Assn. (mem. exec. com. family law sect. 1988-90), Essex County Bar Assn. (mem. exec. com. family law sect. 1988-91). Jewish. Family and matrimonial, Transportation. Office: 101 Eisenhower Pkwy Roseland NJ 07068-1028

**NEWMAN, GLENN,** lawyer; b. N.Y.C., June 3, 1952; s. Stanley Burton and Muriel (Orenstein) N.; m. Anne M. Klaeysen, Jan. 30, 1982; children: Andrew, Emily. BA, SUNY, Albany, 1973; JD, Fordham U., 1978. Bar: N.Y., U.S. Ct. Appeals (2d cir.), U.S. Dist. Ct. (ea. and so. dists.) N.Y. Asst. corp. counsel Corp. Counsel of the City of N.Y., N.Y.C., 1978-88; dep. commr. N.Y.C. Dept. Fin., N.Y.C., 1988-94; ptnr. Roberts & Holland LLP, N.Y.C., 1998—. Treas., trustee Bklyn. Soc. for Ethical Culture, 1995—. Mem. Assn. of the Bar of the City of N.Y. (chair com. on state and local tax. 1998). State and local taxation. Home: 430 6th St Brooklyn NY 11215-3607 Office: Robert & Holland LLP 825 8th Ave Fl 37 New York NY 10019-7498

**NEWMAN, JAMES MICHAEL,** judge, lawyer; b. Bklyn., Apr. 3, 1946; s. Sheldon and Ethel (Silverman) N.; m. Lee Galen; children: Danielle Cari, Matthew Evan, Merrie Lee, Cindy Joy, Bradley Curtis. BA, Queens Coll., 1966; JD, NYU, 1969, LLM, 1975. Bar: N.Y. 1970, N.J. 1977; cert. matrimonial atty., N.J. Assoc. Kramer, Marx, Greenlee & Backus, N.Y.C., 1970-73, Forsyth, Decker, Murray & Broderick, N.Y.C., 1973-74; ptnr. Tommaney & Newman, N.Y.C., 1975-82, Goldzweig, Reilly, Grossman & Newman, Marlboro, N.J., 1978-79, Canarick & Newman, Freehold, N.J., 1979-97, Newman, Scarola & Assocs., Freehold, 1998—; pub. defender Marlboro Twp. (N.J.), 1984-86; judge Marlboro Twp., 1986—, Englishtown Borough, 1990—, Farmingdale Borough, 1991—, Manalapan Township, 1993—, Borough Fair Haven, 1996—. Dep. mayor Marlboro Twp., 1975-79, dir. econ. devel., 1975-79, dir. commuter affairs, 1974; interim commr. Western Monmouth Utilities Authority, 1977; mem. Central N.J. Transp. Bd., 1974-76. Mem. N.J. Bar Assn., Monmouth County Bar Assn. (co-chairperson family law com. 1996-98), Monmouth County Judges Assn. (pres. 1995), Am. Judges Assn., Masons. Jewish. Office: 64 W Main St Freehold NJ 07728-2142

**NEWMAN, JARED SULLIVAN,** lawyer; b. Rockledge, Fla., May 26, 1959; s. Joel Sylvester and Eleanor Mae Newman; m. Cynthia James, Sept. 3, 1995; children: Dustin, Jared, Regan, Taylor. BS in Criminal Justice, U. S.C., 1981, JD, 1989. Bar: S.C. 1989, U.S. Dist. Ct. S.C. 1991, U.S. Ct. Appeals (4th cir.) 1993, U.S. Supreme Ct. 1998. Detective Beaufort County Sheriff's Dept., Beaufort, S.C., 1981-86; asst. solicitor 14th Cir. Solicitor's Office, Beaufort, 1989-92; sole practitioner Beaufort, 1992-95; trial atty. Daugs, Tedder & Newman, Beaufort, 1995—. Mem. ATLA, ABA, S.C. Bar Assn., S.C. Trial Lawyers Assn., Nat. Assn. Criminal Def. Lawyers. Criminal, Civil rights. Home: 12 Planters Cir Beaufort SC 29902-2033 Office: Daugs Tedder & Newman 1 Professional Dr Port Royal SC 29935-1123

**NEWMAN, JOHN DAVID,** lawyer; b. Washington, May 18, 1959; s. John Anderson and Margarita (Maldonado) N.; m. Allison Louise Smith, Mar. 3, 1984; children: Thomas Jonathan, Stacey Caroline. AB, Duke U., 1981, JD, 1984. Bar: Conn. Rschr. Congl. Quar., Washington, 1980-81; assoc. Murthu, Cullina, Richter & Pinney, Hartford, Conn., 1984-88; ptnr. Shipman & Goodwin, Hartford, 1988-92, Cohn & Birnbaum, Hartford, 1992-96, Reid & Riege, Hartford, 1996—. Contbr. articles to Conn. Law Tribune. counsel Animal Friends of Conn., Inc., Hartford, 1984—; bd. dirs. Farmington Valley YMCA. Mem. Nat. Health Lawyers Assn., Am. Assn. Health Plans, Conn. Health Lawyers Assn. Avocations: study of history and politics, distance running, martial arts. Health, Administrative and regulatory. Office: Reid & Riege PC One State St Hartford CT 06105

**NEWMAN, JOHN MERLE,** lawyer; b. Cleve., June 25, 1934; s. Emanuel Robert and Theresa Esther (Dreissinger) N.; 1 child, Thomas Edward; m. Thelma Aitken, July 10, 1992; 1 child, Jennifer Ann Newman-Brazil. AB, Miami U., Oxford, Ohio, 1957; LLB, Cornell U., 1957. Bar: N.J. 1971, U.S. Ct. Appeals (3d cir.) 1961, U.S. Dist. Ct. N.J. 1983, U.S. Dist. Ct. (so. and ea. dists.) N.Y. 1983; cert. civil atty. Supreme Ct. of N.J. Assoc. Bertram Polow, Morristown, N.J., 1960-62; ptnr. Porzio Bromberg & Newman P.C., Morristown, 1962-76, 80—; presiding judge chancery/family divsn. Superior Ct. of N.J., Morristown, 1976-80. Trustee, officer Cmty. Med. Ctr., Randolph Libr., Morristown, 1970-74, Hist. Speedwell Mus., Morristown, 1991—, Family Svc., Morristown, 1988-91; trustee Occupational Tng. Ctr., Morristown, 1965-69. Recipient Cert. of Acad. Performance U. Edinburgh, Scotland, 1956, Trial Bar award N.J. Trial Lawyers Assn., 1997, various certs. for bar and cmty. svcs. Fellow Internat. Soc. Barristers; mem. ABA (litigation sect., environ. subcom., environ. law sect. corp. counsel subcom., vice chair various coms.), N.J. State Bar Assn., Morris County Bar Assn., Omicron Delta Kappa. Avocations: cycling, tennis. Federal civil litigation, State civil litigation, Environmental. Office: Porzio Bromberg & Newman 163 Madison Ave Ste 6 Morristown NJ 07960-7323

**NEWMAN, JON O.,** federal judge; b. N.Y.C., May 2, 1932; s. Harold W. Jr. and Estelle L. (Ormond) N.; m. Martha G. Silberman, June 19, 1953; children: Leigh, Scott, David. Grad., Hotchkiss Sch., 1949; AB magna cum laude, Princeton U., 1953; LLB, Yale U., 1956; LLD (hon.), U. Hartford, 1975, U. Bridgeport, 1980, Bklyn. Law Sch., 1995, N.Y. Law Sch., 1996. Bar: Conn. 1956, D.C. 1956. Law clk. to Hon. George T. Washington U.S. Ct. Appeals, 1956-57; sr. law clk. to chief justice Hon. Earl Warren, U.S. Supreme Ct., 1957-58; ptnr. Ritter, Satter & Newman, Hartford, Conn., 1958-60; counsel to majority Conn. Gen. Assembly, 1959; spl. counsel to gov. Conn., 1959-61; asst. to sec. HEW, 1961-62; adminstrv. asst. to U.S. senator, 1963-64; U.S. atty. Dist. of Conn., 1964-69; pvt. practice law, 1969-71; U.S. dist. judge Dist. of Conn., 1972-79; U.S. cir. judge 2d Cir. Ct. of Appeals, Hartford, 1979-93, chief judge, 1993-97, sr. judge, 1997—. Co-author: Politics: The American Way. With USAR, 1954-62. Recipient Learned Hand medal Fed. Bar Coun., 1987. Fellow Am. Bar Found.; mem. ABA, Am. Law Inst., Conn. Bar Assn., Am. Judicature Soc. Democrat. Office: US Ct Appeals 2d Cir 450 Main St Hartford CT 06103-3022

**NEWMAN, LAWRENCE WALKER,** lawyer; b. Boston, July 1, 1935; s. Leon Bettoney and Hazel W. (Walker) N.; children: Timothy D., Isabel B., Thomas H. A.B., Harvard U., 1957, LL.B., 1960. Bar: D.C. 1961, N.Y. 1965. Atty. U.S. Dept. Justice, 1960-61, Spl. Study of Securities Markets and Office Spl. Counsel on Investment Co. Act Matters, U.S. SEC, 1961-64; asst. U.S. atty. So. Dist. N.Y., 1964-69; assoc. Baker & McKenzie, N.Y.C., 1969-71, ptnr., 1971—; mem. internat. adv. coun. World Arbitration Inst., 1984-87; mem. adv. com. Asia Pacific Ctr. for Resolution of Internat. Trade Disputes, 1987—; mem. adv. bd. Inst. for Transnational Arbitration, 1988—; chmn. U.S. Iranian Claimants Com., 1982—; mem. adv. bd. World Arbitration and Mediation Report, 1993—; mem. bd. adv. to Corporate Counsel's Internat. Adviser, 1995—. Co-author: The Practice of Internat. Litigation, 1992, 93, 2nd edit. 1998, Litigating Internat. Commercial Disputes, 1996; columnist N.Y. Law Jour., 1982—; adv. bd. World Arbitration and Mediation Report; contbr. articles to profl. jours. and books on litigation and internat. arbitration; editor: Enforcement of Money Judgements; chmn. editl. bd. Juris Pub., Inc.; co-editor: Revolutionary Days: The Iran Hostage Crisis and the Hague Claims Tribunal, A Look Back, 1999. Mem. ABA (internat. litigation com., internat. arbitration com.), Internat. Bar Assn. (com. dispute resolution, com. constrn. litigation), Inter-Am. Bar Assn., Fed. Bar Coun., Am. Fgn. Law Assn., Maritime Law Assn. U.S., Assn. Bar City N.Y. (com. on arbitration & alternative dispute resolution 1991-94), Am. Arbitration Assn. (corp. counsel com. 1987—, panel comml. arbitrators), U.S. Coun. Internat. Bus., Ct. Arbitration of Polish Chamber Fgn. Trade (panel of arbitrators), Brit. Col. Internat. Comml. Arbitration Ctr. Federal civil litigation, Private international, Contracts commercial. Office: Baker & McKenzie 805 3rd Ave New York NY 10022-7513

**NEWMAN, MARY LYNN CANMANN,** lawyer; b. Highland Park, Ill.; d. Harry Louis and Elizabeth (Gwinn) C; m. Brian Newman, Nov. 9, 1996. BA, U. Mich., 1986; JD, U. Colo., 1991. Bar: Colo. 1991, Ill. 1992, Nev. 1992, U.S. Dist. Ct. Nev. 1992, U.S. Dist. Ct. Colo. 1994, U.S. Ct. Appeals (9th cir.), Ind. 1998. With No. Trust Bank, Chgo., 1986-88; law clk. to Judge Adams, 2d Jud. Dist. Ct., Reno, Nev., 1991-92; assoc. Jones, Jones, Close & Brown, Reno, 1992-93, Hartman & Armstrong, Reno, 1994-96; ptnr. Dordick, Hopkins & Canmann, Boulder, Colo., 1993-94; assoc. gen. coun. Nev. Indsl. Ins. Systems, Carson City, 1996-98; 2c v.p., asst. gen. counsel Conseco Svcs., LLC, Carmel, Ind., 1998—. Mgr. Colo. Jour. Internat. Environ. Law and Policy, 1990-91. Mem. ABA (young lawyers divsn.), ATLA, Nev. Trial Lawyers Assn., No. Nev. Bankruptcy Bar. Avocations: skiing, tennis, hiking. Insurance, Federal civil litigation, State civil litigation. Office: Conseco Svcs LLC PO Box 1911 11825 N Pennsylvania Carmel IN 46038

**NEWMAN, MICHAEL RODNEY,** lawyer; b. N.Y.C., Oct. 2, 1945; s. Morris and Helen Gloria (Hendler) N.; m. Cheryl Jeanne Anker, June 11, 1967; children: Hillary Abra, Nicole Brooke. Student NASA Inst. Space Physics, Columbia U., 1964; BA, U. Denver, 1967; JD, U. Chgo., 1970. Bar: Calif. 1971, U.S. Dist. Ct. (cen. dist.) Calif. 1972, U.S. Ct. Appeals (9th cir.) 1974, U.S. Dist. Ct. (no. dist.) Calif. 1975, U.S. Supreme Ct. 1978, U.S. Dist. Ct. (so. dist.) Calif. 1979, U.S. Tax Ct. 1979, U.S. Dist. Ct. (ea. dist.) Calif. 1983. Assoc. David Daar, 1971-76; ptnr. Daar & Newman, 1976-78, Miller & Daar, 1978-88, Miller, Daar & Newman, 1988-89, Daar & Newman, 1989—; judge pro-tem L.A. Mcpl. Ct., 1982—, L.A. Superior Ct., 1988—; bd. dirs. Consulegis EEIG; founder, facilitator First, Second and Third Ann. German-Am. Strategic Partnership Conf.; lectr. Ea. Claims Conf., Ea. Life Claims Conf., Nat. Health Care Anti-Fraud Assn., AIA Conf. on Ins. Fraud, Consulegis A.G.M.'s Paris, 1997, Madrid, 1998, Dublin, 1999. mem. L.A. Citizens Organizing Com. for Olympic Summer Games, 1984, mem. govtl. liaison adv. commn., 1984; mem. So. Calif. Com. for Olympic Summer Games, 1984; cert. ofcl. Athletics Congress of U.S., co-chmn. legal com. S.P.A.-T.A.C., chief finish judge; trustee Massada lodge B'nai Brith; mem. fin. and phys. devel. com. U. Haifa. Recipient NYU Bronze medal in Physics, 1962, Maths. award USN Sci., 1963. Mem. ABA (multi-dist. litigation subcom., com. on class actions), L.A. County Bar Assn. (chmn. attys. errors and omissions prevention com., mem. cts. com. litigation sect.), Conf. Ins. Counsel, So. Pacific Assn., TAC (bd. dirs., Disting. Svc. award 1988), Porter Valley Country Club, Breakfast Club. Insurance, Federal civil litigation, State civil litigation. Office: 865 S Figueroa St Ste 2500 Los Angeles CA 90017-2567

**NEWMAN, PAUL A.,** lawyer; b. Cleve., Feb. 27, 1948; s. Robert Stanley and Barbara Esther (Irwin) N.; m. Merrilou, Aug. 14, 1971; children: Jane Elizabeth, Nicole Lynn. BA in Biology, Case Western Reserve U., 1973, MA in English, 1974; JD, Cleve. State U., 1977. Bar: Ohio 1977. Atty. Svete, Hofstetter & Bond, Chardon, Ohio, 1977-81; pvt. practice Chardon, 1981-84; ptnr. Newman, Leary & Brice, Chardon, 1984—. Editor IPSO Jour., 1978-93. Chairman Geauga County Dem. Party, Chardon, 1996-98; pres., trustee Geauga County Pub. Libr., Chardon, 1985—, Geauga County Law Libr., 1980-91; pres. Geauga County Bd. Edn., 1989, 93; mem. Geauga County Bd. Elections, 1996—. Staff Sgt. U.S. Army, 1967-70, Vietnam. Fellow Ohio State Bar Found.; mem. Ohio State Bar Assn., Burton-Middlefield Rotary (pres. 1982—). Avocations: backpacking, farming, photography. General civil litigation, Real property. Office: Newman Leary & Brice 214 E Park St Chardon OH 44024-1214

**NEWMAN, PAULINE,** federal judge; b. N.Y.C., N.Y., June 20, 1927; d. Maxwell Henry and Rosella N. BA, Vassar Coll., 1947; MA, Columbia U., 1948; PhD, Yale U., 1952; LLB, NYU, 1958. Bar: N.Y. 1958, U.S. Supreme Ct. 1972, U.S. Ct. Customs and Patent Appeals 1978, Pa. 1979, U.S. Ct. Appeals (3d cir.) 1981, U.S. Ct. Appeals (fed. cir.) 1982. Research chemist Am. Cyanamid Co., Bound Brook, N.J., 1951-54; mem. patent staff FMC Corp., N.Y.C., 1954-75; mem. patent staff FMC Corp., Phila., 1975-84, dir. dept. patent and licensing, 1969-84; judge U.S. Ct. Appeals (fed. cir.), Washington, 1984—; Disting. prof. George Mason Law Sch., 1995—; bd. dir. Research Corp., 1982-84; program specialist Dept. Natural Scis. UNESCO, Paris, 1961-62; mem. State Dept. Adv. Com. on Internat. Indsl. Property, 1974-84; lectr. in field. Contbr. articles to profl. jours. Bd. dirs. Med. Coll. Pa., 1975-84, Midgard Found., 1973-84; trustee Phila. Coll. Pharmacy and Sci., 1983-84. Mem. ABA (council sect. patent trademark and copyright 1983-84), Am. Patent Law Assn. (bd. dirs. 1981-84), U.S. Trademark Assn. (bd. dirs. 1975-79, v.p. 1978-79), Am. Chem. Soc. (bd. dirs. 1972-81), Am. Inst. Chemists (bd. dirs. 1960-66, 70-76), Pacific Indsl. Property Assn. (pres. 1979-80), Cosmos Club, Vassar Club, Yale Club. Office: US Ct Appeals Nat Cts Bldg 717 Madison Pl NW Washington DC 20439-0002*

**NEWMAN, ROGER,** lawyer; b. Newnan, Ga., Sept. 11, 1954; s. James Taylor and Flora Mae (Rogers) N.; m. Brenda Susan Fleming, Nov. 13, 1993; children: Marisa Len Edge, Samantha Fleming Edge. AAS, Fayetteville Tech. C.C., 1988; BA in Polit. Sci., Fayetteville State U., 1990; JD, Campbell U., 1993. Bar: N.C. 1993, U.S. Dist. Ct. (ea., ctrl. and we. dists.) N.C. 1993. Police officer Fayetteville (N.C.) Police Dept., 1975-79; paralegal Rand, Finch & Gregory, Fayetteville, 1988-90, law clk., 1990-93, atty., 1993-94; atty., sole practitioner Roger Newman, Atty., Fayetteville, 1994—. Bd. dirs. Cumberland County Hospice Assn., Fayetteville, 1994, Cumberland County Health Occupl. Bd., Fayetteville, 1994. Mem. ABA, N.C. Assn. Trial Lawyers Am. Democrat. Avocations: golf, bowling, firearms safety. General civil litigation, Criminal, Workers' compensation. Home: PO Box 42708 Fayetteville NC 28309-2708

**NEWMAN, SANDERS DAVID,** lawyer; b. Bklyn., Nov. 28, 1930; s. Fred and Elsie (Stern) N.; m. Joan Margaret Goodwin, June 14, 1952; children: Jody, Michael, David, Caroline, Jenifer, Mimi. BA, U. Miami, 1952; JD, NYU, 1956. Bar: N.Y. 1956, U.S. Dist. Ct. (ea. dist.) N.Y. 1957, U.S. Supreme Ct. 1958, Pa. 1971, Fla. 1978. Sr. assoc. Otterborg, Steindler, Houston & Rosen, N.Y.C., 1964-67; ptnr. Powers, Greenfield, Newman & Gross, N.Y.C., 1967-70, Blank, Rome, Comisky & McCauley, Phila., 1970-82; bd. dirs. Emons Holdings, Inc., York, Pa., 1982—, R&B Inc., Colmar, Pa., 1990—, Arbor Handling Svcs., Inc., Willow Grove, Pa., 1982—, Love the Children, inc., Quakertown, Pa., 1976—; sr. v.p., sec., gen. counsel, bd. dirs. Obrien Environ Energy Inc. Maj. USAF, 1952-54 (res. 1968—). Mem. ABA, Pa. Bar Assn., Fla. Bar Assn., Phila. Bar Assn. Avocations: sailing, chess. General corporate, Finance, Securities.

**NEWMAN, SANDRA SCHULTZ,** state supreme court justice. BS, Drexel U., 1959; MA, Temple U., 1969; JD, Villanova U., 1972; D (hon.), Gannon U., 1996, Widener U., 1996. Bar: Pa., U.S. Dist. Ct. (ea. dist.) Pa., U.S. Ct. Appeals (3d cir.), U.S. Supreme Ct. Asst. dist. atty. Montgomery County, Pa.; pvt. practice; judge Commonwealth Ct. of Pa., 1993-95; justice Supreme Ct. of Pa., 1995—; past chair bd. consultors Villanova U. Law Sch.; mem. jud. coun. of the Supreme Ct. of Pa., liaison to the 3rd cir. task force on mgmt. of death penalty litigation, liaison to Pa. lawyers fund for client security bd., liaison to domestic rels. procedural rules com., liaison to Pa. Bar Inst.; jud. work group for HHS; mem. adv. com. Nat. Ctr. for State Cts., Am. Law Inst.; mem. Drexel U. Coll. Bus. and Adminstrn.; lectr. and spkr. in field. Author: Alimony, Child Support and Counsel Fees, 1988; contbr. articles to profl. jours. Recipient Phila. award for Super Achiever Pediatric Juvenile Colitis Found. Jefferson Med. Coll. and Hosp., 1979, award for Dedicated Leadership and Outstanding Contbns. to the Cmty. and Law Employment Police Chiefs Assn. of Southeastern Pa., Drexel 100 award, 1993, Medallion of Achievement award Villanova U., 1993, Susan B. Anthony award Women's Bar Assn. Western Pa., 1996, award Justinian Soc., 1996, award Tau Epsilon Law Soc., 1996, Legion of Honor Gold Medallion award Chapel of Four Chaplains, 1997; honored by Women of Greater Phila., 1996; named Disting. Daughter of Pa. Fellow Am. Bar Found., Pa. Bar Found.; mem. Am. Law Inst., Nat. Assn. Women Judges, Montgomery Bar Assn. Office: Supreme Ct Pa Ste 400 100 4 Falls Corporate Ctr West Conshohocken PA 19428

**NEWMAN, SCOTT DAVID,** lawyer; b. N.Y.C., Nov. 5, 1947; s. Edwin Stanley and Evaline Ada (Lipp) N.; m. Judy Lynn Monchik, June 24, 1972; 1 child, Eric. B.A. magna cum laude, Yale U., 1969; J.D., Harvard U., 1973, M.B.A., 1973; LL.M. in Taxation, NYU, 1977. Bar: N.Y. 1974, U.S. Dist. Ct. (so. and ea. dists.) N.Y. 1975, U.S. Ct. Appeals (2d cir.) 1975, U.S. Ct. Claims 1976, U.S. Tax Ct. 1979. Assoc. Dewey, Ballantine, Bushby, Palmer & Wood, N.Y.C., 1973-76, Stroock & Stroock & Lavan, N.Y.C., 1976-78; assoc., ptnr. Zimet, Haines, Moss & Friedman, N.Y.C., 1978-81; tax counsel Phibro-Salomon Inc., N.Y.C., 1981-84; ptnr. Baer, Marks & Upham, N.Y.C., 1984-87; ptnr. Wiener, Zuckerbrot, Weiss & Newman, N.Y.C., 1987-90; ptnr. Whitman & Ransom, N.Y.C., 1990—. Co-author tape cassettes: New Tax Reform Act of 1976, Tax Reform '78, 1978. Tax Reform Act of 1984, 1986, Tax Reform Act of 1986, 1986; contbr. article to profl. jour. Mem. Phi Beta Kappa. Corporate taxation, Personal income taxation, Estate taxation. Home: 21 Kipp St Chappaqua NY 10514-2518 Office: Whitman & Ransom 200 Park Ave Fl 27 New York NY 10166-0005

**NEWMAN, STEPHEN MICHAEL,** lawyer; b. Buffalo, Jan. 12, 1945; s. Howard A. and Mildred (Ballow) N.; m. Gayle Mallon, May 24, 1969; children: Holly, Deborah. AB, Princeton U., 1966; JD, U. Mich., 1969. Bar: N.Y. 1969, Fla. 1976. Assoc. Hodgson, Russ, Andrews, Woods & Goodyear, Buffalo, 1969-73, ptnr., 1973—; lectr. in field. Bd. dirs. Leukemia Soc., United Jewish Fedn. Buffalo Inc., Jewish Ctr. Greater Buffalo Inc., Temple Beth Zion; bd. dirs., chpt. chmn., exec. com. Am. Jewish Com., Buffalo chpt.; active Vol. Action Ctr. United Way of Buffalo and Erie County. Fellow Am. Coll. Trusts and Estates Coun.; mem. ABA (personal svc. corps. com. tax sect.), N.Y. State Bar Assn. (officer), Princeton Club of Western N.Y. (sch. com.). Estate planning, Probate, Pension, profit-sharing, and employee benefits. Office: Hodgson Russ Andrews Woods & Goodyear 1800 One M&T Pla Buffalo NY 14203

**NEWMAN, STUART,** lawyer; b. Hackensack, N.J., June 7, 1947; s. Joseph and Rose (Wilenski) N.; m. Tina Gilson; children: Leslie, Dara, Mindy,

Robert, Jessica. BA, SUNY, Cortland, 1971; JD cum laude, Albany Law Sch., 1974. Bar: N.Y. 1975, Ga. 1978. Assoc. Dewey, Ballantine, Bushby, Palmer & Wood, N.Y.C., 1974-76; from assoc. to ptnr. Jackson, Lewis, Schnitzler & Krupman, Atlanta, 1976—; lectr. U. Ala., Tuscaloosa, 1980-84, Auburn U., 1986—. Dir. Ruth Mitchell Dance Co. of Atlanta, 1986-88. Mem. ABA, Atlanta Bar Assn., Ga. Bar Assn., Lawyers Club Atlanta, Commerce Club, Shakerag Hounds, Inc., Midlands Fox Hounds, Inc., Live Oak Hounds, Ansley Golf Club. Labor. Office: Jackson Lewis Schnitzler & Krupman 1900 Marquis One Tower 245 Peachtree Center Ave NE Atlanta GA 30303-1222

**NEWMAN, THEODORE ROOSEVELT, JR.,** judge; b. Birmingham, Ala., July 5, 1934; s. Theodore R. and Ruth L. (Oliver) N. A.B., Brown U., 1955, LL.D., 1980; J.D., Harvard U., 1958. Bar: D.C. 1958, Ala. 1959. Atty. civil rights div. Dept. Justice, Washington, 1961-62; practiced law in Washington, 1962-70; assoc. judge D.C. Superior Ct., 1970-76; judge D.C. Ct. Appeals, 1976-91, chief judge, 1976-84, sr. judge, 1991—; bd. dirs. Nat. Center for State Cts., v.p., 1980-81, pres., 1981-82. Trustee Brown U. With USAF, 1958-61. Fellow Am. Bar Found.; mem. Nat. Bar Assn. (past pres. jud. coun., C. Francis Stradford award 1984, William H. Hastie award 1988).

**NEWMAN, WILLIAM BERNARD, JR.,** telecommunications executive; b. Providence, Nov. 16, 1950; s. William Bernard and Virginia (Crosby) N.; m. Karen O'Connor, Jan. 11, 1951. BA, Ohio Wesleyan U., 1972; JD, George Mason U., Arlington, Va., 1977; postgrad., Harvard U., 1987. Bar: Va. 1977, D.C. 1978. Atty. com. energy Ho. of Reps., Washington, 1978-81; v.p., Washington counsel Consol. Rail Corp. Dept. Govt. Affairs, Washington, 1981-98; cons. Charles Ross Ptnrs., Washington, Md., 1999—. Bd. dirs. Nat. Coun. for Adoption, 1994-98. Mem. ABA, Va. Bar Assn., D.C. Bar Assn. Home: 1009 Priory Pl Mc Lean VA 22101-2134

**NEWMEYER, ROBERT J.,** lawyer; b. Phila., Dec. 26, 1958; s. Donald and Electa N; m. Cheri L. Matteoni, May 16, 1981; 7 children. BA cum laude, Oral Roberts U., 1981; JD, O.W. Coburn Sch. Law, 1986. Bar: Okla. 1986, Calif. 1991; U.S. Dist Ct. (no. dist.) Okla. 1986, U.S. Dist. Ct. (so. dist.) Calif. 1997, U.S. Dist. Ct. Colo., 1998; U. S. Ct. Appeals (8th cir.) 1999, U.S. Ct. Appeals (9th cir.) 1998, U.S. Ct. Appeals (10th cir.) 1998; U.S. Supreme Ct. 1999, U.S. Ct. Appeals (7th cir.) 1999. Police officer Tulsa Police Dept., 1981-83; law clk. Blackstock, Joyce, et al, Tulsa, 1984; research asst. O.W. Coburn Sch. Law, Tulsa, 1984-85; legal intern McCormick, Andrew & Clark, Tulsa, 1985-86; assoc. McCormick Andrew & Clark, Tulsa, 1986-87; law clk. to U.S. Magistrate Judge Jeffrey S. Wolfe U.S. Dist. Ct., Okla., 1987-91; law clk. to chief U.S. Magistrate Judge Roger C. McKee U.S. Dist. Ct., Calif., 1991-97; assoc. Bopp, Coleson & Bostrom, Terre Haute, Ind., 1997—. Editor Oral Roberts U. Law Rev., 1986. Lctr. Citizen's Crime Commn., Tulsa, 1982-83. Mem. Calif. Bar Assn., Okla. Bar Assn., Christian Legal Soc., Terre Haute Christian Home Educators. Republican. Constitutional, Federal civil litigation, Election. Office: Bopp Coleson & Bostrom PO Box 41 Terre Haute IN 47808-0041

**NEWSOM, JAMES THOMAS,** lawyer; b. Carrollton, Mo., Oct. 6, 1944; s. Thomas Edward and Hazel Love (Mitchell) N.; m. Sherry Elaine Retzloff, Aug. 9, 1986; stepchildren: Benjamin A. Bawden, Holly K. Bawden. AB, U. Mo., 1966, JD, 1968. Bar: Mo. 1968, U.S. Supreme Ct. 1971. Assoc. Shook, Hardy & Bacon, London and Kansas City, Mo., 1972, ptnr., 1976—. Mem. Mo. Law Rev., 1966-68. Lt. comdr. JAGC, USNR, 1968-72. Mem. ABA, Internat. Bar Assn., Kansas City Met. Bar Assn., Lawyers Assn. Kansas City, U. Mo. Law Sch. Law Soc., Kansas City Club, U. Mo. Jefferson Club, Order of Coif, Perry (Kans.) Yacht Club, Stone Horse Yacht Club (Harwich Port, Mass.). Avocations: skiing, sailing, car racing. Product liability, General civil litigation. Office: Shook Hardy & Bacon One Kansas City Pl 1200 Main St Ste 3100 Kansas City MO 64105-2139

**NEWSOME, RANDALL JACKSON,** judge; b. Dayton, Ohio, July 13, 1950; s. Harold I. and Sultana S. (Stony) N. BA summa cum laude, Boston U., 1972; JD, U. Cin., 1975. Bar: Ohio 1975, U.S. Dist. Ct. (so. dist.) Ohio 1977, U.S. Ct. Appeals (6th cir.) 1979, U.S. Supreme Ct. 1981. Law clk. to chief judge U.S. Dist. Ct. (so. dist.) Ohio, 1975-77; assoc. Dinsmore & Shohl, Cin., 1978-82; judge U.S. Bankruptcy Ct. (so. dist.) Ohio, 1982-88, U.S. Bankruptcy Ct. (no. dist.) Calif., Oakland, 1988—; faculty mem. Fed. Jud. Ctr., ALI-ABA, 1987—; mem. Nat. Conf. of Bankruptcy Judges, 1983—, mem. bd. govs., 1987-88, pres., 1999—. Contbg. author: Chapter 11 Theory and Practice, 1994—, Collier on Bankruptcy, 1997—. Fellow Am. Coll. Bankruptcy; mem. Am. Law Inst., Phi Beta Kappa. Democrat. Mem. United Ch. of Christ. Office: US Bankruptcy Ct PO Box 2070 Oakland CA 94604-2070

**NEWTON, ALEXANDER WORTHY,** lawyer; b. Birmingham, Ala., June 19, 1930; s. Jeff H. and Annis Lillian (Kelly) N.; m. Sue Aldridge, Dec. 22, 1952; children: Lamar Aldridge Newton, Kelly McClure Newton Hammond, Jane Worthy Newton, Robins Jeffry Newton. B.S., U. Ala., 1952, J.D., 1957. Bar: Ala. 1957. Pvt. practice law Birmingham; assoc. Hare, Wynn & Newell, Birmingham, 1957; ptnr. Hare, Wynn, Newell & Newton, Birmingham, 1961—; del. U.S. Ct. Appeals (11th cir.) Jud. Conf., 1988, 89, 90, 91; mem. Jefferson County Jud. Nominating Com., 1983-89; mem. Birmingham Airport Authority, 1991—; founding dir. First Comm. Bank. Co-author: (with others) Federal Appellate Procedure, 11th Circuit, 1996. Vice chmn. Birmingham Racing Commn., 1984-87; v.p. U. Ala. Law Sch. Found., 1978-79, pres., 1980-82, exec. com., 1987—; mem. Leadership Ala. Class IV. Capt. inf. U.S. Army, 1952-54. Recipient Disting. Alumnus award Farrah Law Soc. U. Ala., 1982, Sam W. Piples Disting. Alumnus award 1982. Fellow Am. Coll. Trial Lawyers (state chmn. 1983-84, regents' nominatin com. 1984-85), Internat. Soc. Barristers (bd. dirs. 1974-75, sec.-treas. 1976-77, v.p. 1977-78, pres. 1979-80), Internat. Acad. Trial Lawyers; mem. ABA, ATLA, Am. Bar Found., Ala. State Bar (chmn. practices and procedures subsect. 1965, governance com. and pres.'s task force 1984-86, pres.'s com. 1987-88), Birmingham Bar Assn. (exec. com. 1967), Ala. Trial Lawyers Assn. (sec.-treas. 1958-65), Am. Judicature Soc., 11th Cir. His. Soc. (trustee 1988—), Sigma Chi. Democrat. Presbyterian. Clubs: Shoal Creek, Birmingham Country (Birmingham); Capital City (Atlanta); Garden of the God (Colorado Springs, Colo.); University Club (New York). Federal civil litigation, State civil litigation, Personal injury. Home: 2837 Canoe Brook Ln Birmingham AL 35243-5908 Office: Hare Wynn Newell & Newton 800 Massey Bldg 290 21st St N Ste 800 Birmingham AL 35203-3330

**NEWTON, JOHN EDWARD, JR.,** lawyer; b. Chestnut Hill, Jan. 19, 1954; s. John Edward and Corinne (Vahlstrom) N. BA, Wheaton Coll., 1975; MBA, Temple U., 1979, JD, 1982. Bar: Pa. 1982, U.S. Ct. Appeals (4th and 3d cirs.) 1984, U.S. Dist. Ct. (ea. dist.) Pa. 1984. Asst. regional counsel HHS, Phila., 1981-86; assoc. gen. counsel, asst. sec., dir. legal svcs. Franciscan Health System, Aston, Pa., 1986-96; v.p. chief legal counsel Cath. Health Initiatives, Aston, Pa., 1996—; adj. prof. health law and risk mgmt. Phila. Coll. Textiles and Sci., 1993—, LaSalle U., 1995—. Editorial bd. jour. Neumann Report, 1989; contbr. articles to mags. Vice pres., treas. AIDS Task Force of Phila., 1991-92; bd. dirs. Phila. Community Health Alternatives, Phila., 1991; chmn. John Locke Fund, 1993. Mem. Pa. Bar Assn., Beta Gamma Sigma. Health, General corporate. Home: PO Box 2355 Aston PA 19014-0355

**NEWTON, JOHN WHARTON, III,** lawyer; b. Beaumont, Tex., Feb. 18, 1953; s. John Wharton and Katherine (King) N.; children: Martha Garrison, John Wharton IV, Stephen King. BA, U. Tex., 1975; JD, U. Houston, 1978. Bar: Tex. 1979, U.S. Dist. Ct. (ea. dist.) Tex. 1979, U.S. Ct. Appeals (5th cir.) 1981, U.S. Dist. Ct. (so. dist.) Tex. 1987. Ptnr. Orgain, Bell & Tucker, Beaumont, 1984—. Mem. ABA, Tex. State Bar Assn., Tex. Assn. Def. Counsel, Jefferson County Bar Assn., Coll. of State Bar of Tex., Beaumont Club (pres. 1988-89). Episcopalian. Civil rights, General civil litigation, Personal injury. Office: Orgain Bell & Tucker 470 Orleans St Ste 400 Beaumont TX 77701-3076

**NEWTON, MICHAEL DAVID,** lawyer; b. Dearborn, Mich., Feb. 1, 1967; s. Nicholas and Dorothy Marlene (Falk) N. BS, Birmingham-So. Coll., 1989; JD, U. Memphis, 1992. Bar: Tenn. 1992, U.S. Dist. Ct. (ea. dist.) Tenn. 1993. Assoc. J. Troy Wolfe & Assoc., Chattanooga, 1992-93; pvt. practice Chattanooga, 1993—; staff atty. Tenn. Mediation Group, Inc., Chattanooga, 1994—; guest lectr. U. Tenn., Chattanooga. Mem. sponsorship com. March of Dimes, Chattanooga, 1994. Mem. ABA, ATLA, Tenn. Bar Assn., Tenn. Trial Lawyers, Chattanooga Bar Assn. Avocations: golf, hunting, guitar, skiing, music. General civil litigation, Workers' compensation, Personal injury. Home: 2035 Rock Bluff Rd Hixson TN 37343-3172 Office: University Tower Ste 401 851 E 4th St Chattanooga TN 37403

**NEXSEN, JULIAN JACOBS, JR.,** lawyer; b. Columbia, S.C., Sept. 22, 1954; s. Julian J. and Mary Elizabeth (McIntosh) N.; m. Christine Spigner Johnston, Feb. 25, 1984; children: Elizabeth Kincaid, Julian J. III, Sarah Ivey. BA, Washington and Lee U., 1976; JD, U. S.C., 1979. Bar: S.C. 1979, U.S. Ct. Appeals (4th cir.) 1982. Assoc. Nexsen, Pruet, Jacobs & Pollard, Columbia, S.C., 1979-84; assoc. in house counsel, asst. sec. Greenwood (S.C.) Mills, Inc., 1984-95, exec. v.p., 1999—; exec. v.p., COO Greenwood Devel. Corp., 1995-99, pres., CEO, 1999—; exec. v.p. Greenwood Mills, Inc., 1999—; bd. dirs. The County Bank. Bd. visitors Lander Coll., 1985-87; bd. dirs. Edn. Enrichment Found., 1986-89, Greenwood United Way, 1989-92, Greenwood Community Theatre, 1989-93, Greenwood Uptown Devel. Corp., 1991-93; bd. deacons 1st Presbyn. Ch., 1990-93, session, 1993-96; trustee Self Meml. Hosp., 1992-98; bd. dirs. Partnership for a Greater Greenwood, 1999—, Greenwood County Econ. Alliance, 1999—. Mem. ABA, Am. Corp. Counsel Assn., S.C. Bar Assn., Forest Lake Club, Greenwood Country Club, Rotary, S.C. C. of C. (bd. dirs. 1990-93). Presbyterian. General corporate, Land use and zoning (including planning), Real property. Home: 512 E Henrietta Ave Greenwood SC 29649-3142 Office: Greenwood Devel Corp PO Box 1017 Greenwood SC 29648-1017

**NEYDON, ANN ELIZABETH,** lawyer; b. Detroit, July 28, 1947; d. Robert Leonard and Margaret Elizabeth N.; m. Murray David Wilson, Dec. 21, 1990; children: Margret, Steven, Heather. BA, Marygrove Coll., 1968; MA, U. Mich., 1969; JD, Wayne State U., 1974. Tchr. Coll. of St. Theresa, Winona, Minn., 1969-70; investigator U.S. Dept. Labor, Detroit, 1972-74; lawyer Amalgamated Clothing Workers Union Am., N.Y.C., 1974-76; shareholder Sachs, Waldman, O'Hare, Helveston, Bogas & McIntosh, Detroit, 1976—. Pension, profit-sharing, and employee benefits, Labor. Office: Sachs Waldman et al 1000 Farmer St Detroit MI 48226-2834

**NEYMAN, JOSEPH DAVID, JR.,** lawyer; b. Memphis, Feb. 4, 1971; s. Joseph David Sr. and Linda Vaughn Neyman; m. Mary Phillips Johnson, May 17, 1997. BPA cum laude, U. Miss., 1993, JD, 1996. Bar: Miss. 1996, U.S. Dist. Ct. (no. and so. dists.) Miss. 1996, U.S. Ct. Appeals (5th cir.) 1996, Tenn. 1997. Law clk. NLRB, Memphis, 1995; assoc. Walker, Brown & Brown, P.A., Hernando, Miss., 1996—. Participant Leadership DeSoto, Hernando, 1997. Mem. ATLA, Tenn. Bar Assn., Miss. Bar Assn., DeSoto County Bar Assn., DeSoto County Young Lawyers Assn. (pres. 1998—), Optimist Club (v.p./pres. 1997-98). Presbyterian. Avocations: hunting, reading history, shooting, following college athletics. Real property, Personal injury, General civil litigation. Office: Walker Brown & Brown PA PO Box 276 Hernando MS 38632-0276

**NGUYEN, PAUL DUNG QUOC,** lawyer; b. Hung Yen, Vietnam, Feb. 2, 1943; came to U.S., 1975; s. Trac Trong and Do Thi (Vu) N.; m. Kim-Dung T. Dang, Dec. 26, 1967; children: Theresa Thu, Catherine Bao-Chau, Jonathan Hung. LLB, Hue Law Sch., Vietnam, 1965; MA in Pub. Policy Adminstrn., U. Wis., 1973. Bar: N.Y. 1979, U.S. Dist. Ct. (so. and ea. dists.) N.Y. 1979, U.S. Tax Ct. 1979. Prof. law Hue & Can Tho Law Schs., Vietnam, 1973-75; assoc. Proskauer, Rose, Getz & Mendelsohn, N.Y.C., 1979-80; pvt. practice N.Y.C., 1980-81; corp. law specialist Office of Corp. Counsel, City of N.Y., 1981-94; counsel, country rep. Hanoi Rep. Office White & Case, Vietnam, 1994-95; counsel Port Authority of N.Y. and N.J., N.Y.C., 1995—; adj. asst. prof. NYU, 1998—. Bd. dirs. N.Y.C. Indochinese Refugees; hon. chmn. lawyers com. for human rights Vietnamese Legal Protection Fund, 1990-94; legal advisor Indochina Resource Action Ctr., 1990-94; dir. S.E. Asia Resource Action Ctr., 1995-98. Recipient Nat. Legion Honor award Office of Pres., Saigon, 1970. Mem. ABA, Assn. of Bar of City of N.Y. (Outstanding Performance prize com. on mcpl. affairs 1986), Asian Am. Bar Assn. N.Y. (bd. dirs. 1993—), Nat. Asian Pacific Am. Bar Assn. (N.E. regional gov. 1998—). Avocations: tennis, reading, classical music. Office: Port Authority NY & NJ Law Dept One World Trade Ctr New York NY 10048

**NIBLEY, ROBERT RICKS,** retired lawyer; b. Salt Lake City, Sept. 24, 1913; s. Joel and Teresa (Taylor) N.; m. Lee Allen, Jan. 31, 1945 (dec.); children—Jane, Annette. A.B., U. Utah, 1934; J.D., Loyola U., Los Angeles, 1942. Bar: Calif. bar 1943. Accountant Nat. Parks Airways, Salt Lake City, 1934-37, Western Air Lines, Los Angeles, 1937-40; asst. mgr. market research dept. Lockheed Aircraft Corp., Burbank, Calif., 1940-43; asso. firm Hill, Farrer and Burrill, Los Angeles, 1946-53; partner Hill, Farrer and Burrill, 1953-70, of counsel, 1971-78. Served from ensign to lt. comdr. USNR, 1943-46. Mem. ABA, L.A. Bar Assn., Calif. Club, Phi Delta Phi, Phi Kappa Phi, Phi Delta Theta. Home: 4860 Ambrose Ave Los Angeles CA 90027-1866

**NICHOL, GENE RAY, JR.,** university dean; b. Dallas, May 11, 1951; s. Gene R. and Dolores (Dumas) N.; m. Janet Castle, Aug. 20, 1973 (div. 1978); m. Glenn George, Nov. 25, 1984. BA in Philosophy, Okla. State U., 1973; JD, U. Texas, 1976. Bar: Alaska 1978. Assoc. Ely, Guess and Rudd, Anchorage, 1976-78; asst. prof. W.Va. U., Morgantown, 1978-80, assoc. prof., 1980-82; prof. law U. Fla., Gainesville, 1983-84; Cutler prof. law, dir. Inst. of Bill of Rights Law Coll. William and Mary, Williamsburg, W.Va., 1984-88; dean U. Colo. Law Sch., 1988-95; dean, Burton Craige prof. law U. N.C.; host Culture Wars, KBDI T.V., Denver, 1995-96. Author: (with M. Redish) Federal Courts; contbr. articles to profl. jours. Posten research grantee U. W.Va., 1980, 81, 82. Mem. Nat. Lawyers Guild (coms. 1978, vice chair Colo. reapportionment commn.), Am. Law Inst., ACLU (coms. 1978—), Am. Bar Found. Fellows, Order of Coif. Roman Catholic. Avocation: back packing. Office: U N C Chapel Hill Van Hecke-Wettach Hall CB No 3380 Chapel Hill NC 27599-3380*

**NICHOLAS, FREDERICK M.,** lawyer; b. N.Y.C., May 30, 1920; s. Benjamin L. and Rose F. (Nechols) N.; m. Eleanore Berman, Sept. 2, 1951 (div. 1963); children: Deborah, Jan, Tony; m. Joan Fields, Jan. 2, 1983. AB, U. So. Calif., 1947; postgrad., U. Chgo., 1949-50; JD, U. So. Calif., 1952. Bar: Calif. 1952, U.S. Dist. Ct. Calif. 1952, U.S. Ct. Appeals (9th cir.) 1952. Assoc. Loeb & Loeb, L.A., 1952-56; ptnr. Swerdlow, Glikbarg & Nicholas, Beverly Hills, Calif., 1956-62; pvt. practice Beverly Hills, 1962-80; pres., atty. Hapsmith Co., Beverly Hills, 1980—; bd. dirs. Malibu Grand Prix, L.A., 1982-90; gen. counsel Beverly Hills Realty Bd., 1971-79; founder, pres. Pub. Counsel, L.A., 1970-73. Author: Commercial Real Property Lease Practice, 1976. Chmn. Mus. Contemporary Art, L.A., 1987-93, chmn. com. Walt Disney Concert Hall, L.A., 1987-95; trustee Music Ctr. L.A. County, 1987-95, L.A. Philharm. Assn., 1987-95; chmn. Calif. Pub. Broadcasting Commn., Sacramento, 1972-78; pres. Maple Ctr., 1977-79. Recipient Citizen of Yr. award Beverly Hills Bd. Realtors, 1978, Man of Yr. award Maple Ctr., 1980, Pub. Svc. award Coro Found., 1988, The Medici award L.A. C. of C., 1990, Founders award Pub. Counsel, 1990, Trustees award Calif. Inst. Arts, 1993, City of Angels award L.A. Ctrl. Bus. Assn.; named Outstanding Founder in Philanthropy, Nat. Philanthropy Day Com., 1990. Mem. Beverly Hills Bar Assn. (bd. govs. 1970-76, Disting. Svc. award 1974, 81, Exceptional Svc. award 1986), Beverly Hills C. of C. (Man of Yr. 1983). Real property. Home: 1001 Maybrook Dr Beverly Hills CA 90210-2715 Office: Hapsmith Co 9300 Wilshire Blvd Beverly Hills CA 90212-3213

**NICHOLAS, JOSEPH FREDERICK, JR.,** lawyer; b. Cleve., Aug. 23, 1961; s. Joseph F. Sr. and Francis F. Nicholas; m. Kathleen A. Hamper, Aug. 3, 1989; children: Christina M., Maria F., Domenic J. BA, U. Dayton, 1983; JD, Cleveland Marshall Coll. Law, 1986. Bar: Ohio, 1987, U.S. Dist. Ct (no. dist.) Ohio, 1991. Claims rep. Progressive Ins., Mayfied Village, Ohio, 1985-86; regional claims mgr. Transport Ins., Dallas, 1986-91; assoc. Mazanec, Raskin & Ryder Co., Cleve., 1991—. Pres., bd. dirs. Open Door Maternity Home, Euclid, Ohio, 1994-97; mem. booster club Our Lady Mt. Carmel Ch., Wickliffe, Ohio, 1996—. Republican. Roman Catholic. Avocations: golf, football, basketball. Insurance. Office: Mazanec Raskin & Ryder Co 34305 Solon Rd Cleveland OH 44139-2660

**NICHOLAS, WILLIAM RICHARD,** lawyer; b. Pontiac, Mich., June 19, 1934; s. Reginald and Edna Irene (Bartlett) N.; m. Diana Lee Johnson, Aug. 20, 1960; children: Susan Lee, William Richard Jr. BS in Bus., U. Idaho, 1956; JD, U. Mich., 1962. Bar: 1963. Of counsel Latham & Watkins, Los Angeles, 1962-96. Contbr. numerous articles on taxation. Served to lt. (j.g.) USN, 1956-59. Mem. Calif. Bar Assn., Los Angeles County Bar Assn., Am. Coll. Tax Counsel. Home: 1808 Old Ranch Rd Los Angeles CA 90049-2207 Office: Latham & Watkins 633 W 5th St Ste 4000 Los Angeles CA 90071-2005

**NICHOLS, CAROLYN M.,** lawyer; b. Balt., June 21, 1968; d. Joel Mackey and Carolin S. (Sill) Jones; m. Loren B. Nichols, June 8, 1993; 1 child, Maxwell A. BA magna cum laude, U. N.Mex., 1990; JD, Yale U., 1993. Bar: N.Mex. 1993. Sole practitioner Albuquerque, 1993-96; ptnr. Nichols & Oliver, Albuquerque, 1997—. Mem. N.Mex. Criminal Def. Lawyers Assn., Inns of Ct. Avocation: alpine skiing. Criminal, Civil rights. Home: 1122 Central Ave SW Albuquerque NM 87102-2976

**NICHOLS, F(REDERICK) HARRIS,** lawyer; b. Chgo., Jan. 31, 1936; s. Frederick M. and Keturah (Rollinson) N.; div.; children: Rebecca K., Pamela R., Katurah I. BA cum laude, Williams Coll., 1958; LLB, Harvard U., 1961. Bar: N.Y. 1961. Assoc. Cohen Swados Wright Hanifin Bradford & Brett LLP, Buffalo, 1962-65, ptnr., 1965—. Chmn. youth svcs. com. neighborhood svcs. United Way of Erie County, 1998—; membership com., bd. dirs. Buffalo Fine Arts Acad.; chmn. bd. dirs. Child and Family Svcs. Buffalo, 1984-85, bd. dirs., chmn. com., 1983-85; mem. resource mgmt. com. United Way Buffalo and Erie County, 1998—. Fulbright scholar U. Hamburg, Fed. Republic of Germany, 1961-62. Mem. ABA, N.Y. Bar Assn., Erie County Bar Assn., Saturn Club. Republican. Episcopalian. Contracts commercial, General corporate, General practice. Office: Cohen Swados Wright Hanifin Bradford & Brett 70 Niagara St Ste 1 Buffalo NY 14202-3467

**NICHOLS, HENRY ELIOT,** lawyer, savings and loan executive; b. N.Y.C.; m. Frances Griffin Morrison, Aug. 12, 1950 (dec. July 1978); children: Clyde Whitney, Diane Spencer; m. Mary Ann Wall, May 31, 1987. BA, Yale U., 1946; JD, U. Va., 1948. Bar: D.C. 1950, U.S. Dist. Ct. 1950, U.S. Ct. Appeals 1952, U.S. Supreme Ct. 1969. Assoc. Frederick W. Berens, Washington, 1950-52; sole practice, Washington, 1952—; real estate columnist Washington Star, 1966-81; pres., gen. counsel Hamilton Fed. Savs. & Loan Assn., 1971-74; vice chmn. bd. Columbia 1st Bank (formerly Columbia 1st Fed. Savs. & Loan Assn.), Washington, 1974-90, bd. dir.; pres. Century Fin. Corp., 1971-90; regional v.p. Preview, Inc., 1972-78; bd. dir., exec. com. Columbia Real Estate Title Ins. Co., Washington, 1968-78; bd. dir. Greater Met. Bd. Trade, 1974-78, Dist. Realty Title Ins. Co., 1978-86. Nat. adv. bd. Harker Prep. Sch., 1975-80; exec. com. Father Walter E. Schmitz Meml. Fund, Cath. U., 1982-83; bd. dirs. Vincent T. Lombardi Cancer Rsch. Ctr., 1979-84; del. Pres. Johnson's Conf. Law and Poverty, 1967; vice chmn. Mayor's Ad Hoc Com. Housing Code Problems, Washington, 1968-71; mem. Commn. Landlord-Tenant Affairs Washington City Coun., 1970-71; vice chmn. Washington Area Realtors Coun., 1970; exec. com., dir. Downtown Progress, 1970; bd. dirs. Washington Mental Health Assn., 1973, Washington Med Ctr., 1975. Capt. USAAF, 1942-46. Mem. Am. Land Devel. Assn., Nat. Assn. Realtors, Nat. Assn. Real Estate Editors, Washington Bd. Realtors (pres. 1970, Realtor of Yr. 1970, Martin Isen award 1981), Greater Met. Washington Bd. Trade (bd. dirs. 1974-80), U.S. League Savs. Assns. (attys. com. 1971-80), Washington Savs. and Loan League, ABA, D.C. Bar Assn., Internat. Real Estate Fedn., Omega Tau Rho. Episcopalian. Clubs: Yale, Cosmos, Rolls Royce, Antique Auto, St. Elmo. Patentee med. inventions; contbr. articles profl. jours. Real property. Address: 1 Kittery Ct Bethesda MD 20817-2137 Office: 1112 16th St NW Washington DC 20036-4823

**NICHOLS, JOSEPH PATRICK,** lawyer; b. Potsdam, N.Y., Jan. 14, 1958; s. James Alfred and Margaret Helen Nichols; m. Kathleen Marie Sauvageau, Dec. 17, 1984; children: Maureen, Claire, Paul, John. BA, Niagara U., 1979; JD, Union U., Albany, N.Y., 1982. Bar: N.Y. 1983, U.S. Dist. Ct. (we. and no. dists.) N.Y. 1993, U.S. Ct. Claims 1993, U.S. Supreme Ct. 1993. Legis. asst. N.Y. State Assembly, Albany, 1979-83; ptnr. Poissant & Nichols, P.C., Malone, N.Y., 1983—; town atty. Town of Malone, 1987-89. Trustee Wead Libr., Malone. Mem. Kiwanis (bd. dirs. Malone 1998), Elks. Republican. Roman Catholic. Avocations: astronomy, stamp collecting. State civil litigation, Federal civil litigation, Family and matrimonial. Office: Poissant & Nichols PC 55 W Main St Malone NY 12953-1813

**NICHOLS, ROBERT WILLIAM,** lawyer; b. Bogota, Colombia, Feb. 23, 1948; s. William Hansell and Dorothy Marion Nichols; m. Jill Ann Jablon; 1 child, Julie Elizabeth. BA, Baylor U., 1970; JD, U. Okla., 1973. Bar: Colo. 1988, U.S. Dist. Ct. (ea. dist.) Colo. 1973. Atty. U.S. EEOC, Washington, 1973-77, U.S. Senate Judiciary Com. and U.S. Rep. Al Gore, Washington, 1977-81; sr. atty. Consumers Union, Washington, 1981-84, MCI Telecomms., Inc., Washington and Denver, 1984-88; ptnr. Brownstein, Hyatt, Farber & Strickland, Denver, 1988-92; sole practitioner Boulder, Colo., 1992-94; founding shareholder Nichols & Hecht, LLC, Boulder, 1994—; cons. Cmty. TV Bd., Boulder, 1995-97. Precinct co-chair Boulder County Dem. Party, Boulder, 1997—; lectr., workshop leader Unitarian Universalist Assn., Boulder and Washington, 1994—. Lt. USN, 1970-74. Mem. ABA, Fed. Comms. Bar Assn., Colo. Bar Assn. Avocations: reading, golf, hiking. Administrative and regulatory, Communications, Public utilities. Office: Nichols & Hecht LLC 2060 Broadway St Ste 200 Boulder CO 80302-5232

**NICHOLSON, BRADLEY JAMES,** lawyer; b. Montebello, Calif., Sept. 22, 1958; s. Thomas Edwin and Charlotte Elizabeth (Knight) N.; m. Anne Marie Dooley, Oct. 6, 1990. BA, Reed Coll., 1983; JD, U. Pa., 1990. Bar: Calif. 1990, Nev. 1998. Atty. Wilson, Sonsini, Goodrich & Rosati, Palo Alto, Calif., 1990-91; law clk. to Hon. Morris S. Arnold U.S. Dist. Ct., Ft. Smith, Ark., 1991-92; atty. Coudert Bros., San Jose, Calif., 1992-94; law clerk to Hon. Morris S. Arnold U.S. Cir. Ct., Little Rock, 1994-96; atty. Brown & Bain, Palo Alto, Calif., 1997-98; staff atty. ctrl. legal staff Nev. Supreme Ct., Carson City, 1998—. Contbr. articles to profl. jours. Mem. Federalist Soc.(vice chmn. publications Litigation practice group, 1997-98, pres. Little Rock lawyers chpt. 1995-96). Avocations: golf, fishing, music. Office: Nevada Supreme Ct Ctrl Legal Staff Capitol Complex Carson City NV 89710-0001

**NICHOLSON, BRENT BENTLEY,** lawyer, educator; b. Perrysburg, Ohio, Mar. 30, 1954; s. Donald Grant and Wilma Ione (Bentley) N.; m. Ann Elizabeth Loehrke, Sept. 1, 1978; children: Bradley, Lindsay. BS in Bus. Adminstrn., Bowling Green State U., 1976; JD, Ohio State U., 1979. Bar: Ohio 1979, U.S. Dist. Ct. (no. dist.) Ohio 1979, U.S. Tax Ct. 1984. Tax atty. Arthur Young & Co., Toledo, 1979-83; assoc. Cobourn, Smith, Rohrbacher & Gibson, Toledo, 1983-87, ptnr., 1987-88; ptnr. Rohrbacher, Nicholson & Light, Toledo, 1989-90, of counsel, 1990-98; of counsel Rohrbachers, Light, Cron, Zmuda & Trimble, Toledo, 1998—; assoc. prof. legal studies Bowling Green State U., Ohio, 1989—; adj. asst. prof. Bowling Green State U., Ohio, 1984-85, 88. Contbr. articles to profl. jours. Mem. ABA, AICPA, Acad. Legal Studies in Bus., Ohio Bar Assn., Toledo Bar Assn., Bus. Law/Profl. Responsibility Subcom. of Bd. Examiners of AICPA, Perrysburg Ohio Tax Bd. Rev., Pi Sigma Alpha, Beta Gamma Sigma. Republican. Methodist. Avocations: reading, tennis. Probate, Estate planning, Taxation, general. Home: 314 Rutledge Ct Perrysburg OH 43551-5201 Office: Rohrbachers Light Cron Zmuda & Trimble 405 Madison Ave Ste 8 Toledo OH 43604-1207

**NICHOLSON, BRUCE ALLEN,** lawyer; b. Phila., Nov. 12, 1949; s. Charles Glanz and Jean (Billman) N.; m. Linda King Barton, Apr. 22, 1972; children—Jessica Ann, James Barton. B.A., Cornell U., 1971; J.D. cum laude, Boston Coll., 1975. Bar: Pa. 1975. Staff asst. Mass. Bar Assn., Boston, 1973-75; assoc. Duffy, North, Wilson, Thomas & Nicholson, Hatboro, Pa., 1975-78, ptnr., 1978—. pres. Main St. Hatboro Revitalization Com., 1995-98; solicitor Montgomery County Pa. Redevel. Authority, 1993—. Mem. Hatboro Boro Council, 1984-88; chmn. Hatboro Hist. Commn., 1981-83; bd. mgrs. Hatboro Area YMCA, 1984-95, bd. chmn. 1990, 91. Named YMCA Vol. of Yr., 1989, 92. Mem. ABA, Pa. Bar Assn., Montgomery Bar Assn., Greater Hatboro C. of C. (v.p., bd. dirs.), Rotary, Yacht Club of Stone Harbor (N.J.). Republican. Episcopalian. General practice, Real property, Probate. Office: Duffy North Wilson Thomas & Nicholson PO Box 726 104 N York Rd Hatboro PA 19040-2699

**NICHOLSON, CHRISTOPHER MARSHALL,** lawyer, foundation executive; b. Denver; s. John William and Maureen Mida (Marshall) N. BA, U. Mich., 1988; JD, Harvard U., 1991. Bar: Calif. 1991. Assoc. Pillsbury Madison & Sutro, San Francisco, 1991-93; prodr. Legal Video Svcs., Oakland, Calif., 1993-96; devel. officer East Bay Cmty. Found., Oakland, 1997—. Mem. adv. bd. Flaggship Ctr., Hayward, Calif., 1996—; chmn. steering com. Leave A Legacy, Oakland, 1997—. Mem. No. Calif. Planned Giving Coun., Diablo Valley Estate Planning Coun., Rotary, Phi Beta Kappa. Avocations: running, cooking. Office: East Bay Cmty Found 1711 Almond Ave Walnut Creek CA 94596-4307

**NICHOLSON, MARK WILLIAM,** lawyer; b. Newton, Mass., Feb. 6, 1960; s. John Richard and Barbara Ann (Ladd) N. BSFS, Georgetown U., 1982; JD cum laude, Case Western Res. U., 1985. Bar: Ohio 1985. Assoc. Smith & Schnacke, Dayton, 1985-89; assoc. gen. counsel Lexis-Nexis, Dayton, 1989—. Mem. ABA, Ohio Bar Assn. Democrat. Computer, General corporate, Contracts commercial. Home: 2724 Pinegrove Dr Dayton OH 45449-3349 Office: Lexis-Nexis PO Box 933 9443 Springboro Pike Dayton OH 45401-0933

**NICHOLSON, MICHAEL,** lawyer; b. Alexandroupolis, Greece, Nov. 26, 1936; m. Diana Long, June 21, 1964. B.S. in Civil Engring., Northwestern U., 1961; M.S. in Civil Engring., Columbia U., 1963; J.D., St. John's U., 1970. Bar: N.Y. 1971, U.S. Dist. Ct. (ea. dist.) N.Y. 1979, U.S. Ct. Appeals (2d cir.) 1990. Counsel, George A. Fuller Co., N.Y.C., 1970-72, Leonard Wegman Cons. Engrs., N.Y.C., 1972-73; sr. ptnr. Corner, Finn, Nicholson & Charles, Bklyn., 1978—. Bd. dirs. Bklyn. Nephrology Found., 1979, Pelham Bay Gen. Hosp., 1979. Mem. Am. Arbitration Assn., ABA, N.Y. State Bar Assn., N.Y. State Soc. Profl. Engrs., Nat. Soc. Profl. Engrs., Mcpl. Engrs. City of N.Y. (award 1972). Contbr. articles to profl. jours. Government contracts and claims, State civil litigation, Contracts commercial. Office: 75 Livingston St Fl 29 Brooklyn NY 11201-5054

**NICHOLS-YOUNG, STEPHANIE,** lawyer; b. Kansas City, Mo., Dec. 23, 1956; d. Jack Lee and Martha Jayne (Johns) Nichols; m. Roger A Young, Mar. 22, 1980. BA in Radio-TV, U. Ariz., 1978, JD with distinction, 1985. Bar: Ariz. 1985, U.S. Dist. Ct. Ariz. 1985, U.S. Ct. Appeals (9th crct.) 1985. With news and prodn. dept. Sta. KZAZ-TV, Tucson, 1977-79; photgrapher, reporter, coord. weekend news coverage Sta. KVOA-TV, Tucson, 1979-81; coord. news coverage and writing Sta. KNST, Tucson, 1981-82; developer pub. access tng. program Cox Cable Comms., Tucson, 1982-83; rsch. asst. to prof. U. Ariz. Coll. Law, Tucson, 1983; atty. Wentwort & Lundin, P.A., Phoenix, Ariz., 1985-87, Gallagher & Kennedy, P.A., Phoenix, 1987-94; sole practice Phoenix, 1994—; law clk. Wentworth & Lundin, P.A., Phoenix, summer 1984. Vol. Lawyers Program; chair Animal Legal Def. Fund. Mem. Maricopa County Bar Found. (bd. dirs.), U. Ariz. Law Coll. Assn. (bd. dirs.). E-mail: aldf3@aol.com. General civil litigation. Office: 125 E Coronado Rd Phoenix AZ 85004-1512

**NICKEL, GEORGE WALL, JR.,** judge; b. Phila., Nov. 7, 1924; s. George Wall and Florence May (Hemphill) N.; m. Hope Sykes, June 14, 1947 (div. Dec. 1995); m. Jacqueline Mae Davis, Dec. 28, 1995; children: George W. III, Nancy Nickel Groff, Susan Nickel Vancleve. BA in Chemistry, U. Pa., 1948; MS in Chemistry, Va. Poly., 1949. Registered profl. engr.; lic. chem. engr., Pa. Safety dir. Armstrong World Industries, Lancaster, Pa., 1949-85; workers' compensation judge Commonwealth of Pa., Lancaster, 1985—; adj. prof. Millersville (Pa.) U., 1977-91. Mem. Boy Scouts of Am.; bd. dirs., 1987, bd. dirs. Lancaster/Lebanon coun., 190-90; committeeman dist. 11 Rep. Com. Lancaster County, Manheim Twp., 1975-95; pres. Lancaster br. Luth. Brotherhood, 1980-97. Mem. Nat. Safety Coun. (mem. indsl. divsn. 1959-80), Pa. Soc. Profl. Engrs. (past pres.), Rotary Club Lancaster (Paul Harris fellow 1989), Masons (lodge 7641), Valley of Lancaster (lodge of perfection), Tall Cedars of Lebanon (forest # 27), Hamilton Club. Avocations: bridge, fishing, hunting, reading. Home: 46 Valleybrook Dr Lancaster PA 17601-4617 Office: 1661 Old Philadelphia Pike Lancaster PA 17602-2633

**NICKELL, CHRISTOPHER SHEA,** lawyer; b. Paducah, Ky., Mar. 21, 1959; s. Carl Duane and Anna June (Starrett) N. BA, DePauw U., 1981; JD, U. Ky., 1984. Bar: Ky. 1984, U.S. Dist. Ct. (ea. dist.) Ky., 1985, U.S. Dist. Ct. (we. dist.) Ky. 1989. Assoc. Truman L. Dehner, Morehead, Ky., 1984-87; asst. commonwealth atty. 21st Jud. Dist. Ky., 1986-87; assoc. Boehl, Stopher, Graves & Deindoerfer, Paducah, 1989-91, Saladino Law Firm, Paducah, Ky., 1991-97, Nickell Law Firm, Paducah, 1997—; vis. lectr. U. N.C., Chapel Hill, 1987-88; adj. prof. Murray State U., 1989-91. Trustee DePauw U., Greencastle, 1981-84; bd. dirs. N.E. Ky. Legal Svcs., Inc., Morehead, 1985-87, Western Ky. Easter Seal Soc., 1993—. Named to Hon. Order Ky. Cols., 1981. Mem. ABA, Ky. Bar Assn. (Ky. Outstanding Young Lawyer award 1995), McCracken County Bar Assn., Ky. Acad. Trial Attys., Masons (32 deg.) Paducah Lions Club (bd. dirs., chmn. Easter Seals telethon, pres., vice dist. gov.), Elks, Delta Theta Phi. Democrat. E-mail: nlf@ssi-net.net. Personal injury, Workers' compensation, General civil litigation. Office: Nickell Law Firm Old Courthouse Sta 634 Kentucky Ave Paducah KY 42003-1720

**NICKELS, JOHN L.,** state supreme court justice; m. Merita Nickels; 7 children. Bachelor's degree, No. Ill. U.; law degree, DePaul U. Pvt. practice, 20 yrs.; judge Appellate Ct.; cir. judge 16th Jud. Cir.; supreme ct. justice State of Ill., 1992—; bd. dirs. Kane County Bank & Trust Co. Bd. trustees Waubonsee Coll.; mem. adv. coun. and found. Kaneland Sch. Dist.; mem. Kane County Planning Commn., Zoning Bd. Appeals; mem. St. Gall's Parish, Elburn. Office: Illinois Supreme Court Supreme Court Bldg 160 N La Salle St Fl 18 Chicago IL 60601-3106*

**NICKERSON, DON C.,** lawyer. U.S. atty. U.S. Dist. Ct. (So. Dist.), Iowa, 1993—. Office: US Atty So Dist Iowa US CourthouseAnnex 110 E Court Ave Des Moines IA 50309-2044

**NICKERSON, EUGENE H.,** federal judge; b. Orange, N.J., Aug. 2, 1918; m. Marie-Louise Steiner; children—Marie-Louise, Lawrie H., Stephanie W., Susan A. A.B., Harvard U., 1941; LL.B. (Kent scholar), Columbia U., 1943; LL.D. (hon.), Hofstra U., 1970, Bklyn. Law Sch., 1992. Bar: N.Y. 1944, U.S. Supreme Ct. 1948. Law clk. to Judge Augustus N. Hand, 2d circuit U.S. Ct. Appeals, 1943-44; to Chief Justice Harlan F. Stone U.S. Supreme Ct., 1944-46; assoc. Milbank, Tweed, Hope, Hadley & McCloy, 1946-51; ptnr. Hale, Stimson, Russell & Nickerson, 1952-61; county exec. Nassau County, N.Y., 1962-70; ptnr. Nickerson, Kramer, Lowenstein, Nessen, Kamin & Soll, N.Y.C., 71-77; judge U.S. Dist. Ct., Bklyn., 1977-94, sr. judge, 1994—; Counsel N.Y. Gov.'s Com. Pub. Employee Procedures, 1956-58; mem. N.Y. State Law Revision Commn., 1958-59, 77; mem. Met. Regional Council, 1962-70, chmn., 1969-70; mem. adv. council pub. welfare HEW, 1963-65; mem. pub. ofcls. adv. council OEO, 1968. Recipient Emory Buckner award Fed. Bar Coun., 1994. Mem. ABA, Nassau County Bar Assn., Assn. Bar City N.Y. (com. fed. legislation 1971-74, com. on communications 1971-77, com. on judiciary 1974-77), Am. Law Inst., Phi Delta Phi. Office: US Dist Ct US Courthouse 225 Cadman Plz E Brooklyn NY 11201-1818

**NICKERSON, WILLIAM MILNOR,** federal judge; b. Balt., Dec. 6, 1933; s. Palmer Rice and Eleanor (Renshaw) N.; m. Virginia Arlen Bourne, Apr. 25, 1954; children: Carol Lee, Deborah, Susan, Wendy, Laura. BA, U. Va., 1955; LLB, U. Md., Balt., 1962. Bar: Md. 1962. Ptnr. Whiteford, Taylor & Preston, Balt., 1962-85; assoc. judge Cir. Ct. Baltimore County, Towson, Md., 1985-90; judge U.S. Dist. Ct. Md., Balt., 1990—. Served to lt. USCGR, 1955-59. Mem. ABA (judicial adminstrn. div.), Am. Judicature Soc., Fed. Judges Assn., Md. State Bar Assn.. Office: US Dist Ct 101 W Lombard St 3C Baltimore MD 21201-2626

**NICKS, PAUL TODD,** lawyer; b. Sturgis, Ky., Apr. 8, 1964; s. Wesley Allison and Anna Nadine (Ford) N.; m. Julie Alsip. BA in Polit. Sci., U. of the South, 1987; JD, Memphis State U., 1990. Bar: Tenn. 1990, U.S. Dist. Ct. (we. dist.) Tenn. 1991. Assoc. Hill, Boren, Drew & Martindale, Jackson, Tenn., 1990—. Mem. West Tenn. Young Dems., Jackson, 1992. Mem. Assn. Trial Lawyers of Am., Tenn. Trial Lawyers Assn., Tenn. Bar Assn., Madison County Bar Assn., West Tenn. Young Lawyers. Democrat. Methodist. Avocations: golf, softball, basketball, travel. Personal injury, Workers' compensation, Product liability. Office: Hill Boren Drew & Martindale 1269 N Highland Ave Jackson TN 38301-4447

**NICOLAI, DONALD F.,** lawyer; b. Lincoln, Nebr., July 26, 1953; s. Frederick L. and Elizabeth J. (Brinkruff) N.; m. Paula Shill, Aug. 6, 1978; children: Jaclyn, Lauren, Lindsay, Andrea. BA in Polit. Sci., U. Md., 1975; JD, Temple U., 1978. Bar: N.J. 1978, U.S. Dist. Ct. N.J. 1978, U.S. Ct. Appeals (3d cir.) 1979, U.S. Supreme Ct. 1985. Assoc. Lindabury, McCormick & Estabrook, Westfield, N.J., 1978-86, ptnr., 1986—. Decisions published in profl. publs. General civil litigation, Consumer commercial, Health. Office: Lindabury McCormick & Estabrook 53 Cardinal Dr Westfield NJ 07090-1020

**NICOLAI, PAUL PETER,** lawyer; b. Trenton, N.J., Jan. 22, 1953; s. Ernest and Preziosa E. (Cattani) N.; m. Anne Marie Elizabeth LaRochelle, May 14, 1976; children: Caroline Emma, Peter Ernest, Margaret Elizabeth, Alexandra Marie, Elizabeth Anne. BA, Am. Internat. Coll., 1975; JD, Western New Eng. Coll., 1979. Bar: Mass. 1979, U.S. Dist. Ct. Mass. 1980, U.S. Ct. Appeals (1st cir.) 1983, U.S. Supreme Ct. 1984, N.Y. 1987, Washington 1987, U.S. Ct. Appeals (Fed. cir.) 1990, U.S. Tax Ct. 1991. Legal asst. Friendly Ice Cream Corp., Wilbraham, Mass., 1976-79, staff counsel, 1979-81, co. counsel, 1981-88; pres. Nicolai Law Group, P.C., Springfield, Mass., 1984-97; bd. dirs. Video Comms., Inc., Springfield, Packing Machine Co., Inc. Acquisition Corp., Prentics Reed LTC; pres., bd. dirs. Paugus TV, Inc., Manchester, N.H., 1995—, T-W Realty, Inc., Springfield, Mass., 1996—. Bd. dirs. Citizens for Ltd. Taxation, Mass., 1981-84, chmn., 1984-97; mem. we. Mass. exec. com. NCCJ, mem. we. Mass. and Conn. devel. com. 1995-99, nat. trustee, 1991-99; corporator Springfield Day Nursery, Inc., 1995—, mem. mktg. com., 1995-96, Springfield Libr. Mus. Assn., Inc., 1985—; bd. dirs. Pioneer Valley Montessori Soc., Inc., Springfield, 1985-93, v.p., 1988-92, pres., 1992-93; bd. dirs., chmn. Citizens Econs. Rsch. Found., Inc., Boston, 1984-97. Mem. ABA, Am. Arbitration Assn. (arbitration panel 1992—), Mass. Bar Assn. (arbitration panel 1997—), Hampden County Bar Assn. (arbitration and mediation panel 1998—), Boston Bar Assn., Assn. Bar City N.Y., D.C. Bar Assn., Fed. Cir. Ct. Appeals Bar Assn., Am. Internat. Coll. Alumni Assn. (nat. bd. dirs., v.p. 1989-90, pres. 1990-91), Soc. Everett Barney Inc. (treas., clk. 1995-99, dir. 1995—, sec. 1996-99). Roman Catholic. Avocation: reading. Contracts commercial, General corporate, General civil litigation. Home: 24 Venture Dr Springfield MA 01119-2727 Office: Nicolai Law Group PC 146 Chestnut St Ste 1 Springfield MA 01103-1539

**NICOLAIDES, MARY,** lawyer; b. N.Y.C., June 7, 1927; d. George and Dorothy Nicolaides. BCE, CUNY, 1947; MBA with distinction, DePaul U., 1975, JD, 1981. Bar: Ill. 1982, U.S. Dist. Ct. (no. dist.) Ill. 1982, U.S. Patent Office 1983. Sr. design engr. cement subs. U.S. Steel Corp., N.Y.C., then Pitts., 1948-71; sole practice Chgo., 1982—. Mem. ABA. Republican. Greek Orthodox. Elder, Patent, Probate. Address: 233 E Erie St Apt 1804 Chicago IL 60611-2903

**NICOLAS, ANNE EVELINE,** lawyer; b. Liege, Belgium, Feb. 3, 1957; came to U.S. 1979; d. Roger Fernand and Mona (Goldstein) Nicolas. Cand. en Droit with high distinction, U. Liege, 1976, Licence en Droit highest distinction, 1979. Bar: Belgium 1979, Calif. 1981. Legal recruiter Kass Abell & Assocs., L.A., 1984-86; sales mgr. Les Nutons, L.A., 1983-84; assoc. Fine, Perzik & Friedman, L.A., 1981-82; legal recruiter Ziskind, Greene & Assocs., Beverly Hills, Calif., 1987-88; prin. Advocate Legal Search, L.A., 1988—. Avocations: travel, reading, skiing, tennis. Office: Advocate Legal Search 1888 Century Park E Ste 1900 Los Angeles CA 90067-1723

**NICOLOZAKES, WILLIAM ANGELO,** lawyer; b. Cambridge, Ohio, Dec. 22, 1968; s. William G. and Helen B. Nicolozakes. BA, Ohio State U., 1992; JD magna cum laude, Capital U., 1995. Bar: Ohio 1995, U.S. Dist. Ct. (no. and so. dists.) Ohio 1996. Assoc. Kegler, Brown, Hill & Ritter, Columbus, Ohio, 1995-99; v.p., gen. counsel Nicolozakes Trucking & Constrn., Inc., Cambridge, Ohio, 1999—. Mng. editor Capital U. Law Rev., 1994-95. Bd. dirs. Capital U. Law Sch. Alumni Adv. Bd., Columbus, 1998—. Mem. ABA, Columbus Bar Assn., Ohio State Bar Assn., Guernsey County Bar Assn. Greek Orthodox. Construction, General civil litigation, Alternative dispute resolution. Home and Office: PO Box 670 8575 Georgetown Rd 2d Fl Cambridge OH 43725-0670

**NIEHOFF, LEONARD MARVIN,** lawyer; b. St. Louis, Dec. 2, 1957; s. Leonard Marvin and May (Gordon) N.; m. Nancy Wright Blotner, July 31, 1981. BA with high distinction, U. Mich., 1981, JD, 1984, postgrad., 1984. Bar: Mich. 1984, U.S. Dist. Ct. (ea. dist.) Mich., 1985, U.S. Dist. Ct. (we. dist.) Mich. 1985, U.S. Ct. Appeals (6th cir.) 1985, U.S. Supreme Ct. 1988. Research asst. U. Mich. Law Sch., Ann Arbor, 1983; shareholder Butzel Long, Detroit, 1984—; adj. prof. law U. Detroit Law Sch., 1988—, Wayne State U. Law Sch., 1989—. Editor U. Mich. Jour. Law Reform, 1983-84. Bd. advisors C.S. Mott Children's Hosp.; bd. dirs. Mich. Theatre Found. Named to 40 Under 40, Crain's Detroit Bus., 1996. Mem. ABA (forum com. on comms. law 1985—), Fed. Bar Assn. (exec. bd. 1995—), State Bar Mich. (chmn. constl. law com., mem. law and media com., bar jour. adv. bd.), Detroit Bar Assn., Washtenaw Bar Assn. (chmn. trial practice sect.), U. Musical Soc. (bd. dirs.), Mich. Theater Found. (bd. dirs.), CS Mott Children's Hosp. (bd. dirs.). Avocations: music, film, art. General civil litigation, Constitutional, Libel. Office: 350 S Main St Ste 300 Ann Arbor MI 48104-2131

**NIEHOFF, PHILIP JOHN,** lawyer; b. Beaver Dam, Wis., Dec. 31, 1959; s. John Henry and Muriel Jean (Moore) N. BBA with distinction, U. Wis., 1982, JD cum laude, 1985; LLM in Securities Regulation, Georgetown U., 1988. Bar: Wis. 1985, U.S. Dist. Ct. (we. dist.) Wis. 1985, Ill. 1991. Atty. SEC, Washington, 1985-90; assoc. Mayer, Brown & Platt, Chgo., 1990-95, ptnr., 1996—. Co-author: Current Law of Insider Trading, 1990, Public Offerings, securities law handbook, 1997; contbg. author: Securitization of Financial Assets, 1991. Fed. Bar Assn. scholar, 1988. Mem. ABA, State Bar Wis., State Bar Ill., Chgo. Bar Assn., Order of Coif, Golden Key Honor Soc., Beta Gamma Sigma, Phi Kappa Phi, Phi Eta Sigma. Republican. Lutheran. Avocations: fishing, computers, reading, travel. Securities, General corporate. Home: 2800 N Lake Shore Dr Apt 2416 Chicago IL 60657-6248 Office: Mayer Brown & Platt 190 S La Salle St Ste 3100 Chicago IL 60603-3441

**NIELSEN, CHRISTIAN BAYARD,** lawyer; b. San Jose, Calif., May 10, 1954; s. Bayard R. and June (Morgan) N.; m. Kathleen Dearden, Oct. 25, 1980; children: Bayard Douglas, Chandler Kathleen. BA, U. Pacific, Stockton, Calif., 1976; JD, Pepperdine U., 1979. Bar: Calif. 1979, U.S. Dist. Ct. (no. and ea. dists.) Calif. 1979. Sr. ptnr. Robinson & Wood, Inc., San Jose, Calif., 1979—; arbitrator Fed. Panel and State Panel, 1982—; lectr. Calif. Continuing Edn. of the Bar, 1989—. Mem. ABA, Assn. Def. Counsel of No. Calif. (lectr. 1988—), Am. Bd. Trial Advocates (cert. civil trial advocate), Nat. Bd. Trial Advocacy, Def. Rsch. Inst., Internat. Assn. Ins. Counsel, Santa Clara County Bar Assn. Republican. Methodist. E-mail: cbn@r-winc.com. Personal injury, General civil litigation, Product liability. Office: Robinson & Wood Inc 227 N 1st St Fl 2 San Jose CA 95113-1000

**NIELSEN, LELAND C.,** federal judge; b. Vesper, Kans., June 14, 1919; s. Carl Christian and Christena (Larson) N.; m. Virginia Garland, Nov. 27, 1958; 1 child, Christena. A.B., Washburn U., 1946; J.D., U. So. Calif., 1946. Bar: Calif. 1947. Practice law Los Angeles, from 1947; dep. city atty. City of Los Angeles, 1947-51; judge Superior Ct. Calif. San Diego County, 1968-71; judge, now sr. judge U.S. Dist. Ct. (so. dist.) Calif., San Diego, 1971—. Served to maj. A.C., U.S. Army 1941-46. Decorated Purple Heart, Disting. Svc. Cross, Air medal with oak leaf clusters. Mem. Am. Coll. Trial Lawyers. Republican. Presbyterian. Office: US Dist Ct 2160 US Courthouse 940 Front St San Diego CA 92101-8994

**NIELSEN, LYNN CAROL,** lawyer, educational consultant; b. Perth Amboy, N.J., Jan. 11, 1950; d. Hans and Esther (Pucker) N.; m. Russell F. Baldwin, Nov. 22, 1980; 1 child, Blake Nielsen Baldwin. BS, Millersville U., 1972; MA, NYU, 1979; JD, Rutgers U., 1984. Bar: N.J. 1984; cert. tchr. handicapped, reading specialist, learning disability tchr. cons., elem. edn. supr. Instr. Woodbridge (N.J.) Twp. Bd. Edn., 1972-83; legal intern appellate sect. divsn. criminal justice Atty. Gen. State N.J., Trenton, 1983, dep. atty. gen. divsn. civil law, 1985; assoc. Kantor & Kusic, Keyport, N.J., 1984-86, Kantor & Linderoth, Keyport, N.J., 1986-92. Officer Fords (N.J.) Sch. # 14 PTO, 1974-75; elder First Presbyn. Ch. Avenel, N.J., 1985-88, Flemington (N.J.) Presbyn. Ch., 1997—; bd. dirs. New Beginnings Nursery Sch., Woodbridge, 1989-90, Flemington Presbyn. Nursery Sch., 1991-93; elder Flemington Presbyn. Ch., 1997-99; bd. mem. Woodside Farms Homeowners Assn., 1996-99. Mem. ABA, N.J. Bar Assn., Monmouth County Bar Assn., Hunterdon County Bar Assn. Avocations: reading, skiing, sailing. Home and Office: 3 Buchannan Way Flemington NJ 08822-3205

**NIELSEN, NEAL D.,** lawyer. BA, U. Mich., 1971; JD, Detroit Coll. of Law, 1976. Bar: Mich. 1976, U.S. Dist. Ct. 1976. Referee Wayne County Juvenile Ct., Detroit, 1975-76; chief asst. prosecutor Livingston County, Howell, Mich., 1976-81; pvt. practice Brighton, Mich., 1981—. Bd. regents U. Mich., Ann Arbor, 1985-92; pres. Exch. Club, Howell, 1980-84; mem. state com. 6th dist. Mich. State Rep. Party, chmn.-outreach com., chmn. subcom. on ways and means; fin. chmn., sec., chmn. Century Club Livingston County Rep. Com.; mem. Gov.'s Coun.; team leader Gov.'s Gala. Mem. Livingston County Bar Assn. (sec.-treas. 1978-82), Brighton C. of C., Century Club (pres. 1980-84, chmn. 1992-94). State civil litigation, Condemnation, Criminal. Office: 9812 E Grand River Ave Brighton MI 48116-1911

**NIELSEN, WILLIAM FREMMING,** federal judge; b. 1934. BA, U. Wash., 1956, LLB, 1963. Law clk. to Hon. Charles L. Powell U.S. Dist. Ct. (ea. dist.) Wash., 1963-64; mem. firm Paine, Hamblen, Coffin, Brooke & Miller, 1964-91; judge to chief judge U.S. Dist. Ct. (ea. dist.) Wash., Spokane, 1991—. Lt. col. USAFR. Fellow Am. Coll. Trial Lawyers; mem. ABA, Wash. State Bar Assn., Spokane County Bar Assn. (pres. 1981-82), Fed. Bar Assn. (pres. 1988), Spokane County Legal Svcs. Corp. (past pres.), Lawyer Pilot Bar Assn., Assn. Trial Lawyers Am., Wash. State Trial Lawyers Assn., Assn. Def. Trial Attys., Am. Inns of Ct., Charles L. Powell Inn (pres. 1987), The Spokane Club, Rotary, Alpha Delta Phi, Phi Delta Phi. Office: US Dist Ct PO Box 2208 920 W Riverside Ave 9th Fl Spokane WA 99210-2208

**NIEMEYER, JONATHAN DAVID,** lawyer; b. Cin., Feb. 6, 1968; s. Robert Charles and Edwina Gayle Niemeyer; m. Jennifer Miracle, Aug. 7, 1993; children: Alexandra, Benjamin. BA, U. Ky., 1990, JD, 1993. Bar: Ky. 1993, Ohio 1998. Atty. LG&E Energy Corp., Louisville, 1993-96; assoc. Graydon, Head & Ritchey, Cin., 1996-99; asst. gen. counsel Huffy Corp., Miamisburg, Ohio, 1999—. Notes editor Ky. Law Jour., 1992-93. Bd. dirs., sec. Kicks for Kids, Inc., Cin., 1997-98. Mem. Order of Coif. Fax: 937-865-5414. E-mail: jon.niemeyer@huffy.com. Contracts commercial, General corporate, Mergers and acquisitions. Office: Huffy Corp 225 Byers Rd Miamisburg OH 45342-3614

**NIEMEYER, PAUL VICTOR,** federal judge; b. Princeton, N.J., Apr. 5, 1941; s. Gerhart and Lucie (Lenzner) N.; m. Susan Kinley, Aug. 24, 1963; children Jonathan K., Peter E., Christopher J. AB, Kenyon Coll., 1962; student, U. Munich, Federal Republic of Germany, 1962-63; JD, U. Notre Dame, 1966. Bars: Md. 1966, U.S. Dist. Ct. Md. 1967, U.S. Ct. Appeals (4th cir.) 1968, U.S. Supreme Ct. 1970, U.S. Dist Ct. (so. dist.) Tex. 1977, U.S. Ct. Appeals (5th cir.) 1978, U.S. Ct. Appeals (3d cir.) 1980. Assoc. Piper & Marbury, Balt., 1966-74, ptnr., 1974-88; U.S. dist. judge U.S. Dist. Ct. Md., Balt., 1988-90; fed. judge U.S. Ct. Appeals (4th cir.), Balt., 1990—; lectr. advanced bus. law Johns Hopkins U., Balt., 1971-75; lectr. Md. Jud. Conf., Md. Ct. Clks. Assn.; sr. lecturing fellow in appellate advocacy Duke U. Sch. of Law, 1994—; mem. standing com. on rules of practice and procedure cts. appeals, 1973-88, atty. grievance com.-hearing panel, 1978-81, select com.-profl. conduct, 1983-85, adv. com. on Fed. Rules of Civil Procedure, 1993—, chmn., 1996—. Co-author: Maryland Rules Commentary, 1984, supplement, 1988, 2d edit., 1992; contbr. articles to profl. jours. Recipient Spl. Merit citation Am. Judicature Soc., 1987. Fellow Am. Coll. Trial Lawyers, Am. Bar Found., Md. Bar Found., Md. Bar Assn. (Disting. Svc. award litigation sect. 1981), Am. Law Inst.; mem. Wednesday Law Club, Lawyers' Round Table. Republican. Episcopalian. Office: US Cir Ct Md US Courthouse 101 W Lombard St Ste 910 Baltimore MD 21201-2611

**NIER, HARRY K.,** lawyer; b. N.Y.C., Aug. 13, 1925; s. Harry K. Sr. and May O. Nier. LLB, U. Colo., 1950. Pvt. practice Denver, 1952—. Chmn. Denver-Havana Friendship Sister Cities Project, 1990—. Mem. Nat. Lawyers Guild, Colo. Bar Assn., Denver Bar Assn. Avocation: mountaineering. Civil rights, Constitutional, Private international. Home: 1470 S Quebec Way Apt 81 Denver CO 80231-2657 Office: 1700 Lincoln St Ste 3901 Denver CO 80203-4539

**NIERENGARTEN, ROGER JOSEPH,** judge; b. St. Cloud, Minn., Nov. 19, 1925; s. Henry Clarence and Rose (Josephine) N.; m. Dolores Rosalind Lehman, Oct. 4, 1954; children: Therese, Catherine, Mary, Carolyn. BA, St. John's U., Collegeville, Minn., 1948; JD, Marquette U., 1951. Bar: Minn. 1951, U.S. Dist. Ct. Minn. 1951, U.S. Claims Ct., U.S. Supreme Ct. Adminstv. asst. to mayor City of St. Cloud, 1954-56; pvt. practice St. Cloud, 1956-84; judge Minn. Ct. Appeals, St. Paul, 1984-89; sr. ptnr. Hall, Byers, Hanson, Steil & Weinberger Law Offices, St. Cloud, 1989-92; pvt. practice, 1992—; Stearns County atty., St. Cloud, 1962-66. Spl. asst. atty. gen. State of Minn., 1967-71; chmn. Minn. Cath. Conf. Bd. Edn., St. Paul, 1979-83, Cen. Minn. Coun. for Pub. Radio, 1984-87; trustee Minn. Pub. Radio, St. Paul, 1984-87; mem. Minn. Higher Edn. Coordinating Bd., 1989-91. With U.S. Army, 1943-46, 50-51. Mem. ABA, Minn. Bar Assn., Fed. Bar Assn., Assn. Trial Lawyers Am., Minn. Trial Lawyers Assn. Democrat. Roman Catholic. Avocation: reading, writing. Office: PO Box 339 Saint Cloud MN 56302-0339

**NIGH, ROBERT RUSSELL, JR.,** lawyer; b. Enid, Okla., Nov. 1, 1959; s. Robert Russell and Helen Louise (Russell) N.; m. Susan Althadene Placek, Oct. 1, 1989. BA, William Jewell Coll., 1982; JD, U. Okla., 1986. Assoc. Jones, Bryant & Nigh, Enid, 1986-89; asst. pub. defender Tulsa County, Office of Pub. Defender, 1989-92; asst. fed. defender Fed. Pub. Defender's Office, Tulsa, 1992-94, Lincoln, Nebr., 1994-96; pvt. practice Tulsa, 1996—. Mem. Nat. Assn. Criminal Def. Lawyers, Okla. Criminal Def. Lawyers Assn. (bd. dirs. 1991—), Tulsa County Bar Assn. Avocations: hunting, fishing, basketball. Criminal. Office: 2 W 6th St Ste 425 Tulsa OK 74119-1259

**NIGHTINGALE, TRACY IRENE,** lawyer; b. Bloomer, Wis., May 16, 1966; d. Russell L. and Dorothy I. (Bluem) Pederson; m. Brian J. Nightingale, July 16, 1990; children: Austin M., Carson D., Sierra C. BA, U. Wis., Eau Claire, 1988; JD, Hamline U., 1991. Bar: Minn. 1992, U.S. Dist. Minn. 1993, Wis. 1994. Pvt. practice, Mpls., 1991—; atty. Legal Legacy, Ltd., St. Louis Park, Minn., 1996-98; exec. dir. Nat. Assn. Debt Mgrs., St. Louis Park, 1997-98; mediator West Suburban Mediation Ctr., Hopkins, Minn., 1992—. Author: Trust and Estate Planner, 1996. Mem. Minn. Bar Assn., Wis. Bar Assn., Hennepin County Bar Assn. Estate planning, Personal injury, Alternative dispute resolution. Office: Hurwitz Law Firm 6009 Wayzata Blvd Ste 111 Saint Louis Park MN 55416-1223

**NIGRO, RUSSELL M.,** state supreme court justice. Assoc. justice Pa. Supreme Ct., Phila., 1996—. Office: Pa Supreme Ct 1818 Market St Ste 3205 Philadelphia PA 19103-3632*

**NIHILL, JULIAN DUMONTIEL,** lawyer; b. Nairobi, Kenya, Apr. 17, 1950; s. Alan Barclay and Jeannine (Morgan-Davies) N.; m. Catherine Lynn Brittingham, Aug. 28,1977; children: Natalie Penn, Edward Barclay. Student, Ampleforth Coll., Eng., 1967; LLB with honors, Exeter U., Eng., 1972; barrister at law, Inner Temple, Eng., 1973; JD, Boston U., 1977. Bar: Ill. 1977, Tex. 1984, U.S. Tax Ct. 1982. Assoc. McDermott, Will & Emory, Chgo., 1977-79, Baker & McKenzie, Chgo., 1979-83; ptnr. Gardere & Wynne, Dallas, 1984—; chmn. Tex. State Bar Internat. Sect., Internat. Sect. Gardere & Wynne. Contbr. articles to profl. jours. Mem. U.S.-Mex. C. of C., Cavalry and Guards Club. Avocations: Playing piano, sailing, fly-fishing. Private international, Corporate taxation. Office: Gardere & Wynne 3000 Thanksgiving Tower 1601 Elm St Ste 3000 Dallas TX 75201-4761

**NIKAS, RICHARD JOHN,** lawyer; b. Long Beach, Calif., Sept. 9, 1968; s. John Nikolas and Dorothy (Bernardo) N. BA in Internat. Rels., U. So. Calif., 1991, JD, 1995. Bar: Calif. Spl. projects coord. Vessel Assist Assn. Am., Newport Beach, Calif., 1989-94; lawyer Williams Woolley Cogswell Nakazawa & Russell, Long Beach, Calif., 1994—; guest lectr. maritime law U. So. Calif., L.A., 1998—; group chair USCG Working Group on Nat. Maritime Incident Reporting Sys., Washington, 1997—. head football coach Ocean View H.S., Long Beach, 1995; mentor Long Beach Unified Sch. Dist., 1997—. Recipient best oralist award Spong Nat. Invitational Moot Ct., Williamsburg, Va., 1995. Mem. Calif. State Bar Assn., Maritime Law Assn. Avocation: baseball. Admiralty, Federal civil litigation, Transportation. Home: 21720 Wesley Dr Laguna Beach CA 92651-8105 Office: Williams Woolley et al 111 W Ocean Blvd Ste 2000 Long Beach CA 90802-4696

**NIKOLAY, FRANK LAWRENCE,** lawyer; b. Marathon County, Wis., Sept. 1, 1922; s. Jacob and Anna Bertha (Illig) N.; m. Mary Elizabeth Gisvold, Aug. 3, 1958. LLB, U. Wis., 1948. Bar: Wis. 1948, U.S. Dist. Ct. (we. dist.) Wis. 1948, U.S. Supreme Ct. 1961. Dist. counsel Office Price Stabilization, Green Bay, Wis., 1951-52; asst. U.S. atty. U.S. Dist. Ct. (we. dist.) Wis., 1952-53; U.S. atty., 1953-54; mem. assembly State of Wis., 1958-70; ptnr. Nikolay, Jensen, Scott, Gamoke and Grunewald, Colby, 1970—. Mem. bd. regents U. Wis., Madison, 1983-90; mem. Clark County (Wis.) Bd. Suprs., 1949—. Col. U.S. Army, 1948-74. Mem. ABA, Wis. Bar Assn., Am. Legion (post comdr. 1975—), Lions (sec. 1978). Democrat. Roman Catholic. General practice, Criminal, Administrative and regulatory. Office: Nikolay Jensen Scott Gamoke & Grunewald PO Box 465 Colby WI 54421-0465

**NILES, JOHN GILBERT,** lawyer; b. Dallas, Oct. 5, 1943; s. Paul Dickerman and Nedra Mary (Arendts) N.; m. Marian Higginbotham, Nov. 21, 1970; children: Paul Breckenridge, Matthew Higginbotham. BA in History, Stanford U., 1965; LLB, U. Tex., 1968. Bar: Tex. 1968, Calif. 1969, U.S. Dist. Ct. (cen. dist.) Calif. 1973, U.S. Ct. Appeals (9th cir.) 1973, U.S. Dist. Ct. (so. dist.) Calif. 1977, U.S. Supreme Ct. 1979, U.S. Dist. Ct. (no. dist.) Calif. 1983. Assoc. O'Melveny & Myers, Los Angeles, 1973-77, ptnr., 1978—; judge pro tem mcpl. ct. L.A.; spkr., panel mem. Practicing Law Inst., Calif. C.E.B. Served to lt. comdr. USNR, 1968-72, Vietnam. Mem. ABA, Los Angeles County Bar Assn., Am. Judicature Soc. Clubs: Bel-Air Bay (Pacific Palisades, Calif.); Calif. (Los Angeles). Avocation: sailing. Federal civil litigation, State civil litigation, Insurance. Home: 1257 Villa Woods Dr Pacific Palisades CA 90272-3953 Office: O'Melveny & Myers 400 S Hope St Los Angeles CA 90071-2899

**NILLES, JOHN MICHAEL,** lawyer; b. Langdon, N.D., Aug. 20, 1930; s. John Joseph and Isabel Mary (O'Neil) N.; m. Barbara Ann Cook, June 22, 1957; children: Terese M., Daniel J., Marcia L., Thomas M., Margaret J. BA cum laude, St. Johns U., 1955; JD cum laude with distinction, U. N.D., 1958. Bar: N.D. 1958, U.S. Dist. Ct. N.D. 1958, U.S. Ct. Appeals (8th cir.) 1958, Minn. 1991. Shareholder, dir., pres. Nilles, Hansen and Davies, Ltd., Fargo, N.D., 1958-90, of counsel, 1990-95; exec. v.p., gen. counsel Met. Fin. Corp., Mpls., 1990-95, First Bank F.S.B., Mpls., 1995; ret., 1996; pres., bd. dirs. Legal Aid Soc. N.D., Fargo, 1970-76, Red River Estate Planning Coun., 1980-87; vice-chmn. disciplinary bd. Supreme Ct. N.D., 1984-90. Bd. editors N.D. Law Rev., 1957-58. Mem. exec. bd. Red. River Valley coun. Boy Scouts Am., 1959-70; bd. regents U. Mary, Bismarck, N.D., 1967-77; pres., bd. dirs. Cath. Charities, Fargo, 1959-65, Southeast Mental Health Ctr., Fargo, 1972-80. Staff sgt. USAF, 1951-54. Fellow Am. Coll. Trust and Estate Counsel (state dir. 1979-90); mem. ABA, State Bar Assn. N.D., Minn. Bar Assn., Order of Coif. Republican. Roman Catholic. Avocations: tennis, downhill skiing, cross-country skiing, hunting, gun collecting. Banking, General corporate. Home: 10412 Fawns Way Eden Prairie MN 55347-5117

**NILLES, KATHLEEN MARY,** lawyer; b. Fargo, N.D., May 27, 1951; d. J. Gerald and Barbara L. (Accornero) N. BA, U. Santa Clara, 1973; MA, Yale U., 1976; JD, U. Va., 1985; LLM in Taxation, Georgetown U., 1992. Bar: D.C. 1985, U.S. Tax Ct. 1987. Assoc. Patton & Boggs, Washington, 1985-88, Groom & Nordberg, Washington, 1988-90; tax counsel ways and means com. U.S. Ho. of Reps., Washington, 1991-95; ptnr. Gardner, Carton & Douglas, Washington, 1995—; bd. dirs. Tax Coalition, Washington, 1994—; mem. steering com. D.C. Bar Tax Sect., Washington, 1995-97. Co-author: Tax-Exempt Status of Health Care Organizations, 1996. Co-chair fed. club steering com. Human Rights Campaign, Washington, 1997. Avocation: golf, biking. Taxation, general, Native American, Health. Office: Gardner Carton & Douglas 1301 K St NW Ste 900 Washington DC 20005-3317

**NIMETZ, MATTHEW,** lawyer; b. Bklyn., June 17, 1939; s. Joseph L. and Elsie (Botwinik) N.; m. Gloria S. Lorch, June 24, 1975; children: Alexandra Elise, Lloyd. B.A., Williams Coll., 1960, LL.D. (hon.), 1979; B.A. (Rhodes scholar), Balliol Coll., Oxford (Eng.) U., 1962; M.A., Oxford (Eng.) U., 1966; LL.B., Harvard U., 1965. Bar: N.Y. 1966, D.C. 1968. Law clk. to Justice John M. Harlan, U.S. Supreme Ct., 1965-67; staff asst. to Pres. Johnson, 1967-69; assoc. firm Simpson Thacher & Bartlett, N.Y.C., 1969-71; partner Simpson Thacher & Bartlett, 1972-77; counselor Dept. of State, Washington, 1977-80; acting coordinator refugee affairs Dept. of State, 1979-80, under sec. of state for security assistance, sci. and tech., 1980; partner firm Paul, Weiss, Rifkind, Wharton & Garrison, N.Y.C., 1981—; commr. Port Authority N.Y. and N.J., 1975-77; dir. World Resources Inst., chmn., 1982-94; mem. N.Y. State Adv. Coun. on State Productivity, 1990-92; presdl. envoy Greece-Macedonian Negotiations, 1994-95, dep. spl. rep. UN Sec. Gen., 1997—. Trustee William Coll., 1981-96; chmn. UN Devel. Corp., 1986-94; bd. dirs. Charles H. Revson Found., 1990-98, N.Y. State Nature Conservancy, 1997—; chmn. Carnegie Forum in U.S., Greece and Turkey, 1996-98; chmn. Ctr. for Democracy and Reconciliation in S.E. Europe, 1998—; dir. Inst. Pub. Adminstrn., 1999—; mem. internat. adv. com. Ctrl. European U., Budapest, Hungary. Mem. Assn. of Bar of City of N.Y., Coun. on Fgn. Rels. Club: Harvard (N.Y.C.). General corporate, Private international, Securities. Office: Paul Weiss Rifkind Wharton & Garrison Ste 247 1285 Avenue Of The Americas Fl 21 New York NY 10019-6028

**NIMMONS, RALPH WILSON, JR.,** federal judge; b. Dallas, Sept. 14, 1938; s. Ralph Wilson and Dorothy (Tucker) N.; m. Doris Penelope Pickels, Jan. 30, 1960; children—Bradley, Paige, Bonnie. BA, U. Fla., 1960, JD, 1963. Bar: Fla. 1963, U.S. Dist. Ct. (mid. dist.) Fla. 1963, U.S. Ct. Appeals (5th cir.) 1969, U.S. Supreme Ct. 1970. Assoc. Ulmer, Murchison, Ashby & Ball, Jacksonville, Fla., 1963-65, ptnr., 1973-77; asst. pub. defender Pub. Defender's Office, Jacksonville, 1965-69; first asst. state atty. State Atty.'s Office, Jacksonville, 1969-71; chief asst. gen. counsel City of Jacksonville, 1971-73; judge 4th Jud. Cir. Ct., Jacksonville, 1977-83, First Dist. Ct. of Appeal Fla., Tallahassee, 1983-91; judge U.S. Dist. Ct. Mid. Dist. Fla., 1991—; mem. faculty Fla. Jud. Coll., Tallahassee, 1985, 86; mem. Fla. Bar Grievance Com., 1973-76, vice chmn., 1975-76; mem. Fla. Conf. Cir. Judges, 1977-83, mem. exec. com., 1980-83; mem. Met. Criminal Justice Adv. Council, 1977-79; mem. Fla. Gov.'s Task Force on Prison Overcrowding, 1983; mem. Trial Ct. Study Commn., 1987-88. Chmn. lay bd. Riverside Baptist Ch., Jacksonville, 1982; chmn. deacons First Bapt. Ch., Tallahassee, 1988—; trustee Jacksonville Wolfson Children's Hosp., 1973-83. Recipient Carroll award for Outstanding Mem. Judiciary Jacksonville Jr. C. of C., 1980, Disting. Svc. award Fla. Council on Crime and Delinquency, 1981; named Outstanding Judge in Duval County, Jacksonville Bar Assn. Young Lawyers Sect., 1981. Mem. Phi Alpha Delta (pres. chpt. 1962-63), Am. Inns of Ct. (master of bench), Delta Tau Delta (pres. chpt. 1959-60). Office: US Dist Ct 414 US Courthouse 311 W Monroe St Jacksonville FL 32202-4242

**NIMS, ARTHUR LEE, III,** federal judge; b. Oklahoma City, Jan. 3, 1923; s. Arthur Lee and Edwina (Peckham) N.; m. Nancy Chloe Keyes, July 28, 1950; children: Chloe, Lucy. B.A., Williams Coll., 1945; LL.B., U. Ga., 1949; LL.M. in Taxation, NYU, 1954. Bar: Ga. 1949, N.J. 1955. Practice law Macon, Ga., 1949-51; spl. atty. Office Chief Counsel, IRS, N.Y.C. and Washington, 1951-55; assoc. McCarter & English, Newark, 1955-61; ptnr. McCarter & English, 1961-79; judge U.S. Tax Ct., Washington, 1979-88, chief judge, 1988-92. Mem. standing com. Episcopal Diocese of Newark, 1971-75; pres. Colonial Symphony Soc., Madison, N.J., 1975-78. Served to lt. (j.g.) USNR, 1943-46. Recipient Kellogg award Williams Coll., 1990, Career Achievement award The Tax Soc. NYU, 1990. Fellow Am. Coll. Tax Counsel; mem. ABA (sec. sect. taxation 1977-79), N.J. Bar Assn. (chmn. sect. taxation 1969-71, Am. Law Inst., J. Edgar Murdock Am. Inn of Ct. (pres. 1988-92). Office: US Tax Ct 400 2nd St NW Washington DC 20217-0002

**NIRO, CHERYL IPPOLITO,** lawyer; b. Feb. 19, 1950; d. Samuel James and Nancy (Canezaro) Ippolito; m. William Luciano Niro, July 1, 1979; children: Christopher William, Melissa Leigh. BS with highest honors, U. Ill., 1972; JD, No. Ill. U., 1980. Bar: Ill. 1981, U.S. Dist. Ct. (no. dist.) Ill. 1981; cert. negotiator, mediator, facilitator. Dir. Gifted Program/Learning Resource Ctr. Sch. Dist. 45, Villa Park, Ill., 1973-79; assoc. Pope Ballard Sheppard & Fowle, Chgo., 1980-81; ptnr. Partridge and Niro PC; now ptnr. Quinlan & Crisham, Chgo.; spl. counsel to atty. gen. Office of Ill. Atty. Gen.; cons. Ill. Office Edn., 1975; conflict resolution program devel. U.S. Atty. Gen.; pres. Assocs. in Dispute Resolution, Inc.; exec. dir. Com. to Commemorate U.S. Constitution in Ill., 1985-86; coord. Forum on First Amendment, 1986; creator Bicentennial Law Sch. Program; tchg. asst. program instrn. lawyers mediation and negotiation workshops, guest lectr. Harvard U.; mem. appt. panel U.S. Ct. Appeals (7th cir.). Co-editor: Apple Pie, 1975. Mem. Oak Park Women's Connection, 1981—; U. Ill. Spkrs. Bur.; bd. dirs. U. Chgo. Lying-In Hosp., 1982—; chmn. Task Force on Children; co-chair Ill. Conclave on Legal Edn. Ill. State scholar, 1968-72. Mem. ABA, NEA, ATLA, Ill. Trial La Wyers Assn., Ill. Bar Assn. (standing com. legal-related edn. for pub., mem. assembly 1993, bd. govs. 1994-97, treas. 1995-96, 2d v.p. 1997-98, pres. 1999—), Chgo. Bar Assn., DuPage County Bar Assn., Mortar Bd., Phi Kappa Phi, Alpha Lambda Delta, Delta Gamma. Home: 633 N East Ave Oak Park IL 60302-1715 Office: Quinlan & Crisham 30 N LaSalle St Chicago IL 60602*

**NISHI, JIN,** lawyer; b. Torrance, Calif., Mar. 28, 1965; s. Katsuhisa and Kikuko Nishi. BA, UCLA, 1987; JD, U. San Francisco, 1992. Bar: Calif. 1992, Hawaii 1994, U.S. Dist. Ct. (cen. dist.) Calif. 1993, U.S. Dist. Ct. (no. dist.) Calif. 1997. Pvt. practice Gardena, Calif., 1992-93; assoc. Liddi & Rose, Long Beach, Calif., 1993-96; assoc. Erickson Arbuthnot Kilduff Day & Lindstrom, Oakland, Calif., 1996—. Mem. Japanese Bar Assn. (bd. govs. 1993-96). Professional liability, General civil litigation, Insurance. Office: Ericksen Arbuthnot Kilduff Day & Lindstrom 530 Water St # 720 Oakland CA 94607-3746

**NISNEWITZ, DAVID ZALMAN,** judge; b. Bklyn., Sept. 20, 1941; s. Samuel Elias and Lillian Bernice Nisnewitz; m. Judith Poliakoff (div.); m. Carole Ann Gitter, Aug. 17, 1974; children: Michael Louis, Ruth Jean. BA, NYU, 1963, LLM, 1974; JD, Bklyn. Law Sch., 1965. Bar: N.Y., Fla., U.S. Dist. Ct. (ea. dist.) N.Y., U.S. Ct. Appeals (2d cir.), U.S. Supreme Ct. Staff atty. Legal Aid Soc., N.Y.C., 1967-70; litigation atty. Port Authority of N.Y. and N.J., N.Y.C., 1970-71; legal aid soc. and agys. atty. Narcotics Bur./ Queens County Legal Aid Soc., N.Y.C., 1972-79; U.S. adminstrv. law judge U.S. Govt., N.Y.C., 1979—. Contbr. articles to profl. jours. Mem. Kings County Criminal Bar Assn. Democrat. Jewish. Avocations: reading, music, dogs. Office: Office Hearings and Appeals 59-07 175th Pl Fresh Meadows NY 11365

**NISSEN, WILLIAM JOHN,** lawyer; b. Chgo., July 28, 1947; s. William Gordon Jr. and Ruth Carolyn (Banas) N.; m. Patricia Jane Press, Jan. 16, 1971; children: Meredith Warner, Edward William. BA, Northwestern U., 1969; JD magna cum laude, Harvard U., 1976. Bar: Ill. 1976, U.S. Dist. Ct. (no. dist.) Ill. 1976, U.S. Ct. Appeals (7th cir.) 1981. Assoc. Sidley & Austin, Chgo., 1976-83, ptnr., 1983—; gen. counsel Heinold Commodities, Inc., Chgo., 1982-84. Editor Harvard U. Internat. Law Jour., 1974-76. Served to lt. USN, 1969-73. Mem. ABA (co-chmn. futures regulation subcom. on pvt. litig. 1996-98), Chgo. Bar Assn. (chmn. futures regulation com. 1985-86), Am. Legion (comdr. union league post 758 1994-95), Union League Club Chgo. (dir. 1999—). Commodities. Home: 348 Foss Ct Lake Bluff IL 60044-2753 Office: Sidley & Austin 1 First Natl Plz Chicago IL 60603-2003

**NISSENBAUM, DAVID,** lawyer; b. N.Y.C., Sept. 5, 1968. BA in History, SUNY, Albany, 1990; JD, Bklyn. Law Sch., 1993. Bar: N.Y. 1994, N.J. 1996. Legal intern to Senate Daniel P. Moynihan N.Y.C., 1991-92; legal intern N.Y. State Banking Dept., N.Y.C., 1992-93; legal cons. Philip K. Howard, N.Y.C., 1993-94; assoc., Ralph C. Menapace Jr. fellow in urban land use Mcpl. Art Soc. N.Y., Inc., N.Y.C., 1994-96; assoc. Richards & O'Neil LLP, N.Y.C., 1996-98, Schulte Roth & Zabel LLP, N.Y.C., 1998—. Author: (with Connie M. Friesen) Foreign Banks, Debanking & The Growing Use of Alternative Forms, Review of Banking & Financial Services, 1995; contbr. articles to profl. jours. Co-chair, bd. dirs. Bkyn. Pub. Interest Law Found., 1991-92. Edward G. Sparer fellow in pub. interest law, Sparer Found., 1992. Mem. ABA, N.Y. State Bar Assn. (bus. coms. 1990—), Assn. of Bar of City of N.Y. (banking law com.), Nat. Trust for Hist. Preservation. Avocations: urban history, golf, tennis, fishing, music.E-mail: david.nissenbaum@srz.com. Banking, Finance, General corporate. Office: Schulte Roth & Zabel LLP 900 Third Ave New York NY 10022

**NITZE, WILLIAM ALBERT,** government official, lawyer; b. N.Y.C., Sept. 27, 1942; s. Paul Henry and Phyllis (Pratt) N.; m. Ann Kendall Richards, June 5, 1971; children: Paul Kendall, Charles Richards. BA, Harvard U., 1964, JD, 1969; BA, Oxford U., 1966. Bar: N.Y. 1970, U.S. Supreme Ct. 1987. Assoc. Sullivan and Cromwell, N.Y.C., 1970-72; v.p. London Arts, Inc., N.Y.C., 1972-73; counsel Mobil South, Inc., N.Y.C., 1974-76; gen. counsel Mobil Oil Japan, Tokyo, 1976-80; asst. gen. counsel exploration and producing divsn. Mobil Oil Corp., N.Y.C., 1980-87; dep asst. sec. for environment, health and natural resources U.S. Dept. State, Washington, 1987-90; pres. Alliance to Save Energy, Washington, 1990-94; asst. adminstr. for internat. activities U.S. EPA, Washington, 1994—; mem. adv. com. Sch. Advanced Internat. Studies, Washington, 1982-95, professorial lectr., 1993-94; vis. scholar Environ. Law Inst., Washington, 1990; dir. Charles A. Lindbergh Fund, Mpls., 1990-94, Nat. Symphony Orch. Assn., Washington, 1990—. Trustee Aspen Inst., Queenstown, Md., 1988—, Krasnow Inst., Fairfax, Va., 1996—. Mem. Assn. of Bar of City of N.Y., Coun. on Fgn. Rels., Met. Club, Links Club. Republican. Episcopalian. Avocations: running, piano, collecting art. Home: 1537 28th St NW Washington DC 20007-3059 Office: EPA 401 M St SW # 2610R Washington DC 20460-0002

**NIVICA, GJON NELSON, JR.,** lawyer; b. Boston, June 21, 1964; s. Gjon Nelson Sr. and Lynne Rose Nivica; m. Erica Kristin Schlegel. BS, Fla. State U., 1986; JD magna cum laude, Boston U., 1989. Bar: Calif. 1989. Assoc. Gibson Dunn & Crutcher, L.A., 1989-94; sr. counsel AlliedSignal Aerospace, Torrance, Calif., 1994-96; v.p., gen. counsel AlliedSignal Engines, Phoenix, 1996—; bd. dirs. AlliedSignal Techs. Inc., Phoenix. Mem. Defenders of Wildlife, Ctr. for Marine Conservation, Greater Phoenix C. of C. (bd. dirs. 1998). Christian. General corporate. Office: AlliedSignal Engines 111 S 34th St # Ms301229 Phoenix AZ 85034-2802

**NIX, H.E., JR. (CHIP NIX),** lawyer; b. July 26, 1948; s. H.E. and Hazel (Williams) N.; m. Michelle Rundell; children: Trey, Davis. AB in English Lit., Auburn U., 1970; JD, U. Ala., Tuscaloosa, 1973. Law clk. U.S. Dist. Ct., Montgomery, Ala., 1974; assoc. atty. Miller & Hoffman, Montgomery, 1975-76; assoc. atty. Hill, Hill, Carter, Montgomery, 1977-80, ptnr., 1980-89; pres., founder Nix, Holtsford & Vercelli, Montgomery, 1989—. Bd. dirs. YMCA Youth Legislature, Montgomery, 1980—, Fellowship of Christian Athletes, Montgomery, 1996—, Bapt. Healthcare Found., Montgomery, 1989-93. Mem. Montgomery County Bar Assn. (bd. dirs. 1988), Trial Lawyers Am., Internat. Assn. Def. Counsel, Def. Rsch. inst., Ala. Def. Lawyers Assn. (pres. 1990-91), Phi Eta Sigma. Republican. Avocations: song writing, golf. General civil litigation. Home: 3755 Everest Dr Montgomery AL 36106-3336 Office: 300A Water St Montgomery AL 36104-2558

**NIX, ROBERT ROYAL, II,** lawyer; b. Detroit, Mar. 27, 1947; s. Robert R. and Betty Virginia (Karicofe) N.; m. Suzanne Martha Turner, July 11, 1970; children: Christian Michael, Heather Michele. BS, Ea. Mich. U., 1968; JD cum laude, Wayne State U., 1971. Bar: Mich. 1971, U.S. Dist. Ct. (ea. dist.) Mich. 1971, U.S. Ct. Appeals (6th cir.) 1976. Rsch. atty. Mich. Ct. Appeals, Lansing, 1971-72; law clk. to Hon. Charles L. Levin Mich. Ct. Appeals, 1971; law clk. to Hon. S. Jerome Bronson Mich. Ct. Appeals, Detroit, 1972-73; ptnr. Kerr, Russell and Weber, Detroit, 1973—; lectr. in field. Contrb. articles to Michigan Real Property Law Review. Mem. Mich. Land Title Stds. Com., 1990—. Fellow Mich. State Bar Found.; mem. ABA (partnership com. real property, probate and trust law sect., mortgages and secured financing com. corp., banking and bus. law sect., forum constrn. industry sect.), State Bar Mich. (chmn. real property law sect. 1994-95, coun. vice-chmn. 1992-93, chmn. com. on mortgage related financing devices, 1984-87, mem. sect., 1973—, partnership com. 1982—), Oakland County Bar Assn., Detroit Bar Assn., Am. Coll. Real Estate Lawyers, Am. Coll. Mortgage Attys. Republican. Methodist. E-mail: http://www.rrn@krwplc.com. Real property, Contracts commercial, General civil litigation. Office: Kerr Russell and Weber Detroit Ctr Ste 2500 Detroit MI 48226

**NIXON, DAVID L.,** lawyer; b. Concord, Mass., Mar. 19, 1932; s. Louis Gerard and Patricia (Williams) N.; children: Leslie C., Melanie D., Wendy W.N. Branch, Amy W., David Lee Jr., Louis Gerard II. BA cum laude, Wesleyan U., Middletown, Conn., 1953; LLB, U. Mich., 1958. Bar: N.H. 1958, U.S. Dist. Ct. N.H. 1959, U.S. Ct. Appeals (1st cir.) 1961, U.S. Supreme Ct. 1968. Assoc. McLane Carleton Graf Greene & Brown, Manchester, N.H., 1958-61; ptnr. King & Nixon, Manchester, 1961-69, Nixon, Christy & Tessier, Manchester, 1969-76; dir. Brown & Nixon P.A., Manchester, 1976-88; pres. Nixon, Hall & Hess P.A., Manchester, 1988-93, of counsel, 1993-94; pres., dir. Nixon, Raiche, Manning & Casinghino P.A., 1994—; mem. N.H. Supreme Ct. Accreditation Commn., 1985—, N.H. Jud. Coun., 1980-83, 93—. Rep. N.H. Legis., Concord, 1969-74, senate pres., 1973-74; moderator Town of New Boston, N.H., 1964-92. With U.S. Army, 1953-55. Named Trial Lawyer of the Decade, N.H. Trial Lawyers Assn., 1988. Mem. ABA (ho. of dels. 1970-72), Manchester Bar Assn. (pres. 1973-74, named Manchester Lawyer of the Yr. 1995), N.H. Bar Assn. (pres. 1980-81, Disting. Svc. award 1982, award for Professionalism 1993), New Eng. Bar Assn. (pres. 1970-72), Internat. Soc. Barristers (pres. 1996-97), Inner Circle Advs. Personal injury, General civil litigation, General practice. Home: 51 River Front Dr Manchester NH 03102-3243 Office: Nixon Raiche Manning & Casinghino PA 77 Central St Manchester NH 03101-2423

**NIXON, JEREMIAH W. (JAY NIXON),** state attorney general; b. DeSoto, Mo., Feb. 13, 1956; s. Jeremiah and Betty (Lea) N.; m. Georganne Nixon; children: Jeremiah, Will. BS in Polit. Sci., U. Mo., 1978, JD, 1981. Ptnr. Nixon, Nixon, Breeze & Roberts, Jefferson County, Mo., 1981-86; mem. Mo. State Senate from Dist 22, 1986-93; atty. gen. State of Mo., 1993—; chmn. select com. ins. reform.; created video internat. devel. and edn. opportunity program. Honoree, Conservation Fedn. Mo., 1992; named Outstanding Young Missourian, Mo. Jaycees, 1994, Outstanding Young Lawyer, Barrister's Mag., 1993. Mem. Nat. Assn. Attys. Gen. (chair criminal law com., mem. antitrust, consumer protection and environ. and energy coms., chair victim rights working group), Midwest Assn. Attys. Gen. (chmn.), Mo. Assn. Trial Attys. Democrat. Methodist. Office: Atty Gen Office PO Box 899 Jefferson City MO 65102-0899*

**NIXON, JOHN TRICE,** judge; b. New Orleans, La., Jan. 9, 1933; s. H. C. and Anne (Trice) N.; m. Betty Chiles, Aug. 5, 1960 (div. Nov. 1985); children: Mignon Elizabeth, Anne Trice. A.B. cum laude, Harvard Coll., 1955; LL.B., Vanderbilt U., 1960. Bar: Ala. bar 1960, Tenn. bar 1972. Individual practice law Anniston, Ala., 1960-62; city atty. Anniston, 1962-64; trial atty. Civil Rights Div., Dept. Justice, Washington, 1964-69; staff atty., comptroller of Treasury State of Tenn., 1971-76; pvt. practice law Nashville, 1976-77; cir. judge, 1977-78, gen. sessions judge, 1978-80; judge U.S. Dist. Ct. (mid. dist.) Tenn., Nashville, 1980—, now chief judge, 1980—. Served with U.S. Army, 1958. Democrat. Methodist. Clubs: D.U. (Cambridge); Harvard-Radcliffe (Nashville). Office: US Dist Ct 825 US Courthouse Nashville TN 37203

**NIXON, SCOTT SHERMAN,** lawyer; b. Grosse Pointe, Mich., Feb. 7, 1959; s. Floyd Sherman and Marjorie Jane (Quermann) N.; m. Cathryn Lynn Starnes, Aug. 27, 1983; children: Jeffry Sherman, Kelsy Jane, James Robert. BABA, Mich. State U., 1981; JD, U. Denver, 1984. Bar: Colo. 1984, U.S. Dist. Ct. Colo. 1984, U.S. Ct. Appeals (10th cir.) 1984. Assoc. Pryor, Carney & Johnson, P.C., Englewood, Colo., 1984-89, shareholder, 1990-95; pres., shareholder Pryor, Johnson, Montoya, Carney & Karr, P.C., Englewood, 1995—. Officer, bd. dirs. Luth. Brotherhood Br. 8856, Denver, 1993—, Mark K. Ulmer Meml. Native Am. Scholarship Found., Denver, 1994—; officer, mem. coun. Bethan Luth Ch., Englewood, 1993-95. Mem. ABA, Colo. Bar Assn., Denver Bar Assn., Colo. Def. Lawyers Assn. Avocations: music performance, physical fitness, carpentry/construction. Professional liability, Personal injury, Product liability. Home: 6984 S Pontiac Ct Englewood CO 80112-1127 Office: Pryor Johnson Montoya Carney & Karr PC Ste 1313 6400 S Fiddlers Green Cir Englewood CO 80111-4939

**NIZETICH, ANTHONY V.,** lawyer, consultant; b. San Pedro, Feb. 1, 1923; s. Tom B. Nizetich and Zorka Tomas; m. Josephine M. Vitalich, July 19, 1948; children: Lucille, Josetta, Antionette, Tom. AB, U. So. Calif., 1947; LLB, Southwestern Law Sch., 1951. Bar: 1951. Pvt. practice, 1952-60; gen. mgr. legal coun. San Pedro (Calif.) Fisherman's Coop. Assn., 1960-64; dir. pub. affairs Star-Kist Foods, Inc., Terminal Island, Calif., 1964-71, asst. to pres., dir. pub. affairs, 1975-83, cons. pub. affairs, 1983-85; dir. pub. affairs H.J. Heinz Co., Washington, 1971-75; owner Nizetich's Restaurant, San Pedro, 1983-93; internat. fishery cons. San Pedro, 1993—; advisor on internat. fisheries U.S. Dept. of State, 1960-83; mem. Internat. Com. on Atlantic Tunas, 1960-83; mem. Inter-Am. Tropical Tuna Commn., 1960-83. Lt. (j.g.) USNR, 1942-46, PTO. Republican. Roman Catholic. Mem. Calif. State Bar. Avocations: golf, walking, hiking. Home: 1615 Dalmatia Dr San Pedro CA 90732-1346 Office: 839 S Beacon St San Pedro CA 90731-3751

**NIZIN, LESLIE S.,** lawyer; b. N.Y.C., Nov. 21, 1939; s. Albert and Bertha D. Nizin; m. Gail L. Gordon. BA, Queens Coll., 1961; LLB, Bklyn. Law Sch., 1964, JD, 1967. Bar: N.Y. 1964. Atty. Sturim & Nizin, Kew Gardens, N.Y., 1969—. Pres. sch. bd. Half Hollow Hills, Huntington, N.Y., 1977-92. Mem. Queens County Bar Assn. (bd. mgrs., v.p., pres. elect). Criminal, Family and matrimonial. Office: 12510 Queens Blvd Kew Gardens NY 11415-1519

**NOACK, HAROLD QUINCY, JR.,** lawyer; b. San Francisco, May 1, 1931; m. Ann Crosby, Nov. 1952 (div. Sept. 1974); children: Stephen Tracy, Peter Quincy, Andrew Crosby; m. Susan K. Sherwood, Dec. 1975 (div. Jan. 1983); m. Penny Jo Orth, Apr. 2, 1988 (div. May 1989); m. Linda F. Killeen, Mar. 15, 1994 (div. May 1996). BA, U. Calif., Berkeley, 1953; LLB, U. Calif., San Francisco, 1959. Bar: Calif. 1960, Idaho 1969, U.S. Dist. Ct. Idaho 1969. Assoc. Fernoff & Wolfe, Oakland, Calif., 1959-64, Cooley, Crowley, Gaither, Godward, Castro & Huddleson, San Francisco, 1964-65; pvt. practice Oakland, 1965-66; ptnr. Oliphant, Hopper, Stribling & Noack, Oakland, 1966-69; assoc. Eberle, Berlin, Kading & Turnbow, Boise, Idaho, 1969-70; pvt. practice Boise, 1970-83, 85-88; assoc. Anthony Parks, Boise, 1970-75; ptnr. Noack & Korn, Boise, 1970-75, Noack & Hawley, Boise, 1983-85, Lyons & Noack, Boise, 1988-89; pvt. practice law Boise, 1989—. Contbr. articles to profl. jours. Bd. dirs., pres. Idaho Planned Parenthood, Boise, 1970-72; bd. dirs. Idaho Heart Assn., Boise, 1975. 2d lt. U.S. Army, 1954-55. Mem. ABA, Calif. Bar Assn., Idaho Bar Assn. (fee grievance com. 1986—), Boise Bar Assn., Rotary (bd. dirs. Boise club 1980). Avocations: running, walking, fishing, cooking. Bankruptcy, General civil litigation, General practice. Home: PO Box 875 1915 N 24th St Boise ID 83702-0204 Office: 733 N 7th St Boise ID 83702-5500

**NOAH, DOUGLAS TRUE,** lawyer; b. Clearwater, Fla., May 20, 1962; s. Raymond L. and Julia J. (True) N.; m. Seeta M. Noah, Oct. 18, 1986; 1 child, Raymond Eliot. BS, Fla. So. Coll., 1984; JD, Stetson U., 1990. Bar: Fla. 1990, U.S. Dist. Ct. (mid. dist.) Fla., U.S. Ct. Appeals (11th cir.). Lawyer Dempsey & Assocs., P.A., Winter Park, Fla., 1990-91, Dean, Ringers, Morgan & Lawton, P.A., Orlando, Fla., 1991—. Editorial bd. Stetson Law Rev.; contbr. articles to profl. jours. Bd. dirs. Ctr. for Ind. Living in Ctrl. Fla., Inc. Recipient Kraft W. Eidman award Am. Coll. Trial Lawyers, 1990, Victor O. Wehle award in Trial Practice. Mem. ABA, Assn. Trial Lawyers Am., Fla. Def. Lawyers Assn., Orange County Bar Assn., Nat. Order Barristers. State civil litigation, Federal civil litigation, Civil rights. Office: Dean Ringers Morgan & Lawton PA 200 E Robinson St Ste 1020 Orlando FL 32801-1979

**NOAH, PAUL RANDALL,** lawyer; b. Hastings, Mich., Oct. 24, 1961; s. Melvin Laverne and Ellen Kay (Catchick) N.; m. Chen Yin Chow, Aug. 6, 1988; children: Sean, Kelly. BA, Mich. State U., 1983; JD, U. Mich., 1986. Assoc. Catchick & Dodge, Grand Rapids, Mich., 1986-88, Knapp & Vernon, Palo Alto, Calif., 1988-89, Bledsoe, Cathcart, Leahy, Star, San Francisco, 1989-90, Wilson, Sher, Marshall & Peterson, Oakland, Calif., 1990-91; pvt. practice Walnut Creek, Calif., 1991-92; ptnr. Noah & Nerland, Walnut Creek, 1992-95; pvt. practice Orinda, Calif., 1996—. Personal injury, Product liability. Office: 8 Camino Encinas Ste 220 Orinda CA 94563-3350

**NOBLE, FRANK WESLEY, JR.,** lawyer; b. Martins Ferry, Ohio, Nov. 12, 1968; s. Frank Wesley and Ruth Arlene Noble; m. Lisa Ann Dykeman, May 9, 1998. BA in Econs., Bethany (W.Va.) Coll., 1991; JD, Ohio No. U., 1995. Bar: Ohio 1995. Atty. Fisher, Brown, Scarpone, Steubenville, Ohio, 1995-98, Scarpone, LaRue & Assocs., Steubenville, 1998—; atty. Jefferson County Childrens Svcs., Steubenville, 1997—; prosecutor City of Steubenville, 1999—; solicitor Village of Yorkville, 1997—, Village of Tiltonsville, 1999—, Village of Adena, 1999—. Mem. ABA, Ohio State Bar Assn., Jefferson County Bar Assn., Kiwanis Club (pub. rels. com. 1996—). Avocations: reading, sports. Criminal, Personal injury, Probate. Home: 1851 Oregon Ave Steubenville OH 43952 Office: Scarpone LaRue & Assocs 2021 Sunset Blvd Steubenville OH 43952

**NOBLE, HEATHER,** lawyer; b. Princeton, N.J., Dec. 19, 1954; d. Stedman Bennett N.; m. Greg Johnson, Sept. 14, 1992; children: Finn Noble Johnson, Breanna Noble Johnson. BA, U. Calif., Berkeley, 1976; JD, Harvard U., 1982. Bar: Alaska, 1982, U.S. Dist. Ct. Alaska, 1982, U.S. Ct. Appeals (9th cir.), 1983, Idaho, 1987, U.S. Dist. Ct. Idaho, 1987, Wyo., 1991, U.S. Dist. Ct. Wyo., 1992, U.S. Ct. Appeals (10th cir.), 1997, U.S. Supreme Ct., 1997. Staff atty. Alaska Legal Svcs., Anchorage/Barrow/Kotzebue, 1982-86, Idaho Legal Aid, Lewiston, 1987-89; assoc. Spence Moriarty & Schuster, Jackson, Wyo., 1990-97; pvt. practice Jackson, 1997-98. Mem. ABA. Appellate, Personal injury, Federal civil litigation. Office: PO Box 8645 Jackson WY 83002-8645

**NOBLE, LAWRENCE MARK,** federal government agency lawyer; b. N.Y.C., Mar. 30, 1952; s. Hyman S. and Jeanette (Lapides) N.; m. Patricia Fay Bak, Mar. 28, 1981; children: Jonathan, David. BA, Syracuse U., 1973; JD, George Washington U., 1976; Program for Sr. Mgrs. in Govt., John F. Kennedy Sch. Govt., Boston, 1991. Bar: D.C. 1976, U.S. Dist. Ct. 1977, U.S. Ct. Appeals (D.C. cir.) 1977, U.S. Supreme Ct. 1980, U.S. Ct. Appeals (4th cir.) 1989, U.S. Ct. Appeals (5th cir.), 1992. Atty. Aviation Consumer Action Project, Washington, 1976-77; litigation atty. Fed. Election Commn., Washington, 1977-79, asst. gen. counsel for litigation, 1979-83, dep. gen. counsel, 1983-87, gen. counsel, 1987—; mem. ABA election law commn., 1988-93; mem. administrv. conf. U.S., Washington, 1987-96. Contbr. articles to profl. jours.; lectr., spkr. in field. Mem. Coun. on Govt. Ethics Laws (pres. 1997-98), D.C. Bar Assn. Avocations: computer graphics, photography, writing. Home: 9438 Sunnyfield Ct Potomac MD 20854-2090 Office: Fed Election Commn 999 E St NW Washington DC 20463-0002

**NOBLE, RICHARD LLOYD,** lawyer; b. Oklahoma City, Oct. 11, 1939; s. Samuel Lloyd and Eloise Joyce (Millard) N. AB with distinction, Stanford, 1961, LLB, 1964. Bar: Calif. 1964. Assoc. firm Cooper, White & Cooper, San Francisco, 1965-67; assoc., ptnr. firm Voegelin, Barton, Harris & Callister, Los Angeles, 1967-70; ptnr. Noble & Campbell, Los Angeles, San Francisco, 1970—; dir. Langdale Corp., L.A., Gt. Pacific Fin. Co., Sacramento; lectr. Tax Inst. U. So. Calif., 1970; mem. bd. law and bus. program Stanford Law Sch. Contbr. articles to legal jours. Bd. govs. St. Thomas Aquinas Coll. Recipient Hilmer Dehlman Jr. award Stanford Law Sch., 1962; Benjamin Harrison fellow Stanford U., 1967. Mem. ABA, State Bar Calif., L.A. Bar Assn., San Francisco Bar Assn., Commercial Club (San Francisco), Petroleum Club (L.A.), Capitol Hill Club (Washington), Pi Sigma Alpha. Republican. Federal civil litigation, General corporate, Securities. Home: PO Box 67605 Los Angeles CA 90067-0605

**NOBLES, ETHAN CHRISTOPHER,** lawyer; b. Monticello, Ark., June 16, 1969; s. Howard A. and Brenda H. Nobles; m. Lori A. Spencer, June 18, 1994 (div. June 1998). BA, Hendrik Coll., 1991; JD, U. Ark., 1994. Bar: Ark. 1995. Intern reporter Ark. Dem., Little Rock, 1989, 90; news editor, reporter Benton County Daily Record, Bentonville, Ark., 1993-95; ptnr. Nobles & Poore, Fayetteville, Ark., 1995—. Republican. Baptist. Avocations: guitar, Internet, reading. E-mail: ecnobles@arkansas.net. Fax: 501-442-7046. Personal injury, Bankruptcy, Family and matrimonial. Office: Nobles & Poore PO Box 1948 Fayetteville AR 72702-1948

**NOCAS, ANDREW JAMES,** lawyer; b. Los Angeles, Feb. 2, 1941; s. John Richard and Muriel Phyliss (Harvey) N.; 1 child, Scott Andrew. BS, Stanford U., 1962, JD, 1964. Bar: Calif. 1965. Assoc. Thelen, Marrin, Johnson & Bridges, L.A., 1964-71, ptnr., 1972-91; pvt. practice L.A., 1992—; del. Calif. Bar Conv., 1972-92. Served to capt. JAGC, USAR. Fellow Am. Bar Found.; mem. Los Angeles County Bar Assn. (chmn. sect. law office mgmt. 1980-82, chair errors and ommissions com. 1987-88, chair litigation sect. 1988-89), ABA (chmn. arbitration com. 1981), Am. Bd. Trial Advocates, Los Angeles County Bar Found. (trustee 1992—). State civil litigation, Federal civil litigation. Office: 500 S Grand Ave Ste 1200 Los Angeles CA 90071-2624

**NOCERA, JOHN ANTHONY,** lawyer; b. Bklyn., June 15, 1952; s. Anthony Carmine and Louise Margaret (Retta) N.; m. Debralee Marilyn Miller, Sept. 25, 1987. BA, Fordham U., 1974; JD, St. John's U., N.Y.C., 1978. Bar: N.Y. 1979, U.S. Dist. Ct. (so. and ea. dists.) N.Y. 1980, N.J. 1985, U.S. Dist. Ct. N.J. 1985, Pa. 1989, U.S. Ct. Appeals (2nd cir.) 1989. Assoc. Hendler and Murray, N.Y.C., 1978-82, ptnr., 1982-85; ptnr. Rosner and Nocera, N.Y.C., 1985—. Sr. mem. St. John's Law Rev., 1976-77; contbr. articles to profl. jours. V.p. Parkview Condominium Assn., 1982. St. Thomas Moore scholar, 1976-78. Mem. ABA, N.Y. Bar Assn. Avocations: numismatics, skiing. General civil litigation, Banking, Insurance. Office: Rosner and Nocera 90 Washington St New York NY 10006-2214

**NODDINGS, SARAH ELLEN,** lawyer; b. Matawan, N.J.; d. William Clayton and Sarah Stephenson (Cox) Noddings; children: Christopher, Aaron. BA in Math., Rutgers U., New Brunswick, N.J., 1965, MSW, 1968; JD cum laude, Seton Hall U., Newark, 1975; postgrad., UCLA, 1979. Bar: Calif. 1976, Nev. 1976, N.J. 1975, U.S. Dist. Ct. (ctrl. dist.) Calif. 1976, U.S. Dist. Ct. N.J. 1975. Social worker Carteret (N.J.) Bd. Edn., 1970-75; law clk. Hon. Howard W. Babcock, 8th Jud. Dist. Ct., Las Vegas, Nev., 1975-76; assoc. O'Melveny & Myers, L.A., 1976-78; atty. Internat. Creative Mgmt., Beverly Hills, Calif., 1978-81, Russell & Glickman, Century City, Calif., 1981-83; atty. Lorimar Prodns., Culver City and Burbank, Calif., 1983-87, v.p., 1987-93; atty. Warner Bros. TV, Burbank, Calif., 1993—, v.p., 1993—, sr. atty., 1999—. Dir. county youth program, rsch. analyst Sonoma County People for Econ. Opportunity, Santa Rosa, Calif., 1968-69; VISTA vol. Kings County Cmty. Action Orgn., Hanford, Calif., 1965-66; officer, PTA bd. Casimir Mid. Sch. and Arlington Elem. Sch. Mem. Acad. TV Arts and Scis. (nat. awards com. 1994—), L.A. Copyright Soc. (trustee 1990-91), Women in Film, L.A. County Bar Assn. (intellectual property sect.), Women Entertainment Lawyers, Media Dist. Intellectual Propr. Bar Assn. (bd. dirs. 1999—). Avocations: travel, tennis, skiing, bicycling, swimming. Entertainment, Intellectual property, General corporate. Office: Warner Bros TV 300 Television Plz Burbank CA 91505-1372

**NOE, JAMES ALVA,** retired judge; b. Billings, Mont., May 25, 1932; s. James Alva Sr. and Laura Madlen (Parmenter) N.; m. Patricia Arlene Caudill, Aug. 4, 1956; children: Kendra Sue, Jeffrey James, Bradley John, Kirkwood Merle. BA in Polit. Sci., U. Wash., 1954, LLB, 1957; LittD hon., Christian Theol. Sem., 1986. Bar: Wash. 1958, U.S. Dist. Ct. (we. dist.) Wash. 1958, U.S. Ct. Appeals (9th cir.) 1959. Dep. prosecuting atty. King County, Seattle, 1958-61; trial lawyer Williams, Kastner & Gibbs, Seattle, 1961-67; judge Seattle Mcpl. Ct., 1967-71, King County Superior Ct., 1971-96; ret., 1996. Moderator Christian Ch. (Disciples of Christ) in the U.S. and Can., 1977-79. Fellow Am. Bar Found.; mem. ABA (ho. of dels. 1976-78, 82-87, 91-96, bd. govs. 1991-94, chmn. jud. divsn. 1988-89, nat. conf. state trial judges 1981-82), Wash. State Superior Ct. Judges Assn. (pres. 1984-85), Nat. Jud. Coll. (trustee 1988-91, 95—, chair 1999—). Home: 8250 SE 61st St Mercer Island WA 98040-4902

**NOE, RANDOLPH,** lawyer; b. Indpls., Nov. 2, 1939; s. John H. and Bernice (Baker) Reiley; m. Anne Will, Mar. 2, 1968 (div.); children: J.H. Reiley, Anne Will, Randolph, Jonathan Baker. Student Franklin Coll. 1957-60; BS, Ind. State U., 1964; JD, Ind. U., 1967. Bar: Ind. 1968, Ky. 1970. Trust officer Citizens Fidelity Bank & Trust Co., Louisville, 1969-71; sole practice, Louisville, 1971-84; ptnr. Greenebaum, Treitz, Brown & Marshall, 1984-93; of counsel Tilford, Dobbins, Alexander, Buckaway & Black, 1993—; asst. county atty. Jefferson County, 1979-84. Author: Kentucky Probate Methods, 1976, supplement, 1992; editor: Kentucky Law Summary, 1985—. Fellow Am. Coll. Probate Counsel; mem. ABA, Ind. Bar Assn., Ky. Bar Assn. Democrat. Clubs: Pendennis, Wranglers. Probate, Real property, Estate taxation. Home: 3222 Cross Bill Rd Louisville KY 40213-1208

**NOEL, NICHOLAS, III,** lawyer; b. Pottstown, Pa., June 5, 1952; s. Nicholas Jr. and Elaine (Buckwalter) N.; m. Karen Bean Schomp, Oct. 28, 1978; children: Carol Elaine, Nicholas IV. BA magna cum laude, Lehigh U., 1974; JD, U. Detroit, 1977. Bar: Pa. 1977, U.S. Dist. Ct. (ea. dist.) Pa. 1979, U.S. Ct. Appeals (3rd cir.) 1980, U.S. Supreme Ct. 1986, U.S. Dist. Ct. (mid. dist.) Pa. 1989. Assoc. Hahalis Law Office, Bethlehem, Pa., 1977-84; assoc. Teel, Stettz, Shimer & DiGiacomo, Easton, Pa., 1984-87; ptnr. Teel, Stettz, PC, Easton, 1987—, sr. litigation ptnr., 1989—, v.p., 1998—; adj. prof. Northampton County C.C., Bethlehem, 1990, 97; solicitor Chiefs of Police Assn. of Mid. Ea. Pa., 1977—, Palmer Twp. Zoning Hearing Bd., Easton, 1989—; arbitrator Am. Arbitration Assn., 1986—. Contbr. to several books. Trustee Palmer Twp. Moravian Ch., 1985-97, 99—, pres., 1986-92; mem. Moravian Ch. No. Province Ch. and Soc. Com., 1990—, Palmer Moravian Day Sch. bd., 1991-94, 99—. Named Outstanding Young Man Am., 1974. Fellow Pa. Bar Found.; mem. ABA, Pa. Bar Assn. (civil rights chair 1989-92, vice-chmn. legal edn. com. 1992, profl. stds. com. 1983, ho. of delagates 1998-99), Northampton County Bar Assn. (legal ethics and responsibility com. 1987-94, bd. govs. 1991—, treas. 1995, v.p. 1996, pres.-elect 1997, pres. 1998, past pres. 1999), Clinton Budd Palmer Inn of Ct. Avocations: most athletic events, swimming, hiking. Civil rights, General civil litigation, Professional liability. Home: 2840 Green Pond Rd Easton PA 18045-2504 Office: 400 S Greenwood Ave Ste 300 Easton PA 18045-3776

**NOEL, RANDALL DEANE,** lawyer; b. Memphis, Oct. 19, 1953; s. D.A. and Patricia G. Noel; m. Lissa Johns, May 28, 1977; children: Lauren Elizabeth, Randall Walker. BBA with honors, U. Miss., 1975, JD, 1978. Bar: Miss. 1978, U.S. Dist. Ct. (no. and so. dists.) Miss. 1978, Tenn. 1979, U.S. Dist. Ct. (we., mid. and ea. dists.) Tenn. 1979, U.S. Ct. Appeals (5th and 6th cirs.) 1984, U.S. Supreme Ct. 1986. Assoc. Armstrong, Allen, Braden, Goodman, McBride & Prewitt, Memphis, 1978-85; ptnr. Armstrong, Allen, Prewitt, Gentry, Johnston & Holmes, Memphis, 1985—, mgr. litig. practice group, 1990-94, mgmt. com., 1994-97—. Fin. com. Memphis in May Internat. Festival, 1980-81; pres. Carnival Memphis, 1996; bd. dirs. Christ United Meth. Ch., Memphis, 1984-87, 89-91, chmn. bd. trustees, 1995; mem. Leadership Memphis, 1994-95. Fellow Am. Bar Found., Tenn. Bar Found.; mem. ABA (young lawyers divsn., fellow dir. 1988-90, editor The Affiliate newsletter 1987-88, dir. Affiliate Outreach project 1988—, vice-chmn. Award of Achievement com. 1986, ALI-ABA bd. 1992-97, litig. sect. com. chmn.), Am. Counsel Assn. (pres. 1997), Tenn. Bar Assn. (pres. young lawyers divsn. 1990, pres. litig. sect. 1988, bd. govs. 1989—, pres., 1999, Pres.'s Disting. Svc. award 1988-89), Memphis and Shelby Bar Assn. (mem. jud. recommendations, law week nominations and membership coms.), Miss. Bar Assn., Def. Rsch. Inst., Tenn. Def. Lawyers Assn., Am. Judicature Soc. (bd. dirs. 1992-96). Federal civil litigation, State civil litigation, Consumer commercial. Home: 2938 Tishomingo Ln Memphis TN 38111-2627 Office: Armstrong Allen Prewitt Gentry Johnston & Holmes PLLC 80 Monroe Ave Ste 700 Memphis TN 38103-2467

**NOELKE, HENRY TOLBERT (HAL NOELKE),** lawyer; b. Austin, Tex., Aug. 21, 1970; s. Walter Dietrich and Virginia McKimmon Noelke; m. Claire Robertson Carter, Dec. 23, 1994. BA, U. South at Sewanee, 1992; JD, Tex. Tech U., 1995. Bar: Tex. 1996. Intern Ct. Appeals for 3d Dist., Austin, 1995; ind. legal cons., Austin, 1995-96; assoc. Smith, Rose, Finley, Harp & Price, San Angelo, Tex., 1997—. Mem. Tex. Tech Law Rev. Legal Rsch. bd., 1993-95. Regents scholar Tex. Tech U., 1994-95. Mem. State Bar Tex., Coll. State Bar Tex., Tom Green County Young Lawyers Assn. Avocations: ranching, scuba diving, travel. Real property, Oil, gas, and mineral, Estate planning. Office: Smith Rose Finley Et Al 36 W Beauregard Ave Ste 300 San Angelo TX 76903-5883

**NOELKE, PAUL,** lawyer; b. La Crosse, Wis., Feb. 10, 1915; s. Carl Bernard and Mary Amelia (O'Meara) N.; m. Mary Jo Kamps, May 4, 1943; children: Paul William, Mary Nesius, Ann Witt, Kate Helms. A.B. magna cum laude, Marquette U., 1936, J.D. cum laude, 1938; LL.M., U. Chgo., 1947; D.H.L. (hon.), Mt. Senario Coll., 1976. Bar: Wis. 1938, D.C. 1975, U.S. Dist. Ct. (ea. dist.) Wis. 1938, U.S. Supreme Ct. 1960. Assoc. firm Miller, Mack & Fairchild, 1938-40; asst. prof. law Marquette U., 1940-42; spl. agt. FBI, 1942-45; assoc. Quarles & Brady and predecessor firms, Milw., 1943-52, ptnr., 1952-85, of counsel, 1985—. Trustee emeritus Viterbo Coll., LaCrosse, Wis.; mem. adv. bd. Cardinal Stritch Coll., Milw.; past chmn. Pres.'s Coun. Marquette U.; past pres. Serra Internat., Chgo.; past chmn. Bd. Tax Rev., Village of Shorewood, Wis. Recipient Alumnus of Yr. award Marquette U., 1980; recipient Conf. award NCCJ, 1967. Mem. ABA, Wis. State Bar Assn., Milw. Bar Assn., Am. Judicature Soc., Order Holy Sepulchre, Alpha Sigma Nu. Roman Catholic. Home: 2462 N Prospect Ave Milwaukee WI 53211-4451 Office: 411 E Wisconsin Ave Milwaukee WI 53202-4461

**NOFER, GEORGE HANCOCK,** lawyer; b. Phila., June 14, 1926. B.A., Haverford Coll., 1949; J.D., Yale U., 1952. Bar: Pa. 1953. Pvt. practice Phila., 1953—; ret. ptnr. Schnader, Harrison, Segal & Lewis, Phila., 1961-91, sr. counsel, 1992—. Pres. bd. sch. dirs. Upper Moreland Twp., Pa., 1965-73; trustee Beaver Coll., Glenside, Pa., 1969-76; co-trustee and exec. dir. Oberkotter Found.; bd. dirs. Fox Chase Cancer Ctr., Phila., 1989-94; elder, trustee, deacon Abington (Pa.) Presbyn. Ch.; bd. dirs. Phila. Presbyn. Homes, Inc.; bd. dirs. A.G. Bell Assn. for Deaf, Washington, 1992-98. Fellow Am. Coll. Trust and Estate Counsel (regent 1975—, pres. 1983-84, chmn. Pa. 1973-78), Am. Law Inst., Am. Bar Found.; mem. ABA (standing com. on specialization 1980-86, chmn. 1983-86), Pa. Bar Assn., Phila. Bar Assn., Internat. Acad. Estate and Trust Law, Phi Beta Kappa, Phi Delta Phi. Probate, Estate taxation, Non-profit and tax-exempt organizations. Home: 108 Quail Ln Radnor PA 19087-2729 Office: Schnader Harrison Segal & Lewis 1600 Market St Ste 3600 Philadelphia PA 19103-7240

**NOGEE, JEFFREY LAURENCE,** lawyer; b. Schenectady, N.Y., Oct. 31, 1952; s. Rodney and Shirley Ruth (Mannes) N.; m. Freda Carolyn Wartel, Aug. 31, 1980; children: Rori Caitlen, Amara Sonia, Jaden Gwynn. BA cum laude, Bucknell U., 1974; JD, Boston U., 1977. Bar: N.Y. 1978, U.S. Dist. Ct. (so. and ea. dists.) N.Y. 1978. Assoc. Hale Russell & Gray, N.Y.C., 1977-83; sr. atty. Ebasco Services Inc., N.Y.C., 1984-88, dir. Countertrade unit, 1985-88; sr. ptnr. Fogh & Nogee Assocs., 1988; ptnr. Brauner, Baron, Rosenzweig, Bauman & Klein, N.Y.C., 1988-90; sr. ptnr. Nogee & Wartel, 1990—; pvt. counsellor for internat. bus. firms, 1987—. Prin. bassoonist, sec., bd. dirs. The Band of L.I., 1997—; prin. bassoonist Rockway-Five Towns Symphony Orch., 1998—. Trustee Temple Emanu-el of East Meadow, 1995-99, v.p., 1996-97. Mem. ABA, Am. Arbitration Assn., Assn. of Bar of City of N.Y., Nassau County Bar Assn., Internat. Platform Assn., N.Y. New Media Assn., Phi Beta Kappa, Pi Sigma Alpha. Avocations: fencing, bassoon and saxophone music, racquet sports, hiking, bicycling. General civil litigation, Probate, Private international. Office: 900 Ellison Ave Ste 211 Westbury NY 11590-5114

**NOGLE, JAY ANDREW,** lawyer; b. Columbus, Ohio, May 20, 1963; s. James A. and Janis M. Nogle; m. Gretchen Nogle, Dec. 11, 1992; children: Jay Andrew, James Michael. BS, James Madison U., 1985; JD, U. Miami, 1992. Bar: Fla. 1992. Paralegal Thomson Zeder et al, Miami, Fla., 1986-88; paralegal, computer specialist Finnegan Henderson et al, Washington, 1988, Squire Sanders & Dempsey, Miami, 1988-89; computer cons. Litigation Database Design, Miami, 1989-90; legal computer specialist U. Miami Sch. Law, 1990-92; dir. legal sys. Greenberg Traurig, 1992—. Mem. Miami Yacht Club. Office: Greenberg Traurig 1221 Brickell Ave Miami FL 33131-3224

**NOHRDEN, PATRICK THOMAS,** lawyer; b. Santa Cruz, Calif., Mar. 7, 1956; s. Thomas Allen and Roberta Eugenia (Brydon) N.; m. Debora Ann Heintz, Sept. 19, 1981; children: Steven, Laura, Maranda, Patricia. AS, SUNY, Albany, 1980; BA in English with great distinction, San Jose State U., 1984; JD, U. Akron, 1992. Bar: Nev. 1993, U.S. Dist. Ct. Nev. 1993. Regional dir. CareerPro, Inc., Roseville, Calif., 1984-91; cons. Patrick T. Nohrden & Assocs., Youngstown, Ohio, 1991-93; pvt. practice, Las Vegas, Nev., 1993—; bd. dirs. Profl. Resume Svc., Inc., Las Vegas, Las Vegas Diamondbacks, Inc., Old Nev. Fin., Inc., Las Vegas, Clark County Pro Bono Project, Maui Land Devel. Co., Inc., World Internat. Intelligence Bur., Inc.; adj. prof. C.C. So. Nev. Sgt. U.S. Army, 1975-81. Recipient Spirit of Pro Bono award, Meritorious Svc. award. Mem. ATLA, ABA (family law sect.), Fed. Bar Assn., Nev. Trial Lawyers Assn., State Bar Nev. (family law and bankruptcy sects.), Clark County Bar Assn., Phi Kappa Phi. Republican. Roman Catholic. General civil litigation, Bankruptcy, Family and matrimonial. Office: 608 S 8th St Las Vegas NV 89101-7005

**NOLAN, DAVID BRIAN,** lawyer; b. Washington, Jan. 1, 1951; s. John Joseph and Mary Jane Nolan; m. Cheryl Ann Cottle, June 30, 1979; children: John Joseph II, David Brian II, Christopher Dalton. BA, Duke U., 1973; MPA, Am. U., 1975; JD, U. La Verne, 1978; postgrad., Georgetown U., 1981-89. Bar: Calif. 1978, U.S. Dist. Ct. (cen. dist.) Calif. 1979, U.S. Ct. Claims 1981, U.S. Tax Ct. 1981, U.S. Ct. Appeals (D.C. cir.) 1984. Intern Congressman Joel Broyhill, 1971; asst. dir. rsch. Younger-Curb Campaign, L.A., 1978; assoc. L. Rob Werner Law Offices, Encino, Calif., 1979-80; atty. conflicts Office of Pres. Elect, Washington, 1980-81; staff atty. Office of counsel to the Pres. White House, Washington, 1981; staff asst. office of sec. U.S. Dept. Treasury, Washington, 1981-85; spl. asst. office gen. counsel U.S. Dept. Energy, Washington, 1985-90, atty. advisor enforcement div. Office of Nuclear Safety, 1990-91, trial atty. adminstrv. litigation div. Econ. Regulatory Adminstrn., 1991-95, trial atty. Office of Gen. Counsel, 1995—; bd. dirs. Energy Fed. Credit Union. Assoc. editor New Guard Mag., 1983-85. Steering com. L.A. Reps., 1979-80, Reagan for Pres., L.A., 1980; chmn. 39th Assembly, Rep. Ctrl. Com., 1979-80; alt. del. 1972 Rep. Nat. Conv.; pres. N.C. Coll. Rep. Com., 1972-73; nat. treas., bd. dirs. Young Amers. for Freedom, Sterling, Va., 1983-85; corp. dir. Am. Sovereignty Task Force, Vienna, Va., 1984—, State Dept. Watch Ltd., Vienna, 1984—. Charles Edison Youth Found. scholar, 1971; named one of Outstanding Young Men in Am., Jaycees, 1976-86; recipient Mgr. of Yr. honor Dept. Energy Women's Adv. Coun., 1988, Achievement in Equal Opportunity Deptl. award, 1988. Mem. Fed. Bar Assn., Bar Assn. of D.C. (chmn. ethics com. young lawyers div. 1985-87), D.C. Bar, Calif. Bar, U.S. Supreme Ct. Soc., Federalist Soc., U.S. Justice Found. (co-founder, of counsel 1979-80), Conservative Network Club. Home: 8310 Wagon Wheel Rd Alexandria VA 22309-2175 Office: US Dept Energy 1000 Independence Ave SW Washington DC 20585-0001

**NOLAN, DAVID CHARLES,** lawyer, mediator; b. San Mateo, Calif., Oct. 12, 1940; s. Clarence Charles and Leona Henrietta (Lindeman) N.; m. Cynthia Ann James, Feb. 20, 1971; children: Matthew, John, Scott. AB, Stanford U., 1962; JD, U. Calif., Berkeley, 1965. Bar: Calif. 1966, U.S. Ct. Appeals (9th cir.) 1971, U.S. Ct. Appeals (D.C. cir.) 1975, U.S. Dist. Ct. (no. dist.) Calif. 1969, U.S. Dist. Ct. (D.C. cir.) 1970, U.S. Tax Ct., U.S. Supreme Ct. 1972. Ptnr. Graham & James, San Francisco, 1968-93; sole practitioner Walnut Creek, Calif., 1993—. Bd. dirs., officer Family Homes for Retarded, Belmont, Calif., 1978-81; founding dir. Orinda (Calif.) Baseball Assn., 1982-86; commr. Diablo Valley Baseball League, Martinez, Calif., 1983-90. Lt. comdr. USCG, 1965-68. Mem. ABA, Calif. Bar Assn., Contra Costa County Bar Assn., No. Calif. Mediation Assn., Assn. Transp. Practitioners, Commonwealth Club, Maritime Law Assn., Order of Coif. Fax: 925-937-5442. Admiralty, General corporate, Private international. Home: 12 E Altarinda Dr Orinda CA 94563-2406 Office: 1990 N California Blvd Walnut Creek CA 94596-3742

**NOLAN, JAMES P.,** legal translator; b. Albuquerque, Mar. 19, 1946; s. James P. and Maria L. N.; m. Adele L. Nolan, Apr. 5, 1997; children: Catherine, Jamie, Allegra. JD, N.Y. Law Sch., 1992. Translator U.N., N.Y.C., 1977—; linguistic officer Internat. Tribunal for the Law of the Sea, 1998—. Office: UN Room SAB 30 New York NY 10017

**NOLAN, JOHN JOSEPH,** law educator, lawyer; b. Derby, Conn., Nov. 1, 1928; s. Vincent J. and Edna M. (Coté) N.; m. Louise M. McLaughlin, Jan. 18, 1958 (div. Oct. 1974); children: John J., Brian V., Scott R.; m. Adrienne Constance, Aug. 14, 1976; children: Evan G., Alysson C. BS, Holy Cross Coll., 1950; JD, Suffolk U., 1955; LLM, Harvard U., 1962. Assoc. William D. Harlow, Esq., Milford, Conn., 1955-56, Goldstein & Goldstein, Boston, 1956-57; from asst. to full prof. Law Sch. Suffolk U., Boston, 1956-62; prof., 1962-75, 78—; ptnr. Vinci & Nolan, Boston, 1975-78; lectr. Boston U., 1977. Fellow Ford Found., 1961-62. Republican. Roman Catholic. Avocations: skiing, reading, home maintenance and improvement, travel, swimming. Office: Suffolk U Law Sch 120 Tremont St Boston MA 02108-4977

**NOLAN, JOHN MICHAEL,** lawyer; b. Conway, Ark., June 21, 1948; s. Paul Thomas and Peggy (Hime) N. BA, U. Tex., 1970, JD, 1973; LLM in Taxation, George Washington U., 1976. Bar: Tex. 1973, D.C. 1975, U.S. Ct. Mil. Appeals 1973, U.S. Ct. Appeals (D.C. cir.) 1975, U.S. Tax Ct. 1975, U.S. Supreme Ct. 1975. Chief counsel to chief judge U.S. Ct. Mil. Appeals, Washington, 1976-77; assoc. Winstead, McGuire, Sechrest & Minick PC, Dallas, 1977-81; shareholder Winstead Sechrest & Minick PC, Dallas, 1981—. Editor in Chief The Advocate, 1973-76. Capt. JAGC, U.S. Army, 1973-76. Named one of Outstanding Young Men in Am., U.S. Jaycess, 1976. Mem. ABA (real property, probate and trust sect., real property com., partnerships, joint ventrues, and other investment vehicles), Tex. Bar Assn. (real property, probate and trust sect.), D.C. Bar Assn., Dallas Bar Assn. (real estate group), Tex. Coll. Real Estate Lawyers, Coll. State Bar Tex., Real Estate Coun., Salesmanship Club Dallas, Royal Oaks Country Club. Presbyterian. Real property, Bankruptcy, Taxation, general. Home: 6681 Crest Way Ct Dallas TX 75230-2868 Office: Winstead Sechrest & Minick 5400 Renaissance Tower 1201 Elm St Ste 5400 Dallas TX 75270-2199

**NOLAN, LAWRENCE PATRICK,** lawyer; b. Mich., Dec. 31, 1948; s. Gerard P. and Katherine (Gluns) N.; m. Laurel Lee Blasi, Apr. 26, 1980; children: Bridget Blasi, Lawrence Patrick Jr. BA, Western Mich. U., 1971; JD, Thomas M. Cooley Law Sch., 1976. Bar: Mich. 1976, D.C. 1977. Pres. Nolan, Thomsen & Villas, P.C., Eaton Rapids, Mich., 1977—. Pres. Cooley Lawyers Credit Union; bd. dirs. Thomas M. Cooley Law Sch., 1983—; v.p. bd. dirs. Island City Acad.; bd. dirs. Mich. Supreme Ct. Hist. Soc. Named Outstanding Man of Yr., Eaton Rapids Jaycees, 1981. Fellow Mich. Bar Assn. (chmn. young lawyers sect. 1982-83); mem. ABA, D.C. Bar Assn., Eaton County Bar Assn., Ingham County Bar Assn., KC (4th degree). Roman Catholic. Lodges: Rotary (v.p. Eaton Rapids chpt. 1984-85, pres. 1985-86, Paul Harris fellow), K.C. General practice, Personal injury, General civil litigation. Home: 4765 Nakoma Dr Okemos MI 48864-2026 Office: 239 S Main St Eaton Rapids MI 48827-1255

**NOLAN, RICHARD EDWARD,** lawyer; b. N.Y.C., Nov. 28, 1928; m. Agnes F. Gilligan, Jan. 31, 1959; children: Anthony R.G., Christopher W.P., Timothy R.W., Mariana Celeste, Katherine H.L. A.B. cum laude, Holy Cross Coll., 1960; LL.B., Columbia U., 1957. Bar: N.Y. 1958, U.S. Supreme Ct. 1962. Assoc. Davis Polk & Wardwell, N.Y.C., 1957-65; partner Davis Polk & Wardwell, 1966—; sr. counsel, 1990—; Davis Polk & Wardell; dir. N. Atlantic Life Ins. Co., (ret. 1998). Notes editor: Columbia U. Law Rev., 1957. Bd. dirs. United Neighborhood Houses of N.Y., 1970-89. Fellow Am. Coll. Trial Lawyers; Mem. ABA, Fed. Bar Assn., N.Y. Bar Assn., Assn. Bar City N.Y., Am. Law Inst. Lodge: Knights of Malta. Federal civil litigation, State civil litigation, Antitrust. Home: 271 Central Park W New York NY 10024-3020 Office: Davis Polk & Wardwell 450 Lexington Ave New York NY 10017-3911

**NOLAN, TERRANCE JOSEPH, JR.,** lawyer; b. Bklyn., Mar. 29, 1950; s. Terrance Joseph Sr. and Antonia (Pontecorvo) N.; m. Irene M. Rush, Aug. 2, 1980; children: Maryjane Frances, David Anthony. BA, St. Francis Coll., Bklyn., 1971; JD, St. Johns U., Jamaica, N.Y., 1974; LLM, NYU, 1982. Bar: N.Y. 1975, U.S. Dist. Ct. (ea. and so. dists.) N.Y. 1975, U.S. Ct. Appeals (2d cir.) 1975, U.S. Supreme Ct. 1980. Atty. N.Y.C. Transit Authority, Bklyn., 1974-77; specialist labor rels. Pepsi-Cola Co., Purchase,

N.Y., 1977-80; asst. gen. counsel, assoc. dir. labor rels. NYU, N.Y.C., 1980-89, assoc. gen. counsel, dep. dir. labor rels., 1989—. Mem. Am. Corp. Coun. Assn., N.Y. State Bar Assn., Indsl. Rels. Rsch. Assn., Nat. Assn. Coll. and Univ. Attys., Met. Arbitration Group. Labor, Administrative and regulatory, Education and schools. Home: 41 Russell St Lynbrook NY 11563-1135 Office: NYU 70 Washington Sq S New York NY 10012-1091

**NOLEN, SUSAN CARDILLO,** insurance executive, lawyer; b. Rochester, N.Y., July 21, 1960; d. Arnold Edwin and Mary Louise Cardillo; m. Raymond Joseph Nolen, III, Dec. 10, 1988; children: Katherine, Raymond IV, Laura. BA, Bucknell U., 1982; JD, Case Western Res. U., 1985. Bar: Pa. 1986, N.J. 1986. Assoc. Griffith & Burr, PC, Phila., 1985-86; house counsel Physicians Ins. Co., Plymouth Meeting, Pa., 1986-89; asst. v.p., assoc. gen. counsel, asst. sec. Gen. Accident Ins., Phila., 1989-94, v.p. human resources, 1994-97, corp. sr. v.p. bus. svcs., 1997-98; corp. sr. v.p. CGU Ins., Phila., 1998—. Adult edn. instr. St. Francis De Sales, Aston, Pa., 1996—; parent vol. Indian Lane Elem. Sch., Media, Pa., 1998, Girl Scouts of Am., Media, 1998. Mem. ABA, Phila. Bar Assn., Ins. Soc. Phila. (adv. bd. corp. career opportunity program 1994-97), Omicron Delta Kappa, Phi Delta Phi. Republican. Roman Catholic. Avocations: golf, running, photography, music. Home: 380 Olde House Ln Media PA 19063-5320 Office: CGU Ins 436 Walnut St Philadelphia PA 19106-3703

**NOLFI, EDWARD ANTHONY,** lawyer; b. Warren, Ohio, Sept. 30, 1958; s. Eugene Vincent Sr. and Margaret Joyce (Futey) N.; m. Sheri Ann Loue, June 5, 1982. AB, Brown U., 1980; JD, U. Akron, 1983. Bar: Ohio 1983, N.Y. 1986, U.S. Dist. Ct. (no. dist.) Ohio 1987, U.S. Tax Ct. 1987, U.S. Ct. Appeals (6th cir. 1989), U.S. Supreme Ct. 1989. Juggler Miracle Sta., Warren, 1976; instr. Sch. One, Providence, 1980; tech. writer Doctors' Hosp., Massillon, Ohio, 1982; pvt. practice Warren, 1983-84; ptnr. Schubert, Sopkovich & Nolfi, Warren, 1984; assoc. editor Lawyers Coop. Pub. Co., Rochester, N.Y., 1985-87; pvt. practice Akron, Ohio, 1987—; prof. Acad. Ct. Reporting, Akron, 1988-91; prof. Kent State U., 1993, Mt. Aloysius Coll., Cresson, Pa., 1996. Author: The Master Juggler, 1980, Basic Legal Research, 1993, Basic Wills, Trusts, and Estates, 1995; articles editor Am. Law Reports, Fed., 1986-87; law columnist Village Views, 1987-88. Mem. ABA. Roman Catholic. Avocation: juggling. General practice. Home: 1101 E Archwood Ave Akron OH 44306-2857

**NOLLAU, LEE GORDON,** lawyer; b. Balt., Feb. 6, 1950; s. E. Wilson and Carolyn G. (Blass) N.; m. Carol A. Haughney, Aug. 12, 1978; children: Ann G., Catherine E., Margaret C. BA, Juniata Coll., 1972; MAS, Johns Hopkins U., 1975; JD, Dickinson Sch. Law, 1976. Bar: Pa. 1976, U.S. Dist. Ct. (mid. dist.) 1982, U.S. Dist. Ct. (we. dist.) 1988, U.S. Ct. Appeals (3d cir.) 1980, U.S. Supreme Ct. 1982. Instr. Juniata Coll., Huntingdon, Pa., 1976-78; asst. dist. atty. Centre County, Bellefonte, Pa., 1978-80, dist. atty., 1981; assoc. Litke, Lee, Martin, Grine & Green, Bellefonte, 1981-83, Jubelirer & Assocs., State College, Pa., 1983-87; ptnr. Jubelirer, Nollau, Young & Blanarik, Inc., State College, 1988-89, Jubelirer, Rayback, Nollau, Walsh, Young & Blanarik, Inc., State College, 1989-94, Nollau & Young, State Coll., Pa., 1994—; mental health rev. officer Centre County, Bellefonte, 1982—; instr. Pa. State U. Smeal Coll. Bus. Adminstrn., 1995—; lectr. Pa. Bar Inst., 1995—. Mem. ABA, Pa. Bar Assn., Centre Co. Bar, Pa. Assn. Criminal Def. Lawyers. Presbyterian. General civil litigation, Personal injury, Criminal. Office: Nollau & Young 2153 E College Ave State College PA 16801-7204

**NOLLETTI, JAMES JOSEPH,** lawyer; b. Portchester, N.Y., Sept. 20, 1953; s. James Louis and Anne Marie (Mandracchia) N.; children: Jay, Justin, Jamie-Lynn, Jeff. BA, Villanova U., 1975; JD, Fordham U., 1978. Bar: N.Y. 1979, U.S. Dist. Ct. (so. dist.) N.Y., U.S. Supreme Ct. Asst. dist. atty. Westchester County Dist. Atty.'s Office, White Plains, N.Y., 1978-81; assoc. Sirlin & Sirlin, Mamaroneck, N.Y., 1981-84; ptnr. Sirlin, Sirlin & Nolletti, Mamaroneck, 1984—, Pirro, Collier, Cohen & Halpern LLP, White Plains, N.Y.C.; village atty. Village of Mamaroneck, 1985—; mem. adv. bd. Westchester Abstract Co., White Plains, 1985-88; bd. dirs., legal advisor Orienta Beach CLUB, iNC., mAMARONECK, 1986-90. Commr. ABC bd. Westchester County, White Plains, 1984-88, Westchester County Pub. Employees Rels. Bd., 1986-88. Mem. N.Y. State Bar Assn., Westchester County Bar Assn., Westchester County Col. Lawyers Bar Assn. (bd. dirs., v.p. 1989-93). Fax: 914-684-6986/212-696-4064. State civil litigation, Personal injury, Municipal (including bonds). Office: Pirro Collier Cohen & Halpern LLP One North Lexington Ave White Plains NY 10601 also: Pirro Collier Cohen & Halpern LLP 99 Park Ave New York NY 10016-1601

**NOLTE, HENRY R., JR.,** lawyer, former automobile company executive; b. N.Y.C., Mar. 3, 1924; s. Henry R. and Emily A. (Eisele) N.; m. Frances Messner, May 19, 1951; children: Gwynne Conn, Henry Reed III, Jennifer Stevens, Suzanne. BA, Duke U., 1947; LLB, U. Pa., 1949. Bar: N.Y. 1950, Mich. 1967. Assoc. Cravath, Swaine & Moore, N.Y.C., 1951-61; assoc. counsel Ford Motor Co., Dearborn, Mich., 1961, asst. gen. counsel, 1964-71, assoc. gen. counsel, 1971-74, v.p., gen. counsel, 1974-89; v.p., gen. counsel Philco-Ford Corp., Phila., 1961-64; v.p., gen. counsel, sec. Ford of Europe Inc., Warley, Essex, Eng., 1967-69; gen. counsel fin. and ins. subs. Ford Motor Co., 1974-89; sr. ptnr. Miller, Canfield, Paddock & Stone, Detroit, 1989-93, of counsel, 1993—; bd. dirs. Charter One Fin., Inc. Formerly vice chmn. and trustee Cranbrook Ednl. Community; mem. Internat. and Comparative Law Ctr. of Southwestern Legal Found.; bd. dirs. Detroit Symphony Orch.; trustee Beaumont Hosp. Lt. USNR, 1943-46, PTO. Mem. ABA (past chmn. corp. law depts.), Mich. Bar Assn., Assn. Bar City N.Y., Assn. Gen. Counsel, Orchard Lake Country Club, Bloomfield Hills Country Club, Everglades Club (Fla.), Gulfstream Golf Club (Fla.), Ocean Club (Fla.). Episcopalian. Office: Miller Canfield Paddock & Stone 1400 N Woodward Ave Ste 100 Bloomfield Hills MI 48304-2855

**NOLTE, MELVIN, JR.,** lawyer; b. New Braunfels, Tex., Dec. 14, 1947; s. Melvin Sr. and Louise (Beaty) N.; m. Elizabeth C. Tolle, Aug. 26, 1972 (div. June 1980); 1 child, Melvin III; m. Sandra J. Prochazka, Dec. 4, 1984; 1 child, Chad Louis. BA, Southwest Tex. U., 1970; JD, St. Mary's U., San Antonio, 1972. Bar: Tex. 1973. Pvt. practice law New Braunfels, 1973—; mem. adv. coun. Cibolo (Tex.) State Bank, 1982-88; chmn. bd. dirs., pres. Garden Villa, Inc., New Braunfels. Mem. New Braunfels Water Adv. Bd., 1987-88, Comal County Water-Oriented REcreation Dist. Bd., New Braunfels, 1987-89, past pres. Mem. ABA, New Braunfels C. of C., Phi Delta Phi, Pi Gamma Mu. Lodges: Lions, Eagles (past pres. local chpt.). Avocations: hunting, fishing. Real property, Probate, Contracts commercial. Office: 175 N Market St New Braunfels TX 78130-5084

**NOME, WILLIAM ANDREAS,** lawyer; b. Springfield, Ohio, May 21, 1951; s. Reidar Andreas and Nancy Louisa (Smith) N.; m. Carolyn Ruth Johnson, Feb. 7, 1981. BA, Akron U., 1973; JD, Cleve. State U., 1976. Bar: Ohio 1976, U.S. Dist. Ct. (no. dist.) Ohio 1977, U.S. Ct. Appeals (6th cir.) 1985, U.S. Supreme Ct. 1987. Asst. prosecutor Portage County Prosecutor's Office, Ravenna, Ohio, 1977; pvt. practice Ravenna, 1977-82; assoc. Arthur & Clegg, Kent, Ohio, 1982-85; ptnr. Arthur, Nome & Assocs., Kent, Ohio, 1985-96, Arthur, Nome, Can, Szymanski & Clinard, Kent, Cuyahoga Falls, Ohio, 1996-97, Arthur, Nome, Can & Szymanski, Kent, Cuyahoga Falls, Ohio, 1997-98, Arthur, Nome and Szymanski, Kent, Kent, Cuyahoga Falls, Ohio, 1998—; legal advisor Portage Area Regional Transit Authority, Kent, 1986—. Chmn. Highland Home Health Care, Ravenna, 1980, Kent Bd. Bldg. Appeals, 1987, Portage County Mental Health Bd., 1988; trustee Kevin Coleman Mental Health Ctr., 1989-93, pres., 1991-93. Col. Ohio Mil. Res., 1986—. Recipient Cert. of Achievement, Emergency Mgmt. Inst., Fed. Emergency Mgmt. Agy., 1987, 93, 95. Mem. Ohio Bar Assn., Akron Bar Assn., Portage County Bar Assn. (sec.-treas. 1982-85, 98—), Portage County Estate Planning Coun., Delta Theta Phi. Republican. Lutheran. Avocations: gardening, cooking, target shooting, reading. Bankruptcy, Probate, General practice. Office: Arthur Nome & Assocs 1325 S Water St Kent OH 44240-3851

**NONNA, JOHN MICHAEL,** lawyer; b. N.Y.C., July 8, 1948; s. Angelo and Josephine (Visconti) N.; m. Jean Wanda Cleary, June 9, 1973; children: Elizabeth, Caroline, Marianne, Timothy. AB, Princeton U., 1970; JD, NYU, 1975. Bar: N.Y. 1976, U.S. Dist. Ct. (so. dist.) N.Y. 1978, U.S. Ct. Appeals (2d cir.) 1978, U.S. Ct. Appeals (9th cir.) 1980, U.S. Ct. Appeals (5th cir.) 1997, U.S. Dist. Ct. Conn. 1988, U.S. Supreme Ct. 1998. Law asst. to Hon. D.L. Gabrielli N.Y. Ct. Appeals, Albany, 1975-77; assoc. Reid & Priest, N.Y.C., 1977-84; ptnr. Werner & Kennedy, N.Y.C., 1984-99, LeBoeuf, Lamb, Greene & MacRae, 1999—. Contbr. articles to profl. jours. Dep. mayor, trustee Village of Pleasantville, N.Y., 1990-95, mayor, 1995—, acting justice, 1983-89. With USNR, 1970-75. U.S. Olympic Team, Munich, 1972, Moscow, 1980. Fellow Am. Bar Found. (life); mem. ABA (torts and ins. practice sect. com. chair 1986-87, 92-93), N.Y. State Bar Assn. (chair comml. and fed. litigation sect. 1998-99), Assn. Bar City N.Y., N.Y. Fencers Club (pres. 1990-93). Avocations: fencing, running, piano. General civil litigation, Insurance. Office: LeBoeuf Lamb Greene & MacRae 125 W 55th St New York NY 10019-5369

**NOONAN, GREGORY ROBERT,** lawyer; b. Bridgeport, Conn., Dec. 15, 1960; s. John L. and Margaret B. (Petek) N. BA in Acctg. cum laude, N.C. State U., 1982; JD, Wake Forest U., 1985; LLM in Taxation, Villanova U., 1990. Bar: N.C. 1985, Pa. 1986, U.S. Dist. Ct. (ea. dist.) Pa. 1988, U.S. Ct. Claims 1991, U.S. Tax Ct. 1994, U.S. Ct. Appeals (3d cir.) 1994, N.J. 1995, U.S. Dist. Ct. N.J. 1995; CFE, 1995; CPA, N.C.; cert. fraud examiner. Acctg. cons. Ernst & Whinney, Raleigh, N.C., 1985-86; tax atty. Fox, Differ, Norristown, Pa., 1987-90, Solomon Berschler & Warren, Norristown, 1990; tax/bankruptcy atty. Koresko & Noonan, Norristown, 1990-92, Pizonka, Reilley & Bello, King of Prussia, Pa., 1992-94, Deyoung, Walfish & Noonan, King of Prussia, 1994—; instr. acctg., tax and bus. law Pierce Jr. Coll., Phila., 1990-92, Paralegal Inst. Mainline, Phila., 1990; instr. 2d pl. team Mock Trials of Pa. Young Lawyers Divsn. ABA, Norristown, 1989. Mem. ABA, AICPA, Pa. Bar Assn., N.C. Bar Assn., N.J. Bar Assn., Montgomery County Bar Assn., Norristown Jaycees (dir. 1990-94). Republican. Roman Catholic. Avocations: tennis, boating, chess, golf, watching college basketball. Taxation, general, Bankruptcy, General practice. Home: 109 Stony Way Norristown PA 19403-4210 Office: Deyoung Walfish & Noonan PC 144 E Dekalb Pike Ste 200 King of Prussia PA 19406-2150

**NOONAN, JAMES C.,** lawyer, mediator-arbitrator; b. Chgo., July 16, 1928; s. T. Clifford and Ethel (Jennett) N.; m. Carol Colbert, Nov. 24, 1954 (div. June 1975); children: James, Christopher, Mary, Anne, Catherine; m. Ardis Niemann, May 24, 1986. AB, U. Notre Dame, 1953, MA in Criminology, 1954; JD, William Mitchell Coll. Law, St. Paul, 1962. Bar: Minn. 1962, U.S. Dist. Ct. Minn. 1963, U.S. Ct. Appeals (8th cir.) 1971, U.S. Supreme Ct. 1969. Supt. Woodview Detention Home, St. Paul, 1957-63; assoc. Firestone, Fink, Krawetz, Miley, O'Neill, St. Paul, 1963-67; ptnr. Firestone Fink, Krawetz, Miley, Maas and Noonan, St. Paul, 1967-70, Magistad & Noonan, St. Paul, 1971-75; owner James C. Noonan and Assocs., St. Paul, 1975—; probation officer Ramsey County Juvenile Ct., St. Paul. Mem. adv. bd. Home of Good Shepherd, St. Paul, 1958-74; mem. citizen adv. bd. Detention and Corrections Authority, St. Paul, 1966-80. Mem. ABA, Minn. State Bar Assn., Ramsey County Bar Assn., St. Paul Amateur Radio Club, Am. Radio Relay League. Republican. Roman Catholic. Avocation: amateur radio (W9OSN). Estate planning, Probate, Alternative dispute resolution. Home and Office: 339 Summit Ave Saint Paul MN 55102-2176

**NOONAN, JEAN,** lawyer. BA with highest honors, Okla. State U.; JD, U. Tex., Austin. Staff atty. FTC, McLean, Va., 1977-80; mgr. Equal Credit Opportunity Act Enforcement Program FTC, 1980-83, asst. dir. div. credit practices, 1983-86, assoc. dir. credit practices, 1986-91; gen. counsel Farm Credit Adminstrn., 1991—. Office: Farm Credit Adminstrn 1501 Farm Credit Dr Mc Lean VA 22102-5004

**NOONAN, JOHN T., JR.,** federal judge, law educator; b. Boston, Oct. 24, 1926; s. John T. and Marie (Shea) N.; m. Mary Lee Bennett, Dec. 27, 1967; children: John Kenneth, Rebecca Lee, Susanna Bain. B.A., Harvard U., 1946, LL.B., 1954; student, Cambridge U., 1946-47; M.A., Cath. U. Am., 1949, Ph.D., 1951, LHD, 1980; LL.D., U. Santa Clara, 1974, U. Notre Dame, 1976, Loyola U. South, 1978; LHD, Holy Cross Coll., 1980; LL.D., St. Louis U., 1981, U. San Francisco, 1985; student, Holy Cross Coll., 1980, Cath. U. Am., 1980, Gonzaga U., 1986, U. San Francisco, 1986. Bar: Mass. 1954, U.S. Supreme Ct. 1971. Mem. spl. staff Nat. Security Council, 1954-55; pvt. practice Herrick & Smith, Boston, 1955-60; prof. law U. Notre Dame, 1961-66; prof. law U. Calif., Berkeley, 1967-86, chmn. religious studies, 1970-73, chmn. medieval studies, 1978-79; judge U.S. Ct. Appeals (9th cir.), San Francisco, 1985-96, sr. judge, 1996—; Oliver Wendell Holmes, Jr. lectr. Harvard U. Law Sch., 1972, Pope John XXIII lectr. Cath. U. Law Sch., 1973, Cardinal Bellarmine lectr. St. Louis U. Div. Sch., 1973, Ernest Messenger lectr. Cornell U., 1982, John Dewey Meml. lectr. U. Minn., 1986, Baum lectr. U. Ill., 1988, Strassberger lectr. U. Tex., 1989; chmn. bd. Games Rsch., Inc., 1961-76; overseer Harvard U., 1991—. Author: The Scholastic Analysis of Usury, 1957; Contraception: A History of Its Treatment by the Catholic Theologians and Canonists, 1965; Power to Dissolve, 1972; Persons and Masks of the Law, 1976; The Antelope, 1977; A Private Choice, 1979; Bribes, 1984; editor: Natural Law Forum, 1961-70, Am. Jour. Jurisprudence, 1970, The Morality of Abortion, 1970. Chmn. Brookline Redevel. Authority, Mass., 1958-62; cons. Papal Commn. on Family, 1965-66, Ford Found., Indonesian Legal Program, 1968; NIH, 1973, NIH, 1974; expert Presdl. Commn. on Population and Am. Future, 1971; cons. U.S. Cath. Conf., 1979-86; sec., treas. Inst. for Research in Medieval Canon Law, 1970-88; pres. Thomas More-Jacques Maritain Inst., 1977—; trustee Population Council, 1969-76, Phi Kappa Found., 1970-76, Grad. Theol. Union, 1970-73, U. San Francisco, 1971-75; mem. com. theol. edn. Yale U., 1972-77; exec. com. Cath. Commn. Intellectual and Cultural Affairs, 1972-75; bd. dirs. Ctr. for Human Values in the Health Scis., 1969-71, S.W. Intergroup Relations Council, 1970-72, Inst. for Study Ethical Issues, 1971-73. Recipient St. Thomas More award U. San Francisco, 1974, Christian Culture medal, 1975, Laetare medal U. Notre Dame, 1984, Campion medal Cath. Book Club, 1987; Guggenheim fellow, 1965-66, 79-80, Laetare medal U. Notre Dame, 1984, Campion medal, 1987, Alemany medal Western Dominican Province, 1988; Ctr. for advanced Studies in Behavioral Scis. fellow, 1973-74; Wilson Ctr. fellow, 1979-80. Fellow Am. Acad. Arts and Scis., Am. Soc. Legal Historians (hon.); mem. Am. Soc. Polit. and Legal Philosophy (v.p. 1964), Canon Law Soc. Am. (gov. 1970-72), Am. Law Inst., Phi Beta Kappa (senator United chpts. 1970-72, pres. Alpha of Calif. chpt. 1972-73). Office: US Ct Appeals 9th Cir PO Box 193939 San Francisco CA 94119-3939

**NOONAN, MICHAEL DENNIS,** lawyer; b. Rochester, N.Y., Mar. 23, 1941; s. John Francis Noonan and Catherine Teresa (Hock) Cartwright; m. Patricia Quinn, Sept. 30, 1967; children: Michael Jeffrey, Daniel Quinn, Mark Patrick. BSBA, Georgetown U., 1963; JD, Syracuse U., 1966. Bar: N.Y. 1966, Fla. 1974, D.C. 1978. Ptnr.-in-charge real estate sect. Mousaw, Vigdor, Reeves, Heilbronner & Kroll, Rochester, 1966-77; v.p., dep. gen. counsel, asst. sec. Nat. Corp. for Housing Partnerships, Washington, 1977-89; with HUD, Washington, 1989—; justice Town of Mendon (N.Y.) Ct., 1971-74. Mem. bd. Town of Mendon, 1971-74; bd. dirs. Day Care Tng. Ctr. for Handicapped Children, Rochester, 1969-77. Mem. ABA, N.Y. State Bar Assn., Fla. Bar Assn., D.C. Bar Assn., Washington Met. Area Corp. Counsel Assn. Avocations: golf, travel, antique automobiles. Home: 6710 Norview Ct Springfield VA 22152-3055 Office: HUD 451 7th St SW Washington DC 20410-0001

**NOONAN, WILLIAM DONALD,** lawyer, physician; b. Kansas City, Mo., Oct. 18, 1955; s. Robert Owen and Patricia Ruth Noonan. AB, Princeton (N.J.) U., 1977; JD, U. Mo., Kansas City, 1980; postgrad., Tulane U., 1981-83; MD magna cum laude, Oreg. Health Scis. U., 1991. Bar: Mo. 1980, U.S. Ct. Appeals (5th cir.) 1982, U.S. Patent & Trademark Office 1982, U.S. Ct. Appeals (D.C. cir.) 1984, Oreg. 1985, U.S. Ct. Appeals (9th Cir.) 1985. Assoc. Shurgue, Mion, Zinn, Washington, 1983-84, Keaty & Keaty, New Orleans, 1984-85; ptnr. Klarquist, Sparkman, Portland, Oreg., 1985—; intern in internal medicine Portland Providence Med. Ctr., 1993-94; resident in ophthalomology Casey Eye Inst., Portland, 1994-95; adj. prof. patent law Tulane U., New Orleans, 1984-85, U. Oreg., 1992-93. Casenotes editor U. Mo. Law Rev., 1979. Nat. Merit scholar. Mem. ABA, AMA (Leadership award 1994), Alpha Omega Alpha (pres. Oreg. chpt. 1990-91). Republican. Avocation: raising horses, mountain climbing, hiking. Patent. Office: Klarquist Sparkman 121 SW Salmon 1600 World Trade Ctr Portland OR 97201

**NOPAR, ALAN SCOTT,** lawyer; b. Chgo., Nov. 14, 1951; s. Myron E. and Evelyn M. Nopar. BS, U. Ill., 1976; JD, Stanford U., 1979. Bar: Ariz. 1979, U.S. Dist. Ct. Ariz. 1980, U.S. Ct. Appeals (9th cir.) 1980, U.S. Supreme Ct. 1982, Calif. 1989; CPA, Ill. Assoc. O'Connor, Cavanagh, Anderson, Westover, Killingsworth & Beshears P.A., Phoenix, 1979-85, ptnr., 1985-87; of counsel Tower, Byrne & Beaugureau, Phoenix, 1987-88; ptnr. Minutillo & Gorman, San Jose, Calif., 1989-91, Bosco, Blau, Ward & Nopar, San Jose, 1991-96; exec. v.p., gen. counsel, dir. AmeriNet Fin. Systems, Inc., Ontario, Calif., 1996-97; sole practice law San Jose, 1997-99, Palo Alto, Calif., 1999—. Mem. Ariz. Rep. Caucus, Phoenix, 1984-88. Mem. AICPA, ABA (bus. law and law practice mgmt. sects., mem. forum com. on franchising), Ariz. Bar Assn. (bus. law sect.), Calif. State Bar Assn. (bus. law sect.). Avocations: golf, skiing. General corporate, Franchising, Mergers and acquisitions. Office: Ste 100 425 Sherman Ave Palo Alto CA 94306

**NORA, GERALD ERNEST,** lawyer; b. Chgo., May 25, 1951; s. Gerald Edwin and Lois (Billingham) N.; m. Patricia Cunniff, June 19, 1976; children: Gerald Joseph, Thomas More, Mary Elizabeth, John Paul. Student, U. Ill., 1970-71; BA, Georgetown U., 1973, JD, 1978. Bar: Ill. 1978, U.S. Supreme Ct. 1983, U.S. Dist. Ct. (no. dist.) Ill. 1983, U.S. Dist. Ct. Ariz. 1993, U.S. Ct. Appeals (7th cir.) 1996. Asst. state's atty. Cook County Office of State's Atty., Chgo., 1978-86, dep. state's atty., chief spl. prosecutions, 1991-93, exec. asst. policy, 1996—; assoc. Hofeld & Schaffner, Chgo., 1987-91; ptnr. Davidson, Goldstein, Mandell & Menkes, Chgo., 1995-96; sr. lectr. Loyola U. Sch. Law, 1988—; mem. Cook County Revenue Enhancement Com., 1996; former bd. dirs. Chgo. Legal Aid for Incarcerated Mothers. Mem. ABA, ATLA, Ill. State Bar Assn., Nat. Dist. Attys. Assn., Ill. Trial Lawyers Assn., Chgo. Bar Assn., Cath. Lawyers Guild, High Tech. Crime Investigation Assn. General civil litigation, General practice, Criminal. Office: Office of the Cook County States Atty 50 W Washington St Rm 500 Chicago IL 60602-1356

**NORA, WENDY ALISON,** lawyer; b. New Haven, Conn., Feb. 14, 1951; d. James Jackson Nora and Barbara June (Fluhrer) P.; m. Jay Robert Vercauteren, Aug. 21, 1973 (div. Nov. 1981); children: Lucas Jay, Eric Robert. BA, U. Wis., 1971, JD, 1975. Bar: Wis. 1975, U.S. Dist. Ct. (we. dist.) Wis. 1975, Minn. 1985, U.S. Dist. Ct. Minn. 1985, U.S. Supreme Ct. 1986. Pvt. practice Cross Plains, Wis., 1975-81, Madison, Wis., 1981-84, Mpls., 1986-90, Madison, Wis., 1991—; developer, incorporator, pres. Wis. Business Devel. Credit Corp., Madison, 1996—. Atty. State of Wis., 1977-81, asst. pub. defender, 1983-84. Fellow U. Minn. Mem. ABA (vice-chmn. adminstrv. law sect., criminal law and juvenile justice com. 1982—). Finance, Estate taxation, General corporate. Home: 6931 Old Sauk Rd Madison WI 53717-1122

**NORBERG, CHARLES ROBERT,** lawyer; b. Cleve., July 25, 1912; s. Rudolf Carl and Ida Edith (Roberts) N. B.S. in Adminstrv. Engring, Cornell U., 1934; M.A. in Internat. Econs, U. Pa., 1937; LL.B., Harvard U., 1939. Bar: Pa. bar 1940, U.S. Supreme Ct. bar 1946, D.C. bar 1947. Lab. research asst. Willard Storage Battery Co., Cleve., 1934-35; asso. firm Hepburn and Norris, Phila., 1939-42; with Office of Assn. Sec. State for Public Affairs, Dept. State, 1948-51; asst. dir. psychol. strategy bd. Exec. Office of the Pres., 1952-54; mem. staff U.S. Delegation to UN Gen. Assembly, Paris, 1951; adviser U.S. Delegation to UNESCO Gen. Conf., Montevideo, 1954; assoc. firm Morgan, Lewis and Bockius, Washington, 1955-56; individual practice law Washington, 1956—; treas., gen. counsel Inter-Am. Comml. Arbitration Commn., 1968-83, dir. gen., 1983-95, hon. dir. gen., 1995—; hon. mem. Corte Brasileira de Arbitragem Comercial; chief Spl. AID Mission to Ecuador, 1961; spl. Aid Mission to Uruguay, 1961; mem. U.S. delegation to Specialized Inter-Am. Conf. on pvt. internat. law, Panama, 1975. Chmn. Internat. Visitors Info. Service, Washington, 1965-69; chmn. Mayor's Com. on Internat. Visitors, 1971-78; chmn., pres. Bicentennial Commn. of D.C., Inc., 1975-81. Served with USAF, 1942-46. Recipient medal of honor Inter-Am. Comml. Arbitration Commn., 1996. Mem. Phila. Bar Assn., Pa. Bar Assn., Inter-Am. Bar Assn., Washington Fgn. Law Soc. (pres. 1959-63), Am. Soc. Internat. Law, Am. Law Inst., Am. Bar Assn. (chmn. internat. legal exchange program 1974-79), Bar Assn. of D.C. (chmn. internat. law com. 1977-79), Inter-Am. Bar Found. (founder, dir. 1957, pres. 1969-84, chmn. bd. 1984—), Diplomatic and Consular Officers Retired (Washington), Washington Inst. Fgn. Affairs, Academia Colombiana de Jurisprudencia, Inter-Am. Acad. Internat. and Comparative Law, Colegio de Abogados de Quito. Clubs: Met. (Washington); Dacor (Washington); Racquet (Phila.); Harvard (N.Y.C.). Private international, Public international. Home: 3104 N St NW Washington DC 20007-3413 Office: 1819 H St NW Washington DC 20006-3603

**NORBY, MARK ALAN,** lawyer; b. Cadillac, Mich., July 5, 1955; s. Walter Carl and Nadine Kaye (Hunt) N.; m. Connie Lynn Perrine, Feb. 26, 1983. BS in Polit. Sci., Agr., Oreg. State U., 1977; JD, U. Mich., 1980. Bar: Oreg. 1980, U.S. Dist. Ct. Oreg. 1980. Assoc. Stoel, Rives, Boley, Fraser & Wyse, Portland, 1980-86; ptnr. Stoel, RivesLLP, Portland, 1986—. General corporate, Oil, gas, and mineral, Contracts commercial. Office: Stoel Rives LLP 900 SW 5th Ave Ste 2600 Portland OR 97204-1268

**NORCOTT, FLEMING L., JR.,** state supreme court justice; b. New Haven, Oct. 11, 1943. BA, Columbia U., 1965, JD, 1968. Bar: Conn. 1968. Peace corps vol. U. East Africa, Nairobi, Kenya; legal staff Bedford-Stuyvestant Restoration Corp.; asst. atty. gen. Office Atty. Gen., V.I.; judge Superior Ct., 1979-87, Appellate Ct., 1987-92; justice Conn. Supreme Ct., Hartford, 1992—; hearing examiner Conn. Commn. Human Rights and Opportunities; co-founder, exec. dir. Ctr. Advocacy, Rsch. and Planning, Ind., New Haven; lectr. Yale U. Bd. govs. U. New Haven; bd. dirs. Dixwell Community House, Ea. Collegiate Football Ofcls. Assn., New Haven Football Ofcls. Assn., Long Wharf Theatre; assoc. fellow Calhoun Coll., Yale U.; bd. trustees Yale-New Haven Hosp. Mem. Omega Psi Phi. Office: Conn Supreme Ct Drawer N Sta A Hartford CT 06106-1548*

**NORDBERG, JOHN ALBERT,** federal judge; b. Evanston, Ill., June 18, 1926; s. Carl Albert and Judith Ranghild (Carlson) N.; m. Jane Spaulding, June 18, 1947; children: Carol, Mary, Janet, John. Student, Carleton Coll., 1943-44, 46-47; J.D., U. Mich., 1950. Bar: Ill. 1950, U.S. Dist. Ct. (no. dist.) Ill. 1957, U.S. Ct. Appeals (7th cir.) 1961. Assoc. Pope & Ballard, Chgo., 1950-57; ptnr. Pope, Ballard, Shepard & Fowle, Chgo., 1957-76; judge Cir. Ct. of Cook County, Ill., 1976-82; judge U.S. Dist. Ct. (no. dist.) Ill., Chgo., 1982-95, sr. judge, 1995—. Editor-in-chief, bd. editors Chgo. Bar Record, 1966-74. Magistrate of Cir. Ct. and justice of peace Ill., 1957-65. Served with USN, 1944-46; PTO. Mem. ABA, Chgo. Bar Assn., Am. Judicature Soc., Law Club Chgo., Legal Club Chgo., Union League Club of Chgo., Order of Coif. Office: US Dist Ct 219 S Dearborn St Chicago IL 60604-1702

**NORDENBERG, MARK ALAN,** law educator, university official; b. Duluth, Minn., July 12, 1948; s. John Clemens and Shirley Mae (Tappen) N.; m. Nikki Patricia Pirillo, Dec. 26, 1970; children: Erin, Carl, Michael. BA, Thiel Coll., 1970; JD, U. Wis., 1973. Bar: Wis. 1973, Minn. 1974, U.S. Supreme Ct. 1976, Pa. 1985. Atty. Gray, Plant, Mooty & Anderson, Mpls., 1973-75; prof. law Capital U. Law Ctr., Columbus, Ohio, 1975-77; prof. law U. Pitts., 1977—, acting dean Sch. Law, 1985-87, dean Sch. Law, 1987-93, interim univ. sr. vice chancellor and provost, 1993-94, Univ. Disting. Svc. prof., 1994—, interim univ. chancellor, 1995-96, univ. chancellor, 1996—; mem. U.S. Supreme Ct. Adv. Com. on Civil Rules, Washington, 1988-93, Pa. Supreme Ct. Civil Procedure Rules Com., Phila., 1986-92; mem. large and complex case panel Am. Arbitration Assn.; reporter civil justice adv. group U.S. Dist. Ct., Pitts., 1991-96; bd. dirs. Mellon Nat. Bank. Author: Modern Pennsylvania Civil Practice, 1985, 2d edit., 1995. Trustee Thiel Coll., Greenville, Pa., 1987-97; bd. dirs. Inst. for Shipboard Edn. Found., Pitts. Tech. Coun., Pitts. Regional Alliance, Pitts. Digital Greenhouse, Boy Scouts of Allegheny County, Urban League of Pitts., United Way of Allegheny County, World Affairs Coun. of Pitts., The Carnegie Mus., Pitts., Allegheny Conf. on Cmty. Devel., Pitts.; chair Pitts. Coun. on Higher Edn. Named Vectors Pitts. Person of Yr. in Edn., 1996, Person of Yr., 1997. Fellow Am. Bar Found.; mem. ABA, Pa. Bar Assn., Pa. Assn. Colls. and Univs. (bd. dirs.), Allegheny County Bar Assn., Acad. Trial Lawyers Allegheny County, Pitts. Regional Alliance, Pa. Assn. Colls. & Univs., Pitts. Athletic Assn., Law Club Pitts., Univ. Club, Duquesne Club, Wildwood Golf Club. Office: U Pitts Cathedral of Learning Pittsburgh PA 15221-3662

**NORDGREN, GERALD PAUL,** lawyer; b. Chgo., Sept. 3, 1954; s. Donald Alan and Shirlee Ann (Tennyson) N.; m. Nancy Carol DeYoung, May 29, 1976; children: Rachel Katherine, Caleb Donald. BA, U. Ill., 1976; JD, Northwestern U., 1979. Bar: Ill. 1979, U.S. Dist. Ct. (no. dist.) Ill. 1979.

Assoc. Murphy, Putnick, Peters and Davis, Chgo., 1979-80; pvt. practice Chgo., 1980-81; ptnr. Mosher and Nordgren, Chgo., 1981-85; dir. legal svcs. Austin Christian Law Ctr., Chgo., 1983-88; pvt. practice Oak Park, Ill., 1985-90; instr. Roosevelt U., Chgo., 1985, Am. Inst. for Paralegal Studies, Wheaton, Ill., 1988-89; of counsel Koykar, Frejlich & Assocs., Westchester, Ill., 1989, Blair and Cole, Chgo., 1989-90; supv. atty. De Paul Legal Clinic, Chgo., 1990-94; dir. legal svcs. Chgo. Legal Clinic, 1995-99. Contbr. articles to profl. jours. Elder Circle Evang. Free Ch., Oak Park, 1989-93; bd. dirs. Austin Christian Law Ctr., Chgo., 1983-96, Circle Family Care, Chgo., 1987-93. Recipient Pro Bono Publico award Austin Christian Law Ctr., 1989. Mem. Christian Legal Soc., Chgo. Bar Assn., Ill. State B Assn., West Suburban Bar Assn. Avocations: singing, music, sports, history. Family and matrimonial, General civil litigation, Probate. Office: Chgo Legal Clinic 118 N Central Ave Chicago IL 60644-3101

**NORDLING, BERNARD ERICK,** lawyer; b. Nekoma, Kans., June 14, 1921; s. Carl Ruben Ebben and Edith Elveda (Freeburg) N.; m. Barbara Ann Burkholder, Mar. 26, 1949. Student, George Washington U., 1941-43; AB, McPherson Coll., 1947; JD, U. Kans., 1949. Bar: Kans. 1949, U.S. Dist. Ct. Kans. 1949, U.S. Ct. Appeals (10th cir.) 1970. Pvt. practice Hugoton, Kans., 1949—; ptnr. Kramer & Nordling, Hugoton, Kans., 1950—; city atty. City of Hugoton, 1951-87; county atty. Stevens County, Kans., 1957-63; Kans. mem. legal com. Interstate Oil Compact Commn., 1969-93; mem. supply tech. adv. com. nat. gas survey FPC, 1975-77. Editor U. Kans. Law Rev., 1949. Mem. Hugoton Sch. Bds., 1954-68, pres. grade sch. bd., 1957-63; trustee McPherson Coll., 1971-81, mem. exec. com., 1975-81; mem. Kans. Energy Adv. Coun., 1975-78, mem. exec. com., 1976-78. With AUS, 1944-46. Recipient Citation of Merit, McPherson Coll., 1987, Disting. Alumnus award Kans. U. Law Sch., 1993, Lifetime Achievement award Hugoton Kans. Area C. of C., 1994. Fellow Am. Bar Found. (Kans.); mem. ABA, Kans. Bar Assn., S.W. Kans. Bar Assn., Am. Judicature Soc., City Attys. Assn. Kans. (exec. com. 1975-83, pres. 1982-83), Nat. Assn. Royalty Owners (bd. govs. 1980—), S.W. Kans. Royalty Owners Assn. (exec. sec. 1968-94, asst. exec. sec. 1994—), U. Kans. Law Soc. (bd. govs. 1984-87), Kans. U. Endowment Assn. (trustee 1989—), Kans. U. Alumni Assn. (bd. dirs. 1992-97, Fred Ellsworth medallion 1997), Order of Coif, Phi Alpha Delta. Oil, gas, and mineral, Probate, General practice. Office: 209 E 6th St Hugoton KS 67951-2613

**NORDLING, H.G.,** lawyer; b. Neenah, Wis., Sept. 29, 1950; s. H.G. and Mary Isabel (Sullivan) N.; m. Mary J. Ross, July 6, 1984; children: Eva, Sam. JD, U. Wis., 1976. Bar: Wis. 1976, U.S. Dist. Ct. (we. dist.) Wis. 1976. Sole practitioner Washburn, Wis., 1976-86, 93—; dist. atty. Bayfield County, Washburn, Wis., 1987-92, corp. counsel, 1987-90. Bd. dirs. Northern Lites Manor Nursing Home, Washburn, 1996—, New Horizons North, Ashland, Wis., 1980-86. Democrat. Lutheran. Avocations: hunting, fishing, golf, skiing, reading. General civil litigation, Criminal, Real property. Office: 127 W Bayfield St Washburn WI 54891-1131

**NORDLINGER, STEPHANIE G.,** lawyer; b. L.A., 1940. BA, UCLA, 1961, MA, 1969; MA, U. Calif., Berkeley, 1962; JD, Loyola U., 1975. Bar: Calif. 1975, U.S. Dist. Ct. (ctrl. dist.) Calif. 1976, U.S. Ct. Appeals (9th cir.) 1976, U.S. Supreme Ct. 1992. Pvt. practice L.A., 1976-77, 89—; dep. pub. defender L.A. County, 1977-79; adj. prof. Calif. State U., Northridge, 1979; pvt. practice Santa Monica, Encino, Calif., 1979-83; assoc. Baltaxe, Rutkin & Levin, Beverly Hills, Calif., 1983-84; pvt. practice Marina del Rey, Calif., 1984-87; exec. dir. Westside Legal Svcs., Santa Monica, 1988; mem. adv. com. U.S. Ct. Appeals (9th cir.), San Francisco, 1987-90; dir. Joseph Beggs Found., Redlands, Calif., 1992-95. Editor Juvenile Cts. Bar Assn., 1981-82; cons.: (book) CEB California Civil Writ Practice, 1987; editor User Friendly, 1997-98. Bd. dirs., L.A. chpt. pres. ACLU, 1973-74; pres. Westwood Dem. Club, L.A., 1993-95; mem. state ctrl. com. Calif. Dems., 1995-96. Mem. RAND Alumni Assn., L.A. Computer Soc. (pres. 1994, dir., editor), Sierra Club. Avocations: genealogy, gardening, travel. E-mail: snordlinge@aol.com. Appellate, General civil litigation, Probate. Office: PO Box 78757 Los Angeles CA 90016-0757

**NORDLUND, WILLIAM CHALMERS,** lawyer; b. Chgo., Aug. 29, 1954; s. Donald E. and Jane H. (Houston) N.; m. Elizabeth Apell, Oct. 1, 1983; children: William Chalmers Jr., Scott Donald. BA, Vanderbilt U., 1976; JD, Duke U., 1979; MM, Northwestern U., 1990. Bar: Ill. 1979, Md. 1991, Mich. 1992. Assoc. Winston & Strawn, Chgo., 1979-87, ptnr., 1987-90; atty. Constellation Holdings, Inc., 1990-91; v.p., sec., gen. counsel The Oxford Energy Co., Dearborn, Mich., 1991-92, sr. v.p., sec., gen. counsel, 1992-93; gen. counsel Panda Energy Corp., Dallas, 1993-94, v.p. and gen. counsel, 1994-95; v.p., gen. counsel Panda Energy Internat., Inc., Dallas, 1995-96, sr. v.p., gen. counsel, 1996-97, exec. v.p. of fin., 1997-98; prin. Twinbridge Capital Holdings, LLC, Saddle River, N.J., 1999—. Bd. dirs. Orch. of Ill., Chgo., 1983-85; bd. dirs., sec. Literacy Vols. of Am.-Ill., Chgo., 1985-88, treas., 1988-90. Avocations: golf, tennis, skiing. General corporate, FERC practice. Office: Twinbridge Capital Holdings LLC 181 E Saddle River Rd Saddle River NJ 07458-2632

**NORDQUIST, STEPHEN GLOS,** lawyer; b. Mpls., May 13, 1936; s. Oscar Alvin Nordquist and Georgiana (Glos) Ruplin; m. Cynthia Alexandra Turner, Aug. 16, 1958 (div. Aug. 1967); children: Darcy Alden Sullivan, Timothy Turner; m. Regina Frances Stanton, Nov. 1, 1969 (div. May 1996); 1 child, Nicholas Alden. BA cum laude, U. Minn., 1958, LL.B cum laude, 1961. Bar: Minn. 1961, N.Y. 1962. Assoc. Dewey, Ballantine, Bushby, Palmer & Wood, N.Y.C., 1961-69, ptnr., 1969-85; sr. v.p. W.P. Carey & Co., Inc., N.Y.C., 1985-86, exec v.p., sec., 1986-87; ptnr. Cole & Deitz (now Winston & Strawn), N.Y.C., 1988-89; of counsel Dreyer and Traub, N.Y.C., 1990-91; mem. Nordquist & Stern PLLC, N.Y.C., 1996—; pres., bd. dirs. Carey Corp. Property, Inc., Carey-Longmont Inc., Carey-Longmont Real Property, Inc., N.Y.C., 1985-87, 520 East 86th Street, Inc. Mem. Knickerbocker Club (house com.), World Trade Ctr. Club. Republican. Congregationalist. Aviation, Finance, Securities. Home: 211 E 53d St Apt 7D New York NY 10022-4805 also: 6970 Rognaldson Rd SE Brainerd MN 56401-8444 Office: 509 Madison Ave Ste 612 New York NY 10022-5501

**NOREK, FRANCES THERESE,** lawyer; b. Chgo., Mar. 9, 1947; d. Michael S. and Viola C. (Harbecke) N.; m. John E. Flavin, Aug. 31, 1968 (div.); 1 child, John Michael. B.A., Loyola U., Chgo., 1969, J.D., 1973. Bar: Ill. 1973, U.S. Dist. Ct. (no. dist.) Ill. 1973, U.S. Ct. Appeals (7th cir.) 1974. Assoc. Alter, Weiss, Whitesel & Laff, Chgo., 1973-74; asst. states atty. Cook County, Chgo., 1974-86; assoc. Clausen, Miller, Gorman, Caffrey & Witous P.C., 1986—; mem. trial practice faculty Loyola U. Sch. Law, Chgo., 1980—; judge, evaluator mock trial competitions, Chgo., 1978—; lectr. in field. Recipient Emil Gumpert award Am. Coll. Trial Lawyers, 1982. Mem. Chgo. Bar Assn. (instr. fed. trial bar adv. program young lawyer's sect. 1983-84). Office: Clausen Miller Gorman Caffrey & Witous PC 10 S La Salle St Ste 1600 Chicago IL 60603-1098

**NOREK, JOAN I.,** lawyer; b. Chgo., Jan. 26, 1945; d. Michael Stephen and Viola Catherine (Harbecke) N. BA in Chemistry, U. Ill., 1968; JD, DePaul U., 1975. Bar: Ill. 1975, U.S. Dist. Ct. (no. dist.) Ill. 1976, U.S. Ct. Appeals (7th cir.) 1976; registered patent atty. U.S. Patent and Trademark Office. Assoc. William Brinks et al, Chgo., 1975-80; pvt. practice Chgo., 1980—. Mem. Am. Chem. Soc., Chgo. Intellectual Property Law Assn. (mem. bd. mgrs. 1989-91), Chgo. Bar Assn. Intellectual property, Patent, Trademark and copyright. Office: 180 N La Salle St Chicago IL 60601-2501

**NORFOLK, WILLIAM RAY,** lawyer; b. Huron, S.D., Mar. 15, 1941; s. James W. and Helen F. (Thompson) N.; m. Marilyn E. Meadors; children: Stephanie G., Allison T., Meredith H. BA, Miami U., Oxford, Ohio, 1963; student, U. London, 1963-64; LLB, Duke U., 1967. Bar: N.Y. 1968, U.S. Dist. Ct. (so. and ea. dists.) N.Y. 1969, U.S. Ct. Appeals (2d cir.) 1969, U.S. Ct. Appeals (9th cir.) 1977, U.S. Ct. Appeals (5th cir.) 1979, U.S. Ct. Appeals (3d and 11th cirs.) 1981, U.S. Dist. Ct. (ea. dist.) Mich. 1986, U.S. Ct. Appeals (6th and 8th cirs.) 1986, U.S. Ct. Appeals (Fed. cir.) 1990, U.S. Ct. Internat. Trade 1990, U.S. Dist. Ct. (we. dist.) Mich. 1992. Assoc. Sullivan & Cromwell, N.Y.C., 1967-74, ptnr., 1974—. Trustee N.Y. Meth. Hosp. Mem. ABA, N.Y. State Bar Assn. Antitrust, General civil litigation, Mergers and acquisitions. Office: Sullivan & Cromwell 125 Broad St Fl 28 New York NY 10004-2489

**NORGLE, CHARLES RONALD, SR.,** federal judge; b. Mar. 3, 1937. BBA, Northwestern U., Evanston, Ill., 1964; JD, John Marshall Law Sch., Chgo., 1969. Asst. state's atty. DuPage County, Ill., 1969-71, dep. pub. defender, 1971-73, assoc. judge, 1973-77, 78-81, cir. judge, 1977-78, 81-84; judge U.S. Dist. Ct. (no. dist.) Ill., Chgo., 1984—; mem. exec. com. No. Dist. Ill.; mem. 7th Cir. Jud. Coun., 7th Cir. Jud. Conf. planning com., subcom. grant requests Fed. Defender Orgn., Fed. Defender Svcs. Com.; adj. faculty Northwestern U. Sch. Law, John Marshall Law Sch., Chgo.; pres. Atticus Finch Inn Ct. Mem. ABA, Fed. Bar Assn., Ill. Bar Assn., DuPage Bar Assn., Nat. Attys. Assn., DuPage Assn. Women Attys., Chgo. Legal Club, Northwestern Club. Office: US Dist Ct 219 S Dearborn St Ste 2346 Chicago IL 60604-1802

**NORMAN, ALBERT GEORGE, JR.,** lawyer; b. Birmingham, Ala., May 29, 1929; s. Albert G. and Ila Mae (Carroll) N.; m. Catherine Marshall DeShazo, Sept. 3, 1955; children: Catherine Marshall, Albert George III. BA, Auburn U., 1953; LLB, Emory U., 1958; MA, U. N.C., 1960. Bar: Ga. 1957. Assoc. Moise, Post & Gardner, Atlanta, 1958-60, ptnr., 1960-62; ptnr. Hansell & Post, Atlanta, 1962-86, Long, Aldridge & Norman, Atlanta, 1986—; dir. Atlanta Gas Light Co. Served with USAF, 1946-49. Mem. ABA, Ga. Bar Assn., Atlanta Bar Assn., Lawyers Club Atlanta (pres. 1973-74), Am. Law Inst., Am. Judicature Soc. (dir. 1975-78), Old War Horse Lawyers Club, (pres. 1991-92), Cherokee Town and Country Club. Episcopalian. Public utilities, Communications, General civil litigation.

**NORMAN, DAVID JOSEPH,** lawyer; b. Ogdensburg, N.Y., Aug. 25, 1959; s. Richard Joseph and Judith (McDonald) N.; m. Kathryn Ellen Murphy, Mar. 6, 1991; children: Elizabeth, Robert, Teresa. BA, Johns Hopkins U., 1981; D in Law, Cornell U., 1984. Bar: Md. 1985, U.S. Dist. Ct. Md. 1986, U.S. Ct. Appeals (4th cir.) 1988, (D.C. cir.), 1988, U.S. Ct. Appeals (3d cir.) 1989. Assoc. Semmes & Semmes, Balt., 1984-87, Weinberg & Green, Balt., 1987-90; of counsel Montedonico & Mason, Balt., 1990-91; shareholder Mason, Ketterman & Morgan, Balt., 1991-97; gen. counsel, sec. DavCo Restaurants Inc., Crofton, Md., 1997—. Mem. Commn. for Hist. and Archtl. Preservation, Balt., 1985-95, chair, 1991-95. Mem. Phi Alpha Delta. Democrat. Roman Catholic. Franchising, General corporate. Office: DavCo Restaurants Inc 1657 Crofton Blvd Crofton MD 21114-1305

**NORMAN, FORREST ALONZO,** lawyer; b. Renton, Pa., Nov. 21, 1929; s. Forrest Alonzo and Nellie Corley Norman; m. Christine Dende Norman, July 5, 1954; children: Sally, Forrest III, William. BBA, Western Res. U., 1952, LLB, 1954. Bar: Ohio 1954, U.S. Dist. Ct. (no. dist.) Ohio 1956, U.S. Supreme Ct. 1980. Assoc. Hauxhurst, Inglis, Sharp and Cull, Cleve., 1956-64; ptnr. Hauxhurst, Sharp, Mollison & Gallagher, Cleve., 1964-76, Gallagher, Sharp, Fulton and Norman, Cleve., 1976—; pres. Fed. Ins. and Corp. Counsel, Walpole, Mass., 1981-82. Contbr. articles to profl. jours. Gen. chmn. Case Western Res. U. Ann. Fund, 1990-91. With USNR, 1947-52, U.S. Army, 1954-56. Recipient Disting. Svc. award Def. Rsch. Inst., 1983. Fellow Am. Coll. of Trial Lawyers, Ohio State Bar Found., Nat. Assn. R.R. Trial Counsel (bd. dirs. 1986—). Republican. Avocations: golf, gardening, reading. General civil litigation, Federal civil litigation, Insurance. Home: 2977 Courtland Blvd Shaker Heights OH 44122-2803 Office: Gallagher Sharp Fulton & Norman 1501 Euclid Ave Ste 700 Cleveland OH 44115-2108

**NORMAN, MARTHA,** lawyer; b. Birmingham, Ala.; divorced. BS, Elmhurst (Ill.) Coll., 1965; MT, Northwestern Meml. Hosp., Chgo., 1966; JD, John Marshall Law Sch., Chgo., 1994. Bar: Ill. 1994. Atty. Law Offices of Martha Norman, Oak Brook, Ill., 1994—; guest lectr. Elmhurst Coll., 1997-98. Contbr. articles to profl. jours. Mem. ABA, DuPage County Bar Assn. (chair pub. rels. 1997-98, Bd. Dirs. award 1996), Stonehenge, The DuPage Club. Office: 1315 W 22nd St Ste 225 Oak Brook IL 60523-2061

**NORMAN, RICHARD EUGENE,** lawyer; b. Bristol, Pa., Sept. 6, 1968; s. Charles Richard and Diana Linda Norman; m. Sheryl Sipes, Aug. 14, 1993. BA, U. Fla., 1990; JD, Baylor U., 1993. Bar: Tex., U.S. Dist. Ct. (ea., we., so., and no. dists.) Tex. Atty. Crowley Marks & Douglas, Houston, 1993-97; ptnr. Crowley & Douglas, Houston, 1997—. Mem. ABA, Assn. Trial Lawyers Am., Tex. Trial Lawyers Assn. Democrat. Federal civil litigation, Product liability, Personal injury. Office: Crowley & Douglas LLP 1301 Mckinney St Ste 3500 Houston TX 77010-3034

**NORMAN, RICK JOSEPH,** lawyer, writer; b. Baton Rouge, Aug. 27, 1954; s. Merrick Joseph Norman and Ruth Evelyn Bennett; m. Polly Ann Palmer, July 29, 1978; children: Rose, Judson, Joseph. BA, La. State U., 1977, JD, 1979. Bar: La. 1980, Colo. 1990. Asst. U.S. atty. U.S. Dept. Justice, Baton Rouge, 1983-85; mng. ptnr. Woodley & Williams Law Firm, Lake Charles, 1985—; instr. McNeese State U. Lake Charles, 1986-95; atty. City of Lake Charles, 1992-93. Author: Louisiana Corporations, 1983, Louisiana Business Entities, 1998, (novels) Fielder's Choice, 1991, Cross Body Block, 1996. mem. governmental ethics bd. City of Lake Charles, 1991-94. Mem. La. State Bar Assn. (chmn. ethics com. 1994—), Phi Beta Kappa, Phi Kappa Phi. Avocation: baseball. General corporate, Contracts commercial, General practice. Office: Woodley & Williams Law Firm 500 Kirby St Lake Charles LA 70601-5221

**NORRIS, ALAN EUGENE,** federal judge; b. Columbus, Ohio, Aug. 15, 1935; s. J. Russell and Dorothy A. (Shrader) N.; m. Nancy Jean Myers, Apr. 15, 1962 (dec. Jan. 1986); children: Tom Edward Jackson, Tracy Elaine; m. Carol Lynn Spohn, Nov. 10, 1990. BA, Otterbein Coll., 1957, HLD (hon.), 1991; cert., U. Paris, 1956; LLB, NYU, 1960; LLM, U. Va., 1986. Bar: Ohio 1960, U.S. Dist. Ct. (so. dist.) Ohio 1962, U.S. Dist. Ct. (no. dist) Ohio 1964. Law clk. to judge Ohio Supreme Ct., Columbus, 1960-61; assoc. Vorys, Sater, Seymour & Pease, Columbus, 1961-62; ptnr. Metz, Bailey, Norris & Spicer, Westerville, Ohio, 1962-80; judge Ohio Ct. Appeals (10th dist.), Columbus, 1981-86, U.S. Ct. Appeals (6th cir.), Columbus, 1986—. Contbr. articles to profl. jours. Mem. Ohio Ho. of Reps., Columbus, 1967-80. Named Outstanding Young Man, Westerville Jaycees, 1971; recipient Legislator of Yr. award Ohio Acad. Trial Lawyers, Columbus, 1972. Mem. Ohio Bar Assn., Columbus Bar Assn. Republican. Methodist. Lodge: Masons (master 1966-67). Office: US Ct Appeals 328 US Courthouse 85 Marconi Blvd Columbus OH 43215-2823

**NORRIS, BENJAMIN R.,** lawyer; b. N.Y.C., Nov. 26, 1960. BA, Yale U., 1983; JD, Northwestern U., 1986. Bar: Ariz. 1986. Assoc. Brown & Bain, Phoenix, 1986-88; trial atty. U.S. Dept. Justice, Washington, 1989-93; from assoc. to ptnr. Quarles & Brady, LLP, Phoenix, 1993-97, ptnr., 1997—. Mem. ABA, Ariz. Bar Assn., Maricopa County Bar Assn., Nat. Assn. Bankruptcy Trustees. Avocations: running, history, naval history. Bankruptcy, General civil litigation. Office: Quarles & Brady LLC One E Camelback Rd #400 Phoenix AZ 85012

**NORRIS, CHARLES HEAD,** lawyer, manufacturing executive; b. Boston, Sept. 14, 1940; s. Charles Head and Martha Marie N.; BA, U. Pa., 1963, JD, 1968; MA, U. Wash., 1965; m. Diana D. Strawbridge, July 27, 1974 (div. 1994); 1 child, Margaret Dorrance. Bar: Pa. 1968. Mem. firm Morgan, Lewis & Bockius, Phila., 1968-77; pres., chief exec. Artemis Corp., 1978-79; chmn. bd., chief exec., 1979-91; chmn. exec. com., vice-chmn. bd. Remington Rand Corp., 1979-81; ptnr. Artemis Energy Co., 1980-92; chmn., CEO Norris Investment Co., 1992—; chmn. Norris Mfg. Co., 1994—, Garret Precision Products, 1996—; chmn., CEO Precision Technologies, 1996—; trustee maj. stockholders' voting trust Campbell Soup Co., 1987-90; bd. dirs. SBSF Funds, Inc., 1988-91, Del. trust, 1987-91. Bd. dirs. Asprey & Co. Ltd., 1986-97; mem. Harvard U. Bd. Overseas Com. to Visit the Libr., 1989—; mem. Pa. Commn. Crime and Delinquency, 1980-84; mem. Thouron Award Selection Com., 1985-90; mem. Pa. Electoral Coll., 1980; mem. West Pikeland Twp. Suprs., 1969-72; mem. bd. visitors Carnegie Mellon U. Sch. Urban and Pub. Affairs, 1988-90; corp. mem. Belmont Hill Sch., 1990—. Officer USAF, 1960. Mem. ABA, Pa. Bar Assn., Am. Econ. Assn. Clubs: Phila., Knickerbocker, Union League, Vicmead Hunt, Everglades (bd. dirs. 1986-91), Sunningdale Golf (Eng.), The Country (Brookline). Office: PO Box 112 Boston MA 02117-0112

**NORRIS, CHARLES R.,** lawyer; b. Columbia, S.C., Oct. 10, 1954; s. Henry C. and Nancy P. Norris; m. Susan Kilpatrick, Nov. 27, 1993; 1 child. Grad., UCLA, 1976; JD, U. S.C., 1980. Bar: S.C. 1980. Jud. law clk. Winnsboro, S.C., 1980-81; ptnr. Nelson Mullins Riley & Scarborough, Charleston, S.C., 1981—. Mem. Def. Rsch. Inst. (vice-chair 1998), Profl. Liability Underwriters Soc. Professional liability, Libel, Product liability. Office: Nelson Mullins Riley Et Al 151 Meeting St Fl 5 Charleston SC 29401-2239

**NORRIS, DAVID BAXTER,** lawyer; b. Detroit, Sept. 22, 1960; s. Thomas W. and Margaret A. Norris. JD, U. Nebr., 1983, U. San Diego, 1990. Bar: Calif., U.S. Dist. Ct. (so. dist.) Calif., U.S. Supreme Ct., U.S. Ct. Appeals (4th dist.). Assoc. Hillsinger & Costanzo APC, San Diego, 1989-96; pvt. practice, San Diego, 1996—; bd. govs. State Bar Calif., San Francisco, 1998—; bd. dirs. U. San Diego Sch. of Law, San Diego Lawyer mag. Bd. dirs. San Diego Crime Victims Fund, 1996. Mem. Calif. Young Lawyers Assn. (pres. 1998-99), San Diego Barristers Club (pres. 1996), San Diego County Bar Assn. (chmn. disaster preparedness com. 1995—, chmn. 1996, litigation chair 1995-99), Consumer Attys. San Diego, San Diego BBB, San Diego Bar Found. (bd. dirs. 1998—). Fax: 619-232-2691. E-mail: DBN@NorrisLegal.com. General civil litigation, Personal injury. Office: 750 B Street Ste 1740 San Diego CA 92101-8114

**NORRIS, DONALD TERRY,** lawyer, prosecutor; b. West Palm Beach, Fla., Nov. 25, 1946; s. Robert W. and Dorothy B. Norris; m. Regina Ann Raw, Feb. 1, 1966; children: Christi D. Weaver, Paul S. AA, Maple Woods Jr. Coll., Kansas City, Mo., 1972; BA, William Jewell Coll., Liberty, Mo., 1974; JD, U. Mo., Kansas City, 1977. Bar: Mo. 1978. Dep. sheriff Clay County, Mo., 1974-78; asst. prosecutor Clay County, 1979-84; atty. Duncan, Coulson, Schloss et al, Gladstone, Mo., 1984-97, Shull, Norris Beeman & Schloss, Liberty, 1997-99; city prosecutor City of Liberty, 1984-99, City of Pleasant Valley, Mo., 1990-97; mcpl. judge, Pleasant Valley, 1997-99; prosecutor, Clay County, 1999—. Served with USAF, 1966-70. Mem. Mo. Mcpl. and Assoc. Cir. Ct. Prosecutor Assn. (bd. dirs. 1996—), Mo. Mcpl. and Assoc. Cir. Ct. Judges Assn. Democrat. Avocation: golf. Office: Clay County Prosecutors Office Liberty MO 64068

**NORRIS, FLOYD HAMILTON,** lawyer; b. Tahlequah, Okla., Oct. 24, 1908; s. Thomas Franklin and Sudie (Gates) N.; m. Martha B. Norris, July 1944 (dec.); 1 child, Floyd Hamilton II; m. Tania McKnight, June 28, 1991. BS, Northeastern State U., 1932; LLD, Okla. U., 1935. Bar: N.Mex. 1935, Okla. 1935, Calif. 1946. Pvt. practice, L.A., 1935—. Mem. Okla. Legis., Cherokee County, 1936-38. Col. U.S. Army, 1940-46. Decorated Bronze Star medal. Mem. Masons (Shriner). Democrat. Presbyterian. Avocations: gardening, woodworking. Probate, Estate taxation, Consumer commercial. Office: Norris Bldg Inc 714 S Hill St Ste 405 Los Angeles CA 90014-2713

**NORRIS, JAMES MARSHALL,** lawyer, educator; b. Oxnard, Calif., Mar. 9, 1953; s. James Henry Norris; m. Paula Anell Lee, July 17, 1977; children: Nicholas Lee, Matthew Cole. BA, Miss. State U., 1975; JD, U. Miss., 1978. Bar: Miss. 1978. Atty. sr. Miss. Dept. Corrections, Parchman, 1978—; adj. instr. Miss. Delta C.C., Moorhead, 1990—. Baptist. Office: Miss Dept Corrections PO Box 36 Parchman MS 38738-0036

**NORRIS, JOHN HART,** lawyer; b. New Bedford, Mass., Aug. 4, 1942; s. Edwin Arter and Harriet Joan (Winter) N.; m. Anne Kiley Monaghan, June 10, 1967; children: Kiley Anne, Amy O'Shea. BA, Ind. U., 1964; JD, U. Mich., 1967. Bar: Mich. 1968, U.S. Ct. Claims 1975, U.S. Tax Ct. 1979, U.S. Ct. Mil. Appeals 1969, U.S. Supreme Ct. 1974. From assoc. to ptnr. Monaghan, Campbell, LoPrete, McDonald and Norris, 1970-83; of counsel Dickinson, Wright, Moon, Van Dusen & Freeman, 1983-84, ptnr., 1985—; natural gas law counsel to claims mediator Columbia Gas Transmission Corp.; chpt. 11 bankruptcy procs. in Wilmington, Del. Bankruptcy Ct., 1992—; bd. dirs. Prime Securities Corp., Ray M. Whyte Co., Ward-Williston Drilling Co. Contbr. articles to profl. jours. Mem. Rep. State Fin. Com.; founder, co-chmn. Rep. Majority Club; bd. trustees Boys and Girls Clubs of Southeastern Mich., 1979—, Mich. Wildlife Habitat Found., Mercy Coll., Detroit, Detroit Hist. Soc., 1984—; bd. trustees, bd. dirs. African Wildlife Found.; trustee, 1st vice chmn. Salk Inst. With M.I., U.S. Army, 1968-70. Recipient numerous civic and non-profit assn. awards. Fellow Mich. State Bar Found.; mem. ABA (litigation and natural resources sects.), Mich. Oil and Gas Assn. (legal and legis. com.), State Bar Mich. (chmn. environ. law sect. 1982-83, probate and trust law sect., energy conservation task force, oil and gas com.), Oakland County Bar Assn., Detroit Bar Assn. (pub. adv. com.), Am. Arbitration Assn., Fin. and Estate Planning Coun. of Detroit, Def. Orientation Conf. Assn., Detroit Zool. Soc., Blue Key Nat. Hon. Fraternity, Phi Delta Phi. Clubs: Bloomfield Hills Country, Thomas M. Cooley, Detroit Athletic, Econ. (Detroit), Hundred, Prismatic, Turtle Lake, Yondotega. Roman Catholic. Administrative and regulatory, General corporate, Oil, gas, and mineral. Home: 1325 Buckingham Ave Birmingham MI 48009-5881 Office: Dickinson Wright 525 N Woodward Ave Bloomfield Hills MI 48304-2971

**NORRIS, LAWRENCE GEOFFREY,** lawyer; b. Centralia, Ill., June 4, 1926; s. Patrick Iranaeus and Julia Catherine (Lordan) N.; m. Lauretta Shore, Feb. 7, 1953; children: Deborah, Lawrence, David, Steven; m. Barbara H. DeKorte, Sept. 28, 1979. BSEE, U. Ill., 1947; MSEE, Northeastern U., 1962; JD, Boston Coll., 1953. Bar: Mass. 1953, Va. 1968, D.C. 1988. Div. patent counsel GE Co., 1962-69; assoc. patent counsel, sr. corp. atty. Polaroid Corp., 1969-80; v.p., corp. counsel Energy Conversion Devices, Inc., Troy, Mich., 1980-87; ptnr. Rothwell, Figg, Ernst & Kurz, Washington, 1987—. Served with U.S. Army, 1944-46. Mem. ABA, Am. Patent Law Assn., Assn. Corp. Patent Counsel. Club: Fides Soc. Boston Coll. General corporate, Patent. Office: Rothwell Figg Ernst & Kurz Columbia Sq 555 13th St NW Ste 701E Washington DC 20004-1126

**NORRIS, MEGAN PINNEY,** lawyer; b. Mpls., May 20, 1961; d. Rollin Bradford and Margo Pinney N.; m. Howard William Trevor Matthew, May 27, 1989; 1 child, Taylor Norris Matthew. BA, Wesleyan U., 1983; JD, U. Mich., 1986. Bar: Mich. 1986, U.S. Dist. Ct. (ea. dist.) Mich. 1986, U.S. Dist. Ct. (we. dist.) Mich. 1989, U.S. Ct. Appeals (6th cir.) 1998. Assoc. Miller, Confield, Paddock and Stone, P.L.C., Detroit, 1986-94, prin., 1995—; bd. dirs. Detroit Metropolitan Bar Assn.; adv. bd. Inst. Continuing Legal Edn., Ann Arbor, Mich., 1997—. Co-author: Michigan Public Employee Labor Relations Manual, 1994, Employment Discrimination Law Supplement, 1998; contbr. articles to profl. jours. Pres., bd. trustees Deaf, Hearing & Speech Ctr., Detroit, 1996-98, Wayne State Episcopal Chaplanery, Detroit, 1993-98; pres., bd. dirs. Whitlar Sch. Theology, Detroit, 1993-94. Recipient Leadership Detroit award Detroit C. of C., 1996. Mem. Detroit Baristers Assn. (pres. 1994-95), Wesleyan U. bd. trustees nominating com. (1995-97), Episcopal Diocese Mich., Christ Ch. Detroit (sr. warden 1994). Democrat. Avocations: biking, cooking. Labor, Civil rights, General civil litigation. Office: Miller Canfield Paddock and Stone PLC 150 W Jefferson Ave Ste 2500 Detroit MI 48226-4416

**NORRIS, RAYMOND MICHAEL,** lawyer; b. Chgo., Dec. 14, 1948; s. William Patrick and Nellie (Scanlon) N.; m. Maxine Anne Flom, Aug. 16, 1951; children: Michael, Erin, David. BA, U. Toronto, 1977; LLB, York U., Toronto, 1981; MCL, George Washington U., 1982. Bar: Ariz. 1982, U.D. Dist. Ct. Ariz. 1983, U.S. Ct. Appeals (9th cir.) 1985. Assoc. Treon Strick Lucia & Aguirre, Phoenix, 1982-86, shareholder atty., 1986-93; founder, v.p. Norris & O'Daniel, Phoenix, 1993—; judge pro tempore Maricopa County Superior Ct., Phoenix, 1995—. Former pres., bd. dirs. Hope Ctr. for Head Injury, Phoenix, 1985-91; bd. dirs. P.R.I.D.E., Phoenix; mem. vol. lawyers program Pro Bono Legal Svcs., Phoenix, 1994—; mem. legis. com. Gov.'s Coun. on Spine and Head Injuries, 1993—. Mem. ATLA, Ariz. State Bar Assn., Phoenix Trial Lawyers Assn. (bd. dirs.), Ariz. Trial Lawyers Assn. Democrat. Avocations: golf, humor, fitness, little league coaching. Personal injury, Product liability. Home: 106 E Colt Rd Tempe AZ 85284-2386 Office: Norris and O'Daniel PA 2302 N 3rd St Phoenix AZ 85004-1301

**NORRIS, RICK D.,** lawyer; b. Birmingham, Ala., Sept. 16, 1959; s. R.D. and Billie Norris; m. Suzanne Elizabeth Bavker, July 30, 1983; children: Meridith Suzanne, Rick D. III. BA, U. Ala., 1981; JD, Cumberland Sch. Law, 1984. Bar: Ala., S.C., U.S. Dist. Ct. (no. dist.) Ala. Co. rep. Safeco Ins. Co., Birmingham, 1984-86; risk mgmt. staff Willis Corroon Corp., Birmingham, 1986-90; atty. Lamar Nelson Miller, Birmingham, 1990-98; shareholder, atty. Lamar Miller & Norris, Birmingham, 1998—. Named

Outstanding Young Men of Am., 1981. Mem. Ala. State Bar, S.C. State Bar, Ala. Def. Lawyers, Def. Rsch. Inst. Mem. Church of Christ. General civil litigation, Personal injury, Product liability. Home: 3350 Panorama Brook Dr Vestavia Hills AL 35216-4245 Office: Lamar Miller & Norris PC 505 20th St N Birmingham AL 35203-2605

**NORRIS, ROBERT WHEELER,** lawyer, military officer; b. Birmingham, Ala., May 22, 1932; s. Hubert Lee and Georgia Irene (Parker) N.; m. Martha Katherine Cummins, Feb. 19, 1955; children—Lisha Katherine Norris Utt, Nathan Robert. B.A. in Bus. Adminstrn., U. Ala., 1954, LL.B., 1955; LL.M., George Washington U., 1979; postgrad., Air Command & Staff Coll., 1968, Nat. War Coll., 1975. Commd. 2d lt. USAF, advanced through grades to maj. gen.; dep. judge advocate gen. USAF, Washington, 1983-85, judge advocate gen., 1985-88; gen. counsel Ala. Bar Assn., Montgomery, 1988-95; ptnr. London & Yancey, Birmingham, Ala., 1995—. Decorated D.S.M., Legion of Merit, Meritorious Svc. medal. Mem. ABA. Methodist. Military, Ethics, Personal injury. Office: London & Yancey 2001 Park Pl Ste 400 Birmingham AL 35203-2787

**NORRIS, WILLIAM ALBERT,** former federal judge; b. Turtle Creek, Pa., Aug. 30, 1927; s. George and Florence (Clive) N.; m. Merry Wright, Nov. 23, 1974; children: Barbara, Donald, Kim, Alison; m. Jane Jelenko. Student, U. Wis., 1945; B.A., Princeton U., 1951; J.D., Stanford U., 1954. Bar: Calif. and D.C. 1955. Assoc. firm Northcutt Ely, Washington, 1954-55; law clk. to Justice William O. Douglas U.S. Supreme Ct., Washington, 1955-56; sr. mem. firm Tuttle & Taylor, Inc., L.A., 1956-80; judge U.S. Ct. Appeals (9th cir.), L.A., 1980-94, sr. judge, 1994-97; lawyer, mediator Ct. of Appeals Folger, Levin & Kahn, L.A., 1997—; spl. counsel Pres.' Kennedy's Com. on Airlines Controversy, 1961; mem., v.p. Calif. State Bd. Edn., 1961-67. Trustee Calif. State Colls., 1967-72; pres. L.A. Bd. Police Commrs., 1973-74; Democratic nominee for atty. gen. State of Calif., 1974; founding pres. bd. trustees Mus. Contemporary Art, L.A., 1979—; trustee Craft and Folk Art Mus., 1979—. With USN, 1945-47. Home: 1473 Oriole Dr West Hollywood CA 90069-1155 Office: Folger Levin & Kahn 1900 Ave Of Stars Fl 28 Los Angeles CA 90067-4301

**NORSE, KRISTIN A.,** lawyer; b. Newport News, Va., June 21, 1968; d. Edwin M. and Margaret A. (Hammond) N.; m. Jeffrey D. Grabel, July 5, 1997. BA in English, Boston U., 1992, JD, 1992. Bar: Fla. 1992. Assoc. Hampton, Stoddard, Griffin & Runnells, P.A., Brandon, Fla., 1993-96, Harris, Barrett, Mann & Dew, Sun City, Fla., 1997—. Mem. Hillsborough Assn. for Women Lawyers (dir. 1994-96, 98—), Ruskin C. of C. (dir.). State civil litigation, Family and matrimonial, General practice. Office: Harris Barrett Mann & Dew LLP 811 Cypress Village Blvd Ste B Ruskin FL 33573-6724

**NORSTRAND, HANS PETER,** lawyer, real estate investment company executive; b. Cambridge, Mass., Aug. 1, 1940; s. Hans Donald and Marion (Hardy) N.; m. Janet Hoover, Dec. 30, 1967 (div.); children: Rachel Bell, Hans Christopher; m. Katherine Tallman, Feb. 5, 1994. A.B., Dartmouth Coll., 1963; J.D., Boston Coll., 1966. Bar: Mass. 1966; U.S. Supreme Ct., 1994. Asst. atty. gen. Mass., 1966-69; assoc. Sullivan & Worcester, Boston, 1969-74; v.p., gen. csl. Kuras & Co., Inc., Boston, 1974-76; pvt. practice, Boston, 1977-80; v.p., gen. counsel Boston Co. Real Estate Counsel, Inc., 1980-81; prin. Aldrich, Eastman & Waltch, Boston, 1981-91; mng. dir. Sun Capital Advs., Inc., Boston, 1991-93; v.p. State St. Global Advs., 1994-99, v.p. ASB Capital Mgmt., Inc., 1999—; mem. faculty Internat. Council Shopping Ctrs., 1981-88; part-time mem. faculty Boston U. Sch. Mgmt., 1979-82, Boston U. Sch. of Law, 1986-89; corporator West Newton (Mass.) Savs. Bank, 1976-86. Served with USMCR, 1958-61. Mem. ABA, Boston Bar Assn. Democrat. Unitarian. Contbr. articles to legal jours.; speaker in field. Real property. Office: ASB Capital Mgmt Inc 1101 Pennsylvania Ave NW Washington DC 20004-2514

**NORSWORTHY, ELIZABETH KRASSOVSKY,** lawyer; b. N.Y.C., Feb. 26, 1943; d. Leonid Alexander and Wilma (Hudgens) Krassovsky; m. John Randolph Norsworthy, June 24, 1961 (div. 1962), m. Nov. 26, 1977 (div. 1984); 1 child, Alexander. AB magna cum laude, Hunter Coll., CUNY, 1965; MA, U. N.C., 1966; JD, Stanford U., 1977. Bar: D.C. 1978, Mass. 1992, Vt. 1998, U.S. Ct. Appeals (D.C. cir.) 1979. Atty. applications, disclosure rev. and investment adviser regulation, divsn. investment mgmt. SEC, Washington, 1978-79, 80-82, atty. operating brs. and disclosure policy divsn. corp. fin., 1979-80, chief, spl. counsel office of regulatory policy divsn. investment mgmt., 1983-86; assoc. Kirkpatrick & Lockhart, Washington, 1986-90; ptnr. Sullivan & Worcester, Boston, 1990-92; pvt. practice Norfolk, Mass., 1992-95, Concord, Vt., 1996—; pub. arbitrator, chairperson NASD; arbitrator Am. Arbitration Assn. Bd. dirs. First Night, St. Johnsbury; mem. bus. com., chair investment com. North Congl. Ch., St. Johnsbury; mem. adv. bd. Natural Resources, Concord. Fellow Chartered Inst. Arbitrators; mem. ABA (securities com. 1986—, investment adviser investment co. sub-com. 1990 —, alt. dispute resolution cim. 1998—, arbitration sub com., internat. subcom.), N.Y. '40 Acts. Com., Union Club of Boston, Am. Livestock Breek Conservancy, Jacob Sheep Breed Assn., Am. Farmland Trust, Vt. Grass Farmers, Vt. Coverts, Catamount Arts (St. Johnsbury), Athenaeum (St. Johnsbury), College Club (St. Johnsbury), Phi Beta Kappa, Phi Alpha Theta. Democrat. Mem. United Church of Christ. Avocations: farming, swimming, riding, environmental protection. Securities, Private international, Alternative dispute resolution. Office: Winterbrook Farm 1342 Woodward Rd Concord VT 05824-9620

**NORTH, H. DAVIS, III,** lawyer; b. Little Rock, Nov. 23, 1948; s. Hugh Davis and Florence (Harrison) N.; m. Caroline Keener; children: Alexandra, Carter, Harrison. BA, U. N.C., 1970, MAT, 1972; JD, Wake Forest U., 1980. Asst. pub. defender Pub. Defender's Office, Greensboro, N.C., 1980-83; ptnr. Adams, North, Cooke & Landreth, Greensboro, 1983-86, Harrison, North, Cooke & Landreth, Greensboro, 1986—. Recipient Pro Bono award Greensboro Bar Assn., 1996. Mem. Nat. Assn. Criminal Def. Lawyers, N.C. Acad. Trial Lawyers. Avocations: scuba diving, trapshooting, golf. Criminal. Office: Harrison North Cooke Landreth 221 Commerce Pl Greensboro NC 27401-2426

**NORTH, HAROLD LEBRON, JR.,** lawyer; b. Chattanooga, Feb. 17, 1944; s. Harold L. and Frances E. (Starr) N.; m. Teresa L. Hampton, Aug. 29, 1981; children: Harold L. III, Grant Gibson. BA, U. Tenn., 1977; JD, Memphis State U., 1980. Bar: Tenn. 1980, U.S. Dist. Ct. (ea. dist.) Tenn. 1980, U.S. Ct. Appeals (6th cir.) 1984, U.S. Supreme Ct. 1990, D.C. 1991, U.S. Dist. Ct. D.C. 1991, U.S. Ct. Appeals (D.C. cir.) 1992. Assoc. Tanner, Jahn, Atchley, Bridges & Jahn, Chattanooga, from 1980; ptnr. Tanner, Jahn, Anderson, Bridges & Jahn, Chattanooga, Ray & North, P.C., Chattanooga, until 1990, Shumacker & Thompson, P.C., Chattanooga, 1990—. Bd. dirs. Chattanooga Big Bros.-Big Sisters, 1994—, Scenic Land Sch., Chattanooga, 1993-94; bd. dirs. Chattanooga Area Crime Stoppers, Inc., 1984-93, chmn., 1989-90; grad. Leadership Chattanooga, 1988-89; grad. leadership tng. program Chattanooga Resource Found., 1992; mem. Tenn. Rep. Exec. Com., 1990—; chmn. Hamilton County Rep. Party, 1989-91; mem. Hamilton County Election Commn., Chattanooga, 1988-89. Mem. ABA, ATLA, Tenn. Bar Assn., Chattanooga Bar Assn. (chmn. bankruptcy and comml. law sect. 1993-94), D.C. Bar Assn., Tenn. Trial Lawyers Assn., Am. Bankruptcy Inst. Presbyterian. Avocations: golf, hunting, water sports. Bankruptcy, General civil litigation, Contracts commercial. Home: 16 Fairhills Dr Chattanooga TN 37405-4325 Office: Shumacker & Thompson PC First Tennessee Bldg 5th Fl Chattanooga TN 37402

**NORTH, KENNETH E(ARL),** lawyer, educator; b. Chgo., Nov. 18, 1945; s. Earl and Marion (Temple) N.; m. Susan C. Gutzmer, June 6, 1970. AA with high honors, Coll. of DuPage, Glen Ellyn, Ill., 1970; BA with high honors, No. Ill. U., 1971; JD, Duke U., 1974. Bar: Ill. 1974, U.S. Dist. Ct. (no. dist.) Ill. 1974, U.S. Tax Ct., 1975, Guam 1978, U.S. Ct. Appeals (7th cir.), 1978, U.S. Supreme Ct., 1978, U.S. Ct. Internat. Trade 1978, U.S. Ct. Appeals (9th cir.) 1979. Div. chief DuPage County State's Attys. Office, Wheaton, 1976-78; spl. asst. U.S. atty. Terr. of Guam, Agana, 1978-79, atty. gen., 1979-80; prof. sch. law Regent U., Virginia Beach, Va., 1994-98, dir. Ctr. for Leadership Studies, 1995-97; exec. dir. Canon Law Inst., 1998—; cons. Internet and Distance Edn., 1995—, Anglican Canon Law, 1996—; pres., editor, North Pub. Co., 1986-92; adj. prof. law John Marshall Law Sch., Chgo., 1985-90, vis. prof., 1998-99, Keller Grad. Sch. Mgmt. Northwestern U.; instr. Northwestern U. Traffic Inst., 1985-92, Aurora U., 1989-93; cons. Terr. of Guam, 1980-81. Author: Criminal Tax Fraud, 3d edit., 1998; co-author: Criminal and Civil Tax Fraud, 1986, 2d edit., 1993; bd. editors Attorneys' Computer Report, 1986-92; articles editor The Tax Lawyer, 1990-93; contbr. articles to legal publs. Trustee, mem. adv. bd. Ams. for Effective Law Enforcement, 1986-91; v.p. Glen Ellyn Manor Civic Assn., 1981-84, pres., 1984-88; police commr. Village of Glen Ellyn, 1982-89; bd. dirs. YMCA Northeastern DuPage County, 1991-94, 1st v.p. 1994; mem., vestry St. Mark's Episcopal Ch., Glen Ellyn, Ill. Mem. ABA, Assn. Trial Lawyers Am. (sec. criminal sect. 1986-87, 2d vice chair 1987-88, 1st vice chmn. 1989-90, chmn. 1990-91, pres. adv. com. 1991-96), Chgo. Duke Bar Assn. (pres. 1986-87), Computer Law Assn., Mensa. Republican. Episcopalian. Pioneer use of computer in court and delivery of doctoral programs via the internet and world wide web. Computer, Religion. Office: PO Box 3047 Chesapeake VA 23327-3047

**NORTH, STEVEN EDWARD,** lawyer; b. Bklyn., Oct. 16, 1941; s. Irving J. and Barbara (Grubman) N.; m. Sue J. Buznitsky, Dec. 24, 1966; children: Jennifer, Samantha. B.A., CCNY, 1963; J.D., Bklyn. Law Sch., 1966; LLM, NYU, 1967. Bar: N.Y. 1967, U.S. Dist. Ct. (so. and ea. dists.) N.Y. 1970, U.S. Supreme Ct., 1971. Asst. dist. atty. homicide bur. N.Y. County Dist. Attys. Office, N.Y.C., 1967-71; spl. asst. atty. gen., bur. chief N.Y. State Atty. Gen.'s Office, N.Y.C., 1972-75; sole practice, N.Y.C., 1975—; mem. adv. com. Ann. Civil Litigation Inst., Practising Law Inst., 1996; chmn. Assn. Bar Subcom. on Investigation into Imposition of Legis. Limits on Awards for Non-Econ. Damages, 1995; mediator U.S. Dist. Ct. (so. dist.) N.Y., 1994—, apptd. jud. screening program; mem. adv. coms. solo law practice Practising Law Inst., 1991, adv. bd. tort litigation, 1989—; vis. faculty Sch. Law NYU, faculty workshop Cardoza Sch. Law, judge applellate argument, alumni advisor, lectr. in field. Author: Prevention and Detection of Fraud in Industry, 1973, Controlling the Deposition: Winning Your Case Before Trial, 1978, Deposition Strategy, Law and Forms, vol. 1 (Introduction and Law), vol. 5 (Medical Malpractice), vol. 8 (Personal Injury), 1981, (course handbooks) Trial Mechanics, Personal Injury Desbook, 1983, Trial Mechanics and Discovery, 1985, 86, Medical Malpractice Litigation, 1988, Managing the Multi-Million Dollar Case, 1990, Objectifying Brain Damage in Closed Head Injury, 1990, Fundamentals of Medical Malpractice Litigation, 1991, Damage Update, 1992, 93, 94, 95, 96, 97—, Proving & Defending Damages, 1993, Conducting & Defending Depositions, 1993; contbr. chpts. to books; editor Cancer Litigation Bull., 1994—, Fear of Developing Cancer; contbg. editor Law and Order mag.; med.-legal editor Perinatology, 1983; contbr. articles to legal jours.; commentator Eyewitness News, 1994, Court TV, 1994-98, Talk News TV, 1996. Leadership coun. So. Poverty Law Ctr. Mem. ATLA, NOW (benefits com.), U.S. Holocaust Mus. (charter mem.), Am. Bd. Trial Advs., Soc. Med. Jurisprudence, Nat. Conf. Christians and Jews (lawyers divsn., annual dinner com.), N.Y. State Bar Assn. (faculty), N.Y. State Trial Lawyers Assn. (bd. dirs. 1990—), Lotos Club, Nat. Eagle Scout Assn., State Trial Lawyers Assn. (bd. dirs. 1990—, seminar faculty chmn. 1993, faculty decisions program 1991—, Law Day dinner com.), N.Y. County Lawyers Assn. (exec. com. med. malpractice sect., exec. com. gen. tort law sect.), Assn. of Bar of City of N.Y. (civil ct. com. 1980-83, legal and continuing edn. com. 1983—, legal referral svc. com., med. malpractice mediator, 1994—, chmn. subcom. on imposition of legislative limits to awards for non-econ. damages), Vol. Lawyers for the Arts, Mensa. State civil litigation, Personal injury. Home: 6 Saddle Rock Ter Great Neck NY 11023-1921 Office: 148 E 74th St New York NY 10021-3542

**NORTH, WILLIAM T.,** lawyer; b. EMporia, Kans., Feb. 13, 1950; s. Stanley J. and Mildred I. N.; m. Ann K. Winters, Aug. 12, 1972; children: Thomas A., Jennifer A. BA, Emporia State U., 1972; JD, Washburn U., 1976. Bar: Kans., U.S. Supreme Ct., U.S. Dist. Ct. Kans. Ptnr. Masoner & North, Cottonwood Falls, Kans., 1976-91; atty. pvt. practice, Cottonwood Falls, Kans., 1991—. City atty. City of Cottonwood Falls, 1976—, sch. atty. United Sch. Dist. No 248, Chase County, Kans., 1976—. Mem. Kans. Bar Assn., Chase/Lyon County Bar Assn. Republican. Episcopalian. Avocation: golf. Criminal, General practice, Estate planning. Office: 308 Broadway Cottonwood Falls KS 66845

**NORTHCUTT, CLARENCE DEWEY,** lawyer; b. Guin, Ala., July 7, 1916; s. Walter G. and Nancy E. (Homer) N.; m. Ruth Eleanor Storms, May 25, 1941; children: Gayle Marie (Mrs. John J. Young), John E. A.B., U. Okla., 1939, LL.B., 1938. Bar: Okla. 1938. Pvt. practice Ponca City, 1938—; Mem. bd. visitors U. Okla. Served with AUS, 1941-46. Decorated Bronze Star, Air medal with oak leaf cluster., Order St. John of Jerusalem; named Outstanding Citizen of Ponca City, 1982. Fellow Am. Coll. Trial Lawyers, Am. Coll. Trust and Estate Attys., Am. Bar Found.; mem. Acad. Univ. Fellows, Internat. Soc. Barristers, Am. Bd. Advocacy, Internat. Acad. Trial Lawyers, Okla. Bar Assn. (pres. 1975, bd. govs.), Ponca City C. of C. (past pres.). Democrat. Baptist. Clubs: Mason, Kiwanian. Probate, Personal injury. Home: 132 Whitworth Ave Ponca City OK 74601-3438 Office: PO Box 1669 Ponca City OK 74602-1669

**NORTHERN, RICHARD,** lawyer; b. Louisville, Dec. 17, 1948; s. James William and Mary Helen (Barry) N.; m. Mary Lou Grundy, Aug. 28, 1971; children: James Barry, Nancy Hope, Mary Grace. BA in English, U. Louisville, 1970, JD, 1976; MPA, Harvard U., 1977. Bar: Ky. 1976, U.S. Dist. Ct. (we. and ea. dists.) Ky. 1977. Staff writer Courier-Jour., Louisville, 1970-72; dir. planning devel. Jefferson County Govt., Louisville, 1972-76; legis. dir. Office of U.S. Rep. Romano Mazzoli, Washington, 1977-78; spl. asst. U.S. Sec. of Interior, Washington, 1979-80; ptnr. Wyatt, Tarrant & Combs, Louisville, 1980—. Chmn. bd. dirs. Saints Mary and Elizabeth Hosp., Louisville, 1987—. White House fellow, 1979, U.S.-Japan Leadership fellow Japan Soc., Inc., 1988. Democrat. Roman Catholic. General corporate, Administrative and regulatory, Private international. Office: Wyatt Tarrant & Combs 2800 Citizens Plz Louisville KY 40202-2898

**NORTHINGTON, HIAWATHA,** lawyer; b. Natchez, Miss., July 21, 1971; s. Hiawatha and Eunice Northington. BBA, Jackson State U., 1993; JD, U. Tex., 1996. Bar: Tex. 1996, Miss. 1998, U.S. Dist. Ct. (no. and so. dists.) Miss. 1998, U.S. Ct. Appeals (5th and 11th cirs.) 1998. Law clk. Supreme Ct. of Miss., Jackson, 1996-98; assoc. Byrd & Assocs., Jackson, 1998—. Mem. ABA, ATLA, Nat. Bar Assn. Personal injury, Product liability, Appellate. Office: Byrd & Assocs 427 E Fortification St Jackson MS 39202-2341

**NORTHROP, ALBERT WILLIS,** lawyer, judge; b. Paxton, Ill., Nov. 10, 1947; children: Kirstyn Lee, Brian Hale. BA, U. Md., 1969, JD, 1974. Bar: Md. 1974, U.S. Dist. Ct. Md. 1977, U.S. Supreme Ct. 1979. Probation officer State Md., Dept. Juvenile Svcs., Upper Marlboro, Md., 1969-75; ptnr. Northrop, Walsh, Becker, Cclaresi & Spears, Bowie, Md., 1975—; spl. reporter Ct. of Appeals Standing Com. on Rules, Criminal Rules Subcom., 1981; apptd. Prince George's County Orphans' Ct., 1986—; lectr. in field. Author: (lead) Decedents Estates in Maryland, 1994. Instnl. counselor Waxter Children's Ctr., summer 1969; mem. Prince George's County Adv. Youth Action Com., 1972-77, chmn., 1973-77, Prince George's County Child Abuse Task Force, 1973-74, Prince George's County Manpower Adv. Coun., 1974-77, Prince George's County Hotline Pro Backup and Selection Com., 1975-82, bd. mem., 1976-80, treas., 1978-80; mem. adv. bd. Bowie (Md.) Youth Svc. Bur., 1973-77; mem. Prince George's County Juvenile Ct. Adv. Com., 1977-86, chmn., 1978-85; county exec. Citizen Rev. Task Force, 1982-83; active Doncaster Youth Camp Adv. Bd., chair of the aftercare com., 1986-92. Recipient Gladys Noon Spellman award for outstanding contbn. to youth, 1985. Mem. ABA (vice chmn. subcom. juvenile justice 1976-79), Prince George's County Bar Assn. (bd. mem. 1985-86, 87-89, chair CLE, ct. house facilities and newsletter coms., Pres.'s award for outstanding contbn. to cmty. 1987). Avocations: photography, antique and sports cars, sports car racing, horses, western history and memorabilia, skiing. Home: 10721 Mattaponi Rd Upper Marlboro MD 20772-8205 Office: 14300 Gallant Fox Ln Ste 218 Bowie MD 20715-4003

**NORTHROP, EDWARD SKOTTOWE,** federal judge; b. Chevy Chase, Md., June 12, 1911; s. Claudian Bellinger and Eleanor Smythe (Grimke) N.; m. Barbara Middleton Burdette, Apr. 22, 1939; children: Edward M., St. Julien (Mrs. Kevin Butler), Peter. LLB, George Washington U., 1937. Bar: Md. 1937, D.C. 1937. Village mgr. Chevy Chase, Md., 1934-41; pvt. practice, Rockville, Md., Washington, 1937-61; mem. Md. Senate, 1954-61, chmn. fin. com., joint com. taxation fiscal affairs, majority leader, 1959-61; judge U.S. Dist. Ct. Md., Balt., 1961-70; chief judge U.S. Dist. Ct. of Md., Balt., 1970-81, sr. judge, 1981—; mem. Met. Chief Judges Conf., 1970-81; mem. Jud. Conf. Com. on Adminstrn. of Probation System, 1973-79, Adv. Corrections Council U.S., 1976—, Jud. Panel on Multidist. Litigation, 1979—; judge U.S. Fgn. Intelligence Surveillance Ct. of Rev., 1985—. Trustee Woodberry Forest Sch.; founder Washington Met. Area Coun. Govts. & Mass Transp. Agy. Served to comdr. USNR, 1941-45. Decorated Army commendation medal, Navy commendation medal; recipient Profl. Achievement award George Washington U., 1975, Disting. Citizen award State of Md., 1981, Spl. Merit citation Am. Judicature Soc., 1982. Mem. ABA, Md. Bar Assn. (Disting. Svc. award 1982), D.C. Bar Assn., Montgomery County Bar Assn., Barristers, Washington Ctr. Met. Studies. Democrat. Episcopalian. Club: Chevy Chase (Md.). Lodge: Rotary. Office: US Dist Ct 101 W Lombard St Ste 404 Baltimore MD 21201-2626

**NORTHUP, STEPHEN A.,** lawyer; b. N.Y.C., Aug. 20, 1945; s. Robert Edgar and June Sheasby N.; m. Wendy Bauers, Feb. 15, 1969; children: Adam Locke, Maris Rose, Mary Kathleen. BA maxima cum laude, U. Notre Dame, 1967; JD cum laude, Harvard U., 1974. Bar: Pa. 1974, Va. 1977, D.C. 1992, U.S. Supreme Ct. Ptnr. Mays & Valentine, Richmond, Va., 1976—. Chmn. lecal adv. bd. Housing Opportunities Made Equal, Richmond, 1986—; bd. dirs. Prison Family Support Svcs., Richmond, 1996—, St. Gertrude High Sch., Richmond, 1993—. 1st lt. U.S. Army, 1968-71, Vietnam. Avocations: reading, golf, squash. Federal civil litigation, State civil litigation, Banking. Home: 12458 Ashland Vineyard Ln Ashland VA 23005-7446 Office: Mays & Valentine 1111 E Main St Richmond VA 23219-3531

**NORTON, DAVID C.,** federal judge; b. Washington, July 25, 1946; s. Charles Edward and Louise Helen (Le Feber) N.; m. Dee Holmes, June 16, 1973; children: Phoebe Elizabeth, Christine Baron. BA in History, U. of the South, 1968; JD, U. S.C., 1975. Assoc. Holmes & Thomson, Charleston, S.C., 1975-77, 80-82, ptnr., 1982-90; dep. solicitor 9th Jud. Ct., Charleston, 1977-80; U.S. Dist. Ct. judge Charleston, 1990—. With USN, 1969-72. Mem. Fed. Judges Assn., Charleston County Bar Assn. (sec.-treas. 1983-90), S.C. Def. Trial Attys. Assn. (exec. com. 1988-90), S.C. Bar Assn. (Ho. Dels. 1986-90). Episcopalian. Avocations: boating, racquet ball. Office: Hollings Judicial Ctr PO Box 835 Broad & Meeting Sts 3rd Fl Charleston SC 29402-0835

**NORTON, GALE ANN,** lawyer; b. Wichita, Mar. 11, 1954; d. Dale Bentsen and Anna Jacqueline (Lansdowne) N.; m. John Goethe Hughes, Mar. 26, 1990. BA, U. Denver, 1975, JD, 1978. Bar: Colo. 1978, U.S. Supreme Ct. 1981. Jud. clk. Colo. Ct. of Appeals, Denver, 1978-79; sr. atty. Mountain States Legal Found., Denver, 1979-83; nat. fellow Hoover Instn. Stanford (Calif.) U., 1983-84; asst. to dep. sec. USDA, Washington, 1984-85; assoc. solicitor U.S. Dept. of Interior, Washington, 1985-87; pvt. practice law Denver, 1987-90; atty. gen. State of Colo., Denver, 1991-99; atty. Brownstein, Hyatt & Farber, P.C., sr. counsel, 1999—; Murdock fellow Polit. Economy Rsch. Ctr., Bozeman, Mont., 1984; sr. fellow Ind. Inst., Golden, Colo., 1988-90; policy analyst Pres. Coun. on Environ. Quality, Washington, 1985-88; lectr. U. Denver Law Sch., 1989; transp. law program dir. U. Denver, 1978-79. Contbr. chpts. to books, articles to profl. jours. Participant Rep. Leadership Program, Colo., 1988, Colo. Leadership Forum, 1989; past chair Nat. Assn. Attys. Gen. Environ. Com.; co-chair Nat. Policy Forum Environ. Coun.; candidate for 1996 election to U.S. Senate; nat. chair Coalition Rep. Environ. Advs.; chair environ. commn. Rep. Nat. Lawyers Assn. Named Young Career Woman Bus. and Profl. Wome, 1981, Young Lawyer of Yr., 1991, Mary Lathrop Trailblazer award Colo. Women's Bar Assn., 1999. Mem. Federalist Soc., Colo. Women's Forum, Order of St. Ives. Republican. Methodist. Avocation: skiing. Administrative and regulatory, Constitutional, Environmental. Office: Brownstein Hyatt & Farber PC 410 17th St Fl 22 Denver CO 80202-4402

**NORTON, GERARD PATRICK,** lawyer; b. Teaneck, N.J., Aug. 12, 1954. BA, Fordham Coll., 1976; PhD, Mt. Sinai Sch. Medicine, 1987; JD, Fordham U. Sch. Law, 1993. Postdoctoral fellow Merck, Inc., Rahway, N.J., 1986-89; law clk. Pennie & Edmonds, N.Y.C., 1989-92; scientific advisor White & Case, N.Y.C., 1992-93; assoc. Shea & Gould, N.Y.C., 1993-94, Rogers & Wells, N.Y.C., 1994-99, Clifford, Chance, Rogers & Wells, N.Y.C., 1999—. Mem. N.Y. State Bar Assn., N.Y. Intellectual Property Law Assn., Assn. Bar City of N.Y. (com. on sci. and law 1998). Office: Clifford Chance Rogers & Wells 200 Park Ave Fl 8E New York NY 10166-0899

**NORTON, JOHN HISE,** lawyer; b. Kansas City, Mo., Oct. 18, 1952; s. William Harrison and Helen (Gosslee) N.; m. Karen V. Norton, Dec. 16, 1988; children: Elijah Hise, Hunter Jackson, Robbie Norfleet. AB, U. Mo., 1974; JD with distinction, Thomas M. Cooley Law Sch., Lansing, Mich., 1978. Bar: Mo. 1978, U.S. Dist. Ct. (we. dist.) Mo. 1978, U.S. Ct. Appeals (8th cir.) 1978. Pntr. Norton, Pollard & Norton, Kansas City, 1978-89, Norton, White & Norton, Kansas City, 1989-90, Norton & Norton, PC, Kansas City, 1990-96, Norton, Norton & Noland PC, Kansas City, 1996—; bd. dirs. Lawson (Mo.) Bank; mem. 7th Jud. Commn. Mo., 1989-96; frequent lectr. at profl. litigation sems.; presenter in field. Contbr. articles to law jours., chpt. to book. Recipient Lon O. Hocker Meml. Trial Lawyers award Mo. Bar Found., 1988. Mem. ATLA (state del. 1989-95), Mo. Bar Assn., Mo. Assn. Trial Attys. (bd. govs. 1986—, exec. bd., past v.p. and pres.), Clay County Bar Assn. (past pres.), Kansas City Met. Bar Assn. Democrat. Episcopalian. Avocations: golf, flying. Fax: 816-454-5016. Personal injury, Product liability, General civil litigation. Office: Norton Norton & Noland PC 6000 N Oak Trfy Ste 201 Kansas City MO 64118-5176

**NORTON, SALLY PAULINE,** lawyer; b. Elkhart, Ind., Jan. 28, 1964; d. Ronald F. and Peggy Lucille Hale; m. Peter Thomas Norton, Aug. 28, 1993; children: Alexander, Aileen. BA, Ind. U., 1986, JD, 1989. Bar: Ind. 1991, U.S. Dist. Ct. (no. and so. dists.) Ind. 1991. Law clk. Kalamaros & Assocs., South Bend, Ind., 1990-91, assoc., 1991—. Mem. Ind. Bar Assn., St. Joseph County Bar Assn., Def. Trial Counsel Ind., Robert A. Grant Inn of Ct. Avocation: martial arts. Workers' compensation, Insurance, Personal injury. Home: 10628 N Pheasant Cove Dr Granger IN 46530-7576 Office: Kalamoros & Assocs 129 N Michigan St South Bend IN 46601-1603

**NORTON, WILLIAM ALAN,** lawyer; b. Garretsville, Ohio, Apr. 26, 1951; s. Hugh Delbert and Tommie (Leet) N.; m. Denise Ann, May 2, 1991; children: Rachel, Sarah Megan, William Tucker. AA, U. Fla., 1972, BS, 1973, JD, 1976. Bar: Fla. 1977, U.S. Dist. Ct. (so. and mid. dist.) Fla. 1995. Assoc. Law Office of David Paul Horan, Key West, Fla., 1978-79; asst. pub. defender 16th Jud. Cir., Monroe County, Fla., 1979-81, 1st Jud. Cir., Ft. Walton Beach, Fla., 1981-85; assoc. Jones & Foster, P.A., West Palm Beach, Fla., 1985-88, Montgomery Searcy & Denney, West Palm Beach, 1988-89, Searcy Denney Scarola Barnhart & Shipley, P.A., 1989-93; atty./shareholder Searcy Denney Scarola Barnhart & Shipley, P.A., West Palm Beach, 1989—, shareholder; lectr. in civil trial and securities litigation. Bd. dirs. Ctr. for Children in Crisis, West Palm Beach, 1994—. Mem. Fla. Bar Assn. (cert. civil trial litigation), Pub. Investors Arbitration Bar Assn., Palm Beach County Bar Assn., Acad. Fla. Trial Lawyers. Federal civil litigation, General civil litigation, State civil litigation. Home: 8152 Needles Dr Palm Beach Gardens FL 33418-6074 Office: Searcy Denney Scarola et al 2139 Palm Beach Lakes Blvd West Palm Beach FL 33409-6601

**NORTON-LARSON, MARY JEAN,** lawyer, planned giving officer; b. Adrian, Minn., Feb. 18, 1955; d. Robert Eugene and Natalie Norma (Nelson) Norton; m. Richard Allan Larson, Apr. 2, 1977; children: Kathryn, Bennett, Jackson. BA, Bethel Coll., St. Paul, 1977; JD, Hamline U., St. Paul, 1981. Bar: Minn. 1981. Assoc., ptnr. Eastlund, Solstad & Hutchinson, Ltd., Mpls., 1982-95; sole practitioner Cambridge, Minn., 1995-97; planned giving officer Bethel Coll. and Sem., St. Paul, 1997—. Editor notes and comments Hamline Law Rev., 1980-81. Mem. Minn. Women Lawyers. Methodist. Avocations: travel, golf, reading, volleyball. Home: 32299 Jackson Rd NE Cambridge MN 55008-6779 Office: Bethel Coll and Sem 3900 Bethel Dr Saint Paul MN 55112-6902

**NORWITZ, TREVOR S.,** lawyer; b. Cape Town, South Africa, Oct. 21, 1964; came to the U.S., 1989; s. Rubin Gabriel and Marionne Joyce Norwitz; m. Shannon Lieberman, Jan. 19, 1992; children: Raphael Shai, Herschel Sam. B in Bus. Sci., U. Cape Town, 1986; BA in Juris, Oxford (Eng.) U., 1989, MA, 1993; LLM, Columbia U., 1990. Bar: N.Y. 1991. Assoc. Cravath, Swaine & Moore, N.Y.C., 1990-94; ptnr. Walhtell, Lipton, Rosen & Katz, N.Y.C., 1994—. Contbr. articles to profl. jours. Rhodes scholar, 1987. Mem. ABA. General corporate, Mergers and acquisitions, Securities. Office: Wachtell Lipton Rosen & Katz 51 W 52nd St Fl 29 New York NY 10019-6150

**NOSEK, FRANCIS JOHN,** lawyer; b. Evanston, Ill., Apr. 13, 1934; s. Francis J. and Loretto (Brannan) N.; m. Janet Child, Dec. 30, 1964; children: Francis J. III, Peter C. BA in Polit. Sci., U. Idaho, 1956, JD, 1960. Bar: Calif. 1961, U.S. Dist. Ct. (no. dist.) Calif. 1961, U.S. Ct. Appeals (9th cir.) 1961, Alaska 1962, U.S. Dist. Ct. Alaska 1962, D.C. 1978. Pvt. practice Anchorage, 1960-67, 75—; assoc. Bell, Sanders & Tallman, Anchorage, 1961-62; sr. ptnr. Nosek, Bradberry, Wolf and Schlossberg, Anchorage, 1967-75; adj. prof. U. Alaska, Mat-Su C.C., Anchorage, 1976-82; lectr. Anchorage C.C., 1979-83, SBA, 1975-97; editor State of Alaska Real Estate Commn., Anchorage, 1983; presenter numerous lectures and seminars to lawyers, realtors, and bds. of dirs. on real estate and bus. topics. Author: Alaska Mortgage Law, How to Buy and Sell a Business; contbr. articles to law jours. Chair Anchorage Parks and Recreation, 1968-83, IIHF World Jr. Championships, Anchorage, 1988. Mem. Am. Coll. Real Estate Lawyers, Alaska Bar Assn. (chmn. real estate law 1978, mem. internat. law exec. com. 1991-95), Calif. Bar Assn. (real estate law coms.), D.C. Bar Assn. (internat. law com.), Anchorage Bar Assn. Avocations: mountain climbing, ice hockey, antique cars. Real property, Private international. Office: 310 K St Ste 601 Anchorage AK 99501-2041

**NOSLER, MICHAEL D.,** lawyer; b. Denver, July 28, 1947; s. John D. and Jeanette F. Nosler; m. Shirley Beck, Dec. 31, 1983; children: Joshua, Michael J. BA, Colo. State U., 1969; JD, Drake U., 1975. Bar: Colo., U.S. Dist. Ct. Colo., U.S. Ct. Appeals (10th cir.), U.S. Supreme Ct. Staff atty. Mountain States Employers Coun., Denver, 1975-78; assoc. Rothgerber, Appel Powers & Johnson, Denver, 1978-83; ptnr. Rothgerber Johnson & Lyons, Denver, 1983-95, mng. ptnr., 1995-99. Editor Colo. Labor Letter, 1996. Bd. dirs., chmn. Srs. in Cmty. Living, Denver, 1988—. 1st lt. U.S. Army, 1969-73. Mem. Denver Athletic Club. Roman Catholic. Avocations: hunting, fishing, skiing, recreational sports. Labor. Office: Rothgerber Johnson & Lyons One Tabot Ctr 1200 17th St Ste 3000 Denver CO 80202-5855

**NOSSEL, SUZANNE,** lawyer, writer; b. N.Y.C., July 30, 1969; d. Hymie Louis and Renee Judith (Abt) N. AB in Am. and Near Eastern History magna cum laude, Harvard U., 1991, JD magna cum laude, 1996. Bar: N.Y.; cert. mediator Mass., Rep. S. Africa. Human rights vol. advocate Israeli Govt., Jerusalem, 1989; speech writer, corr. sec. Hon Nita M. Lowey Ho. Reps., Washington, 1990 Summer; program coord. Medicare Rights Ctr., N.Y.C., 1991 Summer; law clk. human rights dept. Bell, Dewar & Hull, Johannesburg, South Africa, 1991; overseer S. African Nat. Peace Accord, Johannesburg, South Africa, 1992-93; specialist on observer mission UN, Tsakane Twp., South Africa, 1994; law clk. organized crime and drug task force U.S. Atty.'s Office, Boston, 1995; assoc. Wachtell, Lipton, Rosen & Katz, N.Y.C., 1995, Covington & Burlington, N.Y.C., 1995; assoc. in office of legal advisor U.S. Dept. State, Washington, 1996; law clk. U.S. Ct. Appeals (D.C. Cir.), Washington, 1996-97; Skadden fellow Children's Rights, Inc., N.Y.C., 1997-98; internat. supr. Orgn. for Security and Coop. in Europe, Tuzia, Srebrenica, 1997, 98; cons. Human Rights Watch-Helsinki Watch, Kosovo, Montenegro, Yugoslavia, 1998, McKinsey & Co., N.Y.C., 1999—. Co-author: Presumed Equal: What America's Top Lawyers Really Think About Their Firms, 1997; co-editor-in-chief Harvard Human Rights Jour.; also contbr. articles to U.S. and S. African Jours. Bd. dirs. Michael C. Rockefeller Fellowship, Cambridge, Mass., 1996—; term mem. Coun. on Fgn. Rels., 1997—; trustee Harvard Law Sch. Assn. N.Y.C., 1998—; mem. Am. Friends of Hebrew U.; vol. fund raiser Mark Green campaign for Dem. nomination to run for U.S. Senate, 1998. Recipient Dorot scholarship, Haravard Coll., 1987, Inst. of Politics fellowship, Mark de Wolfe Howe fellowship, Michael C. Rockefeller fellowship, Moot Ct. Competition best brief award 1994, Kaufman fellowship, 1997 Harvard Law Sch., N.Y. Alumni summer fellowship. Mem. N.Y. State Bar Assn., Assn. of Bar of City of N.Y., Phi Beta Kappa. E-mail: SuzanneúNossel@post.Harvard.edu.

**NOTA, KENNETH JOSEPH,** lawyer; b. Providence, Mar. 9, 1962; s. Albert J. and Jean M. (Lepre) N.; m. Patricia A. Matyia, Sept. 16, 1989; children: Adam Edward, Christopher Paul. BA, R.I. Coll., 1985; JD with honors, U. Conn., 1988. Bar: R.I. 1988, Mass. 1989. Paralegal Roberts, Carroll, Feldstein & Peirce, Providence, 1983-85; assoc. Edwards & Angell, Providence, 1988-90; gen. counsel Dryvit Systems, Inc., West Warwick, R.I., 1990—. Mem. R.I. Bar Assn. (vol. lawyers program), Mass. Bar Assn. Avocations: golf, softball, wood-working. General corporate, Contracts commercial, Construction. Office: Dryvit Systems Inc 1 Energy Way West Warwick RI 02893-2322

**NOTARIS, MARY,** lawyer; b. Bklyn., Aug. 20, 1962; d. Antonio Frank and Marie Nancy (Ruggiero) N.; children: Jaime Marie Defelice-Notaris, Jason Stephen Defelice-Notaris. BA in English, Northeastern U., 1988; JD, Franklin Pierce, 1991. Bar: Maine 1992, N.H. 1993, Mass. 1993. Store mgr. Purity Supreme, Billenca, Mass., 1980-94; law clk. Sheehan, Phinney, Bass & Green, Manchester, N.H., 1990; jud. law clk. U.S. Dist. Ct. N.H., Concord, 1990-91, Superior Ct. N.H., Manchester, 1991-92; of counsel Triantafillon & Guerin, Cambridge, Mass., 1992-94; pres. Mary Notaris, Atty. at Law PC, Salem, N.H., 1994—; bd. dirs. N.H. Aids Found., Manchester. Mem. Exch. Club Salem (sec. 1994—). General civil litigation, General practice, Family and matrimonial. Office: 45 Stiles Rd Ste 104 Salem NH 03079-2850

**NOTTINGHAM, EDWARD WILLIS, JR.,** federal judge; b. Denver, Jan. 9, 1948; s. Edward Willis and Willie Newton (Gullett) N.; m. Cheryl Ann Card, June 6, 1970 (div. Feb. 1981); children: Amelia Charlene, Edward Willis III; m. Janis Ellen Chapman, Aug. 18, 1984 (div. Dec. 1998); 1 child, Spencer Chapman. AB, Cornell U., 1969; JD, U. Colo., 1972. Bar: Colo. 1972, U.S. Dist. Ct. Colo. 1972, U.S. Ct. Appeals (10th cir.) 1973. Law clk. to presiding judge U.S. Dist. Ct. Colo., Denver, 1972-73; assoc. Sherman & Howard, Denver, 1973-76, 78-80, ptnr., 1980-87; ptnr. Beckner & Nottingham, Grand Junction, Colo., 1987-89; asst. U.S. atty. U.S. Dept. Justice, Denver, 1976-78; U.S. dist. judge Dist. of Colo., Denver, 1989—. Bd. dirs. Beaver Creek Met. Dist., Avon, Colo., 1980-88, Justice Info. Ctr., Denver, 1985-87, 21st Jud. Dist. Victim Compensation Fund, Grand Junction, Colo., 1987-89. Mem. ABA, Colo. Bar Assn. (chmn. criminal law sect. 1983-85, chmn. ethics com. 1988-89), Order of Coif, Denver Athletic Club, Delta Sigma Rho, Tau Kappa Alpha. Episcopalian. Office: US Dist Ct 1929 Stout St Denver CO 80294-1929

**NOVAK, JOSEPH ANTHONY,** lawyer; b. Detroit; s. Thomas Paul and Mary Cecilia N. AA, Macomb C.C., Warren, Mich., 1984; BA, Oakland U., 1986; JD, Mich. State U., 1991; M Libr. and Info. Sci., Wayne State U., 1998. Intern Wayne County Pub. Defender's Office, Detroit, 1986; intern Office of Jud. Assistance 3d Jud. Ct. Mich., Detroit, 1993, law clk. to Hon. Diane M. Hathaway, intern, 1996. Vol., Vol. Income Tax Assistance Program, Detroit, 1995—; founding sponsor Mich. Vietnam Monument, Lansing, 1997. Recipient Outstanding Vol. Volunteer Income Tax Assistance Program, 1995, 96, 98, 99, The Spirit of Am. Is In the Heart of Its Volunteers IRS, 1995, 96, 97. Mem. Am. Assn. Law Librs., Spl. Librs. Assn., Acctg. Aid Soc. Democrat. Roman Catholic. Avocations: coin and stamp collecting, snow skiing, water skiing, bowling, walking. Home: 36874 Myra Ct Sterling Heights MI 48312-3272

**NOVAK, KARL ERIC,** lawyer; b. Cin., Mar. 18, 1959; s. George and Lois Kathleen Novak; m. Jodi Kay Daniels, July 21, 1986; children: Eric Daniel, Kyle Marie. BA, Coll. of Wooster, 1981; JD, Capital U., 1988. Bar: S.C. 1988, U.S. Dist. Ct. (no. dist.) Ohio, 1989, U.S. Dist. Ct. S.C. 1997. Ptnr. Ness, Motley, Loadholt, Richardson & Poole, Charleston, S.C., 1988—. General civil litigation. Office: Ness Motley Loadholt Et Al 151 Meeting St Ste 600 Charleston SC 29401-2207

**NOVAK, MARK,** lawyer; b. Buffalo, N.Y., Jan. 28, 1952; s. Eugene Francis and Joan (Tross) N.; m. Charlene Mary Ingoglia, Sept. 2, 1972; children: Jason Charles, Jennifer Rose. BA, U. Rochester, 1974; JD, Loyola U., Chgo., 1977. Bar: Ill. 1977, U.S. Dist. Ct. (no. dist.) Ill. 1977, U.S. Ct. Appeals (7th cir.) 1978. Assoc. Anesi, Ozmon & Lewin, Ltd., Chgo., 1977-83; ptnr. Anesi, Ozmon, Rodin, Novak & Kohen, Ltd., Chgo., 1983—. Fundraiser Christmas is for Kids Charity, Chgo., 1992—. Mem. ATLA (product liability sect. 1985—), ABA, Ill. Trial Lawyers Assn., Trial Lawyers for Pub. Justice, Chgo. Bar Assn. (jud. evaluation com. 1995—). Avocations: painting, gardening, traveling. Personal injury, General civil litigation, Product liability. Home: 1212 N Lake Shore Dr Chicago IL 60610-2371 Office: Anesi Ozmon Rodin Novak & Kohen Ltd 161 N Clark St Fl 21 Chicago IL 60601-3206

**NOVARA, MICHAEL J.,** lawyer; b. N.Y.C., May 9, 1960. BA in Politics, Cath. U. Am., 1982; JD cum laude, Bklyn. Law Sch., 1987. Bar: N.Y. 1989, Pa. 1992, U.S. Dist. Ct. (ea. and so. dists.) N.Y. 1989, U.S. Dist. Ct. (we. dist.) Pa. 1992, U.S. Ct. Appeals (3rd cir.) 1994. Intern U.S. Justice Dept., N.Y.C., 1986; law clerk Hon. Gustave Diamond, Pitts., 1987-89, 92-93; assoc. Cahill Gordon & Reindel, N.Y.C., 1989-92; investigator Fed. Pub. Defenders Office, Pitts., 1993, asst. fed. pub. defender, 1993—. Co-founder, chmn. bd. dirs. Pitts. Cares, Pitts., 1992-97. Office: Fed Pub Defenders Office 960 Penn Ave Ste 415 Pittsburgh PA 15222-3811

**NOVASKY, ROBERT WILLIAM,** lawyer; b. Caldwell, Idaho, Sept. 19, 1959; s. Dale Henry and Carole Ann Novasky; m. Kathryn Cheryl James, Aug. 16, 1980; children: Rebekah, Michael, Kristopher. BA, Whitworth Coll., 1981; JD, U. Puget Sound, 1991. Bar: Wash. 1992, U.S. Dist. Ct. (we. dist.) Wash. 1992, U.S. Dist. Ct. (ea. dist.) Wash. 1994. Claims rep. Safeco Ins. Co., Kennewick, Wash., 1983-85, Grange Ins. Co., Wenatchee, Wash., 1985-86; risk assessment adminstr. Kovach & Wilson, Ephrata, Wash., 1986-87; claims rep. Am. States Ins., Seattle, 1987-92; ptnr. Burgess Fitzer, P.S., Tacoma, 1992—. Editor: Motor Vehicle Accident Deskbook, 1995-98; co-author (periodical) Wash. Ins. Law Uptdate, 1994-97. Mem. ABA, Def. Rsch. Inst., Wash. State Bar Assn. (superior ct. liaison com. 1997-98), Wash. Def. Trial Lawyers (ins. law com. 1992-97), Am. Inns of Ct., Puget Sound Inns of Ct. (exec. com. 1996—). Avocations: camping, backpacking, climbing, reading. State civil litigation, Product liability, Estate planning. Office: Burgess Fitzer PS 1501 Market St Ste 300 Tacoma WA 98402-3333

**NOVIKOFF, HAROLD STEPHEN,** lawyer; b. N.Y.C., Apr. 5, 1951; s. Eugene Benjamin and Vivian (Hirsch) N.; m. Amy Pearl, Aug. 20, 1972; children: Sara Heather, Elyse Fana. AB, Cornell U., 1972; JD, Columbia U., 1975. Bar: N.Y. 1976, U.S. Dist. Ct. (so. dist.) N.Y. 1976. Ptnr. Wachtell, Lipton, Rosen & Katz, N.Y.C., 1975—. Mem. ABA, N.Y. State Bar Assn. (bankruptcy com. 1981—), Assn. Bar City N.Y. (bankruptcy and reorgn. com. 1995—), Nat. Bankruptcy Conf. Bankruptcy, Finance. Office: Wachtell Lipton Rosen Katz 51 W 52nd St Fl 29 New York NY 10019-6150

**NOVOTNY, DAVID JOSEPH,** lawyer; b. Melrose Park, Ill., Oct. 3, 1953; s. Joseph F. and Dorothy E. (Erickson) N.; m. Gladys Ruth Korynecky, May 1, 1982. BSc, DePaul U., 1975, JD, 1978. Bar: Ill. 1978, U.S. Dist. Ct. (no. dist.), Ill. 1978, U.S. Ct. Appeals (7th cir.) 1985, U.S. Dist. Ct. (no. dist.), Ind. 1995, U.S. Dist. Ct. (cen. dist.) Ill. 1999. Law clk. to justice Ill. Appellate Ct., Chgo., 1978-80; assoc. Rooks, Pitts & Poust, Chgo., 1980-83; assoc. Peterson, Ross, Schloerb & Seidel (now Peterson & Ross), Chgo., 1983-88, ptnr., 1988—; arbitrator Am. Arbitration Assn., 1987—, Cir. Ct. Cook County Ct.-Annexed Arbitration, 1990—. Exec. editor DePaul Law Rev., 1978. Mem. ABA, Ill. State Bar Assn., 7th Cir. Bar Assn., Soc. Trial Lawyers, Asia-Pacific Lawyers Assn., Lawyer-Pilots Bar Assn., Legal Club Chgo., Def. Rsch. Inst. Federal civil litigation, State civil litigation, Insurance. Office: Peterson & Ross 200 E Randolph St Ste 7300 Chicago IL 60601-7012

**NOVOTNY, F. DOUGLAS,** lawyer; b. Mineola, N.Y., Mar. 10, 1952; s. Frank Joseph and Eleanor Evans (Rose) N.; m. Norma R. Federici, Sept. 7, 1991; children: Nicholas, Christina, Alexander. B.A. cum laude, SUNY-Albany, 1974; postgrad. NYU, Hofstra U., C.W. Post U.; J.D. cum laude, Albany Law Sch., 1979. Bar: N.Y. 1980, U.S. Dist. Ct. (no. dist.) N.Y. 1980. Confidential law asst. Appellate Div. 3d Dept., Albany, 1979-80; ptnr. DeGraff, Foy, Conway, Holt-Harris & Mealey, Albany, 1980-91; pvt. practice, Saratoga, N.Y., 1991-93; supr. atty. Law Offices of F. Douglas Novotny, staff counsel Am. Internat. Group, Inc., 1993—. mem. Albany County Arbitration Pannel, 1984-88. Editor Albany Law Rev., 1978-79; contbr. articles to profl. jours. Mem. Justinian Soc., Assn. Trial Lawyers Am., N.Y. State Trial Lawyers Assn., Capital Dist. Trial Lawyers Assn. Presbyterian. State civil litigation, Federal civil litigation. Home: 27 Mallard Lndg S Waterford NY 12188-1037

**NOVOTNY, PATRICIA SUSAN,** lawyer, educator; b. Omaha, Nov. 22, 1953; d. John Albert and Lauretta Lee (Waters) N. BA, Reed Coll., 1976; JD, U. Wash., 1983. Bar: Wash. 1983, U.S. Supreme Ct. 1995. Staff atty. Wash. Appellate Defender Assn., Seattle, 1989-91, 92-95, asst. dir., 1994-95; spl. counsel Wash. Defender Assn., Seattle, 1991-92; pvt. practice, Seattle, 1986-89, 95—; lectr. U. Wash. Sch. Law, U. Wash. Women Studies, Seattle, 1996—; mem. legal com. N.W. Women's Law Ctr., Seattle, 1990—, chmn., 1995—. Contbr. articles to profl. jours. Recipient individual artist award Seattle Arts Commn., 1990. Mem. Wash. Assn. Criminal Def. Lawyers. Avocations: creative writing, birdwatching, gardening, hiking, jazz. Appellate, Criminal, Family and matrimonial. Office: 4756 U Vill Pl NE Ste 398 Seattle WA 98105-5011

**NOWAK, JOHN E.,** law educator; b. Chgo., Jan. 2, 1947; s. George Edward and Evelyn (Bucci) N.; m. Judith Johnson, June 1, 1968; children: John Edwin, Jeffrey Edward. AB, Marquette U., 1968; JD, U. Ill., 1971. Law clk. Supreme Ct. of Ill., Chgo., 1971-72; asst. prof. U. Ill., Urbana, 1972-75, assoc. prof., 1975-87, law prof., 1978—, grad. coll. faculty, 1982—, Baum Prof. Law, 1993—; chmn. Constl. Law Sch. Sect.; faculty rep. Big Ten Intercollegiate Conf., Schaumburg, Ill., 1981-91; vis. prof. law U. Mich., Ann Arbor, 1985; Lee Disting. vis. prof. Coll. William and Mary, 1993. Co-author: Constitutional Law, 5th edit. 1995, Treatise on Constitutional Law, 1986, 2nd edit., 1992, Story's Commentaries on the Constitution, 1987. Scholar-in-Residence, U. of Ariz., Tucson, 1985, 87. Mem. Assn. of Am. Law Schs. (chm. constl. law sect., accreditation com. 1980-88), Nat. Collegiate Athletic Assn. (mem. infractions com. 1987—), Am. Law Inst., Am. Bar Assn., Ill. Bar Assn., Order of the Coif (Triennial Book award com.). Roman Catholic. Home: 1701 Mayfair Rd Champaign IL 61821-5522 Office: U Ill Coll Law 504 E Pennsylvania Ave Champaign IL 61820-6909

**NOWLAND, JAMES FERRELL,** lawyer; b. Talladega, Ala., Dec. 7, 1942; s. James Franklin and Wilma Delene (Dean) N.; m. Faye Roberts, Aug. 28, 1964; children: Angela Roschelle, James Ferrell II. BS, Jacksonville (Ala.) State U., 1967; BS in Med. Technology, U. Ark., 1972; grad., U. Ark. Med. Ctr., 1974; JD, Oglethorpe U., 1983. Bar: Ga. 1984, U.S. Dist. Ct. (no. dist.) Ga. 1984, U.S. Ct. Appeals (11th cir.) 1984, U.S. Supreme Ct. 1988. Chemist U.S. Army C.E., Marietta, Ga., 1972-97; pvt. practice Cobb County, Ga., 1984—. Capt. USAF, 1967-72. Mem. ABA, Ga. Bar Assn., Cobb County Bar Assn. Environmental, Real property, Personal injury. Home: 50 Mt Calvary Rd Marietta GA 30064-1918 Office: PO Box 1847 Marietta GA 30061-1847

**NOWLIN, JAMES ROBERTSON,** federal judge; b. San Antonio, Nov. 21, 1937; s. William Forney and Jeannette (Robertson) N. B.A., Trinity U., 1959, M.A., 1962; J.D., U. Tex., Austin, 1963. Bar: Tex. 1963, Colo. 1993, U.S. Dist. Ct. D.C. 1966, U.S. Ct. Claims 1969, U.S. Supreme Ct. 1969, U.S. Dist. Ct. (we. dist.) Tex. 1971. Assoc. Kelso, Locke & King, San Antonio, 1963-65; assoc. Kelso, Locke & Lepick, San Antonio, 1966-69; legal counsel U.S. Senate, Washington, 1965-66; propr. Law Offices James R. Nowlin, San Antonio, 1969-81; mem. Tex. Ho. of Reps., Austin, 1967-71, 73-81; judge U.S. Dist. Ct. (we. dist.) Tex., Austin, 1981—; instr. Am. govt. and history San Antonio Coll., 1964-65, 71-73. Served to capt. U.S. Army, 1959-60, USAR, 1960-68. Life fellow State Bar Found; mem. San Antonio Bar Assn., Colo. Bar Assn. Republican. Presbyterian. Avocations: pilot; skiing; hiking; jogging. Office: US Courthouse 200 W 8th St Austin TX 78701-2325

**NOZERO, ELIZABETH CATHERINE,** lawyer; b. Detroit, June 13, 1953; d. Peter J. and Pauline R. (Reeves) N.; m. Stephen A. Catalano, May 23, 1981 (div. May 1993); 1 child: Alexandra L. BA in history, U. Calif., 1975; JD, U. San Diego, 1978. Bar: Calif. 1979, Nev. 1980. Counsel State Industrial Ins. System, Las Vegas, 1980-81; sr. legal counsel Reynolds Elec. & Engring. CO., Las Vegas, 1981-85; asst. gen. counsel U. Nev., Las Vegas, 1985-89; v.p., gen. counsel Harrah's Casino Hotels, Las Vegas, 1989-95; sr. legal counsel Sierra Health Svcs., Inc., 1996-97; gen. counsel Sierra Mil. Health Svcs., Inc., 1997—; owner, pres. Power Staffing Svcs., Inc., 1998—; mem. exec. bd. Nev. Bar Assn. Fee Dispute com. 1982-88, Nev. Law Found., 1980-88. Chairperson S. Nev. Area Health Edn. Ctr., Las Vegas, 1990-94; former chair Nev. Adv. Com. U.S. Commn. on Civil Rights, Nev., 1989-94; gov.'s com. Infrastructive Financing, 1994-95. Recipient Woman of Achievement award Las Vegas C. of C., 1992, Silver State Citizen award Nev. Atty. Gen., 1992. Mem. Nev. Gaming Attys. (v.p. 1994-95), Nev. Resort Assn. (chairperson, regulations com. 1993-95). Administrative and regulatory, Contracts commercial, General corporate. Office: 4648 W Sahara Ave Ste 1 Las Vegas NV 89102-3621

**NOZISKA, CHARLES BRANT,** lawyer; b. Oakland, Calif., Aug. 28, 1953; s. Charles Richard and Shirley Ann (Orme) N. BA, Colo. Coll., 1975; JD magna cum laude, U. San Diego, 1982. Bar: Calif. 1982, U.S. Dist. Ct. (so. dist.) Calif. 1982. Ptnr. Thorsnes, Bartolotta, McGuire & Padilla, San Diego, 1982—. Co-author: Landslide and Subsidence Liability, 1988. Mem. Assn. Trial Lawyers Am., Calif. Trial Lawyers Assn., San Diego Trial Lawyers Assn., San Diego County Bar Assn. Democrat. Avocations: ocean sports. General civil litigation, Insurance. Office: Thorsnes Bartolotta McGuire & Padilla 2550 5th Ave Ste 11 San Diego CA 92103-6612

**NUCCIO, PAUL VINCENT,** lawyer; b. Bklyn., Jan. 10, 1965; s. Paul Lewis and Lucille (Visceglia) N. BBA, Pace U., 1987; JD, Touro Law Sch., 1993. Bar: N.Y. 1994, Pa. 1993, U.S. Dist. Ct. (ea. and so. dists.) N.Y. 1994. Ptnr. Guastaferri & Nuccio LLP. Mem. Kiwanis (sec. 1988-90, v.p. 1993-95, pres. 1995-96). Republican. Roman Catholic. Avocations: camping, hunting, bowling. General practice, Personal injury, Contracts commercial. Office: 32 Court St Ste 904 Brooklyn NY 11201-4404

**NUDELMAN, SIDNEY,** lawyer; b. Cleve., Jan. 16, 1938; s. Ben and Jeanette (Klein) N.; m. Marilyn Rose Caplow, Aug. 23, 1959; children: Jodi, Eric. BS, Ohio State U., 1960, JD summa cum laude, 1963. Bar: Ohio 1963, U.S. Dist. Ct. (no. dist.) Ohio 1964. Assoc. Hahn Loeser & Parks (formerly Hahn, Loeser, Freedheim, Dean & Wellman), Cleve., 1963-70, ptnr., 1971—. Trustee Jewish Family Svc. Assn., Cleveland Heights, Ohio, 1971-85, sec., 1975-79. Named Family of Yr. Fairmount Temple, 1984. Fellow Am. Coll. Trust and Estate Counsel; mem. Ohio Bar Assn. (bd. dirs. probate and trust law sect. 1980—, treas. 1984-87, sec. 1987-89, vice chmn. 1989-91, chmn. 1991-93, chmn. probate law insts. 1989, 90), Cleve. Bar Assn. (chmn. estate planning probate and trust law sect. 1985-86, chmn. estate planning inst. 1989), Order of Coif, Beta Gamma Sigma. Avocations: traveling, running, reading. Estate planning, Probate, Estate taxation. Home: 24553 Dianne Dr Beachwood OH 44122-2309 Office: Hahn Loeser & Parks LLP 3300 BP America Bldg 200 Public Sq Cleveland OH 44114-2303

**NUGENT, ALFRED EMANUEL,** lawyer, educator; b. Boston, Aug. 26, 1928; m. Louise Mary Roche, Apr. 7, 1956; children: Anthony, Christine, Paul, Matthew, Kevin, Helen. AA, Boston U., 1949, JD, 1952. Bar: Mass. 1956. Pvt. practice Law Offices of Menton & Nugent, Watertown, Mass., 1959-60; trial lawyer Pub. Defenders Mass., Boston, 1960-65; pvt. practice Boston, 1965—; trial adv. advisor Harvard Law Sch., Cambridge, Mass., 1980—; judge Boston Coll. Grimes Moot Ct., Newton, Mass., 1985—. Del. Dem. State Com., 1964, 66, 68; chmn. Dem. Town Com., Watertown, 1963-70; civil rights activist. With U.S. Army, 1952-54. Mem. Mass. Trial Lawyers Assn., Nat. Moot Ct. Assn. (judge 1985—). Avocation: reading. Constitutional, Criminal, General practice. Office: 11 Beacon St Boston MA 02108-3002

**NUGENT, EDWARD JAMES, III,** lawyer; b. South Bend, Ind., May 15, 1947; s. Edward J. Jr. and Alma Cecil Nugent; m. Janet S. Nugent, July 4, 1977; children: Kevin C., Elizabeth R. BA, U. Notre Dame, 1969; MA, U. Colo., 1973, JD, 1977. Dep. state pub. defender Colo. State Pub. Defenders Office, Denver, 1977-82; pvt. practice Grand Junction, Colo., 1982—. Mem. Nat. Assn. Criminal Def. Lawyers, Colo. Bar Assn., Colo. Criminal Def. Bar (chair 1998-99), Colo. Lawyer Trust Fund Assn. (pres. 1997—), Colo. Alt. Def. Counsel Commn. (commr. 1996—). Democrat. Avocations: agriculture, raising and hunting Jack Russell terriers, outdoor activities. Criminal, Family and matrimonial. Home: 1038 Q1/2 Rd Mack CO 81525 Office: 225 N 5th St Ste 850 Grand Junction CO 81501-2664

**NUGENT, LORI S.,** lawyer; b. Peoria, Ill., Apr. 24, 1962; d. Walter Leonard and Margery (Frost) Meyer; m. Shane Vincent Nugent, June 14, 1986; 1 child, Justine Nicole. BA in Polit. Sci. cum laude, Knox Coll., 1984; JD, Northwestern U., Chgo., 1987. Bar: Ill. 1987, U.S. Dist. Ct. (no. dist.) Ill. 1988, U.S. Ct. Appeals (7th cir.) 1995. Assoc. Peterson & Ross, Chgo., 1987-94; assoc. Blatt, Hammesfahr & Eaton, Chgo., 1994, ptnr., 1994—. Co-author: Punitive Damages: A Guide to the Insurability of Punitive Damages in the United States and Its Territories, 1988, Punitive Damages: A State-by-State Guide to Law and Practice, 1991, Japanese edit., 1995, Pocket Part, 1999; contbr. articles to law jours. Alternative dispute resolution, Insurance. Office: Blatt Hammesfahr & Eaton 333 W Wacker Dr Ste 1900 Chicago IL 60606-1293

**NUGENT, PAUL ALLEN,** lawyer; b. West Palm Beach, Fla., Feb. 20, 1962; s. Charles Arthur and Barbara Ann (Brewer) N. BA, U. Miami, 1985; JD, Nova U., 1988. Bar: Fla. 1988, U.S. Dist. Ct. (so. dist.) Fla. 1988. Assoc. Wagner, Nugent, Johnson, Roth & Rossin, P.A., West Palm Beach, 1988-89, Reid, Ricca & Rigell, P.A., West Palm Beach, 1989; ptnr. Neal & Nugent, P.A., North Palm Beach, 1990-91; assoc. Bobo, Spicer, Ciotoli, Fulford & Bocchino, P.A., West Palm Beach, 1991—. Mem. ABA, Def. Rsch. Inst., Fla. Def. Lawyers Assn., Palm Beach County Bar Assn. Republican. Roman Catholic. Avocations: golf, basketball, travel, coin and stamp collecting, theatre. Personal injury, State civil litigation, General practice. Office: Bobo Spicer Ciotoli Fulford & Bocchino Esperante 6th Fl 222 Lakeview Ave West Palm Beach FL 33401-6145

**NULL, MICHAEL ELLIOT,** lawyer; b. Chgo., Feb. 14, 1947; s. Samuel Joseph and Rose (Baren) N.; m. Eugenia Irene Frack, Dec. 21, 1969; children: Jennifer Susan, Emily Lauren. B.S. in Psychology, U. Ill., 1969; J.D., Ill. Inst. Tech. Chgo. Kent Law Sch., 1974. Bar: Ill. 1974, U.S. Dist. Ct. (no. dist.) Ill. 1974, U.S. Dist. Ct. (ea. dist.) Mich., 1985, U.S. Dist. Ct. (ea. dist.) Wis., 1986, U.S. Ct. Appeals (7th cir.) 1981, U.S. Ct. Appeals (6th cir.) 1985, U.S. Supreme Ct., 1985. Prin. Michael Null And Assocs., Chgo., 1977—. Author: Truths: A Guide to Practical Metaphysics; composer musical selections. Mem. ABA, 1st Amendment Lawyers Assn. Constitutional, Criminal, Civil rights. Office: 155 N Michigan Ave Chicago IL 60601-7511

**NUNALEE, MARY MARGARET MCEACHERN,** lawyer; b. Wilmington, N.C., July 4, 1970; d. Hugh Alexander Jr. and Mary Lou McEachern; m. Thomas Hervey Nunalee IV, Oct. 3, 1998. BA in Econs., U. N.C., 1992; JD, Campbell U., 1996. Bar: N.C. 1996. Atty. Allen & MacDonald, Wilmington, N.C., 1996-98, Nunalee & Nunalee, LLP, Wilmington, 1998—; dir. Raysand Corp., Wilmington. Mem. Jr. League, Wilmington, 1991—; ex officio mem. Cape Fear Agrl. Park, Wilmington, 1998—; vol. various polit. campaigns; bd. dirs. New Hanover County Arboretum, 1999—. Named Top Fundraiser Leukemia Soc. of Am., 1998, Top 16 Finalist Scribes Nat. Notes Competition, 1994-95, winner 1996. Mem. New Hanover County Bar Assn., N.C. Bar Assn. (young lawyers leadership com.), Inns of Ct. Republican. Methodist. Avocations: running, marathons, cats, boating, golfing. Appellate, Entertainment, General practice. Home: 709 Princess St PO Box 2433 Wilmington NC 28402-2433 Office: Nunalee & Nunalee LLP PO Box 2433 Wilmington NC 28402-2433

**NUNALEE, THOMAS HERVEY, IV,** lawyer; b. Raleigh, Sept. 4, 1969; s. Thomas Hervey III and Linda (Sloop) N.; m. Mary Margaret McEachern, Oct. 3, 1998. BA in Econs. and Bus. Mgmt., N.C. State U., 1991; JD, U. N.C., 1994. Bar: N.C. 1994, U.S. Dist. Ct. (ea. dist.) N.C. 1994. Assoc.

Shanklin & McDaniel LLP, Wilmington, N.C., 1994-98; pvt. practice Wilmington, 1998—. Mem. coun. Pine Valley United Meth. Ch., Wilmington, 1981—, pres. Pine Valley United Meth. Men, Wilmington, 1998. Mem. ABA, N.C. Bar Assn., 5th Jud. Dist. Bar Assn., New Hanover County Bar Assn., C. of C. Democrat. Avocation: sports. General corporate, Estate planning, Real property.

**NUNES, FRANK M.,** lawyer; b. Fresno, Calif., Oct. 25, 1968; s. Marvin Frank and Phyllis Mae Nunes; m. Sharon L. Nunes, July 20, 1996. BS, Calif. State U., Fresno, 1991; JD, San Joaquin Coll. Law, Fresno, 1994. Bar: Calif. 1995, U.S. Dist. Ct. (ea. dist.) Calif. 1995. Dep. dist. atty. Tulare County Dist. Atty., Visalia, Calif., 1995-97; assoc. Marderosian, Oren & Paboojian, Fresno, 1997—. Mem. Fresno County Young Lawyers, Delta Theta Phi, Alpha Gamma Rho (pres. 1990), Alpha Zeta. Roman Catholic. State civil litigation, Personal injury, Real property. Office: Marderosian Oren & Paboojian 1260 Fulton Mall Fresno CA 93721-1916

**NUNES, MORRIS A.,** lawyer; b. Oceanside, N.Y., Apr. 9, 1949; s. Myron A. and Betty Ann (Ecoff) N.; m. Jane S. Chargar, Aug. 30, 1970; 2 children. BA, BS, U. Pa., 1970; JD, Georgetown U., 1975. Bar: Va. 1975, D.C. 1976. Auditor Arthur Young & Co. CPAs, Boston, 1970; controller Sanitary Group, Inc., West Haven, Conn., 1970-72; securities analyst Donatelli, Rudolph & Schoen, Washington, 1972-74; group controller Potomac Electric Power Co., Washington, 1974-77; sole practice Falls Church, Va., 1977—; adj. prof. Cath. U. Law Sch., Georgetown U. Law Sch.; arbitrator Am. Arbitration Assn., Washington, 1980-97; bus. appraiser, pres. Net Worth, Inc., 1988—; hearing officer Va. Supreme Ct., 1996—; bus. adv. bd. James Monroe Bank, 1998—. Author: Operational Cash Flow, 1982, Balance Sheet Mgmt., 1987, The Right Price for Your Business, 1988; co-author: Property Logbook, 1985, Basic Legal Forms for Business, 1989; producer, host TV show Gen. Counsel, 1985-87; contbr. articles to profl. jours. Appointed mem. Va. State Bd. Prof. & Occup. Regulation, 1995-97, chair, 1997—; mem. Fairfax County Edn. Adv. Bd., Va., 1983-87; del. Rep. State Conv., 1993, 94. Mem. Va. State Bar Assn., D.C. Bar Assn., Washington Ind. Writers, Am. Soc. Appraisers, Alpha Lit. and Philosophy Soc., Sigma Chi. Republican. Avocations: racquetball, chess, wargames, music appreciation, squash. Contracts commercial, General corporate, Real property. Office: 7247 Lee Hwy Falls Church VA 22046-3710

**NUNN, KEN,** lawyer; b. Louisville, Mar. 22, 1940; s. Richard and Grace (Lynch) N.; m. Leah K. Blades, Aug. 19, 1962; children: Vicky A., David L. BS in Bus., Ind. U., 1964, JD, 1967. Bar: Ind. 1967, U.S. Dist. Ct. (so. dist.) Ind. 1967, U.S. Ct. Appeals (7th cir.) 1974, U.S. Supreme Ct. 1974. Ptnr. Nunn & Greene, Bloomington, Ind. Personal injury, Product liability. Office: Nunn & Greene 123 S College Ave Bloomington IN 47404-5166

**NUNNENKAMP, KENNETH JOSEPH,** lawyer; b. Amityville, N.Y., Jan. 1, 1961; s. Herbert Adolph and Josephine Mary (Vidiri) N.; m. Giovanna M. Cinelli, Sept. 1, 1984. BA, Ohio Wesleyan U., 1983; JD, Cath. U., 1986. Bar: Va. 1986, D.C. 1989. Clk. Covington & Burling, Washington, 1984-87; commd. 2d lt. USMC, 1983, advanced through grades to 1st lt., 1987; clk. to judge U.S. Ct. Appeals (Fed. cir.), 1988-89; assoc. Finnegan, Henderson et al, Washington, 1991-96; gen. counsel TeraStore, Inc., 1996—; of counsel Reed, Smith, Shaw & McClay, McClean, Va., 1999—. Named one of Outstanding Young Men Am., 1985-86. Mem. Va. State Bar. Home: 11216 Sorrel Ridge Ln Oakton VA 22124-1322

**NURKIEWICZ, DENNIS JOHN, JR.,** lawyer; b. Youngstown, Ohio, May 10, 1966; s. Dennis John Sr. and Carole Dianne N. BS in Adminstrn. Justice, Pa. State U., 1989; JD, Thomas M. Cooley Coll., 1993. Bar: Mich., U.S. Dist. (ea. dist.) Mich. Bd. dirs. Big Bros./Big Sisters, Mt. Pleasant, mich., 1996-97. 1st lt. U.S. Army, 1990-96. Mem. State Bar Mich., Isabella County Bar Assn. (sec./treas. 1994-96). Criminal, Family and matrimonial, Federal civil litigation. Office: 230 N Washington Sq Ste 306 Lansing MI 48933-1312

**NUSSBAUM, HOWARD JAY,** lawyer; b. N.Y.C., Dec. 17, 1951; s. Norman and Ruth (Rand) N.; children: Martin Garrett, Daniel Todd. BA, SUNY, Binghamton, 1972; JD, Boston Coll., 1976. Bar: Fla. 1977, U.S. Dist. Ct. (so. dist. trial and bankruptcy bar) Fla. 1977, U.S. Ct. Appeals (5th and 11th cirs.) 1981. Mng. atty. Legal Aid. Svc., Ft. Lauderdale, Fla., 1976-88; ptnr. Weinstein, Zimmerman & Nussbaum, P.A., Tamarac, Fla., 1988-92; pres. Howard J. Nussbaum, P.A., 1993—; chmn. Legal Aid com. North Broward Bar Assn., Pompano Beach, Fla., 1986-87; cons. Police Acad. of Broward County, Ft. Lauderdale, 1985-87. Author: Florida Landlord/Tenant Law and the Fair Housing Act, 1989. Gen. counsel Registered Apt. Mgrs. Assn. South Fla., 1993—, Wynmoor Cmty. Coun., 1993—, The Accutrack Safety Systems Corp., 1997—, Dominium Mgmt. Svcs, Inc., J&B N. Am. Movers, Inc. Regents scholar N.Y. State, 1968-72, Presdl. scholar Boston Coll. Law Sch., 1973-76. Mem. ABA (litigation sect.), ATLA, Acad. Fla. Trial Lawyers, Broward Bar Assn., Justice Lodge J.C.C. Avocations: softball, tennis, swimming. General civil litigation, Contracts commercial, General corporate. Office: 3029 NW 28th Ave Boca Raton FL 33434-6023

**NUTE, LESLIE F.,** lawyer. BA, Bates Coll., 1963; JD, U. Chgo., 1966. Bar: Ind. 1966, Mich. 1973, Pa. 1998. Sr. v.p., gen. counsel, sec. Bayer Corp., Pitts., 1991—. General corporate. Office: Bayer Corp 100 Bayer Rd Pittsburgh PA 15205-9741

**NUTTER, ROBERT HEINRICH,** lawyer; b. Little Rock, Dec. 23, 1939; s. Robert Alspaugh and Vera (Henry) N.; m. Linda Frances Crunk, June 18, 1960; children: Amy Lynne, Nathan Brook. BS in Pharmacy, U. Fla., 1963; JD, Stetson U., 1970. Bar: Fla. 1970, U.S. Dist. Ct. (mid. dist.) Fla. 1974, U.S. Dist. Ct. Appeals (11th cir.) 1981, U.S. Ct. Appeals (5th cir.), U.S. Supreme Ct. 1978. Pharmacist Walgreen Drug Co., Tampa, Fla., 1964-67; asst. county solicitor Hillsborough County, Tampa, Fla., 1970-73; asst. state's atty. for Hillsborough County, State of Fla., 1973-75; chief asst. spl. prosecutor statewide grand jury, 1974-75; ptnr. Ferlita, Nutter & Rosello, P.A., Tampa, 1975—. Mem. Fla. Bar, Hillsborough County Bar Assn. (grievance com. 1978-81), Assn. Trial Lawyers Am., Acad. Fla. Trial Lawyers, Hillsborough Pharm. Assn. (pres. 1975), Masons. Republican. Avocations: hunting, fishing, reading, family. Fax: (813) 254-6214. Personal injury, General civil litigation, Criminal. Office: Ferlita Nutter & Rosello PA 610 W Azeele St Tampa FL 33606-2206

**NUZUM, ROBERT WESTON,** lawyer; b. Evanston, Ill., Dec. 11, 1952; s. John Weston and Janet Marie (Talbot) N.; m. Julia Ann Abadie, Sept. 16, 1983. BS in Fin., La. State U., 1974, JD, 1977; LLM in Taxation, N.Y.U., 1978. Bar: La. 1977, D.C. 1979. Assoc. Office Chief Counsel, Washington, 1978-81, Jones, Walker, Waechter, Poitevent, Carrere & Denegre, New Orleans, 1981-85; ptnr. Jones, Walker, Waechter, Potevent, Carrere & Denegre, New Orleans, 1985-88, Deutsch, Kerrigan & Stiles, New Orleans, 1988-89, Phelps Dunbar, L.L.P. and predecessor firm, New Orleans, 1989—; prof. law, state and local taxation Tulane U. Sch. Law, New Orleans, 1998—. Editor La. Law Rev., 1977; contbr. articles to profl. jours. Wallace scholar N.Y.U., 1978. Mem. La. Bar Assn. (program chmn. tax sect. 1992-93, sec.-treas. 1993-94, vice-chmn. 1994-95, chmn. 1995-96), Tulane Tax Inst. (planning com. 1993—, tax specialization adv. commn. 1997—), Order of Coif. Republican. Roman Catholic. Avocations: golf, reading, fishing. Taxation, general, Corporate taxation, State and local taxation. Office: Phelps Dunbar LLP 400 Poydras St New Orleans LA 70130-3245

**NYBERG, WILLIAM ARTHUR,** lawyer; b. Chgo., Aug. 27, 1947; s. E. Arthur and Lyna Marie (Palmer) N.; m. Margery Ann Lissner, Mar. 11, 1984. A.B., U. Ill., 1969, J.D., 1975; M.B.A., Columbia U., 1976. Bar: Ill. 1975, U.S. Dist. Ct. (so. and no. dists.) Ill. 1975, U.S. Ct. Appeals (7th cir.) 1975, U.S. Supreme Ct. 1981. Assoc. Winston & Strawn, Chgo., 1976-77; atty. AMSTED Industries, Inc., Chgo., 1977-81, The Richardson Co., Des Plaines, Ill., 1981-82; sr. atty. John Morrell & Co., Northfield, Ill., 1982-84; v.p., gen. counsel United States Can Co., Oak Brook, Ill., 1984-86; assoc. Laser, Schostok, Kolman and Frank, Chgo., 1986-93; counsel Mills Capital Advisors, Inc., Chgo., 1993—. Served with U.S. Army, 1969-72; Vietnam. Decorated Bronze Star, Joint Service Commendation Medal. Mem. ABA, Ill. State Bar Assn., Chgo. Bar Assn. Methodist. General corporate, Mergers and acquisitions, Securities. Home: 533 County Line Rd Highland Park IL 60035-5339

**NYCE, JOHN DANIEL,** lawyer; b. York, Pa., Sept. 7, 1947; s. Harry Lincoln and Dorothy (Wagner) N.; m. Deborah Faith Nyce; children: Joshua David, Laura Kimberly. BA, SUNY-Buffalo, 1970; JD, U. Miami, 1973. Bar: Fla. 1973, U.S. Dist. Ct. (so. dist.) Fla. 1973, U.S. Dist. Ct. (middle dist.) Fla. 1973, U.S. Ct. Appeals (5th and 11th cirs.) 1986, U.S. Supreme Ct. 1984. Assoc. Ralph P. Douglas, Pompano Beach, Fla., 1974, Coleman, Leonard & Morrison, Ft. Lauderdale, Fla., 1975-78; ptnr. Nyce and Smith, Ft. Lauderdale, 1979; sole practice, Ft. Lauderdale, 1980—. co-founder, dir. Rutherford Inst. Author books in field. Bd. dirs. Alliance for Responsible Growth, Inc.; mem. Social Register Ft. Lauderdale, Broward County Right to Life, Operation Rescue, South Fla., Christ's Ministry to the Homeless of Ft. Lauderdale, Fla. Legis. Adv. Coun. on Adoptions, Nat. Right to Life Com., Inc.; mem. exec. com. Broward County Republican Party; bd. dirs. Shepherd Care Ministries, Inc., co-founder Christian Adoption Svcs. of Shepherd Care Ministries, Inc.; cert. trainer Evangelism Explosion III Internat., Inc.; legal counsel and evangelism trainer Coral Ridge Presbyn. Ch., First Bapt. Ch., W. Hollywood, Fla.; mem. U. Miami Broward Citizens Bd., U. Miami. Author: Proof of God's Existence in the Seven C's, and Christian Handbook of Lists. Mem. Broward County Christian Lawyer's Assn. (founder, past pres., bd. dirs.), Atty's. Title Ins. Fund, Christian Legal Soc., Conservative Caucus of Broward County, U.S. Tennis Ctr., Am. Golfer's Club, SUNY Alumni Assn. (Buffalo), Univ. Miami Alumni Assn., Holiday Park Tennis Ctr., Am. Golfer's Club, Sports Fitness Clinic, Univ. Miami Hurricane Club. Republican. Presbyterian. State civil litigation, Family and matrimonial, General practice. Office: Ste 101 4367 N Federal Hwy Fort Lauderdale FL 33308-5213

**NYCUM, SUSAN HUBBELL,** lawyer. BA, Ohio Wesleyan U., 1956; JD, Duquesne U., 1960; postgrad., Stanford U. Bar: Pa. 1962, U.S. Supreme Ct. 1967, Calif. 1974. Sole practice law Pitts., 1962-65; designer, adminstr. legal rsch. sys. U. Pitts., Aspen Sys. Corp., Pitts., 1965-68; mgr. ops. Computer Ctr., Carnegie Mellon U., Pitts., 1968-69; dir. computer facility Computer Ctr., Stanford U., Calif., 1969-72, Stanford Law and Computer fellow, 1972-73; cons. in computers and law, 1973-74; sr. assoc. MacLeod, Fuller, Muir & Godwin, Los Altos, Los Angeles and London, 1974-75; ptnr. Chickering & Gregory, San Francisco, 1975-80; ptnr.-in-charge high tech. group Gaston Snow & Ely Bartlett, Boston, NYC, Phoenix, San Francisco, Calif., 1980-86; mng. ptnr. Palo Alto office Kadison, Pfaelzer, Woodard, Quinn & Rossi, Los Angeles, Washington, Newport Beach, Palo Alto, Calif., 1986-87; sr. ptnr., chmn. U.S. intellectual property/info. tech. practice group Baker & McKenzie, Palo Alto, 1987—, mem. U.S. leadership team, 1987-97, mem. Asia Pacific regional coun., 1995—; trustee EDUCOM, 1978-81; mem. adv. com. for high tech. Ariz. State U. Law Sch., Santa Clara U. Law Sch., Stanford Law Sch., U. So. Calif. Law Ctr., law sch. Harvard U., U. Calif.; U.S. State Dept. del. OECD Conf. on Nat. Vulnerabilities, Spain, 1981; invited speaker Telecom, Geneva, 1983; lectr. N.Y. Law Jour., 1975—, Law & Bus., 1975—, Practicing Law Inst., 1975—; chmn. Office of Tech. Assessment Task Force on Nat. Info. Sys., 1979-80. Author:(with Bigelow) Your Computer and the Law, 1975, (with Bosworth) Legal Protection for Software, 1985, (with Collins and Gilbert) Women Leading, 1987; contbr. monographs, articles to profl. pubs. Mem. Town of Portola Valley Open Space Acquisition Com., Calif., 1977; mem. Jr. League of Palo Alto, chmn. evening div., 1975-76. NSF and Dept. Justice grantee for studies on computer abuse, 1972—. Fellow Assn. Computer Machinery (mem. at large of coun. 1976-80, nat. lectr. 1977—, chmn. standing com. on legal issues 1975—, mem. blue ribbon com. on rationalization of internat. propr. rights protection on info. processing devel. in the '90s 1990—), Coll. Law Practice Mgmt.; mem. ABA (chmn. sect. on sci. and tech. 1979-80), Internat. Bar Assn. (U.S. mem. computer com. of corps. sect.), Computer Law Assn. (v.p. 1983-85, pres. 1986—, bd. dirs. 1975—), Calif. State Bar Assn. (founder first chmn. econs. of law sect., vice chmn. law and computers com.), Nat. Conf. Lawyers and Scientists (rep. ABA), Strategic Forum on Intellectual Property Issues in Software of NAS, Internat. Coun. for Computer Comm. (gov. 1998). Contracts commercial, Trademark and copyright, Computer. Home: 35 Granada Ct Portola Vally CA 94028-7736 Office: Baker & McKenzie PO Box 60309 Palo Alto CA 94306-0309

**NYDEGGER, RICK D.,** lawyer; b. Salt Lake City, Utah, Apr. 24, 1949; s. A. Don and Jean Virginia (Hansen) N.; m. Denise Winegar, Oct. 22, 1970; children: Dan L., Chad E., Kurt D., Brittney, Trent R. BSEE cum laude, Brigham Young U., 1974, JD, 1977. Bar: Utah 1977, U.S. Dist Ct. (ctrl. dist.) Utah 1977, U.S. Patent Office 1977, U.S. Ct. Appeals (5th and 10th cirs.) 1980, U.S. Supreme Ct. 1990, U.S. Ct. Appeals (fed. cir.) 1994. Assoc. Fox, Edwards, & Gardiner, 1977-81, shareholder, dir., 1981-84; founding shareholder, dir., officer Workman, Nydegger & Seeley, Salt Lake City, Utah, 1984—; adj. prof. U. Utah Coll. Law, 1988—, Brigham Young U. Coll. Law, 1998—. Contbr. articles to profl. jours. Mem. ABA, Utah State Bar (chmn. patent, trademark, copyright sect., 1985-87), Am. Intellectual Property Law Assn. (chmn. electronic computer law com., 1990-93; bd. dirs., 1993-96; editorial bd. AIPLA quarterly jour., 1994-98; vice-chmn. ad hoc com. PCT practice, 1994-98; nominations com., 1997, chmn. mid-winter Inst. 2000 planning com.), Fed. Cir. Bar Assn., U.S. Supreme Ct. Hist. Soc. (tenth cir. rep., 1993-94, Utah state rep., 1992-93). Intellectual property. Office: Workman Nydegger & Seeley 60 E South Temple Ste 1000 Salt Lake City UT 84111-1011

**NYE, W. MARCUS W.,** lawyer; b. N.Y.C., Aug. 3, 1945; s. Walter R. and Nora (McLaren) N.; m. Eva Johnson; children: Robbie, Stephanie, Philip, Jennifer. BA, Harvard U., 1967; JD, U. Idaho, 1974. Bar: Idaho 1974, U.S. Dist. Ct. Idaho 1974, U.S. Ct. Appeals (9th cir.) 1980; lic. pilot. Ptnr. Racine, Olson, Nye, Budge & Bailey, Pocatello, Idaho, 1974—; vis. prof. law U. Idaho, Moscow, 1984; adj. prof. Coll. Engring. Idaho State U., 1993—; bd. dirs. Idaho State U. Found., U. Idaho Coll. Law Found. Recipient Alumni Svc. award U. Idaho, 1988. Fellow ABA (mem. ho. dels. 1988—, state chmn. ho. of dels. 1991—, bd. of govs. 1997—), Am. Bar Found. (stat. chmn. 1992-95); mem. Am. Bd. Trial Advs., Am. Coll. Trial Lawyers, Idaho Bar Assn. (commr. 1985—, pres. bd. commrs. 1987-88), Idaho Def. Counsel Assn. (pres. 1982), Idaho State Centennial Found. (commr. 1985-90), 6th Dist. Bar Assn. (pres. 1982). Avocation: flying. General civil litigation, Product liability. Home: 173 S 15th Ave Pocatello ID 83201-4056 Office: Racine Olson Nye Budge & Bailey PO Box 1391 Pocatello ID 83204-1391

**NYERGES, GEORGE LADISLAUS,** lawyer; b. Cleve., Aug. 27, 1925; s. Constantine L. and Irene (Schneider) N.; m. Joanne Mayo, Aug. 2, 1958; children: James George, Susan Joanne. BS, Case Western Reserve U., 1946; LLB, Cleveland-Marshall Law Sch., 1951, LLM, 1956; JD, Cleve. State U., 1969. Bar: Ohio 1951, U.S. Dist. Ct. (no. dist.) Ohio 1954, U.S. Ct. Appeals (6th cir.) 1985, U.S. Supreme Ct. 1991; lic. USCG. Lawyer, sole practice Cleve., 1951—; lectr. legal and med. ethics Cuyahoga C.C., Cleve., 1989; pvt. and ct. interpreter Hungarian lang., 1955—; ind. real estate broker, Ohio, 1960—; cons. to various religious groups, 1985—. Mem. Magyar Club of Cleve., 1952—, sec., 1954-57, pres. 1958; mem. "Night in Budapest Com." in Cleve., 1958-65, Vermilion (Ohio) Yacht Club, 1973—, sec., 1974-76; coach girls baseball Summer Recreational Jr. Girls Baseball, Westlake, Ohio, 1980, coach boys football Fall Recreational Jr. Boys Football, Westlake, 1980-82; former precinct committeeman Dem. Party, Westlake, 1990. Recipient Cert., Am. Judicature Soc., 1961, Plaque Am. Arbitration Assn., 1970, Cert. of Appreciation, Cleve. Bar Assn., 1987-88. Mem. ATLA, ABA, FBA, Ohio State Bar Assn. (Cert. of Appreciation 1991), Phi Gamma Delta. Democrat. Presbyterian. Avocations: former comdr., including lesser chairs and charter mem. of Rocky River Power Squadron. General civil litigation, Personal injury, Probate. Home: 1999 Dover Center Rd Westlake OH 44145-3151 Office: United Office Bldg 2012 W 25th St Ste 803 Cleveland OH 44113-4131

**NYGAARD, RICHARD LOWELL,** federal judge; b. 1940. BS cum laude, U. So. Calif., 1969; JD, U. Mich. Mem. Orton, Nygaard & Dunlevy, 1972-81; judge Ct. Common Pleas, 6th Dist. Pa., Erie, 1981-88, U.S. Ct. Appeals (3d cir.), Erie, Pa., 1988—. Councilman Erie County, 1977-81. With USNR, 1958-64. Mem. ABA, Pa. Bar Assn., Erie County Bar Assn. Office: US Courthouse 717 State St Ste 500 Erie PA 16501-1323*

**NYKANEN, DAVID EDWARD,** lawyer; b. Royal Oak, Mich., June 14, 1970; s. James Floyd and Mary Lynch N.; m. Kelly Ann Powell, Sept. 28, 1996. BA, Oakland U., 1992; JD, Wayne State U., 1995. Bar: Mich. 1995, U.S. Dist. Ct. (ea. dist.) Mich. 1995. Mng. editor Wayne Law Rev., Detroit, 1994-95; assoc. Mason Steinhardt Jacobs Perlman & Pesick, Southfield, Mich., 1995—. contbr. articles to profl. jours. Recipient Alfred G. Wilson award, Oakland U., Rochester, Mich., 1992. Fax: 248-358-3599. E-mail: dnykanen@tir.com. General corporate, Land use and zoning (including planning), Real property. Office: 4000 Town Ctr Ste 1500 Southfield MI 48075-1588

**NYMANN, P. L.,** lawyer; b. Clermont, Iowa, May 18, 1924; s. Jens Christian and Minnie Amalia (Osmundson) N.; m. Charmaine Ann Petersen, Dec. 2, 1951 (div. 1979); children: Michel, Candace, Kimberly, Christopher, Jon (dec.); m. Anne Barrett McDermott, Feb. 15, 1992. BA, U. Iowa, 1949, JD, 1951. Bar: Iowa 1951. Assoc. Louis S. Goldberg, Sioux City, Iowa, 1951-57; ptnr. Goldberg, Nymann & Probasco, Sioux City, 1957-64; v.p., gen. counsel IBP, Inc., Dakota City, Nebr., 1964-72; pvt. practice Sioux City, 1972-74, 83-87; ptnr. Jacobs, Gaul, Nymann & Green, Sioux City, 1974-83, Nymann & Kohl, Sioux City, 1987—. Chmn., Civil Svc. Commn., 1977-79; bd. dirs. United Way Siouxland, 1979-85. With AUS, 1943-46. Mem. ABA, Iowa Bar Assn., Am. Arbitration Assn., Rotary Club. Republican. Avocations: travel, boating, music. Labor, Federal civil litigation, Pension, profit-sharing, and employee benefits. Home: 9364 Decatur Plz Omaha NE 68114-1225 Office: Nymann & Kohl 383390 Orpheum Electric Sioux City IA 51101

**NYS, JOHN NIKKI,** lawyer; b. Duluth, Minn., May 3, 1948; s. Leslie Leo and Kathleen Cecilia (Beaudin) N.; m. Sandra Ann Stephenson, Aug. 20, 1977; 1 child, John Stephenson. BA, Dartmouth Coll., 1970; JD, Stanford U., 1973. Bar: Minn. 1973, U.S. Dist. Ct. Minn. 1973, U.S. Ct. Appeals (8th cir.) 1984, U.S. Dist. Ct. (we. dist.) Wis. 1985, Wis. 1986. Ptnr. Johnson, Killen, Thibodeau & Seiler, Duluth, 1973—. Pres., treas., bd. dirs. Duluth Regional Care Ctr., 1979-85; v.p., bd. dirs. Western Community Coun., 1980-86; cubmaster Lake Superior coun. Boy Scouts Am., 1987-90; mem. state cen. com. Dem. Farmer Labor Party, 1976-78; pres., bd. dirs. Morgan Park Smithville Community Club, 1978-85. Mem. ABA, Duluth Young Lawyers (pres. 1974-75), Minn. State Bar Assn. (chmn. lawyers referral com. 1986-88, bd. govs. 1990-98, pres. 1996-97), 11th Dist. Bar Assn . (pres. 1989-90). Roman Catholic. Banking, Bankruptcy, General corporate. Office: Johnson Killen Thibodeau & Seiler 811 Norwest Ctr Duluth MN 55808

**OAKES, JAMES L.,** federal judge; b. Springfield, Ill., Feb. 21, 1924; m. Evelena S. Kenworthy, Dec. 29, 1973 (dec. Oct. 1997); 3 children; m. Mara A. Williams, Jan. 1, 1999. AB, Harvard U., 1945, LLB, 1947; LLD, New Eng. Coll., 1976, Suffolk U., 1980, Vt. Law Sch., 1995. Bar: Calif. 1949, Vt. 1950. Pvt. practice Brattleboro, Vt.; spl. counsel Vt. Pub. Service Commn., 1959-60; counsel Vt. Statutory Revision Commn., 1957-60; mem. Vt. Senate, 1961-65; atty. gen. Vt., 1967-69, U.S. dist. judge, 1970-71; U.S. cir. judge 2d Cir. Ct. Appeals, Brattleboro, 1971—; chief judge 2d Circuit Ct. Appeals, 1989-92; adj. faculty Duke U. Law Sch., 1985-96, Iowa U. Coll. Law, 1993-97. Office: US Ct Appeals PO Box 696 Brattleboro VT 05302-0696

**OAKES, SUSAN LEIGH,** lawyer; b. Detroit, Apr. 9, 1959; d. Russell Calvin and Grace (Marinelli) Jones; m. Robert Randolph Oakes, Sept. 5, 1987; children: Dana Leigh, Ryan Robert. BA, Kenyon Coll., 1981; JD, U. Mich., 1984. Bar: Colo. 1984. V.p., dir. Ireland Stapleton Pryor & Pascoe, P.C., Denver, 1984-99; ptnr. Holme Roberts & Owen LLP, 1999—; lectr. U. Colo., Boulder, 1991-93. Deacon Cherry Creek Presbyn. Ch., Englewood, Colo., 1990-93, 98—. Mem. ABA, Colo. Bar Assn., Denver Bar Assn., Phi Beta Kappa. Presbyterian. Avocations: bicycling, skiing, reading, choral singing, backpacking. E-mail: oakess@hro.com. Securities, Mergers and acquisitions, General corporate. Home: 5050 S Franklin St Cherry Hl Vlg CO 80110-7035 Office: Holme Roberts & Owen LLP 1700 Lincoln St Ste 4100 Denver CO 80203-4541

**OAKLEY, JOEL NEESE,** lawyer; b. Greensboro, N.C., Jan. 30, 1960; s. Julius H. Oakley and Yvonne P. Berkerly; m. Nancy Calvin, Nov. 25, 1989; 1 child, Erica Danielle. BA, Appalachain State, 1982; JD summa cum laude, N.C. Ctrl. Sch. Law, 1986. Bar: N.C. 1986, U.S. Dist. Ct. (mid. dist.) N.C. 1986. Atty. N.C. Bar, Greensboro, 1986—. Mem. Greensboro Criminal Def. Lawyers Assn. (bd. dirs. 1993—, pres. 1994-95), Guilford Inns Ct., Triad Rugby Dogs. Democrat. Avocation: rugby. Criminal. Office: 322 S Eugene St Greensboro NC 27401-2322

**OAKLEY, JOHN BILYEU,** law educator, lawyer, judicial consultant; b. San Francisco, June 18, 1947; s. Samuel Heywood and Elsie-Maye (Bilyeu) O.; m. Fredericka Barvitz, May 25, 1969; children: Adélie, Antonia. BA, U. Calif., Berkeley, 1969; JD, Yale U., 1972. Bar: Calif. 1972, U.S. Dist. Ct. (no. dist.) Calif. 1974, U.S. Dist. Ct. (ctrl. and ea. dists.) Calif. 1975, U.S. Supreme Ct. 1977, U.S. Ct. Appeals (5th cir.) 1979, U.S. Ct. Appeals (9th cir.) 1992. Rsch. atty. chief justice Donald R. Wright Supreme Ct. of Calif., 1972-73, sr. rsch. atty. chief justice Donald R. Wright, 1974-75; sr. law clk. chief judge M. Joseph Blumenfeld U.S. Dist. Ct. Conn., Hartford, 1973-74; acting prof. law U. Calif., Davis, 1975-79, prof. law, 1979—; reporter Speedy Trial Planning Group, U.S. Dist. Ct., Sacramento, 1977-82, Civil Justice Reform Act Adv. Group, 1991-94, U.S. Jud. Conf. Com. on Fed.-State Jurisdiction, 1991-96, Western Regional Conf. on State-Fed. Jud. Relationships, 1992-93; scholar-in-residence, sr. trial atty. Civil Rights Divsn., U.S. Dept. Justice, Washington, 1979-80; vis. scholar U. Coll., Oxford (Eng.) U., 1982-83; apptd. counsel death penalty appeal Supreme Ct. Calif., 1984-96; cons. Calif. Jud. Coun. Commn. on the Future of the Cts., 1992-93; mem. Calif. Appellate Process task force, 1997—. Co-author: Law Clerks and the Judicial Process, 1980, An Introduction to the Anglo-American Legal System, 1980, 2d edit., 1988, Civil Procedure, 1991, 2d edit., 1996, Federal Courts, 10th edit., 1999; contbr.: Restructuring Justice, 1990. Pub. mem. New Motor Vehicle Bd. Calif., Sacramento, 1976-82, Calif. Jud. Coun. Appellate Process Task Force, 1997—; bd. dirs. Fallen Leaf Lake (Calif.) Mutual Water Co., 1980-82, 94—; western regional assoc., field assoc. Duke U. Primate Ctr., 1986-91, bd. visitors, 1997—. With U.S. Merchant Marine, 1969, Vietnam. Nat. Merit scholar, 1964. Mem. Am. Law Inst. (reporter Fed. Jud. Code Revision Project 1995—), Assn. Am. Law Schs. (chair sect. on civil procedure 1979-80, 96-97), Am. Judicature Soc. (bd. dirs. 1996-98), Phi Beta Kappa. Avocations: aviation, photography, railroads, rugby, running. Office: Univ Calif Sch Law Davis CA 95616

**OAKLEY, TRACY L.,** lawyer; b. Mattoon, Ill., Sept. 6, 1963; s. Max L. and Sharon L. (Freeman) O.; m. Linda M. Tylka, June 30, 1984; children; Jacob, Melissa, Lucs, Tracy, Caroline. BS, U. So. Miss., 1986; JD, U. Miss., 1989. Bar: La. 1989, U. S. Dist. Ct. (ea., mid. and we. dists.) La. 1989, U.S. Ct. Appeals (5th cir.) 1990, Ill. 1991. Assoc. Onebane, Donohoe, Barnard, Torian, Lafayette, La., 1989-92; ptnr. Wilkerson & Oakley, Ruston, La., 1992-94; sole practitioner Ruston, 1994—. Republican. Roman Catholic. Avocations: hunting, fishing, soccer. General civil litigation, Criminal. Address: 1401 Farmerville Hwy Ruston LA 71270-3517

**OATES, CARL EVERETTE,** lawyer; b. Harlingen, Tex., Apr. 8, 1931; s. Joseph William and Grace (Watson) O.; m. Eileen Noble Hudnall; children: Carl William, Gregory Carl Hudnall, Patricia O. Chase, Matthew Noble Hudnall. BS, U.S. Naval Acad., 1955; LLB, So. Meth. U., 1962. Bar: Tex. 1962, D.C. 1977, Nebr. 1985. Assoc. Akin, Gump, Strauss, Hauer & Feld, Dallas, 1962-64, ptnr., 1965-91. Asst. atty. gen. State of Texas, 1992-94, spl. coun., Tex. Dept. Banking, 1994-95, prin. Carl E. Oates, P.C. Chmn. bd. trustees S.W. Mus. Sci. and Tech., Dallas; v.p. S.W. Sci. Mus. Found., Dallas; bd. dirs. Kiwanis Wesley Dental Ctr., Inc., Dallas; pres. Wesley Dental Found., Dallas. Lt. USN, 1955-59. Mem. ABA, D.C. Bar Assn., Tex. Bar Assn., Dallas Bar Assn., Nebr. Bar Assn., Barristers, Northwood Club, Delta Theta Phi. Administrative and regulatory, General corporate, Real property.

**OAXACA, JUAN ROBERTO,** lawyer; b. El Paso, Dec. 27, 1946; s. Javier and Eulalia (Morales) O.; m. Lydia Esther Yañez, May 3, 1969; children: Monica, Miguel, Sara, Belen. BA, U. Tex., El Paso, 1969, MBA, 1975; JD, U. Tex., Austin, 1978. Bar: Tex.; cert. personal injury law. Pvt. practice El Paso, 1979—; ptnr. Oaxaca, Bernal & Assocs., El Paso, 1990—. Sgt. U.S. Army, 1969-71. Avocation: handball. Personal injury, Labor, Insurance. Office: Oaxaca Bernal & Assocs 1515 Montana Ave El Paso TX 79902-5619

**O'BARR, BOBBY GENE, SR.,** lawyer; b. Houston, May 5, 1932; s. Walter Morris and Maggie (Whitt) O'B.; children: Morris Clayton, William Clinton, Candace Jean, Bobby G.; m. Jennifer Ryals, Dec. 5, 1984; 1 child, Richard. BA, U. Miss., 1959, JD, 1958. Bar: Miss. 1958, U.S. Dist. Ct. (no. dist.) Miss. 1958, U.S. Dist. Ct. (so. dist.) Miss. 1966, U.S. Ct. Appeals (5th cir.) 1970, U.S. Supreme Ct. 1971. Pvt. practice Houston, 1958-59; assoc. W.M. O'Barr, Jr., Okolona, Miss., 1959-60; adminstrv. judge Miss. Workmen's Compensation Commn., 1960-65; assoc. Cumbest, Cumbest, O'Barr and Shaddock, Pascagoula, Miss., 1965-68, Hurlbert & O'Barr, O'Barr, Hurlbert and O'Barr, Biloxi, Miss., 1968-80; pvt. practice, owner Bobby G. O'Barr, P.A., Biloxi, 1980—. Mem., pres. Biloxi Port Commn., 1975-90; mem. mgmt. coun. Gulf Mex. Fishery, 1979-82. With USAF, 1951-54. Mem. VFW, State Bar Found., Southeastern Admiralty Law Inst., Miss. Trial Lawyers Assn., Am. Legion, Masons, Shriners. Admiralty, Personal injury, Workers' compensation. Office: PO Box 541 Biloxi MS 39533-0541

**OBER, PAUL RUSSELL,** lawyer; b. Indiana, Pa., Dec. 23, 1945; s. Paul Leo and Florence Elizabeth (Kenly) O.; m. Mary Jo DeSantis, Oct. 3, 1987; children: Joshua P., Michele, Gretchen L., Karl M. BA, Gannon U., 1968; JD, Dickinson U. Sch. Law, 1973. Bar: Pa. 1973, U.S. Dist. Ct. (ea. dist.) Pa. 1973. Assoc. Edelman, Schaeffer, Saylor, Readinger & Poore, Reading, Pa., 1973-77; ptnr. Erickson, Ober & Ober, Reading, Pa., 1977-87, Paul R. Ober & Assocs., Reading, Pa., 1987—. Dir. Berks County Conservancy, Reading, 1985-94, Montessori Children's Home, Reading, 1992-88; pres., dir. Bernville (Pa.) Area Recreation Assn., 1995—. With U.S. Army, 1969-70. Mem. Pa. Bar Assn. (mineral & natural resources com. 1980—, mcpl. law com. 1976—), Berks County Bar Assn., Ducks Unltd. (pres. Middlecreek chpt. 1978-80), Mid. Atlantic Redsetter Club (pres. 1972-80), Nat Redsetter Field Trail Club (pres. 1978-80), Order of Coif, Order of Barristers. Avocations: breading, training and competing with bird dogs, breeding Tennessee walking horses. Environmental, Land use and zoning (including planning), General corporate. Office: 234 N 6th St Reading PA 19601-3300

**OBER, RUSSELL JOHN, JR.,** lawyer; b. Pitts., June 26, 1948; s. Russell J. and Marion C. (Hampson) O.; m. Kathleen A. Stein, Apr. 8, 1972; children: Lauren Elizabeth, Russell John III. BA, U. Pitts., 1970, JD, 1973. Bar: Pa. 1973, U.S. Dist. Ct. (we. dist.) Pa. 1973, U.S. Tax Ct. 1982, U.S. Ct. Appeals (4th cir.) 1976, U.S. Ct. Appeals (3d cir.) 1979, U.S. Ct. Appeals (D.C. cir.) 1985, U.S. Ct. Appeals (2d cir.), 1990, U.S. Ct. Appeals (7th cir.) 1993, U.S. Supreme Ct. 1976. Asst. dist. atty. Allegheny County, Pitts., 1973-75; ptnr. Wallace Chapas & Ober, Pitts., 1975-80, Rose, Schmidt, Hasley & DiSalle, Pitts., 1980-92, Meyer, Unkovic & Scott, Pitts., 1992—. Bd. dirs. Parent and Child Guidance Ctr., Pitts., 1983-90, treas., 1985-86, pres., 1986-88; bd. mgmt. South Hills Area YMCA, 1989-91; mem. Mt. Lebanon Traffic Commn., 1976-81; bd. dirs. Whale's Tale Youth Family Counseling Ctr., 1990-95. Mem. ABA (discovery com. litigation sect. 1982-88, ho. of dels. young lawyers div. 1982-83), Pa. Bar Assn. (ho. of dels. 1983—), Allegheny County Bar Assn. (chmn. young lawyers sect. 1983, bd. govs. 1984, fin. com. 1984-88, mem. coun. civil litigation sect. 1991-93), Nat. Bd. Trial Advocacy (diplomate), Acad. Lawyers Allegheny County (fellow 1983—, bd. govs. 1988-90) U. Pitts. Law Alumni Assn. (bd. govs. 1984-89, v.p. 1985-87, pres. 1987-88), Rivers Club. Federal civil litigation, State civil litigation, Insurance. Office: Meyer Unkovic & Scott 1300 Oliver Bldg Pittsburgh PA 15222

**OBERDANK, LAWRENCE MARK,** lawyer, arbitrator; b. Cleve., Nov. 1, 1935; s. Leonard John and Mary (Pavelich) O.; m. Arlene C. Baldini, Aug. 25, 1962; 1 child, Karen A. BA, Western Res. U., 1958, JD, 1965. Bar: Ohio 1965, U.S. Dist. Ct. (no. dist.) Ohio 1966, U.S. Ct. Appeals (6th cir.) 1968, U.S. Supreme Ct. 1970. Assoc. Law Offices Mortimer Riemer, Cleve., 1965-69; ptnr. Riemer and Oberdank, Cleve., 1969-76; prin. Lawrence M. Oberdank Co., L.P.A., Cleve., 1976—; arbitrator Ohio Employment Rels. Bd., 1985-89, Cleve. Civil Svc. Commn., 1983—, FMHA, 1989—; chmn. mandatory arbitration panel Ct. Common Pleas; mem. Nat. Mediation Bd., 1986—; instr. indsl. rels. law Cleve. State U., 1982-85; instr. labor rels. Cuyahoga C.C., 1983; arbitrator/mediator U.S. Dist. Ct. (no. dist.) Ohio, ea. divsn. fee dispute panel Cleve. Bar Assn.; mem. securities arbitration panel Am. Stock Exch., N.Y. Stock Exch., 1995—. Bd. mediators U.S. EEOC. Mem. ABA (labor and employment sect., labor arbitration, law collective bargaining agreements, alternate dispute resolution sect., fed. ct. annexed/connected programs com., sr. lawyers sect.), Am. Arbitration Assn. (securities arbitrator, nat. labor panel 1973—, comml. arbitration panel, nat. panel of employment arbitrators), Nat. Assn. Securities Dealers, Inc. (bd. mediators), Bar Assn. Greater Cleve. (labor law com.), Cuyahoga County Bar Assn., Am. Judicature Soc., Internat. Soc. Labor Law and Social Legislation, Ohio State Bar Assn. (chmn. labor law sect. 1970-73), Indsl. Rels. Rsch. Assn., Pub. Sector Labor Rels. Assn., Soc. Profls. in Dispute Resolution (bd. dirs. Southwest Ohio chpt.), Nat. Inst. Dispute Resolution (assoc.), Masons, Phi Gamma Delta. Roman Catholic. Avocations: golf, Civil War history. Labor. Home: 8051 Lakeview Ct North Royalton OH 44133-1214 Office: 6450 Rockside Woods Blvd S Cleveland OH 44131-2230

**OBERDIER, RONALD RAY,** lawyer; b. Norwood, Mo., Nov. 11, 1945; s. Albert Jr. and Edith Louise (Vaughn) O.; children: James Myron, Steven Michael; m. Karal Oberdier; children: John Ryan Heffernan, Melissa Ann Heffernan. Student, Ohio State U., 1963-64; AA, SUNY, Albany, 1975; BA, Mary Hardin-Baylor U., 1978; JD, U. Tex., 1980. Bar: Fla. 1981, U.S. Dist. Ct. (no., so. and mid. dists.) Fla. 1981, U.S. Ct. Appeals (5th and 11th cir.) 1981. Enlisted U.S. Army, 1965, served as electronic intelligence specialist, 1965-77; assoc. Mahoney, Hadlow, Jacksonville, Fla., 1981-82, Coker, Myers & Schickel, Jacksonville, 1982-85; pvt. practice, Jacksonville, 1985-86; ptnr. Humphries & Oberdier, Jacksonville, 1987—. Mem. Fed. Bar Assn., Jacksonville Claims Assn., Jacksonville Bar Assn., Jacksonville Assn. Def. Counsel (pres. 1993), Am. Trial Lawyers Assn. (assoc.), Nat. Assn. R.R. Trial Lawyers, Fla. Def. Lawyers Assn. State civil litigation, Personal injury, Insurance. Office: 9550 Regency Square Blvd Jacksonville FL 32225-8191

**OBERDORFER, LOUIS F.,** federal judge; b. Birmingham, Ala., Feb. 21, 1919; s. A. Leo and Stella Maud (Falk) O.; m. Elizabeth Weil, July 31, 1941; children: John Louis, Kathryn Lee, Thomas Lee, William L. A.B., Dartmouth, 1939; LL.B., Yale, 1946. Bar: Ala. bar 1946, D.C. bar 1949. Law clk. to Justice Hugo L. Black, 1946-47; pvt. practice, 1947-51; mem. firm Wilmer, Cutler & Pickering (and predecessors), 1951-61, 65-77; asst. atty. gen. tax div. Dept. of Justice, 1961-65; judge, now sr. judge U.S. Dist. Ct. (D.C. dist.), 1977—; vis. lectr. Yale Law Sch., 1966-71; adv. com. Fed. Rules Civil Procedure, 1962-84; co-chmn. lawyers com. Civil Rights Under Law, 1967-69; adj. prof. law Georgetown U., Washington, 1993—. Editor-in-chief Yale Law Jour., 1941. Served to capt. AUS, 1941-46. Mem. ABA, D.C. Bar Assn. (bd. govs. 1972-77, pres. 1977), Ala. Bar Assns., Am. Law Inst., Yale Law Sch. Assn. (pres. 1971-73). Office: US Dist Ct 333 and Constitution Ave NW Washington DC 20001

**OBERHARDT, WILLIAM PATRICK,** lawyer; b. Chgo., Dec. 12, 1952. BSME, U. Notre Dame, 1975; MD, De Paul U., 1978. Bar: Ill. 1978, U.S. Dist. Ct. (no. dist.) Ill. 1978, U.S. Patent Office 1984, U.S. Ct. Appeals (fed. cir.) 1984, U.S. Claims Ct. 1986, U.S. Ct. Appeals (7th cir.) 1990. Asst. atty. gen. State of Ill., Office Atty. Gen., Consumer Fraud Divsn., Chgo., 1978-84; ptnr. Neuman, Wiliams, Anderson & Olson, Chgo., 1984-90, Roper & Quigg, Chgo., 1990—. Mem. Fed. Cir. Bar Assn., Ill. Bar Assn., Chgo. Bar Assn., Intellectual Property Law Assn. Intellectual property, Patent, Federal civil litigation. Office: Roper & Quigg 200 S Michigan Ave # 1000 Chicago IL 60604-2402

**OBERLY, KATHRYN ANNE,** lawyer; b. Chgo., May 22, 1950; d. James Richard and Lucille Mary (Kraus) O.; m. Daniel Lee Goelzer, July 13, 1974 (div. Aug. 1987); 1 child, Michael W. Student, Vassar Coll., 1967-69; BA, U. Wis., 1971, JD, 1973. Bar: Wis. 1973, D.C. 1981, N.Y. 1995. Law clk. U.S. Ct. Appeals, Omaha, 1973-74; trial atty. U.S. Dept. Justice, Washington, 1974-77, spl. asst., 1977-81, spl. litigation counsel, 1981-82, asst. to Solicitor Gen., 1982-86; ptnr. Mayer, Brown & Platt, Washington, 1986-91; assoc. gen. counsel Ernst & Young LLP, Washington, 1991-94; vice-chair, gen. counsel Ernst & Young LLP, N.Y.C., 1994—; exec. com. CPR Ctr. for Dispute Resolution. Named one of 50 Most Influential Women Lawyers in Am., Nat. Law Jour., 1998. Mem. ABA, Am. Law Inst., Am. Acad. Appellate Lawyers, Wis. Bar Assn., D.C. Bar Assn. Democrat. Office: Ernst & Young LLP 787 7th Ave Fl 14 New York NY 10019-6085

**OBERMAN, MICHAEL STEWART,** lawyer; b. Bklyn., May 21, 1947; s. Hyman Martin and Gertrude O.; m. Sharon Land, Oct. 8, 1975; 1 child, Abigail Land. AB, Columbia U., 1969; JD, Harvard U., 1972. Bar: N.Y. 1973, U.S. Dist. Ct. (so. and ea. dists.) N.Y. 1973, U.S. Ct. Appeals (2d cir.) 1973, U.S. Supreme Ct. 1976, Calif. 1981, U.S. Dist. Ct. (no. dist.) Calif. 1981, U.S. Ct. Appeals (9th cir.) 1981, U.S. Dist. Ct. (so. and cen. dists.) Calif. 1982, U.S. Ct. Appeals (5th cir.) 1989, D.C. 1992, U.S. Ct. Appeals (7th cir.) 1993. Law clk. to Hon. Milton Pollack, U.S. Dist. Ct. (so. dist.) N.Y., 1972-73; assoc. Kramer Levin Naftalis & Frankel LLP, N.Y.C., 1973-79, ptnr., 1980—. Contbr. articles to profl. jours. Recipient Nathan Burkan prize ASCAP, 1973. Mem. N.Y. State Bar Assn. (mem. ho. of dels. 1989-91, exec. com. comml. and fed. litigation sect.). General civil litigation, Intellectual property. Office: Kramer Levin Naftalis & Frankel LLP 919 3rd Ave New York NY 10022-3902

**OBERMAN, STEVEN,** lawyer; b. St. Louis, Sept. 21, 1955; s. Albert and Marian (Kleg) O.; m. Evelyn Ann Simpson, Aug. 27, 1977; children: Rachael Diane, Benjamin Scott. BA in Psychology, Auburn U., 1977; JD, U. Tenn., 1980. Bar: Tenn. 1980, Tenn. Supreme Ct. 1980, Tenn. Criminal Ct. Appeals 1980, U.S. Dist. Ct. (ea. dist.) Tenn. 1980, U.S. Ct. Appeals (4th cir.) 1981, U.S. Ct. Appeals (6th cir.) 1983, U.S. Supreme Ct. 1985. Law clk. Daniel, Duncan & Claiborne, Knoxville, Tenn., 1978-80; assoc. Daniel, Claiborne & Lewallen, Knoxville, Tenn., 1980-82; ptnr. Daniel, Claiborne, Oberman & Buuck, Knoxville, 1983-85, Daniel & Oberman, Knoxville, 1986—; pres., Project First Offender, Knoxville, 1983-86; bd. dirs. Fed. Defender Svcs. Eastern Tenn., Inc., v.p. 1994-97, pres. 1998—; guest instr. U. Tenn. 1988-90; guest lectr. U. Tenn. Law Sch., 1982-88; guest instr. U. Tenn. Grad. Sch. Criminal Justice Program, 1983, 84; guest speaker Ct. Clk's Meeting, Cambridge, Eng., 1984; guest instr. legal clinic, trial advocacy program U. Tenn., 1984—; adj. prof. U. Tenn. Law Sch., 1993— (Forrest W. Lacey award for outstanding faculty contbn. to U. Tenn. Coll. Law Moot Ct. Program, 1993-94; coach U. Tenn. Law Sch. Nat. Trial Team, 1991-96; spl. judge Criminal Divsn. Knox County Gen. Sessions Court; founding mem. Nat. Coll. for DUI Def.; speaker in field. Author: D.U.I.: The Crime and Consequences in Tennessee, 1991, 2d edit., 1997, supplemented annually; co-author: D.W.I. Means Defend With Ingenuity, 1987; contbr. legal articles on drunk driving to profl. jours. Bd. dirs. Knoxville Legal Aid Soc., Inc., 1986-88 (pres. 1990), Arnstein Jewish Community Ctr., 1987-91, pres. 1990; bd. dirs. Knoxville Racquet Club, 1991-93, pres. 1992-93. Col. Aide de Camp Tenn. Gov.'s Staff, 1983, Moot Ct. Bd. Spl. Svc. award, 1995-96. Mem. ATLA, Nat. Assn. Criminal Def. Lawyers (co-chair DUI advocacy com. 1995—), Tenn. Assn. Criminal Def. Lawyers (bd. dirs. 1983-89), Knoxville Bar Assn. Jewish. Criminal, Personal injury. Office: Daniel & Oberman 550 W Main St Ste 950 Knoxville TN 37902-2567

**OBERST, PAUL,** law educator; b. Owensboro, Ky., Apr. 22, 1914; m. Elizabeth Durfee; children—Paul, James, George, Mary, John. A.B., U. Evansville, 1936; J.D., U. Ky., 1939; LL.M., U. Mich., 1941. Bar: Ky. 1938, Mo. 1942. Assoc. firm Ryland, Stinson, Mag & Thomson, Kansas City, Mo., 1941-42; asst. prof. law Coll. of Law, U. Ky., Lexington, 1946-47; prof. Coll. of Law, U. Ky., 1947-82; acting dean, 1966-67; emeritus prof. Coll. of Law, U. Ky., 1982—; vis. prof. U. Chgo., 1954-55, Duke U., 1980; prof., dir. civil liberties program N.Y. U., 1959-61; mem. Nat. Commn. on Acad. Tenure, 1971-73. Contbr. articles to legal jours. Mem. Ky. Commn. on Corrections, 1961-65; mem. Ky. Commn. on Human Rights, 1962-66, 80-90, chmn., 1966-70, 73-76; trustee U. Ky., Lexington, 1963-69, 72-75; mem. Ky. state adv. com. U.S. Civil Rights Commn., 1979-92, chmn., 1982-86. Served to lt. USNR, 1942-46. Mem. Assn. Am. Law Schs. (exec. com. 1970-72), Am., Ky. bar assns., Am. Law Inst., Order of Coif, Phi Delta Phi. Home: 829 Sherwood Dr Lexington KY 40502-2919

**OBERT, KEITH DAVID,** lawyer; b. Talladega, Ala., Nov. 22, 1962; s. Sam R. and Alice M. Obert; m. Alaine Anderson, Aug. 3, 1991; 1 child, Baylor Anderson. BS in Acctg., U. Ala., 1984; JD, U. Miss., 1988. Bar: Miss. 1988, Tenn. 1988, Ala. 1989. Acct. Challenger Lighting Co. Inc., Olive Branch, Miss., 1984-85; atty. Wells, Moore, Simmons, Stufflefield and Neeld, Jackson, Miss., 1988-89, Copeland, Cook, Taylor & Bush, Jackson, 1989-97; shareholder Akers & Obert, P.A., Brandon, Miss., 1997—. Verger, lector, usher, accolyte Chapel of the Cross, Madison, Miss. Mem. ABA, Miss. Bar Assn. (dir. young lawyers divsn., chmn. membership svcs. com. chmn. pub. rels. com., bus. law sect. co-editor newsletter), Rankin County Bar Assn., Hinds County Bar Assn., Tenn. Bar Assn., Ala. State Bar, Bar Assn. of the Fifth Fed. Cir., Miss. Def. Lawyers Assn., Def. Rsch. and Trial Lawyers Assn., Miss. Claims Assn., Jackson Young Lawyers Assn. (pres., v.p., treas., dir.), Hinds County Bar Assn. (dir.),. Avocations: golfing, hunting, skiing. General civil litigation, Product liability, Insurance. Office: Akers & Obert PA 20 Eastgate Dr Ste D Brandon MS 39042-2329

**OBERT, PAUL RICHARD,** lawyer, manufacturing company executive; b. Pitts.; s. Edgar F. and Elizabeth T. Obert. B.S., Georgetown U., 1950; J.D., U. Pitts., 1953. Bar: Pa. 1954, D.C. 1956, Ohio 1972, Ill. 1974, U.S. Supreme Ct. 1970. Sole practice Pitts., 1954-60; asst. counsel H.K. Porter Co., Inc., Pitts., 1960-62, sec., gen. counsel, 1962-71; sec., gen. counsel Addressograph-Multigraph Corp., Cleve., 1972-74; v.p. law Marshall Field & Co., Chgo., 1974-82, sec., 1976-82; v.p., gen. counsel, sec. CF Industries, Inc., Long Grove, Ill., 1982—, also officer, dir. various subs. Served to lt. col. USAF. Mem. ABA (corp. gen. counsel com.), Pa. Bar Assn., Allegheny County Bar Assn., Ill. Bar Assn., Chgo. Bar Assn., Am. Soc. Corp. Secs., Am. Retail Fedn. (bd. dirs. 1977-80), Georgetown U. Alumni Assn. (bd. govs.), Pitts. Athletic Assn., Univ. Club (Chgo.), Delta Theta Phi. General corporate, Administrative and regulatory, Contracts commercial. Office: CF Industries Inc 1 Salem Lake Dr Long Grove IL 60047-8401

**OBNINSKY, VICTOR PETER,** lawyer; b. San Rafael, Calif., Oct. 12, 1944; s. Peter Victor and Anne Bartholdi (Donston) O.; m. Clara Alice Bechtel, June 8, 1969; children: Mari, Warren. BA, Columbia U., 1966; JD, U. Calif., Hastings, 1969. Bar: Calif. 1970. Sole practice, Novato, Calif., 1970—; arbitrator Marin County Superior Ct., San Rafael, 1979—; superior ct. judge pro tem, 1979—; lectr. real estate and partnership law. Author: The Russians in Early California, 1966. Bd. dirs. Calif. Young Reps., 1968-69, Richardson Bay San. Dist., 1974-75, Marin County Legal Aid Soc., 1976-78; baseball coach Little League, Babe Ruth League, 1970-84; mem. nat. panel consumer arbitrators Better Bus. Bur., 1974-88; leader Boy Scouts Am., 1970-84; permanent sec. Phillips Acad. Class of 1962, 1987—; mem. Phillips Acad. Alumni Council, 1991-95; bd. community advisors Buck Ctr. for Rsch. on Aging. Mem. ABA, State Bar Calif., Marin County Bar Assn. (bd. dirs. 1985-91, treas. 1987-88, pres.-elect 1989, pres. 1990), Phi Delta Phi, Phi Gamma Delta. Republican. Russian Orthodox. General practice, General corporate, Probate. Office: 2 Commercial Blvd Ste 103 Novato CA 94949-6121 *An all-out intellectual attempt to understand baseball thoroughly may give sufficient insight to understand oneself; the so-called "designated hitter" rule should be abolished immediately.*

**OBREMSKI, CHARLES PETER,** lawyer; b. Passaic, N.J., Sept. 11, 1946; s. Charles Joseph and Ann (Tichansky) O.; m. Nancy Gail Howell, May 13, 1973; children—Gregory, Christian. B.A., Boston U., 1968; J.D., NYU, 1972. Bar: N.Y. 1972, U.S. Dist. Ct. (so. and ea. dists.) N.Y. 1974, U.S. Ct. Appeals (2d cir.) 1974, U.S. Ct. Claims 1975, U.S. Supreme Ct. 1975. Account specialist IBM Corp., N.Y.C., 1968-69; atty. Home Life Ins. Co., N.Y.C., 1972-73; sole practice, Cornwall, N.Y., 1973—. V.p. Mus. Hudson Highlands, Cornwall-on-Hudson, N.Y., 1975-86; mayor Village of Cornwall, 1977-79. Served to maj. JAGC N.Y. Army N.G. Mem. N.Y. State Bar Assn. Consumer commercial, Real property. Home: PO Box 537 Cornwall NY 12518-0537 Office: 321 Main St Cornwall NY 12518-1503

**O'BRIEN, CHARLES H.,** lawyer, retired state supreme court chief justice; b. Orange, N.J., July 30, 1920; s. Herbert Rodgers and Agnes Sidman (Montanya) O'B.; m. Anna Belle Clement, Nov. 9, 1966; children: Merry Diane, Steven Shawn (dec.), Heather Lynn. LLB, Cumberland U., 1947. Rep. Tenn. Legislature, Memphis, 1963-65, senator, 1965-67; assoc. judge Tenn. Ct. Criminal Appeals, Crossville, 1970-87; assoc. justice Tenn. Supreme Ct., 1987-94, chief justice, 1994-95; ret., 1995; pvt. practice, Crossville, 1995—. Bd. dirs. Lake Tansi Village Property Owners Assn., 1984-89, chmn., 1989. With U.S. Army, 1938-45, ETO, 1950, UN Command, Tokyo. Decorated Bronze Star, Purple Heart with oak leaf cluster. Fellow Tenn. Bar Found.; mem. Tenn. Bar Assn., Cumberland County Bar Assn., Am. Legion, Lake Tansi Village Chowder and Marching Soc. (pres.). Democrat. Avocation: outdoor activities. Estate planning, Finance, Probate.

**O'BRIEN, DANIEL ROBERT,** lawyer; b. Peoria, Ill., May 7, 1951; s. William Patrick and Irene Cornelius O'Brien; m. Eileen Mary Kahn, Aug. 17, 1974; children: Colleen, Patrick, Bridget. BS, No. Ill. U., 1973; JD, Wash. U., St. Louis, 1976. Bar: U.S. Dist. Ct. (so. dist.) Ill. 1977. Ptnr. Smith Moos Schmitt & O'Brien, Peoria, 1976-82, Moos, Schmitt & O'Brien, Peoria, 1982—; lectr. Peoria County Bar Assn., Ill. Continuing Legal Edn., Springfield. Dem. precinct committeeman Dem. Party, 1986. Fellow Ill. Bar Found. (charter mem.). Avocations: coacing children's basketball. Personal injury, Workers' compensation. Office: Moos Schmitt & O'Brien 331 Fulton St Ste 740 Peoria IL 61602-1499

**O'BRIEN, DAVID A.,** lawyer; b. Sioux City, Iowa, Aug. 30, 1958; s. John T. and Doris K. (Reisch) O'B. BA, George Washington U., 1981; JD with distinction, U. Iowa, 1984. Bar: Iowa 1985, U.S. Dist. Ct. (no. dist.) Iowa 1985, Nebr. 1990, U.S. Dist. Ct. Nebr. 1990. Legis. asst. Nat. Transp. Safety Bd., Washington, 1978-81; assoc. O'Brien, Galvin & Kuehl, Sioux City, 1985-88; ptnr. O'Brien, Galvin Moeller & Neary, Sioux City, 1989-94; chair Wage Appeals Bd. & Bd. of Svc. Contract Appeals U.S. Dept. Labor, Washington, 1994-96, acting dir. Office Adminstrv. Appeals, 1995-96, chair adminstrv. review bd., 1996-98; atty. White & Johnson, Cedar Rapids, Iowa, 1998—. Dem. candidate for Congress, 6th dist. of Iowa, Sioux City, 1988; chmn. Woodbury County Dem. Party, Sioux City, 1992-94, chair Iowa campaign Clinton for Pres., Des Moines, 1992; bd. dirs. Mid-Step Svcs. Inc., Sioux City, 1986-91, Mo. River Hist. Devel., Sioux City, 1989-94. Mem. Nat. Assn. Trial Lawyers, Iowa Trial Lawyers Assn. (bd. govs. 1991-94). Roman Catholic. Avocations: sports, politics. E-mail: dobrien@wjpc.com. Personal injury, Workers' compensation, Labor. Office: White & Johnson PO Box 5878 Cedar Rapids IA 52406-5878

**O'BRIEN, DAVID MICHAEL,** law educator; b. Rock Springs, Wyo., Aug. 30, 1951; s. Ralph Rockwell and Lucile O'Brien; m. Claudine M. Mendelovitz, Dec. 17, 1982; children: Benjamin, Sara, Talia. BA, U. Calif., Santa Barbara, 1973, MA, 1974, PhD, 1977. Fulbright lectr. Oxford (Eng.) U., 1987-88; lectr. U. Calif., Santa Barbara, 1976-77; asst. prof. U. Puget Sound, Tacoma, Wash., 1977-79; Spicer prof. U. Va., Charlottesville, 1979—; Fulbright rschr., Tokyo, Kyoto, Japan, 1993-94, Fulbright chair, Bologna, Italy, 1999; jud. fellow U.S. Supreme Ct., Washington, 1982-83; vis. postdoctoral fellow Russell Sage Found., N.Y.C., 1981-82; lectr. USIA, Burma, Japan, France, 1994-95. Author: Supreme Court Watch, 1991—, Constitutional Law and Politics, 2 vols., 3d edit., 1997, Storm Center: The Supreme Court in American Politics, 4th edit., 1996, To Dream of Dreams: Constitutional Politics in Postwar Japan, 1996, To Dream of Dreams: Religious Freedom in Postwar Japan, 1996; editor: Views from the Bench, 1985, Judges on Judging, 1997. Rappatour, jud. selection 20th Century Fund Task Force, N.Y., 1986-87. Tom C. Clark Jud. Fellow, Jud. Fellows Commn., Washington, 1983. Mem. ABA (Silver Gavel award 1987), Am. Judicature Soc., Am. Polit. Sci. Assn., Supreme Ct. Hist. Soc. (editl. bd. 1982—), Internat. Polit. Sci. Assn. Democrat. Avocations: painting, travel. Home: 916 Tilman Rd Charlottesville VA 22901-6338 Office: U Va 232 Cabell Hall Charlottesville VA 22901

**O'BRIEN, DONALD EUGENE,** federal judge; b. Marcus, Iowa, Sept. 30, 1923; s. Michael John and Myrtle A. (Toomey) O'B.; m. Ruth Mahon, Apr. 15, 1950; children: Teresa, Brien, John, Shuivaun. LL.B., Creighton U., 1948. Bar: Iowa bar 1948, U.S. Supreme Ct. bar 1963. Asst. city atty. Sioux City, Iowa, 1949-53; county atty. Woodbury County, Iowa, 1955-58; mcpl. judge Sioux City, Iowa, 1959-60; U.S. atty. No. Iowa, 1961-67; pvt. practice law Sioux City, 1967-78, U.S. Dist. judge, 1978—; chief judge U.S. Dist. Ct. (no. dist.) Iowa, Sioux City, 1985-92, sr. judge, 1992—; rep. 8th cir. dist. ct. judges to Jud. Conf. U.S., 1990-97. Served with USAAF, 1943-45. Decorated D.F.C., air medals. Mem. Woodbury County Bar Assn., Iowa State Bar Assn. Roman Catholic. Office: US Dist Ct PO Box 267 Sioux City IA 51102-0267

**O'BRIEN, DONALD JOSEPH,** lawyer; b. Chgo., Oct. 4, 1913; s. Donald and Julia (Steger) O'B.; m. Helen C. McGinnis, Feb. 26, 1938; children: Donald J. Jr., Nancy S. Brown, Terrence M., Dennis F., Richard M. JD, De Paul U., 1936. Bar: Ill. 1936, U.S. Dist. Ct. (no. dist.) Ill. 1936, U.S. Ct. Appeals (7th cir.) 1936. State senator Ill. Legislature, Chgo., 1950-64; ward committeeman Cook County Dem. Orgn., Chgo., 1953-63, mem. exec. com., 1953-64; judge Cir. Ct., 1964-80; presiding judge Chancery Div. Cook County, Chgo., 1968-80; Senate minority leader Ill. Legislature, 1956-64. Contbr. articles to profl. jours. Disting. service award Nordic Law Club, Chgo., 1972, Celtic Legal Soc., Chgo., 1970, Catholic Lawyers Guild, Chgo., 1978, Chgo. Bar Assn., Young Lawyers 1978. Mem. ABA, Ill. State Bar Assn., Chgo. Bar Assn., Am. Coll. Trial Lawyers, Internat. Acad. Trial Lawyers, Soc. Trial Lawyers Ill., Butterfield Country Club, K.C. Democrat. Roman Catholic. Avocations: fishing, hunting, golf. General civil litigation, General corporate, General practice. Home: 635 E 6th St Hinsdale IL 60521-4712

**O'BRIEN, DUNCAN THOMAS,** lawyer; b. N.Y.C., Nov. 15, 1960; s. Duncan Thomas and Anne Bradshaw O'B.; m. Marlene V. Rehkemp; children: Duncan Thomas, Justin Rehkamp, Regina Rehkamp. AB, Harvard U., 1982, JD, 1985. Bar: N.Y. 1987, U.S. Ct. Appeals (11th cir.) 1987, Mass. 1998. Law clk. to Hon. R. Lanier Anderson, U.S. Ct. Appeals for 11th Cir., Macon, Ga., 1985-86; assoc. Simpson Thacher & Bartlett, N.Y.C., 1986-94, Gibson, Dunn & Crutcher LLP, N.Y.C., 1994-97; ptnr. Sullivan & Worcester LLP, N.Y.C. and Boston, 1997—. Dir. Boston Latin Sch. Assn. Finance, Contracts commercial, Banking. Office: Sullivan & Worcester LLP 1 Post Office Sq Ste 2300 Boston MA 02109-2129

**O'BRIEN, JAMES EDWARD,** lawyer; b. Mpls., June 10, 1937; s. Thomas Edward and Virginia Ann (Balster) O'B.; m. Patricia Jo Ann Cole, Mar. 1, 1958; children: Daniel J., Martin J. BA, U. Alaska, 1962; JD, U. Minn., 1965. Bar: Minn. Assoc. Moss & Barnett, Mpls., 1965—, chmn., CEO. With USAF, 1957-62. Mem. Unilaw (chmn.), Fund for Legal Aid Soc. (bd. dirs.), Kiwanis Internat. (George Hixon fellow 1996), Kiwanis Mpls. (bd. dirs.). Avocations: fishing, boating. General corporate, Mergers and acquisitions, Finance.

**O'BRIEN, JAMES FREEMAN,** lawyer; b. Waltham, Mass., Jan. 23, 1951; s. John Smith and Miriam Anna (Cary) O'B.; m. Norma Jo Greenberg, Feb. 19, 1977 (div. Jan. 1989); 1 stepchild, Nicholas S. Elfner. BA, U. Pa., 1973; JD, Northeastern U., 1978. Bar: Mass., U.S. Dist. Ct. Mass., U.S. Ct. Appeals (1st cir.). Law clk. to the justices Mass. Superior Ct., 1978-79; assoc. Dane, Howe & Brown, Boston, 1979-80, Lawson & Wayne, Boston, 1981-84, Dane & Greenberg, Concord, Mass., 1985-88; ptnr. Dane & Greenberg, Concord, 1988, Dane & O'Brien, Concord, 1988-93; pvt. practice law Concord, 1993—; advisor Harvard Trial Adv. Workshop, Cambridge, Mass., 1992—; trial judge Harvard Ames Moot Ct., Cambridge, 1992—. Actor, dir. numerous amateur and profl. stage plays, 1958—; contbr. articles to profl. jours. Sec., mem. Pub. Ceremonies and Celebrations Com., Concord, 1993—. Named Best Dir., New England Theatre Conf., Brandeis, 1985, 91. Mem. Mass. Bar Assn., Ctrl. Middlesex Bar Assn., Concord Lodge of Elks, Concord Ind. Battery, Frank J. Murray Inn Ct. Avocations: theater, music. General civil litigation, Criminal, Contracts commercial. Office: PO Box 690 Concord MA 01742-0690

**O'BRIEN, JOAN SUSAN,** lawyer, educator; b. New York, Apr. 14, 1946; d. Edward Vincent O'Brien and Joan Therese (Kramer) Quinn; m. Michael P. Wilpan, May 27, 1979; children: Edward B. Wilpan, Anabel T. Wilpan. BA, NYU, 1967; JD, Georgetown U., 1970. Bar: N.Y. 1971, Mass. 1971, U.S. Dist. Ct. (so. and ea. dist.) N.Y. 1972, U.S. Ct. Appeals (2d cir.) 1971. Law clk. to Hon. Frank J. Murray U.S. Dist. Ct. Mass., Boston, 1970-71; asst. U.S. atty. Office of U.S. Atty. U.S. Dist. Ct. (ea. dist.) N.Y., Bklyn., 1972-76; pvt. practice N.Y.C., 1976-79; trial atty. Mendes & Mount, N.Y.C., 1979-84; asst. prof. St. Johns U., Jamaica, N.Y., 1984-90; adminstrv. law judge N.Y. State Workers Compensation Bd., Hempstead, N.Y., 1990-93; appellate atty. Scheine, Fusco, Brandenstein & Rada, Woodbury, N.Y., 1993-97; trial atty. Grey & Grey, L.L.P., Farmingdale, N.Y., 1997—. Editor: Georgetown Law Jour., 1968-70. Pres. Nassau County Dem. Com. Women's Caucus, Westbury, N.Y., 1988-90; leader Girl Scouts Nassau

County, 1990-93. Unitarian-Universalist. Product liability, Personal injury, Workers' compensation. Office: Grey & Grey LLP 360 Main St Farmingdale NY 11735-3592

**O'BRIEN, JOHN GRAHAM,** lawyer; b. N.Y.C., May 12, 1948; s. John Edward and Marian Helen (FitzGerald) O'B.; m. Phyllis Mary Eyth, Apr. 10, 1976; children: John Graham Jr., Jennifer A. BS cum laude, Mt. St. Mary's Coll., Emmitsburg, Md., 1970; JD, Am. U., 1973. Bar: N.J. 1974, D.C. 1974, N.Y. 1982, U.S. Supreme Ct. 1982. Law clk. to Hon. F.C. Kentz and J.H. Coleman, Superior Ct. of N.J., Elizabeth, N.J., 1973-74; assoc. Carpenter, Bennett & Morrissey, Newark, 1975-81; sr. counsel GAF Corp., Wayne, N.J., 1981-90; assoc. gen. counsel Keene Corp., N.Y.C., 1990-93, ISS Internat. Svc. Sys., N.Y.C., 1994-95; cons. GE, Fairfield, Conn., 1993-94; mng. ptnr. Akins & O'Brien LLP, N.Y.C., 1995—. Author: (monograph) Responding to Products Liability Claims, 1986, also supplements; contbg. author: Toxic Torts Practice Guide, 1992. Recipient Disting. Young Alumni award Mt. St. Mary's Coll., 1976. Mem. N.J. Bar Assn., D.C. Bar, Irish Bus. Orgn. N.Y., Echo Lke Country Club (assoc.), Coll. Mens Club. Roman Catholic. General civil litigation, Insurance, Personal injury. Office: Atkins & O'Brien LLP 11 Hanover Sq Ste 2400 New York NY 10005-2819

**O'BRIEN, JOHN NEWELL, II,** lawyer; b. Royal Oak, Mich., July 27, 1961; s. John Newell and Delphine Caroline O.; m. Judith M. Kalpin; children: John III, Matthew. BA, Oakland U., 1983; JD, Detroit Coll. Law, 1987. Bar: Mich. 1987, U.S. Dist. Ct. (ea. dist.) Mich. 1988. Court clerk Oakland County Cir. Ct., Pontiac, Mich., 1984-86; assoc. attorney Barbier & Tolleson, P.C., Troy, Mich., 1986-89; asst. prosecutor Oakland County Prosecutor's Office, Pontiac, 1989-96, chief deputy prosecutor, 1997—; bd. dirs. Child Abuse & Neglect Council, Pontiac, Oakland County Bar Assn., Bloomfield Twp., Mich.; adv. bd. Cmty. Corrections, Pontiac, 1997—; lectr. Nat. Coll. Dist. Attys., Oakland Police Acad., Prosecuting Attys. Assn. Mich. Contbr. author: (with others) Trial Advocacy for Prosecutors, 1996; author The Practical Prosecutor, 1997. Sunday Sch. Tchr. Shrine of the Little Flower, Royal Oak, Mich., 1989—; mem. Royal Oak Cmty. Coalition, 1997—. Recipient Child Advocate of Yr. award Child Abuse & Neglect Council, Pontiac, 1996. Mem. Oakland County Bar Assn., Irish Am. Lawyers Assn., Fraternal Order Police, Detroit Zoological Soc. Republican. Roman Catholic. Avocations: art, windsurfing, scuba diving, travel. Office: Oakland County Prosecutors Office 1200 N Telegraph Rd Pontiac MI 48341-1032

**O'BRIEN, KATHLEEN,** lawyer; b. Billings, Mont., Mar. 27, 1956; d. James Richmond and Joan Mae (Haiston) O'B. BA, Oreg. State U., 1977; JD, U. Oreg., 1980. Bar: Oreg. 1983, U.S. Dist. Ct. Oreg. 1983. Ptnr. Wittrock & O'Brien, Portland, Oreg., 1983—. Co-author: Oregon Women and the Law, 1997. Mem. Oreg. State Bar Assn. (house of dels.), Oreg. Women Lawyers. General practice. Office: 300 SE 80th Ave Portland OR 97215-1526

**O'BRIEN, MURROUGH HALL,** lawyer; b. Portland, Maine, July 23, 1945; s. Francis Massey and Constanze Kathryn (McDonnell) O'B. m. Johannah M. Hart, June 11, 1968; children: John David, Ellen Hart. AB magna cum laude, Harvard U., 1969; JD, U. Maine, 1975. Bar: Maine 1975. Reporter, asst. city editor Evening Express, Portland, Maine, 1970-71; ptnr. firm Dunlap, Wood & O'Brien, Portland, Maine, 1975-80, Dunlap & O'Brien, Portland, Maine, 1980-85, Murrough H. O'Brien, Esquire, Portland, Maine, 1985—; exec. sec. Maine Jud. Coun., Portland, Maine, 1981-97; pres. Portland Book Co. Mem. Keep Maine Scenic Com., 1974-79, So. Coastal Family Planning, Inc., Portland, 1975-79; mem. steering com. Study of the Future of Maine Legal Profession, 1983-89; mem. steering com. Gov.'s Commn. on Land Use Violation, 1983-84; treas. Coalition for Cruise Missile Referendum, 1989; trustee, v.p. Portland Ministry at Large, 1990-96, pres., 1996—. Served with USNR, 1969-70. Mem. ACLU, Cumberland County Bar Assn. Democrat. Pension, profit-sharing, and employee benefits, Real property. Office: 38 High St Portland ME 04101-4532

**O'BRIEN, PATRICK THOMAS,** lawyer; b. Lincoln, Nebr.; s. James Patrick and Monette Mary O'Brien; m. Nancy Louise Butler, Nov. 19, 1966; children: Patrick B., Matthew F. BSBA, U. Nebr., Lincoln, 1967, JD, 1972. Bar: Nebr. 1972, U.S. Ct. Appeals (8th cir.) 1976, U.S. Dist. Ct. Nebr. 1972, U.S. Supreme Ct. 1977. Dep. county atty. Lancaster County Atty. Office, Lincoln, 1972-75; asst. atty. gen. Nebr. Atty. Gen.'s Office, Lincoln, 1975-83, dep. atty. gen., 1983-85; ptnr. Butler, Galter & O'Brien, Lincoln, 1985—. Bd. dirs. Lincoln Cmty. Playhouse, 1977. With USNR, 1961-69, Vietnam. Mem. Nebr. State Bar Assn. Republican. Roman Catholic. General practice, Probate, General civil litigation. Home: 2833 Sheridan Blvd Lincoln NE 68502-4242 Office: Butler Galter & O'Brien 811 S 13th St Lincoln NE 68508-3226

**O'BRIEN, THOMAS GEORGE, III,** lawyer; b. N.Y.C., Aug. 26, 1942; s. Thomas George Jr.and Margaret Patricia (Arctander) O'B.; m. Alison Marie Rich, Aug. 26, 1967; children: Christian Arctander, Kylin Stafford. AB magna cum laude, U. Notre Dame, 1964; LLB, Yale U., 1967. Bar: N.Y. 1967, Fla. 1988. Assoc. Carter, Ledyard & Milburn, N.Y.C., 1971-78; assoc. gen. counsel Frank B. Hall & Co. Inc., Briarcliff Manor, N.Y., 1978-79, v.p., sec., gen. counsel, 1979-86; exec. v.p., sec., gen. counsel CenTrust Savs. Bank, Miami, 1986-87; of counsel Steel Hector & Davis, Miami, 1987-88, ptnr., West Palm Beach, Fla., 1988—; Author: Florida Law of Corporations and Business Organizations, 1990, 92-97. Trustee Bus. Vols. for Arts, Miami, 1986-88, Fla. Repertory Theatre, West Palm Beach, 1989-91, chmn., 1990-91; mem. vestry Episcopal Ch. Bethesda-by-the-Sea, 1991-94, sr. warden, 1992-94; bd. dirs. Bus. Devel. Bd. Palm Beach County, 1991—, sec., 1992-93, chmn., 1993-94; bd. dirs. Palm Beach Fellowship Christians and Jews, 1993-97, sec., 1996-97; bd. dirs. Directions 21st Century, 1995-98, chmn., 1996-98. Lt. USNR, 1967-71, Vietnam. Mem. ABA (com. on legal opinions 1992—), N.Y. State Bar Assn., Fla. Bar (mem. corps./securities law com. 1988—, vice-chmn. 1989-90, chmn. 1990-91, chmn. com. on opinion standards 1988-95, exec. coun. bus. law sect. 1989-93), Am. Soc. Corp. Secs. (sec. N.Y. regional group 1984-86), Palm Beach Yacht Club, PGA Nat. Club. General corporate, Securities, Mergers and acquisitions. Home: 272 Eagleton Estate Blvd Palm Beach Gardens FL 33418-8423 Office: 1900 Phillips Point W 777 S Flagler Dr West Palm Beach FL 33401-6161

**O'BRIEN, WALTER JOSEPH, II,** lawyer; b. Chgo., Apr. 22, 1939; s. Walter Joseph O'Brien and Lorayne (Stouffer) Steele; children: Kelly A., Patrick W., Kathleen; m. Sharon Ann Curling, July 8, 1978; 1 child, John Joseph. BBA, U. Notre Dame, 1961; JD, Northwestern U.-Chgo., 1964. Bar: Ill. 1965, U.S. Dist. Ct. (no. dist.) Ill. 1965, U.S. Supreme Ct. 1973. Assoc. Nicholson, Nisen, Elliott & Meier, Chgo., 1966-70; pres., Capstan Co., Chgo., 1970-73, Walter J. O'Brien II, Ltd., Oak Brook, Ill., 1973-78, O'Brien & Assocs., P.C., Oakbrook Terrace, Ill., 1978—; vice chmn., bd. dirs. Atty. Title Guaranty Fund, Inc., Champaign, Ill., 1979—; arbitrator chairperson 18th Judicial Ct., DuPage County, Ill. Contbr. articles to legal jours. Commr., Oak Brook Plan Commn., 1980-85 ; mem. Oak Brook Zoning Bd. Appeals, 1985-87, Bd. Edn. Elem. Dist. # 53, Oak Brook, Ill., 1991-95; commr. Ill. and Mich. Canal, Nat. Heritage Corridor Commn.; v.p. Oak Brook Civic Assn., 1972; trustee St. Isaac Jogues Ch., Hinsdale, Ill., 1975-76. Served as capt. Q.M.C., U.S. Army, 1964-66. Fellow Ill. Bar Found.; mem. Ill. State Bar Assn. (mem. assembly), DuPage Bar Assn. (bd. dirs. 1987-88, elected Man of Yr. 1988), Am. Inn of Ct. (master DuPage chpt.). Roman Catholic. Club: Butterfield Country (bd. dirs. 1982-88) (Oak Brook). Real property, General corporate, Probate. Office: O'Brien & Assocs PC 17w200 22nd St Oakbrook Terrace IL 60181-4445

**O'BRIEN, WILLIAM J.,** lawyer. BS, Holy Cross Coll., 1965; LLB, Yale U., 1969. Bar: N.Y. 1970, Mich. 1985. Former dep. gen. coun. Chrysler Corp., Highland Park, Mich., former v.p., gen. counsel, sec.; sr. v.p., gen. counsel Chrysler Corp., Highland Park. Office: Daimler Chrysler Corp CIMS 485-14-96 1000 Chrysler Dr Auburn Hills MI 48326-2766

**O'BRIEN, WILLIAM J.,** lawyer, executive assistant; b. N.Y.C., June 9, 1956; s. William J. and rita (Fantry) O'B.; m. Grace Raia O'Brien, July 10, 1982; children: Katherine, Megan. BA, Fordham U., 1978; JD, St. John's U., 1981. Bar: N.Y. 1982, U.S. Dist. Ct. (ea. dist.) N.Y. 1983, U.S. Dist. Ct. (so. dist.) N.Y. 1984. Assoc. Sandback & Birnbaum Esq., Mineola, N.Y., 1982-84; law sec. to judge County Ct./Nassau Ct./Supreme Ct., Mineola, 1984-97, exec. asst. to adminstrv. judge, 1997—. Mem. Kiwanis (charter mem., chair sch. com.). Republican. Roman Catholic. Office: Adminstrv Office 100 Supreme Court Dr Mineola NY 11501-4815

**O'BRIEN, WILLIAM JEROME, II,** lawyer; b. Darby, Pa., Oct. 22, 1954; s. Richard James O'Brien and Margaret (McGill) Hahn. BA in Econ. and Polit. Sci., Merrimack Coll., 1976; JD, Del. Law Sch., 1981. Bar: Pa. 1982, U.S. Dist. Ct. (ea. dist.) Pa. 1983, U.S. Supreme Ct. 1986. Law clk. Commonwealth Ct. of Pa., Harrisburg, 1982-83; assoc. Philips, Curtin and DiGiacomo, Phila., 1983-86, O'Brien & Assocs. PC, Phila., 1986—; bd. dirs. New Manayunk Corp., Phila, counselor, 1987-98. Bd. dirs. North Light Inc., 1986-94, sec., 1988-90, pres., 1990-92; bd. dirs. Manayunk Cmty. Ctr. for Arts, 1988-90, chmn. Chaminouix Mansion, 1989—, chmn., 1991—; spl. asst. to U.S. Senator H. John Heinz, 1976-78; Rep. candidate for Phila. City Coun., 1991, for Phila. City Contr., 1997;mem. Republican State Comm. of PA., 1998—. Mem. Phila. Bar Assn., Pa. Bar Assn., Del. Law Sch. Alumni Assn. (sec. 1985-87), Bus. Assn. Manayunk (bd. dirs. 1987-89), Union League, Racquet Club (mem. com. 1985-87). Roman Catholic. Avocations: squash, court tennis, scuba, golf. General practice, Real property, General corporate. Office: O'Brien & Assocs PC 4322 Main St Philadelphia PA 19127-1421

**O'BRIEN, WILLIAM LAWRENCE,** lawyer; b. Trenton, N.J., July 20, 1951; s. Clarence Leonard and Ruth Hazel O'Brien; m. Roxanne Smith; children: Megan, Colleen, Brendan. BA, Framingham (Mass.) State Coll., 1974; JD, Suffolk U., Boston, 1977. Gen. counsel Nixdorf Computer Engring. Corp., Cambridge, Mass., 1983-91; ptnr. Finneran, Byrnes, Drechsler & O'Brien, Boston, 1991—. Office: Finneran Byrnes et al Eastern Harbor Office Park 50 Redfield St Boston MA 02122-3630

**OBUCHOWSKI, RAYMOND JOSEPH,** lawyer; b. LaGrange, Ill., Oct. 2, 1955; s. Harry John and Betty Lou (Roux) O.; m. Marie Ann Fowler, May 28, 1983; children: Michael Jozef, Brian Matthew. BS, Western Ill. U., 1976; JD, Vt. Law Sch., 1980. Bar: Ill. 1980, Vt. 1982, U.S. Dist. Ct. Ill., U.S. Dist. Ct. Vt., 1983, U.S. Ct. Appeals (7th cir.) 1982; bd. cert. in bus. and consumer bankruptcy law Am. Bankruptcy Bd. of Cert. State's atty. investigator McDonough County Gen. State Atty.'s Office, Macomb, Ill., 1976-77; asst. atty. gen. revenue litigation Ill. Atty. Gen.'s Office, Springfield, Ill., 1981-82; law clk. to Hon. Charles J. Marro U.S. Bankruptcy Ct. Dist. of Vt., Rutland, 1982-83, estate administrator, 1983-84; assoc. Law Office of Jerome Meyers, Springfield, Vt., 1983, Law Office of Joseph C. Palimisano, Barre, Vt., 1984-86; pvt. practice S. Royalton, Vt., 1986—; ptnr. Mayer, Berk & Obuchowski, S. Royalton, 1988-90; pvt. practice Bethel, Vt., 1990-91; ptnr. Obuchowski & Reis, Bethel, 1992-96; pvt. practice Obuchowski Law Office, Bethel, 1997—. Co-author: Vermont Collection Law, 1988, Basic Bankruptcy in Vermont, 1989, Sucessful Creditor's Strategies in Bankruptcy in Vermont, 1990, Foreclosure and Repossession in Vermont, 1991. Mem. Ill. Bar Assn., Vt. Bar Assn. (chmn. bankruptcy com. 1997-99), Nat. Assn. Bankruptcy Trustees, Am. Bankruptcy Inst., Blue Key. Roman Catholic. Avocation: woodworking. Bankruptcy, Consumer commercial. Home: PO Box 25 South Royalton VT 05068-0025 Office: PO Box 60 Bethel VT 05032-0060

**O'CALLAGHAN, ROBERT PATRICK,** lawyer; b. Mpls., Aug. 8, 1924; s. Robert Desmond and Claire Marie (Moe) O'C.; married Albina Julie Sepich, June 4, 1949; children: Michael, Edward, Catherine, Diana, Robert, Daniel. BA, Drake U., 1949; JD, U. Denver, 1951. Bar: Colo. 1951, U.S. Dist. Ct. Colo. 1956, U.S. Tax Ct. 1971, U.S. Ct. Appeals (10th cir.) 1978. Pvt. practice law Denver, 1952-53, Rangely, Colo., 1953-63; real estate broker Grand Junction, Colo., 1963-65; ptnr. Bellinger, Faricy, Tursi & O'Callaghan, Pueblo, Colo., 1965-73; pvt. practice law Pueblo, 1973-76; ptnr. Lattimer, O'Callaghan & Ware P.C., Pueblo, 1978-81; of counsel Quiet & Dice, Denver, 1981-83; pvt. practice law Pueblo, 1983—; atty. Town of Rangely, 1953-63; bd. atty. Pueblo Bd. Realtors, 1971-82; instr. real estate U. Colo., 1968-79; sr. cert. valuer Internat. Real Estate Inst. Pres. Homes for Sr. Citizens Inc., Pueblo, 1978-80; pres. Mt. Carmel Credit Union, 1972-74; adv. bd. dirs. Pueblo Salvation Army, 1987-91. With USNR, 1943-46. Mem. ABA, Colo. Bar Assn., Pueblo County Bar Assn., Nat. Network Estate Planning Attys., Elks (exalter ruler Rangley Lodge No. 1907). Republican. Roman Catholic. Avocation: photography. E-mail: patoc@rmi.net. Real property, Probate, Estate planning. Address: Union Depot 132 W B St Ste 230 Pueblo CO 81003-3407

**OCHS, KALMAN,** lawyer; b. Bklyn., Dec. 6, 1966; s. Fred E. and Marlene P. O.; m. Marsha Fink, June 18, 1990; children: Sarah Leah, Ephraim, Shlomo, Rivka. B in Talmudic Study, Kotler Inst. Higher Learning, Lakewood, N.J., 1990, M in Talmudic Study, 1992; JD, Rutgers U., 1995. Bar: N.J., U.S. Dist. Ct. N.J., U.S. Dist. Ct. (so. dist.) N.Y., U.S. Dist. Ct. (ea. dist.) N.Y. Law clk. Am. Internat. Group, N.Y.C., 1993-95; assoc. Fried Frank Harris Shriver & Jacobson, N.Y.C., 1995—. Mem. ABA, N.Y. State Bar Assn., Assn. of the Bar of the City of N.Y. Bankruptcy. Office: Fried Frank Harris et al 1 New York Plz Fl 22 New York NY 10004-1980

**OCKEY, RONALD J.,** lawyer; b. Green River, Wyo., June 12, 1934; s. Theron G. and Ruby O. (Sackett) O.; m. Arline M. Hawkins, Nov. 27, 1957; children: Carolyn S. Ockey Baggett, Deborah K. Ockey Christiansen, David, Kathleen M. Ocke Hellewell, Valerie Ockey Sachs, Robert. BA, U. Utah, 1959, postgrad., 1959-60; JD with honors, George Washington U., 1966. Bar: Colo. 1967, Utah 1968, U.S. Dist. Ct. Colo. 1967, U.S. Dist. Ct. Utah 1968, U.S. Ct. Appeals (10th cir.) 1969, U.S. Ct. Claims 1987. Missionary to France for Mormon Ch., 1954-57; law clk. to judge U.S. Dist. Ct. Colo., 1966-67; assoc. ptnr., shareholder, v.p., treas., dir. Jones, Waldo, Holbrook & McDonough, Salt Lake City, 1967-91; pres. IntelliTrans Internat. Corp., 1992-94; mem. Utah Ho. of Reps., 1988-90, Utah State Senate, 1991-94; of counsel Mackey Price & Williams, Salt Lake City, 1995-98; asst. atty. gen. Utah, 1998—; trustee SmartUtah, Inc., 1995—, bd. dirs., mem. exec. com., 1995—; trustee Utah Tech. Fin. Corp., 1995-98; lectr. in securities, pub. fin. and bankruptcy law. Mem. editl. bd. Utah Bar Jour., 1973-75; mem. staff and bd. editors George Washington Law Rev., 1964-66; contbr. articles to profl. jours. Stae govtl. affairs chair Utah Jaycees, 1969; del. state Rep. Convs., 1972-74, 76-78, 80-82, 84-86, 94-96, del. Salt Lake County Rep. Conv., 1978-80, 88-92; sec. Wright for Gov. campaign, 1980; legis. dist. chmn. Utah Rep. Party, 1983-87; trustee Food for Poland, 1981-85, pres., trustee Unity to Assist Humanity Alliance, 1992-95; bd. dirs. Utah Opera Co., 1991-94; trustee Utah Info. Tech. Assn., 1991—; . Lt. U.S. Army, 1960-66, to capt. JAG, USAR, 1966-81. Mem. ABA, Utah State Bar Assn. (various coms.), Nat. Assn. Bond Lawyers (chmn. con. on state legislation 1982-85), George Washington U. Law Alumni Assn. (bd. dirs. 1981-85), Order of Coif, Phi Delta Phi. Contracts commercial, Computer, General corporate. Home: 4502 Crest Oak Cir Salt Lake City UT 84124-3825

**OCKLEBERRY, SUZANNE WYNN,** lawyer; b. Morristown, N.J., Sept. 23, 1959; d. James Roswell and Geraldine Wynn; widowed; children: Jordan Leigh, Tyler Jalen. BA, Rutgers U., Camden, 1981, JD, 1984. Bar: Ga. 1994. Assoc. Fain, Gorby, Reeves & Moraitakis, Atlanta, 1984-85; pvt. practice Atlanta, 1985-88; asst. solicitor Solicitors Office Fulton Co., Atlanta, 1988-90, chief sr. asst. dist. atty., dir crimes against women and, 1990-98; regulatory atty. AT&T, Atlanta, 1998—; former co-chair batter subcom. Domestic Violence Protocol Commn., Atlanta. Active mem. Leadership Atlanta, 1996; tutor, mentor E. Lake Elem. Sch. NAAG Program, Atlanta, 1997-98; treas. Canterbury Sch. PTA, Atlanta, 1997-98. Recipient Vol. award Aid to Imprisoned Mothers, 1996. Mem. Ga. Assn. Black Women Attys. (pres. 1996), Ga. Coun. Child Abuse (bd. dirs. 1991—). Avocations: reading, gardening. Home: 4890 Promenade Dr SW Atlanta GA 30331-8721

**O'CONNELL, DANIEL JAMES,** lawyer; b. Evergreen Park, Ill., Aug. 14, 1954; s. Edmund J. and Kathryn J. (Hanna) O'C.; m. Nancy L. Eichler, March 21, 1992; children: Kelly Jacklyn, Kirby Kathryn. BS, Millikin U., 1976; JD, IIT, 1980; postgrad., DePaul U., 1981, U. Mich., 1997, U. Ill., 1999—. Bar: Ill. 1980, U.S. Dist. Ct. (no. dist.) Ill. 1980, U.S. Dist. Ct. Ariz. 1989. Ins. regulatory counsel Kemper Group, Long Grove, Ill., 1980-81, environ. claims counsel, 1981-82; sr. home office claim counsel Zurich Ins. Cos., Schaumburg, Ill., 1982-83; assoc. Clausen, Miller, Gorman et al, Chgo., 1983-86; ptnr. environ. toxic tort litigation O'Connell & Moroney, P.C., Chgo., 1986-90; ptnr. toxic tort litigation Burditt, Bowles & Radzius, Chgo., 1990-91; ptnr. Daniel J. O'Connell & Assocs., P.C., Elgin, 1991—. James S. Kemper Found. scholar, 1972-76. Mem. ABA, APHA, Ill. Bar Assn., Kane County Bar Assn., Def. Rsch. Inst., N.Y. Acad. Scis. Environmental, Insurance, Product liability. Home: 177 Macintosh Ct Glen Ellyn IL 60137-6478

**O'CONNELL, FRANCIS JOSEPH,** lawyer, arbitrator; b. Ft. Edward, N.Y., Mar. 19, 1913; s. Daniel Patrick and Mary (Bowe) O'C.; m. Adelaide M. Nagro, Sept. 27, 1937; children: Chris, Mary Gaynor Lavonas. AB, Columbia U., 1934; JD, Fordham U., 1938; SJD summa cum laude, Bklyn. Law Sch., 1945. Bar: N.Y. 1938, U.S. Dist. Ct. (so. dist.) N.Y. 1942, U.S. Tax Ct. 1941. Counsel and asst. to chmn. exec. com. for labor law and litigation Allied Chem. Corp., N.Y.C., 1942-70; ptnr. Bill & O'Connell and predecessor, Garden City, N.Y., 1970-76; pvt. practice Garden City, N.Y., 1976-85, Cutchogue, N.Y., 1985—; arbitrator, fact-finder, mediator Fed. Mediation and Conciliation Svc., 1970—, N.Y. State Mediation Bd., Am. Arbitration Assn., N.Y. State, Nassau and Suffolk County pub. employment rels. bds., 1970—; adminstrv. law judge N.Y. State Dept. Health, 1979—; instr. labor law and labor rels. Cornell U.; U.S. del. ILO, Geneva, 1948, 59, 69, 72. Author: Labor Law and the First Line Supervisor, 1945, Restrictive Work Practices, 1967, National Emergency Strikes, 1968. Trustee Village of Garden City, 1948-50; mem. bd. edn. Diocese of Rockville Centre (N.Y.), 1972-80; pres. various civic orgns., 1942—. Mem. ABA (labor and internat. law sects.), N.Y. State Bar Assn. (labor com.), Bar Assn. Nassau County (labor and arbitration coms., former chmn. arbitration andlabor law coms.), Mfg. Chemists Assn. (chmn. indsl. rels. com.), U.S. C. of C. (indsl. rels. com.), Southold Indian Mus. (bd. dirs.). Republican. Roman Catholic. Labor, Pension, profit-sharing, and employee benefits. Office: PO Box 819 Cutchogue NY 11935-0819

**O'CONNELL, JOHN JAMES, JR.,** lawyer; b. Winter Park, Fla., Nov. 13, 1957; s. John James and Margaret K. O'Connell; divorced; 1 child, Logan Christian. BA, U. Ariz., 1979; JD, Western State U., San Diego, 1982. Bar: Mont. 1985, Ga. 1992, U.S. Dist. Ct. (no. dist.) Ga. 1992, U.S. Ct. Appeals (11th cir.) 1992, U.S. Dist. Ct. (no. dist.) Calif. 1987, U.S. Dist. Ct. Ariz. 1991, U.S. Ct. Appeals (9th cir.) 1987, U.S. Tax Ct. 1988. Sole practitioner Helena, Mont., Atlanta, 1985-94; sole practitioner, owner firm Atlanta, 1994-97; mng. ptnr. Smith, Furr, Schroeder & O'Connell, Decatur, Ga., 1997-98, Smith, Schroeder & O'Connell, Decatur, 1999—. Mem ABA, ATLA. Avocations: photography, golf, tennis. General civil litigation, Criminal, Personal injury. Office: Smith Schroeder & O'Connell 125 E Trinity Pl Ste 300 Decatur GA 30030-3360

**O'CONNELL, LAWRENCE B.,** lawyer; b. Corpus Christi, Tex., July 18, 1947; s. Lawrence M. and Isabelle Susan (Strawbridge) O.; m. Carolyn Janet Rush, Sept.24, 1967; children: Suzanne Michelle, Elizabeth Danielle, Jason Lawrence. BA, Purdue U., 1970; JD, Ind. U., Indpls., 1975. Bar: Ind. 1975, U.S. Dist. Ct. (no. and so. dists.) Ind. 1975. Chief investigator Consumer Protection Div. Office of the Ind. Atty. Gen., Indpls., 1974-75; dep. atty. gen. Office of the Ind. Atty. Gen., Indpls., 1975; assoc. Schultz, Ewan & Burns Law Firm, Lafayette, Ind., 1975-79; ptnr. Schultz, Ewan, Burns & O'Connell, Lafayette, 1979-82, Gothard, Poelstra & O'Connell, Lafayette, 1982-86, Profl. Assn. Gothard & O'Connell, Lafayette, 1987-93; pvt. practice, 1994—; atty. Tippecanoe County, Lafayette, 1983-95. Edn. cons. Ind. U., 1973-75; treas. Ind. Young Rep. Fedn. 1976-77, chmn. 1977-79; Hoosier Assoc. Ind. Reps., 1980—. Recipient Sagamore of the Wabash citation, Gov. Otis R. Bowen, M.D., Ind. 1978, Gov. Robert D. Orr, Ind. 1980. Mem. ABA, Ind. Bar Assn., Tippecanoe County Bar Assn. (treas. 1976-77), Columbia Club (Indpls.), Ind. Soc. of Chgo., Ind. Mcpl. Lawyers Assn. (bd. dirs. 1989-95, pres. 1994-95). Government contracts and claims, Municipal (including bonds), Private international. Office: Lawrence B O'Connell Esq # 558 223 Main St Lafayette IN 47901-1261

**O'CONNELL, MARGARET SULLIVAN,** lawyer; b. N.Y.C., Feb. 16, 1942; d. Thomas J. and Nora (Ryan) Sullivan; m. Anthony F. O'Connell, May 11, 1968 (dec. Mar. 1975); children: Noreen Anne, Joan Margaret, Alison Marie. Nursing diploma, St. Clare's Hosp. Sch. Nursing, N.Y.C., 1962; BA, Jersey City State Coll., 1973; JD, St. John's U., 1983. Bar: N.Y. 1984, U.S. Dist. Ct. (so. and ea. dists.) 1996; RN, N.Y. Staff nurse St. Clare's Hosp., N.Y.C., 1962-64, head nurse, 1964-67; clin. instr. medicine and surgery St. Clare's Sch. Nursing, N.Y.C., 1967-70; nursing supr. Menorah Home and Hosp., Bklyn., 1974-75; assoc. Costello, Shea & Gaffney, N.Y.C., 1987-95, ptnr., 1995—. Mem. ABA, N.Y. State Bar Assn., Assn. Bar City N.Y. (com. on med. malpractice 1996—), Am. Assn. Nurse Attys., Brehon Law Soc. Personal injury, General civil litigation, Insurance. Office: Costello Shea & Gaffney One Battery Park Pla New York NY 10004

**O'CONNELL, MAURICE DANIEL,** lawyer; b. Ticonderoga, N.Y., Nov. 9, 1929; s. Maurice Daniel and Leila (Geraghty) O'C.; m. Joan MacLure Landers, Aug. 2, 1952; children: Mark M., David L., Ann M., Leila K., Ellen A. Grad., Phillips Exeter Acad., 1946; A.B., Williams Coll., 1950; LL.B., Cornell U., 1956. Bar: Ohio 1956. Since practiced in Toledo; assoc. Williams, Eversman & Black, 1956-60; ptnr. Robison, Curphey & O'Connell, 1961-95, of counsel, 1996—; spl. hearing officer in conscientious objector cases U.S. Dept. Justice, 1966-68; mem. complaint rev. bd. Bd. Commrs. on Grievance and Discipline of Supreme Ct. Ohio, 1987. Mem. Ottawa Hills Bd. Edn., 1963-66, pres., 1967-69; former trustee Toledo Soc. for Handicapped; past trustee Woodlawn Cemetery; past trustee Toledo Hearing and Speech Center, Easter Seal Soc.; mem. alumni council Phillips Exeter Acad. Served to 1st lt. USMCR, 1950-53. Fellow Ohio State Bar Found.; mem. NW Ohio Alumni Assn. of Williams Coll. (past pres.), ABA, Ohio Bar Assn., Toledo Bar Assn. (chmn. grievance com. 1971-74), Kappa Alpha, Phi Delta Phi. Club: Toledo. General corporate, Labor. Home: 3922 W Bancroft St Toledo OH 43606-2533 Office: 9th Flr Four SeaGate Toledo OH 43604

**O'CONNER, LORETTA RAE,** lawyer; b. Denver, Dec. 23, 1958; d. Ronald Lee and Norma Jareene (Warner) Barkdoll; m. George Ellis Bentley, Dec. 31, 1976 (div. 1979); m. Donald Hugh O'Conner, Feb. 3, 1987; children: Justin Lee, Brandon Craig. AS, Denver Acad. Ct. Reporting, 1983; BA summa cum laude, Regis U., 1992; JD, U. Colo., 1996. Bar: Colo., 1996. Ct. reporter Denver, 1983-87; dist. ct. reporter Jud. Dept., State of Colo., Pueblo, 1987-91; ct. reporter Pueblo, 1991-93; student atty. Pueblo County Legal Svcs.; pvt. practice Pueblo, 1997—; contact atty. State of Colo.; contract rep. Jud. Dept., State of Colo. Chief justice Student Govt. Ct., U. So. Colo., Pueblo, 1992; trained facilitator Kettering Found., Pub. Policy Inst., Dayton, Ohio, 1992; sec. So. Colo. Registered Interpretors for Deaf, Pueblo, 1991. President's scholar U. So. Colo., 1991-92, Alumni Assn. scholar, 1991-92; grantee Kettering Found., 1992; Colo. Legislature grantee and scholar Regis U., 1992; Colo. Legislature grantee U. Colo. Sch. Law, 1993-95, Dean's scholar, Dazzo Scholar, King scholar U. Colo. Sch. Law, 1993-96. Mem. ATLA, ABA, Nat. Ct. Reporters Assn., Colo. Trial Lawyers Assn., Colo. Bar Assn., Colo. Womens Bar Assn., Colo. Ct. Reporters Assn., Pueblo County Bas Assn., Boulder Bar Assn., Golden Key Soc., Phi Delta Phi (clk. 1994-95). Avocations: reading, writing novels. Fax: (719) 584-2233. General civil litigation, Criminal, General practice. Home: 15 Mayweed Ct Pueblo CO 81001-1134 Office: O'Conner Law Bldg 426 W 10th St Pueblo CO 81003-2922

**O'CONNOR, CHARLES P.,** lawyer; b. Boston, Sept. 29, 1940; m. Mary Linda Hogan; children: Jennifer, Amy, Austin, Catherine. Bachelors degree, Holy Cross Coll., Worcester, Mass., 1963; LLB, Boston Coll., 1966. Bar: Mass. 1966, D.C. 1968, U.S. Supreme Ct. 1974. Atty., gen. counsel's office NLRB, Washington, 1966-67; assoc. Morgan, Lewis & Bockius, LLP, Washington, 1968-71; ptnr. Morgan, Lewis & Bockius, Washington, 1971—, chmn. labor and employment law sect., 1996-99, mng. ptnr. Washington office, 1995-97; gen. counsel Major League Baseball Player Rels. Com., N.Y.C., 1989-94. Contbr. numerous articles on labor and employment law to law jours. spl. counsel elections com. U.S. Ho. of Reps., Washington, 1968-69. Fellow Coll. Labor and Employment Lawyers; mem. ABA, D.C. Bar Assn., Belle Haven Country Club, N.Y. Athletic Club, Cape Cod Nat. Golf Club. Labor, Entertainment. Home: 6121 Vernon Ter Alexandria VA 22307-1152 Office: Morgan Lewis & Bockius 1800 M St NW Ste 800 Washington DC 20036-5802

**O'CONNOR, EDWARD GEARING,** lawyer; b. Pitts., May 5, 1940; s. Timothy R. and Irene B. (Gearing) O'C.; m. Janet M. Showalter, June 17,

1972; children: Mark G., Susan M. BA, Duquesne U., 1962, JD, 1965. Bar: Pa. 1965, U.S. Dist. Ct. (we. dist.) Pa. 1965, U.S. Ct. Appeals (3d cir.) 1968, U.S. Supreme Ct. 1976. Assoc. Eckert, Seamans, Cherin & Mellott, Pitts., 1965-72, ptnr., 1973—; mem. adv. com. on appellate ct. rules Supreme Ct. Pa., 1986-92, mem. procedures rules com., 1998-01. Editor Duquesne U. Law Rev., 1964-65. Chmn. Hampton (Pa.) Twp. Planning Commn., 1986-87; mem. Hampton (Pa.) Twp. Zoning Hearing Bd., 1997—; bd. dirs. St. Francis Health Sys., Duquesne U.; trustee Noble J. Dick Edn. Fund, 1989—. Recipient Disting. Alumni award Duquesne U. Law Rev., 1985, Disting. Law Alumni award Duquesne U. Sch. Law, 1991, Disting. Svc. award Hampton Twp., 1991, McAnurlty Svc. award Duquesne U., 1992; named Century Club Disting. Alumni, Duquesne U., 1985. Fellow Am. Bar Found., Pa. Bar Found.; mem. Pa. Bar Assn. (ho. of dels. 1985-90), Acad. Trial Lawyers Allegheny County (bd. govs. 1986-89, 98—), Duquesne U. Alumni Assn. (pres. 1980-82, 88-90, bd. govs. 1982-90, bd. dirs. 1988-89), Duquesne Club, Pitts. Athletic Assn., Ally City Bar Found. Republican. Roman Catholic. Federal civil litigation, State civil litigation, Antitrust. Home: 4288 Green Glade Ct Allison Park PA 15101-1202 Office: Eckert Seamans Cherin & Mellott 600 Grant St Ste 44th Pittsburgh PA 15219-2702

**O'CONNOR, EDWARD VINCENT, JR.,** lawyer; b. Yokosuka, Japan, Nov. 9, 1952; s. Edward Vincent and Margaret (Robertson) O'C.; m. Kathy J. Hunt, May 23, 1992. BA, Duke U., 1975; JD, N.Y. Law Sch., 1981. Bar: Va. 1982, D.C. 1983. Assoc. Lewis, Kinsey, Dack & Good, Washington, 1982-87; ptnr. Lewis, Dack, Paradiso & Good, Washington, 1988-89, Lewis, Dack, Paradiso, O'Connor & Good, Washington, 1989-94, The Lewis Law Firm, 1994, Byrd, Mische, Bevis, Bowen, Joseph & O'Connor, Fairfax, Va., 1995—; arbitrator D.C. Superior Ct.; neutral case evaluator and concilliator Fairfax County Cir. Ct.; lectr. Va. Trial Lawyers Assn., Arlington County Bar Assn. Mem. Va. State Bar (lectr., spl. com. on access to legal svcs. 1994—), D.C. Bar, Fairfax County Bar Assn. (lectr., vice chair family law sect. 1995-96, continuing edn. com. 1988-95, chair 1995, mem. pub. svc. com. 1995, chair 1996-98, mem. cir. ct. com. 1994-96, James Keith award for pub. svc. 1999), Legal Svcs. No. Va. (bd. dirs., chmn. pro bono com., sec.-treas. 1998—, pro bono award for outstanding svc. 1997). Family and matrimonial, Probate, Entertainment.

**O'CONNOR, FRANCIS PATRICK,** state supreme court justice; b. Boston, Dec. 12, 1927; s. Thomas Lane and Florence Mary (Hagerty) O'C.; m. Ann Elizabeth O'Brien; children: Kathleen, Francis P., Brien T., Maureen T., Ellen M., Ann E., Jane C., Joyce E., Thomas J., Matthew P. AB, Holy Cross Coll., 1950; LLB, Boston Coll., 1953; JD (hon.), Suffolk U., 1983, New Eng. Sch. Law, 1984. Bar: Mass. 1953. Assoc. Friedman, Atherton, Sisson & Kozol, Boston, 1954-57, Mason, Crotty, Dunn & O'Connor, Worcester, Mass., 1957-73, Wolfson, Moynihan, Dodson & O'Connor, Worcester, 1974-75; judge Mass. Superior Ct., 1976-81; assoc. judge Mass. Supreme Ct., 1981-97, ret., 1997. Office: Mass Supreme Jud Ct Pemberton Sq 1300 New Courthouse Boston MA 02108

**O'CONNOR, GAYLE MCCORMICK,** law librarian; b. Rome, N.Y., July 8, 1956; d. John Joseph and Barbara Jane (Molyneaux) McC. Head libr. Bolling, Walter & Gawthrop, Sacramento, 1987-88, Weintraub, Genshlea & Sproul, Sacramento, 1988-93, Brobeck, Phleger & Harrison, San Diego, 1993-96; legal cons., author, 1996—; owner Automated legal Solutions, 1997—; legal industry mktg. specialist CourtLink, 1998—; instr. law Lincoln U., Sacramento. Assoc. editor, rsch. advisor Alert Publs., Chgo.; contbr. articles to profl. jours. Mem. ABA (tech. show bd.), No. Calif. Assn. Law Librs., So. Calif. Assn. Law Librs., Am. Assn. Law Librs., Spl. Librs. Assn. (chair legal divsn. 1997-98). Avocations: bodybuilding, skiing.

**O'CONNOR, JOSEPH A., JR.,** lawyer; b. N.Y.C., Aug. 12, 1937; s. Joseph A. and Louise G. (Lucht) O'C.; children: Joseph A. III, Edward W. BA, Yale U., 1959; LLB, Columbia U., 1962. Bar: N.Y. 1963, U.S. Supreme Ct. 1968, Pa. 1973, Fla. 1978. Assoc. Davis, Polk & Wardwell, N.Y.C., 1963-72; ptnr. Morgan, Lewis & Bockius, Phila., 1972—. Mem. ABA, N.Y. State Bar Assn., Pa. Bar Assn., Fla. Bar Assn., Phila. Bar Assn., Assn. of Bar of City of N.Y. Roman Catholic. Club: Racquet (Phila.). Office: Morgan Lewis & Bockius LLP 1701 Market St Philadelphia PA 19103-2903

**O'CONNOR, KARL WILLIAM (GOODYEAR JOHNSON),** lawyer; b. Washington, Aug. 1, 1931; s. Hector and Lucile (Johnson) O'C.; m. Sylvia Gasbarri, Mar. 23, 1951 (dec.); m. Judith Ann Byers, July 22, 1972 (div. 1983); m. Eleanor Celler, Aug. 3, 1984 (div. 1986); m. Alma Hepner, Jan. 1, 1987 (div. 1996); children: Blair, Frances, Brian, Brendan. BA, U. Va., 1952, JD, 1958. Bar: Va. 1958, D.C. 1959, Am. Samoa 1976, Calif. 1977, Oreg. 1993. Law clk. U.S. Dist. Ct. Va., Abingdon, 1958-59; practice law Washington, 1959-61; trial atty. U.S. Dept. Justice, Washington, 1961-65; dep. dir. Men's Job Corps OEO, Washington, 1965-67; mem. civil rights div. Dept. of Justice, chief criminal sect., prin. dep. asst. atty. gen., 1967-75, spl. counsel for intelligence coordination, 1975; v.p., counsel Assn. of Motion Picture and Television Producers, Hollywood, Calif., 1975-76; assoc. justice Am. Samoa, 1976, chief justice, 1977-78; sr. trial atty. GSA Task Force, Dept. Justice, 1978-81; insp. gen. CSA, 1981-82; spl. counsel Merit Systems Protection Bd., Washington, 1983-86; U.S. atty. for Guam and the No. Marianas, 1986-89, ret.; pvt. practice Medford, Oreg., 1989—; Am. counsel O'Reilly Vernier Ltd., Hong Kong, 1992-93; ptnr. O'Connor & Vernier, Medford, Oreg., 1993-94; pvt. practice Medford, 1994—. Served with USMC, 1952-55. Mem. Oreg. Bar Assn., D.C. Bar Assn., Va. Bar Assn., Calif. Bar Assn., Am. Samoa Bar Assn., Soc. Colonial Wars, Phi Alpha Delta, Sigma Nu. Federal civil litigation, Criminal, Labor. Home: Box 126 305 N 6th St Jacksonville OR 97530 Office: 916 W 10th St Medford OR 97501-3018

**O'CONNOR, KATHLEEN MARY,** lawyer; b. Camden, Jan. 14, 1949; d. John A. and Marie V. (Flynn) O'C. BA, U. Fla., 1971, JD, 1981. Bar: Fla. 1981, U.S. Ct. Appeals (11th cir.) 1982, U.S. Supreme Ct. 1987. Atty. Walton, Lantaff, Schroeder & Carson, Miami, 1981-84, Thornton, Davis & Murray PA, Miami, 1984-98. Exec. editor U. Fla. Law Rev., 1981; contbr. articles to profl. jours. Legal advocate Miami Project to Cure Paralysis, 1992-97. Mem. ABA, Dade County Bar Assn. (vice-chair appellate cts. com. 1981), Def. Rsch. Inst., Fla. Def. Lawyers Assn. Appellate, Aviation, Insurance.

**O'CONNOR, KEVIN JAMES,** lawyer; b. Hartford, Conn., May 3, 1967; s. Dennis Edmund and Mary Theresa (Leahy) O'Connor. BA, U. Notre Dame, Ind., 1989; JD, U. Conn., Hartford, 1992. Conn. 1992, N.Y. 1993, U.S. Dist. Ct. Conn. (so. and ea. dists.) N.Y. 1994, U.S. Ct. Appeals (2d cir.) 1994. Law clerk Hon. William H. Timbers, U.S. Ct. Appeals (2d cir.), N.Y.C., 1992-93; assoc. Cahill, Gordon & Reindel, N.Y.C., 1993-95; sr. counsel Divsn. Enforcement U.S. Securities & Exchg. Commn., Washington, 1995-97; assoc. LeBoeuf, Lamb, Greene & MacRae, Hartford, Conn., 1997—; adj. prof. George Washington U. Law Sch., Washington, 1996-97, U. Conn. Law Sch., 1998—. Bd. dirs. Old State House, John Rogers African Am. Cultural Ctr., 1999—. Mem. Am. Assn. Bar City of N.Y., Conn. Bar Assn. Republican. Roman Catholic. Home: 34 Dorchester Rd Wethersfield CT 06109-2319 Office: LeBoeuf Lamb Greene & MacRae 225 Asylum St Hartford CT 06103-1516

**O'CONNOR, MARK S.,** judge; b. Bellefontaine, Ohio, June 27, 1944; s. Thomas Edward and Margaret Zettlea O'C.; m. Martha Kennedy, June 15, 1968; children: Timothy, Anne, Brendan. BA, John Carroll U., 1966; JD, Ohio State U., 1969. Bar: Ohio 1969, U.S. Dist Ct. (so. dist.) Ohio 1979. Ptnr. Beck & O'Connor, Bellefontaine, 1970, MacGillivrey, Hadley & O'Connor, Bellefontaine, 1971-79, Thompson, Danley & Heydinger, Bellefontaine, 1979-90; judge Ct. of Common Pleas, Logan County, Bellefontaine, Ohio, 1990—; bd. dirs., sec. West Ctrl. Ohio Jud. Correction Bd., Marysville. Pres. Mary Rutan Hosp., Bellefontaine, 1978, mem. 1975-90; bd. dirs. Logan County Residential Homec Bd., Bellefontaine, 1991—. Mem. Ohio State Bar Assn., Common Pleas Judges Assn., Logan County Bar Assn., Elks (Indian Lakes), Kiwanis (Bellefontaine). Democrat. Roman Catholic. Avocations: history, golf, bridge, fishing. Home: 9027 Oconnors Point Dr Belle Center OH 43310-9300 Office: Ct of Common Pleas 101 S Main St Rm 18 Bellefontaine OH 43311-2055

**O'CONNOR, MICHAEL WILLIAM,** lawyer; b. St. Paul, Apr. 5, 1935; s. Jay P. and Patricia J. (O'Connell) O'C.; m. Anita Woods, 1955; children: Deborah, William, Michelle, Kathleen, Daniel, Thomas. BS, St. Thomas Coll., 1957; BSL, William Mitchell Coll. Law, 1959, LLB, JD, 1961. V.p. Minn. Gas Co., Mpls., 1960-83, Diversified Energies, Mpls., 1983-86; pvt. practice Burnsville and Eagan, Minn., 1986—. Mem. Dakota County Bar Assn. Administrative and regulatory, Criminal, Land use and zoning (including planning). Home: 2609 London Ct Burnsville MN 55337-1028 Office: 1380 Corp Center Curve Ste 214 Eagan MN 55121

**O'CONNOR, PATRICK J.,** lawyer; b. Wilkes-Barre, Pa., Jan. 2, 1943; s. Patrick J. and Helen A. O'Connor; m. Marie M. O'Connor, Mar. 1, 1969; children: Lauren, Edwin, Kara, Paul. BA, Kings Coll., 1964; JD, Villanova U., 1967. Jud. law clk. ea. dist. U.S. Dist. Ct. Pa., Phila., 1967-68; assoc. Pepper Hamilton, Phila., 1968-73; sr. mem. Cozen & O'Connor, Phila., 1973—; bd. cons. law sch. Villanova U. Fellow Am. Coll. Trial Lawyers. Avocations: squash, tennis, golf. Federal civil litigation. Home: 207 Ashwood Rd Villanova PA 19085-1503 Office: Cozen & O'Connor 1900 Market St Philadelphia PA 19103-3527

**O'CONNOR, SANDRA DAY,** United States supreme court justice; b. El Paso, Tex., Mar. 26, 1930; d. Harry A. and Ada Mae (Wilkey) Day; m. John Jay O'Connor, III, Dec. 1952; children: Scott, Brian, Jay. AB in Econs. with great distinction, Stanford U., 1950, LLB, 1952. Bar: Calif., Ariz. Dep. county atty. San Mateo, Calif., 1952-53; civilian atty. Q.M. Market Ctr., Frankfurt am Main, Fed. Republic Germany, 1954-57; pvt. practice Phoenix, 1958-65; asst. atty. gen. State of Ariz., 1965-69; state senator Ariz., 1969-75; chmn. com. on state, county and mcpl. affairs, 1972-73, majority leader, 1973-74; judge Maricopa County Superior Ct., 1975-79, Ariz. Ct. Appeals, 1979-81; assoc. justice U.S. Supreme Ct., 1981—; referee juvenile ct. Maricopa County, 1962-64; chmn. vis. bd. Maricopa County Juvenile Detention Home, 1963-64; mem. Maricopa County Bd. Adjustments and Appeals, 1963-64, Anglo-Am. Legal Exchange, 1980, Maricopa County Superior Ct. Judges Tng. and Edn. Com., 1977-79, Maricopa Ct. Study Com.; chair com. to reorganize lower cts. Ariz. Supreme Ct., 1974-75; faculty Robert A. Taft Inst. Govt.; vice chmn. Select Law Enforcement Rev. Commn., 1979-80; chair Maricopa County Bd. of Adjustments and Appeals, 1963-64; mem. Ariz. Criminal Code Commn., 1974-76; bd. visitors Ariz. State U. Law Sch., 1981; liaison com. on med. edn., 1981. Mem. bd. editors Stanford (Calif.) U. Law Rev. Mem. Ariz. Pers. Commn., 1968-69, Nat. Def. Adv. Com. on Women in Svcs., 1974-76; trustee Heard Mus., Phoenix, 1968-74, 76-81, pres., 1980-81; mem. adv. bd. Phoenix Salvation Army, 1975-81; trustee Stanford U., 1976-81, Phoenix County Day Sch.; mem. citizens adv. bd. Blood Svcs., 1975-77; nat. bd. dirs. Smithsonian Assocs., 1981—, Colonial Williamsburg Found., 1988—; exec. bd. Ctrl. Eastern European Law Initiative, 1990—; past Rep. dist. chmn.; bd. dirs. Phoenix Cmty. Coun., 1969-75, Jr. Achievement Ariz., 1975-79, Blue Cross/Blue Shield Ariz., 1975-79, Channel 8, 1975-79, Phoenix Hist. Soc., 1974-78, Maricopa County YMCA, 1978-81, Golden Gate Settlement; past Rep. dist. chmn., bd. dirs. Phoenix Cmty. Coun.; adv. bd., v.p. Nat. Conf. of Christians and Jews, Maricopa County, 1977-81; bd. dirs., sec. Ariz. Acad., 1969-75, Cathedral chpt. Washington Nat. Cathedral, 1991—. Recipient Ann. award NCCJ, 1975, Disting. Achievement award Ariz. State U., 1980, Sara Lee Frontrunner award 1997; recipient ABA medal, 1997; named Woman of Yr., Phoenix Advt. Club, 1972; inducted, National Women's Hall of Fame, 1995. Mem. ABA, Ariz. Bar Assn. (legal edn., pub. rels. com., lower ct. reorgn. com., select law enforcement revision commn. vice chair 1979-80), Calif. Bar Assn., Maricopa County Bar Assn. (referral svc. chair 1960-62), Soroptimist Club (Phoenix). Lodge: Soroptimists. Office: US Supreme Ct Supreme Ct Bldg 1 First St NE Washington DC 20543

**O'CONNOR, WILLIAM MATTHEW,** lawyer; b. Pensacola, Fla., Apr. 5, 1955; s. William Francis and Rosalind (Shea) O'C.; m. Mary Patricia Keepnews, Oct. 13, 1984; children: William Lawrence, Thomas Patrick, Robert Austin. BS in Psychology, Fordham U., 1977, JD, 1980. Bar: N.Y. 1981, N.J. 1987, U.S. Dist. Ct. N.J. 1987, U.S. Dist. Conn. 1988, U.S. Dist. Ct. (so., ea., no. and we. dists.) N.Y., 1981, U.S. Ct. Appeals (2nd cir.) 1983, U.S. Ct. Appeals (3d cir.) 1996. Intern N.Y. Atty. Gen., N.Y.C., 1978-79; legis. intern Am. Lung Assn., N.Y.C., 1979; assoc. Keane & Butler, N.Y.C., 1979-81, Keane & Beane, White Plains, N.Y., 1981-83, Cooperman, Levitt & Winikoff, P.C., N.Y.C., 1983-86; sr. assoc. Sullivan, Donovan, Hanrahan & Silliere, N.Y.C., 1986-87; ptnr. O'Connor Reddy & Seeler, N.Y.C., 1987-95, Harris Beach & Wilcox LLP, N.Y.C., 1995—. Author: Lobbying Guidebook Am. Lung Assn., 1979. Contbr. articles to profl. jours. Legis. com. pub. schs., White Plains, 1981-82; councilman Town of Pelham, N.Y., 1998—. Mem. ABA, Fed. Bar Coun., N.Y. State Bar Assn. (mem. comml. and fed. litigation sect., creditor's rights com. 1989—), Westchester Bar Assn. (editor in chief Jour. 1983-89, mem. labor law com. 1981—, com. on profl. ethics 1989—), Fordham ILJ Alumni Assn. (bd. dirs. 1984—), New Rochelle Bar Assn. Republican. Roman Catholic. Federal civil litigation, State civil litigation, Banking. Home: 684 Esplanade Pelham NY 10803-2403 Office: Harris Beach & Wilcox LLP 250 Park Ave New York NY 10177-0001

**O'CONNOR QUINN, DEIRDRE,** lawyer; b. N.Y.C., Feb. 19, 1966; d. Raymond and Roisin O'Connor; m. Patrick T. Quinn, Sept. 8, 1990; children: Malachy, Oona. BS in Commerce, U. Va., 1987; JD, Boston Coll., 1990; LLM in Taxation, NYU, 1994. Bar: N.Y.; CPA, VA. Assoc. White & Case, N.Y.C., 1990-95; asst. gen. coun. Prudential Ins., Newark, N.J., 1995—. Mem. AICPA, Assn. of Bar of City of N.Y., N.Y. State Bar Assn. Corporate taxation, Taxation, general. Office: Prudential 213 Washington St Newark NJ 07102-2917

**O'DANIELS, MICHELLE MARIE,** lawyer, associate; b. St. Louis, Sept. 3, 1969; d. Michael Ray and Diane Marie O'Daniels. BS, Creighton U., 1990; JD, Tulane U., 1994. Bar: La. 1994, U.S. Dist. Ct. (ea. dist.) La. 1995, U.S. Ct. Appeals (5th cir.) 1995. Assoc. Jones, Walker, Waechter, Pointevent, Carrere & Denegre, New Orleans, 1995-97, Rice Fowler, New Orleans, 1997—. Editor-in-chief Tulane Maritime Law Jour., 1993-94. Mem. Maritime Law Assn. (assoc. mem.), Navy League. Admiralty, Environmental. Office: Rice Fowler 201 Saint Charles Ave Ste 3600 New Orleans LA 70170-3600

**O'DELL, CHARLENE ANNE AUDREY,** lawyer; b. Warwick, N.Y., Feb. 27, 1963; d. Charles Edward and Stella Ruth (Brazil) O'D. Student, Fordham U., 1981-83; BA summa cum laude with distinction, Boston U., 1985; JD, NYU, 1988. Bar: N.Y. 1989, U.S. Dist. Ct. (so. and ea. dists.) N.Y. 1989, D.C. 1990, Ct. Internat. Trade 1991. Assoc. Winston & Strawn (previously Cole & Deitz), N.Y.C., 1988-90; assoc. Graham & James, N.Y.C., 1990-95, spl. counsel, 1996—. Editor Moot Ct., NYU, 1987-88. Recipient Moot Ct. Advocacy award NYU, 1987. Mem. ABA, N.Y. State Bar Assn. Avocations: reading, tennis, photography. General civil litigation. Office: Graham & James 885 3rd Ave Fl 24 New York NY 10022-4834

**O'DELL, DEBBIE,** lawyer; b. New Eagle, Pa., July 13, 1953; d. John and Margaret (Troncatti) O'D.; m. Anthony J. Seneca, Nov. 1, 1980; 1 child, Mario O'Dell. B, W.Va. U., 1974; JD, Duquesne U., 1977. Bar: Pa. 1977, U.S. Dist. Ct. (we. dist.) Pa. 1977. Sole practice Washington, Pa., 1977-78; sr. ptnr. Seneca & O'Dell, Washington, 1978—; asst. pub. defender Pub. Defenders Office, Washington, 1978; law clk. to presiding judge Washington County Common Pleas, 1978-80; chief of litigation Dist. Atty.'s Office, Washington, 1980-84. Del. Dem. Nat. Convention, San Francisco, 1984; bd. dirs. Daughters of Current Events, Washington, Pa., 1984, 85, 86. Named one of Outstanding Young Women in Am., 1978. Mem. Washington County Bar Assn. (exec. bd. dirs. 1980-84), Pa. Trial Lawyers Assn. (sustaining), Western Pa. Trial Lawyers Assn. (bd. dirs. 1984, 85, 86), Washington Bus. and Profl. Womens Club (pres. 1985-86, corr. sec. 1986—). Avocations: reading, swimming, politics, historic preservation. Family and matrimonial, Criminal, State civil litigation. Home: 335 N Main St Washington PA 15301-4300

**ODELL, HERBERT,** lawyer; b. Phila., Oct. 20, 1937; s. Samuel and Selma (Kramer) O.; m. Valerie Odell; children: Wesley, Jonathan, James, Sarah, Samuel. BS in Econs., U. Pa., 1959; LLB magna cum laude, U. Miami, 1962; LLM, Harvard U., 1963. Bar: Fla. 1963, Pa. 1968. Trial atty. tax div. U.S. Dept. Justice, Washington, 1963-65; assoc. Walton, Lantaff, Schroeder, Carson & Wahl, Miami, Fla., 1965-67; from assoc. to ptnr. Morgan, Lewis & Bockius, Phila., 1967-89; ptnr. Zapruder & Odell, Phila., 1989-98, Odell & Ptnrs., Phila., 1998—; adj. prof. U. Miami, Villanova U.; lectr. various tax insts. Contbr. articles to profl. jours. Ford fellow, 1962-63. Mem. ABA, Fla. Bar Assn., Pa. Bar Assn., Phila. Bar Assn., Phi Kappa Phi, Omicron Delta Kappa, Beta Alpha Psi. Club: Harvard. Avocations: sailing, running, tennis, scuba diving. Corporate taxation, Taxation, general, Personal income taxation. Office: Odell & Ptnrs 401 E City Ave Ste 415 Bala Cynwyd PA 19004-1121

**O'DELL, JOAN ELIZABETH,** lawyer, mediator, business executive; b. East Dubuque, Ill., May 3, 1932; d. Peter Emerson and Olive (Bonnet) O'D.; children: Dominique R., Nicole L. BA cum laude, U. Miami, 1956, JD, 1958. Bar: Fla. 1958, U.S. Supreme Ct. 1972, D.C. 1974, Ill. 1978, Va. 1987; cert. mediator, 1994; lic. real estate broker Ill., Va. Trial atty. U.S. SEC, Washington, 1959-60; asst. state atty. Office State Atty., Miami, Fla., 1960-64; asst. county atty. Dade County Atty.'s Office, Miami, 1964-70; county atty. Palm Beach County Atty.'s Office, West Palm Beach, Fla., 1970-71; regional gen. counsel. U.S. EPA, Region IV, Atlanta, 1971-73, assoc. gen. counsel, Washington, 1973-77; sr. counsel Nalco Chem. Co., Oakbrook, Ill., 1977-78; v.p., gen. counsel Angel Mining, Tenn. and Washington, 1979-96; pres. South West Land Investments, Miami, Fla., 1979-88; v.p., gen. counsel Events U.S.A., Washington, 1990—. Bd. dirs. Tucson Women's Found., 1982-84, U. Ariz. Bus. and Profl. Women's Club, Tucson, 1981-85; bd. dirs. LWV Tucson, 1981-85, pres., 1984-85; bd. dirs. LWV Ariz., 1984-85, chmn. nat. security study; bd. dirs. LWV, Palm Beach County, Fla., 1990-92; mem. Exec. Women's Council, Tucson, 1982-85. Mem. Fla. Bar Assn., D.C. Bar Assn., Va. State Bar Assn. Avocations: camping, hiking, skiing. General corporate, Probate, Appellate.

**ODGERS, RICHARD WILLIAM,** lawyer; b. Detroit, Dec. 31, 1936; s. Richard Stanley and Elsie Maude (Trevarthen) O.; m. Gail C. Bassett, Aug. 29, 1959; children: Thomas R., Andrew B. AB, U. Mich., 1959, JD, 1961. Bar: Calif. 1962. Assoc. Pillsbury, Madison & Sutro, San Francisco, 1961-69, ptnr., 1969-87, 98—; exec. v.p., gen. counsel Pacific Telesis Group, 1987-98. Pres., bd. dirs. Legal Aid Soc. San Francisco; steering com. NAACP Legal Def. Fund; chmn. Legal Cmty. Against Violence; dir., sec./treas. Van Loben Sels Charitable Found. Served with USNR. Fellow Am. Bar Found., Am. Judicature Soc., Am. Coll. Trial Lawyers, Am. Law Inst., Coll. Law Practice Mgmt. E-mail: odgersurw@pillsburylaw.com. Administrative and regulatory, Antitrust, Public utilities. Office: Pillsbury Madison & Sutro 235 Montgomery St Fl 16 San Francisco CA 94104-3074

**ODOM, THOMAS H.,** lawyer; b. N.J., Mar. 8, 1962. BA, Rutgers coll., 1984; JD, U. Pa., 1988. Jud. clk. Hon. Morton I. Greenberg U.S. Ct. Appeals (3d cir.), Phila., 1988-89; assoc. Covington & Burling, Washington, 1989-94; assoc. Arter & Hadden LLP, Washington, 1995-97, ptnr., 1998—; chair, mem. admissions and grievances com., U.S. Ct. Appeals, D.C. cir., Washington, 1992-97. Contbr. articles to profl. jours. Mem. ABA (jud. rev. com., adminstrv. law sect., appellate practice com., litig. sect.), Supreme Ct. Hist. Soc. Appellate, Administrative and regulatory, Constitutional. Office: Arter & Hadden LLP 1801 K St NW Ste 400K Washington DC 20006-1301

**O'DONNELL, BARBARA BOURDONNAY,** lawyer; b. New Orleans, La., Feb. 25, 1961; d. Charles Leon and Doris Maroney Bourdonnay; m. Phillip Arthur O'Donnell, Aug. 13, 1997; 1 child, Darby Guay. BA in Polit. Sci., U. New Orleans, 1982; JD, Tulane U., 1986. Bar: La. 1988, U.S. Dist. Ct. (ea. dist.) La. 1988, U.S. Dist. Ct. (mid. and we. dist.) La. 1990. Atty. W.M. Hingle & Assocs., Slidell, La., 1988-95, Hailey, McNamara, Hall, Larmann & Papale, LLP, Metairie, La., 1995—. Mem. Am. Soc. Law, Medicine and Ethics, Def. Rsch. Inst., La. Assn. Def. Counsel. Office: Hailey McNamara Hall et al Ste 1400 One Galleria Blvd Metairie LA 70001

**O'DONNELL, DANIEL J.,** lawyer; b. Flushing, N.Y., Nov. 17, 1960; s. Edward J. and Roseann (Murtha) O'D.; life partner John J. Banta. BA in Pub. Affairs, George Washington U., 1982; JD, CUNY, 1987. Bar: N.Y. 1987, U.S. Dist. Ct. (ea. and so. dists.) N.Y., U.S. Ct. Appeals (2d cir.), U.S. Supreme Ct. Staff atty. Legal Aid Soc., Bklyn., 1987-94; ptnr. Daniel J. O'Donnell, N.Y.C., 1994—. Mem. Cmty. Bd. 9, N.Y.C., 1995—; pres. Broadway Dems., N.Y.C., 1997-98; founding mem. Morningside Heights Hist. Dist. Com., N.Y.C., 1997—. Office: 2109 Broadway Ste 206 New York NY 10023-2106

**O'DONNELL, DENISE ELLEN,** lawyer. BS in Polit. Sci., Canisius Coll., 1968; MSW, SUNY, Buffalo, 1973, JD summa cum laude, 1982. Bar: N.Y. 1983, U.S. Dist. Ct. (we. dist.) N.Y., 1985, U.S. Ct. Appeals, 1986. Law clerk Hon. M. Dolores Denman U.S. Ct. Appellate Divsn. 4th Dept., Buffalo, 1982-85; asst. U.S. atty. Western Dist. N.Y., Buffalo, 1985-90, appellate chief, 1990-93, 1st asst. U.S. atty., 1993-97, U.S. atty., 1997—; part-time instr. SUNY trial technique program, 1990—; lectr. ethics, evidence & trial practice Office Legal Edn. U.S. Dept. Justice, 1988—; lectr. NITA seminar Western N.Y. Trial Acad., 1994, 98. V.p. U. Buffalo Law Sch. Alumni Assn., 1995—; mem. Vol. Lawyers Program, 1997—, Women's Group, 1994—, Aids Cmty. Svc., 1987-97. Mem. Bar Assn. Erie County (dep. trea. 1992-93, treas. 1993-94), Erie County Bar Found. (co-chair pub. svc. divsn. 1992-93), Women's Bar Assn. State N.Y. (founding mem. Western N.Y. chpt. 1985, local dir., legis. chair, child care com., liaison atty. access com.), Western N.Y. Trial Lawyers Assn., West Side Rowing Club. Office: US Attys Office 138 Delaware Ave Buffalo NY 14202-2404

**O'DONNELL, EDWARD FRANCIS, JR.,** lawyer; b. Waterbury, Conn., May 13, 1950; s. Edward Francis and Dorothy Patricia (Breheny) O'D.; m. Jayne Ann DeSantis, Dec. 29, 1972; children: Ryan Anderson, Brooke Stires. BA, St. Anselm Coll., Manchester, N.H., 1972; JD, U. Conn., 1977. Bar: S.C. 1978, Conn. 1977, U.S. Dist. Ct. S.C. 1978, U.S. Dist. Ct. Conn. 1980, U.S. Ct. Appeals (1st and 2d cirs.) 1980. Assoc. Ogeltree, Deakins, Nash, Smoak & Stewart, Greenville, S.C., 1977-79; ptnr. Siegel, O'Connor, Schiff & Zangari, Hartford, Conn., 1979—. Contbr. articles to profl. jours. Mem. ABA, Conn. Bar Assn., S.C. Bar Assn., Hartford Bar Assn., Wampanoag Country Club, Phi Alpha Theta. Roman Catholic. Labor. Office: Siegel O'Connor Schiff & Zangari 150 Trumbull St Hartford CT 06103-2403

**O'DONNELL, LAWRENCE, III,** lawyer; b. Houston, Dec. 14, 1957; s. Lawrence Jr. and Annell (Haggart) O'D.; m. Dare Boswell, May 22, 1981; children: Linley, Lawrence IV. BS in Archtl. Engring., U. Tex., 1980; JD cum laude, U. Houston, 1983. Bar: Tex. 1983. Assoc. Wood, Campbell, Moody & Gibbs, Houston, 1983-84; ptnr. Campbell & Riggs, Houston, 1984-91; dep. gen. counsel Baker Hughes Inc., Houston, 1991-94; v.p., gen. counsel Baker Hughes Oilfield Ops., Houston, 1993-95; corp. sec. Baker Hughes Inc., Houston, 1991-96, v.p., gen. counsel, 1995—; bd. dirs., mem. exec. com. Spring Br. Edn. Found.; bd. dirs. Am. Arbitration Assn., U. Tex. Med. Br. Trustee Houston Police Activities League. Fellow Tex. Bar Found., Houston Bar Found.; mem. ABA, ASCE, Tex. State Bar (corp. law com. of bus. law sect.), Houston Bar Assn., Am. Corp. Counsel Assn., Am. Soc. Corp. Sec., Tex. Bus. Law Found., Houston Bar Assn., Order of Barons, Phi Delta Phi. Avocations: golf, sailing, skiing. General corporate, Contracts commercial, Mergers and acquisitions. Office: Baker Hughes Inc 3900 Essex Ln Ste 1200 Houston TX 77027-5170

**O'DONNELL, MARTIN J.,** lawyer; b. Boston, Dec. 19, 1936; s. Michael Vincent and Ann Theresa O'Donnell; m. Louise Jaskiel, May 14, 1966; children: Christopher M., Elisabeth L., Leah K. BS, MIT, 1961; JD, Boston Coll. Law, 1964. Bar: Mass. 1964, U.S. Ct. Appeals (1st cir.) 1966, U.S. Ct. Appeals (fed. cir.) 1977, U.S. Supreme Ct. 1984. Assoc. Kenway, Jenney & Hildreth, Boston, 1964-67; assoc., then ptnr. Cesari & McKenna, Boston, 1967—; adj. faculty New Eng. Sch. of Law, Boston, 1974-84; lectr. Mass. Continuing Legal Edn., Boston, 1975—. Mem. vis. com. on humanities MIT, 1993—, chmn. Boston region ednl. coun., 1981—. Mem. IEEE, Boston Patent Law Assn. (pres. 1978-79), Assn. for Computing Machinery. Avocations: language, curling. Patent, Federal civil litigation, Trademark and copyright.

**O'DONNELL, MICHAEL R.,** lawyer; b. Newark, N.J., Feb. 5, 1958; s. William F. and Rosemary F. O'Donnell; m. Jennifer B. O'Donnell; children: William F., Caitlin M. BA in Govt., Notre Dame U., 1980; JD, U. Va., 1988. Bar: N.J. 1988, U.S. Dist. Ct. N.J. 1988, U.S. Ct. Appeals (3rd cir.)

1994. Jud. clk. to presiding judge U.S. Ct. Appeals (fed. cir.), Washington, 1988-89; ptnr. Riker, Danzig, Scherer, Hyland & Perretti, Morristown, N.J., 1989—. Active fundraising Am. Cancer Soc., Parsippany, N.J., 1998. Capt. USMC, maj. USMCR. Mem. FBA, Fed. Cir. Bar Assn., Inns of Ct. Republican. Roman Catholic. Avocations: running, reading. Contracts commercial.

**O'DOWD, PATRICIA JEAN,** deputy attorney general; b. Paterson, N.J., Feb. 10, 1968; d. Joseph Patrick and Patricia Marion (Haring) O'D. BA in History and Polit. Sci., Douglass Coll., 1990; JD, Rutgers U., 1993. Bar: N.J., 1993, N.Y, 1994. Assoc. Noel & Schablik P.A., Parsippany, N.J., 1994; pub. defender Montville (N.Y.) Twp., 1994-98, dep. atty. gen. DYFS sect., 1998—. Douglass fellow, 1986-90. Mem. ABA, N.J. Bar Assn., Morris County Bar Assn. Republican. Roman Catholic. Home: PO Box 183 Pine Brook NJ 07058-0183 Office: 124 Halsey St Newark NJ 07102-3017

**O'DRISCOLL, CORNELIUS JOSEPH,** lawyer; b. Skibbereen, Ireland, Mar. 19, 1936; came to U.S., 1951; s. Cornelius and Catherine O'D.; m. Beverly Elizabeth Brotemarkle, Feb. 4, 1972; children: Cara Suzanne, Catherine Elise. BS, Boston Coll., 1957; LLB, Suffolk U., 1965; postgrad., George Washington U., 1966-67. Bar: Mass. 1965, U.S. Dist. Ct. D.C. 1967, U.S. Dist. Ct. Md. 1968, Ariz. 1969, U.S. Dist. Ct. Ariz. 1969, U.S. Ct. Appeals (9th cir.) 1969, U.S. Supreme Ct. Atty. pvt. practice, Boston, 1965-66, U.S. Govt., Washington, 1966-67; atty. pvt. practice, Washington, 1967-69, Phoenix, 1969—; judge pro tem Phoenix Mcpl. Ct., 1993—. Bd. dirs. Crossroads, Inc., Phoenix, 1993-94, Family Svc. Agy., 1994—, Ctr. for New Directions, 1993-94. Fellow Ariz. Bar Found.; mem. Mass. Bar Assn., D.C. Bar Assn., State Bar Ariz., KC (Grand Knight). Criminal, Personal injury, Product liability. Office: 4630 N 7th St Ste 109 Phoenix AZ 85014-3829

**ODZA, RANDALL M.,** lawyer; b. Schnectady, May 6, 1942; s. Mitchell and Grace (Mannes) O.; m. Rita Ginness, June 19, 1966; children—Kenneth, Keith. B.S. in Indsl. and Labor Relations, Cornell U., 1964, LL.B., 1967. Bar: N.Y. 1967, U.S. Ct. Appeals (2d cir.) 1970, U.S. Dist. Ct. (so. and ea. dists.) N.Y. 1969, U.S. Dist. Ct. (we. dist.) N.Y. 1970, Fed. Dist. Ct. (we. dist.) N.Y. Assoc. Proskauer, Rose, Goetz & Mandelsohn, N.Y.C., 1967-69; assoc. Jaeckle, Fleischmann & Mugel, Buffalo, 1969-72, ptnr., 1972—. Past trustee, legal counsel, past treas. Temple Beth Am. Recipient Honor award Western N.Y. Retail Mchts. Assn., 1980. Mem. Indsl. Relations Rsch. Assn. Western N.Y., ABA, Erie County Bar Assn., N.Y. State Bar Assn. Labor. Office: Jaeckle Fleischmann & Mugel 12 Fountain Plz Rm 700 Buffalo NY 14202-2292

**OECHLER, HENRY JOHN, JR.,** lawyer; b. Charlotte, N.C., Apr. 9, 1946; s. Henry J. and Convere Jones (McAden) O. AB, Princeton U., 1968; JD, Duke U., 1971. Bar: N.Y. 1972, U.S. Ct. Appeals (2d cir.) 1974, U.S. Ct. Appeals (D.C. cir.) 1975, U.S. Ct. Appeals (8th cir.) 1986, U.S. Ct. Appeals (9th cir.) 1995. Assoc. Chadbourne & Parke, N.Y.C., 1971-80, ptnr., 1980—. Avocations: studying airline schedules. General civil litigation, Labor, Transportation. Office: Chadbourne & Parke 30 Rockefeller Plz New York NY 10112-0002

**OEHLER, RICHARD DALE,** lawyer; b. Iowa City, Dec. 9, 1925; s. Harold Lawrence Oehler and Bernito Babb; m. Rosemary Heineman, July 11, 1952, (div.); m. Maria Luisa Holguin-Zea, June 11, 1962; children: Harold D., Richard L. BA in Med. Scis., U. Calif., Berkeley, 1951; JD, Loyola U., L.A., 1961. Bar: Calif. 1962, Fla. 1968. Sales rep. Abbott Labs., Pasadena, Calif., 1951-63; with claims dept. Allstate Ins., Tampa, 1963-70; pvt. practice Tampa, 1970—; instr. Dale Carnegie Courses West Fla. Inst., Tampa, Scott Hitchcock & Assocs., Tampa, 1969—. Pres. U. South Fla. Parents Assn., Tampa, 1986-87. Mem. Fla. Bar Assn., Hillsborough County Bar Assn., Acad. of Fla. Trial Lawyers, Assn. of Trial Lawyers of Am., Masons (32d degree), Shriners, Phi Beta Kappa. Republican. Presbyterian. Avocations: jogging, road races, target shooting, fishing. Personal injury, Probate. Office: 200 N Pierce St Tampa FL 33602-5020

**OETHEIMER, RICHARD A.,** lawyer; b. Teaneck, N.J., July 22, 1956; s. Edward G. and Joan K. (Coakley) O. BA, Boston Coll., 1978; JD, U. Calif., Berkeley, 1981. Bar: Mass. 1981, U.S. Ct. Appeals (1st, 5th and 9th cirs.), U.S. Dist. Ct. Mass., (no. dist.) N.Y., U.S. Supreme Ct. 1985. Assoc. Goodwin, Procter & Hoar LLP, Boston, 1981-88, ptnr., 1988—. Mem. ABA (products liability com. of litigations sect., com. on comml. and banking litigation), Mass. Bar Assn., Boston Bar Assn. Federal civil litigation, General civil litigation. Office: Goodwin Procter & Hoar LLP Exchange Pl Boston MA 02109-2803

**OETTING, ROGER H.,** lawyer; b. Ft. Wayne, Ind., Dec. 17, 1931; s. Martin W. and Valetta E. (Holman) O.; m. Marcia J. Highlands, Aug. 10, 1957; children: Richard H., Susan E., Catherine R. BBA, U. Mich., 1953, MBA, 1956, JD, 1956; LLM in Taxation, Georgetown U., 1958. Ptnr. Touche Ross & Co., Detroit, 1960-80, Warner Norcross & Judd LLP, Grand Rapids, Mich., 1980—; adj. prof. taxation Grand Valley State U., 1984—. Past pres., dir. treas. Chamber Music Soc. Grand Rapids, 1980-89; past dir., treas. Opera Grand Rapids, 1980-87; dir. Porter Hills Presbyn. Village, 1989—, treas., 1990—. Fellow Am. Coll. Tax Lawyers; mem. State Bar Mich. (coun. fed. tax sect. 1991—), Grand Rapids Bar Assn. (chair fin. com. 1983—), Econ. Club (past treas., bd. dirs. 1982-91), Sugar Bush Assn. (dir., sec., treas. 1985—), Kent Country Club, Leland Yacht Club, Univ. Club (bd. dirs., treas.), Rotary (bd. dirs. 1989-93), Delta Kappa Epsilon. Corporate taxation, Personal income taxation, Taxation, general. Office: Warner Norcross & Judd LLP 900 Old Kent Bldg 111 Lyon St NW Grand Rapids MI 49503-2487

**OETTINGER, JULIAN ALAN,** lawyer, pharmacy company executive. BS, U. Ill., 1961; JD, Northwestern U., 1964. Bar: Ill. 1964. Atty. SEC, 1964-67; atty. Walgreen Co., Deerfield, Ill., 1967-72, sr. atty., 1972-78, dir. law, 1978-89, v.p., gen. counsel, corp. sec., 1989—. General corporate, Real property, Securities. Office: Walgreen Co 200 Wilmot Rd Deerfield IL 60015-4616*

**OFFNER, DANIEL O'CONNELL,** lawyer; b. Northampton, Mass., Jan. 23, 1962; s. Elliot Melville and Rosemary (O'Connell) O. BA, Yale U., 1984; JD, Boston U., 1989, MBA, 1990. Bar: Mass. 1989, Calif. 1992. Mgmt. cons. Calif. Environ. Assocs., San Francisco, 1990-92; assoc. Fierst & Neiman, Northampton, Mass., 1992-95; pvt. practice Northampton and L.A., 1995—. Dir. Northampton Ctr. for the Arts, 1992-95, Mass. Vol. Lawyers for the Arts, Boston, 1992-95. Mem. ABA, L.A. County Bar Assn., Beverly Hills Bar Assn. Intellectual property, General corporate, Entertainment. Office: 90 Conz St Northampton MA 01060-3881

**O'FLARITY, JAMES P.,** lawyer; b. Yazoo City, Miss., Oct. 15, 1923; s. James P. and Jessie E. (Marshall) O'F.; m. Betty Reichman, Apr. 9, 1955; children: Michael J., Deborah J. O'Flarity James, Steven M., Pamela G. BS, Millsaps Coll., 1950; postgrad., Miss. Coll. Sch. Law, 1948, 53-54; J.D., U. Fla., 1965. Bar: Miss. 1954, Fla. 1966, U.S. Dist. Ct. (so. dist.) Miss. 1954, U.S. Ct. Mil. Appeals 1957, U.S. Dist. Ct. (so. and mid. dists.) Fla. 1966, U.S. Dist. Ct. (no. dist.) Fla. 1967, U.S. Ct. Appeals (5th cir.) 1957, U.S. Ct. Appeals (11th cir.) 1981, U.S. Supreme Ct. 1957; state ct. cert. arbitrator, mediator. Assoc. law firm Cone, Owen, Wagner, Nugent & Johnson, West Palm Beach, Fla., 1966-69; sole practice law West Palm Beach, 1969—; mem. Supreme Ct. Matrimonial Law Commn. Fla., 1982-85; ABA observer family ct. proc. Nat. Jud. Coll., 1983; mem. U. Fla. Law Ctr. Coun., 1972—, mem. legal edn. com., 1973, chmn. membership and fin. com., 1977-78; lectr. on marital and family law; leader del. for legal exchange on family law to Ministry of Justice, Peoples Republic of China, 1984. Contbr. articles to profl. publs. Mem. U. Fla. Pres.'s Council; mem. U.S Rep. Senatorial Inner Circle, 1988—; col. La. Gov.'s Staff, 1982—. With USAAF, 1942-45. Decorated Air medal with five oak leaf clusters. Fellow Royal Geog. Soc. (life), Am. Bar Found. (life), Roscoe Pound-Am. Trial Lawyers Found. (life), Am. Acad. Matrimonial Lawyers (nat. pres. 1985-86, nat. bd. of govs. 1977-88, founding pres. Fla. chpt. 1976-80, bd. mgrs. Fla chpt. 1976—, hon. permanent pres. emeritus 1982—), Internat. Acad. Matrimonial Lawyers (convenor, founder), Trusler Soc., Fla. Bar Found. (life, exec. dir. screening com. 1976, chmn. projects com. 1976-77, asst. sec. 1973-79, dir. 1977-81); mem. Internat. Soc. Family Law, Internat. Bar Assn. (assoc.), Am. Law Inst. (consultative group law of family dissolution 1990—, Nat. Conf. Bar Pres'. 1991), ABA (chmn. coms. 1973-75, 78-81, 82-83, editor Family Law Newsletter 1975-77, mem. council family law sect. 1976-85, vice-chmn. sect. 1981-82, chmn. sect. 1983-84, mem. conf. sect. chairmen 1982-85, mem. adv. bd. jour. 1978-80), Assn. Trial Lawyers Am. (Fla. State committeeman 1973-75, 1st chmn. family law sect. 1971-72, 72-73), Fla. Supreme Ct. Hist. Soc., Fla. Council Bar Assn. Presidents (life mem.), U. Fla. Law Ctr. Assn. (life), Acad Fla. Trial Lawyers (dir. 1974-77, coll. diplomates 1977), Fla. Bar (exec. council 1973-84, sec.-treas. family law sect. 1973-74, chmn. family law sect. 1974-75, 75-76, guest editor spl. issue jour. 1978, chmn. jour. and news editorial bd. 1978-79, mem. bd. legal specialization and edn. 1982-91, 92-95, jud. nominating procedures com. 1992-93, Family Law Rules com. 1992-95), Palm Beach County Bar Assn. (cir. ct. civil adv. com. 1981, mem. cir. ct. juvenile domestic rels. adv. com. 1971-80, 81-83, adv. com. chmn. 1974-78), Solicitor's Family Law Assn. (Eng.), Gov.'s Club of Palm Beach (founder, life, gov's. coun.), Explorers Club (life, vice chmn. South Fla. chpt. 1990-95), Circumnavigators Club, Travelers Century Club (life), Phi Alpha Delta (life), Sigma Delta Kappa. Family and matrimonial, State civil litigation. Home: 908 Country Club Dr North Palm Beach FL 33408-3714 Office: Ste 960 Esperante 222 Lakeview Ave West Palm Beach FL 33401

**OGBOGU, CECILIA IFY,** lawyer; b. Enugu, Nigeria, Sept. 19, 1964; d. Samuel and Cecilia Ogbogu; 1 child, Jason. BL with honors, Nigerian Law Sch., Lagos, Nigeria, 1986; LLB with honors, Imo State U., Aba, Nigeria, 1985. Bar: Calif. 1996, U.S. Dist. Ct. (ctrl. dist.) Calif. 1996, Nigerian Bar 1986. Staff counsel Cooperative and Commerce, Bank of Nigeria Plc, Enugu, Nigeria, 1988-93; vol. atty. Legal Aid Found. of L.A., 1996, Bet Tzedek Legal Svcs., L.A., 1996; pvt. practice L.A., 1996—. Fellow The Alliance for Children's Rights, L.A., 1998—. Recipient Wiley Manuel award State Bar of Calif., 1997, award of merit Nat. Ctr. for Missing and Exploited Children, 1997. Mem. ABA, Assn. of Trial Lawyers of Am., L.A. County Bar Assn. (barristers' com. mem. 1996—). Democrat. Roman Catholic. Avocations: writing, reading, stamp collecting. Family and matrimonial, General civil litigation, Personal injury. Office: 315 W 9th St Ste 603 Los Angeles CA 90015-4206

**OGBURN, JOHN DENIS,** lawyer; b. Louisville, Mar. 8, 1956; s. William H. and Huberta K. Ogburn; m. Mary Katherine Luckett, July 21, 1979; children: Brian, Jeff, Laura. BA, U. Notre Dame, 1978; JD, U. Louisville, 1984. Bar: Ky. 1984, U.S. Dist. Ct. (ea. and we. dists.) Ky. 1984. Claims mgr. Royal Ins. Co., Louisville, 1979-85, Hanover Ins., Louisville, 1985-89; assoc. Landrum & Shouse, Louisville, from 1989, now ptnr. Maj. JAG, USAR, 1986—. Mem. Ky. Bar Assn., Def. Rsch Inst. Democrat. Roman Catholic. Avocations: golf, running, computers. Insurance, State civil litigation, Federal civil litigation. Home: 3200 Summerfield Dr Louisville KY 40220-3332 Office: Landrum & Shouse 220 W Main St Louisville KY 40202-1395

**OGBURN, THOMAS LYNN, III,** lawyer; b. Winston-Salem, N.C., Sept. 15, 1969; s. Thomas Lynn Jr. and Anita (Hauser) O. BA in Polit. Sci. and Econs., U. N.C., 1992; MBA, JD, Wake Forest U., 1996. Bar: N.C. 1996, S.C. 1996. Assoc. Poyner & Spruill, L.L.P., Charlotte, N.C., 1996-98, with, 1998—. Swim instr. Ctrl. YMCA, Charlotte, 1996-98; CPR instr. ARC, Charlotte, 1996-98. Mem. ABA, N.C. Bar, S.C. Bar, N.C. Bar Orgn. General civil litigation, Consumer commercial. Office: Poyner & Spruill LLP 100 N Tryon St Ste 4000 Charlotte NC 28202-4010

**OGDEN, DAVID WILLIAM,** lawyer; b. Washington, Nov. 12, 1953; s. Horace Greeley and Elaine Celia (Condrell) O.; m. Wannett Smith, 1988; children: Jonathan Smith, Elaine Smith. BA summa cum laude, U. Pa., 1976; JD magna cum laude, Harvard U., 1981. Bar: D.C. 1983, Va. 1986, U.S. Dist. Ct. D.C. 1984, U.S. Dist. Ct. (ea. dist.) Va. 1988, U.S. Ct. Appeals (D.C. cir.) 1984, U.S. Ct. Appeals (4th cir.) 1986, U.S. Ct. Appeals (1st cir. 1989), U.S. Ct. Appeals (10th cir.) 1991, U.S. Supreme Ct. 1987. Law clk. to presiding judge U.S. Dist. Ct. (so. dist.) N.Y., N.Y.C., 1981-82; law clk. to assoc. justice Harry A. Blackmun U.S. Supreme Ct., Washington, 1982-83; assoc. atty. Ennis, Friedman, Bersoff & Ewing, Washington, 1983-85; atty., ptnr. Ennis, Friedman & Bersoff, Washington, 1986-88, Jenner & Block, Washington, 1988-94; legal counsel, dep. gen. counsel U.S. DOD, Washington, 1994-95; assoc. dep. atty. gen. U.S. Dept. Justice, Washington, 1995-97, counselor to the atty. gen., 1997-98, chief of staff to atty. gen., 1998-99, acting asst. atty. gen. for Civil Divsn., 1999—; adj. prof. law Georgetown U. Law Ctr., 1992-95. Author: (with Jerald A. Jacobs) Legal Risk Management for Associations, 1995. Recipient Disting. Pub. Svc. medal Dept. Def., 1995, Atty. Gen.'s medallion, 1999. Mem. ABA, D.C. Bar Assn., Phi Beta Kappa. Democrat. Federal civil litigation, Constitutional.

**OGDEN, JOHN HAMILTON,** lawyer; b. Newport News, Va., Sept. 14, 1951; s. Donald Thomas and Bernice (Hamilton) O.; m. Mary Lynne Vogel, May 11, 1973; children: Amy Elizabeth, Christopher Michael, Andrew David. AB, Villanova U., 1973; JD, Fordham U., 1977. Bar: N.J. 1977, U.S. Dist. Ct. N.J. 1977, U.S. Ct. Internat. Trade 1990. Sr. buyer Consol. Edison of N.Y., N.Y.C., 1973-77; contract mgr. Jersey Cen. Power & Light, Morristown, N.J., 1977-80; atty. Foster Wheeler Corp., Livingston, N.J., 1980-83; gen. counsel Werner & Pfleiderer Corp., Ramsey, N.J., 1983—; corp. sec. Krupp, Werner & Pfleiderer Corp., Ramsey, 1989—; asst. sec., counsel Krupp USA Fin. Svcs. Inc., Ramsey, 1993-98; asst. sec. Krupp USA, Inc., Ramsey, 1998—. Recipient Profl. Lawyer of Yr. award N.J. Commn. on Professionalism in the Law, 1998. Mem. Am. Corp. Counsel Assn. (chair 1990-91, small law dept. subcom., chmn. small law dept. com. 1991-92, bd. dirs. 1991-98, sec. bd. dirs. 1994— chmn. edn. bd. com. 1992-94, exec. com. 1992-98, chair coun. nat. coms. 1994, sec. 1995, treas. 1996, vice chair 1997, founder and chair Leadership Devel. Inst. 1998—), N.J. Corp. Counsel Assn. (bd. dirs. 1992-96, v.p., sec. 1992-93, pres. 1994-95, past pres., editor, contbr. Small Law Department Practitioners Desk Manual, 1993), N.J. State Bar Found. (bd. trustees 1998—, pub. edn. com. 1995—). Contracts commercial, Private international, General corporate. Office: Werner & Pfleiderer Corp 663 E Crescent Ave Ramsey NJ 07446-1287

**OGG, ELTON JERALD, JR.,** educator, academic administrator; b. Springfield, Mo., Aug. 25, 1955; s. Elton Jerald Sr. and Janett Northam O.; m. Mary Jane Nichols, Dec. 28, 1973; children: Jennifer Lauren, Jana Elizabeth. JD, U. Tenn., 1978; MJ, La. State U., 1987; PhD, So. Ill. U., 1994. Bar: Tenn. 1979, La. 1984. Atty. pvt. practice, Baton Rouge, La., 1983-87; asst. prof. comm. U. Tenn., Martin, 1987-97, chmn. dept. comm., 1997—; prof. Tenn. Govs. Sch. Humanities, Martin, 1991-99. Contbr. articles to profl. jours. Pres. Parent-Tchr. Orgn., Martin, 1989-90; coach Martin Girls Softball Assn., 1993-99; dir. Lifeline Blood Svcs., Weadley County, Tenn., 1993-99. Avocations: golf, softball, tennis, reading. Office: U Tenn 305J Gooch Hl Martin TN 38238-0001

**OGG, WILSON REID,** lawyer, poet, retired judge, lyricist, curator, publisher, educator, philosopher, social scientist, parapsychologist; b. Alhambra, Calif., Feb. 26, 1928; s. James Brooks and Mary (Wilson) O. Student, Pasadena Jr. Coll., 1946; AB, U. Calif., Berkeley, 1949; JD, U. Calif., 1952; Cultural D in Philosophy of Law, World U. Roundtable, 1983. Bar: Calif. 1955. Assoc. trust dept. Wells Fargo Bank, San Francisco, 1954-55; pvt. practice Berkeley, 1955—; adminstrv. law judge, 1974-93; real estate broker, cons., 1974—; curator-in-residence, Pinebrook, 1964—; owner Pinebrook Press, Berkeley, 1988—; rsch. atty., legal editor Dept. of Continuing Edn. of Bar U. Calif., 1958-63;instr. 25th Sta. Hosp., Taegu, Korea, 1954, Taegu English Lang. Inst., 1954; trustee World U., 1976-80; dir. admissions Internat. Soc. for Phil. Enquiry, 1981-84; dep. dir. gen. Internat. Biographical Ctr., England, 1986—; dep. gov. Am. Biographical Inst. Rsch. Assn., 1986—. *Judge Ogg's career combines outstanding achievement in the legal profession with a major analysis of the problems of distinguishing co-existence from causality in medicine and science. He has also formulated the two-way flow theory of matter and consciousness under which principles of quantum mechanics, black notes, light, expansion and contraction of manifestation, and physical and biological evolutions are derivative from the basic postulates of the theory.* Contbr. articles to profl. jours.; contbr. poems to mags. With AUS, 1952-54. Elected to Internat. Poetry Hall of Fame Nat. Libr. Poetry, 1997. Mem. VFW, AAAS, ABA, ASCAP, ACLU, Internat. Platform Assn., Internat. Soc. Unified Sci., Internat. Soc. Poets (life), Amnesty Internat., Internat. Soc. Individual Liberty, Internat. Soc. Individual Liberty, State Bar Calif., San Francisco Bar Assn., Am. Arbitration Assnl. (nat. panel arbitrators), Calif. Soc. Psychical Study (pres., chmn. bd. 1963-65), Intertel, Triple Nine Soc., Wisdom Soc., Inst. Noetic Scis., Men's Inner Circle of Achievement, Truman Libr. Inst. (hon.), Am. Legion, City Commons Club (Berkeley), commonwealth Club of Calif., Town Hall Club Calif., Marines Meml. Club, Masons, Shriners, Elks. Unitarian. General practice, Probate, Constitutional. Office: Pinebrook 8 Bret Harte Way Berkeley CA 94708-1611 Office: 1104 Keith Ave Berkeley CA 94708-1607 also: 39231 Liberty St Fremont CA 94538-1501

**OGILBY, BARRY RAY,** lawyer; b. dixon, Ky., Jan. 19, 1947; s. Jess Bryan and Ann (Sutton) O; m. Carolyn Cowser, May 30, 1969 (div. 1973); m. Charlene Marie Coehlo, July 2, 1983; children: Kevin Glenn, Brandon Jesse. BS in Geology, U. Ky., 1969; JD, Memphis State U., 1972. Bar: Tenn. 1972, Tex. 1972, Ky. 1973, Calif. 1985, U.S. Dist. Ct. (cen. and no. dists.) Calif. 1987, U.S. Ct. Appeals (9th cir.) 1989. Litigation atty. Exxon U.S.A., Houston, 1972-74; mktg. atty. Exxon U.S.A., Memphis, 1975-76; labor, environ. atty. Exxon U.S.A., L.A., 1976-78; refinery atty. Exxon U.S.A., Benicia, Calif., 1978-81; counsel Exxon Pipeline Co., Houston, 1981-84; assoc. dv. atty. Exxon Co. USA, Thousand Oaks, Calif., 1985-86; sole practice Calabasas, Calif., 1986-91; gen. counsel Marine Spill Resource Corp., 1991-94; atty. McCutchen, Doyle et al, 1995—; adj. prof. environ. law La Verne Coll., 1989-90; lectr. Am. Labor Inst.-ABA legal Edn. Seminar, San Francisco, 1980, 82. Contbr. articles to profl. jours. Mem. ABA (nat. resources law com., marine resources com. 1998—), Fed. Bar Assn. (labor law com.). Environmental, General civil litigation, FERC practice. Office: McCutchen Doyle et al 3 Embarcadero Ctr San Francisco CA 94111-4003

**OGILVIE, GAIL,** arbitrator, mediator; b. Boston, July 10, 1944; d. Leon Russell and Dorothy Burt Ogilvie. AB in Math., Mount Holyoke Coll., 1966; MEd, Tufts U., 1970; JD, U. Maine, 1977. Bar: Maine 1977, U.S. Dist. Ct. Maine 1977, U.S. Supreme Ct. 1996. Asst. atty. gen. Maine Dept. Atty. Gen., Augusta, 1977-89; worker's compensation commr. Woker's Compensation Commn., Augusta, 1989-94; sr. trial atty. Piampiano & Gavin, Portland, Maine, 1994-96; chair med. malpractice screening panel Maine Superior Ct., Augusta, 1994—. Dir. Richmond Area Health Ctr., 1995—. Mem. Maine State Bar Assn. Avocations: traveling, skiing, sailing, hiking. Home: 25 Gardiner St Richmond ME 04357-1345

**O'GORMAN, PATRICIA ANN,** lawyer; b. Red Wing, Minn., Nov. 3, 1946; d. Robert Pierce and Delores Mathilda (Haas) O'G.; m. L. Scott Harris, June 20, 1970 (div. Oct. 1977). BA in History and Polit. Sci., Coll. of St. Catherine, St. Paul, 1968; JD, U. Minn., 1971. Bar: Minn. 1972, U.S. Dist. Ct. Minn. 1974, Mich. 1977, U.S. Dist. Ct. (ea. dist.) Mich. 1977, U.S. Dist. Ct. (we. dist.) Wis. 1991. Atty. Minn. Dept. Pub. Welfare, St. Paul, 1972-73; asst. county atty. Ramsey County Atty.'s Office, St. Paul, 1974-77; asst. pros. atty. Midland County Pros. Atty.'s Office, Midland, Mich., 1977, chief asst., 1978-79; mem. Morse, Clinton & O'Gorman, Cottage Grove, Minn., 1980-84, Clinton & O'Gorman, PA, Cottage Grove, 1984-91; pres. mem. Patricia A. O'Gorman, PA, Cottage Grove, 1991—; bd. dirs. Minn. Bar Found., Mpls.; mem. adv. com. on family ct. procedures Minn. Supreme Ct., 1986-87, chmn. pro se forms family law subcom., 1997; chmn. pro se forms family ct. litigation com. Minn. Conf. Chief Judges, 1996-98. Citizen's adv. com. Minn. N.G. Armory, Cottage Grove, 1986-90; trustee Law-Polit. Action Com., Mpls., 1988-93; bd. dirs. Family Violence Network, Lake Elmo, Minn., 1989-94. Fellow Am. Acad. Matrimonial Lawyers; mem. Minn. Bar Assn. (bd. govs. 1984-90, chmn. family law sect. 1990-91). Mem. Democrat-Farmer-Labor Party. Roman Catholic. Family and matrimonial, General practice. Office: 8750 90th St S Cottage Grove MN 55016-3389

**O'GRADY, DENNIS JOSEPH,** lawyer; b. Hoboken, N.J., Nov. 16, 1943; s. Joseph A. and Eileen (Broderick) O'Grady; m. Mary Anne Amoruso, Sept. 9, 1966 (div. Apr. 1984); 1 child, Kara Anne. AB, Seton Hall Coll., 1965; MA, U. So. Calif., 1969; JD, Rutgers U., 1973. Bar: N.J. 1973, U.S. Ct. Appeals (3d cir.) 1975, U.S. Dist. Ct. N.J. Ptnr. Riker, Danzig, Scherer, Hyland & Perretti, Newark, Trenton and Morristown, N.J., 1974—; adj. asst. prof. of bus. law St. Peter's Coll., Jersey City, 1973—; adj. prof. law Rutgers U. Law Sch., 1997—. Mem. ABA (bus./bankruptcy sect.), N.J. State Bar Assn. (debtor/creditor sect.), Fed. Bar Assn., Am. Bankruptcy Inst. (health car subcom., bd. profl. cert.), Am. Bd. Cert. (faculty subcom.). Democrat. Roman Catholic. Bankruptcy, Banking, General civil litigation. Office: Riker Danzig Scherer Hyland & Perretti 1 Speedwell Ave Ste 2 Morristown NJ 07960-6823

**OGUL, MICHAEL S.,** lawyer; b. L.A., Mar. 12, 1956; s. Leo Meyer and Sonia Ziba Ogul; married; 2 children. BA in Polit. Sci., U. So. Calif., 1977; JD, U. Calif., San Francisco, 1980. Bar: Calif. 1980, U.S. Dist. Ct. (no. dist.) Calif. 1980. Dep. pub. defender San Joaquin County Pub. Defender, Stockton, Calif., 1981-82; asst. pub. defender Alameda County Pub. Defender, Oakland, Calif., 1982—. Contbr. articles to profl. jours. Mem. Calif. Attys. for Criminal Justice (co-chmn. death penalty com. 1998—, Skip Glen award 1998), Calif. Pub. Defender's Assn. Avocations: bicycling, skiing. Office: Office Pub Defender 1401 Lakeside Dr 4th Fl Oakland CA 94612-4305

**OH, MATTHEW INSOO,** lawyer; b. Seoul, Republic of Korea, Aug. 5, 1938; s. Young Whan and Jeom-soon (Kim) Oh; m. Young Ok, May 24, 1973; children: John Z., Amy J. LLB, Seoul Nat. U., 1963, LLM, 1968; LLM, Columbia U., 1972; JD, William Mitchell Coll. Law, St. Paul, 1982. Bar: Minn. 1982, N.Y. 1988, D.C. 1989. Sr. planning researcher Ministry of Constrn., Seoul, 1968-71; planner Altamaha, Ga. Regional Planning Commn., 1972-74; sole practice St. Paul, Minn., 1982—. Legal advisor Korean Elderly Soc., St. Paul, 1984—; mem. North Korea Human Rights Project, Mpls., 1985-87; chmn. State of Minn. Council on Asian-Pacific Relations, St. Paul, 1985-86; v.p. Minn. Asian Advocacy Coalition, St. Paul, 1983-85; bd. dirs. Urban Concern Workshop, Inc., St. Paul, 1985-86. Fulbright fellow Fulbright Commn., Seoul, 1971. Mem. D.C. Bar Assn., Ramsey County Bar Assn., (Yogi Berra award), Am. Immigration Lawyers Assn., Internat. Assn. Korean Lawyers. Presbyterian. Immigration, naturalization, and customs, Private international. Home: 9 Woodhill Ln Saint Paul MN 55127-2140 Office: 1130 Minn World Trade Ctr 30 7th St E Saint Paul MN 55101-4914

**O'HAGAN, KEVIN MICHAEL,** lawyer; b. Chgo., Aug. 27, 1967; s. James Joseph and Suzanne Elizabeth (Wiegand) O'H.; m. Kathryn Anne Gorham, June 27, 1992; children: Rosemary, Annabel. BA, Coll. of Holy Cross, 1989; JD, DePaul U., 1992. Bar: Ill. 1992, Va. 1995, U.S. Dist. Ct. (no. dist.) Ill. 1992. Asst. fin. analyst Ill. Tool Works Inc., Chgo., 1990-91; atty. Lord Bissell & Brook, Chgo., 1992-94, McGuire Woods Battle & Boothe, Richmond, Va., 1994-95, Waste Mgmt. Inc., Oak Brook, Ill., 1995-98, O'Hagan, Smith & Amundsen, LLC, Chgo., 1998—. Mem. ABA (chair litig. com.). Roman Catholic. Avocations: golf, tennis, biographies, travel. General civil litigation, Mergers and acquisitions, Product liability. Home: 2814 Harrison St Evanston IL 60201-1218 Office: O'Hagan Smith & Amundsen 150 N Michigan Ave Chicago IL 60601-7553

**O'HAGIN, ZARINA EILEEN SUAREZ,** lawyer; b. Ruislip, Eng., Apr. 6, 1954; came to U.S., 1957; d. Harry and Czarina Ruth Suarez O'Hagin; m. Kenneth James Northcott, Oct. 4, 1980 (div. Dec. 1995). AB, U. Chgo., 1976; student, Chgo.-Kent Coll., 1981-82; JD, U. Chgo., 1984. Bar: Ill. 1984. Counsellor Orthogenic Sch., Chgo., 1976-80; assoc. Katten Muchin & Zavis, Chgo., 1984-87, Schiff Hardin & Waite, Chgo., 1987-88, Sidley & Austin, Chgo., 1988-92; employee benefits cons. Price Waterhouse, Chgo., 1992-93; project dir. Chgo. Lawyers Com. for Civil Rights Under the Law, Inc., Chgo., 1993—; mem. adv. bd. FEMALE, Elmhurst, Ill., 1987—. Coauthor: Environmental Liability of Fiduciaries, 1991; contbr. articles to profl. jours. Deacon Episcopal Ch., Chgo., 1998—. Avocations: gardening, pottery, vegetarian cooking. Education and schools, Civil rights. Office: Chgo Lawyers Com for Civil Rights Under Law Inc 100 N La Salle St Ste 600 Chicago IL 60602-2403

**O'HARRA, COLLEEN COLEMAN,** lawyer; b. Orange, Calif., Apr. 9, 1937; d. Walter Logan and Dorothy Lucille (McDonnell) Coleman; m. John Edwin Richardson, Dec. 20, 1959 (div. Oct. 1973); children: Alicia, Laura; m. Lawrence Bland O'Harra, Aug. 25, 1990. BA, Chapman U., 1959; JD, Western State U., 1978. Bar: Calif. 1978. Atty. Greenman, Lacy, Klein, St. John, O'Harra & Heffron, Oceanside, Calif. Pres. Oceanside C. of C., 1986;

mem. Ocean City Coun., 1992—. Recipient Cmty. Svc. award Calif. Women in Govt., San Diego, 1990, Bus. Person of the Yr. award Oceanside C. of C., 1992, Women of Distinction award Soroptimist Internat., Oceanside, 1993. Mem. Bar Assn. No. San Diego County (treas. 1990-92), Womens Resource Ctr. (founder, bd. mem.), Lawyer's Club San Diego. Democrat. Avocations: dancing, reading, crocheting. Home: 600 N The Strand Unit 44 Oceanside CA 92054-1975 Office: Greenman Lacy Klein St John O'Hara & Hefron 900 Pier View Way Oceanside CA 92054-2839

**O'HEARN, MICHAEL JOHN,** lawyer; b. Akron, Ohio, Jan. 29, 1952; s. Leo Ambrose and Margaret Elizabeth (Clark) O'H. BA in Econs., UCLA, 1975; postgrad., U. San Diego, 1977; JD, San Fernando Valley Coll. Law, 1979; postgrad., Holy Apostles Sem., 1993-94. Bar: Calif. 1979, U.S. Dist. Ct. (cen. dist.) Calif. 1979. Document analyst Mellonics Info. Ctr., Litton Industries, Canoga Park, Calif., 1977-79; pvt. practice Encino, Calif., 1979-80; atty. VISTA/Grey Law Inc., L.A., 1980-81; assoc. Donald E. Chadwick & Assocs., Woodland Hills, Calif., 1981-84, Law Offices of Laurence Ring, Beverly Hills, Calif., 1984-85; atty., in-house counsel Coastal Ins. Co., Van Nuys, Calif., 1985-89; atty. Citrus Glen Apts., Ventura, Calif., 1989-92; pvt. practice Ventura County, Calif., 1992—; arbitrator, 1995—; propr., property mgr. Channel Islands Village Mgmt. Co., 1998—. Life mem. Rep. Nat. Com. Recipient Cert. of Appreciation, Agy. for Vol. Svc., 1981, San Fernando Valley Walk for Life, 1988, Cert. of Appreciation, Arbitrator for the Superior and Mcpl. Cts., Ventura County Jud. Dist., 1996. Mem. KC, Ventura County Bar Assn., Ventura County Trial Lawyers Assn., Secular Franciscan Order. Republican. Roman Catholic. Avocation: golf. Estate planning, Insurance, Personal injury. Home: 1941 Fisher Dr Apt B Oxnard CA 93035-3022 Office: 3650 Ketch Ave Oxnard CA 93035-3029

**O'HERN, DANIEL JOSEPH,** state supreme court justice; b. Red Bank, N.J., May 23, 1930; s. J. Henry and Eugenia A. (Sansone) O'H.; m. Barbara Ronan, Aug. 8, 1959; children: Daniel J., Eileen, James, John, Molly. AB, Fordham Coll., 1951; LLB, Harvard U., 1957. Bar: N.J. 1958. Clk. U.S. Supreme Ct., Washington, 1957-58; assoc. Abramoff, Apy & O'Hern, Red Bank, N.J., 1966-78; commr. N.J. Dept. Environ. Protection, 1978-79; counsel to Gov. N.J. Trenton; justice N.J. Supreme Ct., Trenton, 1981—; former mem. adv. com. profl. ethics N.J. Supreme Ct. Past trustee Legal Aid Soc. Monmouth County, (N.J.); mayor Borough of Red Bank, 1969-78, councilman, 1962-69. Served as lt. (j.g.) USNR, 1951-54. Fellow Am. Bar Found.; mem. ABA, N.J. Bar Assn., Monmouth County Bar Assn., Harvard Law Sch. Assn. N.J. (past pres.). Office: NJ Supreme Ct 151 Bodman Pl Red Bank NJ 07701-1070 also: NJ Supreme Ct PO Box 970 Trenton NJ 08625-0970

**OHLANDER, JAN H.,** lawyer; b. Rockford, Ill., July 10, 1954; s. Herbert Eugene Ohlander and Elmina Laura Osen; m. Patricia S. Phillips, June 27, 1976; children: J. Scott, Samuel John, Elle Elyse. BS, U. Ill., 1976; JD, Marquette U., 1979. Bar: U.S. Dist. Ct. (no. dist.) Ill. 1979, U.S. Dist. Ct. (we. and ea. dists.) Wis. 1979, U.S. Ct. Appeals (7th cir.) 1988, U.S. Supreme Ct. 1990. Assoc. Reno & Zahm, Rockford, 1979-81, ptnr., 1982—. Bd. dirs. Rockford Area Crime Stoppers, 1988—. Mem. ATLA, Ill. Trial Lawyers Am., Trial Bar No. Dist. Ill. General civil litigation, Personal injury, Labor. Office: Reno & Zahm 1415 E State St Ste 900 Rockford IL 61104-2394

**OHLY, D. CHRISTOPHER,** lawyer; b. N.Y.C., Nov. 7, 1950; s. Bodo Charles and Ellen Charlotte (Nekolla) O.; m. Karen Vanacek; 1 child, Sara Rebecca. AB, Johns Hopkins U., 1972; JD, U. Va., 1975. Bar: Md. 1975, U.S. Dist. Ct. Md. 1975, U.S. Ct. Appeals (1st, 2d and 4th cirs.), U.S. Tax Ct., U.S. Supreme Ct. Asst. U.S. Atty. U.S. Atty.'s Office, Balt., 1978-81; owner Hazel & Thomas, P.C., Balt., 1989-94; ptnr. Patton Boggs, LLP, Balt., 1994—. Contbr. articles to profl. jours. Mem. ABA (internat. law sect. 1973—), Md. Bar Assn., Am. Soc. Internat. Law, Phi Beta Kappa, Omicron Delta Kappa, Pi Sigma Alpha. Avocations: skiing, computers, amateur radio. Private international, Federal civil litigation, Criminal. Home: 5714 St Albans Way Baltimore MD 21212-2454 also: Village Chalet 5 Middle Ridge Rd South Londonderry VT 05155-9747

**OHMAN, EARL R., JR.,** lawyer. Gen. counsel Occupl. Safety and Health Rev. Commn., Washington. Office: Occupl Safety and Health Rev Commn One Lafayette Centre 1120 20th St NW Washington DC 20036-3406

**O'KEEFFE, CYNTHIA GRISHAM,** lawyer; b. Abilene, Tex., Apr. 24, 1957; d. Robert Douglas and Justine (Digby-Roberts) Grisham; m. Kevin Francis O'Keeffe, June 11, 1988; 1 child, Kevin Patrick. BS, U. Tex., 1979; JD, St. Mary's U., 1982. Bar: Tex., 1982, U.S. Dist. Ct. (we. dist.) Tex., 1986. Assoc. Groce, Locke & Hebdon, San Antonio, 1982-88; pvt. practice San Antonio, 1988—. Contbr. articles to profl. jours. Mem., bd. dirs. Child Guidance Ctr., San Antonio, 1994-97; cmty. bd. dirs. Healy-Murphy Ctr., San Antonio, 1993-97; mem. San Antonio 100, 1996—. Fellow Tex. Bar Found.; mem. ABA, State Bar Tex. (family law sect. 1982—), San Antonio Bar Assn. (family law sect. 1995—). Family and matrimonial. Office: 999 E Basse Rd Ste 180 San Antonio TX 78209-1807

**O'KELLEY, WILLIAM CLARK,** federal judge; b. Atlanta, Jan. 2, 1930; s. Ezra Clark and Theo (Johnson) O'K.; m. Ernestine Allen, Mar. 28, 1953; children: Virginia Leigh O'Kelley Wood, William Clark Jr. AB, Emory U., 1951, LLB, 1953. Bar: Ga. 1952. Pvt. practice Atlanta, 1957-59; asst. U.S. atty. No. Dist. Ga., 1959-61; partner O'Kelley, Hopkins & Van Gerpen, Atlanta, 1961-70; U.S. dist. judge No. Dist. Ga., Atlanta, 1970—, chief judge, 1988-94; mem. com. on adminstrn. of criminal law Jud. Conf. U.S., 1979-82, exec. com., 1983-84, subcom. on jury trials in complex criminal cases, 1981-82, dist. judge rep. 11th cir., 1981-84, mem. adv. com. of fed. rules of criminal procedure, 1984-87; bd. dirs. Fed. Jud. Ctr., 1987-91, adv. com. history program, 1989-91, com. on orientation of newly appointed dist. judges, 1985-88; mem. Com. Jud. Resources, 1989-94; mem. Jud. Coun. 11th Cir., 1990-96, exec. com., 1990-96; mem. Fgn. Intelligence Surveillance Ct., 1980-87; mem. Alien Terrorist Removal Ct., 1996—; corp. sec., dir. Gwinnett Bank & Trust Co., Norcross, Ga., 1967-70. Mem. exec. com., gen. counsel Ga. Republican Com., 1968-70; mem. fin. com. Northwest Ga. Girl Scout Coun., 1958-70; trustee Emory U., 1991-97. Served as 1st lt. USAF, 1953-57; capt. USAFR. Mem. Fed. Bar Assn., Ga. State Bar, Atlanta Bar Assn., Dist. Judges Assn. 5th Cir. (sec.-treas. 1976-77, v.p. 1977-78, pres. 1978-80), Lawyers Club Atlanta, Kiwanis (past pres.), Atlanta Athletic Club, Sigma Chi, Phi Delta Phi, Omicron Delta Kappa. Baptist. Home: 550 Ridgecrest Dr Norcross GA 30071-2158 Office: US Dist Ct 1942 US Courthouse 75 Spring St SW Atlanta GA 30303-3309

**O'KIEF, W. GERALD,** lawyer; b. Portland, Oreg., Feb. 19, 1937; s. William G. and Alice M. (Zilmer) O'K.; m. Sharon M. Moran, June 26, 1966; children: Gregory, Mary, John, Paul. AB, Creighton U., 1960, LLB, 1960; LLM, Harvard U., 1961. Pvt. practice Valentine, Nebr., 1961—; bd. dirs. First Nat. Bank, Valentine, Nebr. Mem. ABA, Nebr. Bar Assn. Estate planning, General practice, Banking. Office: Box 766 111 129 E 3rd St Valentine NE 69201-1809

**OKINAGA, LAWRENCE SHOJI,** lawyer; b. Honolulu, July 7, 1941; s. Shohei and Hatsu (Kakimoto) O.; m. Carolyn Hisako Uesugi, Nov. 26, 1966; children: Carrie, Caryn, Laurie. BA, U. Hawaii, 1963; JD, Georgetown U., 1972. Bar: Hawaii 1972, U.S. Dist. Ct. Hawaii 1972, U.S. Ct. Appeals (9th cir.) 1976. Adminstrv. asst. to Congressman Spark Matsunaga Honolulu, 1964, 65-69; law clk. to chief judge U.S. Dist. Ct. Hawaii, Honolulu, 1972-73; assoc. Carlsmith Ball, Honolulu, 1973-76, ptnr., 1976—; mem. Gov.'s Citizens Adv. Com. Coastal Zone Mgmt., 1974-79; sec. Hawaii Bicentennial Corp., 1975-77, chmn., 1985-87, vice chmn., 1983-85; mem. Jud. Selection Commn., State of Hawaii, 1979-87, vice chmn., 1986; mem. consumer adv. coun. Fed. Res. Bd., 1984-86; chmn. State of Hawaii Jud. Conduct Commn., 1991-94; apptd. mem. Fed. Savings and Loan Adv. Council, Washington, 1988-89; mem. nat. adv. coun. U.S. Small Bus. Adminstrn., 1994—; mem. adv. coun. Fed. Res. Bank of San Francisco, 1995—. Bd. dirs. Moiliili Cmty. Ctr., Honolulu, 1965-68, 73-86; bd. visitors Georgetown U. Law Ctr., 1993—; trustee Kuakini Med. Ctr., 1984-88, 89-96. Capt. USAFR, 1964-72, 74-76. Mem. ABA (ho. of dels. 1991-94, standing com. on jud. selection tenure and compensation 1993-96, standing com. on jud. independence), Hawaii Bar Assn. (sec., bd. dirs. 1981), Am. Judicature Soc. (bd. dirs. 1986—, treas. 1995-97, pres. 1997-99), Georgetown U. Law Alumni Assn. (bd. dirs. 1986-91), Omicron Delta Kappa. Banking, Real property, General corporate. Office: Carlsmith Ball PO Box 656 Honolulu HI 96809-0656

**OKOLIE, CHARLES CHUKWUMA,** lawyer, technology consulting executive, association executive; b. Nze-Enugu, Anambra, Nigeria, Aug. 16, 1943; s. Okwuruora Chiene and Olinandu Nwagu (Mba) O.; m. Tania Nicole Bourbak, Apr. 11, 1968; 1 child, Judith Ngozi. Hon. diploma internat. law and diplomacy, Soviet Acad. Scis. Inst. African Studies, 1966; LL.M., Kieve State U., USSR, 1969; diploma in English and comparative law, 1st class, City of London Coll., 1970; LL.M., U. Calif., 1970, cert. in law and econ. devel., 1971, J.S.D., 1972. Vis. scholar UN Inst. for Tng. and Research, N.Y.C., 1972-73; legal research scholar Harvard U. Law Sch., Cambridge, Mass., 1973-75; prof. law, assoc. dean Lewis U. Coll. Law (now No. Ill. Coll. Law), Glen Ellyn, 1975-77; ptnr. firm Pietrasik, Okolie, Chadwick & Mead, Chgo., 1978-80; UN expert cons. Ctr. on Transnat. Corps., N.Y.C., 1979—; pres. Okolie Internat. Law Chambers: Internat. Tech. Transfer & Trade Cons., Continental Africa C. of C. in Chgo., 1980—; legal counsel, dir. MARSAT Ltd., Lagos, Nigeria, 1981—; vis. prof. law U. Oxford, Eng., 1988-89. Author: Legal Aspects of International Technology Transfer, 1975; International Law Perspectives of the Developing Countries, 1978; International Space Law and Remote Sensing Technology, 1985. Editor: Space Communication and Broadcasting Jour., 1982—. Contbr. numerous articles in field to profl. jours. Bd. dirs. World Without War Council, Chgo., Nat. Coalition on Enterprise Zone, Washington; mem. Nat. Republican. Congl. Com., 1981—. Grad. fellow Hague Acad. Internat. Law, 1970; U. Calif. Sch. Law vis. fellow to EEC, 1970; research fellow Truman Library, Independence, Mo., 1971; individual scholar for policy research in law/econs. Ford Found., 1972; research grantee in space law Dutch Orgn. for Pure Sci. Research, Netherlands, 1980; cert. of recognition Nat. Rep. Congl. Com., 1982; recipient Pres. Medal Merit Rep. Presdl. Task Force, 1985. Fellow Brit. Interplanetary Soc.; mem. ABA, AAAS, Am. Soc. Internat. Law (Jessup Internat. Moot Ct. judge 1973-83), Internat. Law Assn., Internat. Inst. Space Law, Am. Acad. Polit. and Social Scis., N.Y. Acad. Scis., Internat. Bus. Council (Mid Am.), Am. Acad. Polit. Sci. Home: 433 Hill Ave Glen Ellyn IL 60137-4905 Office: Continental Africa Chamber of Commerce in Chgo 1 N La Salle St Chicago IL 60602-3902

**OLAVARRIA, FRANK J.,** lawyer; b. Gainesville, Fla., Nov. 20, 1964; s. E. Pedro Olavarria and Maura Escobio; m. Lynn M. Episcope, June 4, 1994; 1 child, Alexandra Gayle. BA, Boston Coll., 1987; JD, George Washington U., 1990. Asst. state's atty. State of Fla., Miami, 1990-95; assoc. Paul B. Episcope Ltd., Chgo., 1995-97, Williams and Montgomery, Ltd., Chgo., 1997—. Mem. Fla. Bar Assn., Ill. Bar Assn., Trial Bar Assn. Democrat. Roman Catholic. General civil litigation, Personal injury, Criminal. Office: William and Montgomery Ltd 20 N Wacker Dr Chicago IL 60606-2806

**OLD, THOMAS LEIGH,** judge; b. Youngstown, Ohio, Aug. 24, 1946; s. Robert Charles and Martha A. (Herrick) O.; m. Corky L. Stratford; 1 child, Jason T. BA in History, Mt. Union Coll., Alliance, Ohio, 1968; JD, U. Cin., 1973. Bar: Ohio 1973, U.S. Dist. Ct. (no. dist.). Pvt. practice Old & Wean, Warren, Ohio, 1973-87; judge Newton Falls (Ohio) Mcpl. Ct., 1988—; referee Warren (Ohio) Mcpl. Ct., 1977-87; law dir. City of Newton Falls, 1978-87. Trustee 1st Congl. Ch., Newton Falls, 1987-98, Trumbull County Red Cross, Warren, 1990—, Newton Falls Libr. Bd., 1994—, Am. Legion Buckeye Boys State (bd. trustees), Columbus, Ohio, 1995. Sgt. U.S. Army, 1968-70, Vietnam. Mem. Ohio State Bar Assn., Ohio Jud. Conf. (legis. com.), Ohio Mcpl. and County Judges Assn., Trumbull County Bar Assn. Democrat. Avocations: coaching high school soccer, golf. Office: Newton Falls Mcpl Ct 19 N Canal St Newton Falls OH 44444-1370

**OLDENBURG, RONALD TROY,** lawyer; b. Eldora, Iowa, June 2, 1935; s. Lorenz Frank and Bess Louise (Lewis) O.; m. Vickie Yu; children: John, Keith, Mark. BA, U. N.C., 1957; postgrad., Brunnsvik Folkhogskola, Sorvik, Sweden, 1957-58; JD, U. Miss., 1961. Bar: Miss. 1961, Hawaii 1975. Mgr. Continental Travel Svc., Chapel Hill, N.C., 1956-57, Meridian Travel Svc., Raleigh, N.C., 1961, Linmark Internat. Devel., Seoul, 1972-74; fgn. atty. Li Chun Law Office, Taipei, Taiwan, 1965-67; pvt. practice, Taipei, 1967-72, Honolulu, 1975—. Compiler: International Directory of Birth, Death, Marriage and Divorce Records, 1985; contbr. articles on immigration law to legal jours. Capt. JAGC, USAF, 1962-65. Mem. Am. Immigration Lawyers Assn. Immigration, naturalization, and customs. Office: 737 Bishop St Ste 2789 Honolulu HI 96813-3215 also: PO Box 1158 Biloxi MS 39533-1158

**OLDFIELD, E. LAWRENCE,** lawyer; b. Lake Forest, Ill., Dec. 21, 1944; s. W. Ernest and Evelyn Charlotte (Gyllenberg) O.; m. Kaaren Elaine Sabey, Aug. 24, 1974; 1 stepchild, Kimberly Jo; 1 child, Lauren Elizabeth. BA in Polit. Sci., No. Ill. U., 1969; JD, DePaul U., 1973. Bar: U.S. Dist. Ct. (no. dist.) Ill. 1973, U.S. Ct. Appeals (7th cir.) 1974, U.S. Supreme Ct. 1979, U.S. Ct. Appeals (3d cir.) 1985, U.S. Ct. Appeals (10th cir.) 1986, U.S. Ct. Appeals (8th cir.) 1990. Assoc. Ruff & Grotefeld Ltd., Chgo., 1973-77; gen. counsel livestock dept. Hartford Fire Ins. Co., Chgo., 1977-87; prin. E. Lawrence Oldfield & Assocs., Oak Brook, 1987—; mediator, arbitrator U.S. Arbitration and Mediation, 1994-97, Resolute Systems, Inc., 1997—. Trustee Village of Glen Ellyn, 1981-85; committeeman Milton Twp., DuPage County Reps., Wheaton, Ill., 1985-88; publicity chmn. Milton Twp. Reps., Wheaton, 1986-88; mem. Dist. 41 Sch. Bd., 1991-95; elder Christ Ch. of Oak Brook, 1993—; bd. govs. Oak Brook Execs. Breakfast Club, 1993—, 1st v.p., 1997-99, pres., 1999—. Mem. ABA, Ill. Bar Assn., Chgo. Bar Assn., DuPage County Bar Assn., West Suburban Bar Assn., Fed. Trial Bar Assn., Ill. Trial Lawyers' Assn., Assn. Trial Lawyers Am., Safari Club Internat., Am. Legion, VFW, Kiwanis, Moose, Masons, Shriners. Avocations: camping, fishing, hunting, golf, amateur radio. General practice, General civil litigation, General corporate. Home: 1050 Crescent Blvd Glen Ellyn IL 60137-4276 Office: 2021 Midwest Rd Ste 201 Oak Brook IL 60523-1367 also: 1 N La Salle St Ste 1721 Chicago IL 60602-3907

**OLDFIELD, RUSSELL MILLER,** lawyer; b. Salem, Ohio, Aug. 18, 1946; s. Donald W. and Virginia Alice (Harold) O.; m. Mary Lou Kubrin, May 28, 1966; children: Lindsey Marie, Grant Russell. AB, Youngstown State U., 1971; JD, Ohio No. U., 1974. Bar: Ohio 1974, Tenn. 1984. Assoc. counsel Gulf. and Western Industries, Nashville, 1979-83; v.p., gen. counsel, sec. Rogers Group Inc., Nashville, 1983—; vice chmn. coun. of counsel com. Nat. Stone Assn. Served with U.S. Army, 1966-68. Mem. ABA, Nashville Bar Assn., Am. Corp. Counsel Assn. (pres. Tenn. chpt. 1994-95), Samaritan, Inc. (chmn. 1991-92), Univ. Club. Episcopalian. General corporate, Contracts commercial, Construction. Home: 101 Sioux Ct Hendersonville TN 37075-4634 Office: Rogers Group Inc PO Box 25250 Nashville TN 37202-5250

**OLDHAM, J. THOMAS,** lawyer, educator; b. Cleve., Jan. 20, 1948; s. Vern Lawrence and Pauline Adams (Drake) O.; m. Chaille Linn Cooper, Feb. 4, 1995. BA, Denison U., 1970; JD, UCLA, 1974. Bar: Calif. 1974, D.C. 1977, Tex. 1983. Pvt. practice Beverly Hills, Calif., 1974-81; prof. law U. Houston, Beverly Hills, 1981—; vis. prof. law U. Colo., 1984, George Washington (D.C.) U., 1988-89, Cambridge (Eng.) U., 1992. Author: Divorce Separation and the Distribution of Property, 1987, Texas Homestead Law, 1991, Texas Marital Property Rights, 1996, Family Law Cases and Materials, 1998. Pres. Mus. Area Mcpl. Assn., 1986-90; bd. dirs. Main St. Theater, Houston, 1991-97. Mem. Houston Bar Assn. General corporate, Family and matrimonial. Office: U Houston Law Sch 4800 Calhoun St Houston TX 77204-0001

**O'LEARY, DANIEL VINCENT, JR.,** lawyer; b. Bklyn., May 26, 1942; s. Daniel Vincent and Mary (Maxwell) O'L.; m. Marilyn Irene Gavigan, June 1, 1968; children: Daniel, Katherine, Molly, James. AB cum laude, Georgetown U., 1963; LLB, Yale U., 1966. Bar: Ill. 1967. Assoc. Wilson & Mc Ilvaine, Chgo., 1967-75, ptnr., 1975-1987; ptnr. Peterson & Ross, Chgo., 1987-94, Schwartz & Freeman, Chgo., 1994-95; of counsel Davidson, Mandell & Menkes, Chgo., 1995—; pres., bd. dirs. Jim's Cayman Co., Ltd., 1992—, The Lumber Industry's P.G., Inc., 1997—; pres. TV and Radio Purchasing Group Inc.; asst. sec. L.M.C. Ins. Co. Bermuda, 1990—; pres. Wagering Ins. N.Am. Purchasing Group Inc., 1997—. Lt. comdr. USNR, ret. Mem. Kenilworth Sailing Club (commodore 1985-87). Roman Catholic. Avocations: fishing, scuba diving. General corporate, Insurance, Private international. Office: Davidson Mandell & Menkes 303 W Madison St Ste 1900 Chicago IL 60606-3394

**O'LEARY, ELIZABETH STERGION,** lawyer; b. Wellsboro, Pa., Mar. 24, 1949; d. Andrew P. and Elizabeth (Brooks) Stergion; m. Kevin M. O'Leary, Dec. 29, 1973; children: Megan Elizabeth, Colin Austin. BS in Recreation, U. Colo., 1971; MA, U. N. Mex., 1974; JD, Golden Gate U., 1983. Bar: Alaska 1983, U.S. Dist. Ct. Alaska 1985, U.S. Ct. Appeals (9th cir.) 1991; lic. pilot FAA; cert. tchr. Alaska. Tchr. Anchorage Sch. Dist., 1974-80; intern, law clk. Alaska State Supreme Ct., Anchorage, 1982-83; assoc. Giannini & Assoc., Anchorage, 1984-85; hearing officer BBB, Anchorage, 1985-86; pvt. practice, Anchorage, 1985-86; labor law/sch. law uniserv staff NEA-Alaska, Anchorage, 1986-91; asst. U.S. atty. U.S. Atty.'s Office, Anchorage, 1991-99; mem. bankruptcy adv. group Dept. of Justice, Washington, 1996-99; presenter in field. Author: Cooking With Kids, 1978. Health, human svcs. commr. MUN/Anchorage, 1985,86; bd. dirs. Women's Resource Ctr., Anchorage, 1984-86. Mem. Alaska Bar Assn. (mem. bankruptcy bar com. 1991—), Anchorage Bar Assn., Competitive Soccer Club (sec. 1994-96). Avocations: scuba diving, rollerblading, biking, gardening, flying. Office: US Atty's Office 222 W 7th Ave Rm 253 Anchorage AK 99513-7500

**O'LEARY, MICHAEL THOMAS,** lawyer; b. New Rochelle, N.Y., Aug. 26, 1969; s. Joan C. O'Leary. BA, SUNY, Albany, 1991; JD, Fordham U., 1994. Bar: N.J. 1994, N.Y. 1995. Assoc. McMahon Martine & Gallagher, N.Y.C., 1995—. Mem. N.Y. State Bar Assn. (trial lawyers sect., young lawyers sect.). Avocations: rollerblading, skiing, golfing. Personal injury, Insurance, State civil litigation. Office: McMahon Martine & Gallagher 90 Broad St Fl 14 New York NY 10004-2205

**O'LEARY, ROSEMARY,** law educator; b. Kansas City, Mo., Jan. 26, 1955; d. Franklin Hayes and Mary Jane (Kelly) O'L.; m. Larry Dale Schroeder; 1 child, Meghan Schroeder O'Leary. BA, U. Kans., 1978, JD, 1981, MPA, 1982; PhD, Syracuse U., 1988. Bar: Kans. 1981. Gov.'s fellow Office of Gov., Topeka, 1981-82; asst. gen. counsel kans. Corp. Com., Topeka, 1982-83; dir. policy, lawyer Kans. Dept. Health and Environment, Topeka, 1983-85; asst. prof. Ind. U., Bloomington, 1988-90; assoc. prof. Ind. U., Bloomington, 1994—; asst. prof. Syracuse (N.Y.) U., 1990-94. Author: Environmental Change: Federal Courts and the EPA, 1993, Public Administration and the Law, 2d edit., 1996; contbr. more than 50 articles to profl. jours. Bd. govs. U. Kans. Sch. Law, Lawrence, 1980-82, devel. bd., 1981-85; bd. dirs. League Women Voters Syracuse, 1986-88; vol. Habitat for Humanity, Mex., 1990; cons. NSF, 1990; panel mem. Nat. Acad. Scis., Washington, 1990-96. Recipient Outstanding Rsch. award Lily Found., 1992, Best Article award PAR, 1993, 94, Prof. of Yr. award NASPAA, 1996. Mem. ABA (editorial bd. Natural Resources and Environment jour. 1989-95, Award for Excellence 1981), ASPA (exec. com. law and environ. sects., chair environment sect., Rsch. award 1991, Best Conf. Paper award 1991), Am. Polit. Sci. Assn. (nat. chair pub. adminstrn. sect., exec. com. sect. publ.), Acad. Mgmt., Law and Soc. Assn., Assn. Pub. Policy Analysis and Mgmt. Avocations: kayaking, hiking, swimming, canoeing. Office: Ind U SPEA 410J Bloomington IN 47405

**OLECHNY, STEVEN JOHN,** lawyer; b. Hartford, Conn., Aug. 1, 1960; s. John and Felycia (Tomaszek) O. AB, Vassar Coll., 1982; JD, Cornell U., 1985. Bar: Conn. 1985, U.S. Dist. Ct. Conn. 1986, U.S. Dist. Ct. (so. and ea. dists.) N.Y. 1988, U.S. Ct. Appeals (2d cir.) 1988, U.S. Supreme Ct. 1989. Legal intern Chief Pub. Defender State Conn., Hartford, 1983; assoc. Cummings & Lockwood, Stamford, Conn., 1985-89, Hartford, 1989-93; atty. United Techs. Corp.; asst. gen. counsel Otis Elevator Co., 1993-98; dep. gen. counsel The Timberland Co.; v.p., gen. counsel Microflex Corp., 1998—. Active Instrs. of the Handicapped, Manchester, Conn., 1974-88. Recipient Scholastic Achievement award Nat. Emblem Club Am., 1981. Mem. ABA, Conn. Bar Assn. (mem. fed. practice com., fed. civil justice com.), Hartford County Bar Assn., Stamford/Darien Bar Assn., Am. Trial Lawyers Assn., Internat. Anti-Counterfeiting Assn. (bd. dirs.), Internat. Trademark Assn., Am. Corp. Counsel Assn. (v.p. Hartford chpt.), Omicron Delta Epsilon. Avocations: bicycle racing, sailing, photography, skiing, music. General corporate, Private international, Mergers and acquisitions. Home: 3135 Greensburg Cir Reno NV 89509-6889

**OLEISKY, ROBERT EDWARD,** lawyer; b. Mpls., Nov. 23, 1966; s. Allen L. and Marcia E. O. BA, U. Minn., 1989; JD, Hamline U., 1992. Bar: Minn. 1992. Atty. Oleisky & Oleisky P.A., Mpls., 1993—. Bd. dirs. Jewish Family & Children's Svcs., Mpls., 1998-99, vol., 1995-98. Mem. Minn. Assn. Criminal Defense Lawyersm Douglas Andahl Inn of Ct. Democrat. Avocations: basketball, softball, rollerblading, movies, volunteer work. Criminal, Juvenile. Office: Oleisky & Oleisky PA 250 2d Ave S #225 Minneapolis MN 55401

**OLEJKO, MITCHELL J.,** lawyer; b. Jersey City, June 15, 1951; s. Frank Edward and Eugenia Joan Olejko; m. Jill Wolcott, Aug. 5, 1988. AB, Boston Coll., 1973; JD, Washington U., St. Louis, 1977. Bar: Wash. 1977, Oreg. 1992, Calif. 1998, U.S. Dist. Ct. (we. dist.) Wash. 1977, (ea. dist.) Wash. 1978, U.S. Dist. Ct. Oreg. 1992, U.S. Ct. Appeals (9th cir.) 1980. Assoc. Davis, Wright, Todd, Riese & Jones, Seattle, 1977-82; ptnr. Davis, Wright & Jones, Seattle, 1982-92; chief legal officer, sr. v.p. Legacy Health System, Portland, Oreg., 1992-98; ptnr. Morrison & Foerster, San Francisco, 1998—. Contbr. Ambulatory Care Management, 2d edit., 1991. Mem. Am. Acad. Hosp. Attys., Wash. State Soc. Hosp. Attys. (pres. 1991-92). Health, General corporate, Non-profit and tax-exempt organizations. Office: Morrison & Foerster 425 Market St Ste 3100 San Francisco CA 94105-2482

**OLENDER, JACK HARVEY,** lawyer; b. McKeesport, Pa., Sept. 8, 1935; m. Lovell Olender. BA, U. Pitts., 1957, JD, 1960; LLM, George Washington U., 1961. Bar: D.C. 1961, U.S. Supreme Ct. 1965, Md. 1966, Pa. 1985; diplomate Am. Bd. Trial Advocates,Inner Cir. Advocates. Pvt. practice Washington, 1961-79; prin. Jack H. Olender & Assocs., P.C., Washington, 1979—. Contbr. articles to profl. jours. Active World Peace through Law, Washington. Named to Hall of Fame Nat. Assn. Black Women Attys., 1987; recipient Presdl. award Nat. Bar Assn., 1996. Fellow Am. Coll. Trial Lawyers, Internat. Acad. Trial Lawyers and Inner Cir. Advs.; mem. Am. Bd. Profl. Liability Attys. (bd. dirs.), Assn. Trial Lawyers Am., Trial Lawyers Pub. Justice (bd. dirs.), Internat. Assn. Jewish Lawyers and Jurists (bd. dirs.), Bar Assn. of D.C. (pres.). Personal injury. Office: Jack H Olender & Assocs PC 888 17th St NW Fl 4 Washington DC 20006-3939

**OLENICK, MICHAEL HASKEL,** lawyer; b. Panama Canal Zone, Feb. 5, 1952; s. Benson Y. and Evelyn (Weinstein) O.; m. Deborah Recca. BA, Lafayette Coll., 1974; JD, Nova Southeastern U., 1977. Bar: Fla. 1977. Asst. state atty. 17th and 19th Jud. Cirs., Ft. Lauderdale/Ft. Pierce, Fla., 1977-80; asst. county atty., then county atty. Martin County Bd. County Commrs., Stuart, Fla., 1980-86; ptnr. Fry & Olenick, Stuart, 1986-96; gen. counsel Fla. Dept. Edn., Tallahassee, 1996—. Bd. dirs. Easter Seals North Fla., Tallahassee, 1996—; mem. Leon County Airport Adv. Bd., Tallahassee, 1996—; elected sch. bd. mem. Martin County Sch. Bd., 1990-94; pro bono atty. Martin County Children's Svcs. Coun., Stuart, 1986-96. Home: 1143 Conservancy Dr W Tallahassee FL 32312-6745

**OLICK, ARTHUR SEYMOUR,** lawyer; b. N.Y.C., June 15, 1931; s. Jack and Anita (Babsky) O.; m. Selma Ada Kaufman, June 27, 1954; children: Robert Scott, Karen Leslie. B.A., Yale U., 1952, LL.B., J.D., 1955. Bar: N.Y. 1956. Asst. instr. polit sci. Yale U., New Haven, Conn., 1953-55; instr. polit. sci.-bus. law U. Ga., 1955-57; assoc. atty. Casey, Lane & Mittendorf, N.Y.C., 1957-62; asst. U.S. atty. So. Dist. N.Y., 1962-68; chief civil div., 1965-68; partner Otterbourg, Steindler, Houston & Rosen, N.Y.C., 1968-71, Kreindler, Relkin, Olick & Goldberg, N.Y.C., 1971-74; officer, dir. Anderson, Kill & Olick, P.C. and predecessor firms, N.Y.C., 1974—; ptnr. Anderson, Kill & Olick, P.C. and predecessor firms, Washington, 1979—, Phila., 1990—, Newark, 1991—, San Francisco, 1992—, Phila., 1994—, Phoenix, 1994—; lectr. Practicing Law Inst., N.Y.C., 1965—, Bklyn. Bar Assn., Comml. Law League, Nat. Jud. Coll.; lectr., CLE instr. Fordham Law Sch.; candidate N.Y. State Supreme Ct., 1971; counsel Tarrytown (N.Y.) Urban Renewal Agy., 1968-73, 75-77; town atty., Greenburgh, N.Y., 1974; spl. counsel, Town of New Castle, N.Y., 1979-94; village atty., Tarrytown, N.Y., 1968-73, 75-77, Dobbs Ferry, N.Y., 1975-77, North Tarrytown, N.Y.,

1978-81; dir. Westechester County (N.Y.) Legal Aid Soc., 1976-79. Pres. Hartsdale (N.Y.) Bd. Edn., 1968-72; bd. dirs. Westchester County Mcpl. Planning Fedn., 1976-78, Circle in the Sq. Theater, 1978-96; trustee Calhoun Sch., N.Y.C., 1973-80. Served with U.S. Army, 1955-57. Fellow Am. Bankruptcy Coll.; mem. ABA (bus. bankruptcy com., chmn. sect. subcom., ad hoc com. on partnerships in bankruptcy), Am. Bar Found., N.Y. State Bar Assn., Assn. of Bar of City of N.Y. (com. on profl. reposnibility), Fed. Bar Coun., Am. Arbitration Assn. (nat. panel arbitrators), Am. Law Inst., Bklyn. Soc. for Prevention Cruelty to Children (bd. dirs. 1994—), Yale Club, Merchants Club (N.Y.C.), Nat. Lawyers Club (Washington), Rockefeller Ctr. Club, Phi Beta Kappa. Bankruptcy, Federal civil litigation, Insurance. Home: 300 E 54th St New York NY 10022-5018 also: 611 Masters Way Palm Beach Gardens FL 33418-8494 Office: 1251 Avenue Of The Americas New York NY 10020-1104 also: 2000 Pennsylvania Ave NW Washington DC 20006-1812

**OLIENSIS, SHELDON,** lawyer; b. Phila., Mar. 19, 1922. AB with honors, U. Pa., 1943; LLB magna cum laude, Harvard U., 1948. Bar: N.Y. 1949. With Kaye Scholer Fierman Hays & Handler, N.Y.C., 1960—; chmn. N.Y.C. Conflicts of Interest Bd., 1990-98. Pres. Harvard Law Rev., 1948. Trustee Harvard Law Sch. Assn., 1973-77, 1st v.p., 1980-82, pres., 1982-84, trustee, N.Y.C., 1962-65, v.p., 1972-73, pres., 1978-79; nat. chmn. Harvard Law Sch. Fund, 1973-75; mem. Harvard U. overseers com. to visit law sch., 1981-87; spl. master appellate divsn. 1st dept. N.Y. State Supreme Ct., 1983-89, 91—; screening panel appellate divsn. first dept. Capital Def. Office, 1998—; bd. dirs. Legal Aid Soc., 1969-88, pres., 1973-75; vice-chmn. N.Y.C. Cultural Coun., 1968-75; bd. dirs. Cultural Coun. Found., 1968-88, pres., 1968-72, v.p., 1972-82; bd. dirs. Park Assn. N.Y.C., Inc., 1963-73, exec. com., 1967-73, pres., 1965-67; bd. dirs. Gateway Sch., N.Y.C., 1968-83, chmn. bd. trustees, 1968-70; dir. officer Wiltwyck Sch. for Boys, Inc., 1951-71; bd. dirs. East Harlem Tutorial Program, 1972-80, Fund for Modern Cts., 1979-91, N.Y. Lawyers for Pub. Interest, 1980-85, 91-94, Vols. of Legal Svc. Inc., 1984—, pres., 1984-87, trustee Lawyers' Com. for Civil Rights Under Law, 1978-91. Fellow Am. Coll. Trial Lawyers; mem. N.Y. State Bar Assn., N.Y. County Lawyers Assn., Assn. of Bar of City of N.Y. (exec. com. 1961-65, v.p. 1974-75, 86-87, pres. 1988-90, chmn. com. state legis. 1959-61, com. revision of constn. and by-laws 1965-66, com. electric power and environ. 1971-74, com. on grievances 1975-78, com. on access to legal svcs. 1982-87, com. on fee disputes and conciliation 1987-89, nominating com. 1991, mem. task force on N.Y. state constn. conv. 1994-96). Federal civil litigation, State civil litigation, Administrative and regulatory. Office: Kaye Scholer Fierman Hays & Handler 425 Park Ave New York NY 10022-3506

**OLINER, MARTIN,** lawyer, educator; b. Landsberg, Germany, 1947; m. Reva Sumner; children: Harris, Alexander, Charles. BA magna cum laude, CUNY, 1968; JD cum laude, NYU, 1971, LLM in Taxation, 1975. Bar: N.Y. 1972. Pvt. practice N.Y.C.; instr. NYU Sch. Law, 1973-75, asst. prof., 1975-77, adj. prof., 1977—. Mem. ABA (mem. various coms.), N.Y. State Bar Assn. (mem. various coms.), Assn. Bar City of N.Y. Fax: 212-319-8922. Private international, Taxation, general. Office: 375 Park Ave Fl 37 New York NY 10152-0002

**OLIPHANT, CHARLES FREDERICK, III,** lawyer; b. Chattanooga, Sept. 25, 1949; s. Charles Frederick and Jayne (Shutting) O.; m. Nancy Ann Stewart, May 15, 1976; children: James Andrew, Alexander Stewart. AB in Econs., U. N.C., 1971; JD, U. Mich., 1975. Bar: D.C. 1975. Assoc. Miller & Chevalier, Chartered, Washington, 1975-81, mem. firm, 1982—. Bd. adv. Jour. of Taxation of Employee Benefits. Mem. ABA, Bar Assn. D.C. Episcopalian. Avocations: music, reading. Pension, profit-sharing, and employee benefits, Taxation, general. Office: Miller & Chevalier Chartered 655 15th St NW Ste 900 Washington DC 20005-5799

**OLIVAS, DANIEL A.,** lawyer; b. L.A., Apr. 8, 1959; s. Michael A. and Elizabeth M. (Velasco) O.; m. Susan L. Formaker, Oct. 19, 1986; 1 child, Benjamin Formaker-Olivas. BA in English Lit., Stanford U., 1981; JD with honors, UCLA, 1984. Bar: Calif., U.S. Dist. Ct. (cen. dist.) Calif., U.S. Ct. Appeals (9th cir.), U.S. Supreme Ct. Law clk., atty. Hunt & Cochran-Bond, L.A., 1984-88; atty. Heller, Ehrman, White & McAuliffe, L.A., 1988-90; dep. atty. gen. dept. of justice antitrust div. State of Calif., L.A., 1990-91, dep. atty. gen. dept. of justice land law sect., 1991—; state apptd. bd. dirs. Western Ctr. Law and Poverty, L.A., 1988-94; mem. Hispanic employees adv. com. Calif. Dept. Justice, 1990—. Contbr. articles to Los Angeles Daily Jour. Recipeint Atty. Gen.'s award for outstanding achievement in litigation, 1994; named one of Outstanding Young Men of Am., 1984. Mem. Mex.-Am. Bar Assn., Mex.-Am. Bar Found. (bd. dirs. 1993-94), L.A. County Bar Assn. (Jud. Appointments Com 1993-97), Stanford Chicano/Latino Alumni Assn. (pres.-elect 1992-93, pres. 1993-94). Democrat. Jewish. Administrative and regulatory, General civil litigation, Environmental. Office: State of Calif 300 S Spring St Ste 5212 Los Angeles CA 90013-1230

**OLIVER, JAMES JOHN,** lawyer; b. Norristown, Pa., Feb. 18, 1944; s. James Adam and Geraldine M. (Bartlett) O.; m. Judy M. Oliver; children: Justin J., Christine P. BA, St. Mary's U., Halifax, N.S., Can., 1967; LLB, Dalhousie U., Halifax, 1970; student, Harvard U. Law Sch., 1982. Bar: Pa. 1972, U.S. Dist. Ct. Pa. 1973, U.S. Ct. Appeals (3rd cir. 1973). Atty. Nationwide Ins. Co., Phila., 1970-73, Wright, Manning, Kinkead & Oliver, Norristown, Pa., 1974-90; ptnr. Murphy & Oliver, P.C., Norristown, Pa., 1990—. Author/listed in Contemporary Poets of America, 1980, New Voices in American Poetry, 1983. Vice-chmn. East Norristown Bd. Suprs., 1974-79; pres. Am. Cancer Soc., Norristown, 1974-82; chmn. ARC, Norristown, 1975-76; v.p. Child Devel. Found., 1974—; bd. advisor Gwynedd Mercy Coll., 1984-86; dir. Montgomery County Higher Edn. Authority, 1993—. Recipient Spl. Recognition award Montgomery County Assn. for Retarded Citizens, 1993, Individual award of Excellence, 1994, Award for Excellence, Am. Cancer Soc., 1994. Mem. ABA, ATLA, Am. Arbitration Assn. (panel of arbitrators), Montgomery County Bar Assn. (mem. ins. com., med. legal com., trial com.), Pa. Bar Assn. (mem. torts com., med. legal com., trial com.), Pa. Trial Lawyers Assn., Assn. Trial Lawyers of Am., Nat. Coll. Trial Advocacy, Million Dollar Advocates Forum, Tail Twisters/Lions Club. Avocations: sailing, hiking. General civil litigation, Product liability, Personal injury. Office: Murphy & Oliver 43 E Marshall St Norristown PA 19401-4828

**OLIVER, JOHN PERCY, II,** lawyer; b. Alexander City, Ala., Dec. 3, 1942; s. Samuel William and Sarah Pugh (Coker) D.; m. Melissa Vann, June 11, 1966. AB, Birmingham (Ala.) So. Coll., 1964; JD, U. Ala., 1967. Bar: Ala. 1967, U.S. Dist. Ct. (mid. dist.) Ala. 1969, U.S. Supreme Ct. 1971, U.S. Ct. Appeals (5th cir.) 1975, U.S. Ct. Appeals (11th cir.) 1981, U.S. Dist. Ct. (mid. dist.) Ga. 1989. Assoc. Samuel W. Oliver, Atty., Dadeville, Ala., 1967; prin. John P. Oliver II, Atty., Dadeville, 1967-71; ptnr. Oliver & Sims, Attys., Dadeville, 1972-83, Oliver, Sims & Jones, Attys., Dadeville, 1984-85, Oliver & Sims, Attys., Dadeville, 1985—; dir. Bank of Dadeville. Mem. State Dem. Exec. Com., Tallapoosa County, Ala., 1986-94: judge Tallapoosa County Dist. Ct., Dadeville, 1973-76; mcpl. judge, Dadeville, 1976—; spl. probate judge Tallapoosa County Probate Ct., Dadeville, 1987-88. Mem. ABA, Ala. State Bar Assn. (bd. bar commrs. 1992-98), Ala. Trial Lawyers Assn. (exec. com. 1975-77), Tallapoosa County Bar Assn. (pres. 1990). Baptist. Avocations: sailing, skiing. General civil litigation, Real property, Workers' compensation. Office: Oliver & Sims 129 W Columbus St Dadeville AL 36853-1308

**OLIVER, SAMUEL GORDON,** lawyer; b. Vidalia, Ga., Mar. 28, 1960; s. A. Gordon and Louise (Smith) O.; m. Sue Ellen Schiferl, Aug. 25, 1984 (div. Jan. 1986); m. Olga Perminova, Nov. 1, 1999. BA, U. Va., 1982; JD, Stetson U., 1984. Bar: Ga. 1984, Fla. 1984, U.S. Dist. Ct. (so. dist.) Ga. 1984. Sole practice Brunswick, Ga., 1984-86, Darien, Ga., 1986—. Democrat. Methodist. Home: 105 Dogwood St Glennville GA 30427-8939 Office: PO Box 644 Darien GA 31305-0644

**OLIVER, SAMUEL WILLIAM, JR.,** lawyer; b. Birmingham, Ala., Apr. 18, 1935; s. Samuel William and Sarah Oliver; m. Anne Holman Marshall, Aug. 26, 1961; children: Sarah Bradley Oliver Crow, Samuel William III, Margaret Nelson Oliver Little. BS, U. Ala., 1959, JD, 1962. Bar: Ala. 1962, U.S. Dist. Ct. (no. dist.) Ala. 1963. Law clk. Supreme Ct. Ala., Montgomery, 1962-63, U.S. Dist. Ct. (no. dist.) Ala., Birmingham, 1963; assoc. Burr & Forman, Birmingham, 1964-65, ptnr., 1966—, also chmn. bus./corp. law sect., 1990-93; dir. Metalplate Galvanizing Inc., Birmingham; mem. panel arbitrators commercial Am. Arbitration Assn., Atlanta, 1981—. Chmn. bd. govs. The Relay House, Birmingham, 1985-89; mem. Leadership Birmingham, 1990; bd. dirs. Jr. Achievement Greater Birmingham, Inc., 1975—; mem. diocese coun. Episcopal Diocese Ala., Birmingham, 1981-85; chmn. bd. trustees Highlands Day Sch. Found., Inc., Birmingham, 1980-81; bd. dirs. Ala. Kidney Found., Birmingham, 1990-94. With U.S. Army, 1956-58. Mem. ABA (bus. law sect. 1965—, negotiated acquisitions com. 1990—, task force on joint venture and asset purchase agreements 1994—, corp. counsel com. 1994—, sect. internat. law and practice), Internat. Bar Assn. (corp. law sect.), Southeastern Corp. Law Inst. (planning com. 1996—), Birmingham Bar Assn., Ala. Bar Assn., Summit Club (bd. govs., founding mem.), Monday Morning Quarterback Club, Rotary Club, Venture Club. Episcopalian. Contracts commercial, General corporate, Mergers and acquisitions.

**OLIVER, SOLOMON, JR.,** judge; b. Bessemer, Ala., July 20, 1947; s. Solomon Sr. and Willie Lee (Davis) O.; married; 2 children. BA, Coll. of Wooster, 1969; JD, NYU, 1972; MA, Case Western Res. U., 1974. Bar: Ohio 1973, U.S. Dist. Ct. (no. dist.) Ohio 1977, U.S. Ct. Appeals (6th cir.) 1977, U.S. Supreme Ct. 1980. Asst. prof. dept. polit. sci. Coll. of Wooster, Ohio, 1972-75; sr. law clk. to Hon. William H. Hastie U.S. Ct. Appeals (3d cir.), Phila., 1975-76; asst. U.S. atty. U.S. Atty.'s Office, Cleve., 1976-82, chief civil divsn., 1978-82; spl. asst. U.S. atty., chief appellate divsn. Dept. Justice, Cleve., 1982, spl. asst. U.S. atty., 1982-85; prof. law Cleve. State U., 1982-94, assoc. dean faculty and adminstrn., 1991-94; lectr. in law, trial practice Case Western Res. U., Cleve., 1979-82; vis. scholar Stanford U. Coll. Law, 1987; vis. prof. Comenius U., Bratislava, Czechoslovakia, 1991, Charles U., Prague, Czechoslovakia, 1991. Chair O.K. Hoover Scholarship com. Bapt. Ch., 1987-89; trustee Coll. of Wooster, Ohio, 1991-97. Mem. ABA, Nat. Bar Assn. Office: US Dist Ct No Dist Ohio 201 Superior Ave E Ste 250 Cleveland OH 44114-1201

**OLIVER, THOMAS L., II,** lawyer; b. Jackson, Tenn., Apr. 1, 1964; s. Thomas L. and Ruth G. Oliver; m. Denise W. Oliver, May 14, 1988; children: Thomas L. III, Britney W. BS, Auburn U., 1986; JD, Samford U., 1989. Bar: Ala. 1989, U.S. Dist. Ct. Ala. 1989. Assoc. Rives & Peterson, Birmingham, Ala., 1989-94; ptnr. Rives & Peterson, Birmingham, 1995-96; shareholder Carr, Allison, Pugh, Oliver & Sisson, PC, Birmingham, 1997—. Mem. Def. Rsch. Inst. (young lawyer's exec. com. 1996-97), Ala. State Bar (chmn. workers' compensation sect. 1998-99), Ala. Def. Lawyers Assn., Auburn U. Bar Assn. (sec. 1992-93, v.p. 1994-95, pres. 1995-96), Birmingham C. of C. Republican. Roman Catholic. Avocation: golf. Workers' compensation, Professional liability, General civil litigation. Office: Carr Allison Pugh Oliver & Sisson PC 400 Vestavia Pkwy Ste 400 Birmingham AL 35216-3750

**OLIVIERI, JOSÉ ALBERTO,** lawyer; b. San Juan, P.R., Aug. 28, 1957; s. José Juan Olivieri and Carmen Rivera; m. Jeanne Nikolai Olivieri, Aug. 12, 1978; children: Elisa, Lucas, Elena. BA in Polit. Sci. cum laude, Carroll Coll., 1978; JD, Marquette U., 1981. Bar: Wis. 1981. Lawyer Michael, Best & Friedrich, Milw., 1981—; asst. prof. law Marquette U., Milw., 1986-88, adj. prof., 1988—; bd. dirs. Firstar Cmty. Investment Corp., Milw., PR Legal Def. Edn. Found., N.Y.C. Articles editor Marquette Law Rev. Chmn. bd. dirs. Milw. Found., 1998; bd. dirs., pres. United Cmty. Ctr., Milw., 1987-92; mem. U. Wis. Bd. Regents, 1998—. Recipient Pro bono award Posner Found., Milw., 1985, Cmty. Svc. award Future Milw., 1987, Vol. Fundraiser award Nat. Assn. Fundraising Execs., 1993, Leadership award Milw. Civic Alliance, 1995; named Hispanic Man of Yr., United Migrant Opportunity Svcs., Milw., 1998. Mem. ABA, Wis. Hispanic Lawyers Assn. (pres. 1984), Milw. Bar Assn. Avocations: reading, sports. Labor, Immigration, naturalization, and customs, Education and schools. Office: Michael Best & Friedrich 100 E Wisconsin Ave Ste 3300 Milwaukee WI 53202-4108

**OLLEY, MICHAEL JOSEPH,** lawyer; b. Phila., Feb. 7, 1963; s. Francis Robert Olley and Patricia Regina Dougherty; m. Kristine Erin Kelly, Apr. 25, 1998. BS magna cum laude, St. Joseph's U., 1985; JD, Villanova U., 1989. Bar: Pa. 1989, N.J. 1989, U.S. Dist. Ct. (ea. dist.) Pa. 1989, U.S. Dist. Ct. N.J. 1990, U.S. Ct. Appeals (3d cir.) 1992. Rsch. assoc. Chase Econometrics, Bala Cynwyd, Pa., 1985-86; assoc. Marks, Kent & O'Neill, Phila., 1989-92, White and Williams, Phila., 1992-97; sr. trial atty. Coffey & Kaye, Bala Cynwyd, Pa., 1997—. Fellow Acad. of Advocacy; mem. Pa. Bar Assn., St. Joseph's U. Law Alumni Assn. (mem. exec. bd. 1995—), Million Dollar Advocates Forum. Roman Catholic. Avocations: travel, theater, golf. General civil litigation, Personal injury, Product liability. Home: 525 Rock Glen Dr Wynnewood PA 19096-2620 Office: Coffey & Kaye 2 Bala Plz Ste 718 Bala Cynwyd PA 19004-1501

**OLLINGER, GEORGE EDWARD, III,** lawyer, commodities trader; b. Shuri City, Okinawa, Sept. 5, 1951; came to U.S., 1968; s. George Edward and Yoshiko Marie (Tonaki) O.; m. Bonnie Lee Noblet, Aug. 21, 1977; children: Joseph Bryan, Caitlin Marie. BA, UCLA, 1973; JD, U. Detroit, 1977. Bar: Fla. 1977, U.S. Dist. Ct. (mid. dist.) Fla. 1985, U.S. dist. Ct. (so. dist.) Fla. 1980, U.S. Ct. Appeals (5th and 11th cirs.), U.S. Tax. Ct. 1981, U.S. Supreme Ct. File clk. Dickinson, Wright et al, West Bloomfield, Mich., 1976-77; assoc. English, McCaughn & O'Bryan, Ft. Lauderdale, Fla., 1977-78; ptnr. Olds & Titone, P.A., Ft. Lauderdale, 1978; owner Ollinger Law Firm, Melbourne, Ft. Lauderdale, 1978—; legal rschr. Pima County Legal Aid, Tucson, 1995. Author: Ted Peck, 1989. Recipient Pro bono awrd Brevard County Legal Aid, 1996, others; Regents scholar UCLA, 1971-73. Mem. Fla. Bar. Christian. Avocations: golf, genetics, information technology, anthropology, horse breeding. Personal injury, Securities, Criminal. Office: Ollinger Law Firm 100 Rialto Pl Ste 700 Melbourne FL 32901-3072

**OLOFSSON, DANIEL JOEL,** lawyer; b. Chgo., Sept. 29, 1954; s. Joel Gustav and Patricia Marie (Casey) O.; m. Patricia Lynn Severson, Feb. 13, 1987; children: Nicole Lynn, Gustave Daniel, Jonathon Leonard. AA, Thornton Community Coll., 1974; BA, U. Ill., 1976; JD with honors, Chgo.-Kent Coll. Law, Ill. Inst. Tech., 1979. Bar: Ill. 1979, U.S. Dist. Ct. (no. dist.) Ill. 1979, U.S. Ct. Appeals (7th cir.) 1979, U.S. Tax Ct. 1980. Assoc. Jerry L. Lambert, Flossmoor, Ill., 1979-80, John P. Block, Chgo., 1980-82; sole practice, Dolton, Ill., 1982—. Elected trustee Village of Dolton, 1985. James scholar U. Ill., Champaign, 1976. Mem. Chgo. Bar Assn., South Suburban Bar Assn., Ill. State Bar Assn., ABA, Phi Theta Kappa. Democrat. Roman Catholic. Lodges: Rotary, Elks. General civil litigation, Criminal, Family and matrimonial. Home: 15412 Clyde Ave South Holland IL 60473-1913

**OLSCHWANG, ALAN PAUL,** lawyer; b. Chgo., Jan. 30, 1942; s. Morton James and Ida (Ginsberg) O.; m. Barbara Claire Miller, Aug. 22, 1965; children: Elliot, Deborah, Jeffrey. BS, U. Ill., 1963, JD, 1966. Bar: Ill. 1966, N.Y. 1984, Calif. 1992. Law clk. Ill. Supreme Ct., Bloomington, 1966-67; assoc. Sidley & Austin and predecessor firms, Chgo., 1967-73; with Montgomery Ward & Co. Inc., Chgo., 1973-81, assoc. gen. counsel, asst. sec., 1979-81; ptnr. Seki, Jarvis & Lynch, Chgo., 1981-84, dir., mem. exec. com.; exec. v.p., gen. counsel, sec. Mitsubishi Electronics Am. Inc., N.Y.C., 1983-91, Cypress, Calif., 1991—; dir. Mitsubishi Electric Info. Tech. Ctr. Am., Inc. Mem. ABA, Am. Corp. Counsel Assn., Calif. Bar Assn., Ill. Bar Assn., Chgo. Bar Assn., N.Y. State Bar Assn., Bar Assn. of City of N.Y., Am. Arbitration Assn. (panel arbitrators). Contracts commercial, General corporate, Private international. Office: Mitsubishi Electronics Am Inc 5665 Plaza Dr Cypress CA 90630-5023

**OLSEN, ALFRED JON,** lawyer; b. Phoenix, Oct. 5, 1940; s. William Hans and Vera (Bearden) O.; m. Susan K. Smith, Apr. 15, 1979. B.A. in History, U. Ariz., 1962; MS in Acctg., Ariz. State U., 1964; J.D., Northwestern U., 1966. Bar: Ariz. 1966, Ill. 1966, U.S. Tax Ct. 1970, U.S. Supreme Ct. 1970; C.P.A., Ariz., Ill. cert. tax specialist. Acct. Arthur Young & Co., C.P.A.s, Chgo., 1966-68; dir. firm Ehmann, Olsen & Lane (P.C.), Phoenix, 1969-76; dir. Streich, Lang, Weeks & Cardon (P.C.), Phoenix, 1977-78; v.p. Olsen-Smith, Ltd., Phoenix, 1978—; chmn. tax adv. commn. Bd. Legal Specialization, 1990-92. Bd. editors: Jour. Agrl. Law and Taxation, 1978-82, Practical Real Estate Lawyer, 1983-95. Mem. Phoenix adv. bd. Salvation Army., 1973-81. Fellow Am. Coll. Trust and Estate Counsel, Am. Coll. Tax Counsel; mem. AICPA, Ariz. Soc. CPAs, State Bar Ariz. (chmn. tax sect. 1977-78), ABA (chmn. com. on agr., sect. taxation 1976-78, chmn. CLE com. sect. taxation 1982-84), Am. Law Inst. (chmn. tax planning for agr. 1971-82), Cen. Ariz. Estate Planning Coun. (pres. 1972-73), Nat. Cattlemen's Assn. (tax com. 1979-88), Internat. Acad. Estate and Trust Law (exec. coun. 1994—), Sigma Nu Internat. (pres. 1986-88), Phi Beta Kappa, Beta Gamma Sigma, Phi Kappa Phi. Estate planning, Probate, Corporate taxation. Office: 3300 Virginia Financial Pla 301 E Virginia Ave Ste 3300 Phoenix AZ 85004-1218

**OLSEN, HANS PETER,** lawyer; b. Detroit, May 21, 1940; s. Hans Peter and Paula M. (Olsen) O.; m. Elizabeth Ann Gayton, Sept. 14, 1968; children: Hans Peter, Heidi Susanne, Stephanie Elizabeth. BA, Mich. State U., 1962; JD, Georgetown U., 1965; LLM, NYU, 1966. Bar: Mich. 1967, Pa. 1969, R.I. 1974. Law clk. firm Monaghan, McCrone, Campbell & Crawmer, Detroit, 1964; law clk. U.S. Ct. of Claims, Fed. Appellate Ct., Washington, 1966-68; assoc. firm Pepper, Hamilton & Scheetz, Phila., 1968-72; ptnr. firm Hinckley, Allen, & Snyder, Providence and Boston, 1972—; adv. planning com. U. R.I. Fed. Taxation Inst.; continuing legal edn. adv. bd., tax symposium adv. bd. Bryant Coll.; mem. Gov.'s State Task Force, R.I. Pub. Expenditure Coun.; cons. Bur. Nat. Affairs; liaison Bar Assn. and North Atlantic region IRS; tax adminstrs. adv. com. R.I.; lectr. tax insts. and other profl. groups N.Y., L.A., Phila., Boston, R.I.; advisor R.I. Econ. Policy com. Contbr. numerous articles on taxation to legal jours. Fellow Am. Bar Found.; mem. ABA (sect. taxation, exempt orgns. com., subcom. healthcare, corp.-shareholders rels. com., partnerships com.), R.I. Bar Assn. (sect. taxation, sec.-treas. 1977-80, liaison with CPAs, specialization com., mem. various coms.), Providence C. of C., R.I. C. of C. (chmn. com. on bus. taxes and public spending, mem., past chmn. legis. action council), Mich. State Bar, Pa. State Bar. Corporate taxation, Personal income taxation, State and local taxation. Home: 274 Olney St Providence RI 02906-2305 Office: 1500 Fleet Ctr Providence RI 02903

**OLSEN, KENNETH ALLEN,** lawyer; b. Jersey City, June 6, 1953; s. George Anton and Dorothy (Mitschell) O.; m. Andrea M. Olsen. BA in Polit. Sci. and Pre-Law magna cum laude, Rutgers U., 1975; JD, Temple U., 1978. Bar: N.J. 1978, Pa. 1979; U.S. Dist. Ct. N.J. 1978, U.S. Dist. Ct. (mid. dist.) Pa. 1980, U.S. Dist. Ct. (ea. dist.) Pa. 1988; U.S. Ct. Appeals (3d cir.) 1979, U.S. Ct. Appeals (11th cir.) 1981, U.S. Ct. Appeals (D.C. cir.) 1982, U.S. Supreme Ct. 1983. Sole practice; atty. Chgo. Title Ins. Co., Chelsea Title and Guaranty Co., Commonwealth Land Title Co., N.J. Realty Title Ins. Co. Named to Presdl. Classroom Young Ams. Mem. ABA (various sects. and coms.), N.J. State Bar Assn., Pa. Bar Assn., Morris County Bar Assn., Am. Acad. Polit. Sci., Am. Acad. Polit. and Social Sci., Assn. Transp. Practitioners, Temple U. Alumni Assn., Rutgers U. Alumni Assn., Newark Coll. Alumni Assn., Traffic Club Newark Inc., Transp. Lawyers Assn., Phi Beta Kappa, Pi Sigma Alpha. Lutheran. Avocations: tennis, golf, bowling. General practice, Transportation, General civil litigation.

**OLSEN, M. KENT,** lawyer, educator; b. Denver, Mar. 10, 1948; s. Marvin and F. Winona (Wilker) O.; children: Kristofor Anders, Alexander Lee, Nikolaus Alrik, Amanda Elizabeth. BS, Colo. State U., 1970; JD, U. Denver, 1975. Bar: Colo., U.S. Dist. Ct. Colo. 1982, U.S. Tax Ct. Law clk. Denver Probate Ct., 1973-75; assoc. ptnr. Johnson & McLachlan, Lamar, Colo., 1975-80; assoc. Buchanan, Thomas and Johnson, Lakewood, Colo., 1981-82, William E. Myrick, P.C., Denver, 1982-83; referee Denver Probate Ct., Denver, 1983-89; ptnr. Haines & Olsen, P.C., Denver, 1989-95; pvt. practice Denver, 1995—; adv. bd. Denver Paralegal Inst., 1993—, Elder Law Inst., 1994—. Mem. Gov.'s Commn. on Life and the Law, Denver, 1991—; bd. dirs. Adult Care Mgmt., Inc., Denver, 1985-95; bd. dirs. Arc of Denver, Inc., 1990—, pres., 1995-97; bd. dirs. Colo. Guardianship Alliance, Denver, 1990-91; bd. dirs., pres. Colo. Fund for People with Disabilities, 1994—. Recipient Outstanding Vol. Svc. award Adult Care Mgmt., 1990, Outstanding Svc. award The Arc of Denver, 1991, Vol. Svc. award Colo. Gerontol. Soc., 1997, Pres.'s award Arc of Denver, 1998. Mem. ABA, Colo. Bar Assn. (chair probate sect.), Am. Assn. Home for Aging, Nat. Acad. Elder Law Attys., Denver Bar Assn. Episcopalian. Avocations: running, skiing, racquetball, art, hiking. Probate, Estate planning, Estate taxation. Home: 3030 S Roslyn St Denver CO 80231-4153 Office: 650 S Cherry St Ste 1250 Denver CO 80246-3805

**OLSEN, MARY ANN,** lawyer; b. Hoboken, N.J., Aug. 5, 1948; d. Charles Joseph and Margaret Nora (Power) O.; 1 child, Matthew Ellisen. AAS, Purdue U., 1973; BS, St. Peter's Coll., Jersey City, 1973; JD, Rutgers U., 1989. Bar: N.J. 1990, N.Y. 1991. Pvt. practice Bayonne, N.J., 1991—; cons. atty. Hudson County Protective Svc., West New York, N.J., 1993-96. Chmn. money mgmt. com. Bayonne Office on Aging, 1996-97; trustee Jersey City Cmty. Charter Sch.; bd. dirs. St. Joseph's Home for the Blind, Guardianship Assn. N.J., Inc. Mem. N.J. Bar Assn., Hudson County Bar Assn., Hudson Inn of Ct. Family and matrimonial, Probate, Bankruptcy. Office: 8 E 35th St Bayonne NJ 07002-3925

**OLSEN, ROBERT ERIC,** lawyer, public interest litigator; b. Easton, Pa., July 10, 1944; s. Robert Thorvald and Frances (Wallburg) O.; m. Barbara Edith Mackay, July 25, 1992; 1 child, Alexander. AB, Harvard Coll., 1966; MA, U. Pa., 1967; JD, U. Denver, 1975. Bar: Md., Colo. Corp. planner Indsl. Valley Bank, Phila., 1968-73; sr. v.p. First Am. Indsl. Bank and First Am. Leasing Co., Denver, 1973-75; assoc. Calkins, Kramer, Grimshaw & Harring, Denver, 1975-79, Brenman, Epstein, Zerobnick, Raskin & Friedlob, Denver, 1979-80; ptnr. Olsen & Guardi, Denver, 1980-90; fgn. svc. officer U.S. Dept. of State, Washington, 1992-94; of counsel Goldstein & Baron, College Park, Md., 1995-97; atty. OlsenLaw.com., McLean, Va., 1997—; on-air announcer, prodr., critic Sta. KVOD-FM, Denver, 1989-91. Democrat. Avocations: opera, photography, political policy development. Fax: 703-448-8320. E-mail: RobertùEùOlsen@msn.com. Securities, Mergers and acquisitions, Transportation. Home: 922 Ridge Dr Mc Lean VA 22101-1632 Office: OlsenLaw.com 922 Ridge Dr Mc Lean VA 22101-1632

**OLSEN, STEPHEN RAYMOND,** lawyer; b. Livermore, Calif., July 20, 1943; s. Alrae and Wilma F. (Brown) O.; m. Lynn Price, Aug. 25, 1962. AA, Santa Rosa (Calif.) Jr. Coll., 1971; JD, Empire Coll., 1985. Bar: Calif. 1986. Chief assessment stds. County of Sonoma, Santa Rosa, 1978-84, assessor, 1984-86; pvt. practice Santa Rosa, 1986—. Bd. dirs. Bennett Ridge Mut. Water Co., Santa Rosa, 1984-89. Radioman 1/C USN, 1966-70. Mem. Calif. Bar Assn., Sonoma County Bar Assn. (bd. dirs. 1993-98, com. mem. intellectual property sect. 1997—), Santa Rosa C. of C. (edn. com.), Calif. Orgn. of Retired Assessors, Rotary (bd. dirs. 1996—). Avocations: carriage driving (pres. Carriage Assn. Am.). Office: 1301 Farmers Ln Ste 201 Santa Rosa CA 95405-6744

**OLSON, CARL ERIC,** lawyer; b. Center Moriches, N.Y., May 19, 1914; s. August William and Sophie (Maiwald) O.; m. Ila Dudley Yeatts, May 31, 1945; children: Carl Eric, William Yeatts, Nancy Dudley. AB, Union Coll., 1936; JD, Yale, 1940. Bar: Conn. 1941, N.Y. 1947. Assoc. Clark, Hall & Peck, New Haven, 1940-41; assoc. Reid & Priest, N.Y.C., 1946-56, ptnr. 1956-80; pvt. practice, Palm Beach Gardens, Fla., 1981—. Maj. U.S. Army, 1941-45. Mem. Yale Club of the Palm Beaches, PGA Nat. Club. Republican. Congregationalist. General corporate, Private international. Home and Office: 6 Surrey Rd Palm Beach Gardens FL 33418-7088

**OLSON, DENNIS OLIVER,** lawyer; b. Seminole, Tex., Oct. 19, 1947; s. Edwin and Beulah Matilda (Strang) O.; m. leonee Lynn Claud, Jan. 30, 1971; children: James Edwin, Stacy Rae. BA in English, U. Tex., 1969; JD, Tex. Tech U., 1974. Bar: Tex. 1974, U.S. Ct. Mil. Appeals 1974, U.S. Dist. Ct. (no. dist.) Tex. 1978, U.S. Dist. Ct. (we. dist.) Tex. 1978, U.S. Ct. Appeals (5th cir.) 1984, U.S. Supreme Ct. 1985. Commd. USMC, 1969, advanced through grades to capt., 1973, infantry officer various locations including Vietnam, 1969-74; judge advocate USMC, various locations, 1974-78; resigned USMC, 1978; assoc. Carr, Evans, Fouts & Hunt, and predecessor, Lubbock, Tex., 1978-81, ptnr., 1981-85; sole practice Dallas, 1985-88; shareholder, co-chmn. bankruptcy sect. Godwin & Carlton, P.C., Dallas, 1989-94; ptnr. Olson Gibbons Wilbur Nicoud Birne & Gueck, LLP & predecessor, Dallas, 1994—. Bd. dirs. presbyn. Ctr. Doctor's Clinic, Lubbock, 1983-85, United Campus Ministry, Tex. Tech U., Lubbock, 1984-85; elder Canyon Creek Presbyn. Ch., Richardson, Tex.; treas. bd. dirs. Lubbock chpt. ARC, 1975-77; vol. Lubbock United Way, 1978-80. Decorated Bronze Star; named Outstanding Young Man of Am., 1983. Fellow Tex. Bar

Found. (sustaining life); mem. Dallas Bar Assn., Lubbock County Bar Assn. (bd. dirs. 1983-85), Tex. Young Lawyers Assn. (bd. dirs. 1981-83), Judge Advocates Assn. (bd. dirs. 1976-78), Lubbock C. of C. (grad. Leadership Lubbock program 1981), Phi Delta Phi. Bankruptcy, State civil litigation, Banking. Home: 313 Forest Grove Dr Richardson TX 75080-1937

**OLSON, EDWARD M.,** lawyer; b. Detroit, Jan. 30, 1960; s. Kenneth T. and Marjorie O.; m. Margaret L. Olson, July 21, 1984; children: Kathryn, Emily. BA in Polit. Sci., Mich. State U., E. Lansing, 1982; JD, Wayne State U. Law Sch., Detroit, 1985. In house counsel Olde Discount Corp., Detroit, 1985-87, McDonnel Douglas Capital Corp., Troy, Mich., 1987-89; assoc. Cummings, McClorey, Davis & Acho PC, Livonia, Mich., 1989-93, Johnson, Rosati, Galica & Shifman, PC, Farmington Hills, Mich., 1993-96; ptnr. Velardo, Sugamel & Olson PC, Troy, Mich., 1996—. Mem. Mich. Bar, Oakland County Bar Assn., Dist. Ct. Com. General civil litigation, General corporate, Real property. Office: Velardo Sugameli & Olson PC 3150 Livernois Rd Ste 103 Troy MI 48083-5000

**OLSON, JAMES MARK,** lawyer, writer; b. Detroit, Feb. 26, 1945; s. Kenneth John and Mary Helen (Eoff) O.; m. Sally ven Vleck Olson, Sept. 7, 1968 (div. Jan. 21, 1983); children: Hallie Jane, Kathryn Teckla, Jessica Mary; m. Susan J. Grove, May 5, 1989 (div. Jan. 15, 1993); 1 child, James Mark Olson, Jr. BA in Bus., Mich. State U., East Lansing, 1968; JD, Detroit Coll. Law, 1971; LLM in Environ. Law, U. Mich., Ann Arbor, 1977. Bar: Mich. 1971, U.S. Dist. Ct. (we. dist.) Mich. 1973, U.S. Ct. Appeals 1997, Colo. 1987. Law clk. to justice Thomas Brennan Mich. Supreme Ct., Lansing, 1971-72; ptnr. Olson & Dettmer, Traverse City, Mich., 1972-77; pvt. practice, 1977-87; ptnr. Rosi, Olson & Levine P.C., Traverse City, Mich., 1987-92; sr. ptnr. Olson & Noonan, Traverse City, Mich., 1992—; gen. counsel Mich. Land Use Inst. Author: Reindeer and the Easter Bunny, 1981, Michigan Environmental Law, 1981, The Mourd People, 1985; co-author: Cross Border Litigation: Environmental Rights in the Great Lakes Ecosystem, 1986; editor: Christian Ecology Quarterly, 1988-90. Co-founder Environmental Law Com. State Bar of Mich., 1978-79; co-chair Mich. Environmental Law Conf., State Bar of Mich., 1979; coun. mem. Environmental Law Sect.State Bar of Mich., 1980-86; mem. Mich. State Bar Found., Lansing, 1984—. Named Rsch. fellow, 1974-77, Cook fellow, 1974-77 U. Mich. Law Sch.; recipient Award Mich. Coun. of Arts. Mem. State Bar Mich. Avocations: writing, poetry, canoeing, fishing, skiing, travel. Office: Olson & Noonan 420 E Front St Traverse City MI 49686-2614

**OLSON, JAMES WARREN,** lawyer; b. Vermillion, S.D., July 20, 1949; s. Louis Burdette and Mary Cleola (Boden) O.; m. Shirley Mae Dappen, June 21, 1975; children: Neleigh Anne, Ethan Ellsworth. BA, U. S.D., 1971, JD, 1977. Bar: S.D. 1977, Nebr. 1983, U.S. Dist. Ct. S.D. 1977, U.S. Dist. Ct. Nebr. 1987, U.S. Ct. Appeals (8th cir.) 1984, U.S. Supreme Ct. 1984. Assoc. Kirby Law Office, Mitchell, S.D., 1977-78, Bubak Law Office, Tyndall, S.D., 1978; sole practice Armour, S.D., 1978-88; adminstrv law judge City of Salt Lake, 1988—, hearing office chief, 1990-92; adminstrv. law judge City of Spokane, Wash., 1992—; adminstrv. law judge, Spokane, 1992—; states atty. Douglas County, S.D., 1981-84, city atty. Armour S.D., 1979-88; dep. states atty., Charles Mix County, S.D., 1980-84; gen. counsel, Yankton Sioux Tribe, Marty, S.D., 1985-86, various fin. insts., S.D., 1979-84. Active United Ch. of Christ Fin. Com., Armour. Capt. USAR. Mem. ABA (Nat. Conf. Adminstrv. Law Judges), S.D. State Bar Assn., Nebr. State Bar Assn., Assn. Trial Lawyers Am., S.D. Trial Lawyers Assn., S.D. Mcpl. Attys. Assn., Assn. Adminstrv. Law Judges, Armour C. of C., Jaycees, Lions. Republican. Avocations: skiing, racquetball, reading, horseback riding. General civil litigation, General practice, Personal injury. Home: 17207 N Mount Spokane Park Dr Mead WA 99021-9768 Office: 316 W Boone Ave Spokane WA 99201-2354

**OLSON, JOHN KARL,** lawyer; b. Springfield, Mass., Aug. 14, 1949; s. Harold Gunnar and Louise Theodora (Shukis) O.; m. Ann Catherine Sullivan, June 16, 1973; children: Elizabeth Ann, Katherine Louise. AB, Harvard Coll., 1971; JD, Boston Coll., 1975. Bar: Fla. 1975, U.S. Dist. Ct. (mid. and so. dists.) Fla. 1976, U.S. Ct. Appeals (5th cir.) 1979, U.S. Supreme Ct. 1979; U.S. Ct. Appeals (11th cir.) 1981. From assoc. to ptnr. Carlton, Fields, Ward et al., Tampa, Fla., 1975-86; exec. v.p., gen. counsel, dir. Jet Fla., Inc., Miami, 1986-88; ptnr. Stearns Weaver Miller Weissler Alhadeff & Sitterson P.A., Tampa, 1988—. Author: Creditors and Debtors Rights in Florida, 1979, 89, Collier Bankruptcy Practice Guide, 1986. Trustee Tampa Mus. Art, 1992-98. Fellow U. Tampa, 1986—. Mem. ABA (vice-chmn. backruptcy com. 1984-86), Fla. Bar (chmn. bus. law sect. 1988-89), Harvard Club (pres. 1982-84), Turnaround Mgmt. Assn. (Ctrl. Fla. chpt. pres. 1995-96). Bankruptcy, Contracts commercial, General civil litigation. Home: 2632 W Prospect Rd Tampa FL 33629-5358 Office: Sun Trust Fin Ctr 401 E Jackson St Tampa FL 33602-5233

**OLSON, JOHN OLMSTEAD,** lawyer; b. Whitewater, Wis., July 24, 1936; s. Harold Martinus Olson and Esther Louisa Olmstead; m. Marjorie Reed, June 22, 1956 (div. Jan. 1994); children: Sheree, John, Dwight, Lawrence. BBA, U. Wis., 1961, LLB, 1963. Bar: Wis. 1963. Dist. atty. Taylor County, Medford, Wis., 1963-69; U.S. atty. Western Dist. Wis., Madison, 1969-74; ptnr. Braden & Olson, Lake Geneva, Wis., 1974—; instr. U. Wis. Law Sch., Madison, 1975-80. With USAF, 1954-58. Mem. Walworth County Bar Assn. (pres. 1976), Lions. Republican. Mem. United Ch. of Christ. Avocation: wood working. General civil litigation, Criminal, Estate planning. Office: 716 Wisconsin St Lake Geneva WI 53147-1826

**OLSON, KEVIN LORY,** lawyer; b. Berkeley, Calif., Dec. 2, 1956; s. Lorimer Reuben and Norma Carolyn Olson; m. Linda Sue Gladish, June 16, 1978; children: Lisa Marie, Kimberly Ann, Karen Amanda. BS in Math., Ariz. State U., 1977; JD, Yale U., 1980. Bar: Ariz. 1980. Assoc. Lewis and Roca, Phoenix, 1980-85, ptnr., 1985-97; ptnr. Steptoe & Johnson LLP, Phoenix, 1997—. Vice pres., dir. East Valley Partnership, Mesa, Ariz., 1990—. Mem. ABA, State Bar of Ariz., Maricopa County Bar Assn., Tempe C. of C. (pres. 1995-96), Greater Phoenix C. of C. (chmn. transp. com. 1998). Contracts commercial, General corporate, Securities. Office: 40 N Central Ave Ste 2400 Phoenix AZ 85004-4453

**OLSON, KRISTINE,** prosecutor; b. N.Y.C., Aug. 9, 1947; d. Harold John and Arline (Schneider) Olson; children: Karin, Tyler. B.A., Wellesley Coll., 1969, J.D., Yale U., 1972. Bar: Oreg. 1973, U.S. Dist. Ct. Oreg. 1974, U.S. Ct. Appeals (9th cir.) 1975. Asst. U.S. atty. Dept. Justice, Portland, Oreg., 1974-84; vice chair State Indigent Def. Bd., Salem, Oreg., 1985-87; assoc. dean, prof. law Lewis & Clark Coll., 1989-94; U.S. atty. Dept. Justice, Dist. Oreg., Portland, 1994—; adj. prof. Lewis and Clark Coll. Northwestern Sch. Law, 1975-89, U. Oreg. Law Ctr., 1984—; mem. 9th Cir. Task Force on Tribal Cts. Contbr. articles to profl. jours. Bd. dirs., chmn. bd. Oreg. Council on Crime and Delinquency, 1981-87; bd. dirs. State Bd. Police Standards and Tng., 1976-80; chmn. Community Corrections Adv. Bd. Multnomah County, Portland, 1978-80; chmn. women's rights project ACLU Oreg., 1977; mem. World Affairs Council Oreg.; commr., mem. exec. com. Met. Human Relations Commn., mayor's appointee, 1986—. Root Tilden fellow, 1969. Mem. Soc. Am. Archaeology Native Am. Rights Fund, Earthwatch, 1000 Friends of Oreg., Archaeol. Conservancy, Nature Conservancy. Democrat. Clubs: Early Keyboard Soc., City Club of Portland (bd. govs. 1984—, pres.-elect 1995), Multnomah Athletic (Portland). Home: 900 SW 83rd Ave Portland OR 97225-6308 Office: US Dept Justice Mark O Hatfield U S Courthouse 1000 SW 3rd Ave Ste 600 Portland OR 97204-2936*

**OLSON, ROBERT WYRICK,** lawyer; b. Madison, Wis., Dec. 19, 1945; s. John Arthur and Mary Katherine (Wyrick) O.; m. Carol Jean Duane, June 12, 1971; children: John Hagan, Mary Catherine Duane. BA, Williams Coll., 1967; JD, U. Va., 1970. Assoc. Cravath, Swaine & Moore, N.Y.C., 1970-79; asst. gen. counsel Penn Cen. Corp., Cin., 1979-80, assoc. gen. counsel, 1980-82, v.p., dep. gen. counsel, 1982-87; sr. v.p., gen. counsel, sec. Am. Premier Underwriters, Inc. (formerly Penn Cen. Corp.), Cin., 1987-95, Chiquita Brands Internat., Inc., Cin., 1995—. Mem. ABA. General corporate, Securities, Mergers and acquisitions. Office: Chiquita Brands Internat 250 E 5th St Ste 25 Cincinnati OH 45202-4119

**OLSON, WILLIAM JEFFREY,** lawyer; b. Paterson, N.J., Oct. 23, 1949; s. Walter Justus and Viola Patricia (Trautvetter) O.; m. Janet Elaine Bollen, May 22, 1976; children: Robert J., Joanne C. AB, Brown U., 1971; JD, U. Richmond, 1976. Bar: Va. 1976, D.C. 1976, U.S. Ct. Claims 1976, U.S. Ct. Appeals (4th, 9th and D.C. cirs.) 1976, U.S. Supreme Ct. 1982. Assoc. Jackson & Campbell, Washington, 1976-79; ptnr. Gilman, Olson & Pangia, Washington, 1980-92; prin. William J. Olson PC, McLean, Va. and Washington, 1992—; sec., treas. bd. dirs. Victims Assistance Legal Orgn., Virginia Beach, Va., 1979—; presdl. transition team leader Legal Svcs. Corp., Washington, 1980; chmn. and bd. dirs. nat. Legal Svcs. Corp., 1981-82; mem. Pres.'s Export Coun. Subcom. on Export Adminstrn., Washington, 1982-84; spl. counsel bd. govs. U.S. Postal Svc., Washington, 1984-86. Author: Tuition Tax Credits and Alternatives, 1978; co-author: Debating National Health Policy, 1977, Presidential Usurpation, The Law of Executive Orders, 1999. Trustee Davis Meml. Goodwill Industries, Washington, 1980-86, 88-93; chmn. Fairfax County Rep. Com., Fairfax, Va., 1980-82; mem. Rep. State Ctrl. Com., Richmond, Va., 1982-86. Mem. Va. Bar Assn., Assn. Trial Lawyers Am., Va. Trial Lawyers Assn., Christian Legal Soc. Republican. Baptist. Avocation: gardening. Administrative and regulatory, Non-profit and tax-exempt organizations, Government contracts and claims. Office: 8180 Greensboro Dr Ste 1070 Mc Lean VA 22102-3823

**OLVER, MICHAEL LYNN,** lawyer; b. Seattle, June 22, 1950; s. Manley Deforest and Geraldine (Robinson) O.; m. Wendy Kay, July 6, 1974; children: Erin, Christina. BA, U. Wash., 1972; JD, Calif. Western Sch. of Law, 1976. Assoc. Robbins, Merrick & Kraft, Seattle, 1976-77; lawyer, sole practitioner Michael L. Olver, Seattle, 1977-80; ptnr., pres. Merrick & Olver, P.S., Seattle, 1980—; bd. dirs. Found. for Handicapped, Seattle, 1988-93; commr. pro tem Ex part Dept. King County Superior Ct., Seattle, 1992—. Author: Bascomb's Rogue, 1994; editor Calif. Western Internat. Law Jour., 1975-76, contbr. articles to profl. jours. Chmn. Ann. Cath. Appeal, Assumption Parish, Seattle, 1989-90. Mem. Nat. Acad. Elder Law Attys. (dir. Wash. chpt. 1994—), Wash. State Trial Lawyers Assn. Probate, Estate planning, Personal injury. Office: Merrick & Olver PS 9222 Lake City Way NE Seattle WA 98115-3268

**O'MALLEY, CARLON MARTIN,** judge; b. Phila., Sept. 7, 1929; s. Carlon Martin and Lucy (Bol) O'M.; m. Mary Catherine Lyons, Aug. 17, 1957; children: Carlon Martin III, Kathleen B. O'Malley Aikman, Harry Tighe, John Todd, Cara M. BA, Pa. State U., 1951; LLB, Temple U., 1954. Bar: Pa. 1955, Fla. 1973, U.S. Supreme Ct. 1973. Practiced law, 1957-61; asst. U.S. atty. for Middle Dist. Pa., Dept. Justice, 1961-69, U.S. atty., 1979-82; ptnr. O'Malley & Teets, 1970-72, O'Malley, Jordan & Mullaney (and predecessor firms), 1976-79; pvt. practice Pa. and Fla., 1972-79, 82-87; judge Ct. Common Pleas of Lackawanna County (45th Judicial Dist.), 1987-97, sr. judge, 1998—; dir. pub. safety City of Scranton, 1983-86; lectr. Lackawanna Jr. Coll., 1982-86. Editorial bd.: Temple Law Rev, 1952-53. Pres. Lackawanna County (Pa.) unit Am. Cancer Soc., 1966-67; bd. dirs. Pa. Cancer Soc., 1967-68, Lackawanna county chpt. ARC, 1967-69; mem. solicitation team, govtl. divsn. Lackawanna United Fund, 1963-68; chmn. profl. divsn. Greater Scranton (Pa.) YMCA Membership Drives; trustee Everhart Mus., Scranton, 1987—. Pilot USAF, 1955-57, Pa. N.G., 1957-59. Mem. Am. Judges Assn., Nat. Assn. Former U.S. Attys., Pa. Bar Assn., Lackawanna County Bar Assn., Fla. Bar Assn., Country Club of Scranton, Elks (pres. Pa. chpt. 1978-79, judiciary com. 1985-89, justice Grand Forum 1991, 1995-97, chief justice 1992-93, nat. pres. 1997-98), K.C., Phi Kappa (pres.), Delta Theta Phi (pres.). Democrat. Office: Judges Chambers Lackawanna County Courthouse Scranton PA 18503

**O'MALLEY, JAMES TERENCE,** lawyer; b. Omaha, Nov. 24, 1950; s. John Austin and Mayme M. (Zentner) O'M.; m. Colleen L. Kizer, May 22, 1972; children: Erin, Michael, Patrick. BA magna cum laude, U. Notre Dame, 1972; JD, Stanford U., 1975. Bar: Calif. 1975, Tex. 1998. Assoc., then ptnr. Gray Cary Ames & Frye, San Diego, 1975-87; vice chmn., exec. v.p. Noble Broadcast Group, San Diego, 1987-91; ptnr. Gray Cary Ware & Freidenrich, San Diego, 1991—, chmn., CEO, 1996—; bd. dirs. McMillin Cos., LLC, National City, Calif. Bd. dirs. Am. Ireland Fund, San Diego, 1981—, San Diego Regional Econ. Devel., 1997—. Mem. Am. Judicature Soc. Avocations: jogging, music. General corporate, Finance, Real property. Office: Gray Cary Ware Freidenrich 401 B St Ste 1700 San Diego CA 92101-4240

**O'MALLEY, JOHN DANIEL,** law educator, banker; b. Chgo., Dec. 18, 1926; s. William D. and Paula A. (Skaugh) O'M.; m. Caroline Tyler Taylor, July 12, 1958; children: John Daniel, Taylor John. Grad., St. Thomas Mil. Acad., 1945; B.S., Loyola U., Chgo., 1950, M.A., 1952, J.D., 1953; grad., U.S. Army Intelligence Sch., 1962, Command & Gen. Staff Coll., 1965. Bar: Ill. 1953, Mich. 1954, U.S. Supreme Ct. 1962. Asst. prof. law Loyola U., 1953-59, asso. prof., 1959-65; formerly spl. counsel and bond claims mgr. Fed. Ins. Co.; prof. law Loyola U. Grad. Sch. Bus., 1965—, chmn. dept. law, 1968-86; trust officer, v.p. First Nat. Bank Highland Park (Ill.), Marina City Bank, Chgo., Hyde Park Bank & Trust Co., 1970-75; exec. v.p. Harris Bank Winnetka, Ill., 1975-95. Author: Subrogation Against Banks on Forged Checks, 1967, Common Check Frauds and the Uniform Commercial Code, 1969; Contbr. articles to profl. jours. and law revs. Served to maj. AUS, 1945-47, 61-62. Decorated knight grand cross Papal Order of Holy Sepulchre, knight comdr. with star Constantinian Order of St. George (Italy), knight Order of St. Maurice and St. Lazarus (Italy). Mem. ABA, Chgo., Ill., Mich. bar assns., Chgo. Crime Commn., French Nat. Hon. Soc., Am., Chgo. bus. law assns., Mil. Govt. Assn. Home: 1630 Sheridan Rd 6-L Wilmette IL 60091-1830 Office: Loyola U 820 N Michigan Ave Ste 613 Chicago IL 60611-2147

**O'MALLEY, KEVIN FRANCIS,** lawyer, writer, educator; b. St. Louis, May 12, 1947; s. Peter Francis and Dorothy Margaret (Cradick) O'M.; m. Dena Hengen, Apr.2, 1971; children: Kevin Brendan, Ryan Michael. AB, St. Louis U., 1970, JD, 1973. Bar: Mo. 1973, U.S. Ct. Appeals D.C. 1974, U.S. Ct. Appeals (8th cir.) 1979, Ill. 1993. Trial lawyer U.S. Dept. Justice, Washington, 1973-74, Los Angeles, 1974-77, Phoenix, 1977-78; asst. U.S. atty. U.S. Dept. Justice, St. Louis, 1978-83; adj. prof. law St. Louis U., 1979—; lectr. Ctrl. and Ea. European Law Initiative, Russian Fedn., 1996. Author: (with Devitt, Blackmar, O'Malley) Federal Jury Practice and Instruction, 1990, 92; contbr. articles to law books and jours. Community amb. Expt. in Internat. Living, Prague, Czechoslovakia, 1968; bd. dirs. St. Louis-Galway (Ireland) Sister Cities. Capt. U.S. Army, 1973. Recipient Atty. Gen.'s Disting. Service award U.S. Dept. Justice, 1977, John J. Dwyer Meml. Scholarship award, 1967-70. Mem. ABA (chmn. govt. litigation counsel com. 1982-86, chmn. jud. com. 1986-87, chmn. com. on ind. and small firms, chmn. trial practice com. 1991-94, health care litigation 1994-98), Am. Law Inst., Met. Bar Assn. St. Louis (chmn. criminal law sect.), Nat. Inst. Trial Advocacy, Mo. Athletic Club. Roman Catholic. Office: 10 S Brentwood Blvd Ste 102 Saint Louis MO 63105-1694

**O'MALLEY, SUSAN MARIE,** lawyer; b. Evergreen Park, Ill., Apr. 11, 1968; d. Arthur Stephen and Mary Catherine O'Malley. BS, U. N.C., Charlotte, 1990; JD, U. N.C., 1994. Bar: N.C. 1994, D.C. 1996, U.S. Dist. Ct. (ea. dist.) N.C. 1998. Atty. Keel Law Offices, Tarboro, N.C., 1995-98; ptnr. Keel, Kessler & O'Malley, LLP, Tarboro, 1998—. Mem. N.C. Acad. Trial Lawyers (disability adv. sect. edn. chair 1998-99), Jaycees (v.p. 1998-99). Personal injury, Workers' compensation, Pension, profit-sharing, and employee benefits. Office: PO Box 1158 Tarboro NC 27886-1158

**O'MALLEY, TODD J.,** lawyer; b. Scranton, Pa., Dec. 25, 1945; s. Carlon M. O'Malley and Lucy Christian Boland; m. Elizabeth Stocking, Mar. 1, 1968; children: Lucy Christina, Mary Anne. BA, U. Scranton, 1967; JD, U. N.D., 1970. Bar: U.S. Dist. Ct. (mid. dist.) Pa. 1971, U.S. Supreme Ct. 1971, U.S. Ct. Appeals (3rd cir.) 1971. Commd. 2d lt. U.S. Army, 1971; advanced through grades to maj. USNG, 1974; various assignments USNG, Scranton, 1974-92; dep. atty. gen. Bur. Consumer Protection, Commonwealth Pa., Scranton, 1974-75; spl. asst. atty. gen. Dept. Transp., Commonwealth Pa., Scranton, 1975-77; pvt. practice Scranton, 1977—; founding ptnr. O'Malley & Langan, Scranton, 1992—; spl. counsel Dem. State Com., Harrisburg, Pa., 1984-86, Scranton, 1986. Bd. dirs. Citizens Consumer Justice, Harrisburg, 1997-98. Mem. Am. Trial Lawyers Assn. (chair-elect workers compensation div., bd. dirs. workplace injury litig. group 1997—), Pa. Trial Lawyers Assn. (bd. dirs 1996-98), Lackawanna County Bar Assn. Roman Catholic. Workers' compensation, Pension, profit-sharing, and employee benefits, Personal injury. Home: 1107 Richmont St Scranton PA 18509-1725 Office: O'Malley & Langan PC 426 Mulberry St Ste 203 Scranton PA 18503-1509

**OMAN, RALPH,** lawyer; b. Huntington, N.Y., July 1, 1940; s. Henry Ferdinand and Annamarie (Retelsdorf) O.; m. Anne K. Henehan, Oct. 21, 1967; children: Tabitha Russell, Caroline Adams, Charlotte Ericsson. Diploma, Sorbonne U., Paris, 1961; BA, Hamilton Coll., 1962; LLD, Georgetown U., 1973. Bar: D.C. 1973, U.S. Dist. Ct. Md. 1973, U.S. Ct. Appeals (4th cir.) 1974, U.S. Supreme Ct. 1977. Law clk. to U.S. Dist. Ct. judge U.S. Dist. Ct. Md., Balt., 1973-74; trial atty U.S. Dept. Justice, Washington, 1974-75; chief minority counsel patents, trademarks and copyrights subcom. U.S. Senate, Washington, 1975-77; legis. dir. Senator Charles Mathias, Washington, 1977-78; minority counsel judiciary com. U.S. Senate, Washington, 1978-81, chief counsel, staff dir. criminal law subcom., 1981-82, chief counsel patents, copyrights and trademarks subcom., 1982-85; register of copyrights U.S. Copyright Office, Washington, 1985-94; counsel Dechert Price and Rhoads, Washington, 1996—; adj. prof. copyright law George Washington U.; speaker in field. Contbr. numerous articles to profl. jours. Served to lt. USN, 1965-70, Vietnam. Mem. ABA (chair authors com.), Fed. Bar Assn. (past pres. Capitol Hill chpt.). Episcopalian. E-mail: roman@dechert.com. Home: 1110 E Capitol St NE Washington DC 20002-6225 Office: Dechert Price and Rhoads 1775 Eye St NW Ste 1100 Washington DC 20006-2402

**O'MARA, JAMES WRIGHT,** lawyer; b. McComb, Miss., Jan. 7, 1940; s. Junior and Mary Jane (Wright) O'M.; m. Jeanette Walter, June 28, 1963; children: James W. Jr., Angela J. BA, U. Miss., 1962, JD with distinction, 1967. Bar: Miss. 1967. Ptnr. Butler, Snow, O'Mara, Stevens & Cannada, Jackson, Miss., 1967-97, chmn., 1990-97; sr. ptnr. Phelps & Dunbar, Jackson, Miss., 1997—; vis. prof. Jackson Sch. Law, 1970-72. Editor-in-chief Miss. Law Jour., 1966-67. Pres. Jackson Prep. Sch., 1984-85, Woodland Hills Bapt. Acad., Jackson, 1973-84. Capt. U.S. Army, 1962-64. Fellow Miss. Bar Found.; mem. ABA, Miss. Bar Assn., Am. Bankruptcy Inst., Miss. Bankruptcy Conf. (pres. 1980-81). Baptist. Bankruptcy, Contracts commercial, General civil litigation. Home: 1811 Meadowbrook Rd Jackson MS 39211-6526 Office: Phelps & Dunbar PO Box 23066 Jackson MS 39225-3066

**O'MARA, THOMAS FELLERS,** lawyer; b. Elmira, N.Y., May 31, 1963; s. John F. and Ann O'Mara; m. Marilyn Pina, Nov. 9, 1991; 1 child, Caroline. BA, Cath. U. Am., 1987; JD, Syracuse U., 1991. Bar: N.Y. 1991. Asst. dist. atty. N.Y. County, N.Y.C., 1991-94; asst. dist. atty. Chemung County, Elmira, 1997—, dist. atty., 1999—; assoc. Davidson & O'Mara, P.C., Elmira, 1994-99. Bd. dirs. Chemung/Schuyler chpt. ARC, Elmira, 1995—. Criminal. Office: 226 Lake St Elmira NY 14901-3109

**O'MEARA, JOHN FRANCIS,** lawyer; b. Chgo., Apr. 14, 1936; s. John J. and Mary (Joyce) O'M.; children: Marcia A. Hiehle, John A., Timothy D. BS, Loyola U., 1959; JD, Northwestern U., 1960. Bar: Ill. 1961, U.S. Dist. Ct. (no. dist.) Ill. 1964, U.S. Ct. Appeals (7th cir.) 1992. Assoc., ptnr. Lord, Bissell & Brook, Chgo., 1961-74; atty. pvt. practice, Chgo. and Park Ridge, Ill, 1975—; instr. John Marshall Sch. Law, Chgo., 1966-71. Author: Tort Liability of Illinois Land Occupiers, 1968. Bd. dirs. St. Mary of Angels, 1987—; founder, officer Ind. Precinct Orgn., Chgo., 1969-71. With U.S. Army Res., 1960-66. Mem. Holy Name Soc. Roman Catholic. Office: 1737 N Wolcott Ave Chicago IL 60622-1350

**O'MEARA, JOHN J.,** lawyer. Gen. counsel Fed. Retirement Thrift Investment Bd., Washington. Office: Fed Retirement Thrift Investment Bd 1250 H St NW Ste 400 Washington DC 20005-5985*

**OMINSKY, ALAN JAY,** lawyer, medical educator; b. Phila., Apr. 7, 1938; s. Benjamin B. and Ida S. (Snydman) O.; m. Marlene Lachman, Nov. 1, 1992; 1 child, Sara. BA, U. Pa., Phila., 1958, MD, 1962, JD, 1988. Bar: Pa. 1989, U.S. Supreme Ct. 1994; cert. Am. Bd. Anesthesiology, Am. Bd. Psychiatry. Assoc. prof. anesthesiology U. Pa., Phila., 1972-88, assoc. prof. psychiatry, 1975-88; assoc. Bernstein Silver & Agins, Phila., 1089-96. Mem. ABA, Pa. Bar Assn., Phila. Bar Assn. (chair medicolegal com. 1993-95, mem. sr. lawyers, state civil, and computer users coms.), Assn. Trial Lawyers Am., Pa. Trial Lawyers Assn., Phil. Trial Lawyers Assn., Am. Soc. Anesthesiologists, Am. Psychiat. Soc., Lawyers Club Phila., Phi Beta Kappa. Personal injury. Home: 233 S 6th St Apt 701 Philadelphia PA 19106-3751

**OMINSKY, ANDREW MICHAEL,** lawyer; b. Phila., Jan. 8, 1965; s. Albert and Elaine Ominsky; m. Emma G. Ominsky, June 5, 1994; children: Jared, Emily. BA, Duke U., 1987; JD, U. Denver, 1990. Bar: Colo. 1990, U.S Dist. Ct. Colo. 1991, Pa. 1996, U.S. Dist. Ct. (ea. dist.) Pa. 1996. Jud. clk. Colo. Dist. Ct., Englewood, 1989-91; lawyer Burg & Eldredge, P.C., Denver, 1991-96, Ominsky & Messa, P.C., Phila., 1996—; appointed to procedural rules com. Pa. Supreme Ct. Appellate Ct., 1999—. Bd. dirs. Linda Creed Breast Cancer Found., Phila., 1997—, J/CHAI, Phila., 1996—; founder Elaine Ominsky Circle of Friends, Wistar Inst., Gladwyne, Pa., 1997—. Mem. Colo. Bar Assn., Pa. Bar Assn., Pa. Trial Lawyers Assn., Phila. Bar Assn. General civil litigation, Contracts commercial. Office: 1760 Market St Fl 10 Philadelphia PA 19103-4104

**ONDREY GRUBER, WILLIAM MICHAEL,** lawyer; b. Cleve., Oct. 17, 1955; s. Roman Frederick and Mary Margaret (Moriarty) Gruber; m. Lynn Frances Ondrey Gruber, June 16, 1984; children: John Gruber, Elisabeth Gruber. BA, Georgetown U., 1977; JD, Case Western Res. U., 1982. Bar: Ohio 1982, U.S. Dist. Ct. (no. dist.) Ohio 1982. Asst. dir. law City of Cleve., 1982-89, chief asst. dir. law, 1989-99; pvt. practice Shaker Heights, Ohio, 1999—. Chmn. Mi Pueblo Latin Am. Culture Camp; chmn., trustee Concern for Children, Cleve., 1993—. Mem. ABA, Ohio Bar Assn., Cleve. Bar Assn. E-mail: gruberwl@aol.com. Home and Office: 2714 Leighton Rd Shaker Heights OH 44120-1325

**O'NEAL, DALE, JR.,** lawyer; b. Ft. Worth, Nov. 6, 1957; s. Dale O. and Delora (Neal) O'N.; m. Teresa Thompson, June 28, 1986. BBA, U. Tex., 1980; JD, South Tex. Coll., 1983. Bar: Tex. 1983, U.S. Dist. Ct. (no. dist.) Tex. 1988. Pvt. practice Ft. Worth, 1983—; adj. prof. family law U. Tex.; mem. State Bar Tex. Com. for Family Law Revisions, 1994-95. Author: Divorce: Understanding and Preparing for Trial, 1987, Security Agreements for Divorce Collateralization, 1989; asst. editor Tex. Young Lawyers Assn., mem. editl. bd., 1985-86; contbr. articles to profl. jours., convs., and seminars. Mem. Am. Acad. Matrimonial Lawyers, Tex. Young Lawyers Assn. (coun. mem. 1985-86, mem. family law com. 1989), Masons. Avocation: hunting. Family and matrimonial. Office: PO Box 225 Fort Worth TX 76101-0225

**O'NEAL, MICHAEL RALPH,** state legislator, lawyer; b. Kansas City, Mo., Jan. 16, 1951; s. Ralph D. and Margaret E. (McEuen) O'N.; children from a previous marriage: children: Haley Anne, Austin Michael; m. Cindy Wulfkuhle, Apr. 9, 1999. BA in English, U. Kans., 1973, JD, 1976. Bar: Kans. 1976, U.S. Dist. Ct. Kans. 1976, U.S. Ct. Appeals (10th cir.) 1979. Intern Legis. Counsel State of Kans., Topeka, 1975-76; assoc. Hodge, Reynolds, Smith, Peirce & Forker, Hutchinson, Kans., 1976-77; ptnr. Reynolds, Peirce, Forker, Suter, O'Neal & Myers, Hutchinson, 1980-88; shareholder Gilliland & Hayes, P.A., Hutchinson, 1988—; mem. Kans. Ho. of Reps., 1984, chmn. jud. com., 1989-90, 92-96;, 99—; minority whip Kans. Ho. of Reps., 1991-92, majority whip, 1995-96, chmn. edn. com., 1997-98, mem. fiscal oversight com., 1997—; instr. Hutchinson C.C., 1977-88. Vice chmn. Rep. Ctrl. Com., Reno County, Kans., 1982-86; bd. dirs. Reno County Mental Health Assn., Hutchinson, 1984-89, YMCA, 1984-86, Crime Stoppers (ex-officio), Hutchinson; chmn. adv. bd. dirs. Wesley Towers Retirement Cmty., 1984-96; mem. Kans. Travel and Tourism Commn., 1990-94; mem. bd. govs. U. Kans. Law Sch., 1991—; mem. Kans. Sentencing Commn., 1997—. Recipient Leadership award Kans. C. of C. and Industry, 1985; named one of Outstanding Young Men Am., 1986. Mem. ABA, Nat. Conf. State Legislatures (criminal justice com.), Kans. Assn. Def. Counsel, Def. Rsch. Inst., Kans. Bar Assn. (prospective legis. com., Outstanding Svc. award), Hutchinson C. of C. (ex-officio bd. dirs., Leadership award 1984), Am. Coun. Young Polit. Leaders (del. to Atlantic conf. biennial assembly), Kans. Jud. Coun., Commn. on Uniform State Laws. Avocations: basketball, tennis, golf. Home: 8 Windemere Ct Hutchinson KS 67502-2020 Office:

Gilliland & Hayes PA 2d Flr Box 2977 20 W 2nd Ave Hutchinson KS 67501-5246

**O'NEAL, MICHAEL SCOTT, SR.,** lawyer; b. Jacksonville, Fla., Dec. 22, 1948; s. Jack Edwin and Lucille (Colvin) O'N.; m. Barbara Louise Hardie, Jan. 30, 1971 (div. Sept. 1974); 1 child, Jennifer Erin; m. Helen Margaret Joost, Mar. 18, 1985; children: Mary Helen, Angela Marie, Michael Scott O'Neal Jr. AA, Fla. Jr. Coll., 1975; BA in Econs. summa cum laude, U. No. Fla., 1977; JD cum laude, U. Fla., 1979. Bar: Fla. 1980, U.S. Dist. Ct. (mid. dist.) Fla. 1980, U.S. Dist. Ct. (no. dist.) Fla. 1981, U.S. Ct. Appeals (5th and 11th cirs.) 1981, U.S. Supreme Ct. 1986. Assoc. Howell, Liles, Braddock & Milton, Jacksonville, Fla., 1980-83; ptnr. Commander, Legler, Werber, Dawes, Sadler & Howell, Jacksonville, 1983-91, Foley & Lardner, Jacksonville, 1991-93, Howell O'Neal & Johnson, Jacksonville, 1993-96, Howell & O'Neal, Jacksonville, 1996—; pro bono atty. Legal Aid Soc., Jacksonville, 1980—; practicing atty. Lawyers Reference, Jacksonville, 1980—. Pres. Julington Landing Homeowners Assn., Jacksonville, 1980-83. Served to staff sgt. USAF, 1968-74. Mem. ABA, Jacksonville Bar Assn., Fed. Bar Assn., Assn. Trial Lawyers Am., Fla. Def. Lawyers Assn., Northeast Fla. Med. Malpractice Claims Coun. (pres. 1996), Jacksonville Assn. Def. Counsel (pres. 1999), Internat. Assn. Def. Counsel, Def. Rsch. Inst. Republican. Methodist. Clubs: University, San Jose Country (Jacksonville). Avocations: golf, music. Personal injury, Federal civil litigation, State civil litigation. Home: 1299 Norwich Rd Jacksonville FL 32207-7525 Office: Howell O'Neal 200 N Laura St Ste 1100 Jacksonville FL 32202-3500

**O'NEIL, D. JAMES,** lawyer; b. Hudson, N.Y., July 24, 1951; s. Daniel J. and Carolyn J. (Schug) O'N.; m. May 24, 1981; 1 child, Kimberley A. BS, Marist Coll., Poughkeepsie, N.Y., 1973; JD, U. vt., 1977. Bar: N.Y. 1977, U.S. Dist. Ct. (fed., so. and ea. dist.) N.Y. 1978. Asst. dist. atty. Dutchess County Dist. Atty.'s Office, Poughkeepsie, 1977-89; ptnr. Whalen Whalen O'Neil, Poughkeepsie, 1989-91; pvt. practice Poughkeepsie, 1991-93; ptnr. Viglotti & O'Neil, Wappingers Falls, N.Y., 1993—; mem. Arson Task Force, Dutchess County, 1984-86; atty. CJA (Fed. Criminal Panel Def.), 1990-93. Mem. N.Y. State Bar, Dutchess County bar Assn. Criminal, Family and matrimonial, Real property. Home: 5 Taconic View Ct Lagrangeville NY 12540-5517 Office: Viglotti & O'Neil 18 South Ave Wappingers Falls NY 12590-2724

**O'NEIL, JOHN JOSEPH,** lawyer; b. Detroit, July 20, 1943; s. John J. and Dora J. (Collins) O'N.; children: Meghan, Kathryn. BA, Trinity Coll., 1965; LLB, U. Va., 1968. Bar: N.Y. 1969, U.S. Ct. Appeals (2d cir.) 1969, Fla. 1979, D.C. 1982. Assoc. Jackson & Nash, N.Y.C., 1968-71; assoc. Paul, Weiss, Rifkind, Wharton & Garrison, N.Y.C., 1971-77, ptnr., 1977—. Fellow Am. Coll. Trusts and Estates Counsel; mem. ABA (com. on spl. problems of aged), N.Y. State Bar Assn. (com. on taxation, trusts and estates sect.), Assn. Bar City N.Y. (com. on trusts and estates), Pi Gamma Mu. Probate, Family and matrimonial. Office: Paul Weiss Rifkind Wharton & Garrison Ste 1225 1285 Avenue Of The Americas Fl 21 New York NY 10019-6028

**O'NEIL, KENTON R.,** lawyer; b. Roaring Spring, Pa., June 9, 1967; s. Ray E. and Sandra K. O'N.; m. Jill S., Saunders. BSBA in Econs., Clarion U. Pa., 1989; JD, Dickinson Sch. Law, 1992. Bar: Pa. 1992, U.S. Dist. Ct. (mid. dist.) Pa. 1992. Atty. McQuaide Blasko, State College, Pa., 1992-94, Pepicelli, Youngs & Youngs, Meadville, Pa., 1994-96; pvt. practice Clarion, Pa., 1996—. Bd. govs. Pa. State System Higher Edn., 1987-89. Recipient James E. Gemmell award Clarion U. Pa., 1989. Mem. ABA, Am. Acad. Estate Planning Attys., Pa. Bar Assn., Clarion County Bar Assn. Republican. Methodist. Avocations: fishing, hunting, travel. Estate planning, Estate taxation, Probate. Office: 333 W Main St Ste E Clarion PA 16214-1055

**O'NEIL, ROBERT MARCHANT,** university administrator, law educator; b. Boston, Oct. 16, 1934; s. Walter George and Isabel Sophia (Marchant) O'N.; m. Karen Elizabeth Elson, June 18, 1967; children—Elizabeth, Peter, David, Benjamin. AB, Harvard U., 1956, AM, 1957, LLB, 1961; LLD, Beloit Coll., 1985, Ind. U., 1987. Bar: Mass. 1962. Law clk. to Justice William J. Brennan Jr. U.S. Supreme Ct., 1962-63; acting assoc. prof. law U. Calif.-Berkeley, 1963-66, prof., 1966-67, 69-72; exec. asst. to pres., prof. law SUNY-Buffalo, 1967-69; provost, prof. law U. Cin., 1972-73, exec. v.p., prof. law, 1973-75; v.p., prof. law Ind. U., Bloomington, 1975-80; pres. U. Wis. System, 1980-85; prof. law U. Wis.-Madison, 1980-85; prof. law U. Va., Charlottesville, 1985—, pres., 1985-90; gen. counsel AAUP, 1970-72, 91-92. Author: Civil Liberties: Case Studies and the Law, 1965, Free Speech: Responsible Communication Under Law, 2d edit., 1972, The Price of Dependency: Civil Liberties in the Welfare State, 1970, No Heroes, No Villians, 1972, The Courts, Government and Higher Education, 1972, Discriminating Against Discrimination, 1976, Handbook of the Law of Public Employment, 1978, 2d rev. edit., 1993, Classrooms in the Crossfire, 1981, Free Speech in the College Community, 1997; co-author: A Guide to Debate, 1964, The Judiciary and Vietnam, 1972, Civil Liberties Today, 1974. Trustee Tchrs. Ins. and Annuity Assn.; bd. dirs. Commonwealth Fund, Fort James Corp., Sta. WVPT Pub. TV, Am. Law Inst. Home: 1839 Westview Rd Charlottesville VA 22903-1632 Office: Thomas Jefferson Ctr Protection Free Expression 400 Peter Jefferson Pl Charlottesville VA 22911-8691

**O'NEIL, THOMAS FRANCIS, III,** lawyer; b. Fairfield, Conn., Apr. 8, 1957; s. Thomas F. Jr. and Carmen A. (Therrien) O'N.; m. Nancy D., Aug. 14, 1982; children: Caley Elizabeth, Patrick McGee. AB magna cum laude, Dartmouth Coll., 1975-79; JD, Georgetown U., 1979-82. Bar: Md. 1982, U.S. Dist. Ct. Md. 1983, U.S. Ct. Appeals (4th cir.) 1983, D.C. 1992. Legis. asst. Congl. Stewart B. McKinney, Washington, 1980-82; law clk. Hon. Alexander Harvey II U.S. Dist. Ct. Md.; assoc. Venable, Baetjer & Howard, Balt., 1984-86; asst. U.S. atty. U.S. Dept. Justice, Balt., 1986-89; assoc. Hogan & Hartson, Balt., 1990-91, ptnr., 1992-95; chief litigation counsel MCI Comms. Corp., Washington, 1995—; bd. govs. Ged. Bar Assn., Balt., 1992; Walters Art Gallery, ex officio trustee, 1995-96; chairperson William T. Walters Assocs. Recipient Chief Postal Insps. Spl. award U.S. Postal Svc., Washington, 1988, Letter of Commendation award Bur. of Investigation, Washington, 1989, Spl. Achievement award U.S. Dept. Justice, 1989. Mem. Serjeants Inn Law Club. Republican. Roman Catholic. Federal civil litigation, Criminal, Health. Office: MCI Comms Corp 1133 19th St NW Washington DC 20036-3604

**O'NEILL, ALBERT CLARENCE, JR.,** lawyer; b. Gainesville, Fla., Nov. 25, 1939; s. Albert Clarence and Sue Virginia (Henry) O'N.; m. Vanda Marie Nigels, Apr. 26, 1969; 1 child, Heather Marie. B.A. with high honors, U. Fla., 1962; LL.B. magna cum laude, Harvard U., 1965. Bar: Fla. bar 1965. Law clk. to judge U.S. Dist. Ct. (mid. dist.) Fla., Jacksonville, 1965-66; assoc. Fowler, White, Collins, Gillen, Humkey & Trenam, Tampa, Fla., 1966-69; ptnr. Trenam, Simmons, Kemker, Scharf & Barkin, Tampa, 1970-77; mem. firm Trenam, Kemker, Scharf, Barkin, Frye, O'Neill & Mullis (P.A.), Tampa, 1977—, also bd. dirs.; vis. lectr. law Stetson Law Sch., 1970-73. Exec. editor: Harvard Law Rev, 1964-65; contbr. articles to profl. jours. Bd. dirs. Fla. Gulf Coast Symphony, Inc., 1975-86, U. Fla. Found., Inc., 1976-84, 97—, Fla. Orch., 1988-94. Mem. ABA (chmn. tax sect. 1992-93), Am. Law Inst., Am. Coll. Tax Counsel, Fla. Bar (chmn. tax sect. 1975-76), Am. Bar Retirement Assn. (bd. dirs.), Phi Beta Kappa. Taxation, general, Pension, profit-sharing, and employee benefits, General corporate. Office: Trenam Kemker Scharf Barkin Frye O'Neill & Mullis 101 E Kennedy Blvd Ste 2700 Tampa FL 33602-5150

**O'NEILL, ALICE JANE,** lawyer; b. Houston, May 14, 1951; d. Edward John Sr. and Martha Elisabeth (Alford) O'N. BA in Polit. Sci., U. St. Thomas, Houston, 1972, MBA, 1982; MEd in Ednl. Psychology, Tex. A&M U., 1974; JD, South Tex. Coll. Law, 1992. Bar: Tex. 1993, U.S. Dist. Ct. (so. dist.) Tex. 1993, U.S. Dist. Ct. Ariz. 1994. Therapist, supr. Family Svc. Ctr., Houston, 1978-81; personnel coord. Guest Quarters Hotel, Houston, 1981-84; therapist in pvt. practice Houston, 1984-90; law clk. Abraham Watkins Nichols Ballard & Friend, Houston, 1991-93; contract atty. Nelson & Zeidman, Houston, 1994, O'Quinn Kerensky McAninich & Laminanck, Houston, 1994; assoc. Rosen & Newey, Houston, 1994—; mem. adv. bd. Juvenile Justice, Houston, Harris County Detention Ctr., Houston, 1986-93. Mem. ABA, Houston Bar Assn., Assn. for Women Attys., Houston Young Lawyers Assn. Republican. Methodist. Avocations: tennis, dogs, reading, travel. Personal injury, General civil litigation, Family and matrimonial. Home: 403 Euclid St Houston TX 77009-7222 Office: Rosen & Newey 440 Louisiana St Ste 1800 Houston TX 77002-1636

**O'NEILL, HARRIET,** state supreme court justice. Undergrad. degree with honors, Converse Coll.; postgrad., Oxford (Eng.) U.; JD, U. S.C., 1982. Practice law Houston; with Porter & Clements, Morris & Campbell; pvt. practice, 1982-92; judge 152d Dist. Ct., Houston, 1992; justice 14th Ct. Appeals, Houston, 1995, Tex. Supreme Ct., 1998—; Lectr. continuing edn. courses; adv. bd. CLE Inst., 1996; panelist Tex. Ctr. Advanced Jud. Studies., Austin, 1993. Contbr. articles to profl. publs. Mem. U. S.C. academic honors soc.; law sch. rep. ABA. Office: Supreme Ct PO Box 12248 Austin TX 78711*

**O'NEILL, J. NORMAN, JR.,** lawyer; b. L.A., Nov. 12, 1943; s. J. Norman and Helen (Mueller) O'N.; m. Rebecca Wylie, Apr. 19, 1975; children: Kathleen, Taryn, J. Norman III. BA, U. So. Calif., L.A., 1966, MBA, 1969; JD, Southwestern U., L.A., 1974. Bar: Calif. 1977, U.S. Dist. Ct. (cen. dist.) Calif. 1978. Corp. trust adminstr. Title Ins. and Trust Co., L.A., 1971-77; v.p. adminstrn. Nat. Am. Title Ins. Co., L.A., 1977-78; asst. to pres. Hydril Co., L.A., 1978-79; gen. counsel System Parking, Inc., Pasadena, Calif., 1979—. Bd. dirs. Hathaway Home for Children, L.A., 1982-88, Queen of Angeles Med. Ctr., L.A., 1987—, St. Josephs Hosp., San Francisco, 1978—. Mem. ABA, Calif. Bar Assn., L.A. County Bar Assn. (exec. com. corp. law depts. sect. 1990—), Calif. Club (L.A.), Bel Air Bay Club (Pacific Palisades, Calif.), Santa Ana Turf Club (Arcadia, Calif.). Republican. Roman Catholic. Avocations: tennis, stamps. General corporate. Home: 1368 Bedford Rd San Marino CA 91108-2001 Office: System Parking Inc 918 E Green St Pasadena CA 91106-2935

**O'NEILL, JOSEPH DEAN,** lawyer; b. Bayonne, N.J.; s. Austin Joseph and Ann (Lynch) O'N. AB, Allegheny Coll.; JD, N.Y. Law Sch. Bar: N.J. 1968; cert. civil and criminal trial atty. Nat. Bd. Trial Advocacy. Pvt. practice Vineland, N.J.; pres. Cumberland County Legal Aid Soc., Vineland, 1974-87. Contbr. articles to profl. pubs. Assoc. counsel N.J. Jaycees. Recipient Outstanding Contbn. and Leadership award Nat. Assn. Criminal Def. Lawyers, 1978-79. Mem. Assn. Trial Lawyers Am. (pres. N.J. chpt. 1988-89, N.J. legal PAC chmn. 1991-95), Cert. Trial Attys. (bd. dirs. 1988-90). General civil litigation, Criminal. Office: PO Box 847 30 W Chestnut Ave Vineland NJ 08360-5401

**O'NEILL, KEVIN EDGEWORTH,** lawyer; b. Milw., June 17, 1945; s. Charles Arthur and Mary Edgewater O'Neill; m. Jessie Ann Hoyle, Apr. 9, 1980 (div. Jan. 1988); children: Rebecca, Margaret. Degree, St. Norbert Coll.; JD, Marquette U., 1971. Bar: Wis. 1971, Fla. 1971, U.S. Dist. Ct. (ea. and we. dists.) Wis. 1971, U.S. Supreme Ct. 1977. Ptnr. O'Neill & Noonan, Milw., 1971-73; asst. dist. atty. Milwaukee County Dist. Atty. Wis., 1971-72; atty. Law Office William Coffey, Milw., 1973-82; pvt. practice law Milw., 1983—. Mem. Fla. Bar Assn., Wis. Bar Assn., Milw. Bar Assn. Criminal, Family and matrimonial, General civil litigation. Office: 611 N Broadway Ste 510 Milwaukee WI 53202-5004

**O'NEILL, MARK,** lawyer; b. Mpls., Dec. 6, 1925; s. Francis Lawrence and Gertrude Jane (Timmerman) O'N.; m. Edna Charlotte Drexler, Aug. 1, 1953; children: Kevin Francis, David William, Timothy Gareth. BA, Harvard Coll., 1949, JD, 1952. Bar: Ohio 1952, U.S. Dist. Ct. (no. dist.) Ohio 1953, U.S. Ct. Appeals (6th cir.) 1958, U.S. Ct. Appeals (10th cir.) 1974, U.S. Supreme Ct. 1974. Assoc. McConnell Blackmore Cory & Burke, Cleve., 1952-60; ptnr. Weston Hurd Fallon Paisley & Howley, Cleve., 1961—; pres., master bencher Judge Anthony J. Celebrezze Inn of Ct., Cleve., 1987-89. Author: Annual Review of Ohio Tort Law, 1975-85. Chmn. Charter Rev. Commn., University Heights, Ohio, Civil Svc. Commn., University Heights; pres. Task Force on Violent Crime, Cleve., 1990-91. Cpl. USMC, 1944-46. Fellow Am. Coll. Trial Lawyers; mem. ABA, Am. Law Inst., Internat. Assn. Def. Counsel, Ohio State Bar Assn., Cleve. Bar Assn. (pres. 1990-91, Trial Superstar 1988, disting. svc. award 1981-82), Cleve. Assn. Trial Attys. (pres. 1969-70, disting. advocacy award 1983). Avocations: photography, travel. General civil litigation, Personal injury, Professional liability. Office: Weston Hurd Fallon Paisley & Howley 2500 Terminal Tower Cleveland OH 44113

**O'NEILL, PHILIP DANIEL, JR.,** lawyer, educator; b. Boston, Sept. 19, 1951; s. Philip Daniel Sr. and Alice Maureen (Driscoll) O'N.; m. Lisa G. Arrowood, June 25, 1983; children: Alexander Edwin, Sean Matthew, Madeleine Clarice. BA, Hamilton Coll., 1973; JD cum laude, Boston Coll., 1977. Bar: Mass. 1977, N.Y. 1985, R.I. 1988. Assoc. Hale and Dorr, Boston, 1977-83, ptnr., 1983-87; ptnr. Edwards & Angell, Boston, 1987—; adj. rsch. fellow John F. Kennedy Sch. Govt., Ctr. for Sci. and Internat. Affairs Harvard U., 1983-86; adj. prof. law Boston U., 1992, Boston Coll., 1988—; cons. Arms Control and Disarmament Agy. U.S. Dept. Def., 1983-84; guest lectr., commentator Boston Coll. Law Sch., Harvard U. Bus. Sch., Kennedy Sch. Govt., 1985, Boston U. Law Sch., 1990-91, Harvard Law Sch., 1994-95, 98; internat. and domestic comml. arbitrator Am. Arbitration Assn., Hong Kong Ctr. for Internat. Arbitration, N.Am. Free Trade Agreement, Internat. C. of C., Stockholm Arb. Ctr., Euro-Arab C. of C., World Intellectual Property Orgn.; panelist in internat. and domestic legal programs. Contbr. chpts. to books and articles to profl. jours. Fellow Chartered Inst. Arbitrators (Eng.); mem. ABA, Internat. Law Assn. (chmn. am. br. arbitration com. 1985-89, rep. internat. arbitration com. 1989—), Boston Bar Assn. (chmn. internat. law sect. 1994-96, past chmn. internat. litigation and arbitration com.), Am. Soc. Internat. Law. Private international, General civil litigation, General corporate. Home: 11 Blackburnian Rd Lincoln MA 01773-4317 Office: Edwards & Angell 101 Federal St Fl 23 Boston MA 02110-1810

**O'NEILL, RALPH JAMES,** lawyer; b. Berkeley, Calif., Apr. 12, 1958; s. Ralph James and Samantha Ann O'Neill; m. Andrea Lea Yuen, aug. 13, 1989; 1 child, Alyssa. AB, U. Calif., Berkeley, 1982; JD, U. Calif., 1987. Bar: Hawaii 1988, Calif. 1998. Ptnr. Reid Richards & Miyagi, Honolulu, 1993-98, MacDonald Rudy & Byrns, Honolulu, 1998—. Mem. ABA, Hawaii State Bar Assn., Rotary Internat. Avocations: reading, computers, kayaking, running. General civil litigation, Insurance. Office: MacDonald Rudy & Byrns 1001 Bishop St Honolulu HI 96813-3429

**O'NEILL, ROBERT JOSEPH, JR.,** prosecutor, educator; b. Wilmington, Del., Mar. 25, 1959; s. Robert J. Sr. and Helen M. O'Neill. BS, U. Del., 1981; JD, Villanova U., 1985. Bar: Pa. 1985, Del. 1987. Law clk. Del. Superior Ct., Georgetown, 1985-86; dep. atty. gen. State of Del., Wilmington, 1987-95; chief prosecutor Kent County, Dover, Del., 1995—; faculty advisor Nat. Coll. Dist. Attys., Houston, 1993; guest commentator Ct. T.V., N.Y.C., 1996-97. Mem. Wilmington Rugby Club (Chmn. of Yr. 1993). Office: 820 N French St Fl 7 Wilmington DE 19801-3509

**O'NEILL, THOMAS NEWMAN, JR.,** federal judge; b. Hanover, Pa., July 6, 1928; s. Thomas Newman and Emma (Cornpropst) O'N.; m. Jeanne M. Corr., Feb. 4, 1961; children: Caroline Jeanne, Thomas Newman, III, Ellen Gitt. A.B. magna cum laude, Catholic U. Am., 1950; LL.B. magna cum laude, U. Pa., 1953; postgrad. (Fulbright grantee), London Sch. Econs., 1955-56. Bar: Pa. 1954, U.S. Supreme Ct. 1959. Law clk. to Judge Herbert F. Goodrich U.S. Ct. Appeals (3d cir.), 1953-54; to Justice Harold H. Burton U.S. Supreme Ct., 1954-55; assoc. Montgomery, McCracken, Walker & Rhoads, Phila., 1956-63; ptnr. Montgomery, McCracken, Walker & Rhoads, 1963-83; judge U.S. Dist. Ct. (ea. dist.) Pa., 1983—; counsel 1st and 2d Pa. Legis. Reapportionment Commns., 1971, 81; lectr. U. Pa. Law Sch., 1973. Articles editor: U. Pa. Law Rev, 1952-53. Former trustee Lawyers Com. for Civil Rights Under Law; former mem. Gov.'s Trial Ct. Nominating Commn. for Phila. County; former mem. bd. overseers U. Pa. Mus. Fellow Am. Coll. Trial Lawyers; mem. Am. Law Inst. (life), Phila. Bar Assn. (chancellor 1976), Pa. Bar Assn. (gov. 1978-81), U. Pa. Law Alumni Soc. (pres. 1976-77), Pa. Conf. County Bar Officers (pres. 1981-82), Am. Inn of Ct. (founding chmn. U. Pa.), Order of Coif (pres. U. Pa. chpt. 1971-73), Merion Cricket Club, Edgemere Club, Broadacres Trouting Assn., Phi Beta Kappa, Phi Eta Sigma. Office: US Dist Ct 4007 US Courthouse 601 Market St Philadelphia PA 19106-1713

**O'NEILL, THOMAS TYRONE,** lawyer; b. Wichita, Kans., June 9, 1956; s. John Joseph and Dorothy Marie O'Neill; 1 child, Allison Rutherford Jones. BS in Geology, U. Kans., 1983, JD, 1986. Bar: Kans. 1986, U.S. Dist. Ct. Kans. 1986, U.S. Ct. Appeals (10th cir.) 1990. Assoc. Carson & Fields, Kansas City, Kans., 1987-91, ptnr., 1991-96; ptnr. Carson & O'Neill, Kansas City, 1997—. Republican. Avocations: snow skiing, travel. General civil litigation, Personal injury, General practice. Office: Carson & O'Neill 754 Minnesota Ave Ste 302 Kansas City MO 66101

**O'NEILL, TIMOTHY P.,** lawyer; b. Shotts, Scotland, Sept. 23, 1940; came to U.S., 1953; s. Thomas P. and Catherine (O'Connor) O'N.; m. Maria E. Karagianis, May 19, 1982; children: Katherine, Elizabeth. STB, Gregorian U., Rome, 1965; MA, Brandeis U., 1970; JD, Boston U., 1971. Bar: Mass. 1972, U.S. Dist. Ct. Mass. 1982, U.S. Ct. Appeals (1st cir.) 1982. Asst. dist. atty. Suffolk County, Mass., 1972-81; assoc. Driscoll and Gillespie, Lynn, Mass., 1981-83; ptnr. Murphy, DeMarco & O'Neill, Boston, 1983-93, Hanify & King, P.C., Boston, 1993—; clin. supr. Sch. Law Harvard U., Cambridge, Mass., 1976-81; lectr. Mass. Continuing Legal Edn., 1988—. Chmn. fin. com. City of Boston, 1984-86. Recipient Disting. Prosecutor award Citizens for Decency Through Law, Phoenix, 1981. Mem. ABA, Internat. Assn. Defense Coun., Mass. Bar Assn., Inns Ct. Avocations: skiing, reading, classical music. Federal civil litigation, State civil litigation, Personal injury. Home: 145 Dudley Ln Milton MA 02186-4019 Office: Hanify & King PC One Federal St Boston MA 02110

**O'NELL, WILLIAM E.,** lawyer; b. Chgo., Dec. 30, 1960. BA, U. Notre Dame, 1984; MA, U. Calif. San Diego, La Jolla, 1987; JD, U. San Diego, 1996. Bar: Calif. 1996, U.S. Dist. Ct. (so. dist.) Calif. 1996. Lawyer Post Kirby Noonan & Sweat LLP, San Diego. General civil litigation. Office: Post Kirby Noonan & Sweat LLP 11th Fl Am Plaza 600 W Broadway Ste 1100 San Diego CA 92101-3387

**ONGERT, STEVEN WALTER,** lawyer, mediator; b. Palm Springs, Calif., Aug. 9, 1945; m. Kathy D. Dean, July 4, 1991. BA, Hastings (Nebr.) Coll., 1972; JD, South Tex. Coll. Law, 1988. Bar: Tex. 1989, U.S. Dist. Ct. (so. dist.) Tex. 1990. Assoc. Bill De La Garza & Assocs., Houston, 1988-90; ptnr. Dean & Ongert, P.C., Houston, 1990—. Sgt. USAF, 1965-69. Mem. ABA, Houston Bar Assn., Galveston Family Law Bar Assn. (pres. 1993, 94), Assn. Trial Lawyers Am., Tex. Assn. Mediators, Coll. State Bar Tex. Avocations: fishing, collecting antiques. Family and matrimonial, Personal injury. Office: 1020 Bay Area Blvd Ste 220 Houston TX 77058-2628

**OOSTERHUIS, PAUL WILLIAM,** lawyer; b. Webster, Iowa, Nov. 5, 1946; m. Bronson Clayton, Jan. 21, 1978; children: Elizabeth, Christopher. BA, Brown U., 1969; JD, Harvard U., 1973. Bar: D.C. 1973, U.S. Tax Ct. 1989. Staff atty. joint com. on tax. U.S. Congress, Washington, 1973-76, counsel, 1976-78; assoc. Hogan & Hartson, Washington, 1979-80, ptnr., 1981-88; ptnr. Skaddon Arps, Washington, 1988—. Corporate taxation. Office: Skadden Arps 1440 New York Ave NW Ste 600 Washington DC 20005-6000

**OPALA, MARIAN P(ETER),** state supreme court justice; b. Lódz, Poland, Jan. 20, 1921. BSB in Econs., Oklahoma City U., 1957, JD, 1953, LLD (hon.), 1981; LLM, NYU, 1968; HHD, Okla. Christian U. Sci. & Arts, 1981. Bar: Okla. 1953, U.S. Supreme Ct. 1970. Asst. county atty. Oklahoma County, 1953-56; practiced law Oklahoma City, 1956-60, 65-67; referee Okla. Supreme Ct., Oklahoma City, 1960-65; prof. law Oklahoma City U. Sch. Law, 1965-69; asst. to presiding justice Supreme Ct. Okla., 1967-68; administrv. dir. Cts. Okla., 1968-77; presiding judge Okla. State Indsl. Ct., 1977-78; judge Workers Compensation Ct., 1978; justice Okla. Supreme Ct., 1978—, chief justice, 1991-92; adj. prof. law Okla. City U., 1962—, U. Okla. Coll. Law, 1969—; prof. law U. Tulsa Law Sch., 1982—; mem. permanent faculty Am. Acad. Jud. Edn., 1970—; mem. NYU Inst. Jud. Adminstrn.; mem. faculty Nat. Jud. Coll., U. Nev., 1975—; chmn. Nat. Conf. State Ct. Adminstrs., 1976-77; mem. Nat. Conf. Commrs. on Uniform State Laws, 1982—. Co-author: Oklahoma Court Rules for Perfecting a Civil Appeal, 1969. Mem. Adminstrn. Conf. U.S., 1993-95. Recipient Herbert Harley award Am. Judicature Soc., 1977, Disting. Alumni award Oklahoma City U., 1979, Americanism medal Nat. Soc. DAR, 1984, ABA/Am. Law Inst. Harrison Tweed Spl. Merit award, 1987, Humanitarian award NCCJ, 1991, Jour. Record award, 1995, Constn. award Rogers State U., 1996, Jud. Excellence award Okla. Bar Assn., 1997. Mem. AbA (edn. com. appellate judges conf. 1984-93), Okla. Bar Assn. (Earl Sneed Continuing Legal Edn. award 1988, Jud. Excellence award 1997), Okla. County Bar Assn., Am. Soc. Legal History, Oklahoma City Title Lawyers Assn., Am. Judicature Soc. (bd. dirs. 1988-92), Am. Law Inst. (elected), Order of Coif, Phi Delta Phi (Oklahoma City Alumni award). Office: Okla Supreme Ct State Capitol Rm 238 Oklahoma City OK 73105

**OPDAHL, CLARK DONALD,** lawyer; b. St. Paul, June 22, 1956; s. Donald Arthur and Elizabeth Claire O.; m. Cynthia Ann Slipka, Sept. 2, 1977; children: Kyle, Shannon, Kelsey. BA, U. Minn., 1978; JD magna cum laude, William Mitchell Coll. of Law, St. Paul, 1986. Bar: Minn. 1987, U.S. Dist. Ct. Minn. Account exec., v.p. D.A. Opdahl & Assocs., Inc., Roseville, Minn., 1978-86; law clk. David G. Johnson, P.A., North St. Paul, 1984-86; atty. Henson & Efron, P.A., Mpls., 1986—. Baseball coach Blaine/Spring Lake Park Athletic Assn., Blaine, 1987-92, softball coach Spring Lake Park Athletic Assn., 1996-97. Mem. Minn. State Bar Assn., Hennepin County Bar Assn. (co-chmn. cmty. rels. 1989-93, 97-99, co-chmn. publs. com. 1994-97). Avocations: golf, fishing. Mergers and acquisitions, Contracts commercial, General corporate. Office: Henson & Efron PA 1200 Title Ins Bldg Minneapolis MN 55401

**OPPENHEIMER, PETER H.,** lawyer; b. Mineola, N.Y., Mar. 6, 1964; m. Stephanie J. Oppenheimer, Oct. 12, 1996. BA, Yale U., 1986, JD, 1992; MA in Law and Diplomacy, Tufts U., 1992. Staff asst. Coun. on Fgn. Rels., N.Y.C., 1987-88; atty. Bryan Cave LLP, Washington, 1991-99; atty. environ. and natural resources divsn. U.S. Dept. Justice, Washington, 1999—; hon. sec. Am. br. Internat. Law Assn., N.Y.C., 1998-99. Contbr. articles to legal jours. Mem. Natural Resources and Environ. Law Com. Planning Bd., 1997-99. Recipient Hajo Holborn prize Yale U., 1985; German Acd. Exch. Svc. fellow, 1986-87. Mem. Air and Waste Mgmt. Assn., Am. Soc. Internat. Law, Phi Beta Kappa. Avocation: running. Email: peter.Oppenheimer@USDOJ.gov. Office: US Dept Justice 601 D St NW Washington DC 20004-2904 also: PO Box 4390 Ben Franklin Sta Washington DC 20044-4390

**OPPENHEIMER, RANDOLPH CARL,** lawyer; b. N.Y.C., Feb. 5, 1954; s. Bennett and Sandra (Haber) O.; m. Cynthia Ellen Shatkin, June 19, 1976; children: Benjamin David, Adam Jeremy, Jacob Aaron, Jordan Michael, Daniel Corey. BA, U. Vt., 1976; JD, Case Western Res. U., 1979. Bar: N.Y. 1980, U.S. Dist. Ct. (we. dist.) N.Y. 1980, U.S. Dist. Ct. (no. dist.) N.y. 1995, U.S. Bankruptcy Ct. 1980, U.S. Ct. Appeals (2d cir.) 1981. Assoc. Kavinoky & Cook, Buffalo, 1979-84, ptnr., 1984—; instr. legal research, writing and adv., Case Western Res. U., 1978-79. Assoc. editor Case Western Reserve Law Rev., 1977-79. Mem. ABA, N.Y. Bar Assn., Erie County Bar Assn. Contracts commercial, General corporate, Labor. Home: 195 Greenaway Rd Buffalo NY 14226-4165 Office: Kavinoky & Cook 120 Delaware Ave Rm 600 Buffalo NY 14202-2793

**OPPERWALL, STEPHEN GABRIEL,** lawyer; b. Racine, Wis., Aug. 14, 1953; s. Raymond and Helen Bertha Opperwall; m. Kathleen O'Neill, Oct. 27, 1990; children: Christopher Stephen, Scott O'Neill. BA, Calvin Coll., 1975; JD, U. Santa Clara, 1981. Bar: Calif. 1981, U.S. Dist. Ct. (no. and ea. dist.) Calif. 1981, U.S. Tax Ct. 1994, U.S. Ct. Appeals (9th cir.) 1984; cert. specialist in creditor's rights. Tchg. asst. U. Santa Clara (Calif.) Sch. Law, 1979; judge's law clk. U.S. Ct. Appeals, 9th Cir., San Francisco, 1980; assoc. Pitto & Ubhaus, San Jose, Calif., 1980-82, Germino, Layne & Brodie, Palo Alto, Calif., 1982-87, Tarkington, O'Connor & O'Neill, San Jose, 1988-90, Smith & Smith, San Jose, 1990-92; pvt. practice Law Offices of Stephen G. Opperwall, Pleasanton, Calif., 1992—; judge pro tem Santa Clara County Cts., 1986—, Alameda County (Calif.) Cts., 1992—; mem. adv. bd. Fremont (Calif.) Bank, 1996. Editor Santa Clara Law Review, 1980. Mem. bd. dirs. Fremont Symphony, 1994. Mem. Coml. Law League Am., Pleasanton C. of C. Avocations: golf, tennis, computers. Consumer commercial, Bankruptcy. Office: 4900 Hopyard Rd Ste 100 Pleasanton CA 94588-3345

**ORATZ, LISA T.,** lawyer; b. San Diego, Jan. 21, 1961; m. Keith S. Oratz, June 28, 1981. BA, UCLA, 1982, JD, 1986. Bar: Calif. 1986, Wash. 1989. Assoc. Irell & Manella, L.A., 1986-88, Bogle & Gates, Bellevue, Wash., 1988-91, Williams Kastner & Gibbs, Bellevue, 1992-96; of counsel Perkins Coie, Bellevue, 1996—. Contbr. articles to profl. jours. Bd. dirs., mem. assocs. program Corp. Coun. for the Arts, Seattle, 1993—; bd. dirs. Eastside Literacy Coun., Bellevue, 1989-93. Mem. Computer Law Assn., Wash. Software Alliance. Intellectual property, Computer, Trademark and copyright. Office: Perkins Coie 411 108th Ave NE Ste 1800 Bellevue WA 98004-5584

**ORBERSON, WILLIAM BAXTER,** lawyer, educator; b. Jeffersonville, Ind., Aug. 24, 1962; s. William B. and Nancy Lee Orberson; m. Lea Lynn Mater, May 18, 1984; children: Katherine, Madeline, Allyson. BA in Bus. Adminstrn. magna cum laude, Bellarmine Coll., 1983; JD cum laude, U. Louisville, 1986. Bar: Ky. 1986, U.S. Dist. Ct. (ea. dist.) Ky. 1987, U.S. Dist. Ct. (we. dist.) Ky. 1990. Ptnr. Phillips, Parker, Orbersond and Moore P.L.C., Louisville, 1986—; adj. prof. U. Louisville Sch. Law, 1994—. Bd. dirs. Chapel Creek Neighborhood Assn., New Albany, Ind., 1997, v.p., 1998. Mem. ABA, Am. Judicature Soc., Def. Rsch. Inst., Ky. Bar Assn., Louisville Bar Assn. (exec. com. litigation sect. 1994), St. Xavier Legal Soc., Ky. Def. Counsel, U. Louisville Sch. Law Alumni Assn. (class dir. 1994—). Republican. Roman Catholic. Avocations: golf, fishing. Fax: 502-587-1927. General civil litigation, Insurance, Personal injury. Office: Phillips Parker Orbersond Moore PLC Aegon Ctr 716 W Main St Ste 300 Louisville KY 40202-2634

**ORDEN, STEWART L.,** lawyer; b. N.Y.C., Jan. 13, 1953; s. Charles Quigley and Esther (Ash) O.; m. Bonnie Lynn Raymond, Nov. 12, 1988; children: Molly, Justin, Tyler. BA, Clark U., 1975; JD, Bklyn. Law Sch., 1979. Bar: N.Y. 1979. Sr. trial atty. Kings Dist. Atty., Bklyn., 1979-87; ptnr. Orden & Cohen, N.Y.C., 1987-91; pvt. practice, N.Y.C., 1991—; expert on trial techniques and cultural defs. Mem. N.Y. Coun. Def. Lawyers, Assn. Bar City N.Y., N.Y. Criminal Bar Assn., N.Y. State Def. Lawyers Assn., Nat. Assn. Def. Lawyers. Democrat. Avocations: skiing, windsurfing, swimming, rollerblading, biking. Civil rights, Criminal, General civil litigation. Office: 233 Broadway Rm 780 New York NY 10279-0799

**ORDOVER, ABRAHAM PHILIP,** lawyer, mediator; b. Far Rockaway, N.Y., Jan. 18, 1937; s. Joseph and Bertha (Fromberg) O.; m. Carol M. Ordover, Mar. 23, 1961; children: Andrew Charles, Thomas Edward. BA magna cum laude, Syracuse U., 1958; JD, Yale U., 1961. Bar: N.Y. 1961, U.S. Dist. Ct. (so. and ea. dists.) N.Y., U.S. Ct. Appeals (2d cir.), U.S. Supreme Ct. Assoc. Cahill, Gordon & Reindel, N.Y.C., 1961-71; prof. law Hofstra U., Hempstead, N.Y., 1971-81; L.Q.C. Lamar prof. law Emory U., Atlanta, 1981-91; CEO Resolution Resources Corp., Atlanta, 1991—; mediator and arbitrator; vis. prof. Cornell U., Ithaca, N.Y., 1977; vis. lectr. Tel Aviv U., 1989, Am. Law Inst.; team leader nat. program Nat. Inst. Trial Advocacy, Boulder, Colo., 1980, 82, 84, 86, 89, tchr. program Cambridge, Mass., 1979-84, 88, adv. program Gainesville, Fla., 1978-79, northeast regional dir., 1977-81; team leader SE regional program, 1983; team leader Atlanta Bar Trial Tech. Program, 1981-91; lectr. in field; sr. v.p. Resolute Sys. Inc., also bd. dirs. Author: Argument to the Jury, 1982, Problems and Cases in Trial Advocacy, 1983, Advanced Materials in Trial Advocacy, 1988, Alternatives to Litigation, 1993, Cases and Materials in Evidence, 1993, Art of Negotiation, 1994; prodr. ednl. films; contbr. articles to profl. jours. Bd. dirs. Atlanta Legal Aid Soc., 1984-91, 7 Stages Theatre, 1991-96. Recipient Gumpert award Am. Coll. Trial Lawyers, 1984, 85, Jacobsen award Roscoe Pound Am. Trial Lawyer Found., 1986. Fellow Am. Coll. Civil Trial Mediators; mem. ABA, N.Y. State Bar Assn., Assn. Am. Law Schs. (chair litigation sect.), Atlanta Lawyers Club, Am. Law Inst., Am. Acad. of Civil Trial Mediators. Avocation: photography. Office: Resolution Resources Corp 303 Peachtree St Atlanta GA 30308

**O'REGAN, DEBORAH,** association executive, lawyer; b. New Prague, Minn., Aug. 30, 1953; d. Timothy A. and Ermalinda (Brinkman) O'R.; m. Ron Kahlenbeck, Sept. 29, 1984; children: Katherine, Ryan. BA, Coll. of St. Catherine, 1975; JD, William Mitchell Coll. of Law, 1980. Bar: Ala. 1982, Minn. 1980. Asst. city atty. City of Bloomington, Minn., 1978-81, asst. city mgr., 1981-82; CLE dir. Alaska Bar Assn., Anchorage, 1982-84, exec. dir., 1985—; mem. task force on gender equality State Fed. Joint Commn., Anchorage, 1991—; mem. selection com. U.S. Magistrate Judge, U.S. Dist of Ala., 1992; mem. adv. bd. Anchorage Daily News, 1991-93. Mem. Nat. Assn. Bar Execs. (exec. com. 1993-97). Avocations: travel, outdoors, rollerblading. Office: Alaska Bar Assn 510 L St Ste 602 Anchorage AK 99501-1959

**O'REILLY, ANN CATHERINE,** lawyer; b. Rochester, Minn., Dec. 18, 1970; d. Wilfred Gerard and Judith Ann O'Reilly. BA with distinction, U. Wis., 1992; JD cum laude, U. Minn., 1996. Bar: Minn. 1996, U.S. Dist. Ct. Minn. 1998. Law clk. to Hon. John Sommerville Minn. 4th Jud. Dist., Mpls., 1996-97; assoc. atty. LeVander, Gillen & Miller, PA, South St. Paul, Minn., 1997—. Contbr. chpt. to book. Bd. dirs., v.p. Dakota County Legal Assistance, 1997—. Mayo Clinic scholar, 1989. Mem. ABA, Minn. State Bar Assn., Hennepin County Bar Assn., Dakota County Bar Assn., Minn. Women Lawyers. Democrat. Roman Catholic. Avocation: antique refinishing and collecting. E-mail: aoreilly@levander.com. General civil litigation, Criminal, Municipal (including bonds). Office: LeVander Gillen & Miller PA 633 Concord St S Ste 400 South Saint Paul MN 55075-2423

**O'REILLY, EDWARD JOSEPH,** lawyer; b. Boston, June 13, 1953; s. Robert Christopher and Edith Mae (Robbins) O'R.; div.; 1 child, Amelia Mae. BA, U. Mass., 1975; JD, New Eng. Sch. Law, 1981. Bar: Mass. 1982, U.S. Dist. Ct. Mass. 1982. Corrections officer, counselor Mass. Dept. Corrections, Norfolk and Boston, 1976-78; fire fighter Watertown and Gloucester (Mass.) Fire Depts., 1978-81; pvt. practice law Watertown, Gloucester, 1982—. Councillor-at-large Gloucester City Coun., 1982-84; past chmn. Gloucester Sch. Com. Mem. Gloucester Bar Assn. (past pres.), Essex County Bar Assn. Avocations: travel, sailing. Criminal. Home: PO Box 1513 Gloucester MA 01931-1513 Office: 63 Middle St Gloucester MA 01930-5736

**O'REILLY, JAMES THOMAS,** lawyer, educator, author; b. N.Y.C., Nov. 15, 1947; s. Matthew Richard and Regina (Casey) O'R.; children: Jean, Ann. BA cum laude, Boston Coll., 1969; JD, U. Va., 1974. Bar: Va. 1974, Ohio, 1974, U.S. Supreme Ct. 1979, U.S. Ct. Appeals (6th cir.) 1980. Atty. Procter & Gamble Co., Cin., 1974-76, counsel, 1976-79, sr. counsel for food, drug and product safety, 1979-85, corp. counsel, 1985-93, assoc. gen. counsel, 1993-98, adj. prof. in adminstrv. law U. Cin., 1980-97, vis. prof. law, 1998—; cons. Adminstrv. Conf. U.S., 1981-82, 89-90, Congl. Office of Compliance, 1995-96; arbitrator State Employee Relations Bd.; mem. Ohio Bishops Adv. Council, Mayor's Infrastructure Commn, Cin. Environ. Adv. Coun. Author: Federal Information Disclosure, 1977, Food and Drug Administration Regulatory Manual, 1979, Unions' Rights to Company Information, 1980, Federal Regulation of the Chemical Industry, 1980, Administrative Rulemaking, 1983, Ohio Public Employee Collective Bargaining, 1984, Protecting Workplace Secrets, 1985, Emergency Response to Chemical Accidents, 1986, Product Defects and Hazards, 1987, Toxic Torts Strategy Deskbook, 1989; Protecting Trade Secrets Under SARA, 1988, Complying With Canada's New Labeling Law, 1989, Solid Waste Mgmt., 1991, Ohio Products Liability Handbook, 1991, Toxic Torts Guide, 1992, ABA Product Liability Resource Manual, 1993, RCRA and Superfund Practice Guide, 1993, Clean Air Permits manual, 1994, United States Environmental Liabilities, 1994, Elder Safety, 1995, Environmental and Workplace Safety for University and Hospital Managers, 1996, Indoor Environmental Health, 1997, Product Warnings, Defects & Hazards, 1999; contbr. articles to profl. jours.; editorial bd. Food and Drug Cosmetic Law Jour. Mem. Hamilton County Dem. Central Com. Served with U.S. Army, 1970-72. Mem. Food and Drug Law Inst. (chair program com.), ABA (chmn. AD law sect.), Fed. Bar Assn., Leadership Cin. Democrat. Roman Catholic. Administrative and regulatory, Environmental. Office: 24 Jewett Dr Cincinnati OH 45215-2648

**O'REILLY, TIMOTHY PATRICK,** lawyer; b. San Lorenzo, Calif., Sept. 12, 1945; s. Thomas Marvin and Florence Ann (Ohlman) O'R.; m. Susan Ann Marshall, July 18, 1969; children: T. Patrick Jr., Sean M., Colleen K. BS, Ohio State U., 1967; JD, NYU, 1971. Bar: Pa. 1971, U.S. Dist. Ct. (ea. dist.) Pa. 1971, U.S. Dist. Ct. (mid. dist.) Pa. 1972, U.S. Ct. Appeals (3d cir.) 1977, U.S. Supreme Ct. 1988. Ptnr. Morgan, Lewis & Bockius, Phila., 1978—. Editor: Developing Labor Law, 1989; contbr. articles to profl. jours. V.p. Chester Valley Bd. Govs., Malvern, Pa., 1980-85; bd. dirs. Notre Dame Acad. and Devon Preparatory Sch. Mem. ABA (chmn. com. on devel. of the law under the Nat. Labor Relations Act., editor-in-chief The Developing Labor Law jour.), Pa. Bar Assn., Phila. Bar Assn., Ohio State U. Alumni Assn. Avocation: golf. Labor, Pension, profit-sharing, and employee benefits. Home: 1127 Cymry Dr Berwyn PA 19312-2056 Office: Morgan Lewis & Bockius 1701 Market St Philadelphia PA 19103-2903

**O'REILLY, TIMOTHY PATRICK,** judge; b. Bridgeville, Pa., Oct. 2, 1939; s. Alexander James and Marcella Isabel (Rolin) O'R.; m. Maureen Tighe (dec. Nov. 1986); children: Timothy Patrick Jr., Margaret Tighe. BA cum laude, Duquesne U., 1961; JD, Yale U., 1964. Bar: Pa., U.S. Dist. Ct. (we. dist.) Pa., U.S. Ct. Appeals (3d cir.), U.S. Supreme Ct. Atty. NLRB, 1965-69; justice of peace Dist. 05-2-21, Bridgeville, Collier, Heidelberg, South Fayette, Pa., 1970-76; pvt. practice, 1966-95; judge Ct. Common Pleas Allegheny County, 1996—. Staff sgt. USAF, 1964-65; mem. USAFR, 1965-70. Mem. Ancient Order Hibernians, Knights of Equity. Avocations: farming, skiing, writing. Office: Ct Common Please Allegheny County 711 City County Bldg Pittsburgh PA 15219

**ORIE, JANE CLARE,** state representative; d. John R. Orie. BA, Franklin Marshall U.; JD, Duquesne U. Law Sch. Asst. dist. atty. Allegheny County Dist. Atty.'s Office, Pitts., 1989-93; dep. atty. gen. Pa. Office of Atty. Gen., Pitts., 1993-96; state rep. 28th legis. dist. Pa. Ho. of Reps., Harrisburg, 1996—. Republican. Office: 9400 Mcknight Rd Ste 205 Pittsburgh PA 15237-6007

**ORIN, STUART I.,** lawyer. Exec. v.p. corp. affairs, gen. counsel UAL Corp., Elk Grove Village, Ill., 1996—. Office: UAL Corp PO Box 66100 Chicago IL 60666-0100

**ORIOLO, JOSEPH MICHAEL,** lawyer; b. Woodbury, N.J., Jan. 3, 1958; s. Donimic Joseph and Davie Joy Oriolo; m. Margy Grace Courtney, June 2, 1984; children: John, Michael, Luke. BSBA, Georgetown U., 1980; JD, Rutgers U., 1983. Bar: N.J., Pa., U.S. Dist. Ct. N.J. Atty. Ravin, Davis & Sweet, Woodbridge, N.J., 1984-85; atty. Greenbaum Rowe Smith Ravin Davis & Himmel, LLP, Woodbridge, 1985—, ptnr., 1991—. Bd. dirs. Shrewsbury (N.J.) Recreation Com., 1998—. Mem. N.J. State Bar Assn., Middlesex County Bar Assn. (chmn. bus./corp. law com. 1996-99). General corporate, Contracts commercial, Mergers and acquisitions. Home: 253 Williamsburg Dr Shrewsbury NJ 07702-4564 Office: Greenbaum Rowe et al 99 Wood Ave S Iselin NJ 08830-2715

**ORLINSKY, ETHAN GEORGE,** lawyer; b. N.Y.C., Apr. 8, 1964; s. Philip Jack and Rina O. BA, Stanford U., 1986; JD, NYU, 1989. Bar: N.Y. 1990. Assoc. Simpson Thacher & Bartlett, N.Y.C., 1989-92; assoc. counsel Major League Baseball Properties, N.Y.C., 1992-95, dir. legal affairs, 1995-97; v.p., gen. counsel Major League Baseball Enterprises, N.Y.C., 1997—. Intellectual property, Sports, Trademark and copyright. Office: Major League Baseball Enterprises 245 Park Ave New York NY 10167-0002

**ORMASA, JOHN,** retired utility executive, lawyer; b. Richmond, Calif., May 30, 1925; s. Juan Hormaza and Maria Inocencia Olondo; m. Dorothy Helen Trumble, Feb. 17, 1952; children: Newton Lee, John Trumble, Nancy Jean Davies. BA, U. Calif.-Berkeley, 1948; JD, Harvard U., 1951. Bar: Calif. 1952, U.S. Supreme Ct. 1959. Assoc. Clifford C. Anglim, 1951-52; assoc. Richmond, Carlson, Collins, Gordon & Bold, 1952-56, ptnr., 1956-59; with So. Calif. Gas Co., L.A., 1959-66, gen. atty., 1963-65, v.p., gen. counsel, 1965-66; v.p., sys. gen. counsel Pacific Lighting Service Co., Los Angeles, 1966-72; v.p., gen. counsel Pacific Lighting Corp., Los Angeles, 1973-75, v.p., sec., gen. counsel, 1975. Acting city atty., El Cerrito, Calif., 1952. Served with U.S. Navy, 1943-46. Mem. ABA, Calif. State Bar Assn., Richmond (Calif.) Bar Assn. (pres. 1959), Kiwanis (v.p. 1959). Republican. Roman Catholic.

**ORMSBY, CHARLES WILLIAM, JR.,** lawyer; b. Phila.; s. Charles William and Lorraine P. Ormsby; m. Linda A. Deveau, Mar. 21, 1981; children: Charles III, Ashleigh, Brittany. AB, Franklin and Marshall Coll., 1980; JD, George Washington U., 1983. Bar: Pa. 1983, U.S. Supreme Ct. 1998. Assoc. Schnader, Harrison, Segal & Lewis, Phila., 1983-85, Kleinbard, Bell & Brecker, Phila., 1985-89; ptnr. Semanoff, Ormsby & Greenberg, LLP, Jenkintown, Pa., 1989—. Pres. William Tennent Alumni Assn., Warminster, Pa., 1994-98. Republican. Roman Catholic. Avocation: golf. General corporate, Contracts commercial, Real property. Office: Semanoff Ormsby and Greenberg LLP 610 Old York Rd Ste 200 Jenkintown PA 19046-2867

**ORNSTEIN, ALEXANDER THOMAS,** lawyer; b. Detroit, Oct. 11, 1944; s. Charles and Martha (Lichter) O.; m. Harriet Rozenblum, July 5, 1970; children: Charles Allen, Deborah Rena. BS, Washburn U., 1969; postgrad., Detroit Coll. Law, 1970-72; JD, Wayne State U., 1974. Bar: Mich. 1972, U.S. Dist. Ct. (ea. dist.) Mich. 1972, U.S. Ct. Appeals (6th cir.) 1972, U.S. Supreme Ct. 1978. Counselor New Horizons of Oakland County, Pontiac, Mich., 1969-70; staff atty. Mich. Mut. Ins. Co., Detroit, 1973-74; assoc. Chambers, Steiner, Mazur, Ornstein & Amlin P.C., Detroit, 1974-96; pvt. practice Southfield, Mich., 1996—; hearing referee Mich. Dept. Civil Rights, Detroit and Flint, Mich., 1980—. Editor Metro Memo Newspaper, 1984, 86-88; editor-in-chief State Bar of Mich.'s Workers Compensation Law Rev., 1991-93. Pres. Dist. 6, B'nai B'rith; pres. B'nai B'rith Youth Orgn., 1984—; mem. exec. com. B'nai B'rith Internat. Youth Commn.; mem. men's club bd. Congregation Shaarey Zedek; mng. bd. Bais Chabad Farmington Hills, Mich.; pres. Hillel Found. Met. Detroit, 1988-90, chmn. bd.; pres. Centennial Lodge, 1985; internat. v.p. B'nai B'rith, 1996—. Bancroft-Whitney scholar, 1971. Mem. ABA, ATLA, Mich. State Bar Assn. (workers compensation coun.), Detroit Bar Assn., Fed. Bar Assn., Mich. Trial Lawyers Assn., Am. Judicature Soc., Anti Defamation League (co-chair campus com. 1984-86). Avocations: computers, vol. service, flute. Workers' compensation, Personal injury, Securities. Home: 32614 Olde Franklin Dr Farmington Hills MI 48334-1744 Office: 19400 W 10 Mile Rd Ste 111 Southfield MI 48075-2400

**OROL, ELLIOT S.,** lawyer; b. N.Y.C., Feb. 29, 1956; s. Allan and Bernice (Ashkenazy) O.; m. Harriet Orol, June 10, 1984; children: Zoey, Rachel. BS, SUNY, Binghamton, 1977; JD, U. Chgo., 1980, MBA, 1981. Bar: N.Y. 1981. Assoc. Finley, Kumble, Wagner et al, N.Y.C., 1981-83, Paul, Weiss, Rifkind, Wharton & Garrison, N.Y.C., 1983-86; v.p., corp. counsel The Continental Corp., N.Y.C., 1987-96; v.p., gen. counsel, sec. The GRE Ins. Group, N.Y.C., 1996—. Mem. ABA, Am. Corp. Counsel Assn., Am. Soc. of Corp. Secs., Phi Beta Kappa. General corporate, Finance, Private international. Office: 25th Fl 61 Broadway New York NY 10006-2802

**O'RORKE, JAMES FRANCIS, JR.,** lawyer; b. N.Y.C., Dec. 4, 1936; s. James Francis and Helen (Weber) O'R.; m. Carla Phelps, Aug. 6, 1964. A.B., Princeton U., 1958; J.D., Yale U., 1961. Bar: N.Y. 1962. Assoc. Davies, Hardy & Schenck, 1962-69; ptnr. Davies, Hardy, Ives & Lawther, 1969-72, Skadden, Arps, Slate, Meagher & Flom, N.Y.C., 1972—; dir. Clinipad Corp.; mem. adv. bd. Chgo. Title Ins. Co. N.Y. Trustee Mus. Am. Indian-Heye Found., 1977-80; dir. James Lenox House Assn., Inc. Mem. ABA, N.Y. State Bar Assn., Assn. Bar City N.Y., Am. Coll. Real Estate Lawyers, Princeton Club N.Y.C. Real property, Contracts commercial, Finance. Office: Skadden Arps Slate Meagher & Flom 919 3rd Ave New York NY 10022-3902

**O'ROURKE, JAMES LOUIS,** lawyer; b. Bridgeport, Conn., July 5, 1958; s. James G. and Margaret Elizabeth (Fesco) O'R.; m. Margaret C. DiCicco, Sept. 18, 1994. BS, U. Bridgeport, 1984, JD, 1987. Bar: Conn. 1988, U.S. Dist. Ct. Conn. 1989, Mashantucket Pequot Tribal Bar 1995, Supreme Ct. of U.S., 1998. Pvt. practice Stratford, Conn., 1987—. With USN, 1976-79. Mem. ABA, Assn. Am. Trial Lawyers Assn., Conn. Trial Lawyers Assn., Conn. Bar Assn., Greater Bridgeport Bar Assn. Roman Catholic. Avocations: boating, cycling, swimming, golf. Personal injury, General practice, Workers' compensation. Office: The Barnum Profl Bldg 1825 Barnum Ave Stratford CT 06614-5333

**O'ROURKE, RICHARD LYNN,** lawyer; b. Bklyn., Nov. 27, 1949; s. Joseph and Loretta (Casey) O'R.; m. Renee Marie Kupiec, July 17, 1971; children: Shannon, Kathleen. BA, SUNY, Geneseo, 1971; MA, Bowling Green State U., 1972; JD, Pace U. Sch. Law, 1981. Bar: N.Y. 1982, U.S. Ct. Appeals (10th cir.) 1983, U.S. Ct. Appeals (2d cir.) 1994, U.S. Dist. Ct. (all dists.) N.Y. 1982. Dir. career planning Pace U., Pleasantville, N.Y., 1977-81; assoc. Keane & Beane P.C., White Plains, N.Y., 1981-86, ptnr., v.p., 1986—. Judge Village of Brewster, N.Y., 1992—; pres. Brewster Edn. Found., 1992-94; town atty. Southeast Brewster, 1986-89, chmn. zoning bd. appeals, 1986-86; adv. bd. Jr. Achievement West, White Plains, 1977-82. Mem. Putnam County Magistrates Assn. (v.p. 1994-96, pres. 1997—). Avocations: golf, history. Real property, Environmental, General civil litigation. Office: Keane & Beane One N Broadway White Plains NY 10601

**O'ROURKE, WILLIAM ANDREW, III,** lawyer; b. Columbus, Ohio, Jan. 11, 1958; s. William A. Jr. and Jean (Solari) O'R.; m. Sandra Statum; children: Kevin, Melanie, Brian, Patrick. BA, Holy Cross Coll., 1980; JD, Suffolk U., 1983. Bar: Vt. 1984, U.S. Dist. Ct. Vt. 1985. Atty., shareholder Ryan, Smith & Carbine, Rutland, Vt., 1984—. Mem. Vt. Health Policy Coun., Montpelier, 1987, Mt. Saint Joseph Sch. Bd. Mem. ABA, ATLA., Def. Rsch. Inst., Christ the King Sch. Athletic Assn. E-mail: wor@rsclaw.com. Personal injury, Insurance, Workers' compensation. Home: 10 Hilltop Ter Rutland VT 05701-4612 Office: Ryan Smith & Carbine PO Box 310 Rutland VT 05702-0310

**ORR, CYNTHIA HUJAR,** lawyer; b. Panama City, Fla., Oct. 4, 1957; d. Thomas Stanley and Joan Theresa (Sigler) Hujar; m. John David Orr, Aug. 1, 1981. BBA, U. Tex., 1979; JD, St. Mary's U., 1988. Assoc. Goldstein, Goldstein & Hilley, San Antonio, Tex. Mem. Nat. Assn. Women Lawyers (exec. bd. mem.-at-large), Nat. Assn. Criminal Def. Lawyers (co-chair internet com.), San Antonio Criminal Def. Lawyers Assn. (ex-oficio dir.), Tex. Criminal Def. Lawyers Assn. (sec.), Assn. Bd. Cert. Specialists Criminal Law (v.p.). Criminal, Appellate, Antitrust. Home: 2822 Cherry Field Dr San Antonio TX 78245-2601 Office: Goldstein Goldstein & Hilley 29th Fl Tower Life Bldg San Antonio TX 78205

**ORR, DEBRA ANN,** lawyer; b. Twin Falls, Idaho, May 17, 1962; d. Auburn Ray and Loretta Carol Orr. BS, U. Idaho, 1984, JD, 1987. Bar: Idaho 1988, U.S. Dist. Ct. Idaho 1988. Atty. Canyon County Pub. Defender, Nampa, Idaho, 1987-91; ptnr. Orr & Kime, Attys. at Law, Caldwell, Idaho, 1991-95; pvt. practice Caldwell, 1995—. V.p. bd. dirs. Valley Crisis Ctr., Nampa, 1996—; v.p. adminstrv. coun. Caldwell Meth. Ch., 1997—; pres. bd. dirs. 3d dist. CASA Program, Caldwell, 1997—. Recipient Pro Bono award Idaho State Bar, 1997. Mem. Idaho State Bar Assn. (mem. civil rules com. 1995—), Canyon County Lawyers' Club (past pres. 1995-96). Avocations: softball, walking, bicycling. Family and matrimonial, Criminal, Juvenile. Office: PO Box 156 Caldwell ID 83606-0156

**ORR, DENNIS PATRICK,** lawyer; b. N.Y.C., Dec. 29, 1952; s. Gerard Samuel and Mary Ellen (Dowd) O.; m. Laurie Louise Lawless, Jan. 15, 1977; children: Kathryn, Kristen, Megan, Matthew. BA, Boston Coll., 1975; JD, St. John's U., 1978. Bar: N.Y. 1979, U.S. Dist. Ct. (so. and ea. dists.) N.Y. 1979, U.S. Ct. Appeals (2d cir.) 1986. Assoc. Shearman & Sterling, N.Y.C., 1978-86, ptnr., 1987-97; ptnr. Mayer, Brown & Platt, N.Y.C., 1997—. St. Thomas More scholar St. John's Law Sch., Jamaica, N.Y., 1975. Mem. ABA, N.Y. State Bar Assn. Roman Catholic. Antitrust, Securities, Personal injury. Office: Mayer Brown & Platt 1675 Broadway Fl 19 New York NY 10019-5820

**ORR, RICK W.,** lawyer; b. Stevens Point, Wis., July 15, 1957; s. Ward Richard and Jeanne Dorothy O.; m. Cindy Marie Peterson, Feb. 27, 1977; children: Michael, Nicole, Abbie, Alexandra. BS cum laude, U. S.D., 1980, JD with honors, 1983. Bar: S.D. 1983, U.S. Ct. Appeals (8th cir.) 1983, U.S. Dist. Ct. S.D. 1985. Law clk. U.S. Ct. Appeals (8th cir.), Harrison, Ark., 1983-85; assoc. Davenport, Evans, Hurwitz & Smith, Sioux Falls, S.D., 1985-88, ptnr., 1988—. Editor-in-chief U. S.D. Law Rev., 1982-83. Recipient Grand Heart award United Way, Sioux Falls, 1996—. Mem. S.D. State Bar Assn., Phi Beta Kappa. Avocations: golfing, reading. General civil litigation, Insurance, Personal injury. Office: Davenport Evans Hurwitz & Smith 513 S Main Ave Sioux Falls SD 57104-6813

**ORR, ROBERT F.,** state supreme court justice; b. Norfolk, Va., Oct. 11, 1946. AB, U. N.C., 1971, JD, 1975. Bar: N.C. 1975. Pvt. practice Asheville, N.C., 1975-86; assoc. judge N.C. Ct. Appeals, 1986-94; assoc. justice N.C. Supreme Ct., Raleigh, 1994—; mem. N.C. Beverage Control Commn., 1985-86; adj. prof. appellate advocacy N.C. Ctrl. U. Sch. Law, 1989—, adj. prof. N.C. State constl. law, 1998. Mem. Asheville-Revitalization Commn., 1977-81, Asheville-Buncombe Hist. Resources Commn., 1980-81; bd. trustees Hist. Preservation Found. N.C., 1982-85; mem. Nat. Park Sys. Adv. Bd., 1990-95, chmn., 1992-93; bd. visitors U. N.C.-Chapel Hill, 1996—; mem. NCBAs Appellate Rules Study com., 1999—, Gov.'s Crime Commn. With U.S. Army, 1968-71. Mem. N.C. State Bar, 28th Jud. Dist., N.C. Bar Assn. Republican. Office: PO Box 1841 Raleigh NC 27602-1841 also: 304 Justice Bldg 2 E Morgan St Raleigh NC 27601-1428

**ORRICK, WILLIAM HORSLEY, JR.,** federal judge; b. San Francisco, Oct. 10, 1915; s. William Horsley and Mary (Downey) O.; m. Marion Naffziger, Dec. 5, 1947 (dec. Feb. 1995); children: Mary-Louise, Marion, William Horsley III; m. Suzanne Rogers, Jan. 19, 1996. Grad., Hotchkiss Sch., 1933; B.A., Yale, 1937; LL.B., U. Calif.-Berkeley, 1941. Bar: Calif. 1941. Partner Orrick, Dahlquist, Herrington & Sutcliffe, San Francisco, 1941-61; asst. atty. gen. civil div. Dept Justice, 1961-62, antitrust div., 1963-65; dep. under sec. state for adminstrn. Dept. State, 1962-63; practice law San Francisco, 1965-74; former partner firm Orrick, Herrington, Rowley & Sutcliffe; U.S. dist. judge No. Dist. Calif., 1974-85, sr. judge, 1985—. Past pres. San Francisco Opera Assn., Trustee, World Affairs Council; former trustee San Francisco Law Library, San Francisco Found., Children's Hosp. San Francisco, Grace Cathedral Corp. Served to capt. M.I. AUS, 1942-46. Recipient Alumnus of Yr. award Boalt Hall Alumni Assn., U. Calif., 1980. Fellow Am. Bar Found.; mem. Bar Assn. San Francisco (past trustee, treas.). Office: US Dist Ct PO Box 36060 450 Golden Gate Ave San Francisco CA 94102-3482

**ORSATTI, ERNEST BENJAMIN,** lawyer; b. Pitts., Nov. 14, 1949; s. Ernest Ubaldo and Dorothy Minerva (Pfeiffer) O.; m. Ingrid Zalman, May 3, 1975; 1 child, Benjamin E. BA, Marquette U., 1971; JD, Duquesne U., 1974; postgrad., Army Command and Gen. Staff Coll., 1984. Bar: Pa. 1974, U.S. Dist. Ct. (we. dist.) Pa. 1974, U.S. Ct. Appeals (3d cir.) 1977, U.S. Supreme Ct. 1978, U.S. Ct. Appeals (6th cir.) 1992. Assoc. Jubelirer, Pass & Intrieri, Pitts., 1974-81, ptnr., 1981—. Contbg. editor: The Developing Labor Law, 3d edit., 1992. Bd. dirs. Am. Italian Cultural Inst., Pitts. Served to capt. U.S. Army, 1975, lt. col., USAR, ret. Mem. ABA, ACLU, Am. Arbitration Assn., Pa. Bar Assn., Am. Legion. Democrat. Roman Catholic. Labor. Home: 9343 N Florence Rd Pittsburgh PA 15237-4815 Office: Jubelirer Pass & Intrieri 219 Fort Pitt Blvd Pittsburgh PA 15222-1576

**ORTEGO, JIM,** lawyer, legal educator; b. Lake Charles, La., Oct. 6, 1944; s. Yves and Lucille May (Dougay) O. JD, Tulane U., 1969; LLM, U. Toronto, 1973. Bar: La. 1969; bd. cert. family law specialist. Prof. law Dalhousie U., Halifax, N.S., Can., 1974-78; vis. fellow in law U. Chgo., 1978; prof. law Whittier Coll. Law, L.A., 1978-82; cons. Law Reform Commn. of Can., Ottawa, 1975-78, Stats. Can., Ottawa, 1975-80, Law Enforcement Assistance Adminstrn., Washington, 1978-81; vis. prof. law La. State U. Law Ctr., 1980; mem. La. Family Law Adv. Commn.; mem. La. S. Ct. Task Force on Legal Svcs. Co-author: Criminal Law, 1975, Selected Problems in Criminal Law, 1976; editor La. Family Law Newsletter. Mem. ABA (family law sect.), La. State Bar Assn. (chair family law sect., editor La. family law newsletter, Pro Bono award 1994), S.W. La. Bar Assn. Democrat. Family and matrimonial. Address: 1011 Lake Shore Dr Ste 402 Lake Charles LA 70601-9416

**ORTH, PAUL WILLIAM,** lawyer; b. Balt., May 7, 1930; s. Paul W. and Naomi (Howard Bevard) O.; m. Isle Haertle, June 15, 1956; children: Ingrid, Ilse Christine. AB, Dartmouth Coll., 1951; JD, Harvard U., 1954. Bar:

Mass. 1954, Conn. 1957, U.S. Dist. Ct. Conn. 1958, U.S. Ct. Appeals (2d cir.) 1960, U.S. Ct. Appeals (1st cir.) 1983, U.S. Supreme Ct. 1960. Assoc. Hippin, Carey & Powell, Hartford, Conn., 1957-62, ptnr., 1962-86; ptnr. Shipman & Goodwin, Hartford, 1987—; instr. Sch. Law U. Conn., 1959-81. Editor: Every Employee's Guide to the Law, 1993, 96. Chmn. Farmington Conservation Commn., 1982-83; mem. town com. Town of Farmington, 1973-81. With AUS, 1954-56. Fellow Am. Bar Found., Conn. Bar Found.; mem. ABA, Hartford County Bar Assn. (pres. 1983-84), Conn. Bar Assn. (chmn. coms.). Democrat. Labor, General civil litigation, Alternative dispute resolution. Office: Shipman & Goodwin LLP One American Row Hartford CT 06103

**ORTIQUE, REVIUS OLIVER, JR.,** city official; b. New Orleans, June 14, 1924; s. Revius Oliver and Lillie Edith (Long) O.; m. Miriam Marie Victorianne, Dec. 29, 1947; children—Rhesa Marie (Mrs. Alden J. McDonald). AB, Dillard U., 1947; MA, Ind. U., 1949; JD, So. U., 1956; LLD (hon.), Campbell Coll., 1960; LHD (hon.), Ithaca Coll., 1971; LLD (hon.), Ind. U., 1983, Morris Brown Coll., 1992, Loyola U. South, 1993, Dillard U., 1996. Bar: La. 1956, U.S. Dist. Ct 1956, Eastern Dist. La 1956, U.S. Fifth Circuit Ct. of Appeals 1956, U.S. Supreme Ct 1964. Practiced in New Orleans, 1956-78; judge Civil Dist. Ct. for Orleans Parish, 1978-92; assoc. justice La. Supreme Ct., 1993-94; chmn. New Orleans Aviation Bd., 1994—; lectr. labor law Dillard U., 1950-52, U. West Indies, 1986; formerly assoc. gen. counsel Cmty. Improvement Agy.; former gen. counsel 8th Dist. A.M.E. Ch.; former mem. Fed. Hosp. Coun., 1966, Pres.'s Commn. on Campus Unrest, 1970, Bd. Legal Svcs. Corp., 1975-83; chief judge civil cts. Orleans Parish, 1986-87; spkr. in field. Contbr. articles to profl. jours. Former pres. Met. Area Com.; former mem. Bd. City Trusts, New Orleans, New Orleans Legal Assistance Corp. Bd., Ad Hoc Com. for Devel. of Ctrl. Bus. Dist. City of New Orleans; bd. dirs. Cmty. Rels. Coun., Am. Lung Assn.; trustee Antioch Coll. Law, New Orleans chpt. Operation PUSH, 1981-84; pres. Louis A. Martinet Soc., 1959; active World's Fair, New Orleans, 1984, Civil Rights Movement, 1960-79; bd. dirs., mem. exec. com. Nat. Sr. Citizens Law Ctr., L.A., 1970-76, Criminal Justice Coordinating Com., UN Assn. New Orleans, 1980—; former mem. exec. bd. Nat. Bar Found.; mem. exec. com. econ. Devel. Coun. Greater New Orleans; past chmn. Health Edn. Authority of La.; trustee, mem. exec. com. Dillard U.; former mem. bd. mgmt. Flint Goodridge Hosp.; former mem. adv. bd. League Women Voters Greater New Orleans; former mem. men's adv. bd. YWCA; trustee AME Ch., former connectional trustee; former chancellor N.O. Fedn. Chs.; bd. dirs. Nat. Legal Aid and Defender Assn.; bd. trustees Civil Justice Found.; served on over 50 bds., commns. 1st lt. AUS, 1943-47, PTO. Recipient Arthur von Briesen medal Disting. Svcs. Disadvantaged Ams. NLADA, 1971, Weiss award NCCJ, 1975, Brotherhood award NCCJ, 1976, Nat. Black Achievement award, 1979, Poor People's Banner award, 1979, William H. Hastie award, 1983, Outstanding Citizen award Kiwanis of Pontchartrain, 1986, Civil Justice award, 1989, Daniel E. Byrd award NAACP, 1991, A.P. Tureaud Meml. medal La. State NAACP, 1993; Revius O. Ortique Jr. Law Libr. named in his honor, Lafayette, La., 1988; named Outstanding Young Man Nat. Urban League, 1958, Outstanding Person in La. Inst. Human Understanding, 1976, Citizen of Yr. Shreveport, 1993. Mem. ABA (del., Legal Svcs. program, Nat. adv. coun., 1964-71, jud. divsn.), Nat. Bar Assn. (pres. 1965-66, exec. bd., Raymond Pace Alexander award, jud. coun. 1987, William Hastie award 1982, Gertrude E. Rush award 1991), La. State Bar Assn. (former mem. ho. of dels., Lifetime Achievement award 1986), Nat. Legal Aid and Defender Assn. (past pres., mem. exec. bd.), La. District Judges Assn., Am. Judicature Soc. (bd. dirs. 1975-79), Civil Justice Found. (trustee 1989-93), Louis A. Martinet Legal Soc., World Peace Through Law (charter mem.), Blue Key Honor Soc., Phi Delta Kappa, Alpha Kappa Delta. Home: 10 Park Island Dr New Orleans LA 70122-1229 Office: New Orleans Aviation Bd PO Box 20007 New Orleans LA 70141-0007 *In 1989 the National Black Law Journal in cooperation with the UCLA Law Center published: Struggle: A Power Reserved to the People, which was distributed nationwide in commemoration of Black History month, the State of Louisiana thru the office of the Secretary of State has installed a life size portrait of Justice Ortique in the gallery of the State Archives, 1986-1994."With little or no effort on our part, life unfolds with opportunities and rewards, except that we permit our frailties to enslave our ambitions. I am grateful that there are only horizons."*

**ORTIZ, JAY RICHARD GENTRY,** lawyer; b. Washington, Mar. 21, 1945; s. Charles and Catherine Gentry (Candlin) O.; m. Lois Wright Hatcher Greer, June 12, 1982. B.A., Yale U., 1967; postgrad. Stanford U. 1967-68; J.D., U. N.Mex., 1972. Bar: N.Mex. 1973, Mo. 1978, Tenn. 1982, Ga., 1991, U.S. Dist. Ct. N.Mex. 1973, U.S. Ct. Appeals (10th cir. 1973), U.S. Supreme Ct. 1977, U.S. Dist. Ct. (western dist.) Mo. 1978, U.S. Dist. Ct. (no. dist.) Ga. 1991, U.S. Ct. Appeals (8th cir.) 1978, U.S. Ct. Appeals (11th cir.) 1991. Assoc. Rodey, Dickason, Sloan, Akin & Robb, Albuquerque, 1972-75; ptnr. Knight, Sullivan, Villella, Skarsgard & Michael, Albuquerque, 1975-77; litigation atty. Monsanto Co., St. Louis, 1977-81; environ. atty. Eastman Kodak Co., Kingsport, Tenn., 1981-84; sr. atty. AT&T, Atlanta, 1984-91; gen. counsel AMS Group, Inc., 1991-96, 98—; ConsultaAmerica Internat., 1994-97, Vision Net, Inc., 1994—, Constrn. Internat., Inc., 1996-97, Cross Ophthalmic Solutions, LLC, 1996-97, Univest, Ltd., 1996-97; pres. VMS, Inc., 1994—. Precinct vice chmn. Dem. Party, Albuquerque, 1971-77. Served to lt. (j.g.), USN, 1969-70. Mem. ABA, Ga. Bar Assn., N.Mex. Bar Assn., Mo. Bar Assn., Tenn. Bar Assn., Order of Coif, Yale Club of Ga., English Speaking Union, Delta Theta Phi (tribune 1972-77). Episcopalian. Federal civil litigation, Environmental, General corporate. Home: 1000 Buckingham Cir NW Atlanta GA 30327-2704 Office: VMS Inc 1419 Windy Ridge Pky Atlanta GA 30339

**ORTON, JOHN STEWART,** lawyer; b. Cin., Nov. 25, 1949; s. Stewart and Hanni (S.) O.; m. Katharine Fleming Wilson, Aug. 8, 1975; children: Elizabeth Fleming, Virginia Stewart. BA in Polit. Sci., Trinity Coll., 1972; JD, Washington and Lee U., 1975. Bar: Tex. 1975, U.S. Dist. Ct. (so. dist.) Tex. 1976, Colo. 1990. Assoc. Rowland & Keim, Houston, 1976-77, Greenwood & Koby, Houston, 1977-80; assoc., ptnr. Barrow, Bland & Rehmet, Houston, 1980-85; ptnr. Brown, Parker & Leahy, L.L.P., Houston, 1985—. Bd. dirs. Planned Parenthood Houston and S.E. Tex., 1987-96, St. John's Sch. Alumni Assn., Houston, 1991-94, Glassell Sch. Art, Houston, 1988—. Mem. State Bar Tex. Assn., State Bar Colo., Houston Bar Assn., Briar Club, Houston Club, Galveston Country Club. Avocations: tennis, golf, skiing, hiking. Banking, Real property, Contracts commercial. Office: Brown Parker & Leahy LLP 1200 Smith St Ste 3600 Houston TX 77002-4596

**ORTON, R. WILLIS,** lawyer; b. St. George, Utah, Apr. 4, 1954; s. Rulon D. and Laprele (Gubler) O.; m. Deborah Ann Ash, Aug. 20, 1977; children: Jacob, Laurie, Rachel, Nathan, David. BS, Brigham Young U., 1977; JD, U. Utah, 1981. Bar: Utah, Pa., U.S. Dist. Ct. Utah 1981, U.S. Dist. Ct. (no. dist.) Calif. 1989, U.S. Dist. Ct. (we. dist.) Pa. 1991, U.S. Ct. Appeals (10th cir.) 1984, U.S. Ct. Appeals (3rd cir.) 1992. Assoc., shareholder Callister, Nebeker & McCullough, Salt Lake City, 1981-94; assoc. Parson, Davies, Kinghorn & Peters, Salt Lake City, 1995-96, Mackey, Price & Williams, Salt Lake City, 1996-98, Kirton & McConkie, Salt Lake City, 1998—. Mem. Bonneville Knife and Fork Club, Salt Lake City, 1994—. Named to Outstanding Young Men of Am., 1986,. Mem. Rotary. General civil litigation, Federal civil litigation, State civil litigation. Office: Kirton & McConkie 60 E South Temple Salt Lake City UT 84111-1004

**ORWOLL, GREGG S. K.,** lawyer; b. Austin, Minn., Mar. 23, 1926; s. Gilbert M. and Kleonora (Kleven) O.; m. Laverne M. Flentie, Sept. 15, 1951; children: Kimball G., Kent A., Vikki A., Tristen A., Erik G. BS, Northwestern U., 1950; JD, U. Minn., 1953. Bar: Minn. 1953, U.S. Supreme Ct. 1973. Assoc. Dorsey & Whitney, Mpls., 1953-59, ptnr., 1959-60; assoc. counsel Mayo Clinic, Rochester, Minn., 1960-63, gen. counsel, 1963-87, sr. legal counsel, 1987-91, sr. counsel, 1991-92; gen. counsel, dir. Rochester Airport Co., 1962-84, v.p., 1981-84; gen. counsel Mayo Med. Svcs., Ltd., 1972-90; bd. dirs., sec. and gen. counsel Mayo Found. for Med. Edn. and Rsch., 1984-90; gen. counsel Mid-Am. Orthop. Assn., 1984—, Minn. Orthop. Soc., 1985-95; asst. sec./sec. Mayo Found., Rochester, 1972-91; sec. Mayo Emeritus Staff, 1999—; bd. dirs. Charter House, 1986-90; dir., officer Travelure Motel Corp., 1968-86; dir., v.p. Echo Too Ent., Inc.; dir., v.p. Oberhamer Inc.; bd. dirs. Am. Decal and Mfg. Co., 1989-93, sec., 1992-93; adj. prof. William Mitchell Coll. Law, 1978-84. Contbr. articles and chpts. to legal and medico-legal publs.; mem. bd. editors HealthSpan, 1984-93; mem. editl. bd. Minn. Law Rev., 1952-53. Trustee Minn. Coun. on Founds., 1977-82, Mayo Found., 1982-86; trustee William Mitchell Coll. Law, 1982-88, 89-98, mem. exec. com. 1990—; bd. visitors U. Minn. Law Sch., 1974-76, 85-91; mem. U. Minn. Regent Candidate Adv. Coun., 1988—, Minn. State Compensation Coun., 1991-97. With USAF, 1944-45. Recipient Outstanding Svc. medal U.S. Govt., 1991. Mem. ABA, AMA (affiliate), Am. Corp. Counsel Assn., Minn. Soc. Hosp. Attys. (bd. dirs. 1981-86), Minn. State Bar Assn. (chmn. legal/med. com. 1977-81), Olmsted County Bar Assn. (v.p., pres. 1977-79), Rochester C. of C., U. Minn. Law Alumni Assn. (bd. dirs. 1973-76, 85-91), Rochester U. Club (pres. 1977), The Doctors Mayo Soc., Mid Am. Orthop. Assn. (hon.), Mayo Alumni Assn. (hon.), Phi Delta Phi, Phi Delta Theta. Republican. General corporate, Personal injury. Home: 2233 5th Ave NE Rochester MN 55906-4017 Office: Mayo Clinic 200 1st St SW Rochester MN 55905-0002

**ORZEL, MICHAEL DALE,** lawyer; b. Milw., Mar. 6, 1952; s. Stanley and Tekla Mary (Kranski) O.; m. Patti Jayne McGilvray, June 25, 1977. B.A., Marquette U., 1974, J.D., 1977. Bar: Wis. 1977, U.S. Dist Ct. (ea. and we. dists.) Wis. 1977. Assoc. Karius & Kay, Milw., 1977-79, Herman L. Wiernick, S.C., Milw., 1979-81; sole practice, Wauwatosa, Wis., 1981—; Mem. State Bar Wis., Milw. Bar Assn., Waukesha County Bar Assn. Roman Catholic. Criminal, Family and matrimonial, General practice. Home: 3040 S 145th St New Berlin WI 53151-1233 Office: 6525 W Bluemound Rd Milwaukee WI 53213-4073

**OSAKWE, CHRISTOPHER,** lawyer, educator; b. Lagos, Nigeria, May 8, 1942; came to U.S. 1970, naturalized 1979; s. Simon and Hannah (Morgan) O.; m. Maria Elena Amador, Aug. 19, 1982; 1 child, Rebecca E. LLB, Moscow State U., 1967, PhD, 1970; JSD, U. Ill., 1974. Bar: Moscow, 1967. Prof. sch. law Tulane U., New Orleans, 1972-81, 86-88; ptnr. firm Riddle and Brown, New Orleans, 1989—; Eason-Weinmann prof. comparative law, dir. Eason-Weinmann Ctr. for Comparative Law Tulane U., New Orleans, 1981-86; ptnr. Riddle and Brown, 1988—; vis. prof. U. Pa., 1978, U. Mich., 1981, Washington and Lee U., 1986; vis. fellow St. Anthony's Coll., Oxford U., Eng., 1980, Christ Ch. Coll., Oxford U., 1988-89; cons. U.S. Dept. Commerce, 1980-85. Author: The Participation of the Soviet Union in Universal International Organizations, 1972, The Foundations of Soviet Law, 1981, Joint Ventures with the Soviet Union: Law and Practice, 1990, Soviet Business Law, 2 vols., 1991, (with others) Comparative Legal Traditions in a Nutshell, 1982, Comparative Legal Traditions--Text, Materials and Cases, 1985; editor Am. Jour. Comparative Law, 1978-85. Carnegie doctoral fellow Hague Acad. Internat. Law, 1969; Russian rsch. fellow Harvard U., 1972; USSR sr. rsch. exch. fellow, 1982, rsch. fellow Kennan Inst. for Advanced Russian Studies, 1988. Mem. ABA, Am. Law Inst., Am. Soc. Internat. Law, Supreme Ct. Hist. Soc., Soc. de Legislation Comparée, Order of Coif. Republican. Roman Catholic. Home: 339 Audubon Blvd New Orleans LA 70125-4124 Office: 201 S Charles Ave Ste 3100 New Orleans LA 70170

**OSBORN, DONALD ROBERT,** lawyer; b. N.Y.C., Oct. 9, 1929; s. Robert W. and Ruth C. (Compton) O.; m. Marcia Lontz, June 4, 1955; children: David, Judith, Robert; m. Marie A. Johnson, Sept. 11, 1986. BA, Cornell U., 1951; LLB, Columbia U., 1957. Bar: N.Y. 1957, U.S. Tax Ct. 1958, U.S. Ct. Claims 1961, U.S. Ct. Appeals (2d cir.) 1974, U.S. Ct. Appeals (8th cir.) 1974, U.S. Dist. Ct. (so. and ea. dists.) N.Y. 1975, U.S. Supreme Ct. 1975. Assoc. Sullivan & Cromwell, N.Y.C., 1957-64, ptnr., 1964-96, sr. counsel 1997—. Trustee Hamilton Coll., 1978-88, Mus. of Broadcasting, 1975-80; trustee, treas. Kirkland Coll., 1969-78; mem. coun. White Burkett Miller Ctr. Pub. Affairs, 1976-82; bd. dirs., pres. Stevens Kingsley Found., 1967—; sec., treas. Dunlevy Milbank Found., 1974—; bd. dirs. Spanel Found., 1978-88, CBS, Inc., 1975-80. Served with USN, 1951-54. Mem. ABA, N.Y. State Bar Assn., Assn. of Bar of City of N.Y., Am. Bar Found., Scarsdale Golf Club, India House, Regency Whist Club, Country Club of the Rockies. Presbyterian. Private international, Probate, Corporate taxation. Home: 1049 Park Ave New York NY 10028-1061 Office: Sullivan & Cromwell 125 Broad St Fl 28 New York NY 10004-2489

**OSBORN, GERALD T.,** lawyer; b. Kansas City, Mo., Jan. 8, 1956; s. Samuel and Marjory O.; m. Ann C.S. Osborn. BA, Western Washington U., 1979; JD, Willamette U., 1983. Bar: Wash., U.S. Dist. Ct. (we. dist.) Wash. Pvt. practice Anacortes, Wash., 1983—. Mem. Wash. State Trial Lawyers Assn., Rotary Club. Republican. Roman Catholic. General civil litigation, Criminal, Personal injury. Office: PO Box 1216 Anacortes WA 98221-6216

**OSBORN, JOHN EDWARD,** lawyer, pharmaceutical and biotechnology industry executive, former government official, writer; b. Davenport, Iowa, Sept. 4, 1957; s. Edward Richard and Patricia Anne (O'Donovan) O.; m. Deborah Lynn Powell, Aug. 11, 1984; 1 child, Delaney Powell. Student, Coll. William and Mary, 1975-76; BA, U. Iowa, 1979; cert., Georgetown U., 1980; JD, U. Va., 1983; cert., Wadham Coll., Oxford U., 1987; M Internat. Pub. Policy, Johns Hopkins U., 1992; cert., Wharton Sch., U. Pa., 1994-95; postgrad., Princeton U., 1997-99. Bar: Mass. 1985. Law clk. to Hon. Albert V. Bryan U.S. Ct. Appeals (4th cir.), Alexandria, Va., 1983-84; assoc. Hale and Dorr, Boston, 1984-88, Dechert Price & Rhoads, Phila., 1988-89; spl. asst. to legal adviser U.S. Dept. State, Washington, 1989-92; sr. counsel DuPont Merck Pharm. Co., Wilmington, Del., 1992-94, assoc. gen. counsel, 1994-96, v.p., assoc. gen. counsel, asst. sec., 1996-97; v.p. legal affairs Cephalon, Inc., West Chester, Pa., 1997-98, sr. v.p., gen. counsel, sec., 1998—; legal cons. Amnesty Internat. USA, 1987-88; scholar in residence East European studies, Woodrow Wilson Internat. Ctr. for Scholars, Washington, 1991; assoc. scholar Fgn. Policy Rsch. Inst., Phila., 1992—; assoc. William Davidson Inst., U. Mich., Ann Arbor, 1997—; vis. lectr. U. Mich. Bus. Sch., Ann Arbor, 1997—; vis. fellows seminar Ctr. Internat. Studies, Princeton U., 1998; bd. advisors U. Pa. Inst. Law and Econs., Phila., 1999—. Contbr. articles to profl. jours., newspapers and periodicals including N.Y. Times, Wall St. Jour., Wash. Post, Christian Sci. Monitor, Am. Jour. Internat. Law; articles editor: Va. Jour. Internat. Law, 1982-83. Mem. Friends of Child Devel. Ctr., Georgetown U. Med. Sch., Washington, 1999—, Johns Hopkins U. Alumni Coun., Balt., 1997—; mem. U. Va. Law Sch. Bus. Advisory Coun., Charlottesville, 1996—, mem. U. Iowa Endowment Liberal Arts Dean's Adv. Bd., Iowa City, 1999—; rsch. aide, speechwriter George Bush for Pres. Com., 1979-80, 87-88, mem. Del. Rep. State Com., 1995-99, del. to Rep. Nat. Conv., 1996, mem., bd. dirs. Del. Ctr. for the Contemporary Arts, 1994—, v.p. 1997—, Am. Civil Liberties Found. Del., 1995-98, adv. bd. 1998—; trustee Tower Hill Sch., Wilmington, Del., 1997—. Eisenhower fellow, Ireland, 1998. Mem. Am. Corp. Counsel Assn., Am. Soc. Corp. Secs., Atlantic Coun. of the U.S., Mortar Board, Greenville Country Club, Capitol Hill Club, Princeton Club N.Y., Phi Beta Kappa, Phi Delta Phi, Omicron Delta Kappa. Republican. Roman Catholic. Private international, Contracts commercial, General corporate. Home: 5 Doe's Lane Greenville DE 19807-1548 Office: 145 Brandywine Pkwy West Chester PA 19380-4245

**OSBORN, MALCOLM EVERETT,** lawyer; b. Bangor, Maine, Apr. 29, 1928; s. Lester Everett and Helen (Clark) O.; m. Claire Anne Franks, Aug. 30, 1953; children: Beverly, Lester, Malcolm, Ernest. BA, U. Maine, 1952; postgrad. Harvard U. 1952-54; JD Boston U. 1956, LLM, 1961. Bar: Maine 1956, Mass. 1956, U.S. Dist. Ct. Mass. 1961, U.S. Tax Ct. 1961, U.S. Claims 1961, N.C. 1965, U.S. Supreme Ct. 1979, U.S. Ct. Appeals (4th cir.) 1980, Va. 1991. Tax counsel State Mut. Life Assurance Co., Worcester, Mass., 1956-64; v.p., gen. tax counsel Integon Corp. and other group cos., Winston-Salem, N.C., 1964-81; ptnr. House, Blanco & Osborn, P.A., Winston-Salem, 1981-88, v.p., gen. counsel, dir. Settlers Life Ins. Co., Bristol, Va., 1984-89; prin. Malcolm E. Osborn, P.A., Winston-Salem, 1988—; lectr. The Booke Seminars, Life Ins. Co., 1985-87; adj. prof. Wake Forest U. Sch. of Law, Winston-Salem, 1974-82; Disting. guest lectr. Ga. State U., 1965; guest lectr. N.Y.U. Ann. Inst. Fed. Taxation, 1966, 68, 75, 80. Trustee N.C. Council Econ. Edn., 1968-76; bd. dirs. Christian Fellowship Home, 1972-80; co-founder Bereaved Parents Group Winston-Salem, 1978—. Mem. ABA (chmn. com. ins. cos. of taxation sect. 1980-82, chmn. subcom. on continuing legal edn. and publs. 1982-88), Am. Bus. Law Assn. (mem. com. fed. taxation 1968—, chmn. 1972-75), Assn. Life Ins. Counsel (com. on co. tax, tax sect. 1965—), N.C. Bar Assn. (com. taxation 1973—), Fed. Bar Assn. (taxation com. 1973—), Maine State Bar Assn., Va. State Bar Assn., Internat. Bar Assn. (com. on taxes of bus. law sect. 1973—), AAUP, Southeastern Acad. Legal Studies in Bus. Club: Masons (Lincoln, Maine). Com. editor The Tax Lawyer, ABA, 1974-76; author numerous articles in field. Corporate taxation, Personal income taxation, Insurance. Office: PO Box 5192 Winston Salem NC 27113-5192

**OSBORNE, DUNCAN ELLIOTT,** lawyer; b. Orange, N.J., May 24, 1944; s. Walter Dodd Osborne and Anne (Boaz) Treanor; m. Elizabeth May Bachman, Dec. 29, 1965; children: Ellen Osborne Ray, Mark Elliott, Michael Cleveland. BA, Stanford U., 1966; MA, U. Tex., 1968, JD with honors, 1971. Bar: Tex. (cert. estate planning and probate law) 1971, U.S. Supreme Ct. 1975, U.S. Tax Ct. 1975, U.S. Fed. Ct. Claims 1997. Atty. Graves Dougherty, Austin, Tex., 1971-93, Osborne, Lowe, Helman & Smith L.L.P., Austin, 1993—; bd. dirs. Boatmen's Nat. Bank Austin, 1995-97, Hill Country Bank, Austin, 1998. Author, editor: Asset Protection: Domestic and International Law and Tactics; contbr. articles to profl. jours.; mem. adv. bd. Jour. Asset Protection; mem. Tex. Law Rev. Trustee Susan Vaughan Found., Houston, Still Water Found., Austin; chair bd. trustees St. Stephens Episcopal Sch., Austin, 1985-91, St. Andrews Episcopal Sch., Austin, 1978. Fellow Am. Coll. Trust and Estate Counsel, Coll. of State Bar of Tex.; mem. Internat. Tax Planning Assn., Offshore Inst., Internat. Acad. Estate and Tax (exec. com.), Asset Protection Planning Commn. (chair 1996-98)), Order of Coif. Avocation: scuba diving. Estate planning, Non-profit and tax-exempt organizations, Estate taxation. Office: Osborne Lowe Helman & Smith LLP 301 Congress Ave Ste 1900 Austin TX 78701-4041

**OSBORNE, FRANK R.,** lawyer, educator, lecturer; b. Cleve., Dec. 7, 1946; s. Thomas L. and Doris E. O.; m. Charlotte A. Caston, July 8, 1972; children: James, Thomas, Patricia, Janet, Karen, Kathleen, Linda, Jennifer. AB in Polit. Sci., John Carroll U., 1969; JD, Cleve. State U., 1973. Bar: Ohio 1973, U.S. Dist. Ct. (no. dist.) 1975, U.S. Supreme Ct. 1979, U.S. Ct. Appeals (6th cir.) 1979, U.S. Tax Ct. 1980, U.S. Ct. Appeals (7th cir.) 1982. Law clk. to Hon. John V. Corrigan Ohio Ct. Appeals (8th appellate dist.), Cleve., 1973-76; atty. Roudebush, Brown & Ulrich, LPA, Cleve., 1976-86, Arter & Hadden, LPA, Cleve., 1986—; adj. prof. law Ohio civil procedure Cleve. Marshall Coll. Law, Cleve. State U., 1994—; alternative dispute resolution neutral U.S. Dist. Ct. (no. dist.), Cleve., 1990—. Co-author: Civil Discovery Practice in Ohio, 1995. Mem. Ohio State Bar Assn., Cleve. Bar Assn. Fax: 216-696-2645. E-mail: fosborne@arterhadden.com. General civil litigation, Contracts commercial, Appellate. Home: 1278 Croyden Rd Lyndhurst OH 44124-1413 Office: Arter & Hadden LPA 1100 Huntington Bldg Cleveland OH 44115

**OSBORNE, JOHN EDWARDS,** lawyer; b. Tucson, Feb. 10, 1953; s. Earle Dean and Helen Edwards Osborne; m. Diana Kuhel, Apr. 10, 1976; children: Monica, Valerie. AB with honors, Stanford U., 1975; JD, U. Tex., 1981. Bar: Ariz. Supreme Ct. 1981, U.S. Dist. Ct. Ariz. 1981, U.S. Ct. Appeals (9th cir.) 1990, U.S. Supreme Ct. 1994, White Mountain Apache Tribal Ct. Assoc. Chandler, Tullar, Udall & Redhair, Tucson, 1981-85; mng. atty. Tucson br. personal injury dept. Jacoby & Meyers Law Offices, Tucson, 1985-89; mng. ptnr. Goldberg & Osborne, Tucson, 1989—. Referee adminstr. Am. Youth Soccer Orgn., Tucson, 1997—. Fellow Ariz. Bar Found.; mem. ATLA, ABA, Am. Bd. Trial Advs. (assoc. mem., Tucson chpt.), Ariz. Trial Lawyers Assn. (sustaining mem., bd. govs.), State Bar Ariz. (cert. specialist in personal injury and wrongful death, pub. rels. com. 1985-89, trial practice sect. 1988—), Pima County Bar Assn. (pro bono com. 1982-95, v.p. young lawyers divsn. 1987-88). Avocations: private pilot, scuba diving, skiing, hunting, soccer referee. Personal injury, Product liability, Insurance. Office: Goldberg & Osborne 33 N Stone Ave Ste 1850 Tucson AZ 85701-1426

**OSBOURN, MARK A.,** lawyer; b. Louisville, Ky., Aug. 31, 0960; s. Thomas Patrick and Mary Joanne O.; m. Elizabeth Ann Osbourn, May 31, 1985; children: emily Ann, John Patrick. BA, Eastern Ky. U., Richmond, 1982; JD, U. Louisville, 1985. Lawyer, ptnr. Schiller, Osbourn & Barnes, Louisville, Ky., 1986—. Insurance. Office: Schiller Osbourn and Barnes 1100 Ky Home Life Bldg Louisville KY 40202

**O'SCANNLAIN, DIARMUID FIONNTAIN,** judge; b. N.Y.C., Mar. 28, 1937; s. Sean Leo and Moira (Hegarty) O'S.; m. Maura Nolan, Sept. 7, 1963; children: Sean, Jane, Brendan, Kevin, Megan, Christopher, Anne, Kate. BA, St. John's U., 1957; JD, Harvard U., 1963; LLM, U. Va., 1992. Bar: Oreg. 1965, N.Y. 1964. Tax atty. Standard Oil Co. (N.J.), N.Y.C., 1963-65; assoc. Davies, Biggs, Strayer, Stoel & Boley, Portland, Oreg., 1965-69; dep. atty. gen. Oreg., 1969-71; public utility commr. of Oreg., 1971-73; dir. Oreg. Dept. Environ. Quality, 1973-74; sr. ptnr. Ragen, Roberts, O'Scannlain, Robertson & Neill, Portland, 1978-86; judge, U.S. Ct. Appeals (9th cir.), San Francisco, 1986—, mem. exec. com., 1988-89, 1993-94, mem. Jud. Coun. 9th Cir., 1991-93; mem. U.S. Judicial Conf. Com. on Automation and Tech., 1990—; cons. Office of Pres.-Elect and mem. Dept. Energy Transition Team (Reagan transition), Washington, 1980-81; chmn. com. adminstrv. law Oreg. State Bar, 1980-81. Mem. council of legal advisers Rep. Nat. Com., 1981-83; mem. Rep. Nat. Com., 1983-86, chmn. Oreg. Rep. Party, 1983-86; del. Rep. Nat. Convs., 1976, 80, chmn. Oreg. del., 1984; Rep. nominee U.S. Ho. of Reps., First Congl. Dist., 1974; team leader Energy Task Force, Pres.'s Pvt. Sector Survey on Cost Control, 1982-83, trustee Jesuit High Sch.; mem. bd. visitors U. Oreg. Law Sch., 1988—; mem. citizens adv. bd. Providence Hosp., 1986-92. Maj. USAR, 1955-78. Mem. Fed. Bar Assn., ABA (sec. Apellate Judges Conf. 1989-90, exec. com. 1990—, chmn.-elect 1994—), Arlington Club, Multnomah Club. Roman Catholic. Office: US Ct Appeals 313 Pioneer Courthouse 555 SW Yamhill St Ste 104 Portland OR 97204-1370

**OSGOOD, RUSSELL KING,** academic administrator; b. Fairborn, Ohio, Oct. 25, 1947; s. Richard Magee and Mary (Russell) O.; m. Paula Haley, June 6, 1970; children: Mary, Josiah, Micah, Iain. BA, Yale U., 1969, JD, 1974. Bar: Mass. 1974, U.S. Dist. Ct. Mass. 1976. Assoc. Hill & Barlow, Boston, 1974-78; assoc. prof. Boston U., 1978-80; prof. Cornell U., Ithaca, N.Y., 1980-88, dean law sch., 1988-98; pres. Grinnell (Iowa) Coll., 1998—. Lt. USNR, 1969-71. Mem. Am. Soc. for Legal History (editor Law and History Rev. 1982-87), Osgoode Soc., Stair Soc., Selden Soc. Office: Grinnell Coll 1121 Park St Grinnell IA 50112-1640

**O'SHEA, PATRICK JOSEPH,** lawyer, electrical engineer; b. Chgo., Apr. 10, 1950; s. John Raymond and Alta M. (Bauert) O'S.; m. Patricia Ann Dalaker, Aug. 11, 1980; children: Erin, Tarah, Brian, Maghan. BSEE, U. Ill., 1972; JD, John Marshall Law Sch., 1979. Bar: Ill. 1979, U.S. Dist. Ct. (no. dist.) Ill. 1979, U.S. Patent Office 1982. Elec. engr. elec. div. City of Chgo. Police Dept., 1976-79; elec. engr. Commonwealth Edison, Chgo., 1972-76; atty. Patricik Mazza & Assocs., Chgo., 1979-80, Richard E. Alexander & Assocs., Chgo., 1980-81; sole pratice Chgo. and Lombard, Ill., 1981—; spl. asst. states atty. Du. Page County, Ill., 1988; spl. appellate prosecutor, 1989. Elected Rep. committeeman, York Twp., Ill., 1982, chmn. rep. committeeman's orgn., 1996; mem. exec. com. York Twp. Rep. Committeeman's Orgn., vice-chmn., 1992, chmn., 1996; mem. exec. com. DuPage County Bd., 1989—, chmn. landfill com., 1989, 94, vice chmn. legis. com., 1994; commr. Forest Preserve, 1992; gen. counsel Ill. Rep. Party; gen. counsel Ill. Rep. Party. Mem. Ill. Bar Assn., DuPage Bar Assn., Chgo. Bar Assn., Lombard C. of C., Lombard Rotary. Roman Catholic. Avocations: politics, golf, chess. Federal civil litigation, Criminal, Personal injury. Home: 1051 S Fairview Ave Lombard IL 60148-4035 Office: 916 E Saint Charles Rd Lombard IL 60148-2058

**OSHINS, STEVEN JEFFREY,** lawyer; b. Washington, Oct. 21, 1969. BS in Actuarial Stats., U. Calif., Santa Barbara, 1991; JD, U. of the Pacific, 1994. Bar: Calif. 1994, Nev. 1995. Assoc. Law Offices of Oshins & Assocs., Las Vegas, 1994-98, lawyer, shareholder, 1998—. Contbr. articles to profl. jours. and mags. Mem. So. Nev. Estate Planning Coun. (pres. 1998-99). Estate planning, Estate taxation, Probate. Office: Law Offices Oshins & Assocs 1645 Village Center Cir Ste 170 Las Vegas NV 89134-6371

**OSIS, DAIGA GUNTRA,** lawyer; b. Riga, Latvia, July 24, 1943; d. Voldemars and Sandra (Seja) Amatnieks; m. Aivars Osis, Dec. 2, 1967; 1 child, Andre. BA cum laude, CUNY, Bklyn., 1971; JD, U. (Bridgeport) Conn., 1980. Bar: Conn. 1980, U.S. Dist. Ct. Conn. 1981, U.S Ct. Appeals (2d cir.) 1982, U.S. Supreme Ct. 1984. Assoc. DePiano & Palmesi, Bridgeport, 1980-85; ptnr. Gans, Leo & Osis, Bridgeport, 1985-88, Gans, Osis, Reynolds & Riccio, Bridgeport, 1989-90, Gans, Osis & Reynolds, Bridgeport, 1990-94; pvt. practice law Bridgeport, 1994—; asst. prof. law U. Bridgeport, 1982-83. Research editor U. Bridgeport Law Review, 1979-80.

Mem. Bd. Edn., Trumbull, Conn., 1982-84; bd. dirs. Conn. Inst. of Vocal Arts, Southport, Conn., 1984-87. Mem. Conn. Bar Assn., Conn. Trial Lawyers Assn. Democrat. Lutheran. Family and matrimonial, State civil litigation, Personal injury. Home: 175 Middlebrooks Ave Trumbull CT 06611-3016 Office: 1057 Broad St Bridgeport CT 06604-4219

**OSKAM, GERARD LAMBERT,** lawyer; b. East Orange, N.J., June 11, 1956; m. Denise L. Green; children: Monique, Michael, Johnny. AA, Orange Coast Coll., 1985; BS in Fin., U. So. Calif., 1987, AB in Philosophy, 1987; JD, Harvard U., 1990. Bar: Calif. 1990, Nev. 1993, U.S. Dist. Ct. Nev. Atty. Sheppard Mullin Richter and Hampton, Newport Beach, Calif., 1990-91, Stradling Yocca Carlson and Rauth, Newport Beach, 1991-93, McDonald Carano Wilson McCune Bergin Frankovich and Hicks, Reno, 1993—. General corporate, Finance, Securities. Office: McDonald Carano et al 241 Ridge St Fl 4 Reno NV 89501-2028

**OSMAN, EDITH GABRIELLA,** lawyer; b. N.Y.C., Mar. 18, 1949; d. Arthur Abraham and Judith (Goldman) Udem; children: Jacqueline, Daniel. BA in Spanish, SUNY, Stony Brook, 1970; JD cum laude, U. Miami, 1983. Bar: Fla. 1983, U.S. Dist. Ct. (so. dist.) Fla. 1984, U.S. Dist. Ct. (mid. dist.) Fla. 1988, U.S. Ct. Appeals (11th cir.) 1985, U.S. Supreme Ct. 1987, U.S. Ct. Mil. Appeals 1990. Assoc. Kimbrell & Hamann, P.A., Miami, 1984-90, Dunn & Lodish, P.A., Miami, 1990-93; pvt. practice in law Miami, 1993-98; spkr. in field. Mem. adv. com. for Implementation of the Victor Posner Judgement to Aid the Homeless, 1986-89; spkr. small firm and solo practitioner Town Hall Meetings, 1993, 97; spkr. Bridge the Gap Seminar, Comml. Litigation, 1994. Fellow Am. Bar Found.; mem. ABA (product liability com., corp. counsel com., family law), Fla. Bar Assn. (budget com. 1989-92, 97-98, voluntary bar liaison com. 1989-90, spl. com. on formation of All-Bar Conf. 1988-89, chair mid-yr. conv. 1989, mem. long range planning com. 1988-90, bd. govs. 1991-98, spl. commn. on delivery of legal svcs. to the indigent 1990-92, bus. law cert. com. 1995-96, practice law mgmt. com. 1995-96, chair program evaluation com., 1993-94, exec. com. 1992-93, 96—, rules and bylaws com., 1993-94, vice chair disciplinary rev. com. 1994-95, investment com. 1994-95, vice-chair rules com. 1994-95, All-Bar Conf. chair 1997, chair grievance mediation com. 1997-99, pres.-elect 1998-99, pres. 1999-2000, Outstanding Past Voluntary Bar Pres. award 1996, Fawl's Outstanding Achievement award 1997), Dade County Bar Assn. (fed. ct. rules com. 1985-86, chmn. program com. 1988-89, 90-91, 96-97, exec. com. 1987-88), Fla. Assn. Women's Lawyers Assn. (Dade County chpt. bd. dirs. 1984-85, treas. 1985-86, v.p. 1986-87, pres. 1989-90), Fla. Assn. Women Lawyers (v.p. 1988-89, pres. 1989-90), Fla. Bar Found. (dir. 1998—), Nat. Conf. Women's Bar Assn. (dir. nat. conf. 1990-91), Fla. Acad. Trial Lawyers, Dade County Trial Lawyers Assn., Nat. Conf. Bar Pres., So. Conf. Bar Pres. General civil litigation, Contracts commercial, Family and matrimonial. Office: Carlton Fields PA 100 SE 2nd St Ste 4000 Miami FL 33131-2148

**OSNOS, DAVID MARVIN,** lawyer; b. Detroit, Jan. 10, 1932; s. Max and Florence (Pollock) O.; m. Glenna DeWitt, Aug. 10, 1956; children: Matthew, Alison. A.B. summa cum laude, Harvard U., 1953, J.D. cum laude, 1956. Bar: D.C. 1956. Assoc. Arent, Fox, Kintner, Plotkin & Kahn, Washington, 1956-61, ptnr., 1962—, chmn. exec. com., 1978-97; bd. dirs. EastGroup Properties, Jackson, Miss., VSE Corp., Alexandria, Va., Washington Real Estate Investment Trust, Rockville, Md., Washington Wizards Basketball Club, Washington. Trustee Mt. St. Mary's Coll., Emmitsburg, Md., 1981-90; bd. dirs. Greater Washington Jewish Community Found., Rockville, Md., Jewish Community Ctr. Greater Washington, 1964-75. Avocations: tennis, music, enology. Sports, Real property, Taxation, general. Office: Arent Fox Kintner 1050 Connecticut Ave NW Ste 600 Washington DC 20036-5303

**OSOSKI-SLANEC, DARRA,** lawyer; b. Clare, Mich., Sept. 14, 1961; d. Edward Donald and Constance Ruth Ososki; m. Stanton Charles Slanec II, May 16, 1998; 1 child, Shea Delaney Slanec. BA, Mich. State U., 1983; JD, Detroit Coll. Law, 1994. Bar: Mich. 1994. Staff atty. Wayne County Neighborhood Legal Svcs., Detroit, 1994-96; sole practitioner Mt. Clemens, Mich., 1996—; instr. Detroit Coll. Bus., Warren, Mich., 1996—. Bd. dirs. Health Emergency Lifeline Programs, Detroit, 1995-97; marketplace coord. Children's Music Festival, Detroit, 1996, 97. Mem. State Bar Mich., Macomb County Bar Assn., Women Lawyers Assn., Macomb County Probate Bar Assn. Juvenile, Criminal, Probate. Office: 130 Cass Ave Mount Clemens MI 48043-2230

**OSSIP, MICHAEL J.,** lawyer; b. N.Y.C., Nov. 9, 1954; s. William L. and Jeannette (Linial) O.; m. Karen Silverstein, May 28, 1978; 1 child, Brian. BS in Inds. and Labor Rels., Cornell U., 1976; JD, U. Pa., 1979. Bar: Pa. 1979, U.S. Dist. Ct. (ea. dist.) Pa. 1980, U.S. Dist. Ct. (mid. dist.) Pa. 1994, U.S. Ct. Appeals (3d cir.) 1981, U.S. Ct. Appeals (4th cir.) 1982, U.S. Ct. Appeals (8th cir.) 1985, U.S. Ct. Appeals (D.C. cir.) 1986, U.S. Supreme Ct. 1989. Law clk. to judge U.S. Dist. Ct., Wilmington, Del., 1979-80; assoc. Morgan, Lewis & Bockius LLP, Phila., 1980-88, ptnr., 1988—; mem. faculty Cornell U., N.Y.C., 1987—; lectr. Pa. Bar Inst., Phila., Harrisburg and Pitts., 1987—. Pres., bd. dirs. Nat. Tay-Sachs and Allied Diseases Assn. Delaware Valley, Jenkintown, Pa., 1993—; bd. dirs. Nat. Tay-Sachs and Allied Diseases Assn., Brookline, Mass., 1993—. Mem. ABA (com. chair sect. labor law), Pa. Bar Assn., Phila. Bar Assn. Labor, Federal civil litigation, Workers' compensation. Office: Morgan Lewis & Bockius LLP 1701 Market St Philadelphia PA 19103-2903

**O'STEEN, VAN,** lawyer; b. Sweetwater, Tenn., Jan. 10, 1946; s. Bernard Van and Laura Emelyne (Robinson) O.; m. Deborah Ann Elias, May 18, 1974; children—Jonathan Van, Laura Ann. B.A., Calif. Western U., 1968; J.D. cum laude, Ariz. State U., 1972. Bar: Ariz. 1972, U.S. Dist. Ct. Ariz. 1972, U.S. Ct. Appeals (9th cir.) 1973, U.S. Supreme Ct. 1975. Staff atty. Maricopa Legal Aid Soc., Phoenix, 1972-74; atty. Bates & O'Steen, Legal Clinic, Phoenix, 1974-77; atty. O'Steen Legal Clinic, Phoenix, 1977-80; mng. ptnr. Van O'Steen and Ptnrs., Phoenix and Tucson, 1980—; pres. Van O'Steen Mktg. Group, Inc., Phoenix, 1985—. Author numerous self-help legal books. Founding dir. Ariz. Ctr. for Law in the Pub. Interest, 1974-80. Served with USNR, 1963-69. Mem. ABA (chmn. spl. com. delivery legal services 1982-85), Am. Legal Clinic Assn. (pres. 1979), Assn. Trial Lawyers Am. Democrat. Administrative and regulatory, Personal injury. Address: 3605 N 7th Ave Phoenix AZ 85013-3638

**OSTEEN, WILLIAM L., SR.,** federal judge; b. 1931. BA, Guilford Coll., 1953; LLB, U. N.C., 1956. With Law Office of W.H. McElwee, Jr., North Wilkesboro, N.C., 1956-58; pvt. practive Greensboro, N.C., 1958-59; with Booth & Osteen, Greensboro, 1959-69; U.S. atty. U.S. Attys. Office, Greensboro, 1969-74; ptnr. Osteen, Adams & Osteen, Greensboro, 1974-91; fed. judge U.S. Dist. Ct. (mid. dist.) N.C., Greensboro, 1991—. With USAR, 1958-51. Fellow Am. Coll. Trial Lawyers; mem. ABA, N.C. State Bar, N.C. Bar Assn. (mem. and chair subcom. N.C. sentencing commn.), U. N.C. Law Alumni Assn. Office: US Dist Ct PO Box 3485 Greensboro NC 27402-3485

**OSTENDARP, GARY DAVID,** lawyer; b. Cin., Jan. 14, 1945; s. Lawrence A. and Marian H. O.; m. Mary Helen Hubbuch, Dec. 19, 1969; children: Dawn Feltman, Gretchen, Amy, David. BA, Xavier U., 1967; JD, U. Cin., 1971. Bar: Ohio 1971, U.S. Dist. Ct. (so. dist.) Ohio 1972, U.S. Ct. Appeals (6th cir.) 1993, U.S. Supreme Ct. 1994. Law clk. Hon. Timothy S. HOgan U.S. Dist. Ct. (so. dist.) Ohio, Cin., 1971-73; from assoc. to ptnr. Ely & True, Batavia, Ohio, 1973—. Mem. Ohio State Bar Assn., Ohio Assn. Civil Trial Attys., Clermont County Bar Assn., Order of Coif. General civil litigation, Insurance, Personal injury. Office: Ely & True 322 E Main St Batavia OH 45103-3094

**OSTENDORF, LANCE STEPHEN,** lawyer, investor, financial consultant and planner; b. New Orleans, Aug. 16, 1958; 1 child, Christine Marie Ostendorf. BBA summa cum laude, Loyola U., 1976, JD, 1980. Bar: La. 1980, U.S. Dist. Ct. (ea. dist.) La. 1981, U.S. Dist. Ct. La., U.S. Supreme Ct. 1980, U.S. Dist. Ct. (we. and mid. dists.) La. 1983. Ptnr. McGlinchey Stafford Lang, New Orleans, 1980-92, Campbell McCranie Sistrunk, Anzelmo & Hardy, New Orleans, 1992—; treas., CFO Campbell McCranie, New Orleans; owner RCO Internat. Inc.; treas., CFO La. State U. Med. Ctr. Found., New Orleans, 1992—; lectr. Lorman Ednl. Seminars; bd. dirs. La. State U. Med. Ctr. Found., New Orleans, tech. transfer com. Author: Insurance Law; contbr. articles to profl. jours. Mem. ABA, Fed. Bar Assn., Internat. Bar Assn., Metairie Bar Assn., Maritime Law Assn., Comite Maritime Internat., Assn. for Transp. Law, Logistics and Policy, Assn. Average Adjusters of U.S., Jefferson Bar Assn., New Orleans Bar Assn., La. Restaurant Assn., Am. Trial Lawyers Assn., La. Bar Assn., Jefferson Bar Assn., Fifth Cir. Bar Assn., Def. Rsch. Inst., La. Trial Lawyers Assn., Law Def. Lawyers Assn., Houston Mariners Club, Southeastern Adm. Law Inst., St. Thomas Moore Club, La. Notary Soc., Blue Key Honor Soc. Insurance, Finance, Private international. Office: 3445 N Causeway Blvd Ste 800 Metairie LA 70002-3728

**OSTERGAARD, JONI HAMMERSLA,** lawyer; b. Seattle, May 26, 1950; d. William Dudley and Carol Mae (Gillett) Hammersla; m. Gregory Lance Ostergaard, May 22, 1976 (div. 1985); 1 child, Bennett Gillett; m. William Howard Patton, Jan. 1, 1988; 1 child, Morgan Hollis; stepchildren: Colin W., Benjamin C. BS, U. Wash., 1972; MS, Purdue U., 1974; JD, U. Wash., 1980. Bar: Wash. 1980, U.S. Dist. Ct. (we. dist.) Wash. 1980, U.S. Ct. Appeals (9th cir.) 1981, U. S. Ct. Claims 1983. Clin. psychol. intern Yale Med. Sch., 1976-77; law clk. U.S. Ct. Appeals (9th cir.), Seattle, 1980-81; assoc. Roberts & Shefelman, Seattle, 1982-86, ptnr., 1987; ptnr. Foster Pepper & Shefelman, Seattle, 1988-92; sole practitioner Seattle, 1996—. Contbr. articles to profl. jours.; notes and comments editor Wash. Law Rev., 1979-80. Recipient Sophia and Wilbur Albright scholarship U. Wash. Law Sch., 1979-80, law sch. alumni scholarship U. Wash. Law Sch., 1978-79; fellow NIMH. Avocations: gardening, reading. Fax: 206-725-8121. Municipal (including bonds), Public utilities, Appellate.

**OSTERHAGE, LAWRENCE EDWARD,** lawyer; b. Covington, Ky., Dec. 10, 1951; s. Urban Joseph and Dorothy Elizabeth (Bushelman) O.; m. Mary Ann Osterhage, Mar. 1, 1980; children: Jennifer L., Emily E., John J. BA, Thomas More Coll., Crestview Hills, Ky., 1974; JD, U. Louisville, 1977. Bar: Ky. 1977. Reporter Ky. Post, Covington, 1969-74; prosecutor Jefferson County, Louisville, 1977-96; sole practitioner Louisville, 1977—; exec. com. chmn. Jefferson County Drug Ct., Louisville, 1995—. Articles editor, contbr. Jour. Family Law, 1977. Coach, mgr. Jeffersontown Little League, Louisville, 1990—. Ky. Acad. Trial Attys. General practice, Personal injury, Workers' compensation. Office: 310 W Liberty St Ste 204 Louisville KY 40202-3014

**OSTERHOUT, RICHARD CADWALLADER,** lawyer; b. Abington, Pa., Nov. 16, 1945; s. Robert Edward and Charlotte Leedom (Cadwallader) O.; m. Diane Renee Higgins, Sept. 15, 1982; children: Steven M., Schuyler C., Cody R. BA magna cum laude in History, Pa. State U., 1967; JD, Temple U., 1974. Bar: Pa. 1974, U.S. Dist. Ct. (ea. dist.) Pa. 1974, U.S. Ct. Appeals (3d cir.) 1984. Assoc. Wood & Floge, Bensalem, Pa., 1974-77; pvt. practice, Trevose, Pa., 1978-85, Feasterville, Pa., 1985—; solicitor Zoning Hearing Bd., Hulmeville, Pa., 1983—. Contbr. articles to publs. of various hist. socs. Mem. Langhorne Borough Planning Commn. (Pa.), 1974; candidate Rep. Nat. Conv., 1984. WithU.S. Army, 1968-70. Mem. Pa. Bar Assn., Bucks County Bar Assn., Am. Legion, Feasterville Businessmen's Assn. (treas. 1985, 86, v.p. 1987), Kiwanis (pres. Feasterville chpt. 1989-90), Phi Beta Kappa. General practice, State civil litigation, Family and matrimonial. Home: 309 Hemlock Ave Bensalem PA 19020-7331 Office: Richard C Osterhout 1744 Bridgetown Pike Feasterville Trevose PA 19053

**OSTROOT, TIMOTHY VINCENT,** lawyer; b. Hibbing, Minn., June 4, 1960; s. Richard Lloyd and Ramona Joy (Vincent) O.; m. Tina Louise Bahr, Aug. 16, 1980; 1 child, Collin Bryce. AA, Itasca C.C., Grand Rapids, Minn., 1980; BA in Polit. Sci., Idaho State U., 1984; JD cum laude, Hamline U., 1987. Bar: Minn. 1987; U.S. Dist. Ct. Minn. 1987, U.S. Ct. Appeals (8th cir.) Minn. 1992. Assoc. Joseph S. Friedberg, Mpls., 1987-91, Cochrane & Bresnahan, St. Paul, Minn., 1991-92; pvt. practice Champlin, 1992-93; ptnr. Larson, Wilkens & Ostroot, 1992-95; pvt. practice Anoka, Minn., 1995—. Author: Phi Alpha Delta Publs., 1990. Mem. adv. coun. Elk River (Minn.) Early Childhood Edn., 1991-92; diaconate Union Ch. of Christ, Elk River, 1993-96, chair, 1995-96. Schoenecker Leadership scholar Hamline Law Sch., St. Paul, 1986-87, Idaho Press Womens scholar, Pocatello, Idaho, 1984, Verda White Barnes Meml. scholar Idaho State U., Pocatello, 1984; named Itasca Outstanding Citizen, Kiwanis, Grand Rapids, Minn., 1980, Outstanding Young Man of Am., 1988. Mem. ABA, Minn. Bar Assn., Nat. Assn. Criminal Def. Lawyers, Minn. Assn. Criminal Def. Lawyers, Phi Alpha Delta (alumni adv. Monroe chpt. 1990-92, dist. x justice 1990-91, scholar award 1987). Criminal. Home: 19333 Norfolk St NW Elk River MN 55330-1217 Office: 403 Jackson St Ste 300 Anoka MN 55303-2372

**OSTROSKI, RAYMOND B.,** lawyer; b. Wilkes-Barre, Pa., Nov. 24, 1954; s. Joseph Sr. and Lena (Lolli) O.; m. Pamela M. Mullay, Aug. 27, 1994; 1 child, Ray Anthony; stepchildren: Charles R. Suppon, Lauren M. Suppon. Student, Pa. State U., Lehman, 1972-74; BA in Social Scis. summa cum laude, Wilkes Coll., 1976; JD, Temple U., 1983. Bar: U.S. Dist. Ct. (ea. dist.) Pa. 1983. Assoc. Hoegen & Marsh, Wilkes-Barre, Pa., 1983-85; assoc. counsel C-Tec Corp., Wilkes-Barre, 1985-88, corp. counsel, asst. corp. sec., 1988-91, v.p., gen. counsel, corp. sec., 1991-95, exec. v.p., gen. counsel, corp. sec., 1995-97; prin. RBO Consulting, Shavertown, Pa., 1998—; bd. dirs. Mercom, Inc., Princeton, N.J., Cable Mich., Inc., Princeton, N.J. Bd. dirs. Wilkes-Barre YMCA, 1993-94, trustee, 1998—; bd. dirs., v.p. Make-A-Wish Found., Wilkes-Barre, 1990-94. Mem. ABA, Am. Soc. Corp. Secs., Am. Corp. Counsel Assn., Nat. Assn. Corp. Dirs., Pa. Bar Assn., Wilkes-Barre Law & Libr. Assn. Avocations: golf, basketball, softball, guitar. General corporate, Communications, Mergers and acquisitions. Office: 261 Harris Hill Rd Shavertown PA 18708-9684

**OSTROW, MICHAEL JAY,** lawyer; b. Baldwin, N.Y., Apr. 25, 1934; s. Oscar I. and Ethel M. (Morganstern) O.; m. Judith L. Loewenthal, Aug. 25, 1957; children: Thomas L., Kenneth A., Nancy M. BA, Alfred U., 1955; JD, Cornell U., 1958. Bar: N.Y. 1958, U.S. Supreme Ct. 1964, U.S. Dist. Ct. (so. and ea. dists.) N.Y. 1970; diplomate Am. Coll. Family Trial Lawyers. Ptnr. Taylor & Ostrow, Mineola, N.Y., 1961-69, Taylor Atkins & Ostrow, Garden City, N.Y., 1969-96, Ostrow and Taub, Garden City, 1996—; bd. dirs., lectr Advanced Practice Inst. Hofstra Law Sch., Hempstead; lectr. Practicing Law Inst., N.Y.C. Mem. ABA, Acad. Matrimonial Lawyers (pres. N.Y. chpt. 1980-81, sec. nat. acad. 1988-90, nat. v.p. 1990-94, pres.-elect 1995-96, pres. 1996-97), Internat. Acad. Matrimonial Lawyers (bd. govs. 1990-92), N.Y. State Bar Assn. (chmn. family law sect. 1976-78), Nassau County Bar Assn. (pres. 1984-85, chmn. judiciary com. 1992-93), Order of Coif, Zeta Beta Tau, Phi Delta Phi. Family and matrimonial. Home: 8 Randolph Dr Dix Hills NY 11746-8308 Office: Ostrow & Taub 300 Garden City Plz Ste 308 Garden City NY 11530-3359

**O'SULLIVAN, JAMES MICHAEL,** lawyer; b. Boston, Jan. 21, 1958; s. James M. and Edith I. (Fielding) O'S.; m. Mary Ann Hayes, Mar. 28, 1992; children: Mary Elizabeth, Sheila Joanne, Bridget Eileen. BA, U. Mass.; JD, Northeastern U., Boston, 1983. Bar: Mass. 1983, U.S. Ct. Appeals (1st cir.) 1984, U.S. Dist. Ct. Mass. 1984, U.S. Supreme Ct. 1988. Mem. Thayer, Cannon & O'Sullivan, P.C., Quincy, Mass., 1986-90; prin. O'Sullivan & Gizzarelli, P.C., Norwell, Mass., 1990-92, O'Sullivan & Assocs., P.C., Norwell, 1992—; adj. instr. Ea. Nazerene Coll., Quincy, 1992—, New Eng. Banking Ins., Boston, 1989—; examiner Mass. Land Ct. Co-author: Bank Operations, 1990, 2d edit. 1994. Pres., bd. dirs. Cath. Alumni Sodality, Boston, 1984—, South Boston Cmty. Health Ctr., 1982-94; mem. Vols. Lawyers Project. Mem. Mass. Bar Assn., Mass. Conveyancers Assn., KC. Democrat. Roman Catholic. Avocations: running, woodwork, reading. General civil litigation, Probate, Real property. Office: O'Sullivan & Assocs PC 17 Accord Park Dr Norwell MA 02061-1634

**O'SULLIVAN, JUDITH ROBERTA,** lawyer, author; b. Pitts., Jan. 6, 1942; d. Robert Howard and Mary Olive (O'Donnell) Gallick; m. James Paul O'Sullivan, Feb. 1, 1964; children: Kathryn, James. BA, Carlow Coll., 1963; MA, U. Md., 1969, PhD, 1976; JD, Georgetown U., 1996. Editor Am. Film Inst., Washington, 1974-77; assoc. program coord. Smithsonian Resident Assocs., Washington, 1977-78; dir. instl. devel. Nat. Archives, Washington, 1978-79; exec. dir. Md. State Humanities Coun., Balt., 1979-81, 82-84, Ctr. for the Book, Libr. of Congress, Washington, 1981-82; dep. asst. dir. Nat. Mus. Am. Art, Washington, 1984-87, acting asst. dir., 1987-89; pres., CEO The Mus. at Stony Brook, N.Y., 1989-92; exec. dir. Nat. Assn. Women Judges, Washington, 1993; clk. Office Legal Adviser U.S. Dept. State, Washington, 1994-96; summer assoc. Piper & Marbury, Balt., 1995; trial atty. Atty. Gen.'s honors program U.S. Dept. Justice, 1996—; spl. asst. U.S. atty. Ea. Dist. Va., 1999—; chair Smithsonian Women's Coun., Washington, 1988-89; mem. editorial advisory bd. Am. Film Inst., 1979—. Author: The Art of the Comic Strip, 1971 (Gen. Excellence award Printing Industry Am.), Workers and Allies, 1975, (with Alan Fern) The Complete Prints of Leonard Baskin, 1984, The Great American Comic Strip, 1991; editor Am. Film Inst. Catalogue: Feature Films, 1961-70, 1974-77. Trustee Child Life Ctr., U. Md., College Pk., 1971-74; chair Smithsonian Women's Coun., 1988-89. Univ. fellow U. Md., 1967-70, Mus. fellow, 1970-71; Smithsonian fellow Nat. Collection Fine Arts, Washington, 1972-73. Mem. Assn. Assn. Art Mus. Dirs., Am. Assn. Mus., Mid-Atlantic Mus. Conf., AAUW, Md. Bar Assn. Avocations: mystery writing. Home: 17 Ridge Rd # F Greenbelt MD 20770-1749 Office: US Dept Justice Northern Criminal Enforcement Sect Tax Divsn Washington DC 22041

**O'SULLIVAN, LYNDA TROUTMAN,** lawyer; b. Oil City, Pa., Aug. 30, 1952; d. Perry John and Vivian Dorothy (Schreffler) Troutman; m. P. Kevin O'Sullivan, Dec. 15, 1979; children: John Perry, Michael Patrick. BA, Am. U., 1974; JD, Georgetown U., 1978, postgrad; Bar: D.C. 1978; assoc. Chapman, Duff & Paul, Washington, 1978-82, Gadsby & Hannah, Washington, 1983-85; ptnr. Perkins Coie, Washington, 1985-92, Fried, Frank, Harris, Shriver & Jacobson, Washington, 1993-97, Miller & Chevalier, Washington, 1997—; mem. adv. bd. Govt. Contract Costs, Pricing & Acctg. Report; mem. faculty govt. contracts program George Washington U.; lectr. Contbr. articles to profl. jours. Mem. ABA (chair truth in negotiations com. 1991-94, chair acctg., cost and pricing com. 1996—, coun. sect. pub. contract law 1993-95). Government contracts and claims, Federal civil litigation. Office: Miller & Chevalier 655 15th St NW Ste 900 Washington DC 20005-5799

**OSVALD-MRUZ, CHRISTINE,** lawyer; b. Mineola, N.Y., Jan. 27, 1970; d. John and Linda Osvald; m. John Richard Mruz, Jr., Aug. 13, 1994. AB, Princeton U., 1992; JD, Harvard U., 1995. Assoc. Lowenstein Sandler PC, Roseland, N.J., 1995—. General corporate, Mergers and acquisitions, Securities. Office: Lowenstein Sandler PC 65 Livingston Ave Ste 2 Roseland NJ 07068-1791

**OTHS, JOSEPH ANTHONY,** lawyer; b. Valhalla, N.Y., Dec. 6, 1934; s. Joseph William and Martha Mary (Walker) O.; m. Jane Matthews, Aug. 7, 1982; children (previous marriage): Michael, Kathryn, Christine Masson, Jennifer martindill, Amy Montgomery; stepchildren: Debora Roth, Catherine Gravois, Laurie Gaston, Stacey Nicchio. BA, U. Dayton, 1956; LLB/JD, No. Ky. U., 1961. Bar: Ohio 1961, U.S. Dist. Ct. (so. dist.) Ohio 1963, U.S. Supreme Ct. 1971, Fla. 1986, La. 1987, U.S. Ct. Appeals (6th cir.) 1993. Lawyer various ptnrs. and solo practice, Wellston, Ohio, 1961—; sr. ptnr. Oths, Heiser, Regan & Miller, Wellston, 1995—; bd. dirs. First Nat. Bank of Wellston, 1980—. City solicitor City of Wellston, 1965-72; trustee (mem. exec. com.) Rio Grande (Ohio) Coll., 1975-79; mem. Ohio Lottery Commn., 1980-82; chmn. Revolving Loan Fund City of Wellston. Fellow Am. Bar Found.; mem. ABA (coun. dels. 1980-84), Ohio State Bar Assn. (pres. 1979-80), Ohio Acad. Trial Lawyers. Democrat. Avocations: travel, reading, computers. General practice, Appellate, Estate planning. Office: Oths Heiser Regan & Miller 16 E Broadway St Wellston OH 45692-1226

**OTIS, ROY JAMES,** lawyer; b. San Rafael, Calif., May 18, 1946; s. James and Elizabeth Otis; m. Susan Leslie Wish, Aug. 2, 1975; children: Lindsay Elizabeth, Ryan James. BA, Stanford (Calif.) U., 1968; JD, Golden Gate U., 1980. Bar: Calif. 1980, U.S. Dist. Ct. (no. dist.) Calif. 1980; cert. specialist in workman's compensation. Tchr. Albany Children's Ctr., Albany, 1972-77; assoc. atty. Beauzay, Bledsoe, Hammer, et al, San Jose, Calif., 1981-83, Boxer, Elkind & Gerson, Oakland, Calif., 1983-85; assoc. Airola, Williams, Otis et al, San Francisco, 1985-87; ptnr., 1988-92; pvt. practice Walnut Creek, Calif., 1992-93; assoc. Law Offices of Mark Gearheart, Pleasant Hill, Calif., 1993-95; ptnr. Gearheart & Otis, Pleasant Hill, 1996—. Coach childrens' teams MOL Flag Football, 1988-96, CYO Basketball, LMYA Baseball; trek leader Boy Scouts, Sierra Mountains, Calif., Philmont, N.Mex., 1996-98. Mem. Calif. Applications Atty. Assn. (pres. no. Calif. chpt., 1994-96, bd. govs. 1997—), Assn. of Trial Lawyers of Am. (workplace injury litigation group sect. 1996—). Democrat. Avocations: skiing, tennis, bicycle riding, fiction. Workers' compensation. Office: Gearheart & Otis 367 Civic Dr Ste 17 Pleasant Hill CA 94523-1937

**O'TOOLE, AUSTIN MARTIN,** lawyer; b. New Bedford, Mass., Oct. 5, 1935; s. John Brian, Jr. and Helen Veronica O'T.; children: Erin Ann, Austin Martin 2d. BBA, Coll. Holy Cross, 1957; JD, Georgetown U., 1963. Bar: N.Y. 1965, D.C. 1963, Tex. 1975. Law clk. to judge U.S. Ct. Appeals, Washington, 1962-63; assoc. White & Case, N.Y.C., 1963-74; sr. v.p., sr. counsel, sec. Coastal Corp., Houston, 1974—; bd. dirs. A.A. White Dispute Resolution Inst. Bd. editors Georgetown Law Jour., 1962-63. Bd. dirs., pres. Houston Coun. on Alcohol and Drug Abuse Found., 1995—; com. mem. Meth. Health Care Houston Marathon. Officer USMCR, 1957-60. Mem. ABA, Am. Soc. Corp. Secs. (bd. dirs. 1982-85), State Bar of Tex., Houston Bar Assn. (past chmn. corp. counsel sect. 1979-80), Am. Arbitration Assn. (comml. com.). General corporate, Finance, Mergers and acquisitions. Home: 1400 Hermann Dr Unit 14-c Houston TX 77004-7137 Office: Coastal Corp 9 E Greenway Plz Houston TX 77046-0905

**O'TOOLE, DEBORAH SHEA,** lawyer; b. Balt., Sept. 29, 1944; d. Hamilton and Dorothy Hill Shea; m. Dennis Martin O'Toole, Aug. 17, 1963; children: Timothy, Terrence, Patrick, Erin. Student, Coll. William & Mary, 1962-63; BS in Psychology, Va. Commonwealth U., 1973; JD, U. Richmond, 1976. Assoc. McDonald & Crump, Richmond, Va., 1976-77; ptnr. Cowan & Owen, Richmond, Va., 1978—. Dir., treas. Rainbow Games, Inc., Richmond, Va., 1994—. Mem. Met. Richmond Womens Bar assn. (exec. bd. 1996—), Kiwanis. General civil litigation, Labor, Workers' compensation. Office: Cowan & Owen PO Box 35655 1930 Huguenot Rd Richmond VA 23235-4304

**O'TOOLE, GEORGE A., JR.,** judge; b. 1947. AB magna cum laude, Boston Coll., 1969; JD, Harvard U., 1972. Law clerk Arent, Fox, Kintner, Plotkin & Kahn, 1971-72; jr. ptnr. Hale and Dorr, 1972-82; assoc. justice Boston Mcpl. Ct. Dept., 1982-90, Trial Ct. of Mass., 1990-95; dist. judge U.S. Dist. Ct., Mass., 1995—; Contbr. articles to profl. jours. Bd. dirs. Boston Coll. Alumni Assn., 1984-86, Winchester Boat Club, 1988-93. Mem. ABA, Mass. Bar Assn., Boston Bar Assn. Office: US Courthouse 1 Courthouse Way Boston MA 02210-3002

**O'TOOLE, KEVIN MICHAEL,** lawyer; b. Highpoint, N.C., Feb. 20, 1956; s. Theodore Thaddeus and Ellen Regina (O'Shaughnessy) O'T. BA in History, U. Vt., 1978; JD, U. Notre Dame, 1982. Bar: Ill. 1982, Vt. 1984. Assoc. Kavanaugh, Scully, Sudow, White & Frederick, P.C., Peoria, Ill., 1982-83; pvt. practice Pawlet, Vt., 1984-86, Dorset, Vt., 1986—. Pres., trustee Dorset Nusing Assn., 1987-88; active subcom. to review town plan, Dorset, 1987. Mem. ABA, Vt. Bar Assn. Republican. Roman Catholic. Avocations: golf, cross country skiing. Real property, Probate, General practice. Office: PO Box 766 Dorset VT 05251-0766

**O'TOOLE, MARTIN WILLIAM,** lawyer; b. Oswego, N.Y., Nov. 17, 1957; s. Martin Joseph and Jean Patricia (O'Brien) O'T.; m. Susan Ray Rhelan, Aug. 15, 1987. BA, Hamilton Coll., 1980; JD, Cornell U., 1986. Bar: N.Y. 1987. Law clk. to hon. Richard J. Cardamone U.S. Ct. Appeals (2d cir.), Utica, N.Y., 1986-87; atty. Harter, Secrest & Emery, Rochester, N.Y., 1987—. Articles editor Cornell Law Rev., 1985-86. Mem. adv. bd. Genessee Valley chpt. Arthritis Found., Rochester, 1990—. Mem. ABA, Monroe County Bar Assn., N.Y. State Bar Assn., Order of the Coif, Phi Beta Kappa. Estate planning, Probate, Estate taxation. Office: Harter Secrest & Emery 700 Midtown Tower Rochester NY 14604-2006

**O'TOOLE, NEIL D.,** lawyer; b. N.Y.C., Feb. 15, 1945; s. Thomas J. and Electa E. O'Toole; m. Sharyn E. Brown, Mar. 18, 1983; children: Shauna, Melanie, Devin, Kathryn, Patrick, Matthew. BA in Sociology, St. Anselm's Coll., Manchester, N.H., 1966; MA in Social Work, U. Chgo., 1970; JD, U. Pa., 1979. Bar: Colo., N.Y., U.S. Dist. Ct. Colo., U.S. Ct. Appeals (10th cir.), U.S. Supreme Ct. Vol. Peace Corps, South India, 1968-70; rep.

C.A.R.E., Haiti, Cambodia, Mali, 1970-76; assoc. Holmes & Starr, Denver, 1977-80; dep. dist. atty. Jefferson County, Colo., 1980-81; atty. Norton, Miller & O'Toole, Golden, Colo., 1981-85, Dallas, Holland & O'Toole P.C., Denver, 1988-95; sole practitioner Denver, 1985-88, 95—; mem. cervical treatment guidelines task force, shoulder treatment guidelines task force, case mgmt. task force Colo. Dept. Labor. Contbr. articles to profl. jours. Mem. AFL-CIO, ATLA, Colo. Trial Lawyers Assn., Colo. 1st and 2d Jud. Dist. Bar Assns., Workplace Injury Litigation Group (bd. dirs.), Colo. Trial Lawyers Assn., Workers Compensation Edn. Assn. (pres.). Pension, profit-sharing, and employee benefits, Workers' compensation, Personal injury. Office: 226 W 12th Ave Denver CO 80204-3625

**OTOROWSKI, CHRISTOPHER LEE,** lawyer; b. Teaneck, N.J., Nov. 20, 1953; s. Wladyslaw Jerzy and Betty Lee (Robbins) O.; m. Shawn Elizabeth McGovern, Aug. 4, 1978; children: Kirsten, Hilary. BSBA cum laude, U. Denver, 1974, MBA, 1977, JD, 1977. Bar: Wash. 1977, Colo. 1977, U.S. Dist Ct. (we. dist.) D.C. 1977, U.S. Dist. Ct. (we. dist.) Wash. 1978. Asst. atty. gen. Wash. State Atty. Gen., Spokane, 1978-79; atty. Bassett, Gemson & Morrison, Seattle, 1979-81; pvt. practice Seattle, 1981-88; atty. Sullivan, Golden & Otorowski, Seattle, 1988-91, Morrow & Otorowski, Bainbridge Island, 1996—; pvt. practice Morrow and Otorowski, Bainbridge Island, Wash., 1991-96. Contbr. articles to profl. jours. Bd. dirs. Bainbridge Edn. Support Team, Bainbridge Island, 1991-97. Mem. Fed. Bar Assn. We. Dist. Wash. (sec. 1979-82, trustee 1990-93), Wash. State Trial Lawyers Assn. (bd. govs. 1991-93), Assn. Trial Lawyers Am., Seattle Tennis Club, Seattle Yacht Club. Avocations: photography, sailing. General civil litigation, Personal injury. Office: 298 Winslow Way W Bainbridge Is WA 98110-2510

**OTT, ANDREW EDUARD,** lawyer; b. Vancouver, B.C., Can., Sept. 23, 1962; s. Eduard Karl and Elfriede Marie (Petryc) O. BA in English, Seattle U., 1986, JD, 1989; D (hon.), U. Graz, Austria, 1986. Bar: Wash. 1990, U.S. Dist. Ct. (we. dist.) Wash. 1992. Contract atty. Keller Rohrback, Seattle, Lieff Cabraser Heimann & Bernstein, San Francisco, Jamin, Ebell, Schmitt & Mason, Kodiak, Alaska, 1989—; cons. OMNI Tech. Engring., Bothell, Wash., 1986-97. Actor musicals and theater, 1992, 93, 95, 96, 98; musician Cmty. Orch. and Jazz, 1990-98. Mem. ABA, ATLA, Nat. Assn. Self-Employed. Avocations: snow skiing, soccer, bike riding, running, acting. E-mail: Andrew@JESMKOD.com. General civil litigation, Environmental, General practice. Office: Jamin Ebell Schmitt & Mason 323 Carolyn Ave Kodiak AK 99615-6348

**OTT, STEPHEN DOUGLAS,** lawyer; b. Pompton Plains, N.J., Sept. 29, 1967; s. Edward Richard and Grace Rebecca (Williamson) O.; m. Macy R. Robinson, July 31, 1993; 1 child, William Hunter. BA, Mercer U., 1989; JD, Ga. State U ., 1992. Bar: Ga. 1992, U.S. Dist. Ct. (no. dist.) Ga. 1993, U.S. Supreme Ct. 1999. Atty. Killorin & Killorin, Atlanta, 1992-95, Webb, Stuckey & Lindsey, Peachtree City, Ga., 1995—. bd. dirs. Am. Cancer Soc., South Fulton, Fayette. Mem. ABA, Ga. State Bar Assn., Fayette County Bar Assn. (pres. 1999), Kiwanis. Republican. Baptist. Personal injury, Municipal (including bonds), Professional liability. Office: Webb Stuckey & Lindsey 400 Westpark Ct Ste 220 Peachtree City GA 30269-1456

**OTTEN, ARTHUR EDWARD, JR.,** lawyer, corporate executive; b. Buffalo, Oct. 11, 1930; s. Arthur Edward Sr. and Margaret (Ambrusko) O.; m. Mary Therese Torri, Oct. 1, 1960; children: Margaret, Michael, Maureen Staley, Suzanne Hoodecheck, Jennifer. BA, Hamilton Coll., 1952; JD, Yale U., 1955. Bar: N.Y. 1955, Colo. 1959. Assoc. Hodges, Silverstein, Hodges & Harrington, Denver, 1959-64; ptnr. Hodges, Kerwin, Otten & Weeks (predecessor firms), Denver, 1964-73, Davis, Graham & Stubbs, Denver, 1973-86; gen. counsel Colo. Nat. Bankshares, Inc., 1973-93; mem. Otten, Johnson, Robinson, Neff & Ragonetti, P.C., Denver, 1986—; rec. sec. Colo. Nat. Bankshares, Inc., Denver, 1983-93; gen. counsel Regis U., Denver, 1994—; mediator Denver Dist. Ct., 1997—; com. bd. Centura Health, Denver, St. Anthony Hosps., Denver. Lt. USN, 1955-59. Mem. ABA, Colo. Bar Assn., Denver Bar Assn., Am. Arbitration Assn. (panel arbitrators, large complex case panel, mediator panel), Nat. Assn. Securities Dealers (bd. arbitrators), Law club, Univ. Club, Denver Mile High Rotary (pres. 1992-93), Phi Delta Phi. Republican. Roman Catholic. Avocations: hiking, biking, church activities. Banking, General corporate, Education and schools. Home: 3774 S Niagara Way Denver CO 80237-1248 Office: Otten Johnson Robinson Neff & Ragonetti PC 950 17th St Ste 1600 Denver CO 80202-2828

**OTTEN, WESLEY PAUL,** lawyer; b. Duluth, Minn., July 29, 1959; s. Wesley Leo and Mary Ellen Otten; m. Deborah Smoger, Dec. 31, 1987; children: James, Elizabeth. BA, U. Minn., Duluth, 1982; JD, William Mitchell Coll. Law, St. Paul, 1986. Bar: Minn. 1988, U.S. Dist. Ct. Minn. 1990. Pvt. practice Otten Law Offices, Burnsville, Minn., 1988-96; mng. ptnr. Otten & Knutson, P.L.L.P., Burnsville, 1996-98; pres. Otten & Assocs., P.A., Burnsville, 1999—. Chmn. bd. Cmty. Action Coun., Inc., Lakeville, Minn., 1998—. Mem. ATLA, Minn. Bar Assn., Minn. Trial Lawyers Assn., Dakota County Bar Assn. Republican. Lutheran. Avocations: sports, travel. Fax: 612-435-7070. E-mail: wpotten@aol.com. Personal injury, Product liability, Professional liability.

**OTTINGER, PATRICK S.,** lawyer; b. Lake Charles, La., Oct. 12, 1946. BS, U. Southwestern La., 1971; JD, La. State U., 1973. Bar: La. 1974, Tex. 1986, U.S. Dist. Ct. (we. dist.) La. 1977, U.S. Dist. Ct. (mid. dist.) La. 1980, U.S. Ct. Appeals (5th cir.) 1981, U.S. Dist. Ct. (ea. dist.) La. 1986. Ptnr. Ottinger Hebert & Sikes, Lafayette, La.; adj. prof. law Paul M. Hebert Law Ctr., La. State U., 1996—; mem. adv. coun. Mineral Law Inst., 1992-96. Contbr. articles to profl. jours. Fellow La. Bar Found.; mem. La. State Bar Assn. (ho. dels. 1988-96, bd. govs. 1996-97, pres.-elect 1997-98, pres. 1998-99, coun. sect. mineral law 1993-98, sec.-treas. 1995-96, vice chmn. 1996-97, chmn. 1997-98), Lafayette Bar Assn. (bd. dirs. 1978-80, pres.-elect 1991-92, pres. 1992-93). Oil, gas, and mineral, General civil litigation, Contracts commercial. Office: Ottinger Hebert & Sikes LLP 930 Coolidge Blvd PO Box 52606 Lafayette LA 70505-2606*

**OTTINGER, RICHARD LAWRENCE,** dean, law educator; b. N.Y.C., Jan. 27, 1929; s. Lawrence and Louise (Lowenstein) O.; children from previous marriage: Ronald, Randall, Lawrence, Jenny Louise; m. June Godfrey. BA, Cornell U., 1950; LLB, Harvard U., 1953. Assoc. Cleary, Gottlieb, Friendly & Hamilton, N.Y.C., 1955-56; prtnr. William J. Kridel, Law Firm, N.Y.C., 1956-60; second staff mem., dir. programs Peace Corps, L.Am., 1961-64; mem. 89th-91st Congresses, 1965-71, 94th-98th Congresses, 1975-85; prof. Pace U. Sch. Law, White Plains, N.Y., 1985—, dean, 1994—; bd. dirs. Environ. and Energy Study Inst., Washington, Am. Coun. for Energy-Efficient Economy, Washington. Author: Environmental Costs of Electricity, 1990. Contract mgr. Internat. Coop. Adminstrn., 1960-61; organizer Grassroots to Action, 1971-73. Office: Pace U Sch Law 78 N Broadway White Plains NY 10603-3710

**OUDERKIRK, MASON JAMES,** lawyer; b. Des Moines, Feb. 1, 1953; s. Mason George and Florence Astor (Lowe) O.; m. Kari Aune Hormel, May 28, 1983; 1 child, Mason Christopher. BA, Drake U., 1975, JD, 1978. Bar: Iowa 1978, U.S. Dist. Ct. (so. dist.) Iowa 1978, U.S. Ct. Appeals (8th cir.); lic. real estate broker. Assoc. M.G. Ouderkirk Law Office, Indianola, Iowa, 1978-79; ptnr. Ouderkirk Law Firm, Indianola, 1979-96; sr. mem. Ouderkirk, Ouderkirk & Dougherty, P.L.C., Indianola, 1996-98; proprietor Ouderkirk Law Firm, Indianola, Iowa, 1998—; pres. Avanti Realty Co. (formerly Landmark Real Estate, Ltd.), Indianola, 1978—, Avanti Builders Co., Indianola, 1991—; mem. Vol. Lawyers Project of Iowa, 1987-93. Mem. Indianola Police Retirement Bd., 1983-88; instr. Eric Heintz Black Belt Acad., 1988-93, Indianola Parks and Recreation Dept., 1988-93. Mem. ABA, Iowa Bar Assn. (pub. rels. com. 1989-94, family law com. 1989-90), Warren County Bar Assn. (sec., treas. 1985-89, v.p. 1989-90, pres. 1990-92), 5th Jud. Dist. Bar Assn. (sec., treas. 1995), Assn. Trial Lawyers Am., Iowa Trial Lawyers Assn., Nat. Assn. Homebuilders U.S., Home Builders Assn. Iowa, Homebuilders Assn. Greater Des Moines. Episcopalian. Avocations: fishing, hunting, gardening. Personal injury, Family and matrimonial, Probate. Home: 1231 Fulton St Lot 10 Indianola IA 50125-9083 Office: Ouderkirk Law Firm 108 S Howard St PO Box 156 Indianola IA 50125-0156

**OVERFELT, CLARENCE LAHUGH,** lawyer; b. Big Timber, Mont., Apr. 15, 1935; s. Leo and Clara (Drivdahl) O.; m. Joyce Overfelt, Feb. 15, 1959 (div. 1977); children: Kent Leo, Reed Allen; m. Allyce Overfelt, Nov. 21, 1977. BA, U. Mont., 1958, JD, 1968. Bar: Mont. 1968, U.S. Dist. Ct. Mont. 1968. Ptnr. Randono Overfelt & Gianotti, Great Falls, Mont., 1968-73; pvt. practice Overfelt Law Firm, Great Falls, Mont., 1973-91, pres., sr. mem., 1980—; tchr. Cut Bank (Mont.) Pub. Schs., 1959-60, Helena (Mont.) Pub. Schs., 1960-65. Mem. Assn. Trial Lawyers Am., Mont. Trial Lawyers Assn., Civil Justice Found., Meadowlark Country Club, Elks, Kiwanis. Democrat. Episcopalian. Avocations: golf, skiing, music, woodworking, gardening. Workers' compensation, Personal injury, Oil, gas, and mineral. Home: 128 Lower River Rd Great Falls MT 59405-8203 Office: Overfelt Law Firm PC 121 4th St N Ste 2E Great Falls MT 59401-2570

**OVERHOLT, HUGH ROBERT,** lawyer, retired army officer; b. Beebe, Ark., Oct. 29, 1933; s. Harold R. and Cuma E. (Hall) O.; m. Laura Annell Arnold, May 5, 1961; children: Sharon, Scott. Student, Coll. of Ozarks, 1951-53; B.A., U. Ark., 1955, LL.B., 1957. Bar: Ark. 1957. Commd. 1st lt. U.S. Army, 1957, advanced through grades to maj. gen., 1981; chief Criminal Law Div., JAG Sch., Charlottesville, Va., 1971-73; chief personnel, plans and tng. Office of JAG, U.S. Army, Washington, 1973-75; staff judge adv. XVIII Airborne Corps, Ft. Bragg, N.C., 1976-78; spl. asst. for legal and selected policy matters Office of Dep. Asst., 1978-79; asst. judge adv. gen. for mil. law Office of JAG, Washington, 1979-81; asst. judge adv. gen. Office of JAG, 1981-85, judge adv. gen, 1985-89; atty. Ward & Smith, New Bern, N.C., 1989—. Notes and comment editor Ark. Law Rev, 1956-57. Decorated Army Meritorious Service medal with oak leaf cluster, Army Commendation medal with 2 oak leaf clusters., Legion of Merit, Def. Meritorious Service medal, D.S.M. Mem. ABA, N.C. Bar Assn., Ark. Bar Assn., Assn. U.S. Army, Delta Theta Phi, Omicron Delta Kappa, Sigma Pi. Presbyterian. Office: Ward and Smith 1001 College Ct New Bern NC 28562-4972

**OVERMAN, DEAN LEE,** lawyer, investor, author; b. Cook County, Ill., Oct. 9, 1943; s. Harold Levon and Violet Elsa (True) O.; m. Linda Jane Olsen, Sept. 6, 1969; children: Elisabeth True, Christiana Hart. BA, Hope Coll., 1965; student, Princeton Sem. and U., 1965-66; JD, U. Calif., Berkeley, 1969; postgrad. in bus., U. Chgo., 1974, U. Calif. Bar: Ill. 1969, D.C. 1977. Assoc. to ptnr. D'Ancona, Pflaum et al., Chgo., 1970-75; White House fellow, asst. to v.p. Nelson Rockefeller, Washington, 1975-76; assoc. dir. Domestic Council The White House, Washington, 1976-77; sr. ptnr. Winston & Strawn, Washington, 1977—; cons. White House; spl. counsel to Gov. James Thompson, Springfield, Ill.; adj. faculty in secured financing U. Va. Law Sch., Charlottesville; vice chmn. J.F. Forstmann Co.; chmn. Holland Investment Co.; adj. fellow Ctr. for Strategic and Internat. Studies, 1993-95; vis. scholar, officer Harvard U., 1994-95; Templeton scholar Oxford U., 1999—. Author: Toward a National Policy on State and Local Government Finance, 1976, Effective Writing Techniques, 1980, (with others) Financing Equipment, 1973, Sales and Financing Under the Revised UCC, 1975, A Case Against Accident and Self Organization, 1997; monthly newspaper column Chgo. Daily Law Bull.; contbr. articles to profl. jours. Commencement spkr. Hope Coll., Holland, Mich., 1978; bd. dirs. Internat. Bus. Inst., White House Fellows Assn., Cmtys. in Schs., Inc.; adv. bd. The Beacon Group; former bd. dirs. U.S. Decathlon Assn. Reginald Heber Smith fellow U. Pa., 1969-70. Mme. Mensa, Intertel, ABA, Ill. Bar Assn., D.C. Bar Assn., Chgo. Bar Assn., Met. Club (D.C.), Internat. Philos. Enquiry, Triple Nine Soc., Burning Tree Club (Bethesda, Md.), Congl. Country Club (Bethesda), Harvard Club of N.Y.C., Macatawa (Mich.) Bay Yacht Club. Banking, Contracts commercial, General corporate. Office: Winston & Strawn 1400 L St NW Ste 800 Washington DC 20005-3508

**OVERSTREET, MORRIS L.,** state supreme court justice. Judge Tex. Ct. Criminal Appeals. Office: Supreme Court Bldg PO Box 112308 Austin TX 78711

**OVERTON, BENJAMIN FREDERICK,** state supreme court justice; b. Green Bay, Wis., Dec. 15, 1926; s. Benjamin H. and Esther M. (Wiese) O.; m. Marilyn Louise Smith, June 9, 1951; children: William Hunter, Robert Murray, Catherine Louise. B.S. in Bus. Adminstrn., U. Fla., 1951, J.D., 1952; LL.D. (hon.), Stetson U., 1975, Nova U., 1977; LL.M., U. Va., 1984. Bar: Fla. 1952. With Office Fla. Atty. Gen., 1952; with firms in St. Petersburg, Fla., 1952-64; city atty. St. Petersburg Beach, Fla., 1954-57; circuit judge 6th Jud. Circuit Fla., 1964-74, chief judge, 1968-71; chmn. Fla. Conf. Circuit Judges, 1973; justice Supreme Ct. Fla., Tallahassee, 1974—; chief justice Supreme Ct. Fla., 1976-78; past adj. faculty Stetson U. Coll., Law and Fla. St. U. Coll. Law; bd. dirs. Nat. Jud. Coll., 1976-87; mem. Fla. Car Continuing Legal Edn. Com., 1963-74, chmn., 1971-74; 1st chmn. Fla. Inst. Judiciary, 1972; mem. exec. com. Appellate Judges Conf.; chmn. Appellate Structure Commn., 1978-79, Article Rev. Commn., 1983-84, Matrimonial Law Commn., 1982-85; chmn. Jud. Coun. Fla., 1985-89.; chmn. adv. com. for LLM program for appellate judges U. Va., 1985-94. Contbr. legal publs. Past reader, vestryman, sr. warden St. Albans Episcopal Ch., St. Petersburg; chmn. U.S. Constn. Bicentennial Commn. Fla. 1987-91; ch. Family Ct. Commn., 1990-91; ch. Death Case Postconviction Relief Proceeding 1990-91. Fellow Am. Bar Found.; mem. ABA (chmn. criminal justice task force to rev. trial and discovery standards 1991—), Fla. Bar Assn., Am. Judicature Soc. (dir., sec.). Democrat. Lodge: Rotary. Office: Fla Supreme Ct Supreme Court Bldg Tallahassee FL 32399-6556*

**OVROM, ELIZA JANE,** lawyer; b. Keosauqua, Iowa, Feb. 25, 1953; d. Arthur P. and Mary H. (Hamblin) O.; m. Mark R. Schuling, Sept. 4, 1982; children: Charles, Matthew. BA magna cum laude, Coe Coll., 1975; JD, U. Iowa, 1979. Bar: Iowa 1979, U.S. Dist. Ct. Iowa 1983, U.S. Ct. Appeals (8th cir.) 1984, U.S. Supreme Ct. 1985, U.S. Ct. Appeals (5th cir.) 1987. Asst. state atty. gen. State of Iowa, Des Moines, 1979-90; 1st asst. county atty. County of Polk, Iowa, 1991—; mem. civil justice adv. group U.S. Dist. Ct., 1995-99. Trustee Des Moines Pub. Libr., 1996—; bd. dirs. Conservation Found. Polk County, 1995—, Legal Aid Soc. Polk County, 1995—; active Friendship Force Greater Des Moines, 1983—, Plymouth United Congl. Ch., 1991—. Mem. Polk County Bar Assn., Polk County Women Attys., ABA, Iowa County Attys. Assn. Avocations: tae kwon do, golf, reading, bicycling. Home: 500 Glenview Dr Des Moines IA 50312-2526 Office: Polk County Atty Office 111 Court Ave Ste 340 Des Moines IA 50309-2218

**OWEN, H. MARTYN,** lawyer; b. Decatur, Ill., Oct. 23, 1929; s. Honore Martyn and Virginia (Hunt) O.; m. Candace Catlin Benjamin, June 21, 1952; children—Leslie W., Peter H., Douglas P. A.B., Princeton U., 1951; LL.B., Harvard U., 1954. Bar: Conn. 1954. Assoc. Shipman & Goodwin, Hartford, Conn., 1958-61, ptnr., 1961-94, of counsel, 1995-96. Mem. Simsbury (Conn.) Zoning Bd. Appeals, 1961-67, Simsbury Zoning Commn., 1967-79; sec. Capitol Region Planning Agy., 1965-66; bd. dirs. Symphony Soc. Greater Hartford, 1967-73; trustee Renbrook Sch., West Hartford, Conn., 1963-72, treas., 1964-68, pres., 1968-72, hon. life trustee, 1972—; trustee Simsbury Free Library, 1970-84; pres. Hartford Grammar Sch., 1987-98, trustee; corporator Hartford Hosp, 1984-96. Lt. USNR, 1954-57. Mem. ABA, Conn. Bar Assn., Hartford County Bar Assn., Am. Law Inst. Democrat. Episcopalian. Clubs: Princeton (N.Y.C.); Ivy (Princeton, N.J.). General corporate, Antitrust, Municipal (including bonds). Home: 80 Matthew Dr Brunswick ME 04011-3275

**OWEN, JACK EDWARD, JR.,** lawyer; b. Port Arthur, Tex., June 14, 1951; s. Jack Edward and Hessie (Williams) O.; m. Lucy Ross; children: Sean Rhys, MarrGwen Rhys. BS, U.S. Naval Acad., 1973; JD, Harvard U., 1979; MA, U. Tex., 1995. Bar: Tex. 1979, U.S. Ct. Mil. Appeals 1979, U.S. Supreme Ct. 1982. Judge advocate USMC, 1979-83; assoc. prof. U. Tex., Austin, 1983-86; shareholder Graves, Dougherty, Hearon & Moody, Austin, 1986-93; mng. ptnr. Osborne, Lowe, Helman & Smith, LLP, Austin, 1993—. Contbr. articles to profl. jours. Mem. U.S. Naval Acad. Alumni Assn. (trustee 1987-90). Avocation: American military history. Real property, Contracts commercial, Landlord-tenant. Home: 5813 Trailridge Dr Austin TX 78731-4245 Office: Osborne Lowe Helman & Smith 301 Congress Ave Ste 1900 Austin TX 78701-4041

**OWEN, JEFFREY RANDALL,** lawyer; b. Pitts., June 11, 1960; s. Randall J. and Barbara B. Owen; m. Dawn R. Ver Hill, June 5, 1961; children: Jennifer, Rebecca, Kristin. BA in Polit. Sci. and English, Allegheny Coll., 1982; JD, Ohio State U., 1985. Bar: Ohio 1985, U.S. Dist. Ct. (so. dist.) Ohio 1985, Pa. 1986, U.S. Dist. Ct. (we. dist.) Pa. 1986. Atty. Jones Gregg Creehan & Gerace, Pitts., 1986-92; from assoc. to ptnr. to shareholder Reding Rea & Cooper P.C., Pitts., 1992—. Mem. New Hope PCA, Univ. Club. Pitts. General corporate, Franchising, General civil litigation. Office: Reding Rea & Cooper PC 1600 Benedum Trees Bldg 223 4th Ave Pittsburgh PA 15222-1717

**OWEN, JOSEPH GABRIEL,** lawyer, judge; b. Nov. 7, 1933; s. Charls S. and Marie Wolf (Elias) O.; m. Patricia E. Owen, Apr. 28, 1962; children: Elizabeth, Joseph, Ursula, Patrick, Marianne. BA, CCNY, 1955; JD, Fordham U., 1959. Bar: N.Y. 1959, U.S. Dist. Ct. (so. and ea. dists.) N.Y. 1959. With firm Galli, Terhune, Gibbons and Mulvihill, N.Y.C., 1959-63, Alfred Schleider, Goshen, N.Y., 1963-65; ptnr. Schleider and Owen, Goshen, N.Y., 1965-73; sr. ptnr. Joseph G. Owen, Owen & Grogan, Goshen, 1973-84; surrogate Orange County, Goshen, 1985-93; justice N.Y. Supreme Ct. 9th dist., Goshen, 1994—; town justice Town of Wallkill (N.Y.), 1974-84. Past bd. dirs. Hudson Delaware Coun. Boy Scouts Am. Served to maj. U.S. Army N.G. to 1970. Mem. ABA, ATLA, KC, N.Y. State Bar Assn., Orange County Bar Assn., Goshen Bar Assn., Defense Assn. N.Y., Am. Legion, Kiwanis. Republican. Roman Catholic. Home: PO Box 59 Circleville NY 10919-0059 Office: Orange County Govt Ctr Goshen NY 10924-0329

**OWEN, PRISCILLA RICHMAN,** state supreme court justice. BA, Baylor U., JD, 1977. Bar: Tex. 1978, U.S. Ct. Appeals (4th, 5th, 8th and 11th cirs.). Former ptnr. Andrews & Kurth, L.L.P., Houston; justice Supreme Ct. Tex., Austin, 1995—; liaison to Tex. Legal Svcs. for Poor Spl. Supreme Ct. Tex., Supreme Ct. Adv. Com. on Ct.-Annexed Mediations. Named Young Lawyer of Yr., Outstanding Young Alumna, Baylor U. Office: Supreme Ct Tex PO Box 12248 Austin TX 78711-2248

**OWEN, RICHARD,** federal judge; b. N.Y.C., Dec. 11, 1922; s. Carl Maynard and Shirley (Barnes) O.; m. Lynn Rasmussen, June 6, 1960; children: Carl R., David R., Richard. AB, Dartmouth Coll., 1947; LLB, Harvard U., 1950; MusD (hon.), Manhattan Sch. Music, 1989. Bar: N.Y. 1950. Practiced in N.Y.C., 1950-74; assoc. Willkie Owen Farr Gallagher & Walton, 1950-53, Willkie Farr Gallagher Walton & Fitzgibbon, 1958-60; pvt. practice, 1960-65; ptnr. Owen & Aarons, 1965-66, Owen & Turchin, 1966-74; asst. U.S. atty. So. Dist. N.Y., 1953-55; trial atty. antitrust div. U.S. Dept. Justice, 1955-58; U.S. dist. judge So. Dist. N.Y., 1974-89, sr. judge, 1989—; asst. prof. N.Y. Law Sch., 1951-53; adj. prof. law Fordham U. Sch. Law, 1966—. Composer, librettist operas A Moment of War, 1958, A Fisherman Called Peter, 1965, Mary Dyer, 1976, The Death of the Virgin, 1980, Abigail Adams, 1987, Tom Sawyer, 1989, Sadie Thompson, 1997. Trustee Manhattan Sch. Music, N.Y.C.; founder, bd. dirs. Maine Opera Assn., 1975-85; pres., bd. dirs. N.Y. Lyric Opera Co. 1st lt. USAAF, 1942-45. Decorated D.F.C. with oak leaf cluster, Air medal with 3 oak leaf clusters. Mem. ASCAP, Century Assn., Chelsea Yacht Club. Republican. Mem. Soc. of Friends. Office: US Dist Ct US Courthouse Foley Sq New York NY 10007-1501

**OWEN, RICHARD KNOWLES,** lawyer; b. Pitts., July 16, 1945; s. Douglas James Knowles and Sarah Isabelle (McLaren) O. BA, Franklin & Marshall Coll., 1967; MBA, U. Fla., 1971; JD, John Marshall Law Sch., 1975. Bar: Fla. 1977, N.Y. 1983, U.S. Dist. Ct. (so. dist.) Fla. 1980. Sole practice Coral Gables, Fla., 1975—; Pres. Forty Salamanca Corp., 1985-87; dir. Ivory Corp. Mem. ABA, Fed. Trial Bar. Federal civil litigation, State civil litigation, Workers' compensation. Home: 415 E 71st St Apt 3E New York NY 10021-4834 Office: Empire State Bldg 350 5th Ave Ste 7910 New York NY 10118-7999

**OWEN, ROBERT DEWIT,** lawyer; b. St. Louis, Nov. 15, 1948; s. Kenneth Campbell Owen and Mary Elenor (Fish) Luebbers; m. Rebecca Roberts Baxter, June 4, 1977; children: Abigail Mary, James Roy, Charlotte Grace. BA, Northwestern U., 1970; JD cum laude, U. Pa., 1973. Assoc. Sullivan & Cromwell, N.Y.C., 1973-81; ptnr. Towne, Dolgin, Furlaud, Sawyier & Owen, N.Y.C., 1981-83, Owen & Fennell, N.Y.C., 1983-87, Owen & Davis, N.Y.C., 1987—; instr. Nat. Inst. Trial Advocacy, Boulder, Colo., 1988—; faculty mem. ABA Nat. Inst. 1992, 93. Bd. dirs. St. Christopher's-Jennie Clarkson Child Care Svcs., Dobbs Ferry, N.Y., 1991-97. Mem. Assn. Bar City N.Y., Fed. Bar Coun., Nat. Assn. Securities Dealers (bd. arbitrators 1985—), Colonial Springs Club (pres. 1986-94), India House. Episcopalian. Avocations: boating, running. General civil litigation, Contracts commercial, Oil, gas, and mineral. Office: Owen & Davis 805 3rd Ave New York NY 10022-7513

**OWENDOFF, STEPHEN PETER,** lawyer; b. Morristown, N.J., Aug. 1, 1943; m.; 4 children. Student, Bowdoin Coll., 1966; BA, Kent State U., 1966; JD, Georgetown U., 1969. Bar: Ohio 1969. Assoc. Hahn Loeser & Parks and predecessor firms, Cleve., 1969-77; ptnr. Hahn Loeser & Parks (formerly Hahn, Loeser, Freedheim, Dean and Wellman), 1977—; mem. mgmt. com. Hahn Loeser & Parks (formerly Hahn, Loeser, Freedheim Dean); lectr. in field. Active Gesu Ch., University Heights, Ohio; mem. adv. bd. Learning About Bus., Inc.; former pres. Parmadale (Ohio) Adv. Bd.; bd. trustees, mem. community svcs. panel Fedn. Cath. Community Svcs.; rep. United Way Assembly, Parmadale; bd. trustees LeBlond Housing Corp., Health Hill Hosp. Mem. Nat. Assn. Bond Lawyers, Nat. Assn. Coll. and Univ. Attys., Shaker Heights (Ohio) Country Club. Banking, General corporate, Real property. Office: Hahn Loeser & Parks 200 Public Square 3300 American Rd Cleveland OH 44144-2301

**OWENS, A(RNOLD) DEAN,** lawyer; b. Visalia, Calif., June 14, 1943; s. Clarence Cecil and Eula Mae (Boaz) O.; m. Marilyn Joyce Hatfield, Sept. 16, 1967; children: Eric, Rachel. BS, U. Calif., Berkeley, 1966; JD, U. Oreg., 1969. Bar: Oreg. 1969. Assoc. O'Reilly, Anderson, Richmonds & Adkins, Eugene, Oreg., 1969-71; ptnr. Anderson, Richmond & Owens, Eugene, 1971-74, Owens & Loomis, Eugene, 1975-79, Owens & Platt, Eugene, 1982-85; pvt. practice, Eugene, 1979-82, 85—; atty. City of Coburg, Oreg., 1971-79, City of Lowell, Oreg., 1973-79; hearings officer Lane County, Eugene, 1972—. Author: Advising Oregon Business Chpter 13, 1979; editor Lane County Bar News, 1980-87; also articles. Pres. Lane County Muscular Dystrophy Assn., Eugene, 1969-71; chmn. Eugene Human Rights Commn., 1969-71; bd. dirs. Asian Counseling Ctr., Eugene, 1991—; mem. exec. com. Lane County Rep. Party, Eugene, 1993—; mem. Eugene econ. devel. City of Eugene, 1989—; bd. dirs. Eugene-Springfield Met. Partnership, Inc., 1989-90; mem. exec. com. Eugene/Springfield Community Partnership, 1991—. Recipient cert. of appreciation Lane County Law Libr. Adv. Com., 1976-78, Bd. Lane County Legal Aid and Sr. Law Svcs., 1987, 90, spl. award and recognition of vol. svc. Eugene Sports Program, 1982. Mem. Eugene Area C. of C. (bd. dirs. 1986-90, pres. 1989, Disting. Svc. award 1986, 88), Emerald Exec. Assn. (pres. 1984), Eugene Swim and Tennis Club (pres. 1982), Eugene Country Club (chmn. tennis com. 1975-79), Downtown Athletic Club, Tri-Pass Water Ski Club, Eugene Active 20-30 Club (hon. life, editor newsletter 1969-72). Republican. Avocations: tennis, basketball, running, reading, water and snow skiing. State civil litigation, Family and matrimonial, Estate planning. Office: 2160 Oakmont Way Eugene OR 97401-2372

**OWENS, BETTY RUTH,** lawyer; b. Texas City, Tex., Dec. 21, 1951; d. Marvin Lee Jr. and Ellen Frances (Nunnally) O.; m. Robert Foster Geary, Oct. 1, 1994. BS, La State U., 1973, MA, 1975; JD, U. Tex., 1988. Bar: Tex., U.S. Dist. Ct. (so. dist.) Tex. 1989, U.S. Ct. Appeals (5th cir.) 1989. Ptnr. Vinson & Elkins LLP, Houston, 1988—. Author: (with others) ABA Antitrust Law Developments, 4th edit., ABA Annual Review of Antitrust Law Developments, 1992-95; editor ABA Antitrust Summary Judgment Newsletter, 1996-98. Trustee St. Luke's United Meth. Ch., Houston, 1998, mem. adv. com. Senior's Place, 1994-98. Mem. ABA (vice chair civil practice and procedure com., antitrust sect. 1993-98), Am. Law Inst., Tex. Bar Found., Houston Bar Found. Avocations: reading, cooking, travel. General civil litigation, Appellate, Antitrust. Office: Vinson & Elkins LLP 1001 Fannin St Ste 2300 Houston TX 77002-6760

**OWENS, L. DALE,** lawyer; b. Enterprise, Ala., Jan. 26, 1954; s. Lawrence B. Jr. and Helen (Daughdrill) O.; m. Irmina L. Rivero, Aug. 18, 1979; children: Michael L., Andrew C. BA, Emory U., 1975, JD, 1978. Bar: Ga.

1978, U.S. Ct. Appeals (5th cir.) 1978, U.S. Ct. Appeals (11th cir.) 1983, Supreme Ct. 1984. Assoc. Seward & Kissel, Atlanta, 1978-80; assoc. Kilpatrick & Cody, Atlanta, 1980-84, ptnr., 1984-89; ptnr. Booth, Wade & Campbell, Atlanta, 1989-95, Booth Owens & Jospih LLP, Atlanta, 1995-96; pvt. practice Atlanta, 1996-98; of counsel McRae & Bisbee LLP, Atlanta, 1997-98, ptnr., 1998—. Editor-in-chief Ga. State Bar Jour., 1987-89, mem. editl. bd., 1985-87. Fellow Lawyers Found. Ga.; mem. ABA, State Bar of Ga., Atlanta Bar Assn., Mil. and Hospitaller Order of St. Lazarus (officer 1996—), Order of the Coif, Order of Barristers, Lawyers Club of Atlanta. Republican. Episcopalian. Avocations: golf, sailing, coaching little league baseball. General civil litigation, Environmental, Intellectual property. Office: McRae & Bisbee LLP 600 W Peachtree St NW Ste 800 Atlanta GA 30308-3603

**OWENS, ROBERT PATRICK,** lawyer; b. Spokane, Wash., Feb. 17, 1954; s. Walter Patrick and Cecile (Phillippay) O.; m. Robin Miller, Aug. 12, 1978; children: Ryan Barry, Meghan Jane. BA, Wash. State U., 1976; JD, Gonzaga U., 1981; LLM in Admiralty Law, Tulane U., 1983. Bar: Wash. 1982, Alaska 1984, U.S. Dist. Ct. (ea. dist.) Wash. 1982, U.S. Dist. Ct. Alaska 1984, U.S. Ct. Appeals (5th cir.) 1983. Assoc. Groh, Eggers & Price, Anchorage, 1983-88; mng. atty. Taylor & Hintze, Anchorage, 1988-90; Anchorage office mgr. Copeland, Landye, Bennett and Wolf, Anchorage, 1990—; v.p. bd. dirs. Hope Cmty. Resources, Inc., 1999—. Coord. supplies Insight Seminars, Anchorage, 1985-86. Mem. ABA (dist. 27 rep. young lawyers div. 1988-90), Alaska Bar Assn., Wash. State Bar Assn., Anchorage Bar Assn. (pres. 1991-92, v.p. 1990-91, pres. young lawyers sect. 1986-88), Alaska Fly Fishers, Phi Alpha Delta. Roman Catholic. Avocations: fishing, photography, skiing, softball. E-mail: rpowens@micronet.net. Contracts commercial, Environmental, Admiralty. Office: Copeland Landye Bennett & Wolf 701 W 8th Ave Ste 1200 Anchorage AK 99501-3453

**OWENS, RODNEY JOE,** lawyer; b. Dallas, Mar. 7, 1950; s. Hubert L. and Billie Jo (Foust) O.; m. Sherry Lyn Bailey, June 10, 1972; 1 child, Jonathan Rockwell. BBA, So. Meth. U., 1972, JD, 1975. Bar: Tex. 1975, U.S. Dist. Ct. (no. dist.) Tex. 1975, U.S. Tax Ct. 1975, U.S. Ct. Appeals (5th cir.) 1975. Assoc. Durant & Mankoff, Dallas, 1975-78, ptnr., 1978-83; ptnr. Meadows, Owens, Collier, Reed, Cousins & Blau, Dallas, 1983—. Contbr. articles to profl. jours. Baptist. Estate planning, Estate taxation, Taxation, general. Home: 6919 N Jan Mar Dr Dallas TX 75230-3111 Office: Meadows Owens Collier Reed 901 Main St Ste 3700 Dallas TX 75202-3725

**OWENS, WILBUR DAWSON, JR.,** federal judge; b. Albany, Ga., Feb. 1, 1930; s. Wilbur Dawson and Estelle (McKenzie) O.; m. Mary Elizabeth Glenn, June 21, 1958; children: Lindsey, Wilbur Dawson III, Estelle, John. Student, Emory U., 1947-48; JD, U. Ga., 1952. Bar: Ga. 1952. Mem. firm Smith, Gardner & Owens, Albany, 1954-55; v.p., trust officer Bank of Albany, 1955-59; sec.-treas. Southeastern Mortgage Co., Albany, 1959-65; asst. U.S. atty. Middle Dist. Ga., Macon, 1962-65; assoc., then ptnr. Bloch, Hall, Hawkins & Owens, Macon, 1965-72; judge U.S. Dist. Ct. for Mid. Dist. Ga., Macon, 1972—, now sr. U.S. dist. judge. Served to 1st lt., JAG USAF, 1952-54. Mem. State Bar Ga., Macon Bar Assn., Am. Judicature Soc., Phi Delta Theta, Phi Delta Phi. Republican. Presbyterian. Clubs: Rotarian, Idle Hour Golf and Country. Office: US Dist Ct PO Box 65 Macon GA 31202-0065

**OWENS, WILLIAM DEAN,** lawyer; b. Topeka, Kans., July 3, 1931; s. Claude and Melvina Owens; m. Doris McConnell, June 10, 1953; children: Steven D., Susan Bloom, Sarah Steele. BS in Bus., U. Kans., Lawrence, 1953, JD, 1968. Bar: Kans. 1968. Mgr. McConnell Lumber Co., Lawrence, 1955-65; ptnr. Hampton & Royce, L.C., Salina, Kans., 1968—. Trustee, chmn. Kansas Wesleyan U., Salina, 1990—, Salina Regional Health Found., 1986—. Capt. USMC, 1953-55, Japan. Fellow Kans. Bar Found.; mem. ABA, Kans. Bar Assn. Republican. Presbyterian. Avocations: tennis, travel, woodworking. General practice, Real property, General corporate. Home: 2126 Melrose Ln Salina KS 67401-3543 Office: Hampton & Royce LC 119 W Iron Ave Salina KS 67401-2600

**OWNBY, JERE FRANKLIN, III,** lawyer; b. Chicago Heights, Ill., Oct. 1, 1956; s. Jere Franklin Jr. and Emogene (Stephens) O.; m. Melissa Cooley, Mar. 17, 1990. BA, U. Tenn., 1986, JD, 1991. Bar: Tenn. 1991. Assoc. Law Offices of Peter G. Angelos, Knoxville, Tenn., 1991—; mem. Order of Barristers, William B. Spong Invitational Moot Ct. Team. Mem. ABA, Assn. Trial Lawyers Am., Am. Inn of Ct., Tenn. Bar Assn., Knoxville Bar Assn., Tenn. Trial Lawyers Assn., Omicron Delta Epsilon, Pi Sigma Alpha. Democrat. Avocations: gardening, raising dogs, life tng. weekends/Kairos Found. Product liability, Personal injury, Workers' compensation. Home: 3902 Glenfield Dr Knoxville TN 37919-6698 Office: Law Offices Peter G Angelos 2643 Kingston Pike Knoxville TN 37919-3399

**OXMAN, DAVID CRAIG,** lawyer; b. Summit, N.J., Mar. 10, 1941; s. Jacob H. and Kathryn (Grear) O.; m. Phyllis Statter; children—Elena, Lee. A.B., Princeton U., 1962; LL.B., Yale U., 1969. Bar: N.Y. 1970, N.J. 1974, U.S. Dist. Ct. (so. and ea. dists.) N.Y. 1974, U.S. Ct. Appeals (2d cir.) 1974, U.S. Tax Ct. 1977, U.S. Supreme Ct. 1974. Assoc. Davis Polk & Wardwell, N.Y.C., 1970-76, ptnr., 1977-95, sr. counsel, 1995—. Served with USN, 1962-66. Fellow Am. Coll. Trust and Estate Counsel; mem. ABA, N.Y. State Bar Assn., Assn. of Bar of City of N.Y., N.J. Bar Assn., N.Y. County Lawyers Assn. Probate. Office: Davis Polk & Wardwell 450 Lexington Ave New York NY 10017-3911

**OXNER, G. DEWEY,** lawyer; b. Greenville, S.C., Dec. 31, 1933; s. George Dewey and Frances (Ruckman) O.; m. Louise Earle, Sept. 16, 1960; children: Frances, Dewey, Earle. BA, Washington & Lee U., 1956; LLB, U. S.C., 1959. Bar: S.C. 1959, U.S. Dist. Ct. S.C. 1959, U.S. Ct. Appeals (4th cir.) 1959. From assoc. to mng. ptnr. Haynsworth, Marion, McKay & Guerard, Greenville, 1959-98, ptnr., 1998—. Fellow Am. Coll. Trial Lawyers, S.C. Def. Trial Attys. Assn. (pres. 1976), S.C. Bar Assn. (sec. 1997-98, treas. 1998—), Assn. (sec. 1997-98, treas. 1998-99, pres. elect, 1999—). Home: 10 Parkins Lake Rd Greenville SC 29607-3668 Office: Haynsworth Marion McKay & Guerard 75 Beattie Pl Greenville SC 29601-2130

**OZMON, LAIRD MICHAEL,** lawyer; b. Chgo., July 7, 1954; s. Nat Peter and Bette Jean (Rose) O. BA in Polit. Sci. with high honors, Lewis U., 1977; JD, Loyola U., Chgo., 1979. Bar: Ill. 1979, U.S. Dist. Ct. Ill. (no. dist.) 1979, U.S. Ct. Appeals (7th cir.) 1979, Fla. 1980, U.S. Supreme Ct. 1983. Assoc. Anesi, Ozmon, Lewin & Assoc., Chgo., 1979-83; prin. Joliet, Ill., 1983—. Inventor dura file. Mem. ABA, Ill. Bar Assn., Fla. Bar Assn., Chgo. Bar Assn., Assn. Trial Lawyers Am. (committeeman 1988), Ill. Trial Lawyers Assn. (exec. com. 1987, bd. mgrs. 1985—, legis. com., conv. del. 1988). Democrat. Avocations: skiing, weightlifting, horses. Personal injury, State civil litigation. Office: 54 N Ottawa St Joliet IL 60432-4345

**PACE, ROSA WHITE,** lawyer; b. Borger, Tex., Nov. 5, 1932; d. John Herron and Anna Mae (Caldwell) White; m. M. Carroll Pace, Jan. 3, 1968; children: Ann Catherine, Virginia Gale, Mary Jane. BA, William Jewell Coll., 1953; JD, U. Tex., 1956. Bar: Tex. 1956. Ptnr. White & White Attys., Borger, 1956-62, White, White & White Attys., Borger, 1962-65; pvt. practice Borger, 1966—. Co-author: Borger, a History, Hutchinson County History, 1983. Chmn. Hutchinson County Hist. Commn., 1985-94. Recipient Professionalism award Coll. of State Bar of Tex., 1996. Mem. ABA, State Bar Assn. Tex., Borger Bar Assn., DAR (local regent 1975-76), Beta Sigma Phi (women of yr. 1978). Personal income taxation, Probate, General practice. Office: 431 Deahl St Borger TX 79007-4113

**PACE, SAMUEL J., JR.,** lawyer; b. Chester, Pa., Jan. 6, 1954; s. Samuel J. and Mary (Malizia) P.; m. Jeanne M. Pace, Sept. 25, 1992. BS, U. Pa., 1975; JD, Villanova U., 1979. Assoc. Hecher & Maginnis, Phila., 1982-84; assoc. LaBrun & Doak, Phila., 1979-82, 84-86, ptnr., 1986-95; ptnr. Dugan, Brinkmann Maginnis & Pace, Phila., 1995—. Mem. Phila. Futures, 1997—. Fellow Internat. Soc. Barristers; mem. ADTA (exec. coun.). Avocation: golf. Personal injury, Professional liability, General civil litigation. Office: DBMP 1990 Jfk Blvd Ste 1400 Philadelphia PA 19103-1441

**PACE, STANLEY DAN,** lawyer; b. Dayton, Ohio, Dec. 10, 1947; s. Stanley Carter and Elaine (Cutchall) P.; m. Judy Roehm, Sept. 8, 1973; children: Stanley Carter, Barbara Roehm. BA, Denison U., Granville, Ohio, 1970; JD, U. Toledo (Ohio), 1975. Bar: U.S. Dist. Ct. (so. dist.) Ohio 1975, U.S. Dist. Ct. (no. dist.) Ohio 1977, U.S. Ct. Appeals (6th cir.) 1975. Atty. ARMCO Steel Corp., Middletown, Ohio, 1975-77; assoc. Spieth, Bell, McCurdy & Newell, Cleve., 1977-82, dir., 1982—, co-mng. dir., 1987—; bd. mem. Indsl. Rels. Rsch. Assn., Cleve., 1985. Bd. pres. Judson Retirement Community, Cleve., 1985; bd. mem. Arthritis Found. N.E. Ohio, Cleve., 1984, Western Res. Hist. Soc., 1998. Mem. ABA, Ohio Bar Assn., Greater Cleve. Bar Assn., The Country Club, Pepper Pike Club, Tavern Club, Rolling Rock Club. Labor. Office: Spieth Bell McCurdy & Newell 2000 Huntington Bldg Cleveland OH 44115

**PACE, THOMAS,** information services executive, lawyer; b. Teaneck, N.J., July 5, 1951; s. John James and Doris Elizabeth (Ihne) P.; m. Loren Anne Dunn, Sept. 10, 1977; children: Ashley, Ryan, Lindsay. AB with honors, U. N.C., 1973; JD, Washington and Lee U., 1976. Bar: Va. 1976, D.C. 1976, U.S. Ct. Appeals (4th and D.C. cirs.) 1976, U.S. Ct. Appeals (6th cir.) 1978, U.S. Supreme Ct. 1981, N.Y. 1986, U.S. Ct. Appeals (2d cir.) 1986. Assoc. Carr, Jordan, Coyne & Savits, Washington, 1976-79, Arent, Fox, Kintner, Plotkin & Kahn, Washington, 1979-81; communications counsel Dow Jones & Co., Inc., Princeton, N.J., 1981-87; dir. Dow Jones Svc., Princeton, N.J., 1987-91; exec. dir. info. svcs. Dow Jones & Co., Inc., Princeton, N.J., 1991-93; COO DJA Ptnrs., 1994-97; mng. dir., COO EDI Corp., N.Y.C., 1997-98; pres., COO Internat. Fin. Network, Inc., N.Y.C., 1999—; chmn. communications steering com. Dow Jones & Co., Inc., Princeton, 1986-92. Editor Washington and Lee U. Law Rev., 1975-76. Mem. Am. Newspaper Pubs. Assn. (chmn. telecomms. pub. policy com. 1984-88, exec. mem. telecommms. com. 1984-88), Info. Industry Assn. (chmn. telecomms. com. 1985-87, pub. policy and govt. rels. coun. 1987-88, bd. dirs. 1989-92, exec. coun. 1987-88, bd. dirs. 1989-92, exec. com. 1989-92, chmn. 1991). Home: 411 Beacon Blvd Sea Girt NJ 08750-1507

**PACH, LISA ANNE,** lawyer; b. Warren, Mich., Mar. 14, 1968; d. Karen Ruth (Rinkus) P. BS in Fin., Ind. U., 1990; JD, Creighton U., 1993. Bar: Nebr. 1994, Ill. 1994, U.S. Dist. Ct. (no. dist.) Ill. 1995, U.S. Ct. Appeals (7th cir.) 1996. Atty. Luce, Forward, Hamilton & Scripps, Chgo., 1993—. Mem. ATLA, Ill. Trial Lawyers Assn., Women's Bar Assn. Ill., Chgo. Bar Assn. Personal injury, Product liability. Office: Luce Forward Hamilton Scripps 180 N Lasalle St Ste 3110 Chicago IL 60601-2801

**PACHECO, FELIPE RAMON,** lawyer; b. Sagua la Grande, Las Villas, Cuba, Aug. 22, 1924; came to U.S., 1962; s. Felipe and Eugenia America (Rodriguez) P.; m. Maria Infiesta, Apr. 5, 1945; children: Carmen Pacheco Weber, Lilian C. Porter. D in philosophy and art, U. Havana, Cuba, 1947, D of laws, 1953; MS, Syracuse U., 1967; JD, U. Fla., 1975. Bar: Fla. 1975, U.S. Dist. Ct. (mid. dist.) Fla. 1976. Dir. librs. Ctrl. U. Las Villas, Santa Clara, Cuba, 1953-61; asst., assoc. catalog libr. Cornell U., Ithaca, N.Y., 1962-68, asst. law libr., 1969-70; law libr. Carlton, Fields, Tampa, Fla., 1971-75; pvt. practice Tampa, 1976—. Roman Catholic. Contracts commercial, Probate, Real property. Office: 4509 N Armenia Ave Tampa FL 33603-2703

**PACHECO, MICHAEL MAURO,** lawyer, arbitrator; b. Ciudad Juarez, Mex., Nov. 21, 1952; came to U.S., 1959; s. Mauro Miguel and Teresa Pacheco; m. Stacey Susanne Prather, Apr. 12, 1986; children: Michael Cameron, Alexa Susanne. BA with acad. honors, Gonzaga U., 1975; student, Georgetown U. Law Ctr., 1975-76; student in food processing and retail, Willamette U., 1978-87, JD, 1990. Bar: Oreg. 1990, U.S. Ct. Appeals (9th cir.) 1991, U.S. Dist. Ct. Oreg. 1992. Asst. atty. gen. Oreg. Dept. Justice, Salem, 1990-92; dep. dist. atty. Jackson County, Medford, Oreg., 1992-93; vice chmn. parole bd. State of Oreg., Salem, 1993-95; assoc. Vick & Conroyd, LLP, Salem, 1995-98; pvt. practice Salem, 1998—; arbitrator Polk County, Dallas, Oreg., 1996—. Mem. Willamette U. Law Rev., 1989; contbr. articles to law jours. Mem. Oreg. State Hispanic Employees Network, Salem, 1994—; coach Boys and Girls Club, Salem, 1997—. With USMC, 1977. Mem. Oreg. State Bar (uniform civil jury instrns. com. 1997—), Marion County Bar Assn. Avocations: soccer, music, food, health and exercise. Personal injury, General civil litigation, Native American. Office: 338 State St Ste 600 Salem OR 97301-3532

**PACIULLO, MARIA MAESTRANZI,** lawyer; b. Beverly, Mass., May 27, 1968; d. Leo J. and Joanne (Butler) Maestranzi. BA, Fordham Coll., 1990; JD, Boston U., 1993. Bar: Mass. 1993, N.Y. 1994, U.S. Dist. Ct. (ea. and so. dists.) N.Y. 1998. With Maestranzi Bros. Corp., Beverly, 1985-94; law clk. Gloucester divsn. Mass. Dist. Ct., 1994-95; atty. Wagner, Davis & Gold, P.C., N.Y.C., 1995-96, Levitt and Cohen, Williston Park, N.Y., 1996-98, Rivkin, Radler & Kremer, Uniondale, N.Y., 1998—. V.p. New Hyde Park-Stewart Manor Rep. Com.; mem. Fedn. Rep. Women, Nassau County. Mem. Nassau County Bar Assn., Columbia Lawyers' Assn., Fordham Club L.I., L.I. Ctr. for Bus. and Profl. Women. Roman Catholic. Avocations: speaking engagements, writing. General civil litigation, Contracts commercial, General corporate. Home: 1078 Maple Ln New Hyde Park NY 11040-2306 Office: Rivkin Radler & Kremer Eab Plz Uniondale NY 11556-0001

**PACK, LEONARD BRECHER,** lawyer; b. Seattle, Feb. 7, 1944; s. Howard David and Vivian (Brecher) P.; m. Barbara-Jane Lunin (div. Sept. 1978); children: Jesse, Justin; m. Adele Susan Weisman, Jan. 7, 1979; 1 child, Anna Rae. BA, Columbia U., 1966, JD, 1970, MIA, 1970. Bar: N.Y. 1971. Law clk. to judge U.S. Ct. Appeals D.C. Circuit, 1970-71; assoc. Fried, Frank, Harris, Shriver & Jacobson, N.Y.C., 1971-78; sec., assoc. gen. counsel Metromedia, Inc., Secaucus, N.J., 1979-86; sr. v.p., gen. counsel Orion Pictures Corp., N.Y.C., 1986-90; ptnr. Berger Steingut & Stern, N.Y.C., 1990-93; pvt. practice N.Y.C., 1993—. Bd. dirs., v.p. Dance Theatre Workshop. Mem. ABA. Democrat. Jewish. Avocation: music. Fax: 212 354-6468. General corporate, Labor, Entertainment. Office: 1500 Broadway New York NY 10036-4015

**PACKARD, ROBERT CHARLES,** lawyer; b. L.A., Sept. 21, 1919; s. Charles W. and Gertrude (Vern) P.; m. Nanette Taylor, Dec. 21, 1973 (dec.); m. Bettina Van de Kamp. B.S., U. So. Calif., 1941, J.D., 1947. Bar: Calif. 1948. Sr. ptnr. Kirtland & Packard, L.A., 1948-94, of counsel, 1994—. Fellow Am. Coll. Trial Lawyers; mem. ABA, L.A. Bar Assn. (substantive law com.), Intrenat. Bar Assn., Los Angeles County Bar Assn., Lawyer Pilots Bar Assn., Internat. Assn. Ins. Counsel (aviation com.), Am. Bd. Trial Advs., Am. Judicature Soc., Internat. Soc. Barristers, Calif. Club, Los Angeles Country Club, La Quinta Country Club, Phi Delta Phi. Federal civil litigation, State civil litigation, Insurance. Home: 11445 Waterford St Los Angeles CA 90049-3438 Office: 1900 Avenue Of The Stars Los Angeles CA 90067-4301

**PACKARD, STEPHEN MICHAEL,** lawyer; b. Hartford, Conn., Nov. 26, 1953; s. Charles David and Anne (Moriarty) P.; m. Eileen Mary Joyce, May 23, 1981; children: Stephen Michael Jr., Sheila Marie, James Charles, Brian Joseph. BS, Fairfield U., 1975; JD magna cum laude, N.Y. Law Sch., 1981. Bar: N.Y. 1981, U.S. Dist. Ct. (ea. and so. dists.) N.Y. 1981, U.S. Dist. Ct. Conn. 1983, Conn. 1984. Assoc. Mudge, Rose, Guthrie, Alexander & Ferdon, N.Y.C., 1981-83, Wiggin & Dana, New Haven, 1983-87; atty. Aetna Life & Casualty, Hartford, 1987-96; mgr. Andersen Cons., N.Y.C., 1996—; adj. prof. law U. Bridgeport Law Sch., Conn., 1987. Bd. dirs. New Haven Literacy vols., 1985-87. Mem. Conn. Bar Assn., N.Y.C. Bar Assn., Fed. Bar Coun., Conn. Def. Lawyers Assn. Republican. Roman Catholic. General civil litigation, Insurance. Office: Andersen Cons LLP 1345 Avenue Of The Americas New York NY 10105-0302

**PACKENHAM, RICHARD DANIEL,** lawyer; b. Newton, Pa., June 23, 1953; s. John Richard and Mary Margaret (Maroney) P.; m. Susan Patricia Smillie, Aug. 20, 1983. BA, Harvard U., 1975; JD, Boston Coll., 1978; LLM in Taxation, Boston U., 1985. Bar: Mass. 1978, Conn. 1979, U.S. Dist. Ct. Mass. 1979, U.S. Dist. Ct. Conn. 1979, U.S. Ct. Appeals (1st cir.) 1981, U.S. Supreme Ct. 1985. Staff atty. Conn. Superior Ct., 1978-79; ptnr. McGrath & Kane, Boston, 1979-94, Packenham, Schmidt & Federico, Boston, 1994—. Mem. ABA, Mass. Bar Assn., Conn. Bar Assn., Boston Bar Assn., Mass CLE (faculty). Democrat. Roman Catholic. Club: Harvard (Boston). Family and matrimonial, State civil litigation. Home: 1062 North St Walpole MA 02081-2307 Office: Packenham Schmidt & Federico 4 Longfellow Pl Boston MA 02114-2838

**PACKER, MARK BARRY,** lawyer, financial consultant, foundation official, mediator; b. Phila., Sept. 18, 1944; s. Samuel and Eve (Devine) P.; m. Donna Elizabeth Ferguson (div. 1994); children: Daniel Joshua, Benjamin Dov, David Johannes; m. Helen Margaret (Jones) Klinedinst, July, 1995. AB magna cum laude, Harvard U., 1965, LLB, 1968. Bar: Wash. 1969, Mass. 1971. Assoc. Ziontz, Pirtle & Fulle, Seattle, 1968-70; pvt. practice Bellingham, Wash., 1972—; bd. dirs., corp. sec. BMJ Holdings (formerly No. Sales Co., Inc.), 1977—; trustee No. Sales Profit Sharing Plan, 1977—; bd. dirs. Whatcom State Bank, 1995-98. Mem. Bellingham Planning and Devel. Commn., 1975-84, chmn., 1977-81, mem. shoreline subcom., 1976-82; mem. Bellingham Mcpl. Arts Commn., 1986-91, landmark rev. bd., 1987-91; chmn. Bellingham campaign United Jewish Appeal, 1979-90; bd. dirs. Whatcom Cmty. Coll. Found., 1989-92; trustee, chmn. program com. Bellingham Pub. Sch. Found., 1991-98, Heavy Culture classic lit. group, 1991—, Jewish studies group, 1993—; trustee Kenneth L. Kellar Found., 1995—; mng. trustee Bernard M. & Jaffe Found.; Torah reader; pres. Congregation Eytz Chaim, Bellingham, 1998—. Recipient Blood Donor award ARC, 1979, 8-Gallon Pin, 1988, Mayor's Arts award City of Bellingham, 1993. Mem. Wash. State Bar Assn. (sec. environ. and land use law, sec. bus. law, sec. real property, probate and trust, com. law examiners 1992-94). Contracts commercial, Real property, Estate planning. Office: PO Box 1151 Bellingham WA 98227-1151

**PACKERT, G(AYLA) BETH,** lawyer; b. Corpus Christi, Tex., Sept. 25, 1953; d. Gilbert Norris and Virginia Elizabeth (Pearce) P.; m. James Michael Hall, Jan. 1, 1974 (div. 1985); m. Richard Christopher Burke, July 18, 1987; children: Christopher Geoffrey Makepeace Burke Packert, Jeremy Eliot Marvell Packert Burke. BA, La. Tech. U., 1973; MA, U. Ark., 1976; postgrad., U. Ill., 1975-81, JD, 1985. Bar: Ill. 1985, U.S. Dist. Ct. (no. dist.) Ill. 1985, U.S. Ct. Appeals (7th cir.) 1987, Va. 1988, U.S. Dist. Ct. (we. dist.) Va. 1989. Assoc. Jenner & Block, Chgo., 1985-88; law clk. U.S. Dist. Ct. Va. (we. dist.), Danville, 1988-89; asst. commonwealth atty. Commonwealth of Va., Lynchburg, Va., 1989-95; pvt. practice Lynchburg, 1995—. Notes and comments editor U. Ill. Law Rev., 1984-85. Mem. ABA, Phi Beta Kappa. General civil litigation, Criminal, Family and matrimonial. Home: 3900 Faculty Dr Lynchburg VA 24501-3110 Office: PO Box 529 Lynchburg VA 24505-0529

**PACKETT, LARRY FRENCH,** lawyer; b. Richmond, Va., Aug. 18, 1947; s. Arthur Beale and Mary Ellen (French) P.; m. Glady Escobar, Oct. 7, 1978; children: Jessica, Jason. AA, Ferrum (Va.) Jr. Coll., 1967; BA, Chapman Coll., 1970; MA, American U., 1976; JD, George Mason U., 1982. Bar: Va. 1983. Pvt. practice Arlington, Va., 1983—. Co-author: (with others) History of Richmond County, Va., 1976. Lay leader Arlington (Va.) Temple Meth. Ch., 1996; Rep. candidate for Arlington (Va. County Bd., 1988; precinct capt. Arlington County Rep. Com., 1988-92. Recipient Tiger Tail award for tchg. English Arlington Temple Meth. Ch., 1996. Mem. Va. State Bar Assn., Arlington County Bar Assn. Avocations: civil war history, fossil hunting. Criminal, General practice, Juvenile. Home: 879 N Jacksonville St Arlington VA 22205-1323 Office: 2045 15th St N Ste 306 Arlington VA 22201-2614

**PADDISON, DAVID ROBERT,** lawyer; b. Savannah, Ga., May 15, 1949; s. Richard Milton and Josephine Butler (Bowles) P.; m. Frances M. Phares (div. Mar. 1995); children: Hunt, Brian, Margery; m. Jane Ingrid Caddell, Mar. 30, 1996; 1 child, Ethan David. BSBA, La. State U., 1971; JD, Tulane U., 1976. Bar: La. 1976; U.S. Dist. Ct. (ea. dist.) 1976; U.S. Ct. Appeals (5th cir.) 1976; bd. cert. specialist in family law La. State Bar Assn., 1995. Asst. dist. atty. Dist. Atty.'s Office, Covington, La., 1983-86, New Orleans, La., 1978-83; pvt. practice Covington, La., 1986—; advisor Contemporary Arts Ctr., New Orleans, 1978-79; clin. advisor Tulane U. Sch. Law, New Orleans, 1980-81; spl. cons. Dist. Atty.'s Office, New Orleans, 1981. Legal advisor Christ Episcopal Church (sch. planning com., lector, usher). Mem. Covington Bar Assn., La. Trial Lawyers Assn., ATLA. Republican. Episcopalian. Avocations: golf, sailing, snow skiing. Family and matrimonial, Personal injury, Criminal. Office: PO Box 1830 Covington LA 70434-1830

**PADDOCK, MICHAEL BUCKLEY,** lawyer; b. Odessa, Tex., Oct. 13, 1947; s. William B. and Elvira Paddock; children: Mary Katherine, Courtney Anne. BSBA, U. Ark., 1970, JD, 1973. Bar: Tex. 1973, U.S. Ct. Appeals (5th cir.) 1973, U.S. Dist. Ct. (no. dist.) Tex. 1973, U.S. Supreme Ct. 1973. Chief of misdemeanor criminal ct. Tarrant County Dist. Atty., Ft. Worth, 1973-76, chief spl. crime unit, 1973-76, chief criminal divsn., 1973-76; sole practitioner Ft. Worth, 1976—; mem. panel U.S. Steel Workers Arbitration Panel, Dallas, 1982. Trustee Trinity Valley Mental Health Mental Retardation, 1975-79. Mem. ATLA, State Bar Tex., Tex. Trial Lawyers Assn., Tarrant County Trial Lawyers and Family Bar, Tarrant County Bar Assn. (chmn. fee arbitration panel 1984-86). Family and matrimonial, General practice, Insurance. Office: 1300 Summit Ave Ste 400 Fort Worth TX 76102-4418

**PADGETT, GREGORY LEE,** lawyer; b. Greenfield, Ind., May 9, 1959; s. William Joseph and Anna Katherine (Hyre) P.; m. Ruth Anne Dorworth, June 5, 1982; children: Joshua David, William Joel. BA summa cum laude, DePauw U., 1981; JD, Northwestern U., 1984. Bar: Ill., U.S. Dist. Ct. (no. dist.) Ill. 1984, U.S. Ct. Appeals (7th cir.) 1986, Ind. 1988, U.S. Dist. Ct. (no. & so. dists.) Ind. 1988. Assoc. Kirkland & Ellis, Chgo., 1984-88, Baker & Daniels, Indpls., 1988-92; ptnr. Johnson, Lawhead, Buth & Pope, P.C., Indpls., 1992—; adj. prof. Butler U., 1989-90. Mem. Marion County Prosecutor's Rev. Task Force, Indpls., 1991; pres., bd. dirs. Theatre on the Square, Indpls., 1994-95; mem. coun. Hope Evang. Covenant Ch., 1992-96; bd. dirs. Meridian St. Found., 1994-96. Mem. Ind. State Bar Assn., Indpls. Bar Assn. (exec. com. alternative dispute resolution sect.), Pub. Investors Arbitration Bar Assn., Christian Legal Soc., Phi Beta Kappa. Avocations: theatre arts, vocal music, hiking, writing. E-mail: gpadgett@jlbp.com. General civil litigation, Securities, Probate. Office: Johnson Lawhead Buth & Pope PC 8900 Keystone Xing Ste 940 Indianapolis IN 46240-2162

**PADILLA, DAVID JOSEPH,** lawyer, diplomat; b. Detroit, Feb. 9, 1944; s. David J. and Irene C. (Clos) P.; m. Kathryn E. Grant, Apr. 19, 1970; children: Sarah, Elizabeth, Rebecca. BA cum laude, U. Detroit, 1966, JD, 1969; MA, U. Pa., 1974; LLM with highest distinction, George Washington U., 1979; MPA, Harvard U., 1982. Bar: Mich. 1970, D.C. 1975. Tchr. St. Mary's H.S., Detroit, 1969-70; vol. Peace Corps, Venezuela, 1970-72; asst. prosecutor Wayne County Prosecutor's Office, Detroit, 1973; dir. legal svcs. OAS, Washington, 1975-80, asst. exec. sec. Inter-Am. Commn. Human Rights, 1980—, dir. human resources, 1985-86; Adj. prof. Am. U., Washington, 1987-96. Co-author: Municipal Development Institutions in Latin America, 1976; book reviewer Revista Interam. Bibliografía, 1982; contbr. numerous articles to profl. jours., chpts. to books. Pres. Ayuda, Inc., Washington, 1982—. Recipient Best Paper nomination Inter-Am. Bar Assn., 1979; named Outstanding Vol. Ayuda, Inc., 1993. Mem. Mich. Bar Assn., DC Bar Assn., U.S. Supreme Ct. Bar Assn., Theta Xi. Avocations: pilot, marathons, juggling. Home: 6838 Woodland Dr Falls Church VA 22046-2324 Office: OAS 1889 F St NW Washington DC 20006-4493

**PADILLA, JAMES EARL,** lawyer; b. Miami, Fla., Dec. 28, 1953; s. Earl George and Patricia (Bauer) P. BA, Northwestern U., 1975; JD, Duke U., 1978. Bar: Ill. 1978, U.S. Ct. Appeals (5th and 7th cir.) 1978, U.S. Supreme Ct. 1981, Colo. 1982, U.S. Ct. Appeals (10th cir.) 1982, D.C. 1985, N.Y. 1989. Assoc. Mayer, Brown & Platt, Chgo. and Denver, 1978-84; ptnr. Mayer, Brown & Platt, Denver, 1985-87, N.Y.C., 1988-96; private investor, 1996—. Contbg. author: Mineral Financing, 1982, Illinois Continuing Legal Education, 1993. Mem. ABA, Ill. Bar Assn., D.C. Bar Assn., Colo. Bar Assn., N.Y. State Bar Assn. Avocation: golf. Banking, Bankruptcy, Contracts commercial. Office: 1900 Summer St Unit 19 Stamford CT 06905-5024

**PADOVA, JOHN R.,** federal judge; b. 1935. AB, Villanova U., 1956; JD, Temple U., 1959. With Marcu & Marcu, 1960; ptnr. Solo, Bergman & Trommer, 1962-65, Solo, Abrams, Bergman, Trommer & Padova, 1965-71, Solo, Bergman, Trommer, Padova & Albert, 1971-74, Solo, Bergman & Padova, 1974-75, Solo & Padova, 1975-77, 84-86, Solo, Padova & Lisi, 1977-84, Padova & Hinman, 1986-91, Padova & Lisi, 1991-92; fed. judge U.S. Dist. Ct. (ea. dist.) Pa., 1992—. With USNGR, 1959-64, USAR, 1964-68. Mem. ABA, Am. Trial Lawyers Assn., Phila. Bar Assn., Nat. Bd. Trial

Advocacy, Pa. Trial Lawyers Assn., Phila. Trial Lawyers Assn. Office: US Dist Ct 601 Market St Rm 7614 Philadelphia PA 19106-1714*

**PAEZ, RICHARD A.,** judge; b. 1947. BA, Brigham Young U., 1969; JD, U. Calif., Berkeley, 1972. Staff atty. Calif. Rural Legal Assistance, Delano, Calif., 1972-74, Western Ctr. on Law and Poverty, 1974-76; sr. counsel, dir. litigation, acting exec. dir. Legal Aid Found. of L.A., 1976-81; judge L.A. Mcpl. Ct., 1981-94, U.S. Dist. Ct. (ctrl. dist.) Calif., L.A., 1994—. Active Hollywood-Los Feliz Jewish Cmty. Ctr. Mem. Calif. State Bar Assn., L.A. County Bar Assn., Mex.-Am. Bar Assn. L.A. County, Calif. Jud. Coun. Office: US Dist Ct Ctrl Dist Calif Edward R Roybal Ctr & Fed Bldg 255 E Temple St Ste 760 Los Angeles CA 90012-3334

**PAFFORD, JOHN WALTER,** lawyer; b. Parris Island, S.C., Jan. 27, 1949; s. George Gibbs and Eleanor (Lazynski) P.; m. Linda Joyce Norton, Aug. 22, 1970; 1 child, John Walter Jr. BA, Mercer U., 1971, JD, 1976. Bar: Fla. 1977, U.S. Ct. Appeals (11th cir.) 1985, U.S. Dist. Ct. (mid. dist.) Fla. 1977, U.S. Supreme Ct. 1987. Assoc. Mathews, Osborne, Ehrlich, McNatt, Gobelman & Cobb PA, Jacksonville, Fla., 1976-78; asst. state atty. Fla. State Atty.'s Office 4th Jud. Dir., Jacksonville, 1978-80; assoc. Donald W. Matthews, Jacksonville, 1980-81; sole practice Jacksonville, 1981-84; ptnr. Penland, Penland & Pafford PA, Jacksonville, 1984-90, Humphries, Kellogg & Oberdier PA, 1990-91; sr. ptnr. Hurt, Pafford, Carstetter & Gray, P.A., Jacksonville, Fla., 1991-94, Pafford, Carstetter & Gray, P.A., Jacksonville, Fla., 1994—. Sgt U.S. Army, 1971-73. Mem. Acad. Fla. Lawyers, Acad. Fla. Trial Lawyers (Eagles sponsor), Assn. Trial Lawyers Am., Bishop Kenny High Sch. Alumni Assn. (fin. com., chmn. sub.-com.). Democrat. Roman Catholic. Lodges: Masons, Solomon. Avocation: Little League. Personal injury.

**PAGANO, EUGENE SALVATORE ROONEY,** lawyer; b. N.Y.C., Apr. 29, 1951; s. Vito Venero and Virginia Marie (Rooney) P. BA summa cum laude, Spring Hill Coll., Mobile, Ala., 1973; JD, U. Va., 1976; LLM, Harvard U., 1983. Bar: N.Y. 1977, D.C. 1977, U.S. Dist. Ct. (so. dist.) N.Y. 1978, U.S. Dist. Ct. (ea. dist.) N.Y. 1979, U.S. Ct. Appeals (D.C. cir.) 1981, U.S. Ct. Appeals (2d cir.) 1985, U.S. Supreme Ct. 1987. Law clk. to Hon. Stanley S. Harris D.C. Ct. Appeals, Washington, 1976-77; assoc. Donovan Leisure Newton & Irvine, N.Y.C., 1977-81, Farrell, Fritz, Caemmerer, Cleary, Barnosky & Armentano, PC, Mineola, N.Y., 1983-86, Rivkin, Radler & Kremer, Uniondale, N.Y., 1986-92, Matturro, Hirsch & Folks, Carle Place, N.Y., 1992-94, Brody & Fabiani, N.Y.C., 1994-95, Law Offices of Thomas F. Liotti, Garden City, 1995; sr. staff atty. Tower Ins. Co. N.Y., N.Y.C., 1996-97; assoc. Deega & Deegan, LLP, Hempstead, N.Y., 1997-99; self-employed, 1999—. Contbr. articles to profl. jours. Mem. Nassau County Bar Assn. (Pres.'s award 1991). Roman Catholic. Avocation: history. Appellate, General civil litigation.

**PAGE, ALAN CEDRIC,** state supreme court justice; b. Canton, Ohio, Aug. 7, 1945; s. Howard F. and Georgianna (Umbles) P.; m. Diane Sims, June 5, 1973; children: Nina, Georgianna, Justin, Khamsin. BA, U. Notre Dame, 1967; JD, U. Minn., 1978; LLD, U. Notre Dame, 1993; LLD (hon.), St. John's U., 1994, Westfield State Coll., 1994, Luther Coll., 1995, U. New Haven, 1999. Bar: Minn. 1979, U.S. Dist. Ct. Minn. 1979, U.S. Supreme Ct. 1988. Profl. athlete Minn. Vikings, Mpls., 1967-78, Chgo. Bears, 1978-81; assoc. Lindquist & Vennum, Mpls., 1979-85; former atty. Minn. Atty. Gen.'s Office, Mpls., 1985-92; assoc. justice Minn. Supreme Ct., St. Paul, 1993—; cons. NFL Players Assn., Washington, 1979-84. Commentator Nat. Pub. Radio, 1982-83. Founder Page Edn. Found., 1988. Named NFL's Most Valuable Player, 1971, one of 10 Outstanding Young Men Am., U.S. Jaycees, 1981; named to NFL Hall of Fame, 1988, Coll. Football Hall of Fame, 1993. Mem. ABA, Minn. Bar Assn., Hennepin County Bar Assn., Minn. Minority Lawyers Assn., Minn. Assn. Black Lawyers. Avocations: running, biking. Office: 423 Minnesota Judicial Ctr 25 Constitution Ave Saint Paul MN 55155-1500

**PAGE, EDWARD JOHN,** prosecutor; b. Morristown, N.J., Mar. 1, 1956; s. Roy D. and Mary Louise (Klaus) P.; m. Carole A. Blasko, July 18, 192; 1 child, Kevin J. Student, Carson-Newman Coll., 1974-75; BA, U. South Fla., 1978; JD, U. Tulsa, 1981. Bar: Fla. 1981, U.S. Dist. Ct. (mid. dist.) Fla. 1981, U.S. Ct. Appeals (11th cir.) 1982, D.C. 1992; cert. criminal lawyer, Fla.; nat. bd. cert. Criminal Trial Advs. Asst. state atty. State Atty.'s Office, Tampa, Fla., 1981-90; asst. U.S. atty., chief maj. crimes sect. U.S. Atty.'s Office, Tampa, 1990—; sr. assoc. ind. counsel Office Ind. Counsel, Washington, 1995-98; dep. ind. counsel Office of Ind. Counsel Ken Starr, Washington, 1998—. Mem. FBA, Fla. Bar (criminal law cert. com. 1995-96), Hillsborough County Trial Lawyers Assn. (chmn. 1996), Federalist Soc., Am. Inns. Ct. (treas., pres.-elect), Ferguson-White Inn of Ct. (treas. Tampa 1992-96). Republican. Episcopalian. Avocation: flying. Office: Kenneth W Starr Ste 490N 1001 Pennsylvania Ave NW Washington DC 20004-2505

**PAGE, JACK RANDALL,** lawyer; b. Waco, Tex., Aug. 1, 1956; s. Jack Bennett and Mary Elizabeth (Cobbs) P.; m. Shirley Jean Hull, Aug. 5, 1978; children: Anna Christine, Sara Elaine. BBA magna cum laude, Baylor U., 1977, JD, 1980. Bar: Tex. 1980, U.S. Tax Ct. 1985, U.S. Dist. Ct. (we. dist.) Tex. 1987, U.S. Ct. Appeals (5th cir.) 1989; cert. in tax law Tex. Bd. Legal Specialization; CPA, Tex. Acct. Allie B. Gates Jr., CPA, Waco, 1975-78; assoc. Pakis, Giotes, Beard & Page, P.C., Waco, 1980-86, ptnr., 1986—. Chmn. exploring sales team Heart O' Tex. Coun. Boy Scouts Am., 1983, dist. chmn., 1984-85, v.p., 1986-88, coun. commr., 1989-91, coun. pres., 1991-94, asst. coun. commr., 1994—, v.p., 1995-96; mem. adv. coun. dept. acctg. Baylor U., 1993—; co-chmn. Food for Families, 1995—. Recipient Dist. Award of Merit Heart O' Tex. coun. Boy Scouts Am., 1985, Silver Beaver award 1993, Commrs. Key, 1994. Fellow Tex. Bar Found.; mem. AICPA, Tex. Bar Assn., Coll. of State Bar of Tex., Waco-McLennan County Bar Assn., Tex. Soc. CPAs, Waco Estate Planning Coun. (pres. 1983), Rotary (Paul Harris fellow), Order of Demolay (chevalier 1975). Roman Catholic. Avocations: hiking, camping, outdoor activities. Taxation, general, Estate planning, General corporate. Office: Pakis Giotes Beard & Page PC 801 Washington Ave Ste 800 Waco TX 76701-1266

**PAGTER, CARL RICHARD,** lawyer; b. Balt., Feb. 13, 1934; s. Charles Ralph and Mina (Amelung) P.; m. Judith Elaine Cox, May 6, 1978; 1 child by previous marriage: Corbin Christopher. AA, Diablo Valley Coll., 1953; BA, San Jose State U., 1955; LLB, U. Calif., Berkeley, 1964. Bar:Calif. 1965, D.C. 1977, U.S. Supreme Ct. 1976. Law clk. Kaiser Industries Corp., Oakland, Calif., 1963-64, counsel, 1964-70; assoc. counsel Kaiser Industries Corp., Washington, 1970-73; counsel Kaiser Industries Corp., Oakland, Calif., 1973-75; dir. govt. affairs Kaiser Industries Corp., Washington, 1975-76; v.p., sec., gen. counsel Kaiser Cement Corp., Oakland, Calif., 1976-88; cons., gen. counsel Kaiser Cement Corp., San Ramon, 1988-98, cons., 1998—. Author: (with A. Dundes) Urban Folklore from the Paperwork Empire, 1975, More Urban Folklore from the Paperwork Empire, 1987, Never Try to Teach a Pig to Sing, 1991, Sometimes the Dragon Wins, 1996, Why Don't Sheep Shrink When It Rains, 1999. With USNR, 1957-61, to comdr., 1978. Mem. ABA, Contra Costa County Bar Assn., Am. Folklore Soc., Calif. Folklore Soc., Calif. Bluegrass Assn. (founder), Oakland Athletic Club, Univ. Club. Republican. General corporate, Antitrust, Product liability. Home and Office: 17 Julianne Ct Walnut Creek CA 94595-2610

**PAHIDES, ANN-MARIE MACDONALD,** lawyer; b. Ann Arbor, Mich., Dec. 6, 1961; d. Ian Macaulay and Lilian Maria (Diakow) MacDonald; m. Stephen Michael Pahides, Apr. 21, 1989. BA, Albion Coll., 1984; JD, Detroit Coll. of Law, 1988; postgrad., Villanova U. Bar: Pa. 1989, U.S. Dist Ct. (ea. dist.) Pa. 1990, U.S. Ct. Appeals (3d cir.) 1990, U.S. Supreme Ct. 1993. Assoc. Brodie, Techner & Rubinsky Law Offices, Phila. Mem. ABA, Assn. Trial Lawyers Am., Pa. Trial Lawyers Assn., Delaware County Bar Assn., Chester County Bar Assn., Phila. Bar Assn., Pa. Bar Assn. Presbyterian. Avocations: snow skiing, swimming, music, art. Family and matrimonial, Municipal (including bonds), Real property.

**PAINE, JAMES CARRIGER,** federal judge; b. Valdosta, Ga., May 20, 1924; s. Leon Alexander and Josie Carriger (Jones) P.; m. Ruth Ellen Bailey, Sept. 8, 1950; children: James Carriger, Jonathan Jones, JoEllen. B.S., Columbia U., 1947; LL.B., U. Va., 1950, J.D., 1970. Bar: Fla. 1950. Mem. firm Earnest, Lewis, Smith & Jones, West Palm Beach, Fla., 1950-54, Jones Adams Paine & Foster, 1954-60, Jones Paine & Foster, 1960-79; judge U.S. Dist. Ct. (so. dist.) Fla., West Palm Beach, 1979-92, sr. judge, 1992—. Bd. dirs., pres. Children's Home Soc. Fla., 1978-80; mem. bd. Episcopal Diocese S.E. Fla. Served to lt. USNR, 1943-47. Mem. Greater West Palm Beach C. of C. (pres. 1973-74), Palm Beach County Bar Assn. Democrat. Office: US Dist Ct 701 Clematis St West Palm Beach FL 33401-5101

**PAINTER, MARK PHILIP,** judge; b. Cin., Apr. 6, 1947; s. John Philip and Marjorie (West) P.; m. Sue Ann Painter. BA, U. Cin., 1970, JD, 1973. Bar: Ohio 1973, U.S. Dist. Ct. (so. dist.) Ohio 1973, U.S. Supreme Ct. 1980. Assoc. Smith & Schnacke and predecessor firm, 1973-78; sole practice Cin., 1978-82; judge Hamilton County Mcpl. Ct., Cin., 1982-95, Ohio 1st Dist. Ct. Appeals, 1995—; adj. prof. law U. Cin., 1990—; lectr. profl. seminars. Co-author: Ohio DUI Law, 1988, 8th edit., 1999; mem. editl. bd. Criminal Law Jour. Ohio, 1989-92; contbr. articles to profl. jours. Bd. dirs. Citizens Sch. Com., Cin., 1974-76; trustee Freestore Foodbank, Cin., 1984-90, Mary Jo Brueggeman Meml. Found., Cin., 1981-92; bd. commrs. on grievances and discipline Ohio Supreme Ct., 1993-95; mem. Rep. Ctrl. Com., Cin., 1972-82. Recipient Superior Jud. Svc. award Ohio Supreme Ct., 1982, 84, 85. Mem. ABA, Ohio State Bar Assn., Cin. Bar Assn. (trustee 1988-90), Am. Judges Assn., Am. Judicature Soc., Am. Soc. Writers on Legal Subjects, Potter Stewart Inn of Ct. (master of bench emeritus), Bankers Club. Home: 2449 Fairview Ave Cincinnati OH 45219-1170 Office: Ct of Appeals William Howard Taft Law Ctr 230 E 9th St Cincinnati OH 45202-2174

**PAINTER, PAUL WAIN, JR.,** lawyer; b. Cleveland, Tenn., Aug. 10, 1945; s. Paul Wain and Juanita (Davis) P.; m. Judith Ann Babine, Aug. 28, 1971; 1 child, Paul Wain III. BS, Ga. Tech., 1968; JD, U. Ga., 1974. Bar: Ga. 1974, U.S. Dist. Ct. (so. dist.) Ga., U.S. Ct. Appeals (11th cir.). Assoc. Bouhan, Williams & Levy, Savannah, Ga., 1974-79; ptnr. Karsman, Brooks, Painter & Callaway, Savannah, 1979-88, Ellis, Painter, Ratterree & Bart, Savannah, 1988—; faculty mem. Nat. Inst. Trial Advocacy, Emory U. Sch. Law, 1982-90; mem. com. on lawyer qualifications and conduct U.S. Ct. Appeals for 11th Cir., 1995—; mem. ct. adv. com. U.S. Dist. Ct. (so. dist.) Ga., 1992—; mem. Gov.'s Adv. Com. on Tort Reform, Atlanta, 1986; mem. Ga. Bd. Bar Examiners, 1998—. Trustee Ga. Inst. Continuing Legal Edn., Athens, 1992-95; pres. Savannah Arthritis Found., 1982-83; bd. dirs. Ga. Arthritis Found., Atlanta, 1983; grad. Leadership Savannah, 1986-88. Lt. (j.g.) USN, 1968-71. Fellow Am. Coll. Trial Lawyers; mem. ABA, State Bar Ga. (chair trial sect. 1992-93), Def. Rsch. Inst. (Ga. state chmn. 1988-91), Savannah Bar Assn. (pres. 93), Ga. Def. Lawyers Assn. (pres. 1986-87), U. Ga. Law Sch. Assn. (dir. 1997—). Avocations: reading history and fiction, hunting, fishing. Federal civil litigation, General civil litigation. Office: Ellis Painter Ratterree Bart PO Box 9946 Savannah GA 31412-0146

**PAINTON, RUSSELL ELLIOTT,** lawyer, mechanical engineer; b. Port Arthur, Tex., Dec. 5, 1940; s. Clifford Elliott and Edith Virginia (McCutcheon) P.; m. Elizabeth Ann Mullins, July 2, 1965 (div. Dec. 1977); 1 child, Todd Elliott; m. Mary Lynn Weber, May 9, 1981. BS in Mech. Engring., U. Tex.-Austin, 1963, JD, 1972. Bar: Tex. 1972; registered profl. engr., Tex. Engr. Gulf States Utilities, Beaumont, Tex., 1963-66; engr. Tracor, Inc., Austin, Tex., 1966-70, corp. counsel, 1973-83, v.p., gen. counsel, 1983-98, corp. sec., 1991-98; atty. Brown, Maroney, Rose, Baker & Barber, Austin, 1972-73, Childs, Fortenbach, Beck & Guyton, Houston, 1973; corp. sec. Westmark Systems, Inc., Austin, 1990-91. Gen. counsel Paramount Theatre for Performing Arts, 1977-83, 2d vice chmn., 1978-80, 1st vice chmn., 1980-82, chmn. bd., 1982-84, retiring chmn., 1984-85; mem. Centex chpt. ARC; mem. adv. bd. Austin Sci. Acad., 1985-88, 93—; mem. adv. coun. Austin Transp., 1985-88; bd. dirs. Tex. Industries for the Blind and Handicapped, 1988-95, vice chmn., 1990-91. Named Boss of Yr. Austin Legal Secs. Assn., 1981. Mem. ABA, Tex. Bar Assn. (treas. corp. counsel sect. 1982-83), Travis County Bar Assn., Nat. Chamber Litigation Ctr., Better Bus. Bur. (arbitrator 1983—), Am. Electronics Assn. (chmn. Austin coun. 1985-86), Austin Yacht Club (race comdr. 1968-69, treas. 1970-71, sec. 1972, 75, vice commodore 1980, commodore 1981, fleet comdr. 1986), Order Blue Gavel, Houston Yacht Club, Delta Theta Phi. Republican. Episcopalian. General corporate, Securities, Contracts commercial.

**PAJAK, DAVID JOSEPH,** lawyer, consultant; b. Buffalo, N.Y., June 19, 1956; s. William H. and Theresa A. (Granato) P.; m. Peggy J. Fisher, Aug. 1, 1981; children: Andrew J., Karl W. BA, State Coll. Buffalo, 1978; JD, U. Buffalo, 1982. Bar: N.Y. 1983, U.S. Dist. Ct. (we. dist.) N.Y., 1991. Social svcs. counsel Genesee County Dept. Social Svcs., Batavia, N.Y., 1984-93; pvt. practice Corfu, N.Y., 1983—, Buffalo, N.Y., 1993—; town justice Town of Pembroke, N.Y., 1994—; mem. legis. com. N.Y. Fed. on Child Abuse and Neglect, Albany, 1986—, bd. dirs., 1987-89; cons. N.Y. Pub. Welfare Assn., Inc., Albany, 1987-92; pres. Social Svcs. Attys. Assn. N.Y. State, 1990-91; instr. Bill Adam's Martial Arts & Fitness Ctr., Buffalo; cons. Cornell U. Family Life Devel. Ctr., 1993-97. Contbr. articles to profl. jours. Mem. N.Y. State Bar Assn., N.Y. State Magistrate's Assn., Erie County Bar Assn., Genesee County Bar Assn., Genesee County Magistrate's and Peace Officers Assn., Corfu Area Bus. Assn. Republican. Avocations: karate, martial arts. State civil litigation, Family and matrimonial, Legislative. Home: 17 E Main St Corfu NY 14036-9665 Office: 120 Delaware Ave Rm 430 Buffalo NY 14202-2704

**PALACIOS, PEDRO PABLO,** lawyer; b. Santo Tomas, N.Mex., June 29, 1953; s. Luis Flores and Refugio (Hernandez) P.; m. Kelle Haston, July 2, 1983; children: Pedro Pablo II, Charles Rey, Jose Luis. BA, Yale U., 1975; JD, U. N.Mex., 1979. Bar: N.Mex. 1979. Pvt. practice Las Cruces, N.Mex., 1983—. Mem. N.Mex. State Bar Assn. Democrat. Roman Catholic. Avocations: running, coin collecting. Probate, Personal injury, Bankruptcy. Home: PO Box 16335 Las Cruces NM 88004-6335 Office: 1980 E Lohman Ave Ste D-3 Las Cruces NM 88001-3194

**PALADINO, DANIEL R.,** lawyer, beverage corporation executive; B.S., Fordham U., 1965; J.D., NYU, 1968. atty. Simpson Thacher & Bartlett, 1969-76; atty. Davis & Cox, 1976-79; exec. v.p., gen. counsel sec., Joseph Seagram & Sons Inc., N.Y.C., 1979—. General corporate. Office: Joseph Seagram & Sons Inc 375 Park Ave New York NY 10022-6006

**PALAZZO, ROBERT P.,** lawyer, accountant; b. L.A., Apr. 14, 1952; s. Joseph Francis and Mickey Palazzo. BA in Econs., UCLA, 1973; MBA, U. So. Calif., 1976, JD, 1976; postgrad., U. Oxford, 1979. CPA Calif., Nev., Colo.; Bar: Calif. 1976, U.S. Dist. Ct. (so. dist.) Calif. 1977, U.S. Tax Ct. 1977, U.S. Ct. Appeals (9th cir.) 1978, U.S. Supreme Ct. 1980. Assoc. Graham & James, L.A., 1976-78; ptnr. Rader, Cornwall, Kessler & Palazzo CPAs, L.A., 1978-81, Palazzo & Kessler, L.A., 1978-81; pvt. practice L.A., Darwin, Calif., 1981—; judge pro tem L.A. Mcpl. Ct., 1982—; bd. dirs. Cons. Am. Oil Co., Fin. Systems Internat. Inc., Adventures Prodns., Inc.; alumni advisor UCLA, 1977-81, mem. adv. and scholarship com., 1978-81; mem. profl. adv. com. West L.A. Coll., 1993—; lectr. U. Oxford, 1979, U. So. Calif., 1986, Calif. Poly. Inst., Pomona, 1997; hist. cons. A&E Civil War Jour., Death Valley Memories (motion picture), A&E Biography, (history channel) Guns of Infamy; spkr. Calif. State U., Northridge, 1996, Death Valley 49ers Encampment, 1996, 5th Death Valley History Conf., 1999; hist. cons. A&E Biography, Medieval Conf. Plymouth State Coll. U. N.H., 1999; spkr. in field. Author: Darwin, California, 1996; contbg. editor: The Gun Report; prodr. (motion picture) L.A. Bounty; contbr. articles to profl. jours.; featured Tales of the Gun, History Channel, 1998, 99. Founder Ohio History Flight Mus.; bd. dirs. Calif. Cancer Found., L.A., 1978-85, pres., 1979-80; bd. dirs. Friends of William S. Hart Park and Mus., 1990-93, v.p. Mus. Relations; chmn. dist. bd. dirs. Darwin Community Svcs., 1990-92. Mem. L.A. County Bar Assn. (arbitration com., fee dispute resolution program), Italian Am. Lawyers Assn. (bd. govs. 1980—, 1st v.p. 1984-88), Nat. Acad. Rec. Arts and Scis., Western Writers Assn., Century City Bar Assn. (vice-chmn. estate planning, trust and probate com. 1979-80), English Westerners' Soc., Nat. Italian Am. Bar Assn., Am. Numismatic Assn. (dist. rep. Carson City 1981-82, L.A. 1982-83), English Westerners Soc., S.E. Ohio Oil and Gas Assn., Death Valley History Assn. (life, conf. spkr. 1992, 95, 99), Mensa, Wig and Pen Club (London), Omicron Delta Epsilon, Beta Alpha Psi (pres. 1972), Pi Gamma Mu, Phi Alpha Delta, Zeta Phi Eta. Personal income taxation, Corporate taxation, Entertainment. Office: 3002 Midvale Ave Ste 209 Los Angeles CA 90034-3418 also: 230 S Main St Darwin CA 93522

**PALERMO, ANTHONY ROBERT,** lawyer; b. Rochester, N.Y., Sept. 30, 1929; s. Anthony C. and Mary (Palvino) P.; m. Mary Ann Coyne, Jan. 2, 1960; children: Mark Henry, Christopher Coyne, Peter Stuart, Elisabeth Megan McCarthy, Julie Coyne Lawther, Gregg Anthony. BA, U. Mich., 1951; JD, Georgetown U., 1956. Bar: D.C. 1956, N.Y. 1957, U.S. Supreme Ct. 1961. Trial atty. U.S. Dept. Justice, Washington, 1956-58; asst. atty. U.S. Dept. Justice, N.Y.C., 1958-60; asst. U.S. atty. in charge U.S. Dept. Justice, Rochester, N.Y., 1960-61; ptnr. Brennan, Centner, Palermo & Blauvelt, Rochester, 1962-81, Harter, Secrest & Emery, Rochester, 1981-94; ptnr. Hodgson, Russ, Andrews, Woods & Goodyear, LLP, Rochester, 1994-97, of counsel, 1998; of counsel Woods, Oviatt, Gilman, Sturman & Clarke LLP, Rochester, 1999—. Note editor Georgetown Law Jour., 1956. Bd. dirs. McQuaid Jesuit H.S., Rochester, 1978-84, St. Ann's Home for Aged, Rochester, 1974—; bd. dirs., sec. St. Ann's Found., Rochester, 1989—; trustee, charter chmn. Clients' Security Fund N.Y. (now Lawyer's Fund for Client Protection), 1981-90; chmn. Govs. Jud. Screening Com. 4th Jud. Dept., mem. statewide com., 1987-89; chair magistrate selection com. U.S. Dist. Ct. (we. dist.) N.Y., 1995, 98; mem. N.Y. Chief Judge's Commn. on Jud. Salaries, 1997—. Fellow Am. Bar Found., N.Y. State Bar Found. (bd. dirs. 1978-91), Am. Coll. Trial Lawyers; mem. ABA (ho. dels. 1980-98, state del. 1982-85, bd. govs. 1985-88, 1989-93, sec. 1990-93), N.Y. State Bar Assn. (pres. 1979-80, ho. dels. 1973-75, 77—), Monroe County Bar Assn. (pres. 1973), Oak Hill Country Club. Roman Catholic. Avocation: golf. General civil litigation, Estate planning, General practice. Home: 38 Huntington Meadow Rochester NY 14625-1813

**PALERMO, NORMAN ANTHONY,** lawyer; b. Whittier, Calif., Mar. 14, 1937; s. Anthony and Alice Lucille (Ingram) P.; m. Wynne Harrison Kieffer, Apr. 12, 1989; children by previous marriage: David I., Pamela B. BS in Geology, Tulane U., 1958; LLB, Georgetown U., 1966. Bar: Colo. 1966, U.S Dist. Ct. Colo. 1966, U.S. Ct. Appeals (10th cir.) 1966, U.S. Supreme Ct. 1971. Assoc., ptnr. Quigley Wilder & Palermo, Colorado Springs, Colo., 1966-75; v.p. Quigley & Palermo, P.C., Colorado Springs, 1975-85; pres. Norman A. Palermo, P.C., Colorado Springs, 1985—. Chmn. El Paso County Rep. Cen. Com., Colorado Springs, 1985-87; bd. dirs. Goodwill Industries, Colorado Springs, 1973—; mem. State Commn. on Jud. Performance, 1993-97; bd. dirs. Colorado Springs Symphony, 1981-87. Comdr. USNR, 1958-66. Mem. ABA, Colo. Bar Assn., El Paso County Bar Assn., Colorado Springs C. of C. (bd. dirs. 1980-83, 93—, vice-chmn. bd. dirs. 1993-95, chmn. 1996-97), bd. govs. Colo. Bar. Assn., co-chmn. SPRINGS 2000. Republican. Avocations: golf, travel. General corporate, Real property, Estate planning. Home: 1835 Cantwell Grv Colorado Springs CO 80906-6911 Office: 102 E Pikes Peak Ave 5th Fl Colorado Springs CO 80903-1823 also: PO Box 1718 Colorado Springs CO 80901-1718

**PALIOTTA, ARMAND,** lawyer; b. N.Y.C., Mar. 17, 1967; s. Armand R. and Margaret R. Paliotta; m. Amanda M. Dry, Aug. 29, 1992; 1 child, Joshua Armand. BBA, U. Okla., 1989, JD, 1992. Bar: Okla. 1992. Ptnr. Hartzog Conger & Cason, Oklahoma City, Okla., 1992—. General corporate, Corporate taxation, Securities. Office: Hartzog Conger & Cason 1600 Bank of Oklahoma Plz Oklahoma City OK 73102

**PALIZZI, ANTHONY N.,** lawyer, retail corporation executive; b. Wyandotte, Mich., Oct. 27, 1942; s. Vincenzo and Nunziata (Dagostini) P.; m. Bonnie Marie Kirkwood, Mar. 11, 1966; children—A. Michael, Nicholas A. PhB, Wayne State U., 1964, JD, 1966; LLM, Yale U., 1967. Bar: Mich. 1967. Prof. law Fla. State U., Tallahassee, 1967-69; prof. law Tex. Tech U., Lubbock, 1969-71; atty. Kmart Corp., Troy, Mich., 1971-74, asst. sec., 1974-77, asst. gen. counsel, 1977-85, v.p., assoc. gen. counsel, 1985-91, sr. v.p., gen. counsel, 1991-92, exec. v.p., gen. counsel, 1992—. Editor law rev. Wayne State U., 1964-66. Chmn. Brandon Police and Fire Bd., Mich., 1982-87. Mem. ABA, Am. Corp. Counsel Assn., Mich. State Bar Assn. Roman Catholic. General corporate. *

**PALKOVITZ, HERBERT,** lawyer; b. McKeesport, Pa., Dec. 1, 1942. BA, Washington & Jefferson Coll., 1964; JD, Cleve. U., 1968. Bar: Ohio 1969, U.S. Dist. Ct. (no. dist.) Ohio 1970, U.S. Supreme Ct. 1972, U.S. Ct. Appeals (6th cir.) 1982. Pvt. practice Cleve., 1969—; mem. alt. dispute com. Ohio Supreme Ct., Columbus. Chmn. mediation adv. bd. Jewish Family Svc. Assn., Cleve. Fellow Internat. Acad. Matrimonial Lawyers, Am. Acad. Matrimonial Lawyers (pres. Ohio chpt., bd. govs. 1990—); mem. ABA, Cleve. Bar Assn. (chair family law sect.), Cuyahoga County Bar Assn. (chair family law sect.). Family and matrimonial. Office: 1600 Standard Bldg Cleveland OH 44113

**PALL, BRIAN HAROLD,** lawyer; b. S.I., N.Y., May 28, 1959. BS, SUNY at Oswego, 1980; JD, Bklyn. Law Sch., 1985. Bar: N.Y. 1986, N.J. 1986. Real estate mgr. Jamesway Corp., Secaucus, N.J., 1986-87, Great Atlantic & Pacific Tea Co., Montvale, N.J., 1987-88; dir. of real estate Great Atlantic & Pacific Tea Co., Secaucus, N.J., 1988-91, v.p. Waldbaums, 1991-93, corp. v.p. real estate, 1993-97, sr. v.p. devel., 1997—. Mem. Internat. Coun. Shopping Ctrs., N.Y. Bar Assn., N.J. Bar Assn. Office: Great A&P Tea Co Inc 90 Delaware Ave Paterson NJ 07503-1804

**PALLAM, JOHN JAMES,** lawyer; b. Cleve., May 19, 1940; s. James John and Coralia (Gatsos) P.; m. Evanthia Venizelos, Nov. 29, 1969; 1 child, Alethea. BA, Case Western Res. U., 1962; JD, Ohio State U., 1965. Bar: Ohio 1965, U.S. Ct. Claims 1969, U.S. Ct. Mil. Appeals 1969, U.S. Supreme Ct. 1970. Law clk. to presiding justice Cuyahoga County Ct., Cleve., 1965-66; assoc. Burke, Habor & Berick, Cleve., 1970-73; corp. atty. Midland Ross Corp., Cleve., 1973-80, corp. counsel, 1980-87; v.p., gen. counsel Brush Wellman Corp., Cleve., 1987—; guest lectr. Nat. Foundry Assn., Chgo., 1986—. Contbr. articles on labor and environ. matters to jours. Legal advisor Am. Hellenic and Prog. Assn., Cleve., 1966—. Served to capt. JAGC U.S. Army, 1966-70, Vietnam. Decorated Bronze Star with oak leaf cluster. Mem. Ohio Bar Assn. (committeeman 1984—), Cleve. Bar Assn. (merit svc. award 1972), Hellenic Bar Assn., Hellenic Univ. Club, Rowfant. Greek Orthodox. Avocations: history, antiques, golfing, rare books, railroading. Labor, Contracts commercial, Environmental. Office: 17876 Saint Clair Ave Cleveland OH 44110-2602

**PALLANTE, DENISE,** lawyer; b. Camden, N.J., Dec. 28, 1959; d. C. Samuel and Carole J. Micklus; m. Joseph Thomas Pallante, Dec. 31, 1990; children: Augustus Joseph, Gabriel Thomas. BA, Stockton State Coll., inibam B.H., 1980; JD, Temple U., 1984. Bar: Pa. 1984, U.S. Dist. Ct. (ea. dist.) Pa., U.S. Ct. Appeals (3d cir.), Supreme Ct. U.S. Assoc. Berger & Montague, PC, Phila., 1984-87, Sprague & Sprague, Phila., 1988—; bd. dirs. Creative Devel. Internat., Phila., Ctrl. Svcs. Agy., Phila. Articles editor Temple Law Rev., 1983. Mem. ABA, Pa. Bar Assn., Phila. Bar Assn. Roman Catholic. Avocations: gourmet cooking, collecting fine wine, creating children's stories. Home: 327 S 16th St Philadelphia PA 19102-4909 Office: Sprague & Sprague 135 S 19th St Ste 400 Philadelphia PA 19103-4912

**PALLASCH, B. MICHAEL,** lawyer; b. Chgo., Mar. 30, 1933; s. Bernhard Michael and Magdalena Helena (Fixari) P.; m. Josephine Catherine O'Leary, Aug. 15, 1981; children: Bernhard Michael III and Madeleine Josephine (twins). BSS, Georgetown U., 1954; JD, Harvard U., 1957; postgrad., John Marshall Law Sch., 1974. Bar: Ill. 1957, U.S. Dist. Ct. (no. dist.) Ill. 1958, U.S. Tax Ct. 1961, U.S. Ct. Claims 1961, U.S. Ct. Appeals (7th cir.) 1962. Assoc. Winston & Strawn, Chgo., 1958-66; resident mgr. br. office Winston & Strawn, Paris, 1963-65; ptnr. Winston & Strawn, Chgo., 1966-70, sr. capital ptnr., 1971-91; sr. ptnr. B. Michael Pallasch & Assocs., 1991—; dir., corp. sec. Tanis, Inc., Calumet, Mich., 1972—, Greenbank Engring. Corp., Dover, Del., 1976-91, C.B.P. Engring. Corp., Chgo., 1976-91, Chgo. Cutting Svcs. Corp., 1977-88; corp. sec. Arthur Andersen Assocs., Inc., Chgo., 1976—, L'hotel de France of Ill., Inc., Chgo., 1980-85, Water & Effluent Screening Co., Chgo., 1988-91; dir. Bosch Devel. Co., Longview, Tex., 1977-87, Lor Inc., Houghton, Mich., 1977-87, Rana Inc., Madison, Wis., 1978-87, Woodlak Co., Houghton, 1977-87, Zipatone, Inc., Hillside, Ill., 1975-82, Keco Inc., Madison, 1977-81. Bd. dirs. Martin D'Arcy Mus. Medieval and Renaissance Art, Chgo., 1975—; bd. dirs. Katherine M. Bosch Found., 1978—; asst. sec. Hundred Club of Cook County, Chgo., 1966-73, bd. dirs., sec., 1974—. Served with USAFR, 1957-63. Knight of Merit Sacred Mil. Constantinian Order of St. George of Royal House of Bourbon of Two Sicilies, knight comdr. with star Sovereign Mil. Order of Temple of Jerusalem; named youth mayor City of Chgo., 1950; recipient Outstanding Woodland Mgmt. Forestry award Monroe County (Wis.) Soil and Water

Conservation Dist., 1975. Mem. Ill. Bar Assn. (tax lectr. 1961), Advs. Soc., Field Mus. Natural History (life), Max McGraw Wildlife Found., English Speaking Union. Roman Catholic. Clubs: Travellers (Paris); Saddle and Cycle (Chgo.). General corporate, Private international, Contracts commercial. Home: 737 W Hutchinson St Chicago IL 60613-1519 Office: 35 W Wacker Dr Ste 4700 Chicago IL 60601-1614 *Personal philosophy: We define and measure success in various ways: achievement, position, wealth: and attribute it to the application of various attributes but is there any degree of success that we can achieve that is worthier than the knowledge that we have faithfully served those who depend upon and trust in us?.*

**PALLETT, JAMES MCCORMACK,** lawyer, consultant; b. Toronto, Apr. 14, 1950; came to U.S. 1978; s. John Cameron and Mary Virginia (Leuty) P.; m. Melissa Cade, Jan. 19, 1979 (div.); children: Edward James, Nicholas John. BA, Harvard U., 1980; JD, Vermont U., 1984. Bar: Hawaii. Dep. prosecutoer Honolulu, 1984-85; assoc. Winston Mirikitani, Honolulu, 1985-86, Paul Cunney, Honolulu, 1987-90; pvt. practice Honolulu, 1990—. Actor cmty. theater; performances include Grand Hotel, Sweet Charity, A Wonderful Life. Sr. dharma tchr. Kwan Um Zen Sch., 1978-98. Democrat. Zen Buddhist. Avocations: acting, martial arts, music, ice hockey, meditation. Criminal, Entertainment, Environmental. Office: 265 Portlock Rd Honolulu HI 96825-2030

**PALLIARI, RICHARD M.,** lawyer, estate planner; b. L.A., Jan. 5, 1964. BA, U. So. Calif.; JD, U. West Los Angeles, Culver City, Calif. Bar: Calif. 1994. Pvt. practice, L.A., 1994—. Estate planning. Office: 6535 Wilshire Blvd Ste 200 Los Angeles CA 90048-4905

**PALLMEYER, REBECCA RUTH,** federal judge; b. Tokyo, Sept. 13, 1954; came to U.S., 1957; d. Paul Henry and Ruth (Schrieber) P.; m. Dan P. McAdams, Aug. 20, 1977; children: Ruth, Amanda. BA, Valparaiso (Ind.) U., 1976; JD, U. Chgo., 1979. Bar: Ill. 1980, U.S. Ct. Appeals (7th cir.) 1980, U.S. Ct. Appeals 11th and 5th cirs.) 1982. Jud. clk. Minn. Supreme Ct., St. Paul, 1979-80; assoc. Hopkins & Sutter, Chgo., 1980-85; judge administrv. law Ill. Human Rights Commn., Chgo., 1985-91; magistrate judge U.S. Dist. Ct., Chgo., 1991-98, dist. judge, 1998—; mem. jud. resources com. Jud. Conf. of U.S., 1994—. Bd. govs. Augustana Ctr., 1990-91. Mem. Fed. Bar Assn. (bd. mgrs. Chgo. chpt. 1995-99), Womens Bar Assn. Ill. (bd. mgrs. 1995—), Nat. Assn. Women Judges, Fed. Magistrate Judges Assn. (bd. dirs. 1994-97), Chgo. Bar Assn. (chair devel. law com. 1992-93, David C. Hilliard award 1990-91), Valparaiso U. Alumni Assn. (bd. dirs. 1992-94). Lutheran. Avocations: choral music, sewing, running. Office: US Dist Ct 219 S Dearborn St Ste 2178 Chicago IL 60604-1877

**PALLOT, JOSEPH WEDELES,** lawyer; b. Coral Gables, Fla., Dec. 23, 1959; s. Richard Allen Pallot and Rosalind Brown (Wedeles) Spak; m. Linda Fried, Oct. 12, 1956; children: Richard Allen, Maxwell Ross. BS, Jacksonville U., 1981; JD cum laude, U. Miami, Coral Gables, Fla., 1986. Bar: Fla. 1986. Comml. lending officer S.E. Bank, N.A., Miami, 1981-83; ptnr. Steel Hector & Davis, Miami, 1986—. Bd. dirs. MOSAIC: Jewish Mus. Fla., Miami Beach, 1993—; dir. Fla. Grand Opera, 1996—; mem. exec. com. The Beacon Coun. Mem. Miami City Club. Avocations: golf, tennis. Contracts commercial, General corporate, Public utilities. Home: 385 Campana Ave Coral Gables FL 33156-4217

**PALM, GARY HOWARD,** lawyer, educator; b. Toledo, Sept. 2, 1942; s. Clarence William Jr. and Emily Marie (Braunschweiger) P. AB, Wittenberg U., 1964; JD, U. Chgo., 1967. Bar: Ill. 1967, U.S. Dist. Ct. (no. dist.) Ill. 1967, U.S. Ct. Appeals (7th cir.) 1970, U.S. Supreme Ct. 1974. Assoc. Schiff Hardin & Waite, Chgo., 1967-70; dir. Edwin F. Mandel Legal Aid Clinic, Chgo., 1970-91, atty., 1991-98; asst. prof. law U. Chgo., 1970-75, assoc. prof., 1975-83, prof., 1983-91, clin. prof., 1991—; peer rev. reader, clin. edn. grants U.S. Dept. Edn., Washington, 1980, 81, 83, 84, 86, 87, Legal Svcs. Corp., 1986-87; chairperson-elect, chairperson sect. clin. legal edn. Assn. Am. Law Schs., 1985, 86. Vol. ACLU, Chgo., 1968-75. Mem. ATLA, ABA (clin. edn. com. 1974-80, membership com. 1984-85, skills tng. com. 1985-90, accreditation for Law Schs. 1987-94, mem. coun. sect. on legal edn. and admissions to the bar 1994—), Ill. State Bar Assn. (legal edn., admission and competence com. 1985-91, 93—, vice chair 1995-96, chair 1996-97), Chgo. Bar Assn., Chgo. Coun. Lawyers, Assn. Am. Law Sch. (clin. tchg. confs. 1985, 86, 87, 89, recipient Award for Outstanding Contbn. to Clin. Edn., sect. on legal edn. 1989, co-recipient of the award 1994), Clin. Legal Edn. Assn. (ad hoc com. on accreditation 1996, Clin. All Star 1996). Democrat. Home: 2800 N Lake Shore Dr Apt 3706 Chicago IL 60657-6254 Office: U Chgo Law Sch 1111 E 60th St Chicago IL 60637-2776

**PALMA, NICHOLAS JAMES,** lawyer; b. Newark, Oct. 28, 1953; s. James Thomas and Venice Maria (Dibenedetto) P.; m. Mary Jo Cugliari, Sept. 1, 1973; children: Nicholas J., Valerie Michele, James Michael. BS cum laude, William Paterson U., 1975; JD, Seton Hall U., 1979. Bar: N.J. 1979, U.S. Dist. Ct. N.J. 1979, U.S. Ct. Appeals (3d cir.) 1985, N.Y. 1986; cert. firearms expert, Hudson County, N.J. Investigator N.J. Pub. Defender's Office, Essex Region, Newark, 1974-75; investigator Hudson County Prosecutor's Office, Jersey City, 1975-79, asst. prosecutor, 1979-81; ptnr. A.J. Fusco, Jr., P.A., Passaic, N.J., 1981-90; sole practice, Clifton, N.J., 1990—. Recipient Commendation, Dade County Sheriff, Fla., 1976. Mem. Passaic County Bar Assn., N.J. State Bar Assn. Roman Catholic. Criminal, Personal injury, State civil litigation. Home: 221 Cedar St Cedar Grove NJ 07009-1615 Office: 1425 Broad St Clifton NJ 07013-4221

**PALMATEER, LEE ALLEN,** lawyer; b. Catskill, N.Y., Jan. 2, 1962; s. Lawrence Alonzo and Pauline Harriet Palmateer; m. Nancy Elizabeth Albright, May 30, 1987; children: Benjamin Lee, Elliott Timothy, Samuel Lawrence. BSME, Clarkson U., 1984; JD, Albany Law Sch., 1995. Bar: N.Y. 1996, Mass. 1996, U.S. Dist. Ct. (we. dist.) N.Y. 1997, U.S. Dist. Ct. (no., so. and ea. dists.) N.Y. 1998. Engr. GE, Schenectady, N.Y., 1984-92; assoc. Lacy, Katzen, Ryen & Mittleman, Rochester, N.Y., 1995-97, Connor, Curran & Scram, Hudson, N.Y., 1997—. Mem. Zoning Bd. Appeals, Athens, 1992-95. Mem. N.Y. State Bar Assn., Monroe County Bar Assn., Greene County Bar Assn., Columbia County Bar Assn. Democrat. Roman Catholic. Personal injury, Product liability, Land use and zoning (including planning). Office: Connor Curran & Schram PC 441 E Allen St Hudson NY 12534-2422

**PALMER, ALLEN L.,** lawyer, computer software developer; b. Sharon, Pa., May 3, 1953; s. William L. and W. Jean Palmer; m. Sandra E. Heminger, Nov. 26, 1988. BA, U. Pitts., 1975, JD, 1978. Bar: Pa. 1978, U.S. Dist. Ct. (we. dist.) Pa. 1981. Clk. Lawrence County Ct. of Common Pleas, New Castle, Pa., 1979-81; assoc. Gamble, Verterano, Mojock, Piccione & Green, New Castle, 1981-88; ptnr. Gamble, Mojock, Piccione & Palmer, New Castle, 1988—; agt. Lawyers Title Ins. Corp., New Castle, 1989—. Opinion editor Lawrence County Law Jour., 1981-88; developer computer software Perfectly Simple Inheritance Tax, 1998. Bd. dirs. Contact E.A.R.S., New Castle, 1985—. Mem. Pa. Bar Assn., Lawrence County Bar Assn. Democrat. Mem. Christian and Missionary Alliance. Avocations: sport, computers. Real property, Banking, Family and matrimonial. Office: Gamble Mojock Piccione & Palmer 25 N Mill St New Castle PA 16101-3799

**PALMER, ANN THERESE DARIN,** lawyer; b. Detroit, Apr. 25, 1951; d. Americo and Theresa (Del Favero) Darin; m. Robert Towne Palmer, Nov. 9, 1974; children: Justin Darin, Christian Darin. BA, U. Notre Dame, 1973, MBA, 1975; JD, Loyola U., Chgo., 1978. Bar: Ill. 1978, U.S. Supreme Ct. 1981. Reporter Wall Street Jour., Detroit, 1974; freelancer Time Inc. Fin. Publs., Chgo., 1975-77; extern, Midwest regional solicitor U.S. Dept. Labor, 1976-78; tax atty. Esmark Inc., 1978; counsel Chgo. United, 1978-81; ind. contractor Legal Tax Rsch., 1981-89; fin. and legal news contbr. The Chgo. Tribune, 1991—, Bus. Week Chgo. Bur., 1991—, Automotive News, 1993-97, Crain's Chgo. Bus., 1994—, Pioneer Press, 1999—. Mem. Woman's Athletic Club Chgo. Corporate taxation, Taxation, general, Labor. Home: 873 Forest Hill Rd Lake Forest IL 60045-3905

**PALMER, BRUCE C.,** lawyer; b. Stuttgart, Germany, Oct. 5, 1955; s. John C. and Alyce S.; m. Deidre Olive Graham, May 10, 1980; children: Joshua S., MacKenna E. BA in Journalism cum laude, U. Conn., 1981, JD with highest honors, 1985. Mem. fed. and appellate cts. various states. Assoc. Edwards & Angell, Providence, R.I., 1985-88; shareholder Downs Rachlin & Martin Pllc, St. Johnsbury, Vt., 1988—. Bd. dirs. Danville Sch. Bd., Vt., 1990-93, Northeast Kingdom Mental Health Assn., St. Johnsbury, Vt., 1997, Pope Meml. Libr., Danville. Mem. ABA, Caledonia County Bar Assn. (pres. 1990-91), Vt. Bar Assn., N.H. Bar Assn., R.I. Bar Assn., Mass. Bar Assn., Def. Rsch. Inst. Environmental, Insurance, General civil litigation. Office: Downs Rachlin & Martin PPCL PO Box 99 9 Prospect St Saint Johnsbury VT 05819-2212

**PALMER, DENNIS DALE,** lawyer; b. Alliance, Nebr., Apr. 30, 1945; s. Vernon D. Palmer and Marie E. (Nelson) Fellers; m. Rebecca Ann Turner, Mar. 23, 1979; children: Lisa Marie, Jonathan Paul. BA, U. Mo., 1967, JD, 1970. Bar: Mo. 1970, U.S. Dist. Ct. (we. dist.) Mo. 1970, U.S. Ct. Appeals (8th and 10th cirs.) 1973, U.S. Supreme Ct. 1980. Staff atty. Legal Aid Soc. Western Mo., Kansas City, 1970-73; assoc. Shughart, Thomson & Kilroy, P.C., Kansas City, 1973-76, ptnr., bd. dirs., 1976—. Contbr. articles on franchise and employment law to legal jours. Bd. dirs., chmn. legal assts. adv. bd. Avila Coll., Kansas City, 1984-87. 2d lt. U.S. Army, 1970. Mem. ABA (litigation com. 1980, forum com. on franchising 1987), Mo. Bar Assn. (antitrust com. 1975—, civil practice com. 1975—), Kansas City Bar Assn. (chmn. franchise law com. 1987—), Univ. Club. Avocations: jogging, golf, tennis, outdoor activities, reading. Franchising, General civil litigation, Federal civil litigation. Home: 13100 Canterbury Rd Leawood KS 66209-1700 Office: Shughart Thomson & Kilroy 12 Wyandotte Plz 120 W 12th St Fl 16 Kansas City MO 64105-1902

**PALMER, DOUGLAS S., JR.,** lawyer; b. Peoria, Ill., Mar. 15, 1945. AB cum laude, Yale U., 1966; JD cum laude, Harvard U., 1969. Bar: Wash. 1969. Mem. Foster Pepper & Shefelman PLLC, Seattle, 1975—. General corporate, Private international, Real property. Office: Foster Pepper & Shefelman PLLC 1111 3rd Ave Ste 3400 Seattle WA 98101-3299

**PALMER, FLOYD JAMES,** lawyer; b. Stockton, Calif., Oct. 10, 1948; s. William Clyde and Ruth Viola Palmer; m. Susan Marie Aulik, Feb. 28, 1979 (div.); children: Matthew James, Christian Reid. BA, Calif. State U., Hayward, 1973; JD, U. Pacific, 1977; LLM in Labor Law, NYU, 1978. Bar: Calif. 1977. Assoc. Paul, Hastings, Janofsky & Walter, L.A., 1978-79; ptnr. Littler Mendelson P.C., San Francisco, Sacramento, 1979—; mng. shareholder Littler Mendelson P.C., Sacramento, 1984—; labor counsel Families First, Sacramento, 1993—. With USMCR, 1968-69. Mem. ABA, Sacramento Bar Assn. Avocation: golf. Labor, Civil rights. Home: 1080 Wilhaggin Park Ln Sacramento CA 95864-5377 Office: Littler Mendelson 400 Capitol Mall Fl 16 Sacramento CA 95814-4407

**PALMER, JANICE MAUDE,** lawyer; b. Greeley, Colo., Sept. 7, 1951; d. William L. and Cleo E. (White) P.; children: Emilie Halladay, Eileen Halladay, Michael W. Halladay III. BS, Ariz. State U., 1979, JD, 1982. Bar: Ariz. 1983, U.S. Dist. Ct. Ariz. 1983, U.S. Ct. Appeals (9th cir.) 1985. Assoc. Law Office of Guy Buckley, Mesa, Ariz., 1983-86, Slater & Santiquida, Mesa, 1986-89; pvt. practice Phoenix, 1989-92, Mesa, 1992—. Democrat. Family and matrimonial, Bankruptcy, State civil litigation. Office: 1930 S Alma Sch Rd #A-213 2111 E Baseline Rd Ste F8 Tempe AZ 85283-1519

**PALMER, JUDITH GRACE,** university administrator; b. Washington, Ind., Apr. 2, 1948; d. William Thomas and Laura Margaret (Routt) P. BA, Ind. U., 1970; JD cum laude, Ind. U., Indpls., 1973. Bar: Ind. 1974, U.S. Dist. Ct. (so. dist.) Ind. 1974. State budget analyst State of Ind., Indpls., 1969-76, exec. asst. to gov., 1976-81, state budget dir., 1981-85; spl. asst. to pres. Ind. U., 1985-86, v.p. for planning, 1986-91, v.p. for planning and fin. mgmt., 1991-94, v.p., CFO, 1994—; bd. dirs. Ind. Fiscal Policy Inst., Washington Park Cemetery Assn.; bd. dirs. Advanced Rsch. and Tech. Inst., treas. Bd. dirs., sec.-treas. Columbian Found., 1990-94; bd. dirs. Columbia Club, 1989-98, pres. 1995; bd. dirs. Commn. for Downtown, 1984, mem. exec. bd., 1989-92, chmn. cmty. rels. com., 1989-93; mem. State Budget Commn., 1981-85. Named one of Outstanding Young Women in Am., 1978; recipient Sagamore of the Wabash award, 1977, 85, Citation of Merit, Ind. Bar Assn. of Young Lawyers, 1978, Appreciation award, 1980. Mem. ABA, Ind. Bar Assn., Indpls. Bar Assn. Roman Catholic. Office: Ind Univ Bryan Hall Rm 204 Bloomington IN 47405

**PALMER, PHILIP ISHAM, JR.,** lawyer; b. Dallas, June 25, 1929; s. Philip I. and Charlene (Bolen) P.; m. Eleanor Hutson, Mar. 7, 1951; children—Stephen Edward, Michael Bolen. B.B.A., So. Methodist U., 1952; LL.B., U. Tex., 1957. Bar: Tex. 1957, U.S. Dist. Ct. (no. dist.) Tex. 1957, U.S. Ct. Appeals (5th cir.) 1958, U.S. Supreme Ct. 1963, U.S. Dist. Ct. (we. dist.) Tex. 1968, U.S. Ct. Appeals (9th cir.) 1973, U.S. Ct. Appeals (10th cir.) 1974, U.S. Supreme Ct. 1974, U.S. Ct. Appeals (11th cir.) 1981, U.S. Dist. Ct. (ea. dist.) Tex. 1987. Since practiced in Dallas; ptnr. Palmer & Palmer P.C. (and predecessor firms), 1957—; chmn. bd. Carolina Mfg. Corp., 1973—, pres., 1969-73; chmn. bd. Commonwealth Nat. Bank, 1967-69; pres. Pennyrich Corp., 1969-72. Co-author: Texas Creditors Rights; Contbr. articles to profl. jours. Vice consul Republic Costa Rica, 1973—; bd. dirs. Shepherd's Care, 1987—. Fellow Am. Coll. Bankruptcy; mem. Am. Bar Assn., Am. Judicature Soc. Club: City. Bankruptcy, Federal civil litigation. Office: Palmer & Palmer PC 1201 Main St Ste 1510 Dallas TX 75202-3985

**PALMER, RICHARD N.,** state supreme court justice; b. Hartford, Conn., May 27, 1950. BA, Trinity Coll., 1972; JD with high honors, U. Conn., 1977. Bar: Conn. 1977, U.S. Dist. Ct. Conn. 1978, D.C. 1980, U.S. Ct. Appeals (2nd cir.) 1981. Law clk. to Hon. Jon O. Newman U.S. Ct. Appeals (2nd cir.), 1977-78; assoc. Shipman & Goodwin, 1978-80; asst. U.S. atty. Office U.S. Atty. Conn., 1980-83, 87-90, U.S. atty. dist. Conn., 1991, chief state's atty. Conn., 1991-93; ptnr. Chatigny and Palmer, 1984-86; assoc. justice Conn. Supreme Ct., Hartford, 1993—. Mem. Phi Beta Kappa. Office: 231 Capitol Ave Hartford CT 06106-1548

**PALMER, RICHARD WARE,** lawyer; b. Boston, Oct. 20, 1919; s. George Ware and Ruth French (Judkins) P.; m. Nancy Fernald Shaw, July 8, 1950; children: Richard Ware Jr., John Wentworth, Anne Fernald. AB, Harvard U., 1942, JD, 1948. Bar: N.Y. 1950, Pa. 1959. Sec., dir. N.Am. Mfg. Co., Natick, Mass., 1946-48; assoc. Burlingham, Veeder, Clark & Hupper, Burlingham, Hupper & Kennedy, N.Y.C., 1949-57; ptnr. Rawle & Henderson, Phila., 1958-79; ptnr. Palmer, Biezup & Henderson, Phila., 1979-95, of counsel, 1996—; sec. Underwater Technics, Inc., Camden, N.J., 1967-85; adv. on admiralty law to U.S. del. Inter-Govtl. Maritime Consultative Orgn., London, 1967; mem. U.S. Shipping Coordinating Com., mem. Washington legal sub com., 1967—; U.S. del. 30th-34th internat. confs. Titular mem. Comité Maritime Internat.; v.p., sec., bd. dirs. Phila. Belt Line R.R.; bd. dirs. Mather (Bermuda) Ltd. Editor: Maritime Law Reporter. Mem., permanent adv. bd. Tulane Admiralty Law Inst., Tulane U. Law Sch., New Orleans, 1975—; trustee Seamen's Ch. Inst., Phila., 1967—, pres., 1972-84; Harvard Law Sch. Assn., Phila., Pa. (exec. com. 1986—); bd. dirs. Havrford (Pa.) Civic Assn., 1972-85, pres., 1976-79; consul for Denmark in State of Pa., 1980-91, consul emeritus, 1992—. Lt. comdr. USNR. Fellow World Acad. Art and Sci. (treas. 1988—); mem. ABA (former chmn. stdg. com. on admiralty and maritime law 1978-79), N.Y.C. Bar Assn., Phila. Bar Assn., Am. Judicature Soc., Maritime Law Assn. (chmn. limitation liability com. 1977-83, 2d v.p. 1984-86, 1st v.p. 1986-88, pres. 1988-90, immediate past pres. 1990-92), Internat. Bar Assn., Assn. Average Adjusters USA and Gt. Britain, Port of Phila. Maritime Soc., Harvard Law Sch. Assn. of Phila. (exec. com. 1986—), Fgn. Consul assn. of Phila., Danish Order of Dannebrog, Merion Cricket Club, Phila. Club, Rittenhouse Club, India House, Geneal. Soc. Pa. (bd. dirs. 1997—), Harvard Club of N.Y.C. and Phila. (v.p., mem. exec. com. 1983-86, 94-97). Republican. Episcopalian. Admiralty, Private international, Insurance. Home: 432 Montgomery Ave Haverford PA 19041-1559 Office: Palmer Biezup & Henderson Pub Ledger Bldg 620 Chestnut St Philadelphia PA 19106-3413

**PALMER, ROBERT ALAN,** lawyer, educator; b. Somerville, N.J., June 29, 1948. BA, U. Pitts., 1970; JD, George Washington U., 1976. Bar: Va. 1977. Dir. labor relations Nat. Assn. Mfrs., Washington, 1976-79; assoc. gen. counsel Nat. Restaurant Assn., Washington, 1979-85, gen. counsel, 1985-87; assoc. prof. Pa. State U., State College, 1987-88; assoc. prof. Calif. State Poly. U., 1988-92, prof., 1992—. Mem. ABA, Va. State Bar Assn. Home: 557 Fairview Ave Arcadia CA 91007-6736 Office: 3801 W Temple Ave Pomona CA 91768-2557

**PALMER, ROBERT LESLIE,** lawyer; b. Porterville, Calif., Apr. 10, 1957; s. Harrison Rowe and Margaret Elizabeth (Witty) P.; m. Huisuk Kim, Feb. 1, 1986; 1 child, Aaron Rowe. BA, Tulane U., 1979; JD, Georgetown U., 1982. Bar: D.C. 1982, U.S. Ct. Mil. Appeals 1985, Tex. 1987, Ala. 1987, U.S. Dist. Ct. (no. dist.) Ala. 1987, U.S. Ct. Appeals (11th cir.) 1987. Assoc. Lewis Martin Burnett & Dunkle, P.C., Birmingham, Ala., 1987-89, Lewis and Martin, Birmingham, Ala., 1989-90; assoc. Martin, Drummond and Woosley, Birmingham, 1990-91, bd. dirs., 1991-92; bd. dirs. Martin, Drummond, Woosley and Palmer, Birmingham, 1992-95; atty. Environ. Litig. Group, P.C., Birmingham, Ala., 1995—. Ala. del. 6th Joint Conf. between Korea and S.E. U.S., Kyongju, Republic of Korea, 1991, 7th Joint Conf., Atlanta, 1992. Capt. JAGC, U.S. Army, 1983-87, USAR, 1987-91. Recipient commendation Republic of Korea Ministry of Justice, 1984. Mem. ATLA, Christian Legal Soc., Phi Beta Kappa, Omicron Delta Kappa. Republican. Baptist. Environmental, Personal injury, Toxic tort. Home: 1408 E Whirlaway Helena AL 35080-4102 Office: Environ Litig Group PC 3529 7th Ave S Birmingham AL 35222-3210

**PALMER, ROBERT TOWNE,** lawyer; b. Chgo., May 25, 1947; s. Adrian Bernhardt and Gladys (Towne) P.; m. Ann Therese Darin, Nov. 9, 1974; children: Justin Darin, Christian Darin. BA, Colgate U., 1969; JD, U. Notre Dame, 1974. Bar: Ill. 1974, D.C. 1978, U.S. Supreme Ct. 1978. Law clk. Hon. Walter V. Schaefer, Ill. Supreme Ct., 1974-75; assoc. McDermott, Will & Emery, Chgo., 1975-81, ptnr., 1982-86; ptnr. Chadwell & Kayser, Ltd., 1987-88, Connelly, Mustes, Palmer & Schroeder, 1988-89; of counsel Garfield & Merel Ltd., 1990—; mem. adj. faculty Chgo. Kent Law Sch., 1975-77, Loyola U., 1976-78; mem. adv. com. Fed. Home Loan Mortgage Corp., 1988-89; bd. dirs. Ctrl. Fed. Savs. & Loan Assn. of Chgo.; mem. Chgo. Ctr. Adv. Bd. Voyageur Outward Bound Sch., 1988-91. Mem. ABA, Ill. State Bar Assn. (Lincoln award 1983), Chgo. Bar Assn., Internat. Assn. Def. Counsel, Chgo. Club, Dairymen's Country Club, Lambda Alpha. Contbr. articles to legal jours. and textbooks. Federal civil litigation, State civil litigation, Insurance. Office: Garfield & Merel Ltd 211 W Wacker Dr Ste 1500 Chicago IL 60606-1238

**PALMER, THOMAS EARL,** lawyer; b. Columbus, Ohio, July 21, 1939; s. Dwight Miller and Virginia (Gray) P.; children: Bradley Eames, Richard Thomas; m. Victoria Cochrane, July 6, 1985. BA, Denison U., 1961; JD, U. Mich., 1964. Bar: Ohio 1964, U.S. Dist. Ct. (so. dist.) Ohio 1964, U.S. Ct. Appeals (6th cir.) 1968, U.S. Supreme Ct. 1972, U.S. Ct. Appeals (4th cir.) 1973. Assoc. Knepper, White, Richards & Miller, Columbus, 1964-69, ptnr., 1969-72; ptnr. Moritz, McClure & Palmer, Columbus, 1972-74, Gingery & Palmer, Columbus, 1974-80; Squire, Sanders & Dempsey, 1980-91; mng. ptnr. Squire, Sanders & Dempsey, Columbus, 1984-91; v.p., gen. counsel, sec. Mead Corp., Dayton, 1991-99. Bd. dirs. Thurber House, 1990-92; trustee found. bd. Wright State U., 1992-94; trustee Wright State U., 1994—, chmn., 1998—; trustee Dayton Ballet, 1992-94; troop leader Boy Scouts Am., Columbus, 1977-84. Fellow Am. Coll. Trial Lawyers; mem. ABA, Ohio Bar Assn., Dayton Bar Assn., Columbus Bar Assn. (Cmty. Svc. award 1973), Def. Rsch. Inst., Capital Club. Avocations: boating, gardening, woodworking, bicycling. General corporate, Federal civil litigation, Environmental. Address: PO Box 821 Elk Rapids MI 49629-0821

**PALMER, VENRICE ROMITO,** lawyer, educator; b. Springfield, Mass., Jan. 11, 1952; s. Venrice Wellesley and Mildred Adlay (Foster) P. Higher diploma, U. Besançon, France, 1973; AB maxima cum laude, King's Coll., Wilkes-Barre, Pa., 1974; JD, Harvard U., 1977. Bar: N.Y. 1978, U.S. Dist. Ct. (so. and ea. dists.) N.Y. 1979, Ill. 1986, Calif. 1997. Spl. asst. atty. gen. Office N.Y. Atty. Gen., N.Y.C., 1977-79; staff atty. SEC, N.Y.C., 1979-82, br. chief, 1982-83, spl. trial counsel, 1983-85, acting asst. regional adminstr., 1984-85; sr. counsel Sears, Roebuck and Co., Hoffman Estates, Ill., 1985-97, Bank of Am., San Francisco, 1997-99; counsel McCutchen, Doyle, Brown & Enersen, LLP, San Francisco, 1999—; guest lectr. St. John's U. Bus. Sch., N.Y.C., 1984; lectr. Practicing Law Inst., N.Y.C., 1995—, Glasser LegalWorks, Little Falls, N.J., 1997—. Contbr. articles to various law publs. Recipient cert. of appreciation N.Y. State Bar Assn., 1978. Mem. ABA, Am. Soc. Corp. Secs. (lectr. N.Y.C. 1997—). Avocations: opera, ballet, reading. General corporate, Finance, Securities. Home: 1200 Gough St Apt 7A San Francisco CA 94109-6616 Office: McCutchen Doyle Brown & Enersen LLP Three Embarcadero Ctr San Francisco CA 94111

**PALMER, VERNON VALENTINE,** law educator; b. New Orleans, Sept. 9, 1940; s. George Joseph and Juliette Marie (Wehrmann) P. B.A., Tulane U., 1962, LL.B., 1965; LL.M., Yale U., 1966; PhD, Pembroke Coll., Oxford U., 1985. Bar: La. 1965, U.S. Supreme Ct. 1981. Asst. prof. law Ind. Sch. Law, Indpls., 1966-70; lectr. law U. Botswana, Lesotho & Swaziland, Roma, Lesotho, 1967-69; prof. Tulane Law Sch., New Orleans, 1970—; Clarence Morrow research prof. law Tulane Law Sch., 1980—, Thomas Pickles prof. law, 1989—; external examiner Nat. U. Lesotho, Roma, 1978-81; reporter for revision of civil code La. Law Inst. 1979; vis. prof. Faculty Law, U. Strasbourg, 1988, The Sorbonne, U. Paris, 1986, 92, Universite des Antilles, Martinique, 1998, Universidad Ramon Liull, Barcelona, 1998, U. Trento, 1999—. Author: The Roman-Dutch and Lesotho Law of Delict, 1970, The Legal System of Lesotho, 1971, The Paths to Privity, 1992, The Civil Law of Lease in Louisiana, 1997; contbr. numerous articles to profl. jours. Pres. French Quarter Residents Assn., 1973-75, Alliance for Good Govt., 1974-75; del. Nat. Democratic Conv., N.Y.C., 1976. Decorated chevalier L'ordre des Palmes Académiques. Mem. La. Law Inst. Democrat. Roman Catholic. Home: 3311 Coliseum St New Orleans LA 70115-2401 Office: 6329 Freret St New Orleans LA 70118-6231

**PALMER, WAYNE DARWIN,** lawyer; b. Portland, Oreg., Aug. 17, 1955; s. Ronald Darwin and Rena Glee (Morse) P.; m. Cynthia Lee Nelson, Sept. 6, 1975; children: Ryan, Leif, Hillary. BS, Portland State U., 1977; JD, Lewis and Clark U., 1981. Bar: Oreg. 1981, U.S. Dist. Ct. Oreg. 1981. Lawyer Kell, Alterman & Runstein, Portland, 1981—. Mem. Maritime Law Assn. Am., Oreg. Trial Assn., Oreg. State Bar Assn. (mem. exec. com. 1986-87). Avocation: rafting. General civil litigation, Family and matrimonial, Admiralty. Home: 6493 Senorma Cir Milwaukee OR 97267 Office: Kell Alterman & Runstein 1001 SW 5th Ave Ste 1800 Portland OR 97204-1194

**PALMER, WILLIAM D.,** lawyer. BS in Mgmt. with honors, Rensselaer Poly. Inst., 1973; JD cum laude, Boston Coll., 1976. Bar: Fla. 1976, U.S. Dist. Ct. (no., mid. and so. dists.) Fla. 1976; cert. civil mediator, family mediator, arbitrator, Fla. Assoc. Carlton, Fields, Ward, Emmanuel, Smith & Cutler, Orlando, Fla., 1976-82, ptnr., 1982-97; ptnr. Palmer & Palmer, P.A., Orlando, 1997—; arbitrator Am. Arbitration Assn., Ct. Annexed Arbitration Program of the U.S. Dist. Ct. (mid. dist) Fla., Orange County Bar Assn's. Fee Arbitration Com. Past bd. dirs. Fla. Hosp. Found., Life for Kids Adoption Agy.; past chmn. bd. dirs. Ctrl. Fla. Helpline; bd. dirs. Boys and Girls Club of Ctrl. Fla. Mem. ABA (mem. litigation sect., mem. antitrust sect.), Fla. Def. Lawyers Assn., Def. Rsch. Inst., Fla. Bar (mem. litigation, appellate law and family law sects.), Orange County Bar Assn. (chmn. various coms.). General civil litigation. Office: Palmer & Palmer PA 3117B Edgewater Dr Orlando FL 32804-3721

**PALMERI, JOHN M.,** lawyer; b. Denver, Dec. 29, 1958; s. Frank J. and Rosemary Palmeri; m. Camille Weiss, June 26, 1982; children: Nicholas, Winston. AB, Columbia U., 1981; JD, U. Denver, 1984. Bar: Colo. 1984, Wyo. 1994. Shareholder White and Steele, P.C., Denver, 1984—. Editor: Colorado Attorneys' Professional Liability Handbook, 1998. Trustee Denver Area Coun., Boy Scouts Am., Denver, 1997—. Mem. Colo. Def. Lawyers Assn. (pres. 1997-98), Fedn. Ins. and Corp. Cons., Faculty Fed. Advs., Inns of Ct. General civil litigation, Professional liability, Product liability. Office: 950 17th St Fl 21 Denver CO 80202-2815

**PALMERSHEIM, RICHARD J.,** lawyer; b. Milw., Oct. 3, 1929; s. Joseph J. Palmersheim and Loretta Marie Connell; m. Joan S. Benoist, June 7, 1958 (div. June 1976); children: Richard, Mary Jo, James, Thomas, Robert. BS, Marquette U., 1951, LLB, 1957. Bar: Wis. 1957; U.S. Dist. Ct. (ea. dist. Wis.) 1957; U.S. Supreme Ct. 1978. Wis. claims mgr. St. Paul Co.'s, Milw., 1957-65, Wis. gen. counsel, 1965-1990; pvt. practice cons. Milw., 1990—; legal cons. USMC, Milw., 1965-80. 1st. lt. USMC, 1951-53, Korea. Mem.

ABA, Wis. Bar Assn. Republican. Roman Catholic. Avocations: photography, deep sea fishing, gardening, travel. Insurance, Professional liability. Home: 205 S Rolland Rd Brookfield WI 53005-6319

**PALMGREN, NADINE R.,** lawyer; b. Geneseo, Ill., Sept. 9, 1954; d. Wayne A. and Helen L. (Lulich) Stohl; m. Charles F. Palmgren, May 17, 1975; children: Lynn M., Brad M. Student, Black Hawk Coll., 1972-74, No. Ill. U., 1974-76, Augustana Coll., 1975-76; BS, No. Ill. U., 1976; MBA, St. Ambrose U., 1990; JD with honors, Drake U., 1993. Bar: Ill. 1993, Iowa 1993, U.S. Dist. Ct. (cen. dist.) Ill. 1995. Jud. clk. 14th Jud. Cir. Ct., Rock Island, Ill., 1992; ptnr. Stone & Palmgren, Geneseo, 1993—; adj. prof. Black Hawk Coll., Moline, Ill., 1993-97. Author: Understanding Iowa Law, 1993. V.p. Bus. and Profl. Women, Geneseo, 1994; chmn. N & W. Henry County unit Am. Cancer Soc., Geneseo, 1989-90; mem. cmty. devel. com. Jr. Women's Club, Geneseo, 1989-90. Mem. Ill. Bar Assn., Iowa Bar Assn, Henry County Bar Assn. Fax: (309) 944-4629. General practice. Office: Stone & Palmgren 211 S State St Geneseo IL 61254-1454

**PALTER, JOHN THEODORE,** lawyer; b. Berwyn, Ill., Feb. 20, 1960; s. Theodore John and Josephine Sophie P.; m. Kathleen Elizabeth Bagwell Palter, May 17, 1992; children: John Luke, Eliza Kathleen. BS in Fin., No. Ill., 1982; JD, Drake U., 1985. Bar: Tex. 1985, U.S. Dist. Ct. (no. and ea. dists.) Tex. 1989, U.S. Tax Ct. 1987; CPA, Tex. Staff atty. Coopers & Lybrand, Dallas, 1985-87; assoc. Geary, Stahl & Spencer, PC, Dallas, 1987-91, Holmes Millard & Duncan, Dallas, 1991-93; shareholder McCue & Lee, PC, Dallas, 1993-99, Novakou Davis, Dallas, 1999—. Pres. Holy Trinity Sch. Bd., Dallas, 1997—. Mem. Dallas Bar Assn., Assn. Attys. and CPA's. Roman Catholic. Avocation: marathon running. Federal civil litigation, State civil litigation, Contracts commercial. Home: 2712 Amherst St Dallas TX 75225 Office: McCue & Lee PC 5430 Lbj Fwy Ste 1050 Dallas TX 75240-2612

**PAMPHILIS, CONSTANTINE Z.,** lawyer; b. Morristown, N.J., Sept. 9, 1970; s. Nick C. Pamphilis and Theodora M. Carafas. BBA, U. Tex., 1992; JD, Baylor U., 1995. Bar: Tex. 1995, U.S. Dist. Ct. (so., no., we., and ea. dists.) Tex. 1995, U.S. Ct. Appeals (5th cir.) 1998. Rsch. asst. Sch. Pub. Health U. Tex., San Antonio, 1989, 90; legal asst. clk. Baker & Botts, Houston, 1991; project asst. Vinson & Elkins LLP, Houston, 1992-93; summer assoc. Davis & Shank P.C., Houston, 1994, atty., 1995—. Baylor U. scholar, 1993. Mem. ABA, Tex. Assn. Def. Counsel, Tex. Bar Assn., Houston Bar Assn., Def. Rsch. Inst., Beta Gamma Sigma. General civil litigation, Libel, Personal injury. Office: Davis & Shank PC 1415 Louisiana St Ste 4200 Houston TX 77002-7355

**PANDIT, AMY INDRAVADAN,** lawyer; b. Detroit, Mar. 16, 1968; d. Indravadan N. and Devyani I. Pandit; m. Ashis H. Tayal, May 29, 1994; 1 child, Anand Pandit Tayal. Grad., Northwestern U., 1990; JD, Boston U., 1995. Bar: N.Y., Pa. Assoc. Weil Gotshal & Manges LLP, N.Y.C., 1995-97, Buchanan Ingersoll P.C., Pitts., 1997—. G. Joseph Tavro scholar Boston U., 1993. Avocations: snow skiing, swimming, hiking. Mergers and acquisitions, Securities. Home: 43 Mallard Dr Pittsburgh PA 15238-1131 Office: Buchanan Ingersoll One Oxford Centre 301 Grant St Fl 20 Pittsburgh PA 15219-1410

**PANDOLFE, JOHN THOMAS, JR.,** lawyer; b. Neptune, N.J., Dec. 15, 1941; s. John T. and Jeannette R. (Pullen) P.; m. Linda Lee Fritzsche, July 12, 1969; children: Leslie, Matthew. AB, U. Miami, 1965; MS, Monmouth Coll., 1973; JD, U. Miami, 1975. Bar: Fla. 1976, N.J. 1976, U.S. Dist. Ct. N.J. 1976. Ptnr. Pandolfe, Shaw & Rubino, Spring Lake, N.J. Mem. ABA, Fla. Bar Assn., N.J. Bar Assn., Monmouth Bar Assn., Spring Lake Golf Club. General practice. Office: Pandolfe Shaw and Rubino 215 Morris Ave Spring Lake NJ 07762-1360

**PANEBIANCO, THOMAS,** lawyer; b. Camden, N.J., 1951. BA in English with highest honors, Rutgers U., 1973; JD, U. Pa., 1976. Bar: Fla., Pa., D.C. Criminal prosecutor Miami, Fla., 1976-78; staff atty. Office of Gen. Counsel Fed. Maritime Commn., 1978, dep. gen. counsel, gen. counsel, 1997—; mem. Adminstrv. Conf. of the U.S., 1993-95; adj. mem. English dept. Shepherd Coll., Shepherdstown, W.Va. Office: Fed Maritime Commn 800 N Capitol St NW Washington DC 20573-0001*

**PANEK, EDWARD S., JR.,** lawyer; b. Phila., Jan. 10, 1945; s. Edward S. and Clara S. P.; m. Marlene Lazzaro, Sept. 26, 1981; 1 child, Marilyn O. Primiano. BA, St. Joseph's U., Phila., 1966; JD, Villanova U., 1969. Bar: Pa. 1971, U.S. Cir. Ct. (8th cir.) 1976, U.S. Cir. Ct. (3d cir.) 1982. Counsel Phila. Civil Svc. Commn., 1969; trial atty. antitrust divsn. U.S. Dept. Justice, Phila., 1971—. Mem. Logan Sq. Neighborhood Assn., Phila., 1990—. With U.S. Army, 1969-71. Mem. Union League Phila. Roman Catholic. Avocations: sports, investing, wines, real estate, dining. Home: 2137 Race St Philadelphia PA 19103-1009 Office: US Dept Justice Antitrust Divsn 650 Curtis Ctr 7th & Walnut Philadelphia PA 19106

**PANELLI, EDWARD ALEXANDER,** retired state supreme court justice; b. Santa Clara, Calif., Nov. 23, 1931; s. Pilade and Natalina (Della Maggiora) P.; m. Lorna Christine Mondora, Oct. 27, 1956; children: Thomas E., Jeffrey J., Michael P. BA cum laude, Santa Clara U., 1953, JD cum laude, 1955, LLD (hon.), 1986; LLD (hon.), Southwestern U., L.A., 1988. Bar: Calif. 1955. Ptnr. Pasquinelli and Panelli, San Jose, Calif., 1955-72; judge Santa Clara County Superior Ct., 1972-83; assoc. justice 1st Dist. Ct. of Appeals, San Francisco, 1983-84; presiding justice 6th Dist. Ct. of Appeals, San Jose, 1984-85; assoc. justice Calif. Supreme Ct., San Francisco, 1985-94; chief judicial officer JAMS/Endispute, 1995—; instr. Continuing Legal Edn., Santa Clara, 1976-78. Trustee West Valley Community Coll., 1963-72; trustee Santa Clara U., 1963—, chmn. bd. trustees, 1984—. Recipient Citation, Am. Com. Italian Migration, 1969, Community Legal Svcs. award, 1979, 84, Edwin J. Owens Lawyers of Yr. award Santa Clara Law Sch. Alumni, 1982, Merit award Republic of Italy, 1984, Gold medal in recognition of Italians who have honored Italy, Lucca, Italy, 1990, St Thomas More award, San Francisco, 1991, Filippo Mazzei Internat. award, Florence, Italy, 1992; Justice Edward A. Panelli Moot Courtroom named in his honor Santa Clara U., 1989. Mem. ABA, Nat. Italian Bar Assn. (inspiration award 1986), Calif. Trial Lawyers Assn. (Trial Judge of Yr. award Santa Clara County chpt. 1981), Calif. Judges Assn. (bd. dirs. 1982), Jud. Coun. Calif. (vice-chair 1989-93), Alpha Sigma Nu, Phi Alpha Delta Law Found. (hon. mem. Douglas Edmonds chpt.). Republican. Roman Catholic. Avocations: golf, jogging, sailing. Office: JAMS/Endispute Inc 160 W Santa Clara St San Jose CA 95113-1701

**PANICCIA, PATRICIA LYNN,** journalist, writer, lawyer, educator; b. Glendale, Calif., Sept. 19, 1952; d. Valentino and Mary (Napoleon) P.; m. Jeffrey McDowell Mailes, Oct. 5, 1985; children: Alana Christine, Malia Noel. BA in Comm., U. Hawaii, 1977; JD, Pepperdine U., 1981. Bar: Hawaii 1981, Calif. 1982, U.S. Dist. Ct. Hawaii 1981. Extern law clk. hon. Samuel P. King U.S. Dist. Ct., Honolulu, 1980; reporter, anchor woman Sta. KEYT-TV, Santa Barbara, Calif., 1983-84; reporter Sta. KCOP-TV, L.A., 1984-88, CNN, L.A., 1989-93; corr. Cable News Network (CNN), L.A., 1989—; adj. prof. comm. law Pepperdine Sch. Law, 1987, gender & the law, 1994—, adj. prof.; profl. surfer, 1977-81. Recipient Clarion award Women in Comm., Inc., 1988. Mem. ABA (chair of law and media com. young lawyers divsn. 1987-88, nat. conf. com. lawyers and reps. of media 1987-91), Calif. State Bar (mem. com. on fair trial and free press 1983-84, pub. affairs com. 1985-87), Hawaii Bar Assn., Phi Delta Phi (historian 1980-81). Office: PO Box 881 La Canada CA 91012-0881

**PANKEY, LARRY ALLEN,** lawyer, educator; b. Mandaree, N.D., Mar. 18, 1966. BA, U. Ga., 1989; JD, Boston U., 1992. Bar: Ga., 1992, Mass., 1992, Wash., 1999. Ptnr. Pankey, Coffman & Horlock, Decatur, Ga., 1993—; adj. prof. John Marshall Law Sch., Atlanta, 1994—; spkr. Native Am. Consortium, Atlanta, 1996. Mem. ATLA, Ga. Trial Lawyers Assn., DeKalb Bar Assn. (chair Tillman Cup 1998). Civil rights, Labor, Personal injury. Office: Pankey Coffman & Horlock 315 W Ponce De Leon Ave Decatur GA 30030-2441

**PANKOPF, ARTHUR, JR.,** lawyer; b. Malden, Mass., Feb. 1, 1931. BS in Marine Transp., Mass. Maritime Acad., 1951; BS in Fgn. Svc. and Internat. Transp., Georgetown U., 1957, JD, 1965. Bar: Md. 1965, D.C. 1966, U.S. Supreme Ct. 1977. Ea. area mgr. Trans Ocean Van Service of Consol. Freightway, 1958-61; with U.S. Maritime Adminstrn., 1961-65; assoc. firm Preston, Thorgrimson, Ellis & Holman, Washington, 1976-77; minority chief counsel Com. on Mcht. Marine & Fisheries U.S. Ho. of Reps., Washington, 1965-69; minority chief counsel, staff dir. Com. on Commerce, U.S. Senate, 1969-76; mng. dir. Fed. Maritime Commn., 1977-81; pvt. practice Washington, 1981-84; dir. legis. affairs Corp. Pub. Broadcasting, 1984-86, v.p., gen. counsel, sec., 1986-88; pvt. practice Washington, 1988-90, 96—; dir. fed. affairs Matson Navigation Co. Inc., Washington, 1990-95. Mem. Maritime Adminstrv. Bar Assn. (pres. 1995-96), Propeller Club Port of Washington (bd. govs. 1992—). E-mail: a.pankopf@worldnet.alt.net. Administrative and regulatory, Legislative, Transportation. Address: 7819 Hampden Ln Bethesda MD 20814-1108

**PANNEBAKER, JAMES BOYD,** lawyer; b. Middletown, Pa., Mar. 9, 1936; s. Boyd Alton and Kathryn Kennedy (Brindle) P.; divorced; children: Jeffery B., Renee E. Pannebaker Bench, Traci Lee Pannebaker. BS, Elizabethtown Coll., 1958; JD, U. Mich., 1961. Bar: Pa. 1962, U.S. Dist. Ct. (mid. dist.) Pa., U.S. Ct. Appeals (3d cir.), U.S. Supreme Ct. 1969. Pvt. practice, Harrisburg, 1965-86; pres. Pannebaker & Jones, P.C., Middletown, 1986—; mem. regional adv. bd. Mellon Bank, Harrisburg, 1980—. Bd. dirs. Cmty. Gen. Osteo. Hosp., harrisburg, 1970-98; trustee Elizabethtown (Pa.) Coll., 1972-78; mem. adv. bd. Villa Teresa Nursing Home, Harrisburg, 1985—; past chmn. Middletown chpt. ARC; pres. Keystone Area coun. Boy Scouts Am. Capt. U.S. Army, 1962-65. Mem. Am. Legion, Masons, Shriners, Elks. Republican. Methodist. Avocations: skiing, sailing, horseback riding, outdoor activities. Personal injury, Probate, Estate planning. Office: Pannebaker & Jones PC 4000 Vine St Middletown PA 17057-3565

**PANNER, OWEN M.,** federal judge; b. 1924. Student, U. Okla., 1941-43, LL.B., 1949. Atty. Panner, Johnson, Marceau, Karnopp, Kennedy & Nash, 1950-80; judge, now sr. judge U.S. Dist. Ct. Oreg., Portland, 1980—, sr. judge, 1992—. Mem. Am. Coll. Trial Lawyers, Order of Coif. Office: US Dist Ct 1000 SW 3rd Ave Ste 1207 Portland OR 97204-2942

**PANNILL, WILLIAM PRESLEY,** lawyer; b. Houston, Mar. 5, 1940; s. Fitzhugh H. and Mary Ellen (Goodrum) P.; m. Deborah Detering, May 9, 1966 (div. Nov. 1986); children: Shelley, Katherine, Elizabeth. BA, Rice U., 1962; MS, Columbia U., 1963; JD, U. Tex., 1970. Bar: Tex. 1970, U.S. Supreme Ct. 1975, U.S. Ct. Appeals (5th cir.) 1973, U.S. Ct. Appeals (D.C. cir.) 1974, U.S. Ct. Appeals (10th cir.) 1980, U.S. Ct. Appeals (11th cir.) 1981, U.S. Dist. Ct. (so. dist.) Tex. 1975, U.S. Dist. Ct. (no. dist.) Tex. 1991. Assoc. Vinson, Elkins, Searls & Connally, 1970-71; staff asst. Sec. of Treasury, Washington, 1971-72; assoc. Vinson, Elkins, Searls, Connally & Smith, 1972-75; sole practice, 1975-76; ptnr. Pannill and Hooper, Houston, 1977-80; bd. dirs. Reynolds, Allen, Cook, Pannill & Hooper, Inc., Houston, 1980-82; ptnr. Pannill and Reynolds, Houston, 1982-85; sole practice, Houston, 1985-88, ptnr. Pannill, Moser, Mize & Herrmann, Houston, 1988-90, Pannill & Moser, L.L.P., 1990-93, Pannill, Moser & Barnes, L.L.P., 1993—; assoc. editor Litigation Jour. of the Sect. of Litigation, ABA, 1979-81, exec. editor, 1981-82, editor-in-chief, 1982-84, dir. publs., 1984-86, mem. coun., 1986-89; lectr. Southwestern Legal Found., 1980, others. Chmn., Legal Found. Am., 1981-82, bd. dirs., 1983-97. Contbr. articles to profl. jours. With USMCR, 1963-64. Mem. ABA (litigation sect.), Houston Bar Assn., Tex. Bar Assn., Rice Alumni Assn. (bd. dirs. 1989-92), Houston Grand Opera (bd. dirs. 1989-92, adv. bd. 1995—), Houston Symphony Soc. (adv. bd. 1990—), DaCamera Soc. (bd. dirs. 1995-97), Houston Club. Episcopalian. Appellate, Federal civil litigation, State civil litigation.

**PANSEGRAU, PHAEDRA RENÉE,** lawyer; b. Rantoul, Ill., Jan. 19, 1967; d. Robert A. and Shonna Noles Leidecker; m. Timothy L. Pansegrau, Dec. 19, 1992; children: Lauren, Reed. BBA, Baylor U., 1989, JD, 1991. Bar: Tex., U.S. Dist. Ct. (so. dist.) Tex. Assoc. Wesley, Wilson & Herzog, Houston, 1991-95; corp. counsel Compass Group USA, Inc., Charlotte, N.C., 1996—. General corporate, Contracts commercial. Office: Compass Group USA Inc 2400 Yorkmont Rd Charlotte NC 28217-4511

**PANSLER, KARL FREDERICK,** lawyer; b. Canton, Ohio, Sept. 30, 1961; s. Clarence E. and Ruth E. Pansler; m. Heather Ann Craft, Sept. 9, 1985; children: Christopher, Karlene, Chase, Charles. BA, Southeastern Coll., 1982; JD, Oral Roberts U., 1985. Bar: Okla. 1985, Fla. 1987, U.S. Dist. Ct. (mid. dist.) Fla. 1988, U.S. Dist. Ct. (ea. and no. dists.) Okla., U.S. Ct. Appeals (11th cir.). Assoc. Melone & Shepard, Tulsa, Okla., 1985-87, Frost & Purcell, Bartow, Fla., 1987-91; ptnr. Pansler & Moody, Bartow, 1991—; pres. Intrepid Dolphin Investments, Bartow, 1994—. Contbg. author: Christian Ministries and the Law, 1990. Mem. character edn. com. Polk County Pub. Schs., Bartow; pres., bd. chmn. Beacon Christian Sch., Lakeland, Fla., 1991-95. Named Young Alumnus of Yr., Southeastern Coll., Lakeland, 1991. Mem. ATLA, Acad. Fla. Trial Lawyers, Okla. Bar, Fla. Bar, Southeastern Coll. Alumni Assn. (pres. 1998—). Republican. Avocations: Tae Kwon Do, running marathons, golf. Personal injury, Federal civil litigation, General civil litigation. Office: Pansler & Moody PA 575 N Broadway Ave Bartow FL 33830-3919

**PANTEL, GLENN STEVEN,** lawyer; b. Plainfield, N.J., Sept. 25, 1953; s. Donald and Sarah Libby (Pearlman) P.; m. Lisa Pamela Krop, June 28, 1981; 1 child, Adam Scott. AB, Johns Hopkins U., 1975; JD, U. Pa., 1978. Bar: N.J. 1978, U.S. Dist. Ct. N.J. 1978, Pa. 1978, Fla. 1980, U.S. Ct. Appeals (3d cir.) 1982. Law clk. to presiding judge U.S. Dist. Ct. (so. dist.), Miami, Fla., 1978-79; from assoc. to ptnr. Shanley & Fisher P.C., Morristown, N.J., 1979—, also bd. dirs. Trustee Integrity, Inc., Drug and Alcohol Abuse Program, Newark; trustee, mem. scholarship com. 200 Club of Somerset County. Mem. ABA, Fla. Bar Assn., N.J. Bar Assn., Morris County Bar Assn., Phi Beta Kappa. Avocations: skiing, sailing. Real property, Environmental. Home: 3 Cross Way Mendham NJ 07945-3120 Office: Shanley & Fisher PC 131 Madison Ave Morristown NJ 07960-6097

**PANTELOPOULOS, NICHOLAS EVAN,** lawyer; b. Athens, Greece, Oct. 21, 1964; came to U.S., 1970; s. Evan and Helene Pantelopoulos; m. Lea Trataros, June 27, 1993; children: Eleni, Athena. BS, U.S. Merchant Marine Acad., 1986; JD, Union U., 1990; LLM, Fordham U., 1991. Bar: Conn. 1990, N.Y. 1991, D.C. 1991, U.S. Dist. Ct. (no. dist.) N.Y. 1991, U.S. Dist. Ct. (so. and ea. dists.) N.Y. 1995, U.S. Ct. Appeals (2d cir.) 1996. Pvt. practice N.Y./Conn., 1991-95; atty. DeOrchis & Ptnrs., N.Y.C., 1995-97, Biedermann, Hoenig, Massamillo & Ruff, P.C., N.Y.C., 1997—. Mem. Maritime Law Assn. of U.S., N.Y. State Bar Assn. Avocations: sailing, traveling, photography. Aviation, Admiralty, General civil litigation. Home: 1322 Crown Ct Mamaroneck NY 10543-1220 Office: Biedermann Hoenig Massamillo & Ruff PC 90 Park Ave New York NY 10016-1301

**PAOLETTI, JODIE ANN,** lawyer; b. Phila., Apr. 16, 1959. BBA, Temple U., 1987, JD, 1992. Sr. atty. Mellon Bank, N.A., Phila., 1995—. Fax: 215-553-2598. E-mail: MELJAP@aol.com. Office: Mellon Bank NA 8th Fl 1735 Market St Fl 8 Philadelphia PA 19103-7501

**PAPADAKIS, MYRON PHILIP,** lawyer, educator, pilot; b. N.Y.C., Dec. 11, 1940; s. Philip E. and Helen (Eastman) P.; m. Ann Hall, Sept. 1968; children: Wade, Nicholas. BS in Mech. Engring., U. Nebr., 1963; JD, South Tex. Coll. Law, 1974. Bar: Tex. 1975. Pilot, capt. Delta Airlines, Houston, 1970—; pvt. practice Papadakis et al, Houston, 1975-90; of counsel Slack & Davis, Austin, Tex., 1994—; adj. prof. South Tex. Coll. Law, Houston, 1980—; labor law negotiator, airline negotiator. Co-author: Best of Trial-Products Liability, 1991, Aviation Accident Reconstruction and Litigation, 1995; contbr. articles to profl. jours. Lt. USN, 1963-69. Fellow Internat. Soc. Air Safety Investigators (chmn. ethics com. 1986-92); mem. Million Dollar Advocates Forum, ATLA (vice chmn. aviation sect.). Avocations: flying, test flying, photography, fishing. Aviation, Product liability. Office: Slack and Davis Ste 2110 8911 N Capital Of Texas Hwy Austin TX 78759-7200 Address: Papadakis Mp Attorney 5217 Old Spicewood Springs Rd Austin TX 78731-1000

**PAPANICKOLAS, EMMANUEL N.,** lawyer; b. Peabody, Mass., Mar. 19, 1934; s. Nicholas Emmanuel and Catina (Caroulias) P.; m. Georgia Kechris, Sept. 6, 1970; children: Nicholas Emmanuel, Crystal Catina. B.S., Suffolk U., Boston, 1952-59, J.D., 1960. Bar: Mass. 1960, U.S. Dist. Ct. Mass. 1963, U.S. Dist. Ct. R.I. 1974, U.S. Ct. Appeals 1978, U.S. Supreme Ct. 1983. Asst. city solicitor Peabody, Mass., 1962-67; pvt. practice Peabody, 1962—. Chmn. Citizens for Lower Taxes, 1970, Cystic Fibrosis Fund Dr., 1960, Heart Fund Dr., 1960; pres. PanSamian Soc., Pythagoras, 1960. Mem. Assn. Trial Lawyers Am., Mass. Bar Assn., Mass. Acad. Trial Lawyers, Essex Cty. Bar Assn., Peabody Bas Assn. Greek Orthodox. Avocation: boating, gardening/farming, classic literature, painting. Personal injury, Workers' compensation, Criminal. Home: 25 Farm Ave Peabody MA 01960-3901 Office: 16 Chestnut St Peabody MA 01960-5432

**PAPE, STUART M.,** lawyer; b. Paterson, N.J., Dec. 24, 1948. BA, U. Va., 1970, JD, 1973. Bar: Va. 1973, U.S. Ct. Appeals (6th cir.) 1975, U.S. Supreme Ct. 1976, D.C. 1980. Law clk. to Hon. Leonard Braman Superior Ct. D.C., 1973-74; exec. asst. to commr. FDA, 1979; mng. ptnr. Patton Boggs LLP and predecessors, Washington. Mem. ABA (com. food and drug law, sect. adminstrv. law 1973-92), Va. State Bar, D.C. Bar. Addresss: 2950 Chain Bridge Rd NW Washington DC 20016-3408

**PAPER, LEWIS J.,** lawyer, educator; b. Newark, Oct. 13, 1946; s. Sidney and Dorothy (Neiman) P.; m. Jan Clachko, Sept. 4, 1972; children—Lindsay, Brett. B.A., U. Mich., 1968; J.D., Harvard U., 1971; LL.M., Georgetown U., 1972. Bar: D.C. 1971, N.J. 1975, Md. 1984. Fellow, Inst. Pub. Interest Representation, Georgetown U. Law Sch., Washington, 1971-72; staff atty. Citizens Communications Ctr., Washington, 1972-73; legis. counsel to Sen. Gaylord Nelson, U.S. Senate, 1973-75; assoc. atty. Lowenstein, Sandler, Brochin, Kohl & Fisher, Newark, 1975-78; asst. gen. counsel Fed. Communications Commn., Washington, 1978-79, assoc. gen. counsel, 1979-81; ptnr. Grove, Engelberg & Gross, Washington, 1981-86, Keck, Mahin & Cate, 1986-95, Dickstein, Shapiro, Morin & Oshinsky LLP, Washington, 1995—; adj. prof. law Georgetown U. Law Sch., Washington, 1983-86. Author: John F. Kennedy: The Promise and the Performance, 1975, 79, Brandeis: An Intimate Biography, 1983, Empire: William S. Paley and the Making of CBS, 1987. Contbr. articles to newspapers, mags., and profl. jours. Administrative and regulatory, Federal civil litigation, State civil litigation. Office: Dickstein Shapiro Morin & Oshinsky LLP 2101 L St NW Washington DC 20037-1524

**PAPERNIK, JOEL IRA,** lawyer; b. N.Y.C., May 4, 1944; s. Herman and Ida (Titefsky) P.; m. Barbara Ann Barker, July 28, 1972; children: Deborah, Ilana. BA, Yale U., 1965; JD cum laude, Columbia U., 1968. Bar: N.Y. 1969. Assoc. Shea & Gould, N.Y.C., 1968-76, ptnr., 1976-91; ptnr., chmn. corp. and securities dept., mem. mgmt. com. Squadron, Ellenoff, Plesent & Sheinfeld, N.Y.C., 1991—; lectr. various panels. Author: Risks of Private Foreign Investments in the U.S. Served with 11th Spl. Forces, USAR, 1967-73. Mem. ABA (sect. on corp. law, mem. forum on sports and entertainment law), N.Y. State Bar Assn. (lectr. various panels, mem. securities law com.), Assn. of Bar of City of N.Y. (chmn., lectr., mem. corp. law com., mem. securities regulation com. 1992-95(, N.Y. Tri-Bar Opinion Com., Yale Club. General corporate, Securities, Entertainment. Office: Squadron Ellenoff Plesent & Sheinfeld 551 5th Ave Fl 22 New York NY 10176-0049

**PAPPACHEN, GEORGE V., JR.,** lawyer; b. Kerala, India, Mar. 4, 1970; came to the U.S., 1977; s. George V. and Rachel Pappachen; m. Rebekah Sheba Sebastian, June 25, 1994. AA in English Lit., Bob Jones U., 1990; BA in Polit. Sci., U. Fla., 1992; JD, St. John's U., Jamaica, N.Y., 1996. Bar: N.Y. 1997, U.S. Dist. Ct. (ea. and so. dists.) N.Y. 1997. Law clk. Walker & Hill, N.Y.C., 1992-93, Stairs, Dillenbeck, Kelly & Merle, N.Y.C., 1994-96; atty. Wilson Elser Moskowitz Edelman & Dicker, N.Y.C., 1996-98, Fager & Amsler, N.Y.C., 1998—; with Swoorgeeya Dwoni Internat. Literary Firm, Kerala, India. Chief editor (newsletter) Our Times, 1995—. Pres. Pentecostal Youth Fellowship Am., N.Y.,. 1999—; trustee India Charity Fund, N.Y., 1995—. Recipient Am. Jurisprudence award Lawyers Coop., N.Y.C., 1995; Merit scholar Pace U., White Plains, N.Y., 1994. Mem. ABA, N.Y. State Bar Assn., N.Y. County Lawyers Assn., Assn. of the Bar of the City of N.Y. Republican. Pentecostal. Avocations: basketball, tennis, reading, writing. Health, Insurance, General civil litigation. Office: Fager & Amsler 2 Park Ave New York NY 10016-5675

**PAPPAS, CHRIS,** lawyer; b. Bklyn., Oct. 14, 1928; s. Peter Christos and Calliopi Pappas; children: Peter, Nikos, Yannis. BS, Ithaca Coll., 1950; LLB, Bklyn. Law Sch., 1956. Bar: N.Y. 1957, U.S. Dist. Ct. Ct., U.S. Ct. Appeals, U.S. Supreme Ct. 1967. Ptnr. Pappas & Pappas, N.Y.C., 1957-87; pvt. practice Chris Pappas & Assocs., N.Y.C., 1987-97; sr. atty. Marulli Pewarski & Heubel, P.C., N.Y.C., 1997—. Lt. U.S. Army, 1950-53. Decorated Bronze star with oak leaf cluster; recipient Medal of Excellence King of Greece, 1953. Personal injury. Office: Marulli Pewarski & Heubel PC 115 Broadway New York NY 10006-1604

**PAPPAS, DANIEL C.,** lawyer; b. Lincoln, Nebr., Dec. 30, 1948; s. Harry and Margy Margaret Pappas; m. Constance Anne Fouts; children: Allison, Emily, Elizabeth, Rebecca. BS, U. Nebr., 1971; JD, South Tex. Coll. Law, 1974. Bar: Tex. 1974. Assoc. Williams, Kissner et al, Houston, 1974-75, Leo A. Kissner & Assocs., Houston, 1975-80; ptnr. Kissner & Pappas P.C., Houston, 1980-86; prin. Daniel C. Pappas, P.C., Houston, 1986—. Inspector of elections State of Tex.; chmn. sch. bd. St. Agnes Acad., Houston; pres. parish coun. St. Alberts Ch., Houston; pres. Northbrook MUD, Houston. Fellow Houston Bar Assn.; mem. ABA, Coll. of State Bar. Republican. Roman Catholic. General civil litigation, Contracts commercial. Office: Daniel C Pappas PC 4615 Southwest Fwy Ste 600 Houston TX 77027-7106

**PAPPAS, DAVID CHRISTOPHER,** lawyer; b. Kenosha, Wis., Mar. 18, 1936; s. Theros and Marion Lucille (Piperas) P.; m. Laurie Jean Lacaskey, Nov. 26, 1956 (div. 1969); children— Christopher David, Andrea Lynn; m. Nancy Marie Pratt, June 11, 1983. B.S., U. Wis., 1959, S.J.D., 1961. Licensed master mariner. Bar: Wis. 1961, U.S. Dist. Ct. (ea. and we. dists.) Wis. 1965, U.S. Supreme Ct. 1971. Asst. corp. counsel Racine County, Wis., 1961; atty., adviser U.S. Dept. Labor, Washington, 1961-62; staff atty. U.S. Commn. Civil Rights, Washington, 1962-63; asst. city atty. City of Madison, Wis., 1963-65; sole practice, Madison, 1965—. Chmn. Madison Mayor's Citizen Adv. Com., 1964-65; pres. Wis. Cup Assn., Madison, 1965; co-chmn. 2d Congl. Dist. Humphrey for Pres., Madison, 1972. Recipient commendation for Supreme Ct. work Madison City Coun., 1965, commendation resolution City of Madison, 1965. Mem. Wis. Bar Assn., Dane County Bar Assn., Wis. Acad. Trial Lawyers, Am. Assn. Trial Lawyers, Lawyer-Pilot Bar Assn. (master mariner), Gt. Lakes Hist. Soc. Republican. Clubs: Madison; South Shore Yacht (Milw.). *Mr. Pappas was profiled in Madison Magazine, 1988. He is an international sailor, having made small boat crossings of the Atlantic, Pacific, and Indian Oceans with a rounding of Cape Horn east to west. He is a member of the Association of Cape Horners - London and a holder of a commercial pilot's license with instrument and multi-engine ratings. He is also an oil painter with works dispalyed throughout the country. Significant cases include declaring unconstitutional the abortion law in Wisconsin, establishing parity between men and women in divorce property division cases* General civil litigation, General practice, Family and matrimonial. Home and Office: 1787 Strawberry Rd Deerfield WI 53531-9779

**PAPPAS, EDWARD HARVEY,** lawyer; b. Midland, Mich., Nov. 24, 1947; s. Charles and Sydell (Sheinberg) P.; m. Laurie Weston, Aug. 6, 1972; children: Gregory Alan, Steven Michael. BBA, U. Mich., 1969, JD, 1973. Bar: Mich. 1973, U.S. Dist. Ct. (ea. dist.) Mich. 1973, U.S. Dist. Ct. (we. dist.) Mich. 1980, U.S. Ct. Appeals (6th cir.) 1983, U.S. Supreme Ct. 1983. Ptnr. firm Dickinson & Wright, P.L.L.C., Detroit and Bloomfield Hi, Mich., 1973—; mediator Oakland County Cir. Ct., Pontiac, Mich., 1983—; hearing panelist Mich. Atty. Discipline Bd., Detroit, 1983—, chmn., 1987—; mem. bus. tort subcom. Mich. Supreme Ct. Com. Standard Jury Instructions, 1992-94; bd. commrs. State Bar Mich., 1999—. Trustee Oakland Community Coll., Mich., 1982-90, Oakland-Livingston Legal Aid, 1982-90, v.p., 1982-85, pres., 1985-87; trustee, adv. bd. Mich. Regional Anti-Defamation League of B'nai B'rith, Detroit, 1983-90; planning commr. Village of Franklin, Mich., 1987-91, chmn. 1989-91, councilman, 1991-92, chmn. charter com., 1993-94; chmn. State Bar Mich. Long Range Planning com.; pres.-elect Oakland County Bar Assn., 1996-97, pres., 1997-98, chmn. Jud. Selection Task Force, 1997; bd. dirs. Franklin Found., 1989-92; trustee The Oakland Medication Ctr., 1992-96. Master Oakland County Bar Assn. Inn of Ct.; fellow Mich. State Bar Found., Oakland Bar-Adams Pratt Found., ABA Found.; mem. ABA, Fed. Bar Assn., State Bar Mich. (co-chmn. nat. moot ct. competition com. 1974, 76, com. on legal aid, chmn. standing com. on atty. grievances 1989-92, comml. litigation com., civil procedure com. 1992-94, bd. commrs. 1999—), Oakland County Bar Assn. (vice-chmn. continuing legal edn. com., chmn. continuing legal edn. com. 1985-86, mediation com. 1989-90, chmn. mediation com. 1990-91, bd. dirs. 1990-98, chmn. select com. Oakland County cir. ct. settlement week 1991, chmn. strategic planning com. 1992-93, editor Laches monthly mag. 1986-88, co-chair task force to improve justice systems in Oakland County 1993—, pres.-elect, bd. dirs. 1996-97, pres. 1997-98), Am. Judicature Soc., Mich. Def. Trial Lawyers, Def. Rsch. and Trial Lawyers Assn. (com. practice and procedure), B'nai B'rith Barristers. Federal civil litigation, State civil litigation. Home: 32223 Scenic Ln Franklin MI 48025-1702 Office: Dickinson Wright Moon Van Dusen & Freeman 525 N Woodward Ave Bloomfield Hills MI 48304-2971

**PAPPAS, GEORGE FRANK,** lawyer; b. Washington, Oct. 5, 1950; s. Frank George and Lora Marie (Stauber) P.; m. Susan Elizabeth Bradshaw, Apr. 25, 1980; children: Christine Bradshaw, Alexandra Stauber. BA, U. Md., 1972, JD, 1975. Bar: Md. 1976, D.C. 1991, U.S. Dist. Ct. Md. 1976, U.S. Dist. Ct. (D.C. cir.) 1986, U.S. Dist. Ct. (we. dist.) Tex. 1993, U.S. Ct. Appeals (4th cir.) 1976, U.S. Ct. Appeals (D.C. cir.) 1984, U.S. Ct. Appeals (fed. cir.) 1991, U.S. Ct. Appeals (2d cir.) 1993, U.S. Ct. Appeals (6th and 7th cirs.) 1994, U.S. Supreme Ct. 1984, U.S. Ct. of Fed. Claims, 1995. Assoc. H. Russell Smouse, Balt., 1976-81; assoc. Melnicove, Kaufman, Wiener & Smouse, Balt., 1981-83, prin., 1983-88; ptnr. Venable, Baetjer and Howard, Balt., 1988—; lectr. Wash. Coll. Law, Am. U., Washington, 1980-84; mem. moot ct. bd., 1974-75; Master of the Bench , Inn XIII, Am. Inns of Ct., 1989. Founding editor-in-chief Internat. Trade Law Jour., 1974-75. 1st lt. USAF, 1972-76. Mem. ABA, Nat. Assn. R.R. Trial Counsel, Internat. Assn. Def. Counsel, Md. Bar Assn. (chmn. internat. coml. law sect., 1980-81), Am. Intellectual Property Law Assn., U.S. Trademark Assn., Omicron Delta Kappa, Phi Kappa Phi, Phi Beta Kappa. Republican. Greek Orthodox. Club: L'Hirondelle. Federal civil litigation, State civil litigation, Intellectual property. Home: 9 Roland Ct Baltimore MD 21204-3550 Office: Venable Baetjer & Howard 2 Hopkins Plz Ste 2100 Baltimore MD 21201-2982 also: 1201 New York Ave NW Ste 1000 Washington DC 20005-6197

**PAPROCKI, THOMAS JOHN,** lawyer, priest; b. Chgo., Aug. 5, 1952; s. John Henry and Veronica Mary (Bonat) P. BA, Loyola U., Chgo., 1974; student Spanish lang. study, Middlebury Coll., 1976, student Italian lang. study, 1987; M in Divinity, St. Mary of the Lake Sem., 1978; student Spanish lang. study, Instituto Cuannahuac, 1978; Licentiate in Sacred Theology, St. Mary of the Lake Sem., 1979; JD, DePaul U., 1981; JCD, Gregorian U., Rome, 1991. Bar: Ill. 1981, U.S. Dist. Ct. (no. dist.) Ill. 1981, U.S. Supreme Ct. 1994. Assoc. pastor St. Michael Ch., Chgo., 1978-83; pres. Chgo. Legal Clinic, 1981-87, 91—; exec. dir. South Chgo. Legal Clinic, 1981-85, bd. dirs., 1987—; adminstr. St. Joseph Ch., Chgo., 1983-86; vice-chancellor Archdiocese of Chgo., 1985-92, chancellor, 1992-99; adj. faculty Loyola U. of Law, 1999—; senator Presbyteral senate Archdiocese of Chgo., 1985-87, mem. Presbyteral coun., 1992—, mem. Cardinal's cabinet, 1992—, sec. coll. consultors, 1992—; chmn. incardination com., 1991—, chmn. policy devel. com., 1998—, chmn. Fgn. Priests Initiative, 1998—; asst. to the Gen. Sec., Vatican Synod of Bishops, Spl. Assembly for Am., Rome, 1997; bd. dirs. Cath. Conf. Ill., 1985-87; adj. faculty Loyola U. Sch. Law, 1999—. Editorial Adv. Bd. Chicago Catholic Newspaper, 1984-85; contbr. articles to profl. jours. Bd. dirs. United Neighborhood Orgn., Chgo., 1982-85, S.E. Community Youth Svc. Bd., Chgo., 1985, Ctr. for Neighborhood Tech., Chgo., 1986-87, Chgo. Area Found. for Legal Svcs., 1994—; active Chgo. Cmty. Trust Com. on Children, Youth and Families, 1991—, Ill. Family Violence Coordinating Coun., 1994—. Recipient Humanitarian award Polish Am. Congress, 1997; named Man of Yr., Nat. Advs., 1999. Fellow Leadership Greater Chgo.; mem. Ill. Bar Assn., Chgo. Bar Assn. (bd. mgrs. 1999—, Maurice Weigle award 1985), Advs. Soc. (award of merit 1996), Cath. Lawyers Guild, Polish Am. Assn. (bd. dirs. 1998—), The Chgo. Jr. Assn. Commerce and Industry (Ten Outstanding Young Citizens award 1986), Union League Club of Chgo., Pi Sigma Alpha, DePaul U. Alumni Assn. Avocations: hockey, running, reading. Immigration, naturalization, and customs, Non-profit and tax-exempt organizations. Home: 730 N Wabash Ave Chicago IL 60611-2514 Office: Archdiocese of Chgo PO Box 1979 155 E Superior St Chicago IL 60611-2911

**PAQUETTE, STEVEN A.,** lawyer; b. Westport, N.Y., Nov. 30, 1955; s. Ronald A. and Mildred Paquette; m. Cynthia J. Sardino, Sept. 18, 1982; children: Aimee, Sarah, Chelsea. BS in Journalism, Syracuse U., N.Y., 1977, JD, 1979. Bar: N.Y. 1979, U.S. Dist. Ct. (no. dist.) N.Y. 1980, U.S. Dist. Ct. (we. dist.) N.Y. 1986, U.S. Supreme Ct. 1986. Atty. Meggesto Paquette Badera, Syracuse, N.Y., 1979-86, Sardino Paquette, Syracuse, N.Y., 1986—, N.Y. State Dept. Taxation, Syracuse, 1985-91, N.Y. State Assembly, Albany, 1995—; chair Dem. Party Onondaga Cty., Syracuse, 1993—. Mem. alumni bd. Delta Tau Delta Fraternity, Indpls., 1981—; mem. parish coun. St. Michael's Ch., Syracuse, N.Y., 1994—. Mem. N.Y. State Bar Assn., Onondaga Cty. Bar Assn. Democrat. Roman Catholic. Criminal, General civil litigation, General practice. Office: Sardino & Paquette 217 Montgomery St Ste 504 Syracuse NY 13202-1948

**PAQUIN, JEFFREY DEAN,** lawyer; b. Milw., Dec. 7, 1960; s. James DeWayne and Helen Ann (Walter) P. BA, U. Wis., 1983; JD, U. Ky., 1986. Bar: Ga. 1986, U.S. Dist. Ct. (no. dist.) Ga. 1986, U.S. Ct. Appeals (11th cir.) 1986, U.S. Dist. Ct. (mid. dist.) Ga. 1987, D.C. 1989, U.S. Ct. Appeals (D.C. cir.) 1989, U.S. Supreme Ct. 1990. Assoc. Powell, Goldstein, Frazer & Murphy, Atlanta, 1986-94; chief litigation counsel United Parcel Svc., Atlanta, 1994-98; nat. practice leader ADR and litig. mgmt. Price Waterhouse, Atlanta, 1998; nat. practice leader Legal Mgmt. Svcs. Ernst & Young, LLP, Atlanta, 1998—; v.p. Prodn. Values, Inc., Atlanta, 1987-88. Exec. editor U. Ky. Law Rev., 1985-86. Bd. dirs. Children's Motility Disorder Found., 1995—. Mem. ABA, ATLA (assoc.), FBA, Nat. Inst. Dispute Resolution, Am. Corp. Counsel Assn. (bd. dirs. Ga. 1997-98), D.C. Bar Assn., Ga. Bar Assn., Atlanta Bar Assn. (v.p., dir. alternative dispute resolution sect.), Ga. Trial Lawyers Assn., Mortar Board, Phi Delta Phi, Sigma Epsilon Sigma, Psi Chi. Roman Catholic. General civil litigation, Federal civil litigation, State civil litigation. Home: 2100 Glenridge Ct Marietta GA 30062-1879 Office: Ernst & Young LLP 600 Peachtree St Ste 2800 Atlanta GA 30308-2215

**PAQUIN, THOMAS CHRISTOPHER,** lawyer; b. Quincy, Mass., Feb. 12, 1947; s. Henry Frederick and Rita Marie (St. Louis) P.; m. Jean Jacqueline O'Neill, Aug. 5, 1972; children: Martha, Edward. BS in Acctg., Bentley Coll., 1969; JD, U. Notre Dame, 1974. Bar: Mass. 1974, U.S. Dist. Ct. Mass. 1976. Tax atty. Coopers and Lybrand, Boston, 1974-76; assoc. Cargill, Masterman & Cahill, Boston, 1976, Wilson, Curran & Malkasian, Wellesley, Mass., 1976-77; ptnr. Bianchi and Paquin, Hyannis, Mass., 1977-98; shareholder, dir. Quirk and Chamberlain, P.C., Yarmouthport, Mass., 1998—; bd. dirs., chmn. nominating com. Elder Svcs. Cape Cod and Islands, Inc., Dennis, Mass., 1986-91; bd. dirs., corporator Vis. Nurse Assn. Cape Cod Found., Inc., Dennis, 1988-97; pres. Life Svcs. Inc., 1991-95; bd. dirs. Woodside Cemetery Corp. Mem. Bass River Golf Commn., Yarmouth, Mass., 1980-83, chmn., 1982-83; chmn. Yarmouth Golf Course Bldg. Com., 1985-89; mem. hearing com. bd. Bar Overseers of the Supreme Jud. Ct., 1989-95; bd. dirs. Project Coach, Inc., 1990-97; conciliator Barnstable Superior Ct., 1992—. Fellow Mass. Bar Found.; mem. ABA, Mass. Bar Assn. (del. 1986-87, mem. com. on bicentennial U.S. Constn. 1986-88, fee arbitration bd. 1985-86, chmn. spkrs. and writers subcom. 1986-88), Barnstable County Bar Assn. (chmn. seminar com. 1979-83, mem. exec. com. 1981-84, v.p. 1984-86, pres. 1986-87), Estate Planning Coun. Cape Cod (exec. com. 1985-98, sec. 1991-93, pres.-elect 1993-95, pres. 1995-97), Mass. Conveyancers Assn., Mid-Cape Men's Club (v.p. 1992, pres. 1993), Cummaquid Golf Club. Probate, Real property, Estate planning. Office: Quirk and Chamberlain PC PO Box 40 Yarmouth Port MA 02675-0040

**PARA, GERARD ALBERT,** lawyer, real estate broker, consultant; b. Oak Park, Ill., June 27, 1953; s. Bruno Joseph and Bernice Agnes Para; m. Gayle Louise Keegan, Sept. 15, 1979; children; Eric, Teresa. BA with honor, De Paul U., 1973, JD, 1976. Bar: Ill. 1977, U.S. Dist. Ct. (no. dist.) Ill. 1977, U.S. Ct. Appeals (7th cir.) 1977, Fed. Trial Bar. 1984; lic. real estate broker, Ill. Jud. law clk. Ill Appellate Ct. (1st dist.), Chgo., 1977-78; divsnl. counsel Household Internat. Franchisor Divsns., Prospect Heights, Ill., 1978-85; v.p. Bannockburn (Ill.) Pk. Concepts, Inc., 1986-93; dir. real estate ops., asst. gen. counsel Ben Franklin Stores, Carol Stream, Ill., 1994-96; v.p., gen. counsel DiMucci Devel. Corp., Palatine, Ill., 1996-97; gen. counsel Urban Investment Trust Inc., Chgo., 1998—; real estate broker, Long Grove, Ill., 1983—; franchise cons. Elliotts' Off Broadway Deli, Oak Brook, Ill., 1993—. Editor: Medical Malpractice, 1975, Trial Technique, 1975. Asst. coach Little League Buffalo Grove (Ill.) Recreation Assn., 1988—; asst. scoutmaster Boy Scouts Am., Long Grove, 1995—. Mem. ABA, Internat. Coun. Shopping Ctrs., Internat. Corp. Real Estate Execs., Chgo. Bar Assn., Internat. Franchise Assn. Roman Catholic. Avocations: lap swimming, boating, scuba diving, weightlifting. Real property, Franchising, General corporate. Office: Urban Investment Trust Inc 401 N Michigan Ave Chicago IL 60611-4255

**PARADISO, F. JOSEPH,** lawyer; b. Stafford, Conn., Jan. 17, 1935; s. Joseph and Rachele Paradiso; m. Donna Rae Pitkat, Dec. 14, 1970; children: Joseph J., Christopher M., Rachel M. BS, Holy Cross Coll., 1956; JD, Georgetown U., 1959. Asst. state's atty. State of Conn., Rockville, 1962-92, supervisory state's atty., 1990-92; sr. ptnr. Paradisco and Muska, Stafford Springs, Conn., 1992—; corporator Stafford Savs. Bank, 1962—; adv. bd. Stafford Human Svcs., 1993—. Mem. Stafford Bd. of Edn., 1998—; v.p. Dollars for Scholars, Stafford, 1970—; mem. Ct. of Burgess Boro of Stafford Springs, 1960-61. With Army Res. 1959-64. Mem. Rotary Club, K.C., Stafford Fish and Game Club, Conn. Bar Assn. Republican. Roman Catholic. General practice, Real property, State civil litigation. Office: Paradiso & Muska 2 E Main St # 22 Stafford Springs CT 06076-1206

**PARAN, MARK LLOYD,** lawyer; b. Cleve., Feb. 1, 1953; s. Edward Walter and Margaret Gertrude (Ebert) P. AB cum laude in Sociology, Harvard U., 1977, JD, 1980. Bar: Ill. 1980, Mass. 1986, Tex. 1993. Assoc. Wilson & McIlvaine, Chgo., 1980-83, Lurie Sklar & Simon, Ltd., Chgo., 1983-85, Sullivan & Worcester, Boston, 1985-92; pvt. practice, Boston, 1992; pvt. practice, Euless, Tex., 1992—. Mem. ABA, State Bar Tex. Avocations: tornado hunting, observation of severe thunderstorms, photography. Real property, Finance, Securities. Home and Office: 1050 W Ash Ln Apt 1015 Euless TX 76039-2171

**PARANZINO, MICHAEL,** legislative staff member; b. Phila., Feb. 18, 1966; m. Heather Cameron. BA, Yale U., 1988; JD, NYU, 1991. Bar: Ariz. 1991. Atty. Brown & Bain, P.A., Phoenix, 1991-94; rsch. dir. Jon Kyl for U.S. Senate, Phoenix, 1994; legis. dir., press sect. Hon. Matt Salmon, Washington, 1995-97, chief of staff, 1997—. Vol. Salmon for Congress, Ariz. and D.C., 1994, 96, 98. Republican. Roman Catholic. E-mail: mike.paranzino@mail.house.gov.

**PARDIECK, ROGER LEE,** lawyer; b. Seymour, Ind., Mar. 1, 1937; s. Martin W. and Lorna (Wente) P.; m. Mary Ann Purdieck; children: Amy, Andrew, Melissa Duncan. AB, Ind. U., 1959, LLB, 1963. Bar: Ind. 1963, U.S. Dist. Ct. (so. dist.) Ind. 1964, U.S. Ct. Appeals (7th cir.) 1965; diplomate Am. Bd. Trial Advocates. Tchg. asst. Ind. U., Bloomington, 1963-64; spl. prosecutor Jackson County, Ind., 1964-65; ptnr. Montgomery, Elsner and Pardieck, 1965-84; prin. Pardieck, Gill Vargo & MacTavish, PC, Seymour, Ind., 1985—; faculty Nat. Inst. Trial Advocacy, Ind.; lectr. in field. Contbr. articles to profl. jours. Bd. dirs. Seymour Girls Club, 1968-72, Seymour C. of C., 1971-75; bd. dirs. Luth. Comty. Home, 1964-82, pres., 1970; trustee Immanuel Luth. Ch., 1977-80, bd. Immanuel Luth. Sch., 1980-83; adv. bd. Ind. U., Purdue U.-Indpls., 1981-83. Fellow Am. Coll. Trial Lawyers, Ind. Trial Lawyers Assn. (bd. dirs. 1969—, pres. 1975); mem. FBA, ATLA (bd. govs. 1985-88), Ind. State Bar Assn. (bd. govs. 1980-82), Inst. for Injury Reduction (bd. dirs. 1992-95), Nat. Bd. Trial Advocacy, Safety Attys. Fedn. (bd. dirs. 1993-95), Internat. Soc. Primerus Law Firms (bd. dirs. 1995—), Am. Judicature Soc., Inner Cir. Advocates. Personal injury, Federal civil litigation, State civil litigation. Office: 100 N Chestnut St PO Box 608 Seymour IN 47274-0608 also Address: 244 N College Ave Indianapolis IN 46202-3702

**PARDUE, WALLACE DAVID, JR.,** lawyer; b. Bristol, Va., June 30, 1947; s. Wallace D. and Lois B. Pardue; m. Suzanne Pardue, Apr. 19, 1972; children: Joel, Blake, Logan. BA, U. Okla., 1969, JD, 1972. Bar: Okla. 1972. Pvt. practice Oklahoma City, 1972-98; ptnr. Eagleton Nicholson Pordos & Pardue P.C., Oklahoma City, 1998—. Vol. atty. Okla. Lawyers for Children, 1998. Mem. Mens Dinner Club. Presbyterian. General corporate, Consumer commercial, Oil, gas, and mineral. Office: Eagleton Nicholson Pordos 228 Robert S Kerr Ave Oklahoma City OK 73102-5201

**PARIENTE, BARBARA J.,** judge; m. Frederick A. Hazouri. Grad. with high honors, Boston U., 1970; JD with highest honors, George Washington U., 1973. Bar: Fla. 1973; cert. civil trial lawyer Fla. Bar; cert. Nat. Bd. Trial Advocacy. Law clk. to hon. Norman C. Roettger, Jr. U.S. Dist. Ct. (so. dist.) Fla., 1973-75; ptnr. Cone Wagner Nugent, 1975-83, Pariente & Silber, P.A., 1983; pvt. practice; judge U.S. Ct. of Appeals (4th dist.), 1993-97; justice Fla. Supreme Ct., Tallahassee, 1997—; participant Twenty-First Century Justice Conf.; mem. Judicial Cir. Grievance Com., 1989-92, chair, 1990-92; mem. nominating com. U.S. Ct. Appeals (15th cir.), 1980-84. Contbr. articles to profl. jours. Bd. dirs. Fla. Bar Found.; mentor Take Stock in Children; active Palm Beach County Youth Ct. program, 1997, Cities in Schs. mentoring program, 1993, Temple Judea, Palm Beach County Sephardi Fedn., Jewish Cmty. Ctr., Ballet Fla., Palm Beach County Commn. on Status of Women. Recipient award for disting. svc. to the arts Palm Beach County Bar Assn., 1987, Civil Litigation Pro Bono award Legal Aid Soc., 1993. Mem. ABA, Nat. Assn. Women Judges, Am. Inns. of Ct. (founding mem. Palm Beach County chpt.), Acad. Fla. Trial Lawyers (bd. dirs., chair Spkr.'s Bur. program 1984-87, outreach com. 1991-92, co-chair Workhorse Seminar 1991-92), Assn. Trial Lawyers Am. (vice chair profl. rsch. and devel. dept. 1980-82, chair comml. litigation sect. 1984-85, women's trial lawyer caucus 1986-87; mem. ethics com. 1989-90, conv. planning com. 1992-93), Fla. Assn. Women Lawyers. Office: 500 S Duval St Tallahassee FL 32399-6556*

**PARIS, TIMOTHY JOHN,** lawyer, history educator; b. Hammond, Ind., May 7, 1954; s. Lloyd Harold and Evelyn Kaye P.; m. Linda Annette Davis, Aug. 1, 1987. Student, U. St. Andrews, Scotland, 1974-75; BA, Duke U., 1976; JD, Ind. U., 1979; PhD, Cambridge (Eng.) U., 1997. Bar: Calif. 1979, Ariz. 1980, Ind. 1987, U.S. Ct. Appeals (9th cir.) 1979, U.S. Dist. Ct. (ctrl. dist.) Calif. 1979, U.S. Ct. Appeals (3d cir.) 1992, U.S. Dist. Ct. (so. dist.) Ind. 1997. Atty. Thomas, Shafran, Wasser & Childs, L.A., 1980-86; gen. counsel Nat. Property Devel. Corp., Indpls., 1986-90; of counsel Plews, Shadley, Racher & Braun, Indpls., 1990-93, 96—; adj. prof. history Ind. U., Indpls., 1998—. Contbr. articles to profl. jours. Mem. Phi Beta Kappa. Avocations: scuba diving, bicycling, skiing, history. General civil litigation, Environmental, Real property. Office: Plews Shadley Racher & Braun 1346 N Delaware St Indianapolis IN 46202-2415

**PARISH, JAMES RILEY,** lawyer; b. Greenville, S.C., Apr. 21, 1950; s. John James and Martha (Greene) P.; married; 1 child, Katharine S. BA in Polit. Sci., Davidson Coll., 1972; JD, Wake Forest U., 1976. Bar: N.C. 1976, U.S. Dist. Ct. (ea. dist.) N.C. 1981, U.S. Ct. Appeals (4th cir.) 1981. Asst. pub. defender Fayetteville, N.C., 1976-82; lawyer Parish Law Office, Fayetteville, 1982-87; ptnr. Parish Cooke & Weeks, Fayetteville, 1987-89, Parish Cooke & Russ, Fayetteville, 1989-95, Parish Cooke Russ & Bullard, Fayetteville, 1996—; tchr. constl. law Webster U., Fayetteville, 1980-86. Avocations: racquetball, scuba, snorkeling, tennis. Criminal, Appellate. Office: Parish Cooke Russ & Bullard 343 Person St Fayetteville NC 28301-5735

**PARK, KELLEY BARRETT,** lawyer; b. Indpls., Feb. 18, 1968; d. Charles Ronald and Cathy Lee (Pace) Barrett; m. Randall Alan Park, May 29, 1993; 1 child, Samantha Cadian. BA, U. Ga., 1990, JD. Atty. Wiggins & Camp, Carrollton, Ga., 1993-96; corp. atty. Southwire Co., Carrollton, 1996—. Mem. Kiwanis Club. Labor, Pension, profit-sharing, and employee benefits, General corporate. Office: Southwire Co One Southwire Dr Carrollton GA 30119

**PARK, SANG HYUK,** lawyer; b. L.A., June 5, 1968; s. Soo Gil Park and Jung Ja Suh. BA, U. Chgo., 1990; JD, Cornell U., 1993. Bar: N.Y. 1996. Fgn. legal cons. Kim & Chang, Seoul, Rep. of Korea, 1993-96; assoc. Dechert, Price & Rhoads, N.Y.C., 1996—. Mem. Bar Assn. City of N.Y. Avocations: golf, travel, poetry, movies. Mergers and acquisitions, Securities, General corporate. Office: Dechert Price & Rhoads 30 Rockefeller Plz Fl 22 New York NY 10112-2200

**PARK, WILLIAM WYNNEWOOD,** law educator; b. Philadelphia, Pa., July 2, 1947; s. Oliver William and Christine (Lindes) P. BA, Yale U., 1969; JD, Columbia U., 1972; MA, Cambridge U., 1975. Bar: Mass. 1972, D.C. 1980. Law practice Paris, 1972-79; prof. law Boston U., 1979—; counsel Ropes & Gray, Boston; v.p. London Ct. Internat. Arbitration; dir. Boston U. Ctr. Banking Law Studies, 1990-93; vis. prof. U. Dijon, France, 1983-84, Inst. U. Hautes Etudes Internat., Geneva, 1983, U. Hong Kong, 1990; fellow Selwyn Coll., Cambridge, Eng., 1975-77; arbitrator Claims Resolution Tribunal for Dormant Accts., Switzerland. Author: International Chamber of Commerce Arbitration, 1984, 2d edit., 1990, International Forum Selection, 1995, International Commercial Arbitration, 1997, Annotated Guide to the 1998 ICC Arbitration Rules, 1998, Arbitration in Banking and Finance, 1998; contbr. articles and book revs. to profl. jours. Trustee Mass. Bible Soc. Fellow Chartered Inst. Arbitrators (mem. Register). Home: 36 King St Cohasset MA 02025-1304 Office: Boston U Law Sch 765 Commonwealth Ave Boston MA 02215-1401 also: Ropes and Gray 1 International Pl Boston MA 02110-2602

**PARKER, BRET I.,** lawyer; b. N.Y.C., 1968; m. Katharine; 1 child, Matthew. BA, U. Pa., 1990; JD, Fordham U., 1993. Bar: N.Y. 1994, U.S. Dist. Ct. (so. dist.) N.Y., U.S. Dist. Ct. (ea. dist.) N.Y. Law clk. to Hon. K. Michael Moore U.S. Dist. Ct. (so. dist.) Fla., Miami, 1993-94; assoc. Townley & Updike, N.Y.C., 1994-95, Dorsey & Whitney, N.Y.C., 1995-97; sr. atty. Colgate-Palmolive Co., N.Y.C., 1997—. Mem. Internat. Trademarks Assn. (mem. editl. bd. Trademark Reporter 1995—), N.Y.C. Bar Assn. (mem. com. trademarks and unfair competition 1996—). Trademark and copyright, Intellectual property, Private international. Office: Colgate-Palmolive Co 300 Park Ave Fl 8 New York NY 10022-7499

**PARKER, CATHERINE MARIE,** lawyer; b. Thorigni, France, July 4, 1959; came to U.S., 1989; d. Raymond Antoine and Arlette Marie (Laurent) Delarbre; m. Jon Elliott Parker, Jan. 7, 1989; 1 child, William Jacques. JD, U. Paris-Pantheon-Sorbonne, 1980, LLM, 1984. Bar: Paris 1981, Calif. 1990, U.S. Dist. Ct. (ctrl. dist.) Calif. 1990, U.S. Dist. Ct. (no. and so. dist.) Calif. 1991. Atty. Bar Assn. of Paris, 1981-85; counsel/gen. counsel Bail-Equipment, Paris, 1985-89; assoc. Mayer Brown & Platt, L.A., 1990-91, Law Office of Albert S. Golbert, L.A., 1991-92, Pircher Nichols & Meeks, L.A., 1992-95; of counsel Golbert & Assocs., L.A., 1995—. Mem. State Bar of Calif. (advisor 1984-85, exec. com. internat. law sect.), L.A. County Bar Assn. Private international, General corporate, Immigration, naturalization, and customs. Office: Golbert & Assocs 601 W 5th St Los Angeles CA 90071-2004

**PARKER, CHARLES EDWARD,** lawyer; b. Santa Ana, Calif., Sept. 9, 1927; s. George Ainsworth and Dorothy P.; m. Marilyn Esther Perrin, June 23, 1956; children—Mary, Catherine, Helen, George. Student, Santa Ana Coll., U. So. Calif.; J.D., S.W. U.-La. Bar: Calif. 1958, U.S. Dist. Ct. (cen. dist.) Calif. 1958, U.S. Supreme Ct. 1969, D.C. 1971, U.S. Dist. Ct. (no. and so. dists.) Calif. 1981. Prof. law Western State U., Fullerton, Calif., 1973-83; spl. counsel Tidelands, First Am. Title Co., 1980-82; dir. First Am. Fin. Corp., 1981-82. Served to sgt. U.S. Army, 1951-53. Author: (book) Tidelands and The Public Trust, 1991. Mem. ABA (com. improvement land records, sect. real property, mem. com. on title ins. sect. real property), Orange County Bar Assn., Calif. Bar Assn., D.C. Bar Assn. Club: Santa Ana Kiwanis, Lodge: Elks (Santa Ana). Contbr. articles in field to profl. jours. Real property. Office: 18101 Charter Rd Orange CA 92861-2638

**PARKER, CHERIE A.,** lawyer, city councilman; b. St. Petersburg, Fla., Mar. 20, 1951; d. James Moreau and Cornelia Anne (Daly) P.; m. Jerome Jay Weiland, Jan. 1, 1990. BA in English, U. Calif., Berkeley, 1973; JD, U. Calif., San Francisco, 1978. Bar: Calif. 1979, Fla. 1980, Ill. 1989; cert. mediator, Fla. Trial atty. Pub. Defender's Office, San Francisco, 1977-80, Parker & Parker, St. Petersburg, Fla., 1980-82, Defenders, Inc., San Diego, 1982-85; ptnr. Law Offices of C.A. Parker, Santa Ana, Calif., 1985-88; assoc. Goldberg & Goldberg, Chgo., 1989-92, Merkle & Magri, P.A., Tampa, Fla., 1992-96; assoc., ptnr. Parker & Hafner, P.A., Largo, Fla., 1996—; cert. cir. civil mediator Fla. Supreme Ct., 1996—. Author: Extradiction Handbook, 1978. Mem. ABA, ATLA, Acad. Fla. Trial Lawyers, Fla. Bar Assn. (consumer protection com. 1996—), Clearwater Bar Assn. (arbitrator and mediator com. 1996—), Fla. Assn. Women Lawyers. Republican. Avocations: tennis, skiing, windsurfing, piano, chess. Home: PO Box 1692 Clearwater FL 33757-1692 Office: Parker & Hafner PA 2050 W Bay Dr Largo FL 33770-1927

**PARKER, CHRISTOPHER LEE,** lawyer; b. Berea, Ohio, Sept. 11, 1966; s. Lawrence Clinton Parker and Diana Lee (Barhoover) Winkel; m. Lori Anne Himelrigh, Dec. 23, 1955. BS in Econ., Miami U., 1988; JD, U. Dayton, 1991. Bar: Ohio 1991, U.S. Dist. Ct. (no. dist.) Ohio 1996. Atty. Perantinides & Nolan Co., L.P.A., Akron, Ohio, 1991—. Mem. Am. Trial Lawyers Assn., Ohio State Bar Assn., Ohio Trial Lawyers Assn., Akron Bar Assn. Avocations: baseball, softball, exercise, reading, church related activities. Personal injury, Insurance, General civil litigation. Office: Perantinides and Nolan Co LPA 80 S Summit St Akron OH 44308-1732

**PARKER, CHRISTOPHER WILLIAM,** lawyer; b. Evanston, Ill., Oct. 26, 1947; s. Robert H. and Dorothy Boynton P.; m. Mary Ann P., Dec. 28, 1984. BA, Tufts U., 1969; JD, Northeastern U., 1976. Bar: Mass. 1977, U.S. Dist. Ct. Mass. 1977, U.S. Dist. Ct. (we. dist.) Tex. 1986, U.S. Ct. Appeals (1st cir.) 1988, U.S. Supreme Ct. 1988. Law clk. to judge U.S. Bankruptcy Ct. Mass. dist., Boston, 1976-77; assoc. Fletcher, Tilton & Whipple, Worcester, Mass., 1977-79; counsel U.S. Trustee, Boston, 1979-81; assoc. Craig and Macauley P.C., Boston, 1982-84, ptnr., 1984-87; counsel Hinckley, Allen, Snyder & Comen, Boston, 1987-88, ptnr., 1989-91; ptnr. McDermott, Will & Emery, Boston, 1991—. Mem. ABA, Mass. Bar Assn., Am. Bankruptcy Inst. Boston Bar Assn., Comml. Law League. Club: Union Boat (Boston). Bankruptcy, Banking, Federal civil litigation. Home: 11 Tophet Rd Lynnfield MA 01940-1616 Office: McDermott Will & Emery 28 State St Boston MA 02109-1775

**PARKER, DALLAS ROBERT,** lawyer; b. Houston, Oct. 16, 1947; s. Richard Henry and Rosemary (McMillan) P.; m. Ingrid Elayne Thompson, July 1, 1972; children: Robert Jr., Nicholas Mattsson. BA, Vanderbilt U., 1969; JD, U. Tex., 1972. Bar: Tex. 1972. Assoc. Fulbright & Jaworski, Houston, 1972-79, ptnr., 1979-82; ptnr. Brown Parker & Leahy, Houston, 1982—; dir. Amigos de las Americas. Editor U. Tex. Law Rev., 1971. Dir. Odyssey House, Tex., Amigos de las Americas; adv. dir. Houston Tech. Ctr. Named to Chancellors U. Tex. Fellow Houston Bar Found., Tex. Bar Found.; mem. ABA, Tex. Bar Assn., Houston Bar Assn. General corporate, Securities. Office: Brown Parker & Leahy 3600 Two Allen Ctr Houston TX 77002

**PARKER, DONALD SAMUEL,** lawyer; b. Jersey City, July 21, 1948; s. Raymond E. And Alice J. (Gilman) P.; m. Elizabeth F. Dalton, Aug. 11, 1978; children: Luke, Genevieve. AB, Wesleyan U., Middletown, Conn., 1970; JD, U. Chgo., 1973. Bar: N.Y. 1975, U.S. Dist. Ct. (so. dist.) N.Y. 1975, U.S. Ct. Appeals (2d cir.) 1975, U.S. Supreme Ct. 1976, Va. 1989. Assoc. Cahill Gordon & Reindel, N.Y.C., 1974-83; asst. gen. counsel Lever Bros. Co., N.Y.C., 1983-85; dep. gen. counsel Fairchild Industries, Inc., Chantilly, Va., 1985-89, v.p., gen. counsel, 1989-91; v.p., gen. counsel Sprint Internat., 1991-96; sr. v.p. law, regulatory, external affairs, gen. counsel Global One Telecomm., Inc., Brussels, 1996—. Assoc. editor U. Chgo. Law Rev., 1972-73. Mem. ABA, Va. State Bar, N.Y. State Bar Assn., Royal Leopold Club, River Bend Country Club. Private international, Mergers and acquisitions. Office: Global One Telecomm, Rue des Colonies 11, B-1000 Brussels Belgium also: 12490 Sunrise Valley Dr Reston VA 22096-0001

**PARKER, EUGENE LEROY, III,** lawyer; b. Arlington, Mass., Oct. 17, 1949; s. Eugene LeRoy Jr. and Jane Gates (Washburn) P.; m. Jo Ann Williams, June 24, 1978; children: Willis Washburn, Jones Griffith, Alden

Jackson, Eliza Ann. Student, Hampden-Sydney (Va.), 1969; AB, Rutgers U., 1972; JD, Memphis State U., 1976. Bar: Tenn. 1977. Sole practice Etowah, Tenn., 1977—; judge City of Etowah, 1986-95. Regional dir. Am. Youth Soccer Orgn., 1985-95. Mem. Tenn. Trial Lawyers Assn., McMinn County Bar Assn. Republican. Methodist. Avocations: swimming, coaching soccer, scout activities, reading, yard work. Personal injury, Workers' compensation, General practice. Home and Office: PO Box 211 Etowah TN 37331-0211

**PARKER, FRED I.,** federal judge; b. 1938. BA, U. Mass., 1962; LLB, Georgetown U., 1965. With Lyne, Woodworth & Everts, Boston, 1965-66, Office Atty. Gen., Montpelier, Vt., 1969-72, Langrock and Sperry, Middlebury, Vt., 1972-75; ptnr. Langrock, Sperry, Parker & Stahl, Middlebury, 1975-82, Langrock, Sperry, Parker & Wool, Middlebury, 1982-90; fed. judge U.S. Dist. Ct. (Vt. dist.), 1990-91, chief judge, 1991-94; fed. judge U.S. Ct. Appeals (2d cir.), 1994—; mem. conduct bd. Vt. Supreme Ct., 1975-79, jud. conduct bd., 1982-88. Active Vt. Lawyers Project. Mem. Vt. Bar Assn. (chair spl. com. reform of judiciary 1988-89), Chittenden County Bar Assn. Office: US Dist Ct PO Box 392 11 Elmwood Ave Burlington VT 05402-0392 Also: US Dist Court 500 Pearl St Rm 2520 New York NY 10007-1316*

**PARKER, HAROLD ALLEN,** lawyer, real estate executive; b. Denver, Sept. 14, 1924; s. Hyman and Sophia P.; m. Gertrud Parker; children: David, Rodney, Diana, Jesse, Jonathan. JD, Golden Gate U., 1971. Bar: Calif. 1972. Pvt. practice San Francisco; gen. ptnr. Harold Parker Properties, San Francisco; legal cons. San Francisco Craft and Folk Art Mus.; past mem. Bay Area Lawyers for the Arts; spkr. in field; prime developer Union St. Comml. Corridor, San Francisco, 1963—. Pub.: Wolfgang Paalen, His Art and His Writings, 1980, Richard Bowman, Forty Years of Abstract Painting, 1986. Chmn. Fine Arts Commn., Tiburon, Calif., 1976-78. Mem. Family Club (San Francisco). Avocations: music, art, tennis. Office: 1844 Union St San Francisco CA 94123-4308

**PARKER, JAMES AUBREY,** federal judge; b. Houston, Jan. 8, 1937; s. Lewis Almeron and Emily Helen (Stuessy) P.; m. Florence Fisher, Aug. 26, 1960; children: Roger Alan, Pamela Elizabeth. BA, Rice U., 1959; LLB, U. Tex., 1962. Bar: Tex. 1962, N.Mex. 1963. With Modrall, Sperling, Roehl, Harris & Sisk, Albuquerque, 1962-87; judge U.S. Dist. Ct. N.Mex., Albuquerque, 1987—; mem. Standing Commn. on Rules of Practice and Procedures of U.S. Cts., N.Mex. Commn. on Professionalism, 1986—; bd. visitors U. N.Mex. Law Sch., 1996-98. Articles editor Tex. Law Rev., 1961-62. Mem. ABA, Fed. Judges Assn., Am. Judicature Soc., Am. Bd. Trial Advocates, Tex. Bar Assn., N.Mex. Bar Assn., Albuquerque Bar Assn., Order of Coif, Chancellors, Phi Delta Phi. Avocations: ranching, fly fishing, running, skiing. Fax: 505 348-2225. Office: US Dist Judge 333 Lomas Blvd NW Ste 760 Albuquerque NM 87102-2277

**PARKER, JAMES FRANCIS,** lawyer, airline executive; b. San Antonio, Jan. 1, 1947; s. Raymond Francis and Libbie Olivia (Dusek) P.; m. Patricia Elaine Lorang, May 15, 1971; children: James, Jennifer. BA with hons., U. Tex., 1969, JD with hons., 1971. Bar: Tex., U.S. Dist. Ct. (ea., we., so. no. dists.) Tex., U.S. Ct. Appeals (5th and 11th cirs.), U.S. Supreme Ct. Law clk. to presiding judge U.S. Dist. Ct., Austin, Tex., 1972-76; asst. atty. gen. State of Tex., Austin, 1976-79; atty. Oppenheimer, Rosenberg, Kelleher & Wheatley, San Antonio, 1979-86; v.p., gen. counsel SW Airlines Co., Dallas, 1986—. Mem. ABA, Tex. Bar Assn. Democrat. Lutheran. General corporate, Aviation, General practice. Office: SW Airlines Co 2702 Love Field Dr Dallas TX 75235-1908

**PARKER, JEFFREY SCOTT,** law educator, university official; b. Alexandria, Va., Sept. 6, 1952; s. Clarence Franklin and Mary Florence (Partlow) P. B in Indsl. Engring., Ga. Inst. Tech., 1975; JD, U. Va., 1978. Bar: N.Y. 1979, U.S. Dist. Ct. (ea. and so. dists.) N.Y. 1979, U.S. Ct. Appeals (3d cir.) 1981, U.S. Ct. Appeals (2d cir.) 1984, U.S. Supreme Ct. 1984, U.S. Ct. Appeals (fed. cir.) 1985, U.S. Ct. Appeals (4th cir.) 1992, U.S. Ct. Appeals (D.C. cir.) 1997. Assoc. Sullivan & Cromwell, N.Y.C., 1978-86, Sacks Montgomery, N.Y.C., 1986-87; dep. chief counsel U.S. Sentencing Commn., Washington, 1987-88; of counsel Sacks Montgomery, N.Y.C., 1988-90; assoc. prof. of law George Mason U., Arlington, Va., 1990-94; prof. law, assoc. dean acad. affairs George Mason U. Sch. Law, 1994-96, prof. law, 1996—; cons. counsel U.S. Sentencing Commn., Washington, 1988-89. Contbr. articles to law revs.; mem. editorial bd. Va. Law Rev., 1976-78. Mem. ABA, Assn. of Bar of City of N.Y., N.Y. State Bar Assn., Am. Law and Econs. Assn., Am. Econs. Assn., Am. Judicature Soc. Office: George Mason U Sch of Law 3401 Fairfax Dr Arlington VA 22201-4411

**PARKER, JOHN HILL,** lawyer; b. High Point, N.C., Feb. 1, 1944; s. George Edward and Tullia Virginia (Hill) P.; children from previous marriage: Alice Lindsey, Elizabeth Shelby (dec.); m. Lynette Becton Smith, July 7, 1977. BA, U. N.C., 1966; JD, U. Tenn., 1969. Bar: N.C. 1969, U.S. Dist. Ct. (ea dist.) N.C. 1970, U.S. Supreme Ct. Assoc. Sanford, Cannon, Adams & McCullough, Raleigh, N.C., 1969-73; pvt. practice Raleigh, 1974-76; judge N.C. Dist. Ct., Raleigh, 1976-82; ptnr. Cheshire & Parker, Raleigh, 1982—; instr. judges seminars Inst. Govt. Chapel Hill, N.C., 1977-82. Parlementarian Wake County Young Dems., 1971-73; mem. Raleigh Arts Commn., 1981-84, chmn. 1983. Fellow Am. Acad. Matrimonial Lawyers (ethics com. 1995-97, pres. N.C. chap. Am. Acad. of Matrimonial Lawyers, 1999—); mem. ABA, N.C. Bar Assn. (editor family law sect. 1984-85, chmn. 1985-86, 96-97, continuing legal edn. for family law 1979—, chmn. 1985-87, 96-98, chmn. ethics com. 1989-90, chmn. gen. curriculum com. 1989-90), N.C. Acad. Trial Lawyers, Wake County Bar Assn. Episcopalian. Avocations: travel, backpacking, fishing, reading, music. Family and matrimonial, State civil litigation. Home: 1620 Park Dr Raleigh NC 27605-1609 Office: Cheshire & Parker PO Box 1029 133 Fayetteville St Mall Raleigh NC 27601-1356

**PARKER, JOHN VICTOR,** federal judge; b. Baton Rouge, La., Oct. 14, 1928; m. Mary Elizabeth Fridge, Sept. 3, 1949; children: John Michael, Robert Fridge, Linda Anne. B.A., La. State U., 1949, J.D., 1952. Bar: La. 1952. Atty. Parker & Parker, Baton Rouge, 1954-66; asst. parish atty. City of Baton Rouge, Parish of East Baton Rouge, 1956-66; atty. Sanders, Downing, Kean & Cazedessus, Baton Rouge, 1966-79; chief judge U.S. Dist. Ct., Middle Dist. La., Baton Rouge, 1979—; vis. lectr. law La. State U. Law Sch. Served with Judge Adv. Gen.'s Corps U.S. Army, 1952-54. Mem. ABA, Am. Judicature Soc., Am. Arbitration Assn., La. State Bar Assn. (past mem. bd. govs.), Baton Rouge Bar Assn. (past pres.), Order of Coif, Phi Delta Phi. Democrat. Club: Baton Rouge Country. Lodges: Masons (32 deg.); Kiwanis (past pres.). Office: Russell B Long Fed Bldg & Courthouse 777 Florida St Ste 355 Baton Rouge LA 70801-1717

**PARKER, MARY ANN,** lawyer; b. Pitts., Jan. 6, 1953; d. Harry N. Sr. and Mary (Sperl) P.; 1 child, Nickolas Parker Palacios. BS cum laude, SUNY, Buffalo, 1975; JD, U. Tenn., 1977. Bar: Tenn. 1978, U.S. Dist. Ct. (mid. dist.) Tenn. 1978, U.S. Ct. Appeals (5th cir.) 1980, U.S. Supreme Ct. 1982, U.S. Ct. Appeals (6th cir.) 1987. Asst. Dist. Atty. Gen., Ashland City, Tenn., 1977-78; sole practice Nashville, 1978—; instr. Nat. Trial Advocacy Coll., 1983-84. Cmty. svcs. vol. St. Henry's Women's Club, Nashville, 1984-90; mem. stewardship com. Holy Family, 1993—; mem. Women's Polit. Caucus, Nashville, 1986—, Tenn. Dem. Polit. Com., 1988—, Tenn. Dem. Fin. Coun., 1991—; mem. Dem. Leadership Coun., 1991—, bd. dirs., 1992-96. Mem. ABA, ATLA (del. 1983-86, sec. 1985-86, young lawyer's sect. sec. 1982-83, 2d vice chair 1983-84, 1st vice chair 1984-85, chair 1985-86, women's caucus sec. 1981-83, 1st vice chair 1983-84, chair motor vehicles, accidents, premises and govtl. liability sect. 1989-90, sec. torts sect. 1988-89, named Del. of Yr. 1986), Tenn. Trial Lawyers Assn. (bd. govs. 1978-86, chair consumer and victims coalition com. 1986-87), Trial Lawyers Pub. Justice (bd. govs. 1982—, treas. 1990-92, v.p. 1992-93, pres.-elect 1993-94, pres. 1994-95), Nashville Bar Assn. (ethics com. 1983—, chancery and cir. ct. com. 1993—), Tenn. Bar Assn., Pa. Trial Lawyers Assn. Roman Catholic. Avocations: snow and water skiing, tennis, Scuba diving. Personal injury, Environmental, Product liability. Home: 5113 Fountainhead Dr Brentwood TN 37027-5809 Office: Parker & Crofford 209 10th Ave S Ste 511 Nashville TN 37203-0795

**PARKER, MICHAEL DEAN,** district attorney; b. Pinehurst, N.C., Feb. 17, 1964; s. A.B. and Virginia (Britt) P.; m. Carol Denise Ward, Aug. 8, 1986; 1 child, Matthew Grayson. BS, N.C. State U., Raleigh, 1986; JD, U. N.C., 1989. Bar: N.C. 1989. Asst. dist. atty. 20th Prosecutorial Dist. N.C., Monroe, 1989-96, chief asst. dist. atty., 1996—; tchr. N.C. Conf. Dist. Attys., Raleigh, 1995—, Nat. Hwy. Traffic Safety Adminstrn., Washington, 1995—, Fla. Pros. Attys. Assn., Tallahassee, 1995—, N.C. Inst. Govt., Chapel HIll, 1997—. Mem. Vass (N.C.) Rescue Squad, 1977-97; mem. N.C. Prosecutor Tng. Com., 1995—; mem. N.C. Domestic Violence Tng. Com., 1996-98. Mem. Moore County Bar Assn. (prs. 1996-97). Presbyterian. Avocations: farming, teaching, travel, family. Home: PO Box 340 Vass NC 28394-0340 Office: Dist Attys Office PO Box 1065 Monroe NC 28111-1065

**PARKER, RICHARD WILSON,** lawyer; b. Cleve., June 14, 1943; s. Edgar Gael and Pauline (Wilson) P.; m. Helen Margaret Shober, Jan. 3, 1998; children from previous marriage: Brian Jeffrey, Lauren Michelle, Lisa Christine. BA cum laude in Econs., U. Redlands, 1965; JD cum laude, Northwestern U., 1968. Bar: Ohio 1968, Va. 1974. Assoc. Arter & Hadden, Cleve., 1968-71; asst. gen. atty. Norfolk & Western Ry. Co., Cleve. and Roanoke, Va., 1971-74, asst. gen. solicitor, Roanoke, 1974-78, gen. atty., 1978-84; gen. atty. Norfolk So. Corp., 1984-88, sr. gen. atty., Norfolk, Va., 1988-93, asst. v.p. real estate, 1993—. Mem. ABA, Va. State Bar, Va. Bar Assn., Norfolk-Portsmouth Bar Assn. Presbyterian. Real property, Environmental, Contracts commercial. Office: 3 Commercial Pl Norfolk VA 23510-2108

**PARKER, ROBERT M.,** federal judge; b. 1937. BBA, U. Tex., 1961, JD, 1964. Bar: Tex. 1964. Ptnr. Parish & Parker, Gilmer, Tex., 1964-65, Kenley & Boyland, Longview, Tex., 1965, Roberts, Smith & Parker, Longview, 1966-71, Rutledge & Parker, Ft. Worth, 1971-72, Nichols & Parker, Longview, 1972-79; judge U.S. Dist. Ct. (ea. dist.) Tex., 1979-94, chief judge, 1991-94; judge U.S. Ct. Appeals (5th Cir.), Tyler, Tex. Mem. Tex. Bar Assn. Office: 221 W Ferguson St Ste 400 Tyler TX 75702-7200

**PARKER, ROBERT SAMUEL,** lawyer; b. Anoka, Minn., Sept. 6, 1924; s. Raymond Earl and Roberta (Akin) P.; m. Julie Ann Louise Erickson, Aug. 23, 1947; children: John J., Lee C. BS in Law, U. Minn., 1949, LLB, 1950. Bar: Minn. 1951, U.S. Tax Ct. 1972, U.S. Supreme Ct. 1981. Atty. City of Cambridge, Minn., 1950-54, 59-88, Isanti County, 1954-58; mem. firm Parker, Satrom, O'Neil and Benjamin, P.A., Cambridge, 1962—. Staff mem. Minn. Law Rev., 1949-50. Various offices Cambridge Rep. Com. Staff sgt. AUS, 1943-46, PTO. Mem. ABA, Minn. Bar Assn. (bd. govs.), Assn. Trial Lawyers Am., Minn. Trial Lawyers Assn., Am. Legion, VFW, Masons. Methodist. Estate planning, Probate, Personal injury. Home: 1330 357th Ave NW Cambridge MN 55008-8108 Office: Parker Satrom O'Neil Et Al 123 Ashland St S Cambridge MN 55008-1516

**PARKER, ROBIN ROBERT,** lawyer; b. N.Y.C., Dec. 12, 1958; s. Robert Henry and Wylma Mae Parker. BA, Rutgers U., 1980; JD, U. Ill., 1983. Assoc. atty. Law Firm Lemuel H. Blackburn Jr., Trenton, N.J., 1984-85; dep. atty. gen. N.J. Divsn. of Criminal Justice, Trenton, 1985—. Recipient So. Jersey Jewish Law E.C. Assn., 1996, A World of Difference award Anti-Defamation League, 1997, Cmty. Svc. award Burlingtonn County Human Rels. Com., 1998. Mem. NJ State Bar Found. (tolerance subcom.). Office: NJ Divsn of Criminal Justice PO Box 85 Trenton NJ 08625-0085

**PARKER, ROSS GAIL,** lawyer; b. Council Bluffs, Iowa, July 13, 1948; s. Gail Francis and Mildred Julia P.; m. Deborah Jo LeVan, May 5, 1984; children: Sarah LeVan, Alexander LeVan. BS, Iowa State U., 1970; JD, U. Pitts., 1974. Bar: U.S. Dist. Ct. (ea. dist.) Mich. 1975, U.S. Ct. Appeals (6th cir.) 1975. Law clk. to Hon. Michael Cavanagh Mich. Ct. Appeals, Lansing, 1974-75; atty. Fink and LaRene, Detroit, 1975-78; asst. U.S. atty. U.S. Attys. Office, U.S. Dist. Ct. (ea. dist.) Mich., Detroit, 1978—, chief criminal divsn., 1981-89; chief asst. U.S. atty. U.S. Attys. Office, U.S. Dist. Ct. (ea. dist.) Mich., 1989-94; adj. prof. Detroit Coll. Law, 1980-82. Editor-in-chief U. Pitts. Law Rev., 1973-74. Coach Neighborhood Club, Grosse Pointe, Mich., 1998; mgr. SCH Hockey Assn., St. Clair Shores, Mich., 1998—. Recipient Dirs. award U.S. Dept. Justice, 1990. Mem. FBA (Leonard R. Gilman award 1997). Presbyterian. Avocations: reading, coaching, volunteering in church activities. Office: US Attys Office 211 W Fort St Detroit MI 48226-3202

**PARKER, SARAH ELIZABETH,** state supreme court justice; b. Charlotte, N.C., Aug. 23, 1942; d. Augustus and Zola Elizabeth (Smith) P. AB, U. N.C., 1964, JD, 1969; LHD (hon.), Queens Coll., 1998. Bar: N.C. 1969, U.S. Dist. Ct. (mid., ea. and we. dists.) N.C. Vol. U.S. Peace Corps, Ankara, Turkey, 1964-66; pvt. practice Charlotte, 1969-84; former judge N.C. Ct. Appeals, Raleigh; now assoc. justice N. C. Supreme Ct., Raleigh. Bd. visitors U. N.C., Chapel Hill, 1993-97; bd. dirs. YWCA, Charlotte, 1982-85; pres. Mecklenburg County Dem. Women, Charlotte, 1973. Recipient Disting. Woman of N.C. award, 1997, Woman of Achievement award Nat. Fedn. Women's Clubs, 1997. Mem. ABA, Inst. Jud. Adminstrn., N.C. Bar Assn. (v.p. 1987-88), Mecklenburg County Bar (sec.-treas. 1982-84), Wake County Bar Assn., N.C. Internat. Women's Forum, Women Attys. Assn. (Gwyneth David Pub. Svc. award 1986). Episcopalian. Office: NC Supreme Ct PO Box 1841 Raleigh NC 27602-1841

**PARKERSON, HARDY MARTELL,** lawyer; b. Longview, Tex., Aug. 22, 1942; s. James Dee and Winifred Lenore (Robertson) P.; m. Janice Carol Johnson, Aug. 3, 1968; children: James Blaine, Stanley Andrew, Paul Hardy. BA, McNeese State U., Lake Charles, La.; JD, Tulane U., 1966. Bar: La. 1966, U.S. Supreme Ct. 1971. Assoc. Rogers, McHale & St. Romain, Lake Charles, 1967-69; pvt. practice Lake Charles, 1969—; chmn. 7th Congl. Dist. Crime and Justice Task Force, La. Priorities for the Future, 1980; asst. prof. criminal justice La. State U., 1986. Bd. dirs. 1st Assembly of God Ch., Lake Charles, 1980—; bd. regents So. Christian U., Lake Charles, 1993—; mem. La. Dem. State Ctrl. Com., 1992-96, Calcasieu Parish Dem. Com., 1988—, past sec.-treas., exec. com.; former mem. Gulf Assistance Program, Lake Charles; 7th Congl. Dist. La. mem. Imports and Exports Trust Authority, Baton Rouge, 1984-88. Mem. Federal Bar Assn. (chmn. federal courts com., sr. lawyer's divsn.), Pi Kappa Phi Housing Corp. of Lake Charles (bd. dirs., sec.-treas. 1985—), Optimists, Pi Kappa Phi (Beta Mu chpt.). Democrat. Mem. Assembly of God Ch. Avocations: political activist, television talk show host. Federal civil litigation, State civil litigation, Toxic tort. Home: 127 Greenway St Lake Charles LA 70605-6821 Office: The Parkerson Law Firm 807 Alamo St Lake Charles LA 70601-8665

**PARKHURST, BEVERLY SUSLER,** lawyer, former judge; b. Decatur, Ill.; d. Sewell and Marion (Appelbaum) Susler; m. Todd S. Parkhurst, Aug. 15, 1976. BA with honors, U. Ill., 1966, JD, 1969. Bar: Ill. 1969, U.S. Dist. Ct. (no. dist.) Ill. 1969, U.S. Ct. Appeals (7th cir.) 1975, U.S. Supreme Ct. 1980. Assoc. Pope, Ballard, Shepard & Fowle, Chgo., 1969-74; asst. U.S. atty. U.S. Atty.'s Office U.S. Dist. Ct. (no. dist.) Ill., Chgo., 1974-78, exec. asst. U.S. atty., 1978-81; pvt. practice law Offices of Beverly Susler Parkhurst, Chgo., 1982-86; trial judge Cir. Ct. Cook County, 1996-98; of counsel Witwer, Poltrock & Giampietro, Chgo., 1998—; mem. faculty trial advocacy programs Nat. Emory U., Hofstra U.; bd. dirs. Internat. Forum Travel and Tourism Advs., vice chmn. 2d Internat. Conf., Jerusalem, 1986, regional chmn. 3d Internat. Conf., San Francisco, 1987; chmn. inquiry bd. Ill. Atty. Registration and Disciplinary Commn., 1985-87; guest lectr. legal ethics Washington U., St. Louis, 1986; lectr. on travel law, fed. civic procedures and med. malpractice; adj. prof. John Marshall Law Sch., 1999—; mediator Jud. Disput Resolution. Contbr. articles to profl. jours.; spkr. in field. Mem. Ill. Toll Hwy. Adv. Com., 1985-90; bd. dirs. Ill. Soc. for Prevention of Blindness, Cook County Ct. Watchers, Chgo. State U. Found., 1997—. James scholar U. Ill., 1962-66; recipient Spl. Achievement award U.S. Dept. Justice, 1978, Dir.'s award, 1981, Cert. of Profl. Achievement in Mediation, DePaul U. Dispute Resolution Ctr.; U.S. Utility Patent grantee 1984. Mem. ABA (chmn. subcom. alternatives to discovery litigation sect. 1985-87), Ill. Bar Assn. (com. profl. responsibility), Women's Bar Assn., Fed. Bar Assn., Chgo. Bar Assn. (chmn. judiciary commn. 1988-90, bench bar symposium 1988-91, exec. com. Alliance for Women), Nat. Inst. Trial Advocacy (faculty N.E. region), Lincoln Inn of Ct. (v.p.), Legal Club of Chgo. Avocations: scuba diving, swimming, cooking. Computer, Federal civil litigation, General civil litigation. Office: Witwer Poltrock & Giampietro 125 S Wacker Dr Ste 2700 Chicago IL 60606-4402

**PARKINSON, PAUL K.,** lawyer; b. Durango, Colo., Feb. 8, 1952; s. Philip Fulton and Ruth Eloise (Knight) P.; m. Amy Lee Dunham, May 17, 1975; children: Calista R., Karen S. BSE in Psychology, Truman State U., 1977; JD, U. Mo., Kansas City, 1979; LLM in Estate Planning, U. Miami, 1981. Bar: Mo. 1980, U.S. Dist. Ct. (we. dist.) Mo. 1980, U.S. Tax Ct. 1981, Kans. 1989. Assoc. Polsinelli, White, Vardeman & Shelton, Kansas City, Mo., 1981-83; pvt. practice Kansas City, 1984-85; dir. Van Hooser, Olsen & Parkinson, P.C., Kansas City, 1986-89; pvt. practice Overland Park, Kans. and Kansas City, 1989-90; with Hess & Parkinson, Macon, Mo., 1990—; asst. pros. atty. Macon County, 1999—; adj. prof. U. Mo., Kansas City, 1982-85. Pres., dir., program com. chmn. Mid-Am. Planned giving Coun., Kansas City, 1990. Mem. ABA (real property, probate and trust sect. 1980-94), Mo. Bar Assn. (lectr. 1983-90, probate and trust com. 1981—, hosp. law com., banking law com., pres. 41st jud. cir. 1992-94). E-mail: parkfam@istmacen.net. Estate planning, Banking, General corporate. Office: PO Box 405 210 N Rollins St Macon MO 63552-1533

**PARKINSON, THOMAS IGNATIUS, JR.,** lawyer; b. N.Y.C., Jan. 27, 1914; s. Thomas I. and Georgia (Weed) P.; AB, Harvard U., 1934; LLB, U. Pa., 1937; m. Geralda E. Moore, Sept. 23, 1937; children: Thomas Ignatius III, Geoffrey Moore, Cynthia Moore. Admitted to N.Y. bar, 1938, since practiced in N.Y.C.; assoc. Milbank, Tweed, Hope & Hadley, 1937-47, partner, 1947-56; pres. Mar Ltd., 1951—; pres. Breecom Corp., 1972-80, chmn. bd., 1980—; dir., exec. com. Pine St. Fund, Inc., N.Y.C., 1949-83, Trustee State Communities Aid Assn., 1949-83; dir. Fgn. Policy Assn., 1949-53; bd. dirs., exec. com. Milbank Meml. Fund, 1948-84. Mem. Am. Bar Assn., Assn. Bar City N.Y., Pilgrims U.S.A., Brit. War Relief Soc. (officer), Met. Unit Found., Phi Beta Kappa. Clubs: Down Town Assn., Knickerbocker, Union. Office: Windrove Svc Corp 780 3rd Ave Fl 25 New York NY 10017-2024

**PARKISON, JAMES MAX,** trial court administrator, educator; b. Kansas City, Mo., Jan. 12, 1943; s. Amherst Max and Agnes Lorraine (St. George) P.; m. Anne Ruth Hale, Nov. 1, 1969; 1 son, Christopher Hale. BA, Grinnell Coll., 1965; JD, U. Mo.-Kansas City, 1968. Bar: Mo. 1968, U.S. Dist. Ct. (ea. dist.) Mo. 1969. Vol., VISTA, 1969-70; staff atty. St. Louis Legal Aid Soc., 1970-71; cts. program chief Mo. Law Enforcement Assistance Council, Jefferson City, Mo., 1971-73; state ct. adminstr. State of Mo. Supreme Ct., Jefferson City, 1973-81; asst. dir. Inst. Judicial Adminstrn., N.Y.C., 1981-83; trial ct. adminstr. Burlington County, State N.J., Mt. Holly, 1983—; mem. nat. adv. com. Nat. Inst. Law Enforcement and Criminal Justice, Dept. Justice, Washington, 1977-81, nat. adv. com. Inst. for Econ. and Policy Studies, Inc., A Comparative Study of State Ct. Orgns., 1980-83; mem. Nat. State Judicial Info. Systems Com., 1973-81; chmn. systems documentation com., 1976-77; mem. long range planning com. and systems devel. com. Nat. Ctr. for State Cts., Williamsburg, Va., 1976-80; mem. exec. com. Coordinating Council of Nat. Ct. Orgns., 1983-84; cons. Koba Assocs., 1975-83; adj. asst. prof. law NYU Sch. Law, 1982-83; adj. assoc. prof. NYU Sch. Pub. Adminstrn., 1983-85 ; adj. instr. Rutgers Sch. Law, Camden, 1986—; cons. Asian Council for Law and Devel., Colombo, Sri Lanka, Ministry of Justice Sri Lanka, 1982; internat. rapporteur Commn. on Juries, Conf. on Independence of Justice, 1983. Mem. editorial bd. The Justice System Jour., 1983—. Exec. producer Little Theatre, Jefferson City, Mo., 1980-81, bd. dirs., 1979-81, Burlington Co. Footlighters, 1986—. Recipient scholarship U. Mo.-Kansas City Law Sch., 1965. Mem. Am. Judicature Soc. (life), ABA (mem. criminal justice sect. 1981-84), Conf. State Ct. Adminstrs. (nat. exec. com. 1976-81, nat. vice chmn. 1978-79, nat. chmn. 1979-80), Internat. Bar Assn. (vice chmn. com. on adminstrn. of justice, sect. on gen. practice 1982-84), Sigma Delta Chi, Phi Alpha Delta. Methodist. Home: 21 Mountainside Park Ter Montclair NJ 07043-1208

**PARKS, ALBERT LAURISTON,** lawyer; b. Providence, July 18, 1935; s. Albert Lauriston and Dorothy Isabel (Arnold) P.; m. Martha Ann Anderson, Jan. 12, 1961; children: Amy Woodward, George Webster, Reed Anderson. BA, Kent State U., 1958; JD, U. Chgo., 1961. Bar: R.I. 1962, U.S. Dist. R.I. 1963, U.S. Ct. Appeals (1st cir.) 1966, U.S. Supreme Ct. 1980. Assoc. Hanson, Curran, Parks & Whitman, Providence, 1961-65, ptnr., 1966—; town solicitor, North Kingstown, R.I., 1978-80, 97—. Fellow Am. Coll. Trial Lawyers; mem. ABA, R.I. Bar Assn., Maritime Law Assn., Squantum Assn. Republican. Episcopalian. Clubs: Hope and Saunderstown (R.I.) Yacht. State civil litigation, Federal civil litigation, Labor. Home: 40 Hammond Hl Saunderstown RI 02874-3509 Office: The Francis Bldg 146 Westminster St Providence RI 02903-2202

**PARKS, JAMES WILLIAM, II,** public facilities executive, lawyer; b. Wabash, Ind., July 30, 1956; s. James William and Joyce Arlene (Lillibridge) P.; m. Neil Ann Armstrong, Aug. 21, 1982; children: Elizabeth Joyce, Helen Frances, James William III. BS, Ball State U., 1978; JD, U. Miami, 1981. Bar: La. 1981, Fla. 1982, U.S. Dist. Ct. (ea. dist.) La. 1981, U.S. Dist. Ct. (mid. dist.) La. 1982, U.S. Ct. Appeals (5th cir. and 11th cir.) 1981. Atty. Jones, Walker, Waechter, Poitevent, Carrere et al., New Orleans, 1981-83, Foley & Judell, New Orleans, 1983-88, McCollister & McCleary, pc, Baton Rouge, 1988-95; exec. dir. La. Pub. Facilities Authority, Baton Rouge, 1995—. Mem. AICPA, Nat. Assn. Bond Lawyers, La. State Bar Assn., Fla. Bar Assn., Assn. for Gifted and Talented Students, Baton Rouge (treas. 1994-96, pres.-elect 1996-97, pres. 1997-98), Soc. La. CPA (govt. acctg. and auditing com. 1994-95), Nat. Assn. Higher Edn. Facilities Authorities ( bd. dirs. 1996—, v.p. 1997-99, pres. 1999—). Avocations: travel, computers. Home: 5966 Tennyson Dr Baton Rouge LA 70817-2933 Office: La Pub Facilities Authority 2237 S Acadian Thruway Ste 650 Baton Rouge LA 70808-2380

**PARKS, JANE DELOACH,** retired law librarian, legal assistant; b. Atlanta, June 7, 1927; d. John Keller and Martha Lorena (Lee) deLoach; m. James Bennett Parks, Dec. 28, 1951 (dec. Sept. 1983); children: Carrie Anne Parks-Kirby, Susan Jane, Lora Beth Parks-Maury. BA magna cum laude, Vanderbilt U., 1949; postgrad., Emory U., 1950-51; tchr. cert., U. Chattanooga, 1954; postgrad., U. Tenn., Chattanooga, 1971-73. Med. rsch./writing dept. surgery Emory U., Atlanta, 1949-51; sec. to med. dir. Tenn. Tuberculosis Hosp., Chattanooga, 1951-53; tchr. Signal Mountain (Tenn.) Elem. Sch., 1954-55; tchr., dean jr. sch. Cleve. (Tenn.) Day Sch., 1963-70; law firm libr., legal asst. Stophel, Caldwell & Heggie, Chattanooga, 1972-85, Caldwell, Heggie & Helton, Chattanooga, 1985-93, Heiskell, Donelson, Bearman, Adams, Williams & Caldwell, Chattanooga, 1993-94, Baker, Donelson, Bearman & Caldwell, Chattanooga, 1994-99; ret., 1999; tchr. various seminars on legal rsch. and writing, organizing one-person librs. and ch. librs., Chattanooga Legal Secs. Assn., Chattanooga-Hamilton County Bicentennial Libr. Editor (mag.) The Gadfly, 1947-49; editorial asst.: Studio Collotype, 1988 and to profl. jours., 1949—. tchr. Chattanooga Area Literacy Movement, 1984-86; exec. coun. Friends of Chattanooga-Hamilton County Bicentennial Libr., 1989-94; del. Gov.'s Conf.-White House Conf. on Librs. and Info. Svcs., Nashville, 1990; libr. vol. Tenn. Aquarium. Environ. Learning Lab.; allocations com. United Way, 1994—. Mem. Tenn. Paralegal Assn., Chattanooga Area Libr. Assn. (2d v.p. 1989-90, sec. 1992-93), Non-Atty. Profl. Assn. (chmn. 1989-93), Phi Beta Kappa, Mortar Bd. Republican. Methodist. Avocations: genealogy, reading, storytelling, needlework.

**PARR, CAROLYN MILLER,** federal judge; b. Palatka, Fla., Apr. 17, 1937; d. Arthur Charles and Audrey Ellen (Dunklin) Miller; m. Jerry Studstill Parr, Oct. 12, 1959; children: Kimberly Parr Trapasso, Jennifer Parr Turek, Patricia Audrey. BA, Stetson U., 1959; MA, Vanderbilt U., 1960; JD, Georgetown U., 1977; LLD (hon.), Stetson U., 1986. Bar: Md. 1977, U.S. Tax Ct. 1977, D.C. 1979, U.S. Supreme Ct. 1983. Gen. trial atty. IRS, Washington, 1977-81, sr. trial atty. office of chief counsel, 1982; spl. counsel to asst. atty. gen. tax divsn. U.S. Dept. Justice, Washington, 1982-85; judge U.S. Tax Ct., Washington, 1985—. Nat. Def. fellow Vanderbilt U., 1959-60; fellow Georgetown U., 1975-76; recipient Spl. Achievement award U.S. Treasury, 1979. Mem. ABA, Md. Bar Assn., Nat. Assn. Women Judges, D.C. Bar Assn. Office: US Tax Ct 400 2nd St NW Washington DC 20217-0002

**PARR, NANCY GRACE,** lawyer; b. Suffolk, Va., Oct. 22, 1958; d. John Drew and Florence Grace (West) P. BA, U. Va., 1980; JD, U. Richmond, 1983. Bar: Va. 1983. Assoc. David Wm. Shreve & Assocs., Altavista, Va., 1983-84; asst. Commonwealth Atty.'s Office, Suffolk, Va., 1984-87, dep., 1987-94; deputy atty. Commonwealth Atty.'s Office, Chesapeake, Va., 1994-99; acting Commonwealth Atty. Chesapeake, Va., 1999—. Mem. Supporters of Abuse Free Environment, Suffolk, Va., 1985; bd. dirs. Western Tidewater

Friends of Juvenile Ct., Suffolk, 1987-88; edn. chmn. Pilot Club, Suffolk, 1987-88; corr. sec. Polit Club Suffolk, 1998-99; publicity com. Suffolk Peanut Festival, 1988; dir Com. on Literacy, 1987-88; dir. Tidewater Legal Aid Soc., 1998—; dir. Riddick's Folly Mus. Mem. ABA (mem. juvenile justice com. 1986-91, mem. criminal law com. 1991-92), Nat. Dist. Attys. Assn., Suffolk Bar Asns., Va. State Bar Assn. (jud. nominating com. 1997—), Chesapeake Bar Assn. Avocations: travel, reading. Home: 814 General Pickett Dr Suffolk VA 23434-7550 Office: Office of Commonwealth Atty PO Box 15225 Chesapeake VA 23328-5225

**PARRAGUIRRE, RONALD DAVID,** judge; b. Reno, July 8, 1959; s. Paul Charles and Iris Mae (Bleick) P. BBA, San Diego State U., 1982; JD, U. San Diego, 1985. Bar: Pa. 1986, Nev. 1986, D.C. 1987. Legis. asst. U.S. Senator Paul Laxalt, Washington, 1985-86; counsel subcom. on criminal law, judiciary com. U.S. Senate, Washington, 1986-87; lawyer Parraguirre & Parraguirre, Las Vegas, Nev., 1987-91; mcpl. ct. judge Dept. 6 City of Las Vegas, 1991—. Mem. ABA, ATLA, Am. Judges Assn., Nev. Judges Assn., Clark County Bar Assn. (exec. bd. dirs.). Republican. Lutheran. Avocations: skiing, racquetball, hunting, fishing. Office: Las Vegas Mcpl Ct 400 Stewart Ave Las Vegas NV 89101-2927

**PARRIGIN, ELIZABETH ELLINGTON,** lawyer; b. Colon, Panama, May 23, 1932; d. Jesse Cox and Elizabeth (Roark) Ellington; m. Perry G. Parrigin, Oct. 8, 1975. BA, Agnes Scott Coll., 1954; JD, U. Va., 1959. Bar: Tex. 1959, Mo. 1980. Atty. San Antonio, 1960-69; law libr. U. Mo., Columbia, 1969-77, rsch. assoc., 1977-82; atty. pvt. practice, Columbia, 1982—. Elder, clk. of session First Presbyn. Ch., Columbia; mem. permanent jud. commn. Presbyn. Ch. U.S., 1977-83, mem. advisory com. on constitution, 1983-90. Mem. ABA, Mo. Bar Assn. (chmn. sub-com. revision of Mo. trust law 1988-92), Columbia Kiwanis Club (pres. 1997-98). Democrat. Presbyterian. Avocations: music, gardening, reading. Probate, Family and matrimonial, General practice. Home: 400 Conley Ave Columbia MO 65201-4219 Office: 124 N 8th St Columbia MO 65201-4844

**PARRISH, DAVID WALKER, JR.,** legal publishing company executive; b. Bristol, Tenn., Feb. 8, 1923. BA, Emory & Henry Coll., 1948, LLD, 1978; BS, U.S. Merchant Marine Acad., 1950; LLB, U. Va., 1951. Pres. The Michie Co., Charlottesville, Va., 1969-89, vice chmn., 1989-96; pub. cons., 1996—. Home: 114 Falcon Dr Charlottesville VA 22901-2013 Office: 300 Preston Ave Ste 103 Charlottesville VA 22902-5044

**PARRISH, SIDNEY HOWARD,** lawyer; b. Orlando, Fla., Mar. 3, 1940; s. Dallis Matthew and Anne (Cashion) P.; m. Faye Olivia Bass, Aug. 12, 1967; children: Sidney Howard Jr., Christine Olivia. BS, Fla. State U., 1963, JD, 1969. Bar: Fla. 1970, U.S. Dist. Ct. (mid. dist.) Fla. 1973, U.S. Ct. Appeals (11th cir.) 1973, U.S. Supreme Ct. 1973; cert. civil trial lawyer 1983, civil trial advocate 1985. Ptnr. Troutman, Parrish, Williams & Blankenship P.A., Winter Park, Fla., 1970-86, Parrish & Bailey P.A., Orlando, 1986—; asst. atty., prosecutor City of Winter Park, 1970-72; asst. solicitor County of Orange, Fla., 1970-72. Deacon, chmn. bd. of trustees Downtown Bapt. Ch., Orlando, 1986—. With USCGR, 1960-68. Mem. ABA, Orange County Bar Assn. (med./legal com., fed. and state trial practice com.), Assn. Trial Lawyers Am., Acad. Fla. Trial Lawyers, Delta Theta Phi. Federal civil litigation, State civil litigation, Personal injury. Home: 4861 Big Oaks Ln Orlando FL 32806-7826 Office: Parrish Bailey & Morse 116 W America St Orlando FL 32801-3616

**PARROTT, NANCY SHARON,** lawyer; b. Atoka, Okla., Jan. 11, 1944; d. Albert L. and Willie Jo (Parkhill) Furr. BA, Okla. U., 1967; MA, No. Tex. U., 1974; JD, Okla. City U., 1982. Bar: Okla. 1984, U.S. Supreme Ct. 1984. Ptnr. Champman & Chapman, Oklahoma City, 1984-85; chief legal asst. marshal Okla. Supreme Ct., Oklahoma City, 1985—. Mem. Leadership Oklahoma, Leadership Oklahoma City; bd. dirs. Youth Leadership Exch. Mem. ABA, Okla. Bar Assn., Okla. County Bar Assn. Briefcase, Am. Adjudicature Soc., Okla. Bar Assn. (chmn. awards com.). Office: Okla Supreme Ct State Capital Bldg 245 Oklahoma City OK 73105

**PARRY, PAUL STEWART,** lawyer; b. London, Sept. 16, 1938; came to U.S., 1949; s. William and Winifred Parry; m. Deborah J. Backhaut, May 20, 1958; children: Alan, Susan, Joan. BA, San Fernando State U., 1965; MBA, Pepperdine U., 1978; JD, Calif. So. Law Sch., Riverside, 1985. Bar: Calif., U.S. Dist. Ct. (ctrl. and so. dists.) Calif. Pvt. practice Palm Springs, Calif.; bd. dirs. Arthritis Found., Coachella Valley, Calif., Bet Chesid Legal Svcs., Palm Springs. Mem. personnel commn. City of Palm Springs, 1996-98, rent control commn., 1998—. Mem. ABA, Calif. Bar. Assn., Riverside County Bar Assn., Desert Bar Assn. (family law sect. 1995—). Avocations: boating, tennis, swimming. Family and matrimonial, Bankruptcy, Personal injury. Office: Law Offices of Paul S Parry Ste 200 777 E Tahquitz Canyon Way Palm Springs CA 92262-6797

**PARRY, STANLEY WARREN,** lawyer; b. Cedar City, Utah, May 7, 1949; s. Dixon C. Parry and Majorie (Miller) Dubois; m. Carol Lynne Wright; children: Heidi, John, Mathis, Joseph, Tyler. BA, So. Utah U., 1974; JD, Brigham Young U., 1977. Bar: Nev. 1977. Dep. dist. atty. County of Clark, Las Vegas, 1977-83; trial atty. U.S. Dept. Justice Strike Force, Las Vegas, 1983-89; pvt. practice Las Vegas, 1989—; ptnr. K. Michael Leavitt, Las Vegas, 1991-94, Curran & Parry, Las Vegas, 1994—; pres. Grand West Devel., Las Vegas, 1992-96. Chmn. Las Vegas Ethics Rev. Bd., 1992-95. Mem. Keystone Club (bd. dirs. 1995-97). Mem. LDS Ch. Real property, Land use and zoning (including planning), General civil litigation. Office: Curran & Parry 601 S Rancho Dr Ste C-23 Las Vegas NV 89106-4825

**PARRY, WILLIAM DEWITT,** lawyer; b. Hartford, Conn., June 4, 1941; s. William Brown and Mary Elizabeth (Caton) p.; m. Andrea Hannah Lewis, June 30, 1973; children: Sara, Jessica. BA, U. Mass., 1963; JD, U. Pa., 1966. Bar: N.J. 1987, Pa. 1967, U.S. Dist. Ct. (ea. dist.) Pa. 1974, U.S. Ct. Appeals (3d cir.) 1980, U.S. Ct. Appeals (9th cir.) 1998, U.S. Supreme Ct. 1980. Assoc. Shapiro, Cook & Bressler, Phila., 1966-67; asst. dir. ABA joint com on continuing legal edn. Am. Law Inst., Phila., 1967-73; assoc. Lowenschuss Assocs., Phila., 1973-85; of counsel Weiss, Golden & Pierson, Phila., 1985-88; pvt. practice Phila., 1988; ptnr. Rubin, Quinn, Moss & Patterson, Phila., 1989-93; pvt. practice Phila., 1993—. Author: Understanding and Controlling Stuttering: A Comprehensive New Approach Based on the Valsalva Hypothesis, 1994; editor U. Pa. Law Rev., 1964-66, The Practical Lawyer, 1967-73. Founder Phila. area chpt. Nat. Stuttering Project, 1985—, dir. Nat. Stuttering Project, 1996—; trustee Unitarian Soc. Germantown, Phila., 1983-86. Mem. ABA, Assn. Trial Lawyers Am., Pa. Bar Assn., Phila. Bar Assn., Pa. Trial Lawyers Assn. (Phila. chpt.). Democrat. Avocations: writing, lecturing. Personal injury, Federal civil litigation, State civil litigation. Home: 520 Baird Rd Merion Station PA 19066-1302 Office: 1608 Walnut St Ste 900 Philadelphia PA 19103-5451

**PARSON, CONNIE WALTER,** lawyer; b. Birmingham, Ala., Dec. 5, 1946; d. Matthew and Lorene (Ross) P.; m. Linda Jean Robinson, May 31, 1969; children: Nyya, Connyse. B.A., U. Ala., Birmingham, 1978; J.D., Miles Sch. Law, Fairfield, Ala., 1982. Bar: Ala. 1984. Ctr. mgr. United Parcel Service, Birmingham, 1970-76; auditor Days Inn Motel, Bessemer, Ala., 1976-79; terminal mgr. Express Transport, Chattanooga, 1979-81; dist. mgr. Mercury Motor Express, Tampa, Fla., 1981—; cons. TSI, Birmingham, 1981—. Vol., ARC, Birmingham, 1979—. Served with U.S. Army, 1967-70. Mem. ABA, Nat. Bar Assn., Ala. Bar Assn., Assn. Trial Lawyers Am., NAACP, Delta Theta Phi. Baptist. Lodge: Masons. Office: 517 Tuscaloosa Ave SW Birmingham AL 35211-1674

**PARSON, JASON A.,** lawyer; b. Madisonville, Ky., Jan. 30, 1963; s. Dewey Allen and Peggy Sue Parson; m. Valerie Ann Schmidt, Mar. 28, 1992; 1 child, Samuel Ayres. BA, Ind. Ctrl. U., Indpls., 1985; JD, Washington U., St. Louis, 1988. Bar: Ill. 1989, U.S. Dist. Ct. (no. dist.) Ill. 1991. Fed. clk. to Hon. John F. Nangle U.S. Dist. Ct. (ea. dist.) Mo., St. Louis, 1988-90; assoc. Lord, Bissell & Brook, Chgo., 1990-98, ptnr., 1998—. Editor-in-chief Washington U. Law Quar., 1987-88; contbr. articles to profl. jours. Hagelskamp scholar, 1984. Mem. Ill. State Bar Assn., Def. Rsch. Inst., Ill. Assn. Healthcare Attys., Ill. Assn. Def. Trial Counsel. Avocation: vocal music. Health, State civil litigation, Federal civil litigation. Office: Lord Bissell & Brook 115 S Lasalle St Ste 3200 Chicago IL 60603-3972

**PARSONS, A. PETER,** lawyer; b. Norwood, Mass., May 29, 1945; s. Charles A.A. and Elizabeth P. (Coombs) P.; children: A. Peter, Christopher P.; m. Elizabeth A. Lee, Aug. 24, 1991; 1 child Alex W. AA, Palm Beach Jr. Coll., 1968; BS Fla. Atlantic U., 1969; JD, Duke U., 1973. Bar: Wash. 1973, U.S. Dist. Ct. (ea. and we. dists.) Wash. 1974, U.S. Ct. Appeals (9th cir.) 1974; CPA, Fla., Wash. Acct., Haskins & Sells, Ft. Lauderdale, 1969-70; tax cons. Arthur, Young & Co., Portland, Oreg., 1972; law clk. Wash. Supreme Ct., 1973-74; atty. Perkins, Coie, Seattle, 1974-77; mem., mng. dir. Weinrich, Gilmore & Adolph, Seattle, 1978-87; ptnr. Davis Wright Tremaine LLP, 1988—; adj. prof. U. Puget Sound, 1974-75; lectr. U. Wash., 1978-81. Mem. editorial bd. Duke U. Law Jour., 1971-73. Contbr. articles to legal jours. Chmn. bd. dirs. PIVOT, non-profit corp., Seattle, 1975-78; Group Theater, Seattle, 1984-86; chmn. bd. dirs. MIT Enterprise Forum, Seattle, 1984-92 ; Wash. State Biotechnology Assn. 1991-94, Washington Software Alliance, Bellevue, 1996-98, Midisoft Corp., Issaquah, 1996-98, Info. Technol. World Congress N.Am., 1998—, BC Softworld Soc., 1998—. Served with USAF, 1963-67. Mem. ABA, Wash. Bar Assn., Am. Intellectual Property Law Assn., Computer Law Soc., Am. Inst. CPAs, Wash. Soc. CPAs, Seattle-King County Bar Assn., Am. Coll. of Mediators, Rainier Club, Seattle Yacht Club. Technology, Securities, Intellectual property. Home: 1864 Broadmoor Dr E Seattle WA 98112-2312 Office: Davis Wright Tremaine LLP 2600 Century Sq 1501 4th Ave Ste 2600 Seattle WA 98101-1688

**PARSONS, CHARLES ALLAN, JR.,** lawyer; b. Mpls., July 16, 1943; s. Charles Allan and Grace Adelaide (Covert) P.; m. JoAnne Ruth Russell, Oct. 16, 1965; children: Charles, Daniel, Nancy. BS, U. Minn., 1965, JD cum laude, 1972. Bar: Minn. 1972, U.S. Dist. Ct. Minn. 1972, U.S. Supreme Ct. 1995. Ptnr. Moss & Barnett, P.A., 1972—. Bd. dirs. Legal Advice Clinics Ltd., Mpls., 1975-93; chair steering com. S.E. Asian Legal Assistance Project, Mpls., 1988-93. Named Vol. Atty. of Yr., Legal Advice Clinics, Ltd., Mpls., 1990. Mem. ABA, Am. Coll. Real Estate Lawyers, Minn. State Bar Assn. (co-chair legis. com. real property sec. 1986—, coun. mem. 1986—, chair real property sect. 1993-94), Hennepin County Bar Assn. (chair real property sect. 1988-89). Roman Catholic. Avocations: reading, walking, biking, hiking. Real property, Finance. Office: Moss & Barnett PA 4800 Norwest Ctr 90 S 7th Minneapolis MN 55402-4119

**PARSONS, DONALD FRANCIS,** lawyer; b. Phila., June 28, 1948. BSEE cum laude, Lehigh U., 1970, MA, 1972; JD, Georgetown ., 1977. Bar: Del. 1977. Law clk. to Hon. James L. Latchum U.S. Dist. Ct. Del., 1977-79; ptnr. Morris, Nichols, Arsht & Tunnell, Wilmington, Del., 1979—. Case and note editor Georgetown Law Jour., 1976-77. Mem. ABA, N.Y. Patent Law Assn., Phila. Patent Law Assn., Am. Intellectual Property Law Assn., Del. Bar Assn. (pres. 1999—). E-mail: dparsons@mnat.com. Intellectual property. Office: Morris Nichols Arsht & Tunnell PO Box 1347 1201 N Market St Wilmington DE 19899-1347*

**PARSONS, INGA LORRAINE,** law educator; b. Jackson Hole, Wyo., Oct. 24, 1962; m. Roger Talkov, Sept. 6, 1992; children: Ara Rose, Ethan Charles. AB in Govt., Harvard U., 1985; JD, Columbia U., 1986. Bar: N.Y. 1990. Legis. intern U.S. Senate, Washington, 1983; summer assoc. Spence, Moriarity & Schuster, Jackson Hole, 1986-89; legis. intern Office Atty. Gen., N.Y.C., 1987-89; fed. jud. law clerk USDC CDCA, L.A., 1989-90; asst. fed. defender Legal Aid Soc., N.Y.C., 1990-95; acting asst. prof. clin. law NYU, N.Y.C., 1995—; guest commentator Ct. TV, N.Y.C., 1993—, Fox News, 1998—; instr. trial advocacy Harvard U., 1993—, Fordham U., 1993—, Rutgers U., 1993—, Cordozo U., 1993—. Head coach Jackson Hole Little League, 1986-89. Recipient Jane Marks Murphy prize Columbia U., 1989, Cmty. Recognition NYU Law Student Body, 1996; G.G. Michelson fellow Helena Rubenstein Found., 1992-93. Mem. ABA, Nat. Assn. Criminal Def. Lawyers, N.Y. Women's Bar Assn. Avocations: skiing, reading, gardening, cooking. Office: NYU Sch Law 249 Sullivan St New York NY 10012-1079

**PARSONS, JAMES BOWNE,** lawyer; b. Mineola, N.Y., Mar. 21, 1954; s. Edward Finch and Elizabeth (Hubbell) P.; m. Carol Anne Sherfy, Dec. 30, 1977. BA in Polit. Sci., U. Puget Sound, 1976; JD, Lewis and Clark Coll., 1980. Bar: Oreg. 1980, Wash. 1982, Bar of No. Mariana Islands 1990, U.S. Dist. Ct. (we. dist.) Wash. 1986, U.S. Ct. Appeals (9th cir.) 1990, U.S. Dist. Ct. (Oreg.) 1990, U.S. Dist. Ct. (No. Mariana Islands) 1990, U.S. Tax Ct. 1985. Sole practice Oregon City, Oreg., 1980-83; assoc. Copenbarger et al, Seattle, 1983-84, Holman & Monahan, Seattle, 1984-86; pvt. practice Seattle, 1986-90; asst. atty. gen. Commonwealth of the No. Mariana Islands, 1990-92; corp. counsel, pres. Secure Benefits, Inc., 1993-96; mng. ptnr. Parsons Law firm, Bellevue, Wash., 1996—; bd. dirs., sec.-treas., spkr. Eastside Legal Assistance Program. Speaker various non-profit orgns. regarding estate planning, charitable giving and bus. formation. Mem. ABA (real property, probate and trust, bus. law sect., com. on fed. regulation of securities), Wash. State Bar Assn. (spkr., real property, probate and trust sects., bus. sect., com. on interprofl. rels.). Democrat. Episcopalian. Avocations: traveling, skiing, scuba diving, wine, music. General corporate, Estate planning, Securities. Home: 8704 NE 21st Pl Bellevue WA 98004-2440 Office: Parsons Law Firm 10655 NE 4th St Ste 707 Bellevue WA 98004-5037

**PARSONS, RODNEY HUNTER,** lawyer; b. Pasadena, Calif., Feb. 4, 1947; s. Clarence Eugene and Agnes Prentice (Hunter) P.; m. Deneise Renee Trebotich, Aug. 2, 1980; children: Shannon, Justin, Ryan, Renee, Morgan. BA, UCLA, 1968, JD, 1975. Bar: Calif. 1975, U.S. Dist. Ct. (cen. dist.) Calif. 1980. Assoc. Law Offices Manley Freid, L.A., 1975-78, Robert P. Lawton Inc., Brea, Calif., 1978-79; ptnr. Lether & Parsons, Brea, Calif., 1979-84; owner, pres. Rodney H. Parsons Inc., Fullerton, Calif., 1984—; judge pro tem Superior Ct., 1989—. Bd. dirs. Brea C. of C., 1979-88, pres., 1980-82; bd. dirs. Brea Found., 1990. Mem. Orange County Bar Assn. (family law sect.), Rotary (bd. dirs. 1979-81). Avocations: golf, youth sports, model trains, writing. Family and matrimonial. Office: 285 Imperial Hwy Fullerton CA 92835-1048

**PARTLOW, JAMES JUSTICE,** lawyer; b. Sanford, Fla., Apr. 3, 1970; s. Patrick Grieder Partlow and Deborah Justice Partridge; m. Chandra Denise Partlow, Sept. 27, 1997. BS in Criminology cum laude, Fla. State U., 1991; JD, Miss. Coll., 1994. Bar: Fla. 1994, U.S. Dist. Ct. (mid. dist.) Fla. 1996, U.S. Supreme Ct. 1998. Atty. Stenstrom, McIntosh, Colbert, Whigham & Simmons, P.A., Sanford, 1994—; city atty. Code Enforcement Bd., Sanford, 1997—, Nuisance Abatement Bd., Sanford, 1997—, Code Enforcement Bd., DeBary, Fla., 1997—. Coach baseball and flag football City of Sanford Dept. Recreation, 1998—. Mem. Fla. Bar Assn. (trial lawyer sect., family and matrimonial law sect.), Seminole County Bar Assn. (family law sect., trial lawyers sect., treas. 1998). Republican. Baptist. Avocations: whale watching, classic cars, scuba diving, travel. Family and matrimonial, General civil litigation. Home: 57 Lake Dr Debary FL 32713-2873 Office: 200 W 1st St Ste 22 Sanford FL 32771-1204

**PARTNOY, RONALD ALLEN,** lawyer; b. Norwalk, Conn., Dec. 23, 1933; s. Maurice and Ethel Marguerite (Roselle) P.; m. Diane Catherine Keenan, Sept. 18, 1965. B.A., Yale U., 1956; LL.B., Harvard U., 1961; LL.M., Boston U., 1965. Bar: Mass. 1962, Conn. 1966. Atty. Liberty Mut. Ins. Co., Boston, 1961-65; assoc. counsel Remington Arms Co., Bridgeport, Conn., 1965-70; gen. counsel Remington Arms Co., 1970-88, sec., 1983-93; sr. counsel E.I. du Pont de Nemours & Co., Wilmington, Del., 1985-95. Served with USN, 1956-58; to capt. USNR (ret.). Mem. ABA, Sporting Arms and Ammunition Mfrs. Inst. (chmn. legis. and legal affairs com. 1971-86), Am. Judicature Soc., U.S. Navy League (pres. Bridgeport coun. 1975-77, nat. dir., Conn. pres. 1977-80, v.p. Empire region 1980-85), Naval Res. Assn. (3d dist. pres., nat. exec. com. 1981-85, nat. v.p. 1997—), Chancery Club, Harvard Club of Boston, Harvard Club of Phila., Yale Club of N.Y.C., Assn. of Yale Alumni (del. 1997—). General corporate, Contracts commercial, Antitrust. Home: 616 Bayard Rd Kennett Square PA 19348-2504

**PARTOYAN, GARO ARAKEL,** lawyer; b. Toledo, Dec. 6, 1936; s. Garo and Vartoohi (Yessayan) P.; m. Kathleen D. Valencia, Apr. 1, 1981; children: Garo Linck, Elizabeth Margaret, Martin Joseph. BS in Chem. Engring., Northwestern U., 1959; JD, U. Mich., 1962; LLM, NYU, 1964. Bar: N.Y. 1963, U.S. Dist. Cts. (so. dist.) N.Y. 1964, U.S. Ct. Claims 1966, U.S. Ct. Appeals (2nd cir.) 1966, U.S. Dist. Ct. (ea. dist.) N.Y. 1968. Ptnr. Curtis, Morris & Safford, N.Y.C., 1962-76; gen. counsel mktg. and tech. Mars, Inc., McLean, Va., 1976-98; atty. Mgmt. of Intellectual Property, Sarasota, Fla., 1998—. Mem. Dobbs Ferry (N.Y.) Bd. Edn., 1972-76, pres., 1975-76; chmn. Fairfax Citizens Group, Fairfax County, Va., 1988-90. Mem. ABA, Am. Intellectual Property Law Assn., N.Y. Intellectual Property Law Assn., Internat. Trademark Assn. (pres. 1990-91, bd. dirs. 1983—), Intellectual Property Owners (bd. dirs. 1992—). Avocations: sailing, curling. Private international, Patent, Trademark and copyright. Office: 7385 Regina Royale Sarasota FL 34238-4545

**PARTRIDGE, MARK VAN BUREN,** lawyer, educator, writer; b. Rochester, Minn., Oct. 16, 1954; s. John V.B. and Constance (Brainerd) P.; m. Mary Roberta Moffitt, Apr. 30, 1983; children: Caitlin, Lindsay, Christopher. BA, U. Nebr., 1978; JD, Harvard U., 1981. Bar: Ill. 1981, U.S. Dist. Ct. (no. dist.) Ill. 1981, U.S. Dist. Ct. (ea. dist.) Mich. 1983, U.S. Ct. Appeals (fed. cir.) 1983, U.S. Ct. Appeals (4th cir.) 1986, U.S. Ct. Appeals (5th cir.) 1993, U.S. Ct. Appeals (3rd cir.) 1998. Assoc. Pattishall, McAuliffe, Newbury, Hilliard & Geraldson, Chgo., 1981-88, ptnr., 1988—; adj. prof. John Marshall Law Sch., Chgo., 1990—; arbitrator Cook County Mandatory Arbitration Program, 1989—; v.p. Harvard Legal Aid Bur., 1980-81; mediator no. dist. Ill. Voluntary Mediation Program, 1997—. Contbr. articles to profl. jours.; mem. editl. bd. The Trademark Reporter, 1994-97; adv. bd. IP Litigator, 1995—. Vol. Chgo. Vol. Legal Svcs., 1983—. Mem. ABA (com. chmn. 1989-91, 94-99), Internat. Trademark Assn. (com. vice chmn. 1996), World Intellectual Property Orgn. (experts panel internet domain name process 1998-99), Am. Intellectual Property Law Assn. (com. chmn. 1989-91, 96-98, bd. dirs. 1998—), Intellectual Property Law Assn. Chgo. (com. chmn. 1993-96), Brand Names Ednl. Found. (moot ct. regional chmn. 1994-96, nat. vice-chmn. 1997-98, nat. chmn. 1998-99), Legal Club (v.p. 1998), Execs. Club, Union League Club. Avocations: writing, genealogy, travel, computers. Trademark and copyright, Federal civil litigation, Private international. Office: Pattishall McAuliffe Newbury Hilliard & Geraldso 311 S Wacker Dr Ste 5000 Chicago IL 60606-6631

**PASAHOW, LYNN H(AROLD),** lawyer; b. Ft. Eutiss, Va., Mar. 13, 1947; s. Samuel and Cecelia (Newman) P.; m. Leslie Aileen Cobb, June 11, 1969; 1 child, Michael Alexander. AB, Stanford U., 1969; JD, U. Calif., Berkeley, 1972. Bar: Calif. 1972, U.S. Ct. Appeals (9th cir.) 1972, U.S. Dist. Ct. (no. dist.) Calif. 1973, U.S. Dist. Ct. (cen. dist.) Calif. 1974, U.S. Supreme Ct. 1976, U.S. Dist. Ct. (ea. dist.) Calif. 1977, U.S. Ct. Appeals (fed. cir.) 1990. Law clk. judge U.S. Dist. Ct. (no. dist.) Calif., San Francisco, 1972-73; assoc. McCutchen, Doyle, Brown & Enersen, Palo Alto, Calif., 1973-79; ptnr. McCutchen, Doyle, Brown & Enersen, San Francisco, 1979—; attys. adv. panel Bay Area Biosci. Ctr., 1993—; mem. adv. bd. Berkeley Ctr. for Law and Tech., 1998—. Author: Pretrial and Settlement Conferences in Federal Court, 1983; co-author: Civil Discovery and Mandatory Disclosure: A Guide to Effective Practice, 1994; contbr. articles to profl. jours. Mem. ABA, Calif. Bar Assn., Am. Intellectual Property Law Assn. Democrat. Patent, Trademark and copyright, Federal civil litigation. Office: McCutchen Doyle Brown & Enersen 3150 Porter Dr Palo Alto CA 94304-1212 *Notable cases include: duPont vs. Cetus, PCR patent litigation, nicotine patch patent litigation, University of California & Vysis v. Oncor FISH litigation.*

**PASCAL, ROBERT ALBERT,** lawyer; b. Fort Lauderdale, Fla., Sept. 29, 1965; s. Albert and Maria Pascal. BA, Loyola U., 1987; JD, Nova Southeastern U., 1991. Bar: Fla. 1991. Pvt. practice Fort Lauderdale, Fla., 1991—. Editor E-Mag., 1997, Ibl.com.. Vol. Broward Lawyers Care, Ft. Lauderdale, 1992-97, Lawyer for Arts, Ft. Lauderdale, 1993-98; v.p. Quantum Resource Mgmt. Internat., Ft. Lauderdale, 1992—. Avocations: cycling, swimming, travel, linguistics. Immigration, naturalization, and customs, Criminal, Private international. Home: 1506 SE 12th St Fort Lauderdale FL 33316-1410 Office: Pascal L Proff Offices 300 Ave of Arts Fort Lauderdale FL 33316

**PASCHKE, JERRY BRYAN,** lawyer; b. Palmdale, Calif., Aug. 6, 1965; s. Donald Joseph and Diana Marie (Scott) P. BS, St. John's U., Collegeville, Minn., 1988; JD, Hamline U., St. Paul, 1991. Bar: Minn. 1991, Army Ct. Mil. Rev. 1992, U.S. Magistrates Ct. 1993. Commd. 1st lt. U.S. Army, 1992, advanced through grades to capt., 1992; post judge advocate U.S. Army-Sierra Army Depot, Herlong, Calif., 1992-94; brigade trial counsel U.S. Army-Camp Stanley, Uijongbu, South Korea, 1994-95; legal instr. U.S. Army-Ft. Huachuca, Sierra Vista, Ariz., 1995-97, chief criminal law, 1997-98, mil. magistrate, 1995-97; acct. Accts.-On-Call, Mpls., 1998—; adminstrv. law officer USAR, Ft. Snelling, Minn., 1998—. Mem. landlord-tenant hotline Minn. Pub. Interest Rsch. Group, Mpls., 1989; advisor DeMolay, Reno, 1992-94. Decorated Army Commendtion medal, Meritorious Svc. medal. Mem. Masons, Order St. Barbara. Avocations: hiking, chess, travel, bowling. Home: 4450 Minnetonka Blvd Apt 103 Saint Louis Park MN 55416-5816

**PASCOTTO, ALVARO,** lawyer; b. Rome, Mar. 8, 1949; came to U.S., 1984; s. Antonio and Anna Ludovica (Habig) P.; m. Linda Haldan, July 20, 1985. JD, U. Rome, 1973. Bar: Italy 1976, Calif. 1987, U.S. Dist. Ct. (cen. dist.) Calif. 1987, U.S. Ct. Appeals (9th cir.) 1987. Ptnr. Studio Legale Pascotto, Rome, 1976-86, Pascotto, Gallavotti & Gardner, L.A. and Rome, 1986-90, Pascotto & Gallavotti, L.A., 1990—; of counsel Irell & Manella LLP, L.A., 1994—; ofcl. counsel Consulate Gen. Italy, L.A., 1987—. Mem. ABA, Calif. Bar Assn., Italian-Am. Bar Assn., Am. Mgmt. Assn., Consiglio dell'Ordine Degli Avvocati e Procuratori di Roma. Clubs: Circolo del Golf (Rome); Malibu (Calif.) Racquet Club, Regency Club (L.A.), L.A. Country Club. Private international, Entertainment, Aviation. Home: 6116 Merritt Dr Malibu CA 90265-3847 Office: Pascotto & Gallavotti 1800 Avenue Of The Stars Los Angeles CA 90067-4211

**PASEK, JEFFREY IVAN,** lawyer; b. Pitts., Apr. 4, 1951; m. Kathryn Ann Hirsh, Aug. 17, 1975; children: Joshua, Benjamin, Michael. BA, U. Pitts., 1973; JD, U. Pa., 1976. Bar: Pa. 1976, U.S. Dist. Ct. (ea. dist.) Pa. 1976, U.S. Ct. Appeals (3d cir.) 1976, U.S. Dist. Ct. (we. dist.) Pa. 1977, U.S. Supreme Ct. 1980, U.S. Dist. Ct. (mid. dist.) Pa. 1984, N.Y. 1988, N.J. 1988, U.S. Dist. Ct. N.J. 1988, U.S. Dist. Ct. (so. and ea. dists.) N.Y. 1989, U.S. Ct. Appeals (2d cir.) 1989, U.S. Dist. Ct. Vt. 1990. Assoc. Cohen, Shapiro, Polisher, Shiekman & Cohen, Phila., 1976-84; ptnr. Cohen Shapiro Polisler Shiekman and Cohen, Phila., 1985-95; sr. mem. Cozen and O'Connor, Phila., 1995—; lectr. Pa. Bar Inst., Harrisburg, 1980-83, 86, 95, 96, 97, 98, 99, course planner, 1986; instr. Inst. for Paralegal Tng., Phila., 1981-82. Mem. nat. governing coun. Am. Jewish Congress, N.Y.C., 1985, 88-96, pres. Pa. region, 1992-95; co-chmn. Commn. on Law and Social Action, Phila., 1985-92; bd. dirs. Jewish Employment and Vocat. Svc. Phila., 1982—, asst. treas., 1986-87, v.p., 1987-95, pres., 1995-98; bd. dirs. Fairmount Geriatric Ctr., 1986-88, sec., 1985-87, v.p., 1987-88; bd. dirs. Pa. Legal Svcs. Ctr., 1987-88, treas., 1988. Mem. ABA (equal employment opportunity law com., labor law sect.), Pa. Bar Assn., Phila. Bar Assn. (co-chmn. labor and employment law com. 1997), Indsl. Rels. Rsch. Assn., Pa. Chamber of Bus. and Industry (exec. com. 1991-96, bd. dirs. 1988—, chmn. indsl. rels. com. 1984-87, chmn. edn. com. 1988-91). Labor, Civil rights, General civil litigation. Office: Cozen and O'Connor 1900 Market St Philadelphia PA 19103-3527

**PASICH, KIRK ALAN,** lawyer; b. La Jolla, Calif., May 26, 1955; s. Chris Nick and Iva Mae (Tormey) P.; m. Pamela Mary Woods, July 30, 1983; children: Christopher Thomas, Kelly Elizabeth, Connor Woods. BA in Polit. Sci., UCLA, 1977; JD, Loyola Law Sch., L.A., 1980. Bar: Calif. 1980, U.S. Dist. Ct. (no., so., ea. and cen. dists.) Calif. 1981, U.S. Ct. Appeals (9th cir.) 1982, U.S. Ct. Appeals (1st cir.) 1992. Assoc. Paul, Hastings, Janofsky & Walker, L.A., 1980-88, ptnr., 1988-89; ptnr. Troop Steuber Pasich Reddick & Tobey, LLP, L.A., 1989—. Author: Casualty and Liability Insurance, 1990, 96; co-author: Officers and Directors: Liabilities and Protections, 1996, The Year 2000 and Beyond: Liability and Insurance for Computer Code Problems, 1999; contbg. editor: West's California Litigation Forms: Civil Procedure Before Trial, 1996; entertainment law columnist, ins. law columnist L.A. and San Francisco Daily Jour., 1989—; contbr. articles to profl. jours. Active bd. dirs. Nat. Acad. Jazz, L.A., 1988-89, chmn. bd. dirs. Woody Herman Found., L.A., 1989-92, active L.A. City Atty's. Task Force for Econ. Recovery, 1992-93. Named to Calif's. Legal Dream Team as 1 of state's top 25 litigators, Calif. Law Bus., 1992, as one of the nation's top 45 lawyers under age 45, The Am. Lawyer, 1995. Mem. ABA (mem. Task Force on Complex Insurance Coverage Litigation). General civil litigation,

Entertainment, Insurance. Office: 2029 Century Park E Los Angeles CA 90067-2901

**PASSER-MUSLIN, JULIETTE MAYABELLE,** lawyer. MusB, Manhattan Sch. Music, 1981, MA in Music Edn., 1984; postgrad., NYU, 1985-86, Columbia U., 1988-89; JD cum laude, Yeshiva U., 1990. Bar: N.Y. 1990. Solist, music dir. mus. theater cos. in U.S. and Europe, 1977-87; dir. admissions and pub. rels. St. Sergius Sch., N.Y.C., 1981-83; tchg. asst. edn. dept. NYU, N.Y.C., 1985-86; assoc. Debevoise & Plimpton, N.Y.C., 1990-94, Patterson, Belknap, Webb & Tyler, LLP, N.Y.C., 1994-96; pres., gen. counsel Internat. Project Devel. Group, LLC, N.Y.C., 1996—; adj. lectr. Hunter Coll. CUNY, and Hunter Coll. H.S., 1981-82; tchg. asst., substitute lectr. Manhattan Sch. Music, N.Y.C., 1981-83; judge numerous music competitions, including Bklyn. Acad. Music, 1985, 86. Contbr. numerous articles to law and other publs.; performer, dir. musicals, including Camelot, Sound of Music, Fantasticks, Grease, West Side Story, Show Boat, Little Night Music, Carousel, King and I, and Jewus Christ Superstar; spl. guest 3d Internat. Festival Contemporary Music, Leningrad, USSR, 1988. Bd. dirs. Coun. for Trade and Econ. Cooperation, U.S.-Uzbekistan Coun., St. Petersburg Found. Scholar Jewish Found. for Edn. Women, 1977-78, Manhattan Sch. Music. Mem. Internat. Law Soc., N.Y. State Bar Assn., Bar Assn. City N.Y., Women in Internat. Trade, Coun. on Fgn. Rels. Fax: 212-541-2486. Private international, Finance, General corporate. Office: Internat Project Devel Group 666 5th Ave Fl 37 New York NY 10103-3799

**PASTER, ROBERT W.,** lawyer; b. St. Louis, Apr. 3, 1966; s. Phillip J. and Flora A. Paster; children: Steven P., Leah D. BA, U. Pa., 1987; JD, Washington U., 1990. Bar: Mo. 1991, Ill. 1991. Assoc. Reid, Murphy & Tobben, St. Louis, Zeircher & Horker, St. Louis. Contbr. articles to profl. jours. Pres. Am. Jewish Congress, St. Louis, 1997—. Mem. Bar Assn. Met. St. Louis, Estate Planning Coun. St. Louis, St. Louis County Bar Assn. Estate planning, General corporate, Probate. Office: Ziercher & Hocker 231 S Bemiston Ave Fl 8 Saint Louis MO 63105-1914

**PASTOOR, MARIA K.,** lawyer; b. Grand Rapids, Mich., Nov. 18, 1959. BA, St. Olaf Coll., 1981; JD, U. Minn., 1985. Bar: Minn. 1985. Law clk. Minn. Ct. of Appeals, St. Paul, 1985-86; pvt. practice St. Paul, 1986-94, 96—; staff atty. Battered Women's Legal Advocacy Project, St. Paul, 1994-96; adminstrv. law judge State of Minn. Office of Adminstrv. Hearings, Mpls., 1996-99. Mem. ABA, Minn. Women Lawyers, Minn. State Bar Assn. Family and matrimonial, Appellate. Office: Pastoor Law Office Ltd 332 Minnesota St Ste E1434 Saint Paul MN 55101-1324

**PASTORIZA, JULIO,** lawyer; b. Havana, Cuba, Sept. 22, 1948; came to U.S., 1960; s. Julio S. and Emilia (Bardanca) P.; m. Gloria M. Alvarez-Pedroso, Jan. 5, 1974; 1 child, Gloria Cristina. AA, Miami Dade C.C., 1967; BA, U. Fla., 1969; JD, U. Miami, 1973. Bar: Fla. 1973, U.S. Tax Ct. 1974, U.S. Supreme Ct. 1977. Assoc. Miguel A. Suarez P.A., Miami, Fla., 1973-77; ptnr. Sulli, Pastoriza & Hill, Miami, 1977-82; shareholder Julio Pastoriza, P.A., Coral Gables, Fla., 1982-85; ptnr. LaCapra & Wiser, Miami, 1985-87; pvt. practice Coral Gables, 1987—; agent Attys. Title Ins. Fund, Miami, 1979—; instr. Biscayne Coll., Miami, 1972-76. Spkr. pre-marital conf. St. Theresa Cath. Ch., Coral Gables, 1981-88, mem. adv. bd., 1987-89; mem. adv. bd. Our Lady of Lourdes Acad., Miami, 1991-95. Democrat. Avocations: fishing, photography. Real property, Bankruptcy, Family and matrimonial. Home: 2601 San Domingo St Coral Gables FL 33134-5534 Office: 250 Bird Rd Ste 216 Coral Gables FL 33146-1424

**PATAKI, LEONARD IGNATIUS,** lawyer; b. Palmerton, Pa., Oct. 2, 1953; s. Ignatz and Olga Pataki; m. Kathleen Harrison, Nov. 29, 1981; 1 child, Alexander. BS, U. Pitts., 1975; JD with honors, Okla. City U., 1977. Bar: Okla. 1978, U.S. Dist. Ct. (no. dist.) Okla. 1978, U. S. Dist. Ct. (ea. dist.) Okla. 1993, U.S. Ct. Appeals (10th cir.) 1981, U.S. Supreme Ct. 1985. Law clk. Hon. Allen Barrow U.S. Dist. Ct., Tulsa, 1978-79, law clk. Hon. Fred Daugherty, 1979, sr. law clk. Hon. James O. Ellison, 1979-82; ptnr. Doerner, Saunders, Daniel & Anderson, Tulsa, 1982—. Pres., trustee Tulsa CASA, Inc., 1997-98. Unitarian. Bankruptcy, Labor, Federal civil litigation. Home: 1024 E 19th St Tulsa OK 74120-7415 Office: Doerner Saunders Daniel & Anderson 320 S Boston Ave Ste 500 Tulsa OK 74103-3725

**PATE, STEPHEN PATRICK,** lawyer; b. Beaumont, Tex., May 6, 1958; s. Gordon Ralph and Shirley Jean (Riley) P.; m. Jean Janssen; 1 child, Teddy. BA, Vanderbilt U., 1980, JD, 1983. Bar: Tex. 1984, U.S. Dist. Ct. (ea. dist.) Tex. 1984, U.S. Dist. Ct. (so. dist.) Tex. 1985. Law clk. to judge Joe J. Fisher U.S. Dist. Ct. Tex., Beaumont, 1983-84; ptnr. Fulbright & Jaworski, Houston. Contbr. articles to profl. jours. Fellow Houston Bar Found., Tex. Bar Found.; mem. ABA (vice chmn. property ins. com. tort and ins. practice sect. 1994—), Tex. Bar Assn., Tex. Young Lawyers Assn. (bd. dirs. 1992-94), Houston Young Lawyers Assn. (bd. dirs. 1990-92, sec. 1992-93, chmn. professionalism com., mem. sunset rev. com. 1990), Manitoba Master Angler, Billfish Found. (Top Angler 1993), Knight of Momus, The Briar Club, Phi Beta Kappa. Republican. Roman Catholic. Avocations: hunting, fishing. Insurance, General civil litigation, Personal injury. Home: 2740 Arbuckle St Houston TX 77005-3932 Office: Fulbright & Jaworski 1301 Mckinney St Houston TX 77010-3031

**PATE, WILLIAM AUGUST,** lawyer; b. Selma, Ala., Dec. 9, 1942; s. William Herbert and Shirley Rosemary (DeMattie) P.; m. Wanda Arlene Whaley, Feb. 2, 1973. BA in Polit. Sci., Citadel, 1964; JD, U. Miss., 1972. Bar: Miss. 1972, U.S. Dist. Ct. (no. dist.) Miss. 1972, U.S. Dist. Ct. (so. dist.) Miss. 1973. Sole practice Gulfport, Miss., 1972—. Mem. Saucier (Miss.) Vol. Fire Dept., Harrison County Pk. Commn., 1980-88, Harrison County Fire Commn.; bd. dirs. Harrison County Mental Health Assn., Christmas in April, Miss. Coast. Capt. USAF, 1965-69. Mem. ABA, Miss. State Bar, Harrison County Bar Assn., Miss. Trial Lawyers Assn., Gulfport Yacht Club, F and AM. General practice, Personal injury, Consumer commercial. Home: 23179 Saucier Lizana Rd Saucier MS 39574-9147 Office: 2017 20th Ave Gulfport MS 39501-3041

**PATEL, MARILYN HALL,** judge; b. Amsterdam, N.Y., Sept. 2, 1938; d. Lloyd Manning and Nina J. (Thorpe) Hall; m. Magan C. Patel, Sept. 2, 1966; children: Brian, Gian. B.A., Wheaton Coll., 1959; J.D., Fordham U., 1963. Bar: N.Y. 1963, Calif. 1970. Mng. atty. Benson & Morris, Esq., N.Y.C., 1962-64; sole practice N.Y.C., 1964-67; atty. U.S. Immigration and Naturalization Svc., San Francisco, 1967-71; sole practive San Francisco, 1971-76; judge Alameda County Mcpl. Ct., Oakland, Calif., 1976-80, U.S. Dist. Ct. (no. dist.) Calif., San Francisco, 1980—; now chief judge U.S. Dist. Ct. for No. Dist. Calif., San Francisco, 1998—; adj. prof. law Hastings Coll. of Law, San Francisco, 1974-76. Author: Immigration and Nationality Law, 1974; also numerous articles. Mem. bd. visitors Fordham U. Sch. Law. Mem. ABA (litigation sect., jud. adminstrn. sect.), ACLU (former bd. dirs.), NOW (former bd. dirs.), Am. law Inst., Am. Judicature Soc. (bd. dirs.), Calif Conf. Judges, Nat. Assn. Women Judges (founding mem.), Internat. Inst. (bd. dirs.), Advs. for Women (co-founder), Assn. Bus. Trial Lawyers (bd. dirs.). Democrat. Avocations: piano playing; travel. Office: US Dist Ct Rm 19-5356 450 Golden Gate Ave San Francisco CA 94102-3661

**PATER, MICHAEL JOHN,** lawyer; b. Natrona Heights, Pa., Aug. 22, 1957; s. Clifford Donald and Alice (Lehmann) P.; m. Kathy Jo Pollack, Apr. 17, 1982. BA in Acctg., BA in Bus. Adminstrn., Grove City (Pa.) Coll., 1979; MSBA, Robert Morris Coll., 1983; JD, Duquesne U., 1988. Bar: Pa. 1988, U.S. Dist. Ct (we. dist.) Pa. 1988. Credit and fin. mgr. Penreco divsn. Pennzoil, Butler, Pa., 1981-88; tax atty. Arthur Young, Pitts., 1988-89; ptnr. Hergenroeder & Heights P.C., Butler, Pitts., 1989—. Campaign treas. Pa. State Senator Melissa A. Hart, 1990—; bd. dirs. Am. Cancer Soc., Four Corners unit, Pitts., 1989-96, New Dirs. Am. Cancer Soc., Pitts., 1988—. Mem. ABA, Pa. Bar Assn., Butler County Bar Assn. (treas. 1991—), Allegheny County Bar Assn. Republican. Avocation: sports. Real property, Probate, General practice. Home: 3128 Primrose Ln Natrona Heights PA 15065-1830 Office: Hergenroeder & Heights 101 E Diamond St Ste 202 Butler PA 16001-5944

**PATIENT, ROBERT J.,** lawyer; b. St. Paul, Dec. 26, 1946; s. Earl Louis and Annabelle L. Patient; m. Elizabeth A. Plunkett, Mar. 16, 1982 (div. Feb. 1990); 1 stepchild, Melissa A. Larson; m. Rebecca Ann Larson, Feb. 16, 1994. Student, Santa Monica Coll., 1969-71; BA in English, U. Minn., 1975; postgrad., Hamline U., 1976-78; JD, William Mitchell Coll. Law., 1980. Bar: Minn. 1980, U.S. Dist. Ct. Minn. 1980, Wis. 1987, U.S. Ct. Appeals (8th cir.) 1996. Pvt. practice, St. Paul, 1980—; arbitrator, mediator Creative Dispute Resolution, Mpls., 1991—. Mem. FBA, Am. Arbitration Assn. (arbitrator, mediator), U.S. Arbitration and Mediation (arbitrator, mediator), ATLA, Minn. Trial Lawyers Assn. (legis. com., chair fire loss litig. com. 1998—), Wis. State Bar Assn., Minn. Trial Lawyers Assn., Minn. State Bar Assn. (cert. civil trial specialist 1989), Ramsey County Bar Assn. Avocations: golf, travel, reading, early 20th century antiques. Personal injury, General civil litigation. Home: 1483 Albert St N Saint Paul MN 55108-2301 Office: 55 5th St E Saint Paul MN 55101-2701

**PATMAN, PHILIP FRANKLIN,** lawyer; b. Atlanta, Nov. 1, 1937; s. Elmer Franklin and Helen Lee (Miller) P.; m. Katherine Sellers, July 1, 1967; children: Philip Franklin, Katherine Lee. BA, U. Tex., 1959, LLB, 1964; MA, Princeton U., 1962. Bar: Tex. 1964, U.S. Supreme Ct. 1970, U.S. Dist. Ct. (so. dist.) Tex. 1971, U.S. Dist. Ct. (we. dist.) Tex. 1975. Atty. office of legal adviser Dept. State, Washington, 1964-67; dep. dir. office internat. affairs HUD, Washington, 1967-69; pvt. practice Austin, Tex., 1969—. Contbr. articles to legal jours. Ofcl. rep. of Gov. Tex. to Interstate Oil Compact Commn., 1973-83, 87-91. Woodrow Wilson fellow, 1959. Fellow Tex. Bar Found.; mem. ABA, Tex. Bar Assn., Tex. Ind. Prodrs. and Royalty Owners Assn., Tex. Oil and Gas Assn., Tex. Law Rev. Assn., Austin Club, Headliners Club, Westwood Country Club, Rotary, Phi Beta Kappa, Phi Delta Phi. Administrative and regulatory, Oil, gas, and mineral, Environmental. Office: Patman & Osborn 515 Congress Ave Ste 1704 Austin TX 78701-3503

**PATRICK, CHARLES WILLIAM, JR.,** lawyer; b. Monroe, N.C., Oct. 9, 1954; s. Charles William and Louise (Nisbet) P.; m. Celeste Hunt, June 5, 1976; children: Laura Elizabeth, Charles William III. BA magna cum laude, Furman U., 1976; JD, U. S.C., 1979. Bar: S.C. 1979, U.S. Dist. Ct. S.C. 1981, U.S. Ct. Appeals (11th cir.) 1981, U.S. Ct. Appeals (10th cir.) 1983, U.S. Ct. Appeals (4th cir.) 1986. Law clk. to presiding judge 9th Cir. Ct. State of S.C., Charleston, 1979-80; assoc. Ness, Motley, Loadholt, Richardson and Poole and predecessor firm Blatt and Fales, Charleston, 1980—; assoc. Motley, Loadholt, Richardson and Poole and predecessor firm Blatt and Fales, Charleston, 1980-84, ptnr., 1984—. Exec. editor S.C. Law Review, 1978; contbr. articles to profl. jours. Mem. ABA, Assn. Trial Lawyers Am., S.C. Assn. Trial Lawyers, Trial Lawyers for Pub. Justice, Phi Beta Kappa. Democrat. Presbyterian. Avocations: boating, skiing, fishing. Product liability, Personal injury, General civil litigation. Home: 38 Church St Charleston SC 29401-2742 Office: Ness Motley Loadholt Richardson & Poole 151 Meeting St PO Box 1137 Charleston SC 29402-1137

**PATRICK, DANE HERMAN,** lawyer; b. San Antonio, Oct. 18, 1960; s. Kae Thomas and Joyce Lynn (von Scheele) P.; m. Kelly Marie Carlson, May 17, 1986. BA in Econs. with honors, U. Tex., 1983; JD, So. Meth. U., 1987. Assoc. Law Office of Earl Luna, Dallas, 1987-88, Veitch & Davis, San Antonio, 1988-91; pvt. practice, San Antonio, 1991—. Mem. ATLA, San Antonio Trial Lawyers Assn. (bd. dirs.), San Antonio United Shareholder Assn. (chmn. 1988-92). Democrat. Methodist. Avocations: weight lifting, hunting, martial arts. Personal injury, Insurance, General civil litigation. Office: 111 Soledad St Ste 300 San Antonio TX 78205-2298

**PATRICK, H. HUNTER,** judge; b. Gasville, Ark., Aug. 19, 1939; s. H. Hunter Sr. and Nelle Frances (Robinson) P.; m. Charlotte Anne Wilson, July 9, 1966; children: Michael Hunter, Colleen Annette. BA, U. Wyo., 1961, JD, 1966. Bar: Wyo. 1966, U.S. Dist. Ct. Wyo. 1966, Colo. 1967, U.S. Supreme Ct. 1975. Mcpl. judge City of Powell (Wyo.), 1967-68; sole practice law Powell, 1966-88; atty. City of Powell, 1969-88; justice of the peace County of Park, Wyo., 1971-88; bus. law instr. Northwest Community Coll., Powell, 1968-98; dist. judge State of Wyo. 5th Jud. Dist., 1988—; mem. Wyo. Dist. Judges Conf., sec.-treas., 1993-94, vice chair, 1994-95, chair, 1995-96. Editor: Bench Book for Judges of Courts of Limited Jurisdiction in the State of Wyoming, 1980-90. Dir. cts. Wyo. Girls State, Powell, 1982-85, 89-98; elder, deacon, moderator of deacons Powell Presbyn. Ch., 1997; mem. Wyo. Commn. Jud. Conduct & Ethics, 1997—. Recipient Wyo. Crime Victims Compensation Commn. Judicial award, 1995. Fellow Am. Bar Found., Wyo. Jud. Adv. Coun.; mem. ABA (Wyo. state del. to ho. of dels. 1994—, Wyo. del. judicial adminstrn. divsn., exec. com. nat. conf. trial ct. judges representing Wyo., Colo., Kans., Nebr., Pub. Svc. award for ct.-sponsored Law Day programs 1990, 92), Wyo. Bar Assn., Colo. Bar Assn., Park County Bar Assn. (sec. 1969-70, pres. 1970-71), Wyo. Assn. Cts. Ltd. Jurisdiction (pres. 1973-80), Am. Judicature Soc., Nat. Coun. Juvenile and Family Ct. Judges, Nat. Conf. Trial Ct. Judges (exec. com., rep. Wyo., Colo., Nebr., and Kans. 1997—). Avocations: photography, travel, fishing, camping, bicycling. Home: PO Box 941 Powell WY 82435-0941 Office: PO Box 1868 Cody WY 82414-1868

**PATRICK, JAMES DUVALL, JR.,** lawyer; b. Griffin, Ga., Dec. 28, 1947; s. James Duvall and Marion Wilson (Ragsdale) P.; m. Cynthia Hill, Jan. 19, 1991. BS in Indsl. Mgmt., Ga. Inst. Tech., 1970; JD, U. Ga., 1973. Bar: Ga. 1973, U.S. Dist. Ct. (mid. dist.) Ga. 1973, U.S. Dist. Ct. (so. dist.) Ga. 1983, U.S. Ct. Appeals (5th cir.) 1974, U.S. Supreme Ct., U.S. Ct. Appeals (11th Cir.) 1981, U.S. Tax Ct. 1985. Assoc. Cartledge, Cartledge & Posey, Columbus, Ga., 1973-74; ptnr. Falkenstrom, Hawkins & Patrick, Columbus, 1975, Falkenstrom & Patrick, Columbus, 1975-77; sole practice, Columbus, 1977—; instr. bus. law Chattahoochee Valley C.C., Phenix City, Ala., 1975-77; instr. paralegal course Columbus Coll., 1979, 84; del. U.S./China Joint Session on Trade, Investment, and Econ. Law, Beijing, 1987, Moscow Conf. on Law and Bilateral Econ. Rels., Moscow, 1990. Mem. Hist. Columbus Found., Mayor's Com. for the Handicapped, 1987-88; local organizer, worker Joe Frank Harris for Gov. Campaign, Columbus, 1982; bd. dirs. Columbus Symphony Orchestra, 1988-94. Mem. ATLA, ABA, Am. Judicature Soc., State Bar Ga., Ga. Trial Lawyers Assn., Columbus Young Lawyers Club, Columbus Lawyers Club, Columbus Kappa Alpha Alumni Assn. (sec.), Phi Delta Phi, Kappa Alpha. Methodist. Clubs: Civitan (bd. dirs. 1975-77), Country of Columbus, Georgian (Atlanta), Buckhead, Chattahouchee River Club (local chpt.). State civil litigation, General practice, Personal injury. Office: 831 2nd Ave Columbus GA 31901-2703

**PATRICK, MARTY,** lawyer; b. N.Y.C., May 10, 1949; s. Harry and Evelyn (Beroza) P.; m. Madelaine Joyce Benjamin, Dec. 2, 1984; 1 child, Jason; BS, L.I. U., 1971; Cert. Inst. for Leadership Devel., Jerusalem, 1974; JD, Nova Southeastern U., 1981. Exec. dir. Zionist Orgn. Am., Miami Beach, Fla., 1975-78; pres. Enigma Enterprises, Inc., Miami, Fla., 1978-82; ptnr. firm Martin Howard Patrick, P.A. Miami Beach, 1982—; pres. Patrick Law Ctr., Miami Beach, 1983-89; pres. First Fla. Title & Abstract Co., Miami, 1983—; chief exec. officer Atlantic Coast Title Co., 1989—; CEO Laughing in the Dark Prodns., 1994—. Horovitz scholar, 1980. Mem. ABA, Ga. Bar Assn., Fla. Bar Assn. Lodges: Mensa. Contbr. articles to profl. jours. Real property, Estate planning. Home: 12910 Oleander Rd Miami FL 33181-2356 Office: 1141 Kane Concourse Bay Harbor Is FL 33154-2012

**PATRICK, PAULA ANTOINETTE,** lawyer; b. Phila., Jan. 28, 1968; d. Levander and Mattie Marie Patrick. BA, Bennett Coll., Greensboro, N.C., 1990; JD, Tex. So. U., Houston, 1993. Bar: Pa. 1994, U.S. Dist. Ct. (ea. dist.) Pa. 1994, U.S. Dist. Ct. Md. 1996, U.S. Ct. Appeals (3d cir.) 1994. Sole practitioner Phila., 1994—; with City of Phila.-CompSvcs., Inc., 1997—. Mem. ABA, ATLA, Nat. Bar Assn. (women lawyers divsn.). Democrat. Avocations: reading, cooking. Workers' compensation, Personal injury, Family and matrimonial. Home: 225 S 15th St Ste 502 Philadelphia PA 19102

**PATRICK, PHILIP HOWARD,** lawyer; b. Bridgend, Wales, Aug. 12, 1946; s. Frederick Harry and Phyllis Mair (Vaulters) P.; m. Rosalind Elizabeth Davies, Aug. 5, 1969. MusB, U. Wales, 1969; MFA, Princeton U., 1971, PhD, 1973; JD, Washington (D.C.) Coll. Law, 1980. Bar: D.C. 1980, Md. 1981. Asst. prof. Am. U., Washington, 1973-77; cons., Washington, 1978-81; pvt. practice, Silver Springs, Md., 1980-89; pres. Computing Community Services Corp., Silver Springs, 1980-89; gen. counsel The Orcutt Group Ltd., Rockville, Md., 1989-92; dir. contracts FileTek, Inc., Rockville, Md., 1992—. Founder, sec. Nat. Welsh-Am. Found., Washington, 1981-84, mem. adv. coun., 1984—. Mem. D.C. Computer Law Forum. Computer, General corporate. Home: 2523 Oakenshield Dr Potomac MD 20854-2926 Office: FileTek Inc 9400 Key West Ave Rockville MD 20850-3322

**PATRICK, VICTOR PHILLIP,** lawyer; b. Lake Forest, Ill., Jan. 7, 1958; s. Rodger Ralph Patrick and Phyllis Elaine Bachler; m. Elizabeth Fletcher, Aug. 9, 1985; children: Kathryn Elaine, Stephen James, Diane Elizabeth, Marie Christine, Thomas Grant, John Wallace. AB in Politics magna cum laude, Princeton U., 1982; JD cum laude, Harvard U., 1985. Bar: D.C. 1986, N.Y. 1986, U.S. Ct. Appeals (10th cir.) 1986. Law clk. U.S. Ct. Appeals 10th Cir., Denver, 1985-86; assoc. Cleary, Gottlieb, Steen & Hamilton, Washington, 1986-88, 92-94, Brussels, 1988-91; asst. gen. counsel Allied-Signal Inc., Morristown, N.J., 1994-95, assoc. gen. counsel, 1996-97; v.p., gen. counsel AlliedSignal Aerospace Equipment Sys., Torrance, Calif., 1997-99; dep. gen. counsel AlliedSignal, Inc., Morristown, N.J., 1999—; officer, dir. various AlliedSignal subsidiaries, worldwide, 1994—; asst. sec. Allied-Signal Inc. Mem. ABA. Mem. LDS Ch. Mergers and acquisitions, General corporate, Finance.

**PATRICK, WENDY LYNN,** prosecutor; b. Orange, Calif., Oct. 19, 1968. BA, UCLA, 1990; JD, Calif. Western Sch. of Law, 1994. Bar: Calif. 1994, U.S. Dist. Ct. (so. dist.) Calif. 1994, U.S. Ct. Appeals (9th cir.) 1995. Lawyer San Diego Pub. Defender's Office, 1994-97, San Diego Dist. Atty.'s Office, 1997—. Mem. Law Review Calif. Western Law Sch. Mem. San Diego County Bar Assn., Am. Cancer Soc. (bd. dirs.), San Diego Barristers Club (bd. dirs.), Soc. Club (bd. dirs.), Lincoln Club, Inns of Ct., Thomas More Soc., Lincoln Club. Roman Catholic. Avocations: skiing, concert violinist, travel, karate. Office: San Diego Dist Atty 2851 Meadow Lark Dr San Diego CA 92123-2709

**PATRICK, WILLIAM BRADSHAW,** lawyer; b. Indpls., Nov. 29, 1923; s. Fae William and Mary (Bradshaw) P.; m. Ursula Lantzsch, Dec. 28, 1956; children: William Bradshaw, Ursula, Nancy. AB, The Principia, 1947; LLB, Harvard U., 1950. Bar: Ind. Supreme ct. 1950, U.S. Dist. Ct. (so. dist.) Ind. 1950, U.S. Ct. Apls. (7th cir.) 1961. Ptnr., Patrick & Patrick, Indpls., 1950-53; pvt. practice, Indpls., 1953—; gen. counsel Met. Planning Commn. Marion County and Indpls., 1955-66; dep. proscecutor Marion County, Ind., 1960-62; past pres., dir. The Cemetery Co., operating Meml. Park Cemetery, Indpls.; sec., dir. Rogers Typesetting Co., Indpls., 1966-85. Pres. Indpls. Legal Aid Soc., 1963. Lt. (j.g.) USNR, 1942-46. Recipient DeMolay Legion of Honor. Mem. ABA, Ind. Bar Assn., Indpls. Bar Assn., Lawyers Assn. Indpls., Indpls. Estate Planning Coun., Am. Legion, SAR (sec. Ind. Soc. 1953-59), Svc. Club Indpls., U.S. Navy League, Mil. Order Loyal Legion (comdr. Ind. Soc. 1979), Mason (33d degree), Shriner. Probate, Estate taxation, General corporate. Address: 7 N Meridian St Indianapolis IN 46204-3000

**PATT, HERBERT JACOB,** lawyer; b. Chgo., Feb. 12, 1935; s. Abraham and Esther Blanch (Kuchinsky) P.; m. Yvonne Phyllis Shavell, Oct. 9, 1958 (dec. Mar. 1986); children: Alon Wayne Patt, Bradley Earl, Colette Emile; m. Lynn Cheryl Feingold, December 26, 1993. BA, Northwestern U., 1956, JD, 1958. Bar: Ill. 1959, U.S. Dist. Ct. (no. dist.) Ill. 1959, U.S. Supreme Ct. 1977, Calif. 1986, U.S. Dist. Ct. (ctrl. and so. dists.) Calif. 1987, U.S. Ct. Appeals (9th cir.) 1987. Assoc. Andres & Andres, Santa Ana, Calif. Pres. Jewish Nat. Fund Orange Co., Santa Ana, 1994-95, chmn., 1996-98, nat. bd. dirs., N.Y., 1994-98; pres. Temple Judea, Laguna Hills, Calif., 1992-93. General civil litigation, Personal injury, Probate. Office: Andres & Andres 322 W 3rd St Santa Ana CA 92701-5226

**PATTE, GEORGE DAVID, JR.,** lawyer; b. Batavia, N.Y., Dec. 16, 1945; s. George David and Patricia Elmira (O'Cain) P.; m. Mary Christine Crass, Dec. 28, 1969; children: Chesua Conkling, George David V. BA in Internat. Relations, Ithaca Coll., 1967; JD, U. Louisville, 1974. Bar: N.Y. 1976, U.S. Dist. Ct. (no. dist.) N.Y. 1976. Tchr. spl. studies Dryden (N.Y.) High Sch., 1970-72; sole practice Ithaca, N.Y., 1976-80, 88—; ptnr. Greenburg & Patte, Ithaca, 1981-88; lectr. bus. law Ithaca Coll., 1985-86. Author: (with Greenburg) A Legal View of Your Rights if Injured on the Job, 1986. Pres. Tompkins County Soc. for Prevention Cruelty to Animals, Ithaca, 1980, bd. dirs. 1977-81; mem. Instl. Animal Care and Use Com., Cornell U., Ithaca, 1986-88; bd. dirs. United Way of Tompkins County, 1987-94; trustee Ithaca Coll., 1991-96. Mem. N.Y. State Bar Assn., Tompkins County Bar Assn., N.Y. Trial Lawyers Assn. (pres. so. tier affiliate 1987-89, bd. dirs. 1987-95), Ithaca Coll. Alumni Assn. (bd. dirs. 1990—, chmn. nominations com. 1985, pres. 1990-93, Disting. Alumni award 1997). Roman Catholic. Avocation: stream fishing for trout. State civil litigation, Construction. Home: 1167 Taughannock Blvd Ithaca NY 14850-9573 Office: 121 E Buffalo St Ithaca NY 14850-4222

**PATTEN, BRENDA L.,** lawyer, urban planner; b. Long Beach, Calif., Feb. 15, 1948; d. Benjamin Joseph and Evelyn Jeanette Lott; m. Louis Alan Valla, Jan. 10, 1971 (div. July 1975); m. Robert Bruce Patten, Oct. 9, 1993; 1 child, Ariel Solomon. BA in Polit. Sci., U. Fla., 1970, JD with honors, 1983; M in Urban Planning, Mich. State U., 1978. Bar: Fla. 1983; cert. in city, county and local govt. law; lic. pvt. pilot. Urban planner North Ctrl. Fla. Regional Planning Coun., Gainesville, 1974-76, City of Jacksonville, Fla., 1978-79, State of N.Y., Albany, 1979-80; atty. Winderweedle, Haines, Ward & Woodman, Orlando, Fla., 1983-86; gen. counsel The Emmer Group, Gainesville, 1988-89; dep. county atty., acting gen. counsel Sarasota County Govt., Sarasota, Fla., 1989-97; shareholder, atty. Kirk-Pinkerton, P.A., Sarasota, 1997—; bd. dirs. Sarasota Coastal Credit Union, 1990-97; legal counsel Gov.'s Growth Mgmt. Adv. Com., 1986-87. Contbg. author: Perspectives on Florida's Growth Management Act of 1985, 1986; contbr. articles to profl. jours. Bd. dirs. Marie Selby Bot. Gardens, Sarasota, 1998—; mem. corp. bd. dirs. Ringling Sch. Art and Design, Sarasota, 1997—. Mem. Am. Planning Assn., Fla. Planning and Zoning Assn., Sarasota C. of C. (bd. dirs., com. for econ. devel. 1997—). Avocation: flying. Administrative and regulatory, Environmental, Land use and zoning (including planning). Office: Kirk-Pinkerton PA 720 S Orange Ave Sarasota FL 34236-7773

**PATTEN, THOMAS LOUIS,** lawyer; b. St. Joseph, Mo., Oct. 3, 1945; m. Sherry V. Patten; children: Elizabeth, Caroline, Brooke. BS, U. Mo., 1967, JD, 1969. Bar: Mo. 1969, D.C. 1972, U.S. Dist. Ct. D.C. 1972, U.S. Claims Ct. 1972, U.S. Ct. Appeals (fed. cir.) 1972, U.S. Supreme Ct. 1972, U.S. Ct. Appeals (9th cir.) 1974, U.S. Ct. Appeals (4th cir.) 1981, Va. 1983, U.S. Dist. Ct. (ea. and we. dists.) Va. 1983. Ptnr Latham & Watkins, Washington. Fellow Am. Coll. Trial Lawyers. Government contracts and claims, Federal civil litigation, Criminal. Office: Latham & Watkins Ste 1300 1001 Pennsylvania Ave NW Washington DC 20004-2585

**PATTERSON, CHRISTOPHER NIDA,** lawyer; b. Washington Courthouse, Ohio, Apr. 17, 1960; s. Donis Dean and JoAnne (Nida) O.; children: Travis, Kirsten. BA, Clemson U., 1982; JD, Nova U., 1985. Bar: Fla. 1985, U.S. Dist. Ct. (mid. dist.) Fla. 1985, U.S. Ct. Mil. Rev. 1986, U.S. Ct. Mil. Appeals 1987, U.S. Dist. Ct. (ea. dist.) Va. 1987, U.S. Supreme Ct. 1990, U.S. Ct. Appeals (11th cir.) 1992, U.S. Dist. Ct. (no. dist.) Fla. 1992, U.S. Dist. Ct. (so. dist.) Tex. 1995; cert. criminal trial lawyer Fla. Bar. and Nat. Bd. Trial Advocacy. Prosecutor Fla. State Attys. Office, Orlando, Fla., 1985; spl. asst. U.S. Atty. U.S. Dist. Ct. (ea. dist.) Va., 1987-90; ptnr. Patterson & Hauversburk, Panama City, Fla., 1992—; adj. prof. law Gulf Coast Coll.; family law mediator, dependency law mediator Fla. Supreme Ct. Author: Queen's Pawn, 1996, Treasure Trove, 1997; contbr. Nat. DAR Mag., the Defender mag. Chancellor St. Thomas Episcopal Ch. Capt. JAGC, U.S. Army, 1986-92, Desert Storm. Mem. Nat. Assn. Criminal Def. Lawyers (life), Fla. Assn. Criminal Def. Lawyers, Acad. Fla. Trial Lawyers, Assn. Fed. Def. Attys., Fla. Acad. Profl. Mediators, Fla. Bar (criminal law sect., mil. law standing com., del. 11th cir. jud. conf. 1999, Pro Bono Svc. award, nominee Jefferson award for pub. svc. 1999), Bay County Bar Assn., The Ret. Officers' Assn., Christian Legal Soc., Am. Legion, Fellowship of Christian Athletes, Nat. Triathlon Fedn. Episcopalian. Avocations: athletics, triathlons. Criminal. Office: PO Box 1368 1021 Grace Ave Panama City FL 32401-2420

**PATTERSON, CYNTHIA J.,** lawyer; b. Albuquerque, N. Mex., Oct. 18, 1956; d. William E. and Janet R. Walker. BS in Bus., U. N. Mex., 1991; JD, Whittier Law Sch., L.A., 1994. Bar: N. Mex. 1994. Lawyer pvt. practice, Albuquerque, N. Mex., 1994—. Mem. Golden Key, Phi Beta Kappa. Personal injury, Professional liability, Family and matrimonial. Office: Law

Offices Cynthia J Patterson 2014 Central Ave SW Albuquerque NM 87104-1467

**PATTERSON, DONALD ROSS,** lawyer, educator; b. Sept. 9, 1939; s. Sam Ashley and Marguerite (Robinson) P.; m. Peggy Ann Schulte, May 1, 1965; children: D. Ross, Jerome Ashley, Gretchen Anne. BS, Tex. Tech U., 1961; JD, U. Tex., 1964; LLM, So. Meth. U., 1972. Bar: Tex. 1964, U.S. Ct. Claims 1970, U.S. Ct. Customs and Patent Appeals 1970, U.S. Ct. Mil. Appeals 1970, U.S. Supreme Ct. 1970, U.S. Dist. Ct. (ea. dist.) Tex. 1982, U.S. Ct. Appeals (5th cir.) 1991, U.S. Ct. Appeals (D.C. cir.) 1994; bd. cert. in immigration and naturalization law, Tex. Commd. lt. (j.g.) USN, 1964, advanced through grades to lt. comdr., 1969; asst. officer in charge Naval Petroleum Res., Bakersfield, Calif., 1970-72; staff judge adv. Kenitra, Morocco, 1972-76; officer in charge Naval Legal Svcs. Office, Whidbey Island, Wash., 1976-79; head mil. Justice divsn., Subic Bay, The Philippines, 1979-81; ret. USN, 1982; pvt. practice Tyler, Tex., 1982—; instr. U. Md., 1975, Chapman Coll., 1977-79, U. LaVerne, 1980-81, Tyler Jr. Coll., 1990—, Jarvis Christian Coll., 1990—, U. Tex., Tyler, 1993—. Mem. East Tex. Estate Planning Coun. Mem. Coll. of State Bar of Tex., Tex. Bar Assn., Smith County Bar Assn., Am. Immigration Lawyers Assn., Masons, Rotary (pres.), Shriners, Toastmasters (past pres.), Phi Delta Phi. Republican. Baptist. Immigration, naturalization, and customs, Consumer commercial, Bankruptcy. Home: 703 Wellington St Tyler TX 75703-4666 Office: 777 S Broadway Ave Ste 106 Tyler TX 75701-1648

**PATTERSON, JAMEE JORDAN,** lawyer; b. L.A., Sept. 28, 1955; d. James Joseph Jr. and Marie Antanette (Kunz) Jordan; m. Timothy Raymond, Aug. 6, 1983; 1 child, Joseph Thomas. BA, UCLA, 1977; JD, Loyola U., L.A., 1981. Bar: Calif. 1981, U.S. Dist. Ct. (ctrl. dist.) Calif. 1981, U.S. Dist. Ct. (so. dist.) Calif. 1982, U.S. Supreme Ct. 1986, U.S. Ct. Appeals (9th cir.) 1991. Dep. atty. gen. Atty. Gen.'s Office, L.A., 1981-83, San Diego, 1983—; liaison to Calif. Coastal Com. Co-chair Women Employees Adv. Com., San Diego, 1986-87. Regents scholar UCLA, 1973-77, regents fellow, 1977-78; recipient Disting. Legal Svc. award Assn. of Calif. State Attys, 1996. Mem. Assn. Deps. Atty. Gen. (pres. 1987, 94), San Diego County Bar, Lawyers Club San Diego (co-chair reproductive rights com. 1990). Avocations: reading, running, skiing, cross country skiing, cooking. Office: Calif Atty Gen PO Box 85266 110 W A St Ste 1100 San Diego CA 92101-3702

**PATTERSON, JOHN DE LA ROCHE, JR.,** lawyer; b. Schenectady, N.Y., July 8, 1941; s. John de la Roche Sr. and Jane C. (Clay) P.; m. Michele F. Demarest, Nov. 28, 1987; children: Daniel C., Sara R., Amy C. BA, Johns Hopkins U., 1963; LLB, Harvard U., 1966. Bar: Mass. 1968. Vol. Peace Corps, Chad, 1966-67; assoc. Foley, Hoag & Eliot, Boston, 1967-73, ptnr., 1974—, exec. com., 1989-97. Chmn. Kodaly Ctr. Am. Inc., Newton, Mass., 1977-87. Mem. ABA, Boston Bar Assn. Democrat. Avocations: sailing, tennis, travel, reading. General corporate, Intellectual property, Mergers and acquisitions. Office: Foley Hoag & Eliot 1 Post Office Sq Ste 1700 Boston MA 02109-2170

**PATTERSON, MICHAEL P.,** prosecutor. BA, Tulane U.; JD, U. Fla., 1973. Bar: Fla. 1974. Pvt. practice, 1974-81; asst. state atty. First Jud. Cir. Ct., Fla., 1981-91; U.S. atty. U.S. Dist. Ct. (no. dist) Fla., 1993—; com. mem. U.S. Atty. Gen. Adv. Com. of U.S. Attys., 1995—. Office: US Attorney No Dist Florida 315 S Calhoun StSte 510 Tallahassee FL 32301-1841 Office: U S Attorney 114 E Gregory St Pensacola FL 32501-4972*

**PATTERSON, PATRICIA ANNE,** law librarian; b. Phila., May 12, 1938; d. Stanley J. and Jane T. (Walsh) Compton; m. Keith C., Mar. 11, 1972; 1 child, Brian J. BA, St. Mary Coll., 1970; MLS, U. Denver, 1980. Tax librarian Baker & McKenzie, Chgo., 1981-82; reference librarian Schiff Hardin & Waite, Chgo., 1982-84, law librarian, 1984-87, dir. legal info. svcs., 1987—; mem. faculty Am. Bankers Assn., Nat. Grad. Trust Sch., Evanston, Ill., 1987—; bd. mem. West Pub. Co., St. Paul, 1987—. Reviewer books include American Law Publishing, 1984, Commercial Law, 1987; contbr. articles to profl. jours. Mem. ABA, Am. Assn. Law Librs. (exec. bd.), Chgo. Assn. Law Librs., Spl. Librs. Assn., Assn. Records Mgrs. and Adminstrs., Beta Phi Mu. Roman Catholic. Office: Schiff Hardin & Waite 7200 Sears Tower Chicago IL 60606

**PATTERSON, ROBERT DEWEY,** lawyer; b. Tupelo, Miss., Oct. 2, 1925; s. Dewey D. and Louise Catherine (Sullivan) P.; m. Jan Ella Pegues, Sept. 11, 1950; children: Robert, Jan Lee, Victoria, Mary Reed. BA, LLB, JD, U. Miss., 1950. Bar: Miss. 1950, U.S. Ct. Appeals (5th cir.) 1955, U.S. Supreme Ct., 1956. Prosecuting atty. Monroe County, Aberdeen, Miss., 1956-60; city atty. City of Aberdeen, 1996-98. With U.S. Army, 1944-46. Mem. Miss. Bar Found. (pres. 1982-83). Democrat.

**PATTERSON, ROBERT PORTER, JR.,** federal judge; b. N.Y.C., July 11, 1923; s. Robert Porter and Margaret (Winchester) P.; m. Bevin C. Daly, Sept. 15, 1956; children: Anne, Robert, Margaret, Paul, Katherine. AB, Harvard U., 1947; LLB, Columbia U., 1950. Bar: N.Y. 1951, D.C. 1966. Law clk. Donovan, Leisure, Newton & Lumbard, N.Y.C., 1950-51; asst. counsel N.Y. State Crime Commn. Waterfront Investigation, 1952-53; asst. U.S. atty. Chief of Narcotics Prosecutions and Investigations, 1953-56; asst. counsel Senate Banking and Currency Com., 1954; assoc. Patterson, Belknap, Webb & Tyler, N.Y.C., 1956-60, ptnr., 1960-88; judge U.S. Dist. Ct. (so. dist.) N.Y., 1988—; counsel to minority select com. pursuant to house resolution no. 1, Washington, 1967; mem. Senator's Jud. Screening Panel, 1974-88, Gov.'s Jud. Screening Panel, 1975-82, Gov.'s Sentencing Com., 1978-79. Contbr. articles to profl. jours. Chmn. Wm. T. Grant Found., 1974-94, Prisoners' Legal Services N.Y., 1976-88; dir. Legal Aid Soc., 1961-88, pres., 1967-71; chmn. Nat. Citizens for Eisenhower, 1959-60, Scranton for Pres., N.Y. State, 1964; bd. mgrs. Havens Relief Fun Soc., 1994—, Millbrook Sch., 1966-78, Vera Inst. Justice, 1981—, New Sch. for Social Rsch., 1986-94, George C. Marshall Found., 1987-93; mem. exec. com. Lawyers Com. for Civil Rights Under Law, 1968-88; mem. Goldman Panel for Attica Disturbance, 1972, Temporary Commn. on State Ct. System, 1971-73, Rockefeller U. Council, 1986-88, exec. com. N.Y. Vietnam Vets. Meml. Commn., 1982-85, Mayor's Police Adv. Com., 1985-87. Served to capt. USAAF, 1942-46. Decorated D.F.C. with cluster, Air medal with clusters. Mem. ABA (ho. of dels. 1976-80), N.Y. State Bar Assn. (pres. 1978-79), Assn. Bar City N.Y. (v.p. 1974-75), N.Y. County Lawyers Assn., Am. Law Inst., Am. Judicature Soc. (bd. dirs. 1979). Republican. Episcopalian. Home: Fair Oaks Farm Cold Spring NY 10516 Office: US Dist Ct So Dist NY US Court House 500 Pearl St New York NY 10007-1316

**PATTERSON, RUDOLPH N.,** lawyer; b. Poulan, Ga., Feb. 6, 1939. AB, Mercer U., 1961, JD, 1963. Bar: Ga. 1962. Ptnr. Westmoreland, Patterson & Moseley, Albany, Ga.; pres. elect State Bar Ga. Mem. ABA, Macon Bar Ass. (pres. 1967), ATLA, State Bar Ga. (sec. 1996-98, bd. govs., chmn. gen. practice and trial sect. 1985-87), Inst. Continuing Legal Edn. (trustee 1988—), Ga. Trial Lawyers Assn. (disciplinary bd., state budget com.), Macon Trial Lawyers Assn., Nat. Orgn. Social Security Claimants' Reps. (pres. 1982-83, exec. com. 1979—). Pension, profit-sharing, and employee benefits, Probate, Personal injury. Office: Westmoreland Patterson & Moseley 235 W Roosevelt Ave Albany GA 31701-2640*

**PATTI, ANTHONY PETER,** lawyer; b. Bethpage, N.Y., Jan. 28, 1966; s. Anthony Victor and Beatrice Mary Patti; m. Helen Frances Winn, Dec. 28, 1991; children: Anthony Michael, Gabriella Maria, Francesca Claudia. BA cum laude, U. Mich., 1987; JD, U. Notre Dame, 1990. Bar: Mich. 1990, U.S. Dist. Ct. (ea. dist.) Mich. 1990, U.S. Dist. Ct. (we. dist.) Mich. 1996, U.S. Ct. Appeals (6th cir.) 1991. Assoc. atty. Hooper, Hathaway, Price, Beuche & Wallace, Ann Arbor, Mich., 1990-96, ptnr., 1996—; parliamentarian clk. and cons. Conv. II, Inc., Washington, 1985-86; lectr. Lawyer-Tchr. Partnership, Ann Arbor, 1994—; guest lectr. Adult Legal Edn., Adult Edn. Program. Contbr. chpts. to books, contbr. articles to profl. jours. Bd. dirs., founder Ann Arbor Cath. Forum, 1994—; participant Queensland Law Soc. Recipient grants and awards. Mem. State Bar Mich. (mem. litigation and internat. sects.), Fed. Bar Assn., Washtenaw County Bar Assn., Washtenaw Trial Lawyers Assn., Nat. Italian-Am. Bar Assn., Italian-Am. Bar Assn. Mich., Cath. Lawyers Guild. Avocations: family, choral and solo singing, international travel. General civil litigation, Trademark and copyright, Personal injury. Office: Hooper Hathaway et al 126 S Main St Ann Arbor MI 48104-1945

**PATTISHALL, BEVERLY WYCKLIFFE,** lawyer; b. Atlanta, May 23, 1916; s. Leon Jackson and Margaret Simkins (Woodfin) P.; children by previous marriage: Margaret Ann Arthur, Leslie Hansen, Beverly Wyckliffe, Paige Terhune Pattishall Watt, Woodfin Underwood; m. Dorothy Daniels Mashek, June 24, 1977; 1 stepchild, Lyssa Mashek Piette. BS, Northwestern U., 1938; JD, U. Va., 1941. Bar: Ill. 1941, D.C. 1971. Pvt. practice law Chgo., 1946—; ptnr. Pattishall, McAuliffe, Newbury, Hilliard & Geraldson and predecessor firms, Chgo.; dir. Juvenile Protective Assn. Chgo., 1946-79, pres., 1961-63, hon. dir., 1979—; dir. Vol. Interagy. Assn., 1975-78, sec., 1977-78; U.S. del. Diplomatic Confs. on Internat. Trademark Registration Treaty, Geneva, Vienna, 1970-73, Diplomatic Conf. on Revision of Paris Conv., Nairobi, 1981; mem. U.S. del. Geneva Conf. on Indsl. Property and Consumer Protection, 1978; adj. prof. trademark, trade identity and unfair trade practices law Northwestern U. Sch. Law, Chgo. Author: (with David C. Hilliard) Trademarks, Trade Identity and Unfair Trade Practices, 1974, Unfair Competition and Unfair Trade Practices, 1985, Trademarks, 1987, Trademarks and Unfair Competition, 1994, 3d edit., 1998; contbr. articles to profl. jours. Bd. dirs. Constl. Rights Found. Chgo., 1996-98. Lt. comdr. USNR, WWII, ETO, PTO, ATO, ret. comdr USNR. Fellow Am. Coll. Trial Lawyers (bd. regents 1979-83); mem. ABA (chmn. sect. patent, trademark copyright law 1963-64), Internat. Patent and Trademark Assn. (pres. 1955-57, exec. com. 1955—), Assn. Internat. Pour La Protection Propriete Indsl. (mem. of honor), Ill. Bar Assn., Chgo. Bar Assn., D.C. Bar Assn., Chgo. Bar Found. (dir. 1977-83), U.S. Trademark Assn. (dir. 1963-65), Legal Club, Law Club (pres. 1982-83), Econ. Club, Chikaming Country Club, Univ. Club, Mid-Am. Club, U. Va. Lile Law Soc. (sr. counselor), Selden Soc. (London, Ill. rep.). Trademark and copyright, Federal civil litigation, State civil litigation. Office: Pattishall McAuliffe Newbury Hilliard & Geraldson 311 S Wacker Dr Ste 5000 Chicago IL 60606-6631

**PATTISON, DAPHNE LYNN,** lawyer; b. Baytown, Tex., Oct. 29, 1965; d. Thomas Benjamin and Cora (Love) Everage; m. T.W. Pattison, Jr., Nov. 2, 1996. BS, So. Meth. U., 1988; JD, U. Houston, 1991. Bar: Tex. 1991, Miss., 1995. Mem. JAG corps U.S. Navy, Gulfport, Miss., 1991-95; assoc. Rushing and Guice, Biloxi, Miss., 1995-96, Law Offices of Robert Pritchard, Pascagoula, Miss., 1996-97; lawyer pvt. practice, Ocean Springs, Miss., 1997—; bd. dirs. Constrn. Battalion Ctr. Credit Union, Gulfport, Miss., 1994-95. Vol. coach for Ocean Springs H.S. Mock Trial Team, 1998, 99. Lt. cmmdr. USN, 1991-95. Mem. Miss. Bar Assn. (young lawyers divsn., women and law com.), Jackson County Bar Assn. (treas.), Jackson County Young Lawyers (chair speech competition), Rotary Club. Democrat. Episcopalian. Avocation: tennis. Criminal, Personal injury, General civil litigation. Office: PO Box 904 Ocean Springs MS 39566-0904

**PATTISON, GEORGE EDGAR,** lawyer; b. Beaver Falls, Pa., May 25, 1944; s. John Norwood and Rosemary (Smith) P.; m. Marsha Wildermuth, June 8, 1968; children: Geoffrey, Megan. BS, Ohio State U., 1967; JD, U. Cin., 1972. Bar: Ohio 1972, U.S. Dist. Ct. (so. dist.) Ohio 1973, U.S. Supreme Ct. 1980. Legal editor W.H. Anderson Legal Pub., Cin., 1972-75; asst. pros. County of Clermont, Batavia, Ohio, 1975-80, pros. atty., 1981-89; pvt. practice Batavia, 1975—. Mem. ABA, Assn. Trial Lawyers Am. (winner environ. law essay 1972), Ohio State Bar Assn., Clermont County Bar Assn., Ohio Trial Lawyers Assn., Clermont County Citizens Law Enforcement Assn., Clermont County C. of C., Masons. Republican. Methodist. Criminal, General civil litigation, Real property. Home: 1091 Raintree Dr Milford OH 45150-9653 Office: 285 E Main St Batavia OH 45103-3072

**PATTON, BRUCE M.,** law educator; b. Terre Haute, Ind., Oct. 14, 1956; s. William Eugene and Carol Ann P.; m. Diana McLain Smith, Oct. 21, 1994. AB, Harvard COll, 1977, JD, 1984. Bar: Mass. Co-founder, assoc. dir. Harvard Negotiation Project, Cambridge, Mass., 1979-84, dep. dir., 1984—; co-founder, assoc. dir. Program on Negotiation at Harvard Law Sch., Cambridge, Mass., 1983—; co-founder, ptnr. Vantage Partners, LLC, Cambridge, 1997—; co-founder, prin. Conflict Mgmt. Inc., Cambridge, 1984—; co-founder, dir. Conflict Mgmt. Group, Cambridge, 1984—; Thaddeus R. Beal lectr. Harvard Law Sch., Cambridge, 1985—. Co-author: The Mainstream of Alegbra and Trigonometry, 2d edit., 1980, Getting To Yes, 2d edit., 1991, Difficult Conversations, 1999; contbr. articles to profl. jours. Avocations: squash, hiking. E-mail: bpatton@law.harvard.edu. Office: Harvard Negotiation Project Harvard Law Sch Pound Hall 524 Cambridge MA 02138

**PATTON, CHARLES HENRY,** lawyer, educator; b. Asheville, N.C., Jan. 1, 1953; s. Charles Robert and Sarah (Gulledge) P. BA, Memphis State U., 1975, JD, 1979. Bar: Tenn. Assoc. Holt, Bachelor, Spicer & Ryan, Memphis, 1979-80; fin. exec. Felsenthal Planning Service Co., Memphis, 1980-81; sole practice Memphis, 1981—; prof. Memphis State U., 1982—. Planned giving dir. Christ United Meth. Ch., Memphis, 1986; mem. Planned Giving Coun. Memphis. Mem. S.E. Regional Bus. Law Professors Assn., Memphis Bar Assn., Estate Planning Coun. Memphis. Republican. Avocations: classic automobile restoration, model trains. Estate planning, Probate, Estate taxation. Office: 5100 Poplar Ave Ste 2701 Memphis TN 38137-4000

**PATTON, DAVID ALAN,** lawyer; b. Oakland, Calif., Nov. 14, 1960; s. Douglas Kieth and Joan Erlene P.; m. Renee Theresa, Nov. 21, 1987 (div. Dec. 1996); children: Thomas, Joseph. BA, U. Calif., Berkeley, 1983; JD, Santa Clara U., 1987. Bar: Calif. 1988. Atty. Collins & Schlothaver, San Jose, 1988-93; ptnr. Lonich & Patton, San Jose, 1993—; judge pro tem Santa Clara Superior Ct., San Jose, 1996—, arbitrator, 1994—. Insurance, General civil litigation. Office: Lonich & Patton 111 W Saint John St Ste 600 San Jose CA 95113-1105

**PATTON, JAMES LEELAND, JR.,** lawyer; b. Wilmington, Del., Sept. 28, 1956; s. James L. Patton and Eleanor Phillips Crawford Brown; m. Kathleen Long Patton, May 29, 1981; children: Kathryn Stuart, Diana Lantz. BA in Philosophy, Davidson (N.C.) Coll., 1979; JD, Dickinson Sch. Law, Carlisle, Pa., 1983. Bar: Del. 1983, U.S. Dist. Ct. Del. 1983, U.S. Ct. Appeals (3rd cir.) 1988, U.S. Supreme Ct. 1991. Ptnr., chair Bankruptcy Dept. Young Conaway Stargatt & Taylor, Wilmington, 1983—; trustee Pvt. Panel Bankruptcy Trustees, 1985-88. Contbr. (ref. ency.): Fletcher Corporate Bankruptcy, Reorganization and Dissolution, 1992. Mem. ABA, Del. State Bar Assn. (bankruptcy law subcom. chmn. 1986—). Avocation: photography, sailing. Bankruptcy, Contracts commercial, General corporate. Office: Young Conaway Stargatt & Taylor PO Box 391 11th & Market Wilmington DE 19899

**PATTON, JAMES RICHARD, JR.,** lawyer; b. Durham, N.C., Oct. 27, 1928; s. James Ralph and Bertha (Moye) P.; m. Mary Margot Maughan, Dec. 29, 1950; children: James Macon, Lindsay Fairfield. AB cum laude, U. N.C., 1948; postgrad., Yale U., 1948; JD, Harvard U., 1951. Bar: D.C. bar 1951, U.S. Supreme Ct. 1963. Attache of Embassy; spl. asst. to Am. ambassador to, Indochina, 1952-54; with Office Nat. Estimates, Washington, 1954-55; atty. Covington & Burling, Washington, 1956-61; founding ptnr., chmn. exec. com. Patton Boggs, LLP, Washington, 1962—; Lectr. internat. law Cornell Law Sch., 1963-64, U.S. Army Command and Gen. Staff Coll., 1967-68; Mem. Nat. Security Forum, U.S. Air War Coll., 1965, Nat. Strategy Seminar, U.S. Army War Coll., 1967-70, Global Strategy Discussions, U.S. Naval War Coll., 1968, Def. Orientation Conf., 1972; mem. Com. of 100 on Fed. City, Washington; mem. adv. council on nat. security and internat. affairs Nat. Republican Com., 1977-81; bd. dirs. Security Nat. Bank (Wash.), Signet, N.A., Madeira Sch., Greenway, Va., 1975-81, Lawyers Com. for Civil Rights Under Law, Washington, Legal Aid Soc. Washington; mem. Industry Policy Adv. Com. for Trade Policy Matters, 1984-87; mem. visiting com. Ackland Art Mus. U. N.C., 1987—, Nat. Coun. Anderson Ranch Arts Ctr., 1987—. Adv. coun. mem. Johns Hopkins U. Sch. Advanced Internat. Studies, 1989-92; nat. bd. dirs. Aspen Mus., 1987-90; nat. coun. mem. Whitney Mus., 1992—; bd. dirs., exec. com. Nat. Mus. Natural History, Smithsonian, 1992—; bd. dirs. Smithsonian Nat. Bd., 1999—; trustee Aspen Music Festival and Sch., 1993—. Fellow U.N.C. Wilson Library, 1996—. Mem. ABA (past com. chmn.), Inter-Am. Bar Assn. (past del.), Internat. Law Assn. (past com. chmn.), Am. Soc. Internat. Law (treas., exec. coun.), Washington Inst. Fgn. Affairs, Nat. Gallery (collectors com. 1988-91), Gerrard Soc., Met. Club (Washington), Phi Beta Kappa, Alpha Epsilon Delta. General corporate, Private international, Public international.

**PATTON, JOHN MICHAEL,** lawyer; b. Washington, Sept. 3, 1947; s. Earl Richard and Frances Anne (Basar) P. BA in History, George Washington U., 1969, JD, 1974; BS in Acctg., U. Md., 1982. Bar: D.C. 1974. Atty. exempt orgns. tech. divsn. IRS, 1972—. With USAR, 1969-75. Mem. AICPA. Roman Catholic. Avocation: calendar date history of world events. Home: 3725 Macomb St NW Apt 112 Washington DC 20016-3841

**PATTON, PETER MARK,** lawyer; b. Chgo., Dec. 23, 1955; s. James T. and Dorothy R. Patton; m. Anne E. Castimore, Oct. 12, 1985; 1 child, William James. AB, Harvard Coll., 1977; JD, U. Calif., Berkeley, 1985. Bar: Pa. 1987, U.S. Dist. Ct. (ea. dist.) Pa. 1987, U.S. Ct. Appeals (4th cir.) 1986, U.S. Ct. Appeals (3rd cir.) 1988. Law clk. U.S. Ct. Appeals (4th cir.), Richmond, Va., 1985-87; assoc. Galfand, Berger, Phila., 1987-93, ptnr., 1993—. Committeeman Dem. Orgn., Delaware County, 1998. Reciient Profl. Responsibility award Am. Jurisprudence, 1985. Mem. Pa. Trial Lawyers Assn., Phila. Trial Lawyers Assn., Million Dollar Advocates Forum. Avocation: running. Personal injury, Product liability. Office: Galfand Berger 1818 Market St Ste 2300 Philadelphia PA 19103-3629

**PATTON, ROBERT CHARLES,** lawyer; b. Newark, N.J., July 28, 1943; s. Orville Miller and Martha Rich Patton; m. Virginia Jacqueline Southgate, Apr. 3, 1969; childen: Gregory Charles, Lisa Farris, Morgan Lea. BS, Western Mich. U., 1965; JD, U. Ky., 1968. Bar: Ky. 1968, U.S. Dist. Ct. (no. dist.) Ky. 1989, U.S. Ct. Appeals (6th cir.) 1969. Atty. City of Silver Grove, Ky., 1969-74; asst. commonwealth atty. County of Newport, Ky., 1978; asst. county atty,. County of Newport, 1969-78, Campbell county pub. defender, 1991—. Mem. Ky. Assn. of Trial Attys., Ky. Assn. Criminal Def. Lawyers. Democrat. Office: 14 W 4th St Newport KY 41071-1063

**PATTON, ROGER WILLIAM,** lawyer, educator; b. Spokane, Apr. 18, 1945; s. Kenneth Randall and Dorothy (Mostoller) P.; m. Susan L. Budd, June 15, 1968; 1 child, Michael Andrew. BS, Oreg. State U., 1968; JD, U. Calif., San Francisco, 1971. Bar: Wash. 1971, Calif. 1972. Asst. pub. defender Alameda County Pub. Defender, Oakland, Calif., 1972-78; counsel Kaiser Engrs. Internat., Oakland, 1978-79; ptnr. Patton, Wolan & Boxer, Oakland, 1979—; assoc. prof. law Armstrong Law Sch., Berkeley, Calif., 1976-84; adj. prof. Calif. State U., Hayward, 1984-87; assoc. prof. law Oakland Law Sch., 1990—. Capt. U.S. Army Res., 1968-72. Mem. Calif. State Bar (adminstrn. of justice com. 1989—), Fed. Bar No. Calif., Asian Law Caucus, Dem. Lawyers Club, Alameda Divers (pres. 1990-91). Democrat. Avocations: scuba diving, bicycling, astronomy, adventure travel, watching baseball and basketball. Civil rights, General civil litigation, Criminal. Office: Patton Wolan & Boxer 80 Grand Ave Ste 600 Oakland CA 94612-3744

**PATULA, RODNEY RICHARD,** lawyer; b. Berwyn, Ill., Nov. 19, 1949; s. Henry Biel and Irene Patricia Paula; m. Judith A. Brey, June 10, 1972 (div. Dec. 1977)); m. Marilyn K. Thieme, Apr. 25, 1982; 1 stepchild, Aaron M. Thieme. AB, U. Chgo., 1970; JD, U. Denver, 1973. Bar: Colo. 1974, U.S. Dist. Ct. Colo. 1074, U.S. Ct. Appeals (10th cir.) 1977, U.S. Supreme Ct. 1981, U.S. Ct. Appeals (5th cir.) 1989, U.S. Ct Appeals (9th cir.) 1993, Calif., 1996, U.S. Dist. Ct. (no., ctrl., ea. and so. dists.) 1996. Sr. law clk. to chief judge U.S. Dist. Ct. for Colo., Denver, 1974-75; assoc. Davis Graham & Stubbs, Denver, 1975-79; shareholder, dir. Pryor Carney & Johnson P.C., Englewood, Colo., 1979-95; ptnr., chmn. nat. litigation practice group Graham & James, LLP, San Francisco, 1995—. Contbr. articles to law jours. Bd. dirs. Mile High United Way, Denver, 1990-92; mem. Lawyers' Com. for Civil Rights, San Francisco, 1995—. Mem. ABA, Colo. Bar Assn. (ethics com. 1987-89), State Bar Calif., Denver Bar Assn. (Vol. Lawyer of Yr. award 1986), Bar Assn. San Francisco. Avocations: hiking, wines. Federal civil litigation, Private international, Alternative dispute resolution. Office: Graham & James LLP One Maritime Plz 3d Fl San Francisco CA 94111

**PATURIS, E. MICHAEL,** lawyer; b. Akron, Ohio, July 12, 1933; s. Michael George and Sophia (Manos) P.; m. Mary Ann Toompas, Febr. 28, 1965. BS, U. N.C., 1954, JD with Honors, 1959, attended, 1959-60. Bar: N.C. 1959, D.C. 1969, Va. 1973; CPA. Acct. Charlotte and Wilmington, N.C., 1960-63; assoc. Poyner, Geraghty, Hartsfield & Townsend, Raleigh, N.C., 1963-64; atty. advisor Chief Counsel's Office, Washington, 1964-66; sr. trial atty. Chief Counsel's Office, Richmond, Va., 1966-69; ptnr. Reasoner, Davis & Vinson, Washington, 1969-78; sole practitioner Alexandria, 1978—; acctg. instr. U. N.C., Chapel Hill, 1959-60; acctg., econs. instr. N.C. State U., Raleigh, 1963-64; business law instr. George Mason U., Fairfax County, Va., 1978-79. Mem. bd. editors U. N.C. Law Rev. With U.S. Army, 1954-56. Mem. Phi Beta Kappa., Beta Gamma Sigma. Corporate taxation, Estate taxation, General corporate. Home: 6326 Stoneham Ln Mc Lean VA 22101-2345 Office: Law Offices of EM Paturis 431 N Lee St Alexandria VA 22314-2301

**PAUCA, JANET FRANCES,** lawyer; b. Hemel Hempstead, Eng., June 13, 1941; came to U.S., 1968; d. Leonard and Kathleen Emily (Finnemore) Thearle; m. Alfredo Lazo Pauca, Aug. 28, 1965; children: Leonard, Rosemary, Deanna. BA, Wake Forest Univ., 1979, JD, 1982. Bar: N.C. 1983. Sr. library asst. Royal Postgrad. Med. Sch., London, 1961-67; sole practice law Winston-Salem, N.C., 1983—. Mem. Winston-Salem Conv. Ctr. Commn., 1984-89. Mem. N.C. Bar Assn. (Hispanic lawyers com.), N.C. Assn. Women Attys. Democrat. Roman Catholic. Avocations: ice skating, reading, music. Criminal, Family and matrimonial, Juvenile.

**PAUCIULO, JOHN WILLIAM,** lawyer; b. N.Y.C., Nov. 6, 1965; m. Johanna Choate; children: Michael, Nina. BA, Villanova U., 1987; JD, Temple U., 1990. Staff atty. U.S. Securities and Exch. Commn., N.Y.C., 1990-92; assoc. Lamb, Windle & McErlane, West Chester, Pa., 1992-96; assoc. counsel Pep Boys, Phila., 1996-98; assoc. White & Williams, Phila., 1998—. Judge of elections Chester County, Pa., 1995—. Mem. Pa. Bar Assn. General corporate, Securities, Real property. Home: 17 Beverly Ave Malvern PA 19355-3005 Office: White & Williams 1800 One Liberty Pl Philadelphia PA 19103

**PAUL, ADAM CRAIG,** lawyer; b. Ft. Dix, N.J., May 18, 1972. BA cum laude, James Madison U., 1994; JD cum laude, Cath. U. Am., 1997. Bar: Va. 1997, U.S. Dist. Ct. (ea. dist.) Va. 1997, U.S. Ct. Appeals (4th cir.) 1997), Md. 1998, U.S. Dist. Ct. Md. 1998. Legal intern ABA, Washington, 1995; law clk. Senate Jud. Commn., Washington, 1996, U.S. Dept. Justice, Washington, 1996; assoc. Gold Stanley Morrison & Laughlin, P.C., Alexandria, Va., 1997—; Bar: Va., Md., U.S. Dist Ct. (ea. dist.) Va. 1997, U.S. Dist. Ct. Md. 1998, U.S. Ct. Appeals (4th cir.) 1997. Mem. No. Va. Bankruptcy Bar Assn., Phi Delta Phi. Bankruptcy, Consumer commercial. Office: Gold Stanley et al 1800 Diagonal Rd Ste 300 Alexandria VA 22314-2840

**PAUL, DAVID AARON,** lawyer; b. West Orange, N.J., Dec. 18, 1969; s. Mike S. and Stephanie E. (Kelsh) P.; m. Melissa Lynne Haralson. BS, Stetson U., 1991, JD with honors, 1994. Bar: Fla. 1994, U.S. Dist. Ct. (mid. dist.) Fla. 1994. Atty. Fisher, Rushmer et al, Orlando, Fla., 1994-97, Justin C. Johnson, St. Petersburg, Fla., 1997-98, Maher, Gibson & Guiley, Orlando, 1998—. Bd. dirs. Orange County Children's Safety Village, Orlando, 1996-97, Ctrl Fla. YMCA, Orlando, 1996-97, YMCA Camping Svcs., Orlando, 1996-97. Named Best Advocate in the Nationa ABA/Am. Coll. Trial Lawyers, 1993, Nat. Champion, Nat. Trial Competition, 1993. Mem. ATLA, Acad. Fla. Trial Lawyers (dir. young lawyers 1998), Order of Barristers. General civil litigation, Personal injury. Office: Maher Gibson & Guiley 90 E Livingston St Ste 200 Orlando FL 32801-1597

**PAUL, EVE W.,** lawyer; b. N.Y.C., June 16, 1930; d. Leo I. and Tamara (Sogolow) Weinschenker; m. Robert D. Paul, Apr. 9, 1952; children: Jeremy Ralph, Sarah Elizabeth. BA, Cornell U., 1950; JD, Columbia U., 1952. Bar: N.Y. 1952, Conn. 1960, U.S. Ct. Appeals (2nd cir.) 1975, U.S. Supreme Ct. 1977. Assoc. Botein, Hays, Sklar & Herzberg, N.Y.C., 1952-54; pvt. practice Stamford, Conn., 1960-70; staff atty. Legal Aid Soc., N.Y.C., 1970-71; assoc. Greenbaum, Wolff & Ernst, N.Y.C., 1972-78; v.p. legal affairs Planned Parenthood Fedn. Am., N.Y.C., 1979—, v.p., gen. counsel, 1991—; bd. dirs. Ctr. for Gender Equality, Inc. Contbr. articles to legal and health publs. Trustee Cornell U., Ithaca, N.Y., 1979-84; mem. Stamford Planning Bd., Conn., 1967-70; bd. dirs. Stamford League Women Voters, 1960-62, Ctr. for Gender Equality, 1995—. Harlan Fiske Stone scholar Columbia Law Sch., 1952. Mem. ABA, Conn. Bar Assn., Assn. of Bar of City of N.Y., Stamford/Norwalk Regional Bar Assn., U.S. Trademark Assn. (chairperson dictionary listings com. 1988-90), Phi Beta Kappa, Phi Kappa Phi. Nonprofit and tax-exempt organizations, Intellectual property, Health. Office: Planned Parenthood Fedn 810 7th Ave New York NY 10019-5818 *The ability to plan the number and timing of my children has made it possible for me to enjoy career, marriage and family.*

**PAUL, HERBERT MORTON,** lawyer, accountant, taxation educator; b. N.Y.C.; s. Julius and Gussie Paul; m. Judith Paul; children: Leslie Beth, Andrea Lynn. BBA, Baruch Coll.; MBA, NYU, LLM; JD, Harvard U. Ptnr. Touche Ross & Co., N.Y.C.; assoc. dir.-tax Touche Ross & Co., dir. fin counseling; mng. ptnr. Herbert Paul, P.C., N.Y.C., 1983—; prof. taxation, trustee NYU. Author: Ordinary and Necessary Expenses; editor: Taxation of Banks; adv. tax editor The Practical Acct.; mem. adv. bd. Financial and Estate Planning, Tax Shelter Insider, Financial Planning Strategist, Tax Shelter Litigation Report; bd. dirs. Partnership Strategist, The Business Strategist; cons. Profl. Practice Mgmt. Mag.; mem. panel The Hot Line; advisor The Partnership Letter, The Wealth Formula; cons. The Insider's Report for Physicians; mem. tax bd. Business Profit Digest; cons. editor physician's Tax Advisor; bd. fin. cons. Tax Strategies for Physicians; tax and bus. advisor Prentice Hall; contbg. editor. Jour. of Accountancy; mem. editl. bd. Family Bus. Advisor. Trustee NYU, mem. bd. overseers Grad. Sch. Bus.; mem. com. on trusts and estates Rockefeller U.; trustee Alvin Alley Am. Dance Theatre, Assoc. Y's of N.Y.; co-chmn. accts. divsn. Fedn. Philanthropies; mem. adv. bd. Family Bus. Advisor; pres. coun. NYU. Mem. NYU Alumni Assn. (pres., bd. dirs.). Mem. ABA, Inst. Fed. Taxation (adv. com. chmn.), Internat. Inst. on Tax and Bus. Planning (adv. bd.), Assn. Bar City N.Y., NYU Tax Soc. (pres.), Bur. Nat. Affairs-Tax Mgmt. (adv. com. on exec. compensation), Am. Inst. CPAs (com. on corp. taxation), Tax Study Group, N.Y. County Lawyers Assn., N.Y. State Soc. CPAs Dir. (chmn. tax div. com. on fed. taxation, gen. tax com., furtherance com., com. on rels. with IRS, bd. dirs.), Nat. Assn. Accts., Assn. of Bar of City of N.Y., Accts. Club of Am., Pension Club, Nat. Assn. Estate Planners (bd. dirs.), N.Y. Estate Planning Coun. (bd. dirs.), N.Y. C. of C. (tax com.), Grad. Sch. Bus. of NYU Alumni Assn. (pres.), NYU Alumni Assn. (pres.). Clubs: Wall St., City Athletic (N.Y.C.), Inwood Country. Corporate taxation, Personal income taxation, Estate planning. Office: Mahoney Cohen Paul & Co PC 370 Lexington Ave Rm 1001 New York NY 10017-6503

**PAUL, JAMES WILLIAM,** lawyer; b. Davenport, Iowa, May 3, 1945; s. Walter Henry and Margaret Helene (Hillers) P.; m. Sandra Kay Schmid, June 15, 1968; children: James William, Joseph Hillers. BA, Valparaiso U., 1967; JD, U. Chgo., 1970. Bar: N.Y. 1971, U.S. Ct. Appeals (2d cir.) 1971, U.S. Dist. Ct. (so. and ea. dists.) N.Y. 1972, U.S. Supreme Ct. 1977, U.S. Ct. Appeals (6th cir.) 1981, Ind. 1982, U.S. Dist. Ct. (no. dist.) Ind. 1982, U.S. Claims Ct. 1989, U.S. Dist. Ct. (ea. dist.) Mich. 1989, U.S. Ct. Appeals (fed. cir.) 1991. Assoc. Rogers & Wells, N.Y.C., 1970-78, ptnr., 1978—; dir., officer Musica Sacra, Inc., 1972-81. Bd. dirs. Turtle Bay Music Sch., Am. Lutheran Publicity Bur. Recipient Disting. Alumnus award Valparaiso U., 1994. Mem. ABA (antitrust sect. ins. com.), Assn. Bar City N.Y. (com. on legal and jud. ethics, com. on civil ct.), Fed. Bar Council. Democrat. Clubs: Quaker Hill Country (Pauling, N.Y.). Antitrust, General civil litigation, Labor. Home: 360 E 72nd St Apt A-710 New York NY 10021-4755 also: 5 Curtis Dr Sherman CT 06784-1220 Office: Rogers & Wells 200 Park Ave Ste 5200 New York NY 10166-0005

**PAUL, MAURICE M.,** federal judge; b. 1932. BSBA, U. Fla., 1954, LLB, 1960. Bar: Fla. 1960. Assoc. Sanders, McEwan, Mims & MacDonald, Orlando, Fla., 1960-64; ptnr. Akerman, Senterfitt, Eidson, Mesmer & Robinson, Orlando, 1965-66, Pitts, Eubanks, Ross & Paul, Orlando, 1968-69; judge U.S. Cir. Ct. (9th cir.) Fla., 1973-82; judge, now sr. judge U.S. Dist. Ct. (no. dist.) Fla., 1982—. Office: US Dist Ct 401 SE 1st Ave Gainesville FL 32601-6899

**PAUL, RICHARD MONROE, III,** lawyer; b. Orange, Calif., Nov. 12, 1970; s. Richard M. Jr. and Linda L. (Spurrier) P.; m. Jayme Rochelle, May 16, 1992; children: Cassidy Elise, Barrett Monroe. BA, U. Mo., 1992, JD, 1995. Bar: Mo. 1995, Kans. 1996, U.S. Ct. Appeals (8th, 9th and cirs.) 1996. Jud. law clk. Mo. Supreme Ct., Jefferson City, 1995, Mo. Ct. Appeals, Kansas City, 1996; assoc. Shughart, Thomson & Kilroy, P.C., Kansas City, Mo., 1996—. Assoc. mng. editor Mo. Law Rev., 1994-95. Mem. Kansas City (Mo.) Bar Assn., Lawyers Assn. Kansas City, Federalist Soc. Antitrust, Appellate, General civil litigation. Office: Shughart Thomson & Kilroy 120 W 12th St Ste 1700 Kansas City MO 64105-1923

**PAUL, RICHARD STANLEY,** lawyer; b. Whitefish, Mont., Apr. 26, 1941; s. Richard C. and Esther (Shenefelt) P.; m. Elizabeth Headley, May 28, 1966; children: Christopher, Matthew. BA in History, U. Mont., 1963; MA in Am. History, U. Minn., 1964; JD, U. Pa., 1969. Bar: Del. 1969, Conn. 1988. Assoc. gen. counsel Xerox Corp., Stamford, Conn., 1980-88; dep. gen counsel Xerox Corp., Stamford, 1988-89, v.p., gen. counsel, 1989-91, sr. v.p., gen counsel, 1992—. Chmn. exec. com. Ctr. for Pub. Resources, Mfg. Alliance Law Coun. Mem. ABA, Del. Bar Assn., Conn. Bar Assn., Am. Corp. Cousnel Assn., Assn. Gen. Counsel. Republican. Lutheran. Office: Xerox Corp 800 Long Ridge Rd Stamford CT 06902-1288

**PAUL, RICHARD WRIGHT,** lawyer; b. Washington, May 23, 1953; s. Robert Henry Jr. and Betty (Carey) P.; m. Paula Ann Coolsaet, July 25, 1981; children: Richard Haven, Timothy Carey, Brian Davis. AB magna cum laude, Dartmouth Coll., 1975; JD, Boston Coll., 1978. Bar: Mich. 1978, U.S. Dist. Ct. (ea. dist.) Mich. 1978, U.S. Ct. Appeals (6th cir.) 1982, U.S. Supreme Ct. 1989, U.S. Dist. Ct. (we. dist.) Mich. 1991. Assoc. Dickinson, Wright, Moon, Van Dusen & Freeman, Detroit, 1978-85, ptnr., 1985—; mediator Wayne County Cir. Ct., Oakland County Dist. Ct. Co-author, Barbarians At The Gate: Daubert Two Years Later, 1995; contbr. articles to profl. publs. Mem. ABA, State Bar of Mich. (treas. litigation sect.), Def. Rsch. Inst., Detroit Bar Assn., Mich. Def. Trial Counsel, Dartmouth Lawyers Assn., Oakland County Bar Assn., Assn. Def. Trial Counsel, Alumni Coun. Dartmouth Coll., Dartmouth Detroit Club (pres. 1980—). Avocations: tennis, cycling. General civil litigation, Professional liability, Product liability.

**PAUL, ROBERT,** lawyer; b. N.Y.C., Nov. 22, 1931; s. Gregory and Sonia (Rijock) P.; m. Christa Holz, Apr. 6, 1975; 1 child, Gina. BA, NYU, 1953; JD, Columbia U., 1958. Bar: Fla. 1958, N.Y. 1959. From assoc. to ptnr. Paul, Landy, Beiley & Harper, P.A., Miami, 1964-94; counsel Republic Nat. Bank Miami, 1967-95. Past pres. Fla. Philharm., Inc., 1978-79; trustee U. Miami. Mem. ABA, N.Y. Bar Assn., Fla. Bar Assn., Fla. Zool. Soc., French-Am. C. of C. of Miami (pres. 1986-87). Private international, Banking, General corporate. Home: 700 Alhambra Cir Miami FL 33134-4808

**PAUL, ROBERT CAREY,** lawyer; b. Washington, May 7, 1950; s. Robert Henry and Betty Jane (Carey) P. AB, Dartmouth Coll., 1972; JD, Georgetown U., 1978. Assoc. Milbank, Tweed, Hadley & McCloy, N.Y.C., 1978-85; ptnr. Dechert Price & Rhoads, N.Y.C., 1986-89, Kelley Drye & Warren, Brussels, 1989-93; counsel Rockefeller & Co., Inc., N.Y.C., 1995—. Private international, Finance, Real property. Home: 310 E 46th St Apt 9B New York NY 10017-3023 Office: Rockefeller & Co Inc 30 Rockefeller Plz 56th Fl New York NY 10112-0256

**PAUL, THOMAS FRANK,** lawyer; b. Aberdeen, Wash., Sept. 23, 1925; s. Thomas and Loretta (Ounstead) P.; m. Dolores Marion Zaugg, Apr. 1, 1950; chilren: Pamela, Peggy, Thomas Frank. BS in Psychology, Wash. State U., 1951; JD, U. Wash., 1957. Bar: Wash. 1958, U.S. Dist. Ct. (no. and so. dists.) Wash. 1958, U.S. Ct. Appeals (9th cir.) 1958, U.S. Supreme Ct. 1970. Ptnr., shareholder, dir. LeGros, Buchanan & Paul, Seattle, 1958—; lectr. on admiralty and maritime law. Mem. ABA (chmn. com. on admiralty and maritime litigation 1982-86), Wash. State Bar Assn., Maritime Law Assn. U.S.A. (com. on nav. and C.G. matters 1981-82, com. on U.S. Mcht. Marine program 1981-82, com. on practice and procedure 1982-86, com. on limitation of liability 1982-86, com. on maritime legislation 1982—, nom. com. 1998—), Asia Pacific Lawyers Assn., Rainier Club, Columbia Tower Club. Republican. Product liability, Admiralty, General civil litigation. Home: 1323 Willard Ave W Seattle WA 98119-3460 Office: LeGros Buchanan & Paul 701 5th Ave Ste 2500 Seattle WA 98104-7051

**PAUL, VIVIAN,** lawyer; b. N.Y.C., July 3, 1925; d. A. Spencer and Simonson Feld; m. M.B. Paul, Sept. 10, 1966; children: Leslie Vivian, Melissa Beth. BA, U. Miami, 1944; LLB, U. So. Calif., 1949. Bar: Calif. 1949, U.S. Dist. Ct. (so. dist.) Calif. 1950. Pvt. practice, Cathedral City, Calif., 1949—. Editor-in-chief U. So. Calif. Law Rev., 1944. Los Angeles County Bar Assn. Democrat. Insurance, Personal injury. Home and Office: 69864 Via Del Norte Cathedral City CA 92234-1726

**PAUL, WILLIAM GEORGE,** lawyer; b. Pauls Valley, Okla., Nov. 25, 1930; s. Homer and Helen (Lafferty) P.; m. Barbara Elaine Brite, Sept. 27, 1963; children—George Lynn, Alison Elise, Laura Elaine, William Stephen. B.A., U. Okla., 1952, LL.B., 1956. Bar: Okla. bar 1956. Pvt. practice law Norman, 1956; ptnr. Oklahoma City, 1957-84; with Crowe & Dunlevy, 1962-84, 96—; sr. v.p., gen. counsel Phillips Petroleum Co., Bartlesville, Okla., 1984-95; ptnr. Crowe & Dunlevy, Oklahoma City, 1996—; assoc. prof. law Oklahoma City U., 1964-68; adv. bd. Martindale Hubbell, 1990—. Author: (with Earl Sneed) Vernon's Oklahoma Practice, 1965. Bd. dirs. Nat. Ctr. for State Cts., 1993-99, Am. Bar Endowment, 1986—. 1st lt. USMCR, 1952-54. Named Outstanding Young Man Oklahoma City, 1965, Outstanding Young Oklahoman, 1966. Fellow Am. Bar Found. (chmn. 1991), Am. Coll. Trial Lawyers; mem. ABA (bd. govs. 1995—, pres. 1999), Okla. Bar Assn. (pres. 1976), Oklahoma County Bar Assn. (past pres.), Nat. Conf. Bar Pres. (pres. 1986), U. Okla. Alumni Assn. (pres. 1973), Order of Coif, Phi Beta Kappa, Phi Delta Phi, Delta Sigma Rho. Democrat. Presbyterian. Federal civil litigation, State civil litigation, General corporate. Home: 13017 Burnt Oak Rd Oklahoma City OK 73120-8919 Office: Crowe & Dunlevy 1800 Mid-Am Tower 20 N Broadway Ave Ste 1800 Oklahoma City OK 73102-8273

**PAUL, WILLIAM MCCANN,** lawyer; b. Cambridge, Mass., Feb. 9, 1951; s. Kenneth William and Mary Jean (Lamson) P.; m. Janet Anne Forest, Feb. 25, 1984; children: Emily L'Engle, Andrew Angwin, Elizabeth Seton. Student, U. Freiburg, Fed. Republic of Germany, 1971-72; BA, Johns Hopkins U., 1973; JD, U. Mich., 1977. Bar: D.C. 1978, U.S. Dist. Ct. D.C. 1978, U.S. Ct. Claims 1984, U.S. Ct. Appeals (4th cir.) 1980, U.S. Ct. Appeals (fed. cir.) 1983, U.S. Tax Ct. 1990. Law clk. to judge U.S. Ct. Appeals (5th cir.), Austin, Tex., 1977-78; assoc. Covington & Burling, Washington, 1978-87, ptnr., 1987-88, 89—; dep. tax legis. counsel U.S. Treasury Dept., 1988-89. Mem. ABA (asst. sec. tax sect. 1995-97, sec. 1997—), D.C. Bar Assn., Am. coll. Tax Counsel, Order of Coif. Presbyterian. Corporate taxation, Personal income taxation. Home: 5604 Chevy Chase Pky NW Washington DC 20015-2520 Office: Covington & Burling PO Box 7566 1201 Pennsylvania Ave NW Washington DC 20004-2401

**PAULISICK, GERRI VOLCHKO,** lawyer; b. Pitts., June 12, 1969; m. Gerald Michael and Judith F. Volchko; m. Joseph R. Paulisick, Jr., May 3, 1997. BA, Pa. State U., 1991; JD, Duquesne U., 1994. Bar: Pa. 1994, U.S. Dist. Ct. (we. dist.) Pa. 1994. Law clk. Butler County Ct. of Common Pleas, Butler, Pa., 1994-95; assoc. Murrin, Taylor & Flach, Butler, 1995—. Mem. Am. Cancer Soc. (bd. dirs., v.p. 1996—), Pa. Bar Assn., Butler County Bar Assn., Vis. Nurse Assn. (bd. dirs. 1998—), Soroptimist. Democrat. Roman Catholic. Family and matrimonial, Probate, General practice. Office: Murrin Taylor & Flach 110 E Diamond St Butler PA 16001-5982

**PAULSON, TERRY CLAYTON,** lawyer, consultant, educator; b. Coronado, Calif., Aug. 31, 1954; d. Lee Arthur and Shay (Foshee) Clayton; m. Walter Alfred Paulson, June 9, 1978; children: Melissa Shay, Veronica Lee; 1 stepchild, Stephen Blake. BA, U. Ark., Fayetteville, 1976; JD, U. Ark., Little Rock, 1979. Bar: Ark. 1980, U.S. Dist. Ct. Ark. 1980, U.S. Ct. Appeals (8th cir.) 1980. Law clk. Hon. Robert F. Fussell, Little Rock, 1978-79; assoc. atty. House, Holmes & Jewell, P.A., Little Rock, 1979-84; cons. Little Rock, 1984-92; dir., instr. A.E.G.I.S.-L.R. Law, Little Rock, 1992; instr. U. Ark. Little Rock Sch. Law, 1992; adj. assoc. prof. Coll. Bus. Adminstrn./ U. Ark. at Little Rock, 1993-95, vis. asst. prof., 1995-96, asst. prof., 1996—; mem. pers. action team Little Rock Sch. Dist. Strategic Initiative Task Force, 1996; mem. Little Rock Sch. Dist. Facilities Rev. Com., 1996-97. Editor: Arkansas Environmental Law Handbook, 1997; contbr. articles to profl. jours. Bd. dirs. Ark. affiliate Am. Heart Assn., Little Rock, 1997; advisor, bd. dirs. 20th Century Club Hope Lodge, Inc., Little Rock, 1993-96; vol. Vols. in Pub. Schs., Little Rock, 1986—; mem. Leadership Greater Little Rock, 1997—. Named Outstanding Vol., Am. Heart Assn., Ark., 1997; Ark. Real Estate Found. grantee, 1995. Mem. Ark. Assn. Women Lawyers (pres.), Acad. Legal Studies in Bus. Avocations: golf, gourmet cooking, reading. Office: U Ark at Little Rock Coll Bus Adminstrn 2801 S University Ave Little Rock AR 72204-1000

**PAULSRUD, ERIC DAVID,** lawyer; b. Ft. Randall, Wash., May 16, 1960; s. David G. and Joan E. (Swanson) P.; m. Deborah Mae Thompson, Aug. 7, 1982. BA, St. Olaf Coll., Northfield, Minn., 1982; JD, Hamline U., 1985. Bar: Minn. 1985, Mo. 1988, U.S. Ct. Appeals (8th cir.) 1988, Ill. 1989, U.S. Ct. Appeals (7th cir.) 1989, U.S. Dist. Ct. (ea. dist.) Mo. 1988, U.S. Dist. Ct. (so. dist.) Ill. 1989, U.S. Supreme Ct. 1990. Law clk. Honorable Edward Bearse, Anoka, Minn., 1985-86, Honorable J. Smith Henley, 8th cir., Harrison, Ark., 1986-88; assoc. Lewis, Rice & Fingersh, St. Louis, 1988-97, Leonard, Street and Deinard, Mpls., 1997—. Mem. ABA (media law sect. 1991—, antitrust sect. 1991—), Internat. Trademark Assn. Lutheran. Avocations: bicycling, woodwork, gardening. Libel, Antitrust, General civil litigation. Office: Leonard Street & Deinard 150 S 5th St Ste 2300 Minneapolis MN 55402-4238

**PAUPP, TERRENCE EDWARD,** research associate, educator; b. Joliet, Ill., Aug. 10, 1952; s. Edward Theodore and Mary Alice (Combs) P. BA in Social Scis., San Diego State U., 1974; ThM, Luth. Sch. Theology, 1978; JD, U. San Diego, 1990. Instr. philosophy San Diego City Coll., 1983-86, Southwestern Coll., Chula Vista, Calif., 1980-83; law clerk Sch. Law U. San Diego, 1987-88; law clerk Office of Atty. Gen., San Diego, 1988-89; rsch. assoc. Frank & Milchen, San Diego, 1989, Dougherty & Hildre, San Diego, 1990-95; sr. rsch.-assoc. Inst. for Ctrl. and Ea. European Studies, San Diego State U., 1996—; cons. Cmty. Reinvestment Act, San Diego, 1993-95; sr. rsch. assoc. Inst. Ctrl. and Ea. European Studies San Diego State U., 1994-95; adj. faculty in criminal justice and polit. sci. Nat. U. Contbr. articles to law jours. Cons. Neighborhood House 5th Ave., 1994-95, Bethel Baptist Ch., 1994-95, PBS Frontline documentary The Nicotine Wars, 1994. Mem. ATLA, N.Y. Acad. Scis. Democrat. Lutheran. Avocation: tennis. Office: San Diego State University Inst Ctrl & Ea European Study 4430 North Ave Apt 9 San Diego CA 92116-3980

**PAVALON, EUGENE IRVING,** lawyer; b. Chgo., Jan. 5, 1933; m. Lois M. Frenzel, Jan. 15, 1961; children: Betsy, Bruce, Lynn. BSL, Northwestern U., 1954, JD, 1956. Bar: Ill. 1956. Sr. ptnr. Pavalon & Gifford, Chgo., 1970—; mem. com. on discovery rules Ill. Supreme Ct., 1981—; lectr., mem. faculty various law schs.; bd. dirs. ATLA Mut. Ins. Co. Former mem. state bd. dirs. Ind. Voters Ill; bd. overseers Inst. Civil Justice, Rand Corp., 1993-99; mem. vis. com. Northwestern U. Law Sch., 1990-96. Capt., USAF, 1956-59. Fellow Am. Coll. Trial Lawyers, Internat. Soc. Barristers, Internat. Acad. Trial Lawyers, Roscoe Pound Found. (life fellow, pres. 1988-90); mem. ABA, Chgo. Bar Assn. (bd. mgrs. 1978-79), Ill. Bar Assn., Ill. Trial Lawyers Assn. (pres. 1980-81), Trial Lawyers for Pub. Justice (founding mem., v.p. 1991-92, pres.-elect 1992-93, pres. 1993-94), Assn. Trial Lawyers Am. (parlimentarian 1983-84, sec. 1984-85, v.p. 1985-86, pres. elect 1986-87, pres. 1987-88), Am. Bd. of Profl. Liability Attys. (diplomate), Am. Bd. Trial Advocates, Chgo. Athletic Assn., Standard Club. Author: Human Rights and Health Care Law, 1980, Your Medical Rights, 1990; contbr. articles to profl. jours., chpts. in books. Personal injury, Federal civil litigation, State civil litigation. Home: 1540 N Lake Shore Dr Chicago IL 60610-6684 Office: Pavalon Gifford et al 2 N La Salle St Chicago IL 60602-3702

**PAVIA, GEORGE M.,** lawyer; b. Genoa, Italy, Feb. 14, 1928; s. Enrico L. and Nelly (Welisch) P.; m. Ellen Salomon, June 15, 1952; children—Andrew, Alison; m. 2d, Antonia Pearse, Dec. 2, 1976; children—Julian, Philippa. B.A., Columbia U., 1948, LL.B., 1951; postgrad. U. Genoa, 1954-55. Bar: N.Y. 1951, U.S. Supreme Ct. 1956, U.S. Dist. Ct. (so. and ea. dists.) N.Y. 1956. Assoc., Fink & Pavia, N.Y.C., 1955-65; sr. ptnr. Pavia & Harcourt, N.Y.C., 1965—. Served to capt. JAGC, U.S. Army, 1951-54. Mem. ABA, Internat. Law Soc., Consular Law Soc. Private international, General corporate. Home: 18 E 73rd St New York NY 10021-4130 Office: 600 Madison Ave New York NY 10022-1615

**PAVITT, WILLIAM HESSER, JR.,** lawyer; b. Bklyn., Dec. 9, 1916; s. William Hesser and Elsie (Haring) P.; m. Mary Oden, June 19, 1937; children: William, Howard, Gale, Bruce. BA, Columbia U., 1937; JD, 1939. Bar: N.Y. 1939, Philippines 1945, Md. 1946, D.C. 1947, Ohio 1955, Calif. 1958. Law clk. to judge N.Y. Ct. Appeals, 1939-40; assoc. Spence, Windels, Walser, Hotchkiss & Angell, N.Y.C., 1940-44; contracting officer Office of Rsch. and Inventions (now Office of Naval Rsch.), Washington, 1946-48; assoc. Richard Whiting, Whiting and Pavitt, Washington, 1948-54, Toulmin & Toulmin, Dayton, Ohio, 1954-57, Smyth & Roston, L.A., 1957-59; ptnr. Smyth, Roston & Pavitt, L.A., 1960-81; sr. ptnr. Beehler & Pavitt, L.A., 1981—. Mem. L.A. Intellectual Property Law Assn. (pres. 1969-70, chmn. Calif. state bar patent sect. 1971-72). Intellectual property, Federal civil litigation. Office: 100 Corporate Pointe Ste 300 Culver City CA 90230-8738

**PAWELCZYK, RICHARD,** lawyer; b. N.Y.C.. BA, SUNY, Stony Brook, 1990; JD, St. Johns Sch. of Law, 1996. Bar: N.Y. 1997, Conn. 1996, U.S. Dist. Ct. (ea. and so. dist.) N.Y. 1997. Atty. Jacobson & Colfin, N.Y.C., 1996—; cons. Fifth Ave Media, N.Y.C., 1996—; vis. lectr. CUNY-Baruch Coll., 1998—; assoc. pub. Cover Mag., 1998—. Mem. ABA (coms. on trademarks and the internet, copyrights and the internet, broadcasting and sound recording), N.Y. County Lawyers Comms. and Entertainment (intellectual property sect.), N.Y. State Bar Assn. (coms. on copyrights and trademarks). Avocations: music, sports, literature. Environmental, Intellectual property. Office: Jacobson & Colfin PC 156 5th Ave Ste 434 New York NY 10010-7002

**PAWLIK, JAMES DAVID,** lawyer, historian; b. Cleve., May 26, 1958; s. Eugene Joseph and Eleanor Therese Marie (Gorzelanczyk) P. BA cum laude, Ohio State U., 1980, MA, 1991; JD cum laude, Harvard U., 1983. Bar: Calif. 1984, U.S. Ct. Appeals (9th cir.), 1985, U.S. Dist. Ct. (no. dist.) Calif. 1984, U.S. Dist. Ct. (ctrl. and ea dists.), Calif. 1986, Ohio 1980. Intern Dept. Def., Washington, 1980; assoc. Chandler, Wood, Harrington & Maffly, San Francisco, 1983-87, ptnr., 1988-89; teaching assoc. Ohio State U., 1990-91; pvt. practice Law Offices of James D. Pawlik, Cleve., 1991-93; ind. contractor Gallagher, Sharp, Fulton & Norman, Cleve., Ohio, 1992-93; jud. law clk. to Hon. Robert J. Krupansky U.S. Ct. Appeals (6th cir.), Cleve., 1993—; instr. dept. history Cuyahoga C.C., Parma, Ohio, 1993—; instr. dept. polit. sci. Lourdes Coll., Sylvania, Ohio, 1993. Mem. staff Harvard Internat. Law Jour., 1981-83. Campaign mgr. for city coun. candidate, Westerville, Ohio, 1977; bd. trustees Midpark H.S. Alumni Assn., 1999—. William Green Meml. scholar 1979, Kosciuszko scholar 1989-91; Ohio State U. fellow, 1989-90; named Midpark H.S. Acad. Hall of Fame, 1997. Mem. ABA, State Bar Ohio, Mensa, Ohio State U. Alumni Assn., Harvard Alumni Assn., Phi Beta Kappa, Phi Kappa Phi, Phi Alpha Theta.

**PAYNE, LUCY ANN SALSBURY,** law librarian, educator, lawyer; b. Utica, N.Y., July 5, 1952; d. James Henry and Dorothy Eileen (Seavy) Salsbury; m. Albert E. Payne, June 2, 1973 (div. 1983); 1 child, Joni Eileen. MusB, Andrews U., 1974; MA, Loma Linda (Calif.) U., 1979; JD, U. Notre Dame, Ind., 1988; MLS, U. Mich., 1990. Bar: Ind. 1988, Mich. 1988, U.S. Dist. Ct. (no. and so. dists.) Ind. 1988, U.S. Ct. Appeals (7th cir.) 1992. Rsch. specialist Kresge Libr. Law Sch. U. Notre Dame, 1988-90, asst. libr., 1990-91, assoc. libr., 1991-96, librarian, 1996—. Contbr. articles to profl. jours. Mem. ABA, Am. Assn. Law Librs., Mich. Bar Assn., Ind. Bar Assn., Ohio Regional Assn. Law Librs., Mich. Assn. Law Librs., St. Joseph County Bar Assn. Adventist. Office: U Notre Dame Law Sch Kresge Law Libr Notre Dame IN 46556

**PAYNE, MARGARET ANNE,** lawyer; b. Aug. 10, 1947; d. John Hilliard and Margaret Mary (Naughton) P. Student, Trinity Coll., Washington, 1965-66; BA magna cum laude, U. Cin., 1969; JD, Harvard U., 1972; LLM in Taxation, NYU, 1976. Bar: N.Y. 1975, U.S. Dist. Ct. (so. dist.) N.Y. 1975, Calif. 1979, U.S. Dist. Ct. (so. dist.) Calif. 1979. Assoc. Mudge, Rose, Guthrie, and Alexander, N.Y.C., 1972-75, Davis, Polk and Wardwell, N.Y.C., 1976-78, Seltzer, Caplan, Wilkins and McMahon, San Diego, 1978-79; assoc. Higgs, Fletcher and Mack, San Diego, 1980-82, ptnr., 1983-90, of counsel, 1991—; adj. prof. grad. tax program U. San Diego Sch. Law, 1979-89, Calif. Western Sch. Law, San Diego, 1980-82; judge pro tem Mcpl. Ct., San Diego Jud. Dist., 1983, 92. Bd. dirs. Artist Chamber Ensemble, Inc., 1983-86, Libr. Assn. La Jolla, Calif., 1983-86, San Diego County Crimestoppers, Inc., 1993-95, San Diego Crime Commn., 1994-95, St. Augustine's H.S., 1994-95, San Diego Hist. Soc., 1993-95. Mem. ABA, Calif. State Bar Assn., San Diego County Bar Assn., Mortar Bd., Guidon Soc., Charter 100, Phi Beta Kappa. Probate, Estate taxation, Estate planning. Office: Higgs Fletcher & Mack 401 W A St Ste 2600 San Diego CA 92101-7913

**PAYNE, MARY LIBBY,** judge; b. Gulfport, Miss., Mar. 27, 1932; d. Reece O. and Emily Augusta (Cook) Bickerstaff; m. Bobby R. Payne; children: Reece Allen, Glenn Russell. Student, Miss. Univ. Women, 1950-52; BA in Polit. Sci. with distinction, U. Miss., 1954, LLB, 1955. Bar: Miss. 1955. Ptnr. Bickerstaff & Bickerstaff, Gulfport, 1955-56; sec. Guaranty Title Co., Jackson, Miss., 1957; assoc. Henley, Jones, & Henley, Jackson, Miss., 1958-61; freelance rschr. Pearl, Miss., 1961-63; solo practitioner Brandon, Miss., 1963-68; exec. dir. Miss. Judiciary Commn., Jackson, 1968-70; chief drafting & rsch. Miss. Ho. Reps., Jackson, 1970-72; asst. atty. gen. State Atty. Gen. Office, Jackson, 1972-75; founding dean, assoc. prof. Sch. Law Miss. Coll., Jackson, 1975-78, prof., 1978-94; judge Miss. Ct. Appeals, Jackson, 1995—; bd. disting. alumnae Miss. U. Women, 1988-97. Contbr. articles to profl. jours. Founder, bd. dirs. Christian Conciliation Svc., Jackson, 1983-93; counsel Christian Action Com. Rankin Bapt. Assn., Pearl, 1968-92; advisor Covenant Ministerial Fellowship, 1995—. Recipient Book of Golden Deeds award Pearl Exch. Club, 1989, Excellence medallion Miss. U. Women, 1990; named Woman of Yr. Miss. Assn. Women Higher Edn., 1989, Power of One honoree Miss. Govs. Conf., 1996, Miss. Coll. Lawyer of the Yr., Mis. Coll. Sch. Law Alumni Assn., 1998, Outstanding Woman Lawyer, Miss. Women Lawyers Assn., 1999. Fellow Am. Bar Found.; mem. Miss. Bar Found., Christian Legal Soc. (nat. bd. dirs. 1992—, regional membership coord.), Margaret Brent League. Baptist. Avocations: public speaking, travel, needlepoint, sewing, reading. Office: Ct Appeals PO Box 22847 Jackson MS 39225-2847

**PAYNE, ROBERT E.,** federal judge; b. 1941. BA in Polit. Sci., Washington and Lee U., 1963; LLB magna cum laude, Washington & Lee U., 1967. Assoc., ptnr. McGuire, Woods, Battle & Boothe, Richmond, Va., 1971-92; fed. judge U.S. Dist. Ct. (ea. dist.) Va., 1992—. Notes editor Wash. & Lee U. Law Rev. Capt. U.S. Army, 1967-71. Mem. ABA, Va. Bar Assn., Va. State Bar Assn., Va. Assn. Def. Attys. (chmn. comml. litigation sect. 1989-91), Richmond Bar Assn., Order of Coif. Episcopalian. Fax: 804-916-2669. Office: Lewis F Powell Jr US Courthouse 1000 E Main St Ste 334 Richmond VA 23219-3525

**PAYNE, ROY STEVEN,** judge; b. New Orleans, Aug. 30, 1952; s. Fred J. and Dorothy Julia (Peck) P.; m. Laureen Fuller, Sept. 8, 1973; children: Julie Elizabeth, Kelly Kathryn, Alex Steven, Michael Lawrence. BA with distinction, U. Va., 1974; JD, La. State U., 1977; LLM, Harvard U., 1980. Bar: La. 1977, U.S. Dist. Ct. (we. dist.) La. 1980, U.S. Ct. Appeals (5th cir.) 1980, U.S. Supreme Ct. 1983. Law clk. to judge U.S. Dist. Ct., Shreveport, La., 1977-79; assoc. Blanchard, Walker, O'Quin & Roberts, Shreveport, 1980-83, ptnr., 1984-87; U.S. Magistrate judge, We. Dist. La., Shreveport, 1987—; instr. New Eng. Sch. Law, Boston, 1979-80. Contbr. articles to profl. jours. Chmn. Northwest La. Legal Svcs. Assn., Shreveport, 1984-85. Mem. 5th Cir. Bar Assn., 5th Cir. Jud. Coun. (magistrate judges com. 1992—), La. State Bar Assn. (editorial bd. Forum jour., 1983-87, legal aid com.), Fed. Magistrate Judges Assn., Shreveport Bar Assn., La. Assn. Def. Counsel (bd. dirs. 1987), Harry V. Booth Am. Inn of Ct. (pres. elect 1994-95, pres. 1996-98), Order of Coif, Rotary, Phi Kappa Phi, Phi Delta Phi. Methodist. Home: 12494 Harts Island Rd Shreveport LA 71115-8505 Office: US Courthouse 300 Fannin St Ste 4300 Shreveport LA 71101-3122

**PAYNE, R.W., JR.,** lawyer; b. Norfolk, Va., Mar. 16, 1936; s. Roland William and Margaret (Sawyer) P.; m. Gail Willingham, Sept. 16, 1961; children: Darrell, Preston, Darby, Clinton. BA in English, U. N.C., 1958, LLB, 1961; LLB, Stetson U., 1962. Bar: Fla. 1963, U.S. Dist. Ct. (so. dist.) 1964, U.S. Ct. Appeals (11th cir.) 1965, U.S. Supreme Ct. 1970. Assoc. Roney & Beach, St. Petersburg, Fla., 1963-64, Nichols, Giather, Beckham, Miami, Fla., 1964-67; ptnr. Spence, Payne, Masington, Miami, 1967-95, Payne, Leeds, Colby & Robinson, P.A., Miami, 1995-97; pvt. practice Miami, 1997, 98; ptnr. McLuskey, McDonald & Payne, P.A., Miami, 1999—; presenter numerous profl. convs. and seminars. Contbr. articles to legal jours., legal edn. books. Mem. Ottawa Roughriders, Can. Football League, fall 1958; capt. football team U. N.C., 1957, bd. dirs., v.p. alumni bd., 1984-92, bd. dirs. ednl. found., 1988-92; bd. dirs. Chem. Dependency Tng. Inst.; past pres. Coral Gables (Fla.) Sr. H.S. Athletic Boosters Club; past bd. dirs. Coral Gables War Meml. Youth Ctr., bd. trustees 1st United Meth. Ch. Coral Gables; past mem. gov.'s coun. on phys. fitness and sports, Fla.; past assoc. mem. Jr. Orange Bowl Com. With USMC, 1959. Fellow Am. Coll. Trial Lawyers, Internat. Acad. Trial Lawyers; mem. ABA, ATLA, Am. Bd. Trial Advocates, Fla. Bar Assn., Acad. Fla. Trial Lawyers (past mem. bd. govs.), Dade County Bar Assn. (past bd. dirs.), Dade County Trial Lawyers Assn. (founder, past pres.), Bankers Club, Miami Club, Univ. Club, Coral Reef Yacht Club, Order of Golden Fleece, Order of Old Well, Sigma Chi, Phi Delta Phi. Avocations: boating, golf, diving. General civil litigation, Personal injury, Product liability. Office: McLuskey, McDonald & Payne PA Two Datran Ctr 19th Flr 9130 S Dadeland Blvd Miami FL 33156-7818

**PEABODY, BRUCE R.,** lawyer; b. Pitts., June 20, 1956; s. Robert B. and Mary (Brawdy) P. BA in Am. Studies cum laude, Yale U., 1978; JD, U. Va., 1981. Rsch. atty., lectr. Legal Data Resources, Inc., Hartford, Conn., 1981-83; atty. Hogan, Rini & Mednick, New Haven, 1984-87, 90-94, Berchem & Moses, P.C., Milford, Conn., 1987-90; owner, atty. Bruce R. Peabody, Esquire, New Haven, 1994—. Bd. dirs., pres. New Haven Chorale, Inc., 1983-95; mem. adv. bd. Mems. of Yale Art Museums, New Haven, 1997—, pres., 1999—; bd. dirs. East Rock Inst., New Haven, 1998—; trustee First and Summerfield United Meth. Ch., 1986-89; elder First Presbyn. Ch., 1996—. Avocation: choral singing. General corporate, Real property, Contracts commercial. Home: 73 Sleeping Giant Dr Hamden CT 06518-2120 Office: 110 Whitney Ave New Haven CT 06511

**PEACOCK, JUDITH ANN** See **ERWIN, JUDITH ANN**

**PEAR, CHARLES E., JR.,** lawyer; b. Macon, Ga., June 18, 1950; s. Charles Edward and Barbara Jane P.; m. Linda Sue King; children: Jennifer Sue, Charles Edward III, Stephanie Sue. BA, U. Hawaii, 1972 with honors; JD, U. Calif., Berkeley, 1975. Bar: Hawaii 1976, Fla. 1977, Colo. 1994, U.S. Ct. of Appeals (9th cir.). Assoc. Rush, Moore, Craven, Sutton, Morry & Beh, Honolulu, 1976-77, of counsel, 1987-90; assoc., ptnr. Carlsmith & Dwyer, Honolulu, 1977-82; ptnr. Burke, Sakai, McPheeters, Bordner & Gilardy, Honolulu, 1983-87; vis. prof. law and computers U. British Columbia, 1990-93; of counsel Holland & Hart, Denver, 1993-96; counsel, ptnr. McCorriston, Miho, Miller& Mukai, Honolulu, 1996—; mem. Hawaii Real Estate Commn. com. on condominium and resort real estate legis., 1978-79; spl. counsel to consumer protection com. Hawaii State Ho. of Reps., 1981-82; chair real property and fin. svcs. sect. Hawaii State Bar Assn., ABA. Editor-in-Chief Hawaii Conveyance Manual II, 1987; editor Hawaii Commercial Real Estate Manual, 1988; bd. editors Hawaii Inst. of Continuing Legal Edn.; co-author: Nat. Assn. of Real Estate Licensing Law Officials and Nat. Timesharing Coun. Model Timesharing Act, 1981-82; contbg. author: Winning With Computers, 1992, Hawaii Real Estate Manual, 1997; lectr. in field, 1981—. Mem. ABA (document assembly interest group, expert sys. interest group, hypermedia interest group). Real property, Computer, Finance.

**PEARCE, CARY JACK,** lawyer; b. Copeville, Tex., Aug. 28, 1934; s. James Zebulon and Lillian (Graves) P.; m. Joyce Selette Hulsey, Oct. 17, 1959; children: Janet, Joseph, Alissa, Gale. BA, Baylor U., 1955; LLB, So. Methodist U., 1962. Bar: Tex. 1962, D.C. 1971. Asst. chief pub. counsel sec. antitrust divsn. U.S. Dept. Justice, Washington, 1967-70; dep. gen. counsel White House Office Consumer Affairs, Washington, 1970-71; pvt. practice, Washington, 1971—; pres., dir. OSI Mgmt, Inc. Contbr. articles to profl. jours. Bd. trustees All Souls Unitarian Ch., Washington. Mem. ABA. Unitarian. Antitrust, Private international, Administrative and regulatory. Office: 1730 K St NW Ste 304 Washington DC 20006-3839

**PEARCE, HARRY JONATHAN,** lawyer; b. Bismarck, N.D., Aug. 20, 1942; s. William R. and Jean Katherine (Murray) P.; m. Katherine B. Bruk, June 19, 1967; children: Shannon Pearce Baker, Susan J., Harry M. BS, USAF Acad., Colorado Springs, Colo., 1964; JD, Northwestern U., 1967; Degree in Engring. (hon.), Rose-Hulman Inst. Tech., 1997; LLD (hon.), Northwestern U., 1998. Bar: N.D. 1967, Mich. 1986. Mcpl. judge City of Bismarck, 1970-76, U.S. magistrate, 1970-76, police commr., 1976-80; sr. ptnr. Pearce & Durick, Bismarck, 1970-85; assoc. gen. counsel GM, Detroit, 1985-87, v.p., gen. counsel, 1987-92, exec. v.p., gen. counsel, 1992-94, exec. v.p., 1994-95, vice chmn., 1996—; bd. dirs. GM Corp., Hughes Electronics Corp., GM Acceptance Corp., Delphi Automotive Sys. Corp., Alliance of Automobile Mfrs. of Marriott Internat. Inc., Econ. Strategy Inst., Theodore Roosevelt Medora Found., MDU Resources Group, Inc., Nat. Def. U. Found., Detroit Investment Fund. Mem. law bd. Sch. Law, Northwestern U.; mem. bd. visitors U.S. Air Force Acad.; chmn. Product Liability Adv. Coun. Found.; founding mem. minority counsel demonstration program Commn. on Opportunities for Minorities in the Profession, ABA; chmn. The Sabre Soc., USAF Acad.; trustee Howard U., U.S. Coun. for Internat. Bus., New Detroit, Inc.; mem. The Mentor's Group Forum for U.S.-European Union Legal-Econ. Affairs, The Conf. Bd., Network of Employers for Traffic Safety's Leadership Coun., Pres.'s Coun. on Sustainable Devel., World Bus. Coun. for Sustainable Devel., World Economic Forum Coun. Innovative Leaders in Globalization. Capt. USAF, 1964-70. Named Michiganian of Yr., The Detroit News, 1997; Hardy scholar Northwestern U., Chgo., 1964-67, recipient Alumni Merit award, 1991. Fellow Am. Coll. Trial Lawyers, Internat. Soc. Barristers; mem. Am. Law Inst. Avocations: amateur radio, woodworking, sailing. General corporate. Office: GM Corp 100 Renaissance Center PO Box 100 Detroit MI 48265-1000

**PEARCE, JOHN Y.,** lawyer; b. New Orleans, Mar. 26, 1948; s. John Young II and Marina (Harris) P.; m. Marjorie Pamela Doyle, May 22, 1971 (div.); children: Andrea Elizabeth, Roger Wellington. BA, La. State U., 1973, JD, 1976. Bar: La. 1977, U.S. Dist. Ct. (ea., mid. and we. dists.) La., U.S. Ct. Appeals (5th and 11th cirs.). Assoc. Doyle, Smith & Doyle, New Orleans, 1977-79, ptnr., 1979-80, mng. ptnr., 1980-84; ptnr. Montgomery, Barnett, Brown, Read, Hammond & Mintz, New Orleans, 1984—. Sgt. U.S. Army, 1969-71. Mem. ABA (ho. dels. 1998-99), La. Bar Assn. (chmn. mineral law coun. 1994-95), New Orleans Bar Assn. (exec. com., pres. 1997-98). Republican. Episcopalian. Oil, gas, and mineral, Environmental, General civil litigation. Office: Montgomery Barnett Brown Read Hammond & Mintz 1100 Poydras St New Orleans LA 70163-1101

**PEARCE, MARGARET TRANNE,** law librarian; b. San Bernardino, Calif., Mar. 20, 1946; d. Paul Nelson and Margaret (Buchanan) Gregory; m. Ronald Wayne Pearce, Jan. 13, 1973; 1 child, Alice. BA in Edn., U. Kans., 1968; MLS, Emporia State U., 1969; postgrad., Washington U., 1982-83. Asst. libr. Kans. State U., Manhattan, 1969-73; assoc. law libr. Washington U., St. Louis, 1974-80; ct. libr. Mo. Ct. Appeals (ea. dist.), St. Louis, 1981-83; libr. 8th Cir. Libr., Kansas City, Mo., 1983—. Guardian ad litem Ct. Appointed Spl. Advocates, Johnson County, Kans., 1984-88. Mem. Am. Assn. Law Librs., Mid-Am. Assn. Law Librs., Kansas City Assn. Law Librs. (bd. dirs. 1992-93, sec. 1995—). Home: 8408 W 113th St Overland Park KS 66210-2438 Office: US Cts Libr 811 Grand Blvd Kansas City MO 64106-1904

**PEARCE, MARK DOUGLAS,** lawyer; b. Shreveport, La., Apr. 4, 1962; s. Frank and Marie Elise (Schaaf) P.; m. Theresa Marie VanAsselberg, June 4, 1984; children: Mark D. Jr., Chelsea Nicole. BS in Mech. Engring., La. Tech. U., 1984; JD, La. State U., 1992. Bar: La. 1992, U.S. Dist. Ct. (ea., we., and cen. dists.) La. 1992. Engr. Tex. Instruments, Dallas, 1984; project engr. Bingham-Willamette Co., Shreveport, 1984-85; sr. engr. Ctrl. La. Elec. Co., Pineville, La., 1986-89; atty. Stafford, Stewart & Potter, Alexandria, La., 1992—. Commr. Cenla Civitan, Alexandria, 1996. Mem. ASME, La. State Bar Assn., Alexandria Bar Assn., Kiwanis Club Alexandria. Baptist. Avocations: golf, fishing. Product liability, Insurance, Estate planning. Home: 818 W Shore Dr Alexandria LA 71303-2077 Office: 3112 Jackson St Alexandria LA 71301-4746

**PEARCE, MARK GASTON,** lawyer; b. Bklyn., Aug. 15, 1953; s. Gaston Roden and Patricia Louise Pearce; m. Nancy B. McCulley, Oct. 13, 1984; 1 child. BA, Cornell U., 1975; JD, SUNY, Buffalo, 1978. Bar: N.Y. 1979, U.S. Dist. Ct. (we. dist.) N.Y. 1980. Field atty. Nat. Labor Rels. Bd., Buffalo, 1979-92, dist. trial specialist, 1992-94; assoc. Lipsitz, Green, Fahringer, Roll, Salisbury & Cambria, Buffalo, 1994-98, ptnr., 1998—. Mem. mcpl. legis. regional com. Erie County, Buffalo, 1997-98. Mem. N.Y. State Bar Assn. (com. chmn. labor law sect. 1994—), Minority Bar Assn. of Western N.Y. (pres. 1992-94), Indsl. Rels. Rsch. Assn. of Western N.Y. (adv. bd. 1994—). Avocations: oil painting, skiing, golf. Labor. Office: Lipsitz Green Fahringer Roll Salisbury & Cambria 42 Delaware Ave Ste 300 Buffalo NY 14202-3857

**PEARCE, RICHARD LEE,** lawyer; b. Racine, Wis., Apr. 11, 1959; s. John Wallace and Betty Jane (Anthony) P.; m. Cynthia Diane Davis, June 11, 1983; 1 child, Melissa Lauren. BS in Chemistry, U. S.C., 1981, JD, 1984. Bar: S.C. 1984, U.S. Dist. Ct. S.C. 1985, U.S. Ct. Appeals (4th cir.) 1985. Law clk. to resident cir. judge Edward B. Cottingham, 1984-85; assoc. Fox, Zier, Burkhalter & Verenes, Aiken, S.C., 1985-86; ptnr. Toole & Toole, Aiken, 1986-96; asst. pub. svcs. dir., legis. liaison S.C. Bar, 1996-98; city solicitor, staff atty. City of Aiken, 1998—; instr. Am. Banking Inst., Nat. Advocacy Ctr., Nat. Dist. Attys. Assn.; guest lectr., adj. instr. U. S.C., Aiken. Emcee Sch. Bd. Acad. Tournament, Aiken, 1986; bd. dirs. Tri-Devel. Ctr., Aiken, 1985-86; spl. events com. Downtown Aiken Devel. Corp.; fundraiser com. Am. Cancer Soc., 1985-88; legal advisor Children's Place, Inc.; judge mock trial high sch. competition, 1991-96; trustee Aiken, Barnwell, Banberg, and Edgefield Libr. Sys. Mem. S.C. Bar Assn. (ho. of dels. 1989-95, pro bono program 1989-97, resolution of fee disputes bd., lawyers' fund for client protection, task force on justice for all, ethics adv. com., unauthorized practice law com., co-editor Legis. Update, editor Ethics Adv. Opinion Summaries, coord. annual jud. evaluation), Aiken County Bar Assn. (pres. 1990-92), Aiken C. of C. (legal liaison 1986), Internat. Mcpl. Lawyers Assn., Nat. Dist. Attys. Assn., S.C. Solicitors Assn., Rotary Internat. (bd. dirs. 1994-96, pres.-elect 1994-95, pres. 1995-96, group study exch. coord., Aiken-Llandrindod, Wales, U.K., Exch. Program, Paul Harris fellow, Sustaining Paul Harris fellow), Omicron Delta Kappa, Hitchcock Woods Axe Club. Presbyterian. Avocations: camping, outdoor activities, historical research, cycling. General practice, Personal injury, State civil litigation. Office: City of Aiken PO Box 1177 Aiken SC 29802-1177

**PEARCE, RICHARD WARREN,** law educator, lawyer; b. Glen Ellyn, Ill., Jan. 26, 1924; s. William Hemingsly Pearce and Alice Heald (dec. June 3, 1993); m. Neva Mae Brook, Sept. 8, 1945; children: Richard W. Jr., Karen Gail. BA, Stetson U., 1950, MA, 1955, JD, 1957; LLD (hon.), Fla. Southern Coll., 1973; HHD (hon.), Meth. Coll., 1991; LLD (hon.), Bethune Cookman Coll., 1998. Bar: Fla. 1950. Atty., 1950-62; prof. Stetson Univ., Deland, Fla., 1958-68; sr. lectr. Stetson Univ., Deland, 1984—; v.p., dean Fla. Southern Coll., Lakeland, 1968-73; pres. Meth. Coll., Fayetteville, N.C., 1973-83. Author: (textbook) Law and Society, 1966. Trustee Fla. Meth. Children Home, 1962-66, Fla. United Meth. Ch.; vice chmn. Volusia County Sch. Bd., Deland, 1962-68; conf. lay leader N.C. Annual Conf. United Meth. Ch., Raleigh, N.C., 1977-83; del. World Meth. Conf., 1979, '84; secr., treas. Ctrl. Fla. League of Small Municipalities, 1961-68. With USN, 1943-46. Democrat. Methodist. Avocations: golf, travel, electronics. Office: Dept Bus 421 N Woodland Blvd Dept Bus Deland FL 32720-3760

**PEARE, DAN C.,** lawyer; b. Wichita, Kans., Nov. 9, 1960; s. Robert E. and Helen A. (Kraft) P.; m. Valory S. Innes, Sept. 12, 1992; children: Robert Jordan, Regan Elizabeth, Reilly Nicole. BS in Fin., Wichita State U., 1982, MBA, 1985; JD, U. Kans., 1988. Bar: Kans. 1988; U.S. Ct. Appeals (10th cir.). Mem. Hinkle, Eberhart & Elkori, LLC, Wichita, 1988—; dir., trustee The Morrison Found., Wichita, 1993—; dir./officer DUI Victim Ctr. of Kans., Wichita, 1992-97; mem. planned giving com. Via Christi Found., Wichita, 1996—. Author: (with others) Kansas Estate Adminstration Handbook, 1992. Recipient award for top paper, Am. Jurisprudence, U. Kans. Sch. of Law, 1988. Mem. Wichita Estate Planning Coun., Wichita Estate Planning Forum, Kans. Bar Assn. (exec. com. mem. 1996—). Roman Catholic. Avocations: sports, photography, woodworking. Estate planning, Estate taxation. Home: 1420 N Sport Of Kings Ct Wichita KS 67230-7151 Office: Hinkle Eberhart Elkoun LLC 301 N Main St Ste 2000 Wichita KS 67202-4820

**PEARLBERG, IRVAN A.,** lawyer; b. Bklyn., Feb. 2, 1951; s. Lawrence and Marion Pearlberg; m. Patricia Lynn Lacy, Nov. 11, 1994; children: Erica, Richard; 1 stepchild, Scott Pearson. BS, Long Island U., 1973; JD, John Marshall Law Sch., Atlanta, 1976. Bar: Ga. 1976, U.S. Dist. Ct. (no. dist.) Ga. 1977, U.S. Ct. Appeals (5th cir.) 1981, U.S. Ct. Appeals (11th cir.) 1981, U.S. Supreme Ct. 1980. Assoc. atty. Richard L. Powell, Esquire, Marietta, 1976-78; ptnr. Van Pearlberg & Assocs., Marietta, 1978-83; ptnr., atty. Manheim & Pearlberg, Marietta, 1985-86; asst. dist. atty. Dist. Atty.'s Office of Cobb County, Marietta, Ga., 1983-84, 90—; assoc. judge Mcpl. Ct. City of Marietta, 1990; instr. North Ctrl. Ga. Law Enforcement Acad., Marietta. Author poetry. Trustee Cobb Landmarks and Hist. Soc., Cobb County, 1998. Served with USCGR, 1969-76. Mem. Cobb County Bar Assn., Nat. Dist. Attys. Assn., Nat. Assn. Trial Advocates, Old War Horse Lawyers Club, Kiwanis of Marietta, Inc. : 383 Church St NW Marietta GA 30060-1357 Office: Office of Dist Atty 10 E Park Sq Marietta GA 30090-0115

**PEARLMAN, MICHAEL ALLEN,** lawyer; b. Phila., Sept. 22, 1946; s. William and Mary (Stark) P.; m. Ann Gerald, June 1, 1969; children: Benjamin, Amy. BA, Duke U., 1968, JD, 1970. Bar: N.C. 1970, D.C. 1971, U.S. Dist. Ct. (mid. dist.) N.C. 1973, N.Y. 1982, Ct. Internat. Trade 1982. Atty. FTC, Washington, 1970-73; assoc. gen. counsel, asst. sec. Fieldcrest Mills, Inc., Eden, N.C., 1973-81; counsel GE, Syracuse, N.Y., 1981-85; corp. counsel Eastman Kodak Co., Rochester, N.Y., 1985-96; internat. counsel Eastman Kodak Co., Rochester, 1997-98, dir. legal affairs L.Am. region, 1998—; pres. ctrl. and western N.Y. chpt. Am. Corp. Counsel Assn., 1992-93. Pres. Rockingham County Arts Coun., N.C., 1979-80. Mem. Duke Law Sch. Alumni Assn. (bd. dirs. 1994-97), Temple Sinai (treas. 1994-96). General corporate, Private international, Mergers and acquisitions. Home: 3045 NE 208th St Aventura FL 33180-3625 Office: Eastman Kodak Co 8600 NW 17th St Ste 200 Miami FL 33126-1034

**PEARLMAN, PETER STEVEN,** lawyer; b. Orange, N.J., June 11, 1946; s. Jack Kitchener and Tiela Josephine (Fine) P.; m. Joan Perlmutter, June 19, 1969; children: Heather, Christopher, Megan. BA, U. Ill., 1967; JD, Seton Hall U., 1970. Bar: N.J. 1970, U.S. Dist. Ct. N.J. 1970, U.S. Tax Ct. 1973, U.S. Supreme Ct. 1974, U.S. Ct. Appeals (2d cir.) 1981, U.S. Ct. Appeals (3d cir.) 1983, U.S. Ct. Appeals (7th cir.) 1985, U.S. Ct. Appeals (D.C. cir.) 1998; cert. civil trial atty., 1982. Assoc. Cohn & Lifland, Esquires, Saddle Brook, N.J., 1970-72; ptnr. Cohn, Lifland, Pearlman, Herrmann & Knopf, Saddle Brook, 1972—; lectr. Nat. Inst. Trial Advocacy, Hempstead, N.Y., 1988—; active trial advocacy program Weidner Law Sch.; adj. faculty mem. trial advocacy program Hofstra Law Sch.; master C. Willard Heckel Inn of Ct.; guest lectr. appellate advocacy Roger Williams Law Sch., 1995—; mem. panel arbitrators Am. Arbitration Assn.; lectr. for Inst. Continuing Legal Edn. for State of N.J. Mem. ABA, ATLA, N.J. Bar Assn. Federal civil litigation, State civil litigation, General corporate. Home: 9 Harvey Dr Short Hills NJ 07078-1122 Office: Cohn Lifland Pearlman Herrmann & Knopf 1 Park 80 Plz W Ste 4 Saddle Brook NJ 07663-5808

**PEARLMAN, SAMUEL SEGEL,** lawyer; b. Pitts., May 28, 1942; s. Merle Maurice and Bernice Florence (Segel) P.; m. Cathy Schwartz, Aug. 16, 1964; children: Linda P. Kraner, Caren E. AB, U. Pa., 1963, LLB magna cum laude, 1966. Bar: Pa. 1966, Ohio, 1967, U.S. Ct. Appeals (3d cir.) 1967. Law clk. U.S. Dist. Ct. (Ea. dist.) Pa., 1966-67; assoc. Burke, Haber & Berick, Cleve., 1967-72, prin., 1973-86, prin. Berick, Pearlman & Mills, 1986—; lectr. law Case Western Res. U. Sch. Law, 1978-82; mem. registration com. Ohio Div. Securities, 1979-89; adv. dir. Midland Title Security, Inc. Trustee Realty ReFund Trust (NYSE), 1990-98. Mem. ABA, Ohio State Bar Assn., Greater Cleve. Bar Assn. (chmn. securities law sect. 1985-86), Order of Coif. Republican. Jewish. Author: Cases, Forms and Materials for Modern Real Estate Transactions, 1978, 82. General corporate, Real property, Finance. Office: 1111 Superior Ave 1350 Eaton Ctr Cleveland OH 44114

**PEARLMUTTER, FREDI L.,** lawyer, educator; b. Paterson, N.J., Nov. 15, 1946; d. Paul and Rose H. Pearlmutter; m. Paul D. Cohen, Oct. 18, 1987. AB cum laude, Brown U., 1968; JD, Harvard U., 1971. Bar: N.J. 1987, N.Y. 1972, U.S. Dist. Ct. N.J. 1987, U.S. Dist. Ct. (so. dist.) N.Y. 1973, U.S. Dist. Ct. (ea. dist.) N.Y. 1973). Assoc. Fried, Frank, Harris, Shriver & Jacobson, N.Y.C., 1971-74; atty. U.S. Mktg. and Refining divsn. Mobil Oil Corp., N.Y.C., 1974-80; asst. gen. counsel Amerada Hess Corp., N.Y.C., 1980-86; adj. prof. Seton Hall U. Sch. Law, Newark, 1994—; of counsel Cooper, Rose & English, Summit, N.J., 1987—. Contbr. articles to profl. jours. Mem. Warren Twp. (N.J.) Environ. Commn.; mem. ad. hoc com. on land use Warren Twp. Mem. ABA, N.J. State Bar Assn. (chair environ. law sect. 1997-98, founder and co-chair environ. ins. com.), Assn. Bar City N.Y. (com. on energy law, com. on adminstrv. law). Environmental, Insurance, Administrative and regulatory. Office: Cooper Rose & English LLP 480 Morris Ave Summit NJ 07901-1523

**PEARLSTEIN, BRIAN K.,** lawyer; b. Pitts., Aug. 29, 1966; s. Morris Alvin and Shirley Elaine P.; m. Miriam Karin Mevorah, Apr. 1, 1995; 1 child, Noah Benjamin. BA, U. Mich., 1995; JD, Am. U., 1991. Bar: Md. 1991, DC 1992, U.S. Dist. Ct. Md. 1992, U.S. Ct. Appeals (4th cir.) 1992. Assoc. Leftwich & Douglas, Washington, 1991-95, Brodsky Greenblatt & Renehan, 1995—. Bd. dirs. Am. Liver Found., 1998—. Avocations: squash, skiing, outdoor activities. General civil litigation, Family and matrimonial. Office: Brodsky Greenblatt & Renehan 16061 Comprint Cir Gaithersburg MD 20877-1321

**PEARLSTEIN, PAUL DAVIS,** lawyer; b. Berlin, N.H., Jan. 3, 1938; s. Victor and Sophia (Davis) P.; m. Patricia Hurston, June 1964 (div.); children: Laura Sue, David Seth; m. Marilyn Mills, Jan. 11, 1981; children: Adam Lowell, Susanna Lee. AB, U. Pa., 1959; LLB, U. Va., 1962. Bar: Va. 1962, D.C. 1963, Md. 1990, U.S. Supreme Ct. 1970; cert. bankruptcy splst. Commercial Law League of Am. Acad., arbitrator Am. Arbitraton Assn., Nat. Assn. Securities Dealers. Atty. HUD, Washington, 1964-66; adminstr. contrn. and purchasing activities Cafritz Co. and affiliated cos., Washington, 1966-68; pvt. practice Washington, 1968-96; ptnr. Pearlstein & Jacques, Washington, 1989—, Pearlstein & Assocs., 1997—; chair adv. rules com. U.S. Bankruptcy Ct. for D.C.; bankruptcy trustee, Washington and Va., 1973-90; speaker numerous orgns. Editor: Real Estate Practice in DC, Md. and Va. ; contbr., editor articles and book revs. to legal jours. Bd. mgrs. Washington Hebrew Congregation, 1979-85, pres. brotherhood, 1974-75; mandolinist and guitarist Takoma Mandoleers, 1971—, Orgn. Anacostia Rowing and Scullings, Coun. for Ct. Excellence; bd. dirs., sec. Met. Washington, DC Trial Lawyers Found., 1991-96; mem. inter group rels. com. Jewish Cmty. Coun., 1973-90; bd. dirs. DC chpt. Am. Diabetes Assn., 1987-89. Capt. U.S. Army, 1962-64. Fellow Am. Bar Found.; mem. ABA (real probperty and probate sects.), Bar Assn. D.C. (chmn. real property law com. 1976-78, Chmn. of Yr. award 1977, Spl. Projects award, 1987, pres. rsch. found.), Jud. Conf. D.C., Washington Assn. Realtors, Washington Estate Planning Coun., D.C. Land Title Assn. (v.p. 1989-90). Democrat. Avocations: kyaking, hiking, mandolin, guitar, rowing. Real property, Bankruptcy, Probate. Office: 1730 Rhode Island Ave NW Washington DC 20036-3102

**PEARLSTINE, NEAL R.,** lawyer; b. Sellersville, Pa., Nov. 15, 1954; s. Jules Pearlstine; m. Sharon L. Pearlstine, Nov. 15, 1980. BSBA, U. Denver, 1976; JD, Cumberland Sch. Law, 1980; LLM, Villanova U., 1989. Bar: Pa. 1980, Fla. 1981, U.S. Dist. Ct. (ea. dist.) Pa. 1991. Staff atty., ptnr. Pearlstine-Salkin Assocs., Lansdale, Pa., 1980-95; shareholder Pearlstine & Assocs., P.C., Lansdale, 1995—. Mem. North Penn C. of C. (sec. 1993—). Estate planning, Real property, General corporate. Office: Pearlstine & Assocs PC 2422 N Broad St #789 Lansdale PA 19446

**PEARMAN, JOEL EDWARD,** lawyer; b. Knoxville, Tenn., Jan. 12, 1949; s. Jess Edward and Ozell (Huff) P.; m. Barbara White, July 17, 1991; children: Joshua Edward, Paul Jonathan, Lindsley Margiotta. BA, Bryan Coll., 1971; JD, U. Tenn., 1973. Bar: Tenn. 1974, U.S. Dist. Ct. (no. dist.) Tenn. 1974. Atty. Foster Care Rev. Com., Kingston, Tenn., 1978-80, Child Abuse Rev. Team, 1984-90; commr. Roane County Election Commn., Kingston, 1982-90, Lockheed Martin Energy Sys., Procurement Policies and Procedures, 1991—; mem. steering com. Leadership Roane County, Kingston, 1986-88. Named one of Outstanding Young Men, 1975-76. Mem. Nat. Contract Mgmt. Assn., Tenn. Bar Assn., Roane County Bar Assn. (pres. 1983—), Rotary (Harriman pres. 1982-83). Republican. Nuclear power, Government contracts and claims. Office: PO Box 2002 Oak Ridge TN 37831-6501

**PEARMAN, JOHN STEWART,** lawyer; b. Paris, Ill., May 13, 1970; s. Ralph S. and Mary Ann Pearman. BA, Loyola U., Chgo., 1992; JD, So. Ill. U., 1995. Bar: Ill. 1995. Policy and program specialist Ill. Atty. Gen.'s Office, Chgo., 1995, exec. asst. atty. gen., 1995-97; polit. dir. Citizens for Jim Ryan, Chgo., 1997-98; assoc. Asher, Smith & Isaf, 1998—. Mem. Ill. Bar Assn., Chgo. Bar Assn., Chgo. Area Runners Assn., Tau Kappa Epsilon, KC (3d degree). Republican. Roman Catholic. Avocation: marathon running. Workers' compensation, Personal injury, Product liability. Office: 236 W Court St Paris IL 61944-1721

**PEARMAN, SHAUN,** lawyer; b. Denver, Mar. 4, 1960; s. Edwin E. and Nina J. (Callaway) P.; m. Terri M. Harris, Mar. 15, 1986; children: Brandon, Adam, Jordan, Macey, Ian. BBA, U. Denver, 1982, JD, 1986. Bar: Colo. 1987, U.S. Dist. Ct. Colo. 1988. Assoc. Scheffel & Assocs. P.C., Denver, 1988—; expert witness atty. fee disputes and bank collateral verification, Colo. and Wyo., 1994—. Pres. Action Recycling Ctr., Wheat Ridge, Colo., 1988—; elder Trinity Bapt. Ch., Wheat Ridge, 1993—; legis. liaison Inst. Scrap Recycling Industries, 1996—. Mem. Attys. Title Guaranty Fund (agent 1989—), Golden Key (life). Republican. Avocations: bicycling, midget car racing. E-mail: spearman@tnslaw.com. Criminal, Real property. Office: Scheffel & Assocs P.C. 3801 E Florida Ave Ste 600 Denver CO 80210-2544

**PEARSON, CHARLES THOMAS, JR.,** lawyer; b. Fayetteville, Ark., Oct. 14, 1929; s. Charles Thomas and Doris (Pinkerton) P.; m. Wyma Lee Hampton, Sept. 9, 1988; children: Linda Sue, John Paddock. B.S., U. Ark., 1953, J.D., 1954; postgrad., U.S. Naval Postgrad. Sch., 1959; A.M., Boston U., 1963. Bar: Ark. bar 1954. Practice in Fayetteville, 1963—; dir. officer N.W. Comms., Inc., Dixieland Devel., Inc., Jonlin Investments, Inc., World Wide Travel Svc., Inc., Okliania Farms, Inc., N.W. Arl. Land & Devel., Inc., Garden Plaza Inns, Inc. Word Data, Inc., M.P.C. Farms, Inc., Fayetteville Enterprises, Inc., NWA Devel.Co., Delta Comm., Inc.; past. dir., organizer N.W. Nat. Bank. Adviser Explorer Scouts, 1968—; past pres. Washington County Draft Bd.; past pres. bd. Salvation Army. Served to comdr. Judge Adv. Gen. Corps USNR, 1955-63. Mem. ABA, Ark. Bar Assn., Washington County Bar Assn., Judge Advs. Assn., N.W. Ark. Ret. Officers Assn. (past pres.), Methodist Men (past pres), U. Ark. Alumni Assn. (past dir.), Sigma Chi (past pres. N.W. Ark. alumni, past chmn. house corp.), Alpha Kappa Psi, Phi Eta Sigma, Delta Theta Phi. Republican. Methodist. Clubs: Mason (32 deg., K.T., Shriner), Moose, Elk, Lion, Metropolitan. Personal injury, Real property, General practice. Office: 36 E Center St Fayetteville AR 72701-5301

**PEARSON, HENRY CLYDE,** judge; b. Ocoonita, Lee County, Va., Mar. 12, 1925; s. Henry James and Nancy Elizabeth (Seals) P.; m. Jean Calton, July 26, 1956; children—Elizabeth, Frances, Timothy Clyde. Student Union Coll., 1947-49; LL.B., U. Richmond, 1952. Bar: Va. 1952, U.S. Ct. Appeals (4th cir.) 1957, U.S. Supreme Ct. 1958. Sole practice, Jonesville, Va., 1952-56; asst. U.S. atty. Western Dist. Va., Roanoke, 1956-61; ptnr. Hopkins, Pearson & Engleby, Roanoke, 1961-70; judge U.S. Bankruptcy Ct. Western Dist. Va., Roanoke, 1970—; participant Va. Continuing Edn. Seminars; mem. adv. com. fed. rules bankruptcy procedure. Mem. Va. Ho. of Reps., 1954-56, Va. Senate, 1968-70; Republican nominee Gov. of Va., 1961. Served with USN, 1943-46; PTO. Mem. Va. State Bar, ABA, Va. Trial Lawyers Assn., Assn. Trial Lawyers Am., Am. Judicature Soc., Am. Judges Assn., Fed. Bar Assn., Delta Theta Phi, Tribune Jefferson Senate, Am. Legion,

VFW. Methodist. Clubs: Masons, Shriners. Editorial bd. Am. Survey Bankruptcy Law, 1979. Office: 1910 Mcvitty Rd Salem VA 24153-7406

**PEARSON, JOHN EDWARD,** lawyer; b. Jamaica, N.Y., Aug. 20, 1946; s. Stanley Charles and Rose Margaret (Manning) P.; m. Laura Marie Johannes, Dec. 28, 1968; children: Laura Rose, Jack. BA, Manhattan Coll., 1968; JD, St. John's U., 1972. Bar: N.Y. 1973, Fla. 1981, U.S. Dist. Ct. (so. dist.) N.Y. 1977, U.S. Dist. Ct. (so. dist.) Fla. 1982, U.S. Ct. Appeals (11th cir.) 1982, U.S. Ct. Appeals (5th cir.) 1982. Assoc. Sage, Gray, Todd & Sims, N.Y.C., 1972-78, ptnr., 1979; ptnr. Sage, Gray, Todd & Sims, Miami, Fla., 1980-87; ptnr. Hughes, Hubbard & Reed, Miami, 1987-91, 94-98, counsel, 1998—; ptnr. Hughes, Hubbard & Reed, N.Y.C., 1992-93. Author jour. article (Best Article award 1971). With USMCR, 1968-69. Mem. ABA, Fla. Bar Assn., N.Y. State Bar Assn., Assn. Bar City N.Y., Dade County Bar Assn., N.Y. County Lawyers Assn., Greater Miami C. of C. (trustee). Republican. Roman Catholic. Avocations: sailing, running. Finance, Real property. Home: 276 Sea View Dr Key Biscayne FL 33149-2504 Office: Hughes Hubbard & Reed 201 S Biscayne Blvd Ste 2500 Miami FL 33131-4305

**PEARSON, JOHN Y., JR.,** lawyer; b. Norfolk, Va., July 23, 1942. BA, Washington & Lee U., 1964; JD, U. Va., 1971. Bar: Va. 1971. Atty. Willcox & Savage P.C., Norfolk, Va. Bd. editors: Va. Law Rev., 1969-71. Fellow Am. Coll. Trial Lawyers; mem. ABA (mem. litigation, tort and ins. practice sects.), Va. Assn. Def. Attys., Order of Coif. General civil litigation, Professional liability, Product liability. Office: Willcox & Savage PC 1800 NationsBank Ctr Norfolk VA 23510-2197

**PEARSON, PAUL DAVID,** lawyer, mediator; b. Boston, Jan. 22, 1940; s. Bernard J. and Ruth (Bayla) Horblit; m. Carol A. Munschauer; children: David Todd, Lisa Kari, Grant M. BA, Bucknell U., 1961; LLB, U. Pa., 1964. Bar: Mass. 1966, N.Y. 1987. Staff atty., tech. assoc. lab. cmty. psychiatry dept. psychiatry Med. Sch. Harvard U., Boston, 1966-68; assoc. Snyder Tepper & Berlin, Boston, 1968-71; ptnr., 1971-77; with Hill & Barlow, 1977-87, ptnr., chmn. family law dept., 1987-96; with Hodgson, Russ, Andrews, Woods and Goodyear, Buffalo, 1987-96; ptnr. chmn. family law dept. Hodgson, Russ, Andrews, Woods and Goodyear; of counsel Sullivan & Oliverio, 1996—; lectr. Mass. Con. Legal Edn., New Eng. Law Inst., dept. psychiatry SUNY, Buffalo, 1989—; instr. law and mental health Boston Psychoanalytic Soc. and Inst., 1975-87; lectr. in field. Contbr. articles to profl. jours. Founding mem. Alliance for Dispute Resolution, 1996; bd. dirs. Jewish Cmty. Ctr. Greater Buffalo, 1991-96, Am. Jewish Com. Buffalo, 1991—, pres., 1995-97, nat. bd. govs., 1997—, Arts Coun. Buffalo and Erie County, 1992-99, bd. dirs., legal coord. Parent Edn. And Custody Effectiveness program N.Y. 8th jud. dist.; trustee, legal counsel Wayland (Mass.) Townhouse; trustee Family counseling Svc. (region West); mem., chmn., clk. Wayland Zoning Bd. Appeals; v.p., counsel Arts Wayland Zoning Bd. Appeals; v.p., counsel Arts Wayland Found., 1982-87; vis. fellow Woodrow Wilson Found., 1985-87, Mass. Gov.'s Spl. Commn. on Divorce, 1985-87. Capt. Mil. Police Corps USAR. Fellow Am. Acad. Matrimonial Lawyers (pres., bd. mgrs. Mass); mem. ABA (family law and ADR coms.), Mass. Bar Assn. (chmn. family law sect.), Acad. Family Mediators, N.Y. State Coun. on Divorce Mediation, Assn. Family and Conciliation Cts., Boston Bar Assn. (family law com., legis. chmn.), N.Y. Bar Assn. (family law com., ADR com.), Erie County Bar Assn. (chmn. alternative dispute resolution com., family law com.). Family and matrimonial, Probate, Alternative dispute resolution. Home: 605 Lebrun Rd Amherst NY 14226-4232 Office: 600 Main Place Tower Buffalo NY 14202-3706

**PECA, PETER SAMUEL,** judge; b. Monterrey, Calif., Nov. 28, 1942; s. Peter Samuel and Ellen (Daly) P.; m. dorothy burnham, Jan. 5, 1983; children: Samuel, Meredith. BSCE, N.Mex. State U., 1972; JD, Cleve. State U., 1977. Bar: Ohio 1977, Tex. 1978. Dist. judge 171st Dist. Ct. Tex., El Paso, 1986-98; judge El Paso County Ct., 1998—. Democrat. Roman Catholic. Avocation: golf. Office: El Paso County Ct #7 500 E San Antonio Ave El Paso TX 79901-2419

**PECCARELLI, ANTHONY MARANDO,** lawyer; b. Newark, Apr. 12, 1928; s. Adolph and Mary (Marano) P.; m. Mary Dearborn Hutchison, Dec. 23, 1953; children: Andrew Louis, David Anthony, Laura Elizabeth. BS, Beloit Coll., 1953; JD, John Marshall Law Sch., 1959; M in Jud. Studies, U. Nev., 1990. Bar: Ill. 1961, U.S. Dist. Ct. (no. dist.) Ill., U.S. Supreme Ct. Supr. real estate and claims Gulf Oil Corp., Chgo., 1956-61; asst. state's atty. DuPage County, Wheaton, Ill., 1961-65; first asst. state's atty. DuPage County State's Atty., Wheaton, Ill., 1965-69; mem.-del. Ill. Constnl. Conv., Springfield, 1969-70; exec. dir. Ill. State's Atty. Assn., Elgin, 1970-71; ptnr. Barclay, Damisch & Sinson, Chgo., 1971-79; assoc. cir. judge 18th Jud. Cir. Ct., Wheaton, 1979-82, cir. judge, 1982-93, chief judge, 1989-93, presiding judge domestic rels. divsn., 1982-83, presiding judge law divsn., 1987-89, chief judge, 1989-93; justice 2nd dist. Ill. Appellate Ct., Wheaton, 1993-94; state's atty. DuPage County, Wheaton, Ill., 1995-96; assoc., of counsel Ottosen Treuarthen Britz Dooley & Kelly, Ltd., Wheaton, Ill., 1996—; exec. Conflict Resolution Ltd.; chair Ill. Jud. Conf. Ill. Supreme Ct., Springfield, 1987-89. Contbr. articles to profl. jours. Bd. dirs., treas. DuPage Coun. for Child Devel.; bd. dirs. Ctrl. DuPage Pastoral Counseling Ctr.; chair Wheaton Com. for Jud. Reform, 1962; trustee Midwestern U., 1993—, vice chmn., bd. trustees 1997-99. Cpl. USMC, 1946-48. Mem. DuPage County Bar Assn. (pres. 1972-73), DuPage County Legal Assistance Fedn. (pres. 1973-74), DuPage County Lawyer Referral Svc. (pres. 1972),. Congregationalist.

**PECKERMAN, BRUCE MARTIN,** lawyer; b. Milw., Sept. 28, 1949; s. Joseph and Doris (Kassel) P.; m. Jeanette Chrustowski. BA, U. Wis., 1971; JD, Washington U., St. Louis, 1973. Bar: Wis. 1974, U.S. Dist. Ct. (we. dist.) Wis. 1974, U.S. Ct. Appeals (7th cir.) 1977. Sole practice Milw., 1985—. Recipient young leadership award Milw. Jewish Fedn. Mem. ABA, Wis. Bar Assn. (past chmn. family law sect.), Milw. Bar Assn. (bench/bar com. 1987-88), Am. Acad. Matrimonial Lawyers (past pres.). Family and matrimonial. Office: 920 E Mason St Milwaukee WI 53202-4015

**PECORARO, STEVEN JOHN,** lawyer; b. N.Y.C., Apr. 27, 1961; m. Frances P. Ferraro, Feb. 18, 1996. BA in Polit. Sci., CUNY, Flushing, 1982; JD, St. John's U., Jamaica, N.Y., 1985. Bar: N.Y. 1986, U.S. Dist. Ct. (so. and ea. dists.) N.Y. 1993. Asst. dist. atty. Dist. Atty.'s Office, Queens County, N.Y., 1985-87; sr. staff atty. Law Offices of Stewart H. Friedman, Lake Success, N.Y., 1987-91; sr. trial atty. Alio & Caiati, N.Y.C., 1991-95; ptnr. Pecoraro & Schiesel, N.Y.C., 1995—. Mem. N.Y. State Bar Assn. Avocations: hunting, fishing, outdoor activities. Personal injury. Office: Pecoraro & Schiesel Ste 1800 One Whitehall St New York NY 10004

**PEDATA, MARTIN ANTHONY,** lawyer; b. Moonachu, N.J., Feb. 14, 1959; m. Deborah Lauren Pedata, May 26, 1990; children: Joshua, Matthew, Alexis. BA, William Paterson Coll., 1981; MA, U. South Fla., 1984; JD, Mercer U., 1987. Bar: Fla., U.S. Supreme Ct., U.S. Ct. Appeals (11th cir.), U.S. Ct. Appeals (3d cir.), U.S. Ct. Appeals (fed. cir.), U.S. Dist. Ct. (fed. dist.), U.S. Dist. Ct. (mid. dist.) Fla. Atty. John T. Allen, P.A., St. Petersburg, Fla., 1987-88; pvt. practice Palm Harbor, Fla., 1989-97; atty. Pedata and Taylor P.A., St. Petersburg, 1997—. Aviation, Trademark and copyright, General civil litigation. Office: Pedata and Taylor PA 3550 Morris St N Saint Petersburg FL 33713-1629

**PEDDIE, COLLYN ANN,** lawyer; b. Houston, Jan. 14, 1957; d. George Henry and Wanda June P. BA, Rice U., 1979; JD, George Washington U., 1982. Bar: Washington D.C. 1982, Tex. 1983, U.S. Dist. Ct. (so. dist.) Tex. 1984, U.S. Ct. Appeals (5th, 11th, and D.C. cirs.). Law clerk Judge John R. Brown, Houston, 1982-83; atty. Vinson & Elkins, LLP, Houston, 1983-88; shareholder, v.p. Jenkens & Gilchrist, PC, Houston, 1988-91; ptnr. Moriarty & Peddie, LLP, Houston, 1991-93; prin. Collyn A. Peddie, PC, Houston, 1993-99; of counsel Weil Gotshal & Manges, LLP, Houston, 1999—; adj. prof. U. Houston Law Ctr., 1996-97. Contbr. articles to profl. jours. Mem. trustees coun. Dem. Nat. Com., 1988-93; bd. dirs. Interfaith Ministries for Greater Houston, 1986-96, exec. com. 1987-96, counsel 1990-96; bd. dirs. Planned Parenthood Houston and Southeast Tex., 1997—. Wallace fellow Ctr. Study Presidency, 1979-80. Fellow Houston Bar Found; mem. Phi Beta Kappa. Appellate, Federal civil litigation, State civil litigation. Office: Weil Gotshal & Manges LLP 700 Louisiana St Ste 1600 Houston TX 77002-2722

**PEDERSON, JANET CLAIRE,** lawyer; b. Buffalo Center, Iowa, Oct. 9, 1958. BA with distinction, U. Iowa, 1980; JD with honors, Drake U., 1984. Bar: Iowa 1984, U.S. Dist. Ct. (no. dist.) Iowa 1986, Tex. 1990, U.S. Dist. Ct. (no. dist.) Tex. 1990, U.S. Dist. Ct. (ea. dist.) Tex. 1992. Ptnr. Lemke & Pederson, McKinney, Tex., 1990—. Mem. Collin County Bar Assn. (pres. 1999—), Plano Bar Assn., Grayson County Bar Assn. Bankruptcy. Office: Lemke & Pederson 201 S Mcdonald St Ste E Mc Kinney TX 75069-5624

**PEDRAZA, MIGUEL A., JR.,** lawyer; b. Springfield, Mass., Sept. 26, 1960; s. Miguel Angel and Dolores (Eldy) P.; m. Kerry Lynn Lee, Aug. 6, 1983; children: Bridget Ana, Brennan John. BA, U. Notre Dame, 1982; JD, U. Cin., 1985. Bar: Ohio 1985, U.S. Dist. Ct. (so. dist.) Ohio 1986. Assoc. Katz, White & Pedraza, Cin., 1986-89, Schwer, Taggart, Wehler, Emerich & Winks, Springfield, Ohio, 1989-92; ptnr. Strozdas & Pedraza, Springfield, 1992-98, Geyer, Strozdas & Pedraza, Springfield, 1998—. Pres., bd. dirs. Alzheimers Assn. of Clark, Champaign and Logan Counties, Springfield, 1992-94; bd. dirs. Clark County chpt. Am. Cancer Soc., 1991-94. Roman Catholic. Avocations: travel, golf. Banking, Labor, Real property. Office: Geyer Strozdas Pedraza LLP 22 S Limestone St Ste 330 Springfield OH 45502-1232

**PEDUTO, MARK B.,** lawyer; b. Pitts., Apr. 11, 1966; s. Frank G. and Carmella Peduto; divorced; 1 child, Rose Marie. BS with honors, St. Vincent Coll., Latrobe, Pa., 1988; JD, Duquesne U., 1991. Bar: Pa. 1991, U.S. Dist. Ct. (we. dist.) Pa. 1991. Probate and file clk. Allegheny County Register of Wills, Pitts., 1989; clk. pro tem. Duquesne U., Pitts., 1990-91; assoc. atty. Am. Bankruptcy Ctr., Pitts., 1996-97; sole practitioner Pitts., 1991—. Mem. St. Vincent Coll. Alumni Coun., Latrobe, 1995—. Mem. ABA, Pa. Bar Assn., Allegheny County Bar Assn., Pa. Assn. Notaries, Nat. Notaries Assn., Am. Bankruptcy Inst., St. Thomas More Soc., Fort Pitt Assembly # 0912, K.C. (fin. sec. Allegheny Coun. 285, Faithful Navigator, dist. warden). Fax: 412-761-2525. E-mail: MBPJD@aol.com. Bankruptcy, Probate, Estate planning. Office: 3313 Brighton Rd Pittsburgh PA 15212-2333

**PEET, MARIA LARA,** lawyer; b. Santa Clara, Cuba, Jan. 25, 1962; came to U.S., 1970; d. Marcos Antonio and Juana Caridad Lara; m. Edgar Anton Peet, Jan. 29, 1983; children: Anjelica Helena, Marcos Anton, Miranda Laraine. BA in Polit. Sci. magna cum laude, U. South Fla., 1983; JD cum laude, Stetson U., 1986. Bar: Fla. 1986, U.S. Dist. Ct. (mid. dist.) Fla. 1989, U.S. Ct. Appeals (11th cir.) 1992. Law clk. 2d Dist. Ct. Appeal, Tampa, Fla., 1986-90; assoc. Shropp, Buell & Elligett, P.A., Tampa, 1990-94; pvt. practice, Ft. Myers, Fla., 1996—; prof. Edison C.C., Ft. Myers, 1997. Asst. author: (update) Florida Civil Practice, 1992. Com. mem. Child Watch Lee County, Fla., 1998—, Lee County Dem. Com., 1997—; mem. com. on professionalism Lee County, 1998—; vol. atty. Guardian Ad Litem, Lee County, 1999. Scholar Stetson U. Coll. Law, 1985-86. Mem. Fla. Bar, Fla. Assn. Women Lawyers (chpt. rep. 1997—, cert. 1998), Lee County Bar Assn., Lee County Assn. Women Lawyers (pres. 1997). Appellate, General civil litigation, Criminal. Home: 1342 Bougainvillea St Fort Myers FL 33901-6700 Office: PO Box 2980 Fort Myers FL 33902-2980

**PEET, RICHARD CLAYTON,** lawyer, consultant; b. N.Y.C., Aug. 24, 1928; s. Charles Francis and Florence L. (Isaacs) P.; m. Barbara Jean McClure, Mar. 17, 1956 (div. July, 1988); children: Victoria Clementine, Alexandra Constance, Elizabeth Erica, Clarissa Barbara. JD, Tulane U., 1953. Bar: La. 1955, D.C. 1955. Law clk. Melvin M. Belli, San Francisco, 1954; with The Calif. Co., Standard Oil of Calif., 1955; atty. appellate sect. Lands div. Dept. Justice, Washington, 1956; asst. to dep. gen. counsel Dept. Commerce, 1957; legis. asst. Republican policy com. U.S. Senate, 1958; legis. asst. U.S. Senate minority leader William F. Knowland, 1958; asso. counsel House Judiciary Com., 1959-62; asso. minority counsel House Pub. Works Com., 1969-74; pres. Citizens for Hwy. Safety, 1978-84; practiced in Washington, 1962-68; prin. Richard Clayton Peet & Assos., 1972—; ptnr. Anderson, Pendleton, McMahon, Peet & Donovan, 1977-80, Anderson, Peet & Co., 1980-84; pres., mng. dir. Lincoln Rsch. Ctr., 1965-72; v.p. Oil East Corp., 1978-83. Author: Goals for a Constructive Opposition, 1966; contbg. editor: Congressional Digest, 1960-61, Jour. Def. and Diplomacy, 1983-86, Senate Rep. Week, 1991; (weekly radio show) Across the Aisle, 1992; composer: song Stand Up For America, 1971 (George Washington medal Freedom's Found. 1971), A Monologue With God, 1996, Remembrance House. Chmn. bd. Workshop Library on World Humor. With U.S. Army, 1946-47, with USAFR, 1950-55. Nominated for Rockefeller Public Svcs. Awd. Mem. Phi Delta Phi, Pi Kappa Alpha. Conceived Highway Safety Act of 1973 with Cong. Wm. Harsha, OH, establishing road safety improvement programs, created (with congress) Natl. Bicentennial Highway Safety Year to promote, organized and chaired (with Pres. Ford) White House Conf. on Highway Safety, 1976. Appellate, Constitutional, Legislative. Home: PO Box 971 Mc Lean VA 22101-0971

**PEGALIS, ANDREW MARK,** business executive, lawyer; b. Jamaica, N.Y., June 19, 1968; s. Steven Elliot Pegalis and Laura Ann Thaler. BA in Econs., Emory U., 1990; JD, Am. U., 1995. Bar: Md. 1996. Risk mgmt. specialist Prudential Ins. of Am., Newark, N.J., 1990-92; legal clk. USEPA-Office of Adminstrv. Law Judges, Washington, 1992-93; contract atty. U.S. Trade Rep., Geneva, 1996, MCI Metro, Vienna, Va., 1997; pres. Next Millennium Cons., Bethesda, 1997—. Author: Y2K Risk Management, 1999. Vol. Nat. Capital chpt. ARC, Washington, 1996-98. Mem. ABA, Soc. for Info. Mgmt. Year 2000 Working Group, Md. State Bar Assn. Office: Next Millennium Cons 5541 Nicholson Ln # 304 Rockville MD 20852-3113

**PEGRAM, JOHN BRAXTON,** lawyer; b. Yeadon, Pa., June 29, 1938; s. William Bement and Marjorie (Rainey) P.; m. Patricia Jane Narbeth; Aug. 21, 1965; children: Catherine, Stephen. AB in Physics, Columbia U., 1960; LLB, NYU, 1965. Bar: N.Y. 1965, U.S. Dist. Ct. Del. 1994, U.S. Dist. Ct. (ea. and so. dists.) N.Y. 1994, U.S. Supreme Ct. 1971. Engr. Fairchild Camera and Instrument Corp., Clifton, N.J., 1960-66; assoc. Hoxie Faithfull and Hapgood, LLP, N.Y.C., 1966-71; ptnr. Davis Hoxie Faithfull and Hapgood, N.Y.C., 1972-95; prin. Fish & Richardson P.C., 1995—; mem. intellectual property litig. adv. com. U.S. Dist. Ct. for the Dist. Del., 1994-96; mem. neutral evaluation and mediation panels U.S. Dist. Ct. for the Eastern Dist. of N.Y., 1994-97; mem. mediation panel U.S. Dist. Ct. for the So. Dist. N.Y., 1994-97. Editor The Trademark Reporter jour., 1984-86, mem. editorial adv. bd., 1986—; contbr. articles to profl. jours. Fellow Am. Bar Found. (life); mem. IEEE, ABA (chmn. antitrust law sect. com. on patents, trademarks and know how 1986-89, mem. legal econs. sect., bus. law sect., chmn. intellectual property law divsn. IV 1995-96), Am. Phys. Soc. (life), Fed. Bar Coun., Fed. Cir. Bar Assn., N.Y. State Bar Assn., Assn. of Bar of City ofN.Y., Am. Intellectual Property Law Assn. (chmn. fed. practice and procedure com. 1974-76, chmn. unauthorized practice com. 1977-79, chmn. trade secrets com. 1992-94, mem. Japan practice com. 1992—, mem. editl. bd. Quar. Jour., 1994-95, chmn. fed. litig. com. 1995-97, chmn. internat. com. 1998—), N.Y. Intellectual Property Law Assn. (sec. 1981-84, dir. 1984-86, pres. 1989-90), U .S. Bar/Japan Patent Office Liaison Coun. (del. 1990—), Inst. Trade Mark Agts. (overseas mem.), Am. Judicature Soc., Internat. Intellectual Property Soc., Internat. Patent and Trademark Assn. (U.S. group AIPPI), Internat. Trademark Assn. (bd. dirs. 1985-87, fin. com. 1987-95, pub. com. 1997-98). Patent, Trademark and copyright, Intellectual property. Office: Fish & Richardson PC 45 Rockefeller Plz Fl 28 New York NY 10111-2889

**PEIKES, LAWRENCE DAVID,** lawyer; b. N.Y.C., Jan. 5, 1963; s. Meyer Joshua and Sheila Carol P.; m. Jeanne Marie Feore, Sept. 24, 1989; children: Joelle Simone, Ethan Michael. BS, U. Md., 1984; JD, George Washington U., 1987. Bar: U.S. Dist. Ct. (no. dist.) Calif. 1987, U.S. Ct. Appeals (9th cir.) 1987, U.S. Dist. Ct. (ea. dist.) Calif. 1988, Conn. 1990, U.S. Dist. Ct. (ctrl. dist.) Conn. 1991, U.S. Dist. Ct. (so. dist.) N.Y. 1992, U.S. Ct. Appeals (9th cir.) 1993, U.S. Dist. Ct. (ea. dist.) N.Y. 1995, N.Y. 1996. Atty. Littler Mendelson, San Francisco, 1987-90, Paul, Hastings, Janofsky & Walker, Stamford, Conn., 1990-95, Roberts & Finger, LLP, N.Y.C., 1995-97, Epstein, Becker & Green, P.C., N.Y.C., 1997—. Trustee scholar George Washington U., 1986-87. Mem. ABA, State Bar Calif. Labor. Office: Epstein Becker & Green PC 250 Park Ave Ste 1200 New York NY 10177-1211

**PEIRCE, FREDERICK FAIRBANKS,** lawyer; b. Torrington, Conn., Jan. 28, 1953; s. Everett L. and Frederica (Fairbanks) P.; m. Sandra Marie MacMillan, Dec. 16, 1989. BS with high honors, Colo. State U., 1975; JD, U. Colo., 1979. Bar: Colo. 1979, U.S. Dist. Ct. Colo. 1979. Assoc. Bratton & Zimmerman, Gunnison, Colo., 1979-80; staff atty. Holland & Hart, Aspen, Colo., 1980-82; assoc. Austin, McGrath & Jordan, Aspen, 1982-84, Austin & Jordan, Aspen, 1984-87; ptnr. Austin, Jordan, Young & Peirce, Aspen, 1987-89, Austin & Peirce, Aspen, 1989-92, Austin, Peirce & Smith, P.C., Aspen, 1992—. Bd. dirs. Aspen Nordic Coun. Inc., 1985-88, Aspen Velo Club Inc., 1986-88, Aspen Cycling Club, Inc., 1988-93; bd. dirs. Aspen Ctr. for Environ. Studies, 1991-97, v.p., 1992-94, pres., 1994-97; bd. dirs. Pitkin County Pks. Assn., Inc., 1990-98, v.p., 1991-92, pres., 1992-95; mem. Aspen Valley Land Trust, 1990-98, v.p., 1991-92, pres., 1992-95; mem. bd. edn. Aspen Sch. Dist., 1997—. NSF grantee, 1975. Mem. Colo. Bar Assn. (bd. govs. 1989-93, exec. coun. 1993-95, v.p. 1995-96, ethics com., 1995-97), Pitkin County Bar Assn. (v.p. 1985-86, pres. 1986-88, bd. govs. rep. 1989-93), Phi Kappa Phi. Avocations: skiing, hiking, fly fishing, cycling, flying. Real property, General corporate, Landlord-tenant. Office: Austin Peirce & Smith PC Ste 205 600 E Hopkins Ave Aspen CO 81611-2933

**PEKELIS, ROSSELLE,** judge. Former judge Wash. Superior Ct. King County; now chief judge divsn. I Wash. Ct. Appeals, Seattle; founding ptnr. Jud. Dispute Resolution, Seattle. Office: Jud Dispute Resolution 1411 4th Ave Ste 200 Seattle WA 98101-2244

**PELAVIN, MICHAEL ALLEN,** lawyer; b. Flint, Mich., Sept. 5, 1936; s. B. Morris and Betty (Weiss) P.; m. Natalie Katz, June 18, 1960; children: Mark, Gordon. Student, U. Mich., 1954-55, Wayne State U., 1955-57; JD, Detroit Coll. Law, 1960. Bar: Mich. 1960, U.S. Tax Ct. 1966, U.S. Ct. Appeals (6th cir.) 1969, N.Y. 1989. Assoc. Pelavin & Powers, P.C. (now Pelavin, Powers & Behm P.C.), Flint, 1960-63, ptnr., 1963-71, pres., 1980—; trustee Nat. Jewish Cmty. Rels. Adv. Coun., 1986-89, now Jewish Coun. Pub. Affairs. Chmn. young leadership cabinet United Jewish Appeal, 1973; pres. Flint Jewish edn., 1974-77; chmn. Bishop Internat. Airport Authority, 1990—. Recipient Herbert Lehman Young Leadership award United Jewish Appeal, Sydney B. Melet Humanitarian award Urban Coalition Greater Flint, Donald Riegle Cmty. Svc. award & Pres. award Flint Jewish Fedn., Disting. Svc. award Genesee County Bar Assn. Mem. ABA, N.Y. State Bar Assn. Democrat. General corporate, Probate, Personal income taxation. Home: 7776 Talavera Pl Delray Beach FL 33446-4319 Office: Pelavin Powers & Behm PC 801 S Saginaw St Ste 100 Flint MI 48502-1580

**PELL, DANIEL MAX,** lawyer; b. N.Y.C., July 19, 1949; s. Joseph C. and Hazel (Kowitz) P.; m. Joan Kohler, 1982 (dec. 1985); 1 child, Max Andrew. BA in Psychology, Lafayette Coll., 1971; JD, DePaul U., 1975. Bar: Pa., Md., Ill. U.S. Dist. Ct. (mid. and ea. dists.) Pa., U.S. Ct. Appeals (3d cir.), U.S. Supreme Ct. Pvt. practice, York, Pa.; bd. dirs., mem. exec. com. Ctrl. Pa. Legal Svcs., Lancaster, 1988-94; mem. fed. pub. defender's panel U.S. Dist. Ct. for Mid. Dist. Pa., 1985—; gen. counsel Wireless Telecom., Inc., York, 1994—. Active Internat. Campaign for Tibet, 1994-95. Mem. Pa. Bar Assn., York County Bar Assn. (pro bono rep. Chinese detainees of Golden Venture 1994—). Avocation: photography. Criminal, Personal injury, General corporate. Office: 425 W Market St York PA 17404-3803

**PELL, WILBUR FRANK, JR.,** federal judge; b. Shelbyville, Ind., Dec. 6, 1915; s. Wilbur Frank and Nelle (Dickerson) P.; m. Mary Lane Chase, Sept. 14, 1940 (dec. 1996); children: Wilbur Frank III, Charles Chase. A.B., Ind. U., 1937, LL.D. (hon.), 1981; LL.B. cum laude, Harvard U., 1940; LL.D., Yonsei U., Seoul, Korea, 1972, John Marshall Sch. Law, 1973. Bar: Ind. 1940. Pvt. practice Shelbyville, 1940-42, 45-70; spl. agt. FBI, 1942-45; sr. ptnr. Pell & Good, 1949-56, Pell & Matchett, 1956-70; judge U.S. Ct. Appeals (7th cir.), 1970—, now sr. judge; mem. 3 judge spl. divsn. U.S. Ct. Appeals (D.C. cir.), appointing ind. counsel, 1987-92; dep. atty. gen., Ind., 1953-55; dir., chmn. Shelby Nat. Bank, 1947-70. Bd. dirs. Shelbyville Community Chest, 1947-49, Shelby County Fair Assn., 1951-53; dir. Shelby County Tb Assn., 1948-70, pres., 1965-66; dist. chmn. Boy Scouts Am., 1956-57; mem. pres.'s council Nat. Coll. Edn., 1972-87; dir. Westminster Found., Ind. U.; hon. dir. Korean Legal Center. Fellow Am. Coll. Probate Counsel, Am. Bar Found.; mem. ABA (judge Edward R. Finch Law Day USA Speech award 1973), Ind. Bar Assn. (pres. 1962-63, chmn. ho. of dels. 1968-69), Fed. Bar Assn., Ill. Bar Assn., Shelby County Bar Assn. (pres. 1957-58), 7th Fed. Cir. Bar Assn., Am. Judicature Soc., Am. Coun. Assn., Shelby County C. of C., Nat. Conf. Bar Pres.'s, Riley Meml. Assn., Ind. Soc. Chgo. (pres. 1978-79), Harvard Law Soc. Ill. (pres. 1980-81), Rotary (dist. gov. 1952-53, internat. dir 1959-61), Union League, Legal Club (pres. Chgo. 1976-77), Law Club (pres. Chgo. 1984-85), Kappa Sigma, Alpha Phi Omega, Theta Alpha Phi, Tau Kappa Alpha, Phi Alpha Delta (hon.). Republican. Presbyterian (elder, deacon). Office: US Ct Appeals 7th Cir 219 S Dearborn St Ste 2760 Chicago IL 60604-1803

**PELLECCHIA, JOHN MICHAEL,** lawyer; b. Orange, N.J., Dec. 6, 1958. BA, Lafayette Coll., 1980; JD cum laude, Tulane U., 1983. Bar: N.J. 1983, U.S. Dist. Ct. N.J. 1983, U.S. Supreme Ct. 1994. Assoc. Pitney, Hardin, Kipp & Szuch, Morristown, N.J., 1983-86; asst. counsel to gov. Thomas H. Kean State of N.J., Trenton, 1986-88; ptnr. Riker, Danzig, Scherer, Hyland & Perretti, LLP, Morristown and Trenton, 1988—; mem. mgmt. com. Riker, Danzig, Scherer, Hyland & Perretti LLP, Morristown and Trenton, 1995—; jud. extern to fed. dist. ct. judge, U.S. Dist. Ct., New Orleans, 1982-83; sr. fellow Tulane Law Sch., 1982-83, mem. N.J. Supreme Ct. Com. on Tax Ct., 1993-96; mem. bus. and fin. svcs. task force of Gov. Whitman's Econ. Master Plan Commn., 1994. Trustee, v.p. Leukemia Soc. Am. North Jersey chpt., 1991—; trustee N.J. Shakespeare Festival, 1996—. Vol. of Yr., Leukemia Soc. Am. North Jersey chpt., 1994. General civil litigation, Legislative, Administrative and regulatory. Office: Riker Danzig Scherer Hyland & Perretti LLP 50 W State St Ste 1010 Trenton NJ 08608-1220

**PELLECCHIO, RALPH L.,** lawyer. BA, Princeton U., 1971; JD, Columbia U., 1976. Assoc. Cravath, Swaine & Moore, 1976-80; mng. dir., gen. counsel instnl. securities bus. Morgan Stanley Dean Witter, N.Y.C., 1980—. Mem. ABA (bus. law sect., com. on fed. regulation securities, subcom. market regulations), Nat. Assn. Securities Dealers (corp. fin. com.), Securities Industry Assn. (chair, capital markets com.). Securities, General corporate, Finance. Office: Morgan Stanley Dean Witter 1585 Broadway New York NY 10036-8200

**PELLEGRIN, GILLES GEORGE,** lawyer; b. Paris, Mar. 8, 1952; s. Jacques Robert Pellegrin and Nicole Deret; m. Litzie E. Gozlan, Dec. 22, 1981; children: Vanessa, Raphael. Cert., Inst. for Internat. and Fgn., Trade Law/Georgetown U., 1977; Dess de Droit des Rels. Comml. Indsl., U. Paris, 1977; M Comparative Jurisprudence, NYU, 1978. Assoc. Mudge, Rose, Guthrie & Alexander, N.Y.C., 1977, Debost, Borel, Carpentier & Falques, Paris, 1978; European counsel Tex. Instruments, Villeneuve-Louvet, France, 1980-84; legal advisor of the chmn. and CEO Honda France, Marne-La-Vallee, France, 1984-87; gen. counsel Sema Group, Montrouge, France/London, 1987-90; corp. gen. counsel Bull S.A., Paris, 1990—. Avocations: tennis, fencing, swimming, skiing, theater. Computer, Private international. Office: Bull HN Info Systems Inc 300 Concord Rd Billerica MA 01821-4186

**PELLETT, JON MICHAEL,** lawyer; b. Orlando, Fla., Nov. 16, 1961; s. Milton Francis and Jean Ellen (Avery) P.; m. Karen Walker, July 21, 1984 (div. Sept. 1990). BS in Biology, U. Ctrl. Fla., Orlando, 1984, BS in Stats., 1985; JD, Fla. State U., 1993. Bar: Fla. 1995, U.S. Dist. Ct. (mid. dist.) Fla. 1996. Legal trainee Dept. Bus. and Profl. Regulation, Tallahassee, 1993-95; staff atty. Agy. for Health Care Adminstrn., Tallahassee, 1995-96; assoc. Freeman, Hunter & Malloy, Tampa, Fla., 1996—; vol. guardian ad litem Guardian ad Litem Program, Tallahassee, 1991-95. Bd. dirs. Friends of the Arboretum, Orlando, 1998—. Mem. ABA, ATLA, Hillsborough County Bar Assn. Avocations: racquetball, beach volleyball. Administrative and regulatory, Health, Appellate. Office: Freeman Hunter and Malloy 201 E Kennedy Blvd Ste 1950 Tampa FL 33602-5829

**PELLETTIERI, RUTH RABSTEIN,** lawyer; b. N.Y.C., Apr. 18, 1913; d. Samuel Aaron and Molly (Krock) Rabstein; m. Manuel Cantor, June 22, 1942 (div.); m. George Pellettieri, May 6, 1949. LLB, Rutgers U., 1934. Bar: N.J., 1935. Ptnr. Pellettieri, Rabstein, & Altman, Princeton, N.J., 1935—. Bd. govs. Am. Jewish Com., N.J., 1982; bd. overseers U. Pa. Grad. Sch. Edn., 1990; bd. dirs. Greenwood House Home for Aged, George Pellettieri Home for Aged, Women's Rsch. Found., Legal Aid Soc. Mercer County. Mem. ABA, N.J. Bar Assn., Mercer County Bar Assn., Jewish Fedn. Ctrl. Jersey. Home: 50 Governors Ln Princeton NJ 08540-3670 Office: Pellettieri Rabstein Altman Ste 111 Nassau Park Blvd Princeton NJ 08540

**PELLINO, CHARLES EDWARD, JR.,** lawyer; b. Chgo., May 2, 1943; s. Charles Edward Sr. and Ella Pellino; m. Melinda Poorman, Aug. 20, 1966; children: Charles, Tracy, William. BA, Drake U., 1965; JD, U. Wis., 1968. Bar: Wis. 1968, U.S. Dist. Ct. (we. dist.) Wis. 1972, U.S. Tax Ct. 1984, U.S. Dist. Ct. (ea. dist.) Wis. 1985, U.S. Ct. Appeals (7th cir.) 1985, U.S. Supreme Ct. 1985, U.S. Dist. Ct. Hawaii, 1996, U.S. Dist. Ct. Del. 1997. Assoc. McAndrews, Fritschler & Huggett, Madison, Wis., 1968-70; ptnr. Fritschler, Ross, Pellino & Protzman, Madison, 1970-73, Fritschler, Pellino & Assocs., Madison, 1973-76, Fritschler, Pellino, Schrank & Rosen, Madison, 1976-88, Fritschler, Pellino, Rosen and Mowris, Madison, 1988—. Contbr. articles to profl. jours. Mem. ABA, Wis. Bar Assn., Nat. Assn. Criminal Def. Lawyers, Wis. Acad. Trial Lawyers, Wis. Assn. Criminal Def. Lawyers (sec.-elect 1987—). Avocations: flying, golf. General corporate, Criminal, Taxation, general. Office: Pellino Rosen Mowris & Kirkhuff PC 131 W Wilson St Ste 1201 Madison WI 53703-3245

**PELOQUIN, LOUIS OMER,** lawyer; b. Tracy, Quebec, Can., June 15, 1957; came to U.S., 1986; s. Gilles and Andree (Gelinas) P.; m. Carole Plante, Aug. 21, 1987; children: Louis-Alexandre, Valerie. BBA, Laval U., Quebec City, Can., 1980; LLB, U. Montreal, Can., 1984; LLM, NYU, 1987. Bar: Que. 1985, N.Y. 1988. Assoc. Martineau Walker, Montreal, Que., Can., 1985-86, Paul, Weiss, Rifkind, Wharton & Garrison, N.Y.C., 1987-89, Shearman & Sterling, N.Y.C., 1989-91, McCarthy Tetrault, Montreal, 1991-93; v.p., gen. counsel, sec. Golden Star Resources Ltd., Denver, 1993—. Contbr. articles to profl. jours. Recipient Richard de Boo prize in Taxation, 1984. Mem. ABA, N.Y. Bar Assn., Quebec Bar Assn., Assn. Am. Corp. Counsel, Rocky Mountain Mineral Law Found. Avocations: golf, skiing, reading, painting. General corporate, Private international, Mergers and acquisitions. Home: 5300 E Nichols Dr Littleton CO 80122-3892 Office: Golden Star Resources Ltd 1660 Lincoln St Ste 3000 Denver CO 80264-3001

**PELSTER, WILLIAM CHARLES,** lawyer; b. St. Louis, May 11, 1942; s. William R. and Marie C. (Graefe) P.; m. Terry C. Cuthbertson, Aug. 9, 1969. BA, Oberlin Coll., 1964; JD, U. Mich., 1967. Bar: Mo. 1967, N.Y. 1968, U.S. Dist. Ct. (so. dist.) N.Y. 1968, U.S. Ct. Appeals (2d cir.) 1968, U.S. Supreme Ct. 1972. Law clk. to judge Lenord P. Moore U.S. Ct. Appeals (2d cir.), N.Y.C., 1967-68; assoc. Donovan, Leisure, Newton & Irvine, N.Y.C., 1968-75; ptnr. Skadden, Arps, Slate, Meagher & Flom, LLP, N.Y.C., 1976—. Trustee Cancer Care Inc., N.Y.C., 1975—. Mem. ABA, Assn. of Bar of City of N.Y. Antitrust. Office: Skadden Arps Slate Meagher & Flom LLP 919 3rd Ave New York NY 10022-3902

**PELTIN, SHERWIN CARL,** lawyer; b. Milw., Aug. 2, 1929; s. Alvin Leonard and Rebecca (Weisfeldt) P.; m. Julie Marion Stern, Mar. 15, 1953; children: Laurie Peltin Merar, Steven, William. BBA, U. Wis., 1950, LLB, 1952; LLM in Taxation, NYU, 1955; SJD, George Washington U., 1962. Bar: Wis. 1952, U.S. Tax Ct. 1958, U.S. Fed. Claims Ct. 1960; CPA, Wis. Atty. U.S. Tax Ct., Washington, 1955-58; lawyer Offices of Louis L. Meldman, Milw., 1958-62; ptnr. Laikin, Swietlik & Peltin, Milw., 1962-68, Peregrine, Marcuvitz & Peltin, Milw., 1968-87, Weiss, Berzowski, Brady & Donahue, Milw., 1987—. Elected trustee Village Bd. Trustees, Bayside, 1967-73. Capt. U.S. Army, 1952-54, Korea. Mem. ABA, State Bar Wis., Milw. Bar Assn., Estate Counselors' Forum, Profl. Inst. Tax Study. Taxation, general, Estate planning, Probate. Office: Weiss Berzowski Brady & Donahue 700 N Water St Milwaukee WI 53202-4206

**PELTON, ROBERT O.,** lawyer; b. Abilene, Tex., Jan. 25, 1946; s. Oland W. and Eva (Cox) P.; m. Judith Pelton; 1 child, Robert C. BBA, McMurry Coll., 1970; JD, So. Tex. Coll. of Law, 1975. Bar: Tex. 1975, U.S. Dist. Ct. So. Dist. 1975. Lawyer pvt. practice, Houston, 1975—; pres. Cmty. Svc. Option Program, Houston, 1985. Former editor: Docket Call; author: Voice For the Defense; contbr. articles to profl. jours. With USNG, 1966-72. Mem. Harris Co. Criminal Lawyer Assn. (pres.), Tex. Criminal Defense Lawyers Assn. (assoc. dir.). Baptist. Avocation: motorcycle. Office: 1908 N Memorial Way Houston TX 77007-8319

**PELTON, RUSSELL MEREDITH, JR.,** lawyer; b. Chgo., May 14, 1938; s. Russell Meredith and Mildred Helen (Baumrucker) P.; m. Patty Jane Rader, Aug. 12, 1961; children: James, Thomas, Michael, Margaret. BA, DePauw U., 1960; JD, U. Chgo., 1963. Bar: Ill. 1963, U.S. Supreme Ct. 1979. Assoc., Peterson, Ross, Schloerb & Seidel, Chgo., 1966-72, ptnr., 1972-90; ptnr. Oppenheimer, Wolff & Donnelly, 1990—, Chgo. mng. ptnr., 1992-95, 98—; co-founder, gen. counsel Chgo. Opportunities Industrialization Ctr., 1969-83; gen. counsel Delta Dental Plan Ill., 1979-96; bd. dirs. First United Life Ins. Co., 1979-82; gen. counsel Am. Assn. Neurol. Surgeons, 1981—. Pres. Wilmette Jaycees, 1970; chmn. Wilmette Sch. Bd. Caucus, 1970-71; Wilmette Dist. 39 Bd. Edn., 1972-80. Bd. dirs. Wilmette United Way, 1980-86, campaign chmn., 1983-85, pres., 1985-86; Wilmette Zoning Bd. Appeals, 1989—, chmn., 1990—. Served to capt. USAF, 1963-66. Mem. Chgo. Bar Assn., Ill. Bar Assn., ABA, Soc. Trial Lawyers. Federal civil litigation, State civil litigation, Labor. Office: Oppenheimer Wolff & Donnelly Two Prudential Plz 45th Fl 180 N Stetson Ave Chicago IL 60601-6710

**PELUSO, MATTHEW A.,** lawyer; b. Norfolk, Va., June 9, 1964; s. Angelo R. and Eileen K. Peluso; m. Christine Cascio, May 25, 1996; 1 child, Olivia Page. BA in Philosophy, George Washington U., 1988; JD, U. Miami, 1991. Bar: N.J., Pa., Fla., U.S. Dist. Ct. N.J., U.S. Ct. Appeals (3rd cir.). Profl. baseball player Chgo. White Sox, 1986; asst. prosecutor Mercer County Pros Office, Trenton, N.J., 1991; assoc. Slimm & Goldberg, Westmont, N.J., 1992-94; in-house counsel The Robert Plan, Edison, N.J., 1994-96; assoc. Cuyler Burk, Parsippany, N.J., 1997, Wilbraham, Lawler & Buba, Haddonfield, N.J., 1998—. Avocations: history, langs. Federal civil litigation, State civil litigation, Environmental. Home: 61 Elm St Lambertville NJ 08530-1510

**PEMBERTON, ROBERT HARNSON,** lawyer; b. Waco, Tex., Oct. 30, 1966; s. Stanton Bethay and Jo Ann Pemberton. BBA, Baylor U., 1989; JD, Harvard U., 1992. Bar: Tex. 1992, U.S. Dist. Ct. (so. dist.) Tex., U.S. Ct. Appeals (5th cir.). Assoc. Baker & Botts, Houston, 1993-98; briefing atty. Supreme Ct. Tex., Austin, 1992-93, rules atty., 1998—. Active Austin Big Bros.-Big Sisters, 1998—. Mem. Travis County Bar Assn., Young Men's Bus. League. Office: Supreme Ct Tex 201 W 14th St Austin TX 78701-1614

**PEÑA, AARON, JR.,** lawyer; b. Austin, Tex., June 8, 1959; s. Lionel Aron and Sylvia (Alamia) P.; m. Monica Solis, Mar. 29, 1991; children: Adrienne, Aaron, John, Alyssa, Anthony. BA in Liberal Arts, U. Tex., 1984; JD, Tex. So. U., 1987. Bar: Tex. 1988. Legis. asst. Tex. Legislature, Austin; mem. staff Tex. Dem. Party, Austin, Tex. U.S. Senator Bob Krueger, Austin; tchr. Austin Ind. Sch. Dist.; ptnr. Peña, McDonald, Prestia & Ornelas, Edinburg, Tex., 1988-90, Aaron Peña & Assocs., Edinburg, 1990—. Author, spkr. published rec.: Million Dollar Arguments, 1997. Mem. ABA, ATLA, State Bar Tex., Nat. Employment Lawyers Assn. Roman Catholic. Avocations: travel, golf. Civil rights, State civil litigation, Personal injury. Home: 2709 Lakeshore Dr Edinburg TX 78539-7713 Office: Aaron Peña & Assocs 1110 S Closner Blvd Edinburg TX 78539-5662

**PENA, GUILLERMO ENRIQUE,** lawyer; b. Miami Beach, Fla., Aug. 16, 1963; s. Gustavo A. and Rosa Amelia (LeRiverend) P.; m. Jacqueline Torre, Sept. 11, 1993; children: Austin Jake, Allison Lee. BBA, Austin Peay State U., Clarksville, Tenn., 1988; JD, Fla. State U., 1991. Bar: Fla. 1991, U.S. Dist. Ct. (no. and so. dists.) Fla. 1991, U.S. Ct. Appeals (11th cir.) 1991, U.S. Supreme Ct. 1996; cert. in criminal trial law Criminal Trial Law Found. Assoc. Boehm, Brown, Rigdon & Seacrest, P.A., Tallahassee, 1990-92, Raia & Preira, Miami Beach, Fla., 1992-95, Jeffrey S. Weiner, P.A., Miami, Fla., 1995-96; pvt. practice Miami, 1996—; guest judge U. Miami Sch. Law-Most Ct. Camp, 1996-97. Sgt. U.S. Army, 1984-86, ETO. Young pres. Mt. Sinai Hosp., Miami Beach, Fla. Recipient Recognition award Legal Svcs. Greater Miami, 1996, Pro Bono Svc. award Dade County Bar Assn., Miami, 1995, Young Pres. award Mt. Sinai Hosp., 1999. Mem. ABA (criminal justice sect.), Cuban Am. Bar Assn. (Pro Bono Project 1996), Nat. Assn. Criminal Def. Lawyers, Am. Judicature Soc., Am. Inns of Ct. (barrister), Fla. Assn. Criminal Def. Lawyers, Fla. Bar (cert. as specialist in criminal law), Young Pres. Club. Criminal. Office: 444 Brickell Ave Ste 928 Miami FL 33131-2407

**PENA, RICHARD,** lawyer; b. San Antonio, Feb. 13, 1948; s. Merced and Rebecca (Trejo) P.; m. Carolyn Sarah Malley, May 25, 1979; 1 stepchild, Jason Charles Schubert. BA, U. Tex., 1970, JD, 1976. Bar: Tex. 1976, Colo. 1986. Pvt. practice law Austin, Tex., 1976—; instr. bus. law St. Edwards U., Austin, 1983, Austin C.C., 1981-82; broker Tex. Real Estate Commn., 1980—; sports editor Austin Light, 1982. Bd. dirs. Ctr. for Battered Women, Austin, 1979-82, Austin Assn. Retarded Citizens, 1980-82; chmn. Austin Travis County Mental Health/Mental Retardation Pub. Responsibility Com., 1979-84; chmn. pvt. facilities monitoring com. Austin Assn. Retarded Citizens, 1981; bd. dirs. Boys Club of Austin, 1987-88; chair Homeless Task Force Austin, 1999—. Named to Outstanding Young Men. of Am., 1982. Fellow Tex. Bar Found. (sustaining life; trustee 1994, sec., treas. 1994, vice chair 1995, chair 1996); mem. State Bar Tex. (bd. dirs. Dist. 9 1991—, exec. com. 1992—, chmn. minority representation com. 1991-92, pres. 1998-99, chmn. profl. devel. com. 1991-92, policy manual com. 1993, fed. jud. appts. com. 1984-86, opportunities for minorities in the profession com. 1990-91, mem. advt. rev. com., pres.-elect 1997), Travis County Bar Assn. (trustee lawyer referral svc. 1984-85, bd. dirs. 1986-88, sec. 1988, pres. 1990-91, chmn. jud. screening com. 1987, chmn. 1988-89, ins. com. 1988, 89, chmn. law day banquet com. 1988-89, lawyer referrel svc. com. 1983-84, trustee 1984-86, membership com. 1989), Capitol Area Mex. Am. Lawyers (pres. 1985, Outstanding Hispanic Lawyer Austin 1989), Legal Aid Soc. Ctrl. Tex. (bd. dirs. 1984), Austin Young Lawyers Assn., Tex. Trial Lawyers Assn., Austin C. of C. (Leadership Austin 1985-86). Democrat. Personal injury, Workers' compensation. Home: 107 Top O The Lake Dr Austin TX 78734-5234 Office: 901 S Mo Pac Expy Austin TX 78746-5776

**PENALTA, C. RICHARD,** prosecutor; b. Matanzas, Cuba, May 27, 1959; m. Carol Ann Sogan, Nov. 14, 1992; children: Lance Alexander, Gabrielle Alexa. Student, Brunel U. West London, 1991, U. Madrid, 1991; JD, Washburn Sch. Law, 1991. Bar: U.S. Dist. Ct. (no., mid. and so. dist.) Fla., U.S. Ct. Appeals (11th cir.), U.S. Ct. Internat. Trade, U.S. Ct. Appeals (armed forces cir.); lic. real estate agt., Fla. Adminstrn. specialist IBM, Boca Raton, Fla., 1985, Miami, Fla., 1985-86, Gainesville, Fla., 1986-88; assoc. comml. litigation divsn. Kinsey Vincent Pyle, P.A., Daytona Beach, Fla., 1992; asst. state atty. Office of State Atty. 7th Jud. Cir. Fla., Daytona Beach, 1992-96, Office of State Atty. 15th Jud. Cir. Fla., West Palm Beach, 1997—; assoc. Eubank, Hassel & Assocs., P.A., Daytona Beach, 1996-97; instr. Penalta & Assocs., P.A., Fla., 1994—; dir., owner Knights of Neptune, Dive & Travel, 1988—; adj. faculty, instr. U. Fla., Gainesville, 1987-88; corp. instr. Unemployment Ins. Corp., Boca Raton, Fla., 1999—; lectr. in field. Mem. Volusia County Domestic Violence Task Force,1 993-94. Recipient Outstanding Instr. award U. Fla. Mem. ABA, ATLA, Nat. Dist. Attys. Assn., Fla. Bar Assn., Palm Beach County Bar Assn., Hispanic Bar Assn., Fla. Pros. Attys. Assn. (DUI trial sch. staff, edn. com.), Fla. Def. Lawyers Assn., Def. Rsch. Inst., Aircraft Owners and Pilots Assn., World Underwater Fedn., Nat. Assn. Underwater Instrs., Profl. Assn. Diving Instrs., Nat. Assn. Cave Diving, U.S. Navy League. Avocations: flying, scuba diving, golf, tennis, running. Home: 2128 Tarpon Lake Way West Palm Beach FL 33411-5766 Office: Office of State Atty. 401 N Dixie Hwy West Palm Beach FL 33401-4209

**PENCE, MARTIN,** federal judge; b. Sterling, Kans., Nov. 18, 1904; m. Eleanor Fisher, Apr. 12, 1975. Bar: Calif. 1928, Hawaii 1933. Practice law Hilo, Hawaii, 1936-45, 50-61; judge 3d Circuit Ct., Hawaii, 1945-50; chief judge U.S. Dist. Ct., Hawaii, 1961-74; sr. judge U.S. Dist. Ct., 1974—. Office: US Dist Ct 300 Alamonana Blvd Rm C423 Honolulu HI 96850-0423

**PENDELL, TERRY ASHLEY,** lawyer, mediator; b. Great Bend, Kans., July 26, 1937; d. John J. and Ida Berniece (Littrell) Ashley; m. George M. Pendell Jr., June 25, 1960 (div. July 1977); children: George III, Wade A.; m. Cal K. Moser, Feb. 18, 1994. BA, U. Okla., 1960, MEd, 1965; JD, Oklahoma City Univ., 1967. Bar: Okla. 1967, U.S. Dist. Ct. (we. dist.) Okla. 1967, U.S. Dist. Ct. (no. dist.) Okla. 1972, U.S. Supreme Ct. 1980. Ptnr. Pendell & Pendell Lawyers, Oklahoma City, 1967-73; assoc. Pritchett & Pendell, Oklahoma City, 1973-75; judge Oklahoma City Mcpl. Ct., Oklahoma City, 1975-90, Okla. Worker's Compensation Ct., State of Okla., Oklahoma City, 1990-96; ptnr. Pritchett, Snyder & Pendell, Oklahoma City, 1996; adj. law prof. Okla. City U., 1998; pvt. mediator, Oklahoma City, 1995—. Dir. Cmty. Coun. Okla., Oklahoma City, 1980—; co-chair Heartland Com., Oklahoma City, 1997-98; chmn. TB Task Force to the Homeless, Oklahoma City, 1997-99. Mem. Okla. City U. Law Alumni Assn. (bd. dirs. 1997-99, Outstanding Law Sch. Alumni award 1994), Nat. Assn. Women Judges (bd. dirs. 1982-84), Ruth Bader Ginsberg Inn of Ct. (officer 1995—), Iota Tau Tau, Zeta Phi Eta (Outstanding Svc. award 1975-87), Gamma Phi Beta. E-mail: oktap@yahoo.com. Alternative dispute resolution, Labor, Probate. Office: Pritchett Snyder & Pendell 1140 NW 63rd St Ste 301 Oklahoma City OK 73116-6511

**PENDYGRAFT, GEORGE WILLIAM,** lawyer; b. Jeffersonville, Ind., Nov. 3, 1946; s. George Benjamin and Norma Jean (Hall) P.; m. Melissa Ann Pendygraft, 1977 (div. Sept. 1990); children: Alexandrea Jean, Ryan Samuelson; m. Jacqueline Sue Samuelson, Jan. 15, 1991. AB in Chemistry, Franklin Coll., 1968; PhD in Phys. Organic Chemistry, U. Ky., 1972; JD, Columbia U., 1975. Bar: N.Y. 1976, Ind. 1976, U.S. Patent and Trademark Office 1976, U.S. Dist. Ct. (ea. and so. dists.) N.Y. 1980, U.S. Ct. Appeals (D.C. cir.) 1980. Lectr. in chemistry U. Ky., Lexington, 1968-70; assoc. Watson, Leavenworth, Kelton & Taggart, N.Y.C., 1975-76; ptnr. Baker and Daniels, Indpls., 1976-88, Pendygraft, Plews & Shadley, Indpls., 1988-90; prin., pres. George W. Pendygraft, P.C., Indpls., 1990—. Contbr. articles to profl. jours. Bd. trustees Franklin Coll., 1982-86, nat. chmn. ann. fund, 1981. NDEA fellow, NSF fellow; Franklin Coll. scholar. Environmental, Patent. Office: 1000 Waterway Blvd Indianapolis IN 46202-2155 also: 10723 Chase Ct Fishers IN 46038-9433 also: 1000 Waterway Blvd Indianapolis IN 46202-2155

**PENN, JOHN GARRETT,** federal judge; b. Pittsfield, Mass., Mar. 19, 1932; s. John and Eugenie Gwendolyn (Heyliger) P.; m. Ann Elizabeth Rollison, May 7, 1966; children: John Garett II, Karen Renee, David Brandon. BA, U. Mass., 1954; LLB, Boston U., 1957; postgrad., Princeton U., 1967-68. Bar: Mass 1957, D.C. 1970. Trial atty. U.S. Dept. Justice, Washington, 1961-65, atty. tax divsn., 1961-70; then reviewer, asst. chief gen. litigation sect., assoc. judge Superior Ct. of D.C., Washington, 1970-79; judge U.S. Dist. Ct. D.C., Washington, 1979—, chief judge, 1992-97, sr. judge. Ex-officio dir. day care program D.C. Dept. Recreation, 1978—. With JAGC, U.S. Army, 1958-61. Nat. Inst. Pub. Affairs fellow, 1967. Mem. Nat. Bar Assn., Mass. Bar Assn., Washington Bar Assn., D.C. Bar Assn., Bar Assn. D.C. (hon.), Am. Judicature Soc., Boston U. Law Sch. Alumni Assn. Episcopalian. Office: US Dist Ct DC US Courthouse 333 Constitution Ave NW Washington DC 20001-2802

**PENN, PHILIP JULIAN,** lawyer; b. Anchorage, May 11, 1955; s. Percy Junius and Jeanne Naomi (Johnson) P.; m. Rita Elaine Edwards, Feb. 20, 1993. AB, Duke U., 1977; JD, N.C. Ctrl. Law Sch., 1981. Bar: N.C. 1981. Law clerk Henry E. Moss/Paul C. Bland, Durham, N.C., 1981; pvt. practice Durham, 1981, 83-84; ptnr. Sloan, Moss & Penn, Durham, 1982; assoc. atty. Malone, Brown & Matthewson, P.A., Durham, 1982; fed. jud. law clerk U.S. Dist. Ct., Greensboro, N.C., 1982-83; appeals referee N.C. Employment Security Commn., Winston-Salem, N.C., 1984-87; asst. pub. defender 26th Defender Dist., Charlotte, N.C., 1987-92; asst. atty. gen. Virgin Islands Govt., St. Croix, 1992-93; mgr. Know Bookstore, 1995; pvt. practice Charlotte, 1996-98; staff atty. Children's Law Ctr., Charlotte, 1998—; bd. dirs. chmn. legis. and legal issues com. N.C. Gov's. Waste Mgmt. Bd., Raleigh, N.C., 1991-92; adv. bd. mem. Mecklenburg Community Corrections, Charlotte, 1992. Author: Colorblind is a Spiritual State of Mind, 1993. Bd. dirs. Neighborhood Justice Ctr., Winston-Salem, 1987, Recovery Inc., Charlotte, 1994, Portraits of Color, 1996; alt. del. N.C. Rep. Party, Winston-Salem, 1987; mentor Queens Coll., Charlotte, 1990-92; facilitator New Options for Violent Actions, Mecklenburg County, N.C., 1992. Recipient African-Am. Image award Queens Coll., 1992; named to Outstanding Young Men of Am., 1983, 86. Mem. Tuskegee Airmen, Inc., Kappa Alpha Psi (lt. strategus 1990). Democrat. Roman Catholic. Avocations: aviation, photography, art, sports, history. Address: PO Box 34204 Charlotte NC 28234-4204

**PENNAMPED, BRUCE MICHAEL,** lawyer; b. Kearney, Nebr., July 16, 1948; s. Matthew Paul and Betty Fern (Harper) P.; mm. Victoria A. Crull, May 13, 1972 (div. Dec. 1980); 1 child, Katheryn A.; m. Melissa J. Barth, July 22, 1985. BS in Mgmt., Ind. U., 1970, JD, 1972. Bar: Ind. 1972, U.S. Dist. Ct. (no. and so. dists.) Ind. 1972, U.S. Ct. Appeals (7th cir.) 1978. Assoc. Rocap Rocap Reese & Young, Indpls., 1972-76; pvt. practice Indpls., 1976-78, 88-91; ptnr. Forbes & Pennamped, Indpls., 1978-88, Lowe Gray Steele & Hoffman, Indpls., 1991-96, Lowe Gray Steele & Darko, Indpls., 1996—; chair and panelist Ind. Continuing Legal Edn. Forum; mem. Ind. Child Custody and Support Adv. Commn. Contbr. articles to profl. jours. Majority atty. Ind. Ho. of Reps., Indpls. Cpl. USMCR, 1967-69. Fellow Am. Acad. Matrimonial Lawyers. Family and matrimonial. Home: 9662 Decatur Dr Indianapolis IN 46256-9654 Office: Lowe Gray Steele & Darko 4600 Bank One Tower Indianapolis IN 46204-5146

**PENNELL, WILLIAM BROOKE,** lawyer; b. Mineral Ridge, Ohio, Oct. 28, 1935; s. George Albert and Katherine Nancy (McMeen) P. AB, Harvard U., 1957; LLB cum laude, U. Pa., 1961; m. Peggy Polsky, June 17, 1958; children: Katherine, Thomas Brooke. Bar: N.Y. 1963, U.S. Dist. Ct. (so. dist.) N.Y. 1964, U.S. Dist. Ct. (ea. dist.) N.Y. 1964, U.S. Ct. Appeals (2d cir.) 1966, U.S. Claims 1966, U.S. Tax Ct. 1967, U.S. Supreme Ct. 1967. Clk. U.S. Dist. Ct., (so. dist.) N.Y., N.Y.C., 1961-62; assoc. Shearman & Sterling, N.Y.C., 1962-71, ptnr., 1971-91. Recent case editor U. Pa. Law Rev., 1960-61. Bd. govs. Bklyn. Heights Assn., 1964-74, pres., 1969-71; chmn. bd. Willoughby House Settlement, 1972-95. Served with U.S. Army, 1957. Fellow Salzburg Seminar Am. Studies, 1965. Mem. Rembrandt Club. Federal civil litigation, State civil litigation, Private international. Office: PO Box 249 Canaan NY 12029-0249

**PENNEY, CHARLES RAND,** lawyer, civic worker; b. Buffalo, July 26, 1923; s. Charles Patterson and Gretchen (R) P. BA, Yale U., 1945; JD, U. Va., 1951; DFA (hon.), SUNY, 1995. Bar: Md. 1952, N.Y. 1958, U.S. Supreme Ct. 1958. Law sec. to U.S. Dist. Ct. Judge W.C. Coleman, Balt., 1951-52; dir. devel. office Children's Hosp., Buffalo, 1952-54; sales mgr. Amherst Mfg. Corp., Williamsville, N.Y., 1954-56, also; Delevan Electronics Corp., East Aurora, N.Y.; mem. firm Penney & Penney, Buffalo, 1958-61; pvt. practice, Niagara County, N.Y., 1961—. Numerous contemporary art collection exhbns. include Mus. Modern Art, N.Y.C., 1962, Whitney Mus. Am. Art, N.Y.C., 1963, 79, 80, Burchfield-Penney Art Ctr., 1973, 92-96, Meml. Art Gallery, Rochester, 1976, 78, 83, 88, U. Iowa, 1978, Columbus (Ohio) Gallery Fine Arts, 1979, Whitte Meml. Mus., San Antonio, 1979, U. N.C., 1979, Ga. Mus. Art, 1979, Hunter Mus. Art, Chattanoga, Tenn., 1980, Brooks Meml. Art Gallery, Memphis, 1980, Portland (Maine Mus. Art), 1980, Arts Ctr., South Bend, Ind., 1980, The Bowers Mus., Santa Ana, Calif., 1980, Beaumont (Tex.) Art Mus., 1981, 88, Meadows Mus. Art, Shreveport, La., 1981, 88, Cedar Rapids (Iowa) Mus. Art, 1983, Roland Gibson Art Gallery, Potsdam, N.Y., 1983, 84, Met. Mus. Art, 1984, San Jose Mus. Art, 1985, Tampa Mus., 1986, Boston Athenaeum, Mass., 1986, The New Britain (Conn.) Mus. Art, 1986, Currier Gallery Art, Manchester, N.H., 1987, Miss. Mus. Art, Jackson, 1987, others; selected works from art collections exhibited at Met. Mus. Art, N.Y. Hist. Soc., 1987, San Francisco Mus. Art, 1963, Walker Art Ctr., Mpls., 1963, Pa. Acad. Fine Arts, 1964, and 25 U.S. Embassies, 1965-72, U. Ariz., Tucson, 1965, 66, Albright-Knox Art Gallery, Buffalo, 1967, 87, Cleve. Mus., Art, 1972, Indpls. Mus. Art, 1973, Whitney Mus. Am. Art, N.Y., 1979, 80, Milw. Mus. Art, 1984, Wadsworth Atheneum, Hartford, 1986, Corcoran Gallery Art, Washington, 1987, U. Mich., 1993, Terra Mus. Am. Art, 1993. Bd. dirs. Buffalo State Coll. Found.; hon. life trustee Burchfield-Penney Art Ctr.; mem. Kenan Ctr., Lockport, N.Y., Hallwalls Contemporary Arts Ctr., Buffalo, N.Y., Landmark Soc. of Niagara Frontier, Buffalo Indsl. Heritage Com., Carnegie Art Ctr., North Tonawanda, N.Y., Peterson Soc. of Buffalo State Coll. 2d lt. U.S. Army, 1943-46. Recipient Pres.'s Disting. Svc. award Buffalo State Coll., 1991, Disting. Svc. to Culture award Coll. Arts and Scis., SUNY, Potsdam, 1983; named Disting. fellow Cultural Studies of the Burchfield-Penney Art Ctr., 1994, Outstanding Individual Philanthropist, Nat. Soc. Fund Raising Execs. Western N.Y., 1996, Individual Patron of the Arts award Buffalo and Erie County Arts Coun. and Buffalo C. of C., 1997, Citation for Outstanding Achievements and Svc. to Lockport Cmty., N.Y. State Assembly, 1997; awarded Key to City of Lockport, 1997. Fellow The Explorers Club: mem. AARP, Albright-Knox Art Gallery Buffalo (life), Buffalo Mus. Sci. (life), Buffalo and Erie County Hist. Soc. (life), Niagara County Hist. Soc. (life), Old Ft. Niagara (life), Buffalo Soc. Artists (hon. trustee), Hist. Lockport (life), Landmark Soc. Western N.Y. (life), Nat. Trust Hist. Preservation, Am. Ceramic Cir., Hist. Lewiston (life), Friends of U. Rochester Librs. (life) Meml. Art Gallery U. Rochester (hon. bd. mgrs., hon. life), Winslow Homer Soc. of Dirs. Cir. (hon. life), Smithsonian Instn. (benefactors cir.), Rochester Hist. Soc. (life), Am. Hist. Print Collectors Soc. (life), Burchfield Homestead Soc. (hon. life), Archives Am. Art, Mark Twain Soc. (hon.), Landmark Soc. of the Niagara Frontier, U. Rochester's Pres.'s Soc. (hon. life), U. Iowa's Pres.'s Club (hon. life), Va. Law Found., Nat. Geog. Soc. (life), World's Fair Collectors Soc., Heisey Collectors Am., Brit. Commemorative Collectors, Hist. Soc. of Tonawandas (life), Pres.'s Cir. Buffalo State Coll. (hon. life), Peanut Pals, Grolier Club, Pan Am. Expo Collectors Soc., Columbus (Ohio) Mus. of Art, Castellani Art Mus./Niagara U., Landmark Soc. Niagara Frontier, Buffalo Indsl. Heritage Com., Peterson Soc. (life), Yale Club of N.Y.C., Roycrofters-at-Large Assn. (life), Arctic Circle Club, Order of the Alaska Walrus, Chi Psi, Phi Alpha Delta. Clubs: Automobile (Lockport); Zwicker Aquatic, Niagara County Antiques (hon.); Rochester Art (hon. life). General practice. Office: 538 Bewley Building Lockport NY 14094-2944 *I have tried to strive for excellence in whatever I undertake, be it small or large. What success I may have achieved has required initiative, imagination, and dedication to the task at hand. Satisfaction comes from the hard work that leads to an objective. In all that I do I adhere to the Golden Rule and to fairness, honesty, and understanding in human relationships. I try to maintain a sense of humor at all times. And I enjoy living in a small community because it is from such areas that the strength of America comes.*

**PENNINGER, WILLIAM HOLT, JR.,** lawyer; b. Springfield, Mo., May 4, 1954; s. William Holt Sr. and Marjorie Marie (Emanuel) P.; m. Una Lee McLeer, Aug. 8, 1981; children: Una Lee, William Holt III. BS, MIT, 1976; JD, MBA, Tulane U., 1981; LLM, Tulane, 1983. Bar: La. 1981, N.Y. 1984, Mo. 1987. Customer service rep. CIT Fin. Services, Inc., Springfield, Mo., 1976-77; lexis rep. Mead Data Cen., New Orleans, 1981-83; assoc. Hill, Betts & Nash, N.Y.C., 1983-85, Cole & Deitz, N.Y.C., 1985-86; fin. planner IDS Fin. Services Inc., Springfield, Mo., 1986-87; assoc. Farrington & Curtis, Springfield, 1987-90; legal counsel Med. Def. Assocs., Springfield, 1990—; bd. dirs. Med. Def. Ins. Co., Med. Def. Assoc. Composer, performer: The Accessible Penninger, 1991, Man/Machine/Music, 1991, Fdt=mdv, 1992, The Coyote, The Scorpion & The Goat, 1993. Mem. Greene County Estate Planning Coun., 1987-91; bd. dirs. Springfield Regional Opera, 1989-93. Mem. ABA, Mo. Bar Assn. (ins. law com.), Springfield Met. Bar Assn., Nat. Assn. Securities Dealers (lic. 1986-89). Republican. Presbyterian. Avocations: sailing, skin and scuba diving, theoretical physics, electronic music composition, photography. General corporate, Insurance, Administrative and regulatory. Home: 2705 S Patterson Ave Springfield MO 65804-3913 Office: Legal Counsel Med Def Assoc 1311 E Woodhurst Dr Springfield MO 65804-4282

**PENNINGTON, JOHN WESLEY, III,** lawyer, school system administrator; b. Peoria, Ill., Apr. 1, 1943; s. John W. Jr. and Clara Media (Hicks) P.; m. Marcia Gebhard, July 11, 1964; children: John W. IV, Joshua Wallace, Jennifer Kate. BSE with honors, U. South Fla., 1971; MS in Mgmt., Fla. Internat. U., 1974; JD, U. Miami, 1981. Bar: Fla. 1982; registered profl. engr., Fla., Md. Supr. construction Dade County Sch. Bd., Miami, Fla., 1972-79; dir. planning and constrn. U. Miami, 1979-81, M.R. Harrison Constrn. Co., Miami, 1981-85; v.p. ops., corp. counsel M.R. Harrison Constrn. Co., Miami, Fla., 1987-90; exec. v.p., corp. counsel Harvesters Group Inc., 1985-87; pres., CEO Am. Consolidated Group, Inc., Miami, 1987-90; asst. supt., staff atty. Dade County Sch. Bd., Miami, 1990—; vis. prof. Fla. Internat. U., Miami, 1978; mgmt. trustee Trowel Trades Union Funds, Miami, 1983-85; speaker in field. Editor (short stories) Clara Media Hicks

Pennington, 1992; contbr. articles to profl. jours. V.p. Kendale Lakes (Fla.) Condominium Assn., 1973-75; tchr. high sch. class Kendale United Meth. Ch., South Dade, Fla., 1988. Capt. USMC, 1961-68, Vietnam, ret. med. disability. Mem. Am. Inst. Indsl. Engrs. (sr.), Am. Arbitration Assn. (aribrator), Fla. Bar Assn., Dade County Bar Assn., Omicron Delta Kappa (pres. 1970-71), Pi Mu Epsilon, Phi Kappa Phi, Tau Beta Phi. Construction, Contracts commercial, General practice. Home: 8567 SW 137th Ave Miami FL 33183-4075 Office: Office of Staff Atty 1450 NE 2nd Ave Ste 428 Miami FL 33132-1308

**PENN-JENKINS, MONIQUE LORAE,** lawyer; b. L.A., June 15, 1966; d. Leamond Franklin Penn and Irene (Watts) Jenkins, stepfather Theodore Jenkins; m. Michael Craig Watson, June 28, 1997. BA, U. Va., 1987; JD cum laude, Howard U., 1994. Bar: Pa. 1994, D.C. 1995, U.S. Ct. Appeals (D.C. cir.) 1995. Lease adminstr. MCI Telecomms. Corp., Washington, 1988-91; lawyer Grammer Kissel Robbins Skancke & Edwards, Washington, 1994-97, Sutherland, Asbill & Brennan LLP, Washington, 1997-98, Fed. Energy Regulatory Commn., Washington, 1998—. Trainer Washington Literacy Coun., Washington, 1997—; bd. dirs. Push Literacy Action Now, Washington, 1997-98. Mem. Fed. Energy Bar Assn., Am. Assn. of Blacks in Energy. Avocations: horseback riding, literacy tutor, reading, Mary Kay. Administrative and regulatory, Appellate, FERC practice. Office: Fed Energy Regulatory Commn 888 1st St NE Washington DC 20426-0002

**PENNOYER, JAMES ESTEN,** judge; b. St. Louis, Aug. 16, 1949; s. James and Miriam Hinsdale (Mellon) P.; m. Ann Marie Robins, Apr. 19, 1986. BA in Philosophy, Hobart Coll., 1971; JD, U. Puget Sound, 1975. Bar: Mo. 1975, U.S. Dist. Ct. (ea. and we. dist.) Mo. 1975. Ptnr. Hugh C. Roberts, Jr., Farmington, Mo., 1975-77, Stevenson, Pennoyer & Ray, Farmington, 1977-79; 1st trial asst. pros. atty. St. Francois County, Farmington, 1975-79; assoc. circuit judge, 1979—. Bd. dirs. S.E. Mo. Community Treatment Ctr., Farmington, 1978—, chmn. 1986-87, 92-96. Mem. Assn. Trial Lawyers Am., Assn. Probate and Assoc. Circuit Judges (bd. dirs. 1979-82), St. Francois Country Club, Elks. Democrat. Home: PO Box 508 Bonne Terre MO 63628-0508 Office: Cir Ct Div III Courthouse 2d Fl Farmington MO 63640

**PENNY, WILLIAM LEWIS,** lawyer; b. Memphis, Sept. 4, 1953; s. Charles B. and Dorothy R. (Rivers) P.; m. Linda Brown, Sept. 8, 1979; 1 child, Joseph Martin. BA, U. Tenn., 1975; JD, Nashville Sch. Law, 1981. Bar: Tenn. 1981, U.S. Ct. Appeals (6th cir.) 1981. Program evaluator Office of Comptroller, State of Tenn., Nashville, 1975-80; mgr. compliance and audit Tenn. Dept. Edn., Nashville, 1980-82; chief environ. counsel Tenn. Dept. Health and Environment, Nashville, 1982-84, asst. commr., gen. counsel, 1984-91; gen. counsel Tenn. Dept. Environment and Conservation, Nashville, 1991-92; prin. Law Firm of Manier, Herod, Hollabaugh & Smith, Nashville, 1992-98; counsel Wyatt, Tarrant & Combs, Nashville, 1998—. Bd. dirs. Hosp. Hospitality House, chmn., 1993. Mem. ABA (vice chair of pubs., solid waste com., sec. Nat. Resources Energy and Environ. law), Tenn. Bar Assn. (chmn. environ. law sect. 1991, 92, exec. com. 1992—), Nashville Bar Assn. (chair environ. law com.), Assn. Govt. Accts. (editor newsletter, Nashville 1977-79, sec. Nashville chpt. 1979-80, bd. dirs. chpt. 1980-84). Methodist. Avocations: music, bluegrass guitar, hiking, coaching little league sports. Administrative and regulatory, Environmental, Health. Home: 6501 Cornwall Dr Nashville TN 37205-3041 Office: Wyatt Tarrant & Combs 1500 W Nashville City Ctr 511 Union St Nashville TN 37219-1733

**PENSINGER, JOHN LYNN,** lawyer; b. Hagerstown, Md., June 5, 1949; s. Linford Snider and Marguerite Joan (McNeal) P.; m. Eileen Sue Howard, Nov. 7, 1972. BA, U. Md., 1971; JD, U. Balt., 1976; LLM, George Washington U., 1987. Bar: Md. 1976, D.C. 1977, U.S. Ct. Claims 1977, U.S. Tax Ct. 1977, U.S. Dist. Ct. Md. 1978, U.S. Dist. Ct. D.C. 1978, U.S. Ct. Appeals (4th cir.) 1978, U.S. Ct. Mil. Appeals 1978, U.S. Ct. Appeals (D.C. cir.) 1978, U.S. Customs Ct. 1979, U.S. Supreme Ct. 1980, U.S. Ct. Internat. Trade 1981, U.S. Ct. Appeals (fed. cir.) 1982, U.S. Ct. Appeals (5th cir.) 1986, U.S. Ct. Appeals (3d cir.) 1988, U.S. Army Ct. Mil. Rev. 1989. Mgr., E.M. Willis & Sons, Washington, 1977-79; pvt. practice, Rockville, Md., 1978-79; atty. Amalgamated Casualty Ins. Co., Washington, 1979-86; asst. gen. counsel Legal Svcs. Corp., Washington, 1986-88, sr. litigation counsel, 1988-95; atty. Office Justice Programs U.S. Dept. Justice, 1995-96, assoc. gen. counsel, 1996—. Mem. ABA, Am. Soc. Internat. Law, Fed. Bar Assn., Md. Bar Assn. Roman Catholic. Administrative and regulatory, Federal civil litigation, Government contracts and claims. Home: 4 Stratton Ct Rockville MD 20854-6227

**PEOTTER, SARA JO,** lawyer; b. Green Bay, Wis., June 9, 1948; d. Marvin Harold and Florence Agnes Peotter; divorced; children: Randolph William, Matthew James. AD, U. Minn., 1981, BA, 1984; JD, William Mitchell Coll. Law, 1991. Bar: Minn. 1991, Wis. 1992, U.S. Dist. Ct. Minn. 1993. Acct. Econs. Labs., St. Paul, 1975-77; office adminstr., bookkeeper Collins, Buckley et al, St. Paul, 1977-81, paralegal, 1981-86, paralegal, law clk., 1986-91; sole practitioner St. Paul, 1991—; co-chair mentor program Minn. Women Lawyers, Mpls., 1994-96. Del., Dem. Labor Party, St. Paul, 1994-95. Mem. ABA (chair-elect solo small firm com. 1998—), Minn. State Bar Assn. (bd. govs.), 1st Dist. Bar Assn. (sec.-treas. 1998—), Ramsey County Bar Assn. (chair continuing legal edn. 1997—), Rotary Internat. (subchair group study 1998—). Roman Catholic. Avocations: biking, walking, stamp collecting, reading, swimming. General practice, General civil litigation, Sports. Home: 2111 Patricia St Saint Paul MN 55120-1326 Office: Peotter Law Firm PO Box 21603 2110 S Lexington Eagan MN 55121

**PEPE, LOUIS ROBERT,** lawyer; b. Derby, Conn., Mar. 7, 1943; s. Louis F. and Mildred R. (Vollaro) P.; m. Carole Anita Roman, June 8, 1969; children: Marissa Lee, Christopher Justin, Alexander Drew. B in Mgmt. Engring., Rensselaer Poly. Inst., 1964, MS, 1967; JD with distinction, Cornell U., 1970. Bar: Conn. 1970, U.S. Dist. Ct. Conn. 1970, U.S. Ct. Appeals (2d cir.) 1971, U.S. Supreme Ct. 1975, U.S. Ct. Claims 1978. Assoc. Alcorn, Bakewell & Smith, Hartford, Conn., 1970-75; ptnr. Alcorn, Bakewell & Smith, Hartford, 1975-82; sr. ptnr. Pepe & Hazard, Hartford, 1983—; adj. assoc. prof. Hartford Grad. Ctr., 1972-87; dir. BayBank Conn., 1987-93; Adv. coun. Cornell Law Sch., 1990—. Mem. New Hartford Housing Authority, 1971-72, New Hartford Planning Zoning Commn., 1973-84, chmn., 1980-84, New Hartford Inland Wetlands Commn., 1975-78; mem. adv. coun. Cornell Law Sch., 1990—; dir. Capitol Area Found. Equal Justice, 1993—. 1st lt. U.S. Army, 1964-66. Decorated Army Commendation medal. Fellow Am. Bar Found.; mem. ABA, Am. Coll. Trial Lawyers, Am. Bd. Trial Advocates, Conn. Bar Assn. (chmn. constrn. law sect. 1989-92), Conn. Trial Lawyers Assn., Hartford County Bar Assn., Phi Kappa Phi. Construction, Federal civil litigation, State civil litigation. Home: 3 Metacom Dr Simsbury CT 06070-1851 Office: Goodwin Sq Hartford CT 06103-4300

**PEPE, STEVEN DOUGLAS,** federal magistrate judge; b. Indpls., Jan. 29, 1943; s. Wilfrid Julius and Roselda (Gehring) P.; m. Janet L. Pepe. BA cum laude, U. Notre Dame, 1965; JD magna cum laude, U. Mich., 1968; postgrad., London Sch. Econs. and Polit. Sci., 1970-72; LLM, Harvard U., 1974. Bar: Ind. 1968, U.S. Dist. Ct. Ind. 1968, D.C. 1969, U.S. Dist. Ct. D.C. 1969, mass. 1973, Mich. 1974, U.S. Dist. Ct. (ea. dist.) Mich., 1983. Law clk. Hon. Harold Leventhal U.S. Cir. Ct. Appeals, Washington, 1968-69; staff atty. Neighborhood Legal Svcs. Program, 1969-70; cons. Office of Svcs. to Aging, Lansing, Mich., 1976-77, Adminstrn. Aging, Dept. Health and Human Svcs., 1976-78; U.S. magistrate judge Eastern Dist., Ann Arbor, Mich., 1983—; mem. Biregional Older Am. Advocacy Assistance Resource and Support Ctr., 1979-81; cons., bd. dirs. Ctr. Social Gerontology (1988-93); clin. prof. law, dir. Mich. Clin. Law Program, U. Mich. Law Sch., 1974-83; adj. prof. law Detroit Mercy Sch. Law, 1985; lectr. U. Mich. Law Sch., 1985-97. Editor Mich. Law Rev.; contbr. articles to profl. jours. Recipient Reginald Heber Smith Cmty. Lawyer fellowship, 1969-70; Mich.-Ford Internat. Studies fellow, 1970-72, Harvard Law Sch. Clin. Teaching fellow, 1972-73. Mem. State Bar Mich., State Bar Ind., D.C. Bar, Fed. Bar Assn., Washtenaw County Bar Assn., Vanzetti M. Hamilton Bar Assn., Am. Inn Court XI, U. Detroit Mercy, Pi Sigma Alpha, Order of Coif. Office: US District Court PO Box 7150 Ann Arbor MI 48107-7150

**PEPER, CHRISTIAN BAIRD,** lawyer; b. St. Louis, Dec. 5, 1910; s. Clarence F. and Christine (Baird) P.; m. Ethel C. Kingsland, June 5, 1935 (dec. Sept. 1995); children: Catherine K. Peper Larson, Anne Peper Perkins, Christian B.; m. Barbara C. Pleiter, Jan. 25, 1996. AB cum laude, Harvard U., 1932; LLB, Washington U., 1935; LLM, Yale U., 1937. Bar: Mo. 1934. Pvt. practiced St. Louis; of counsel Blackwell Sanders Peper Martin LLP; lectr. various subjects Washington U. Law Sch., St. Louis, 1943-61; ptnr. A.G. Edwards & Sons, 1945-67; pres. St. Charles Gas Corp., 1953-72; bd. dirs. St. Louis Steel Casting Inc., Hydraulic Press Brick Co., El Dorado Paper Bag Mfg. Co., Inc. Editor: An Historian's Conscience: The Correspondence of Arnold J. Toynbee and Columba Cary-Elwes, 1986. Contbr. articles to profl. jours. Mem. vis. com. Harvard Div. Sch., 1964-70; counsel St. Louis Art Mus. Sterling fellow Yale U., 1937. Mem. ABA, Mo. Bar Assn., St. Louis Bar Assn., Noonday Club, Harvard Club, East India Club (London), Order of Coif, Phi Delta Phi. Roman Catholic. General corporate, Estate planning. Home: 1454 Mason Rd Saint Louis MO 63131-1211 Office: Blackwell Sanders Peper Martin LLP 720 Olive St Saint Louis MO 63101-2338

**PEPPEL, HOWARD REX,** lawyer, educator; b. Pitts., Dec. 7, 1948; s. Howard C. and Virginia Card P.; m. Barbara Ann Hunt, Dec. 21, 1970; children: Susan E., Jennifer A., David R. BS, U. Tenn., 1970, JD, 1973. Bar: Tenn. 1973, U.S. Ct. Mil. Appeals 1974, U.S. Dist. Ct. (we. dist.) Tenn. 1978, U.S. Supreme Ct. 1980. Commd. 2d lt. USAF, 1973, advanced through grades to lt. col., 1991; asst. staff judge adv. USAF, Keesler AFB, Miss., 1973-76, area def. counsel HQ, 1976-77; asst. staff judge adv. USAF, Eaker AFB, Ark., 1978-92, Eglin AFB, Fla., 1993—; with Peppel, Gomes & MacIntosh, PC, Memphis, 1977—; asst. prof. U. Memphis, 1984—; recruiting USAF lawyer The Judge Adv. Gen., USAF, 1991—. Lt. col. USAFR, 1973—. Mem. Comml. Law League Am. Republican. Southern Baptist. Consumer commercial, Contracts commercial, Military. Office: Peppel Gomes & MacIntosh PC 474 Perkins Ext Ste 205 Memphis TN 38117-3803

**PEPPER, ALLAN MICHAEL,** lawyer; b. Bklyn., July 5, 1943; s. Julius and Jeanette (Lasovsky) P.; m. Barbara Benjamin, Aug. 30, 1964; children—Leslie Anne, Joshua Benjamin, Adam Richard, Robert Benjamin. B.A. summa cum laude, Brandeis U., 1964; LL.B. magna cum laude, Harvard U., 1967. Bar: N.Y. 1968, U.S. Dist. Ct. (so. and ea. dists.) N.Y. 1968, U.S. Ct. Appeals (2d cir.) 1968, U.S. Supreme Ct. 1988. Law clk. U.S. Ct. Appeals for 2d Circuit, N.Y.C., 1967-68; assoc. Kaye, Scholer, Fierman, Hays & Handler, N.Y.C., 1968-74, ptnr., 1975—; lectr. in field. Mem. exec. com., assoc. nat. chmn. Brandeis U. Alumni Fund, 1979-82, nat. chmn., 1982-85, chmn. 25th Reunion gift com., 1989, devel. com., trustee, 1982-85, pres., councillor, 1980—, mem. 35th Reunion gift com., 1999; trustee Brandeis U., 1985-95, sec., 1992-93, budget and fin. com., 1988-95, chmn. com. strategic plan, 1990-91, acad. affairs com., 1985-92, student life and phys. facilities com., 1985-89, vice chmn. ad hoc by-laws com., 1988-89, long range planning com., 1989-91, chmn. audit com., 1991-95, exec. com., 1990-91, mem. 35th Reunion gift com., 1999; bd. dirs. Styles Brook Homeowners Assn., 1990—, exec. com., 1994—; nominating com. Edgemont Sch. Bd., 1992-93; trustee Edgemont Sch. Found., 1994—; mem. 30th reunion gift com. Harvard Law sch., 1996-97. Recipient Henry Jones-Golda Meier Bnai Brith Youth Services award, 1986, L.I. Press Valedictory medal, 1960; Felix Frankfurter scholar Harvard U. Law Sch., 1964-65; Louis D. Brandeis hon. scholar Brandeis U., 1964. Mem. ABA, Assn. of Bar of City of N.Y. (mem. law firm mgmt. com. 1987-91, litigation com, 1998—), N.Y. State Bar Assn. (comml. and fed. lit. sect., vice chmn. com. on discovery 1993-97), Brandeis U. Alumni Assn. (exec. com. 1982-97, alumni giving strategic planning com., 1992, Alumni Svc. award 1988), Phi Beta Kappa (L.I. Alumni award 1960). Democrat. Jewish. Lodge: B'nai B'rith (pres. Henry Jones Lodge 1982-84, mem. Westchester-Putnam council 1982-85, bd. govs. dist. 1, 1985-86). Federal civil litigation, State civil litigation, Antitrust. Office: Kaye Scholer Fierman Hays & Handler LLP 425 Park Ave New York NY 10022-3506

**PEPYNE, EDWARD WALTER,** lawyer, psychologist, former educator; b. Springfield, Mass., Dec. 27, 1925; s. Walter Henry and Frances A. (Carroll) P.; m. Carol Jean Dutcher, Aug. 2, 1958; children—Deborah, Edward, Jr., Susan, Byron, Shari, Randy, David, Allison, Jennifer. B.A., Am. Internat. Coll., 1948; M.S., U. Mass., 1951, Ed.D., 1968; postgrad., NYU, 1952-55; prof. diploma, U. Conn., 1964; J.D., Western New Eng. Coll., 1978. Bar: Mass. 1978, U.S. Supreme Ct. 1981. Prin., tchr. Gilbertville Grammar Sch., Hardwick, Mass., 1948-49; sch. counselor West Springfield High Sch., Mass., 1949-53; instr. NYU, 1953-54; supt. schs. New Shoreham, R.I., 1954-56; asst. prof. edn. Mich. State U., 1956-58; sch. psychologist, guidance dir. Pub. Sch. System, East Long, Mass., 1958-62; lectr. Westfield State Coll., 1961-65; dir. pupil services Chicopee Pub. Sch., 1965-68; assoc. prof. counselor edn. U. Hartford, West Hartford, Mass., 1968-71, prof., 1971-85, dir. Inst. Coll. Counselors Minority and Low Income Students, 1971-72, dir. Div. Human Services, 1972-77; cons. Aetna Life & Casualty Co., Hartford, 1962-75; hearing officer Conn. State Bd. Edn., 1980-99; exec. dir. Sinapi Assocs., 1959-78; pvt. practice, Ashfield, Mass., 1978—. Co-author: Better Driving, 1958; assoc. editor: Highway Safety and Driver Education, 1954; chmn. editorial com.: Man and the Motor Car, 5th edit., 1954; contbr. numerous articles to profl. jours. Chief Welfare Svcs. Civil Def., Levittown, N.Y., 1953-54; chmn. Ashfield Planning Bd., Mass., 1979-83; moderator Town of Ashfield, 1980-81, town counsel, Charlemont, Mass., 1983-84; mem. jud. nominating coun. Western Regional Com., 1993—; mem. Mohawk Regional Sch. Com., 1999—. Mem. ABA, APA, Mass. Bar Assn., Mass. Acad. Trial Attys., Am. Pers. and Guidance Assn., New Eng. Pers. and Guidance Assn. (bd. dirs.), New Eng. Ednl. Rsch. Orgn. (pres. 1971), Am. Assn. Sch. Adminstrs., Am. Ednl. Rsch. Assn., Mt. Tom Amateur Radio Assn., Franklin County Amateur Radio Club, Elks, Kiwanis (pres. 1988-89, lt. gov. div. 12, 1991-92), Masons (master 1994-96), Shriners, Phi Delta Kappa. General practice, Administrative and regulatory, Real property. Home: PO Box 31 134 Ashfield Mountain Rd Ashfield MA 01330-9622 Office: PO Box 345 134 Ashfield Mountain Rd Ashfield MA 01330-9622

**PERAGINE, PAUL FRANCIS,** lawyer; b. Englewood, N.J., Nov. 23, 1953; s. Paul G. and Ann Peragine; m. Eva Gilmer, Aug. 15, 1998. BBA, Pace U., 1981; JD, Touro Law Sch., 1984. Bar: N.Y. 1986, N.J. 1986, U.S. Tax Ct. 1986. Assoc. Wollin Assocs., Ft. Lee, N.J., 1984-88; ptnr. Ballon Stolll Bader & Nadler, N.Y.C., 1988-97, Fromme Schwartz Newman & Cornicello LLP, N.Y.C., 1997—; bd. dirs. Altzheimers Assn., Ft. Lee. Real property, General corporate, Taxation, general. Office: Fromme Schwartz Newman & Cornicello LLP 233 Broadway Rm 2702 New York NY 10279-2799

**PERDUE, JIM MAC,** lawyer; b. Dallas, Dec. 6, 1938; s. Otis Lloyd and Juanita (Percy) P.; m. Carole Diane Phillips, Nov. 27, 1966 (div. Aug. 1989); children: Jim M. Jr., Joe N., William Jeffrey. BA, U. Houston, 1961, JD, 1963. Bar: Tex. 1963, U.S. Dist. Ct. (so. dist.) Tex. 1964, U.S. Supreme Ct. 1970; diplomate Am. Bd. Profl. Liability Attys. Assoc. Fulbright Crooker, Houston, 1965-68; ptnr. Miller, Gann & Perdue, Houston, 1968-80, Perdue, Turner & Berry, Houston, 1980-90, Perdue & Todesco, Houston, 1990-98, Perdue & Clore L.L.P., Houston, 1993-98, The Perdue Law Firm L.L.P., Houston, 1999—; health law bd. mem. U. Houston Coll. Law, 1987-95. Author: The Law of Texas Medical Malpractice, 1975, The Law of Texas Medical Malpractice, 2d. edit., 1985, Medical Malpractice Handbook, 1988, Who Will Speak for the Victim: A Treatise on Plaintiff's Jury Argument, 1989, (with J. Sales) The Law of Strict Tort Liability, 1977; contbr. articles to profl. jours., book chpts. Steering com. Gulf Coast Legal Found., 1996. Commdr. USNR, 1965-73. Recipient Outstanding Alumnus award U. Houston Coll. Law, 1977. Fellow Am. Coll. Trial Lawyers, Tex. Bar Found.; mem. Am. Coll. Legal Medicine (assoc.), Am. Bd. Trial Advocates (pres. Houston chpt. 1984-85), Tex. Trial Lawyers Assn. (malpractice com. chmn. 1965-76, dir. 1988-91), State Bar Tex. (com. profl. ethics 1985, com. continuing legal edn. 1988-89, pattern jury charge III rev. 1988-93, jud. qualifications com. 1988-91, qualifications, tenure & compensation state jud. 1988-91, Gene Cavin Outstanding Contbn. Legal Edn. award 1995), Supreme Ct. Tex. Task Force Standardized Discovery Malpractice Cases, Houston Bar Assn. (grievance com. 1971-73, spl. com. professionalism 1988-89, Outstanding Com. Chmn. Yr. 1974-75), Houston Med. Legal Soc. (pres. 1995-96), Order of Coif, Inner Cir. Advocates. Personal injury, Product liability, Toxic tort. Home: 2929 Buffalo Speedway Unit 1002 Houston TX 77098-1709 Office: The Perdue Law Firm LLP 2727 Allen Pkwy Ste 800 Houston TX 77019-2100

**PERELLA, MARIE LOUISE,** lawyer; b. Akron, Ohio, Feb. 5, 1967; d. Manuel James and Jean Ann (Nalencz) P. BA in Spanish, John Carroll U., 1989; student, Univ. Ibero Americana, Mexico City, 1988; JD, Akron U., 1992. Bar: Ohio 1992, U.S. Dist. Ct. (no. dist.) Ohio 1993, U.S. Supreme Ct. 1996. Law clk. Akron Law Dept., 1990; legal intern Cuyahoga Falls (Ohio) Law Dept., 1990-92; law clk. Ticktin, Baron, Koepper & Co. LPA, Cleve., 1992, assoc. atty., 1992—; commed. to take marriage licence applications at penal instns. Probate Ct. of Cuyahoga County, 1994—. Guest spkr. Cleve. Legal Secs. Assn. meeting, 1995. John Carroll U. scholar, 1988-89, Presdl. Honor scholar, 1985-89, Am. Values scholar, 1985-89, others. Mem. Ohio State Bar Assn., Cuyahoga County Bar Assn. (family law sect.), Centro Cultural Hispano, Justinian Forum, Phi Alpha Delta (clk. law sch./grant chpt. 1991-92), Sigma Delta Pi. Avocations: sports, travel, flute. General practice, Family and matrimonial, State civil litigation. Office: Ticktin Baron Koepper & Co LPA 1621 Euclid Ave Cleveland OH 44115-2107

**PERERA, LAWRENCE THACHER,** lawyer; b. Boston, June 23, 1935; s. Guido R. and Faith (Phillips) P.; m. Elizabeth A. Wentworth, July 5, 1961; children: Alice V. Perera Lucey, Caroline F. Perera Barry, Lucy E., Lawrence Thacher. B.A., Harvard U., 1957, LL.B., 1961. Bar: Mass. 1961, U.S. Supreme Ct. 1973. Clk. Judge R. Ammi Cutter, Mass. Supreme Jud. Ct., Boston, 1961-62; assoc. Palmer & Dodge, Boston, 1962-69; ptnr. Palmer & Dodge, 1969-74; judge Middlesex County Probate Ct., East Cambridge, Mass., 1974-79; ptnr. Hemenway & Barnes, Boston, 1979—; mem. faculty and nat. coun. Hon. Nat. Jud. Coll., Reno, prof./pres. Mass. Continuing Legal Edn., Inc., 1988-90. Chmn. Boston Fin. Commn., 1969-71; overseer Brigham and Women's Hosp., Boston, Boston Lyric Opera; chmn. bd. overseers Boston Opera Assn.; chmn. Back Bay Archtl. Commn., 1966-72; trustee emeritus Sta. WGBH Ednl. Found., Boston Athenaeum, Wang Ctr. Performing Arts; trustee Social Law Libr., Boston. Fellow Am. Acad. Matrimonial Lawyers, Am. Coll. Trust and Estate Counsel; mem. ABA, Am. Bar Found., Am. Law Inst., Mass. Bar Assn., Mass. Bar Found., Boston Bar Assn.. Probate, Family and matrimonial, General practice. Home: 18 Marlborough St Boston MA 02116-2101 Office: 60 State St Boston MA 02109-1800

**PEREY, RON,** lawyer; b. Cleve., Feb. 2, 1943; s. John Perecinsky and Anne (Nagy) Disman; 1 child, Page Suzanne; m. Janice Ash, Aug. 19, 1995. BA in Polit. Sci., Miami U., Oxford, Ohio, 1965; JD cum laude, Ohio State U., 1968. Bar: Wash. 1968, U.S. Dist. Ct. (we. dist.) Wash. 1968, U.S. Ct. Appeals (9th cir.) 1973, U.S. Supreme Ct. 1985. Assoc. Reed McClure, Seattle, 1968-71, ptnr., 1971-82; ptnr. Perey & Smith, Seattle, 1982-86, Perey Langley, Seattle, 1986-92; owner Law Offices of Ron Perey, Seattle, 1992—; lectr. in field of personal injury and trial practice. Contbr. articles to profl jours. Fellow Roscoe Pound Found.; mem. ATLA (state del. 1989-90), ABA (litigation sect.), King County Bar Assn. (chmn. med.-legal com. 1989-90), Wash. State Trial Lawyers Assn. (bd. govs. 1983-85, 89-91), Am. Bd. Trial Advs. (diplomate; nat. bd. rep. 1996—, treas. 1998, v.p. 1999), Wash. State Bar Assn. (bd. govs. 1994-97), Damage Attys. Round Table. Democrat. Avocations: travel, reading, weight lifting, tennis, hiking, jogging. Personal injury, General civil litigation. Office: Market Place Tower 2025 1st Ave Ste 250 Seattle WA 98121-2147

**PEREYRA-SUAREZ, CHARLES ALBERT,** lawyer; b. Paysandu, Uruguay, Sept. 7, 1947; came to U.S., 1954, naturalized, 1962; s. Hector and Esther (Enriquez-Sarano) P.-S.; m. Susan H. Cross, Dec. 30, 1983. BA in History magna cum laude, Pacific Union Coll., 1970; postgrad., UCLA, 1970-71; JD, U. Calif., Berkeley, 1975. Bar: Calif. 1975, D.C. 1980. Staff atty. Western Ctr. Law and Poverty, Inc., Los Angeles, L.A., 1976; trial atty. civil rights div. U.S. Dept. Justice, Washington, 1976-79; asst. U.S. atty., criminal div. U.S. Dept. Justice, Los Angeles, L.A., 1979-82; sr. litigation assoc. Gibson, Dunn & Crutcher, Los Angeles, L.A., 1982-84; sole practice Los Angeles, L.A., 1984-86; ptnr. McKenna & Cuneo, Los Angeles, L.A., 1986-95, Davis Wright Tremaine, L.A., 1995-98; pvt. practice L.A., 1998—. Democrat. Avocations: tennis, jogging, travel. Federal civil litigation, State civil litigation, Criminal.

**PEREZ, DANIEL FRANCISCO,** lawyer, educator; b. Amarillo, Tex., Dec. 3, 1958; s. Jose Alexander and Mary Louise (Lucero) P.; m. Suzanna Odette Sanchez, Mar. 31, 1988; children: Maya Christine, Anthony Daniel. BS in Chem. Engring., Tex. Tech. U., 1981; JD, U. Tex., 1987. Bar: Calif. 1988, Tex. 1989, U.S. Patent Office 1989, U.S. Dist. Ct. (no. dist.) Tex. 1989, (we. dist.) Tex. 1993. Engr. Amoco Prodn. Co., Tex., 1981-85; atty. Workman, Nydegger & Jensen, La Jolla, Calif., 1987-88, Baker, Mills & Glast, Dallas, 1989-90, Jones, Day, Reavis & Pogue, Dallas, 1990-92, Johnson & Gibbs, Dallas, 1992-93; ptnr. Warren & Perez, Dallas, 1993—; adj. prof. U. Tex. Law Sch. Author and lectr. in field. Vol. Rape Crisis Ctr., Lubbock, Tex. 1983-86, Counselor for Homeless, San Diego, 1988-90; active Opportunity Dallas Greater Dallas C. of C., 1991, Hispanic Bus. Forum, Dallas, 1992. Recipient Community Svc. award Greater Dallas Chamber Community Devel. Div., 1992. Fellow Tex Bar Found.; mem. Mexican-Am. Bar Assn. (chair scholarship com. 1992-93), State Bar Tex. (opportunity for minorities com. 1991-94, task force on future of alt. dispute resolution 1992), Tex. Young Lawyers Assn. (chair alt. dispute resolution com. 1991-92, chair juvenile justice com. 1992-93, dir. 1991-93), Dallas Bar Assn. (community dispute resolution com. 1992), Dallas Assn. Young Lawyers (dir. 1991-93), U. Tex. Law Sch. Alumni Assn. (dir. 1992-95). Democrat. Roman Catholic. Avocations: fitness, music. Patent, Federal civil litigation, Trademark and copyright. Home: 3112 Cornell Ave Dallas TX 75205-2932 Office: Warren & Perez 1601 Elm St Ste 3000 Dallas TX 75201-4757

**PEREZ, LUIS ALBERTO,** lawyer; b. Havana, Cuba, Dec. 22, 1956; came to U.S., 1961; s. Alberto and Estela (Hernandez) P. BBA cum laude, Loyola U., New Orleans, 1978, JD, 1981. Car: La. 1981, U.S. Dist. Ct. (ea. and mid. dists.) La. 1981, U.S. Ct. Appeals (5th and 11th cirs.) 1981, U.S. Dist. Ct. (we. dist.) La. 1983, D.C. 1989, U.S. Dist. Ct. (D.C. cir.) 1989, U.S. Ct. Appeals D.C. 1989, U.S. Supreme Ct. 1989, Tex. 1994. Ptnr. Adams and Reese, New Orleans, 1981—; chmn. internat. practice team Adams & Reese. Mem. ABA, La. Bar Assn., Fed. Bar Assn., Interamerican Bar Assn., D.C. Bar Assn., State Bar Tex., Hispanic Lawyers Assn. La. (pres. 1988-94), Beta Gamma Sigma. Avocations: scuba diving, racquetball. Federal civil litigation, Contracts commercial, General corporate. Office: Adams and Reese 4500 One Shell Sq New Orleans LA 70139-4501

**PEREZ, RICHARD LEE,** lawyer; b. L.A., Nov. 17, 1946; s. Salvador Navarro and Shirley Mae (Selbrede) P.; m. Yvonne Perez; children: Kristina, Kevin, Ryan. BA, UCLA, 1968; JD, U. Calif., Berkeley, 1971. Bar: U.S. Dist. Ct. (no. dist.) Calif. 1974, U.S. Ct. Appeals (9th cir.) 1974, U.S. Dist. Ct. (ea. dist.) Calif. 1982, U.S. Dist. Ct. (no. dist.) Tex. 1984, U.S. Dist. Ct. (so. dist.) Calif. 1991. Assoc. McCutchen, Doyle, Brown & Enersen, San Francisco, 1972-74, John R. Hetland, Orinda, Calif., 1974-75; ptnr. Lempres & Wulsfberg, Oakland, Calif., 1975-82, Perez & McNabb, Orinda, 1982—; speaker real estate brokerage and computer groups and seminars; mem. adv. bd. Computer Litigation Reporter, Washington, 1982-85, Boalt Hall High Tech. Law Jour., 1984-90. Assoc. editor U. Calif. Law Rev., 1970-71. Served to capt. U.S. Army, 1968-79. Mem. ABA, Alameda County Bar Assn., Contra Costa County Bar Assn. Federal civil litigation, State civil litigation, Computer. Office: Perez & McNabb 140 Brookwood Rd Orinda CA 94563-3035

**PEREZ-ABREU, JAVIER,** lawyer; b. Havana, Cuba, Aug. 20, 1960; came to U.S., 1961; s. Gustavo and Martha (Caballero) Perez-Abreu; m. Dulce Maria Fernandez, Jan. 25, 1986; children: Carla, victor. BA in English and Bus. Adminstrn., Fla. State U., 1982; JD, U. Miami, 1985. Bar: Fla. 1985; cert. in marital and family law, family mediator, civil mediator. Atty./law clk. Antonio J. Pineiro, Jr., P.A., Miami, Fla., 1982-85; assoc. Manuel Alonso-Poch, P.A., Coral Gables, Fla., 1986-87; ptnr. Perez-Abreu, & Martin-Lavielle, PA, Coral Gables, 1987—; vice chmn. fla. Bar grievance Com. 11-B, Miami, 1993-97; barrister First Family chpt. Inns of Ct., Miami, 1995—; panel mem. Mediator qualifications Adv. Panel, Miami, 1994—. Author/editor: (seminar materials) Temporary Support Middle Income Divorce, 1994. Guardian ad litem pro-bono Dade County Bar, Miami, 1985—, pro-bono project mem., 1985—. Mem. Cuban Am. Bar Assn. (former v.p. and dir.), Dade County Bar Assn., Fla. Trial Lawyers Assn. Republican. Avocations: tennis, jogging, gym. Family and matrimonial,

Alternative dispute resolution. Office: Perez-Abreu & Martin-Lavielle 901 Ponce De Leon Blvd Ste 502 Miami FL 33134-3073

**PEREZ-GIMENEZ, JUAN MANUEL,** federal judge; b. San Juan, P.R., Mar. 28, 1941; s. Francisco and Elisa (Gimenez) P.; m. Carmen R. Ramirez, July 16, 1964; children: Carmen E., Juan C., Jorge E., Jose A., Magdalena. BBA, U. P.R., 1963, JD, 1968; MBA, George Washington U., 1965. Bar: P.R. 1968. Ptnr. Goldman, Antonetti & Davila, San Juan, 1968-71; asst. U.S. atty. San Juan, 1971-75, U.S. magistrate, 1975-79; judge U.S. Dist. Ct. P.R., San Juan, 1979—. Mem. ABA, Fed. Bar Assn., Colegio de Abogados. Roman Catholic.

**PERKIEL, MITCHEL H.,** lawyer; b. N.Y.C., Oct. 26, 1949; s. Frank and Ella Perkiel; m. Lois E. Perkiel, June 24, 1984; children: Joshua L., Alexa Kim, Griffin. BA, SUNY, Stony Brook, 1971; JD, New York Law Sch., 1974. Bar: N.Y. 1975, U.S. Dist. Ct. (so. and ea. dists.) N.Y. 1975, U.S. Ct. Appeals (2d cir.) 1975, Conn. 1988. Law clk. to presiding justice N.Y. County Civil Ct., 1975; assoc. Levin & Weintraub & Crames, N.Y.C., 1975-80, ptnr., 1980-90; ptnr. Kaye, Scholer, Fierman, Hayes & Handler, N.Y.C., 1990—. Notes and comments editor New York Law Rev., 1973-74. With USAR, 1969-73. Mem. ABA, Assn. of Bar of City of N.Y., Am. Bankruptcy Inst., Turnaround Mgmt. Assn. (dir.). Bankruptcy. Office: Kaye Scholer Fierman Hayes & Handler LLP 425 Park Ave New York NY 10022-3506

**PERKINS, ALVIN BRUCE, II,** lawyer; b. Alexandria, La., Dec. 21, 1959; s. Alvin B. and Nyla Jean (Humbles) P.; m. Lisa Lynn Adams, Oct. 1, 1983; children: Alvin Bruce III, Katherine Camille. BA, La. Coll., 1982; JD, So. Univ., 1990. Bar: La., U.S. Dist. Ct. (we. dist.) La. Salesman Al's A/Sales, Alexandria, La., 1976-80, mgr., 1980-86; cons. Dealer's Auto Auction, Pineville, La., 1982-84; assoc. Sheffield Law Offices, Alexandria, La., 1990-91; sole practitioner A. Bruce Perkins Law Office, Alexandria, La., 1991-92; mng. ptnr. Lavespere & Perkins, Alexandria, La., 1992-98; sole practitioner Alvin Bruce Perkins Law Offices, Alexandria, La., 1998—; atty. Pro-Bono of Ctrl. La., Alexandria, 1992—. Precinct chmn. Campaign Election/Pineville City Ct., 1996-97. Mem. Trial Lawyers Assn., Ctrl. La. Bar Assn., La. State Bar Assn. Avocations: hunting, fishing, boating, restoring older high performance vehicles. Criminal, Personal injury, Family and matrimonial. Office: 1718 Lee St Alexandria LA 71301-6238

**PERKINS, JON SCOTT,** lawyer; b. Covington, Va., Oct. 14, 1965; s. Edgar Leroy and Linda (Scott) P. BBA, Coll. William and Mary, 1989; JD, Washington and Lee U., 1996. Bar: Va. 1996; CPA, Va. Sr. assoc., acct. Coopers & Lybrand, Richmond, Va., 1989-93; assoc. Mays & Valentine, L.L.P., Richmond, 1993—. Mem. membership com. Greater Richmond Tech. Coun., 1998—; bd. dirs. Charterhouse Sch., Inc. Mem. The Tribe Club (trustee 1987—). Avocations: martial arts, boating. General corporate, Finance, Mergers and acquisitions. Office: Mays & Valentine LLp 1111 E Main St Richmond VA 23219-3531

**PERKINS, JOSEPH JOHN, JR.,** lawyer; b. Pitts., Feb. 22, 1954; s. Joseph John Sr. and Joan Elizabeth (Challingsworth) P.; m. Rebecca Ellen Graham, Apr. 7, 1984; children: Benjamin Joseph, Nathaniel Graham. BS in Geol. Engring. magna cum laude, Princeton U., 1976; JD, U. Denver, 1979. Bar: Alaska 1979, U.S. Dist. Ct. Alaska 1979, U.S. Ct. Appeals (9th cir.) 1983, U.S. Supreme Ct. 1986. Assoc. Guess & Rudd, P.C., Anchorage, 1979-84, shareholder, 1984—; pres. Guess & Rudd, P.C., 1997—. Trustee Rocky Mountain Mineral Law Found., Denver, 1988—. Mem. ABA (vice chmn. hard mineral com., sect. on natural resources, energy and environ. law 1992-93, ethics com., sect. on natureal resources, energy and environ. law 1997-98), Alaska Bar Assn. (chmn. natural resources law sect. 1984-88), Sigma Xi, Tau Beta Pi. Republican. Protestant. Avocations: swimming, biking, Boy Scouts, gardening, travel. Contracts commercial, Oil, gas, and mineral, Natural resources. Home: 7202 Hunter Cir Anchorage AK 99502-4185 Office: Guess & Rudd PC 510 L St Ste 700 Anchorage AK 99501-1959

**PERKINS, ROBERT ANTON,** judge; b. Laredo, Tex., Oct. 27, 1947; s. William Anton and Carol (Salisbury) P.; m. Yoland Velasquez, June 7, 1969 (div. 1979); 1 child, Javier; m. Cyndy Allen, Aug. 2, 1980; children: Allen, Ana. BA in Govt., U. Tex., 1970, JD, 1973. Bar: Tex. 1973. Pvt. practice Austin, Tex., 1973-75; justice of the peace County of Travis, Austin, 1975-80, judge county ct., 1980-82; judge 331st Dist. Ct., Austin, 1982—; adminstrv. judge Criminal Dist. Judges, Austin, 1991—. Mem. City Human Rels. Commn., Austin, 1976-79, Austin Mediation Ctr. Bd., 1983-84; mem., pres. Pan-Am. Recreation Ctr., Austin, 1975—; bd. dirs. Ctr. for Battered Women, Austin, 1978-80. Mem. Mex.-Am. Bar Assn., Tex. Bar Assn. (jud. sect.), Travis County Bar Assn. (criminal law and procedure com.), Sierra. Democrat. Roman Catholic. Avocations: jogging, hiking. Home: 2633 Deerfoot Trl Austin TX 78704-2764 Office: PO Box 1748 Austin TX 78767-1748

**PERKINS, ROGER ALLAN,** lawyer; b. Port Chester, N.Y., Mar. 4, 1943; s. Francis Newton and Winifred Marcella (Smith) P.; m. Katherine Louise Howard, Nov. 10, 1984; children: Marshall, Morgan, Matthew, Justin, Ashley. BA, Pa. State U., 1965; postgrad., U. Ill., 1965-66; JD with honors, George Washington U., 1969. Bar: Md. 1969, Mass. 1975. Trial atty. Nationwide Ins. Co., Annapolis, Md., 1969-72; assoc. Arnold, Beauchemin & Huber, PA, Balt., 1973; from assoc. to ptnr. Goodman & Bloom, PA, Annapolis, 1973-76; ptnr. Luff and Perkins, Annapolis, 1976-78; pvt. practice Anapolis, 1978—; temp. adminstrv. hearing officer Anne Arundel County, 1984—; asst. city atty., Annapolis, 1980-82; atty. Bd. Appeals of City of Annapolis, 1986—; mem. Appellate Jud. Nominating Commn., 1995—. Editl. adv. bd. Daily Record, 1996-97. Mem. Gov.'s Task Force on Family Law, 1991-94; adv. coun. on family legal need of low income persons MLSC, 1991; coach youth sports. Fellow Am. Acad. Matrimonial Lawyers, Am. Bar Found., Md. Bar Found. (bd. dirs. 1992-95); mem. ABA (ho. dels. 1991-93, 94-96, standing com. on solo and small firm practitioners 1993-97, chair 1996-97), Md. State Bar Assn. (pres. 1992-93, treas. 1988-91, bd. govs. 1985-87, chair spl. com. on lawyer profl. responsibility 1994-95, family and juvenile law sect. coun. 1983-89, chair 1987-88), Anne Arundel County Bar Assn. (pres. 1984-85). Republican. Methodist. Family and matrimonial, State civil litigation. Home: 503 Bay Hills Dr Arnold MD 21012-2001 Office: The Courtyards 133 Defense Hwy Ste 202 Annapolis MD 21401-8907

**PERKINS, ROSWELL BURCHARD,** lawyer; b. Boston, May 21, 1926. AB cum laude, Harvard U., 1945, LLB cum laude, 1949; LLD (hons.), Bates Coll., 1988. Bar: Mass. 1949, N.Y. 1949. Assoc. Debevoise, Plimpton & McLean, N.Y.C., 1949-53; ptnr. Debevoise & Plimpton and predecessor firm, N.Y.C., 1957-96; of counsel, head rep. office Debevoise & Plimpton LLC, Moscow, 1997—; asst. sec. U.S. Dept. Health, Edn. and Welfare, 1954-56; counsel to Gov. Nelson A. Rockefeller State of N.Y., 1959; asst. counsel spl. subcom. Senate Commerce Com. to investigate organized crime in interstate commerce, 1950; chmn. N.Y.C. Mayor's Task Force on Transp. Reorgn., 1966; mem. Pres.'s Adv. Panel on Pers. Interchange, 1968, chmn. adv. com. Medicare Adminstrn. Contracting, Subcontracting HEW, 1973-74; dir. Fiduciary Trust Co., N.Y., 1963—; trustee Bowery Savs. Bank, 1975-82; mem. legal com. to bd. dirs. N.Y. Stock Exch., 1995—. Author: The New Federal Conflict of Interest Law; editor Harvard Law Rev. Mem. N.Y. Lawyers Com. Civil Rights, 1970-73; mem. nat. exec. com., 1973—, co-chmn. 1973-75; mem. adv. coun. Woodrow Wilson Sch. Pub. and Internat. Affairs, Princeton U., 1967-69; bd. dirs. The Commonwealth Fund, 1974—, Sch. Am. Ballet, 1974-85, chmn. bd. 1976-80; dir., sec. N.Y. Urban Coalition, 1967-74; trustee Pomfret Sch., 1961-76; The Brearly Sch., 1969-75; dir. Salzburg Seminar Am. Studies, 1970-80; mem. overseers vis. com. Kennedy Sch. Govt., Harvard U., 1971-77, Harvard and Radcliffe Colls., 1958-64, 1971-77. Recipient Spl. Merit citation Am. Judicature Soc., 1989, Harvard Law Sch. Assn. award, 1994. Mem. ABA (commn. on law and economy, 1975-79, mem. house of dels. 1980-93), N.Y. State Bar Assn., Assn. of the Bar of the City of N.Y. (chmn. spl. com. on fed. conflict of interest laws 1958-60). Assn. Harvard Alumni (pres. 1970-71), Am. Law Inst. (mem. coun. 1969, pres. 1980-93, chmn. coun. 1993—), Am. Arbitration Assn. (bd. dirs. 1966-71). General corporate, Private international, Mergers and acquisitions. Home: 1120 5th Ave New York NY 10128-0144 Office: Debevoise & Plimpton 875 3rd Ave Fl 23 New York NY 10022-6256 Other: Debevoise & Plimpton LLC, Bolshoi Palashevsky Tr 13/2, 103104 Moscow Russia

**PERL, JUSTIN HARLEY,** lawyer; b. Mpls., Sept. 30, 1957; s. Norman and Addie Perl; m. Lynn Goldman, Feb. 23, 1985; children: Alexandra, Phillip. BA, U. Mich., 1980, JD, 1983. Summer assoc. Fried, Frank, Harris, Shriver & Jacobson, N.Y.C., 1982; assoc. Maslon Edelman Borman & Brand, LLP, Mpls., 1983-88, ptnr., 1988—; adj. faculty mem. Civil Practice Clinic, William Mitchell Coll. Law, St. Paul, 1987-91; presenter in field. V.p., trustee, mem. pers. com. Adath Jeshurun Congregation, Minnetonka, Minn., 1996—. Mem. Am. Arbitration Assn. (abitrator), Hennepin County Bar Assn. (investigator 1991—, dist. IV ethics com. 1991—, lawyers vol. com. 1991—, immigrant projects com. 1996—)., Advanced Dispute Resolution, Inc., Conflict Mgmt. and Dispute Resolution. General civil litigation, Family and matrimonial, Intellectual property. Office: Maslon Edelman Borman & Brand LLP 3300 Norwest Ctr Minneapolis MN 55402

**PERLBERGER, RALPH,** lawyer; b. Amsterdam, The Netherlands, Feb. 9, 1931; s. Oscar and Claire (Untermans) P.; m. Carol Sue Riner, July 23, 1967; children: Jody, Jillian. BA, Stanford U., 1953; JD, Harvard U., 1956. Bar: N.Y. 1957, D.C. 1959, U.S. Supreme Ct. 1960. Assoc. Lewis & McDonald, N.Y.C., 1957-59, Nordlinger Riegelman Benetar & Charney, N.Y.C., 1959-61. Mem. Village of Saltaire Recreation Com., Fire Island, N.Y., 1976-78; active Nat. Ski Patrol Systems Inc.; coach jr. soccer team; instr. windsurfing, Village of Saltaire, Fire Island, N.Y. Mem. Assn. of the Bar of the City of N.Y. (sec. com. on state cts. of superior jurisdiction), N.Y. County Lawyers Assn., MENSA. Jewish. Club: Harvard (N.Y.), Saltaire Yacht. Contracts commercial, General corporate, Private international. Home: 19 E 88th St New York NY 10128-0557 Office: 225 Broadway New York NY 10007-3001

**PERLING, LESTER J.,** lawyer; b. St. Paul, Minn., July 31, 1955; s. Joseph and Doris Perling. BA, Ga. State U., 1976, M in Health Adminstrn., 1980; JD, U. Miami, 1994. Bar: Fla. 1994, U.S. Dist. Ct. (so. dist.) Fla. 1995. Adminstr. Intracoastal Cardiology, Delroy Beach, Fla., 1990, Nat. Medical Enterprises, various, 1985-90, Charter Medical Corp., Ft. Lauderdale, Fla., 1994—; instr. Nova Southeastern U., Ft. Lauderdale, 1997—; speaker in field. Mem. Am. Health Lawyers Assn. Health. Office: Broad and Cassel 500 E Broward Blvd Ste 1130 Fort Lauderdale FL 33394-3077

**PERLIS, MICHAEL FREDRICK,** lawyer; b. N.Y.C., June 3, 1947; s. Leo and Betty F. (Gantz) P.; children: Amy Hannah, David Matthew; m. Angela M. Rinaldi, Dec. 23, 1988. BS in Fgn. Svc. , Georgetown U., 1968, JD, 1971. Bar: D.C. 1971, N.Y. 1993, U.S. Dist. Ct. D.C. 1971, U.S. Ct. Appeals 1971, D.C. Ct. Appeals 1971, Calif. 1980, U.S. Dist. Ct. (no. dist.) Calif. 1980, U.S Dist. Ct. (cen. dist.) Calif. 1985, U.S. Ct. Appeals (9th cir.) 1980, U.S. Supreme Ct., 1980, N.Y. 1993. Law clerk D.C. Ct. Appeals, Washington, 1971-72; asst. corp. counsel D.C., Washington, 1972-74; counsel U.S. SEC, div. enforcement, Washington, 1974-75, br. chief, 1975-77, asst. dir., 1977-80; ptnr. Pettit & Martin, San Francisco, 1980-89, Stroock & Stroock & Lavan, L.A., 1989—; adj. prof. Cath. U. Am., 1979-80. Mem. ABA (co-chmn. subcom. securities and commodities litigation 1982-83), D.C. Bar Assn., Calif. State Bar Assn. Federal civil litigation. Office: Stroock & Stroock & Lavan 2029 Century Park E Ste 1800 Los Angeles CA 90067-3086

**PERLMAN, BURTON,** judge; b. New Haven, Dec. 17, 1924; s. Phillip and Minnie Perlman; m. Alice Weihl, May 20, 1956; children: Elizabeth, Sarah, Nancy, Daniel. B.E., Yale U., 1945, M.E., 1947; LL.B., U. Mich., 1952. Bar: Ohio, 1959, N.Y. 1953, Conn. 1952, U.S. Dist. Ct. (so. and ea. dists.) N.Y. 1954, U.S. Ct. Appeals (2d cir.) 1953, U.S. Ct. Appeals (6th cir.) 1959, U.S. Dist. Ct. (so. dist.) Ohio 1959. Assoc. Armand Lackenbach, N.Y.C., 1952-58; pvt. practice, Cin., 1958-61; assoc. Paxton and Seasongood, 1961-67; ptnr. Schmidt, Effton, Josselson and Weber, 1968-71; U.S. magistrate U.S. Dist. Ct. (so. dist.) Ohio, 1971-76; U.S. bankruptcy judge, 1976—; chief bankruptcy judge so. dist. Ohio, 1986-93; adj. prof. U. Cin. Law Sch., 1976—. Served with U.S. Army, 1944-46. Mem. ABA, Fed. Bar Assn., Am. Judicature Soc., Cin. Bar Assn. Office: US Bankruptcy Ct Atrium 2 8th Fl 221 E 4th St Cincinnati OH 45202-4124

**PERLMAN, RICHARD BRIAN,** lawyer; b. N.Y.C., Aug. 19, 1951; s. William H. and Beryl N. (Cohen) P.; m. Virginia Merrill, Aug. 1, 1976; 1 child, Jason Eric. BA, Franklin and Marshall Coll., 1973; JD, Temple U., 1976. Bar: Pa. 1976, U.S. Dist. Ct. (ea. dist. ) Pa. 1977, U.S. Supreme Ct. 1982, Fla. 1999; cert. family mediator Fla. Supreme Ct., 1996. Assoc. Law Offices of Peter N. Harrison, Doylestown, Pa., 1976-77, Zion & Klein, Bryn Mawr, Pa., 1977-78; founder, owner The Law Ctr., Norristown, Pa., 1978-96, West Chester, Pa., 1982-96. Pres. Mothers Against Drunk Driving, Chester and Delaware Counties, Pa., 1987-89, 90-92; bd. dirs. Big Bros./Big Sisters, Montgomery County, Pa., 1979-85. Avocations: music, classic cars, tennis, golf, boating. Family and matrimonial, Bankruptcy, General practice.

**PERLOFF, JEAN MARCOSSON,** lawyer; b. Lakewood, Ohio, June 25, 1942; d. John Solomon and Marcella Catherine (Borngen) Marcosson; m. Lawrence Storch, Sept. 8, 1991. BA magna cum laude, Lake Erie Coll., 1965; MA in Italian, UCLA, 1967; JD magna cum laude, Ventura Coll. Law, 1976. Bar: Calif. 1976, U.S. Dist. Ct. (cen. dist.) Calif. 1978. Assoc. in Italian U. Calif.-Santa Barbara, 1967-70; law clk., paralegal Ventura County Pub. Defender's Office, Ventura, Calif., 1975; sole practice, Ventura, 1976-79; coprin. Clabaugh & Perloff, A Profl. Corp., Ventura, 1979-82; sr. jud. atty. to presiding justice 6th div. 2d Dist. Ct. Appeals, L.A., 1982-97; instr. Ventura Coll. Law, 1976-79. Pres., bd. dirs. Santa Barbara Zool. Gardens, 1987-88; bd. trustees Lake Erie Coll., 1993—. Named Woman of Yr., 18th Senatorial dist. and 35th Assembly dist. Calif. Legislature, 1992; recipient Disting. Alumnae award Lake Erie Coll., 1996. Mem. Calif. Bar Assn. (mem. appellate ct. com. 1993-95) Kappa Alpha Sigma. Democrat. Club: Fiesta City. Avocations: tennis, jogging, biking, reading, music. Home: 1384 Plaza Pacifica Santa Barbara CA 93108-2877

**PERLS, N. LYNN,** lawyer; b. Chgo., 1961; d. Stephen R. and Rae D. P.; life ptnr. Brenda A. Broussard. BA, Pitzer Coll., 1982; JD, U. N. Mex., 1989. Bar: N. Mex. 1989, U.S. Dist. Ct. N. Mex. 1990. Assoc. Kanter & Everage, PA, Albuquerque, 1989-93; pvt. practice Law Offices of Lynn Perls, Rio Rancho, N. Mex., 1993—. Mem. state ctrl. com. Dem. Party, N. Mex., 1997—; referee FIFA 8. Mem. ABA, Sandoval County Bar Assn. (treas. 1993—), N. Mex. Women's Bar Assn. Family and matrimonial, Estate planning, General practice. Home: Law Offices of Lynn Perls 4111 Barbara Loop Ste E-1 Rio Rancho NM 87124

**PERLSTEIN, WILLIAM JAMES,** lawyer; b. N.Y.C., Feb. 7, 1950; s. Justin Sol and Jane (Goldberg) P.; m. Teresa Catherine Lotito, Dec. 20, 1970; children—David, Jonathan. B.A. summa cum laude, Union Coll., 1971; student London Sch. Econs., 1969-70; J.D., Yale U., 1974. Bar: Conn. 1974, D.C. 1976, U.S. Dist. Ct. D.C. 1977, U.S. Ct. Appeals (D.C. cir.) 1978, U.S. Supreme Ct. 1993. Law clk. Judge Marvin Frankel, U.S. Dist. Ct., N.Y.C., 1974-75; assoc. Wilmer, Cutler & Pickering, Washington, 1975-82, ptnr., 1982—, mem. mgmt. com. 1995—, chmn. 1998—. Mng. editor Yale Law Jour., 1973-74; contbg. author The Workout Game, 1987. Mem. ABA (bus. bankruptcy com. 1983—, vice-chmn. executory contracts subcom. of bus. bankruptcy com. 1988-90, bankruptcy cts. subcom. 1990-97, chmn. legislation subcom. 1997—), Am. Bankruptcy Inst. (chmn. legis. com. 1986-89, bd. dirs. 1989-93, 97—), Am. Law Inst., Am. Coll. Bankruptcy (at-large regent), Union Coll. Alumni Coun., Phi Beta Kappa. Jewish. Bankruptcy, Legislative.

**PERRI, AUDREY ANN,** lawyer; b. Oxnard, Calif., Feb. 2, 1936; d. Zafon A. and Francis M. (Sandblom) Hartman; m. Frank M. Perri, Aug. 10, 1958; children: Michael H., Michelle F. Conte. BA, U. Redlands, 1958; JD, U. La Verne, 1976. Bar: U.S. Dist. Ct. (ctrl. dist.) 1977, Calif., 1976. Tchr. Corona (Calif.) Unified Sch. Dist., 1958-60, Chaffey H.S. Dist., Upland, Atta Loma, Calif., 1960-64, 70-71, Claremont (Calif.) H.S. Dist., 1967-68, Oak Park (Ill.)-River Forrest H.S., 1971-72; dep. dist. atty. Dist. Atty.'s Office, San Bernardino, Calif., 1976-81; with career criminal prosecution unit Dist. Atty.'s Office, San Bernardino, 1979-81; assoc. Civington & Crowe LLP, Ontario, Calif., 1981-85; ptnr. Civington & Crowe LLP, Ontario, 1986—; dept. mgr. family law, 1995—; tchr. ESL, Reykjavik, Iceland, 1971-72; judge pro tem, mediator San Bernardino County Superior Ct., 1983—, L.A. County Superior Ct. East Dist., 1983—; seminar panelist. Bd. dirs. Am. Field Svc., 1965-69, Nat. Conf. Christians and Jews, 1977-82; trustee U. LaVerne Law Sch. Found.; mem. state ctrl. com. Dem. Party, 1981-82. Recipient Boss of Yr. award, Ontario-Inland Valley Legal Secs. Assn., 1989, Susan B. Anthony Women of Yr. award San Bernardino County Commn. Status of Women, 1992, Disting. Alumnus of Yr. award U. La Verne Law Sch., 1993. Mem. ABA, AAUW (past-pres. chpt., Disting. Cmty. Svc. award 1983), Calif. Bar Assn. (family law sect. 1977—, del. conf. dels. 1977-96, exec. com. conf. dels. 1985-88, commr. legal svc. fund 1993-95, commr. jud. nominees evaluation commn. 1995-98), San Bernardino County Bar Assn. (trustee 1981-83, 84-86, chair legis., resolution com. 1980-81, mem. bench, bar, media com. 1980-85, mem. jud. evaluation com. 1986-95), Western San Bernardino County Bar Assn. (bd. dirs. 1992-95), Assn. Cert. Family Law Specialists, Inland County Women at Law (founding pres. 1981-82), Calif. Women Lawyers (bd. dirs. 1980-81, 82-84, first v.p. 1983-84, bylaws com. 1980-81, jud. evaluation com. 1981-82, co-chair legis. com. 1982-83), East-West Family Coun. Family and matrimonial. Home: 8373 Camino Sur Cumirosur Rancho Cucamonga CA 91730 Office: Covington & Crowe 1131 W 6th St Ontario CA 91762-1121

**PERRIN, EDWARD PATTERSON,** lawyer; b. Spartanburg, S.C., Sept. 19, 1925; s. Lewis Wardlaw and Elizabeth (Patterson) P.; m. Anne Porcher Zeigler, Apr. 7, 1951; children: Anne Perrin Flynn, Sallie Perrin White, Edward Patterson Jr. BS, U. Va., 1948; JD, U. S.C., 1950. Ptnr. Perrin, Perrin, Mann & Patterson, Spartanburg, S.C., ret.; chmn. Spartanburg Bank and Trust Co., 1970-72, 1st State Savs. and Loan Assn., Spartanburg, 1980-86; bd. dirs. Carolina Cash Co., Spartanburg. Deacon 1st Presbyn. Ch., Spartanburg, 1954-65, elder, 1966—; trustee Spartanburg County Found., 1982-88, chmn., 1987. Cpl. U.S. Army Air Corps, 1944-45. Mem. S.C. Bar Found. (bd. dirs. 1986-91, pres. 1988-89), Spartanburg Rotary Club (pres. 1972-73, Cert. of Honor 1988-89), Country Club of Spartanburg (bd. dirs. 1993-95, pres. 1993-94). Avocations: tennis, traveling, reading history.

**PERRIN, JAMES KIRK,** lawyer; b. Saginaw, Mich., Feb. 10, 1940; s. Robert Wallace and Elizabeth (Kirk) P.; m. Harriet Halteman, June 12, 1962; children: Mark, Rob, Jane, Jim. BA, Ohio Wesleyan U., 1962; JD, U. Mich., 1965. Bar: Ill. 1965, U.S. Dist. Ct. (no. dist.) Ill. 1965, U.S. Ct. Appeals (7th cir.) 1976, U.S. Supreme Ct. 1977. Assoc. McKenna Storer Rowe White & Haskell, Chgo., 1965-70, ptnr., 1970-75; founding ptnr. Haskell & Perrin, Chgo., 1975—, sr. ptnr., 1989—. Contbr. over 30 articles to profl. jours.; spkr. in field. Commr. Deerfield (Ill.) Plan Commn., 1970-72. Mem. ABA (trial techniques com., task force on delay in litigation), Internat. Assn. Def. Counsel, Soc. Trial Lawyers, Ill. Assn. Def. Trial Counsel, Phi Beta Kappa. Federal civil litigation, State civil litigation, Product liability. Office: Haskell & Perrin 200 W Adams St Ste 2600 Chicago IL 60606-5284

**PERRIN, SARAH ANN,** lawyer; b. Neoga, Ill., Dec. 13, 1904; d. James Lee and Bertha Frances (Baker) Figenbaum; m. James Frank Perrin, Dec. 24, 1926. LLB, George Washington U., 1941, JD, 1964. Bar: D.C. 1942. Assoc. atty. Mabel Walker Willebrandt, law office, Washington, 1941-42; atty. various fed. housing agys., 1942-69, asst. gen. counsel FHA, Washington, 1959-60, asst. gen. counsel HUD, Washington, 1960-69; sec. Nat. Housing Conf., Washington, 1970-80; rsch. cons. housing and urban devel., Palmyra, Va., 1970-76; acting sec. Nat. Housing Rsch. Coun., Washington, 1973-80; bd. dirs. Nat. Housing Conf., 1972—. Mem. Rep. Presdl. Adv. Commn., 1991-92, Senatorial Com.; trustee Found. for Coop. Housing, 1975-80; mem. Blue Ridge Presbytery Div. Mission, Presbyn. Ch., 1979-80, Friends of Fluvanna County Libr. Mem. ABA, Fed. Bar Assn., Women's Bar Assn. D.C. (pres. 1959-60), Nat. Assn. Women Lawyers, George Washington Law Assn., Charlottesville Area Women's Bar Assn., Fluvanna County Bar Assn., Fluvanna County Hist. Soc. (pres. 1973-75, exec. com. 1985-89), Order Eastern Star, Presbyn. Women (pres. Fork Union chpt. 1972-80, sec. 1980-94), Phi Alpha Delta (internat. pres. 1955-57, internat. adv. bd.). Home: Solitude Plantation Palmyra VA 22963

**PERRIS, TERRENCE GEORGE,** lawyer; b. L.A., Oct. 18, 1947; s. Theodore John Grivas and Penny (Sfakianos) Perris. BA magna cum laude, U. Toledo, 1969; JD summa cum laude, U. Mich., 1972. Bar: Ohio 1972, U.S. Tax Ct. 1982, U.S. Ct. Claims 1983, U.S. Supreme Ct. 1983. Law clk. to judge U.S. Ct. Appeals (2d cir.), N.Y.C., 1972-73; law clk. to Justice Potter Stewart U.S. Supreme Ct., Washington, 1973-74; assoc. Squire, Sanders & Dempsey LLP, Cleve., 1974-80; ptnr. Squire, Sanders & Dempsey, Cleve., 1980—; v.p., trustee SS&D Found., Cleve., 1984—; nat. coord. Taxation Practice Area, 1987—, mem. mgmt. com., 1996—; chmn. Cleve. Tax Inst., 1993; vis. prof. law U. Mich., 1996; lectr. in field. Mem. vis. com. U. Mich. Law Sch., 1986—. Capt. U.S. Army, 1974. Mem. ABA, Ohio Bar Assn., Cleve. Bar Assn. (subchpt. C of internal revenue code task force), Supreme Ct. Hist. Soc., Tax Club Cleve., Order of Coif, Union Club of Cleve., U. Mich. Club of Cleve., The Club of Cleve., Pres.'s Club (Ann Arbor, Mich.), Phi Kappa Phi. Republican. Eastern Orthodox. Avocation: landscape gardening. Corporate taxation, Personal income taxation, Constitutional. Office: Squire Sanders & Dempsey LLP 4900 Key Tower 127 Public Sq Cleveland OH 44114-1216

**PERRONE, JOSEPH JOSEPH,** laywer; b. Queens, N.Y., June 19, 1965; s. Joesph John and Marion T. P.; m. Susan M. Lynch, Aug. 5, 1995. BS, St. John's U., 1985, JD, 1988. Assoc. McDonald, Hebermann & Fenzel, N.Y.C., 1988-93, Law Offices of Peter D. Fenzel, N.Y.C., 1993-96; ptnr. Fenzel & Perrone P.C., N.Y.C., 1997—. Admiralty, Aviation. Office: Fenzel & Perrone 63 Wall St New York NY 10005-3001

**PERRY, BRIAN DREW, SR.,** lawyer, career officer; b. New Orleans, Feb. 3, 1955; s. Donald Roy and Helen Magaret P.; m. Karla Leigh, Mar. 17, 1984; children: Ashleigh, Brain-Drew, Morgan, Max, Emmaline, Kevin. BS, Our Lady of Holy Cross, 1985; JD, Loyola U., 1989. Bar: La. Asst. city atty. City of New Orleans, 1989-91; adv. Saudi Arabian Oil Co., Dhahran, Saudi Arabia, 1991-98; pvt. practice New Orleans, 1998—; bd. govs. Saudi Aramco Employees Assn., Dhahran, Saudi Arabia, 1984-88. Pub.: New Orleans Legis. Digest, 1990; author: Algiers Point, 1999. Mem. Saudi Aramco Sch. Bd., New Orleans, 1995-98. Lt. Col. U.S. Army, 1973—. Mem. La. State Bar Assn. Catholic. Fax: 504-482-8244. E-mail: bdp@mail.usa.com. General civil litigation, General practice, Private international. Home: 38 Park Timbers New Orleans LA 70131 Office: Law Office Brian D Perry Sr 4041 Tulane Ave New Orleans LA 70119-6849

**PERRY, EDWIN CHARLES,** lawyer; b. Lincoln, Nebr., Sept. 29, 1931; s. Arthur Edwin and Charlotte C. (Peterson) P.; m. Joan Mary Hanson, June 5, 1954; children: Mary Mills, Judy Phipps, James Perry, Greg Perry, Jack Perry, Pricilla Perry. BS, U. Nebr., 1953, JD, 1955. Bar: Nebr. 1955; U.S. Dist. Ct. Nebr., 1955; U.S. Ct. Appeals Nebr., 1968. Prin. Perry, Guthery, Haase & Gessford, P.C., Lincoln, 1957—. Chmn. Lincoln Lancaster County Planning Com., Madonna Rehab. Hosp. Fellow Am. Bar Found., Nebr. Bar Found.; mem. Nebr. State Bar Assn. (chair ho. dels. 1987-88, pres. 1991-92), Nebr. Coun. Sch. Attys. (pres. 1978-79), Lincoln Bar Assn. (pres. 1982-83). Republican. Roman Catholic. Banking, Education and schools, Estate planning. Office: Perry Guthery Haase & Gessford PC 1400 US Bank Bldg Lincoln NE 68508

**PERRY, GEORGE WILLIAMSON,** lawyer; b. Cleve., Dec. 4, 1926; s. George William and Melda Patricia (Arther-Holt) P. BA in Econs., Yale U., 1949; JD, U. Va., 1953. Bar: Ohio 1953, D.C. 1958, U.S. Supreme Ct. 1958, U.S. Ct. Appeals (D.C. cir.) 1959. Atty. U.S. Dept. Justice, Washington, 1954-56; assoc. Roberts and McInnis, Washington, 1957-59; atty. assoc. counsel Com. on Interstate Fgn. Commerce, U.S. Ho. Reps., Washington, 1960-65; atty., advisor ICC, Washington, 1965-68; assoc. dir. devel. Yale U., New Haven, 1968-70; trust officer The No. Trust Co., Chgo., 1970-71; dir. tax rsch. Pan Am. World Airways, N.Y.C., 1973-75; hearing officer Indsl. Commn. Ohio, Cleve., 1978-81; sole practice Cleve., 1981—. With U.S. Army, 1945-46. Mem. Soc. Cin. in State of Conn., Phi Delta Phi. Episcopalian. Administrative and regulatory, General practice.

**PERRY, JON ROBERT,** lawyer; b. Kane, Pa., May 14, 1965; s. James Felix and Judith Rose (Zelina) P.; m. Joni Lee Detrick, Aug. 10, 1991; children: Alex Joseph, Trevor James. BA summa cum laude, Pa. State U., 1987; JD magna cum laude, Duquesne U., 1991. BAr: Pa. 1991, U.S. Dist. Ct. (we. dist.) Pa. 1991, U.S. Ct. Apppeals (3d, 6th, 7th and fed. cirs.). Assoc. Reed Smith Shaw & McClay, Pitts., 1990-94; ptnr. Betts & Perry, Pitts., 1994-97, Kapetan Meyers Rosen & Louik, Pitts., 1998—; bd. dirs. Flying Pig Theatre, Pitts., J's Place, Inc., Kane, RBCI, Inc., Cranberry, Pa., CDS, Inc., Pitts.

Exec. editor Duquesne Law Rev., 1991. Vol. mentor/spkr. elem. and high schs., Pitts. area, 1992—. Mem. ATLA, Pa. Trial Lawyers Assn., Pa. Bar Assn., Allegheny County Bar Assn., Phi Beta Kappa. Personal injury, Product liability, General civil litigation. Office: Kapetan Meyers et al 437 Grant St Pittsburgh PA 15219-6002

**PERRY, LEE ROWAN,** retired lawyer; b. Chgo., Sept. 23, 1933; s. Watson Bishop and Helen (Rowan) P.; m. Barbara Ashcraft Mitchell, July 2, 1955; children: Christopher, Constance, Geoffrey. BA, U. Ariz., 1955, LLB, 1961. Bar: Ariz. 1961. Since practiced in Phoenix; clk. Udall & Udall, Tucson, 1960-61; mem. firm Carson, Messinger, Elliott, Laughlin & Ragan, 1961-99. Mem. law rev. staff, U. Ariz., 1959-61. Mem. bd. edn. Paradise Valley Elementary and High Sch. Dists., Phoenix, 1964-68, pres., 1968; treas. troop Boy Scouts Am., 1970-72; mem. Ariz. adv. bd. Girl Scouts U.S.A., 1972-74, mem. nominating bd., 1978-79; bd. dirs. Florence Crittenton Services Ariz., 1967-72, pres., 1970-72; bd. dirs. U. Ariz. Alumni, Phoenix, 1968-72, pres., 1969-70; bd. dirs. Family Service Phoenix, 1974-75; bd. dirs. Travelers Aid Assn. Am., 1985-89; bd. dirs. Vol. Bur. Maricopa County, 1975-81, 83-86, pres., 1984-85; bd. dirs. Ariz. div. Am. Cancer Soc., 1978-80, Florence Crittenton div. Child Welfare League Am., 1976-81; bd. dirs. Crisis Nursery for Prevention of Child Abuse, 1978-81, pres., 1978-80; Ariz. dir. Devereux Found., 1996—, vice chmn. 1996-98. 1st lt. USAF, 1955-58. Mem. State Bar Ariz. (conv. chmn. 1972), Rotary (dir. 1971-77, 95-96, pres. 1975-76, West Leadership award 1989), Ariz. Club (bd. dirs. 1994—, pres.-elect 1997-98, pres. 1998-99), Phoenix Country Club, Phi Delta Phi, Phi Delta Theta (pres. 1954). Republican. Episcopalian. E-mail: imlerp@att.net. Real property, Finance, General corporate. Home: 106 N Country Club Dr Phoenix AZ 85014-5443

**PERRY, MATTHEW J., JR.,** federal judge; b. 1921. BS, S.C. State U., 1948, LLB, 1951. Bar: S.C. Atty. Spartanburg, S.C., 1951-61, Columbia, S.C., 1961-76; judge U.S. Ct. Mil. Appeals, Washington, 1976-79; judge U.S. Dist. Ct., Columbia, 1979-95, sr. judge, 1995—; instr. law U. S.C., 1973-75. Office: US Dist Ct 1845 Assembly St Columbia SC 29201-2431

**PERRY, RONALD,** lawyer; b. Pitts., Feb. 20, 1952; s. Joseph E. and Margaret (Majhan) P.; m. Deborah Lauer, July 19, 1975; children: Meredith Lyn, Erin Michelle. BA in Polit. Sci., Ind. U., Pa., 1974; JD, Western New Eng. U., 1978; LLM in Taxation, Temple U., 1982. Bar: Pa. 1978, U.S. Dist. Ct. (mid. dist.) Pa. 1979, U.S. Tax Ct. 1980, U.S. Supreme Ct. 1984. Pvt. practice York, Pa., 1978-82; ptnr. Carn, Vaughn & Perry, York, 1982-85, Countess, Gilbert, Andrews, York, 1985—; asst. dist. atty., York County, 1982-85. Pres. Self-Help Counseling, York, 1978-84; bd. dirs. West York (Pa.) Sch. Dist., 1983-85, York County Jr. Achievement, 1998—, dir. White Rose Invitational track and Field Meet, 1998—; solicitor West York Zoning Bd., 1987-88; chmn. Manchester Twp. Planning Commn., 1992-98; pres. York County Literacy Coun., 1992-98; bd. dirs. Jr. Achievement York County. Mem. ABA, Pa. Bar Assn., York County Estate Planning Coun. (bd. dirs. 1986-91), Rotary Club. Avocation: music. Contracts commercial, Corporate taxation, Taxation, general. Office: Countess Gilbert Andrews 29 N Duke St York PA 17401-1204

**PERRY, ROTRAUD MEZGER,** lawyer; b. Berlin, Aug. 29, 1927; came to U.S., 1927; d. Fritz and Luise (Scheuerle) M.; m. John Wilson Perry, Sept. 9, 1950; children: Erik David, Julia Louise, Kathleen Anne, Duncan Gerrit, Ellen Eva. AB, Bryn Mawr Coll., 1948; JD, U. Mich., 1952. Bar: D.C. 1954, Md. 1974, U.S. Supreme Ct. 1962. Various positions Library of Congress, Washington, 1947-50; atty. USN, Washington, 1955-56; sole practice Washington, 1957-78; ptnr. Perry & Perry, Washington, 1978-97; retired. Mem. Bar Assn. D.C., D.C. Bar Assn., Women's Bar Assn. D.C. (pres. 1975-76). Democrat. Probate, General practice, Public international. Home: 3511 Idaho Ave NW Washington DC 20016-3151

**PERRY, SHERRYL ROSENBAUM,** lawyer; b. Binghampton, N.Y., Mar. 5, 1941; d. Arthur J.S. and Miriam (Kantor) Rosenbaum; m. David Perry, June 24, 1962. BS in Biochemistry, Drexel U., 1963; MA in English, U. Pa., 1964; JD, Villanova U., 1979. Bar: Pa. 1979, U.S. Dist. Ct. (ea. dist.) Pa. 1979, U.S. Ct. Appeals (3d cir.) 1980. Assoc. Pepper, Hamilton & Scheetz, Phila., 1979-83; ptnr. Perry, Fialkowski & Perry, Phila., 1983—; lectr. Am. Law Inst. symposiums, 1983-86. Co-author: Planning, Financing and Construction Health Care Facilities, 1983. Mem. ABA (lectr. symposia 1983-86), ATLA, Pa. Bar Assn., Phila. Bar Assn., Def. Rsch. Inst. Republican. Avocations: photography, skiing,. Product liability, Personal injury, Professional liability. Home: 431 Boxwood Rd Bryn Mawr PA 19010-1254 Office: 1 Penn Sq W Ste 1600 Philadelphia PA 19102-4826 *Notable cases include: 1st punitive damage award against a hosp. in the Commonwealth of Pa., 1985; multimillion dollar verdict against 2 hosps. and 2 physicians, hosp. corp. liability a key allegation, 1987; one of largest multimillion dollar settlements in a med. malpractice case in State of N.J., 1990.*

**PERRY, TIMOTHY A.,** criminal justice educator; b. San Diego, Apr. 11, 1939; s. Sidney Lilburn and May (Babler) P.; m. Sherry Grace Maxwell, Apr. 8, 1972. BA in Police Sci. and Adminstrn., Seattle U., 1976. Cert. coll. prof., vocat. instr., Wash. Police officer Seattle Police Dept., 1966-77, tng. officer, 1977-84, narcotics detective, 1985-90; chief of police Clyde Hill (Wash.) Police Dept., 1984-85; prof. criminal justice Shoreline C.C., Seattle, 1990—, dir. criminal justice edn., 1993—; appeared on nat. programs, include King TV, King Radio, Kiro TV, Kiro Radio, Komo TV; cons. with attys. in civil law suits involving police issues; v.p., author Palladium Publs., Seattle, 1984-92; expert witness, cons. in field, 1988—; appointed Bd. Law Enforcement Tng., Stds. and Edn., Wash., 1997—; adv. bd. Police Corps., Wash., 1997. Author: Basic Patrol Procedures, The Practical Mockscene Manual, The Art of Criminal Investigation. Mem. Wash. Assn. Police Trainers, Wash. State Law Enforcement Educators Assn., Pacific Assn. Law Enforcement Educators, Internat. Assn. Chiefs of Police. Office: Shoreline CC 16101 Greenwood Ave N Seattle WA 98133-5667

**PERSCHBACHER, DEBRA BASSETT,** lawyer; b. Pleasanton, Calif., Oct. 28, 1956; d. James Arthur and Shirley Ann (Russell) Bassett; m. Rex Robert Perschbacher, June 4, 1989. BA, U. Vt., 1977; MS, San Diego State U., 1982; JD, U. Calif., Davis, 1987. Bar: Calif. 1987, D.C. 1990, U.S. Dist Ct. (no. and ea. dists.) Calif. 1988, U.S. Ct. Appeals (9th cir.), 1988, U.S. Supreme Ct., 1991. Guidance counselor Addison Cen. Supr. Union, Middlebury, Vt., 1982-83, Milton (Vt.) Elem. Sch., 1983-84; assoc. Morrison & Foerster, San Francisco, 1986; jud. clk. U.S. Ct. Appeals (9th cir.), Phoenix, 1987-88; assoc. Morrison & Foerster, San Francisco and Walnut Creek, Calif., 1988-92; sr. atty. Calif. Ct. Appeal (3d appellate dist.), Sacramento, 1992-99; tutor civil procedure, rsch. asst. U. Calif., Davis, 1985-87; instr. U. Calif. at Davis Ext., 1995—; lectr. law U. Calif., Davis, 1997—; adj. prof. law McGeorge Sch. Law, 1998-99; dir., legal process, McGeorge Sch. Law, 1999—. Sr. articles editor U. Calif. Law Rev., Davis, 1986-87; editor, 1985-86. Mem. Mozart Acad., 1998—, Sacramento Opera Chorus, 1998—. Mem. AAUW, ABA (vice chmn. ethics com. young lawyers divsn. 1989-91, exec. com. labor and employment law com. 1989-90), Sacramento County Bar Assn., Women Lawyers of Sacramento. Democrat. Avocations: music, tennis, travel, hiking. Home: 1541 39th St Sacramento CA 95816-6720 Office: McGeorge Sch Law 3200 5th Ave Sacramento CA 95817-2799

**PERSCHBACHER, REX ROBERT,** dean, law educator; b. Chgo., Aug. 31, 1946; s. Robert Ray and Nancy Ellen (Beach) P.; m. Debbie Bassett Hamilton; children: Julie Ann, Nancy Beatrice. AB in Philosophy, Stanford U., 1968; JD, U. Calif., Berkeley, 1972. Bar: Calif. 1972, U.S. Dist. Ct. (no. dist.) Calif. 1973, U.S. Dist. Ct. (so. dist.) Calif. 1979, U.S. Ct. Appeals (9th cir.) 1980, U.S. Dist. ct. (ea. dist.) Calif. 1985. Law clk. to judge U.S. Dist. Ct. (no. dist.) Calif., San Francisco, 1973-74; asst. prof. law U. Tex., Austin, 1974-75; assoc. Heller, Ehrman, White & McAuliffe, San Francisco, 1975-78; asst. prof. law U. San Diego, 1978-79, assoc. prof. law, 1980-81; mem. faculty Inst. on Internat. and Comparative Law, London, 1984—; acting prof. law U. Calif., Davis, 1981-85, prof., 1988—, assoc. dean, 1993-98, dean Law Sch., 1998—; dir. clin. edn. Univ. Calif., Davis, 1981-93, acad. senate, law sch. rep., 1989-91; vis. prof. law Univ. Santa Clara (Calif.), summer 1986. Co-author: California Civil Procedure, 1987, California Legal Ethics, 1992, Problems in Legal Ethics, Cases and Materials on Civil Procedure; contbr. articles to legal jours. Bd. dirs. Legal Svcs. of No. Calif., 1990—. Mem. ABA, Calif. Bar Assn., Am. Assn. Law Schs., Inn of Ct. Democrat. Avocations: hiking, travel. Office: U Calif Sch Law King Hall Davis CA 95616*

**PESHKIN, SAMUEL DAVID,** lawyer; b. Des Moines, Oct. 6, 1925; s. Louis and Mary (Grund) P.; m. Shirley R. Isenberg, Aug. 17, 1947; children—Lawrence Allen, Linda Ann. BA, State U. Iowa, 1948, JD, 1951. Bar: Iowa 1951. Ptnr. Bridges & Peshkin, Des Moines, 1953-66, Peshkin & Robinson, Des Moines, 1966-82; Mem. Iowa Bd. Law Examiners, 1970—. Bd. dirs. State U. Iowa Found., 1957—, Old Gold Devel. Fund, 1956—, Sch. Religion U. Iowa, 1966—. Fellow Am. Bar Found., Internat. Soc. Barristers; mem. ABA (chmn. standing com. membership 1959—, ho. of dels. 1968—, bd. govs. 1973—), Iowa Bar Assn. (bd. govs. 1958—, pres. jr. bar sect. 1958-59, award of merit 1974), Inter-Am. Bar Assn., Internat. Bar Assn., Am. Judicature Soc., State U. Iowa Alumni Assn. (dir., pres. 1957). Private international, General corporate, Corporate taxation. Home: 6445 E Winchcomb Dr Scottsdale AZ 85254-3356

**PESIKOFF, BETTE SCHEIN,** lawyer; b. N.Y.C., Oct. 9, 1942; d. Stephen and Ethel (Barrett) Schein; m. Richard B. Pesikoff, June 7, 1964; children: David, Josh, Daniel. BS, NYU, 1963, MA, 1964; JD, U. Houston, 1974. Bar: Tex. 1974, U.S. Dist. Ct. (so. dist.) Tex. 1975, U.S. Patent & Trademark. Tchr. N.Y.C. Bd. Edn., 1964-68; pvt. practice Houston, 1977—. Chmn. social action com. Cong. Emam El, Houston, 1985-87, bd. dirs., sec., 1986-88; mem. community rels. com. Jewish Fedn. Houston, 1986-88; mem. Tex. Supreme Ct. Child Support Guidelines Commn., 1986-87. Fellow Tex. Bar Found.; mem. ABA, Houston Bar Assn. (sec. family law sect. 1986-87), Gulf Coast Family Law Specialists. Democrat. Family and matrimonial, Probate, General practice. Office: 1715 North Blvd Houston TX 77098-5413

**PESTA, BEN W., II,** lawyer, writer; b. Hagerstown, Md., Oct. 15, 1948; s. Ben W. and Ethel Irene (Kirkpatrick) P.; m. Monique Raphel High, Dec. 24, 1987. AB, UCLA, 1969; JD, U. Calif., Berkeley, 1972. Assoc. pub. Weider Health & Fitness, Woodland Hills, Calif., 1984-90. Contbr. Esquire, Playboy, Rolling Stone, Sport, TV Guide, Cosmopolitan, L.A. Style mags. and profl. jours. Capt. USAF., 1973. Criminal, Appellate. Office: 10000 Santa Monica Blvd Ste 320 Los Angeles CA 90067-7007

**PETAK, DEVERA L.,** lawyer; b. Paterson, N.J., Oct. 22, 1953; d. Joseph Andrew and Margaret Victoria Petak. BA, Calif. State U. Stanislaus, Turlock, 1975; JD, Western State U., Fullerton, Calif., 1979. With Beam Dicaro D'Anthny, L.A., 1984-89, Kornblum Ferry & Frye, San Francisco, 1989-92; ptnr. Presthoet, Patrak, Kleeger Fidone & Villasenn, San Francisco, 1992-96, Zelle & Larsos LLp, L.A., 1996—. Mem. Calif. Bar Assn., L.A. Bar Assn., San Francisco Bar Assn., L.A. Women Lawyers Assn., So. Calif. Def. Lawyers, Rotter Group. Insurance. Office: Zelle & Larson LLP 11601 Wilshire Blvd Fl 6 Los Angeles CA 90025-1770

**PETER, ARNOLD PHILIMON,** lawyer, business executive; b. Karachi, Pakistan, Apr. 3, 1957; came to U.S., 1968; s. Kundan Lal and Irene Primrose (Mall) P. BS, Calif. State U., Long Beach, 1981; JD, Loyola U., L.A., 1984; MS, Calif. State U., Fresno, 1991. Bar: Calif. 1985, U.S. Dist. Ct. (ea., so., no. and cen. dists.) Calif. 1986, U.S. Ct. Appeals (9th cir.) 1989, U.S. Ct. Appeals (11th cir.) 1990. Law clk. appellate dept. Superior Ct., L.A., 1984-85, U.S. Dist. Ct. (ea. dist.) Calif., Fresno, 1986-88; assoc. Pepper, Hamilton & Scheetz, L.A., 1988-89, McDermott, Will & Emery, P.A., L.A., 1989-90, Cadwalader, Wickersham & Taft, L.A., 1990-91; labor and employment counsel City of Fresno, Calif., 1991-94; atty. Littler Mendelson, L.A., 1999—; v.p. legal and bus. affairs Universal Studios, Hollywood, Calif., 1994—; adj. prof. law San Joaquin (Calif.) Sch. Law, 1993—; adj. prof. law Calif. State U., Fresno, 1993—, acad. inquiry officer, 1993—. Contbr. articles to profl. jours. Mem. ABA, L.A. County Bar Assn. (mem. conf. of dels., com. on fed. cts.), Calif. State Bar Assn. (chmn. com. on fed. cts., chmn. exec. com. labor and employment law sect.), L.A. Athletic Club, Friars Club. Federal civil litigation, Labor, State civil litigation. Office: Universal Studios 100 Universal City Plz Universal Cty CA 91608-1002

**PETER, LAURA ANNE,** lawyer; b. Santa Monica, Calif., June 17, 1964; d. Gabriel George Pitta and Barbara Joyce (Leomazzi) P. BS, Cornell U., 1986; MA, U. Chgo., 1988; JD, Santa Clara U., 1992; LLM, U. London, 1994. Bar: U.S. Patent and Trademark Office, 1989, Calif. 1992, U.S. Dist. Ct. (ctrl. and no. dists.) Calif. 1992, U.S. Ct. Appeals (9th cir.) 1992. Assoc. Law Offices of Rafael Chodos, Santa Monica, 1995-97; mgr. Rancho de Vino, Monterey, Calif., 1991-93; adj. prof. Santa Clara U. Contbr. articles to profl. jours. Fellow The UN Grad. Study Programme, Geneva, Switzerland, 1987; recipient Hague (The Netherlands) Acad. Internat., 1993. Mem. ABA, Internat. Bar Assn., Internat. Lit. and Artistic Assn., Licensing Execs. Soc. Fax: (415) 576-0300. E-mail: lap@townsend.com. Intellectual property, Entertainment, Private international. Office: Townsend & Townsend & Crew 2 Embarcadero Ctr Lbby 8 San Francisco CA 94111-3822

**PETER, PHILLIPS SMITH,** lawyer; b. Washington, Jan. 24, 1932; s. Edward Compston and Anita Phillips (Smith) P.; m. Jania Jayne Hutchins, Apr. 8, 1961; children: Phillips Smith Peter Jr., Jania Jayne Hutchins Stone. BA, U. Va., 1954, JD, 1959. Bar: Calif. 1959. Assoc. McCutchen, Doyle, Brown, Enerson, San Francisco, 1959-63; with GE (and subs.), various locations, 1963-94; v.p. corp. bus. devel. GE (and subs.), 1973-76; v.p. GE (and subs.), Washington, 1976-79, v.p. corp. govtl. rels., 1980-94; counsel, head govt. rels. dept. Reed Smith Shaw & McClay, Washington, 1994—; chmn. bd. govs. Bryce Harlow Found., 1990-92, bd. dirs. Mem. editl. bd. Va. Law Rev., 1957-59. Trustee Howard U., 1981-89; bd. dirs., exec. com. Nat. Bank of Washington, 1981-86; v.p. Fed. City Coun., Washington, 1979-85; bd. dirs. Carlton, 1987-90, 95-98, pres., 1995-96. With transp. corps U.S. Army, 1954-56. Mem. Calif. Bar Assn., Order of Coif, Wee Burn Club, Ea. Yacht Club, Farmington Country Club, Ponte Vedra Club, Lago Mar Club, Landmark Club, Congl. Country Club, Georgetown Club, Chevy Chase Club, Pisces Club, F Street Club, Fairfax Club, Carlton Club (bd. dirs. 1990—), Coral Beach and Tennis Club, Johns Island Club, The Windsor Club, Omicron Delta Kappa. Episcopalian. General corporate, Public international, Corporate taxation. Home: 10805 Tara Rd Potomac MD 20854-1341 also: Johns Island 1000 Beach Rd & 690 Ocean Vero Beach FL 32963-3429

**PETERMAN, ROGER LEE,** lawyer; b. Yasilati, Mich., Oct. 26, 1953; s. Lloyd Edward and Agnes Eloise Peterman; m. Mary Margaret Galuardi, Aug. 23, 1975; children: Christina, Elizabeth, Robert. BA in Econs., U. Ky., 1975, JD, 1979. Exec. dir. Ky. Devel. Fin. Authority, Frankfort, 1981-83; ptnr. Peck, Shaffer & Williams LLP, Covington, Ky., 1983—. Contbr. articles to profl. jours. Chmn. No. Ky. Port Authority, Ft. Mitchel, 1975—; bd. mem. Tri-County Econ. Devel. Corp., Ft. Mitchel, 1992-98; city councilman City of Ft. Thomas, 1999—. Mem. ABA, Ky. Bar Assn., Leadership Ky. Alumni Assn. Home: 129 Riverside Pkwy Fort Thomas KY 41075-1142 Office: Pecke Shaffer & Williams LLP 118 W 5th St Covington KY 41011-1481

**PETERMANN, TONYA C.,** lawyer; b. Ft. Walton Beach, Fla., Dec. 17, 1967; d. Thomas Earl and Janice Anita (Bulger) Collins; m. June 3, 1995 (div. Oct. 1997); m. Steven Craig Petermann, May 5, 1998. AA, Okaloosa Waltam C.C., Niceville, Fla., 1987; BA, U. West Fla., 1990; JD, Cumberland Sch. Law, 1993. Bar: Fla. 1993. Atty. John P. Townsend, P.A., Ft. Walton Beach, 1993-95, Stephen Poche, P.A., Shalinar, Fla., 1995—. Family and matrimonial. Office: PO Box 130 Shalimar FL 32579-0130

**PETERS, AULANA LOUISE,** lawyer, former government agency commissioner; b. Shreveport, La., Nov. 30, 1941; d. Clyde A. and Eula Mae (Faulkner) Pharis; m. Bruce F. Peters, Oct. 6, 1967. BA in Philosophy, Coll. New Rochelle, 1963; JD, U. So. Calif., 1973. Bar: Calif., 1974. Sec., English corr. Publimondial, Spa, Milan, Italy, 1963-64, Fibramianto, Spa, Milan, 1964-65, Turkish del. to Office for Econ. Cooperation & Devel., Paris, 1965-66; adminstrv. asst. Office for Econ. Cooperation & Devel., Paris, 1966-67; assoc. Gibson, Dunn & Crutcher, L.A., 1973-80, ptnr., 1980-84, 88—; commr. SEC, Washington, 1984-88; bd. dirs. 3M Corp., Merrill Lynch & Co., Mobil Corp., Northrop Grumman, Callaway Golf Co. Recipient Disting. Alumnus award Econs. Club So. Calif., 1984, Washington Achiever award Nat. Assn. Bank Women, 1986, Critics Choice award nat. Women's Econ. Alliance, 1994, Women in Bus. award HOllywood C. of C., 1995. Mem. ABA, State Bar of Calif. (civil litigation cons. group 1983-84), Los Angeles County Bar Assn., Black Women Lawyers Assn. L.A., Assn. Bus. Trial Lawyers (panelist L.A. 1982), Women's Forum, Washington. Administrative and regulatory, Federal civil litigation, General civil litigation. Office: Gibson Dunn & Crutcher 333 S Grand Ave Ste 4400 Los Angeles CA 90071-3197

**PETERS, DANIEL WADE,** lawyer; b. Carroll, Iowa, Sept. 5, 1969; s. Howard B. and Madelyn R. Peters; m. Tamra J. Schmeidler, Oct. 13, 1990; children: Leighton D., Dylan L. BBA in Econs. and Fin., Washburn U., 1991; JD, U. Denver, 1994. Bar: Kans. 1994, Mo. 1997. Gen. counsel Medstaff Mgmt. Corp., Topeka, 1994-95; assoc. Holbrook, Heaven & Osborn, Kansas City, Kans., 1996—; lectr. in field. Mem. ABA, Healthcare Fin. Mgmt. Assn., Am. Health Lawyers Assn., Kans. Bar Assn., Mo. Bar Assn. Health, General corporate, Contracts commercial. Office: Holbrook Heaven & Osborn PO Box 17192 757 Armstrong Ave Kansas City KS 66101-2701

**PETERS, ELLEN ASH,** state supreme court justice; b. Berlin, Mar. 21, 1930; came to U.S., 1939, naturalized, 1947; d. Ernest Edward and Hildegard (Simon) Ash; m. Phillip I. Blumberg; children: David Bryan Peters, James Douglas Peters, Julie Peters Haden. BA with honors, Swarthmore Coll., 1951, LLD (hon.), 1983; LLB cum laude, Yale U., 1954, MA (hon.), 1964, LLD (hon.), 1985; LLD (hon.), U. Hartford, 1983; Georgetown U., 1984; LLD (hon.), Yale U., 1985, Conn. Coll., 1985, N.Y. Law Sch., 1985; HLD (hon.), St. Joseph Coll., 1986; LLD (hon.), Colgate U., 1986, Trinity Coll., 1987, Bates Coll., 1987, Wesleyan U., 1987, DePaul U., 1988; HLD (hon.), Albertus Magnus Coll., 1990; LLD (hon.), U. Conn., 1992; LLD, U. Rochester, 1994. Bar: Conn. 1957. Law clk. to judge U.S. Circuit Ct., 1954-55; assoc. in law U. Calif., Berkeley, 1955-56; prof. law Yale U., New Haven, 1956-78, adj. prof. law, 1978-84; assoc. justice Conn. Supreme Ct., Hartford, 1978-84, chief justice, 1984-96, sr. justice, 1996—. Author: Commercial Transactions: Cases, Texts, and Problems, 1971, Negotiable Instruments Primer, 1974; contbr. articles to profl. jours. Bd. mgrs. Swarthmore Coll., 1970-81; trustee Yale-New Haven Hosp., 1981-85, Yale Corp., 1986-92; mem. conf. Chief Justices, 1984—, pres., 1994; hon. chmn. U.S. Constl. Bicentennial Com., 1986-91; mem. Conn. Permanent Commn. on Status of Women, 1973-74, Conn. Bd. Pardons, 1978-80, Conn. Law Revision Commn., 1978-84; bd. dirs. Nat. Ctr. State Cts., 1992-96, chmn., 1994, Hartford Found., 1997—. Recipient Ella Grasso award, 1982, Jud. award Conn. Trial Lawyers Assn., 1982, citation of merit Yale Law Sch., 1983, Pioneer Woman award Hartford Coll. for Women, 1988, Disting. Svc. award U. Conn. Law Sch. Alumni Assn., 1993, Raymond E. Baldwin Pub. Svc. award Quinnipiac Coll. Law Sch., 1995, Disting. Svc. award Conn. Law Tribune, 1996, Nat. Ctr. State Cts., 1996; named Laura A. Johnson Woman of Yr. Hartford Coll., 1996. Mem. ABA, Conn. Bar Assn. (Jud. award 1992, Spl. award 1996), Am. Law Inst. (coun.), Am. Acad. Arts and Scis., Am. Philos. Soc. Office: Conn Supreme Ct Drawer N Sta A 231 Capitol Ave Hartford CT 06106-1548

**PETERS, FRANK AUGUST,** lawyer; b. Seattle, Aug. 12, 1919; s. Carl A. and Ellen (Fagerquist) P.; m. Gertrude B. Peters, July 20, 1946 (dec. Sept. 1986); m. Bonnie D. Peters. BA, U. Wash., 1940, LLB, 1946. Bar: Wash. 1946, U.S. Dist. Ct. (Wash.) 1946, U.S. Ct. Appeals (9th cir.) 1946, U.S. Supreme Ct. 1964. Law clk. to presiding justice U.S. Ct. Appeals (9th cir.), San Francisco, 1946-47; sole practice Tacoma and Puyallup, Wash., 1947—. Contbr. articles to legal and other jours. Pres. Puyallup Rotary Club, 1950. Served to lt. USN, 1942-46, PTO. Mem. Nat. Assn. Criminal Def. Attys., Assn. Trial Lawyers Am., Wash. State Bar Assn. (disciplinary hearing officer Tacoma chpt. 1985—), Wash. State Trial Lawyers Assn. Lodge: Elks. Criminal, Personal injury, Probate. Home: 3507 NE 182nd St Lk Forest Park WA 98155-4221 Office: PO Box 1738 Tacoma WA 98401-1738

**PETERS, FREDERICK WHITTEN,** lawyer; b. Omaha, Aug. 20, 1946; s. Jordan Holt and Elizabeth (O'Bryant) P.; m. Mary Gores Peters, Jan. 2, 1969; children: Mary Irvin, Elizabeth Holt, Margaret Etheridge. BA magna cum laude, Harvard U., 1968; MS with distinction, London Sch. Econs., 1973; JD magna cum laude, Harvard U., 1976. Bar: D.C. 1978, U.S. Dist. Ct. D.C. 1978, U.S. Dist. Ct. Md., 1994, U.S. Ct. Appeals (3d and D.C. cirs.) 1979, U.S. Ct. Claims 1981, U.S. Ct. Appeals (11th cir.) 1986, U.S. Ct. Mil. Appeals 1993. Law clk. to presiding judge U.S. Ct. Appeals (D.C. cir.), Washington, 1976-77; law clk. to justice William J. Brennan U.S. Supreme Ct., Washington, 1977-78; assoc. Williams & Connolly, Washington, 1978-84, ptnr., 1984-95; prin. dep. gen. counsel Dept. of Defense, 1995-97, undersec., acting sec. USAF, 1997-99, sec. USAF, 1999—; mem. legal ethics com. D.C. Bar, 1988-94, chmn. rules rev. com., 1991-96; rules com. U.S. Ct. Mil. Appeals, 1993-95. Pres. Harvard Law Rev., 1975-76. Bd. dirs. Cleveland Park Hist. Soc., Washington, 1986-91, Washington Area Lawyers for the Arts, 1987-93; mem. adv. com. on streamlining procurement laws DOD, 1991-93. Lt. USNR, 1969-72. Fellow Am. Bar Found.; mem. ABA. Democrat. Episcopalian. Avocations: sailing, tennis, computer sci. Criminal, Federal civil litigation, Computer. Home: 3250 Highland Pl NW Washington DC 20008-3231 Office: Undersec USAF Rm 4E886 1670 Air Force Pentagon Washington DC 20330-1670

**PETERS, JOAN SCHLUMP,** lawyer; b. Plainfield, N.J., June 19, 1961; d. John A. and Angela C. (Casciano) Schlump; married June 24, 1989; children: Jonathan, Jeremy, Gillian. BA cum laude, Wellesley Coll., 1983; JD, Georgetown U., 1986. Bar: N.Y. 1987, U.S. Dist. Ct. P.R. 1991, U.S. Ct. Appeals (1st cir.) 1987. Judicial clk., Hon. Juan R. Torruella 1st Circuit Ct. Appeals, Boston, 1986-87; assoc. Stroock, Stroock & Lavan, N.Y.C., 1987-89; judicial clk., Hon. Hector Laffitte Fed. Dist. Ct. P.R., San Juan, 1990-91; assoc., litigation Nachman, Guillemard & Rebollo, San Juan, 1992—. Home and Office: 37 Highview Ave Old Greenwich CT 06870-1703

**PETERS, KEVIN RICHARD,** lawyer; b. Evergreen Park, Ill., Mar. 18, 1952; s. Robert and LaVergne Agnes Peters; m. Darlene Aurelia Kmiec, May 29, 1988; 1 child, Darcy. BA, Millikin U., 1974; JD, John Marshall Law Sch., 1983. Bar: U.S. Dist. Ct. (no. dist.) Ill. 1983, U.S. Dist. Ct. (mid. dist.) 1994. Asst. states atty. Dekalb County, Sycamore, Ill., 1983-84; asst. pub. defender Cook County Pub. Defender, Chgo., 1984-94; pvt. practice Chgo., 1994—. Mem. Chgo. Bar Assn., Nat. Assn. Criminal Def. Lawyers. Avocations: camping, basketball. Criminal, Civil rights. Office: 542 S Dearborn St Ste 750 Chicago IL 60605-1525

**PETERS, LEE IRA, JR.,** public defender; b. Jamestown, N.Y., Dec. 17, 1946; s. Lee Ira and Carrie Irene (Roberson) P.; m. Mabel Luisa Thompson, June 21, 1969; children: Tammy M., Lee III, Ryan J. BA in Criminology, Fla. State U., 1971; JD, U. Fla., 1984. Bar: Fla. 1984, U.S. Dist Ct. (mid. dist.) Fla. 1989. Sr. intern Pub. Defender State of Fla., Gainesville, Fla., 1983; spl. asst. U.S. Atty No. Dist. Fla., Tallahassee, 1987-89; asst. states atty. 3d cir. State's Atty. Office, Live Oak, Fla., 1984-89; asst. pub. defender, felony divsn. chief 3rd cir. Pub. Defender's Office, Live Oak, 1989—; spl. agt. crim. investigation Bur. ATF- U.S. Treas., Anniston, Ala., Boise, Idaho, 1971-77, resident agt.-in-charge Portland, Oreg., 1977-81; assoc. counsel (pro bono) Nat. Assn. Treas. Agts., 1993—. With USN, 1965-67, Vietnam, U.S. Army Res., 1981-95. Recipient Disting Svc. award Fla. Coun. Crime & Delinquency, Chpt. XV, 1989; Meritorious Svc. Sec. Army U.S., 1997. Mem. ACLU, Fla. Assn. Criminal Def. Lawyers, Fla. Bar Assn. (3d cir. grievance com. 1993-96), Acad. Fla. Trial Lawyers, 3d Cir. Bar Assn., Am. Legion (fin. officer post 107, Live Oak), McAlpin Comty. Club (pres. 1990-96), Rotary Club, Elks, Phi Alpha Delta. Avocation: cattle and Arabian horse raising. Office: Third Cir Pub Defender 106 Ohio Ave S Live Oak FL 32060-3212

**PETERS, R. JONATHAN,** lawyer, chemical company executive; b. Janesville, Wis., Sept. 6, 1927; m. Ingrid H. Varvayn, 1953; 1 dau., Christina. B.S. in Chemistry, U. Ill., 1951; J.D., Northwestern U., 1954. Bar: Ill. 1954. Chief patent counsel Englehard Industries, 1972-82, Kimberly-Clark Corp., Neenah, Wis., 1982-85; gen. counsel Lanxide Corp., Newark, Del., 1985-87; pvt. practice Chgo., 1985—. Served with CIC, U.S. Army, 1955-57. Patentee in field. Mem. ABA, Am. Intellectual Property Law Assn., Lic. Execs. Soc., Assn. Corp. Patent Counsel. Clubs: North Shore Golf (Menasha, Wis.), Masons, Scottish Rite, Shriners. Patent, Trademark and copyright.

**PETERS, RICHARD,** lawyer; b. Bklyn., June 6, 1945; s. Edmund Richard and Louise (Parks) P. BA, Tulane U., 1967; MA, Fla. State U., 1968, PhD, 1985; JD, Calif. Western, 1988. Bar: Calif. 1989. Instr. English U. San Diego, 1991, San Diego City Coll., 1989—, San Diego Mesa Coll., 1989—; panel atty. Appellate Defenders, Inc., San Diego, 1989—. Author: (poetry) On Aging, 1991. Mem. ABA, San Diego County Bar Assn. Office: Richard Peters Atty 5690 Greenshade Rd San Diego CA 92121-4230

**PETERS, ROBERT TIMOTHY,** judge; b. Memphis, Dec. 28, 1946; s. Rhulin Earl and Bertie Nichols (Moore) P.; m. Ruth Audrey Allen, Dec. 11, 1973; children: Lindsay Elizabeth, Christopher Andrew. AA, St. Petersburg Jr. Coll., 1969; BA, U. Fla., 1971, JD, 1973. Bar: Fla. 1973, U.S. Dist. Ct. (mid. dist.) Fla. 1977, U.S. Ct. Appeals (5th cir.) 1981; cert. real estate lawyer. Ptnr. Goza, Hall & Peters P.A., Clearwater, Fla., 1973-84; sole practice Clearwater, 1984-95; apptd. cir. judge Fla., 1995—; Gov. Fla.'s appointee Condominium Study Commsn., Clearwater, 1990-91. Columnist Clearwater Sun newspaper, 1985—. 1st Lt. U.S. Army, 1966-68, Vietnam. Decorated Silver Star, Purple Heart, Bronze Star with oak leaf cluster. Mem. Fla. Bar (condominium and planned devel. com.), Clearwater Bar Assn. Avocations: reading, exercise. Office: 14250 49th St N Clearwater FL 33762-2800 Address: PO Box 6316 Clearwater FL 33758-6316

**PETERS, SAMUEL ANTHONY,** lawyer; b. N.Y.C., Oct. 25, 1934; s. Clyde and Amy (Matterson) P.; m. Ruby M.Mitchell, Apr. 28, 1962; children: Robert, Samuel, Bernard. BA, NYU; LLB, Fordham U. Bar: N.Y. 1961, Calif. 1973, U.S. Supreme Ct. 1967. Trial atty. Dept. Justice, 1961-68; staff atty. Lawyer's Com. for Civil Rights Under Law, 1968-69; atty. legal dept. Atlantic Richfield Co., L.A., 1970, litigation counsel, price and wage control counsel, 1970-73, labor counsel, 1972-79, sr. counsel pub. affairs, 1980-85; assoc. law prof. Rio Hondo Coll.; bd. dirs. Weingart Ctr. Assn., Women's Transitional Living Ctr. With U.S. Army, 1955-58. Mem. ABA (mem. approval commn., standing com. on legal assts.), Langston Bar Assn., L.A. County Bar Assn., Toastmasters Internat. (v.p. edn. chpt. 1391), Alpha Phi Alpha. Education and schools, General practice, Alternative dispute resolution. Home: 11471 Kensington Rd Los Alamitos CA 90720-3803

**PETERS, STEPHEN JAY,** lawyer; b. Jeffersonville, Ind., Apr. 15, 1955; s. Jerome Humphrey and Mildred Mae (Cooper) P.; m. Paula Gail Zaremba, Oct. 12, 1985; 1 child, Kirsten Alexandra. BA cum laude, Amherst Coll., 1977; JD, Ind. U., 1980. Bar: Ind. 1981, U.S. Dist. Ct. (so. dist.) Ind. 1981, U.S. Ct. Appeals (7th cir.) 1982, U.S. Dist. Ct. (no. dist.) Ind. 1983, U.S. Supreme Ct. 1985. Assoc. Stewart, Irwin, Gilliom, Fuller & Meyer, Indpls., 1980-85, Stewart, Irwin, Gilliom, Meyer & Guthrie, Indpls., 1985-87; ptnr. Stewart & Irwin, Indpls., 1987—. Author, editor: (book) Litigating Insurance Claims in Indiana, 1992. Named Outstanding Young Man in Am., U.S. Jaycees, 1984. Mem. ABA, Def. Rsch. Inst., Ind. State Bar Assn., 7th Cir. Bar Assn., Ind. Def. Lawyers Assn., Lawyers Club Indpls. General civil litigation, Insurance, Labor. Office: 251 E Ohio St Ste 1100 Indianapolis IN 46204-2147

**PETERS, THOMAS HARRY,** lawyer; b. Stephenville, Nfld., Can., Apr. 6, 1966; s. Bruce H. and Nancy J. Peters. BA, Trinity U., San Antonio, 1988; JD, Duke U., 1992. Bar: Calif. 1992, U.S. Dist. Ct. (ctrl., no., so. and ea. dists.) Calif. 1993, U.S. Ct. Appeals (9th cir.) 1993. Assoc. Breidenbach, Swainston, Crispo & Way, L.A., 1992-94, Fogel, Feldman, Ostrov, Ringler & Klevens, L.A., 1994—. Mem. ACLU. Recipient Wiley W. Manuel award for pro bono legal svcs. State Bar of Calif., 1997. Mem. ATLA, Consumer Attys. of Calif., Consumer Attys. Assn. of L.A. (bd. govs. 1996—). Personal injury, Product liability, Professional liability. Office: Fogel Feldman Ostrov Ringler & Klevens 1620 26th St Ste 100 Santa Monica CA 90404-4059

**PETERS, THOMAS P., II,** lawyer; b. Lewiston, Maine; s. Nelson M.J. and Wilma G. P.; m. Jeanne; children: William, Sarah, John. BA, Bates Coll., 1972; MS in Edn., U. Maine, Gorham, 1975; JD, Franklin Pierce Law Sch., 1983. Bar: Maine 1983. Owner Peters & Randlett, Attys., Lewiston, 1983-96; pres., owner Thomas P. Peters II & Assocs., P.A., Lewiston, 1996—; Dir. svcs. Tri-County Mental Health, Lewiston, 1976-80; chmn. Andruscoggin Head Start, Lewiston, 1985-91; corporator Ctrl. Maine Med. Ctr., Lewiston, 1992-96; complaint justice State Maine, 1990—; prof. law Lewiston Regional Tech. Ctr., 1990—. Recipient Kenneth Jordan award for outstanding citizen, 1993, 96; Fed. Rsch. grantee NIH, 1968. Mem. Maine Trial Lawyers Assn., Andruscoggin County Bar. Personal injury, Probate, Family and matrimonial. Office: Thomas P Peters II & Assocs PA 937 Main St Lewiston ME 04240-5154

**PETERS, VICTORIA L.,** prosecutor; b. Detroit, Feb. 16, 1956; d. Leslie L. and Elizabeth J. (Mullen) P. BA, George Washington U., 1979; JD, U. Denver, 1984. Bar: Colo. 1984, U.S. Ct. Appeals (D.C. cir.) 1992. Assoc. Goldsmith & Luby P.C., Denver, 1984-88; asst. atty. gen. Atty. Gen.'s Office, Denver, 1988-92, sr. asst. atty. gen., 1992—. Recipient Regional Adminstr.'s award for coop. excellence EPA, Denver, 1989, Cert. of Appreciation, Sierra Club, 1993. Avocation: horses. Home: 2025 Field St Lakewood CO 80215-1721 Office: Atty Gen's Office 1525 Sherman St Denver CO 80203-1714

**PETERS, WILLIAM JAMES,** lawyer; b. Washington, Jan. 12, 1967; s. Richard Jacob and Concepcion Valera Peters; m. Maria Christine Peters, July 19, 1992; children: Matthew James, Natalie Christine. BA, UCLA, 1990; JD, Loyola U., 1994. Corp. counsel MCI Systemhouse, L.A., 1994-96; assoc. Milbank, Tweed, Hadley & McCloy, L.A., 1996-99; dir. legal Exult, Irvine, 1999—. Computer, Intellectual property.

**PETERSEN, BENTON LAURITZ,** paralegal; b. Salt Lake City, Jan. 1, 1942; s. Lauritz George and Arleane (Curtis) P.; m. Sharon Donnette Higgins, Sept. 20, 1974 (div. Aug. 9, 1989); children: Grant Lauritz, Tashya Eileen, Nicholas Robert, Katrina Arleane. AA, Weber State Coll., 1966, BA, 1968; BA, Weber State Coll., 1968; M of Liberal Studies, U. Okla., 1980; diploma, Nat. Radio Inst. Paralegal Sch., 1991; JD, Monticello U., 1999. Registered paralegal. Announcer/news dir. KWHO Radio, Salt Lake City, 1968-70, KDXU Radio, St. George, Utah, 1970-73, KSOP Radio, Salt Lake City, 1973-76; case worker/counselor Salvation Army, Midland, Tex., 1976-84; announcer/news dir. KBRS Radio, Springdale, Ark., 1984-86; case worker/counselor Office of Human Concern, Rogers, Ark., 1986-88; announcer KAZM Radio, Sedona, Ariz., 1988-91; paralegal Benton L. Petersen, Manti, Utah, 1991—; cons. Sanpete County Srs., Manti, 1992—. Award judge Manti City Beautification, 1992-96; treas. Manti Destiny Com., 1993-98; tourism com. Sanpete County Econ. Devel., Ephraim, Utah, 1993-96. Served with U.S. Army N.G., 1959-66. Mem. Nat. Assn. Federated Tax Preparers, Nat. Paralegal Assn., Am. Assn. Christian Counselors. Mem. LDS Ch. Avocations: reading, participating in Doctor Who role playing games. Home: 470 E 120 N Manti UT 84642-0011

**PETERSEN, ELISABETH SARANEC,** lawyer; b. New Haven, July 25, 1947; d. Edmund Carl and Phyllis Marie (Ross) Saranec; m. (div.); children: Erika Anne, Aili Kristina. AB, Vassar Coll., 1969; JD, Duke U., 1972. Bar: N.C. 1972, U.S. Dist. Ct. (mid. and ea. dists.) N.C. 1972, U.S. Ct. Appeals (4th cir.) 1976, U.S. Supreme Ct. 1979. Assoc. W. Paul Pulley, Durham, N.C., 1972-75; pvt. practice Durham, 1975—; panel trustee U.S. Bankruptcy Ct., mid. dist., N.C., 1978—. Mem. ABA, Nat. Assn. Consumer Bankruptcy Attys. (sec. 1994-96), N.C. Bar Assn., Nat. Assn. Bankruptcy Trustees, N.C. Women Lawyers Assn., Vassar Club. Democrat. Roman Catholic. Bankruptcy, Consumer commercial. Office: Ste 110B 3326 Durham Chapel Hill Blvd Durham NC 27707-6241

**PETERSEN, JAMES LEO,** lawyer; b. Bloomington, Ill., Feb. 3, 1947; s. Eugene and Cathryn Theresa (Hemmele) P.; m. Helen Louise Moser, Nov. 20, 1971; children: Christine Louise, Margaret Theresa. BA, Ill. State U., 1970; MA, U. Ill., Springfield, 1973; JD magna cum laude, Ind. U., 1976. Bar: Ind. 1976, Fla. 1980, U.S. Dist. Cts. (no. and so. Ind.), U.S. Ct. Appeals (7th cir.), U.S. Supreme Ct. Admissions officer U. Ill., Springfield, 1970-71, asst. to v.p., 1971-72, registrar, 1972-73; assoc. Ice Miller Donadio & Ryan, Indpls., 1976-83, ptnr., 1983—. Pres. United Cerebral Palsy of Ctrl. Ind., 1981-83, pres. Found., 1988-90. Mem. ABA, Fla. Bar Assn., Ind. Bar Assn., Internat. Assn. Def. Counsel, Ill. State U. Alumni Assn. (pres. 1990-92), Ind. U. Law Alumni Assn. (bd. dirs. 1992—, pres. 1998-99), Order of Coif. General civil litigation, Franchising, Product liability. Home: 11827 Sea Star Dr Indianapolis IN 46256-9400 Office: Ice Miller Donadio & Ryan PO Box 82001 One American Sq Indianapolis IN 46282

**PETERSHACK, RICHARD EUGENE,** lawyer; b. Milw., Nov. 17, 1953; s. Richard Victor and Dolores Barbara (Weitzer) P.; m. Michele Elaine Carrier, Aug. 6, 1977; children: Benjamin, Katherine. BA, Oberlin Coll., 1975; JD, U. Wis., 1982. Bar: Wis. 1982, U.S. Dist. Ct. (we. dist.) Wis. 1982, U.S. Dist. Ct. (ea. dist.) Wis. 1992. Legis. aide Wis. State Senate, Madison, 1978-79; exec. dir. Wis. Dist. Atty. Assn., Madison, 1980-82; law clk. Wis. Surpeme Ct., Madison, 1982-83; assoc. Herz, Levin, Teper, Summer & Croysdale, Milw., 1983-85, Easton & Harms, Madison, 1985-88, Axley Brynelson, Madison, 1988-90; ptnr. Axley Brynelson, LLP, Madison, 1991—; pres. Wis. Energy Conservation Corp., Madison, 1993-96. Campaign mgr. Al Baldus for Congress, Eau Claire, Wis., 1978, Justice Roland Day for Supreme Ct., Madison, 1986; campaign treas. Bill Bablitch for Supreme Ct., Madison, 1983. Mem. Order of Coif. Banking, Finance, Real property. Home: 307 Farwell Dr Madison WI 53704-6023 Office: Axley Brynelson LLP 2 E Mifflin St Ste 200 Madison WI 53703-2860

**PETERSON, ALLEN JAY,** lawyer, educator; b. Los Alamos, N.C., Oct. 26, 1949; s. Lyle Jay and Lois May (Richards) P.; m. Beverly White, May 27, 1989; children: Elizabeth Bishop, Adam Bryant. AA, St. Petersburg Jr. Coll., 1969; BA, Davidson Coll., 1971; postgrad., Harvard U., 1972; JD, U. N.C., 1976. Bar: N.C. 1974, U.S. Dist. Ct. (we. dist.) N.C. 1976. Ptnr. James, McElroy & Diehl, Charlotte, N.C., 1976-84, Howell & Peterson, Burnsville, N.C., 1984-87, Norris & Peterson, Burnsville, N.C., 1987-94; v.p., gen. counsel North State Foods, Inc., 1995—; constnl. law instr. U. N.C., Charlotte, 1977-78. Sunday sch. tchr. Higgins Meml. Meth. Ch., Burnsville, 1991-93, mem. adminstrv. bd., 1990-93. Mem. Am. Assn. Trial Lawyers, N.C. Acad. Trial Lawyers. Avocation: trout fishing. Home: RR 6 Box 944 Burnsville NC 28714-9632

**PETERSON, ANNE LINNEA,** law librarian, lawyer; b. Canton, Ohio, May 1, 1954; d. Norman Harry and Rhea Mae (Woody) P. BA, Coll. of Wooster, 1976; MLS, U. Ill., 1977; JD, U. Akron, 1984. Bar: Ohio 1984. Cataloguer U. Ill. Libr., Champaign, 1977-78; reference libr. U. Akron (Ohio) Libr., 1978-89; assoc. libr. Squire, Sanders & Dempsey, Cleve., 1989-94; libr. Benesch, Friedlander, Coplan & Aronoff, Cleve., 1994—. Mem. LA, Am. Assn. Law Librs. Office: Benesch Friedlander Et Al 2300 American Rd Cleveland OH 44144-2301

**PETERSON, BRADLEY LAURITS,** lawyer; b. Mpls.; m. Christine Elizabeth Stoutner, Sept. 16, 1989; children; Alexandra May, Elizabeth K. MBA, U. Chgo., 1982; JD, Harvard U., 1988. Bar: Ill. 1988. Mktg. rep. IBM, Chgo., 1982-85; assoc. Kirkland & Ellis, Chgo., 1988-93, Wildman & Harrold, Chgo., 1993-95; ptnr. Mayer Brown & Platt, Chgo., 1995—. Author: The Smart Way to Buy Information Technology: How to Maximize Value and Avoid Costly Pitfalls, 1998. Computer, General corporate, Communications. Office: Mayer Brown & Platt 190 S Lasalle St Ste 3100 Chicago IL 60603-3441

**PETERSON, BROOKE ALAN,** lawyer; b. Omaha, Dec. 6, 1949; s. Lloyd Earl and Priscilla Anne (Bailey) P.; m. Diane Louise Tegmeyer, Aug. 19, 1990. BA, Brown U., 1972; JD, U. Denver, 1975. Bar: Colo. 1975, U.S. Dist. Ct. Colo. 1975. Assoc. Garfield & Hecht, Aspen, Colo., 1975-77, Robert P. Grueter, Aspen, 1977-78; ptnr. Wendt, Grueter & Peterson, Aspen, 1978-79; prin. Brooke A. Peterson, P.C., Aspen, 1979-93; prin. Kaufman & Peterson, 1994—; mcpl. judge, Aspen, 1980—. Chmn. election commn., Pitkin County, 1979—. Mem. ABA, Colo. Bar Assn. (bd. govs. 1984-86, exec. council 1986-87), Pitkin County Bar Assn. (pres. 1981-83), Am. Trial Laywers Assn., Colo. Trial Lawyers Assn. Avocations: skiing, surfing, cycling, golf, music. General practice, Real property, General corporate. Home: 222 Roaring Fork Dr Aspen CO 81611-2239 Office: 315 E Hyman Ave Aspen CO 81611-1946

**PETERSON, DAVID EUGENE,** lawyer; b. Ft. Wayne, Ind., Dec. 29, 1957; s. Earl Eugene and Gloria Anne (Richardson) P.; m. Cynthia Elaine Davis, Aug. 5, 1958; children: Sarah Kirsten, Philip Conrad. AB in Econs., U. Mich., 1980, JD, 1983. Bar: Fla. 1983. Atty. Lowndes, Drosdick, Doster, Kantor & Reed, P.A., Orlando, Fla., 1983—. Bankruptcy, Consumer commercial, General civil litigation. Home: 1445 Granville Dr Winter Park FL 32789-1424 Office: Lowndes Drosdick Doster Kantor & Reed 215 N Eola Dr Orlando FL 32801-2095

**PETERSON, EDWIN J.,** retired supreme court justice, law educator; b. Gilmanton, Wis., Mar. 30, 1930; s. Edwin A. and Leora Grace (Kitelinger) P.; m. Anna Chadwick, Feb. 7, 1971; children: Patricia, Andrew, Sherry. B.S., U. Oreg., 1951, LL.B., 1957. Bar: Oreg. 1957. Assoc. firm Tooze, Kerr, Peterson, Marshall & Shenker, Portland, 1957-61; mem. firm Tooze, Kerr, Peterson, Marshall & Shenker, 1961-79; assoc. justice Supreme Ct. Oreg., Salem, 1979-83, 91-93, chief justice, 1983-91; ret., 1993; disting. jurist-in-residence, adj. instr. Willamette Coll. of Law, Salem, Oreg., 1994—; chmn. Supreme Ct. Task Force on Racial Issues, 1992-94; mem. standing com. on fed. rules of practice and procedure, 1987-93; bd. dirs. Conf. Chief Justices, 1985-87, 88-91. Chmn. Portland Citizens Sch. Com., 1968-70; vice chmn. Young Republican Fedn. Orgn., 1951; bd. visitors U. Oreg. Law Sch., 1978-83, 87-93, chmn. bd. visitors, 1981-83. Served to 1st lt. USAF, 1952-54. Mem. Oreg. State Bar (bd. examiners 1963-66, gov. 1973-76, vice chmn. profl. liability fund 1977-78), Multnomah County Bar Assn. (pres. 1972-73), Phi Alpha Delta, Lambda Chi Alpha. Episcopalian. Home: 3365 Sunridge Dr S Salem OR 97302-5950 Office: Willamette Univ Coll Law 245 Winter St SE Salem OR 97301-3916

**PETERSON, FRANKLIN DELANO,** lawyer; b. Braham, Minn., Nov. 11, 1932; s. John Erick and Myrtle M. (Anderson) P.; m. Beverly Ann Crabb, Aug. 2, 1958; children: Heidi, Durward, Heather. Student, Augsburg Coll., 1950-51; BA, St. Cloud State Coll., 1955; LLB, William Mitchell Coll. Law, 1961. Bar: Minn. 1961. Field claims adjuster Farmers Mut. Ins. Co., St. Paul, 1955-57; asst. dist. claims mgr. Minn. Farmers Ins. Group, Mpls., 1957-62; sole practice Kenyon, Minn., 1963—; atty. City of Kenyon, 1964-82; v.p. Kenyon Devel. Corp., bd. dirs.; sec. Tri-Valley Constrn. Co., Kenyon, bd. dirs. Chmn. Goldwater for Pres. campaign, Village of Kenyon Reps., 1964, Goodhue County LeVander for Gov., 1966, Goodhue County Reps, 1969-70; sec. Goodhue Selective Service Bd., 1968—; pres. Mineral Springs Chem. Dependency Ctr., 1974-85; mem. Kenyon Pub. Sch. Bd. Edn., 1976-82, treas. 1980-82, Kenyon Booster Club (charter), v.p. 1983; mgr. mgr. Kenyon Legion Baseball, 1979—; bd. dirs. Kenyon Roseview Apts., 1967—, pres. 1985—. Served with USAF, 1950-52. Mem. ABA, Minn. Bar Assn. (jud. dist. del., pres. 1st dist. 1979-80), Goodhue County Bar Assn., Minn. Assn. Plaintiffs Attys., Nat. Assn. Claimants Counsel, Sons of Norway (pres. Kenyon lodge 1969), Kenyon Comml. Club, Kenyon Country Club (pres. Osman Shrine Clowns 1993), Masons, Shriners, Lions (pres. Kenyon chpt.). Lutheran. General practice, Estate planning, Probate. Home: RR Box B Kenyon MN 55946 Office: 634 2nd St Kenyon MN 55946-1334

**PETERSON, H. DALE,** lawyer; b. Stevens Point, Wis., Jan. 4, 1951; s. Harold C. and Eva I. (Hansen) P.; m. Julie A. Goplin, Jan. 1, 1995; children: Matt, David, Alex, Ellen. BS with honors, U. Wis., Stevens Point, 1973; JD cum laude, U. Wis., 1978. Bar: U.S. Dist. Ct. (we. dist.) Wis., U.S. Ct. Appeals (7th cir.) Wis. Rsch. analyst U.S. Dept. Justice, Washington, 1973-75; ptnr. Stroud, Willink & Howard, LLC, Madison, Wis., 1978—; dir. Wis. Farm Bur. Svc. Bd., Inc., Madison, 1994—. Co-author: Contract Law in Wisconsin, 1995. Mem. Dane County Bar Assn. (dir./treas. 1987-91). General corporate, General civil litigation, Contracts commercial. Office: Stroud Willink & Howard LLC PO Box 2236 Madison WI 53701-2236

**PETERSON, HOWARD COOPER,** lawyer, accountant; b. Decatur, Ill., Oct. 12, 1939; s. Howard and Lorraine (Cooper) P.; BEE, U. Ill., 1963; MEE, San Diego State Coll., 1967; MBA, Columbia U., 1969; JD, Calif. Western Sch. Law, 1983; LLM in Taxation NYU, 1985. Bar: Calif., cert. fin. planner.; CPA, Tex.; registered profl. Engr., Calif.; cert. neuro-linguistic profl. Elec. engr. Convair divsn. Gen. Dynamics Corp., San Diego, 1963-67, sr. electronics engr., 1967-68; gen. ptnr. Costumes Characters & Classics Co., San Diego, 1979-86; v.p., dir. Equity Programs Corp., San Diego, 1973-83; pres., dir. Coastal Properties Trust, San Diego, 1979-89, Juno Securities, Inc., 1983-96, Juno Real Estate Inc., 1974—, Scripps Mortgage Corp., 1987-90, Juno Transport Inc., 1988—; CFO, dir. Imperial Screens of San Diego, 1977-96, Heritage Transp. Mgmt. Inc., 1989-91, A.S.A.P. Ins. Svcs. Inc., 1983-85. Mem. ABA, Interam. Bar Assn., Nat. Soc. Public Accts., Internat. Assn. Fin. Planning, Assn. Enrolled Agts. Estate planning, Real property, Taxation, general.

**PETERSON, JAN ERIC,** lawyer; b. Seattle, Apr. 28, 1944; s. Theodore Dare and Dorothy Elizabeth (Spofford) P.; children: Nels Andrew, Anne Elizabeth; m. Marguerite Victoria Caggiano, Mar. 31, 1984. AB in History, Stanford U., 1966; JD, U. Wash., 1969. Bar: Wash. 1969, U.S. Dist. Ct. (we. and ea. dists.) Wash. 1970, U.S. Ct. Appeals (9th cir.) 1970. Gen. counsel ACLU, Seattle, 1969-71; assoc. Daniel F. Sullivan, Seattle, 1972-73; sr. ptnr. Peterson, Young, Putra, Fletcher and Zeder, Seattle, 1973—. Drafter (state statute) Tap Water Regulation Act, 1983. Mem. ABA (editor assoc. 1976-78), Damages Attys. Round Table (founding, pres. 1997-98), ATLA (del. 1985-86), Am. Coll. Trial Lawyers, Wash. State Trial Lawyers Assn. (bd. 1973-85, pres. 1982-83, Trial Lawyer of Yr. 1999), Wash. State Bar Assn. (jud. selection 1985-87, bd. govs. 1992-95, pres. elect. 1999—), Am. Bd. Trial Adv. (diplomate, pres. Wash. chpt. 1990), ACLU, Bd. Legal Found. Wash. Democrat. Avocations: piano, baseball, basketball, golf. Personal injury, Product liability, Professional liability. Office: Peterson Young Putra Fletcher & Zeder 1501 4th Ave Ste 2800 Seattle WA 98101-1664

**PETERSON, JEANNE LOUISE,** lawyer; b. Washington, Apr. 21, 1945; d. Carl W. and Olive M. (Foerster) Tiller; m. John E. Peterson, Sept. 14, 1968 (div. Apr. 1983); m. James R. Flanigan, March 21, 1998; children—Kristin, Ian, Karin. B.A. in History, Kalamazoo Coll., 1966; M.A. in African History, U. Edinburgh (Scotland), 1967; J.D. cum laude, Mich. State U., 1980. Bar: Mich. 1980. Acting head history dept. Milton Margai Tchrs. Coll., Freetown, Sierra Leone, 1971-73; lectr. history dept. U. Sierra Leone, Freetown, 1973-75; cons., tchr. Dickinson-Iron Counties Head Start Program, Iron Mountain, Mich., 1975-76; atty. Mich. State Housing Devel. Authority, Lansing, 1980-99; exec. dir. Calif. Tax Credit Allocation Com., Sacramento, 1999—. Trustee Grand Ledge Bd. Edn. (Mich.), 1982-83, v.p., 1983-84, pres., 1984-85. Mem. ABA, Mich. Bar Assn., Women Lawyers Assn. Mich. Democrat. Home: 1616 6th St Sacramento CA 95814-6306 Office: Calif Tax Credit Allocation Com 915 Capitol Mall Rm 485 Sacramento CA 95814-4801

**PETERSON, KIMBERLEY JEAN,** lawyer; b. Livermore, Calif., Mar. 10, 1965; d. Lester Albert and Wanda Muriel Peterson. BSBA, U. Calif., Berkeley, 1987; JD, U. Ariz., 1992. Bar: Calif. 1992. Fin. analyst Hewlett-Packard Co., Palo Alto, Calif., 1987-89; sr. assoc. Deloitte & Touche LLP, San Jose, Calif., 1992-95; atty. Office Chief Counsel Dept. Treas. Ctrl. Calif., San Jose, 1995—. Mem. Calif. Bar Assn., Santa Clara County Bar Assn. (exec. com. bus. law sect. 1994—). Avocations: wine tasting, golf, skiing, college sports. Office: Dept Treas Office Chief Counsel Ctrl Calif 55 S Market St Ste 505 San Jose CA 95113-2385

**PETERSON, MARTIN LEE,** lawyer; b. Lawton, Okla., Jan. 20, 1956; s. Russell Warren Peterson and Allegra Evangeline (Pedersen) Stehr; m. Sandra Lynn Gibson, May 24, 1986; 1 child, Blaine Linley. Student, Tarleton State U., 1974-75; BA, U. Tex., Arlington, 1976; JD, U. Tex., 1979. Bar: Tex. 1979, U.S. Supreme Ct. 1991. Staff atty. McMillan & Lewellen, P.C., Stephenville, Tex., 1979-89; pvt. practice Stephenville, 1990-96. Contbr. articles to profl. jours. Mem. Asst. Dist. Atty. 220th Jud. Dist., 1996—. Avocations: sailing, stamp collector. State civil litigation, Criminal, General practice. Home and Office: RR 2 Box 12 Hico TX 76457-9717

**PETERSON, OSLER LEOPOLD,** lawyer; b. Mpls., Oct. 19, 1946; s. Osler Luther and Delores (Kealy) P.; m. Sandra Ann Freeto, Jan. 2, 1971 (div. Dec. 1983); m. Deborah Jean Bero, July 30, 1989. BA, Brown U., 1969; JD cum laude, Suffolk U., 1976. Bar: Mass. 1976, U.S. Dist. Ct. Mass. 1976. Pvt. practice Newton, Mass., 1976-84; ptnr. Freeto, Peterson & Scoll, Newton, 1984—. Bd. mem. Riverside Cmty. Care (formerly Neww Ctr., Inc.), 1976-96, clk., 1978-84, pres., 1984-89; bd. mem. Lasell Coll. (formerly Lasell Jr. Coll.), 1983-97, 98—, clk., 1984-91; bd. mem. Lasell Village, Inc., 1990—, chmn., 1992—; bd. mem. Medfield Zoning Bd. Appeals, 1993—. Mem. ABA, ATLA, Mass. Bar Assn., Mass. Conveyancers Assn. Personal injury, General civil litigation, Real property. Home: 10 Copperwood Rd Medfield MA 02052-1034 Office: Freeto Peterson & Scoll 580 Washington St Newton MA 02458-1416 also: Medfield Profl Bldgs 5 N Meadows Rd Ste 27 Medfield MA 02052-2317

**PETERSON, PAUL AMES,** lawyer; b. Los Angeles, Feb. 17, 1928; s. Ames and Norma (Brown) P.; m. Cynthia Peterson, June 21, 1953 (div.); children: Daniel C., Andrew G., Matthew A., James F.; m. Barbara J. Henderson, Sept. 12, 1976. BS in Econs., U. Calif., Berkeley, 1953, JD, 1956. Bar: Calif. 1956, U.S. Ct. Appeals (9th cir.) 1956, U.S. Supreme Ct. 1964. Assoc. Law Offices of George W. Phillips, Castro Valley, Calif., 1956-57; ptnr. Peterson & Price, San Diego, 1958—; assoc. prof. Calif. Western Coll. Law, San Diego, 1960-63, U. San Diego Law Sch., 1958-60, U. Calif., San Diego, 1984—; bd. trustees U. Calif. Found., San Diego, 1988-92. Contbr. articles to profl jours. Bd. dirs. San Diego County Water Authority, 1984-90, San Diego Conv. Ctr. Corp., 1985-90. Served as tech. sgt. U.S. Army, 1946-48, Korea. Fellow Am. Judicature Soc.; mem. Fed. Bar Assn., State Bar of Calif., Phi Beta Kappa, Order of Coif. Democrat. Avocation: hiking. Administrative and regulatory, Environmental, Real property. Home: 7020 Neptune Pl La Jolla CA 92037-5328 Office: Peterson & Price 530 B St Ste 1700 San Diego CA 92101-4405

**PETERSON, RICHARD WILLIAM,** judge, lawyer; b. Council Bluffs, Iowa, Sept. 29, 1925; s. Henry K. and Laura May (Robinson) P.; m. Patricia Mae Fox, Aug. 14, 1949; children: Katherine Ilene Peterson Sherbondy, Jon Eric, Timothy Richard. BA, U. Iowa, 1949, JD with distinction, 1951; postgrad., U. Nebr.-Omaha, 1972-80, 86. Bar: Iowa 1951, U.S. Dist. Ct. (so. dist.) Iowa 1951, U.S. Supreme Ct. 1991, U.S. Ct. Appeals (8th cir.) 1997. Pvt. practice law Council Bluffs, 1951—; U.S. commr. U.S. Dist. Ct. (so. dist.) Iowa, 1958-70; part-time U.S. magistrate judge U.S. Dist. Ct. (so. dist.) Iowa, 1970—; mem. nat. faculty Fed. Jud. Ctr., Washington, 1972-82; emeritus trustee Children's Square, U.S.A.; verifying ofcl. Internat. Prisoner Transfer Treaties, Mexico City, 1977, La Paz, Bolivia, 1980, 81, Lima, Peru, 1981. Author: The Court Moves West: A Study of the United States Supreme Court Decision of Appeals from the United States Circuit and District Court of Iowa, 1846-1882, 1988, West of the Nishnabotna: The Experiences of Forty Years of a Part-Time Judicial Officer as United States Commissioner, Magistrate and Magistrate Judge, 1958-1998, 1998; co-author: (with George Mills) No One is Above the Law: The Story of Southern Iowa's Federal Court, 1994; contbr. articles to legal publs. Bd. dirs. Pottawattamie County (Iowa) chpt. ARC, state fund chmn., 1957-58; state chmn. Radio Free Europe, 1960-61; dist. chmn. Trailblazer dist. Boy Scouts Am., 1952-55; mem. exec. coun. Mid-Am. Coun., 1976—. With inf. U.S. Army, 1943-46. Decorated Purple Heart, Bronze Star; named Outstanding Young Man Council Bluffs C. of C., 1959. Fellow Am. Bar Found. (life); mem. ABA, Am. Judicature Soc., Iowa Bar Assn. (chmn. com. fed. practice 1978-80, probate and trust coun. and sect. 1997—), Pottawattamie County Bar Assn. (pres. 1979-80), Fed. Bar Assn., Inter-Am. Bar Assn., Supreme Ct. Hist. Soc., Fed. Magistrate Judges Assn. (pres. 1978-79), Iowa Conf. Bar Assn. Pres. (pres. 1985-87), Hist. Soc. of U.S. Cts. Eighth Jud. Cir. (pres. 1989-99), Kiwanis (pres. Council Bluffs club 1957), Masons, Phi Delta Phi, Delta Sigma Rho, Omicron Delta Kappa. Republican. Lutheran. Home: 1007 Arbor Ridge Cir Council Bluffs IA 51503-5000 Office: PO Box 248 25 Main Pl Ste 200 Council Bluffs IA 51503-0790

**PETERSON, RONALD ROGER,** lawyer; b. Chgo., July 27, 1948; married; children: Elizabeth G., Ronald W. AB, Ripon, 1970; JD, U. Chgo., 1973. Bar: Ill. 1974, U.S. Dist. Ct. (no. dist.) Ill. 1974, U.S. Ct. Appeals (7th cir.) 1974, U.S. Dist. Ct. (ea. dist.) Wis. 1975, U.S. Dist. Ct. (no. dist.) Ind. 1978, U.S. Dist. Ct. (cen. dist.) Ill. 1980, U.S. Ct. Appeals (8th cir.) 1984, U.S. Ct. Appeals (6th cir.) 1990, U.S. Ct. Appeals (9th cir.) 1996. Ptnr. Jenner & Block, Chgo., 1974—; commd. 2d lt. U.S. Army, 1968, advanced through grades to 1st lt., 1973, ret., 1978, with mil. intelligence, 1968-78. Mem. ABA, Chgo. Bar Assn., Internat. Soc. Insolvency Practitioners, Comml. Law League, Am. Bankruptcy Inst., Am. Coll. Bankruptcy Lawyers. Avocation:

skiing. Bankruptcy, Contracts commercial, State and local taxation. Office: Jenner & Block 1 E Ibm Plz Fl 4000 Chicago IL 60611-7603

**PETERSON, STEPHEN D.,** lawyer; b. St. Paul, Sept. 13, 1969; s. Duane A. and Carol J. Peterson; m. Torin Galley Stokes. BA, King Coll. cum laude, 1991; JD, Emory U., 1994. Ptnr. Paris and Peterson, P.C., Atlanta, 1984-98; assoc. Roberts, Isaf and Summers, Atlanta, 1998—. Adult Sunday sch. tchr. Ch. of the Apostles, 1998. Mem. Ga. Trial Lawyers Assn., Atlanta Bar Assn. (small firms sect.). Avocations: backpacking, history, golf. General civil litigation.

**PETERSON, STEVEN A.,** lawyer; b. Princeton, Minn., Sept. 9, 1953; s. Albin Arthur and Patricia Ann (Samuelson) P.; m. Michelle Behring, Jan. 11, 1980; children: Michael Charles, Stephanie Rose. BA, U. Minn., 1975; JD, Hamline U., 1978. Bar: Minn. 1978, U.S. Dist. Ct. Minn. 1979. Pvt. practice Milaca, Minn., 1978-92, Chanhassen, Minn., 1984—. Mem. Minn. Bar Assn. Republican. Lutheran. General practice, Real property, Probate. Home: 8021 Dakota Ave Chanhassen MN 55317-9638 Office: 80 W 78th St Ste 101 Chanhassen MN 55317-8716

**PETERSON, WILLIAM ALLEN,** lawyer; b. Marshall, Mo., Oct. 1, 1934; s. R.O. and Marjorie E. (Mallot) P.; m. Mary Kay Moore, July 26, 1958; children: Laura, Clayton, Mary M., Sarah. BS, Drury Coll., Springfield, Mo., 1958; JD, Washington U., 1963. Bar: Mo. 1963, U.S. Dist. Ct. (ea. dist.) Mo. 1964, U.S. Dist. Ct. (we. dist.) Mo. 1965, U.S. Supreme Ct. 1967. Assoc. Riddle, O'Herin & Newberry, Malden, Mo., 1963-65; asst. atty. gen. State of Mo., Jefferson City, 1965-70; legislator Mo. Ho. Reps., Jefferson City, 1970-74; pvt. practice Marshall, 1974—; atty. City of Marshall, 1976-78, City of Slater, Mo., 1988-89; judge mcpl. divsn. State Cir. Ct., Marshall, 1979-80, Slater, 1990-94; pros. atty. County of Saline, Marshall, 1979-80, 84-88. With USN, 1954-56. Mem. ABA, Mo. Bar Assn., Assn. Trial Lawyers Am., Am. Legion, VFW. Methodist. General civil litigation, Workers' compensation, Probate. Home: 503 E Eastwood St Marshall MO 65340-1535 Office: 54 W Arrow St PO Box 9 Marshall MO 65340-0009

**PETERZELL, BETSY VANCE,** lawyer; b. Winston-Salem, N.C., May 23, 1958; d. Robert Livingston and Jean (Blanding) Vance; m. Marc L. Peterzell, Dec. 19, 1987; children: Michael, Stephen. BA, Salem Coll., 1980; JD, Emory U., 1985. Bar: Ga. 1985. Paralegal Arnall, Golden & Gregory LLP, Atlanta, 1982-84; assoc. Powell, Goldstein, Frazer & Murphy LLP, Atlanta, 1985-89, Sutherland, Asbill & Brennan LLP, Atlanta, 1989-92; ptnr. Meadows, Ichter & Trigg, P.C., Atlanta, 1992—; dir., acting CEO AIMED Corp., Atlanta, 1997—; dir. Atlanta Brewing Co., 1993-97. Vice-chmn. bd. Am. SIDS Inst., Atlanta, 1994—. Mem. ABA, Ga. Bar Assn., Atlanta Bar Assn. Avocations: physics, piano, tennis. Mergers and acquisitions, General corporate, Finance. Office: Meadows Ichter & Trigg PC 8 Piedmont Ctr NE Ste 300 Atlanta GA 30305-1533

**PETH, HOWARD ALLEN,** lawyer, educator; b. Calif., Apr. 20, 1955; s. Howard Allen and Diane Marie (Munyan) P.; m. Gloria Gene Stockton, Aug. 9, 1992; children: Andrew Howard, Rachel Gloria. BA, U. Calif., San Diego, 1980; MD, U. Santiago, 1984; JD, U. Mo., 1991. Bar: Calif. 1993, U.S. Ct. Appeals (9th cir.) 1993, U.S. Ct. Claims, U.S. Ct. Appeals (fed. cir.) 1993, U.S. Dist. Ct. (so. dist.) Calif. 1993, U.S. Supreme Ct. 1997; diplomate Am. Bd. Internal Medicine, Am. Bd. Emergency Medicine; lic. physician, Calif., Mo., Wis. Asst. prof. U. Mo. Sch. Medicine, Columbia, 1997—. Fellow Am. Coll. Legal Medicine; mem. AMA, ABA (health law sect.), ACP, Am. Coll. Emergency Physicians. Republican. Episcopalian. Office: U Mo Hosp and Clinic One Hospital Dr Columbia MO 65212

**PETILLON, LEE RITCHEY,** lawyer; b. Gary, Ind., May 6, 1929; s. Charles Ernest and Blanche Lurene (Mackay) P.; m. Mary Anne Keeton, Feb. 20, 1960; children: Andrew G., Joseph R. BBA, U. Minn., 1952; LLB, U. Calif., Berkeley, 1959. Bar: Calif. 1960, U.S. Dist. Ct. (so. dist.) Calif. 1960. V.p. Creative Investment Capital, Inc., L.A., 1969-70; corp. counsel Harvest Industries, L.A., 1970-71; v.p., gen. counsel, dir. Tech. Svcs. Corp., Santa Monica, Calif., 1971-78; ptnr. Petillon & Davidoff, L.A., 1978-92, Gipson Hoffman & Pancione, 1992-93; pvt. practice Torrance, Calif., 1993-94; ptnr. Petillon & Hansen, Torrance, Calif., 1994—. Co-author: R&D Partnerships, 2d edit., 1985, Representing Start-Up Companies, 1992, 6th edit., 1999, Chapter 9, California Transaction Forms, 1996. Chmn. Neighborhood Justice Ctr. Com., 1983-85, Middle Income Co., 1983085; active Calif. Senate Commn. on Corp. Governance, State Bar Calif. Task Force on Alternative Dispute Resolution, 1984-85; chmn. South Bay Sci. Found., Inc.; vice-chmn. Calif. Capital Access Forum, Inc. Recipient Cert. of Appreciation L.A. City Demonstration Agy., 1975, United Indian Devel. Assn., 1981, City of L.A. for Outstanding Vol. Svcs., 1984. Mem. ABA, Calif. State Bar Assn. (pres., Pro Bono Svcs. award 1983), L.A. County Bar Found. (bd. dirs. 1986-89), L.A. County Bar Assn. (chmn. law tech. sect., alt. dispute resolution sect. 1992-94, trustee 1984-85, Griffin Bell Vol. Svc. award 1993). Avocations: backpacking, reading, music, painting. General corporate, Securities. Home: 1636 Via Machado Palos Verdes Estates CA 90274-1930 Office: Petillon & Hansen 21515 Hawthorne Blvd Ste 1260 Torrance CA 90503-6503

**PETITTI, MICHAEL JOSEPH, JR.,** lawyer; b. Canton, Ohio, July 25, 1955; s. Michael Joseph and Shirley Darlene Petitti; m. Anita Jean Charley, Aug. 27, 1977; 1 child, Michael Joseph III. BA in Edn., Ari. State U., 1982, JD cum laude, 1987. Bar: Ariz. 1987, U.S. Dist. Ct. Ariz. 1987, U.S. Ct. Appeals (9th cir.) 1987. Social worker Tempe (Ariz.) Ctr. for the Handicapped, 1982-84; atty. Evans, Kitchel & Jenckes, P.C., Phoenix, 1987-88, Bevs, Gilbert & Morrill, P.C., Phoenix, 1988-90, David F. Gomez, P.C., Phoenix, 1990—; spkr. in field. Pedrick scholar, 1984, 85, 86. Mem. ABA, State Bar Ariz., Maricopa County Bar Assn., Nat. Employment Lawyers Assn., Ariz. Employment Lawyers Assn. Democrat. Labor, Federal civil litigation, State civil litigation. Office: David F Gomez PC 2525 E Camelback Rd Ste 860 Phoenix AZ 85016-4279

**PETIX, STEPHEN VINCENT,** lawyer; b. Detroit, Oct. 29, 1942. Honors AB, Xavier U., Ohio, 1964; JD, U. Mich., 1967. Bar: Mich. 1968, Calif. 1972, U.S. Dist. Ct. (ea. dist.) Mich. 1968, U.S. Dist. Ct. (so. dist.) Calif. 1972, U.S. Ct. Claims 1996, U.S. Ct. Appeals (9th cir.) 1974, U.S. Supreme Ct. 1980. Law clk. to Hon. Gordon Thompson Jr. U.S. Dist. Judge for So. Dist. Calif., 1972-73; asst. U.S. atty. criminal divsn. U.S. Atty.'s Office, San Diego, 1974-78, asst. chief civil divsn., 1978-94; ptnr. Quinton & Petix, San Diego, 1994—. With JAGC USNR, 1968-71. Mem. State Bar Calif. (conf. dels. 1995-99, litigation sect. 1995-98), San Diego County Bar Assn. (chairperson pub. lawyers com. 1989, vice-chairperson 1987-88, fed. ct. com. 1995-99), San Diego Trial Lawyers Assn. (environ. law seminar, govtl. immunities seminar), San Diego Bar Assn. (aviation sect.), Orange County Bar Assn. (aviation sect.), Mission Bay Yacht Club (past dir.). Avocations: youth sports coach (soccer, baseball), golf, yachting. Federal civil litigation, Personal injury, Product liability. Office: Quinton and Petix Attys at Law Koll Ctr 501 W Broadway Ste 710 San Diego CA 92101-3544

**PETOSKEY, ELIZABETH M.,** lawyer; b. Chgo., Apr. 20, 1957. BS in Bus., Ind. U., 1979; MBA, Ea. Mich. U., 1981; JD, Thomas M. Cooley Law Sch., Mich., 1985. Bar: Mich. 1985. Ptnr. Conlin, McKenney & Philbrick, P.C., Ann Arbor, Mich., 1985—. Dir. Jr. League Ann Arbor, 1989; pres. Mich. Theater Found., Ann Arbor, 1995. Mem. ABA, State Bar Mich., Washtenaw County Bar Assn. Estate planning, Probate, Estate taxation. Office: Conlin McKenney & Philbrick PC Ste 400 350 S Main St Ann Arbor MI 48104-2131

**PETRASICH, JOHN MORIS,** lawyer; b. Long Beach, Calif., Oct. 13, 1945; s. Louis A. and Margaret A. (Moris) P.; children from previous marriage: Jason, Jacquelyn; m. Mary T. Nevin, Aug. 22, 1997. BA, U. So. Calif., 1967, JD, 1970. Bar: Calif. 1971, U.S. Dist. Ct. (cen. dist.) 1971, U.S. Ct. Appeals (9th cir.) 1973, U.S. Dist. Ct. (no. dist.) Calif. 1974, U.S. Ct. Appeals (ea. dist.) Calif. 1976. Assoc. Fulop, Rolson, Burns & McKittrick, Beverly Hills and Newport Beach, Calif., 1971-74, ptnr., 1975-82; ptnr., head litigation McKittrick, Jackson, DeMarco & Peckenpaugh, Newport Beach, 1983-93; shareholder, head litigation Jackson, DeMarco & Peckenpaugh, Newport Beach, 1993—; also bd. dirs. McKittrick, Jackson, DeMarco & Peckenpaugh, Newport Beach. Mem. editorial staff U. So. Calif. Law Rev., 1969-70. Mem. ABA, Beverly Hills Bar Assn., L.A. Bar Assn., Assn. Trial Lawyers Am., Orange County Bar Assn., Lawyers Club L.A., Order of Coif. General civil litigation, Insurance, Real property. Office: Jackson DeMarco Peckenpaugh PO Box 19704 Irvine CA 92623-9704

**PETREY, R. CLAYBOURNE, JR.,** lawyer; b. Kingsport, Tenn., June 19, 1951; s. Robert C. and Helen Kabrich P.; m. Suzanne Van Zandt, Oct. 22, 1977; children: Caleb Claybourne, Elizabeth Anne. BS, Mich. State U., 1972; MS, U. Tenn., 1976; JD, U. Mich., 1983. Computer systems analyst IRS, Washington, 1977-78; rsch. assoc. NSF, Washington, 1978-80; assoc. Dearborn & Ewing, Nashville, 1983-89, ptnr., 1989-92; of counsel Boult, Cummings, Conners, Nashville, 1992-94; assoc. gen. counsel Am. Health Ctrs., Parsons, Tenn., 1994-97; sec., gen. counsel Ayers Asset Mgmt., Parsons, Tenn., 1998—. Bd. dirs. Nashville Bd. Zoning Appeals, 1993-98, chmn., 1995. Real property, Contracts commercial, Land use and zoning (including planning). Office: Ayers Asset Mgmt Inc 68 W Main St Parsons TN 38363-2012

**PETRIE, BRUCE INGLIS,** lawyer; b. Washington, Nov. 8, 1926; s. Robert Inglis and Marion (Douglas) P.; m. Beverly Ann Stevens, Nov. 3, 1950 (dec. Oct. 1993); children: Laurie Ann Roche, Bruce Inglis, Karen Elizabeth Medsger. BBA, U. Cin., 1948, JD, 1950. Bar: Ohio 1951, U.S. Dist. Ct. (so. dist.) Ohio 1951, U.S. Ct. Appeals (6th cir.) 1960, U.S. Supreme Ct. Assoc. Kunkel & Kunkel, Cin., 1950-51; assoc. Graydon, Head & Ritchey, 1951-57, ptnr., 1957—. Exec. prodr. (sch. video) Classical Quest; contbr. articles to legal jours. Mem. bd. Charter Com. Greater Cin., 1952—; mem. bd. edn. Indian Hill Exempted Village Sch. Dist., 1965-67, pres., 1967; mem. adv. bd. William A. Mitchell Ctr., 1969-86; mem. Green Areas adv. com. Village of Indian Hill, Ohio, 1969-80, chmn., 1976-80; mem. Ohio Ethics Com., 1974-75; founder Sta. WGUC-FM; mem. WGUC-FM Cmty. Bd., 1974—, chmn., 1974-76; bd. dirs. Murray Seasongood Good Govt. Fund, 1975—, pres., 1989—; bd. dirs. Nat. Civic League, Cin. Vol. Lawyers for Poor Found., Linton Music Series, Amernet Chamber Music Soc.; parents as tchrs. Metro Housing Authority Commn., 1991—; elder, trustee, deacon Knox Presbyn. Ch.; a prin. advocate merit selection judges, Ohio. Recipient Pres.'s award U. Cin., 1976, Disting. Alumnus award, 1995. Fellow Am. Bar Found.; mem. ABA, Ohio Bar Assn., Cin. Bar Assn. (pres. 1981), Am. Judicature Soc. (Herbert Lincoln Harley award 1973, dir.), Nat. Civic League (Disting. Citizen award 1985, coun. 1984—), Am. Law Inst., Ohio State Bar Assn. Found. (Outstanding Rsch. in Law and Govt. award 1986, Charles P. Taft Civic Gumption award 1988, Ohio Bar medal 1988), Cincinnatus Assn., Order of Coif, Lit. Club, Univ. Club, Cin. Club. Avocations: tennis, squash, woodworking, writing, horticulture, music. General corporate, Estate planning, Real property. Home: 2787 Walsh Rd Cincinnati OH 45208-3428 Office: Graydon Head & Ritchey 1900 Fifth 3d Ctr 511 Walnut St Ste 1900 Cincinnati OH 45202-3157

**PETRIN, HELEN FITE,** lawyer, consultant, mediator; b. Bklyn., June 22, 1940; d. Clyde David and Connie Marie Keaton; m. Michael Richard Petrin, June 29, 1963; children: Jennifer Lee, Michael James, Daniel John. BS, Rider Coll. (now Rider U.), 1962, MA, 1980; postgrad., Glassboro (N.J.) Coll. (now Rowan U.), 1981; JD, Widener U., 1987. Bar: Pa. 1989, N.J. 1990, U.S. Dist. N.J. 1990. Tchr. bus. edn. Pennsville (N.J.) Meml. High Sch., 1962-66; asst. prof. Salem Community Coll., Carney's Point, N.J., 1977-81; asst. prof. Brandywine Coll. Widener U., Wilmington, Del., 1981-87, asst. prof., adminstr., dir. paralegal program, 1987-88; dir. continuing legal edn. Widener U. Sch. Law, Brandywine, 1987-88; pvt. practice computer cons. Del., Pa., N.J., Del., Pa., N.J., 1988—; pvt. practice law Salem, N.J., 1989—; prosecutor Pilesgrove Township, N.J., 1990-91; dep. surrogate Salem County, N.J., 1991—; word processing cons. New Castle County (Del.) Pers. Dept., 1983; mem. dist. I ethics com. N.J. Supreme Ct., 1993-96; instr. N.J. Inst. for CLE, 1995—; adv. com. on minority concerns Ct. N.J. Vicinage 15, 1995—; judge mock trial N.J. State Bar, 1994—. Pres. bd. Salem County YMCA, 1983, bd. dirs., 1980-98; dir. mediator Salem County YMCA Mediation Svcs., 1995—; vol. atty. Phila. Vols. for Indigent Program, 1990-95, Camden Legal Svcs., Inc. for Salem County, 1990—; bd. dirs. United Way Salem County, 1991-97, treas., 1994-95; bd. dirs. United Ways of Pa. & N.J., 1994-97; mem. Hope III com. (Home Ownership and Opportunity for People Everywhere), Salem, N.J., 1992—; vol. atty. Salem County N.J. Office Aging Sr. Law Day, 1991—, vol. dir. Guardianship Monitoring Program, 1993—; bd. dirs. Stand Up for Salem, Inc., 1991—, sec.-treas., 1997—. Mem. ABA (chmn. young lawyers econs. com. 1990-93, vice chmn. mktg. legal svcs. com. gen. practice sect. 1993-98), N.J. State Bar Assn. (exec. com. young lawyers divsn. 1990-93, trustee 1998—, pro bono com. 1998—), Pa. Bar Assn., Phila. Bar Assn. (probate adv. panel 1992-94), Salem County Bar Assn. (treas. 1991-92, sec. 1992-93, v.p., pres.-elect 1993-94, pres. 1994-95, dir. of Salem County, N.J. YMCA Family Ct. Mediation program 1995—), Delta Pi Epsilon (sec. bd. dirs. 1980-82). Avocations: swimming, music, walking, reading. General practice, Probate, Civil rights. Home: 99 Marlton Rd Woodstown NJ 08098-2722 Office: 51 Market St Salem NJ 08079-1909

**PETRO, JAMES MICHAEL,** lawyer, politician; b. Cleve., Oct. 25, 1948; s. William John and Lila Helen (Janca) P.; m. Nancy Ellen Bero, Dec. 16, 1972; children: John Bero, Corbin Marie. BA, Denison U., 1970; JD, Case Western Res., 1973. Bar: Ohio 1973, U.S. Dist. Ct. (no. dist.) Ohio 1974, U.S. Ct. Appeals (6th cir.) 1981. Spl. asst. U.S. senator W.B. Saxbe, Cleve., 1972-73; asst. pros. atty. Franklin County, Ohio, 1973-74; asst. dir. law City of Cleve., 1974; ptnr. Petro & Troia, Cleve., 1974-84; dir. govt. affairs Standard Oil Co., Cleve., 1984-86; ptnr. Petro, Rademaker, Matty & McClelland, Cleve., 1986-93, Buckingham, Doolittle & Burroughs, Cleve., 1993-95. Mem. city coun. Rocky River, Ohio, 1977-79, dir. law, 1980; mem. Ohio Ho. of Reps., Columbus, 1981-84, 86-90; commr. Cuyahoga County, Ohio, 1991-95; Auditor of State of Ohio, 1995—. Mem. ABA, Ohio State Bar Assn., Cleve. Bar Assn. Republican. Methodist. Home: 1021 Linworth Village Dr Columbus OH 43235-5026 Office: 88 E Broad St Columbus OH 43215-3506

**PETROS, RAYMOND LOUIS, JR.,** lawyer; b. Pueblo, Colo., Sept. 19, 1950. BS, Colo. Coll., 1972; JD, U. Colo., 1975. Bar: Colo. 1975. Jud. clk. to Justice Paul V. Hodges Colo. Supreme Ct., Denver, 1975-77; assoc. Bermingham, White, Burke & Ipsen, Denver, 1977-78; from assoc. to ptnr. Hall & Evans, Denver, 1978-81; ptnr. Kirkland & Ellis, Denver, 1981-86; mem. Holme, Roberts & Owen, Denver, 1986-96, Petros & White, LLC, 1996—. Contbr. articles to profl. jours. Bd. dirs. Rocky Mountain Poison Control Found., Denver, 1988-94. Real property, Land use and zoning (including planning). Office: Petros & White LLC Ste 820 730 Seventeenth St Denver CO 80202-3518

**PETROSKY, ROBERT,** lawyer; b. BelleVernon, Pa., Sept. 10, 1953; s. Peter and Jennie N. (Morycz) P.; m. Karen A. Crnovic, Nov. 3, 1979; 1 child: Kristin Nicole. BS, Indiana U. of Pa., 1975; JD, Temple U., 1978. Bar: Pa. 1978, U.S. Dist. Ct. (we. dist.) Pa. 1978. Staff atty. Laurel Legal Svcs., Inc., Kittanning, Pa., 1978-83; pvt. practice law Kittanning, Pa., 1983—. Mem. Pa. Bar Assn., Pa. Assn. Trial Lawyers. Personal injury, Probate, Real property. Home: 318 Oak Dr Kittanning PA 16201-2037 Office: 303 Arch St Kittanning PA 16201-1515

**PETROSKY, SARA LYNN,** lawyer, township commissioner; b. Lancaster, Pa., Apr. 18, 1960; d. Joseph Paul and Iona (Piper) P.; m. Stanley Ervin, July 4, 1986; children: Jarek Ervin, Danika Ervin. BA magna cum laude, Messiah Coll., 1982; JD cum laude, Temple U., 1987. Atty. Pepper, Hamilton & Scheetz, Phila., 1987-89, Sprecher, Felix, Visco, Hutchison & Young, Phila., 1989-90, Morgan, Lewis & Bockius, Phila., 1993-95, McCann, Mailey & Geschke, Phila., 1995—; coord. Delaware County Mock Trial Competition, 1990-91. Mem. fin. com. Wallingford-Swarthmore Sch. Dist., 1992; bd. dirs. Family and Cmty. Svc. of Delaware County, 1995—; commr. Nether Providence Twp., 1994—, pres. 1996; mem. Delaware County Leadership Group, 1994-96. Mem. Pa. Bar Assn. (commn. on women in legal profession 1994—), Phila. Bar Assn. (chancellor's commn. on children at risk 1994-95). Home: 214 Sykes Ln Wallingford PA 19086-6350

**PETRUCELLI, JAMES MICHAEL,** judge; b. Fresno, Calif., Dec. 28, 1949; s. Gene Vincent and Josephine Marie (Frediani) P.; m. Toby Laura Petrucelli; 1 child, Vincent Michael. BS, Fresno State Coll., 1972; JD, San Joaquin Coll., 1989. Bar: Calif. 1989, U.S. Dist. Ct. (ea. dist.) Calif. 1989, U.S. Dist. Ct. (no. dist.) Calif. 1990, U.S. Ct. Appeals (9th cir.) 1990, U.S. Supreme Ct., 1993. Dep. sheriff Fresno County Sheriff's Dept., 1974-89; pvt. practice Fresno, 1989-98; judge Fresno County Superior Ct., Fresno, 1999—; del. State Bar Conf. of Dels., Fresno, 1990-98; State Bar Law Practice Mgmt. Sect., 1994-98, dir. Commn. For Adv. Calif. Paralegal Specialation Inc., 1995—. Pres. San Joaquin Coll. Law Alumni Assn., Fresno, 1990-96; mem. exec. com. San Joaquin Coll. Law, 1990-91, 20th anniversary com., 1990-91; trustee Kerman (Calif.) Unified Sch. Dist., 1982-88; bd. dirs. North Cen. Fire Protection Dist., Kerman, 1990-98. Mem. ABA, Am. Trial Lawyers Assn., Consumer Attorney of Calif., Calif. Bar Assn., Fresno County Bar Assn., Inns of Ct. Office: Fresno Co Courthouse 1100 Van Ness Ave Fresno CA 93724-0001

**PETRUSH, JOHN JOSEPH,** lawyer; b. Rochester, Pa., Oct. 15, 1942; s. Joseph Anthony and Helen Rosemarie (Klucarich) P.; children: John Joseph, Joshua Laurence. AB cum laude, Princeton U., 1964; LLB, Stanford U., 1967. Bar: Calif. 1967, Pa. 1970. Assoc. Bernard Petrie, San Francisco, 1967-68; law clk. to judge Common Pleas Ct. Beaver County, Pa., 1969; assoc. Buchanan, Ingersoll, Rodewald, Kyle & Buerger, Pitts., 1970-75; pvt. practice Beaver, Pa., 1976—. Mem. Beaver Town Coun., 1973-88; bd. dirs. Beaver County unit Am. Cancer Soc., 1976-90, United Way of Beaver County, 1986-92; trustee Beaver Area Sch. Dist. Edn. Found. With USMCR, 1961-63. Mem. ABA, ATLA, Pa. Bar Assn., Pa. Trial Lawyers Assn. (bd. govs. western chpt. 1984-90), Allegheny County Bar Assn., Beaver County Bar Assn. (treas. 1987—). Republican. Personal injury, Workers' compensation, State civil litigation. Home: 331 Wilson Ave Beaver PA 15009-2323 Office: 348 College Ave Beaver PA 15009-2209

**PETTEY, WILLIAM HALL, JR.,** lawyer; b. New Orleans, Apr. 22, 1958; s. William Hall and Jeanie Nelson (Hewes) P.; m. Kimberly Ann Mosley, Apr. 25, 1992; children: William Hall III, Philip Thomas Hewes. BS, U. So. Miss., 1980; JD, U. Miss., Oxford, 1983. Bar: Miss. 1983, U.S. Dist. Ct. (no. dist.) Miss. 1983, U.S. Ct. Appeals (5th cir.) 1984, U.S. Dist. Ct. (so. dist.) Miss. 1984. Lawyer Dukes Dukes Keating & Faneca, Gulfport, Miss., 1984-96; pvt. practice Gulfport, 1996—. V.p. Miss. Railway Mus., Hattiesburg, 1983-87; elder Westminster Presbyn. Ch., Gulfport, 1992, steering com. Covenant Christian Sch., 1994—. Mem. Miss. Bar Assn., Harrison County Bar Assn., Louisville & Nashville Hist. Soc., Ill. Ctrl. Hist. Soc., Trinity United Meth. Ch., Nat. Railway Hist. Soc. Avocations: railroading, model railroading, photography. Real property, State civil litigation, Transportation. Home: 323 2nd St Gulfport MS 39507-1016 Office: 1225 31st Ave Gulfport MS 39501-1847

**PETTIBONE, PETER JOHN,** lawyer; b. Schenectady, N.Y., Dec. 11, 1939; s. George Howard and Caryl Grey (Ketchum) P.; m. Jean Kellogg, Apr. 23, 1966; children: Stephen, Victoria. AB summa cum laude, Princeton U., 1961; JD, Harvard U., 1964; LLM, NYU, 1971. Bar: Pa. 1965, D.C. 1965, N.Y. 1968, U.S. Supreme Ct. 1974, Russia (fgn. legal cons.) 1995. Lectr. Heidelberg (Fed. Republic Germany) U., 1965-67; assoc. Cravath, Swaine & Moore, N.Y.C., 1967-74, Lord Day & Lord, Barrett Smith, N.Y.C., 1974-76; ptnr. Lord Day & Lord, Barrett Smith, N.Y.C. and Washington, 1976-94, Patterson, Belknap, Webb & Tyler LLP, N.Y.C. and Washington, 1994—; pres. 1158 Fifth Ave. Corp., N.Y.C., 1991-94; pres. North Ferry Co., Shelter Island, N.Y., 1987-90; bd. dirs., vice-chmn. N.Y. State Facilities Devel. Corp., N.Y.C., 1983-89. Editor USSR Legal Materials, 1990-92. Trustee, treas. Hosp. Chaplaincy Inc., N.Y.C., 1980-86, Civitas, N.Y.C., 1984-92; mem. Coun. Fgn. Rels., 1993—; trustee Union Chapel, Shelter Island, N.Y., 1990—, CEC Internat. Ptnrs., 1996—; bd. dirs., vice chmn. Geonomics Inst., Middlebury, Vt., 1991-98; mem. vestry Ch. of Heavenly Rest, N.Y.C., 1987-93; mem. Nat. Adv. Coun. Harriman Inst. Columbia U., 1996—; mem. Russia com. Episcopal Diocese of N.Y. Capt. U.S. Army, 1965-67, Heidelberg, Germany. Mem. ABA, Assn. Bar City N.Y. (chmn. com. on CIS affairs 1991-94), U.S.-USSR Trade and Econ. Coun. Inc. (U.S. co-chmn. legal com. 1980-92), U.S.-Russia Bus. Coun. (bd. dirs.), Soc. of Cin., Anglers Club N.Y.C., Shelter Island Yacht Club, Amateur Ski Club N.Y. (pres. 1980-82), Canterbury Choral Soc. (pres. 1983-84), Phi Beta Kappa. Episcopalian. General corporate, Private international, Securities. Home: 1158 5th Ave New York NY 10029-6917 also: 10 Wesley Ave Shelter Island Heights NY 11965 Office: Patterson Belknap Webb & Tyler LLP 1133 Avenue Of The Americas New York NY 10036-6710

**PETTIETTE, ALISON YVONNE,** lawyer; b. Brockton, Mass., Aug. 16, 1952. Student Sorbonne, Paris, 1971-72; BA, Sophie Newcomb Coll., 1972; MA, Rice U., 1974; JD, Bates Coll., 1978. Bar: Tex. 1979, U.S. Dist. Ct. (so. dist.) Tex. 1980, U.S. Ct. Appeals (5th cir.) 1981. Ptnr. Harvill & Hardy, Houston, 1979-83; pvt. practice, Houston, 1983-84; assoc. O'Quinn & Hagans, Houston, 1984-86, Jones & Granger, Houston, 1986-88; pvt. practice, Houston, 1988—. Editor Houston Law Rev. U. Houston, 1976-78. Exercise instr. YWCA, Houston, 1976-81, U. St. Thomas, Houston. NDEA fellow Rice U., Houston, 1972-74; Woodrow Wilson scholar, Tulane U., New Orleans, 1972. Mem. ABA, Assn. Trial Lawyers Am., Tex. Trial Lawyers Assn., Houston Trial Lawyers Assn., Phi Delta Phi, Phi Beta Kappa. Personal injury, Product liability, Federal civil litigation. Home: PO Box 980847 Houston TX 77098-0847

**PETTIGREW, EDWARD W.,** lawyer; b. Aurora, Ill., July 16, 1943. AB, Kenyon Coll., 1965; JD, U. Mich., 1968. Bar: Wash. 1970, Mich. 1971, U.S. Ct. Appeals (9th cir.) 1971, U.S. Dist. Ct. (we. and ea. dists.) Wash. 1971. Shareholder Graham & Dunn, Seattle, 1970—. Mem. Fed. Bar Assn. (pres. western dist. Wash. 1987-88). General civil litigation, Contracts commercial. Office: Graham & Dunn 1420 5th Ave Fl 33 Seattle WA 98101-4087

**PETTIS, DAVID WILSON, JR.,** lawyer; b. Montgomery, Ala., Jan. 28, 1945; s. David W. and Mildred R. Pettis; m. Jacquelyn C. Johnson, June 4, 1966; children: Kelly S. Thomas, Amy K. BS in Chemistry, Tulane U., 1966; JD, U. Ga., 1973. Bar: Ga. 1973, Fla. 1974, U.S. Dist. Ct. (mid. dist.) Fla. 1974, U.S. Ct. Appeals (11th cir.) 1981, U.S. Ct. Appeals (fed. cir.) 1983, U.S. Dist. Ct. (no. dist.) Fla. 1987. Assoc. Stein & Orman, PA, Tampa, Fla., 1973-76; shareholder Duckworth, Allen, Dyer & Pettis, PA, Tampa, 1976-86, Pettis & McDonald, PA, Tampa, 1986-96, David W. Pettis Jr., PA, Tampa, 1997, Pettis & Van Royen, PA, Tampa, 1998—. Lt. USN, 1966-70, Vietnam. Mem. Am. Intellectual Property Law Assn. Intellectual property, Patent, Trademark and copyright. Office: Pettis & Van Royen PA 501 E Kennedy Blvd Ste 700 Tampa FL 33602-5200

**PETTUS, E. LAMAR,** lawyer; b. 1945; m. Donna C.; children: Evan Lamar, Carrie Anne, Samuel Chase. BSME, U. Ark., 1968, JD with honors, 1973. Bar: U.S. Dist. Ct. 1974 Ark., U.S. Ct. Appeals (8th cir.) 1974, Ark. Supreme Ct. 1974, U.S. Supreme Ct. 1979. Canton works plant engr. trainee Internat. Harvester, 1971; assoc. Pearson & Woodruff Law Firm, 1973; pvt. practice Pettus Law Firm, Fayetteville, Ark., 1974—; city atty. Farmington, 1981; mem. com. bar examiners Ark. Supreme Ct., 1986, chmn., 1988-89. Bus. mgr. Ark. Law Rev.; participant: televised "Ask Your Lawyer Program", 1981-83. Mem. Washington County Health Adv. Com., 1981-83; fin. chair Ctrl. United Meth. Ch., 1994-96, vice chair adminstrv. bd., 1997—; mem. Washington County Dem. Ctrl. Com., 1986-90; bd. dirs. Abilities Unltd. N.W. Ark., Inc., 1982-84, legal counsel; mem. Fayette Sch. Bd., 1991-97; counselor/tchr. Jr. High Meth. Youth Fellowship, 1985; active Friend Head Start Econ. Opportunity Agy., 1985-93, Assn. Voluntary Lawyers for Elderly, 1990-93. Comdr. USN, 1968-71, Vietnam, res. 1971-86. Recipient Navy Achievement medal, Navy Commendation medal. Mem. ABA, Ark. Bar Assn (pres. 1993-94, various positions and coms.), Ark. Trial Lawyers Assn., Washington County Bar Assn. (pres. 1989-90, v.p. 1989-90, sec.-treas. 1978-79), Fayetteville C. of C. (legis. com. 1994—), Rotary Internat. (various coms.). General corporate, Real property, Consumer commercial. Office: PO Box 1665 151 W Dickson St Fayetteville AR 72702

**PETTYJOHN, SHIRLEY ELLIS,** lawyer, real estate executive; b. Liberty, Ky., Aug. 16, 1935; d. Wesley Barker and Ada Lou (Bryant) Ellis; m. Flem D. Pettyjohn, Sept. 24, 1955; children: Deena Renee, Ellisa Denise. BS in Commerce, U. Louisville, 1974, JD, 1977. Bar: Ky. 1978, Ind. 1988; lic. real estate broker, Ky., Ind.; cert. mediator. Pres. Universal Devel. Corp., Ky. and Fla., 1984—, Pettyjohn Inc., Ky. and Ind., 1967—, Ind. Mediation Svcs., Inc., 1990—, Ky. Mediation Svcs., Inc., 1991—; v.p. Continental Investments Corp., 1986—; sr. ptnr. Pettyjohn & Assocs., Attys., 1987—. Editor Law-Hers Jour. Vice chmn. Louisville and Jefferson County Planning

Commn., 1971-75; mem. Gov.'s Conf. on Edn., 1977, jud. nominee, 1981, Met. Louisville Women's Polit. Caucus, Bluegrass State Skills Corp., 1992-96, Ky. Opera Assn. Guild; elected mem. Ky. State Dem. Exec. Com., 1988-92; del. Nat. Dem. Conv. and Dem. Nat. Platform Com., 1988; bd. dirs. Ky. Dem. Hdqs., Inc., 1988-92, Pegasus Rising, Inc.; chmn. Okolona Libr. Task Force; mem. Clinton-Gore Nat. Steering Com., 1995. Recipient Mayor's Cert. Recognition, 1974, Mayor's Fleur de lis award, 1969-73, Excellence in Writing award Arts Club Louisville, 1986, 87, 93, 99; inducted into Casey County Alumni Hall of Fame, 1997. Mem. ABA, NAFE, Nat. Assn. Adminstrv. Law Judges, Ky. Bar Assn., Louisville Bar Assn., Women Lawyers Assn. of Jefferson County, Am. Judicature Soc., Clark County Bar Assn., Ind. Bar Assn., Ind. Assn. Mediators, Am. Inst. Planners, Women's C. of C. of Ky. (past bd. dirs., chmn. legis. com.), Am. Legion (aux.), Fraternal Order Police Assn. (award 1982), Louisville Legal Secs. (past pres., editor Law-Hers Jour.), Coun. of Women Pres. (past pres., Woman of Achievement award 1974), Louisville Visual Arts Assn. (former bd. dirs.), Louisville Ballet Guild (chair audience devel. 1989-91), Dem. Leadership Coun., Casey County Alumni Assn. (pres. 1998—), Jefferson County Dem. Women's Club (past v.p.), Nat. Fedn. Dem. Women's Clubs, Spirit of 46th Club, Mose Green Club, North End Club, 12th Ward Club, S. End Club, 3rd Ward Club, Highland Pk. Club, Grass Roots Club, Harry S. Truman Club, Beargrass Club, Arts Club of Louisville (past pres.), Sigma Delta Kappa (life), Chi Thi Theta, Century 2000 Democrat Club. General practice, Probate, Administrative and regulatory. Home: 6924 Norlynn Dr Louisville KY 40228-1471 Office: 4500 Poplar Level Rd Louisville KY 40213-2124

**PETZOLD, JOHN P.,** judge; b. 1938. BA, U. Maine, 1961; LLB, Washington & Lee U., 1962. Bar: Ohio 1962. Judge Montgomery County Common Pleas Ct., Dayton, Ohio. Mem. ABA, Ohio State Bar Assn. (bd. govs., former chairperson young lawyers sect., chairperson pub. rels. com., vice chairperson lawyers assistance com., eminent domain com., banking, comml., and bankruptcy law com., pres.-elect 1998-99), Dayton Bar Assn., Common Pleas Judge Assn. Avocations: golf, swimming, writing, teaching, reading, genealogy. Office: Montgomery County Common Pleas Ct 41 N Perry St Dayton OH 45402-1431

**PEYTON, GORDON PICKETT,** lawyer; b. Washington, Jan. 22, 1941; s. Gordon Pickett and Mary Campbell (Grasty) P.; m. Marjorie G. Parish, June 9, 1962 (div.); children: Janet Porter, William Parish; m. Jean Nye Groseclose, Oct. 20, 1979. BA cum laude, U. of the South, 1962; JD, Duke U., 1965. Bar: Va. 1965, U.S. dist. Ct. (ea. dist.) Va. 1966, U.S. Ct. Appeals (4th cir.) 1975, U.S. Ct. Mil. Appeals 1980. Asst. city atty. Alexandria, Va., 1966-69; pvt. practice Alexandria, 1966-82, 88—; v.p. Peyton, Prendergast and Shapiro, Ltd., Alexandria, 1982-84; pres. Peyton & Shapiro, Ltd., 1985-88. Asst. commr. accounts Alexandria Cir. Ct., 1978—; bd. trustees U. of the South, 1972-76, Ch. Schs. in Diocese of Va., 1974-84; sr. warden Immanuel Ch.-on-the-Hill, 1990-91. 1st lt. USAF Res. ret. Fellow Am. Bar Found.; mem. ABA, 4th Cir. Jud. Conf., Va. Bar Assn., Va. State Bar (chmn. 8th dist. grievance com. 1988-90, chmn. disciplinary bd. 1996-97), Va. Trial Lawyers Assn., Alexandria Bar Assn. (pres. 1982-830, Am. Judicature Soc., Va. Conf. Commrs. of Accts., Alexandria C. of C. (v.p., dir. 1974-77). Episcopalian. Bankruptcy, Probate. Office: 908 King St Ste 201 Alexandria VA 22314-3067

**PEYTON, WALTER BURDETTE,** lawyer; b. Burnsville, N.C., Sept. 29, 1915; s. Wythe M. and Flora (Bogart) P.; m. Margaret Parsons (dec. Apr. 1983); 1 child, Robert Vance. LLB, Wake Forest U., 1939. Bar: N.C. 1940, N.Y. 1947, U.S. Dist. Ct. (no. dist.) N.Y. 1949. Assoc. Clark & Welch, N.Y.C., 1945-48; assoc. and ptnr. Palmer & Hankin, Binghamton, N.Y., 1948-86; pvt. practice law Binghamton, 1987—. Past pres., dir. Broome Co. Taxpayers Assn., Binghamton, 1965—, United Taxpayers of N.Y. State, Utica, 1976—; past dist. chmn., exec. bd. dirs. Susquenango coun. Boy Scouts of Am. 1st lt. U.S. Army, 1941-45. Recipient cert. of appreciation for 50 yrs. svc. N.C. State Bar, 1990. Mem. ABA, Broome Co. Bar Assn. (bd. dirs. 1954), N.Y. State Bar Assn., Am. Judicature Soc., The Soc. Med. Jurisprudence, Peyton Soc. Va., Masons, Johnson City Lodge (past master), Unity Daylight (chaplain 1985, 88), CNY York Rite Coll. (past gov.), York Rite Sovereign Coll. of NA (assoc. regent). Estate planning, Real property, Probate. Office: 88 Hawley St Binghamton NY 13901-3904

**PEZZILLO, BRIAN JAMES,** lawyer; b. Albuquerque, Aug. 29, 1970; s. Niel James and Patricia Gail Pezzillo. BBA, U. N.Mex., 1992, JD, 1996. Bar: New Mex. 1996, U.S. Dist. Ct. N. Mex. 1997. Audit asst. N.Mex. Credit Union League, Albuquerque, 1990-91; enrollment counsel Kaplan Ednl. Ctr., Albuquerque, 1992-93; law clk. Albuquerque City Atty.'s Office, 1995; atty. Stratton & Cavin, P.A., Albuquerque, 1996—. Mem. ABA, Federalist Soc. General civil litigation, General corporate, Administrative and regulatory. Office: Stratton & Cavin PA 40 First Plaza Ctr NW Ste 610 Albuquerque NM 87102-5801

**PFAELZER, MARIANA R.,** federal judge; b. L.A., Feb. 4, 1926. AB, U. Calif., 1947; LLB, UCLA, 1957. Bar: Calif. 1958. Assoc. Wyman, Bautzer, Rothman & Kuchel, 1957-69, ptnr., 1969-78; judge U.S. Dist. Ct. (ctrl. dist.) Calif., 1978—; mem. Jud. Conf. Adv. Com. on Fed. Rules of Civil Procedure. pres., v.p., dir. Bd. Police Commrs. City of L.A., 1974-78. UCLA Alumnus award for Profl. Achievement, 1979, named Alumna of Yr., UCLA Law Sch., 1980, U. Calif. Santa Barbara Disting. Alumnus award, 1983. Mem. ABA, Calif. Bar Assn. (local adminstrv. com., spl. com. study rules procedure 1972, joint subcom. profl. ethics and computers and the law coms. 1972, profl. ethics com. 1972-74, spl. com. juvenile justice, women's rights subcom. human rights sect.), L.A. County Bar Assn. (spl. com. study rules procedure state bar 1974). Office: US Dist Ct 312 N Spring St Ste 152 Los Angeles CA 90012-4703

**PFAFF, ROBERT JAMES,** lawyer; b. Pitts., Jan. 12, 1943; s. William Michael and Elizabeth (Ludwig) P.; m. Carol Pillich, June 18, 1977. BS in Edn., Slippery Rock U., 1965; JD, Duquesne U., 1973. Bar: Pa. 1973, U.S. Dist. Ct. (we. dist.) Pa. 1973, U.S. Supreme Ct. 1980. Tchr. secondary schs. Norwin and Jeanette, Pa., 1965-66; suit group supr. Liberty Mut. Ins. Co., Pitts., 1966-70; assoc. Egler, McGregor & Reinstadtler, Pitts., 1973-76; ptnr. Leopold, Eberhardt & Pfaff, Altoona, Pa., 1976-80; sr. ptnr. Meyer, Darragh, Buckler, Bebenek & Eck, Pitts., 1980-84, Pfaff, McIntyre, Dugas & Hartye, Hollidaysburg, Pa., 1984—. Bd. dirs. Blair County Legal Services, Altoona. Mem. ABA, Internat. Assn. Def. Counsel, Def. Rsch. Inst., Pa. Bar Assn., Blair County Bar Assn., Allegheny County Bar Assn., Pa. Assn. Mut. Ins. Cos. (claims com.), Pa. Def. Inst., Altoona Area Claims Assn. Republican. Roman Catholic. Avocations: golf, music, licensed pilot. Insurance, State civil litigation, General civil litigation. Home: 405 Kingsberry Cir Pittsburgh PA 15234-1065 Office: Pfaff McIntyre Dugas & Hartye PO Box 533 Hollidaysburg PA 16648-0533

**PFANNKUCHE, CHRISTOPHER EDWARD KOENIG,** lawyer; b. Chgo., May 1, 1955; s. Edward Louis and Barbara (Koenig) P. BA in Polit. Sci., Loyola U., Chgo., 1977, BS in Edn., 1978, JD, 1980. Bar: Ill. 1980, U.S. Dist. Ct. (no. dist.) Ill. 1980, U.S. Ct. Claims 1984, U.S. Ct. Internat. Trade 1984, U.S. Tax Ct. 1983, U.S. Ct. Mil. Appeals 1983, U.S. Ct. Appeals (7th cir.) 1983, U.S. Ct. Appeals (D.C. cir.) 1984, U.S. Supreme Ct. 1983. Asst. states atty. State's Atty.'s Office, Cook County, Skokie, Ill., 1981—, Macon County, Decatur, Ill., 1981. Author: Traffic Trial Procedure Handbook, 1981. Mem. ABA, Ill. Bar Assn., Chgo. Bar Assn., Decatur Bar Assn., N.W. Suburban Bar Assn. (membership chmn. 1982-83, law day chmn. 1982-86, bd. govs. 1985—), Nat. Dist. Attys. Assn., Assn. Trial Lawyers Am., Am. Judicature Soc., Ill. Trial Lawyers Assn., Phi Alpha Delta. Roman Catholic. Avocations: pilot, scuba diving. Home: 7220 W Greenleaf Ave Chicago IL 60631-1013 Office: States Attys Office Cook County 5600 Old Orchard Rd Skokie IL 60077-1051

**PFEFFER, DAVID H.,** lawyer; b. N.Y.C., Mar. 15, 1935. B. Chem. Engring., CCNY, 1956; J.D., NYU, 1961, LL.M. in Trade Regulation, 1967. Bar: N.Y. 1961. With patent dept. U.S. Rubber Co., Wayne, N.J., 1957-61; assoc. Watson, Leavenworth, Kelton & Taggart, N.Y.C., 1961-63; assoc. Morgan & Finnegan, N.Y.C., 1963-70, ptnr., 1971—; village prosecutor Roslyn Harbor, N.Y., 1976-78, village justice, 1979—; panel of arbitrators Am. Arbitration Assn. Mem. ABA (litigation sect.), N.Y. State Bar Assn., Assn. Bar City N.Y., Nassau County Bar Assn. (coms. on patent and trademarks, fed. practice), Am. Intellectual Property Law Assn. (com. alt. dispute resolution), N.Y. Intellectual Property Law Assn. (com. on jud. selection), N.Y. State Magistrates Assn., Nassau County Magistrates Assn., Order of Coif. Patent, Trademark and copyright, Antitrust. Office: Morgan & Finnegan LLP 345 Park Ave Fl 22 New York NY 10154-0053

**PFEFFER, ROBERT E.,** lawyer; b. White Plains, N.Y., June 24, 1966. BA in Econs., U. Chgo., 1989, JD, 1995. Bar: Ill., N.Y., U.S. Ct. Appeals (7th cir.). Clk. U.S. Ct. Appeals (7th cir.), Chgo., 1995-97; assoc. Weil, Godshal & Manges, N.Y.C., 1997-98, Paul, Weiss et al, N.Y.C., 1998—. General civil litigation, Criminal. Office: 1285 Avenue Of The Americas New York NY 10019-6028

**PFEIFER, GREGORY J.,** lawyer; b. Tulsa, Okla., May 5, 1965; s. James Francis and Sheila Kathleen Pfeifer; m. Debra Alfone, Aug. 17, 1991; children: Lauren, James. BS cum laude, U. Tex., Austin, 1987, JD, 1992. Bar: Tex. Oil and gas prodn. engr. Kerr, Lafayette, La., 1987-88, ARCO Oil & Gas, Midland, Tex., 1988-89; lawyer Tex. Natural Conservation Commn., Austin, 1992-97, Kirkpatrick & Lockhart, Pitts., 1997—. Mem. Soc. Petroleum Engrs. Environmental, General civil litigation, Administrative and regulatory. Office: Kirkpatrick & Lockhart 1500 Oliver Building Pittsburgh PA 15222-2312

**PFEIFER, PAUL E.,** state supreme court justice; b. Bucyrus, Ohio, Oct. 15, 1942; m. Julia Pfeifer; children: Lisa, Beth, Kurt. BA, Ohio State U., 1963, JD, 1966. Asst. atty. gen. State of Ohio, 1967-70; mem. Ohio Ho. of Reps., 1971-72; asst. prosecuting atty. Crawford County, 1973-76; mem. Ohio Senate, 1976-92, minority floor leader, 1983-84, asst. pres. pro-tempore, 1985-86; ptnr. Cory, Brown & Pfeifer, 1973-92; justice Ohio Supreme Ct., 1992—; chmn. jud. com. Ohio Senate, 10 yrs. Mem. Grace United Meth. Ch., Bucyrus. Mem. Bucyrus Rotary Club. Office: Supreme Court of Ohio 30 E Broad St Fl 3 Columbus OH 43266-0419

**PFEIFFER, MARGARET KOLODNY,** lawyer; b. Elkin, N.C., Oct. 7, 1944; d. Isadore Harold and Mary Elizabeth (Brody) K.; m. Carl Frederick Pfeiffer II, Sept. 2, 1968. BA, Duke U., 1967; JD, Rutgers U., 1974. Bar: N.J. 1974, N.Y. 1976, D.C. 1981, U.S. Supreme Ct. 1979. Law clk. to Hon. F.L. Van Dusen U.S. Ct. Appeals 3d cir., Phila., 1974-75; assoc. Sullivan & Cromwell, N.Y.C. and Washington, 1975-82, ptnr., 1982—. Contbr. articles to profl. jours. Mem. ABA, Internat. Bar Assn., D.C. Bar Assn., N.Y. State Bar Assn., Assn. of Bar of City of N.Y. Avocations: hiking, reading, music. Antitrust, Federal civil litigation, Intellectual property. Office: Sullivan & Cromwell 1701 Pennsylvania Ave NW Washington DC 20006-5866

**PFEUFFER, ROBERT TUG,** lawyer, mediator; b. New Braunfels, Tex., May 15, 1937; s. Tug Somers and Laura Mildred Pfeuffer; m. Jean Louise Hillje, Mar. 24, 1959; children: Michael Somers, David Gregory, Susan Gode. BA, Tex. A&M U., 1959; JD, U. Tex., 1962. Bar: Tex., U.S. Dist. Ct. (we. dist.) Tex., U.S. Supreme Ct. Asst. staff judge advocate USAF, Dover AFB, 1962-65; assoc. Bartram, Reagan & Burrus, New Braunfels, Tex., 1965-70; ptnr. Bartram, Reagan Burrus & Pfeuffer Attys., New Braunfels, Tex., 1970-73; state dist. judge 207th Dist. Ct. Tex., New Braunfels, Tex., 1973-95; sr. dist. judge Tex. State Jud., New Braunfels, Tex., 1995—; mediator, arbitrator Brazel & Pfeuffer Attys., New Braunfels, Tex., 1995—. Pres. Comal County Fair Assn., New Braunfels, 1977. Fellow Tex. Bar Found. (life); mem. Comal County Bar Assn. (pres. 1972), Lions (pres. New Braunfels club 1973). Democrat. Methodist. Alternative dispute resolution, Real property, Probate. Home: 3735 River Rd New Braunfels TX 78132-3123 Office: Brazel & Pfeuffer Attys 170 E San Antonio St New Braunfels TX 78130-4534

**PFLAUMER, KATRINA C.,** lawyer. BA in English Lit. cum laude, Smith Coll.; MA in Teaching English, Columbia U.; JD, NYU. Tchr. English and Am. Lit. Westtown Sch., Pa., 1970-72; staff atty. Seattle King County Defender Assn., 1975-77, Fed. Pub. Defender's Office, Seattle, 1977-80; pvt. practice, 1980-93; U.S. atty. Dept. Justice (we. dist.) Washington, 1993—; pro tem judge King County Superior Ct.; adj. prof. U. Puget Sound Sch. Law; guest lectr. U. Washington, Hastings, Cardozo, Nat. Inst. Trial Advocacy programs; lawyer rep. 9th Cir. Jud. Conf.; named to Atty. Gen. Adv. Com., 1994-95. Mem. Fire Brigade Emergency Response Team. Mem. FBA (pres. we. dist. Washington 1991, chair implementation of gender task force report com.), Nat. Assn. Criminal Def. Lawyers (mem. nominating com.), U.S. Sentencing Commn. (practitioners adv. group), Am. Civil Liberties Union (mem. legal com.), Seattle-King County Bar Assn. (mem. jud. conf. com.), Washington Assn. Criminal Def. Lawyers (pres. 1988-89), State Bench Bar (mem. press com.), Phi Beta Kappa. Fax: 206-553-0882. Office: US Dept Justice SeaFirst5th Ave Plaza 800 5th Ave Ste 3600 Seattle WA 98104-3187*

**PFROMMER, MICHAEL PAUL,** lawyer; b. Dallas, Nov. 19, 1965; s. Paul E. and Doris J. Pfrommer; m. Kelly A. Kitabchi, Aug. 23, 1996; 1 child, Hannah Grace. BBA in Mktg., U. Tenn., 1991; JD, U. Memphis, 1995. Bar: Tenn. Assoc. Blount Law Firm, Memphis, 1996-98, Castle and Assocs., PLC, Memphis, 1998—. Legal Methods fellow U. Memphis Law Sch., 1993-94. Mem. ABA, ATLA, Tenn. Bar Assn., Memphis Bar Assn. Avocations: fishing, hiking, gardening, reading, skiing. Personal injury, Workers' compensation, General civil litigation. Office: Castle and Assocs PLC 6555 Quince Rd Ste 319 Memphis TN 38119-8220

**PHAIR, JOSEPH BASCHON,** lawyer; b. N.Y.C., Apr. 29, 1947; s. James Francis and Mary Elizabeth (Baschon) P.; m. Bonnie Jean Hobbs, Sept. 04, 1971; children: Kelly I., Joseph B., Sean P. BA, U. San Francisco, 1970, JD, 1973. Bar: Calif., U.S. Dist. Ct. (no. dist.) Calif., U.S. Ct. Appeals (9th cir.). Assoc. Berry, Davis & McInerney, Oakland, Calif., 1974-76, Bronson, Bronson & McKinnon, San Francisco, 1976-79; staff atty. Varian Assocs., Inc., Palo Alto, Calif., 1979-83, corp. counsel, 1983-86, sr. corp. counsel, 1986-87, assoc. gen. counsel, 1987-90, v.p., gen. counsel, 1990-91, v.p., gen. counsel, sec., 1991—. Mem. devel. bd. St. Vincent de Paul Devel. Coun., San Francisco, 1992—. Mem. Bay Area Gen. Counsel, Silicon Valley Assn. Gen. Counsel, The Olympic Culb. Roman Catholic. General corporate, Mergers and acquisitions, Securities. Office: Varian Med Systems Inc M/S V-250 3100 Hansen Way Palo Alto CA 94304-1030

**PHAN, NHAT D.,** lawyer. BSE, U. Pa., 1989; JD, Am. U., 1995. Bar: Va. 1995, U.S. Ct. Appeals (fed. cir.) 1997, U.S. Dist. Ct. (ea. dist.) Va. 1998. Patent examiner U.S. Patent and Trademark Office, Washington, 1990-95; assoc. Burns Doane Swecker & Mathis, Alexandria, Va., 1995—. Editor: Am. U. J. Internat. Law and Policy, 1994-95. Mem. ABA, Am. Intellectual Property Assn. Patent, Federal civil litigation. Office: Burns Doane Swecker & Mathis 1737 King St Ste 500 Alexandria VA 22314-2727

**PHARIS, JAMES ANDREW, JR.,** lawyer; b. Pineville, La., Dec. 25, 1925; s. James Andrew and Florie Elizabeth (Humble) P.; m. Jo Anne Mohon, Aug. 24, 1951; children: Anne Kathleen, James Richard, Jonathan Scott. BS, USLI, Lafayette, La., 1947. Bar: La. 1962. Pvt. practice Alexandria, La. Author: Tales from the Izzard of Was, 1993; author of poetry. Mem. editl. com. U. Tex. M.D. Anderson Cancer Ctr.-Anderson Network, Houston, 1997—, mem. referral telephone contact, 1997—. Mem. Alexandria Bar Assn. (pres. 1973). General civil litigation, Condemnation, Estate planning. Office: 831 Desoto St Alexandria LA 71301-7634

**PHELAN, CHARLES SCOTT,** retired lawyer; b. Saranac Lake, N.Y., Mar. 21, 1926; m. Ruth Rene Kuntzleman, Sept. 4, 1948; children: Susan P. Moser, Donna K. Merrick, Barbara K. Glumac. BSEE, Pa. State U., 1949; LLB, George Washington U., 1954. Bar: N.Y. 1955, D.C. 1956, U.S. Patent Office, 1956, U.S. Ct. Appeals (fed. cir.) 1982. Elec. engr. GE, Schenectady, N.Y., 1949-52, patent asst., 1950-54; sr. atty. AT&T Bell Labs., Whippany, N.J. and other cities, 1954-86; pvt. practice patent law, Millington, N.J., 1987-95. Mem. Passaic Twp. (N.J.) Bd. Edn., 1962-64. 2d lt. U.S. Army, 1944-47. Mem. ABA, Am. Intellectual Property Law Assn., N.J. Patent Law Assn. (pres. 1964-65), Tau Beta Pi, Eta Kappa Nu. Avocations: fishing, hiking, sketching. Patent, Personal income taxation.

**PHELAN, ROBIN ERIC,** lawyer; b. Steubenville, Ohio, Dec. 28, 1945; s. Edward John and Dorothy (Borkowski) P.; m. Melinda Jo Ricketts, May 27, 1995; children: Travis McCoy, Tiffany Marie, Trevor Monroe. BSBA, Ohio State U., 1967, JD, 1970. Bar: Tex. 1971, U.S. Ct. Appeals (5th cir.) 1981, U.S. Ct. Appeals (11th cir.) 1981, U.S. Ct. Appeals (6th cir.) 1986, U.S. Ct. Appeals (10th cir.) 1988, U.S. Supreme Ct. Ptnr. Haynes and Boone, Dallas, 1970—. Co-author: Bankruptcy Practice and Strategy, 1987, Cowans Bankruptcy Law and Practice, 1987, Annual Survey of Bankruptcy Law, 1988, Bankruptcy Litigation Manual; contbr. articles to profl. jours. Mem. ABA (chmn. bankruptcy litigation subcom. 1990-95, chmn. unconventional bankruptcy issues), Internat. Bar Assn., Am. Bankruptcy Inst. (dir., past pres.), Am. Coll. Bankruptcy, State Bar Tex. (chmn. bankruptcy law com. sect. bus. law 1989-91), Dallas Bar Assn. Roman Catholic. Avocation: athletics. Bankruptcy. Home: 4214 Woodfin St Dallas TX 75220-6416

**PHELPS, ROBERT FREDERICK, JR.,** lawyer; b. Evanston, Ill., Aug. 20, 1956; s. Robert F. and Hanna (Kulej) P.; m. Joan Ann Brisky, Oct. 6, 1984; children: Jennifer Katherine, William Robert. BA, Trinity Coll., Hartford, Conn., 1978; JD cum laude, U. Mich., 1981; LLM, NYU, 1987. Bar: Conn. 1981, U.S. Tax Ct. 1987. Atty. Cummings & Lockwood, Stamford, Conn., 1981-87; atty. Day, Berry & Howard, Stamford, 1987-91; v.p. J.P. Morgan, N.Y.C., 1991—; cons. Conn. Safe Deposit Assn., 1983-87; mem. Fairfield County Estate Planning Coun., 1987-98; mem. Conn. Tax and Estate Planning Coun., 1990-92, Dallas Estate Planning Coun., Estate Planning Coun. North Tex., 1998—. Contbr. articles to profl. jours. Bd. dirs. Greenwich Coun. on Youth and Drugs, Inc., 1985-89; elder Noroton Presbyn. Ch., Darien, Conn., 1990-93; mem. Rep. Town Meeting, Darien, 1992-95; res. elder Highland Park Presbyn. Ch., 1998—. Mem. ABA (real property and probate sect., tax sect.), Conn. Bar Assn. (estates sect., tax and real property sects.), Middlesex Club, Northwood Country Club, Phi Beta Kappa. Republican. Avocation: tennis. Estate planning, Probate, Estate taxation. Home: 3816 Greenbrier Dr Dallas TX 75225-5217 Office: JP Morgan Texas 300 Crescent Ct Ste 400 Dallas TX 75201-7847

**PHELPS, ROBERT J.,** lawyer; b. Davenport, Iowa, Apr. 20, 1946; s. Lowell Dean and Helen Berniece (Hall) P.; m. Cheryl Ann O'Brien, Sept. 3, 1966 (div. Nov. 1983); children: Kristin Marie, Randall L.; m. Lauren Gail McNaughton, June 16, 1984. BA in History, U. Iowa, 1971; MA in Internat. Relations, U. Ark., 1972; JD, U. Tulsa, 1974. Bar: Okla. 1975, U.S. Dist. Ct. (no. dist.) Okla. 1975, Iowa 1987, U.S. Dist. Ct. (so. dist.) Iowa 1987. Assoc. Drummond and Raymond, Pawhuska, Okla., 1975; from assoc. to ptnr. Byers and Phelps, Cleve., 1975-83; sole practice Cleve., 1983-87, Davenport, Iowa, 1987—. Mem. Pawnee County Rep. Cen. Com., Cleve., 1986; bd. dirs. Cleve. Area Health Care Found., 1977-87; mem. Davenport City Rep. Party Cen. Com., 1987-89. Served as sgt. USAF, 1968-72. Mem. ABA, Okla. Bar Assn., Iowa Bar Assn., Scott County Bar Assn., Davenport C. of C., Cleve. C. of C. (chmn. indsl. devel. com. 1986-87). Avocations: reading, swimming, tennis. Consumer commercial, General practice, Criminal. Office: 1622 E Lombard St Davenport IA 52803-2448

**PHILIP, AMANDA,** prosecutor, consultant; b. Bklyn., Dec. 20, 1968; d. Irma Y (Lewis) Philip. BS in Econs., Franklin Pierce Coll., Rindge, N.H., 1990, BA in Mass. Comm., 1990; MBA in Econs., Syracuse U., 1995, JD, 1995. Bar: N.Y. 1995. Law clk. N.Y. State Atty. Gen., N.Y.C., summer 1993; law clk. to Judge Brian Hedges Family Ct., Syracuse, N.Y., summer 1994; prosecutor Queens (N.Y.) Dist. Atty.'s Office, 1995—. Democrat. Home: 29 Tiffany Pl Apt 2L Brooklyn NY 11231-2997

**PHILIP, JOHN B.,** lawyer; b. Oct. 14, 1948; s. Willis Douglas Jr. and Frances Harriet (Moore) P.; m. Georgia M. Avent, May 3, 1975; 1 child, Audrey Lane. BS, U. Memphis, 1971, JD, 1974. Bar: Tenn. 1974. Ptnr. Crislip, Philip & Assocs., Memphis; bd. dirs. Memphis Area Legal Svcs., Memphis, 1985-89. Mem. Tenn. Bar Assn., Memphis Bar Assn. (bd. dirs. 1988-89), Nat. Assn. Lawyers, Optimist Club of White Station (past pres.). Presbyterian. Avocation: golf. Bankruptcy, Family and matrimonial, General civil litigation. Office: Crislip Philip & Assocs 147 Jefferson Ave # 300 Memphis TN 38103-2200

**PHILIPPART, HOWARD LOUIS, JR.,** lawyer; b. Detroit, Aug. 20, 1927; s. Howard Louis Philippart and Helen Agnes Carr; married, June 1952; children: Michelle, Mary Elizabeth, Howard III, Timothy, Matthew, Lisa Marie, Rose Marie. LLB, U. Detroit, 1952. Pvt. practice Mich., 1952—; asst. prosecuting atty. Wayne County Prosecutors, Mich., 1964-94, dep. chief out country, 1994; magistrate, atty. 17th Dist. Ct., Redford, Mich., 1997—. Founder Down River Irish Am., 1994. With USN. Mem. Am. Legion, Mich. Assn. Dist. Ct. Magistrates, Wayne County Mich. Assn. of Chiefs of Police, Wayne County Detectives Assn. (life), K.C. (advocate). Criminal, General practice, Personal injury. Home: 14645 Lenore Redford MI 48239-3350

**PHILIPS, ABE L., JR.,** lawyer; b. Columbus, Ga., Dec. 31, 1934; s. Abram Lewis and Mary Louise (Rice) P.; m. Frances Carolyn Tingen, Aug. 23, 1957; children: A. Lewis III, Sidney Tingen, Scott Rice, L. Bradley. Student, Auburn U., 1953-55; BA, U. Ala., Tuscaloosa, 1957, JD, 1959. Bar: Ala. 1959, U.S. Dist. Ct. (so., mid., no. dists.) Ala. 1961, U.S. Ct. Appeals (5th cir.) 1967, U.S. Supreme Ct. 1970, U.S. Ct. Appeals (11th cir.) 1982. Assoc. Reams, Philips, Brooks et. al., Mobile, Ala., 1959-66, ptnr., 1966-98, mng. ptnr., 1976-98; ptnr. Pierce, Ledyard, Latta & Wasden PC, Mobile, 1998—. Mem. Gov.'s Indsl. Com., Ala.; mem. world trade com. C. of C., Mobile; mem. exec. com. Mobile County Dems., 1963; gen. chmn. Am. Jr. Miss Program, Mobile, 1968; pres. Jr. C. of C., 1969. Mem. Maritime Law Assn. U.S. (proctor), Southeastern Admiralty Law Inst., Mobile Bar Assn. (mem. admirality com.), Mystics Time, Soc. Les Bon Vivants. Methodist. Avocations: tennis, scuba diving, quail hunting, youth sports coach. Fax: 334-344-9696. Admiralty, Federal civil litigation, General practice. Home: 4160 Carmel Dr N Mobile AL 36608-2405 Office: Pierce Ledyard Latta & Wasden PC 400 Colonial Bank Centre 41 N Beltline Hwy Mobile AL 36608-1204

**PHILIPSBORN, JOHN TIMOTHY,** lawyer, author; b. Paris, Oct. 19, 1949; s. John David and Helen (Worth) P. AB, Bowdoin Coll., 1971; MEd, Antioch Coll., 1975; JD, U. Calif., Davis, 1978. Bar: Calif. 1978, U.S. Dist. Ct. (no. and ea. dists.) Calif. 1978, U.S. Ct. Appeals (9th cir.) 1985, U.S. Supreme Ct. 1985; cert-specialist in criminal law State of Calif., 1985. VISTA vol. Office of Gov. State of Mont., Helena, 1972-73; cons. U.S. Govt., Denver, 1974; lectr. Antioch New Eng. Grad. Sch., Keene, N.H., 1973-75, U. N.H., Durham, 1973-75; ptnr. Philipsborn & Cohn, San Jose, Calif., 1978-80; atty., supr. Defenders Inc., San Diego, 1980-83; assoc. Garry, Dreyfus & McTernan, San Francisco, 1983-87; pvt. practice, San Diego and San Francisco, 1987—; cons. Nicaraguan ct. evaluation projects, 1987-88, UN Internat. Tribunal, 1995—; coord. Internat. Conf. Adversarial Sys., Lisbon, Portugal, 1990; mem. adj. faculty New Coll. Law, San Francisco, 1991—; legal asst. project refugee camps S.E. Asia, 1992—, legal edn. projects, Cambodia, 1995—; cons. on continuing edn. of bar, 1995—. Bd. editors Champion, Forum; contbr. articles to profl. jours., chpts. to book. Founder trial program San Francisco Schs., 1986; bd. dirs. Calif. Indian Legal Svcs., 1990-96. Fulbright scholar, Portugal, 1989. Mem. Nat. Assn. Criminal Def. Lawyers (assoc., co-chmn. death penalty impact litigation group 1989, co-chmn. govtl. misconduct com. 1990-92, vice chmn. task force on emerging democracies 1990-91), Calif. State Bar (evaluation panel criminal law specialists 1986—, com. on continuing edn. of bar 1991-94, criminal law subcom. state bd. legal specialists 1995-96), Calif. Attys. for Criminal Justice (bd. govs. 1989-94, assoc. editor jour. 1987—, chmn. Amicus Curiae com. 1992—, co-chmn. govtl. misconduct com. 1989-92), World Affairs Coun. Criminal, Public international. Office: Civic Ctr Bldg 507 Polk St Ste 250 San Francisco CA 94102-3337

**PHILLIPS, ALMARIN,** economics educator, consultant; b. Port Jervis, N.Y., Mar. 13, 1925; s. Wendell Edgar and Hazel (Billett) P.; m. Dorothy Kathryn Burns, June 14, 1947 (div. 1976); children: Almarin Paul, Frederick Peter, Thomas Rock, David John, Elizabeth Linett, Charles Samuel; m. Carole Cherry Greenberg, Dec. 19, 1976. B.S., U. Pa., 1948, M.A., 1949; Ph.D., Harvard, 1953. Instr. econs. U. Pa., 1948-50, 51-53, asst. prof. econs., 1953-56, prof. econs. and law, 1963-91; Hower prof. pub. policy U. Pa. 1983-91; chmn. dept. econs. U. Pa., 1968-71, 72-73, assoc. dean Wharton Sch., 1973-74, dean Sch. Pub. and Urban Policy, 1974-77, chair faculty senate, 1990-91; teaching fellow Harvard, 1950-51; assoc. prof. U. Va, 1956-61, prof., 1961-63; vis. prof. U. Hawaii, summer 1968, U. Warwick, London

Grad. Sch. Bus. Studies, 1972, Ohio State U., McGill U., 1978, Calif. Inst. Tech, Northwestern U., 1980, Ariz. Coll. Law, 1987, Inst. Europeén d'Adminstrn. des Affairs (INSEAD), France, spring 1990; co-dir. Pres.'s Commn. Fin. Structure and Regulation, 1970-71; mem. Nat. Commn. Electronic Fund Transfers, 1976-77; chmn. bd. Econsult Corp., 1990-96. Author: (with R.W. Cabell) Problems in Basic Operations Research Methods for Management, 1961, Market Structure, Organization and Performance, 1962, Technology and Market Structure: A Study of the Aircraft Industry, 1971, (with P. Phillips and T.R. Phillips) Biz Jets: Technology and Market Structure in the Corporate Jet Aircraft Industry, 1994; Editor: Perspectives on Antitrust Policy, 1965, (with O.E. Williamson) Prices: Issues in Theory, Practice and Policy, 1968, Promoting Competition in Regulated Markets, 1975 ; editor Jour. Indsl. Econs., 1974-90; Contbr. articles to tech. lit. Served with AUS, 1943-45. Decorated Purple Heart, Bronze Star. Fellow Am. Statis. Assn., AAAS; mem. Am. Econ. Assn., Econometric Soc., European Econ. Assn., Internat. Telecommunications Soc. (bd. dirs. 1990—). Home: 1115 Remington Rd Wynnewood PA 19096-4021

**PHILLIPS, ANTHONY FRANCIS,** lawyer; b. Hartford, Conn., May 18, 1937; s. Frank and Lena Phillips; m. Rosemary Karran McGowan, Jan. 28, 1967; children: Karran, Antonia, Justin. BA, U. Conn., 1959; JD, Cornell U., 1962. Bar: N.Y. 1964, U.S. Dist. Ct. (so. dist., ea. dist.) N.Y. 1965, (ctrl. dist.) Calif. 1980, U.S. Tax Ct. 1981, U.S. Ct. Appeals (2nd cir.) 1967, (3d cir.) 1985, (4th cir.) 1983, (5th cir.) 1972, (7th cir.) 1987, (9th cir.) 1983, (10th cir.) 1983, U.S. Supreme Ct. 1971. Assoc. Willkie, Farr & Gallagher, N.Y.C., 1963-69, ptnr., 1969—. Mem. adv. com. Cornell U. Law Sch., 1994—. Fellow Am. Bar Found.; mem. ABA, N.Y. State Bar Assn., N.Y. County Bar Assn. (bd. dirs. 1989-95), Assn. of Bar of City of N.Y. Federal civil litigation, State civil litigation. Home: 3 Elm Rock Rd Bronxville NY 10708-4202 Office: Willkie Farr & Gallagher 787 7th Ave Lbby 2 New York NY 10019-6018

**PHILLIPS, BARNET, IV,** lawyer; b. New York, N.Y., July 5, 1948; s. Barnet III and Isabelle (Auriema) P.; m. Sharon Walsted Packey, Jan. 2, 1981; children: Victoria Ilonka, Caroline Walsted. BA, Yale U., 1970; JD, Fordham U., 1973; LLM, NYU, 1977. Bar: N.Y. 1974. Assoc. Hughes Hubbard & Reed, N.Y.C., 1973-76; assoc. Skadden, Arps, Slate, Meagher & Flom, N.Y.C., 1977-81, ptnr., 1981—; adj. assoc. prof. Forham U., N.Y.C., 1987-88; articles editor The Tax Lawyer, 1989-91. Co-author: Structuring Corporate Acquisition - Tax Aspects. Bd. dirs Student/Sponsor Partnership, N.Y.C., 1990-95; bd. cons. Portsmouth (R.I.) Abbey Sch., 1991-96, chmn., 97—. Republican. Avocations: skiing, opera, triathlons. Corporate taxation, Taxation, general, Personal income taxation. Home: 6 Hycliff Rd Greenwich CT 06831-3223 Office: Skadden Arps Slate Meagher & Flom 919 3rd Ave New York NY 10022-3902

**PHILLIPS, BRUCE HAROLD,** lawyer; b. Little Rock, Feb. 5, 1962; s. Philip Kirkland and Jayne (Jack) L.; m. Nancy Lee Williams, Nov. 12, 1994. BA in Bus. Adminstrn., U. Ark., Little Rock, 1988; JD, U. Ark., Fayetteville, 1993. Bar: Ark. 1993, Tenn. 1994, U.S. Dist. Ct. (mid. dist.) Tenn. 1994, U.S. Ct. Appeals (6th cir.) 1995. Golf profl. Internat. Golf, Little Rock, 1982-85, Tee-to-Green Golf, Little Rock, 1985-89; assoc. Jack, Lyon & Jones, P.A., Nashville, 1993—. Mem. Phi Alpha Delta. Avocation: golf. General civil litigation, Entertainment, Intellectual property. Office: Jack Lyon & Jones PA 11 Music Cir S Nashville TN 37203-4335

**PHILLIPS, CONNIE SULLIVAN,** judge; b. Campbellsville, Ky., Feb. 25, 1957; d. Murrell and Hazel Mae Sullivan; m. Roy V. Phillips. BS in Polit. Sci. and History, Campbellsville Coll., 1980; JD, U. Ky., 1983. Pub. defender Dept. Pub. Advocacy, Frankfort, Ky., 1984-86, 92-93; atty. William Colvin, Atty., Greensburg, Ky., 1986-87; law ptnr. Colvin & Phillips, Greensburg, 1987-91; pvt. practice law Campbellsville, 1991-94; dist. judge Adminstrv. Office of the Cts., Frankfort, 1994-98, 98—. Mem. Ky. Bar Assn. Office: PO Box 4189 203 Court St Campbellsville KY 42719

**PHILLIPS, CYRUS EASTMAN, IV,** lawyer; b. Charlottesville, Va., Oct. 2, 1944; s. Cyrus Eastman, III and Sue (Irving) P.; m. Shirley Ruth Hunter, June 11, 1967; children: Cyrus Eastman V, Kathryn G., Susan L., William H. A.B. with honors U. Ill., 1966; J.D., Coll. William and Mary, 1968. Bar: Va. 1968, U.S. Ct. Claims 1969, U.S. Supreme Ct. 1971, U.S. Ct. Appeals (4th cir.) 1976, U.S. Ct. Appeals (fed. cir.) 1982. Atty., adviser, trial atty. Def. Logistics Agy. Def. Constrn. Supply Ctr., Columbus, Ohio, 1968-80; adminstrv. judge Bd. Contract Appeals GSA, Washington, 1980-87, dep. vice chmn., 1984-86, vice chmn., 1986-87; of counsel, McGuire, Woods, Battle and Boothe, Washington, 1987-88, ptnr., 1989—; lectr. Legal Edn. Inst., Dept. Justice, Washington, 1982—, GSA Trail Boss Program, 1988—. Rsch. editor William and Mary Law Rev., 1968. Contbr. articles to profl. jours. Chmn. Plain Township Zoning Commn., New Albany, Ohio, 1978-80. Recipient Meritorious Civilian Svc. award Def. Logistics Agy., Dept. Def., 1980. Mem. ABA, Va. Bar Assn., Va. Trial Lawyers Assn., Fed. Bar Assn. (pres. Columbus chpt. 1974-75, vice chmn. bd. contracts appeals com. 1981), Nat. Conf. Bds. of Contract Appeal, Fed. Circuit Bar Assn., Computer Law Assn., Nat. Muzzle Loading Rifle Assn. (Friendship, Ind.). Republican. Presbyterian. Home: 5405 Jamie Ct Fredericksburg VA 22407-1617 Office: McGuire Woods Battle & Boothe Army and Navy Club Bldg 1627 I St NW Ste 1000 Washington DC 20006-4007

**PHILLIPS, DANA WAYNE,** lawyer; b. Corpus Christi, Tex., Oct. 5, 1951; s. David Wayne and Mildred (Elliott) P.; m. Dene' Elaine Batelaan, July 21, 1973 (div. 1981); m. Susan Jeanne Predmore, Mar. 23, 1985; 1 child Tristan Reid Phillips, step daughter: Lindsey Ann Midgley. Student, So. Meth. U., Dallas, 1969-70; BA, U. Calif., Santa Barbara, 1973; JD, U. San Diego, 1976. Bar: Calif. 1976, U.S. Dist. Ct. (ctrl. dist.) Calif. 1977. Atty. Pell & Phillips, Ventura, Calif., 1976-80, Drucker & Steinschriber, Sherman Oaks, Calif., 1980-82; gen. counsel Pension Vest, Inc., Montrose, Calif., 1982-85; atty. Drucker & Steinschriber, Sherman Oaks, Calif., 1985-86; gen. counsel Sacramento Housing & Redevelopment Agy., Sacramento, 1986—; bd. mem. Nat. Assn. Pvt. Pracement Syndicators, L.A., 1984-85; chmn., bd. dirs. Calif. Housing Authority Risk Mgmt. Agy., Oakland. Mem. ABA, Sacramento County Bar Assn., Sacramento Mother Lode Govt. Atty. Assn. Office: Sacramento Housing & Redevelopment Agy 630 I St Sacramento CA 95814-2404

**PHILLIPS, DOROTHY KAY,** lawyer; b. Camden, N.J., Nov. 2, 1945; d. Benjamin L. and Sadye (Levinsky) Phillips; children: Bethann P., David M. Schaffzin. BS in English Lit. magna cum laude, U. Pa., 1964; MA in Family Life and Marriage Counseling and Edn., NYU, 1975; JD, Villanova U., 1978. Bar: Pa. 1978, N.J. 1978, U.S. Dist. Ct. (ea. dist.) Pa. 1978, U.S. Dist. Ct. N.J., 1978, U.S. Ct. Appeals (3d cir.), 1984, U.S. Supreme Ct. 1984. Tchr., Haddon Twp. High Sch. (N.J.), and Haddon Heights High Sch. (N.J.), 1964-70; lectr., counselor Marriage Council of Phila.; lectr. U. Pa. and Hahnemann Med. Schs., Phila., 1970-75; atty. Adler, Barish, Daniels, Levin & Creskoff, Phila., 1978-79, Astor, Weiss & Newman, Phila., 1979-80; ptnr. Romisher & Phillips, P.C., Phila., 1981-86; prin. Law Office of Dorothy K. Phillips, 1986—; faculty Sch. of Law Temple U. Guest speaker on domestic rels. issues on radio and TV shows; featured in newspaper and mag. articles; contbr. articles to profl. jours. Rosenbach Found., Philadanco, Fedn. Allied Jewish Appeal (lawyers. div.), World Affairs Coun.; bd. mem. Anti-Defamation League of B'nai B'rith, Nat. Mus. Jewish History, mem. friends' circle, Athenaeum, Phila., shareholder. Mem. ABA, ATLA (membership com. 1990-91, co-chair 1989-90), Pa. Trial Lawyers Assn. (chair membership com. family sect. 1989-90, presenter ann. update civil litigators-family law, author procedures practice of family law Phila. County Family Law Litigation Sect. County practiced database 1991), Pa. Bar Assn. (continuing legal edn. com. 1990-92, faculty, lectr. Pa. Bar Inst. Continuing Legal Edn. 1990, panel mem. summer meeting 1991), N.J. Bar Assn., Phila. Bar Assn. (chmn. early settlement program 1983-84, mem. custody rules drafting com. for Supreme Ct. Pa., spl. events speaker on pensions, counsel fees, written fee agreements 1989-91, co-chair and moderator of panel mandatory continuing legal edn. 1994), Phila. Trial Lawyers Assn., Montgomery County Bar Assn., Lawyers Club. E-mail: dkphil@aol.com. Family and matrimonial, State civil litigation, Appellate. Address: 121 S Broad St Ste 21 Philadelphia PA 19107-4534

**PHILLIPS, DWIGHT WILBURN,** lawyer; b. Detroit, Dec. 19, 1951; s. Wilburn Raymond and Inez Marie (Sims) P. BA, U. San Francisco, 1973; JD, U. Mich., 1976. Bar: Mich. 1976. Assoc. Ronald Crenshaw and Assocs., Detroit, 1976-81; ptnr. Patterson, Phifer & Phillips, Detroit, 1981—. chmn. bd. Eastside Br. YMCA, 1987-90. Mem. ABA, Mich. Bar Assn. (workers compensation sect., panel chmn., atty. discipline bd.), Wolverine Bar Assn. (treas. 1979-81), Assn. Trial Lawyers Am., Alpha Phi Alpha. Avocation: model trains. Workers' compensation, Personal injury. Home: 1233 Audubon Rd Grosse Pointe MI 48230-1151 Office: Patterson Phifer & Phillips PC 1274 Library St Ste 500 Detroit MI 48226-2283

**PHILLIPS, ELIZABETH JASON,** lawyer; b. Boston, Sept. 3, 1936; d. Richard Eliot and Elizabeth Harding (McClure) Jason; m. William Morris Phillips Jr., Mar. 2, 1991; children: Meredith Rowe, William Morris Phillips III, Eleanor Anne, Robert J., Lee B. Stewart. BA in History, U. Mass., 1958; MEd, U. Hartford, 1969; JD, Western New Eng. Coll., Springfield, Mass., 1977. Bar: Mass. 1977, U.S. Dist. Ct. Mass. 1978, Va. 1981, U.S. Dist. Ct. (ea. dist.) Va. 1981, U.S. Dist. Ct. D.C. 1981, U.S. Dist. Ct. (we. dist.) Va. 1982, U.S. Ct. Appeals (4th cir.) 1982, U.S. Supreme Ct. 1984. Ptnr. firm Thompson & Stewart, Ludlow, Mass., 1977-80; adminstr. Office Atty. Gen., Commonwealth of Va., Richmond, 1980-82, asst. atty. gen., 1982-84; dep. Commr. Indsl. Commn. Va., 1984-91; dep. commr., mgr. dispute resolution divsn. Va. Workers' Compensation Commn., Richmond, 1991—. Trustee Ludlow Hosp., 1979-80. Mem. ABA, Richmond Bar Assn., Va. Bar Assn., Va. Assn. Adminstrv. Law Judges and Hearing Officers (pres.-elect 1999), Va. Exec. Inst., Ludlow C. of C. (pres. 1980). Episcopalian. Home: Cedar Shade 3859 Raymond Walker Rd Hayes VA 23072-4620 Office: Va Workers Compensation Commn 1000 Dmv Dr Richmond VA 23220-2036

**PHILLIPS, ELLIOTT HUNTER,** lawyer; b. Birmingham, Mich., Feb. 14, 1919; s. Frank Elliott and Gertrude (Zacharias) P.; m. Gail Carolyn Isbey, Apr. 22, 1950; children—Elliott Hunter, Alexandra. A.B. cum laude, Harvard U., 1940, J.D., 1947. Bar: Mich. 1948. Since practiced in Detroit; ptnr. Hill Lewis (formerly Hill, Lewis, Adams, Goodrich & Tait), 1953-89, of counsel, 1989-96; of counsel Clark Hill, 1996—; chmn. bd. dirs. Detroit & Can. Tunnel Corp.; pres., dir. Detroit and Windsor Subway Co.; mem. Mich. Bd. Accountancy, 1965-73. Contbr. to legal and accounting jours. Chmn. bd. dirs. Southeastern Mich. chpt. ARC; pres., trustee McGregor Fund; trustee Boys Republic, Detroit Inst. for Children, United Way Southeastern Mich., Univ. Liggett Sch.; mem. nat. maj. gifts com. Harvard U., Harvard Pres.'s Assocs., 1974—; Pres.'s Coun., 1990, mem. overseers com. to visit Law Sch., overseers com. univ. resouces, Mich. chmn. Harvard Coll. Fund; trustee, pres. Ch. Youth Svc.; mem. Detroit Area coun. Boy Scouts Am. Lt. comdr. USNR, 1946. Recipient Spitzley award Detroit Inst. for Children, 1986, Harvard Alumni Assn. Disting. Svc. award, 1991. Fellow Mich. State Bar Found. (life), Am. Bar Found. (life); mem. ABA, State Bar Mich., Detroit Bar Assn., Lincoln's Inn Soc., Soc. Colonial Wars in Mich. and Fla., Country Club Detroit, Detroit Club (pres. 1988-89), Yondotega Club, Grosse Pointe Club, Harvard Ea. Mich. Club (pres. 1955-56, Disting. Alumnus award 1992), Harvard Club N.Y.C., John's Island Club. Episcopalian (vestryman, sr. warden). Pension, profit-sharing, and employee benefits, General corporate, Non-profit and tax-exempt organizations. Home: 193 Ridge Rd Grosse Pointe MI 48236-3554 Office: 333 W Fort St Detroit MI 48226-3115

**PHILLIPS, ELVIN WILLIS,** lawyer; b. Tampa, Fla., Feb. 27, 1949; s. Claude Everett and Elizabeth (Willis) P.; m. Sharon Gayle Alexander, June 20, 1970; children: Natasha Hope, Tanya Joy, Trey Alexander. BA, U. Fla., 1971; MA, Western Carolina U., 1974, EdS, 1975; JD, Stetson U., 1980. Bar: Fla. 1980, U.S. Dist. Ct. (mid. dist.) Fla. 1981, U.S. Dist. Ct. (so. dist.) Fla. 1982, U.S. Ct. Appeals (11th cir.) 1988. Tchr. Monroe County Schs., Key West, Fla., 1970-73; asst. prin. Habersham County Schs., Clarksville, Ga., 1973-77; assoc. Dixon, Lawson & Brown, Tampa, Fla., 1980-81, Yado, Keel, Nelson et al, Tampa, Fla., 1981; ptnr. Lawson, McWhirter, Grandoff & Reeves, Tampa, Fla., 1981-88, Williams, Parker, Harrison, Dietz & Getzen, Sarasota, Fla., 1988—. Leadership Devel. Program fellow Southern Regional Coun., Atlanta, 1975. Mem. ABA (forum com. constrn. industry 1989-96), Fla. Bar (chmn. 1991-92, vice chmn. 1990-91, mem. benefits com.), Sarasota County Bar Assn., Phi Kappa Phi, Phi Alpha Delta, Phi Delta Kappa. Democrat. Baptist. Construction, Government contracts and claims, State civil litigation. Home: 3310 Del Prado Ct Tampa FL 33614-2721 Office: Williams Parker Harrison Dietz & Getzen 200 S Orange Ave Sarasota FL 34236-6802

**PHILLIPS, FLORENCE TSU,** lawyer, choreographer, dance educator; b. Taipei, Republic of China, May 2, 1949; came to U.S., 1957; d. Victor Z.M. and Dulcie (Ling) Tsu; m. Patrick J. Phillips; 1 child, Roderick James. Student, NYU, 1967-69; BA summa cum laude, UCLA, 1971, JD, 1974. Bar: Calif. 1974. Dancer Imperial Japanese Dancers, N.Y.C., 1965-70, Ballet de Paris, Paris and Montreal, Que., Can., 1967-68, Grands Ballets Canadiens, Montreal, 1968-69; atty. HUD, Washington, 1974, L.A. Pub. Defender's Office, 1975-77; owner, dir. Danceworks Studio, L.A., 1978—; atty. Minami, Lew & Tamaki, LLP, San Francisco, 1997—; choreographer, dir. Sinay Ballet, L.A., 1979—. Choreographed over 30 ballets, 1979—; consulting editor Dance Tchr. Now Mag. Mem. Bar Assn. San Francisco, Phi Beta Kappa, Pi Gamma Mu. Avocations: pets, gardening, needle crafts. Personal injury, Family and matrimonial, General civil litigation.

**PHILLIPS, GEORGE LANDON,** prosecutor; b. Fulton, Miss., May 24, 1949; s. Gilbert L. and Grace (Staker) P. BS, U. So. Miss., 1971; JD, U. Miss., 1973. Bar: Miss. 1973. Assoc. Johnson, Pittman & Pittman, Hattiesburg, Miss., 1980-94; ptnr. Norris & Phillips, 1975-76; county pros. atty. Forrest County, Miss., 1976-80; U.S. atty. So. Dist. Miss., Jackson, Miss., 1980-94; chmn. investigative agys. subcom. U.S. Atty. Gen.'s Adv. Com., 1983-86, mem. law enforcement coordination subcom. and budget subcom., 1986-88; spl. coun. U.S. Senator T. Cochran, 1995—; chmn. AGAC subcom. law enforcement cooperation and victim/witness assistance, 1989-94; instr. Hattiesburg Police Acad., 1977. Bd. dirs. Forrest County Youth Ct.; pres. South Ctrl. chpt. ARC, 1980-81; bd. dirs. Pine Burr Area coun. Boy Scouts Am.; mem. Atty. Gen.'s Adv. Com., 1981-82, 89-91; bd. dirs. Jackson Zoo, 1989-91. Mem. Miss. Prosecutors Assn. (pres.), Fed. Bar Assn., Miss. Bar Assn. (v.p. southern region), Am. Criminal Justice Assn., Nat. Dist. Attys. Assn., Miss. Trial Lawyers, Miss. Quarter Horse Assn. (pres.), Kiwanis. Baptist. Office: Spl Counsel Office of US Sen T Cochran 188 E Capital Ste 614 Jackson MS 39201-2125

**PHILLIPS, JAMES DICKSON, JR.,** federal judge; b. Scotland County, N.C., Sept. 23, 1922; s. James Dickson and Helen (Shepherd) P.; m. Jean Duff Nunalee, July 16, 1960; children: Evelyn, James Dickson, III, Elizabeth Duff, Ida Wills. BS cum laude, Davidson Coll., 1943; JD, U. N.C., 1948. Bar: N.C. 1948. Asst. dir. Inst. Govt., Chapel Hill, N.C., 1948-49; ptnr. firm Phillips & McCoy, Laurinburg, N.C., 1949-55, Sanford, Phillips, McCoy & Weaver, Fayetteville, N.C., 1955-60; from asst. prof. to prof. law U. N.C., 1960-78, dean Sch. Law, 1964-74; circuit judge U.S. Ct. Appeals (4th cir.), 1978—; Mem. N.C. Wildlife Resources Commn., 1961-63; mem. N.C. Cts. Commn., 1963-75; also vice chmn.; chmn. N.C. Bd. Ethics, 1977-78. Served with parachute inf. U.S. Army, 1943-46. Decorated Bronze Arrowhead, Bronze Star, Purple Heart; recipient John J. Parker Meml. award, Thomas Jefferson award, Disting. Alumnus award U. N.C., 1993. Mem. Am. Law Inst. Democrat. Presbyterian.

**PHILLIPS, JERRY JUAN,** law educator; b. Charlotte, N.C., June 16, 1935; s. Vergil Ernest and Mary Blanche (Wade) P.; m. Anne Butler Colville, June 6, 1959; children: Sherman Wade, Dorothy Colville. B.A., Yale U., 1956, J.D., 1961; B.A., Cambridge (Eng.) U., 1958, M.A. (hon.), 1964. Bar: Tenn. bar 1961. Assoc. firm Miller & Martin, Chattanooga, 1961-67; asst. prof. law U. Tenn., 1967-72, assoc. prof., 1972-73, prof., 1973—, W.P. Toms prof., 1980—; advisor Tenn. Law Revision Commn., 1968-70; mem. Tenn. Jud. Council, 1970-74; adv. Fed. Interagy. Task Force on Products Liability, 1976-77; lectr. in field. Author: Products Liability in a Nutshell, 5th edit., 1998, Products Liability Cases and Materials on Torts and Related Law, 1980, Products Liability Treatise, 3 vols., 1986, Cases and Materials on Tort Law, 1992, 2d edit., 1997, Products Liability-Cases, Materials, Problems, 1994; advisor Tenn. U. Law Rev., 1977—. U. Tenn. grantee, 1978. Mem. ABA, Am. Law Inst., Knoxville Bar Assn., Am. Assn. Law Schs., Order of Coif, Phi Beta Kappa. Democrat. Episcopalian. Club: Knoxville Racquet. Office: 1505 Cumberland Ave Knoxville TN 37996-0001

**PHILLIPS, JOHN BOMAR,** lawyer; b. Murfreesboro, Tenn., Jan. 28, 1947; s. John Bomar Sr. and Betty Blanche (Primm) P.; m. Ellen Elizabeth Ellis, Aug. 9, 1969; children: John Bomar III, Anna Carroll, Ellis Elizabeth. BS, David Lipscomb Coll., 1969; JD, U. Tenn., 1974. Bar: Tenn. 1974, U.S. Dist. Ct. (ea. dist.) Tenn. 1975, U.S. Tax Ct. 1976, U.S. Ct. Appeals (6th cir.) 1980. Assoc. Stophel, Caldwell & Heggie, Chattanooga, 1974-79; ptnr. Caldwell, Heggie & Helton, Chattanooga, 1979-91, Miller & Martin, Chattanooga, 1991—. Author: Tennessee Employment Law, 1989, Employment Law Desk Book for Tennessee Employers, 1989; editor: The Tennessee Employment Law Update, 1986—; mem. nat. moot ct. team U. Tenn. Law Rev. Pres. Chattanooga State coll. Found., 1992-94, Boys Club of Chattanooga, 1983-84; sec. Tenn. Aquarium, 1989—; chmn. Chattanooga Conv. and Visitors Bur., 1996-97; bd. dirs. Vol. Comty. Sch., Chattanooga, 1980-85, Coun. for Alcohol and Drug Abuse, Chattanooga, 1981-83, Creative Discovery Mus., 1994-99, Girls Prep. Sch., 1997—, Allied Arts of Gtr. Chattahooga, 1997—; mem. Hamilton County Juvenile Ct. Commn., 1995-99. Fellow Tenn. Bar Found., Chattanooga Bar Found.; mem. ABA (labor law sect.), Tenn. Bar Assn. (chair labor law sect. 1992-93, Justice Joseph W. Henry award 1986-87), Chattanooga Bar Assn. (bd. govs. 1978-79), Chattanooga C. of C. (bd. dirs. 1998—), Order of Coif, Fairyland Country Club (Lookout Mountain, Tenn.), Walden Club (bd. govs. 1992-95), Mountain City Club, Kiwanis (pres. Chattanooga 1986-87). Mem. Disciples of Christ. Avocations, reading, writing. Labor, Libel. Home: 1107 E Brow Rd Lookout Mountain TN 37350-1015 Office: Miller & Martin 832 Georgia Ave Ste 1000 Chattanooga TN 37402-2289

**PHILLIPS, JOHN C.,** lawyer; b. Staten Island, N.Y., June 6, 1948; s. John D. G. and Eleanor (Stier) P.; m. Karen Francis McKenna, June 5, 1971; children: James, Thomas, Robert. AB in Govt., Cornell U., 1970; MA in Polit. Sci., Rutgers U., 1972, JD, 1975. Bar: N.J. 1975, U.S. Dist. Ct. N.J. 1975, N.Y. 1982, U.S. Supreme Ct. 1985, U.S. Ct. Appeals (3d cir.) 1985, Fla. 1988. Assoc. Carpenter, Bennett & Morrisey, Newark, 1975-79, Buttermore, Mullen & Jeremiah, Westfield, N.J., 1979-80; mng. ptnr. Buttermore, Mullen, Jeremiah & Phillips, Westfield, 1981-85, 87—; with DeVos, Phillips & Co. PC, 1986-87; trustee, dir. Animal Care Fund Inc., East Smithfield, Pa., 1983-98. Author: (with others) New Jersey Transactins, Zoning and Planning, 1993. Dir., coach Police Athletic League, Berkeley Heights, N.J., 1967—; mem. Kappa Alpha Literary Soc., 1967—, trustee Kappa Alpha Assn., 1974-90, v.p. Kappa Alpha Assn. Found., 1978-87, vice-chmn., 1983, chmn., 1984; dir. Youth Soccer Club, Berkeley Heights, 1983-94; mem. Berkeley Heights Twp. Com., 1985-87, dep. mayor, 1986, 87; Twp. atty., Berkeley Heights, 1989, 91, 94—; planning bd. atty. Twp. Warren, 1987—; mem. N.J. Hotel and Multiple Dwelling Safety Bd., 1988—, vice chmn., 1998—; mem. Rep. Mcpl. Com., 1985—, vice chmn., 1990-92, 98—, mem. dist. XII Ethics Com., 1993-97, Dist. XII Fee Arbitratin Com., 1998—. Recipient award for Assistance and Dedication to youth, Police Athletic League, Berkeley Heights, 1975, Dedicated Svc. award Berkeley Heights Twp. Com., 1983. Mem. ABA, Assn. Trial Lawyers Am., Assn. Trial Lawyers N.J., N.J. State Bar Assn., Union County Bar Assn., Urban Land Inst., Jaycees (sec. New Providence-Berkeley Heights chpt. 1982, Jaycee of Yr. 1982), Fedn. of Planning Ofcls., Inst. of Mcpl. Attys., Canoe Brook Country Club. Republican. Methodist. Land use and zoning (including planning), Personal injury, State civil litigation. Home: 56 Emerson Ln Berkeley Heights NJ 07922-2414 Office: Buttermore Mullen Jeremiah & Phillips 445 E Broad St Westfield NJ 07090-2123

**PHILLIPS, JOHN T., II,** legal and cultural history educator, publisher; b. San Diego, Mar. 24, 1954; s. John T. and Caroline P. Phillips. BS in Econ., N.C. State U., 1975; JD, George Washington U., 1978; postgrad., U. Va. Bar: D.C. 1978, Va. 1980, U.S. Dist. Ct. (D.C. dist.) 1979, U.S. Dist. Ct. (ea. dist.) Va. 1993. Of counsel Pitts, Wike and Wingfield, Washington and Va., 1978-79; pvt. practice Washington and Va., 1980-96; instr. history George Mason U., Fairfax, Va., 1996—, Fairfax Tchr. Acad., 1996—, Shenandoah U., Leesburg, Va., 1997—; pub. Goose Creek Prodns., Leesburg, Va., 1995—; instr. legal/cultural history U. Va., Charlottesville, 1999—; cons. historian Native Am. TV. Author: Colonial Laws of Virginia and County Court Orders, 1996; editl. bd. Essays in History, Charlottesville; editor, pub. Morley-The Intimate Story of Virginia's Governor & Mrs. Westmoreland Davis, 1998, The Bulletin of the Historical Society of Loudoun County, Virginia, 1957-76; contbr. articles, revs. to profl. publs. Cons. historian Courthouse Renovation, Leesburg, Va.; chmn. Rep. Caucus, Leesburg; fundraiser, acquisitions Balch Libr., Leesburg. Mem. No. Va. Assn. for History (bd. dirs. 1999—), Assocs. of the Libr. of Congress, Phi Delta Phi. Republican. Episcopalian. Office: Colonial Laws Project PO Box 776 Leesburg VA 20178-0776

**PHILLIPS, J(OHN) TAYLOR,** judge; b. Greenville, S.C., Aug. 20, 1921; s. Walter Dixon and Mattie Sue (Taylor) P.; m. Mary Elizabeth Parrish, Dec. 18, 1954; children: John Allen, Susan, Linda-Lea, Julia. AA, Glenville State Coll., 1952; JD, Mercer U., 1955; LLD, Asbury Coll., 1992. Bar: Ga. 1954, U.S. Supreme Ct. 1969. Mem. Ho. of Reps. State of Ga., Atlanta, 1959-62, Senate, 1962-64. With USMC, 1942-51. Methodist. Home: 1735 Winston Dr Macon GA 31206-3241 Office: State Ct Bibb County PO Box 5086 Macon GA 31213-0001

**PHILLIPS, JOSEPH BRANTLEY, JR.,** lawyer; b. Greenville, S.C., Dec. 5, 1931. B.S. in Bus. Adminstrn., U. S.C., 1954, J.D., 1955. Bar: S.C. 1955. Assoc. Leatherwood, Walker, Todd & Mann, Greenville, 1958-63, ptnr., 1963—. Chmn. bd. deacons Presbyterian Ch., 1970-71, pres. Men of Ch., 1968-69, chmn. Christian Service Ctr., 1972-73; bd. dirs. Greenville Urban Ministry, 1978. Mem. ABA, S.C. Bar Assn., Greenville Bar Assn., Greenville Young Lawyers Club (pres. 1961-62), Lawyers Pilots Bar Assn., Kiwanis (pres. 1973). Clubs: Greenville Country (pres. 1977). Antitrust, General corporate, Aviation. Home: 207 Butler Springs Rd Greenville SC 29615-2261 Office: PO Box 87 Greenville SC 29602-0087

**PHILLIPS, KAREN BORLAUG,** economist, association executive; b. Long Beach, Calif., Oct. 1, 1956; d. Paul Vincent and Wilma (Tish) Borlaug. Student Cath. U. P.R., 1973-74; B.A., U. N.D., 1977, B.S., 1977; postgrad. George Washington U., 1978-80. Research asst. research and spl. programs adminstrn. U.S. Dept. Transp., Washington, 1977-78, economist, office of sec., Washington, 1978-82; profl. staff mem. (majority) Com. Commerce, Sci., Transp., U.S. Senate, Washington, 1982-85, tax economist (majority) com. on fin., 1985-87, chief economist (minority) senate com. on fin., 1987-88; commr. Interstate Commerce Commn., 1988-94; v.p. legislation Assn. Am. Railroads, Washington, 1994-95, sr. v.p. policy, legis. & comm., 1995-98; pres. Policy & Advocacy Assocs., Alexandria, Va., 1998—. Contbg. author studies, publs. in field. Recipient award for Meritorious Achievement, Sec. Transp., 1980, Spl. Achievement awards, 1978, 80, Outstanding Performance awards, 1978, 80, 81. Mem. Am. Econ. Assn., Women's Transp. Seminar (Woman of Yr. award 1994), Transp. Research Forum, Assn. Transp. Law, Logistics & Policy, Tax Coalition, Blue Key, Phi Beta Kappa, Omicron Delta Epsilon. Republican. Lutheran. Office: Policy and Advocacy Associates 1800 Diagonal Rd Ste 600 Alexandria VA 22314-2840

**PHILLIPS, LARRY EDWARD,** lawyer; b. Pitts., July 5, 1942; s. Jack F. and Jean H. (Houghtelin) P.; m. Karla Ann Hennings, June 5, 1976; 1 son, Andrew H.; 1 stepson, John W. Dean IV. BA, Hamilton Coll., 1964; JD, U. Mich., 1967. Bars: Pa. 1967, U.S. Dist. Ct. (we. dist.) Pa. 1967, U.S. Tax Ct. 1969. Assoc. Buchanan, Ingersoll, Rodewald, Kyle & Buerger, P.C. (now Buchanan Ingersoll P.C.), Pitts., 1967-73, mem., 1973—. Mem. Am. Coll. Tax Counsel, Tax Mgmt. Inc. (adv. bd.), Pitts. Tax Club, ABA (sect. taxation, com. on corp. tax and sect. real property, probate and trust law), Allegheny County Bar Assn., Pa. Bar Assn., Duquesne Club. Republican. Presbyterian. Corporate taxation, Estate taxation, Personal income taxation. Office: Buchanan Ingersoll PC One Oxford Ctr 301 Grant St Fl 20 Pittsburgh PA 15219-1410

**PHILLIPS, LEO HAROLD, JR.,** lawyer; b. Jan. 10, 1945; s. Leo Harold and Martha C. (Oberg) P.; m. Patricia Margaret Halcomb, Sept. 3, 1983. BA summa cum laude, Hillsdale Coll., 1967; MA, U. Mich., 1968, JD cum laude, 1973; LLM magna cum laude, Free U. of Brussels, 1974. Bar: Mich. 1974, N.Y. 1975, U.S. Supreme Ct. 1977, D.C. 1979. Fgn. lectr. Pusan Nat. U., Korea, 1969-70; assoc. Alexander & Green, N.Y.C., 1974-77; counsel Overseas Pvt. Investment Corp., Washington, 1977-80, sr. counsel,

1980-82, asst. gen. counsel, 1982-85; asst. gen. counsel Manor Care, Inc., Gaithersburg, Md., 1985-91, asst. sec., 1988—, assoc. gen. counsel, 1991—, v.p., 1996—; vol. Peace Corps, Pusan, 1968-71; mem. program for sr. mgrs. in govt. Harvard U., Cambridge, Mass., 1982. Contbr. articles to legal jours. Chmn. legal affairs com. Essex Condominium Assn., Washington, 1979-81; deacon Chevy Chase Presbyn. Ch., Washington, 1984-87, moderator, 1985-87, supt. ch. sch., elder, trustee, 1987-90, pres., 1988-90, mem. nominating com., 1995-96. Recipient Alumni Achievement award Hillsdale Coll., 1980; Meritorious Honor award Overseas Pvt. Investment Corp., 1981, Superior Achievement award, 1984. Mem. ABA (internat. fin. transactions com., vice-chmn. com. internat. ins. Law), Am. Soc. Internat. Law (Jessup Internat. Law moot ct. judge semi-final rounds 1978-83, chair corp. counsel com. 1993-97), Internat. Law Assn. (Am. br.; com. sec. 1982), D.C. Bar, N.Y. State Bar Assn., Royal Asiatic Soc. (Korea br.), State Bar Mich., Washington Fgn. Law Soc. (sec.-treas. 1980-81, bd. dirs., program coord. 1981-82, v.p. 1982-83, pres.-elect 1983-84, pres. 1984-85, chmn. nominating com. 1986, 88), Washington Internat. Trade Assn. (bd. dirs. 1984-87), Assn. Bar City N.Y., Hillsdale Coll. Alumni Assn. (co-chmn. Washington area 1977-90), Univ. Club (N.Y.C.). Private international, General corporate, Contracts commercial. Home: 4740 Connecticut Ave NW Apt 702 Washington DC 20008-5632 Office: Manor Care Inc 11555 Darnestown Rd Gaithersburg MD 20878-3200

**PHILLIPS, MARTY ROY,** lawyer; b. Sardis, Tenn., Oct. 22, 1966; s. Jerry Lynn and Oleta Ann (Hayes) P.; m. Sybile Gaye Martin, June 17, 1989; children: Zachary Lynn, Jonathan Martin. BA in English, Union U., Jackson, Tenn., 1988; JD, U. Tenn., 1991. Bar: Tenn. 1991, U.S. Dist. Ct. (we. dist.) Tenn. 1991, U.S. Dist. Ct. (cen. dist.) 1996, U.S. Ct. Appeals (6th cir.) 1995. Atty. Rainey, Rizer, Butler, Reviere & Bell, Jackson, 1991—. Adv. bd. West Tenn. Bus. Coll., 1997, bd. dirdsd. Birth Choice, Inc., Jackson, 1994—. Mem. Jackson-Madison County Bar Assn. (v.p. 1996-97). Republican. Baptist. General civil litigation, Personal injury, Product liability. Office: Rainey Kizer Butler Reviere & Bell 105 S Highland Ave Jackson TN 38301-6107

**PHILLIPS, MARY KLEYLA,** lawyer; b. Cleve., Apr. 29, 1946; d. Paul Archer and Mary Catherine (Gabele) Kleyla; m. Philip B. Phillips, Apr. 10, 1976; 1 child: Grant E. Cert., Jackson Meml. Hosp. Sch. Nursn, 1967; BA magma cum laude, Fla. St. U., 1973; JD cum laude, U. Fla. Coll. Law, 1975. Bar: Fla. 1975; RN, Fla. Assoc. Bedell, Dittmar, DeVault, Pillans & Gentry, Jacksonville, Fla., 1976-86, Gentry, Phillips & Hodak, P.A., Jacksonville, Fla., 1986—; mem. Acad. Fla. Trial Lawyers (coll. diplomates, 1984—, bd. dirs. 1984-86, Amicus Curiae com. 1983-86, constl. by-laws com. 1984-86, seminar com. 1984-86, pub. rels. com. 1985-86, spkrs. com. 1985-86, chmn. ethics com. 1989-90); mem. Fla. Bar Assn. (civil procedure rules com. 1980-86, grievance com. 1980-84 (chmn. 1983-84), bd. cert., designation advt. 1985-86, vice-chmn. continuing legal edn. com. 1989-91, rules jud. adminstrn. com. 1994-96); mem. Fla. Laega Svcs., 1984-87 (bd. dirs. 1984-87, treas. 1985-87, pers. com. 1985-86); mem. Jacksonville Bar Assn., 1981-87 (bd. govs. 1981-87, pres. young lawyers section 1981-82, pres. 1986-87); spkr. numerous legal and nursing engagememts, Fla., 1990—. Mem. bd. dirs. Girls Clubs Jacksonville, Inc., 1983-86; trustee Jessie Ball duPont Reiligious, Chasritable and Ednl. Fund, 1986—; Master Bench Chester Bedell Inn Ct., 1985-98 (emeritus 1998—); trustee Chester Debell Meml. Found., 1988-96; trustee U. Fla. Law Ctr. Assn., Inc., 1988—; mem. 4th Jud. Cir. Jud. Nominating Commn., 1991-95, chair 1993-94; dean search com. U. Fla. Coll. Law, 1995-96; pres. Jacksonville Women's Network, 1997. Mem. ABA, ATLA, Am. Bd. Trial Advs., Am. Judicature Soc., Am. Soc. Law Medicine, ANA, Am. Assn. Nurse Attys. Personal injury. Office: Gentry Phillips & Hodak PA 6 E Bay St Ste 400 Jacksonville FL 32202-5420

**PHILLIPS, PAMELA KIM,** lawyer; b. San Diego, Feb. 23, 1958; d. John Gerald and Nancy Kimiko (Tabuchi) Phillips; m. R. Richard Zanghetti, Sept. 16, 1989. BA cum laude, The Am. U., 1978; JD, Georgetown U., 1982. Bar: N.Y. 1983, U.S. Dist. Ct. (so. dist.) N.Y. 1983, Fla. 1994, U.S. Dist. Ct. (mid. dist.) Fla. 1994. Assoc. Curtis, Mallet-Prevost, Colt & Mosle, N.Y.C., 1982-84; assoc. LeBoeuf, Lamb, Greene & MacRae, N.Y.C., 1984-90, ptnr., 1991—. Mng. editor The Tax Lawyer, Georgetown U. Law Sch., Washington, 1980-81. Mem. coun. The Fresh Air Fund, 1991-94; bd. dirs. Jacksonville Zool. Soc., Inc., 1996—, sec., 1997—; pres. First Coast Venture Capital Group, Inc., 1996-98. Am. Univ. scholar, Washington, 1976-78. Mem. ABA, Bar Assn. City N.Y. (sec. young lawyers com. 1987-89, chmn. 1989-91, second century com. 1990-93, banking law com. 1991-94), Jacksonville Bar Assn., N.Y. Athletic Club, River Club. Democrat. Roman Catholic. Avocations: tennis, travel. Banking, Contracts commercial, Mergers and acquisitions. Home: 109 Carriage Lamp Way Ponte Vedra Beach FL 32082-1903 Office: LeBoeuf Lamb Greene & MacRae 125 W 55th St New York NY 10019-5369 also: 50 N Laura St Ste 2800 Jacksonville FL 32202-3656

**PHILLIPS, ROBERT JAMES, JR.,** lawyer, corporate executive; b. Houston, Aug. 4, 1955; s. Robert James and Mary Josephine (Bass) P.; m. Nancy Norris, Apr. 24, 1982; 1 child, Mary Ashton. BBA, So. Meth. U., 1976, JD, 1980. Bar: Tex. 1980. Vp., gen. counsel Aegis Shipping Ltd., London, 1980-81; assoc. Bishop, Larrimore, Lamsens & Brown, 1981-82; pres. Phillips Devel. Corp., Ft. Worth, Tex., 1982—; pvt. practice Ft. Worth, 1982-87, 89—; assoc. Haynes and Boone, Ft. Worth, 1988-89; sr. v.p. Am. Real Estate Group, 1989-93, Am. Savs. Bank, N.A., New West Fed. Savs. and Loan Assn., 1989-93, Am. Savs. Bank, Ft. Worth, 1991-92; chmn., CEO creative risk control Environ. Risk Mgmt. Inc., Ft. Worth, 1992-94; pres., CEO Pangburn Candy Co., 1996-99; exec. v.p. Ancor Holdings, 1999—; bd. dirs. Tex. Heritage, Inc. Bd. dirs., exec. com. Ft. Worth Ballet Assn., 1984-85, Van Cliburn Found.; v.p. planning, bd. dirs., exec. com. Ft. Worth Symphony Orch., 1984-85; bd. dirs. Mus. Modern Art, 1986—; bd. dirs., exec. com., chmn. investment com. Tex. Boys Choir, 1983-85. Mem. ABA, Tex. Bar Assn., Ft. Worth Bd. Realtors, Crescent Club, Phi Delta Phi, Kappa Sigma, Beta Gamma Sigma. Clubs: River Crest Country, Ft. Worth. Avocations: hunting, fishing, photography. General practice, Estate planning, Real property. Home and Office: PO Box 470099 Fort Worth TX 76147-0099

**PHILLIPS, RONALD FRANK,** academic administrator; b. Houston, Nov. 25, 1934; s. Franklin Jackson and Maudie Ethel (Merrill) P.; m. Jamie Jo Bottoms, Apr. 5, 1957 (dec. Sept. 1996); children: Barbara Celeste Phillips Oliveira, Joel Jackson, Phil Edward. BS, Abilene Christian U., 1955; JD, U. Tex., 1965. Bar: Tex. 1965, Calif. 1972. Bldg. contractor Phillips Homes, Abilene, Tex., 1955-56; br. mgr. Phillips Weatherstripping Co., Midland and Austin, Tex., 1957-65; corp. staff atty. McWood Corp., Abilene, 1965-67; sole practice law Abilene, 1967-70; mem. adj. faculty Abilene Christian U., 1967-70; prof. law Pepperdine U., Malibu, Calif., 1970—, dean Sch. Law, 1970-97, dean emeritus, 1997—, vice chancellor, 1995—. Deacon North A and Tenn. Ch. of Christ, Midland, 1959-62; deacon Highland Ch. of Christ, Abilene, 1965-70; elder Malibu Ch. of Christ, 1978-95; mgr., coach Little League Baseball, Abilene, Huntington Beach and Malibu, 1968-78, 90-95; coach Youth Soccer, Huntington Beach, Westlake Village and Malibu, 1972-80, 85-86, 91. Recipient Alumni citation Abilene Christian U., 1974. Fellow Am. Bar Found. (life); mem. ABA, State Bar Tex., State Bar Calif., Christian Legal Soc., L.A. Bar Assn., Assn. Am. Law Schs. (chmn. sect. on adminstrn. law schs. 1982, com. on cts. 1985-87), Am. Law Inst., Nat. Conf. Commrs. on Uniform State Laws. Republican. Office: Pepperdine U 24255 Pacific Coast Hwy Malibu CA 90263-0002

**PHILLIPS, STANTON EARL,** lawyer; b. Maybrook, N.Y., Dec. 6, 1954; s. Donald J. and Florence R. (Mintz) P.; m. Debra A. Goldenberg, May 27, 1990; children: Kayla Elise, Dylan, Maxwell. BA in Polit. Sci., Am. U., 1976; JD, George Mason U., 1980. Bar: Va. 1980, D.C. 1981, U.S. Dist. Ct. (ea. dist.) Va. 1983, U.S. Dist. Ct. D.C. 1986. Rsch. asst. to Senator Mike Gravel (Alaska) U.S. Senate, 1974; prin. Law Office Stanton Phillips, Arlington, Va., 1980—; spl. analysis team Associated Press, Washington, 1976. Author: Adoption Law, Procedure and Practice, 1995; co-author: Adoption Law in Virginia, 1996; contbg. author: Adoption Law and Practice, 1991-94; editor: Adoption Law Jour., 1990-92; contbr. articles to newspapers and profl. jours. Youth coord. Herb Harris for U.S. Ho. of Reps., Alexandria, Va., 1974; polit. cons. Sargent Shriver for Pres., Washington, 1976, Bruce Bradley for U.S. Senate, Bethesda, Md., 1976, Sharon Metz for Rep., Green Bay, Wis., 1980; LBJ Congl. intern, 1978; legal cons. D.C. Com. for Placement of Children in Family Homes, Washington, 1984-87, legal mem., 1987—; chairperson adoption rules com. D.C. Superior Ct., Washington, 1992. Recipient W.Va. Gov.'s Cup, W.Va. Ski Counsel, 1984, Southeastern Ski Club Championship, 1984, 1992, 1st Pl. team Subaru Ski Club Challenge, 1991. Mem. Am. Acad. Adoption Attys. (sec. 1990-91, trustee 1990-91), Am. Assn. Polit. Cons., Families for Pvt. Adoption, Arlington County Bar Assn., Resolve. Democrat. Jewish. Avocations: ski racing, international travel, back-packing. Family and matrimonial. Home: 3600 Launcelot Way Annandale VA 22003-1360 Office: 2009 14th St N Ste 510 Arlington VA 22201-2514

**PHILLIPS, THOMAS ROYAL,** state supreme court chief justice; b. Dallas, Oct. 23, 1949; s. George S. and Marguerite (Andrews) P.; m. Lyn Bracewell, June 26, 1982; 1 son, Daniel Austin Phillips; 1 stepson, Thomas R. Kirkham. BA, Baylor U., 1971; JD, Harvard U., 1974; LLD (hon.), Tex. Tech. U., 1997; DHL (hon.), St. Edwards U., 1998. Bar: Tex. 1974; cert. in civil trial law Tex. Bd. Legal Specialization. Briefing atty. Supreme Ct. Tex., Austin, 1974-75; assoc. Baker & Botts, Houston, 1975-81; judge 280th Dist. Ct., Houston, 1981-88; chief justice Supreme Ct. Tex., Austin, 1988—; mem. com. on fed.-state rels. Jud. Conf. U.S., 1990-96; chair Tex. Jud. Dists. Bd., 1988—; mem. State Judges Mass Tort Litig. Com., 1991-96; bd. dirs. Elmo B. Hunter Citizens Ctr. for Jud. Selection, 1992-94, Southwestern Legal Found.; mem. Nat. Conf. Chief Justices, 1988—, pres., 1997-98; adv. dir. Rev. of Litig., U. Tex. Law Sch., 1990—; chair Nat. Mass Tort Conf. Planning Com., 1993-94. Bd. advisors Ctr. for Pub. Policy Dispute Resolution, U. Tex. Law Sch., 1993—; mem. planning com. South Tex. Coll. of Law Ctr. for Creative Legal Solutions, 1993—. Recipient Outstanding Young Lawyer award Houston Young Lawyers Assn., 1986, award of excellence in govt. Tex. C. of C., 1992; named Appellate Judge of Yr., Tex. Assn. Civil Trial and Appellate Specialists, 1992-93, Disting. Alumnus, Baylor U., 1998. Mem. ABA (task force lawyers polit. contbns. 1997-98), Am. Law Inst. (advisor Fed. Jud. Code Project 1996—), Nat. Ctr. for State Ctrs. (chair, bd. dirs. 1997-98), State Bar Tex. (chmn. pattern jury charges IV com. 1985-87, vice chmn. adminstrn. justice com. 1986-87), Am. Judicature Soc. (bd. dirs. 1989-95, 99—, exec. bd. 1995-96), Tex. Philol. Soc., Houston Philol. Soc., Houston Bar Assn., Travis County Bar Assn. Republican. Episcopalian. Office: Tex Supreme Ct PO Box 12248 Austin TX 78711-2248

**PHILLIPS, W. ALAN,** entertainment lawyer, educator; b. Mobile, Ala., Aug. 26, 1963; s. Billy Ray and Clara Joanne (Andrews) P.; m. Molly Melissa Stocks, Nov. 3, 1984; children: Abigail Alston, James Andrew. MusB, James Madison U., 1985; JD, U. Richmond, 1994. Bar: Tenn., 1994, U.S. Dist. Ct. (mid. dist.) Tenn., 1995. Mktg. mgr. Silver Bells Music, Nashville, 1986; field rep. ASCAP, Richmond, Va., 1986-88; regional sales mgr. Independence Comm., Richmond, 1988-91; law clerk Press, Jones & Waechter, Richmond, 1992-93; law clerk Jack, Lyon & Jones, P.A., Nashville, 1993, assoc., 1995—; atty. OrNda Health Corp., Nashville, 1994-95; adj. prof. copyright Middle Tenn. State U., Murfreesboro, 1996—, Belmont U., Nashville, 1997-98. Assoc. editor: U. Richmond Law Rev., 1992-94; contbr. articles to profl. jours. Mem. ABA (chmn. arts, entertainment and sports law com. young lawyers divsn. 1997-98), Nashville Bar Assn. (chmn. intellectual property com. 1997-98), Country Music Assn., Copyright Soc. of South, Internat. Entertainment Buyers Assn. (gen. coun. 1998—), Friends Against Musical Exploitation Artists (gen. counsel 1998—). Baptist. Avocation: computers. Fax: 615-259-4668. Entertainment, Trademark and copyright, Federal civil litigation. Office: Jack Lyon & Jones PA 11 Music Cir S Ste 202 Nashville TN 37203-4335

**PHILLIPS, WILLIAM RUSSELL, SR.,** lawyer; b. N.Y.C., June 4, 1948; s. Samuel Russell and Annie Laura (Galloway) P.; m. Dorothy Elizabeth Lowery, Apr. 10, 1976; 1 child, William Russell Jr. BS, Washington & Lee U., 1970; JD, Georgetown U., 1974. Bar: Va. 1975, Ga. 1977, U.S. Dist. Ct. (no. dist.) Ga. 1977, U.S. Ct. Appeals (11th cir.) 1979. Law clk., atty. advisor EPA, Washington, 1973-75; asst. regional counsel region IV EPA, Atlanta, 1976-85, assoc. regional counsel region IV, 1986-90; sr. assoc. Thompson, Mann & Hutson, Atlanta, 1990-91; of counsel Peterson, Dillard, Young, Asselin & Powell, Atlanta, 1992-97; chief dep. atty. gen. State of Ga., 1997—, sr. asst. atty. gen., 1998—. Editor: Environmental Desk Manual, 1992, 94. Apptd. by gov. to Legis. Wetlands Study Com., 1992; cubmaster Cub Scouts Am., Lilburn, Ga., 1989-92; pres. Wyndemere Neighborhood Assn., Stone Mountain, Ga., 1990-94; v.p. Meth. Men's Fellowship, Glenn Meml. United Meth. Ch., 1989, pres., 1990. 1st lt. U.S. Army, 1972. Mem. Ga. Bar Assn. (sec. environ. law sect. 1985, vice chmn. 1986, chmn. 1987), Va. Bar Assn., Lawyers Club Atlanta. Avocations: golf, tennis, church service. Environmental. Office: Peterson Dillard Young Asselin Powell & Wilson 230 Peachtree St NW Atlanta GA 30303-1534

**PHILP, P. ROBERT, JR.,** lawyer; b. Frankfurt, Germany, Apr. 24, 1958; came to U.S., 1959; s. P. Robert Sr. and Katherine Fowler P. BA, U. Tenn., 1983; JD, Calif. Western U., 1986; grad. Ctr. Trial and Appellate Adv., U. Calif., 1989. Bar: Calif. 1987, U.S. Dist. Ct. (so. dist.) Calif. 1987. Jud. clk. to Hon. Robert C. Coates, 1985; assoc. to Bruce W. Lorber, Lorber, Grady, Farley & Volk, San Diego, 1987-90; sr. assoc. to Edward Chapin and Peter Ward, Chapin, Fleming & Winet, San Diego, 1990-93; pvt. practice La Jolla and San Diego, Calif., 1993—. Notes and comments editor Calif. Western Law Rev., 1985-86; staff writer Calif. Western Internat. Law Jour., 1984-85. Dir. San Diego Ecology Ctr., Inc., 1985-89, sec., 1986-87, mem. exec. com., 1986-89, chmn. toxic hazards com., 1986; dir. I Love A Clean San Diego County, Inc., 1986-89; mem. mus. art coun. San Diego Mus. Contemporary Art, 1988-92, mem. after five com., 1990; mentor Walden Family Svcs.; cochair facility expansion event Libr. Assn. La Jolla, 1990; vol. Helen Woodward Animal Ctr., 1990; usher St. James-by-the-Sea Episcopal Ch., La Jolla, 1989-93, mem. planned giving com., 1989-95; sponsor Christian Children's Fund, 1985-94. Recipient Disting. Vol. Svc. award The Calif. Republican Party, 1988. Mem. State Bar Calif. (vol. in parole 1989-90, del. 1989, mentor solo and gen. practice sect. 1994—), San Diego County Bar Assn. (mem. literacy coun. 1989-90, mem. fast track bench/bar com. 1990), Delta Kappa Epsilon. Episcopalian. Avocations: reading, art, music, outdoors, running. E-mail: philplaw@earthlink.net. General civil litigation, Personal injury, Construction. Office: La Jolla Shores Plz 2223 Avenida De La Playa La Jolla CA 92037-3200

**PHIPPS, DAVID LEE,** lawyer; b. Fairfield, Iowa, Jan. 11, 1945; s. Sherman Richard and Dorothy Helen (Butterfield) P.; children: Rachelle, Martin, Robin, Kelly. BA, Drake U., 1967, JD with honors, 1969. Bar: Iowa 1969, U.S. Dist. Ct. (so. dist.) Iowa, 1969, U.S. Dist. Ct. (no. dist.) Iowa 1974, U.S. Ct. Appeals (8th cir.) 1975. Assoc. Whitfield & Eddy, Des Moines, 1969-74, ptnr., 1974—. Contbr. articles to profl. jours. Mem. ABA, Internat. Assn. Def. Counsel, Am. Coll. Trial Lawyers, Am. Bd. Trial Advocates, Iowa State Bar Assn., Iowa Def. Counsel Assn. (past pres.), Def. Rsch. Inst., Iowa Acad. Trial Lawyers, Polk County Bar Assn. Mem. Reorganized Ch. of Jesus Christ of Latter Day Saints. Avocations: reading, woodworking, collecting, biking. General civil litigation, Federal civil litigation, Insurance. Office: Whitfield & Eddy PLC 317 6th Ave Ste 1200 Des Moines IA 50309-4112

**PHIPPS, ROBERT MAURICE,** lawyer; b. Detroit, Apr. 24, 1929; s. James Marion Phipps and Emma Holmes; m. Darleen Marie Rehbein, Aug. 23, 1952; children: David M., Robert Maurice II., Christina M. BS in Chemistry, U. Ala., 1954; JD, Akron U., 1959. Bar: Ohio 1960, U.S. Patent Office 1963, U.S. Supreme Ct. 1964, Mo. 1966, Can. Patent Office, 1967, U.S. Dist. Ct. (ea. dist.) Mo. 1968, D.C. 1969, Mich. 1971, U.S. Dist. Ct. (ea. dist.) Mich. 1974, Ill. 1977, U.S. Dist. Ct. (we. dist.) N.Y. 1981, N.Y. 1982. Patent atty. various cos., 1962-74; patent counsel, asst. sec. Velsicol Chem. Corp., Chgo., 1974-78; hearing officer dept. welfare State of Ill., Chgo., 1979; sr. patent counsel Bausch and Lomb Inc., Rochester, N.Y., 1980-84; pvt. practice Penfield, N.Y., Mayfield, Ky., 1984—. Trustee Westbury Manor, Chesterfield, Mo., 1968-69; elder, trustee, deacon Presbyn. Ch., Penfield; trustee Hicks Cemetery Assn., Mayfield, Ky., 1975—. Sgt. U.S. Army, 1948-51. Mem. Am. INtellectual Property Law Assn., Rochester Intellectual Property Law Assn. (sec. 1983, v.p. 1989). Republican. Patent, Trademark and copyright. Office: 106 Arbor Ridge Dr Mayfield KY 42066-1238

**PICADIO, ANTHONY PETER,** lawyer; b. Latrobe, Pa., Dec. 7, 1941; s. Peter J. and Elsie M. (Caldarelli) P.; m. Lynette Norton. BA, U. Pitts., 1965, JD, 1970. Bar: Pa. 1970, U.S. Dist. Ct. (we. dist.) Pa. 1970, U.S. Ct. Appeals (3d cir.) 1971, U.S. Supreme Ct. 1998. Asst. atty. gen. Dept. Environ Protection Commonwealth Pa., 1970-72; ptnr. Reding, Blackstone, Rea & Sell, Pitts., 1972-75, Tucker, Arensberg, P.C., Pitts., 1975-85; founder, sr. ptnr. Picadio, McCall, Miller & Norton, Pitts., 1985—; gen. counsel Seven Fields Devel. Co., 1988—; gen. counsel, v.p., dir. Info. Renaissance, 1996—. Editor U. Pitts. Law Rev. Dir. Inst. For Conservation Leadership, Washington, 1993-95, Pa. Environ. Coun., Phila., 1993-96; post-chmn., dir. Alleghany Land Trust, Pitts., 1995—. Mem. Order of Coif. Environmental, Construction, General civil litigation. Office: Picadio McCall Miller & Norton USX Tower 600 Grant St Ste 46 Pittsburgh PA 15219-2703

**PICARIELLO, PASQUALE,** lawyer; b. Norristown, Pa., May 26, 1959; s. Pasquale J. and Helen Irene (Delpizzo) P.; m. Claudia Coulter. BA, Columbia U., 1981; JD, Rutgers U., 1984. Bar: N.J. 1984, U.S. Dist. Ct. N.J. 1984, N.Y. 1985, U.S. Ct. Appeals (3d cir. 1985), Pa. 1994, U.S. Dist. Ct. (ea. dist.) Pa. 1995. Assoc. Slimm, Dash & Goldberg, Westmont, N.J., 1984-89, Ballen and Gertel, Camden, N.J., 1989-93; pvt. practice, Hammonton, N.J., 1993-95; litigation atty. Jacoby & Meyers Law Offices, Phila., 1995-98; pvt. practice, Voorhees, N.J., 1999—. Mem. N.J. State Bar Assn., Camden County Bar Assn. (young lawyer com. 1987-90), Delta Phi. Civil rights, Professional liability, Federal civil litigation. Home: 901 Central Ave Hammonton NJ 08037-1116 Office: PO Box 287 Hammonton NJ 08037-0287

**PICAZIO, KIM LOWRY,** lawyer; b. Greenville, N.C., Jan. 8, 1969; d. Harry Etheridge and Marion Thomas Lowry; m. Michael James Picazio, Mar. 25, 1995; 1 child, Sonny Michael. JD, Fla. State U., 1995. Bar: Fla. 1995. Lawyer Heinrich, Gordon, Hargrove, Weihe & James, P.A., Ft. Lauderdale, Fla., 1995-96, Law Offices of Robert D. Hertzberg, P.A., Miami, Fla., 1996—. Mem. ATLA, Am. Acad. Matrimonial Lawyer, Dade County Bar Assn., First Family Law Inns Ct. Family and matrimonial, General civil litigation, Personal injury. Office: 100 SE 2nd St Ste 3550 Miami FL 33131-2150

**PICCO, STEVEN JOSEPH,** lawyer; b. N.Y.C., Sept. 9, 1948; s. Carl and Constance (Speers) P.; m. Ada T. Ryan, July 15, 1972; children: Christopher, Timothy, Kaitlin. BS, Rider Coll., Lawrenceville, N.J., 1970; JD, Seton Hall U., 1975. Bar: N.J. 1975, U.S. Dist. Ct. N.J. 1975, U.S. Ct. Appeals (3d cir.) 1975. Data processing programmer-sys. engring. N.J. Dept. Labor and Industry, Trenton, 1970-75; project specialist N.J. Dept. Environ. Protection, Trenton, 1975-76, dir. regulatory and govtl. affairs, 1976-78, acting dep. commr., 1979-80, asst. commr., 1979-81; asst. commr. N.J. Dept. Energy, Newark, 1978-79; ptnr. Greenstone & Sokol, Trenton, 1981-87, Picco Mack Herbert Kennedy Jaffe & Yoskin, Trenton, 1988-97, Reed Smith Shaw & McClay, LLP, Trenton, 1997—. Chmn. bd. dirs. Northeast-Midwest Inst.; bd. dirs. N.J. Coun. Urban Econ. Devel., Pennington Sch., Boheme Soc.; chmn. bd. dirs. Robert Wood Johnson Health Care Corp. at Hamilton; mem. George Washington coun. Boy Scouts Am.; treas. N.J. Orgn. for a Better State; mem. N.J. Seed. Mem. ABA, N.J. State Bar Assn., Mercer County Bar Assn. Avocations: golf, reading, community volunteer work. Environmental, Administrative and regulatory. Office: Reed Smith Shaw & McClay LLP Princeton Forrestal Village 136 Main St Ste 250 Princeton NJ 08540-5789

**PICCOLO, GERARD ANTHONY,** lawyer; b. Omaha, Oct. 11, 1955; s. Salvatore and Maria Rose Piccolo. BSBA, Creighton U., 1977, JD, 1979. Bar: Nebr. 1979, U.S. Dist. Ct. Nebr. 1979, U.S. Supreme Ct. 1983. Pvt. practice Omaha, 1984-88; dep. pub. defender Hall County Pub. Defender's Office, Grand Island, Nebr., 1988-90, pub. defender, 1990—. Judge advocate USAF, 1980-84. Republican. Roman Catholic. Avocations: chess, basketball, running. Home: 1524 Coventry Ln Apt 66 Grand Island NE 68801-7063 Office: Hall County Pub Defender 117 E 1st St Ste 2 Grand Island NE 68801-6022

**PICKARD, HOWARD BREVARD,** law educator, consultant; b. Mangum, Okla., Mar. 6, 1917; s. Charles Brevard and Leila Maude (Davis) P.; m. Georgia Lela Martin, Dec. 24, 1940 (dec. Dec. 1973); children: Virginia Ann Robertson, Karen Sue Oliver; m. Sylvia Claudine Thomas, Dec. 27, 1974. BA, U. Okla., 1938, LLB, 1940; LLM, George Washington U., 1948. Bar: Okla. 1940, U.S. Supreme Ct. 1958. From atty. to supervising atty. Office of Gen. Counsel USDA, Washington, 1940-70, dir. consumer svc. div. Office of Gen. Counsel, 1970-72; prof. Cecil C. Humphrey Sch. of Law Memphis State U., 1972-87, prof. emeritus Cecil C. Humphrey Sch. of Law, 1987-98. Author: (chpt.) Agricultural Law, 1981. Lt. USN, 1942-45. Mem. Lions Internat. (pres. Arlington, Va. chpt. 1965-66, dist. gov. 1970-71, pres. Germantown, Tenn. chpt. 1975-76, 87-88, dist./state chmn. com. 1972-95), Order of Coif, Phi Beta Kappa. Democrat. Avocations: fishing, golf, painting, carpentry. Home: 2075 Thorncroft Dr Memphis TN 38138-4016

**PICKARD, JOHN ALLAN,** lawyer; b. White Plains, N.Y., Sept. 4, 1940; s. Victor and Rhoda (Walinshinsky) P. BA, The Am. U., 1963; JD, Washington Coll. Law, 1966. Bar: N.Y. 1987, Oreg. 1969, U.S. Ct. Appeals (9th cir.) 1970, U.S. Ct. Appeals (2d cir.) 1988, U.S. Dist. Ct. Oreg. Dep. dist. atty., 1970, criminal appeals atty., 1967-71; tax law specialist IRS, Washington, 1966-67; dep. dist. atty. Clachamus County, Oregon City, Oreg.; atty. pvt. practice fed. appeals Oreg., 1972—; with Arnold, Fortan & Porter, 1964-65. Advisor Mental Health Law Project, N.Y.C., 1984—, ACCESS Inc. Homeless. Appt. to Lawyers Conf. on Appellate Cts. ABA. Fellow Roscoe Pound Found.; mem. ABA (litigation sect., sole practice and adminstrv. law sects., jud. adminstrv. sec., health law forum, legal edn. and bar admissions), ATLA (civil rights litigation sect., social security and disability sect.), Am. Jud. Soc. Democrat. Avocation: politics. Criminal, Federal civil litigation, Constitutional. Home: 90 Bryant Ave Apt 3B White Plains NY 10605-1952 Office: PO Box 1907 White Plains NY 10602-1907

**PICKERING, CHARLES W., SR.,** federal judge; b. 1937. BA, U. Miss., 1959, JD, 1968; Hon. Doctorate, William Carey Coll. Ptnr. Gartin, Hester and Pickering, Laurel, Miss., 1961-71; judge Laurel Mcpl. Ct., 1969; pvt. practice Laurel, 1971-72, 80; ptnr. Pickering and McKenzie, Laurel, 1973-80, Pickering and Williamson, Laurel, 1981-90; judge U.S. Dist. Ct. (so. dist.) Miss., Hattiesburg, 1990—. Contbr. articles to Mississippi Law Journal. Mem. ABA, Miss. Bar Assn., Jones County Bar. Assn., State 4-H Adv. Coun., Assn. Trial Lawyers in Am., Miss. Trial Lawyers Assn., U. Miss. Alumni Assn., Jones County Jr. Coll., Jones County Farm Bur., Kiwanis Club. Office: US Courthouse 701 N Main St Ste 228 Hattiesburg MS 39401-3478

**PICKERING, GRETCHEN ANDERSON,** lawyer; b. Phila., May 12, 1963; d. J. Pierce and Molly E. A.; m. James H. Pickering Jr., May 11, 1996. BA, Kenyon Coll., 1985; JD, Temple U., 1988. Bar: Pa. 1988, N.J. 1988, U.S. Dist. Ct. (ea. and mid. dists.) Pa. 1988, U.S. Dist. Ct. N.J. 1988, U.S. Ct. Appeals (3d cir.) 1988. Assoc. Clark, Ladner, Fortenbrugh & Young, Phila., 1988-93; counsel Elf Atochem N.Am., Inc., Phila., 1993-97, sr. counsel, 1998—. Environmental, Administrative and regulatory. Office: Elf Atochem NAm Inc 2000 Market St Ste 2200 Philadelphia PA 19103-3399

**PICKERING, JOHN HAROLD,** lawyer; b. Harrisburg, Ill., Feb. 27, 1916; s. John Leslie and Virginia Lee (Morris) P.; m. Elsa Victoria Mueller, Aug. 23, 1941 (dec. Nov., 1988); children: Leslie Ann, Victoria Lee; m. Helen Patton Wright, Feb. 3, 1990. AB, U. Mich., 1938, JD, 1940, LLD, 1996; LLD, D.C. Sch. Law, 1995. Bar: N.Y. 1941, D.C. 1947. Practiced in N.Y.C., 1941, practiced in Washington, 1946—; assoc. Cravath, de Gersdorff, Swaine & Wood, 1941; law clk. to Justice Murphy, Supreme Ct. U.S., 1941-43; assoc. Wilmer & Broun, 1946-48, ptnr., 1949-62; ptnr. Wilmer, Cutler & Pickering, 1962-79, Wilmer & Pickering, 1979-81; ptnr. Wilmer, Cutler & Pickering, 1981-88, sr. counsel, 1989—; vis. lectr. U. Va. Law Sch., 1958; mem. com. visitors U. Mich. Law Sch., 1962-68, chmn. devel. com., 1973-81; mem. com. on adminstrn. of justice U.S. Ct. Appeals (D.C. cir.), 1966-72, chmn. adv. com. on procedures, 1976-82, chmn. mediation project, 1988—; bd. govs. D.C. Bar, 1975-78, pres., 1979-80; dir. Nat. Ctr. for State Cts., 1987-93. Lt. comdr. USNR, 1943-46. Recipient Outstanding Achievement award U. Mich., 1978, Disting. Svc. award Nat. Ctr. for State Cts., 1985, 50 Yr. award from Fellows Am. Bar Found., 1993, Paul C. Reardon award Nat. Ctr. for State Cts., 1994, Pro Bono award NAACP Legal Def. Fund, 1990, Am. Bar Assn. medal, 1999, Justice William J. Brennan Jr. award, D.C. Bar, 1998, Justice Potter Stewart award, Coun. for

Court Excellence, 1999, numerous other awards. Mem. ABA (state del. 1984-93, chmn. commn. on legal problems of elderly 1985-93, sr. advisor 1993-95, chmn. 1995-96, commr. emeritus 1996—, chmn. sr. lawyers divsn. 1996-97), D.C. Bar Assn. (Lawyer of the Yr. 1996), Am. Law Inst., Barristers Washington, Lawyers Club, Met. Club, Chevy Chase Club, Wianno Club, Order of Coif, Phi Beta Kappa, Phi Kappa Phi. Democrat. Mem. United Ch. Christ. Administrative and regulatory, Federal civil litigation, Libel. Home: 5317 Blackistone Rd Bethesda MD 20816-1822 Office: 2445 M St NW Ste 8 Washington DC 20037-1435

**PICKERSTEIN, HAROLD JAMES,** lawyer; b. Bridgeport, Conn., July 9, 1946; s. Maurice L. and Sylvia (Kornblut) P.; m. Marjorie S. Feldman, Aug. 11, 1968; children: Andrew Louis, Michael Robert, Edward Jeffrey (dec. 1999). AB, U. Pa., 1967; JD, Boston U., 1970. Bar: Conn. 1970, D.C. 1992, U.S. Tax Ct. 1971, U.S. Ct. Appeals (2d, 8th, 9th and 10th cirs.) 1971, U.S. Ct. Appeals (D.C. cir.), 1992, U.S. Ct. Appeals (Fed. cir.) 1992, U.S. Dist. Ct. Conn. 1972, U.S. Supreme Ct. 1973, U.S. Dist. Ct. Ariz. 1997, U.S. Dist. Ct. (so. dist.) N.Y. 1998. Trial atty. U.S. Dept. Justice, Washington, 1970-72; asst. U.S. atty. for Conn. U.S. Dept. Justice, Bridgeport, 1972-74; U.S. atty. U.S. Dept. Justice, New Haven, 1974-75; chief asst. U.S. atty. U.S. Dept. Justice, Bridgeport, 1975-86; ptnr. Pepe & Hazard, L.L.P., Hartford, Southport, Conn., 1986-96. Fellow Am. Coll. Trial Lawyers. Criminal, Federal civil litigation, General civil litigation. Office: Pepe & Hazard LLP 30 Jelliff Ln Southport CT 06490-1482

**PICKETT, WALLACE JAMES, III,** lawyer, consultant; b. Birmingham, Ala., Feb. 6, 1949; s. Wallace James and Mary Frances (Cochran) P.; children: Joanna Carol, Wallace James IV, John Zachary. BS in Chemisty, Birmingham So. Coll., 1971; MS in Physiology and Biophysics, U. Ala. Birmingham, 1974; MD, U. S. Ala., 1977; JD, La Salle U., 1996. Pres. Sanford (Fla.) Diagnostics, 1985-90; CEO Fla. Mobile Imaging, Sanford, 1987-89; pres., CEO Ctrl. Fla. Radiology, Lake Mary, 1990—; pres. J.P. Resources; cons. W. James Pickett III P.A., Longwood, Fla., 1985—. Major U.S. Army, 1977-83. Jewish. Home: 13132 Cog Hill Way Orlando FL 32828-8845

**PICKHOLZ, JASON R.,** lawyer; b. N.Y.C., Jan. 10, 1970; s. Marvin Gerald and Joyce (Merrick) P. BA, Colgate U., 1991; JD, NYU, 1994. Bar: N.Y. 1995, U.S. Dist. Ct. (so. dist.) N.Y. 1995. Law clk. Hon. Kevin Thomas Duffy, U.S. Dist. Ct., So. Dist., N.Y.C., 1994-95; assoc. Morvillo Alramowitz, Grand Iason & Silberberg, P.C., N.Y.C., 1995-97, Paul, Weiss, Rifkind, Wharton & Garrison, N.Y.C., 1997—. Chair law fifth yr. reunion com. NYU, 1998-99. Mem. ABA (contbr. article to newsletter com. on pretrial practice of discovery sect. litigation 1998), Assn. Bar of City of N.Y., NYU Law Alumni Assn. (dir. 1997—), N.Y. Athletic Club. Federal civil litigation, State civil litigation, Criminal. Office: Paul Weiss Rifkind Wharton & Garrison Rm 200 1285 Avenue Of The Americas New York NY 10019-6065

**PICKLE, JERRY RICHARD,** lawyer; b. Paris, Tex., Feb. 2, 1947; s. Joseph Rambert and Martha Marie (Biggers) P.; m. Helen Leigh Russell, May 3, 1975; children: Jonathan Russell, Sarah Elizabeth. BA in History, U. Houston, 1969, JD, 1971. Bar: Tex. 1972, U.S. Dist. Ct. (no. dist.) Tex. 1974, U.S. Dist. Ct. (we. dist.) Tex. 1989. Mem. Luna, Ballard & Pickle, Garland, Tex., 1972-74; assoc. Hightower & Alexander, Dallas, 1974-76, Cuba & Johnson, Temple, Tex., 1976-77; sr. corp. counsel Scott & White Clinic, Temple, 1977—; asst. prof. Tex. A&M U. Coll. of Medicine, Temple, 1986—. Contbr. articles to profl. jours. V.p. The Caring House, Temple, 1989, Tex. divsn. Am. Cancer Soc., Temple, 1976-77; adv. bd. R.R. & Pioneer Mus., Temple, 1982-84; hist. preservation bd. City of Temple, 1979-90; chmn. Bell County Hist. Commn., 1980-82; bd. dirs. Bell County Mus., 1992-96, Temple Coord. Child Care Coun., 1991-93, Sr. Citizens Activites Ctr., Temple, 1993-94, pres., 1994-95; bd. dirs. Temple Cultural Activities Ctr., 1992-98, pres., 1994-95; chair Heart o'Tex. Coun., Chisholm Trail Dist., Boy Scouts Am., 1987-88. Mem. ABA, State Bar Tex. (health law sect. councilman 1980-84, 85-87, chmn. 1983-84), Tex. Young Lawyers Assn., Tex. Bar Found., State Bar Coll., Bell-Lampasas-Mills Counties Bar Assn. (bd. dirs. 1985-90, pres. 1988-89), Bell-Lampasas-Mills Counties Young Lawyers Assn. (pres. 1980-81), Am. Health Lawyers Assn., Temple C. of C. (bd. dirs. 1983-85, 88-90), Rotary (chpt. dir. 1981-85, 86-87), Jaycees (chpt. dir. 1977-78). Democrat. Episcopalian. Avocations: reading, golf, music. Fax: 254-724-4501. Health, General corporate, Insurance. Office: Scott & White Clinic 2401 S 31st St Temple TX 76508-0001

**PICKLE, L. SCOTT,** lawyer; b. Koscoisko, Miss., Jan. 21, 1965; m. Shelia G. Pickle, Mar. 13, 1993; children: Griffin, Taylor. BBA, U. Miss., 1987, JD, 1990. Bar: Miss. 1990. Judge Kosciusko Mcpl. Ct., 1995—; pvt. practice, Kosciusko, 1990—. Real property, General practice, Federal civil litigation. Office: PO Box 701 Kosciusko MS 39090-0701

**PICKLE, ROBERT DOUGLAS,** lawyer, footwear industry executive; b. Knoxville, Tenn., May 22, 1937; s. Robert Lee and Beatrice Jewel (Douglas) P.; m. Rosemary Elaine Noser, May 9, 1964. AA summa cum laude, Schreiner Mil. Coll., Kerrville, Tex., 1957; BSBA magna cum laude, U. Tenn., 1959, JD, 1961; honor grad. seminar, Nat. Def. U., 1979; hon. grad., U.S. Army JAG Sch., U.S. Army Logistics Mgmt. Sch.; grad., U.S. Army Inf. Sch., Army Command-Gen. Staff Coll. Bar: Tenn. 1961, Mo. 1964, U.S. Ct. Mil. Appeals 1962, U.S. Supreme Ct. 1970. Atty. Brown Shoe Co., Inc., St. Louis, 1963-69, asst. sec., atty., 1969-74, sec., gen. counsel, 1974-85; v.p., gen. counsel, corp. sec. Brown Shoe Co., Inc. (formerly Brown Group, Inc.), St. Louis, 1985—; indiv. mobilization augmentee, asst. army judge adv. gen. civil law The Pentagon, Washington, 1984-89. Provisional judge Municipal Ct., Clayton, Mo., summer 1972; chmn. Clayton Region attys. sect., profl. div. United Fund Greater St. Louis Campaign, 1972-73, team capt., 1974-78; chmn. City of Clayton Parks and Recreation Commn., 1985-87; liaison admissions officer, regional and state coordinator U.S. Mil. Acad., 1980—. Col. JAGC, U.S. Army, 1961-63. Decorated Meritorious Svc. medal; 1st John W Green law scholarship; recipeitn Cold War Recognition cert. Sec. Def. Fellow Harry S. Truman Meml. Library; mem. ABA, Tenn. Bar Assn., Mo. Bar Assn., St. Louis County Bar Assn., Bar Assn. Met. St. Louis, St. Louis Bar Found. (bd. dirs. 1979-81), Am. Corp. Counsel Assn., Am. Soc. Corp. Secs. (treas. St. Louis regional group 1976-77, sec. 1977-78, v.p. 1978-79, pres. Quarter-Century Club 1979-80), U. Tenn. Gen. Alumni Assn. (pres., bd. dirs. St. Louis chpt. 1974-76, 80-84, bd. govs. 1982-89), U.S. Trademark Assn. (bd. dirs. 1978-82), Tenn. Soc. St. Louis (bd. dirs. 1980-88, treas., sec., v.p. 1984-87, pres. 1987-88), Smithsonian Nat. Assocs., World Affairs Coun. St. Louis, Inc., Am. Legion, University Club (v.p., sec. St. Louis chpt. 1976-81, bd. dirs. 1976-81), Stadium Club, West Point Soc. St. Louis (hon. mem., bd. dirs. 1992—), Conf. Bd. (coun. chief legal officers), Fontbonne Coll. Pres.'s Assocs. (O'Hara Soc.), St. Louis U. Billiken Club, St. Louis U. DuBourg Soc. (hon. dean), Scabbard and Blade, Kappa Sigma, Phi Delta Phi, Phi Theta Kappa, Beta Gamma Sigma, Phi Kappa Phi. Republican. Presbyterian. Avocations: reading, spectator sports. Antitrust, General corporate, Securities. Home: 214 Topton Way Saint Louis MO 63105-3638 Office: Brown Group Inc 8300 Maryland Ave Saint Louis MO 63105-3645

**PIDGEON, STEVEN D.,** lawyer; b. Norwood, Mass., Mar. 28, 1957; s. Norman L. and Dorothy H. Pidgeon; m. Kathryn A. Pierson, Sept. 12, 1981; children: Tyler Steven, Gregory Michael, Austin Robert. BA, U. Miami, 1978, JD, 1981. Ptnr. Streich, Lang, P.A., Phoenix, 1981-94, Snell & Wilmer, LLP, Phoenix, 1994—; bd. dirs. Enterprise Network, Phoenix, 1986—; mem. Ariz. Securities Coun., Phoenix, 1995—. Author articles. Mem. ABA, State Bar Ariz., Maricopa County Bar Assn. Avocation: golf. General corporate, Securities. Office: Snell & Wilmer LLP 400 E Van Buren St Phoenix AZ 85004-2223

**PIEDMONT, RICHARD STUART,** lawyer; b. Niskayuna, N.Y., Mar. 28, 1948; s. Henry Stuart and Lucille (Gagnon) P.; m. Marcia J. Quick, Apr. 11, 1981; m. Denise Nicole Rochette, Michael Norman Rochette, Alexandria Q. BA, U. Notre Dame, 1971. Bar: N.Y. 1977, U.S. Dist. Ct. (no. dist.) N.Y. 1977. Pres. Phoenix Abstract Corp., Albany, N.Y., 1979-84, v.p., 1984-89; ptnr. Piedmont & Rutnik, Albany, 1980-85, Devine, Piedmont & Rutnik, Albany, 1985-89; pvt. practice Piedmont Law Firm, 1990-95; ptnr. Harris Beach & Wilcox LLP, Albany, 1995—. Founding bd. dirs. Make-a-Wish Found. of Northeastern N.Y.; former trustee Empire State Aerosci. Mus.; mem. parish coun. St. John the Evangelist Ch. Mem. N.Y. State Bar Assn., N.Y. State Land Title Assn., Ea. N.Y. Land Surveyors Assn., Schenectady County Bar Assn., Albany County Bar Assn., Aircraft Owners and Pilots Assn., Notre Dame Club Northeastern N.Y. (bd. dirs.). Democrat. Roman Catholic. Real property, Probate, Administrative and regulatory. Home: 1016 N Country Club Dr Niskayuna NY 12309-5405 Office: 20 Corporate Woods Blvd Albany NY 12211-2396

**PIEPER, DAROLD D.,** lawyer; b. Vallejo, Calif., Dec. 30, 1944; s. Walter A. H. and Vera Mae (Ellis) P.; m. Barbara Gillis, Dec. 20, 1969; 1 child, Christopher Radcliffe. AB, UCLA, 1967; JD, USC, 1970. Bar: Calif. 1971. Ops. rsch. analyst Naval Weapons Ctr., China Lake, Calif., 1966-69; assoc. Richards, Watson & Gershon, L.A., 1970-76, ptnr., 1976—; spl. counsel L.A. County Transp. Commn., 1984-93, L.A. County Met. Transp. Authority, 1993-94; commr. L.A. County Delinquency and Crime Commn., 1983-94, pres., 1987-94; chmn. L.A. County Delinquency Prevention Planning Coun., 1987-90. Contbr. articles to profl. jours. Peace officer Pasadena (Calif.) Police Res. Unit, 1972-87, dep. comdr., 1979-81, comdr., 1982-84; chmn. pub. safety commn. City of La Canada Flintridge, Calif., 1977-82, commr. 1977-88; bd. dirs. La Canada Flintridge Coordinating Council, 1975-82, pres. 1977-78; exec. dir. Cityhood Action Com., 1975-76; active Calif. Rep. Party, Appellate Circle of Legion Lex U. So. Calif.; chmn. Youth Opportunities United, Inc., 1990-96, vice-chmn. 1988-89, bd. dirs. 1988-96; mem. L.A. County Justice Systems Adv. Group, 1987-92; trustee Lanterman Hist. Mus. Found., 1989-94, Calif. City Mgmt. Found., 1992—. Recipient commendation for Community Service, L.A. County Bd. Suprs., 1978, Commendation for Svc. to Youth, 1996. Mem. La Canada Flintridge C. of C. and Cmty. Assn. (pres. 1981, bd. dirs. 1976-83), Navy League U.S., Pacific Legal Found., Peace Officers Assn., L.A. County, UCLA Alumni Assn. (life), U. So. Calif. Alumni Assn. (life), L.A. County Bar Assn., Calif. Bar Assn., ABA, U. So. Calif. Law Alumni Assn. Government contracts and claims, Construction. Office: Richards Watson & Gershon 333 S Hope St Fl 38 Los Angeles CA 90071-1406

**PIERAS, JAIME, JR.,** federal judge; b. San Juan, P.R., May 19, 1924; s. Jaime Pieras and Ines Lopez-Cepero; m. Elsie Castaner, June 6, 1953; 1 child, Jaime Pieras Castaner. AB in Econs., Catholic U. Am., 1945; JD, Georgetown U., 1948. Bar: P.R. Pvt. practice San Juan, 1949-82; judge U.S. Dist. Ct. for P.R., San Juan, 1982—, now sr. judge; mem. Com. on the Bicentennial of the Constitution, Judicial Conf. U.S.; mem. Puerto Rico Commn. on the Bicentennial of the U.S. Constituion. Contbr. article to Cath. U. Law Rev., 1986. Chmn. fin. Statehood Republican Party, San Juan, 1963-64; Rep. nat. committeeman for P.R., San Juan 1967-80. 2nd Lt. U.S. Army (Mediterranean) 1946-47, MTO; Res., 1949. Mem. ABA (exec. bd., Nat. Conf. Fed. Trial Judges), P.R. Bar Assn., D.C. Bar Assn. Lodge: Rotary. Office: 1200-A Chase Manhattan Bldg 254 Munoz Rivera Ave Hato Rey San Juan PR 00918-1703*

**PIERCE, DONALD FAY,** lawyer; b. Bexley, Miss., Aug. 28, 1930; s. Percy O. and Lavada S. (Stringfellow) P.; m. Norma Faye Scribner, June 5, 1954; children: Kathryn Pierce Peake, D. F. Jr., John S., Jeff G. BS, U. Ala., 1956, JD, 1958. Bar: Ala. 1958, U.S. Ct. Appeals (5th cir.) 1958, U.S. Dist. Ct. (no., mid. and so. dists.) Ala. 1958, U.S. Ct. Appeals (11th cir.) 1982. Law clk. to presiding judge U.S. Dist. Ct. (so. dist.) Ala., 1958-59; ptnr. Hand, Arendall, Bedsole, Greaves & Johnston, Mobile, Ala., 1964-91, Pierce, Carr, Alford, Ledyard & Latta, P.C., Mobile, 1991—. Trustee, UMS Prep. Sch., 1980-87; mem. Products Liability Adv. Coun., 1990—; bd. overseers The Vanderbilt Cancer Ctr., 1994—. 1st lt. U.S. Army, 1951-53. Mem. Ala. Def. Lawyers Assn. (past pres.), Fedn. Ins. and Corp. Counsel, Am. Acad. Hosp. Attys., Internat. Assn. Def. Counsel, Def. Counsel Trial Acad. (bd. dirs. 1983-84), Def. Research Inst. (pres. 1987, chmn. 1988). Baptist. Contbr. articles to profl. jours. Federal civil litigation, Health, Environmental. Home: 4452 Winnie Way Mobile AL 36608-2221 Office: Pierce Ledyard Latta & Wasden P.C. Colonial Bank Ctr 41 N Beltline Hwy Ste 400 Mobile AL 36608-1291

**PIERCE, DONNA L.,** lawyer; b. Bermuda, Dec. 25, 1952; came to U.S., 1953; d. William R. and Joyce (Brewer) P.; 1 child, Dylan Pierce Austin. AS, Greenville (S.C.) Coll., 1976; BS, U. S.C., 1978, JD, 1980. Bar: S.C. 1981, U.S. Dist. Ct. (ea. dist.) Tenn. 1981, U.S. Ct. Appeals (4th, 5th, 6th, 11th cirs.) 1981, Tenn. 1982. Trial atty. Tenn. Valley Authority, Knoxville, Tenn., 1981-84; litigation ptnr. Chambliss & Bahner, Chattanooga, 1985-93, Chattanooga Human Rights and Rels. Comsn., 1993; gen. counsel U. of the South, Sewanee, Tenn., 1994; dir. S.E. Tenn. Legal Svcs., Chattanooga, 1988-92; advisor Cleve. State Coll., 1988-92. Mem. Tenn. Supreme Ct. Commn. on CLES and Specialization, 1993-98, Tenn. Supreme Ct. Commn. on Gender Fairness, 1994-96. Mem. ABA, S.C. Bar Assn., S.E. Tenn. Lawyers Assn. for Women (pres. 1990), Tenn. Lawyers Assn. for Women (bd. dirs. 1988-90), Tenn. Bar Assn., Chattanooga Bar Assn. (bd. govs. 1988-93, pres. 1992-93), Order of Coif. Federal civil litigation, State civil litigation, Pension, profit-sharing, and employee benefits. Office: U of the South 735 University Ave Sewanee TN 37383-0001

**PIERCE, JOHN GERALD (JERRY PIERCE),** lawyer; b. Winter Haven, Fla., Jan. 12, 1937; s. Francis E. and Margaret (Butler) P.; m. Kathleen E.; children: Kathleen M. Cooke, Nancy A., John Gerald Jr., Michael J. B in Chem. Engring., U. Fla., 1959, JD with honors, 1965. Bar: Fla. 1966, U.S. Dist. Ct. (mid. dist.) Fla., U.S. Ct. Appeals (11th cir.). Assoc. Anderson & Rush, Dean & Lowndes, Orlando, Fla., 1966-68, Arnold, Matheny & Eagen, Orlando, 1968-70; ptnr. Pierce, Lewis & Dolan, Orlando, 1970-74; sole practice Orlando, 1974—. Served to 1st lt. U.S. Army, 1959-62. Mem. ABA, Fla. Bar Assn., Orange County Bar Assn. Republican. Roman Catholic. Avocations: golf, boating, skiing. E-mail: jerryaty@aol.com. General corporate, Real property, Securities. Home: 605 Fox Valley Dr Longwood FL 32779-2417 Office: 800 N Ferncreek Ave Orlando FL 32803-4172

**PIERCE, LAWRENCE WARREN,** retired federal judge; b. Phila., Dec. 31, 1924; s. Harold Ernest and Leora (Bellinger) P.; m. Wilma Taylor (dec.); m. Cynthia Straker, July 8, 1979; children: Warren Wood, Michael Lawrence, Mark Taylor. BS, St. Joseph's U., Phila., 1948, DHL, 1967; JD, Fordham U., 1951, LLD, 1982; LLD, Fairfield U., 1972, Hamilton Coll., 1987, St. John's U., 1990. Bar: N.Y. State 1951, U.S. Supreme Ct. 1968. Civil law practice N.Y.C., 1951-61; asst. dist. atty. Kings County, N.Y., 1954-61; dep. police commr. N.Y.C., 1961-63; dir. N.Y. State Div. for Youth, Albany, 1963-66; chmn. N.Y. State Narcotic Addiction Control Commn., 1966-70; vis. prof. criminal justice SUNY, Albany, 1970-71; U.S. dist. judge So. dist. N.Y., 1971-81; judge U.S. Fgn. Intelligence Surveillance Ct., 1979-81; apptd. U.S. cir. judge for 2d Cir., 1981-89, sr. U.S. cir. judge for 2d Cir., 1990-95, ret., 1995; dir. Cambodian ct. tng. project Internat. Human Rights Law Group, 1995. Past bd. dirs. CARE, Fordham U., Havens Fund. Soc., Lincoln Hall for Boys, S-R N.Y. Chpt., Cath. Interracial Coun., Inst. Jud. Adminstrn., Am. Law Inst.; bd. dirs. St. Joseph's U., Phila., Practising Law Inst. Mem. ABA (site evaluation com., sec. legal edn. 1996-98, alt. observer U.S. Mission to UN 1988-90), Coun. Fgn. Rels. Home: PO Box 2234 Sag Harbor NY 11963-0111

**PIERCE, MORTON ALLEN,** lawyer; b. Liberec, Czechoslovakia, June 25, 1948; m. Nancy Washor, Dec. 14, 1975; children: Matthew J., Nicholas L. BA, Yale Coll., 1970; JD, U. Pa., 1974; postgrad. Oxford U., 1974-75. Bar: N.Y. 1975. Assoc. Reid & Priest, N.Y.C., 1975-83, ptnr., 1983-86; ptnr. Dewey Ballantine, N.Y.C., 1986—. Contbr. articles to profl. jours. Mem. Internat. Bar Assn., ABA (chairman subcom. internat. securities matters 1986-91), Assn. Bar City of N.Y. Mergers and acquisitions, Securities, Private international. Home: 188 E 76th St New York NY 10021-2826 Office: Dewey Ballantine 1301 Ave Of The Americas New York NY 10019-6022

**PIERCE, PHYLIS MISE,** lawyer; b. Middlesboro, Ky., Aug. 25, 1937; d. Clabe M. and Gladys (Orr) Mise; m. John T. Pierce, Dec. 20, 1959; children: John, Mary. BA, Berea (Ky.) Coll., 1960; MA, Ea. Tenn. State U., 1973; JD, U. Tenn., 1980. Bar: Tenn., 1980. Atty. advisor Social Security Adminstrn., Kingsport, Tenn., 1980-84, supervisory atty. advisor, 1984-86; solo practice Kingsport, 1986-88; atty. Social Security Adminstrn., Kingsport, Tenn., 1990-98, supervisory atty. advisor, 1998—. Administrative and regulatory. Home: PO Box 3762 Kingsport TN 37664-0762

**PIERCE, RICHARD WILLIAM,** lawyer; b. Detroit, Sept. 30, 1941; s. Donald Allen and Sarah Elizabeth (Giffen) P. BA, Ohio Wesleyan U., 1963; JD, Northwestern U., 1966. Bar: Mich. 1967, U.S. Dist. Ct. (ea. dist.) Mich., U.S. Ct. Appeals (6th cir.). Assoc. Tinkham, Snyder & MacDonald, Wayne, Mich., 1967-68; asst. pros. atty Washtenaw County, Ann Arbor, Mich., 1968-70; ptnr. Ellis, Talcott & Ohlgren, Ann Arbor, 1971-82; sole practice Ann Arbor, 1982—. Mem. Mich. Tech. Council, Ann Arbor, 1983-98; bd. dirs. Ann Arbor Area Council for Internat. Bus., 1984-87. Mem. Mich. Bar Assn. (chmn. dist. H subcom. character and fitness 1984-93), Washtenaw County Bar Assn. (pres. 1976-77), Am. Immigration Lawyers Assn. (chmn., I.N.S. liaison com. 1997-99). Presbyterian. Lodge: Kiwanis (local pres. 1978-79). Avocations: tennis, jogging. Immigration, naturalization, and customs, General corporate, Trademark and copyright. Office: 709 W Huron Ste 200 Ann Arbor MI 48103

**PIERCE, RICKLIN RAY,** lawyer; b. Waukegan, Ill., Sept. 16, 1953; s. Forest Ellsworth and Mildred Colleen (Cole) P. BBA in Acctg., Washburn U., 1975; BA in Econs., 1978, JD, 1978. Bar: Kans. 1978, U.S. Dist. Ct. Kans. 1978, U.S. Ct. Appeals (10th cir.) 1981, U.S. Supreme Ct. 1986. Assoc. Law Firm of C. C. Whittaker, Jr., Eureka, Kans., 1978-79; trust officer Smith County State Bank & Trust Co., Smith Center, Kans., 1979-80; staff atty. Northwest Kans. Legal Aid Soc., Goodland, 1980-81; assoc. Jochems, Sargent & Blaes, Wichita, Kans., 1981-82, Garden City, Kans., 1982-83; pvt. practice, Garden City, 1983-88; atty. County of Finney, 1988-93; pvt. practice, Garden City, 1993—. Pres., chmn. bd. dirs. Volunteers, Inc. of Finney County. Mem. Western Kans. Coun. Estate Planning & Giving. Mem. ABA, Assn. Trial Lawyers Am., Kans. Bar Assn., Southwest Kans. Bar Assn., Kans. Trial Lawyer Assn., Finney County Bar Assn. (treas.). Republican. Methodist. Criminal, General corporate, State civil litigation. Home: 2015 Campus Dr Garden City KS 67846-3706 Office: 206 W Pine St Garden City KS 67846-5347

**PIERCE, SHARON IRENE,** judge, lawyer; b. Atlanta, Oct. 12, 1951; d. Hugh Delano and Nellie Thelma Pierce. AB, Ga. State U., 1973; JD, Atlanta Law Sch., 1981, LLM, 1982. Bar: Ga. 1982, U.S. Ct. Appeals Ga., 1982, Ga. Supreme Ct. 1982, U.S. Dist. Ct. (no. dist.) Ga. 1982, U.S. Ct. Appeals (11th cir.) 1982. Dir. registration and conv. svcs. Atlanta Conv. and Visitors Bur., 1974-77; sec. to dist. dir. Nat. Assn. Securities Dealers, Atlanta, 1978-80; alumni rels./libr. Atlanta Law Sch., 1980-82; pvt. practice law Fayetteville, Ga., 1982—; mcpl. ct. judge City of Fayetteville, 1988—, Town of Tyrone, Ga., 1989—; mcpl. ct. judge pro tem City of Peachtree City, Ga., 1992—; pres. Easy Enterprises, Inc., Fayetteville, 1989—. Bd. mem. United Way Fayette County, Ga., 1983—. Mem. Leadership Ga. Methodist. Avocations: Tai Chi, travel, needlework, paper crafts. Office: 175 Bradford Sq Ste A Fayetteville GA 30215-1967

**PIERCY, JAMES R.,** lawyer; b. Sharon, Pa., Apr. 19, 1948; s. James Edward and Ursula Marie P.; m. Rebecca Lee Sharp, May 23, 1970; children: D. Stefan, Jillian Marie. BA, Pa. State U., 1970; JD, Case Western Reserve U., 1973. Bar: Ohio 1973. Asst. atty. gen. Office Atty. Gen. of Ohio, Columbus, 1973-79; atty., shareholder E.S. Gallon & Assocs. L.P.A., Dayton, 1979—; lectr. Ohio Continuing Legal Edn. Inst., Columbus, 1997-98. Mem., past chmn. City of Vandalia (Ohio) Planninc Com., 1970—. Mem. ATLA, Ohio Acad. Trial Lawyers, Ohio State Bar Assn. (workers' compensation com. 1983—), Dayton Bar Assn., Miami Valley Trial Lawyers Assn., Phi Alpha Theta. Avocations: exercise, weight lifting. Workers' compensation. Office: ES Gallon & Assocs 2200 Forty W Fourth Ctr 40 W 4th St Ste 1100 Dayton OH 45402-1874

**PIERETTI, GINO G., JR.,** lawyer; b. Portland, Oreg., Dec. 12, 1934; s. Gino G. and Alice (Pellegrini) P.; m. Kathryn Mary Karp, July 6, 1969 (div. 1990); children: Tony, Micheal, Mark, Gina; m. Astrid Viola Withers, Nov. 25, 1994. BA, Willamette U., 1956, JD, 1958. Bar: Oreg. 1958. From assoc. to sr. ptnr. Schwabe, Williamson & Wyatt, Portland, 1959-85; pvt. practice Portland, 1991—. Pres. Oreg. chpt. Multiple Sclerosis Soc., Portland, 1979; trustee Parry Ctr. for Children, Portland, 1975, Ryles Ctr. for Mentally Ill, Portland, 1996. 1st lt. U.S. Army, 1958-64. Mem. Tuscan Assn. Oreg. (v.p. 1996-97), Jazz Soc. Oreg. (trustee 1993-97), Multnomah Athletic Club. Democrat. Avocations: handball, travel, music, wine, food. Office: 1100 SW 6th Ave Portland OR 97204-1020

**PIERLUISI, PEDRO R.,** lawyer; b. San Juan, P.R., Apr. 26, 1959; s. Jorge A. and Doris (Urrutia) P.; children: Anthony, Michael, Jacqueline, Rafael. BA, Tulane U., 1981; JD, George Washington U., 1984. Bar: D.C. 1984, U.S. Dist. Ct. D.C. 1985, U.S. Ct. Appeals (D.C. cir.) 1985, P.R. 1990, U.S. Supreme Ct. 1990, U.S. Dist. Ct. P.R., 1990, U.S. Ct. Appeals (1st cir.), 1993. Assoc. Verner, Liipfert, Bernhard, McPherson & Hand, Washington, 1984-85, Cole, Corette & Abrutyn, Washington, 1985-90; ptnr. Pierluisi Pierluisi & Mayol-Bianchi, San Juan, 1990-93; atty. gen. Govt. of P.R., 1993-96; ptnr. O'Neill & Borges, San Juan, 1997—. Mem. ABA (ho. of dels. 1995-96, standing com. on substance abuse 1995-98, coordinating com. on gun violence, 1998—), Nat. Assn. Attys. Gen. (chair eastern region 1996), George Washington U. Internat. Law Soc. (pres. 1982-83), Phi Alpha Delta (hon., Munoz chpt.), N.Y. Stock Exch. (arbitrator), Nat. Assn. Securities Dealers, (arbitrator) 1998—. Avocation: jogging. General civil litigation, General corporate, Administrative and regulatory. Office: O'Neill & Borges 250 Ave Munoz Rivera Am Internat Plz San Juan PR 00918-1808

**PIERNO, ANTHONY ROBERT,** lawyer; b. Uniontown, Pa., Apr. 28, 1932; s. Anthony M. and Mary Jane (Saporita) P.; m. Beverly Jean Kohn, June 20, 1954; children: Kathryn Ann Pierno, Robert Lawrence Pierno, Linda Jean Pierno, Diane Marie Leonard. BA with highest honors, Whittier Coll., 1954; JD, Stanford U., 1959. Bar: Calif. 1960, D.C. 1979, Tex. 1994. Assoc. Adams, Duque & Hazeltine, L.A.; ptnr. Poindexter & Barger, L.A.; chief dep. commr. State of Calif., 1967-69, commr. of corps., 1969-71; ptnr. Wyman, Bautzer, Rothman & Kuchel, Beverly Hills, Calif.; sr. ptnr. Memel, Jacobs, Pierno & Gersh, L.A., 1976-86; ptnr. Pillsbury, Madison & Sutro, L.A., 1986-89; sr. v.p., gen. counsel MAXXAM, Inc., L.A. and Houston, 1989-97. Author: Corporate Disaggregation, 1982; editor Stanford U. Law Rev. Trustee Whittier Coll., 1977—, chmn. bd. trustees, 1994—, chmn. presdl. selection com., 1989-90; chmn. Marymount Coll., Palos Verdes, Calif., 1989-92, trustee, 1976-93; past mem. Los Angeles County Children's Svcs. Commn. With U.S. Army, 1954-56. Recipient Emcalian award Marymount Palos Verdes Coll., 1983. Mem. ABA, Los Angeles County Bar Assn., State Bar Calif. (chmn. com. on corps. 1971-75, advisor to com. on corps. 1975-76, mem. exec. com. bus. law sect. 1976-80, chmn. spl. com. on franchise law), Calif. Club (L.A.). Republican. Roman Catholic. General corporate, Alternative dispute resolution, Administrative and regulatory. Office: 3625 DelAmo Blvd Ste 360 Torrance CA 90503 also: 74361 Hwy 111 Ste 1 Palm Desert CA 92260

**PIERSOL, LAWRENCE L.,** federal judge; b. Vermillion, S.D., Oct. 21, 1940; s. Ralph Nelson and Mildred Alice (Millette) P.; m. Catherine Anne Vogt, June 30, 1962; children: Leah C., William M., Elizabeth J. BA, U. S.D., 1962, JD summa cum laude, 1965. Bar: S.D. 1965, U.S. Ct. Mil. Appeals, 1965, U.S. Dist. Ct. S.D. 1968, U.S. Supreme Ct. 1972, U.S. Dist. Ct. Wyo. 1980, U.S. Dist. Ct. Nebr. 1986, U.S. Dist. Ct. Mont. 1988. Ptnr. Davenport, Evans, Hurwitz & Smith, Sioux Falls, S.D., 1968-93; judge U.S. Dist. Ct., Sioux Falls, 1993—; chief judge Dist. of S.D., 1999—; mem. budget com. Jud. Conf. U.S.; chmn. tribal ct. com. 8th Cir. Jud. Coun. Majority leader S.D. Ho. of Reps., Pierre, 1973-74, minority whip, 1971-72; del. Dem. Nat. Conv., 1972, 76, 80; S.D. mem. del. select commn. Dem. Nat. Com., 1971-75. Mem. ABA, State Bar S.D., Fed. Judges Assn. (bd. dirs., v.p.). Roman Catholic. Avocations: reading, running, painting, mountaineering. Office: US Dist Ct 400 S Phillips Ave Sioux Falls SD 57104-6824

**PIERSON, GREY,** lawyer; b. Abilene, Tex., Dec. 31, 1950; s. Don and Annette (Grubbs) P. Student in history Baylor U., 1971, JD, 1974; student in internat. law Coll. William and Mary, Exeter, Eng., summer 1973. Bar: Tex. 1974, U.S. Dist. Ct. (no. dist.) Tex. 1974, U.S. Ct. Appeals (5th cir.) 1983, U.S. Supreme Ct. 1984. Assoc. Law Office of Tom Sneed, Odessa, Tex., 1974-76, Duke, Duke, & Jelinek, Arlington, Tex., 1976-78; ptnr. Duke & Pierson, Arlington, 1978-79, Pierson & Galyen, Arlington, 1983-88, Pierson, Baker & Ray, 1988-95, Pierson & Behr, 1995—; sole practice, Arlington, 1979-83; gen. counsel Mercer Internat. Transp., Ft. Worth, 1979-

84; sr. legal adviser Dominica Caribbean Freeport Authority, Roseau, W.I., 1979; ptnr. Sta. KVMX-FM, Eastland, Tex., 1981-86. Contbr. articles to City Digest mag., 1979-80. Pres. Eastland Youth Council, 1967, Arlington Community Theatre, 1979; mem. Tarrant 2000 Commn. on Civil Justice, 1988; chmn. Tarrant County Rep. Jud. Recruitment Com., 1988; del. Rep. Nat. Conv., New Orleans, 1988. Recipient Disting. Svc. award Nat. Assn. Disabled Ams., Washington, 1982. General corporate, Private international, Real property. Office: Pierson & Behr Ste 105 101 E Randol Mill Rd Arlington TX 76011-5800

**PIERSON, W. DEVIER,** lawyer; b. Pawhuska, Okla., Aug. 12, 1931; s. Welcome D. and Frances (Ratliff) P.; m. Shirley Frost, Feb. 1, 1957; children—Jeffrey, Elizabeth, Stephen. A.B., U. Okla., 1953, LL.B., 1957. Bar: Okla. 1957, U.S. Dist. Ct. Okla. 1957, U.S. Supreme Ct. 1966, U.S. Ct. Appeals D.C. 1969, U.S. Ct. Appeals (5th cir.) 1972, U.S. Ct. Appeals (10th cir. 1975), U.S. Ct. Appeals (2d cir.) 1996. Assoc., Duval & Head, Oklahoma City, 1957-59; sole practice, Oklahoma City, 1959-65; chief counsel Joint Com. on Orgn. of Congress, 1965-67; assoc. spl. counsel to Pres. and Counselor of White House Office, 1967-68; spl. counsel to Pres. U.S., 1968-69; ptnr. Pierson Semmes and Bemis and predecessor firms, Washington, 1969—. Trustee U. Okla. Found., 1996—; chmn. bd. visitors U. Okla. Coll. of Law; mem. bd. visitors U. Okla. Internat. Programs Ctr.; dir. Atlantic Coun. of U.S., 1995—. Served to 1st lt. U.S. Army, 1953-54. Recipient Outstanding Alumnus award U. Okla., 1995. Mem. ABA, D.C. Bar Assn., Fed. Bar Assn., Okla. Bar Assn., City Tavern Club (Washington), Met. Club (Washington). Alternative dispute resolution, Appellate, General civil litigation. Home: 5326 Chamberlin Ave Chevy Chase MD 20815-6661 Office: Pierson Semmes and Bemis 1054 31st St NW Ste 300 Washington DC 20007-6600

**PIERSON, WILLIAM GEORGE,** lawyer; b. Pontiac, Mich., Oct. 13, 1951; s. Robert D. and Elizabeth C. (Brode) P.; m. Mary K. Grossa, Sept. 25, 1986; children: Megan Ewing, Robert John. BBA, Cen. Mich. U., 1973; JD, Detroit Coll. Law, 1980. Bar: Mich. 1980, U.S. Dist. Ct. (ea. dist.) Mich. 1982, U.S. Supreme Ct. 1985. Sr. assoc. Kohl, Secrest, Wardle, Lynch, Clark & Hampton, Farmington Hills, Mich., 1980-89, Schwartz & Jalkanen, Southfield, Mich., 1989-90; sole practice Howell, Mich., 1991-99; counsel Oakland County Corp., Pontiac, Mich., 1999—. Mem. ABA, Mich. Bar Assn. (negligence sect., elected to rep. assembly 1999—), Oakland County Bar Assn (dist. ct. com. 1983-84, cir. ct. com. 1984-85, negligence com. 1987—, med.-legal com. 1989—), Livingston County Bar Assn. Avocations: golf, skiing, boating, camping. Personal injury, Insurance, State civil litigation. Home: 2153 Ridge Rd White Lake MI 48383-1742 Office: Oakland County Dept Corp Counsel Dept 419 1200 N Telegraph Rd Dept 419 Pontiac MI 48341-1032

**PIETZ, LYNNE PEPI,** lawyer; b. Rochester, N.Y., Mar. 1, 1952; d. Irvine Manne and Ethel Bernhardt (Jacobsen) Kriegsfeld; m. Jeffrey Thomas Pietz, June 29, 1975; children: Morgan Elliott, Brynna Michelle. AB cum laude, Washington U., St. Louis, 1973, JD, 1977. Bar: Mo. 1977, Calif. 1986, Ohio 1991, U.S. Dist. Ct. (so. dist.) Ohio 1991, U.S. Ct. Appeals (D.C. cir.) 1978. Congl. fellow U.S. Congl. Office of Tech. Assessment-Health Program, Washington, 1977-78; contracts specialist OTA-Adminstrv. Office, Washington, 1978-80; assoc. Rinos & Packer, Santa Ana, Calif., 1986-90, Louis & Froelich Co., LPA, Dayton, Ohio, 1990-92; pvt. practice Dayton, Ohio, 1992—; exec. dir. The Disability Found., Inc., 1999—; vol. instr. elder law U. Dayton-Inst. for Learning in Retirement, Dayton, 1995—; spkr. elder law Sr. Network Alzheimers Assn., Dayton, 1993—. Mem. City of Irvine (Calif.) Childcare Com., 1985-88; trustee Life Essentials, Inc., Dayton, 1993-99; vol. McGovern Presdl. Campaign, Cleve., 1967. Mem. Nat. Acad. Elder Law Attys., Ohio State Bar Assn., Calif. State Bar Assn., D.C. Bar Assn., Mo. Bar Assn., Phi Beta Kappa. Avocations: piano, walking, attending kids' sports events. Estate planning, Probate, Elder. Office: 124 E 3rd St Ste 300 Dayton OH 45402-2177 also: care The Dayton Found 2100 Kettering Tower Dayton OH 45423-1002

**PIETZSCH, MICHAEL EDWARD,** lawyer; b. Burlington, Iowa, Aug. 1, 1949; s. Walter E. and Leanna (Moore) P.; children: Christine E., Catherine M. AB, Stanford U., 1971; JD, U. Chgo., 1974. Bar: Ill. 1974, Ariz. 1976. Assoc. Schwartz & Freeman, Chgo., 1974-75; ptnr. McCabe & Pietzsch, Phoenix, 1975-90, Pietzsch & Williams, Phoenix, 1990-95, Polese, Pietzsch, Williams & Nolan, Phoenix, 1995—. Contbr. articles to profl. jours.; speaker at profl. confs. Del. White House Conf. Small Bus., Washington, 1986, Nat. Saver Summit, 1998; chmn. bd. trustees Ariz. Sci. Ctr., 1994—; pres. The Group, Inc., 1995—. Fellow Am. Coll. Tax Counsel, Am. Coun. on Tax Policy; mem. ABA (chmn. personal svc. orgns. com. tax sect. 1986-90), Stanford Phoenix Club (pres. 1982-84). General corporate, Pension, profit-sharing, and employee benefits, Health. Home: PO Box 44405 Phoenix AZ 85064-4405 Office: 2702 N 3d St Ste 3000 Phoenix AZ 85004-4607

**PIGG, JAMES STEVEN,** lawyer; b. Oklahoma City, Okla., Mar. 16, 1950; s. James Lewis and Betty Jo (Lorance) P.; m. Connie Dean Walker, June 2, 1973; children: Karli Jai, James Scott. BA, Washburn U., 1972, JD, 1976. Bar: Kans. 1976, U.S. Dist. Ct. Kans. 1976, U.S. Ct. Appeals (10th cir.) 1976. Dep. city atty. City of Topeka, 1976-78; assoc. Fisher, Patterson, Sayler & Smith, Topeka, 1978-81, ptnr., 1981—; adj. asst. prof. Washburn U. Sch. Law, 1998—; lectr. seminar materials Kans. Bar Assn. Employment Law Institute, 1995, 98, Labor and Employment Law, N.B.I., 1990, 91. Author: Washburn Law Institute, 1992. Past pres. Topeka Tennis Assn., 1989-94. Mem. Kans. Assn. Def. Counsel (pres. 1996-97), Kans. Bar Assn., Def. Rsch. Inst., Am. Inns of Ct. (chmn. edn. com. Topeka chpt. 1995-96). Avocations: tennis, water skiing, gardening. Civil rights, Labor, Personal injury. Home: 5600 SW 9th Ter Topeka KS 66606-2334 Office: Fisher Patterson Sayler & Smith PO Box 949 3550 SW 5th St Topeka KS 66606-1998

**PIGMAN, JACK RICHARD,** lawyer; b. Fostoria, Ohio, June 5, 1944; s. Jack R. and A. Ada (McDevitt) P.; m. Judy Lynn Price, June 19, 1968 (div. 1983); m. Carolyn Ruth Parker, May 31, 1986; children: Shaeney E. Pigman Craig, J. Ryan, Adam Parker. BA, U. Notre Dame, 1966; JD cum laude, Ohio State U., 1969. Bar: Ohio 1969, U.S. Ct. Mil. Appeals 1970. Law clk. Ohio Supreme Ct., Columbus, 1969-70; assoc. Wright, Harlor, Morris & Arnold, Columbus, 1970, 74-76; ptnr. Porter, Wright, Morris & Arthur and predecessor firms, Columbus, 1977—; speaker, continuing legal edn. programs and profl. orgns. Trustee Ctr. for New Directions, 1990-96, treas., 1996; trustee United Cerebral Palsy of Columbus and Franklin County, 1976-82, pres., 1980. Capt. JAG U.S. Army, 1970-74. Mem. ABA, Ohio State Bar Assn., Columbus Bar Assn. (chmn. bankruptcy com. 1982-84), Columbus Met. Club (trustee 1980-87, pres. 1985-86). Republican. Avocations: tennis, skiing, reading, cooking, photography, travel. Banking, Bankruptcy, Finance. Office: Porter Wright Morris & Arthur 41 S High St Ste 2800 Columbus OH 43215-6194

**PIGOTT, BRAD,** prosecutor; b. McComb, Miss., Aug. 3, 1954; m. Margaret Scheppke; children: David, Chris. BA summa cum laude, Duke U.; JD, U. Va. Ptnr. Watkins, Ludlam & Stennis, Jackson, Miss., 1987-90, Maxey, Pigott, Wann & Begley, Jackson, 1990-94; U.S. atty. for so. dist. Miss. Dept. Justice, Jackson, 1994—. Vice chmn. Miss. Bd. Edn., 1989-94. Office: US Dept Justice 188 E Capitol St Ste 500 Jackson MS 39201-2126

**PIKE, GEORGE HAROLD,** law librarian; b. Dubuque, Iowa, Aug. 5, 1959; s. George Harold and Pauline Elizabeth (Blair) P.; m. Deborah Rene Martin, May 29, 1994. BA, Coll. Idaho, 1982; JD, U. Idaho, 1985; MLS, U. Wash., 1988. Staff atty. Idaho Legal Aid Svcs., Idaho Falls, 1985-86; acting assoc. libr. U. Idaho Coll. of Law, Moscow, 1986-87; reference libr. Northwestern Sch. of Law of Lewis & Clark Coll., Portland, Oreg., 1988-91, dep. dir. of law libr., 1991-94; dir. of law libr. U. Pitts., 1994—; cons. in field, Portland, 1989-93. Mem. ALA, Am. Assn. Law Librs., Idaho Bar Assn., Western Pa. Law Librs. Assn. (v.p. 1997-2000). Avocations: golf, stamp collecting, aviation. Office: U Pitts 3900 Forbes Ave Pittsburgh PA 15213

**PIKE, ROBERT WILLIAM,** insurance company executive, lawyer; b. Lorain, Ohio, July 25, 1941; s. Edward and Catherine (Stack) P.; m. Linda L. Feitz, Dec. 26, 1964; children: Catherine, Robert, Richard. BA, Bowling Green State U., 1963; JD, U. Toledo, 1966. Bar: Ohio 1966, Ill. 1973. Ptnr. Cubbon & Rice Law Firm, Toledo, 1968-72; asst. counsel Allstate Ins. Co., Northbrook, Ill., 1972-74, assoc. counsel, 1974-76, asst. sec., asst. gen. counsel, 1976-77, asst. v.p., asst. gen. counsel, 1977-78, v.p., asst. gen. counsel, 1978-86, sr. v.p., sec., gen. counsel, bd. dirs., 1987-99, exec. v.p., 1999—; bd. dirs. Allstate subs. Bd. dirs., exec. com. Assn. Calif. Ins. Cos., Nat. Assn. Ind. Insurers; mem. bd. overseers Inst. for Civil Justice. Served to capt. inf. U.S. Army, 1966-68. Mem. ABA, Ill. Bar Assn., Ohio Bar Assn., Ivanhoe (Ill.) Club. Roman Catholic. Home: 811 Hawthorne Pl Lake Forest IL 60045-2210 Office: Allstate Ins Co 2775 Sanders Rd Ste F8 Northbrook IL 60062-6127

**PILAND, JOHN CHARLES,** lawyer; b. Paxton, Ill., Dec. 6, 1961; s. Joseph C. and Jo Anne (Hortin) P.; m. Debra Ann Stewart, July 28, 1984; children: Jacqueline Prince, David Lincoln. BSBA, U. Ill., 1984, JD, 1987. Bar: Ill. 1987, U.S. Dist. Ct. (cen. dist.) 1988, U.S. Ct. Appeals (7th cir.) 1988, U.S. Supreme Ct. 1991. Atty. Heyl, Royster, Voelker & Allen, Urbana, Ill., 1987-95; spl. legal counsel to Ill. House Rep. Leader, 1993-94; state's atty. Champaign County, 1995—; mem. nat. adv. coun. SBA, Washington, 1988-89; mem. gov.'s adv. bd., Springfield, Ill., 1988-90; mem. Ill. Truth-in-Sentencing Commn., 1995-98. Fl. page U.S. Ho. of Reps., Washington, 1979-80; legis. aide Ill. Ho. of Reps., Springfield, 1981-82. Harry S. Truman Found. scholar, 1982. Fellow Am. Bar Found.; mem. ABA, SAR, Ill. State Bar Assn. (bd. govs. 1995—), Champaign County Bar Assn., Nat. Dist. Attys. Assn., Ill. States Attys. Assn. (exec. com. 1995—), Lions, Masons, Rotary, Phi Alpha Delta. Republican. Criminal. Office: Champaign County States Atty PO Box 785 Urbana IL 61803-0785

**PILATO, LOUIS PETER,** lawyer; b. Rochester, N.Y., May 6, 1944; s. Patsy and Rose (Pandolfo) P.; m. Marie Matacchiera, Aug. 2, 1969; children—Tristen, Tara. B.A., U. Miami, 1967; J.D., SUNY-Buffalo, 1973. Bar: N.Y. 1973, U.S. Dist. Ct. (we. dist.) N.Y. 1975. Sole practice law, Rochester, N.Y., 1973-74; asst. dist. atty. Monroe County, Rochester, N.Y., 1974-76, spl. asst. dist. atty., 1976-85, chief spl. investigation unit, 1984-85; ptnr. Fero, Collins & Pilato, 1986-87—, Fero & Pilato, 1987—; legal counsel Gates Little League, Rochester, 1974-76; instr. Brighton Police Dept., Rochester, N.Y., 1978. Served with AUS, 1969-72. Mem. Monroe County Bar Assn., N.Y. State Dist. Atty.'s Assn., St. Thomas More Lawyers Guild, Italian Am. Bus. Assn. Republican. Roman Catholic. Lodge: Moose (v.p.). Home: 134 Oak Ln Rochester NY 14610-3136 Office: Fero & Pilato 183 Main St E Rochester NY 14604-1612

**PILCHEN, IRA A.,** editor; b. Chgo., Jan. 17, 1964; s. Bernard J. and Erna (Lee) P. BA in History, U. Ill., 1986. Assoc. editor Judicature jour., Chgo., 1991-98; dir. comms. Am. Judicature Soc., Chgo., 1991-98; editor Student Lawyer mag. ABA Publishing, Chgo., 1999—; mem. adv. coun. Ill. State Justice Commn., 1995. Vol. interpretive guide Friends of the Chicago River, 1991—. Named Vol. of Yr., Friends of Chicago River, 1993. Avocations: swimming, bicycling, Chicago history. Office: ABA Publishing 750 N Lake Shore Dr Fl 8 Chicago IL 60611-4403

**PILCHER, DEBRA EVELYN,** lawyer; b. Groton, Conn., Jan. 16, 1967; d. Imon Lester and Dorothy Evelyn (Cole) Pilcher. BS in Speech Comm., Oreg. State U., 1989; JD, U. Oreg., 1993. Bar: U.S. Dist. Ct. (fed. dist.) Oreg. 1996, Oreg. 1999. Law clk. Hon. Pierre L. Van Ryselberghe, Eugene, Oreg., 1993-94; assoc. Speer, Hoyt, Jones, Poppe & Wolf, Eugene, Oreg., 1994-98, Hyundai Semiconductor Am., Inc., Eugene, Oreg., 1998—. Mem. Eugene Active 20/30, 1997—. Mem. Oreg. State Bar (chair law sch. outreach com. new lawyers divsn. 1995-97), Oreg. Women Lawyers (bd. dirs. 1996-98, treas. 1998—), Lane County Bar Assn. (new lawyers com. 1993-98, program com. 1994—), Eugene/Springfield Tax Assn. (sec. 1997-98), Profl. Women's Forum, Eugene C. of C. (leadership class pres. 1996-97, govt. and legis. affairs steering com. 1997—). Avocations: backpacking, brewing. General corporate. Office: Hyundai Semiconductor Am 1830 Willow Creek Cir Eugene OR 97402-9146

**PILCHER, JAMES BROWNIE,** lawyer; b. Shreveport, La., May 19, 1929; s. James Reece and Martha Mae (Brown) P.; m. Lorene Pilcher; children: Lydia, Martha, Bradley. BA, La. State U., 1952; JD summa cum laude, John Marshall Law Sch., 1955; postgrad., Emory U., 1957. Bar: Ga. 1955. Legal aide to Spkr. of Ho. of Reps. Washington, 1961-64; assoc. city atty. City of Atlanta, 1964-69; pvt. practice law Atlanta, 1969—. Exec. committeeman Dem. Exec. Com. of Fulton County, Ga., 1974-86; bd. dirs. Whitehead Boys Club, 1961-89; trustee Ga. Inst. Continuing Legal Edn., 1988-89. Fellow Lawyers Found. Ga., 1996—. Fellow Lawyers Found. Ga.; mem. ABA, State Bar Ga. (chmn. 1988-89, gen. practice and trial sect., chmn. criminal law sect. 1986-87), Ga. Assn. Criminal Def. Lawyers (pres. 1980-82), Ga. Trial Lawyers (mem. exec. com. 1980—), Ga. Claimants Attys. Assn. (pres. 1983-84), Nat. Assn. Criminal Def. Lawyers (bd. dirs. 1980-85), Ga. Inst. Trial Advocacy (bd. dirs. 1986-89), South Fulton Bar Assn. (pres. 1987-88), Am. Bankruptcy Inst., Nat. Assn. Consumer Bankruptcy Attys., Trial Lawyers for Pub. Justice, Kiwanis (Peachtree, Atlanta pres. 1983-84, gov. Ga. dist. 1992-93). Presbyterian. Criminal, Personal injury. Home: 1195 W Wesley Rd NW Atlanta GA 30327-1407 Office: One Northside 75 Atlanta GA 30318-7715

**PILLANS, CHARLES PALMER, III,** lawyer; b. Orlando, Fla., Feb. 22, 1940; s. Charles Palmer Jr. and Helen (Scarborough) P.; m. Judith Hart, July 6, 1963; children: Charles Palmer IV, Helen Hart. BA, U. Fla., 1962, JD, 1966. Bar: Fla. 1967, U.S. Dist. Ct. (mid. dist.) Fla. 1967, U.S. Ct. Appeals (2d cir.) 1968, U.S. Supreme Ct. 1971, U.S. Ct. Appeals (3d cir.) 1976, U.S. Ct. Appeals (5th and 11th cirs.) 1981. Assoc. Bedell, Bedell, Dittmar, Smith & Zehmer, Jacksonville, Fla., 1966-70; asst. state atty. 4th jud. cir. Jacksonville, 1970-72; asst. gen. counsel City of Jacksonville, 1972; ptnr. Bedell, Dittmar, DeVault Pillans & Coxe, P.A., Jacksonville, 1972—; mem. Fla. Bd. Bar Examiners, Tallahassee, 1979-84, chmn., 1983-84; mem. Jud. Nominating Commn., 1988-92, chmn., 1990-91, 1st Dist. Ct. Appeal, Tallahassee, 1988-92, chmn., 1990-91. Master Chester Bedell Inn of Ct.; fellow Am. Coll. Trial Lawyers, ABA; mem. Am. Bar Found., Fla. Bar Assn. (chmn. profl. ethics com. 1998—). Methodist. Federal civil litigation, State civil litigation, Criminal. Home: Villa 110 6740 Epping Forest Way N Jacksonville FL 32217-2687 Office: Bedell Dittmar DeVault Pillans & Coxe PA Bedell Bldg 101 E Adams St Jacksonville FL 32202-3303

**PILLING, GEORGE WILLIAM,** lawyer; b. Reading, Pa., Mar. 25, 1942; s. Hugh Aiken and Lillian Elenor (Hannah) P.; m. Susan Genung, Sept. 5, 1973 (div. 1975); 1 dau., Jocelyn Kay. B.A., Kalamazoo Coll., 1963; J.D. with distinction, U. Mich., 1966. Bar: Mich. 1968, Calif. 1969, U.S. Dist. Ct. (cen. dist.) Calif. 1969. Clk., Montgomery McCracken, Walker & Rhoads, Phila., summer 1966, Cooper White & Cooper, San Francisco, summer 1968; assoc. Pollock & Palmer, L.A., 1968-70; staff atty. Western Ctr. on Law and Poverty, L.A., 1970-72; ptnr. Shapiro Posell & Pilling, Los Angeles, 1972-73; sole practice, Los Angeles, 1973—; chmn. bd. L.G. & N. Enterprises, L.A., 1978—; bd. dirs. Newell Sports Enterprises, L.A., Audiofile, Inc., La Jolla, Calif., Innovative Adventures, Inc., L.A. Mem. ACLU (exec. com. So. Calif. div. 1971, 72). Democrat. State civil litigation, Family and matrimonial, General practice. Home: 18000 Coastline Dr Malibu CA 90265-5730

**PILLION, MICHAEL LEITH,** lawyer; b. Sept. 4, 1957. BS, Pa. State U., 1979; JD, Villanova U., 1985. Bar: Pa. 1985, N.J. 1986. Ptnr. Morgan, Lewis & Bockius LLP, Phila. General corporate, Intellectual property, Landlord-tenant. Office: Morgan Lewis & Bockius LLP 1701 Market St Philadelphia PA 19103-2903

**PIMENTEL, JULIO GUMERESINDO,** lawyer, accountant; b. Chgo., Aug. 11, 1961; s. Julio Caesar and Jeannie Irene (Jakovac) P.; m. Margaret Mary O'Donnell, July 5, 1987 (div. Jan. 1995); children: Ashley Adel, Benjamin Maximillion. BS in Commerce, DePaul U., 1983, M of Accountancy, 1984; JD, John Marshall Law Sch., 1991. Bar: Ill. 1992; CPA, Ill.; cert. internal auditor. Deli clk. Jewel Food Stores, Chgo., 1978-84; field auditor Harris Bank, Chgo., 1984-85; asset-based lending field auditor Chase Comml. Corp., Chgo., 1985-86; acct. Allstate Ins., Northbrook, Ill., 1986-87; revenue agt. IRS, Chgo., 1987-91, estate tax atty., 1991—; pvt. practice, acct. Chgo., 1992—. Ill. State scholar, 1979. Mem. ATLA, Inst. Internal Auditors, Chgo. Bar Assn., IRS Bowling League (Most Polite award 1994-95), Freemen. Avocations: weightlifting, martial arts, gun collecting, old cars, archery. Estate planning, Family and matrimonial, Personal injury. Home and Office: PO Box A3761 Chicago IL 60690-3761

**PINCUS, ANDREW J.,** lawyer. Gen. counsel Dept. Commerce, Washington. Office: Dept Commerce General Councel 14th And Constitution Ave NW Washington DC 20230-0001

**PINCUS, SHELDON HOWARD,** lawyer; b. Bklyn., May 4, 1952; s. Nat and Frances P.; m. Sherry A. Beltramini, July 11, 1982; children: Matthew A., Lauren N. BS with distinction, Pa. State U., 1973; JD, Rutgers Sch. Law, 1977. Bar: N.J. 1977, DC 1981. Assoc. Goldberg & Simon, P.A., Clifton, N.J., 1978-81; sr. ptnr. Bucceri, Pincus, Clifton, N.J., 1981—. Dir. Mental Health Assn. Essex County, Montclair, N.J., 1993-98, Friends Montclair Co-Op, 1996-97. Avocations: skiing, backpacking, home renovation. Labor, Education and schools, General practice. Office: Bucceri & Pincus 1200 Rte 46 Clifton NJ 07013-2440

**PINCZOWER, KENNETH EPHRAIM,** lawyer; b. N.Y.C., Aug. 24, 1964; s. Joachim and Dinah Pinczower; m. Julie Rieder. BA, Queens Coll., 1985; postgrad., Rabbinical Sem. of Am., N.Y.C., 1983-86; JD, Benjamin N. Cardozo Sch. Law, 1989. Bar: N.Y. 1990, N.J. 1990, D.C. 1991, Fla. 1993, U.S. Dist. Ct. (so. and ea. dist.) N.Y. 1990, U.S. Dist. Ct. N.J. 1990. Auditor Seidman & Seidman/B.D.O., N.Y.C., 1986-87; summer assoc. U.S. Attys. Office, So. Dist. N.Y., N.Y.C., 1988; Alexander jud. fellow U.S. Dist. Judge, So. Dist. N.Y., N.Y.C., 1987-88; asst. corp. counsel N.Y.C. Law Dept., 1989-95; atty. Barron, McDonald, Carroll & Cohen, N.Y.C., 1995—. Editor Cardozo Arts & Entertainment Law Jour., 1988-89. Vol. instr. Jewish Edn. Program, N.Y.C., 1983-86; instr. Aish Ha Torah, 1994-98; chmn. Torah Chesed Fund, Yeshiva U., 1995—; Talmud assoc. Artscroll Mesorah Heritage Found., 1993—; com. mem. Nat. Conf. Synagogue Youth, 1991—. Avocations: Talmudic law, tennis, basketball. Home: 3950 Blackstone Ave Bronx NY 10471-3703 Office: Barron McDonald et al 1 Whitehall St New York NY 10004-2109

**PINDER, ANNETTE L.,** marketing administrator; b. Bklyn., Aug. 19, 1949; s. Abe and Sonia Laufe; m. John E. Pinder, Sept. 11, 1981; 1 child, Amy Lauren. BA, SUNY, Buffalo, 1985. Sales info. specialist/writer Barrister Info. Sys. Corp., Buffalo, 1985-87; dir. clint svcs., mktg. dir. Damon & Morey LLP, Buffalo, 1987—. Contbr. articles to profl. jours. Troop leader Girl Scouts of Buffalo and Erie County, 1994-96; group leader Ride for Roswell, Roswell Park Cancer Inst., Buffalo, 1997, 98; group leader corp. challenge Blind Assn., 1997, 98; mem. ad hoc com. De Graff Meml. Hosp., Tonawanda, N.Y., 1995. Mem. ABA (law practice mgmt. sect.), Assn. Legal Adminstrs., Legal Mktg. Assn. Democrat. Jewish. Office: Damon & Morey LLP 1000 Cathedral Pl 298 Main St Ste 1000 Buffalo NY 14202-4096

**PINDYCK, BRUCE EBEN,** lawyer, corporate executive; b. N.Y.C., Sept. 21, 1945; s. Sylvester and Lillian (Breslow) P.; m. Mary Ellen Schwartz, Aug. 18, 1968; children: Ashley Beth, Eben Spencer, Blake Michael Lawrence. AB, Columbia U., 1967, JD, 1970, MBA, 1971. Bar: N.Y. 1971, Wis. 1987. Assoc. Olwine, Connelly, Chase, O'Donnell & Weyher, N.Y.C., 1971-80; asst. gen. counsel Peat, Marwick, Mitchell & Co., N.Y.C., 1980-82; ptnr. Hollyer, Jones, Pindyck, Brady & Chira, N.Y.C., 1983-87; pres., CEO Meridian Industries, Inc., Milw., 1985—; also chmn. bd. dirs. Meridian Industries, Inc.; CEO Majilite Corp., Dracut, Mass., 1987—; also chmn. bd. dirs. Majilite Corp.; mem. capital campaign com. Columbia U., 1984-87. Bd. dirs. Harambee Cmty. Sch., 1991-96, Milw. Ballet Co., 1993-97, Milw. Pub. Mus., 1994-98. Mem. Columbia Coll. Alumni Assn. (regional dir. 1988-94, v.p. 1994-98, exec. com., 1994-98) , World Pres.'s Orgn. General corporate, General civil litigation. Address: 100 E Wisconsin Ave Milwaukee WI 53202-4107

**PINEAU, JOHN KENNETH,** lawyer; b. Detroit, July 2, 1960; s. Kenneth John and Rosemary Louise P.; m. Cynthia Pineau, Aug. 3, 1991. Student, U. Mich., 1981; BA with honors, Oberlin Coll., 1982; JD, U. Colo., 1994. Bar: Colo. 1994, U.S. Dist. Ct. Colo. 1994. Adminstrv. hearings advocate Wayne Legal Svcs., Detroit, 1984-91; atty. of counsel Lawrence S. Mertes P.C., Boulder, Colo., 1995—; pvt. practice Boulder, 1994—; ct. appointed counsel for Boulder County, Office of Pub. Defender, Boulder, 1995. Recipient Am. Jurisprudence award Lawyer Coop. Pub., Boulder, 1993, 94. Mem. Colo. Bar Assn., Colo. Trial Lawyers Assn., Boulder Crime Def. Bar. Criminal, General civil litigation. Office: Lawrence S Mertes PC 3050 Broadway St Ste 201 Boulder CO 80304-3154

**PINEDA, DAYNA JAYNE,** lawyer; b. Lake View Terrace, Calif., Jan. 26, 1963. BS in Biochemistry/Molecular Biology, U. Calif., Santa Barbara, 1985; JD, U. San Diego, 1993. Bar: Calif. 1993. With Amgen, Inc., Thousand Oaks, Calif., 1985-89, Alliance Pharm. Corp., San Diego, 1989-93; assoc. Gray Cary Ware & Freidenrich, San Diego, 1993—; mem. Biocom Legis. Com. Mem. Calif. State Bar assn., San Diego County Bar Assn. Intellectual property, General corporate. Office: Gray Cary Ware & Freidenrich 4365 Executive Dr San Diego CA 92121-2123

**PINGREE, BRUCE DOUGLAS,** lawyer; b. Salt Lake City, June 6, 1947; s. Howard W. and Lois (Ivie) P.; m. Lorraine Bertelli, Oct. 11, 1981; children: Christian James, Matthew David, Alexandra Elizabeth, Meredith Gillian, Lauren Ashley, Geoffrey Nicholas. BA in Philosophy, U. Utah, 1970, JD, 1973. Bar: Ariz. 1973, Tex. 1990. Ptnr. Snell & Wilmer, Phoenix, 1973-89; shareholder Johnson & Gibbs, Dallas, 1989-93; ptnr. Gardere & Wynne, Dallas, 1993-95, Baker & Botts, L.L.P., Dallas, 1995—; lectr. in field of taxation. Contbr. articles to profl. jours. Served to capt. USAR. Mem. ABA (tax sect., past chair employee benefits com., past vice chair, past chmn. various sub-coms., 1993-94, chair joint com. on employee benefits 1994-95), Tex. State Bar Assn. (vice-chair, tax sect. benefits and compensation com. 1998-99), S.W. Benefits Conf., Nat. Assn. Stock Plan Profls., Order of Coif. Episcopalian. Pension, profit-sharing, and employee benefits, Corporate taxation, Personal income taxation. Home: 4065 Bryn Mawr Dr Dallas TX 75225-7032 Office: Baker & Botts LLP 2001 Ross Ave Ste 600 Dallas TX 75201-2980

**PINKERTON, ALBERT DUANE, II,** lawyer; b. Portland, Oreg., Aug. 28, 1942; s. Albert Duane and Barbara Jean Pinkerton; 1 child, Albert Duane III; m. Mary-Clare Bittle, 1993. BA, Willamette U., 1964, JD, 1966. Bar: Oreg. 1966, U.S. Dist. Ct. Oreg. 1966, U.S. Ct. Appeals (9th cir.) 1966, Alaska 1985, Calif. 1986, U.S. Dist. Ct. Calif. 1987. Gen. practice Springfield, Oreg., 1966-69, Burns, Oreg., 1969-86, Concord, Calif., 1986-88; assoc. Sellar Hazard Fitzgerald McNeely Alm & Manning, Walnut Creek, Calif., 1988—. Mem. Oreg. State Bar (com. Uniform Jury Instrns. sec. 1972-73, 82-83, chmn. 1973-74, 83-84; com. Procedure and Practice sec. 1985-86, chmn. 1986-87), Am. Judicature Soc., Masons (master 1980-81), Grand Lodge of Oreg. (dist. dep. 1983-86). State civil litigation, Insurance, General practice. Home: PO Box 21347 Concord CA 94521-0347 Office: 1111 Civic Dr Ste 300 Walnut Creek CA 94596-3894

**PINKERTON, C(HARLES) FREDERICK,** lawyer; b. Salt Lake City, Mar. 7, 1940; s. Charles Frederick II and Margaret L. (McDowell) P.; m. Joyce Montelione; children: Charles Frederick, John Dale. BA, Calif. Luth. Coll., 1964; JD, U. Oreg., 1967. Bar: Nev. 1968, U.S. Dist. Ct. Nev. 1968, U.S. Ct. Appeals (9th cir.) 1976. Dep. dist. atty Washoe County Dist. Atty.'s Office, Reno, 1968-71, chief chmn. dep. dist. atty., 1971. Served as cpl. USMC, 1959-62. Fellow ATLA, Am. Coll. Criminal Lawyers; mem. ABA, Am. Coll. Trial Lawyers, Nat. Assn. Criminal Def. Lawyers, No. Nev. Trial Lawyers Assn., Am. Inns of Ct. (pres. Bruce R. Thompson chpt. 1995-96). Office: 203 S Arlington Ave Reno NV 89501-1702

**PINKUS, I(RVING) MARSHALL,** lawyer; b. Indpls., June 24, 1947; s. Seymour Samuel and Virginia (Schwartz) P.; m. Marilyn J. Shelby, July 15, 1973 (div. June 30, 1989); children: Brandi, Jared, Cara; m. Julie K. Blaschke, Jan. 20, 1990; children: Gabriel Paul, Rachel Catherine. BA magna cum laude, Butler U., 1969; JD, Ind. U., 1973. Pub. defender Marion County Superior Ct., Indpls., 1974-90; pvt. practice Zinkan O'Hara Pinkus, Indpls., 1979-93, Dutton Overman, Indpls., 1993—; judge pro-tem various cts. Marion County; spkr. in field. Mem. Ind. Bar Assn., Assn. Am. Trial Attys. Republican. Avocations: bridge, chess, marine biology, archeology, sports. Criminal, Family and matrimonial, Personal injury. Office: Dutton Overman 36 S Pennsylvania St Ste 710 Indianapolis IN 46204-3688

**PINNEY, SIDNEY DILLINGHAM, JR.,** lawyer; b. Hartford, Conn., Nov. 17, 1924; s. Sydney Dillingham and Louisa (Griswold) Wells P.; m. Judith Munch, Sept. 30, 1990; children from previous marriage: William Griswold, David Rees. Student, Amherst Coll., 1941-43, Brown U., 1943; also, M.I.T., 1943-44; BA cum laude, Amherst Coll., 1947; LLB, Harvard U., 1950. Bar: Conn. 1950. Pvt. practice Hartford, 1950; assoc. Shepherd, Murtha and Merritt, Hartford, 1950-53; ptnr. Shepherd, Murtha and Merritt (name changed to Murtha, Cullina, Richter and Pinney 1967), 1953-92, of counsel, 1993—; lectr. on estate planning. Contbr. to: Estate Planning mag. Bd. dirs. Greater Hartford Area TB and Respiratory Diseases Health Soc., 1956-69, pres., 1966-67; mem. Wethersfield (Conn.) Town Coun., 1958-62; trustee Hartford Conservatory Music, 1967-71, 75-81; trustee, pres. Historic Wethersfield Found., 1961-81; bd. dirs. Hartford Hosp., 1971-80, adv. bd., 1980—; mem. adv. com. Jefferson House, 1978-82; mem. Mortensen Libr. Bd. of Visitors U. Hartford, 1984—; corporator Hartford Pub. Libr., 1969—, Renbrook Sch., West Hartford, Conn., 1970-75. 1st lt. USAF, 1943-46. Fellow Am. Coll. Trust and Estate Counsel; mem. ABA, Nat. Acad. Elder Law Attys., Conn. Bar Assn. (exec. com. elder law sect.), Hartford County Bar Assn. Republican. Congregationalist. Estate planning, Probate, Estate taxation. Office: City Place 185 Asylum St Hartford CT 06103-3408

**PINNISI, MICHAEL DONATO,** lawyer, educator; b. Buffalo, N.Y., Oct. 12, 1960; s. Frank Joseph and Dolores Ann Pinnisi; m. Donna Lynn Heilweil, July 13, 1986; children: Kerry Lynn, Rose. AB cum laude, Cornell U., 1982, JD, 1985. Bar: N.Y. 1986, U.S. Dist. Ct. (so. dist.) N.Y. 1987, U.S. Dist. Ct. (no. dist.) N.Y. 1991, U.S. Dist. Ct. (we. dist.) N.Y. 1993, , U.S. Ct. Appeals (2d. cir.) 1988, U.S. Ct. Appeals (D.C. cir.) 1998. Trial atty. honor program U.S. Dept. of Justice, Washington, 1985-87; assoc. atty. Shearman & Sterling, N.Y.C., 1987-88; asst. U.S. atty. U.S. Atty., So. Dist. N.Y., N.Y.C., 1988-91; assoc. atty. Cleary, Gottlieb, Steen & Hamilton, Washington, 1991-92; prin. atty. Pinnisi, Wagner et al, Ithaca, N.Y., 1992-97, Brown, Pinnisi and Michaels, Ithaca, 1997—; adj. prof. law Cornell Law Sch., Ithaca, 1992—; cert. arbitrator U.S. Dist. Ct. No. Dist. N.Y., 1993—; spkr. in field. Dir. Ithaca Cmty. Childcare, 1993-94, F.I.R.S.T., Phila., 1996-97. Mem. ABA, N.Y. State Bar Assn., Tompkins County Bar Assn., Phi Delta Phi. General civil litigation, Intellectual property, Appellate. Office: Brown Pinnisi & Michaels PC 400 M & T Bank Bldg 118 N Tioga St Ste 400 Ithaca NY 14850-4343

**PINNIX, JOHN LAWRENCE,** lawyer; b. Reidsville, N.C., Oct. 8, 1947; s. John Lawrence and Esther (Cobb) P.; m. Sally Auman, June 15, 1985; children: Jennifer Elizabeth Haigwood, William C. Haigwood. BA, U. N.C., Greensboro, 1969; JD, Wake Forest U., 1973; MA, U. N.C., Greensboro, 1975. Bar: N.C. 1973, D.C. 1981; U.S. Dist. Ct. (ea. dist.) N.C. 1977, U.S. Dist. Ct. (mid. and we. dists.) N.C. 1981; U.S. Ct. Appeals (4th cir.) 1981; U.S. Supreme Ct. 1981. Assoc. Fagg, Fagg & Nooe, Eden, N.C., 1973-74; spl. counsel Adminstrv. Office of the Cts., Morganton, N.C., 1975-76; ptnr. Allen and Pinnix (formerly Barringer, Allen & Pinnix), Raleigh, N.C., 1977—; adj. N.C. Ctrl. U. Sch. Law, 1997; sr. lecturing fellow Duke U. Sch. Law, 1999—. Contbr. articles to profl. jours. Alt. del. Dem. Nat. Conv., Miami, 1972, mem. rules com., Washington and Atlanta, 1988; bd. dirs. Farmworkers Legal Svcs., Raleigh, 1990-92. Mem. Am. Immigration Lawyers Assn. (founding mem. Carolinas chpt. 1980, chpt. chair 1984-85, 87-88, nat. bd. govs. 1993—, sec. nat. exec. com. 1997-99, 2d v.p. 1999—), Am. Immigration Law Found. (trustee 1992-97, vice chair 1994-97), N.C. Bar Assn. (chmn. immigration and nationality law com. 1989-91), N.C. State Bar (bd. cert. immigration specialist, immigration law specialty com. bd. legal specialization 1996—), U. N.C. Greensboro Alumni Assn. (bd. dirs. 1975-76, bd. dirs. Excellence Found. 1995-97), Internat. Focus Inc. (bd. dirs. 1998-99), N.C. Bar Assn. (internat. law sect. coun. 1999—). Baptist. Avocations: photography, film, reading. Immigration, naturalization, and customs. Home: 125 Ammons Dr Raleigh NC 27615-6501

**PINSKY, BRADLEY M.,** lawyer; b. Syracuse, N.Y., July 18, 1968; s. Philip Carlin and Marilyn (Levin) P.; m. Allison Michelle Seidberg. BA, Brandeis U., 1991; M of Health Adminstrn., Tulane U., 1995, JD, 1995. Bar: N.Y. 1996. Law clk. to presiding justice N.Y. State Claims Ct., Binghamton, 1995-97; assoc. Pinsky & Skandalis, Syracuse, 1997—; atty. Regional Emergency Med. Svcs. Coun. Bd. dirs. PROBE, Binghamton, 1995-96, Jewish Family Svc., Syracuse, 1998&, Youth Cts. of Broome County, Binghamton, 1995-98, Home Aides Ctrl. N.Y., 1999— mem. Leadership Greater Syracuse Class of 1998. Mem. Am. Health Lawyers Assn. Avocation: golf. Health, Real property, General practice. Office: Pinsky & Skandalis PO Box 250 5790 Widewaters Pkwy Syracuse NY 13214-1850

**PINSKY, MICHAEL S.,** lawyer; b. Chgo., July 25, 1945; s. Joseph and Irene (Sodakoff) P.; m. Judy R. Rabin, Sept. 29, 1974; children: David, Susie, Jodie. BS, U. Ill., 1967; JD, DePaul U., 1971. Bar: Ill. 1971. Conferee, revenue agt. IRS, Chgo., 1967-72; ptnr. Levenfeld & Kanter, Chgo., 1972-80, Levenfeld, Eisenberg Janger, Chgo., 1980-84, Vedder Price, Kaufman & Kammholz, Chgo., 1984-88, Gottlieb & Schwartz, Chgo., 1989-92; with Levin & Schreder, Chgo., 1993-97, Altheimer & Gray, Chgo., 1997—. Bd. dirs. Better Boys Found., Chgo., 1989-94; mem. planned giving com. Am. Soc. for Technion, 1997—. Mem. Am. Bar Assn., Assn. of Bar of State of Ill., Assn. of Bar of City of Chgo. (com. chmn. 1984-86). Taxation, general, Corporate taxation, Estate planning. Office: 10 S Wacker Dr Ste 4000 Chicago IL 60606-7407

**PINSON, JERRY D.,** lawyer; b. Harrison, Ark., Sept. 7, 1942; s. Robert L. and Cleta (Keeter) P.; m. Jane Ellis, Sept. 11, 1964; 1 child, Christopher Clifton. BA, U. Ark., 1964, JD, 1967. Bar: Ark. 1967, U.S. Ct. Appeals (8th cir.) 1967, U.S. Supreme Ct. 1967, U.S. Dist. Ct. (ea. and we. dists.) Ark. 1968. Dep. atty. gen. State of Ark., Little Rock, 1967-70; ptnr. Pinson & Reeves, Harrison, 1973-88; sole practice Harrison, 1970-73, 88—; mem. Ark. Supreme Ct. com. on the unauthorized practice of law in Ark., 1979-91, chmn. 1990-91; spl. justice Ark. Supreme Ct., 1991, 94; active state bd. law examiners, 1997—. Pres. United Way Boone County, Harrison, 1974. Mem. ABA, Am. Judicature Soc., Assn. Trial Lawyers Am., Ark. Bar Assn., Boone County Bar Assn., Harrison C. of C. (sec. bd. dirs. 1977). Lodge: Rotary (bd. dirs. 1975, v.p. 1976, pres. 1977). State civil litigation, Personal injury, General practice. Office: Atty at Law PO Box 1111 Harrison AR 72602-1111

**PIOMBINO, ALFRED ERNEST,** law consultant, writer; b. Poughkeepsie, N.Y., Oct. 9, 1962; s. Alfred Raymond and Barbara Jean (Elmendorf) P. AS, Dutchess Community Coll., Poughkeepsie, 1983; BS, Marist Coll., 1986, MPA, 1988. Notary pub., Fla., N.J., N.Y., Maine. Instr. Ulster Community Coll., Stone Ridge, N.Y., 1986-88; pres. Piombino Corp., Poughkeepsie, 1987-94; commr. of deed for Conn. in N.Y., 1991-94, for Fla. in N.Y., 1992-94; mem. Acad. of Legal Studies in Bus.; adj. faculty L.I. U., 1988-94, Pratt Inst., 1989-93; Dedimus Justice, State of Maine, 1995—; founder, chmn. Maine Magistrate's Coun.; fair hearing officer City of Portland, Maine, 1997—; civil svc. commr. City of Portland, 1999—. Author: Notary Public Handbook: A Guide for New York, 1989, Notary Public Handbook: A Guide for New Jersey, 1991, Notary Public Handbook: A Guide for Maine, 1992, Notary Public Handbook: A Guide for Florida, 1993, Notary Public Register and Recordkeeping Protocols, 1993, Notary Public Handbook: A Guide for Vermont Notaries, Commissioners and Justices of the Peace, 1995, Notary Public Handbook: A Guide for California Notaries and Commissioners, 1997, Notary Public Handbook: Principles, Practices & Cases, nat. edit., 1997. Mem. faculty Am. Heart Assn., Dutchess County, N.Y., 1983-88; bd. dirs. ARC, Dutchess County, 1977-82; trustee Nat. Multiple Sclerosis Soc. (Maine chpt.); Ky. Col. Gubernatorial Commn., 1997. Master, lic. officer Merchant Marine. Recipient Nat. First Aid award Johnson & Johnson, 1978, Jefferson award, 1993, Vt. Sec. of State Commendation, 1995, Ark. Traveler Gubernatorial award, 1996. Mem. ABA (jud. adminstrn. divsn., info. security com.), ASPA (v.p. Dutchess County chpt. 1979-86), Am. Soc. Notaries (life, bd. dirs., cybernotary com.), Nat. Spkrs. Assn., Nat. Judges Assn., Nat. Assn. Parliamentarians, Am. Inst. Parliamentarians, Nat. Conf. Adminstrv. Law Judges, N.Y. State Assn. Notaries Pub. (founder, pres.), Northeastern Regional Acad. Legal Studies in Bus., Nat. Conf. Adminstrv. Law Judges, Italian Heritage Ctr. Portland, Propeller Club. Republican. Roman Catholic. Avocations: amateur radio, traveling, private pilot, boating, maritime history and lighthouse preservation. Fax: 800-366-6302. E-mail: piombino@abanet.org. Office: PO Box 778 Portland ME 04104-0778

**PIPER, JAMES WALTER,** lawyer; b. Mpls., Apr. 28, 1950; s. Mansell Garrett and Maxine (Sorenson) P.; m. Connie Lee Moore (div.); m. Jane Marie Quentan, May 27, 1995. BBA, Baylor U., 1971; JD, U. Tex., 1974. Bar: Tex. 1974, U.S. Dist. Ct. (we. dist.) Tex. 1976, U.S. Ct. Appeals (5th cir.) 1978, U.S. Supreme Ct. 1980; bd. cert. in family law. Atty. Legal Aid Soc. Ctrl. Tex., Austin, 1974-76, mng. atty., 1976-84; ptnr. Piper & Powers, L.L.P., Austin, 1984—; mem. faculty Tex. Coll. Trial Advocacy, Houston, 1980. Founding mem. Family PAC, Austin, 1998. Mem. Travis County Bar Assn. (sec.-treas. family law sect. 1989-90), Coll. of State Bar of Tex., Tex. Acad. Family Law Specialists, Travis County Family Law Advocates. Avocations: reading, hiking, boating, music. Family and matrimonial. Office: Piper & Powers LLP 2206 Lake Austin Blvd Austin TX 78703-4548

**PIPER, JULIAN M.,** lawyer; b. N.Y.C., Mar. 25, 1942; s. William and Esther P.; m. Carol Marsha Segal, June 19, 1965; children: David, Stephanie, Diane. BA, U. South Fla., 1963; JD, U. Fla., 1965. Bodily injury claims advisor Allstate Ins. Co., St. Petersburg, Fla., 1966-70; assoc. Harrison Mann Davenport Rowe & Stanton, St. Petersburg, 1970-76; sr. ptnr. Goldner Reams Marger Davis Piper & Bartlett, St. Petersburg, 1977-92; mng. ptnr. Piper Ludin Howie & Werner, St. Petersburg, 1992—. Mem. ABA, Fla. Bar Assn., Acad. Fla. Trial Lawyers, St. Petersburg Bar Assn. Avocations: tennis, travel. Office: Piper Ludin et al 5720 Central Ave Saint Petersburg FL 33707-1719

**PIPKIN, MARVIN GRADY,** lawyer; b. San Angelo, Tex., Nov. 15, 1949; s. Raymond Grady and Lillie Marie (Smith) P.; m. Dru Cheatham, July 24, 1971; children: Lacey Elizabeth, Matthew Todd. BBA, U. Tex., 1971, JD, 1974. Bar: Tex. 1974, U.S. Dist. Ct. (we. dist.) Tex. 1979, U.S. Ct. Appeals (5th cir.) 1983. Assoc. Green & Kaufman, San Antonio, 1974-79, ptnr., 1979-82; ptnr. Kendrick & Pipkin, San Antonio, 1982-93, Drought & Pipkin L.L.P., San Antonio, 1993-98, Pipkin and Oliver, 1998—; mem. coms. on ethics and admissions Tex. Supreme Ct., admissions com.; adv. dir. Trinity Nat. Bank, San Antonio, 1983; bd. dirs. Allied Am. Bank, San Antonio, First Interstate Bank, San Antonio. Bd. dirs. Monte Vista Hist. Assn., San Antonio, 1975-78. Fellow Tex. Bar Found., San Antonio Bar Found.; mem. ABA, Tex. Assn. Def. Counsel, Tex. Bar Assn., San Antonio Bar Assn. Republican. Methodist. Avocations: sports, outdoor activities. General civil litigation, Real property, General corporate. Home: 2 Dorchester Pl San Antonio TX 78209-2203 Office: Drought & Pipkin LLP 112 E Pecan St Ste 2600 San Antonio TX 78205-1528

**PIPKIN, WILLIAM A.,** lawyer; b. Seminole, Okla., June 25, 1934; s. James W. and Ruth E. P.; m. Anna L. Roberts, Oct. 20, 1978. LLB, Samford U., 1957. Bar: Okla., U.S. Dist. Ct. (10th cir.), U.S. Supreme Ct. Pvt. practice Moore, Okla., 1957—. Administrative and regulatory, Criminal, Family and matrimonial. Office: 110 W Main St Moore OK 73160-5106

**PIRCHER, LEO JOSEPH,** lawyer; b. Berkeley, Calif., Jan. 4, 1933; s. Leo Charles and Christine (Moore) P.; m. Phyllis McConnell, Aug. 4, 1956 (div. April 1981); children: Christopher, David, Eric; m. Nina Silverman, June 14, 1987; B.S., U. Calif.-Berkeley, 1954, J.D., 1957. Bar: Calif. 1958, N.Y. 1985; cert. specialist taxation law Calif. Bd. Legal Specialization. Assoc. Lawler, Felix & Hall, L.A., 1957-62, ptnr., 1962-65, sr. ptnr., 1965-83; sr. ptnr. Pircher, Nichols & Meeks, L.A., 1983—; adj. prof. Loyola U. Law Sch., L.A., 1959-61; corp. sec. Am. Metal Bearing Co., Gardena, Calif., 1975—, dir. Varco Internat. Inc., Orange, Calif.; speaker various law schs. and bar assns. edn. programs. Author: (with others) Definition and Utility of Leases, 1968. Chmn. pub. fin. and taxation sect. Calif. Town Hall, Los Angeles, 1970-71. Mem. Calif. State Bar, N.Y. State Bar, Los Angeles County Bar Assn. (exec. com. comml. law secton), ABA, Nat. Assn. Real Estate Investment Trusts Inc. (cert. specialist taxation law). Republican. Club: Regency (L.A.). Real property, General corporate, Corporate taxation. Office: Pircher Nichols & Meeks 1999 Avenue Of The Stars Los Angeles CA 90067-6022

**PIRRO, JEANINE FERRIS,** lawyer; b. Elmira, N.Y., June 2, 1951; d. Esther Ferris; m. Albert J. Pirro, Aug. 23, 1975; children: Christi, Alexander. BA, U. Buffalo, 1972; JD, Albany Law Sch., 1975. Bar: N.Y. 1975. Legis. aide N.Y. State Senate, Albany, 1973-75; asst. dist. atty. Westchester County Dist. Atty. Office, White Plains, N.Y., 1975-78, chief Victim Witness Unit,, 1978-79, chief domestic violence/child abuse bur., 1978-90, dist. atty., 1994—; county judge Westchester County, White Plains, 1990-93. Contbr. articles to profl. jours. Chair Gov. Pataki's N.Y. State Commn. on Domestic Violence Fatalities Rev. Bd., 1996; bd. dirs. My Sister's Place, 1990—; bd. vis. Pace U. Sch. Law, 1994—. Mem. N.Y. State Dist. Attys. Assn. (pres. 1999—), Nat. Mus. Women's History (bd. adv.). Republican. Roman Catholic. Office: Westchester County Dist Atty County Courthouse 111 Dr ML King Jr Blvd White Plains NY 10601-2507

**PIRTLE, H(AROLD) EDWARD,** lawyer; b. Detroit, Apr. 6, 1948; s. Edward Bensen Pirtle and Lorraine Virginia (La Pointe) Schwartz; m. Maxine Mary Stencel, June 10, 1971 (div. May 1981); children: Kimberly, Jeffrey, Michelle; m. Betsy Yvonne Mark, Sept. 1, 1984. AS, Macomb County Cmty. Coll., Warren, Mich., 1977; B in applied sci., Siena Heights Coll., 1983; JD, U. Toldeo, 1990. Bar: Mich. 1990, U.S. Dist. Ct. (ea. dist.) Mich. 1990, U.S. Ct. Appeals (6th cir.) 1997. Assoc. Beaman & Beaman, Jackson, Mich., 1990-91; pvt. practice, H. Edward Pirtle, Atty. at Law, Detroit, 1991-96; assoc. Calligaro & Meyering, PC, Taylor, Mich., 1996-97; pvt. practice, Detroit, 1997—. With U.S. Navy, 1967-72. Mem. ABA, Criminal Def. Attys. of Mich., Macomb County Bar Assn., Met. Detroit Bar Assn., Am. Mensa (gen. rep. 1984-85, legal counsel Mensa Edn. and Rsch. Found., trustee, found. sec.). Avocations: camping, hunting, fishing. Contracts commercial, Criminal, Bankruptcy. Office: 1805 Ford Bldg 615 Griswold Detroit MI 48226-3901

**PISANO, VINCENT JAMES,** lawyer; b. Englewood, N.J., Sept. 12, 1953; s. Vincent Paul and Georgette (Cernek) P.; m. Lissa Roth, May 4, 1996; 1 child, Catherine Callahan Steele. BA, Vassar Coll., 1975; JD, St. Johns U., 1978. Bar: N.Y. 1979. With Skadden, Arps, Slate, Meagher and Flom, N.Y.C., 1978—; ptnr. Skadden, Arps, Slate and Meagher, N.Y.C., 1986—. Bd. dirs. Make a Wish Found. Met. N.Y., 1988-90. Mem. N.Y. Bar Assn., N.Y.C. Bar Assn., Vassar Coll. Alumni Assn. Securities, General corporate, Mergers and acquisitions. Office: Skadden Arps Slate Meagher & Flom 919 3rd Ave New York NY 10022-3902

**PISCIOTTA, DONNA MARIA,** lawyer; b. Oyster Bay, N.Y., Mar. 2, 1961; d. Joseph Diego and Mary (Guido) P.; m. John Gerard Balzer, June 30, 1990. JD, New Eng. Sch. Law, 1988. Bar: Mass. 1988, U.S. Ct. Appeals (1st cir.) 1988. Assoc. Goldenberg, Walters & Lipson, Brookline, Mass., 1989-92, Barron & Stadfeld, Boston, 1992-95, Anzuoni & Assocs., 1994-98, Colucci & Assocs., 1998—; instr. Newbury Coll., Boston, 1991-94. Democrat. Avocation: physical fitness. Real property. Home: 77 Old Right Rd Ipswich MA 01938-1063

**PISCITELLI, FRANK E., JR.,** lawyer; b. Richmond Heights, Ohio, Mar. 11, 1967; s. Frank E. Sr. and Janet (Dunn) P.; m. Denise A. Carthuff, Dec. 29, 1995. BA in Comms., Cleve. State U., 1990, JD, 1993. Sole practitioner Cleve., 1996-98; atty. Timothy A. Shimko & Assocs., Cleve., 1993-96, 98—. Mem. ATLA, Ohio Acad. Trial Lawyers. General civil litigation, Personal injury. Office: 925 Euclid Ave Ste 2010 Cleveland OH 44115-1407

**PISCITELLI, PETER,** lawyer; b. N.Y.C., Apr. 9, 1930; s. Antonio and Mary Domenica Piscitelli; m. Frances Marie Defina, Sept. 12, 1954; 1 child, Anthony. AB, CCNY, 1952; JD, St. John's Law Sch., 1958. Bar: N.Y. 1959, U.S. Dist. Ct. (so. and ea. dists.) N.Y. 1969, U.S. Supreme Ct. 1963. Atty. Dwyer & Lawler, Bklyn., 1959-61; chief investigator N.Y.C. Dept. Investigation, 1961-66; counsel to legis. rep. Mayor's Office, N.Y.C. and Albany, 1966-70; legis. rep. N.Y.C. Bd. of Edn., Bklyn., 1970-79; legis. rep. Mayor's Office, N.Y.C., 1978-79, dir. inter-govtl. rels., 1979-82; ptnr. Condello, Ryan & Piscitelli, N.Y.C. and Albany, 1982-90, Bower & Gardner, N.Y.C., 1990-94, Wilson, Elser, Moskowitz, Edelman & Dicker, N.Y.C., 1994—; comdg. officer N.Y. Naval Militia, 1978-79; chmn. N.Y.C. Water Bd., 1985-88, Tchrs. Retirement Bd., N.Y.C., 1982-85; mem. Com. on Character & Fitness, 1992—. Del. Dem. Nat. Conv., Chgo., 1968; mem. Columbus Citizens Found., 1986—. Lt. USNR, 1952-55. Mem. Columbian Lawyers 1st Dept. Democrat. Roman Catholic. Avocations: reading, traveling, government. Legislative, Administrative and regulatory, Land use and zoning (including planning). Office: Wilson Elser Moskowitz Edelman & Dicker 150 E 42d St New York NY 10017

**PITEGOFF, JEFFREY I.,** lawyer; b. Ft. Leonardwood, Mo., Jan. 5, 1968; s. Alan Pitegoff and Linda Ellen Meyerson; m. Dona R. Newcomb; children: Kianna Jordan, Jaron Imrie. BS, U. Evansville, 1990; JD, Oklahoma City U., 1994. Bar: Nev., 1994, U.S. Dist. Ct. Nev., 1994, U.S. Ct. Appeals (9th cir.) 1999. Assoc. Albregts & Albregts, Las Vegas, Nev., 1994-95, Earley Savage, Las Vegas, Nev., 1995—. Avocations: skiing, racquetball, cycling, pool. General civil litigation, Consumer commercial, Personal injury. Office: Earley Savage 7251 W Lake Mead Blvd Ste 550 Las Vegas NV 89128-8351

**PITEGOFF, PETER ROBERT,** lawyer, educator; b. N.Y.C., Mar. 6, 1953; s. Joseph and Libbie (Shapiro) P.; m. Ann Casady, Mar. 22, 1986; children: Maxwell Jacob, Elias Samuel. AB, Brown U., 1975; JD, NYU, 1981. Bar: Mass 1981, N.Y. 1988; cert. tchr., R.I. Tchr. Hope High Sch., Providence, 1974-75; community organizer Nat. Assn. for So. Poor, Petersburg, Va., 1975-76, Citizens Action League, Oakland, Calif., 1976-78; gen. counsel ICA Group, Boston, 1981-88; ptnr. Arrington & Pitegoff, Somerville, Mass., 1986-88; prof. law SUNY, Buffalo, 1988—, acad. vice dean law sch., 1998—; adj. asst. prof. law NYU, 1986-88; instr. Harvard Law Sch., 1985; cons. in field, 1978—; legal counsel cmty. devel. worker purchases of bus. corp. fin. dem. corp. structures child care policy and welfare policy. Contbr. to profl. publs. Root-Tilden scholarship NYU, 1978; grantee Pub. Interest Law Found., N.Y.C., 1981. Democrat. Jewish. Avocations: athletics, travel, music. Office: SUNY Sch of Law 507 Obrian Hall Buffalo NY 14260-0116

**PITT, GEORGE,** lawyer, investment banker; b. Chgo., July 21, 1938; s. Cornelius George and Anastasia (Geocaris) P.; m. Barbara Lynn Goodrich, Dec. 21, 1963 (div. Apr. 1990); children: Elizabeth Nanette, Margaret Leigh; m. Pamela Ann Pittsford, May 19, 1990. BA, Northwestern U., 1960, JD, 1963; hon. grad., U.S. Army Intelligence Sch., Ft. Holabird, Md., 1964. Bar: Ill. 1963. Assoc. Chapman and Cutler, Chgo., 1963-67; ptnr. Borge and Pitt, and predecessor, 1968-87, Katten Muchin & Zavis, Chgo., 1987-97; sr. mng. dir. Banc One Capital Markets, Inc. (formerly First Chgo. Capital Markets, Inc.), 1998—; conf. chmn. Bond Buyer's 3d Ann. Midwest Pub. Fin. Conf., 1994; conf. co-chmn. Bond Buyer's 8th Ann. Midwest Pub. Fin. Conf., 1999. editor notes and comments Northwestern U. Law Rev., 1962-63. 1st lt. AUS, 1964. Fellow Am. Coll. of Bond Counsel; mem. Ill. State Bar Assn., The Monroe Club, Univ. Club. Chgo., Michigan City Yacht Club, Ind. Soc. of Chgo., Eta Sigma Phi, Phi Delta Phi, Phi Gamma Delta. Municipal (including bonds). Home: 600 N McClurg Ct Chicago IL 60611-3044 Office: Banc One Capital Markets Inc Mail Ste IL1 0534 One First National Plz Chicago IL 60670-0534

**PITT, REDDING,** lawyer; b. Decatur, Ala., Mar. 29, 1944; s. Charles Kermit and Dorothea Rowena (Slaughter) P.; m. Jane Hanify, Sept. 20, 1969 (div. Dec. 1980); 1 child, William Rivers; m. Abigail P. van Alstyne, Aug. 24, 1985. Student, U. Ams., Mexico City, 1963; BA, U. Ala., 1967; JD, Boston Coll., 1977. Staff asst. to chmn. FDIC, Washington, 1977-79; staff asst. to comptr. of currency U.S. Treasury Dept., Washington, 1979-80; asst. atty. gen. State of Ala., Montgomery, 1981-94, counsel to sec. of state, 1981-84, asst. legal adviser to dir. fin., 1984-86, chief dep. atty. gen., 1987-91, counsel to atty. gen., 1991-94; U.S. atty. U.S. Dist Ct. (Mid. Dist.) Ala., Montgomery, 1994—; mem. Ala. Juvenile Justice Coordinating Coun. Supreme Ct. Ala., Montgomery, 1992-94. Editor: Powers and Duties of State Attorneys General, 1988. Mem. Ala. Gov. Drug Adv. Bd., Montgomery, 1994—; mem. adv. bd. Blackburn Inst. U. Ala., 1996—. Capt. U.S. Army, 1969-72. Recipient Pres. award Nat. Assn. Attys. Gen., 1988. Mem. ABA, ATLA, Fed. Bar Assn. (pres. 1995—), Ala. Law Inst. (mem. reform adv. com. 1982-93), Ala. Bar Assn. (mem. com. bench & bar rels. 1994-95). Democrat. Episcopalian. Avocations: history, golf. Office: US Atty Mid Dist Ala 1 Court Sq Ste 201 Montgomery AL 36104-3538*

**PITTMAN, EDWIN LLOYD,** state supreme court justice; b. Hattiesburg, Miss., Jan. 2, 1935; s. Lloyd H. and Pauline P.; m. Virginia Lund, 1996; children: Melanie, Win, Jennifer. BS, U. So. Miss.; JD, U. Miss., 1960. Bar: Miss. Practiced law until, 1964; mem. Miss. Senate, 1964-72; treas. State of Miss., Jackson, 1976-80, sec. of state, 1980-84, atty. gen., 1984-88; justice Supreme Ct. Miss., Jackson, 1989—. Trustee William Carey Coll. 2nd lt., Inf. U.S. Army. Mem. U. Miss. Alumni Assn., U. So. Miss. Alumni Assn., Miss. Jaycees (past state dir.), ABA, South Central Miss. Bar Assn. Democrat. Baptist. Clubs: Lions, Masons. Office: Miss Supreme Ct Gartin Justice Bldg Jackson MS 39205-0117*

**PITTMAN, VIRGIL,** federal judge; b. Enterprise, Ala., Mar. 28, 1916; s. Walter Oscar and Annie Lee (Logan) P.; m. Floy Lasseter, 1944; children—Karen Pittman Gordy, Walter Lee. B.S., U. Ala., 1939, LL.B., 1940. Bar: Ala. bar 1940. Spl. agt. FBI, 1940-44; practice law Gadsden, Ala., 1946-51; judge Ala. Circuit Ct., Circuit 16, 1951-66; U.S. dist. judge Middle and So. Dist. Ala., 1966-71; chief judge U.S. Dist. Ct. for Ala. So. Dist., 1971-81, sr. judge, 1981—; periodically sits as judge U.S. Ct. Appeals 11th Cir., 1981—; lectr. bus. law, econs. and polit. sci. U. Ala. Center, Gadsden, 1948-66. Author: Circuit Court Proceedings in Acquisition of a Tract of Right of Way, 1959, A Judge Looks at Right of Way Condemnation Proceedings, 1960, Technical Pitfalls in Right of Way Proceedings, 1961. Mem. Ala. Bd. Edn., 1951; trustee Samford U., 1974-90, 92—. Lt. (j.g.) USN, 1944-46. Mem. Ala. State Bar, Etowah County Bar Assn. (pres. 1949), Omicron Delta Kappa. Democrat. Baptist. Office: US Dist Ct PO Box 465 Mobile AL 36601-0465

**PITTS, GARY BENJAMIN,** lawyer; b. Tupelo, Miss., Aug. 23, 1952; s. Dexter Derward Pitts and Eva Margaret (Holcomb) Bush; m. Nicole Palmer; children: Andrew Ross, Caitlan Taylor. Student, U. Miss., Oxford, 1970-71, Coll. Charleston (S.C.), 1971-73; BA, McGill U., Montreal, Que., Can., 1973-74; JD, Tulane U., New Orleans, 1979. Bar: Tex. 1979, U.S. Ct. Appeals (5th cir.) 1980, U.S. Supreme Ct. 1983. Assoc. Julian & Seele, Houston, 1979-84, Ogletree, Pitts & Collard, Houston, 1984-85; ptnr. Pitts & Collard LLP, Houston and Dallas, 1985-96; owner Pitts & Assocs., Houston, 1996—. Organizer, legal counsel for Neighborhood Watch Coalition. Capt. USNG, 1975-87. Mem. ATLA, Maritime Law Assn. (Proctor in Admiralty 1980—). Personal injury, Workers' compensation, Admiralty. Office: Pitts & Assocs 8866 Gulf Fwy Ste 117 Houston TX 77017-6528

**PITTS, MICHAEL STUART,** lawyer; b. Charlotte, N.C., Dec. 23, 1969; s. H. Marshall and Peggie B. Pitts. BA, U. N.C., Chapel Hill, 1992; JD, U. S.C., 1996. Bar: S.C. 1996, N.C. 1998, U.S. Dist. Ct. S.C. 1996, U.S. Ct. Appeals (4th cir.) 1996. Assoc. Grant, Leatherwood & Pitts, Greenville, S.C., 1996—. Mem. S.C. Def. Trial Attys. Assn., Phi Beta Kappa. General civil litigation, Insurance. Office: Grant Leatherwood & Pitts 306 E North St Greenville SC 29601-2114

**PITZER, JEFF SCOTT,** lawyer; b. Pitts., Sept. 8, 1963; s. George Earl and Billie Raye Pitzer; m. Tricia Ann Shelley, Nov. 1, 1997. BA in Chemistry, U. Kans., 1986; Jd, U. Wis., 1990. Assoc. Jenner & Block, Chgo., 1990-97, ptnr., 1997—. mem. ABA, Fed. Trial Bar, Chgo. Coun. Lawyers. General civil litigation, Criminal. Home: 3714 N Marshfield Ave Chicago IL 60613-3622 Office: Jenner & Block One IBM Plaza Chicago IL 60611

**PITZNER, RICHARD WILLIAM,** lawyer; b. Fond du Lac, Wis., Sept. 19, 1946; s. Robert J. and Almira (Wurtz) P.; m. Georgene J. Thuerwachter, July 6, 1968 (div. 1991); children: Christie, Kyle; m. Ricki L. Mundstock, Jan. 4, 1998. BBA, U. Wis., 1968, MBA, 1969, JD, 1972. Bar: Wis. 1972, U.S. Dist. Ct. (we. dist.) Wis. 1972, U.S. Tax Ct. Ptnr. Murphy & Desmond, Madison, Wis., 1972—; tchr. U. Wis., Madison, 1975-78. Mem. ABA, AICPA, Nat. Assn. Accts., Wis. Inst. CPAs, State Bar Wis., Wis. Inst. CPAs, Nakoma Golf Club, Madison Club, Order of Coif, Beta Gamma Sigma. Avocations: golf, swimming. Corporate taxation, Estate taxation,

Probate. Home: 1305 Boundary Rd Middleton WI 53562-3843 Office: Murphy & Desmond 2 E Mifflin St Madison WI 53703-2889

**PIZZULLI, FRANCIS COSMO JOSEPH,** lawyer, bioethicist; b. Bklyn., May 16, 1950; s. Dominick Lawrence and Rose Nancy (Ieracitano) P. BA in Math. with high honors, U. Calif.-Santa Barbara, 1971; JD, U. So. Calif., 1974. Bar: Calif. 1975. NEH postdoctoral fellow Inst. of Soc., Ethics and the Life Scis., Hastings Ctr., Hastings-on-Hudson, N.Y., 1974-75; law clk. U.S. Ct. Appeals (9th cir.), 1975-76; sole practice, Santa Monica, Calif., 1981—; speaker, lectr., panelist in bioethics field. Editor So. Calif. Law Rev., 1973-74. Contbr. articles to profl. publs. Spl. cons. Nat. Commn. for Protection Human Subjects of Biomed. and Behavioral Research, Washington, 1976-77. Mem. Italian-Am. Lawyers Assn., Order of Coif. Roman Catholic. Lodge: KC. General civil litigation, Constitutional, Entertainment. Office: 718 Wilshire Blvd Santa Monica CA 90401-1708

**PLAEGER, FREDERICK JOSEPH, II,** lawyer; b. New Orleans, Sept. 10, 1953; s. Edgar Leonard and Bernice Virginia (Schiwetz) P.; m. Kathleen Helen Dickson, Nov. 19, 1977; children: Douglas A., Catherine E. BS, La. State U., 1976, JD, 1977. Bar: La. 1978, Tex. 1999, U.S. Dist. Ct. (ea. dist.) La. 1978, U.S. Ct. Appeals (5th cir.) 1981, U.S. Supreme Ct. 1989. Law clk. U.S. Dist. Ct. (ea. dist.) La., New Orleans, 1977-79; assoc. Milling, Benson, Woodward, Hillyer, Pierson & Miller, New Orleans, 1979-85, ptnr., 1985-89; v.p., gen. counsel, corp. sec. La. Land and Exploration Co., New Orleans, 1989-97; v.p., gen. counsel Burlington Resources Inc., Houston, 1997—. Bd. dirs. New Orleans Speech and Hearing Ctr., 1985-91, pres., 1988-90; bd. dirs. Children's Oncology Svcs. La. (Ronald McDonald House of New Orleans), 1987-90; selected mem. Met. Area Com. Leadership Forum, 1986; bd. dirs. Soc. Environ. Edn., La. Nature and Sci. Ctr., 1992-94; bd. dirs. New Orleans City Park Assn., 1996-97. Recipient Service to Mankind award Sertoma, 1989. Mem. ABA, La. Bar Assn., Am. Corp. Counsel Assn. (bd. dirs. New Orleans chpt. 1995-98), Am. Petroleum Inst. (mem. gen. commn. law), Univ. Club, Lakeside Country Club. Republican. Avocations: golf, hunting, fishing. General corporate, Oil, gas, and mineral, General practice. Home: 5105 Longmont Dr Houston TX 77056-2417 Office: Burlington Resources Inc 5051 Westheimer Rd Ste 1400 Houston TX 77056-5686

**PLAGER, S. JAY,** federal judge; b. Long Branch, N.J., May 16, 1931; s. A.L. and Clara L. Plager; children: Anna Katherine, David Alan, Daniel Tyler. A.B., U. N.C., 1952; J.D., U. Fla., 1958; LL.M., Columbia U., 1961. Bar: Fla. 1958, Ill. 1964. Asst. prof. law U. Fla., 1958-62, assoc. prof., 1962-64; assoc. prof. law U. Ill., Champaign-Urbana, 1964-65, prof., 1965-77; dir. Office Environ. and Planning Studies, 1972-74, 75-77; dean, prof. law Ind. U. Sch. Law, Bloomington, 1977-84; prof. law Ind. U. Sch. Law, 1984-90; counselor to undersec. U.S. Dept. Health and Human Svcs., 1986-87; assoc. dir. Office of Mgmt. and Budget Office of Mgmt. and Budget, 1987-88; adminstr. info. and regulatory affairs Exec. Office of the Pres., 1988-89; cir. judge U.S. Ct. Appeals (fed. cir.), 1989—; vis. research prof. law U. Wis., 1967-68; vis. scholar Stanford U., 1984-85. Author: (with others) Water Law and Administration, 1968, Social Justice Through Law-New Approaches in the Law of Property, 1970, (with others) Florida Water Law, 1980. Chmn. Gainesville (Fla.) Planning Commn., 1962-63; mem. Urbana Plan Commn., 1966-70; mem. nat. air pollution manpower devel. adv. com., 1971-75; cons. Ill. Inst. for Environ. Quality, U.S. EPA; chmn. Ill. Task Force on Noise, 1972-76; vice chmn. Nat. Commn. on Jud. Discipline and Removal, 1991-93. With USN, 1952-55. Office: US Ct Appeals for Fed Cir The National Courts Bldg 717 Madison Pl NW Washington DC 20439-0002

**PLAINE, LLOYD LEVA,** lawyer; b. Washington, Nov. 3, 1947. BA, U. Pa., 1969; postgrad., Harvard U.; JD, Georgetown U., 1975. Bar: D.C. 1975. Legis. asst. to U.S. Rep. Sidney Yates, 1971-72; with Sutherland, Asbill & Brennan, Washington, 1975-82, ptnr., 1982—. Fellow Am. Bar Found., Am. Coll. Trust and Estate Counsel (past regent), Am. Coll. Tax Counsel; mem. ABA (past chmn. real property, probate and trust law sect.). Estate planning, Probate, Estate taxation. Office: Sutherland Asbill & Brennan 1275 Pennsylvania Ave NW Washington DC 20004-2404

**PLANT, PAUL BRUNSON,** lawyer; b. Andalusia, Ala., Apr. 11, 1944; s. Arthur Earl and Sara Inis Plant; m. Cherie Harwell, June 15, 1968; children: Sara Cherie Plant Williams, Jonathan Paul. AA, Pensacola (Fla.) Jr. Coll., 1964; B in Music Edn., George Peabody Coll. Tchrs., Nashville, 1967; JD, Samford U., 1974. Bar: Tenn. 1974, U.S. Dist. Ct. (ctrl. dist.) Tenn. 1976, U.S. Ct. Appelas (6th cir.) 1986, U.S. Supreme Ct. 1992. Ptnr. Harwell & Plant, Lawrenceburg, TN; bd. dirs. Cmty. Bank and Trust, Lawrenceburg, Tenn.; chmn. SGA Systems, Ltd. Editor Cumberland-Samford Law Rev. 1973-74. Lay leader Coleman Meml. United Meth. Ch., past chmn. adminstrv. bd.; charter mem. 21st Century Coun. Lawrence County; host pres. Babe Ruth Baseball World Sries, 1978; charter mem. Leadership Lawrence County; chmn. LAWRENCEBURG 175; dir., condr. Lawrence County Oratorio Soc. Ann. Christmas Pops Concert. Fellow Tenn. Bar Found.; mem. ABA (sects. on gen. practice, econs. of practice of law), ATLA, Am. Judicature Soc., Am. Bd. Trial Advocates, Tenn. Bar Assn. (bd. govs. 1989-91, ho. of dels.. 1981, sec. 1985-87, dep. spkr. 1987-89, spkr. 1989-91), Tenn. Trial Lawyer's Assn., Lawrence County Bar Assn. (pres. 1993-94), Cumberland Nat. Alumni Assn. (v.p. 1987-89), Masons (past pres. Lawrence County Scottish Rite club), Shriners (past pres. Lawrence County club), Kiwanis (past pres. Lawrenceburg chpt., Kiwanian of Yr. award 1978), Lawrence County C. of C. (past pres., Citizen of Yr. award 1995). Democrat. Methodist. Avocation: music. General civil litigation, General practice, Insurance. Office: Harwell & Plant 225 N Mahr Ave Lawrenceburg TN 38464-3231

**PLASSE, ANDREW FREDERICK,** lawyer; b. Manhasset, N.Y., Dec. 5, 1955; s. Herman and Sherley (Puner) P.; m. Karen A. Bishop, Jan. 8, 1984. B.A., SUNY-Stony Brook, 1977; J.D., Syracuse U., 1981; LL.M., Boston U., 1983. Bar: N.Y. 1982, Mass. 1982, Fla. 1984, U.S. Dist. Ct. (no. dist.) N.Y. 1984. Assoc. Davoli, McMahon & Kublick, P.C., Syracuse, N.Y., 1981—. Mem. ABA, N.Y. State Bar Assn., Onondaga County Bar Assn., Mass. Bar Assn. Democrat. Jewish. Office: 225 W 34th St Ste 1204 New York NY 10122-1299

**PLASTARAS, THOMAS EDWARD,** lawyer; b. N.Y.C., Aug. 8, 1957; s. Joseph Edward and Lois Jean (Brady) P. BS in Hosp. Adminstrn., Ithaca Coll., 1979; JD cum laude, Calif. Western Sch. Law, 1982. Bar: Calif. 1982, U.S. Dist. Ct. (so. dist.) Calif. 1982, N.Y. State 1983, U.S. Dist. Ct. (ea. and so. dists.) N.Y. 1984, U.S. Tax Ct. 1984, Minn. 1984, D.C. 1989. Law clk. to presiding justice U.S. Dist. Ct. (so. dist.) Calif., San Diego, 1981-82; assoc. Kelly, Rode, Kelly & Burke, Westbury, N.Y., 1982-87; sole practice Smithtown, N.Y., 1988—; appointed referee Suffolk County Supreme Ct., N.Y. Mem. N.Y. State Bar Assn., N.Y. State Trial Lawyers Assn., Nassau/Suffolk County Bar Assn. Lodge: Rotary (bd. dirs. Nesconset club). State civil litigation, Personal injury, Federal civil litigation. Office: Gallagher Walker Bianco & Plastaras 98 Willis Ave Mineola NY 11501-2611

**PLASZCZAK, ROMAN THADDEUS,** lawyer; b. San Diego, Oct. 3, 1943; s. Thaddeus Roman and Lorrine (Wiedenfeld) P. BA, Western Mich. U., 1965; JD, Detroit Coll., 1968. Bar: Mich. 1968, U.S. Supreme Ct, 1974, U.S. Dist. Ct. (we. dist.) 1979. Asst. pros. atty. Muskegon (Mich.) County, 1970-72; ptnr. Jerkins, Plaszczak, Hurley & Bauhof, Kalamazoo, 1972-79, Plaszczak & Bauhof P.C., Kalamazoo, 1979—. Leader Legal Explorer Scouts, Kalamazoo, 1975-77; vol. Cath. Family Services, Kalamazoo, 1982-83. Served as capt. U.S Army, 1968-70, Vietnam. Decorated Bronze Star; recipient Civil Rights Litigation award ACLU, 1986, Raymond W. Fox Advocacy Achievement award, 1990. Mem. ATLA, Mich. Bar Assn. (state trial cts. com. 1980-85, investigator Mich. atty. grievance com. 1980—), Mich. Trial Lawyers Assn., Greater Paw Paw C. of C. (pres. 1990-97). Republican. Avocations: offshore power boat racing, travel. Personal injury, Federal civil litigation, State civil litigation. Home: 729 Mapleview Dr Paw Paw MI 49079-1185 Office: Plaszczak & Bauhof PC 137 N Park St Ste 203 Kalamazoo MI 49007-3769

**PLATNER, MICHAEL GARY,** lawyer; b. Forest Hills, N.Y., June 18, 1957; s. Alan and Norma Platner; children: Marissa, Amanda, Carina. AB in Econs. cum laude, Washington U., St. Louis, 1979; JD, Emory U., 1982, MBA, 1982. Bar: Fla. 1983, Ga. 1983. Ptnr. Gunster, Yoakley, Valdes-Fauli & Stewart, P.A., Ft. Lauderdale, Fla., 1983—. Mem. legal affairs com. Internat. Franchise Assn. Mem. ABA, Fla. Bar Assn. (computer law sub-com.), Computer Law Assn., Real Estate Securities and Syndication Inst. (pres. S.E. Fla. chpt. 1987). General corporate, Securities, Mergers and acquisitions. Home: 1401 S Ocean Blvd Apt 908 Pompano Beach FL 33062-7385 Office: 500 E Broward Blvd Ste 1400 Fort Lauderdale FL 33394-3076

**PLATSIS, GEORGE JAMES,** lawyer; b. Khaniá, Crete, Nov. 8, 1937; came to U.S., 1938; s. Artemi and Marika (Siradakis) Platsidakis; m. Barbara Jean Spor, Aug. 16, 1964; children: Christina Mary, Maria Elizabeth. BA, U. Mich., 1962, JD, 1967. Bar: D.C. 1969, Mich. 1969, U.S. Ct. Appeals, U.S. Ct. Appeals (6th cir.), U.S. Dist. Ct. (we. dist.) Mich. Atty. FTC, Washington, 1967-69; asst. atty. gen. Mich. Dept. Atty. Gen., Lansing, 1969-75; spl. asst. atty. gen. Mich. Dept. Atty. Gen., Okemos, 1975-89; pvt. practice, Okemos, 1975—. Bd. dirs., v.p., treas. Holy Trinity Greek Orthodox Ch., Lansing, 1980-84, 94-95. With U.S. Army, 1963-65. Mem. Am. Hellenic Ednl. and Progressive Assn. (local officer 1975—, dist. gov. 1980—, supreme counsellor 1989-90), Pancretau Assn. Am. (legal advisor 1984-86), Kiwanis. Avocations: sailing, travel, archaeology. General civil litigation, Condemnation, Personal injury. Office: 2019 Shagbark Ln Okemos MI 48864-3631

**PLATT, DAVID M.,** lawyer; b. Lansing, Mich., June 9, 1955; s. Earl C. and Katherine A. P.; m. Kathleen S. Spencer Platt, Nov 10, 1979; children: Katherine Jean, Joan Ellen. BA, Mich. State U., E. Lansing, 1975, MA, 1976; JD, Thomas A. Cooley LS, Lansing, Mich., 1980. Bar: Mich. 1980; U.S. Dist. Ct. (we. dist.) 1990, Fla. 1992. Instr. Mich. State U., E. Lansing, 1977-79; counsel Proaction Inst. MSU, E. Lansing, Mich., 1979-83, K.A. Knapp & Co., Grand Rapids, Mich., 1983-84, Centennial Group, Lansing, Mich., 1984-89; atty. Farhat & Story, East Lansing, Mich., 1989—; dir. IAFP-MID Mich., Lansing, 1991-94, Highfields, Lansing, 1996—. Co-author: Preparation for Work in Michigan, 1979, Preparation for Work in Changing Economy. Estate planning, Probate, General corporate. Office: Beacon Place 4572 S Hagadorn Rd Ste 3 East Lansing MI 48823-5385

**PLATT, GARY R.,** lawyer; b. Elizabeth, N.J., June 18, 1948. BA in English, Lafayette Coll., 1970; JD, U. Md., 1973. Bar: N.J. 1974. Law sec. to Hon. V. William DiBuono and Cuddie E. Davidson Superior Ct. N.J., 1973-74; asst. prosecutor Office of the Union County Prosecutor, Elizabeth, 1974-75, Office of the Passaic (N.J.) County Prosecutor, 1975-76; assoc. Einhorn & Harris, Denville, N.J., 1976-81; mem. Einhorn, Harris & Platt, Denville, N.J., 1981-88; pvt. practice law Cedar Knolls & Morristown, N.J., 1988-92; mem. Ullman, Furhman, Platt & Koy, P.C., Morristown, 1992-99, Ullman, Furhman, Broeman & Platt, P.C., Morristown, 1999—. Mem. ABA, N.J. State Bar Assn., Lafayette Coll. Alumni Leadership Coun. Avocations: scuba diving, genealogy, civil war study. Land use and zoning (including planning), Real property, Contracts commercial. Office: Ullman Furhman Broeman & Platt PC 89 Headquarters Plz N-12 Morristown NJ 07960-6834

**PLATT, HAROLD KIRBY,** lawyer; b. Southampton, N.Y., Nov. 7, 1942; s. William Bangs and Edith (Guldi) P.; m. Joan Pritchard, June 20, 1970; 1 child, Timothy Ross. B.S. in Foreign Service, Georgetown U., 1964; J.D., Fordham U., 1971. Bar: N.Y. 1972, U.S. Supreme Ct. 1976, U.S. Dist. Ct. (ea. dist.) N.Y. 1988. Sole practice, Southampton, 1972-77; ptnr. Platt & Platt, Southampton, 1977-80, Platt, Platt & Platt, Southampton, 1980—. Articles editor Fordham Law Review, N.Y.C., 1970-71. Bd. dirs., sec. Southampton Hosp. Assn., 1979-85. Served with Mil. Police, U.S. Army, 1965-67; Germany. Mem. Suffolk County Bar Assn. (fee disputes com. 1974-82, chmn. 1981-82, mem. real property law commn. 1975-78, mem. law office econ. com. 1981-82, mem. taxation com. 1984-85, 92-93), N.Y. State Bar Assn., ABA. Real property, Probate, General practice. Home: 9 Dovas Path Southampton NY 11968-2830 Office: Platt Platt & Platt 99 Sanford Pl Southampton NY 11968-3338

**PLATT, LESLIE A.,** lawyer; b. Bronx, N.Y., Aug. 7, 1944; s. Harold and Ann (Bienstock) P.; m. Marcia Ellin Berman, Aug., 1969; 1 son, Bill Lawrence. B.A., George Washington U., 1966; J.D., N.Y.U., 1969. Bar: N.Y. 1970, U.S. Dist. Ct. D.C. 1972. Atty. advisor Office Gen. Counsel, HUD, Washington, D.C., 1971-72, legis. atty., 1972-75, asst. gen. counsel for legis. services, 1975-78, assoc. gen. counsel for legis., 1978-80; dep. gen. counsel-legal counsel HEW (HHS 1980), Office Gen. Counsel, Washington, 1980-81, legal counsel and staff dir. White House Agent Orange working group, 1980-81; pvt. practice law, Washington, 1982-91; exec. asst. to dir. NIH, 1991-92; exec. v.p./chief operating officer/gen. counsel, The Institute for Genomic Rsch, Gaithersburg, Maryland, 1992-95; sr. v.p. strategic devel., gen. counsel Am. Type Culture Collection, Manassas, Va., 1996-98, pres, dir. Foundation for Genetic Medicine, Inc., 1997—. Patentee in field. Chmn. community adv. bd. Fairfax Hosp. Assn. Cameron Glen Facility; chair steering com. Reston/Herndon Bus.-High Schs. partnership. Recipient Disting. Service award HUD, 1978. Mem. ABA, Fed. Bar Assn., Am. Jud. Soc., Fed. Sr. Exec. Service (charter), Internat. Bar Assn. Health, Legislative, Administrative and regulatory. Home: 11901 Triple Crown Rd Reston VA 20191-3015 Office: 10801 University Blvd Manassas VA 20110-2204

**PLATT, THOMAS COLLIER, JR.,** federal judge; b. N.Y.C., N.Y., May 29, 1925; s. Thomas Collier and Louise Platt; m. Ann Byrd Symington, June 25, 1948; children: Ann Byrd, Charles Collier, Thomas Collier, III, Elizabeth Louise. B.A., Yale U., 1947, LL.B., 1950. Bar: N.Y. 1950. Assoc. Root, Ballantine, Harlan, Bushby & Palmer, N.Y.C., 1950-53; asst. U.S. atty. Bklyn., 1953-56; assoc. Bleakley, Platt, Schmidt, Hart & Fritz, N.Y.C., 1956-60, ptnr., 1960-74; judge U.S. Dist. Ct. (ea. dist.) N.Y., Uniondale, 1974—; chief judge U.S. Dist. Ct. (ea. dist.) N.Y., Bklyn., 1988-95; former dir. Phoenix Mut. Life Ins. Co., RAC Corp., McIntyre Aviation, Inc.; atty. Village of Laurel Hollow, N.Y., 1958-74; acting police justice Village of Lloyd Harbor, N.Y., 1958-63. Alt. del. Republican Nat. Conv., 1964, 68, 72; del. N.Y. State Rep. Conv., 1966; trustee Brooks Sch., North Andover, Mass., 1968-82, pres., 1970-74. Served with USN, 1943-46. Mem. Fed. Judges Assn. (sec., bd. dirs. 1982-91). Episcopalian. Clubs: Phelps Assn. (New Haven) (bd. govs. 1960-98); Cold Spring Harbor Beach (N.Y.) (bd. mgrs. 1964-70); Yale of N.Y.C. Office: US Dist Ct 2 Uniondale Ave/Hempstead T Uniondale NY 11553

**PLATT, WILLIAM HENRY,** judge; b. Allentown, Pa., Jan. 25, 1940; s. Henry and Genevieve (McElroy) P.; m. Maureen Hart, Nov. 29, 1969; children: Meredith H., William H., James H. AB, Dickinson Coll., 1961; JD, U. Pa., 1964. Bar: Pa. 1967, U.S. Supreme Ct. 1971. Ptnr. Yarus and Platt, Allentown, 1967-77; asst. pub. defender Lehigh County (Pa.), 1972-75, chief pub. defender, 1975-76, dist. atty., 1976-91; ptnr. Eckert, Seamans, Cherin & Mellott, 1991-95; city solicitor City of Allentown, Pa., 1994-95; judge Ct. Common Pleas of Lehigh County, Allentown, 1996—; mem. criminal procedural rules com. Supreme Ct. Pa., 1982-92, chmn., 1986-92. Mem. Gov.'s Trial Ct. Nominating Commn. Lehigh County, 1984-87; mem. Pa. Commn. on Crime and Delinquency Victim Services Adv. Com., 1983-91. Served with M.P., U.S. Army, 1964-66. Mem. ABA, Pa. Bar Assn., Lehigh County Bar Assn., Nat. Assn. Dist. Attys. (state dir. 1982-84), Pa. Assn. Dist. Attys. (pres. 1983-84, exec. com. 1980-86, tng. inst. mem. 1986-91, chmn. 1986-87), Pa. Bar Inst. (bd. dirs. 1989—, exec. com. 1994—, pres. 1997-98), Pa. Conf. of State Trial Judges (edn. com. 1997-99). Office: Lehigh County Courthouse 455 W Hamilton St Allentown PA 18101-1614

**PLATTNER, RICHARD SERBER,** lawyer; b. N.Y.C., Aug. 10, 1952; s. Milton and Sallee Sarah (Serber) P.; m. Susan M. Madden, June 4, 1976 (div. June 1979); m. Susan K. Morris, Mar. 30, 1983; children: Samuel Morris, Katherine Elise. BA cum laude, Mich. State U., 1973; JD, Ariz. State U., 1977. Bar: Ariz. 1977, U.S. Dist. Ct. Ariz. 1977, U.S. Ct. Appeals (9th cir.) 1987; cert. specialist personal injury and wrongful death. Assoc. Wolfe & Harris, Pa., 1977-79, Monbleau, Vermeire & Turley, Phoenix, 1979-81, Phillips & Lyon, Phoenix, 1981; sole practice Phoenix, 1982-91; ptnr. Plattner Verderame, P.C., 1991—; Posse comdr. Maricopa County Sheriff Adj. Posse, 1986—; judge pro tem Maricopa County Superior Ct., 1986—, Ariz. Ct. Appeals, 1993—. Editor: Trial Judges of Maricopa County, 1985; co-editor Jury Verdict Research newsletter, 1982-83. Mem. Am. Bd. Trial Advs. (assoc. 1997—), Assn. Trial Lawyers Am. (sustaining mem.), Ariz. Trial Lawyers Assn. (sustaining mem., editor Ariz. Appellate Highlights, 1985—, bd. dirs., 1987—, pres. 1991), Ariz. Bar Assn. (mem. civil practice and procedure com. 1988-91, 92—, civil jury instrn. com. 1991), Maricopa County Bar Assn., Phoenix Trial Lawyers Assn. (bd. dirs. 1983—, pres. 1986-87), Ariz. Bus. and Profl. Assn. (pres. 1984-86). Product liability, Insurance, Personal injury. Office: PO Box 36570 Phoenix AZ 85067-6570

**PLAVE, ERICA FROHMAN,** lawyer; b. N.Y.C., Dec. 20, 1962; d. Lawrence A. and Barbara H. Frohman; m. Mitchell Plave, July 7, 1985; children: Aaron, Leah. BA, Wesleyan U., Middletown, Conn., 1985; JD, George Washington U., 1989. BAr: Md. 1989, D.C. 1990, U.S. Dist. Ct. D.C., U.S. Ct. Appeals (D.C. cir.). Atty. Arnold & Porter, Washington, 1990-97, Marriott Internat., Bethesda, Md., 1997-98; sr. atty. Sodexho Marriott Svcs., Gaithersburg, Md., 1998—. Mem. Bar of D.C., Women's Bar Assn. D.C., Order of Coif, Phi Beta Kappa. General corporate, General civil litigation. Office: Sodexho Marriott Svcs 9801 Washington Blvd Gaithersburg MD 20878

**PLAX, KAREN ANN,** lawyer; b. St. Louis, June 29, 1946; d. George J. and Evelyn G. Zell; m. Stephen E. Plax, Dec. 19, 1968; 1 child, Jonathan. BA magna cum laude, U. Mo., St. Louis, 1969; JD with distinction, U. Mo., Kansas City, 1976. Bar: Mo. 1976, U.S. Supreme Ct. 1980. Atty. Thayer, Gum & Wickert, Grandview, Mo., 1976-84, Plax & Cochet, Kansas City, Mo., 1984-87; pvt. practice Kansas City, 1987—; chair family access com. Jackson County Family Ct., 1998; chair divsn. 3, region IV Mo. Supreme Ct. Com. to review ethical conduct of attys., 1997-98. Author: Missouri Bar Practical Skills, 1998; asst. editor: Racial Integration in the Inner Suburb, 1990; contbr. articles to profl. law jours. Recipient Pub. Svc. award U. Mo. Kansas City Law Found., 1998, Woman of Yr. award Assn. Women Lawyers of Greater Kansas City, 1999. Fellow Am. Acad. Matrimonial Lawyers (pres.-elect Mo. chpt. 1998); mem. ABA (family law sect. 1996-98), Kansas City Met. Bar Assn., Mo. Bar Family Law (legis. chair 1997-98, exec. coun. 1997-98, Spl. Commendation for Legis. Role in Family Law 1998). Avocations: creative writing, drama. Family and matrimonial. Office: 1310 Carondelet Dr Kansas City MO 64114-4803

**PLEASANT, JAMES SCOTT,** lawyer; b. Anniston, Ala., July 14, 1943; s. James C. and Barbara (Scott) P.; m. Susan M. Pleasant, May 17, 1966; children: Deborah Kaye, Carol Ann, Julie Ruth. BS, Oreg. State U., 1965; JD summa cum laude, Willamette U., 1972. Bar: Tex. 1972, U.S. Dist. Ct. (no. dist.) Tex. 1973, U.S. Ct. Appeals (5th cir.) 1975, U.S. Supreme Ct. 1977. Ptnr. Gardere & Wynne LLP, Dallas, 1972—. Mem. Smithsonian Assn., Washington, 1985—, Dallas Mus. of Art, 1987—. Capt. U.S. Army, 1966-69, Vietnam. Mem. ABA (partnership law sect. 1969—), Tex. Bar Assn. (partnership law sect. 1989—), Vietnam Pilots Assn., Dustoff Assn. Real property, General corporate, Securities. Office: Gardere & Wynne LLP 1601 Elm St Ste 3000 Dallas TX 75201-4761

**PLEBAN, SARAH SHELLEDY,** lawyer; b. York, Nebr., June 13, 1956; d. James Edwin and Mary Patricia (Cornwall) Shelledy; m. C. John Pleban, Sept. 26, 1981; children: Jonathan Cornwall, Meredith Shelledy, Jacob Stevens. BA in Psychology, Quincy Coll., 1977; JD, St. Louis U., 1981. Bar: Mo. 1981, Ill. 1982, U.S. Dist. Ct. (we. dist.) Mo. 1981. Dir. placement Law Sch. St. Louis U., 1981-82; chief trial atty. St. Louis County Pub. Defenders Office, Clayton, Mo., 1982-89; pvt. practice St. Louis, 1989—. Mem. planning and devel. bd. dirs. Franciscan Charities, St. Louis, 1988—; Affton Sch. Dist. Bd. Edn., 1996—; pres. St. Michael's Sch. Bd., Shewsbury, Mo., 1991-94.. Mem. Ill. Bar Assn., Mo. Bar Assn. Criminal, Juvenile, Family and matrimonial. Office: 100 S 4th St Ste 600 Saint Louis MO 63102-1822

**PLESS, LAURANCE DAVIDSON,** lawyer; b. Jacksonville, Fla., Dec. 22, 1952; s. James William Pless III and Anne (Dodson) Martin; m. Dana Halberg, June 20, 1980; children: Anna Amesbury, William Davidson, Deane Ahlgren. AB cum laude with distinction, Duke U., 1975; JD, U. N.C., Chapel Hill, 1980. Assoc. Neely & Player, P.C., Atlanta, 1980-86, ptnr., 1986-92; ptnr. Welch, Spell, Reemsnyder, Pless & Davis, P.C., Atlanta, 1992—. Contbr. articles to profl. jours.; mem. staff N.C. Law Rev. Vol. Saturday Vol. Lawyer's Found., Atlanta, 1980-92. Mem. ABA, Lawyer's Club of Atlanta, Atlanta Bar Assn., Capital City Club, Lake Rabun Assn. Democrat. Episcopalian. Avocations: hiking, tennis, coaching kid's sports, canoeing. E-mail: ldp@welchspell.com. General corporate, Mergers and acquisitions, General practice. Home: 25 Palisades Rd NE Atlanta GA 30309-1530 Office: Welch Spell Reemsnyder Pless & Davis PC 400 Colony Sq NE Ste 2020 Atlanta GA 30361-6305 also: PO Box 428 Lakemont GA 30552-0008

**PLETZ, THOMAS GREGORY,** lawyer; b. Toledo, Oct. 3, 1943; s. Francis G. and Virginia (Connell) P.; m. Carol Elizabeth Connolly, June 27, 1969; children: Anne M., John F. BA, U. Notre Dame, 1965; JD, U. Toledo, 1971. Bar: Ohio 1971, U.S. Ct. Appeals (6th cir.) 1978, U.S. Supreme Ct. 1985. Ct. bailiff Lucas County Common Pleas Ct., Toledo, 1967-71; jud. clk. U.S. Dist. Ct. (no. dist.) Ohio, Toledo, 1971-72; assoc. Shumaker, Loop & Kendrick, Toledo, 1972-76, litigation ptnr., 1976—; acting judge Sylvania (Ohio) Mcpl. Ct., 1990—; mem. Ohio Bar Bd. Examiners, 1993—, chmn., 1996-99. Active Toledo Parish Coun., 1987-99; chmn., trustee Kiroff Trial Adv. Com., Toledo, 1982-91. With USNR, 1965-92; ret. CDR. Recipient Toledo Jr. Bar award, 1995. Mem. ABA, Ohio State Bar Assn., Toledo Bar Assn. (trustee 1981-93), Diocesan Attys. Bar Assn., 6th Cir. Jud. Conf. (life), Nat. Conf. Bar Examiners Com. Roman Catholic. General civil litigation, Education and schools, Libel. Office: Shumaker Loop & Kendrick 1000 Jackson St Toledo OH 43624-1573

**PLEUS, ROBERT J., JR.,** lawyer; b. Orlando, Fla., Jan. 9, 1936; s. Robert J. Sr. and Virginia T. Pleus; m. Marie T. Pleus, June 8, 1963; children: Lawrence, Robert III, Michael, Maria, Melissa, Sean. BA, U. Notre Dame, 1957; JD, U. Fla., 1962. Bar: Fla., U.S. Dist. Ct. Fla. Assoc. Rush, Read & Marshall, Orlando, 1962-65; ptnr. Smathers, Tepper & Pleus, Orlando, 1965-68, Carlton Fields, Orlando, 1968-80, Pleus, Adams & Spears, Orlando, 1980-95; of counsel Akerman, Senterfitt & Eidson, Orlando, 1995—; pres. young lawyers divsn. Fla. Bar, Tallahassee, 1970-72, bd. govs., 1976-82. Mem. town coun. Town of Windermere, Fla., 1972-74, mayor, 1987-93; pres. Tri-County League of City of Orlando, 1991-92. Lt. USN, 1957-65. Mem. Am. Coll. Real Estate Lawyers, Am. Coll. Mortgage Attys., Orange County Bar Assn. (pres. 1975-76, Legal Aid Soc. award of excellence 1992). Republican. Roman Catholic. Real property, Contracts commercial. Home: 522 W 2nd Ave Windermere FL 34786-8513 Office: Akerman Senterfitt and Eidson 255 S Orange Ave Ste 1000 Orlando FL 32801-3483

**PLEVY, ARTHUR L.,** lawyer; b. N.Y.C., May 26, 1936; s. Louis and Sarah (Aronowitz) P.; student Bklyn. Coll., 1953-57; BEE, CCNY, 1959; LLB, JD, Bklyn. Law Sch., 1967; children—Scott Eric, Robert Todd. Design engr. I T & T Labs., Nutley, N.J., 1959-60; project engr. Westrex, N.Y.C., 1960-62; sr. mem. tech. staff RCA N.Y.C., 1962-65, patent counsel, RCA Research Center, Princeton, 1965-70; admitted to N.Y. State bar, 1965, N.J. bar, 1970, Supreme Ct. bar, 1970, Ct. Customs and Patent Appeals bar; pvt. practice patent law, Edison, N.J., 1970-91; sr. ptnr. Plevy & Assocs., 1991—; cons. electronic firms; pres. New Ventures, Edison, N.J., 1970—; arbitrator Am. Arbitration Assn. Mem. ABA, N.J. Patent Law Assn., Fed. Bar Assn., N.Y. Bar Assn., N.J. Bar Assn., IEEE, CCPA, Mason. Contbr. numerous articles on electronics, patent and trademark law to profl. jours.; patentee field of electronics. E-mail: aplevy@greenbaumlaw.com. Fax: (732) 549-1881. Patent, Trademark and copyright. Home: 77 Colfax Rd Skillman NJ 08558-2310 Office: Greenbaum Rowe Smith Ravin Davis & Himmel LLP PO Box 5600 Woodbridge NJ 07095-0988

**PLEWS, DENNIS JAMES,** lawyer; b. Grand Rapids, Mich., Feb. 5, 1948; s. Kenneth J. and Mary Frances (Weiks) P. AA, St. Petersburg Jr. Coll., 1970; BA in Polit. Sci., U. West Fla., 1972; JD cum laude, Fla. State U., 1974. Bar: Fla. 1975; U.S. Dist. Ct. (mid. dist.) Fla. 1975; Fla. Pub. Svc. Commn. 1977. Staff counsel Fla. energy joint house/senate com. Fla. Energy Com., Joint House/Senate Fla. Legislature, Tallahassee, 1973-74; spl. asst. pub. defender Pub. Defender 2nd Jud. Cir. Ct. Fla., Tallahassee, 1974; asst. pub. defender Pub. Defender 12th Jud. Cir. Ct. Fla., Sarasota, 1975-77; assoc. Law Office of Robert Hill Schultz, Bradenton, Fla., 1977-80; pvt. practice, Brandenton, 1980—. Co-author: Energy in Florida, 1974. With U.S. Army, 1967-69, Vietnam. Mem. AAAS, ATLA (Outstanding Mem. recognition), Fla. Bar, Acad. Fla. Trial Lawyers (chmn. dist. 9 speaker's bur. 1987—), Local Group Deep Sky Observers (founding), So. Poverty Law Ctr., Planetary Soc., Vietnam Vets. Sarasota and Manatee, Amnesty Internat.,

Am. Inns of Ct. Democrat. Avocations: astronomy, physics, cosmology, fishing, tennis. General civil litigation, Personal injury, Product liability. Office: 1111 9th St W Bradenton FL 34205-7332

**PLISKA, EDWARD WILLIAM,** lawyer, retired judge; b. Rockville, Conn., Apr. 13, 1935; s. Louis Boleslaw and Constance (Dombrowski) P.; m. Luisa Anne Crotti, Nov. 29, 1958; children: Gregory, John, Thomas, Laura. AB, Princeton (N.J.) U., 1956; LLB, U. Conn., 1964; LLD (hon.), San Mateo (Calif.) U., 1975. Bar: Calif. 1965. Dep. dist. atty. Santa Barbara (Calif.) County, 1965; dep. dist. atty. San Mateo County Dist. Atty., Redwood City, Calif., 1965-71, chief trial dep., 1970-71; pvt. practice San Mateo, 1971-72; judge San Mateo County Mcpl. Ct., 1973-86; ptnr. Corey, Luzaich, Manos & Pliska, Millbrae, Calif., 1986—; officer Am. Judges Assn., 1983-86; prodr. and host (TV and Radio show) Justice Forum, 1973-78; prof. criminal and constitutional law San Mateo Law Sch., 1971-76; leader People to People legal delegations to Europe, India, Nepal, 1985, 87, 91. Editor Ct. Rev., 1981-88. Leader People to People Legal Delegations, Europe, India, Nepal, 1985, 87, 91; trustee Belmont (Calif.) Sch. Dist., 1987-91, pres., 1990; chmn. San Mateo County Cultural Arts Commn., 1987-90; mem. Peninsula Comty. Found. Arts Fund, 1988—; officer Hillbarn Theatre, 1989—. With U.S. Army, 1957. NEH grantee, 1975, 80. Mem. Calif. Judges Assn., Calif. State Bar Assn., Nat. Assn. Criminal Def. Lawyers, Calif. Attys. for Criminal Justice, San Mateo County Bar Assn., Bohemian Club. Democrat. Roman Catholic. Avocations: acting and directing plays, reading, sports spectator. Criminal, General civil litigation, Alternative dispute resolution. Home: 1567 Escondido Way Belmont CA 94002-3634 Office: Corey Luzaich Manos Pliska PO Box 669 700 El Camino Real Millbrae CA 94030-2009

**PLOTNICK, PAUL WILLIAM,** lawyer; b. Chgo., Mar. 16, 1947; s. Sam and Mary (Price) P.; m. Eleanor Levy, Jan. 18, 1970; 1 child, Sarah Jennie. BA, So. Ill. U., 1969; JD, DePaul U., 1974. Bar: Ill. 1974., U.S. Dist. Ct. (no. dist.) Ill. 1974, U.S. Ct. Appeals (7th cir.) 1974, U.S. Tax Ct. 1975, U.S. Supreme Ct. 1977. Tchr. Chgo. Pub. Schs., 1969-74; pvt. practice Chgo., 1974-75; pres. Paul W. Plotnick, Ltd., Skokie, Ill., 1979—; asst. pub. defender Cook County Pub. Defender's Office, Chgo., 1975-79; felony asst. Cook County Pub. Defender's Office, Evanston, Ill., 1976-79. Contbr. articles, poem to profl. publs. Pres. Budlong Woods Civic Group, Chgo., 1982-83; candidate for judge Circuit Ct. Cook County, 1998. Staff sgt. U.S. Army, 1969. Named Man of the Yr. Midwest Fedn. Men's Clubs, 1995; recipient Disting. Svc. award Chgo. Vol. Legal Svcs., 1995. Mem. ABA, ATLA, Ill. State Bar Assn., Chgo. Bar Assn., N.W. Suburban Bar Assn., N. Suburban Bar Assn., Kiwanis (pres. Skokie Valley chpt. 1989-90, Disting. Sec. award 1987, Disting. Pres. award 1991, Lay Person of the Yr. I.I. Dist. divsn. 7), Beth Hillel Men's Club (pres. 1991-93), Decalogue Soc. State civil litigation, Real property, Criminal. Office: Paul W Plotnick Ltd 9933 Lawler Ave Ste 312 Skokie IL 60077-3706

**PLOTNIK, KATYA MICHELE,** lawyer; b. N.Y.C.; d. Arthur and Meta (Von Borstel) P. BA, U. Wis., 1990; JD, CUNY, Queens, 1994. Bar: N.J. 1994, N.Y. 1995. Assoc. Law Office of Bruno Joseph Bembi, Hempstead, N.Y., 1994-96; founding ptnr. Rodriguez & Plotnik, N.Y.C., 1996—. Mem. Am. Immigrtion Lawyers Assn., N.Y. County Lawyers Assn., N.Y. State Bar Assn. Democrat. Avocation: martial arts. Office: Rodriguez & Plotnik 299 Broadway Rm 712 New York NY 10007-1901

**PLOTTEL, ROLAND,** lawyer; b. N.Y.C., Oct. 1, 1934; s. Charles and Frances (Banner) P.; m. Jeanine Parisier, June 3, 1956; children—Claudia, Michael, Philip. B.A., Columbia U., 1955, LL.B., 1958, M.S. in E.E., 1964. Bar: N.Y. 1958, U.S. Patent Office 1962, U.S. Ct. Appeals 1964, U.S. Supreme Ct. 1964. House counsel Radiotronix Communications Labs., N.Y.C., 1958-61; patent atty. Bendix Corp., Teterboro, N.J., 1961-64; internat. patent atty. Western Electric Co., N.Y.C., 1964-70; sole practice, N.Y.C., 1970—; of counsel Frishauf, Holtz, Goodman & Woodward, N.Y.C.; lectr. patent law Practising Law Inst.; arbitrator Civil Ct., 1964—. Harlan Fiske Stone fellow. Mem. ABA, N.Y. County Lawyers Assn., Am. Intellectual Property Law Assn., N.Y. Patent Trademark and Copyright Law Assn., IEEE, Internat. Soc. Hybrid Microelectronics, Am. Arbitration Assn. Club: City N.Y. Patent, Trademark and copyright, Intellectual property. Home: 50 E 77th St New York NY 10021-1836 Office: 45 Rockefeller Plz New York NY 10111-0100

**PLUCIENNIK, THOMAS CASIMIR,** lawyer, former assistant county prosecutor; b. Irvington, N.J., Apr. 8, 1947; s. Casimir Stanley and Helen Victoria (Sienicki) P.; m. Maria Anne Soriano, June 16, 1974. BS in Acctg., Seton Hall U., 1969, JD, 1983; MA in Criminal Justice, CUNY, 1976. Bar: N.J. 1983, U.S. Ct. Mil. Appeals 1986, U.S. Dist. Ct. N.J. 1983, D.C. 1994, U.S. Supreme Ct. 1995, N.Y. 1996, U.S. Ct. Appeals (3rd cir.), U.S. Dist. Ct. (so., ea., fed. dists.) N.Y. 1998; cert. criminal trial atty., mil. trial atty.; lic. pvt. investigator. Mng. ptnr. Joe Bell's Tavern & Restaurant, Newark, 1979; police officer City of Newark, 1972-79; criminal investigator Essex County Prosecutor, Newark, 1980-84, asst. prosecutor, 1984-88; sr. asst. prosecutor Warren County, N.J., 1988-89; atty. Voorhees & Acciavatti Esq., Morristown, N.J., 1989-94; defense atty. Picillo Caruso, 1994-96; assoc. Netchert, Dineen & Hillman, 1996-97; litigator Francis J. Dooley, 1998-99; pvt. practice, 1999—; cert. instr. N.J. State Police Tng. Commn., Trenton, 1984; asst. dir. instruction Officers Candidate Sch. N.J. Mil. Acad., Sea Girt. Committeeman South Orange Republican Club, N.J., 1978-83; treas., founder Tuxedo Park Neighborhood Assn., South Orange, 1977; fin. sec. J. T. Kosciusko Assn., Irvington, N.J., 1979. Served to 1st lt. U.S. Army, 1969-71, maj. (ret.) JAGC, 1985-90. Recipient Class C. Commendations, Newark Police Dept., 1973, 74, 75, Command Citations, 1973, 74, 75, 77, 78. Mem. ATLA, ABA, Worrall F. Mountain Inn of Ct. (master), Trial Attys. N.J., N.J. State Bar Assn., N.J. Def. Assn., Morris County Bar Assn., N.Y. State Bar Assn., Washington D.C. Bar Assn., Am. Legion, Officers Club (pres. Sea Girt, N.J. 1979-81), Ret. Officers Assn., Picatinny Officers Club, South Orange Lions Club (charter mem.), Polish Univ. Club. Republican. Roman Catholic. General civil litigation, Criminal, Insurance. Home: 11 Laurel Ln Morris Plains NJ 07950-3216

**PLUIMER, EDWARD J.,** lawyer; b. Rapid City, S.D., 1949. BA cum laude, U. S.D., 1971; JD cum laude, NYU, 1974. Bar: Minn. 1975. Law clk. to Hon. Robert A. Ainsworth, Jr. U.S. Ct. Appeals (5th cir.), 1974-75; ptnr. Dorsey & Whitney, Mpls.; mem. Minn. Supreme Ct. ADR Task Force, 1988-92. Editor N.Y. U. Law Rev. Mem. Order of the Coif. General civil litigation, Franchising, Securities. Office: Dorsey & Whitney LLP 220 S 6th St Ste 2200 Minneapolis MN 55402-1498

**PLUMB, ROBERT THOMPSON, II,** lawyer; b. San Diego, 1951; s. Robert T. and Elsie Jane (Burket) P.; m. Rita Robbins. BA, Coll. Idaho, 1973; JD, Thomas Jefferson Sch. Law, 1977. Bar: Calif. 1979; cert. legal specialist in family law. Pvt. practice Law Offices of Robert T. Plumb II, Coronado, Calif., 1979—. Mem. Rotary. Avocations: golf, bridge, travel. Office: PO Box 180734 Coronado CA 92178-0734

**PLUNK, JOHN MATTHEW,** lawyer; b. Athens, Ala., Apr. 14, 1953; s. Leonard B. and Jane Starkey Plunk; m. Molly Maund, July 22, 1971; children: Molly, Jennifer. BS, U. Ala., Tuscaloosa, 1975, JD, 1978. Bar: Ala. 1978, U.S. Dist. Ct. (no. div.) Ala., U.S. Ct. Appeals (11th cir.). Ptnr. Alexander, Corder, Plunk, Baker, Shelly & Shipman, P.C., Athens, 1978—; dist. atty. 39th Jud. Circuit, Limestone County, Ala., 1981-82; bd. dirs. 1st Am. Bank, Decatur, Ala. Mem. Limestone County Dem. Exec. Com., 1994—; trustee U. Mobile, Ala., 1996—. Mem. Ala. Trial Lawyers Assn. (exec. com. 1989—, chmn. pub. rels. com. 1995-96). Baptist. Avocation: golf. Real property, Personal injury, Probate. Office: Alexander Corder Et Al PO Box 809 Athens AL 35612-0809

**PLUNKETT, PAUL EDMUND,** federal judge; b. Boston, July 9, 1935; s. Paul M. and Mary Cecilia (Erbacher) P.; m. Martha Milan, Sept. 30, 1958; children: Paul Scott, Steven, Andrew, Kevin. BA, Harvard U., 1957, JD, 1960. Ptnr. Mayer Brown & Platt, Chgo., 1960-63, 78-83; asst. atty. U.S. Atty.'s Office, Chgo., 1963-66; ptnr. Plunkett Nisin et al, Chgo., 1966-78; judge U.S. Dist. Ct. (no. dist.) Ill., Chgo., 1983—; adj. faculty John Marshall Law Sch., Chgo., 1964-76, 82—, Loyola U. Law Sch., Chgo., 1977-82. Mem. Fed. Bar Assn. Clubs: Legal, Law, Union League (Chgo.). Office: US Dist Ct Everett McKinley Dirksen Bldg 219 S Dearborn St Ste 1446 Chicago IL 60604-1705

**PLUNKETT, STEPHEN OLIVER,** lawyer; b. St. Paul, Feb. 7, 1963; s. Robert William and Mary Jane Plunkett; m. Barbara McCarthy, Oct. 13, 1990; children: Connor, Anne. BA, U. Minn., 1985, JD, 1989. Ptnr. Rider, Bennett, Egan & Arundel, Mpls., 1989—. Product liability, Insurance, General civil litigation. Office: Rider Bennett Egan & Arundel 2000 Metro Ctr 333 S 7th St Minneapolis MN 55402-2414

**PLUSS, EDWARD ALLEN,** lawyer; b. Denver, May 9, 1955; s. Norman and Barbara Pluss; m. Janis Pluss, Sept. 2, 1984; 1 child, Maxwell. BBA, U. Tex., 1977; JD, U. Denver, 1980. Bar: Colo. U.S. Dist. Ct. Colo., U.S. Ct. Appeals (10th cir.). Pub. defender Colo. State Pub. Defender, Denver, 1980-85; assoc. Haligam & Loltner, P.C., Denver, 1985-89; pvt. practice law Denver, 1989—. Criminal. Office: 1741 High St Denver CO 80218-1320

**PLUTA, TOM,** lawyer; b. Ludlow, Mass., Oct. 16, 1950; s. John J. and Stella M. (Gruszka) P. Cert., A. Mickiewicz U., Poznań, Poland, 1971, Gosudarstvenniy U., St. Petersburg, Russia, 1972; BA, Boston U., 1972; JD, Boston Coll., 1975; cert., Harvard U., 1975. Bar: Mass. 1975, D.C. 1977, U.S. Ct. Internat. Trade 1981, U.S. Supreme Ct. 1981. Fgn. svc. officer U.S. Dept. State, Washington and Helsinki, Finland, 1976-81; lawyer Arlington, Va., 1981-83; counsel, Bd. Vets. Appeals U.S. Dept. Vets. Affairs, Washington, 1983—. Editor Boston Coll. Jour. Internat. Law, 1974-75. Republican. Roman Catholic. Avocations: history, politics, foreign travel, beaching. Home: 5610 Durbin Rd Bethesda MD 20814-1014 Office: 810 Vermont Ave NW Washington DC 20420-0001

**PLUYMEN, BERT W.,** lawyer; b. Hoensbroek, Holland, Oct. 3, 1948; s. Harry and Paula Pluymen. BA, Rice U., 1971; JD with honors, U. Tex.-Austin, 1974. Bar: Tex. 1974, U.S. Dist. Ct. (ea. dist.) Tex. 1976, U.S. Dist. Ct. (we. dist.) Tex. 1978, U.S. Supreme Ct. 1978, U.S. Ct. Appeals (5th cir.) 1974, U.S. Ct. Appeals (11th cir.) 1982, U.S. Dist. Ct. (no. dist.) Tex. 1986. Asst. atty. gen. State of Tex., 1974-78; assoc. Byrd, Davis & Eisenberg, Austin, 1978-81, ptnr., 1982; ptnr. Pluymen & Jenkins, P.C. and predecessors, Austin, 1982—. Bd. dirs., v.p. Austin Dem. Forum, 1987-89; bd. dirs. Travis Assn. for the Blind, 1986-89, Tex. Consumer Assn., 1987—; bd. dirs.. Unity Ch. of Austin, 1988—, Dispute Resolution Ctr., 1988-89, Austin Parks and Recreation Dept., 1988-89. Fellow Tex. Bar Found.; mem. Tex. Young Lawyers Assn. (bd. dirs. 1983-84), Austin Young Lawyers Assn. (pres. 1981-82, named outstanding young lawyer 1985), Travis County Bar Assn. (bd. dirs. 1982-83), Assn. Trial Lawyers Am., Tex. Trial Lawyers Assn. (assoc. bd. dirs. 1980-83, bd. cert. personal injury trial law, Tex. bd. legal specialization), Order of Coif. Personal injury, Workers' compensation. Office: Pluymen & Jenkins PC 8140 N Mo Pac Expy Ste 150 Austin TX 78759-8837

**PLYMALE, RONALD E.,** lawyer; b. Huntington, W.Va.; s. Arthur L. and R. Ellene Plymale; m. Nancy L. Papp, June 21, 1989. BA, Ohio State U., 1963, JD, 1968. Bar: Ohio 1968, U.S. Dist. Ct. (so. dist.) Ohio 1969, U.S. Ct. Appeals (6th cir.) 1973, U.S. Supreme Ct. 1976; cert. civil trial lawyer. Lawyer Barkan & Neff, Columbus, Ohio, 1968-70; city atty. City of Grove City, Ohio, 1971-79; lawyer Plymale & Assocs., Columbus, Ohio, 1980—. Fellow Roscoe Pound Found.; mem. Assn. of Trial Lawyers of Am., Nat. Bd. of Trial Advocacy, Million Dollar Advocates Forum. General civil litigation, Personal injury, Professional liability. Office: Plymale & Assocs 350 S High St Columbus OH 43215-4510

**POCIUS, JAMES EDWARD,** lawyer; b. Scranton, Pa., Mar. 26, 1952; s. Edward Leonard and Aldona Petronella Pocius; m. Kristine Marie Mauck, Aug. 5, 1978; 1 child, Victoria Marie. BA, Pa. State U., 1973; JD, Duquesne U., 1978. Bar: Pa., U.S. Dist. Ct. (mid. dist.) Pa. 1978, U.S. Ct. Appeals (3rd cir.) 1991. Law clk. to hon. Judge James Walsh Scranton, 1978-79; assoc. Lenahan & Dempsey, Scranton, 1979-87; pvt. practice Scranton, 1987-92; regional supervising atty. Marshall Dennehey Warner Coleman and Goggin, Scranton, 1992—; spkr. in field. Contbr. articles to profl. jours. V.p. St. Francis Soup Kitchen, Scranton, 1989—. Mem. Lackawanna Bar Assn. (com. mem.). Workers' compensation, Insurance, Administrative and regulatory. Office: Marhsll Dennehey Warner Coleman and Goggin 507 Linden St Scranton PA 18503-1608

**PODBOY, ALVIN MICHAEL, JR.,** law library director, lawyer; b. Cleve., Feb. 10, 1947; s. Alvin Michael and Josephine Esther (Nagode) P.; m. Mary Ann Gloria Esposito, Aug. 21, 1971; children: Allison Marie, Melissa Ann. AB cum laude, Ohio U., 1969; JD, Case Western Res. U., 1972, MLS, 1977. Bar: Ohio 1972, U.S. Dist. Ct. (no. dist.) Ohio 1973, U.S. Supreme Ct. 1992. Assoc. Joseph T. Svete Co. LPA, Chardon, Ohio, 1972-76; dir. pub. services Case Western Res. Sch. Law Libr., Cleve., 1974-77, assoc. law libr., 1977-78; libr. Baker & Hostetler, LLP, Cleve., 1978-88, dir. librs., 1988—; instr. Notre Dame Coll. of Ohio, Cleve., 1991—. Am. Inst. Paralegal Studies, Cleve., 1991-96. Bd. overseers Case Western Res. U., 1981-87, mem. vis. com. sch. libr. sci., 1980-86, mem. Westlaw adv. bd., 1987-92, bd. govs. law sch. alumni assn., 1992-95, West's Legal Directory Ohio Adv. Panel, 1990-91; mem. adv. com. West's Info. Innovators Inst., 1995-97; chmn. Case We. Res. Libr. Sch. Alumni Fund, 1979-80. Rep. precinct committeeman Cuyahoga County, Cleve., 1981-95, mem. exec. com., 1984-87. 1st lt. USAF, 1972. Mem. ABA, Ohio State Bar Assn. (chmn. libraries com. 1989-91), Cleve. Bar Assn., Am. Assn. Law Librs. (cert., chmn. pvt. law librs. spl. interest sect. 1994-95), Ohio Regional Assn. Law Librs. (pres. 1985), Case We. Res. U. Libr. Sch. Alumni Assn. (pres. 1981), Arnold Air Soc., Am. Legion, KC, Pi Gamma Mu, Phi Alpha Theta. Roman Catholic. Avocation: alpine skiing. Home: 5705 Deer Creek Dr Willoughby OH 44094-4185 Office: Baker & Hostetler LLP 3200 National City Ctr Cleveland OH 44114-3485

**PODGOR, ELLEN SUE,** lawyer, educator; b. Bklyn., Jan. 30, 1952; d. Benjamin and Yetta (Shilensky) Podgor. BS magna cum laude, Syracuse U., 1973; JD, Ind. U., Indpls., 1976; MBA, U. Chgo., 1987; LLM, Temple U., 1989. Bar: Ind. 1976, N.Y. 1984, Pa. 1987. Dep. prosecutor Lake County Prosecutor's Office, Crown Point, Ind., 1976-78; ptnr. Nicholls & Podgor, Crown Point, 1978-87, instr. Temple U. Sch. Law, 1987-89; assoc. prof. law sch. St. Thomas U., Miami, Fla., 1989-91, Ga. State U., Atlanta, 1991—. Author: (with Israel) White Collar Crime In A Nutshell, (with Israel and Borman) White Collar Crime: Law and Practice; assoc. editor Ind. Law Rev., 1975-76; contbr. articles to legal jours.; mem. adv. bd. BNA Criminal Practice Manual. Del. Ind. Dem. Conv., 1982. Mem. ABA, NACDL, Am. Law Inst., Ind. Bar Assn. Democrat. Jewish. Office: Ga State U Coll Law PO Box 4037 Atlanta GA 30302-4037

**PODGORSKY, ARNOLD BRUCE,** lawyer; b. Glen Cove, N.Y., Feb. 8, 1951; s. Stanley Morton and Lillian (Cantor) P.; m. Jean Carol Levine, June 17, 1972; children: Anna, Carolyn. BA, Alfred (N.Y.) U., 1972; JD, Syracuse (N.Y.) U., 1975. Bar: D.C. 1975, U.S. Ct. Appeals (7th and 8th cirs.) 1977, U.S. Ct. Appeals (2d, 4th and 9th cirs.) 1978, U.S. Supreme Ct. 1979, U.S. Ct. Appeals (5th cir.) 1980, U.S. Dist. Ct. D.C. 1980. Atty. NLRB, Washington, 1975-79; with Cadwalader, Wickersham & Taft, Washington, 1979-86, Gerst, Heffner, Carpenter & Podgorsky, Washington, 1986-92, Wright & Talisman, P.C., Washington, 1992—. Mem. ABA, Pi Gamma Mu. Avocations: horseback riding, youth pony club. Labor, Antitrust, General civil litigation. Office: Wright & Talisman PC 1200 G St NW Ste 600 Washington DC 20005-3838

**PODHURST, AARON SAMUEL,** lawyer; b. N.Y.C., Apr. 29, 1936; s. Louis and rae (Pomerantz) P.; m. Dorothy Ellen Podhurst, Sept. 7, 1958; children: Karen Beth Dern, Laura Koffsky, Julie Weinberg. BBA, U. Mich., 1957; JD, Columbia U., 1960. Bar: Fla., 1961, N.Y., 1961. Assoc. Nichols, Gaither, Miami, Fla., 1962-67; founding ptnr. Podhurst, Orseck, Josefsberg, Eaton, Meadow, Olin & Perwin, P.A., Miami, 1967—. Vice pres. Miami Coalition for Safe Cmty., 1994—; mem. Orange Bowl Com., Miami, 1996—. Recipient Nat. Medallion award NCCJ, 1994; Harlan Fiske Stone scholar, 1960. Mem. ABA (aviation com.), Internat. Acad. Trial Lawyers (pres. 1990), Acad. Fla. Trial Lawyers (pres. 1978, aviation com.), Am. Coll. Trial Lawyers, Assn. Trial Lawyers Am. (bd. govs., aviation com.), Internat. Soc. Barristers, Inner Cir. of Advocates. Aviation, Personal injury, Consumer commercial. Office: Podhurst Orseck Josefsberg Eaton Meadow Olin & Perwin PA 25 W Flagler St Miami FL 33130-1712

**PODLEWSKI, JOSEPH ROMAN, JR.,** lawyer; b. Chgo., Jan. 8, 1953; s. Joseph Roman Podlewski Sr. and Marie Catherine Fischer; m. Heidi Elizabeth Hanson, May 3, 1986; children: Drew, William. BA, No. Ill. U., 1975; JD, IIT, 1978. Bar: Ill. 1978, U.S. Dist. Ct. (no. dist.) Ill. 1978. Law clk. to Hon. Tobias G. Barry Ill. Appellate Ct. (3rd dist.), Ladd, 1978-81; atty./advisor Ill. Environ. Protection Agy., Springfield and Maywood, 1981-89; atty. Rosenthal & Schanfield, Chgo., 1989—; mem. adj. faculty Moraine Valley C.C., Palos Hills, Ill., 1991—. Lead articles editor: Chgo.-Kent Coll. Law Rev. Mem. ABA, Ill. State Bar Assn., Chgo. Bar Assn. (chmn. environ. law com. 1993-94), Govs. Small Bus. Environ. Task Force. Environmental, General civil litigation. Home: 4721 Franklin Ave Western Springs IL 60558-1720 Office: Rosenthal & Schanfield 55 E Monroe St Fl 46 Chicago IL 60603-5713

**POFF, FRANKLIN ALBRIGHT, JR.,** lawyer; b. Hot Springs, Ark., Sept. 27, 1956; s. Franklin Albright and Carolyn Virginia (Hanson) P.; m. Theresa Ann Wolf, Aug. 19, 1978; children: Franklin A. III, William Wolf, Christopher Curtis. BA in History and Polit. Sci., Hendrix Coll., 1979; JD, U. Ark., 1982. Bar: Ark. 1982, U.S. Dist. Ct. Ark. 1982, U.S. Ct. Appeals (8th cir.) 1982, U.S. Supreme Ct. 1988, Tex. 1990, U.S. Ct. Appeals (5th cir.) 1990, U.S. Dist. Ct. Tex. 1990. Atty. Walker & Poff, Little Rock, 1982-90; assoc. Gooding & Dodson, Texarkana, Tex., 1990-92; mem. exec. com. Gooding & Dodson, P.C., Texarkana, 1992-98; of counsel Crisp, Jordan & Boyd, Texarkana, 1998—. Bd. dirs. Boys and Girls Club of Texarkana, Inc., 1996-98, Easter Seals of Texarkana, Inc., 1995—, vice chmn., 1999—, Texarkana Resources for Disabled, 1999—, Teen Ct. of Texarkana, 1999—. Mem. Ark. Bar Assn., Tex. Bar Assn., S.W. Ark. Bar Assn., N.W. Tex. Bar Assn., Texarkana Bar Assn. Fax: 903-832-8489. General civil litigation, Insurance, Toxic tort. Office: Crisp Jordan & Boyd PO Box 6297 Texarkana TX 75505-6297

**POFF, RICHARD HARDING,** state supreme court justice; b. Radford, Va., Oct. 19, 1923; s. Beecher David and Irene Louise (Nunley) P.; m. Jo Ann R. Topper, June 24, 1945 (dec. Jan. 1978); children: Rebecca, Thomas, Richard Harding; m. Jean Murphy, Oct. 26, 1980. Student, Roanoke Coll., 1941-43; LL.B., U. Va., 1948, LL.D., 1969. Bar: Va. 1947. Partner law firm Dalton, Poff, Turk & Stone, Radford, 1949-70; mem. 83d-92d congresses, 6th Dist. Va.; justice Supreme Ct. Va., 1972-89, sr. justice, 1989—; Vice chmn. Nat. Commn. on Reform Fed. Crime Laws; chmn. Republican Task Force on Crime; sec. Rep. Conf., House Rep. Leadership. Named Va.'s Outstanding Young Man of Year Jr. C. of C., 1954; recipient Nat. Collegiate Athletic Assn. award, 1966, Roanoke Coll. medal, 1967, Distinguished Virginian award Va. Dist. Exchange Clubs, 1970, Presdl. certificate of appreciation for legislative contbn., 1971, legislative citation Assn. Fed. Investigators, 1969, Thomas Jefferson Pub. Sesquicentennial award U. Va., 1969, Japanese Am. Citizens League award, 1972, Carrio Professionalism award Va. State Bar Assn. Criminal Law Sect., 1998; named to Hall of Fame, Am. Legion Boys State, 1985; fellow Va. Law Found., 1997. Mem. Bar Assn., VFW, Am. Legion, Pi Kappa Phi, Sigma Nu Phi. Clubs: Mason, Moose, Lion. Office: Va Supreme Ct 100 N 9th St Richmond VA 23219-2335 *When you know you are right, fight. When you are in doubt, wait. When you know you are wrong, admit your mistake and correct it.*

**POGREBIN, BERTRAND B.,** lawyer; b. Bklyn., Apr. 10, 1934; s. Abraham and Esther Pogrebin; m. Letty Cottin; children: Abagail, Robin, David. AB, Rutgers U., 1955; LLB, Harvard U., 1958. Bar: N.Y. 1959, U.S. Dist. Ct. (ea. and so. dists.) N.Y. 1963, U.S. Ct. Appeals (2d cir.) 1965, U.S. Ct. Appeals (4th cir.) 1965, U.S. Ct. Appeals (6th cir.) 1970, U.S. Ct. Appeals (9th cir.) 1987. Pres. Rains & Pogrebin, P.C., N.Y.C., 1959—; adj. prof. law NYU, 1975-90, Hofstra Law Sch., 1980-82, 86-91, 97-98; vis. lectr. Yale Law Sch., 1983. Co-author: Labor Relations: The Basic Process, Law and Practice, 1988, 2d edit., 1999. Mem. Am. Jewish Congress; v.p., bd. dirs. Appleseed Found. Mem. ABA, N.Y.C. Bar Assn., Nassau County Bar Assn., Suffolk County Bar Assn., Indsl. Rels. Rsch. Assn. Pension, profit-sharing, and employee benefits, Education and schools, Labor. Home: 33 W 67th St New York NY 10023-6224 Office: 210 Old Country Rd Mineola NY 11501-4218 also: 375 Park Ave New York NY 10152-0002

**POGUE, L(LOYD) WELCH,** lawyer; b. Grant, Iowa, Oct. 21, 1899; s. Leander Welch and Myrtle Viola (Casey) P.; m. Mary Ellen Edgerton, Sept. 8, 1926; children: Richard Welch, William Lloyd, John Marshall. AB, U. Nebr., 1924; JD, U. Mich., 1926; SJD, Harvard U., 1927. Bar: Mass., N.Y., D.C., Ohio, U.S. Supreme Ct. Assoc. Ropes, Gray, Boyden and Perkins, 1927-33; ptnr. affiliated firm Searle, James and Crawford, N.Y.C., 1933-38; asst. gen. counsel CAB, 1938-39, gen. counsel, through 1941, chmn. bd., 1942-46; mem., mng. ptnr. Pogue & Neal, Washington, 1946-67; Washington mng. ptnr. Jones, Day, Reavis & Pogue, Washington, 1967-79, ret., 1981; Lindbergh Meml. lectr. Nat. Air and Space Mus., Smithsonian Inst., 1991; presenter essay 50th Ann. Internat. Civil Aviation Orgn., Montreal, 1994; spkr. in field. Author: International Civil Air Transport Transition Following WW II, 1979, Pogue/Pollock/Polk Genealogy as Mirrored in History, 1990 (1st pl. in Anna Ford Family history book contest 1991, Nat. Genealogical Soc. award for excellence genealogy and family history 1992, William H. and Benjamin Harrison Book award Coun. Ohio Genealogists 1992, Outstanding Achievement award County and Regional History category Ohio Assn. Hist. Socs. and Mus. 1992, 1st pl. award Iowa Washington County Geneal. Soc. 1994, cert. commendation Am. Assn. State and Local History 1994, 1st place award Lake Havasu Geneal. Soc. 1996); contbr. articles to profl. pubs. Mem. U.S. dels., Chgo. Internat. Civil Aviation Conf., 1944; vice chmn. Bermuda United Kingdom-U.S. Conf., 1946; vice chmn. Assembly Provisional Internat. Civil Aviation Orgn., 1946; mem. Internat. Civil Aviation Orgn. Assembly, 1947. With AUS, 1918. Recipient Elder Statesman of Aviation award Nat. Aeronautic Assn., Golden Eagle award Soc. Sr. Aerospace Execs., 1st annual recipient of L. Welch Pogue award for Aviation Achievement, McGraw-Hill Orgn.'s Aviation Week Group, 1994; fellow Am. Helicopter Soc., Benjamin Franklin fellow Royal Soc. Arts. Fellow Royal Aero. Soc.; mem. AIAA (hon.), Am. Air Mus. (founding mem. in Britain) Can. Aeronautics and Space Inst., Nat. Aeronautic Assn. (pres. 1947), Nat. Air and Space Soc. (founder), Nat. Geneal. Soc., New Eng. Hist. Geneal. Soc. (life, former trustee), Ohio Geneal. Soc. (life), Md. Geneal. Soc. (life), Provincial Families of Md., First Families of Ohio, Helicopter Assn. Internat. (hon. mem. for life), Met. Club, Univ. Club, Wings Club (hon., N.Y.C.), Bohemian Club (San Francisco), Cosmos Club, Masons, Order of the First World War (charter), Aero Club of Washington. Aviation, General corporate, Finance. Home: 5204 Kenwood Ave Chevy Chase MD 20815-6604 Office: Jones Day Reavis & Pogue 51 Louisiana Ave NW Washington DC 20001-2113

**POHL, MICHAEL A.,** lawyer; b. Cleve., Oct. 25, 1942; s. Irwin P. and Ruth B. (Bishko) P.; m. Ellen Durchslag, Dec. 12, 1970 (div. 1982); children: Matthew E., Andrew F. BA, Amherst Coll., 1965; JD, Case Western Res. U., 1968. Bar: Ohio 1968, Fla. 1972, U.S. Supreme Ct. 1974. Atty. NLRB, 1971-72; asst. state's atty. for Dade County State of Fla., Miami, 1973-74; asst. dir. of law City of Cleve., 1979-83; instr. employment discrimination law and Title VII Cleve. State U., 1982-83; litigation mgr. Leader Nat. Ins. Co., 1985-90, Ins. Inst. Am., 1990—; with Mazanec, Raskin & Ryder Co., L.P.A., Cleve., 1991-95, Ulmer & Berne, Cleve., 1995-96, Reid, Berry & Stanard, Cleve., 1997-98; asst. v.p. Aon Risk Services, Cleve., 1998—. Mem. Ohio State Bar Assn., The Fla. Bar. Avocations: opera, golf. Fax: 216-623-4171. Insurance, Personal injury, General civil litigation. Home: 3104 Woodbury Rd Shaker Heights OH 44120 Office: Aon Risk Services Skylight Office Tower 1660 W 2nd St Ste 650 Cleveland OH 44113-1419

**POHLEN, PATRICK ALAN,** lawyer; b. Sheldon, Iowa, Jan. 20, 1959; s. George William and Karroll Kae Pohlen; m. Laura Marie Gaber, July 31, 1981; children: Ashley Mae, Andrew Patrick, Austin John. BA, Iowa State U., 1981; JD, U. Iowa, 1984. Bar: N.Y. 1985, Mo. 1993, Calif. 1997. Assoc. Willkie Farr & Gallagher, N.Y.C., 1984-92; ptnr. Stinson, Mag & Fizzell, Kansas City, Mo., 1992-96, Cooley Godward LLP, Palo Alto, Calif., 1996—; sec. Megabios Corp., Millbrae, Calif., 1997—; lectr. Bay Area Legal Secs. Forum, 1998. Author: Securities Offerings, 1997, 98. Pres. Visitation Sch. PTA, Kansas City, 1993-94; lector Visitation Ch., Kansas City, 1993-96, Nativity Ch., Menlo Park, Calif., 1996—; bd. dirs. Atherton (Calif.) Civic Interest League, 1997—; head coach Menlo-Atherton Little League, 1997, 98, 99. Mem. N.Y. State Bar Assn., Mo. Bar Assn., Calif. Bar Assn., Phi Beta Kappa. Republican. Roman Catholic. Avocations: golf, sports, music. General corporate, Mergers and acquisitions, Securities. Office: Cooley Godward LLP 5 Palo Alto Sq Palo Alto CA 94306-2122

**POHLMANN, WILLIAM HOWARD,** lawyer; b. N.Y.C., Dec. 16, 1944; m. Linda Marie Fata, Nov., 1973; children: Craig, Christopher, Darren. BBA, Bernard M. Baruch Sch. Bus. and Pub. Adminstrn., 1966; JD, St. John's U., 1968; postgrad., NYU, 1970. Bar: N.Y. 1968, U.S. Supreme Ct. 1972, U.S. Dist. Ct. (ea. and so. dists.) N.Y. 1975, U.S. Ct. Appeals (2d cir.) 1975. Pvt. practice Bronx, N.Y., 1968-69; asst. to justices appellate divsn. N.Y. State Supreme Ct., 1969-74, sr. law asst., 1974-76; jud. asst. to justice N.Y. State Supreme Ct., White Plains, 1976—; pres. Ardsley Engine Co. No. 1; adj. prof. law Iona Coll. Sch. Bus., 1982-83; asst. to chmn. Westchester County Bd. Legislators, 1990-95, legis. counsel to county bd., 1995-96, asst. to county exec., 1996-97; lectr. in field. Acting Village Justice, 1983-91; chmn. Greenburgh Rep. Town Com., 1995-99. Lt. col. USAR, 1981—. Mem. N.Y. State Bar Assn., Westchester County Bar Assn., White Plains Bar Assn., N.Y. State Magistrates Assn., Westchester County Magistrates Assn. State civil litigation, Criminal, Estate taxation. Office: 214 Mamaroneck Ave White Plains NY 10601-5301

**POINTER, SAM CLYDE, JR.,** federal judge; b. Birmingham, Ala., Nov. 15, 1934; s. Sam Clyde and Elizabeth Inzer (Brown) P.; m. Paula Purse, Oct. 18, 1958; children: Minge, Sam Clyde III. A.B., Vanderbilt U., 1955; J.D., U. Ala., 1957; LL.M., NYU, 1958. Bar: Ala. 1957. Ptnr. Brown, Pointer & Pointer, 1958-70; judge U.S. Dist. Ct. (no. dist.) Ala., Birmingham, 1970-82, chief judge, 1982—; judge Temp. Emergency Ct. Appeals, 1980-87; mem. Jud. Panel Multi-dist. Litigation, 1980-87; mem. Jud. Conf. U.S., 1987-90; mem. Jud. Coun. 11th Cir., 1987-90, mem. standing com. on rules, 1988-90, chmn. adv. com. on civil rules, 1990-93. Bd. editors: Manual for Complex Litigation, 1979-91. Mem. ABA, Ala. Bar Assn., Birmingham Bar Assn., Am. Law Inst., Am. Judicature Soc., Farrah Order of Jurisprudence, Phi Beta Kappa. Episcopalian. Office: US Dist Ct 882 US Courthouse 1729 5th Ave N Birmingham AL 35203-2000

**POIS, JOSEPH,** lawyer, educator; b. N.Y.C., Dec. 25, 1905; s. Adolph and Augusta (Lesser) P.; m. Rose Tomarkin, June 24, 1928 (dec. May 1981); children: Richard Adolph (dec.), Robert August, Marc Howard.; m. Ruth Livingston, Nov. 27, 1983 (div. 1984). A.B., U. Wis., 1926; M.A., U. Chgo., 1927, Ph.D., 1929; J.D., Chgo.-Kent Coll. Law, 1934. Bar: Ill. 1934, Pa. 1978. Staff mem. J.L. Jacobs & Co., Chgo., 1929-35; jr. partner J.L. Jacobs & Co., 1946-47; gen. field supr. Pub. Adminstrn. Service, Chgo., 1935-38; chief adminstrv. studies sect. U.S. Bur. Old Age and Survivors Ins., 1938-39; chief adminstrv. and fiscal reorgn. sect. U.S. Bur. Budget Exec. Office of Pres., 1939-42; dir. finance State of Ill., 1951-53; counsel, asst. to pres., v.p., treas., dir. Signode Corp., 1947-61; prof. U. Pitts., 1961-76, emeritus, 1976—, chmn. dept. pub. adminstrn., 1961-71, asso. dean, 1973-75; dir. Vision Service Plan of Pa., 1984-85; cons. ECA, 1948, Dept. State, 1949, 62-65, U.S. Dept. Def., 1954, Brookings Instn., 1962-63, AID, 1965, Indian Inst. Pub. Adminstrn., 1972, Commn. on Operation Senate, 1976, Pitts. Citizens' Task Force on Refuse Disposal, 1976-78; mem. cons. panel Comptroller Gen. of U.S., 1967-75. Author: The School Board Crisis: a Chicago Case Study, 1964, Financial Administration in the Michigan State Government, 1938, Kentucky, Handbook of Financial Administration, 1937, Public Personnel Administration in the City of Cincinnati, 1936, (with Edward M. Martin and Lyman S. Moore) The Merit System in Illinois, 1935, Watchdog on the Potomac: A Study of the Comptroller General of the United States, 1979; contbg. author: The New Political Economy, 1975, State Audit-Developments in Public Accountability, 1979. Mem. Chgo. Bd. Edn., 1956-61; pres. Chgo. Met. Housing and Planning Council, 1956-57, Immigrants Service League, Chgo., 1960-61; dir. Pitts. Council Pub. Edn., 1965-67; mem. citizens bd. U. Chgo., 1958-78; mem. Pitts. Bd. Pub. Edn., 1973-76; bd. dirs. Pitts. Center for Arts, 1977-85, World Federalist Assn. Pitts., 1984-97, emeritus, 1997—; bd. dirs. Pitts. dist. Zionist Orgn. Am., 1979-81, mem. Hunger Action Coalition, Pitts., 1985-86; mem. Allegheny County Bd. Assistance, 1981-90, chmn. 1981-87. Served from comdr. to capt. USCGR, 1942-46. Decorated Navy Commendation medal; recipient alumni citation for pub. service U. Chgo., 1960; award for pub. service U.S. Gen. Accounting Office, 1971. Mem. ABA, FBA, ASPA (award for pub. svc. Pitts. area chpt. 1989), Am. Polit. Sci. Assn., Ctr. for Study of the Presidency, Govt. Fin. Officers Assn., Fin. Execs. Inst., Inst. Mgmt. Accts., Chgo. Bar Assn., U. Chgo. Alumni Club (pres. Pitts. chpt. 1981-84), Army and Navy Club, Allegheny County Bar Assn., Phi Beta Kappa, Pi Lambda Phi, Phi Delta Phi. Home: 825 Morewood Ave Pittsburgh PA 15213-2950

**POJMAN, PAUL J.,** lawyer; b. Cleve., Aug. 22, 1917; s. Joseph F. and Cecilia Pojman; widower; children: Paul E., Marianne, Jeanne, Raymond, Richard, Elizabeth. BS in Tchg., Baldwin Wallace U., 1943; MA, Case Western Res. U., 1948, LD, 1942; PhB, John Carroll U., 1939. Pvt. practice Parma Heights, Ohio, 1942—. Mem. coun. Walton Hills Village, 1950-51. Mem. Cleve. Bar Assn., Parma Bar Assn. Probate, Estate taxation, Personal income taxation. Office: 5851 Pearl Rd Ste 302 Parma Heights OH 44130-2112

**POLAN, DAVID JAY,** lawyer; b. Chgo., Feb. 16, 1951; s. Julius and Jeanne Warsaw (Fox) P.; m. Terri Susan Lapin, Aug. 3, 1980; children: Adam Michael, Daniel Jacob, Jennifer Leigh. BA, U. Ill., 1972; JD, John Marshall Law Sch., Chgo., 1975. Bar: Ill. 1975, Ariz. 1990, U.S. Dist. Ct. (no. dist.) Ill. 1975, U.S. Dist. Ct. Ariz. 1990, U.S. Ct. Appeals (7th cir.) 1977. Atty. Pritzker & Glass, Ltd., Chgo., 1975-78, Barnett, Ettinger, Glass, Berkson & Braverman, Chgo., 1978-79; gen. mgr. Y.P. Aurora, Ltd., Ill., 1979-83; gen. ptnr.orp. sec. THC Ptnrs., Chgo., 1980—; counsel, corp. sect. JP Comms. Co., Tucson, 1981-90; gen. mgr. Sta. KPOL-TV, Tucson, 1986-90; gen. counsel Northtown Bus. Svc., Ltd., Lincolnwood, Ill., 1975-88; gen. ptnr. THC Ptnrs., Chgo., 1980—; sta. mgr. KPOL-TV, Tucson, 1983-86, gen. mgr., 1986-90; gen. counsel Northtown Bus Svc., Ltd., Lincolnwood, Ill., 1975-88; co-owner LV Pictures, Las Vegas, 1984-86. Active Orchard Village Assn. for Handicapped, Skokie, Ill., 1981-87; mem. Soviet Jewry commn. Jewish Fedn. Ariz., Tucson, 1984, leadership devel. program, 1984-87, chmn., 1985-87, bd. dirs., 1985-91, mem. nat. com. for leadership devel., 1986-91, chmn. western area, 1988-91, active various coms.; bd. dirs. Congregation Anshei, Israel, 1993—, treas., 1995-97, pres., 1997-99, immediate past pres., 1999—; assoc. mem. Hadassah, Tucson, 1984; bd. dirs. Jewish Family and Children's Svcs., 1986-92, also sec., 1988-89, v.p., 1989-92; bd. dirs. Jewish Cmty. Found., 1987-91, Tucsonans Say No to Drugs, 1986-87; bd. dirs., vice-chmn. Ping-Welch's Championship LPGA Tournament, 1992. Recipient Cmty. Svc. award Jewish Fedn. So. Ariz., 1987, Meritorious Svc. award, 1988, Gary I. Sarver Young Man of Yr. award, 1989. Mem. Ariz. State Bar, Pima County Bar Assn., Tucson Pks. Found. (bd. dirs.), Volk Jewish Cmty. Ctr. Club, Rockford Lightning Continental Basketball Assn. (co-owner 1986-91), Diehard Cubs Fan Club, Ventana Canyon Golf and Raquet Club. Family and matrimonial, Bankruptcy, Federal civil litigation. Office: 1100 E Ajo Way Ste 211 Tucson AZ 85713-5055

**POLAND, RICHARD CLAYTON,** law educator; b. Hartland, Maine, June 23, 1947; s. Richard and Viola (Gardiner) P.; m. Judy Raithel, Feb. 2, 1978; 1 child, Brooke. BA, Taylor U., 1969; MS in Bus., Thomas Coll., 1993; JD, Northeastern U. Sch. Law, 1974. Bar: Maine, U.S. Dist. Ct. Maine, U.S. Supreme Ct. Sole practice law Skowhegan, Maine, 1974-94; prof. law, dir. pre-law program Flagler Coll, St. Augustine, Fla., 1994—; real estate developer; probate judge Somerset County, Skowhegan, 1977-94, Maine Family Ct. Commn., Augusta, 1981; mem. Maine Jud. Coun., Portland, 1989-93. Cpl. Maine Nat. Guard, 1970-76. Mem. So. Assn. Pre-Law Advisors (v.p.). Republican. Avocations: travel, reading. Home: 48 Ocean Ct Saint Augustine FL 32084-7938 Office: Flagler Coll 74 King St Saint Augustine FL 32084-4342

**POLAND, RICHARD L.,** lawyer; b. N.Y.C., Aug. 14, 1948; s. William and Nancy B. (Landi) P. AB, Duke U., Durham, N.C., 1970; JD, U. Tex., 1973. Bar: Ill. 1973, Calif. 1974, N.J. 1988. Assoc. Mayer, Brown & Platt, Chgo., 1973-74, Cox, Castle, Nicholson & Weeks, L.A., 1974; atty. County of L.A. Pub. Defender, L.A., 1975-76; assoc. Charles Gangloff & Assocs., Long Beach, Calif., 1976-80; pvt. practice Long Beach, 1980—. Criminal. Office: 333 W Broadway Ste 200 Long Beach CA 90802-4439

**POLANSKY, LARRY PAUL,** court administrator, consultant; b. Blkyn., July 24, 1932; s. Harry and Ida (Gershgom) P.; m. Eunice Kathryn Neun; children: Steven, Harriet, Bruce. BS in Acctg., Temple U., 1958, JD, 1973. Bar: Pa. 1973, U.S. Dist. Ct. (ea. dist.) Pa. 1973, U.S. Ct. Appeals (3d cir.) 1973, D.C. 1978, U.S. Supreme Ct. 1980. Acct., systems analyst City of Phila., 1956-63; data processing mgr. Jefferson Med. Coll. and Hosp., Phila., 1963-65; systems engr. IBM Corp., Phila., 1965-67; dep. ct. adminstr. Common Pleas Cts. of Phila., 1967-76; dep. state ct. adminstr. Pa. Supreme Ct., Phila., 1976-78; exec. officer D.C. Cts., Washington, 1979-90; presdl. appt. to bd. dirs. State Justice Inst., 1985-89; bd. dirs. Search Group, Inc. Author: A Primer for the Technologically Challenged Judge, 1995; contbr. articles to profl. jours. Served as cpl. U.S. Army, 1951-53, Korea. Fellow Inst. for Ct. Mgmt., Denver, 1984; recipient Reardon award Nat. Ctr. for State Cts., 1982, Disting. Svc. award Nat. Ctr. for State Cts., 1986, Justice Tom C. Clark award Nat. Conf. of Metro. Cts., 1991, award of merit Nat. Assn. Ct. Mgmt., 1996. Mem. ABA (jud. adminstrn. divsn., chmn. tech. com. 1991-93, 95, exec. com. lawyers conf. 1985-98, chmn. 1991-92, JAD coun. 1994-97), Conf. State Ct. Adminstrn. (bd. dirs. 1980-86, pres. 1984-85). Republican. Jewish. Avocations: tennis, skiing, computers, golf. Home and Office: PO Box 752 Lake Harmony PA 18624-0752

**POLANSKY, STEVEN JAY,** lawyer; b. Phila., Nov. 21, 1956; s. Larry P. and Eunice K. (Neun) P.; m. Kathleen Diane Spofford; children: Michelle, Jeffrey, Scott. BBA magna cum laude, Temple U., 1978; JD magna cum laude, Syracuse U., 1981. Bar: Pa. 1981, N.J. 1981, D.C. 1983; cert. civil trial atty., N.J. Assoc. Cozen, Begier and O'Conner, Phila., 1981-85, LaBrum and Doak, Woodbury (N.J.) and Phila., 1985-88; ptnr. Ostrager, Fieldman & Zucker, Moorestown (N.J.), Bala Cynd (Pa.), 1988-92; shareholder Spector Gadon & Rosen P.C., Moorestown, 1992—. Elected mem. Cherry Hill Bd. of Edn., 1990-93; trustee Georgetowne Condo Assn., Lindenwold, N.J., 1982-83. Mem. ABA, N.J. Bar Assn., Pa. Bar Assn., Phila. Bar Assn., Pa. Def. Inst., Camden County Bar Assn., Def. Research Inst. Jewish. Avocations: skiing, carpentry. Personal injury, Insurance, State civil litigation. Office: Spector Gadon & Rosen PC 309 Fellowship Rd PO Box 1001 Moorestown NJ 08057-0950

**POLE, DEBRA E.,** lawyer; b. Birmingham, Ala.; m. Robert H. Brown. BA, Dickinson Coll., 1973; JD, U. Fla., 1975. Guest lectr. U. Fla. Coll. Law, Gainesville, 1975-76; asst. state atty. State Atty.'s Office, West Palm Beach, Fla., 1976-80; assoc., ptnr. Haight, Dickson, Brown & Bonesteel, Santa Monica, Calif., 1980-88; founding ptnr. Dickson, Carlson & Campillo, Santa Monica, 1988-95; ptnr. Brobeck, Phleger & Harrison LLP, L.A., 1995—. Fellow Am. Coll. Trial Lawyers; mem. FICC. Fax: 213-745-3345. E-mail: dpole@brobeck.com. Office: Brobeck Phleger & Harrison LLP 550 S Hope St Los Angeles CA 90071-2627

**POLIAKOFF, GARY A.,** lawyer, educator; b. Greenville, S.C, Nov. 25, 1944; s. Herman and Dorothy (Ravitz) P.; m. Sherri D. Dublin, June 24, 1967; children: Ryan, Keith. BS, U. S.C., 1966; JD, U. Miami, 1969. Bar: Fla. 1969, D.C. 1971, Colo. 1999. Founding prin., sr. ptnr., pres. Becker & Poliakoff, P.A., Hollywood, Miami, Naples, Sarasota, West Palm Beach, Clearwater, Tampa, Ft. Myers, Boca Raton, St Petersburg, Orlando, Ft. Walton Beach, Fla., Prague and Beijing, 1973—; adj. prof. condominium law and practice Nova Southeastern U.; panelist Nat. Confs. Community Assns.; testified before coms. of the U.S. Senate on Condominiums; lectr. ann. condominium seminars Fla. Bar; participant Fla. Law Revision Council; cons. to State Legis. and the White House in drafting Condominium and Coop. Abuse Relief Act, 1980; mem. condominium study commn. State of Fla., 1990; chmn. State of Fla. Advisory Coun. on Condominiums, 1992, 93. Author: The Law of Condominium Operations, 1988; co-author: Florida Condominium Law and Practice, 1982, The Florida Bar Continuing Legal Education, 1982; contbr. articles to legal jours. Recipient Judge Learned Hand award Am. Jewish Com. for devel. of co-ownership housing law. Mem. Fla. Bar (co-chmn. legis. sub-com. condominium and coop. law), Coll. Cmty. Assn. Lawyers (bd. govs.), Scribes. Real property.

**POLICY, VINCENT MARK,** lawyer; b. Warren, Ohio, Mar. 29, 1948; s. Vincent James and Anna Marie (Berardi) P.; m. Katherine Anne Veazey; children: Nicholas, Katherine Nicole. BA, U. Md., 1970; JD, Georgetown U., 1973. Bar: N.Y. 1974, D.C. 1975, U.S. Supreme Ct. 1977. Assoc. Cahill Gordon & Reindel, Washington and N.Y.C., 1973-78, Hogan & Hartson, Washington, 1978-85; prin. Pohoryles & Greenstein PC, Washington, 1985-89, Greenstein, Delorme & Luchs, P.C., Washington, 1989—. Author: Speedy Trial, A Constitutional Right in Search of Definition, 1973. Mem. D.C. Bar Assn. (chmn. rental housing com. 1985-88), D.C. Assn. Realtors (speaker 1984—), Apt. and Office Bldg. Assn. (lectr. 1985—), Greater Washington Bd. Trade (subcom. on initiatives, econ. growth com.), D.C. Builders Assn. (legis. affairs com.), Phi Beta Kappa, Omicron Delta Kappa. Democrat. Roman Catholic. Lodge: KC. Avocation: sailing. Real property, Banking, State civil litigation. Office: Greenstein DeLorme & Luchs 1620 L St NW Ste 900 Washington DC 20036-5613

**POLIN, ALAN JAY,** lawyer; b. N.Y.C., Sept. 5, 1953; s. Mortin and Eleanor (Clarke) P.; m. Sharon Lynn Hirschfeld, Oct. 10, 1976; children: Jay Michael, Meryl Beth. Student, Cornell U., 1971-74; BA cum laude, Seton Hall U., 1978; JD, Nova U., 1981. Bar: Fla. 1981, N.Y. 1990; lic. athlete agt., Fla. Assoc. Berryhill, Avery, Williams & Jordan, Esq., Ft. Lauderdale, Fla., 1981-82, Greenspoon & Marder, P.A., Miami, Fla., 1982-83; pvt. practice Ft. Lauderdale, 1983-86; ptnr. Mousaw, Vigdor, Reeves & Hess, Ft. Lauderdale, 1986-90; pvt. practice Coral Springs, Fla., 1990—; adj. faculty mem. Nova U.; mem. grievance com. Fla. Bar, 1989-92, vice chair, 1990-91, chair, 1991-92. Chmn. Broward County Crct. Ct. Handbook, 1988; contbr. chpt. to Bridge the Gap Attorney's Handbook, 1987. Dir. Temple Beth Am., Margate, Fla., 1991-93; mem. Anti-Defamation League, Fla. Regional Bd., 1994-96; mem. exec. com. Broward County Dem., 1989-96; vice mayor City of Coral Springs, 1994-96, commr., 1991—; mem. bd. dirs. Fla. Regional Bd. of Anti-Defamation League, 1994—, Children's Cardiac Rsch. Found., Inc., 1996—, The Irving Fryer Found., Inc., 1995-96, Am. Heart Assn., 1997—. Recipient Am. Jurisprudence award Nova U. Law Ctr., 1981. Mem. Fla. Bar Assn. (bd. govs. young lawyers divsn. 1987-89), Broward County Bar Assn. (exec. com. young lawyers sect. 1986-87), North Broward Assn. Realtors, Inc. (affiliate, std. contract forms com. 1989-95, atty./realtor rels. com. 1989-91), Kiwanis (Key Club advisor 1990-91). Estate planning, Contracts commercial, Real property. Office: 3300 N University Dr Ste 601 Coral Springs FL 33065-4132

**POLINER, BERNARD,** lawyer; b. Middleton, Conn., Nov. 18, 1931; s. Harry and Rose (Poliner) P.; m. Judith R. Protass, July 14, 1957; children: Howard, Debra. BA, U. Conn., 1954; LLB, Boston U., 1957. Bar: Conn. 1958, Mass. 1958, U.S. Dist. Ct. 1958. Assoc. Hartford, Conn., 1958—. Chmn. Zoning Bd. Appeals, Bloomfield, Conn., 1969-85; town atty. Bloomfield, 1985-90. Mem. Hartford County Bar Assn. (pres. 1985-86), Conn. Trial Lawyers Assn. (bd. govs. 1981-97), Conn. Bar Assn. (house of dels.). Democrat. Workers' compensation, Personal injury, Product liability. Home: 13 Carpenter Ln Bloomfield CT 06002-1839 Office: Poliner Poliner & Antin 516 Main St Ste 4 Middletown CT 06457-3355

**POLISHOOK, LEWIS A.,** lawyer; b. Englewood, N.J., Mar. 22, 1970; s. Irwin H. and Sheila S. Polishook. AB, Brown U., 1992; JD, Harvard U., 1995. Bar: N.J. 1995, N.Y. 1996, Mass. 1997. Law clk. to Judge Bruce Selya U.S Ct. Appeals (1st cir.), Providence, 1995-96; assoc. Winthrop, Stimson, Putnam & Roberts, N.Y.C., 1996-98, Kornstein, Veisz & Wexler, LLP, N.Y.C., 1998—. Contbr. articles to profl. jours. Mem. ABA, Assn. Bar City N.Y. General civil litigation, Private international, Insurance. Office: Kornstein Veisz & Wexler 757 3d Ave New York NY 10017

**POLITAN, NICHOLAS H.,** federal judge; b. Newark, Nov. 13, 1935; m. Marian E. Politan; children: Nicholas H. Jr., Vincent J. Bar: N.J. 1961, U.S. Dist. Ct. N.J. 1961, U.S. Ct. Appeals (2d cir.) 1969, U.S. Ct. Appeals (3d cir.) 1971, U.S. Tax Ct. 1972, U.S. Supreme Ct. 1973. Law clk. to Hon. Gerald McLaughlin U.S. Ct. Appeals (3d cir.), Newark, 1960-61; sr. ptnr. Cecchi and Politan, Lyndhurst, N.J., 1961-64, 72-87; litigation ptnr. Krieger, Chodash & Politan, Jersey City, 1964-72; dir., chmn. exec. com. County Trust Co., Lyndhurst, 1980-87; judge U.S. Dist. Ct. N.J., 1987—; instr. legal rsch. and writing Rutgers U. Law Sch., 1963. Mng. editor Rutgers Law Rev., 1959; contbr. articles to profl. jours. Office: US Dist Ct King Bldg Box 999 Newark NJ 07101-0999

**POLITI, STEPHEN MICHAEL,** lawyer, educator; b. Mass., Mar. 30, 1948; s. Selvi J. and Anne (Gargiulo) P.; m. Joan Spignesi, June 29, 1985. AB in Econs. cum laude, U. Mass., 1970; JD, Boston U., 1973, LLM in Taxation, 1974. Bar: Mass. 1973, U.S. Tax Ct. 1977, U.S. Dist. Ct. Mass. 1977. Counsel Joint Legis. Com. on Taxation, Boston, 1973-74; staff atty. Mass. Dept. Revenue, Boston, 1974-79, chief counsel, 1979-83; pvt. practice Boston, 1983-86; ptnr. Hennessy, Killgoar & Politi, Boston, 1986—; prof. Bentley Coll. Grad. Sch. of Taxation, Waltham, Mass., 1977—. Contbr. articles to profl. jours. Former chmn. Lexington Mass. Bd. of Selectman; former pres. Lexington Hist. Soc.; chmn. Lexington Hist. Dists. Commn., 1990—. Mem. Mass. Bar Assn., Boston Bar Assn. State and local taxation, General practice. Office: Hennessy Killgoar & Politi 11 Beacon St Boston MA 02108-3002

**POLITIS, MICHAEL JOHN,** lawyer; b. Queens, N.Y., Sept. 12, 1961; s. John and Theodora P.; m. Rania, Sept. 12, 1998.; BS, U. Fla., 1983; JD, Nova U. Law Sch., 1988. Bar: U.S. Dist. Ct. (mid. dist.) Fla. Chief of homicide State Atty's. Office, Daytona Beach, Fla., 1992-95; ptnr. Vasilaros & Politis, P.A., Daytona Beach, 1993—; v.p. Extreme Sports, Inc., Daytona Beach, 1993—. Mem. Volusia County Bar Assn. Greek Orthodox. Avocations: motorcycling, surfing, water skiing, snow skiing. General civil litigation, Criminal. Office: Vasilaros & Politis PA 154 S Halifax Ave Daytona Beach FL 32118-4480

**POLITZ, HENRY ANTHONY,** federal judge; b. Napoleonville, La., May 9, 1932; s. Anthony and Virginia (Russo) P.; m. Jane Marie Simoneaux, Apr. 29, 1952; children: Nyle, Bennett, Mark, Angela, Scott, Jane, Michael, Henry, Alisa, John, Nina. BA, La. State U., 1958, JD, 1959. Bar: La. 1959. Assoc., then ptnr. firm Booth, Lockard, Jack, Pleasant & LeSage, Shreveport, 1959-79; judge U.S. Ct. Appeals (5th cir.), Shreveport, 1979-99, chief judge, 1992-99; vis. prof. La. State U. Law Center; bd. dirs. Am. Prepaid Legal Services Inst., 1975—; mem. La. Judiciary Commn., 1978-79; mem. U.S. Jud. Conf., 1992-99, exec. com., 1996-99. Mem. editl. bd. La. State U. Law Rev., 1958-59. Mem. Shreveport Airport Authority, 1973-79, chmn., 1977; bd. dirs. Rutherford House, Shreveport, 1975—, pres., 1978; pres. Caddo Parish Bd. Election Suprs., 1975-79; mem. Electoral Coll., 1976. Served with USAF, 1951-55. Named Outstanding Young Lawyer in La., 1971, Outstanding Alumnus La. State U. Law Sch., 1991; inducted in La. State U. Hall of Distinction, 1992. Mem. Am. Bar Assn., Am. Judicature Soc., Internat. Soc. Barristers, La. Bar Assn., La. Trial Lawyers Assn., Shreveport Bar Assn., Justinian Soc., K.C., Omicron Delta Kappa. Democrat. Roman Catholic. Office: US Ct Appeals 300 Fannin St Ste 5226 Shreveport LA 71101-3120

**POLITZ, NYLE ANTHONY,** lawyer; b. Lake Charles, La., May 7, 1953; s. Henry Anthony and Jane Marie (Simoneaux) P.; m. Catherine Bordelon, May 28, 1977; children: Brandon, Jared, Caroline. Student, La. State U., Shreveport, 1971-72, U. Guadalajara, 1972, La. State U., 1972-74; JD, La. State U., 1977. Bar: La. 1978, U.S. Dist. Ct. (ea., mid. and we. dists.) La. 1978, U.S. Ct. Appeals (5th cir.) 1979. Assoc. Booth, Lockard, Jack, Pleasant & LeSage, Shreveport, La., 1978-79; ptnr. Booth, Lockard, Politz, LeSage & D'Anna, L.L.C., Shreveport, 1979-96; assoc. Pendley Law Firm, Plaquemine, La., 1996-98; ptnr. Jones, Odom, Spruiell, Davis & Politz, LLP, Shreveport, 1998—; lectr. La. State Univ., Shreveport. Resolutions com. La. Dem. Party, 1980; bd. dirs. Liberty Bank & Trust, Greenwood, La., 1980-86. Mem. ABA, ATLA, La. State Bar Assn. (ho. of dels. 1986-98), La. Trial Lawyers Assn. (bd. govs. 1983-94), Shreveport Bar Assn. (exec. com. 1983-85, 93-94, bd. dirs. pro bono project, chmn. 1993-94), N.W. La. Trial Lawyers Assn. (treas. 1987-90), KC. Democrat. Roman Catholic. Avocations: whitetail deer and wild turkey hunting, golf. General civil litigation, Personal injury, Toxic tort. Office: Jones Odum et al PO Drawer 1320 Shreveport LA 71164-1320

**POLK, LEE THOMAS,** lawyer; b. Chgo., Feb. 25, 1945; s. Lee Anthony and Mary Josephine (Lane) P.; m. Susan Luzader, Mar. 21, 1975; children: Adam, Angela. AB, Coe Coll., 1967; JD, U. Chgo., 1970. Bar: Ill. 1970, U.S. Dist. Ct. (no. dist.) Ill. 1970, U.S. Ct. Mil. Appeals 1972, U.S. Dist. Ct. (ea. dist.) Mich. 1983, U.S. Claims Ct. 1983, U.S. Ct. Appeals (7th cir.) 1984, U.S. Ct. Appeals (6th cir.) 1987, U.S. Tax Ct. 1987, U.S. Ct. Appeals (3rd cir.) 1989, U.S. Dist. Ct. (ea. dist.) Wis. 1998. Assoc. firm Vedder, Price, Kaufman & Kammholz, Chgo., 1970-72, 75-77, ptnr., 1977-86; ptnr. Murphy, Smith & Polk, 1986-98, Ogletree, Deakins, Murphy, Smith & Polk, 1999—. Author: ERISA Practice & Litigation, 1993, updated annually; contbr. articles on employee benefits and health law to profl. jours. Served to capt. JAGC, U.S. Army, 1972-75. Mem. ABA (sects. on real property, trust and probate, tax and bus., vice chair ESOP com.), Ill. Bar Assn., Chgo. Bar Assn. (chmn. employee benefits com. 1987-88), Midwest Pension Conf. (chmn. Chgo. chpt. 1986), Am. Health Lawyers Assn., Phi Beta Kappa, Phi Kappa Phi, Union League Club. Roman Catholic. Pension, profit-sharing, and employee benefits, General corporate, Health. Home: 820 Sheridan Rd Evanston IL 60202-2513 Office: Ogletree Deakins Murphy Smith & Polk 2 1st Nat Plz Fl 25 Chicago IL 60603

**POLKING, PAUL J.,** lawyer. BS, U. Notre Dame, 1959, JD, 1966. Bar: Iowa 1966, N.C. 1978. Atty. office of comptroller of currency Dept. of Treasury, 1966-70; gen. counsel NationsBank Corp., Charlotte, N.C. Office: Bank of Am NationsBank Corp Ctr (Bank) NC1-007-56-11 Charlotte NC 28255

**POLLACK, DAVID L.,** lawyer; b. Madison, Wis., May 1, 1956; s. Sidney Solomon and Elta Elizabeth (Spaulding) P.; m. Avery Elizabeth Schneider, July 14, 1986; children: Elsbeth Rose, Mollie Brown, Samantha Louise. AB, Haverford (Pa.) Coll., 1978; JD, Yale U., 1989. Bar: Pa. 1989, U.S. Dist. Ct. (we. dist.) Pa. 1989. Atty. Kirkpatrick & Lockhart LLP, Pitts., 1989-98, Gefsky and Lehman, P.C., Pitts., 1998—. Non-profit and tax-exempt organizations, Taxation, general, Mergers and acquisitions. Office: Gefsky and Lehman PC 1 Ppg Pl Ste 2301 Pittsburgh PA 15222-5401

**POLLACK, HOWARD JAY,** lawyer; b. Cheltenham, Pa., Oct. 31, 1965; s. Barry Allen and Karen Elizabeth (Plone) P.; m. Lisa Marie Fitzgerald, Oct. 24, 1993. BA in Economics, U. Del., 1987; JD cum laude, Syracuse U., 1991. Bar: Del. 1991, U.S. Dist. Ct. Del. 1991, Pa. 1992. Atty. Richards, Layton & Finger, Wilmington, Del., 1990-94, Brownstein Hyatt Farber & Strickland, P.C., Denver, 1994—. Contbr. articles to profl. jours. Bd. dirs. Del. Jewish Cmty. Ctr., Wilmington, 1993-94; active Del. Rep. Party, Wilmington, 1991-94. Recipient Robert Anderson Writing award, 1991. Mem. ABA (planning bd. Young Lawyers Divsn. real estate law divsn., com. on law and tech., com. on joint ventures, partnerships, 1993—), Del. Bar Assn., Order of Coif. Republican. Jewish. Avocations: skiing, mountaineering, reading, squash. Real property, Contracts commercial. Home: 956 Olive St Denver CO 80220-4816 Office: Brownstein Hyatt Farber & Stickland 410 17th St Ste 2200 Denver CO 80202-4468

**POLLACK, MICHAEL,** lawyer; b. N.Y.C., July 14, 1946; s. Irving and Bertha (Horowitz) P.; m. Barbara Linda Shore, Aug. 23, 1970; children: Matthew, Ilana. BEng, Cooper Union, 1967; MS, U. Pa., 1970; JD, Temple U., 1974. Bar: Pa. 1974, U.S. Dist. Ct. (ea. dist.) Pa. 1974. Rsch. scientist Pa. Rsch. Assocs., Phila., 1968-69; engr. GE Co., Valley Forge, Pa., 1969-70, Burroughs Corp., Great Valley, Pa., 1970-71; assoc. Blank, Rome, Comisky & McCauley, Phila., Pa., 1974-82; ptnr. Blank, Rome, Comisky & McCauley, Phila., 1982—; chmn. dept. real estate Blank, Rome, Comisky & McCauley, 1997—; lectr., course planner Pa. Bar Inst., Phila., chmn. real estae dept. Mem. ABA, Pa. Bar Assn., Phila. Bar Assn., Internat. Assn. Attys. and Execs. in Corp. Real Estate, Eta Kappa Nu, Tau Beta Pi. Republican. Avocations: music, tennis. Real property. Office: Blank Rome Comisky & McCauley 1 Logan Sq Fl 3 Philadelphia PA 19103-6998

**POLLACK, MILTON,** federal judge; b. N.Y.C., Sept. 29, 1906; s. Julius and Betty (Schwartz) P.; m. Lillian Klein, Dec. 18, 1932 (dec. July 1967); children—Stephanie Pollack Singer, Daniel A.; m. Moselle Baum Erlich, Oct. 24, 1971. A.B., Columbia U., 1927, J.D., 1929. Bar: N.Y. 1930. Assoc. Gilman & Unger, N.Y.C., 1929-38; ptnr. Unger & Pollack, N.Y.C., 1938-44; propr. Milton Pollack, N.Y.C., 1945-67; dist. judge U.S. Dist. Ct. (so. dist.) N.Y., 1967—, sr. status, 1983; mem. com. on ct. adminstrn. Jud. Conf., 1968-87, mem. Jud. Panel on Multi-dist. Litigation, 1983-95. Mem. Prospect Park So. Assn., Bklyn., pres., 1948-50, counsel, 1950-60, bd. dirs., 1945-60; mem. local SSS, 1952-60; chmn. lawyers div. Fedn. Jewish Philanthropies, 1957-61, vice chmn., 1954-57; chmn. lawyers div. Am. Jewish Com., 1964-66, bd. dirs., from 1967; hon. dir. Beth Isreal Hosp.; trustee Temple Emanu-El, from 1977, v.p., from 1978. Decorated chevalier Legion of Honor (France); recipient Learned Hand award Am. Jewish Com., 1967, Proskauer medal lawyers divsn. Fedn. Jewish Philanthropies, 1968, Disting. Svc. medal N.Y. County Lawyers Assn., 1991, Fordham-Stein Prize award, 1994, Devitt award Disting. Svc. to Justice, 1995. Mem. ABA, N.Y. State Bar Assn., Assn. of Bar of City of N.Y., Columbia Law Sch. Alumni Assn. (pres. 1970-72), Harmonie Club (bd. trustees). Office: US Dist Ct US Courthouse Foley Sq New York NY 10007-1501

**POLLACK, STANLEY P.,** lawyer; b. N.Y.C., Apr. 23, 1928; s. Isidor and Anna (Shulman) P.; m. Susan Aronowitz, June 16, 1974; 1 child, Jane. BA, NYU, 1948; JD, Harvard U., 1951; LLM in Taxation, NYU, 1959. Bar: N.Y. 1951, U.S. Dist. Ct. (so. dist.) N.Y. 1955. Sole practice N.Y.C., 1955-61; v.p., gen. counsel James Talcott, Inc., N.Y.C., 1961-73; sr. exec. v.p. Rosenthal & Rosenthal Inc., N.Y.C., 1973—. Served to j.g. lt. USNR, 1951-54. Mem. Bklyn. Bar Assn. (banking com., bankruptcy com.), Fed. Bar Council, Assn. Comml. Fin. Atty.'s (pres. 1968), Factors Chain Internat. Club: Harvard (N.Y.C.). Banking, Contracts commercial. Home: 6 Peter Cooper Rd New York NY 10010-6701 Office: Rosenthal & Rosenthal Inc 1370 Broadway # 2 New York NY 10018-7302

**POLLAK, CATHY JANE,** lawyer; b. Newark, Nov. 15, 1951; d. Seymour and Ruth Norma (Seidler) P.; m. Steven Michael Rosner, Aug. 12, 1976; children: Jessica Dori, Elizabeth Meryl. BA magna cum laude, Cedar Crest Coll., 1973; JD, Rutgers U., 1976. Bar: N.J. 1976, U.S. Dist. Ct. N.J. 1976, N.Y. 1990. Law clk., assoc. atty. O'Brien Daaleman & Liotta, Elizabeth, N.J., 1974-78; assoc. atty., ptnr. Feinberg, Dee & Feinberg, Bayonne, N.J., 1978-84; sr. assoc. Stoldt & Horan, Hackensack, N.J., 1984-93; atty. pvt. practice, Woodcliff Lake, N.J., 1993—; mem. bd. trustees, sec. Bergen County Task Force on Women and Addictions, Paramus, N.J., 1993—; mem. Bergen County Dist. Domestic Violence Legal Advocacy Project, Hackensack, 1993—. Mem. Hebrew sch. exec. com. Temple Beth Or, Washington Twp., N.J., 1993—. mem. sisterhood. Mem. N.J. State Bar Assn. (family law com.), Bergen County Bar Assn. (family law com.). Avocations: reading, dancing. Family and matrimonial, General practice, State civil litigation. Office: 188 Broadway Woodcliff Lk NJ 07675-8067

**POLLAK, JAY MITCHELL,** lawyer; b. Chgo., Apr. 5, 1937; s. Bertram L. and Florence (Molner) P.; m. Patricia Pollak, May 11, 1963; children: Mitchell Emery, John Andrew. BS, Miami U., Oxford, Ohio, 1959; JD, Northwestern U., 1962. Bar: Ill. 1962, U.S. Dist. Ct. (no. dist.) Ill. 1971, U.S. Ct. Appeals (7th cir.) 1982, U.S. Supreme Ct. 1982. V.p. Pollak & Hoffman LTD, Chgo., 1963—; atty. Counsel to Northbrook (Ill.) Hist. Soc.; prosecutor Village of Northbrook; mem. Page Ctr. for Entrepreneurship. Pres. Northbrook Hockey League, 1986-88; mem. bus. adv. coun. Miami U., mem. adv. bd. Mem. ABA (anti-trust law sect.), Ill. Bar Assn., Chgo. Bar Assn., Forum Com. on Franchising, Atty. Gen.'s Ill. Franchise Adv. Bd. Franchising, General corporate, Probate. Home: 846 Dundee Rd Northbrook IL 60062-2705 Office: Pollak and Hoffman Ltd 1200 Shermer Rd Ste 301 Northbrook IL 60062-4563

**POLLAK, LOUIS HEILPRIN,** judge, educator; b. N.Y.C., Dec. 7, 1922; s. Walter and Marion (Heilprin) P.; m. Katherine Weiss, July 25, 1952; children: Nancy, Elizabeth, Susan, Sarah, Deborah. A.B., Harvard, 1943; LL.B., Yale, 1948. Bar: N.Y. bar 1949, Conn. bar 1956, Pa. bar 1976. Law clk. to Justice Rutledge U.S. Supreme Ct., 1948-49; with Paul, Weiss, Rifkind, Wharton & Garrison, N.Y.C., 1949-51; spl. asst. to Amb. Philip C. Jessup State Dept., 1951-53; asst. counsel Amalgmated Clothing Workers Am., 1954-55; mem. faculty Yale Law Sch., 1955-74, dean, 1965-70; Greenfield prof. U. Pa., 1974-78, dean Law Sch., 1975-78, lectr., 1980—; judge U.S. Dist Ct. (ea. dist.) Pa., Phila., 1978—, now sr. judge; vis. lectr. Howard U. Sch. Law, 1953; vis. prof. U. Mich. Law Sch., 1961, Columbia Law Sch., 1962. Author: The Constitution and the Supreme Court: A Documentary History, 1966. Mem. New Haven Bd. Edn., 1962-68; chmn. Conn. adv. com. U.S. Civil Rights Commn., 1962-63; mem. bd. NAACP Legal Def. Fund, 1960-78, v.p., 1971-78; chmn. New Haven Human Rights Com., 1963-64. Served with AUS, 1943-46. Mem. ABA (chmn. sec. individual rights 1970-71), Fed. Bar Assn., Phila. Bar Assn., Am. Law Inst. (coun. 1978—). Office: US Dist Ct 16613 US Courthouse 601 Market St Philadelphia PA 19106-1713

**POLLAK, MARK A.,** lawyer, trade association executive; b. New Brunswick, N.J., Nov. 30, 1954; s. Ernest George and Martha Helen (Kaplan) P. BA, Tufts U., 1975; JD, Am. U., 1978. Bar: D.C. 1978, U.S. Ct. Appeals (D.C. cir.) 1978, N.J. 1979, U.S. Dist. Ct. D.C. 1979, U.S. Dist. Ct. N.J. 1979. Legal editor, labor rels. reporter BNA, Washington, 1978-79; staff atty. Merit Systems Protection Bd., Washington, 1980-82, exec. asst. to chmn., 1982-83; asst. to pres. Cosmetic, Toiletry and Fragrance Assn., Washington, 1983-85, v.p. adminstrn., 1985-88, v.p. mem. rels., 1988—. Mem. ABA (editor labor and employment law reports 1980-83). Home: 6404 Kenhowe Dr Bethesda MD 20817-5446 Office: Cosmetic Toiletry Assn 1101 17th St NW Washington DC 20036-4704

**POLLAK, STEPHEN JOHN,** lawyer; b. Chgo., Mar. 22, 1928; s. Maurice August Pollak and Laura (Kramer) Fisher; m. Ruth Scheinfeld, June 22, 1951; children: Linda Jan, David Michael, Roger Lincoln, Eve Juliette. BA, Dartmouth Coll., 1950; LLB, Yale U., 1956. Bar: Ill. 1956, D.C. 1957. Assoc. Covington & Burling, Washington, 1956-61; asst. to solicitor gen. Dept. Justice, Washington, 1961-64; legal counsel to Pres.'s Task Force War Against Poverty, Washington, 1964; dep. gen. counsel Office Econ. Opportunity, Washington, 1964-65; 1st asst. to asst. atty. gen. Civil Rights Divsn. Dept. Justice, Washington, 1965-67; advisor to Pres. for Nat. Capital Affairs Washington, 1967; spl. asst. to atty. gen. Dept. Justice, Washington, 1967, asst. atty. gen. Civil Rights Divsn., 1967-69; ptnr. Shea & Gardner, Washington, 1969—; counsel, assoc. ind. counsel to ind. counsel James C. McKay Franklyn C. Nofziger Matters, Washington, 1987-88, 89-90; mem. panel mediators U.S. Ct. Appeals and Dist. Ct., Washington, 1989—; bd. dirs. Draper and Kramer, Inc., Chgo. Mem. Hist. Soc. D.C. Cir., bd. dirs., 1993—, chair oral history project, 1993—; chair D.C. Cir. Jud. Conf. Com. on the Adminstrn. of Justice Under Emergency Conditions, 1971-73, chair com. on pro bono legal svcs., 1997—; pres. Housing Devel. Corp., 1976-80, NAACP Legal Def. and Ednl. Fund, Inc., Washington, 1987-95; bd. dirs., chair Black Student Fund, Washington, 1976-80, trustee, 1969—. Recipient Wiley A. Branton award Washington Lawyers' Com. for Civil Rights Under the Law, 1992, Whitney North Seymour award, 1994, Svc. of Justice award D.C. Legal Aid Soc., 1994. Mem. ABA, D.C. Bar Assn. (pub. svcs. activities rev. com. 1990-92, chair, 1989-95, bd. govs. 1972, 73, 81-82, sec. 1974-75, pres.-elect 1979-80, pres. 1980-81, Frederick B. Abramson award 1992, 94), D.C. Jud. Nomination Commn. (sec. 1986-88, acting chair 1988-89, chair 1989-90), Am. Law Inst., Order of Coif, Phi Beta Kappa. Federal civil litigation, Labor, Alternative dispute resolution. Office: Shea & Gardner Ste 800 1800 Massachusetts Ave NW Washington DC 20036-1872

**POLLARD, CAROLINE PRAY,** legal assistant; b. Wellesley, Mass., Oct. 14, 1957; d. W. Howard and Margaret Louise (Sasseville) P.; m. Joseph W. Cialini, Jr., May 12, 1979; 1 child, Laura Anne. BS in Journalism, Boston U., 1979; cert. completion in gen. practice, Inst. for Paralegal Tng., Phila., 1981. Prodn. coord. E. Bruce Harrison Co., Washington, 1979-80; legal asst. Ballard, Spahr, Andrews & Ingersoll, Phila., 1981-83, sr. legal asst. for asbestos, 1983-89, gen. sr. legal asst., 1989-96, litigation support coord., 1996—. Vol. Phila. Folk Festival, Schwenksville, Pa., 1981—; vol. info. booth Pa. Hort. Soc. Flower Show, Phila., 1996—. Mem. Legal Asst. Mgmt. Assn. (chmn. Phila. chpt. 1988—, chmn. conf. com. 1998-99), Assn. Legal Adminstrs. Office: Ballard Spahr Andrews Et Al 1735 Market St 51st Fl Philadelphia PA 19103-7501

**POLLARD, DENNIS BERNARD,** lawyer, educator; b. Phila., May 12, 1968. BS in Psychology, Pa. State U., 1990; JD, Ohio State U., 1993; postgrad., U. Mich., 1996. Bar: Ohio 1993, U.S. Dist. Ct. (no. dist.) Ohio 1994, U.S. Ct. Appeals (6th cir.) 1994. Staff atty. The Legal Aid Soc. Cleve., 1993-95; atty. student affairs, student life Pa. State U., 1995-96; acad. adminstrv. intern U. Mich. Law Sch., Ann Arbor, 1996-97; asst. dean student affairs U. Tenn. Coll. Law, Knoxville, 1997-98; program dir. tenants' rights unit Tenants' Action Group of Phila., 1998—. Mem. ABA, Ohio State Bar Assn., Phi Delta Phi. Avocation: biking. Home: 506 S White Horse Pike Apt D9 Stratford NJ 08084-1550 Office: Tenants' Action Group of Philadelphia 21 S 12th St Fl 12 Philadelphia PA 19107-3610

**POLLARD, EDWARD NEAL,** lawyer; b. Raleigh, N.C., Sept. 19, 1960; s. Robert Burns and LaRue Taylor Pollard; m. Mary Sheehan, Aug. 1, 1992; 1 child, Daniel Edward. BSCE, N.C. State U., 1982; JD, Wake Forest U., 1993. Bar: N.C. 1993, U.S. Dist. Ct. (ea., mid. and we. dists.) N.C.; registered profl. engr., S.C. Civil engr. Charleston (S.C.) Naval Shipyard, 1982-86; structural engr. Naval Facility Engring. Command, Charleston, 1986-90; jud. law clk. to Judge Hiram H. Ward, Winston-Salem, N.C., 1993-96; assoc. Bugg & Wolf, P.A., Durham, N.C., 1996—. Mem. N.C. Bar Assn. (adminstrn. of justice task force 1998—). Construction, General civil litigation. Office: Bugg & Wolf PA PO Box 2917 Durham NC 27715-2917

**POLLARD, FRANK EDWARD,** lawyer; b. Framingham, Mass., Oct. 26, 1932; s. Frank E. and Marjorie G. (Bayer) P.; m. Joyce A. Angell, June 4, 1955; children: Gary R., Jeffrey F., Donald B., Edward D., Laurie J. AB, Northeastern U., 1954; JD, Boston U., 1956. Bar: Conn. 1956, Mass. 1956, Fla. 1959, U.S. Dist. Ct. Mass., U.S. Supreme Ct. 1969. Ptnr., atty. Lee & Pollard, Westfield, Mass., 1958-80; pvt. practice Westfield, 1980-96; pres. Pollard & Pollard P.C., 1997—. Pres. Westfield 2000 Redevel. Corp., 1978, counsel, 1980—; atty. City of Westfield, 1970-71; parlimentarian Mass. Jr. C. of C., 1964; pres. Boys Club Greater Westfield, Inc., 1972-73. Recipient Distinguished Svc. award U.S. Jaycees, Westfield, 1966. Mem. Westfield C. of C. (pres. 1975, counsel 1975—), Westfield Boys and Girls Club (pres. 1972-73, Man and Boy award 1973), Kiwanis (life mem., lt. gov. 1977-78, Westfield pres. 1967-68). Avocations: golf, photography, carpentry. Probate, Real property, Estate planning. Home: 419 Southwick Rd Apt 10C Westfield MA 01085-4764 Office: 48 E Silver St # 1 Westfield MA 01085-4449

**POLLARD, HENRY ROBINSON, IV,** lawyer, investor; b. Richmond, Va., Aug. 5, 1943; s. Henry Robinson III and Esther Roy (Nichols) P.; m. Jeanette Gay Baker, Aug. 6, 1964 (div. Sept. 1983); children: Henry R., Braxton B., Coleman W., Elizabeth Berkeley; m. Julia Harris Whitlock, July 15, 1984. BS, Hampden-Sydney Coll., 1964; LLB, U. Richmond, 1967. Bar: Va. 1967, N.C., U.S. Dist. Ct. (ea. dist.) Va. 1977, U.S. Dist. Ct. (we. dist.) Va. 1988, U.S. Ct. Appeals (4th cir.) 1979. Pvt. practice Richmond, Va., 1967-72; pres. Parker, Pollard & Brown, Richmond, Va., 1972—; Sec., bd. dirs. Fidelity Fed. Savs. Bank, Richmond, BB&T Fin. of Va., Virginia Beach, Home Builders Assn., Richmond, among others. Inventor Base for Post, (software) Activity Chase Sys. Mem. adv. bd. HealthSouth Med. Ctr., Richmond, 1994-96; bd. dirs. Boys and Girls Clubs of Richmond. Mem. ABA (real property sect., probate and trust law sect., litig. sect., legal econs. sect.), ATLA, Va. Bar Assn. (coun. 1988-92, med. malpractice rev. panel 1977-90, long range planning com. 1989-96, chmn. long range planning com. 1992-96), N.C. Bar Assn., Va. Trial Lawyers Assn., Richmond Bar Assn. (fin. com.), Am. Inns of Ct. (Richmond chpt.), Henrico County Bar Assn. (real estate law com. 1977-78, law practice mgmt. sect.), Omicron Delta Kappa (Leadership award 1964), Phi Delta Phi. Presbyterian. Avocations: golf, fishing, jogging. General civil litigation, Contracts commercial, Real property. Home: 2906 Leffingwell Pl Richmond VA 23233-6901 Office: Parker Pollard & Brown PC 5511 Staples Mill Rd Richmond VA 23228-5422

**POLLARD, MICHAEL ROSS,** lawyer, health policy researcher and consultant; b. Flint, Mich., Apr. 14, 1947; s. Gail Winton Pollard and Evelyn Georgeanna (LeMire) Goplen; m. Penelope Brigham, Aug. 22, 1970. AB in Polit. Sci., U. Mich., 1969; JD, Harvard U., 1972, MPH, 1974. Bar: Mass. 1972, D.C. 1975. Profl. assoc. for program devel. Nat. Acad. Scis. Inst. Medicine, Washington, 1974-77, dir. law and ethics div., 1977-78; atty. advisor Office of Policy Planning, FTC, Washington, 1978-81, asst. dir. Bur. Consumer Protection, 1981-83; dir. Office of Policy Analysis, Pharm. Mfrs. Assn., Washington, 1983-88; exec. dir. Am. Pharm. Inst., Washington, 1988-89; counsel Michaels, Wishner & Bonner, P.C. (now Michaels & Bonner PC), Washington, 1988-89, ptnr., 1989—; cons. Nat. Ctr. for Health Svcs. Rsch., Rockville, Md., 1975-80, Office Tech. Assessment U.S. Congress, 1984-95; dir. Inst. for Health Policy Solutions, 1992—. Contbr. articles to profl. jours. Treas. Nat. Leadership Coalition on AIDS, 1988-93; treas. and dir.-at-large Nat. Commn. on Cert. of Physician Assts., 1991-97, James B. Angell scholar U. Mich., 1967, 68, 69. Mem. ABA, Phi Beta Kappa, Pi Sigma Alpha. Democrat. Avocations: running, cycling, gardening, architectural drawing. Antitrust, Health, Administrative and regulatory. Home: 7300 Maple Ave Chevy Chase MD 20815-5108 also: 29 Paradise Lane West Southport ME 04576 Office: Michaels & Bonner 1140 Connecticut Ave NW Ste 900 Washington DC 20036-4009

**POLLARD, OVERTON PRICE,** state agency executive, lawyer; b. Ashland, Va., Mar. 26, 1933; s. James Madison and Annie Elizabeth (Hutchinson) P.; m. Anne Aloysia Meyer, Oct. 1, 1960; children—Mary O., Price, John, Anne, Charles, Andrew, David. AB in Econs., Washington and Lee U., 1954, JD, 1957. Bar: Va. Claims supr. Travelers Ins. Co., Richmond, Va., 1964-67; asst. atty. gen. State of Va., Richmond, 1967, 70-72; spl. asst. Va. Supreme Ct., Richmond, 1968-70; exec. dir. Pub. Defender Commn., Richmond, 1972—; ptnr. Pollard & Boice and predecessor firms, Richmond, 1972-87; bd. govs. Va. Criminal Law Sect., Richmond, 1970-72, 91-93; chmn. prepaid legal services com. Va. State Bar, Richmond, 1982-85; pres. Met. Legal Aid, Richmond, 1978. Del. to State Dem. Cong., Richmond, 1985; mem. Va. Commn. on Family Violence Prevention, 1995; bd. dirs. Henrico Cmty. Housing Corp., 1999. With USN, 1957-59. Recipient service award Criminal Law Bd. of Govs. for Pub. Defender Study, 1971. Mem. ABA, Va. Bar Assn. (chmn. criminal law sect. 1991-93), Richmond Bar Assn., Nat. Legal Aid and Defender Assn. (Reginald Heber Smith award 1991), Va. Bar Assn. (Pro Bono Publico award 1995). Democrat. Baptist. Avocation: fishing. Home: 7726 Sweetbriar Rd Richmond VA 23229-6622 Office: Pub Defender Commn 701 E Franklin St Ste 1416 Richmond VA 23219-2510

**POLLEY, TERRY LEE,** lawyer; b. Long Beach, Calif., June 2, 1947; s. Frederick F. and Geraldine E. (Davis) P.; m. Patricia Yamanoha, Aug. 4, 1973; children: Todd, Matthew. AB, UCLA, 1970; JD, Coll. William and Mary, 1973. Bar: Calif. 1973, U.S. Tax Ct. 1974, U.S. Supreme Ct. 1987. Assoc. Loeb & Loeb, L.A., 1973-78; ptnr. Ajalat, Polley & Ayoob, L.A., 1978—; lectr. taxation law U. So.Calif., 1978-94. Author (with Charles R. Ajalat) California's Water's Edge Legislation, 1987; contbr. articles to profl. jours, legal jours.; editorial bd. William and Mary Law Rev. Chmn. bd. dirs. Greater Long Beach Christian Schs., 1988-92, sec., 1994—; elder Grace Brethren Ch., Long Beach, 1988—. Mem. ABA (state and local tax com. 1973-92), Calif. Bar Assn. (chmn. taxation sect. 1990-91, exec. com. 1987-92, state and local tax com. 1975—, taxation sect., recipient V. Judson Klein award 1993), L.A. County Bar Assn. (exec. com. 1980-87, chmn. exec. com. 1985-86, taxation sect.), Nat. Assn. State Bar Tax Sects. (exec. com. 1990—, chmn. 1995-96, treas. 1998—). Republican. State and local taxation. Office: Ajalat Polley & Ayoob 643 S Olive St Ste 200 Los Angeles CA 90014-1651

**POLLI, ROBERT PAUL,** lawyer; b. Miami, Fla., Nov. 22, 1947; s. Silas Frederick and Ann Martha (Papada) P.; m. Carolyn Jane Albritton, June 13, 1974. BA, U. South Fla., 1969, MA, 1971, 78; JD, Stetson U., 1983. chmn. grievance com. Fla. Bar. Tchr. Project Headstart, various locations, 1968-69; exceptional child educator Hillsborough County Schs., Tampa, Fla., 1974-76; guidance counselor Hillsborough County Schs., 1976-80; profl. photographer Tampa, 1972—; assoc. Bennie Lazzara, Jr., P.A., Tampa, 1983-87; ptnr. Lazzara, Caskey, Polli and Paul, Tampa, 1987-91; pvt. practice, Tampa, 1991—. Contbr. articles to profl. jours. Mem. ABA, Fla. Bar Assn., Fla. Assn. Criminal Def. Lawyers, Hillsborough County Assn. Criminal Def. Lawyers (pres.). Democrat. Roman Catholic. Criminal. Home: PO Box 411 Anna Maria FL 34216-0411 Office: 101 E Kennedy Blvd Ste 3130 Tampa FL 33602-5151

**POLLIHAN, THOMAS HENRY,** lawyer; b. St. Louis, Nov. 15, 1949; s. C.H. and Patricia Ann (O'Brien) P.; m. Donna M. Bickhaus, Aug. 25, 1973; 1 child, Emily Christine. BA in Sociology, Quincy U., 1972; JD, U. Notre Dame, 1975; Exec. Masters in Internat. Bus., St. Louis U., 1992. Bar: Mo. 1975, Ill. 1976. Jud. law clk. to judge Mo. Ct. of Appeals, St. Louis, 1975-76; from assoc. to ptnr. Greenfield, Davidson, Mandelstamm & Voorhees, St. Louis, 1976-82; asst. gen. counsel Kellwood Co., St. Louis, 1982-89, gen. counsel, sec., 1989-93, v.p., sec., gen. counsel, 1993—. Trustee Quincy (Ill.) U., 1987-93, 97—, pres. alumni bd., 1986-87; pres. S.W. Neighborhood Improvement Assn., St. Louis, 1984, Quincy (Ill.) U. Found., 1993-94, 97—; dir., sec. New Piasa Chautauqua, Ill., 1996-97. Named Quincy U. Alumnus of Yr., 1997. Mem. Bar Assn. Met. St. Louis. Roman Catholic. Avocations: soccer, cycling. General corporate, Contracts commercial, Real property. Home: 415 Spring Ave Saint Louis MO 63119-2634 Office: Kellwood Co 600 Kellwood Pkwy Ste 300 Chesterfield MO 63017-5897

**POLLINGER, WILLIAM JOSHUA,** lawyer; b. Passaic, N.J., Dec. 14, 1944; s. Irving R. and Ethel (Groudan) P.; m. Helen Rizzo, May 30, 1977; children: Samantha, Zachary. BA, Rutgers U., 1966; JD, Am. U., 1969. Bar: N.J. 1969, U.S. Dist. Ct. N.J. 1969, N.Y. 1981, U.S. Supreme Ct. 1982, U.S. Ct. Appeals (3d cir.) 1986; cert. Civil Trial Atty. N.J. Supreme Ct., 1983. Assoc. Krieger & Klein, Passaic, 1969-75; ptnr. Delorenzo & Pollinger, Hackensack, N.J., 1975-84; pres. William J. Pollinger, P.A., Hackensack, 1984-88, Pollinger, Fearns & Kemezis, P.A., 1988-90, Pollinger & Fearns, P.A., Hackensack, 1990-92, William J. Pollinger P.A., Hackensack, N.J., 1992—; mem. Bergen County Ethics Com., N.J., 1984-88; lectr. ins. N.J.-ICLE, master Robert L. Clifford Am. Inn of Court. Arbitrator Better Bus. Bur. of Bergen and Rockland Counties, Paramus, N.J., 1983-89, Am. Arbitration Assn., 1983—. Assoc. of Yr. award Builders Assn. No. N.J., Paramus, 1981. Master Justice Robert L. Clifford Am. Inn of Ct.; mem. N.J. State Bar Assn., Passaic County Bar Assn., Bergen County Bar Assn., Assn. Trial Lawyers Am., Trial Attys. N.J., Am. Arbitration Assn., Def. Research Inst., Phi Delta Phi. Lodge: Masons (past master). Avocation: track and field officiating (certified). State civil litigation, Personal injury, Insurance. Office: 302 Union St Hackensack NJ 07601-4303

**POLLOCK, BRADLEY NEIL,** lawyer; b. St. Charles, Ill., Sept. 23, 1970; s. Neil Edward and Karen Irene Pollock; m. Tara Lynne Kozlowski, Aug. 23, 1997. BA with distinction, U. Ill., 1992; JD, Loyola U., Chgo., 1995. Bar: Ill. 1995, U.S. Dist. Ct. (no. dist.) Ill. 1995. Assoc. Williams & Montgomery, Ltd., Chgo., 1995, Robert N. Wadington & Assocs., Chgo., 1995—. Recipient Am. Jurisprudence award in Appellate Practice Lawyers Coop. Pub., 1993. Mem. ATLA, Ill. Bar Assn., Chgo. Bar Assn., Ill. Trial Lawyers Assn. Avocations: fly fishing, backpacking, other outdoor activities. Personal injury, Product liability, Professional liability. Home: IN281 Prairie Ave Glen Ellyn IL 60137 Office: Robert N Wadington & Assocs 111 W Washington St Ste 1460 Chicago IL 60602-2767

**POLLOCK, BRUCE GERALD,** lawyer; b. Providence, Feb. 18, 1947; s. Reuben and Stella (Reitman) P.; m. Sheri Barbara Tepper, Dec. 21, 1969; children: Dawn, Meah. BA, U. R.I., 1968; JD, Suffolk U., 1974. Bar: R.I. 1974, U.S. Supreme Ct. 1978, U.S. Dist. Ct. R.I. 1980. Law clk. R.I. Superior Ct., Providence, 1974, adminstrv. asst. to chief justice, 1975; asst. pub. defender R.I. Dept. Pub. Defender, Providence, 1975-80; pvt. practice Warwick and West Warwick, R.I., 1980—; adj. instr. So. N.E. Law Sch., New Bedford, Mass., 1990. Dist. chmn. Narragansett Coun. Shawomet Dist. Boy Scouts Am., 1996-98. Fellow R.I. Bar Found. (bd. dirs. 1990—); mem. ABA, Nat. Conf. Bar Pres., New Eng. Bar Assn. (del. 1991-93), R.I. Bar Assn. (pres. 1992-93, award of merit 1995). Democrat. Avocations: golf, skiing, stained glass craftsman, bicycling, Tai Chi. General practice, Criminal, Personal injury. Office: 45 Providence St West Warwick RI 02893-3714

**POLLOCK, DAVID SAMUEL,** lawyer; b. Altoona, Pa., Dec. 11, 1949; s. Arthur Edgar and Judith Jaffee Pollock; m. Rita Lee, June 27, 1971; children: Adam, Joshua. BA, Pa. State U., 1970; JD, Duquesne U., 1974. Bar: Pa. 1974, U.S. Dist. Ct. (we. dist.) Pa. 1974. Law clk. Ct. Common Pleas, Pitts., 1974-76; assoc. Jubelirer, Pass & Intrieri PC, Pitts., 1976-82; prin. Pollock & Adams, Pitts., 1982-92; ptnr. Wittlin Goldston Caputo & Pollock PC, Pitts., 1992-94, Reed Smith Shaw & McClay LLC, Pitts., 1994-98; prin. David S. Pollock & Assocs., Pitts., 1998—; lectr. in field. Contbr. articles to law revs., jours. and presentations. Bd. dirs. Jewish Comty. Ctr., 1988-97, sec., 1993-95, treas., 1992-93, asst. treas. 1991-92, exec. com. 1990-98, chair Emma Kaufmann Camp, 1991-94, other offices; past bd. dirs., founding dir., atty. Oakland Bus. and Civic Assn.; intergenerational choir, past mem. brotherhood, bd. trustees Temple Sinai. With USAR, 1970-76. Recipient Ida and Samuel Latterman Vol. Mitzvah award Jewish Comty. Ctr., 1989. Fellow Am. Acad. Matrimonial Lawyers (co-chmn. membership com., bd. examiners Pa. chpt. 1993-95, 97-98, mem. program com. Pa. chpt. 1993-96); mem. ABA (family law sect.), Am. Inns of Matrimonial Cts. (Master 1995-96, 97—), Pa. Bar Assn. (various offices family law sect., coun. mem. 1987-91, 92-95, co-chair program com. 1984-87, 88-89, 91-95, editor-in-chief Pa. Family Lawyer 1996—, task force on family ct. reform 1997—, Outstanding Contbn. award 1988-89, Spl. Achievement award 1993, 94, 95, 96, 97, 98), Pa. Futures Commn. (family law task group 1996-97), Washington County Bar Assn. (family law sect.), Allegheny County Bar Assn. (coun. mem. family law sect. 1984-87, 88-91, 92-95, 96—, co-chair rules com. 1996-97, co-chair ct. rels. com. 1994-95, opinions com. 1993—, co-chair procedures and rulees com. 1985-88), Washington County Bar Assn. (family law sect.), Duquesne U. Law Alumni Assn. (bd. govs. 1993-96). Avocations: snow and water skiing, swimming, jogging, bicycling, canoeing. Fax: (412) 471-9001. E-mail: dpollock@dsplaw.com. Family and matrimonial. Office: 420 Frick Bldg 437 Grant St Pittsburgh PA 15219-6002

**POLLOCK, JEFFREY LAWRENCE,** lawyer; b. Phila., June 12, 1962; s. Burton Harold and Marolee (Morrison) P. BA, U. Pa., 1984; JD, U. Pitts., 1987. Bar: Pa. 1987, U.S. Dist. Ct. (we. dist.) Pa. 1987. Assoc. Feldstein, Grinberg, Stein & McKee, Pitts., 1987-89; pvt. practice, Pitts., 1989—. Bd. dirs. Leukemia Soc. Western Pa. 1992-94; chmn. Jewish Cmty. Ctr. Theatre, 1992-96. Mem. Pa. Bar Assn. (Michael K. Smith award 1999), Allegheny County Bar Assn. (bd. govs. 1994-99, judiciary com. 1999, chmn. young lawyers sect. 1995, 97), Family Mediation Coun. W. Pa. Avocations: golf, theatre, softball, basketball, charity work. Criminal, Family and matrimonial, Entertainment. Office: 1516 S Negley Ave Ste 300 Pittsburgh PA 15217-1420

**POLLOCK, JEFFREY MORROW,** lawyer; b. Morristown, N.J., Sept. 23, 1961; s. Stewart G. and Penelope (Morrow) P.; m. Holly Ann Tinkham, Jan. 21, 1988; 1 child, Jeffrey Wentworth. BA, Hamilton Coll., 1984; JD, NYU, 1987. Bar: N.J. 1987, D.C. 1988, U.S. Dist. Ct. N.J. 1988. Jud. law clk. to Chief Judge Donald P. Lay U.S. Ct. Appeals 8th Cir., St. Paul, 1987-88; assoc. Pitney, Hardin, Kipp & Szuch, Morristown, 1988-94; ptnr. Sills Cummis, Newark, 1994—; mem. underground storage tank task force N.J. Dept. Environ. Protection and Energy, Trenton, 1992; mem. com. on complementary dispute resolution N.J. Supreme Ct., Trenton, 1992, chmn. complex cases working group. Mem. editorial bd. N.J. Lawyer; contbr. articles to profl. jours. Mem. N.J. State Bar Assn. (dir. and sec. environ. law sect.), Worrall F. Mountain Inn of Ct. Quaker. Avocation: fly fishing. Environmental, Product liability. Home: 11 Liberty Hills Ct Long Valley NJ 07853-3087 Office: Sills Cummis One Riverfront Plz Newark NJ 07102

**POLLOCK, JOHN PHLEGER,** lawyer; b. Sacramento, Apr. 28, 1920; s. George Gordon and Irma (Phleger) P.; m. Juanita Irene Gossman, Oct. 26, 1945; children: Linda Pollock Harrison, Madeline Pollock Chiotti, John, Gordon. A.B., Stanford U., 1942; J.D., Harvard U., 1948. Bar: Calif. 1949, U.S. Supreme Ct. 1954. Ptnr. Musick, Peeler & Garrett, L.A., 1953-60, Pollock, Williams & Berwanger, L.A., 1960-80; ptnr. Rodi, Pollock, Pettker, Galbraith & Cahill, L.A., 1980-89, of counsel, 1989—. Contbr. articles to profl. publs. Active Boy Scouts Am.; trustee Pitzer Coll., Claremont, Calif., 1968-76, Pacific Legal Found., 1981-91, Fletcher Jones Found., 1969—, Good Hope Med. Found., 1980—. Mem. ABA, Los Angeles County Bar Assn. (trustee 1964-66). State civil litigation, Federal civil litigation, Estate planning. Home: 30602 Paseo Del Valle Laguna Niguel CA 92677-2317 Office: 444 S Flower St Ste 1700 Los Angeles CA 90071-2901

**POLLOCK, MELANY TAWANDA,** paralegal, legal assistant; b. Washington, Nov. 12, 1971; d. William Calvin Jr. and Brenda Lee (Bullock) P. BA, Radford U., 1993; MA, Am. U., 1998. Adminstrv. asst. Fed. Dept. Ins. Corp., Washington, 1992, 93, 94; asst. physician recruiter Humana Group Health Plan, Washington, 1995; paralegal specialist Legal Svc. No. Va., Falls Church, Va., 1995-96; legal asst. King & Spalding Law Firm, Washington, 1996—. Mem. Nat. Black Am. Paralegal Assn., Nat. Capital

Area Paralegal Assn., Nat. Coun. Negro Women, Nat. Press Club, Women in Video & Film, Women in Comm., Alpha Kappa Alpha. Baptist. Avocations: sewing, writing, reading, pottery, running. Home: 11109 Ascot Cir Fredericksburg VA 22407-5059 Office: King & Spalding Law Firm Ste 1200 1730 Pennsylvania Ave NW Washington DC 20006-4706

**POLLOCK, STACY JANE,** lawyer; b. Palmerton, Pa., Dec. 24, 1969; d. Charles Paul Pollock and Marianne (Kovatch) Althouse. BA, Allentown Coll. St. Francis, Center Valley, Pa., 1991; postgrad., U. De Las Americas, Puebla, Mex., 1991; JD with honors, George Wash. U., 1994. Bar: Pa. 1995, D.C. 1996, U.S. Ct. Appeals (11th cir.) 1996. Assoc. Arnold & Porter, Washington, 1994-95, 96—; jud. clk. U.S. Ct. Appeals, 11th Cir., Montgomery, Ala., 1995-96. Bd. dirs. Palisade Gardens Condominiums, Arlington, Va., 1998-99. Democrat. Roman Catholic. General civil litigation, Product liability, Federal civil litigation. Office: Arnold and Porter 555 12th St NW Washington DC 20004-1206

**POLLOCK, STEWART GLASSON,** lawyer, former state supreme court justice; b. East Orange, N.J., Dec. 21, 1932. BA, Hamilton Coll., 1954, LLD (hon.), 1995; LLB, NYU, 1957; LLM, U. Va., 1988. Bar: N.J. 1958. Asst. U.S. atty. Newark, 1958-60; ptnr. Schenck, Price, Smith & King, Morristown, N.J., 1960-74, 76-78; commr. N.J. Dept. Pub. Utilities; counsel to gov. State of N.J., Trenton, 1978-79; assoc. justice N.J. Supreme Ct., Morristown, 1979-99; of counsel Riker Danzig Hyland & Perretti, Morristown, 1999—; mem. N.J. Commn. on Investigation, 1976-78; chmn. coordinating coun. on life-sustaining med. treatment decision making Nat. Ctr. for State Cts., 1994-96; bd. dirs. Law Ctr. Found., Inst. of Jud. Adminstrn. Assoc. editor N.J. Law Jour.; contbr. articles to legal jours. Trustee Coll. Medicine and Dentistry, N.J., 1976. Mem. ABA (chmn. appellate judges conf. 1991-92), N.J. Bar Assn. (trustee 1973-78), Am. Judicature Soc. (dir. 1984-88), Morris County Bar Assn. (pres. 1973). Office: Riker Danzig Scherer Hyland & Perretti One Speedwell Ave Morristown NJ 07962-0900

**POLOZOLA, FRANK JOSEPH,** federal judge; b. Baton Rouge, Jan. 15, 1942; s. Steve A. Sr. and Caroline C. (Lucito) P.; m. Linda Kay White, June 9, 1962; children: Gregory Dean, Sheri Elizabeth, Gordon Damian. Student bus. adminstrn., La. State U., 1959-62, JD, 1965. Bar: La. 1965. Law clk. to U.S. Dist. Ct. Judge E. Gordon West, 1965-66; assoc. Seale, Smith & Phelps, Baton Rouge, 1966-68, ptnr., 1968-73; part-time magistrate U.S. Dist. Ct. (mid. dist.) La., Baton Rouge, 1972-73, magistrate, 1973-80, judge, 1980—, chief judge, 1998—; adj. prof. Law Ctr., La. State U., 1977-95. Bd. dirs. Cath. High Sch. Mem. La. Bar Assn., Baton Rouge Bar Assn., Fed. Judges Assn., 5th Cir. Dist. Judges Assn., La. State U. L Club, KC, Wex Malone Inns of Ct., Omicron Delta Kappa. Roman Catholic. Office: US Dist Ct Russell B Long Fed Bldg & US Courthouse 777 Florida St Ste 313 Baton Rouge LA 70801-1717

**POLSKY, HOWARD DAVID,** lawyer; b. Phila., Sept. 10, 1951; s. Herman and Meriam (Ternoff) P. BA, Lehigh U., 1973; JD, Ind. U., 1976. Bar: Pa. 1976, N.J. 1977, D.C. 1978, U.S. Ct. Appeals (D.C. cir.) 1976. Atty. FCC, Washington, 1976-79; assoc. Kirkland & Ellis, Washington, 1979-83; ptnr. Wiley, Rein & Fielding, Washington, 1983-92; v.p. fed. policy and regulation COMSAT Corp., Bethesda, Md., 1992—; adj. prof. law Del. Law Sch. Widner U., 1981-84. Mem. ABA, Fed. Bar Assn., Fed. Com. Bar Assn. Administrative and regulatory, Public utilities, Communications.

**POLSTON, RONALD WAYNE,** law educator; b. Raymond, Ill., Nov. 1, 1931; s. Joseph M. and Minnie V. (Wilson) P.; m. Mary Ann Campbell, Aug. 5, 1961; children—Anne Campbell, Joseph Harrison. B.S., Eastern Ill. U., 1953; LL.B., U. Ill., 1958. Bar: Ill. 1959, Ind., 1967, U.S. Supreme Ct. 1964. Assoc. Craig & Craig, Mt. Vernon, Ill., 1958-64; ptnr., 1964-65; asst. prof. Ind. U. Sch. Law, Indpls., 1965-68, assoc. prof., 1968-71, asst. dean, 1968-71, prof. 1971-95, prof. emeritus, 1995—; vis. prof. Monash U., Melbourne, Australia, 1972-73. Trustee Eastern Mineral Law Found., 1985—. Served to cpl. U.S. Army, 1953-55. Democrat. Methodist. Home: 311 S McGown Raymond Raymond IL 62560 Office: Indiana Univ Sch Law 735 W New York St Indianapolis IN 46202-5222

**POLSTRA, LARRY JOHN,** lawyer; b. Lafayette, Ind., June 28, 1945; s. John Edward and Elizabeth (Vandergraff) P.; m. Joan Marie Blair Rozier, Sept. 2, 1972 (dec.); 1 stepchild, Shawn M. Rozier; m. Barbara Dominy, Mar. 18, 1988; stepchildren: Tobi Shawn Porter, Teri Lane Kelly. BS in Bus. Mgmt., Bob Jones U., 1968; JD, Atlanta Law Sch., 1976, LLM, 1977. Bar: Ga. 1976, U.S. Dist. Ct. (no. dist.) Ga. 1976, U.S. Ct. Appeals (11th cir.) 1990, U.S. Supreme Ct. 1994. Mktg. dir. N.Am. Security, Atlanta, 1972-73; acctg. supr. Allstate Ins. Co., Atlanta, 1973-76; sole practice Atlanta, 1976-77; ptnr. Law Smith (formerly Smith & Polstra), Atlanta, 1977-94, of counsel, 1995; of counsel England & McKnight, 1996—, Hays & Maysilles, P.C., 1997—; arbitrator Fulton County Superior Ct., Atlanta, 1986. Served to 1st lt. USMC, 1968-71, Vietnam. Mem. ATLA, Atlanta Bar Assn., Ga. Assn. Trial Lawyers, Ga. Assn. Criminal Def. Lawyers, Marine Corps Assn. Ga. Lawyers. Avocation: golf. State civil litigation, Family and matrimonial, Criminal. Home: 2081 Hampton Trl SE Conyers GA 30013-2347 Office: PO Box 450909 1979 Lakeside Pkwy Ste 220 Tucker GA 30084-5813

**POLZIN, CHARLES HENRY,** lawyer; b. Saginaw, Mich., June 9, 1954; s. James William and Dorothy Marie (Koski) P.; m. Roberta Anne Zaremba, May 26, 1984; children: Alexander James, Matthew Robert, Madelyn Marie. BA magna cum laude, Western Mich. U., 1975; JD cum laude, U. Mich., 1979. Bar: Mich. 1979. Assoc. Hill, Lewis, Adams, Goodrich & Tait, Detroit, 1979-81, Martin, Axe, Buhl & Schwartz, Bloomfield Hills, Mich., 1981-83, Hill, Lewis, Adams, Goodrich & Tait, Birmingham, Mich., 1983-86; ptnr. Hill Lewis, Birmingham, 1986-96; mem. Clark Hill P.L.C., Birmingham, 1996—. Mem. founders jr. coun. bd. Detroit Inst. Arts, 1986-92, treas., 1988-89, pres., 1989-91; bd. dirs. Coalition on Temporary Shelter, 1992—, pres., 1997—. Waldo Sangren scholar Western Mich. U., 1974. Mem. ABA, Oakland County Bar Assn. (chmn. continuing legal edn. com. 1986-88). General civil litigation, Municipal (including bonds). Office: Clark Hill PLC 255 S Old Woodward Ave Fl 3D Birmingham MI 48009-6182

**POMBERT, JEFFREY LAWRENCE,** lawyer; b. Kankakee, Ill., Feb. 6, 1968; s. Lawrence G. Pombert and Alice E. Spencer; m. Winifred Lisa Beebe, Jan. 13, 1990; children: Josiah Lincoln, Winifred Jeneé, Abigail Lawren, Jeffrey Lawson. BA, Ea. Ill. U., 1990; JD, U. Mich., 1995. Bar: Ga. 1996. Intern Congressman Joe Barton, Washington, 1990; supply specialist U.S. Army Tank-Automotive Command, Warren, Mich., 1991-93; clk. Conlin, McKenney & Philbrick, P.C., Ann Arbor, Mich., 1994-96; atty. Bird & Assocs., P.C., Atlanta, 1996—. Editor-in-chief Mich. Law and Policy Rev., 1994-95. Scholar Kiwanis Club Kankakee, 1986, Pres. scholar Ea. Ill. U., Charleston, 1989, Parents' Club scholar Ea. Ill. U. Parents' Club, Charleston, 1989. Mem. Nat. Lawyers Assn., Christian Legal Soc., Ga. Bar. Republican. Baptist. General civil litigation, General corporate, Non-profit and tax-exempt organizations. Office: Bird & Assocs PC 1150 Monarch Plaza 3414 Peachtree Rd NE Atlanta GA 30326-1153

**POMERANTZ, JERALD MICHAEL,** lawyer; b. Springfield, Mass., July 9, 1954; s. Lawrence Louis Pomerantz and Dolores (Barez) Chaudoir. BA in Econs. cum laude, Brandeis U., 1976; JD, Vanderbilt U., 1979; student, Am. Inst. Banking, 1983-99. Atty. McAllen, Tex., 1979-80, Weslaco, Tex., 1980-85; gen. counsel, sec. Tex. Valley Bancshares, Inc., Weslaco, 1985-87; atty. for Hidalgo County Rural Fire Prevention Dist., Tex., 1982-88; atty. SBA, Harlingen, Tex., 1987; pvt. practice Weslaco, Tex., 1987-88, 89—, Dallas, 1988-89; atty. Security Bank Shares, F.M., Dallas, 1988-89; adv. dir. South Tex. Fed. Credit Union, 1995-98; atty. Elsa (Tex.) Housing Authority, Weslaco (Tex.) Housing Authority, 1997—. Mem. Weslaco Charter Review Com., 1981-82,; drafted S.B. 139 (amending Tex. bus. and commerce code sect. 9.402(g)) regular session Tex. Legislature), 1989, S.B. 140, 1989, enacted as H.B. 2005 (amending Tex. Credit Code sect. 1.06) regular session Tex. Legislature, 1993. Recipient continuing edn. award Banking Law Inst., 1992. 17269656. Assn. Bank Counsel (bd. dirs. 1993-96, 1997—), State Bar Tex., Conf. on Consumer Fin. Law, Coll. State Bar Tex. (bd. dirs. 1990-95), Hidalgo County Bar Assn. (law libr. com. 1999—), Rio Grande Valley Bankruptcy Attys. Assn. Banking, Real property, Consumer commercial. Home and Office: PO Box 10 Weslaco TX 78599-0010

**POMEROY, CHRISTOPHER DONALD,** lawyer; b. Waterbury, Conn., Nov. 11, 1970. BS in Biology cum laude, Fairfield (Conn.) U., 1992; JD with high honors, George Washington U., 1996. Bar: Va. 1996, U.S. Dist. Ct. (ea. and we. dists.) Va. 1997, U.S. Ct. Appeals (4th cir.) 1997. Assoc. atty. Williams, Mullen, Christian & Dobbins, Richmond, Va., 1996-98, McGuire, Woods, Battle & Boothe LLP, Richmond, 1998—; bd. govs. environ. law sect. Va. State Bar, 1999—. Environmental. Office: McGuire Woods Battle & Boothe 901 E Cary St Richmond VA 23219-4057

**POMEROY, GREGG JOSEPH,** lawyer; b. Flushing, N.Y., June 22, 1948; s. George Bart and Dianne (Marshall) P.; m. Deborah Christina Pomeroy, Feb. 16, 1985 (div.); children: Christopher William, Glenn David; m. Suzanne R. Pomeroy, July 25, 1992; children: Adam Barton, Sarah Nicole. BA, U. Fla., 1971; JD, Samford U., 1974. Bar: Fla. 1974, U.S. Dist. Ct. Fla. 1974, U.S. Ct. Appeals (5th and 11th cirs.) 1974. Asst. pub. defender 17th Jud. Cir., Ft. Lauderdale, Fla., 1974-75; ptnr. Pomeroy, Pomeroy & Pomeroy, Ft. Lauderdale, 1976-86, Pomeroy & Pomeroy, P.A., Ft. Lauderdale, 1987-96; pvt. practice Fort Lauderdale, 1996—. Served to specialist class 4 USNG, 1970-76. Mem. ABA, Def. Research Inst., NRA, Coral Ridge Power Squadron, Harleys Owners Group. Roman Catholic. Clubs: Boat U.S., NRA. Avocations: boating, motorcycling. Personal injury, Insurance, Product liability. Office: 2787 E Oakland Park Blvd # 350-6 Fort Lauderdale FL 33306-1647

**POMEROY, HARLAN,** lawyer; b. Cleve., May 7, 1923; s. Lawrence Alson and Frances (Macdonald) P.; m. Barbara Lesser, Aug. 24, 1962; children: Robert Charles, Caroline Macdonald, Harlan III. BS, Yale U., 1945; JD, Harvard U., 1948. Bar: Conn. 1949, U.S. Supreme Ct. 1954, U.S. Ct. Appeals (fed. cir.) 1954, Ohio 1958, U.S. Dist. Ct. (no. dist.) Ohio 1958, U.S. Claims Ct. 1958, U.S. Ct. Appeals (6th cir.) 1958, U.S. Tax Ct. 1958, D.C. 1975, Md. 1981, U.S. Dist. Ct. (D.C. dist.) 1984, U.S. Ct. Internat. Trade 1984, U.S. Ct. Appeals (D.C. cir.) 1986; cert. county ct. mediator, Fla. Atty. trial sect. tax div. Dept. Justice, Washington, 1952-58; assoc. Baker & Hostetler, Cleve., 1958-62, ptnr., 1962-75; ptnr. Baker & Hostetler, Washington, 1975-92; gen. chmn. Cleve. Tax Inst., 1971; fgn. legal advisor to Romanian Securities Mkts., 1997, Macedonia, 1998; lectr. on tax and comml. law. Author: (monographs) The Privatization Process in Bulgaria; Bulgarian Government Structure and Operation-An Overview; contbr. articles to profl. jours. Treas. Shaker Heights (Ohio) Dem. Club, 1960-62; trustee, mem. exec. com. 1st Unitarian Ch. Cleve., 1965-68; trustee River Road Unitarian Ch., Bethesda, Md., 1988-90; gen. counsel, former asst. treas. John Glenn Presdl. Com., 1983-87; participant Vol. Lawyers Project, Legal Counsel for Elderly, Washington, 1983-92; vol. Guardian Ad Litem Program, Sarasota, Fla., 1990-92, GED-H.S. Equivalency Program, Sarasota, 1990-92; participant Guardianship Monitoring program 12th Jud. Cir., Fla., 1996-97; vol. exec. fgn. legal advisor Internat. Exec. Svc. Corps. with Privatization Ministry, Prague, Czech Republic, 1994-95; mem. spl. mission to Bulgarian Ministry of Fin., U.S. Dept. Treasury, 1995. Mem. ABA (resident liaison Bulgaria for Ctrl. and East European Law Initiative 1992-93), Am. Arbitration Assn. (arbitrator 1992—), Nat. Assn. of Securities Dealers (arbitrator 1992—), N.Y. Stock Exch. (arbitrator 1995—), Multistate Tax Commn. (arbitrator 1996—, mem. neutral roster IRS mediation program), D.C. Bar Assn., The Field Club (Sarasota, Fla.), Columbia Country Club (Bethesda, Md.), Yale Club (pres.), Harvard Club, Ivy League Club of Sarasota. Public international, Taxation, general, Private international. Home: 7336 Villa D Este Dr Sarasota FL 34238-5648 Office: Baker & Hostetler 1050 Connecticut Ave NW Ste 11 Washington DC 20036-5307 also: 3200 National City Ctr Cleveland OH 44414-3485

**POMPA, RENATA,** lawyer; b. N.Y.C., Sept. 8, 1961. BA, Columbia U., 1983; JD, St. John's U., 1986. Bar: N.Y. 1987. Assoc. atty. employee benefits Shea & Gould, N.Y.C., 1989-94; assoc. atty. employee benefits, exec. compensation and corp. securities Thacher, Proffitt & Wood, N.Y.C., 1994—. Mem. Nat. Assn. Stock Plan Profls., Am. Compensation Assn., Assn. Bar City N.Y. Pension, profit-sharing, and employee benefits, Labor, Securities. Home: 350 W 57th St Apt 10G New York NY 10019-3762 Office: Thacher Proffitt & Wood Two World Trade Ctr New York NY 10048

**PONDER, LESTER MCCONNICO,** lawyer, educator; b. Walnut Ridge, Ark., Dec. 10, 1912; s. Harry Lee and Clyde (Gant) P.; m. Sallie Mowry Clover, Nov. 7, 1942; children—Melinda, Constance; m. Phyllis Gretchen Harting, Oct. 14, 1978. B.S. summa cum laude in Commerce, Northwestern U., 1934; J.D. with honors, George Washington U., 1938. Bar: Ark. 1937, Ind. 1948. Atty. Ark. Dept. Revenue, Little Rock, 1939-41; atty. IRS, Chgo. and Indpls., 1941-51; ptnr. Barnes & Thornburg and predecessor Barnes, Hickam, Pantzer & Boyd, Indpls., 1952—; adj. prof. Sch. Law, Ind. U., Bloomington, 1951-54, Sch. Law, Ind. U., Indpls., 1954-63; lectr. polit. sci. Ind. U., Indpls., 1982-85. Author: United States Tax Court Practice & Procedure, 1976. Bd. dirs., vice chmn., chmn. Ind. chpt. The Nature Conservancy, 1981-89; mem. adv. coun. Ind. Dept. Natural Resources, 1986—; past bd. mem. Sigma Chi Found. Served with USN, 1942. Fellow Am. Bar Found., Ind. State Bar Found., Ind. Bar Found., Am. Coll. Tax Counsel; mem. ABA (coun., taxation sect. 1970-73, chair sr. lawyers div. 1993-94, adv. coun. Commr. Internal Revenue 1964—), Ind. State Bar Assn., Indpls. Bar Assn., Assn. of Seventh Fed. Cir. Republican. Presbyterian. Club: Meridian Hills Country (Indpls.). Lodge: Rotary (past bd. dirs.). Corporate taxation, Personal income taxation, Estate taxation. Office: Barnes & Thornburg Merchants Bank Bldg Ste 1313 Indianapolis IN 46204-3506

**PONITZ, JOHN ALLAN,** lawyer; b. Battle Creek, Mich., Sept. 7, 1949; m. Nancy J. Roberts, Aug. 14, 1971; children: Amy, Matthew, Julie. BA, Albion Coll., 1971; JD, Wayne State U., 1974. Bar: Mich. 1974, U.S. Dist. Ct. (ea. dist.) Mich. 1975, (we. dist.) Mich. 1986, U.S. Ct. Appeals (6th cir.) Mich. 1981, U.S. Supreme Ct. 1992. Assoc. McMachan & Kaichen, Birmingham, Mich., 1973-75; atty. Grand Trunk Western R.R., Detroit, 1975-80, sr. trial atty., 1980-89; gen. counsel, 1990-95; ptnr. Hopkins & Sutter, Detroit, 1995—. V.p. Beverly Hills (Mich.) Jaycees, 1981. Served to capt. USAR, 1974-82. Mem. Mich. Bar Assn., Nat. Assn. R.R. Trial Counsel, Oakland County Bar Assn. Lutheran. Avocation: golf. Federal civil litigation, General corporate, Personal injury. Office: Hopkins & Sutter 2800 Livernois Rd Ste 220 Troy MI 48083-1220

**PONOROFF, LAWRENCE,** law educator, legal consultant; b. Chgo., Sept. 10, 1953; s. Charles Melvin and Jean Eileen (Kramer) P.; m. Monica J. Moses, July 25, 1981; children: Christopher J., Devon E., Laura J., Scott C. AB, Loyola U., Chgo., 1975; JD, Stanford U., 1978. Bar: Colo. 1978, Ohio 1988, U.S. Dist. Ct. Colo., U.S. Dist. Ct. (no. dist.) Ohio, U.S. Ct. Appeals (10th cir.). Assoc. Holme Roberts & Owen, Denver, 1978-84, ptnr., 1984-86; asst. prof. law U. Toledo, 1986-88, assoc. prof. coll. of law, 1988-90, prof. law, assoc. dean academic affairs, 1990-92, prof., 1990-95; prof. Tulane U. Sch. Law, New Orleans, 1995—, vice dean, 1998—; vis. prof. Wayne State U. Law Sch., 1993, U. Mich. Law Sch., 1997, lectr. fed. juc. ctr.; cons. long range planning subcom. of com. on adminstrn. of bankruptcy system Jud. Conf. of the U.S. Co-author: (with S.E. Snyder) Commercial Bankruptcy Litigation, 1989, (with J. Dolan) Basic Concepts in Commercial Law, 1998. Mem. ABA, ABI, Am. Law Inst. Home: 6025 Pitt St New Orleans LA 70118-6010 Office: Tulane Law Sch Coll Law 6329 Freret St New Orleans LA 70118-6231

**PONSOLDT, WILLIAM RAYMOND, JR.,** lawyer; b. Westwood, N.J., July 6, 1966; s. William Raymond and Marriane (Kannegeiger) P.; m. Kimberly Rae Waller, Sept. 4, 1993. BS, U. Fla., 1988, JD, 1992. Bar: Fla. 1993, U.S. Dist. Ct. (mid. and so. dists.) Fla. 1993. Assoc. Kohl, Bobko, McKey, McManus et al, Stuart, Fla., 1992-93, Kohl, Metzger, Spotts, PA, Stuart, Fla., 1993-96; shareholder Kohl, Metzger, Spotts, Ponsoldt & Tapper, PA, Stuart, Fla., 1997—; bd. dirs. Regency Affiliates, Denver. V.p. Treas. Coast Leaders, Stuart, 1992-96; active Leadership Martin County, Stuart, 1993-96; mem. bd. adjustments Stuart County, 1993-96; chmn. Stuart Law Libr. Com., 1994—; bd. dirs. Martin County Bd. Code Enforcement. mem. Mem. Martin County Bar Assn. Avocations: sports, reading. Securities, General civil litigation, Construction. Office: Kohl Metzger Spotts PA 50 Kindred St Stuart FL 34994-3040

**PONSOR, MICHAEL ADRIAN,** federal judge; b. Chgo., Aug. 13, 1946; s. Frederick Ward and Helen Yvonne (Richardson) P.; chidren from previous marriage, Anne, Joseph; 1 stepchild, Christian Walker; m. Nancy L. Coiner, June 30, 1996. BA magna cum laude, Harvard Coll., 1969; BA second class honors, Oxford U., 1971, MA, 1979; JD, Yale U., 1975. Bar: Mass., U.S. Dist. Ct. Mass., U.S. Ct. Appeals (1st cir.), U.S. Supreme Ct. Tchr. Kenya Inst. Administrn., Nairobi, 1967-68; law clk. U.S. Dist. Ct., Boston, 1975-76; assoc. Homans, Hamilton, Dahmen & Lamson, Boston, 1976-78; ptnr. Brown, Hart & Ponsor, Amherst, Mass., 1978-83; U.S. magistrate judge U.S. Dist. Ct., Springfield, Mass., 1984-94, U.S. dist. judge, 1994—; adj. prof. Western N.E. Coll. Sch. Law, Springfield, 1988—, Yale Law Sch., New Haven, 1989-91; presenter in field. Rhodes scholar Oxford U., 1969. Mem. Mass. Bar Assn., Hampshire County Bar Assn., Boston Bar Assn. Office: US Dist Ct Rm 539 1550 Main St Springfield MA 01103-1422

**PONTAROLO, MICHAEL JOSEPH,** lawyer; b. Walla Walla, Wash., Sept. 1, 1947; s. Albert and Alice Mary (Fazzari) P.; m. Elizabeth Louise Onley, July 18, 1970; children: Christie, Amy, Nick, Angela. BA, Gonzaga U., 1969, JD, 1973. Bar: Wash. 1973, U.S. Dist. Ct. (ea. dist.) Wash. 1974. Assoc. Mullin & Etter, Spokane, Wash., 1973-74, William Iunker, Spokane, 1974-75, Delay, Curran & Boling, Spokane, 1975-77; prin. Delay, Curran, Thompson & Pontarolo, P.S., Spokane, 1977-97, Delay, Curran, Thompson, Pontarolo & Walker, Spokane, 1997—; mem. Spokane County Med. Legal Com., 1987-88, 91; chmn. liaison com. Superior Ct., 1987-88, 94-97, chair, 1994-95, mem. arbitration bd., 1987—; mem. Bench Bar Com., 1987-88; bd. govs., nom. com., superior ct. judge adv. com. to Gov. Locke, Wa.; adj. prof. Gonzaga U. Sch. Law, 1987—. Bd. dirs. Community Ctrs. Found., Spokane, 1986-89; active Spokane C.C. Legal Secretary Adv. Com.; mem. adv. bd. Spokane C.C., 1992—. Recipient Cert. of Recognition, Superior Ct. Clk., Spokane, 1986. Mem. ABA, Wash. State Bar Assn. (interprofl. com. 1987-90, character and fitness com. 1991-94, com. chair 1993-94, spl. dist. counsel 1984—, mem. jud. recommendation com. 1994-98, co-chair jud. recommendation com. 1996—, chair judicial recommendation com. 1997-98), Wash. State Trial Lawyers Assn. (v.p. east 1979-80, Cert. Appreciation 1982, 90, 92, Leadership award 1984, CLE program chmn. 1984, mem. awards com. 1995-99, chair 1995-96), Assn. Trial Lawyers Am., Spokane County Bar Assn. (v.p., sec.-treas. 1986-89, pres. 1989-90, trustee 1984-86, membership com. chair 1992-93), Alpha Sigma Nu. Workers' compensation, Personal injury, Insurance. Office: Delay Curran Thompson & Pontarolo 601 W Main Ave Ste 1212 Spokane WA 99201-0684

**PONTIFF, PAUL E.,** lawyer; b. Bklyn., June 6, 1930; s. Louis J. and Catherine A. (Menig) P.; m. Judy A. Dufour, June, 13, 1998; children: Kathy Braley, Shawna Braley, Lynn Lafond, Paul L., Thomas M., Matthew J. BBA in Acctg., St. Johns U., N.Y.C., 1954, JD, 1959. Bar: N.Y. 1959, U.S. Tax Ct. 1962, U.S. Dist. Ct. (no. dist.) N.Y. 1974. Acctg. tax mgr. Ball George & Co. CPAs, Glens Falls, N.Y., 1960-62; lawyer Bartlett, Pontiff Stewart & Rhodes PC, Glens Falls, 1962—. Bd. dirs. IACA World Awareness Children's Mus., 1986—. Served with U.S. Army, 1954-56. Mem. Warren County Bar Assn. (pres. 1977-78), Eastate Planning Coun. Eastern N.Y. (v.p. 1999—), Glens Falls Elks, Glens Falls Rotary Club (past pres.). Avocations: mountain climbing, tennis, golf. Corporate taxation, Probate, Contracts commercial. Office: Bartlett Pontiff et al PO Box 2168 One Washington St Glens Falls NY 12801

**POOCK, STEVEN DOYLE,** lawyer; b. Columbus, Ohio, Jan. 21, 1956; m. Mildred Gaviño, Dec. 22, 1990; 1 child, Jesse. BS in Psychology, Miami U., Oxford, Ohio, 1979; MS in Linguistics, San Diego State U., 1988; JD cum laude, Tex. Tech U., 1995. Bar: Tex. 1995, U.S. Dist. Ct. (so. dist.) Tex. 1997. Counselor U. Houston, 1988-94; pvt. practice, Houston, 1995—. Lt. comdr. USN, 1979-86. Mem. ABA, ATLA, State Bar Tex., Tex Trial Lawyers Assn. General civil litigation, Consumer commercial, Real property. Office: PO Box 984 Sugar Land TX 77487-0984

**POOLE, SHARON ALEXANDRA,** lawyer; b. Hollywood, Calif., Jan. 31, 1950; d. James Earl and Lolly L. (Solo) P.; m. Larry E. Greenberger, July 4, 1972 (div. 1983); m. John Oren, Feb. 2, 1996. BS in Communications, Fla. State U., 1977; JD, Stetson Coll., 1980; LLM in Admiralty, Tulane U., 1982; postgrad., Oxford (Eng.) U., 1980. Bar: Fla. 1981, U.S. Dist. Ct. (mid. dist.) Fla. 1982. Ptnr. Cushman & Poole, St. Augustine, Fla., 1982-83; pvt. practice law St. Augustine, 1983—. Bd. dirs., sec. St. Augustine Humane Soc., St. Augustine, 1988—. Mem. Fla. Bar Assn., St. John's Bar Assn. Family and matrimonial, Admiralty, General practice. Office: 10 Mc Millan St # 1 Saint Augustine FL 32084-1618

**POOLER, DELIA BRIDGET,** lawyer; b. Augusta, Maine, Mar. 3, 1963; d. Gerard H. Sr. and Carolyn Luosey Pooler; m. Paul Crowley, Jr., Oct. 15, 1994. Degree in Econs., Harvard U., 1985; JD, U. Maine, Portland, 1989. Bar: Maine, Mass. Law intern, assoc. Black, Lambert, Coffin & Haines, Portland, 1988-90; assoc. Bornstein & Hovermale, Portland, 1990-91; pvt. practice law Portland, 1991—. Regional interviewer Harvard Admissions, Portland, 1993—. Mem. Maine State Bar Assn., Cumberland Bar Assn., Women's Law Sect. Roman Catholic. Personal injury, Pension, profit-sharing, and employee benefits, Workers' compensation. Office: PO Box 7032 Portland ME 04112-7032

**POOLER, ROSEMARY S.,** federal judge; b. 1938. BA, Brooklyn Coll., 1959; MA, Univ. of Conn., 1961; JD, Univ. of Mich. Law Sch., 1965. With Crystal, Manes & Rifken, Syracuse, 1966-69, Michaels and Michaels, Syracuse, 1969-72; asst. corp. counsel Dir. of Consumer Affairs Unit, Syracuse, 1972-73; common counsel City of Syracuse N.Y. Public Interest Rsch. Group, 1974-75; chmn., exec. dir. Consumer Protection Bd., 1975-80; commr. N.Y. State Public Services Commn., 1981-86; staff dir. N.Y. State Assembly, Com. on Corps., Authorities and Commns., 1987-94; judge Supreme Ct., 5th Judicial Dist., 1991-94; district judge U.S. Dist. Ct. (N.Y. no. dist.), 2nd circuit, Syracuse, 1994—; cir. judge U.S. Dist. Ct. (N.Y. no. dist.), 2nd circuit; vis. prof. of law Syracuse Univ. Coll. of Law, 1987-88; v.p. legal affairs Atlantic States Legal Found., 1989-90. Mem. Onondaga County Bar Assn., N.Y. State Bar Assn., Women's Bar Assn. of the State of N.Y., Assn. of Supreme Ct. Justices of the State of N.Y. Office: Federal Bldg PO Box 7395 100 S Clinton St Syracuse NY 13261-6100

**POORE, JAMES ALBERT, III,** lawyer; b. Butte, Mont., June 28, 1943; s. James A. Jr. and Jesse (Wild) P.; m. Shelley A. Borgstede, Feb. 12, 1989; children: James IV, Jeffrey. AB, Stanford U., 1965; JD with honors, U. Mont., 1968. Bar: Mont. 1968, U.S. Dist. Ct. Mont. 1968, U.S. Ct. Appeals (9th cir.) 1972, U.S. Supreme Ct. 1973. Assoc. Poore, Poore, McKenzie & Roth, Butte, 1968-74; prin., v.p. Poore, Roth & Robinson, P.C., Butte, 1974-96; ptnr. Knight, Masar & Poore, LLP, Missoula, Mont., 1996-98, Poore & Hopkins PLLP, Missoula, Mont., 1998—; speaker in field. Assoc. editor U. Mont. Law Rev., 1967-68; contbg. editor Product Liability Desk Reference, 1999—; contbr. articles to profl. publs. Dist. dir. Boy Scouts Am., S.W. Mont., 1969; dir. YMCA, Butte, 1981-83; founding bd. dirs. Hospice of Butte, 1982-85, Butte Community Theater, 1977-80; pres. Butte Uptown Assn., 1974; dir. Butte Silverbow Am. Cancer Soc. Bd., 1992-95. Fellow Am. Bar Found.; mem. ABA, State Bar Mont., Am. Judicature Soc., Silver Bow Bar Assn., Western Mont. Bar Assn., Phi Delta Phi. General civil litigation, Environmental, Native American. Home: 910 Greenough Dr W Missoula MT 59802-3739 Office: Poore & Hopkins PLLP 210 E Pine St Missoula MT 59802-4513

**POORE, SHANNON LEIGH,** lawyer; b. Wurzberg, Germany, June 9, 1969; parents U.S. citizens; d. David Robert and Sandra A. (Guess) P. BA, U. Ark., 1991, JD, 1994. Bar: Ark. 1995, U.S. Dist. Ct. (we. dist.) Ark. 1995. Pvt. practice Fayetteville, Ark., 1995-96; assoc. Nobles, Poore & Jones, P.A., Fayetteville, 1996, Nobles & Poore, Fayetteville, 1997-99, Ball & Mourton, Ltd., PLLC, Fayetteville, 1999—. Mem. Washington County Dem. Ctrl. Com., Fayetteville, 1996-98. Recipient Law Sch. award Bur. Nat. Affairs, 1994. Mem. Washington County Bar Assn., Fayetteville C. of C. Democrat. Avocations: outdoor activities, reading. Family and matrimonial, Juvenile, Criminal. Office: Ball & Mourton Ltd PO Box 1948 Fayetteville AR 72702-1948

**POPE, ANDREW JACKSON, JR. (JACK POPE),** retired judge; b. Abilene, Tex., Apr. 18, 1913; s. Andrew Jackson and Ruth Adelia (Taylor) P.; m. Allene Esther Nichols, June 11, 1938; children: Andrew Jackson III, Walter Allen. BA, Abilene Christian U., 1934, LLD (hon.), 1980; LLB, U. Tex., 1937; LLD (hon.), Pepperdine U., 1981, St. Mary's U., San Antonio,

1982, Okla. Christian U., 1983. Bar: Tex. 1937. Practice law Corpus Christi, Corpus Christi, 1937-46; judge 94th Dist. Ct., Corpus Christi, 1946-50; justice Ct. Civil Appeals, San Antonio, 1950-65; justice Supreme Ct. of Tex., Austin, 1965-82, chief justice, 1982-85. Author: John Berry & His Children, 1988; chmn. bd. editors Appellate Procedure in Tex., 1974; author numerous articles in law revs. and profl. jours. Pres. Met. YMCA, San Antonio, 1956-57; chmn. Tex. State Law Libr. Bd., 1973-80; trustee Abilene Christian U., 1954—. Seaman USNR, 1944-46. Recipient Silver Beaver award Alamo council Boy Scouts Am., 1961, Distinguished Eagle award, 1983; Rosewood Gavel award, 1962, St. Thomas More award, St. Mary's U., San Antonio, 1982; Outstanding Alumnus award Abilene Christian U., 1965; Greenhill Jud. award Mcpl. Judges Assn., 1980; Houston Bar Found. citation, 1985; San Antonio Bar Found. award, 1985; Disting. Jurist award Jefferson County Bar, 1985; Outstanding Alumnus award U. Tex. Law Alumni Assn., 1988; George Washington Honor medal Freedom Found., 1988; Disting. Lawyer award Travis County, 1992. Fellow Tex. Bar Found. (Law Rev. award 1979, 80, 81); mem. ABA, State Bar Tex. (pres. jud. sect. 1962, Outstanding Alumnus 1994, Outstanding Fifty Years Lawyer award 1994), Tex. Bar Found., Order of Coif, Nueces County Bar Assn. (pres. 1946), Travis County Bar Assn., Bexar County Bar Assn., Tex. Philos. Soc., Austin Knife and Fork (pres. 1980), Am. Judicature Soc., Tex. State Hist. Assn., Tex. Supreme Ct. Hist. Soc. (v.p.), Sons of Republic of Tex., Statesmanship award State Bar Tex., 1998, Christian Chronicle Coun. (chmn.), Masons, K.P. (grand chancellor 1946), Alpha Chi, Phi Delta Phi, Pi Sigma Alpha. Mem. Ch. of Christ. Home: 2803 Stratford Dr Austin TX 78746-4626

**POPE, DAVID BRUCE,** lawyer; b. Nov. 15, 1945; s. Thomas Bass and Nathalie Jane (Estill) P.; m. Martha McEvoy, Aug. 26, 1967; children: John Brandon, Nora Katharine. BA, Tex. Tech. U., 1968; JD, U. Houston, 1971. Bar: Tex. 1971, U.S. Ct. Appeals (5th cir.) 1973, U.S. Ct. Appeals (11th cir.) 1981, U.S. Ct. Appeals (10th cir.) 1990, U.S. Supreme Ct. 1975, Colo. 1990. Briefing atty. 1st Ct. Civil Appeals, Houston, 1971-72; assoc. Lynch, Chappel, Allday & Aldridge, Midland, Tex., 1972-76; atty. Texaco, Inc., Houston, 1976-80, Midland, Tex., 1980-82; chief atty. Texaco, Inc., Midland, 1982-84, sr. atty., 1985; sr. atty. Texaco, Inc., Denver, 1989—. Environmental, Oil, gas, and mineral, Administrative and regulatory. Home: 15853 E Crestridge Cir Aurora CO 80015-4215 Office: Texaco Inc 4601 DTC St PO Box 2100 Denver CO 80201-2100

**POPE, HAROLD D.,** lawyer; b. Newton, N.J., Aug. 29, 1955; s. Harold Clark and Gertrude Melvine (Taylor) P.; m. Renay Anita Quarles, Aug. 11, 1979; children: Daman Mitchell, Ebony Aisha. BA summa cum laude, Concordia Coll., Moorhead, Minn., 1976; JD, Duke U., 1980. Bar: N.J. 1980, U.S. Dist. Ct. Mich. 1980, U.S. Ct. Appeals 1982. Assoc. Lamb, Hutchinson, Chappel, Ryan & Harting, Jersey City, 1980-84; assoc. Lewis, White & Clay, P.C., Detroit, 1984-88, shareholder, 1989-94; ptnr. Segue & Fair, Detroit, 1994-95; mem. Segue, Fair, Adams & Pope, Detroit, 1996-98, Adams & Pope, PLLC, 1998-99, Jaffe, Raitt, Heuer & Weiss Profl. Corp., Detroit, 1999—. Bd. dirs. Mich. chpt. Am. Diabetes Assn., 1997—; mem. exec. bd. Detroit Pub. Schs. Student Motivational Program, 1988-90, treas., 1988-89; bd. dirs., Pontiac Area Transitional Housing, sec., 1990-91. Mem. Mich. State Bar Assn., N.J. Bar Assn. (environ. law co.), Garden State Bar Assn. (trustee 1982-84), Wolverine Bar Assn., Nat. Bar Assn. (pres. elect, 1998-99, v.p. region 1994-98, pres. 1999—, exec. com. 1992-94, bd. dirs. 1992-94, chair comml. law sect. 1990-92), Pi Gamma Mu, Alpha Phi Alpha. General civil litigation, Consumer commercial, Product liability. Office: Jaffe Raitt Heuer & Weiss 1 Woodward Ave Ste 2400 Detroit MI 48226

**POPE, HENRY RAY, JR.,** ; b. Franklin, Pa., Oct. 17, 1916; s. Henry Ray and Gail Inda (Bigelow) P.; m. Mary Louise Smith, Dec. 27, 1940; children: Henry Ray III, Kent Smith. BA, MA, Pa. State U., 1938; LLD, U. Pa., 1941. Bar: Pa. 1942, U.S. Dist. Ct. (we. dist.) Pa. 1948, U.S. Supreme Ct. 1961. Hwy. counsel Pa. Dept. Hwys., 1941-45; asst. counsel Pa. Pub. Utility Commn., 1945-48; sole practice Clarion, Pa., 1948-79; judge Ct. Common Pleas of Clarion County, 1979; of counsel Pope & Drayer; lectr. med. and legal seminars. Mem. ABA, Am. Coll. Trial Lawyers and Probate, Clarion County Bar Assn., Pa. Bar Assn. Presbyterian. Administrative and regulatory, Personal injury, Probate. Office: Pope and Drayer 10 Grant St Apt A Clarion PA 16214-1023

**POPE, JOHN WILLIAM,** judge, law educator; b. San Francisco, Mar. 12, 1947; s. William W. and Florence E. (Kline) P.; m. Linda M. Marsh, Oct. 23, 1970 (div. Dec. 1996); children: Justin, Ana, Lauren. BA, U. N.Mex., 1969, JD, 1973. Bar: N.Mex. 1973, U.S. Dist. Ct. N.Mex. 1973, U.S. Ct. Appeals (10th cir.) 1976. Law clk. N.Mex. Ct. of Appeals, Santa Fe, 1973; assoc. Chavez & Cowper, Belen, N.Mex., 1974; ptnr. Cowper, Bailey & Pope, Belen, 1974-75; pvt. practice law Belen, 1976-80; ptnr. Pope, Apodaca & Conroy, Belen, 1980-85; dir. litigation City of Albuquerque, 1985-87; judge State of N.Mex., Albuquerque, 1987-92, Dist. Ct. (13th jud. dist.), N.Mex., 1992—; instr. U. N.Mex., Albuquerque, 1983—, prof. law , 1990—; lectr. in field. Mem. state cen. com. Dem. Party, N.Mex., 1971-85; state chair Common Cause N.Mex., 1980-83; pres. Valencia County Hist. Soc., Belen, 1981-83; active Supreme Ct. Jury (UJI civil instructions com., state bar hist. com., bench and bar com.). Recipient Outstanding Jud. Svc. award N.Mex. State Bar, 1996; named City of Belen Citizen of Yr. 1995, Excellence in Tchg. award 1998. Mem. Valencia County Bar, Albuquerque Bar Assn. Avocations: swimming, golf, photography, historical research. Home: 400 Godfrey Ave Belen NM 87002-6313 Office: Valencia County Courthouse PO Box 1089 Los Lunas NM 87031-1089

**POPE, MARK ANDREW,** lawyer; b. Munster, Ind., May 22, 1952; s. Thomas A. and Eleanor E. (Miklos) P.; m. Julia Risk Pope, June 15, 1974; children: Brent Andrew, Bradley James. BA, Purdue U., 1974; JD cum laude, Ind. U., 1977. Bar: Ind. 1977, U.S. Dist. Ct. (so. dist.) Ind. 1977, U.S. Ct. Appeals (7th cir.) 1984. Assoc. Johnson & Weaver, Indpls., 1977-79, Rocap, Rocap, Reese & Young, Indpls., 1980-82, Dutton & Overman, Indpls., 1982-88; ptnr. Dutton & Overman, 1988-89; asst. gen. counsel Lincoln Nat. Corp., Fort Wayne, Ind., 1989-91, sr. counsel, 1991-95, v.p. govt. rels., 1995—; bd. dirs. Ft. Wayne Bicentennial Coun.; pres., bd. dirs. ARCH, Inc., 1994—. Bd. editors, devel. editor Ind. U. Law Rev., 1976-77. Mem. pres.'s coun. Purdue U., 1977—; applied eoncs. cons. Jr. Achievement, 1989; bd. dirs. Jr. Achievement of No. Ind., 1992-94; pres., bd. dirs. ARCH, Inc., 1995—; grad. Leadership, Fort Wayne, 1992; mem. parish coun. St. Elizabeth Ann Seton Ch., 1993—. Named Disting. Hoosier, Gov. of Ind., 1974. Fellow Ind. Bar Found., Indpls. Bar Found. (disting.); mem. ABA (dist. rep. young lawyers divsn. 1981-83, dir. 1983-84, liaison coord. 1985-86, 87-88, exec. coun. 1981-88, cabinet 1982-88, gen. practice sect. coun. mem. 1986—, membership chmn. 1987-89, chmn. career and family com. 1990-92, dir. 1991—), Indpls. Bar Assn. (v.p. 1983, chmn. young lawyers divsn. 1981), 500 Festival Assocs. (vice-chmn. of 500 festival parade 1985-89), Orchard Ridge Country Club (bd. dirs. 1995—, sec. 1996—). Avocations: tennis, golf, running. Insurance, State civil litigation, General corporate. Office: Lincoln Nat Corp 200 E Berry St Fort Wayne IN 46802-2706

**POPE, ROBERT DANIEL,** lawyer; b. Screven, Ga., Nov. 29, 1948; s. Robert Verlyn and Mae (McKey) P.; children: Robert Daniel Jr., Veronica Teres, Jonathan Chase, Byron Christopher, Jessica Victoria. BS in Criminal Justice magna cum laude, Valdosta (Ga.) State Coll., 1975; JD, John Marshall Law Sch., Savannah, Ga., 1980. Bar: Ga. 1981, U.S. Dist. Ct. (no., mid. and so. dist.) Ga. 1983, U.S. Ct. Appeals Ga. 1982. Pvt. practice Cartersville, 1981—; mem. Valdosta Indigent Def. Atty. Panel, 1981-83, Bartow County Indigent Def. Panel, Cartersville, 1987-91, So. Dist. of Ga. Indigent Def. Panel, Brunswick, 1982-84; mem. Cobb County Cir. Defender's Panel for Indigent Criminal Def., Marietta, Ga., 1986—. Recognized as one of most successful criminal def. lawyers Cobb County Cir. Defenders Office, 1994. Mem. Ga. Assn. Criminal Def. Lawyers, Ga. Bar Assn. (criminal law sect.), Am. Criminal Justice Orgn. (Valdosta chpt. pres. 1974-75). Criminal, Personal injury, Product liability. Home: 74 Spruce Ln SE Cartersville GA 30121-7643 Office: PO Box 1111 Cartersville GA 30120-1111

**POPE, SHAWN HIDEYOSHI,** lawyer; b. Jacksonville, Fla., July 19, 1962; s. Robert George Pope and Michiyo (Nagano) Pope-Griffin. AA with honors, Fla. C.C., Jacksonville, 1983; BBA, U. North Fla., Jacksonville, 1986; JD, Mercer U., Macon, Ga., 1990. Bar: Fla. 1990, U.S. Dist. Ct. (mid. dist.) Fla. 1991, U.S. Ct. Appeals (11th cir.) 1991, U.S. Supreme Ct., 1996. Math. tutor Fla. C.C. of Jax, Jacksonville, 1981-83; heavy equipment operator Sears Roebuck, Jacksonville, 1982-87; actuary technician Am. Heritage Life Ins. Co., Jacksonville, 1986-87; assoc. Boyler, Tanzler & Boyer, P.A., Jacksonville, 1990-91, Penland & Penland, P.A., Jacksonville, 1991-94; pvt. practice Law Office of Shawn H. Pope, Jacksonville, 1994-96, Shawn H. Pope, P.A., Jacksonville, 1997—; pro bono counsel Jax Area Legal Aid, Inc., Jacksonville, 1990—. Coord. United Way, Jacksonville, 1987, Jacksonville Blood Bank, 1986. Mem. ABA, ATLA, Fla. Bar, Jacksonville Bar, Acad. Fla. Trial Lawyers, Phi Delta Phi (vice magister). Avocations: surfing, traveling, fishing, reading, foreign langs. General civil litigation, Personal injury, Workers' compensation. Office: 233 E Bay St Ste 615 Jacksonville FL 32202-3447

**POPE, WILLIAM L.,** lawyer, judge; b. Brownsville, Tex., Nov. 5, 1960; s. William E. and Maria Antonieta P.; m. Sandra Solis, May 16, 1992; children: Ana Lauren, William E.H. AA, Tex. Southmost Coll., 1980; postgrad., U. Tex., 1980-81, Tex. Christian U., 1982, Tex. Coll. Osteo. Medicine, 1982-83; JD, Baylor U., 1986; MD (hon.), Cosmopolitan U. & Rsch. Inst., Vina del Mar, Chile, 1998. Bar: Tex. 1986, U.S. Dist. Ct. (so. dist.) Tex. 1988, U.S. Supreme Ct. 1990. Assoc. Adams & Graham, Harlingen, Tex., 1986-91, ptnr., 1991—; mcpl. ct. judge City of La Feria, Tex., 1987—. Mem. ABA, Tex. State Bar Assn., Cameron County Bar Assn. Mem. Ch. of Christ. General civil litigation, Workers' compensation, Health. Office: Adams & Graham L L P PO Box 1429 Harlingen TX 78551-1429

**POPKIN, ALICE BRANDEIS,** lawyer; b. N.Y.C.; d. Jacob H. and Susan Brandeis Gilbert; m. Jordan J. Popkin; children: Susan Cahn, Anne, Louisa. AB magna cum laude, Radcliffe Coll., 1949; JD, Yale U., 1953. Bar: N.Y. 1953, U.S. Dist. Ct. (so. dist.) N.Y. 1956, U.S. Ct. Appeals (2nd cir.) 1959, U.S. Supreme Ct. 1962, D.C. 1972, Mass. 1987. Assoc. Cahill Gordon & Reindel, 1953-61; dir. internat. programs Peace Corps, 1961-63; project co-dir. Georgetown Inst. Criminal Law and Procedure, 1967-72; spl. counsel Senate Sub-Com. to Investigate Juvenile Delinquency, 1972-74; atty., prof. Antioch Sch. Law, 1974-77; assoc. adminstr. EPA, 1977-79; pvt. practice cons. on internat. environ. issues, 1979-81, practicing atty., 1981-87; of counsel Toabe and Riley, Chatham, Mass., 1987—. Fellow Brandeis U.; bd. trustees Radcliffe Coll.; mem. Chatham Harbor Mgmt. Com.; trustee Eldredge Pub. Libr., 1994—. Mem. Mass. Bar Assn., Barnstable County Bar Assn., Estate Planning Coun. Cape Cod, Planned Giving Coun. Cape Cod. Estate planning, Probate. Office: Toabe & Riley Box 707 154 Crowell Rd Chatham MA 02633-2800

**POPOWITZ, NEIL MICHAEL,** lawyer; b. Bklyn., Nov. 29, 1963; s. Leonard and Rochelle (Garfen) P. AB, U. Calif., Berkeley, 1985; JD, Loyola Marymont U., 1988. Bar: Calif. 1989. Assoc. atty. Rushfeldt, Shelley & Drake, Sherman Oaks, Calif., 1989-90, Fisher & Prager, L.A., 1990-91, Ibold & Anderson, L.A., 1991-92, Dickson, Carlson & Campillo, Santa Monica, Calif., 1992-95, Wilner, Klein & Siegel, Beverly Hills, Calif., 1995-98; sole practitioner L.A., 1998—. Mem. ABA, Fed. Bar Assn., San Fernando Valley Bar Assn., Assn. Bus. Trial Lawyers, L.A. County Bar Assn., Phi Alpha Delta. Democrat. Jewish. Avocations: skiing, photography. General civil litigation, Contracts commercial, Real property. Office: 515 S Flower St Ste 3500 Los Angeles CA 90071-2203

**POPP, GREGORY ALLAN,** lawyer; b. Miami, Fla., Oct. 28, 1948; s. raymond S. and Lila E. Morrow) P.; m. Kimberly Ann Popp, Aug. 16, 1975 (div. Aug. 1996); children: Gregory, Adam; m. Joan Hyde Peterson, Nov. 21, 1996; 1 child, Gregory Adam. AA, Miami-Dade Jr. Coll., Miami, 1968; BA, Fla. Atlantic U., 1972; JD, U. Miami, 1976. Bar: Fla. 1976, U.S. Dist. Ct. (mid. dist.) Fla. 1977. Assoc. Spielvogel Goldman, Merritt Island, Fla., 1976-77; pvt. practice Cocoa, Merritt Island, 1977-86; spl. ptnr., branch mgr. Blackwell, Walker, Melbourne and Miami, 1986-90; assoc. Reinman, Harrell et al, Melbourne, 1991-94; gen. counsel The Heritage Cos., Cape Canaveral, Fla., 1994-98; of counsel Lowndes, Drosdick, Doster, Kantor & Reed, Orlando, 1998—; adj. prof. Embry-Riddle Aero. U., Datona Beach, Fla., 1995—, Webster U., Merritt Island, 1997—, U. Ctrl. Fla., Cocoa, 1991—, Brevard C.C., 1980-93; atty. Brevard County Code Enforcement Bd., 1983-91. Chmn., bd. dirs. Titusville-Cocoa Airport Authority, 1995-98, mem. 1995—; legal officer Merritt Island Sr. Squadron/Civil Air Patrol, 1994—; mem. Brevard County Civilian Mil. Affairs Coun., 1999; pres. Brevard County Legal Aid, Inc., 1984-87, sec.-treas., 1981-84, dir., 1980-87. Mem. The Fla. Bar, Brevard County Bar Assn. (A. Max Brewer Meml. award for cmty. svcs. 1984), Cape Kennedy Area Bd. Realtors (assoc.), Cocoa Beach Boating Club (hon., legal advisor 1977-95), Cocoa Beach Area Ski Club (founder, pres. 1990-93), Aircraft Owners and Pilots Assn. (legal plan panel atty. 1990—), Brevard Aviation Assn. (pres. 1992-94). Republican. Presbyterian. Avocations: flying, sailing, golf, snow and water skiing. Fax: (407) 452-9625. E-mail: gapop@aol.com. General corporate, Real property. Home: 470 Cheyenne Trl Merritt Island FL 32953-7803 Office: Lowndes Drosdick Doster Kantor & Reed 215 N Eola Dr Orlando FL 32801-2095

**POPP, TERI E.,** lawyer; b. Riverhead, N.Y., Oct. 14, 1957; d. Ronald J. and Elsa G. (Bode) Shaw; m. William J. Popp. BA, U. Minn., 1983; JD, Hamline U., 1988. Bar: Minn. 1988, U.S. Dist. Ct. Minn. 1989. Spl. asst. atty. gen. State of Minn., St. Paul, 1988-89; sole practice Golden Valley, Minn., 1989—. Sec. exec. bd. Hamline U., St. Paul, 1996—, trustee, 1995—; chmn. symphony ball WAMSO-Minn. Orch. Vol. Assn., 1998, v.p. membership com. 1995-97; troop leader Greater Mpls. coun. U. S. Girl Scouts, 1992—, svc. unit mgr. Prairie Stars svc. unit, 1993-95; chmn. New Year's Eve gala for Salvation Army, Harbor Light Endowment Fund and Greater Twin Cities Youth Symphonies, 1994-96. Mem. ABA, Minn. State Bar Assn. Avocations: volunteer work, cross-stitch, computers. Labor. Office: 620 Mendelssohn Ave N Golden Valley MN 55427-4310

**POPPER, ROBERT,** law educator, former dean; b. N.Y.C., May 22, 1932; s. Walter G. and Dorothy B. (Kluger) P.; m. Mary Ann Schaefer, July 12, 1963; children: Julianne, Robert Gregory. BS, U. Wis., 1953; LLB, Harvard U., 1956; LLM, NYU, 1963. Bar: N.Y. 1957, U.S. Dist. Ct. (so. dist.) N.Y. 1962, U.S. Ct. Appeals (2d cir.) 1962, U.S. Supreme Ct. 1962, U.S. Dist. Ct. (ea. dist.) N.Y. 1969, U.S. Ct. Appeals (7th cir.) 1970, U.S. Ct. Appeals (8th cir.) 1971, Mo. 1971, U.S. Dist. Ct. (we. dist.) Mo. 1973. Trial atty. criminal br. N.Y.C. Legal Aid Soc., 1960-61; asst. dist. atty. N.Y. County, 1961-64; assoc. Seligson & Morris, N.Y.C., 1964-69; mem. faculty School of Law, U. Mo., Kansas City, 1969-96, prof., 1973-96, acting dean, 1983-84, dean, 1984-93, dean and prof. emeritus, 1996—; cons. and lectr. in field. Author: Post Conviction Remedies in a Nutshell, 1978, De-Nationalizing the Bill of Rights, 1979; contbr. articles to profl. jours. Fellow ABA; mem. Mo. Bar, Kansas City Met. Bar Assn., Mo. Inst. of Justice. Home: 6229 Summit St Kansas City MO 64113-1556 Office: U Mo Kansas City Sch Law 500 E 52nd St Kansas City MO 64110-2467

**POPPLER, DORIS SWORDS,** lawyer; b. Billings, Mont., Nov. 10, 1924; d. Lloyd William and Edna (Mowre) Swords; m. Louis E. Poppler, June 11, 1949; children: Louis William, Kristine, Mark J., Blaine, Claire, Arminda. Student, U. Minn., 1942-44; JD, Mont. State U., 1948. Bar: Mont. 1948, U.S. Dist. Ct. Mont. 1948, U.S. Ct. Appeals (9th cir.) 1990. Pvt. practice law Billings, 1948-49; sec., treas. Wonderpark Corp., Billings, 1959-62; atty. Yellowstone County Attys. Office, Billings, 1972-75; ptnr. Poppler and Barz, Billings, 1972-79, Davidson, Veeder, Baugh, Broeder and Poppler, Billings, 1979-84, Davidson and Poppler, P.C., Billings, 1984-90; U.S. atty. Dist. of Mont., Billings, 1990-93; field rep. Nat. Indian Gaming Commn., Washington, 1993—. Pres. Jr. League, 1964-65; bd. dirs., pres. Yellowstone County Metre Bd., 1982; trustee Rocky Mt. Coll., 1984-90, mem. nat. adv. bd., 1993—; mem. Mont. Human Rights Commn., 1988-90; bd. dirs. Miss Mont. Pageant, 1995—. Recipient Mont. Salute to Women award, Mont. Woman of Achievent award, 1975, Disting. Svc. award Rocky Mt. Coll., 1990, 1st ann. U. Montana Law Sch. Disting. Female Alumna award, 1996. Mem. AAUW, Mont. Bar Assn., Nat. Assn. Former U.S. Attys., Nat. Rep. Lawyers Assn., Internat. Women's Forum, Yellowstone County Bar Assn. (pres. 1990), Alpha Chi Omega. Republican. Office: Nat Indian Gaming Commn 1441 L St NW Fl 9 Washington DC 20005-3512

**POPPLETON, MILLER JOHN,** lawyer; b. Bethesda, Md., Mar. 18, 1950; s. Miller John and Dorothy May (Hood) P.; m. Janet Perry, Mar. 30, 1999; children: Ashley Lynn, Aubrey Paige. AA, U. Charleston, 1972, BA, 1974; JD, Cath. U. of Am., 1977. Bar: Va. 1977, Md. 1978, D.C. 1979; U.S. Dist. Ct. Md. 1978, U.S. Dist. Ct. D.C. 1979, U.S. Dist. Ct. Va. 1978, U.S. Ct. Appeals (D.C. cir.) 1979, U.S. Ct. Appeals (4th cir.) 1978; U.S. Supreme Ct. 1977; U.S. Ct. of Claims, 1978. Atty. Protas & Spivok, Bethesda, 1977-82, prin., ptnr., 1982-95; sr. ptnr. Poppleton, Garrett & Polott, Bethesda, 1995—. Vice-pres. Luth. Ch. Shephard's Care, Olney, Md., 1997. With USN, 1967-73. Mem. Bar Assn. of Montgomery County, Md., Bar Assn. of Fairfax County, Va. Democrat. Lutheran. Avocations: restoration of classic automobiles, snow skiing, carpentry. E-mail: mpoppleton@p6plaw.com. Contracts commercial, Construction, General civil litigation. Home: 5719 Stanbrook Ln Laytonsville MD 20882-1715 Office: Poppleton Garrett & Polott 6430 Rockledge Dr Ste 500 Bethesda MD 20817-1886

**PORCELLI, FRANK PAUL,** lawyer; b. Wilmington, Del., Sept. 15, 1947; s. Attilio F. and Evelyn S. (Feingold) P.; m. Carol M. Stenger Porcelli, Sept. 29, 1972; children: Regan, Erik, Ryan. AB in English Lit., Boston Coll., Chestnut Hill, Mass., 1968; JD, Harvard U., 1971; MS in Chemistry, Northeastern U., 1981. Bar: Mass. 1971, Del. Assoc. Fish & Richardson, Boston, 1971-78, ptnr., 1979-94; prin. Fish & Richardson PC, Boston, 1995—; vis. prof. intellectual property law, Harvard Law Sch., Cambridge, Mass., 1999. Co-author: (book chpt.) State Trademark and Unfair Competition Law, 1987; contbr. articles to profl. jours. Capt. U.S. Army Res., 1968-73. Mem. ABA, Am. Intellectual Property Law Assn., Fed. Ct. Bar Assn., Boston Patent Law Assn. Avocations: golf, running, downhill skiing, history, spectator of college football and basketball. Office: Fish & Richardson PC 225 Franklin St Fl 32 Boston MA 02110-2809

**PORES, JOEL MICHAEL,** lawyer; b. Bklyn., Aug. 9, 1951. BA, Bklyn. Coll., 1973; JD, Pepperdine U., 1976. Bar: Calif., U.S. Ct. Appeals (4th dist.) Calif. Sole practice Newport Beach, Calif., 1985—; presiding arbitrator State Bar Calif., L.A., 1997—. Contbr. articles to profl. jours. Mem. Calif. Bar Assn. (co-chmn. client rels. com. 1992—; presiding arbitrator mandatory fee arbitration com. 1992—; ethics professionalism com., L.A. 1997—). Professional liability, Personal injury. Office: 110 Newport Center Dr Newport Beach CA 92660-6902

**PORFILIO, JOHN CARBONE,** federal judge; b. Denver, Oct. 14, 1934; s. Edward Alphonso Porfilio and Caroline (Carbone) Moore; m. Joan West, Aug. 1, 1959 (div. 1983); children: Edward Miles, Joseph Arthur, Jeanne Kathrine; m. Theresa Louise Berger, Dec. 28, 1983; 1 stepchild, Katrina Ann Smith. Student, Stanford U., 1952-54; BA, U. Denver, 1956, LLB, 1959. Bar: Colo. 1959, U.S. Supreme Ct. 1965. Asst. atty. gen. State of Colo., Denver, 1962-68, dep. atty. gen., 1968-72, atty. gen., 1972-74; U.S. bankruptcy judge Dist. of Colo., Denver, 1975-82; judge U.S. Dist. Ct. Colo., Denver, 1982-85, U.S. Ct. Appeals (10th cir.), Denver, 1985—; instr. Colo. Law Enforcement Acad., Denver, 1965-70, State Patrol Acad., Denver, 1968-70; guest lectr. U. Denver Coll. Law, 1978. Committeeman Arapahoe County Republican Com., Aurora, Colo., 1968; mgr. Dunbar for Atty. Gen., Denver, 1970. Mem. ABA. Roman Catholic. Office: US Ct Appeals Byron White US Courthouse 1823 Stout St Denver CO 80257-1823

**PORITZ, DEBORAH T.,** state supreme court chief justice, former attorney general. Atty. gen. State of N.J., 1994-96; chief justice Supreme Ct. N.J., Trenton, 1996—. Office: Supreme Ct NJ Richard J Hughes Complex CN 023 Trenton NJ 08625-0023*

**PORTELLO, WILLIAM LESLIE, III,** lawyer; b. San Francisco, Dec. 20, 1965; s. William Leslie and Mary Alison Portello; m. Cammie Christine La Rue, Oct. 3, 1998. BA in History, U. Calif., Davis, 1989; JD, U. Oreg., 1993. Bar: Calif. 1993, U.S. Dist. Ct. (ea. dist.) Calif. 1993, Oreg. 1994. Pvt. practice law Davis, 1993-95; assoc. Thompson, Meade and Nielsen, Sacramento, 1995-97; sr. assoc. Guichard, Jones and Tarkoff, Sacramento, 1997—. Commr. Davis Sr. Citizens Commn., 1994—. Mem. Rotary Club Davis-Sunrise. Avocations: American history, skiing, fishing. State civil litigation, Personal injury, Insurance. Office: Guichard Jones and Tarkoff 400 Capitol Mall Fl 11 Sacramento CA 95814-4407

**PORTEOUS, G. THOMAS, JR.,** judge; b. 1946. BA, La. State U., 1968, JD, 1971. Spl. counsel, atty. gen., 1971-73; asst. dist. atty. Dist. Atty. Office Parrish of Jefferson, 1973-75; ptnr. Edward, Porteous & Amato, Grenta, La., 1973-74, Edwards, Porteous & Lee, Grenta, 1974-76, Porteous, Lee & Mustakas, 1976-80, Porteous & Mustakas, Metairie, La., 1980-84; city atty. City of Harahan, La., 1982-84; dist. ct. judge divsn. A State of La., 1984-94; dist. judge U.S. Dist. Ct. (ea. dist.), La., 1994—. Mem. ABA, Fed. Bar Assn., La. State Bar Assn., 4th and 5th Cir. Judges Assn., Jefferson Bar Assn., Am. Judges Assn., La. Dist. Atty. Assn. Office: US Dist Ct E Dist LA 500 Camp St Rm C-206 New Orleans LA 70130-3313

**PORTER, CHARLES, JR.,** writer, mediator, business executive; b. Austin, Tex., Oct. 31, 1951; s. Charles R. and Ruby S. Porter; children: Chuck, David, Mary Margaret. B of Bus. in Fin., U. Tex., 1974; student, Dispute Resolution Ctr., Austin, 1993. Exec. v.p. Unicenter Properties, Inc., Houston, 1977-81; pres. Porter Plumb, Inc., Houston, 1981-92; pres., chmn. Houston Data Transmission, 1988-92; pres. Judgment Svcs. Co., Austin, 1992—. Author: How to Collect Your Judgment in Texas, 1998, How to Collect Hot Checks in Texas, 1998, Preparing for Small Claims Court for Non-Attorneys, 1998. Mem. Austin Assn. Mediators, Soc. Cert. Debt Collectors, Ex Students Assn. U. Tex. (bd. dirs. 1987-90), Omicron Delta Kappa, Phi Gamma Delta. Office: 2630 Exposition Blvd Ste G16 Austin TX 78703-1757

**PORTER, J. ANDREW,** lawyer; b. Macon, Ga., Sept. 9, 1947; s. Truett A. and Cleo C. P.; m. Mary Lynn Porter, Apr. 28, 1979; children: Shelley, Beth. BA, Wake Forest U., 1969, JD, 1975. Bar: N.C.; U.S. Dist. Ct. (mid. and we. dists. N.C.) 1975, U.S. Ct. Appeals (4th cir.). Assoc. Sanders & London, Charlotte, N.C., 1975-86, Crowell & Porter, Salisbury, N.C., 1986—; v.p. Rowan County Bar Assn., Salisbury, N.C., 1991, pres. 1992. Chmn. bd. trustees 1st Bapt., Salisbury, 1992; bd. dirs., legal advisor Good Shepards Clinic, Salisbury, 1994—; pres. CHADD, Salisbury, 1992-94. Estate planning, General corporate, General practice. Office: Crowell & Porter 120 N Jackson St Salisbury NC 28144-4235

**PORTER, JAMES KENNETH,** retired judge; b. Newport, Tenn., Apr. 6, 1934; s. John Calhoun and Bessie Betis (Crouch) P.; m. Evelyn Janet Rhodes, Sept. 17, 1955; children: Jane Caroline, James Kenneth Jr. BS, U. Tenn., 1955, JD, 1957. Bar: Tenn. 1957, U.S. Dist. Ct. (ea. dist.) Tenn. 1958, U.S. Ct. Appeals (6th cir.) 1971. Ptnr. Porter, Porter & Dunn, Porter & Porter, Newport, 1957-74; state rep. Tenn. Gen. Assembly, Nashville, 1961-65, minority fl. leader, 1963-65; county atty. Cocke County, Tenn., 1961-63, commr. County Election Commn., 1966-72, chmn., 1968-70; mem. Tenn. Senate, Nashville, 1972-74; state cir. judge 4th Jud. Cir., Newport, 1974-93; ret., 1993; state presiding judge 4th Jud. Cir., Newport, 1984-86, 88-90, 1992-93; judgeship nominee U.S. Dist. Ct. (ea. dist.), Tenn., 1986; Tenn. Ct. Appeals nominee, 1990; del. S.E. Law Rev. Conf., Durham, N.C., 1957, Nat. Conf. State Legislator Leaders, Boston, 1963; discussion leader Nat. Jud. Coll., Reno, 1981, faculty adviser, 1982; mem. Gov.'s Correction Overcrowding Commn., Nashville, 1985-86. Contbr. articles to U. Tenn. Law Rev., 1956-57, editor in chief, 1957. Active Farm Bur., 1962-82; mem. adv. coun., trustee Walters State Community Coll., Morristown, Tenn., 1975-86. Mem. ABA (Tenn. jud. del. 1984), Tenn. Jud. Conf. (v.p. 1980-81), Tenn. Trial Judges Assn. (bd. dirs. 1976-86, pres. 1982-85), Tenn. Bar Assn. (spl. trial counsel 1973-76), Cocke County Bar Assn., Smoky Mountain Country Club (bd. dirs. 1964-67, v.p. 1966-67), Order of Coif, Sigma Alpha Epsilon (Highest Effort Law award 1986), Phi Delta Phi. Republican. Baptist. Avocations: golf, gardening, guitar. Home: 306 North St Newport TN 37821-2413 Office: 106 S Mims Ave Newport TN 37821-3125

**PORTER, JAMES MORRIS,** judge; b. Cleve., Sept. 14, 1931; s. Emmett Thomas and Mary (Connell) P.; m. Helen Marie Adams, May 31, 1952; children: James E., Thomas W., William M., Daniel J. A.B., John Carroll U., 1953; J.D., U. Mich., 1957. Bar: Ohio 1957. Assoc. firm M.B. & H.H. Johnson, Cleve., 1957-62, McAfee, Hanning, Newcomer, Hazlett & Wheeler, Cleve., 1962-67; ptnr. firm Squire, Sanders & Dempsey, Cleve., 1967-92; judge Ohio Ct. Appeals, 8th Dist., Cleve., 1993—. 1st lt. U.S. Army, 1953-55. Fellow Am. Coll. Trial Lawyers; mem. Best Lawyers in Am., Union

Club, The Club, The Country Club (Cleve.). Republican. Roman Catholic. Office: Lakeside Courthouse Ct Appeals Lakeside Ave Cleveland OH 44113-1082

**PORTER, JAMES SCOTT,** lawyer; b. Syracuse, N.Y., Sept. 3, 1959; s. James Franklin and Janice Litchfield P.; m. Susan Clark, Jan. 16, 1993; 1 child, Catherine Clare. BA in Broadcasting & History, SUNY, Oswego, 1981; JD, Syracuse U., 1985. Bar: N.Y. 1988, U.S. Ct. Appeals (2d cir.) 1987, U.S. Dist. Ct. (we. dist.) N.Y. 1987, U.S. Dist. Ct. (no. dist.) N.Y. 1991, U.S. Supreme Ct. 1995. Staff atty. Niagara County Legal Aid Soc., Niagara Falls, N.Y., 1986-87; atty. Frank Hiclock Legal Aid Soc., Syracuse, N.Y., 1987-91, pvt. practice, Syracuse and Seneca Falls, N.Y., 1991—. Niagara County Legal Aid Soc. fellow, 1985-86. Mem. Nat. Assn. Criminal Defense Lawyers, N.Y. State Bar Assn. Independent. Roman Catholic. Criminal, Appellate, Juvenile. Home: 1 Elwell St Seneca Falls NY 13148-1260 Office: PO Box 365 141 Fall St Seneca Falls NY 13148-1511

**PORTER, JOSEPH EDWARD, III,** lawyer, music recording industry consultant; b. Kansas City, Kans., Feb. 15, 1946; s. Joseph Edward Porter Jr.; m. Christina Leslie Braysher; 1 child, Jospeh Edward IV. BS, Calif. State U., L.A., 1968; JD, U. So. Calif., 1971. Bar: Calif. 1972, D.C. 1980, U.S. Ct. Appeals (9th cir.) 1972, U.S. Dist. Ct. (ctrl. dist.) Calif. 1972, U.S. Dist. Ct. (so. dist.) Calif. 1978, U.S. Dist. Ct. Hawaii 1997, U.S. Supreme Ct. 1978. Assoc. Kaplan Livingston Goodman & Beck, Beverly Hills, Calif., 1971; asst to chmn. bd. Motown Records, Hollywood, Calif., 1971-73; dir. bus. affairs Am. Internat. Pictures, Beverly Hills, Calif., 1973-75; pvt. practice Beverly Hills, Calif., 1975-85, Seal Beach, Calif., 1985—. Contbr. articles to profl. jours. Trustee Westerly Sch. Long Beach, Calif., 1997; mem. Environ. Quality Control Bd., Seal Beach, 1998; v.p. Human Rels. Commn., L.A., 1980-82. 2d lt. USMC, 1966-68. Mem. Black Entertainment and Sports Lawyers Assn. (founder, dir. 1975—), Black Am. Law Students Assn. (founder 1968), KC (dist. dep. 1989-91, Man of Yr. 1991). Avocations: golf, family, reading, cycling. Entertainment, Criminal. Office: 206 3rd St Seal Beach CA 90740-6009

**PORTER, KIRBY HUGH,** lawyer; b. Oklahoma City, Okla., May 5, 1960; s. H. Hugh and Marguerite Nokes Porter; m. Jennifer Mary Nelson, May 22, 1993; children: Christine Victoria, John (Jack) Kirby. BS, Radford (Va.) U., 1982; JD, George Mason U., 1988. Bar: Va. 1989, U.S. Ct. Appeals (4th cir.) 1989, U.S. Dist. Ct. (ea. dist.) Va. 1989, U.S. Ct. Appeals (D.C. cir.) 1990, U.S. Supreme Ct. 1995. Assoc. Lukas, McGowan, Nace & Gutierrez, Washington, 1989-90; asst. Commonwealth's Atty.'s Office, City of Richmond, 1990-92; sr. asst. Commonwealth's Atty.'s Office, City of Hanover, Va., 1992-95; assoc. Duane and Shannon, P.C., Richmond, 1995—; instr. Hanover County Sheriff's Office, 1992—. Mem. Hanover Ruritan, Hanover, 1998—, Mechanicsville (Va.) Businessmens Assn., 1998—. Mem. Hanover Bar Assn., Richmond Bar Assn., Richmond Criminal Bar Assn., Ashland/Hanover C. of C. Republican. Methodist. Avocations: community volunteer, woodworking, camping. Criminal, General civil litigation. Home: 7132 Mill Valley Rd Mechanicsville VA 23111-5219 Office: Duane and Shannon PC 10 E Franklin St Richmond VA 23219-2131

**PORTER, MICHAEL PELL,** lawyer; b. Indpls., Mar. 31, 1940; s. Harold Troxel and Mildred Maxine (Pell) P.; m. Alliene Laura Jenkins, Sept. 23, 1967 (div.); 1 child, Genevieve Natalie, Porter Eason; m. Janet Kay Smith Hayes, Feb. 13, 1983 (div.). Student, DePauw U., 1957-58; BA, Tulane U., 1961, LLB, 1963. Bar: La. 1963, U.S. Ct. Mil. Appeals 1964, N.Y. 1969, Hawaii 1971. Clk. U.S. Ct. Appeals (5th cir.), New Orleans, 1963; assoc. Sullivan & Cromwell, N.Y.C., 1968-71; assoc. Cades Schutte Fleming & Wright, Honolulu, 1971-74, ptnr., 1975-94; mem. faculty Addis Ababa (Ethiopia) U. Sch. Law, 1995-99; sr. regulatory advisor Egyptian Capital Market Authority, Cairo, 1999—; legal advisor St. Matthews Anglican Ch. Addis Ababa, 1995-99; cons. Rep. of Yemen, 1997; mem. deans coun. Law Sch. Tulane U., 1981-88; dep. vice chancellor Episcopal Diocese Hawaii, 1980-88, chancellor, 1988-94; chancellor Episcopal Ch., Micronesia, 1988-95. Author: Hawaii Corporation Law & Practice, 1989; Hawaii reporter State Limited Partnership Laws, 1992-94. Bd. dirs. Jr. Achievement Hawaii, Inc., 1974-84, Inst. Human Svcs., Inc., 1980-88; donor Michael P. Porter Dean's Scholarstic Award, U. Hawaii Law Sch., 1977—. With JAGC, U.S. Army, 1963-66, Vietnam. Fulbright scholar, 1997-99; Tulane U. fellow, 1981; lectorship named in his honor, Addis Abba, 1994-97; established Michael P. Porter Prizes on Ethnic Harmony and Religious Tolerance in a Dem. Soc. at Addis Ababa, 1995. Mem. ABA, Hawaii State Bar Assn. Republican. General corporate, Securities.

**PORTER, ROBERT CARL, JR.,** lawyer; b. Cin., Sept. 21, 1927; s. Robert Carl and Lavinia (Otte) P.; m. Joanne Patterson, July 5, 1952; children: Robert Carl III, David M., John E. BA with distinction, U. Mich., 1949; JD, Harvard U., 1952. Bar: Ohio 1952, U.S. Dist. Ct. (so. dist.) Ohio 1954, U.S. Ct. Appeals (6th cir.) 1954, U.S. Ct. Mil. Appeals 1956, U.S. Supreme Ct. 1956, U.S. Tax Ct. 1980. Ptnr., Porter & Porter, Cin., 1953-54; sole practice, Cin. 1954-63; sr. ptnr. Porter & McKinney, Cin., 1963-88; sr. ptnr. Porter & Porter, 1989—; dir. and officer numerous cos.. Served with JAGC, USAF, 1952-53. Mem. ABA, Ohio State Bar Assn., Cin. Bar Assn., Phi Beta Kappa. Presbyterian. Clubs: Cin. Country, University, U. Mich., Harvard Law Sch. Assn., Masons (Scottish Rite), Shriners (Cin.). Probate, General corporate, Taxation, general. Home: 2365 Bedford Ave Cincinnati OH 45208-2656 Office: Porter & Porter 2100 4th and Vine Tower Cincinnati OH 45202

**PORTER, VERNA LOUISE,** lawyer; b. May 31, 1941. BA, Calif. State U., 1963; JD, Southwestern U., 1977. Bar: Calif. 1977, U.S. Dist. Ct. (ctrl. dist.) Calif. 1978, U.S. Ct. Appeals (9th cir.) 1978. Ptnr. Eisler & Porter, L.A., 1978-79, mng. ptnr., 1979-86; pvt. practice, 1986—; judge pro-tempore L.A. Mcpl. Ct., 1983—, L.A. Superior Ct., 1989—, Beverly HIlls Mcpl. Ct., 1992—; mem. subcom. landlord tenant law, State Calif., panelist conv.; mem. real property law sect. Calif. State Bar, 1983; mem. client rels. panel, vol. L.A. County Bar Dispute Resolution; ct. appointed arbitrator civil cases, fee arbitrator L.A. Superior Ct. Editl. asst., contbr. Apt. Bus. Outlook, Real Property News, Apt. Age. Mem. adv. coun. Freddie Mac Vendor, 1995—; mem. World Affairs Coun. Mem. ABA, L.A. County Bar Assn. (client-rels. vol. dispute resolution fee arbitration 1981—), L.A. Trial Lawyers Assn. Wilshire Bar Assn. Women Lawyers' Assn., Landlord Trial Lawyers Assn. (founding, pres.), Camera Soc. Republican. Real property, Landlord-tenant, Consumer commercial. Office: 2500 Wilshire Blvd Ste 1226 Los Angeles CA 90057-4365

**PORTMAN, GLENN ARTHUR,** lawyer; b. Cleve., Dec. 26, 1949; s. Alvin B. and Lenore (Marsh) P.; m. Katherine Seaborn, Aug. 3, 1974 (div. 1984); m. Susan Newell, Jan. 3, 1987. BA in History, Case Western Res. U., 1968; JD, So. Meth. U., 1975. Bar: Tex. 1975, U.S. Dist. Ct. (no. dist.) Tex. 1975, U.S. Dist. Ct. (so. dist.) Tex. 1983, U.S. Dist. Ct. (we. and ea. dists.) Tex. 1988. Assoc. Johnson, Bromberg & Leeds, Dallas, 1975-80, ptnr., 1980-92; ptnr. Arter, Hadden, Johnson & Bromberg, Dallas, 1992-95, Arter & Hadden LLP, Dallas, 1996—; chmn. bd. dirs. Physicians Regional Hosp., 1994-96; mem. exec. bd. So. Meth. U. Sch. Law, 1994-99; lectr. bankruptcy topics South Tex. Coll. Law, State Bar Tex. Asst. editor-in-chief Southwestern Law Jour., 1974-75; contbr. articles to profl. jours. Firm rep. United Way Met. Dallas, 1982-92; treas. Lake Highlands Square Homeowners Assn., 1990-93. Mem. ABA, Am. Bankruptcy Inst., State Bar Tex. Assn., Dallas Bar Assn., So. Meth. U. Law Alumni Assn. (council bd. dirs., v.p. 1980-86, chmn. admissions com., chmn. class agt. program 1986-89, chmn. fund raising 1989-91), 500 Club Inc., Assemblage Club. Republican. Methodist. Real property, Bankruptcy, Contracts commercial. Home: 9503 Winding Ridge Dr Dallas TX 75238-1451 Office: Arter & Hadden 1717 Main St Ste 4100 Dallas TX 75201-7389

**PORTMAN, MARK E.,** lawyer, mediator; b. Cleve., Mar. 16, 1951; s. Harry S. and Beatrice P.; m. Jan Simmons, Apr. 10, 1994; 1 child, Allison. BA, Ohio State U., 1973; JD, Case Western Res. U., 1976. Bar: Calif. 1977. Legal aid atty. San Jose (Calif.) Legal Aid, 1977-79; pvt. practice DiFranza & Portman, San Jose, 1980-94; law and mediation family law practice San Francisco, 1994—. Co-author: (legislation) Domestic Violence Prevention Laws, 1978, (court rules) Family Court, 1981. Pro bono svc. Santa Clara Pro Bono Project, San Jose, 1982-94. Mem. Santa Clara County Bar (leader 1977-94), No. Calif. Mediation Assn. (bd. dirs. 1997-99, treas. 1997-99), Acad. Family Mediators. Family and matrimonial. Office: PO Box 5758 Novato CA 94948-5758

**PORTMAN, SUSAN NEWELL,** lawyer; b. El Dorado, Kans., Sept. 12, 1953; d. Richard and Denise (Beaudequin) Newell; m. Glenn A. Portman, Jan. 2, 1987. BS in Math., U. Okla., 1975; JD summa cum laude, Am. U., 1982. Bar: Tex. 1983, U.S. Dist. Ct. (no. dist.) Tex. 1983. Math. statistician U.S. Dept. Labor Bur. Labor Statistics, Washington, 1975-76; assoc. Johnson, Bromberg & Leeds, Dallas, 1983-87; div. counsel Nat. Gypsum Co., Dallas, 1987-88, corp. counsel, 1988-91, sr. corp. counsel and asst. sec., 1991-93. Treas. Lake Highlands Square Homeowners Assn., Dallas, 1991-93. Named Deans fellow Am. U., recipient Mussey Prize. Mem. So. Meth. U. Sch. Law Corp. Coun., 500 Inc. Club, Pi Mu EPsilon, Alpha Lambda Delta. Democrat. Presbyterian. Antitrust, Contracts commercial, Securities. Home and Office: 9503 Winding Ridge Dr Dallas TX 75238-1451

**PORTNOY, ELLIOTT IVAN,** lawyer; b. Morgantown, W.Va., Nov. 1, 1965; s. Donald Charles and Enid Joan (Pallant) P.; m. Estee Renee Mermelstein, Sept. 6, 1992; 1 child, Joshua Brandon. BA, Syracuse U., 1986; JD, Harvard U., 1992; DPhil, Oxford (Eng.) U., 1995. Bar: Md. 1992, D.C. 1993. Staff asst., cons. dem. policy com. U.S. Senate, Washington, 1985-88; assoc. Arent Fox Kintner Plotkin & Kahn, Washington, 1992—; atty. Clinton-Gore presdl. transition, Washington, 1992-93. Author: Guide to Congress, 1991. Founder, pres. bd. dirs. Kids Enjoy Exercise Now Found., Washington, Oxford, 1987—; bd. dirs. Jewish Social Svcs. Agy., Washington, 1996—; exec. com. Dem. Young Lawyers Com., Washington, 1996—. Rhodes scholar, 1986. Government contracts and claims, Education and schools. Home: 11305 Commonwealth Dr North Bethesda MD 20852 Office: Arent Fox Kintner Plotkin & Kahn 1050 Connecticut Ave NW Ste 500 Washington DC 20036-5339

**PORTO, STEVEN MICHAEL,** lawyer; b. Des Moines, Sept. 2, 1952; s. Anthony Francis and Genevieve (Greco) P. Student, Regis Coll., 1970-71, Loyola U., Rome, 1971-72; BA, Creighton U., 1974, postgrad., 1974-75; JD, Drake U., 1977. Bar: Iowa 1977, U.S. Dist. Ct. (so. dist.) Iowa 1978. Pvt. practice Polk County, Iowa, 1977—. Mem. ABA (internat. law practice sect.), Iowa Bar Assn. (com. prepaid legal svcs. 1986-88). Avocations: ice hockey, bicycling, skiing. Office: 1200 Valley West Dr Ste 407 West Des Moines IA 50266-1905

**POSCH, ROBERT JOHN, JR.,** lawyer; b. Levittown, N.Y., Feb. 24, 1950; s. Robert John and Maryrose (Finnegan) P.; m. Mary Lou Collins, July 28, 1974; children: Judith Ann, Robert III, Eric. BA, Manhattan Coll., 1972; JD, Hofstra U., 1975, MBA, 1981. Bar: N.Y. 1977, U.S. Ct. Appeals (2d cir.) 1977. Legal asst. Doubleday & Co., Inc., Garden City, N.Y., 1975-77; staff counsel Doubleday & Co., Inc., Garden City, 1977-82, assoc. counsel, 1982-87; sec., counsel Doubleday Book & Music Clubs, Inc., Garden City, 1987-99; v.p. legal postal and govt. affairs Crossings, Doubleday Online, DSI and Lit. Express, Garden City, 1989—; instr. Nassau C.C., Hempstead, N.Y., 1984—; mem. adv. bd. real estate symposium Hofstra U.; bd. dirs. Crossings, Inc.; v.p. Literary Express sect. Profl. Book Clubs Inc. Author: Direct Marketer's Legal Adviser, 1983, What Every Manager Needs to Know About Marketing and the Law, 1984, Marketing and the Law, 1988, Cumulative Supplement, 1989, 90, (with others) The Direct Marketing Handbook, 1984, 91; columnist: Direct Marketing, 1981—; contbr. articles to profl. jours.; speaker in field. Mem. ABA, Am. Corp. Counsel Assn. (newsletter editor 1988-92, bd. dirs. Greater N.Y. chpt.), Third Class Mail Assn. (bd. dirs. and exec. comm.), Direct Mktg. Assn. (privacy, use tax and legal lobbying groups, various coms. 1986—), Christian Legal Soc., Nassau Bar Assn. (various coms. 1977—, AAP Postal Affairs), L.I. Assn., N.Y. State Bus. Coun., Alpha Mu Alpha, Beta Gamma Sigma. Republican. General corporate, Antitrust, Entertainment. Home: 3151 Grand Blvd Baldwin NY 11510-4826 Office: Doubleday Direct 401 Franklin Ave Ste 100 Garden City NY 11530-5945

**POSCOVER, MAURY B.,** lawyer; b. St. Louis, Jan. 13, 1944; s. Edward and Ann (Chapnick) P.; m. Lorraine Wexler, Aug. 14, 1966; children: Michael, Daniel, Joanna. BA, Lehigh U., 1966; JD, Washington U., 1969. Bar: Mo. 1969. Assoc. Husch & Eppenberger, St. Louis, 1969-75, ptnr., 1975—; lectr. Washington U., St. Louis, 1972-79. Editor-in-chief: The Business Lawyer, 1995-96; contbr. articles to profl. jours. Bd. dirs. Childhaven, St. Louis, 1978-92, pres. 1986; pres. Jewish Community Rels. Coun., 1990-92. Mem. ABA (bd. govs. 1999—, chmn. comml. fin. svcs. com. bus. law sect. coun., chair bus. law sect. 1997-98, editor-in-chief jour.), Bar Assn. Met. St. Louis (pres. 1983-84), Mo. Bar Assn. (bd. govs. 1979-81), Am. Judicature Soc. (dir. 1981-87), Washington U. Alumni Law Assn. (pres. 1980-81), Mo. Athletic Club, Am.-Israel C. of C. (pres. 1999—). Jewish. E-mail: mbposcover@SL.husch.com. Contracts commercial, General corporate, Banking. Office: Husch & Eppenberger 100 N Broadway Ste 1300 Saint Louis MO 63102-2789

**POSEY, JANETTE ROBISON,** lawyer; b. Gentry, Mo., Mar. 5, 1939; d. John Otto and Daphne Elainee (Ross)ü Robison; m Walter Daniel Posey, July 6, 1958; children: Sheree Lanae Posey Tyner, Jennifer, Renee. AA, Fullerton (Calif.) C.C., 1967; BA, Calif. State U., Fullerton, 1970, MA, 1971; JD, Western State U., Fullerton, 1976. Bar: Calif. 1976, U.S. Dist. Ct. (so. and ctrl. dists.) Calif. 1977, U.S. Ct. Appeals (9th cir.) 1977, U.S. Supreme Ct. 1977; life C.C. tchr. credential, Calif. Pvt. practice, Anaheim, Calif., 1977—; pvt. practice, owner Posey and Posey, Tustin, Calif., 1977—; cofounder Orange County Women's Law Ctr., Fullerton, 1973-76; adj. prof. law Am. Coll. Law, Brea, Calif., 1991-93, Western State U. Coll. Law, 1993-96. 2d v.p. Villa Park (Calif.) Women's League, 1988-89, 3d v.p., 1989-90; educator smile project VISTA, Yorba Linda, Calif., 1972. Mem. State Bar Calif., Orange County Bar Assn., Orange County Women Lawyers Assn. (bd. dirs. 1977-78), L.A. Bar Assn. Presbyterian. Avocations: writing, ballroom dancing, swimming, traveling. Personal injury, Probate. Office: 17671 Irvine Blvd Ste 208 Tustin CA 92780-3129

**POSEY, TERRY WAYNE,** lawyer; b. Springfield, Ohio, Nov. 9, 1950; s. William Eugene and Nancy Lougene (Lakins) P.; m. Deborah Lynn Henson, Oct. 4, 1977; children: Terry Wayne Jr., Ryan Christopher. BS, U. Dayton, 1983; JD, Capital U. Sch. Law, 1988. Bar: Ohio 1988, U.S. Dist. Ct. (so. dist.) Ohio 1988, U.S. Supreme Ct. 1992. Police officer Dayton (Ohio) Police Dept., 1968-87; pvt. practice law Dayton, 1987—. Recipient Mem. of Yr. award Fraternal Order of Police of Ohio, 1987. Mem. ABA, Ohio State Bar Assn., Dayton Bar Assn., Scottish Rite (trustee), Masons (Dayton pres. bd. dirs., 33 degree), Shriners. Personal injury, Family and matrimonial, Criminal. Home: 7842 Winding Way N Tipp City OH 45371-9243 Office: 7460 Brandt Pike Dayton OH 45424-3240

**POSGAY, MATTHEW NICHOLS,** lawyer; b. Ft. Lauderdale, Fla., Sept. 23, 1970; s. Raymond Joseph and Mary Lynn P. BA in Polit. Sci., U. Fla., 1991, JD, 1994. Bar: Fla. 1995. Assoc. Kubicki Draper, West Palm Beach, Fla., 1995—. Mem. Fla. Bar Spkrs. Bur., 1997—. Mem. ABA, Fla. Bar Assn., Fla. Defense Lawyers Assn., Defense Rsch. Inst., U. Fla. Coll. Law Alumni Assn., Phi Alpha Delta, Phi Kappa Phi, Sigma Phi Epsilon, Fla. Blue Key. Democrat. Methodist. Avocations: scuba diving, golf, weight lifting. General civil litigation, Insurance, Product liability. Office: Kubicki Draper Ste 1100 1645 Palm Beach Lakes Blvd West Palm Beach FL 33401-2209

**POSNER, ALAN B.,** lawyer; b. Green Bay, Wis., Dec. 27, 1951; s. Sam and Celia Posner; m. Dawn V. Bates, July 20, 1974. BA, Wayne State U., 1974; JD, UCLA, 1977. Bar: Mich. 1977, Calif. 1980, U.S. Dist. Ct. (ea. dist.) Mich. 1978, U.S. Supremee Ct. 1988. Assoc. Kelman Loria, Detroit, 1978-83, ptnr., 1984-94, mng. ptnr., 1995—; mediator Wayne County Mediation, Detroit, 1986—. Author: (novel) Basehit, 1997. Mem. Mich. Trial Lawyers Asn. Democrat. Personal injury, Civil rights, Product liability. Office: Kelman Loria 2300 First Nat Bldg Detroit MI 48226

**POSNER, DAVID S.,** lawyer; b. Pitts., Dec. 27, 1945; s. Mortimer B. and Lillian P.; m. Marilyn Hope Ackerman, Aug. 14, 1966; children: Morton J., Jennifer L. BS, Carnegie Mellon U., 1969; JD, U. Pitts., 1972. Bar: Pa. 1972, U.S. Supreme Ct. 1981. Ct. adminstr. Washington County, Pa., 1972-76; asst. dist. atty. Washington County, 1976-79; ptnr. Goldfarb & Posner, Washington, Pa., 1979-97, Goldfarb, Posner, Beck, DeHaven & Drewitz, Washington, 1997—; pres. Pa. Council of Trial Ct. Adminstrs., 1972-76; solicitor Clk. of Cts., Washington, 1983—. Mem. sect. 85 YMCA, Washington, 1980-85; bd. dirs. United Way, Washington, 1979-85; pres. Beth Israel Congregation, 1992-94. With USAR, 1966-72. Mem. ABA, Pa. Bar Assn. (ho. of dels. 1995-97), Washington County Bar Assn. (treas. 1982-83, pres. 1995), B'nai B'rith (past pres.). Real property, Banking, Contracts commercial. Home: 149 S Wade Ave Washington PA 15301-4926 Office: Goldfarb Posner Beck DeHaven & Drewitz 26 S Main St Ste 200 Washington PA 15301-6812

**POSNER, ERNEST GARY,** lawyer; b. Nashville, July 2, 1937; s. Alvin Joseph and Bertha (Halpern) P.; m. Gretel Roberta Tishler, Dec. 22, 1963; children: Suzanne Lyn, Deborah Ariel. BChE, Vanderbilt U., 1959; postgrad., Suffolk U., 1963-64; JD, Am. U., 1967. Bar: Va. 1967, Pa. 1968, U.S. Dist. Ct. (ea. dist.) Pa. 1969, U.S. Patent Office 1970, U.S. Supreme Ct. 1975. Advanced through grades to lt. comdr., 1967; commd. U.S. Navy, 1959, ret., 1967; staff Interagy. Com. Oceanography, Washington, 1967-68; patent lawyer Atlantic Richfield Co., Phila., 1968-72; v.p., gen. counsel, corp. sec. PQ Corp., Valley Forge, Pa., 1972—. Commr., vice chmn. Govt. Study Commn., Upper Merion, Pa., 1975-76. Served to capt. USNR. Mem. ABA, Soap & Detergent Assn. (legal com. 1974—), Am. Intellectual Property Law Assn., Internat. Bus. Forum (spkr.), Lic. Exec. Soc. (trustee 1993—, v.p. 1997—), Am. Corp. Counsel Assn., Masons, B'nai B'rith (sec. 1974-76, chpt. founder). General corporate, Private international, Patent. Office: PQ Corp Swedesford Rd PO Box 840 Valley Forge PA 19482-0840

**POSNER, LOUIS JOSEPH,** lawyer, accountant; b. N.Y.C., May 29, 1956; s. Alex Pozner and Hilda G. (Gottlieb) Weinberg; m. Betty F. Osin, June 21, 1986; 1 child, Daniel. BS in Acctg., Drexel U., 1979; MS in Taxation, Pace U., 1985; JD, N.Y. Law Sch., 1989. Bar: N.Y. 1990, N.J. 1990, U.S. Dist. Ct. (so. and ea. dists.) N.Y., 1990, D.C. 1991, U.S. Ct. Appeals (2d cir.) 1993, U.S. Supreme Ct. 1994. Auditor Arthur Andersen & Co., CPAs, Phila., 1979-81; tax sr. Kenneth Leventhal & Co., CPAs, N.Y.C., 1981-82; tax mgr. Mann Judd Landau, CPAs, N.Y.C., 1983-86; tax dir. Integrated Resources, Inc., N.Y.C., 1986-89; pvt. practice N.Y.C., 1989—; spkr. in field. Producer, dir. TV show Your Legal Rights. Mem. ABA, AICPA, Assn. Bar City N.Y., N.Y. State Soc. CPA's (tax com. 1985-90, mem. faculty N.Y.C. chpt. Found. for Acctg. Edn. 1989-90), N.Y. County Lawyers Assn. (trusts and estates sect.), N.Y. State Bar Assn. (trusts and estates sect.),Assn. of Atty. CPA's.Mensa (coord. spl. interest group N.Y.C. chpt. 1978-90). Taxation, general, Estate planning, Bankruptcy. Home: 160 E 48th St Apt 12T New York NY 10017-1225 Office: 635 Madison Ave Ste 400 New York NY 10022-1009

**POSNER, MARTIN LOUIS,** lawyer; b. N.Y.C., June 8, 1948; s. Carl and Evelyn Rachel P.; m. Jane Yvonne Kaplowitz, June 7, 1970. BA in Biology, CCNY, 1970, MA in Environ. Edn., 1975; JD, Pace U., 1984, LLM in Environ. Law, 1993. Bar: N.Y. 1985, U.S. Dist. Ct. (ea. and so. dists.) N.Y. 1991. Tchr. N.Y. Pub. Sch. Sys., N.Y.C., 1970-84; assoc. Law Offices of Henry Greenburg, White Plains, N.Y., 1984-85; ptnr. Posner, Posner & Assocs. PC, White Plains, N.Y., 1985—. Commr. Patterson (N.Y.) Environ. Conservation Commn., 1989-93; mem. Putnam County Environ. Mgmt. Coun., Carmel, N.Y., 1990-93, Town of Patterson, 1996—. Mem. ABA, N.Y. State Bar Assn., White Plains Bar Assn., Westchester Bar Assn. Real property, Bankruptcy, Environmental. Office: Posner Posner & Assocs PC 399 Knollwood Rd White Plains NY 10603-1931

**POSNER, MICHAEL HOFFMAN,** lawyer; b. Chgo., Nov. 19, 1950; s. Harry Randolph and Elizabeth (Hoffman) P.; m. Deborah Korzenik, Dec. 12, 1986. Children: Alexander Korzenik Posner, Hannah Korzenik Posner. BA with honors, U. Mich., 1972; JD, U. Calif., Berkeley, 1975. Bar: Calif. 1975, Ill. 1976, U.S. Dist Ct. (no. dist.) Ill. 1976. Research asst. Internat. Commn. Jurists, Geneva, 1974; assoc. Sonnenschein, Carlin, Nath & Rosenthal, Chgo., 1975-78; exec. dir. Lawyers Com. for Human Rights, N.Y.C., 1978—; bd. dirs. Amnesty Internat., 1982-84; vis. lectr. Yale Law Sch., New Haven, 1981-84, Columbia Law Sch., N.Y.C., 1984—. Contbr. articles to profl. jours. Mem. Council Fgn. Relations, N.Y.C. Mem. ABA. Democratic. Jewish. Avocations: tennis, skiing, hiking. Office: Lawyers Com for Human Rights 333 7th Ave New York NY 10001-5004

**POSNER, RICHARD ALLEN,** federal judge; b. N.Y.C., Jan. 11, 1939; s. Max and Blanche Posner; m. Charlene Ruth Horn, Aug. 13, 1962; children: Kenneth A., Eric A. AB, Yale U., 1959, LLD (hon.), 1996; LLB, Harvard U., 1962; LLD (hon.), Syracuse U., 1986, Duquesne U., 1987, Georgetown U., 1992, U. Pa., 1997; D honoris causa, U. Ghent, 1995. Bar: N.Y. 1963, U.S. Supreme Ct. 1966. Law clk. Justice William J. Brennan Jr. U.S. Supreme Ct., Washington, 1962-63; asst. to commr. FTC, Washington, 1963-65; asst. to solicitor gen. U.S. Dept. Justice, Washington, 1965-67; gen. counsel Pres.'s Task Force on Communications Policy, Washington, 1967-68; assoc. prof. Stanford U. Law Sch., Calif., 1968-69; prof. U. Chgo. Law Sch., 1969-78, Lee and Brena Freeman prof., 1978-81, sr. lectr., 1981—; circuit judge U.S. Ct. Appeals (7th cir.), Chgo., 1981—, chief judge, 1993—; research assoc. Nat. Bur. Econ. Research, Cambridge, Mass., 1971-81; pres. Lexecon Inc., Chgo., 1977-81. Author: Antitrust Law: An Economic Perspective, 1976, Economic Analysis of Law, 5th edit., 1998, The Economics of Justice, 1981, (with William M. Landes) The Economic Structure of Tort Law, 1987, The Problems of Jurisprudence, 1990, Cardozo: A Study in Reputation, 1990, Sex and Reason, 1992, The Essential Holmes, 1992, (with Tomas J. Philipson) Private Choices and Public Health: The AIDS Epidemic in Economic Perspective, 1993, Overcoming Law, 1995, Aging and Old Age, 1995, The Federal Courts: Challenge and Reform, 1996, Law and Legal Theory in England and America, 1996, The Federal Courts: Challenge and Reform, 1997, Law and Literature, revised and enlarged edit., 1998, The Problematics of Moral and Legal Theory, 1999; pres. Harvard Law Rev., 1961-62; editor Jour. Legal Studies, 1972-81. Fellow AAAS, Am. Law Inst., Brit. Acad.; mem. Am. Econ. Assn., Am. Law and econ. Assn. (pres. 1995-96). Office: US Ct Appeals 7th Cir 219 S Dearborn St Chicago IL 60604-1702

**POSS, STEPHEN DANIEL,** lawyer; b. Buffalo, Jan. 13, 1955; s. Gilbert H. and Bernice L. (Lippman) P. BA magna cum laude, Amherst Coll., 1978; JD, U. Chgo., 1981. Bar: N.Y. 1982, Mass. 1988; U.S. Dist. Ct. (so. dist.) N.Y. 1984, U.S. Dist. Ct. Mass. 1988; U.S. Tax Ct. 1983; U.S. Supreme Ct. 1986; U.S. Ct. Appeals (1st cir.) 1989, U.S. Ct. Appeals (fed. cir.) 1992. Assoc. Cravath, Swaine & Moore, N.Y.C., 1981-87, Goodwin, Procter and Hoar, Boston, 1988-89; ptnr. Goodwin, Procter & Hoar LLP, Boston, 1989—; teaching asst. to prof. Henry Steele Commager, 1977; lectr. Mass. Continuing Legal Edn., 1987—, Mass. Bar Assn. Ednl. Seminars, 1992-94; seminar chmn. SEC Inst. II, 1998; lectr. Nasdaq Exec. Forum, 1998; mem. civil litigation curriculum com. Mass. Continuing Legal Edn., 1997—. Advisor campaign Bill Guy for U.S. Senate from N.D., 1974, Quentick Burdick for U.S. Senate, N.D., 1976, Bill Bradley for U.S. Senate, N.J., 1978, Gary Hart for U.S. Senate, Colo., 1980, Jeff Bingaman for U.S. Senate, N.Mex., 1982; pro bono counsel to Dem. Nat. Com., 1986-87; bd. dirs. Internat. Forum, N.Y.C., 1984; counsel of N.Y. Law Assocs., N.Y.C., 1985; mem. fin. com. Campaign to re-elect U.S. Senator John Kerry, 1990; bd. dirs. Mass. Audubon Soc., 1997—. John Woodruff Simpson fellow, 1978. Mem. ABA, Boston Bar Assn., Mass. Bar Assn. (panelist biotech. com. 1990, vice chair bus. litigation com. 1992-94), Internat. Churchill Soc. General civil litigation, Securities, Mergers and acquisitions. Office: Goodwin Procter & Hoar LLP Exchange Pl Boston MA 02109-2803

**POSSÉ, OLGA ALICIA,** lawyer, educator; b. Havana, Cuba, July 22, 1957; came to U.S., 1962; d. Florentino Posse and Maria Olga (Solis) Casal. BA, NYU, 1981; MS, Tex. Womans U., 1984; MA, Bklyn. Coll., 1991; JD, Bklyn. Law Sch., 1994. Bar: N.Y. 1995. Chemistry fellow Tex. Womans U., Houston, 1983-84; spl. litigation clk. The Legal Aid Soc. N.Y., N.Y.C., 1992-93; felony appeals atty. The Legal Aid Bur. of Buffalo, Inc., 1994-98; with Bouvier, O'Connor, Buffalo, 1998—. Lt. USN, 1985-91. Recipient scholarship NYU, 1977-81, Chemistry Tchg. fellowship Tex. Womans U., 1983-84. Mem. ABA, N.Y. State Bar Assn., Erie Bar Assn., Assn. Trial Lawyers Am. Republican. Roman Catholic. Avocations: writing, sailing, gardening. Criminal, General civil litigation, Personal injury. Home: 712 Main St Apt 312 Buffalo NY 14202-1717 Office: Bouvier O'Connor Main Place Tower 350 Main St Ste 1400 Buffalo NY 14202-3702

**POST, RUTH-ELLEN,** lawyer, educator; b. Audubon, N.J., Mar. 6, 1946; d. Theodore J. and Margaret E. Post; m. D.R. Karklin (div. 1981); 1 child, Kenneth D. Karklin; m. Dale H. Corliss, May 23, 1984; 1 child, Rebecca Post Corliss. BA, Montclair State U., 1967; JD, Rutgers U., Camden, N.J., 1975. Gen. practice law William V. Eisenberg, Esq., Haddonfield, N.J., 1975-76; sole practitioner Medford, N.J., 1976-78, Pittsfield, Mass., 1983-84, Pelham, N.H., 1987-88; prof., chmn. dept. Rivier Coll., Nashua, N.H., 1988—; mem. certifying bd. Nat. Assn. Legal Assts., Tulsa, 1994-98; bd. dirs. Am. Assn. for Paralegal Edn., Overland Park, Kans., 1970-91. Author: (textbook) Paralegal Internships: Finding, Managing, and Transitioning Your Career, 1999; co-author: (manual) Preventing Unauthorized Practice of Law: For the Paralegal in New Hampshire, 1998. Mem. Pelham Planning Bd., 1986-88. Named Atty. of Yr., Paralegal Assn. N.H., 1996. Mem. N.H. Bar Assn. (chair paralegal task force 1994, mem. com. on unauthorized practice of law 1996—). Office: Rivier Coll 420 S Main St Nashua NH 03060-5043

**POSTAL, DAVID RALPH,** lawyer; b. Grand Rapids, Mich., Jan. 12, 1945; s. Ralph Bernard and Eleanor Postal; children: Bryan Charles, Stephanie Lynn. BA, Mich. State U., 1967; JD cum laude, U. Mich., 1974. Bar: Ariz. 1975, U.S. Dist. Ct. Ariz. 1975, U.S. Ct. Appeals (9th cir.) 1981. Assoc. Powers, Boutell, Fannin & Kurn, Phoenix, 1974-75; staff atty. Ariz. Supreme Ct., Phoenix, 1975-76; sole practice Phoenix, 1976-78, 83—; ptnr. Holland & Postal, Phoenix, 1978-83; lectr. in real estate, 1976. Pres. New Hope for the Blind, Phoenix, 1976-82; chmn. bd. dirs. Trinity United meth. Adminstrn., Phoenix, 1980; trustee New Beginnings Transitional Home, 1995—; bd. dirs. Westside Foodbank, 1998—. Served to 1st lt., U.S. Army, 1969-72. Mem. Maricopa County Bar Assn., Kiwanis (pres. Phoenix 1984-85). Republican. Real property, Contracts commercial, General civil litigation. Office: 3601 N 7th Ave Phoenix AZ 85013-3638

**POSTERARO, DAVID ROBERT,** lawyer; b. N.Y.C., Nov. 10, 1952; s. Anthony Francis and Lygia Maria Posteraro. BA, Fordham U., 1974; JD, Case Western Res. U., 1981. Bar: Ohio. Legal counsel ELTECH Systems Corp., Boca Raton, Fla., 1981-87; ptnr. Weston, Hurd, Fallon, Paisley & Howley, Cleve., 1987-96; v.p., gen. counsel Nat. Auto Credit, Solon, Ohio, 1996-97; ptnr. Roetzel & Andress, Cleve., 1997—. Bd. mem. AIDS Taskforce of Greater Cleve. Mem. Ohio Bar Assn., Cleve. Bar Assn. (intellectual property com.; seminar presenter 1990-91), Licensing Execs. Soc., Cleve. Restoration Soc., Ohio City Devel. Assn. Democrat. Roman Catholic. General corporate, Intellectual property. Home: 3904 Bridge Ave Cleveland OH 44113-3316 Office: Roetzel & Andress 1375 E 9th St Cleveland OH 44114-1724

**POSTLEWAITE, WILLIAM NEAL, SR.,** lawyer; b. Columbus, Ohio, Apr. 12, 1918; s. David Neal and Savannah E. (Marshall) P.; m. Margaret J. M. Chapman, Feb. 3, 1945; children: Margaret M., Elizabeth A., William N. Jr., Susan C., Charles C., John P. AB with honors, Williams Coll., 1940; JD, Ohio State U., 1947. Bar: Ohio, 1947. Ptnr. Postlewaite & Jordan, Columbus. Pres. parish council St. Catherine's Ch., Columbus, 1982-84; trustee St. Ann's Hosp., Columbus, 1963-93. Served to lt. comdr. USNR, 1942-54. Mem. ABA, Ohio Bar Assn., Columbus Bar Assn. Clubs: Columbus Country, University (Columbus) (trustee 1978-81). General corporate, Probate, Estate taxation. Home: 106 S Harding Rd Columbus OH 43209-1935 Office: Postlewaite & Jordan 3040 Riverside Dr Ste 122 Columbus OH 43221-2578

**POSTNER, MARYA A.,** lawyer; b. Bronx, Feb. 24, 1966; d. William J. and Marie H. Postner; m. Tito A. Serafini, May 22, 1993; 1 child, Arianna. BS, Georgetown U., 1987; PhD, Princeton U., 1993; JD, U. Calif., Berkeley, 1996. Bar: Calif. 1996, U.S. Dist. Ct. (no. dist.) Calif. 1996, U.S. Ct. Appeals (9th cir.) 1996, U.S. Patent and Trademark Office 1998. Assoc. Cooley Godward LLP, Palo Alto, Calif., 1996—. Intellectual property, Patent. Office: Cooley Godward LLP 5 Palo Alto Sq Palo Alto CA 94306-2122

**POSTON, ANITA OWINGS,** lawyer; b. Sylacauga, Ala., Sept. 24, 1949; d. John T. and Margaret (Cochran) Owings; m. Charles E. Poston, June 9, 1973; children: Charles E. Jr., John W., Margaret Elizabeth. BA, U. Md., 1971; JD, Coll. William & Mary, 1974. Bar: Va. 1974. Atty. Vandeventer Black LLP, Norfolk, Va., 1974—; substitute judge Norfolk (Va.) Gen. Dist. Cts., 1982-90; mem. Bar Examiners Bd. Mem. bio ethics adv. com. Children's Hosp., Norfolk, 1985—; mem. State Bd. for Community Colls., Richmond, 1985-90, chmn. 1988-89; mem. Norfolk Sch. Bd., 1990—, chmn., 1997—. Mem. ABA, Va. Bar Assn. (exec. com., pres.-elect 1999), Norfolk-Portsmouth Bar Assn. (pres. 1998-99), Am. Inn of Ct. Fax: 757-446-8670. E-mail: aposton@vanblk.com. General corporate, Health, Estate planning. Office: Vandeventer Black & Martin 500 World Trade Ctr Norfolk VA 23510-1679

**POSTON, BEVERLY PASCHAL,** lawyer; b. Birmingham, Ala., Aug. 21, 1955; d. Arthur Buel and Nellie Jo (Weaver) P.; m. Richard F. Poston, Aug., 1992. BA with honor, U. North Ala., 1976; JD, Birmingham Sch. Law, 1982. Bar: Ala. 1982, U.S. Dist. Ct. (no. dist.) Ala. 1982, U.S. Ct. Appeals (11th cir.) 1983. Assoc. St. John & St. John, Cullman, Ala., 1982-84; pvt. practice Cullman, 1984-85, 92—; ptnr. Paschal & Collins, Cullman, 1986-92. Pres. Cullman County Hist. Soc., 1986-87, bd. dirs., 1996—. Named one of Outstanding Young Women Am., 1984; recipient Citiation of Honor, Young Career Women Program, 1989. Mem. ABA, ATLA, Ala. Trial Lawyers Assn., Cullman County Bar Assn. (sec. tres. 1997-98, v.p. 1998-99, pres. 1999—), Pilot Club Internat. (Sweetheart award Cullman 1985), Cullman Bus. and Profl. Women's Assn. (young careerist award), Cullman Home Builder Assn. Avocations: horseback riding, rodeos, farming, writing. Criminal, State civil litigation, Family and matrimonial. Home: 1797 County Road 972 Cullman AL 35057-5861 Office: 905 2nd Ave SW Ste D 905 Cullman AL 35055-4224

**POSTON, ELLERBY DELANCE,** lawyer, real estate broker; b. Johnsonville, S.C., Mar. 25, 1934; s. Percy Delance and Fairalee Roberta (Johnson) P.; m. Linda Sue Howard, Mar. 29, 1959; children: Leslie Howard, Ellerby Delance II. BS in BA, U. S.C., 1960, JD, 1970. Bar: S.C. 1960, U.S. Dist. Ct. (ea. dist.) S.C. 1960, U.S. Ct. Appeals (4th cir.) 1989. Pvt. practice Johnsonville, S.C.; pres. Johnsonville Realty Co., 1965—; atty. City of Johnsonville, 1962-85. Mayor City of Johnsonville, 1964-66, chmn. Planning and Zoning Commn.; chmn. Johnsonville Recreation Commn., 1966-70; mem. florence County Recreation Commn., 1966-70; pres. PTA, Johnsonville, 1967-70; chmn. Johnsonville-Hemingway Coun. on Alcohol and Drug abuse, 1972-74; co-founder The Lighthouse Alcohol and Drug Abuse Counseling Ctr., Hemingway, S.C., 1971; mem. Florence County Hosp. Commn., 1969-70, Florence County Devel. Bd., 1964-66. Mem. ABA, ATLA, S.C. State Bar, Florence County Bar Assn. Baptist. Avocations: boating, antique car restoration. Criminal, General civil litigation, Labor. Home: PO Drawer 779 482 Country Club Dr Johnsonville SC 29555-6609 Office: 114 Seaboard Ave Johnsonville SC 29555

**POSTON, REBEKAH JANE,** lawyer; b. Wabash, Ind., Apr. 20, 1948; d. Bob E. and April (Ogle) P. BS, U. Miami, 1970, JD, 1974. Bar: Fla. 1974, Ohio 1977, U.S. Dist. Ct. (so. and mid. dists.) Fla., U.S. Dist. Ct. (ea. dist.) Wis., U.S. Dist. Ct. (no. dist.) Ohio, U.S.Dist. Ct. (no. dist.) Mich., U.S.Ct. Appeals (5th, 6th, 7th and 11th cirs.). Asst. U.S. atty. U.S. Atty.'s Office, Miami, Fla., 1974-76; spl. atty. organized crime and racketeering sect. Strike Force, Cleve., 1976-78; ptnr. Fine, Jacobson, Schwartz, Nash & Block, Miami, 1978-94, Steel Hector & Davis, Miami, 1994—; adj. prof. U. Miami Law Sch., Coral Gables, 1986; mem. U.S. sentencing guidelines com. So. Dist. of Fla., Miami, 1987-88. Mem. Fla. Bar Assn., Nat. Assn. Criminal Def. Attys., Nat. Directory Criminal Lawyers, Am. Immigration Lawyers Assn., Dade County Bar Assn. Democrat. Lutheran. Avocations: power boat racing, swimming. Criminal, Immigration, naturalization, and customs, Private international. Home: 1541 Brickell Ave Apt 3706 Miami FL 33129-1229 Office: 200 SE 2nd St Miami FL 33131

**POTENZA, JOSEPH MICHAEL,** lawyer; b. Stamford, Conn., June 27, 1947; s. Michael Joseph Sr. and Rose Elizabeth (Coppola) P.; m. Wendy Ann David, Dec. 19, 1971 (div. Jan. 1978); m. Karen Louise Yankee, Jan. 28, 1978; children: Wendy Lynn, Chiara Micol. BSEE cum laude, Rochester Inst. Tech., 1970; JD, Georgetown U., 1975. Bar: Va. 1975, D.C. 1976, U.S. Dist. Ct. D.C., U.S. Ct. Appeals (fed. cir.), U.S. Ct. Appeals (6th cir.), U.S. Supreme Ct. Patent examiner U.S. Patent and Trademark Office, Arlington, Va., 1970-74, law clk. bd. appeals, 1974-75, law clk. to presiding judge 6th cir. U.S. Ct. Appeals, 1975-76; assoc. Banner, Birch, McKie & Beckett, Washington, 1976-80, ptnr., 1980—; adj. prof. Georgetown U. Law Ctr., Washington, 1985—; faculty Nat. Inst. Trial Advocacy--Patent Inst., 1996—. Editor (monographs) Sorting Out Ownership Rights in Intellectual Property, 1980, Recent Developments in Licensing, 1981. Bd. dirs. Found. for a Creative Am., 1991—. Recipient Patent and Trademark Office Superior Performance award Dept. Commerce, 1973-75. Fellow Am. Bar Found.; mem. ABA (young lawyers divsn. exec. coun. 1979—, chmn. legis. action com. 1980—, chmn. patent trademark and copyright com. 1977—, house of dels. 1984-86, sci. and tech. sect., coun. mem. 1985—, membership chmn. 1985—, budget co-chmn. 1987—, budget officer 1988—, vice chmn. 1991—, chmn.-elect 1992-93, chmn. 1993, chmn. standing com. on pub. oversight, 1996—, fed. practice and procedure com. intellectual property law sect. 1995-96, spring CLE program 1997-98, chmn. summer CLE 1999, chair fed. practice and procedure com. div. chmn., div. VI IP law sec. 1995-97), IEEE, AAAS (nat. conf. lawyers and scientists), Am. Intellectual Property Law Assn. (chmn. unfair competition com. 1980-81), D.C. Bar Assn. (sec. patent, trademark, copyright sect.), Va. Bar Assn., Wash. Patent Lawyers Club (pres. 1988-89), Am. Inns of Ct. (founding mem. and exec. com. Giles S. Rich 1991—, v.p. 1997, pres. 1998-99), Phi Sigma Kappa, Alpha Sigma (pres. 1979-80), Tau Beta Pi. Patent, Trademark and copyright, State civil litigation. Home: 1238 Gilman Ct Herndon VA 20170-2418 Office: Banner & Witcoff 1001 G St NW Ste 1100 Washington DC 20001-4545

**POTTER, CLEMENT DALE,** district attorney general; b. McMinnville, Tenn., Dec. 22, 1955; s. Johnnie H. and Elnora (Harvey) P.; children: Cory, Sarah, John Warren. BS, Middle Tenn. State U., 1984; JD, U. Tenn., 1987; cert., Tenn. Law Enforcement Acad., 1980. Bar: Tenn. 1987, U.S. Dist. Ct. (ea. dist.) Tenn. 1989. Pvt. practice law McMinnville, 1987-89; city judge City of McMinnville, Tenn., 1988-89; pub. defender 31st Dist. State Tenn., McMinnville, 1989-98, dist. atty. gen., 1999—. Asst. to gen. editor Tools for the Ultimate Trial, 1st edit., 1985. Mem. Leadership McMinnville, 1989, chmn., 1995, 96. Staff sgt. USAF, 1974-80. Named McMinnville Warren County C. of C. Vol. of Yr., 1995; recipient D. Porter Henegar & Fred L. Hoover Sr. Bell Ringer award, 1995. Mem. ABA, Cheer Mental Health Assn. (dir. 1988—, pres. 1991-96), Harmony House Inc. (dir. 1993-95), Noon Exch. Club McMinnville (dir. 1992-94, sec. 1994, pres.-elect 1995, pres. 1996-97), Kiwanis Club of Warren County (pres. 1986-87), Tenn. Secondary Schs. Athletic Assn. (h.s. football referee 1988—), Am. Legion. Avocations: computers, gardening, coaching youth softball. Office: Dist Atty Gen 31st Dist PO Box 510 455 N Chancery Mc Minnville TN 37111

**POTTER, DAVID JIMMIE,** lawyer, real estate developer; b. Texarkana, Tex., Feb. 15, 1943; s. Jimmie Jackson and Mary Wilma Potter; m. Martha Elizabeth Miller, 1971 (div.) children: David Jimmie II, Stephanie Elizabeth, Jackson Miller; m. Charlotte Post, June 30, 1989. BBA, Tulane U., 1965, MBA, 1966; JD, U. Ark., 1970. Bar: Ark., Tex., U.S. Dist. Ct. (we. dist.) Ark., U.S. Dist. Ct. (ea. and no. dists.) Tex., U.S. Ct. Appeals (5th and 8th cirs.), U.S. Ct. Internat. Trade, U.S. Supreme Ct. V.p. B. Rosenberg & Sons, New Orleans, 1966; mgmt. cons. Solidar, Malmo, Sweden, 1966; pres. ProTeck Indsl. Footwear, Texarkana, Ark., 1967; mgmt. cons. Deutesprecken Gesellschaft, West Germany, 1968; sole practitioner Texarkana, Tex., 1970—; bd. dirs., officer Two States Constrn. Co., Texarkana, Tex. and Ark., 1980-85; bd. dirs., pres. Potter Properties, Texarkana, Ark., 1997—; pres., bd. dirs. Western Ark. Rock Inc., 1996—. Mem. Ark. Red River Commn., 1993—. Mem. ATLA, Tex. Trial Lawyers Assn., Ark. Trial Lawyers Assn., Lions Club (bd. dirs. 1970—), Texarkana C. of C. Methodist. Avocations: travel, real estate and business development, sports, scuba diving, hunting. General practice, General civil litigation, Personal injury. Office: David J Potter & Assocs 901 N Stateline Dr Texarkana TX 75501

**POTTER, ERNEST LUTHER,** lawyer; b. Anniston, Ala., Apr. 30, 1940; s. Ernest Luther and Dorothy (Stamps) P.; m. Gwyn Johnston, June 28, 1958; children: Bradley S., Lauren D. A.B., U. Ala., 1961, LL.B., 1963, LL.M., 1979. Bar: Ala. 1963, U.S. Dist. Ct. (no. dist.) Ala. 1964, U.S. Ct. Appeals (5th cir.) 1965, U.S. Supreme Ct. 1972, U.S. Ct. Appeals (11th cir.) 1982. Assoc. Burnham & Klinefelter, Anniston, Ala., 1963-64; assoc. Bell, Richardson, Cleary, McLain & Tucker, Huntsville, Ala., 1964-66, ptnr., 1967-70; ptnr. Butler & Potter, Huntsville, 1971-82; pvt. practice, Huntsville, 1983—; bd. dirs. VME Microsystems Internat. Corp., Inc.; mem. faculty Inst. Bus. Law and Polit. Sci., U. Ala.-Huntsville, 1965-67. Contbg. author: Marital Law, 1976, 2d edit. 1985. V.p. No. Ala. Kidney Found., 1976-77; treas. Madison County Dem. Exec. Com., 1974-78; bd. dirs. United Way Madison County, 1982-87, Girls Inc., Huntsville, 1988—, pres., 1991. Mem. Ala. Law Inst., ABA, Ala. Bar Assn., Madison County Bar Assn., Phi Beta Kappa, Order of Coif. Episcopalian. General practice, Family and matrimonial, Estate planning. Home: 1284 Becket Dr SE Huntsville AL 35801-1670 Office: 200 Clinton Ave W Huntsville AL 35801-4918

**POTTER, GARY THOMAS,** lawyer; b. Boulder, Colo., Nov. 12, 1941; s. Ralph Boyce Potter and Patricia Jamie O'Rourke; m. Pamela Closson, Aug. 3, 1963; children: Matthew, Michael, Andrew, Katie. BA, Regis Coll., 1963; JD, U. Colo., 1966. Atty. Kayne Watson Potter, Boulder, 1966-67, State of Colo. Dept. of Law, Denver, 1967-68; trust atty. First Nat. Bank of Denver, 1968-77; mktg. v.p. Integrated Resource, Denver, 1977-78; pvt. practice Denver, 1978—. Pres. Lakewood Jr. Basketball, 1977-78; athletic dir. St. Bernadettes, Lakewood, 1992-93; bd. dirs., pres. Tchrs. Award Found., Denver, 1974-75; bd. dirs. Craig Hosp., Denver, 1977-80. Mem. U.S. Golf Assn. (sectional affairs com. 1980-98), Colo. Golf Assn. (bd. govs. 1974-88), Trans-Miss. Golf Assn. (trustee 1980—), Pacific Coast Golf Assn. (past pres. 1977, 88), Denver. C. of C. (pres. 1994-95). Roman Catholic. Probate, Estate planning, General corporate. Office: 1700 Broadway Ste 1217 Denver CO 80290-1201

**POTTER, JOHN WILLIAM,** federal judge; b. Toledo, Ohio, Oct. 25, 1918; s. Charles and Mary Elizabeth (Baker) P.; m. Phyllis May Bihn, Apr. 14, 1944; children: John William, Carolyn Diane, Kathryn Susan. PhB cum laude, U. Toledo, 1940; JD, U. Mich., 1946. Bar: Ohio 1947. Assoc. Zachman, Boxell, Schroeder & Torbet, Toledo, 1946-51; ptnr. Boxell, Bebout, Torbet & Potter, Toledo, 1951-69; mayor city of Toledo, 1961-67; asst. atty. gen. State of Ohio, 1968-69; judge 6th Dist. Ct. Appeals, 1969-82; judge U.S. Dist. Ct., Toledo, 1982—, sr. judge, 1992—; presenter in field. Sr. editor U. Mich. Law Rev., 1946. Pres. Ohio Mcpl. League, 1965; past assoc. pub. mem. Toledo Labor Mgmt. Commn.; past pres., bd. dirs. Commn. on Rels. with Toledo (Spain); past bd. dirs. Cummings Sch. Toledo Opera Assn., Conlon Ctr.; past trustee Epworth United Meth. Ch.; hon. chmn. Toledo Festival Arts, 1980. Capt. F.A., U.S. Army, 1942-46. Decorated Bronze Star; recipient Leadership award Toledo Bldg. Congress, 1965, Merit award Toledo Bd. Realtors, 1967, Resolution of Recognition award Ohio Ho. of Reps., 1982, Outstanding Alumnus award U. Toledo, 1966, conf. rm. named in his honor, U.S. Courthouse, Toledo, 1998; named to Field Arty. Officer Candidate Sch. Hall of Fame, 1999. Fellow Am. Bar Found., Am. Judicature Soc., 6th Jud. Cir. Dist. Judges Assn., Fed. Judges Assn.; mem. ABA, Ohio Bar Assn. (Found. Outstanding Rsch. award 1995), Toledo Bar Assn. (exec. com. 1962-64, award 1992), Lucas County Bar Assn., Toledo Area C. of C. (v.p. 1973-74), U. Toledo Alumni Assn. (past pres.), Toledo Zool. Soc. (past bd. dirs.), Old Newsboys Club, Toledo Club, Kiwanis (past pres.), Phi Kappa Phi. Home: 2418 Middlesex Dr Toledo OH 43606-3114 Office: US Dist Ct 307 US Courthouse 1716 Spielbusch Ave Toledo OH 43624-1363

**POTTER, KEVIN,** lawyer. Former dist. atty. Wood County, Wis.; former chmn. Wis. Tax Appeals Commn., Wis. Labor and Indsl. Review Commn.; U.S. Atty. We. Dist. Wis., Madison, 1991-93; mem. Brennan Steil Basting and MacDougall S.C., Madison, 1993—. Office: Brennan Steil Basting and MacDougall PO Box 990 22 E Mifflin St Ste 400 Madison WI 53701-0990

**POTTER, RICHARD CLIFFORD,** lawyer; b. Providence, Nov. 25, 1946; s. Peter Rex Potter and Helen Louise (McDevitt) St. Onge; children: Catherine Anne, David Henry. BA, U. N.C., 1968; JD cum laude, Ind. U., 1973. Bar: Ill. 1973, U.S. Dist. Ct. (no. dist.) Ill. 1973, U.S. Ct. Appeals (8th cir.) 1975, U.S. Ct. Appeals (3d cir.) 1978, U.S. Ct. Appeals (4th and 5th cirs.) 1979, U.S. Ct. Appeals (9th cir.) 1980, U.S. Supreme Ct. 1979. Assoc. Kirkland & Ellis, Chgo., 1973-75; atty. and ptnr. Bell, Boyd & Lloyd, Chgo., 1975-89; of counsel Sidney & Austin, 1989-93; ptnr. Oppeheimer, Wolfe & Donnelly, 1993—; lobbyist Boise Cascade Corp., Washington, 1981-84. Assoc. editor, exec. officer Ind. Law Jour., 1972-73; author various publs. Bd. dirs. Northbrook (Ill.) Park Dist. adv. council, 1982. Mem. ABA (vice chmn. internat. law and practice com. on internat. aspects litigation 1986-88, chmn. internat. law and pracitce subcom. on settlement and ADR 1987-88, sec. patent, trademark and copyright), Internat. Bar Assn. (internat. computer and tech.com., vice-chmn. com. R.), Legal Club Chgo., Law Club Chgo., Am. Intellectual Property Law Assn., Japan-Am. Soc. Chgo., Am. Arbitration Assn. (comml. arbitrator), Licensing Execs. Soc. (chmn. Japan com.), French-Am. C. of C. (past exec. v.p.), Am. Swiss C. of C. (past sec.), Univ. Club (Chgo.). Private international, Federal civil litigation, Computer. Home: 1580 Tara Ln Lake Forest IL 60045-1221 Office: Oppenheimer et al 180 N Stetson Ave Fl 45 Chicago IL 60601-6710

**POTTER, ROBERT DANIEL,** federal judge; b. Wilmington, N.C., Apr. 4, 1923; s. Elisha Lindsey and Emma Louise (McLean) P.; m. Mary Catherine Neilson, Feb. 13, 1954; children: Robert Daniel, Mary Louise, Catherine Ann. AB in Chemistry, Duke U., 1947, LLB, 1950; LLD (hon.), Sacred Heart Coll., Belmont, N.C., 1982. Bar: N.C. 1951. Pvt. practice law Charlotte, N.C., 1951-81; chief judge U.S. Dist. Ct. (we. dist.) N.C., 1984-91, dist. judge, 1991-94, now sr. judge. Commr. Mecklenburg County, Charlotte, 1966-68. Served as 2d lt. U.S. Army, 1944-47, ETO. Mem. N.C. Bar Assn. Republican. Roman Catholic. Club: Charlotte City. Office: US Courthouse 250 Federal Bldg 401 W Trade St Charlotte NC 28202-1619

**POTTER, TANYA JEAN,** lawyer; b. Washington, Oct. 30, 1956; d. John Francis and Tanya Agnes (Kristof) P.; m. Howard Bruce Adler; 1 child, Alexandra Potter Adler. BA, Georgetown U., 1978, JD, 1981. Bar: D.C. 1982, U.S. Ct. Appeals (D.C. cir.), U.S. Ct. Appeals (fed. cir.), U.S. Dist. Ct. (D.C. dist.), U.S. Ct. Internat. Trade. Assoc. Ragan and Mason, Washington, 1981-88; atty.-adviser Office of Chief Counsel for Import Adminstrn., U.S. Dept. Commerce, Washington, 1989-92; mediator D.C. Superior Ct., 1982-84. Author: Practicing Before the Federal Maritime Commission, 1986, supplement, 1988, Preferentiality Under the Proposed Commerce Department Regulations, 1990, Oil Refining in U.S. Foreign-Trade Zones, 1990. Rep. Avenel Homeowners Adv. Coun., 1994-97; dir. Avenel Bd. Dirs., 1997, 98, 99—. Recipient Cmty. Svc. Recognition award ARC, Washington, 1986. Mem. ABA, Bar Assn. of D.C. (exec. coun. ad law sect. 1985-89). Avocations: sports, travel, visiting museums and art galleries. Administrative and regulatory, Private international.

**POTTS, BERNARD,** lawyer; b. Balt., Aug. 22, 1915; s. Phillip Louis and Anna (Novey) P.; m. Frieda Hochman, 1948; children: Phillip Louis, Neal Allen, Bryan H., Andrea Maria. ABA, Balt. Coll. Commerce, 1936; LLB, Eastern U., Balt., 1949; JD, U. Balt., Balt., 1950. Bar: Md. 1950. Tax cons. Balt., 1936-49, pvt. practice, 1949—; ptnr., sr. counsel Potts & Potts, PA, Balt., 1975—. Founder, counsel Gamber Community Vol. Fire Co., 1963; founder, pres. Mary Dopkin's Children's Fund, 1950-60; founder Police Cmty. Rels. Coun. Md., 1956; founder, v.p. Boys Town Homes Md., 1965-80; founder, chmn. Accident and Prevention Bur. Md., 1965-75; pres. Safety First Club Md., 1966-68; mem. Md. bd. NCCJ, 1976-80; bd. dirs. NCCJ-Md. Conf. Social Concern, 1976-80; co-founder, co-chmn. Greater Balt. Mental Health Coun., 1980; founder E. Balt. Children's Fund, Coun. Ind. Self-Help, Police Community Rels. Couns., Crime Prevention Bur. Md., 1960-75; founder Md. chpt. Boys & Girls Club Am., 1988; pro bono adviser, bd. dirs. Patterson Emergency Food Ctr. & Soup Kitchen, Bea Gaddy Homes for Homeless Women & Children Inc.; pro bono atty. Trancare, Inc., Md. Vernon Youth Ctr. Served with AUS, 1943. Recipient cert. police cmty. rels. Mich. State U., 1961, Disting. Citizens award Office Gov. Md., 1971, Presdl. citation Balt. City Coun., 1977, Outstanding Alumnus award Mt. Vernon Law Sch., Eastern U., 1970, Wheel Master's award Metro Civic Assn., 1963, Cert. Appreciation Balt. Police Dept., 1972, Cert. of Appreciation Gov. Schaefer, 1991, Cert. award Balt. City Sheriff, 1994, Cert. of Appreciation and Congratulations, Congressman Ben Cardin, 1994; numerous awards B'nai B'rith, Safety First Club; Bernard Potts Day proclaimed by Gov. Md., 1980. Am. Bar Assn., Fed. Bar Assn., Am. Trial Lawyers Assn., Balt. Bar Assn., Met. Civic Assn. Balt. (v.p. 1968-80), Humanitarian Assn. Md. (v.p.), Jewish War Vets. (past post comdr.), Masons, B'nai B'rith (past pres. Balt. 1965, internat. commr. community svcs. 1972—, sec. CVS exec. commn.). Estate planning, Probate, Taxation, general. Home: 3206 Midfield Rd Baltimore MD 21208-4420 Office: Ste 1102 Court Sq Bldg Baltimore MD 21202

**POTTS, DENNIS WALKER,** lawyer; b. Santa Monica, Calif., Dec. 17, 1945; s. James Longworth and Donna (Neely) P.; m. Chung Wan; children: Brandon Earl Woodward, Trevor Shipley. BA, U. Calif., Santa Barbara, 1967; JD, U. Calif., San Francisco, 1970. Bar: Hawaii 1971, Calif. 1971, U.S. Dist. Ct. Hawaii 1971, U.S. Ct. Appeals (9th cir.) 1973, U.S. Supreme Ct. 1978, U.S. Dist. Ct. (cen. dist.) Calif. 1983. Assoc. Chuck Mau, Honolulu, 1971-74; sole practice Honolulu, 1974—; mem. litigation com. ACLU Hawaii, 1977-82; former mem. Hawaii Acad. Plaintiff's Attys. Recipient cert. Coll. of Advocacy, Hastings Coll. Law, U. Calif., San Francisco-Sch. Law Loyola U., San Francisco, 1973. Mem. ATLA (sustaining), ACLU Hawaii (Disting. Svc. cert. 1974), Consumer Lawyers Hawaii, Honolulu Club. Federal civil litigation, State civil litigation, Personal injury. Office: 2700 Pacific Tower 1001 Bishop St Honolulu HI 96813-3429

**POTUZNIK, CHARLES LADDY,** lawyer; b. Chgo., Feb. 11, 1947; s. Charles William and Laverne Frances (Zdenek) P.; m. Mary Margaret Quady, Jan. 2, 1988; children: Kylie Brommell, Kathryn Mary. BA with high honors, U. Ill., 1969; JD cum laude, Harvard U., 1973. Bar: Minn. 1973. Assoc. Dorsey & Whitney LLP, Mpls., 1973-78, ptnr., 1979—. Mem. Minn. State Bar Assn. (chmn. state securities law subcom., 1987—), Hennepin County Bar Assn., Minn. Securities Adv. Com., Phi Beta Kappa. Mem. Evang. Free Ch. Avocations: hunting, fishing, camping, canoeing, foreign travel. Securities, Finance. Office: Dorsey & Whitney LLP Pillsbury Ctr S 220 S 6th St Ste 2200 Minneapolis MN 55402-1498

**POUND, JOHN BENNETT,** lawyer; b. Champaign, Ill., Nov. 17, 1946; s. William R. and Louise Catherine (Kelly) P.; m. Mary Ann Hanson, June 19, 1971; children: Meghan Elizabeth, Matthew Fitzgerald. BA, U. N.Mex., 1968; JD, Boston Coll., 1971. Bar: N. Mex. 1971, U.S. Dist. Ct. N. Mex. 1971, U.S. Ct. Appeals (10th cir.) 1972, U.S. Supreme Ct., 1993. Law clk. to Hon. Oliver Seth, U.S. Ct. Appeals, 10th Cir., Santa Fe, 1971-72; asst. counsel Supreme Ct. Disciplinary Bd., 1977-83, dist. rev. officer, 1984—; mem. Supreme Ct. Com. on Jud. Performance Evaluation, 1983-85; bd. dirs. Archdiocese Santa Fe Cath. Social Svcs., 1995—. Contbr. articles to profl. jours. Pres. bd. dirs. N.Mex. Ind. Coll. Fund, Santa Fe; chmn. N.Mex. Dem. Leadership Coun., 1991—; bd. dirs. Santa Fe Boys Club, 1989-92; rules com. N.Mex. Dem. Party, 1982—; v.p. Los Alamos Nat. Lab. Comm. Coun., 1985-90; fin. chmn. N.Mex. Clinton for Pres. campaign, 1992; co-chmn. Clinton-Gore Re-election Campaign, N.Mex., 1996. Fellow Am. Bar Found., Am. Coll. Trial Lawyers, N.Mex. Bar Found.; mem. ABA, Am. Bd. Trial Advocates, N.Mex. Bar Assn. (health law sect. 1987—), Santa Fe County Bar Assn. Democrat. Roman Catholic. Avocations: history, foreign language, literature, swimming, baseball. General civil litigation, Health, General corporate. Office: Herrera Long & Pound PA PO Box 5098 2200 Brothers Rd Santa Fe NM 87505-6903

**POVICH, DAVID,** lawyer; b. Washington, June 8, 1935; s. Shirley Lewis and Ethyl (Friedman) P.; m. Constance Enid Tobriner, June 14, 1959; children: Douglas, Johanna, Judith, Andrew. BA, Yale U., 1958; LLB, Columbia U., 1962. Bar: D.C. 1962, U.S. Ct. Appeals (4th cir.) 1980, U.S. Tax Ct. 1981, U.S. Ct. Appeals (5th and 11th cirs.) 1984, U.S. Dist. Ct. Md., U.S. Ct. Appeals (3d cir.) 1997. Law clk. to assoc. judge D.C. Ct. Appeals, Washington, 1962-63; ptnr. Williams & Connolly, Washington, 1963—, mem. exec. com., 1986-87. Bd. dirs., officer Lisner Home for Aged. Mem. D.C. Bar Assn., ABA, Bar Assn. D.C., Barristers (exec. com. 1992-93). Federal civil litigation, Criminal, Personal injury. Office: Williams & Connolly 725 12th St NW Washington DC 20005-5901

**POWELL, BARRY L.,** public accountant, tax lawyer; b. Texarkana, Mar. 26, 1951; s. John C. and Pearl (Thatcher) P.; m. Shelley Tucker, June 22, 1975; children: Aaron N., Lewis M. BA, U. Tex., 1973; JD, IIT, Chgo.,

1980. CPA, Ill. Mgr. food svc. U. Tex., Austin, 1970-73; acctg. supr. Realco Svcs., Inc., Chgo., 1973-75; CPA Altschuler, Melvoin & Glasser, Chgo., 1975-77, Peat, Marwick & Mitchell, Chgo., 1977-80; assoc. Pitler & Mandell, Chgo., 198-83; CPA Arthur Young, Chgo., 1983-84; CPA, ptnr. Altschuler, Melvoin & Glasser, Chgo., 1984-93; exec. v.p., gen. counsel 1st Security Holding Corp., Chgo., 1993—; chmn. AM&G Fin. Svcs. Ind. Group, Chgo. Treas., bd. dirs. Northbrook (Ill.) Symphony Orchestra; sec., bd. dirs. Assn. for K.I.D.S., Chgo., 1984-87. Mem. AICPA, ABA, Ill. State Bar Assn., Chgo. Bar Assn., Ill. CPA Soc. Avocations: creative writing, photography. Office: First Security Holding Corp 150 S Wacker Dr Ste 1100 Chicago IL 60606-4103

**POWELL, CHARLES LAW,** lawyer; b. Abington, Pa., Apr. 25, 1958; s. Thomas Richards Jr. and Margaret Mowry (Estes) P.; m. Margaret Louise Thomas, July 6, 1985; children: John Richards, Daniel Robert, Olivia Grace. BA cum laude, Dickinson Coll., 1980; JD, Villanova U., 1983. Bar: Pa. 1983, U.S. Dist. Ct. (ea. dist.) Pa. 1983. Litigation assoc. Swartz, Campbell & Detweiler, Phila., 1983-92, ptnr., 1992—; speaker in field. Editor Coopertown SCOOP, Bryn Mawr and Haverford, Pa., 1989-91; contbr. articles to profl. publs. Mem. Coopertown Civic Assn., Bryn Mawr and Haverford, 1986—; chmn. stewardship com. Bryn Mawr Presbyn. Ch., 1993. Mem. Union League Phila., Pa. Def. Inst., Pa. Bar Assn., Def. Rsch. Inst., Comml. Law League Am., Phi Kappa Psi. Republican. Avocations: reading, family and church activities, running, gardening. Federal civil litigation, State civil litigation, Contracts commercial. Office: Swartz Campbell & Detweiler 1600 Land Title Bldg Philadelphia PA 19110

**POWELL, DURWOOD ROYCE,** lawyer; b. Raleigh, N.C., Nov. 21, 1951; s. Albert Royce and Powell; m. Leej Ida Copperfield, Mar. 1, 1980. BS, U. N.C., 1974, JD, 1979; LLM in Taxation, Emory U., 1985. Bar: N.C. 1979, U.S. Dist. Ct. (ea., mid. and we. dists.) N.C. 1981, U.S. Tax Ct. 1981, U.S. Ct. Appeals (4th cir.) 1984, U.S. Ct. Claims 1984, U.S. Supreme Ct. 1984, D.C. 1988, U.S. Ct. Appeals (D.C. cir.) 1988, N.Y. 1989. Mgmt. analyst GAO, Norfolk, Va., 1974-76; tax staff Arthur Andersen & Co., Washington, 1979-80; assoc. Biggs, Meadows, Etheridge & Johnson, Rocky Mount, N.C., 1980-82, Biggs Law Firm, Rocky Mount, 1982-83; ptnr. Maupin, Taylor, Ellis & Adams, Raleigh, N.C., 1985—, also bd. dirs.; adj. prof. corp. taxation Grad. Sch. Bus., U. N.C., Chapel Hill, 1989-92; faculty Duke U. Tax and Estate Planning Conf., 1991; mem. negotiation project Harvard U., Cambridge, Mass., 1992. Contbr. articles to profl. jours. Tax reform com. Duke U., Washington, 1988. Mem. ABA (tax, corp., banking and securities sects.), N.C. Bar Assn. (tax and corp. sects.), Phi Beta Kappa, Phi Eta Sigma. Corporate taxation, Mergers and acquisitions, Securities. Home: 7616 Wingfoot Dr Raleigh NC 27615-5485 Office: Maupin Taylor Ellis & Adams 3200 Beech Leaf Ct Ste 500 Raleigh NC 27604-1064

**POWELL, ERIC KARLTON,** lawyer, researcher; b. Parkersburg, W.Va., July 23, 1958; s. James Milton and Sarah Elizabeth (Gates) P. BA in History, W.Va. U., 1980, BSBA, 1981; JD, Western State U., Fullerton, Calif., 1987. Bar: Ga. 1992, W.Va. 1993, U.S. Dist. Ct. (we. dist.) W.Va. 1993. Reference libr. Western State U., 1984; tchr. acctg. Rosary H.S., Fullerton, 1984-85; law clk. Zonni, Ginnochio Taylor, Santa Ana, Calif., 1986-93; temp. law sch. Gibson, Dunn & Crutcher, Irvine, Calif., 1993; pvt. practice, Parkersburg, 1993—. Asst. scoutmaster Boy Scouts Am., Parkersburg, 1981-83. Mem. ABA, ATLA, W.Va. Trial Lawyers Assn., Nat. Eagle Scout Assn., Elks, Delta Theta Phi. Republican. Presbyterian. Avocations: hiking, reading, canoeing, chess, astronomy. Criminal, Juvenile, Personal injury. Home: 2002 20th St Parkersburg WV 26101-3606 Office: 500 Green St Parkersburg WV 26101-5131

**POWELL, J. R.,** lawyer, judge; b. Woodbury, N.J., Feb. 1, 1954; s. Jeremiah Robbins and Elaine Claire (Gardner) P.; m. Dianne M. Gilds, Feb. 20, 1983; children: Sarah Laine, Jillian Ruth. BA summa cum laude, Glassboro (N.J.) State Coll., 1976; JD, Rutgers U., Camden, N.J., 1979. Bar: Pa. 1980, N.J. 1981, U.S. Dist. Ct. N.J. 1981, U.S. Supreme Ct. 1989. Assoc. Falciani, Fletcher, Woodbury, 1980-83, Weber & Marcus, Woodbury, 1983-84; pvt. practice, Woodbury, 1984-95, Pitman, 1995—; presiding mcpl. ct. judge Vicinage 15 Boroughs of Glassboro, Clayton, Pitman, Paulsboro, Twps. of Harrison and South Harrison, N.J., 1986—, East Greenwich, Greenwich, and Gloucester City, 1996—, Deptford, 1997—; instr. Conf. Mcpl. Ct. Judges, Trenton, 1988—, chmn. conf., 1992-94; trustee Gloucester County Bar Found., 1988-94; mcpl. ct. com. Supreme Ct., N.J. Supreme Ct., Trenton, 1987—, com. on interpreters in the cts., 1996—; del. Rules of Evidence Conf., New Brunswick, 1992; faculty Nat. Jud. Coll., Reno, 1995—, Rowan U., Glassboro, N.J., 1997. Author, compiler: Benchbook for Municipal Court Judges, 1992; also articles. Mem. Mantua Twp. Sch. Bd., Barnsboro, N.J., 1984-86; pres. Harrison Twp. Jaycees, Richwood, N.J., 1974-75; trustee Mt. Zion United Meth. Ch., 1988—. With U.S. Army, 1972-74. Mem. Gloucester County Bar Assn. (trustee 1986-94), sec. 1994-95), Gloucester County Mcpl. Judges Assn. (treas., v.p., pres. 1987—). Avocations: golf, reading, music. General civil litigation, Education and schools, Personal injury. Office: 708 Lambs Rd Pitman NJ 08071-2038

**POWELL, J(AMES) C(ORBLEY),** lawyer, engineer; b. Parkersburg, W.Va., Sept. 29, 1955; s. James Milton and Sarah Lou (Gates) P. BSME, W.Va. U., 1977, JD, 1981. Bar: W.Va. 1981, U.S. Dist. Ct. (no. and so. dists.) W.Va. 1981, Pa. 1987, U.S. Supreme Ct. 1990, U.S. Ct. Appeals (4th cir.) 1992. With An. Cyanamid, Willow Island, W.Va., 1977-78; ptnr. Hardman & Powell, Parkersburg, 1981-89, Hunt & Powell, Charleston, W.Va., 1989-92; sole practitioner Charleston, 1992—. Republican candidate for W.Va. Ho. of Dels., Wood County, 1982, 84. Mem. ABA (sect. litigation com. on products liability 1988-91), ATLA (breast implant sect. 1993—), W.Va. State Bar (com. of criminal law 1987-94, com. law and medicine 1988-97, com. on sole and gen. practitioner), Kanawha County Bar Assn., Atty. Info. Exch. Assn., Soc. Automotive Engrs., W.Va. Head Injury Assn., W.Va. Trial Lawyers Assn. Presbyterian. Product liability, Personal injury, General civil litigation. Office: 405 Capitol St Ste 505 Charleston WV 25301-1730

**POWELL, JAMES M.,** lawyer, singer; b. Ashtabula, Ohio, May 27, 1939; s. Gerald and Lois Powell; m. Judith M. Powell, Aug. 12, 1961; children: Janai Lane, Jennifer Ernst, Julene Zizza. BS, U.S. Mcht. Marine Acad., 1961; JD, U. Mich., 1964. Bar: Alaska 1965, U.S. Dist. Ct. Alaska 1965, U.S. Ct. Appeals (9th cir.) 1965. Law clk. Alaska Supreme Ct., Fairbanks, 1964-65; ptnr. Hughes Thorsness Powell Huddleston & Bauman, Anchorage, 1965—. Mem. Alaska Bd. Govs., Anchorage, 1979-74; capt. CAP, 1997-98. Presbyterian. Avocations: flying, singing. Aviation, Personal injury, General civil litigation. Home: 2143 Churchill Dr Anchorage AK 99517-1311 Office: Hughes Thorsness Et Al 550 W 7th Ave Ste 1100 Anchorage AK 99501-3563

**POWELL, KATHLEEN LYNCH,** lawyer, real estate executive; b. N.Y.C., Dec. 30, 1949; d. Daniel Francis and Mary Margaret (Flynn) L.; m. P. Douglas Powell. BA in Math. cum laude, Coll. of Mt. St. Vincent, 1970; postgrad., U. Pa., 1976-77; JD cum laude, U. Md., 1977; LL.M. in Taxation, NYU, 1991. Bar: Pa. 1977, N.J. 1978, N.Y. 1984, D.C. 1985, Conn. 1995, U.S. Ct. Appeals (3d cir.) 1980, U.S. Supreme Ct. 1981. Research analyst, claims rep. Social Security Adminstrn., Balt., 1973-76; assoc. Drinker, Biddle & Reath, Phila., 1977-84, ptnr., 1984-86; v.p., gen. counsel M. Alfieri Co., Inc., Edison, N.J., 1987-89; v.p., counsel Berwind Property Group, Phila., 1992—; instr. Inst. for Paralegal Tng., Phila. 1984—. Vol. atty. Support Ctr. for Child Advocates, Phila., 1979-86, Queen Village Neighbors Assn., Phila., 1984-86; pres. Soc. Hill Towers Buyers Assn., Phila., 1979-80; bd. dirs. Soc. Hill Civic Assn., 1980. Mem. ABA, Pa. Bar Assn., Phila. Bar Assn. (chair zoning and land use com. 1985-86), Conn. Bar Assn.

**POWELL, KENNETH EDWARD,** investment banker; b. Danville, Va., Oct. 5, 1952; s. Terry Edward and C. Anne (Wooten) P.; m. Cicely Grandin Moorman, Jan. 3, 1976; children: Tanner, Priscilla. Student, Hampden-Sydney Coll., 1971-73; BA in Polit. Sci., U. Colo., 1975; JD, U. Richmond, 1978; LLM in Taxation, Coll. of William and Mary, 1982. Bar: Va. 1978, U.S. Dist. Ct. (ea. dist.) Va. 1979, U.S. Tax Ct. 1980. Ptnr. Maloney, Yeatts & Barr, Richmond, Va., 1978-87; ptnr., owner Hazel & Thomas, P.C., Richmond, 1987-94, mem. bus./tax team, internat. bus. team; v.p. Legg Mason, Richmond, Va., 1994—. Vice chmn. Sci. Mus. Va., Richmond, 1984-91; chmn. Va. Police Found., Inc., 1987; bd. dirs. State Edn. Assistance Authority, 1991—; mem. adv. bd. Va. Opera, 1991—; candidate U.S. Congress, Va., 1986. Recipient Disting. Svc. award Fraternal Order of Police, 1986; named Outstanding Young Man of the Yr., Jaycees, 1981, Outstanding Young Alumni, U. Colo., 1982. Mem. ABA, Va. Bar Assn. (chmn. profl. responsibility com. 1989-92, chmn. com. on legal edn. and admission to the Bar 1991—), Richmond Bar Assn., Richmond C. of C. (bd. dirs. 1988), Va. Econ. Developers Assn. (gen. counsel), Va. Econ. Bridge Initiative. Episcopal. Office: Legg Mason Wood Walker Inc Riverfront Plz East Tower 951 E Byrd St Ste 810 Richmond VA 23219-4039

**POWELL, LARRY SCOTT,** lawyer; b. Atlanta, Sept. 1, 1969; s. Larry Cassium and Jean (Schwingal) P.; m. Kristi Alane Van Matre, Dec. 3, 1994; 1 child, Kelsie Joy. BBA, Ohio U., 1991; JD, U. Detroit, 1994. Bar: Ohio. Law clk. Meigs County Common Pleas Ct., Pomeroy, Ohio, 1991, Meigs County Pub. Defenders, 1992; law clk. Meigs County Prosecutor's Office, 1993, asst. prosecutor, 1994—; assoc. Little, Sheets & Warner, Pomeroy, 1994-95; ptnr. Tenoglia & Powell, Pomeroy, 1995—; coord. Meigs County Mock Trial, 1994—. Mem. Pomeroy Gun Club, Eagles. Avocations: hunting, fishing, euchre, golfing. Office: Tenoglia & Powell 200 E 2d St Pomeroy OH 45769

**POWELL, ROGER NORMAN,** lawyer; b. Balt., Sept. 26, 1942; s. Philip C. and Roslyn (Goldberger) P.; m. Michele Rae Cohen, Aug. 10, 1965 (div. 1978); children: Alan, Tamara; m. Iris Sandra Quirmbach, Oct. 15, 1978. BA, U. Md., 1965; JD, U. Balt., 1970. Bar: Md. 1971. Pvt. practice Pikesville, Md., 1971—; atty. Md. State Fireman's Assn., Annapolis, 1974—. Editor: Fire Laws of Maryland, 1982-99, 8th edit. Bd. dirs. Md. affiliate Am. Diabetes Assn., 1988-90; founder, dir. Reister's Towne Festival. Named Vol. of Yr. Pikesville Vol. Fire Co., 1974. Mem. Md. Bar Assn., Md. State Fireman's Assn., Balt. County Bar Assn. Democrat. Jewish. General civil litigation, General practice. Office: 107 Old Court Rd Baltimore MD 21208-4011

**POWELL, RUSSELL ALAN,** lawyer; b. Lerwick, Scotland, Dec. 13, 1960; came to U.S., 1993; s. Caleb and Annkina (Merchant) P. BA in Astronautics, U. London, 1980; LLB, U. Glasgow, Scotland, 1984; JD, Harvard U., 1995. Bar: Grey's Ct., U.K. 1985, U.S. Ct. Appeals (11th cir.) 1995. Barrister Orr & Assocs., London, 1985-89; engr. European Space Agy., Paris, 1989-93; assoc. Reynolds, Baugh & Mills, Boston, 1995; ptnr. Powell & Assocs., Pigeon Forge, Tenn., 1995—; cons. Brit. Parliament, London, 1987-89; advocate Grey's Ct., London, 1986-88. Author: Man and Law, 1987, (periodical) Operation of Rocket, 1991; patentee ground tire sparer. Child counselor Youth of Am., N.C., 1993-94, Tenn., 1996-97. Lt. Royal Army, 1981-84. Winner World Cruiserweight Boxing Championship, 1994. Mem. ABA, Fed. Bar Assn., Internat. Bar Assn. Republican. Avocations: music, chess, research. Constitutional, Civil rights. Office: 3152 Parkway Ste 13-122 Pigeon Forge TN 37863-3340

**POWELL, STEPHEN WALTER,** judge; b. Hamilton, Ohio, Jan. 25, 1955; s. Walter E. and Bobbi M. (Powell) P.; m. Kathryn Powell; children: Eric R.W., S. Michael; stepchildren: Greggory A., Garrett A. BA, Heidelberg Coll., 1977; JD, U. Dayton, 1981. Bar: Ohio 1981, U.S. Dist. Ct. (so. dist.) Ohio 1982. Referee Common Pleas Ct., Juvenile, Domestic and Probate, Hamilton, 1984-88; ptnr. Powell, Napier, Carmella and Allen, Hamilton, 1986-91; judge Area II Ct., Butler County, Ohio, 1989-91; judge probate div. Butler County Common Pleas Ct., Hamilton, 1991-95; presiding judge Ohio Ct. Appeals, 12th Appellate Dist., Middletown, 1995-97, adminstrv. judge, 1997-98, presiding judge, 1999—; agt. Commonwealth Land Title, Louisville, 1988-90; parliamentarian Judges Assn. Ohio Ct. Appeals, 1995—. Sec. Butler County Rep. Cen. Com., 1982-88; trustee Union Twp., Butler County, West Chester, 1979-88; bd. dirs. United Way Hamilton Area, 1986-90. Named Man of the Day Sta. WMOH, Hamilton, 1986; recipient Meritorious Svc. award Ohio Assn. Probate Judges, 1992, 93, 94. Mem. ABA, Ohio Bar Assn., Butler County Bar Assn. Presbyterian. Office: Ohio Ct Appeals 12th Appellate Dist 1 City Centre Plz # 1009 Middletown OH 45042-1901

**POWER, JOHN BRUCE,** lawyer; b. Glendale, Calif., Nov. 11, 1936; m. Sandra Garfield, Apr. 27, 1998; children by previous marriage: Grant, Mark, Boyd. AB magna cum laude, Occidental Coll., 1958; JD, NYU, 1961; postdoctoral, Columbia U., 1972. Bar: Calif. 1962. Assoc. O'Melveny & Myers, L.A., 1961-70, ptnr., 1970-97; resident ptnr. O'Melveny & Myers, Paris, 1973-75; Sheffelman disting. lectr. Sch. Law, U. Wash., Seattle, 1997; mem. Social Svcs. Commn. City of L.A., 1993, pres., 1993; pres. circle, exec. com. Occidental Coll., 1979-82, 91-94, chair, 1993-94. Contbr. articles to jours. Bd. dirs. Met. L.A. YMCA, 1988—, treas., 1998—; mem. bd. mgrs. Stuart Ketchum Downtown YMCA, 1985-92, pres., 1989-90; mem. Los Angeles County Rep. Ctrl. Com., 1962-63; trustee Occidental Coll., 1992—, vice chmn., 1998—. Root Tilden scholar. Fellow Am. Coll. Comml. Fin. Lawyers (bd. regents 1999—); mem. ABA (vice chmn. internat. fin. subcom. 1984-91, comml. fin. svcs. com., com. 3d party legal opinions, UCC com., bus. law sect.), Am. Bar Found. (life), Calif. Bar Assn. (chmn. partnerships and unincorporated assns. com. 1982-83, chmn. uniform commn. code com. 1984-85, exec. com. 1987-91, chmn. bus. law sect. 1990-91, chmn. coun. sect. chairs 1992-93, liaison to state bar commn. on future of legal profession and state bar), L.A. County Bar Assn. (exec. com. comml. law and bankruptcy sect. 1970-73, 86-89), Internat. Bar Assn., Fin. Lawyers Conf. (bd. govs. 1982—, pres. 1984-85), Exec. Svc. Corps (sec. 1985—, trustee 1994—), Occidental Coll. Alumni Assn. (pres. 1967-68), Phi Beta Kappa. General corporate, Private international, Securities. Office: O'Melveny & Myers 400 S Hope St Los Angeles CA 90071-2899

**POWERS, BRIDGET BROWN,** lawyer, educator; b. Huntsville, Ala., July 24, 1966; d. Roy Elbert and Nancy Anne Elizabeth Brown; m. Carl Frederick Powers, June 16, 1994; 1 child, Kelly Elizabeth Mary. BA, U. N.C., 1989; JD, Detroit Coll. of Law, 1992. Assoc. Pointner & Joseph, P.C., Charlevoix, Mich., 1992-94; owner, ptnr. Smith and Powers, Petoskey, Mich., 1994—; adj. instr. North Ctrl. Mich. Coll., Petoskey, 1996—; asst. city atty. City of Petoskey, 1995—; v.p., bd. dirs. Charlevoix Fed. Credit Union, 1996—. Mem. Women's Resource Ctr., Petoskey, 1992—. Recipient Sheriff's Appreciation award Charlevoix City Sheriff, 1995; named Outstanding Jaycee of Yr. Petoskey Area Jaycees, 1994-95. Mem. C. of C. Republican. Roman Catholic. Avocations: reading, tennis, golf, hiking, camping. General civil litigation, Real property, Probate. Office: Smith and Powers 618 Howard St Petoskey MI 49770-2724

**POWERS, EDWARD HERBERT,** lawyer; b. Jersey City, N.J., June 21, 1942; s. Samuel and Ruth (Handman) P.; m. Phyllis Elinor Alpern, May 29, 1966; children: Alexander, Jill, Annette. BA, U. Mich., 1964, JD, 1967. Bar: Mich. 1968, U.S. Dist. Ct. (ea. dist.) Mich. 1968, U.S. Ct. Appeals (6th cir.) 1989, U.S. Supreme Ct. 1990. Owner, mem. Pelavin, Powers & Behm PC., Flint, Mich., 1968—; instr. Mott Adult Edn., Flint, 1970-74 Chmn. region XI U. Mich. Law Sch. Fund, 1980-81; v.p. Flint Jewish Fedn., 1978-82; chmn. Flint United Jewish Appeal, 1978; v.p. Congregation Beth Israel, 1979-82. Mem. Assn. Trial Lawyers Am., Mich. Trial Lawyers Assn., State Bar Mich., ABA (forum on constrn. industry), Genesee County Bar Assn., Am. Mensa Soc., Univ. Club (Flint). Real property, Contracts commercial, General practice. Home: 1071 Briarcliffe Dr Flint MI 48532-2102 Office: Pelavin Powers & Behm PC 200 Phoenix Bldg Flint MI 48502

**POWERS, ELIZABETH WHITMEL,** lawyer; b. Charleston, S.C., Dec. 16, 1949; d. Francis Persse and Jane Coleman Cotten (Wham) P.; m. John Campbell Henry, June 11, 1994 (dec. Jan. 1997). AB, Mt. Holyoke Coll., 1971; JD, U. S.C., 1978. Bar: S.C. 1978, N.Y. 1979. Law clk. to justice S.C. Cir. Ct., Columbia; assoc. Reid & Priest, N.Y.C., 1978-86, ptnr., 1986-97; of counsel LeBoeuf, Lamb, Greene & MacRae, N.Y.C., 1997—. Exec. editor S.C. Law Rev., Columbia, 1977-78. Bd. dirs. The Seamen's Ch. Inst., 1996—, sec., 1999—; vol. N.Y. Jr. League, N.Y.C., 1983—; bd. trustees Ch. Club, 1991-94, 97—, v.p. 1992-94. Mem. ABA, S.C. Bar Assn., Nat. Soc. Colonial Dames of Am. (parliamentarian 1994—), Nat. Soc. Colonial Dames in State of N.Y. (pres. 1992-95). Avocations: bridge, tennis. Public utilities, General corporate, Securities.

**POWERS, JOHN KIERAN,** lawyer; b. Schenectady, Aug. 2, 1947; s. Paul Joseph and Anne Marie (Leahy) P.; children: Erin Kelly, Megan Kerry. BS, U. Notre Dame, 1969; JD, Union U., Albany, N.Y., 1972. Bar: N.Y. 1973, U.S. Dist. Ct. (no. dist.) N.Y. 1973, U.S. Dist. Ct. (so., ea., we. dists.) N.Y. 1982, U.S. Ct. Appeals (2d cir.) 1984, U.S. Supreme Ct. 1985, U.S. Dist. Ct. Vt. 1988. Assoc. Medwin and McMahon, Albany, 1973-77; pvt. practice law, Albany, 1973-80; pres. John K. Powers, P.C., Albany, 1980-87; ptnr. Powers and Santola, 1987—; trustee N.Y. State Lawyers Polit. Action Com., 1983-88, treas., 1989-93, chair, 1993—; trustee ATLA Pol. Action Com., 1995-98. Contbr. articles to publs. Fellow Roscoe Pound Found. Mem. ABA (sustaining, vice-chair, legis. subcom., automobile law com., trial and ins. practice sect., state leader com. on state legis. sect.), Nat. Coll. Adv. (co-founder), Assn. Trial Lawyers Am. (life, state del. 1990, bd. govs. 1990—, exec. com. 1995—), Am. Bd. Trial Advocates (advocate), N.Y. State Bar Assn. (sustaining, lectr., exec. com. and chmn. legis. com. trial lawyers sect.), N.Y. State Trial Lawyers Assn. (sustaining, bd. dirs. 1983-88, chmn. key person legis. com., chmn. pubs. com., chmn. atty. referral com., exec. com. 1986—, treas. 1988-89, v.p. 1989-91, 1st v.p. 1990-91, pres.-elect 1991-92, pres. 1992-93, award of merit, 1990, 94, award of excellence 1991, Pres. award 1995, 96, 98, dist. svc. award 1997), N.Y. Trial Lawyers Inst. (lectr. and program chmn. 1981—, treas. 1988-89, pres. 1992-93), (life) N.Y. State Head Injury Assn. (co-counsel 1983-85, bd. dirs. 1992-93, 1st v.p. 1993—), Capitol Dist. Trial Lawyers Assn. (bd. dir. 1979-81, v.p. 1983-85, pres. 1985-86), Pa. Trial Lawyers Assn., Alban County Bar Assn. (lectr.), Chief Judge's Com. to Improve Availability of Legal Svcs., Chief Judge's Pro-Bono Monitoring Com., Civil Justice Found. (guest lectr. Law Sch. NYU, Albany Law Sch., U. Syracuse Law Sch., Albany Med. Coll.), Trial Lawyers for Pub. Justice, Lions (pres. Scotia, N.Y. chpt. 1979-80). Democrat. Roman Catholic. Federal civil litigation, State civil litigation, Personal injury. Home and Office: 39 N Pearl St Albany NY 12207-2785

**POWLESS, KENNETH BARNETT,** lawyer; b. Creal Springs, Ill., Mar. 11, 1917; s. George Newton and Sarah Maud (Barnett) P.; m. Emily Mary Cygnar, July 17, 1943; children: Linda Carol, James Kenneth, David Griffin, Catherine Celeste. BS, U. Ill., 1938, JD, 1940. Bar: Ill. 1940. Pvt. practice Marion, Ill., 1940-41, 52-58, Marion, 1963-64; ptnr. Powless and Winters, Marion, 1946-52, Winters, Powless & Morgan, Marion, 1958-63, Powless Law Office, Marion, 1974-82; arbitrator Indsl. Commn. Ill., 1983-90; ret. counsel, dir. 1st Bank & Trust Co. of Williamson County. Chmn. bd. Marion Meml. Hosp., 1956-76, bd. dirs. emeritus, 1976—; spl. asst. atty. gen. State of Ill., 1954-58, 73-82; state's atty. Williamson County, 1968-72, former arbitrator Indl. Commn., 1980-889. Capt. U.S. Army, 1941-46, ETO. Mem. Am. Soc. Hosp. Attys., Ill. State Bar Assn., Williamson County Bar Assn., Egyptian Illini Club, Marion Kiwanis Club (dist. lt. gov. 1971), Elks Club (exalted ruler 1951), Masons, Shriners. Republican. Methodist. Condemnation, Real property. Home: 905 N Van Buren St Marion IL 62959-2255

**POZNER, LOUIS-JACK,** lawyer; b. N.Y.C., Dec. 12, 1946; s. Harry Bear and Regina (Lindsey) P.; m. Rona Judkowitz, June 9, 1968; children: Samantha Brooke, Jo-Ellen, Zachary Blair. BA with honors in History, U. Rochester, 1968; JD, Bklyn. Law Sch., 1971. Bar: N.Y. 1972, U.S. Dist Ct. (no. dist.) N.Y. 1972, U.S. Dist. Ct. (so. and ea. dists.) N.Y. 1991, U.S. Supreme Ct. 1983. Law clk. N.Y. State Supreme Ct. Appellate Divsn. 3rd Dept., Albany, 1971-72; law clk. to Judge James Gibson N.Y. State Ct. Appeals, Albany, 1972; assoc. DeGraff Foy Conway Holt-Harris & Meeley, Albany, N.Y., 1973-74; pvt. practice Albany, N.Y., 1974—; pres. Louis-Jack Pozner, P.C., Albany, N.Y., 1993—; judge Albany Law Sch. Moot Ct. Competition, 1979, 80, 84, 86, 89—; advisor in 1982 State Mock Trial Tournament. Pres. Electronic Body Art Inc., 1979-80, bd. dirs., 1976-79; trustee Temple Israel Albany, 1976-82, 98—, v.p., 1980-82, exec. v.p., 1995-96, pres., 1996-98; bd. dirs. Friends of Albany Pub. Libr., 1982-84, Greater Albany Jewish Fedn., 1979-85, Horizon House, 1982-83, Bet Shraga Hebrew Acad. the Capital Dist., 1978-88, v.p., 1980-85, pres., 1985-88; co-chmn. cmty. rels. com. Greater Albany Jewish Fedn., 1980-82; trustee Daus. of Sarah Found., 1983—, v.p., 1988-90, pres., 1990-93; bd. trustees Greater Jewish Fedn. Northeastern N.Y., 1999—, bd. govs. endowment fund, 1999—. Recipient of Greater Albany Jewish Fedn. Samuel E. Aronowitz Young Leadership award, 1981. Mem. ABA (mem. character and fitness coms. 3d dist. 1990-99, mem. com. on profl. stds. 1999—), Albany County Bankruptcy Bar Assn., Albany County Bar Assn., Assn. Trial Lawyers Am., N.Y. State Bar Assn., N.Y. State Trial Lawyers Assn. (family law sect.). General civil litigation, General practice, Family and matrimonial. Home: 258 Lenox Ave Albany NY 12208-1408 Office: 11 N Pearl St Apt 1405 Albany NY 12207-2709

**POZO-DIAZ, MARTHA DEL CARMEN,** lawyer; b. Miami, Fla., May 24, 1965; d. Eduardo Esteban and Martha Josefina (Coll) Pozo; m. Ramon Jorge Diaz, Jan. 7, 1989; children: Ramon Eduardo, Martha del Carmen, Eduardo Manuel. BBA, U. Miami, 1986, JD, 1990. Bar: Fla. 1991. Owner, pres. Martha Pozo-Diaz, P.A., Miami, 1990—. Mem. ABA, Dade County Bar Assn., Cuban Am. Bar Assn. Republican. Roman Catholic. Real property, General corporate. Office: 8000 W Flagler St Ste 203 Miami FL 33144-2153

**POZZUOLI-BUECKER, RENEE M.,** lawyer; b. Wellsville, N.Y., Sept. 21, 1964; d. Orlando R. and Jennet R. Pozzuoli; m. Allan P. Buecker Jr., Oct. 12, 1990; 2 children. BA/BS in Acctg. and Polit. Sci., Cabrini Coll., 1986; JD, Villanova U., 1989. Bar: N.J. 1989, Pa. 1989, U.S. Dist. Ct. (ea. dist.) Pa. 1989, U.S. Dist. Ct. N.J. 1989. Assoc. Hughes & Hendrix, W. Trenton, N.J., 1989-96, Goldbeck, McCafferty & McKeever, Westmont, N.J., 1996—. Mem. adv. bds. United Way. Mem. ABA, N.J. Bar Assn., Pa. Bar Assn. Republican. Roman Catholic. Bankruptcy, Consumer commercial, State civil litigation. Office: Goldbeck McCafferty & McKeever 216 Haddon Ave Ste 420 Westmont NJ 08108-2812

**PRAGER, BETTY RUTH,** lawyer, medical technician; b. Phila., July 11, 1932; d. Marcus and Lydia (Nickespark) Tecker. AB, Temple U., 1954; JD, U. West L.A., 1980. Bar: Calif. 1989. Med. technician, L.A., 1955—, pvt. practice,, 1989—. Office: 12304 Santa Monica Blvd Los Angeles CA 90025-2551

**PRAGER, SUSAN WESTERBERG,** law educator, provost; b. Sacramento, Dec. 14, 1942; d. Percy Foster Westerberg and Aileen M. (McKinley) P.; m. James Martin Prager, Dec. 14, 1973; children: McKinley Ann, Case Mahone. AB, Stanford U., 1964, MA, 1967; JD, UCLA, 1971. Bar: N.C. 1971, Calif. 1972. Atty. Powe, Porter & Alphin, Durham, N.C., 1971-72; acting prof. law UCLA, 1972-77, prof. Sch. Law, 1977—, Arjay and Frances Fearing Miller prof. of law, 1992—, assoc. dean Sch. Law, 1979-82, dean, 1982-98; provost Dartmouth Coll., Hanover, N.H., 1999—; bd. dirs. Pacific Mut. Life Ins. Co., Newport Beach, Calif. Editor-in-chief, UCLA Law Rev., 1970-71. Trustee Stanford U., 1976-80, 87-97. Mem. ABA (council of sect. on legal edn. and admissions to the bar 1983-85), Assn. Am. Law Schs. (pres. 1986), Order of Coif. Address: Dartmouth College Office of the Provost 6004 Parkhurst Hall Rm 204 Hanover NH 03755-3529

**PRAGUE, RONALD JAY,** lawyer; b. N.Y.C., May 1, 1963; s. Martin Malcolm Prague and Betty Mae Sorrin; m. Jerilyn Semon; children: Haley Sara, Jessica Nikki. BS, Cornell U., 1985; JD, Northwestern U., Chgo., 1988. Bar: N.Y. 1988, U.S. Dist. Ct. (so. and ea. dists.) N.Y. Assoc. Richards & O'Neil, N.Y.C., 1988-92, Haythe & Curley, N.Y.C., 1992-98; corp. counsel Dialogic Corp., Parsippany, N.J., 1998—. Mem. N.Y. State Bar Assn. (trademark and unfair competition com. 1997—). Contracts commercial, General corporate, Intellectual property. Home: 1160 3d Ave Apt 4E New York NY 10021 Office: Dialogic Corp 1515 Route 10 Parsippany NJ 07054-4538

**PRANSKY, JOAN E.,** lawyer, community organizer; b. N.Y.C., Apr. 26, 1946; d. John and Sharon (Harris) P.; 1 child, Leah. BS, Syracuse U., 1967; JD, Seton Hall U., 1974. Bar: N.J. 1974, U.S. Dist. Ct. N.J. 1974. Social worker Dept. Social Svcs., N.Y.C., 1967; elem. sch. tchr. V.I. Bd. Edn., St. Thomas, 1968; lawyer Essex-Newark Legal Svcs., 1974-83; supervising trial atty. Urban Legal Clinic, prof. Rutgers U. Sch. Law, Newark, 1983-86; atty. in pvt. practice Montclair, N.J., 1986—; atty., N.J. State Bar fellow Seton Hall Law Sch. Ctr. for Social Justice, Newark, 1992-94; legal counsel N.J. Tenant Orgn., 1984—; legal counsel, advisor City-wide Tenant Orgns., East Orange, Newark, Paterson, Elizabeth, Orange, Jersey City, 1976-90; adv. mem. N.J. State Com. on Rent Control, , N.J. State Com. on Multifamily Dwellings, 1983-85. Editor, co-founder Shelterforce, 1976-85; contbr. articles to N.Y. Times, others. Bd. dirs. N.J. Citizen Action, 1990-94; mem. budget adv. com. Montclair Bd. Edn., 1996; co-founder Support Integrated Pub. Edn., Montclair, 1996; co-founder, mem. steering com. Montclair Civil

Rights Coalition, 1997. Recipient Equal Justice medal Legal Svcs. of N.J., 1989, Ronald B. Atlas Meml. award N.J. Tenant Assn., 1988. Mem. N.J. State Bar, N.J. Nat. Lawyers Guild, N.J. Rainbow Coalition (Fannie Lou Hamer br.). Avocations: singing in chorus, hiking, whitewater rafting, jogging. Home: 11 Stephen St Montclair NJ 07042-5031 Office: 460 Bloomfield Ave Montclair NJ 07042-3552

**PRASHER, GREGORY GEORGE,** lawyer; b. Akron, Ohio, Oct. 4, 1948; s. George and Pauline Grace (Marcum) P.; m. Patricia Jolyn Siepel, Aug. 22, 1970 (div. Aug. 1993); children: Angela Katheryn, Michael Gregory. BA, Ohio State U., 1969; JD, Duke U., 1972. Bar: U.S. Dist. Ct. (we. and ea. dists.) Mich. 1972, U.S. Ct. Appeals (6th cir.) 1974, U.S. Supreme Ct. 1980. Assoc. Warner, Norcross & Judd, Grand Rapids, Mich., 1972-76; shareholder Clary, Nantz & Wood, Grand Rapids, 1976-84; shareholder, officer Schenk, Boncher & Prasher, Grand Rapids, 1984—; legal counsel Wetlands Found. of West Mich., Grand Rapids, 1985—. Bd. dirs., officer Grand Rapids Summerfest, 1987-94; bd. dirs. Grand Rapids Ballet, 1990-93; precinct del. Rep. Party, Kent County, Mich., 1985-86, Mich. State del., 1986. Mem. Elks. Roman Catholic. Avocations: golf, carpentry, cycling. General corporate, General civil litigation, Probate. Office: Schenk Boncher & Prasher 601 3 Mile Rd NW Grand Rapids MI 49544-1601

**PRASHKER, AUDREY EVE,** lawyer; b. N.Y.C., Nov. 11, 1958; d. Eugene Ira and Roberta Phyllis (Frank) P.; m. Alexander Oldham Clarke, July 11, 1992. Attended, Dartmouth Coll., 1978-79; BA, Wellesley Coll., 1980; JD, Columbia U., 1983. Bar: N.Y. 1984. Assoc. Reavis & McGrath, N.Y.C., 1983-85; assoc. Paul Weiss Rifkind Wharton & Garrison, N.Y.C., 1985-90, 94-95, Tokyo, 1990-94; sr. atty. internat. wireline, video, mergers & acquisitions Bell Atlantic Corp., N.Y.C., 1995—. Bd. dirs. Surprise Lake Camp, N.Y.C., 1989—. Mem. Fgn. Women Lawyers Assn. (pres. 1993-94, treas. 1992-93), Bar Assn. City of N.Y. (Asian affairs com.). Avocations: swimming, tennis, computers. General corporate, Mergers and acquisitions, Private international. Office: Bell Atlantic Corp 1095 Ave of Americas New York NY 10036

**PRATHER, JOHN CHRISTOPHER,** lawyer; b. Bushnell, Fla., Nov. 19, 1951; s. John Gibson and Mary McCarley Prather; m. Beth Elaine Lindberg, May 31, 1986; children: Ashley Ann, Lucy Amalia. BA, U. N.C., 1974, JD, 1974. Bar: N.C. 1977, N.Y. 1983, U.S. Dist. Ct. (we. dist.) N.C. 1980, U.S. Ct. Appeals (4th cir.) 1979. Asst. atty. gen. N.C. Atty. Gen.'s Office, Raleigh, 1977-82; asst. dist. atty. N.Y. County Dist. Atty.'s Office, N.Y.C., 1982-96, dep. bur. chief, 1989-92, sr. investigative counsel, 1992-96; 1st asst. inspector gen. N.Y.C. Sch. Constrn. Aux., Bronx, 1996—. Recipient Cert. of Appreciation, Motion Picture Assn. of Am., 1993. Office: NYC Sch Constrn Auth 188 W 230th St Bronx NY 10463-5215

**PRATHER, JOHN GIDEON, JR.,** lawyer; b. Lexington, Ky., Sept. 10, 1946; s. John Gideon Sr. and Marie Jeanette (Moore) P.; m. Hilma Elizabeth Skonberg, Aug. 4, 1973; children: John Hunt, Anna Russell. BS in Acctg., U. Ky., 1968, JD, 1970. Bar: Ky. 1971, U.S. Dist. Ct. (ea. dist.) Ky. 1978, U.S. Dist. Ct. (we. dist.) Ky. 1984, U.S. Ct. Appeals (6th cir.) 1988, U.S. Supreme Ct. 1988. Ptnr., prin. Law Offices John G. Prather, Somerset, Ky., 1972—; bd. dirs. Lawyers Mutual Ins. Co. Ky., 1989—, treas., 1995—. Bd. dirs. United Way, 1978—; mem. state cen. com. Ky. Young. Dems., Frankfort, 1972. Served to 1st lt. USAF, 1971-72, JAG, 1972. Mem. ABA (house dels.), ATLA, Am. Bd. Trial Advs., Am. Coll. Trial Lawyers, Ky. Acad. Trial Attys., Ky. Bar Assn. (ho. of dels. 1984-85, bd. govs. 1985-91, v.p. 1991-92, pres.-elect 1992-93, pres. 1993-94, lectr.), Coun. Sch. Bd. Attys. (state pres., bd. dirs. 1986—, lectr.), Ky. Def. Coun. (bd. dirs. 1987-91), Pulaski County Indsl. Found. (bd. dirs. 1982-95), Phi Delta Phi. Mem. Christian Ch. Avocations: boating, flying. General practice, Personal injury, Probate. Home: 510 N Main St Somerset KY 42501-1434 Office: PO Box 616 Somerset KY 42502-0616

**PRATHER, KENNETH EARL,** lawyer; b. Detroit, May 9, 1933; s. Earl and Agnes (Mesanko) P.; m. Shirley Armstrong, Dec. 26, 1955; children: Eric, Kimberly, Jon, Laura, Lisa; m. Jeanette M. Elder, June 30, 1973; 1 child, Kenneth. PhB, U. Detroit, 1955, JD 1960. Bar: Mich. 1960. Assoc. Kenney, Radom, Rockwell & Kenney, Detroit, 1960-66; ptnr. Kenney, Kenney, Chapman & Prather, Detroit, 1966-76; pvt. practice, Detroit, 1976-82; ptnr. Prather, Hilborn & Harrington, P.C., Detroit, 1982, Prather & Assocs., P.C., Detroit, 1982—; adj. prof. law U. Detroit. Fellow Am. Acad. Matrimonial Lawyers (bd. govs. 1988-89), Internat. Acad. Matrimonial Lawyers (bd. mgrs. 1989); mem. Am. Coll. Family Law Trial Lawyers, State Bar Mich. (chairperson family law sect. 1983-84), Detroit Athletic. Contbr. articles to legal jours. Family and matrimonial, Personal injury. Home: 5 Stratford Pl Grosse Pointe MI 48230-1907 Office: Prather & Assocs PC 3800 Penobscot Bldg Detroit MI 48226

**PRATHER, LENORE LOVING,** state supreme court chief justice; b. West Point, Miss., Sept. 17, 1931; d. Byron Herald and Hattie Hearn (Morris) Loving; m. Robert Brooks Prather, May 30, 1957; children: Pamela, Valerie Jo, Malinda Wayne. B.S., Miss. Univ. Women, 1953; JD, U. Miss., 1955. Bar: Miss. 1955. Practice with B. H. Loving, West Point, 1955-60, sole practice, 1960-62, 65-71, assoc. practice, 1962-65; mcpl. judge City of West Point, 1965-71; chancery ct. judge 14th dist. State of Miss., Columbus, 1971-82; supreme ct. justice State of Miss., Jackson, 1982-92, presiding justice, 1993-97, chief justice, 1998—; v.p. Conf. Local Bar Assn., 1956-58; sec. Clay County Bar Assn., 1956-71. 1st woman in Miss. to become chancery judge, 1971, and supreme ct. justice, 1982. Mem. ABA, Miss. State Bar Assn., Miss. Conf. Judges, DAR, Rotary, Pilot Club, Jr. Aux. Columbus Club. Episcopalian. Office: Miss Supreme Ct PO Box 117 Jackson MS 39205-0117

**PRATT, GEORGE CHENEY,** law educator, retired federal judge; b. Corning, N.Y., May 22, 1928; s. George Wollage and Muriel (Cheney) P.; m. Carol June Hoffman, Aug. 16, 1952; children: George W., Lise M., Marcia Pratt Burke, William T. BA, Yale U., 1950, JD, 1953. Bar: N.Y. 1953, U.S. Supreme Ct. 1964, U.S. Ct. Appeals 1974. Law clk. to Charles W. Froessel (Judge of N.Y. Ct. Appeals), 1953-55; assoc. then ptnr. Sprague & Stern, Mineola, N.Y., 1956-60; ptnr. Andromidas, Pratt & Pitcher, Mineola, 1960-65, Pratt, Caemmerer & Cleary, Mineola, 1965-75; partner Farrell, Fritz, Pratt, Caemmerer & Cleary, 1975-76; judge U.S. Dist. Ct. (Eastern Dist. of N.Y.), 1976-82, U.S. Circuit Ct. Appeals for 2d circuit (Uniondale), N.Y., 1982-93; sr. circ. judge U.S. Cir. of Appeals for 2d Cir., N.Y., 1993-95; prof. Touro Law Sch., Huntington, N.Y., 1993—; counsel Parnon & Pratt L.L.P., N.Y.C., 1995—. Mem. ABA, N.Y. State Bar Assn., Nassau County Bar Assn., Soc. Am. Law Tchrs. Mem. United Ch. of Christ. Office: Touro Law Ctr 300 Nassau Rd Huntington NY 11743-4346

**PRATT, ROBERT WINDSOR,** lawyer; b. Findlay, Ohio, Mar. 6, 1950; s. John Windsor and Isabelle (Vance) P.; m. Catherine Camak Baker, Sept. 3, 1977; children: Andrew Windsor, David Camak, James Robert. AB, Wittenberg U., Springfield, Ohio, 1972; JD, Yale U., 1975. Bar: Ill. 1975, U.S. Dist. Ct. (no. dist.) Ill. 1976, U.S. Dist. Ct. (we. dist.) Mich. 1995, U.S. Ct. Appeals (fed. cir.) 1984, U.S. Ct. Appeals (7th cir.) 1996. Assoc. Keck, Mahin & Cate, Chgo., 1975-81, ptnr., 1981-97; pvt. practice Wilmette, Ill., 1998—. Bd. dirs. Chgo. region ARC, 1985-96, vice chmn., 1988-92, chmn., 1992-96, bd. dirs. Mid-Am. chpt., 1992-96. Mem. ABA, Chgo. Bar Assn., Yale Club (Chgo.). Antitrust, Finance, Contracts commercial.

**PRATTE, GEOFFREY LYNN,** lawyer, arbitrator; b. Bonne Terre, Mo., Sept. 14, 1940; s. Charles John and Ruth Jane (Thornton) P.; m. Gretchen Ann Westendorf, Mar. 15, 1969; children: Stephen Charles, Geoffrey Marc, Nicole Elizabeth, Gregory Lynn, Robert Wendell. BA in Philosophy, Kilroe Coll., 1963; MA in French, St. Louis U., 1967; JD, Wash. U., 1974. Bar: Mo. 1974, U.S. Dist. Ct. (ea. dist.) Mo. Tchr. Divine Heart Sem., Donaldson, Ind., 1963-65; analyst CIA, McLean, Va., 1967-71; assoc. Roberts & Roberts, Farmington, Mo., 1974-87; pvt. practice Farmington, Mo., 1987—; asst. pros. atty. St. Francis County, Farmington, Mo., 1987-93; city pros. atty. Bonne Terre, Mo., 1988—; labor arbitrator Fed. Mediation and Conciliation Svc., Washington, 1988—. Bd. dirs. Terre du Lac Property Owners Assn., 1976-87. Mem. Order of the Coif, KC. Roman Catholic. Avocations: jogging, gardening. Office: 205 E Liberty St Farmington MO 63640-3129

**PRATUM, MICHAEL JAMES,** lawyer; b. Bellingham, Wash., Oct. 14, 1955; s. Rolf Hoyendahl Pratum. BS in Chemistry, U. Puget Sound, 1979, BA in Philosophy, 1980, JD, 1984. Bar: Wash. 1986, U.S. Dist. Ct. (we. dist.) Wash. 1986. Pvt. practice Federal Way, Wash., 1987—. Mem. Wash. Bar Assn., Seattle-King County Bar Assn., Wash. Trial Lawyers Assn., Assn. Trial Lawyers Am., Fed. Way C. of C. (ambassador 1987-90). Labor, General civil litigation, General practice. Office: 33516 9th Ave S # 5B Federal Way WA 98003-6322

**PRAVEL, BERNARR ROE,** lawyer; b. Feb. 10, 1924. BSChemE, Rice U., 1947; JD, George Washington U., 1951. Bar: D.C. 1951, Tex. 1951, U.S. Supreme Ct. 1951. Ptnr. Pravel, Hewitt, Kimball and Krieger, Houston, 1970-99; sr. counsel Akin, Gump, Houston, 1999—. Patent editor George Washington U. Law Rev., 1950. Precinct chmn. Houston Rep. Com., 1972-74. Served to lt. (j.g.) USNR. Fellow Am. Bar Found., Tex. Bar Found.; mem. ABA (chair intellectual property sect. 1991-92), Tex. Bar Assn. (chmn. patent, trademark sect. 1968-69, bd. dirs. 1976-79, Outstanding Contbn. 1982), Nat. Coun. Patent Law (chmn. 1970-71), Am. Intellectual Property Law Assn. (pres. 1983-84), Houston Intellectual Property Law Assn. (pres. 1983-84, Outstanding Svc. award 1986), Order of Coif, Kiwanis, Tau Beta Pi. Patent, Intellectual property, Trademark and copyright. Home: 10806 Oak Hollow St Houston TX 77024-3017 Office: Akin Gump South Tower 1900 Pennzoil Pl Houston TX 77002

**PRAVEL, JAMES W.,** lawyer; b. Houston, Oct. 14, 1957; s. Bernarr Roe and Retta (Atkinson) P. BSME, U. Tex., 1980; JD, Calif. Western Sch. Law, San Diego, 1991. Design/project engr. FMC Wellhead Equipment Divsn., Houston, 1980-84; pres. Pravel Offshore, Inc., Houston, 1984-90; assoc. Mason, Mason & Albright, Arlington, Va., 1991-94; prin. Pravel Intellectual Property Law, P.C., Alexandria, Va., 1994—. Mem. Am. Intellectual Property Law Assn. (chair subcom. on trademarks 1992-93), Toastmasters (pres., treas. 1998). Avocations: hunting, fishing, running, scuba. Intellectual property. Office: Pravel Intellectual Property Law 200 Daingerfield Rd Ste 400 Alexandria VA 22314-2884

**PRAY, DONALD EUGENE,** foundation administrator, lawyer; b. Tulsa, Jan. 16, 1932; s. Clyde Elmer and Ruth Annette (Frank) P.; m. Margaret Morrow, June 12, 1953; children: Melissa, Susan; m. Lana J. Dobson, Nov. 18, 1985. BS in Petroleum Engring., U. Tulsa, 1955; LLB with honors, U. Okla., 1963. Bar: Okla. 1963, U.S. Dist. Ct. (no. dist.) Okla. 1965, U.S. Supreme Ct. 1965. Assoc. firm Fuller, Smith, Mosberg, Davis & Bowen, Tulsa, 1963-65; ptnr. firm Schuman, Deas, Pray & Doyle, Tulsa, 1965-68, Pray, Scott & Livingston, and predecessor firm Pray, Scott, Williamson & Marlar, Tulsa, 1968-79; chmn., mem. exec. com. firm Pray, Walker, Jackman, Williamson & Marlar (merged with firm Walker & Jackman), Tulsa, 1979-95; exec. dir. Donald W. Reynolds Foundation, Tulsa, 1993—. Bd. dirs. Grace & Franklin Bernsen Found., U. Tulsa, St. Johns Med. Ctr., Philbrook Art Mus, Tulsa Ballet Theater., exec. v.p. Served to capt. USAF, 1955-57. Fellow Am. Bar Found.; mem. ABA (econs. com.), Tulsa Estate Planning Forum (pres.), Tulsa Mineral Lawyers Sect. (pres.). Republican. Presbyterian. Clubs: Summit (pres.). Office: 1701 Village Center Cir Las Vegas NV 89134-6303

**PREECE, LYNN SYLVIA,** lawyer; b. Birmingham, Eng., June 13, 1955; d. Norman and Sylvia Florence (James) Preece. LLB, Leeds (Eng.) U., 1976; postgrad., Washington U., St. Louis, 1978-79; JD, Loyola U., 1981. Bar: Ill., 1981. Assoc. Barnes Richardson, Chgo., 1980-86; from assoc. to ptnr. Burditt & Radzius, Chgo., 1986-88; ptnr. Katten Muchin & Zavis, Chgo., 1988-96, Baker & McKenzie, Chgo., 1996—; adj. prof. John Marshall Law Sch., 1998—. Contbr. articles to profl. jours. Chair customs com. Chgo. Bar Assn., 1986-87, Am. Bar Sect. Internat. Law, Washington, 1993-95, practitioners workshop bd., 1995-97; sec., dir. Women in Internat. Trade, Chgo., 1986-89, British Am. C. of C., Chgo., 1990; dir. Chgo. Internat. Sch., 1994-96. Recipient Gold medal Duke of Edinurghs award Scheme, London, 1973. Mem. ABA (coun. mem., newsletter editor 1996-98), Ct. Internat. Trade Bar Assn., Internat. Bar Assn. Avocations: gardening, emroidery, genealogy. Office: Baker & McKenzie 130 E Randolph Dr Ste 3700 Chicago IL 60601-6342

**PREGERSON, HARRY,** federal judge; b. L.A., Oct. 13, 1923; s. Abraham and Bessie (Rubin) P.; m. Bernardine Seyma Chapkis, June 28, 1947; children: Dean Douglas, Kathryn Ann. B.A., UCLA, 1947; LL.B., U. Calif.-Berkeley, 1950. Bar: Calif. 1951. Pvt. practice Los Angeles, 1951-52; Assoc. Morris D. Coppersmith, 1952; ptnr. Pregerson & Costley, Van Nuys, 1953-65; judge Los Angeles Mcpl. Ct., 1965-66, Los Angeles Superior Ct., 1966-67, U.S. Dist. Ct. Central Dist. Calif., 1967-79, U.S. Ct. Appeals for 9th Circuit, Woodland Hills, 1979—; faculty mem., seminar for newly appointed distr. Judges Fed. Jud. Center, Washington, 1970-72; mem. faculty Am. Soc. Pub. Adminstrn., Inst. for Ct. Mgmt., Denver, 1973—; panelist Fed. Bar Assn., L.A. chpt., 1989, Calif. Continuing Edn. of Bar, 9th Ann. Fed. Practice Inst., San Francisco, 1986, Internat. Acad. Trial Lawyers, L.A., 1983; lect. seminars for newly-appointed Fed. judges, 1970-71. Author over 450 published legal opinions. Mem. Community Rels. Com., Jewish Fedn. Coun., 1984—, Temple Judea, Encino, 1955—; bd. dirs. Marine Corps Res. Toys for Tots Program, 1965—, Greater Los Angeles Partnership for the Homeless, 1988—; bd. trustees Devil Pups Inc., 1988—; adv. bd. Internat. Orphans Inc., 1966—, Jewish Big Brothers Assn., 1970—, Salvation Army, Los Angeles Met. area, 1988—; worked with U.S. Govt. Gen. Svcs. to establish the Bell Shelter for the homeless, the Child Day Care Ctr., the Food Partnership and Westwood Transitional Village, 1988. 1st lt. USMCR, 1944-46. Decorated Purple Heart, Medal of Valor Apache Tribe, 1989; recipient Promotion of Justice Civic award, City of San Fernando, 1965, award San Fernando Valley Jewish Fedn. Coun., 1966, Profl. Achievement award Los Angeles Athletic Club, 1980, Profl. Achievement award UCLA Alumni Assn., 1985, Louis D. Brandeis award Am. Friends of Hebrew U., 1987, award of merit Inner City Law Ctr., 1987, Appreciation award Navajo Nation and USMC for Toys for Tots program, 1987, Humanitarian award Los Angeles Fed. Exec. Bd., 1987-88, Grateful Acknowledgement award Bet Tzedek Legal Svcs., 1988, Commendation award Bd. Suprs. Los Angeles County, 1988, Others award Salvation Army, 1988, numerous others. Mem. ABA (vice-chmn., com. on fed. rules of criminal procedure and evidence sect. of criminal 1972—, panelist Advocacy Inst., Phoenix, 1988), L.A. County Bar Assn., San Fernando Valley Bar Assn. (program chmn. 1964-65), State Bar Calif., Marines Corps Res. Officers Assn. (pres. San Fernando Valley 1966—), DAV (Birmingham chpt.), Am. Legion (Van Nuys Post),. Office: US Ct Appeals 9th Cir 21800 Oxnard St Ste 1140 Woodland Hills CA 91367-7919

**PREGO, MAYDA,** lawyer; b. N.Y.C., Oct. 21, 1966. BA, Yale U., 1988; JD, U. Mich., 1992. Bar: N.Y. 1993, Mass. 1993, U.S. Dist. Ct. (so. and ea. dists.) N.Y. 1993. Ptnr. Anderson Kill Olick & Oshinsky, P.C., N.Y.C. Contbg. editor: U. Mich. Jour. Law Reform, 1990-92. Mem. ABA, Hispanic Nat. Bar Assn., Phi Delta Phi. Insurance, Environmental, General civil litigation. Home: 1865 Brickell Ave Miami FL 33129-1621

**PREM, F. HERBERT, JR.,** lawyer; b. N.Y.C., Jan. 14, 1932; s. F. Herbert and Sybil Gertrude (Nichols) P.; m. Patricia Ryan, Nov. 18, 1978; children from previous marriage: Julia Nichols, F. Herbert III. AB, Yale U., 1953; JD, Harvard U., 1959. Bar: N.Y. 1960. Assoc. Whitman & Ransom, N.Y.C., 1959-66, ptnr., 1967-93, co-chmn. exec. com., 1988-92, chmn., 1993; chmn. Whitman Breed Abbott & Morgan LLP, N.Y.C., 1993—; bd. dirs. Fuji Photo Film U.S.A., Inc., Fuji Med. Sys. U.S.A., Inc., Noritake Co., Inc., Seiko Instruments America, Inc., The HealthCare Chaplaincy, Inc. Bd. dirs. Bagaduce Music Lending Libr., Inc., 1988-95, pres., 1989-93; bd. dirs. Cmty. Action for Legal Svc. Inc., 1967-70, treas., Legal Aid Soc. N.Y.C., 1967-70. Lt. (j.g.) USNR, 1953-56. Mem. ABA, Assn. of Bar of City of N.Y. (sec. 1967-69), N.Y. State Bar Assn., Am. Law Inst. (life), Am. Soc. Internat. Law, Yale Club. Episcopalian. Private international, General corporate. Office: Whitman Breed Abbott Morgan LLP 200 Park Ave New York NY 10166-0005

**PRENTICE, EUGENE MILES, III,** lawyer; b. Glen Ridge, N.J., Aug. 27, 1942; s. Eugene Miles and Anna Margaret (Kiernan) P.; m. Katharine Kirby Culbertson, Sept. 18, 1976; children: Eugene Miles IV, Jessie Kirby, John Francis. BA, Washington and Jefferson Coll., Pa., 1964; JD, U. Mich., 1967. Bar: N.Y. 1973, U.S. Dist. Ct. (so. dist.) N.Y. 1973, U.S. Dist. Ct. (ea. dist.) N.Y. 1974, U.S. Ct. Appeals (2d cir.) 1974, N.Y. Supreme Ct. 1973. With Morgan Guaranty Trust, N.Y.C., 1967-68, 71-73; assoc. White & Case, N.Y.C., 1973-78; assoc. Windels, Marx et al, N.Y.C., 1978-80, ptnr., 1980-84; ptnr. Brown & Wood, N.Y.C., 1984-93, Piper & Marbury, N.Y.C., 1993-96; pres. Midland (Tex.) Sports, Inc., 1990—; ptnr. Bryan Cave LLP, N.Y.C., 1996—; bd. dirs. Nat. Life Ins. Co., Montpelier, Vt., Tex. League Profl. Baseball, 1990—. Trustee Vt. Law Sch., 1984—, Washington and Jefferson Coll., Pa., 1985—, Nat. Assn. Profl. Baseball Leagues, 1992—, vice chmn. of bd., 1995—, St. Hilda's and St. Hugh's Sch., N.Y.C., 1993—, pres. of bd., 1995—. Capt. U.S. Army, 1968-70. Mem. ABA, Assn. of Bar of City of N.Y., Links Club, Union League Club, N.Y. Athletic Club, Spring Lake Bath & Tennis Club, Lake Mansfield Trout Club (Vt.). Republican. Banking, General corporate, Private international. Home: 34 W 95th St New York NY 10025-6701 Office: Bryan Cave LLP 245 Park Ave Rm 2801 New York NY 10167-2897

**PRENTKE, RICHARD OTTESEN,** lawyer; b. Cleve., Sept. 8, 1945; s. Herbert E. and Melva B. (Horbury) P.; m. Susan Ottesen, June 9, 1974; children: Catherine, Elizabeth. BSE, Princeton U., 1967; JD, Harvard U., 1974. Assoc. Perkins Coie, Seattle, 1974-80, ptnr., 1981—, CFO, 1989-94. Author: School Construction Law Deskbook, 1989, rev. 2d edit. 1998; contbr. articles to profl. jours. Pres., trustee Seattle County Day Sch., 1990-95; trustee Pocock Rowing Found., 1996—. With USN, 1967-70. Fellow Leadership Tomorrow, Seattle, 1985-86. Mem. ABA, Wash. State Bar Assn. (mem. jud. screening com. 1985-91, chmn. 1987-91), Seattle-King County Bar Assn. (chmn. jud. task force 1990-93), Am. Arbitration Assn. (arbitrator 1988—), Princeton U. Rowing Assn. (pres. 1993—, trustee 1976—), Rainier Club, Princeton Club Wash. (trustee 1986—, pres. 1990-92), Seattle Tennis Club. Avocations: art, carpentry, travel, rowing, sports. Computer, Construction. Office: Perkins Coie 1201 3rd Ave Fl 40 Seattle WA 98101-3029

**PRESKA, LORETTA A.,** federal judge; b. 1949. BA, Coll. St. Rose, 1970; JD, Fordham U., 1973; LLM, NYU, 1978. Assoc. Cahill, Gordon & Reindel, N.Y.C., 1973-82; ptnr. Hertzog, Calamari & Gleason, N.Y.C., 1982-92; fed. judge U.S. Dist. Ct. (so. dist.) N.Y., N.Y.C., 1992—. Mem. ABA, N.Y. State Bar Assn., N.Y. County Lawyers Assn., Fed. Bar Coun., Fordham Law Alumni Assn. (v.p.). Office: US Courthouse 500 Pearl St Rm 1320 New York NY 10007-1316

**PRESKI, BRIAN JOSEPH,** lawyer; b. Phila., Apr. 25, 1965; s. Henry John and Dolores (Domanski) Przybyszewski; m. Kelly Ann McKeon, June 2, 1989; children: Dennis, Lauren. BA, St. Joseph's U., 1987; JD, Widener U., 1992. Bar: Pa. 1992. Asst. dist. atty. Dist. Atty.'s Office, Phila., 1989-95; chief counsel jud. com. Ho. of Reps., Harrisburg, Pa., 1995—. Republican. Roman Catholic. Office: Ho of Reps Jud Com 25 Capitol Annex Harrisburg PA 17120

**PRESLAR, HOLLY ANN,** lawyer; b. Grants Pass, Oreg., June 27, 1966; d. Gary L. and Phyllis J. (Gardner) P.; m. Lloyd A. Wilson, May 1, 1992. BA, So. Oreg. State Coll., 1988; JD, U. Oreg., 1991. Bar: Oreg. 1992. Assoc. Myrick, Seagraves et al, Grants Pass, 1992-95, ptnr., 1995-96; pvt. practice, Grants Pass, 1996—. Bd. dirs. Women's Crisis Support Team, Grants Pass, 1994—; coach mock trial team Illinois Valley H.S. Cave Junction, Oreg., 1996-99; mem. adv. bd. Cmty. Dispute Resolution, Grants Pass, 1997—; mem. adv. bd. Josephine County Mental Health, 1997—. Mem. Oreg. State Bar (law related edn. com. new lawyer divsn. 1993, local profl. responsibility com. 1995—), Josephine County Bar Assn. (pres. 1996, pro-tem judge 1998—), Jobs Daus. (exec. coun., guardian 1994-96). Democrat. Methodist. Avocations: collecting antiques, gardening. Family and matrimonial, Criminal, General civil litigation. Office: 245 NW B St Grants Pass OR 97526-2031

**PRESON, STEPHEN W.,** lawyer; b. Atlanta, May 30, 1957. BA, Yale U., 1979; Dipl., U. Dublin, 1980; JD, Harvard U., 1983. Bar: D.C. 1983, also fed. cts. Law clk. U.S. Ct. Appeals (11th cir.), Savannah, Ga., 1983-84; vis. fellow Ctr. for Law in the Pub. Interest, Washington, 1984-85; assoc., ptnr. Wilner, Cutler & Pickering, Washington, 1986-93; prin. dep. gen. counsel Dept. of Def., Washington, 1993-95; dep. asst. atty. gen. U.S. Dept. Justice, Washington, 1995-98; gen. counsel Dept. of Navy, Washington, 1998—. Recipient Disting. Pub. Svc. medal Dept. of Def., 1995. Mem. ABA.

**PRESS, MICHAEL S.,** lawyer; b. N.Y.C., Oct. 30, 1948; s. Irving E. and Florence C. (Mandel) P.; m. Priscilla E. Campo, Oct. 4, 1980; children: Michael S. Press Jr., Priscilla Dorothy. AB, Dartmouth Coll., 1971; JD cum laude, U. Miami, 1974. Bar: N.Y. 1975, U.S. Dist Ct. (so. dist.) N.Y. 1975, (we dist.) N.Y. 1983, (ea. dist.) N.Y. 1987, U.S. Dist. Ct. (ea. dist.) Mich. 1986, U.S. Ct. Appeals (1st cir.) N.Y. 1987, (2nd cir.) N.Y. 1980, (federal cir.) N.Y. 1988, U.S. Tax Ct. 1993, U.S. Supreme Ct. 1985. Assoc. Whitman & Ransom, N.Y.C., 1974-84, ptnr., 1984-93; atty. Neumair & Riad, P.C., N.Y.C., 1996—. Mem. bd. editors U. Miami Law Rev., 1973-74. Capt. USAF, 1971-83. Recipient Am. Jurisprudence award U. Miami, 1972, 73. Mem. Piping Rock Club, Hyannisport Club, Beaver Dam Winter Sports Club, Assn. Bar City N.Y., Fed. Bar Coun., Phi Kappa Phi. Republican. Roman Catholic. General civil litigation, Securities. Home: 36 Harbor Rd Oyster Bay NY 11771-1702

**PRESSER, STEFAN,** lawyer, educator; b. Bklyn., Apr. 30, 1953; s. Sidney and Sydonia (Cohen) P.; m. Sandra B. Sherman, Sept. 21, 1988; children: David, Natania, Rachel Sherman-Presser. BA in Sociology magna cum laude, Yale U., 1976; JD, NYU, 1979. Staff counsel Civil Rights Bur. N.Y. State Office of the Atty. Gen., 1979-80; staff counsel Greater Houston chpt. ACLU, 1981-84; legal dir. ACLU of Pa., Phila., 1985—; clin. adj. prof. Temple U. Sch. Law, 1990—; vis. lectr. Bryn Mawr Coll. Grad. Sch. of Social Work & Social Rsch., 1997, 98. Co-author: The Rights of Single People, 1985; contbr. articles to profl. jours. Recipient award for meritorious svc. in field of corrections Prison Soc., 1994, Liberty Bell award Bar Assn. Lehigh County, 1996, Andrew Hamilton award Phila. Bar Assn. 1997; named Disting. Advocate, Support Ctr. for Child Advocates, Phila., 1996; Root-Tilden scholar NYU Sch. Law, 1976-79; Arthur Garfield Hays fellow, 1978-79. Jewish. Office: ACLU of Pa 125 S 9th St Ste 701 Philadelphia PA 19107-5194

**PRESSER, STEPHEN BRUCE,** lawyer, educator; b. Chattanooga, Aug. 10, 1946; s. Sidney and Estelle (Shapiro) P.; m. Carole Smith, June 18, 1968 (div. 1987); children: David Carter, Elisabeth Catherine; m. ArLynn Leiber, Dec. 13, 1987; children: Joseph Leiber, Eastman Leiber. A.B., Harvard U., 1968, J.D., 1971. Bar: Mass. 1971, D.C. 1972. Law clk. to Judge Malcolm Richard Wilkey U.S. Ct. Appeals (D.C. cir.), 1971-72; assoc. Wilmer, Cutler & Pickering, Washington, 1972-74; asst. prof. law Rutgers U., Camden, N.J., 1974-76; vis. assoc. prof. U. Va., 1976-77; prof. Northwestern U., Chgo., 1977—, class 1940 rsch. prof., 1992-93, Raoul Berger prof. legal history, 1992—, assoc. dean acad. affairs Sch. Law, 1982-85; adj. prof. mgmt. and strategy Kellogg Grad. Sch. Mgmt., Northwestern U., Chgo., 1992—. Author: (with Jamil S. Zainaldin) Law and Jurisprudence in American History, 1980, 3d edit., 1995, Studies in the History of the United States Courts of the Third Circuit, 1983, The Original Misunderstanding: The English, The Americans and the Dialectic of Federalist Jurisprudence, 1991, Piercing the Corporate Veil, 1991, revised ann., (with Ralph Ferrara and Meridith Brown) Takeovers: A Strategist's Manual, 2d edit., 1993, Recapturing the Constitution, 1994, (with Douglas W. Kmiec) The American Constitutional Order: History, Cases, and Philosophy, 1998; assoc. articles editor Guide to American Law, 1985. Mem. acad. adv. bd. Washington Legal Found. Recipient summer stipend NEH, 1975; Fulbright Sr. scholar Univ. Coll., London Sch. Econs. and Polit. Sci., 1983-84, Inst. Advanced Legal Studies, 1996; Adams fellow Inst. U.S. Studies, London, 1996. Mem. Am. Soc. Legal History (bd. dirs. 1979-82), Am. Law Inst., Univ. Club Chgo. (bd. dirs. 1997—, sec., 1999—), Legal Club Chgo., Reform Club (London). Home: 785 Willow Rd Winnetka IL 60093-3847 Office: Northwestern U Law Sch 357 E Chicago Ave Chicago IL 60611-3069

**PRESSLEY, FRED G., JR.,** lawyer; b. N.Y.C., June 19, 1953; s. Fred G. Sr. and Frances (Sanders) P.; m. Cynthia Denise Hill, Sept. 5, 1981. BA cum laude, Union Coll., 1975; JD, Northwestern U., 1978. Bar: Ohio 1978, U.S. Dist. Ct. (so. dist.) Ohio 1979, U.S. Dist. Ct. (no. dist.) Ohio 1985, U.S. Dist. Ct. (ea. dist.) Wis. 1980, U.S. Ct. Appeals (6th cir.). Assoc. Porter, Wright, Morris & Arthur, Columbus, Ohio, 1978-85, ptnr., 1985—. Bd.

dirs. Columbus Area Leadership Program, 1981-84, Franklin County Bd. Mental Retardation and Devel. Disabilities, Columbus, 1989-97, Union Coll., Schenectady, N.Y., 1992—. Recipient Civic Achievement award Ohio Ho. of Reps., 1988. Mem. ABA. Avocations: jogging, golf, basketball, military history. Labor, Civil rights. Office: Porter Wright Morris & Arthur 41 S High St Ste 2800 Columbus OH 43215-6194

**PRESSMAN, GLENN SPENCER,** lawyer; b. Phila., May 25, 1952; s. Albert and Elaine (Coffae) P.; m. Laura Feldman, Sept. 5, 1982; children: Alexandra, Daniel. BS, Pa. State U., 1974; JD with honors, Drake U., 1981. Bar: Colo. 1981, U.S. Dist. Ct. Colo. 1981, U.S. Ct. Appeals (10th cir.) 1981. Ptnr. Melat Pressman Ezell & Higbie, Colorado Springs, Colo., 1981—. Recipient Order of the Coif, 1981. Democrat. Jewish. Avocations: skiing, mountain climbing. Personal injury, Product liability, General civil litigation. Office: Melat Pressman Ezell Higbie 711 S Tejon St Colorado Springs CO 80903-4049

**PRESSON, WILLIAM RUSSELL,** lawyer; b. Memphis, Dec. 10, 1955; s. Russell Barnes and Mary Louise (Ford) P.; m. Rae Nell Hunter, June 28, 1986. BA, Millsaps Coll., 1977; M in Pub. Affairs, JD, U. Tex., 1981. Bar: Miss. 1981, U.S. Dist. Ct. (so. dist.) Miss. 1981, U.S. Ct. Appeals (5th cir.) 1985, U.S. Dist. Ct. (no. dist.) Miss. 1986. Assoc. Gerald, Brand, Watters, Cox & Hemleben, Jackson, Miss., 1981-84, Satterfield & Allred, Jackson, 1984-90, Harper, Bellan, McWhorter & Williams, 1990-92; pvt. practice Jackson, 1992—. Mem. ABA, Miss. State Bar Assn., Hinds County Bar Assn., Miss. Oil and Gas Lawyers Assn., Miss. Bankruptcy Conf. Democrat. Episcopalian. Oil, gas, and mineral, Real property, Probate. Home: 1607 Laurel St Jackson MS 39202-1244 Office: 4551 Office Park Dr PO Box 4170 Jackson MS 39296-4170

**PRESTI, GERALYN MARIE,** lawyer; b. Cleve., July 15, 1955; d. Joseph Carl Presti and Josephine Joanne Ambrogio; m. John Reid Sedor, Aug. 16, 1980; 2 children. BMus, Ohio U., 1978; M of Social Sci. Adminstrn., Case Western Res. U., 1988, JD, 1988. Bar: Ohio 1989. Music therapist Bellefaire, Cleve., 1978-79, The Cleve. Music Sch. Settlement, Cleve., 1979-84; assoc. gen. counsel Forest City Enterprises, Inc., Cleve., 1989—; admissions counsellor Case Western Res. U., Cleve., 1993-96, adv. bd. LLM degree fgn. students, 1998—; rsch. asst., adj. law prof. Forest City Enterprise, Inc., Cleve., 1994-96. Trustee Homeowners Assn., Bentleyville, Ohio, 1992-94, Cleve. Music Sch. Settlement, 1999—; co-chmn. ann. fund U. Sch., Shaker Heights, Ohio, 1998—; dir. Ohio U. Sch. of Music, Athens, 1985-86; project mem. Reorgn. of the Cuyahoga County Dept. Human Svcs., Cleve., 1985. Recipient Greater Cleve. Woman of Profl. Excellence award YWCA, 1996. Mem. Ctr. for Profl. Ethics, Cleve. Bar Assn., Order of Coif. Avocations: pianist, travelling, art, reading, films. Office: Forest City Enterprise Inc 50 Public Sq Cleveland OH 44113-2202

**PRESTON, BRUCE MARSHALL,** lawyer, educator; b. Trinidad, Colo., Feb. 24, 1949; s. Marshall Caldwell and Juanita (Killgore) P.; m. Mariannina Erra, Aug. 10, 1974; children: Charles Marshall, Robert Arthur. BS summa cum laude, Ariz. State U., 1971; MA, U. Ariz., 1972, JD, 1975. Bar: Ariz. 1975, U.S. Ct. Appeals (9th cir.) 1976, U.S. Ct. Claims 1983, U.S. Tax Ct. 1983, U.S. Supreme Ct. 1983; cert. fin. planner. Atty. Maricopa County Office of Pub. Defender, Phoenix, 1975-84; ptnr. Simonsen & Preston, Phoenix, 1985-86, Simonsen, Preston, Sargeant & Arbetman, Phoenix, 1986; atty. office of atty. gen. State of Ariz., 1987-90; assoc. Broening, Oberg and Woods, Phoenix, 1989-96, ptnr., 1997—; judge pro tem Mcpl. Ct., Phoenix, 1984-86; licensee in sales Ariz. Dept. Real Estate, Phoenix, 1981-87; adj. faculty Phoenix Coll. for Fin. Planning, Denver, 1984-87, Maricopa County Community Coll. Dist., Phoenix, 1985-87, Ariz. State U. Coll. of Bus., Tempe, 1986-87, Ottawa U., Phoenix, 1986. Chmn. com., treas., pres. bd. dirs. Kachina Country Day Sch., 1982-90; bd. dirs. Family Svc. Agy., Phoenix, 1988—, treas., 1990-91; bd. dirs. Clearwater Hills Homeowners Assn., Paradise Valley, Ariz., 1989—, v.p., 1990, treas., 1991; bd. dirs. Phoenix Boys Choir, 1989-90. Mem. Ariz. Assn. Def. Counsel, Ariz. Bar Assn. (cert. specialist criminal law 1982-84), Maricopa County Bar Assn., Ariz. State U. Coll. Liberal Arts Alumni Assn. (bd. dirs. 1978-80, 87-88), Phi Kappa Phi. Avocations: computers, skiing, boating, running. Insurance, Personal injury, General civil litigation. Home: 7247 N Black Rock Trl Paradise Valley AZ 85253 Office: Broening Oberg & Woods 1122 E Jefferson St Phoenix AZ 85034-2224

**PRESTON, CHARLES GEORGE,** lawyer; b. Fairbanks, Alaska, Nov. 11, 1940; s. Charles William and Gudveig Nicoline (Hoem) P.; m. Hilde Delphine van Stappen, Mar. 12, 1970; children: Charles William, Stephanie Delphine, Christina Nicoline. BA, U. Wash., 1963, MPA, 1968; JD, Columbia U., 1971. Bar: Wash. 1971, D.C. 1981, U.S. Dist. Ct. D.C. 1981, U.S. Dist. Ct. (we. dist.) Wash. 1971, U.S. Ct. Appeals (9th cir.) 1972, U.S. Ct. Appeals (4th cir.) 1979, U.S. Ct. Appeals (5th cir., D.C. cir.) 1978, U.S. Ct. Appeals (2d cir.) 1980, U.S. Ct. Appeals (11th cir.) 1981, U.S. Supreme Ct. 1977, U.S. Ct. Claims 1982, U.S. Ct. Appeals (fed. cir.) 1982, U.S. Ct. Appeals (1st cir.) 1984, U.S. Ct. Appeals (3d, 6th & 7th cirs.) 1987, Va. 1987, U.S. Dist. Ct. (ea. dist.) Va. 1989, U.S. Dist. Ct. (we. dist.) Wash. 1971, U.S. Dist. Ct. (no. dist.) Calif. 1981, U.S. Bankruptcy Ct. Va. 1990. Assoc. Jones, Grey, Bayley & Olson, Seattle, 1971-72; atty. and asst. counsel for litigation Officer of Solicitor, U.S. Dept. Labor, Seattle, 1972-76, Washington, 1976-81; atty. Air Line Pilots Assn., Washington, 1981-82; mng. ptnr. MacNabb, Preston & Waxman, Washington, 1981-86, Preston & Preston, Great Falls, Va., 1986-95, Charles G. Preston, P.C., 1995—; pres. Preston Group, Inc. 1989—. Lectr. seminars. Mem. ABA, Wash. State Bar, D.C. Bar Assn., Va. Bar Assn., Tng. Law Inst. (pres. 1985—), Gt. Falls Bus. and Profl. Assn. (pres. 1990), The Serbian Crown, Va. (pres. 1989—). Real property, General corporate, State civil litigation. Office: Charles G Preston PC 774C Walker Rd Great Falls VA 22066-2639

**PRESTON, CHARLES MICHAEL,** lawyer; b. Balt., Oct. 11, 1945; s. Carlton Edward and Jeannette Thorn (Baker) P.; m. Carol Ann Armacost, June 21, 1969 (div. Dec. 1978). BA, Western Md. Coll., 1967; JD, U. Balt., 1970. Bar: Md. 1970, U.S. Dist. Ct. Md. 1972, U.S. Supreme Ct. 1974, U.S. Dist. Ct. (trial bd.) 1984. Law clk. to Hon. E.O. Weant, Jr. Westminster, Md., 1970-71; assoc. Hoffman & Hoffman, Westminster, 1972-75; ptnr. Hoffman, Hoffman & Preston, Westminster, 1976-77, Hoffman, Stoner & Preston, Westminster, 1978-79; ptnr., v.p. Stoner, Preston & Boswell Chartered, Westminster, 1980—; rev. bd., panel mem. Atty. Grievance Commn., Annapolis, Md., 1978-95; mem. Md. Ct. Appeals Commn. on alternate dispute resolution, 1998—. Contbr. articles to profl. jours. Mem. Carroll County Gen. Hosp., Westminster, 1983—; trustee Raymond I. Richardson Found., Middleburg, Md., 1979-93; bd. dirs. Carroll County Agrl. Ctr., Westminster, 1975—; dir. N.W. dist. ARC, Balt., 1987-95; trustee Balt. Opera Co., 1998—. With U.S. Army, 1970-71. Fellow Md. Bar Found., Am. Bar Found.; mem. ABA (del. ho. of dels.), Md. State Bar Assn. (treas., bd. govs. 1991-97, pres.-elect 1997, pres. 98), Carroll County Bar Assn. (pres. 1985), People's Pro Bono Action Com., Inc., Elks. Presbyterian. Avocations: snow skiing, ice skating, woodworking, music, travel. Office: Stoner Preston & Boswell PO Box 389 188 E Main St Westminster MD 21157-5017

**PRESTON, COLLEEN ANN,** lawyer; b. Monterey, Calif., Oct. 11, 1955; d. Howard Houston and Catherine (Reid) Harrison; m. Raymond C. Preston Jr., June 12, 1982. BA, U. Fla., 1975, JD, 1978; LLM, Georgetown U., 1985. Bar: Fla. 1979, U.S. Ct. Claims 1979, U.S. Ct. Appeals (fed. cir.) 1979. Assoc. Akerman, Senterfitt & Eidson, Orlando, Fla., 1978-79; atty. advisor, office of gen. counsel Sec. USAF, 1979-83; counsel com. on armed svcs. U.S. Ho. Reps., Washington, 1983-89, gen. counsel, 1990-93; spl. asst. to Sec. Def. for legal matters Dept. Def., Washington, 1993, dep. under sec. of def. for acquisition reform, 1993-97; cons. Preston & Assocs., 1997—. Capt. USAF, 1979-83. Avocations: golf, tennis, cross country and downhill skiing, water skiing.

**PRESTON, DAVID RAYMOND,** lawyer; b. Harlingen, Tex., Feb. 12, 1961; s. Raymond C., Jr. and Janet (Bowman) P. BS, U. Fla., 1983, MS, 1985, PhD, 1989; JD, George Mason Sch. Law, 1996. Bar: Calif., U.S. Patent and Tradmark Office. Postdoctoral rsch. U.S. Army, Frederick, Md., 1989-90; patent examiner U.S. Patent and Trademark Office, Washington, 1990-94; tech. devel. specialist Nat. Cancer Inst., NIH, Bethesda, Md., 1994-96; intern for Judge Rader U.S. Ct. Appeals (fed. cir.), Washington, 1995; patent attorney Campbell & Flores, San Diego, 1996-97; asst. patent counsel Aurora Bioscis. Corp., San Diego, 1997-98; pres. David R. Preston & Assocs., San Diego, 1999—. Judge internat. sci. fair U.S. Patents and Trademark Office, 1991. NIH fellow, 1987, Pres.'s fellow Am. Soc. Microbiology, 1988. Mem. AAAS, ABA, Am. Intellectual Property Law Assn., Fed. Cir. Bar Assn., San Diego Intellectual Property Law Assn. Republican. Avocations: tennis, golf, skiing, surfing, windsurfing. Intellectual property, Patent. Office: Ste 104 11404 Sorrento Valley Rd San Diego CA 92122

**PRESTON, JAMES YOUNG,** lawyer; b. Atlanta, Sept. 21, 1937; s. James William and Mary Lou (Young) P.; m. Elizabeth Buxton Gregory, June 13, 1959; children: Elizabeth P. Carr, Mary Lane P. Lennon, James Brenton Preston. BA in English, U. N.C., 1958, JD with high honors, 1961. Bar: N.C. 1961. Assoc. to ptnr. Parker, Poe, Adams & Bernstein L.L.P. and predecessors, Charlotte, N.C., 1961—. Pres. Charlotte Area Fund, 1968, Cmty. Sch. of Arts, 1976-78; pres. Arts and Sci. Coun. Charlotte/ Mecklenburg, Inc., 1986-87, chair The Nat. Conf. for Cmty. and Justice, Charlotte, 1996—, Wildacres Leadership Initiative, 1994—; vice chair N.C. Dance Theatre, 1995-97. Mem. ABA (ho. dels. 1988-92, 95-97), N.C. State Bar (pres. 1987-88), Am. Law Inst., Nat. Conf. Bar Presidents (exec. coun. 1989-92), Phi Beta Kappa, Phi Eta Sigma. Democrat. Episcopalian. Avocations: travel, tennis, profl. and civic activities. Taxation, general, Estate planning, General corporate. Office: Parker Poe Adams Bernstein LLP 201 S College St 2500 Charlotte Plz Charlotte NC 28244

**PRESTON, ROBERT F.,** lawyer; b. N.Y.C., Jan. 10, 1961; s. Robert B. and Margarita (Figueredo) P.; m. Kimberly Anne Mills, Sept. 19, 1987; children: Kelsey Anne, J. Tyler. BA, U. Va., 1983; JD, Villanova U., 1987. Bar: Pa. 1987, N.J. 1987, U.S. Dist. Ct. (ea. dist.) Pa. 1988, U.S. Dist. Ct. N.J. 1987, U.S. Ct. Appeals (ed. and fed. cirs.) 1988, U.S. Claims Ct. 1987. Assoc. Rosenthal & Ganister, West Chester, Pa., 1987-89; atty. Am. Home Products Corp., St. Davids, Pa., 1989-95, sr. atty., 1995—. Mem. Phi Delta Phi (pres. 1986-87), Phi Sigma Iota. Private international, General corporate, Mergers and acquisitions. Office: Law Dept-Internat 170-3 N Radnor-Chester St Saint Davids PA 19087-5252

**PRESTON, STEPHEN W.,** lawyer. BS summa cum laude, Yale U., 1979; postgrad., Trinity Coll., U. Dublin, 1980; JD magna cum laude, Harvard U., 1983. Bar: D.C. Law clk. to Hon. Phyllis A. Kravitch U.S. Ct. Appeals (11th cir.), 1983-84; vis. fellow Ctr. for Law in Pub. Interest, Washington, 1984-85; ptnr. Wilmer, Cutler & Pickering, Washington, 1986-93; dep. gen. counsel, prin. dep. gen. counsel, acting gen. counsel Dept. of Defense, 1993-95; dep. asst. atty. gen. Dept. Justice, 1995-98; gen. counsel Dept. Navy, 1998—. Office: Office of Gen Counsel Dept of Navy 1000 Navy Pentagon Washington DC 20350-1000*

**PRESTRIDGE, PAMELA ADAIR,** lawyer; b. Delhi, La., Dec. 25, 1945; d. Gerald Wallace Prestridge and Louis Baugh and Peggy Adair (Arender) Martin. BA, La. Poly. U., 1967; M in Edn., La. State u., 1968, JD, 1973. Bar: U.S. Dist. Ct. (mid. dist.) La. 1975, U.S. Dist. Ct. (so. dist.) Tex. 1982, U.S. Ct. Appeals (5th cir.) 1982, U.S. Supreme Ct. 1990. Law clk. to presiding justice La. State Dist. Ct., Baton Rouge, 1973-75; ptnr. Breazeale, Sachse & Wilson, Baton Rouge, 1975-82, Hirsch & Westheimer P.C., Houston, 1982-92; pvt. practive, Houston, 1992—. Counselor Big Bros./Big Sisters, Baton Rouge, 1968-70; legal cons., bd. dirs. Lupus Found. Am., Houston, 1984-93; bd. dirs. Quota Club, Baton Rouge, 1979-82, Speech and Hearing Found., Baton Rouge, 1981-82, The Actors Workshop, Houston, 1988-93; active Tex. Accts. and Attys. for the Arts. Recipient Pres.'s award Lupus Found. Am., 1991, cert. of appreciation Assn. Atty. Mediators, 1992, Outstanding Profl. Woman of Houston award Fedn. Profl. Women, 1984. Mem. ABA, La. Bar Assn., Tex. Bar Assn., Houston Bar Assn., Houston Bar Found., Assn. Atty. Mediators (bd. dirs. 1994-96, Citation for Outstanding Mems. 1993), Profl. Atty.-Mediators Coop. (v.p. 1994, bd. dirs. 1994-96, pres. 1995), Phi Alpha Delta. Eckankar. Avocations: acting, ultralite flying. General civil litigation, Bankruptcy, Alternative dispute resolution. Home: 1701 Hermann Dr Unit 2603 Houston TX 77004-7330 Office: 3300 Phoenix Tower PO Box 130987 Houston TX 77219-0987

**PRESTRIDGE, ROGERS MEREDITH,** lawyer; b. Crowville, La., July 31, 1934; s. James Ivy and Vergie (Rogers) P.; m. Kathryn Sinclair, July 3, 1968; children: Dana, Zachary, Kathryn, Bennett. BA, N.E. La. U., 1961; JD, La. State U., 1966. Bar: La. 1966. Atty. for Inheritance Collector Bossier Parish, La., 1966-72; asst. dist. atty. 26th Jud. dist., 1969-72; pvt. practice Bossier City, La., 1966-89; coord. of legal and govtl. affairs La. State U. Med. Sch., Shreveport, 1989—; judge Bossier City, 1973-75; mem. La. Commn. Law Enforcement and Adminstrn. of Criminal Justice, 1973-75. Mem. La. Bd. Regents for Higher Edn., 1975-81; mem. Caddo-Bossier Port Commn., 1976-97, pres., 1987-89; bd. dirs. River Cities High Tech., Inc.; chmn. Shreveport, Bossier Mil. Affairs Com., 1987; chmn. Riverside Community Hosp., 1987-91; bd. dirs., 1987; bd. dirs. La. Assn. for Blind. Capt. USAF, 1954-58, 61-62. Mem. Am. Judges Assn., La. State Bar Assn. (ho. of dels.), Bossier C. of C. (pres. 1986), Nat. Councile Juvenile Ct. Judges, Bossier Jaycees (past pres.), Phi Alpha Delta. Democrat. Episcopalian. Education and schools, Health. Office: LSU Sch of Med PO Box 33932 Shreveport LA 71130-3932

**PRESTWOOD, ALVIN TENNYSON,** lawyer; b. Roeton, Ala., June 18, 1929; s. Garret Felix and Jimmie (Payne) P.; m. Sue Burleson Lee, Nov. 27, 1974; children: Ann Celeste Prestwood Peeples, Alison Bennett, Cynthia Joyce Lee Koplos, William Alvin Lee, Garret Courtney. BS, U. Ala., 1951, LLB, 1956, JD, 1970. Bar: Ala. 1956, U.S. Ct. Appeals (6th and 11th cirs.) 1981, U.S. Supreme Ct. 1972. Law clk. Supreme Ct. Ala., 1956-57; asst. atty. gen. Ala., 1957-59; commr. Ala. Dept. Pensions and Security, 1959-63; pvt. practice Montgomery, Ala., 1963-65, 77-82; ptnr. Volz, Capouano, Wampold, Prestwood & Sansone, 1965-77, Prestwood & Rosser, 1982-85, Capouano, Wampold, Prestwood & Sansone, 1986-94, Volz, Prestwood & Hanan, 1995—; chmn. Gov.'s Com. on White House Conf. on Aging, 1961; mem. adv. com. Dept. Health, Edn. and Welfare, 1962; sec. Nat. Coun. State Pub. Welfare Adminstrs., 1962. Mem. editorial bd. Ala. Law Rev., 1955-56; contbr. articles to profl. jours. Pres. Morningview Sch. P.T.A., 1970; chmn. Am. Nursing Home Assn. Legal Com., 1972; bd. dirs. Montgomery Bapt. Hosp., 1958-65; chmn. bd. mgmt. East Montgomery YMCA, 1969; chmn. deacons Cloverdale Bapt. Ch., 1994, 95, 98. Served to 1st lt., inf. AUS, 1951-53. Decorated Combat Inf. Badge.; recipient Sigma Delta Kappa Scholastic Achievement award U. Ala. Sch. Law, 1956, Law Day Moot Ct. award U. Ala. Sch. Law, 1956. Mem. ABA (chmn. com. on jud. preformance and conduct 1996, chmn. Judiciary's Image Evaluation Task Force), Ala. Bar Assn. (chmn. adminstrv. law sect. 1972, 78, 83, 97), Montgomery County Bar Assn. (chmn. exec. com. 1971), Farrah Order Jurisprudence, Eleventh Cir. Jud. Conf., Am. Trial Lawyers Assn., Am. Judicature Soc., Kappa Sigma. Civil rights, Administrative and regulatory, Federal civil litigation. Home: 1431 Magnolia Curv Montgomery AL 36106-2043 Office: Volz Prestwood & Hanan 350 Adams Ave Montgomery AL 36104-4204

**PRETTYMAN, HOWARD CROSS, JR.,** lawyer; b. Charleston, S.C., Aug. 26, 1940; s. Howard and Ruth (Minott) P.; m. Andrea Riederhof, Dec. 29, 1959; 1 child, Rhett Marie Prettyman Gray. JD, U. S.C., 1964. Bar: S.C. Sole practice Summerville, S.C., 1964—. With USMCR, 1959-65. General practice, Family and matrimonial, Real property. Home: 1960 Marsh Oak Ln Johns Island SC 29455-6305 Office: 207 S Main St Summerville SC 29483-6009

**PREUS, CHRISTIAN ANDREW,** lawyer; b. St. Louis, Dec. 18, 1959; s. Robert David and Donna Mae (Rockman) P.; m. Cynthia Kay Chase, July 23, 1983; children: Erika C., Luke C., Caleb M., Kristiana N. Student, Luther Sem., Adelaide, Australia; BS in Mktg., Ind. U., 1981; JD, U. N.D., 1985. Legis. asst. N.D. Legislature, Bismarck, 1985; law clk. N.D. Supreme Ct., Bismarck, 1985-86; ptnr. Meagher & Geer, Mpls., 1986—. Mem. city coun. City of Plymouth, Minn., 1996-98, planning commn., 1994-95; bd. regents Concordia Coll., St. Paul, Minn., 1989-92; bd. dirs. Luth. Ch. Mo. Synod, St. Louis, 1995—. Mem. N.D. Bar Assn., Wis. Bar Assn. Republican. Labor, Insurance, Antitrust. Home: 16205 5th Ave N Plymouth MN 55447-3630 Office: Meagher & Geer 4200 Multifoods Tower 33 S 6th St Ste 4200 Minneapolis MN 55402-3788

**PREWOZNIK, JEROME FRANK,** lawyer; b. Detroit, July 15, 1934; s. Frank Joseph and Loretta Ann (Parzych) P.; m. Marilyn Ruth Johnson, 1970; 1 child, Frank Joseph II. AB cum laude, U. Detroit, 1955; JD with distinction, U. Mich., 1958. Bar: Calif. 1959. Pvt. practice, Calif., 1960-91. Served in U.S. Army, 1958-60. Mem. ABA, State Bar Calif. Republican. Home: 431 Georgina Ave Santa Monica CA 90402-1909

**PREZYNA, ANN ELIZABETH,** lawyer; b. Beaufort, S.C., Apr. 10, 1951; d. Anthony Paul and Louise Ann (Moscato) P. BS in Natural Resources, Cornell U., 1973; JD, George Washington U., 1976; MS in Water Resources, U. Wis., 1978. Bar: D.C. 1976, Alaska 1978, Wash. 1987, U.S. Dist. Ct. Alaska 1979, U.S. Dist. Ct. (we. dist.) Wash. 1990, U.S. Ct. Appeals (9th cir.) 1979, U.S. Ct. Appeals (D.C. cir.) 1977, U.S. Supreme Ct. 1982. Asst. atty. gen. Alaska Dept. Law, Juneau, 1979-80; atty. Std. Oil Co., Anchorage, 1981; asst. atty. gen. Alaska Dept. Law, Anchorage, 1982-86; asst. regional counsel U.S. EPA Region 10, Seattle, 1987-89, assoc. regional counsel, 1989-95, dep. regional counsel, 1995—. Avocations: weightlifting, flying, bicycling, birdwatching, running. Home: 2031 Fairview Ave E Seattle WA 98102-3591 Office: US EPA ORC-158 1200 6th Ave Ste 900 Seattle WA 98101-3188

**PRIBANIC, VICTOR HUNTER,** lawyer; b. McKeesport, Pa., Apr. 7, 1954; s. John Edward and Marlene Cecilia (Hunter) P. B.A., Bowling Green State U., 1976; J.D., Duquesne U., 1979. Bar: Pa. 1979, U.S. Dist. Ct. (we. dist.) Pa. 1979, U.S. Ct. Appeals (3d cir.) 1979, U.S. Supreme Ct. 1989, U.S. Ct. Claims 1990. Law clk. to presiding justice Pa. Ct. Common Pleas, Pitts., 1982-85; asst. dist. atty. Office of Dist. Atty., Pitts., 1980-82; pvt. practice, Pitts. and McKeesport, 1982—; pres. Pribanic & Pribanic, P.C., 1987—. Mem. Nat. Assn. Criminal Def. Lawyers, Assn. Trial Lawyers Am., Acad. Trial Lawyers Allegheny County, Pa. Trial Lawyers Assn. Democrat. Roman Catholic. Personal injury, State civil litigation, Criminal. Home: 100 Victoria Dr Mc Keesport PA 15131-1224 Office: 1735 Lincoln Way White Oak PA 15131-1715 Address: 513 Court Pl Pittsburgh PA 15219-2002

**PRICE, CHARLES STEVEN,** lawyer; b. Inglewood, Calif., June 10, 1955; s. Frank Dean Price and Ann (Rounds) Bolling; m. Sandra Helen Laney, Feb. 26, 1983; children: Katherine Laney, Courtney Ann, Diana Emily. BA, U. Calif., Santa Barbara, 1976; JD, U. Chgo., 1979. Bar: Ariz. 1980, U.S. Dist. Ariz. 1980, U.S. Ct. Appeals (9th cir.) 1982. Assoc. Brown & Bain P.A., Phoenix, Ariz., 1979-85, ptnr., 1985-96; ptnr. Allen & Price P.L.C., Phoenix, Ariz., 1996—. Antitrust, Health, Securities. Office: Allen & Price PLC 3131 E Camelback Rd Ste 110 Phoenix AZ 85016

**PRICE, DANIEL MARTIN,** lawyer; b. St. Louis, Aug. 23, 1955; s. Albert and Edith S. (Werner) P.; m. Kim Ellen Heebner, July 15, 1984; children: Emma Rachel, Joseph Armin, Joshua Simon. BA, Haverford Coll., 1977; diploma in law, Cambridge U., 1979; JD, Harvard U., 1981. Bar: D.C. 1981, Pa. 1987. Assoc. Drinker, Biddle & Reath, Phila., 1981-82, 86-89; dep. gen. counsel Office of U.S. Trade Rep., Washington, 1989-92; ptnr. Powell, Goldstein, Frazer & Murphy, Washington, 1992—; atty., adviser Dept. State, Washington, 1982-84; dep. agt. U.S. Iran-U.S. Claims Tribunal, Hague, The Netherlands, 1984-86; lectr. Haverford Coll., 1982. Articles editor Harvard Law Rev., 1980-81; contbr. Am. Jour. Internat. Law, Internat. Lawyer, Internat. Fin. Law Rev., Internat. Banking and Fin. Law. Am. Keasbey scholar Cambridge U., 1977-78. Mem. ABA (co-chmn. trade com. on N.Am. Free Trade Agreement), Internat. Bus. Forum (legal adv. bd. 1987-89), Am. Arbitration Assn. (panel arbitrators), Internat. C. of C. (arbitrator), Orgn. for Internat. Investment (counsel), Phi Beta Kappa. Private international, Public international. Office: 1001 Pennsylvania Ave NW Washington DC 20004-2505

**PRICE, GRIFFITH BALEY, JR.,** lawyer; b. Lawrence, Kans., Aug. 15, 1942; s. Griffith Baley and Cora Lee (Beers) P.; m. Maria Helena Martin, June 29, 1968 (div.); children: Andrew Griffith, Alexandra Helena; m. Nancy Culver Rhodes, Aug. 17, 1997. AB (cum laude), Harvard U., 1964; LLB, NYU, 1967. Bar: N.Y. 1967, U.S. Ct. Appeals (6th cir.) 1975, U.S. Ct. Appeals (2nd cir.) 1978, U.S. Ct. Appeals (3d, 5th and 11th cirs.) 1981, U.S. Ct. Appeals (fed. cir.) 1984, D.C. 1991. Assoc. Dewey, Ballantine, Bushby, Palmer & Wood, N.Y.C., 1967-75; ptnr. Milgrim Thomajan & Lee, N.Y.C., 1976-86, of counsel, ptnr. Finnegan, Henderson, Farabow, Garrett & Dunner, Washington, 1987—; adj. prof., lectr. George Washington U. Law Ctr., Washington, 1989-93; frequent lectr. ABA, Practicing Law Inst., Law & Bus., 1982—. Author: (with others, treatise) Milgrim on Trade Secrets, 1986; contbr. articles to publs. Root-Tilden scholar NYU Law Sch., 1964-67. Mem. ABA (intellectual property sect., com. chmn.), Internat. Trademark Assn. (bd. dirs., com. chmn.), Am. Intellectual Property Law Assn. (com. chmn.), Licensing Execs. Soc., N.Y. Athletic Club, Harvard Club (Washington), Cosmos Club. Presbyterian. Intellectual property, Trademark and copyright, Federal civil litigation. Office: Finnegan Henderson Farabow Garrett & Dunner 1300 I St NW Ste 700 Washington DC 20005-3314

**PRICE, HENRY J.,** lawyer; b. LaGrange, Ind., Mar. 26, 1937; m. Jeri L. Price; 1 child, Craig H. AB cum laude, Wittenberg U., Springfield, Ohio, 1959; JD, U. Mich., 1962; LLM, Georgetown U., 1963. Bar: D.C. 1962, Ind. 1963, U.S. Supreme Ct., U.S. Ct. Appeals (7th cir.), U.S. Dist. Ct. (no. and so. dists.) Ind., U.S. Dist. Ct. (D.C. dist.) Ptnr. Barnes & Thornburg, Indpls., 1963-85, Townsend, Yosha Cline & Price, Indpls., 1985-86, Henry J. Price, P.C., 1986, Price & DeLaney, Indpls., 1987-89, Price & Shula, Indpls., 1989-91, Price & Barker, Indpls., 1991-96, Price & Findling, Indpls., 1996-97, Price, Kuss & Mellowitz, Indpls., 1997-99, Price, Potter & Mellowitz, Indpls., 1999—; faculty, prof. dir. Ind. Nat. Inst. Trial Advocacy, Indpls., 1983-89; lectr. in field. Co-author: Law and Tactics in Federal Criminal Cases, 1964, Condemnation in Indiana, 1976. Pres. Ind. Civil Liberties Union, 1980-89. Mem. ATLA, ABA, Ind. Bar Assn., Indpls. Bar Assn., Bar Assn. 7th fed. Cir., Am. Bd. Trial Advs., Internat. Soc. Barristers (bd. dirs. 1990-95), Ind. Trial Lawyers Assn. (bd. dirs. 1989—, mem. exec. com. 1997—), Indpls. Am. Inn Ct. Avocations: tennis, flying, snow skiing. Product liability, General civil litigation, Personal injury. Office: Price Potter & Mellowitz 301 Massachusetts Ave Indianapolis IN 46204-2108

**PRICE, JAMES TUCKER,** lawyer; b. Springfield, Mo., June 22, 1955; s. Billy L. and Jeanne Adele Price; m. Francine Beth Warkow, June 8, 1980; children: Rachel Leah, Ashley Elizabeth. BJ, U. Mo., 1977; JD, Harvard U., 1980. Bar: Mo. 1980. Assoc. firm Spencer Fane Britt & Browne, Kansas City, 1980-86; ptnr. Spencer Fane Britt & Browne LLP, Kansas City, 1987—, chair environ. practice group, 1994—, mem. exec. com., 1997—; mem. steering com. Kansas City Bi-State Brownfields Initiative, 1997—. Contbr. to monographs, other legal publs. Mem. ABA (coun. sect. natural resources, energy and environ. law 1992-95, vice chmn. solid and hazardous waste com. 1985-90, chmn. 1990-92, chmn. brownfields task force 1995-97, vice chmn. environ. transactions and brownfield com. 1998—), Mo. Bar Assn., Kansas City Met. Bar Assn. (chmn. environ. law com. 1985-86), Greater Kansas City C. of C. (co-chair Brownfields Working Group, 1996-98, chmn. energy and environ. com. 1987-89). Environmental, Federal civil litigation, State civil litigation. Office: Spencer Fane Britt & Browne LLP 1000 Walnut St Ste 1400 Kansas City MO 64106-2140

**PRICE, JOHN ALEY,** lawyer; b. Maryville, Mo., Oct. 7, 1947; s. Donald Leroy and Julia Catherine (Aley) P.; m. Deborah Diadra Gunter, Aug. 12, 1995; children: Theodore John, Joseph Andrew. BS, N.W. Mo. State U., 1969; JD, U. Kans., 1972. Bar: Kans. 1972, U.S. Dist. Ct. Kans. 1972, U.S. Ct. Appeals (10th cir.) 1972, Tex. 1984, U.S. Ct. Appeals (5th cir.) 1984, U.S. Supreme Ct., 1987; cert. civil trial law Tex. Bd. Legal Specialization, 1989—. Law clk. U.S. Dist. Ct. Kans., Wichita, 1972-74; assoc., then ptnr. firm Weeks, Thomas and Lysaught, Kansas City, Kans., 1974-82; ptnr. Winstead, Sechrest & Minick, Dallas, 1982-96, litigation sect. coord., 1990-92, intellectual property sect. litigation coord., 1993-95; gen. counsel Travelhost, Inc., Dallas, 1996—; spl. prosecutor Leavenworth County Dist. Atty., 1970-71, Sedgwick County Dist. Atty., Wichita, Kans., 1971-72. Author: Our Boundless Self (A Call to Awake), 1992, A Gathering of Light: Eternal Wisdom for a Time of Transformation, 1993; co-author: Soular Reunion: Journey to the Beloved, 1997; editor (mag.) Academic Analyst, 1968-69; assoc. editor U. Kans. Law Rev., 1971-72, Dallas Bus. Jour.; author legal publs. Co-dir. Douglas County Legal Aid Soc., Lawrence, Kans., 1971-72; co-pres. Northwood Hills PTA, Dallas, 1984, Westwoood Jr. H.S. PTA,

1989-90; founder New Frontiers Found., 1993; co-founder Wings of Spirit Found., 1994, dir., v.p., 1994—. Mem. ABA, Kans. Bar Assn. (mem. task force for penal reform; Pres.'s Outstanding Svc. award 1981), Tex. Bar Assn., Pro Bono Coll., State Bar Tex., 1992—, World Bus. Acad., Inst. Noetic Scis., UN Assn. (humans rights com. Dallas chpt. 1991-93, bd. dirs. 1991-93), Campaign for the Earth (chpt. coord. Global Report 1991-92, coord. govt. and politics area 1991-92), Blue Key, Order of Coif, Phi Delta Phi, Sigma Tau Gamma (v.p. 1968-69). Mem. Unity Ch. Federal civil litigation, Trademark and copyright, Antitrust. Office: Travelhost Inc 10701 N Stemmons Fwy Dallas TX 75220-2419 *Individually, each person creates his or her reality every moment of existence. Collectively, we hold within ourselves a boundless capacity to co-create a world filled with love, compassion and abundance for all sentient beings. The key to a new order of the ages lies within our own hearts, minds and souls.*

**PRICE, JOHN LOUIS,** judge; b. Chgo., Oct. 9, 1937; s. John Oscar Price and Ferne (Logsdon) Braddy.; m. Julia A. Price, Dec. 24, 1960; 1 child, Lynette Dianne. BS in Social Sci., Ball State U., 1961, MASociology, 1969; JD, Ind. U., 1968. Teacher Clarks Pt., Alaska, 1962-64; bill reader, asst. Ind. Ho. Reps., Indpls., 1965; chief probation officer Marion County Criminal Cts., Indpls., 1965-66; bailif Marion County Mcpl.Cts., Indpls., 1966-67; tchr. Greenfield (Ind.) Pub. Schs., 1967-68; criminal ct. commissioner Marion Superior Cts., Indpls., 1968-81; assoc. prof. Ind. U., Indpls., 1968-86; pvt. law practice Indpls., 1968-81; judge Marion county Municipal Cts., Indpls., 1982-94, Marion County Superior Ct, 1994-00; assoc. prof. Ind. U., Purdue U., Indpls., 1968-86; tchr. Nat. Judicial Coll., Reno, 1988-94. Bd. dirs. Crossroads council Boys Scouts Am., 1982—, Buchanan Counselling Svc., Indpls., 1986—; deacon 2d Presby. Ch., Indpls., 1977-79. Fellow Ball State U., Indpls. Bar Foun.; mem. Kiwanis Club Indpls. (bd. dirs. 1983—, pres. 1991-92). Democrat. Avocations: reading, camping, scouting. Office: Superior Ct #11 1421 City County Bldg Indianapolis IN 46204

**PRICE, JOHN RICHARD,** lawyer, law educator; b. Indpls., Nov. 28, 1934; s. Carl Lee and Agnes I. P.; m. Suzanne A. Leslie, June 22, 1963; children: John D., Steven V. B.A. with high honors, U. Fla., 1958; LL.B. with honors, NYU, 1961. Bar: Calif. 1962, Wash. 1977, U.S. Ct. Appeals (9th cir.), U.S. Dist. Ct. (we. dist.) Wash. Assoc. McCutchen, Doyle, Brown & Enersen, San Francisco, 1961-69; prof. law U. Wash., Seattle, 1969-97, dean, 1982-88; of counsel Perkins Coie, Seattle, 1976—. Author: Contemporary Estate Planning, 1983, Price on Contemporary Estate Planning, 1992. Served with U.S. Army, 1953-55. Root-Tilden fellow NYU Sch. Law, 1958-61. Fellow Am. Coll. Trust and Estate Counsel (former regent); mem. ABA, Am. Law Inst., Internat. Acad. of Estate and Trust Law, Order of Coif, Phi Beta Kappa. Congregationalist. Home: 3794 NE 97th St Seattle WA 98115-2564 Office: 1201 3rd Ave Fl 40 Seattle WA 98101-3099

**PRICE, LIONEL FRANKLIN,** lawyer; b. New Orleans, Mar. 14, 1940; s. Samuel and Anna Estelle (Harris) P.; m. Cory Jean Smith, Nov. 15, 1974; children: Daniel Saxon, Cassia Amber, Darby Killeen. BA, La. State U., 1963; JD, Tulane U., 1971; Bar: La. 1971, U.S. Dist. Ct. (ea. dist.) La. 1971, U.S. Ct. Appeals (5th cir.) 1971. Assoc. Flanders & Flanders, New Orleans, 1971-74; sole practice, Slidell, La. and New Orleans, 1974—; pres., chmn. bd. D&P Pub. Co., Inc.; dir. Gulf Caribe Transport, Inc., New Orleans; pres. Pripub Enterprises Inc. Actor (film) JFK, (TV) Unsolved Mysteries, others; tchr. filmmaking Delgado C.C., 1996, 97; actor, writer, prodr., dir. (pilot radio series) The Captain; author: Little Gods and Angry Men, 1986; editor: Lousiana Entertainment Maganews; contbr. articles to profl. publs. Bd. dirs. Jefferson Mil. Coll. Found., 1983-84; trustee Bankruptcy Ct. Ea. Dist. La. Served to comdr. USNR, 1963—. Recipient Editor's Choice award Nat. Libr. Poetry, 1996. Mem. ABA, La. Bar Assn., Naval Res. Assn. (chpt. v.p. 1978-80), Slidell Bar Assn., Internat. Platform Assn., Am. Fedn. T.V. & Radio Artists, Delta Theta Phi (Outstanding Student award 1971). Admiralty, Entertainment, Personal injury. Home: PO Box 5961 Slidell LA 70469-5961 Office: 60346 Lilac Dr Lacombe LA 70445-3008

**PRICE, PAUL L.,** lawyer; b. Chgo., Apr. 21, 1945; s. Walter S. and Lillian (Czerepkowski) L.; m. Dianne L. Olech, June 3, 1967; children: Kristen, Kathryn. BBA, Loyola U., Chgo., 1967; JD with honors, Ill. Inst. Tech., 1971. Bar: Ill. 1971, U.S. Dist. Ct. (no. dist.) Ill., U.S. Ct. Appeals (7th cir.). Tax acct. Arthur Anderson & Co., Chgo., 1970-71; assoc. Doyle & Tarpey, Chgo., 1971-75, Gordon & Assocs., Chgo., 1975-76; from assoc. to ptnr. Pretzel & Stouffer, Chartered, Chgo., 1976-96; ptnr. Price, Tunney, Reiter & Bruton, Chgo., 1996—. With USMC, 1969-70. Fellow Am. Coll. Trial Lawyers; mem. ABA, Ill. Bar Assn., Soc. Trial Lawyers, Ill. Assn. Def. Trial Counsel (pres. 1990-91), Fedn. Ins. and Corp. Counsel (pres.), Def. Rsch. Inst. (bd. dirs.), Lawyers for Civil Justice (bd. dirs.), Assn. Def. Trial Attys., Ill. Inst. Tech.-Chgo. Kent Coll. Law Alumni Assn. (pres. 1989-90). Roman Catholic. General civil litigation, Product liability. Office: Price Tunney Reiter & Bruton 200 N Lasalle St Ste 3050 Chicago IL 60601-1014

**PRICE, PHILLIP VINCENT,** lawyer; b. Indpls., Jan. 2, 1949; s. Frank A. and Gertrude E. (Maloney) P.; m. Patricia A. Quinn, May 18, 1974; children: William Quinn, Richard Frank, Colleen Elizabeth. Student, Purdue U., 1967-68; BA in Polit. Sci., U. Wis., 1971; JD, Ind. U., Indpls., 1975. Bar: Ind. 1975, U.S. Ct. Appeals (7th cir.) 1983, U.S. Dist. Ct. (so. dist.) Ind. 1975, U.S. Dist. Ct. (no. dist.) Ind. 1985, U.S. Supreme Ct., 1985. Legal advisor Marion County Sheriff Dept., Indpls., 1975-77; assoc. Yarling, Tunnell, Robison & Lamb, Indpls., 1977-78; sole practice Indpls., 1978—; lectr. in field. Mem. ABA, Ind. Bar Assn., Indpls. Bar Assn., Nat. Orgn. Social Security Claimants Reps., U. Wis. Alumni Club (pres. 1983-84). Democrat. Roman Catholic. Avocations: fly fishing, computing, Boy Scouts, furniture kit building. Pension, profit-sharing, and employee benefits, Administrative and regulatory, Probate. Office: 4249 Lafayette Rd Indianapolis IN 46254-2409

**PRICE, PINE SCOTT,** lawyer; b. Kenosha, Wis., Dec. 21, 1957; s. Lewis Hall P. and Gladys Margie Dutt; m. Vicki Lynn McDannel, June 8, 1980; children: Sarah Chantelle, Richelle Christine. BS in Zoology, So. Ill. U., 1989, MBA, 1993, JD, 1993. Bar: Ill. 1993, Fla. 1994, U.S. Dist. Ct. (mid. dist.) Fla. 1995. Asst. pub. defender Pub. Defender of 20th Jud. Cir. Ct., Punta Gorda, Fla., 1994-98; atty. pvt. practice, Punta Gorda, Fla., 1998—. Avocations: kayaking, camping, rock climbing, canoeing, chess. Criminal, Personal injury, General practice. Office: 201 W Marion Ave Ste 207 Punta Gorda FL 33950-4401

**PRICE, RICHARD LEE,** judge; b. N.Y.C., Sept. 19, 1940; s. Saul and Claire (Bernstein) P.; m. Laura Shapiro; children: Lisa, Howard, Alex. BA in Polit. Sci., Roanoke Coll., 1961; LLB, N.Y. Law Sch., 1964; LLD (hon.), Shaw U., 1980. Bar: N.Y. 1965, U.S. Ct. Internat. Trade 1965, U.S. Dist. Ct. (so. and ea. dists.) N.Y. 1966, U.S. Ct. Appeals (2d cir.) 1967, U.S. Supreme Ct. 1974. Assoc. Law Office Harry H. Lipsig, N.Y.C., 1967-69; law sec. to judge Civil Ct., N.Y.C., 1969-76, chief law asst., 1976-80, judge, 1980—; acting justice Bronx (N.Y.) County Supreme Ct.; chmn. com. setting support amount Gov.'s Commn. on Child Support, com. on gender bias 12th Jud. Dist.; mem. curriculum devel. com. office of ct. administrn. Contbr. articles to profl. jours. Exec. officer Lt. 7th Precinct Auxiliary Police, 1980; chairperson East River Housing Com., 1969, 74-75, 77-81, mem. 1966-69, 71-73, 76; mem. Coordinating Council Coops., 1973—, Citizens Com. ERA, B'nai B'rith Career and Counseling Services (adv. bd.); trustee Bialystoker Synagogue, 1966-79; bd. dirs. East Side Torah Ctr., Grand St. Consumers Soc., 1972—, Fedn. Coops., 1974—, Lower East Side Businessmen's Assn., 1977-80, City Coalition on Child Sexual Abuse, chairperson pub. relations com.; treas. Am. Judges Found. Recipient Pub. Service award Lower East Side Jewish Festival, 1985. Mem. ABA (task force law related edn.), N.Y. State Bar Assn. (past chairperson com. on dist. city village and town cts., citizenship edn. and cts. and community coms., chairperson subcom. pub. events and edn.), Assn. of Bar of City of N.Y. (coun. on jud. adminstrn. women in the cts. coms.), Black Bar Assn., N.Y. Women's Bar Assn. (criminal law, children's rights and legal rights of battered women planning coms., co-chmn. com. on gender bias), N.Y.C. Criminal and Civil Cts. Bar Assn. (v.p.), Met. Women's Bar Assn. (bd. dirs. 1998—, chairperson task force on discrimination of women in cts.), N.Y. County Lawyers Assn. (chairperson law related edn. com.), N.Y. State Trial Lawyers Assn. (chairperson jud. adminstrn. and procedure com. 1982), Am. Judges Assn. (pres., 1st v.p., 2d v.p., asst. treas., bd. govs.), NOW, East Side C. of C., Bronx Womans Bar Assn. (treas.). Lodge: B'nai B'rith (past pres. lawyers unit). Office: Supreme Ct 851 Grand Concourse Ste 918 Bronx NY 10451-2937

**PRICE, ROBERT ALLAN,** lawyer; b. Phila., Dec. 25, 1946; s. Harold James and Marie (Werner) P.; m. Margaret Price (div. 1972); 1 child, Karen Elaine Price Vretto; m. Donna Elaine Walding, Nov. 22, 1975; children: Robert Allan Jr., Jamie Leigh. BS, Troy State U., Dothan, Ala., 1989; JD, Jones Sch. Law, Montgomery, Ala. Bar: Ala. Enlisted man U.S. Army, 1967, advanced through grades to CW 4, pilot; ret., 1987; with Lear Siegler Svcs., Ft. Rucker, Ala., 1987—; pvt. practice, Enterprise, Ala., 1994—. Decorated DFC. Mem. ABA, Ala. Bar Assn. Avocations: golf, fishing. Family and matrimonial, Personal injury, Bankruptcy. Office: PO Box 310968 Enterprise AL 36331-0968

**PRICE, ROBERT DEMILLE,** lawyer; b. N.Y.C., Oct. 11, 1915; s. Willard DeMille Price and Eugenia Reeve; m. Newell Potter, Aug. 15, 1940 (div. May 1946); 1 child, Jonathan; m. Ruth Bentley, July 5, 1946; children: Katharine, Susannah, Rebecca. AB in Econs. with honors, Cornell U., 1936; JD, Harvard U., 1940; MBA, Clark U., 1973. Bar: Mass. 1940, U.S. Dist. Ct. Mass. 1941, U.S. Tax Ct. 1977, U.S. Supreme Ct. 1978. Assoc. Ropes & Gray, Boston, 1940-43, 1946-50; ptnr. Vaughan, Esty, Crotty & Mason, Worcester, Mass., 1950-53, Sibley, Blair & Mountain, Worcester, 1953-70, Corbin, Sarapas, Madaus & Arakelian, Worcester, 1970-73, Price & Madaus, Worcester, 1973-87; pres. Robert D. Price, PC, Holden, Mass., 1987—; Dir. Appian Way Pizza, Ltd., Worcester, 1951-61, Food Specialties, Inc., Worcester, 1951-61, James Monroe Wire and Cable Co., S. Lancaster, Mass., 1973—; mem. Fin. Com., Holden, 1989—. Moderator (TV series) Am. Bar Assn. Jr. Bar Assn., 1947-50. Dir., treas. Friends Gale Free Librs. Inc., Holden, 1988—; mem. adv. bd. Met. Dist. Commn., 1990-96; pres. Humanist Chaplaincy at Harvard, 1995—. Lt. USNR, 1943-51. Mem. Worcester County Bar Assn., Worcester Club (dir. 1953—). Avocations: museum and art show, photography, alpine climbing, sailing. Estate planning, Estate taxation, General corporate. Office: 2 Malden St Holden MA 01520-1827

**PRICE, ROBERT ERNEST,** lawyer; b. Athens, Ohio, Dec. 24, 1954; s. Ernest and Cora (Pugh) P.; m. Linda Carol Jordan, Jan. 30, 1983; children: Sarah Catherine, David Ernest. BSBA, U. N.C., 1977, JD, 1980. Bar: U.S. Dist. Ct. (mid. dist.) N.C. 1982, U.S. Dist. Ct. (ea. dist.) N.C. 1987, U.S. Ct. Appeals (4th cir.) 1987, U.S. Supreme Ct. 1987. Assoc. Davis & Brewer, Clemmons, N.C., 1980-83; pvt. practice Rowland, N.C., 1984-86, 90—; ptnr. Price & McIntyre, Rowland, 1987-89. Recipient Disting. Svc. award Robeson County Jaycees, 1989. Mem. Rowland C. of C. (sec.), Phi Beta Kappa, Phi Eta Sigma, Beta Gamma Sigma. Democrat. Presbyterian. Real property, General practice. Home and Office: PO Box 369 Rowland NC 28383-0369

**PRICE, STEVEN,** lawyer, communications executive; b. N.Y.C., Feb. 14, 1962; s. Robert and Margery (Wiener) P.; m. Tina Gitlin, 1991. BA, Brown U., 1984; LLD, Columbia U., 1989. Reporter The Gainesville (Fla.) Sun, 1983; mergers analyst Goldman Sachs and Co., N.Y.C., 1984-86; v.p. PriCellular, Inc., N.Y.C.; v.p. Price Communications Corp., N.Y.C., 1986-89, also bd. dirs.; spl. asst. to chief del. to nuclear and space talks U.S. Dept. State, Washington and Geneva, 1989-90, cons. nuclear space talks del., 1990-91; assoc. Davis, Polk & Wardwell Attys., 1990-93; pres., CEO PriCellular Corp., 1993—; bd. dirs. N.Y. Law Jour. Co., PriCellular Corp. Mem. Phi Beta Kappa. Communications, General corporate.

**PRICE, STUART WINSTON,** lawyer; b. Pasadena, Calif., Jan. 20, 1962; s. Frank Dean and Ann Browning (Rounds) P.; m. Lynne Marie Bowman, May 26, 1996. BA, U. Calif., Santa Barbara, 1983; JD, UCLA, 1986. Assoc. Drummy Garrett King & Harrison, Costa Mesa, Calif., 1986-91; assoc., ptnr. McDermott, Will & Emery, Newport Beach, Calif., 1991—. Federal civil litigation, State civil litigation. Office: McDermott Will & Emery 1301 Dove St Ste 500 Newport Beach CA 92660-2444

**PRICE, WILLIAM RAY, JR.,** state supreme court judge; b. Fairfield, Iowa, Jan. 30, 1952; s. William Ray and Evelyn Jean (Darnell) P.; m. Susan Marie Trainor, Jan. 4, 1975; children: Emily Margret, William Joseph Dodds. BA with distinction, U. Iowa, 1974; postgrad., Yale U., 1974-75; JD cum laude, Washington and Lee U., 1978. Bar: Mo. 1978, U.S. Dist. Ct. (we. dist.) Mo. 1978, U.S. Ct. Claims 1978, U.S. Ct. Appeals (8th cir.) 1985. Assoc. Lathrop & Norquist, Kansas City, Mo., 1978-84, ptnr., 1984-92, chmn. bus. litigation sect., 1987-88, 90-92, exec. com., 1989-92; judge Supreme Ct. Mo., Jefferson City, 1992—, chief justice, 1999—; G.L.V. Zumwalt monitoring com. U.S. Dist. Ct. (we. dist.) Mo., Kansas City. Pres. Kansas City Bd. Police Commrs.; mem. Together Ctr. & Family Devel. Ctr., Kansas City; chmn. merit selection com. U.S. marshal Western Dist. of Mo., Kansas City; bd. dirs. Truman Med. Ctr., Kansas City. Rockefeller fellow, 1974-75; Burks scholar Washington & Lee U., 1976. Mem. Christian Ch. Office: Supreme Ct Mo 101 High St Jefferson City MO 65102-0150*

**PRICKETT, GREGORY L.,** judge; b. Torrance, Calif., May 3, 1956; m. Laura Suzanne Arthur, Sept. 12, 1981; children: Jennifer, Sean. BA, U. So. Calif., L.A., 1978; JD, Southwestern U., 1981. Dep. dist. atty. L.A. County, 1981-83; dep. dist. atty. Orange County, Santa Ana, Calif., 1983-91, sr. dep. dist. atty., 1991-95; mcpl. ct. judge Fullerton, Calif., 1995-98; judge Superior Ct., Fullerton, 1998—; lectr. in field. Contbr. articles to profl. jours. Adv. bd. Canning Hunger, Orange, Calif., 1995—, Friends Ctr.-Azusa (Calif.) Pacific U., 1990—; chairperson missions com. S.W. Yearly Meeting, Whittier, Calif., 1998. Named Disting. Lectr. Calif. Dist. Atty. Assn., 1989. Mem. Am. Judges Assn. Mem. Soc. of Friends. Office: Superior Ct Judge 1275 N Berkeley Ave Fullerton CA 92832-1206

**PRIDE, KENNETH RODNEY,** lawyer, consultant; b. L.A., Dec. 31, 1953; s. James Allen and Mable Louise (Jones) P.; divorced; children: Kenneth Rodney II, Jason Alexander. AA, Los Angeles Harbor Coll., 1975; BA, U. So. Calif., 1977; JD, Loyola U., Los Angeles, 1982; MBA, Pepperdine U., 1988. House counsel Mark Industries, Long Beach, Calif., 1982—; chmn. Am. Equipment Ins. Ltd., Cayman Islands; bd. dirs. Mark Credit Corp, Powered Mobile Platforms Corp, Mark Comml. Fin. Corp, Mark Industries Corp.; cons. Am. Mgmt. Advisers, Ltd.; sports agt. Profl. Stars, Inc. Active Los Angeles County Cen. Com., 1974-79, State Cen. Com., Calif., 1975-78; asst. scout master Boy Scouts Am. Served with USAF, 1971-73. Recipient Outstanding Community Service Resolution Calif. State Legis., 1975. Mem. Farm and Indsl. Equipment Inst. (legal and legis. com. 1983—). Roman Catholic. Avocations: camping, travel, akiing. Home: 8121 W Manchester Ave # 523 Playa Del Rey CA 90293-8728

**PRIEST, GEORGE L.,** law educator; b. 1947. BA, Yale U., 1969; JD, U. Chgo., 1973. Assoc. prof. U. Puget Sound, Tacoma, 1973-75; law and econ. fellow U. Chgo., 1975-77; prof. U. Buffalo, 1977-80, UCLA, 1980-81, Yale U., New Haven, 1981—; dir. program in civil liability; John M. Olin prof. law and econs., 1986—. Mem. Pres.' Com. on Privatization, 1987-88. Office: PO Box 208215 New Haven CT 06520-8215

**PRIEST, MELISSA LENORE,** lawyer; b. New Orleans, Mar. 26, 1962; d. Wayne Patrick and Nancy Ann (Dague) P. BA magna cum laude, Southwestern U., 1983; JD, U. Tex., 1986. Bar: Tex. 1986. Asst. dist. atty. Bexar County Dist. Attys. Office, San Antonio, 1987-90, chief grand jury sect., 1990—. Chair, bd. dirs. Good Samaritan Ctr., San Antonio, 1988-98; vestry mem. St. Stephen's Episc. Ch., San Antonio, 1991-94; vol. mediator Bexar County Dispute Resolution Ctr., San Antonio, 1994-99. Mem. San Antonio Young Lawyers' Assn., Bexar County Women's Bar Assn. (bd. dirs. 1990-91, sec. 1992, Belva Lockwood Outstanding Young Lawyer award 1990), Jr. League of San Antonio. Democrat. Avocations: music, choir, reading, movies, computers. Office: Bexar County Dist Attys Office 300 Dolorosa San Antonio TX 78205-3005

**PRIEST, PETER H.,** lawyer; b. Norwood, Mass., Sept. 12, 1955; s. William G. and Mary E. (Horne) P.; children: William, Sarah. BSEE, U. Maine, Orono, 1977; JD, U. Maine, Portland, 1980. Bar: N.Y. 1981, N.C., 1996, U.S. Dist. Ct. (so., ea. dists.) N.Y. 1981, U.S. Patent Office 1981, U.S. Ct. Appeals (Fed. cir.) 1987. Assoc. Davis, Hoxie, Faithfull, Hapgood, N.Y.C., 1980-88, ptnr., 1989-95; pvt. practice, Chapel Hill, N.C., 1995—. Mem. ABA, Am. Intellectual Property Law Assn., Fed. Cir. Bar Assn., Internat. Intellectual Property Soc., Union Internat. Avocats. Patent. Office: 529 Dogwood Dr Chapel Hill NC 27516-2807

**PRIEST, TROY ALFRED-WILEY,** lawyer; b. Balt., Oct. 5, 1968; s. Roy Otis and Sudie Mae (Payton) P.; m. Françoise Borja Santos, Aug. 10, 1991; 1 child, Gabrielle Borja. BA, Brown U., 1990; JD, Northeastern U., 1993. Bar: Md. 1993, D.C. 1994, U.S. Dist. Ct. Md. 1994, U.S. Dist. Ct. D.C. 1995. Law clk. Hon. Annice M. Wagner chief judge D.C. Ct. of Appeals, Washington, 1993-94; assoc. Houston & Howard, Washington, 1994-96, Mason, Ketterman & Morgan, Balt., 1996-99; exec. v.p., chief legal officer The Consortium of Med. Dirs., Inc., Silver Spring, Md., 1999—; dist. counselor Omega Psi Phi Fraternity, Inc., New Eng., Providence, R.I., 1991-93. Mem. ABA, Am. Health Lawyers Assn., Nat. Bar Assn., Md. Bar Assn., Bar Assn. D.C., Defense Rsch. Inst. Democrat. Baptist. General corporate, Health, Labor. Home: 1306 Canyon Rd Silver Spring MD 20904-1406 Office: The Consortium of Med Dirs Inc 9606 Colesville Rd Silver Spring MD 20901

**PRIM, JOSEPH ANTHONY,** lawyer; b. Phila., June 29, 1944; s. Joseph A. and Leila A. P.; children: Joseph A. III, Jennifer L.; m. Jeanne C. Mullen, May 29, 1992; 1 child, Marian S. BA, U. Pa., 1967; JD, Boston U., 1970. Bar: Pa. 1970, U.S. Dist. Ct. (ea. dist.) Pa. 1970, U.S. Ct. Appeals (3d cir.) 1974, U.S. Supreme Ct. 1991. Assoc. O'Halloran, Stack & Smith, Phila., 1970-73, Stephen A. Sheller & Assocs., Phila., 1980-87; pvt. practice Phila., 1974-80; ptnr. Duca & Prim, Phila., 1987—. Mem. Pa. Bar Assn., Phila. Bar Assn. (chmn. worker's compensation com. 1993-94, treas. 1994—), Union League Phila. Workers' compensation. Office: 1500 Walnut St Ste 900 Philadelphia PA 19102-3505

**PRIMAS, EMMETT E., JR.,** lawyer; b. Camden, N.J., Feb. 28, 1958; s. Emett E. Sr. and Joanne Primas; m. Toni Marie Primas; children: Falone, Mitchell. BA, Rutgers U., 1981, JD, 1987. Bar: U.S. Ct. Appeals 1994, N.J. 1998, U.S. Dist. Ct. N.J. 1998. Casino analyst N.J. Casino control Commn., Atlantic City, 1981-84; assoc. Harvey Johnson, Camden, 1988-89; staff atty. N.J. Office of Pub. Defender, Trenton, 1989-91; ptnr. Smith and Primas, Camden, 1991-97, Emmett E. Primas Sr., Woodbury, N.J., 1997—; mem. ethics com. N.J. Supreme Ct., Trenton, 1998. Counsel Elliott Heart Meml. Fund, Mullica Hill, N.J., 1995—, Camden Renaissance, 1996—; advisor Ruthers U., Camden, 1995-98. Mem. Assn. Criminal Def. Lawyers, N.J. State Bar Assn. (mcpl. ct. com. 1997—), Gloucester County Bar Assn., Kappa Alpha Psi, Masons. Baptist. Avocation: golf. General practice. Office: 20 E Centre St Woodbury NJ 08096-2416

**PRIMPS, WILLIAM GUTHRIE,** lawyer; b. Ossining, N.Y., Sept. 8, 1949; s. Richard Byrd and Mary Elizabeth (Guthrie) P.; m. Sophia Elizabeth Beutel, Aug. 25, 1973; children: Emily Ann, Elizabeth Armstrong, William Andrew. BA, Yale U., 1971; JD, Harvard U., 1974. Bar: N.Y., 1975. Assoc. LeBoeuf, Lamb, Leiby & MacRae, N.Y.C., 1974-82; ptnr. LeBoeuf, Lamb, Greene & MacRae, N.Y.C., 1983—; counsel to Bd. Zoning Appeals, Bronxville, 1988-89, chmn., 1989-91. Mem. class coun. Yale U., New Haven, 1986-91; trustee Village of Bronxville, 1991—, dep. mayor, 1995—; deacon Reformed Ch. Bronxville, 1989-94. Mem. ABA, N.Y. State Bar Assn., Assn. Yale Alumni (class rep. 1986-91), Yale Club, Bronxville Field Club. Republican. Federal civil litigation, Antitrust, Insurance. Home: 71 Summit Ave Bronxville NY 10708-1815 Office: LeBoeuf Lamb Greene & MacRae 125 W 55th St New York NY 10019-5369

**PRINCE, CHARLES O., III,** lawyer; b. 1950. BA, U. So. Calif., 1971, MA, JD, 1975. Bar: Pa. 1975, Md. 1979, Minn. 1982. Formerly gen. counsel Commercial Credit Co.; exec. v.p., gen. counsel, sec. Traveler's Group, N.Y.C., 1986-98; co-gen. counsel, sec. Citigroup (merger of Traveler's Group and Citibank), N.Y.C., 1998—. Office: Citigroup 153 E 53rd St New York NY 10043*

**PRINCE, DAVID CANNON,** lawyer; b. Hawkinsville, Ga., July 4, 1950; s. Carl Willis and Carobel (Cannon) P.; m. Mary MacIntyre, June 30, 1973. BA in Econs., Clemson U., 1972; JD, St. John's U., Jamaica, N.Y., 1980. Bar: N.Y. 1981, Ga. 1982, U.S. Dist. Ct. (no. dist.) Ga. 1982. Atty. enforcement SEC, Atlanta, 1981-86; regional counsel Shearson Lehman Bros. Inc., Atlanta, 1986-92; gen. counsel Robinson-Humphrey Co., Inc., Atlanta, 1992—. Capt. USAF, 1972-78. Mem. ABA (co-chairperson young lawyers div. 1986-88). Democrat. Avocations: sailing, running. Securities, Administrative and regulatory, Federal civil litigation. Home: 1824 Lenox Rd NE Atlanta GA 30306-3031 Office: 3333 Peachtree Rd NE Atlanta GA 30326-1070

**PRINCE, TIMOTHY PETER,** lawyer; b. San Bernardino, Calif., July 11, 1965; s. Ralph H. and Alexine C. Prince. BA in Polit. Sci., U. Calif., Berkeley, 1987; JD, U. Calif., San Francisco, 1990. Bar: Calif., U.S. Dist. Ct. (ctrl. dist.) Calif. Asoc. Wilson, Borror, Dunn & Scott, San Bernardino, Calif., 1990-98; ptnr. Tomlinson, Nydam & Prince, San Bernardino, 1998—. Law rev. editor Hastings Constnl. Law Quar., 1989-90; contbr. articles to profl. jours. bd. dirs. Am. Lung Asn. of the Indland Counties, 1993-96, sec., 1994-96; chmn. Citizens for Accountable City Govt., San Bernardino, 1997. Calif. Alumni scholar, 1983-87, Gannett Found. scholar, 1983-87. Mem. North End Neighborhood Assn. (v.p. 1998—), Rotary Club (chmn. scholarship program), Inland C's Calif. Berkeley Alumni Club (pres. 1995). Democrat. Presbyterian. Achievements include being candidate in primary and general elections for Mayor of San Bernardino; writing ordinance restricting tobacco use adopted by City Council of San Bernardino. Avocations: hiking, jogging, music, travel, politics. General civil litigation, Product liability, Personal injury. Office: Tomlinson Nydam & Prince 290 N D St Ste 807 San Bernardino CA 92401-1704

**PRINCE, WILLIAM TALIAFERRO,** federal judge; b. Norfolk, Va., Oct. 3, 1929; s. James Edward and Helen Marie (Taliaferro) P.; m. Anne Carroll Hannegan, Apr. 12, 1958; children: Sarah Carroll Prince Pishko, Emily Taliaferro, William Taliaferro, John Hannegan, Anne Martineau Thompson, Robert Harrison. Student, Coll. William and Mary, Norfolk, 1947-48, 49-50; AB, Williamsburg, 1955, BCL, 1957, MLT, 1959. Bar: Va. 1957. Lectr. acctg. Coll. William and Mary, 1955-57; lectr. law Marshall-Wythe Sch. Law, 1957-59; assoc. Williams, Kelly & Greer, Norfolk, 1959-63, ptnr., 1963-90; U.S. magistrate judge Eastern Dist. of Va., Norfolk, 1990—; pres. Am. Inn of Ct. XXVII, 1987-89. Bd. editors: The Virginia Lawyer, A Basic Practice Handbook, 1966. Bd. dirs. Madonna Home, Inc., 1978-93, Soc. Alumni of Coll. William and Mary, 1985-88. Fellow Am. Coll. Trial Lawyers, Am. Bar Found., Va. Law found. (bd. dirs. 1976-90); mem. ABA (ho. of dels. 1984-90), Am. Judicature Soc. (bd. dirs. 1984-88), Va. State Bar (coun. 1973-77, exec. com. 1975-80, pres. 1978-79). Roman Catholic. Home: 1227 Graydon Ave Norfolk VA 23507-1006 Office: Walter E Hoffman US Courthouse 600 Granby St Ste 181 Norfolk VA 23510-1915

**PRING, CYNTHIA MARIE,** lawyer; b. Colorado Springs, Colo., Mar. 24, 1948; d. Roy I. and Charlotte M. (Myers) P.; m. Ross A. Wilson, Oct. 2, 1976 (div. 1987); children: Alexander Pring-Wilson, Jessica and Maggie Pring-Wilson (twins); m. Eugene R. Griffith Jr., Oct. 21, 1993. BA, Stanford U., 1970; JD, U. Denver, 1974. Bar: Colo. 1974, U.S. Dist. Ct. Colo. 1974. Dep. dist. atty. State of Colorado, Colorado Springs, 1974-77, chief dep. dist. atty., 1977-78; sole practice Colorado Springs, 1978—. Mem. Colo. Bar Assn., El Paso County Bar Assn., Assn. Trial Lawyers Am., Colo. Trial Lawyers Assn., Nat. Orgn. Social Security Claimant's Reps., Workers' Compensation Edn. Assn. Republican. Avocations: horses, computers, lit. Workers' compensation, Pension, profit-sharing, and employee benefits, Personal injury. Home: 1329 Wood Ave Colorado Springs CO 80903-2342 Office: 802 S Tejon St Colorado Springs CO 80903-4149

**PRINS, MARTIN DOUGLAS,** legal health care consultant; b. Independence, Mo., Jan. 23, 1958; s. Martin and Patricia (Robertson) P.; m. Roma Lynn Umsted, Sept. 18, 1982; children: Martin Alexander, Angela Michelle. BA, U. Mo., Kansas City, 1980, JD, 1982. Bar: Mo. 1982, U.S. Dist. Ct. (we. dist.) Mo. 1982. Atty. Humphrey and Farrington P.C., Independence, 1982-85; ptnr. Humphrey, Farrington, Prins and McClain, Independence, 1985-86; pvt. practice Lee's Summit, Mo., 1986-89; v.p. Med. Rev. Consultants, Inc., Independence, 1989-93, sr. v.p., 1993-97, pres. profl.

svcs. divsn., 1997—; seminar presenter and hosp. cons., Med. Rev. Consultants, 1989; presenter seminars, 1989-95. Trustee Glennwood Park United Meth. Ch., Independence, 1959-97; mem. United Meth. Men, Independence, 1990-97. Mem. Am. Health Lawyers Assn. (mem. alt. dispute resolution panel), Mo. Bar Assn., Eastern Jackson County Bar Assn., Kansas City Bar Assn., Healthcare Fin. Mgrs. Assn. Fax: 816-795-6734. Office: Med Appeals and Cons PO Box 3079 Independence MO 64055-8079

**PRITCHARD, CLYDE BASIL,** lawyer; b. Pawhuska, Okla., Jan. 25, 1937; s. William Henderson and Hester Nealie (Olive) P.; m. Seglinda Kelle, July 6, 1963; 1 child, Benjamin Christian. BS, Okla. State U., 1960; JD, U. Tulsa, 1965. Bar: Mich., U.S. Dist. Ct. (ea. dist.) Mich. 1974, U.S. Ct. Appeals (6th cir.) 1974, U.S. Supreme Ct. 1974. Atty., regional counsel IRS, Dallas, 1967-70; trial atty. organized crime divsn. Dept. of Justice, Washington, 1970-75; sole practitioner Franklin, Mich., 1975—. Mem. Planning Commn., Franklin Village, Franklin, Mich., 1988. Lt. col. USAF, 1970-80. Mem. Birmingham Country Club, Phi Delta Phi, Sigma Chi (bd. dirs. 1956-60). Presbyterian. Avocations: golf, gardening, sailing. Criminal, Federal civil litigation. Home: 24700 Pritchard Ln Franklin MI 48025-2204 Offfce: PO Box 250677 Franklin MI 48025-0677

**PRITCHARD, LLEWELYN G.,** lawyer; b. N.Y.C., Aug. 13, 1937; s. Llewelyn and Anne Mary (Streib) P.; m. Joan Ashby, June 20, 1959; children: David Ashby, Jennifer Pritchard Vick, Andrew Harrison, William Llewellyn. AB with honors, Drew U., 1958; LLB, Duke U., 1961. Ptnr. Helsell & Fetterman, Seattle. Trustee, corp. counsel Allied Arts Found.; pres. Allied Arts Seattle, 1974-76; trustee Meth. Ednl. Found., 1970—, pres., 1991-92; life trustee Patrons of Pacific N.W. Civil, Cultural and Charitable Orgns., 1969—, pres., 1972-73; bd. dirs. Planned Parenthood of Seattle/King County, 1972-78; trustee Seattle Symphony Orch., 1979-83, chmn. bd., 1980-82, hon. trustee; trustee U. Puget Sound., 1972-99, mem. exec. com., chmn. bd. visitors to Law Sch., 1984-88; chancellor Pacific N.W. Ann. conf. United Meth. Ch., 1969—. Fellow Am. Bar Found. (life, state chmn. 1988—); mem. ABA (bd. govs. 1986-89, chmn. program com. 1988-89, exec. com. 1988-89, Ho. of Dels. 1979—, nat. dir. young lawyers divsn. 1971, chmn. sect. of individual rights and responsibilities 1975-76, exec. coun. family law sect. 1992-98, chair standing com. on legal aid and indigent defendants 1973-75, chair legal needs study 1995-98, chair adv. com. to pro bono immigration project 1995—), Wash. State Bar Assn. (bd. govs. King County 1972-75), King County Bar Assn. (chair young lawyers sect. 1970). Avocations: reading, art collector. Family and matrimonial, General practice. Home: 5229 140th Ave NE Bellevue WA 98005-1024 Office: Helsell & Fetterman 1500 Puget Sound Plz Seattle WA 98101

**PRITCHARD, THOMAS ALEXANDER,** lawyer, paralegal educator; b. Coral Gables, Fla., May 5, 1949; s. John Alexander and Blodwyn Ellen (Lett) P.; m. Maureen M. Rider, Mar. 14, 1979. B.A. in History, U. Fla., 1971; J.D., U. Miss., 1974. Bar: Miss. 1974, U.S. Dist. Ct. (no. dist.) Miss. 1974, U.S. Dist. Ct. (so. dist.) Miss. 1976, U.S. Ct. Appeals (5th and 11th cirs.) 1981. Ptnr. Deen & Pritchard, Gulfport Miss., 1976-77, Joseph, Pritchard, Smith, Biloxi & Gulfport, 1981-83; assoc. C.E. Morris, Jr., Biloxi, 1977-81; sole practice, Biloxi, 1983—; instr. paralegal program Phillips Coll., Gulfport, 1980-82. Editor Jour. Space Law, U. Miss. Sch. Law, 1974. Dir. dependent youth activities Keesler AFB, Harrison County, Miss., 1979-82. Served to 1st lt. U.S. Army, 1975. Mem. Assn. Trial Lawyers Am., Miss. Trial Lawyers Assn. (bd. govs. 1990-92), Harrison County and Biloxi Bar Assn., Delta Theta Phi. Democrat. Lutheran. Personal injury, Workers' compensation, General civil litigation. Home: 3507 Courtney Cir Ocean Springs MS 39564-3401 Office: 175C Lameuse St Biloxi MS 39530-3803

**PRITCHETT, MICHAEL EUGENE COOK,** lawyer; b. Louisiana, Mo., Mar. 14, 1960; s. Lloyd Thornton and Wanda Maxine P.; m. Lila Sue Cook, July 30, 1983; children: Andrew Jacob, Courtney Elizabeth. BA in Econs. & Polit. Sci., U. Mo., 1982, MA in Econs., 1983, JD, 1986. Law clk. Supreme Ct. Mo., Jefferson City, 1986-88; assoc. Inglish, Monaco, Riner & Lockenvitz, Jefferson City, 1988-89; asst. atty. gen. Mo. Atty. Gen.s. Office, Jefferson City, 1989—. Gregory fellow U. Mo., 1982-83. Mem. Mo. Bar Assn. Office: Atty Gen's Office PO Box 899 Jefferson City MO 65102-0899

**PRITCHETT, RUSSELL WILLIAM,** lawyer, educator; b. Missoula, Mont., Feb. 16, 1951; s. Floyd Wiley and Mary Almeda (Brewer) P.; m. Meg Jesse Jacobson, June 23, 1974; 1 child, Arundel B. BA in History, U. Wash., 1974; JD, Northwestern Sch. of Law, 1977; LLM Maritime & Internat., U. London, 1979. Bar: Wash. 1978, Alaska 1979, U.S. Dist. Ct. Alaska 1979, U.S. Ct. Appeals (9th cir.) 1980, U.S. Dist. Ct. (we. dist.) Wash. 1984. In-house counsel Steamship Mut. Underwriting Assn., Ltd., London, 1978; assoc. Graham & James, Anchorage, 1978-81, Braun, Moriya, Hoashi & Kubota, Tokyo, 1981-83; pvt. practice Bellingham, Wash., 1983-95; ptnr. Pritchett & Jacobson, Bellingham, Wash., 1995-98; adj. prof. internat. trade Western Wash. U., Bellingham, 1986—. Contbr. articles to profl. jours. Pres. Bellingham Maritime Found., 1985. Mem. Maritime Law Assn. U.S. (com. on fisheries 1985—, proctor), Am. Immigration Lawyers Assn. Avocations: cross country skiing, hiking. Admiralty, Immigration, naturalization, and customs, Private international. Home and Office: 870 Democrat St Bellingham WA 98226-8829

**PRITIKIN, JAMES B.,** lawyer, employee benefits consultant; b. Chgo., Feb. 18, 1939; s. Stan and Anne (Schwartz) P.; m. Barbara Cheryl Demovsky, Apr. 20, 1968 (dec. 1988); children: Gregory, David, Randi; m. Mary Szatkowski, July 7, 1990; 1 child, Peyton. BS, U. Ill., 1961; JD, DePaul U., 1965. Bar: Ill. 1965, U.S. Dist. Ct. (no. dist.) Ill. 1965, U.S. Supreme Ct. 1985; cert. matrimonial arbitrator. Pvt. practice, Chgo., 1965-68, 1984—; ptnr. Sudak, Grubman, Pritikin, Rosenthal & Feldman, Chgo., 1969-80, Pritikin & Sohn, Chgo., 1980-84, Nadler, Pritikin & Mirabelli, Chgo., 1997—; pres. Prepaid Benefits Plans Inc., Chgo., 1978—; exec. dir. The Ctr. for Divorce Mediation Ltd. Fellow Internat. Acad. Matrimonial Lawyers, Am. Acad. Matrimonial Lawyers (pres.-elect); mem. ABA, Am. Acad. Matrimonial Lawyers (pres. Ill. chpt.), Ill. Bar Assn., Chgo. Bar Assn. (cir. ct. Cook County liaison com.), Chgo. Pub. Schs. Alumni Assn. (v.p. 1984—). Family and matrimonial. Office: 1 Prudential Plz 130 E Randolph Dr Chicago IL 60601-6207

**PRIVETERA, LORA MARIE,** lawyer; b. Toms River, N.J., July 6, 1967; d. Joseph Alfred and Gloria Estelle (Perez) P. BA, Georgian Ct. Coll., 1989; JD, Temple U., 1992. Bar: N.J. 1992, Pa. 1992. Visitation counsellor Ocean County Superior Ct., Toms River, N.J., 1992-93; lawyer Tanner & Tanner, Barnegat, N.J., 1993-95. Mem. ABA. Republican. Roman Catholic. General practice, Family and matrimonial, Estate planning. Office: 703 Mill Creek Rd Ste F-2 Manahawkin NJ 08050-3828

**PRIVETT, CARYL PENNEY,** lawyer; b. Birmingham, Ala., Jan. 7, 1948; d. William Kinnaird Privett and Katherine Speake (Binford) Ennis. BA, Vanderbilt U., 1970; JD, NYU, 1973. Bar: Ala. 1973, U.S. Dist. Ct. (so. dist.) Ala. 1973, U.S. Dist. Ct. (no. dist.) Ala. 1974, U.S. Ct. Appeals (5th cir.) 1974, U.S. Ct. Appeals (11th cir.) 1981. Assoc. Crawford & Blacksher, Mobile, Ala., 1973-74, Adams, Baker & Clemon, Birmingham, 1974-76; asst. U.S. atty. no. dist. Ala. U.S. Atty.'s Office, U.S. Dept. Justice, Birmingham, 1976-92, 93-94, first asst. U.S. atty., 1992-93, U.S. atty., 1995-97, chief asst., 1997-98; pvt. practice Mountain Brook, Ala., 1999—; city prosecutor City of Mountain Brook, 1999—. Bd. dirs. Legal Aid Soc., Birmingham, 1986-88, pres., 1988; sec., founder Lawyers for Choice, Ala., 1989-92; bd. dirs. Planned Parenthood Ala., Birmingham, 1998—, v.p., 1986-91; chair domestic violence com. City of Birmingham, 1989-91; sustaining mem. Jr. League Birmingham; active Downtown Dem. Club, Birmingham, Photography Guild, Birmingham Mus. Art. Recipient Cert. in Color Photography U. Ala., Birmingham, 1989, Commr.'s Spl. citation Food and Drug Adminstrn.; named one of Outstanding Young Women Am., 1977, 78. Mem. ABA, Fed. Bar Assn. (pres. Birmingham chpt. 1979), Birmingham Bar Assn. (mem. exec. com. 1996-98), Ala. Bar Assn. (chmn. com. women in the profession 1997-99, chair womne's sect. 1999—), Birmingham Bar Found., Ala. Acad. Atty. Mediators, Ala. Dispute Resolution Found., Summit Club, Altamont Alumni Assn. (bd. dirs.). Presbyterian. Avocation: photography. Home: 30 Norman Dr Birmingham AL 35213-4310 Office: 115 Office Park Dr Ste 320 Birmingham AL 35223-2426

**PRO, PHILIP MARTIN,** judge; b. Richmond, Calif., Dec. 12, 1946; s. Leo Martin and Mildred Louise (Beck) P.; m. Dori Sue Hallas, Nov. 13, 1982; 1 child, Brenda Kay. BA, San Francisco State U., 1968; JD Golden Gate U., 1972. Bar: Calif. 1972, Nev. 1973, U.S. Ct. Appeals (9th cir.) 1973, U.S. Dist. Ct. Nev. 1973, U.S. Supreme Ct. 1976. Pub. defender, Las Vegas, 1973-75; asst. U.S. atty., Dist. Nev., Las Vegas, 1975-78; ptnr. Semenza, Murphy & Pro, Reno, 1978-79; dep. atty. gen. State of Nev., Carson City, 1979-80; U.S. magistrate U.S. Dist. Ct. Nev., Las Vegas, 1980-87; U.S. dist. judge, 1987—; instr. Atty. Gen.'s Advocacy Inst., Nat. Inst. Trial Advocacy, 1992; chmn. com. adminstrn. of magistrate judge system Jud. Conf. U.S., 1993—. Bd. dirs. NCCJ, Las Vegas, 1982—, mem. program com. and issues in justice com. Mem. ABA, Fed. Judges Assn. (bd. dirs. 1992—), Nev. State Bar Assn., Calif. State Bar Assn., Nev. Judges Assn. (instr.), Assn. Trial Lawyers Am., Nev. Am. Inn Ct. (pres. 1989—), Ninth Cir. Jury (instructions com.), Nat. Conf. U.S. Magistrates (sec.), Nev. Am. Inn of Ct. (pres. 1989-91). Republican. Episcopalian. Office: US Dist Ct 341 Fed Bldg 300 Las Vegas Blvd S Ste 4650 Las Vegas NV 89101-5883

**PROBUS, MICHAEL MAURICE, JR.,** lawyer; b. Louisville, Jan. 26, 1963; s. Michael Maurice and Jerilyn Ann (Burks) P.; m. Luz Marie Probus, May 22, 1985; children: Michael Julian, Lauren Michael. BA, U. Dallas, 1985; JD, U. Tex., 1988. Bar: Tex. 1988, U.S. Dist. Ct. (we. dist.) Tex. 1990, U.S. Ct. Appeals (5th cir.) 1993. Jud. law clk. to chief judge U.S. Dist. Ct. Tex., Houston, 1988-90; assoc. Law Offices of Michael A. Wash, Austin, Tex., 1990-97; pvt. practice, Austin, 1997—. Pro bono atty. Vol. Legal Svcs., Austin, 1994—. Mem. Travis County Bar Assn. (mem. CLE com. 1993—). Democrat. Roman Catholic. Personal injury, Product liability, Professional liability. Office: 1000 First State Bank Tower 400 W 15th St Austin TX 78701-1600

**PROCHNOW, HERBERT VICTOR, JR.,** lawyer; b. Evanston, Ill., May 26, 1931; s. Herbert V. and Laura (Stinson) P.; m. Lucia Boyden, Aug. 6, 1966; children: Thomas Herbert, Laura. A.B., Harvard U., 1953, J.D., 1956; A.M., U. Chgo., 1958. Bar: Ill. 1957, U.S. Dist. Ct. (no. dist.) Ill. 1961. With 1st Nat. Bank Chgo., 1958-91, atty., 1961-70, sr. atty., 1971-73, counsel, 1973-91, adminstrv. asst. to chmn. bd., 1978-81; pvt. practice, 1991—. Author: (with Herbert V. Prochnow) A Treasury of Humorous Quotations, 1969, The Changing World of Banking, 1974, The Public Speaker's Treasure Chest, 1986, The Toastmaster's Treasure Chest, 1988; also articles in legal publs. Mem. ABA, Ill. Bar Assn., Chgo. Bar Assn. (chmn. com. internat. law 1970-71), Am. Soc. Internat. Law, Phi Beta Kappa. Clubs: Harvard (N.Y.C.); Chicago (Chgo.), Legal (Chgo.), Law (Chgo.), Onwentsia, Economic (Chgo.), University (Chgo.). Banking, Private international. Home: 949 Woodbine Pl Lake Forest IL 60045-2275 Office: 155 N Michigan Ave Chicago IL 60601-7511

**PROCHNOW, THOMAS HERBERT,** lawyer; b. Chgo., May 29, 1967; s. Herbert Victor Jr. and Lucia (Boyden) P. AB, Harvard U., 1989; JD, Yale U., 1993; student, U. London, 1989, U. Paris Sorbonne, 1990. Bar: N.Y. 1994, U.S. Dist. Ct. (so. and ea. dists.) N.Y. 1994, U.S. Dist. Ct. (no. dist.) N.Y. 1995, U.S. Ct. Appeals (fed. cir.) 1998. Assoc. Debevoise & Plimpton, N.Y.C., 1993—. Contbr. chpt. to book, articles to profl. jours. Vol. atty., asylum program Lawyers Com. for Human Rights, N.Y.C., 1994-98; fundraiser, assocs. campaign Legal Aid Soc., N.Y.C., 1997-98. Recipient award of Excellence, Vol. Lawyers for the Arts, 1996. Mem. ABA (intellectual property sect.), Assn. Bar City N.Y. Intellectual property, Computer. Office: Debevoise & Plimpton 875 3d Ave New York NY 10022

**PROCOPIO, JOSEPH GUYDON,** lawyer; b. Paterson, N.J., May 1, 1940; s. Joseph A. and V. Genevieve (Kievitt) P.; m. Joanne Julia Roccato, June 30, 1962 (div. Aug. 1980); children: Jennifer Tehani Tyler, Joseph Christian; m. Frances Mary Hansen Schmieder, Apr. 16, 1988 (div. Oct. 1998); stepchildren: Timothy James Schmieder, Julie Ann Schmieder. BS, U.S. Naval Acad., 1962; MS in Ops. Rsch., Naval Postgrad. Sch., 1971; JD, Cath. U. Am., 1979; LLM, George Washington U., 1987. Bar: Va. Commd. ensign USN, 1962, served to comdr., 1978, ret., 1983; gen. counsel, sec. Presearch, Inc., Fairfax, Va., 1983-85; dir. bus. devel., then v.p. corp. communications ERC Internat., Fairfax, Va., 1985-90; pres., CEO Advanced Engring. Group, Inc., Fairfax, 1990-92; chmn., CEO JP Fin. Group Ltd., Fairfax, 1992—; prin. The Poretz Group, 1996-98; bd. dirs. Solomon Group; prin. The Millenium Group, Ltd. (formerly Ashley-Boden-Keenan, Inc.); v.p. Valuation Techs., LLC. Decorated Bronze Star, Meritorious Svc. medal, 3 Joint Svc. Commendation medal, Nat. Def. medal (Cambodia), Navy Achievement medal, Combat Action ribbon. Mem. Internat. Inst. Strategic Studies, Va. Bar Assn., The Atlantic Coun., World Affairs Coun. Washington, George Washington U. Law Alumni Assn., U.S. Naval Acad. Alumni Assn., U.S. Naval Acad. Class of 1962 Assn. (bd. dirs. 1978-80, 87—, spl. asst. to pres. 1984-87), Nat. Eagle Scout Assn., The Met. Club. Avocations: reading, history (legal, military, naval, economic). Finance, Private international, General corporate. Home: 237 Cherry St Castle Rock CO 80104-3206

**PROCTOR, DAVID RAY,** lawyer; b. Nashville, Apr. 18, 1956; s. Raymond Douglas and Margaret Florence (Coffey) P.; m. Robbin Lynn Fuqua, May 12, 1984 (div.); children: Rachael Lynne, Benjamin David. AA in Polit. Sci., Cumberland Jr. Coll., 1976; BA in Polit. Sci., Vanderbilt U., 1978; JD, Cumberland Sch. Law, 1981; LLM in Taxation, U. Fla., 1983. Bar: Ala. 1981, Tenn. 1983, U.S. Tax Ct. 1983. Law clk. to presiding justice Ala. Supreme Ct., Montgomery, 1981-82; assoc. Thrailkill & Goodman, Nashville, 1983-84; v.p. taxes Alfa Mut. Ins. Co., Montgomery, 1984—. Contbg. editor Cumberland Law Rev., 1980-81; contbr. articles to profl. jours. Tchr. Rsch. Bd., Birmingham, Ala., 1980; active Montgomery Area United Way, 1985—; mem. stewardship com. Montgomery Bapt. Assn., 1995-96; treas. Taylor Rd. Bapt. Ch., 1994-95, asst. treas., 1996, treas., 1997-98. Mem. ABA, Nat. Assn. Mut. Ins. Cos. (tax com. 1988—, chmn. 1997—), Ala. Bar Assn., Tenn. Bar Assn., Sunrise Exch. Club Montgomery (treas. 1989-91), Phi Alpha Delta, Pi Sigma Alpha. Baptist. Avocations: running, music, sports, charities. Corporate taxation, Personal income taxation, State and local taxation. Home: 317 Arrowhead Dr Montgomery AL 36117-4142 Office: Alfa Mut Ins Co 2108 E South Blvd Montgomery AL 36116-2015

**PROCTOR, EDWARD GEORGE,** lawyer; b. Chgo., July 16, 1929; s. Harold Proctor and Catherine Elliott; m. Kathleen Friend, Apr. 4, 1959; children: Brian, Diana, Edward, Laurel, Abigail, John. BS, Loyola U., Chgo., 1951; JD, Loyola U., 1953. Bar: Ill. 1953. From assoc. to ptnr. Kirkland & Ellis, Chgo., 1953-78; ptnr. Reuben & Proctor, Chgo., 1978-87, Isham, Lincoln, Beale (merger with Reuben & Proctor), Chgo., 1987-88, Hinshaw & Culbertson, Chgo., 1988—; adj. prof. Loyola U. Sch. of Law; past trustee Loyola U.; chmn. bus. dept. Hinshaw & Culbertson. Co-chmn. Com. to Elect Mary Ann McMorrow to Ill. Supreme Ct., 1991-92; mem. Legal Assistance Found. Friends Com. Chgo.; former tchr. CCD classes St. Barnabas Ch., Chgo.; former fundraiser Mt. Carmel H.S., Morgan Park Acad., St. Ignatius Coll. Prep. Recipient Medal of Excellence Loyola U. Sch. Law, 1989, plaque of Appreciation Cath. Charities, 2 plaques of Appreciation Loyola Alumni Assn. Fellow ABA (life); mem. Ill. Bar Assn., Chgo. Bar Assn. (comml. fin. and transactions coms.), Bankruptcy Inst., Loyola Law Alumni Assn. (past pres.), Olympia Fields Country Club (past pres.), Lambda Alpha Internat. Roman Catholic. Avocation: golf. Real property, General corporate, Contracts commercial. Office: Hinshaw & Culbertson 222 N La Salle St Ste 300 Chicago IL 60601-1081

**PROM, STEPHEN GEORGE,** lawyer; b. Jacksonville, Fla., July 8, 1954; s. George W. and Bonnie M. (Porter) P.; divorced; children: Ashley Brooke, Aaron Jacob, Adam Glenn; m. Charlotte Rutter. AA in Polit. Sci. with high honors, Fla. Jr. Coll., 1974; BA in Polit. Sci. with high honors, U. Fla., 1977, JD with honors, 1979. Bar: Fla. 1980, U.S. Dist. Ct. (mid. dist.) Fla. 1980, U.S. Dist. Ct. (no. dist.) Fla. 1981, U.S. Tax Ct. 1982, U.S. Ct. Appeals (11th cir.) 1985, U.S. Supreme Ct. 1985. Assoc. Rogers, Towers, Bailey, Jones & Gay, Jacksonville, 1979-83, Foley & Lardner, Jacksonville, 1983-86; ptnr. Christian & Prom, Jacksonville, 1986-87, Prom, Korn & Zehmer, P.A., Jacksonville, 1987-95, Brant, Moore, MacDonald & Wells, P.A., 1995—. Sr. mgmt. editor U. Fla. Law Rev., 1978-79. Mem. Leadership Jacksonville, 1984, Jacksonville Cmty. Coun. Inc., 1985-86; bd. dirs. Mental Health Resource Ctr., Jacksonville, 1984-87, Mental Health Resource Foun., Jacksonville, 1985-87, Mental Health Found., Inc., 1987-89, mem. cmty. bd., 1989-91; bd. dirs. Youth Crisis Ctr., Jacksonville, 1984-86, Young Profls. Bd. Multiple Sclerosis Soc., 1988-89; bd. dirs. The Team, Inc., 1992-94; vol. Jacksonville, Inc., 1993-96, Jacksonville Found., Inc., 1993-96, Positively Jacksonville!, Inc., 1993-95. Mem. ABA (tax, health law sects.), Fla. Bar Assn. (tax, health law bd., bd. govs. young lawyers sect. 1983-87), Jacksonville Bar Assn. (chmn. health law sect.), Am. Acad. Healthcare Attys., Am. Hosp. Assn., Nat. Health Lawyers Assn., Fla. Acad. Healthcare Attys. (bd. dirs. 1994-97), Jacksonville Sailing Found., Inc. (bd. dirs. 1997—), N.E. Fla. Sailboat Rating Assn., Inc. (bd. dirs. 1997-98, chair 1998), Epping Forest Yacht Club (bd. govs., rear commodore sail), Ponte Vedra Club, North Fla. Cruising Club, Phi Beta Kappa, Phi Theta Kappa, Phi Kappa Phi. Republican. Baptist. Avocations: sailing, surfing, weightlifting, tennis, jogging. Health, Contracts commercial. Office: Brant Moore MacDonald & Wells PA 50 N Laura St Jacksonville FL 32202-3664

**PROMISLO, DANIEL,** lawyer; b. Bryn Mawr, Pa., Nov. 15, 1932; s. Charles and Pearl (Backman) P.; m. Estelle Carasso, June 10, 1961; children: Mark, Jacqueline, Steven. BSBA, Drexel U., 1955; JD magna cum laude, U. Pa., 1966. Bar: Pa. 1966. Pres., owner Hist. Souvenir Co., Phila., 1957—; assoc. Wolf, Block, Schorr & Solis-Cohen, Phila., 1966-70, ptnr., 1977-94, exec. com., 1987-89, of counsel, 1994—, mng. dir., 1997—; founder, pres. dir. Inst. for Paralegal Tng., Phila., 1970-75, cons., 1975-77. Editor: Corporate Law, 1970, Real Estate Law, 1971, Estates and Trusts, 1971, Civil Litigation, 1972, Employee Benefit Plans, 1973, Criminal Law, 1974; contbr. articles in field to profl. jours. bd. dirs. Phila. Drama Guild, 1977-95, chmn., 1982-86; bd. dirs. Phila. Israel Econ. Devel. Program, 1983-88, Inst. for Arts in Edn., 1990-93, WHYY, Inc., 1994—, vice-chmn., 1995-96, chmn., 1996-97; bd. dirs. U.S. Physicians, Inc., 1995—; trustee Resource Asset Investment Trust, 1997—. Mem. Order of Coif, Drexel U. 100, Blue Key, Phi Kappa Phi. Democrat. Jewish. Avocations: movies, basketball, tennis. General corporate, Mergers and acquisitions, Securities. Office: Wolf Block Schorr & Solis-Cohen 1650 Arch St Fl 21 Philadelphia PA 19103-2097

**PROPST, ROBERT BRUCE,** federal judge; b. Onatchee, Ala., July 13, 1931; s. Franklin Glenn and Mildred (Moore) P.; m. Elma Jo Griffin, Dec. 29, 1962; children: Stephen, David, Joanne. B.S., U. Ala., 1953, J.D., 1957. Pvt. practice law Wilson, Propst, Isom, Jackson, Bailey & Bott, 1957-80; Judge U.S. Dist Ct. (no. dist.) Ala., Birmingham, 1980-96; sr. judge U.S. Dist Ct. (no. dist.) Ala., Anniston, 1996—. Served to 1st lt. U.S. Army, 1953-55. Mem. ABA, Ala. Bar Assn., Birmingham Bar Assn., Calhoun County Bar Assn., Jaycees (pres. 1954-60). Methodist. Club: Exchange (Anniston, Ala.). Avocation: golf. Home: 500 Webster Rd Lot 102 Auburn AL 36832-4214 Office: US Dist Ct 581 US Courthouse 1729 5th Ave N Birmingham AL 35203-2000

**PROSSER, DAVID THOMAS, JR.,** state supreme court justice, former state representative; b. Chgo., Dec. 24, 1942; s. David Thomas Sr. and Elizabeth Averell (Patterson) P. BA, DePauw U., 1965; JD, U. Wis., 1968. Bar: Wis. 1968,. Lectr. Ind. U., Indpls., 1968-69; advisor U.S. Dept. Justice, Washington, 1969-72; adminstrv. asst. to U.S. Rep. Harold V. Froehlich, Washington, 1973-74; pvt. practice Washington, 1975, Appleton, Wis., 1976; dist. atty. Outagamie County, Appleton, 1977-78; state rep. State of Wis., Madison, 1979-96; commr. Tax Appeals Commn., 1996-98; justice Supreme Ct. Wis., 1998—; commr. Nat. Conf. Commrs. on Uniform State Laws, Madison, 1982-96; mem. Wis. Sesquecentennial Commn., Madison, 1993; minority leader Wis. Assembly. Chmn. Rep. Assembly Campaign com., Madison, 1989—. Mem. Wis. Bar Assn., Outagamie Bar Assn., Fox Cities C. of C. Presbyterian. Avocation: art collector of American prints. Home: 2904 N Meade St Appleton WI 54911-1561 Office: Supreme Ct Wis PO Box 1688 Madison WI 53701*

**PROTHRO, JERRY ROBERT,** lawyer; b. Midland, Tex., Dec. 22, 1946; s. Jack William Prothro and Nita Marie (Stovall) Milligan; m. Leslie Joan Lepar, Aug. 15, 1970 (div. 1994); children: Laura Kay, Evan Jackson. BA, Southwestern U., 1969; JD, U. Tex. Sch. Law, 1972. Lawyer, capt. U.S. Army, JAGC, 1972-76; ptnr. Turpin, Smith & Dyer, Midland, 1975-85, Boyd, Sanders, Wade, Cropper & Prothro, Midland, 1985-91; pvt. practice Dallas and Midland, Tex., 1991—; mem. admissions com. M/O div. U.S. Dist. Ct. for Western Dist. Tex., 1987—; speaker in field. *Jerry Prothro has extensive experience in banking and contract litigation, family law, probate and real estate matters. He is currently engaged in the practice of commercial and civil litigation in Dallas and North Texas, and frequently volunteers to represent clients through the Dallas Legal Hospice and various Gay and AIDS related non-profit groups. He is interested in representing Client's in the field of gay rights, relationship issues, discrimination and equal protection.* Treas., v.p. Southwestern U. Alumni Bd., Georgetown, Tex., 1980-90, pres.-elect, 1991, pres., 1992-94; trustee, Southwestern U., 1992-94; adminstrv. bd. First United Meth. Ch., Midland, 1989-96; vice chmn. Permian Basin AIDS Coalition Bd., 1994; active Midland County Hist. Commn., 1980-85. Named Univ. scholar Southwestern U., 1969; recipient Disting. Svc. medal U.S. Army, 1974. Mem. Midland County Young Lawyers (pres. 1979-80), Midland County Bar Assn., 5th Cir. Bar Assn., Pi Kappa Alpha Social Frat., Blue Key Leadership Frat., Pi Gamma Mu Social Sci. Frat. Methodist. Avocations: antique collecting, camping, men's movement activity. E-mail: prothro@msn.com. Office: 6003 Maple Ave Ste 109 Dallas TX 75235-6520

**PROTIGAL, STANLEY NATHAN,** lawyer; b. Wilmington, Del., June 3, 1950; s. Bernard Protigal. BS in Aircraft Maintenance Engring., Northrop U., 1973; JD, Vt. Law Sch., 1978. Bar: U.S. Patent Office 1977, D.C. 1978. Assoc. Sixbey F. & L., Arlington, Va., 1978-79, atty., 1979-82; patent atty. Allied-Signal Bendix Aerospace, Teterboro, N.J., 1982-88; patent counsel Micron Tech., Inc., Boise, Idaho, 1988-94; pvt. practice, Boise, Idaho, 1994-96, Seattle, 1996-98; assoc. Sabath and Truong, San Jose, Calif., 1998—. Mem. IEEE, Mensa. Avocations: pvt. pilot, bicycling, skiing. Patent, Legislative, Government contracts and claims.

**PROVENGHI, RUGGERO,** lawyer; b. Honolulu, Hawaii, Apr. 30, 1955; s. Bruno Calitti and Agustina (Salinas) P.; m. Tracy Lynn Savage, Sept. 2, 1995;1 child, Nicholas Bruno; children by previous marriage: Dominique, Alexandria. BA in Polit. Sci., U. Tex., El Paso, 1978; JD, Tex. Tech. U., 1980. Cert. in personal injury trial law, Tex. Bd. of Legal Specialization. Assoc. Leeton & Leeton, Midland, Tex., 1981-83; atty. pvt. practice, Midland, 1983-95, El Paso, Tex., 1995—; atty. Lone Star Abstract & Title, Midland, Tex., 1984-92. Assoc. judge Mcpl. Ct., Midland, 1990-93. With U.S. Navy, 1972-74. Mem. ATLA, Tex. Trial Lawyers Assn., El Paso Bar Assn. (com. mem. 1996—), State Bar of Tex. Avocations: family activities, jogging, racquetball, golf, tennis. Personal injury, General civil litigation, Real property. Office: 1420 Geronimo Dr Ste B120 El Paso TX 79925-1899

**PROVENZANO, RONALD CASPER,** lawyer; b. Chgo., Feb. 25, 1966; s. Casper Patrick and Muriel (Spialek) P. BS in Acctg., U. Ill., 1988, JD, 1991. Bar: Ill. 1991, U.S. Dsit. Ct. (no. dist.) Ill. 1992. Law clk. Hon. Anthony A. Alaimo U.S. Dist. Ct., Brunswick, Ga., 1991-92; assoc. Kirkland & Ellis, Chgo., 1992-97, ptnr., 1997-98; v.p., assoc. gen. coun. True North Comms. Inc., 1999—. Mem. Chgo. Bar Assn., U. Ill. Alumni Assn. (adv. bd.). Fax: 312-425-6337. E-mail: rprovenzano@truenorth.com. Trademark and copyright. Home: 2642 N Seminary Ave # 3 Chicago IL 60614-1344 Office: True North Comms Inc 101 E Erie St Chicago IL 60611-2812

**PROVINE, JOHN C.,** lawyer; b. Asheville, N.C., May 15, 1938; s. Robert Calhoun and Harriet Josephine (Thoms) P.; m. Martha Ann Monson, Aug. 26, 1966 (div. Jan. 1975); m. Nancy Frances Lunsford, Apr. 17, 1976 (div. Mar. 1996); children: Robert, Frances, Harriet. AB, Harvard U., 1960; JD, U. Mich., 1966; MBA, NYU, 1972, LLM in Taxation, 1975. Bar: N.Y., Tenn., U.S. Dist. Ct. (so. and ea. dists.) N.Y., U.S. Ct. Appeals (2nd and 6th cirs.), U.S. Dist. Ct. (mid. dist.) Tenn., U.S. Supreme Ct. From assoc. to ptnr. White & Case, N.Y.C., 1966-74, ptnr., 1974-81, 92-94; ptnr. White & Case, Jakarta and Ankara, 1982-91; counsel Dearborn & Ewing, Nashville, Tenn., 1982. Lt. USN, 1960-63. Mem. ABA, N.Y. Bar Assn., Tenn. Bar Assn., Assn. of Bar of City of N.Y. Avocations: bluegrass music, rural activities. Private international, General corporate, Contracts commercial. Home and Office: 6630 Manley Ln Brentwood TN 37027-3401

**PROVINZINO, JOHN C.,** lawyer; b. Long Prairie, Minn., Apr. 30, 1947; s. John T. and Jean M. Provinzino; m. Jannine M. Provinzino, Dec. 29, 1970;

children: Alan, Laura, Anne. BA, St. John's U., 1969; JD, U. Minn., 1972. Bar: Minn. 1972, U.S. Dist. Ct. Minn. 1972. Ptnr. Murphy, Neils & Provinzino, St. Cloud, Minn., 1972-76, Reichert, Wenner, Koch & Provinzino, St. Cloud, 1976—. Mem. St. Cloud Newman Ctr., 1992-94, Epilepsy Found., 1975-80. Capt. Army N.G., 1969-77. Mem. Minn. Bar Assn., Stearns-Benton County Bar Assn., St. Cloud C. of C., Kiwanis. Avocations: racquetball, golf. Fax: 320-252-2678. State civil litigation, Pension, profit-sharing, and employee benefits, Criminal. Office: Reichert Wenner Koch & Provinzino 501 W Saint Germain St Saint Cloud MN 56301-3605

**PROVIS, TIMOTHY ALAN,** lawyer; b. Chgo., July 13, 1948; s. William Harold Sr. and Dorothy Louise P. BA, U. Wis., 1974; JD, Santa Clara U., 1981. Bar: Calif. 1982, U.S. Dist. Ct. (no. dist.) Calif. 1982, U.S. Ct. Appeals (9th cir.) 1983, U.S. Supreme Ct. 1987, U.S. Ct. Appeals (7th cir.) 1992, Wis. 1992, U.S. Dist. Ct. (we. dist.) Wis. 1995, U.S. Dist. Ct. (ea. dist.) Wis. 1996. Atty. pvt. practice, Madison, Wis., 1982—. Sgt. USAF, 1968-71. Appellate, Criminal, Civil rights. Office: 1920 Birge Ter Apt 1 Madison WI 53705-2372

**PROVORNY, FREDERICK ALAN,** lawyer, educator; b. Bklyn., Sept. 7, 1946; s. Daniel and Anna (Wurm) P.; m. Nancy Ileene Wilkins, Nov. 21, 1971; children: Michelle C., Cheryl A., Lisa T., Robert D. BS summa cum laude, NYU, 1966; JD magna cum laude, Columbia U., 1969. Bar: N.Y. 1970, U.S. Supreme Ct. 1973, D.C. 1975, Mo. 1977, Md. 1987, Calif. 1989; CPA, Md., Mo. Law clk. to Judge Harold R. Medina U.S. Ct. Appeals (2d cir.), N.Y.C., 1969-70; asst. prof. law Syracuse (N.Y.) U., 1970-72; assoc. Debevoise, Plimpton, Lyons & Gates, N.Y.C., 1972-75, Cole & Groner P.C., Washington, 1975-76; with Monsanto Co., St. Louis, 1976-86, asst. co. counsel, 1978-86; pvt. practice Washington, 1986-89; ptnr. Provorny & Jacoby, Washington, 1989-91; counsel Shaw, Pittman, Potts & Trowbridge, Washington, 1991-93; ptnr. Tydings & Rosenberg, Balt., 1993-94; pvt. practice Balt., 1994-95, Washington, 1995-98; Harold R. Tyler prof. of sci. and tech., law and director Sci. and Tech. Law Ctr., Albany (N.Y.) Law Sch., 1998—; lect. Bklyn Law Sch., 1973-74; adj. prof. U. Balt. Sch. of Law, 1996-98; pres. Sci. and Tech. Assocs., Inc., 1986-91. Contbr. articles to profl. jours. Trustee Christian Woman's Benevolent Assn. Youth Home, 1979-83. Mem. ABA, Am. Law Inst., Am. Arbitration Assn. (panel comml. abitrators), Philo-Mt. Sinai Lodge 968, Masons, Beta Gamma Sigma. Jewish. General corporate, Administrative and regulatory, Environmental. Home: 11803 Kemp Mill Rd Silver Spring MD 20902-1511 Office: Albany Law School 80 New Scotland Ave Albany NY 12208-3434

**PROVOST, JAMES H(ARRISON),** law educator; b. Washington, Oct. 15, 1939; s. Oscar A. and Mary (Howe) P. BA, Carroll Coll., 1959; STB, U. Louvain (Belgium), 1963, MA, 1963; JCD, Lateran U., Rome, 1967. Chancellor Diocese of Helena, Mont. Roman Cath. Ch. and officialis (presiding judge of Diocesan Tribunal), Helena, 1967-79; prof. canon law Cath. U. Am., 1979—, also chmn. dept. Canon law, 1987-98; exec. coord. Canon Law Soc. Am., Washington, 1980-86. Mng. editor The Jurist, 1980—. Mem. Cath. Theol. Soc. Am., Canon Law Soc. Am., Can. Canon Law Soc., Canon Law Soc. Gt. Brit. and Ireland, Canon Law Soc. Australia & New Zealand, Societe Internationale de droit religieuses et comparees, Consociatio Internationalis. Office: Cath U Am Dept Of Canon Law Washington DC 20064-0001

**PROZAN, MICHAEL WILLIAM,** lawyer; b. Albuquerque, Dec. 9, 1959; s. George Bernard and Sylvia Jean (Simmons) P. AB, Columbia U., 1982; JD with honors, U. San Francisco, 1986; LLM, Georgetown U., 1990. Bar: Calif. 1986, D.C. 1988, U.S. Dist. Ct. (no. dist.) Calif. 1986, U.S. Ct. Appeals (9th cir.) 1986. Atty. U.S. SEC, Washington, 1987-91; spl. asst. U.S. Atty., 1988-89; assoc. Schwabe, Williamson & Wyatt, Portland, Oreg., 1991—. Contbr. articles to profl. jours. Mem. ABA, Calif. Bar Assn., D.C. Bar Assn., Fed. Bar Assn. Avocations: skiing, hiking, cooking, reading.

**PRUELLAGE, JOHN KENNETH,** lawyer; b. St. Louis, Feb. 4, 1941; s. John H. P. and Bertha Kunkel; m. Patricia Marré, Dec. 30, 1966 (div. Apr. 1993); children: Jill Shannon Pruellage Hunt, John Kenneth, Jr., William Marré; m. Vicky L. Fehl, Aug. 29, 1993. BS, St. Louis U., 1962; JD, U. Mo., 1965; LLM, George Washington U., 1968. Tax staff Coopers & Lybrand, St. Louis, 1965-66; ptnr., chmn. Lewis, Rice & Fingersh, LLC, St. Louis, 1970—; bd. dirs. Unity Health Sys., St. Louis. Bd. dir. St. Anthony's Med. Ctr., St. Louis, 1996—; trustee St. Louis U., 1998—. Capt. USAF, 1966-70. Mem. ABA, Mo. Bar Assn., St. Louis Bar Assn., Noonday Club (v.p., bd. dirs. 1996—), Old Warson Country Club (v.p., bd. dirs. 1997—). Office: Lewis Rice Fingersh LLC 500 N Broadway Ste 2000 Saint Louis MO 63102-2147

**PRUESSNER, DAVID MORGAN,** lawyer; b. Corpus Christi, Tex., May 13, 1955; s. Harold Trebus and Alma (Morgan) P.; m. Becky McKinney, May 21, 1977; children: Jennifer, Daniel, Heather. BA cum laude, Baylor U., 1977, JD cum laude, 1980. Bar: Tex. 1980, U.S. Dist. Ct. (no. dist.) Tex. 1980, U.S. Ct. Appeals (5th cir.) 1986, U.S. Supreme Ct. 1989. Atty. Coke & Coke, Dallas, 1980-83, Shank, Irwin & Conant, Dallas, 1983-90, Pettit & Martin, Dallas, 1990-92, Fletcher & Springer, Dallas, 1992-98, Pruessner & Shilling, Dallas, 1999—; instr. legal assts. program So. Meth. U., Dallas, 1989-91. Assoc. editor Baylor Law Rev., 1980. Avocations: world religions, history, chess. Fax: (214) 378-7401. E-mail: david@pruessner-shilling.com. Appellate, Insurance, General civil litigation. Office: Pruessner & Shilling 10300 N Central Expy Ste 285 Dallas TX 75231-4363

**PRUGH, WILLIAM BYRON,** lawyer; b. Kansas City, Mo., Jan. 3, 1945; s. Byron E. and Helen Prugh; m. Linda Stuart, Aug. 12, 1968; 1 child, K. Niccole. BA, U. Mo., Kansas City, 1966, JD, 1969, LLM in Taxation, 1971. Bar: Mo. 1969, U.S. Tax Ct. 1975, U.S. Supreme Ct. 1975, Kans. 1982. Assoc. Shughart Thomson & Kilroy, P.C., Kansas City, 1969—. Author, editor: Missouri Corporation Law and Practice, 1985, Missouri Taxation Law and Practice, 1987, 3d edit., 1996. Mem. ABA, Mo. Bar (chmn. taxation com. 1988-90, chmn. computer tech. com. 1989-91), Kansas City Met. Bar Assn. (chmn. tax com. 1989-90, chmn. computer law com. 1989-91, Pres. award 1988). Republican. Methodist. Taxation, general, State and local taxation, Estate planning. Office: Shughart Thomson & Kilroy 12 Wyandotte Plz 120 W 12th St Fl 18 Kansas City MO 64105-1902

**PRUITT, ROBERT RANDALL,** lawyer; b. Rockledge, Fla., May 27, 1965; s. Clarence Robert and Susan Pruitt; m. Lisl S. Pruitt, Aug. 18, 1990. BBA in Mgmt. and Mktg., Baylor U., 1987; JD, South Tex. Coll. of Law, 1990. Bar: Tex. 1990. Restaurant mgr. Pappas Restaurants, Inc., Houston, 1987-89; atty. Giessel, Stone, Barker & Lyman P.C., Houston, 1990-92; shareholder Chalker, Bair, P.C., Houston, 1992-98; assoc. gen. counsel Gulf States Toyota, Inc., 1998—. Mem. ABA, ACCA, Houston Bar Assn., Tex. Young Lawyers Assn., Houston Young Lawyers Assn., Tex. Assn. of Responsible Nonsubscribers (treas. 1996—). Avocations: golf, snow skiing. General corporate, Contracts commercial, General civil litigation. Office: Gulf States Toyota Inc 7701 Wilshire Place Dr Houston TX 77040-5399

**PRUNA, LAURA MARIA,** lawyer; b. La Habana, Cuba, Apr. 23, 1954; came to U.S., 1961; d. Max and Martha Luz P. BBA, U. Miami, 1976; JD, Fla. State U., 1988. Bar: Fla. 1989, U.S. Ct. Appeals (11th cir.), U.S. Ct. Mil. Appeals, Ill. 1989. Law clk. Dept. Profl. Regulation, State of Fla., Tallahassee, 1987-88; atty. Carl Di Bernardo, P.A., South Miami, Fla., 1989-90, Pruna & Milian, Miami, Fla., 1991-93, Pruna Law Offices, Miami, 1993—. Atty., Fundacion Centro Americana, Miami, 1997-98. Mem. Colombian Am. Bar (bd. dirs. 1997-98), Cath. Lawyers Guild (pres. 1989-92). Republican. Avocations: fishing, reading. Immigration, naturalization, and customs, Family and matrimonial, Private international. Office: Pruna Law Offices 2525 SW 3d Ave Ste 205 Miami FL 33129-2057

**PRUSAK, MAXIMILIAN MICHAEL,** lawyer; b. Granite City, Ill., Mar. 22, 1943; s. Max Emil and Catherine Theresa (Jakich) P.; m. Carolyn Irene Pinkel, July 2, 1966; children: Scott Michael, Stephanie K. BS in Math., U. Ill., 1965, JD, 1968. Bar: Ill. 1968, U.S. Dist. Ct. (so. dist.) Ill. 1973. Staff atty. Atty.'s Title Guaranty Fund, Champaign, Ill., 1968-69; ptnr. Goldsworthy, Fifield & Prusak, Peoria, Ill., 1973-80, Nicol, Newell, Prusak & Winne, Peoria, 1980-83, Prusak & Winne, Peoria, Ill., 1983-88, Prusak, Winne & Wombacher, Peoria, 1988-93, Prusak & Winne, Ltd., Peoria, 1993—. Contbr. articles to profl. publs. Bd. dirs. Human Svc. Ctr., Peoria, 1970's, Friendship House, Peoria, 1980, Southside Mission, Peoria, 1988-89; pres. adminstrv. bd. 1st United Meth. Ch., Peoria, 1990—. Capt. USAF, 1969-73. Mem. Ill. State Bar Assn., Peoria County Bar Assn. (bd. dirs. 1982, 94, 98, 99), Union League Club Chgo., Ill. Valley Yacht Club. Avocations: computers, sailing, reading. Personal injury, General civil litigation, Insurance. Home: 5821 N Mar Vista Dr Peoria IL 61614-3850 Office: Prusak & Winne Ltd 704 Jefferson Bldg 331 Fulton St Peoria IL 61602-1499

**PRUZANSKY, JOSHUA MURDOCK,** lawyer; b. N.Y.C., Mar. 16, 1940; s. Louis and Rose (Murdock) P.; m. Susan R. Bernstein, Aug. 31, 1980; 1 child, Dina Gabrielle. BA, Columbia Coll., 1960, JD, 1965. Bar: N.Y., 1965, U.S. Dist. Ct. (ea. and so. dists.) N.Y., 1968, U.S. Supreme Ct., 1980. Ptnr. Scheinberg, DePetris & Pruzansky, Riverhead, N.Y., 1965-85, Greshin, Ziegler & Pruzansky, Smithtown, 1985—; mem. exec. coun. N.Y. State Conf. Bar Leaders, 1984—, chmn., 1988-89; mem. grievance com. Appellate Divsn. 10th Judicial Dist., 1992-96; mem. adv. bd. Ticor Title Guarantee Co., 1992—; mem. L.I. adv. bd. HSBC Bank, 1995—; dir. N.Y. State Com. for Modern Cts., 1998—; mem. adv. task force N.Y. Dept. State corps., 1998—. Trustee Evan Frankel Found., 1993—; mem. bd. visitors Columbia Law Sch., 1989—; chair bd. visitors Touro Law Sch., 1998—; dir. The Mus. Stony Brook, 1998—. Fellow ABA Found., N.Y. State Bar Found. (bd. dirs. 1994—); mem. ABA (ho. of dels. 1997—, probate and real property sect., ho. of dels. 1996—, standing com. on solo and small firm practitioners 1998—), N.Y. State Bar Assn. (ho. dels. 1982—, pres. 1997-98, exec. com. 1992-99, spl. com. women and law 1986-91, task force om small firms 1991-92, trusts and estates sect., gen. practice, elder law), Suffolk County Bar Assn. (bd. dirs. 1979-89, pres. 1985-86), N.Y. County Lawyers Assn., Nassau County Bar Assn. Probate, General corporate, Real property. Office: Greshin Ziegler & Pruzansky 199 E Main St Smithtown NY 11787-2892

**PRYCE, JEFFREY FREMONT,** lawyer; b. Washington; s. William T. and Joan M. (MacClurg) P. BA in Philos., Wesleyan U., 1982; MPhil, Cambridge U., 1986; JD, Yale U., 1991. Bar: Pa. 1993, D.C. 1996. Fellow Sen. Kennedy U.S. Senate, Washington, 1982-83; legis. asst. Rep. Markey, U.S. Ho. of Reps., Washington, 1983-85, 86-88; law clk. Justice B.R. White, U.S. Supreme Ct., Washington, 1991-93; spl. counsel DoD Gen. Counsel, Washington, 1993-94; counselor Office of Sec. of Defense, Washington, 1994—. Office: OUSDP 4-e 808 Pentagon Washington DC 20301-0001

**PRYE, STEVEN MARVELL,** lawyer; b. Memphis, Nov. 13, 1952; s. John Allen and Thelma Inez (Buckner) P. BA, Yale U., 1974; JD, Harvard U., 1978; LLM in Taxation, NYU, 1985. Bar: N.Y. 1979, U.S. Dist. Ct. (ea. and so. dists.) N.Y. 1981, U.S. Tax Ct. 1984. Assoc. Stroock, Stroock & Lavan, N.Y.C., 1978-83, DeForest & Duer, N.Y.C., 1983-86, Phillips, Nizer, Benjamin, Krim & Ballon, N.Y.C., 1986-89; atty., instr. NYU, 1989-93; instr. Vt. Law Sch., 1993—. Sr. editor Harvard Civil Rights and Civil Liberties Law Rev., 1977-78. Named one of Outstanding Young Men of Am., U.S. Jaycees, 1983. Mem. ABA (estate taxation of lifetime transfers com., real property probate and trust law sects.), N.Y. State Bar Assn. (legis., estate planning coms., trust and estates law sect.), Assn. Bar of City of N.Y. (young lawyers com. 1985-89), NAACP, ACLU, Common Cause Com. Democrat. Avocations: opera, reading, theater, travel. Estate planning, Probate, Estate taxation. Home: 509 W Green St Champaign IL 61820-5051 Office: Vt Law Sch Chelsea St South Royalton VT 05068

**PRYOR, DAVID W.,** lawyer, law educator; b. Columbus, Ohio, Apr. 5, 1956; s. George M. and Marcia H. (Halliday) P.; m. Diana Lynn Dysart, Aut. 8, 1987; children: Stephen, Michael, Elizabeth. BA, Miami U., Oxford, Ohio, 1979; JD, Capital U., 1984; LLM, U. Ark., 1985. Bar: Ohio, 1984, D.C. 1986, U.S. Dist. Ct. (so. dist.) Ohio 1986. Assoc. Hamilton Kramer Myers & Cheek, Columbus, 1986-90, ptnr., 1990-96; mng. ptnr. Gallagher Bradigan Gams & Pryor, Columbus, 1996—; adj. prof. Law Sch. Capital U., Columbus, 1987—. Contbr. articles to profl. jours. Bd. dirs. The Open Shelter, Columbus, 1995-98; mem. Charity Newsies, Columbus, 1993—. Recipient Outstanding Citizenship award Columbus Jaycees, 1992. Mem. ABA (chmn. agrl. law 1996-99), Ohio St. Bar Assn. (v.p. agrl. law 1997-99), Columbus Bar Assn. (chmn. agrl. law 1994-96). Presbyterian. Avocations: skiing, platform tennis, farming. General civil litigation, Real property, Agriculture. Office: Gallagher Bradigan Gams Pryor & Littrel 471 E Broad St Ste 1900 Columbus OH 43215-3842

**PRYOR, KATHRYN ANN,** lawyer; b. Fayetteville, Ark., Oct. 27, 1960; d. Neil Birnie Pryor and Judy Martha Trice. BA in Journalism, U. Ark., 1983; JD, U. Ark., Little Rock, 1989. Bar: Ark. 1989, U.S. Dist. Ct. (ea. dist.) Ark. 1989, U.S. Dist. Ct. (we. dist.) Ark. 1989, U.S. Ct. Appeals (8th cir.) 1989. Dir. radio and TV rels. U. Ark., Little Rock, 1983-84; law clk. Rose Law Firm, Little Rock, 1987-88; ptnr. Wright, Lindsey & Jennings, Little Rock, 1989—. Active Jr. League of Little Rock, 1990-94, Friends of the Ark. Repertory Theatre, 1993-94. Mem. ABA, Ark. Bar Assn., Pulaski County Bar Assn., Ark. Assn. Def. Coun., Ark. Assn. Women Lawyers. Democrat. Episcopalian. Avocations: theater, skiing, biking, music. Product liability, Insurance, Personal injury. Office: Wright Lindsey & Jennings 200 W Capitol Ave Ste 2200 Little Rock AR 72201-3699

**PRYOR, MARK LUNSFORD,** state attorney general; b. Fayetteville, Ark.; m. Jill Pryor; children: Adams, Porter. BA in History, U. Ark., 1985, JD, 1988. Pvt. practice Wright, Lindsey & Jennings, Little Rock, 1988-97; mem. Ark. Ho. of Reps., 1990, chmn. Freshman Caucus, mem. judiciary com., com. on aging and legis. affairs; atty. gen. State of Ark., 1999—. Office: Office of Attorney General State Capitol Little Rock AR 72201-1088*

**PRYOR, SHEPHERD GREEN, III,** lawyer; b. Fitzgerald, Ga., June 27, 1919; s. Shepherd Green Jr. and Jeffie (Persons) P.; m. Lenora Louise Standifer, May 17, 1941 (dec.); m. Ellen Wilder, July 13, 1984; children from previous marriage: Sandra Pryor Clarkson, Shepherd Green IV, Robert Stephen, Patty Pryor Smith (dec.), Alan Persons, Susan Lenora Pryor. BSAE, Ga. Inst. Tech., 1947; JD, Woodrow Wilson Coll. Law, Atlanta, 1974. Bar: Ga. 1974, U.S. Dist. Ct. (no. dist.) Ga. 1974, U.S. Ct. Appeals (5th cir.) 1974, U.S. Ct. Appeals (11th cir.) 1982, U.S. Supreme Ct. 1977; registered profl. engr. Ga., comml. pilot. engr. Hartford Accident and Indemnity Co., 1947-56, nuclear engr. Lockheed Ga. Co., 1956-64, research and tech. rep., 1964-87, real estate salesman Cole Realty Co. and Valient Properties, 1955-74, Sole practice of law, Atlanta, 1974—. Past pres. Loring Heights Civic Assn.; past mem. Sandy Springs Civic Assn. Devonwood Br.; former trustee Masonic Children's Home of Ga.; bd. advisors Reinhardt Coll.; mem. North Springs Homeowners Assn.; chmn. bd. Bd. Equalization, Fulton County, Ga. Capt. U.S. Army, 1942-45, USAFR, 1942-55. Mem. Ga. Bar Assn., Ga. Trial Lawyers Assn., Mensa, Intertel, Soc. Automotive Engrs., Assn. Old Crows, The Old Guard of the Gate City Guard (commandant), Masons, Shriners, Sigma Delta Kappa, Pi Kappa Phi, Kappa Kappa Psi, Republican. Methodist. General practice, General corporate, Real property. Address: 135 Spalding Dr NE Atlanta GA 30328-1912

**PRYOR, WILLIAM C.,** judge; b. Washington, May 29, 1932. BA, Dartmouth Coll., 1954; LLB with honors, Georgetown U., 1959. Bar: D.C. 1959, Ohio 1964, U.S. Supreme Ct. 1965. With U.S. Dept. Justice, Washington, 1959-68; judge D.C. Dist. Ct., Washington, 1968—; former chief judge; now sr. judge DC Ct. of Appeals, Washington, 1993—; instr. Georgetown U., Washington, 1969, 71, Potomac Law Sch., 1976—. Bd. dirs. YMCA, St. Albans Sch., Opportunities Industrialization Ctr., Am. Cancer Soc. Lt. USAS, 1955-56. Mem. ABA, Washington Bar Assn., D.C. Bar, Washington Athletic Club. Office: Dist of Columbia Ct of Appeals 500 Indiana Ave NW Washington DC 20001-2131

**PRYOR, WILLIAM HOLCOMBE, JR.,** state attorney general; b. Mobile, Ala., Apr. 26, 1962; s. William Holcombe Sr. and Laura Louise (Bowles) P.; m. Kristan Camille Wilson, Aug. 15, 1987; children: Caroline Elizabeth, Victoria Camille. BA in Legal Studies with honors, N.E. La. U., 1984; JD with honors, Tulane U., 1987. Law clk. U.S. Ct. Appeals (5th cir.), Judge John Minor Wisdom, New Orleans, 1987-88; assoc. Cabaniss, Johnston, Gardner, Dumas & O'Neil, Birmingham, Ala., 1988-91, Walston, Stabler, Wells, Anderson & Bains, Birmingham, 1991-95; dep. atty. gen. State of Ala., Montgomery, 1995-97, atty. gen., 1997—; adj. prof. Samford U. Cumberland Sch. Law, Birmingham, 1989-94. Bd. student editors Tulane Law Rev., 1985-86, editor-in-chief 1986-87, bd. advisory editors, 1995—. La. nat. com. Young Rep. Nat. Fedn., 1984-86; mem. Ala. Rep. Exec. Com., 1994-95. Order of Coif, Phi Kappa Phi, Omicron Delta Kappa. Roman Catholic. Office: Office Atty Gen 11 S Union St Montgomery AL 36130-2103

**PRZEKOP-SHAW, SUSAN,** lawyer; b. Grand Rapids, Mich., July 1, 1952; d. Charles Peter P. and Stella Anastasia Niedzwiecki; m. William Francis Shaw, Sept. 3, 1977; children: William, Jonathan, Michael. BS in Pharmacy, U. Mich., 1975; postgrad., U. Tenn., 1977; JD, Thomas Cooley Law Sch., 1979. Bar: Mich.; registered pharmacist. Drug analyst Upjohn Drug Co., Portage and Ann Arbor, Mich., 1974; pharmacy intern, pharmacist Meijer Thrifty Acres Pharmacy, Grand Rapids, Ypsilanti, Lansing, Mich., 1972-81; analyst funds adminstrn. silicosis and disease fund Bur. Workers Compensation Dept. Labor State of Mich., Lansing, 1977-78; student liaison for com. on advtsg. cert., specialization State Bar Mich., Lansing, 1977-78; assoc. Sinas, Dramis, Brake, Boughton, McIntyre & Reising, P.C., Lansing, 1979-89; asst. atty. gen. corrections divsn. Mich. Dept. Atty. Gen., Lansing, 1989-97, mem. litigation adv. bd., 1992-98, asst. atty. gen. Mich. Civil Svc. Commn., 1997—; legal advisor gov.'s adv. group on mental health and corrections Office of Gov. State of Mich., Lansing, 1991-93; mem. labor and employment sect. State Bar Mich. Prodr. plays Lansing Catholic Ctrl. Drama Dept. Prodns., 1998—. Chairperson pub. rels. com. Boys and Girls Club Lansing, 1985-87, bd. dirs., 1985-91, sec., 1987-88, first v.p., 1988-90, pres., 1989-90; co-chairperson, raffle ticket chairperson St. Gerard Cath. Ch., Lansing, 1989—, mem. edn. commn. 1993—, chairperson parent-student activity day, 1993—, chairperson fin., 1993-95, co-chairperson fin. Parish Spring Festival, 1998. Fellow Mich. State Bar Found.-State Bar Mich., 1998. Mem. Nat. Assn. Attys. Gen. (spkr. on consent decrees and injunctions 1992, constitutionality of prison litigation reform act 1997), Mich. Trial Lawyers Assn. (bd. dirs. 1983-85). Avocation: theatre. Fax: (517) 373-6434. E-mail: przekopshaws@ag.state.mi.usa. Home: 5914 Claremont Ct Lansing MI 48917-5125 Office: Mich Dept Atty Gen 525 W Ottawa Ste 640 Lansing MI 48913-0001

**PUCCINELLI, ANDREW J.,** lawyer; b. Elko, Nev., July 21, 1935. BA cum laude, U. of the Pacific, 1975, JD, 1978. Bar: Nev. 1978. Ptnr. Puccinelli & Puccinelli, Elko, Nev.; bus. law adj. prof. No. Nev. C.C., 1982-93; legal advisor Nev. Home Health Svcs., 1980-88. Bd. dirs. Nev. Legal Svcs., 1986-93. Mem. ATLA, Nev. Trial Lawyers Assn., Nev. State Bar Assn. (bd. govs. 1993—, v.p. 1996-97, pres.-elect 1997-98, pres. 1998-99, No. Nev. disciplinary bd. 1988-93, CLE com. 1981-85), Elko County Bar Assn. (pres. 1985-86), Phi Delta Phi. Office: Puccinelli & Puccinelli 700 Idaho St Elko NV 89801-3824*

**PUCILLO, ANTHONY ERNEST,** lawyer; b. Oak Park, Ill.; s. Daniel William Sr. and Carol Elaine Pucillo; m. Shirley Marie Pucillo, Dec. 24, 1989; 1 child, Adam Christian. BA, U. Ill., 1971; JD, U. Iowa, 1973; LLM in Internat. and Comparative Law, Georgetown U., 1994. Bar: Fla. 1974, U.S. Dist. Ct. (mid. dist.) Fla. 1998, U.S. Dist. Ct. (so. dist.) Fla. 1975, U.S. Ct. Appeals (5th cir.) 1978, U.S. Ct. Appeals (11th cir.) 1981, U.S. Supreme Ct. 1981. Law clk. Squire Sanders & Dempsey, Cleve., 1973; assoc. Jones, Paine & Foster, West Palm Beach, Fla., 1974-79; ptnr., founder Anthony E. Pucillo P.A., West Palm Beach, Fla., 1979—. Mem. editl. bd. Iowa Law Rev., 1973-74; contbr. articles to profl. jours. Mem. Masons. General civil litigation, Private international, Contracts commercial.

**PUCKETT, ELIZABETH ANN,** law librarian, law educator; b. Evansville, Ind., Nov. 10, 1943; d. Buell Charles and Lula Ruth (Gray) P.; m. Joel E. Hendricks, June 1, 1964 (div. June 1973); 1 child, Andrew Charles; m. Thomas A. Wilson, July 19, 1985. BS in Edn., Eastern Ill. U., 1964; JD, U. Ill., 1977, MS in L.S., 1977. Bar: Kans. 1978, Ill. 1979. Acquisitions/reader services librarian U. Kans. Law Library, Lawrence, 1978-79; asst. reader services librarian So. Ill. U. Law Library, Carbondale, 1979-81, reader services librarian, 1981-83; assoc. dir. Northwestern U. Law Library, Chgo., 1983-86, co-acting dir., 1986-87; dir./assoc. prof. South Tex. Coll. Law Library, Houston, 1987-89; dir./prof. South Tex. Coll. Law Libr., Houston, 1990-94, U. Ga. Law Libr., Athens, 1994—. Co-author: Evaluation of System-Provided Library Services to State Correctional Centers in Illinois, 1983; co-editor Uniform Commercial Code: Confidential Drafts, 1993. Mem. ABA, Am. Assn. Law Librs. (mem. exec. bd. 1993-96). Avocations: reading, antiques. Office: U Georgia Law Libr Athens GA 30602-6018

**PUCKETT, LAWRENCE HOWARD,** judge; b. Bristol, Va., May 7, 1951; s. Thomas Samuel and Anna Lee (Browning) P.; m. Patricia Kathleen Baker, July 19, 1975; children: Andrew, Anna, Elizabeth. BA in History, Bryan Coll., 1973; JD, U. Memphis, 1979. Bar: Tenn. 1980, U.S. Dist. Ct. (so. dist.) Tenn. 1980, U.S. Ct. Appeals (6th cir.) 1994. Assoc. atty. Conrad Finnell P.C., Cleveland, Tenn., 1980-87, 92-97; assoc. atty., ptnr. Bell & Assocs., Cleveland, 1987-92; asst. atty. gen. 10th jud. dist. Office of Dist. Atty. Gen., Cleveland, 1997; cir. ct. judge 10 jud. dist. Bradley County Courthouse, Cleveland, 1997—. Mem. ABA, Tenn. Bar Assn., Tenn. Trial Judges Conf., Bradley County Bar Assn. Republican. Baptist. Avocations: history, geneology. Home: 3814 Northwood Dr NW Cleveland TN 37312-3805 Office: Bradley County Courthouse 155 N Ocoee St Cleveland TN 37311-5068

**PUCKETT, PAUL WALTER,** lawyer; b. Honolulu, July 31, 1946; s. Paul James and Jean Haruko (Tsuda) P.; m. Peggy Hope, Nov. 29, 1969; children: Christopher, Paul Casey, Curtis James. BA, Colo. U., 1971, JD, 1974. Bar: Colo., U.S. Dist. Ct. Colo., U.S. Ct. Appeals (10th cir.). Right-of-way coord. Colo.-Ute Elec. Co., Montrose, 1975-76; pvt. practice Gunnison & Crested Butte, Colo., 1976-86, Denver, 1986-92; asst. prosecutor Glendale, Colo., 1988-92; asst. city atty. City and County of Denver, 1992—. Bd. dirs. Rocky Mountain Ski Assn., Denver, 1978-82; pres., bd. dirs. Concerned Lawyers, Inc., Wheat Ridge, Colo., 1987-92; bd. dirs., v.p. Mile High Coun. on Alcohol and Drug Abuse, Denver, 1990-92. Home: 2701 S Utica St Denver CO 80236-2102 Office: City Atty's Office 303 W Colfax Ave Ste 500 Denver CO 80204-2623

**PUCKETT, TONY GREG,** lawyer; b. Oklahoma City, Okla., Mar. 28, 1961; s. Tony Gene and Sandra Claire P.; m. Jennifer Ann Tubb, Aug. 8, 1987. BA, Colo. Coll., 1983; JD with distinction, U. Okla., 1988. Bar: U.S. Supreme Ct., 10th Cir. Ct. Appeals, 8th Cir. Ct. Appeals, U.S. Dist. Ct. Okla. (we. dist.), U.S. Dist. Ct. Okla. (no. dist.), U.S. Dist. Ct. Okla. (ea. dist.), U.S. Dist. Ct. Tex (No. Tex. dist.). Law clk. Lytle Soule & Curlee, Oklahoma City, Okla., 1986-88, assoc., 1988-92; shareholder Lytle Soule & Curlee, Oklahoma City, 1993-97, McAfee & Taft, Oklahoma City, Okla., 1998—. Author: Supreme Court Broadens Liability for Harassment, 1998, Supreme Court Dicples Same-Sex Sexual Harassment Issue, 1998; contbg. author: Age Discrimination in the Workplace: A Primer for Human Resources Professionals, 1999. Trustee McAfee & Taft Found., Oklahoma City, 1998-99. Mem. ABA (labor and employment law sect.), Okla. Bar Assn. (labor and employment sect., chmn. 1997-98), Okla. County Bar Assn., Okla. Assn. Muncipal Attys., Soc. for Human Resources. Republican. Presbyterian. Avocations: soccer coaching and playing, kids. Labor. Office: McAfee & Taft 211 N Robinson Ave Ste S1000 Oklahoma City OK 73102-7103

**PUERNER, PAUL RAYMOND,** lawyer; b. Milw., Mar. 27, 1927; s. Bertram Harvey and Carmen Marie (Sousa) P.; m. Rae Harriet Smart, Aug. 19, 1950; children: John, Pamela, Thomas, James, Jane, Michael, Susan. BS in Mech. Engring., U. Wis., 1949; JD, Harvard U., 1955. Bar: Ill. 1955, Wis. 1956, U.S. Dist. Ct. (ea. dist.) Wis. 1956, U.S. Ct. Appeals (7th cir.) 1957, U.S. Supreme Ct. 1960, U.S. Ct. Appeals (fed. cir.) 1982. Engr. Lago Oil & Transport Co., Aruba, The Netherlands, West Antilles, 1949-52; atty. Vapor Heating Corp., Chgo., 1955-56; assoc. Michael, Best & Friedrich, Milw., 1956-64, ptnr., 1964-87; pvt. practice Milw., 1987—. Bd. dirs. Mequon-Thiensville (Wis.) Union High Sch. Dist. 1, 1968—. With USNR, 1945-46. Mem. ABA, Wis. Bar Assn., Milw. Bar Assn., Milw. Patent Law Assn. (pres. 1970-71), Wis. Intellectual Property Law Assn., Alpha Chi Rho. Methodist. Patent, Federal civil litigation, Trademark and copyright. Home: 335 E Antoine Dr Port Washington WI 53074-1398 Office: 633 W Wisconsin Ave Milwaukee WI 53203-1918 *Notable cases include: Phillips Industries, Inc. vs. State Stove and Mfg. Co. Inc., 1975; Busse, et al vs. U.S., 1977; State Industries, Inc. vs. Rheem Mfg. Co., 1985; State Industries, Inc. vs. Mor-Flo Industries, Inc. and Am. Appliance Mfg. Corp., 1989.*

**PUGH, DAVID EDWARD,** lawyer; b. Union, N.Y., July 3, 1950; s. William and Arline (Loudenburg) P.; m. Karin L. Brooks, Sept. 27, 1980; children: Jonathan, Brian, Catherine. Student, Syracuse U., 1968-69; BA, SUNY, Binghamton, 1972; JD, Bklyn. Law Sch., 1975. Bar: N.Y. 1976, U.S. Dist. Ct. (ea. and so. dists.) N.Y. 1977; cert. family mediator, Fla. Sole practice N.Y.C., 1976-81; assoc. Wallman & Kramer, N.Y.C., 1981-83, ptnr., 1984-92; ptnr. Warshaw, Burstein, Cohen, Schlesinger & Kuh, LLP, N.Y.C., 1992-94; counsel Banks Pickett Gruen & Shapiro, LLP, Mt. Kisco, N.Y., 1994-97, Randal G. Lawrence & Assocs., Katonah, N.Y., 1997-99; negotiator Steven A. Bagen & Assocs., Gainesville, Fla., 1999—; lectr. Women's Survival Space, Bklyn., 1978-81; cons. Playcare, Inc., Katonah, N.Y., 1983—. Mem. ABA (family law sect.), N.Y. State Bar Assn. (family law sect.), Assn. Trial Lawyers Am., N.Y. Trial Lawyers Assn. Republican. Presbyterian. Family and matrimonial, State civil litigation. Home: 1429 NW 48th Ter Gainesville FL 32605-4566

**PUGH, FRANCIS LEO,** lawyer; b. Detroit, Dec. 8, 1934; s. Charles Herbert and Elizabeth Sonetta (Brown) P.; m. Mary Louise Hake, Oct. 4, 1958; children: Jane Marie, Thomas Scott, Francis Leo II, Patrick Kevin. BS, Auburn U., 1957; MS, St. Louis U., 1959; JD, Ventura Coll Law, 1979. Bar: Calif., U.S. Dist. Ct. (cen. dist.) Calif. 1980, U.S. Ct. Appeals (9th cir.) 1981, U.S. Tax Ct. Atty. sole practitioner, Somis, 1980-83, Masci & Pugh, Inc., Thousand Oaks, Calif., 1983-85, sole practitioner, Camarillo, Calif., 1985—; adj. faculty So. Calif. Inst. Law, Ventura, 1982-85; mem. oversight com. Lawyer Referral Svc., Ventura, 1994—; mem. Estate Planning Coun., 1983—, past pres. and dir.; chmn. Multidisciplinary Estate Planning reg. workshops, 1998-99; notary public State of Calif. Ventura County, 1992—. Mem. editl. bd. Citations monthly mag. of Ventura Bar Assn. Dir., v.p., pres. Dos Caminos Plaza Assoc., Camarillo, 1994-98; dir., pres. Ponderosa Heights HOA, 1989-97; lay min. Work Furlough, Corrections, Camarillo, 1987—. Capt. USAF, 1959-62. Mem. AIAA (sr.), Fed. Bar Assn., Calif. Bar Assn., Calif. Bar Tax Sect., Lawyer Pilots Bar Assn. Republican. Roman Catholic. Avocations: commercial pilot, certified flight instructor. Taxation, general, Estate planning. Office: 2460 Ponderosa Dr N #A110 Camarillo CA 93010-2375

**PUGH, KEITH E., JR.,** lawyer; b. L.A., Mar. 17, 1937; s. Keith Emerson and Serena (Reynolds) P.; m. Kathleen Perry, Aug. 28, 1958 (div. Mar. 1973); children—Linda, Lisa, Scott; m. Pamela Carolyn Winberry, May 20, 1973; children—Alexander, Caroline. Student, Principia Coll., 1955-58; J.D., U. So. Calif., 1962. Bar: Calif. 1962, D.C. 1969, U.S. Supreme Ct. 1976, U.S. Ct. Internat. Trade 1983, U.S. Ct. Appeals (fed. cir.) 1994. Dep. atty. gen. antitrust sect. Office Calif. Atty. Gen., San Francisco, 1962-65; assoc. Broad, Busterud & Khourie, San Francisco, 1965-66, Office Joseph Alioto, San Francisco, 1966-68, Howrey & Simon, Washington, 1968-69; ptnr. Howrey & Simon, 1970-98, also mem. mgmt., 1980-98. Mem. State Bar Calif., D.C. Bar Assn., Annapolis Yacht Club, Ocean Reef Club, Phi Delta Phi. Avocation: boating. Antitrust, Federal civil litigation, Mergers and acquisitions. Home: 100 Anchor Dr # 443 Key Largo FL 33037-5277 Office: Howrey & Simon 1299 Pennsylvania Ave NW Ste 1 Washington DC 20004-2420

**PUGH, RANDALL SCOTT,** lawyer; b. Jamestown, N.Y., Mar. 31, 1950; s. H. Theodore and Jeanne M. (Crossley) P.; m. Christie S., Sept. 3, 1978; 1 child, Theodore Clifford. BA, Hobart Coll., 1972; JD, U. Richmond, 1976. Bar: Va. 1976, U.S. Dist. Ct. Va. 1982, U.S. Bankruptcy Ct. 1982. Law clk. to justice Supreme Ct., Richmond, Va., 1976-77; asst. county atty. Prince William County, Manassas, Va., 1977; assoc., ptnr. Whitticar, Sokol, Ledbetter & Haley, Fredericksburg, Va., 1978-87; prin. R. Scott Pugh, Fredericksburg, 1987—; pres. Lawyer Assistance and Support Svc., Fredericksburg, 1987—; dep. county atty. Spotsylvania County, Va., 1988-90; instr. criminal law Rappahannock Criminal Justice Acad., 1978-90. Editor Cir. Writer, 1991—. Bd. dirs. Rappahannock Boy Scouts Am., Fredericksburg, 1982-86, Big Bros. & Sisters, 1978-81; chmn. Spotsylvania County Dem. Com., 1987-91; mem., chair Spotsylvania County Sch. Bd., 1993-96; mem. Spotsylvania County Bd. of Zoning Appeals, 1997—; television host and panelist Rappahannock Rev., 1997—. Mem. ABA, Va. Trial Lawyers Assn., Fredericksburg Area Bar Assn., Fredericksburg C. of C., Fredericksburg Area Jaycees (bd. dirs. 1978-82), Hobart Coll. Alumni, U. Richmond Alumni Assn. Democrat. Methodist. Avocation: computers. General civil litigation, Consumer commercial, Appellate. Office: 9108 Courthouse Rd Spotsylvania VA 22553-1902

**PUGH, STEPHEN HENRY, JR.,** lawyer; b. Chgo., Oct. 17, 1942; s. Stephen Henry Pugh Sr. and Mardella (James) Barran; children: Preston L. Leslie. AB in Classics/Philosophy, Loyola U., Chgo., 1968, JD, 1973. Summer clk. U.S. Atty. for No. Dist., Chgo., 1972; law clk. Hon. James B. Parsons, Chgo., 1973-74; spl. trial atty. U.S. Dept. Justice, Chgo., 1974-77; assoc. Chapman & Cutler, Chgo., 1978-83, prin., 1983-91; ptnr., shareholder Pugh, Jones & Johnson, P.C., Chgo., 1991—. Bd. mem. Emergency Fund for Needy People, Chgo.; mem. Character and Fitness Commn., Chgo., Atty. Registration and Disciplinary Commn., Chgo. Sgt. USAF, 1970. Named Bd. Mem. of Yr., Parkway Cmty. House/Hull Assn., 1986; recipient cert. appreciation ISBA Practicing Lawyers Bus. Fair, 1988, Testimonial of Appreciation, Loyola U. Sch. Law, 1994. Mem. ABA, Nat. Bar Assn., Ill. State Bar Assn., Cook County Bar Assn., Chgo. Bar Assn., Monroe Club, Hyde Park Athletic Club. Avocations: golf, tennis. General civil litigation, Real property, Finance. Office: Pugh Jones & Johnson PC 180 N La Salle St Ste 2910 Chicago IL 60601-2700

**PUGH, WILLIAM WALLACE,** lawyer; b. Flushing, N.Y., Sept. 13, 1941; s. Wallace Raymond and Martha (Greenewald) P.; m. Joyce Curry, Dec. 17, 1977; children: James Thomas, Kristin Anne, Katherine Elizabeth. BS in Physics, Bucknell U., 1963; MS in Ops. Research, NYU, 1966; JD, Cath. U., 1972. Bar: D.C. 1973, U.S. Dist. Ct. D.C. 1976, U.S. Ct. Appeals (D.C. cir.) 1977, U.S. Supreme Ct. 1977, U.S. Ct. Appeals (5th cir.) 1987. Electronics engr. Grumman Aircraft Engring. Corp., Beth Page, N.Y., 1964-65; mem. tech. staff TRW Systems Group, McLean, Va., 1966-69; advertising examiner FTC, Washington, 1970-72; assoc. Keller & Heckman, Washington, 1972-75; gen. counsel Nat. Motor Freight Traffic Assn., Alexandria, Va., 1975—. Mem. ABA, D.C. Bar Assn., Fed. Bar Assn., Transp. Lawyer Assn., Assn. Transp. Law Practitioners, Delta Theta Phi. Administrative and regulatory, Federal civil litigation, Transportation. Home: 3404 Kimberly Dr Falls Church VA 22042-3748 Office: Nat Motor Freight Traffic Assn 2200 Mill Rd Alexandria VA 22314-4654

**PUGH, WILLIAM WHITMELL HILL,** lawyer; b. Baton Rouge, La., June 25, 1954; s. George Willard and Jean (Hemphill) P.; m. Beth Smith, Mar. 12, 1983; children: Brendan Kelly, Bryan Clayton, Katharine Elaine. BA, U. Va., 1976; JD, La. State U., 1979. Bar: La. 1979, U.S. Supreme Ct. 1986, U.S. Ct. Appeals (5th and 11th cirs.) 1983. Law clk. to presiding justice U.S. Ct. Appeals (5th cir.), New Orleans, 1979-80. Editor-in-chief La. Law Rev., 1978-79. Mem. Maritime Law Assn., La. Assn. Def. Counsel, La. State Bar Assn., Coun. of La. State Law Inst. (young lawyers rep. 1988-91, mem. 1992—). Admiralty, General civil litigation, Insurance. Office: Liskow & Lewis One Shell Sq 50th Fl New Orleans LA 70139-5001

**PUGLIESE, ROBERT FRANCIS,** lawyer, business executive; b. West Pittston, Pa., Jan. 15, 1933. BS, U. Scranton, 1954; LLB, Georgetown U., 1957, LLM, 1959; grad. advanced mgmt. program Harvard U., 1976. Bar: D.C. 1957, U.S. Dist. Ct. 1957, U.S. Ct. Claims 1958, U.S. Tax Ct. 1957, U.S. Ct. Appeals 1957. Assoc. Hedrick & Lane, Washington, 1957-60; tax counsel Westinghouse Electric Corp., Pitts., 1961-70, gen. tax counsel, 1970-75, v.p., gen. tax counsel, 1975-76, v.p., gen. counsel, sec., 1976-86, sr. v.p., 1987, exec. v.p., 1988-92; spl. counsel Eckert, Seamans, Cherin & Mellott, Pitts., 1993—; bd. dirs. Internat. Tech. Corp. Mem. Assn. Gen. Counsel. General corporate. Office: Eckert Seamans Cherin & Mellott 600 Grant St Ste 45 Pittsburgh PA 15219-2703

**PUGSLEY, ROBERT ADRIAN,** law educator; b. Mineola, N.Y., Dec. 27, 1946; s. Irvin Harold and Mary Catherine (Brusselars) P. BA, SUNY-Stony Brook, 1968; JD, NYU, 1975, LLM in Criminal Justice, 1977. Instr. sociology New Sch. Social Rsch., N.Y.C., 1969-71; coordinator Peace Edn. programs The Christophers, N.Y.C., 1971-78; assoc. prof. law Southwestern U., L.A., 1978-81, prof., 1981—, program dir., prof. law program Vancouver, B.C., Can., 1998; adj. asst. prof. criminology and criminal justice Southampton Coll.-Long Island U., 1975-76; acting dep. dir. Criminal Law Edn. and Rsch. Ctr., NYU, 1983-86; bd. advisors Ctr. Legal Edn. CCNY-CUNY, 1978, Sta. KPFK-FM, 1985-86; founder, coordinator The Wednesday Evening Soc., L.A., 1979-86; vis. prof. Jacob D. Fuchsberg Law Ctr. Touro Coll., L.I., N.Y., summers 1988, 89; lectr. in criminal law and procedure Legal Edn. Conf. Ctr., L.A., 1982-96; lectr., dir. Comparative Criminal Law and Procedure Inst. U. B.C., Vancouver, summers 1994, 98, 99; lectr. legal profl. responsibility West Bar Rev. Faculty, Calif., 1996-98; legal analyst/commentator for print and electronic media, 1992—. Creative advisor Christopher Closeup (nationally syndicated pub. svc. TV program), 1975-83; host Earth Alert, Cable TV, 1983-87; producer, moderator (pub. affairs discussion program) Inside L.A., Sta. KPFK-FM, 1979-86, Open Jour. program, Sta. KPFK-FM, 1991-94; contbr. articles to legal jours. Founding mem. Southwestern U. Pub. Interest Law com., 1992—; mem. L.A. County Bar Assn. Adv. Com. on Alcohol & Drug Abuse, 1991-95, co-chair, 1993-95; mem. exec. com. non-govtl. orgns. UN Office of Pub. Info., 1977; mem. issues task force L.A. Conservancy, 1980-81, seminar for law tchrs. NEH UCLA, 1979; co-convener So. Calif. Coalition Against Death Penalty, 1981-83, convener, 1983-84; mem. death penalty com. Lawyer's Support Group, Amnesty Internat. U.S.A.; founding mem. Ch.-State Coun., L.A., 1984-88. Robert Marshall fellow Criminal Law Edn. and Rsch. Ctr., NYU Sch. Law, 1976-78; bd. dirs. Equal Rights Sentencing Found., 1983-85, Earth Alert Inc., 1984-87; mem. adv. bd. First Amendment Info. Resources Ctr., Grad. Sch. of Libr. and Info. Sci., UCLA, 1990—; mem. coun. Friends UCLA Libr., 1993—, pres., 1996—; mem. adv. bd. Children Requiring A Caring Kommunity, 1998—. Mem. Am. Legal Studies Assn., Am. Soc. Polit. and Legal Philosophy, Assn. Am. Law Schs., Inst. Soc. Ethics and Life Scis., Soc. Am. Law Tchrs., Internat. Platform Assn., Internat. Soc. Reform of Criminal Law, The Scribes. Democrat. Roman Catholic. Office: Southwestern U Sch Law 675 S Westmoreland Ave Rm 410 Los Angeles CA 90005-3905 Address: PO Box 440 East Hampton NY 11937-0440

**PULLANO, RICHARD L.,** lawyer; b. Chgo., Feb. 20, 1957; s. Eugene C. and Mary Louise Pullano; m. Candace Ann Haberkorn; children: Michael, Olivia. BBA, U. Notre Dame, 1979; JD, DePaul U., 1982. Asst. state's atty. Cook County State's Atty. Office, Chgo., 1982-87; atty. Robert A. Clifford and Assocs., Chgo., 1987-98; prin., pvt. practice law Chgo., 1998—; adj. prof. U. DePaul Coll. Law, Chgo., 1990-94; lectr. in field. Mem. ATLA, Ill. Trial Lawyers Assn., Ill. Bar Assn., Chgo. Bar Assn. Personal injury, Product liability, Aviation. Office: 100 W Monroe St Fl 19 Chicago IL 60603-1967

**PULLEN, RICHARD OWEN,** lawyer, communications company executive; b. New Orleans, Nov. 6, 1944; s. Roscoe LeRoy and Gwendolen Sophia Ellen (Williams) P.; m. Frances G. Eisenstein, Jan. 24, 1976 (div. 1986). B.A. in Econs., Whitman Coll., 1967; J.D., Duke U., 1972. Bar: D.C. 1973. Fin. mgmt. trainee Gen. Electric Co., Lynn, Mass., 1967-69; sr. atty. domestic facilities div. Common Carrier Bur., FCC, Washington, 1972-79, atty. advisor Office of Opinions and Rev., 1979-81; chmn. definitions and terminology of joint industry, govt. com. for preparation of U.S. Proposals 1977 Broadcasting Satellite World Adminstrv. Radio Conf.; v.p. Washington office Contemporary Comm. Corp., New Rochelle, N.Y., 1981-91; v.p., gen. counsel Comm. Innovations Corp., New Rochelle, 1991—. With USCGR, 1967-75. Mem. ABA, Fed. Comm. Bar Assn., Fed. Bar Assn., Internat. Platform Assn. Republican. Unitarian. Administrative and regulatory, Communications, Public utilities.

**PULLEY, LEWIS CARL,** lawyer; b. Oklahoma City, Aug. 19, 1954; s. Harriet Ruth (Meyers) P.; foster sons: Tuan Le, Chien Hoang. Student, Oxford U., England, 1974; BA with high honors, U. Okla., 1976; JD, Am. U., 1979. Bar: Pa. 1981, U.S. Ct. Mil. Appeals 1982, U.S. Ct. Appeals (D.C. cir.) 1985, U.S. Supreme Ct. 1985, D.C. 1987. Commd. 1st lt. USAF, 1982, advanced through grades to capt., 1982, judge advocate, 1982-88; atty. Def. Logistics Agy., Alexandria, Va., 1988-90; atty. EEO br. mass media bur. FCC, 1990-97, supr. atty. EEO br. mass media bur., 1997—. Contbr. over 500 articles to 11 newspapers and mags. (recipient Investigative Reporting award, Okla. City Gridiron Found., 1975, Media award for Econ. Understanding, Dartmouth Bus. Sch., 1980). Vol. Nat. Pub. Radio, Washington, 1989-90, Connections, 1990-98, White House, 1993-94; mem. Ams. for Med. Progress Ednl. Found. Ewing Found. fellow, 1975. Mem. Pa. Bar Assn., D.C. Bar Assn. Democrat. Jewish. Avocations: travel, collecting polit. paraphernalia. Office: FCC Mass Media Bur EEO Br 445 12th St SW Washington DC 20554-0001

**PULOS, WILLIAM WHITAKER,** lawyer; b. Hornell, N.Y., Aug. 29, 1955; s. William Leroy and Juanita (Whitaker) P. BA magna cum laude Econs., Alfred U., 1977; JD, Union U., 1980. Bar: N.Y. 1982, U.S. Bankruptcy Ct. 1982, U.S. Supreme Ct. 1987. Pvt. practice Alfred U., Alfred, N.Y., 1981-90; adj. prof. law Alfred U., 1981-90; prof. bus. adminstrn. SUNY-Alfred, 1982-84; tutor Empire State Coll., 1982-85; atty. Town of Alfred, 1982—, Village of Almond (N.Y.), 1983-98, Town of West Almond (N.Y.), 1987-97, Town of West Union (N.Y.), 1992-98, Town of Birdsall (N.Y.), 1993-97; mem. Allegany County and Steuben County Assigned Counsel Program for Indigent Defendants, 1982-85; spl. prosecutor Allegany County, 1984—; asst. counsel N.Y. State Assembly, 1980; hearing officer N.Y. state Small Claims Assessment Rev., 1983-87. Active Alfred Sta. Vol. Fireman's Assn., Inc., 1985-98, 2d chief, 1988-92, pres. 1994-96; treas. Alfred Community Organizers and Renovators, 1985—. Recipient Outstanding Young Man Am. award U.S. Jaycees, 1982, 86. mem. ABA, Assn. Trial Lawyers Am., N.Y. State Bar Assn., Steuben County Bar Assn., Alfred Lions Club, Inc. (pres. 1988-89, Melvin Jones fellow 1991, Lions of Yr. 1990) State Sheriff's Assn. (hon.), U.S. Jaycees, Lions, Elks, Delta Sigma Phi. State civil litigation, Federal civil litigation, Personal injury. Office: 44 N Main St PO Box 334 Hornell NY 14843-0334

**PULVERMACHER, LOUIS CECIL,** lawyer; b. N.Y.C., May 10, 1928; s. Joseph and Lucille Lottie (Meyer) P.; m. Jo Kuchai, May 17, 1974; children: Lewis, Andrew, Stanley, Robin. Grad., Horace Mann Sch., 1945; AB, Franklin and Marshall Coll., 1948; JD, U. Pa., 1951. Bar: N.Y. 1955. Ptnr. Port & Pulvermacher, N.Y.C., 1956-68; sole practice Louis C. Pulvermacher P.C., 1968—; lawyer; b. N.Y.C., May 10, 1928; s. Joseph and Lucille Lottie (Meyer) P.; grad. Horace Mann Sch., 1945; AB, Franklin and Marshall Coll., 1948; JD, U. Pa., 1951; m. Jo Kuchai, May 17, 1974; children: Lewis, Andrew, Stanley, Robin. Admitted to N.Y. bar, 1955; ptnr. law firm Port & Pulvermacher, N.Y.C., 1956-68; sole practice law Louis C. Pulvermacher P.C., 1968—. Pro bono panel U.S. Dist. Ct. (so. and ea. dists.) N.Y. Served with USNR, 1951-54. Mem. ABA (co-chmn. econs. law), Found. Fed. Bar Coun. (v.p. 1978-90, chmn. bd. 1990-92), Fed. Bar Coun. (chmn. bd. dirs. 1983-88), Dutchess County Bar Assn. (exec. com. 1995-98), mem. Sch. Bd. Millbrook Ctrl. Sch. Dist., 1995-98. Jewish. Mem. pro bono panel U.S. Dist. Ct. (so. and ea. dists.) N.Y. Served with USNR, 1951-54, sch. bd. Millbrook Ctrl. Sch. Dist., 1995-98. Mem. ABA (co-chmn. econs. law), Found. Fed. Bar coun. (v.p. 1978-90, chmn. bd. 1990-92), Fed. Bar. Coun. (chmn. bd. dirs. 1983-88), Dutchess County Bar Assn. (exec. com. 1995-98). Jewish. Federal civil litigation, State civil litigation, General practice. Address: 2214 Harbour Court Dr Longboat Key FL 34228-4174

**PUMPHREY, GERALD ROBERT,** lawyer; b. Flushing, N.Y., May 31, 1947; s. Fred Paul and Anne (Afferman) P.; m. Joann DeLillo, Oct. 6, 1968; children: Gerald, Christopher, Elena. BBA, St. John's U., 1969, MBA, 1974; JD, Nova U., 1978. Bar: Fla. 1978. Assoc. Walden & Walden, Dania, Fla., 1978; v.p. legal svcs. Golden Bear, Inc., North Palm Beach, Fla.; v.p. legal svcs. Jack Nicklaus & Assocs., Air Bear, Inc., also bd. dirs.; v.p., sec. Triple P., Inc., 1978-83; pvt. practice, 1983—. Bd. advdisor Benjamin Sch. Found. Athletics Assn., 1980-83; coord. Benjamin Sch. Found., Inc.; mem. golf com. St. Clare's Sch.; pres. Home and Sch. Assn., 1983-84; bd. dirs. Deaf Svc. Ctr. Palm Beach County Inc., 1988-89. Mem. ABA, Palm Beach County Bar Assn., North Palm Beach County Bar Assn. (pres. 1991-92), Palm Beach Gardens C. of C. (counsel 1983-87), Kiwanis (charter mem., bd. dirs. Palm Beach Gardens 1983-87), Rotary North Palm Beach (bd. dirs. 1998—, sec. 1999-2000), Phi Alpha Delta. Fax: 561-626-4824. General civil litigation, Real property, General practice. Office: Ste 300 11000 Prosperity Farms Rd Palm Beach Gardens FL 33410-3462

**PURCELL, BRIAN CHRISTOPHER,** lawyer, associate; b. Charlottesville, Va., Sept. 3, 1968; s. Harold Walton and Anita (Balicky) P.; m. Susan J. Dixon, Oct. 30, 1993. BS in Commerce, U. Va., 1990, JD, 1994, MS in Acctg., 1995. Bar: Va. 1994; CPA, 1997. Assoc. Clark & Stant, P.C., Virginia Beach, Va., 1995—. Vol. Am. Heart Assn., Virginia Beach, 1995. Mem. Virginia Beach Bar Assn., Va. State CPA Assn. (bd. mem. Tidewater chpt.), U. Va. Club of Tidewater (bd. mem. 1996—), Beta Gamma Sigma. Avocations: American antique furniture, music, sports. Corporate taxation, Mergers and acquisitions, Taxation, general. Office: Clark & Stant PC 900 One Columbus Ctr Virginia Beach VA 23462

**PURCELL, JOHN JOSEPH, III,** lawyer, consultant; b. Washington, Aug. 4, 1969; s. John Joseph Jr. and Georgia (O'Brien) P.; m. Lindsay Anne Elizabeth Newbold, Mar. 9, 1996; 1 child, John W. BA, Dartmouth Coll., 1991; MBA, Washington U., St. Louis, 1995, JD, 1996. BAr: Ill. 1996, U.S. Dist. Ct. (no. dist.) Ill. 1996. Assoc. Price Waterhouse, St. Louis, 1991-93, Skadden, Arps, Slate, Meagher & Flom, Chgo., 1996-98; gen. counsel, corp. sec. Georgeson & Co. Inc., N.Y.c., 1998—. Contbr. chpt. to book. Avocations: writing, golf, fishing. General corporate, Securities. Office: Georgeson & Co Inc Wall St Plz 88 Pine St Fl 30 New York NY 10005-1801

**PURCELL, WILLIAM PAXSON, III,** university policy center administrator; b. Phila., Oct. 25, 1953; s. William Paxson Jr. and Mary (Hamilton) P.; m. Deborah Lee Miller, Aug. 9, 1986; 1 child, Jesse Miller. AB, Hamilton Coll., 1976; JD, Vanderbilt U., 1979. Bar: Tenn. 1979, U.S. Ct. Appeals (6th cir.) 1985, U.S. Supreme Ct. 1986. Staff atty. West Tenn. Legal Svcs., Jackson, Tenn., 1979-81; asst. pub. defender Metro Pub. Defender, Nashville, Tenn., 1981-84, sr. asst. pub. defender, 1984-85; assoc. Lionel R. Barrett, P.C., Nashville, 1985-86; ptnr. Farmer, Berry & Purcell, Nashville, 1986-90; mem. Tenn. Ho. of Reps., Nashville, 1986-96, also majority leader, 1990-96; dir. child and family policy ctr. Vanderbilt Inst. for Pub. Policy Studies, Vanderbilt U., Nashville, 1996—; chmn. select com. on children and youth Tenn. Gen. Assembly, 1989-96; exec. dir. Vanderbilt Legal Aid Soc., 1978-79; chmn. NCSL Assembly of State Issues, 1995; chmn. policy makers' program adv. bd. Danforth Found. Mem. exec. com. exec. com. 6th dist. Dems., Nashville, 1986-88, mem. Tenn. State Gen. Assembly, Nashville, 1986-96, Majority leader, 1990-96, chmn. human svcs.com. Nat. Conf. State Legislatures, Washington, 1993; mem. Dem. Nat. Com. exec. com., 1994-97; chmn. Dem. Legislative Campaign Com., 1994-96. Toll fellow Coun. State Govts., 1988; named Legislator of Yr. Dist. Attys.' Gen. Conf. 1989, Tenn. Conservation League, 1991. Mem. ABA, Tenn. Bar Assn., Nashville Bar Assn. Methodist. Office: 1207 18th Ave S Nashville TN 37212-2807

**PURCUPILE, JOHN STEPHEN,** lawyer; b. Ventura, Calif., Nov. 8, 1954; s. John Charles and Sylvia Marie (Pilgrim) P.; m. Anna Marie Leone, June 20, 1981; children: John Justin, Jessica Marie. BA, Case Western Reserve U., 1980; JD, Duquesne U., 1983. Bar: Pa. 1983, U.S. Dist. Ct. (we. dist.) Pa. 1983, U.S. Ct. Appeals (3rd cir.) 1997, U.S. Supreme Ct. 1987. Lawyer Stone & Stone, Pitts., 1983-85; law clk. Ct. of Common Pleas Hon. Livingstone M. Johnson, Pitts., 1985-88; lawyer Egler, Garrett & Egler, Pitts., 1988—. General civil litigation, General practice. Home: 335 Kennedy Rd Prospect PA 16052-2505 Office: Egler Garrett & Egler 428 Forbes Ave Ste 2100 Pittsburgh PA 15219-1695

**PURNELL, CHARLES GILES,** lawyer; b. Aug. 16, 1921; s. Charles Stewart and Ginevra (Locke) P.; m. Jane Carter; children: Mimi, Sarah Elizabeth, Charles H., John W. Student, Rice Inst., 1938-39; BA, U. Tex., 1941; student, Harvard Bus. Sch., 1942; LLB, Yale U., 1947. Bar: Tex. 1948. Ptnr. Locke, Purnell, Boren, Laney & Neely, Dallas, 1947-89; ptnr. Locke, Purnell, Rain & Harrell, Dallas, 1989-90, of counsel, 1990-99; of counsel Locke, Liddell & Sapp, Dallas, 1999—; exec. asst. to Gov. of Tex., Austin, 1973-75. Bd. dirs. Trinity River Authority of Tex., 1975-81; vice chmn. Tex. Energy Adv. Council, 1974. Served to lt. U.S. Navy, 1942-45; PTO. Mem. ABA, Tex. Bar Assn., Tex. Bar Found, Yale Club, Dallas Country Club, Dallas Petroleum Club, La Jolla (Calif.) Beach and Tennis Club. Episcopalian. General practice, Condemnation. Home: 1 Saint Laurent Pl Dallas TX 75225-8128 Office: Locke Lidell & Sapp 2200 Ross Ave Ste 2200 Dallas TX 75201-2748

**PURNELL, OLIVER JAMES, III,** law librarian, lawyer; b. Richmond, Va., Jan. 18, 1949; s. Oliver James Jr. and Margaret Helen (Hodges) P.; m. Cheryl Naomi Williams, June 30, 1973; children: Oliver James IV, Amy Susan. AA, U. Hartford, 1969; AB, Middlebury Coll., 1972; MSLS, Case Western Reserve U., 1976; JD, Western New England Sch. Law, 1982. Bar: Conn. 1982, U.S. Dist. Ct. (fed. dist.) Conn. 1982. Dir., pharmacy libr. U. Conn. Sch. Pharmacy, Storrs, Conn., 1977-81; assoc. Lavitt, Hutchinson & Kaplan, Vernon, Conn., 1981-84, DuBeau & Ryan, Vernon, Conn., 1984-87, Howard, Kohn Sprague & Fitzgerald, Hartford, Conn., 1987-89; pvt. practice Vernon, 1989-92; reference librarian U. Conn. Sch. Law, Hartford, 1992-98; regional information mgr. Lexis-Nexis, Vernon, 1998-99. Contbr. articles to profl. jours. Scoutmaster Boy Scouts of Am., Rockville, Conn., 1990—. Recipient Eagle Scout award Boy Scouts of Am., 1964. Mem. Am. Assn. Law Libraries, So. New England Law Libr. Assn. (pres. 1998-99), Moose Lodge, A.F. & A.M. (master Fayette Lodge 1970). Avocations: skiing, camping, hiking, church organist. Office: 6 Forestview Dr Vernon Rockville CT 06066-4807

**PURSER, DONALD JOSEPH,** lawyer; b. Chgo., Apr. 21, 1954; s. Donald Cornelius and Mary Alice (Fashingbauer) P. BS, U. Utah, 1975; MS, Reid Coll., 1976; JD, George Mason U., 1980; postdoctoral, Georgetown U., 1981. Bar: Va. 1980, U.S. Tax Ct. 1980, U.S. Ct. Appeals (4th and 10th cirs.) 1980, Utah 1981, U.S. Supreme Ct, 1987; Nat. Bd. Trial Advocacy. Spl. agt. U.S. Dept. of State, Washington, 1976-80; law clk. to judge U.S. Dist. Ct., Alexandria, Va., 1980-81; assoc. Richards, Brandt, Miller & Nelson, Salt Lake City, 1981-83; sole practice Salt Lake City, 1983-85; ptnr. Fowler & Purser, Salt Lake City, 1985-87, Purser & Edwards LLC, Salt Lake City, 1987—; owner Advent Wealth Strategies Group LLC; judge pro tem Salt Lake County Cir. Ct., 1981-85; adj. faculty U. Phoenix, Salt Lake City, 1984—; advance staff office of v.p. of U.S., Washington, 1986; bd. dirs. Ameralex Risk Retention Group Chgo., Am. Western Life Ins. Co., Tarzana, Calif.; chmn. Rep. Congl. Dist. Utah. Active fin. com. Snelgrove for Congress campaign, 1988. Maj. JAGC, USAR. Mem. ABA (litigation sect., torts and ins. practice sect.), Am. Bd. Trial Advocates, Am. Inn of Ct. II (barrister), Phi Delta Theta, Delta Theta Pi. Republican. Roman Catholic. Clubs: Blue Goose (Salt Lake City), Utah Elephant Lodge: K.C. Avocations: skiing, stock market, reading, Aikido. Insurance, Personal injury, General civil litigation. Home: 3054 Kennedy Dr Salt Lake City UT 84108-2123

**PURSLEY, RICKY ANTHONY,** law librarian; b. Wareham, Mass., July 11, 1954; s. Gene Everett and Evelyn May (Silveira) P.; m. Susan Elizabeth Scott, Nov. 27, 1982 (div.); children: Carinda Elizabeth, Julia Rayner, Rianna Susan. BA in Polit. Sci., Boston U., 1976; postgrad., Southwestern U., 1976-78. Notary public, D.C., 1991—. Law librarian Graham & James, Los Angeles, 1977-79; legal copy editor Arnold & Porter, Washington, 1980-85; rsch. libr., info. svcs. mgr. Fisher Wayland Cooper Leader & Zaragoza LLP, Washington, 1985—, law libr., 1985-97, accounts mgr., 1990; jury commr. Circuit Ct. of Arlington County and City of Falls Church, Va., 1993. Bd. deacons Little Falls Presbyn. Ch., Arlington, Va., 1995-97, elder, mem. session, 1998—; mem. Nottingham Elem. Sch. PTA Capital Improvement Plan adv. com., 1995—, legis. coord., 1996—; mem. Arlington, Va. Pub. Schs. Vocat., Career and Adult Edn. adv. com., 1996—, adv. coun. on Sch. Facilities and Capital Programs, 1996—. Named one of Outstanding Young Men in Am. U.S. Jaycees, 1978. Mem. Am. Assn. Law Librs., Law Librs.' Soc. Washington, Am. Soc. Notaries. Democrat. Presbyterian. Avocations: music, writing, carpentry. Home: 2704 N Sycamore St Arlington VA 22207-1132 Office: Fisher Wayland Cooper Leader & Zaragoza LLP 2001 Pennsylvania Ave NW Washington DC 20006-1851

**PURTELL, LAWRENCE ROBERT,** lawyer; b. Quincy, Mass., May 2, 1947; s. Lawrence Joseph and Louise Maria (Loria) P.; m. Cheryl Lynn Tymon, Aug. 3, 1968; children: Lisa Ann, Susan Elizabeth. AB, Villanova U., 1969; JD, Columbia U., 1972. Bar: N.Y. 1973, N.J. 1978, Conn. 1988. Assoc. White & Case, N.Y.C., 1972-73; judge advocate USMC, Washington, 1973-76; assoc. White & Case, N.Y.C., 1977-79; corp. counsel Great Atlantic & Pacific Tea Co., Montvale, N.J., 1979-81; asst. gen. counsel United Techs. Corp., Hartford, Conn., 1981-84, assoc. gen. counsel, 1984-92, sec., gen. counsel, 1989-92; v.p., gen. counsel and sec. Carrier Corp., 1992-93; sr. v.p., gen. counsel and corp. sec. Mc Dermott Internat., New Orleans, La., 1993-96; sr. v.p., gen. counsel Koch Industries, Wichita, Kans., 1996-97; exec. v.p., gen. counsel Alcoa, Pitts., 1997—. Capt. USMC, 1973-76. Roman Catholic. Avocations: running. Mergers and acquisitions, Securities, Finance. Home: 1220 Bennington Ave Pittsburgh PA 15217-1135 Office: Alcoa 201 Isabella St Pittsburgh PA 15212*

**PURVINES, VERNE EWALD, JR.**, lawyer; b. St. Louis, Feb. 13, 1945; s. Verne Ewald and Gertrude (Griese) P.; m. Mary Garland Adams, Dec. 16, 1987. BS, U. Wash., 1966; JD, NYU, 1971. Bar: N.Y. 1973, D.C. 1979, U.S. Ct. Appeals (4th and D.C. cirs.) 1979, Mo. 1982, U.S. Supreme Ct. 1983, U.S. Ct. Appeals (8th cir.) 1983. Assoc. LeBoeuf, Lamb, Leiby & MacRae, N.Y.C., 1971-75; atty. Chesapeake & Potomac Telephone, Washington, 1975-76, Geico Corp., Washington, 1976-81; v.p., gen. counsel, sec. Navco Cos., St. Louis, 1981—; bd. dirs. Navco Corp., St. Louis, Nat. Gen. Ins. Co., St. Louis, Nat. Gen. Assurance Co., St. Louis, Nat. Gen. Mktg., Inc., St. Louis. Mem. Forest Park Forever, St. Louis. Mem. ABA, St. Louis Bar Assn., Mo. Bar Assn. Republican. Insurance, General corporate, Administrative and regulatory. Office: Navco Cos 1 National General Plz Hazelwood MO 63045-1313

**PURVIS, JOHN ANDERSON**, lawyer; b. Aug. 31, 1942; s. Virgil J. and Emma Lou (Anderson) P.; m. Charlotte Johnson, Apr. 3, 1976; 1 child, Whitney; children by previous marriage: Jennifer, Matt. BA cum laude, Harvard U., 1965; JD, U. Colo., 1968. Bar: Colo. 1968, U.S. Dist. Ct. Colo. 1968, U.S. Ct. Appeals (10th cir.) 1978. Dep. dist. atty. Boulder, Colo., 1968-69; asst. dir., dir. legal aid U. Colo. Sch. Law, 1969; assoc. Williams, Taussig & Trine, Boulder, 1969; head Boulder office Colo. Pub. Defender Sys., 1970-72; assoc., ptnr. Hutchinson, Black, Hill, Buchanan & Cook, Boulder, 1972-85; ptnr. Purvis, Gray, Schuetze and Gordon, 1985-98, Purvis, Gray & Gordon, LLP, 1999—; acting Colo. State Pub. Defender, 1978; adj. prof. law U. Colo., 1981, 84-88, 94, others; lectr. in field; chmn. Colo. Pub. Defender Commn., 1979-89; mem. nominating commn. Colo. Supreme Ct., 1984-90; mem. com. on conduct U.S. Dist. Ct., 1991-97, chmn., 1996-97; chmn. Boulder County Criminal Justice Com., 1975-81. Recipient Ames award Harvard U., 1964, Outstanding Young Lawyer award Colo. Bar Assn., 1978, Dist. Achievement award U. Colo. Law Sch. Alumni Assn., 1997. Mem. Internat. Soc. Barristers, Internat. Acad. Trial Lawyers, Am. Bd. Trial Advocates, Am. Coll. of Trial Lawyers (state chmn. 1998—), Colo. Bar Assn. (chair litigation sect. 1994-95), Boulder County Bar Assn., Colo. Trial Lawyers Assn., Am. Trial Lawyers Assn., Trial Lawyers for Pub. Justice, Colo. Bar Found., Am. Bar Found., Supreme Ct. Hist. Soc. (state chmn. 1998—), Faculty of Fed. Advocates (bd. dirs. 1999—). Democrat. Personal injury, State civil litigation, Federal civil litigation. Address: 1050 Walnut St Ste 501 Boulder CO 80302-5144

**PURVIS, RANDALL W. B.**, lawyer; b. Summit, N.J., Mar. 2, 1957; s. Merton B. and Marjory L. (Baker) P.; m. Robin Head Intemann Purvis; children: Zachary, Timothy, Andrew. BS, Ohio State U., 1979; JD, Georgetown U., 1982. Bar: Colo. 1983, U.S. Dist. Ct. Colo. 1983, U.S. Ct. Appeals (10th cir.) 1983. Pvt. practice Colorado Springs, Colo., 1983—; bd. dirs. Nova Resources Corp., Dallas, 1985-88. Councilman Colorado Springs City Coun., 1987-99, re-elected 1991, 95; mem. steering com. Nat. League of Cities, Washington; elder 1st Presbyn. Ch., Colorado Springs, 1987-91; bd. trustees Meml. Hosp. Colorado Springs, 1991—. Mem. Colo. Bar Assn., El Paso County Bar Assn. (com. chmn. 1986), Colorado Springs C. of C. (com. chmn. 1986), Colorado Springs Bridge Club, Phi Beta Kappa. Republican. Avocations: bridge, woodworking. General civil litigation, Real property, Probate. Office: 13 S Tejon Ste 201 Colorado Springs CO 80903-1520

**PUSATERI, JAMES ANTHONY**, judge; b. Kansas City, Mo., May 20, 1938; s. James A. and Madeline (LaSalle) P.; m. Jacqueline D. Ashburne, Sept. 1, 1962; children—James A., Mark C., Danielle L. B.A., U. Kans., 1960, LL.B., 1963. Bar: Kans. 1963, U.S. Dist. Ct. Kans. 1963, U.S. Ct. Appeals (10th cir.) 1964. Assoc. Payne, Jones, Chartered, Olathe, Kans., 1963-65; assoc. James Cashin, Prairie Village, Kans., 1965-69; asst. U.S. atty. Dept. Justice, Kansas City, Kans., 1969-76; judge U.S. Bankruptcy Ct. Dist. Kans., Topeka, 1976—. Mem. Prairie Village City Council, 1967-69. Mem. Kans. Bar Assn., Topeka Bar Assn., Nat. Conf. Bankruptcy Judges, Am. Bankruptcy Inst. Office: US Bankruptcy Ct 444 SE Quincy St Topeka KS 66683

**PUSATERI, LAWRENCE XAVIER**, lawyer; b. Oak Park, Ill., May 25, 1931; s. Lawrence E. and Josephine (Romano) P.; m. Eve M. Graf, July 9, 1956; children: Joanne, Lawrence F., Paul L., Mary Ann, Eva. JD summa cum laude, DePaul U., 1953. Bar: Ill. 1953. Asst. state's atty. Cook County, 1957-59; ptnr. Newton, Wilhelm, Pusateri & Naborowski, Chgo., 1959-77; justice Ill. Appellate Ct., Chgo., 1977-78; ptnr. Peterson, Ross, Scloerb & Seidel, Chgo., 1978-95; of counsel Peterson & Ross, 1996—; pres. Conf. Consumer Fin. Law, 1984-92, chmn. gov. com., 1993—; mem. Ill. Supreme Ct. Com. on Pattern Jury Instrns., 1981-96; mem. adv. bd. Ctr. for Analysis of Alt. and Dispute Resolution, 1999—; mem. U.S. Senate Jud. Nominations Commn. State Ill., 1993, 95; exec. dir. State of Ill. Jud. Inquiry Bd., 1995-96; panel chmn. Cook County mandatory arbitration, 1990—, judicate Am. Arbitration; mem. Merit Selection Panel for U.S. Magistrate; lectr. law DePaul U., Chgo., 1962, Columbia U., N.Y.C., 1965, Marquette U., Milw., 1962-82, Northwestern U. Law Sch., Def. Counsel Inst., 1969-70; apptd. by U.S. Senator Paul Simon to Merit Screening Com. Fed. Judges, U.S. Atty. and U.S. Marshal, 1993, others; mem. task force indigent appellate def. Cook County Jud. Adv. Coun., 1992-95; mem. Ill. Gen. Assembly, 1964-68. Contbr. articles to profl. jours. Chmn. Ill. Crime Investigating Commn., 1967-68, chmn. Ill. Parole and Pardon Bd., 1969-70; bd. dirs. Ill. Law Enforcement Commn., 1970-72; chmn. Com. on Correctional Facilities and Services; exec. v.p. and gen. counsel Ill. Fin. Svcs. Assn., 1980-95; chmn. law forum Am. Fin. Svcs. Assn., 1975-76; mem. spl. commn. on adminstrn. of justice in Cook County, Ill. (Greylord Com.) 1984-90, bd. dirs. Chgo. Crime Commn., 1986-91; mem. Ill. Supreme Ct. Spl. Commn. on the Adminstrn. of Justice, Ill. Supreme Ct. Appointment, 1991. Served to capt. JAGC, AUS, 1955-58. Named One of Ten Outstanding Young Men in Chgo., Chgo. Jr. Assn. Commerce and Industry, 1960, 65; recipient Outstanding Legislator award Ill. Gen. Assembly, 1966. Mem. ABA (com. consumer fin. svcs. 1975—, ho. dels. 1981-90, judicial adminstrn. divsn. 1980-95, mem. exec. com. lawyer's conf. 1994-95, mem. bench and bar rels. com. 1994-96, mem. adv. com. to Ill. State Del., Jud. Adminstrn. Divsn. in Recognition of Leadership in Improvement of Adminstrn. of Justice award 1993), Ill. State Bar Assn. (pres. 1975-76, com. on fed. jud. and related appointments; Abraham Lincoln Legal Writing award 1959, mem. adv. com., state del., 1994—, bd. dirs.), Chgo. Bar Assn. (bd. mgrs. 1965-66), Fred B. Snite Found. (sec., counsel 1976-90), Gertrude and Walter Swanson Found. (sole trustee 1995—), Mid-Am. Club Chgo. Republican. Roman Catholic. Finance.

**PUSHINSKY, JON**, lawyer; b. N.Y.C., May 30, 1954; s. Paul and Harriet (Rosenberg) P.; m. M. Jean Clickner, July 31, 1982; children: Matthew Clickner-Pushinsky, Jeremy Clickner-Pushinsky. BA, U. Pa., 1976, MA, 1976; JD, U. Pitts., 1979. Bar: Pa. 1979, U.S. Dist. Ct. (we. dist.) Pa. 1979, U.S. Ct. Appeals (3rd cir.) 1980, U.S. Supreme Ct. 1988. Staff counsel W.Va. Legal Svcs. Plan, Wheeling, 1979-80; pvt. practice Pitts., 1980—. Dem. candidate Superior Ct. Pa., 1993, 95; solicitor Cmty. Human Svcs. Corp., Pitts., 1992—; consulting lawyer ARC-Allegheny, Pitts., 1981—. Recipient Civil Libertarian award ACLU of Pa., 1994, Cmty. Citation of Merit Allegheny County Mental Health/Mental Retardation Bd., 1992, Cert. Appreciation Pitts. Commn. on Human Rels., 1992. Mem. Pa. Trial Lawyers Assn., Allegheny County Bar Assn. (appellate practice com., civil rights com.). Democrat. Avocations: reading, hiking, movies. Civil rights, Constitutional, General practice. Office: 429 4th Ave Pittsburgh PA 15219-1500

**PUSTILNIK, DAVID DANIEL**, lawyer; b. N.Y.C., Mar. 10, 1931; s. Philip and Belle (Gerberholtz) P.; m. Helen Jean Todd, Aug. 15, 1959; children: Palma Elyse, Leslie Royce, Bradley Todd. BS, NYU, 1952, JD, 1958, LLM, 1959; postgrad., Air War Coll., 1976. Bar: N.Y. 1959, U.S. Supreme Ct. 1962, Conn. 1964. Legis. tax atty. legis. and regulations div. Office Chief Counsel, IRS, Washington, 1959-63; atty. Travelers Ins. Co., Hartford, Conn., 1963-68; assoc. counsel Travelers Ins. Co., Hartford, 1968-73, counsel, 1973-75, assoc. gen. counsel, 1975-87, dep. gen. counsel, 1987-93; mem. adv. coun. Hartford Inst. on Ins. Taxation, 1978-93, vice chmn., 1991-92, chmn., 1992-93. Grad. editor NYU Tax Law Rev., 1958-59. Trustee Hartford Coll. for Women, 1985-91; life sponsor Am. Tax Policy Inst.; dir. Congregation Beth Yam, 1996—. Served to col. USAFR. Kenneson fellow NYU, 1958-59. Fellow Am. Coll. Tax Counsel; mem. ABA (chmn. ins. cos. com. 1976-78), Am. Coun. Life Ins. (chmn. co. tax com. 1982-84), Am. Ins. Assn. (chmn. tax com. 1979-81), Assn. Life Ins. Counsel (chmn. tax sect. 1991-93), Twentieth Century Club, Sea Pines Country Club (co-chair social com. 1997—). Corporate taxation, Pension, profit-sharing, and employee benefits.

**PUTMAN, (JAMES) MICHAEL**, lawyer; b. San Antonio, May 12, 1948; s. Harold David and Elizabeth Finley (Henderson) P.; m. Kris J. Bird. B.B.A., S.W. Tex. State U., 1969; J.D., St. Mary's U., 1972. Bar: Tex. 1972, U.S. Dist. Ct. (we. dist.) Tex. 1980, U.S. Ct. Appeals (5th and 11th cirs.) 1981; cert. personal injury trial law specialist Tex. Bd. Legal Specialization. Ptnr. Putman & Putman (inc. 1981), San Antonio, 1972-81, officer, dir., 1981—. Mem. ATLA, State Bar Tex., Nat. Employment Lawyers Assn., Tex. Trial Lawyers Assn. (assoc. dir. 1995, dir. 1996—), San Antonio Trial Lawyers Assn. (dir., officer 1975—), Am. Bd. Trial Advocates. Personal injury, Product liability, Labor. Office: 310 S Saint Marys St Fl 27 San Antonio TX 78205-3113

**PUTMAN, PHILIP A.**, lawyer, consultant, real estate broker; b. Erie, Pa., Mar. 25, 1935; m. Mimi Putman, July 7, 1957; children: Ben, Linda. Student, Long Beach (Calif.) Coll., 1961; BS, U. Calif., Long Beach, 1963, MS, 1967; JD, Pepperdine U., Westminster, Calif., 1971. Bar: Calif.; real estate broker, Calif.; cert. bus. opportunity appraiser. Mfg. liaison engr. Autonetics, Anaheim, Calif., 1962-63; mfg. engr. Douglas Aircraft Co., Long Beach, 1959-61, econs. advisor to v.p. plans, 1964-73; sr. trial atty. Putman & Assocs. Law Offices, Huntington Beach, Calif., 1973—; sr. broker A+ Properties, Huntington Beach, 1978-88; pres., CEO Nucleus Engring., Bell Gardens, Calif., 1988-91; sr. cons. Exodus Cons. Svcs., Huntington Beach, 1994—; CEO, cons. Allied Profl. Network, Costa Mesa, Calif., 1998—; judge pro tem Calif. State Bar, Santa Ana, 1985. Author: Discom Economic Model, 1969, Do Your Own Copyright, 1975, Strive to Be Happy, 1991, Forgiven Gospel Songs, 1993. Mem. Huntington Beach Econs. Adv. Coun., 1974. Served with USAF, 1954-58, Japan. Mem. ABA, Calif. Trial Laweyrs Assn. Republican. Christian. Avocations: guitar, writing and singing gospel music. Administrative and regulatory, Immigration, naturalization, and customs, Appellate. Office: Allied Prof Network 666 Baker St # 215 Costa Mesa CA 92626-4428

**PUTMAN, TIMOTHY JOSEPH**, lawyer; b. Massilon, Ohio, Mar. 17, 1954; s. Norman Joseph and Phyllis (Kraft) P. BA, Ohio State U., 1977; JD, U. Akron, 1984. Bar: Ohio 1985, U.S. Dist. Ct. (no. dist.) Ohio 1986, U.S. Ct. Appeals (6th dist.) 1986. Auditor Pub. Utilities Commn. Ohio, Columbus, 1977-78; adminstrv. asst. Ohio Senate, Columbus, 1978-79; v.p. Canton (Ohio) Indsl. Pk., Ltd., 1979-85; pres. Putman Properties, Inc., Canton, 1985—; pvt. practice Canton, 1985—. Active Leadership Canton, 1988, constrn. div. United Way, Cen. Stark County, Ohio, 1987; mem. YMCA; exec., Rep. committeeman, Stark County, 1980—. Mem. ABA, Ohio State Bar Assn., Stark County Bar Assn. Contracts commercial, Real property, General corporate. Home: 1486 Alexandria Pkwy SE Canton OH 44709-4814 Office: 4810 Munson St NW Canton OH 44718-3613

**PUTNAM, RICHARD JOHNSON**, federal judge; b. Abbeville, La., Sept. 27, 1913; s. Robert Emmett and Mathilde (Young) P.; m. Dorethea Gooch, Jan. 27, 1940; children: Richard Johnson, Claude Robert, Mary Stacy, Cynthia Anne. BS cum laude, Springhill Coll., Mobile, 1934; LLB, Loyola U., New Orleans, 1937. Bar: La. 1937. Pvt. practice law Abbeville, 1937-54; dist. atty. 15th Jud. Dist., La., 1948-54; judge 15th Jud. Dist. Ct., La., 1954-61; dist. judge U.S. Dist. Ct. (we. dist.) La., La., 1961-75; sr. U.S. dist. judge Lafayette, La., 1975—; temporary judge U.S. Ct. Appeals for 5th cir., 1983; rep. fed. cts. Coun. La Law Inst., 1976-89, sr. mem. inst. coun., 1989—; liaison judge for we. dist. 5th Cir. Archives - Hist. Com. , 1980; chmn. sr. judges adv. bd. Fed. Judges Assn., 1983—. Served from ensign to lt. USNR, 1942-45. Recipient Student Coun. Key Loyola U., 1937. Mem. Dist. Judges Assn., ABA, La. Bar Assn., Fifth Cir. Dist. Judges Assn., Am. Legion, VFW, St. Thomas Moore Soc. (Svc. award 1937), Delta Theta Phi. Lodge: KC. Office: US Dist Ct 300 Fed Bldg 800 Lafayette St Ste 3900 Lafayette LA 70501-6800

**PUTNEY, LAURA LEA**, lawyer; b. Mpls., Aug. 28, 1970; d. Harold Lee and Lorraine Ellen Putney. BA, Furman U., 1992; JD, Harvard U., 1995. Bar: Ga. 1995, N.Y. 1997. Assoc. Alston & Bird, Atlanta, 1995-96, Kauff, McClain & McGuire, N.Y.C., 1996—. Labor. Office: Kauff McClain & McGuire 950 3d Ave Ste 1500 New York NY 10022

**PUTNEY, WAINSCOTT WALKER**, lawyer; b. Pitts., Nov. 10, 1957; s. Charles Walker and Karen (Albright) P.; m. Sharon Lynn Smith, Apr. 11, 1982. BS in Physics, Va. Mil. Inst., 1978; JD, U. Tulsa, 1981; LLM, George Washington U., 1991. Bar: Fla. 1981, D.C. 1990, Va. 1993, U.S. Dist. Ct. (mid. dist.) Fla. 1981, U.S. Ct. Appeals (11th cir.) 1984, U.S. Dist. Ct. (so. dist.) Fla. 1985, U.S. Ct. Appeals (D.C. cir.) 1987, U.S. Dist. Ct. (ea. and we. dists.) Va. 1995, U.S. Ct. Appeals (4th cir.) 1993, U.S. Ct. Fed. Claims, 1989, U.S. Ct. Appeals (fed. cir.) 1990, U.S. Supreme Ct. 1985. Assoc. Sanders, McEwan, Mims & Martinez, Orlando, Fla., 1981-85; pvt. practice Orlando, 1985-89; trial atty. U.S. Dept. Justice, Washington, 1989—; bankruptcy trustee, Orlando, 1985-89; lectr. comml. law Mary Washington coll., Fredericksburg, Va., 1997—. Contbr. articles to profl. jours. Precinct committeeman Orange County Rep. Exec. Com., 1987-88. Recipient cert. of appreciation Legal Aid Soc., 1988. Mem. Fla. Bar Assn. (bd. govs. young lawyers divsn. 1991-93), IEEE. Bankruptcy, Taxation, general, Criminal.

**PUTTER, DAVID SETH**, lawyer; b. N.Y.C., Mar. 11, 1944; s. Norton Seth and Ruth Crystal P.; m. Lee Dow, Apr. 26, 1987. BA in Biology, Beloit Coll., 1965; student, U. Granada, Spain, 1964; JD, Syracuse U., 1968. Bar: Vt. 1970, N.Y. 1971, U.S. Dist. Ct. Vt. 1970, U.S. Ct. Appeals (2d cir.) 1973, U.S. Ct. Claims 1998. Atty. Putter & Carrington, Arlington, Vt., 1970-73; Bennington County pub. defender State of Vt., Bennington, 1973-76; law clk. to Superior Ct. judges State of Vt., Burlington, 1976-78; asst. atty. gen. State of Vt., Montpelier, 1979-81; lawyer Putter & Unger, Montpelier, 1981-88, Saxer, Anderson, Wolinsky & Sunshine, Montpelier, 1988—. Contbr. articles to profl. jours. acting Superior Ct. judge, 1997—; chair legal panel ACLU Vt., 1988—; sponsored advisor on assembly, free press, free speech USIA, Lusaka, Zambia, Kampala, Uganda, 1996. Recipient Jonathan Chase award ACLU Vt., 1991, 97. Avocations: hiking, camping, theater, travel, music (folk and rock). Appellate, General civil litigation, Constitutional. Home: 6 Towne St Montpelier VT 05602-4231 Office: Saxer Anderson Wolinsky & Sunshine PC 15 E State St Montpelier VT 05602-3010

**PUTTOCK, JOHN LAWRENCE**, lawyer; b. Santa Barbara, Calif., Apr. 15, 1949; s. Lawrence Marion and Kathleen Puttock; m. Erika Sakurai, Oct. 7, 1978; children: Lucas A., Eric. BA in Anthropology, U. Calif., Santa Barbara, 1971; JD, Golden Gate U., 1976. Bar: Calif. 1977, U.S. Dist. Ct. (cen. dist.) Calif. 1981, U.S. Ct. Appeals (3d cir.) 1997. Assoc. Law Offices of Fujii & Toda, Tokyo, 1977-81; dir. chief counsel Tokio Marine Mgmt., Inc., Los Angeles, 1981—; bd. dirs. Champion SAE House Corps. Editor, translator: Products Liability in the U.S., 1983. Founder, pres. Roy and Roxie Campanella Physical Therapy Scholarship Foun., 1996—; founder, chmn. Forgotten Heroes Found., 1999—. Alexander Bee scholar, 1973-74, Calif. State scholar, 1967-71. Mem. ABA, Sigma Alpha Epsilon. E-mail: forgottenheroes@msn.com. Intellectual property, Personal injury, Private international.

**PYATT, JOYCE A.**, lawyer; b. St. Louis, Sept. 21, 1958; d. Louie Kenneth and E. Jean Pyatt; m. Richard Michael Vreeland (div. June 1987); 1 child, Elizabeth Lauren Vreeland. BS in Edn., U. Mo., St. Louis, 1984; JD, St. Louis U., 1993. Bar: Mo. 1993. Pvt. practice Hillsboro, Mo., 1993—. Family and matrimonial, Criminal, Personal injury. Office: PO Box 207 10626 Highway 21 Hillsboro MO 63050-5039

**PYFER, JOHN FREDERICK, JR.**, lawyer; b. Lancaster, Pa., July 25, 1946; s. John Frederick and Myrtle Ann (Greiner) P.; m. Carol Trice, Nov. 25, 1970; children: John Frederick III, Carol Lee. Grad. cum laude, Peddie Sch., 1965; BA in Polit. Sci. and Econs., Haverford Coll., 1969; JD, Vanderbilt U., 1972. Bar: Pa. 1972, U.S. Dist. Ct. (ea. dist.) Pa. 1973, U.S. Tax Ct. 1975, U.S. Supreme Ct. 1975, U.S. Dist. Ct. (mid. dist.) Pa. 1984, U.S. Ct. Appeals (3d cir.) 1986. Law clk. to presiding justice Ct. Common Pleas, Lancaster, Pa., 1972-74; assoc. Xakellis, Perezous & Mongiovi, 1972-76; founding ptnr. Allison & Pyfer, Lancaster, 1976-85, pres. Pyfer & Assocs., 1986-88, Pyfer & Reese, 1988—; prof. para-legal tng. Pa. State Extension Service, 1989-93; fed. ct. mediator, 1992—. Pres. Lancaster-Lebanon Coun. Boy Scouts Am. 1989-93, coun. commr. 1987-89, mem. nat. com., 1996—, Eagle Scout with 3 palms, God and Country award, God and Svc. award, Wood Badge, Scouter's Key, Vigil Honor, Order of Arrow, Disting. Commnr. award, Silver Beaver award, West fellow, 1910 Soc., Nat. Jamboree, 1960, 64, 85, 89, 93, 97, World Jamboree, 1967, 87, 95, 98, Japan Jamboree, 1990, Can. Jamboree, 1993; bd. dirs. World of Scouting Mus. Fellow Am. Bd. Criminal Lawyers, Lancaster Heritage Ctr.; mem. ABA (First prize Howard C. Schwab Nat. Essay Contest in Writing, 1972), ATLA, SAR, Nat. Assn. Criminal Def. Lawyers, Pa. Trial Lawyers Assn., Pa. Criminal Def. Lawyers Assn., Am. Arbitration Assn., Pa. Bar Assn., Lancaster Bar Assn., Inns Ct. (founder, pres. W. Hensel Brown, 1993-94), Christian Lawyers Soc., Train Collector Assn. (divsn. pres. 1984), Am. Orchid Soc. (affiliate pres. 1998). Republican. United Ch. of Christ (elder, pres. 1989, 95). Clubs: Lions (pres. 1980-82) (Willow Street, Pa.); Masons (Lancaster). Contbr. articles to law revs., law treatises. Criminal, Family and matrimonial, General practice. Home: 1100 Little Brook Rd Lancaster PA 17603-6116 Office: Pyfer & Reese 128 N Lime St Lancaster PA 17602-2951

**PYKE, JOHN SECREST, JR.**, lawyer, polymers company executive; b. Lakewood, Ohio, July 11, 1938; s. John S. and Elma B. Pyke; student Haverford Coll., 1956-58; BA, Columbia Coll., 1960, postgrad. Columbia Sch. Grad. Faculties, 1960-61; JD, Columbia Law Sch., 1964; m. Judith A., Dec. 26, 1970; 1 child, John Secrest, III. Bar: N.Y. 1965. Assoc. firm Townsend & Lewis (now Thacher, Proffit & Wood), N.Y.C., 1964-68; atty. M.A. Hanna Co., Cleve., 1968—, sec., 1973—, v.p., gen. counsel, 1979—. Trustee, Western Res. Acad., Hudson, Ohio, 1976—. Mem. ABA, Assn. Bar City N.Y., Am. Soc. Corp. Secs., Am. Corp. Counsel Assn., Union Club, Clifton Club, Cleve. Yachting Club. Author: Landmark Preservation, 1969, 2d edit., 1972. General corporate, Mergers and acquisitions, Securities. Office: MA Hanna Co 200 Public Sq Ste 36-5000 Cleveland OH 44114-2304

**PYLE, KURT H.**, lawyer; b. Oakland, Calif., Mar. 11, 1941; s. Thomas H. and Jean W. P.; m. Beth R., Apr. 30, 1977; children: Christopher, Brendan, Hilary. BS, U. Calif., Berkeley, 1962; JD, Hastings Coll. Law, 1965. Bar: Calif. 1966, U.S. Dist. Ct. (ctrl. dist.) Calif. 1966, D.C. 1972, U.S. Ct. Appeals (9th cir.) 1978, U.S. Dist. Ct. (no. and so. dists.) Calif. 1982, U.S. Dist. Ct. (ea. dist.) Calif. 1983, U.S. Claims Ct. 1984, U.S. Tax Ct. 1984. Capt., judge advocate USAF, Wright-Patterson AFB, Ohio, 1962-65; from atty. to mng. ptnr. Schramm & Raddue, Santa Barbara, Calif., 1965-96; ptnr. Reicker, Clough, Pfau & Pyle, Santa Barbara, 1996—. Bd. dirs. Santa Barbara Counseling Ctr., 1996—. Mem. ATLA, Santa Barbara County Bar Assn., Assn. Bus. Trial Lawyers, Consumers Attys. Calif., Santa Barbara Inn of Ct. General civil litigation, Labor, Personal injury. Home: 520 Grove Ln Santa Barbara CA 93105-2428 Office: Reicker Clough Pfau & Pyle PO Box 1470 Santa Barbara CA 93102-1470

**PYLE, LUTHER ARNOLD**, lawyer; b. Pontotoc County, Miss., Dec. 5, 1912; s. Thomas Luther and Lillie Dean (Reynolds) P.; m. Elizabeth McWillie Browne, Aug. 9, 1941; children—William A., Robert Bradford, Ben Cameron. LL.B., Cumberland U., 1936, J.D., 1960. Bar: Miss. 1936, D.C. 1974, U.S. Dist. Ct. (no. dist.) Miss. 1936, U.S. Dist. Ct. (so. dist.) Miss. 1946, U.S. Ct. Apls. (5th cir.) 1946, U.S. Ct. Appeals (11th cir.) 1981, U.S. Supreme Ct. 1959. Sole practice, New Albany, Miss., 1936-42; pros. atty. Union County, Miss., 1940-42; assoc. Cameron & Wills, Jackson, Miss., 1946-52; chancellor 5th chancery ct. dist. Miss., 1952-58; ptnr. Watkins, Pyle, Ludlam, Winter & Stennis, Jackson, 1958-80; ptnr. Barnett, Alagia & Pyle, Jackson, 1981-83; of counsel Pyle, Dreher, Mills & Dye, 1993—; participant World Law Conf., Manila, 1977, Madrid, 1979; bd. dirs. Miss. Bar Commn., 1959-63. Mem. exec. bd. Andrew Jackson council Boy Scouts Am., 1946; bd. govs. Jackson Little Theatre, 1964-67; pres. Jackson Jr. C. of C., 1949; chmn. downtown div. United Givers, Mental Health Assn. Served to lt. col. JAG Corps, U.S. Army, 1942-46. Recipient Silver Beaver award Boy Scouts Am. Fellow Miss. Bar Found.; mem. Fed. Bar Assn., ABA (chmn. continuing legal edn. 1958-74), Am. Judicature Soc. (dir.), Hinds County Bar Assn., Miss. Bar Assn. (chmn. jud. adminstrn. com. 1966-70), U.S. Supreme Ct. Hist. Soc., U.S. C. of C., Jackson C. of C. (dir. 1960-63), Miss. Dept. Res. Officers Assn. (pres. 1950), Am. Legion (past comdr.). Episcopalian. Clubs: University (dir. 1972-92), Jackson Country, Annandale Golf. Contbr. articles to profl. jours. Federal civil litigation, State civil litigation, General practice. Home: 1803 E Northside Dr Jackson MS 39211-6029

**PYLE, WALTER K.**, lawyer; b. Chgo.; s. Garland K. and Agnes G. (O'Connor) P.; m. Frances S. Kaminer; children: Michael K., James B., Isaac David. JD, Loyola U., Chgo., 1964; postgrad, NYU, 1964-65. Bar: Ill. 1965, Calif. 1981, U.S. Supreme Ct. 1972, U.S. Ct. Appeals (1st cir.) 1979, U.S. Ct. Appeals (7th cir.) 1992, U.S. Ct. Appeals (8th cir.) 1977, U.S. Ct. Appeals (9th cir.) 1980, U.S. Dist. Ct. (no. dist.) Ill. 1965, U.S. Dist. Ct. (no. dist.) Calif. 1981, U.S. Dist. Ct. (ea. dist.) Calif. 1982, U.S. Dist. Ct. (cen. dist.) Calif. 1989, U.S. Dist. Ct. (so. dist.) Calif. 1991; cert. specialist Appellate Law, State Bar Calif., Bd. Legal Specialization. Asst. state's atty. Criminal Div. Cook County (Ill.) State's Atty.'s Office, Chgo., 1967-69; asst. atty. gen. Ill. Atty. Gen.'s Office, Chgo., 1969-78; pvt. practice law Chgo., 1978-80, San Francisco, 1981-88, Berkeley, Calif., 1988—; arbitrator Alameda County (Calif.) Superior Ct., 1993—; judge pro tempore Oakland (Calif.) Mcpl. Ct., 1989—. Mem. ABA, Calif. Bar Assn., Ill. Bar Assn., Alameda County Bar Assn. (dir. 1992-93), DuPage County Bar Assn., Bar Assn. San Francisco, Chgo. Bar Assn., Calif. Assn. Toxicologists. Avocations: running, cooking. Construction, Criminal, General civil litigation. Office: 2039 Shattuck Ave Ste 202 Berkeley CA 94704-1150

**PYM, BRUCE MICHAEL**, lawyer; b. Alameda, Calif., Sept. 29, 1942; s. Leonard A. and Willamay (Strandberg) P. B.B.A., U. Wash., 1964, J.D., 1967. Bar: Wash. 1967, U.S. Dist. Ct. (we. dist.) Wash. 1968, U.S. Ct. Appeals (9th cir.) 1968, U.S. Tax Ct. 1969, U.S. Supreme Ct. 1971. Law clk. Wash. State Supreme Ct., Olympia, 1967-68; assoc. Graham & Dunn, Seattle, 1968-73, shareholder, 1973-92; ptnr. Heller, Ehrman, White & McAuliffe, Seattle, 1992—; mng. ptnr. Northwest Offices, 1994-99. Bd. dirs. United Way of King County, 1986-92, chmn., 1990. Mem. ABA, Wash. State Bar Assn., King County Bar Assn. (pres. 1984-85). General corporate, Securities, Mergers and acquisitions. Office: Heller Ehrman White & McAuliffe 701 5th Ave Ste 6100 Seattle WA 98104-7098

**PYUN, MATTHEW SUNG KWAN**, lawyer; b. Honolulu, Mar. 21, 1937; s. Matthew S.K. and Elsie S.O. (Chee) P.; m. Mary Ann Kagawa, Feb. 26, 1959; children: Leslie S.H., Anne K. BBA, U. Hawaii, 1959; LLB, Drake U., 1963. Bar: Hawaii 1964, U.S. Ct. Appeals (9th cir.) 1964. Law clk., bailiff U.S. Dist. Ct. Hawaii, 1964; dep. corp. counsel City and County of Honolulu, 1965; atty. Legal Aid Soc. Hawaii, 1965-68; sole practice Honolulu, 1968—; judge Honolulu Dist. Ct. 1st cir., 1981-84. Mem. Rep. Nat. Com. Served with USAF, 1960-61. Mem. ABA, ATLA, Am. Judicature Soc., Honolulu Club, Phi Alpha Delta, Phi Kappa Pi. Episcopalian. Consumer commercial, General civil litigation, General practice. Office: 615 Piikoi St Ste 1107 Honolulu HI 96814-3141

**QIAN, JIN**, law librarian; b. Shanghai, China; came to the U.S., 1987; s. Bingchun and Shiyi Qian. BA, Shanghai Tchrs. U., ;, 1981; MA, Fordham U., 1988; MLS, St. John's U., 1990. Libr. trainee N.Y. Pub. Libr., N.Y.C., 1988; reference asst. N.Y. Hist. Soc., N.Y.C., 1989-90; asst. libr. Wilson, Elser et al., N.Y.C., 1990-92, head libr., 1992—. Presdl. scholar Fordham U., 1987. Mem. Law Libr. Assn. Greater N.Y., Am. Assn. Law Librs., Spl. Libr. Assn., ALA. Home: PO Box 811 New York NY 10163-0811 Office: Wilson Elser & Moskowitz 150 E 42nd St New York NY 10017-5612

**QUACKENBUSH, JUSTIN LOWE**, federal judge; b. Spokane, Wash., Oct. 3, 1929; s. Carl Clifford and Marian Huldah (Lowe) Q.; m. Marie McAtee; children: Karl Justin, Kathleen Marie, Robert Craig. BA, U. Idaho, 1951; LLB, Gonzaga U., Spokane, 1957. Bar: Wash. 1957. Dep. pros. atty.

Spokane County, 1957-59; ptnr. Quackenbush, Dean, Bailey & Henderson, Spokane, 1959-80; dist. judge U.S. Dist. Ct. (ea. dist.) Wash., Spokane, 1980—, now sr. judge; part-time instr. Gonzaga U. Law Sch., 1960-67. Chmn. Spokane County Planning Commn., 1969-73. Served with USN, 1951-54. Mem. Wash. Bar Assn., Spokane County Bar Assn. (trustee 1976-78), Internat. Footprint Assn. (nat. pres. 1967), Spokane C. of C. (trustee, exec. com. 1978-79), Shriners. Episcopalian. Office: US Dist Ct PO Box 1432 Spokane WA 99210-1432

**QUADE, VICTORIA CATHERINE,** editor, writer, playwright, producer; b. Chgo., Aug. 15, 1953; d. Victor and Virginia (Uryasz) Q.; m. Charles J. White III, Feb. 15, 1986 (div. Aug. 1996); children: Michael, David, Catherine. BS in Journalism, No. Ill. U., 1974. Staff reporter news divsn. The News-Tribune, LaSalle, Ill., 1975-77; staff writer news divsn. The News-Sun, Waukegan, Ill., 1977-81; staff writer ABA Jour., Chgo., 1981-85; mng. editor ABA Press, Chgo., 1985-90, editor, 1990—, sr. editor, 1994—. Author: (poetry) Rain and Other Poems, 1976, Laughing Eyes, 1979, Two Under the Covers, 1981; playwright Late Nite Catechism: Saints, Sisters & Ejaculation, 1993, (with Maripat Donovan) Room for Advancement, 1994, Mr. Nanny, 1997, (musical) Lost in Wonderland, 1998; producer Late Nite Catechism and Mr. Nanny; contbr. to numerous anthologies and publs. Recipient numerous awards from Soc. Nat. Assn. Publs., AP, UPI. Mem. Am. Soc. Bus. Press Editors (award), Chgo. Newspaper Guild (award), Am. Soc. Assn. Execs. (Gold Circle award 1989, 90). Avocations: traveling, photography. Office: ABA 750 N Lake Shore Dr Chicago IL 60611-4403

**QUADRI, FAZLE RAB,** lawyer, government official; b. Dacca, Pakistan, Aug. 5, 1948; came to U.S., 1967; s. Gholam Moula and Jehan (Ara) Q.; children: Ryan F., Tania M. AA, Western Wyo. Coll., 1969; BA, Calif. State U., 1972; JD, Western State U., 1978; postgrad. cert. in criminal advocacy, U. Calif., San Francisco, 1988. Bar: Calif. 1981. Sr. adminstrv. analyst San Bernardino County, Calif., 1978-82, acting legis. adv., 1982, sr. legis. analyst, 1982-90, county legis. analyst, 1990-93, acting pub. defender, 1984; dist. counsel Mojave Desert Air Quality Mgmt. Dist., Victorville, Calif., 1993—; dist. cousnel Antelope Valley Air Pollution Control Dist., 1997—; local gov. rep. State Hazardous Waste Mgmt. Council, Sacramento, Calif., 1982-84; chmn.'s rep. County Projects Selection Coms., San Bernardino, 1983-91; county rep. South Coast Air Quality Mgmt. Dist., El Monte, Calif., 1983-87. Advisor Mcpl. Adv. Couns., San Bernardino, 1984-87; mem. Law Libr. Bd. Trustees, 1984-85, 93-95. Mem. ABA, Calif. Bar Assn., Calif. State U. Alumni Assn. (bd. dirs. 1985-86), Masons, Shriners. Republican. Islamic. Avocations: personal computers, reading, music, karate, water sports. Home: 535 E Mariposa Dr Redlands CA 92373-7351 Office: Mojave Desert AQMD 15428 Civic Dr Ste 300 Victorville CA 92392-2383

**QUALE, ANDREW CHRISTOPHER, JR.,** lawyer; b. Boston, July 7, 1942; s. Andrew Christopher and Luella (Meland) Q.; m. Sally Sterling Ellis, Oct. 15, 1977; children: Andrew, Addison. BA magna cum laude, Harvard U., 1963, LLB cum laude, 1966; postgrad., Cambridge (Eng.) U., 1966-67. Bar: Mass. 1967, N.Y. 1971. Fellow Internat. Legal Ctr., Bogota, Colombia, 1967-68; cons. Republic of Colombia, Bogota, 1968-69; assoc. Cleary, Gottlieb, Steen and Hamilton, N.Y.C., 1969-75; ptnr. Coudert Brothers, N.Y.C., 1975-82, Sidley and Austin, N.Y.C., 1982—; adj. prof. Sch. of Law U. Va., Charlottesville, 1976-88; cons. privatizations World Bank, UN, Harvard Inst. Internat. Devel., 1982—. Contbr. to profl. publs. Pres. Bronxville (N.Y.) Sch. Bd., 1991-93; founder, bd. dirs. Bronxville Sch. Found., 1991-95, 96—; bd. dirs. Coun. The Ams. Mem. ABA, Assn. Bar City N.Y., N.Y. State Bar Assn., N.Y.C. Bar Assn. (chmn. Inter-Am. affairs com. 1982-85), Colombian-Am. Assn. (v.p., bd. dirs.), Bronxville Field Club, Norfolk (Conn.) Country Club, Doolittle Lake Co. (Norfolk, bd. dirs.). Banking, Mergers and acquisitions, Private international. Office: Sidley & Austin 875 3rd Ave Fl 14 New York NY 10022-6293

**QUALLS, ALVIE EDWARD, II,** lawyer; b. Huntington, W. Va., Dec. 3, 1960; s. Alvie Edward and Marion Inez (Clay) Q. BA, Marshall U., 1984, MA, 1986; JD, U. Tulsa, 1992. Bar: W. Va. 1992, U.S. Dist. Ct. (so. dist.) W. Va. 1992. Legal asst. Rood and Mills, Legal Corp., Huntington, W. Va., 1982-84; law clerk W. Va. Supreme Ct. of Appeals, Huntington, W. Va., 1992-94; attorney W. Va. Pub. Defender Office, Huntington, W. Va., 1994—. Vol. U. Tulsa Coll. Law; mem. City of Huntington Forces 2000 com., 1984, Covall County Democratic Party. Kevin Russell Bowen scholar Marshall U. Student Govt., Huntington, 1982. Mem. U. Tulsa Coll. Law Regional Alumni Bd., Cabell County Democratic Women's Club, Cabell County Bar Assn., Phi Alpha Delta, Pi Sigma Alpha, Pi Alpha Theta. Mem. Ch. of God. Avocations: working out, reading, travel, sports. Office: Mundy and Adkins 422 9th St Huntington WV 25701-1485

**QUALLS, STEVEN DANIEL,** lawyer; b. Detroit, May 24, 1967; s. Hugh Pharris Qualls and Lenora Ann Allen; m. Elizabeth Lynn Crosier, June 21, 1990; children: Joshua Michael, Emily Elizabeth. BS, Tenn. Tech. U., 1992; JD, Nashville Sch. Law, 1996. Law clk. Cameron & Chaffin, Cookeville, Tenn., 1992-96; atty. Cameron & Chaffin, Cookeville, 1996-98; atty., sr. ptnr. Qualls & Fry PLLC, Cookeville, 1998—; mem. adv. bd. First Am. Nat. Bank, Cookeville, 1996-98; cons. Jackson Nat. Bank, Cookeville, 1996-98. Bd. dirs. Montessori Childrens Sch., Cookeville, 1993-98; treas. State Senate Charlotte Burks, Cookeville, 1998; active Dem. Party Putnam County, Cookeville, 1998. Mem. Noun Day Lions Clu b(v.p. 1996-98). Avocations: racquetball, tennis, golf. Family and matrimonial, Real property, Criminal. Home: 4900 Rocky Point Rd Cookeville TN 38506-8542 Office: Qualls & Fry PLLC 16 S Washington Ave Cookeville TN 38501-3980

**QUANDT, JOSEPH EDWARD,** lawyer, educator; b. Port Huron, Mich., May 21, 1963; s. Herbert Raymond and Mary Katherine (West) Q.; m. Christine Ann Reilly, Aug. 21, 1993. BA, Oakland U., 1990; JD, Thomas M. Cooley Law Sch., Lansing, Mich., 1993. Bar: Mich. 1994, U.S. Dist. Ct. (ea. and we. dists.) Mich. 1994. Exec. dir. Lord & Taylor, Sterling Heights, Mich., 1985-90; compliance and enforcement specialist Mich. Dept. Environ. Quality, Lansing, 1990-93, adv. bd., 1997—; assoc. Stowe, Draling & Boyd, Traverse City, Mich., 1993-94, Smith & Johnson, Traverse City, 1994-98; ptnr. Menmuir, Zimmerman, Kuhn, Taylor and Quandt, Traverse City, 1998—; lectr., commentator Inst. CLE, Ann Arbor, Mich., 1994—; adj. prof. Thomas M. Cooley Law Sch., 1997—. Contbr. articles to profl. jours. Bd. dirs. Involved Citizens Enterprises, Traverse City, 1995—. Mem. Nat. Honor Soc. for Polit. Scientists, Ancient Order Hibernians, Pi Sigma Alpha. Republican. Roman Catholic. Avocations: ice hockey, golf, fly fishing. Environmental, Natural resources, Real property. Office: Menmuir Zimmerman Kuhn et al 122 W State St Traverse City MI 49684-2404

**QUARLES, JAMES LINWOOD, III,** lawyer; b. Huntington, W.Va., Oct. 12, 1946; s. James Linwood Jr. and Beatrice (Hardwick) Q.; m. Sharon Taft, Dec. 20, 1969; children: Jessica, Matthew. BS cum laude, Denison U., 1968; JD cum laude, Harvard U., 1972. Bar: Mass. 1974, U.S. Dist. Ct. Mass. 1975, U.S. Ct. Appeals (D.C. cir.) 1975, U.S. Ct. Appeals (6th cir.) 1979, U.S. Supreme Ct. 1980, D.C. 1981, U.S. Ct. Appeals (2d cir.) 1981, U.S. Ct. Appeals (1st and 4th cirs.) 1983, Md. 1985. Law clk. to presiding justice U.S. Dist. Ct. Md., Balt., 1972-73; with Watergate Spl. Pros. Force, Washington, 1973-75; from assoc. to sr. ptnr. Hale and Dorr, Boston and Washington, 1975—. Mem. Am. Law Inst. Democrat. Federal civil litigation, Intellectual property, Securities. Office: Hale & Dorr Ste 1000 1455 Pennsylvania Ave NW Washington DC 20004-1085

**QUARLES, WILLIAM DANIEL,** judge; b. Balt., Jan. 16, 1948; s. William Daniel and Mabel (West) Q.; m. Deborah Ann Grant, Oct. 7, 1969 (div. Aug. 1976); 1 child, Eloise. BS, U. Md., 1976; JD, Cath. U., 1979. Bar: D.C. 1979, Md. 1991. Law clk. to presiding judge U.S. Dist. Ct. Md., Balt., 1979-81; assoc. Finley Kumble, Washington, 1981-82; asst. U.S. atty. U.S. Dept. Justice, Balt., 1982-86; assoc., then ptnr. Venable, Baetjer, Howard & Civiletti, Washington, 1986-96, head litigation group, 1993-94; apptd. assoc. judge Cir. Ct. for Balt. City, 1996; permanent mem. U.S. 4th Cir. Jud. Conf., Richmond, Va., 1986—; mem. D.C. Law Revision Commn., 1989-91; nominated to U.S. Dist. Ct., Dist. Md., 1992; mem. Md. Gov.'s Commn. on Volunteerism Svc., 1994-95, 96—. Author: Summary Adjudication: Dispositive Motions and Summary Trials, 1991. Coord. Presdl. Regional Task Force on Organized Crime and Drug Law Enforcement, 1984-85. Home: 1 E Chase St Baltimore MD 21202-2526 Office: Circuit Court Bar for Baltimore City 111 N Calvert St Ste 324 Baltimore MD 21202-1966

**QUATTLEBAUM, GUY ELLIOT,** lawyer; b. West Palm Beach, Fla., Jan. 9, 1969; s. Guy Earl and Phyllis Ann Quattlebaum; m. Amy Strickland, June 3, 1995. BA, Fla. State U., 1991; JD, St. Thomas U., 1996. Bar: Fla. 1996, U.S. Dist. Ct. (so. dist.) Fla. 1997, U.S. Ct. Appeals (11th cir.) 1997. Assoc. Peterson, Bernard, Vandenberg, Zei, Geisler & Martin, P.A., West Palm Beach, 1996—. Legal writing fellow St. Thomas U. Sch. Law, Miami, Fla., 1995-96. Mem. ABA, Fla. Bar Assn., Palm Beach County Bar Assn. (exec. bd. mem. young lawyers sect. 1998-99), Cath. Lawyers Guild (exec. bd. mem. 1998-99). Republican. Roman Catholic. Fax: 561-471-5603. E-mail: guy.quattlebaum@wpb-law.com. General civil litigation, Insurance, Personal injury. Home: 322 Valencia Rd West Palm Beach FL 33401-7932 Office: Peterson Bernard et al 1550 Southern Blvd # 300 West Palm Beach FL 33406-3240

**QUATTRO, MARK HENRY,** lawyer, developer; b. Waterbury, Conn., June 23, 1955; s. Mario Peter and Elizabeth (Musco) Q.; m. Linda Ann DeVito, Sept. 13, 1986; children: Alana Rene, Nicholas Mark. BA in Urban Planning summa cum laude, U. Conn., 1978; JD, Georgetown U., 1981. Bar: Conn. 1981. Assoc. Updike, Kelley & Spellacy, Hartford, Conn., 1981-86; v.p., gen. counsel Assoc. Devel. Corp., Hartford, 1986-88, pres., 1989; pres. Mark H. Quattro, P.C., Middletown, Conn., 1989—, Quattro Devel. Corp., Middletown, 1989—, Lex Mgmt. Co., Middletown, 1989—; mng. ptnr. Middletown Profl. Park, 1989—; mng. ptnr. Middlesex Surg. Ctr., Middletown Golf Club. Vice chmn. Charter Revision Commn., Waterbury, 1978; staff dir. joint com. on environment Conn. State Legislature, 1975-78; exec. v.p. bd. govs. U. conn., Storrs, 1976-77; chmn. Canton Bd. Assessment Appeals, 1992—, chmn. Canton Econ. Devel. Agy., 1994—; mem. Canton Dem. Town Com., 1989—. Eric S. Lund scholar, 1977. Mem. Hartford County Bar Assn., Middlesex County Bar Assn., Kiwanis, Phi Beta Kappa, Phi Kappa Phi. Roman Catholic. Avocations: golf, skiing. Real property, Health, Contracts commercial. Office: 540 Saybrook Rd Middletown CT 06457-4711

**QUAY, THOMAS EMERY,** lawyer; b. Cleve., Apr. 3, 1934; s. Harold Emery and Esther Ann (Thomas) Q.; divorced; children: Martha Wyndham, Glynis Cobb, Eliza Emery; m. Winnifred B. Cutler, May 13, 1989. A.B. in Humanities magna cum laude (Univ. scholar), Princeton U., 1956; LLB (Univ. scholar), U. Pa., 1963. Bar: Pa. 1964. Assoc. Pepper, Hamilton & Scheetz, Phila., 1963-65; with William H. Rorer, Inc., Ft. Washington, Pa., 1965—; sec., counsel William H. Rorer, Inc., 1974-79, v.p., gen. counsel, sec., 1979-88; v.p. legal planning and adminstrn. Rorer Group, 1988-90; counsel Reed Smith Shaw and McClay, Phila., 1991-93; v.p., gen. counsel Athena Inst., Chester Springs, Pa., 1993—. Bd. dirs. Main Line YMCA, Ardmore, Pa., 1971-73, chmn. bd., 1972-73; editor 10th Reunion Book Princeton Class of 1956, 1966, 25th Reunion Book, 1981—, class sec., 1966-71, class v.p., 1971-81, pres., 1981-86. Lt. (j.g.) USNR, 1957-60. Recipient Svc. Commendation Main Line YMCA, 1973. Mem. ABA, Pa. Bar Assn., Phila. Bar Assn., Pharm. Mfrs. Assn. (chmn. law sect. 1983), Pa. Biotech. Assn. (chmn. legis. com., mem. exec. com. 1991-93), Phila. Drug Exch. (chmn. legis. com. 1975-78), Cannon Club of Princeton U., Sharswood Law Club of U. Pa., Princeton Club of Phila. Democrat. Presbyterian. General corporate, Intellectual property, Antitrust. Office: 601 Swedesford Rd Ste 201 Malvern PA 19355-1573

**QUAYLE, MARILYN TUCKER,** lawyer, wife of former vice president of United States; b. 1949; d. Warren and Mary Alice Tucker; m. J. Danforth Quayle, Nov. 18, 1972; children: Tucker, Benjamin, Corinne. BA in Polit. Sci., Purdue U., 1971; JD, Ind. U., 1974. Pvt. practice atty. Huntington, Ind., 1974-77; ptnr. Krieg, DeVault, Alexander & Capehart, Indpls., 1993—. Author: (with Nancy T. Northcott) Embrace the Serpent, 1992, The Campaign, 1996. General corporate, Health, Public international. Office: Quayle 2000 2929 E Camelback Rd Ste 124 Phoenix AZ 85016-4425

**QUELLO, SANDRA GAIL,** lawyer, consultant; b. Melrose Park, Ill., Mar. 28, 1954; d. Louis P. and Dorothy M. Q.; m. Joseph P. Tiscareno, Apr. 19, 1975 (div. Mar. 1986). BA, DePaul U., 1990; JD, John Marshall Law Sch., 1995. Atty. Bldg. Dept., City of Chgo., 1996; assoc. atty. Ernest T. Rossiello & Assocs., Chgo., 1997-98; pvt. practice Schaumburg, Ill., 1996—. Vol. atty. Legal Assistance Found., Chgo., 1996-98, Cook County Bar Assn., Chgo., 1997. Mem. Ill. State Bar Assn., Chgo. Bar Assn. Avocations: reading, civic activities, theater, dining, music. Office: 1821 Walden Office Sq Ste 400 Schaumburg IL 60173-4273

**QUIAT, GERALD M.,** lawyer; b. Denver, Jan. 9, 1924; s. Ira L. and Esther (Greenblatt) Q.; m. Roberta M. Nicholson, Sept. 26, 1962; children: James M., Audrey R., Melinda A., Daniel P., Ilana L., Leonard E. AA, U. Calif., Berkeley, 1942; AB, LLB, U. Denver, 1948, changed to JD, 1970. Bar: Colo. 1948, Fed. Ct. 1948, U.S. Dist. Ct. Colo. 1948, U.S. Ct. Appeals (10th cir.) 1948, U.S. Surpeme Ct. 1970. Dep. dist. atty. County of Denver, Colo., 1949-52; partner firm Quiat, Seeman & Quiat, Denver, 1952-67, Quiat & Quiat (later changed to Quiat, Bucholtz & Bull, P.C.), 1968; pres. Quiat, Bucholtz & Bull & Laff, P.C. (and predecessors), Denver, 1968-85; pvt. practice Denver, 1985—; bd. dirs., chmn. audit com. Guaranty Bank & Trust Co., Denver; past bd. dirs. and chmn. bd. ROMED, RMD, Inc. Past trustee Holding Co., Rose Med. Ctr., Denver, pres., chmn. bd. dirs., 1976-79; mem. Colo. Civil Rights Com., 1963-71, chmn., 1966-67, 69-70, hearing officer, 1963-71; bd. dirs. Am. Cancer Rsch. Ctr., Denver, chmn. bd., 1991-93; chmn. bd. Am. Med. Ctr., 1993-95; mem. nat. civil rights com., hon. mem. nat. exec. com., hon. nat. commr. Anti-Defamation League, B'nai B'rith, mem. exec. com., chmn. bd. Mountain States region, 1980-82. With inf. U.S. Army, 1942-45. Decorated Combat Infantry Badge, Bronze Star. Mem. ABA, Colo. Bar Assn., Colo. Trial Lawyers Assn. (pres. 1970-71), Am. Legion (comdr. Leyden-Chiles-Wickersham post 1 1955-56, past judge adv. Colo. dept.). Probate, Real property. Home: 8130 E Lt William Clark Rd Parker CO 80134-5825 Office: Penthouse Suite 1720 S Bellaire St Denver CO 80222-4304

**QUIAT, MARSHALL,** lawyer; b. Denver, Mar. 10, 1922; s. Ira Louis and Esther Quiat; m. Ruth Laura Saunders, Nov. 26, 1950 (dec. Nov. 1995); 1 child, Matthew Philip; m. Jane Cooley, May 1, 1996. BA, U. Colo., 1947, JD, 1948. Bar: Colo. 1949, U.S. Dist. Ct. Colo. 1949, U.S. Ct. Appeals (10th cir.) 1968. Pvt. practice, Denver, 1949—; judge Gilpin County (Colo.) Ct., 1956, 1st Jud. Dist. Ct., Golden, Colo., 1959; mem. com. on jud. reform Colo. Legis. Commn., 1958. Mem. Colo. Ho. of Reps., Denver, 1949-51; bd. dirs. Luth. Med. Ctr., Denver, 1961-87. 1st lt. F.A., U.S. Army, 1941-46, MTO, ETO. Mem. Am. Radio Relay League (nat. bd. dirs. 1986-99), Pi Gamma Mu, Delta Sigma Rho, Phi Alpha Delta. Avocations: amateur radio, skiing, mathematics, history. Family and matrimonial, State civil litigation, Communications. Home: 714 Pontiac St Denver CO 80220-5540 Office: PO Box 200878 Denver CO 80220-0878

**QUICK, ALBERT THOMAS,** law educator, dean; b. BattleCreek, Mich., June 28, 1939; s. Robert and Vera Quick; m. Brenda Jones; children: Lori, Traci, Becki, Breton, Regan, Leigh. BA, U. Ariz., 1962; MA, Cen. Mich. U., 1964; JD, Wayne State U., 1967; LLM, Tulane U., 1974. Bar: Mich. 1968, Ky. 1987. Asst. prosecutor Calhoun County, Marshall, Mich., 1968-69; assoc. Hatch & Hatch, Marshall, 1969-70; asst. prof. U. Maine, Augusta, 1970-73; prof. law U. Louisville, 1974-87, spl. asst. to univ. provost, 1983-87; dean, prof. law Ohio No. U., Ada, 1987-95; prof. law, dean U. Toledo, Ohio, 1995-99. Co-author: Update Federal Rules of Criminal Procedure; contbr. articles to profl. jours. Recipient Medallion of Justice Nat. Bar Assn., 1995. Mem. ABA, Assn. Am. Law Schs. (criminal justice sect.), Ky. State Bar Assn., Mich. State Bar Assn., Willis Soc., Ohio State Bar Assn., Toledo Bar Assn., Rotary, Phi Kappa Phi. Episcopalian. Avocations: racquetball, tennis, art, reading. Office: Univ Toledo Coll Law 2801 W Bancroft St Toledo OH 43606-3390

**QUIDD, DAVID ANDREW,** paralegal; b. Chicago Heights, Ill., Sept. 8, 1954; s. John Richard and Mary (Wingate) Q. BA in Polit. Sci., U. New Orleans, 1976; postgrad., La. State U., 1976-79; paralegal cert., U. New Orleans, 1990. Coord. vols. Carter/Mondale Re-election Commn., New Orleans, 1980; paralegal Kitchen & Montagnet, New Orleans, 1981-84, Herman, Herman, Katz & Cotlar, New Orleans, 1985-92; freelance paralegal Metairie, La., 1992—. Pres. Alliance for Good Govt., Jefferson Parish, La., 1982, Young Dems. La., 1975-77; mem. Jefferson Parish Dem. Exec. Com., 1983-87, 89-96, chmn., 1990-93, treas., 1994, vice chmn., 1995; mem. Dem. State Ctrl. Com., 1996—; chmn. Jefferson Dem. Alliance, 1997—. Mem. Nat. Fedn. Paralegal Assns. (primary rep. 1995-97, secondary rep. 1998-99), New Orleans Paralegal Assn. (treas. 1991-94), Gretna Hist. Soc. (parliamentarian 1998-99). Roman Catholic. Avocation: jogging. Home: 1141 Papworth Ave Metairie LA 70005-2338

**QUIGLEY, LEONARD VINCENT,** lawyer; b. Kansas City, Mo., June 21, 1933; s. Joseph Vincent and Rosemary (Cannon) Q.; m. Lynn Mathis Pfohl, May 23, 1964; children: Leonard Matthew, Cannon Louise, Daniel Pfohl, Megan Mathis. A.B., Coll. Holy Cross, 1953; LL.B. magna cum laude, Harvard U., 1959; LL.M. in Internat. Law, NYU, 1962. Bar: N.Y. 1960. Assoc. Cravath, Swaine & Moore, N.Y.C., 1959-67; ptnr. Paul, Weiss, Rifkind, Wharton & Garrison, N.Y.C., 1968—; gen. counsel Archaeol. Inst. Am., Boston. Served to lt. USN, 1953-56. Mem. ABA, Can. Bar Assn., N.Y. State Bar Assn., Coun. Fgn. Rels., Assn. Bar City N.Y., Harvard Club (N.Y.C.), West Side Tennis Club (Forest Hills, N.Y.). General corporate, Private international, Oil, gas, and mineral.

**QUIGLEY, ROBERT ANDREW,** lawyer; b. Meadowbrook, Pa., Dec. 22, 1966; s. Francis H. and Mary Ann Quigley; m. Suzanne L. Foreman, May 20, 1995; 1 child, Colin F. BSBA, Slippery Rock U., 1988; JD, George Washington U., 1996. Bar: Pa. 1997, U.S. Dist. Ct. (mid. dist.) Pa. 1997. Asst. counsel Highmark Inc., Camp Hill, PA., 1996-99; assoc. duane, Morris & Hecksher, LLP, Harrisburg, Pa., 1999—. Mem. Am. Health Lawyers Assn., Pa. Soc. Healthcare Attys., Pa. Bar Assn. Health, Professional liability, Labor. Home: 118 Parkview Rd New Cumberland PA 17070-1727 Office: Duane Morris & Heckscher LLP 305 N Front St Fl 5 Harrisburg PA 17101-1216

**QUIGLEY, THOMAS J.,** lawyer; b. Mt. Carmel, Pa., July 22, 1923; s. James S. and Helen C. (Laughlin) Q.; m. Joan R. Reifke, Aug. 11, 1956; children: Thomas J., Jr., Joan E., James S. AB, Bucknell U., 1947; LLB, Yale U., 1950. Bar: Ohio, U.S. Dist. Ct. Ohio, U.S. Ct. Appeals (6th and D.C. cirs.). With Squire, Sanders & Dempsey, 1950—, adminstr. labor dept., 1971-80, mng. ptnr., Washington, 1980-85; nat. vice chmn., 1985-86; nat. chmn., 1986-90. Past pres., dir. exec. com. Nat. Symphony Orch., nat. trustee Musical Arts Assn. Cleve.; bd. dirs. Call for Action, Belgian Am. C. of C. 1st lt. USAAF, 1942-45. Decorated D.F.C., Air medal with oak leaf cluster, Belgium's Order of the Crown. Mem. ABA, Ohio Bar Assn., D.C. Bar Assn., Cleve. Bar Assn., Fed. City Coun., Yale Law Sch. Alumni. Assn. Roman Catholic. Clubs: Yale (N.Y.C.), Edgartown Yacht (Mass.), Chevy Chase, Metropolitan (Wash.). Labor. Office: Squire Sanders & Dempsey PO Box 407 1201 Pennsylvania Ave NW Washington DC 20004-2491 also: Key Tower Bldg Cleveland OH 44114

**QUILLEN, CECIL DYER, JR.,** lawyer, consultant; b. Kingsport, Tenn., Jan. 21, 1937; s. Cecil D. and Mary Louise (Carter) Q.; m. Vicey Ann Childress, Apr. 1, 1961; children: Cecil D., Ann C. BS, Va. Poly. Inst., 1958; LLB, U. Va., 1962. Bar: Va. 1962, N.Y. 1963, Tenn. 1974. Atty. patent dept. Eastman Kodak Co., Rochester, N.Y., 1962-65, atty. patent sect. Tenn. Eastman Co. (div. Eastman Kodak), Kingsport, Tenn., 1965-69, mgr., 1969-72, mgr. licensing, 1972-74, sec. and asst. chief counsel, 1974-76, dir. patent litigation Eastman Kodak, 1976-82, dir. antitrust litigation Eastman Kodak, 1978-82, v.p. and chief counsel Tenn. Eastman, 1983-85, v.p., and assoc. gen. counsel Eastman Kodak, 1986, sr. v.p., gen. counsel, dir., 1986-92; sr. adv., Putnam, Hayes & Bartlett, Inc., Washington, 1992—. Mem. ABA, Va. State Bar, Am. Intellectual Property Law Assn., Va. Poly. Inst. Com. of 100, Assn. of Gen. Counsel. Intellectual property, Antitrust, General civil litigation.

**QUILLEN, CECIL DYER, III,** lawyer; b. Rochester, N.Y., Aug. 15, 1963; s. Cecil Dyer, Jr and Vicey Ann (Childress) Q.; m. Mary Stuart Humes, Oct. 20, 1990; 1 child, Caroline. AB magna cum laude, Harvard U., 1985; JD, U. Va., 1988. Bar: N.Y. 1989, D.C. 1991, U.S. Ct. Appeals (4th cir.) 1989. Law clk., Sr. Cir. Judge U.S. Ct. Appeals (4th cir.), Richmond, Va., 1988-89; assoc. Sullivan & Cromwell, N.Y.C., 1989-95; assoc. Linklaters & Paines, N.Y.C., 1995-96, ptnr., 1996—; spkr. various profl. confs. Notes editor Va. Law Rev., 1987-88. Mem. ABA, N.Y. State Bar Assn., Assn. Bar City of N.Y., Raven Soc., Order of Coif, Phi Beta Kappa. Securities, Banking, Private international. Office: Linklaters & Paines 1345 Avenue Of The Americas New York NY 10019-5374

**QUINA, MARION ALBERT, JR.,** lawyer; b. Mobile, Ala., Apr. 18, 1949; s. Marion Albert Sr. and Tallulah (Dunlap) Q.; children: Marion Albert III, Elliott Richardson; m. Jamie Mayhall Curtis, May 2, 1998. BS, U. Ala., 1971; JD, Samford U., 1974. Bar: Ala. 1974, U.S. Dist. Ct. (so. dist.) Ala. 1975, U.S. Ct. Appeals (5th cir.) 1977, U.S. Ct. Appeals (11th cir.) 1981. Assoc. Lyons, Pipes & Cook, Mobile, 1974-77, ptnr., 1978-87; shareholder Lyons, Pipes & Cook, P.C., Mobile, 1988—. Past mem., bd. dirs. Mobile Touchdown Club, Presch. for the Sensory Impaired; mem. United Way, 1989—; mem. adv. bd. Cumberland Sch. of Law, Birmingham; sec., treas., vice chmn., chmn. Southeastern Admiralty Law Inst., Athens, Ga., 1996—. 1st lt. U.S. Army. Mem. ABA, Ala. Bar Assn., Mobile Bar Assn. (chmn. admiralty and maritime law com.), Maritime Law Assn. U.S. (assoc.), Ala. Wildlife Fedn. (past dir.), Mobile Area C. of C. (past vice chmn., gen. counsel), Kiwanis (past dir.), Mobile County Wildlife Assn., Mobile Propeller Club, Mobile Area C. of C. Diplomat Club, among others. Avocations: hunting, fishing. Admiralty, General corporate, Contracts commercial. Office: Lyons Pipes & Cook PC 2 N Royal St Mobile AL 36602-3896

**QUINCE, PEGGY A.,** state supreme court justice; b. Norfolk, Va., Jan. 3, 1948; m. Fred L. Buckine; children: Pegga LaVerne, Laura LaVerne. BS in Zoology, Howard U., 1970; JD, Cath. U. of Am., 1975. Hearing officer Rental Accomodations Office, Washington; pvt. practice Norfolk, 1977-78, Bradenton, Fla., 1978-80; asst. atty. gen. criminal divsn. Atty. Gen.'s Office, 1980; apptd. 2d Dist. Ct. of Appeals, 1994-98; state supreme ct. justice Fla. Supreme Ct., 1998—; lectr. in field. Asst. Sunday sch. tchr., mem. #3 usher bd. New Hope Missionary Bapt. Ch.; active Jack and Jill of Am., Inc., Urban League, NAACP, Tampa Orgn. for Black Affairs. Recipient award Cath.'s Neighborhood Legal Svcs. Clinic. Mem. Nat. Bar Assn., Fla. Bar, Va. State Bar, George Edgecomb Bar Assn., Hillsborough County Bar Assn., Fla. Assn. Women Lawyers, Hillsborough Assn. Women Lawyers, Tampa Bay Inn of Ct., Alpha Kappa Alpha. E-mail: supremecourt@mail.flcourts.org. Office: 500 S Duval St Tallahassee FL 32399-1925*

**QUINLAN, GUY CHRISTIAN,** lawyer; b. Cambridge, Mass., Oct. 28, 1939; s. Guy Thomas and Yvonne (Carver) Q.; m. Mary-Ella Holst, Apr. 18, 1987. AB, Harvard Coll., 1960, JD, Harvard U., 1963. Bar: N.Y. 1964, U.S. Dist. Ct. (so. and ea. dists.) N.Y. 1965, U.S. Ct. Appeals (2d cir.) 1967, U.S. Supreme Ct. 1969, U.S. Ct. Appeals (8th cir.) 1973, (10th cir.) 1977, (4th cir.) 1993, (11th cir.) 1995, U.S. Tax Ct. 1977. Assoc. Rogers & Wells, N.Y.C., 1963-70, ptnr., 1970-90, of counsel, 1991—. Past pres. Unitarian Universalist Svc. Com., Yorkville Common Pantry; past pres. Unitarian Universalist Dist. of Met. N.Y.; mem. adv. council on ministerial studies Harvard U. Div. Sch. Mem. ABA, N.Y. State Bar Assn., Fed. Bar Coun., Am. Judicature Soc., Am. Assn. Internat. Commn. Jurists, Lawyers Alliance for World Security, Lawyers Com. on Nuclear Policy. Democrat. Club: Harvard (N.Y.C.). Antitrust, Environmental, Insurance. Office: Rogers & Wells 200 Park Ave Fl 8E New York NY 10166-0800

**QUINLAN, WILLIAM ALLEN,** lawyer, writer; b. Chgo., Oct. 14, 1909; s. William Hiner and Alice Gertrude (Burns) Q.; m. Grace Elizabeth Anderson, 1936 (dec. 1967); children: William A. Jr., John R., Michael A.; m. Elizabeth Mary Hayes, 1968. PhB, U. Chgo., 1932, JD, 1933. Bar: Ill. 1936, Md. 1957, U.S. Supreme Ct. 1944. Asst. to chmn. Nat. Bakers Coun., Chgo., 1933-35; in chg. pub./indsl. rels., editor, gen. counsel Am. Bakers Assn., Chgo. and Washington, 1935-43; bd. dirs., ctrl. v.p. Pvt. Truck Coun. of Am., Inc., Chgo. and Washington, 1939-43; counsel Biscuit and Cracker Mfrs. Assn. of U.S., Washington, 1942-43; pvt. practice Washington, Riva, Md., 1943-93; gen. counsel/spl. counsel Nat. Candy Wholesalers Assn., Inc., Pvt. Truck Coun. of Am., Inc., Retail Bakers of Am., Retail Jewelers of Am., U.S. Wholesale Grocers Assn., Inc.; Washington counsel Campbell

Taggart Assoc. Bakeries, Gen. Baking Co., Helms Bakeries, J.S. Hershey Baking Co., Omar, Inc., Taylor Food Co., Ward Baking Co. Editor, pub.: The Quinlan Private Truck Law Report; editor-in-chief La Critique, U. Chgo. Student Literary Mag. Mem. County Bd. of Appeals, Montgomery County, Md., 1953-60; co-founder, past pres. Commodore John Barry divsn. Anne Arundel County Divsn. 1, Ancient Order of Hibernians in Am.; founder, past pres. Right to Life Conf. of Anne Arundel County; lector, hosp. visitor, Eucharistic minister Anne Arundel Med. Ctr.; past pres. St. Vincent de Paul Soc., St. Mary's Ch., Annapolis, Md., Holy Name Soc. Our Lady of Mercy Ch., Potomac, Md. Mem. Nat. Press Club (hon. life), Ancient Order of Hibernians (chpt. pres. 1982), K.C. (advocate), Sigma Chi (hon. life). Republican. Roman Catholic. General corporate, Government contracts and claims. Home and Office: 15300 Pine Orchard Dr Silver Spring MD 20906-1358

**QUINN, ANDREW PETER, JR.,** lawyer, insurance executive; b. Providence, Oct. 22, 1923; s. Andrew Peter and Margaret (Canning) Q.; m. Sara G. Bullard, May 30, 1952; 1 child, Emily H. AB, Brown U., 1945; LLB, Yale U., 1950. Bar: R.I. 1949, Mass. 1960, U.S. Tax Ct. 1960, U.S. Supreme Ct. 1986. Pvt. practice Providence, 1950-59, Springfield, Mass., 1959-88; ptnr. Letts & Quinn, 1950-59; with Mass. Mut. Life Ins. Co., 1959-88, exec. v.p., gen. counsel, 1971-88; of counsel Day, Berry & Howard, Hartford, Conn. and Boston, 1988—; pres., trustee MML Series Investment Fund, 1971-88; bd. dirs. Sargasso Mut. Ins. Co., Ltd., 1986-95, pres., 1986-89, chmn. bd. dirs., 1989-93. Trustee, MacDuffie Sch., 1974-87, chmn. bd., 1978-85; trustee Baystate Med., Springfield, 1977-80. Lt. (j.g.) USNR, 1944-46. Mem. ABA (co-chmn. nat. conf. lawyers and life ins. cos. 1973), Assn. Life Ins. Counsel (pres. 1983-84), Am. Coun. Life Ins. (chmn. legal sect. 1971), Life Ins. Assn. Mass. (chmn. exec. com. 1975-77), Brown U. Alumni Assn. (bd. dirs. 1969-72), N.Y. Yacht club, Longmeadow Country Club, Dunes Club, Hillsboro Club, Conn. Valley Brown U. (past pres.). General corporate, Insurance. Home: 306 Ellington Rd Longmeadow MA 01106-1559 Office: Day Berry & Howard City Pl Hartford CT 06103-3499

**QUINN, CHARLES NORMAN,** lawyer; b. Abington, Pa., Nov. 5, 1943; s. Charles Ransom and Lela Josephine (Cooper) Q.; m. Mary Bernadette Bradley, Oct. 4, 1975 (div. Oct. 1976); m. Vicki Lou Erickson Heinze, Nov. 11, 1978; stepchildren: Scott L., Kymbra Lynn Kaznay. BSME, Purdue U., 1965; ME, Pa. State U., 1970; JD, Villanova (Pa.) U., 1973. Bar: U.S. Dist. Ct. (ea. dist) Pa. 1974, U.S. Ct. Appeals (fed. cir.) 1984. Systems engr. GE Co., King of Prussia, Pa., 1965-70; atty. Paul and Paul, Phila., 1973-75, Penwalt Corp., Phila., 1976-80, A.R. Miller, P.C., Phila., 1981-85; ptnr. Miller & Quinn, Phila., 1986-91; atty., of counsel Dann Dorfman Herrell & Skill, Phila., 1992—. Contbr. articles to profl. jours. Mem. ABA, Phila. Patent Law Assn. (treas. 1980-83, gov. 1987-89), Phila. Intellectual Property Law Assn., Am. Intellectual Property Law Assn., Phila. Bar Assn. Avocations: golf, classical music, personal computers. E-mail: cquinn@wahs.com. Patent, Trademark and copyright. Home: 617 Marydell Dr West Chester PA 19380-6328 Office: Dann Dorfman Herrell & Skillman 1601 Market St Ste 720 Philadelphia PA 19103-2307

**QUINN, FRANCIS XAVIER,** arbitrator, mediator, author, lecturer; b. Dunmore, Pa., June 9, 1932; s. Frank T. and Alice B. (Maher) Q.; m. Marlene Stoker Quinn; children: Kimberly, Catherine, Cameron, Lindsay, Megan, Savannah. BA, Fordham U., 1956, MA, 1958; STB, Woodstock Coll., 1964; MS in Indsl. Rels., Loyola U., Chgo., 1966; PhD in Indsl. Rels., Calif. Western U., 1966. Assoc. dir. Inst. Indsl. Rels. St. Joseph's Coll., Phila., 1966-68; Manpower fellow Temple U., Phila., 1969-74, asst. to dean Sch. Bus. Adminstrn., 1972-78; arbitrator Fed. Mediation and Conciliation Svc., Nat. Mediation Bd., Am. Arbitration Assn., Nat. Assn. Railroad Referees, Dem. Nat. Steering Com.; ; apptd. to Rail Emergency Bd., 1975, to Fgn. Service Grievance Bd., 1976, 78, 80; chmn. Hall of Fame com. Internat. Police Assn., 1980—, Tulsa City-County Mayor's Task Force to Combat Homelessness, 1991-92; mem. exec. bd. Tulsa Met. Ministries, 1990-92, Labor-Religion Coun. Okla., 1990—. Author: The Ethical Aftermath of Automation, 1963, Ethics and Advertising, 1965, Population Ethics, 1968, The Evolving Role of Women in the World of Work, 1969, Developing Community Responsibility, 1970; editor: The Ethical Aftermath Series; contbr. articles to profl. jours. V.p. Dem. Nat. Steering Com. 1998-2000; chmn. Hall of Fame com. Internat. Police Assn., 1990—, Tulsa City-County Mayor's Task Force to Combat Homelessness, 1991-92; mem. exec. bd. Tulsa Met. Ministries, 1990-92, Labor-Religion Coun. Okla., 1990—. Named Tchr. of Yr. Freedom Found., 1959; recipient Human Rels. award City of Phila., others. mem. Nat. Acad. Arbitrators (v.p. 1999—), Indsl. Rels. Rsch. Assn., Assn. for Social Econs., Soc. for Dispute Resolution, Am. Arbitration Assn. (arbitrator), Nat. Assn. Railroad Refs. (v.p. 1996—, arbitrator), Internat. Soc. Labor Law and Social Security, Internat. Ombudsman Inst. Democrat. Home: 230 Hazel Blvd Tulsa OK 74114-3926

**QUINN, JAMES W.,** lawyer; b. Bronxville, N.Y., Oct. 1, 1945; s. James Joseph Quinn and Marie Joan (Blossy) Tisi; m. Kathleen Manning, Kellianne, Christopher, Tierney, Kerrin. AB cum laude, U. Notre Dame, 1967; JD, Fordham U., 1971. Bar: N.Y. 1972, U.S. Dist. Ct. (so. and ea. dists.) N.Y. 1973, U.S. Ct. Appeals (2nd cir.) 1976, U.S. Supreme Ct. 1984, U.S. Ct. Appeals (3rd, 7th and 9th cirs.) 1985, U.S. Ct. Appeals (8th cir.) 1991. Assoc. Weil, Gotshal & Manges, N.Y.C., 1971-77, 78-79, ptnr., 1979—; ptnr. Fleisher & Quinn, N.Y.C., 1977-78; adj. assoc. prof. law Fordham U., N.Y.C., 1985-87. Editor Fordham U. Law Rev., 1969-71; contbr. articles to legal jours. Mem. ABA (litigation sect., co-chmn. subcom. alternate means of dispute resolution of com. corp. counsel, program chmn. trial practice com., sports and entertainment forum), Assn. of Bar of City of N.Y. (com. of state jurisdiction, com. on entertainment sports, com. on anti-trust regulation, chmn. sports law com.). Federal civil litigation, State civil litigation. Home: 1 Maple Way Armonk NY 10504-2602

**QUINN, JOHN PETER,** lawyer, software designer; b. Bay City, Mich., Aug. 20, 1944; s. William Joseph and Helen Marie (Darland) Q.; m. Dana Elizabeth Hillman, June 1969 (div. 1974); 1 child, Adrianne; m. Sharon Margaret Goode, June 27, 1981; children: William, Catherine, Mary Margaret, John, Daniel. BS in Chemistry, Xavier U. La., New Orleans, 1968; JD cum laude, U. Mich., 1972. Bar: Mich. 1974, U.S. Dist. Ct. (ea. dist.) Mich. 1977, U.S. Ct. Appeal (6th cir.) 1977, U.S. Supreme Ct. 1985. Police officer Detroit Police Dept., 1973-74; counsel Detroit Bd. Police Commrs., 1974-76; chair bd. dirs. Quinn & Budaj, P.C., Detroit, 1977-85; asst. corp. counsel Detroit Law Dept., 1976-77, prin./supervising asst. corp. counsel, 1985—; def. mediator Mediation Tribunal Assn., Detroit, 1995—. Contbr. articles to profl. jours. Chair bd. dirs. S.W. Alliance of Neighborhoods, Detroit, 1995—; founding mem. bd. dirs. S.W. Cmty. and Neighborhood Devel. Orgn., Detroit, 1990. With U.S. Army, 1968-70, Munich. Recipient Spirit of Detroit award Detroit City Coun., 1979. Mem. Detroit Bar Assn. (pub. adv. com., mediator, vice chair dist. ct. sect.), Assn. Def. Trial Counsel. Roman Catholic. Avocations: cottage living, camping, woodworking, classical languages. Office: City of Detroit Law Dept 1650 First Nat Bldg Detroit MI 48226

**QUINN, LINDA C.,** lawyer; b. Rockville Centre, N.Y., 1948. BA, Mt. Holyoke Coll., 1969; JD, Georgetown U., 1972. Bar: N.Y. 1973. Law clk. Hon. J. Joseph Smith U.S. Ct. Appeals (2d cir.), 1972-73; dir. divsn. corp. fin. SEC; ptnr. Shearman & Sterling, N.Y.C. Named one of 50 Top Women Lawyers Nat. Law Jour., 1998. Mem. ABA. E-mail: lquinn@shearman.com. Banking, Securities, General corporate. Office: Shearman & Sterling 599 Lexington Ave Fl 16 New York NY 10022-6069*

**QUINN, MICHAEL S.,** lawyer; b. N.Y.C., Nov. 17, 1962; s. Alan H. and Ruth B. (Ney) Q.; m. Krista A. Landerholm, Nov. 18, 1989; 1 child, Jack. BA in Internat. Affairs, George Washington U., 1984; JD, NYU, 1987. Bar: N.Y. 1988, D.C. 1990, Colo. 1994. Assoc. Chary Gottlieb Steent, N.Y.C., 1988-90, 92-94, Mattias Stephen Joques, Sydney, Australia, 1991; assoc. Holland & Hart, Denver, 1994-96, ptnr., 1996—; asst. prof. law Denver U., 1996. Bd. dirs. World Trade Orgn., Denver, 1997—. Private international, Legislative, Securities. Office: Holland and Hart LLP 555 17th St # 3200 Denver CO 80202-3950

**QUINN, R. JOSEPH,** judge; m. Carole Quinn. BA, St. John's U.; JD, Hamline U. Minn. State rep., 1983-90; judge Minn. Supreme Ct., 1991—. Office: Anoka County Court 325 E Main St Anoka MN 55303-2483

**QUINN, THOMAS GERARD,** lawyer; b. Bklyn., Feb. 11, 1950; s. Thomas J. and Catherine A. Quinn; m. Barbara A. Ferrara, June 30, 1973; 1 child, Bret T. BS in Chemistry, SUNY, Stony Brook, 1972; JD, U. Calif., Berkeley, 1976. Bar: N.Y. 1977, Calif. 1977, U.S. Dist. Ct. (so. and ea. dist.) N.Y. 1977. Assoc. Fish & Neane, N.Y.C., 1976-79, Satterlee & Stephens, N.Y.C., 1979-80; assoc. gen. counsel ICPI, Westport, Conn., 1980-81; atty. AT&T, N.Y. and N.J., 1981-96; corp. counsel Lucent Techs., Liberty Corner, N.J., 1996—; sec.-treas. Product Liability Adv. Coun., Reston, Va., 1990—; bd. dirs. Lawyers for Civil Justice, Washington, 1990—. Avocations: travel, wine, cooking. Product liability, Toxic tort, Communications. Office: Lucent Techs Inc 283 King George Rd Rm C3d02 Warren NJ 07059-5134

**QUINN, THOMAS JOSEPH,** lawyer; b. Worcester, Mass., May 26, 1954; s. John Peter and Winifred Agnes (McDonough) Q.; children: Meghan, Conor, Alexander. BA summa cum laude, St. Francis Coll., Biddeford, Maine, 1975; JD, U. Notre Dame, 1978. Bar: Maine 1978, Mass. 1979, U.S. Dist. Ct. Maine 1978, U.S. Ct. Appeals (1st cir.) 1991. Rsch. asst. to prof. Alan Dershowitz Harvard Law Sch., Cambridge, Mass., 1977; law clk. to Hon. Charles A. Pomeroy Supreme Jud. Ct. of Maine, Portland, 1978-79; assoc., ptnr. Douglas, Whiting, Quinn & Denham, Portland, 1979-93; ptnr. Beals & Quinn, Portland, 1993-98; litigation counsel UNUM Life Ins. Co., Portland, 1998—; instr. U. So. Maine, Portland, 1982-86. Author: (screenplay) Choice of Law, 1992; notes editor, author Jour. of Legislation, 1978-79; contbg. author Maine Lawyers Rev. Mem. City of Portland Historic Preservation Com., 1993-95. Mem. Am. Bd. Trial Advocates, Maine Bar Assn., Cumberland County Bar Assn., Maine Trial Lawyers Assn., Million Dollar Advocates Forum. Avocations: painting, travel, writing. General civil litigation, Product liability, Personal injury. Home: 415 Brighton Ave Portland ME 04102-2326 Office: UNUM Life Ins Co 2211 Congress St Portland ME 04102-1941

**QUINN, TIMOTHY CHARLES, JR.,** lawyer; b. Caro, Mich., Mar. 3, 1936; s. Timothy Charles and Jessie (Brown) Q.; m. Linda Ricci, June 21, 1958; children: Gina M., Samantha E., Timothy Charles III. BA, U. Mich., 1960; JD, Columbia U., 1963. Bar: N.Y. 1963, U.S. Dist. Ct. (so. and ea. dists.) N.Y. 1965, U.S. Ct. Appeals (2d cir.) 1967. Assoc. Clark, Carr & Ellis, N.Y.C., 1963-69, Casey, Tyre, Wallace & Bannerman, N.Y.C., 1969-71, Arsham & Keenan, N.Y.C., 1971; assoc. Conboy, Hewitt, O'Brien & Boradman, N.Y.C., 1972-74, ptnr., 1975-83, mem. exec. com., 1981-83; ptnr. Quinn, Cohen, Shields & Bock, N.Y.C., 1983-88, Quinn & Suhr, White Plains, N.Y., 1988-95, Quinn, Marantis & Rosenberg, White Plains, N.Y., 1995-97, Dickerson & Reilly, N.Y.C., 1997—; arbitrator N.Y.C. Civil Ct., 1982-88 , Am. Arbitration Assn., N.Y.C., 1966—, 9th Jud. Dist., 1988—. Mem. ABA, N.Y. State Bar Assn., Westchester County Bar Assn., Assn. of Bar of City of N.Y., N.Y. State Trial Lawyers Assn., Nat. Assn. R.R. Trial Counsel, Conf. Freight Loss and Damage Counsel, N.Y. Law Inst., Def. Rsch. Inst., Westchester Country Club. Avocation: golf. General practice, Federal civil litigation, State civil litigation. Office: Dickerson & Reilly 780 3rd Ave New York NY 10017-2024 Address: 70 W Red Oak Ln White Plains NY 10604-3602

**QUINTIERE, GARY GANDOLFO,** lawyer; b. Passaic, N.J., Nov. 26, 1944; s. Benjamin and Sadie (Riotto) Q.; m. Judy Rosenthal, Aug. 16, 1966; children: Karen, Geoffrey. AB in Govt., Lafayette Coll., 1966; JD, George Washington U., 1969. Bar: Va. 1969, D.C. 1970. Law clk. to Judge Philip Nichols, Jr. U.S. Ct. Appeals (Fed. cir.), Washington, 1969-70; from assoc. to ptnr. Miller & Chevalier, Washington, 1970-85; ptnr. Morgan, Lewis & Bockius, Washington, 1985—. Mem. ABA, D.C. Bar Assn., Va. Bar Assn. Avocations: tennis, skiing, golf. Pension, profit-sharing, and employee benefits. Home: 14 Mercy Ct Potomac MD 20854-4540 Office: Morgan Lewis & Bockius 1800 M St NW Washington DC 20036-5802

**QUIRANTES, ALBERT M.,** lawyer; b. Cuba, Jan. 25, 1963; came to U.S., 1966; s. Alberto adn Haydee (Mendez) Q. B in Bus., U. Miami, Fla., 1984; JD, U. Fla., 1987. Bar: Fla. 1988, U.S. Dist. Ct. (so. dist.) Fla. 1990, U.S. Dist. Ct. (mid. dist.) Fla. 1990, U.S. Ct. Appeals (11th cir.) 1990, U.S. Supreme Ct. 1991, U.S. Dist. Ct. Ariz. 1991. Pub. defender Ct. 8th cir., Gainsville, Fla., 1988-89; pvt. practice Miami, Fla., 1989—; sr. ptnr. Ticket Law Ctr., P.A., Miami, Fla., 1990—. Mem. Fla. Traffic Ct. Rules Com., Tallahassee, 1991—. Mem. Fla. Assn. Criminal Def. Attys., Dade Bar (cts. com. 1992—, criminal cts. com. 1992—), Latin C. of C., Jaycees. Criminal, Administrative and regulatory, Health. Home and Office: 1800 NW 7th St Miami FL 33125-3504

**QUIRK, FRANK EDWARD,** lawyer; b. Cambridge, Mass., Nov. 24, 1932; s. Frank Thomas and Eleanor J. (McDermott) Q.; m. Joyce Keath, June 30, 1956; 1 child, John F.; m. Patricia L. Kelly, Dec. 10, 1972; children: Elizabeth J., Michael W. BS, Ohio State U., 1957, JD, 1959. Bar: Ohio 1959, Colo. 1998, U.S. Dist. Ct. (no. dist.) Ohio 1959; U.S. Ct. Appeals (6th cir.) 1972. Partner Roetzel, Hunsicker & Michaels, Akron, Ohio, 1959-70; partner Brouse & McDowell, Akron, 1970—, mng. ptnr., 1989-97. Mem. Akron Bar Assn. (pres. 1983-84), Akron Bar Found. (pres. 1989-90), Akron City Club (pres. 1980), Akron Golf Charities (pres. 1966), Akron Jaycees (pres. 1962-63). Avocations: skiing, biking, outdoor activities, reading. General civil litigation, General corporate, Environmental. Home: 1675 Brookwood Dr Akron OH 44313-5065 Office: Brouse & McDowell 500 First National Tower Akron OH 44308

**QUIRK, MICHAEL L.,** lawyer; b. Milw., July 3, 1946; s. Charles Michael and Paula E. Q.; m. Kathleen Mary Klug, June 28, 1970; children: Monica, Rosemary, Emily, Martha, Thomas. BA, Notre Dame U., 1968; JD, Marquette U., 1971. Bar: Wis. 1971, U.S. Dist. Ct. (ea. and we. dists.) Wis. 1971, U.S. Ct. Mil. Appeals 1973, U.S. Supreme Ct. 1974, U.S. Ct. Appeals (7th cir.) 1978. Lawyer U.S. Army Judge Adv., Ft. Eustis, Va., 1971-73; lawyer Def. Appellate Div. U.S. Army, Arlington, Va., 1973-75; assoc. Arnold, Murray & O'Neill, Milw., 1975-90; shareholder O'Neill, Schimmel, Quirk & Carroll S.C., Milw., 1990—. Capt. U.S. Army, 1971-75. Mem. ABA (litig. sect.), Def. Rsch. Inst., Milw. Met. Assn. Commerce. Insurance, Personal injury, Probate. Office: O'Neill Schimmel Et Al 312 E Wisconsin Ave Ste 616 Milwaukee WI 53202-4305

**QUIST, GORDON JAY,** federal judge; b. Grand Rapids, Mich., Nov. 12, 1937; s. George J. and Ida F. (Hoekstra) Q.; m. Jane Capito, Mar. 10, 1962; children: Scot D., George J., Susan E., Martha J., Peter K. BA, Mich. State U., 1959; JD with honors, George Washington U., 1962. Bar: D.C. 1962, Ill. 1964, U.S. Dist. Ct. (no. dist.) Ill. 1964, U.S. Supreme Ct. 1965, Mich. 1967, U.S. Dist. Ct. (we. dist.) Mich. 1967, U.S. Ct. Appeals (6th cir.) 1967. Assoc. Hollabaugh & Jacobs, Washington, 1962-64, Sonnenschein, Levinson, Carlin, Nath & Rosenthal, Chgo., 1964-66; assoc. Miller, Johnson, Snell & Cummiskey, Grand Rapids, 1967-72, ptnr., 1972-92, mng. ptnr., 1986-92; judge U.S. Dist. Ct. (we. dist.) Mich., Grand Rapids, 1992—. Bd. dirs. Wedgewood Acres-Ch. Youth Home, 1968-74, Mary Free Bed Hosp., 1979-88, Christian Ref. Publs., 1968-78, 82-88, Opera Grand Rapids, 1986-92, Mary Free Bed Brace Shop, 1988-92, Better Bus. Bur., 1972-80, Calvin Theol. Sem., 1992-93; bd. dirs. Indian Trails Camp, 1970-78, 82-88, pres., 1978, 88. Mem. Am. Indicature Soc., Univ. Club Grand Rapids, Order of Coif, Fed. Bar Assn. Avocations: reading, travel. Office: 482 Ford Fed Courthouse 110 Michigan St NW Grand Rapids MI 49503-2313

**QUITTMEYER, PETER CHARLES,** lawyer; b. Charlottesville, Va., Oct. 9, 1957; s. Charles L. and Maureen (Rankin) Q.; children: Charles Lake, Laura Slater. BA with high distinction, U. Va., 1979, JD, 1982. Bar: Ga. 1985. Assoc. King & Spalding, Atlanta, 1982-87; shareholder Trotter, Smith & Jacobs, Atlanta, 1987-91; ptnr. Nelson Mullins Riley & Scarborough, Atlanta, 1991—; adj. prof. computer law Emory U. Sch. Law, Atlanta, spring 1996, 98. Author: Computer Software Agreements, 1985—; mem. Va. Law Rev., 1981-82; contbr. articles to law jours. Mem. ABA, Computer Law Assn., Ga. Bar Assn., Raven Soc., Order of Coif, Phi Beta Kappa. Computer, Intellectual property, General corporate. Office: Nelson Mullins Riley & Scarborough 999 Peachtree St NE Ste 1400 Atlanta GA 30309-4422

**RAAB, IRA JERRY,** lawyer, judge; b. N.Y.C., June 20, 1935; s. Benjamin and Fannie (Kirschner) R.; m. Regina Schneider, June 4, 1957 (div. 1978); children: Michael, Shelley; m. Katie Rachel McKeever, June 30, 1979 (div. 1991); children: Julie, Jennifer, Joseph; m. Gloria Silverman, Nov. 7, 1996; children: Jill, Todd, John. BBA, CCNY, 1955; JD, Bklyn. Law Sch., 1957; MPA, NYU, 1959, postgrad., 1961; MS in Pub. Adminstrn., L.I. U., 1961; MBA, Adelphi U., 1990. Bar: N.Y. 1958, U.S. Dist. Ct. (so. and ea. dists.) N.Y. 1960, U.S. Supreme Ct. 1967, U.S. Tax Ct. 1976, U.S. Ct. Appeals (2d cir.) 1977. Pvt. practice Woodmere, N.Y., 1958-96; agt. Westchester County Soc. Prevention of Cruelty to Children, White Plains, N.Y., 1958; counsel Dept. Correction City of N.Y., 1959, trial commr. Dept. Correction, 1976, asst. corp. counsel Tort divsn., 1963-70; staff counsel SBA, N.Y.C., 1961-63; counsel Investigation Com. on Willowbrook State Sch., Boro Hall, S.I., N.Y., 1970; gen. counsel Richmond County Soc. Prevention of Cruelty to Children, Boro Hall, 1970-81; pro bono counsel N.Y.C. Patrolmen's Benevolent Assn., 1974-81; rep. to UN Internat. Criminal Ct., 1977-78; arbitrator Small Claims Ct. Day Cts., N.Y.C., 1970-96; arbitrator L.I. Better Bus. Bur., 1976-93; arbitrator Nassau County Dist. Ct., 1978-93, arbitrator Small Claims Ct., 1978-96; spl. master N.Y. County Supreme Ct., 1977-96; judge N.Y.C. Parking Violations Bur., 1991-93; small claims arbitrator N.Y.C. Civil Ct., 1970-96; arbitrator U.S. Dist. Ct. (ea. dist.) N.Y., 1986-96; lectr. comty. and ednl. orgns.; instr. paralegal course Lawrence Sch. Dist., N.Y., 1982-84; law prof. Briarcliff Coll., Bethpage, N.Y., 1997. Chmn. Businessmen's Luncheon Club, Wall St. Synagogue, 1968-79; exec. sec. Cmty. Mediation Ctr., Suffolk County, 1978-80, exec. v.p., 1980-81; vice chmn. Woodmere Inc., Com., 1980-81; mem. adv. bd. Nassau Expressway Com., 1979-80; bd. dirs. Woodmere Mchts. Assn., 1979-80, v.p., 1979-83, chmn., 1984-93; candidate for dist. ct. judge Nassau County, 1987, 88, 89, 91, 93, 94; candidate for supreme ct. justice Nassau and Suffolk Counties, 1995, 98, candidate for presiding judge of Nassau County Dist. Ct., ; elected judge Nassau County Dist. Ct., 1997—; candidate for county ct., Nassau County, 1997; candidate for presiding judge dist. ct., 1999; sec. Congregation Aish Kodesh, Woodmere. Recipient Consumer Protection award FTC, 1974, 76, 79, Recognition award Pres. Ronald Reagan, 1986, Man of Yr. award L.I. Coun. of Chambers, 1987. Mem. ABA (chmn. cts. and comty. com. 1988-93, exec. com. jud. adminstrn. divsn. lawyers conf. 1989-95), Am. Judges Assn. (bd. govs. 1973-78, 82-88, 89-96, 97—, nat. treas. 1978-82, chmn. civil ct. ops. com. 1975-76, chmn. ednl. film com. 1974-77, editl. bd. Ct. Rev. mag. 1975-79, 82-86, chmn. spkrs. bur. com. 1976-77, chmn. legis. com. 1983-95, chmn. resolutions com. 1995-98, chan. jud. concerns com. 1997—, historian 1988—, William H. Burnett award 1983), Am. Judges Found. (pres. 1977-79, chmn. bd. trustees 1979-83, treas. 1974-75, 76-77, trustee 1983-97), Assn. Arbitrators of Civil Ct. City of N.Y. (past pres.), N.Y. State Bar Assn. (sec. dist., city, town and villages cts. com.), Nassau County Bar Assn. (criminal cts. com., matrimonial and family ct. com., ct. com., ethics com.), Profl. Group Legal Svc. Assn. (past pres.), Internat. Assn. Jewish Lawyers and Jurists (com. to draft Internat. Bill of Rights to Privacy 1982, coun. 1981-95, bd. govs. 1984-95), adv. bd. comty. dispute ctr. 1979-81), K.P. (past chancellor comdr.). Democrat. Fax: (516) 572-2507. General practice, State civil litigation, Personal injury. Home: 375 Westwood Rd Woodmere NY 11598-1624 Office: District Court 99 Main St Hempstead NY 11550-2405

**RAAB, SHELDON,** lawyer, Bklyn. Nov. 30, 1937; s. Morris and Eva (Shereshevsky) R.; m. Judith Deutsch, Dec. 15, 1963; children: Michael Kenneth, Elisabeth Louise, Andrew John. AB, Columbia U., 1958; LLB cum laude, Harvard U., 1961. Bar: N.Y. 1961, U.S. Ct. Appeals (2d cir.) 1963, U.S. Dist. Ct. (so. and ea. dists.) 1967. Dep. asst. atty. gen. State of N.Y., 1961-63, asst. atty gen., 1963-64; assoc. Fried, Frank, Harris, Shriver & Jacobson and predecessor firm, N.Y.C., 1964-69, ptnr., 1970-81, inc. ptnr., 1981—. Mem. exec. com. lawyers' div. United Jewish Appeal, 1982—. Mem. ABA, Am. Law Inst., N.Y. State Bar Assn. (trial lawyers sect. 1968—), Assn. of Bar of City of N.Y. (adminstrv. law com. 1968-71, spl. com. electric power and environment 1971-73, chmn. energy com. 1974-79, fed. cts. com. 1981-84, state superior cts. juris. com. 1985-88). Democrat. General civil litigation, Appellate, Securities. Office: Fried Frank Harris Shriver & Jacobson 1 New York Plz Fl 22 New York NY 10004-1980

**RAAS, DANIEL ALAN,** lawyer; b. Portland, Oreg., July 6, 1947; s. Alan Charles and Mitzi (Cooper) R.; m. Deborah Ann Becker, Aug. 5, 1973; children: Amanda Beth, Adam Louis. BA, Reed Coll., 1969; JD, NYU, 1972. Bar: Wash. 1973, Calif. 1973, U.S. Dist. Ct. (we. dist.) Wash. 1973, U.S. Ct. Appeals (9th cir.) 1975, U.S. Supreme Ct. 1977, U.S. Tax Ct. 1983, U.S. Ct. Claims 1984. Atty. Seattle Legal Svcs, VISTA, 1972-73; reservation atty. Quinault Indian Nation, Taholah, Wash., 1973-76; reservation atty. Lummi Indian Nation, Bellingham, Wash., 1976-97, spl. counsel, 1997—; mem. Raas, Johnsen & Stuen, P.S., Bellingham, 1982—; cons. Falmouth Inst., Fairfax, Va., 1992—, Nat. Am. Ind. Ct. Judges Assn., McLean, Va., 1976-80. Rules chmn. Whatcom County Dem. Conv., Bellingham, 1988, 92, 94, 96; bd. dirs. Congregation Beth Israel, Bellingham, 1985—, pres., 1990-92; mem. adv. com. legal asst. program Bellingham Vocat. Tech. Inst., 1985-91; trustee Whatcom County Law Libr., 1978—; pres. Vol. Lawyer Program, 1990-93, bd. dirs., 1988-94; pres. Cliffside Cmty. Assn., 1978-80, bd. dirs., 1977-89; bd. dirs. Friends Maritime Heritage Ctr., 1983-86, Samish Camp Fire Coun., 1988-94, pres. 1991-94, v.p., 1989-91, regional v.p. Union Am. Hebrew Congregations, 1986-93, nat. trustee, exec. com., 1995-99, sec. Pacific N.W. region, 1993-95, pres., 1995-99. John Ben Snow scholar, NYU, 1969-70, Root-Tilden scholar, NYU, 1970-72. Mem. Wash. State Bar Assn. (trustee Ind. law sect. 1989-95, Pro Bono award 1991), Whatcom County Bar Assn. (v.p. 1981, pres. 1982, Pro Bono award 1991), Grays Harbor Bar Assn. (v.p. 1976). Native American, General civil litigation, Consumer commercial. Home: 1929 Lake Crest Dr Bellingham WA 98226-4510 Office: Raas Johnsen & Stuen PS 1503 E St Bellingham WA 98225-3007

**RABB, BRUCE,** lawyer; b. Cambridge, Mass., Oct. 4, 1941; s. Maxwell M. and Ruth (Cryden) R.; m. Harriet Rachel Schaffer, Jan. 4, 1970; children: Alexander Charles, Katherine Anne. AB, Harvard U., 1962; Cert. d'Etudes Politiques, Institut d'Etudes Politiques, Paris, 1963; LLB, Columbia U., 1966. Bar: N.Y. 1966. Law clk. to judge U.S. Ct. Appeals (5th cir.), 1966-67; assoc. Stroock & Stroock & Lavan, N.Y.C., 1967-68, 71-75, ptnr., 1976-91; ptnr. Kramer, Levin, Naftalis & Frankel, N.Y.C., 1991—; staff asst. to Pres. U.S., 1969-70; vice-chmn. Lawyers Com. Human Rights, 1977-95, nat. coun., 1996—; bd. dirs. Chiquita Italia, SpA; supr. bd. dirs. Agora-Gazeta, sp.zo.o., 1993-98, Agora-Druk, sp.zo.o., 1995-98; pub. mem. Adminstrv. Conf. U.S., 1982-86, 89-92, spl. counsel, 1986-88. sec. Lehrman Inst., 1978-88; bd. dirs. Citizens Union of N.Y., 1981-87, 88-94, 95—, Am. Friends of Alliance Israelite Universelle, 1987—, Human Rights Watch, 1987—, Welfare Law Ctr., 1997—; mem. Human Rights Watch/Ams., 1982—, Human Rights Watch/Helsinki, 1985-97, Fund for Free Expression, 1987-97, Human Rights Watch/Middle East, 1989—, vice chmn., 1990—; mem. internat. adv. com. Internat. Parliamentary Group for Human Rights in the Soviet Union, 1984-88, Prin. of the Coun. for Excellence in Govt., 1990—; adv. coun. Doctors of the World USA, 1996—. Mem. ABA (adv. panel Internat. Human Rights Trial Observer project), Am. Law Inst., Assn. of Bar of City of N.Y. (fed. legis., internat. law chair 1992-95, internat. human rights, civil rights, legal edn. and admission to bar, internat. trade coms., coun. on fgn. affairs), Harvard Club N.Y.C., Met. Club of Washington. Private international, Finance, General corporate. Office: Kramer Levin et al 919 3rd Ave New York NY 10022-3902

**RABB, HARRIET SCHAFFER,** government official, lawyer, educator; b. Houston, Sept. 12, 1941; d. Samuel S. and Helen G. Schaffer; m. Bruce Rabb, Jan. 4, 1970; children: Alexander, Katherine. BA in Govt., Barnard Coll., 1963; JD, Columbia U., 1966. Bar: N.Y. 1966, U.S. Supreme Ct. 1969, D.C. 1970. Instr. seminar on constl. litigation Rutgers Law Sch., 1966-67; staff atty. Center for Constl. Rights, 1966-69; spl. counsel to commr. consumer affairs N.Y.C. Dept. Consumer Affairs, 1969-70; sr. staff atty. Stern Community Law Firm, Washington, 1970-71; asst. dean urban affairs Law Sch., Columbia U., N.Y.C., 1971-84, prof. law, dir. clin. edn., 1984—; George M. Jaffen prof. law and social responsibility Law Sch., Columbia U., 1991-99, vice dean, 1992-99; gen. counsel Dept. Health and Human Svcs., Washington, 1993—; mem. faculty employment and tng. policy Harvard Summer Inst., Cambridge, Mass., 1975-79. Author: (with Agid, Cooper and Rubin) Fair Employment Litigation Manual, 1975, (with Cooper and Rubin) Fair Employment Litigation, 1975. Bd. dirs. Ford Found., 1977-89, N.Y. Civil Liberties Union, 1972-83, Lawyers Com. for Civil Rights Under Law, 1978-86, Legal Def. Fund NAACP, 1978-93, Mex. Am. Legal Def. and Edn. Fund, 1986-90, Legal Aid Soc., 1990-93; mem. exec. com. Human Rights Watch, 1991-93; trustee Trinity Episcopal Sch. Corp., 1991-93. Office: Dept Health and Human Svcs 200 Independence Ave SW Rm 722A Washington DC 20201-0004

**RABBITT, DANIEL THOMAS, JR.,** lawyer; b. St. Louis, Sept. 19, 1940; s. Daniel Thomas and Charlotte Ann (Carpenter) R.; m. Susan Lee Scherger, July 26, 1969. BA in Commerce, St. Louis U., 1962, JD cum laude, 1964. Bar: Mo. 1964, U.S. Supreme Ct. 1970. Assoc. Moser, Marsalek, Carpenter, Cleary, Jaeckel, Keaney & Brown and predecessor, St. Louis, 1964-68; ptnr. Moser, Marsalek, Carpenter, Cleary, Jaeckel, Keaney & Brown, St. Louis, 1969-81; mem. Brown, James & Rabbitt, P.C., St. Louis, 1981-91, Rabbitt, Pitzer & Snodgrass, P.C., St. Louis, 1991—; instr., St. Louis U. Sch. Law, 1968-70. Recipient Lon Hocker Meml. Trial Atty. award Mo. Bar Found., 1975. Fellow Am. Coll. Trial Lawyers; mem. ABA (chmn. young lawyers sect. 1973-74), Am. Judicature Soc., Mo. Bar Assn., Internat. Assn. Def. Counsel (product liability adv. coun.), Bar Assn. Met. St. Louis, Mo. Athletic Club (gov. 1978-81, v.p. 1980-81). Federal civil litigation, State civil litigation, Product liability. Office: 800 Market St Ste 2300 Saint Louis MO 63101-2506

**RABECS, ROBERT NICHOLAS,** lawyer; b. Scranton, Pa., Mar. 19, 1964; s. Nicholas and Anne Marie (Stull) R. BA summa cum laude, U. Scranton, 1986; JD cum laude, Georgetown U., 1990. Bar: Pa. 1990, D.C. 1992. Assoc. Reed Smith Shaw & McClay, Washington, 1990-94, Hogan & Hartson, Washington, 1994—. Columnist Managed Healthcare News, Belle Meade, N.J., 1994-98. Fulbright scholar, 1986-87; NEH undergrad. fellow, 1985. Mem. ABA, Am. Health Lawyers Assn., Pa. Bar Assn. (health law com.), D.C. Bar Assn. (health law sect.), Alpha Sigma Nu. Roman Catholic. Health. Home: 3401 38th St NW Apt 914 Washington DC 20016-3045 Office: Hogan & Hartson 555 13th St NW Washington DC 20004-1161

**RABEKOFF, ELISE JANE,** lawyer; b. N.Y.C., June 26, 1959; d. Sidney and Natalie (Kaufman) R.; m. Christopher Gladstone, June 7, 1986; children: Katherine, Nicholas. AB, Princeton U., 1980; JD, Yale U., 1986. Bar: Pa. 1986, D.C. 1988, U.S. Dist. Ct. (fed. dist.) D.C. 1988. Legis. asst. Sen. D.P. Moynihan, Washington, 1980-83; law clk. judge Charle R. Richey U.S. Dist. Ct. D.C., Washington, 1986-88; assoc. Shea & Gardner, Washington, 1988-93; v.p., gen. counsel Quadrangle Devel. Corp., Washington, 1993—. Bd. dirs. Chelsea Sch., Silver Spring, Md., 1990-95. General corporate, Real property, Labor. Office: Quadrangle Devel Corp 1001 9th St NW Washington DC 20001-4311

**RABENSEIFNER, HANNA CAMILLE,** lawyer; b. Rymarov, Czechoslovakia, May 8, 1957; d. Slavoj V. and Vera L. (Valouch) R.; m. John K. Pepper Jr., Sept. 19, 1986. JD, U. Zurich, Switzerland, 1982; LLM, U. Miami, 1984, JD, 1987. Bar: Fla. 1988, U.S. Dist. Ct. (so. dist.) Fla. 1992. Contr. Internat. Bus. Corp., Miami, 1987-89; pvt. practice Miami, 1989—. Immigration, naturalization, and customs, Real property. Office: 905 Brickell Bay Dr Apt 1831 Miami FL 33131-2928

**RABIN, AVRUM MARK,** lawyer; b. Chgo., Jan. 6, 1941; s. Harold Saul Rabin and Sylvia Silbert; m. Barbara Bennett, May 21, 1964; children: Daniel, Rebecca, Susan, Jordana, Alex, Robert. BS, Western Ill. U., 1962; JD, John Marshall Law Sch., 1965. Bar: Ill. 1965, U.S. Dist. Ct. (ctrl. dist.) Ill. 1966, U.S. Tax Ct. 1977. Asst. states atty. Sangamon County, Springfield, Ill., 1965-66; legal advisor Sec. of State, Springfield, 1966-68; pvt. practice Springfield, 1966-91, Rabin, Myers & Hanken, Springfield, 1991—. Brigadier gen. Ill. Air N.G., 1966—. Mem. N.G. Assn. of U.S., Ill. State Bar Assn., Masons. Jewish. Avocations: backpacking, fly fishing, photography. Contracts commercial, Probate, Real property. Office: Rabin Myers & Hanken PC 1300 S 8th St Springfield IL 62703-2519

**RABIN, GILBERT,** judge, lawyer; b. Tarrytown, N.Y., June 10, 1923; s. Charles and Jeanette (Kalman) R.; m. Zita Segall, June 18, 1950; children—Jill, Corey, Marni. LL.B., NYU, 1948, LL.M., 1950; LL.D. (hon.), Mercy Coll., 1981. Bar: N.Y. 1948. Assoc., Raphael & Conlon, N.Y.C., 1948-50; sr. ptnr. Rabin & Green, N.Y.C., 1950-73; sole practice, Yonkers, N.Y., 1974-82; judge, chief judge City of Ct. Yonkers, 1982-94; lectr. N.Y. State Jud. Sems.; jud. hearing officer N.Y. Supreme Ct., 9th Jud. Dist., 1994—; legis. advisor to mem. N.Y. Assembly, Yonkers, 1966-70; justice City of Yonkers, 1970-82. Co-founder C.H.E.A.R. (Children's Hearing Edn. and Research), Yonkers, 1969—, named Man of Yr., 1972. Recipient numerous awards Israel Bonds, Big Bros., others. Mem. N.Y. State Bar Assn., West County Bar Assn., Yonkers Lawyers Assn., N.Y. State City Ct. Judges Assn., N.Y. State Magistrates Assn. Jewish.

**RABINOVITZ, JOEL A.,** lawyer; b. Brookline, Mass., Oct. 18, 1962. AB, Harvard U., 1984, JD, 1987. Bar: Mass. 1988, U.S. Ct. Appeals (2d, 4th and 5th cirs.) 1989, U.S. Ct. Appeals (7th cir.) 1991, D.C. 1993, U.S. Ct. Appeals (D.C. cir.) 1994. Jud. clk. to Hon. Ann Aldrich U.S. Dist. Ct., Cleve., 1987-88; trial atty. tax divsn. appellate sect. U.S. Dept. Justice, Washington, 1988-93; assoc. Harkins Cunningham, Washington, 1993-98; atty., advisorWireless Telecommunications Bureau, Pub. Safety and Private Wireless Divsn. Federal Comm. Commn., Washington, 1998—. Federal civil litigation, Administrative and regulatory, Communications. Office: Federal Comm Commn 445 12th St SE Rm 3-a421 Washington DC 20003-2238

**RABINOWITZ, STUART,** dean, law educator. BA cum laude, CCNY, 1966; JD magna cum laude, Columbia U., 1969. Bar: N.Y. 1970. Assoc. in law Sch. Law Columbia U., N.Y.C., 1969-71; assoc. litigation dept. Rosenman, Colin, Kaye, Petschek, Freund & Emil, N.Y.C., 1971-72; asst. prof. law Hofstra U. Sch. Law, Hempstead, N.Y., 1972-75, assoc. prof. law, 1975-83, prof. law, 1983—, Alexander M. Bickel Disting. prof. law, 1985-97, Andrew Boas and Mark Claster Disting. Prof. Civil Procedure, 1997—, assoc. dean, 1976-79, vice dean, 1982-86, dean, 1989—, chair local budget adv. com.; pvt. cons., 1972-89. Mem. commn. on govt. revision Nassau County, 1993—, chairperson local budget adv. com. Recipient UJA Fedn. Leadership award, Disting. Svc. in the Cause of Justice award Legal Aid Soc., 1995, Martin Luther King Living the Dream award Equal Opportunity Commn., 1995. Mem. ABA, Am. Arbitration Assn. (mem. adv. com.), Fund for Modern Cts. (bd. dirs.), Am. Law Inst., N.Y. State Bar Assn., Nassau County Bar Assn. (proclamation for outstanding svc. to both the legal profession and the cmty. 1991), Suffolk County Bar Assn., Inns of Ct., Phi Beta Kappa. Office: Hofstra U Sch Law 121 Hofstra University Hempstead NY 11549-1210*

**RABKIN, PEGGY ANN,** lawyer; b. Buffalo, Apr. 13, 1945; d. Anthony J. and Margaret G. (Catuzzi) Marano; m. Samuel S. Rabkin, June 29, 1969. BA, SUNY, Buffalo, 1967, MEd, 1970, MA, 1972, JD, PhD, 1975. Tchr. Buffalo Pub. Schs., 1967-69; grad. teaching asst. SUNY, Buffalo, 1969-72; case analyst U.S. Equal Employment Opportunity Com., 1974; dir. affirmative action U. Louisville, 1975-78, adj. prof. of law, 1976-77; atty. office for labor and employment HEW, N.Y.C., 1978; atty. for civil rights Am. Home Products Corp., N.Y.C., 1978-86, sr. atty., 1986—. Author: Fathers to Daughters, 1980; editor: Buffalo Law Rev., 1974-75; contbr. articles to profl. jours. Commr. Louisville & Jefferson Co. Human Relations Com., Louisville, 1977-78. Recipient Christopher Baldy fellow, SUNY at Buffalo Law Sch., 1974-75, Regents Coll. Scholarship N.Y. State Bd. of Regents, 1963-67. Mem. ABA, Assn. of Bar of City of N.Y., Am. Corp. Counsel Assn., Soc. of Human Resources Mgmt., U.S. C. of C. (labor com. 1991—). Avocations: skiing, reading, cooking, and nutrition. Labor, Civil rights. Office: Am Home Products Corp 5 Giralda Farms Madison NJ 07940-1027

**RABORN, JAMES RAY,** lawyer; b. L.A., Dec. 8, 1945; m. Jonell Y. Raborn. BA, La. State U., 1968, JD, 1974. Bar: Tex. 1974, La. 1974. Pvt. practice Houston. Pension, profit-sharing, and employee benefits.

**RABUNSKI, ALAN E.,** lawyer; b. N.Y.C., Jan. 18, 1948; s. Leo and Noima (Alperovich) R.; children: Jonathan Sandler, Benjamin Jacob. BA, CUNY, 1971; JD with honors, John Marshall Law Sch., 1975; LLM in Taxation, NYU, 1978. Bar: N.Y. 1975, Ill. 1975, U.S. Tax Ct. 1981. Law clk. Hon. Allan Stouder Ill. Appellate Ct., Kankakee, 1975-76; pvt. practice law N.Y.C., 1976-94; ptnr. Rabunski & Katz, LLP, N.Y.C., 1994—; lectr. NYU Sch. of Continuing Edn., N.Y.C., 1985-89; lectr. in field. Coach Little League, Larchmont, N.Y., 1988-91; mem. Bd. Assessment Rev., Larchmont, 1992-94; arbitrator Civil Ct. of City of N.Y. Mem. ABA, N.Y. State Bar Assn. (trusts and estates law sect. com. taxation, tax sect. com. on estates, trusts, practice and procedure). Taxation, general, Estate planning, Probate. Home: 151 Fenimore Rd Mamaroneck NY 10543-3538 Office: Rabunski & Katz LLP 630 3rd Ave New York NY 10017-6705

**RABY, KENNETH ALAN,** lawyer, retired army officer; b. Dec. 29, 1935; s. Carl George and Helen Josette (Milne) R.; m. Shirley Rae Nelson, June 2, 1957; children: Randolph Carlton, Shelly Ann. BA, U. S.D., 1957, JD, 1960; grad. with honors, Command and Gen. Staff Coll., 1975, U.S. Army War Coll., 1981. Bar: S.D. 1960, Ga. 1988. Commd. 2d lt. U.S. Army, 1957, advanced through grades to col. JAGC, 1979, ret., 1987; dep. staff judge adv. Am. Divsn., Chu Lai, Vietnam, 1968-69; chief legal team U.S. Army Inf. Sch., Ft. Benning, Ga., 1969-71; team chief, acting divsn. chief adminstrv. law divsn. Office JAG, Dept. Army, 1971-74; staff judge adv. Hdqs. 24th Inf. Divsn., Ft. Stewart, Ga., 1974-79; staff judge adv. U.S. Army Armor Ctr., Ft. Knox, Ky., 1979; chief criminal law divsn. Office of JAG, Washington, 1981-84; sr. judge Army Ct. Mil. Rev., Falls Church, Va., 1984-87; law asst. Ga. Ct. Appeals, 1987—; former chmn., mem. Joint Service Com. on Mil. Justice, 1981-84; mem. Mil. Justice Act of 1983 Adv. Commn., 1984-87; army liaison to criminal law sect. ABA, 1981-84; chief mil. def. counsel U.S. vs. Calley. Decorated Legion of Merit, Bronze Star with oak leaf cluster, Meritorious Svc. medal with 2 oak leaf clusters, Joint Svc. Commendation medal, Air medal, Army Commendation medal with oak leaf cluster, Army Achievement medal. Mem. FBA (chmn. law enforcement liaison com. 1986-87), Assn. U.S. Army, Ga. Bar Assn., Order Ea. Star (worthy grand patron, grand chpt. Ga. 1999—), Masons, Shriners, Scottish Rite, Delta Theta Phi, Theta Xi. Home: 575 Spender Trce Atlanta GA 30350-5017 Office: Staff Atty Ga Ct Appeals Jud Bldg Rm 306 Capitol Sq Atlanta GA 30334-9003

**RACHIE, CYRUS,** lawyer; b. Willmar, Minn., Sept. 5, 1908; s. Elias and Amanda (Lien) R.; m. Helen Evelyn Duncanson, Nov. 25, 1936; children: John Burton Rachie, Janice Carolyn MacKinnon, Elisabeth Dorthea Becker. Student, U. Minn., 1927-28; JD, George Washington U., 1932, William Mitchell Coll. Law, 1934. Bar: Minn. 1934, U.S. Supreme Ct. Atty. Minn. Hwy. Dept., 1934-43; spl. asst. atty. gen. Minn., 1946-50; counsel Luth. Brotherhood (fraternal life ins. co.), 1950-61; pvt. practice law Mpls., 1961-62; v.p., counsel Gamble-Skogmo, Inc., Mpls., 1962-64; v.p., gen. counsel Aid Assn. Lutherans, Appleton, Wis., 1964-70; sr. v.p., gen. counsel Aid Assn. Lutherans, 1970-73; with Rachie & Rachie, 1973-83; pvt. practice, 1983—; part-time spl. master Minn. 4th Jud. Dist., 1977. Councillor Nat. Luth. Coun., 1959-66, sec., 1962-64, mem. exec. com., 1965-66; United Luth. Ch. in Am. del. to 4th Assembly Luth. World Fedn., Helsinki, 1963; past pres. Luth. Welfare Soc. Minn.; past chmn. Mpls. Mayor's Com. on Human Rels.; chmn. finance United Fund drive, 1967-68; past mem. bd. dirs. Mpls. YMCA; trustee emeritus William Mitchell Coll. Law Augsburg Coll. With USNR, 1943-46. Recipient Disting. Alumnus award William Mitchell Coll. Law, 1987. Mem. ABA Minn. Bar Assn., Am. Legion, Minn. Fraternal Congress (past pres.). Lutheran. Club: Rotarian. Probate. Home: 7500 York Ave S Apt 101 Minneapolis MN 55435-4736 *I always try to keep in mind that the Christian Cross consists of both vertical and horizontal lines. The vertical is the longest line and represents a direct line from all of us on the bottom to God on the top and we must commune with Him. The horizontal represents an encompassing line that takes in all of mankind. If my life activities do not include the implementation of both lines of the cross, I will not have a balanced and Christian life.*

**RACHLIN, ALAN SANDERS,** lawyer; b. N.Y.C., Mar. 14, 1942; s. Irving Louis and Blanche (Klein) R.; m. Gail S. Kaufman, June 11, 1972 (dec. Apr. 1987); m. Charlotte D. Moslander, Aug. 15, 1992. BA, CCNY, 1965; MPA, CUNY, 1971; JD, N.Y. Law Sch., 1975. Bar: N.Y. 1976, U.S. Dist. Ct. (so. and ea. dists.) 1976, U.S. Supreme Ct. 1983. Atty. N.Y. State Dept. Ins., N.Y.C., 1976-79, sr. atty., 1979-81, assoc. atty., 1981-87, supervising atty., 1987-96, prin. atty., 1996—. With U.S. Army, 1966-67. Mem. ABA (chair com. on pub. reg. tips), N.Y. State Bar Assn., N.Y. County Lawyers Assn., Med. Jurisprudence. Democrat. Jewish. Avocations: science fiction, mysteries. Office: NY State Ins Dept 25 Beaver St New York NY 10004-2310

**RACHLIN, LEILA,** lawyer; b. Boston, Dec. 8, 1965; d. Howard C. and Nahid Mehri Rachlin; m. Greg M. Zipes, Aug. 21, 1994. BA, Cornell U., 1988; JD, Fordham U., 1991. Bar: N.Y. 1992, U.S. Dist. Ct. (so. and ea. dist.) N.Y. 1992. Assoc. dir. continuing legal edn. Court TV, N.Y.C., 1991-92; assoc. Zeichner, Ellman & Kruase, N.Y.C., 1992-94, Cleary, Gottlieb, Steen & Hamilton, N.Y.C., 1994-97; sr. corp. assoc. White & Case, LLP, N.Y.C., 1998—; rsch. asst., law jour. mem. Fordham Internat., 1989-91. Editor Cornell Praxis Literary mag., 1986-88. Mem. Vol. Lawyers for the Arts, 1995—. Mem. Assn. of the Bar of the City of N.Y., (assn. night com.), New York Women's Bar Assn., Corp. (mem. corp. banking and intellectual property coms., liaison for lawyer mentor program). Avocations: museums, theater, film. Banking, Contracts commercial, General corporate. Home: 415 E 80th St Apt 5F New York NY 10021-0637 Office: White & Case LLP 1155 Avenue Of The Americas New York NY 10036-2711

**RACINE, BRIAN AUGUST,** intellectual property lawyer; b. Evanston, Ill., Feb. 13, 1963; s. Frank M. and Kathryn Racine; m. Gail E. Ekstrom, Oct. 3, 1992. BA, U. No. Iowa, 1986; JD, U. Miss., 1989; LLM in Intellectual Property, John Marshall Law Sch., 1995. Authorized house counsel, Fla., Ill. Assoc. legal GTE Air Fone Inc., Oakbrook, Ill., 1990-93; counsel GRI Inc., Chgo., 1993-94, sr. counsel intellectual property, 1994-96; sr. intellectual property counsel NCCI, Inc., Boca Raton, Fla., 1996—. Rsch. asst. Loyola Law Jour., U.-5th Cir. Decisions, 1987. Mem. ABA, Computer Law Assn., Licensing Exec. Soc. Avocation: golf. Home: 3503 SE Fairway Oaks Trl Stuart FL 34997-4711 Office: NCCI Inc 750 Park Of Commerce Dr Boca Raton FL 33487-3696

**RADCLIFFE, WILLIAM LOUIS,** lawyer; b. L.A., Oct. 15, 1958; s. John Albert and Rose Marie Radcliffe; m. Bonita Gemma Van Daalen Meyer, Aug. 11, 1986; 1 child, Andrew William. Student, San Diego State U., 1977-79; BS in Law, Western State U., 1980, JD, 1982. Bar: Calif. 1983, U.S. Dist. Ct. (cen. dist.) Calif. 1983. Pvt. practice Covina, Calif., 1983—. Mem. L.A. Trial Lawyers Assn., Eastern Bar Assn., L.A. County Bar Assn., Toastmasters (treas. 1987). Avocations: basketball, public speaking. Bankruptcy, Personal injury, Family and matrimonial. Office: 4195 Chino Hills Pky Chino Hills CA 91709-2618

**RADDING, ANDREW,** lawyer; b. N.Y.C., Nov. 30, 1944; m. Bonnie A. Levinson, Oct. 7, 1972; children: Judith Lynne, Joshua David. BBA, CCNY-Baruch Sch., 1965; JD, Boston U., 1968. Bar: N.Y. 1968, Md. 1977, D.C. 1977, U.S. Supreme Ct. Grad. fellow Northwestern U. Sch. Law, 1968-69; asst. counsel U.S. Ho. of Reps. Select Com. on Crime, 1969-72; asst. U.S. atty. for Dist. Md., 1972-77; ptnr. Francomano, Radding & Mannes, Balt., 1977-80, Burke, Gerber, Wilen, Francomano & Radding, Balt., 1980-85, Blades & Rosenfeld P.A., Balt., 1985-97, Adelberg, Rudow, Dorf, Hendler and Sameth LLC, Balt., 1997—; mem. adj. faculty clin. practice skills, criminal law, fed. criminal practice U. Balt. Sch. Law, 1980—; mem. trial experience com. U.S. Dist. ct., 1986-88; apptd. by gov. State Adminstrv. Bd. of Election Laws, 1995-96. Bd. dirs. Copper Hill Condominium, 1979-82, pres., 1981-82; subcom. Md. Republican Conv., 1981; sen. C.M. Mathias Jud. Selection com., 1986, chmn. U.S. Dist. Ct. Bicentennial Program, 1989-90. Mem. ABA, Md. Bar Assn., Balt. City Bar Assn. (jud. selection com. 1990-92, 94—, chmn. 1996-97, exec. coun. 1998-99, co-chmn. membership com. 1999—), Fed. Bar Assn. (Balt. chpt. pres. 1986-87), U.S. Atty. Alumni Assn. Md. (pres. 1978—), Md. Inst. Continuing Profl. Edn. for Lawyers (bd. govs. 1987-92, inquiry panel atty. grievance com. 1991—), U.S. Arbitration and Mediation and Nat. Arbitration Forum (mediator and arbitrator), Nat. Arbitration Forum (arbitrator). Jewish. Federal civil litigation, State civil litigation, Criminal. Office: Adelberg Rudow et al LLC 2 Hopkins Plz Baltimore MD 21201-2930

**RADER, DIANE CECILE,** lawyer; b. San Francisco, Sept. 8, 1949; d. Dale A. and Genevieve A. (Couture) R. BA, Portland State U., 1987; JD, Lewis and Clark Coll., 1990. Bar: Oreg. 1990, Idaho 1992, U.S. Dist. Ct. Idaho 1992, U.S. Dist. Ct. Oreg. 1995. Founder, cons. D.C. Rader & Assocs., Portland, 1972-88; real estate broker Rader Realty, Portland, 1982—; pvt. practice law Boise, 1992—; with Rader and Rader, Ontario, Oreg., 1990—; bd. dirs. Criminal Justice Adv. Bd., Malheur County, Oreg. Asst. mng. editor: Internat. Legal Perspectives, 1989-90. Polit. cons. and fundraiser various parties and campaigns, Oreg., 1972-88; fundraiser, cons. charitable orgns., Oreg., 1972—, others. Mem. ABA, ATLA, Nat. Assn. Criminal Def. Lawyers, Oreg. Trial Lawyers Assn., Oreg. Criminal Def. Lawyers Assn., Oreg. State Bar (pub. svc. and info. com. 1994-97, chmn. pub. rels. subcom. 1994—), Phi Alpha Delta. Avocations: music, writing, arts, outdoor sports, travel. Criminal, General practice, Personal injury. Office: Rader & Rader 381 W Idaho Ave Ontario OR 97914-2344

**RADER, PHILIP SPENDELOW,** lawyer; b. Columbia, S.C., Mar. 2, 1952; s. John Frank and Helen Heald Rader; m. Ellen Louise Gordon, Nov. 10, 1985; 1 child, Isaac Clark. BA, U. S.C., 1976, JD, 1981. Bar: N.H. 1981. Assoc. Michael, Jones & Wensley, Rochester, N.H., 1982-85, ptnr., 1985-97; assoc. Cooper, Deans & Cargill, North Conway, N.H., 1997-98, shareholder, dir., 1998—. Auditor Town of Lee, N.H., 1990-95. Mem. Rochester C. of C. (pres. 1992). General practice, Family and matrimonial. Home: PO Box 970 Intervale NH 03845-0970 Office: Cooper Deans & Cargill 92 Pine St PO Box 450 North Conway NH 03860-0450

**RADER, RALPH TERRANCE,** lawyer; b. Clarksburg, W.Va., Dec. 5, 1947; s. Ralph Coolidge and Jeanne (Cover) R.; m. Rebecca Jo Vorderman, Mar. 22, 1969; children: Melissa Michelle, Allison Suzanne. BSME, Va. Poly. Inst., 1970; JD, Am. U., Washington, 1974. Bar: Va. 1975, U.S. Ct. Customs and Patent Appeals 1977, U.S. Dist. Ct. (ea. dist.) Mich. 1978, Mich. 1979, U.S. Ct. Appeals (6th cir.) 1979, U.S. Dist. Ct. (we. dist.) Mich. 1981, U.S. Ct. Appeals (fed. cir.) 1983. Supervisory patent examiner U.S. Patent Office, Washington, 1970-77; patent atty., ptnr. Cullen, Sloman, Cantor, Grauer, Scott & Rutherford, Detroit, 1977-88; ptnr., Dykema, Gossett, 1989-96; ptnr. Rader, Fishman & Grauer, 1996—. Contbr. articles to profl. jours. Mem. adminstrv. bd. First United Methodist Ch., Birmingham, Mich., 1980—. With U.S. Army, 1970-76. Recipient Superior Performance award U.S. Patent Office, Washington, 1971-77. Mem. Am. Patent Law Assn., ABA, Mich. Patent Law Assn., Mich. Bar. (mem. governing council patent trademark and copyright law sect. 1981-84), Engring. Soc. Detroit, Masons, Tau Beta Pi, Pi Tau Sigma, Phi Kappa Phi. Methodist. Patent, Trademark and copyright, Federal civil litigation. Home: 4713 Riverchase Dr Troy MI 48098-4186 Office: Rader Fishman & Grauer 1533 N Woodward Ave Ste 140 Bloomfield Hills MI 48304-2862

**RADER, RANDALL RAY,** federal judge; b. 1949. BA magna cum laude, 1974; JD with honors, George Washington U., 1978. Bar: D.C., U.S. Ct. Appeals (fed. cir.) 1990, U.S. Claims Ct., U.S. Supreme Ct. Legis. asst. to Congresswoman Virginia Smith U.S. Ho. of Reps., 1975-78; mem. staff Ways and Means Com. U.S. Ho. Reps., 1978-81; chief counsel subcom. on Constn. U.S. Senate Judiciary Com., chief counsel, staff dir. subcom. on patents, copyrights and trademarks, 1981-87; counsel to Senator Orrin Hatch, 1981-87; judge U.S. Ct. Claims, Washington, 1988-90, U.S. Ct. Appeals (fed. cir.), Washington, 1990—; lectr. patent law U. Va. Sch. Law; lectr. trial advocacy, lectr. George Washington U. Nat. Law Ctr., Washington; lectr. comparative patent law Georgetown U. Law Ctr., Washington. Co-author: Patent Law, 1997; co-editor: Criminal Justice Reform, 1983; contbr. articles to prof. jours. Mem. FBA. Office: US Ct Appeals Fed Cir 717 Madison Pl NW Ste 913 Washington DC 20439-0002

**RADER, STEVEN PALMER,** lawyer; b. Charlotte, N.C., Dec. 30, 1952; s. Alvin Marion Jr. and Shirley Ninabelle (Palmer) R. AB, Duke U., 1975; postgrad., Stetson U., 1975-76; JD, Wake Forest U., 1978. Bar: N.C. 1978, U.S. Dist. Ct. (ea. dist.) N.C. 1979. Assoc. Wilkinson and Vosburgh, Washington, N.C., 1978-81; pvt. practice Washington, 1981-88; spl. asst. to sec. N.C. Dept. Human Resources, Raleigh, 1988-89, asst. dir. office legal affairs, 1989-91, gen. counsel, 1991-93; ptnr. Wilkinson & Rader, P.A., Washington, 1993—; commr. Nat. Conf. Commrs. on Uniform State Laws, 1985-93; gen. counsel N.C. Rep. Party, 1992-97; commr. N.C. Rules Rev. Commn., 1997—. Mem., sec. City of Washington Human Rels. Coun., 1981-83; chmn. Beaufort County Rep. party, Washington, 1983-87, 1st Congl. Dist. Rep. party, N.C., 1985-92; v.p. East Main St. Area Neighborhood Assn., 1983-85; del. Rep. Nat. Conv., 1984, 88, 92. Mem. N.C. State Bar, 2d Jud. Dist. Bar, Beaufort County Hist. Soc. (v.p. 1981-85, pres. 1985-86). Lutheran. Avocations: boating, classic automobiles, travel. Home: PO Box 1901 Washington NC 27889-1901 Office: Wilkinson & Rader PA PO Box 732 Washington NC 27889-0732

**RADEY, DONA LYNN,** lawyer; b. N.Y.C., Nov. 28, 1959; d. Richard Gregor and Abigail Elizabeth (Irvin) R. BA, U. Pa., 1981; JD, U. So. Calif., 1987. Bar: N.Y. 1990. Assoc. Winthrop, Stimson, Putnam & Roberts, N.Y.C., 1987—. Pro bono atty. Lawyer's Com. for Human Rights, N.Y., 1991. Mem. ABA. Mergers and acquisitions, General corporate, Securities. Office: Winthrop Stimson Putnam & Roberts One Battery Park Plz New York NY 10004

**RADIN, SAM,** lawyer, estate planner; b. N.Y.C., Aug. 1, 1951; s. Clarence and Marjorie (Rembar) R.; m. Pamela Anderson, Sept. 13, 1981; children: Clarence Anderson, Elizabeth Rebecca. BA, Columbia U., 1973; JD, Boston U., 1976. Bar: N.J. 1976, U.S. Dist. Ct. N.J. 1976, N.Y. 1978, U.S. Dist. Ct. (so. dist.) N.Y. 1978, U.S. Ct. Appeals (D.C. cir.) 1978, U.S. Supreme Ct. 1980. Assoc. Burns, Van Kirk, N.Y.C., 1976-79, Lovejoy Wasson successor to Burns, Van Kirk, N.Y.C., 1979-80; pvt. practice, N.Y.C., 1980-84; v.p., gen. counsel Nat. Madison Group, Inc., N.Y.C., 1984—. Contbg. author: Executive Compensation Answer Book, 1998; contbg. author, editor: Estate and Retirement Planning Answer Book, 1999; also articles. Bd. dirs. Student Athletes Inc., N.Y.C., 1992-98, Westchester Conservatory Music, White Plains, N.Y., 1995-97. Recipient Nathan Burkan Meml. prize ASCAP, 1975. Mem. ABA (subcom. on life ins. tax sect. 1996—), N.Y. State Bar Assn., Assn. Bar City N.Y. Avocations: salt water fly fishing, collecting books, skiing, running. Estate planning, Estate taxation. Home: 71 Greenacres Ave Scarsdale NY 10583-1442 Office: Nat Madison Group Inc 355 Lexington Ave New York NY 10017-6603

**RADIN, STEVEN S.,** lawyer; b. Newark, N.J.; s. Morris and Sara Radin; m. Karen Burman; children: Jonathan, Elizabeth Radin Jacobs. AB, Seton Hall U., 1957; LLB, JD, Columbia Law Sch., 1960. Atty. Sills Cummis Radin Tischman Gross & Epstein, Newark. 2d lt. U.S. Army. Insurance, Bankruptcy, Banking. Office: Sills Cummis Radin Tischman Gross & Epstein One Riverfront Plaza Newark NJ 07102

**RADLER, MONTE PHILIP,** lawyer; b. Torrington, Conn., Feb. 25, 1952; s. Albert Gabriel and Hazel Dawn (Schneider) R.; m. Christine Anne Gatti, Aug. 22, 1982; children: Matthew Abraham Idan, Ethan Alexander. BA, Northwestern U., 1974; JD, U. Conn., 1978; MS, So. Conn. State, 1985. Bar: Conn. 1979, U.S. Dist. Ct. 1980, U.S. Supreme Ct. 1993. Fund raiser Nat. Assn. March of Dimes, Chgo., 1974-75; assoc. Albert E. Goring, Jr., P.C., Torrington, 1979-80, Goldman & Rosen, P.C., Bridgeport, Conn., 1980-82, McHugh & McKeon, P.C., Westport, Conn., 1982-85; sr. asst. pub. defender State of Conn., Stamford, 1985-98, supr. asst. pub. defender, 1998—. Mem. Nat. Assn. Criminal Def. Lawyers, Conn. Assn. Criminal Def. Lawyers. Office: State of Conn Pub Defenders Office Psychiat Def Unit CVH PO Box 351 Middletown CT 06457-7023

**RADMER, MICHAEL JOHN,** lawyer, educator; b. Wisconsin Rapids, Wis., Apr. 28, 1945; s. Donald Richard and Thelma Loretta (Donahue) R.; children from previous marriage: Christina Nicole, Ryan Michael; m. Laurie J. Anshus, Dec. 22, 1983; 1 child, Michael John. B.S., Northwestern U., Evanston, Ill., 1967; J.D., Harvard U., 1970. Bar: Minn. 1970. Assoc. Dorsey & Whitney, Mpls., 1970-75, ptnr., 1976—; lectr. law Hamline U. Law Sch., St. Paul, 1981-84; gen. counsel, rep., sec. 147 federally registered investment cos., Mpls. and St. Paul, 1977—. Contbr. articles to legal jours. Active legal work Hennepin County Legal Advice Clinic, Mpls., 1971—. Mem. ABA, Minn. Bar Assn., Hennepin County Bar Assn. Club: Mpls. Athletic. General corporate, Securities. Home: 4329 E Lake Harriet Pky Minneapolis MN 55409-1725 Office: Dorsey & Whitney Pillsbury Ctr S 220 S 6th St Ste 2200 Minneapolis MN 55402-1498 *A key to a successful and happy life is achieving a balance. Intellectual, academic and vocational goals are important, but their pursuit should be balanced with ample time spent with family and friends, travel and enjoying reading, music, art and sports. Don't be afraid to try something new; realize that education should be a lifelong pursuit. Much frustration can be avoided by realizing that life is full of trade-offs. You can't experience the joy of raising children and have the complete freedom of the child-free. Finally, while you should strive for* *perfection, be content with less. We are only human, and live in an imperfect, yet wonderful, world.*

**RADNOR, ALAN T.,** lawyer; b. Cleve., Mar. 10, 1946; s. Robert Clark and Rose (Chester) R.; m. Carol Sue Hirsch, June 22, 1969; children: Melanie, Joshua, Joanna. B.A., Kenyon Coll., 1967; M.S. in Anatomy, Ohio State U., 1969, J.D., 1972. Bar: Ohio 1972. Ptnr., Vorys, Sater, Seymour & Pease, Columbus, Ohio, 1972—; adj. prof. law Ohio State U., Columbus, 1979—. Contbr. articles to profl. jours. Bd. dirs., trustee Congregation Tifereth Israel, Columbus, 1975—, pres., 1985-87; trustee Columbus Mus. Art, 1995-98. Named Boss of Yr., Columbus Assn. Legal Secs., 1983. Fellow Am. Coll. of Trial Lawyers; mem. ABA, Ohio State Bar Assn., Columbus Bar Assn., Def. Research Inst., Internat. Assn. Def. Counsel, Ohio Hosp. Assn. Democrat. Jewish. Avocations: reading; sculpture. Personal injury, Product liability. Home: 400 S Columbia Ave Columbus OH 43209-1629 Office: Vorys Sater Seymour & Pease 52 E Gay St PO Box 1008 Columbus OH 43216-1008

**RADOGNO, JOSEPH ANTHONY,** lawyer; b. Chgo., Dec. 7, 1958; s. Nunzio Concetto and Bernice M. Radogno; m. Randi Ellen Weinberg, Sept. 28, 1991; 1 child, Celestina Nicole. BA, U. Ill., 1980; JD, Ill. Inst. Tech., 1984. Bar: Ill. 1984. Claim litig. atty. Allstate Ins. Co., Northbrook, Ill., 1989—. Insurance.

**RADON, JENIK RICHARD,** lawyer; b. Berlin, Jan. 14, 1946; came to U.S., 1951, naturalized, 1956; s. Louis and Irmgard (Hinz) R.; m. Heidi B. Duerbeck, June 10, 1971; 1 child, Kaara H.D. BA, Columbia Coll., 1967; MCP, U. Calif., Berkeley, 1971; JD, Stanford U., Berkeley, 1971. Bar: Calif. 1972, N.Y. 1975, U.S. Ct. Appeals (2d cir.) 1975, U.S. Dist. Ct. (so. dist.) N.Y. 1975. Atty. Radon & Ishizumi, N.Y.C., Berlin and Tokyo, 1981—; counsel Walter, Conston, Alexander & Green, N.Y.C., 1991—; lectr. Polish Acad. Scis., 1980, Tokyo Arbitration Assn., 1983, Japan External Trade Orgn., 1983, 86, Japan Mgmt. Assn., 1983, 90, Japan Inst. Internat. Bus. Law, 1983-84, Va. Ctr. World Trade, 1985, UN Indsl. Devel. Orgn., Warsaw, 1987, Wichita World Trade Coun., 1987, Inst. Nat. Economy of Poland, 1987, Hungarian Econ. Roundtable, 1987, Tallinn, 1988, USSR Com. on Sci. and Tech., 1988, USSR Fgn. Trade Ministry, 1988, Tallinn Tech. Inst., 1988, Tartu State U., 1988, U. Ottawa, 1988-89, Palm Beach World Trade Coun., 1988, Fla. Atlantic U., 1988, Bus. Assn. Latin Am. Studies, 1989—, Assn. France-Poland, 1989, Russian and East European Studies Inst. Stanford U., 1989, Ukrainian Profl. Assn. N.Y. and N.J., 1989, Columbia U. Harriman Inst., 1989, Inst. East-West Security Studies, 1989, Friedrich-Schiller U. Jena, East Germany, 1990, East European Inst. Free U. Berlin, numerous others; bd. dirs. Gland Pharma Ltd., India, 1996—, HTM Sport, Estonia, 1993—; pub. Baltic Rev., 1993—, City Paper (Baltic), 1993—; mem. exec. com. Vetter Group, Germany. Editor-in-chief Stanford Jour. Internat. Studies, 1970-71; contbr. The International Acquisitions Handbook, 1987, Negotiating and Financing Joint Ventures Abroad, 1989, How to Form and Manage Successful Strategic Alliances, 1990, Risks Management in International Business, 1991, Comrade Goes Private, 1992, Investing in Reform, 1991, Fordham Internat. Law Jour., 1996, various jours. in U.S., Germany, Canada. Active Am. Coun. on Germany, N.Y.C., 1978—; vice-chmn. U.S.-Polish Econ. Coun., 1989-93; mem. exec. com. Afghanistan Relief Com., N.Y.C., 1980-95; bd. dirs. Columbia Coll. Alumni Assn., 1988-92, nat. coun., 1996—, Freedom Medicine, 1987-94, chmn., 1989-94; trustee Direct Relief Internat., Santa Barbara, Calif., 1987-89; founder and dir. Eesti and Eurasian Fellowship of Columbia U., 1990—; profl., advisor (assoc.) Columbia Harriman Inst., 1993—; advisor Estonian Ministry of Economy, Reform and Justice, 1991-95; adv. Prime Min. of Crimea, Ukraine, 1994-95; adv. to Parliament Republic of Georgia, 1996-98, advisor Min. of Fin. of Georgia, 1998—, Georgian Internat. Oil Corp., 1998—; chmn. Estonian-Am. C. of C., 1990-93, Deutsche Stiftung fuer internationale rechtliche Zusammenarbeit, Estonia Commn., Beirat, 1992-94. Mem. ABA, Asia-Pacific Lawyers Assn., German-Am. Law Assn. Roman Catholic. Private international, General corporate, Banking. Office: Radon & Ishizumi 269 W 71st St New York NY 10023-3701

**RAE, JOHN JOSEPH,** lawyer; b. Battle Creek, Mich., Sept. 11, 1935; s. James Gordon and Mary Kathryn (McGrail) R.; m. Patricia Ann Rae, Dec. 30, 1961; children: Elizabeth, Susan, Mary. BS in Social Sci. cum laude, John Carroll U., Cleve., 1957; JD, DePaul U., Chgo., 1961. Bar: Ill. 1961, Mich. 1965. Assoc. McDermott, Will & Emery, Chgo., 1961-65; pvt. practice Battle Creek, Mich., 1965-75; pros. atty. Calhoun County, Marshall, Mich., 1975-76; city atty. City of Midland, Mich., 1977-95; mem. State Bar Ethics Com., Lansing, Mich., 1994. Editor Calhoun County Bar Assn. Newsletter; contbr. articles to profl. jours. Chairperson bd. trustees Mid-Mich. Dispute Resolution Ctr., Saginaw, 1995. Capt. U.S. Army, 1959-69. Mem. State Bar Mich., Midland County Bar Assn. Roman Catholic. Avocations: reading, music.

**RAE, MATTHEW SANDERSON, JR.,** lawyer; b. Pitts., Sept. 12, 1922; s. Matthew Sanderson and Olive (Waite) R.; m. Janet Hettman, May 2, 1953; children: Mary-Anna, Margaret Rae Mallory, Janet S. Rae Dupree. AB, Duke, 1946, LLB, 1947; postgrad., Stanford U., 1951. Bar: Md. 1948, Calif. 1951. Asst. to dean Duke Sch. Law, Durham, N.C., 1947-48; assoc. Karl F. Steinmann, Balt., 1948-49, Guthrie, Darling & Shattuck, L.A., 1953-54; nat. field rep. Phi Alpha Delta Law Frat., L.A., 1949-51; research atty. Calif. Supreme Ct., San Francisco, 1951-52; ptnr. Darling, Hall & Rae (and predecessor firms), L.A., 1955—; mem. Calif. Commn. Uniform State Laws, 1985—, chmn., 1993-94; chmn. drafting com. for revision Uniform Prin. and Income Act of Nat. Conf., 1991-97, Probate and Mental Health Task Force, Jud. Coun. Calif., 1996—. Vice pres. L.A. County Rep. Assembly, 1959-64; mem. L.A. County Rep. Ctrl. Com., 1960-64, 77-90, exec. com., 1977-90; vice chmn. 17th Congl. Dist., 1960-62, 28th Congl. Dist., 1962-64; chmn. 46th Assy. Dist., 1962-64, 27th Senatorial Dist., 1977-85, 29th Senatorial Dist., 1985-90; mem. Calif. Rep. State Ctrl. Com., 1966—, exec. com., 1966-67; pres. Calif. Rep. League, 1966-67; trustee Rep. Assocs., 1979-94, pres., 1983-85, chmn. bd. dirs., 1985-87. 2d lt. USAAF, WWII. Fellow Am. Coll. Trust and Estate Counsel; academician Internat. Acad. Estate and Trust Law (exec. coun. 1974-78); mem. ABA, L.A. County Bar Assn. (chmn. probate and trust law com. 1964-66, chmn. legis. com. 1980-86, chmn. program com. 1981-82, chmn. membership retention com. 1982-83, trustee 1983-85, dir. Bar Found., 1987-93, Arthur K. Marshall award probate and trust law sect. 1984, Shattuck-Price Meml. award 1990), South Bay Bar Assn., State Bar of Calif. (chmn. state bar jour. com. 1970-71, probate com. 1974-75; exec. com. estate planning trust and probate law sect. 1977-83, chmn. legis. com. 1977-89; co-chmn. 1991-92; probate law cons. group Calif. Bd. Legal Specialization 1977-88; chmn. conf. dels. resolutions com. 1987, exec. com. conf. dels. 1987-90), Lawyers Club L.A. (bd. govs. 1981-87, 1st v.p. 1982-83), Am. Legion (comdr. Allied post 1969-70), Legion Lex (bd. dirs. 1964-99, pres. 1969-71), Air Force Assn., Aircraft Owners and Pilots Assn., Town Hall (gov. 1970-78, pres. 1975), World Affairs Coun., Internat. Platform Assn., Breakfast Club (law, pres. 1989-90), Commonwealth Club, Chancery Club (pres. 1996-97), Rotary, Phi Beta Kappa (councilor Alpha Assn. 1983—, pres. 1996), Omicron Delta Kappa, Phi Alpha Delta (supreme justice 1972-74, elected to Disting. Svc. chpt. 1978), Sigma Nu. Presbyterian. Probate, Estate taxation, Estate planning. Home: 600 John St Manhattan Beach CA 90266-5837 Office: Darling Hall & Rae 520 S Grand Ave Fl 7 Los Angeles CA 90071-2600

**RAEDER, MYRNA SHARON,** lawyer, educator; b. N.Y.C., Feb. 4, 1947; d. Samuel and Estelle (Auslander) R.; m. Terry Oliver Kelly, July 13, 1975; children: Thomas Oliver, Michael Lawrence. BA, Hunter Coll., 1968; JD, NYU, 1971; LLM, Georgetown U., 1975. Bar: N.Y. 1972, D.C. 1972, Calif. 1972. Spl. asst. U.S. atty. U.S. Atty.'s Office, Washington, 1972-73; asst. prof. U. San Francisco Sch. Law, 1973-75; assoc. O'Melveny & Myers, L.A., 1975-79; assoc. prof. Southwestern U. Sch. Law, L.A., 1979-82, prof., 1983—, Irwin R. Buchalter prof. law, 1990; mem. faculty Nat. Judicial Coll., 1993—. Prettyman fellow Georgetown Law Ctr., Washington, 1971-73. Author: Federal Pretrial Practice, 2d edit., 1995; co-author: Evidence, State and Federal Rules in a Nutshell, 3d edit., 1997, Evidence, Cases, Materials and Problems, 2d edit., 1998. Fellow Am. Bar Found.; mem. ABA (criminal justice sect. 1994-97, vice-chair planning 1997-98, chair elect 1997-98, chair 1998-99, trial evidence com. litigation sect. 1980—, adv. to nat. conf. com-mrs. uniform state laws drafting com. uniform rules of evidence 1996—), Assn. Am. Law Schs. (chair elect evidence sect. 1996, chair 1997, com. on sects. 1984-87, chair women in legal edn. sect. 1982), Nat. Assn. Women Lawyers (bd. dirs. 1991-98, pres.-elect 1993, pres. 1994-96), Women Lawyers Assn. L.A. (bd. dirs., coord. mothers support group 1987-96), Order of Coif, Phi Beta Kappa. Office: Southwestern U Sch Law 675 S Westmoreland Ave Los Angeles CA 90005-3905

**RAFALOWICZ, JOSEPH,** lawyer; b. Berlin, Germany, Aug. 31, 1946; came to U.S., 1952; s. Leon and Rose (Shabason) R.; m. Karen Jo Price, June 1981; children: Benjamin Jacob, Adam Russell. AB, U. Pa., 1968; JD, Harvard U., 1971. Bar: Mass. 1971, U.S. Dist. Ct. Mass. 1972, N.Y. 1978, U.S. Dist. Ct. (ea. and so. dists.) N.Y. 1979. Assoc. Lourie & Cutler, Boston, 1971-73, Ellison & Lessess, Boston, 1973-77; gen. counsel Ticketron, N.Y.C., 1977-87; pvt. practice N.Y.C., White Plains, N.Y., 1987—. Mem. ABA, N.Y. State Bar Assn. Estate planning, Estate taxation, Probate. Home: 24 Taymil Rd New Rochelle NY 10804-2802 Office: 401 Broadway Ste 400 New York NY 10013-3005

**RAFEEDIE, EDWARD, SR.,** federal judge; b. Orange, N.J., Jan. 6, 1929; s. Fred and Nabeeha (Hishmeh) R.; m. Ruth Alice Horton, Oct. 8, 1961; children: Fredrick Alexander, Jennifer Ann. BS in Law, U. So. Calif., 1957, JD, 1959; LLD (hon.), Pepperdine U., 1978. Bar: Calif. 1960. Pvt. practice Santa Monica, Calif., 1960-69; mcpl. ct. judge Santa Monica Jud. Dist., 1969-71; judge Superior Ct. State of Calif., L.A., 1971-82; dist. judge U.S. Dist. Court (cen. dist.) Calif., L.A., 1982-96, sr. judge, 1996—. With U.S. Army, 1950-52, Korea. Office: US Dist Ct RM 244P 312 N Spring St Ste 244P Los Angeles CA 90012-4704

**RAFFERTY, CATHERINE MARY,** lawyer; b. Washington, Aug. 20, 1966; d. Joseph Patrick and Angene George Rafferty. BA in Pub. Policy Studies, U. Chgo., 1988, MA in Internat. Rels., 1988; JD, Cath. U., 1991; LLM in Tax, Georgetown U., 1994. Bar: D.C. 1991, U.S. Tax Ct. 1992, U.S. Dist. Ct. D.C. 1992, U.S. Ct. Appeals (C.C. cir.) 1992, Md. 1994. Atty. Office Assoc. Chief Counsel (Internat.) IRS, Washington, 1991-92; atty. Kelly & Nicolaides, Chevy Chase, Md., 1992-94; pvt. practice Chevy Chase, 1994-95; mem. Rafferty & Farmakides, LLC, Washington, 1995; mng. mem. Rafferty & Rafferty, PLLC, Washington, 1995—; chairwoman Montgomery/Prince George's County Tax Study Group, Md., 1998—. Chair various events Philoptochos Soc. St. Sophia Greek Orthodox Cathedral, Washington, 1994—, asst. treas., 1999—. Mem. ABA, Md. State Bar Assn., D.C. Bar, Bar Assn. D.C., Women's Bar Assn. D.C., Montgomery County Bar Assn. Greek Orthodox. Estate planning, Probate, Estate taxation. Office: Rafferty & Rafferty PLLC 4730 Massachusetts Ave NW Washington DC 20016-2306

**RAFFERTY, EDSON HOWARD,** lawyer, consultant; b. Newark, Jan. 7, 1943; s. Martin James and Amber Louise (Leach) R.; m. Sharon S. Margulies; children: Ethan Eric, Heather Knowles, Lydia Manela, Jillian Margulies. Degree in Chemistry, Syracuse U., BS in Mech. Engring., 1966; MS in Bio-engring., U. Tex., 1982; JD, Hamline Law Sch.; M in Mgmt., MIT. Bar: Mass. 1982. Chief engr. Artificial Heart Project, VA Hosp., Houston and Syracuse, N.Y., 1966-68; prin. scientist, mgr. Artificial Heart Program Applied Sci. divsn. Litton Industries, Inc., Mpls., 1968-70; COO, exec. v.p., dir. Bio-Medicus, Inc., Mpls., 1970-78, acting pres., 1970-73; sr. ptnr. Consultus, Inc., Cambridge, Mass., 1978—; mng. ptnr. Attys. at Law-Rafferty & Associates, Cambridge, Mass., 1982—; pres., CEO Neuro-Genesis, Inc., 1996—. Over 50 patents and inventions in field; contbr. articles to profl. jours. Nat. coord. med. exch. between U.S. and USSR, Mpls., 1975-79; chmn. corp. fin. Coun. on U.S./USSR Health Care Exch., Mpls., 1975-79; participant numerous TV spls. on artificial heart, 1968-78. Recipient IR-100 award Indsl. Rsch. Inc., 1972, Bachner award Plastic Industry Trade Orgn., 1976. Mem. ABA, ATLA (chmn. Theophylline Litigation Group 1990—, chmn. Automatic Door Litigation Group 1992—), Mass. Bar Assn. General civil litigation, Personal injury, Product liability. Office: Rafferty & Associates 66 Long Wharf 3rd Floor Boston MA 02110

**RAFFERTY, JAMES GERARD,** lawyer; b. Boston, July 9, 1951; s. James John and Helen Christine (Kennedy) R.; m. Rhonda Beth Friedman, May 17, 1981; children: Jessica Faith, Evan Louis Quinn. BA, Brown U., 1974; MA, Princeton U., 1980; JD, Georgetown U., 1984. Bar: Md. 1985, D.C. 1985, U.S. Tax Ct. 1988, U.S. Ct. Appeals (4th cir.) 1989, U.S. Ct. Appeals (3d cir.) 1992. Assoc. Piper & Marbury, Washington, 1984-91, Pepper, Hamilton & Scheetz, Washington, 1991-92; founding ptnr. Harkins Cunningham, Washington, 1992—. Contbr. articles to legal jours. Brown U. Club of Boston scholar, 1969-70. Mem. ABA (chmn. com. on affiliated and related corps. tax sect. 1994-95). Roman Catholic. Avocation: golf. Corporate taxation, General corporate, Mergers and acquisitions. Office: Harkins Cunningham Ste 600 801 Pennsylvania Ave NW Washington DC 20004

**RAGAN, CHARLES OLIVER, JR.,** lawyer; b. Knoxville, Tenn., Dec. 23, 1935; s. Charles Oliver and Jeanette (Butler) R.; m. Pauline Iona Kimsey, Apr. 19, 1958. B.S. in Bus. Adminstrn., U. Tenn., 1958, J.D., 1963. Bar: Tenn. 1964, U.S. Dist. Ct. (ea. dist.) Tenn. 1965; cert. consumer bankruptcy specialist. Staff atty. State of Tenn., Chattanooga, 1964-69; atty. Bean & Phillips, Chattanooga, 1969-73; sr. ptnr. Ragan & Schulman, Chattanooga, 1973-75, Ragan & Littleton, Chattanooga, 1975-80, Ragan & Wulforst, Chattanooga, 1980-84; pvt. practice, Chattanooga, 1984—; Tenn. commnr. Nat. Conf. Commrs. on Uniform State Laws, 1976-80. Campaign treas. for Democratic candidates. Mem. ABA, Assn. Trial Lawyers Am., Tenn. Bar Assn., Tenn. Trial Lawyers Assn. (bd. govs. 1977-81), Chattanooga Trial Lawyers Assn. (pres. 1977), Chattanooga Bar Assn. (bd. govs. 1979-80). Democrat. Methodist. Personal injury, General practice, Bankruptcy. Home: 185 Woodcliff Cir Signal Mountain TN 37377-3142 Office: 707 Georgia Ave Ste 300 Chattanooga TN 37402-2047

**RAGAZZO, CORINA-MARIA,** lawyer; b. Santiago de Cuba, Cuba, May 23, 1967; came to U.S., 1971; d. Hugo Cecilio and Juana Maria Artime; m. Robert Allen Ragzzo, Nov. 16, 1996. BA, U. St. Thomas, 1989; JD, U. Houston, 1992. Bar: Tex. 1992, U.S. Dist. Ct. (so. dist.) Tex. 1994, U.S. Ct. Dist. Ct. (ea. and no. dists.) Tex. 1997, U.S. Ct. Appeals (5th cir.) 1997. Staff atty. U. Houston Legal Aid Clinic, 1983-93; law clk. to presiding justice U.S. Dist. Ct. (so. dist.) Tex., Houston, 1993-94; assoc. Mehaffy & Weber, Houston, 1994, Phelps Dunbar, Houston, 1995-97; atty. Marathon Oil Co., Houston, 1997—. Editor Houston Jour. Internat. Law, 1991-92. Mem. Hispanic Bar Assn. (bd. dirs. 1998—). Republican. Roman Catholic. Avocations: travel, theater, fine arts. Oil, gas, and mineral, Contracts commercial. Office: Marathon Oil Co 5555 San Felipe St Houston TX 77056-2723

**RAGER, RUDOLPH RUSSELL,** lawyer; b. Miles City, Mont., Jan. 15, 1932; s. Harry E. and Esther (Anderson) R.; m. Sharon E. Keeling, Dec. 30, 1959; children: Sean, Kurt, Quita, Elani, Valari, Jordan. BBA, U. N.D., 1956; JD, U. N.Mex., 1958. Bar: N.Mex. 1958, U.S. Dist. Ct. N.Mex. 1959. Sole practice Albuquerque, 1958—; atty. Village of Corrales, 1971-81; bd. dirs. Anderson Devel. Corp., Albuquerque, Anderson We. Corp., Albuquerque. Pres., bd. dirs. Albuquerque Tutoring Assn., 1967; bd. dirs. Luth. Coordinating Council, Albuquerque, 1975, Corrales Hist. Soc., 1988-94; bd. dirs., sec. Maxie L. Anderson Found., Albuquerque, 1984—; adv. bd. dirs. Albuquerque City Balloon Mus.; bd. dirs., treas. San Pedro Creek Homeowner's Assn., Anderson Charitable Found. Gold Seal scholar, 1949. Mem. N.Mex. Bar Assn., Albuquerque Bar Assn. Republican. Lutheran. Lodge: Kiwanis (pres. Albuquerque chpt. 1966). Real property, Contracts commercial, General corporate. Home: 20 Canada Vista Dr Sandia Park NM 87047-9645 Office: Ste 550E 6400 Uptown Blvd NE Albuquerque NM 87110-4226

**RAGER, SUSAN GODMAN,** lawyer. AA, Averett Coll., 1966; BA cum laude, Va. Commonwealth U., 1984; JD, U. Richmond, 1987. Bar: Va. 1990, Md. 1990, D.C. 1993. Pvt. practice Coles Point, Va., 1990—. Mem. 15th Judicial Cir. Bar Assn. (pres. 1995), Northern Neck Bar Assn. Criminal, Family and matrimonial, General practice. Office: Susan Godman Rager PC PO Box 117 Coles Point VA 22442-0117

**RAGGI, REENA,** federal judge; b. Jersey City, May 11, 1951. BA, Wellesley Coll., 1973; JD, Harvard U., 1976. Bar: N.Y. 1977. U.S. atty. Dept. Justice, Bklyn., 1986; ptnr. Windels, Marx, Davies & Ives, N.Y.C., 1987; judge U.S. Dist. Ct. (ea. dist.) N.Y., Bklyn., 1987—. Office: US Courthouse 225 Cadman Plz E Brooklyn NY 11201-1818

**RAGLAND, ROBERT ALLEN,** lawyer; b. Bartlesville, Okla., Apr. 18, 1954; s. Thomas Martin and Joan Ethel (Murphy) R. BA, U. Md., 1976; JD, George Mason Sch. of Law, 1980. Dir. regulatory reform and govt. orgn. Nat. Assn. Mfrs., Washington, 1979-82, asst. v.p. taxation, 1983-86; mgr. congl. relations The Clorox Co., Oakland, Calif., 1982-83; dir. tax rsch. U.S. C. of C., Washington, 1988—; chief tax counsel, mng. dir. Nat. Chamber Found., Washington, 1989—; v.p. Trust First Union Nat. Bank, 1995—. Author: Transportation Reform, 1980, Employee Stock Ownership Plans, 1989, Taxation of Foreign Source Income, Distributional Impact of Excise Taxes, 1990; editor: Taxation of Intercorporate Profits, 1990, Jour. Regulation and Social Costs, 1992—. Active Boy Scouts Am., Washington, 1967— (Eagle Scout 1970, bd. dirs. nat. capital area coun.); dep. dir. duPont for Pres., 1987-88; v.p. Nat. Chamber Found. U.S. C. of C., 1989-93. Republican. Roman Catholic. Home: PO Box 65667 Washington DC 20035-5667

**RAGOSTA, VINCENT A.F.,** judge; b. Providence, Feb. 12, 1924; s. Domenic and Rosa (Bottis) R.; m. Carmela C. Bruno, Oct. 3, 1953; children: Vincent Jr., Paul D., Dominic L., Peter J. BS in Acctg., U. R.I., 1949; JD, Boston Coll., 1951. Bar: R.I. 1951, U.S. Ct. Appeals (1st cir.) 1962. Asst. city solicitor City of Providence, 1953-66, city pros., 1953-60, commr. Bur. of Lics., 1977-78; assoc. judge Dist. Ct. R.I., 1978-86; assoc. justice Superior Ct. R.I., 1986—; pvt. practice Providence, 1966-77. State pres. Arthritis Found., 1978. Staff Sgt. U.S. Army, 1943-46, PTO. Recipient Star of Italian Solidarity award Rep. of Italy, 1973. Mem. ABA, ATLA, R.I. Bar Assn., Order Sons of Italy in Am. (state pres. 1971-77), Phi Kappa Phi, Beta Gamma Sigma. Roman Catholic. Avocations: physical fitness, travel, reading, sports. Home: 161 Gentian Ave Providence RI 02908-1131 Office: RI Superior Ct 250 Benefit St Providence RI 02903-2719

**RAHAMAN, VINCENT N.,** lawyer; b. Dublin, Ireland, July 12, 1960; came to the U.S., 1980; s. Sheer S. Rahaman and Clare M. Deweid; 1 child, Ryan. BAS, Our Lady of the Lake U., 1985; MBA, Gonzaga U., 1990; JD, Thomas M. Cooley Law Sch., 1994. Bar: Colo. Assoc. Retherford, Mullen, Johnson & Bruce, Colorado Springs, Colo., 1997-98; pvt. practice Colorado Springs, 1998—. Mem. ABA (family law sect.), Colo. Bar Assn. (family law sect.). Family and matrimonial. Office: 415 Sahwatch St Colorado Springs CO 80903-3815

**RAHM, DAVID ALAN,** lawyer; b. Passaic, N.J., Apr. 18, 1941; s. Hans Emil and Alicia Katherine (Onuf) R.; m. Susan Eileen Berkman, Nov. 23, 1972; children: Katherine Berkman, William David. AB, Princeton U., 1962; JD, Yale U., 1965. Bar: N.Y. 1966, D.C. 1986. Assoc. Paul, Weiss, Rifkind & Wharton, N.Y.C., 1965-66, 1968-69; asst. counsel N.Y. State Urban Devel. Corp., N.Y.C., 1969-72, assoc. counsel, 1972-75; counsel real estate div. Internat. Paper Co., N.Y.C., 1975-80; ptnr. Stroock & Stroock & Lavan, N.Y.C., 1980-83, sr. ptnr., 1984—; mem. legis. com. Real Estate Bd. N.Y., 1988-92; lectr. Old Dominion Coll., Norfolk, Va., 1967-68, NYU, 1986—; mem. editl. bd. Comml. Leasing Law and Strategy, 1988-95; mem. N.Y.C. bd. advisors Commonwealth Land Title Ins. Co., 1996—. Contbr. articles to profl. jours. Fund raiser corp. com. N.Y. Philharm., N.Y.C., 1980-84; trustee Manhattan Sch. Music, 1989—, treas., 1991-94, chmn., 1994—. Mem. ABA (comml. leasing com. 1987-88, 94—, pub./pvt. devel. com. 1989—, real property sect.), Assn. of Bar of City of N.Y. (housing and urban devel. com. 1977-80, 81-84, real property com. 1989-92), Princeton Club. Democrat. Presbyterian. Avocations: music, reading, travel. Real property, Landlord-tenant. Office: Stroock Stroock & Lavan 180 Maiden Ln New York NY 10038-4925

**RAI, ARTI K.,** law educator; b. Kanpur, India, Nov. 17, 1966; came to U.S., 1973; s. J.P.Srivastava and Jagdish Bains. AB, Harvard U., 1983-87, JD, 1991; student, Harvard Med. Sch., 1987-88. Bar: D.C. 1991, Pa. 1991. Law clk. to Hon. Marilyn Hall Patel U.S. Dist. Ct., San Francisco, 1991-92; atty. Jenner & Block, Washington, 1992-94, U.S. Dept. Justice, Washington, 1994-95; lectr. law and medicine U. Chgo., 1995-96; faculty fellow Harvard U., Cambridge, Mass., 1996-97; assoc. prof. law U. San Diego Law Sci., 1997—; mem. governing bd. Consortium for Healthcare Quality, San Diego, 1997—. Co-author: Law and Mental Health System, 1999; contbr. articles to profl. jours. John Harvard scholar, 1986, 87; Wilson, Sonsini, Goodrich & Rosati Internet scholar, 1998. Mem. Am. Soc. Law and Medicine. Office: U San Diego Law Sch 5998 Alcala Park San Diego CA 92110-2429

**RAIGN, MICHAEL STEPHEN,** lawyer; b. Glendale, Ariz., Mar. 11, 1960; s. Phillip Harry and Stephenie Elizabeth (Medoff) R.; m. Sherie Leslie Gee, July 2, 1995; 1 child, Kelsie Gee. BBA in Acctg., U. Tex., 1982, BA in Govt., 1983; JD, St. Mary's U., San Antonio, 1986. Bar: Tex. 1987; cert. in criminal law Tex. Bd. Legal Specialization, 1997. Prosecutor Bexar County Dist. Atty.'s Office, San Antonio, 1987-95; pvt. practice, San Antonio, 1995—; player San Antonio Soccer Assn.; referee San Antonio Soccer Referee's Assn. Candidate for bd. dirs. Edwards Aquifer Authority, San Antonio, 1996. Mem. Tex. Criminal Def. Lawyers Assn., Tex. Dist. and County Attys. Assn. Republican. Roman Catholic. Avocations: music, soccer, backpacking, photography, antiques. Criminal. Office: 313 S Main Ave San Antonio TX 78204-1016

**RAIKES, CHARLES FITZGERALD,** retired lawyer; b. Mpls., Oct. 6, 1930; s. Arthur FitzGerald and Margaret (Hawthorne) R.; m. Antonia Raikes, Dec. 20, 1969; children: Jennifer Catherine, Victoria Samantha. B.A., Washington U., 1952; M.A., Harvard U., 1955, LL.B., 1958. Bar: N.Y. State 1959. Assoc. White & Case, N.Y.C., 1958-69; assoc. gen. counsel Dun & Bradstreet, Inc., N.Y.C., 1969-72; v.p., gen. counsel Dun & Bradstreet, Inc., 1972-73; v.p., gen. counsel The Dun & Bradstreet Corp., N.Y.C., 1973-76, sr. v.p., gen. counsel, 1976-94, of counsel, 1994-95; ret., 1995; cons. Bd. Govs. Fed. Reserve System, 1958-95. Served with U.S. Army, 1952-54. Woodrow Wilson fellow, 1952. Mem. Assn. Bar City of N.Y., Harvard Club, Sky Club, Phi Beta Kappa. General corporate. Home: 26 Crooked Trl Rowayton CT 06853-1106

**RAILTON, WILLIAM SCOTT,** lawyer; b. Newark, July 30, 1935; s. William Scott and Carolyn Elizabeth (Guiberson) R.; m. Karen Elizabeth Walsh, Mar. 31, 1979; 1 son, William August; children by previous marriage: William Scott, Anne Greenwood. BSEE, U. Wash., 1962; JD with honors, George Washington U., 1965. Bar: D.C. 1966, Md. 1966, Va. 1993, U.S. Patent Office 1966. Assoc., then ptnr. Kemon, Palmer & Estabrook, Washington, 1966-70; sr. trial atty. Dept. Labor, Washington, 1970-71, asst. counsel for trial litigation, 1971-72; chief counsel U.S. Occupational Safety and Health Rev. Commn., Washington, 1972-77; acting gen. counsel U.S. Occupational Safety and Health Rev. Commn., 1975-77; ptnr. Reed, Smith, Shaw & McClay, Pitts., 1977—; lectr. George Washington U. Law Sch., 1977-79, seminar chmn. Occupational Safety and Health Act, Govt. Inst., 1979-96; lectr. Practicing Law Inst., 1976-79. Author: (legal handbooks) The Examination System and the Backlog, 1965, The OSHA General Duty Clause, 1977, The OSHA Health Standards, 1977; OSHA Compliance Handbook, 1992; contbg. author: Occupational Safety and Health Law, 1988, 93. Regional chmn. Montgomery County (Md.) Republican party, 1968-70; pres. Montgomery Sq. Citizens Assn., 1970-71; bd. dirs., pres. Foxvale Farms Homeowners Assn., 1979-82; pres. Orchards on the Potomac Homeowners Assn., 1990-92; dir. Great Falls Hist. Soc., 1991-94; scoutmaster Troop 55 Boy Scouts Am., 1993-98. With USMC, 1953-58. Recipient Meritorious Achievement medal Dept. Labor, 1972, Outstanding Service award OSHA Rev. Commn., 1977, elected fell. Coll. Labor and Employment Lawyers, 1998. Fellow Coll. Labor and Employment Lawyers; mem. ABA (mgmt. co-chmn. occupational safety and health law com. 1995-98), Md. Bar Assn., Va. Bar Assn., Bar Assn. D.C. (vice chmn. young lawyers sect. 1971), Order of Coif, Sigma Phi Epsilon, Phi Delta Phi. Labor, Patent, Federal civil litigation. Home: 10102 Walker Lake Dr Great Falls VA 22066-3502 also: East Tower 1301 K St NW # 1100 Washington DC 20005-3317 *Lawsuits are won by pre-trial preparation. A litigator should be candid with his clients and honest in his dealings with associates, opponents and the courts; an attorney should also volunteer his service to the community of which he is a part.*

**RAIMO, BERNARD (BERNIE RAIMO),** lawyer; b. Kansas City, Mo., May 29, 1944; m. Sharon Marie Brady, Aug. 23, 1974; children: Sarah Elizabeth, Peter Bernard. BA, U. Notre Dame, 1965; MA, U. Md., 1967; JD with honors, George Washington U., 1972. Bar: D.C. Staff asst. to Sen. Stuart Symington Mo., 1968-72; asst. corp. counsel D.C., Washington, 1972-76; legis. analyst Am. Petroleum Inst., 1976-78; counsel Permanent Select Com. Intelligence U.S. Ho. Reps., Washington, 1978-91, chief counsel Ho. Com. Standards of Official Conduct, 1991-95; minority counsel Ho. Com. Standards of Official Conduct, 1995-97; counsel to Dem. leader U.S. Ho. of Reps., 1997—. Office: Office of the Dem Leader H-204 The Capitol Washington DC 20515-0001

**RAIMONDI, JOSEPHINE ANN,** lawyer; b. Indpls., Dec. 3; d. Anthony Leonard and Catherine Ann (Mascari) R. BS, Georgetown U., 1980; JD, U. Mich., 1987. Staff acct. Arthur Andersen & Co., Chgo., 1980-81; cons. Peterson & Co., Chgo., 1982-84; atty. LeBoeuf, Lamb Greene & MacRae, N.Y.C., 1987-92; gen. cousnel Midwest Employers Gas Co., St. Louis, 1993-97; asst. v.p., sr. counsel W.R. Berkley Corp., Greenwich, Conn., 1997—. Mem. Westport (Conn.) Young Women's League. General corporate, Mergers and acquisitions, Securities. Home: 473 Main St Westport CT 06880-2159 Office: WR Bekeley Corp 165 Mason St Greenwich CT 06830-6608

**RAINBOLT, JOHN VERNON, II,** lawyer; b. Cordell, Okla., May 24, 1939; s. John Vernon (Mike) and Mary Alice (Power) R.; m. Janice Glaub, Oct. 2, 1976; children—John Vernon, III, Sara McLain, Charles Joseph. B.A., Okla. U., 1961, LL.B., 1964; postgrad. George Washington U. 1971-73. Bar: Okla. 1964, D.C. 1971, U.S. Supreme Ct. 1971. Legis. counsel, adminstrv. asst. U.S. Rep. Graham Purcell, Washington, 1967-72; counsel agr. com. U.S. Ho. of Reps., Washington, 1972-74, chief counsel, 1975; commr. Commodity Futures Trading Commn., Washington, 1975-78; sole practice, Washington, 1978—; ptnr. Miles & Stockbridge, Washington, 1982-86; advisor agr. policy Tokyo Roundtable White House, 1978-81; mem. Adminstrn. Conf., U.S., 1976-79; mem. CFTC Adv. Com. on Regulatory Coord. Author and draftsman Commodity Futures Trading Commn. Act, 1974; contbr. articles to legal jours. Served to 1st lt. Inf., U.S. Army, 1964-67. Vice chmn. Commodity Futures Trading Commn., 1975-78. Mem. ABA (chmn. subcom. on fgn. markets and traders 1982-85, chmn. subcom. internat. issues 1996-97), U.S. Futures Industry Assn. (assoc., internat. com., Japan chpt.), Vietnam Vets. Clubs: Commodity of Washington. Banking, Securities, Private international. Office: Rainbolt Law Office 1200 G St NW Ste 800 Washington DC 20005-3814

**RAINER, G. BRADLEY,** lawyer; b. Phila., June 5, 1947; s. Francis J. and Ruth J. Rainer; m. Joan Klamkin, Mar. 27, 1949; children: Daniel, Julia. BA, Wesleyan U., Middletown, Conn., 1969; JD, Temple U., 1972. Bar: Pa. 1972, U.S. Dist. Ct. (ea. dist.) Pa. 1972. Assoc. Duryea, Larzelere & Hepburn, Ardmore, Pa., 1972-74, ptnr., 1975-76; sole practitioner Haverford, Pa., 1976-79; ptnr. Hecker Rainer and Brown, Phila., 1980-88; shareholder Rubin Quinn Moss & Patterson PC, Phila., 1988-93; shareholder, chair bus. dept., mem. exec. com. Eckell, Sparks, Levy, Auerbach & Monte, PC, Media, Pa., 1993—; pres. Phila. Bar Edn. Ctr., 1998—; adj. prof. Temple U. Sch. Law, Phila., 1995—; spkr. at seminars. Pres. Voyage House, Phila., 1992-94; bd. dirs. Crisis Intervention Network, Phila., 1983-89; pres. A Better Chance in Lower Merion, Ardmore, 1977-79. Mem. Assn. Profl. Responsibility Lawyers. General corporate, Estate planning, Ethics. Office: Eckell Sparks et al 344 W Front St Media PA 19063-2632

**RAINEY, GORDON FRYER, JR.,** lawyer; b. Oklahoma City, Okla., Apr. 26, 1940; s. Gordon F. and Esther (Bliss) R.; m. Selina Norman, Aug. 3, 1968; children: Kate, Melissa, Gordon III. BA in English, U. Va., 1962, LLB, 1967. Bar: Okla. 1967, Va. 1968. Assoc. Rainey, Flynn, Wallace, Ross & Cooper, Oklahoma City, 1967-68; assoc. Hunton & Williams, Richmond, Va., 1968-75, ptnr., 1975—; chmn. of exec. com. Hunton & Williams; bd. dirs. Bon Secours Richmond Health Sys., Inc.; dir. Crestar Fin. Corp., Weidmuller North Am., Inc., Meml. Regional Med. Ctr., Inc. Bd. mgrs., pres. U. Va. Alumni Assn.; trustee Colonial Williamsburg Found., Va. Found. Ind. Colls.; mem. Gov. Gilmore's Blue Ribbon Comm. on Higher Edn.; campaign chmn. United Way of Greater Richmond, 1982, trustee, 1981-84; bd. dirs., past pres. Sheltering Arms Hosp., 1984; trustee Sheltering Arms Found.; chmn. Gov.'s Econ. Devel. Adv. Coun. Dist. 12; mem. Gov. Gilmore Transition Adv. Com.; mem. Gov.'s Adv. Com. for Va. Strategy on Econ. Devel.; mem. Bd. Housing and Cmty. Devel.; past mem. bd. govs. St. Catherine's Sch.; past chmn. bd. dirs. Leadership Met. Richmond.; mem. Mayor's Emergency Shelter Task Force, 1981; past pres., bd. dirs. Met. Bus. Found. 1st lt. U.S. Army, 1962-64, Korea. Recipient Disting. Grad. award Casady Sch., Comm. and Leadership award toastmasters Internat., 1983. Mem. ABA (sect. on bus. law, banking law com., mem. com. on devel. in investment svcs.), Richmond Metro C. of C. (bd. dirs., past chmn.), Commonwealth Club, Country Club of Va., The Brook (N.Y.C.), Forum Club (Richmond). Republican. Episcopalian. Banking, Finance, General corporate. Office: Hunton & Williams Riverfront Plz East Tower PO Box 1535 Richmond VA 23218-1535

**RAINEY, JOHN DAVID,** federal judge; b. Freeport, Tex., Feb. 10, 1945; s. Frank Anson and Jewel Lorene (Hortman) R.; m. Judy Davis, Aug. 17, 1968; children, John David Jr., Jacob Matthew, Craig Thomas. BBA, So. Meth. U., 1967, JD, 1972. Bar: Tex. 1972, U.S. Dist. Ct. (no. dist.) Tex. 1974, U.S. Tax Ct. 1974, U.S. Ct. Appeals (5th cir.) 1981, U.S. Supreme Ct. 1981, U.S. Dist. Ct. (so. dist.) Tex. 1986. Assoc. Taylor, Mizell, Price, Corrigan & Smith, Dallas, 1973-79; ptnr. Gilbert, Gilbert & Rainey, Angleton, Tex., 1979-82, Rainey & LeBoeuf, Angleton, 1982-86; judge 149th Dist. Ct., Brazoria County, Tex., 1987-90, U.S. Dist. Ct. (so. dist.) Tex., 1990—; bd. dirs. Angleton Bank of Commerce. Mem. City of Angleton Planning and Zoning Commn., 1981-84; mem. Angleton Charter Rev. Commn., 1984, chmn. 1982. Served with U.S. Army, 1969-70. Mem. ABA, State Bar Tex., Brazoria County Bar Assn. (pres. 1983-84). Methodist. Lodge: Lions (pres. Angleton 1986-87). Avocations: hunting, fishing, woodworking. Office: US Dist Ct 515 Rusk St Ste 8613 Houston TX 77002-2603

**RAINEY, WILLIAM JOEL,** lawyer; b. Flint, Mich., Oct. 11, 1946; s. Ralph Jefferson and Elsie Matilda (Erickson) R.; m. Cynthia Hetsko, June 15, 1968; children: Joel Michael, Allison Elizabeth. AB, Harvard U., 1968; JD, U. Mich., 1971. Bar: N.Y. 1973, Wash. 1977, Ariz. 1987, Mass. 1992, Kans. 1997, U.S. Dist. Ct. (so. and ea. dists.) N.Y. 1973, U.S. Ct. Appeals (2nd cir.) N.Y. 1973, U.S. Dist. Ct. (we. dist.) Wash. 1977, U.S. Supreme Ct. 1976, U.S. Ct. Appeals (9th cir.) Wash. 1978, U.S. Dist. Ct. Ariz. 1987, U.S. Dist. Ct. Mass. 1992. Assoc. atty. Curtis, Mallet-Prevost, Colt & Mosle, N.Y.C., 1971-76; atty., asst. corp. sec. Weyerhaeuser Co., Tacoma, Wash., 1976-85; v.p., corp. sec., gen. counsel Southwest Forest Industries Inc., Phoenix, 1985-87; sr. v.p., corp. sec., gen. counsel Valley Nat. Corp. and Valley Nat. Bank, Phoenix, 1987-91; v.p., gen. counsel Cabot Corp., Boston, 1991-93; exec. v.p., gen. coun., corp. sec. Fourth Fin. Corp., Wichita, Kans., 1994-96; sr. v.p., gen. counsel, corp. sec. Payless ShoeSource, Inc., Topeka, 1996—. Editor U. Mich. Jour. Law Reform, 1970-71. Bd. dirs. Big Bros./Big Sisters, 1994-96. Maj. USAR, 1970-91. Mem. ABA (chmn. task force 1984-91), Wash. State Bar Assn., State Bar of Ariz., Assn. Bank Holding Cos. (steering com. 1989-91, chmn. lawyers com. 1990-91), Harvard Club of Phoenix (bd. dirs. 1989-91). Avocations: backpacking, running, fishing, bicycling. General corporate, Securities, Pension, profit-sharing, and employee benefits. Home: 901 Deer Run Dr Lawrence KS 66049-4731 Office: Payless ShoeSource Inc PO Box 1189 Topeka KS 66601-1189

**RAINONE, MICHAEL CARMINE,** lawyer; b. Phila., Mar. 4, 1918; m. Ledena Tonioni, Apr. 10, 1944; children: Sebastian, Francine. LLB, U. Pa., 1941. Bar: Pa. 1944, U.S. Dist. Ct. Pa. 1944, U.S. Supreme Ct. 1956. del. 3d cir. Jud. Conf., 1984-95. Bd. dirs. C.C., Phila. 1970-85; past pres. Nationalities Svc. Ctr., hon. bd. dirs.; commr. Fellowship Commn., 1973-82; bd. dirs., mem. govt. rels. com. Mental Health Assn. Southeastern Pa., 1979-91; pres. Columbus Civic Assn. Pa., Inc., 1984-91; chmn. Lawyers' Biog. Com. Hist. Soc., U.S. Dist. Ct.; trustee Balch Inst. for Ethnic Studies, 1989-92; regional v.p. Nat. Italian-Am. Found.; pres. Seaview Harbor Civic Assn., 1990-95, pres. emeritus, 1996—; apptd. judge Final Law Sch. Trial Advocacy Program for the Northeast, 1996; counsel, v.p. Piccula Opera Com., Phila., 1997—. Recipient Disting. Svc. award Nationalities Svc. Ctr., 1975, Man of Yr. award Columbus Civic Assn., 1969, Legion of Honor, Chapel of Four Chaplains, 1979, Bronze Medallion award, 1982, commendation Pa. Senate, 1982, Villanova Law Sch. Appreciation award 1993, Syracuse U. Achievement award 1994, Hon. Lifetime award KC, 1997; Resolution of Praise, pres. City Coun. of Phila., 1999. Mem. ABA, ATLA, Internat. Acad. Law and Sci., Justinian Soc. (bd. govs. 1980-83), Pa. Bar Assn., Pa. Trial Lawyers Assn. (bd. govs. 1982-84), N.Y. Trial Lawyers Assn. (assoc.), Phila. Bar Assn. (bd. dirs. 1980-83, asst. sec. 1983, 84, created the Beccaria award), Lawyers Club Phila. (pres. 1982-84), Phila. Trial Lawyers Assn. (pres. 1982-83), Nat. Italian-Am. Bar Assn. (bd. govs. 1985-90, historian 1987-90, pres. 1991-93, bd. chmn. 1993-95), Am. Arbitration Assn. (arbitrator 1950—), Sons of Italy (Man of Yr. award 1995). General civil litigation, Contracts commercial, Estate planning. Home: 2401 Pennsylvania Ave Philadelphia PA 19130-3061 Office: 1530 Chestnut St Fl 4 Philadelphia PA 19102-2739

**RAINS, M. NEAL,** lawyer; b. Burlington, Iowa, July 26, 1943; s. Merritt and Lucille (Lepper) R.; m. Jean Baldwin, July 26, 1980 (div. 1995); children: Robert Baldwin, Kathleen Kellogg. B.A. in Polit. Sci. with honors, U. Iowa, 1965; J.D., Northwestern U., 1968. Bar: Ohio 1968. Assoc. Arter & Hadden, Cleve., 1968-76, ptnr., 1976—, mem. exec. com., 1981—, mem. mgmt. com., 1987-90, mng. ptnr., 1990-92; master bencher Inns of Ct., 1990—; lectr. on profl. topics, including alternative dispute resolution, distbn. law, litigation practice and procedure, and antitrust. Contbr. articles to profl. jours. Former trustee Legal Aid Soc. Cleve.; trustee Cleve. Play House, mem. adv. coun., 1988—; trustee Citizens League Greater Cleve., Cleve. Art Assn. With U.S. Army, 1968-70. Fellow Am. Bar Found.; mem. ABA, Ohio Bar Assn., Bar Assn. Greater Cleve. (chmn. young lawyers sect. 1975-76, recipient cert. merit 1975), Def. Rsch. Inst., Internat. Assn. Def. Counsel, Ohio Assn. Civil Trial Attys., Cleve. Bar Found. (trustee 1999—), Harold H. Burton Am. Inn Ct. (pres. 1999—), Union Club, Cleve. Skating Club, City Club, Print Club, Rowfant Club, Phi Beta Kappa, Omicron Delta Kappa, Phi Delta Phi. Antitrust, General civil litigation. Home: 12546 Cedar Rd Cleveland Heights OH 44106 Office: Arter & Hadden 1100 Huntington Bldg Cleveland OH 44115

**RAINVILLE, CHRISTINA,** lawyer; b. N.Y.C., Feb. 7, 1962; d. Dewey and Nancy Rainville; m. Peter S. Greenberg, May 1994; children: Jeremy, Catharine. BS, Northwestern U., 1984, JD, 1988. Atty. Schnader Harrison Segal & Lewis, Phila., 1988—. Mem. ABA, Nat. Assn. Criminal Def. Lawyers. Presbyn. Federal civil litigation, Civil rights, Criminal. Office: Schnader Harrison et al Ste 3600 1600 Market St Philadelphia PA 19103-7240

**RAISLER, KENNETH MARK,** lawyer; b. New Rochelle, N.Y., May 15, 1951; s. Herbert A. and Norma (Glaubach) R.; m. Sara Ann Kelsey, June 11, 1978; children: Caroline Elisabeth, Katharine Kelsey, David Mark. BSBA, Yale Coll., 1973; JD, NYU, 1976. Bar: N.Y. 1977, D.C. 1977, U.S. Dist. Ct. (so. dist.) N.Y. 1977, U.S. Dist. Ct. D.C. 1977, U.S. Ct. Appeals (2d cir.) 1977, U.S. Ct. Appeals (D.C. cir.) 1977, U.S. Ct. Appeals (7th cir.) 1982, U.S. Ct. Appeals (10th cir.) 1983, U.S. Supreme Ct. 1985. Law clk. U.S. Dist. Ct. (so. dist.) N.Y., N.Y.C., 1976-77; asst. U.S. atty., Washington, 1977-82; dep. gen. counsel Commodity Futures Trading Commn., Washington, 1982-83, gen. counsel, 1983-87; ptnr. Rogers & Wells, N.Y.C., 1987-92, Sullivan & Cromwell, N.Y.C., 1992—. Mem. Assn. of Bar of City of N.Y. (chair futures regulation com. 1988-91). Office: Sullivan & Cromwell 125 Broad St Fl 28 New York NY 10004-2489

**RAK, LORRAINE KAREN,** lawyer; b. Trenton, N.J., Jan. 8, 1959; d. Charles Walter and Lottie Mary (Debiec) R. BA in Polit. Sci., Seton Hall U., South Orange, N.J., 1981; JD, Cornell U., 1984. Bar: N.J. 1986, N.Y. 1986, U.S. Dist. Ct. N.J. 1986, U.S. Dist. Ct. (so. and ea. dists.) N.Y. 1988, U.S. Dist. Ct. (no. dist.) N.Y. 1991, U.S. Ct. Appeals (4th cir.) 1989, U.S. Ct. Appeals (2d cir.) 1990, U.S. Ct. Appeals (3d cir.) 1991. Assoc. Shearman & Sterling, N.Y.C., 1984-91, Robinson, St. John & Wayne, N.Y.C., 1992-93; dep. atty. gen. State of N.J., Newark, 1993—. Active Lawyers' Com. for Human Rights, N.Y.C. Mem. ABA, ACLU, LWV, Cornell Law Assn., Amnesty Internat., Polish Arts Club Trenton. Democrat. Roman Catholic. Federal civil litigation, General civil litigation, State civil litigation. Office: State of NJ Divsn of Law Pub Trans Sect One Penn Plaza East Newark NJ 07105

**RAKER, IRMA STEINBERG,** judge; b. Bklyn.; m. Samuel K. Raker, Apr. 3, 1960; children: Mark, Stefanie, Leslie. BA, Syracuse U., 1959; cert. of attendance (hon.), Hague (The Netherlands) Acad. Internat. Law, 1959; JD, Am. U., 1972. Bar: Md. 1973, D.C. 1974, U.S. Dist. Ct. Md. 1977, U.S. Ct. Appeals (4th cir.) 1977. Asst. state's atty. State's Atty.'s Office of Montgomery County, Md., 1973-79; ptnr. Sachs, Greenebaum & Tayler, Washington, 1979-80; judge Dist. Ct. Md., Rockville, 1980-82, Cir. Ct. for Montgomery County, Md., 1982-94, Ct. of Appeals of Md., 1994—; adj. prof. Washington Coll. Law, Am. U., 1980—; faculty seminar leader child abuse course Nat. Coll. Dist. Attys. at U. Mass., 1977; mem. faculty Md. Jud. Inst., Nat. Criminal Def. Inst., 1980, 81, 82; instr. litigation program Georgetown Law Ctr.-Nat. Inst. Trial Advocacy; mem. legis. com. Md. Jud. Conf., mem. exec. com., 1985-89, mem. commn. to study bail bond and surety industry in Md.; mem. spl. com. to revise article 27 on crimes and punishment State of Md., 1991—; mem. inquiry com. atty. Grievance Commn. Md., 1978-81; chairperson jud. compensation com. Md. Jud. Conf., 1997—. Past editor Am. U. Law Rev. Treas., v.p. West Bradley Citizens Assn., 1964-68; mem. adv. com. to county exec. on child abuse Montgomery County, 1976-77, mem. adv. com. to county exec. on battered spouses, 1977-78, mem. adv. com. on environ. protection, 1980; mem. citizens adv. bd. Montgomery County Crisis Ctr., 1980. Recipient Robert C. Heeney award Md. State Bar Assn., 1993, Dorothy Beatty Meml. award Women's Law Ctr., 1994, Rita Davidson award Women's Bar Md., 1995, Margaret Brent Trailblazers award ABA Commn. on Women in the Profession/Women's Bar Assn. Md., 1995, Elizabeth Dole Woman of Achievement award ARC, 1998, others. Fellow Md. Bar Found.; mem. ABA (chairperson criminal justice stds. com. 1995-96, mem. coun. criminal law sect. 1997—, del. nat. conf. state trial judges, active various coms.), Md. State Bar Assn. (chairperson coun. criminal law and practice sect., mem. bd. govs. 1981, 82, 85, 86, 90, mem. coun. litigation sect., active coms., chairperson com. to draft pattern jury instrns. in civil and criminal cases 1980—), Nat. Assn. Women Judges, Internat. Acad. Trial Judges, Am. Law Inst., Montgomery County Bar Assn. (chairperson criminal law sect. 1978-79, mem. exec. com. 1979-80, active other coms.), Montgomery County Bar Leaders, Women's Bar Assn. Md., Women's Bar Assn. D.C., Hadassah Women's Orgn. (life), Pioneer Women Na'amat (hon. life, Celebration of Women award 1985), Pi Sigma Alpha. Avocations: photography, tennis, needlework. Office: Ct of Appeals of Md 50 Maryland Ave Rockville MD 20850-2320

**RAKESTRAW, GREGORY ALLEN,** lawyer; b. Findlay, Ohio, Jan. 20, 1949; s. Russell E. and Genevieve (Might) R.; m. Sandra Sue Steegman, July 17, 1971; children: Adam Edwin, Seth Allen, Ashley Marie. BA, Wittenberg U., 1971; postgrad., Ohio State U., 1972; JD with distinction, Ohio No. U., 1974. Bar: Ohio 1974, U.S. Dist. Ct. (no. dist.) Ohio 1974, U.S. Ct. Appeals (6th cir.) 1992. Assoc. Russell E. Rakestraw, Findlay, 1974-78; ptnr. Rakestraw & Rakestraw, Findlay, 1978—; referee Findlay Mcpl., 1974-75; spl. prosecutor Marion Twp., Hancock County, Ohio, 1976—. Contbr. to Ohio Divorce, 1981. Mem.-at-large Findlay City Coun., 1975-76, Hancock County Human Rights Commn., Findlay, 1978-84. Fellow Ohio State Bar Found.; mem. ABA, Ohio State Bar Assn., N.W. Ohio Bar Assn., Findlay-Hancock County Bar Assn. (past pres.), Assn. Trial Lawyers Am., Ohio Assn. Trial Lawyers, Internat. Platform Assn., Findlay AAA (bd. dirs.), Lambda Chi Alpha (past pres.). Republican. Lutheran. Avocations: sailing and power boating, building , remodeling. General civil litigation, Family and matrimonial, General practice. Home: 11595 County Road 40 Findlay OH 45840-9029 Office: Rakestraw & Rakestraw 119 E Crawford St Findlay OH 45840-4887

**RALEY, CHARLES EDWARD,** lawyer; b. Washington, May 3, 1946; s. Irving James and Rosalie Alice (Kennedy) R.; m. Phyllis Marie Mann, June 10, 1968; children: Brian Kennedy, Adam Chrisman. BA, U. Va., 1968; JD, George Washington U., 1972. Bar: D.C. 1973, U.S. Dist. Ct. D.C. 1973, U.S. Ct. Appeals (D.C. cir.) 1973, U.S. Ct. Claims 1973, U.S. Ct. Appeals (fed. cir.) 1982, U.S. Ct. Appeals (1st cir.) 1985, U.S. Ct. Appeals (6th cir.) 1987, U.S. Supreme Ct. 1987. Dir. Israel & Raley, Chartered, Washington, 1972-94; sr. ptnr. Watt, Tieder, Hoffar, LLP, Mc Lean, Va., 1994—. 2d lt. U.S. Army, 1968-69. Mem. ABA, Univ. Club Washington, River Bend Golf & Country Club, Va. Student Aid Found., U. Va. Alumni Assn., Phi Delta Phi. Avocations: golf, running. Federal civil litigation, Construction, Government contracts and claims. Office: Watt Tieder & Hoffar LLP 7929 Westpark Dr Ste 400 Mc Lean VA 22102-4224

**RALEY, JOHN W., JR.,** lawyer; b. May 23, 1932; s. John Wesley and Helen Thames; children: John Wesley III, Robert Thames. AB, Okla. Baptist U., 1954; JD, U. Okla., 1959. Bar: Okla. 1959, U.S. Supreme Ct. 1973, U.S. Ct. Appeals (10th cir.), 1962, U.S. Dist. (we. dist.) 1961, U.S. Dist. Ct. (no. dist.) 1988, U.S. Dist. Ct. (ea. dist.) 1989 Okla. Asst. U.S. atty. We. Dist. Okla. U.S. Dept. Justice, 1961-69; ptnr. Northcutt, Raley, Clark and Gardner, Ponca City, Okla., 1969-90; U.S. atty. Ea. Dist. Okla. U.S. Dept. Justice, 1990-97; of counsel Northcutt, Clark, Gardner & Hron, Ponca City, 1997—. Mayor of Ponca City, Okla., 1980-83. Capt. USNR, 1950-84, ret. Recipient George Washington Honor medal Freedoms Found. at Valley Forge, 1971, Spl. Initiative award U.S. Dept. Justice, 1994, Outstanding Alumni Achievement award Okla. Bapt. U., 1981, Outstanding Citizen award Ponca City, 1984. Fellow Am. Coll. Trial Lawyers; mem. ABA, Am. Bd. Trial Advs., Okla. Bar Assn. (mem. bd. govs.), Kay County Bar Assn. (pres. 1980), Am. Legion, Mason, Reserve Officers Assn., Naval Reserve Assn., VFW. Republican. So. Baptist. Office: 400 E Central Ave Ste 401 Ponca City OK 74601-5428 Address: PO Box 1412 Ponca City OK 74602-1412

**RALEY, JOHN WESLEY, III,** lawyer; b. Oklahoma City, Oct. 19, 1959; s. John Wesley Raley Jr. and Mary Lane Mallett; m. Kelly Elaine Williams, Sept. 22, 1984; children: Katherine Elise, William Thomas, James Wesley. BA summa cum laude, U. Okla., 1981, JD, 1984; LLM, U. Aberdeen, Scotland, 1988. Bar: Tex. 1985, U.S. Dist. Ct. (so. dist.) Tex. 1985, U.S. Ct. Appeals (5th cir.) 1985; bd. cert. personal injury trial law Tex. Bd. Legal Specialization. Assoc., participating assoc. Fulbright & Jaworski, LLP, Houston, 1985-96, ptnr., 1996—; lectr. civil litigation U. Houston CLE, 1995—. Deacon Meml. Dr. Bapt., Houston, 1986—; on-air spokesman Houston Pub. TV, 1996—; laborer Habitat for Humanity, Houston, 1998. Fellow Tex. Bar Found. (life); mem. ABA, State Bar Tex., Houston Bar Assn. (interdisciplinary ednl. alliance 1977—, spkrs. bur. 1987—), U. Okla. Varsity O Club, Phi Beta Kappa. Democrat. Avocations: basketball, golf, tennis, local amateur drama performances. General civil litigation, Personal injury, Intellectual property. Home: 5 Falling Leaf Ln Houston TX 77024-4513 Office: Fulbright & Jaworski LLP 1301 Mckinney St Ste 5100 Houston TX 77010-3031

**RALLO, DOUGLAS,** lawyer; b. Orange, N.J., Nov. 22, 1953; s. Vito and Mary (Spiduro) R. BA, Montclair (N.J.) State Coll., 1975; cert., Inst. Internat. and Comparative Law, 1977; JD, John Marshall Law Sch., 1978. Bar: Ill. 1979, U.S. Dist. Ct. (no. dist.) Ill. 1979, Wis., 1998, U.S. Ct. Appeals (7th cir.) 1979, U.S. Dist. Ct. (ea. dist.) Wis. 1995. Corp. lawyer Bendix Corp., N.Y.C., 1979-81; assoc. David T. Rallo & Assocs., Ltd., Chgo., 1981-83, Horwitz & Assocs., Ltd., Chgo., 1983-84, Semmelman & Bertucci Ltd., Lake Forest, Ill., 1984-98; pvt. practice Law Offices of Douglas Rallo, Libertyville, Ill., 1998—; Notable cases include: Sherrod vs. Berry, 629F. Supp. 159 (1985) and 589F Supp. 433 (1984); rsch. asst. A Functional Analysis of the Criminal Code Reform Act of 1978 for U.S. Congress; panel atty. Ill. state appellate defender's office, 1980; profiled in Newsweek mag., 1989, Chgo. Tribune, 1989; tchr. adult legal edn. programs Libertyville (Ill.) High Sch., 1988-90, Mundelein (Ill). High Sch., 1989. Contbr. articles to profl. jours. Commr. Libertyville Youth Commn., 1990-94; bd. dirs. Civic Ctr. Found., Libertyville; v.p. Lake County chpt. N.W. Ill. MADD, 1989-91. Mem. Ill. State Bar Assn. (lectr. on hedonic damages, civil practice and procedure, seminar on expert witnesses, 1989), Lake County Bar Assn., Ill. Trial Lawyers Assn., State Bar Wis., Libertyville/Mundelein/Vernon Hills C. of C., State Bar of Wis., Pi Sigma Alpha. Avocations: water sports, swimming, softball. Personal injury, Product liability, Workers' compensation. Office: Law Offices Douglas Rallo 611 S Milwaukee Ave Libertyville IL 60048-3256

**RALSTON, ROBERT W.,** lawyer; b. Phila., Nov. 11, 1947; s. Robert and Virginia M. Ralston; m. Nancy Ellen Harshman, June 14, 1969; children: Brian, Timothy, Kevin. BA in Polit. Sci., Ursinus Coll., 1969; JD, Dickinson U., 1972. Bar: Del., U.S. Dist. Ct. Del. Atty. Prickett, Jones, Elliott, Kristol & Schnee, Wilmington, Del., 1972-87; pvt. practice Robert W. Ralston, Esq., Wilmington, Del., 1987—. Mem. Del. State Bar Assn. (asst. sec. 1973-74, sec. 1974-75). Democrat. Methodist. Workers' compensation, Personal injury. Home: 6 Tenby Dr Wilmington DE 19803-2619 Office: Robert W Ralston Esq 10 E 13th St Wilmington DE 19801-3202

**RAMBO, RICK LYNN,** lawyer; b. New Orleans, Aug. 21, 1967; s. Jerald Von and Ruth Payne R. BS in Computer Sci., U. New Orleans, 1988; MBA, A.B. Freeman, 1994; JD, Tulane U., 1994. Bar: Tex. 1994, U.S. Dist. Ct. (all dists.) Tex., 1994, D.C. 1996, Colo. 1997. Software engr. T.L. James & Co., Inc., St. Rose, La., 1988-89; project leader Bell Avon, Inc., Picayune, Miss., 1991; pres., co-owner Software Systems Devel., Inc., La Place, La., 1989-91; law clk. Office of Dist. Atty., New Orleans, 1992, O'Niel, Eichin, Miller & Breckenridge, New Orleans, 1992; assoc. Fulbright & Jaworski, Houston, 1993—. Mem. Tex. Bar Assn., Houston Bar Assn., Maritime Law Assn., Order of Coif, Beta Gamma Sigma, Phi Delta Phi. General civil litigation, Admiralty, Insurance. Office: Fulbright & Jaworski 1301 Mckinney St Ste 5100 Houston TX 77010-3031

**RAMBO, SYLVIA H.,** federal judge; b. Royersford, Pa., Apr. 17, 1936; d. Granville A. and Hilda E. (Leonhardt) R.; m. George F. Douglas, Jr., Aug. 1, 1970. BA, Dickinson Coll., 1958; JD, Dickinson Sch Law, 1962; LLD (hon.), Wilson Coll., 1980, Dickinson Sch. Law, 1993, Dickinson Coll., 1994, Shippensburg U., 1996, Widener U., 1999. Bar: Pa. 1962. Atty. trust dept. Bank of Del., Wilmington, 1962-63; pvt. practice Carlisle, 1963-76; from public defender to chief public defender Cumberland County, Pa., 1974-76; judge Ct. Common Pleas, Cumberland County, 1976-78, U.S. Dist. Ct. (mid. dist.) Pa., Harrisburg, 1979-92; chief judge U.S. Dist. Ct. (mid. dist.) Pa., Pa. & Md., 1992—; asst. prof., adj. prof. law Dickinson Sch. Law, 1974-76. Mem. Nat. Assn. Women Judges, Phi Alpha Delta. Democrat. Presbyterian. Office: US Dist Ct Federal Bldg PO Box 868 Harrisburg PA 17108-0868

**RAMER, BRUCE M.,** lawyer; b. Teaneck, N.J., Aug. 2, 1933; s. Sidney and Anne S. (Strassman) R.; children: Gregg B., Marc K., Neal I. BA, Princeton U., 1955; LLB, Harvard U., 1958. Bar: Calif. 1963, N.J. 1958. Assoc., Morrison, Lloyd & Griggs, Hackensack, N.J., 1959-60; ptnr. Gang, Tyre, Ramer & Brown, Inc., L.A., 1963—. Exec. dir. Entertainment Law Inst., Law Ctr. of U. So. Calif.; bd. of councilors Law Ctr. U. So. Calif.; chmn., nat. bd. govs. Am. Jewish Com., 1995-98, nat. v.p., 1982-88, pres., 1998—, L.A. chpt., 1980-83, chair Western region, 1984-86, comty. svc. award, 1987, nat. pres., 1998—, adv. bd. Skirball Inst. on Am. Values, 1998—; chmn. Asia Pacific Rim Inst., 1989-98; trustee Loyola Marymount U., L.A. Children's Mus., 1986-89; vice chair United Way, 1991-93, corp. bd. dirs., 1981-93, chair coun. pres. 1989-90, mem. cmty. issues coun., 1989-90, chair discretionary fund distbn. com., 1987-89; bd. dirs., chair Geffen Playhouse, 1995-98, founding chair, 1998—; bd. dirs. L.A. Urban League, 1987-93, 96—, Jewish Fedn. Coun. of Greater L.A. (mem. Cmty. Rels. com., bd. dirs., exec. com.), Jewish TV Network, Sta. KCET-TV; mem., bd. dirs. Rebuild L.A., 1992-96; mem. bd. govs. Calif. Cmty. Found., 1988-98; recipient Ann. Brotherhood award NCCJs, 1990; mem. Fellows of Am. Bar Found.; mem. econ. strategy panel State Calif., 1997—; bd. dirs. Shoah Visual History Found., Righteous Persons Found., L.A. 2012 Bid Com. for the So. Calif. Olympic Games; bd. dirs. Jewish Fedn. Coun. Greater L.A., mem. exec. com., cmty. rels. com. Pvt. U.S. Army, 1958-59, 2d lt., 1961-62. Mem. ABA (mem. spl. com. jud. ind.), L.A. County Bar Assn., Calif. Bar Assn., Beverly Hills Bar Assn. (Exec. Dirs. award 1988, Entertainment Lawyer of Yr. award 1996), L.A. Copyright Soc. (pres. 1974-75), Calif. Copyright Conf. (pres. 1973-74), Princeton Club (pres. 1975-78). Entertainment. Office: Gang Tyre Ramer & Brown Inc 132 S Rodeo Dr Beverly Hills CA 90212-2415

**RAMEY, CARL ROBERT,** lawyer; b. Binghamton, N.Y., Feb. 15, 1941; s. Clinton W. and Hester May (Wisdom) R.; m. Maryan Sitzenkopf, Aug. 11, 1962 (div. Sept. 1987); children: Mark Alan, Christian David; m. Karen

Reichard, Nov. 28, 1987. AB, Marietta Coll., 1962; MA, Mich. State U., 1964; JD, George Washington U., 1967. Bar: D.C. 1968, U.S. Dist. Ct. D.C. 1968, U.S. Ct. Appeals (D.C., 2d, 3d, 4th, 5th, 7th and 9th cirs.), U.S. Supreme Ct. 1972, Md. 1999. Assoc. McKenna, Wilkinson & Kittner, Washington, 1967-71, ptnr., 1971-86; ptnr. Wiley, Rein & Fielding, Washington, 1986—. Contbr. articles to profl. jours., chpt. to Copyright Law Symposium, 1969; editorial staff George Washington Law Rev., 1965-67. Recipient First Prize award Nat. Nathan Burkan Meml. Writing Competition, ASCAP, 1969. Mem. ABA, Fed. Communications Bar Assn. (treas. 1977-78, co-chair editl. adv. bd. Fed. Comms. Law Jour. 1993-96), D.C. Bar Assn., Md. Bar Assn. Republican. Episcopalian. Avocations: skiing, tennis, boating, biking. Administrative and regulatory, Communications, Constitutional. Office: Wiley Rein & Fielding 1776 K St NW Washington DC 20006-2304

**RAMEY, DENNY L.,** bar association executive director; b. Portsmouth, Ohio, Feb. 22, 1947; s. Howard Leroy and Norma Wylodine (Richards) R.; m. Jeannine Gayle Dunmyer, Sept. 24, 1971 (div. Nov. 1991); children: Elizabeth Michelle, Brian Michael. BBA, Ohio U., 1970; MBA, Capital U., 1976. Cert. assn. exec. Adminstrv. mgr. Transit Warehouse div. Elston Richards Storage Co., Columbus, Ohio, 1970-73; mgr. continuing profl. edn. Ohio Soc. CPA's, Columbus, 1973-79; exec. dir. Engrs. Found. of Ohio, Columbus, 1979-80; asst. exec. Ohio State Bar Assn., Columbus, 1980-86, exec. dir., sec., treas., 1986—; treas., exec. com., bd. dirs. Ohio Bar Liability Ins. Co., Columbus, 1986—; treas. Ohio State Bar Found., 1986—; treas. Ohio Legal Ctr. Ins., Columbus, 1988-91; sec. Ohio Printing Co., Ltd., 1991; v.p. Osbanet, Inc., 1993—. Mem. Nat. Assn. Bar Execs. (chmn. various coms.), Am. Soc. Assn. Execs., Ohio Soc. Assn. Execs., Heritage Golf Club, The Player's Club. Methodist. Avocations: tennis, golf, sports memorabilia, wine appreciation. E-mail: dramey@ohiobar.org. Office: Ohio State Bar Assn 1700 Lake Shore Dr PO Box 16562 Columbus OH 43216-6562

**RAMEY, MARK S.,** lawyer; b. Huntington, W.Va., Jan. 29, 1958; s. Alva and Wanda Ramey; m. Lori Summers, Sept. 1, 1979 (div. 1986); 1 child, Christopher Michael; m. Lynn Van Ilyning, May 11, 1991; children: Payton Renee, Cameron Nicole. BA in Polit. Sci., U. Ctrl. Fla., 1984; JD, Stetson U., 1987. Bar: Fla., U.S. Ct. Appeals (11th cir.), U.S. Dist. Ct. (mid. dist.) Fla., U.S. Supreme Ct. Asst. state atty. 6th cir. Office of State's Atty.'s Office, Pinellas County, Fla., 1987-92; assoc. atty. Haas Austin Ley Rof & Patsko PA, Tampa, Fla., 1992-94; atty., shareholder Haas Ramey & Beik PA, Tampa, 1994-98, Ramey Ramey & Kampf PA, Tampa, 1998—. Insurance, Personal injury, State civil litigation. Office: Ramey Ramey & Kampf PA 1901 N 13th St Tampa FL 33605-3612

**RAMIL, MARIO R.,** state supreme court justice; b. Quezon City, The Philippines, June 21, 1946; came to U.S., 1956; s. Quintin A. and Fausta M. (Reyes) R.; m. Judy E. Wong, Nov. 6, 1971; children: Jonathan, Bradley. BA in Polit. Sci., Calif. State U., Hayward, 1972; JD, U. Calif., San Francisco, 1975. Bar: Calif. 1976, Hawaii 1976, U.S. Dist. Ct. Hawaii, U.S. Dist. Ct. (no. dist.) Calif., U.S. Ct. Appeals (9th cir.). Law clk. San Francisco Neighborhood Legal Aid Found., 1973-75; legal counsel Sandigan-Newcomers Svcs., Inc., San Francisco, 1975-76; dep. atty. gen. Dept. Labor and Indsl. Rels., 1976-79; dep. atty. gen. cen. adminstrn. U. Hawaii, 1979-80; staff atty. house majority atty.'s office Hawaii Ho. of Reps., 1980; pvt. practice, 1980-82; dep. atty. gen. adminstrv. div. State of Hawaii, 1982-84, ins. commr., 1984-86; dir. Hawaii State Dept. Labor and Indsl. Rels., Honolulu, 1986-91; of counsel Lyons, Brandt, Cook and Hiramatsu, 1991-93; assoc. justice Hawaii Supreme Ct., Honolulu, 1993—. Bd. dirs. Hawaii Youth-At-Risk, 1989; co-chair state conv. Dem. Party State of Hawaii, 1984; mem. Adv. Coun. on Housing and Constrn., State of Hawaii, 1981; pres., bd. dirs. Hawaii Non-Profit Housing Corp.; exec. sec., chmn. adminstrv. budget com. Oahu Filipino Community Coun.; bd. dirs, legal advisor Oahu Filipino Jaycees, 1978-81. Office: Ali'iolani Hale Hawaii Supreme Ct 417 S Kinga St Honolulu HI 96813-2902 Address: PO Box 2560 Honolulu HI 96804-2560*

**RAMIREZ, ANTHONY BENJAMIN,** lawyer; b. Frizell, Kans., Jan. 17, 1937; s. Jesus Ruiz Ramirez and Francisca Lopez; m. Jeanette Marilyn Lee, Sept. 19, 1964; children: Christopher Benjamin, Andrew Anthony. BA, St. Benedict's Coll., Atchison, Kans., 1959; JD, St. Louis U., 1967. Bar: Mo. 1967, U.S. Dist. Ct. (ea. dist.) Mo. 1968. Legal staff probate divsn. St. Louis City Cir. Ct., 1967-72; atty. various law offices St. Louis, St. Louis, 1972-81; ptnr. Coleman, Ross, Goetz, Robert & Ramirez, 1981-86; pvt. practice St. Louis, 1986—; legal advisor Mexican Consulate in St. Louis, 1979—; adj. prof. law Webster U., St. Louis, 1988-93. Editor (newsletter) DeNuevo, 1978-80; co-host Latin Rhythms radio program KDHX FM, 1992-93. Bd. dirs. Confluence St. Louis, 1990-96, ARC, Bi-State chpt. St. Louis, 1990-94, Springboard to Learning, 1996—; mem. Coro Fellows Program, 1994-95; facilitator Hispanic Leaders Group Greater St. Louis, 1985-93, sec., 1993-95, chmn., 1995—; Mo. del. White House Conf. on Small Bus., 1986; mem. SBA St. Louis Dist. Adv. Coun., 1985-93; mem. Fordyce Two Leadership Summit, 1990; commr. Mo. Commn. on Human Rights, 1983-87; charter mem. Gov.'s Coun. on Hispanic Affairs, 1980. Staff sgt. U.S. Army, 1959-60, 61-64. Named Mo. Minority Advocate of Yr. U.S. SBA, St. Louis, 1984; recipient Pres. award Hispanic C. of C., St. Louis, 1986, St. Louis Cmty. award of merit KPLR-TV, St. Louis, 1989. Mem. ABA, Nat. Assn. Criminal Def. Attys., Mo. Bar Assn., Bar Assn. Metro St. Louis, Law Alumni Assn. St. Louis U. Sch. Law (v.p. 1984-88), Hispanic C. of C. Met. St. Louis (co-founder, pres. 1982-85, chmn. bd. 1983-88). Republican. Roman Catholic. Criminal, Personal injury, General civil litigation. Office: 1221 Locust St Ste 503 Saint Louis MO 63103-2380

**RAMIREZ, FRANK TENORIO,** lawyer; b. Fresno, Calif., July 16, 1952; s. Ramon and Connie Ramirez; m. Teresa Gonzales, Apr. 15, 1978; children: Irene, Isabel, Francesca. BS, Calif. State U., Fresno, 1974; JD, U. Calif., Berkeley, 1977. Bar: Calif. 1978, U.S. Dist. Ct. (ea. dist.) Calif. 1978, U.S. Dist. Ct. (so. dist.) Calif. 1983, U.S. Ct. Appeals (9th cir.), 1984. Staff atty. Calif. Rural Legal Assistance, Inc., Madera, 1977-81; regional counsel Calif. Rural Legal Assistance, Inc., Fresno, 1982-84; trustee Calif. Rural Legal Assistance, Inc., San Francisco, 1986-98; pub. defender Fresno County Pub. Defender's Office, Fresno, 1982; ptnr. Hernandez & Ramirez, Fresno, 1984—; trustee Fresno County Law Libr., 1998. Mem. Fresno County Bar Assn., Madera County Bar Assn. (pres. 1996), La Raza Lawyers Assn. (pres. San Joaquin Valley chpt. 1983). Democrat. Roman Catholic. Personal injury, State civil litigation, Criminal. Office: Hernandez & Ramirez 6103 N 1st St Ste 102 Fresno CA 93710-5406

**RAMO, ROBERTA COOPER,** lawyer; b. Denver, Aug. 8, 1942; d. David D. and Martha L. (Rosenblum) Cooper; m. Barry W. Ramo, June 17, 1964. BA magna cum laude, U. Colo., 1964, LHD (hon.), 1995; JD, U. Chgo., 1967; LLD, U. Mo., 1995, U. Denver, 1995. Bar: N.Mex. 1967, Tex. 1971. With NC. Fund, Durham, 1967-68; nat. tchg. fellow Shaw U., Raleigh, N.C., 1968-70; mem. Sawtelle, Goode, Davidson & Troilo, San Antonio, 1970-72, Rodey, Dickason, Sloan, Akin & Robb, Albuquerque, 1972-74; sole practice law Albuquerque, 1974-77; dir., shareholder Poole, Kelly & Ramo, Albuquerque, 1977-93; shareholder Modrall, Sperling, Roehl, Harris & Sisk, Albuquerque, 1993—; lectr. in field. Co-author: New Mexico Estate Administration System, 1980; editor: How to Create a System for the Law Office, 1975; contbg. editor: Tex. Probate Sys., 1974; contbr. articles to profl. jours., chpts. to books. Bd. dirs., past pres. N.Mex. Symphony Orch., 1977-86; bd. dirs. Albuquerque Cmty. Found., N.Mex. First, 1987-90; bd. regents U. N.Mex., 1989-94, pres., 1991-93, chmn. presdl. search com., 1990; mem. vis. com. U. Chgo. Law Sch., 1987-90, 96—; mem. steering com. World Conf. Domestic Violence, 1996—; mem. Am. Law Inst. Coun., 1997—, Martindale-Hubbell Legal Adv. Bd., 1997—; chmn. bd. Cooper's Inc., 1999—. Recipient Disting. Pub. Svc. award Gov. of N.Mex., 1993. Fellow Am. Bar Found.; mem. ABA (pres. 1995, bd. govs. 1994-97, chmn. London 2000 com. 1997—, Asia Law Initiatives Coun. 1999—, others), Albuquerque Bar Assn. (bd. dirs., pres. 1980-81), N.Mex. Bar Assn. (Outstanding Contbn. award 1981, 84), Am. Bar Retirement Assn. (bd. dirs. 1990-94), Am. Judicature Soc. (bd. dirs. 1988-91), Law Inst. Coun., Am. Arbitration Assn. (bd. dirs. 1997—, bd. trustees Global Ctr. Dispute Resolution Rsch. 1999—), Greater Albuquerque C. of C. (bd. dirs., exec. com. 1987-91). Pension, profit-sharing, and employee benefits, Probate, Real property. Address: Modrall Sperling Roehl Harris & Sisk PO Box 2168 Albuquerque NM 87103-2168

**RAMOS, CARLOS E.,** law educator; b. Caguas, P.R., Oct. 20, 1952; s. Francisco E. and Olga (Gonzalez) R.; m. Lesbia Hernandez, July 30, 1988; children: Carlos Francisco, Isabel Maria, Macarena Eugenia. BA, U. P.R., 1974, JD, 1978; diploma, U. Stockholm, 1975; LLM, U. Calif., Berkeley, 1987. Bar: P.R. 1978, U.S. Dist. Ct. P.R. 1978, U.S. Ct. Appeals (1st cir.) 1979. Staff atty. P.R. Legal Svcs., San Juan, P.R., 1978-79; asst. prof. law InterAm. U. P.R., San Juan, 1979-86, assoc. prof., 1986-93, dean, prof. law, 1993—; exec. dir. Santurce Law Firm, San Jose, 1983-86. Co-author: Derecho Constitucional de Puerto Rico y los Estados Unidos, 1990, Teoria y Practica de la Litigacion en Puerto Rico. Mem. ABA, ATLA, Am. Judicature Soc., P.R. Bar Assn. Office: InterAm U PR Sch Law Office of Dean PO Box 70351 San Juan PR 00936-8351

**RAMPELL, PAUL,** lawyer; b. West Palm Beach, Fla., Jan. 2, 1956; m. Rita Bubis, Aug. 31, 1986; 1 child, Palmer. BA, Princeton U., 1977; JD, U. Fla., 1980. Bar: Fla. 1980. Atty. Schulte Roth & Zabel, Palm Beach and N.Y.C., 1980-87; pvt. practice, Palm Beach, 1987—. Author: Immortality Made Easy, 1998. Chmn. Palm Beach Code Enforcement Bd. Mem. Princeton Club N.Y., Mar-a-Lago Club. Estate planning, Real property. Office: 125 Worth Ave Ste 202 Palm Beach FL 33480-4466

**RAMSAUR, ALLAN FIELDS,** lawyer, lobbyist; b. Rocky Mount, NC, Dec. 30, 1951; s. Carl Hamilton and Celestine (Fields) R.; m. Jimmie Lynn Brewer, Sept. 2, 1972; children: Katherine Celeste, Benjamin Allan. BA in Polit. Sci., Lambuth U., 1974; JD, U. Tenn., 1977. Bar: Tenn. 1977. Staff atty. Tenn. Dept. Mental Health, Nashville, 1977-80; dir. Tenn. Assn. Legal Services, Nashville, 1980-86; campaign dir. Steve Cobb, Nashville, 1986; exec. dir. Nashville Bar Assn., 1986-98, Tenn. Bar Assn., 1999—. Pres. Woodland-in-Waverly Neighborhood Assn., Nashville, 1985; bd. dirs. SAGA, Nashville, 1984-86, Bethlehem Center, Nashville, 1990-96 (sec. 1992, v.p. 1994-95). Recipient Leadership Nashville award, 1988. Mem. ABA (liaison to standing com. on legal aid and indigent defendants 1984-86, spl. com. on prepaid legal svcs. 1988-89, standing com. on lawyer referral and info. svc. 1990-92), Nat. Assn. Bar Execs. (chair edn. com.), Tenn. Bar Assn. (pres. young lawyers divsn. 1985-86), Nat. Legal Aid and Defender Assn. (chmn. legis com. 1984-86), Nashville Bar Assn. (exec. dir. 1986-98). Democrat. Methodist. E-mail: aramsaur@tnbar.org. Home: 1417 Beddington Park Nashville TN 37215-5815

**RAMSAY, LOUIS LAFAYETTE, JR.,** lawyer, banker; b. Fordyce, Ark., Oct. 11, 1918; s. Louis Lafayette and Carmile (Jones) R.; m. Joy Bond, Oct. 3, 1945; children: Joy Blankenship, Richard Louis. JD, U. Ark., 1947; LLD (hon.), U. Ark., Fayetteville, 1988, U. Ark., Pine Bluff, 1992. Bar: Ark. 1947, U.S. Dist. Ct. Ark. 1947, U.S. Ct. Appeals (8th cir.) 1948, U.S. Supreme Ct. 1952. Of counsel Ramsay, Bridgforth, Harrelson & Starling and predecessor firm Ramsay, Cox, Lile, Bridgforth, Gilbert, Harrelson & Starling, Pine Bluff, Ark., 1948—; pres. Simmons First Nat. Bank, Pine Bluff, Ark., 1970-78, CEO, chmn. bd. dirs., 1978-83; chmn. exec. com., bd. dirs. Blue Cross-Blue Shield of Ark., Usable Life Ins. Co.; chmn. exec. com. Simmons First Nat. Corp. Mem. bd. Econ. Devel. Alliance of Jefferson County; mem. ofcl. bd. First United Meth. Ch. With USAF, 1942-45, maj. Res., 1945-49. Recipient Disting. Alumnus award U. Ark., 1982, Outstanding Lawyer award Ark. Bar Assn./Ark. Bar Found., 1966, 87. Mem. ABA (mem. spl. com. on presdl. inability and vice presdl. vacancy 1966), Ark. Bar Assn. (pres. 1963-64), Ark. Bar Found. (pres. 1960-61, Joint Bar Assn.-Bar Found. Outstanding Lawyer award 1966, Lawyer Citizen award 1987), Ark. Bankers Assn. (pres. 1980-81), Pine Bluff C. of C. (pres. 1968), Rotary (pres. Pine Bluff 1954-55). Methodist. General corporate, Probate. Office: Ramsay Bridgforth Harrelson & Starling 11th Fl Simmons 1st Nat Bldg 501 S Main St Pine Bluff AR 71601-4327

**RAMSEY, DAVID WADE,** lawyer; b. Toronto, Ont., Oct. 9, 1962; came to U.S., 1968; s. David Harold and Marion Elizabeth R. BS, Auburn U., 1986, MBA, 1988; JD, Birmingham Sch. Law, Birmingham, 1996. Bar: Ala. Nat. acct. rep. AT&T, Dallas and Birmingham, 1988-92; mortgage banker SouthTrust Mortgage, Birmingham, 1992-94, Compass Bank, Birmingham, 1994-97; mem. Acres & Ramsey, LLC, Birmingham, 1997-99, Ramsey & Assocs. LLC, Birmingham, 1999—. Mem. Ala. State Bar Assn., Birmingham Bar Assn. Avocations: auto restoration, sailing, golf, motorcycling, bicycling. Real property, Intellectual property, Trademark and copyright. Office: 300 Office Park Dr Ste 309 Birmingham AL 35223-2473

**RAMSEY, EDWARD LAWRENCE,** judge; b. Dothan, Ala., Dec. 9, 1941; s. Joseph Robert and Hilda (Hawkins) R.; m. Pamela Thuss, 1971 (div. 1976); 1 child, Matthew Edward. Student, Emory U., 1960-62; BA, U. Ala., Tuscaloosa, 1965, JD, 1966. Bar: Ala. 1966, Calif. 1970, U.S. Ct. Appeals (5th and 11th cirs.) 1972. Dep. dist. atty. Office of Dist. Atty., San Diego, 1970-72; pvt. practice Birmingham, Ala., 1972-94; judge civil divsn. Cir. Ct. Jefferson County, Birmingham, 1995—. Bd. dirs. Firehouse Shelter, Birmingham, 1993—. Capt. USMC, 1967-70. Mem. Exchange Club (past pres.). Republican. Episcopalian.

**RAMSEY, HENRY, JR.,** university official, lawyer, retired judge; b. Florence, S.C., Jan. 22, 1934; s. Henry Ramsey and Mary Ann Brunson; reared by Charles Arthur and Nellie Tillman; m. Evelyn Yvonne Lewis, June 11, 1961 (div. Sept. 1967); children: Charles, Githaiga, Robert, Ismail; m. Eleanor Mason Ramsey, Sept. 7, 1969; children: Yetunde, Abeni. Student, Howard U.; BA, U. Calif., Riverside, 1960; LLB, U. Calif., 1963; student Inst. Edn. Mgmt., Harvard U., 1992; LLD (hon.), William Mitchell Coll. Law, 1996. Bar: Calif., 1964, U.S. Supreme Ct., 1967. Dep. dist. atty. Contra Costa County, Calif., 1964-65; pvt. practice Ramsey & Rosenthal, Richmond, Calif., 1965-71; prof. law U. Calif., Berkeley, 1971-80; judge Superior Court County of Alameda State Calif., Oakland, 1980-90; dean Sch. Law, Howard U., Washington, 1990-96, v.p. for legal affairs, acting gen. counsel, 1994-95, ret.; vis. prof. law U. Tex., Austin, 1977, U. Colo., Boulder, 1977-78, Am. Indian Law Ctr., U. N.Mex., 1980; mem., pres. Coun. Legal Edn., Opportunity, Washington, 1987-93; chair Law Sch. Admission Coun.-Bar Passage Rate Study Group, 1990-93; mem. Fellows of Am. Bar Found. Adv. Rsch. Com., 1995—; mem. Coun. for Ct. Excellence, D.C. Jury Project, 1996-97; panelist Washington, D.C. region Ctr. for Pub. Resources, Institute for Dispute Resolution. Mem. City Coun. Berkeley, 1973-77, Criminal Justice Planning Bd., County of Alameda, 1973-76; trustee City of Berkeley Libr., 1973-74, Fibreboard Asbestos Compensation Trust, 1994—; bd. dirs. Redevel. Agy., Berkeley, 1971-73; dir. Rosenberg Found., San Francisco, 1999—. With USAF, 1951-55. Recipient Jefferson Jurist award Calif. Assoc. Black Lawyers, 1986, Disting. Alumnus award U. Calif., 1987, Disting. Svc. award Wiley Manuel Law Found., 1987. Mem. ABA (mem. sect. legal edn. and admissions to bar 1982—, chair 1991-92, mem. standards rev. com. 1992-95), Nat. bar Assn., Nat. Ctr. State Cts. (mem. commn. trial ct. performance stds. 1987-95, Dist. Svc. award 1990), Am. Law Inst., Am. Judicature Soc., Calif. Judges Assn., Cosmos Club, Fed. City Club, Alpha Phi Alpha. Democrat. Avocations: cooking, reading, gardening, travel.

**RAMSEY, JAMES E.,** lawyer; b. Worcester, Mass., Feb. 22, 1968; s. Edward and Margaret R.; m. Meredith, 1996; 1 child, Rebecca. BS, Northeastern U., 1991, MS, 1992; JD, Suffolk U., 1995. Bar: Mass. 1996, Conn. 1996. Law clk. Conn. Superior Ct., New Haven, 1995-96; assoc. O'Connor & Grace, Boston, 1996—. Mem. Mass. Bar Assn. Avocations: golf, softball, biking. General civil litigation, Insurance, Product liability. Office: O'Connor & Grace 126 State St Ste 300 Boston MA 02109-2305

**RAMSEY, NATALIE D.,** lawyer; b. Greenville, Tenn., Dec. 6, 1959; d. William Trent and Nancy Elizabeth (Maupin) R. BS, U. Del., 1981; JD, Villanova U., 1984. Bar: Pa. 1984, U.S. Dist. Ct. (ea. dist.) Pa. 1985, U.S. Ct. Appeals (3rd cir. and 11th cirs.) 1989. Assoc. atty. Frederick L. Reigle, Esq. and Assocs., Reading, Pa., 1984-85, Montgomery, McCracken, Walker & Rhoads, LLP, Phila., 1985-93; ptnr. Montgomery, McCracken, Walker & Rhoads, Phila., 1993—; chair programs com. East. Dist. of Pa. Bankruptcy Conf., 1999—. Co-author: (manual) Pennsylvania Bar Association Seminar-The 1994 Bankruptcy Act, 1995. Mem. Comml. Law League, Turnaround Mgmt. Assn. Presbyterian. Avocations: swimming, travel, reading. Bankruptcy, Federal civil litigation. Office: Montgomery McCracken Walker & Rhoads LLP 123 S Broad St Fl 24 Philadelphia PA 19109-1099

**RAMUNNO, L. VINCENT,** lawyer; b. Italy, Oct. 7, 1939; came to U.S., 1948; m. Marian Capano Ramunno, June 10, 1973; children: Vincent, Louis, Lisa. BA, U. Del., 1961; JD, Georgetown U., 1965. Bar: Del. 1965. 1st asst. U.S. atty. Dist. of Del., Wilmington, 1966-68; pvt. practice law Wilmington, 1969—. Personal injury. Office: Ramunno & Ramunno PA 903 N French St Wilmington DE 19801-3371

**RANA, HARMINDERPAL SINGH,** lawyer; b. Bombay, July 4, 1968; came to U.S., 1970; s. Baljit Singh and Devinder (Kaur) R.; m. Aasjot Kaur Sidhu, Mar. 8, 1998. BS in Fgn. Svc., cert. in Asian studies, Georgetown U., 1990; JD, honors cert. in internat. law, Rutgers U., Camden, N.J., 1994. Bar: N.J. 1994, U.S. Dist. Ct. N.J. 1994, N.Y. 1995, U.S. Dist. Ct. (so. and ea. dists.) N.Y. 1995. Pvt. practice, Warren, N.J., 1994—; assoc. staff analyst N.Y.C. Dept. Mental Health, Bklyn., 1995-97, borough coord., Bklyn. and S.I., 1997—; pool atty. family law litigation N.J. Office Pub. Defender, Middlesex and Somerset counties, 1995—. Mem. traffic safety com. Warren Twp. (N.J.) Coun., 1997-99. NYU Trustees scholar, 1986, N.Y. State Regents scholar, 1986. Mem. ABA, N.J. Bar Assn., Assn. Bar City N.Y. (health law com. 1997—, liaison to joint subcom. on human cloning). Sikh. Avocations: literature, philosophy, world affairs, athletic cross training, public service. General practice, Immigration, naturalization, and customs, Contracts commercial. Office: 3 Krausche Rd Warren NJ 07059

**RANDA, RUDOLPH THOMAS,** judge; b. Milw., July 25, 1940; s. Rudolph Frank and Clara Paula (Kojis) R.; m. Melinda Nancy Matera, Jan. 15, 1977; children—Rudolph Daniel, Daniel Anthony. B.S., U. Wis.-Milw., 1963; J.D., U. Wis.-Madison, 1966. Bar: Wis. 1966, U.S. Dist. Ct. (ea. and we. dists.) Wis., 1966, U.S. Ct. Appeals (7th cir.) 1973, U.S. Supreme Ct. 1973. Sole practice, Milw., 1966-67; prin. city atty. Office Milw. City Atty., 1970-75; judge Milw. Mcpl. Ct., 1975-79, Milwaukee County Circuit Ct., 1979-81, 1982-92, Appellate Ct., Madison, Wis., 1981-82; federal judge U.S. Dist. Ct. (ea. dist.) Wis., 1992—; chmn. Wis. Impact, Milw., 1980—; lectr. Marquette U. Law Sch., Milw., 1980—. Served to capt. U.S. Army, 1967-69, Vietnam. Decorated Bronze Star medal. Mem. Milw. Bar Assn., Wis. Bar Assn., Trial Judges Wis., Am. Legion (adjutant Milw. 1980), Thomas More Lawyers Soc. (former pres. Milw.), Milw. Hist. Soc., Phi Alpha Theta. Roman Catholic. Office: US Courthouse 517 E Wisconsin Ave Rm 247 Milwaukee WI 53202-4504

**RANDALL, EVAN LEVY,** lawyer; b. San Antonio, Jan. 4, 1971. BBA, U. Tex., 1992; JD, MA in Urban Planning, U. Kans., 1998. Bar: Mo. 1998, U.S. Dist. Ct. (we. dist.) Mo. 1998. Assoc. Spencer Fane Britt & Browne LLP, Kansas City, Mo., 1998—. Mem. Order of Coif, Phi Kappa Phi. Environmental, Real property. Office: Spencer Fane Britt & Browne 1000 Walnut St Ste 1400 Kansas City MO 64106-2140

**RANDALL, JAMES GRAFTON,** lawyer, consultant; b. Lake Forest, Ill., Dec. 2, 1951; s. John Albert Jr. and Barbara Blanche (Coen) R.; m. Valerie Sue Skinner, Oct. 18, 1980; children: William Douglas and Michael Coen (twins). AA in Speech, Chaffey Jr. Coll., 1971; BS, SUNY, Albany, 1977; JD, Western State U., 1980. Bar: Mont. 1985, Calif. 1986, U.S. Dist. Ct. Mont. 1986, U.S. Dist. Ct. (cen. dist.) Calif. 1987, U.S. Dist. Ct. (so. dist.) Calif. 1992. Pvt. practice law Orange, Calif., 1985-87; assoc. Samuel Gabriel & Assocs., Long Beach, Calif., 1987-90; pvt. practice law, cons., 1990-93; sr. trial counsel Early Maslach Price, 1993—; instr. Am. Coll. Law, 1985; spkr. Consumer Attys. Assn., 1999. Author: California Personal Injury Forms, 1987; contbr. numerous articles profl. jours. U.S. Army, 1969-71, 73-76. Decorated Vietnam Cross of Gallantry with palm. Mem. Am. Trial Lawyers Assn. (Belli seminar conv. speaker 1990-92), Calif. Trial Lawyers Assn., L.A. Trial Lawyers Assn., San Diego Trial Lawyers Assn. (seminar speaker 1987). Democrat. Avocations: writing, local politics. Personal injury, Product liability. Home: 136 N Edgemar Cir Anaheim CA 92807-3107

**RANDALL, KENNETH C.,** dean, law educator. JD, Hofstra U., 1981; Master's, Yale U., 1982, Columbia U., 1985; Doctorate, Columbia U., 1988. Practice law Simpson Thacher & Bartlett, N.Y.C., 1982-84; with faculty U. Ala. Sch. Law, Tuscaloosa, 1985—, vice dean, 1989-93, dean, 1993—. Author book on international law; contbr. articles to law jours. and revs. W. Bayard Cutting Jr. fellow of internat. law Columbia U. Sch. Law, 1984-85. Office: U Ala Law Sch PO Box 870382 Tuscaloosa AL 35487-0382*

**RANDELS, ED L.,** lawyer; b. Albuquerque, Nov. 17, 1953; s. James L. and Betty J. (Ridgeway) R.; m. Kathryn J. Eddleman, July 11, 1975; children: Nancy L., Joshua L. BA, Mid-Am. Nazarene Coll., Olathe, Kans., 1975; JD, U. Kans., 1982. Bar: Kans. 1982, U.S. Dist. Ct. Kans. 1982, U.S. Ct. Appeals (10th cir.) 1994. Asst. county atty. Montgomery County, Indpendence, Kans., 1982-85, Miami County, Paola, Kans., 1985-86; asst. city atty. City of Wichita, Kans., 1986-92; asst. county counselor Sedgwick County, Wichita, Kans., 1992—; law day dir. Miami County Bar Assn., Paola, Kans., 1985-86. Contbr. articles to profl. jours. Mem. ABA, Kans. Bar Assn., Wichita Bar Assn. (chair law in edn. com. 1999—, mem. mcpl. practice com.), Christian Legal Soc. (pres. Wichita chpt. 1998-99). Republican. Nazarene. Office: Sedgwick County Counselor 525 N Main St Ste 359 Wichita KS 67203-3731

**RANDICK, MARLYS ANN,** legal secretary; b. Titonka, Iowa, June 8, 1937; d. Henry Lewis and Margaret Jean (Sleper) Stecker; m. Robert Andrew Randick, Jr., July 10, 1970; children: Alyson Margaret, Suzanne Elizabeth. AA, Wartburg Coll., 1956. Cert. CTC, ICTA. Sec. Dept. of State, Washington, 1962-66; sec. Am. Embassy, Beirut, 1963-65, Manila, 1965-66; sec. to dean U. San Francisco, 1968-72; seamstress Carolyn Parker Designs, Lafayette, Calif., 1978-80; travel agt. Golden Gate Tours, Lafayette, 1981-91; legal sec. Bradford Pers., Walnut Creek, Calif., 1992-95, Guidotti & Lee, Orinda, Calif., 1995—; self-employed Marlys Randick Sec. & Graphic Design, 1995—. Active Nat. Charity League, 1988-92; vol. ch. activities. Democrat. Lutheran. Avocations: graphic design, crafts, quilting. Home: 524 Dawkins Dr Lafayette CA 94549-5410

**RANDOLPH, ARTHUR RAYMOND,** federal judge; b. Riverside, N.J., Nov. 1, 1943; m. Eileen J. O'Connor, May 18, 1984; children: John Trevor, Cynthia Lee. BS, Drexel U., 1966; JD summa cum laude, U. Pa., 1969. Bar: Calif. 1970, D.C. 1973, U.S. Supreme Ct. 1973. Law clk. to hon. judge Henry J. Friendly U.S. Ct. Appeals, 2d Cir., N.Y.C., 1969-70; asst. to solicitor gen. U.S. Dept. Justice, Washington, 1970-73, dep. solicitor gen., 1975-77; ptnr. Sharp, Randolph & Green, Washington, 1977-83, Randolph & Truitt, Washington, 1983-87, Pepper, Hamilton & Scheetz, Washington, 1987-90; judge U.S. Ct. Appeals (D.C. cir.), Washington, 1990—; spl. asst. atty. gen. State of Mont., 1983-90, State of N.Mex., 1985-90, State of Utah, 1986-90; mem. adv. panel Fed. Cts. Study Com., 1989-90; spl. counsel Com. on Stds. of Ofcl. Conduct, U.S. Ho. of Reps., 1979-80; adj. prof. law Georgetown U. Law Ctr., 1974-78; exec. sec. Atty. Gen.'s Com. on Reform of Fed. Jud. System, 1975-77; mem. com. on Fed. Rules of Evidence U.S. Justice Dept., 1972; chmn. Com. on Govtl. Structures, McLean, Va., 1973-74; adj. prof. law sch. George Mason U., 1992, disting. prof., 1998; mem. com. codes conduct Jud. Conf. U.S., 1993-98, chmn., 1995-98. Recipient Spl. Achievement award U.S. Dept. Justice, 1971. Mem. Am. Law Inst., Calif. Bar Assn., D.C. Bar Assn., Order of Coif. Office: US Ct Appeals 333 Constitution Ave NW Washington DC 20001-2866

**RANDOLPH, CHRISTOPHER CRAVEN,** lawyer; b. Washington, May 26, 1956; s. William Barksdale and Elizabeth Page (Craven) R.; m. Linda Bubernak Dressler, June 6, 1982; children: Alexander Dressler, Brian Donovan. BA summa cum laude, U. Va., 1978; JD cum laude, Harvard U., 1982. Bar: D.C. 1983, N.Y. 1983. Assoc. Debevoise & Plimpton, N.Y.C., 1982-86, Washington, 1987-92; atty. advisor Agy. for Internat. Devel., Washington, 1992-95; investor, entrepreneur Vienna, Va., 1995—. Editor Harvard Law Rev., 1980-82; contbr. articles to profl. jours. Mem. ABA, D.C. Bar Assn., Phi Beta Kappa. Republican. Episcopalian. Avocations: travel, reading, sports. Securities, General corporate, Government contracts and claims. Home and Office: 2619 Five Oaks Rd Vienna VA 22181-5436

**RANDOLPH, JEROME C.,** lawyer; b. Cin., Mar. 21, 1948; s. Henry J. and Martha T. (Dannenfelser) R.; m. Patricia M. McNamara, June 15, 1968; children: Peter, Ben, Michael. BA in Polit. Sci., Xavier U., 1970; JD, U.

Chgo., 1973. Bar: Ill. 1973, Ohio 1978. With Keating, Muething & Klenkamp, Cin. Mem. ABA, Fed. Bar Assn., Ohio Bar Assn., Cin. Bar Assn. Democrat. Roman Catholic. Avocations: coaching youth baseball, tennis. General civil litigation, Environmental. Office: Keating Muething & Klenkamp 1800 Provident Tower Cincinnati OH 45202-3752

**RANDOLPH, KENNETH E.,** lawyer. Sr. v.p., gen. counsel Dynegy Inc. (formerly NGC Corp.), Houston, 1987—. Office: Dynegy Inc 1000 Louisiana St Ste 5800 Houston TX 77002-5050*

**RANDOLPH, ROBERT MCGEHEE,** lawyer; b. San Antonio, June 15, 1936; s. Nowlin and Marjorie (McGehee) R.; m. Jeanette Harrison, Feb. 10, 1962; children: Jeanette, Anne, Nowlin. BA, Tex. Christian U., Ft. Worth, 1957; LLB, U. Tex., 1961. Bar: Tex. 1961, U.S. Dist. Ct. (no. dist.) Tex. 1963, U.S. Supreme Ct. 1972, U.S. Ct. Appeals (5th cir.) 1981. Litigation sect. chief Law, Snakard & Gambill, Ft. Worth, 1963—. Bd. visitors St. Thomas More Coll. 1st lt. U.S. Army. Fulbright scholar, 1957-58. Fellow Tex. Bar Found.; mem. Tex. Assn. Def. Counsel, Ft. Worth-Tarrant County Bar Assn., River Crest Country Club, Ft. Worth Club, Alpha Chi. Federal civil litigation, General civil litigation, State civil litigation. Office: Law Snakard & Gambill 500 Throckmorton St Ste 3200 Fort Worth TX 76102-3859

**RANKIN, CLYDE EVAN, III,** lawyer; b. Phila., July 3, 1950; s. Clyde Evan, Jr. and Mary E. (Peluso) R.; m. Camille Cozzone, Aug. 24, 1997; A.B., Princeton U., 1972; J.D., Columbia U., 1975; postgrad. Hague Acad. Internat. Law, 1975. Bar: N.Y., N.J., D.C., U.S. Supreme Ct. Law clk. to judge U.S. Dist. Ct. So. Dist. N.Y., 1975-77; assoc. Debevoise, Plimpton, Lyons & Gates, N.Y.C., 1977-79; assoc. Coudert Bros., N.Y.C., 1979-83, ptnr., 1984—. Trustee The Rensselaerville (N.Y.) Inst., 1989—, Coun. on Fgn. Rels., 1996—. Stone scholar, 1974. Mem. ABA, Assn. of Bar of City of N.Y., N.Y. State Bar Assn., D.C. Bar Assn., N.J. Bar Assn. Roman Catholic. Club: Amateur Comedy (N.Y.C.). Contbr. article to legal jour. General corporate, Private international. Office: Coudert Bros 1114 Ave of Americas New York NY 10036-7703

**RANKIN, GENE RAYMOND,** lawyer; b. Madison, Wis., Sept. 29, 1940; s. Eugene Carleton and Mildred Florence (Blomster) R.; m. Katherine E. Hundt, Aug. 25, 1979; 1 child, Abigail Hundt. BS, U. Wis., 1966, MS in Planning, 1973, JD, 1980. Bar: Wis. 1980, U.S. Dist. Ct. (we. dist.) Wis. 1980, U.S. Ct. Appeals (7th cir.) 1992. Systems analyst U. Wis. Primate Research Ctr., Madison, 1967-72; planner Dane County Regional Planning Commn., Madison, 1973-79; pres. Mendota Rsch., 1978—; with Risser and Risser, Madison, 1980-89; dir. land regulation and records dept. Dane County, Madison, 1984-89; pvt. practice Madison, Wis., 1989—; dir. bd. examiners Wis. Supreme Ct., Madison, 1994—; planning cons., Madison, 1973-77; guest lectr. land use, ethics and admiralty law Law Sch. U. Wis., 1982, 86, 93, 94, 95, 96, guest lectr. land econs. Planning Sch., 1973-81; guest lectr. various legal subjects U. Wis. Ext., 1988—. Author: Historic Preservation Law in Wisconsin, 1982; The First Bite at the Apple: State Supreme Court Takings Jurisprudence Antedating First English, 1990; (with others) Boundary Law in Wisconsin, 1991; contbr. articles to profl. jours. Bd. dirs. Madison Trust for Hist. Preservation, 1984-87, Madison Zoning Bd. of Appeals, 1986-94, Dane County Humane Soc., 1988-90, Dane County Housing Devel. Corp., 1975-79; spl. counsel City of Fitchburg, 1983-84, Nat. Trust for Hist. Preservation, 1989-90, City of Shullsburg, 1990-98; gen. counsel Cat Fanciers' Assn. Midwestern Region, 1990-95, Hist. Madison, Inc., 1981—, Wis. Lead Region Hist. Trust, Inc., 1992—; mem. legis. coun. Spl. Com. on Condo. Issues, Madison, 1984-85; commr. and vice-chmn. Dane County Housing Authority, 1979-84; chmn. Wis. Chamber Orch. Bd., 1979-81; state chmn. McCarthy 1976 campaign, Madison, 1974-76. With USCGR, 1958-60. Fellow Nat. Endowment for the Arts and Humanities, 1972; Olympic finalist for Internat. 470 yachting competition, 1976. Mem. Am. Planning Assn., Urban Land Inst., Urban and Regional Info. Sys. Assn., Wis. Bar Assn. (bd. dirs., treas., founder environ. law sect.), Dane County Bar Assn., Coun. Bar Admission Adminstrs., U. Wis. Hoofers Sailing Club (vice commodore 1972), Meml. Union Club, U.S. Yacht Racing Union, Downtown Madison Rotary. Avocations: sailing, racquet sports, music, skating, motorcycling. Environmental, Real property, Land use and zoning (including planning). Home: 2818 Ridge Rd Madison WI 53705-5224 Office: 715 Tenney Bldg 110 E Main St Madison WI 53703-3395

**RANKIN, JAMES WINTON,** lawyer; b. Norfolk, Va., Sept. 9, 1943; s. Winton Blair and Edith (Griffin) R.; m. Donna Lee Carpenter, June 25, 1966 (dec.); children—Thomas James, William Joseph, Elizabeth Jeanne; m. JoAnne Katherine Murray, Feb. 11, 1978. A.B. magna cum laude, Oberlin Coll., 1965; J.D. cum laude, U. Chgo., 1968. Bar: Ill. 1968, U.S. Dist. Ct. (no. dist.) Ill. 1969, U.S. Ct. Appeals (7th cir.) 1971, U.S. Ct. Appeals (5th cir.) 1979, U.S. Supreme Ct. 1975, Calif. 1986. Law clk. U.S. Dist. Ct. (no. dist.) Ill., 1968-69; assoc. Kirkland & Ellis, Chgo., 1969-73, ptnr., 1973—. Mem. ABA, Order of Coif, Mid-Am. Club, Univ. Club, Mich. Shores Club, Kenilworth Club, Ephriam Yacht Club. Presbyterian. Antitrust, Federal civil litigation, Health. Home: 633 Kenilworth Ave Kenilworth IL 60043-1070 Office: Kirkland & Ellis 200 E Randolph St Fl 54 Chicago IL 60601-6636

**RANSBOTTOM, JENNIFER DICKENS,** lawyer; b. Pontiac, Mich., Oct. 7, 1966; d. David Noel and Suzanne Lynch Dickens; m. Barry Don Ransbottom, July 4, 1997. BS, Marshall U., 1988; JD, W.Va. U., 1994. Bar: Ga. 1994, W.Va. 1994, U. S. Dist. Ct. (so. dist.) W.Va. 1994. Assoc. Tyson & Tyson, Huntington, W.Va., 1995—. Mem. ABA, Ga. Bar Assn., W.Va. Bar Assn. (family law com. 1997—), Cabell County Bar Assn. Republican. Roman Catholic. Family and matrimonial, Education and schools, Juvenile. Office: Tyson & Tyson PO Box 1096 Huntington WV 25713-1096

**RANSOM, CLIFTON LOUIS, JR.,** lawyer, real estate investor; b. Houston, May 25, 1935; s. Clifton Louis and Birdelle (Wykoff) R.; m. Dorothy Ellen Peterson, Dec. 25, 1974. BS in Math., Tex. So. U., 1956; BA in Philosophy, St. Joseph's Coll., Rensselaer, Ind., 1964; MA in Bibl. Theology, St. Louis U., 1970; JD, Tex. So. U., 1974; LLM in Taxation, Washington Law Sch., Salt Lake City, 1991. Bar: Tex. 1974, U.S. Dist. Ct. (so. dist.) Tex. 1976, U.S. Ct. Appeals (5h cir.) 1980, U.S. Supreme Ct. 1980, U.S. Tax Ct. 1991; ordained priest Roman Cath. Ch., 1968. Priest Diocese of Galveston-Houston, 1968-74; atty. Tex. Welfare Dept., Houston, 1975-80, Gulf Coast Legal Found., Houston, 1980—. Bd. dirs. Hope Is Victory AIDS Found., Houston, 1993-96. Lt. (j.g.) USN, 1957-60. Democrat. Family and matrimonial, General civil litigation. Home: 3919 Point Clear Dr Missouri City TX 77459-3710 Office: Gulf Coast Legal Found 1415 Fannin St Ste 300 Houston TX 77002-7632

**RAPHAEL, DAVID COLEMAN,** lawyer; b. New Orleans, Apr. 22, 1968; s. David Coleman and Rita Bares R.; m. Diana Lorena Rubio, June 7, 1997; 1 child, Amanda Elise; 1 stepchild, Corey Moody Jr. BS, La. State U., 1989, JD, 1993. Bar: La. 1994, U.S. Dist. Ct. (ea. dist.) 1996. V.p., gen. counsel Fig Tree Foods, Inc., Metairie, La., 1995; assoc. Michael L. Eckstein, New Orleans, 1995—. Mem. New Orleans Bar Assn. Contracts commercial, General corporate, Estate planning. Office: Michae L Eckstein 1515 Poydras St Ste 2195 New Orleans LA 70112-3753

**RAPOPORT, DAVID E.,** lawyer; b. Chgo., May 27, 1956; s. Morris H. and Ruth (Teckteil) R.; m. Andrea Gail Albun; children: Alyson Faith, Steven Andrew. BS in Fin., No. Ill. U., 1978; JD with high honors, Ill. Inst. Tech., 1981; cert. trial work, Lawyers Postgrad. Inst., Chgo., 1984; cert. civil trial specialist, Nat. Bd. Trial Adv., 1991. Bar: Ill. 1981, Wis. 1995, U.S. Dist. Ct. (no. dist.) Ill. 1981, U.S. Dist. Ct. (trial bar) Ill. 1993, U.S. Dist. Ct. (so. and ctrl. dists.), U.S. Ct. Appeals (7th cir.) 1981, U.S. Ct. Appeals (7th cir.) 1981, U.S. Ct. Appeals (4th cir.) 1996. Assoc. Katz, Friedman, Schur & Eagle, Chgo., 1981-90, of counsel, 1990—; ptnr. Baizer & Rapoport, Chgo.; of counsel Baizer & Rapoport, Highland Park, Ill., 1990-95; founder, pres. Rapoport Law Offices, P.C. (formerly Rapoport & Kupets P.C.), 1995—; instr. legal writing Ill. Inst. Tech.-Kent Coll. Law, Chgo., 1981, guest lectr., 1985—; instr. Ill. Inst. CLE, 1995—; arbitrator Cir. Ct. Cook County, Ill., Million Dollar Advs. Forum, 1995—; state coord., lead trial counsel, mem. plaintiff's steering com. In Air Disaster at Charlotte Douglas Airport, 1994; mem. lead counsel com. In Air Disaster at Morrisville, N.C., 1994; lead trial counsel, In The Air Disaster at Sioux Gateway Airport, 1989. Bd. dirs. Congregation Beth Judea, Long Grove, Ill. Fellow Roscoe Pound Found.; mem. ABA, ATLA (sustaining mem.), Ill. Bar Assn., Ill. Trial Lawyers Assn., Chgo. Bar Assn., Ill. Inst. for CLE, Trial Lawyers for Pub. Justice, Trial Lawyers for Pub. Justice, Trial Lawyers for Civil Justice, Lake County Bar Assn. Personal injury, Product liability, Aviation. Office: Rapoport & Kupets Law Offices 77 W Washington St Fl 20 Chicago IL 60602-2801 also: O'Hare Internat Ctr 10275 W Higgins Rd Ste 370 Rosemont IL 60018-3885

**RAPOSA, PAMELA ADRIENNE,** legal executive; b. Manchester, Conn., Sept. 13, 1946; d. Delphis and Minerva (Chappel) LaBonte; m. Gerald Silvio Brunette, Oct. 10, 1970 (div. Jan. 10, 1981); m. Richard Anthony Raposa, Mar. 8, 1991. AA, Greater Harford C.C., Conn., 1983; BA, U. Conn., West Hartford, Conn., 1986; JD, Western New Eng. Sch. Law, Springfield, Mass., 1990. Bar: Conn. 1990, Oreg. 1991, Am. Bar Assn., U.S. Ct. Appeals (9th cir.) Oreg. Exec. sec. Fairbanks Morse Divsn., St. Johnsbury, Vt., 1964-66, Colt Industries, Inc., West Hartford, Conn., 1966-70; contract adminstr. Dynamic Controls Corp., South Windsor, Conn., 1970-72; adminstrv. asst. Am. Postal Workers, East Hartford, Conn., 1972-91; asst. pub. defender Southwestern Oreg. Pub. Defenders, Coos Bay, Oreg., 1991-92, Multnomah Defenders, Inc., Portland, Oreg., 1992-93; chief, planning and rsch. unit State of Conn. Divsn. of Spl. Revenue, Newington, Conn., 1993—; adjunct prof. Southwestern Oreg. C.C., North Bend, 1991-92, Lynnfield Coll., Portland, 1992-93. Officer, dir. Conn. Breast Cancer Found./Coalition, Thomaston, 1994—. Recipient Profl. Achievement award Conn./Mass. Postal Workers, 1986-88. Roman Catholic. Avocations: golf, reading, travel. Home: 21 Bantle Rd East Hartford CT 06118-2833 Office: State Conn Divsn of Spl Revenue 555 Russell Rd Newington CT 06111-1523

**RAPP, GERALD DUANE,** lawyer, manufacturing company executive; b. Berwyn, Nebr., July 19, 1933; s. Kenneth P. and Mildred (Price) R.; children: Gerald Duane Jr., Gregory T., Amy Frances Wanzek. B.S., U. Mo., 1955; J.D., U. Mich., 1958. Bar: Ohio bar 1959. Practice in Dayton, 1960—; ptnr. Smith & Schnacke, 1963-70; asst. gen. counsel Mead Corp., Dayton, 1970, v.p. human resources and legal affairs, 1973, v.p., corp. sec., 1975, v.p., gen. counsel, corp. sec., 1976, v.p., gen. counsel, 1979, sr. v.p., gen. counsel, 1981-91, counsel to bd. dirs., 1991-92; of counsel Bieser, Greer & Landis, 1992—; pres. R-J Holding Co., Weber Canyon Ranch, Inc. Sr. editor U. Mich. Law Rev., 1957-58. Past chmn. Oakwood Youth Commn.; past v.p., bd. dirs. Big Bros. Greater Dayton; mem. pres.'s visitors com. U. Mich. Law Sch.; past trustee Urbana Coll.; past pres., trustee Ohio Ctr. Leadership Studies, Robert K. Greenleaf Ctr., Indpls.; past pres. bd. trustees Dayton and Montgomery County Pub. Libr.; past. mem. bd. visitors Law Schs. of Dayton. 1st lt. U.S. Army, 1958-60. Mem. ABA, Ohio Bar Assn., Dayton Bar Assn., Moraine Country Club, Dayton Racquet Club, Dayton Lawyers Club, Met. Club Washington, Phi Kappa Psi, Phi Delta Phi, Beta Gamma Sigma. Presbyterian. Fax: 937-224-0403. Antitrust, General corporate. Office: 108 Green St Dayton OH 45402-2835

**RAPP, STEPHEN JOHN,** prosecutor; b. Waterloo, Iowa, Jan. 26, 1949; s. Spurgeon John and Beverly (Leckington) R.; m. Donna J.E. Maier, 1981; children: Alexander, Stephanie. AB cum laude, Harvard U., 1970; JD with honors, Drake U., 1973. Bar: Iowa 1974, U.S. Dist. Ct. (no. and so. dists.) Iowa 1978, U.S. Ct. Appeals (8th cir.) 1979, U.S. Supreme Ct. 1979. Rsch. asst. Office of U.S. Senator Birch Bayh, Ind., 1970; community program asst. HUD, Chgo., 1971; mem. Iowa Ho. Reps., 1972-74, 79-83, Coun. to Majority Caucus, Iowa Ho. Reps., 1975; staff dir., counsel subcom. on juvenile delinquency U.S. Senate, Washington, 1977-78; ptnr. Rapp & Gilliam, Waterloo, 1979-83; pvt. practice Waterloo, 1983-93; U.S. atty. U.S. Dist. Ct. (no. dist.) Iowa, 1993—. Del., mem. com. Dem. Nat. Conv., 1976, 80, 84, 88, 92; mem. Dem. Nat. Adv. Com. on Econ., 1982-84, chmn. Black Hawk Dem. Com., 1986-91; mem. Iowa Dem. Com., 1990-93, chair 2d C.D. Dem. Com., 1991-93. Mem. ABA, Iowa Bar Assn., Order of Coif. Methodist. Home: 219 Highland Blvd Waterloo IA 50703-4229

**RAPPAPORT, BRET ANDREW,** lawyer; b. Chgo., Apr. 24, 1961; s. Earle Samuel and Nancy (Karzen) R.; m. Virginia McKenney, June 9, 1984; children: Jeremy, Conor, Chandler, Cassidy. BS in Fin., Ind. U., 1983; JD, John Marshall Law Sch., Chgo., 1986. Bar: Ill. 1986, U.S. Dist. Ct. (no. dist.) Ill. 1986, U.S. Ct. Appeals (7th cir.) 1986, U.S. Supreme Ct. 1989. Asst. atty. gen. Ill. Atty. Gen.'s Office, Chgo., 1986-89; assoc. Schwartz, Cooper, Greenberger & Krauss, Chgo., 1989-95, ptnr., 1996—; adj. prof. John Marshall Law Sch., Chgo., 1989-94. Contbr. articles to profl. jours.; editor John Marshall Law Rev., 1985; field editor Wildflower Mag., 1997. Chmn. bd. commrs. Deerfield (Ill.) Bannockburn Fire Protection Dist., 1990—; commr. Union Drainage Dist., Lake County, Ill., 1995—; pro-bono counsel ACLU, Chgo., 1989-95; pres. Wild Ones Natural Landscapers, Milw., 1996—. Named Atty. of the Year, Constnl. Rights Found., Chgo., 1990. Mem. Ill. Appellate Lawyers Assn., Ill. Bar Assn. Avocations: gardening, conservation. Appellate, General civil litigation, Labor. Home: 1440 Montgomery Rd Deerfield IL 60015-2063 Office: Schwartz Cooper Greenberger & Krauss 180 N La Salle St Ste 2700 Chicago IL 60601-2757

**RAPPAPORT, STUART RAMON,** lawyer; b. Detroit, Apr. 13, 1935; s. Reuben and Zella (Golechen) R.; m. Anne M. Plotnick; children: Douglas, Erica Rappaport Witt. BA in History, U. Mich., 1956; JD, Harvard U., 1959. Bar: Calif. 1962. Trial lawyer, chief trials, bur. chief, chief. asst. pub. defender L.A. County Pub. Defender's Office, L.A., 1962-87; pub. defender Santa Clara County, San Jose, Calif., 1987-95; pvt. practice, 1995—; mem. standing adv. com. on criminal law Jud. Coun. Calif., San Francisco, 1993—; mem. discipline evaluation com. State Bar of Calif. Contbr. articles to profl. jours. Recipient Lifetime Achievement award Calif. Attys. for Criminal Justice. Mem. Calif. Pub. Defenders Asn. (pres. 1982-83, Lifetime Achievement award), L.A. County Pub. Defenders Assn. (pres.). Democrat. Jewish. Address: PO Box 960 Mendocino CA 95460-0960

**RAPPARD, GARY DONALD,** lawyer; b. Ottawa, Kans., Jan. 9, 1956; s. Donald Earl and Eldred Lenore (Fisher) R.; m. Laura Louise Murray, Oct. 20, 1984. BA, Ottawa U., 1977; JD, U. Kans., 1980. Bar: Kans. 1981, Mo. 1983, U.S. Dist. Ct. Kans. 1981, U.S. Dist. Ct. (we. dist.) Mo. 1983. Claims atty. CIGNA Corp., Overland Park, Kans., 1981-83; from staff atty. to gen. counsel Black & Veatch Engrs., Kansas City, Mo., 1983-87; sole practice law Kansas City, 1987—. Trustee United Meth. Ch., Shawnee, Kans., 1990-93. Fax: 913-894-5100. Workers' compensation, Personal injury, Probate. Office: 12760 W 87th Street Pkwy Lenexa KS 66215-2878

**RASHKIND, ALAN BRODY,** lawyer; b. N.Y.C., June 6, 1947; s. Julian and Eleanor (Brody) R.; m. Suzette DeBell, July 9, 1972; children: Graham Brody, Douglas Cormack. BA, Randolph-Macon Coll., 1969; JD, U. Va., 1972. Bar: Va. 1972, U.S. Dist. Ct. (ea. dist.) Va. 1972, U.S. Ct. Appeals (4th cir.) 1980, U.S. Supreme Ct. 1992. Assoc. Furniss, Davis and Sachs, Norfolk, Va., 1972-75; ptnr., shareholder Furniss, Davis Rashkind and Saunders P.C. and predecessors, Norfolk, 1976—; mem. faculty Va. State Bar Professionalism Course, 1996-99. Co-author: Virginia Insurance Case Finder, 1994; contbr. articles to profl. jours. Trustee Randolph-Macon Coll., Ashland, Va., 1991—, pres. Soc. of Alumni, 1987-89; trustee, mem. exec. com. Chesapeake Bay Acad., Virginia Beach, Va., 1989—, vice chmn., 1996—. Mem. ABA, Va. State Bar Assn., Va. Bar Assn., Fed. Bar Assn., Norfolk-Portsmouth Bar Assn., Virginia Beach Bar Assn., Va. Assn. Def. Attys., Def. Rsch. Inst., Fedn. Ins. and Corp. Counsel, Boyd Graves Conf. (chmn. 1995-97). General civil litigation, Insurance, Personal injury. Office: Furniss Davis et al 6160 Kempsville Cir Norfolk VA 23502-3933

**RASHKIND, PAUL MICHAEL,** lawyer; b. Jamaica, N.Y., May 21, 1950; s. Murray and Norma (Dorfman) Weinstein; m. Robin Shane, Dec. 20, 1975; children: Adam Charles, Noah Hamilton, Jennifer Elizabeth. AA, Miami-Dade Jr. Coll., 1970; BBA, U. Miami, Coral Gables Fla., 1972, JD, 1975. Bar: Fla. 1975, D.C. 1981, N.Y. 1981, U.S. Dist. Ct. (so. dist.) Fla. 1975, U.S. Ct. Appeals (5th cir.) 1976, U.S. Supreme Ct. 1978, U.S. Dist. Ct. (mid. dist.) Fla. 1979, U.S. Ct. Appeals (2d and 11th cirs.) 1981, U.S. Ct. Appeals (4th and 6th cirs.) 1986, U.S. Dist. Ct. (no. dist.) Fla. 1987, U.S. Dist. Ct. (no dist.) Calif. 1989; diplomate Nat. Bd. Trial Advocacy-Criminal Law (bd. examiners), bd. cert. Criminal Trial Law, Fla. Bar. Asst. state atty. Dade County State Attys. Office, Miami, Fla., 1975-78, chief asst. state atty. in charge of appeals, 1977-78; atty. Sams, Gerstein & Ward, P.A., Miami, 1978-83; ptnr. Bailey, Gerstein, Rashkind & Dresnick, Miami, 1983-92, supr. asst. Fed. Defender Chief of Appeals, Miami, 1992—; spl. master Ct. Appointment, Miami, 1982-83; arbitrator Dade County Jail Inmates Grievance Program, Miami, 1981-92; mem. Fla. Bar Unauthorized Practice of Law Com. C, 11th Jud. Cir., Miami, 1980-84, Fed. Ct. Practice Com., 1992—; mem. So. Dist. Fla. Fed. Ct. Rules Com., 1996—. Contbr. articles on ethics and criminal law to profl. jours. Pres., bd. dirs. Lindgren Homeowners Assn., Miami, Fla., 1981-86. Fellow Am. Bd. Criminal Lawyers (bd. govs. 1980-86; mem. ABA (ethics com. criminal justice sect. 1979-92, vice chmn. 1985-87, chmn. 1987-89, ethics advisor to chair, 1992-97, criminal justice sect. coun., 1998—), Fla. Bar Assn. (commn. on Lawyer professionalism 1988-89, criminal law cert. com. 1989-94, standing com. on professionalism 1989-94), N.Y. Bar Assn., D.C. Bar Assn., Dade County Bar Assn., Assn. Trial Lawyers Am., Acad. Fla. Trial Lawyers (chmn. criminal law sect. 1985-86, diplomate 1986—), Nat. Assn. Criminal Def. Lawyers, Soc. Bar and Gavel, Iron Arrow, Hon. Order Ky. Cols., Omicron Delta Kappa, Delta Sigma Rho-Tau Kappa Alpha, Pi Sigma Alpha, Phi Rho Pi, Delta Theta Phi. Democrat. Jewish. Criminal, Constitutional, Appellate. Office: Fed Pub Defender's Office SD FL 150 W Flagler St Ste 1500 Miami FL 33130-1555

**RASKIN, JAMIN BEN,** law educator; b. Dec. 13, 1962; s. Marcus Goodman and Barbara Judith (Bellman) R.; m. Sarah Bloom, Aug. 11, 1990; children: Hannah Grace, Thomas Bloom, Tabitha Claire. BA, Harvard U., 1983, JD, 1987. Tchg. fellow govt. dept. Harvard U., Cambridge, Mass., 1985-87; asst. atty. gen. Commonwealth of Mass., Boston, 1987-89; gen. counsel Nat. Rainbow Coalition, Washington, 1989-90; prof. law Washington Coll. Law Am. U., Washington, 1990—, co-dir. program on law and govt., 1990—. Contbr. articles to profl. jours.; featured guest on nat. and local tv and radio shows including Crossfire, C-Span, Diane Rehm Show, NPR, others. Mem. 1992 Clinton-Gore Transition Team Justice Dept. Civil Rights Cluster, Washington, 1992; bd. dirs. Washington area Nat. Rainbow Coalition, 1992—. Mem. ABA (co-chair sect. on adminstrv. law, com. on election law 1998—). Office: Am U Washington Coll Law 4801 Massachusetts Ave Washington DC 20016

**RASMUS, JOHN CHARLES,** trade association executive, lawyer; b. Rochester, N.Y., Dec. 27, 1941; s. Harold Charles and Myrtle Leota (Dybevik) R.; m. Elaine Green Reeves, Mar. 19, 1982; children: Kristin, Stuart, Karin. A.B., Cornell U., 1963; J.D., U. Va., 1966. Bar: Va. 1970, U.S. Supreme Ct. 1974. Spl. agt. Def. Dept., Washington, 1966-70; v.p., adminstrv. officer, legis. research counsel U.S. League Savs. Instns., Washington, 1970-83; asst. to exec. v.p. Nat. Assn. Fed. Credit Unions, 1983-84; sr. fed. adminstrv. counsel, mgr. regulatory and trust affairs Am. Bankers Assn., 1985—. Mem. ABA, Fed. Bar Assn. (disting. service award 1980, 82, past chmn. long range planning com., past chmn. council fin. instns. and economy), Univ. Club, Exchequer Club, Masons. Home: 303 Kentucky Ave Alexandria VA 22305-1739

**RASMUSSEN, DAVID L.,** lawyer; b. Rochester, N.Y., Apr. 20, 1958; s. Verlin L. and Betty B. Rasmussen; m. Debra J. Rasmussen, Oct. 8, 1993; children: Daniel, Megan, Peter, Colleen. BS in Bus., Miami U., 1980; JD, Syracuse U., 1985. Internal auditor Union Pacific R.R., Omaha, 1980-82; assoc. Lacy Katzen Ryen & Mittliana, Rochester, 1985-87; assoc. Harris Beach & Wilcox, Rochester, 1987-92, ptnr., 1993—. Avocations: skiing, mountain biking, kayaking. Bankruptcy, Contracts commercial, Consumer commercial. Office: Harris Beach & Wilcox 130 E Main St Rochester NY 14604-1687

**RASMUSSEN, DOUGLAS JOHN,** lawyer; b. Mt. Clemens, Mich., Jan. 18, 1941; s. Kenneth Edward and Laura Jean (Fletcher) R.; m. Andrea Marie Smart, Aug. 22, 1964; children: Mark Douglas, Michael Andrew. BBA, U. Mich., 1962, MBA, JD, 1965. Bar: Mich. 1965, U.S. Dist. Ct. (ea. dist.) Mich. 1965, U.S. Tax Ct. 1973, U.S. Ct. Appeals (6th cir.) 1973. Assoc. Clark Hill PCL, Detroit, 1965-73, mem., 1973—; CEO Clark Hill PCL, 1994—. Trustee Community Found. for S.E. Mich., Holley Found., bd. dirs. S.E. chpt. ARC, Detroit, 1987—, chmn., 1994-96; bd. dirs. YMCA of Metro Detroit, chmn., 1992-93; unit chmn. United Way, Detroit, 1987-92; bd. dirs. Detroit Symphony Orch., 1999—. Recipient Outstanding Vol. award Mich. Chpt. Nat. Assn. Fund Raising Execs., 1988, Fundraiser Yr. award Nat. ARC, 1997, Stanley S. Kresge award Rotary Club. Fellow Am. Coll. Trust and Estate Counsel (regent 1987-93); mem. ABA, State Bar Mich., Detroit Bar Assn., Internat. Acad. Estate and Trust Law, Fin. and Estate Planning Coun. Detroit (pres. 1986-87), Detroit Athletic Club (bd. dirs. 1992, pres. 1997). Republican. Presbyterian. Avocations: music, photography, Nordic skiing, golf. Probate, Estate planning, Taxation, general. Home: 466 Lakeland St Grosse Pointe MI 48230-1655 Office: Clark Hill PLC 500 Woodward Ave Ste 3500 Detroit MI 48226-3435

**RASMUSSEN, RICHARD ROBERT,** lawyer; b. Chgo., July 5, 1946; s. Robert Kersten Rasmussen and Marisa Bruna Batistoni; children: Kathryn, William. BS, U. Oreg., 1970, JD, 1973. Bar: Oreg. 1973. Atty. U.S. Bancorp, Portland, Oreg., 1973-83, 95—, v.p. law divsn., 1983-87, mgr. law divsn, 1983-95, sr. v.p., 1987-95, mgr. corp. sec. divsn., 1990-94. Mem. editl. bd. Oreg. Bus. Law Digest, 1979-81, Oreg. Debtor/Creditor newsletter, 1980-84; contbr. articles to profl. jours. Chmn. mgmt. com. YMCA of Columbia-Willamette, Portland, 1978-79; bd. dirs. Camp Fire, 1988-89, v.p., 1990-91; bd. dirs. Portland Repertory Theatre, 1994-96. Mem. Oreg. State Bar Assn. (chmn. corp. counsel com. 1979-81, debtor/creditor sect. 1982-83; sec. com. on sects. 1982-83), ABA, Multnomah County Bar Assn., Am. Bankers Assn. (bank counsel com. 1996-99), Beta Gamma Sigma. Club: Founder's (Portland). Avocations: mountaineering, white-water rafting, tennis, basketball. Banking, Finance. Office: US Bancorp Legal Dept 111 SW 5th Ave Portland OR 97204-3604

**RASMUSSEN, THOMAS VAL, JR.,** lawyer, small business owner; b. Salt Lake City, Aug. 11, 1954; s. Thomas Val and Georgia (Smedley) R.; m. Donita Gubler, Aug. 15, 1978; children: James, Katherine, Kristin. BA magna cum laude, U. Utah, 1978, JD, 1981. Bar: Utah 1981, U.S. Dist. Ct. Utah 1981, U.S. Supreme Ct. 1985, U.S. Ct. Appeals (10th cir.) 1999. Atty. Salt Lake Legal Defender Assn., Salt Lake City, 1981-83, Utah Power and Light Co., Salt Lake City, 1983-89; of counsel Hatch, Morton & Skeen, Salt Lake City, 1989-90; ptnr. Morton, Skeen & Rasmussen, Salt Lake City, 1991-94, Skeen & Rasmussen, Salt Lake City, 1994-97; pvt. practice, Salt Lake City, 1997—; co-owner, developer Handi Self-Storage, Kaysville, Utah, 1984-93; instr. bus. law Brigham Young U., Salt Lake City, 1988-90. Adminstrv. editor Jour. Contemporary Law, 1980-81, Jour. Energy Law and Policy, 1980-81. Missionary Ch. of Jesus Christ of Latter-Day Sts., Brazil, 1973-75. Mem. Utah, Salt Lake County Bar Assn., Intermountain Miniature Horse Club (pres. 1989, 2d v.p. 1990), Phi Eta Sigma, Phi Kappa Phi, Beta Gamma Sigma. Avocations: tennis, scuba diving, showing horses, travel, collecting art. General civil litigation, Juvenile, Criminal. Home: 3094 Whitewater Dr Salt Lake City UT 84121-1561 Office: 4659 Highland Dr Salt Lake City UT 84117-5137

**RASMUSSEN, WAYNE ROGER,** law educator, consultant; b. Sioux Falls, S.D., May 8, 1936; s. Ezra Christian and Loretta Mae Belle (Schlafer) R.; m. Carol Joy Longsdorf Prue, June 4, 1960 (div. May 1973); children: Joy, Corbin; m. Mary Dee Fowlkes, May 20, 1973; children: Thomas, Frances, Heather. BA, ThB, St. Paul Bible Coll., 1963; JD, John Marshall Law Sch., Atlanta, 1989. Bar: Ga. 1989, Calif. 1992; CPCU. Claims adjuster Travelers Ins. Co., St. Paul, 1966-70; claims supr. Travelers Ins. Co., Washington, 1970-72; asst. mgr. claims Travelers Ins. Co., Atlanta, 1972-77; asst. v.p. Continental Ins. Co., N.Y.C., 1977-82; mgr. state claims Continental Ins. Co., Charlotte, N.C., 1982-86; pvt. practice, Atlanta, 1989—; prof. law John Marshall Law Sch., 1989—; ins. cons., Atlanta, 1990—. Aux. police officer N.Y. Police Dept., N.Y.C., 1978-82. With USAF, 1954-58. Named Outstanding Prof. of Yr., John Marshall Law Sch., 1992. Mem. Soc. of CPCU (treas. 1980), Soc. of CLU. Avocations: skiing, walking.

**RASMUSSON, THOMAS ELMO,** lawyer; b. Lansing, Mich., Dec. 5, 1941; s. William and Mary Jane Rasmusson; m. Alice Wolo, Oct. 1, 1989; children: David, Jane. BA, Mich. State U., 1963; JD, U. Mich., 1966; MA, Fletcher Sch., 1988. Bar: Mich. 1967, U.S. Ct. Appeals (6th cir.) 1982, U.S. Supreme Ct. 1982. Law clk. to presiding justice Mich. Supreme Ct., Lansing, 1966-68; asst. prosecutor Ingham Prosecutor's Office, Lansing, 1968-72, criminal divsn. chief, 1972-75; spl. prosecutor Ingham County, Lansing, 1975-76; pvt. practice Lansing, 1975—; Fulbright prof. U.S. Info. Svc., Washington, 1986-88; cons. U.S. AID, Monrovia, Liberia, 1989-90; contractor U.S. Dept. of

State, Monrovia, 1987-90; adj. prof. Cooley Law Sch., Lansing, 1991-97; rsch. assoc. program on negotiation Harvard U., Cambridge, 1987-88; mem. Ct. Rule Com., Lansing, 1979-81. Editor: Jurisprudence and System Science, 1986, Interactive Systems, 1988, (series) Liberian Law Reports, 1988-90; contbr. articles to profl. jours. Chair fin. Ingham Rep. Party, Lansing, 1994-98, mem. exec. com., 1994—; mem. 8th Congl. Com., Lansing, 1997—. Recipient Outstanding Svc. award U.S. Edn. Found., 1987; grantee U.S. Edn. Found., 1987. Mem. AAAS, State Bar Mich. Republican. Methodist. Avocations: physics, history of science. State civil litigation, Federal civil litigation, Criminal. Home: 3715 Delta River Dr Lansing MI 48906-3476 Office: Rasmusson and Assoc. 501 S Capitol Ave Ste 305 Lansing MI 48933-2331

**RASSEL, RICHARD EDWARD,** lawyer; b. Toledo, Jan. 10, 1942; s. Richard Edward and Madonna Mary (Tuohy) R.; m. Elizabeth Ann Frederick, Dec. 5, 1967 (wid. June 1977); children: Richard III, Elizabeth; m. Dawn Ann Lynch, Sept. 17, 1983; children: Lauren, Brian. BA, U. Notre Dame, 1964; JD, U. Mich., 1966. Bar: Mich. 1966, U.S. Dist. Ct. (ea. dist.) Mich. 1969, U.S. Ct. Appeals (6th cir.) 1971, U.S. Supreme Ct. 1980. Law clk. to presiding judge Mich. Ct. Appeals, Detroit, 1966; shareholder, chmn. CEO Butzel & Long, Detroit, 1970—; bd. dirs. Lex Mundi Law Firm Alliance, Robertson-Jamieson Corp. Contbr. articles to profl. jours.; lectr. in field. Past pres., bd. dirs. Birmingham Cmty. House; mem. bd. advisors U. Detroit Grad. Sch. Bus.; mem. steering com. Friends of Legal Aid; pres. Rosa Parks Scholarship Found., Detroit, Detroit Police Athletic League, S.E.E.D. Found.; bd. dirs. Met. Affairs Coalition, Mich. Jobs Commn., Detroit Legal News. Fellow Am. Coll. Trial Lawyers, Mich. Bar Found.; mem. ABA (forum com., vice chmn. law and media com. tort and ins. practice sect.), Am. Arbitration Assn., Fed. Bar Assn., State Bar Mich. (past chmn. media and the law com., chmn. TV in the cts. com.), Detroit Bar Assn. (exec. com., U.S dist. cts. com.), Libel Def. Resource Ctr. (vice chmn. def. counsel sect.), Detroit C. of C. (bus. attraction and expansion coun. southeast Mich.), Leadership Detroit Alumni Assn., U.S. Navy League, Detroit Athletic Club, Birmingham Athletic Club, Otsego Club, Village Club. Roman Catholic. Libel, Federal civil litigation, General civil litigation. Home: 1601 Quarton Rd Birmingham MI 48009-1037 Office: Butzel Long 150 W Jefferson Ave Ste 900 Detroit MI 48226-4416

**RASTIGUE, KERRY ANN,** lawyer; b. Detroit, May 21, 1965; d. Robert Kenneth and Joan Patricia Anderson; m. John Nicholas Rastigue, Apr. 25, 1997. B in Gen. Studies, U. Mich., 1987; JD, Wayne State U., 1990. Bar: Ill. 1990, Mich. 1994. Assoc. Sidley & Austin, Chgo., 1990-94, Clark Hill, PLC, Detroit, 1994-96; shareholder Buydens & Anderson P.C., Detroit, 1996—. Contbr. articles to profl. jours. Mem. ABA. Pension, profit-sharing, and employee benefits. Office: Buydens & Anderson PC 333 W Fort St Ste 1920 Detroit MI 48226-3162

**RATAJ, EDWARD WILLIAM,** lawyer; b. St. Louis, Oct. 14, 1947; m. Elizabeth Spalding, July 4, 1970; children: Edward, Suzanne, Anne, Thomas, Charles. BS in Acctg., St. Louis U., 1969, JD, 1972. Assoc. Bryan, Cave, McPheeters & McRoberts, St. Louis, 1972-82, ptnr., 1983—. Pension, profit-sharing, and employee benefits. Office: Bryan Cave McPheeters & McRoberts 211 N Broadway Saint Louis MO 63102-2733

**RATCLIFFE, J. RICHARD,** lawyer; b. Pawtucket, R.I., Aug. 15, 1956; s. J. Richard and Edith J. (Kerrigan) R.; m. Margaret M. Pfeiffer, Aug. 27, 1988; children: James, Nicholas. BA, Providence Coll., 1978; JD, Washington U., 1981. Bar: R.I. 1981, Mass. 1981, U.S. Dist. Ct. R.I. 1982, U.S. Ct. Appeals (1st cir.) 1982, U.S. Dist. Ct. Mass. 1983. Law clk. R.I. Supreme Ct., Providence, 1981-83; assoc. Zisson & Veara, Boston, 1983-86; pvt. practice Boston, 1987; asst. atty. gen. R.I. Dept. Atty. Gen., Providence, 1988-95; assoc. Temkin & Assocs. Ltd., Providence, 1995-98; ptnr. Ratcliffe & Burke LLP, Providence, 1999—. Mem. R.I. Bar Assn. (chair criminal bench bar com. 1995—, mem. ho. of dels. 1997—), Common Cause (mem. gov. bd.), Save The Bay, The Haitian Project (sec. 1990—), Am. Inns of Ct. Avocations: tennis, skiing. General civil litigation, Criminal. Home: 7 Holly Ln Cumberland RI 02864-3328 Office: Ratcliffe & Burke LLP BankBoston Plz Providence RI 02903

**RATCLIFFE, PHYLLIS ANN,** lawyer, antique dealer; b. Fordville, N.D., May 30, 1933; d. Elwood S. and Ruth Eileen (Wilson) R.; m. Ernest Fred Senne, Sept. 8, 1962 (div. July, 1982); 1 child, Scott Craig; m. Merril Berg, Jan. 8, 1983. BA, U.N.D., 1956, LLB, 1958, JD, 1985. States atty. McKenzie County, N.D., 1967-74; city atty. Watford City, N.D., 1960-74; states atty. Grant County, N.D., 1987-91, Griggs County, 1993-99; city atty. Cooperstown, N.D., 1994—; pvt. practice Watford City, N.D., 1958-74, Carson, Flasker, N.D., 1985-91, Cooperstown, N.D., 1991—; instr. Law Enforcement Ctr., Bismark, N.D., 1983, Bismark Jr. Col., 1984, Grant County, 1989-90. Bd. dirs. Trinity Lutheran Ch. Coun., Cooperstown, N.D., 1992-96, Griggs County (N.D.) Arts Coun., 1993; pres. Cooperstown (N.D.) Cmty. Club. Mem. N.D. Bar Assn., Nat. Dist. Attys. Assn., N.D. States Atty. Assn., Nat. Assn. Tax Practitioners, Red River Valley Estate Planning Coun. Avocations: antiques dealer. Office: 501 9th St SE Cooperstown ND 58425-7426

**RATH, FRANCIS STEVEN,** lawyer; b. N.Y.C., Oct. 10, 1955; s. Steven and Elizabeth (Chorin) R.; m. Denise Stephania Thompson, Aug. 2, 1980. BA cum laude, Wesleyan U., Middletown, Conn., 1977; JD cum laude, Georgetown U., 1980; postgrad., Harvard U., 1999. Bar: D.C. 1980, U.S. Dist. Ct. D.C. 1981, U.S. Ct. Appeals (D.C. cir.), 1981, U.S. Supreme Ct. 1987, Va. 1988. Atty., advisor Comptr. of the Currency, Washington, 1980-84; assoc. Verner, Liipfert, Bernhard, McPherson & Hand, Washington, 1984-85; founding mem. Wolf, Arnold & Monroig (merged with Burnham, Connolly, Oesterly & Henry), Washington, 1986-88; pvt. practice Great Falls, Va., 1989—; internat. cons. Fried, Frank, Harris, Shriver and Jacobson, 1991-95; counsel Seward & Kissel, Washington, 1995-98; counsel, Squire Sanders & Dempsey, Washington, 1998—. Editor: Law and Policy in Internat. Bus., 1979-80; contbg. author Business Ventures in Eastern Europe and Russia; contbr. articles to profl. jours. Trustee Dunn Loring (Va.) Vol. Fire Dept., 1986. Mem. ABA, D.C. Bar Assn., Va. Bar Assn., Bar of U.S. Supreme Ct., U.S. Combined Tng. Assn. (legal com. 1989-91, 96—, safety com. 1990-91, 96—, bd. govs. 1995-98). Private international, General corporate, Public international. Home and Office: 1051 Kelso Rd Great Falls VA 22066-2032

**RATHBUN, RANDALL KEITH,** lawyer; b. Miami Beach, Fla., Aug. 24, 1953; s. Ronald K. and Betty L. (Stockstill) R.; m. Janet Sue Meyer, Oct. 8, 1983; children: Zachary Keith, Joshua George, Kelsea Rebecca. BS, Kans. State U., 1975; JD, Washburn U., 1978. Bar: Kans.. 1978, U.S. Dist. Ct. Kans. 1978, U.S. Ct. Appeals (10th cir.) 1985. Assoc. Curfman, Harris, Bell, Weigand & Depew, Wichita, Kans., 1978-80; ptnr. Depew, Gillen & Rathbun, Wichita, 1980-93; U.S. atty. U.S. Dept. of Justice, Wichita, Kans., 1993-96; ptnr. Depew & Gillen, Wichita, Kans., 1996—. Bd. dirs. Washburn Law Jour., 1977-78. Chair 4th Congressional Dist. Democrats, Kans., 1986-88; exec. com. State Dem. Party, Topeka, 1986-88; del. Dem. Nat. Conv., Atlanta, 1988; treas. State Dem. Party, 1991—; officer, bd. dirs. Sedgwick County unit Am. Cancer Soc.-Wichita, 1984-90; bd. dirs. Kans. div. Am. Cancer Soc., Wichita, 1987-90. Mem. Wichita Bar Assn. (sec.-treas. 1991-92), Wichita Young Lawyers (pres. 1983-84), Kans. Bar Assn. Democrat. Methodist. Environmental. Office: Depew & Gillen 151 N Main St Ste 800 Wichita KS 67202-1409*

**RATHJEN, JON LAURENCE,** lawyer, mediator; b. Elizabeth, N.J., June 28, 1951; s. Theodore A. Rathjen and Marie Betty Ahrendtsen; 1 child, Daniel Laurence. AB, Brown U., 1973; JD, U. Calif., Berkeley, 1977. Bar: Calif. 1978, U.S. Dist. Ct. (no. dist.) Calif. 1980. Atty. Paul & Baker, Oakland, Calif., 1979-81, Warwick, Gardner & Rathjen, Oakland, 1981-88, Pearce & Rathjen, Walnut Creek, Calif., 1988—. Cons. Bay Area Lawyers for the Arts, San Francisco, 1981-85; bd. dirs. Dancer's Repertory Theater, Oakland, 1978-81. Mem. Contra Costa County Bar Assn. (family law sect., mediation sub-sect.). Family and matrimonial, Bankruptcy, General civil litigation. Office: 1333 N California Blvd Ste 525 Walnut Creek CA 94596-4576

**RATHKOPF, DAREN ANTHONY,** lawyer; b. Lynbrook, N.Y., May 12, 1933; s. Arden Herman and Florence Marie (Gortikov) R.; m. Mira Torgersen, Mar. 30, 1963; children: Ann, Erika. BA, Columbia U., 1955, LLB, 1958. Bar: N.Y. 1958, U.S. Dist. Ct. (ea., so. dists.) N.Y. 1962. Assoc. Mendes & Mount, N.Y.C., 1961-62, Rathkopf & Rathkopf, N.Y.C., 1962-66; ptnr. Rathkopf & Rathkopf, Glen Cove, N.Y., 1966-81, Payne, Wood & Littlejohn, Glen Cove and Melville, N.Y., 1982-98; of counsel Payne, Wood & Littlejohn, Melville, Bridgehampton, Locust Vly, N.Y., 1999—. Author: (with others) The Law of Zoning and Planning, 4th edit., 1977. Mem. N.Y. State Bar Assn., Nassau County Bar Assn. Land use and zoning (including planning). Home: 149 Turkey Ln Cold Spring Harbor NY 11724-1712 Office: Payne Wood & Littlejohn 290 Broadhollow Rd Melville NY 11747-4818

**RATLIFF, WILLIAM D., III,** lawyer; b. Ft. Worth, Aug. 25, 1949; s. William D. and Barbara (Warner) R.; m. Julie Martin, Oct. 4, 1980; children: William D., Emily Martin. B.B.A., U. Tex., 1971, J.D., 1974; LL.M., So. Meth. U., 1975. Law clk. U.S. Tax Ct., Washington, 1975-77; mem. Cantey, Hanger, Gooch, Munn & Collins, Ft. Worth, 1977-84, Haynes and Boone, Ft. Worth, 1984—. Fellow Am. Coll. Trust and Estate Counsel, Tex. Bd. Legal Specialization (cert.), Tex. Bar Found.; mem. ABA, State Bar Tex. Republican. Clubs: Ft. Worth, Rivercrest Country. Banking, Probate, Real property. Office: Haynes and Boone 1300 Burnett Plz Fort Worth TX 76102

**RATNER, DAVID LOUIS,** retired law educator; b. London, Sept. 2, 1931. AB magna cum laude, Harvard U., 1952, LLB magna cum laude, 1955. Bar: N.Y. 1955. Assoc. Sullivan & Cromwell, N.Y.C., 1955-64; assoc. prof. Cornell Law Sch., Ithaca, N.Y., 1964-68, prof., 1968-82; prof. law U. San Francisco Law Sch., 1982-99, dean, 1982-89, prof. emeritus, 1999—; exec. asst. to chmn. SEC, Washington, 1966-68; chief counsel Securities Industry Study, Senate Banking Com., Washington, 1971-73; vis. prof. Stanford (Calif.) U., 1974, Ariz. State U., Tempe, 1974, U. San Francisco, 1980, Georgetown U., Washington, 1989-90, U. Calif., Hastings, San Francisco, 1992; mem. Larkspur (Calif.) Planning Commn., 1992—. Author: Securities Regulation: Cases and Materials, 6th edit., 1998, Securities Regulation in a Nutshell, 6th edit., 1998, Institutional Investors: Teaching Materials, 1978. Fulbright scholar Monash U., Australia, 1981. Fellow Royal Soc. Arts (London); mem. Am. Law Inst., Cosmos Club (Washington), Harvard Club of San Francisco (pres. 1999—), Phi Beta Kappa. E-mail: dlratner@aol.com. Home and Office: 84 Polhemus Way Larkspur CA 94939-1928

**RATTERREE, RYBURN CLAY,** lawyer; b. Atlanta, Sept. 2, 1949; s. Joseph Duffie and Zaida Clay Ratterree; m. Katherine Carr Jones, Mar. 15; children: Joseph Duffie, Katherine Carr. BA, U. Va., 1972; JD cum laude, U. Ga., 1977. Bar: Ga. 1977, U.S. Dist. Ct. (no. dist.) Ga. 1977, U.S. Dist. Ct. (so. dist.) Ga. 1981. Assoc. Smith, Cohen, Ringel, Kehler Martin, Athens, 1977-79, Overten, Heyl & Bostrom, Englewood, Colo., 1979-81; assoc., ptnr. Karsman, Brooks, Painter, Callaway, Savannah, Ga., 1981-88; ptnr. Painter, Ratterree & Bart, Savannah, Ga., 1988-96, Ellis, Painter, Ratterree & Bart, Savannah, 1996—; bd. dirs. Hospice Savannah, Inc. Grad. Leadership Savannah, 1990; mem. Mayors Task Force on Drainage, Savannah, 1986; vestryman Christ Ch., Savannah, 1990, 93, 96—. Mem. Rotary Savannah, Soc. of Profls. in Dispute Resolution, Internat. Acad. of Mediators (founding assoc.). Republican. Episcopalian. Avocations: golf, boating, coaching youth soccer. Alternative dispute resolution, State civil litigation, Federal civil litigation. Home: 10 Wild Thistle Ln Savannah GA 31406-7208 Office: Ellis Painter Ratterree & Bart 2 E Bryan St Fl 10 Savannah GA 31401-2655

**RATTIGAN, JOHN E., JR.,** lawyer; b. Quincy, Mass., July 3, 1957; m. Carole J. O'Shaughnessy, June 12, 1982; children: Christopher, Michael, Timothy. BA, Merrimack Coll., 1979; JD, U. Va., 1982. Bar: Mass. 1982, U.S. Dist. Ct. Mass. 1982, U.S. Ct. Appeals (1st cir.) 1982. Assoc. Palmer & Dodge LLP, Boston, 1982-89, ptnr., 1990—; mem. adv. bd. MIT Ctr. for Real Estate, Cambridge, Mass., 1990—. Bd. dirs., mem. exec. com. Trust for City Hall Plz., Boston, 1995—, Downtown Crossing Assn., Boston, 1991—; mem. Mayor's Washington St. Adv. Com., Boston, 1997. Recipient Disting. Svc. award Downtown Crossing Assn., 1997. Mem. Order of Coif. Real property, Transportation. Office: Palmer & Dodge LLP 1 Beacon St Ste 22 Boston MA 02108-3190

**RATTRAY, JAMES BAILEY,** lawyer; b. Watertown, N.Y., July 26, 1950; s. Clifford M. and Dora M. (Bailey) R.; m. Paula Cataldi, Nov. 30, 1998. AB cum laude, Syracuse U., 1972; JD, Coll. William and Mary, 1975, MLT, 1982. Bar: Va. 1975, D.C. 1976. Assoc. firm Ernest C. Consolvo, Norfolk, Va., 1975; dep. city atty. City of Hampton (Va.), 1976-92; exec. dir. Hampton (Va.) Redevel. and Housing Authority, 1992—; instr. St. Leo Coll., Tidewater Center, Langley AFB, Va., 1982—, Golden Gate U., Resident Ctr., Langley AFB, 1978-82, Hampton U., Va., 1985-90. Mem. ABA, D.C. Bar Assn., Va. Bar Assn., Local Govt. Attys. of Va., Nat. Assn. Housing and Redevel. Ofcls., Pub. Housing Authority Dirs. Assn. Episcopalian. Contbr. articles to profl. jours. Home: PO Box 146 Hampton VA 23669-0146 Office: PO Box 280 Hampton VA 23669-0280

**RAU, LEE ARTHUR,** lawyer; b. Mpls., July 22, 1940; s. Arthur W. and Selma A. (Lund) R.; m. Janice R. Childress, June 27, 1964; children: Brendan D., Patrick C., Brian T. BSB, U. Minn., 1962; JD, UCLA, 1965. Bar: Calif. 1966, D.C. 1972, Va. 1986, U.S. Dist. Ct. D.C. 1973, U.S. Dist. Ct. (ea. dist.) Va. 1988, U.S. Ct. Mil. Appeals 1966, U.S. Ct. Appeals (D.C. cir.) 1972, U.S. Ct. Appeals (3d cir.) 1975, U.S. Ct. Appeals (6th cir.) 1980, U.S. Ct. Appeals (4th cir.) 1988, U.S. Supreme Ct. 1971. Trial atty. evaluation sect. antitrust div. U.S. Dept. Justice, Washington, 1965-66, appellate sect., 1970-72; assoc. Reed Smith Shaw & McClay, Washington, 1972-74, ptnr., 1975—; former mem. constl. and adminstrv. law adv. com. Nat. Chamber Litigation Ctr. Inc.; sec., bd. dirs. Old Dominion Land Co., Inc. Contbr. articles to profl. jours. Sec. bd. dris. Reston Found., 1982-93; bd. dirs. Reston Interfaith Inc., 1973-89, pres, 1984-88; bd. dirs. Greater Reston Arts Ctr., 1988-96, pres., 1989-91, sec., 1991-95; mem. Washington Dulles Task Force, 1982-91; mem. exec. com. and ops. com. Fairfax-Falls Ch. United Way, mem. regional coun., 1988-92. Capt. JAGC, U.S. Army, 1966-70. Named Restonian of Yr., 1990; decorated Commendation with oak leaf cluster; recipient Best of Reston award. Mem. ABA (antitrust, adminstrv. law, corp. banking and bus., sci. and tech. sects.), D.C. Bar Assn. (past chmn. energy study group), Calif. Bar Assn., U.S. C. of C. (antitrust policy com.). Democrat. Lutheran. Antitrust, Administrative and regulatory, General corporate. Home: 11654 Mediterranean Ct Reston VA 20190-3401 Office: Reed Smith Shaw & McClay 8251 Greensboro Dr Ste 1100 Mc Lean VA 22102-3844

**RAUCCI, FRANCIS JOSEPH,** lawyer, business executive. AB, St. Joseph's U., 1958; JD, Georgetown U., 1965. Bar: Mont. 1965, Pa. 1976, D.C. 1988. V.p., labor counsel Buttrey Food & Drug Co., 1968-76, exec. v.p., gen. counsel, 1981-86; corp. v.p., gen. counsel Acme Markets, Inc., 1976-81; sr. v.p., gen. counsel Alpha Beta Co., 1986-89; chief labor counsel Am. Stores Co., Salt Lake City, 1989-95, exec. v.p., chief labor officer, 1995—. Dir. Pa. Crime Commn., 1976-81; chmn. Prepaid Legal Svcs. Commn., 1981-86. Office: Am Stores Co 709 E South Temple Salt Lake City UT 84102-1205

**RAUDONIS, VALERIE CHRISTINE,** lawyer; b. Nashua, N.H., July 30, 1953; d. Alphonse J. and Sophie C. (Raucykevich) R.; m. Joseph W. Kenny, Aug. 28, 1976; children: Ryan, Laura. BA, Boston Coll., 1975; JD, New England Sch. Law, Boston, 1978. Bar: N.H. 1978, U.S. Dist. Ct. N.H. 1978, U.S. Tax Ct. 1979, U.S. Ct. Appeals (1st cir.) 1979. Pvt. practice Nashua, N.H., 1978—; mem. part-time faculty Rivier Coll. Paralegal Studies, Nashua 1984-86, 91-92, mem. adv. bd., 1993—, chairperson, 1999. Bd. dirs. Nashua Children's Assn., 1980-88, v.p., 1982-84, pres., 1984-85, assoc., 1988—; bd. dirs. YWCA, 1979-84, mem. YM-YW coun., 1981-84, 2d v.p., 1983-84; trustee Mt. St. Mary Sem., 1981-86, Tacy House, Inc., 1981-86; bd. dirs. Nashua Youth Coun., 1982-83, Adult Learning Ctr., 1995—; mem. N.H. Action Com. for Foster Children, 1983-86; mem. adv. com. to bd. dirs. Souhegan Theatre Coun., 1990—; mem. St. Casimir's Ladies Guild, 1981-86. Recipient N.H. Young Career Woman, Nat. Fed. Bus. and profl. Women, Catherine M. McAuley award. Fellow N.H. Bar Found.; mem. ABA (custody com. family law sect. 1983-84), N.H. Bar Assn. (chmn. com. on juvenile problems and family law 1980-81, 82-83, com. on needs of children 1984-85), Nashua Bar Assn., Nat. Fedn. Bus. and Profl. Women (chmn. young career woman com. 1982-83, 2d v.p. Nashua 1983-85, pres. 1985-86, N.H. Young Career Woman award 1982). Avocations: downhill skiing, children. Probate, Family and matrimonial, General civil litigation. Office: 7 Auburn St Nashua NH 03064-2615

**RAUL, ALAN CHARLES,** lawyer; b. Bronx, N.Y., Sept. 9, 1954; s. Eugene and Eduarda (Müller-Mañas) R.; m. Mary Tinsley, Jan. 30, 1988; children: Caroline Tinsley, William Eduardo Tinsley, Alexander Tinsley. AB magna cum laude, Harvard U., 1975, MPA, 1977; JD, Yale U., 1980. Bar: N.Y. 1982, D.C. 1982, U.S. Ct. Appeals (D.C. cir.) 1982, U.S. Dist. Ct. D.C. 1986, U.S. Ct. Internat. Trade 1988, U.S. Claims Ct. 1988, U.S. Ct. Appeals (fed. cir.) 1988, U.S. Supreme Ct. 1988, U.S. Ct. Appeals (9th cir.) 1991, U.S. Ct. Appeals (4th cir.) 1994, U.S. Ct. Appeals (11th cir.) 1996. Law clk. to judge U.S. Ct. Appeals (D.C. cir.), Washington, 1980-81; assoc. Debevoise & Plimpton, N.Y.C., 1981-86; White House assoc. counsel Pres. Reagan, Washington, 1986-88; gen. counsel Office Mgmt. and Budget, Washington, 1988-89, USDA, Washington, 1989-93; prin. Beveridge & Diamond P.C., Washington, 1993-97; ptnr. Sidley & Austin, Washington, 1997—; cons. Reagan-Bush campaign, N.Y.C., 1984; com. mem. Food and Drug Law Inst. Co-chairperson, co-founder Lawyers Have Heart; chmn. bd. USDA Grad. Sch., 1991-93; bd. dirs. Am. Heart Assn., Nations Capital Affiliate, 1993-97; treas., dir. Citizens Assn. Georgetown, 1993-97; mem. Nat. Policy Forum's Environ. Policy Coun. Recipient Disting. Achievement award Am. Heart Assn., 1991, Vol. of Yr. award, 1993. Mem. ABA (coun. sect. internat. law and practice 1992-98, chmn. com. on nat. security and internat. law 1990-92, standing com. on election law 1995—, sect. internat. law and practice govt. affairs officer 1996-98), Assn. of Bar of City of N.Y. (chmn. subcom. on Cen. Am. issues 1985, mem. com. on inter-Am. affairs 1983), Federalist Soc. (mem. nat. practitioners adv. coun., chair environ. and property rights practice group), FDA Reform Group, Coun. on Fgn. Rels. Administrative and regulatory, Environmental, Private international. Office: Sidley & Austin 1722 Eye St NW Fl 7 Washington DC 20006-3795

**RAUM, ARNOLD,** federal judge; b. Lynn, Mass., Oct. 27, 1908; s. Isaac and Ida (Ross) R.; m. Muriel Leidner Slaff, Jan. 26, 1944 (div.); m. Violet Gang Kopp, Apr. 26, 1957; stepchildren—Robert E., Elizabeth A., Katherine F. AB summa cum laude, Harvard, 1929, LLB magna cum laude, 1932. Bar: Mass. 1932, U.S. Supreme Ct. 1935, D.C. 1935, bars of various other fed. cts 1935. Sheldon fellow Cambridge U., Eng., 1932; atty. for RFC, 1932-34; spl. asst. to atty. gen. U.S., 1934-50; spl. prosecutor in connection with fed. grand jury investigation of corruption La., 1939; 1st dep. solicitor gen. U.S., also occasional acting, 1939-1950; directed litigation of all Fed. tax cases as well as other types of cases in U.S. Supreme Court, 1939-1950; made arguments in numerous Supreme Ct. cases, including Calif. Tidelands case; judge U.S. Tax Ct., Washington, 1950—; lectr. on taxation Yale Law Sch., 1937-38; mem. faculty Harvard Law Sch., 1947. Editor Harvard Law Rev. 1930-32. Served as lt. comdr. USCGR, World War II. Hon. mem. D.C. Bar Assn., Fed. Bar Assn.; mem. Am. Law Inst., Phi Beta Kappa. Club: Cosmos (Washington). Home: 2622 31st St NW Washington DC 20008-3519 Office: US Tax Ct 400 2nd St NW Washington DC 20217-0002

**RAVEN, ROBERT DUNBAR,** lawyer; b. Cadillac, Mich., Sept. 26, 1923; s. Christian and Gladys L. (Dunbar) R.; m. Leslie Kay Erickson, June 21, 1947; children: Marta Ellen, Matt Robert, Brett Lincoln. AB with honors, Mich. State U., 1949; LLB, U. Calif., Berkeley, 1952. Bar: Calif. 1953. Assoc. Morrison & Foerster and predecessor, San Francisco, 1952-56, ptnr., 1956-94, sr. of counsel, 1994—; chmn. Morrison & Foerster (and predecessor), San Francisco, 1974-82; mem. Jud. Coun. of Calif., 1983-87. Bd. dirs. Bay Area USO, 1964-73, pres., 1968-70; mem. San Francisco Mayor's Criminal Justice Coun., 1971-72; co-chmn. San Francisco Lawyer's Com. for Urban Affairs, 1976-78; bd. dirs. Lawyers Com. for Civil Rights Under Law, 1976-96. With USAAF, 1942-45. Decorated Air medal with oak leaf cluster. Mem. ABA (pres. 1989, mem. standing com. fed. judiciary 1975-80, chmn. 1978-80, chmn. standing com. on legal aid and indigent defendants 1981-83, chair standing com. dispute resolution 1991-93, chair sect. dispute resolution 1993-94), FBA, Am. Arbitration Assn. (bd. dirs. 1988-96), CPR Inst. for Dispute Resolution (mem. exec. com.), Internat. Acad. Trial Lawyers, State Bar Calif. (gov. 1978-81, pres. 1981), Bar Assn. San Francisco (pres. 1971), Am. Law Inst., Am. Bar Found., Am. Judicature Soc., Boalt Hall Alumni Assn. (pres. 1972-73), World Trade Club (San Francisco), Order of Coif. Democrat. Antitrust, Federal civil litigation, State civil litigation. Home: 1064 Via Alta Lafayette CA 94549-2916 Office: Morrison & Foerster 425 Market St San Francisco CA 94105-2482

**RAVJI, AAMER,** lawyer; b. Karachi, Pakistan, May 29, 1964; came to U.S., 1989; s. Shaukat and Dilshad Ravji; m. Sherin Thawer, June 7, 1998. Student, Aga Khan Med. Coll. and Univ., Karachi, 1986-89; BS in Criminal Justice, Northeastern U., Boston, 1993; JD, Syracuse U., 1996. Bar: Tex. 1997. Law clk. Tex. Natural Resources Conservation Commn., Austin, 1995; chief jud. intern U.S. Bankruptcy Ct., Houston, 1995-96; law clk. to chief counsel Creative Music Entertainment, Houston, 1996; assoc. Carmodys, Tex. Trial Lawyer, Dallas, 1997—. Vol., mem. legal com. Aga Khan Found., Dallas, 1997—; mem. Metroport Rep. Group, Ft. Worth, 1997—. Mem. Tex. Young Lawyers Assn., Dallas Lawyers Assn. Islamic. General civil litigation, Personal injury. Office: Carmodys Tex Trial Lawyers 5000 Bank One Ctr 1717 Main St # Lb50 Dallas TX 75201-4605

**RAWL, A. VICTOR, JR.,** lawyer; b. Charleston, S.C., May 14, 1969; s. A. Victor and Laura (Hamilton) R. BA, Wofford Coll., Spartanburg, S.C., 1991; JD, U. S.C., 1995, M of Internat. Bus., 1995. Bar: S.C. 1995, U.S. Dist. Ct. S.C. 1998. Law clk. to Hon. P. Michael Duffy U.S. Dist. Ct. S.C., Charleston, 1995-97; assoc. McNair Law Firm, Columbia, S.C., 1997—. Articles editor S.C. Lawyers Mag., 1996-98. Mem. Leadership Charleston, 1997. Mem. ABA (exec. coun. young lawyers divsn. 1999—), S.C. Bar Assn. (exec. coun. Young Lawyers divsn. 1995—), World Trade Ctr. Federal civil litigation, General civil litigation, Private international. Office: McNair Law Firm PO Box 11390 Columbia SC 29211-1390

**RAWLES, EDWARD HUGH,** lawyer; b. Chgo., May 7, 1945; s. Fred Wilson and Nancy (Hughes) R.; m. Margaret Mary O'Donoghue, Oct. 20, 1979; children: Lee Kathryn, Jacklyn Ann. BA, U. Ill., 1967; JD summa cum laude, Ill. Inst. Tech., 1970. Bar: Ill., 1970, Colo. 1984, U.S. Dist. Ct. (cen. dist.) Ill. 1970, U.S. Ct. Appeals (7th cir.) 1983, U.S. Supreme Ct. 1973. Assoc. Reno, O'Byrne & Kepley, Champaign, Ill., 1970-73, ptnr., 1973-84; pres. Rawles, O'Byrne, Stanko & Kepley P.C., Champaign, 1984-98, pres., 1990-97; mem. student legal svc. adv. bd. U. Ill., Urbana, 1982—; hearing officer Ill. Fair Employment Practice Commn., Springfield, 1972-74; mem. rules com. U.S. Dist. Ct. for Ctrl. Dist. Ill., 1994—. Diplomate Nat. Bd. Trial Advocacy. Fellow Ill. State Bar Found., 1984. Mem. Ill. Bar Assn., Bar Assn. 7th Fed. Cir., Rules Com. U.S. Dist. Court (ctrl. dist. Ill.), Assn. Trial Lawyers Am., Ill. Trial Lawyers Assn., Colo. Trial Lawyers Assn., Kent Soc. Honor Men, Phi Delta Theta. Roman Catholic. Federal civil litigation, State civil litigation, Personal injury. Home: 6 Alice Dr White Heath IL 61884-9747 Office: Rawles O'Byrne Stanko & Kepley PC 501 W Church St Champaign IL 61820-3412

**RAWLINGS, BOYNTON MOTT,** lawyer; b. El Paso, Tex., Dec. 6, 1935; s. Junius Mott and Laura Bassett (Boynton) R.; m. Nancy Mary Peay, Aug. 24, 1962 (div. 1973); children: Laura Bassett, James Mott; m. Judith Reed, Dec. 10, 1977; 1 child, William Reed. AB, Princeton U., 1958; LLB, Stanford U., 1961; Diploma, U. Strasbourg (France), 1963. Bar: Calif., 1962, D.C., 1980, Conseil Juridique Paris, 1973, Avocat Paris, 1992. Assoc. Broad, Busterud & Khourie, San Francisco, 1963-65, Homer G. Angelo, Brussels, 1966; assoc., ptnr. S.G. Archibald, Paris, 1967-74; ptnr. Boynton M. Rawlings, Paris, Los Angeles, 1974-84, Kevorkian & Rawlings, Paris, 1984-90; ptnr. Oppenheimer, Wolff and Donnelly, Paris, 1990—. Contbr. articles to profl. jours. Mem. Los Angeles Bar Assn. (bd. dirs. sect. internat. law 1975-82), French Am. C. of C. L.A. (bd. dirs. 1985—). Republican. Episcopalian. Avocations: music; tennis; skiing; hiking. Contracts commercial, General corporate, Private international. Office: Oppenheimer Wolff Donnelly, 53 Ave Montaigne, 75008 Paris France also: 211 King St Ste 101 Charleston SC 29401-3175

**RAWLINS, DONALD R.,** lawyer; b. Dyersburg, Tenn., Apr. 28, 1965; s. Dal M. and Rebecca S. Rawlins. BBA, U. Memphis, 1987; JD, Am. U., 1990. Bar: Tenn., 1990. Asst. gen. counsel, asst. sec. AutoZone, Inc., Memphis, 1990—. Recipient Best Brief award ATLA, 1990. General corporate, Securities. Office: AutoZone Inc 123 S Front St Memphis TN 38103-3618

**RAWLS, CHARLES RICHARDSON,** lawyer, government official; b. Raleigh, N.C.; m. Deanne Elizbeth Maynard. BA in Bus. Mgmt., N.C. State U., 1979; JD, Campbell U., 1982. Bar: N.C. 1982. Counsel to subcom. on forests, family farms, and energy Ho. of Reps., Washington, 1983-85, assoc. gen. counsel com. on agr., 1985-88, legis. dir. Congressman Martin Lancaster, 1988-90, adminstrv. asst., 1991-93; asst. to dep. sec. agr. Richard Rominger USDA, Washington, 1993-98, gen. counsel, 1998—. Office: USDA/Office Gen Counsel 1400 Independence Ave SW Washington DC 20250-0002

**RAWLS, FRANK MACKLIN,** lawyer; b. Suffolk, Va., Aug. 24, 1952; s. John Lewis and Mary Helen (Macklin) R.; m. Sally Hallum Blanchard, June 26, 1976; children: Matthew Christopher, John Stephen, Michael Andrew. BA cum laude in History, Hampden Sydney Coll., 1974; JD, U. Va., 1977. Bar: Va. 1977, U.S. Dist. Ct. (ea. dist.) Va. 1977, U.S. Ct. Appeals (4th cir.) 1977. Assoc. Rawls, Habel & Rawls, Suffolk, 1977-78, ptnr., 1978-91; ptnr. Ferguson & Rawls, 1991-96, Ferguson, Rawls, MacDonald, Overton & Grissom, P.C., 1996-98, Ferguson, Rawls, MacDonald & Overton, P.C., Suffolk, 1999—; sec., bd. dirs. Suffolk Title Ltd., 1986-95; bd. dirs Old Dominion Investors Trust, Inc. 1994—, Secure Title, Inc., 1996—. Deacon Westminster Reformed Presbyn. Ch., Suffolk, 1979-83, elder, clk. of session, 1984-91, 94—; chmn. bd. dirs. Suffolk Crime Line, 1982-90, Suffolk Cheer Fund, 1982—, Covenant Christian Schs., Suffolk, 1982-84; bd. dirs. Norfolk Christian Schs., 1990—, v.p., 1998—; pres. Parent Tchr. Fellowship, 1995-97, vice-chmn. steering com. for capital campaign, 1996—, v.p., 1997—; mem. adv. bd. dirs. Salvation Army, Suffolk, 1977-95, chmn., 1989-90; chmn. Suffolk Com. on Affordable Housing, 1989-90; bd. dirs. Suffolk YMCA, 1988-90, Suffolk Youth Athletic Assn., 1999—. Mem. ATLA, Suffolk Bar Assn. (past pres.), Va. State Bar, Va. Bar Assn., Christian Legal Soc., Va. Trial Lawyers Assn., Suffolk Bar Assn., Rotary (bd. dirs. 1998—). General practice, Personal injury, General corporate.

**RAWLS, JOHN D.,** lawyer; b. Jacksonville, Fla., Sept. 16, 1943; s. Hugh Miller Sr. and Katherine (Dickenson) R. BA, Williams Coll., 1965; JD, Fla. State U., Tallahassee, 1974. Bar: Fla. 1975, La. 1986, U.S. Dist. Ct. (mid. dist.) Fla. 1975, U.S. Dist. Ct. (ea. dist.) La. 1986, U.S. Dist. Ct. (no. dist.) Fla. 1989, U.S. Dist. Ct. (we. dist.) La. 1996, U.S. Ct. Appeals (5th cir.) 1986. Assoc. Foerster & Hodge, Jacksonville Beach, Fla., 1975-78; ptnr. Thames, Rawls & Skinner, Jacksonville, 1978-80; pvt. practice, Jacksonville, 1980-85; pres. At Your Svc. Supply Co., New Orleans, 1985-86; assoc. Oestreicher, Whalen & Hackett, New Orleans, 1986-87; pvt. practice, New Orleans, 1987—; charter mem. Fla. Commn. on Ethics, Tallahassee, 1974-75. Mem. Fla. State U. Law Rev., 1973-74. Bd. dirs. Celebration '86, New Orleans, 1985-86; vol. NO/AIDS Task Force, New Orleans, 1986—; bd. dirs. La. Lesbian and Gay Polit. Action Caucus, New Orleans, 1987-89, Nat. Lesbian and Gay Law Assn., Washington, 1992-94, Supreme Ct. of La. Hist. Soc., New Orleans, 1992-96; founder, sec., bd. dirs. La. Electorate of Gays and Lesbians, New Orleans, 1993-96; chair La. Gov.'s Commn. on HIV and AIDS, Baton Rouge, 1994-95; unofcl. advisor on Gay and AIDS issues Gov. of La., Baton Rouge, 1992-96. Capt. U.S. Army, 1968-72, Vietnam. Nat. Merit scholar, 1961. Fellow La. Bar Found.; mem. New Orleans Bar Assn. Democrat. Episcopalian. Avocation: reading. Personal injury. Office: 400 Magazine St Ste 100 New Orleans LA 70130-2439

**RAWLS, R. STEVEN,** lawyer; b. St. Petersburg, Fla., Oct. 22, 1956; s. Ronald Radcliffe Rawls and Kathryn Faye Henson; m. Beth Ellen Mauer, Apr. 25, 1989; children: Sean, Erin. BIS, U. S. Fla., 1987; JD, U. Fla., 1991. Bar: Fla. 1992, U.S. Dist. Ct. (mid. dist.) Fla. 1993, U.S. Dist. Ct. (no. dist.) Fla. 1998. Assoc. Butler, Burnette & Pappas, Tampa, 1991-98, ptnr., 1999—. Co-author: Discovery Issues and Bad Faith Cases, 1996; contbr. articles to profl. jours. Mem. ABA, Hillsborough County Bar Assn., Def. Rsch. Inst. Insurance, Toxic tort, Personal injury. Office: Butler Burnett Pappas Ste 1100 6200 W Courtney Campbell Cswy Tampa FL 33607-5946

**RAWSON, MARJORIE JEAN,** lawyer; b. Okolona, Miss., Dec. 5, 1939; d. E.P. and Marjorie J. R. BS, U. Miss., 1961; MS, Ind. U., 1969; JD, John Marshall Law Sch., 1977. Bar: Ind. 1977, U.S. Dist. Ct. (no. dist.) Ind. 1977, U.S. Ct. Appeals (7th cir.) 1983, U.S. Supreme Ct. 1983, Fla. 1988, U.S. Dist. Ct. (mid. dist.) Fla. 1991, U.S. Ct. Mil. Appeals, 1995. Tchr. Munster (Ind.) High Sch., 1966-77; atty. pvt. practice, Munster, 1977-90; deputy prosecutor Lake County Juvenile Ct., Gary, Ind., 1978-90; pvt. practice Naples, Fla., 1991—; adj. prof. Ind. U., Gary, 1984-87, Purdue U., Hammond, Ind., 1988-90, John Marshall Law Sch., Chgo., 1984-87, U. South Fla., Ft. Myers, 1992-97; compliance specialist Collier County Pub. Schs., Naples, 1997—. Editor: Handbook for Legal Assistants, 1987. Past pres. Women's Polit. Caucus, Naples, 1995-97, Women's Rep. Club, Naples, 1992-94; mem. adv. bd. Naples Alliance Children, 1997—. Mem. AAUW, LWV, Collier County Bar Assn. (bd. dirs. 1996—), Naples C. of C. (bd. dirs. 1997—), Zonta Club. Republican. Avocations: jogging, swimming, music. Family and matrimonial, Education and schools. Office: 400 5th Ave S Ste 300 Naples FL 34102-6556

**RAWSON, RICHARD J.,** lawyer; b. N.Y.C., May 23, 1946. BA, Columbia U., 1968; MA, U. Calif., Berkeley, 1969, PhD, 1975; JD, Harvard U., 1978. Bar: N.Y. 1979, U.S. Dist. Ct. (so. dist.) N.Y. 1985, U.S. Ct. Appeals (2d and 3rd cirs.). Sr. v.p., gen. counsel RJR Nabisco, Inc., N.Y.C., 1998—. Mem. ABA (sr. v.p., gen. counsel). Mergers and acquisitions, General corporate. Office: RJR Nabisco Inc Rm 200 1301 Avenue Of The Americas Fl 33 New York NY 10019-6054*

**RAY, BETTY JEAN G.,** lawyer; b. New Orleans, June 7, 1943; d. William E. George and Iris U. (Berthold) Grizzell; m. Gerald L. Ray, June 9, 1962; children: Gerald L. Ray, Jr., Brian P. BS Psychology, La. State U., 1976, JD, 1980. Bar: La., 1980; U.S. Dist. Ct. (ea., mid. and we. dists.) La. 1981; U.S. Ct. Appeal (5th cir.) 1981. Jud. law clk. 19th Jud. Dist. Ct., Baton Rouge, 1980-81; atty. Jean G. Ray, Baton Rouge, 1981-83; counsel Gulf Stream, Inc., Baton Rouge, 1982-83; staff atty. La. Dept. Justice, Baton Rouge, 1983-84, asst. atty. gen., 1984-87; staff atty. FDIC, Shreveport, La., 1987-88, mng. atty., 1988-94; spl. dep. receiver Receivership Office, La. Dept. Ins., Baton Rouge, 1994-95; spl. counsel Brook, Pizza & van Loon, L.L.P., Baton Rouge, 1995—. Mem. La. Bar Assn., Baton Rouge Bar Assn., Baton Rouge Assn. Women Attys., Order of Coif, Phi Beta Kappa, Phi Delta Phi (scholar 1980). Episcopalian. General civil litigation, Consumer commercial, Government contracts and claims. Home: 1143 Oakley Dr Baton Rouge LA 70806-7925 Office: Brook Pizza & van Loon Ste 402 9100 Bluebonnet Centre Blvd Baton Rouge LA 70809-2985

**RAY, BRUCE DAVID,** lawyer; b. Denver, Dec. 19, 1955; s. John Denver Ray and Jane (Guiney) Mitchell; m. Faith Theofanus, Aug. 20, 1978; children: Ellena, Constance, Christian, Zoe. BA magna cum laude, U. Colo., 1978; JD, Union U., Albany, N.Y., 1981. Bar: Colo. 1981. Spl. environ. counsel URS-Berger, San Bernardino, Calif., 1982-84; asst. regional counsel EPA, Denver, 1984-90; spl. asst. U.S. atty. U.S. Dept. Justice, Denver, 1987-90; sr. environ. counsel Johns-Manville, Denver, 1990—. Asst. editor Natural Resources and Environment, 1989—; contbr. articles to legal jours. First v.p. St. Catherine Greek Orthodox Ch. of S.E. Denver, 1994-95. Recipient bronze medal EPA, 1986, 91, gold medal, 1989, Environ. Excellence award, 1987, Best Article award, 1988, Roasch prize Albany Law Sch., 1981. Mem. ABA (sect. on natural resources, energy and environ. law), Colo. Bar Assn. (environ. law coun. 1987—, chmn. 1995-96), Aurora Bar assn., Environ. Law Inst., Air and Waste Mgmt. Assn., World Tae Kwon Do Fedn. (yellos belt), Phi Beta Kappa. Avocation: German language and literature, modern Greek. E-mail: bdr@jm.com. Environmental. Office: Johns-Manville 717 17th St Denver CO 80202-3330

**RAY, DAVID P.,** lawyer; b. Eastport, Maine, July 21, 1952; s. Ralph S. and Fae B. Ray; m. Kay Loftus, Aug. 25, 1989; 1 child, Cyrilla Jane. BS, U. Maine, 1974; JD, Cornell U., 1977. Bar: Maine 1977, U.S. Dist. Ct. Maine 1977, U.S. Ct. Appeals (1st cir.) 1977. Assoc. Jensen, Baird, Gardner & Henry, Portland, Maine, 1977-80; counse. to Senator George J. Mitchell, U.S. Senate, Washington, 1980-82; ptnr. Amerling & Burns, P.A., Portland, 1982-97, Burns, Ray & DeLano, Portland, 1997—. Bd. dirs., v.p. Ctr. for Cultural Exch., Portland. Mem. ABA, Maine Bar Assn., Maine Bar Found. Construction, Contracts commercial, Insurance. Office: Burns Ray & DeLano PA 193 Middle St Portland ME 04101-4076

**RAY, FRANK ALLEN,** lawyer; b. Lafayette, Ind., Jan. 30, 1949; s. Dale Allen and Merry Ann (Fleming) R.; m. Carol Ann Olmutz, Oct. 1, 1982; children: Erica Fleming, Robert Allen. BA, Ohio State U., 1970, JD, 1973. Bar: Ohio 1973, U.S. Dist. Ct. (so. dist.) Ohio 1975, U.S. Supreme Ct. 1976, U.S. Tax Ct. 1977, U.S. Ct. Appeals (6th cir.) 1977, U.S. Dist. Ct. (no. dist.) Ohio 1980, Pa. 1983, U.S. Dist. Ct. (ea. dist.) Mich. 1983, U.S. Ct. Appeals (1st cir.) 1986; cert. civil trial adv. Nat. Bd. Trial Advocacy. Asst. pros. atty. Franklin County, Ohio, 1973-75; chief civil counsel Franklin County, 1976-78; dir. econ. crime project Nat. Dist. Attys. Assn., Washington, 1975-76; assoc. Brownfield, Kosydar, Bowen, Bally & Sturtz, Columbus, Ohio, 1978, Michael F. Colley Co., L.P.A., Columbus, 1979-83; pres. Frank A. Ray Co., L.P.A., Columbus, 1983-93, Ray & Todaro Co., LPA, Columbus, 1993-94, Ray, Todaro & Alton Co., L.P.A., Columbus, 1994-96, Ray, Todaro, Alton & Kirstein Co., L.P.A., Columbus, 1996, Columbus, Ray, Alton & Kirstein Co., L.P.A., 1996-98; sr. ptnr. Ray & Alton, L.L.P., 1998—; mem. seminar faculty Nat. Coll. Dist. Attys., Houston, 1975-77; mem. nat. conf. faculty Fed. Jud. Ctr., Washington, 1976-77; bd. editors Man. for Complex Litigation, Fed. Jud. Ctr., 1999—; bd. mem. bar examiners Ohio Supreme Ct., 1992-95, Rules Adv. Com., 1995-99. Editor: Economic Crime Digest, 1975-76; co-author: Personal Injury Litigation Practice in Ohio, 1988, '91; bd. editors Manual for Complex Litigation, 1999—. Mem. fin. com. Franklin County Rep. Orgn., Columbus, 1979-84; trustee Ohio State U. Coll. Humanities Alumni Soc., 1991-93, Nat. Coun. Ohio State U. Coll. Law Alumni Assn., 1998—; mem. Legal Aid Soc. of Columbus Capital Campaign Fund Cabinet, 1998. 1st lt. inf. U.S. Army, 1973. Named to Ten Outstanding Young Citizens of Columbus, Columbus Jaycees, 1976; recipient Nat. award of Distinctive Svc., Nat. Dist. Attys. Assn., 1977. Fellow Am. Coll. Trial Lawyers, Internat. Soc. Barristers, Columbus Bar Found., Roscoe Pound Found., Ohio Acad. Trial Lawyers, Ohio State Bar Found.; mem. ABA, Am. Bd. Trial Advocates (sec. Ohio chpt. 1999—), Columbus Bar Assn. (sec.-treas. 1999—, Profl. award 1997), Million Dollar Advs. Forum, Ohio State Bar Assn. (com. negligence law 1990-97), Assn. Trial Lawyers Am. (state del. 1990-92), Ohio Acad. Trial Lawyers (pres. 1989-90, Pres.' award 1986), Franklin County Trial Lawyers Assn. (pres. 1987-88, Pres.'s award 1990), Inns of Ct. (pres. Judge Robert M. Duncan chpt. 1993-94), Million Dollar Advs. Forum. Presbyterian. Personal injury, General civil litigation, Product liability. Home: 2030 Tremont Rd Columbus OH 43221-4330 Office: 175 S 3rd St Ste 350 Columbus OH 43215-5188

**RAY, HUGH MASSEY, JR.,** lawyer; b. Vicksburg, Miss., Feb. 1, 1943; s. Hugh Massey and Lollie Landon (Powell) R.; m. Florence Hargrove, Sept. 3, 1966; children—Hugh, Hallie. BA, Vanderbilt U., 1965, JD, 1967. Bar: Tex. 1967, U.S. Dist. Ct. (so. dist.) Tex. 1967, U.S. Dist.Ct. (we. dist.) La. 1979, U.S. Dist. Ct. (we. dist.) Tex. 1979, U.S. Dist Ct. (no. dist.) Tex. 1980, U.S. Ct. Appeals (11th cir.) 1982, U.S. Dist. Ct. (no. dist.) Calif. 1989, N.Y. 1992; cert. Tex. Bd. Legal Specialization. Asst. U.S. atty. So. Dist. Tex., 1967-68; assoc. Andrews & Kurth, Houston, 1968-77, ptnr., 1977—; lectr. Ctrl. and Ea. European Law Initiative, Vilnius, Lithuania, 1996. Co-author: Bankruptcy Investing, 1992, Enforcing Debts and Judgments, vol. 1 & 2, 1998; editor-in-chief Creditor's Rights in Texas, 1975; contbr. articles to profl. jours. Mem. ABA (chmn. real property practice com. 1975-77, chmn. continuing legal edn. com. young lawyers divsn. 1976-78, vice-chmn. 1979, chmn. oil and gas subcom. bus. bankruptcy com. 1985-89, chmn. executory contracts subcom. 1989-93, chmn. bus. bankruptcy com. 1993-96, chmn. com. on trust indentures and indenture trustees 1995-97, mem. standing com. on jud. selection, tenure and compensation 1996-97, coun. mem. bus. law sect. 1997—, chmn. ad hoc com. on bankruptcy ct. structure 1996—), FBA, Houston Bar Assn., Tex. Bar Assn. (chmn. bankruptcy com. 1985-88), Am. Law Inst., Houston Country Club, Tex. Club, Houston Club. Episcopalian. Bankruptcy, Federal civil litigation, State civil litigation. Home: 5785 Indian Cir Houston TX 77057-1302 Office: Andrews & Kurth 600 Travis St Ste 4200 Houston TX 77002-2910

**RAY, JEANNE CULLINAN,** lawyer, insurance company executive; b. N.Y.C., May 5, 1943; d. Thomas Patrick and Agnes Joan (Buckley) C.; m. John Joseph Ray, Jan. 20, 1968 (dec. Mar. 1993); children: Christopher Lawrence, Douglas James. Student, Univ. Coll., Dublin, Ireland, 1963; AB, Coll. Mt. St. Vincent, Riverdale, N.Y., 1964; LLB, Fordham U., 1967. Bar: N.Y. 1967. Atty. Mut. Life Ins. Co. N.Y. (MONY), N.Y.C., 1967-68, asst. counsel, 1969-72, assoc. counsel, 1972-73, counsel, 1974-75, asst. gen. counsel, 1976-80, assoc. gen. counsel, 1981-83, v.p. pension counsel, 1984-85, v.p. area counsel group and pension ops., 1985-87, v.p. sector counsel group and pension ops., 1988, v.p., chief counsel exec. and corp. affairs, 1988-89; v.p. law, sec. MONY Securities Corp., N.Y.C., 1980-85, MONY Advisers, Inc., N.Y.C., 1980-88; sec. MONYCO, Inc., N.Y.C., 1980-85; v.p., counsel MONY Series Fund, Inc., Balt., 1984-87; v.p., assoc. gen. counsel Tchrs. Ins. and Annuity Assoc. Coll. Ret. Equities Fund (TIAA-CREF), N.Y.C., 1989-91, v.p., chief counsel ins., 1991-99. Contbr. articles to legal jours. Cubmaster, den mother Greater N.Y. coun. Boy Scouts Am., N.Y.C., 1978-84, mem. bd. rev. and scouting com., 1985-99. Mem. ABA (chmn. employee benefits com. tort and ins. practice sect. 1981-82, vice-chmn. 1983-96), Assn. Life Ins. Counsel (chmn. policy holders tax com. tax sect. 1982-91, vice chmn. tax sect. 1991-93, chmn. 1993-99), Assn. Bar City N.J. (chmn. employee benefits com. 1992-95), Investment Co. Inst. (mem. pension com. 1993-99), Am. Coun. Life Ins. (chmn. fiduciary task force of pension com. 1990-99), Am. Coun. Life Ins. Democrat. Roman Catholic. Pension, profit-sharing, and employee benefits, Securities, General corporate. Address: 304 E 20 St #3E New York NY 10003

**RAY, JENNIFER SMITH,** lawyer; b. Cin., Nov. 8, 1968; d. Raymond Allen Smith and Mary Ann Cabrera; m. Adam Dean-Marcel Ray, June 8, 1996. BA summa cum laude, So. Meth. U., 1990; JD, Stanford U., 1995. Bar: Calif. 1995. Assoc. Brobeck, Phleger & Harrison LLP, San Francisco, 1995—. Mem. ABA, Calif. Bar Assn., San Francisco Bar Assn. Democrat. Product liability. Office: Brobeck Phleger & Harrison Spear Tower 1 Market St San Francisco CA 94105-1420

**RAY, MARY LOUISE RYAN,** lawyer; b. Houston, Dec. 8, 1954; d. Cornelius O'Brien and Mary Anne (Kelley) R.; m. Marshall Ransome Ray, Jan. 30, 1982; children: Siobhan Elisabeth Kelley, Johanna Frances Morris, Jonathan Jordan Willson. BA with honors, U. Tex., 1976; JD, St. Mary's Univ., San Antonio, Tex., 1980. Bar: Tex. 1980, U.S. Dist. Ct. (so. dist.) Tex. 1981, U.S. Ct. Appeals (5th cir.) 1993, U.S. Supreme Ct. 1994. Assoc. Kelley & Ryan, Houston, 1980-82, R.W. Armstrong, Brownsville, Tex., 1982-83; ptnr. Armstrong & Ray, Brownsville, Tex., 1983-87; shareholder Ransome and Ray, P.C., Brownsville, Tex., 1987—. Bd. dirs. Brownsville Soc. for Crippled Children, 1984-95, pres., 1992-93; bd. dirs. Valley Zool. Soc., 1990—, sec., 1999; bd. dirs. United Way of Southern Cameron County, 1989-95, pres., 1994; bd. dirs. Crippled Children's Found., Brownsville, 1989—; bd. dirs. Episcopal Day Sch. Found., 1995—, pres., 1995—. Fellow Tex. Bar Found.; mem. Tex. Bar Assn., Cameron County Bar Assn. (bd. dirs. 1990—, pres. 1998), Tex. Assn. Bank Counsel, Brownsville C. of C. (bd. dirs. 1998-99). Episcopalian. General civil litigation, Probate, General corporate. Office: Ransome & Ray PC 550 E Levee St Brownsville TX 78520-5343

**RAY, PAUL DUBOSE,** lawyer; b. Barnwell, S.C., July 1, 1966; s. Albert DuBose and Harriet Jane (LaMaster) R. BA, Furman U., 1988; JD, U. S.C., 1991. Bar: S.C. Asst. contracts atty. County of Charleston, S.C., 1992-94; projects officer County of Charleston, 1994; pres. Palmetto Practice Systems, Charleston, 1994—. Mem. Phi Beta Kappa. Computer, Estate planning, Probate. Office: Palmetto Practice Systems 21 Broad St Charleston SC 29401-3001

**RAY, PAULA MARIE,** lawyer; b. Denver, Oct. 16, 1951; d. Paul Eugene and Della (Brancucci) R. BA, U. No. Colo., 1974; JD, Creighton U., 1981. Bar: Colo. 1981. Jud. law clk. Colo. Ct. Appeals, Denver, 1981-82; assoc. Beck & Cassinis, Aurora, Colo., 1982-83; dep. dist. atty. Adams County Dist. Atty.'s Office, Brighton, Colo., 1983-85; assoc. Wood, Ris & Hames, Denver, 1985-87; asst. U.S. Atty. Dist. Colo. U.S. Atty.'s Office, Denver, 1987—. Lead articles editor Creighton Law Rev., 1980-81. Mem. FBA (past pres. 1992).

**RAY, RONALD DUDLEY,** lawyer; b. Hazard, Ky., Oct. 30, 1942. BA in Psychology and English, Centre Coll., 1964; JD magna cum laude, U. Louisville, 1971. Assoc. Greenebaum, Doll & McDonald, 1971-75, ptnr., 1975-84, 85-86; ptnr. Ray & Morris, Louisville, 1986-89; mng. ptnr. Ronald Ray Attys., Louisville, 1990—; dep. asst. sec. def. Pentagon, Washington, 1984-85; adj. prof. law U. Louisville Sch. Law, 1972-80; commr. Presdl. Commn. on Assigment of Women in Mil., 1992. Author: Military Necessity & Homosexuality, 1993; sr. legal editor: Personnel Policy Manual, Bank Supervisory Policies, The Bank Employee Handbook, 1985-86; mil. historian. State fin. chmn. Nat. Fin. Com. for George Bush for Pres.; chmn. Vietnam Vets. Leadership Program in Ky., 1982-85, Ky. Vietnam Vets. Meml. Fund, 1985-91; trustee Marine Corps Command and Staff Found., 1985-92; mem. exec. com. State Cen. Com., Ky. Rep. Party, 1986-90; mem. Am. Battle Monuments Commn., 1990-94; spokesman Coalition of Am. Vets., 1998—, chmn., 1999—. With USMC, 1964-69; col. USMCR (ret.). Decorated Silver Star medal with gold star, Bronze Star medal, Purple Heart, Vietnamese Cross of Gallantry, Vietnamese Honor Medal; recipient Nat. Eagle award Nat. Guard Assn., 1985. Mem. Naval Inst. (life), Marine Corps Res. Officers' Assn. General civil litigation, Government contracts and claims, Labor. Home: Halls Hill Farm 3317 Halls Hill Rd Crestwood KY 40014-9523

**RAY, STEPHEN ALAN,** academic administrator, lawyer; b. Oklahoma City, Aug. 26, 1956; s. Thompson Eugene and Dorothea Hodges. BA summa cum laude, St. Thomas Sem., 1978; PhD, Harvard U., 1986; JD, U. Calif., Hastings, 1990. Bar: Calif. 1990, Mass. 1994. Assoc. Richards, Watson & Gershon, L.A., 1990-93; lectr. theology Boston Coll., Chestnut Hill, Mass., 1993-95; staff counsel Houghton Miffin Co., Boston, 1995-96; asst. dean acad. affairs Harvard Law Sch., Cambridge, 1998—, dir. acad. affairs, 1996-98; vis. lectr. religion Harvard Divinity Sch., spring 1995; adv. bd. Harvard Native Am. Program, 1999—. Author: The Modern Soul, 1987. Vol. AIDS action com., Boston, 1994-96; atty. vol. AIDS Project L.A., 1991-93. Mem. ABA, Cherokee Nation Okla. E-mail: aray@law.harvard.edu. Office: Harvard Law Sch Griswold Hall 209 Cambridge MA 02138

**RAY, TAMBER,** lawyer; b. Valparaiso, Ind., Dec. 4, 1968. BA, Radford U., 1990; JD, Howard U., 1993; LLM in Intellectual Property, Geroge Washington U., 1998. Bar: Va. 1994. Program dir. WVRU-FM, Radford, Va., 1987-90; pub. info. specialist FCC, Washington, 1990-91; legal intern Nat. Assn. Broadcasters, Washington, 1992-93; assoc. Besozzi, Gavin, Craven & Schmitz, Washington, 1994-96, Ginsburg, Feldman & Bress, Washington, 1996-98, Shook, Hardy & Bacon, Washington, 1998-99, Kraskin, Lesse & Cosson LLP, Washington, 1999—. Contbr. articles to profl. publs. Vestry mem. St. James' Episcopal Ch., Washington, 1996-98. Mem. Va. State Bar Assn., Fed. Comms. Bar Assn. (co-chair young lawyers com. 1995-96, exec. com. 1996-97). Intellectual property, Communications. Office: Kraskin Lesse & Cosson LLP 2120 L St NW Ste 520 Washington DC 20037-1527

**RAYBURN, RALPH F.,** lawyer; b. Evansville, Ind., Apr. 6, 1954. BA, U. Wis., 1976; JD, U. Nebr., 1980. Assoc. Spears Ludersky, Portland, Oreg., 1982-83, Whipple Jolander, Portland, 1983-86; ptnr. McClain & Rayburn, Portland, 1986-95, Amburgey & Rubin, Portland, 1995—. Mem. Oreg. State Bar Assn., Multnomah Bar Assn. (professionalism com.). Labor, General civil litigation. Office: Amburgey & Rubin 1750 SW Harbor Way Ste 450 Portland OR 97201-5182

**RAYE-WONG, CATHERINE,** lawyer, sole practitioner; b. Redwood City, Calif., Oct. 26, 1961; d. Gerald Francis and Barbara Jean Raye; m. Arnold C. Wong, July 20, 1991; 1 child, Stephen Raye Wong. BA in English, Coll. of Notre Dame, Belmont, Calif., 1988; JD, San Francisco Law Sch., 1993; LLM in Taxation, Golden Gate Sch. Law, 1997. Bar: Calif. 1993. Assoc. Law Office of David J. Palmer, San Carlos, Calif., 1993-95; probate rsch. atty. San Mateo County Superior Ct., Redwood City, 1995-98; assoc. Law Office of Richard W. Henson, San Carlos, 1998; sole practitioner Law Office of Richard W. Hanson, San Carlos, 1998—; sec. San Mateo County Barristers, Redwood City, 1993-97. Editor, co-author: Estate Planning Concepts, 1998; author: (booklet) Do's and Don't's of Probate, 1995. Mem. San Francisco Law Sch. alumni bd., 1993-96, Coll. Notre Dame alumni bd., 1993-96; sr. law atty. Legal Aid Soc., San Mateo County, 1993-95; bd. mem. Caring Cupboard Sr. Food Program, San Carlos, 1995. Recipient Woman of Yr. in Self-Devel. award, County of San Mateo Women in Mgmt., 1997, Outstanding Achievement in Am. Jurisprudence award West Pub., San Francisco, 1993. Mem. State Bar of Calif. (estate planning, probate and trust sect. 1993—), San Mateo County Bar Assn. (probate sect. 1993—, conf. of dels. 1995, 99), San Carlos Lions Club (past 3d v.p.), Delta Theta Phi. Democrat. Presbyterian. Avocations: hiking, reading, listening to music, singing. Estate planning, Probate, Estate taxation. Office: Law Office of Richard W Henson 909 Laurel St San Carlos CA 94070-3916

**RAYLESBERG, ALAN IRA,** lawyer; b. N.Y.C., Dec. 6, 1950; s. Daniel David and Sally Doris (Mantell) R.; m. Caren Thea Coven, Nov. 20, 1983; children: Lisa Maris, Jason Todd. BA, NYU, 1972; JD cum laude, Boston U., 1975. Bar: N.Y. 1976, U.S. Dist. Ct. (so. dist.) N.Y. 1976, U.S. Dist. Ct. (ea. dist.) N.Y. 1978, U.S. Tax Ct. 1981, U.S. Ct. Appeals (2d and 5th cirs.) 1982, U.S. Ct. Appeals (1st cir.) 1986, U.S. Ct. Appeals (9th cir.) 1996. Assoc. Orans, Elsen & Polstein, N.Y.C., 1975-77; assoc. Guggenheimer & Untermyer, N.Y.C., 1977-83, ptnr., 1983-85; ptnr. Rosenman & Colin, N.Y.C., 1985—; co-chmn. litigation dept. Rosenman & Colin, 1998-99, chmn. litigation dept., 1999—; adj. instr. N.Y. Law Sch., 1980-83; instr. Nat. Inst. of Trial Advocacy; mem. adv. group comml. divsn., mediation panel N.Y. State Supreme Ct.; mem. arbitration panel U.S. Dist. Ct. (ea. dist.) N.Y. Bd. dirs. Fund for Modern Cts., 1994—. Mem. ABA, Fed. Bar Coun., Assn. Bar City N.Y., N.Y. County Lawyers Assn. (bd. dirs. 1995-98, 99—, fed. ct. com. 1988—, appellate ct. com. 1990—, co-chmn. appellate ct. com. 1992-93, chair appellate ct. com. 1993-96), N.Y. County Lawyers Assn. Found. (bd. dirs. 1998—), N.Y. State Bar Assn. (ho. delegates 1996—), Securities Industry Assn. (legal and compliance divsn) N.Y. Coun. Def. Lawyers, Town Club of Newcastle (mem. exec. com. 1987-91). Democrat. Jewish. Federal civil litigation, State civil litigation, Criminal. Office: Rosenman & Colin 575 Madison Ave Fl 26 New York NY 10022-2585

**RAYMOND, DAVID WALKER,** lawyer; b. Chelsea, Mass., Aug. 23, 1945; s. John Walker and Jane (Beck) R.; m. Sandra Sue Broadwater, Aug. 12, 1967 (div.); m. Margaret Byrd Payne, May 25, 1974; children: Pamela Payne, Russell Wyatt. BA, Gettysburg Coll., 1967; JD, Temple U., 1970. Bar: Pa. 1970, D.C. 1971, Ill. 1975, U.S. Dist. Ct. (no. dist.) Ill. 1981, U.S. Supreme Ct. 1974. Govtl. affairs atty. Sears, Roebuck and Co., Washington, 1970-74; atty. Sears Hdqrs. law dept. Sears, Roebuck and Co., Chgo., 1974-80, asst. gen. counsel advt., trademarks and customs, 1981-84, asst. gen. cousnel adminstrn., 1984-86, mgr. planning and analysis corp. planning dept., 1986-89, sr. corp. cousnel pub. policy corp. law dept., 1989-90; assoc. gen. counsel litigation and adminstrn. law dept. Sears Mdse. Group, 1990-92, dep. gen. counsel, 1992-93, v.p., gen. cousnel, 1993-95; v.p. law Sears Roebuck and Co., 1996; of cousnel Winston & Strawn, Washington, 1996—. Mem. staff Temple Law Quar., 1968-69, editor, 1969-70. Trustee No. Ill. U., 1996-98; mem. bd. visitors Christopher Newport U., 1999—. Mem. ABA, Nat. Assn. Coll. and Univ. Attys., Assn. Governing Bds., Phi Alpha Delta. Presbyterian. General corporate, Administrative and regulatory, Legislative. Office: Winston & Strawn 1400 L St NW Ste 800 Washington DC 20005-3508

**RAYNOLDS, WILLIAM F., II,** lawyer; b. San Antonio, Feb. 7, 1948; s. William F. and Doris Raynolds; m. Kathryn Raynolds, July 11, 1987; children: Lisa Chipman, Mike Chipman, Casey Raynolds. BS, U. Tulsa, 1973, JD, 1976. Atty. Hood & Raynolds, Tulsa, 1987—; adj. prof. legal assistant program U. Tulsa, 1993—, adj. prof. coll. law, 1995—. Editor Okla. Family Law Jour., 1995. Fellow Am. Acad. Matrimonial Lawyers; mem. ABA (family law sect.), Tulsa County Bar Assn. (family law sect., pres. 1993, 94, 95, 96, 97), Okla. Bar Assn. (family law sect.). Roman Catholic. Family and matrimonial. Office: Hood & Raynolds 1914 S Boston Ave Tulsa OK 74119-5222

**RAYNOVICH, GEORGE, JR.,** lawyer; b. Pitts., Dec. 30, 1931; s. George Sr. and Zora (Mamula) R.; m. Mary Ann Senay, July 11, 1953; children: George III, Andrew. BS, U. Pitts., 1957; JD, Duquesne U., 1961. Bar: Pa. 1962, U.S. Dist. Ct. (we. dist.) Pa. 1962, U.S. Patent and Trademark Office 1962, U.S. Supreme Ct. 1966, U.S. Ct. Appeals (fed. cir.) 1986. Patent agt. Consolidation Coal Co., Library, Pa., 1959-62; ptnr. Stone & Raynovich, Pitts., 1962-75; atty. Wheeling-Pitts. Steel Corp., Pitts., 1975-77, gen. counsel, sec., 1978-85, v.p., 1980-85; sr. atty. Buchanan Ingersol P.C., Pitts., 1986-88, 89-96; ptnr. Price & Raynovich, Pitts., 1988-89; of counsel Gorr Moser Dell and Loughney, 1997—. Councilman Borough of Baldwin, Allegheny County, Pa., 1972-75, govt. study commr., 1973. 1st lt. USAF, 1952-56. Mem. Allegheny County Bar Assn., Pitts. Intellectual Property Law Assn., Acad. Trial Lawyers Allegheny County. Democrat. Mem. Serbian Orthodox Ch. Patent, Real property, Federal civil litigation. Home: 335 Jean Dr Pittsburgh PA 15236-2511 Office: Gorr Moser Dell & Loughney 1300 Frick Bldg Pittsburgh PA 15219

**RAZZANO, FRANK CHARLES,** lawyer; b. Bklyn., Feb. 25, 1948; s. Pasquale Anthony and Agnes Mary (Borgia) R.; m. Stephanie Anne Lucas, Jan. 10, 1970; children: Joseph, Francis, Catherine. BA, St. Louis U., 1969; JD, Georgetown U., 1972. Bar: N.Y. 1973, U.S. Dist. Ct. (so. dist.) N.Y. 1973, U.S. Dist. Ct. (es. dist.) N.Y. 1973, N.J. 1976, D.C. 1981, Va. 1984, U.S. Dist. Ct. N.J. 1976, U.S. Dist. Ct. Md. 1977, U.S. Dist. Ct. (no. dist.) Calif. 1981, U.S. Dist. Ct. D.C. 1982, U.S. Dist. Ct. (ea. dist.) Va. 1989, U.S. Dist. Ct. (we. dist.) Va. 1990, U.S. Ct. Appeals (2d cir.) 1973, U.S. Ct. Appeals (3d cir.) 1975, U.S. Ct. Appeals (D.C. and 5th cirs.) 1983, U.S. Ct. Appeals (4th cir.) 1984, U.S. Ct. Appeals (6th cir.) 1990, U.S. Supreme Ct. 1976. Assoc. Shea & Gould, N.Y.C., 1972-75; asst. U.S. atty. Dist. of N.J., Newark, 1975-78; asst. chief trial atty. SEC, Washington, 1978-82; ptnr. Shea & Gould, Washington, 1982-94, mng. ptnr., 1991-92; ptnr. Camhy Karlinsky Stein Razzano & Rubin, Washington, 1994-96, Dickstein, Shapiro, Morin & Oshinsky, Washington, 1996—; lectr. in field; adv. bd. Securities Litigation Reform Act Reporter, Securities Regulation Law Jour.; adj. prof. law U. Md. Sch. Law. Civil law editor Rico Law Reporter; mem. adv. bd. Corp. Confidentiality and Disclosure Letter; hon. adv. com. Jour. Internat. Law and Practice, Detroit Coll. Law; contbr. articles to legal jours. Scoutmaster Vienna coun. Boy Scouts Am., 1984. Recipient spl. achievement award Justice Dept., 1977, spl. commendation, 1978, Outstanding Achievement award Detroit Coll. of Law, 1993. Mem. ABA (chmn. criminal law com., sect. bus. law 1996—), Va. Bar, D.C. Bar (chmn. litigation sect. 1987-89, vice-chmn. coun. sects. 1988-89), Assn. Securities & Exch. Commn. Alumni (pres. 1993-95), Phi Beta Kappa, Eta Sigma Phi. Roman Catholic. Federal civil litigation, State civil litigation, Securities. Home: 1713 Paisley Blue Ct Vienna VA 22182-2326

**RAZZANO, PASQUALE ANGELO,** lawyer; b. Bklyn., Apr. 3, 1943; s. Pasquale Anthony and Agnes Mary (Borgia) R.; m. Maryann Walker, Jan. 29, 1966; children: Elizabeth, Pasquale, Susan, ChristyAnn. BSCE, Poly. Inst. Bklyn., 1964; student law, NYU, 1964-66; JD, Georgetown U., 1969. Bar: Va. 1969, N.Y. 1970, U.S. Ct. Appeals (2d, 3d, 7th, 9th and fed. cirs.), U.S. Supreme Ct., U.S. Dist. Ct. (so., ea. and western dists.) N.Y., U.S. Dist. Ct. (we. dist.) Tex., U.S. Dist. Ct. Hawaii, U.S. Dist. Ct. Conn. Examiner U.S. Patent Office, 1966-69; assoc. Curtis, Morris & Safford, P.C., 1969-71, ptnr., 1971-91; ptnr. Fitzpatrick, Cella, Harper & Scinto, 1991—; guest lectr. U.S. Trademark Assn., Am. Intellectual Property Law Assn., Practicing Law Inst., NYU Law Ctr., ABA, N.Y. Intellectual Property Law Assn. Mem. bd. editors Licensing Jour., 1986—; mem. bd. editors Trademark Reporter, 1987—, book rev. editor, 1989-91, pub. articles editor, 1991-94, domestic articles editor, 1992-93, 95, editor-in-chief 1996—. Rep. committeeman Rockland County. Recipient Robert Ridgeway award, 1964. Mem. ABA (guest lectr.), Fed. Bar Assn. (chmn. trademark law com. 1997—), N.Y. Intellectual Property Law Assn. (bd. dirs. 1985—, sec. 1988-91, pres. 1994-95), Licensing Exec. Soc. (chmn. N.Y. chpt. 1996—), Internat. Trademark Assn. (bd. dirs. 1996—), Am. Intellectual Property Law Assn., N.Y. Bar Assn., N.Y. Coun. Bar Leaders (exec. coun. 1993-94), Va. Bar Assn., Italian Am. Bar Assn., Bar Assn. City N.Y., Columban Laws Assn., N.Y. Athletic Club, Minute Man Yacht Club, Shorehaven Golf Club. Republican. Roman Catholic. Patent, Trademark and copyright, Federal civil litigation. Address: 21 Covelee Dr Westport CT 06880-6407 also: 14 Deerwood Trl Lake Placid NY 12946-1834

**RE, EDWARD DOMENIC,** law educator, retired federal judge; b. Santa Marina, Italy, Oct. 14, 1920; s. Anthony and Marina (Maetta) R.; m. Margaret A. Corcoran, June 3, 1950; children: Mary Ann, Anthony John, Marina, Edward, Victor, Margaret, Matthew, Joseph, Mary Elizabeth, Mary Joan, Mary Ellen, Nancy Madeleine. BS cum laude, St. John's U., 1941, LLB summa cum laude, 1943, LLD (hon.), 1968; JSD, NYU, 1950; DPed, Aquila, Italy, 1960; LL.D. (hon.), St. Mary's Coll., Notre Dame, Ind., 1968, Maryville Coll., St. Louis, 1969, N.Y. Law Sch., 1976, Bklyn. Coll., CUNY, 1978, Nova U., 1980, Roger Williams Coll., 1982, Dickinson Sch. Law, Carlisle, Pa., 1983, Seton Hall U., 1984, Stetson U., 1990, William Mitchell Coll. Law, 1992, St. Francis Coll., Bklyn., 1993; L.H.D. (hon.), DePaul U., 1980, Coll. S.I., CUNY, 1981, Pace U., 1985, Am. U. of Rome, 1995; D.C.S. (hon.), U. Verona, Italy, 1987; J.D. (hon.), U. Bologna, Italy, 1988, U. Urbino, Italy, 1994. Bar: N.Y. 1943. Appointed faculty St. John's U., N.Y., 1947, prof. law, 1951-69, adj. prof. law, 1969-80, Disting. prof., from 1980; vis. prof. Georgetown U. Sch. Law, 1962-67; adj. prof. law N.Y. Law Sch., 1972-82, Martin disting. vis. prof., 1982-90; spl. hearing officer U.S. Dept. Justice, 1956-61; chmn. Fgn. Claims Settlement Commn. of U.S., 1961-68; asst. sec. ednl. and cultural affairs U.S. Dept. State, 1968-69; judge U.S. Customs Ct. (now U.S. Ct. Internat. Trade), N.Y.C., 1969-91, chief judge, 1977-91, chief judge emeritus, 1991—; mem. Jud. Conf. U.S., 1986-91, adv. com. on appellate rules, 1976-88, com. on internat. jud. rels., 1994-97; chmn. adv. com. on experimentation in the law Fed. Jud. Ctr., 1978-81; mem. bd. higher edn. City of N.Y., 1958-69, emeritus, 1969—; Jackson lectr. Nat. Coll. State Trial Judges, U. Nev., 1970. Author: Foreign Confiscations in Anglo-American Law, 1951, (with Lester D. Orfield) Cases and Materials on International Law, rev. edit., 1965, Selected Essays on Equity, 1955, Brief Writing and Oral Argument, 6th edit., 1987, (with Joseph R. Re) 7th edit., 1993, (with Zechariah Chafee Jr.) Cases and Materials on Equity, 1967, Cases and Materials on Equitable Remedies, 1975; (with Joseph R. Re) Law Students' Manual on Legal Writing and Oral Argument, 1991; chpt., freedom in internat. soc. Concept of Freedom (editor Rev. Carl W. Grindel), 1955; Cases and Materials on Remedies, 1982, (with Joseph R. Re) 4th edit., 1996; contbr. articles to legal jours. Served with USAAF, 1943-47; col. JAGC, ret. Decorated Grand Cross Order of Merit Italy; recipient Am. Bill of Rights citation; Morgenstern Found. Interfaith award; USAF commendation medal; Distinguished service award Bklyn. Jr. C. of C., 1956. Mem. ABA (ho. of dels. 1976-78, chmn. sect. internat. and comparative law 1965-67), Am. Fgn. Law Assn. (pres. 1971-73), Am. Law Inst., Fed. Bar Coun. (pres. 1973-74), Am. Soc. Comparative Law (pres. 1969-91), Am. Justinian Soc. Jurists (pres. 1974-76), Internat. Assn. Jurists: Italy-USA (pres. 1991—), Internat. Assn. Judges (prin. rep. to UN 1993—), Scribes Am. Soc. Writers on Legal Subjects (pres. 1978). Office: 305 B 147th St Neponsit NY 11694

**REA, WILLIAM J.,** judge; b. 1920. BA, Loyola U., 1942; LLB, U. Colo., 1949. With U.S. Census Bur., Denver, 1949-50; adjuster Farmers Ins. Group, L.A., 1950; pvt. practice law L.A., 1950-64, Santa Ana, Calif., 1964-68; judge Superior Ct., L.A., 1968-84; judge U.S. Dist. Ct. (cen. dist.) Calif., L.A., 1984—, sr. judge. Past pres. L.A. chpt. Nat. Exec. Com.; chmn. Constrn. and By-Law Com. With USN, WWII. Mem. L.A. County Bar Assn. (Outstanding Jurist award 1985), So. Calif. Def. Counsel Assn. (Disting. Svc. award 1982), Internat. Acad. Trial Lawyers (Trial Judge of Yr. 1982), L.A. Trial Lawyers Assn., Am. Bd. Trial Advs. (nat. pres.), L.A. County Bar Assn. (Trial Judge of Yr. 1985). Office: US Dist Ct 312 N Spring St Los Angeles CA 90012-4701

**READ, NICHOLAS CARY,** lawyer; b. Florence, Italy, Nov. 9, 1951; came to U.S., 1952; s. Forrest Godfrey III and Virginia (Cary) R.; m. Anne Parker Renfro, May 16, 1976; children: Sarah, Joanna. BFA, U. N.C., 1974; MA in History, U. Va., 1979, JD, 1982. Bar: Mass., U.S. Dist. Ct. Mass. Assoc. Craig & Mocauley, Boston, 1982-85; counsel N.E. Merchants Leasing Co., Boston, 1985-87; sr. counsel Boston Safe Deposit and Trust Co., Boston, 1987—. Banking, Consumer commercial, Contracts commercial. Office: Boston Safe Deposit & Trust Co 1 Boston Pl Boston MA 02108-4407

**READY, WILLIAM ALVA, III,** lawyer; b. Columbia, S.C., Jan. 11, 1955; s. William A. Jr. and Susie Ready; m. Deborah Boyles Gresham, May 21, 1977 (div. Dec. 1990); children: Rebekah Lynn, Deborah Leigh; m. Diana Carol Cook, Sept. 13, 1997. BA, Clemson U., 1977; JD, U. S.C., 1980. Bar: S.C. 1980, U.S. Dist. Ct. S.C. 1984, U.S. Ct. Appeals (4th cir.) 1986. Asst. solicitor Lexington (S.C.) County Solicitor's Office, 1980-84; asst. atty. gen. Office of the Atty. Gen., Columbia, 1984-87; staff counsel S.C. Dept. Health and Environ. Control, Columbia, 1987—; organizer, dir. S.C. 1st Juvenile Arbitration Program for 1st Offenders, Lexington, 1983-84. Mem. Nat. Assn. Atty. Gens., S.C. Bar Assn., Phi Kappa Phi. Baptist. Avocations: reading, spending time with family, movies, church. Administrative and regulatory, Environmental, Health. Home: 1205 Baffin Bay Rd Columbia SC 29212-3308 Office: SC Dept Health Environ Control 2600 Bull St Columbia SC 29201-1708

**REAGAN, GARY DON,** state legislator, lawyer; b. Amarillo, Tex., Aug. 23, 1941; s. Hester and Lois Irene (Marcum) R.; m. Nedra Ann Nash, Sept. 12, 1964; children: Marc, Kristi, Kari, Brent. BA, Stanford U., 1963, JD, 1965. Bar: N.Mex. 1965, U.S. Dist. Ct. N.Mex., 1965, U.S. Supreme Ct. 1986. Assoc. Smith & Ransom, Albuquerque, 1965-67; ptnr. Smith, Ransom, Deaton & Reagan, Albuquerque, 1967-68, Williams, Johnson, Houston, Reagan & Porter, Hobbs, N.Mex., 1968-77, Williams, Johnson, Reagan, Porter & Love, Hobbs, 1977-82; pvt. practice, Hobbs, 1982—; city atty. City of Hobbs, 1978-80, 97—, City of Eunice, N.M., 1980—; mem. N.Mex. State Senate, 1993-96; instr. N.Mex. Jr. Coll. and Coll. of S.W., Hobbs, 1978-84; N.Mex. commr. Nat. Conf. Commrs. Uniform State Laws, 1993-96; adv. mem. N.Mex. Constl. Revision Commn., 1993-95. Mayor, City of Hobbs, 1972-73, 76-77, city commr., 1970-78; pres., dir. Jr. Achievement of Hobbs, 1974-85; pres., trustee Landsun Homes, Inc., Carlsbad, N.Mex., 1972-84; trustee Lydia Patterson Inst., El Paso, Tex., 1972-84, N.Mex. Conf. United Meth. Ch., 1988—, Coll. of S.W., Hobbs, 1989—; chmn. County Democratic Com., 1983-85. Mem. ABA, State Bar N.Mex. (coms. 1989-96, v.p. 1992-93, pres. 1994-95), Lea County Bar Assn. (pres. 1976-77), Hobbs C. of C. (pres. 1989-90), Rotary (pres. Hobbs 1985-86), Hobbs Tennis (pres. 1974-75). Home: 200 E Eagle Dr Hobbs NM 88240-5323 Office: 501 N Linam St Hobbs NM 88240-5715

**REAGAN, HARRY EDWIN, III,** lawyer; b. Wichita, Kans., Sept. 9, 1940; s. Harry E. II and Mary Elizabeth (O'Steen) R.; m. Marvene R. Rogers, June 17, 1965; children: Kathleen, Leigh, Mairen. BS, U. Pa., 1962, JD, 1965. Bar: Pa. 1965, U.S. Dist. Ct. (ea. dist.) Pa. 1965, U.S. Ct. Appeals (3d cir.) 1965. From assoc. to ptnr. Morgan, Lewis & Bockius, Phila., 1965-98. Chmn. Northhampton Twp. Planning Commn., Bucks County, Pa., 1974-79; mem. Warwick Twp. Planning Commn., 1980-95, chmn., 1994; supr. Warwick Twp., 1996-98; chmn. San Miguel County (Colo.) Open Space Commn., 1998—, Town of Telluride Open Space Commn., 1999—. Mem. ABA (labor sect.), Pa. Bar Assn. (labor sect.), Phila. Bar Assn. (labor sect.), Indsl. Rels. Assn. (pres. Phila. chpt. 1990-91). Republican. Presbyterian. Avocations: coaching rugby, skiing, raising horses, bicycling. Labor, Pension, profit-sharing, and employee benefits. Home and Office: 12350 McKenzie Springs Rd Placerville CO 81430

**REAGLE, JACK EVAN,** lawyer; b. Sharon, Pa., Feb. 26, 1957; s. James Leroy and Barbara (Sarchet) R. BA, Edinboro State Coll., 1979; student, Calif. Western U., 1979-80; JD, U. Akron, 1982. Bar: Pa. 1982, U.S. Dist. Ct. (we. dist.) Pa. 1983, U.S. Supreme Ct. 1988. Pvt. practice Hermitage, Pa., 1982-84; atty. Northwestern Legal Svcs., Coudersport, Pa., 1984—; pvt. practice Coudersport, 1988—; pub. defender Potter County, Coudersport, 1984-87. Contbr. articles to profl. jours. Mem. ABA, Pa. Bar Assn., Assn. Trail Lawyers Am., Phi Alpha Delta. Republican. Criminal, Family and matrimonial, General practice. Office: 37418 Legends Trail Dr Farmington Hills MI 48331

**REAL, CATHERINE WILLIAMS,** lawyer; b. Detroit, Dec. 5, 1946. BA, Fla. Atlantic U., 1967, postgrad.; JD, Stetson U., 1978. Bar: Fla. 1979, U.S. Dist. Ct. (mid. dist.) Fla., U.S. Ct. Appeals (11th cir.). Staff dir. Fla. Senate, Tallahassee; asst. state atty. 13th Jud. Circuit, Tampa, Fla.; mng. ptnr. Muga & Real, PA, Tampa, 1981-98; pvt. practice, Tampa, 1998—; staff dir. health and rehab. svc. com. Fla. Senate, Tallahassee; Founder CourtWatch Hillsborough County Inc., Tampa, 1996—; bd. dirs. The Spring, Tampa. Recipient award for outstanding victim advocacy Victim's Voice, Tampa, 1993, 95; cert. of appreciation Ctr. for Women, Tampa, 1994, 96, Outstanding Vol. award, 1995. Mem. ATLA, Am. Acad. Trial Lawyers, Hillsborough County Bar Assn. Family and matrimonial. Office: 2110 W Platt St Tampa FL 33606-1759

**REAL, MANUEL LAWRENCE,** federal judge; b. San Pedro, Calif., Jan. 27, 1924; s. Francisco Jose and Maria (Mansano) R.; m. Stella Emilia Michalik, Oct. 15, 1955; children: Michael, Melanie Marie, Timothy, John Robert. B.S., U. So. Calif., 1944, student fgn. trade, 1946-48; LL.B., Loyola Sch. Law, Los Angeles, 1951. Bar: Calif. 1952. Asst. U.S. Atty.'s Office, Los Angeles, 1952-55; pvt. practice law San Pedro, Calif., 1955-64; U.S. atty. So. Dist. Calif., 1964-66; judge U.S. Dist. Ct. (cen. dist.) Calif., L.A., 1966—. Served to ensign USNR, 1943-46. Mem. Am., Fed., Los Angeles County bar assns., State Bar Calif., Am. Judicature Soc., Chief Spl. Agts. Assn., Phi Delta Phi, Sigma Chi. Roman Catholic. Club: Anchor (Los Angeles). Office: US Dist Ct 312 N Spring St Ste 217P Los Angeles CA 90012-4704

**REAM, DAVIDSON,** law publications administrator, writer; b. Ossining, N.Y., May 2, 1937; s. Joseph H. and Anita (Biggs) R.; m. Judith Krampitz, Oct. 1, 1966; children: Michael E., Caitlin D. BA, Yale U., 1961; JD, U. Va., 1964; LLM, U. Calif., Berkeley, 1971. Bar: D.C. 1972. Spl. asst. Supreme Ct. of Pakistan, 1964-65; law program developer The Asia Found., San Francisco and Sri Lanka, 1966-69; rsch. atty. Continuing Edn. of the Bar, Berkeley, 1970-75; publ. dir. ABA, Chgo., 1975-78; publ. mgr. Callaghan & Co., Wilmette, Ill., 1978-83; publs. dir. Def. Rsch. Inst., Chgo., 1984—. Editor: Condemnation Practice in California, 1973, Landslide and Subsidence Liability, 1974, Attorney's Guide to Professional Responsibility, 1978, Products Liability Pretrial Notebook, 1989, Product Liability Defenses, 1992; editor For The Defense, 1984—. Pres. Ridgeville Assn., Evanston, Ill., 1977-81, Mental Health Assn., Evanston, 1992-95; alderman City of Evanston, 1983-87; bd. dirs. Dem. Party Evanston, 1978-90. Mem. ABA, D.C. Bar Assn. Avocations: hiking, camping, travel, community affairs. Home: 214 Oak Grove St Apt 203 Minneapolis MN 55403-3312 Office: Def Rsch Inst 150 N Michigan Ave Chicago IL 60601-7553

**REAMS, BERNARD DINSMORE, JR.,** lawyer, educator; b. Lynchburg, Va., Aug. 17, 1943; s. Bernard Dinsmore and Martha Eloise (Hickman) R.; m. Rosemarie Bridget Boyle, Oct. 26, 1968 (dec. Oct. 1996); children: Andrew Dennet, Adriane Bevin. BA, Lynchburg Coll., 1965; MS, Drexel U., 1966; JD, U. Kans., 1972; PhD, St. Louis U., 1983. Bar: Kans. 1973, Mo. 1986, N.Y. 1996. Instr., asst. librarian Rutgers U., 1966-69; asst. prof. law, librarian U. Kans., Lawrence, 1969-74; mem. faculty law sch. Washington U., St. Louis, 1974-95, prof. law, 1976-95, prof. tech. mgmt., 1990-95, librarian, 1974-76, acting dean univ. libraries, 1987-88; prof. law, assoc. dean, dir. Law Libr. St. John's U. Sch. Law, Jamaica, N.Y., 1995-97; assoc. dean acad. affairs St. John's U. Sch. Law, Jamaica, 1997-98; prof. law St. John's U. Sch. Law, Jamaica, N.Y., 1998—; vis. fellow Max-Planck Inst., Hamburg, 1995, 97, 98; vis. prof. law Seton Hall U., 1999—. Author: Law For The Businessman, 1974, Reader in Law Librarianship, 1976, Federal Price and Wage Control Programs 1917-1979: Legis. Histories and Laws, 1980, Education of the Handicapped: Laws, Legislative Histories, and Administrative Documents, 1982, Housing and Transportation of the Handicapped: Laws and Legislative Histories, 1983, Internal Revenue Acts of the United States: The Revenue Act of 1954 with Legislative Histories and Congressional Documents, 1983 Congress and the Courts: A Legislative History 1978-1984, 1984, University-Industry Research Partnerships: The Major Issues in Research and Development Agreements, 1986, Deficit Control and the Gramm-Rudman-Hollings Act, 1986, The Semiconductor Chip and the Law: A Legislative History of the Semiconductor Chip Protection Act of 1984, 1986, American International Law Cases, 2d series, 1986, Technology Transfer Law: The Export Administration Acts of the U.S., 1987, Insider Trading and the Law: A Legislative History of the Insider Trading Sanctions Act, 1989, Insider Trading and Securities Fraud, 1989, The Health Care Quality Improvement Act of 1989: A Legislative History of P.L. No. 99-660, 1990; The National Organ Transplant Act of 1984: A Legislative History of P.L. No. 98-507, 1990, A Legislative History of Individuals with Disabilities Education Act, 1994, Federal Legislative Histories: An Annotated Bibliography and Index to Officially Published Sources, 1994, Electronic Contracting Law, 1996, Health Care Reform, 1994, The American Experience: Clinton and Congress, 1997, The Omnibus Anti-Crime Act, 1997; co-author: Segregation and the Fourteenth Amendment in the States, 1975, Historic Preservation Law: An Annotated Bibliography, 1976, Congress and the Courts: A Legislative History 1787-1977, 1978, Federal Consumer Protection Laws, Rules and Regulations, 1979, A Guide and Analytical Index to the Internal Revenue Acts of the U.S., 1909-1950, 1979, The Numerical Lists and Schedule of Volumes of the U.S. Congressional Serial Set: 73d Congress through the 96th Congress, 1984, Human Experimentation: Federal Laws, Legislative Histories, Regulations and Related Documents, 1985, American Legal Literature: A Guide to Selected Legal Resources, 1985, The Constitution of the United States: A Guide and Bibliography, 1987, The Congressional Impeachment Process and the Judiciary, 1987, Tax Reform 1986: A Legislative History of the Tax Refrom Act of 1986, 1988, The Constitutions of the States: A State by State Guide and Bibliography, 1988, Executive and Professional Employment Contracts, 1988, The Legislative History of the Export Trading Company Act of 1982 Including the Foreign Trade Antitrust Improvements Act, 1989, Federal Deficit Control, 1989, The Legislative History of the Export Trading Company Act of 1982 Including the Foreign Trade Antitrust Improvements Act, 1989, United States-Canada Free Trade Act: A Legislative History, 1990, Trade Reform Legislation 1988: A Legislative History of the Omnibus Trade and Competitiveness Act of 1988, 1992, Disability Law in the United States, 1992, Bankruptcy Reform Amendments, 1992, The Law of Hospital and Health Care Administration: Case and Materials, 1993, The Civil Rights Act of 1991: A Legislative History, 1994, The North American Free Trade Agreement, 1994, Catalonia, Spain, Europe, and Latin America: Regional Legal Systems and their Literature, 1995, A Legislative History of the Prison Litigation Reform Act of 1996, 1997, Federal Backruptcy Law: A Legislative History of the Bankruptcy Reform Act of 1994, 1998, A Legislative History of the International Antitrust Enforcement Assistance Act of 1994, 1998. Bd. trustees Quincy Found. for Med. Rsch. Charitable Trust, San Francisco. Fellow Am. Bar Foun.; recipient Thornton award for excellence Lynchburg Coll., 1986, Joseph L. Andrews Bibliog. award, 1995; named to Hon. Order Ky. Cols., 1992. Mem. ABA, Am. Law Inst., ALA, Am. Soc. Law and Medicine, Nat. Health Lawyers Assn., Am. Assn. Higher Edn., Spl. Librs. Assn., Internat. Assn. Law Libr. Coll. and Univ. Attys., Order of Coif, Phi Beta Kappa, Sigma Xi, Beta Phi Mu, Phi Delta Phi, Phi Delta Epsilon, Kappa Delta Pi, Pi Lambda Theta. Office: Seton Hall U Sch Law One Newark Ctr Newark NJ 07102-5210

**REARDON, FRANK EMOND,** lawyer; b. Providence, May 22, 1953; s. J. Clarke and Dorothy (Emond) R.; m. Deborah Walsh, Sept. 30, 1978; children: Kathleen Elizabeth, Brendan Francis, William James, Sean Patrick. BA, Holy Cross Coll., Worcester, Mass., 1975; JD, Suffolk U., 1978; MS, Harvard U., 1981. Bar: Mass. 1978, R.I. 1978, U.S. Dist. Ct. Mass. 1980, U.S. Dist. Ct. R.I. 1980, U.S. Supreme Ct. 1986. Counsel Nat. Assn. Govtl. Employment and Internat. Brotherhood Police Officers, Cranston, R.I., 1978-81; asst. gen. counsel Brigham and Women's Hosp., Boston, 1981-84; litigation counsel Risk Mgmt. Found. Harvard Med. Instns., Cambridge, Mass., 1984-87; ptnr. Hassan and Reardon, Boston, 1987—; chmn. bd. dirs. St. Monica's Nursing Home, 1984-89, Med. Area Fed. Credit Union, 1984-89; clk., trustee Deaconness Glover Hosp., Needham, Mass.; ethics com. Boston Children's Hosp., 1993-96. Contbr. articles to profl. jours. Chmn. fin. com. Town of Needham, Mass.; mem. pres.'s council Coll. Holy Cross, 1985—. Beuilacqua scholar, 1978. Mem. ABA, Mass. Bar Assn. (chmn. health law sect. 1987—), Assn. Trial Lawyers Am., Am. Soc. Law and Medicine (cmty. rep. children's hosp. ethics com.). Democrat. Roman Catholic. Avocations: tennis, sailing, golf, writing. Health, General civil litigation, Labor. Home: 44 Sargent St Needham MA 02492-3434 Office: Hassan & Reardon 535 Boylston St Boston MA 02116-3720

**REARDON, JAMES PATRICK,** lawyer; b. Milw., Apr. 7, 1936; s. Paul C. and Elinor C. (Hupfer) R.; m. Mary M. King; children: Tim, Kathleen, Dan, Patty, Kevin, Colleen, Brian. BS, Marquette U., MIlw., 1957, JD, 1960. Bar: Wis. 1960, U.S. Dist. Ct. (ea. dist.) Wis. 1960, U.S. Dist. Ct. (we. dist.) Wis. 1982, U.S. Ct. MIl. Appeals 1967, U.S. Supreme Ct. 1967, U.S. Ct. Appeals (7th Cir.) 1972. Assoc. Kasdorf, Lewis & Swietlik, S.C. and predecessor firms, Milw., 1960—. Bd. dirs. Woolsack Soc.-Marquette U. Law Sch., Milw., 1994-99. Lt. comdr. USNR, 1966-88. Fellow Am. Coll. Trial Lawyers (com. mem. 1993-95); mem. Civil Trial Counsel Wis. (pres.), Wis. Bar Assn., 7th Cir. Ct. Appeals Bar Assn. Roman Catholic. Avocations: fishing, boating, skiing, snowmobiling. Workers' compensation, Personal injury, State civil litigation. Office: Kasdorf Lewis & Swietlik SC 1551 S 108th St Milwaukee WI 53214-4020

**REARDON, MARK WILLIAM,** lawyer; b. Englewood, N.J., June 7, 1956; s. Matthew Francis and Rose Mary (Snyder) R.; m. Patricia Louise Powers, Apr. 19, 1985. BA, Knox Coll., 1977; JD, Seton Hall U., 1980. Bar: N.J. 1980, U.S. Dist. Ct. N.J. 1980, U.S. Ct. Mil. Appeals 1981, Wash. 1987, U.S. Supreme Ct. 1987, U.S. Ct. Appeals (fed. cir.) 1988, Ct. of Fed. Claims 1997. Atty. The Boeing Co., Seattle, 1986—. Capt. JAGC, U.S. Army, 1981-86. Maj. JAGC USAR, 1986-95. Mem. ABA, Wash. Bar Assn. Republican. Roman Catholic. Avocations: jogging, swimming. Government contracts and claims, Computer, Federal civil litigation. Office: The Boeing Co MC 13-08 PO Box 3707 Seattle WA 98124-2207

**REARDON, ROBERT IGNATIUS, JR.,** lawyer; b. N.Y.C., Nov. 28, 1945; s. Robert I. and Mildred (Lomax) R.; m. Lise Hofffman; children: Colleen Brooke, Kelly Elizabeth. BS in Econs., Boston Coll., 1967; JD, Fordham U., 1970. Bar: Conn. 1970, U.S. Dist. Ct. Conn. 1974, U.S. Ct. Mil. Appeals 1971, U.S. Ct. Appeals (2d cir.) 1974, U.S. Supreme Ct. 1974, U.S. Ct. Claims 1986. Ptnr. Shapiro & Reardon, P.C., New London, Conn., 1973-83; pres. Reardon Law Firm P.C., New London, 1983—; state trial referee Conn. Supreme Ct., 1985—. Chmn. Bd. Fin. Town of Waterford, Conn., 1974-79; mem. Bd. Edn. Town of East Lyme, Conn., 1981-84; trustee Eugene O'Neill Meml. Theater, Inc., 1978-84. Served as capt. USMC, 1970-73. Mem. ABA (award of achievement young lawyers sect. 1975), ATLA (bd. dirs. 1998—), Conn. Trial Lawyers Assn. (pres. 1997-98), Conn. Bar Assn. (bd. govs. 1979-81, ho. of dels. 1975-79), New London County Bar Assn. (mem. exec. com. 1975-79). General civil litigation, Personal injury, Product liability. Home: 95 Quarry Dock Rd Niantic CT 06357-1908 Office: 160 Hempstead St New London CT 06320-5638

**REARDON, THOMAS MICHAEL,** lawyer; b. Meadville, Pa., Apr. 14, 1946; s. John Joseph and Agnes Devon R.; m. Anne J. Hezzey; children: Jennifer, Marion, Elizabeth, Eric. BA cum laude, Alfred U., 1968; JD, Harvard U., 1971. Bar: Mass., U.S. Dist. Ct. Mass. Atty. pvt. practice, 1971—; pres. ML Strategies, Inc.; mem. exec. com. Mintz, Levin, Chon, Ferris, Glovsky & Popeo. Co-author: Managed Care Answer Book, 1998; contbr. articles to profl. jours. Avocations: reading, horseback riding, skiing, jogging. Health. Office: Mintz Levin Cohn Ferris Glousky & Popeo 1 Fin Ctr Boston MA 02111

**REARDON, TIMOTHY P.,** lawyer; b. Milw., Dec. 11, 1962; s. James P. and Mary M. Reardon; m. Ann E. Horning, June 6, 1987; children: Patrick, Megan, Michael, Kevin. BS, Marquette U., 1985, JD, 1988. Bar: Wis. 1988. Atty. Reinhart, Boerner, Van deuren, Norris & Rieselbach, S.C., Milw., 1988—. Author comment Marquette Law Rev., 1988. Bd. dirs. Family Svc. of Milw., 1998—. Mem. Marquette H.S Alumni Assn. (bd. dirs., pres.). General corporate, Mergers and acquisitions, Corporate taxation. Office: Reinhart Boerner et al 1000 N Water St Ste 2100 Milwaukee WI 53202-3197

**REASER, WILLIAM JOHN, JR.,** lawyer; b. Stroudsburg, Pa., Apr. 8, 1949; s. William J. and Henrietta (Biggs) R.; m. Elizabeth Hintze, Aug. 2, 1969; children: Matthew Ryan, Megan Michelle. AB cum laude, Muhlenberg Coll., 1971; JD, Dickinson Sch. Law, 1974. Bar: Pa. 1974. Pvt. practice Stroudsburg, 1978—. Democrat. Lutheran. Home: RR 3 Box 3196 Stroudsburg PA 18360-9336 Office: 111 N 7th St # A Stroudsburg PA 18360-2111

**REASONER, BARRETT HODGES,** lawyer; b. Houston, Apr. 16, 1964; s. Harry Max and Macey (Hodges) R.; m. Susan Hardig; children: Matthew Joseph, Caroline Macey, William Harry. BA cum laude, Duke U., 1986; Grad. Dipl., London Sch. Econs., 1987; JD with honors, U. Tex., 1990. Bar: Tex. 1990, U.S. Dist. Ct. (so., we., and no. dists.) Tex. 1993, U.S. Ct. Appeals (5th cir.) 1993, U.S. Supreme Ct. 1997. Asst. dist. atty. Harris County Dist. Atty.'s Office, Houston, 1990-92; ptnr. Gibbs & Bruns, L.L.P., Houston, 1992—. Fellow Tex. Bar Found., Houston Bar Found.; mem. Am. Judicature Soc. (bd. dirs. 1994—, exec. com. 1997—), State Bar Tex. (jud. rels. com. 1998—), Houston Bar Assn., Houston Young Lawyers Assn. (pub. schs. and pub. edn. com. 1994—, chmn. pub. schs. and pub. edn. com. 1997—, outstanding com. chair 1999), Order of Barristers. Episcopalian. General civil litigation. Office: Gibbs & Bruns LLP 1100 Louisiana St Ste 5300 Houston TX 77002-5215

**REASONER, HARRY MAX,** lawyer; b. San Marcos, Tex., July 15, 1939; s. Harry Edward and Joyce Majorie (Barrett) R.; m. Elizabeth Macey Hodges, Apr. 15, 1963; children: Barrett Hodges, Elizabeth Macey Reasoner Stokes. BA in Philosophy summa cum laude, Rice U., 1960; JD with highest honors, U. Tex., 1962; postgrad., U. London, 1962-63. Bar: Tex., D.C., N.Y. Law clk. U.S. Ct. Appeals (2d cir.), 1963-64; assoc. Vinson & Elkins, Houston, 1964-69, ptnr., 1970—, mng.ptnr., 1992—; vis. prof. U. Tex. Sch. Law, 1971, Rice U., 1976, U. Houston Sch. Law, 1977; chair adv. group U.S. Dist Ct. (so. dist.) Tex.; mem. adv. com. Supreme Ct. Tex. Author: (with Charles Alan Wright) Procedure: The Handmaid of Justice, 1965. Trustee U. Tex. Law Sch. Found., Southwestern Legal Found., 1990—, Rice U., Baylor Coll. Medicine; chair Tex. Higher Edn. Coordinating Bd., 1991; bd. dirs. Houston Music Hall Found. Bd., 1996—; mem. Houston Annenberg Challenge Child Centered Schs. Initiative Bd., 1997—. Rotary Found. fellow 1962-63; named Disting. Alumnus, U. Tex., 1997, U. Tex. Sch. Law, 1998. Fellow Am. Coll. Trial Lawyers, Internat. Acad. Trial Lawyers, Internat. Soc. Barristers, ABA Found., Tex. Bar Found.; mem. ABA (chmn. antitrust sect. 1989-90), Houston Bar Assn., Assn. Bar City N.Y., Am. Law Inst., Houston Com. Fgn. Rels., Houston Philos. Soc., Philos. Soc. Tex., Am. Bd. Trial Advocates, Century Assn. N.Y.C., Houston Country Club, Eldorado Country Club (Calif.), Castle Pines Golf Club (Colo.), Cosmos Club (D.C.), Galveston Artillery Club, Chancellors, Barristers, Phi Beta Kappa, Phi Delta Phi. Antitrust, Federal civil litigation, State civil litigation. Office: Vinson & Elkins 2800 First City Tower 1001 Fannin St Houston TX 77002-6760

**REASONER, STEPHEN M.,** federal judge; b. 1944. BA in Econs., U. Ark., 1966, JD, 1969. Mem. firm Barret, Wheatley, Smith & Deacon, Jonesboro, Ark., 1969-88; from judge to chief judge U.S. Dist. Ct. (ea. dist.) Ark., Little Rock, 1988—; bd. dirs. U. Ark. Law Rev.; mem. judicial coun. 8th cir., 1990-93. Trustee Craighead-Jonesboro Pub. Libr., 1972—, chmn. 1984-88; bd. dirs. Jonesboro C. of C., 1981-84, Ark. IOLTA, 1987—, Abilities Unltd., 1974-81; mem. St. Marks Episcopal Ch. Vestry, 1976-79, sr. warden, 1979. With USAR, 1969-73. Mem. ABA, Am. Counsel Assn., Am. Judicature Soc., Ark. Bar Assn. (exec. com., ho. of dels. 1984-87), Craighead County Bar Assn. (pres. 1983-84). Avocation: flying. Office: Courthouse 600 W Capitol Ave Ste 560 Little Rock AR 72201-3327

**REATH, GEORGE, JR.,** lawyer; b. Phila., Mar. 14, 1939; s. George and Isabel Duer (West) R.; children from a previous marriage: Eric (dec. 1995), Amanda; m. Ann B. Rowland, 1990. BA, Williams Coll., 1961; LLB, Harvard U., 1964. Bar: Pa. 1965, U.S. Dist. Ct. (ea. dist.) Pa. 1966, U.S. Ct. Appeals (3d cir.) 1996. Assoc. Dechert Price & Rhoads, Phila., 1964-70, Brussels, 1971-74; atty. Pennwalt Corp., Phila., 1974-78, mgr. legal dept., asst. sec., 1978-87, sr. v.p.-law, sec., 1987-89; sr. v.p., gen. counsel, sec. Elf Atochem N.Am., Inc. (formerly Pennwalt Corp.), Phila., 1990-92; sr. v.p., gen counsel, sec. Legal Triage Svcs., Inc., Phila., 1993-98; sr. v.p., gen. counsel, sec. Triage Mediation Svcs., Inc., Phila., 1999—; bd. dirs. Internat. Bus. Forum, Inc., 1978-91; arbitrator Am. Arbitration Assn. Trustee Children's Hosp., Phila., 1974—, sec., 1980-81, vice chmn., 1984-97; bd. mgrs. Phila. City Inst. Libr., 1974—, treas., 1981-88, pres., 1989-99; bd. dirs. Phila. Festival Theatre for New Plays, 1983-94, Ctrl. Phila. Devel. Corp., 1987-93; bd. dirs. Bach Festival Phila., 1990-98, v.p., 1992-93; bd. dirs. Crime Commn. Delaware Valley, 1st vice chmn., 1992-94, chmn., 1994-96; exec. com., 1996—; bd. coun. mem. Episcopal Cmty. Svcs. 1999—. Mem. ABA, Am. Arbitration Assn., Pa. Bar Assn., Phila. Bar Assn., Penllyn Club, Winter Harbor Yacht Club, Am. Corp. Counsel Assn., Penn Club, Soc. Profls. in Dispute Resolution (assoc.), Phi Beta Kappa. General corporate, Contracts commercial, Alternative dispute resolution.

**REAVES, CRAIG CHARLES,** lawyer, educator; b. Pickstown, S.D., May 28, 1952; s. Charles William and Yvonne Joan (Ericson) R.; m. Val Gulbranson, Dec. 28, 1971; children: Nathan, Aaron. BA in Bus. and Polit. Sci., U. Kans., 1975, JD, 1978. Bar: Kans. 1978, U.S. Dist. Ct. Kans. 1978, Mo. 1980, U.S. Dist. Ct. (we. dist.) Mo. 1980, U.S. Tax Ct. 1984; CLU; chartered fin. cons.; cert. elder law atty. Nat. Elder Law Found. Counsel, agt., mgr., dir. mktg. John Hancock Life Ins. Co., Kansas City, Mo., 1972-80; officer, instr. Creative Fin. Cons., Inc., Overland Park, Kans., 1979-96; sole practice Kansas City, 1980-84, 88-90; mem., officer, dir. Crews, Smart, South, Whitehead, Reaves & Waits P.C., Kansas City, 1984-88; pres., dir. Reaves & Haynes, P.C., Kansas City, 1990-92, Reaves Law Firm, P.C., Kansas City, 1992—; founder Reaves Ednl. Sys., 1997—. Dir., officer Respite Care Svcs., 1988—; bd. dirs., sec. Greater Kansas City Arthritis Found., 1988-97, Mid-Am. Planned Giving Coun., 1988-91; chmn. Planned Giving Com., 1997—; bd. dirs., pres. Life Care Planning, 1988—; bd. dirs. Kansas City Fellowship Christian Athletes, 1979-86, chmn. bd. dirs., 1982-85; com. chmn. Kansas City Arts Festival, 1985. Mem. Nat. Acad. Elder Law Attys., Am. Acad. Estate Planning Attys., CLU Assn. (instr. 1980—, com. chmn. 1985), Estate Planning Soc. Kansas City, Phi Alpha Delta (justice 1976-78), Delta Sigma Pi (sec. 1974-75). Republican. Presbyterian. Estate planning, General corporate, Probate. Office: Reaves Law Firm 4400 Madison Ave Kansas City MO 64111-3407

**REAVLEY, THOMAS MORROW,** federal judge; b. Quitman, Tex., June 21, 1921; s. Thomas Mark and Mattie (Morrow) R.; m. Florence Montgomery Wilson, July 24, 1943; children—Thomas Wilson, Marian, Paul Stuart, Margaret. B.A., U. Tex., 1942; J.D., Harvard, 1948; LL.D., Austin Coll., 1974, Southwestern U., 1977, Tex. Wesleyan, 1982; LL.M., U. Va., 1983; LLD, Pepperdine U., 1993. Bar: Tex. 1948. Asst. dist. atty. Dallas, 1948-49; mem. firm Bell & Reavley, Nacogdoches, Tex., 1949-51; county atty. Nacogdoches, 1951; with Collins, Garrison, Renfro & Zeleskey, 1951-52; mem. firm Fisher, Tonahill & Reavley, Jasper, Tex., 1952-55; sec. state Tex., 1955-57; mem. firm Powell, Rauhut, McGinnis & Reavley, Austin, Tex., 1957-64; dist. judge Austin, 1964-68; justice Supreme Ct., Tex., 1968-77; counsel Scott & Douglass, 1977-79; judge U.S. Ct. Appeals (5th cir.), Austin, 1979-90; now sr. judge U.S. Ct. Appeals (5th cir.), Austin, TX, 1990—; lectr. Baylor U. Law Sch., 1976-94; adj. prof. U. Tex. Law Sch., 1958-59, 78-79, 88-95. Chancellor S.W. Tex. conf. United Meth. Ch., 1972-93, chancellor emeritus, 1993—. Lt. USNR, 1943-45. Club: Mason (33 deg.). Office: US Ct Appeals Homer Thornberry Judicial Bldg 903 San Jacinto Blvd Ste 434 Austin TX 78701-2450

**REBACK, JOYCE ELLEN,** lawyer; b. Phila., July 11, 1948; d. William and Sue (Goldstein) R.; m. Itzhak Brook, Aug. 2, 1981; children: Jonathan Zev, Sara Jennie. BA magna cum laude, Brown U., 1970; JD with honors, George Washington U., 1976. Bar: D.C. 1976, U.S. Dist. Ct. D.C. 1976, U.S. Ct. Appeals (D.C. cir.) 1976, U.S. Ct. Appeals (3d cir.) 1983, U.S. Ct. Appeals (Fed. cir.) 1985. Assoc. Fulbright & Jaworski, Washington, 1976-84, ptnr., 1984-87; legal cons. IMF, Washington, 1987—. Contbr. articles to profl. jours. Mem. ABA, D.C. Bar Assn., Phi Beta Kappa. Jewish. Office: Internat Monetary Fund 700 19th St NW Washington DC 20431-0001

**REBACK, RICHARD NEAL,** lawyer; b. Knoxville, Tenn., Feb. 9, 1954; s. Theodore and Delores (Robinson) R.; m. Kathryn Ann Gellens, Aug. 7, 1988; children: Jessica, Joshua, Matthew. BA magna cum laude, Duke U., 1976; JD with honors, U. Tex, 1979. Bar: Tex. 1980, U.S. Ct. Appeals (5th cir.) 1980, D.C. 1981, U.S. Ct. Appeals (D.C. cir.). Law clk. to assoc. judge U.S. Ct. Appeals (5th cir.), Austin, Tex., 1979-80; assoc. Wilmer, Cutler & Pickering, Washington, 1981-83, Swidler & Berlin, Washington, 1984-87; asst. U.S. atty. Washington, 1987-95; chief of staff, counselor to Insp. Gen. U.S. Dept. Interior, Washington, 1995-99, counsel Insp. Gen., 1999—; Mem. Ballston Ptnrship., Arlington, Va., 1986-89. Note editor: Tex. Law Rev., 1978-79. Mem. Ballston-Va. Sq. Civic Assn., Arlington, 1985-89, Am. Israel Pub. Affairs Com., Washington, 1984—; pres. Vernon Sq. Assn., Arlington, 1986-89. Mem. ABA, D.C. Bar Assn., Tex. Bar Assn., Pi Sigma Alpha, Phi Eta Sigma. Democrat. Jewish. Avocations: athletics, civic and political activities. Federal civil litigation, Administrative and regulatory. Home: 11209 Korman Dr Potomac MD 20854-2049

**REBANE, JOHN T.,** lawyer; b. Bamberg, Germany, Oct. 29, 1946; s. Henn and Anna (Inna) R.; m. Linda Kay Morgan, Sept. 22, 1972; children: Alexis Morgan, Morgan James. BA, U. Minn., 1970, JD, 1973. Bar: Minn. 1973. Atty. Land O'Lakes, Inc., Arden Hills, Minn., 1973-80; assoc. gen. counsel Land O'Lakes, Inc., Arden Hills, 1983, v.p., gen. counsel, 1984—; sec. Cenex Land O'Lakes Agronomy Co.; sec., dir. Land O' Lakes Internat. Devel. Corp. Mem. ABA, Minn. Bar Assn., Hennepin County Bar Assn., Nat. Coun. Farm Coop. (exec. com. chmn.). General corporate, Contracts commercial, Mergers and acquisitions. Office: Land O'Lakes Inc PO Box 64101 Saint Paul MN 55164-0101

**REBER, DAVID JAMES,** lawyer; b. Las Vegas, Nev., Mar. 1, 1944; s. James Rice and Helen Ruth (Cusick) R.; m. Jacqueline Yee, Aug. 31, 1968; children: Emily, Brad, Cecily. BA, Occidental Coll., L.A., 1965; JD, Harvard U., 1968. Bar: Calif. 1969, Hawaii 1975, U.S. Dist. Ct. Hawaii, U.S. Ct. Appeals (9th cir.), U.S. Supreme Ct. Asst. prof. law U. Iowa, Iowa City, 1968-70; assoc. Sheppard Mullin Richter & Hampton, L.A., 1970-75, Goodsill Anderson Quinn & Stifel, Honolulu, 1975-76; ptnr. Goodsill Anderson Quinn & Stifel, 1976—. Dir. Oahu Econ. Devel. Bd., Honolulu, Hawaii Appleseed Pub. Interest Law Ctr., Honolulu. Mem. ABA (bus., antitrust and pub. utilities sects.), Hawaii Bar Assn. Avocations: golf, tennis, softball, travel. Mergers and acquisitions, Securities, General corporate. Office: Goodsill Anderson Quinn & Stifel 1099 Alakea St Honolulu HI 96813-4511

**REBER, JOSEPH E.,** lawyer; b. Butte, Mont., Aug. 9, 1940; s. Joseph B. and Marie Terry (Tauriainen) R. BA in Hist., U. Mont., 1962, JD, 1965; LLM in Tax, NYU, 1982. Bar: Mont. 1965, U.S. Supreme Ct. 1970, N.Y. 1980, Calif. 1989. Law clk. Mont. Supreme Ct., Helena, 1965; ptnr. Heron & Reber, Helena, 1965-70; pvt. practice Helena, 1970-80; assoc. various law firms, N.Y.C., 1980-84; v.p. Pension & Actuarial Co., Colorado Springs, Colo., 1984-89; gen. counsel Great Am. Life Ins., L.A., 1989-90; pvt. practice Marina Del Rey, Calif., 1990—; presenter in field. Author: Trust and Tax Estate Planning, 1993; editor law rev. U. Mont., 1964-65; contbr. articles to Fin. Planning Mag., 1987-89. State chmn. Robert F. Kennedy for Pres., Mont., 1968, Senator Frank Church for Pres., 1976; del. platform com. Dem. Nat. Conv., 1976-80; active endowment steering com. L.A. Philharmonic, 1992—; dir. SOM Found., 1995—. Capt. USMSC, 1966-72. Mem. ABA (minorities vice-chmn., internat. law com. 1995—), Nat. Acad. Elder Law Attys., Calif. Bar Assn. (trust com. 1992—), Mont. State Hist. Soc. (v.p. 1979-80), Marina-Culver City Bar Assn. (pres. 1994-95), L.A. County Bar Assn. (ho. of dels.). Avocations: art, history, skiing, music, scuba. Estate planning, Estate taxation, Probate.

**REBOLLO-LOPEZ, FRANCISCO,** territory supreme court justice. Justice Supreme Ct. of Puerto Rico, San Juan, 1992—. Office: Supreme Court PO Box 2392 San Juan PR 00902-2392*

**RECABO, JAIME MIGUEL,** lawyer; b. Manila, Philippines, Oct. 6, 1950; came to U.S., 1969; s. Matthew M. and Luisa (De Leon) R.; children: James M., Danielle M.; m. Maureen Susan Ward, Dec. 1980; children: Matthew J., Maura E., Joseph A., Olivia M. BA, Fordham U., 1973, JD, 1988; MBA in Fin., St. John's U., 1977. Bar: N.Y. 1989, N.J. 1989, Conn. 1989. Bus. office mgr. Eger Nursing Home Inc., S.I., N.Y., 1974-77; sr. acct. Kingsbrook Jewish Med. Ctr., Bklyn., 1977-78; asst. compt. Jewish Home & Hosp. for the Aged, Bronx, N.Y., 1978-79; dir. fiscal svcs. Frances Schervier Home & Hosp., Bronx, 1979-86; exec. v.p. finance & legal affairs Franciscan Health System N.Y., Bronx, 1986-89; mgmt. cons., health and immigration atty. N.Y.C., 1989—; co-founder, exec. v.p., legal counsel Profl. Healthcare Assocs., Bronxville, N.Y., 1994—. Bd. dirs. Frances Schervier Home and Hosp., Bronx, 1987-90, Bklyn. United Meth. Ch. Home, 1991-94, Hudson Valley Med. Ctr. Found., Peekskill, N.Y., 1998—; vice-chmn. NYAHSA Contrs. Com., N.Y.C., 1985-86, N.Y. Archdiocese Contrs. Coun., N.Y.C., 1980-83. Mem. ABA, Am. Immigration Lawyers Assn., N.J. Bar Assn., N.Y. Bar Assn., Conn. Bar Assn., Healthcare Fin. Mgmt. Assn., Nat. Health Lawyers Assn., Filipino Am. Lawyers Assn. Roman Catholic. Health, Immigration, naturalization, and customs. Office: 34 Palmer Ave Bronxville NY 10708-3404

**RECILE, GEORGE B.,** lawyer; b. New Orleans, Feb. 14, 1954; s. Sam J. Recile and Annie Mary Ciolino; m. Kathryn Nicole Morgan, July 1, 1995; children: Ashley, Bryan. BA, Tulane U., 1975; JD, Loyola U., 1978. Bar: La. 1978, U.S. Dist. Ct. (ea. dist.) La. 1979, U.S. Ct. Appeals (5th cir.) 1979, U.S. Dist. Ct. (we. and mid. dists.) 1989. Staff atty. La. State Atty. Gen., New Orleans, 1978-80; assoc. Tucker & Schonekas, New Orleans, 1980-82, Law Offices Charles McHale, New Orleans, 1982-83; atty. Recile & Gould, Metairie, La., 1983-87, George B. Recile & Assocs., New Orleans, 1987-95; ptnr. Chehardy, Sherman, Ellis, Breslin & Murray, Metairie, 1995—. Past mem. New Orleans Alcoholic Beverage Control Bd., La. State Bd. Pvt. Investigators. Mem. Am. Trial Lawyers Assn., La. Trial Lawyers Assn., Acad. New Orleans Trial Lawyers, La. State Bar Assn. (ho. of dels., 24th jud. dist.). Republican. Roman Catholic. General civil litigation, Personal injury. Office: Chehardy Sherman Ellis Breslin & Murray 1 Galleria Blvd Ste 1100 Metairie LA 70001-2033

**RECTOR, JOHN MICHAEL,** association executive, lawyer; b. Seattle, Aug. 15, 1943; s. Michael Robert and Bernice Jane (Allison) R.; m. Mary Kaaren Sueta Jolly, Feb. 8, 1977 (div. 1994); m. Carmen D. Nouri, 1995; children: Christian Phillip, Ciera Rose, Zachary Ryan. BA, U. Calif., Berkeley, 1966; JD, U. Calif., Hastings, 1969; PharmD (hon.), Ark. State Bd. Pharmacy, 1991. Bar: Calif. 1970, U.S. Supreme Ct. 1974. Trial atty. civil rights div. Dept. Justice, 1969-71; dep. chief counsel judiciary com. U.S. Senate, 1971-73, counsel to Sen. Birch Bayh, 1971-77, chief counsel, staff dir., 1973-77; confirmed by U.S. Senate as assoc. adminstr. to Law Enforcement Assistance Adminstn. and adminstr. of Office Juvenile Justice Dept. Justice, 1977-79; spl. counsel to U.S. Atty. Gen., 1979-80; dir. govt. affairs Nat. Assn. Retail Druggists, Washington, 1980-85; sr. v.p. govt. affairs, gen. counsel Nat. Assn. Retail Druggists, 1986—; chmn. adv. bd. Nat. Juvenile Law Center, 1973-77; mem. Hew panel Drug Use and Criminal Behavior, 1974-77; mem. cons. panel Nat. Commn. Protection Human Subjects of Biomed. and Behavioral Research, 1975-76; mem. bd. Nat. Inst. Corrections, 1977-79; chmn. U.S. Interdepartmental Council Juvenile Justice, 1977-79; mem. bd. com. civil rights and liberties Am. Democratic Action, 1976-80, Pres.'s Com. Mental Health-Justice Group, 1978; com. youth citizenship ABA, 1978-84; mem. Pharm. Industry Adv. Com.; exec. dir., treas. polit. action com. Nat. Pharmacists Assn., 1981—; exec. dir. Retail Druggist Legal Legis. Def. Fund, 1985—, founder, chmn. Washington Pharmacy Industry Forum; mem. numerous fed. narcotic and crime panels and coms.; owner Second Genesis, an antique and furniture restoration co. Mem. editorial bd. Managed Care Law; contbr. articles to profl. jours. Exec. com. small bus. and fin. couns. Dem. Nat. Com., 1988-92; dir. Dem. Leadership Coun.'s Network, 1989-92, bd. advisers, 1992-94, Clinton-Gore Washington Bus. adv. com.; bd. dirs. Small Bus. Legis. Coun., 1987—, sec., 1999—; bd. dirs. Nat. Bus. Coalition for Fair Competition, 1984—. Perry E. Towne scholar, 1966-67; mem. U.S. Atty. Gen.'s Honors Program, 1968-71; recipient Children's Express Juvenile Justice award, 1981. Mem. Calif. Bar Assn., Nat. Health Lawyers Assn., Am. Soc. Assn. Execs. (govt. affrs sect.), Washington Coun. Lawyers, Assn. of Former Senior Senate Aides, Vinifera Wine Growers Assn. Va. (life), Health R Us, Am. League of Lobbyists, Theta Chi. Democrat. Avocation: collecting antique furniture, books and documents. Office: Nat Assn Retail Druggists 205 Daingerfield Rd Alexandria VA 22314-2885

**REDD, ANDREW W.,** lawyer; b. Albany, Ga., Nov. 25, 1950; s. N.L. W. and Bobbie G. Redd; m. Susan A. Waters, Sept. 9, 1972; children: Andrew Gaines, Amy Melissa, Erin Grace. BS, Auburn U., 1973; JD, Birmingham U., 1979. Bar: Ala., U.S. Dist. Ct. Ala., U.S. Ct. Appeals (6th cir.), U.S. Ct. Appeals (11th cir.), U.S. Supreme Ct. Claims examiner Social Security Adminstrn., Birmingham, 1973-79; pvt. practice Machen, Redd & Dobson, Sylacauga, Ala., 1979-86; asst. gen. counsel, gen. counsel Ala. Dept. of Corrections, 1986—; com. Bar Com. on Corrections, Montgomery, 1990—, Civil Justice Reform Com., Montgomery, 1997-98, Ala. Com. on Sentencing, 1997—. With USAF Res., 1970-76. Mem. Nat. Assn. of A.G. Corrections, Ala. State Bar Assn. Methodist. Avocations: hunting, fishing, living historian, woodworking. Office: Ala Dept Corrections 101 S Union St Montgomery AL 36130-3022

**REDD, CHARLES APPLETON,** lawyer; b. Quincy, Ill., Aug. 13, 1954; s. Charles Lambert and Julia (Harrell) R.; m. Susan Backer, June 2, 1978; children: Elizabeth Appleton, Christopher O'Leary, Thomas Charles, Daniel Louis. BA, St. Louis U., 1976, JD, 1979. Bar: Wis. 1979, U.S. Dist. Ct. (ea. and we. dists.) Wis. 1979, Mo. 1980, Ill. 1991. Trust adminstr. First Wis. Trust Co., Milw., 1979-80; asst. counsel Centerre Trust Co. of St. Louis (now Bank of Am., N.A.), 1980-83; assoc. Armstrong, Teasdale, Schlafly & Davis, St. Louis, 1983-85; ptnr. Armstrong, Teasdale, Schlafly, Davis & Dicus and predecessor firm, St. Louis, 1986-94; chmn. trust and estates dept., 1993-94; former adj. prof. law in estate planning St. Louis U. Sch. Law. Mem. bd. editors: Mo. Lawyers Weekly. Mem. Estate Planning Coun. of St. Louis; bd. dirs. Life Crisis Svcs., Inc.; mem. bequest and gift coun. St. Louis U. Recipient Mo. Bar Pres.'s award, 1991. Fellow Am. Coll. of Trust and Estate Counsel (mem. fiduciary litig. comn., estate and gift tax com.); mem. ABA (taxation sect., real property, probate and trust law sect.), Wis. Bar Assn., Mo. Bar Assn. (coun. mem. probate and trust com.), Ill. State Bar Assn., Bar Assn. Met. St. Louis (past chmn. probate and trust sect.). Probate, Estate taxation, Estate planning. Home: 7245 Maryland Ave University City MO 63130 Office: Sonnenschein Nath & Rosenthal 1 Metropolitan Sq Ste 3000 Saint Louis MO 63102-2741

**REDDEN, JAMES ANTHONY,** federal judge; b. Springfield, Mass., Mar. 13, 1929; s. James A. and Alma (Cheek) R.; m. Joan Ida Johnson, July 13, 1950; children: James A., William F. Student, Boston U., 1951; LL.B., Boston Coll., 1954. Bar: Mass., 1954, Oreg., 1955. Pvt. practice Mass., 1954-55; title examiner Title & Trust Ins. Co., Oreg., 1955; claims adjuster Allstate Ins. Co., 1956; mem. firm Collins, Redden, Ferris & Velure, Medford, Oreg., 1957-73; treas. State of Oreg., 1973-77; atty. gen., 1977-80; U.S. dist. judge, now sr. judge U.S. Dist. Ct. Oreg., Portland, 1980—. Chmn. Oreg. Pub. Employee Relations Bd.; mem. Oreg. Ho. of Reps., 1963-69, minority leader, 1967-69. With AUS, 1946-48. Mem. ABA, Mass. Bar Assn., Oreg. State Bar. Office: US Dist Ct 1527 US Courthouse 1000 SW 3d Ave Portland OR 97204-2902

**REDDEN, ROGER DUFFEY,** lawyer; b. Washington, Dec. 19, 1932; s. Layman J. and Elizabeth (Duffey) R.; m. Gretchen Sause, July 14, 1962. AB, Yale Coll., 1954; LLB, U. Md., 1957. Bar: Md. 1958, U.S. Dist. Ct. Md. 1958, U.S. Ct. Appeals (4th cir.) 1958, U.S. Supreme Ct. 1965. Law clk. to judge U.S. Ct. Appeals (4th cir.), 1957-58; assoc. Smith, Somerville & Case, Balt., 1959-63, ptnr., 1965-68; asst. atty. gen. State of Md., 1964-65; ptnr. Piper & Marbury, Balt., 1969-97, ptnr. emeritus, 1998—; bd. dirs. Peoples Water Svc. Co.; draftsman Md. State Dept. Legis. Reference, 1958; counsel Md. Savs. and Loan Study Commn., 1960-61; mem. Gov.'s Commn. to revise testamentary laws of Md., 1965-70; mem. standing com. on rules of practice and procedure Md. Ct. Appeals, 1969-73, 88-91, Md. code revision com., 1970—, Appellate Jud. Nominating Commn., 1975-79, Commn. to study Md. Tax Ct., 1978-79, Gov.'s Task Force on Energy, 1991-95; chmn. Task Force on Permits Simplification, 1979-81. Editor in chief Md. Law Rev., 1956-57; contbr. articles to legal jours. Served with U.S. Army, 1958-59, 61-62. Fellow Am. Bar Found., Md. Bar Found.; mem. Md. State Bar Assn. (chmn. probate and estate law sect. 1966-68, chmn. long range planning com. 1972-73, chmn. com. on laws 1988-89, council sect. adminstrv. law 1980-82, council sect. bus. law 1978-81), Balt. City Bar Assn. (chmn. com. on continuing legal edn. 1976-77, chmn. com. on judiciary 1978-79, chmn. com. on by-laws 1981-82), ABA, Jud. Conf. U.S. Ct. Appeals for 4th Cir. (conf. study com. 1982-83). Democrat. Episcopalian. Public utilities, Municipal (including bonds), Administrative and regulatory. Office: Piper & Marbury 36 S Charles St Baltimore MD 21201-3020

**REDDER, THOMAS JOSEPH,** lawyer, judge, legislator, federal administrator; b. Marshall, Minn., June 18, 1955; s. Lester J. and Ardell S. (Hentges) R. BA, Colo. State U., 1978; JD, U. Colo., 1981. Bar: Colo. 1981, U.S. Dist. Ct. Colo. 1981, U.S. Ct. Appeals (10th cir.) 1982, D.C. 1983, U.S. Supreme Ct. 1985. Pvt. practice Fort Collins, Colo., 1981-91; mcpl. judge Wellington, Colo., 1983-88, Timnath, Colo., 1985-88; elected Colo. Ho. of Rep. 58th Gen. Assy., 1991-93; region VIII adminstr. U.S. Sml. Bus. Adminstrn., Denver, 1993-98; v.p. sales, mktg., bus. devel. Cytomation, Inc., Ft. Collins, Colo. Mem. advance staff White House, Washington, 1977, 78, 80, 93; staff asst. U.S. Senator Daniel Patrick Moynihan, Washington, 1977; advance staff Mondale for Pres., Washington, 1984; trip dir. for Dukakis/Bentsen presdl. campaign, Boston, 1988; Dem. nominee for U.S. House of Reps., 4th Congrl. Dist. of Colo., 1992. Mem. ABA, Colo. Bar Assn., Larimer County Bar Assn. Democrat. Roman Catholic. E-mail: tjredder@aol.com. General practice, General civil litigation, Criminal. Home and Office: PO Box 9626 Fort Collins CO 80525-0503

**REDDIEN, CHARLES HENRY, II,** lawyer, corporate executive, consultant; b. San Diego, Aug. 27, 1944; s. Charles Henry and Betty Jane (McCormick) R.; m. Paula Gayle, June 16, 1974; 1 child, Tyler Charles. BSEE, U. Colo., Boulder, 1966; MSEE, U. So. Calif., 1968; JD, Loyola U., L.A., 1972. Bar: Calif. 1972, Colo. 1981, U.S. Dist. Ct. 1981. Mgr., Hughes Aircraft Co., 1966-81; pvt. practice, 1972—; pres., broker R&D Realty Ltd., 1978-91; mem. spl. staff, co-dir. tax advantage group OTC Net Inc., 1981-82; pres., chmn. Heritage Group Inc., investment banking holding co., 1982-84, Plans and Assistance Inc., mgmt. cons., 1982-83, Orchard Group Ltd., investment banking holding co., 1982-84, J.W. Gant & Assocs., Inc., investment bankers, 1983-84; mng. ptnr., CEO J.W. Gant & Assocs., Ltd., 1984-85; chmn. bd. Kalamath Group Ltd., 1985-87, Heritage group Ltd. Investment Bankers, 1985-87; dir. Virtusonics Corp., 1985-92; v.p., dir. Heritage Fin. Planners Inc., 1982-83; pres., chmn. PDN Inc., 1987-89; pub., exec. v.p., dir. World News Digest Inc., 1987-90, LeisureNet Entertainment, Inc., 1989-90; chief exec. officer, Somerset Group Ltd., 1988-93, Inland Pacific Corp., 1989-91, World Info. Network, Inc., 1990-92, pres., CEO, chmn., Europa Cruises Corp., 1992-94; CEO, chmn. Casino World Inc., 1993-97, Miss. Gaming Corp., 1993-97; pres., chmn., CEO Chart Group Ltd., 1997—. Recipient tchg. internship award, 1964. Mem. Calif. Bar Assn., Nat. Assn. Securities Dealers, IEEE (chmn. U. Colo. chpt. 1965), AIAA, Phi Alpha Delta, Tau Beta Pi, Eta Kappa Nu. Contbr. articles to profl. jours. General corporate. Office: PO Box 6133 Diamondhead MS 39525-6002

**REDDING, JOSEPH E.,** lawyer; b. West Allis, Wis., May 20, 1969. BS, U. Wis., Platteville, 1991; JD, Marquette U., 1994. Bar: Wis. 1994, U.S. Dist. Ct. (ea. dist.) Wis. 1994. Atty. Glojek Ltd., West Allis, 1994—. Bd. dirs. Wis. Parents Coalition for the Retarded, Oconomowoc, 1995—. Criminal, Appellate. Office: Glojek Ltd 6212 W Greenfield Ave West Allis WI 53214-5088

**REDDING, ROBERT ELLSWORTH,** lawyer, association executive; b. South Bend, Ind., Mar. 23, 1919; s. Harry Ellsworth and Lorraine (Livengood) R.; m. Blanche Breisch, Apr. 14, 1941 (div.); children—Rosemary, Robert Ellsworth, Douglas; m. A. Virginia Boender, July 22, 1972. A.B., Ohio State U., 1940; LL.B., J.D., Georgetown U., 1946. Bar: D.C. 1946, Md. 1949, U.S. Supreme Ct. 1950. Legal asst. to mem. CAB, Washington, 1949-51; mem. Bradshaw Shearin Redding & Thomas, Silver Spring, Md., 1951-59; v.p., gen. counsel Transp. Assn. Am., Washington, 1960-69; dir. Office Facilitation, Dept. Transp., Washington, 1970-76; sole practice, Washington, 1976—; sec. Cert. Claims Profl. Accreditation Council, Washington, 1981-85; chief judge Appeal Tax Ct., Rockville, Md., 1953-55; dir. fed. affairs Shippers Nat. Freight Claim Council, Washington, 1979-89; cons. UN Devel. Program, N.Y.C., 1980-81. Author: Community Planning for Air Transportation, 1960. Washington editor Handling and Shipping mag., 1976-81. Pres. Allied Civic Group (50 assns.), Silver Spring, 1956-68; chmn. research com. Md. Republican Com., 1965-70; chmn. fin. adv. com. to county council, Rockville, 1965-70; exec. dir. Montgomery County Taxpayers League. Served to 2d lt. U.S. Army, 1943-46. Mem. Phi Beta Kappa, Phi Alpha Delta (supreme justice 1966-68, exec. v.p. Pub. Service

Ctr. 1984-91. Episcopalian. Club: Univ. (bd. govs.) (Washington). Lodges: Masons, Scottish Rite. Transportation, Legislative, Estate planning. Home: 9105 Falls Chapel Way Potomac MD 20854-2452

**REDDY, LAKSHMI YEDDULA,** lawyer; b. Hyderabad, India, May 29, 1970; came to U.S., 1972; d. Yeddula Ramachandra and Mani Yedula Reddy; m. Venkat Ramana, Aug. 12, 1993. BS in Biology, Vanderbilt U., 1992; JD cum laude, Ind. U., Indpls., 1997. Bar: Ind. 1997, U.S. Dist. Ct. (no. and so. dists.) Ind. 1997. Rsch. asst. dept. infectious diseases Vanderbilt U., Nashville, 1992-94; rsch. asst. Ctr. for Law and Health, Indpls., 1995-95; jud. law clk. to Hon. Frank Sullivan Jr. Ind. Supreme Ct., Indpls., 1997-98; assoc. Zeigler Carter Cohen & Koch, Indpls., 1998—. Notes dept. editor Ind. Law Rev., 1996-97, assoc. editor, 1995-96. Personal injury, Health. Office: Zeigler Carter et al 8500 Keystone Xing Ste 510 Indianapolis IN 46240-2461

**REDENBACHER, GARY,** lawyer; b. 1955; m. Renae Nielsen Fish, June 15, 1985; children: Mikayla and Bryce (twins). BA, U. Calif., Santa Cruz, 1977; MA, Calif. State U., 1982; JD, U. Calif., Hastings, 1990. Bar: Calif. 1990, U.S. Dist. Ct. (no. dist.) Calif. 1995. Dir. phys. edn. YMCA, Cupertino, Calif., 1978-81; lectr. dept. phys. edn. Calif. State U., Fresno, 1982-87; gen. contractor Fresno, 1986-93; mktg. spokesman Orville Redenbacher's Popcorn, Fullerton, Calif., 1987-94; atty. pvt. practice, Santa Cruz, Calif., 1990—. Bd. dirs. Coun. Children, U. San Diego, 1996—; chmn. bd. Legal Svcs. Children, San Francisco, 1991-95; bd. dirs. Child Abuse Prevention Coun., Santa Cruz, 1993-96. Mem. ATLA, Santa Cruz Trial Lawyers Assn. Avocations: volleyball, woodworking, soccer. Education and schools, Construction, General civil litigation. Office: 5610 Scotts Valley Dr # 35 Santa Cruz CA 95066-3476

**REDFEARN, PAUL L., III,** lawyer; b. Camp Cook, Calif., Oct. 1, 1951; s. Paul Leslie Jr. and Alice Ruby Redfearn; children: Ashley, Lauren; m. Denise Jean Davis, July 24, 1993. BS, S.W. Mo. State U., 1973; JD, Oklahoma City U., 1976. Bar: Mo. 1977, U.S. Dist. Ct. (we. and ea. dists.) Mo., U.S. Dist. Ct. Kans., U.S. Dist. Ct. N.D., U.S. Dist. Ct. Mont., U.S. Ct. Appeal (8th ant 11th cirs.); bd. cert. civil trial advocate. Assoc. Sheridan, Sanders & Simpson, P.C., 1977-79, William H. Pickett, P.C., 1979-84; ptnr. Redfearn & Brown, P.C., Kansas City, Mo., 1984—; lectr. and presenter in field. Contbr. chpts. to books. Bd. govs. S.W. Mo. State U., 1998—. Mem. ABA, ATLA, Mo. Bar Assn., Mo. Assn. Trial Attys. (bd. govs. 1986-94, exec. com. 1990—, pres. 1992), Am. Bd. Trial Advocates (charter, pres. chpt. 1996-97), Kansas City Met. Bar Assn., East Jackson County Bar Assn. Democrat. Christian. Avocation: tennis. Personal injury, Product liability. Office: Redfearn & Brown PC 1125 Grand Blvd Ste 814 Kansas City MO 64106-2518

**REDIGER, RICHARD KIM,** lawyer; b. Glendale, Calif., Sept. 10, 1950; s. Richard Lee and Alba Clare (Burt) R.; m. Linda Lee Olsen, Mar. 21, 1981; children: Susan Elizabeth, Kathryn Rose, Erin Marie. BA, UCLA, 1975; JD, Loyola U., 1978. Bar: Calif. 1978, Colo. 1979, U.S. Ct. Appeals (9th and 10th cirs.) 1979, U.S. Dist. Ct. (cen. dist. L.A.) 1979, Utah 1993, U.S. Dist. Ct. Utah 1993. Assoc. Gray, Gorham & Paul, L.A., 1976-79; dep. dist. atty. 4th Jud. Dist., Colorado Springs, Colo., 1979-83; asst. atty. gen. Office Atty. Gen., Denver, 1983-84; assoc. Hall & Evans, Denver, 1984-88; of counsel George L. Vamos, Denver, 1988-89, Manville Corp., Denver, 1989-91, Cook & Fitch, Denver, 1992—; spl. asst. county atty. El Paso County, 1983-84; spl. pros. 20th Jud. Dist., 1984; instr. State of Colo., 1981-83, lectr., 1984. Contbr. DUI/DWAI Manual State of Colorado, 1981. Mem. ABA, Colo. Bar Assn., Calif. Bar Assn., Utah Bar Assn., Denver Bar Assn., Salt Lake County Bar Assn. Avocations: vocal instruction and performance. General civil litigation, Insurance, Workers' compensation. Office: Cook & Fitch 7887 E Belleview Ave Ste 375 Englewood CO 80111-6057

**REDING, JOHN ANTHONY,** lawyer; b. Orange, Calif., May 26, 1944. AB, U. Calif., Berkeley, 1966, JD, 1969. Bar: Calif. 1970, U.S. Dist. Ct. (no., ctrl. ea. and so. dists.) Calif., U.S. Claims Ct., U.S. Supreme Ct. Formerly mem. Crosby, Heafey, Roach & May P.C., Oakland, Calif.; now ptnr. Paul, Hastings, Janofsky & Walker, LLP, San Francisco. Mem. ABA (chmn. West Coast litigation dept., sects. on litigation, intellectual property, and natural resources, energy and eviron. law, coms. on bus. torts, internat. law, trial practice and torts and insurance), Am. Intellectual Property Law Assn., State Bar Calif. (sect. on litigation), Bar Assn. San Francisco, Assn. Bus. Trial Lawyers. General civil litigation, Environmental, Intellectual property. Office: Paul Hastings Janofsky & Walker LLP 345 California St San Francisco CA 94104-2606

**REDLEAF, DIANE LYNN,** lawyer; b. N.Y.C., Dec. 3, 1954; d. Paul David and Rhoda Eileen (Rosen) Redleaf; m. Anatoly S. Libgober, June 28, 1987; children: Brian Daniel, Jonathan Alan. BA, Carleton Coll., Northfield, Minn., 1976; JD, Stanford U., 1979. Bar: Ill. 1979, U.S. Ct. Appeals (7th cir.) 1989, U.S. Dist. Ct. (no. dist.) 1979. Staff atty. 18th St. Office, Chgo., 1979-81; staff atty. women's law project Legal Assistance Found. of Chgo., 1981-84, supr. children's law and policy project, 1984—; lectr. child welfare law U. Chgo. Law Sch., 1994-96. Contbr. articles to profl. jours. Chmn. Neon St. Adv. Bd., Chgo., 1988-90; founding mem. Ill. Task Force on Child Support, Chgo., 1982—; coord. adv. bd. Children's Rights Project, Chgo., 1985—; bd. dirs. Nat. Coalition Child Protection Reform. Recipient Equal Justice award Legal Assistance Found. Chgo., 1990, 94. Mem. Chgo. Coun. Lawyers. Avocations: piano, violin. Civil rights. Address: 36 S Wabash Oak Park IL 60302

**REDLICH, MARC,** lawyer; b. N.Y.C., Nov. 25, 1946; s. Louis and Mollie R.; m. Janis Redlich, Jan. 16, 1982; children: Alison, Suzanne, Rachel. BA, Queens Coll., 1967; JD, Harvard U., 1971. Bar: Mass. 1971, U.S. Dist. Ct. 1971, U.S. Ct. Appeals (1st cir.) 1974, U.S. Ct. Appeals (5th cir.) 1984. Assoc. Rubin & Rudman, Boston, 1971-75; mem., sr. dir. Widett, Slater & Goldman, Boston, 1975-84; prin. Law Offices of Marc Redlich, Boston, 1984—; seminar chmn. Mass. Continuing Legal Edn., Inc., 1996. Mem. Mass. Bar Assn. (governing coun. civil litigation sect., participant/panelist chpt. 93A in the bus. context seminar 1996), Cambridge Bar Assn., Nat. Assn. Coll. and Univ. Attys., Harvard Sq. Bus. Assn. (bd. dirs. 1989-92, 93-94), Friends of Switzerland Inc. (bd. dirs. 1984-94, assoc. pres. 1991-93, pres. 1993—), German Am. Bus. Club of Boston (exec. com. 1997—), Harvard Club Boston (co-chair music com. 1997-98, chair 1998—), Phi Beta Kappa. General practice, General civil litigation, General corporate. Office: Three Center Plz Boston MA 02108

**REDLICH, NORMAN,** lawyer, educator; b. N.Y.C., Nov. 12, 1925; s. Milton and Pauline (Durst) R.; m. Evelyn Jane Grobow, June 3, 1951; children: Margaret Bonny-Claire, Carrie Ann, Edward Grobow. AB, Williams Coll., 1947, LLD (hon.), 1976; LLB, Yale U., 1950; LLM, NYU, 1955; LLD (hon.), John Marshall Law Sch., 1990. Bar: N.Y. 1951. Practiced in N.Y.C., 1951-59; assoc. prof. law NYU, 1960-62, prof. law, 1962-74, assoc. dean Sch. Law, 1974-75, dean Sch. Law, 1975-88, dean emeritus, 1992—, Judge Edward Weinfeld prof. law, 1982—; counsel Wachtell, Lipton, Rosen & Katz, N.Y.C., 1988—; editor-in-chief Tax Law Rev., 1960-66; mem. adv. com. Inst. Fed. Taxation, 1963-68; exec. asst. corp. counsel, N.Y.C., 1966-68, 1st asst. corp. counsel, 1970-72, corp. counsel, 1972-74; asst. counsel Pres. Commn. on Assassination Pres. Kennedy, 1963-64; mem. com. on admissions and grievances U.S. 2d Circuit Ct. Appeals, 1978—, chmn., 1978-87. Author: Professional Responsibility: A Problem Approach, 1976, Constitutional Law, Cases and Materials, 1983, rev. edit., 1996, Understanding Constitutional Law, 1995; contbr. articles in field. Chmn. commn. on law and social action Am. Jewish Congress, 1978—, chmn. governing coun., 1996; mem. Borough Pres.'s Planning Bd. Number 2, 1959-70, counsel N.Y. Com. to Abolish Capital Punishment, 1958-77; mem. N.Y.C. Bd. Edn., 1969; mem. bd. overseers Jewish Theol. Sem., 1973—; trustee Law Ctr. Found. of NYU, 1975—, Freedom House, 1976-86, Vt. Law Sch., 1977—, Practicing Law Inst., 1980—; trustee Lawyers Com. for Civil Rights Under Law, 1976—, co-chmn., 1979-81; bd. dirs. Legal Aid Soc., 1983-88, NAACP Legal Def. Fund, 1985—, Greenwich House, 1987—. Decorated Combat Infantryman's Badge. Mem. ABA (coun. legal edn. and admissions to bar 1981—, vice chmn. 1987-88, chmn. 1989-90, equal opportunities in legal profession 1986-92, ho. of dels. 1991—), Assn. of Bar of City of N.Y. (exec. com. 1975-79, professionalism com. 1988-92). Office: 51 W 52nd St Fl 30 New York NY 10019-6119

**REDMAN, CLARENCE OWEN,** lawyer; b. Joliet, Ill., Nov. 23, 1942; s. Harold F. and Edith L. (Read) R.; m. Barbara Ann Pawlan, Jan. 26, 1964 (div.); children: Scott, Steven; m. 2d, Carla J. Rozycki, Sept. 24, 1983. BS, U. Ill., 1964, JD, 1966, MA, 1967. Bar: Ill. 1966, U.S. Dist. Ct. (ea. dist.) Ill. 1970, U.S. Ct. Appeals (7th cir.) 1973, U.S. Ct. Appeals (4th cir.) 1982, U.S. Supreme Ct. 1975. Assoc. Keck, Mahin & Cate, Chgo., 1969-73, ptnr., corp. ptnr., 1973—, CEO, 1986-97; of counsel Lord, Bissell & Brook, Chgo., 1997—; spl. asst. atty. gen. Ill., 1975-8; bd. dirs. AMCOL Internat. Corp. Mem. bd. visitors U. Ill. Coll. of Law, 1991-95. Capt. U.S. Army, 1967-69. Decorated Bronze Star. Mem. Ill. State Bar Assn. (chmn. young lawyers sect. 1977-78, del. assembly 1978-81, 84-87), Chgo. Bar Assn., Seventh Cir. Bar Assn. General corporate, Federal civil litigation, Labor. Office: Lord Bissell & Brook 115 S Lasalle St Ste 3200 Chicago IL 60603-3972

**REDMANN, JOHN WILLIAM,** lawyer, consultant; b. New Orleans, Sept. 10, 1963; s. William Vincent and Ana Maria (Macouzet) R. BA in Psychology, BA in French, Loyola U. of the South, 1986, JD, 1989. Bar: La. 1990, U.S. Dist. Ct. (ea. dist.) La. 1990; cert. notary pub., La. Litigation law clk. Orleans Sewerage and Water Bd., New Orleans, 1989-90; law clk. to Hon. Judge Connolly Orleans Civil Dist. Ct., New Orleans, 1990-92; atty. Exnicios & Nungesser, New Orleans, 1992-94; prin. Law Offices of John W. Redmann, New Orleans, 1994—; v.p. L'Ecole Maternelle, 1998—, also bd. dirs.; v.p., gen. counsel Meridian Group, L.L.C., New Orleans, 1998—; v.p. L'Ecole Maternelle, 1998, also bd. dirs.; v.p., gen. counsel Meridian Group, L.L.C., New Orleans, 1998—; charter mem. alumni com. Loyola Law Sch. Moot Ct., 1991-96, also chmn. 1980's decade ann. fund campaign. Charter mem. Loyola Law Sch. Moot Ct. Alumni Com., New Orleans, 1991-96; 1980's decade chmn. 1995 Loyola Law Ann. Fund Campaign, New Orleans; charter mem./officer Lawyers Against Crime, Inc., New Orleans, 1995—. Mem. ATLA (traumatic brain injury litigation group 1997—), Nat. Inst. Trial Advocacy (diplomate), La. Trial Lawyers Assn. (mem. leadership and membership coms. 1994-96), Assn. of New Orleans Trial Lawyers, Supreme Ct. of La. Hist. Soc. (charter), So. Trial Lawyers Assn. (bd. dirs. 1998—), La. Hispanic C. of C. (bd. dirs. 1998—), Young Leadership Counsel, Bards Bohemia (mem. exec. bd. 1998-99), Celtic Club of New Orleans (pres. 1997-98). Roman Catholic. Avocations: travel, foreign languages. Personal injury, Admiralty, General civil litigation. Home: 1327 Short St New Orleans LA 70118-4043 Office: 9701 Lake Forest Blvd Ste 101 New Orleans LA 70127-5403

**REDMOND, CHRISTOPHER JOHN,** lawyer; b. Oakland, Calif., May 8, 1947; s. Owen Joseph and Josephine Alice (Hanswirth) R.; m. Rosalyn Lee Finney, June 8, 1970; children: Kirk, Renee, Megan. BA, U. Kans., 1968, JD, 1970. Bar: Kans. 1970, U.S. Dist. Ct. Kans. 1970, U.S. Ct. appeals (10th cir.) 1973, U.S. Supreme Ct. 1974. Mem. Husch & Eppenberger LLC, Wichita, Kans., 1970—. Assoc. editor Am. Bankruptcy Inst. Jour. Mem. ABA (chmn., subcom. internat. law, bus. bankruptcy com., 1995—), Wichita Bar Assn. (bd. govs.). Private international, Bankruptcy, Federal civil litigation. Office: Husch & Eppenberger LLC 1200 Main St Ste 1700 Kansas City MO 64105-2100

**REDMOND, DARLENE LEOLA,** lawyer; b. Chgo., Nov. 17, 1963; d. Frank Ester and Darlene (Adams) R. B of Bus., Loyola U., 1986; JD, U. Iowa, 1991. Bar: Ill. 1991, U.S. Dist. Ct. (no. dist.) Ill. 1991. Staff auditor Nat. Futures Assn., Chgo., 1986-87; paralegal Rivkin, Radler, Dunne & Bayh, Chgo., 1987-88; intern U.S. Dept. of Justice, Washington, summer 1990; asst. pub. defender Cook County Pub. Defender, Chgo., 1991—. Mem. Black Women Lawyers Assn. Baptist. Avocations: swimming, reading. Home: 5424 S Cornell Ave Apt 319 Chicago IL 60615-5600

**REDMOND, LAWRENCE CRAIG,** lawyer; b. Chgo., Mar. 17, 1943; s. Lawrence Craig and Marie Alberta (Campbell) R.; m. Bess Peoples, Mar. 16, 1967 (div. Sept. 1980); children: Masai, Maya; m. Luanne Marie Bethke, May 23, 1986; children: Geneva Marie, Sarai Bernice, Darcy Milita, Abina Grace, Leni Louise. BA, U. Ill., Chgo., 1973; JD, John Marshall Law Sch., 1983. Pvt. practice Chgo., 1986—; panel atty. Capital Litigation divsn. State Appellate Defender, Chgo., 1992—; computer cons. Chgo., 1986—. Mayoral nominee Harold Washington Party, Chgo., 1995, Cook County state's atty. nominee, 1996, 49th Ward Com., 1996; Ill. gubernatorial cand. Reform Party, 1997; elected chmn. Reform Party of Ill., 1999. With USAF, 1960-64. Avocations: creative writing, African drums, martial arts, photography. Criminal, General civil litigation, Election.

**REDMOND, PATRICIA ANN,** lawyer; b. Phila., Mar. 17, 1950; d. John Charles and Mildred Muriel (Smith) R.; m. Jerry M. Markowitz, Oct. 19, 1985; 1 child, Lisa Dawn. BA, U. Miami (Fla.), 1975, JD, 1979. Bar: Pa. 1979, Fla. 1979, U.S. Dist. Ct. (so. dist.) Fla. 1980, U.S. Ct. Appeals (11th cir.) 1985. Assoc. Britton, Cohen, Kaufman, et al, Miami, 1980-81; pvt. practice law Miami, 1981—; lectr., advisor Legal Svcs., Greater Miami, 1985—; ethics panelist Nat. Conf. of Bankruptcy Judges, 1990; adj. prof. St. Thomas U. Sch. Law. Mem. ABA, Bankruptcy Bar Assn. So. dist. Fla. (pres. 1988-89, chmn. legal edn. com. 1990-91), Norton Inst., Am. Bankruptcy Inst. (local rules com. 1990, 91), Bankruptcy Law Inst. (local rules com.), Comml. Law League (vice chmn. speaker bur.). Democrat. Avocations: aerobics, water sports, walking. Bankruptcy. Office: Two Datran Ctr 9130 S Dadeland Blvd Miami FL 33156-7818

**REDMOND, RICHARD ANTHONY,** lawyer; b. Chgo., Oct. 4, 1947; s. Richard Aloysius and Mary Jane (Berger) R.; m. Merrilee Clark, May 5, 1984; children: Richard William, Michael Clark. BA, U. Notre Dame, 1969; JD, Cornell U., 1972. Bar: Ill. 1972, U.S. Dist. Ct. (no. dist.) Ill. 1972, U.S. Ct. Appeals (7th cir.) 1975, U.S. Supreme Ct. 1976. Assoc. Freeman & Tingler, Chgo., 1972-75; from assoc. to ptnr. Kennedy, Golan & Morris, Chgo., 1975-81; ptnr. Walsh, Case, Coale & Brown, Chgo., 1981-89, McBride, Baker and Coles, Chgo., 1989—; mem. com. of profl. responsibility Ill. Supreme Ct., 1983-97, chmn., 1993-97. Trustee Chgo. Acad. Sci., 1986-95, chmn. bd. trustees, 1990-94. Mem. ABA, Chgo. Bar Assn. (chmn. eminent domain subcom. 1982—), Law Club Chgo., Mich. Shores Club. Roman Catholic. Condemnation, Federal civil litigation, State civil litigation. Office: McBride Baker & Coles Northwestern Atrium Ctr 500 W Madison St Chicago IL 60661-2511

**REDMOND, ROBERT,** lawyer, educator; b. Astoria, N.Y., June 18, 1934; s. George and Virginia (Greene) R.; m. Georgine Marie Richardson, May 21, 1966; children: Kelly Anne, Kimberly Marie, Christopher Robert. BA, Queens Coll., 1955; MPA, CUNY, 1962; JD, Georgetown U., 1970. Bar: D.C. 1971, Va. 1974, U.S. Supreme Ct. 1974. Commd. 2d lt. USAF, 1955, advanced through grades to lt. col., 1972, ret., 1978; served as spl. investigations officer Korea, Vietnam, W. Germany; adj. prof., acad. dir. mil. dist. Washington Resident Ctr. Park U., Parkville, Mo., 1977—; pvt. practice Falls Church, Va., 1980—. Precinct capt. Fairfax County Rep. Party, Va., 1981-87; pres. PTO, Falls Church, 1984-86; treas. Fedn. Cath. Schs. PTO, 1986-87; bd. dirs. Chaconas Home Owners Assn., 1984—, Social Ctr. Psychiat. Rehab., 1987-93. Mem. ATLA, Va. Trial Lawyers Assn., Fairfax Bar Assn., Assn. Former Air Force Office Spl. Investigations Agts. (chpt. pres. 1984-86, nat. membership com. 1986—), Comml. Law League, Delta Theta Phi, K.C. (4th deg.). Roman Catholic. General practice, Personal injury, Consumer commercial. Home: 7802 Antiopi St Annandale VA 22003-1405 Office: Ste 900-N 7799 Leesburg Pike Falls Church VA 22043-2413

**REDSTONE, SUMNER MURRAY,** entertainment company executive, lawyer; b. Boston, May 27, 1923; s. Michael and Belle (Ostrovsky) R.; m. Phyllis Gloria Raphael, July 6, 1947; children: Brent Dale, Shari Ellin. BA, Harvard U., 1944, LLB, 1947; LLD (hon.), Boston U., 1994; LHD (hon.), N.Y. Inst. Tech., 1996. Bar: Mass. 1947, U.S. Ct. Appeals (1st cir.) 1948, U.S. Ct. Appeals (8th cir.) 1950, U.S. Ct. Appeals (9th cir.) 1948, D.C. 1951, U.S. Supreme Ct. 1952. Law sec. U.S. Ct. Appeals for 9th Circuit, San Francisco, 1947-48; instr. law and labor mgmt. U. San Francisco, 1947; spl. asst. to U.S. Atty. Gen., Washington, 1948-51; ptnr. Ford, Bergson, Adams, Borkland & Redstone, Washington, 1951-54; pres., CEO Nat. Amusements Inc., Dedham, Mass., 1967—, chmn. bd., 1986—; chmn. bd. Viacom, Inc., N.Y.C., 1987—; CEO Viacom, Inc., 1996; prof. Boston U. Law Sch., 1982, 85-86; bd. dirs. TV Acad. Arts and Scis. Found.; vis. prof. Brandeis U., Waltham, Mass.; lectr. Harvard Law Sch., Cambridge, Mass.; Judge on Kennedy Libr. Found., (sel. comm. John F. Kennedy Profile in Courage award). Chmn. met. divsn. NE Combined Jewish Philanthropies, Boston, 1963; mem. exec. bd. Combined Jewish Philanthropies of Greater Boston; mem. corp. New Eng. Med. Ctr., 1967—, Mass. Gen. Hosp. Corp.; trustee Children's Cancer Rsch. Found.; founding trustee Am. Cancer Soc.; chmn. Am. Cancer Crusade, State of Mass., 1984-86; Art Lending Libr.; sponsor Boston Mus. Sci.; chmn. Jimmy Fund Found., 1960; v.p., mem. exec. com. Will Rogers Meml. Fund; bd. dirs. Boston Arts Festival; bd. overseers Dana Farber Cancer Ctr., Boston Mus. Fine Arts; mem. presdl. adv. com. on arts John F. Kennedy Libr. Found., also judge ann. John F. Kennedy Profile in Courage Award com.; chmn. Corp. Commn. on Edn. Tech., 1996—, presdl. apptd. chmn., 1996. 1st lt. AUS, 1943-45. Decorated Army Commendation medal; named 1 of 10 Outstanding Young Men in New Eng., Boston Jr. C. of C., 1958; recipient William J. German Human Rels. award Am. Jewish Com. Entertainment/Comm. Divsn., 1977, Silver Shingle award Boston U. Law Sch., 1985, Variety New Eng. Humanitarian award, 1989, Golden Plate award Am. Acad. Achievement, 1993, 32d Ann. Salute to Excellence Program, 1993, Bus. Excellence award U. So. Calif. Sch. Bus. Adminstrn., 1994, The Stephen S. Wise award The Am. Jewish Congress, 1994, Man of Yr. award MIPCOM, the Internat. Film and Programme Market for TV, Video, Cable and Satellite, 1994, The Legends in Leadership award Emory U., 1995, Allan K. Jonas Lifetime Achievement award Am. Cancer Soc., 1995, Humanitarian award Variety Club Internat., 1995, Expeditioner's award N.Y.C. Outward Bound Ctr., 1996, Patron Arts award Songwriter's Hall Fame, 1996, Vision 21 award N.Y. Inst. Tech., 1996, Trustees award NATAS, 1997, Ripple of Hope award Robert F. Kennedy Meml., 1998, Humanitarian award Nat. Conf. Christians and Jews, 1998; named Communicator of Yr., B'nai B'rith Comm./Cinema Lodge, 1980, Man of Yr., Entertainment Industries Divsn. of UJA Fedn., 1988, Pioneer of Yr., Motion Picture Pioneers, 1991, Grad. of Yr., Boston Latin Sch., 1989, Honoree 7th ann. fundraiser Montefiore Med. Ctr., 1995, Hall of Fame award Broadcasting and Cable mag., 1995. Mem. ABA, Nat. Assn. Theatre Owners (chmn. bd. dirs. 1965-66, exec. comm. 1995—), Theatre Owners Am. (asst. pres. 1960-63, pres. 1964-65), Motion Picture Pioneers (bd. dirs.), Boston Bar Assn., Mass. Bar Assn., Harvard Law Sch. Assn., Am. Judicature Soc., Masons, Univ. Club, Harvard Club. Home: 98 Baldpate Hill Rd Newton MA 02459-2825 Office: Nat Amusements Inc PO Box 9126 Dedham MA 02027-9126

**REE, MICHELE LEE,** lawyer, nurse; b. Upland, Pa., Dec. 5, 1962; d. MaryLee (Sitkoski) Colflesh. BSN magna cum laude, LaSalle U., 1991; JD, Widener U. Law Sch., 1996. Mgr. ICU, CCU, hemodialysis U. Pa. Presbyn. Med. Ctr., Phila., 1991-95, staff nurse, 1995-96; nurse atty. McKissock & Hoffman, Phila., 1996-97, Anapol, Schwartz, Weiss & Cohan, Phila., 1997—. Mem. ABA, Phila. Bar Assn., Pa. Bar Assn., Phila. Trial Lawyers Assn. Avocations: bridge, fishing, reading mystery novels, sports. Home: 5 Dana Ct Aston PA 19014-3356 Office: Anapol Schwartz Weiss & Cohen 1900 Delancey Pl Philadelphia PA 19103-6612

**REECE, LAURENCE HOBSON, III,** lawyer; b. Ft. Bragg, N.C., Oct. 29, 1952; s. Laurence Hobson Jr. and Zora (Brannan) R.; m. Patricia Lynne Manson, May 11, 1991; 1 child, Jonathan Tucker. SB, MIT, 1974; JD, U. Va., 1978. Bar: Mass. 1978, U.S. Dist. Ct. Mass. 1979, U.S. Ct. Appeals (1st cir.) 1979. Assoc. Nutter, McClennen & Fish, Boston, 1978-83, jr. ptnr., 1984; prin. Gelb, Heidlage & Reece, P.C., Boston, 1985-87, Heidlage & Reece, P.C., Boston, 1987-98; ptnr. Lucash, Gesmer & Updegrove, LLP, Boston, 1998—; trial adviser, trial advocacy program Harvard U. Law Sch.; panelist for computer and high tech. programs of ABA, Mass. Continuing Legal Edn., Inc., also others; mem. Interest on Lawyers' Trust Accounts funds com. Boston Bar Found., 1991-97; mem. civil litigation curriculum adv. com. Mass. Continuing Legal Edn., Inc., 1992—. Contbr. numerous articles to legal jours. Mem. ABA (computer and internet litigation com. 1986—, assoc. editor Computer Litigation Jour. 1989-94, editor-in-chief 1994-97, co-chair 1997—), Boston Bar Assn. (computer and internet law com. 1984—), Phi Beta Kappa. Avocations: sailing, reading, travel. Computer, Federal civil litigation, State civil litigation. Home: 32 Clifton Heights Ln Marblehead MA 01945-2750 Office: Lucash Gesmer & Updegrove LLP 40 Broad St Ste 325 Boston MA 02109-4310

**REED, BARRY C., JR.,** lawyer; b. Oct. 9, 1958. BS, Holy Cross Coll., Worcester, Mass., 1980; JD, Suffolk U., 1983. Bar: Mass., U.S. Dist. Ct. Mass. Atty. Reed, O'Reilly & Brett, Boston, 1983—. Personal injury, Product liability. Office: 101 Tremont St Boston MA 02108-5004

**REED, BETTY ANN,** lawyer; b. Jacksonville, Ill., Aug. 17, 1943; d. Robert George and Betty Mae Hills; m. Wayne M. Michael, Sept. 13, 1980 (div. 1992); children: Marla Reed Brandt, Thomas Edward Reed. BA, Douglass Coll., New Brunswick, N.J., 1965. Sole practitioner Modesto, Calif. Avocation: bird watching. Family and matrimonial, Probate. Office: 804 14th St Modesto CA 95354-1023

**REED, D. GARY,** lawyer; b. Covington, Ky., June 4, 1949; m. Mary Elizabeth Goetz, May 20, 1972; children: Mark, Stacey. BA, Xavier U., 1971; JD, Catholic U. Am., 1974. Bar: Ohio 1974, Ky. 1975, U.S. Ct. Appeals (6th cir.) 1975, U.S. Dist. Ct. (so. dist.) Ohio 1974, U.S. Dist. Ct. (ea. dist.) Ky. 1977, U.S. Dist. Ct. (we. dist.) Ky. 1980. Law clk. to judge U.S. Dist. Ct. (so. dist.) Ohio, Cin., 1974-75; assoc. Dinsmore & Shohl, Cin., 1976-82, ptnr., 1982-90; dir. legal svcs. Choice Care Health Plans, Inc., 1991-96; asst. gen. coun., 1996-97; ins. counsel Humana, Inc., Louisville, 1998—; asst. sec. Choice Care Found., 1996-97. Contbg. author: Woodside, Drug Product Liability, vol. 3, 1987. Asst. sec. The Choice Care Found., 1996-97. Mem. ABA, Ky. Bar Assn., Ohio Bar Assn., Nat. Health Lawyers Assn., No. Ky. C. of C. (Leadership award 1988), Greater Cin. Coun. for Epilepsy (bd. dirs. 1990-97), Leadership No. Ky. Alumni Assn. Health, Insurance, General corporate. Office: Humana Inc Insurance Cons-Law Dept 500 W Main St Ste 300 Louisville KY 40202-4268

**REED, EDWARD CORNELIUS, JR.,** federal judge; b. Mason, Nev., July 8, 1924; s. Edward Cornelius Sr. and Evelyn (Walker) R.; m. Sally Torrance, June 14, 1952; children: Edward T., William W., John A., Mary E. BA, U. Nev., 1949; JD, Harvard U., 1952. Bar: Nev. 1952, U.S. Dist Ct. Nev. 1957, U.S. Supreme Ct. 1974. Atty. Arthur Andersen & Co., 1952-53; spl. dep. atty. gen. State of Nev., 1967-79; judge U.S. Dist. Ct. Nev., Reno, 1979—, chief judge, now sr. judge. Former vol. atty. Girl Scouts Am., Sierra Nevada Council, U. Nev., Nev. Agrl. Found., Nev. State Sch. Adminstrs. Assn., Nev. Congress of Parents and Teachers; mem. Washoe County Sch. Bd., 1956-72, pres. 1959, 63, 69; chmn. Gov.'s Sch. Survey Com., 1958-61; mem. Washoe County Bd. Tax Equalization, 1957-58, Washoe County Annexation Commn., 1968-72, Washoe County Personnel Com., 1973-77, chmn. 1973; mem. citizens adv. com. Washoe County Sch. Bond Issue, 1977-78, Sun Valley, Nev., Swimming Pool Com., 1978, Washoe County Blue Ribbon Task Force Com. on Growth, Nev. PTA (life); chmn. profl. div. United Way, 1978; bd. dirs. Reno Siver Sox, 1962-65. Served as staff sgt. U.S. Army, 1943-46, ETO, PTO. Mem. ABA (jud. adminstrn. sect.), Nev. State Bar Assn. (adminstrv. com. dist. 5, 1967-79, lien law com. 1965-78, chmn. 1965-72, probate law com. 1963-66, tax law com. 1962-65), Am. Judicature Soc. Democrat. Baptist. Office: US Dist Ct 400 S Virginia St Ste 606 Reno NV 89501-2182

**REED, GREGORY RUSSELL,** lawyer; b. Allentown, Pa., Nov. 19, 1946; s. Vernon Paul and Emma Jane (Horning) R.; m. Kathryn Adele Shute, Sept. 16, 1978; children: Douglas J., Jason T., Christopher M., Jessica M. BA, Lehigh U., 1968; JD, Temple U., 1975. Bar: Pa. 1975. Sole practice Nazareth, Pa., 1975—. Served with U.S. Army, 1968-70. Mem. Pa. Bar Assn., Northampton County Bar Assn. Democrat. Avocations: collector of antique phonographs and records. Fax: 610-746-3633. Estate planning, Probate. Office: 141 S Broad St Nazareth PA 18064-2119

**REED, JAMES A.,** lawyer; b. Muncie, Ind., Aug. 28, 1956; s. Ralph E. and Thelma M. R.; m. Kristina N. Martin, Apr. 1, 1978; children: Mark, Allison, Anna. AB, Ind. U., Bloomington, 1978; JD, Ind. U. Sch. Law, Indpls., 1983. Bar: Ind. 1983, U.S. Ct. Appeals (so. dist.) 1983. Atty. Buch, Berry et al, Indpls., 1983-90, Shiles & Reed, Indpls., 1990-96, Bingham, Summers, Welsh & Spilman, Indpls., 1996—; pres., bd. dirs. Indpls. City Market, 1994-97; mentor, bd. dirs. Behavior Corp., Carvel, Ind., 1996—. Mem., bd. dirs. Chistel Deltaan Family Found., Indpls., 1997—, Christel House, Inc., 1997—. Omdpls. Bar Assn., Phi Beta Kappa. Mem. LDS Ch. Family and matrimonial. Office: Bingham Summers et al 10 W Market St Ste 2700 Indianapolis IN 46204-4900

**REED, JAMES ALEXANDER, JR.,** lawyer; b. Rochester, N.Y., Feb. 7, 1930; s. James Alexander and Rose Winifred (Nellist) R.; m. Dora Anne DeVries, Feb. 17, 1972 (div. Mar. 1983); children: Geoffrey M., Diane E. BA cum laude, Amherst Coll., 1952; JD, Harvard U., 1955. Bar: N.Y. 1958, U.S. Dist. Ct. (we. dist.) N.Y. 1959, U.S. Dist. Ct. (no. dist.) N.Y. 1960. Assoc. Osborn, Reed, & Burke, Rochester, 1958-63, ptnr., 1964-96, of counsel, 1997—; dep. atty. Town of Pittsford, N.Y., 1976-77, atty., 1977-95. Served to lt. USNR, 1955-58. Mem. ABA, N.Y. State Bar Assn., Monroe County Bar Assn., Am. Judicature Assn. Republican. Episcopalian. State civil litigation, Federal civil litigation, Insurance. Home: 8 Greenwood Park Pittsford NY 14534-2912 Office: Osborn Reed & Burke 1 Exchange St Rochester NY 14614-1403

**REED, JOHN SQUIRES, II,** lawyer; b. Lexington, Ky., Mar. 20, 1949; s. John Squires and Mary Alexander (O'Hara) R.; m. Nancy Claire Battles, Dec. 29, 1973; children: Alexandra Simmons, John Squires III. AB in Polit. Sci., U. Ky., 1971; JD, U. Va., 1974. Bar: Ky. 1974, U.S. Dist. Ct. (we. dist.) Ky. 1975, U.S. Ct. Appeals (6th cir.) 1975, U.S. Dist. Ct. (ea. dist.) Ky. 1979, U.S. Supreme Ct. 1980, U.S. Ct. Appeals (fed. cir.) 1985. Assoc. Greenebaum Doll & McDonald, Louisville, 1974-79, ptnr., 1979-87; ptnr. Hirn, Doheny, Reed & Harper, Louisville, 1987-96, Reed Weitkamp Schell & Vice PLLC, Louisville, 1996—. Mem. Leadership Louisville, 1982, treas., mem. exec. com. Leadership Louisville Alumni Assn., 1984, pres., 1985; bd. dirs. Econs. Am. in Ky., 1985—, Nat. Assn. Community Leadership, 1986-91, treas. 1987-88, v.p. 1988-89, pres., 1989-90, Leadership Louisville Found., Inc., 1986-92, Greater Louisville Econ. Devel. Partnership, 1987-97; chair. Leadership USA, Inc., 1997, Louisville Collegiate Sch., 1996—. 1st lt. U.S. Army, 1974. Mem. ABA (antitrust, intellectual property, litig. sects.), Ky. Bar Assn., Louisville Bar Assn. (bd. dirs. 1985-86, treas. 1988, sec. 1989, v.p. 1990, pres. 1992), Louisville Boat Club, Valhalla Golf Club, Phi Beta Kappa. Democrat. Presbyterian. Antitrust, Federal civil litigation, Patent. Office: Reed Weitkamp Schell & Vice PLLC 2400 Citizens Plz Louisville KY 40202

**REED, JOHN WESLEY,** lawyer, educator; b. Independence, Mo., Dec. 11, 1918; s. Novus H. and Lilian (Houchens) R.; m. Imogene Fay Vonada, Oct. 5, 1946 (div. 1958); m. Dorothy Elaine Floyd, Mar. 5, 1961; children: Alison A., John M. (dec.), Mary V., Randolph F., Suzanne M. AB, William Jewell Coll., 1939, LLD, 1995; LLB, Cornell U., 1942; LLM, Columbia U., 1949, JSD, 1957. Bar: Mo. 1942, Mich. 1953. Assoc. Stinson, Mag, Thomson, McEvers & Fizzell, Kansas City, Mo., 1942-46; assoc. prof. law U. Okla., 1946-49; assoc. prof. U. Mich., 1949-53, prof., 1953-64, 68-85, Thomas M. Cooley prof., 1985-87, Thomas M. Cooley prof. emeritus, 1987—; dean, prof. U. Colo., 1964-68; dean, prof. Wayne State U., Detroit, 1987-92, prof. emeritus, 1992—; vis. prof. NYU, 1949, U. Chgo., 1960, Yale U., 1963-64, Harvard U., 1982, U. San Diego, 1993; dir. Inst. Continuing Legal Edn., 1968-73; reporter Mich. Rules of Evidence Com., 1975-78, 83-84; mem. faculty Salzburg Sem., 1962, chmn., 1964. Author: (with W.W. Blume) Pleading and Joinder, 1952; (with others) Introduction to Law and Equity, 1953, Advocacy Course Handbook series, 1963-81; editor in chief Cornell Law Quar., 1941-42; contbr. articles to profl. jours. Pres. bd. mgrs. of mins. and missionaries benefit bd. Am. Bapt. Chs. U.S.A., 1967-74, 82-85, 88-94; mem. com. visitors JAG Sch., 1971-76; trustee Kalamazoo Coll., 1954-64, 68-70. Recipient Harrison Tweed award Assn. Continuing Legal Edn. Adminstrs., 1983, Samuel E. Gates award Am. Coll. Trial Lawyers, 1985, Roberts P. Hudson award State Bar Mich., 1989. Fellow Internat. Soc. Barristers (editor jour. 1980—); mem. ABA (mem. coun. litigation sect.), Assn. Am. Law Schs. (mem. exec. com. 1965-67), Am. Acad. Jud. Edn. (v.p. 1978-80), Colo. Bar Assn. (mem. bd. govs. 1964-68), Mich. Supreme Ct. Hist. Soc. (bd. dirs. 1991—), Sci. Club Mich., Order of Coif. Office: U Mich Sch Law Ann Arbor MI 48109-1215

**REED, JONATHAN SETH,** lawyer; b. Ridgewood, N.J., May 10, 1958; s. Lawrence and Leila Sandgrund Reed; m. Reesa Hoffman, Nov. 2, 1986; children: Ethan Henry, Alexander Saul, Hannah Beth. BA, Franklin & Marshall Coll., 1980; JD, U. Colo., 1983. Bar: N.J. 1984, U.S. Dist. Ct. N.J. 1984, U.S. Ct. Appeals (3d cir.) 1984. Assoc. DeMaria Ellis & Hunt, Newark, 1984-90, ptnr., 1990-95; ptnr. Traub Eglin Lieberman Straus, Hackensack, N.J., 1996—. Contbr. articles to profl. jours. County committeeman Bergen County Dem. Party, Upper Saddle River, N.J., 1996—; dir. Upper Saddle River Quality of Life Com., 1998—. Mem. ABA, N.J. Bar Assn., Bergen County Bar Assn. Democrat. Jewish. Avocations: hiking, reading, sports, theatre. Insurance, Labor, Professional liability. Office: Traub Eglin Lieberman Straus 505 Main St Hackensack NJ 07601-5900

**REED, KEITH ALLEN,** lawyer; b. Anamosa, Iowa, Mar. 5, 1939; s. John Ivan and Florence Lorine (Larson) R.; m. Beth Illana Kesterson, June 22, 1963; children: Melissa Beth, Matthew Keith. BBA, U. Iowa, 1960, JD, 1963. Bar: Ill. and Iowa 1963. Ptnr. Seyfarth, Shaw, Fairweather & Geraldson, Chgo., 1963—. Co-author: Labor Arbitration in Healthcare, 1981; co-editor: Chicagoland Employment Law Manual, 1994, Employment and Discrimination, 1996, Federal Employment Law and Regulations, 1989-99; co-contbr. articles to Am. Hosp. Assn. publs., 1986-89. Trustee Meth. Hosp. Chgo., 1985—, Trinity Ch. North Shore, Wilmette, Ill., 1983—; mem. ad hoc labor adv. com. Am. Hosp. Assn., Chgo., 1980—; bd. dirs. Lyric Opera Chgo. Ctr. for Am. Artists, pres., 1983-86. Mem. ABA (bd. dir. health law forum 1979-82), Chgo. Bar Assn. (labor and employment law com. 1978—), Union League Club Chgo. (bd. dirs. 1985-88), Sunset Ridge Country Club (Northbrook, Ill.). Republican. Methodist. Avocations: music, community theater, tennis, golf. Health, Labor. Office: Seyfarth Shaw Fairweather & Geraldson 55 E Monroe St Ste 4200 Chicago IL 60603-5863

**REED, LOWELL A., JR.,** federal judge; b. Westchester, Pa., 1930; s. Lowell A. Sr. and Catherine Elizabeth R.; m. Diane Benson; four children. BBA, U. Wis., 1952; JD, Temple U., 1958. Bar: Pa. 1959, U.S. Dist. Ct. (ea. dist.) Pa. 1961, U.S. Ct. Appeals (3d cir.) 1962, U.S. Supreme Ct. 1970. Corp. trial counsel PMA Group, Phila., 1958-63; assoc. Rawle & Henderson, Phila., 1963-65, gen. ptnr., 1966-88; judge U.S. Dist Ct., Phila., 1988-99; sr. judge U.S. Dist. Ct., Phila., 1999—; lectr. law Temple U., 1965-81, faculty Acad. Advocacy, 1988—, Pa. Bar Inst., 1972—. Contbr. articles to profl. jours. Elder Abington (Pa.) Presbyn. Ch.; past. mem. Pa. Senate Select Com. Med. Malpractice; past pres., bd. dirs. Rydal Meadowbrook Civic Assn.; bd. dirs. Abington Sch. Bd., 1971, World Affairs Coun. Phila., 1983-88; trustee Abington Health Care Corp., 1983-88, 90-93. Lt. comdr. USNR, 1952-57. Recipient Alumni Achievement award Temple U. 1988. Mem. ABA, Phila. Bar Assn. (chmn. medico legal com. 1975, constl. bicentennial com. 1986-87, commn. on jud. selection and retention 1983-87), Temple Am. Inn of Ct. (pres. 1990-93, master of bench 1990—), Am. Judicature Soc., Temple U. Law Alumni Assn. (exec. com. 1987-90, 99—), Hist. Soc. U.S. Supreme Ct., Hist. Soc. U.S. Dist. Ct. Ea. Dist. Pa. Republican. Office: US Dist Ct 11614 US Courthouse Independence Mall W Philadelphia PA 19106

**REED, REX HOWARD,** foundation executive, lawyer; b. Joliet, Ill., Dec. 7, 1935; s. Howard Odin and Edith Frances (Gray) R.; m. Elizabeth Marie Hvizdos, May 4, 1968; children: Jennifer, Steven, Julia, Roger. BS, U. Ill., 1958; JD, So. Meth. U., 1961. Bar: Tex. 1961, D.C. 1965, U.S. Supreme Ct. 1965. Atty. Fed. Power Co. Commn., Washington, 1965-66, NLRB, Houston, 1966-68; asst. gen. counsel exchange service U.S. Army and USAF, Dallas, 1968-71; exec. v.p., legal dir. Nat. Right to Work Legal Def. Found., Springfield, Va., 1971—. Served to capt. USAF, 1962-65, served to lt. comdr. USNR, 1968-75. Mem. D.C. Bar Assn. Republican. Home: 1819 St Boniface St Vienna VA 22182-3352 Office: Nat Right to Work Legal Def Found 8001 Braddock Rd # 600 Springfield VA 22151-2110

**REED, ROBERT PHILLIP,** lawyer; b. Springfield, Ill., June 14, 1952; s. Robert Edward and Rita Ann (Kane) R.; m. Janice Leigh Kloppenburg, Oct. 8, 1976; children: Kevin Michael, Matthew Carl, Jennifer Leigh, Rebecca Ann. AB, St. Louis U., 1974; JD, U. Ill., 1977. Bar: Ill. 1977, U.S. Dist. Ct. (ctrl. dist.) Ill. 1979, U.S.Ct. Appeals (7th cir.) 1983, U.S. Dist. Ct. (so. dist.) Ill. 1992, Colo. 1993. Intern Ill. Legislature, Springfield, 1977-78; assoc. Traynor & Hendricks, Springfield, 1979-80; ptnr. Traynor, Hendricks & Reed, Springfield, 1981-88; pvt. practice Springfield, 1988—; pub. defender Sangamon County, Ill., Springfield, 1979-81; hearing examiner Ill. State Bd. Elections, Springfield, 1981-88; spl. asst. atty. gen. State of Ill., Springfield, 1983—; instr. Lincoln Land Community Coll., Springfield, 1988. Trustee Springfield Pk. Dist., 1985-89. Mem. Nat. Assn. Securities Dealers, Inc. (arbitrator 1996—), Comml. Law League Am., Ill. State Bar Assn., Colo. Bar Assn., Attys. Title Guaranty Fund, Inc., Phi Beta Kappa. Roman Catholic. General civil litigation, Probate, Real property. Office: 1129 S 7th St Springfield IL 62703-2418

**REED, RONALD ERNST,** lawyer; b. Frankfort, Ky., Mar. 24, 1958; s. Thomas B. and Gerhild M. Reed; m. Lisa J. Hayden, Mar. 7, 1994; 1 child, Spencer Thomas. BA, U. Fla., 1980, JD, 1983. Bar: Fla. 1983, U.S. Dist. Ct. (mid. dist.) Fla. 1987. Asst. states atty. State Atty.'s Office, Jacksonville, Fla., 1983-86; ptnr. Fallin & Reed, Jacksonville, 1986-87, Bullock, Childs, Pendley & Reed, P.A., Jacksonville, 1987—. Democrat. Methodist. Avocations: golfing, reading, sports. Personal injury, Insurance, Product liability. Office: Bullock Childs Pendley & Reed PA Ste 711 Blackstone Bldg 2333 E Bay St Jacksonville FL 32202

**REED, STEVEN CHARLES,** lawyer; b. Des Moines, Dec. 19, 1948; s. Charles Norland and Jeanette Theresa (Greiner) R.; m. Janice Elaine Waters, Dec. 20, 1969; children: Nicole Leanne, Jennifer Michelle. BSE with honors, Drake U., 1970, JD with honors, 1974. Iowa 1975, Nebr. 1975. Assoc. Fitzgerald, Brown, Schorr, Strom & Barmettler, Omaha, 1975-76; prin. Reed, Lenihan & Holzworth, Des Moines, 1976-89; pvt. practice West Des Moines, Iowa, 1989—; bd. mem. St. Pius X Bd. of Edn., Des Moines, 1985-87, First Iowa Community Credit Union, West Des Moines, 1987-88. Mem. Iowa State Bar Assn. (chair comml. and bankruptcy law sect., editor comml. and bankruptcy law newsletter), ATLA, Polk County Bar Assn., Order of Coif, Urbandale-Des Moines C. of C., Friendly Sons of St. Patrick, Des Moines (treas. 1985-86, v.p. 1986-87). Republican. Roman Catholic. Home: 9920 Hammontree Dr Des Moines IA 50322-1307 Office: 1741 Grand Ave West Des Moines IA 50265-5076

**REED, THOMAS A.,** laweyr, judge; b. Yonkers, N.Y., Feb. 4, 1934; s. John A. and Helen A. Reed; m. Margaret S. Reed, Apr. 20, 1967; children: Danielle S., Jennifer A. BS, Fordham U., 1963; LLB, Cornell U., 1966. Bar: N.Y. 1966. Ptnr. Reed & Reed, Poughkeepsie, N.Y., 1966-97; owner Thomas A. Reed, Esq., Poughkeepsie, 1998—; bd. dirs. Taconic Resources for Independence, Poughkeepsie, 1988—, Lighthouse-Mid Hudson Region, Poughkeepsie, 1991-96. Town justice Town of Pleasant Valley, N.Y., 1972—. Mem. N.Y. State Bar Assn., Dutchess County Bar Assn., N.Y. State Magistrates Assn., Dutchess County Magistrates Assn. (pres. 1977), Pleasant Valley Lions Club (pres., bd. dirs.). Avocation: tennis. Family and matrimonial, Probate, Real property. Office: 94 Market St Poughkeepsie NY 12601-4014

**REEDER, DONALD R.,** lawyer; b. Columbus, Ohio, May 14, 1952; s. William W. and Helen M. Reeder; children: Matthew L., Zachary R. BA in Polit. Sci., Ohio State U., 1974; JD, Capital U., 1981. Pvt. practice law Powell, Ohio, 1982—. Pres. Hyatts Cmty. Park, Inc., Powell, 1988—; chmn. Liberty Twp. Bd., Powell, 1994—. Mem. Delaware County Bar Assn. (v.p. 1998—). Home: 2379 Hyatts Rd Delaware OH 43015-7989 Office: PO Box 174 35 N Liberty St Powell OH 43065-9289

**REEDER, F. ROBERT,** lawyer; b. Brigham City, Utah, Jan. 23, 1943; s. Frank O. and Helen H. (Heninger) R.; m. Joannie Anderson, May 4, 1974; children: David, Kristina, Adam. JD, U. Utah, 1967. Bar: Utah 1967, U.S. Ct. Appeals (10th cir.) 1967, U.S. Ct. Mil. Appeals 1968, U.S. Supreme Ct. 1972, U.S. Ct. Appeals (D.C. and 5th cirs.) 1979. Shareholder Parsons, Behle & Latimer, Salt Lake City, 1968—, bd. dirs., 1974-92. Bd. dirs. Holy Cross Found., 1981-90, chmn., 1987-90; bd. dirs. Holy Cross Hosp., 1990-93, treas., 1986-87, vice chmn., 1987-93; bd. dirs. Holy Cross Health Svcs. Utah, 1993-94, treas., 1993-94; bd. dirs., vice chmn. Salt Lake Regional Med. Ctr., 1995—; trustee Univ. Hosp. Found., 1995; hon. col. Salt Lake City Police, Salt Lake County Sheriff. Served with USAR, 1967-73. Mem. ABA, Utah State Bar, Salt Lake County Bar (ethic adv. com. 1989-94), Cottonwood Country Club (bd. dirs. 1978-82, 83-86, pres. 1981-82), Rotary. Public utilities, Contracts commercial, General civil litigation. Office: Parsons Behle & Latimer PO Box 45898 Salt Lake City UT 84145-0898

**REEDER, JAMES ARTHUR,** lawyer; b. Baton Rouge, June 29, 1933; s. James Brown and Grace (Britt) R.; m. Mary Leone Guthrie, Dec. 30, 1958; children: Mary Virginia, James Jr., Elizabeth Colby. BA, Washington and Lee U., Lexington, Va., 1955; LLB, U. Tex., 1960; JD, La. State U., 1961. Ptnr. Booth, Lockard, Jack et al, Shreveport, La., 1961-72; pres. and mgng. ptnr. Shreveport Broadcasting Co., 1972-86; CEO, mng. gen. ptnr. Radio USA Limited, Houston, 1986-89; pres. SW subsidiaries Sun Group, Inc., Houston, 1990-92; atty. Patton & Boggs, LLP, Washington, 1991-94; ptnr. Patton, Boggs LLP, Washington, 1994—; dir. ABC Radio Sta. Affiliates adv. bd., N.Y.C., 1978-84. Dir. Boys Country, Houston, 1986-90; pres. Holiday in Dixie, Shreveport, 1968; chmn. Ambassadors Club, Shreveport, 1979. 1st Lt. U.S. Army, 1955-57. Named La. Outstanding Young Man, La. Jaycees, 1969. Mem. ABA (bd. dirs. young lawyers sect. 1967-68, Gavel awards com. 1980), La. Bar Assn. (pres. young lawyers sect. 1966, La. Outstanding Young Lawyer award 1968), D.C. Bar Assn., Tex. Bar Assn., Nat. Assn. Broadcasters, Houston Country Club, Demoiselle Club (Shreveport), Allegro Club (Houston). Roman Catholic. Legislative.

**REEDER, ROBERT HARRY,** retired lawyer; b. Topeka, Dec. 3, 1930; s. William Harry and Florence Mae (Cochran) R. AB Washburn U., 1952, JD, 1960. Bar: U.S. Dist. Ct. Kans. 1960, Kans. 1960, U.S. Supreme Ct. 1968. Rsch. asst. Kans. Legis. Council Rsch. Dept., Topeka, 1955-60; asst. counsel Traffic Inst., Northwestern U., Evanston, Ill., 1960-67, gen. counsel, 1967-92; exec. dir. Nat. Com. on Uniform Traffic Laws and Ordinances, Evanston, 1982-90. Co-author: Vehicle Traffic Law, 1974; The Evidence Handbook, 1980. Author: Interpretation of Implied Consent by the Courts, 1972. Served with U.S. Army, 1952-54. Mem. Com. Alcohol and Other Drugs (chmn. 1973-75). Republican. Methodist. Criminal.

**REEDOM, JAMES PATRICK,** paralegal, educator; b. New Iberia, La., July 18, 1949; s. Marshall and Dorothy (Lewis) R. BA in Polit. Sci., Grambling State U., 1972; MA in Polit. Sci., SUNY, Albany, 1973. Dep. dir. criminal justice Grambling (La.) State U., 1975-76; instr. constnl. prelaw Schenectady (N.Y.) C.C., 1977-78; instr. polit. sci., pub. adminstrn. Lincoln U., Jefferson City, Md., 1978-80; instr. govt. Tex. Christian U., Ft. Worth, 1981-82; exec. dir. Help Is On The Way, Ft. Worth, 1988—, pres. bd. dirs., 1994—. Author: Prose Law Manual, 1996. SUNY tchg. fellow, 1975, 76, 77. Mem. Ft. Worth C. of C. Democrat. Roman Catholic. Avocation: computer programming. Home and Office: 3024 Mount Vernon Ave Ste 2 Fort Worth TX 76103-2956

**REEG, KURTIS BRADFORD,** lawyer; b. St. Louis, Sept. 1, 1954; s. Jay Flory and Mary Louise (Braun) R.; m. Cynthia Diane Wable, June 25, 1994. BA cum laude, DePauw U., 1976; JD, St. Louis U., 1979. Bar: U.S. Dist. Ct. (ea. dist.) Mo. 1979, U.S. Dist. Ct. (so. dist.) Ill. 1981, U.S. Ct. Appeals (8th cir.) 1984, U.S. Ct. Appeals (7th cir.) 1986, U.S. Dist. Ct. Ariz. 1994, U.S. Ct. Appeals (2d cir.) 1994, U.S. Supreme Ct. 1994. Law clk. to presiding justice Ill. Appellate Ct. (5th dist.), Granite City, 1979-80; assoc. Coburn, Croft & Putzell, St. Louis, Mo. and Belleville, Ill., 1980-86, ptnr., 1986-91; ptnr., chmn. tort and ins. group, co-chmn. litigation dept. Gallop, Johnson & Neuman, L.C., St. Louis, 1991-98; mem. compensation com. Gallop, Johnson & Neuman, L.C., Belleville, 1991-97; mem. mgmt. com. Gallop, Johnson & Neuman, L.C., St. Louis, Ill., 1991-98; mng. ptnr. Gallop, Johnson & Neuman, L.C., Belleville, Ill., 1997-98; ptnr. Sonnenschein Nath & Rosenthal, St. Louis, 1998—; chmn. Nationwide Products Liability Grp., St. Louis Tort and Ins. Grp., instr. legal research and writing St. Louis U., 1979-80. Mem. Police, Fire Commns., City of Town and Country, Mo., 1987-89; Rep. committeeman 24th ward, St. Louis, 1980. Mem. ABA, Ill. State Bar Assn., Mo. Bar Assn., Bar Assn. of Met. St. Louis, Internat. Assn. Def. Counsel, Ill. Assn. Def. Trial Counsel, Fedn. ins. and Corp. Counsel, Def. Rsch. Inst., Midwest Environ. Claims Assn., Phi Alpha Delta, Pi Sigma Alpha. Republican. Avocations: hunting, fishing, golf, astronomy. E-mail: kbr@sonnenschein.com. Insurance, Product liability, Toxic tort. Home: 12720 Willowyck Dr Saint Louis MO 63146-3726 Office: Sonnenschein Nath & Rosenthal Ste 3000 One Metropolitan Sq Saint Louis MO 63102

**REES, JAMES BRENNAN,** lawyer; b. Cinn., Jan. 23, 1954; s. Samuel Dewitt and Jane Elizabeth R. BA in Political Sci., U. Ky., 1976; JD, N. Ky. U., 1979. Bar: Ky. 1979, W. Va. 1991, U.S. Ct. Appeals (6th cir.), U.S. Ct. Appeals (4th cir.), U.S. Dist. Ct. N.D., Ky. (ea. dist.) 1979, U.S. Dist. Ct. S.D., W. Va. (so. dist.) 1991. Pvt. practice Burlington, N.Y., 1979-89; chief pub. defender Pub. Defense Corp. 12th Cir., Fayetteville, W. Va., 1989—; instr. W. Va. Inst. Tech., Montgomery, W. Va., 1992-96. Office: Public Defender Corp 12 Cir PO Box 239 Fayetteville WV 25840-0239

**REES, THOMAS DYNEVOR,** lawyer; b. S.I., N.Y., Sept. 25, 1949; s. Thomas and Caroline (Bridgman) R.; m. Josephine Stephanie Madej, Apr. 8, 1978; 1 child, Thomas D. III. AB in Polit. Sci., Stanford U., 1971; JD, U. Pa., 1975. Bar: N.Y. 1976, Pa. 1977, U.S. Supreme Ct. 1982. Assoc. Lovejoy, Wasson, Lundgren & Ashton, N.Y.C., 1975-77, Morgan, Lewis & Bockius, Phila., 1977-81; dep. gen. counsel Office of Gov. of Pa., Harrisburg, 1981-85; counsel High Swartz, Roberts & Seidel, Norristown, Pa., 1985-86, ptnr., 1987—; CLE course planner, faculty mem. Pa. Bar Inst., 1990—; employment panel arbitrator Am. Arbitration Assn., Phila., 1991—. Solicitor Upper Merion Twp., King of Prussia, Pa., 1987-88, 90-95, Abington (Pa.) Twp., 1986-87; pres. Gladwyne (Pa.) Civic Assn., 1995-97. Mem. ABA, Pa. Bar Assn. (chair mcpl. law sect. 1993-95), Montgomery County Bar. Assn. (co-chair employment law com. 1996-97), King of Prussia C. of C. (solicitor 1996—). Republican. Episcopalian. Labor, Land use and zoning (including planning), Education and schools. Office: High Swartz Roberts & Seidel LLP 40 E Airy St Norristown PA 19401-4803

**REESE, KIRK DAVID,** lawyer; b. Rochester, Minn., Jan. 8, 1948; s. Orville Arnold and Alta Matilda (Borgen) R.; m. Shan G. Kovatch, Aug. 1, 1974; children: Nels E., Hannah M., Ingrid M. BA, Beloit Coll., 1970; JD, Ohio No. U., 1983. Bar: Wis. 1983, U.S. Dist. Ct. (we. and ea. dists.) Wis. 1985, U.S. Ct. Appeals (7th cir.) 1986. Instr. Ohio No. U., Ada, 1983-84; pvt. practice, Rhinelander, Wis., 1984-85; assoc. Eckert Law Office, Rhinelander, 1985-91; commr. Oncida County Family Ct., Rhinelander, 1991—; pvt. practice Reese Law Office, Rhinelander, 1991—. Rsch. editor Ohio No. U. Law Rev., 1981-82. Chmn. bd. dirs. White Pines Community Broadcasting, Rhinelander, 1991—, Rhinelander Soccer Assn., 1990—. Recipient Book award Am. Jurisprudence, 1983. Mem. Kiwanis. Estate planning, Probate, Workers' compensation. Office: PO Box A Rhinelander WI 54501-0076

**REEVES, GENE,** judge; b. Meridian, Miss., Feb. 27, 1930; s. Clarence Eugene and May (Philyaw) R.; m. Brenda Wages, Sept. 26, 1980. JD, John Marshall U., 1964; cert. judge spl. ct. jurisdiction; postgrad., U. Nev., 1995. Bar: Ga. 1964, U.S. Ct. Appeals (11th cir.) 1965, U.S. Supreme Ct. 1969. Ptnr. Craig & Reeves, Lawrenceville, Ga., 1964-71; sole practice Lawrenceville, 1971-85; prin. Reeves Law Firm, 1985-94; judge City Ct., Lawrenceville, 1969-70, Magistrate Ct. of Gwinnett County, Ga., 1994—. Sgt. USAF, 1951-54. Mem. ABA, ATLA, GTLA, Am. Jud. Soc., Gwinnett County Bar Assn. (pres. 1970-72), Criminal Def. Lawyers Assn., Atlanta Bar Assn. Baptist. Home: 221 Pineview Dr Lawrenceville GA 30045-6035 Office: 75 Langley Dr Lawrenceville GA 30045-6935

**REEVES, PAMELA,** lawyer; b. Marion, Va., July 21, 1954. BA, U. Tenn., 9176, JD, 1979. Bar: Tenn. 1979, U.S. Dist. Ct. (ea. and mid. dists.) Tenn. 1979, U.S. Ct. Appeals (6th cir.), U.S. Supreme Ct. Ptnr. Watson Hollow & Reeves, PLC, Knoxville; lectr. employment related issues, ethics, and professionalism and civil procedure Knoxville Bar Assn., Tenn. Bar Assn., 1991—. Mem. U. Tenn. Law Rev., 1976; contbr. articles to profl. jours. Mem. ABA, Tenn. Bar Found., Tenn. Bar Assn. (pres. 1998, pres. young lawyers cons. 1989-90, ho. dels. 1987-92), Knoxville Bar Assn. (pres. Knoxville barristers 1983, sec. 1994-96), Am. Inns of Ct. (master of the bench, adminstr. 1994), Phi Beta Kappa. E-mail: swaneeves@mindpsring.com. Office: Watson Hollow & Reeves PC 1700 First Tennessee Plz 800 S Gay St Ste 1700 Knoxville TN 37929-1700*

**REEVES, ROSS CAMPBELL,** lawyer; b. Raleigh, N.C., Oct. 15, 1948; s. Ralph Bernard Jr. and Frances Campbell R.; m. Robin Fuller Neuschel, June 20, 1970; children: Cameron Fuller, Peter C. BA, Yale U., 1970; JD, U. Va., 1973. Bar: Va. 1973 (chmn. bus. laws com. 1984-86), U.S. Cir. Ct. (4th cir.) 1973; cert. specialist bus. bankruptcy ABBI. Staff atty. Adminstrv. Conf. U.S., Washington, 1973-74; assoc. Kaufman Oberndorfer & Spainhour, Norfolk, Va., 1974-79; ptnr. Kaufman Oberndorfer & Spainhour, Norfolk, 1979-82, Willcox & Savage, P.C., Norfolk, 1982—; dir. Heritage Bank & Trust Co., Norfolk, 1993—, Va. Venture Capital Forum, Norfolk, 1996—; lectr. in field. Chmn. adv. com. Chrysler Mus. Art, Norfolk, 1985-87. Mem. Norfolk Assembly (sec.-treas. 1996-98, pres. 1999—), Norfolk Hist. Soc. (dir. 1995—), Harbor Club (dir. 1998—). Bankruptcy, Contracts commercial, General corporate. Office: Willcox & Savage PC 1800 Nations Bank Ctr Norfolk VA 23510

**REGAN, JOHN MANNING, JR.,** lawyer; b. Phila., Feb. 6, 1958; s. John Manning and Sheila Hogan Regan; m. Rhonda Doreen Cartner, Apr. 17, 1982; 1 child, Timothy Joseph. BA, U. Windsor, Ont., Can., 1979; JD, Villanova U., 1988. Bar: N.Y. 1988, U.S. Dist. Ct. (we. dist.) N.Y., U.S. Bankruptcy Ct. (we. dist.) N.Y., U.S. Ct. Appeals (2d cir.). Confidential law asst. to Hon. Richard C. Wesley, N.Y. State Supreme Ct., Rochester, 1988-89; ptnr. Reyes & Regan, P.C., Rochester, 1989-92; ptnr., pres. Regan & Regan, P.C., Rochester, 1992—. Contbr., editor The Chancellor, newsletter, 1996-98. Rep. candidate for U.S. Ho. of Reps. from 30th Congl. Dist. N.Y., 1990. Lt. comdr. USN, 1981-85. Mem. St. Thomas More Lawyers Guild (bd. govs. Rochester). Roman Catholic. Avocations: tennis, skiing, theology, philosophy. General civil litigation, Personal injury, Appellate. Office: 13 S Fitzhugh St Ste 330 Rochester NY 14614-1422

**REGAN, MICHAEL PATRICK,** lawyer; b. Bklyn., Feb. 22, 1941; s. Cornelius Francis and Marguerite (Cann) R.; m. Susan Ann Light, July 13, 1974; children: Michael Patrick, Brian Christopher, Mark Dennis. BA in English, U. Notre Dame, 1963; LLB, Albany Law Sch., Union U., 1967, JD, 1968. Bar: N.Y. 1967, Va. 1975. Assoc. Medwin & McMahon, Albany, N.Y., 1967-69; asst. dist. atty. Albany County, N.Y., 1969; corp. atty. Mohasco Corp., Amsterdam, N.Y., 1969-74; asst. gen. csl. Dan River Inc., Danville, Va., 1975, assoc. gen. counsel, 1981-84, assoc. gen. counsel, asst. sec., 1984, acting gen. counsel, asst. sec., 1988, gen. counsel, asst. sec., 1989, assoc. gen. counsel, asst. sec. Dan River Holding Co., 1984-88, acting gen. counsel, asst. sec., 1988, gen. counsel, asst. sec., 1989—; assoc. gen. counsel, asst. sec. Dan River Svcs. Corp. of Va., 1984-88; gen. counsel, 1989, Wunda Weve Carpets, Inc., Greenville, S.C., 1990-93; mng. dir. Law Offices Michael P. Regan, P.C., 1990—. Sec. Dan Pac, polit. action com., Danville; clarinetist, saxophonist Tightsqueeze Philharm. Band; leader: The Dance-Notes; sec. Dan Pac Polit. Action Com., 1976-89. Mem. ABA, N.Y. State Bar Assn., Va. Bar Assn., Danville Bar Assn., Union Internationale des Avocats. Republican. Roman Catholic. Club: Rotary (Danville). General corporate, Pension, profit-sharing, and employee benefits, Trademark and copyright. Home: 236 Cambridge Cir Danville VA 24541-5233 Office: 703 Patton St Danville VA 24541-1905

**REGAN, PAUL MICHAEL,** lawyer; b. Detroit, May 8, 1953; s. Timothy J. and Adele (Anthony) R. BA, Duke U., 1975; JD, Cath. U., 1979. Bar: N.Y. 1983. Clearance officer, counsel Ticor Title Guarantee Co., Syracuse, N.Y., 1980-84; assoc. Van Epps & Shulman, Syracuse, 1984-87, Shulman Law Firm, Syracuse, 1987-91; ptnr. Shulman Curtin Grundner Regan & Snyder, P.C., Syracuse, 1992—; speaker Nat. Bus. Inst., 1991, N.Y. State Bar Seminars, 1990-94. Vestry Christ Ch., Malius, N.Y., 1991-96; bd. dirs. Cazenovia (N.Y.) Childrens House, 1990-94; counsel Save Our Cmty., Inc., Cazenovia, 1989-93. Mem. N.Y. State Bar Assn., Onondaga County Bar Assn. (chmn. real estate contract com. 1990-96, com. on title standards 1990-96, spkr. 1998). Real property, Environmental. Office: Shulman Curtin Grundner Regan & Snyder 250 S Clinton St Syracuse NY 13202-1263

**REGAN, RICHARD ROBERT,** lawyer; b. Somerville, Mass., Aug. 2, 1960; s. Robert Richard and Helene Marie Regan; m. Mary Theresa Hart; children: Abigail Hart Regan, Aidan Hart Regan. BA, Bates Coll., 1982; MA, U. Va., 1984; JD, U. Maine, 1994. Tcht. Iolani Sch., Honolulu, 1985-89,

Wilbraham (Mass.) & Monson Acad., 1989-91; title abstractor Cloutier Barrett Conley Cloutier, Portland, Maine, 1993-94; atty. Hart & Regan, Bath, Maine, 1994—. Contbr. articles to profl. jours. Pres. Smalls Brook Crossing Homeowners Assn., Cumberland, Maine, 1997—. Mem. Maine Trial Lawyers Assn. (publs. editor, legis. com. 1995—), Bath Brunswick Bar Assn. (sec. 1997—). Avocations: cooking, beer making, sports, rock music. Personal injury, Criminal, Probate. Office: Hart & Regan 37 Court St Bath ME 04530-2017

**REGAN, ROBERT TERRENCE,** lawyer; b. Teaneck, N.J., Mar. 27, 1951; s. Raymond T. and Elizabeth V. (Oates) R.; m. Marilyn C. Spadola, Feb. 7, 1981. BA, Fordham U., 1973; JD, U. Toledo, 1976. Bar: N.J. 1976, N.Y. 1984, U.S. Dist. Ct. N.J. 1976, U.S. Supreme Ct. 1983. Law clk. to Hon. Kevin M. O'Halloran Superior Ct. of N.J., Hackensack, 1976-77; assoc. Randall, Randall & McGuire, Westwood, N.J., 1977-79; ptnr. McGuire & Regan, P.A., Westwood, 1980-90; owner Robert T. Regan, P.C., Westwood, 1990—; borough atty. Borough of Edgewater (N.J.), 1979—, Borough of Upper Saddle River (N.J.), 1989—, Borough of Midland Park (N.J.), 1994—; counsel Leonia (N.J.)Planning Bd., 1985—, Montvale (N.J.) Planning Bd., 1993—. Lectr. at various symposiums. Elected county com. Upper Saddle River Borough, 1992—. Mem. Bergen County Bar Assn. (chair 1995—, mcpl. law com., land use com.). Republican. Roman Catholic. Avocations: bicycling, wine collecting. Municipal (including bonds), Real property, Land use and zoning (including planning). Home: 35 Ridge Rd U Saddle Riv NJ 07458-2140 Office: 345 Kinderkamack Rd Westwood NJ 07675-1600

**REGAN, SUSAN GINSBERG,** lawyer; b. N.Y.C., Oct. 20, 1947; d. Irwin Arthur and Sylvia (Rosen) Ginsberg; m. Neil A. Goldberg, Jan. 24, 1975 (div. May 1987); children: Jane Goldberg, Rafael Goldberg; m. Edward Van Buren Regan, Oct. 12, 1991. BA, U. Mich., 1969; JD, SUNY, Buffalo, 1974. Bar: N.Y. 1975. Asst. county atty. Erie County, Buffalo, N.Y., 1975-78; ptnr. Magavern, Magavern & Grimm LLP, Buffalo, N.Y., 1982-98; assoc. gen. counsel Vis. Nurse Svc. N.Y., N.Y.C., 1998—; mem., chair establishment com. N.Y. State Pub. Health Coun., 1996—; clin. asst. prof. SUNY Sch. Medicine and Biomed. Scis., Buffalo, 1997—. Mem. Nat. Health Lawyers Assn., N.Y. State Bar Assn. (health law com., com. on profl. ethics, N.Y.C., 1984-87). Avocation: skiing. Health, Non-profit and tax-exempt organizations. Office: Vis Nurse Svc NY 107 E 70th St New York NY 10021-5006

**REGENBOGEN, ADAM,** judge; b. Steyer, Austria, June 12, 1947; s. William and Pauline (Feuerstein) R.; m. Paula Ruth Rothenberg, June 27, 1970 (div. Oct. 1992); children: Stacy, Candice; m. Helen Busuttil Drwal, Apr. 20, 1996; 1 stepchild, Jason A. Drwal. BA, Temple U., 1969; MSW, U. Pa., 1972; JD, Temple U., 1980. Bar: N.Y. 1983. Social worker VA, Coatesville, Pa., 1974-78; supr. VA, Northport, N.Y., 1978-80, quality assurance dir., 1980-87; dir. quality assurance N.Y. State Office Mental Health, Willard, 1987-91; conciliator, acting judge N.Y. State Workers Compensation Bd., Binghamton, 1992-98; judge Ithaca, Binghamton and Elmira, 1998—; pvt. practice N.Y., 1983-98; conciliator, acting judge Workers Compensation Bd., N.Y., 1992-98, judge, 1998—. Organizer/incorporator Ithaca (N.Y.) Reform Temple, 1992; organizer Parents Without Partners, Ithaca, 1992. Recipient Pro Bono Svc. award Suffolk County Bar Assn., 1986. Mem. Tompkins County Bar Assn. Home: PO Box 2234 14 Grant St Port Dickinson Binghamton NY 13902-2234 Office: Workers Compensation Bd 44 Hawley St Binghamton NY 13901-4434

**REGENSTREIF, HERBERT,** lawyer; b. N.Y.C., May 13, 1935; s. Max and Jeannette (Hacker) R.; m. Patricia Friedman, Dec. 20, 1967 (div. July 1968); m. Charlotte Lois Levy, Dec. 11, 1980; 1 child, Cara Rachael. BA, Hobart Coll., 1957; JD, N.Y. Law Sch., 1960; MS, Pratt Inst., 1985. Bar: N.Y. 1961, Ky. 1985, U.S. Dist. Ct. (ea. and so. dists.) N.Y. 1962, U.S. Dist. Ct. (ea. dist.) Ky. 1998, U.S. Tax Ct. 1967, U.S. Ct. Appeals (2d cir.) 1962, U.S. Supreme Ct. 1967. Ptnr. Fried & Regenstreif, P.C., Mineola, N.Y., 1963—; reservist atty. Fed. Emergency Mgmt. Agy., 1998—; cons. in field; arbitrator Dist. Ct., Nassau County, N.Y., 1989—, N.Y.C. Civil Ct., 1984-86; sec.-treas. Sta. WAHY-FM, Inc., 1998—. Contbr. articles to profl. jours. County committeeman Dem. Com., Queens County, N.Y., 1978-79. Mem. Bar Assn. Nassau County, Ky. Bar Assn., Phi Delta Phi, Beta Phi Mu, Hobart Club of N.Y. (gov. 1968-69). General practice, Religion.

**REGNIER, JAMES,** state supreme court justice; b. Aurora, Ill.; m. Linda Regnier; 3 children. BS, Marquette U., 1966; JD, U. Ill., 1973. Judicial Fellow ACTL, Internat. Soc. Barristers; completed atty. mediator tng., Atty.-Mediator Tng. Inst., Dallas, 1993. Lawyer pvt. practice, Rochelle, Ill., 1973-78; co-founder, ptnr. Regnier, Lewis and Boland, Great Falls, Mont., 1979-91; lawyer pvt. practice, Missoula, Mont., 1991-97; justice Mont. Supreme Ct., Helena, 1997—; appt. Mont. Supreme Ct. Commn. on Civil Jury Instrn.; appt. lawyer-rep. to 9th Cir. Judicial Confs., 1987, 88, 89, chair Mont. lawyer delegation, 1989; lectr. U. Mont. Sch. Law, numerous continuing legal edn. seminars. Contbr. Mont. Pattern Jury Instrns. for Civil Cases, 1985. Co-founder Mont. chpt. Am. Bd. Trial Advocates, 1989—, pres. Officer USN, Vietnam. Office: Montana Supreme Ct Justice Bldg 215 N Sanders St Helena MT 59601-4522

**REGNIER, RICHARD ADRIAN,** lawyer; b. Portland, Oreg., Aug. 23, 1931; s. Augustus Jerome and Marietta (Howland) R.; m. Maria Teresa Arguindegui, Oct. 12, 1957; children: Richard Adrian Jr., Lisa Marina, Augustus Jerome II, Teresa Lynn; m. Georgianna Pennington, Aug. 5, 1993. Student, Harvard U., 1949-50; BS, U.S. Mil. Acad., 1955; LLB, U. Calif., Berkeley, 1962. Bar: Calif. 1963, U.S. Dist. Ct. (so. dist.) Calif. 1963, U.S. Supreme Ct. 1968. Commd. 2d lt. USAF, 1955, advanced through grades to capt., res., 1959; dep. dist. atty. Ventura County, Calif., 1963-65; assoc. Ferguson, Regnier & Paterson, Oxnard, Calif., 1965-68, ptnr., 1968-90; pvt. practice Oxnard, Calif., 1990—; instr. criminal law and evidence Ventura County Jr. Coll. and Ventura County Sheriff's Acad., 1963-65; judge pro tem Superior Ct. Ventura County, 1971—. Speaker Right to Life League So. Calif., Ventura County, 1973—; campaign chmn. MacIntyre for Assessor, Ventura County, 1986; pres. Oxnard Coll. Found., 1994—; bd. advisors Red Cloud Indian Sch. Named Extraordinary Minister of Holy Eucharist, Archbishop of Los Angeles, Ventura, 1971—. Mem. ABA, Am. Bd. Trial Advocates, Calif. Bar Assn. (group ins. com. 1973-76, com. bar examine site rev. team), Ventura County Bar Assn. (exec. com. 1987-89), Assn. Trial Lawyers Am., Consumer Attys. Calif. (recognition of experience certs. various areas), Ventura County Trial Lawyers Assn. (pres. 1971, 86, lectr. trial law), Am. Judicature Soc., Ventura County Legal Aid Assn. (pres. 1968), Am. Arbitration Assn. (arbitrator 1966—), Nat. Bd. Trial Adv. (diplomate, cert.), Ventura Inns of Ct., Saticoy Country Club (pres. 1992). Republican. Lodges: Rotary (pres. 1982-83, Paul Harris fellow 1986), K.C. Avocations: golf, running, weight lifting, skiing. State civil litigation, Personal injury, Federal civil litigation. Office: Law Offices Richard Regnier 301 N A St Oxnard CA 93030-4901

**REHBERGER, ROBERT LEE,** lawyer, educator; b. St. Louis, Apr. 2, 1949; s. W.R. and Ruth (Grimmer) Schoolfield. BS, Benedictine Coll., Atchison, Kans., 1971; MBA, U. Puget Sound, 1971, MPA, 1975; JD, U. Mo., Kansas City, 1980. Bar: Mo. 1981, U.S. Dist. Ct. (we. dist.) Mo. 1981, Ill. 1981, U.S. Dist. Ct. (so. dist.) Ill. 1985, Okla. 1983, U.S. Dist. Ct. (we. dist.) Okla 1983, D.C. 1985, U.S. Ct. Appeals (10 cir.) 1986, Ga. 1988, U.S. Dist. Ct. (no. dist.) Ga. 1988, U.S. Dist. Ct. (so. dist.) Ga. 1990, U.S. Dist. Ct. (mid. dist.) Ga. 1991, Fla. 1990, U.S. Supreme Ct. Comptr. cir. ct. Madison County, Edwardsville, Ill., 1976-77, law clk. to presiding justice, 1981, asst. states atty., 1981-82; prof. Southwestern Okla. State U., Weatherford, 1982-86; corp. cons. Olympia Produce, 1988-90; pvt. practice law Stockbridge, Ga., 1988—; instr. U. Mo., St. Louis, spring 1982; faculty advisor Alpha Kappa Psi Southwestern Okla. State U., Weatherford, 1982-86; adj. prof. Clayton State Coll., 1991—. With U.S. Army, 1972-75. Mem. ABA, Okla. Bar Assn., Assn. Trial Lawyers Am., Ill. Bar Assn., Met. Bar Assn. St. Louis, Met. Bar Assn. Kansas City, D.C. Bar Assn., Madison County Bar Assn., Alpha Kappa Psi, Delta Phi. Lodge: Moose, Masons, Optimists. Avocations: water and snow skiing, horse back riding. Home: 451 Stagecoach Rd Stockbridge GA 30281-1927 Office: Robert Rehberge & Assocs 5025 N Henry Blvd Stockbridge GA 30281-3538

**REHBOCK, RICHARD ALEXANDER,** lawyer; b. New Haven, Sept. 12, 1946; s. Morton J. and Evelyn (Norris) R.; m. Nanette DiFalco, June 5, 1997; 1 stepchild: Gregory. BA, Fairleigh Dickinson U., 1968; JD, St. John's U., 1973. Bar: N.Y. 1974, U.S. Dist. Ct. (ea. and so. dists.) N.Y. 1974, U.S. Ct. Appeals (2d cir.) 1977, U.S. Ct. Appeals (3d cir.) 1996, U.S. Supreme Ct. 1978, U.S. Dist. Ct. (we. dist.) N.Y. 1983, Fla. 1987. Atty. criminal div. Legal Aid Soc., N.Y.C., 1973-77; staff atty. U.S. Dist. Ct. N.Y. Legal Aid Soc., Bklyn., 1977-79; ptnr. Rehbock, Fishman & Kudisch, Kew Gardens, N.Y., 1979-83; pvt. practice law, N.Y.C., 1983—. Staff sgt. U.S. Army, 1969-70, Vietnam. Fellow Am. Bd. Criminal Lawyers; mem. Criminal Ct. Bar Assn. (bd. dirs. Queens County chpt.), Am. Trial Lawyers Assn., Nat. Assn. Criminal Def. Attys. (vice chmn. legis. com.), Nat. Assn. Trial Attys., Fed. Bar Coun., N.Y. State Bar Assn., Queens Bar Assn., N.Y. County Lawyers Assn., N.Y. State Assn. Criminal Def. Attys. (chair fed. legis. com.), Fla. Bar Assn. Criminal, Federal civil litigation, Contracts commercial. Home and Office: 1 Maple Run Dr Jericho NY 11753-2827

**REHM, JOHN BARTRAM,** lawyer; b. Paris, Nov. 23, 1930; s. George and Mary (Torr) R.; m. Diana Mary Aed, Dec. 19, 1959; children: David Bartram, Jennifer Aed. AB, Harvard U., 1952; LLB, Columbia U., 1955; M.T.S., Wesley Sem., 1990. Bar: N.Y. 1955, D.C. 1969, U.S. Dist. Ct. D.C. 1971, U.S. Ct. Internat. Trade 1980, U.S. Supreme Ct. 1988. Assoc. Willkie, Owen, Farr, Gallagher & Walton, N.Y.C., 1955-56; atty.-advisor U.S. Dept. State, Washington, 1956-62, asst. legal advisor for econ. affairs, 1962-63; gen. counsel Office of Spl. Trade Rep., Washington, 1963-69; ptnr. Busby, Rivkin, Sherman, Levy & Rehm, Washington, 1969-77, Busby, Rehm and Leonard, Washington, 1977-87, Dorsey & Whitney, Washington, 1988—. Democrat. Episcopalian. Administrative and regulatory, Private international, Legislative. Home: 5005 Worthington Dr Bethesda MD 20816-2748 Office: Dorsey & Whitney 1330 Connecticut Ave NW Washington DC 20036-1704

**REHNQUIST, WILLIAM HUBBS,** United States supreme court chief justice; b. Milw., Oct. 1, 1924; s. William Benjamin and Margery (Peck) R.; m. Natalie Cornell, Aug. 29, 1953; children: James, Janet, Nancy. BA, MA, Stanford U., 1948; MA, Harvard U., 1949; LLB, Stanford U., 1952. Bar: Ariz. Law clk. to former justice Robert H. Jackson, U.S. Supreme Ct., 1952-53; with Evans, Kitchel & Jenckes, Phoenix, 1953-55; mem. Ragan & Rehnquist, Phoenix, 1956-57; ptnr. Cunningham, Carson & Messenger, Phoenix, 1957-60, Powers & Rehnquist, Phoenix, 1960-69; asst. atty.-gen. office of legal counsel Dept. of Justice, Washington, 1969-71; assoc. justice U.S. Supreme Ct., 1971-1986, chief justice, 1986—; mem. Nat. Conf. Commrs. Uniform State Laws, 1963-69. Author: The Supreme Court: How It Was, How It Is, 1987, Grand Inquests: The Historic Impeachments of Justice Samuel Chase and President Andrew Johnson, 1992, All the Laws But One, 1999; contbr. articles to law jours., nat. mags. Served with USAAF, 1943-46, NATOUSA. Mem. Fed., Am. Maricopa (Ariz.) County bar assns., State Bar Ariz., Nat. Conf. Lawyers and Realtors, Phi Beta Kappa, Order of Coif, Phi Delta Phi. Lutheran. Office: Supreme Ct US 1 1st St NE Washington DC 20543-0001

**REICH, DEBORAH ZISKIND,** public relations and legal marketing executive; b. Pitts., Mar. 4, 1961; d. Gerald N. and Norma Jean (Morris) Ziskind; m. Manuel D. Reich, Nov. 11, 1989. BA in Internat. Rels., Tufts U., 1983. Litigation specialist, sr. case mgr., pub. affairs and client devel. assoc. Weil, Gotshal & Manges, N.Y.C., 1989-94; mgr. mktg. Reed Smith Shaw & McClay, Pitts., Phila., N.Y.C., Washington and Princeton, N.J., 1994-96; pres., CEO, Deborah Ziskind Reich Pub. Rels., Pitts., 1996—; founder, chmn. The Global Conf. Inst., 1996—; pub. rels. cons. Pitts. Chamber Music Soc., U. Pitts. dept. music, 1983-85; antitrust case mgr. cons. Dickie, McCamey & Chilcote, 1985-87; exec. May Corp., Pitts., 1987-89. Contbg. columnist The Chronicle, Pitts., 1977—; columnist Resident Publs., N.Y.C., 1991-94, Actor's Resource, N.Y.C., 1992-94; bd. editors Strategies: The Journal of Legal Marketing; mem. Legal Mktg. Assn., 1992—; exec. editor Designate for Yr. 2000, Stretegies, The Jour. Legal Mktg. Mem. exec. com. New Leadership bd. Pitts. Symphony Orch., 1994—. MacJannet scholar in internat. law and economics Tufts U. and Ctr. for European Studies, Talloires, France, 1981. Mem. Tufts Media and Comm. Group, Pitts. Filmmakers (bd. dirs. 1996-99), Tufts Media and Comms. Group. Avocations: international politics, music, writing, piano performance, legal ethics. Office: 4415 5th Ave Pittsburgh PA 15213-2654

**REICH, LARRY SAM,** lawyer; b. Bklyn., Sept. 24, 1946; s. Sidney and Regina (Brown) R.; m. Patricia S. Neustein, Aug. 18, 1968; children: Ilysa Jill, Shari Beth. BA, Hofstra U., 1969; JD, Bklyn. Law Sch., 1973. Bar: N.Y. 1974, U.S. Dist. Ct. (so. and ea. dists.) N.Y. 1974, U.S. Ct. Appeals (2d cir.) 1974, U.S. Supreme Ct. 1980. Assoc. S. Edward Orenstein PC, N.Y.C., 1973-78; ptnr. Herzfeld & Rubin PC, N.Y.C., 1978—; arbitrator U.S. Dist. Ct. for Ea. Dist. N.Y., Bklyn., 1986—. Mem. ABA, N.Y. State Bar Assn. (chmn. com. on supreme cts. 1986-89, chmn. com. on jud. adminstrn. 1989-92, com. jud. adminstrn. 1989-94), N.Y. County Bar Assn., Nassau County Bar Assn., Assn. Trial Lawyers Am., N.Y. State Trial Lawyers Assn. Avocations: running, rowing, biking, reading. Federal civil litigation, State civil litigation. Office: Herzfeld & Rubin PC 40 Wall St Fl 56 New York NY 10005-2349

**REICH, PETER LESTER,** legal educator, legal and historical consultant; b. L.A., Mar. 20, 1955; s. Jack Edward and Lillian (Lerner) R.; m. Alisa Schulweis, Sept. 8, 1985; children: Gabriel, Eli. BA in History, UCLA, 1976, PhD in History, 1991; JD, U. Calif., Berkeley, 1985. Bar: Calif. 1985, U.S. Dist. Ct. (ctrl. dist.) Calif. 1986. Rsch. atty. Calif. Ct. Appeal, Ventura, 1985-86; assoc. Parker, Milliken et al, L.A., 1986-88; asst. prof. law Whittier Law Sch., L.A., 1988-91, assoc. prof. law, 1991-93; prof. law Whittier Law Sch., Costa Mesa, Calif., 1993—; vis. prof. of history U. Calif., Irvine, 1999. Author: Mexico's Hidden Revolution, 1995; mem. editl. bd. Western Legal History, 1995—; contbr. articles to profl. jours. Recipient Hubert Herring Meml. award Pacific Coast Coun. on Latin Am. Studies, 1991, Ray A. Billington award Western History Assn., 1995; Fulbright-Hays fellow, 1979-80; Rocky Mountain Mineral Law Found. rsch. grantee, 1993, 95, 99; Huntington Libr. fellow Andrew Mellon Found., 1997. Mem. Am. Soc. for Legal History, Assn. Am. Law Scs. (sec.-treas. immigration sect.), Calif. Supreme Ct. Hist. Soc. Democrat. Jewish. Avocations: sea kayaking, hiking, ice skating. Office: Whittier Law Sch 3333 Harbor Blvd Costa Mesa CA 92626-1501

**REICH, SAMUEL JOSEPH,** lawyer; b. Pitts., Sept. 8, 1935; s. Jack M. and Esther L. (Landaw) R.; m. Diane Marchase; children: Stephen, Hillary. BA, U. Pitts., 1957; LLB, U. Pa., 1960. Bar: D.C. 1960, Pa. 1961, Pa. Supreme Ct. 1961, U.S. Supreme Ct., U.S. Ct. Appeals (3rd cir.), U.S. Dist. Ct. Atty. criminal div. U.S. Dept. Justice, Washington, 1960-61; asst. U.S. atty. U.S. Atty.'s Office, Pitts., 1961-64, 1st asst., 1964-66; ptnr. Cooper, Schwartz, Diamond & Reich, Pitts., 1966-75; pvt. practice Pitts., 1975-83, 85-87; ptnr. Rothman, Gordon, Foreman & Groudine, Pitts., 1983-85, Hess, Reich, Georgiades, Wile & Homyak, Pitts., 1986-92, Reich, Werner & Alexander, 1992—; adj. prof. law Duquesne U., Pitts., 1975-87; speaker in criminal law field. Bd. dirs. Chartiers Valley Sch., Pitts., 1969-75, pres. bd., 1975; bd. dirs. Alzheimer's Disease Alliance, Pitts., 1983—; active various youth and sports orgns. Mem. Allegheny County Bar Assn. (judiciary com. 1981-84, 87—, chmn. 1989, pres. 1995), Pa. Trial Lawyers Assn., Am. Judicature Soc., Assn. Lawyers Criminal Cts. Allegheny County (chmn. 1971-74), Nat. Assn. Criminal Def. Attys., Am. Trial Lawyers Assn., Western Pa. Trial Lawyers Assn., Pitts. Athletic Assn., South Hills Bnai Brith (pres.). Democrat. Jewish. Avocation: sports. Fax: 412-391-5323. E-mail: RWA@acba.org. Criminal, Family and matrimonial, Entertainment. Home: 5030 5th Ave Apt 206 Pittsburgh PA 15232-2179 Office: Reich Werner & Alexander 4960 USx Twr Pittsburgh PA 15219

**REICHARD, WILLIAM EDWARD,** lawyer, consultant; b. Lorain, Ohio, Dec. 6, 1938; s. Russell E. and Regina C. (Bartinique) R.; m. Patricia J. Mooney, Apr. 20, 1963; children: Ann E. Reichard McHugh, John B., William M., Margaret C., Kathryn M. (dec.), Patrick M., Elizabeth T., Daniel C., Michael C. BS in Physics, Coll. Holy Cross, 1961; JD, NYU, 1968. Bar: Ohio 1968, Fla. 1975, U.S. Dist. Ct. (no. dist.) Ohio 1968. Law clk. to Hon. William J. Thomas U.S. Dist. Ct. (no. dist.) Ohio, Cleve., 1968-69; atty. Spieth, Bell, McCurdy & Newell, Cleve., 1969-73; ptnr. Conway, Patton, Bouhall & Reichard, Cleve., 1973-97; pvt. practice Westlake, Ohio, 1997—; bd. dirs. Sachem, Inc., Austin, Tex., Alloy Engring. Co., Berea, Ohio. Trustee Magnificat H.S., Rocky River, Ohio, 1985—, St. Ignatius H.S., Cleve., 1995—. Mem. Fla. Bar Assn., Ohio Bar Assn., Cleve. Bar Assn., Cuyahoga County Bar Assn., Westwood Country Club. Republican. Roman Catholic. Avocations: tennis, golf, wine collecting. Estate planning, General corporate, Pension, profit-sharing, and employee benefits. Home: 18560 High Pkwy Rocky River OH 44116-2831 Office: William E Reichard Co A Legal Profl Assn 25109 Detroit Rd Ste 300 Westlake OH 44145-2544

**REICHBACH, GUSTIN LEWIS,** state supreme court justice; b. Bklyn., Oct. 9, 1946; s. Herman and Lee (Klein) R.; m. Ellen Meyers, Oct. 24, 1984; 1 child, Hope Isadora. BA with high honors in Polit. Sci., SUNY, Buffalo, 1967; JD, Columbia U., 1970. Bar: N.Y. 1972, U.S. Dist. Ct. (ea. and so. dists.) N.Y. 1972, Calif. 1975, U.S. Dist. Ct. (ea. and no. dists.) Calif. 1975, U.S. Supreme Ct. 1984. Pvt. practice, N.Y., 1972-90; pvt. practice Calif., 1975-90; judge Civil Ct. City of N.Y., Bklyn., 1991-98; justice Supreme Ct. N.Y., Bklyn., 1990—; counsel to commr. Calif. Agrl. Labor Rels. Bd., Sacramento, 1975-76. Co-author: The Bust Book, 1970, Litigating Electronic Surveillance Claims in Criminal Cases, 1977. Recipient David Michael award N.Y. State Bar Assn., 1992. Mem. Phi Beta Kappa. Office: Supreme Ct State NY 120 Schermerhorn St Brooklyn NY 11201-5108

**REICHE, FRANK PERLEY,** lawyer, former federal commissioner; b. Hartford, Conn., May 8, 1929; s. Karl Augustus and LaFetra (Perley) R.; m. Janet Taylor, Sept. 26, 1953; children: Cynthia Reiche Schumacker, Dean S. AB, Williams Coll., 1951; LLB, Columbia U., 1959; MA, George Washington U., 1959; LLM in Taxation, NYU, 1966. Bar: N.J. 1960, D.C. 1981. Assoc. Stryker, Tams & Dill, Newark, 1959-61; assoc. Smith, Stratton, Wise & Heher, Princeton, N.J., 1962-64, ptnr., 1964-79; commr. Fed. Election Commn., Washington, 1979-85; chmn. Fed. Election Commn., 1982; ptnr. Katzenbach, Gildea & Rudner, Lawrenceville, N.J., 1986-93; pvt. practice law Princeton, N.J., 1993-97; of counsel Schragger, Lavine & Nagy, West Trenton, N.J., 1997—. Trustee Westminster Choir Coll., Princeton, 1974-86, Ctr. Theol. Inquiry, Princeton, 1991-97, Wells Coll., Aurora, N.Y., 1994—; mem. planned giving com. Williams Coll., Williamstown, Mass., 1973-87, nat. chmn. planned giving, 1983-87. Lt. USN, 1952-56. Mem. ABA, D.C. Bar Assn., N.J. Bar Assn., Am. Coll. Trust and Estate Counsel (N.J. state chair 1995—). Republican. Presbyterian. Clubs: Washington Golf and Country, Capitol Hill. Estate planning, Probate, Estate taxation.

**REICHEL, AARON ISRAEL,** lawyer, rabbi, editor; b. N.Y.C., Jan. 30, 1950; s. Oscar Asher and Josephine Hannah (Goldstein) R. BA, Yeshiva U., 1971, MA, 1974; JD, Fordham U., 1976. Bar: N.J. 1977, N.Y. 1978; ordained rabbi, 1975. Atty. editor Securities Regulation Prentice-Hall, Englewood Cliffs, N.J., 1977-78; editor, founder govt. disclosure service Prentice-Hall, Paramus, N.J., 1978-82; atty. editor fed. taxation Prentice-Hall, Paramus, 1982-89; tech. editor Warren, Gorham & Lamont, Practical Acct., N.Y.C., 1989-90; assoc. Firm A. Edward Major, N.Y.C., 1990-91, Firm Allen L. Rothenberg, N.Y.C., 1991-93; pvt. practice N.Y.C., 1993—. Author: The Maverick Rabbi, 1984, 2d edit. 1986, Back to the Past for Inspiration for the Future—West Side Institutional Synagogue Jubilee 1937-87, 1987; co-author (manual) Style and Usage, 1984; contbr. The 1986 Jewish Directory and Almanac, 1986, The 1987-88 Jewish Almanac, 1988; contbg. editor Complete Guide to the Tax Reform Act of 1986, Prentice-Hall's Explanation of the Tax Reform Act of 1986, Prentice Hall's Complete Guide to the Tax Law of 1987, 1988, Prentice Hall's Explanation of the Technical & Miscellaneous Revenue Act of 1988, 1988, Guide to Equal Employment Practices, 1997; contbr. articles to profl. jours. bd. dirs. Union Orthodox Jewish Congregations Am., N.Y.C., 1973-74, Harry and Jane Fischel Found., N.Y.C., 1977—, West Side Instl. Synagogue, 1987-98, Amalgamated Dwellings, Inc., 1992-96; nat. pres. YAVNEH, N.Y.C., 1973-74; mem. youth commn. Am. Jewish Congress, N.Y.C., 1973-76. Mem. ABA, N.Y. State Bar Assn. (various coms.), N.Y. County Lawyers Assn. (various coms.), Am. Soc. Access Profls. (founder, 1st chmn. N.Y. chpt.), Nat. Jewish Commn. on Law and Pub. Affairs (family law com.), Yeshiva U. Alumni Assn. (exec. com. 1971-87, editor-in-chief Bull. 1974-78). Avocations: writing, baseball, tennis, compiling proverbs. Personal injury, General practice, Civil rights. Home: 83-28 Abingdon Rd Kew Gardens NY 11415-1714

**REICHERT, BRENT LARRY,** lawyer; b. Crookston, Minn., Dec. 17, 1956; s. Garfield G. and Juanne C. Reichert; m. Sandra Lee Smith, Apr. 25, 1987; children: Blake L., Brian L. BA summa cum laude, Concordia Coll., 1979; JD, U. Minn., 1982. Bar: Minn. 1982, U.S. Dist. Ct. Minn. 1982, U.S. Ct. Appeals (8th cir.) 1983, U.S. Tax Ct. 1983, Tex. Supreme Ct. 1990, U.S. Dist. Ct. (no. dist.) Tex. 1990, U.S. Dist. Ct. (we. dist.) Mich. 1998. Legal writing instr. U. Minn. Law Sch., Mpls., 1980-81, appellate advocacy instr., 1981-82; assoc. Robins, Kaplan, Miller & Ciresi L.L.P., Mpls., 1982-89, ptnr., 1989—; presenter in field. Chmn. music and worship com. Normandale Luth. Ch., 1998-99. Mem. ATLA, ABA (torts and ins. practice sect.), Minn. State Bar Assn., Minn. Trial Lawyers Assn., Tex. State Bar Assn., Hennepin County Bar Assn., Dallas County Bar Assn., Internat. Assn. Arson Investigators. Avocations: music, tennis, hunting, fishing, coaching youth sports teams. General civil litigation, Insurance, Product liability. Home: 6416 Glacier Pl Edina MN 55436-1808 Office: Robins Kaplan Miller & Ciresi LLP 2800 LaSalle Plaza 800 Lasalle Ave Minneapolis MN 55402-2015

**REICHMAN, ADELLE E.,** lawyer; s. Joseph and Gizella (Wieder) R.; m. Moshe Gottlieb, Aug. 28, 1984. BA, Bklyn. Coll.; MA, MEd, Columbia U., JD, 1987. Bar: N.Y., U.S. Dist. Ct. (so. and ea. dists.) N.Y., U.S. Ct. Appeals. Fiscal officer Counterforce, Bklyn.; sole practitioner Bklyn. Recipient Nat. Bus. and Labor award. Mem. N.Y. State Law Assn. General civil litigation, Contracts commercial, Real property. Office: 1253 E 6th St Ste 2368 Brooklyn NY 11235-6201

**REICHMAN, DAWN LESLIE,** lawyer, educator, deputy sheriff; b. Portsmouth, Va., Feb. 15, 1951; d. Stanley J. and Ernestine Enid (Kaiserman) Greif; m. James Richard Smith, Apr. 27, 1975 (div. July 1978); m. Victor I. Reichman, Nov. 24, 1979; children: Mark Heath, Margo Ilene, Shelley Renee. BA, U. Calif., L.A., 1972; cert. dep. sheriff, Sheriff Acad., 1974; JD, Whittier Coll., 1988. Bar: Calif. 1988, U.S. Dist. Ct. (ea. and cen. dists.) Calif. 1988. Dep. sheriff L.A. County Sheriff's Dept., 1973-81; substitute tchr. Palmdale (Calif.) Sch. Dist., 1988-90; pvt. practice law Palmdale, 1988—; alt. def. counsel, 1990-91; vol. arbitrator L.A. Superior and Mcpl. Cts., 1995—; vol. mediator L.A. Superior Ct., 1997—, vol. judge pro tem, 1998—. Spokesperson Ana Verde Homeowners Assn., Palmdale, 1989-95; assoc. Alpha Charter Guild of Antelope Valley Hosp.; bd. dirs. Palmdale Cmty. Assn., 1992; mem. prins. adv. com. Highland H.S., 1994-95, mock trial coach, 1997-98; bd. dir. Families Caring for Families, 1995-98; v.p., bd. dirs. Desert Haven Enterprises, 1996-97; mem. strategic planning task force Antelope Valley Hosp. Med. Ctr., 1996; mem. Career Prep Coun. Law and Govt. Adv. Com., 1994-98; pres. Primary Source Profl. Referral Bd., 1995-96; mem. gala com. Antelope Valley Hosp. Gift Found., 1995. Mem. High Desert Criminal Def. Bar Assn. (v.p. 1993, former sec.), Antelope Valley Bar Citizens Law Sch. (chmn. 1991-97), Encouraging Potential in Children (co-chmn. 1991), Phi Alpha Delta. Avocations: reading, crosswords, cryptograms. Criminal, Family and matrimonial. Office: 520 E Palmdale Blvd # C Palmdale CA 93550-4603

**REICIN, ERIC DAVID,** lawyer; b. Chgo., Aug. 12, 1969; s. Ronald Ian and Alyta Reicin; m. Jodi Wise, Sept. 3, 1994. Student, Regent Coll., England, 1990; AB in Econs. and Polit. Sci., U. Mich., 1991; JD cum laude, U. Ill., 1994. Bar: Ill. 1994, U.S. Dist. Ct. (no. dist.) Ill. 1994, D.C. 1995, U.S. Dist. Ct. D.C. 1995, U.S. Ct. Appeals (D.C. cir.) 1995, U.S. Dist. Ct. Md. 1997, U.S. Ct. Appeals (4th cir.) 1997, U.S. Supreme Ct. 1998. Intern U.S. Senator Robert W. Kasten, Washington, 1989; intern Office of Policy Devel. White House, Washington, 1990; intern U.S. Congressman Carl Pursell, Washington, 1991; law clk. State's Atty.-Champaign County, 1994; assoc. Laner Muchin Dombrow Becker Levin and Tominberg, Chgo., 1994-95, Birch Horton Bittner and Cherot, Washington, 1995-99; asst. gen. counsel Sallie Mae, Inc., Reston, Va., 1999—. Co-editor: Employment Discrimination Law, 3d edit., 1999. Harno scholar, 1993-94, Congrl. scholar, 1986; Pub. Interest Law Found. fellow. Mem. ABA (exec. lt. gov. 1993-94, EEO com. nat. co-chmn. regional liaison program 1997—, nat. co-chmn. govt. liaison program 1998, nat. co-chmn. ABA/EEOC joint tng. partnership 1997—), D.C. Bar Assn. (litigation, labor and employment sect.) Soc. for Human Resource Mgmt., Met. Washington Employment Lawyers Assn. (sec., bd. dirs. 1997—), Mortar Bd., Pi Sigma Alpha, Omicron Delta Epsilon, Sigma

Iota Rho, Alpha Epsilon Pi (Arnold B. Hoffman award 1990). Republican. Labor, General corporate, Administrative and regulatory. Office: Sallie Mae Inc 11600 Sallie Mae Dr Ste 1200 Reston VA 20193-0001

**REICIN, RONALD IAN,** lawyer; b. Chgo., Dec. 11, 1942; s. Frank Edward and Abranita (Rome) R.; m. Alyta Friedland, May 23, 1965; children: Eric, Kael. BBA, U. Mich., 1964, MBA, 1967, JD cum laude, 1967. Bar: Ill. 1967, U.S. Tax Ct. 1967; CPA, Ill. Mem. staff Price Waterhouse & Co., Chgo., 1966; ptnr. Jenner & Block, Chgo., 1967—. Bd. dirs. Nat. Kidney Found., Ill., 1978—, v.p., 1992-95, pres., 1995-98; bd. dirs. Ruth Page Found., 1985—, v.p., 1990—; bd. dirs. Scoliosis Assn. Chgo., 1981-90, Kohl Children's Mus., 1991-95. Mem. Chgo. Bar Assn., Internat. Conf. Shopping Ctrs., ABA, Ill. Bar Assn., Chgo. Mortgage Attys. Assn., Phi Kappa Phi, Beta Gamma Sigma, Beta Alpha Psi. Clubs: Executive, Legal (Chgo.). Real property, General practice, General corporate. Office: Jenner & Block 1 E Ibm Plz Fl 38 Chicago IL 60611-7693

**REID, BENJAMINE,** lawyer; b. Concord, N.C., Jan. 11, 1950; s. Fred Herndon and Frances Barnhardt Reid; m. Jennie Lou Divine, Dec. 19, 1970; children: Elisabeth Divine, Margaret Hethcox, Benjamine Joseph. AB, U. N.C., 1971; JD cum laude, U. Ga., 1974. Bar: Fla., Ga., U.S. Ct. Appeals (3rd, 5th and 11th cirs.), U.S. Supreme Ct. Atty., shareholder Kimbrell & Hamann, Miami, Fla., 1974-90; shareholder Popham Haik, Miami, 1990-97, Carlton Fields, Miami, 1997—; bd. dirs. Product Liability Adv. Coun., Washington. Sr. editor U. Ga. Law Rev.; contbr. articles to profl. jours. Vice-chair, exec. com. mem. Greater Miami Chamber; pres. Dade Pub. Edn. Fund; chair Leadership Miami. Fellow Am. Bar Found.; mem. ABA (coun./com. chair litigation sect.), U. N.C. Gen. Alumni Assn. (bd. dirs.), U. N.C. Nat. Devel. Coun. (Miami chair), Phi Kappa Phi. Democrat. Episcopalian. Avocations: golf, history, travel. Federal civil litigation, Product liability, State civil litigation.

**REID, DAVID G.,** lawyer; b. N.Y.C., Oct. 28, 1948; s. Donald D. and Charlotte A. (Marois) R. BA, McGill U., Montreal, 1970; JD, Boston U., 1973. Bar: Vt. 1973, U.S. Dist. Ct. Vt. 1973, Mass. 1977, U.S. Supreme Ct. 1978, U.S. Ct. Appeals (2d cir.) 1978, U.S. Dist. Ct. Mass. 1991. Pub. defender Orleans, Caledonia, Essex counties, St. Johnsbury, Vt., 1973-75, Bennington (Vt.) County, 1975-79, Windham County, Brattleboro, Vt., 1979-89; ptnr. Reid & Rudgers, Brattleboro, 1989—. Personal injury, Criminal. Office: Reid & Rodgers 8 Williston St Brattleboro VT 05301-3202

**REID, DONNA LAKE,** lawyer; b. Ft. Bragg, N.C., Sept. 19, 1964; d. Michael Johnson and Lynda Lake (Reese) R. BS in Accounting and Bus. Admin., U. Kans., 1986, JD, 1990. Bar: Ga. 1991. Internat. contract coord. Turner Internat., Atlanta, 1991-92, mgr., CNN internat. contracts, 1992-93, dir., network contracts admin., 1993-94; assoc. gen. counsel Liberty Sports, Inc., Dallas, 1994-96; gen. counsel and dir. bus. affairs Fox Sports Internat. and Fox Sports Ams., L.A., 1996-97; gen. counsel, v.p. bus. and legal affairs Fox Sports Internat., Fox Sports Ams., Fox Sports World, L.A., 1997—. Leader Young Life, L.A., 1997. General corporate, Sports. Office: Fox Sports Internat 10000 Santa Monica Blvd Ste 333 Los Angeles CA 90067-7007

**REID, EDWARD SNOVER, III,** lawyer; b. Detroit, Mar. 24, 1930; s. Edward S. Jr. and Margaret (Overington) R.; m. Carroll Grylls, Dec. 30, 1953; children: Carroll Reid Highet, Richard Gerveys, Jane Reid McTique, Margaret Reid Boyer. B.A., Yale U., 1951; LL.B. magna cum laude (Sheldon fellow), Harvard U., 1956. Bar: Mich. 1957, N.Y. 1958, D.C. 1982, Gaikokuho jimu-bengoshi, Tokyo 1991-96. Asso. Davis, Polk & Wardwell, N.Y.C., 1957-64; partner Davis, Polk & Wardwell, 1964-95, sr. counsel, 1996—; dir. Gen. Mills, Inc., 1974-89. Mem. N.Y.C. Bd. Higher Edn., 1971-73; trustee Bklyn. Inst. Arts and Scis., 1966-93, chmn., 1974-79; trustee Bklyn. Mus., 1973-93, 94—; bd. dirs. Bklyn. Bot. Garden Corp., 1977-92, 96—, Bargemusic Ltd., 1990-93. Lt. USMCR, 1951-53. Mem. ABA, N.Y. State Bar Assn., Assn. of Bar of City of N.Y., Am. Law Inst., Internat. Bar Assn., Inter-Pacific Bar Assn., Heights Casino Club, Rembrandt Club, Century Assn. Club, Yale Club, L.I. Wyandanch Club, Quoque Beach Club, Shinnecock Yacht Club, Quoque Field Club. General corporate, Mergers and acquisitions, Securities. Home: PO Box 39 Quogue NY 11959-0039 Office: Davis Polk & Wardwell 450 Lexington Ave New York NY 10017-3911

**REID, INEZ SMITH,** lawyer, educator; b. New Orleans, Apr. 7, 1937; d. Sidney Randall Dickerson and Beatrice Virginia (Bundy) Smith. BA, Tufts U., 1959; LLB, Yale U., 1962; MA, UCLA, 1963; PhD, Columbia U., 1968. Bar: Calif. 1963, N.Y. 1972, D.C. 1980. Assoc. prof. Barnard Coll. Columbia U., N.Y.C., 1972-76; gen. counsel youth div. State of N.Y., 1976-77; dep. gen. counsel HEW, Washington, 1977-79; inspector gen. EPA, Washington, 1979-81; chief legis. and opinions, dep. corp. counsel Office of Corp. Counsel, Washington, 1981-83; corp. counsel D.C., 1983-85; counsel Laxalt, Washington, Perito & Dubuc, Washington, 1986-90, ptnr., 1990-91; counsel Graham & James, 1991-93, Lewis, White & Clay, P.C., 1994-95; assoc. judge D.C. Ct. Appeals, 1995—. William J. Maier, Jr. vis. prof. law W.Va. U. Coll. Law, Morgantown, 1985-86. Author: Together Black Women, 1972; contbr. articles to profl. jours. and publs. Bd. dirs. Homeland Ministries Bd. United Ch. of Christ, N.Y.C., 1978-83, vice chmn., 1981-83; chmn. bd. govs. Antioch Law Sch., Washington, 1979-81; chmn. bd. trustees Antioch U., Yellow Springs, Ohio, 1981-82; bd. trustees Tufts U., Medford, Mass., 1988-98, Lancaster (Pa.) Sem., 1988—; bd. govs. D.C. Sch. Law, 1990-96, chmn., 1991-95. Recipient Emily Gregory award Barnard Coll., 1976, Arthur Morgan award Antioch U., 1982, Service award United Ch. of Christ, 1983, Disting. Service (Profl. Life) award Tufts U. Alumni Assn., 1988. Office: DC Ct Appeals 500 Indiana Ave NW Ste 6 Washington DC 20001-2131

**REID, JEAN MARGO,** lawyer; b. Lockport, N.Y., Aug. 31, 1945; m. Richard P. Brief, Jan. 12, 1980; 1 child, Kristin Reid Brief. BA, Wells Coll., 1967; JD, Harvard U., 1970. Atty. Nat. Housing and Econ. Devel. Law Project, Berkeley, Calif., 1970-72; counsel CEDC, Inc., Hempstead, N.Y., 1972-76, Am. Women's Econ. Devel. Corp., N.Y.C., 1977-79; asst. prof. NYU, 1981-88; atty. Sanford C. Bernstein & Co Inc, N.Y.C., 1988-92, assoc. counsel, 1992-96, gen. counsel, 1997—. Office: Sanford C Bernstein & Co Inc 767 5th Ave New York NY 10153-0023

**REID, JUSTUS WEBB,** lawyer; b. Fairfield, Iowa, June 11, 1943; m. Phyllis C. Horne, June 11, 1966; children: Heather, Jebb, Erica, Payton. BA, Fla. State U., 1965; JD, U. Fla., 1968. Bar: Fla. 1968. Assoc. Fisher, Prior, Pruitt, West Palm Beach, Fla., 1968-71, Cone, Wagner, Nugent, West Palm Beach, 1971-74, Howell, Kirby, et al, West Palm Beach, 1974-79; ptnr. Magill Sevier & Reid, West Palm Beach and Miami, 1979-85, Reid Ricca & Rigell, West Palm Beach, 1985-93, Reid Metgger & Assocs., West Palm Beach, 1993—. Bd. dirs. Boys and Girls Clubs, West Palm Beach, 1996—. Mem. U.S. Polo Assn. Avocation: polo. Home: 12297 Plantation Ln North Palm Beach FL 33408 Office: Reid Metgger & Assocs 250 S Australian Ave West Palm Beach FL 33401-5018

**REID, LINDA KATHRYN,** lawyer, nurse administrator; b. Pitts., Mar. 22, 1957; d. Clarence G. and M. Kathryn (Haines) R.; m. James R. Kelly, Dec. 21, 1991. BS in Nursing, U. Pitts., 1979, MS in Nursing Edn., 1984; JD, Duquesne U., 1990. Bar: Pa., 1990; cert. BLS instr., EMT. Nurse's aide Presbyn. U. Hosp., Pitts., 1977-78, staff nurse, 1979—, relief supr., 1983—, clin. instr., 1985-87; grad. student asst. U. Pitts., 1981; dir. staff devel. Butler (Pa.) Meml. Hosp., 1987-91; pvt. practice atty. Pitts., 1991—. Mem. Duquesne Law Rev., 1987. EMT Wilkinsburg (Pa.) Emergency Med. Svcs., 1986-90; bd. dirs. Am. Heart Assn. Butler (Pa.) br. 1988-91; advisor Butler County Vo-Tech. Health Assistants Program 1988-91. Mem. ANA, ABA, Pa. Nurses Assn. (mem. continuing edn. approval unit 1990—), Sigma Theta Tau, Phi Eta Sigma, U. Pitts. Alumni Assn. Republican. Avocations: sailing, boating, tennis, piano,. Home: 7448 Schoyer Ave Pittsburgh PA 15218-2316 Office: PO Box 82561 Pittsburgh PA 15218-0561

**REID, LORINE MAY,** lawyer; b. Toledo, Ohio, Apr. 29, 1932; d. Edwin McKechnie and Eleanora Mary (DeMars) R. B.A. in Speech, Wayne State U., 1958; M. Social Work, U. Mich., 1965; J.D., U. Toledo, 1969. Bar: Ohio 1973. Exec. dir. Mental Health Bd., 1970-72; planning dir. Pilot Cities Project, Dayton, Ohio, 1972-75; sole practice, Dayton, 1974—; legal dir. Childrens Service Bd., 1977-81; tchr. U. Dayton, 1977-80. Citizens adv. bd. Dayton Mental Health Ctr., 1978-85. Recipient Mental Health Service award Gov. of Ohio, 1984. Mem. Dayton Women Voters League, ABA, Ohio State Bar Assn., Dayton Bar Assn., Nat. Assn. Women Lawyers. Democrat. Club: Altrusa Internat. (pres. 1985—). Avocation: community theatre.

**REID, LYLE,** former state supreme court justice; b. Brownsville, Tenn., June 17, 1930; m. Elizabeth W.; children: Betsy, Martha Lyle. BSBA, U. Tenn., JD, 1956. Bar: Tenn. 1957, U.S. Ct. Appeals (6th cir.). Asst. state atty. gen. State of Tenn., Nashville, 1961-63; county atty. Haywood County, Brownsville, Tenn., 1964-86; atty. Reid & Banks, Brownsville, Tenn., 1963-66; assoc. judge Tenn. Ct. Criminal Appeals, Tenn., 1987-90; chief justice Tenn. Supreme Ct., Nashville, 1990-94; v.p. litigation Columbia/HCA, Nashville, 1998—; deputy commr. Dept. Commerce & Ins., Tenn. With USAF, Korea. Mem. ABA, Am. Bar Found., Tenn. Bar Assn. Democrat. Methodist. Office: Columbia/HCA 1 Park Plz Nashville TN 37203-1548

**REID, ROBERT C.,** lawyer; b. Ft. Pierce, Fla., Apr. 4, 1951; s. George H. and Caroline (Paul) R.; m. Marian M. Reid, May 19, 1979; stepchildren: Jessica, Matthew, Adam Morgan. BA, Memphis State U., 1973, JD, 1976; LLM in Taxation, U. Fla., 1985. Bar: Tenn. 1976, Fla. 1989. State coordinator Tenn. Assn. Legal Svcs. and Legal Aid Projects, Nashville, 1976-77; sole practice Nashville, 1977; tax counsel, v.p., asst. corp. counsel Corroon & Black Benefits, Inc., Nashville, 1977-84; tax atty. Baker, Worthington, Crossley, Stansberry & Woolf, Nashville, 1985-89; mem. Bryant, Miller and Olive, Tallahassee, Fla., 1989—. Contbr. articles to law jours. Bd. dirs. Coordinating Counsel for Community Concerns, Nashville, 1979, pres., 1980. Mem. Fla. Bar Assn., Nat. Assn. Bond Lawyers. Democrat. Avocations: photography, scuba diving. Finance, Municipal (including bonds), Taxation, general. Office: Bryant Miller and Olive 201 S Monroe St Ste 500 Tallahassee FL 32301-1879

**REID, WILLIAM JOSEPH,** lawyer; b. Batesville, Miss., Jan. 3, 1970; s. W. Joe and Sally Greenlee Reid; m. Stephanie Lynn Tilton, July 26, 1997. BA, U. Miss., 1992, JD, 1995. Bar: Miss. 1995, U.S. Dist. Ct. (no. and so. dists.) Miss. 1995, U.S. Ct. Appeals (5th cir.) 1995. Atty. Liston/Lancaster, Winona, Miss., 1995—. Mem. ATLA, Miss. Bar Assn., Miss. Trial Lawyers Assn., Montgomery County Bar Assn. Methodist. Avocations: basketball, golf, snow skiing. General civil litigation, Personal injury, Product liability. Office: Liston/Lancaster PO Box 645 126 N Quitman St Winona MS 38967-2229

**REIDENBERG, JOEL R.,** law educator; b. 1961. AB in Govt., Dartmouth, 1983; JD, Columbia U., 1986; Diplôme d'études approfondies dr.int.eco., U. Paris-Sorbonne, 1987. Bar: N.Y. 1986, D.C. 1988. Friedmann fellow PROMETHEE, Paris, 1986-87; assoc. Debevoise & Plimpton, Washington, 1987-90; prof. law, dir. grad. program acad. affairs Fordham U. Sch. Law, N.Y.C., 1990—; cons. FTC, Washington, 1997—; expert advisor European Commn., Luxembourg, 1993-96, Brussels, 1997-98. Co-author: Data Privacy Law, 1996, Online Services and Data Protection and Privacy: Regulatory Responses, 1998; contbr. articles to profl. jours. Mem. Assn. Am. Law Schs. (chair sect. law and computers 1997, chair sect. defamation and privacy 1998). Fax: 212-636-6899.

**REIDENBERG, LOUIS MORTON,** lawyer; b. Phila., Dec. 1, 1939; s. Bernard and Beatrice (Rauer) R.; children: Daniel J., Jeffrey B. BBA, U. Miami, Fla., 1961; JD, U. Minn., 1965. Bar: Minn. 1965. Law clk. Minn. Supreme Ct., St. Paul, 1965-66; assoc. Katz, Burstein & Galbraith, Mpls., 1966-70; ptnr. Burstein & Reidenberg, Mpls., 1970-71; pvt. practice Mpls., 1971-78, 81-83; ptnr. Reidenberg & Eagon, Mpls., 1978-81, Reidenberg & Jaycox, Bloomington, Minn., 1983-85, Reidenberg & Ormond, Mpls., 1985-87; pvt. practice Mpls., 1988-91; ptnr. Reidenberg & Arrigoni, Mpls., 1991—; lectr. Minn. Continuing Legal Edn., 1976, 75, 76, 77, 83, 86, Minn. Inst. Legal Edn., 1987. Mem. Am. Acad. Matrimonial Lawyers, Minn. State Bar Assn. (mem. family law com.), Hennepin County Bar Assn. (family law com. 1971-83). Family and matrimonial. Office: Reidenberg & Arrigoni 625 Pillsbury Ctr 200 S 6th St Ste 625 Minneapolis MN 55402-1887

**REIFF, HELEN HAYSLETTE,** lawyer, editor; b. Chgo., Feb. 8, 1925; widowed. BA, Oberlin Coll., 1946; JD, Vt. Law Sch., 1990. Bar: Vt. 1991. Owner Maxi Editorial Svc., Middlebury, Vt., 1982—. Family and matrimonial, Probate, Real property. Home and Office: 23 S Gorham Ln Middlebury VT 05753-1002

**REIFF, JEFFREY MARC,** lawyer; b. Phila., Jan. 24, 1955; s. Morton William and Phyliss (Rubin) R.; m. Dominiqus F. Edrei, June 3, 1979; children—Justin Alexander, Collin Michael. B.S., B.A. magna cum laude in Mktg. Fin., Am. U., 1976; J.D., Temple U., 1976. Bar: Pa. 1979, U.S. Dist. Ct. Pa. 1975, N.Y. 1985. Ptnr. Sablosky, Wertheimer & Reiff, Phila., 1979-82, Mozenter, Durst & Reiff, Phila., 1982-85; prin., founder Reiff, Haaz and Assocs. and predecessor firms, Phila., 1985—. Mem. young leadership bd. Fedn. Jewish Agys., Phila., 1982—; bd. dirs. Golden Slipper Charities, Phila., 1979—, Solomon Schecker Schs., Phila., 1984. Mem. Phila. Bar Assn. (com. chmn. 1984—), Pa. Bar Assn. (com. chmn., mem. lawyers reference com. young lawyers div. 1980—), Am. Trial Lawyers Assn., Pa. Trial Lawyers Assn., Phila. Trial Lawyers Assn. Clubs: Locust, Golden Slipper (bd. dirs. 1980—), Abington Country (Phila.). Personal injury, Criminal, Entertainment. Office: Jeffrey M Reiff & Assocs 1429 Walnut St Fl 12 Philadelphia PA 19102-3218

**REILLY, CHARLES JAMES,** lawyer, educator, accountant; b. Pawtucket, R.I., Oct. 10, 1950; s. Thomas Joseph and Florence Marie (McKenna) R.; m. Barbara Bouffard, Aug. 7, 1971; children: Kristen, Elizabeth. BSBA, Providence Coll., 1972; JD, Suffolk U., 1979. Bar: R.I. 1979, U.S. Dist. Ct. R.I. 1979, U.S. Ct. Appeals (1st cir.) 1979, U.S. Supreme Ct. 1984, U.S. Ct. Claims, 1985; CPA, R.I. Agt. IRS, Providence, 1972-75; appellate conferee U.S. Dept. Treasury, Boston, 1976-81; ptnr. Arcaro & Reilly, Providence, 1981-91, Reilly Law Assocs., Providence, 1991—; assoc. prof. Grad. MST program Bryant Coll., Smithfield, R.I., 1983—. Mem. Am. Inst. CPA's, R.I. Soc. CPA's, ABA, R.I. Bar Assn. (chair tax sect. 1996—). Democrat. Roman Catholic. Club: R.I. Country. Avocation: golf. Corporate taxation, Personal income taxation, State and local taxation. Office: Reilly Law Assocs 1040 Turks Head Bldg Providence RI 02903

**REILLY, EDWARD ANTHONY, JR.,** lawyer; b. N.Y.C., Sept. 6, 1954; s. Edward A. and Jane M. Reilly; m. Diane M. Blair, Oct. 11, 1980 (div. July 1997); children: Edward A. III, Kathryn F., Jennifer L., Michael J. BA, U. Notre Dame, 1976; JD, Columbia U., 1979. Bar: Conn. 1979. Ptnr. Cummings & Lockwood, Hartford, Conn., 1979-91, LeBoeuf, Lamb, Greene & MacRae, LLP, Hartford, 1991—. Mem. Wampanoag Country Club. General corporate, Finance, Mergers and acquisitions. Home: 84 Steele Rd West Hartford CT 06119-1154 Office: LeBoeuf Lamb Greene & MacRae LLP 225 Asylum St Hartford CT 06103-1516

**REILLY, EDWARD FRANCIS, JR.,** former state senator, federal agency administrator; b. Leavenworth, Kans., Mar. 24, 1937; s. Edward F. and Marian C. (Sullivan) R. BA, U. Kans., 1961. V.p. Reilly & Sons, Inc., Leavenworth, 1967-92; pres. Yllier Lake Estates, Inc., Easton, Kans., 1965-89; mem. Kans. Ho. of Reps., 1963-64; mem. Kans. State Senate, 1964-92, asst. majority leader, 1977-80, vice-chmn. govtl. orgn., chmn. ins. subcom., chmn. fed. and state affairs com. Mem. Nat. Commn. on Accreditation of Law Enforcement Agys.; chmn. U.S. Parole Commn. Dept. of Justice, Md., 1992—; former commr. ex officio U.S. Sentencing Commn., Washington; del. to Rep. Nat. Conv., Miami Beach, Fla., 1968; chmn. Leavenworth County Radio Free Europe Fund, 1972; bd. dirs. St. John's Hosp., Leavenworth, 1970-79, sec.; bd. dirs. Leavenworth Assn. for Handicapped, 1968-69, ARC, Leavenworth chpt., Kans. Blue Cross/Blue Shield, 1969-72; apptd. by Pres. Reagan Nat. Hwy. Safety Adv. Com.; active Trinity Nat. Leadership Roundtable, Cath. Campaign Am., Kans. Adv. Bd. Juvenile Offenders, Nat. Com. Cmty. Corrections. Recipient Cmty. Leaders of Am., 1971, 85, 86, Hallpac Pub. Svc. award, 1988, Am. Police Hall of Fame award, 1990, Good Samaritan award Order of Michael the Arch Angel Police Legion, 1990, Commendation award mayor and city commn. of Leavenworth, Kans., 1990, Carnegie Hero Fund Commn. award and medallion, 1991, Silver Angel award Kans. Cath. Conf., 1992; named Outstanding Young Men Am., 1965-76. Mem. Nat. Inst. Corrections (adv. bd.), Am. Paroling Authorities Internat., Am. Correctional Assn., Am. Probation and Paroling Assn., Leavenworth C. of C. (hon. dir. 1970-73), No. Assn. Chiefs Police, Assn. U.S. Army (Henry Leavenworth award 1960), Kansas City (Kans.) C. of C., Leavenworth Hist. Soc. (dir. 1968-73), John Carroll Soc., Native Sons of Kansas City, Ancient Order of Hibernians, U.S. Supreme Ct. Hist. Soc., Kiwanis (dir. 1969-70, Connelly award 1991, Legion of Honor award 1996), K.C., Elks, Eagles, Order of Malta, Equestrian Order Holy Sepulchre Jerusalem. Republican. Roman Catholic.

**REILLY, FRANCIS X.,** lawyer, consultant; b. Westborough, Mass., Sept. 18, 1916; s. Francis Xavier and Blanche Marie (Marshall) R.; m. Beverly E. Blackwell, Oct. 7, 1941 (dec. July 1982); children: Martha J. Reilly Hinchman, John F. AB, Dartmouth Coll., 1938; JD, Harvard U., 1941. Bar: Mass. 1941, Ill. 1954. Atty., treas. Wilson & Co., Inc., Chgo., 1963-67; v.p. LTV Corp., Dallas, 1967-70; v.p., treas. B. F. Goodrich Co., Akron, Ohio, 1970-73; gen. counsel, v.p. Rollins Burdick Hunter, Chgo., 1973-84; pvt. practice law and cons. Barrington, Ill., 1984—. Lt. comdr. USNR, 1943-46. Mem. ABA, U. Club of Chgo. General practice. Home and Office: 420 Elm Rd Barrington IL 60010-3124

**REILLY, GEORGE,** lawyer; b. Waukegan, Ill., Nov. 29, 1934; s. James M. and Hilda Clara (Van Heirseele) R.; m. Dadee Bruce, Dec. 23, 1957; children: Laurene Beth, Theresa Ann. BA, Ill. Coll., 1956; MS, S.D. State U., 1958; JD, U. Minn., 1964. Bar: Minn. 1964, U.S. Dist. Ct. Minn. 1964, U.S. Ct. Appeals (8th cir.) 1965. Assoc. Leonard, Street and Deinard, Mpls., 1964-70, ptnr., 1973-82, mng. ptnr., 1983-91, ptnr., chair of bus. divsn., 1991-96; chief dep. atty. gen. State of Minn., St. Paul, 1971-72; chief counsel Minn. Housing and Fin. Agy., St. Paul, 1972-80. Campaign chair Spannaus for Atty. Gen. com., 1974, 78, Spannaus for Gov., 1982. Mem. ABA, Minn. State Bar Assn., Citizens League, Variety Childrens Assn. (bd. dirs.). Democrat. Avocations: travel, sports. General corporate, Contracts commercial, Communications. Office: Leonard Street & Deinard 150 S 5th St Ste 2300 Minneapolis MN 55402-4238

**REILLY, JOHN B.,** lawyer; b. Bangor, Maine, Sept. 12, 1947; s. Louis J. and Evelyn I. (Lindsay) R.; children: Carolyn, Bridget. BA, U. R.I., 1970; JD cum laude, Suffolk U., 1976. Bar: R.I. 1976, U.S. Dist. Ct. R.I. 1976, U.S. Claims Ct. 1980, U.S. Supreme Ct. 1983, U.S. Ct. Appeals (1st and 2d cirs.) 1984, Mass. 1985, U.S. Dist. Ct. Mass. 1985, U.S. Ct. Appeals (3rd cir.) 1985, U.S. Dist. Ct. Conn. 1995; cert. fraud examiner. Sole practice, Providence, 1976-81, Warwick, R.I., 1981-83; sr. ptnr. John Reilly & Assocs. predecessor firms, Warwick, 1984-89. Mem. Def. Rsch. Inst., Gov's Automobile Ins. Reform Task Force, 1992-93. Mem. ABA, R.I. Assn. Auto Theft and Arson Investigators (sec. 1995-96, pres. 1997—), R.I. Bar Assn., Trucking Ind. Def. Assn., Pi Sigma Alpha, Phi Kappa Psi. General civil litigation, Environmental, Insurance. Home: 80 Paterson Ave Warwick RI 02886-9110 Office: John Reilly & Assoc 300 Centerville Rd Warwick RI 02886-0200

**REILLY, MARIE SAMBOR,** lawyer; b. Phila., July 11, 1961; d. Gregore James and Mary Rita (Villari) Sambor; m. John F. Reilly, Nov. 17, 1990. BS, St.Joseph's U., Phila., 1984; JD, Villanova U., 1988. Bar: Pa. 1988, N.J. 1988, U.S. Dist. Ct. (ea. dist.) Pa. 1988, U.S. Dist. Ct. N.J. 1988. Law clk. U.S. Dist. Ct./Ea. Dist. Pa., Reading, 1988-90; assoc. Lavin, Coleman, Finarelli & Gray, Phila., 1990-92, Margolis, Edelstein & Scherlis, Phila., 1992-95, Monaghan & Gold, P.C., Elkins Park, Pa., 1995-98, Gregory J. Sutton, Marlton, N.J., 1998-99, Mark J. Hill & Assocs., Phila., 1999—. Contbr. chpt. to book. Mem. ABA, Pa. Bar Assn., Phila. Bar Assn. Avocation: home renovation projects. Personal injury, General civil litigation, Civil rights. Office: Mark J Hill & Assocs P C 2 Penn Center Plz Ste 200 Philadelphia PA 19102-1721

**REILLY, THOMAS F.,** state attorney general; b. Springfield, Mass.; m. Ruth Reilly; 3 children. BA, Am. Internat. Coll., 1964; JD, Boston Coll., 1970. Atty. Civil Rights divsn. Atty. Gen.'s Office; dist. atty. Middlesex County Dist. Atty. Office, 1991-99; atty. gen. State of Mass., Springfield, 1999—. Founder The Cmty. Based Justice Program. Office: 436 Dwight St Springfield MA 01103-1317 also: One Ashburton Pl Boston MA 02108-1698*

**REINBOLT, DONNA MCNULTY,** lawyer; b. N.Y.C., Apr. 16, 1961; d. Robert Joseph and Hannah Theresa McNulty; m. Paul Christian Reinbolt; children: Robert, Jake. BA, SUNY, Albany, 1983; JD, Western New Eng. U., 1986. Bar: Conn. 1987, N.Y. 1988, Pa. 1993. Assoc. Gallagher and Gallagher, Garden City, N.Y., 1986-87, Bachner Tally, N.Y.C., 1987-88, Wagner Davis and Gold, N.Y.C., 1988-92; assoc. counsel Zamagias Properties, Pitts., 1992-95, dir. ops., legal counsel, 1995—; bd. dirs. County Fair Air Conditioning Corp., Westbury, N.Y., 1986—. Mem. Allegheny County Bar Assn. (coun. real estate sect. 1993-97, treas. 1997-98). Avocations: travel, skiing, reading, charity work. Home: 10 Middlefield, London NW8 6NE, England

**REINER, LEONA HUDAK,** consultant, attorney; b. Cleve., Apr. 7; d. Stephen and Anna (Ilko) Hudak; 1 child, Eric. BA, Case Western Res. U.; MA in Libr. Sci., U. Wis., MA in Spanish; JD, LLM, Cleve. State U., 1971; LLM, Yale U., 1987, D in Jurisprudential Law, 1991. Bar: Pa. 1973. Pres. Reiner Assocs., New Haven, 1971—, Ctr. for Jud. Accountability, New Haven, 1994—. Author: (book) Early American Women Printers & Publishers, 1978, Lehrnfreiheit: Freedom to Learn, 1991; contbr. articles to profl. jours. Sterling fellow Yale Law Sch., 1981-83, 87-91; Regent's Scholar U. Wis. Mem. Phi Beta Kappa, Beta Phi Mu. Avocation: collecting embroidered and needlepoint artwork. Federal civil litigation, Family and matrimonial. Home and Office: 65 Judwin Ave New Haven CT 06515-2312

**REINERT, CYNTHIA,** lawyer; b. Lansing, Mich., July 1957; d. Robert Relf and Patricia Boone; 1 child, Melanie Elayne Nickless. BA, Ind. U., 1994, JD, 1997. Bar: Ind. 1997. Pvt. practice Indpls., 1997—. Bd. dirs. Ind. Coalition Against Domestic Violence, 1998—. Mem. ABA, ATLA, NOW, Ind. Bar Assn., Ind. Trial Lawyers Assn., Indpls. Bar Assn. Democrat. Avocation: pro bono work with substance abusers. E-mail: famlaw@quest.net. Family and matrimonial. Home: 402 Majestic Bldg 47 S Pennsylvania St Indianapolis IN 46204

**REINGLASS, MICHELLE ANNETTE,** lawyer; b. L.A., Dec. 9, 1954; d. Darwin and Shirley (Steiner) R. Student, U. Calif., Irvine, 1972-75; BSL, Western State U., 1977, JD, 1978. Bar: Calif. 1979, U.S. Dist. Ct. (ctrl. dist.) Calif. 1979, U.S. Ct. Appeals (9th cir.) 1981, U.S. Dist. Ct. (so. dist.) Calif. 1989. Pvt. practice employee litig. Laguna Hills, Calif., 1979—; instr. Calif. Continuing Edn. of Bar, 1990—, Western State Coll., 1991, Rutter Group, 1994—; chmn. magistrate selection com. U.S. Dist. Ct. (ctrl. dist.) Calif., L.A., 1991, 93, 94, 95, mem. commn., 1997; lectr. in field. Contbr. articles to profl. jours. Pres. Child or Parental Emergency Svcs., Santa Ana, Calif., 1990-92; bd. dirs. Pub. Law Ctr., Santa Ana, 1982-92, Coalition for Justice; mem. exec. com. CHOC Follies. Recipient Jurisprudence award Anti-Defamation League, 1997; named to Hall of Fame, Western State U., 1993. Mem. State Bar Calif., Orange County Bar Assn. (del. to state conv. 1980—, bd. dirs. 1983-94, chmn. bus. litigation sect. 1989, sec. 1990, treas. 1991, pres.-elect 1992, pres. 1993), Orange County Trial Lawyers Assn. (bd. dirs. 1987-89, Bus. Trial Lawyer of Yr. award 1995), Orange County Women Lawyers (Lawyer of Yr. award 1996), Vols. in Parole (chmn. adv. com. 1990-91), Peter Elliot Inns Ct. (master), Am. Bd. of Trial Advocates. Avocations: distance running, skiing. Federal civil litigation, State civil litigation, Labor. Office: 23161 Mill Creek Dr Ste 170 Laguna Hills CA 92653-1649

**REINHARD, PHILIP G.,** federal judge; b. LaSalle, Ill., Jan. 12, 1941; s. Godfrey and Ruth R.; married Virginia Reinhard; children: Bruce, Brian, David, Philip. BA, U. Ill., Champaign, 1962, JD, 1964. Asst. state atty. Winnebago County, 1964-67; atty. Hyer, Gill & Brown, 1967-68; state atty. Winnebago County, 1968-76; judge 17th Jud. Cir., 1976-80, Appellate Ct., 1980-92, U.S. Dist. Ct. (no. dist.) Ill., 1992—; mem. security, space and facilities com. U.S. Jud. Conf. Mem. Am. Acad. Jud. Edn., Winnebago County Bar Assn. Office: US Courthouse 211 S Court St Rockford IL 61101-1219

**REINHARD, STEVEN IRA,** lawyer; b. Schenectady, N.Y., June 9, 1961; s. Arnold and Lenore (Bluthe) R.; m. Susan Marie Parham, June 15, 1986; children: Laura Suzanne, Samuel Jacob. BSBA, U. N.C., Chapel Hill, 1982, JD, 1985. Bar: N.C. 1985, U.S. Dist. Ct. (ea. dist.) N.C. 1985, U.S. Dist. Ct. (mid. dist.) N.C. 1989. Assoc. Graham & James, Raleigh, N.C., 1985-93, Johnson, Mercer, Hearn & Vinegar, PLLC, Raleigh, N.C., 1994-97, Ragsdale & Liggett, PLLC, Raleigh, N.C., 1997—. Mem. N.C. Bar Assn. (chair real property sect. 1998—), Wake County Real Property Lawyers Assn. (pres. 1994-95). Real property, General corporate. Office: Ragsdale & Liggett PLLC 2840 Plaza Pl Ste 400 Raleigh NC 27612-6345

**REINHARDT, BENJAMIN MAX,** lawyer, arbitrator, mediator; b. N.Y.C., Dec. 29, 1917; s. Meyer and Miriam (Fischer) R.; children: Dennis, Dixie, Sara, Shawn. BA, Harvard U., 1940; JD magna cum laude, Southwestern U., L.A., 1956. Bar: Calif. 1956, U.S. Supreme Ct. 1960. Pvt. practice Van Nuys, Calif., 1957-87, Palm Desert, Calif., 1987—; chief legal counsel Northridge (Calif.) Hosp. Found., 1965-75; atty. Calif. Psychol. Assn., San Francisco, 1965-70; tchr. law Los Angeles County Bd. Edn., L.A., 1965-73; instr. law U. So. Calif., L.A., 1963-69, Coll. of Desert, Palm Desert, Calif., 1992-94; arbitrator Superior Ct. Calif., Palm Springs, 1994—; atty. Sr. T.V., Indian Wells, Calif., 1992—. Mem. Palm Desert Police Adv. Com., 1993-98; mem. adv. bd. Ret. Sr. Vol. Program, Palm Desert, 1994-96; instr. law Elderhostel, Indian Wells, Calif., 1993-98. Capt. U.S. Army, 1941-46. Mem. State Bar Calif., Desert Bar Assn. Republican. Avocations: golf, reading. State civil litigation, General practice, Probate. Office: 73450 Country Club Dr Spc 280 Palm Desert CA 92260-8617

**REINHARDT, STEPHEN ROY,** federal judge; b. N.Y.C., Mar. 27, 1931; s. Gottfried and Silvia (Hanlon) R.; children: Mark, Justin, Dana. B.A. cum laude, Pomona Coll., 1951; LL.B., Yale, 1954. Bar: Calif. 1958. Law clk. to U.S. Dist. Judge Luther W. Youngdahl, Washington, 1956-57; atty. O'Melveny & Myers, L.A., 1957-59; partner Fogel Julber Reinhardt Rothschild & Feldman (L.C.), L.A., 1959-80; judge U.S. Ct. Appeals (9th cir.), L.A., 1980—; Mem. exec. com. Dem. Nat. Com., 1969-72, nat. Dem. committeeman for Calif., 1976-80; pres. L.A. Recreation an dParks Commn., 1974-75; mem. Coliseum Commn., 1974-75; mem. L.A. Police Commn., 1974-78, pres., 1978-80; sec., mem. exec. com. L.A. Olympic Organizing com., 1980-84; bd. dirs. Amateur Athletic Found. of L.A., 1984-92; adj. prof. Loyola Law Sch., L.A., 1988-90. Served to 1st lt. USAF, 1954-56. Mem. ABA (labor law coun. 1975-77).

**REINHART, RICHARD PAUL,** lawyer; b. Cleve., Sept. 1, 1954; s. Richard A. and Carole F. (Kaspar) R.; m. Debra Rae Hitchcock, June 20, 1976; children: Geoffrey, Richelle Marie. BA with honors, Rollins Coll., 1976; JD with distinction, Emory U., 1979. Bar: Ga. 1979, Fla. 1980. Ptnr. Morris, Manning & Martin, Atlanta, 1979-89; officer McMillen Reinhart and Voght, P.A., Orlando, Fla., 1989—, also bd. dirs. Mem. ABA, ATLA, Fla. Bar Assn., Ga. Bar Assn., Orange County Bar Assn., Acad. Fla. Trial Lawyers, Order of Coif, Omicron Delta Kappa. Federal civil litigation, State civil litigation. Office: McMillen Reinhart and Voght PA Ste 700 20 N Orange Ave Orlando FL 32801-3438

**REINHART, ROBERT ROUNTREE, JR.,** lawyer; b. Chgo., Oct. 21, 1947; s. Robert Rountree and Ruth (Duncan) R.; m. Elizabeth Aileen Plews, July 26, 1969; children: Andrea Jean, Jessica Elizabeth, Rebecca Jill. BA, Northwestern U., 1968; JD, U. Mich., 1971. Bar: Ill. 1971, Mich. 1972, Minn. 1973, U.S. Supreme Ct. 1976. Law clk. to judge U.S. Dist. Ct. (we. dist.) Mich., Grand Rapids, 1971-73; assoc. Oppenheimer Wolff & Donnelly, Mpls., 1973-77, ptnr., 1978-96, chair labor and employment bus. group, 1985-92; ptnr. Dorsey & Whitney, Mpls., 1996—; co-chair Upper Midwest Employment Law Inst., Mpls., 1984—. Mem. ABA (labor and employment, civil litigation sects.), Minn. Bar Assn. Labor, General civil litigation. Office: Dorsey & Whitney 1400 Pillsbury Ctr S 220 S 6th St Ste 2200 Minneapolis MN 55402-1498

**REINKE, STEFAN MICHAEL,** lawyer; b. Concord, Calif., May 7, 1958; s. Albert Richard and Patricia Eleanor (Stefan) R.; m. Lisa Elaine Williams, June 7, 1997. AA, Bakersfield Coll., 1978; AB, U. So. Calif., 1981; JD, U. Calif., Davis, 1984. Bar: Hawaii 1984, U.S. Dist. Ct. Hawaii 1984, U.S. Ct. Appeals (9th and Fed. cirs.) 1985. Assoc. Carlsmith, Wichman, Case, Mukai & Ichiki, Honolulu, 1984-86; dir. Lyons, Brandt, Cook & Hiramatsu, Honolulu, 1986—; lectr. Windward C.C., 1995-98; lawyer rep. 9th Cir. Jud. Conf., 1995; lawyer rep. Jud. Conf. for the U.S. Dist. Ct. Hawaii, 1996-98. Bd. dirs. Hawaii Ctrs. for Ind. Living, Honolulu, 1985-91, Prevent Child Abuse Hawaii, 1995—, v.p., 1999—. Mem. ABA, FBA (pres. Hawaii chpt. 1994-96, 98-99), Hawaii Bar Assn., Am. Arbitration Assn. (arbitrator and mediator), Def. Rsch. Inst., Hawaii State Cycling Assn. (bd. dirs. 1998—), Phi Beta Kappa, Phi Alpha Delta. General civil litigation, Insurance, Labor. Office: Lyons Brandt Cook & Hiramatsu 841 Bishop St Ste 1800 Honolulu HI 96813-3918

**REINKE, WILLIAM JOHN,** lawyer; b. South Bend, Ind., Aug. 7, 1930; s. William August and Eva Marie (Hein) R.; m. Sue Carol Colvin, 1951 (div. 1988); children: Sally Sue Taelman, William A., Andrew J.; m. Elizabeth Beck Lockwood, 1991. AB cum laude, Wabash Coll., 1952; JD, U. Chgo., 1955. Bar: Ind. 1955. Assoc. Barnes & Thornburg and predecessors, South Bend, Ind., 1957-61; ptnr. Barnes & Thornburg and predecessors, 1961-96, of counsel, 1996—; former chmn. compensation com., former mem. mgmt. com. Trustee Stanley Clark Sch., 1969-80, pres., 1977-80; mem. adv. bd. Salvation Army, 1973—, pres., 1990-92; bd. dirs. NABE Mich. chpt., 1990-94, pres. 1993-94, Isaac Walton League, 1970-81, United Way, 1979-81; pres. South Bend Round Table, 1963-65; trustee First Meth. Ch., 1976-70. Served with U.S. Army, 1955-57. Recipient Outstanding Local Pres. award Ind. Jaycees, 1960-61, Boss of Yr. award, 1979, South Bend Outstanding Young Man award, 1961. Mem. ABA, Ind. State Bar Assn., St. Joseph County Bar Assn., Ind. Bar Found. (patron fellow), Am. Judicature Soc., Ind. Soc. Chgo., Summit Club (past gov., founders com.), Rotary (bd. dirs. 1970-73, 94-97). General civil litigation, Contracts commercial, Construction. Home: 51795 Waterton Square Cir Granger IN 46530-8317 Office: Barnes & Thornburg 600 1st Source Bank Ctr 100 N Michigan St Ste 600 South Bend IN 46601-1632

**REINSTEIN, JOEL,** lawyer; b. N.Y.C., July 23, 1946; s. Louis and Ruth Shukovsky; children: Lesli, Louis, Mindy. BSE, U. Pa., 1968; JD cum laude, U. Fla., 1971; LLM in Taxation, NYU, 1974. Bar: Fla. 1971, U.S. Tax Ct. 1973, U.S. Dist. Ct. (so. dist.) Fla. 1976. Atty., office of chief counsel IRS, 1971-74; ptnr. Capp, Reinstein, Kopelowitz and Atlas, P.A., Ft. Lauderdale, Fla., 1975-85; dir., ptrn. Greenberg, Traurig, Hoffman, Lipoff, Rosen & Quentel, P.A., Ft. Lauderdale, 1985-92; gen. counsel Internat. Magnetic Imaging, Inc., Boca Raton, Fla., 1992-94; prin. Law Offices of Joel Reinstein, Boca Raton, 1993—; lectr. Advanced Pension Planning, Am. Soc. C.L.U.s; lectr. in field. Mem. editl. bd. U. Fla. Law Rev. 1970-71; contbr. articles to profl. jours. Mem. Fla. Bar Assn. (tax sect.), ABA (tax sect.), Order of Coif, Phi Kappa Phi, Phi Delta Pi. Corporate taxation, General corporate, Estate planning. Office: The Plaza 5355 Town Center Rd Ste 801 Boca Raton FL 33486-1069

**REINSTEIN, ROBERT J.,** dean, law educator; b. Balt., Mar. 17, 1945; m. Mary Taylor Aspinwall; children: Ellen, Thomas. BS in Engring. Physics with distinction, Cornell U., 1965; JD cum laude, Harvard U., 1968. Bar: Md. 1969, Pa. 1982, U.S. Supreme Ct. 1971. Law clk. to Hon. Frank A. Kaufman U.S. Dist. Ct. Md., 1968-69; from asst. prof. to assoc. prof. Sch. Law Temple U., Phila., 1969-73, prof. Sch. Law, 1973—; sr. atty. appellate sect. Civil Rights Divsn., U.S Dept. Justice, 1977-78, chief litigation sect., 1979-80; chief legal officer Temple U., 1982-89, dean Sch. Law, 1989—; vis. prof. law Hastings Coll. Law, San Francisco, 1975, Georgetown U., 1978-79; cons. atty. NAACP Spl. Contbn. Fund, 1970-77. Contbr. articles to profl. jours. Chair civil rights com. B'nai Brith Anti-Defamation League, Phila. Mem. ABA, Pa. Bar Assn. Office: Temple U Sch Law 1719 N Broad St Philadelphia PA 19122-6002

**REINTHALER, RICHARD WALTER,** lawyer; b. N.Y.C., Feb. 27, 1949; s. Walter F. and Maureen C. (Tully) R.; m. Mary E. Maloney, Aug. 8, 1970; children: Brian, Scott, Amy. BA in Govt. magna cum laude, U. Notre Dame, 1970, JD summa cum laude, 1973. Bar: N.Y. 1974, U.S. Dist. Ct. (so. and ea. dists.) N.Y. 1974, U.S. Ct. Appeals (2d cir.) 1974, U.S. Ct. Appeals (9th cir.) 1976, U.S. Ct. Appeals (5th cir.) 1978, U.S. Ct. Appeals (11th cir.) 1981, U.S. Supreme Ct. 1977. Assoc. White & Case, N.Y.C., 1973-81, ptnr., 1981-95; ptnr. Dewey Ballantine LLP, N.Y.C., 1995—; mem. adv. group U.S. Dist. Ct. (ea. dist.) N.Y., 1992—, chairperson subgroup on ethics, 1993—. Contbr. articles to profl. jours. Served to 1st lt. U.S. Army, 1974. Fellow Am. Bar Found.; mem. ABA (2d cir. chmn. discovery com. 1982-87, program coord. 1986, ann. meeting litigation sect., vice chmn. com. on fed. procedure 1988-89, co-chmn. com. on profl. responsibility 1989-92, vice chmn. securities litigation com. 1993-94, vice chair Hong Kong meeting 1995, co-chair energy litigation com. 1996-97, co-chair antitrust litigation com. 1997—), N.Y. State Bar Assn., Assn. of Bar of City of N.Y. (mem. com. to enhance diversity in the profession 1990—, mem. Orison S. Marden Meml. Lectrs. com. 1994—, chair 1997—, spl. com. on mergers, acquisitions and corp. control contests 1995—), Scarsdale Golf Club (Hartsdale, N.Y., bd. govs. 1994—), Capital Hill Club (Washington). Republican. Roman Catholic. Avocations: golf, tennis. Federal civil litigation, Securities, Antitrust. Office: Dewey Ballantine LLP 1301 Avenue Of The Americas New York NY 10019-6022

**REIS, WERNER ADAM,** lawyer, pathologist; b. Tamm, Germany, June 6, 1948; came to U.S., 1951; s. Josef John and Magdalena (Troll) T.; m. Annalisa Bromley, Feb. 14, 1997; children: Sarah, Jennifer, Christine. MD, Med. Coll. Wis., 1973; BS, Marquette U., 1969, JD, 1983. Bar: Wis. 1983, U.S. Dist. Ct. (ea. dist.) Wis. 1983. Resident Presbyn. Hosp., San Francisco, 1973-74, St. Josephs Hosp., Milw., 1974-75, Milw. Co. Gen. Hosp., Milw., 1975-77; pathologist St. Francis Hosp., Milw., 1977-80; atty., phys. Warshafsky Law Firm, Milw., 1980—; asst. clin. prof. Med. Coll. Wis., Milw., 1977-80; mem. adv. bd. Present Music, Milw., 1995—; jud. cons., Milw., 1983—. Contbr. articles to profl. publs. Mem. lawyers bd. dirs. Wis. Civil Liberty Union, Milw., 1985-92. Fellow NSF, 1967. Fellow Am. Coll. Clin. Pathology, Am. Coll. Legal Medicine. Avocations: music, hiking, literature, auto repair, film. Personal injury. Office: Warshafsky Law Firm 839 N Jefferson St Milwaukee WI 53202-3740

**REISENMAN, DEBRA JILL,** lawyer; b. Bronx, N.Y., May 15, 1969; d. Robert and Linda Reisenman; m. Richard Renert, Nov. 5, 1995. BA magna cum laude, SUNY, New Paltz, 1991; JD cum laude, Albany Law Sch., 1994. Bar: N.Y. 1995. Law clk. to Magistrate Smith U.S. Dist. Ct., Albany, N.Y., 1992; legal asst. Legal Aid Soc., Forest Hills, N.Y., 1993; trial atty. Finkelstein, Lenne, Gittelsohn & Ptnrs., Newburgh, N.Y., 1995-98, mng. atty., 1998—. Mem. N.Y. State Bar Assn. Democrat. Jewish. Avocations: racquetball, reading. Personal injury. Home: 23 Laurel Rd New City NY 10956-4829 Office: Finkelstein Lenne Gittelsohn & Ptnrs 436 Robinson Ave Newburgh NY 12550-3341

**REISING, RICHARD P.,** lawyer. BA, Stanford U.; JD, U. Mo. Bar: Ill. 1970. Asst. gen. counsel, sec. Archer-Daniels-Midland Co., Decatur, Ill., v.p., sec., gen. counsel, 1991-97, sr. v.p., 1997—. General corporate. Office: Archer-Daniels-Midland Co 4666 E Faries Pky Decatur IL 62526-5666

**REISKE, PETER FRANCIS,** lawyer; b. Milw., Mar. 28, 1941; s. Francis Hugo and Louise Hanna (Ulrich) R.; m. Judith Marie Bonny, Aug. 22, 1964; children: Bonny Louise, Scott Peter, Michelle Kathleen. BSBA, Marquette U., 1963, JD, 1965. Bar: Wis. 1965, U.S. Dist. Ct. (ea. dist.) Wis. 1965. Pvt. practice Milw., 1965—. Pres. Bay View-St. Francis Jaycees, 1966-67, Bay View Bus. Assn., 1973-74. Mem. State Bar of Wis., Milw. Bar Assn., South Shore Yacht Club (Sportsmanship trophy 1996, Competitor of Yr. 1996), Sertoma (pres. 1986-87). Roman Catholic. Avocations: sailing, hunting, fishing, walking. General practice, Probate, Real property. Home: 3058 S Superior St Milwaukee WI 53207-3064 Office: Reiske & Reiske Attys 230 W Wells St Ste 600 Milwaukee WI 53203-1866

**REISMAN, JASON ERIC,** lawyer; b. Atlanta, Feb. 15, 1969; s. Stuart Ronald and Donna Faye Reisman; m. Suzanne Gail Barrett, Dec. 31, 1994. BS in Econs. summa cum laude, U. Pa., 1991; JD cum laude, Georgetown U., 1994. Bar: Pa. 1994, N.J. 1994, U.S. Dist. Ct. (ea. dist.) Pa. 1994, U.S. Dist. Ct. N.J. 1994, U.S. Ct. Appeals (8th cir.) 1998, U.S. Ct. Appeals (3d cir.) 1999. Lawyer Obermayer Rebmann Maxwell & Hippel LLP, Phila., 1994—. Vol. lawyer Homeless Advocacy Project, Phila., 1994—; vol. basketball coach Ridley Jr. ABA, Ridley Park, Pa., 1995—; vol. co-leader Explorers Program, Phila., 1997-98. Mem. ABA, Pa. Bar Assn., Phila. Bar Assn. Democrat. Jewish. Avocations: sports, family, coaching kids. Labor. Office: Obermayer Rebmann Maxwell & Hippel LLP One Penn Ctr 19th Fl 1617 Jfk Blvd Ste 1950 Philadelphia PA 19103-1895

**REISMAN, JOANNE,** lawyer; b. Walnut Creek, Calif., May 16, 1958; d. Elias and Leorita R. BA cum laude, UCLA, 1980; JD, Lewis and Clark Coll., 1983. Bar: Oreg. 1983. With Harrington, Anderson & DeBlasio, Portland, 1984-85, Case & Dusterhoff, Portland, 1985-86; assoc. Shannon & Johnson PC, Portland, 1986-87; pvt. practice Portland, 1987—; spkr. in field. Author, pub. (newsletter) Councilor, 1990—; contbr. articles to profl. jours. Organizer profl. women's network event Powertea, 1993-96. Mem. Am. Mensa (SIGHT coord. 1992—). E-mail: midnitdr@teleport.com. Family and matrimonial, Estate planning, Personal injury. Office: 732 SW 3rd Ave Ste 304 Portland OR 97204-2409

**REISS, JOHN BARLOW,** lawyer; b. London, Aug. 29, 1939; came to U.S., 1963; s. James Martin and Margaret Joan (Ping) R.; m. Mary Jean Maudsley, Aug. 6, 1967 (div. 1978); m. Kathleen Strouse, Aug. 2, 1979; 1 child, Juliette Blanche. BA with honors, Exeter U., Devon, Eng., 1961; AM, Washington U., St. Louis, 1966, PhD, 1971; JD, Temple U., 1977. Bar: Pa. 1977, N.J. 1977, U.S. Dist. Ct. N.J. 1977, D.C. 1980, U.S. Supreme Ct. 1981, U.S. Dist. Ct. D.C. 1982. Economist Commonwealth Econ. Com., London, 1962-63; asst. prof. Allegheny Coll., Meadville, Pa., 1967-71; assoc. prof. Stockton State Coll., Pomona, N.J., 1971-75; asst. health commr. State of N.J., Trenton, 1975-79; dir. office of health regulation U.S. Dept. HHS, Washington, 1979-81; assoc. Baker & Hostetler, Washington, 1981-82; assoc. Dechert Price & Rhoads, Phila., 1982-86, ptnr., 1986-93, asst. chair health law group, 1984-91, chmn. health law group, 1991-93; ptnr. Saul, Ewing, Remick & Saul, Phila., 1993—, chmn. health law dept., 1995—. Mem. editl. bd. Topics in Hosp. Law, 1985-86, Hosp. Legal Forms Manual, 1985—, Jour. Health Care Tech., 1984-86; contbr. Hosp. Contracts Manual, 1983—; contbr. articles to profl. jours., chpts. to books. Bd. dirs. Gateway Sch. Little Children, Phila., 1986-99, ECRI, Plymouth Meeting, Pa., 1994—; mem. vestry All Saints Ch., Wynnewood, Pa., 1993, 96—; mem. The Union League of Phila., 1995—; mem. Univ. Barge Club, 1997—, British Officers Club of Phila., 1999—. Pub. Health Svc. fellow, 1979-81, English Speaking Union fellow, 1963-66, Econ. Devel. Adminstr. fellow Washington U., 1966-67. Mem. Nat. Health Lawyers Assn., N.J. Soc. Hosp. Attys., Phila. Bar Assn., Am. Hosp. Assn., N.J. Hosp. Assn., Brit. Am. C. of C. of Greater Phila. (bd. dirs. 1991), Brit. Officers Club of Phila. Avocations: gardening, house restoring, reading, philately. Health, General corporate, Administrative and regulatory. Home: 415 Wister Rd Wynnewood PA 19096-1808 Office: Saul Ewing Remick & Saul 3800 Centre Sq W Philadelphia PA 19102

**REISS, SIDNEY H.,** judge; b. Passaic, N.J., Nov. 2, 1926; s. Theodore and Mollie (Holder) R.; m. Anester Feld, Apr. 3, 1955; children: Theodore F., Marci. BS, U.S. Mcht. Marine Acad., 1949; JD, Rutgers U., Newark, 1955; BA (hon.), Passaic County Coll., Paterson, N.J., 1976. Bar: N.J. 1956, U.S. Dist. Ct. N.J. 1956, U.S. Supreme Ct. 1957. Pvt. practice, Passaic, 1956-65; sr. ptnr. Reiss & Scancarella, Passaic, 1965-76; judge Superior Ct., State of N.J., Paterson, 1976—, criminal assignment judge, 1983—. Counsel Passaic County Bd. Social Svcs.; councilman City of Passaic, 1967-71; freeholder Passaic County, 1971-76, freeholder dir., 1974-75. Lt. USN, 1945-51, PTO, Korea. Recipient Disting. Svc. award Passaic C. of C. 1970, trustees outstanding achievement citation Passaic County Children's Shelter, 1973, outstanding svc. citation as criminal assigment judge Assn. Criminal Def. Lawyers of N.J., 1990. Mem. ABA, N.J. Bar Assn., Passaic County Bar Assn., Am. Legion, Masons, Lions (pres. Passaic 1964-65). Home: 85 Elmwood Ave Passaic NJ 07055-2408 Office: Passaic County Ct House Paterson NJ 07505

**REITER, ALLEN GARY,** lawyer; b. Bronx, N.Y., Jan. 6, 1950; s. Leo and Anna (Lenchis) R.; m. Karen Kozac, Sept. 16, 1979. BA, SUNY, Albany, 1972; JD, U. Pa., 1975. Bar: N.Y. 1976, U.S. Dist. Ct. (so. dist.) N.Y. 1977, U.S. Dist. Ct. (ea. dist.) N.Y. 1980, U.S. Supreme Ct. 1983, U.S. Ct. Appeals (2d cir.) 1988. Asst. dist. atty. N.Y. County, N.Y.C., 1975-79; assoc. Skadden, Arps, Slate, Meagher & Flom, N.Y.C., 1979-85; ptnr. Schonwald, Schaffzin & Mullman, N.Y.C., 1985-89, Siller & Wilk LLP, N.Y.C., 1989-98, Cooperman, Levitt, Winikoff, Lester & Newman, N.Y.C., 1998—. Mem. Assn. of Bar of City of N.Y. Democrat. Jewish. Federal civil litigation, State civil litigation, General civil litigation. Home: 35 Seton Rd Larchmont NY 10538-1517 Office: Cooperman Levitt Winikoff Lester & Newman 800 3rd Ave New York NY 10022-7604

**REITER, JOSEPH HENRY,** lawyer, retired judge; b. Phila., Mar. 21, 1929; s. Nicholas and Barbara (Hellmann) R.; m. Beverlee A. Bearman, Nov. 8, 1993. AB, Temple U., 1950, LLB, 1953. Bar: D.C. 1953, Pa. 1954. Atty. advisor U.S. Army, 1955-61; asst. U.S. atty. Ea. Dist. Pa., 1961-63, asst. U.S. atty. in charge of civil div., 1963-69; chief organized crime and racketeering strike force Western N.Y. State, U.S. Dept. Justice, 1969-70, sr. trial atty. tax div. 1970-72, regional dir. office of drug abuse law enforcement, 1972-73; dep. atty. gen., dir. Drug Law Enforcement Office of Pa., 1973-77; ptnr. Stassen, Kostos and Mason, Phila. 1978-85, Kostos Reiter & Lamer, 1985-89; judge Armed Svcs. Bd. of Contract Appeals, Falls Church, Va., 1989-95; of counsel Kostos & Lamer, Phila., 1995—; mem. adv. com. Joint State Commn. on Procurement; lectr. in field. Contbr. articles to profl. jours. Mem. Citizens Crime Commn. Pa. With U.S. Army, 1953-55. Recipient Meritorious Svc. award U.S. Atty. Gen. Clark, 1967, Spl. Commendation Asst. U.S. Atty. Gen. Tax Div., 1969, Outstanding Performance award U.S. Atty. Gen. Richardson, 1973. Mem. ABA, Fed. Bar Assn., D.C. Bar Assn., Pa. Bar Assn., Phila. Bar Assn., Am. Legion, Vesper Club, Downtown Club. Government contracts and claims. Office: Kostos & Lamer 1608 Walnut St Ste 1300 Philadelphia PA 19103-5407

**REITZELL, WILLIAM R.,** lawyer; b. Worcester, Mass., Sept. 20, 1952; m. Ann Butler, Nov. 28, 1982. AB, Colgate U., 1974; JD, Suffolk U., 1977. Bar: Mass. 1977, U.S. Dist. Ct. Mass. 1979. Trial atty. Travelers Ins. Co., Worcester, 1977-85; atty. Fuller, Reitzell, Rosenberg, Worcester, 1985-93, Donahue & Rauscher, Worcester, 1993—; arbitrator Am. Arbitration Assn., Boston, 1985—. Mem. MAss. Bar Assn., Worcester County Bar Assn., Worcester Club. Personal injury, Workers' compensation, General civil litigation. Office: 23 Harvard St Worcester MA 01609-2835

**REIVER, JOANNA,** lawyer; b. Oct. 20, 1946; d. Julius and Iona (Peterson) R.; m. Robert E. Schlusser, July 16, 1982; children: Amelia, Daniel. Student, U. Del., 1964-65; AB, W. Va. U., 1968; JD, Catholic U. Am., 1976. Bar: Del. 1976. Reporter Del. State News, Dover, 1968-69, San Deigo Evening Tribune, 1969-71; asst. editor Epilepsy Found. Am., Washington, 1972-73; asst. to dean Cath. U. Am. Law Sch., Washington, 1973-76; assoc. Murdoch & Walsh, P.A., Wilmington, Del., 1976-81, dir., 1980-82; ptnr. Schlusser & Reiver, Wilmington, Del., 1982-87, Schlusser, Reiver, Hughes and Sisk, Wilmington, Del., 1987-94; dir. Schlusser & Reiver, P.A., Wilmington, Del., 1995—; adj. prof. Delaware Law Sch. Widener U., 1987—; bd. dirs. ARC of Del. Pres. Estate Law Specialist Bd., Inc., 1998-99; v.p. Del. Care Plan, Inc., 1999. Fellow Am. Coll. Trust and Estate Counsel; mem. Del. Bar Assn. (sec. estates and trusts sect. 1982-84, vice chmn. 1984-85, chmn. 1985-86), Estate Planning Council Del. (bd. dirs. 1983-85, chmn. membership com. 1983-84, 1987-88, pres. 1991-92), Nat. Assn. Estate Coun. (bd. dirs. 1993, treas. 1998-99). Estate planning, Probate, Estate taxation. Office: Schlusser & Reiver PA 1700 W 14th St Wilmington DE 19806-4012

**REJAN, JEFFREY NEIL,** lawyer; b. Bronx, N.Y., Apr. 15, 1955; s. Gilbert and Shirley Rejan; m. Lisa M. Tidball, Dec. 5, 1986; children: Andrew M., Gregory J. AB, Columbia U., 1977; JD, Boston U., 1980. Bar: N.Y. 1981, U.S. Dist. Ct. (ea. and so. dists.) N.Y. 1982. Assoc. Bower & Gardner, N.Y.C., 1980-81; assoc. Kroll, Rubin & Fiorella LLP, N.Y.C., 1981-89, ptnr., 1990—. Mem. Assn. Bar City N.Y. Personal injury, Insurance, Product liability. Office: Kroll Rubin & Fiorella LLP 520 Madison Ave New York NY 10022-4213

**RELIN, LEONARD,** lawyer; b. Rochester, N.Y., Nov. 8, 1936; s. Benjamin W. and Bernice L. Relin; 1 child, David S. BS in Econ., U. Pa., 1957; JD, Albany Law Sch., 1961. Assoc. Lacy, Katzen, Green & Jones, Rochester, 1962-63; pvt. practice Rochester, 1963—; bd. dirs. First Nat. Bank of Rochester, 1978-92, Atlanta Nat. Bank, 1986-92; v.p. Tramell Crow Co., 1st Am. Bank, Palm Bch. Sgt. USAFR, 1960-65. Named for Best of TV, Bank Mktg. Assn., 1987, for Best of Print Media, Bank Mktg. Assn., 1990. Mem. Monroe County Bar Assn., N.Y. State Bar Assn., N.Y. State Trial Lawyers Assn., U. Pa. Alumni Assn. (pres. western N.Y. chpt. 1979, trustee spl. trust). Republican. Jewish. Avocations: boating, travel, tennis. Bankruptcy, Real property, General civil litigation. Home: 2165 East Ave Rochester NY 14610-2607 Office: 1 Main St E Rochester NY 14614-1807

**RELKIN, ELLEN,** lawyer; b. Bronx, N.Y., Aug. 27, 1959; d. Joseph and Marjorie Relkin; m. Alan Rojer, June 20, 1981; children: Rebecca, Isaac, Aurora. BA in History cum laude, Cornell U., 1980; JD, Rutgers U., 1984. Bar: N.J. 1985, U.S. Dist. Ct. (so., ea. no. and we. dists.) N.Y. 1985, D.C. 1986, U.S. Ct. Appeals (3d cir.) 1986. Law clk. to Hon. Sylvia B. Pressler appellate divsn. N.J. Superior Ct., 1984-85; assoc. Porzio, Bromberg, Newman & Baumeister, N.Y.C., 1985-88, Baumeister & Samuels, PC, N.Y.C., 1988-92, Weitz & Luxenberg, PC, N.Y.C., 1997—; of counsel Karl Asch, P.A., Clark, N.J., 1992-93, Sybil Shainwald, PC, N.Y.C., 1993-96; bd. advisors BNA Toxics Law Reporter, Washington, 1990—, BNA Products Liability Law Reporter, Washington, 1995—; trustee Nat. Pre-Suit Mediation Program, Washington, 1997-98. Contbr. articles to profl. jours. Troop leader Girl Scouts U.S., Maplewood, N.J., 1993-98. Mem. ABA (vice chair com. on toxic torts and environ. law 1991-97), ATLA (1st vice chair sect. toxic, environ. and pharm. torts 1999), N.Y. Bar Assn. (co-chair toxic tort com. environ. law sect. 1990-94, 98). Product liability, Personal injury, Environmental. Office: Weitz & Luxenberg PC 180 Maiden Ln New York NY 10038-4925

**REMAR, ROBERT BOYLE,** lawyer; b. Boston, Nov. 19, 1948; s. Samuel Roy and Elizabeth Mary (Boyle) R.; m. Victoria A. Greenhood, Nov. 11, 1979; children: Daniel A.G., William B.G. BA, U. Mass., 1970; JD, Boston Coll., 1974. Bar: Ga. 1974, Mass. 1975, U.S. Ct. Appeals (5th cir.) 1978, U.S. Ct. Appeals (11th cir.) 1981, U.S. Ct. Appeals (2d cir.) 1995, U.S. Supreme Ct. 1981. Staff atty. Ga. Legal Svcs. Program, Savannah, 1974-76, Western Mass. Legal Svcs., Greenfield, 1976-77; sr. staff atty. Ga. Legal Svcs. Program, Atlanta, 1977-82; ptnr. Remar & Graettinger, Atlanta, 1983-95, Kirwan, Parks, Chesin & Remar PC, Atlanta, 1993-96, Rogers & Hardin, Atlanta, 1996—; bd. dirs., exec. com. ACLU, N.Y.C., pres. Ga. chpt., 1985-87, gen. counsel, 1980-83; hearing officer Ga. Pub. Svc. Commn., Atlanta, 1985-98; adj. prof. Ga. State U., Atlanta, 1984-98, spl. asst. atty. gen., 1990—; bd. experts Lawyers Alert, Boston, 1985-94. Mem. Ga. Energy Regulatory Reform Commn., Gov. of Ga., 1980-82, Ga. Consumer Adv. Bd., 1981-82; pres. Ga. Consumer Ctr. Inc., 1988-91; bd. dirs., exec. com. Ga. Resource Ctr.; v.p. Ga Ctr. Law Pub. Inst., 1991-94. Mem. ABA (chmn. individual rights access to civil justice com.), ATLA, Ga. Bar Assn. (chmn. individual rights sect. 1981-83, co-chmn. consumer rights and remedies com. 1979-83, chmn. death penalty re. com. 1993—, mem. legis. adv. com. 1994-97), Gate City Bar Assn., Lawyers Club Atlanta, Lamar Inn of Ct. (master of the bench). Democrat. Avocations: golf, gardening. Administrative and regulatory, Federal civil litigation, Labor. Home: 1714 Meadowdale Ave NE Atlanta GA 30306-3114 Office: Rogers & Hardin Internat Tower Peachtree Ctr 229 Peachtree St NE Ste 2700 Atlanta GA 30303-1638

**REMINGER, RICHARD THOMAS,** lawyer, artist; b. Cleve., Apr. 3, 1931; s. Edwin Carl and Theresa Henrietta (Bookmyer) R.; m. Billie Carmen Greer, June 26, 1954; children: Susan Greer, Patricia Allison, Richard Thomas. AB, Case-Western Res. U., 1953; JD, Cleve. State U., 1957. Bar: Ohio 1957, Pa. 1978, U.S. Supreme Ct. 1961. Pers. and safety dir. Motor Express, Inc., Cleve., 1954-58; mng. ptnr. Reminger & Reminger Co., L.P.A., Cleve., 1958-90; mem. nat. claims couns. adv. bd. Comml. Union Assurance Co., 1980-90; lectr. transp. law Fenn Coll., 1960-62; lectr. bus. law Case Western Res. U., 1962-64; lectr. products liability U. Wirtschaft at Schloss Gracht, Erfstadt-Liblar, Germany, 1990-91, Bar Assn. City of Hamburg, Germany, 1990; mem. faculty Nat. Inst. for Trial Advocacy, 1992. One-man shows include Gates Mills Art Show (Jury), Cleve., 1993, 99, Orange Art Show, Cleve., Greater Cleve. Bar Assn., Cafe du Parc, Palm

Beach, Fla., 1993-95, The Island Nat. Bank, Palm Beach, 1993, The Intown Club Gallery, Cleve., 1993, St. Paul Gallery, Cleve., 1994, New Orgn. for the Visual Arts, Cleve., 1994, The Everglades Club, Palm Beach, 1990-97, The Lost Tree Club, 1992-97, Mass. Coll. Art, Boston, 1994, Ursuline Coll., Cleve., 1994, Oil Painters Am., Chgo., 1994, 95, Cleve. Playhouse Gallery, 1995, 20th Ann. Russell Art Show, Cleve., 1995, The Wolfhope Gallery, Cleve., 1995, Good Samaritan Med. Ctr., West Palm Beach, Fla., 1995, Norton Gallery of Art, Palm Beach, 1996, Key Trust Co. Fla. Exhbn., North Palm Beach, 1996, 97, Blue Moon Gallery, Cleve., 1996, 22nd Ann. Russell Art Show, Cleve., 1997, The Oriel Gallery, Dublin Ireland, 1997, Bohemian Club Gallery, San Francisco, 1996, 97, 98, Martha Lincoln Gallery, Vero Beach, Fla., 1997, Alzgalerie, Munich, 1998, Ann Norton Gallery, Palm Beach, 1999, Galerie im OSRAM-Haus, Munich, 1999, Internat. Soc. Marine Painters, Cleve., 1999; represented in numerous private collections worldwide. Mem. joint com. Cleve. Acad. Medicine-Greater Cleve. Bar Assn.; trustee Cleve. Zool. Soc., mem. exec. com., 1984-89, v.p., 1987-89; trustee Andrew Sch., 1984-96; Meridia Huron Hosp., Cleve., Cleve. Sch. for Blind, 1987-88, Cerebral Palsy Assn., 1984-87; trustee Intracoastal Health Sys., Palm Beach, Fla., 1992—. With AC, USNR, 1950-58. Mem. ABA (com. on law and medicine, profl. responsibility com. 1977-90), FBA, ATLA, Fedn. Ins. and Corp. Counsel, Internat. Bar Assn., Ohio Bar Assn. (coun. dels. 1987-90, internat. law com. 1990-91), Pa. Bar Assn., Cleve. Bar Assn. (chmn. med.-legal com. 1978-79, prof. liability com. 1977-90), Transp. Lawyers Assn., Cleve. Assn. Civil Trial Attys., Am. Soc. Hosp. Attys., Soc. Ohio Hosp. Attys., Ohio Assn. Civil Trial Attys., Am. Judicature Soc., Def. Rsch. Inst., Maritime Law Assn. U.S., Am. Coll. Law and Medicine, 8th Jud. Bar Assn. (life Ohio dist.), Internat. Ins. Law Soc., Palm Beach County Bar Assn., Oil Painters Am., Internat. Soc. Marine Painters (profl. mem., v.p.), North Shore Arts Assn., Rockport Art Assn., Lost Tree Property Owners Assn., Mayfield Country Club (pres. 1980-82), Union Club, Hermit Club (pres. 1973-75), Lost Tree Club (bd. govs. 1991-94), Everglades Club (Fla.), Kirtland Counry Club, Rolling Rock Club (Pa.), The Bohemian Club (Calif.), Salmagundi Club (N.Y.C.). Federal civil litigation, State civil litigation, Personal injury.

**REMINGTON, CLARK A.,** lawyer, educator; b. Mpls., Oct. 16, 1955; s. Lawrence J. Remington. BM, Ind. U., 1978, BS, 1980, MM, 1980; JD, Columbia U., 1987. Bar: N.Y. 1989. Law clk. to Hon. Robert H. Bork U.S. Ct. Appeals for D.C. Cir., Washington, 1987-88; rsch. asst. to Hon. Robert H. Bork Am. Enterprise Inst., Washington, 1988; assoc. Debevoise & Plimpton, N.Y.C., 1988-93; asst. prof. law Bklyn. Law Sch., 1993—. Contbr. articles to profl. jours. Mem. ABA, Assn. Bar City N.Y. Office: Bklyn Law Sch 250 Joralemon St Brooklyn NY 11201-3700

**REMPE, STEPHEN M. R.,** lawyer; b. DeKalb, Ill.; s. George A. and Mary E. (Brown) R.; m. Becky Banks, Aug. 15, 1970 (div. Mar. 1996); children: Meggie, Blaise, Annie. BA, U. Ariz., 1969; JD, St. Mary's U., San Antonio, 1972. Bar: Tex. 1972, Ariz. 1973. Assoc. Sullivan, Mahoney & Tang, Phoenix, 1975-85; lawyer Maricopa County Pub. Defender, Phoenix, 1972-75, 85—. Pres. St. Thomas More Soc., 1980-85. Mem. NACLD, Ariz. Attys. for Criminal Justice, Brophy Coll. Prep. Alumni Assn. (v.p. 1979-80), Sigma Alpha Epsilon. Office: Maricopa County Pub Defender 11 W Jefferson St Ste 5 Phoenix AZ 85003-2302

**RENBERG, MICHAEL LOREN,** lawyer; b. San Francisco, Apr. 19, 1962; s. Charles and Margret Renberg; m. Shelley Maher, Oct. 19, 1991; children: Kristen, Kyle, Brian, Lauren. BA, UCLA, 1985; JD, U. San Francisco, 1988. Bar: Calif. 1988. Law clk. U.S. Dist. Ct. (ea. dist.) Calif., Fresno, 1988-89; assoc. Adams, Duque & Hazeltine, L.A., 1989-94; ptnr. Parichan, Renberg, Crossman & Harvey, Fresno, 1994—. Mem. Rotary (sec. Fresno 1996—). Avocations: basketball, golf. General civil litigation, Personal injury, Construction. Office: Parichan Renberg Et Al 2350 W Shaw Ave Ste 130 Fresno CA 93711-3400

**RENCH, STEPHEN CHARLES,** lawyer; b. Coffeyville, Kans., Oct. 11, 1930; s. Stephen and Gladys Mae (Carpenter) R.; m. Loraine Pennock, Oct. 11, 1966. B.A. in Econs., U. Kans., 1952; J.D., Georgetown U., 1959. Bar: Colo. 1959, U.S. Dist. Ct. Colo. 1959, U.S. Ct. Appeals (10th cir.) 1961, U.S. Supreme Ct. 1979. Law clk. to judge U.S. Ct. Appeals (10th cir.), Denver, 1959; law clk. to chief judge U.S. Dist. Ct. Colo., Denver, 1960-61; assoc. Tippit and Haskell, Denver, 1961-63; clk. Probate Ct., Denver, 1964-65; dep. state pub. defender, Denver, 1966-74; tng. dir. Colo. State Pub. Defender System, Denver, 1974-77, tng. dir. as ind. contractor tng. seminars, 1980-82; sole practice, Denver, 1977—; mem. permanent lecturing faculty for summer sessions and seminars Nat. Coll. Criminal Def., Houston, 1974—, course dir., 1977; instr. trial tactics and strategy, evidence courses U. Denver Law Sch., 1979-91; lectr. in field throughout U.S. Served to 1st lt. USAF, 1952-56. Mem. Colo. Trial Lawyers Assn., Colo. Criminal Def. Bar, Nat. Assn. Criminal Def. Lawyers, Nat. Legal Aid and Defenders Assn., Nat. Practice Inst., Assn. Trial Lawyers Am., Denver Bar Assn., Colo. Bar Assn., ABA. Author: Fingertip Law for Colorado Public Defenders, 1975; Strategy for Colorado Public Defenders, 1979; The Rench Book, Trial Tactics and Strategy, 1980; Courtbook, 1982; monthly columnist Trade Secrets of a Trial Lawyer, Washington Memo, 1977-78; contbr. articles to profl. publs. Criminal, General civil litigation, Appellate.

**RENDELL, MARJORIE O.,** federal judge; m. Edward G. Rendell. BA, U. Pa., 1969; postgrad., Georgetown U., 1970-71; JD, Villanova U., 1973; LLD (hon.), Phila. Coll. Textile and Sci., 1992. Ptnr. Duane, Morris & Heckscher, Phila., 1972-93; judge U.S. Dist. Ct. (ea. dist.) Pa., 1994—, U.S. Ct. Appeals (3d cir.), Phila.; asst. to dir. annual giving Dept. Devel., U. Pa., 1973-78; mem. adv. bd. Chestnut Hill Nat. Bank/East Falls Adv. Bd.; mem. alternative dispute resolution com. mediation divsn. Ea. Dist. Pa. Bankruptcy Conf. Active Acad. Vocal Arts, Market St. East Improvement Assn., Pa.'s Campaign for Choice, Phila. Friends Outward Bound; vice chair Ave. of Arts, Inc.; vice chair bd. trustees Vis. Nurse Assn. Greater Phila. Mem. ABA, Am. Bankruptcy Inst., Pa. Bar Assn., Phila. Bar Assn. (bd. dirs. young lawyers sect. 1973-78), Phila. Bar Found. (bd. dirs.), Forum Exec. Women, Internat. Women's Forum, Phi Beta Kappa. Office: US Courthouse 601 Market St Rm 21613 Philadelphia PA 19106-1715

**RENDER, JOHN CLIFFORD,** lawyer; b. Logansport, Ind., Aug. 16, 1943; s. John Clifford and Joan Helen (O'Connor) R.; m. Mary Jane Allison, Aug. 12, 1967 (div. Apr. 1975); children: Allison A. Render Porter, Meredith M.; m. Diane Lois Dougherty, July 30, 1976. BS, Butler U., 1966; JD, Ind. U., 1971. Tchr. English Indpls. Pub. Schs., 1966-69; dir. of planning Ind. Hosp. Assn., Indpls., 1969-71; atty., dir. Hall, Render, Killian, Heath & Lyman, P.C., Indpls., 1971—; gen. counsel Ind. Hosp. and Health Assn., Indpls., 1982—. Named Sagamore of Wabash, Gov. State of Ind., 1989. Mem. Columbia Club, Skyline Club, Indpls. Athletic Club. Avocations: golf, traveling, reading. Health. Office: Hall Render Killian Heath & Lyman # 2000 One American Sq Indianapolis IN 46282

**RENDON, JOSEFINA MUNIZ,** judge, mediator, arbitrator; b. San Juan, P.R., June 17, 1949; d. Francisco V. Muniz-Souffront and Gloria (Vazquez de) Muniz; m. Ruben Rendon, June 29, 1974; children: Daniel Ruben, Raquel Ischel. Student, U. Tex., 1967-68, Universidad Interamericana, San Juan, 1968-69; BA, U. Houston, 1972, JD, 1976. Bar: Tex. 1977, U.S. Dist. Ct. (so. dist.) Tex. 1979, U.S. Ct. Appeals (5th cir.) 1979. Legal process clk. Pub. Defenders Office, San Francisco, 1977-78; ptnr. Rendon & Rendon, Houston, 1978-83; mcpl. ct. judge City of Houston, 1983—; pvt. practice, 1997—; commr., vice-chmn. Civil Service Commn., Houston, 1980-83; spkr. Congl. Justice com. Newspaper legal columnist, La Voz de Houston, 1980-83; mem. editl. bd. The Houston Lawyer, 1996—, Tex. Bar Law Jour., 1999—. Bd. dirs. Pub. Interest Advocacy Coun., Houston, 1979-81; pres. SER-Jobs for Progress Bd., Houston, 1983-86; dist. legal adviser League United L.Am. Citizens, Houston, 1980-83; former co-chair Hispanic-Jewish Dialogue com.; edn. com. mem. Houston Mus. Fine Arts. Recipient awards League United L.Am. Citizens, Outstanding Svc. to Cmty. award City of Houston, 1983, award for legal excellence NAACP, 1999; named One of Houston's Most Interesting People, Houston City Mag., 1984. Mem. ABA, Nat. Inst. Dispute Resolution Edn. Network, Am. Judges Assn., Tex. Mcpl. Cts. Assn., Tex. Bar Assn. (dispute resolution sect.), Houston Bar Assn. (dispute resolution sect.), Mex.-Am. Bar Assn., Acad. Family Mediators, Victim Offender Mediation Assn., Soc. Profls. in Dispute Resolution (Houston chpt. bd. dirs. 1997—), Family Mediation Network. Office: 909 Kipling St Houston TX 77006-4314

**RENFREW, CHARLES BYRON,** lawyer; b. Detroit, Oct. 31, 1928; s. Charles Warren and Louise (McGuire) R.; m. Susan Wheelock, June 28, 1952 (div. June 1984); children: Taylor Allison Ingham, Charles Robin, Todd Wheelock, James Bartlett; m. Barbara Jones Orser, Oct. 6, 1984; 5 stepchildren. AB, Princeton U., 1952; JD, U. Mich., 1956. Bar: Calif. 1956. Assoc. Pillsbury, Madison & Sutro, San Francisco, 1956-65, ptnr., 1965-72, 81-82; U.S. dist. judge No. Dist. Calif., San Francisco, 1972-80; dep. atty. gen. U.S. Washington, 1980-81; instr. U. Calif. Boalt Hall Sch. Law, 1977-80; v.p. law Chevron Corp. (formerly Standard Oil Co. Calif.), San Francisco, 1983-93, also bd. dirs.; ptnr. LeBoeuf, Lamb, Greene & McRae, San Francisco, 1994-97; pvt. practice San Francisco, 1998—; mem. exec. com. 9th Cir. Jud. Conf., 1976-78, congl. liaison com. 9th Cir. Jud. Council, 1976-79, spl. com. to propose standards for admission to practice in fed. cts. U.S. Jud. Conf., 1976-79; chmn. spl. com. to study problems of discovery Fed. Jud. Ctr., 1978-79; mem. council on role of cts. U.S. Dept. Justice, 1978-83; mem. jud. panel Ctr. for Pub. Resources, 1981—; head U.S. del. to 6th UN Congress on Prevention of Crime and Treatment of Offenders, 1980; co-chmn. San Francisco Lawyers Com. for Urban Affairs, 1971-72, mem., 1983—; bd. dirs. Internat. Hospitality Ctr., 1961-74, pres., 1967-70; mem. adv. bd. Internat. Comparative Law Ctr., Southwestern Legal Found., 1983-93; trustee World Affairs Council No. Calif., 1984-87, 94—, Nat. Jud. Coll., 1985-91, Grace Cathedral, 1986-89. Contbr. articles to profl. jours. Bd. fellow Claremont U., 1986-94; bd. dirs. San Francisco Symphony Found., 1964-80, pres., 1971-72; bd. dirs. Coun. Civic Unity, 1962-73, pres., 1971-72; bd. dirs. Opportunity Through Ownership, 1969-72, Marin County Day Sch., 1972-74, No. Calif. Svc. League, 1975-76, Am. Petroleum Inst., 1984—, Nat. Crime Prevention Coun., 1982—; alumni trustee Princeton U., 1976-80; mem. vis. com. u. chgo. Law Sch., 1977-79, u.Mich. Law Sch., 1977-81; bd. visitors J. Reuben Clark Law Sch., Brigham Young U., 1981-83, Stanford Law Sch., 1983-86; trustee Town Sch. for Boys, 1972-80,pres. 1975-80; gov. San Fransciso Symphony Assn., 1974—; mem. nat. adv. bd. Ctr. for Nat. Policy, 1982—; bd. dirs. Nat. Coun. Crime and Deliquency, 1981-82, NAACP Legal Def. and Edn. Fund, 1982—; parish chancellor St. Luke's Episcopal Ch., 1968-71, sr. warden, 1974-76; mem. exec. coun. San Francisco Deanery, 1969-70; mem. diocesan coun. Episcopal Diocese of Calif., 1970; chmn. Diocesan Conv., 1977, 78, 79. Served with USN, 1946-48, 1st lt. U.S. Army, 1952-53. Fellow Am. Bar Found.; mem. ABA (coun. mem. sect. antitrust law 19778-82, vice c hmn. sect. antitrust law 1982-83), San Francisco Bar Assn. (past bd. dirs.), Assn. Gen. Counsel, State Bar Calif., Am. Judicature Soc., Am. Coll. Trial Lawyers (pres. 1995-96), Am. Law Inst., Coun. Fgn. Rels., Order of Coif, Phi Beta Kappa, Phi Delta Phi. General corporate, Federal civil litigation. Office: 710 Sansome St San Francisco CA 94111-1704

**RENFRO, WILLIAM LEONARD,** futurist, lawyer, inventor, entrepreneur; b. West Palm Beach, Fla., Sept. 9, 1945; s. Ernest Leonard and Oine Warren (McAdams) R. BS in Physics, Rensselaer Poly. Inst., 1967, MS in Nuclear Engring., 1972; postgrad., Yale U., 1967-68; JD, U. Conn., 1972. Bar: Conn. 1973. Physicist Compustion Engring., Windsor Locks, Conn., 1968-69; pvt. practice law, Hartford, Conn., 1973-74; sr. rsch. assoc. The Futures Group, Glastonbury, Conn., 1973-76; analyst futures rsch. Congl. Rsch. Svc., U.S. Congress, Washington, 1976-80; pres. Policy Analysis Co., Inc., Washington, 1980—; vis. fellow Ark. Inst.; guest lectr. Georgetown U., Brookings Inst., Nat. War Coll.; adj. prof. George Washington U., Indsl. Coll. Armed Forces Nat. Def. U.; mem. nat. foresight network U.S. Congress. Author: (with others) The Futures Research Handbook, 1997, Anticipatory Democracy, 1978, The Public Affairs Handbook, 1983, The Legislative Role of Corporations, 1982, Applying Methods and Techniques of Futures Research, 1983, Future Research and the Straegic Planning Process, 1985, Non-Extrapolative Forecxasting in Business, 1988, Futures Research Methodology: The UN Millennium Project, 1999; author: Issue Management in Stratetic Planning, 1993; editor Futures Rsch. Quar. World Futures Soc.; issues mgmt. editor the Futurist, 1982—, Tech. Analysis and Strategic Mgmt. Mem. long range planning com. United Way; chmn. Nat. Millennium Found.; trustee World Tech. Found. Mem. AAAS, ABA, Pub. Rels. Soc. Am., Issues Mgmt. Assn. (bd. dirs. 1981—, v.p. 1986-88, pres. 1988-96(, World Futures Soc., Internat. Pub. Rels. Assn., Conn. Bar Assn., Hartford County Bar Assn., English Speaking Union (trustee), Clan Hamilton Soc., St. Andrews Soc. Episcopalian.

**RENFROW, JAY ROYCE,** lawyer; b. Canon City, Colo., Feb. 19, 1943; s. J.F. and Fern W. Renfrow; m. Evelyn Lee Renfrow, July 25, 1964; children: Seadon T., Stephanie J. BS in Bus., U. Colo., 1964, JD, 1969. Bar: Colo. 1969, U.S. Dist. Ct. Colo. 1969, U.S. Ct. Appeals (10th cir.) 1970, U.S. Supreme Ct. 1970. Pres. J. Royce Renfrow, P.C., Colorado Springs, Colo., 1969-96, Speedway Gas and Oil Co., Colorado Springs, 1969—, Wine Corp. of N.Am., Colorado Springs, 1982-88; v.p., gen. counsel MedLogic Global Corp., Colorado Springs, 1991-92; sec., gen. counsel InnterCircle Group, Inc., Colorado Springs, 1996-97; mgr. J. Royce Renfrow PLLC, Mt. Crested Butte, Colo., 1997-98, Renfrow & Frazier PLLC, Mt. Crested Butte, 1998—. Patentee in field. Bd. dirs. ARC, Colorado Springs, 1970-94, Colo. Opera Festival, Colorado Springs, 1990-96. Mem. Winter Night Club. Avocations: skiing, backpacking, astronomy, food and wine, hunting. General corporate, Estate planning, Real property. Office: Renfrow & Frazier PLLC PO Box 5444 600 Gothic Rd Crested Butte CO 81225

**RENKENS, MADELINE A.,** lawyer. BA, U. Rochester, N.Y., 1973; MLS, Queens Coll., 1974; JD cum laude, Fordham U., 1979. Bar: N.Y. 1980, Conn. 1981, Wash. 1984, Alaska 1986, U.S. Dist. Ct. Alaska, U.S. Dist. Ct. (so. dist.) N.Y., U.S. Dist. Ct. (we. dist.) Wash., U.S. Ct. Appeals (9th cir.), U.S. Supreme Ct. Tchr., library media specialist Southampton (N.Y.) Pub. Schs., 1974-76; law clk. U.S. Dept. Justice, 1978-79, trial atty. anti-trust div., 1979-82; assoc. Willkie Farr & Gallagher, N.Y.C., 1982-84, Barokas & Martin, Seattle, 1984-87; pvt. practice, Snohomish, Wash., 1988—. Mem. St. James Cathedral Choir, Snohomish County Hist. Soc. Mem. Washington Women Lawyers. Home and Office: 329 Ave C Snohomish WA 98290-2732

**RENNER, CURTIS SHOTWELL,** lawyer; b. Paris, France, June 24, 1958. BA, Wesleyan U., Middletown, Conn., 1981; JD cum laude, Harvard U., 1988. Bar: Mass. 1988, D.C. 1995. Assoc. Crowell & Moring, Washington, 1988-95; ptnr. Watson & Renner, Washington, 1995—. Contbr. articles to profl. jours. Mem. ABA, D.C. Bar Assn., Phi Beta Kappa. Toxic tort, Product liability, General civil litigation. Office: Watson & Renner 2000 M St NW Ste 330 Washington DC 20036-3307

**RENNER, JOHN ROBERT,** lawyer; b. Cleve., July 10, 1964; s. John William and Gail Medora (Eaton) R. AB, Dartmouth Coll., 1986; JD, U. Calif. Berkeley, 1990. Bar: Calif. 1990, U.S. Dist. Ct. (no. dist.) Calif. 1990, (cen. dist.) Calif. 1992, U.S. Ct. Appeals (9th cir.) 1990, U.S. Dist. Ct. (so. dist.) Calif. 1997. Law clk. Hon. Oliver W. Wanger U.S. Dist. Ct. Ea. Dist., Fresno, Calif., 1991; dep. atty. gen. Calif. Dept. Justice, L.A., 1991-95; assoc. Coudert Brothers, L.A., 1995—. Republican. General civil litigation, Private international, State civil litigation. Office: Coudert Brothers 1055 W 7th St Fl 20 Los Angeles CA 90017-2577

**RENNER, ROBERT GEORGE,** federal judge; b. Nevis, Minn., Apr. 2, 1923; s. Henry J. and Beatrice M. (Fuller) R.; m. Catherine L. Clark, Nov. 12, 1949; children: Robert, Anne, Richard, David. BA, St. John's U., Collegeville, Minn., 1947; JD, Georgetown U., 1949. Bar: Minn. 1949. Pvt. practice Walker, 1949-69; U.S. atty. Dist. of Minn., 1969-77, U.S. magistrate, 1977-80, U.S. dist. judge, 1980-92, assumed sr. status, 1992—. Mem. Minn. Ho. of Reps., 1957-69. Served with AUS, 1943-46. Mem. FBA. Roman Catholic. Office: US Dist Ct 748 US Courthouse 316 Robert St N Saint Paul MN 55101-1495

**RENNICK, KYME ELIZABETH WALL,** lawyer; b. Columbus, Ohio, Dec. 27, 1953; d. Robert Leroy and Julie (Allison) Wall; m. Ian Alexander Rennick, Oct. 15, 1983; children: Daniel Alexander, Julie Ellen. BA, Centre Coll., 1975; MA, Ohio State U., 1978; JD, Capital U., 1982. Bar: Ohio 1982, U.S. Dist. Ct. (no. and so. dists.) Ohio 1983. Legal intern Ohio Dept. Natural Resources, Columbus, 1981-83, gen. counsel, 1983-86, chief counsel, 1986-95, dep. dir., 1995—. Editor: Baldwin's Ohio Revised Code Annotated, Title 15 Conservation of Natural Resources, 1984. Presbyterian. Avocations: running, biking, crafts. Office: Ohio Dept Natural Resources Fountain Sq Bldg 3D Columbus OH 43224

**RENO, JANET,** federal official, lawyer; b. Miami, Fla., July 21, 1938; d. Henry and Jane (Wood) R. A.B. in Chemistry, Cornell U., 1960; LL.B., Harvard U., 1963. Bar: Fla. 1963. Assoc. Brigham & Brigham, 1963-67; ptnr. Lewis & Reno, 1967-71; staff dir. judiciary com. Fla. Ho. of Reps., Tallahassee, 1971-72; cons. Fla. Senate Criminal Justice Com. for Revision Fla.'s Criminal Code, spring 1973; adminstrv. asst. state atty. 11th Jud. Circuit Fla., Miami, 1973-76, state atty., 1978-93; ptnr. Steel Hector and Davis, Miami, 1976-78; atty. gen. Dept. Justice, Washington, 1993—; mem. jud. nominating commn. 11th Jud. Circuit Fla., 1976-78; chmn. Fla. Gov.'s Council for Prosecution Organized Crime, 1979-80. Recipient Women First award YWCA, 1993. Mem. ABA (Inst. Jud. Adminstrn. Juvenile Justice Standards Commn. 1973-76), Am. Law Inst., Am. Judicature Soc. (Herbert Harley award 1981), Dade County Bar Assn., Fla. Pros. Atty.'s Assn. (pres. 1984-86). Democrat. Office: Office of the Attorney General Rm 10-130 950 Pennsylvania Ave NW Dept Justice Washington DC 20530-0001

**RENO, OTTIE WAYNE,** former judge; b. Pike County, Ohio, Apr. 7, 1929; s. Eli Enos and Arbannah Belle (Jones) R.; A in Bus. Adminstrn., Franklin U., 1949; LLB, Franklin Law Sch., 1953; JD, Capital U., 1966; grad. Coll. Juvenile Justice, U. Nev., 1973; m. Janet Gay McCann, May 22, 1947; children: Ottie Wayne II, Jennifer Lynn, Lorna Victoria. Admitted to Ohio bar, 1953; practiced in Pike County; recorder Pike County, 1957-73; common pleas judge Probate and Juvenile divs. Pike County, 1973-79. Mem. adv. bd. Ohio Youth Services, 1972-74. Mem. Dem. Central Com. Camp Creek precinct, 1956-72, 83-90; sec. Pike County Central Com., 1960-70, 83-87; chmn. Pike County Dem. Exec. Com., 1971-72, 1988-90; del. Dem. Nat. Conv., 1972, 96; mem. Ohio Dem. Central Com., 1969-70; Dem. candidate 6th Ohio dist. U.S. Ho. of Reps., 1966, 88th Dist. Ohio Ho. of Reps., 1992; pres. Scioto Valley Local Sch. Dist., 1962-66. Recipient Distinguished Service award Ohio Youth Commn., 1974; 6 Outstanding Jud. Service awards Ohio Supreme Ct.; 15 times Ala. horseshoe pitching champion; named to Nat. Horseshoe Pitchers Hall of Fame, 1978; mem. internat. sports exchange, U.S. and Republic South Africa, 1972, 80, 82. Mem. Ohio, Pike County (pres. 1964) Bar Assns., Nat. Council Juvenile Ct. Judges, Am. Legion. Mem. Ch. of Christ in Christian Union. Author: Story of Horseshoes, 1963; Pitching Championship Horseshoes, 1971, 2d rev. edit., 1975; The American Directory of Horseshoe Pitching, 1983, Ohio vs. Smith, Murder, 1990, Reno and Apsaalooka Survive Custer, 1996. Home: 148 Reno Rd Lucasville OH 45648-9580

**RENTENBACH, PAUL ROBERT,** lawyer; b. Detroit, June 30, 1945; s. Robert Frederick and Elizabeth Alberta (Henderson) R.; m. Jacqueline Sue Lang, July 29, 1967; children: Eric, Lauren, Erin. BA, U. Mich., 1967; JD, Harvard U., 1972. Bar: Mich. 1972. Tchr. Detroit Pub. Schs., 1968-69, Univ. Liggett Sch., Grosse Pointe, Mich., 1969-70; ptnr. Dykema Gossett PLLC, Detroit, 1972—; bd. dirs. Crowley, Milner & Co., Detroit. Trustee Attic Theatre, Inc., Detroit, 1987-91. Mem. ABA, Detroit Bar Assn. Mergers and acquisitions, Securities, Finance. Office: Dykema Gossett 400 Renaissance Ctr Ste 3800 Detroit MI 48243-1603

**RENWICK, EDWARD S.,** lawyer; b. L.A., May 10, 1934. AB, Stanford U., 1956, LLB, 1958. Bar: Calif. 1959, U.S. Dist. Ct. (cen. dist.) Calif. 1959, U.S. Ct. Appeals (9th cir.) 1963, U.S. Dist. Ct. (so. dist.) Calif. 1973, U.S. Dist. Ct. (no. dist.) Calif. 1977, U.S. Dist. Ct. (ea. dist.) Calif. 1981, U.S. Supreme Ct. 1985. Ptnr. Hanna and Morton LLP, L.A.; mem., bd. vis. Stanford Law Sch., 1967-69; mem. environ. and natural resources adv. bd. Stanford Law Sch. Bd. dirs. Calif. Supreme Ct. Hist. Soc. Fellow Am. Coll. Trial Lawyers, Am. Bar Found.; mem. ABA (mem. sect. on litigation, antitrust law, bus. law, chmn. sect. of nat. resources, energy and environ. law 1987-88, mem. at large coord. group energy law 1989-92, sect. rep. coord. group energy law 1995-97, Calif. del. legal com., interstate oil compact com.), Calif. Arboretum Assn. (trustee 1986-92), L.A. County Bar Assn. (chmn. natural resources law sect. 1974-75), The State Bar of Calif., Chancery Club (pres. 1992-93), Phi Delta Phi. Office: Hanna and Morton LLP 600 Wilshire Blvd Fl 17 Los Angeles CA 90017-3212

**REPPER, GEORGE ROBERT,** lawyer; b. Topeka, Dec. 22, 1954; s. George Vincent Jr. and Maria Magdalena (Bullert) R.; m. Helen Linda Zeichner, Aug. 23, 1981; children: Brian Lawrence, Kevin Michael, Michelle Suzanne. BS, SUNY, Albany, 1977; JD, Albany Law Sch., 1981. Bar: N.Y. 1982, D.C. 1982, U.S. Patent and Trademark Office 1984, U.S. Ct. Appeals (fed. cir.) 1989. V.p. Rothwell, Figg, Ernst & Kurz, Washington, also bd. dirs. Contbr. articles to profl. jours. including Patent World. Mem. ABA (patents, trademarks and copyrights sect.), D.C. Bar Assn. (patents, trademarks and copyrights sect.), Am. Intellectual Property Law Assn., Internat. Intellectual Property Assn., Internat. Fedn. Indsl. Property Attys., Intellectual Property Owners, Internat. Trademark Assn. Republican. Patent, Trademark and copyright, Mergers and acquisitions. Office: Rothwell Figg Ernst & Kurz 555 13th St NW Ste 701E Washington DC 20004-1126

**REPPETO, WILLIAM M., III,** lawyer; b. Dallas, Jan. 8, 1966; s. William M. Jr. and Mary Elizabeth (Carpenter) R.; m. Deveri Marie Darilek, Aug. 22, 1992. BA, U. Tex., 1988; JD, So. Meth. U., 1992. Bar: Tex., U.S. Dist. Ct. (we. dist.) Tex. Atty. Gordon Hollon, Boerne, Tex., 1992, Bobbitt & Holter, Boerne, Tex., 1993-94, Reppeto & Geistweidt, Boerne, Tex., 1994—. Dir. police activities City of Boerne, 1994—. Mem. Kendall County Bar Assn. (officer, dir. 1994—), Rotary (officer, dir. 1994—). Republican. Methodist. Avocations: physical fitness, fly fishing, travel, western art, golf. Criminal, Family and matrimonial, General practice. Office: Reppeto & Geistweidt 106 W Blanco Rd Boerne TX 78006-2014

**RESKE, STEVEN DAVID,** lawyer, writer; b. Mpls., May 31, 1962; s. Albert Edgar Reske and Florence Mae Altland. BA with distinction, St. Olaf Coll., Northfield, Minn., 1985; JD cum laude, Boston U., 1988. Bar: Ill. 1988, Minn. 1989, D.C. 1998, U.S. Dist. Ct. Minn. 1991, U.S. Ct. Appeals (5th cir.) 1989, (7th and 8th cir.) 1992, (D.C. circuit) 1998, U.S. Supreme Ct. 1993. Intern U.S. Senator Durenberger, Washington, 1981-82, Citizens for Ednl. Freedom, Washington, D.C., 1981-82, Abbott-Northwestern Hosp., Mpls., 1984, U.S. Dist. Ct. Judge Magnuson, St. Paul, 1986; summer assoc. Faegre & Benson, Mpls., 1987; assoc. Sidley & Austin, Chgo., 1988; law clk. to Hon. Judge Politz U.S. Ct. Appeals 5th cir., Shreveport, La., 1988-89; pvt. practice, 1989—, writer, 1989—. Contbr. CD Rev., 1993-95, JAZZIZ, 1996—, Skyway News, 1997—; contbr. articles to profl. jours.; mem. Am. Jour. Law and Medicine, 1986-87, editor, 1987-88; legal editor-at-large Minn. Law and Politics, 1998—; columnist Twin Cities Revue, 1998—. Recipient Minn. Super Lawyer award, 1998, Am. Jurisprudence award, 1988; Edward F. Hennessey scholar, 1988, G. Joseph Tauro scholar, 1986. Mem. ABA (antitrust divsn.), Minn. State Bar Assn., Hennepin County Bar Assn., Am. Econ. Assn., Am. Philos. Assn. Federal civil litigation, Antitrust, Constitutional. Office: 3422 Douglas Dr N Crystal MN 55422-2414

**RESMINI, RONALD JOSEPH,** lawyer; b. Providence, June 16, 1942; s. Joseph Andrew and Corrine Marie (Barrette) R.; m. Paula Oliver, July 1, 1979; children: R. Jason, Adam Joseph, Andrew Oliver. BA, Providence Coll., 1965; JD, Suffolk U., 1968. Bar: R.I. 1969, U.S. Dist. Ct. R.I. 1972, U.S. Supreme Ct. 1972, U.S. Ct. Mil. Appeals 1981, Mass. 1984. Substitute tchr. pub. schs., Cranston, Providence, R.I., 1968-69; law clk. to justice R.I. Supreme Ct., Providence, 1971; pvt. practice Providence, 1981—; mem. faculty R.I. Trial Inst., 1988-89; instr. bus. law Roger Williams U., Providence, 1969-73; asst. town solicitor Town of Coventry (R.I.), 1970-72; lectr. continuing legal edn. program R.I. Bar Assn., 1978—; lectr. Roger William Sch. Law, 1996; instr. R.I. Law Inst.; mem. R.I. Continuing Legal Edn. Com., 1992; lectr. personal injury Nat. Bus. Inst., 1988. Author: Handbook on Uninsured-Underinsured Motorist Coverage, 1984, Bad Faith Litigation, 1985, Soft Tissue Injury Handbook, 1986, R.I. Tort Series, 1988, Tort Law and Personal Injury Practice, 2 vols., 1988, R.I. Action and Remedies, 1992, Domestic Relations Encyclopedia, 1996. Bd. dirs. Providence chpt. ARC, 1974-78; campaign fin. chmn. for R.I. atty. gen., 1986; coach Barrington (R.I.) Little League, 1988, 93, 94, 95; coach Sr. League and All Stars, 1990, 91, 92, 93, 94; soccer coach McDonald's All Stars, 1995; pres. Parent-Child Indian Guide Orgn., Barrington YMCA, 1988; Eucharistic min. St. Lukes, Orchard View Nursing Home. Served to capt.

U.S. Army, 1969-71; USAR, 1971-77, ret. Decorated Meritorious Svc. medal; recipient Arbitration award, Am. Arbitration Assn., 1987. Fellow R.I. Bar Found.; mem. Interest Lawyer's Trust Accounts (founder, chmn. 1984), R.I. Trial Lawyers Assn. (treas. 1975-85, bd. govs. 1986—), Nat. Bd. Trial Advocacy (bd. examiner 1990), Univ. Club, R.I. Country Club, Turks Head Club, Crestwood Country Club. Roman Catholic. General civil litigation, Personal injury. Home: 43 Riverside Dr Barrington RI 02806-3615 Office: 155 S Main St Ste 400 Providence RI 02903-2963 also: 41 Mink St Seekonk MA 02771-5914

**RESNECK, WILLIAM ALLAN,** lawyer; b. Memphis, Oct. 21, 1945; s. William Saul and Charlotte Helen (Mayer) R.; m. Ellen Diamond, July 27, 1979; children: Joshua, Rachel. AB, Oberlin Coll., 1967; JD, Ind. U., 1970. Bar: Calif. 1971. Assoc. Steinhart, Goldberg, San Francisco, 1970-75; sole practice San Francisco, Berkeley and Oakland, Calif., 1975—; adminstrv. law judge State of Calif., Berkeley, 1977—; prof. St. Mary's Paralegal Program, Oakland, Calif., 1979-85; part time dep. atty. City of Berkeley, 1985-87. Mem. Order of Coif. Avocation: whitewater rafting. State civil litigation, Personal injury, Workers' compensation. Office: 2 Theatre Sq Ste 234 Orinda CA 94563-3346

**RESNICK, ALICE ROBIE,** state supreme court justice; b. Erie, Pa., Aug. 21, 1939; d. Adam Joseph and Alice Suzanne (Spizarny) Robie; m. Melvin L. Resnick, Mar. 20, 1970. PhB, Siena Heights Coll., 1961; JD, U. Detroit, 1964. Bar: Ohio 1964, Mich. 1965, U.S. Supreme Ct. 1970. Asst. county prosecutor Lucas County Prosecutor's Office, Toledo, 1964-75, trial atty., 1965-75; judge Toledo Mcpl. Ct., 1976-83, 6th Dist. Ct. Appeals, State of Ohio, Toledo, 1983-88; instr. U. Toledo, 1968-69; justice Ohio Supreme Ct., 1989—; co-chairperson Ohio State Gender Fairness Task Force. Trustee Siena Heights Coll., Adrian, Mich., 1982—; organizer Crime Stopper Inc., Toledo, 1981—; mem. Mayor's Drug Coun.; bd. dirs. Guest House Inc. Mem. ABA, Toledo Bar Assn., Lucas County Bar Assn., Nat. Assn. Women Judges, Am. Judicature Soc., Toledo Women's Bar Assn., Ohio State Women's Bar Assn. (organizer), Toledo Mus. Art, Internat. Inst. Toledo. Roman Catholic. Home: 2407 Edgehill Rd Toledo OH 43615-2321 Office: Supreme Ct Office 30 E Broad St Fl 3 Columbus OH 43266-0001*

**RESNICK, JEFFREY LANCE,** federal magistrate judge; b. Bklyn., Mar. 5, 1943; s. Bernard and Selma (Monheit) R.; m. Margery O'Connor, May 27, 1990. BA, U. Conn., 1964; LLB, U. Conn., West Hartford, 1967. Bar: Conn. 1967, N.Y. 1968, U.S. V.I. 1968, D.C. 1979, U.S. Ct. Appeals (3d cir.) 1979. Assoc. Office of J.D. Marsh, Christiansted, St. Croix, V.I., 1967-69; asst. atty. gen. Dept. Law, Christiansted, 1969-73; ptnr. James & Resnick, Christiansted, 1973-89; magistrate judge U.S. Dist. Ct. V.I., Christiansted, 1989—. Active V.I. Bridge Team, 1971—. Jewish. Avocations: writing poetry and palindromes. Office: US District Court 3013 Est Golden Rock Christiansted VI 00820-4256

**RESNICK, STEPHANIE,** lawyer; b. N.Y.C., Nov. 12, 1959; d. Diane Gross. AB, Kenyon Coll., 1981; JD, Villanova U., 1984. Bar: Pa. 1984, N.J. 1984, U.S. Dist Ct. (ea. dist.) Pa. 1984, U.S. Dist Ct. N.J. 1984, N.Y. 1990, U.S. Ct. Appeals (3d cir.) 1993, U.S. Dist. Ct. (so. dist.) N.Y. 1996, U.S. Supreme Ct. 1998. Assoc. Cozen and O'Connor, Phila., 1984-87; assoc. Fox, Rothschild, O'Brien & Frankel, Phila., 1987-92, ptnr., 1992—. Mem. Vols. for Indigent Program, Phila., 1987-92. Mem. ABA, Pa. Bar Assn. (disciplinary bd. and study com. 1989-91, prof. liability com. 1991-92, commr. on Women in the Profession, 1997—), Phila. Bar Assn. (profl. responsibility com. 1992—, profl. guidance com. 1992-96, investigative divsn. Commn. on Jud. Selection and Retention 1988-94, women's rights com. 1993—, co-chair 1995, 96, Women in the Profession com. 1993—, Comm. on Jud. Selection and Retention 1995—, vice-chair 1996, chair 1997), N.J. Bar Assn., N.Y. Bar Assn., Womens Way (bd. dirs. 1997—, co-chair campaign 1998—). General civil litigation, Insurance, Federal civil litigation. Home: 233 S 6th St Apt 2306 Philadelphia PA 19106-3756 Office: Fox Rothschild O'Brien & Frankel 2000 Market St Ste 10 Philadelphia PA 19103-3231

**RESOR, STANLEY ROGERS,** lawyer; b. N.Y.C., Dec. 5, 1917; s. Stanley Burnet and Helen (Lansdowne) R.; m. Jane Lawler Pillsbury, Apr. 4, 1942 (dec.); children: Stanley R., Charles P., John L., Edmund L., William B., Thomas S., James P.; m. Louise Mead Walker, May 1, 1999. BA, Yale U., 1939, LLB, 1946. Bar: N.Y. 1947. Assoc., then ptnr. firm Debevoise & Plimpton, N.Y.C., 1946-65, 71-73, 79-87, of counsel, 1988-90; undersec. Dept. Army, 1965, sec., 1965-71, ambassador negotiations for Mut. and Balanced Force Reductions in Central Europe, 1973-78; undersec. for policy Dept. Def., 1978-79. Fellow Yale Corp., 1979-86. Served to maj. AUS, 1942-45. Decorated Silver Star, Bronze Star, Purple Heart; recipient George C. Marshall award Assn. U.S. Army, 1974, Sylvanus Thayer award Assn. Graduates of U.S. Mil. Acad., 1984. Mem. ABA, Assn. of Bar of City of N.Y. (chmn. com. internat. arms control and security affairs 1983-86), Atlantic Coun. (bd. dirs.), Arms Control Assn. (chmn. bd.), UN Assn. U.S.A. (nat. coun.), Coun. Fgn. Rels., Lawyers Alliance for World Security (bd. dirs.), Internat. Inst. Strategic Studies. Republican. Episcopalian. Home: 809 Weed St New Canaan CT 06840-4023 Office: Debevoise & Plimpton 875 3rd Ave Fl 23 New York NY 10022-6256

**RESSA, GREGORY JOHN,** lawyer; b. Rockville Centre, N.Y., Oct. 3, 1962; s. Ames D. and Roslyn Maguire Ressa; 1 child, Margo Avallone. BA, Tufts U., 1984; JD, Fordham U., 1987. Bar: N.Y. 1987. Ptnr. Simpson Thacher & Bartlett, N.Y.C., 1987—. Real property, General corporate. Office: Simpson Thacher & Bartlett 425 Lexington Ave Fl 15 New York NY 10017-3954

**RESSING, THOMAS GARRETT,** lawyer; s. Clinton P. and Georgiana (Quackenbush) R.; m. Sharon Ressing, July 19, 1980; 1 child, Garrett L. BS, Muskingam Coll., New Concord, Ohio, 1963; JD, Ohio No. U., 1966. Bar: Ohio 1966, U.S. Supreme Ct. 1972, U.S. Dist. Ct. Ohio 1973. Pvt. practice Mount Vernon, Ohio, 1966—. Active YMCA. Mem. C. of C., Rotary. Presbyterian. Office: 10 E Vine St Mount Vernon OH 43050-3226

**RETAMAR, RICHARD E.,** lawyer; b. Miami, Fla., Mar. 28, 1964; s. Henry and Alicia Retamar; m. Susan D. Retamar, Jan. 26, 1991; children: Alexander J., Grant Everett. BS, Fla. State U., 1985; JD, St. Thomas U., Miami, 1988. Bar: Fla. 1990. Assoc. Kind, Rosenthal & Zane, Boca Raton, Fla., 1990-92; ptnr. Kind, Rosenthal, Mosick and Retamar, Boca Raton, 1992-95; assoc. The Glick Law firm, Boca Raton, 1995; ptnr. Glick & Retamar, Boca Raton, 1995—. Bd. dirs. Sun Flower Condo Assn., Boca Raton, 1991-92, Riviera Civil Assn., Boca Raton, 1995, Future Vision Youth Devel., Boca Raton, 1998—. Mem. Fla. Bar Assn., South Palm Beach County Bar Assn., Hispanic Bar Assn., Palm Beach County Bar Assn., Palm Beach County Trial Lawyer Assn., Acad. Fla. Trial Lawyers, Hispanic Am. Bus. Club (bd. dirs. 1996—). Avocations: boating, fishing, mountain biking, tennis, basketball. State civil litigation, Insurance, Personal injury. Office: Glick & Retamar 2424 N Federal Hwy Ste 460 Boca Raton FL 33431-7747

**RETHORE, KEVIN WATT,** lawyer; b. Willingboro, N.J., Aug. 2, 1967; s. Bernard Gabriel and Marilyn Watt Rethore. BA in English, Boston Coll., 1989; JD, Pa. State U., 1994. Bar: Pa. 1994, N.J. 1994, R.I. 1995. Assoc. Bingaman, Hess, Coblentz & Bell, P.C., Reading, Pa., 1994—. Editor Berks County Law Jour., 1995—. Fax: 610-376-3105. E-mail: kwrethore@bhcb.com. General civil litigation, Appellate, Trademark and copyright. Office: Bingaman Hess Coblentz & Bell PC 601 Penn St Ste 660 Reading PA 19601-3549

**RETSON, NICHOLAS PHILIP,** lawyer, military officer; b. Appleton, Wis., Oct. 20, 1947; s. Philip Nicholas and Catherine Retson; m. Birgit Maria Abromaitis, Dec. 30, 1977; children: Philip N., Kathryn L., Nicholas Peter. BA in Chemistry, Ripon Coll., 1969; JD, Marquette U., 1972; LLM in Govt. Procurement, George Washington U., 1983. Bar: Wis. 1972, U.S. Dist. Ct. (ea. and we. dists.) Wis. 1972. Commd. 2nd lt. U.S. Army, 1969, advanced through grades to col., 1990; ops. officer Trial Def. Svc., Falls Church, Va., 1976-78; prof. contract law Judge Adv. Gen.'s Sch., Charlottesville, Va., 1979-82; trial team chief Office Chief Trial Atty., Falls Church, 1983-86; chief contract law divsn. Hdqrs. U.S. Army Europe, Heidelberg, Germany, 1986-90; chief counsel U.S. Army Test and Evaluation Command, Aberdeen Proving Ground, Md., 1990-93; chief contract law divsn. Office Judge Adv. Gen., Washington, 1993-95; army chief trial atty. U.S. Army Litigation Ctr., Arlington, Va., 1995—. Mem. ABA (vice chair alternative disputes resolution subcom. sect. on pub. contract law 1995—), State Bar Wis. (dir. non resident lawyers divsn. 1980—), Ripon Coll. Alumni Assn. (dir. 1995—). Greek Orthodox. Avocations: travel, stocks, scouting. Office: US Army Litigation Ctr 901 N Stuart St Arlington VA 22203-1821

**REUBEN, DON HAROLD,** lawyer; b. Chgo., Sept. 13, 1928; s. Michael B. and Sally (Chapman) R.; m. Evelyn Long, Aug. 27, 1948 (div.); children: Hope Reuben Boland, Michael Barrett, Timothy Don, Jeffrey Long, Howard Ellis; m. Jeannette Hurley Haywood, Dec. 13, 1971; stepchildren: Harris Hurley Haywood, Edward Gregory Haywood. BS, Northwestern U., 1949, JD, 1952. Bar: Ill. 1952, Calif. 1996. With firm Kirkland & Ellis, Chgo., 1952-78, sr. ptnr., until 1978; sr. ptnr. Reuben & Proctor, Chgo., 1978-86, Isham, Lincoln & Beale, Chgo., 1986-88; sr. counsel Winston & Strawn, 1988-94; of counsel Altheimer & Gray, Chgo., 1994—; spl. asst. atty. gen. State of Ill., 1963-64, 69, 84; gen. coun. Tribune Co., 1965-88, Chgo. Bears Football Club, 1965-88, Cath. Archdiocese of Chgo., 1975-88; coun. spl. session Ill. Ho. of Reps., 1964, for Ill. treas. for congl., state legis. and jud. reapportionment, 1963; spl. fed. ct. master, 1968-70; dir. Lake Shore Nat. Bank, 1973-93; dir. Heitman Fin., 1993-98; mem. citizens adv. bd. to sheriff County of Cook, 1962-66, mem. jury instrn. com., 1963-68; rules com. Ill. Supreme Ct., 1963-73; mem. pub. rels. com. Nat. Conf. State Trial Judges; mem. com. study caseflow mgmt. in law div. Cook County Cir. Ct., 1979-88; mem. adv. implementation com. U.S. Dist. Ct. for No. Dist. Ill., 1981-82; mem. Chgo. Better Schs. Com., 1968-69, Chgo. Crime Commn., 1970-80; mem. supervisory panel Fed. Defender Program; gen. counsel Palm Springs Air Mus., 1996—; dir. News-Gazette, Champaign, Ill., 1997-99; lectr. on libel, slander, privacy and freedom of press. Bd. dirs. Lincoln Park Zool. Soc., 1972-84 ; trustee Northwestern U., 1977—; mem. vis. com. U. Chgo. Law Sch., 1976-79. Mem. Ill. Bar Assn., Chgo. Bar Assn. (chmn. subcom. on propriety and regulation of contingent fees com. devel. law 1966-69, subcom. on media liaison 1980-82, mem. com. on profl. info. 1980-82), ABA (standing com. on fed. judiciary 1973-79, standing com. on jud. selection, tenure and compensation 1982-85), Am. Law Inst., Am. Judicature Soc., Fellows Am. Bar Found., Am. Coll. Trial Lawyers (Rule 23 com. 1975-82, judiciary com. 1987-91), Am. Arbitration Assn. (nat. panel arbitrators), Calif. Bar Assn., Desert Bar Assn., Internat. Acad. Trial Lawyers, Union League Club (Chgo.), Tavern Club, Mid-Am. Club, Law Club, Casino Club, The Springs Club, Desert Riders of Palm Springs, The Chgo. Club, Phi Eta Sigma, Beta Alpha Psi, Beta Gamma Sigma, Order of Coif. General civil litigation, Libel, Constitutional. Home: 20 Jill Ter Rancho Mirage CA 92270-2635

**REUBEN, LAWRENCE MARK,** lawyer; b. Akron, Ohio, Apr. 5, 1948; s. Albert G. and Sara I. (Rifkin) R. Student, London Sch. Econs., 1969; BS, Ind. U., 1970; JD, Ind. U., Indpls., 1973. Bar: Ind. 1973, U.S. Dist. Ct. (so. dist.) Ind. 1973, U.S. Dist. Ct. (no. dist.) Ind. 1975, U.S. Ct. Appeals (7th cir.) 1975, U.S. Supreme Ct. 1976, U.S. Ct. Appeals (9th cir.) 1978, U.S. Ct. Appeals (D.C. cir.) 1994, U.S. Ct. Appeals (fed. cir.) 1999. Ptnr. Atlas, Hyatt & Reuben, Indpls., 1976-87, Atlas & Reuben, Indpls., 1987-90; chief counsel Ind. Dept. Ins., 1990-91; gen. counsel Ind. Dept. Transp., 1991-93; chief deputy Ind. Atty. Gen., Indpls., 1993-94; gen. counsel State Lottery Commn. Ind., Indpls., 1994-97; pvt. practice Indpls., 1997—. V.p. Ind. Civil Liberties Union, 1975-84; sec., bd. dirs. Indpls. Humane Soc., 1974-85; fellow Indpls. C. of C.-Lacey Leadership Program, 1982; sec., v.p., bd. dirs. Julian Ctr., Inc., 1983-89; mem. ch.-state commn. Nat. Jewish Community Relations Adv. Council, N.Y.C., 1982-89; bd. dirs. Indpls. Consumer Credit Counseling Bur., 1983-89; pres. Bur. Jewish Edn., 1984-86; parliamentarian Ind. State Dem. Party, 1985-86; mem. Indpls. Police Community Relations Rev. Com., 1983. Recipient Robert Risk award Ind. Civil Liberties Union, 1981, David M. Cook Meml. award Indpls. Jewish Community Rels. Coun., 1982; L.L. Goodman Leadership award, Jewish Fed. Indpls., 1989. Mem. ABA, Fed. Bar Assn., Ind. Bar Assn., Indpls. Bar Assn. Democrat. Jewish. Federal civil litigation, Labor, General practice. Office: Jefferson Plaza 1 Virginia Ave Ste 600 Indianapolis IN 46204-3671

**REUM, JAMES MICHAEL,** lawyer; b. Oak Park, Ill., Nov. 1, 1946; s. Walter John and Lucy (Bellegay) R. BA cum laude, Harvard U., 1968, JD cum laude, 1972. Bar: N.Y. 1973, D.C. 1974, U.S. Dist. Ct. (so. dist.) N.Y. 1974, Ill. 1979, U.S. Dist. Ct. (no. dist.) Ill. 1982. Assoc. Davis Polk & Wardwell, N.Y.C., 1973-78; assoc. Minority Counsel Com. on Judiciary U.S. Ho. of Reps., Washington, 1974; ptnr. Hopkins & Sutter, Chgo., 1979-93, Winston & Strawn, Chgo., 1994—. Midwest advance rep. Nat. Reagan Bush Com., 1980; nominee commr. Securities and Exchange Comm., Pres. Bush, 1992. Served to SP4 USAR, 1969-75. Recipient Harvard U. Honorary Nat. Scholarship, 1964-72. Mem. Monte Carlo Country Club (Monaco), Univ. Club (N.Y.C.). Republican. Mergers and acquisitions, Banking, Finance. Home: 12 E Scott St Chicago IL 60610-2320 Office: Winston & Strawn 35 W Wacker Dr Ste 4200 Chicago IL 60601-1695

**REUTIMAN, ROBERT WILLIAM, JR.,** lawyer; b. Mpls., June 4, 1944; s. Robert William and Elsbeth Bertha (Doering) R.; m. Virginia Lee Traxler, June 25, 1983; children: Robert James, Joseph Lee. BA magna cum laude, U. Minn., 1966, JD, 1969. Bar: Minn. 1969, U.S. Ct. Mil. Appeals 1969, U.S. Dist. Ct. Minn. 1973, U.S. Ct. Appeals (8th cir.) 1976, U.S. Tax. Ct. 1979. Mem. Armstrong, Phleger, Reutiman & Vinokour, Ltd., Wayzata, Minn., 1973-76; ptnr. Phleger & Reutiman, Wayzata, 1976-81; pvt. practice Wayzata, 1981—. Chmn. Spring Pk. Planning Commn., 1978. Capt. U.S. Army, 1969-73. Decorated Army Commendation medal. Mem. ABA, Minn. Bar Assn., Hennepin County Bar Assn., Am. Arbitration Assn. (panel of arbitrators), Phi Beta Kappa. Lutheran. Avocations: fishing, rose growing. General civil litigation, Personal injury, Consumer commercial. Home: 11610 3rd Ave N Plymouth MN 55441-5919 Office: 305 Rice St E Wayzata MN 55391-1615

**REVELEY, WALTER TAYLOR, III,** dean; b. Churchville, Va., Jan. 6, 1943; s. Walter Taylor and Marie (Eason) R.; m. Helen Bond, Dec. 18, 1971; children: Walter Taylor, George Everett Bond, Nelson Martin Eason, Helen Lanier. AB, Princeton U., 1965; JD, U. Va., 1968. Bar: Va. 1970, D.C. 1976. Asst. prof. law U. Ala., 1968-69; law clk. to Justice Brennan U.S. Supreme Ct., Washington, 1969-70; fellow Woodrow Wilson Internat. Ctr. for Scholars, 1972-73; internat. affairs fellow Coun. on Fgn. Rels., N.Y.C., 1972-73; assoc. Hunton & Williams, Richmond, Va., 1970-76, ptnr., 1976-98, mng. ptnr., 1982-91; dean William and Mary Law Sch., 1998—; lectr. Coll. William and Mary Law Sch., 1978-80. Author: War Powers of the President and Congress: Who Holds the Arrows and Olive Branch, 1981; mem. editl. bd. Va. Law Rev., 1966-68; contbr. articles to profl. jours. Trustee Princeton U., 1986—, Presbyn. Ch. (U.S.A.) Found., 1991-97, Va. Hist. Soc., 1991-96, Union Theol. Sem., 1992—, Andrew W. Mellon Found., 1994—, Va. Mus. Fine Arts, 1995—, pres. 1996-99, St. Christopher's Sch., 1996—; bd. dirs. Fan Dist. Assn., Richmond, Inc., 1976-80, pres., 1979-80; bd. dirs. Richmond Symphony, 1980-92, pres., 1988-90, pres. symphony coun., 1994-99; bd. dirs. Presbyn. Outlook Found. and Book Svc., 1985—, pres., 1992-95; bd. dirs. Va. Mus. Found., 1990—; elder Grace Covenant Presbyn. Ch.; bd. dirs. New Covenant Trust Co., 1997-99. Mem. ABA, Va. Bar Assn., D.C. Bar Assn., Richmond Bar Assn., Am. Soc. Internat. Law, Am. Judicature Soc., Am. Bar Found., Va. Bar Found., Princeton Assn. Va. (bd. dirs. 1981—, pres. 1983-85), Edn. Lawyers (bd. govs. 1992—, chmn. Va. State Bar sect. 1992-95), Raven Soc., Phi Beta Kappa, Omicron Delta Kappa. Home: 2314 Monument Ave Richmond VA 23220-2604 Office: Hunton & Williams Riverfront Pla East Tower PO Box 1535 Richmond VA 23218-1535

**REVERCOMB, HORACE AUSTIN, III,** judge; b. Richmond, Va., Sept. 22, 1948; s. Horace Austin Jr. and Mary Virginia (Kelley) R.; m. Annie S. Anthony, July 10, 1976; children: Brian Austin, Suzanne Melanie. BA, Pembroke State U., 1971; JD, George Mason U., 1977. Bar: Va. 1978. Pvt. practice law King George, Va., 1978-82; ptnr. Revercomb & Revercomb, King George, 1982-90; judge Gen. Dist. Cts. of 15th Jud. Dist. Va., 1990-99, Cir. Ctr. 15th Jud. Dist. Va., 1999—. Mem. Va. Bar Assn. Methodist. Avocation: music. Home: PO Box 216 King George VA 22485-0216

**REW, LAWRENCE B.,** lawyer; b. Eugene, Oreg., June 22, 1936. BA, Whitman Coll., 1958; JD, Willamette U., 1961. Bar: Oreg. 1961. Ptnr. Corey, Byler, Rew, Lorenzen & Hojem, LLP, Pendleton, Oreg. Mem. ABA, Oreg. State Bar Assn. (pres.-elect., Pub. Svc. award 1991, bd. bar examiners 1975-79, bd. govs. 1996—). Agriculture, Estate planning, Real property. Office: Corey Blyer Rew Lorenzen & Hojem LLP PO Box 218 222 SE Dorion Ave Pendleton OR 97801-2553*

**REYES, LILLIAN JENNY,** lawyer; b. Covington, Ky., June 23, 1955; d. Luis and Lillian Ann (Barroso) R.; m. Robert Timothy Joyce, May 16, 1986. BA magnum cum laude, U. Miami, Fla., 1977; JD with honors, U. Fla., 1980. Bar: Fla. 1980, U.S. Dist. Ct. (mid. dist.) Fla. 1981, U.S. Ct. Appeals (11th cir.) 1981. Assoc. Carlton, Fields, Ward, Emmanual, Smith & Cutler, Tampa, Fla., 1980-87; ptnr. Joyce & Reyes, Tampa, 1987—. Bd. dirs. Suncoast counsel Girl Scouts Am., 1981-83; bd. dirs., past chmn. aging rsch. unit, chmn. ombudsman counsel project, community rsch. devel. bd., pub. affairs com., legis. breakfast com. Jr. League Tampa. Recipient George W. Milan award U. Fa. Law Rev.; named Ms. Clearwater, Fla., Miss Am. Pageant, 1973, princess Orange Bowl Com., 1977. Mem. ATLA, Fla. Bar Assn., Hillsborough County Bar Assn. (probate and guardianship rules com. 1981-87, asst. chmn. law week 1984-85, bd. dirs. young lawyers sect. 1985-87, law week chmn. 1987-88, bd. dirs. 1987-97), Fla. Trial Lawyers Assn., Bay Area Legal Svcs. Vol. Lawyers Program, U. Fla. Law Rev. Alumni Assn. Democrat. Roman Catholic. Avocations: acting, travel. Personal injury. Office: Joyce & Reyes 101 E Kennedy Blvd Ste 3875 Tampa FL 33602-5812

**REYNA, ROSE MARIE GUERRA,** lawyer, judge; b. McAllen, Tex.; d. Antonio and Rebecca (Flores) Guerra; m. Daniel Reyna, Nov. 27, 1985; children: Daniel Joshua, Anthony Jacob. BA, Pan Am. U., 1981; JD, U. Tex., 1983. Bar: Tex. 1984, U.S. Dist. Ct. (so. dist.) Tex. 1984, U.S. Ct. Appeals (5th cir.) 1984, U.S. Supreme Ct. 1994. Ptnr. Skaggs, Reyna & Garza, LLP (and predecessor firms), McAllen, Tex., 1986-98; judge 206th Dist. Ct. Hidalgo County, Edinburg, Tex., 1999—. Mem. Tex. Assn. Def. Counsel, Hidalgo County Bar Assn. (past dir., pres. 1992-93), State Bar Tex. (dist. 12b grievance com. 1989-92), Tex. Young Lawyers Assn. (bd. dirs. 1988-90). Office: Skaggs Reyna & Garza LLP 710 Laurel Mcallen TX 78501

**REYNARD, MURIEL JOYCE,** lawyer; b. Miami Beach, Fla., May 20, 1945; d. Hyman and Faye (Feinstein) Friedkin; m. Brian Patrick Delaney, Nov. 27, 1983; children: Kelly, Charlotte. BA, SUNY, Stony Brook, 1967, MS, 1973; JD cum laude, Yeshiva U., 1983. Bar: N.Y. 1984, U.S. Dist. Ct. (so. and ea. dists.) N.Y. 1984. Health planner Nassau-Suffolk RMP/CHP, Centereach, N.Y., 1972-74; adminstr. N.Y.C. Health and Hosps. Corp., 1974-75; health planner AFSCME Dist. Coun. 37, N.Y.C., 1975-76; adminstr. Inst. Emergency Medicine Albert Einstein Coll. Medicine, N.Y.C., 1977-80; asst. atty. U.S. Atty.'s Office (so. dist.) N.Y., N.Y.C., summer 1982; assoc. Skadden, Arps, Slate, Meagher & Flom, N.Y.C., 1983-85, Paskus, Gordon & Mandel, N.Y.C., 1985-86; v.p., sr. assoc. counsel The Chase Manhattan Bank, N.A., N.Y.C., 1986-96; v.p. assoc. gen. counsel Citicorp Credit Svcs. Inc., N.Y.C., 1997—. Notes and comments editor Cardozo Law Rev.; contbr. numerous articles to law jours. Mem. ABA, N.Y.C. Bar Assn., N.Y. State Bar Assn. Consumer commercial, Advertising, Intellectual property. Office: Citicorp Credit Services Inc One Court Square New York NY 11120

**REYNOLDS, H. GERALD,** lawyer; b. Alexander City, Ala., July 16, 1940; s. James H. and Melba V. (Scott) R.; m. Mary Alice McGiboney, Sept. 3, 1960; children—Cathy, Gerre, Amy, Richie. B.A., Auburn U., 1962; J.D., Cumberland Sch. Law, 1965. Bar: Ala. 1965, Fla. 1977. Ptnr. King and Reynolds, Alexander City, 1965-66; sole practice, Alexander City, 1966-71; corp. counsel U.S. Pipe and Foundry, Birmingham, Ala., 1971-72; environ. counsel Jim Walter Corp., Tampa, Fla., 1972-87, Walter Industries Inc., 1988— ; judge Ct. Common Pleas, Tallapoosa County, Ala., 1967-68; mem. faculty Alexander City State Jr. Coll., 1966-71; ad hoc instr. Coll. Pub. Health Grad. Sch. U. South Fla., 1988-90. Mem. Ala. Constl. Revision Commn., 1970-75; mem. Ala. Democratic Exec. Com., 1970-72. Mem. Fla. Bar Assn. (chmn. eviron. and land use law sect. 1981-82, vice chmn. continuing legal edn. com. 1980-94). Methodist. Contbr. articles to legal jours. *As a young lawyer practicing solo in Alabama, he joined the Jaycees. A couple years later, became state governmental affairs chairman. He returned home from a 1979 Washington seminar with an idea from Congressman Bill Steiger, Wisconsin. He suggested that they look at the need for state constitutional reform. From his suggestion Mr. Reynolds decided to pursue revising the Alabama Constitution,then the longest state constitution in the USA. The Jaycees lobbied to create a state constitutional revision commission. After the bill became law, Mr. Reynolds was appointed the youngest memeber of a commission of 25 to prepare a proposed revised constitution to be submitted to legislature.* Environmental, Health.

**REYNOLDS, JOHN W.,** federal judge; b. Green Bay, Wis., Apr. 4, 1921; s. John W. and Madge (Flatley) R.; m. Patricia Ann Brody, May 26, 1947 (dec. Dec. 1967); children: Kate M. Reynolds Lindquist, Molly A., James B.; m. Jane Conway, July 31, 1971; children: Jacob F., Thomas J., Frances P., John W. III. PhB, U. Wis., 1946, LLB, 1949. Bar: Wis. 1949. Since practiced in Green Bay, dist. dir. price stblzn., 1951-53, U.S. commr., 1953-58, atty. gen. of Wis., 1958-62; gov. State of Wis., 1963-65; U.S. dist. judge Ea. Dist. Wis., Milwa., 1965-71, chief judge, 1971-86, sr. judge, 1986—. Served with U.S. Army, 1942-46. Mem. State Bar Wis., Am. Law Inst., Fed. Judges Assn., Former Govs. Assn. Office: US Dist Ct 296 US Courthouse 517 E Wisconsin Ave Milwaukee WI 53202-4500

**REYNOLDS, MICHAEL TIMOTHY,** lawyer; b. N.Y.C., June 29, 1968; s. Timothy John and Patricia Mary Reynolds. AB in History magna cum laude, Dartmouth Coll., 1990; MPhil in Medieval History, Cambridge (Eng.) U., 1991; JD, Yale U., 1995. Bar: N.Y. 1996, U.S. Dist. Ct. (so. and ea. dists.) N.Y. 1996. Law clk. to Hohn. Diarmuid F. O'Scannlain, U.S. Ct. Appeals for 9th Cir., Portland, Oreg., 1995-96; litigation assoc. Cravath, Swaine & Moore, N.Y.C., 1996—. Exec. editor Yale Law Jour., 1994-95. Keasbey Found. scholar Cambridge U., 1990-92. Mem. Assn. Bar City N.Y. (com. on non-profit orgns. 1997—), Phi Beta Kappa. General civil litigation, Antitrust, Non-profit and tax-exempt organizations. Office: Cravath Swaine & Moore 825 8th Ave Fl 38 New York NY 10019-7475

**REYNOLDS, RICHARD LOUIS,** lawyer; b. Baton Rouge, Sept. 10, 1953; s. Louis Baker and Mildred (Close) R.; m. Wendie Daigle, Nov. 23, 1978; children: Lindsey Michelle, Keith Richard. BS, La. State U., 1975; JD, Loyola U., New Orleans, 1978. Bar: La. 1978, U.S. Dist. Ct. (ea. dist.) La. 1978, U.S. Ct. Appeals (5th cir.) 1982, U.S. Supreme Ct. 1982. Law clk. 22nd Jud. Dist. Ct., Covington, La., 1978-79; ptnr. Liberto and Reynolds, Covington, 1979-80; contract atty. Mental Health Advocacy Service, Baton Rouge, 1982-83; pvt. practice Covington, 1980-88; dir. Richard Reynolds and Assocs., Covington and Metairie, La., 1988—; asst. dist. atty. Covington, 1984-86, 87-93; instr. Delgado C.C., New Orleans, 1986-87; cons. NBKA, 1988; pres. Statewide Title and Appraisal Svcs., Inc. (formerly Strategic Title and Appraisal Svcs., Inc.). Columnist: The Northshore Journal. Bd. dirs. Alpha House, Covington, 1986-90, River Forest Acad. Sch.; campaign mgr. for candidate for La. Senate, 1983; mem. exec. com. St. Tammany Parish Dem. Com., 1983; active La. Dem. Ctrl. Com., 1983; Webelos den leader Den 2, Pack 112, Istrouma coun. Boy Scouts Am., 1995-96, com. mem. Troop 110, 1997. Mem. ABA, La. Bar Assn., Covington Bar Assn., Assn. Trial Lawyers Am., La. Trial Lawyers Assn., St. Tammany Bd. Realtors, St. Tammany Home Bldrs. Assn., Rotary (Paul Harris fellow 1987, pres. 1988-89), Optimists. Avocations: photography, travel, camping. Real property, Probate, General civil litigation. Office: Richard Reynolds & Assocs PO Box 2439 Covington LA 70434-2439

**REYNOLDS, TIMOTHY GERARD,** lawyer; b. Bronx, N.Y., 1955. BS, Fordham U., 1976, JD, 1980. Bar: N.Y. 1981. Law clk. to Judge William H. Mulligan U.S. Ct. Appeals (2d cir.), 1980-81; with Skadden, Arps, Slate, Meagher & Flom LLP, N.Y.C., 1981—, ptnr., 1992—. Writing and rsch. editor: Fordham Law Rev. Insurance, General civil litigation. Office: Skadden Arps Slate Meagher & Flom LLP 919 3rd Ave New York NY 10022-3902

**REYNOLDS, WILLIAM MACKENZIE, JR.,** lawyer; b. Sumter, S.C., June 9, 1921; s. William MacKenzie and Helen (Janes) R.; m. Nancy Nash, Apr. 14, 1950; children: Helen Janes, William MacKenzie III. BS, The Citadel, 1942; JD, U. S.C., 1975. Bar: S.C. 1975. Commd. 2d lt. USAF, 1942, advanced through grades to col., 1963, ret., 1971; assoc. Nash & Chappell, Sumter, 1975-78; ptnr. Reynolds & Reynolds, Sumter, 1978—; bd. dirs. Sumter Casket Co.; master in equity County of Sumter, 1984-93. Decorated Legion of Merit, Disting. Flying Cross, Air medal. Mem. Sumter County Bar Assn., U.S. Law Sch. Alumni Assn. (bd. dirs. 1979-89), Order of Daedalians. Episcopalian. Probate, Real property. Home: 1 Gadsden Way Apt 45 Charleston SC 29412-3563 Office: Reynolds & Reynolds 3 Law Range PO Box 396 Sumter SC 29151-0396

**REYNOLDS, ZACKERY E.,** lawyer; b. Eureka, Kans., Dec. 19, 1957. BA, U. Kans., 1979; JD with honors, Washburn U., 1982. Bar: Kans. 1982, Mo. 1992. Pvt. practice Fort Scott, Kans. Mem. ABA (exec. coun., young lawyers divsn. 1991-92), ATLA, Kans. Bar Assn. (pres.-elect 1998-99, v.p. 1997-98, sec.-treas. 1996-97, chair profl. ethics grievance com. 1993-95, pres. young lawyers sect. 1986-87, Oustanding Svc. award 1992), Mo. Bar Assn., Kans. Trial Lawyers Assn., Phi Delta Phi. Insurance, Product liability, Personal injury. Office: Reynolds Law Firm PA PO Box 32 102 S Jordan Fort Scott KS 66701*

**RHAME, HAROLD ELLIS, JR.,** law educator; b. El Paso, July 3, 1926; s. Harold Ellis and Ethel Clara (Dunagan) R.; m. Joan Williams, Feb. 14, 1955; children: Lucy S., Ann B., Ellis W. AB, Princeton U., 1946; MD, George Washington U., 1950; JD, U. Bridgeport, 1990. Bar: Conn. 1991. Intern Barnes Hosp., St. Louis, 1951, resident, 1952; resident NYU-Bellevue Med. Ctr., N.Y.C., 1952-56; pvt. med. practice Bridgeport, Conn., 1956-88; law educator Quinnipac Coll. Law, Bridgeport, 1994.

**RHEE, ALBERT,** lawyer, author; b. Pa., June 25, 1958; s. S.K. and B.C. (Chun) R.; m. I.Y. Choi, June, 1992. AB, Wabash (Ind.) Coll., 1980; JD, U. So. Calif., 1985; M Jurisprudence, U. Calif., Berkeley, 1990; postgrad., Oxford U., 1999—. Bar: N.Y. 1986. Fellow Bryn Mawr (Pa.) Coll., 1985-87; instr. U. Calif. Boalt Hall Sch. Law, 1987-95, Oxford U., 1999—. Editor: Patent Law in Korea, 1994, Intellectual Property in Korea, 1995. Recipient Franklin award U. So. Calif. Law Sch., L.A., 1985, grad. fellowship Bryn Mawr Coll., 1985-87, grad. law fellowship U. Calif. Berkeley Boalt Hall Law Sch., 1988-90, Boalt Hall fellowship, 1990-92. Mem. N.Y. County Lawyers Assn. Avocations: music, fine arts, zen. Public international, Private international.

**RHEINSTEIN, PETER HOWARD,** government official, physician, lawyer; b. Cleve., Sept. 7, 1943; s. Franz Joseph Rheinstein and Hede Henrietta (Neheimer) Rheinstein Lerner; m. Miriam Ruth Weissman, Feb. 22, 1969; 1 child, Jason Edward. BA with high honors, Mich. State U., 1963, MS, 1964; MD, Johns Hopkins U., 1967; JD, U. Md., 1973. Bar: Md., D.C.; diplomate Am. Bd. Family Practice; cert. added qualifications in geriatric medicine. Intern USPHS Hosp., San Francisco, 1967-68; resident in internal medicine USPHS Hosp., Balt., 1968-70; practice medicine specializing in internal medicine Balt., 1970—; instr. medicine U. Md., Balt., 1970-73; med. dir. extended care facilities CHC Corp., Balt., 1972-74; dir. drug advt. and labeling div. FDA, Rockville, Md., 1974-82, acting dep. dir. Office Drugs, 1982-83, acting dir. Office Drugs, 1983-84, dir. Office Drug Standards, 1984-90; dir. medicine staff, Office Health Affairs FDA, 1990—; chmn. Com. on Advanced Sci. Edn., 1978-86, Rsch. in Human Subjects Com., 1990-92; adj. prof. forensic medicine George Washington U., 1974-76; WHO cons. on drug regulation Nat. Inst. for Control Pharm. and Biol. Products, People's Republic of China, 1981—; advisor on essential drugs WHO, 1985—; FDA del. to U.S. Pharmacopeial Conv., 1985-90, coord. com. for assessment and transfer of tech. NIH, 1990—, health care fin. adminstrn. tech. adv. com., 1990—, Nat. Adv. Coun. on Healthcare Policy, Rsch. and Evaluation, 1990—, Healthy People 2000/2010 Steering Com., 1990—, CDC and Prevention Task Force on Cmty. Preventive Svcs., 1996—, Nat. Task Force on Industry/Provider CME Collaboration, 1992—. Co-author: (with others) Human Organ Transplantation, 1987; spl. editorial advisor Good Housekeeping Guide to Medicine and Drugs, 1977—; mem. editorial bd. Legal Aspects Med. Practice, 1981-89, Drug Info. Jour., 1982-86, 91-95; contbr. articles to profl. jours. Recipient Commendable Svc. award FDA, 1981, Group award of merit, 1983, 88, Group Commendable Svc. award 1989, 92, 93, 95, 99, Commr.'s Spl. citation, 1993. Fellow Am. Coll. Legal Medicine (bd. govs. 1983-93, treas., chmn. fin. com. 1985-88, 90-91, chmn. publs. com. 1988-93, jud. coun. 1993-95; Pres.'s awards 1985, 86, 89, 90, 91, 93), Am. Acad. Family Physicians; mem. Am. Acad. Pharm. Phys. (bd. trustees 1998—), AMA, ABA, Drug Info. Assn. (bd. dirs. 1982-90, pres. 1984-85, 88-89, v.p. 1986-87, chmn. ann. meeting 1991, 94, steering com. Ams. 1991—, Outstanding Svc. award 1990), Fed. Bar Assn. (chmn. food and drug com. 1976-79, Disting Svc. award 1977), Med. and Chirurgical Faculty Md., Balt. City Med. Soc., Johns Hopkins Med. and Surg. Assn., APHA, Md. Bar Assn., Math. Assn. Am., Soc. Indsl. and Applied Math., Mensa (life), U. Md. Alumni Assn. (life), Fed. Exec. Inst. Alumni Assn. (life), Johns Hopkins U. Alumni Assn., Mich. State U. Alumni Assn. (life), Mich. State U. Honors Coll. Alumni Assn. (bd. dirs. 1998—), Chartwell Golf and Country Club, Annapolis Yacht Club, Johns Hopkins Club, Delta Theta Phi. Avocations: boating, electronics, physical fitness, real estate investments. Home: 621 Holly Ridge Rd Severna Park MD 21146-3520 Office: FDA Office of Health Affairs Dir Medicine Staff 5600 Fishers Ln Rockville MD 20857-0001

**RHIND, JAMES THOMAS,** lawyer; b. Chgo., July 21, 1922; s. John Gray and Eleanor (Bradley) R.; m. Laura Haney Campbell, Apr. 19, 1958; children: Anne Constance, James Campbell, David Scott. Student, Hamilton Coll., 1940-42; A.B. cum laude, Ohio State U., 1944; LL.B. cum laude, Harvard U., 1950. Bar: Ill. bar 1950. Japanese translator U.S. War Dept., Tokyo, Japan, 1946-47; congl. liaison Fgn. Operations Adminstrn., Washington, 1954; atty. Bell, Boyd & Lloyd, Chgo., 1950-53, 55—, ptnr., 1958-92, of counsel, 1993—; Bd. dirs. Kewaunee Scientific Corp., Statesville, N.C., Lindberg Corp., Rosemont, Ill., Griffith Labs., Inc., Alsip, Ill. Commr. Gen. Assembly United Presbyn. Ch., 1963; life trustee Ravinia Festival Assn., Hamilton Coll., Clinton, N.Y., U. Chgo.; Northwestern Univ. Assocs.; chmn. Cook County Young Republican Orgn., 1957; Ill. Young Rep. nat. committeeman, 1957-58; v.p., mem. bd. govs. United Rep. Fund Ill., 1965-84; pres. Ill. Childrens Home and Aid Soc., 1971-73, life trustee; bd. dirs. E.J. Dalton Youth Center, 1966- 69; governing mem. Chgo. Symphony Orch., Chgo.; mem. Ill. Arts Council, 1971-75; mem. exec. com. div. Met. Mission and Ch. Extension Bd., Chgo. Presbytery, 1966-68; trustee Presbyn. Home, W. Clement and Jessie V. Stone Found., U. Chgo. Hosps. Served with M.I. AUS, 1943-46. Mem. ABA, Ill. Bar Assn., Chgo. Bar Assn. (bd. mgrs. 1967-69), Fed. Bar Assns., Chgo. Council on Fgn. Relations, Japan Am. Soc. Chgo., Legal Club Chgo., Law Club Chgo., Phi Beta Kappa, Sigma Phi. Clubs: Chicago, Glen View (Ill.), Commercial (Chgo.), Mid-Day Club (Chgo.), Economic (Chgo.). General corporate, Securities. Home: 830 Normandy Ln Glenview IL 60025-3210 Office: Bell Boyd & Lloyd 3 First National Pla 70 W Madison St Ste 3200 Chicago IL 60602-4244

**RHOADES, DANA CHRISTINE,** lawyer; b. Leavenworth, Kans., July 21, 1970; d. Bert Allen Barnes and Freya Christine Roberts; m. Kerry Lane Rhoades, Jan. 1, 1994; 1 child, Thomas Mitchell. BS, Ill. State U., 1992; JD, Loyola U., Chgo., 1995. Bar: Ill. 1995. Assoc. Hugh Finson Law Office, Monticello, Ill., 1996; ptnr. Shonkwiler, Ayers & Rhoades, Monticello, 1997—. Campaign mgr. Com. to Elect Pat Rhoades, Monticello, 1997-98; county coord. Com. to Elect Judge Thomas Appleton, Piatt County, Ill., 1998. Mem. ABA, Piatt County Bar Assn. (pres. 1996—). Republican. Methodist. Avocation: reading. General practice, Probate, Real property. Office: Shonkwiler Ayers & Rhoades 114 S Charter St Monticello IL 61856-1853

**RHOADES, JOHN SKYLSTEAD, SR.,** federal judge; b. 1925; m. Carmel Rhoades; children: Mark, John, Matthew, Peter, Christopher. AB, Stanford U., 1948; JD, U. Calif., San Francisco, 1951. Prosecuting atty. City of San Diego, 1955-56, dep. city atty., 1956-57; pvt. practice San Diego, 1957-60; ptnr. Rhoades, Hollywood & Neil, San Diego, 1960-85; judge U.S. Dist. Ct. (so. dist.) Calif., San Diego, 1985—. With USN, 1943-46. Office: US Dist Ct 940 Front St San Diego CA 92101-8994

**RHOADS, CARL LYNN,** lawyer, retired military officer; b. Covert, Mich., Aug. 17, 1914; s. Lloyd George and Ida Elizabeth (Cooper) R.; m. Irene Ann Carlson, Dec. 27, 1938; 1 child, Douglas Carroll (dec.). BS, We. Mich. U., 1938; JD, Wayne State U., 1951. Bar: Mich., U.S. Dist. Ct. Mich., U.S. Ct. Appeals (3rd cir.), U.S. Ct. Appeals (6th and 9th cirs.), U.S. Dist. Ct. Mil. Appeals, U.S. Supreme Ct. Commd. 2d lt. U.S. Army, 1943; advanced through grades to col. USAR, various assignments, 1943-53; staff judge adv., mil. justice instr. USAR, Detroit, 1954-74; ret., 1974; pvt. practice Ecorse, Mich., 1951—. Democrat. Avocation: gardening. Bankruptcy, General civil litigation, Criminal. Office: Carl L Rhoads and Assocs PO Box 9001 4073 W Jefferson Ave Ecorse MI 48229-1736

**RHOADS, NANCY GLENN,** lawyer; b. Washington, Oct. 15, 1957; d. Donald L. and Gerry R. R.; m. Robert A. Koons, June 23, 1984. BA, Gettysburg Coll., 1980; JD, Temple U., 1983. Bar: Pa., U.S. Dist. Ct. (ea. dist.) Pa. 1983. Rsch. asst. Prof. Mikochick, Phila., 1982-83; law clk. Phila. Ct. of Common Pleas, 1983-85; assoc. Post and Schell P.C., Phila., 1985-90, Sheller, Ludwig and Badey, Phila., 1990—. Co-author: Aging and the Aged: Problems, Opportunities, Challenges, 1980. Vol. Spl. Olympics. Mem. Phila. Bar Assn. (med. legal com.), Phi Beta Kappa, Phi Alpha Theta, Pi Delta Epsilon, Eta Sigma Phi. Avocations: classical piano, horticulture, swimming. Personal injury. Home: 401 Audubon Ave Wayne PA 19087-4006 Office: Sheller Ludwig and Badey 1528 Walnut St Philadelphia PA 19102-3604

**RHOADS, ROBERT K.,** lawyer, retail executive; b. 1954. BA, U. Ark, 1976, JD, 1980. Bar: Ark. 1980. Asst. gen. counsel Wal-Mart Stores Inc., Bentonville, Ark., 1980-85, gen. counsel, sec., 1985-88, sr. v.p., gen. counsel, sec., 1988—. Office: Wal-Mart Stores Inc 702 SW 8th St Bentonville AR 72716-6299

**RHODE, DEBORAH LYNN,** law educator; b. Jan. 29, 1952. BA, Yale U., 1974, JD, 1977. Bar: D.C. 1977, Calif. 1981. Law clk. to judge U.S. Ct. Appeals (2d cir.), N.Y.C., 1977-78; law clk. to Hon. Justice Thurgood Marshall U.S. Supreme Ct., D.C., 1978-79; asst. prof. law Stanford (Calif.) U., 1979-82, assoc. prof., 1982-85, prof., 1985—; dir. Inst. for Rsch. on Women and Gender, 1986-90, Keck Ctr. of Legal Ethics and The Legal Profession, 1994—; sr. counsel jud. com. Ho. of Reps., Washington, 1998; trustee Yale U., 1983-89; pres. Assn. Am. Law Schs., 1998; Ernest W. McFarland prof. Stanford Law Sch., 1997—; sr. counsel com. on the jud. U.S. Ho. of Reps., 1998. Author: Justice and Gender, 1989, (with Geoffrey Hazard) the Legal Profession: Responsibility and Regulation, 3d edit., 1993, (with Annette Lawson) The Politics of Pregnancy: Adolescent Sexuality and Public Policy, 1993, (with David Luban) Legal Ethics, 1995, (with Barbara Allen Babcock, Ann E. Freedman, Susan Deller Ross, Wendy Webster Williams, Rhonda Copelon, and Nadine H. Taub) Sex Discrimination and the Law, 1997, Speaking of Sex, 1997, Professional Responsibility: Ethics by the Pervasive Method, 1998; editor: Theoretical Perspectives on Sexual Difference, 1990; contbr. articles to profl. jours. Office: Stanford U Law Sch Crown Quadrangle Stanford CA 94305

**RHODEN, WILLIAM GARY,** lawyer; b. Aiken, S.C., June 20, 1955; s. Thomas Gary and Catherine (Moseley) R.; m. Paula Jean Henderson, Aug. 8, 1981. BS in Psychology, U. S.C., Aiken, 1977; JD, U. S.C., 1980. Bar: S.C. 1981, U.S. Dist. Ct. S.C. 1982, U.S. Ct. Appeals (4th cir.) 1985. Lab. asst. psychology dept. U. S.C., Aiken, 1975-77; asst. dir. Greer (S.C.) YMCA, 1977-78; law clk. U.S. Atty. Office, Greer, 1977-78; intern U.S. Justice Dept., Columbia, S.C., 1980-81; staff atty. Office of Atty. Gen. State of S.C., Florence, 1981; asst. atty. gen. Office of Atty. Gen. State of S.C., Charleston, S.C., 1981-83; asst. solicitor 7th Jud. Cir., Spartanburg, S.C., 1984-86; pvt. practice Gaffney, S.C., 1986—. Bd. dirs. Cherokee Children's Home, S.C. Peach Festival. Mem. ABA, Cherokee County Bar Assn. (sec.-treas. 1988-96, pres. 1996—), Rotary (Paul Harris fellow), Phi Alpha Delta. Avocations: tennis, golf, racquetball. General practice. Home: 119 College Dr Gaffney SC 29340-3002 Office: 221 E Floyd Baker Blvd PO Box 1937 Gaffney SC 29342-1937

**RHODES, ARTHUR DELANO,** benefits administrator; b. Phila., Nov. 26, 1960; s. A.D. and Mary (McNair) R.; m. Angela Marie Jolly, May 21, 1988. AA, Miss. Delta Jr. Coll., Moorhead, 1980; BA in Polit. Sci., Millsaps Coll., 1982; JD, U. Miss., 1985. Bar: Miss. 1985, U.S. Dist. Ct. (no. and so. dist.) Miss. 1985. Intern asst. dist. atty. Dist. Atty's Office, Hernando, Miss., 1985; counsel Child Support Unit, Dept. of Human Svcs., Brookhaven, Miss., 1985-87; assoc. Prewitt & Bradley, Jackson, Miss., 1987-88; chief of staff Congressman Mike Parker, Washington, 1988-98; pres., CEO Ch. of God Benefits Bd., Cleveland, Tenn., 1999—. Republican. Mem. Ch. of God. Avocations: travel, reading. Home: 2014 Woodchase Way NE Cleveland TN 37311-1461 Office: The Benefits Bd PO Box 4608 Cleveland TN 37320-4608

**RHODES, ERIC FOSTER,** arbitrator, employee relations consultant, writer; b. Luray, Va., Feb. 5, 1927; s. Wallace Keith and Bertha (Foster) R.; m. Barbara Ellen Henson, Oct. 19, 1946; children: Roxanne Jane, Laurel Lee; m. Lorraine Endresen, July 29, 1972; m. Daisy Chun, May 31, 1980. AA, George Washington U., 1949, AB, 1950, MA, 1952, EdD, 1967. Tchr. high sch. Arlington, Va., 1950-52; counselor Washington Lee High Sch., Arlington, Va., 1952-53, dir. publs., 1953-54, chmn. dept. English, 1954-55; exec. sec. Arlington Edn. Assn., Arlington, Va., 1952-53, Montgomery County (Md.) Edn. Assn., Rockville, Md., 1955-57; lectr. edn. George Washington U., Washington, 1955-60, 65-70; salary cons. NEA, Washington, 1957-58, asst. dir. membership div., 1958-60; dir. N.Y. regional office, N.Y.C., 1960-64; ednl. cons. Ednl. Rsch. Svcs., White Plains, N.Y., 1964-65; pres. Ednl. Svc. Bur., Inc., Arlington, Va., 1965-72, chmn. bd., 1972-80; pres. Negotiations Consultation Svcs., Inc., Arlington, 1969-80, Eastern States Advt. Inc., Arlington, 1970-79, EFR Corp., Arlington, 1972-90; exec. dir. Assn. Negotiators and Contract Adminstrs., 1981-89; area coord. U.S. Legal Protection Co., 1989-95; pres. Employee Futures Rsch., Colorado Springs, Colo., 1980—, Waterfront Only Real Estate, New Port Richey, Fla., 1988-92, Inst. for Negotiations Tng., New Port Richey, 1989-95, Asset Protection Co., 1991—; asst. supt. for adminstrn. Brighton Schs., Rochester, N.Y., 1983-88; owner Frederick Foster Galleries, Arlington, 1974-80; cons. Va. Dept. Community Colls., Richmond, 1965-77; vice chancellor Va. Community Coll. System, 1970-71; employee rels. ofcl. City of Orlando, 1980-83; lectr. edn. Frostburg (Md.) State Coll., 1967. Author: Negotiating Salaries, 41 Ways to Cut Budget Costs, Making Good Things Happen Through Negotiation; editor: Inside Negotiations, Wages and Benefits, Employers' Negotiating Service. Mem. Civil Rights Commn., Franklin Twp., N.J., 1962-64; mem. Sr. victim assistance team Colorado Springs Police Dept., 1997—; mem. Franklin Twp. Bd. Edn., 1964-65; mem. adv. bd. Keep Am. Beautiful, 1964-75, nat. chmn., 1968; bd. dirs., v.p. Unitarian-Universalist Ch., Tarpon Springs, Fla., 1990-95, pres., 1994-95. With U.S. Army, 1945-47. Mem. Am. Assn. Sch. Adminstrs., Internat. Assn. Sch. Bus. Officials, NEA, Edn. Press Assn., Nat. Assn. Ednl. Negotiators (exec. dir. 1971-81), Am. Arbitration Assn. (labor arbitrator), Indsl. Rels. Rsch. Assn., United C. of C. of Pasco County (sec., treas. 1989-90, exec. dir. 1990-91), Am. Legion, Fed. Schoolmen's Club, N.Y. Schoolmen's Club, Lions (v.p. N.Y.C. club 1964-65), Kiwanis (pres. West Pasco club 1991-93), Order of St. John of Jerusalem, Phi Delta Kappa (chpt. pres. 1959-60). Home: 1994 Copper Creek Dr Colorado Springs CO 80910-1867 Office: PO Box 15236 Colorado Springs CO 80935-5236

**RHODES, GEORGE FREDERICK, JR.,** lawyer; b. Houston, Nov. 2, 1952; s. George F. and Marion Kathleen Rhodes; m. Bebe Lyn Burns, Nov. 30, 1980; 1 child, Elizabeth Kathleen. BS, U. Tex., 1974; JD, U. Houston, 1991. Bar: Tex. 1991, U.S. Dist. Ct. (all dists.) Tex. 1992. Reporter KTBC-TV, Austin, 1974-76; reporter KHOU-TV, Houston, 1977-79, KTVI-TV, St. Louis, 1979-82; dir. pub. rels. Inn on the Park Four Season Hotel, Houston, 1982-84; editor in chief Houston City Mag., 1984-86; dir. pub. affairs Tex. Children's Hosp., Houston, 1986-88; assoc. Hirsch & Westheimer, P.C., Houston, 1991-94, Haynes and Boone, LLP, Houston, 1994-99, Gibson Gruenert & Hebert LLP, 1999—. Co-author: Annual Survey of Texas Privacy and Related Claims Against the Media, 1996-98. Pres. The Park People, Houston, 1987-88; bd. dirs. U. Houston Law Alumni Assn., 1994-96; adminstrv. bd. St. Paul's United Meth. Ch., Houston, 1998—. Avocations: reading, traveling. Libel, General civil litigation, Consumer commercial. Office: 3003 South Loop W Ste 320 Houston TX 77054-1311

**RHODES, JESSE THOMAS, III,** lawyer; b. Memphis, Jan. 1, 1955; s. J. Thomas Sr. and Carolyn (Ross) R.; m. Joye Beth, May 28, 1983; children: Jessica Elizabeth, Robert Thomas. BA magna cum laude, Southwest Tex. State U., 1977, JD, 1980. Bar: Tex. 1980, U.S. Dist. Ct. (so. dist.) Tex. 1984; diplomate Am. Bd. Profl. Liability Attys.; bd. cert. in personal injury trial law. Assoc. Southers & Lyons, San Antonio, 1980-94; ptnr. Lyons & Rhodes, San Antonio, 1994—; mem. adv. coun. Nat. Jud. Coll. Fellow Tex. Bar Found. (life), Coll. State Bar; mem. San Antonio Bar Assn., San Antonio Trial Lawyers Assn. (pres. 1994). Personal injury, Toxic tort, Professional liability. Office: Lyons & Rhodes 126 Villita St San Antonio TX 78205-2735

**RHODES, RALPH BEAUFORD,** lawyer; b. Charleston, S.C., Jan. 31, 1933; s. Elree Beauford and Sophie (O'Brien) R.; m. Sheila Marie Nelson, Apr. 12, 1958; children: Stacy Marie Cullen, Lisa Ellen, Morgan E. Brazelton, Shannon N. BA, U. Va., 1955; JD, U. Denver, 1961; MA, U. Colo., 1970. Bar: Colo. 1962, U.S. Dist. Ct. Colo. 1962, U.S. Ct. Appeals (10th cir.) 1962, U.S. Supreme Ct. 1972. Engrng. geologist Va. Dept. Hwys., Richmond, 1955-57; asst. engrng. geologist Colo. Dept. Hwys., Denver, 1958-61; contract specialist Martin Marietta Cary, Waterton, Colo., 1962-67; pvt. practice Denver, 1967—. With U.S. Army, 1957-58. Mem. Colo. Bar Assn., Denver Bar Assn. Avocations: auto racing, scuba diving, traveling. State civil litigation, Criminal, Appellate. Office: 1748 High St Denver CO 80218-1306

**RHODES, THOMAS WILLARD,** lawyer; b. Lynchburg, Va., Mar. 9, 1946; s. Howard W. and Ruth R.; m. Ann Bloodworth, May 31, 1975; children: Mildred, Andrew. AB, Davidson (N.C.) Coll., 1968; JD, U. Va., 1971. Bar: Ga. 1971. Assoc. Smith, Gambrell & Russell and predecessor firms, Atlanta, 1971-76, ptnr., 1976—; dir., pres. Atlanta Vol. Lawyers Found., 1984-89, Fed. Defender Program, Atlanta, 1989-94. Contbr. articles to profl. jours. Capt. USAR, 1971-72. Recipient Heiner award, Atlanta Vol. Lawyers Found., 1989. Fellow Am. Law Inst.; mem. Ga. Bar Assn. (past chmn. antitrust law sect.), ABA. Antitrust, General civil litigation, Bankruptcy. Office: Smith Gambrell & Russell Promenade II 1230 Peachtree St NE Ste 3100 Atlanta GA 30309-3592

**RHODES-DEVEY, MICHAEL,** lawyer; b. Elmhurst, N.Y., Sept. 18, 1958; s. Donald P. and Ellen (Brett) Devey; m. Alison A. Rhodes, June 7, 1980; children: Rachel, Brian N. BA, SUNY, Oneonta, 1980; JD, Union U., 1985. Bar: N.Y. 1986, U.S. Dist. Ct. (no dist.) N.Y. 1986, U.S. Dist. Ct. (so. dist.) N.Y. 1987, U.S. Dist. Ct. (we. dist.) N.Y. 1990, St. Regis Mohawk Tribal Ct. House parent Helderberg House, Altomont, N.Y., 1980-82; assoc. O'Connell & Aranowitz, Albany, N.Y., 1985-89; asst. atty. gen. State of N.Y. Dept. Law, Albany, 1989-91; assoc. Kingsley & Towne, P.C., Albany, 1991-95; prin. Breeze & Rhodes-Devey, Slingerlands, N.Y., 1995—; gen. counsel St. Regis Mohawk Tribe, Akwesasne, N.Y., 1994—. Active Capital region ACLU, Albany, 1985-89. Mem. N.Y. State Bar Assn., Albany County Bar Assn., Capital Regional Bankruptcy Bar Assn., Capital Region Trial Lawyers Assn. Avocations: fishing, motorcycling, coaching youth hockey and lacrosse. Native American, Consumer commercial, Real property. Home: 80 Iroquois Trl Slingerlands NY 12159-9436 Office: Breeze & Rhodes-Devey 1397 New Scotland Rd Slingerlands NY 12159-7204

**RHYNE, CHARLES SYLVANUS,** lawyer; b. Charlotte, N.C., June 23, 1912; s. Sydneyham S. and Mary (Wilson) R.; m. Sue Cotton, Sept. 16, 1932 (dec. Mar. 1974); children: Mary Margaret, William Sylvanus; m. Sarah P. Hendon, Oct. 2, 1976; children: Sarah Wilson, Elizabeth Parkhill. BA, Duke U., 1934, LLD, 1958; JD, George Washington U., 1937, DCL, 1958; LLD, Loyola U., Calif., 1958, Dickinson Law Sch., 1959, Ohio No. U., 1966, De Paul U., 1968, Centre, 1969, U. Richmond, 1970, Howard U., 1975, Belmont Abbey, 1982. Bar: D.C. 1937. Pvt. practice Washington; sr. ptnr. Rhyne & Rhyne; gen. counsel Nat. Inst. Mcpl. Law Officers, 1937-88, of counsel; prof. govt. and aviation law George Washington U., 1948-53; prof. govt. Am. U., 1939-44; gen. counsel Fed. Commn. Jud. and Congl. Salaries, 1953-54; spl. cons. Pres. Eisenhower, 1957-60; Dir. Nat. Savs. & Trust Co., 1941-76, ACCIA Life Ins. Co., 1966-84; Mem. Internat Commn. Rules Judicial Procedures, 1959-61, Pres.'s Commn. on UN, 1969-71; spl. ambassador, personal rep. of Pres. U.S. to UN High Commr. for Refugees, 1971-73. Author: Civil Aeronautics Act, Annotated, 1939, Airports and the Courts, 1944, Aviation Accident Law, 1947, Airport Lease and Concession Agreements, 1948, Cases on Aviation Law, 1950, The Law of Municipal Contracts, 1952, Municipal Law, 1957, International Law, 1971, Renowned Law Givers and Great Law Documents of Humankind, 1975, International Refugee Law, 1976, Law and Judicial Systems of Nations, 1978, Law of Local Government Operations, 1980, (autobiography) Working for Justice in America and Justice in the World, 1996; editor Mcpl. Atty., 1937-88; contbr. articles to profl. jours. Trustee George Washington U., 1957-67, Duke U., 1961-85, now trustee emeritus. Recipient Freedoms Found. award for creation Law Day-U.S.A., 1959; Alumni Achievement award George Washington U., 1960; Nat. Bar Assn. Stradford award, 1962; 1st Whitney M. Young award, 1972; Harris award Rotary, 1974; U.S. Dept. State appreciation award, 1976; Nansen Ring for refugee work, 1976, 1st Peacemaker award Rotary Internat., 1988. Mem. ABA (life mem. ho. dels., pres. 1957-58, chmn. ho. dels. 1956-58, chmn. commn. world peace through law 1958-66, chmn. com. aero. law 1946-48, 51-54, chmn. internat. and comparative law sect. 1948-49, chmn. UN com., chmn. commn. on nat. inst. justice 1972-76, nat. chmn. Jr. Bar Conf. 1944-45, ABA Gold Medal 1966), D.C. Bar Assn. (pres. 1955-56, Disting. Svc. award, 1975, Grotius Peace award 1958), Inter-Am. Bar Assn. (v.p. 1957-59), Am. Bar Found. (pres. 1957-58, chmn. fellows 1958-59), Internat. Bar (founder patron 1947, v.p. 1957-58), Am. Judicature Soc. (dir. life), Am. Law Inst. (life), Am. Soc. Internat. Law (life), World Peace Through Law Ctr. (pres. 1963-89), World Jurist Assn. (pres. 1989-91, hon. pres. for life), Nat. Aero. Assn. (bd. dirs. 1945-47), Washington Bd. Trade, Duke U. Alumni Assn. (chmn. nat. coun. 1955-56, pres. 1959-60), Barristers, Met. Club (life), Nat. Press Club, Congl. Country Club (life), Nat. Lawyers Club (life), Univ. Club, Order of Coif (life), Scribes, Delta Theta Phi (life), Omicron Delta Kappa. Private international, Constitutional, General practice. Home and Office: 1404 Langley Pl Mc Lean VA 22101-3010

**RHYNEDANCE, HAROLD DEXTER, JR.,** lawyer, consultant; b. New Haven, Conn., Feb. 13, 1922; s. Harold Dexter and Gladys (Evans) R.; m. Barbara Ann Hall (dec.); 1 child, Harold Dexter III; m. Ruth Cosline Hakanson. BA, Cornell U., 1943, JD, 1949; grad., U.S. Army Command and Gen. Staff Coll., 1961, U.S. Army War Coll., 1970. Bar: N.Y. 1949, D.C. 1956, U.S. Tax Ct. 1950, U.S. Ct. Mil. Appeals 1954, U.S. Supreme Ct. 1954, U.S. Ct. Appeals (D.C. cir.) 1956, (2d cir.) 1963, (3rd cir.) 1965, (4th cir.) 1973, (5th cir.) 1968, (7th cir.) 1973, (9th cir.) 1964, U.S. Temporary Emergency Ct. Appeals 1975, U.S. Dist. Ct. D.C. 1956, U.S. Dist. Ct. (so. and ea. dist.) N.Y. 1963. Pvt. practice Buffalo, Eggertsville, N.Y., 1949-50; examiner/gen. atty. ICC, Washington, 1950-51; atty.-advisor Subversive Activities Control Bd., Washington, 1951-52; trial atty., spl. asst. to atty. gen., asst. U.S. atty. U.S. Dept. Justice, Washington, 1953-62; sr. trial atty., asst. gen. counsel, gen. counsel FTC, Washington, 1962-73; counsel Howrey & Simon, Washington, 1973-76; mng. atty., asst. gen. counsel, corp. counsel Washington Gas Light Co., 1977-87; counsel Conner & Wetterhahn, 1987-90; cons. Fairview, N.C., 1990—; exec. sec. adv. coun. on rules of practice and procedures FTC; mem. Jud. Conf. (D.C. Cir.), 1967—; chmn. legal and regulatory subcom. Solar Energy Com., Am. Gas Assn., Washington, 1978-84; lectr. George Washington U. Law Ctr., 1974; faculty moderator Def. Strategy Seminar Nat. War Coll., 1973; participant spl. programs Indsl. Coll. of Armed Forces, 1962, 69, Armed Forces Staff Coll., 1964. V.p. bd. dirs. Peninsula Symphony Assn., Palos Verdes Peninsula, Calif., 1989-94; bd. dirs. Help-The-Homeless-Help-Themselves, Inc., Palos Verdes Peninsula, 1991-93. 1st lt. U.S. Army, 1943-46, PTO; col. AUS, 1982—. Mem. ABA, Fed. Bar Assn., D.C. Bar Assn., Bar Assn. of D.C., Washington Met. Area Corp. Counsel Assn. (bd. dirs. 1981-84), Cornell Lawyers Club D.C. (pres. 1959-61), The Selden Soc. (London), Biltmore Forest Country Club (Asheville, N.C.), Montreat (N.C.) Scottish Soc., Res. Officers Assn. (life), Mil. Order Carabao, U.S. Army War Coll. Alumni Assn. (life), Leadership Asheville Forum, Downtown Club Asheville (bd. dirs. 1998—), Cornell Alumni Assn., Am. Legion (life), Sigma Chi, Phi Delta Phi. Republican. Episcopalian. Administrative and regulatory, Antitrust, Federal civil litigation. Home and Office: Eagles View 286 Sugar Hollow Rd Fairview NC 28730-9559

**RIBLE, MORTON,** financial services and manufacturing executive; b. Los Angeles, July 30, 1938; s. Ulysses Floyd and Ruth (Morton) R.; m. Ann Martin, June 22, 1963; children: Kimberly, Kristen. AB cum laude, Princeton U., 1961; JD, Stanford U., 1964; MBA, U. So. Calif., 1973. Bar: Calif. 1964. Ptnr. Darling, Mack, Hall & Call, L.A., 1965-69; v.p., gen.

counsel, sec. The Leisure Group Inc., L.A., 1969-76; sr. v.p., gen. counsel, dir. Calif. Life Corp., L.A., 1976-78; v.p., gen. counsel, sec. Pacific S.W. Airlines, San Diego, 1978-85, v.p. human resources and adminstrn., 1985-87; v.p., gen. counsel, sec. PS Group Inc., San Diego, 1978-87; sr. v.p., gen. counsel, chief adminstrv. officer AM Internat., Inc., Chgo., 1988-94; chmn. San Diego Travel Group, Inc., 1994—; dir. Simpact Inc., San Diego, 1995—, chmn., 1995-96; pres., CEO Bus. Backers' Mgmt. Corp., San Diego, 1996—. Bd. dirs. San Diego C. of C., 1983-86, Rancho Santa Fe (Calif.) Cmty. Found., 1981-89, Internat. Forum for Corp. Dirs., 1997—, The Chmn.'s Round Table, 1997—; pres. Palos Verdes (Calif.) Cmty. Arts Assn., 1976-77; trustee Rancho Santa Fe Youth Inc., 1980-82. Fellow ABA; mem. Calif. Bar Assn. Avocations: running, skiing. Address: PO Box 945 Rancho Santa Fe CA 92067-0945

**RICCIARDI, LAWRENCE R.,** lawyer. BA, Fordham U., 1962; JD, Columbia U., 1965; course in executive program, Stamford U., 1978. Bar: N.Y. 1967. Assoc. Gilbert, Segall & Young, 1965-69; counsel Overseas Pvt. Invest Corp/US Dept. State Internat. Devel., 1969-73; internat. counsel Am. Express, 1973-75; gen. counsel Internat. Banking Corp., 1975-77, Travel Related Svcs., 1977-89; exec. v.p., gen. counsel RJR Nabisco, Inc., N.Y.C., 1989-93, pres., 1993-1995; sr. v.p. & gen. council IBM, Armonk, N.Y, 1995—. Mem. Assn. of Bar of City of N.Y. Office: IBM New Orchard Rd Armonk NY 10504*

**RICCIO, FRANK JOSEPH,** lawyer, educator; b. Somerville, Mass.. BS, Boston Coll., 1973; DMD, Boston U., 1977; JD, Suffolk U., 1985. Bar: Mass. 1985, U.S. Dist. Ct. Mass. 1986, U.S. Ct. Appeals (1st cir.) 1986. Dentist Lowell, Mass., 1977-83, Metheun, Mass., 1983-84; assoc. Sugarman & Sugarman, Boston, 1985-87; pvt. practice Braintree, Mass., 1987; clin. instr. oral medicine Harvard U., Boston, 1995—. Dental extern USPHS, 1976. Mem. Am. Assn. Trial Attys., Mass. Bar Assn., Mass. Acad. Trial Attys., Million Dollar Advocates Forum. Personal injury. Office: Law Offices of Frank J Riccio PC 25 Braintree Hill Park Ste 208 Braintree MA 02184-8702

**RICE, BRADLEY HAROLD,** lawyer; b. Genoa, Ohio, Dec. 12, 1957; s. Eugene Reed and Audrey Ann Rice; m. Laura Lynn Hipple, Aug. 7, 1981; children: Justin, Amanda. BA, U. Toledo, 1979; JD, So. Meth. U., 1982. Bar: Tex. 1982, U.S. Dist. Ct. (no. dist.) Tex. 1982, U.S. Dist. Ct. (so. dist.) Tex. 1991, U.S. Dist. Ct. (ea. and we. dists.) Tex. 1992, U.S. Ct. Appeals (5th cir.) 1991, U.S. Supreme Ct. 1991. Lawyer Decker, Jones, McMackin, McClane, Hall & Bates, Ft. Worth, 1982—. Fellow Tex. Bar Found.; mem. Coll. of the State Bar Tex., Tex. Assn. Def. Counsel, Ft. Worth Tarrant County Young Lawyers (pres. 1986). Methodist. General civil litigation, Contracts commercial, Construction. Office: Decker Jones McMackin et al 2500 Bank One Tower 500 Throckmorton St Fort Worth TX 76102-3708

**RICE, CANICE TIMOTHY, JR.,** lawyer; b. St. Louis, Apr. 4, 1950; s. Canice Timothy and Elizabeth Jane (Tobin) R. AB, Holy Cross Coll., 1972; JD, U. Mo., 1976. Bar: Mo. 1976, Ill. 1977, U.S. Dist. Ct. (cen. and so. dists.) Ill. 1977, U.S. Ct. Appeals (7th and 8th cirs.) 1977, U.S. Dist. Ct. (ea. dist.) Mo., US. Ct. Appeals (2d cir.) 1991. Pvt. practice law St. Louis, 1976—. Mem. ATLA, Bar Assn. Met. St. Louis (chair fed. litigation and practice com. 1996-97, co-chair 1997—), Ill. Bar Assn., Mo. Assn. Trial Attys., Lawyers Assn. Federal civil litigation, State civil litigation, Personal injury. Home: 6624 Kingsbury Blvd Saint Louis MO 63130-4605 Office: 408 Olive St Ste 200 Saint Louis MO 63102-2721

**RICE, DARREL ALAN,** lawyer; b. Denver, Jan. 8, 1947; s. Dale Harvey and Dorothy (Enewold) F.; m. Jeffrey Lynn Taylor, May 31, 1970; children: Ashley, Justin, Chandler. BSIE, U. Ark., 1969; JD, So. Meth. U., 1972. Bar: Tex. 1972. Assoc. Butler & Binion, Houston, 1972-75, Winstead, McGuire, Sechrest & Minick, P.C., Dallas, 1975-78; shareholder Winstead Sechrest & Minick, P.C., Dallas, 1978—. Trustee 1st Presbyn. Ch. Found., Dallas, 1982-94; adv. dir. Spl. Camps for Spl. Kids, Dallas, 1987-90, bd. dirs., mem. exec. com., 1990—; bd. dirs. Tex. Bus. Law Found., 1989—, Jubilee Park and Cmty. Ctr. Corp.; bd. dirs., mem. exec. com. Dallas CASA, 1989—; bd. dirs. Dallas Opera, 1997—; mem. exec. bd. So. Meth. U. Law Sch., 1991-97. Mem. ABA, Tex. Bar Assn., State Bar Tex. (chmn. legal opinions com. 1989-92, mem. coun. bus. law sect. 1992-94), Dallas Bar Assn., Tex. Assn. Bank Counsel. General corporate, Securities, Mergers and acquisitions. Office: Winstead Sechrest & Minick PC 5400 Renaissance Tower 1201 Elm St Dallas TX 75270-2199

**RICE, DENIS TIMLIN,** lawyer; b. Milw., July 11, 1932; s. Cyrus Francis and Kathleen (Timlin) R.; children: James Connelly, Tracy Ellen. A.B., Princeton U., 1954; J.D., U. Mich., 1959. Bar: Calif. 1960. Practiced in San Francisco, 1959—; assoc. firm Pillsbury, Madison & Sutro, 1959-61, Howard & Prim, 1961-63; prin. firm Howard, Rice, Nemerovski, Canady, Falk & Rabkin, 1964—; bd. dirs. Gensler & Assocs., Inc., Vanguard Airlines; chmn., mng. com. San Francisco Inst. Fin. Svcs., 1983-92. *Mr. Rice has been listed in "Best Lawyers in America" since 1987. He is Founder and Chair of the Committee on Cyberspace Law of the California Bar Business Law Section. He has also spoken and published extensively on the Internet and Cyber securities.* Councilman, City of Tiburon, Calif., 1968-72, mayor, 1970-72; dir. Marin County Transit Dist., 1970-72, 77-81, chmn., 1979-81; supr. Marin County, 1977-81, chmn., 1979-80; commr. Marin Housing Authority, 1977-81; mem. San Francisco Bay Conservation and Devel. Commn., 1977-83; bd. dirs. Planning and Conservation League, 1981—, Marin Symphony, 1984-92, Marin Theatre Co., 1987-97, Marin Conservation League, 1995—, Digital Village Found., 1995—, pres., 1997—; mem. Met. Transp. Commn., 1980-83; mem. bd. visitors U. Mich. Law Sch. 1st lt. AUS, 1955-57. Recipient Freedom Found. medal, 1956. Fellow Am. Bar Found.; mem. ABA (fed. regulation of securities com., chair Asia-Pacific Bus. Law Com.), State Bar Calif. (editor 1978-80, vice chair sect. bus. law 1978-80, chair com. adminstrn. justice 1997-98, chair com. cyberspace law 1997—), San Francisco Bar Assn., Am. Judicature Soc., Bankers Club, Tiburon Peninsula Club, Nassau Club, Olympic Club, Order of Coif, Phi Beta Kappa, Phi Delta Phi. General civil litigation, General corporate, Securities. Office: 3 Embarcadero Ctr Ste 700 San Francisco CA 94111-4003

**RICE, GEORGE LAWRENCE, III (LARRY RICE),** lawyer; b. Jackson, Tenn., Sept. 24, 1951; s. George Lawrence Jr. and Judith W. (Pierce) R.; m. Joy Gaia, Sept. 14, 1974; children: George Lawrence IV (Nick), Amy Colleen. Student, Oxford U., 1972-73; BA with honors, Rhodes Coll., 1974; JD, U. Memphis, 1976; Nat. Coll. Advocacy, ATLA, 1978. Bar: Tenn. 1977, U.S. Supreme Ct. 1980. Assoc. Rice, Rice, Smith, Bursi, Veazey, Admundsen & Jewell LLPC, 1976-81, ptnr., 1981—, acting sr. ptnr., 1995. Author: Divorce Practice in Tenn., 1987, 2d edit., 1987, Family Law, 1988, Winning for Your Client, 1988, Divorce Practice A to Z, 1989, Divorce Lawyer's Handbook, 1989, (video) Divorce: What You Need to Know When it Happens to You, 1990, Rice's Divorce Practice Manual, 1990, Child Custody in Tennessee, 1992, The Complete Guide to Divorce Practice, 1992, Divorce Trial, Tribulations, Tactics and Triumphs, 1993, The Complete Guide to Divorce Practice, 1993, 2d edit., 1998, Divorce Practice Made Easier, 1993, Divorce Practice, 1994, Visual Persuasion, AIDS 1996 Clients, Prenuptial Agreements, 1996, The Ethical Effective Lawyer: Divorce and Personal Injury, 1996, In Pursuit of the Perfect Personal Injury Practice, 1997, Wiley Family Law Update, Discovery Supplement, 1997, Tennessee Evidence Workshop Handbook, 1997, Hot Topics in Family Law, 1997, Child Custody and Visitation in Tennessee, 1998, Larry Rice on Divorce: How to Run an Efficient and Effective Divorce Practice and Improve Client Satisfaction, 1998, Client Communications, 1998, Post Nuptial Agreement A Proposal for Consideration, 1998, Larry Rice of Divorce, 1998; mem. bd. editors Matrimonial Strategist, 1995-99, Hunt, Hide Shoot--a Guide to Paintball, 1996; contbr. articles to profl. jours. Founding chair Student Legal Assistance Program, 1975, active Supreme Ct. Child Support Guidelines Commn., 1989, Family Law Revision Commn., 1990-91, 98—; mem. Timberwolves Paintball Team; exec. com. Rhodes Coll. Red and Black Soc., 1999. Named One of Best Lawyers in Am., 1993, 94; recipient Excellence in Edn. award PESI, 1997; Outstanding intern supr. Rhodes Coll., 1997-98, Mentor award Amicus Cuni Family Laws Sect. Wilson-Wilson, 1997-98. Mem. ABA (conv. lectr. 1993, 94, 98, 99), ATLA, Tenn. Bar Assn. (chmn., co-founder family law sect. 1987-88), Memphis Bar Assn. (founding chmn. family law sect.), Tenn. Trial Lawyers Assn. (chair-legal asst. adv. com. 1997-98). Family and matrimonial, Personal injury. Office: Rice Rice Smith Bursi et al 44 N 2nd St Fl D10 Memphis TN 38103-2251

**RICE, JAMES BRIGGS, JR.,** lawyer; b. Kansas City, Mo., Dec. 31, 1940; s. James Briggs and Oma J. (Smoyer) R.; m. Carolyn Ryan, Aug. 11, 1962 (div.); children: James Briggs III, Cynthia L.; m. Beverly Sue, Oct. 24, 1980. AB, U. Mo., 1962, JD, 1965. Bar: Mo. 1965, U.S. Dist. Ct. (we. dist.) Mo. 1968. Assoc., Rogers, Field & Gentry, Kansas City, 1967-72; ptnr. Wesner, Wesner & Rice, Sedalia, Mo., 1972-75, Rice & Romines, Sedalia, 1975-80; pvt. practice, Sedalia, 1980—; atty. Sedalia Area Devel. Corp., 1976-79. Chmn., Police Pers. Bd., Sedalia, 1976. Served as capt. U.S. Army, 1965-67; Vietnam. Mem. ABA, Mo. Bar Assn., Pettis County Bar Assn. (pres. 1975), , Am. Judicature Soc., Mo. Assn. Trial Atty.'s, VFW, Vietnam Vets. of Pettis County. Republican. Methodist. Lodges: Kiwanis (pres. 1975), Noon-day Optimist, Masons, Shriners. General practice, Personal injury, Workers' compensation. Home: 1610 W 11th St Sedalia MO 65301-5219 Office: 701 S Ohio Ave Sedalia MO 65301-4415

**RICE, JULIAN CASAVANT,** lawyer; b. Miami, Fla., Dec. 31, 1923; s. Sylvan J. and Maybelle (Casavant) R.; m. Dorothy Mae Haynes, Feb. 14, 1958; children—Scott B., Craig M. (dec.), Julianne C., Linda D., Janette M. Student, U. San Francisco, 1941-43; JD cum laude, Gonzaga U., 1950. Bar: Wash. 1950, Alaska 1959, U.S. Tax Ct. 1988. Pvt. practice law Spokane, 1950-56, Fairbanks, Alaska, 1959—; prin. Law Office Julian C. Rice (and predecessor firms), Fairbanks, 1959; mem. Fairbanks dist. adv. bd. Key Bank, Anchorage; founder, gen. counsel Mt. McKinley Mut. Savs. Bank, Fairbanks, 1965—, chmn. bd., 1979-80; v.p., bd. dirs., gen. counsel Skimmers, Inc., Anchorage, 1966-67; gen. counsel Alaska Carriers Assn., Anchorage, 1960-71, Alaska Transp. Conf., 1960-67. Mayor City of Fairbanks, 1970-72. Served to maj. USNG and USAR, 1943-58. Decorated Bronze Star, Combat Infantryman's Badge. Fellow Am. Bar Found. (life); mem. ABA, Wash. Bar Assn., Alaska Bar Assn., Transp. Lawyers Assn., Spokane Exchange Club (pres. 1956). E-mail: service@ptz.alaska.net. Estate planning, Family and matrimonial, Transportation. Office: PO Box 70516 Fairbanks AK 99707-0516

**RICE, KOLLIN LAWRENCE,** lawyer; b. Painesville, Ohio, Nov. 4, 1970; s. Lawrence and Carolyn R.; m. Manda R., July 3, 1993. BA cum laude, U. Toledo, JD cum laude. Pvt. practice Toledo, Ohio, 1997—. Mem. Toledo Bar Assn. Criminal, Labor, Personal injury. Office: 3730 Lipton Ave Toledo OH 43613

**RICE, NANCY E.,** state supreme court justice; b. Boulder, Colo., June 2, 1950; 1 child. BA cum laude, Tufts U., 1972; JD, U. Utah, 1975. Law clerk U.S. Dist. Ct. of Colo., 1975-76, dep. state pub. defender, appellate divn., 1976-77; asst. U.S. atty. Dist. of Colo., 1977-87; dep. chief civil divn. U.S. Attorney's Office, 1985-87; judge Denver Dist. Ct., 1987-98; apptd. judge Colo. Supreme Ct., 1998—. Contbr. articles to profl. jours. Mem. Denver Bar Assn., Colo. Bar Assn. (bd. govs. 1990-92, exec. coun., 1991-92), Women's Bar Assn., Rhone-Brackett Inn of Ct. (master 1993-97), Women Judges Assn. (co-chair nat. conf. 1990). Office: Colo Supreme Ct Colo State Judicial Bldg 2 E 14th Ave Fl 4 Denver CO 80203-2115*

**RICE, PAUL JACKSON,** lawyer, educator; b. East St. Louis, Ill., July 15, 1938; s. Ray Jackson and Mary Margaret (Campbell) R.; m. Carole Jeanne Valentine, June 6, 1959; children: Rebecca Jeanne Ross, Melissa Ann Hansen, Paul Jackson Jr. BA, U. Mo., 1960, JD, 1962; LLM, Northwestern U., 1970; student, Command and Gen. Staff Coll., 1974-75, Army War Coll., 1982-83. Bar: Mo. 1962, Ill. 1969, U.S. Dist. Ct. (no. dist.) Ill. 1970, U.S. Supreme Ct. 1972, U.S. Ct. Appeals (D.C. cir.) 1991, D.C. 1993. Commd. 1st lt. U.S. Army, 1962, advanced through grades to col., 1980; asst. judge advocate 4th Armored Div., Goeppingen, Fed. Republc Germany, 1966-69; dep. staff judge advocate 1st Cavalry Div., Republic Vietnam, 1970-71; inst., prof. The Judge Adv. Gen. Sch., Charlottesville, Va., 1971-74, commdt., dean, 1985-88; br. chief Gen. Law Br., Pentagon, 1975-78; chief adminstrv. law div. Office Judge Adv. Gen., Pentagon, Washington, 1978-79; staff judge adv. 1st Inf. Div., Ft. Riley, Kans., 1979-82, V Corps U.S. Army, Frankfurt, Fed. Republic Germany, 1983-85, USACAC, Ft. Leavenworth, Kans., 1989-90; faculty Indsl. Coll. Armed Forces, 1988-89; chief counsel Nat. Hwy. Traffic Safety Adminstrn., Washington, 1990-93; ptnr. Arent Fox Kintner Plotkin & Kahn, Washington, 1993—. Contbr. articles to profl. jours. Granted Legal Svc. award State of Hessen, Weisbaden, Fed. Republic Germany, 1985, Cert. Merit U. Mo. Alumni Assn., 1987. Mem. ABA, Mo. Bar Assn., Ctr. For Law and Nat. Security, U. Va. Sch. Law (1985-89), Lion Tamers, Phi Delta Phi. Methodist. Avocations: writing, reading, sports. Transportation, Administrative and regulatory, Product liability. Home: 7835 Vervain Ct Springfield VA 22152-3107 Office: Arent Fox Kintner Plotkin & Kahn 1050 Connecticut Ave NW Ste 500 Washington DC 20036-5339

**RICE, SHAWN G.,** lawyer; b. Milw., Aug. 11, 1968; s. Jeremiah K. and Catherine (Fountain) R.; m. Liesl M. Testwuide, July 6, 1996. BA, Creighton U., 1990; JD, Marquette U., 1993. Bar: Wis. 1993, U.S. Dist. Ct. (ea. dist.) Wis. 1993, U.S. Dist. Ct. (we. dist.) Wis. 1995. Jud. intern Wis. Ct. Appeals, Waukesha, 1992, U.S. Bankruptcy Ct. (ea. dist.) Wis., Milw., 1992-93; assoc. Kohner, Mann & Kailas, S.C., Milw., 1993-97; gen. coun. Schreier Malting Co., Sheboygan, Wis., 1997-98; assoc. Godfrey & Kahn, S.C., Milw., 1998—; pres., gen. coun. Wis. Zeta Alumni Corp., Sigma Phi Epsilon, Marquette U., 1994-98; mng. mem., bd. dirs. T.R. Testwuide & Assocs., Ltd., Sheboygan, 1998—. Law Class of 1948 and Stellman scholar, Marquette U., 1992-93; recipient Alumni of Yr. award Sigma Phi Epsilon Frat., Milw., 1996. Republican. Roman Catholic. Avocations: golf, politics. General corporate, Mergers and acquisitions, Health. Home: 610 Highland Ter Sheboygan WI 53083-4205 Office: Godfrey & Kahn SC 780 N Water St Fl 15 Milwaukee WI 53202-3512

**RICE, THOMAS O'CONNOR,** lawyer. BS, Fordham U., 1966; JD, St. John's U., 1968; LLM, NYU, 1977. Asst. dist. atty. Kings County; assoc. Wingate, Kearney & Cullen, 1970—; adj. assoc. prof. law L.I. U., 1977-78. Mem. Cath. Child Care Soc., Diocese Bklyn., trustee, 1983—, mem. exec. com. wills and estates planning program; mem. coun. regents St. Francis Coll., Bklyn.; trsutee Xavieran H.S., L.I. Philharm. Orch. Mem. N.Y. State Bar Assn. (exec. and jud. selection coms., trusts and estates com., bus. law sect., chair fin. com., treas. 1993—, pres.-elect 1998-99, pres. 1999—), Bklyn. Bar Assn. Banking, General corporate, Contracts commercial. Office: 32 Court St Brooklyn NY 11201 also: 445 Broad Hollow Rd Melville NY 11747

**RICE, VERNON RAWL,** lawyer; b. Garland, Utah, Apr. 4, 1939; s. Rawl S. Rice and Leona Buist; m. Loretta Chambers, Sept. 13, 1962; children: Robyn, Scott, Diane, Susan, Kimberly, Debra. BS in Chemistry, Utah State U., 1963; LLB, George Washington U., 1966. Bar: Va. 1967, U.S. Patent Ct. Patent atty. DuPont Co., Wilmington, Del., 1967-71, sr. supervisory atty., 1971-77, group counsel, 1977-81, managing counsel, 1981-94, assoc. gen. counsel, 1994-98, assoc. gen. counsel, chief intellectual property counsel, 1998—. Mem. Rotary Club Wilmington (chmn. bd. charter sch. Wilmington 1996—). Environmental, Patent. Office: DuPont Co 1007 Market St # 2 Wilmington DE 19898-0001

**RICE, WALTER HERBERT,** federal judge; b. Pitts., May 27, 1937; s. Harry D. and Elizabeth L. (Braemer) R.; m. Bonnie Rice; children: Michael, Hilary, Harry, Courtney Elizabeth. BA, Northwestern U., 1958; JD, MBA, Columbia U., 1962; LLD (hon.), U. Dayton, 1991. Bar: Ohio 1963. Asst. county prosecutor Montgomery County, Ohio, 1964-66; assoc. Gallon & Miller, Dayton, Ohio, 1966-69; 1st asst. Montgomery County Prosecutor's Office, 1969; judge Dayton Mcpl. Ct., 1970-71, Montgomery County Ct. Common Pleas, 1971-80; judge U.S. Dist. Ct. (so. dist.) Ohio, 1980-95, chief judge, 1996—; adj. prof. U. Dayton Law Sch., 1976—, bd. visitors, 1976—; chmn. Montgomery County Supervisory Council on Crime and Deliquency, 1972-74; vice chmn. bd. dirs. Pretrial Release, Inc., 1975-79. Author papers in field. Pres. Dayton Area Coun. on Alcoholism and Drug Abuse, 1971-73; chmn. bd. trustees Stillwater Health Ctr., Dayton, 1976-79, Family Svc. Assn. Dayton, 1978-80; chmn. RTA in 2000 Com., 2003 Com. Designed To Bring Nat. Park to Dayton To Honor Wright Bros. and Birth of Aviation; chmn. Martin Luther King Jr. Meml. Com., Dayton Aviation Heritage Commn.; trustee Montgomery County Vol. Lawyers Project, Miami Valley Cultural Alliance, Sinclair Community Coll. Found., U.S. Air & Trade Show, Barbara Jordan Com. Racial Justice. Recipient Excellent Jud. Service award Ohio Supreme Ct., 1976, 77, Outstanding Jud. Service award, 1973, 74, 76, Man of Yr. award Disting. Service Awards Council, Dayton, 1977, Outstanding Jurist in Ohio award Ohio Acad. Trial Lawyers, 1986, Pub. Ofcl. of Yr. award Ohio region of Nat. Assn. Social Workers, 1992, Humanitarian award NCCJ, 1993, City Mgr.'s Cmty. Svc. award City of Dayton, 1994, Paul Laurence Dunbar Humanitarian award, 1996, Pres.' award NAACP, 1996. Mem. Dayton Bar Assn., Carl D. Kessler Inn of Ct. (founder, former chmn.).

**RICE, WINSTON EDWARD,** lawyer; b. Shreveport, La., Feb. 22, 1946; s. Winston Churchill and Margaret (Coughlin) R.; m. Barbara Reily Gay, Apr. 16, 1977; 1 child, Andrew Hynes; children by previous marriage: Winston Hobson, Christian MacTaggart. Student, Centenary Coll. La., 1967; JD, La. State U., 1971. Bar: La. 1971, Colo. 1990, Tex. 1992. Cons. geologist Gulfport, Miss., 1968-70; ptnr. Phelps, Dunbar, New Orleans, 1971-88; sr. ptnr. Rice, Fowler, New Orleans, Houston, Miami, Fla., London and Bogota, 1988—; instr. law La. State U., Baton Rouge, 1970-71. Assoc. editor La. Law Rev., 1970-71. Mem. La. Bar Assn., Colo. State Bar Assn., Tex. State Bar, New Orleans Bar Assn., Canadian Transp. Lawyers Assn., New Orleans Assn. Def. Counsel, La. Assn. Def. Counsel, Fedn. Ins. and Corporate Counsel, Com. Maritime Internat. (titulary mem.), Maritime Law Assn. U.S. (chmn. subcom. on offshore exploration and devel. 1985-88, vice chmn. com. internat. law of the sea 1988-91, chmn. 1991-95, mem. sec. 1998—), Assn. Average Adjusters U.S., Assn. Average Adjusters (U.K.), Soc. Ins. Trainers and Educators, Ctr. Transp. Law and Policy, Trucking Ind. Defense Assn., Mariners Club (treas. 1974-75, 78-79, sec. 1975-76, v.p. 1976-77, pres. 1977-78), Boston Club, Stratford Club, New Orleans Country Club, Coral Beach and Tennis Club, Order of Coif, Phi Delta Phi, Phi Kappa Phi, Kappa Alpha. Republican. Episcopalian. Admiralty, Insurance, Private international. Office: 201 Saint Charles Ave Ste 3600 New Orleans LA 70170-3600

**RICH, BEN ARTHUR,** lawyer, educator; b. Springfield, Ill., Mar. 27, 1947; s. Ben Morris and Betty Lorraine (Ingalls) R.; m. Caroline Rose Castle, Oct. 4, 1984 (div. Nov. 1988); m. Kathleen Mills, Aug. 17, 1991. Student, U. St. Andrews, Scotland, 1967-68; BA, DePauw U., 1969; JD, Washington U., 1973; PhD, U. Colo., 1995. Bar: Ill. 1973, N.C. 1975, Colo. 1984. Rsch. assoc. U. Ill. Coll. Law, Urbana, 1973-74; staff atty. Nat. Assn. Attys. Gen., Raleigh, N.C., 1974-76; prin. Hollowell, Silverstein, Rich & Brady, Raleigh, 1976-80; dep. commr. N.C. Indsl. Commn., Raleigh, 1980-81; counsel N.C. Meml. Hosp., Chapel Hill, 1981-84; assoc. univ. counsel U. Colo. Health Scis. Ctr., Denver, 1984-86; gen. counsel U. Colo., Boulder, 1986-89, spl. counsel to the regents, 1989-90; asst. clin. prof. U. Colo. Sch. Medicine, 1992-94; asst. prof. U. Colo. Health Scis. Ctr., 1995—, asst. dir. program in healthcare ethics, humanities and law, 1995—; asst. prof. attendent U. Colo. Sch. Medicine, 1986-91, adj. instr. Sch. Law, 1988-95, adj. prof., 1996—; vis. assoc. prof., 1990-91; lectr. U. Denver Coll. Law. Contbr. articles to jours., chpt. to book. Mem. Am. Coll. Legal Medicine (assoc.-in-law 1987), Am. Philos. Assn., Am. Soc. Bioethics and Humanities, Am. Soc. Law, Medicine and Ethics (health law tchrs. sect.), Toastmasters Internat. (pres. Raleigh chpt. 1978). Unitarian. Avocations: sailing, jogging, tennis. Home: 222 S Elm St Denver CO 80246-1133 Office: Univ Colo Health Scis Ctr Box B137 4200 E 9th Ave Denver CO 80220-3700

**RICH, FREDERIC CARL,** lawyer; b. Elizabeth City, N.C., 1956. AB, Princeton U., 1977; JD, U. Va., 1981. Ptnr., head global project fin. group Sullivan & Cromwell, N.Y.C., 1981—; pres. Scenic Hudson Land Trust, Inc.; dir. Lila Acheson and DeWitt Wallace Fund Hudson Highlands, Hudson River Found., Scenic Hudson Inc. Keasby fellow King's Coll., Cambridge, Eng., 1978. Office: Sullivan & Cromwell 125 Broad St Fl 28 New York NY 10004-2489

**RICH, GILES SUTHERLAND,** federal judge; b. Rochester, N.Y., May 30, 1904; s. Giles Willard and Sarah Thompson (Sutherland) R.; m. Gertrude Verity Braun, Jan. 10, 1931 (dec.); 1 child, Verity Sutherland Grinnell (Mrs. John M. Hallinan); m. Helen Gill Field, Oct. 10, 1953. SB, Harvard, 1926; LLB, Columbia, 1929; LLD (hon.), John Marshall Law Sch., Chgo., 1981, George Washington U., 1989, Franklin Pierce Law Ctr., 1993, George Mason U., 1998. Bar: N.Y. 1929, U.S. Patent Office 1934. Pvt. practice N.Y.C., 1929-56; ptnr. specializing patent and trademark law Williams, Rich & Morse, 1937-52, Churchill, Rich, Weymouth & Engel, 1952-56; assoc. judge U.S. Ct. Customs and Patent Appeals, 1956-82; cir. judge U.S. Ct. Appeals (Fed. cir.), 1982—; lectr. patent law Columbia, 1942-56, N.Y. Law Sch., 1952; adj. prof. Georgetown U. Law Sch., 1963-69. Contbr. articles to profl. jours. Recipient Jefferson medal N.J. Patent Law Assn., 1955, Kettering award Patent Trademark and Copyright Inst. George Washington U., 1963, Founder's Day award for disting. govt. svcs., 1970, Freedom Found. award Am. Inst. Chemists, 1967, Eli Whitney award Conn. Patent Law Assn., 1972, Columbia U. Sch. Law medal for Excellence, 1994, Licensing Execs. Soc. of U.S.A. and Can. award, 1994; recognized by Chief Justice as oldest active fed. judge in U.S. history, 1997. Mem. ABA, Assn. of Bar of City of N.Y., Am. Intellectual Property Law Assn., N.Y. Patent Law Assn. (pres. 1950-51), Rochester Patent Law Assn. (hon. life), L.A. Patent Law Assn. (hon.), San Francisco Patent Law Assn. (hon. life). Clubs: Harvard (Washington), Cosmos. Office: US Ct Appeals Fed Cir 717 Madison Pl NW Washington DC 20439-0002 *Died June 9, 1999.*

**RICH, MICHAEL JOSEPH,** lawyer; b. N.Y.C., June 19, 1945; s. Jesse and Phyllis (Sternfeld) R.; m. Linda Christine Kubis, July 19, 1969; children: David Lawrence, Lisa Diane. BA, Gettysburg Coll., 1967; JD, Am. U., 1972. Bar: Del. 1973, U.S. Dist. Ct. Del. 1973, U.S. Supreme Ct. 1976, Pa. 1981. Law clk. Del. Supreme Ct., Georgetown, 1972-73; assoc. Tunnell & Raysor, Georgetown, 1973-76; ptnr. Dunlap, Holland & Rich, P.A., Georgetown, 1976-80; gen. counsel Pearlette Fashions, Inc., Lebanon, Pa., 1981-83; assoc. Morris, Nichols, Arsht & Tunnell, Georgetown, 1983-86, ptnr., 1987-91; ptnr. Twilley, Street, Rich, Braverman & Hindman, P.A., Dover, Del., 1991-95; state solicitor, 1995—; mem. Bd. Bar Examiners, Del., 1986-97, chmn., 1996-97; minority counsel Del. Ho. of Reps., Dover, 1977-79; mem. Del. Gov's Magistrate Commn., 1980, 83-86; sec. Del. Gov's. Jud. Nominating Commn., 1986-89. Bd. dirs. People's Place II, Inc., Milford, Del., 1973-77; pres. Bi-County United Way, Inc., Milford, 1977-78; mem. Partnership Greater Milford Commn., 1987-89, Friends Milford Library. Served to 1st lt. U.S. Army, 1967-69, Vietnam. Dean's fellow Am. U., 1971-72. Mem. ABA, Am. Judicature Soc., Del. Bar Assn. (pres. 1990-91), Sussex County Bar Assn. (pres. 1987-89). Republican. Office: Dept Justice 820 N French St Wilmington DE 19801-3520

**RICH, MICHAEL LOUIS,** lawyer; b. Dover, N.J., Sept. 23, 1959; s. Ronald G. and Florence L. (Ripatrazone) R.; m. Virginia Hourigan, Nov. 16, 19991; 1 child, Michael James. BA magna cum laude, Gettysburg Coll., 1981; JD cum laude, Am. U., 1984. Bar: N.J. 1984, U.S. Supreme Ct. 1989. Assoc. Dillon, Bitar & Luther, Morristown, N.J., 1984-89, ptnr., 1989—; commr. Morris County Housing Authority, Morristown, 1991-97. General civil litigation, Appellate, General corporate. Office: Dillon Bitar & Luther 53 Maple Ave Morristown NJ 07960-5219

**RICH, R(OBERT) BRUCE,** lawyer; b. N.Y.C., Oct. 28, 1949; s. John J. and Sylvia (Berkenblit) R.; m. Melissa Jo Saxe; children—Megan, Alexander. A.B., Dartmouth Coll., 1970; J.D., U. Pa., 1973. Bar: N.Y. 1974, U.S. Dist. Ct. (so. and ea. dists.) N.Y. 1974, U.S. Ct. Appeals (2d cir.) 1980, U.S. Supreme Ct. 1980, U.S. Ct. Appeals (D.C. cir.) 1985. Assoc. firm Weil, Gotshal & Manges, N.Y.C., 1973-81, ptnr., 1981—. Contbg. author: Cultivating the Wasteland: Can Cable Put the Vision Back in TV?, 1983, The International Libel Handbook, 1995. Contbr. articles to profl. jours.; coeditor: Business and Legal Guide to Online-Internet Law, 1997. Mem. ABA (antitrust law sect., forum com. on communications law), Assn. Bar City N.Y. (com. on trade regulation 1982-85, communications law com. 1985-88), Phi Beta Kappa. Antitrust, Federal civil litigation, Trademark and copyright. Office: Weil Gotshal & Manges 767 5th Ave Fl Concl New York NY 10153-0119

**RICH, ROBERT STEPHEN,** lawyer; b. N.Y.C., Apr. 30, 1938; s. Maurice H. and Natalie (Priess) R.; m. Myra N. Lakoff, May 31, 1964; children: David, Rebecca, Sarah. AB, Cornell U., 1959; JD, Yale U., 1963. Bar:

N.Y. 1964, Colo. 1973, U.S. Tax Ct. 1966, U.S. Supreme Ct. 1967, U.S. Ct. Claims 1968, U.S. Dist. Ct. (so. dist.) N.Y. 1965, U.S. Dist. Ct. (ea. dist.) N.Y. 1965, U.S. Dist. Ct. Colo. 1980, U.S. Ct. Appeals (2d cir.) 1964, U.S. Ct. Appeals (10th cir.) 1978; conseil juridique, Paris, 1968. Assoc. Shearman & Sterling, N.Y.C., Paris, London, 1963-72; ptnr. Davis, Graham & Stubbs, Denver, 1973—; adj. faculty U. Denver Law Sch., 1977—; adv. bd. U. Denver Ann. Tax Inst., 1985—; adv. bd. global bus. and culture divsn. U. Denver, 1992—, Denver World Affairs Coun., 1993—; bd. dirs. Clos du Val Wine Co. Ltd., Danskin Cattle Co., Areti Wines, Ltd., Taltarni Vineyards, Christy Sports, Copper Valley Assn., pres.; bd. dirs. several other corps.; mem. Colo. Internat. Trade Adv. Coun., 1985—, tax adv. com. U.S. Senator Hank Brown; mem. Rocky Mountain Dist. Export Coun. U.S. Dept. Commerce, 1993—. Author treatises on internat. taxation; contbr. articles to profl. jours. Bd. dirs. Denver Internat. Film Festival, 1978-79, Alliance Francaise, 1977—; actor, musician N.Y. Shakespeare Festival, 1960; sponsor Am. Tax Policy Inst., 1991—; trustee, sec. Denver Art Mus., 1982—; mem. adv. bd. Denver World Affairs Coun., 1993—, Anschutz Family Found. Capt., AUS, 1959-60. Fellow Am. Coll. Tax Counsel (bd. regents 10th cir. 1992—); mem. ABA, Internat. Bar Assn., Colo. Bar Assn., N.Y. State Bar Assn., Assn. of Bar of City of N.Y., Asia-Pacific Lawyers Assn., Union Internationale des Avocats, Internat. Fiscal Assn. (pres. Rocky Mt. br. 1992—, U.S. regional v.p. 1988—), Japan-Am. Soc. Colo. (bd. dirs. 1989—, pres. 1991-93), So. Boulder Park Ecological Assn. (pres. 1999—), Confrerie des Chevaliers du Tastevin, Rocky Mountain Wine & Food Soc., Meadowood Club, Denver Club, Mile High Club, Cactus Club Denver, Yale Club, Denver Tennis Club. Corporate taxation, Private international, Taxation, general. Office: Cherry Creek Sta PO Box 61429 Denver CO 80206-8429 also: Antelope Co 555 17th St Ste 2400 Denver CO 80202-3941

**RICH, WILLIAM HAGOOD BELLINGER,** lawyer; b. Lexington, Ky., Sept. 9, 1970; s. William H.B. and Sara Rosemary (O'Daniel) R.; m. Stephanie S. Rich. BS in Acctg., U. Ky., 1992; JD, Regent U., 1996. Bar: Ky. 1996, U.S. Dist. Ct. (ea. and we. dists.) Ky. 1997, U.S. Ct. Appeals (6th cir.) 1997. Assoc. Robinette & Assocs., Pikeville, Ky., 1996-97; corp. counsel Lexington-Fayette Urban County Govt., 1997-98; assoc. Andrews & Assocs., Lexington, 1998—. Republican. Consumer commercial, General practice, General civil litigation. Office: Andrews & Assocs PO Box 1179 333 W Vine St 16th Fl Lexington KY 40588-1179

**RICHARD, BARRY,** lawyer. BA, U. Miami, 1964, JD, 1967. Bar: Fla. 1967, N.Y., D.C., U.S. Dist. Ct. (no., mid., and so. dists.) Fla, U.S. Ct. Appeals (5th, 11th, and D.C. cirs.), U.S. Ct. Mil. Appeals, U.S. Supreme Ct. Atty. Judge Advocate Gen.'s Corps USN; pvt. practice Miami; asst. atty. gen., dep. atty. gen. State of Fla.; shareholder Roberts, Baggett, LaFace & Richard, Tallahassee, 1978-91, Greenberg, Traurig, Tallahassee, 1991—; spl. counsel Gov. Fla., Fla. Legis., Fla. Atty. Gen., Fla. Sec. of State, Fla. Ins. Comms. Mem. Fla. Bar Assn. (gen. litig. counsel), Fla. Acad. Trial Lawyers. Office: Greenberg Traurig PA PO Drawer 1838 101 E College Ave Tallahassee FL 32302

**RICHARDS, ALLAN MAX,** lawyer, educator; b. Marshalltown, Iowa, June 11, 1954; s. Eldon M. Richards and Nancy Ann Stellner Mitchell. BA, Luther Coll., Decorah, Iowa, 1976; postgrad., Mankato (Minn.) State U., 1981; JD, Whittier Coll., 1989; LLM, U. Ark., 1991. Bar: Iowa 1990. Account exec. J. Osgood, CPA, Hollywood, Calif., 1986-88; pers./claims dir. Royal Parking, L.A., 1988-89; coll. instr. Buena Vista Coll., Marshalltown, 1991—; sole practitioner of law Cedar Rapids and Tama, Iowa, 1991—; bd. dirs. Cedar Rapids Homebuilder. Mem. state ctrl. com. Dem. Party Iowa, 1994-96, Tama County chair, 1992—. USDA nat. grad. fellow, 1990. Mem. Am. Agrl. Law Assn., Christian Legal Soc., Eagles (pres. 1993-94, 95-97, legal advisor 1993—). Methodist. Avocations: wrestling, stamp collecting. Agriculture, Taxation, general, General practice. Home: 305 S Main Montour IA 50173 Office: 305 2nd St SE Ste 500 Cedar Rapids IA 52401-1703

**RICHARDS, BARBARA L.,** paralegal. Student, Okla. State U. Tech. Inst., 1984-87; paralegal, Ind. U. Purdue U. Indpls., 1993. Adminstrv. asst. Volt Info. Scis., Inc., Indpls., 1987-88; pre-claims rep. United Student Aid Funds, Indpls., 1988-89; mgr. office Asset Conservation Enterprises, Inc., Indpls., 1989-90; paralegal Carmel, Ind., 1991—. Mem. LWV Ind. (health care, domestic violence, juvenile justice coms.), LWV Hamilton County (treas., sec., chairperson domestic violence), Paralegal Soc. Ind. (ethics com.), Hamilton County Paralegal Assn. (treas.), Hamilton County Coalition Against Family Violence, Prevail, Inc. (victim advocate). Home and Office: 934 Shea Ct Apt H Carmel IN 46032-1575

**RICHARDS, CHARLES FRANKLIN, JR.,** lawyer; b. Evergreen Park, Ill., Jan. 30, 1949; s. Charles Franklin and Mary Corinne (Joyce) R.; m. Maureen Patricia Duffy, June 17, 1972 (div. Mar. 1989); m. Deborah Ann Murphy, May 20, 1991; children: Patrick, Corrine, Meghan, Shannon, Nicole. BA, St. Mary's of Minn., 1971; JD, U. Ill., 1974. Bar: Minn. 1974, U.S. Dist. Ct. Minn. 1974, Ariz. 1985, U.S. Dist. Ct. Ariz. 1985, U.S. Ct. Appeals (9th cir.) 1985; cert. civil trial adv. Nat. Bd. Trial Advocacy. Asst. city atty. City of Rochester, Minn., 1974-76; assoc., then ptnr. O'Brien, Ehrick, Wolf, Deaner & Downing, Rochester, 1976-85; assoc., shareholder Gallagher & Kennedy, PA, Phoenix, 1985-94; pvt. practice, Phoenix, 1994—; judge pro tem Ariz. Ct. Appeals, 1994. Contbr. articles to legal pubs. Bd. dirs. St. Mary's Hosp., Rochester, 1983-85; del. Dem. Nat. Conv., San Francisco, 1984. Mem. ABA, ATLA, State Bar Ariz. (exec. coun. trial practice sect. 1994-99, mem. civil jury instrns. com. 1994—, co-editor Trial Practice Newsletter 1990-99), Minn. Bar Assn. Roman Catholic. Avocations: golf, bicycling, hiking, reading, astronomy. General civil litigation, Personal injury, Insurance. Office: 5308 N 12th St Ste 401 Phoenix AZ 85014-2903

**RICHARDS, DAVID ALAN,** lawyer; b. Dayton, Ohio, Sept. 21, 1945; s. Charles Vernon and Betty Ann (Macher) R.; m. Marianne Catherine Del Monaco, June 26, 1971; children: Christopher, Courtney. BA summa cum laude, Yale U., 1967, JD, 1972; MA, Cambridge U., 1969. Bar: N.Y., 1973. Assoc. Paul, Weiss, Rifkind, Wharton & Garrison, N.Y.C., 1972-77, Coudert Bros., N.Y.C., 1977-80, ptnr., 1981-82; ptnr., head real estate group Sidley & Austin, N.Y.C., 1983—; gov. Anglo-Am. Real Property Inst. U.S./U.K., 1983-88, chair, 1993; mem. Chgo. Title N.Y. Realty Adv. Bd., 1992—. Contbr. articles to profl. jours. Trustee Scarsdale Pub. Libr., 1984-89, pres., 1988-89; co-chair N.Y. Lawyers for Clinton/Gore, 1996. Fellow Am. Bar Found.; mem. ABA (real property, probate and trust sect., coun. 1982-88, chair 1991-92), Am. Coll. Real Estate Lawyers (gov. 1987-93), Assn. of Bar of City of N.Y. (real property com. 1978-80, 84-87), Kipling Soc. (N.Am. rep.), Shenorock Shore Club (Rye, N.Y.), The Grolier Club (N.Y.C.). Democrat. United Ch. of Christ. Real property. Home: 18 Forest Ln Scarsdale NY 10583-6464 Office: Sidley & Austin 875 3rd Ave Fl 14 New York NY 10022-6293

**RICHARDS, GATES THORNTON,** lawyer; b. Rochester, N.Y., Aug. 15, 1938; s. C. Elton Richards and Muriel I. Gates; m. Margaret M. Kyte, Oct. 2, 1971; children: Gates, Brady, Mara. BA in English, Va. Mil. Inst., 1961; LLB, U. Ga., 1964. Bar: Ohio 1969, Ky. 1989, U.S. Dist. Ct. (no. dist.) Ky., U.S. Dist. Ct. (so. dist.) Ohio, U.S. Ct. Appeals (6th cir.), U.S. Supreme Ct. Assoc. Beirne and Wirthlin, Cin., 1968-78; pvt. practice law Cin., 1978—; adj. prof. Chase Coll. Law, No. Ky. State U.; lectr./presenter in field. Bd. mem., treas. Vol. Lawyers for the Poor; alumni bd. Summit Country Day Sch.; com. mem. St. Xavier H.S.; devel. com. Ursuline Acad.; active Heritage Soc. U. Ga., Inst. Soc. Va. Mil. Inst.; past bd. mem. May Festival Assn.; charter mem. parents coun. Georgetown U. Coll. Arts and Sci., Washington. Capt. Army Intelligence Security, 1966-68. Fellow Am. Bd. Trial Advs. (life, adv.); mem. ATLA, ABA (litigation com., contbg. editor Federal Rules of Evidence, the Law in the States), Ohio State Bar Assn. (chair negligence law com., chmn. ad hoc product liability com., select com. on the rules of evidence, editor negligence law newsletter), Ohio Acad. Trial Lawyers (governing trustee, treas., sec., v.p. elect, local editor Ohio Trial mag.), Ohio Assn. Civil Trial Attys., Ky. Def. Coun., Ky. Acad. Trial Lawyers, Cin. Bar Assn. (chair joint com. with Acad. Medicine, negligence law com., ethics com., professionalism and grievance com.), Nat. bd. Trial Advocacy (bd. cert. civil trial adv., charter mem. Cin. chpt.), Million Dollar Forum, Assn. Profl. Responsbility Attys., Def. Rsch. Inst., Roscoe Pound Found., Civil Justice Found. (founding sponsor), Soc. Col. Wars, Cin. Country Club, Queen City Club, Cin. Athletic Club, VFW (life), George K. Siemer VFW. General civil litigation. Home: Five Grandin Ln Cincinnati OH 45208 Office: 3807 Carew Tower 441 Vine St Ste 441 Cincinnati OH 45202-2813

**RICHARDS, GERALD THOMAS,** lawyer, consultant, educator; b. Monrovia, Calif., Mar. 17, 1933; s. Louis Jacquelyn Richards and Inez Vivian (Richardson) Hall; children: Patricia M. Richards Grauf, Laura J., Dag Hammarskjold; m. Mary Lou Richards, Dec. 27, 1986. BS magna cum laude, Lafayette Coll., 1957; MS, Purdue U., 1963; JD, Golden Gate U., 1976. Bar: Calif. 1976, U.S. Dist. Ct. (no. dist.) Calif. 1977, U.S. Patent Office 1981, U.S. Ct. Appeals (9th cir.) 1984, U.S. Supreme Ct. 1984. Computational physicist Lawrence Livermore (Calif.) Nat. Lab., 1967-73, planning staff lawyer, 1979, mgr. tech. transfer office, 1980-83, asst. lab. counsel, 1984-93; sole practice, Livermore, 1976-78, Oceanside, Calif., 1994-97; emeritus atty. pro bono participant Calif. State Bar, Concord, 1998—, Contra Costa Sr. Legal Svcs., 1998—; constrn. law instr. Contrs. State License Schs., Van Nuys, Calif., 1998; mem. exec. com., policy advisor Fed. Lab. Consortium for Tech. Transfer, 1980-88; panelist, del. White House Conf. on Productivity, Washington, 1983; del. Nat. Conf. on Tech. and Aging, Wingspread, Wis., 1981. Commr. Housing Authority, City of Livermore, 1977, vice chairperson, 1978, chairperson, 1979; pres. Housing Choices, Inc., Livermore, 1980-84; bd. dirs. Valley Vol. Ctr., Pleasanton, Calif., 1983, pres., 1984-86. Recipient Engring. award Gen. Electric Co., 1956. Maj. U.S. Army, 1959-67. Mem. ABA, Calif. State Bar (conv. alt. del. 1990-92), Alameda County Bar Assn., Eastern Alameda County Bar Assn. (sec. 1978, bd. dirs. 1991-92, chair lawyers referral com. 1992-93), Santa Barbara County Bar Assn., San Diego County Bar Assn., Bar Assn. of Northern San Diego County, San Francisco Bar Assn., Phi Beta Kappa, Tau Beta Pi, Sigma Pi Sigma. General practice, Contracts commercial, Probate. Home: 2505 Whitetail Dr Antioch CA 94509-7744

**RICHARDS, MARTA ALISON,** lawyer; b. Memphis, Mar. 15, 1952; d. Howard Jay and Mary Dean (Nix) Richards; m. Jon Michael Hobson, May 5, 1973 (div. Jan. 1976); m. 2d, Richard Peter Massony, June 16, 1979 (div. Apr. 1988); 1 child, Richard Peter Massony, Jr. Student Vassar Coll., 1969-70; AB cum laude, Princeton U., 1973; JD, George Washington U., 1976. Bar: La. 1976, U.S. Dist. Ct. (ea. dist.) La. 1976, U.S. Ct. of Appeals (5th cir.) 1981, U.S. Supreme Ct. 1988, U.S. Dist. Ct. (mid. dist.) La., 1991. Assoc. Phelps, Dunbar, Marks, Claverie & Sims, New Orleans, 1976-77; assoc. counsel Hibernia Nat. Bank, New Orleans, 1977-78; assoc. Singer, Hutner, Levine, Seeman & Stuart, New Orleans, 1978-80, Jones, Walker, Waechter, Poitevent, Carrere & Denegre, New Orleans, 1980-84; ptnr. Mmahat, Duffy, & Richards, 1984, Montgomery, Barnett, Brown, Read, Hammond & Mintz, 1984-86, Montgomery, Richards & Ballin, 1986-89, Gelpi, Sullivan, Carroll and Laborde, 1989; gen. counsel Maison Blanche Inc., Baton Rouge, 1990-92; gen. counsel La. State Bond Commn., 1992-97; pvt. law practice, cons., 1998—; lectr. paralegal inst. U. New Orleans, 1984-89, adj. prof., 1989. Contbr. articles to legal jours. Treas. alumni coun. Princeton U., 1979-81. Mem. ABA, La. State Bar Assn., New Orleans Bar Assn., Baton Rouge Bar Assn., Nat. Assn. Bond Lawyers, Princeton Alumni Assn. New Orleans (pres. 1982-86). Episcopalian. General corporate, Contracts commercial, Municipal (including bonds). Home and Office: 4075 S Ramsey Dr Baton Rouge LA 70808-1653

**RICHARDS, MAURICE,** lawyer; b. Tremonton, Utah, Apr. 16, 1922; s. Bernard M. and Lula (Winchester) R.; m. Sophie Reed, Sept. 6, 1944 (div. Sept. 1977); children: Sheree, Reed, Brett, Tina, Joanne, J.R., Jeff; m. Suzie Bisel, Oct. 9, 1977. AA, Weber Coll., 1942; BA, BL, U. Utah, 1950, JD, 1967; postgrad., Yale U., 1951. Bar: Utah 1951. Atty. City of Clinton and North Ogden, Utah, 1950; atty. Weber County, Ogden, Utah, 1951-63, commr., 1965-68, pub. defender, chief trial atty., 1972—; ptnr. Richards, Caine & Allen, Ogden, 1953—. Served to capt. U.S. Army, 1943-47; as col. Utah N.G. Decorated D.F.C., Air medal with three bronze oak leaf clusters. Democrat. Mormon. Home: 4152 N 350 W Ogden UT 84414-1181 Office: Richards Caine & Allen 2568 Washington Blvd Ste 6 Ogden UT 84401-3114

**RICHARDS, PAUL A.,** lawyer; b. Oakland, Calif., May 27, 1927; s. Donnell C. and Theresa (Pasquale) R.; m. Ann Morgans, May 20, 1948 (dec. 1984); 1 child: Paul M.; m. Elise Hall, Dec. 6, 1996. Practiced law Reno, Nev., 1953—; settlement judge settle conf. program Supreme Ct. State of Nev., 1998—. General civil litigation, General corporate, Environmental. Office: 248 S Sierra St Reno NV 89501-1908

**RICHARDS, RICHARD,** lawyer, political consultant; b. Ogden, Utah, May 14, 1932; s. Blaine Boyden and Violet Geneva (Williams) R.; m. Frances Annette Bott, Jan. 15, 1954; children: Julie R. Dockter, Richard Albert, Jan R. Stevenson, Amy R. Hartvigsen, Brian Lee. AS, Weber Jr. Coll., Ogden, Utah, 1959; JD, U. Utah, 1962; DHum (hon.), Coll. Boca Raton, Fla., 1982. Journeyman sign painter Richards Sign Co., Ogden, 1958-62; legis. asst. Congressman from Utah, Washington, 1962-63, adminstrv. asst., 1963-64; lawyer Froerer, Parker, Richards, Ogden, 1964-69; polit. dir. Rep. Nat. Com., Washington, 1969-70, dep. chmn., 1971; lawyer Mecham & Richards & Self, Ogden, 1972-80; pres. Commerce Cons. Internat., Washington, also Utah, 1984—; we. Presdl. coord. for Nixon, Rep. Party, Washington, 1972; we. coord. Reagan Campaign, Washington, 1980; headed transition team for Reagan Adminstrn. at Dept. Interior, 1980; Rep. nat. chmn. Rep. Nat. Com., Washington, 1981-83. Utah state chmn. Rep. Party, Salt Lake City, 1965-67, 75-77; mem. Ogden ARts Coun., 1961. 2d lt. U.S. Army, 1952-55. Named Outstanding Young Man, Ogden Jaycees, 1967, State of Utah Jaycees, 1968. Mem. Ogden Rotary Club. Republican. Mormon. Avocations: art--working in oils, water color and acrylics, golf. Home: 5273 Daybreak Dr Ogden UT 84403-4594

**RICHARDS, SUZANNE V.,** lawyer; b. Columbia, S.C., Sept. 7, 1927; d. Raymond E. and Elise C. (Gray) R. AB, George Washington U.,. 1948, JD with distinction, 1957, LLM, 1959. Bar: D.C., 1958. Sole practice, Washington, 1974—; lectr. in family and probate law. Recipient John Bell Larner award George Washington U., 1958; named Woman Lawyer of the Yr., Women's Bar Assn. D.C., 1977. Mem. Bar Assn. D.C. (pres. 1989-90), Women's Bar Assn. (pres. 1977-78), Trial Lawyers Assn. of D.C. (bd. govs. 1978-82, 85—, treas. 1982-85), D.C. Bar, Fed. Bar Assn., Nat. Assn. Women Lawyers, ABA (mem. ho. dels. 1988-90), D.C. Jud. Conf., 1976-99. General practice, Probate, Family and matrimonial. Home: 530 N St SW Washington DC 20024-4546 Office: PO Box 65466 Washington DC 20035-5466

**RICHARDS, THOMAS H.,** lawyer, arbitrator; b. Exeter, N.H., May 29, 1942; s. Frank F. and Ella (Higgins) R.; m. Barbara M. Blackmer, Mar. 23, 1975; children: Daniel, Matthew. BA cum laude, U. N.H., 1964; JD, NYU, 1967. Bar: N.H. 1967, U.S. Dist. Ct. N.H., U.S. Ct. Appeals (1st cir., D.C. cir.) 1987. Assoc. to v.p. Sheehan Phinney Bass & Green, Manchester, N.H., 1967-68, 70—. Mem. N.H. Jud. Coun., Concord, 1988-90; mem. long range planning com. N.H. Supreme Ct., 1989-90, mem. profl. conduct com., 1989-90. Capt. 25th inf. divsn., U.S. Army, 1968-69. Root-Tilden fellow. Fellow Am. Bar Found., Am. Coll. Trial Lawyers, Internat. Soc. Barristers, N.H. Bar Found. (chmn. 1991-92); mem. Manchester Bar Assn. (bd. govs. 1975-80), New Eng. Bar Assn. (bd. govs. 1989-92), N.H. Bar Assn. (bd. govs. 1985-87, pres. 1989-90), Nat. Conf. Bar Pres., Phi Beta Kappa. Avocations: carpentry, collecting and restoring antique tools. Federal civil litigation, Environmental, Product liability. Home: 377 Briar Hill Rd Hopkinton NH 03229-2869 Office: Sheehan Phinney Bass & Green 1000 Elm St Ste 1801 Manchester NH 03101-1792

**RICHARDSON, ARTHUR WILHELM,** lawyer; b. Glendale, Calif., Apr. 3, 1963; s. Douglas Fielding and Leni (Tempelaar-Lietz) R.; m. Noriko Satake, Nov. 14, 1998. AB, Occidental Coll., 1985; student, London Sch. Econs., 1983; JD, Harvard U., 1988. Bar: Calif. 1989. Assoc. Morgan, Lewis and Bockius, L.A., 1988-90; staff lawyer U.S. SEC, L.A., 1990-92, br. chief, 1992-96, sr. counsel, 1996—. Mem. ABA, Calif. Bar Assn., L.A. County Bar Assn., Harvard/Radcliffe Club So. Calif., Town Hall Calif., L.A. World Affairs Coun., Sierra Club, Phi Beta Kappa. Presbyterian. Home: 2615 Canada Blvd Apt 209 Glendale CA 91208-2078 Office: US SEC 5670 Wilshire Blvd Fl 11 Los Angeles CA 90036-5679

**RICHARDSON, BETTINA JIMISE,** lawyer, religious organization administrator; b. Madrid, Sept. 29, 1962; d. James Williams and Betty Joan (Lisle) Abbe; m. Terry Wayne Richardson, Aug. 9, 1980; children: Tiffany Renae, Tara Delyce. AA, Southwestern Assemblies God U., 1981; BA, Calif. State U., 1990; JD, South Tex. Coll., 1992. Asst. dist. atty. Harris County Dist. Atty., Houston, 1993-96; assoc. Fulbright & Jaworski, L.L.P., Dallas, 1996-97; pvt. practice Houston, 1997—; dir. women's ministries South Tex. Dist. Coun. Assemblies God, Houston, 1997—; dir. House Hope Maternity Home, Houston, 1997—. Mem. Tex. State Bar Assn., Dallas Bar Assn., Houston Bar Assn. Republican. Avocations: public speaking, reading, snow skiing, traveling. Office: 1201 Louisiana St Ste 3300 Houston TX 77002-5609

**RICHARDSON, BETTY H.,** prosecutor; b. Oct. 3, 1953. BA, U. Idaho, 1976; JD, Hastings Coll. Law, 1982. Staff aid U.S. Senator Frank Church, 1976-77; teaching asst. Hastings Coll. Law, 1980-82, tchg. asst., 1980-82; legal rsch. asst. criminal divsn. San Francisco Superior Ct., 1982-84; jud. law clk. Chamber of Idaho Supreme Ct. Justice Robert C. Huntley Jr., 1984-86; atty. U.S. Dept. Justice, Boise, Idaho, 1993—; instr. Boise State U., 1987, 89; mem. U.S. Atty. Gen.'s Adv. Com. subcoms. on environ., juvenile justice, civil rights and native Am. issues, others; mem. hon. adv. bd. for Crime Victims Amendment in Idaho, 1994; mem. Dist. of Idaho Judges and Lawyer Reps. com., gender fairness com., Civil Justice Reform Act com. and criminal adv. com. Mem. Idaho Indsl. Commn., 1991-93, chmn., 1993; bd. dirs. Parents and Youth Against Drug Abuse; adv. bd. of the Family and Workplace Consortium. Tony Patino fellow Hastings Coll. Law, 1982. Mem. Idaho State Bar Assn. (Pro Bono Svc. award 1988—, mem. governing coun. Govt. and Pub. Sectors Lawyers sect.), Idaho State Prosecuting Attys. Assn. Office: US Attys Office PO Box 32 Boise ID 83707-0032

**RICHARDSON, DANIEL RALPH,** lawyer; b. Pasadena, Calif., Jan. 18, 1945; s. Ralph Claude and Rosemary Clare (Lowery) R.; m. Virginia Ann Lorton, Sept. 4, 1965; children: Brian Daniel, Neil Ryan. BS, Colo. State U., 1969; MBA, St. Mary's Coll. of Calif., 1977; JD, JFK U., 1992. Bar: Calif. Systems engr. Electronic Data Systems, San Francisco, 1972-73; programmer/analyst Wells Fargo Bank, San Francisco, 1973-74; systems analyst Crown-Zellerbach Corp., San Francisco, 1974; programming mgr. Calif. Dental Svc., San Francisco, 1974-75, Fairchild Camera and Inst., Mountain View, Calif., 1975-77; sr. systems analyst Bechtel Corp., San Francisco, 1977; pres. Richardson Software Cons., Inc., San Francisco, 1977—; pvt. practice San Francisco, 1993—; instr. data processing Diablo Valley Coll., Concord, Calif., 1979-80. Author: (book) System Development Life Cycle, 1976, (computer software) The Richardson Automated Agent, 1985. Asst. scoutmaster Boy Scouts Am., Clayton, Calif., 1983-91; soccer coach Am. Youth Soccer League, Clayton, 1978-83. 1st lt. USAF, 1966-72. Mem. ABA, State Bar Calif., Computer Law Assn., Acad. Profl. Cons. and Advisers (cert. profl. cons.), Assn. Systems Mgrs. Avocations: travel, reading, writing, computer repair. Intellectual property, Computer, General civil litigation. Office: 870 Market St Ste 400 San Francisco CA 94102-3010

**RICHARDSON, DENNIS MICHAEL,** lawyer, educator; b. L.A., July 30, 1949; s. Ralph Lee and Eva Catherine (McGuire) R.; 1 child from previous marriage, Scott Randol; m. Catherine Jean Coyl, July 27, 1973; children: Jennifer Eve, Valerie Jean, Rachel Catherine, Nicole Marie, Mary Rose, Marie Christina, Laura Michelle, Alyssa Rose. BA, Brigham Young U., 1976, JD, 1979. Bar: Oreg. 1979. Owner Dennis Richardson & Assocs., P.C., Central Point, Oreg., 1979-96; pvt. practice law, 1996—; CEO IMPEX U.S. Corp., 1999—; guest lectr. in field. Contbr. articles to profl. jours. Bd. dirs. Oreg. Lung Assn., 1980, Shakespearean Festival, Ashland, 1981, Jackson County Legal Services, 1982; chmn. GOP Oreg. 2d. Congl. Dist., 1996—, treas. GOP Oreg. Exec. Com., 1999—. Served as helicopter pilot U.S. Army, 1969-71, Vietnam. Decorated Vietnamese Cross Gallantry. Republican. E-mail: randa@grrtech.com. Personal injury, Product liability. Office: Dennis Richardson & Assocs PC 55 S 5th St Central Point OR 97502-2474

**RICHARDSON, DONALD V.,** lawyer; b. Florence, S.C., Jan. 14, 1936; s. Donald V. and Margaret R. R.; m. Elizabeth Nelson Richardson, June 21, 1958; children: Anne, Dean, Don. BA, U. S.C, Columbia, LLB. Bar: S.C. 1960, U.S. Cir. Ct. (4th cir.); Internat. Assn. Def. Coun., 1967. Ptnr. Wahley, McCutchen, Blanton & Richardson, Columbia, S.C., 1960-73, Richardson, Plowden, Carpenter & Robinson, Columbia, S.C., 1973—; chmn. Grievence Com., Columbia, S.C., 1980-85; mediation Harvard U., Boston, 1996. Contbr. article to profl. jours. Episcopalean. Alternative dispute resolution, Personal injury, General civil litigation. Home: 4774 Heath Hill Rd Columbia SC 29206-4611 Office: Richardson Plowden Carpenter & Richardson PO Drawer 7788 1600 Marion St Columbia SC 29201-2913

**RICHARDSON, DOUGLAS FIELDING,** lawyer; b. Glendale, Calif., Mar. 17, 1929; s. James D. and Dorothy (Huskins) R.; m. Leni Tempelaar-Lietz, June 26, 1959; children—Arthur Wilhelm, John Douglas. A.B., UCLA, 1950; J.D., Harvard U., 1953. Bar: Calif. 1953. Assoc. O'Melveny & Myers, Los Angeles, 1953-68, ptnr., 1968-86, of counsel, 1986—. Author: (with others) Drafting Agreements for the Sale of Businesses, 1971, Term Loan Handbook, 1983. Bd. govs. Town Hall of Calif., L.A., 1974-87, sec., 1977, v.p., 1978-79, pres., 1984, mem. adv. coun., 1987—, chmn. sect. on legis. and adminstrn. of justice, 1968-70, pres. Town Hall West, 1975, mem. exec. bd., 1973-93; bd. dirs. Hist. Soc. Calif., 1976-82, pres., 1980-81; bd. dirs. Alliance Francaise de Pasadena, 1993-98, treas., 1993-95. Mem. ABA (com. on devels. in bus. financing, com. state regulation of securities, com. corp. law and acctg., com. employee benefits and exec. compensation of sect corp. banking and bus. law.), Calif. Bar Assn., Los Angeles County Bar Assn. (chmn. com. Law Day 1968, exec. com. comml. law sect. 1974-78, exec. com. corp. law sect. 1975-86), Kiwanis, Phi Beta Kappa. Republican. Presbyterian (elder). Clubs: California, Harvard So. Calif. General corporate, Municipal (including bonds), Securities. Home: 1637 Valley View Rd Glendale CA 91202-1340 Office: O'Melveny & Myers 400 S Hope St Los Angeles CA 90071-2899

**RICHARDSON, GARY L.,** lawyer; b. Caddo, Okla., Feb. 5, 1941; s. William and Madeline (Joines) R.; m. Sandra G. Rogers; children: Charles L. Richardson, Chadwick R. Richardson, Chandra A. Ford. BS in Edn., Bethany Nazarene Coll., 1963; JD, S. Tex. Coll. Law, Houston, 1972. Asst. dist. atty. Muskogee County Ct., Muskogee, Okla., 1976-78; pvt. atty. Okla. Bar Assn., Muskogee, 1979-81; U.S. atty. Ea. Dist. Okla., Muskogee, 1982-84; pvt. practice Okla. Bar Assn., Tulsa, 1984—. Author: (tape series) Winning in the Courtroom, 1994. Office: 6555 S Lewis Ave Tulsa OK 74136-1010

**RICHARDSON, HARRISON LAMBERT, JR.,** lawyer; b. Bangor, Maine, Jan. 26, 1930; s. Harrison Lambert and Janet Lovejoy Richardson; m. Elsa Chapin (div.); children: Janet Chapin, Harrison lambert III, James Brooks; m. Melody Ann (div.); m. Catherine Adams, Feb. 23, 1991. BA, U. Maine, 1953; JD, U. Calif., San Francisco, 1959. Bar: U.S. Dist. Ct. (no. dist.) Ill. 1959, Maine, 1963. Assoc. Hinshaw, Culbertson, Moelmann & Hoban, Chgo., 1959-63; ptnr. Robinson, Richardson & Leddy, Portland, Maine, 1963-70, Richardson & Troubh, Portland, 1970-95; sr. ptnr. Richardson, Whitman, Large & Badger, Portland and Bangor, 1995—; trustee U. Maine Sys., Bangor, 1980-92, chair, 1988-90; dir., trustee Am. U. Bulgaria, Blagoevgrad, 1993—. Ho. of reps. Maine Legislature, Augusta, 1965-70, majority leader, 1967-70, Maine senate, 1974-75. Capt. USMC, 1953-56, Korea. Office: Richardson Whitman Large & Badger 465 Congress St Ste 900 Portland ME 04101-3540

**RICHARDSON, JAY,** lawyer; b. Vernal, Utah, June 24, 1957; s. Harold H. and Norma (Anderson) R.; 1 child, Bryce Cameron. BS, Brigham Young U., 1979; JD, Willamette U., 1982. Bar: Oreg. 1982; CPA, Oreg.; CMA. Sr. tax. specialist Peat Marwick Mitchell, Portland, Oreg., 1982-85; assoc. Zalutsky, Klarquist and Johnson, P.C., Portland, 1985-88; tax mgr. Coopers & Lybrand, Portland, 1988-91; mgr. N.W. group Price Waterhouse, Portland, 1991-92; ind. benefits cons., 1993—; vice chmn. Northwest Tax Inst., Portland, 1988. Contbr. articles to profl. jours. and The Oregonian. Mem. planning com. Oreg. Mus. Sci. and Industry, 1985-88. Mem. ABA, AICPA, Oreg. Soc. CPAs (chmn. joint atty. com. 1996—), Nat. Assn. Accts. Republican. Avocations: astronomy, sociobiology, photography, running, golf. Corporate taxation, Pension, profit-sharing, and employee benefits, General corporate. Home and Office: 7100 SW Windemere Loop Portland OR 97225-6168

**RICHARDSON, JOEL GLENN,** lawyer; b. Houston, Jan. 25, 1955; s. Joseph Gerald and June (Sneddon) R. BA in Am. Studies, Southwestern U., Georgetown, Tex., 1976; JD, Regent U., Virginia Beach, Va., 1987, South Tex. Coll. Law, Houston, 1988. Bar: Tex. 1989, U.S. Ct. Appeals (5th cir.) 1991, U.S. Supreme Ct. 1991. Pvt. practice San Antonio. With USMCR, 1978-79; with USNR, 1979-90. Mem. State Bar Tex. Juvenile, General practice, Appellate. Office: PO Box 780254 San Antonio TX 78278-0254

**RICHARDSON, JOHN CARROLL,** lawyer, tax legislative consultant; b. Mobile, Ala., May 3, 1932; s. Robert Felder and Louise (Simmons) R.; m. Cicely Tomlinson, July 27, 1961; children: Nancy Louise, Robert Felder III, Leslie. BA, Tulane U., 1954; LLB cum laude, Harvard U., 1960. Bar: Colo. 1960, N.Y. 1965, D.C. 1972. Assoc. Holland & Hart, Denver, 1960-64; legal v.p. Hoover Worldwide Corp., N.Y.C., 1964-69; v.p., gen. counsel Continental Investment Corp., Boston, 1969; dep. tax legis. counsel U.S. Dept. Treasury, Washington, 1970-71, tax legis. counsel, 1972-73; ptnr. Brown, Wood, Ivey, Mitchell & Petty, N.Y.C., 1973-79, LeBoeuf, Lamb, Leiby & MacRae, N.Y.C., 1979-88, Morgan, Lewis & Bockius, N.Y.C., 1988-93; ret., 1993; tax legis. cons., Orford, N.H., 1993—; adj. prof. Law Sch. Fordham U., 1990-94. Served to lt. comdr. USN, 1954-57. Mem. ABA (chmn. com. adminstrv. practice tax sect. 1984-86), N.Y. State Bar Assn. (exec. com. tax sect. 1975-84), D.C. Bar Assn., Am. Coll. Tax Counsel, N.Y. Athletic Club, Royal Automobile Club. Corporate taxation.

**RICHARDSON, KATHLEEN HARRIS,** lawyer; b. Louisville, Apr. 13, 1948; d. John Manville and Roberta Jane (Burgess) Harris; m. Bruce Warren Richardson, June 17, 1972; children: Suzanne Elizabeth, John Kenneth. BA, U. Wash., 1972; JD, Creighton U., 1977. Bar: Mont. 1977. Assoc. Morrison, Ettien & Barron, Havre, Mont., 1977-79; dep. atty. Hill County, Havre, 1979-82; sole practice, Havre, 1982-85; assoc. Young, Brown & Richardson, Havre, 1986-89, ptnr., 1990-96; gen. counsel Northern Mont. Hosp., 1996—; instr. bus. law Northern Mont. Coll., Havre, 1980. Dir. Human Resources Devel. Coun., Havre, 1978-80, chmn., 1979, 80; dir. Children's House, Havre, 1981-82, sec., 1981-82; dir. Mont. Law Found., 1987—, pres., 1990—; trustee State Bar Mont., 1986—. Named Woman of Year, Beta Sigma Phi, 1981. Mem. ABA, Mont. Bar Assn. (trustee 1986—, pres. health care law sect., 1998-99), 12th Jud. Dist. Bar Assn. (v.p. 1983, treas. 1982, pres. 1984). Republican. Club: Alpha Xi Delta. General civil litigation. Office: 30 13th St Havre MT 59501-5222

**RICHARDSON, PATRICK WILLIAM,** lawyer; b. Huntsville, Ala., Oct. 5, 1925; s. Schuyler Harris and Suzane Agnes (Smith) R.; m. Martha Alice Holliman, Dec. 23, 1949; m. Mary McAlpine Moore, Oct. 9, 1970; children: Schuyler Harris, III, James Holiman. BS, U. Ala., 1946, JD, 1948, LLD (hon.), 1976. Bar: Ala. 1948, U.S. Ct. Appeals (5th cir.) 1955, U.S. Sup. Ct. 1957, U.S. Ct. Appeals (11th cir.) 1981. Assoc. Bell, Richardson, Smith & Callahan, P.A. and predecessors, Huntsville, 1948, ptnr., then pres., 1971—; spl. cir. solicitor 23d Cir. Ala., 1951. Bd. dirs. U. Ala. Huntsville Found., 1962—, pres., 1952-74. Fellow Am. Coll. Trial Lawyers; mem. ABA, Ala. State Bar (pres. 1969-70), Huntsville-Madison County Bar Assn. (pres. 1966-67), Am. Law Inst., Ala. Law Inst. (council), Am. Coll. Mortgage Attys. (regent 1975-77). Democrat. Methodist. Club: Rotary. General civil litigation, Probate, Real property. Office: 116 Jefferson St S Huntsville AL 35801-4818

**RICHARDSON, RALPH HERMAN,** lawyer; b. Detroit, Oct. 12, 1935; s. Ralph Onazime and Lucinda Ollie (Fluence) R.; m. Arvie Y., June 1, 1956 (div. 1961); children: Cassandra, Tanya, Arvie Lynn; m. Julia A., Sept. 16, 1962 (div. 1982); children: Traci, Theron. BA, Wayne State U., 1964, JD, 1970. Bar: Mich., U.S. Ct. Appeals (6th cir.), Supreme Ct. U.S., 1970. Postal transp. clk. U.S. P. O., Detroit, 1954-56; clk. pub. aid worker City Detroit, 1956-65; sr. labor relations rep. Ford Motor Co., Ypsilanti, Mich., 1965-70, wage admins., 1966, labor relations rep., 1967; atty. Brown Grier, Richardson P.C., Detroit, 1970-71; atty Richardson, Grier P.C., Detroit, 1971-73; ptnr. Stone, Richardson P.C., Detroit, 1973—; bd. dirs. Legal Aid, Defender Assn. Detroit, 1985-86; apptd. hon. spl. agt. Office of Investigations, Office Inspector gen., U.S. Printing Office, 1997. Mem. bd. dirs. YMCA Fisher Branch; Boy Scouts Am.; apptd. to Bd. Appeals for Hosp. Bed Reduction by Gov. State of Mich., 1982, apptd. Spl. Asst. Atty. Gen., by Frank J. Kelley, Atty Gen. for the State Mich., May 23, 1984, apptd. to Task Oriented Com. to review the issue in-home child care by Detroit City Council Mem., Maryann Mahaffey. With U.S. Army, 1964. Mem. NAACP (life), Am. Arbitration Assn., Legal Aid Defender Assn., Mich. State Bar Fellows, Optimists, Masons, Shriners (imperial legal advisor, gen. counsel 1994-97, Right Eminent Grand Comdr. of the Knights Templar, State of Mich. 1997—), Phi Alpha Delta, Kappa Alpha Psi. Democrat. General corporate, Criminal, Condemnation. Office: Stone Richardson PC 2910 E Jefferson Ave Detroit MI 48207-4208

**RICHARDSON, ROBERT ALLEN,** lawyer, educator; b. Cleve., Feb. 15, 1939; s. Allen B. and Margaret C. (Thomas) R.; m. Carolyn Eck Richardson, Dec. 9, 1968. BA, Ohio Wesleyan U., 1961; LLB, Harvard U., 1964. Bar: Ohio 1964, Hawaii 1990. Ptnr. Caffee, Halter & Griswold, Cleve., 1968-89; counsel Mancini, Rowland & Welch (formerly Case & Lynch), Maui, Hawaii, 1990—; lectr., affirmative action officer, atty., exec. com. Maui (Hawaii) C.C., 1989—; chmn. gov. fin. dept., chmn. cmty. svc. com., mem. oper. com. Caffee, Halter & Griswold; past lectr. Sch. Law Cleve. State U.; counsel Maui C. of C., Kahului, 1994—. Pres. trustee Big Bros., Big Sisters of Maui, 1990-94; v.p., trustee, pres. Ka Hole A Ke Ole Homeless Resource Ctr., 1990—; trustee Maui Acad. Performing Arts, 1990-97, Maui Symphony, Maul Counseling Svc., 1990-96, Kapalua Music Festival, Friends of Children Advocate Ctr., Legal Aid Soc. Hawaii, pres., 1998-88; v.p., trustee, chmn. devel. com. Cleve. Playhouse, 1984-89; trustee, mem. exec. com., program chmn. Cleve. Coun. World Affairs, 1970-89; past model UN chmn. Cleve. Com. on Fgn. Rels.; trustee, mem. exec. com., budget chmn. Neighborhood Ctrs. Assn., 1980-89. Mem. Rotary Club of Maui, Maui Country Club, Roufant Club (adv.), Cleve. Skating Club. General practice, Education and schools, General corporate. Home: 106 Poohina Rd Kula HI 96790-9724 Office: Mancini Rowland & Welch 33 Lono Ave Kahului HI 96732-1633

**RICHARDSON, WILLIAM WINFREE, III,** lawyer; b. Williamsburg, Va., Aug. 12, 1939; s. William Winfree Jr. and Ellen Blanche (Johnson) R.; m. Constance Diane Niver (div. July 1985); children: Christine Marie, Kenneth Erik. BA, Coll. William and Mary, 1963, Bachelor of Civil Law, 1966, JD, 1967. Bar: Va. 1968. Pvt. practice Providence Forge, Va., 1968—; commr. accounts New Kent Cir. Ct., Providence Forge, 1968—, atty. correctional field unit, 1968—; asst. commr. accounts Charles City Cir. Ct., Providence Forge, 1970—; bd. dirs. C.H. Evelyn Piling Co. Inc., Providence Forge. Advisor Selective Svc. System, New Kent County, Va., 1972. Internat. Order Kings Daus. and Sons scholar, 1957. Mem. ABA, Williamsburg Bar Assn., Va. Trial Lawyers Assn., Am. Judicature Soc., Internat. Platform Assn., Colonial Bar Assn., Phi Alpha Delta, Sigma Pi. Avocations: hist. restoration, collecting antiques. General practice, Probate, Real property. Home: Chelsea Plantation West Point VA 23181 Office: PO Box 127 Providence Forge VA 23140-0127

**RICHDALE, DAVID ALLEN,** lawyer; b. Seattle, Sept. 16, 1937; s. David William and Nan Mary (Morrison) R.; m. Beverly Eastman, Aug. 28, 1959 (div. Oct. 1980); children: Victoria, David; m. Pamela Rae Haester, Apr. 10, 1981. BA in Econs., U. Wash., 1959, JD, 1962. Bar: Wash. 1963. Assoc. Reed McClure Moceri Thown, 1963-68; ptnr. Treece Richdale Malone Corning Abbott, Inc., Seattle, 1969—. Avocations: skiing, fishing. Personal injury, Product liability, Real property. Office: Treece Richdale Malone Corning Abbott Inc 1718 NW 56th St Seattle WA 98107-5227

**RICHELSON, HARVEY,** lawyer, educator; b. N.Y.C., Sept. 5, 1951; s. Nathan Eli and Rose (Michalofsky) R. BS in Bus., U. Ariz., 1973; JD, Southwestern U., L.A., 1977; Diploma in Postgrad. Studies Taxation, U. San Diego, 1986, LLM in Taxation cum laude, 1988. Bar: Calif. 1978, Ariz. 1978, U.S. Dist. Ct. (ctrl. dist.) Calif. 1978, U.S. Tax Ct. 1978, U.S. Dist. Ct. (so. dist.) Calif. 1988, U.S. Ct. Appeals (9th cir.) 1986. Pvt. practice Ventura, Calif., 1978-79; ptnr. Hughes & Richelson, Thousand Oaks, Calif., 1979-84; corp. counsel Consolidated Energy Sys., Inc., Thousand Oaks, 1986-91; pvt. practice Thousand Oaks, 1984—; prof. bus. law Moorpark (Calif.) C.C., 1981-93, Calif. C.C., 1981; pres. Consul-Tax Corp., Inc., 1979-81. Screenwriter (theatrical movie) Punk Vacation, 1986. Exec. dir. Scrub Oaks Self-Help Housing, 1984-86, trustee, 1983-88; mem. citizens adv. com. City of Thousand Oaks, 1984-85. Recipient Am. Jurisprudence Book award, West Pub. Co., 1976. Mem. Calif. State Bar Assn., Ariz. State Bar Assn. Professional liability. Office: 223 E Thousand Oaks Blvd Thousand Oaks CA 91360-5803

**RICHEY, KENT RAMON,** lawyer; b. Churubusco, Ind., Jan. 9, 1960; m. Robin Kamen, Sept. 23, 1989; children: Jacob, Henry. BA, MA, Northwestern U., 1982; JD, Harvard U., 1986. Bar: N.Y. 1987. Law clk. to Judge Walter Mansfield U.S. Ct. Appeals (2d cir.), N.Y.C., 1986-87; assoc. Cravath, Swaine & Moore, N.Y.C., 1987-93, sr. atty., 1993-97; gen. counsel Allegro Resorts Corp., N.Y.C., 1997—. Mem. ABA. Real property, Securities, Mergers and acquisitions. Office: Allegro Resorts Corp care of Westbrook Ptnrs LLC 599 Lexington Ave Rm 3800 New York NY 10022-6030

**RICHICHI, JOSEPH,** lawyer; b. Stamford, Conn., May 12, 1946; s. Dominick and Santa (Palermo) R.; m. Elizabeth Hamill Vance, Aug. 19, 1972; children: Danielle Joie, Jon Joseph. BA, U. Conn., Storrs, 1968; JD, U. Conn., West Hartford, 1972. Bar: Conn. 1973, U.S. Dist. Ct. Conn. 1973, U.S. Dist. Ct. (so. dist., ea. dist.) N.Y. 1980, N.Y. 1990. Assoc. D'Andrea and Selsberg, Stamford, 1972-77; ptnr. Sherman and Richichi, Stamford, 1977—; lectr. bus. law Norwalk C.C., 1980-82; bd. dirs. Stamford Ambulance Corp. With USAR, 1968-74. Mem. ABA, N.Y. State Bar Assn., Conn. Bar Assn., Conn. Real Estate Commn., Stamford Welfare Commn. (sec. 1974-77), Stamford Film Commn., Stamford Regional Bar Assn., U. Conn. Alumni Assn. (pres. So. Conn. chpt. 1975-76), Italian Ctr. Stamford (treas. 1988—). Avocations: travel, photography, golf, tennis, boating. Real property, Land use and zoning (including planning), General practice. Home: 208 Jonathan Dr Stamford CT 06903-1507 Office: Sherman and Richichi 27 5th St Stamford CT 06905-5082

**RICHINS, KENT ALAN,** lawyer; b. Evanston, Wyo., Oct. 13, 1959; s. Robert H. and Betty L. (Evert) R.; m. Rosie Ramos, May 27, 1978; children: Mike, Jason, Jennifer. BS in Psychology, Polit. Sci., Utah State U., 1982; JD, Washburn U., 1985. Bar: Kansas 1985, U.S. Dist. Ct. Kans. 1985, Wyo. 1986, U.S. Dist. Ct. Wyo. 1986, U.S. Tax Ct. 1987. Sole practice Worland, Wyo., 1985—; v.p. Cloud Peak Investment, Inc., Worland, 1983—, also bd. dirs. City atty. City of Worland, 1989—. Mormon. Avocation: oil painting, golf. Criminal, General practice, Real property. Office: 721 Big Horn Ave PO Box 1858 Worland WY 82401-1858

**RICHINS, NORMA JEAN,** judge; b. Lordsburg, N.Mex., Feb. 15, 1928; d. William Henry and Lillie Mae (Hanner) Helbig; m. Clyde L. Richins, July 7, 1957; children: C. Wesley, Donald W. Cert. Tchr., N.Mex. State U., 1946; postgrad., Western N.Mex. U., 1948, Ea. N.Mex. U., 1989. Program asst. U.S. Dept. Agr., Lordsburg, 1956-57; bookkeeper Richins Bros., Inc., Animas, N.Mex., 1957-88; probate judge Hidalgo County Probate Ct., Lordsburg, 1993—; bd. dirs. Commn. on Aging, 1997—. Author (song-music and words) I Don't Need You Anymore, Lover of Mine, 1987, (song-music) Arabian Camel Walk, 1990, (song-music and words) 100 Years of Glory, 1994. Mem. OES, Sage and Sand Ext. Club (pres. 1994-96). Republican. Methodist. Avocations: writing music and words. Home: 309 Cedar Lordsburg NM 88045 Office: Hidalgo County Probate Judge 300 Shakespeare St Lordsburg NM 88045-1939

**RICHMAN, JOEL ESER,** lawyer, mediator, arbitrator; b. Brockton, Mass., Feb. 17, 1947; s. Nathan and Ruth Miriam (Bick) R.; m. Elaine R. Thompson, Aug. 21, 1987; children: Shawn Jonah, Jesse Ray, Eva Rose. BA in Psychology, Grinnell Coll., 1969; JD, Boston U., 1975. Bar: Mass. 1975, U.S. Dist. Ct. Mass. 1977, U.S. Supreme Ct. 1980, U.S. Ct. Appeals (1st cir.) 1982, Hawaii 1985, U.S. Dist. Ct. Hawaii 1987. Law clk. Richman & Perenyi, Brockton, Mass., 1973-75, atty., 1975-77; atty. pvt. practice, Provincetown, Mass., 1977-82, Paia, Hawaii, 1985—; arbitrator Am. Arbitration Assn., Paia, 1992—, mediator, 1994—. Pres. Jewish Congregation Maui (Hawaii), 1989-97, bd. dirs., 1984-89; bd. dirs. Pacific Primate Ctr., 1991—, pres., 1994—. Avocations: windsurfing, youth soccer, T'ai Chi. Real property, Construction, Contracts commercial. Office: PO Box 46 Paia HI 96779-0046

**RICHMAN, MICHAEL PAUL,** lawyer; b. New Rochelle, N.Y., Mar. 12, 1953; m. Elizabeth Fried, July 10, 1977; children: Joseph, Peter. AB, Vassar Coll., 1975; JD, Columbia U., N.Y.C., 1979. Bar: D.C. 1979, U.S. Dist. Ct. D.C. 1980, U.S. Ct. Appeals (D.C. cir.) 1980, N.Y. 1985, U.S. Ct. Appeals (so. and ea. dist.) N.Y. 1985, U.S. Ct. Appeals (2d cir.) 1989, U.S. Ct. Appeals (9th cir.) 1992, U.S. Dist. Ct. Ariz. 1995, U.S. Dist. Ct. (no. dist.) Ill. 1996, U.S. Dist. Ct. (we. dist.) Mich. 1998. Assoc. Covington & Burling, Washington, 1979-84, Shoeman, Marsh, Updike & Welt, N.Y.C., 1984-86, Rosenman & Colin, N.Y.C., 1986-89; assoc. Mayer, Brown & Platt, N.Y.C., 1989-92, partner, 1993—; dir. Am. Bankruptcy Inst., Alexandria, Va., 1996—. Berger award and Harlan Fiske Stone scholar Columbia U. Sch. of Law, N.Y.C., 1978. Mem. ABA, N.Y. State Bar Assn., Assn. of Bar City of N.Y. Avocations: music, running, tennis. Bankruptcy. Home: 17 Eck Pl New Rochelle NY 10804-4605 Office: Mayer Brown & Platt 1675 Broadway Fl 19 New York NY 10019-5820

**RICHMAN, STEPHEN EDWARD,** lawyer; b. Phila., Aug. 3, 1956; s. Sidney and Bernice Audrey (Eubank) R.; m. Cynthia Ann James, Apr. 21, 1989; children: Catherine Therese, Samuel Ethan. BA with high hons., U. Fla., 1978; JD cum laude, Hastings Coll. of Law, 1982. Assoc. O'Connor & Cavanagh, Phoenix, 1982-95, sr. mem., 1995—. Trustee Ariz. Theatre Co., Phoenix, 1993—. Mem. State Bar of Ariz. (sec. constrn. law sect. 1994—), Ariz. Builders Alliance (mem. legal adv. coun. 1990—), Ariz. Contractors Assn. (mem. legal adv. coun. 1990—), Thurston Soc., Phi Beta Kappa. Avocations: running, scuba diving, theatre, computers. Construction, General civil litigation. Office: 1 E Camelback Rd Ste 1100 Phoenix AZ 85012-1656

**RICHMAN, STEPHEN I.,** lawyer; b. Washington, Pa., Mar. 26, 1933; m. Audrey May Gefsky. BS, Northwestern U., 1954; JD, U. Pa., 1957. Bar: Pa. 1958, U.S. Dist. Ct. (we. dist.) Pa. With McCune Greenlee & Richman, 1960-63, Greenlee Richman Derrico & Posa, 1963-84, ptnr. Richman, Smith Law Firm, P.A., Washington, 1985—; bd. dirs. Three Rivers Bank; lectr. U. South Fla. Sch. Medicine, Mine Safe Internat. Chamber of Mines of Western Australia, W.Va. U. Med. Ctr. Grand Rounds, Am. Coll. Chest Physicians, Pa. Thoracic Soc., Am. Thoracic Soc., The Energy Bur., Coll. of Am. Pathologists, Allegheny County Health Dept., APHA, Internat. Assn. Ind. Accident Bds. and Commns., Indsl. Health Found., Nat. Coun. Self-Insurers Assn., Am. Iron and Steel Inst., Can. Thoracic Soc., I.L.O./N.I.O.S.H., Univs. Associated for Rsch. and Edn. in Pathology, Am. Ceramics Soc., Nat. Sand Assn.; mem. adv. com. U.S. Dist. Ct. Western Dist. Pa., 1994—; lectr. in field. Author: Meaning of Impairment and Disability, Chest, 1980, Legal Aspects for the Pathologist, in Pathology of Occupational and Environmental Lung Disease, 1988, A Review of the Medical and Legal Definitions of Related Impairment and Disability, Report to the Department of Labor and the Congress, 1986, Medicolegal Aspects of Asbestos for Pathologists, Arch. Pathology and Laboratory Medicine, 1983, Legal Aspects of Occupational and Environmental Disease, Human Pathology, 1993, Impairment and Disability in Pneumoconiosis, State of the Art Reviews in Occupational Medicine-The Mining Industry, 1993, other publs. and articles; author House Bills 2103 and 885 co-author Act 44 and 57 amending Pa. Workmen's Compensation Act. Mem. legal com. Indsl. Health Found., Pitts.; bd. dirs. Pitts. Opera Soc., 1994—, Pitts. Jewish Fedn., 1994-97; dir. Jewish Family and Children's Svc., Pitts., 1995—. Mem. ABA (former vice chair workers compensation and employers liability law com., toxic and hazardous substance and environ. law com., lectr.), ATLA, Pa. Bar Assn. (former mem. coun. of worker's compensation sect., lectr., contbg. author bar assn. quarterly 1992, 93), Pa. Chamber Bus. and Industry (workers' compensation com., chmn. subcom. on legis. drafting, lectr.). Workers' compensation, Personal injury, Toxic tort. Home: 820 E Beau St Washington PA 15301-2906 Office: Washington Trust Bldg Ste 200 Washington PA 15301

**RICHMAN, THEODORE CHARLES,** lawyer; b. Bklyn., Feb. 24, 1951; s. Albert H. Richman and Miriam Mesnik; m. Johanna Goscinsky, Aug. 29, 1976; children: Michael, Jonelle. BA, Ohio U., 1973; JD, NYU, 1977. Bar: N.Y. 1978, U.S. Dist. Ct. (ea. and so. dists.) N.Y. 1980, U.S. Supreme Ct. 1986. Assoc. Pillerdorf & Nassy, N.Y.C., 1978-79; ptnr. Solomon, Richman, Greenberg, P.C., Lake Success, N.Y., 1980—. Bd. dirs., pres. South Shore Jewish Cmty. Ctr., Oceanside, N.Y., 1987—; bd. dirs., sec. United Jewish Ys of L.I., Plainview, N.Y., 1988—. Mem. ABA, N.Y. State Bar Assn., N.Y. State Trial Lawyers, N.Y. County Bar Assn. Contracts commercial, Construction, General corporate. Office: Solomon Richman Greenberg 3000 Marcus Ave New Hyde Park NY 11042-1012

**RICHMOND, DAVID WALKER,** lawyer; b. Silver Hill, W.Va., Apr. 20, 1914; s. David Walker and Louise (Finlaw) R.; m. Gladys Evelyn Mallard, Dec. 19, 1936; children: David Walker, Nancy L. LL.B., George Washington U., 1937. Bar: D.C. 1936, Ill. 1946, Md. 1950. Partner firm Miller & Chevalier, Washington; lectr. fed. taxation. Contbr. to profl. jours. Served from ensign to lt. comdr. USNR, 1942-46. Decorated Bronze Star; recipient Disting. Alumni Achievement award George Washington U., 1976. Fellow Am. Bar Found., Am. Coll. Trial Lawyers, Am. Coll. Tax Counsel; mem. ABA (chmn. taxation sect. 1955-57, ho. of dels. 1958-60), Am. Law Inst., Lawyers' Club of Washington, Union League (Chgo.), Masons. Republican. Methodist. Corporate taxation, Legislative. Home: 7979 S Tamiami Trl Apt 359 Sarasota FL 34231-6819 Office: 655 15th St NW Washington DC 20005-5701

**RICHMOND, DIANA,** lawyer; b. Milw., July 5, 1946; d. William Lee and Laurel Jean (Bohlmann) Schultz; 1 child, Kavana. BA, U. Chgo., 1967; JD with highest honors, Golden Gate U., 1973. Bar: Calif. 1973, U.S. Dist. Ct. (no. dist.) Calif. 1973. Assoc. Stern, Stotter & O'Brien, San Francisco, 1973-77; sole practice, San Francisco, 1977-80, 83—; ptnr. Richmond & Kadushin, San Francisco, 1981-82; chmn. exec. com. family law sect. Calif. State Bar, 1984-85. Editor: California Marital Termination Settlements, 1988; editl. cons. Calif. Family Law Practice, 1984—; cons. editor: California Family Law Practice and Procedure II, 1995—. Recipient Outstanding Alumna award Golden Gate U. Sch. of Law, 1985. Fellow Am. Acad. Matrimonial Lawyers (pres. No. Calif. chpt. 1988-89), Barrister Club San Francisco (pres. 1979), Bar Assn. San Francisco (bd. dirs. 1983-84, cert. of merit 1977). Democrat. Family and matrimonial, Alternative dispute resolution, Appellate. Office: 180 Sutter St Fl 3 San Francisco CA 94104-4001

**RICHMOND, HAROLD NICHOLAS,** lawyer; b. Elizabeth, N.J., Apr. 5, 1935; s. Benjamin I. and Eleanor (Turbowitz) R.; m. Elaine Zemel, June 16, 1957 (div. Nov. 1972); children: Bonnie J. Ross, Michele Weinfeld; m. Marilyn A. Wenrich, Aug. 26, 1973; children: Eric L., Kacy L. BA, Tulane U., 1957; LLB, NYU, 1961, LLM in Taxation, 1965. Estate tax examiner IRS, Newark, 1963-65; tax mgr. Puder & Puder/Touche Ross & Co., CPAs, Newark, 1965-73; ptnr. Sodowick Richmond & Crecca, Newark, 1973-84; prin. Harold N. Richmond, West Orange, N.J., 1984-86; ptnr. Wallerstein Hauptman & Richmond, West Orange, 1986-91, Hauptman & Richmond, West Orange, 1992—. With U.S. Army, 1959-60. Mem. ABA (tax sect. closely held bus. com., real property and probate sect.), N.J. Bar Assn. (tax, real property and probate sects.), Essex County Bar Assn. (chmn. tax com. 1989, real property and probate sect.). Avocations: running, tennis. Corporate taxation, Estate planning, Taxation, general. Office: Hauptman & Richmond 200 Executive Dr Ste 130 West Orange NJ 07052-3389

**RICHMOND, JAMES G.,** lawyer; b. Sacramento, Feb. 20, 1944; s. James Gibbs and Martha Ellen (Glidden) R.; m. Lois Marie Bennett, Oct. 22, 1988; 1 child, Mark R. BS in Mgmt., Ind. U., 1966, postgrad., 1966-69, JD, 1969. Bar: Ind. 1969, Ill. 1991, U.S. Dist. Ct. (no. dist.) Ind. 1971, U.S. Dist. Ct. (so. dist.) Ind., 1969, U.S. Ct. Appeals (7th cir.) 1975, U.S. Tax Ct. 1980. Spl. agent FBI, 1970-74; spl. agent Criminal Investigation Divsn. IRS, 1974-76; asst. U.S. atty. no. dist. U.S. Atty. Office, Ind., 1976-80; assoc. Galvin, Stalmack & Kirschner, Hammond, Ind., 1980-81; pvt. practice Highland, Ind., 1981-83; ptnr. Goodman, Ball & Van Bokkelen, Highland, Ind., 1983-85; U.S. atty. no. dist. State of Ind., Hammond, 1985-91; spl. counsel to dep. atty. gen. of the U.S. U.S. Dept. Justice, Washington, 1990-91; mng. ptnr. Ungaretti and Harris, Chgo., 1991-92, ptnr., 1995—; exec. v.p., gen. counsel Nat. Health Labs., 1992-95; practitioner in residence Ind. U. Sch. Law, Bloomington, 1989. Minority counsel senate republicans October Surprise Hearings, 1992. Fellow Am. Coll. Trial Lawyers. Republican. Avocation: fishing. Office: Ungaretti & Harris 3500 Three First National Plz Chicago IL 60602-4283

**RICHMOND, TANYA GOFF,** lawyer; b. Camden, Maine, Jan. 22, 1967; d. Frederick George and Patricia Ann Goff; m. Stewart S. Richmond, Jr., June 15, 1991; 1 child, Samuel S. BA, Colby Coll., 1989; JD, Franklin Pierce Law Sch., 1993. Bar: N.H. 1993, U.S. Dist. Ct. N.H. 1993. Atty. Crisp & Assocs., Concord, N.H., 1994—. Contbr. articles to profl. jours. Mem. ABA, ATLA, N.H. Bar Assn. (sec. family law sect. 1995-97), William F. Batchelder Inn Ct. (sec. 1997—). Contracts commercial, Family and matrimonial, Personal injury. Office: Crisp & Assocs 2 Loudon Rd Ste 403 Concord NH 03301-5301

**RICHMOND, WILLIAM PATRICK,** lawyer; b. Cicero, Ill., Apr. 5, 1932; s. Edwin and Mary (Allgier) R.; m. Elizabeth A., Jan. 9, 1954 (div.); children: Stephen, Janet, Timothy; m. Magda, June 8, 1992. AB, Albion Coll., 1954; JD, U. Chgo., 1959. Bar: Ill. 1959, N.Y. 1985. Assoc. Sidley & Austin, Chgo., 1960-67, ptnr., 1967-98, counsel, 1998—. Served with U.S. Army, 1954-56. Fellow Am. Coll. Trial Lawyers; mem. ABA, Soc. Trial Lawyers, Chgo. Bar Assn., Dessert Forest Golf Club (Carefree, Ariz.), Ruth Lake Country Club (Hinsdale, Ill.). Republican. Methodist. Federal civil litigation, State civil litigation, Personal injury. Home: 4 Tartan Ridge Burr Ridge IL 60521-8904 Office: Sidley & Austin 1 First Natl Plz Chicago IL 60603-2003

**RICHTER, DONALD PAUL,** lawyer; b. New Britain, Conn., Feb. 15, 1924; s. Paul John and Helen (Racoske) R.; m. Jane Frances Gumpright, Aug. 10, 1946; children: Christopher Dean, Cynthia Louise. A.B., Bates Coll., 1947; LL.B., Yale U., 1950. Bar: N.Y. 1951, Conn. 1953. Assoc. Winthrop, Stimson, Putnam & Roberts, N.Y.C., 1950-52; ptnr. Murtha, Cullina, Richter and Pinney, Hartford, Conn., 1954-94, counsel, 1994—. Trustee Bates Coll., 1962-94, Manchester (Conn.) Meml. Hosp., 1963-94, Hartford Sem., 1973-85; trustee Suffield Acad., 1974—, pres., 1982-89; bd. dirs. Met. YMCA Greater Hartford, 1970-94, pres., 1976-81, trustee, 1994—; mem. nat. coun. YMCA, 1978-82; bd. dirs. Church Homes, 1967-81; trustee, v.p., Silver Bay Assn., 1971-96. With USNR, 1943-46. Fellow Am. Coll. Trust and Estate Counsel; mem. ABA, Conn. Bar Assn., Univ. Club, Hartford Club, 20th Century Club, Rotary (Paul Harris fellow 1996), Phi Beta Kappa, Delta Sigma Rho. Congregationalist. General corporate, Estate planning. Home: 140 Boulder Rd Manchester CT 06040-4508 Office: Murtha Cullina Richter & Pinney City Place I 185 Asylum St & 29th St Hartford CT 06103-3469

**RICHTER, LISA SHERRILL,** lawyer; b. Moon Twp., Pa., Aug. 3, 1969; d. Larrymore and Kay Johnson Sherrill; m. Timothy J. Richter, Oct. 17, 1998. BA with honors, U. Tenn., 1990, JD, 1994. Bar: Tenn. 1994, U.S. Dist. Ct. (mid. dist.) Tenn. 1995. Assoc. Larry D. Wilks, Springfield, Tenn., 1994—. Bd. dirs. Am. Heart Assn. Mem. Tenn. Bar Assn., Robertson County Bar Assn. Democrat. Methodist. Avocation: football. Family and matrimonial, General practice. Office: Larry D Wilks Law Office 509 W Court Sq Springfield TN 37172-2413

**RICHTER, PAUL DAVID,** lawyer; b. Champaign, Ill., Nov. 21, 1969; s. David Jerome and Bonnie Lee (Hess) R.; m. Julie Anne Guevara, Mar. 1, 1997. BA in Liberal Arts and Scis., U. Ill., 1992; JD, DePaul U., 1996. Bar: Ill. 1996. Assoc. Rapoport Law Offices, P.C., Chgo., 1996—. Mem. ATLA, Lawyers-Pilots Bar Assn., Ill. Trial Lawyers Assn. Avocations: pvt. pilot, jet skiing, snow skiing, hiking. General civil litigation, Personal injury, Aviation. Home: 1607 Reading Cir Carpentersville IL 60110-3106 Office: Rapoport Law Offices PC 10275 W Higgins Rd Ste 270 Rosemont IL 60018-3884

**RICHTER, TOBIN MARAIS,** lawyer; b. Washington, Dec. 31, 1944; s. Vivian Craig and Leora Chapelle (Aultman) R.; m. Elizabeth Mills Dunlop, July 11, 1970; children: Ian, Lauren. B in City Planning, U. Va., 1967, JD, 1973. Bar: Ill. 1973, U.S. Dist. Ct. (no. dist.) Ill. 1973, U.S. Ct. Appeals (7th cir.) 1977, U.S. Supreme Ct. 1979, U.S. Dist. Ct. (ea. dist.) Wis. 1987. Assoc. Ross & Hardies, Chgo., 1973-80, ptnr., 1981-84; ptnr. Spindell, Kemp & Kimball, Chgo., 1984-89; pvt. practice Chgo., 1989—; adj. instr. U. Wis., Osh Kosh, 1976. Co-author: Federal Land Use Regulation, 1977; contbr. articles to profl. jours. Legal counsel 44th Ward Community Zoning Bd., Chgo., 1980; v.p., Aux. Bd. Chgo. Architecture Found., 1983; pres., bd. dirs. Landmarks Preservation Council Ill., Chgo., 1986. 1st lt. U.S. Army, 1968-70, Vietnam. Mem. ABA, Ill. Bar Assn. (judge Lincoln Writing awards contest 1982), Chgo. Bar Assn., Soc. Am. Mil. Engrs. (v.p. 1980, 84, 86), Am. Planning Assn., Econ. Club (Chgo.), Dunham Woods Club (Wayne, Ill.). Avocations: tennis, pottery. Federal civil litigation, State civil litigation, Real property. Office: 33 N Dearborn St Ste 1401 Chicago IL 60602-3107

**RICKERD, DONALD SHERIDAN,** foundation executive; b. Smiths Falls, Ont., Can., Nov. 8, 1931; s. Harry M. and Evaline Mildred (Sheridan) R.; m. Julie Rekai, Dec. 14, 1968; 1 child, Christopher. Student, St. Andrews U., Scotland, 1951-52; BA, Queen's U., Can., 1953; LLD, Queen's U., 1985; BA (Rotary Found. fellow), Balliol Coll., Oxford U., Eng., 1955; MA, Oxford U., Eng., 1963; DCL, Mount Allison U., Can., 1985; LLD, Trent U., Can., 1986; LLB, York U., Can., 1991. Bar: Ont. 1959; apptd. Queen's Counsel, 1978. Assoc. Fasken & Calvin, Toronto, 1957-61; registrar, lectr. history, asst. prof. law Faculty of Adminstrv. Studies York U., Toronto, 1961-68; pres. Donner Can. Found., Toronto, 1968-89, W.H. Donner Found., Inc., N.Y.C., 1971-87, Max Bell Found., Toronto, 1989-97, Zavikon Found., 1997—; chmn. bd. dirs. Draeger Can. Ltd.; former bd. dirs. ICWI Found., Kingston, Jamaica. Former chmn. Coun. Ontario Coll. Art, Toronto; past chmn. Ctrl. Hosp., 1993-96; mem. Royal Commn. concerning activities of Royal Canadian Mounted Police, 1977-81; former bd. govs. Upper Can. Coll., Toronto, trustee, vice chmn. bd. trustees, Queen's U.; former mem. bd. regents Mt. Allison U; chair, pres. Wellesley Ctrl. Hosp., Toronto. Decorated Order of Can. Mem. County of York Law Assn., Toronto Lawyers Club, Bd. Trade Met. Toronto, Univ. Club.

**RICKS, J. BRENT,** lawyer, book publisher; b. Chgo., Nov. 11, 1949; s. Paul Brent R. and Marthe (Forte) Tremaine; m. Louise Perry (div. 1988); 1 child, Benjamin Brent; m. Valerie Swearingen, July 28, 1957; 1 child, Abigail Dawn. BA, Johns Hopkins U., 1971; JD, U. N.Mex., 1974. Bar: N.Mex. 1974, U.S. Dist. Ct. N.Mex. 1974, U.S. Supreme Ct. 1979. Pvt. practice atty. Albuquerque, 1974—; gallery dir. Adobe Gallery, Albuquerque, 1984-87; book pub. Avanyu Pub. Inc., Albuquerque, 1984—; mft. Southwest Composites Inc., Albuquerque, 1989-93. Magistrate judge cand. Dem. Party, Albuquerque, 1978. Democrat. Avocation: whitewater rafting. Personal injury, Real property, Alternative dispute resolution. Home: 2835 Trellis Dr NW Albuquerque NM 87107-2933 Office: PO Box 27134 Albuquerque NM 87125-7134

**RICKS, JOYCIA CAMILLA,** investigator, lawyer; b. Atlanta, Feb. 17, 1949; d. George Palmer and Johnnie Mae (Ricks) Redd. BBA, Albany State Coll., 1971; MS, Ga. State U., 1977; JD, Woodrow Wilson Coll. Law, Atlanta, 1979, LLM, 1987. Bar: Ga. 1979, U.S. Dist. Ct. (no. dist.) Ga. 1979, U.S. Ct. Appeals (5th cir.) 1979. Acctg. clk. Gulf Oil Corp., Atlanta, 1971; clk. EEOC, Atlanta, 1971-73, paralegal specialist, 1973-79, investigator, 1979-91; gen. counsel Albany State Coll. Alumni Assn., 1986-90. Mem. NAACP, Atlanta, 1983—. Recipient Presdl. citation award Equal Opportunity in Higher Edn., Washington, 1981, Spl. Achievement award EEOC, Atlanta, 1982-84, 86-89, Employee of Yr., 1997. Mem. ABA, Atlanta Bar Assn., Ga. Assn. Black Women Attys., Albany State Coll. Alumni Assn. (pres. Atlanta chpt. 1983-85, gen. counsel 1986-90), ATLA, Ga. State U. Alumni Assn., Woodrow Wilson Coll. Law Alumni Assn., Women of the Ch. Presbyn. (hon. life), Am. Bus. Women's Assn. (Woman of Yr., Tara chpt. 1985, 91), Spreading Oak Cmty. Club. Democrat. Presbyterian. Office: EEOC 100 Alabama St Ste 4R30 Atlanta GA 30303

**RIDDICK, WINSTON WADE, SR.,** lawyer; b. Crowley, La., Feb. 11, 1941; s. Hebert Hobson and Elizabeth (Wade) R.; m. Patricia Ann Turner, Dec. 25, 1961;1 child, Winston Wade. BA, U. Southwestern La., 1962; MA, U. N.C., 1963; PhD, Columbia U., 1965; JD, La. State U., 1973. Bar: La. 1974, U.S. Dist. Ct. (so., mid. and we. dists.) La., U.S. Ct. Appeals (5th cir.), U.S. Supreme Court. Asst. prof. gov., dir. Inst. Gov. Research, La. State U., Baton Rouge, 1966-67; dir. La. Higher Edn. Facilities Commn., Baton Rouge, 1967-72; exec. asst. state supt. La. Dept. Edn., Baton Rouge, 1972-73; law ptnr. Riddick & Riddick, Baton Rouge, 1973—; asst. commnr., gen. counsel La. Dept. Agr., Baton Rouge, 1981-82; cons. Riddick & Assoc., Baton Rouge, 1973—; part-time law faculty mem. So. Univ. Law Ctr., Baton Rouge, 1974-95; assoc. prof. SULC, 1995—, exec. asst. atty. gen. State of La., 1987-91. Spl. asst. to Gov. John J. McKeithen on Adv. Ctr. for Edn. in Politics Fellowship, 1966-67; state campaign mgr. Gillis W. Long for Gov., Baton Rouge, 1971; mem. East Baton Rouge Parish Dem. Exec. Com., 1981-84. Mem. La. Trial Lawyers Assn. (bd. govs. 1978-80), real estate investor and property mgr., 1975—. Presbyterian. Health, Constitutional, Insurance. Office: Riddick & Riddick 1563 Oakley Dr Baton Rouge LA 70806-8622

**RIDDLE, CHARLES ADDISON, III,** state legislator, lawyer; b. Marksville, La., June 8, 1955; s. Charles Addison Jr. and Alma Rita (Gremillion) R.; m. Margaret Susan Noone, Mar. 24, 1978; children: Charles Addison IV, John H., Michael J. BA, La. State U., 1976, JD, 1980. Bar: La. 1980, U.S. Dist. Ct. (mid. and we. dists.) La. 1983, U.S. Ct. Appeals (5th cir.) 1988, U.S. Supreme Ct. 1991, U.S. Ct. Vets. Appeals 1994. Assoc. Riddle & Bennett, Marksville, 1980; pvt. practice Marksville, 1981—; mem. La. Ho. of Reps., Baton Rouge, 1992—; reelected La. House of Reps., Baton Rouge, 1995-. Elected La. State Dem. Cen. com., Avoyelles Parish, 1983-87, Parish Exec. Demo. Com. 1987-91. Mem. Avoyelles Bar Assn. (pres. 1987-88), Bunkie Rotary (bd. dirs.), Marksville Lions, Marksville C. of C. (pres. 1988-92). E-mail: criddle777@aol.com. Office: 208 E Mark St Marksville LA 71351-2416

**RIDDLE, DON RAMON,** lawyer; b. Abilene, Tex., Dec. 28, 1937; s. Glen Boyce and Pauline (Price) R.; m. Jenny Lu Brunton, Apr. 27, 1963; children: Stacy, Todd. BA, Baylor U., 1960; LLB cum laude, U. Houston, 1966. Assoc. Brown Kronzer Abraham Watkins & Steely, Houston, 1966-69, ptnr., 1969-74; ptnr. Riddle, Murphrey, O'Quinn & Cannon, Houston, 1974-79; prin. Riddle & Assocs., Houston, 1979-94; ptnr. Riddle & Baumgartner, Houston, 1994—; mem. Tex. State Bar grievance Com., Houston, 1975-78. Sgt. USMC, 1960-66. Mem. Tex. Trial Lawyers Assn. (dir. 1971-73). Personal injury. Office: Riddle & Baumgartner 6810 Fm 1960 Rd W # 200 Houston TX 77069-3804

**RIDDLE, MICHAEL LEE,** lawyer; b. Oct. 7, 1946; s. Joy Lee and Francis Irene (Brandes) R.; m. Suzan Ellen Shaw, May 25, 1969 (div.); m. Carol Jackson, Aug. 13, 1977; 1 child, Robert Andrew. BA, Tex. Tech U., 1969, JD with honors, 1972. Bar: Tex. 1972, U.S. Dist. Ct. (no. dist.) Tex. 1972, U.S. Ct. Appeals (5th cir.) Tex. 1972. Assoc. Geary Brice Barron & Stahl, Dallas, 1972-75; ptnr. Baker Glast Riddle Tuttle & Elliott, Dallas, 1975-80; ptnr., mng. ptnr. Middleburg, Riddle & Gianna, 1980—; chmn. bd. dirs. Provident Bancorp Tex., 1987-90. bd. dirs. U.S.A. Film Festival, pres., 1984-86. Mem. ABA, Tex. Bar Assn., Dallas Bar Assn., Coll. of State Bar of Tex., Lakewood Country Club, Crescent Club. Democrat. Lutheran. Banking, Real property.

**RIDEOUT, JOI HUCKABY,** lawyer; b. Nashville, Nov. 9, 1960; d. Melvyn Everett and Ellena Stone Huckaby; m. Rex Kendall Rideout, Oct. 24, 1992. BA, Wellesley Coll., 1982; JD, Harvard U., 1985. Bar: N.Y. Assoc. corp. fin. Cahill Gordon & Reindel, N.Y.C., 1985-88; assoc. entertainment Beldock Levine & Hoffman, N.Y.C., 1988-90; dir. bus. legal affairs Dick Scott Entertainment, N.Y.C., 1990-93, v.p., gen. counsel, 1990-93; ptnr. Rideout & Green, N.Y.C., 1993-96; dir. bus. affairs Waldrision Enterprises, Inc., N.Y.C., 1996—; pres., bd. dirs. Women Make Movies, Inc., N.Y.C., 1989-95; v.p., bd. dirs. Black Entertainment and Sports Lawyers, 1996—; instr. Practising Law Inst., N.Y.C., 1995—. Mem. Bar of the City of N.Y. Avocations: tennis, dance, filmmaking, crafts. Entertainment, Intellectual property. Home: 534 Harmon Cove Tower Secaucus NJ 07094-1754

**RIDER, BRIAN CLAYTON,** lawyer; b. San Antonio, Oct. 8, 1948; s. Ralph W. and Emmie Rider; m. Patsy Anne Ruppert, Dec. 27, 1970; children: Christopher, David, James, Andrew. BA, Rice U., 1969; JD, U. Tex., 1972. Bar: Tex. 1972. Assoc. then ptnr. Dow, Cogburn & Friedman, Houston, 1972-83; ptnr. Brown, McCarroll & Oaks Hartline, Austin, Tex., 1983-96; adj. prof. law U. Tex., 1997—. Contbr. articles to profl. jours.; lectr. in field. Mem. Am. Coll. Real Estate Lawyers, Travis County Bar Assn. (bd. dirs. 1986-88, chmn. Travis County real estate sect. 1986-88), State Bar of Tex. (coun. real estate and probate sect. 1992-96). Real property, Finance, Environmental. Home: 2906 Hatley Dr Austin TX 78746-4613 Office: 1300 S Mopac Austin TX 78746

**RIDER, MARK MCMASTER,** lawyer; b. Oneonta, N.Y., Dec. 21, 1947; s. Charles Colburn and Eleanor (McMaster) R.; m. Mary Ellen Hammel, Dec. 29, 1969; children: Heather, Tara, Robert. BA, U. Rochester, 1969; JD, Union U., Albany, N.Y., 1975. Bar: N.Y. 1976, U.S. Dist. Ct. (no. dist.) N.Y. 1976. County atty. Saratoga County, Ballston Spa, N.Y.; mem. N.Y. State Com. on Profl. Stds., Albany, 1995—. Chmn. Ballston Spa Ednl. Found., 1996-98. Sgt. U.S. Army, 1969-71. Recipient Disting. Svc. award Legal Aid Soc., Albany, 1992. Mem. N.Y. State Bar Assn. (nominating com. 1995—, President's Pro Bono award 1996), N.Y. State Bar Assn. Found., Saratoga County Bar Assn. (sec., treas. v.p., pres. 1991-95). Republican. Avocations: golf, tennis, racquetball, genealogy, refinishing. Office: Saratoga County Atty's Off 40 Mcmasters St Ballston Spa NY 12020-1980

**RIDLEY, CLARENCE HAVERTY,** lawyer; b. Atlanta, June 3, 1942; s. Frank Morris Jr. and Clare (Haverty) R.; m. Eleanor Horsey, Aug. 22, 1969; children: Augusta Morgan, Clare Haverty. BA, Yale U., 1964; MBA, Harvard U., 1966; JD, U. Va., 1971. Bar: Ga. 1971. Assoc. King & Spalding, Atlanta, 1971-77, ptnr., 1977—; bd. dirs. Haverty Furniture Cos., Inc., mem. exec. com., 1992—, vice chmn. bd. dirs., 1996—. Author: Computer Software Agreements, 1987, 2d edit., 1993; exec. editor Va. Law Rev., 1970-71. Chmn. St. Joseph's Hosp. Found., Atlanta, 1986-89; trustee St. Joseph's Health Svcs., 1987—, chmn. fin. com., 1992-96, vice chmn. bd. trustees, 1996—. Roman Catholic. Home: 2982 Habersham Rd NW Atlanta GA 30305-2854 Office: King & Spalding 191 Peachtree St SW Atlanta GA 30303-3637

**RIEGER, MICHAEL IRA,** lawyer; b. N.Y.C., Oct. 19, 1952; s. Joseph and Adrienne R. BA in Sociology, SUNY, Buffalo, 1973; JD, George Mason U., 1977. Bar: Va. 1977. Pvt. practice Fairfax, Va., 1977—; lectr. in field. Mem. Va. State Bar Assn., Fairfax Bar Assn. co-chmn. com. law related edn. 1996-97, co-chmn. com. continuing legal edn. 1995-96, chmn. subcom. gen. dist. ct. criminal law 1993-95, com. mem.). Criminal. Office: 3975 University Dr Ste 330 Fairfax VA 22030-2520

**RIEGER, MITCHELL SHERIDAN,** lawyer; b. Chgo., Sept. 5, 1922; s. Louis and Evelyn (Sampson) R.; m. Rena White Abelmann, May 17, 1949 (div. 1957); 1 child, Karen Gross Cooper; m. Nancy Horner, May 30, 1961 (div. 1972); stepchildren: Jill Levi, Linda Hanan, Susan Perlstein, James Geoffrey Felsenthal; m. Pearl Handelsman, June 10, 1973; stepchildren: Steven Newman, Mary Ann Malarkey, Nancy Halbeck. *Wife, Pearl H. Rieger, born in Chicago (1928), received a B.A. degree in Speech and Language Pathology from the University of Michigan (1948) and an M.A. degree in Educational Psychology from the University of Chicago (1974). Since then she has been in private practice as a psychoeducational diagnostician. In January, 1997 she became a consultant at the Rush Neurobehavioral Center, Skokie, Illinois. In 1997, the Center established the Pearl H. Rieger award to honor a pioneer in the field of neurobehavioral disorders in children. On November 13, 1997 Pearl Rieger became the first recipient of the award named after her.* AB, Northwestern U., 1944; JD, Harvard U., 1949. Bar: Ill. 1950, U.S. Dist. Ct. (no. dist.) Ill. 1950, U.S. Supreme Ct. 1953, U.S. Ct. Mil. Appeals 1953, U.S. Ct. Appeals (7th cir.) 1954. Legal asst. Rieger & Rieger, Chgo., 1949-50, assoc., 1950-54; asst. U.S. atty. No. Dist Ill., Chgo., 1954-60; 1st asst. No. Dist Ill., 1958-60; assoc. gen. counsel SEC, Washington, 1960-61; ptnr. Schiff Hardin & Waite, Chgo., 1961—, sr. counsel, 1998—; instr. John Marshall Law Sch. Chgo., 1952-54. *Notable cases: before federal court juries (Chicago) for U.S. convictions in 1st vote fraud trial (U.S. v Louis Nathan, 1955), and last income tax evasion trial involving post WWII sale of new automobiles for unreported amounts exceeding price control (U.S. v. Leonard Bernard, 1959); for SEC first judicial opinion interpreting SEC's then Statement of Policy about literature used in mutual fund shares sales (Boruski v. SEC, U.S. Court Appeals, 2nd Circuit, 1961); successfully represented 35 investment banking firms in one of 1st class action jury trials involving legality of initial public offering (Bisgeier v. Fotomat Corp., (federal court, San Diego, 1976).* Contbr. articles to profl. jours. Active Chgo. Crime Commn., bd. dirs., 1998—; pres. Park View Home for Aged, 1969-71; Rep. precinct committeeman, Highland Park, Ill., 1964-68; bd. dirs. Spertus Mus. Judaica, 1987-91, vis. com., 1991—. Served to lt. (j.g.) USNR, 1943-46, PTO. Fellow Am. Coll. Trial Lawyers; mem. ABA, FBA (pres. Chgo. chpt. 1959-60, nat. v.p. 1960-61), Chgo. Bar Assn., Ill. Bar Assn., Am. Judicature Soc., 7th Circuit Bar Assn., Standard Club, Law Club Chgo., Vail Racquet Club, Phi Beta Kappa. Jewish. Avocations: photography, skiing, sailing. Professional liability. Home: 4950 S Chicago Beach Dr Chicago IL 60615-3207 Office: Schiff Hardin & Waite 6600 Sears Tower Chicago IL 60606

**RIEGERT, ROBERT ADOLF,** law educator, consultant; b. Cin., Apr. 21, 1923; s. Adolf and Hulda (Basler) R.; m. Roswitha Victoria Bigalke, Oct. 28, 1966; children: Christine Rose, Douglas Louis. BS, U. Cin., 1948; LLB cum laude, Harvard U., 1953; Doctoris Juris Utriusque magna cum laude, U. Heidelberg, Germany, 1966; postgrad., U. Mich., Harvard U., Yale U., MIT. Bar: D.C. 1953, Cts. Allied High Commn. Germany 1954. Mem. Harvard Legal Aid Bur., 1952-53; sole practice Heidelberg, 1954-63; vis. assoc. prof. So. Meth. U. Law Sch., Dallas, 1967-71; prof. law Cumberland Law Sch., Samford U., Birmingham, Ala., 1971-97; prof. emeritus Cumberland Law Sch., Samford U., Birmingham, 1997—; dir. Cumberland Summer Law Program, Heidelberg, 1981-94; Disting. vis. prof. Salmon P. Chase Coll. Law, 1983-84. Author: (With Robert Braucher) Introduction to Commercial Transactions, 1977, Documents of Title, 1978; contbr. articles to profl. jours. Served to 1st lt. USAAF, 1943-46. Grantee Dana Fund for Internat. and Comparative Law, 1979; grantee Am. Bar Found., 1966-67; German Acad. Exchange, 1953-55, mem. Harvard Legal Aid Bur., Salmon P. Chase Coll. law scholar, 1950; Pres.'s scholar U. Cin., 1941. Mem. ABA (com. on new payment systems), Internat. Acad. Comml. and Consumer Law, Am. Law Inst., Ala. Law Inst. (coun.), Assn. Am. Law Schs. (sect. internat. legal exchs., subcom. on com. laws), German Comparative Law Assn., Acad. Soc. German Supreme Cts., Army-Navy Club (Washington). Office: Samford U Cumberland Law Sch Birmingham AL 35229-0001

**RIEKE, FORREST NEILL,** lawyer; b. Portland, Oreg., May 26, 1942; s. Forrest Eugene and Mary Neill (Whitelaw) R.; m. Madonna Bernardi, Apr. 2, 1966; children: Mary Jane, Forrest Ermelindo. AB in Polit. Sci., Stanford U., 1968; JD, Willamette U., 1971. Bar: Oreg. 1971, U.S. Dist. Ct. Oreg. 1974, U.S. Ct. Appeals (9th cir.) 1975, U.S. Supreme Ct. 1977. Sr. dep. dist. atty. Multnomah County, Portland, 1971-76; ptnr. Rieke & Savage P.C., Portland, 1977—; instr. Oreg. State Police Acad., Ft. Rilea, 1979—. Contbr. editor Williamette U. Law Rev., 1971. Chmn. legis. com. Council Great Schs., Washington, 1985-92, dir., 1985-91, pres., 1992-93; trustee Emanuel Hosp. Found., 1987-93; bd. dirs. Portland Pub. Schs., 1978-93, Columbia Willamette United Way, Portland, 1983-94; organizer Oreg. Conservation and Devel. Found., Portland, 1986-90. Mem. ABA, Oreg. Bar Assn. (indigent accused def. com., chmn. law related edn. com. 1985, bd. dirs. criminal law sect. 1979-84, mem. pub. info. com. 1987-90, ho. dels. 1995—), Nat. Criminal Def. Lawyers Assn., Multnomah County Bar Assn., Oreg. Criminal Def. Lawyers Assn. Republican. Presbyterian. Club: Multnomah Athletic. Lodge: Rotary. Avocations: skiing, reading, coaching youth sports. Personal injury, Criminal, General civil litigation. Home: 820 SW 2nd Ave Apt 6 Portland OR 97204-3085 Office: Rieke & Savage PC 820 SW 2nd Ave Ste 200 Portland OR 97204-3087

**RIEKE, PAUL VICTOR,** lawyer; b. Seattle, Apr. 1, 1949; s. Luvern Victor and Anna Jane (Bierstedt) R.; m. Judy Vivian Farr, Jan. 24, 1974; children: Anna Katharina, Peter Johann. BA, Oberlin Coll., 1971; postgrad. U. Wash., 1971, Shoreline C.C., 1972-73; JD, Case Western Res. U., 1976. Bar: Wash. 1976, U.S. Dist. Ct. (we. dist.) Wash. 1976, U.S. Tax Ct. 1978. Assoc. Hatch & Leslie, Seattle, 1976-82, ptnr., 1982-91; ptnr. Foster, Pepper & Shefelman, PLLC, 1991—. Exec. notes editor Case Western Res. U. Law Rev., 1975-76. Mem. exec. bd. dist. council N. Pacific dist. Am. Luth. Ch., Seattle, 1978-83, council pres. 1983, Am. Luth. Ch. pub. bd., 1984-87; v.p. Northwest Wash. Synod of Evangelical Luth. Ch. Am., Seattle, 1988-90, mem. Synod Coun., 1990-92, del. ELCA Nat. Assembly, 1991, ELCA Northwest Synod Regional Rep., 1992-96, region one coun. pres., 1994-96. Mem. ABA, Wash. State Bar Assn., Seattle-King County Bar Assn., Order of Coif. Democrat. Lodge: Seattle Downtown Central Lions. General corporate, Probate, Real property. Home: 321 NE 161st St Shoreline WA 98155-5741 Office: Foster Pepper & Shefelman PLLC 34th Fl 1111 3rd Ave Seattle WA 98101

**RIES, CHARLES WILLIAM,** lawyer; b. Mankato, Minn., June 1, 1952; s. William Charles and Margaret Theresa Ries; m. Carol Jean Kaduce; children: Ryan Charles, Thalia Anne, William John Michael. BS in Acctg. cum laude, Mankato State Coll., 1974; JD cum laude, William Mitchell Coll. Law, 1981. Bar: Minn. 1981, U.S. Dist. Ct. Minn. 1981, U.S. Ct. Appeals (8th cir.) 1990; CPA, Minn. Law clk. Lamm, Lamm & Nelson, Mankato, 1979; law clk. Farrish, Johnson & Maschka, PLLP, Mankato, 1979-81, assoc., 1981-84, ptnr., 1984—. Staff sgt. U.S. Army, 1970-76. Mem. Minn. State Bar Assn. (bankruptcy sect., pres. 1994-95), Madison Lake Am. Legion (adjutant), Mankato Area Girls Fastpitch Assn. (dir., pres. 1996-97). Roman Catholic. Bankruptcy. Office: Farrish Johnson & Maschka PLLP PO Box 550 201 N Broad St Mankato MN 56002-0550

**RIES, WILLIAM CAMPBELL,** lawyer; b. Pitts., Apr. 8, 1948; s. F. William and Dorothy (Campbell) R.; m. Mallory Burns, Oct. 26, 1968; children: William Sheehan, Sean David. AB, Cath. U. Am., 1970; JD, Duquesne U., 1974; cert. Grad. Sch. Indsl. Adminstrn., Carnegie Mellon U., 1980. Bar: Pa. 1974, U.S. Dist. Ct. (we. dist.) Pa. 1974, U.S. Supreme Ct. 1979. Atty., then mng. counsel trust and investment svc. Mellon Bank, N.A., Pitts., 1974-90; ptnr. Dickie, McCamey and Chilcote, Pitts., 1990-98; mem. Sweeney, Metz, Fox, McGrann & Schermer, LLC, 1998—; mem. adv. com. decedents' estates and trust law Pa. Joint State Govt. Commn., 1981—; adj. prof. Duquesne U., 1984—. Author: The Regulation of Investment Management and Fiduciary Services West, 1997. Pres. McCandless Twp. Civic Assn., Pitts., 1981—, McCandless Town Coun., chair pub. safety com., vice chair fin com.; sec. McCandless Indsl. Devel. Auth.; liaison McCandless zoning hearing bd. Fellow Am. Bar Found.; mem. ABA (chmn. fiduciary svcs. subcom.), Pa. Bar Assn., Allegheny County Bar Assn., Pitts. Estate Planning Coun., Am. Bankers Assn. (co-chmn. nat. conf. lawyers and corp. fiduciaries, chmn. trust counsel com.), Pa. Bankers Assn. (trust com., trust legis. com.), Rivers Club, Treesdale Golf and Country Club. Republican. Avocations: golf, sailing, cross-country skiing, fitness. Banking, Securities, Pension, profit-sharing, and employee benefits. Home: 9602 Fawn Ln Allison Park PA 15101-1737

**RIESELBACH, ALLEN NEWMAN,** lawyer; b. Milw., June 2, 1931; s. Allen Saxe and Renee (Newman) R.; m. Patricia Fried, May 27, 1956; children: Anne, William. AB, Harvard U., 1953, LLB, 1956. Bar: Wis. 1956, Fla. 1971, Colo. 1986. Shareholder Reinhart, Boerner, Van Deuren, Norris & Rieselbach, S.C., Milw., 1959-99, sr. counsel, 1999—; gov. Am. Coll. Real Estate Lawyers, 1989-92. Editor: Wisconsin Condominium Law, 1980. Mem. exec. bd. Milw. County Boy Scouts, 1975-92, 99—; bd. dirs. Milw. Repertory Theater, 1984-90, 99—; pres. Milw. Symphony Orch., 1995-98, mem. exec. com., 1992—. Mem. Rotary. Avocations: sailing, biking. Real property, Construction, Land use and zoning (including planning). Office: Reinhart Boerner Van Deuren Norris & Rieselbach 1000 N Water St Ste 2100 Milwaukee WI 53202-3197

**RIESS, GEORGE FEBIGER,** lawyer, educator; b. New Orleans, Oct. 22, 1943; s. Frank and Jane (Kelleher) R.; m. June 22, 1968 (div. June 1976); 1 child, Katherine Cody; m. Maida Magee, Aug. 23, 1980; children: Frank Henry, Carson Magee, Maida Jean. BA, Tulane U., 1965; JD, La. State U., 1969. Bar: La. 1969, Mich. 1972, U.S. Dist. Ct. (ea., we. and mid. dists.) La. 1970. Mng. ptnr. Johnson & Riess Law Firm, New Orleans, 1970-76; ptnr. Monroe & Lemann Law Firm, New Orleans, 1976-96, Polack, Rosenberg, Endom & Riess, L.L.P., New Orleans, 1996—; bd. dirs. Plaquemines Oil and Devel. Corp., New Orleans; adj. prof. law Tulane U. Law Sch., New Orleans, 1987-94. Sec. of vestry St. Martin Episcopal Ch., Metairie, La., 1992—. Recipient Ford Found. grant, 1969. Fellow La. State Bar Found.; mem. ABA, Am. Judicature Soc., Fed. Bar Assn., La. Assn. Def. Counsel, La. State Bar Assn., New Orleans Assn. Def. Counsel, So. Yacht Club, New Orleans Lawn Tennis Club. Product liability, Personal injury, Admiralty. Office: Polack Rosenberg Edom & Riess LLP 938 Lafayette St Ste 100 New Orleans LA 70113-1067

**RIFKIND, ROBERT S(INGER),** lawyer; b. N.Y.C., Aug. 31, 1936; s. Simon H. and Adele (Singer) R.; m. Arleen Brenner, Dec. 24, 1961; children: Amy, Nina. BA, Yale U., 1958; JD, Harvard U., 1961; LHD (hon.), Jewish Theol. Sem. Am., 1998. Bar: N.Y. 1961, U.S. Supreme Ct. 1965. Asst. to solicitor gen. Dept. Justice, 1965-68; assoc. firm Cravath, Swaine & Moore, N.Y.C., 1962-65, 68-70; ptnr. Cravath, Swaine & Moore, 1971—. Trustee Dalton Sch., N.Y.C., 1975-83, hon. trustee, 1983—, pres., 1977-79; trustee Brandeis U., 1998—, The Loomis Inst., 1987-95, Citizens Budget Commn.; bd. dirs. Charles H. Revson Found., 1991—, chmn., 1997—; bd. dirs. Jewish Theol. Sem. Am., 1983—, Leo Baeck Inst., 1999—, Benjamin N. Cardozo Sch. Law, 1984-89; pres. Am. Jewish Com., 1994-98, hon. pres., 1998—. Fellow Am. Coll. Trial Lawyers, Am. Bar Found.; mem. ABA, Coun. Fgn. Rels., Am. Law Inst., Assn. of Bar of City of N.Y., Phi Beta Kappa. Democrat. Antitrust, Federal civil litigation, State civil litigation. Office: Cravath Swaine & Moore Worldwide Pla 825 8th Ave Fl 38 New York NY 10019-7475

**RIGBY, AMANDA YOUNG,** paralegal firm executive; b. Yokosuka, Japan, Nov. 15, 1961; d. James Linton Young, Philip T. (stepfather) and Serena Margaret (Murray) Poisson; m. D'Arcy A. Rigby, Apr. 6, 1991; children: Ian A., Helen E. Cert. paralegal, U. San Diego, 1989; AA in Social Sci., Miramar Coll., 1990. Cert. domestic violence counselor, Calif. Sec. Martin & Branfman, Solana Beach, Calif., 1988-89; sr. paralegal DiGennaro & Davis, San Diego, 1989-91; owner, pres. paralegal firm AR & Co., San Diego, 1989—. Author poetry in Taking Chances mag., 1992. Vol. clinic coord. San Diego Vol. Lawyer Program, 1989-96; vol. asst. to abuse victims San Diego Police Dept., 1992—; parliamentarian Mira Mesa Town Coun., San Diego, 1992-95; founding mem. Scripps Ranch High Found., San Diego, 1992-95; sec., and nat. and state rep. Pomerado Hosp. Mothers of Twins, Poway, Calif., 1994—; mem. Vista (Calif.) Unified Sch. Dist. Common Ground Task Force, 1995-97; staff paralegal San Diego Vol. Lawyer Program, 1994-95; bd. dirs. So. Calif. Mothers of Twins, Inc., 1996—; legal clinic trainer, speaker Community Resource Ctr., 1996—. Mem. ABA. Republican. Methodist. Avocations: reading, writing, sailing, exercising, working on the house. Office: AR & Co 615 Cabezon Pl Fl 2 Vista CA 92083-6309

**RIGBY, KENNETH,** lawyer; b. Shreveport, La., Oct. 20, 1925; s. Samuel and Mary Elizabeth (Fearnhead) R.; m. Jacqueline Carol Brandon, June 8, 1951; children: Brenda, Wayne, Glen. BS magna cum laude, La. State U., 1950, JD, 1951. Bar: La. 1951, U.S. Ct. Appeals (5th cir.) 1966, U.S. Supreme Ct. 1971, U.S. Tax Ct. 1981, U.S. Ct. Appeals (11th cir.) 1982. Ptnr. Love, Rigby, Dehan & McDaniel, 1951—; adj. prof. of law LSU Law Ctr., 1990—; mem. Marriage-Persons Com. La. Law Inst., 1981—, mem. council, 1988—; mem. La. Supreme Ct. Jud. Coun., 1999—. Sec. mandatory continuing legal edn. com. La. Supreme Ct., 1987-95, mem. jud. coun., 1999—. Served with USAAF, 1943-46. Fellow Am. Acad. Matrimonial Lawyers, Am. Coll. Trial Lawyers; mem. ABA, Shreveport Bar Assn. (pres. 1973-74), La. State Bar Assn. (chmn. com. on continuing legal edn. 1974-75, chmn. family law sect. 1981-82, bd. of govs. 1986-88). Methodist. Contbr. articles to profl. jours. Family and matrimonial, State civil litigation, Personal injury. Office: Transcontinental Tower 330 Marshall St Ste 1400 Shreveport LA 71101-3018

**RIGBY, ROBERT GLEN,** lawyer; b. Shreveport, La., Feb. 14, 1958; s. Kenneth and Jacqueline (Brandon) R.; m. Deena Lee Digirolamo, Oct. 27, 1990; children: Anna, Benjamin, Olivia. BS summa cum laude., Duke U., 1980; MA, So. Ill. U., 1984; JD, La. State U., 1988. Bar: La. 1988, Tex., 1989, U.S. Dist. Ct. (so. dist.) Tex., U.S. Ct. Appeals (5th and D.C. cirs.). Tchr. Caddo Parish Sch. Bd., Shreveport, 1980-81, Yonkers (N.Y.) Sch. Bd., 1984-85; assoc. Vinson & Elkins, Houston, 1988-96; ptnr. Vinson & Elkins

L.L.P., Houston, 1996—. Adminstrv. counsel Bay Harbour United Meth. Ch., League City, Tex., 1998—. Mem. Tex. Bar Assn., La. Bar Assn., Houston Bar Assn., Order of Coif, Phi Beta Kappa. Avocation: flying. Appellate, General civil litigation, Aviation. Office: Vinson & Elkins LLP 1001 Fannin St Ste 2300 Houston TX 77002-6760

**RIGDON, JAY ALDEN,** lawyer; b. Syracuse, Ind., Apr. 7, 1960; s. Jay A. and Elsie B. R.; m. Brenda Jo Rhodes, Nov. 17, 1984; children: Jay, Chelsea, Isaac. BA in Polit. Sci and Econs., George Washington U., 1981; JD, Ind. U., 1984. Bar: Ind. 1984. Ptnr. Rockhill, Pinnick, Pequignot, Helm, Landis & Rigdon, Warsaw, Ind., 1984—. Mem. Ind. Domestic Violence Coun., Indpls., 1990-96; pres., bd. dirs. Kosciusko County United Way, Warsaw, 1992-96; v.p. Bd. Aviation Commrs. Mem. ABA, Ind. Bar Assn. Democrat. Episcopalian. General practice, State civil litigation, Family and matrimonial. Office: Rockhill Pinnick Et Al 105 E Main St Warsaw IN 46580-2742

**RIGGIO, NICHOLAS JOSPEH, SR.,** lawyer; b. St. Louis, Oct. 1, 1930; s. Joseph and Anna (Trapani) R.; m. Etta G. Riggio, Nov. 6, 1954; children: Nicholas Jr., Michael John, Joy Ann. BS, St. Louis U., 1953; LLB, Washington U., 1959, JD, 1968. Pvt. practice St. Louis, 1959—. Founder Hill 2000 Orgn., St. Louis. Inducted into St. Louis Soccer Hall of Fame, 1985. Condemnation, General civil litigation, Consumer commercial. Office: 5149 Shaw Ave Saint Louis MO 63110-3039

**RIGGS, ARTHUR JORDY,** retired lawyer; b. Nyack, N.Y., Apr. 3, 1916; s. Oscar H. and Adele (Jordy) R.; m. Virginia Holloway, Oct. 15, 1942 (dec.); children: Arthur James (dec.), Emily Adele Riggs Freeman, Keith Holloway, George Bennett; m. Priscilla McCormack, Jan. 16, 1993. AB, Princeton U., 1937; LLB, Harvard U., 1940. Bar: Mass. 1940, Tex. 1943; cert. specialist in labor law. Assoc. Warner, Stackpole, Stetson & Bradlee, Boston, 1940-41; staff mem. Solicitors Office U.S. Dept. Labor, Washington, Dallas, 1941-42; mem. Johnson, Bromberg, Leeds & Riggs, Dallas, 1949-81; of counsel Geary & Spencer, Dallas, 1981-91. Mem. ABA, State Bar Tex., Phi Beta Kappa. Avocations: Maya archeology, history, photography. Labor, Pension, profit-sharing, and employee benefits. Home and Office: 2110 Antibes Dr Carrollton TX 75006-4326

**RIGGS, M. DAVID,** lawyer, rancher; b. Nov. 29, 1937; s. James Ray and Thelma Beatrice (Fisher) R.; m. Dora Arleen Hoppes, Dec. 31, 1959; children: Lisa René, Michael Eric, Jennifer Lee, Andrea Lynn, Aaron David. BA, Phillips U., Enid, Okla., 1959; MA, Okla. U., 1962; JD, Tulsa U., 1968. Bar: Okla. 1969, U.S. Dist. Ct. (no., we. and ea. dists.) Okla. Mem. Okla. Ho. of Reps., Oklahoma City, 197-84, Okla. Senate, Oklahoma City, 1985-88; founder, shareholder Riggs, Abney, Neal, Turpen, Orbison and Lewis, Oklahoma City, Muskogee, Denver, 1972—. Democrat. Avocation: farming/ranching. Alternative dispute resolution, General civil litigation, Personal injury. Home: HC 67 Box 798 Skiatook OK 74070-9140 Office: Riggs Abney 502 W 6th St Tulsa OK 74119-1016

**RIGGS, R. WILLIAM,** state judge. Grad., Portland State U., 1961; JD, U. Oreg., 1968. Atty. Willner Bennet & Leonard, 1972-78; judge circuit ct. 4th Judicial Dist. Multonmah County, 1978; judge Oreg. Ct. of Appeals, 1988-98, Oreg. Supreme Ct., 1998—. Active mem. Cmty. Law Poject; founder Integra Corp. Capt. USNR. Office: 1163 State St Salem OR 97310-1331

**RIGGSBEE, LUNDAY ADAMS,** lawyer; b. Hendersonville, N.C., Jan. 19, 1954; d. Hoyle Brannock Jr. and Katherine (Durham) Adams; m. George Frederick Riggsbee, Feb. 8, 1986. BA in Math, Lenoir Rhyne Coll., Hickory, N.C., 1976; JD, U. N.C., 1984. Bar: N.C. 1984. Assoc. Tim Hubbard Law Firm, Pittsboro, N.C., 1984-86; pvt. practice, 1986—; bd. dirs. North State Legal Svcs. Bd. dirs. United Way, Chatham County, N.C., 1988-91. Mem. N.C. Bar Assn., ABA, Chatham County Bar Assn. (sec., treas. 1985-86, v.p. 1986-87, pres. 1987-88), N.C. Acad. Trial Lawyers, Susie Sharp Inns of Ct. Democrat. Episcopalian. Avocations: canoeing, horseback riding, sports. General practice, Juvenile, Real property. Office: 49 Hillsboro St Pittsboro NC 27312-5891

**RIGNANESE, CYNTHIA CROFOOT,** lawyer; b. Chgo., Aug. 8, 1965; d. Fred Ralph and Hazel Jean Crofoot; m. Stephen Mark Rignanese, Nov. 24, 1990. Student, Richmond Coll., London, 1986; BSBA, U. Fla., Gainesville, 1987; student, U. Siena, Florence, Italy, 1987; JD, U. Fla., Gainesville, 1990. Bar: Fla., U.S. Dist. Ct. (mid. dist.) Fla. Atty. Peterson & Myers, PA, Lake Wales, Fla., 1990-94, Law Office of J. Kelly Kennedy, Winter Haven, Fla., 1994—; adj. prof. Webber Coll., Babson Park, Fla., 1994—. Contbr. articles to profl. jours. Mem. Estate Planning Coun. of Polk County, Exec. Womens Club, Winter Haven, Fla.; mentor U. Fla., Gainesville. Mem. ABA, Fla. Bar (scholarship com., speakers bureau, mem. property, probate and trust law sect.), Winter Haven C. of C., Lake Wales C. of C. (dir. 1998—, leadership class IV 1999), Lake Wales Kiwanis Club (past pres., dir. 1990—, spkrs. bur., named Kiwanian of Yr. 1995); founding mem. Winter Haven Women's Bar Assn. (pres. 1997—). Avocations: art, travel, reading, growing orchids. Estate planning, Real property, General corporate. Home: 3507 White Oak Ct Lake Wales FL 33853-8554 Office: Law Office J Kelly Kennedy 198 1st St S Winter Haven FL 33880-3004

**RIGOLOSI, ELAINE LA MONICA,** lawyer, educator, consultant; b. Astoria, N.Y., Oct. 12, 1944; d. Richard Anthony and Caroline La Monica; m. Robert Salvatore Rigolosi, June 15, 1997; children: Robert, Rebecca, Luke, Laura. BS, Columbia Union Coll., Takoma Park, Md., 1964; MN, U. Fla., 1967; EdD, U. Mass., 1975; JD, Benjamin N. Cardozo Sch. Law, N.Y.C., 1993. Bar: N.J. 1994, N.Y. 1994, D.C. 1995; RN, N.Y. Chair dept. nursing edn. Tchrs. Coll., Columbia U., N.Y.C., 1988-91, prof. nursing edn., 1982-96, acting chair dept. nursing edn., 1994-96, prof. dept. orgn. and leadership, 1996—, dir. Inst. Rsch. in Nursing, 1981—; health care mgmt. cons. in pvt. practice, N.Y.C., 1974—; bd. dirs. Hooper Holmes, Inc., Basking Ridge, N.J., 1989—; cons. Delaware Valley Transplant Program, Phila., 1998, U. Tenn. Coll. Pharmacy, Memphis, 1995-98. Author: The Nursing Process: A Humanistic Approach, 1979 (Am. Jour. Nursing Book of Yr. 1979), Management in Health Care, 1994. Dept. HHS grantee, 1977-80, 80-83. Fellow Am. Acad. Nursing; mem. ABA, Assn. Bar City N.Y. (com. on health law 1994-97), Am. Health Lawyers Assn., Am. Assn. Nurse Attys., Am. Coll. Legal Medicine, Sigma Theta Tau. Avocations: tennis, skiing, needlepoint, interior design. Home: 158 Summit Dr Paramus NJ 07652-1312 Office: Tchrs Coll Columbia U 525 W 120th St New York NY 10027-6625

**RIGOR, BRADLEY GLENN,** lawyer; b. Cheyenne Wells, Colo., Aug. 9, 1955; s. Glenn E. and Lelia (Teed) R.; m. Twyla G. Helweg, Sept. 4, 1983; children: Camille, Brent, Tiffany, Lauren. BS in Mktg., Ft. Hays State U., 1977; JD, Washburn U., 1980. Bar: Kans. 1980, U.S. Dist. Ct. Kans. 1980, U.S. Tax Ct. 1981, U.S. Ct. Appeals (10th cir.) 1982, U.S. Supreme Ct. 1986, Colo. 1990, Tex. 1991, U.S. Dist. Ct. Colo. 1991, Mo. 1993, Fla. 1998; cert. trust and fin. advisor Inst. Cert. Bankers. Ptnr. Zuspann & Rigor, Goodland, Kans., 1980-82; city atty. Goodland, 1981-82; asst. county atty. Wallace County, Sharon Springs, Kans., 1982-84, county atty., 1984; city atty. Sharon Springs, 1983-84; judge Mcpl. Ct., Goodland, 1988-93; ptnr. Fairbanks, Rigor & Irvin, P.A., Goodland, 1982-93; v.p., mgr. personal trusts Merc. Bank, St. Joseph, Mo., 1993-96; sr. v.p., mgr., personal trust adminstr. SunTrust Bank, Naples, Fla., 1996-98, Bond Schoeneck & King P.A., Naples, Fla., 1998—. Mem. Kans. Bar Assn., Tex. Bar Assn., Mo. Bar Assn., Colo. Bar Assn., Fla. Bar Assn., Collier County Bar Assn. (trust and estates sect.). Republican. Baptist. Estate planning. Office: Bond Schoeneck & King PA 4001 Tamiami Trl N Ste 404 Naples FL 34103-3555

**RIGSBY, LINDA FLORY,** lawyer; b. Topeka, Kans., Dec. 16, 1946; d. Alden E. and Lolita M. Flory; m. Michael L. Rigsby, Aug. 14, 1963; children: Michael L. Jr., Elisabeth A. MusB, Va. Commonwealth U., 1969; JD, U. Richmond, 1981. Bar: Va. 1981, D.C. 1988. Assoc. McGuire, Woods, Battle & Boothe, Richmond, Va., 1981-85; dep. gen. counsel and corp. sec. Crestar Fin. Corp., Richmond, 1985-99, gen. counsel, corp. sec., 1999—. Recipient Disting. Svc. award U. Richmond, 1987; named Vol. of Yr. U. Richmond, 1986, Woman of Achievement, Met. Richmond Women's Bar, 1995. Mem. Va. Bar Assn. (exec. com. 1993-96), Richmond Bar Assn. (bd. dirs. 1992-95), Va. Bankers Assn. (chair legal affairs 1992-95), U. Richmond Estate Planning Coun. (chmn. 1990-92). Roman Catholic. Avocations: music, gardening. Home: 10005 Ashbridge Pl Richmond VA 23233-5402 Office: Crestar Fin Corp 919 E Main St Richmond VA 23219-4625

**RIGTRUP, KENNETH,** state judge, arbitrator, mediator; b. Burley, Idaho, Jan. 13, 1936; s. Robert Peter and Bessie Viola (Price) R.; m. Susanne Joan Remund, May 15, 1964; children: Mark Robert, Michael James, Scott Kenneth, Melissa Ann, Jennifer Marie. BS in Acctg., U. Utah, 1960, JD, 1962. Bar: Utah 1962; U.S. Dist. Ct. Utah, 1962. Clk. Utah Supreme Ct., Salt Lake City, 1962; ptnr. Rigtrup & Hadley, Salt Lake City, 1962-68; pvt. practice, Salt Lake City, 1968-72; admin. law judge Indsl. Commn., Salt Lake City, 1972-77; mem. Pub. Svc. Commn., Salt Lake City, 1977-80; judge 3d Dist. Ct., Salt Lake City, 1980-97; active sr. judge Utah Cts., Salt Lake City, 1997—; chmn. Bd. Sr. Judges, 1998-99; mem. adv. com. on rules of juvenile procedure Utah Supreme Ct., Salt Lake City, 1993-95. Copy and rsch. editor Utah Law Rev., 1961-62. Chmn. Utah White House Conf. on Handicapped Individuals, Salt Lake City, 1976-77; mem. Utah Gov.'s Com. on Employment of Handicapped, 1976-80, vice chmn. and acting chmn. 1977-80; mem. citizens evaluation and selection com. to rev. pvt. non-profit orgn. applications for urban mass transit authority grants, 1975-77, dir., vice chair. Utah Assistive Tech. Found., 1991—. Recipient Disting. Svc. award Utah Rehab. Counseling Assn., Salt Lake City, 1976-77; Nat. Citation award Nat. Rehab. counseling Assn., 1977; Maurice Warshaw Golden Key award, Utah Gov.'s Com. on Employment of Handicapped, 1975. Mem. ABA, ATLA, Utah Bar Assn. (exec. com. family sect. 1980-90, lawyers helping lawyers com., alt. dispute resolution com.), Nat. Ass. Regulatory Utility Commns. (water com. 1977-78, gas com. 1978-80), Am. Judicature Soc. Republican. Mem. LDS Ch. Home: 1961 Millbrook Rd Salt Lake City UT 84106-3853 Office: Arbitration/Mediation Svcs 3098 Highland Dr Ste 399 Salt Lake City UT 84106-6004

**RIHERD, JOHN ARTHUR,** lawyer; b. Belle Plaine, Iowa, Sept. 1, 1946; s. William Arthur and Julia Elizabeth Riherd; m. Mary Blanche Thielen, July 5, 1969; children: Elizabeth, Teresa. BA, U. Iowa, 1968, JD, 1974; MA, Gonzaga U., 1992. Bar: Wash. 1974, Iowa 1974, U.S. Dist. Ct. (ea. dist.) Wash. 1974, U.S. Ct. Appeals (9th cir.) 1980, U.S. Dist. Ct. (we. dist.) Wash. 1981. Ptnr. Woods & Riherd, Spokane, Wash., 1974-83, Richter-Wimberley, Spokane, 1983-88, Workland, Witherspoon, Riherd & Brajcich, Spokane, 1988-94; sr. v.p., gen. counsel Med. Svc. Corp. Ea. Wash., 1994-95; ptnr. Perkins Coie, Spokane, 1995-96, Riherd & Sherman P.S., Spokane, 1996—; adj. prof. Whitworth Coll., Spokane, 1988-90; permanent deacon Cath. Diocese of Spokane. Bd. dirs. Salvation Army, 1976—, chmn., 1996-98; bd. dirs. Mead Sch. Dist., Spokane, 1986-95, pres., 1992-94; bd. dirs. Mayor's Leadership Prayer Breakfast, Spokane, 1986-90, Hospice of Spokane, 1984-87, 91-94, mem. bishop's fin. coun. Cath. Diocese of Spokane, 1993-99, chmn. 1997-98; pres. Spokane County Sch. Dirs. Assn., 1991-92. Mem. ABA, Wash. Bar Assn. (mem. coun. pub. procurement and constrn. law sect. 1986-89, sec.-treas. gen. practice sect. 1989-92), Nat. Health Lawyers Assn., Am. Arbitration Assn. (panel mem. 1988—), North Spokane Exch. Club (pres. 1981), Spokane Country Club. Health, Insurance, Estate planning. Home: 1309 W Crestwood Ct Spokane WA 99218-2918 Office: Riherd & Sherman PS 1212 N Washington St Ste 210 Spokane WA 99201-2401

**RIKLEEN, SANDER A.,** lawyer; b. N.Y.C., Jan. 2, 1953; s. Alexander Sander and Rebecca F. Rikleen; m. Lauren Stiller, May 25, 1975; children: Alex, Ilyse. BA, Clark U., 1973; JD, Boston Coll., 1976. Bar: Mass. 1977, U.S. Dist. Ct. Mass. 1977, U.S. Ct. Appeals (1st cir.) 1977, U.S. Supreme Ct. 1985, U.S. Dist. Ct. Appeals (D.C. cir.) 1985, U.S. Tax Ct. 1990, U.S. Dist. Ct. (D.C.) Dist. 1994. Assoc. Rich, May, Bilodgau & Flaherty, Boston, 1976-82, ptnr., 1983-91; ptnr. Widett, Slater & Goldman, Boston, 1991-92, Hutchins, Wheeler & Dittmar, Boston, 1992—; adj. faculty New Eng. Sch. Law, Boston, 1977-85. Bd. dirs. Temple shir Tikva, Wayland, Mass., 1987—. General civil litigation, Securities. Office: Hutchins Wheeler & Dittmar 101 Federal St Boston MA 02110-1817

**RIKON, MICHAEL,** lawyer; b. Bklyn., Feb. 2, 1945; s. Charles and Ruth (Shapiro) R.; m. Leslie Sharon Rein, Feb. 11, 1968; children: Carrie Rachel, Joshua Howard. BS, N.Y. Inst. Tech., 1966; JD, Bklyn. Law Sch., 1969; LLM, NYU, 1974. Bar: N.Y. 1970, U.S. Dist. Ct. (so. and ea. dists.) N.Y. 1971, U.S. Ct. Appeals (2d cir.) 1972, U.S. Supreme Ct. 1973, U.S. Ct. Appeals (5th and 11th cirs.) 1981. Asst. corp. counsel City of N.Y., 1969-73; law clk. N.Y. State Ct. Claims, 1973-80; ptnr. Rudick and Rikon, P.C., N.Y.C., 1980-88; pvt. practice, N.Y.C., 1988-94; ptnr. Goldstein, Goldstein and Rikon, P.C., N.Y.C., 1994—. Contbr. articles to profl. jours. Pres. Village Greens Residents Assn., 1978-79; chmn. bd. Arden Heights Jewish Ctr., Staten Island, N.Y., 1976-77; pres. North Shore Republican Club, 1977; mem. community bd. Staten Island Borough Pres., 1977. Fellow Am. Bar Found.; mem. ABA (chair com. Condemnation), ATLA, TLPJ Found., N.Y. State Bar Assn. (spl. com. of condemnation law), Suffolk County Bar Assn., N.Y. County Lawyers Assn. (chair Condemnation com.), Republican. Jewish. Avocations: collecting stamps, photography, collecting miniature soldiers. Condemnation, State civil litigation, Real property. Home: 133 Avondale Rd Ridgewood NJ 07450-1301 Office: 80 Pine St New York NY 10005-1702

**RILEY, ANTHONY DALE,** lawyer; b. Sheffield, Ala., Mar. 31, 1964; s. Dan Richard and Virginia (Harris) R.; m. Jennifer Leah Misner, Mar. 12, 1988; children: Elizabeth Anne, Sarah Katherine, Emma Caroline. BA, U. Ala., 1985, JD, 1988. Bar: Ala. 1989, U.S. Dist. Ct. (no. dist.) Ala. 1990. Sole practice Tuscumbia, Ala., 1989-93, Muscle Shoals, Ala., 1993—. Treas. Shoals Republican Club, Florence, Ala., 1994—, Muscle Shoals Civil Svc. Bd., 1997—, chmn. 1998—. Mem. Colbert County Bar Assn. (v.p. 1996-98, pres. 1999—). Southern Baptist. Avocations: politics, fishing, Sunday sch. tchr. General practice, Probate, Pension, profit-sharing, and employee benefits. Office: 1705 Gusmus Ave Muscle Shoals AL 35661-2459

**RILEY, ARCH WILSON, JR.,** lawyer; b. Wheeling, W.Va., Jan. 15, 1957; s. Arch W. Sr. and Mary List (Paull) R.; m. Sally Ann Goodspeed, Aug. 9, 1980; children: Ann Jerome, Sarah Paull. BA in French and Econs., Tufts U., 1979; JD, W.Va. U., 1982. Bar: W.Va. 1982, U.S. Dist. Ct. (no. and so. dists.) W.Va. 1982. Assoc. Riley & Yahn, Wheeling, 1982, Riley & Broadwater, Wheeling, 1982-83; ptnr. Riley & Riley, L.C., Wheeling, 1983-92, Bailey, Riley, Buch & Harman, L.C., Wheeling, 1993—; bd. dirs. Wheeling Health Right, Inc.; mem. nat. coun. W.Va. U. Coll. Law. Pres. Upper Ohio Valley Crisis Hotline Inc., Wheeling, 1987-88; chmn. Human Rights Commn., Wheeling, 1985; committeeman Ohio County Dem. Execs., Wheeling, 1984-88; bd. dirs., pres. Northwood Health Sys., Inc., Wheeling, 1988-89;bd. dirs. Ohio Valley ARC, Wheeling, 1988; del. 1988 Dem. Nat. Conv. Mem. Am. Bankruptcy Inst., Am. Health Lawyers Assn., W.Va. State Bar (mem. continuing edn. commn., bankruptcy law com., mental health law com.), W.Va. Bar Assn., Ohio County Bar Assn. (sec. 1983-84), Wheeling Country Club. Presbyterian. Bankruptcy, Health, Real property. Office: Bailey Riley Buch & Harman PO Box 631 Wheeling WV 26003-0081

**RILEY, BENJAMIN KNEELAND,** lawyer; b. Pompton Plains, N.J., June 3, 1957; s. Christopher Sibley and Katharine Louise (Piper) R.; m. Janet Welch McCormick, Sept. 15, 1984; children: Keith McCormick, Jamin McCormick. AB, Dartmouth Coll., 1979; JD, U. Calif., Berkeley, 1983. Bar: Calif. 1983, U.S. Dist. Ct. (no. dist.) Calif. 1983, U.S. Ct. Appeals (9th cir.) 1983, U.S. Dist. Ct. (ea. dist.) Calif. 1985, U.S. Dist. Ct. (cen. dist.) Calif. 1987. Assoc. McCutchen, Doyle, Brown & Enerson, San Francisco, 1983-84; ptnr. Cooley Godward LLP, San Francisco, 1984—; lectr. Boalt Hall Sch. Law, 1989; mem. San Francisco Legal Svcs. Clinic, 1983—; mem. adv. bd. Berkeley Ctr. for Law and Tech., 1998—. Assoc. editor Calif. Law Rev. Spl. asst. dist. atty., San Francisco, 1988; chair, commr. Orinda Pks. & Recreation Commn., 1992-97; mem. City Orinda Task Force, Heart of Orinda Commn., Gateway and Cmty. Ctr. Renovation, 1990-97; bd. dirs. Children's Garden, 1987-92; v.p., mem. Orinda Assn., chmn. Orinda's 4th of July celebration, planning com. Orinda Union Sch. Dist., 1998. ABA, Calif. Bar Assn., San Francisco Bar Assn., Barrister of San Francisco Club. Democrat. E-mail: briley@cooley.com. Real property, General civil litigation, Intellectual property. Office: Cooley Godward 1 Maritime Plz Fl 20 San Francisco CA 94111-3404

**RILEY, DANIEL JOSEPH,** lawyer, educator; b. Amarillo, Tex., Jan. 14, 1947; s. Roy Weldon and Joette Aline (Winger) R.; m. Glenda Joy Hoel, Apr. 15, 1947; children: Carla Annette, Ragan Patrick. BA cum laude, U. Tex., 1969, JD summa cum laude, 1971. Bar: Tex. 1971, U.S. Ct. Fed. Claims 1974, U.S. Supreme Ct. 1979, U.S. Ct. Appeals (fed. cir.) 1982. Ptnr. Baker & Bolts LLP, Washington, 1993—; adj. prof. grad. sch. U. Dallas, 1983-94. Assoc. editor U. Tex. Law Rev., 1970. Mem. constitution rev. com. State of Tex., Austin, 1978. Mem. ABA (uniform state procurement code com. 1980), Nat. Contract Mgmt. Assn. (bd. advisors), Tex. Bar Found., Tex. Bar Assn., Dallas Bar Assn., Order of Coif, Phi Beta Kappa. Republican. Government contracts and claims, Private international, General corporate. Home: 712 W Braddock Rd Alexandria VA 22302-3601 Office: Baker & Bolts LLP 1299 Pennsylvania Ave NW Washington DC 20004-2400

**RILEY, EDWARD PATTERSON, JR.,** lawyer; b. Greenville, S.C., Oct. 16, 1928; s. Edward Patterson Riley and Martha Elizabeth Dixon; m. Nancy Ann Hale, June 12, 1954; children: Edward Patterson Riley, III, Elizabeth Anne Riley Boswell. AB1, Furman U., 1950; postgrad., U. S.C., 1952-54; JD, Mercer U., 1956. Bar: S.C. 1956, U.S. Dist. Ct. (we. dist.) S.C. 1959, U.S. Supreme Ct. 1978. Ptnr. Riley & Riley, Greenville, 1956-79, Riley Riley Laws & Stewart, Greenville, 1979-87, Nelson Mullins, Greenville, 1987-95; of counsel Nelson Mullins, Riley & Scarborough and predecessors, Greenville, 1995—; mem. adv. bd. Palmetto Bank & Trust, Simpsonville, S.C., 1969—. Bd. trustees Greenville Meml. Auditorium, S.C. Mus.; bd. dirs. Cmty. Coun., Phillis Wheatley Ctr.; chmn. Am. Heart Fund. Cpl. U.S. Army, 1950-52. Mem. S.C. Bar Assn. (mem. house of dels.), Kiwanis (charter pres. Simpsonville), Am. Legion (comdr. post # 3). Democrat. Methodist. Avocations: walking, reading. Real property. Home: 219 McDaniel Ave Greenville SC 29601-3709 Office: Nelson Mullins Riley & Scarborough PO Box 10084 301 N Main St Greenville SC 29601-2122

**RILEY, JAMES KEVIN,** lawyer; b. Nyack, N.Y., July 21, 1945; s. Charles A. and Mary Lenihan R.; m. Joan Leavy Riley, Oct. 4, 1969; children: Carolyn, Tara, Sean. AB, Fordham Coll., 1967; JD, Rutgers U., 1970. Bar: N.Y. 1971, N.J. 1983, U.S. Supreme Ct. 1984; cert. fin. planner., estate planner. Asst. dist. atty. Rockland County, New City, N.Y., 1973-74; ptnr. Amend & Amend, N.Y.C., 1974-78, O'Connell & Riley, Pearl River, N.Y., 1978—; pub., pres. 1099 Express Software, 1099 Express Ltd., Pearl River, 1987-97; adj. prof. estate planning Pace Univ., White Plains, N.Y.; atty. Town of Orangetown. Bd. dirs. United Way of Rockland County, N.Y., 1974-80, Rockland Family Shelter for Victims of Domestic Violence, 1981-85, literacy vols. Rockland County, 1989—; chmn. bd. dirs. New Hope Manor, Barryville, N.Y., 1985-88. Mem. ABA, Am. Soc. Hosp. Attys., Nat. Coun. Sch. Dist. Attys., N.Y. State Bar Assn. (ho. of dels. 1988-92), Rockland County Bar Assn. (bd. dirs. 1986—, pres. 1997-98), Internat. Platform Assn., Rotary Club of Pearl River (pres. 1999—). Democrat. Roman Catholic. Estate planning, Education and schools, Municipal (including bonds). Home: 145 Franklin Ave Pearl River NY 10965-2510 Office: O'Connell & Riley 144 E Central Ave Pearl River NY 10965-2532 also: 103 Chestnut Ridge Rd Montvale NJ 07645-1801

**RILEY, JOHN FREDERICK,** lawyer; b. Salisbury, N.C., Oct. 18, 1938; s. John Horace and Beatrice (Williams) R.; m. Jan Colby, June 20, 1965; children: John Michael, Jennifer Lynn, Julia Grace. BA, Wake Forest U., 1960; JD, U. N.C., 1967. Bar: N.C. 1967. Law clk. to presiding justice N.C. Supreme Ct., Raleigh, 1967-68; assoc. Leroy, Wells, Shaw & Hornthal, Elizabeth City, N.C., 1968-70; ptnr. Leroy, Wells, Shaw, Hornthal & Riley, Elizabeth City, N.C., 1970-85, Hornthal, Riley, Ellis & Maland, Elizabeth City, N.C., 1985—. Chmn. adv. bd. Salvation Army, Elizabeth City, 1976-77; trustee Elizabeth City State U., 1981-86. Hankins scholar Wake Forest U., Winston-Salem, N.C., 1956. Mem. ABA, N.C. Bar Assn. (bd. dirs. real property sect. 1979-83), N.C. Land Title Assn., Elizabeth City Bar Assn. (pres. 1973-74), 1st Jud. Dist. Bar Assn. (pres. 1985-86). Democrat. Methodist. Club: Harbor Club (Norfolk, Va.), Pine Lakes Country (Elizabeth City, N.C.). Rotary. Avocations: golf, tennis, boating. Real property, General corporate, Probate. Home: 101 Inlet Dr Elizabeth City NC 27909-3225 Office: Hornthal Riley Ellis & Maland 301 E Main St # 220 Elizabeth City NC 27909-4425

**RILEY, MICHAEL HYLAN,** lawyer; b. Ardmore, Okla., Oct. 26, 1951; s. Paul Emerson and Anne (Hylan) R. AB cum laude, Harvard U., 1973; JD, Northeastern U., 1978. Bar: Mass. 1978, U.S. Dist. Ct. Mass. 1980, U.S. Ct. Appeals (1st cir.) 1980. Assoc. White, Inker, Aronson, Boston, 1979-83, Chaplin & Milstein, Boston, 1984-86, Goldstein & Manello, Boston, 1986-91; ptnr. Goldstein & Manello, P.C., Boston, 1992-95; of counsel King & Navins, P.C., Wellesley, Mass., 1995—; lectr. Met. Coll. Boston U., 1986-92. Author: Estate Administration, 1985, 2d edit., 1993. Mem. ABA, Boston Bar Assn. Democrat. Avocations: books, music, food, wine, backpacking. Estate planning, Probate, Estate taxation. Home: 83 Grove Hill Ave Newton MA 02460-2336 Office: King & Navins PC 20 William St Wellesley MA 02481-4102

**RILEY, PAUL E.,** judge; b. 1942. BS, St. Louis U., 1964, JD, 1967. Hearings examiner motor carrier divsn. Ill. Commerce Commn., 1967-69; from asst. pub. defender to chief pub. defender Office of Pub. Defender, 1969-82; prin. Law Office of Paul Riley, Edwardsville, Ill., 1969-72, Mudge Riley and Lucco, Edwardsville, 1972-85; assoc. judge State of Ill., 1985, cir. judge, 1986; judge U.S. Dist. Ct. (so. dist.) Ill., East St. Louis, 1994—. Mem. ABA, Ill. State Bar Assn. (mem. assembly), Madison County Bar Assn. (pres. 1975). Office: US Dist Ct So Dist Ill Fed Courthouse 750 Missouri Ave East Saint Louis IL 62201-2954

**RILEY, PETER JAMES,** lawyer; b. Teaneck, N.J., June 7, 1956; s. John Bernard and Mary Ann (Lannig) R.; m. Laura Willson Latham, June 12, 1982; children: Peyton Lannig, Rachel Malone. BBA, U. Tex., 1978; JD, So. Meth. U., 1981. Bar: Tex. 1981, U.S. Dist. Ct. (no. dist.) Tex. 1981. Sr. shareholder Thompson & Knight, Dallas, 1981—. Mem. ABA, Dallas Bar Assn, Tower Club, Brook Hollow Golf Club. Republican. Presbyterian. Avocation: golf. General corporate, Bankruptcy. Home: 6606 Glendora Ave Dallas TX 75230-5220 Office: Thompson & Knight 3300 1st City Ctr Dallas TX 75201

**RILEY, SCOTT C.,** lawyer; b. Bklyn., Oct. 5, 1959; s. William A. and Kathleen (Howe) R.; m. Kathleen D. O'Connor, Oct. 6, 1984; children: Matthew, Brendan. BA, Seton Hall U., South Orange, N.J., 1981; JD, Seton Hall U., Newark, 1984. Bar: N.J. 1985, U.S. Dist. Ct. N.J. 1985. Assoc. Dwyer, Connell & Lisbona, Montclair, N.J., 1985-87; assoc. gen. counsel, v.p. Consolidated Ins. Group, Wilmington, Del., 1987-91; counsel Cigna Ins. Group, Phila., 1991-94; assoc. gen. counsel KWELM Cos., N.Y.C., 1994-98, head U.S. legal ops., 1998—. Mem. ABA (com. on environ. ins. coverage), Fedn. of Ins. and Corp. Counsel, Excess and Surplus Lines Claims Assn., N.J. State Bar Assn., Profl. Liability Underwriting Soc. Insurance, Environmental, Toxic tort. Office: KWELM Companies 599 Lexington Ave New York NY 10022-6030

**RILEY, STEVEN ALLEN,** lawyer; b. Nashville, Tenn., Oct. 2, 1952; s. Harris DeWitt Jr. and Margaret (Barry) R.; m. Laura Anne Trickett, Mar. 15, 1980; children: Mary Louise, Margaret Reed, Allen Trickett. BA, Vanderbilt U., 1974, JD, 1978. Bar: Tenn. 1978, U.S. Dist. Ct. (mid. dist.) Tenn., U.S. Ct. Appeals (6th cir.), U.S. Supreme Ct. Ptnr. Bass, Berry & Sims, Nashville, 1978-96, Bowen Riley Warnock & Jacobson, PLC, Nashville, 1996—. Mem. ABA (litig. bus. and antitrust sects.), Tenn. Bar Assn., Nashville Bar Assn. Presbyterian. General civil litigation, Health, Antitrust. Office: Bowen Riley Warnock & Jacobson PLC 1906 W End Ave Nashville TN 37203-2309

**RILEY, THOMAS JACKSON,** lawyer; b. New Hebron, Miss., July 19, 1933; s. James Arthur and Mary (Baker) R.; m. Helen Gayle Anderson, Feb. 1, 1958 ;(dec. Mar. 1981); m. Billie Anderson, Nov. 1, 1981; children: Thomas Jackson Jr., Mark Riley, Franklin Lawrence. BS, U. So. Miss., 1958; LLB, U. Miss., 1961, JD, 1968. Bar: Miss. 1961, U.S. Dist. Ct. Miss. 1965, U.S. Ct. Appeals (5th cir.) 1965. Atty. State of Miss., 1961—; sch. bd. atty. Perry County Schs., New Augusta, Miss., 1975—, Richton (Miss.) Schs., 1970—. Prosecutor City of Hattiesburg, 1965, Forrest County, Hattiesburg, 1969; bd. dirs. YMCA, pres., 1972-74. With U.S. Army, 1953-56. Republican. Baptist. Avocations: fishing, hunting, gardening. Home: 54 Cabin Rd Hattiesburg MS 39401-8853

**RILEY, WILLIAM JAY,** lawyer; b. Lincoln, Nebr., Mar. 11, 1947; s. Don Paul and Marian Frances (Munn) R.; m. Norma Jean Mason, Dec. 27, 1965; children: Brian, Kevin, Erin. BA, U. Nebr., 1969, JD with distinction, 1972. Bar: Nebr. 1972, U.S. Dist. Ct. Nebr. 1972, U.S. Ct. Appeals (8th cir.) 1974; cert. civil trial specialist Nat. Bd. Trial Advocacy. Law clk. U.S. Ct. Appeals (8th cir.), Omaha, 1972-73; assoc. Fitzgerald, Schorr Law Firm, Omaha, 1973-79, ptnr., 1979—; adj. prof. trial practice Creighton U. Coll. Law, Omaha, 1991—; chmn. fed. practice com. Fed. Ct., 1992-94. Scoutmaster Boy Scouts Am., Omaha, 1979-89, scout membership chair Mid Am. Coun., 1995-98. Recipient Silver Beaver award Boy Scouts Am., 1991. Fellow Am. Coll. Trial Lawyers (chair state com. 1997-99), Nebr. State Bar Found.; mem. Am. Bd. Trial Advs. (treas., v.p. 1998—), Nebr. State Bar Assn. (chmn. ethics com. 1996-99, mem. ho. of dels. 1998—), Omaha Bar Assn. (treas. 1997-98), Robert M. Spire Inns of Ct. (master 1994—, counselor 1997-98), Order of Coif, Phi Beta Kappa. Republican. Methodist. Avocations: reading, hiking, cycling. General civil litigation, Federal civil litigation, State civil litigation. Office: Fitzgerald Schorr Law Firm 1100 Woodmen Tower Omaha NE 68102

**RILL, JAMES FRANKLIN,** lawyer; b. Evanston, Ill., Mar. 4, 1933; s. John Columbus and Frances Eleanor (Hill) R.; m. Mary Elizabeth Laws, June 14, 1957; children: James Franklin, Roderick M. AB cum laude, Dartmouth Coll., 1954; LLB, Harvard, 1959. Bar: D.C. bar 1959. Legis. asst. Congressman James P. S. Devereux, Washington, 1952; pvt. practice Washington, 1959-89; assoc. Steadman, Collier & Shannon, 1959-63; ptnr. Collier, Shannon & Rill, 1963-69, Collier, Shannon, Rill & Scott, 1969-89; asst. atty. gen., antitrust div. U.S. Dept. Justice, Washington, 1989-92; ptnr. Collier, Shannon, Rill & Scott, Washington, 1992—; co-chair internat. competition policy adv. com. U.S. Dept. Justice, 1997—; pub. mem. Adminstrv. Conf. of U.S., 1992-94; coun. prin. Coun. for Excellence in Govt.; mem., advisor panel Office of Tech. Assessment of Multinat. Firms and U.S. Tech. Base. Contbr. articles to profl. jours. Trustee emeritus Bullis Sch., Potomac, Md. Served to 1st lt. arty. AUS, 1954-56. Fellow Am. Bar Found.; mem. ABA (antitrust law sect., past chmn.), D.C. Bar Assn., Phi Delta Theta, Met. Club, Loudon Valley Club. Home: 7305 Masters Dr Potomac MD 20854-3850 Office: Collier Shannon Rill & Scott 3050 K St NW Ste 400 Washington DC 20007-5100

**RINEHART, WILLIAM JAMES,** lawyer; b. Kansas City, Mo., June 2, 1948; s. Jim Hugh and Julia Eilene (Tolbert) R; m. Mary Kathleen Jones Bishop (div.); children: Jamie Michell, Kari Dawn, William Michael; m. Linda Kay Holland, Mar. 20, 1977; children: Heather Lynn, James Freeman. AA, El Reno Jr. Coll., 1978; BA in Criminal Justice, Ctrl. State U., 1979; JD, Oklahoma City U., 1985. Bar: Okla. 1989, U.S. Dist. Ct. (we. dist.) Okla. 1990, U.S. Dist. Ct. (ea. dist.) Okla. 1991, U.S. Dist. Ct. (no. dist.) Okla. 1992, U.S. Ct. Appeals (10th cir.) 1993), U.S. Supreme Ct. 1994. Private practice William Rinehart, Atty. at Law, El Reno, Okla., 1989—; atty., litig. Okla. Dept. Transp., Oklahoma City, 1990—. Bd. pres. El Reno Sch. Bd. Capt. USAR, 1967-96, ret. Avocation: Web authoring. General civil litigation, General practice, Condemnation. Office: State of Okla Dept Transp 200 NE 21st St Oklahoma City OK 73105-3204

**RING, LEONARD M.,** lawyer; b. Taurage, Lithuania, May 11, 1923; came to U.S., 1930, naturalized, 1930; s. Abe and Rose (Kahn) R.; m. Donna R. Cecrle, June 29, 1959; children—Robert Steven, Susan Ruth. Student, N.Mex. Sch. Mines, 1943-44; LLB, DePaul U., 1949, JD; LLD (hon.), Suffolk U., 1990. Bar Ill. 1949. Spl. asst. atty. gen. State Ill., Chgo., 1967-72; spl. atty. Ill. Dept. Ins., Chgo., 1967-73; spl. trial atty. Met. San. Dist. Greater Chgo., 1967-77; lectr. civil trial, appellate practice, tort law Nat. Coll. Advocacy, San Francisco, 1971, 72; chmn. and spl. atty. com. jury instrns. Ill. Supreme Ct., 1967—; nat. chmn. Attys. Congl. Campaign Trust, Washington, 1975-79. Author: (with Harold A. Baker) Jury Instructions and Forms of Verdict, 1972. Editorial bd. Belli Law Jour., 1983—; adv. bd. So. Ill. U. Law Jour., 1983—. Contbr. chpts. to books including Callaghan's Illinois Practice Guide, Personal Injury, 1988 and chpt. 6 (Jury Selection and Persuasion) for Masters of Trial Practice, also numerous articles to profl. jours. Trustee, Roscoe Pound-Am. Trial Lawyers Found., Washington, 1978-80; chmn. bd. trustees Avery Coonley Sch., Downers Grove, Ill., 1974-75. Served with U.S. Army, 1943-46. Decorated Purple Heart. Fellow Am. Coll. Trial Lawyers, Internat. Acad. Trial Lawyers, Internat. Soc. Barristers, Inner Circle Advs.; mem. Soc. Trial Lawyers, Am. Judicature Soc., Appellate Lawyers Assn. (pres. 1974-75), Assn. Trial Lawyers Assn. (nat. pres. 1973-74), Ill. Trial Lawyers Assn. (pres. 1966-68), Trial Lawyers for Pub. Justice (founder, pres. 1990-91), Chgo. Bar Assn. (bd. mgrs. 1971-73, 2d v.p. 1993), ABA (coun. 1983—, chair tort and ins. sect. 1989—, fed. jud. standing com. 7th cir. 1991—), Ill. Bar Assn., Kans. Bar Assn. (hon., life), Lex Legion Bar Assn. (pres. 1976-78), Met. Club, Plaza Club, Meadow Club, River Club, Monroe Club. State civil litigation, Personal injury, Federal civil litigation. Home: Ginger Creek 6 Royal Vale Dr Oak Brook IL 60521 Office: Ill Supreme Ct PO Box 4987 Oak Brook IL 60522-4987

**RING, LUCILE WILEY,** lawyer; b. Kearney, Nebr., Jan. 2, 1920; d. Myrtie Mercer and Alice (Cowell) W.; m. John Robert Ring, Mar. 28, 1948; children: John Raymond, James Wiley, Thomas Eric. AB, U. Nebr. at Kearney, 1944; JD, Washington U., 1946. Bar: Mo. 1946, U.S. Dist. Ct. (ea. dist.) Mo. 1947, U.S. Ct. Appeals (8th cir.) 1972. Atty.-adviser, chief legal group adjudications br. Army Fin. Ctr., St. Louis, 1946-52; exec. dir. lawyer referral service St. Louis Bar, 1960-70; pvt. practice, St. Louis, 1960—; staff law clk. U.S. Ct. Appeals (8th cir.), St. Louis, 1970-72; exec. dir. St. Louis Com. on Cts., 1972-85; legal advisor Mo. State Anat. Bd., 1965-95; adj. prof. adminstrv. law Webster Coll., Webster Groves, Mo., 1977-78; mem. Mo. Profl. Liability Rev. Bd., State of Mo., 1977-79. Author, editor: Guide to Community Services - Who Do I Talk To, 1974, 75, 1976-79; St. Louis Court Directories, 1972, 73, 74, 75; Felony Procedures in St. Louis Courts, 1975; author: Breaking Barriers: The St. Louis Legacy of Women in Law 1869-1969, 1996; author (series): Women Lawyers in St. Louis History, 1996, Women Breaking Barriers, 1998; contbr. articles to profl. jours. Mem. Mo. Mental Health Authority, 1964-65; bd. dirs., v.p. Drug and Substance Abuse Council, met. St. Louis, 1976-83; mem. adv. council St. Louis Agy. on Tng. and Employment, 1976-83; mem. Mayor's Jud. Reform Subcom., St. Louis, 1974-76. Washington U. Sch. Law scholar, 1944-46; 1st Mo. woman nominated for St. Louis Ct. Appeals, Mo. Appellate Commn., 1972; 1st woman nominated judgeship Mo. Non-Partisan Ct. Plan, 1972; recipient letter of commendation Office of Chief of Fin., U.S. Army, 1952, Outstanding Alumni award U. Nebr. Kearney, 1994. Mem. Bar Assn. Met. St. Louis (v.p. 1975-76), Legal Services of Eastern Mo., Inc. (v.p. 1978-79, dir.), Legal Aid Soc. of St. Louis City and County (bd. dirs. 1977-78), HUD Women and Housing Commn. (commr. 1975), Women's Bar Assn. (treas. St. Louis chpt. 1949-50), Mo. Assn. Women Lawyers (treas. 1959-60, pres. 1960-61), Pi Kappa Delta, Sigma Tau Delta, Xi Phi, Washington U. Dental Faculty Wives (pres. 1972-74). Methodist. General practice. Home and Office: 2041 Reservoir Loop Rd Selah WA 98942-9616

**RING, RENEE ETHELINE,** lawyer; b. Frankfurt, Germany, May 29, 1950; arrived in U.S., 1950; d. Vincent Martin and Etheline Bergetta (Schoolmeesters) R.; m. Paul J. Zofnass, June 24, 1982; Jessica Renee, Rebecca Anne. BA, Catholic U. Am., 1972; JD, U. Va., 1976. Bar: N.Y. 1977. Assoc. Whitman & Ransom, N.Y.C., 1976-83; assoc. Carro, Spanbock, Fass, Geller, Kaster & Cuiffo, N.Y.C., 1983-86, ptnr., 1986; ptnr. Finley Kumble Wagner et. al., N.Y.C., 1987; of counsel Kaye, Scholer, Fierman, Hays & Handler, N.Y.C., 1988; ptnr. Kaye, Scholer, Fierman, Hays & Handler, LLP, N.Y.C., 1989-97, Hunton & Williams, N.Y.C., 1997—. Mem. exec. com. Lawyers for Clinton, Washington, 1991-92; team capt. Clinton Transition Team, Washington, 1992-93; mem. Nat. Lawyers Coun. Dem. Nat. Com., 1993-98; trustee The Clinton Legal Expense Trust, 1998—; mem. Alumni Coun. U. Va. Sch. of Law, 1997—. Mem. ABA, N.Y. Women's Bar Assn. Democrat. Roman Catholic. General corporate, Securities, Banking. Office: Hunton & Williams 200 Park Ave Rm 4400 New York NY 10166-0091

**RING, RONALD HERMAN,** lawyer; b. Flint, Mich., Nov. 30, 1938; s. Herman and Lydia (Miller) R.; m. Joan Kay Whitener, Aug. 5, 1966. AB, U. Mich., 1961, LLB, 1964. Bar: Mich. 1964, U.S. Dist. Ct. (ea. dist.) Mich. 1966. Assoc. Beagle, Benton & Hicks, Flint, 1964-69; ptnr. Beagle & Ring, Flint, 1970-80, Beagle, Ring & Beagle, Flint, 1980-85, Ring, Beagle & Busch, Flint, 1985-93, Ronald H. Ring, P.C., Flint, 1993-95; pvt. practice Flint, 1991—. Mem. meml. com. Crossroads Village, Flint, 1981; pres. Family Service Agy., Genesee County, Mich., 1986. Mem. ABA, Assn. Trial Lawyers Am., Mich. Bar Assn. (delivery of legal service com. 1986, med. malpractice panel 1986), Genesee County Bar Assn. (pres. 1980-81, bd. dirs. 1979-82, cir. ct. mediation panel 1986). Club: Ostego Ski (Gaylord, Mich.). Avocations: skiing, sailing. State civil litigation, Personal injury, General practice. Office: 11083 Bussa Rd Rapid City MI 49676-9662

**RINGEL, DEAN,** lawyer; b. N.Y.C., Dec. 12, 1947; m. Ronnie Sussman, Aug. 24, 1969; children: Marion, Alicia. BA, Columbia Coll., 1967; JD, Yale U., 1971. Bar: N.Y. 1972, U.S. Ct. Appeals (6th cir.) 1972, U.S. Ct. Appeals (2d and D.C. cirs.) 1974, U.S. Supreme Ct. 1976, U.S. Ct. Appeals (10th cir.) 1982, U.S. Ct. Appeals (11th cir.) 1997. Law clk. to Judge Anthony J. Celebrezze U.S. Ct. Appeals (6th cir.), 1971-72; assoc. Cahill Gordon & Reindel, N.Y.C., 1972-79; ptnr. Cahill, Gordon & Reindel, N.Y.C., 1979—. Mem. ABA (vice chmn. com. on freedom of speech and press 1978-79), Assn. Bar City N.Y. (commn. com., fed. litigation, antitrust and trade regulation), N.Y. State Bar (chmn. antitrust com., sect. comml. and fed. litigation 1994-96, co-chmn. fed. judiciary com. 1997—, media law com.), Pub. Edn. Assn. (trustee, sec.). Federal civil litigation, Antitrust, Libel. Office: Cahill Gordon & Reindel 80 Pine St Fl 17 New York NY 10005-1790

**RINGEL, FRED MORTON,** lawyer; b. Brunswick, Ga., July 19, 1929; s. Phil S. and Louise (Pfeiffer) R.; m. Toby Markowitz, Mar. 18, 1962; children: Andrew Franklin, Douglas Eric, Michael Stanley, Edrea Janet Piper. A.B., U. Ga., 1950; LL.B. magna cum laude, Harvard U. (mem. bd. Law Rev. 1954-55), 1955. Bar: Ga. 1951, Fla. 1955, N.Y. 1956. Research asst. Am. Law Inst., N.Y.C., 1955-56; assoc. firm Cravath, Swaine & Moore, N.Y.C., 1956-59; atty. W.R. Grace & Co., N.Y.C., 1959-60; mem. firm Rogers, Towers, Bailey, Jones & Gay, P.A., Jacksonville, Fla., 1961—; also treas. Rogers, Towers, Bailey, Jones & Gay, P.A. Contbr. articles to legal jours. Bd. govs. Fla. Nature Conservancy, 1962-69. Served with USAF, 1951-53; 1t. Col. Res. Recipient Oak Leaf award Nature Conservancy, 1974. Mem. Am. Bar Assn., Am. Law Inst., Phi Beta Kappa. General corporate, State and local taxation. Home: 4478 Craven Rd W Jacksonville FL 32257-8049 Office: Rogers Towers Bailey Jones & Gay 1301 Gulf Life Dr Ste 1500 Jacksonville FL 32207-1811

**RINGER, DARRELL WAYNE,** lawyer; b. Elizabeth, N.J., Apr. 14, 1948; s. Darrell Wayne and Elva (Brown) R.; m. Mary Kay Williamson, Mar. 6, 1970 (div. May 1977); 1 child, Daniel Benjamin; m. Rebecca Ruth Bonner, Feb. 23 1979; 1 child, Darren Wayne. BS in Physics, W.Va. U., 1971; MBA, U. N.D., 1975; JD, W.Va. U., 1978. Bar: W.Va. 1978, U.S. Dist. Ct. (no. and so. dists.) W.Va. 1978. Assoc. Jones, Williams, West & Jones, Clarksburg, W.Va., 1978-80, Moreland & Ringer, Morgantown, W.Va., 1980-83, Reeder, Shuman, Ringer & Wiley, Morgantown, 1983-91, Ringer Law Offices, Morgantown, 1991—; 1st asst. prosecutor Monongalia County, W.Va., 1985-87; host W.Va. Pub. TV, PBS Pub. Affairs Programming, 1991—. Bd. dirs. Monongalia County (W.Va.) Mental Health Assn., Morgantown, 1981-83; mem. W.Va. U. Animal Care and Use Com., 1985—. Capt. USAF, 1971-75. Mem. ABA, ATLA, W.Va. Bar Assn. (pres. 1999-2000), Monongalia County Bar Assn. (sec. 1980-92), W.Va. Trial Lawyers Assn. (bd. govs. 1982-91). Democrat. Avocation: amateur radio. General corporate, Criminal, Personal injury. Home: 18 W Front St Morgantown WV 26501-4507 Office: 68 Donley St Morgantown WV 26501-5907

**RINGLE, BRETT ADELBERT,** lawyer, petroleum company executive; b. Berkeley, Calif., Mar. 17, 1951; s. Forrest A. and Elizabeth V. (Darnall) R.; m. Sue Kinslow, May 26, 1973. BA, U. Tex., 1973, JD, 1976. Bar: Tex. 1976, U.S. Dist. Ct. (no. dist.) Tex. 1976, U.S. Supreme Ct. 1980, U.S. Ct. Appeals (5th cir.) 1984. Ptnr., Shank, Irwin & Conant, Dallas, 1976-86, Jones, Day, Reavis & Pogue, Dallas, 1986-96; v.p. Hunt Petroleum Corp., Dallas, 1996—; adj. prof. law So. Meth. U., Dallas, 1983. Author: (with J.W. Moore and H.I. Bendix) Moore's Federal Practice, 2nd edit., Vol. 12, 1980, Vol. 13, 1981, (with J.W. Moore) Vol. 1A, 1982, Vol. 1A Part 2, 1989. Mem. Dallas Bar Assn. Federal civil litigation, State civil litigation, General practice. Home: 3514 Gillon Ave Dallas TX 75205-3220 Office: Hunt Petroleum Corp 1601 Elm St 5000 Thanksgiving Tower Dallas TX 75201

**RINGLER, JEROME LAWRENCE,** lawyer; b. Detroit, Dec. 26, 1948. BA, Mich. State U., 1970; JD, U. San Francisco, 1974. Bar: Calif. 1974, U.S. Ct. Appeals (9th cir.) 1974, U.S. Dist. Ct. (no. dist.) Calif. 1974, U.S. Dist. Ct. (ctrl. dist.) Calif. 1975, U.S. Dist. Ct. (so. dist.) Calif. 1981. Assoc. Parker, Stansbury et al, L.A., 1974-76; assoc. Fogel, Feldman, Ostrov, Ringler & Klevens, Santa Monica, Calif., 1976-80, ptnr., 1980—; arbitrator L.A. Superior Ct. Arbitration Program, 1980-85. Named Verdictum Juris Trial Lawyer of Yr., 1996. Mem. ATLA, ABA, State Bar Calif., L.A. County Bar Assn. (litigation sect., exec. com. 1994—), L.A. Trial Lawyers Assn. (bd. govs. 1981—, treas. 1988, sec. 1989, v.p. 1990, pres.-elect 1991, pres. 1992, Trial Lawyer of the Yr. 1987), Calif. Trial Lawyers Assn., Am. Bd. Trial Advs. (assoc. 1988, adv. 1991), Inns of Ct. (master). Avocations: skiing, tennis. Personal injury, General civil litigation, Product liability. Office: Fogel Feldman Ostrov Ringler & Klevens 1620 26th St # 100S Santa Monica CA 90404-4013

**RINGO, ROBERT GRIBBLE,** lawyer; b. Spokane, Wash., Aug. 18, 1924; s. Floyd V. and Claire (Williams) R.; m. Kathryn Reese, May 24, 1953; children: Molly, Robert, Charles, Julie Ann, Mary Ellen. BS, U. Oreg., 1949; LLB, N.W. Coll. Law, Portland, Oreg., 1951. Bar: Oreg. 1951, U.S. Ct. Mil Appeals 1969, U.S. Supreme Ct. 1970, U.S. Ct. Appeals (9th Cir.) 1969. Dep. dist. atty. Benton Co., Corvallis, Oreg., 1951-53; ptnr. Ringo & Walton, Corvallis, 1953-85, Ringo, Stuber, Ensor & Hadlock P.C., Corvallis, 1986—. Bd. dirs. Good Samaritan Hosp., Corvallis, 1988—. Lt. col. USAFR, 1972. Mem. ABA, Benton County Bar Assn. (pres. 1964-65), Oreg. Bar Assn. (bd. govs. 1980-83, sec. 1982-83), ATLA (bd. govs. 1982-90), Oreg. Trial Lawyers Assn. (pres. (1979-80), Am. Bd. Trial Advs. (diplomat, nat. exec. com. 1982), State of Oreg. Profl. Responsibility Bd, State of Oregon Jud. Fitness Commn., Oregon Law Found. (Pres. 1994). Democrat. Episcopalian. General civil litigation, Personal injury, Product liability. Office: Ringo Stuber Ensor & Hadlock PC PO Box 1108 Corvallis OR 97339-1108

**RINI, ALICE GERTRUDE,** law educator, lawyer, nursing educator; b. N.Y.C.; d. John W. and Jacqueline F. (Dilworth) Anderson; m. Leonard Paul Rini; children: Alice Marie, Paul William, Anthony John. BS, Adelphi U., 1961, MS, 1966; postgrad., St. John's U., 1975-79; JD, No. Ky. U., 1988. Bar: Ky. 1989. Prof. nursing Nassau C.C., Garden City, N.Y., 1966-79; chair dept. nursing No. Ky. U., Highland Heights, N.Y., 1980-87; assoc. prof. nursing No. Ky. U., 1980—; of counsel Wasson, Braden, Heeter & King, Newport, N.Y., 1996-97; adj. prof. law No. Ky. U., Highland Heights, 1987—. Author: (with others) Core Curriculum Gerontology Nursing, 1995, Core Curriculum Advanced Nursing Practice, 1997, Nursing Documentation: Legal Focus Across Practice Settings, 1998; contbr. articles to profl. jours. Bd. dirs. Brighton Ctr., Newport, Ky., 1983-99; mem. adv. bd. Inst. for Health Freedom, Washington. Mem. Am. Assn. Nurse Attys. (bd. dirs. 1989-92), Nat. Gerontology Nurses Assn. (mem. editl. bd. 1996—), No. Ky. Bar Assn. (sect. officer 1989—, health law com. officer 1992—), Sigma Theta Tau (nominating com. 1991, rsch. com. 1997—). Home e-mail: rinia@email.msn.com. Office e-mail: rini@nku.edu. Home: PO Box 176 Alexandria KY 41001-0176

**RINSKY, JOEL CHARLES,** lawyer; b. Bklyn., Jan. 29, 1938; s. Irving C. and Elsie (Millman) R.; m. Judith L. Lynn, Jan. 26, 1963; children: Heidi M., Heather S., Jason W. BS, Rutgers U., 1961, LLB, 1962, JD, 1968. Bar: N.J. 1963, U.S. Dist. Ct. N.J. 1963, U.S. Supreme Ct. 1967, U.S. Ct. Appeals (3d cir.) 1986; cert. civil trial atty., N.J. Pvt. practice, Livingston, N.J., 1964-97; sr. ptnr. Rinsky & Marley L.L.C., Livingston, 1997-98; of counsel Gonzalez and Weichert P.C., Livingston, 1999—. Committeeman Millburn-Short Hills (N.J.) Dem. Com., 1982-97, vice chmn., 1983-87; trustee Student Loan Fund, Millburn, 1983-91. Fellow Am. Acad. Matrimonial Lawyers; mem. N.J. Bar Assn., Essex County Bar Assn. (exec. com. sect. family law). Jewish. Avocations: tennis, chess, golf, piano. Family and matrimonial, Personal injury, Real property. Home: 87 Sullivan Dr West Orange NJ 07052-2262 Office: 127 East Mount Pleasant Ave Livingston NJ 07039

**RINTAMAKI, JOHN M.,** lawyer. BBA, U. Mich., 1964, JD, 1967. Bar: Mich. 1968, Pa. 1973. Sr. atty. internat. Ford Motor Co., 1978-84, assoc. counsel corp. and financings, 1984-86, asst. sec., assoc. counsel, 1986-92, sec., asst. gen. counsel, 1993-98, v.p., gen. counsel, sec., 1999—. Office: Ford Motor Co Office of Gen Counsel The American Rd Dearborn MI 48121-1899*

**RINTELMAN, DONALD BRIAN,** lawyer; b. Madison, Wis., May 25, 1955; s. Donald Carl Rintelman and Eugenie Elizabeth Kroll; m. Ann Marie Gall, Aug. 2, 1980; children: Katherine Ann, Brian James. BA, U. Wis., 1976; JD, U. Mich., 1980. Bar: Wis. 1980, U.S. Dist. Ct. (ea. dist.) Wis. 1980, U.S. Dist. Ct. (we. dist.) Wis. 1984. Assoc. Whyte & Hirschboeck, S.C., Milw., 1980-86, shareholder, 1986—; mng. dir. Whyte Hirschboeck Dudek, S.C., Milw., 1994—; chmn. comml. practice group Am. Law Firm Assn. Internat., L.A., 1998—. Bd. mem. Ozaukee County United Way Allocations, Mequon, Wis., 1986-88; treas. Cedarburg (Wis.) Cmty. Scholarship Fund, 1991-93; coun. pres. Advent Luth. Ch., Cedarburg, 1996-97. Mem. ABA, Wis. Bar Assn., Milw. Bar Assn. Republican. Avocations: travel, golf, enjoying children's soccer, swimming. General corporate, Contracts commercial, Mergers and acquisitions. Home: N108w7365 Balfour St Cedarburg WI 53012-3248 Office: Whyte Hirschboeck Dudek SC 111 E Wisconsin Ave Ste 2100 Milwaukee WI 53202-4861

**RINTOUL, DAVID SKINNER,** lawyer; b. Westport, Conn., July 11, 1961; s. Stephen Rich and Eve Clark (Green) R.; m. Judy Mae Duncan, Aug. 7, 1988; children: Emily Grace, Maxwell Duncan. BA, Johns Hopkins U., 1983; JD with high honors, U. Conn., Hartford, 1986. Bar: Ill. 1986, Conn. 1989, U.S. Dist. Ct. (no. dist.) Ill. 1987, U.S. Dist. Ct. Conn. 1989, U.S. Ct. Appeals (2d cir.) 1997. Atty. Schwartz & Freeman, Chgo., 1986-89, Levin & D'Agostino, Hartford, Conn., 1989-91; ptnr. Rintoul & Rintoul, Rocky Hill, Conn., 1991-95, Rosenblatt, Rintoul & Rintoul, West Hartford, Conn., 1996-99, Rintoul & Rintoul, Glastonbury, Conn., 1999—. Mem. Nat. Employment Lawyers Assn., Conn. Employment Lawyers Assn. (bd. dirs. 1996—). Democrat. Episcopalian. Avocations: rowing, cycling, singing. Labor. Home: 73 Hunter Ln Glastonbury CT 06033-1440 Office: Rintoul & Rintoul 136 New London Tpke Glastonbury CT 06033-2234

**RIOPELLE, BRIAN CHARLES,** lawyer; b. Brockville, Ont., Can., Dec. 15, 1961; s. Harold Francis and Alice Oetjen Riopelle; m. Elizabeth Eshelman, Sept. 2, 1990; children: Fain, Kyle. BA in English, Yale U., 1984; JD, U. Va., 1989. Bar: Calif., Va. Assoc. Morgan Stanley & Co. Inc., N.Y.C., 1984-86; law clk. The Honorable Stephen V. Wilson, L.A., 1989-90; atty. Latham & Watkins, L.A., 1990-93, McGuire, Woods, Battle & Boothe LLP, Richmond, Va., 1993—; adj. prof. law T.C. Williams Sch. Law, Richmond, 1994-97. Ordained elder River Rd. Presbyn. Ch., Richmond, 1997—. Avocations: soccer, chess, military history. E-mail: bcriopel@mwbb.com. Fax: 804-698-2150. Intellectual property, Federal civil litigation, Antitrust. Office: McGuire Woods Battle & Boothe LLP 901 E Cary St Richmond VA 23219-4057

**RIORDAN, DEBORAH TRUBY,** lawyer; b. Georgetown, S.C., May 29, 1968; d. David Charles and Vickie (Turner) Truby; m. Gary Ray Riordan, Aug. 26, 1995; 1 child, Katherine Spencer. BA, U. Ark., 1990; JD, Vanderbilt U., 1993. Bar: Ark. 1993, U.S. Dist. Ct. (ea. and we. dists.) Ark. 1993. Law clk. various law firms, Little Rock, 1991-92; assoc. Shults & Ray LLP, Little Rock, 1993-99; dir. Hill, Gilstrap, Perkins & Warner, Little Rock, 1999—. Staff writer Interaction mag., 1997-98. Vol. Ctrl. Ark. Legal Svcs., Little Rock, 1993-97; vol. coord. Ark. Arts Ctr., Little Rock, 1993-95; tng. com., sec., yearbook editor Jr. League, Little Rock, 1996—; pastor parish rev. com. Trinity United Methodist Ch., Little Rock, 1998—. Mem. ABA, Arkansas County Bar Assn., Pulaski County Bar Assn. Avocations: tennis, walking, reading, Arkansas Razorbacks football, spending time with daughter. Contracts commercial, Real property, Communications. Home: 8 Auriel Dr Little Rock AR 72223-9111 Office: Hill Gilstrap Perkins & Warner 1 Information Way Ste 200 Little Rock AR 72202

**RIPPLE, KENNETH FRANCIS,** federal judge; b. Pitts., May 19, 1943; s. Raymond John and Rita (Holden) R.; m. Mary Andrea DeWeese, July 27, 1968; children: Gregory, Raymond, Christopher. AB, Fordham U., 1965; JD, U. Va., 1968; LLM, George Washington U., 1972, LLD (hon.), 1992. Bar: Va. 1968, N.Y. 1969, U.S. Supreme Ct. 1972, D.C. 1976, Ind. 1984, U.S. Ct. Appeals (7th cir.), U.S. Ct. Mil. Appeals, U.S. Dist. Ct. (no. dist.) Ind. Atty. IBM Corp., Armonk, N.Y., 1968; legal officer U.S. Supreme Ct., Washington, 1972-73, spl. asst. to chief justice Warren E. Burger, 1973-77; prof. law U. Notre Dame, 1977—; judge U.S. Ct. Appeals (7th cir.), South Bend, 1985—; reporter Appellate Rules Com., Washington, 1978-85; commn. on mil. justice U.S. Dept. Def., Washington, 1984-85; cons. Supreme Ct. Ala., 1983, Calif. Bd. Bar Examiners, 1981; cons. Anglo-Am. Jud. Exch., 1977, mem., 1980; adv. com. Bill of Rights to Bicentennial Constn. Commn., 1989; mem. adv. com. on appellate rules Jud. Conf. U.S., 1985-90, chmn., 1990-93; chmn. adv. com. on appellate judge edn. Fed. Jud. Ctr., 1996—. Author: Constitutional Litigation, 1984. Served with JAGC, USN, 1968-72. Mem. ABA, Am. Law Inst., Phi Beta Kappa. Office: US Ct of Appeals 208 US Courthouse 204 S Main St South Bend IN 46601-2122 also: Fed Bldg 219 S Dearborn St Ste 2660 Chicago IL 60604-1803

**RIPPLINGER, GEORGE RAYMOND, JR.,** lawyer; b. East St. Louis, Ill., Apr. 19, 1945; s. George Raymond and Virginia Lee (Toupnot) R. AB, U. Ill., 1967, JD, 1970. Bar: Ill. 1970, U.S. Dist. Ct. (so. dist.) Ill. 1970, U.S. Ct. Appeals (7th cir.) 1970, U.S. Dist. Ct. (cen. dist.) Ill. 1972, U.S. Tax Ct. 1971, U.S. Claims Ct. 1973, U.S. Ct. Mil. Appeals 1985, U.S. Supreme Ct. 1973, U.S. Ct. Internat. Trade 1973, U.S. Dist. Ct. (ea. dist.) Mo. 1977, U.S. Ct. Appeals (8th cir.) 1977. Assoc. Meyer & Meyer, Belleville and Greenville, Ill., 1970-72; assoc. Meyer & Kaucher, Belleville and Highland, Ill., 1972-73; sole practice Belleville, 1974; ptnr. Ripplinger & Walsh, Clayton, Mo., 1974-76, Ripplinger, Dixon & Johnston, Belleville, Ill., St. Louis, Scott AFB, and Bellvue, Neb., 1976-94; prin. George Ripplinger & Assoc., Belleville, Ill., 1994—. Bd. visitors Coll. of Law U. Ill., 1979-86, pres., 1983-84; chmn. Southwestern Ill. chpt. ACLU, 1971-74, 76-80; mem. exec. com. Sierra Club, 1981-85. Lt. col. USAR, 1970—. Fellow Am. Bar Found., Ill. Bar Found. (bd. dirs. 1994—, treas. 1998—); mem. ABA (ho. of dels. 1989-93, 95-99, chmn. workers compensation com. 1985-88, divsn. dir. 1988-89, 95-99, mem. coun. 1989-93, sec. 1999— gen. practice/solo and small firm sect.), ATLA, Lawyers Trust Fund Ill. (bd. dirs. 1988-94), Ill. Bar Assn. (bd. govs. 1981-83, 87-93, sec. 1991-92), St. Clair County Bar Assn., Met. St. Louis Bar Assn., Mo. Bar Assn., Ill. Trial Lawyers Assn. (bd. advs. 1993—), Land of Lincoln Legal Assistance Found. (bd. dirs. 1982-88, vice chmn. 1987-88), Res. Officers Assn. Democrat. E-mail: ripplinger@prodigy.net. Personal injury, Professional liability, Product liability. Office: George Ripplinger & Assoc 2215 W Main St Belleville IL 62226-6668

**RISI, JOSEPH JOHN,** lawyer; b. N.Y.C., Oct. 4, 1956; m. Karen Ann Janusz; children: Joseph, Christopher, Kathryn. BA in Govt., St. John's U., 1978; JD, Widener U., 1982. Bar: N.Y. 1983, U.S. Ct. Mil. Appeals 1986, U.S. Tax Ct. 1988, U.S. Supreme Ct. 1994. Prin. law asst. N.Y. State Ct. System, Kew Gardens, 1983-88; mng. atty. Risi & Santospirito, L.I. City, N.Y., 1988-96, Risi & Assocs., L.I. City, N.Y., 1996—; arbitrator Civil Ct. N.Y.C., 1988—; mem. adv. bd. Chgo. Title Ins. Co., Mineola, N.Y., 1990—. Mem. adv. bd. Aviation Adv. Bd., Queens County, N.Y., 1990—, Caring & Sharing, Queens County, 1995—. Mem. N.Y. State Bar Assn., Queens County Bar Assn. (chmn. law & legis. 1997—), L.I. City Lawyers Assn. (past pres., grievance com. 1994—). General civil litigation, Contracts commercial, Estate planning. Office: Risi & Assocs 23-19 31st St Long Island City NY 11105

**RISTAU, KENNETH EUGENE, JR.,** lawyer; b. Knoxville, Tenn., Feb. 14, 1939; s. Kenneth E. and Frances (Besch) R.; m. Mary Emily George, Nov. 27, 1967 (div. Apr. 1985); children: Heidi, Mary Robin, Kenny, Michael, Robert; m. Emily Pettis, Mar. 31, 1990; 1 child, James Patrick. BA, Colgate U., 1961; JD, NYU, 1964. Bar: U.S. Ct. Appeals (9th cir.) 1968, U.S. Ct. Appeals (D.C. cir.) 1974, U.S. Supreme Ct. 1974, U.S. Dist. Ct., Southern Dist. of Calif., 1993. Assoc. Gibson, Dunn & Crutcher, L.A., 1964-69; ptnr. Gibson, Dunn & Crutcher, Irvine, Calif., 1969—. Fellow Coll. Labor and Employment Lawyers (charter); mem. Employers Group (adv. bd.), Orange County Indsl. Rels. Rsch. Assn. (pres. 1992-93), Big Canyon Country Club, Rancho Las Palmas Country Club, Newport Beach Tennis Club, Santa Fe

Hunt M.F.H. (pres., bd. dirs.). Administrative and regulatory, Labor. Office: Gibson Dunn & Crutcher Jamboree Ctr 4 Park Plz Irvine CA 92614-8557

**RISTAU, MARK MOODY,** lawyer, petroleum consultant; b. Warren, Pa., Mar. 21, 1944; s. Harold J. and Eleanor K. (Moody) R. BA, Pa. Mil. Coll., 1966; BA, Widner Coll., 1966; JD, Case Western Res. U., 1969. Bar: Pa. 1970, D.C. 1972, U.S. Supreme Ct. 1973, N.Y. 1982. Pvt. practice, Warren, 1970-85, Warren and Vancouver, B.C., Can., 1976-85, Jamestown, N.Y., 1982-85, sr. ptnr. Ristau & McKeirnan, Warren, 1986—; sr. dir. Pa. Allied Oil Producers, 1972-78, atty. for Pa. Field Producers, 1981-85; ptnr. SAR Devel., 1984-91, Slagle Almendinger & Ristau, 1983-89; dir. Try-M Fin. Co., 1978-81; counsel United Refining Co., Pennbank, Enchanced Oil Recovery, Consol. Services, 1982-84; chmn. bd. Comml. Service Corp., U.S. interim trustee, 1979-88, bankruptcy trustee, 1988-98; CEO, Silicon Electro-physics Corp., Inc., 1988-91, Phoenix Materials Corp., Inc., 1988-91; chmn. bd. dirs. Warren Industries, Inc., 1991-94; bd. dirs. Petrex, Inc., A & A Metal Fabricating; U.S. counsel Brazilian Promotions, Inc. of Brazilian Govt., 1981-85; v.p. Daytona Apts., Inc., Daytona Beach, Fla.; sec. Daytona Devel. League. Mem. Warren County Bd. Pub. Assistance, 1970-71, chmn., 1971-72; mem. Broward County (Fla.) Devel. League, 1981-83; mem. Fla. Profl. Recruitment Assn., 1980-83. Recipient Tate Meml. award, 1981; Sambas award, 1981. Mem. Assn. Trial Lawyers Am., Am. Arbitration Assn., Warren County Bar Assn. (past pres.). Clubs: Eagles (hon. life); Ipanema (Brazil); Conewango (Warren). Contbr. articles on law to profl. jours.; case reporter Legal Intelligencer, 1972-79. Banking, Bankruptcy, Contracts commercial. Home and Office: 203 W 3d Ave Warren PA 16365-2331

**RISTUBEN, KAREN R.,** lawyer; b. Malden, Mass., Sept. 28, 1956; d. James Francis and Jane Dale Ristuben; m. Eric N. Starkoff, Apr. 16, 1988 (div. Apr. 12, 1994); 1 child, James Hunter. BFA, Tufts U., 1982; JD, Suffolk U., 1987. Bar: Mass., U.S. Dist. Ct. Mass. 1987. Paralegal Parker Coulter Daley & White, Boston, 1982-83; paralegal Meehan Boyle & Cohen, Boston, 1983-87, assoc., 1987-94, dir., 1994—; chair, bd. dirs. Ctr. for Health Care Negotiation, Boston. Author: Containing and Using Medical Records in Massachusetts, 1993; contbr. articles to profl. jours. Bd. govs. Sch. of the Mus. of Fine Arts, 1996-97. Mem. ABA (vice chair medicine and law com. 1995—), Mass. Bar Assn. (budge and fin. com. 1998, chair health law sect. coun. 1996-98), Mass. Acad. of Trial Attys. (bd. govs. 1995—), Womens Bar Assn. Avocations: sea kayaking, biking, running, art, music. Personal injury, Health, Alternative dispute resolution. Office: Meehan Boyle & Cohen 2 Center Plz Ste 600 Boston MA 02108-1922

**RITCHIE, ALEXANDER BUCHAN,** lawyer; b. Detroit, Apr. 19, 1923; s. Alexander Stevenson and Margaret (May) R.; m. Sheila Spellacy, June 1998; 1 child, Barbara Ritchie Drolshagen. BA, Wayne State U., 1947, JD, 1949. Bar: Mich. 1949. Pvt. practice Detroit, 1949-52, 84—; asst. gen. counsel, asst. v.p. Maccabees Mutual Life Ins. Co., Detroit, 1952-65; v.p., sec., gen. counsel Maccabees Mutual Life Ins. Co., Southfield, Mich., 1977-84; sec., house counsel Wayne Nat. Life Ins. Co., Detroit, 1966-67; ptnr. Fenton, Nederlander, Dodge & Ritchie, Detroit, 1967-77; spl. asst. atty. gen. State Mich., 1974-77. Bd. mem. Detroit Bd. Edn., 1971-77, Detroit Ctrl. Bd. Edn., 1971-73; bd. Police Commrs., Detroit, 1974-77; bd. dirs. Doctor's Hosp., Detroit, 1974-89. With U.S. Army, 1943-46. Recipient Key to the City of Detroit, Mayor Coleman Young, 1977. Mem. Mich. State Bar Assn. Avocations: reading, golf, theatre, gourmet. Home: 29255 Laurel Woods Dr Apt 201 Southfield MI 48034-4647

**RITCHIE, STAFFORD DUFF, II,** lawyer; b. Buffalo, June 13, 1948; s. Stafford Duff Ritchie and A. Elizabeth Smith Cavage; m. Rebecca P. Thompson, June 27, 1975; children: Stafford D. III, Thompson C., Glynis A. Student, Rensselaer Poly. Inst., Troy, N.Y., 1966-68; BS in Econs., U. Pa., 1970, JD, 1974. Bar: N.Y. 1975. Atty./advisor, asst. gen. counsel, spl. asst. gen. counsel Adminstrv. Office of U.S. Cts., Washington, 1974-82, assoc. gen. counsel, to 1982; gen. counsel Cavages, Inc., Buffalo, 1982-94; pvt. practice Buffalo, 1994—; counsel Coms. of Jud. Conf. of U.S., Jud. Conf. Com., Jud. Conf. of 9th Cir. of U.S.; spl. counsel for major procurement Supreme Ct. of U.S. Trustee Calasanctius Sch., Buffalo, 1990-92; dir. Crisis Svcs. Inc., Buffalo, 1997—. Sgt. USMCR, 1970-76. Mem. ABA, ATLA, N.Y. State Bar Assn. Avocation: computers. Contracts commercial, Real property, General practice. Office: 200 Olympic Towers 300 Pearl St Buffalo NY 14202-2501

**RITH, DAVID J., II,** lawyer; b. Cape Girardeau, Mo., July 4, 1961; s. David J. and Carol A. (Bennett) R. BA, Concordia Coll., 1983; JD, U. Mo., 1989. Bar: Mo. 1989, U.S. Dist. Ct. (we. dist.) Mo. 1989, U.S. Tax Ct. 1993. Law clk. Supreme Ct. Mo., Jefferson City, 1989-90; atty. Lowes & Drusch, Cape Girardeau, Mo., 1990—. Bd. dirs. Luth. Family & Children's Svcs., Cape Girardeau, 1996—, Southeast Mo. Legal Svcs., Charleston, 1998—. Lutheran. Insurance, General civil litigation, Criminal. Office: Lowes & Dusch 2913 Independence St Cape Girardeau MO 63703-8320

**RITHER, ALAN CRAIG,** lawyer; b. Mpls., May 14, 1947; s. Clifford Lawrence and Martha (Kirstine) R.; m. Kathy Lorene Richardson, Sept. 12, 1969; children: David, Sara. BA in Polit. Sci., U. Wash., 1969, JD, 1972. Bar: Wash. 1973, U.S. Dist. Ct. (ea. dist.) Wash. 1976. Sr. atty. Battelle, Pacific N.W. divsn., Richland, Wash., 1973—; chmn. Export Control Coord. Orgn., 1994-95. V.p. Radiant Light Broadcasting, Richland, 1989—. Major, USAFR. Fellow Nat. Contract Mgmt. Assn. (cert.); mem. Wash. State Bar Assn. (chmn. internat. practice sect. 1995-96). Mem. Assemblies of God. Avocations: bowhunting, astronomy, camping. Government contracts and claims, Private international, Intellectual property. Office: Battelle Pacific Northwest Divsn 902 Battelle Blvd Richland WA 99352-1793

**RITT, ROGER MERRILL,** lawyer; b. N.Y.C., Mar. 26, 1950; m. Mimi Santini, Aug. 25, 1974; children: Evan Samuel, David Martin. BA, U. Pa., 1972; JD, Boston U., 1975, LLM, 1976. Bar: Mass. 1977, Pa. 1975, U.S. Tax Ct. Sr. ptnr. Hale and Dorr, Boston, 1984—; adj. prof. grad. tax program Boston U., 1979-92; panelist Am. Law Inst., Mass. Continuing Legal Edn., World Trade Inst., NYU Inst. on Fed. Taxation; mem. exec. com. Fed. Tax Inst. New Eng. Treas. Found. for Tax Edn. Mem. ABA (tax sect.), Boston Bar Assn. Corporate taxation, Taxation, general, Personal income taxation. Office: Hale and Dorr 60 State St Boston MA 02109-1816

**RITTENBERRY, KELLY CULHANE,** lawyer; b. Rockville Centre, N.Y., May 29, 1969; d. William and Eileen Patricia Culhane; m. Bryan Alex Rittenberry, July 8, 1995. BA, U. Okla., 1991; postgrad., So. Meth. U., 1993-94; JD, Marquette U., 1994. Bar: Tex. 1994, Wis. 1994, U.S. Dist. Ct. (no. dist.) Tex. 1994, U.S. Dist. Ct. (ea. dist.) Wis. 1994. Law clk. Gibson, Dunn & Crutcher, Dallas, summer 1992; summer assoc. Arter, Hadden, Johnson & Bromberg, Dallas, 1993-94, assoc., 1994-95; assoc. Akin, Gump, Strauss, Haver & Feld, Dallas, 1995—. Pro bono lawyer Martin Luther King Ctr., Dallas, 1997-98, Housing Crisis Ctr., Dallas, 1997-98, Legal Svcs. North Tex., Dallas, 1997-98, SMU Immigration Clinic, Dallas, 1997-98. Mem. FBA (bd. mem. young lawyers divsn. 1994—, nat. sec. young lawyers divsn. 1997-98, nat. treas. 1998—), State Bar Tex. (Coll.), Dallas Bar Assn. (judiciary com. 1996-98, media rels. com. 1996-98, entertainment com. 1996-98). Republican. Roman Catholic. Avocations: travel, skiing, reading, outdoor activities. Insurance, General civil litigation, Franchising. Office: Akin Gump Strauss Haver & Feld LLP 1700 Pacific Ave Ste 4100 Dallas TX 75201-4675

**RITTER, ANN,** lawyer; b. Gainesville, Fla.; d. Herbert David and Mary Ellen Kimmel; m. H.N. Ritter III, Apr. 28, 1985; 1 child, Kristy Ann. BS, Fla. State U., 1980; JD, U. Tenn., 1982. Assoc. Gilreath & Rowland, Knoxville, 1982-83, Law Office D.A. Speights, Hampten, S.C., 1983-84; assoc. Nessmotley Loadholt Richardson Poole (formerly Blatt & Fales, Charleston, 1984-92, ptnr., 1992—. Product liability. Home: 936 White Point Blvd Charleston SC 29412-4322

**RITTER, ANN L.,** lawyer; b. N.Y.C., May 20, 1933; d. Joseph and Grace (Goodman) R. BA, Hunter Coll., 1954; JD, N.Y. Law Sch., 1970; postgrad. Law Sch., NYU, 1971-72. Bar: N.Y. 1971, U.S. Ct. Appeals (2d cir.) 1975, U.S. Supreme Ct. 1975. Writer, 1954-70, editor, 1955-66, tchr., 1966-70; atty. Am. Soc. Composers, Authors and Pubs., N.Y.C., 1971-72, Greater N.Y. Ins. Co., N.Y.C., 1973-74; sr. ptnr. Brenhouse & Ritter, N.Y.C., 1974-78; sole practice N.Y.C., 1978—. Editor N.Y. Immigration News, 1975-76. Mem. ABA, Am. Immigration Lawyers Assn. (treas. 1983-84, sec. 1984-85, vice-chair 1985-86, chair 1986-87, chair program com. 1989-90, chair spkrs. bur. 1989-90, chair media liaison 1989-90), N.Y. State Bar Assn., N.Y. County Lawyers Assn., Assn. Trial Lawyers Am., N.Y. State Trial Lawyers Assn., N.Y.C. Bar Assn., Watergate East Assn. (v.p., asst. treas. 1990—). Democrat. Jewish. Immigration, naturalization, and customs, Family and matrimonial, Personal injury. Home: 47 E 87th St New York NY 10128-1005 Office: 420 Madison Ave Rm 1200 New York NY 10017-1171

**RITTER, JEFFREY BLAKE,** lawyer; b. Iowa City, Iowa, Sept. 13, 1954; s. Charles Clifford and Patricia Ann (Wise) R.; m. Rita L. Soronen, Jan. 1, 1977; children: Jordan, Chelsea. BA, MA, Ohio State U., 1976; JD, Duke U., 1979. Bar: Ky. 1979, D.C. 1980, Ohio 1983. Assoc. Barnett & Alagia, Louisville, 1979-82, Schwartz, Kelm, Warren & Rubenstein, Columbus, Ohio, 1982-90; of counsel Vorys, Sater, Seymour & Pease, Columbus, 1991-94; U.S. legal adviser for facilitation UN Working Party, Geneva, 1990-96; dir. ECLIPS, Columbus, 1994-98, Document Authentication Sys., Inc., Balt., 1998—. Chair Adv. Group on Internat. Trade, Columbus, 1990. Mem. ABA (chair sect. of bus. law com. on cyberspace law, 1995-98, reporter, subcom. on scope of uniform comml. code 1990-91). Democrat. Avocations: cycling, jazz, poetry. Computer, General corporate, Private international. Office: Document Authentication Sys Inc 351 W Camden St Ste 800 Baltimore MD 21201-2479

**RITTER, ROBERT THORNTON,** lawyer; b. N.Y.C., Nov. 4, 1956; s. Robert J. and Barbara W. (Foust) R.; m. Rebecca L. Grubbs, July 25, 1981; children: Sarah, Luke, Robert R. BA, Duke U., 1979; JD, Washington U., 1984. Bar: Mo., 1984, U.S. Dist. Ct. (ea. dist.) Mo., 1985. Assoc. William Brown, Atty. at Law, Bridgeton, Mo., 1984-85, Kopsky & Vouga, Chesterfield, Mo., 1986; pvt. practice Clayton, Mo., 1987-89; ptnr. Ritter & Gusdorf, Clayton, 1990-96; mem. Ritter & Gusdorf L.C., Clayton, 1997—. Treas. Campaign Election of State Rep. Steve Moore, 1988; coach Little League Baseball. Mem. Mo. Bar Assn., Bar Assn. Met. St. Louis, St. Loius Assn. Christian Attys. (bd. dirs. 1994—). Republican. Avocation: tennis. Personal injury, Family and matrimonial, Real property. Office: Ritter & Gusdorf LC 225 S Meramec Ave Ste 1220 Clayton MO 63105-3596

**RITVO, ELIZABETH ANN,** lawyer; b. Washington, July 14, 1951; d. Martin and Zelma Ritvo; m. Robert G. Kunzendorf, June 5, 1971; children: Jennifer, Rebecca. AB, Yale Coll., 1973; JD, U. Va., 1976. Bar: Va. 1976, D.C. 1978, U.S. Dist. Ct. D.C. 1978, Mass. 1980, U.S. Ct. Appeals (D.C. cir.), U.S. Dist. Ct. Mass. 1980, U.S. Ct. Appeals (1st cir.) 1980, U.S. Supreme Ct. 1987. Staff atty. Dept. Transp., Washington, 1976-77; assoc. Kirlin Campbell & Keating, Washington, 1977-79; assoc. Brown Rudnick Freed & Gesmer, Boston, 1980-84, ptnr., 1985—. Mem. Women's Bar Found. (trustee 1994-99). General civil litigation, Appellate, Libel. Office: Brown Rudnick Freed & Gesmer One Financial Ctr Boston MA 02111

**RITZ, STEPHEN MARK,** financial advisor, lawyer; b. Midland, Mich., Aug. 23, 1962; s. Alvin H. and Patricia M. (Padway) R. BA, Northwestern U., 1985; JD, Ind. U., 1989. Bar: Ill. 1990, U.S. Dist. Ct. (no. dist.) Ill. 1990, Ind. 1996. Atty. Chapman & Cutler, Chgo., 1990-93; pres., CEO S.M. Ritz and Co., Inc., Indpls., 1994-97; CEO Newport Pension Mgmt. LLC, 1997—; dir. Indsl. Logistics, Inc., Indpls., 1994-96. Mem. ABA, Inst. CFPs, Registry CFPs, Internat. Assn. Fin. Planners. Office: Newport Pension Mgmt 9465 Counselors Row Ste 108 Indianapolis IN 46240-3816

**RIVA, DAVID MICHAEL,** lawyer; b. Herrin, Ill., Sept. 19, 1948; s. Charles David and Maryann (Peek) R.; m. Paula Jean Calvert, July 31, 1971; children: Allison, Jennifer, Katie, Sarah. BA, Knox Coll., 1970; JD, Washington U., 1974. Bar: Ill. 1974, U.S. Dist. Ct. (so. dist.) Ill. 1974. Pvt. practice West Frankfort, Ill., 1974—. Officer West Frankfort Bd. Edn., 1983-93; bd. dirs. West Frankfort Recreation Assn. Mem. Masons. Avocation: coaching girls fast pitch softball. General practice, Probate, Real property. Home: 1270 Ramsey Heights Rd West Frankfort IL 62896-4971 Office: 226 E Main St West Frankfort IL 62896-2406

**RIVARD, DEBRA LYNN,** legal secretary; b. Pottsville, Pa., Apr. 22, 1957; d. Marlin Milton and Eileen Louise (Wagner) Nagle; m. James Thomas Conlogue, Jr., July 21, 1979 (div. Aug. 1988); 1 child, James Thomas Conlogue III; m. Joseph Crawford Rivard, Dec. 3, 1988; children: Andrea, Andrew, Amber Renee. Grad., Del. Technical & C.C., Dover, 1998. Listing sec. John Holmes Yacht Broker, Georgetown, Md., 1975-76; inside sales mgr. So. States Co-op Inc., Middletown, Smyrna, Del., 1976-79; ins. salesman John Hancock, Wilmington, Del., 1979-80; salesperson Wide World Imports, Dover, Del., 1980-81; divsnl. mgr./buyer Leggett Dept. Store, Dover, Seaford, Del., 1981-86; distbr./mktg. dir. Ocean Air Syss. I & II (Rexair), Dover, Glasgow, Del., 1986-91; store mgr. Dress Barn Inc., Wilmington, Dover, Rehoboth Beach, Del., 1991-95; legal sec. House of Reps.-Legis. Hall, Dover, 1996—; advisor Assn. Info. Tech. Profls.- Del Tech, Dover. Religious instr. St. Bernadettes Cath. Ch., Harrington, Del., 1995-97; computer trainer Help Yourself Tech., Harrington, 1997—. Recipient Contbn. award Student Support Svcs., 1997; named to All-Del. Acad. Team, Del. C.C. Bd., 1998. Mem. Assn. Info. Tech. Profls. (v.p., acting pres. 1997—, Contbn. award 1998), Phi Theta Kappa (cons., All-USA Acad. Team 1998—), Alpha Beta Gamma. Republican. Roman Catholic. Avocations: reading, exercising. Fax: 302-398-9779. Home E-mail: joedee1@bellatlantic.net. Office E-mail: lrivard@legis.state.de.us. Home: 226 Delaware Ave Harrington DE 19952-1202 Office: House of Reps Court St Dover DE 19901

**RIVELLESE, VINCENT WOODROW,** lawyer; b. Smithtown, N.Y., Apr. 27, 1969; s. Vincent Joseph and Lynne Joan R.; m. Nadine Mary-Cecille Rapacioli, Oct. 25, 1997. AB, Harvard U., 1991; JD, Am. U., 1994. Bar: N.Y. 1995, U.S. Dist. Ct. (so. dist.) N.Y. 1998. Asst. dist. atty. Manhattan Dist. Attys. Office, N.Y.C., 1994—. Mem. N.Y. County Lawyers Assn. Avocations: jazz, saxophone, science fiction, puzzles. Office: Dist Attys Office 1 Hogan Pl New York NY 10013-4311

**RIVERA, JOSE DE JESUS,** prosecutor; b. Zacatecas, Mex., 1950; m. Nina Rivera; three children, two stepchildren. BA, No. Ariz. U.; JD, Ariz. State U. Atty. civil rights divsn. Dept. of Justice, 1976-77; asst. U.S. atty. Dist. Ariz., 1977-81; with Langerman, Beam, Lewis and Marks, 1981-84; ptnr. Rivera, Scales and Kizer, 1984—; atty. City of El Mirage; U.S. atty. Ariz. dist. U.S. Dept. Justice, 1998—. Bd. dirs. Inst. Cmty. Initiatives; mem. com. Los Abogados, Phoenix Planning and zoning Commn.; coach Little League. With N.G. Mem. Ariz. State Bar. (bd. govs.). Democrat. Avocation: reading. Office: Rm 4000 230 N 1st Ave Phoenix AZ 85025-0085*

**RIVERA, OSCAR R.,** lawyer, corporate executive; b. Havana, Cuba, Dec. 8, 1956; s. Alcibiades R. and Marian (Fernandez) R.; m. Diana J. Bartnett; children: Peter, Taylor. BBA, U. Miami, 1978; JD, Georgetown U., 1981. Bar: Fla. 1981, U.S. Dist. Ct. (so. dist.) Fla. 1982, U.S. Tax Ct. 1982. Assoc. Corrigan, Zelman & Bander P.A., Miami, Fla., 1981-83; ptnr. Siegfried, Rivera, Lerner & De La Torre P.A., Miami, 1984—; adj. prof. law U. Miami, 1987—. Asst. mgr. campaign to elect Michael O'Donovan, Miami, 1976; mem. youth adv. bd., Miami, 1975-78, youth planning council Dade County, Miami, 1975-78. Mem. ABA, Cuban Am. Bar Assn., Internat. Coun. Shopping Ctrs. (v.p. Fla. polit. action com., v.p. Fla. govtl. affairs com., state dir. Fla.), Little Havana Kiwanis, Orange Key, Omicron Delta Kappa, Phi Kappa Phi. Avocations: photography, skiing. Real property, Landlord-tenant, General corporate.

**RIVERA, RANFI R.,** lawyer; b. Mt. Vernon, N.Y., Jan. 13, 1967; s. Ann. L. Rivera; m. Mariangela Premoli, June 18, 1994; 1 child, Andrew M. BS in Computer Sci., NYU, 1988; JD, Fordham U., 1991. Bar: N.Y., N.J. Assoc. atty. Biedermann, Hoenig, Massamillo & Ruff, N.Y.C., 1992-95; sr. assoc. atty. Oppenheimer, Wolff & Donnelly, N.Y.C., 1995—. Mem. ABA, Nat. Hispanic Bar Assn., N.Y. State Bar Assn., Assn. Bar City of N.Y. Roman Catholic. Avocations: golf, music. Fax: 212-486-0708. E-mail: rrivera@owdlaw.com. Office: Oppenheimer Wolff & Donnelly 153 E 53d St New York NY 10022

**RIVERA, WALTER,** lawyer; b. N.Y.C., Jan. 18, 1955; s. Marcelino and Ana Maria (Reyes) R. BA, Columbia U., 1976; JD, U. Pa., 1979. Bar: N.Y. 1979. Law clk. to cen. legal research staff N.Y. State Ct. Appeals, Albany, 1979-81; asst. atty. gen. State of N.Y., N.Y.C., 1981-85; sole practice N.Y.C., 1985-88; shareholder Rivera & Muniz, P.C., N.Y.C., 1988-93, Law Offices of Walter Rivera P.C., 1994-97; ptnr. Rivera, Hunter, Colon & Dobshinsky, LLP, N.Y.C., 1998—; chmn. Third World Lawyers Caucus, N.Y. State Atty. Gen.'s Office, N.Y.C., 1984; arbitrator City Ct. N.Y.C., 1985. Mem. ABA, Puerto Rican Bar Assn., Nat. Hispanic Bar Assn., N.Y. State Bar Assn., Assn. Bar City N.Y. (past chmn. com. on small law firm mgmt.). Avocations: camping, travel. State civil litigation, General civil litigation, Federal civil litigation. Home: 2 Nob Hill Dr Elmsford NY 10523-2417 Office: Rivera Hunter Colon & Dohshinsky LLP 61 Broadway Rm 1030 New York NY 10006-2701

**RIVERS, KENNETH JAY,** retired judicial administrator, consultant; b. N.Y.C., Feb. 13, 1938; s. Alexander Maximillian and Albertina Ray (Gay) R.; m. Leah B. Files, Sept. 21, 1957 (div.); children: Londa Denise, Nancy Laura, Terrie Ruth, Kenneth J. Jr. AAS in Criminal Justice, St. Francis Coll., Bklyn., 1978, BS in Criminal Justice, 1978; MPA, L.I. Univ., 1981. Correction officer N.Y.C. Dept. Correction, 1965-69; ct. officer N.Y. State Unified Ct. System, N.Y.C., 1969-71, asst. ct. clk., 1971-73, sr. ct. clk., 1973-85, assoc. ct. clk., 1985-88, prin. ct. clk., 1988-90, dep. chief clk., 1991-93; ret., 1993; tng. instr. N.Y. State Unified Ct. System, N.Y.C., 1985—, pers. assessor, 1985—; lectr. John Jay Coll. NYU, N.Y.C., 1987. Author: Juvenile Crime Survey, 1982, New York State Jury Selection, 1984. Bd. dirs. Parkway Consumers Med. Coun., Bklyn., 1983—, Cen. Bklyn. Tenant's Rights, 1988—. Recipient Leadership award Tribune Soc., N.Y. State Cts., 1987, Svc. award, 1988, Cert. of Merit award Fedn. Afro-Am. Civil Svc. Orgns., 1987. Mem. ASPA, Internat. Pers. Mgmt. Assn., Acad. Polit. Sci., Conf. Minority Pub. Adminstrs., Masons. Democrat. Methodist. Avocation: jazz musician.

**RIVET, DIANA WITTMER,** lawyer, developer; b. Auburn, N.Y., Apr. 28, 1931; d. George Wittmer and Anne (Jenkins) Wittmer Hauswirth; m. Paul Henry Rivet, Oct. 24, 1952; children: Gail, Robin, Leslie, Heather, Clayton, Eric. BA, Keuka Coll., 1951; JD, Bklyn. Law Sch., 1956. Bar: N.Y. 1956, U.S. Dist. Ct. (e. and so. dists.) N.Y. 1975. Sole practice Orangeburg, N.Y., 1957—; county atty. Rockland County (N.Y.), 1974-77; asst. to legis. chmn. Rockland County, 1978-79; counsel, adminstr. Indsl. Devel. Agy., Rockland County, 1980-91, Rockland Econ. Devel. Corp., 1981-90; counsel, exec. dir. Pvt. IndustryCoun. Rockland county, 1980-90; pres., CEO Environ. Mgmt. Ltd., Orangeburg, 1980-98; mem. air mgmt. adv. com. N.Y. State Dept. Environ. Conservation 1984-92, Orangetown Planning Bd., 1993—. Pres. Rockland County coun. Girl Scouts U.S., 1981-84; chmn. Rockland County United Way, 1996-97, mem. campaign com., 1983-84, 88-89, 93, sec., 1997—, bd. dirs., 1988-94, 95—; mem. Leadership Rockland, 1991-94. Recipient Cmty. Svc. award Keuka Coll., 1965, Disting. Svc. award Town of Orangetown, 1970, Disting. Svc. award Rockland County, 1989, Econ. Devel. award Rockland Econ. Devel. Corp., 1990; named Businessperson of Yr. Jour. News, Rockland County, 1982. Mem. ABA, N.Y. State Bar Assn. (mcpl. law sect. exec. com. 1976-83, environ. law sect. exec. com. 1974-86), Rockland County Bar Assn. (chair environ. law com. 1994-96), Rockland Bus. Assn. (bd. dirs. 1981-97, small bus. adv. com. 1998, gov. affairs com. 1998—), Rockland Computer Users' Group (bd. dirs. 1998—). Democrat. Mem. Religious Soc. of Friends. Environmental, Real property, Municipal (including bonds). Home: 1 Lester Dr Orangeburg NY 10962-2316

**RIVETTE, FRANCIS ROBERT,** lawyer; b. Syracuse, N.Y., May 1, 1952; s. Francis Patrick and Barbara Parker (Smith) R. BA, Allegheny Coll., 1974; JD, Syracuse U., 1977. Bar: N.Y. 1978, D.C. 1980, U.S. Dist. Ct. (no. dist.) N.Y. 1978, U.S. Supreme Ct. 1993. Ptnr. Rivette & Rivette P.C., Syracuse, 1978—; corp. counsel Fangand Enterprises Ltd., 1978—. Mem. ATLA, N.Y. State Trial Lawyers Assn., Syracuse Corvette Club (pres. 1985-86), Sportscar Vintage Racing Assn., Nat. Corvette Restorers Soc. (nat. judge, 1985, 88, 95, 97), Phi Delta Phi, Phi Gamma Mu. Republican. General practice, Personal injury, General corporate. Home: 200 Old Liverpool Rd Liverpool NY 13088-6354 Office: Rivette & Rivette PC 224 Harrison St Ste 306 Syracuse NY 13202-3067

**RIVKIN, JOHN LAWRENCE,** lawyer; b. Hewlett, N.Y., Dec. 16, 1955; s. Leonard Lambert and Lenore Diana R.; m. Nancy Jean Sandarg, July 26, 1987; children: Erika, Diana, Michael. BA summa cum laude, Union Coll., 1978; JD, U. Va., 1981. Bar: N.Y. 1982, U.S. Dist. Ct. (ea. and so. dists.) N.Y. 1982, Fla. 1983, D.C. 1985, U.S. Claims Ct. 1985, U.S. Ct. Appeals (3rd, 5th, 11th cirs.) 1992, U.S. Supreme Ct. 1983. Sr. ptnr. Rivkin, Radler & Kremer, Uniondale, N.Y., 1981—; disting. lectr. law, mem. nat. litig. panel U. Va. Sch. Law; lectr. law Practising Law Inst., N.Y., 1986; mem. adv. coun. Touro Law Sch., Huntington, N.Y.; mem. coun. overseers L.I. U., Old Brookville, N.Y.; spkr. in field. Contbr. articles to profl. jours. Nott scholar Union Coll., 1978. Mem. N.Y. State Trial Lawyers Assn., Fedn. Ins. Corp. Counsel, Def. Rsch. Inst., Huntington Yacht Club, Alpha Delta Phi. Avocation: yachting. Fax: 516-357-3333. E-mail: www.rivkinradler.com. Federal civil litigation, Insurance, Environmental. Office: Rivkin Radler & Kremer Eab Plz Uniondale NY 11556-0001

**RIVKIN, STEVEN ROBERT,** lawyer; b. Boston, Jan. 11, 1937; s. Bernard Morris and Ruth (Lasker) R.; m. Mary Stimpson Seckinger, Aug. 17, 1975; children: Caroline Seckinger Carlson, Robert Edward Seckinger, Sarah Edith Rivkin, Jesse Stimpson Rivkin. AB, Harvard U., 1958, LLB, 1962. Bar: Mass. 1963, D.C. 1967, Md. 1992, U.S. Supreme Ct. 1968. Analyst Weapons Systems Evaluation Group, Washington, 1958-59; tech. asst. for legal affairs White House Staff and Exec. Office of Pres., Washington, 1961-65; assoc. Foley Hoag & Eliot, Boston, 1965-67, Fisher Sharlitt & Gelband, Washington, 1967-68; counsel, ptnr. Nicholson & Carter, Washington, 1971-75; ptnr. Rivkin & Lewis, Washington, 1982-83; pvt. practice, Washington, 1968-70, 75-81, 83—; vis. fellow Progressive Policy Inst. of Dem. Leadership Coun., Washington, 1992; counsel Sloan Commn. on Cable Comms., N.Y.C., 1970-71. Author, editor 5 books; contbr. articles to profl. jours. With USAR, 1962-67. Recipient Travel and Study award Ford Found., 1970. Democrat. Jewish. Avocations: amateur cellist. E-mail: srrivkin@msn.com. Fax: 202-628-7630. FERC practice, Securities, Environmental. Home: 8013 Maple Ridge Rd Bethesda MD 20814-1307

**RIVLIN, LEWIS ALLEN,** lawyer, entrepreneur; b. N.Y.C., Oct. 15, 1929; s. Benjamin and Lena (Levy) R.; m. Alice Mitchell Rivlin, June 28, 1955 (div. Sept. 1977); children: Catherine Amy, Allan Mitchell, Douglas Gray; m. Dianne M. Farrington, Oct. 7, 1977; children: Benjamin, Leigh. BA, Swarthmore Coll., 1951; JD, Harvard Law Sch., 1957. Bar: D.C. 1957, U.S. Ct. Appeals (D.C. cir.) 1957, U.S. Supreme Ct. 1960. From ensign to commdr. U.S. Naval Reserve, 1951-71; atty. patent sect., civil divsn. U.S. Dept. Justice, Washington, D.C., 1957-59, sr. trial atty. gen. litigation sect., antitrust divsn., 1959-64; advanceman Hubert H. Humphrey For V.P. Campaign, 1964; ptnr. O'Connor, Green, Thomas, Walters & Kelly, Washington, D.C., 1965-68; del. coord. Hubert H. Humphrey For Pres. Campaign, Washington, D.C., 1968; Humphrey-Muskie campaign coord. Pa. Dem. Nat. Com., Harrisburg, Pa., 1968; founding ptnr. Peabody, Rivlin, Lambert & Meyers, Washington, D.C., 1969-81; chmn. & CEO New Venture Capital Corp., Rockville, Md., 1981—; founding ptnr. Rivlin, Velarde & Taylor, LLP, Washington, D.C., 1995-98; chmn. bd. dirs., CEO Tribal Funding Devel. and Mgmt. Corp., Rockville, Md., 1984—; pres. Gen. Internat. Fin. Corp., Rockville, 1985—; dir., exec. v.p., gen. counsel Hainan Zhonge Refinery, People's Rep. China, 1996—;. Co-author: (book) Report of the D.C. Circuit Judicial Conference Committee on ABA Standards for the Administration of Criminal Justice, 1973. Mem. ABA, Fed. Comms. Bar Assn., Fed. Bar Assn. Avocations: tennis, classical music, travel, sailing. Antitrust, Legislative, Public international. Office: Law Offices of Lewis A Rivlin PC 1825 Eye St NW Ste 400 Washington DC 20006-5415

**RIZOWY, CARLOS GUILLERMO,** lawyer, educator, political analyst; b. Sarandi Grande, Uruguay, Mar. 5, 1949; came to U.S., 1973, naturalized, 1981; s. Gerszon and Eva (Visnia) R.; m. Charlotte Gordon, Mar. 14, 1976; children: Brian Isaac, Yael Deborah, Michal Evie. BA, Hebrew U., Jerusalem, 1971; MA, U. Chgo., 1975, PhD, 1981; JD, Chgo. Kent Coll. Law, Ill. Inst. Tech., 1983. Bar: Ill. 1983, U.S. Dist. Ct. (no. dist.) Ill. 1983,

U.S. Ct. Appeals (7th cir.) 1983. Asst. prof. polit. sci. Roosevelt U., Chgo., 1982-89, chmn. dept. polit. sci., 1983-86, dir. internat. studies program, 1986-89; mng. ptnr. Ray, Rizowy & Fleischer, Chgo., 1983-90; ptnr. corp. law dept. Gottlieb and Schwartz, 1990-92; ptnr. Levenfeld, Eisenberg, Janger, Glassberg, Samotny & Halper, 1993-94; of counsel Sonnenschein, Nath & Rosenthal, 1994—; dir. Midwest Am. Friends of Hebrew U., 1997—; hon. consul of Uruguay, Chgo., 1994—; adj. assoc. prof. Spertus Coll. Judaica, Chgo., 1984—; weekly polit. analyst on Middle East, internat. law and fgn. policy, resource specialist Sta. WBEZ Pub. Radio and BBC Latin Am. Author: Avoiding Premises Liability Suits by Improving Security, 1991, Middle East Security: Five Areas to Watch, 1997. V.p., resource specialist to exec. com. Orgn. Children of Holocaust Survivors, Chgo., 1982; pres. Assn. Children Holocaust Survivors, 1986-91; pres. bd. dirs. Soviet Jewry Legal Advocacy Ctr., 1986-88; rsch. com. Nat. Strategy Forum, bd. dirs. UN Assn. U.S., 1985-89; mem. cmty. rels. com. Jewish Fedn. Met. Chgo., 1983-84; mem. adv. bd., chmn. internat. affairs commn. Am. Jewish Congress, Chgo., 1983-85, chmn. subcom. for Israel, 1986-88; mem. Nat. Spkrs. Bur. United Jewish Appeal, Nat. Spkrs. Bur. Devel. Corp. for Israel; mem. adv. bd. Chgo. Action for Soviet Jewry, 1983-85; bd. dirs. Am. Friends of Hebrew U., Chgo., 1984-86, Florence Heller Jewish Cmty. Ctr., 1986-88, Soviet Jewry Legal Advocacy Ctr., 1986-88; mem. human rights com. Anti-Defamation League, 1986, bd. dirs., 1989—; bd. dirs. Bd. Jewish Edn., 1989-91, Hispanic Coalition for Jobs, 1991-94; chmn. univ. educators divsn. Jewish United Fund, 1988-90; mem. consular corp. adv. bd. Internat. Vis. Ctr. Chgo., 1995—, com. fgn. affairs Chgo. Coun. Fgn. Rels., 1994—. Scholar Hebrew U., 1967-72, U. Chgo., 1972-78, Hillman Found., 1978, Peter Volid Found., 1980; recipient Globalist award Heritage Internat. Trade Assn., 1997. Mem. ATLA, ABA (chmn. bus. com. 1993-95), Assn. Ibero-Am. Consuls of Chgo., Ill. State Bar Assn., Chgo. Bar Assn. (internat. trade com.), Latin Am. Bar Assn., Nat. Hispanic Bar Assn., Am. Immigration Lawyers Assn., Am. Polit. Sci. Assn., Am. Judicature Soc., Exec. Club Chgo., Internat. Platform Assn., Wexner Heritage Found., Am. Forum, Latin Am. C. of C. (bd. dirs. 1991—, gen. counsel 1992—), Anshe Emet Congregation, Masons. Private international, Public international, Mergers and acquisitions. Office: Sonnenschein Nath & Rosenthal 8000 Sears Tower Chicago IL 60606

**RIZZARDI, KEITH WILLIAM,** lawyer; b. Bayshore, N.Y., June 21, 1969; s. William D. and Elenaor D. R. B of Govt., U. Va., 1991; JD, U. Fla., 1994; MPA, Fla. Atlantic U., 1998. Bar: Fla. 1994, U.S. Dist. Ct. (so. dist.) Fla. 1998. Paralegal Grumman Corp., Bethpage, N.Y., 1989-92; atty. South Fla. Water Mgmt. Dist., West Palm Beach, 1995—. Bd. dirs. Govs. Coun. Cmty. Health Partnerships, West Palm Beach, 1998—; cons., grant writer Sandoway House Nature Ctr., Delray Beach, Fla., 1998—. Mem. Phi Alpha Delta. Democrat. Lutheran. Avocations: golf, softball, stunt kites. Office: South Fla Water Mgmt Dist 3301 Gun Club Rd West Palm Beach FL 33406-3007

**RIZZO, JAMES GERARD,** lawyer; b. Hartford, Conn., Nov. 6, 1962; s. Thomas Dignan and Jean Kathryn (Foley) R.; m. Patricia Marie Conrad, Oct. 5, 1996; children: Madeleine Patrice, Abigail Rose. AB, Georgetown U., 1984; JD, Fordham U., 1990. Bar: Conn. 1990, N.Y. 1991, U.S. Dist. Ct. (ea. and so. dists.) N.Y. 1991, D.C. 1996, U.S. Supreme Ct. 1998. Assoc. Bower & Gardner, N.Y.C., 1990-93, Mudge, Rose, Guthrie, Alexander & Ferdon, N.Y.C., 1993-94, O'Melveny & Myers LLP, N.Y.C., 1994-97; ptnr. Carr Goodson Warner, Washington, 1997—. Hon. usher St. Patrick's Cathedral, N.Y.C., 1984—; v.p. St. Joseph's Parish Coun., Bronxville, N.Y., 1988-90. Mem. Bar Assn. D.C., Soc. of the Friendly Sons of St. Patrick, John Carroll Soc., Lowes Island Club, Sea Island Club. Republican. Roman Catholic. Environmental, General civil litigation, Product liability. Office: Carr Goodson Warner 1301 K St NW Ste 400 Washington DC 20005-3317

**RIZZO, JAMES S.,** lawyer; b. Rome, N.Y., July 3, 1969; s. James and Mary Ann R.; m. Lucy J. Giardino, Aug. 19, 1995; 1 child, Julia Reneé. BA in English, SUNY, Potsdam, 1991; JD, Union U., 1995. Bar: N.Y. 1996, U.S. Dist. Ct. (no. dist.) N.Y. 1996, U.S. Ct. Appeals (2d cir.) 1997, U.S. Supreme Ct. 1999. Asst. corp. counsel City of Rome, 1996, first asst. corp. counsel, 1996—. Mem. ABA, N.Y. State Bar Assn. (exec. com. alt. young lawyers sect. 1997-99, editor-in-chief Perspective Mag. young lawyers sect. 1999—), Oneida County Bar Assn., City Rome Bar Assn. (dir. 1998—). State civil litigation, Civil rights, Land use and zoning (including planning). Home: 1015 Jervis Ave Rome NY 13440-2338 Office: Corp Counsel City Hall City of Rome 198 N Washington St Rome NY 13440-5815

**RIZZO, JOHN JOSEPH,** lawyer; b. Blue Island, Ill., June 6, 1968; s. Joseph and Marie Susan Rizzo; m. Maureen Lyn Carter, Dec. 9, 1995; 1 child, Gianna Isabella. BA, Loyola U., Chgo., 1990; JD, Creighton U., 1994. Bar: Ill. 1994. Assoc. ptnr. Decker & Linn, Waukegan, Ill. Recipient Am. Legion merit award, 1982. Mem. Ill. State Bar Assn., Lake County Bar Assn., Chgo. Bar Assn., Ill. Trial Lawyers Assn., Workers Compensation Lawyers Assn., Justinian Legal Soc. (sec. 1999—), Sons of Italy (state del. 1996—). Workers' compensation, Personal injury, Libel. Home: 7191 Pennsbury Ln Gurnee IL 60031-9114 Office: Decker and Linn Ltd 215 N Utica St Waukegan IL 60085-4235

**RIZZO, RONALD STEPHEN,** lawyer; b. Kenosha, Wis., July 15, 1941; s. Frank Emmanuel and Rosalie (Lo Cicero); children: Ronald Stephen Jr., Michael Robert. BA, St. Norbert Coll., 1963; JD, Georgetown U., 1965, LLM in Taxation, 1966. Bar: Wis. 1965, Calif. 1967, Ill. 1999. Assoc. Kindel & Anderson, L.A., 1966-71, ptnr., 1971-86; ptnr. Jones, Day, Reavis & Pogue, L.A., 1986-93, Chgo., 1993—; bd. dirs. Guy LoCicero & Son Inc., Kenosha, Wis. Contbg. editor ERISA Litigation Reporter; mem. internat. adv. editl. bd. Jour. Pensions Mgmt. and Mktg. Schulte zur Hausen fellow Inst. Internat. and Fgn. Trade Law, Georgetown U., 1966. Fellow Am. Coll. Tax Counsel; mem. ABA (chmn. com. on employee benefits sect. on taxation 1988-89, vice chair com. on govt. submissions 1995-99), Los Angeles County Bar Assn. (chmn. com. on employee benefits sect. on taxation 1977-79, exec. com. 1977-78, 90-92), State Bar Calif. (co-chmn. com. on employee benefits sect. on taxation 1980), West Pension Conf. (steering com. L.A. chpt. 1980-83). Avocations: reading, golf, travel. Pension, profit-sharing, and employee benefits, Corporate taxation. Home: 1040 N Lake Shore Dr Apt 19C Chicago IL 60611-6164 Office: Jones Day Reavis & Pogue 77 W Wacker Dr Ste 3500 Chicago IL 60601-1692

**ROACH, ARVID EDWARD, II,** lawyer; b. Detroit, Sept. 6, 1951; s. Arvid Edward and Alda Elizabeth (Buckley) R. BA summa cum laude, Yale U., 1972; JD cum laude, Harvard U., 1977. Bar: D.C. 1978, N.Y. 1978, U.S. dist. ct. D.C. 1978, U.S. dist. ct. (so. dist.) N.Y. 1978, U.S. Ct. Appeals (10th cir.) 1980, U.S. Ct. Appeals (2d cir.) 1981, U.S. Ct. Appeals (D.C. cir.) 1981, U.S. Ct. Appeals (7th and 9th cirs.) 1982, U.S. Supreme Ct. 1983, U.S. Dist. Ct. Md., 1985, U.S. Ct. Appeals (3d, 4th, 5th, 6th, 8th, 11th cirs.) 1988, U.S. Ct. Appeals (1st cir.) 1992. Law clk. to judge U.S. Dist. Ct., 1977-78; assoc. Covington & Burling, Washington, 1978-85, ptnr., 1985—. Mem. ABA, Am. Law Inst. Contbr. articles to legal jours. Administrative and regulatory, Federal civil litigation, Pension, profit-sharing, and employee benefits. Office: Covington & Burling PO Box 7566 Washington DC 20044-7566

**ROACH, B. RANDALL,** lawyer, city council member; b. Dayton, Ohio, July 24, 1968; s. B.C. and Wanda Ruth (Hickey) R.; m. Julie Ann Herman, Aug. 24, 1996. BA in Psychology, Political Science, U. Dayton, 1991, JD, 1995. Adminstrv. asst. Office Lt. Gov., Columbus, 1989-91; law clerk Office Atty. Gen., Columbus, 1992-94; trial atty. Leonard & Roach, Bellbrook, Ohio, 1995-96, Cornyn, Roach & Hughes, Springboro, Ohio, 1997; vice chair Greene Co. Bd. Elections, Xenia, Ohio, 1995-96; bd. mem. Green Co. Bar Assn., 1997. Chmn. Greene Cty. Dem. Party, Xenia, 1994—; city councilman City Fairborn, 1995—; bd. mem. Fairborn Sr. Ctr., 1997—, Fairborn Neighborhood Ctr., 1994—. Mem. ABA, Am. Trial Lawyers Assn., Federal Bar Assn. Roman Catholic. Federal civil litigation, Labor, Government contracts and claims. Home: 51 Sunburst Dr Fairborn OH 45324-2530

**ROACH, EDGAR MAYO, JR.,** lawyer; b. Pinehurst, N.C., June 2, 1948; s. Edgar Mayo Sr. and Rhuamer (Richardson) R.; m. Deborah Day, Oct. 10, 1970; children: Edgar Mayo III, John Clifton. BA, Wake Forest U., 1969; JD with honors, U. N.C., 1974. Bar: N.C. 1974, Va. 1976, U.S. Ct. Appeals (4th cir.) 1976. Law clk. to judge U.S. Ct. Appeals (4th cir.), Abingdon, Va., 1974-75; assoc. Hunton & Williams, Richmond, Va., 1975-80; ptnr. Hunton & Williams, Raleigh, N.C., 1981-94; sr. v.p. Va. Power, Richmond, 1994-97; exec. v.p., CFO Dominion Resources, Inc. now Va. Electric & Power Co., Richmond, 1997—. Public utilities, Nuclear power. Home: 3142 Monument Ave Richmond VA 23221-1457 Office: Va Electric & Power Co 1 James River Plz PO Box 26666 Richmond VA 23261-6666

**ROACH, JON GILBERT,** lawyer; b. Knoxville, June 17, 1944; s. Walter Davis and Lena Rose (Chapman) R.; m. Mintha Marie Evans, Oct. 22, 1977; children: Jon G., II, Evan Graham. B.S., U. Tenn., 1967, J.D., 1969. Bar: Tenn. 1970, D.C. 1981, U.S. Ct. Appeals (6th cir.). Assoc. Stone & Bozeman, Knoxville, 1970-71; pvt. practice, Knoxville, 1971-83; city atty., dir. of law, Knoxville, 1976-83; ptnr. Peck, Shaffer & Williams, Knoxville, 1983-90, Watson, Hollow & Reeves, P.L.C., 1990—; mem. faculty Knoxville Bus. Coll., 1973-74; mem. Tenn. Commn. on Continuing Legal Edn. and Specialization of Tenn. Supreme Ct.; mem. bd. Bapt. Health Sys. Found. Mem. ABA, Tenn. Br Assn. (mem. ho. of dels.), Knoxville Bar Assn., D.C. Bar Assn. Democrat. Baptist. Club: Kiwanis (East Knoxville). Municipal (including bonds), General civil litigation, Probate. Home: 1701 River Shores Dr Knoxville TN 37914-6023 Office: Watson Hollow & Reeves PLC PO Box 131 1700 Tennessee Ave Knoxville TN 37921-2639

**ROACH, ROBERT MICHAEL, JR.,** lawyer; b. Bronxville, N.Y., May 27, 1955; s. Robert M. and Mary Dee R.; m. Marcia E. Backus, June 14, 1986. BA, Georgetown U., 1977; JD, U. Tex., 1981. Bar: Tex. 1981, U.S. Dist. Ct. (so. dist.) Tex. 1982, U.S. Ct. Appeals (5th cir.) 1982, U.S. Dist. Ct. (we. dist.) Tex. 1984, U.S. Supreme Ct. 1986, U.S. Dist. Ct. (ea. dist.) 1986, U.S. Dist. Ct. (no. dist.) Tex. 1988. Assoc. Vinson & Elkins, Houston, 1981-83, Ryan & Marshall, Houston, 1983, Mayor, Day & Caldwell, Houston, 1983-88; ptnr. Mayor, Day, Caldwell & Keeton, Houston, 1989-93; founding ptnr. Cook & Roach LLP, Houston, 1993—; dir. appellate advocacy U. Houston Law Ctr., 1994—; adj. prof. law U. Houston, 1990; lectr. continuing legal edn. U. Houston Law Ctr., 1989—; lectr. continuing legal edn. State Bar Tex., U. Tex., South Tex. Coll. Law, So. Meth. U., ABA; rschr., editor U.S. Senate Com. on Nutrition, 1975, 76, 77; rschr. U.S Supreme Ct., Washington, 1977; mem. Tex. Law Rev., 1979-81. Editor Def. Counsel Jour., 1990-93. Active U.S. Supreme Ct. Hist. Soc. Mem. Internat. Assn. Def. Counsel, Fedn. Ins. and Corp. Counsel, Def. Rsch. Inst. (grievance com.), Tex. Assn. Def. Counsel, State Bar Tex. (appellate sect. coun. officer 1989—), Houston Bar Assn. (officer, appellate sect.), Houston Club, Houston Met. Racquet Club, Houston Ctr. Club. Avocations: music, travel, oenology, tennis. General civil litigation, Personal injury, Product liability. Office: Cook & Roach LLP Texaco Heritage Plz 1111 Bagby St Ste 2650 Houston TX 77002-2543

**ROADES, JOHN LESLIE,** lawyer; b. El Campo, Tex., Mar. 29, 1951; s. Ora E. and Carolyn Elizabeth (Roten) R.; m. Therese Carol Pavlas, Mar. 20, 1982; children: Leslie Carol, Elizabeth Ann. AA, Wharton (Tex.) Coll., 1971; BBA, U. Tex., 1973, JD, 1975. Bar: Tex. 1976. Assoc. Manske and Hajovsky, El Campo, Tex., 1976-77; county atty. Wharton County, 1981-83; dist. atty. 23rd Jud. Dist., Wharton and Matagorda counties, 1983-84; pvt. practice law Wharton, 1977—. Chmn. Wharton County Dem. Party, 1978-79, 91-95, state exec. com., 1981-82; state pres. Young Dems., 1981-82. Mem. Tex. Bar Assn. (coun. mem. gen., solo and small firm sect., 1995—, local bar svcs. com. 1990-95), Wharton County Bar Assn. (pres. 1989-90), Lions (v.p. 1992-94, pres. 1994-95). Methodist. Family and matrimonial, General practice, Personal injury. Office: 1201 N Alabama Rd PO Box 1219 Wharton TX 77488-1219

**ROAF, ANDREE LAYTON,** judge; b. Mar. 31, 1941; m. Clifton G. Roaf; 4 children. BS in Zoology, Mich. State U., 1962; JD with high honors, U. Ark., 1978; LLD (hon.), Mich. State U., 1996. Bar: Ark. 1978. Bacteriologist Mich. Dept. Health, Lansing, 1963-65; rsch. biologist FDA, Washington, 1965-69; staff asst. Pine Bluff (Ark.) Urban Renewal Agy., 1971-75; biologist Nat. Ctr. for Toxicological Rsch., Jefferson, Ark., 1978-79; assoc. Walker, Roaf, Campbell, Ivory & Dunklin, Little Rock, 1979-86, ptnr., 1986-95; assoc. justice Ark. Supreme Ct., Little Rock, 1995-96; appellate judge Ark. Ct. Appeals, 1997—. Editor Ark. Law Rev. Mem. PTA bd. Forest Park Elem. Sch., 1972-74, 34th Ave Sch., 1974-76, 80-83, Southeast Jr. High, 1976-77; mem. ad hoc com. for voter registration Jefferson County, 1972-73; bd. dirs. Ark. Coun. on Human Rels., 1972-73, Ark. for Arts, 1983, Ark. Student Loan Authority, 1977-81, Vocals, 1989—; bd. trustees Southeast Ark. Arts and Sci. Ctr., 1972-75, sec., 1974-75; sec. Pine Bluff OIC Bd., 1972-78, Pine Bluff Police-Cmty. Rels. Task Force, 1973; mem. Jefferson County Com. on Black Adoptions, 1973-75, chmn., 1974-75; mem. Ark. Code of Ethics Commn., 1987, Friends of Sta. KRLE-FM, 1982-88, 90-94, pres., 1985-86; mem. Jefferson County Dem. Com., 1980-82; trustee Winthrop Rockefeller Found., 1990-94; mem. vestry Grace Episcopal Ch., 1995—. Recipient disting. alumni award Mich. State U., 1996; inducted Ark. Black Hall of Fame, 1996; named Gayle Pettus Pontz outstanding Ark. woman lawyer, 1996. Mem. ABA, Ark. Bar Assn. (chmn. youth edn. com. 1979-80), Pulaski County Bar Assn. (chmn. hist. com. 1986-87), Jefferson County Bar Assn., W. Harold Flowers Law Soc. Office: Justice Bldg 625 Marshall St Ste 1230 Little Rock AR 72201-1052

**ROAN, FORREST CALVIN, JR.,** lawyer; b. Waco, Tex., Dec. 18, 1944; s. Forrest Calvin and Lucille Elizabeth (McKinney) R.; m. Vickie Joan Howard, Feb. 15, 1969 (div. Dec. 1983); children: Amy Katherine, Jennifer Louise; m. Leslie D. Hampton Roan, Jan. 2, 1999. BBA, U. Tex., Austin, 1976. Bar: Tex. 1976, U.S. Dist. Ct. (we. dist.) Tex. 1977, U.S. Dist. Ct. (so. dist.) Tex. 1998, U.S. Ct. Appeals (5th cir.) 1977, U.S. Supreme Ct. 1979, U.S. Ct. Appeals (11th cir.) 1981, U.S. Ct. Appeals (fed. cir.) 1998, U.S. Ct. Internat. Trade, 1998. Prin. Roan & Assocs., Austin, 1969-71; counsel, com. dir. Tex. Ho. of Reps., 1972-75; assoc. Heath, Davis & McCalla, Austin, 1975-78; prin. Roan & Gullahorn, P.C., Austin, 1978-85, Roan & Autrey (formerly Roan & Simpson), P.C., 1986-99; sr. ptnr. Cantey, Hanger, Roan & Autrey, 1999—. Bd. dirs. Lawyers Credit Union, chmn., 1982-83; bd. dirs. pub. law sect. State Bar Tex., 1980-84; dir. Am. Bankers Gen. Agy. With Tex. Army N.G., 1966-74. Fellow Tex. Bar Found.; mem. ABA, Tex. Assn. Def. Counsel, Def. Rsch. Inst., Travis County Bar Assn., Tex.-Mexico Bar Assn., Knights of the Symphony (vice chancellor 1997—), Tex. Lyceum Assn. (v.p., bd. dirs. 1983-87), Austin C. of C., Met. Club, Austin Club, Headliners Club, Masons, Shriners (Parsons Masonic master 1976-77). Methodist. Administrative and regulatory, Insurance, General corporate. Office: Cantey Hanger Roan & Autrey 200 Norwest Bank Tower 400 W 15th St Austin TX 78701-1600

**ROBB, DEAN ALLEN, SR.,** lawyer, farmer; b. Feb. 26, 1924; s. Zenas Allan and Mary Dorothy (Cunningham) R.; m. Barbara Gulley, Aug. 24, 1947 (div.); children: Laura, Dean Allen Jr., Blair M.; m. Cindy Mathias, 1983; 1 child, Matthew Zenas, 1 stepson, Ben. BS, U. Ill., 1946; JD, Wayne State U., 1949. Bar: Mich. 1949, U.S. Dist. Ct. (ea. dist.) Mich. 1950, U.S. Dist. Ct. (we. dist.) Mich. 1960, U.S. Dist Ct. Appeals (6th cir.) 1960, U.S. Dist. Ct. (no. dist.) Ind. 1962, U.S. Dist. Ct. (no. dist.) Ohio 1968, U.S. Supreme Ct. Sr. ptnr. Goodman, Crockett, Eden & Robb, Detroit, 1950-71; sole practice, owner Dean A. Robb, P.C., Traverse City, Mich., 1971-76; pres. Robb, Dettmer & Phillips, Traverse City, 1976-81, Robb, Dettmer, Messing & Thompson, P.C., Traverse City, 1983-86, Robb, Messing, Palmer & Dignan PC, Traverse City, 1986-96, Dean Robb Law Firm, Traverse City, 1997—; lectr. various nat., state and local bar assns.; guest lectr. Detroit Coll. Law, Thomas Colley Law Sch., U. Detroit Law Sch., U. Mich., U. Miss.; mem. faculty Nat. Coll. Advocacy Assn. Trial Lawyers Am., Practicing Law Inst., N.Y.C., Inst. Continuing Legal Edn., Ann Arbor, Mich.; apptd. to jud. selection com. we. dist. U.S. Dist. Ct. Mich., 1986-93; designated counsel for Brotherhood of Locomotive Engrs., 1989-92; bd. dirs. NW Mich. br. ACLU, Rehab. Inst. Detroit ; vol. atty. Penrickton Nursery Sch. for Visually Handicapped Children, Taylor, Mich.;. Co-author: Lawyers Desk Reference, 1964-75; co-editor Rights of Railroad Workers, 1973; contbr. articles to legal publs. Mem. Traverse City and Leelanau Players; exec. sec. Met. Detroit Fair Employment Practices Coun., Dodge Cmty. House; pres. Grand Traverse Hist. Soc., 1987-91; contbr., bd. trustees Traverse City Civic Players, 1973-78; active supporter Traverse Area Found.; active supporter 3d level Crisis Invention Ctr., bd. dirs., 1996; Dem. nominee Mich. Supreme Ct., 1986; intern Presbyn. Ch., 1946-47; exec. bd. dirs. Boys & Girls Club, Grand Traverse. Served with USN, 1942-44. Recipient Lawyer of Yr. award Wayne State U., 1975-76, Outstanding Lawyers Alum award, 1975; Champion of Justice award State Bar of Mich., 1994. Fellow Am. Coll. Trial Lawyers; mem. ABA, DAV, NOW, NAACP (life), Trial Lawyers for Pub. Justice (nat. pres.), Assn. Trial Lawyers Am. (past nat. co-chmn. nat. com. on civil rights, past chmn. R.R. law sect.), Mich. Trial Lawyers Assn. (past pres.), Nat. Lawyers Guild (mem.-at-large), Grand-Traverse-Leelanau-Antrim County Bar Assn., Mich. Bar Assn., Nat. Assn. Ciminal Def. Lawyers, Actors Equity, Wayne State U. Alumni Assn. (exec. bd.), Sierra Club, Friends of the Earth, Amnesty Internat., Grand Traverse Area C. of C., U. Ill. Alumni Assn. General civil litigation, Personal injury, Product liability. Office: Dean Robb Law Firm PO Box 879 416 St Joseph St Suttons Bay MI 49682

**ROBBINS, DALE ROBERT,** lawyer; b. Billings, Mont., Feb. 20, 1958; s. Jack Dale and Rosemary Robbins; m. Barbara Jean Tucker, Aug. 18, 1990; 1 child, James Andrew. BA, U. Mont., 1980, MBA, 1987, JD, 1988; MEd, Mont. State U., 1984. Bar: Mont. 1988, U.S. Dist. Ct. Mont. 1988. Atty. Social Security Adminstrn., Billings, Mont., 1991-95, sr. atty., 1995-98; atty. Social Security Adminstrn., Billings, 1998—. Regional v.p. Nat. Treasury's Employee Union, Billings, 1998; cub master Boy Scouts Am., 1998. Mem. K.C. (pres. 1998, 4th degree sec. 1995-98), Order of the Arrow. Roman Catholic. Avocations: hemeopathic and natural medicine, Tae-Kwon-Do. Office: Office of Hearings and Appeals 2900 4th Ave N Ste 500 Billings MT 59101-1271

**ROBBINS, ELLEN SUE,** lawyer, educator; b. Chgo., Mar. 15, 1967; d. Sheldon Neal and Barbara Lynn (Corenman) R. BS in Bus. Adminstrn. summa cum laude, U. Ill., 1988; JD magna cum laude, Harvard U., 1991. Bar: Ill. 1991. Jud. clk. to Judge Charles Kocoras U.S. Dist. Ct., Chgo., 1991-92; atty. Sidley & Austin, Chgo., 1992—; adj. prof. law DePaul Coll. Law, Chgo., 1997—. Mem. ABA, Chgo. Bar Assn. Avocations: jogging, golf, sports. Office: Sidley & Austin One First Nat Plz Chicago IL 60603-2003

**ROBBINS, FRANK EDWARD,** retired lawyer; b. Hamilton, Ont., Can., Nov. 25, 1924; came to U.S., 1938; s. Frank E. and Mary Swann (Boyd) R.; m. Beatrice Noback, Dec. 20, 1944; children: R. Bruce (dec.), Mary E. Robbins Collina, B. Joanne Robbins Hicken, Frank E. Jr., Jacqueline, John C., George R. B Chem. Engring., Rensselaer Poly. Inst., 1944; JD, George Washington U., 1953. Bar: D.C. 1953, U.S. Ct. Appeals (fed. cir.) 1982, N.Y. 1958, Ill. 1968. Ptnr. Beale & Jones, Washington, 1953-56; pvt. practice, Rochester, N.Y., 1956-60; gen. counsel Photostat div. Itek Corp., Rochester, 1960-63; dir. patents and licensing Kennecott Corp., N.Y.C., 1963-66; patent and trademark counsel CPC Internat., Inc., N.Y.C., 1966-76; assoc. Irons & Sears, Washington, 1976-79, ptnr., 1979-81; sr. ptnr. Robbins & Laramie, Washington, 1981-90; ptnr. Venable, Baetjer, Howard & Civiletti, Washington, 1990-94; sr. of counsel Roylance, Abrams, Berdo & Goodman, Washington, 1994-98; ret., 1998. Author: The Defense of Prior Invention, 1977; author, editor: Candor in Prosecution, 1985. Treas. Quaint Acres Civic Assn., Silver Spring, Md., 1984-89. Lt. (j.g.) USNR, 1944-47. Mem. ABA, Am. Arbitration Assn., Assn. Corp. Patent Counsel, Am. Intellectual Property Law Assn., Md. Patent Law Assn. (past pres., bd. govs. 1985-98), D.C. Bar Assn., Assn. Bar D.C. Democrat. Unitarian. Avocation: gardening. Patent, Trademark and copyright, Federal civil litigation.

**ROBBINS, JACK WINTON,** lawyer; b. Flemington, Mo., Nov. 1, 1919; s. Winnie and Opal (Pitts) R.; m. Hilda Haynes, Feb. 2, 1946; children: Randel Bliss Brodrique, Mark Haynes Robbins. BS, U. North Tex., 1941; JD, Columbia U., 1943. Bar: N.Y. 1944, Pa. 1956, U.S. Supreme Ct. 1953. Law clk. N.Y. Ct. of Appeals, Albany, 1943-44; assoc. atty. Cravath, Swaine & Moore, N.Y.C., 1944-53; prosecutor Nuremberg (Germany) War Crimes Trials, 1946-48; counsel Pitcairn Trust Co., Jenkintown, Pa., 1953—. Bd. dirs. Upper Dublin Twp. Sch. Bd., Ft. Washington, Pa., 1960-73, Ursinus Coll., Collegeville, Pa., 1984—. Mem. ABA, Pa. Bar Assn., Phila. Bar Assn. Republican. Methodist. General practice, General corporate, Estate planning. Home: 1206 Spring Ave Fort Washington PA 19034-1522 Office: Pitcairn Trust Co 165 Township Line Rd Jenkintown PA 19046-3531

**ROBBINS, NORMAN NELSON,** lawyer; b. Detroit, Sept. 27, 1919; s. Charles and Eva (Gold) R.; m. Pamela Anne Eldred, June 22, 1946; children: Susan, Aimee. LLB, JD, Wayne State U., 1943. Bar: Mich. 1943. Pvt. practice Birmingham, Mich., 1943—; chmn. Mich. Bd. for Marriage Counselors, 1971-75; lectr. Inst. Continuing Legal Edn. Editor Mich. Family Law Jour., 1974—; mem. editorial bd. Am. Jour. Family Law; co-editor: Michigan Family Law, 2 vols., 1988; contbr. 600 articles to legal publs. Chmn. Wayne County unit Am. Cancer Soc., Detroit, 1971-76, Mich. Dept. Vets. Trust Fund, 1977-8. Capt. USMCR, 1943-46, PTO. Recipient Gov.'s award State of Mich., Cert. of Appreciation, Gov. of Mich., Cert. of Recognition, Detroit Common Coun. award Mich. Assn. Marriage Counselors, Lifetime Achievement award Mich. Family Law Sect. Mem. ABA (mem. family law coun. 1993-95, exec. editor ABA Family Adv. 1991—), Mich. Bar Assn. (chmn. family law sect. 1974-75), Oakland County Bar Assn., Am. Acad. Matrimonial Lawyers (pres. Mich. chpt. 1982), Am. Legion (judge adv. Mich. dept. 1968-69, comdr. Detroit chpt. 1970-71). Family and matrimonial. Home and Office: 5543 Tadworth Pl West Bloomfield MI 48322-4016

**ROBBINS, RACHEL F.,** lawyer; b. Trenton, N.J., Oct. 30, 1950. BA, Wellesley Coll., 1972; JD, NYU, 1976. Bar: N.Y. 1977. Mng. dir., gen. counsel J.P. Morgan & Co., Inc., N.Y.C. Mng. editor Ann. Survey Am. Law. Mem. ABA, Assn. of the Bar of the City of N.Y., N.Y. State Bar Assn., Order of the Coif. E-mail: robbinsúrachel@jpmorgan.com. Office: JP Morgan & Co Inc 60 Wall St New York NY 10260-0001*

**ROBBINS, STEPHEN J. M.,** lawyer; b. Seattle, Apr. 13, 1942; s. Robert Mads and Aneita Elberta (West) R.; children: Sarah E.T., Alicia S.T. AB, UCLA, 1964; JD, Yale U., 1971. Bar: D.C. 1973, U.S. Dist. Ct. D.C. 1973, U.S. Ct. Appeals (D.C. cir.) 1973, U.S. Ct. Appeals (3d cir.) 1973, U.S. Dist. Ct. (ea. and no. dists.) Calif. 1982, U.S. Dist. Ct. (cen. dist.) Calif. 1983, Supreme Ct. of Republic of Palau, 1994. Pres. U.S. Nat. Student Assn., Washington, 1964-65; dir. scheduling McGovern for Pres., Washington, 1971-72; assoc. Steptoe & Johnson, Washington, 1972-75; chief counsel spl. inquiry on food prices, com. on nutrition and human needs U.S. Senate, Washington, 1975; v.p., gen. counsel Straight Arrow Pubs., San Francisco, 1975-77; dep. dist. atty. City and County of San Francisco, 1977-78; regional counsel U.S. SBA, San Francisco, 1978-80; spl. counsel Warner-Amex Cable Communications, Sacramento, 1981-82; ptnr. McDonough, Holland and Allen, Sacramento, 1982-84; v.p. Straight Arrow Pubs., N.Y.C., 1984-86; gen. legal counsel Govt. State of Koror, Rep. of Palau, Western Caroline Islands, 1994-95; pvt. practice law, 1986—. Staff sgt. U.S. Army, 1966-68. Mem. ABA (sect. urban, state and local govt. law-land use, planning and zoning com., sect. real property, probate and trust law, sect. natural resources energy, environ. law, forum com. on affordable housing and cmty. devel.), Internat. Mcpl. Lawyers Assn., D.C. Bar, State Bar of Calif., Urban Land Inst. (mem. steering com. Sacramento dist.), Am. Hist. Assn., Am. Planning Assn. (planning and law divsn., internat. divsn.), Internat. Urban Devel., Law Assn. for Asia and the Pacific (LawAsia), Chamber Music Soc. of Sacramento, Oreg. Shakespeare Festival, Shaw Island Hist. Soc. Unitarian. Avocations: theatre, art, hiking. Environmental, Real property, Land use and zoning (including planning). Office: 2150 3rd Ave Sacramento CA 95818-3102

**ROBBINS, VERNON EARL,** lawyer, accountant; b. Balt., Aug. 16, 1921; s. Alexander Goldborough and Anne Jeanette (Bubb) R.; m. Ruth Adele Holland, Oct. 21, 1941; m. 2d, Alice Sherman Meredith, Feb. 17, 1961; 1 dau., Sharon R. Fick; 1 stepdau., Susan V. Henry. A.B.A., Md. Sch. Acctg., 1941; J.D., U. Balt., 1952. Bar: Md. 1952. Internal revenue agt. IRS, Balt., 1945-52; ptnr. Robbins, Adam & Co., C.P.A. firm, Cambridge, Md., 1952—; sole practice law, Cambridge, 1952—; bd. dirs. Bank of Eastern Shore. Served with U.S. Maritime Service, 1941-45. Named Boss of Yr., Tidewater chpt. Nat. Secs. Assn., 1978. Mem. ABA, Md. bar Assn., Am. Inst. C.P.A.s, Md. Assn. C.P.A.s, Am. Assn. Atty.-C.P.A.s, Am. Judicature Soc., Navy League, Dorchester County Hist. Soc., Dorchester Art Center. Democrat. Methodist. Club: Cambridge Yacht. Lodges: Elks, Masons, Shriners. Corporate taxation, Estate taxation, Personal income taxation. Office: PO Box 236 126 Market Sq Cambridge MD 21613-1860

**ROBERSON, BRUCE H.,** lawyer; b. Wilmington, Del., Mar. 7, 1941; s. A. L. and Virginia Amelia (Heerdt) R.; m. Mary E. Abrams; children: Cheryl Anne, David B., Douglas M. BS cum laude, Washington and Lee U., 1963; JD, U. Va., 1966. Bar: Va. 1966, Del. 1966, Fla. 1969. Assoc. Morris, Nichols, Arsht & Tunnell, Wilmington, 1966-67; assoc. Holland & Knight LLP, Tampa, Fla., 1969—; ptnr. Holland & Knight, Tampa, Fla., 1975—. Contbg. editor Warren, Gorham and Lamont Banking and Lending Institution Forms, 1992-99. Capt. U.S. Army, 1967-69. Decorated Bronze Star U.S. Army, 1969. Fellow Am. Bar Found., Fla. Bar Found.; mem. ABA (bus. law sect. com. on consumer fin. svcs. 1976—, banking law com. 1980—, savs. instns. com. 1989-96), Am. Judicature Soc., Fla. Bar Assn. (corp. banking and bus. law sect. exec. coun. 1978-86, chmn. banking law com. 1982-84), Del. Bar Assn., Va. Bar Assn., Hillsborough County Bar Assn., Univ. Club, Tampa Yacht and Country Club, Lambda Chi Alpha. Republican. Methodist. Banking, General corporate, Consumer commercial. Office: Holland & Knight LLP PO Box 1288 Tampa FL 33601-1288

**ROBERSON, G. GALE, JR.,** lawyer, arbitrator; b. Chgo., Mar. 22, 1933; s. G. Gale and Charlotte D. R.; m. Ann Griesedieck, Jan. 3, 1957; children: Michael G., Christine R. Hurd. BA, Dartmouth Coll., 1955; LLB, Harvard U., 1960. Bar: Ill. 1960, U.S. Dist. Ct. (no. dist.) Ill. 1961. Assoc. Leibman, Williams, etc., Chgo., 1960-65; asst. counssel Fed. Res. Bank, Atlanta, 1965-66; ptnr., assoc. Quinn, Jacobs & Barry, Chgo., 1966-81; ptnr. McBride Baker & Coles, Chgo., 1981—; arbitrator, mediator NASD, N.Y.C., 1998—; lectr. in field. Contbr. articles to profl. jours. Bd. dirs. Jobs For Youth/Chgo., Inc., 1979—, pres., 1980-95; mem., chmn. Zoning Bd. Appeals, Wilmette, Ill., 1979-91. Lt. j.g. USN, 1955-57. Mem. ABA, Ill. State Bar Assn., Chgo. Bar Assn., Mich. Shores club. Securities, General corporate, General civil litigation. Home: 1351 Ashland Ave Wilmette IL 60091-1607 Office: McBride Baker & Coles 500 W Madison St Fl 40 Chicago IL 60661-2511

**ROBERSON, LINDA,** lawyer; b. Omaha, July 15, 1947; d. Harlan Oliver and Elizabeth Aileen (Good) R.; m. Gary M. Young, Aug. 20, 1970; children: Elizabeth, Katherine, Christopher. BA, Oberlin Coll., 1969; MS, U. Wis., 1970, JD, 1974. Bar: Wis. 1974, U.S. Dist. Ct. (we. dist.) Wis. 1974. Legis. atty. Wis. Legis. Reference Bur., Madison, 1974-76, sr. legis. atty., 1976-78; assoc. Rikkers, Koritzinsky & Rikkers, Madison, 1978-79; ptnr. Koritzinsky, Neider, Langer & Roberson, Madison, 1979-85, Stolper, Koritzinsky, Brewster & Neider, Madison, 1985-93, Balisle & Roberson, Madison, 1993—; lectr. U. Wis. Law Sch., Madison, 1978—. Co-author: Real Women, Real Lives, 1981, Wisconsin's Marital Property Reform Act, 1984, Understanding Wisconsin's Marital Property Law, 1985, A Guide to Property Classification Under Wisconsin's Marital Property Act, 1986, Workbook for Wisconsin Estate Planners, 2d edit., 1993, 3rd edit., 1997, 4th edit., 1999, Look Before You Leap, 1996, Family Estate Planning in Wis., 1992, rev. edit. 1996, The Marital Property Classification Handbook, 1999. Fellow Am. Acad. Matrimonial Lawyers, Am. Bar Found.; mem. ABA, Wis. Bar Assn., Dane County Bar Assn., Legal Assn. Women, Nat. Assn. Elder Law Attys. Estate planning, Probate, Family and matrimonial. Office: Balisle and Roberson PO Box 870 Madison WI 53701-0870

**ROBERTS, ALFRED WHEELER, III,** lawyer, law firm executive; b. N.Y.C., Aug. 3, 1938; s. Alfred Wheeler and Florence Henley (Kirk) R.; m. Pamela Anne Stover, June 29, 1967; children: Ashley Anne, Alfred Kirk, Michael Tyler. BA, Dartmouth Coll., 1960, MBA, 1961. CPA, N.Y. With Arthur Young & Co., N.Y.C., 1961-89, ptnr., 1971-89, vice chmn., 1982-88; ptnr. RFE Investment Ptnrs., New Canaan, Conn., 1989-90; exec. dir. Winthrop, Stimson, Putnam & Roberts, N.Y.C., 1991-98; dir. The Peterson Cos., Inc., 1998-99. Bd. dirs., treas. Legal Aid Soc. N.Y., 1981-88; bd. dirs. YMCA of Greater N.Y., 1983-89, vice chmn., 1987-89. Mem. AICPA, Univ. Club. Congregationalist.

**ROBERTS, BRIAN MICHAEL,** lawyer; b. Cin., May 28, 1957; s. Shearl Joseph and Mary Ruth (Christian) R.; m. Carol Denise Zimmerman, July 28, 1979; children: Nicholas Brian, Mary Katelin, Kevin Matthew. BS in Bus., Miami U., Oxford, Ohio, 1979; JD, U. Dayton, 1982. Bar: Ohio 1982, U.S. Dist. Ct. (so. dist.) Ohio 1983, U.S. Ct. Appeals (6th cir.) 1984, U.S. Supreme Ct. 1988. Ptnr. Jablinski, Folino, Roberts & Martin Co. LPA, Dayton, 1982—. Organizer, scheduler legal presentations to engaged couples Family Life Office, Archdiocese of Cin., Dayton, 1982-92. Mem. Ohio State Bar Assn., Ohio Acad. Trial Lawyers, Dayton Bar Assn., Miami Valley Trial Lawyers Assn., Assn. Trial Lawyers Am. Republican. Roman Catholic. E-mail: jfrm@msn.com. Estate planning, Probate, State civil litigation. Home: 3830 Gardenview Pl Dayton OH 45429-4517 Office: Jablinski Folino Roberts & Martin Co LPA PO Box 1266 Dayton OH 45402-9766

**ROBERTS, BURK AUSTIN,** lawyer; b. Albuquerque, Apr. 8, 1968; s. Thomas Franklin Jr. and Judy Jane Roberts; m. Cindy Rene Breaux, June 6, 1998. BA, U. Tex., 1989; JD, Baylor U., 1991. Bar: Tex. 1992. Ptnr. Roberts & Roberts LLP, Killeen, Tex., 1992—; city atty. City of Harker Heights, Tex., 1994—; co-chair region 5 devel. Tex. Ctr. Legal Ethics & Professionalism, Austin, 1998-99. mem. adv. bd. Killeen Salvation Army, 1993—, chair, 1996. Named Outstanding Young Man of Am., 1998. Fellow Tex. Bar Found., mem. Coll. State Bar Tex. Family and matrimonial, State civil litigation. Office: Roberts & Roberts LLP 324 E Avenue C Killeen TX 76541-5233

**ROBERTS, BURTON BENNETT,** lawyer, retired judge; b. N.Y.C., July 25, 1922; s. Alfred S. and Cecelia (Schanfein) R.; m. Gerhild Ukryn. B.A., NYU, 1943, LL.M., 1953; LL.B., Cornell U., 1949. Bar: N.Y. 1949. Asst. dist. atty. New York County, 1949-66; chief asst. dist. atty. Bronx County, Bronx, N.Y., 1966-68; acting dist. atty. Bronx County, 1968-69, dist. atty., 1969-72; justice Supreme Ct. State N.Y., 1973-98, adminstrv. judge criminal br. Bronx County 12th Jud. Dist., 1984-98, adminstrv. judge civil br. Bronx County 12th Dist., 1988-98; ret., 1998; counsel Fischbein, Badillo, Wagner & Harding, 1999—. Pres. Bronx div. Hebrew Home for Aged, 1967-72. With U.S. Army, 1943-45. Decorated Purple Heart, Bronze Star with oak leaf cluster. Mem. Assn. Bar City N.Y., Am. Bar Assn., N.Y. Bar Assn., Bronx County Bar Assn., N.Y. State Dist. Attys. Assn. (pres. 1971-72). Jewish (exec. bd. temple). Home: 215 E 68th St Apt 19A New York NY 10021-5727 Office: Fischbein Badillo et al 909 3rd Ave New York NY 10022-4731

**ROBERTS, CHRISTOPHER CHALMERS,** lawyer; b. Washington, Oct. 12, 1950; s. Chalmers McGeagh and Lois (Hall) R.; m. Mary Hammond Higgins, Apr. 23, 1983; children: Kevin, Morgan, Rachel, Sarah. BA, Amherst Coll., 1972; JD, Georgetown U., 1975, MLT, 1981. Bar: Md. 1975, D.C. 1976, U.S. Dist. Ct. Md. 1978, U.S. Ct. Appeals (4th cir.) 1979, U.S. Dist. Ct. D.C. 1980, U.S. Ct. Appeals (D.C. cir.) 1980. Law clk. to presiding justice Ct. Appeals of Md., Annapolis, 1974-76; assoc. Shulman, Rogers, Gandal, Pordy & Ecker, P.A., Rockville, Md., 1978-83, ptnr., 1984—; counsel Montgomery County Students Automotive Trades Found., Md., 1984—. Editor Jour. Georgetown Law, 1973-75; contbr. articles to legal jours. Bd. dirs. CPC Health Corp., 1988—. Mem. Amherst Alumni Assn. Washington (past officer, pres.). Mergers and acquisitions, General corporate, Securities. Office: Shulman Rogers Gandal Pordy & Ecker 11921 Rockville Pike Ste 300 Rockville MD 20852-2743

**ROBERTS, DAVID AMBROSE,** lawyer; b. Pascagoula, Miss., Apr. 27, 1962; s. James Elmer and Edna Louise (Scott) R.; m. Elizabeth Anne Knecht, June 29, 1990. BA, U. Miss., 1985, JD, 1988. Bar: Miss. 1988, U.S. Dist. Ct. (no. dist.) Miss. 1988, U.S. Ct. Appeals (5th cir.) 1991, U.S. Dist. Ct. (so. dist.) Miss. 1991, U.S. Supreme Ct. 1996. Asst. dist. atty. Office of Dist. Atty., State of Miss., Pascagoula, 1988-90; ptnr. Gordon, Myers, Frazier & Roberts, Pascagoula, 1991-94; pvt. practice Pascagoula, 1994—. Recipient Am. Jurisprudence award, 1988; named to Outstanding Young Men in Am. Mem. ATLA, Miss. Bar Assn., Jackson County Bar Assn., 5th Cir. Bar Assn., Nat. Assn. Criminal Def. Lawyers, Miss. Trial Lawyers Assn., Elks. Consumer commercial, General practice, Criminal. Office: PO Box 2009 Pascagoula MS 39569-2009

**ROBERTS, DAVID MACE,** lawyer, consultant; b. N.Y.C., Feb. 23, 1964; s. Seymour and Maida Lia Roberts; m. Laurie Patriece Cheatham, June 30, 1995. Student, London Sch. Econs., 1985; BA with highest honors, NYU, 1986; JD, Emory U., 1989. Bar: Tex. 1989, D.C. 1992, U.S. Dist. Ct. (no. dist.) Tex. 1989, U.S. Ct. Appeals (5th cir.) 1992, U.S. Supreme Ct. 1992. Atty. Bickel & Brewer, Dallas, 1989-92, Ronquillo & DeWolf, LLP, Dallas, 1992-97, Langley & Branch, P.C., Dallas, 1997-99, Winstead, Sechrest & Minick P.C., Dallas, 1999—. Mem. regional bd. dirs. Anti Defamation League, Dallas, 1996—. Mem. ABA, Tex. Bar Assn., D.C. Bar, Dallas Bar Assn. General corporate, Securities, Private international. Office: Winstead Sechrest & Minick PC 5400 Renaissance Tower 1201 Elm St Dallas TX 75270-2199

**ROBERTS, DELMAR LEE,** editor; b. Raleigh, N.C., Apr. 9, 1933; s. James Delmer and Nellie Brockelbank (Tyson) R. BS in Textile Mgmt., N.C. State U., 1956; MA in Journalism, U. S.C., 1974. Product devel. engr. U.S. Rubber Co. (Uniroyal), Winnsboro, S.C., 1959-64; process improvement engr. Allied Chem. Co., Irmo, S.C., 1965-67; assoc. editor S.C. History Illustrated Mag., Columbia, 1970; editor-in-chief, editl. v.p. Sandlapper-The Mag. of S.C., Columbia, 1968-74; mng. editor, art dir. Legal Econs. mag. of the ABA, Chgo., 1975-89, Law Practice Mgmt. mag. of the ABA, Chgo., 1990—. Editor: The Best of Legal Economics, 1979; freelance editor and/or designer of over 35 books. Active World Affairs Coun. Columbia, 1997—; 1st v.p. English-Speaking Union, 1996-97, pres. 1997—. With U.S. Army, 1956-58. Hon. fellow Coll. of Law Practice Mgmt., Golden, Colo., 1995—. Mem. Soc. Profl. Journalists, Capital City Club (Columbia), Phi Kappa Tau, Kappa Tau Alpha. Avocations: European travel, Turkish carpet/Kilim collecting, antique collecting.

**ROBERTS, HARRY MORRIS, JR.,** lawyer; b. Dallas, June 10, 1938; s. Harry Morris and La Frances (Reilly) R.; m. Nancy Beth Johnson, Mar. 7, 1964; children: Richard Whitfield, Elizabeth Lee. BBA, So. Meth. U., 1960; LLB, Harvard U., 1963. Bar: Tex. 1963, U.S. Dist. Ct. (no. dist.) Tex. 1964, U.S. Ct. Appeals (5th cir.), 1972, U.S. Supreme Ct. 1971. Assoc. Thompson & Knight, Dallas, 1963-69, ptnr., 1970-75, sr. ptnr., 1975—; chmn. real estate, probate and trust law sect. State Bar Tex., 1984-85; vis. scholar U. Tex. Law Sch., 1986. Contbr. articles to legal jours. Trustee Shelter Ministries of Dallas, 1982— (chmn. bd. trustees 1992-95). Mem. ABA, Dallas Bar Assn. (chmn. real estate sect. 1981), Am. Bar Found., Tex. Bar Found., Dallas Bar Found., Am. Coll. Real Estate Lawyers, Tex. Coll. Real Estate Attys. (vice chair, bd. dirs. 1990-93). Episcopalian. Clubs: Salesmanship (Dallas), Dallas Country. Finance, Landlord-tenant, Real property. Office: Thompson & Knight 1700 Pacific Ave Ste 3300 Dallas TX 75201-4693

**ROBERTS, J. WENDELL,** federal judge; b. Somerset, Ky., May 1, 1943; s. Earl C. and Dorothy (Whitaker) R.; children: Stephen A., Shannon L. BA, Ea. Ky. U., 1964; JD, U. Ky., 1966. Bar: Ky. 1966, U.S. Dist. Ct. (we. dist.) Ky. 1978, U.S. Ct. Appeals (6th cir.) 1983. Atty. Ky. Dept. Revenue, Frankfort, 1966; law clk. Ky. Supreme Ct., Frankfort, 1966-67; atty. Charles A. Williams & Assocs., Paducah, Ky., 1967, Westberry & Roberts, Marion, Ky., 1968-87; city atty. City of Marion, 1968-84; judge U.S. Bankruptcy Ct. Western Dist. Ky., Louisville, 1987—, chief judge, 1988-95. Vice chmn. Pennyrile Area Devel. Dist., Hopkinsville, Ky., 1968-72; vol. Habitat for Humanity and Ctr. for the Arts, Louisville. Mem. Ky. Bar Assn., Louisville Bar Assn., Nat. Conf. Bankruptcy Judges (bd. govs. 1991-94), Mcpl. Attys. Assn. Ky. (pres. 1983). Methodist. Avocations: volunteer work. Office: US Bankruptcy Ct US Courthouse 601 W Broadway Ste 528 Louisville KY 40202-2238

**ROBERTS, JAMES DONZIL,** lawyer; b. St. Louis, Mo., Apr. 4, 1957; s. Donzil D. and Barbara V. Malona; m. Jody A. Garcia, Dec. 7, 1985; children: James D. Jr., Jessica E. Student, Calif. State U., Northridge, 1976-79, Calif. State U., Dominguez Hills, 1981; JD, U. LaVerne, 1985. Bar: Calif. 1985, U.S. Dist. Ct. (ctrl. dist.) Calif. 1986. Staff and supr. atty. Bollington Stilz & Bloeser, Woodland Hills, Calif., 1985-90; mng. atty. Bollington and Roberts, Long Beach, Calif., 1990—; judge pro tem Long beach Mcpl. Ct., Long Beach, 1992—; lectr. extension program UCLA, 1994—. Trustee U. LaVerne San Fernando Valley Coll. Law, Encino, 1984-85; active West L.A. County Coun., Boy Scouts Am., West Hills, Calif., 1995. Mem. Assn. Calif. House Counsel (founding mem.); mem. L.A. County Bar Assn., Long Beach Bar Assn., Assn. So. Calif. Def. Counsel, Long Beach Barristers Assn., Am. Inn Ct. (Long Beach, barrister). Avocations: baseball/softball, bowling, golf. General civil litigation, Insurance, Personal injury. Office: Bollington & Roberts 3780 Kilroy Airport Way Ste 540 Long Beach CA 90806-6803

**ROBERTS, JAMES L., JR.,** state supreme court justice; b. June 8, 1945; m. Rose D. Roberts. BA, Millsaps Coll., 1967; MBA, Miss. State U., 1968; JD, U. Miss., 1971; grad., Nat. Jud. Coll., 1988. Pvt. practice Pontotoc County, Miss., 1971-84; chancellor 1st Chancery Ct. Dist., Miss., 1988-92; assoc. justice Miss. Supreme Ct., Jackson, 1992-99; prosecuting atty. Pontotoc County, 1972-84; speaker in field. Commr. pub. safety State of Miss., 1984-88; mem. Northeast Mental Health-Mental Retardation Commn., 1972-88; chmn. task force hearings Gov.'s Alliance Against Drugs, 1986-87; Sunday sch. leader, ch. officer Pontotoc United Meth. Ch.; candidate for Gov. of Miss., 1999—. Recipient Herman C. Galzier award Miss chpt. Am. Soc. Pub. Adminstrn., 1985. Mem. ABA (jud. divsn.), Miss. Bar Assn., 1st Jud. Dist. Bar Assn., Pontotoc County Bar Assn., Miss. Conf. of Judges, Nat. Coun. Juvenile and Family Ct. Judges, Nat. Coll. Probate Judges, Millsaps Coll. Alumni Assn., Miss. State U. Alumni Assn., U. Miss. Alumni Assn., Rotary Club, Omicron Delta Kappa, Delta Theta Phi, Alpha Kappa Psi, Kappa Sigma, Pi Alpha Alpha (hon.).

**ROBERTS, JARED INGERSOLL,** lawyer; b. Phila., Mar. 20, 1946; s. Brooke and Anna (Ingersoll) R.; m. Katherine Sherwood, May 17, 1986; children: Eleanor, Bayard. BA, Princeton U., 1968; JD, U. Va., 1974. Bar: Pa. 1974, U.S. Dist. Ct. (ea. dist.) Pa. 1975, U.S. Ct. Appeals (3rd cir.) 1975, U.S. Supreme Ct. 1977. Assoc. Duane, Morris & Heckscler, Phila., 1974-82; spl. counsel Fed. R.R. Adminstrn., Washington, 1982-84; assoc. gen. counsel Amtrak, Washington, 1984—. Lt. (j.g.) USNR, 1968-70. Contracts commercial, Environmental. Office: Amtrak Law Dept 60 Massachusetts Ave NE Washington DC 20002-4285

**ROBERTS, JEAN REED,** lawyer; b. Washington, Dec. 19, 1939; d. Paul Allen and Esther (Kishter) Reed; m. Thomas Gene Roberts, Nov. 26, 1958; children: Amy, Rebecca, Nathanial. AB in Journalism, U. N.C., 1966; JD, Ariz. State U., 1973. Bar: Ariz. 1974. Pvt. practice Jean Reed Roberts P.C., Scottsdale, Ariz.; judge pro tem Superior Ct., Maricopa County, Ariz., 1979-92; judge pro tem Ariz. Ct. Appeals, 1995—; chmn., adv. endowment bd. City of Scottsdale, Ariz., 1994-98; past pres. Charter 100 of Phoenix. Mem. Nat. Acad. Elder Law, Ariz. Bar Assn., Ariz. Women's Town Hall, Scottsdale Bar Assn. Democrat. Jewish. E-mail: jrr@jeanreedroberts.com. Estate planning, Elder, Probate. Office: 8669 E San Alberto Dr Ste 101 Scottsdale AZ 85258-4309

**ROBERTS, JOHN DERHAM,** lawyer; b. Orlando, Fla., Nov. 1, 1942; s. Junius P. and Mary E. Roberts; m. Malinda K. Swineford, June 11, 1965; 1 child, Kimberlyn Amanda. Cert., Richmond (Va.) Bus. Coll., 1960; BS, Hampden-Sydney (Va.) Coll., 1964; LLB, Washington & Lee U., 1968. Bar: Va. 1968, Fla. 1969, U.S. Supreme Ct. 1969, U.S. Ct. Customs and Patent Appeals 1970, U.S. Tax Ct. 1970, U.S. Ct. Appeals (5th cir.) 1970, U.S. Ct. Appeals (9th cir.) 1974, U.S. Supreme Ct. 1969. Law clk. U.S. Dist. Ct., Jacksonville, Fla., 1968-69; assoc. Phillips, Kendrick, Gearhart & Aylor, Arlington, Va., 1969-70; asst. U.S. Atty. mid. dist. Fla. U.S. Dept. Justice, Jacksonville, 1970-74; asst. U.S. Atty. Dist. of Alaska, Anchorage, 1974-77, U.S. magistrate judge, 1977—. Bd. dirs. Teen Challenge Alaska, Anchorage, 1984-93; chmn. Eagle Scout Rev. Bd., 1993—; bd. dirs. Alaska Youth for Christ, 1993-96; govs.'s Prayer Breakfast Com., 1994—, vice-chair, 1998—. Recipient Citizenship award DAR, Anchorage, 1984, plaque, U.S. Navy, Citizen Day, Adak, Alaska, 1980. Mem. ABA, Nat. Conf. Spl. Ct. Judges (exec. bd. 1985-92), 9th Cir. Conf. Magistrates (exec. bd. 1982-85, chmn. 1984-85), Alaska Bar Assn., Anchorage Bar Assn., Chi Phi, Psi Chi, Phi Alpha Delta. Republican. Office: US Magistrate Judge 222 W 7th Ave Unit 46 Anchorage AK 99513-7563

**ROBERTS, JOHN M.,** law educator, former prosecutor; 2 children. Attended, Tenn. Technological U., Cookeville, 1954-57; degree, U. Tenn., Knoxville, 1960. Atty. Tenn. Valley Authority, 1960-62, Livingston, Tenn., 1962-77; gen. sessions judge, probate & juvenile judge Overton County, 1969-74; assoc. prof. criminal justice Tenn. Technol. U., 1974-85; dist. atty. gen. 13th judicial dist. State of Tenn., 1977-90, asst. atty. gen., co-dir. enforcement divsn., 1990-92; dep. dir. Dist. Attys. Gen. Conf., 1990-92; U.S. atty. State Tenn. (mid. dist.), 1993-98; assoc. prof. of law Cumberland U., Lebanon, Tenn., 1998—. Mem. Tenn. Bar Assn., Livingston Exchg. Club, Overton County, City of Livingston C. of C. (exec. dir.). Office: US Attorney Mid District TN 222 E Main St Livingston TN 38570-1904

**ROBERTS, LAUREL LEE,** lawyer; b. Lowell, Mass., Oct. 31, 1944; d. Angus Henry and Lorraine (Thompson) R. BA in History and Sociology, U. Calif., Santa Barbara, 1966, MA in Counseling, 1969, BA in Film Studies, 1973; PhD, U. So. Calif., 1976; JD, U. West L.A., 1982. Bar: Calif. 1984, U.S. Ct. Appeals 1985, U.S. Dist. Ct. (ctrl. dist.) Calif. 1985, U.S. Ct. Appeals (9th cir.) 1985; cert. secondary educator, Calif.; credential in pupil personnel svcs., Calif. Dormitory head resident U. Calif., Santa Barbara, 1964-69; counselor Foothill Elem. Sch., Goleta, Calif., 1968; univ. counselor U. Calif., Santa Barbara, 1969-73; adj. lectr. Grad. Sch. of Edn. U. So. Calif., L.A., 1975; asst. dean academic affairs Office of the Chancellor Calif. State U., Long Beach, 1976-86; atty. Law Office of Laurel Roberts, Hermosa Beach, Calif., 1984—; cons. U. So. Calif./Ind. U. Consortium on Instrnl. Devel., L.A., 1975, Nat. Commn. on Indsl. Innovation, Pasadena, Calif., 1986; lectr. Assn. for Devel. of Computer-based Instructional Systems, 1978. Author: (slide-tape presentation) CSU Educational Policy, 1980. Home legal svc. for elderly and infirmed, 1984—; participant Lt. Gov. Mike Curb's USA-Mexico Exch. Program, Fullerton, Calif., 1984; legal aid vol. U. West L.A., Culver City, 180-84; mem. Supt. of Pub. Instrn. Assessment Adv. Com., Sacramento, 1985. Recipient Am. Jurisprudence award Lawyers Coop. Pub. Co., 1982. Mem. Irish-Am. Bar Assn., Women Lawyers Assn. of L.A., L.A. County Bar Assn., Fed. Bar Assn. Republican. Roman Catholic. Avocations: travel, tennis, film, the arts. Probate, Family and matrimonial, General practice. Office: PO Box 594 Hermosa Beach CA 90254-0594

**ROBERTS, MARK SCOTT,** lawyer; b. Fullerton, Calif., Dec. 31, 1951; s. Emil Seidel and Theda (Wymer) R.; m. Sheri Lyn Smith, Sept. 23, 1977; children: Matthew Scott, Meredith Lyn, Benjamin Price. BA in Theater, Pepperdine U., 1975; JD, Western State U., 1978; cert. civil trial advocacy program, U. Calif., San Francisco, 1985; cert. program of instrn. for lawyers, Harvard U., 1990. Bar: Calif. 1980, U.S. Dist. Ct. (cen. dist.) Calif. 1980, U.S. Supreme Ct. 1989, U.S. Ct. Mil. Appeals 1989, U.S. Tax Ct. 1990. Concert mgr. Universal Studios, Hollywood, Calif., 1973-74; tchr. Anaheim (Calif.) Union Sch Dist., 1979-80; prin. Mark Roberts & Assocs., Fullerton, Calif., 1980—; instr. bus. law Biola U., La Mirada, Calif., 1980-84; judge pro tem Orange County Superior Ct., Santa Ana, 1989—. Co-author: Legacy-Plan, Protect and Preserve Your Estate, 1996, Generations Plan Your Legacy, 1999. Mem. Calif. State Bar Assn., Orange County Bar Assn., Nat. Network Estate Planning Attys. Avocations: snow and water skiing. Estate planning, Probate. Office: Mark Roberts & Assocs 1440 N Harbor Blvd Ste 900 Fullerton CA 92835-4122

**ROBERTS, MICHAEL JAMES,** lawyer; b. Salisbury, Md., Nov. 2, 1936; s. Wilmer C. Roberts and Augusta (Dayton) Doukas; m. Jean Murray, June 7, 1958; children: Mark William, Lisa Marie. BA, Duke U., 1958; JD, Am. U., 1965. Bar: D.C. 1966, Md. 1966, U.S. Dist. Ct. D.C., U.S. Ct. Appeals D.C. cir., U.S. Supreme Ct. Mem. staff U.S. congressman Carlton R. Sickles (Md.), Washington, 1963-64; assoc. Verner, Liipfert, Bernhard & McPherson, Washington, 1965-70; ptnr., mem. Verner, Liipfert, Bernhard, McPherson & Hand, Washington, 1970—, pres., mng. atty., 1987—. Vestry Christ Episcopal Ch., Stevensville, Md., 1984-86. Lt. USN, 1958-62, PTO. Democrat. Avocation: boating. Administrative and regulatory, Aviation. Home: 300 Roberts Ln Stevensville MD 21666-2860 Office: Verner Liipfert Bernhard McPherson & Hand 901 15th St NW Ste 600 Washington DC 20005-2306

**ROBERTS, MICHAEL LEE,** lawyer; b. Gadsden, Ala., Feb. 26, 1952; s. Edwin Bruce and May Ann Roberts; m. Mary Lee Brown. BA, Samford U., 1974; JD, Cumberland Sch. of Law, 1977. Bar: Ala. 1977, U.S. Dist. Ct. (no. dist.) Ala. 1977, U.S. Ct. Appeals (5th and 11th cir. 1979), U.S. Supreme Ct. 1996. Law clk. Ct. of Civil Appeals, Montgomery, Ala., 1977-78; atty. Floyd, Keener, Cusimano and Roberts, Gadsden, Ala., 1978-97, Cusimano, Keener, Roberts and Kimberley, Gadsden, 1997—. Author: Alabama Tort Law, 2d edit., 1996, Alabama Tort Law Handbook, 1990. Mem. Ala. Trial Lawyers Assn., Assn. of Trial Lawyers of Am. General civil litigation, Personal injury, Product liability. Office: Cusimano Keener Roberts & Kimberley 153 S 9th St Gadsden AL 35901-3645

**ROBERTS, ROBERT, III,** lawyer; b. Shreveport, La., July 22, 1930; s. Robert and Mary Hodges (Marshall) R.; m. Susan F. Forrester, Mar. 16, 1974; children: Robert (dec.), Marshall, Francis T. Kalmbach Jr., Ellen K. Tizian, Lewis K.F. Kalmbach, Samuel A. Kalmbach. BA, La. State U., 1951, JD, 1953. Bar: La. 1953, U.S. Dist. Ct. (we. dist.) La. 1958, U.S. Ct. Appeals (5th cir.) 1966, U.S. Supreme Ct. 1975. Assoc., then ptnr. and shareholder Blanchard, Walker, O'Quin & Roberts and predecessor, Shreveport, 1955—. Former pres. Family Coun. and Children's Svcs.; former mem. Peabody study com. Caddo Parish Schs.; former chmn. legal div. United Way. 1st lt JAGC, U.S. Army, 1953-55. Mem. ABA, La. State Bar Assn. (former chmn. mineral law sect., former mem. ho. dels., former mem. bd. govs.), La. State Law Inst. (sr. officer, law reform agy. coun. 1962—, mineral code adv. com., civil code lease adv. com.), Soc. Bartolus, Shreveport Bar Assn. (pres. 1981), Shreveport Club. General corporate, Oil, gas, and mineral. Office: Blanchard Walker O'Quin & Roberts PO Box 1126 Shreveport LA 71163-1126

**ROBERTS, RONALD,** lawyer, mediator; b. Campbellville, Ontario, Can., June 1, 1925; came to U.S., 1948, naturalized, 1955; s. Jane C. Crowley, Sept. 10, 1949. BBA, U. Mich., 1952, LLB, 1956. Bar: Tex., Ill. Counsel Old Republic Life Ins. Co., Chgo., 1956-61; counsel, asst. gen. mgr. Am. Nat. Ins. Co., Dallas, 1961-70; sr. v.p. Am. Nat. Ins. Co., Galveston, Tex., 1970-76; pres. Ronald Roberts & Assocs. Inc., Dallas, 1976-91; pvt. practice mediation Dallas, 1992—; pro bono mediation svcs. Dispute Mediation Svc., 1993—; pres., chmn. bd. Consumer Credit Ins. Assn., Chgo., 1967-69. Bd. dirs. Hockey Canada, Ottawa, Ontario, 1974-79. Pilot officer RCAF, 1943-45. Recipient Arthur J. Morris award Consumer Credit Ins. Assn., 1983. Mem. ABA, Tex. Bar Assn., Dallas Bar Assn., Ill. Bar Assn., Chgo. Bar Assn., Assn. Atty.-Mediators, Am. Arbitration Assn., Soc. Profls. in Dispute Resolution, Phi Kappa Phi, Beta Gamma Sigma. Avocations: golf, skiing, reading, travelling. Alternative dispute resolution, Insurance, Sports. Home: 5818 Club Oaks Ct Dallas TX 75248-1118

**ROBERTS, SCOTT RAYMOND,** lawyer; b. Ft. Worth, July 30, 1969; s. Virgil and Martha (Sewell) R.; m. Kimberly Jean Roberts, Aug. 10, 1996. BA in Econs., So. Meth. U., 1991; JD, Baylor U., 1995. Bar: Tex. 1996, U.S. Dist. Ct. (no. dist.) Tex. 1996, U.S. Dist. Ct. (we. and ea. dists.) Tex. 1997. Briefing atty. to Judge Sam Cummings U.S. Dist. Ct. for No. Dist. Tex., Lubbock, 1995-96; assoc. Baker & McKenzie, Dallas, 1996-97, Bracewell & Patterson, L.L.P., Dallas, 1997—. Del. Tex. Rep. Conv., Ft. Worth, 1998. Mem. Dallas Bar Assn. Republican. Presbyterian. Federal civil litigation, General civil litigation, State civil litigation. Office: Bracewell & Patterson LLP 500 N Akard St Ste 4000 Dallas TX 75201-3387

**ROBERTS, STEVEN DILLON,** lawyer; b. San Antonio, June 10, 1968; s. Henry Dillon and Carolyn Ann Roberts; m. Anna Lee Bilhartz, Feb. 29, 1992; children: Rachel Marie, Steven Dillon II, James Dillon. AB in Politics, Princeton U., 1990; JD, So. Meth. U., 1993. Bar: Tex. 1993, U.S. Dist. Ct. (all dists.) Tex. 1993. Law clk. Hitt & Assocs., Dallas, 1991-93, assoc., 1993-94; assoc. Cooper, Aldous & Scully, Dallas, 1994-97; shareholder Cooper & Scully, Dallas, 1998—; Com. mem., subcom. chmn. for bond proposal Duncanville (Tex.) Ind. Sch. Dist., 1996-97; alumni schs. com. mem. Princeton U., Dallas, 1997-98. Mem. Tex. Assn. Def. Counsel, Dallas Bar Assn., Princeton Alumni Assn. Dallas/Fort Worth (judge Princeton book awards 1997-98). Roman Catholic. Personal injury, Insurance, Family and matrimonial. Office: Cooper & Scully PC 900 Jackson St Ste 100 Dallas TX 75202-4426

**ROBERTS, THOMAS ALBA,** lawyer; b. Ft. Wayne, Ind., Sept. 7, 1946; s. Jack and Elizabeth (Wallace) R.; m. Mary Alice Buckley, Aug. 11, 1973; children: Kaitrin M., John A., Kara B. BA, Georgetown U., 1969, JD, 1972. Bar: N.Y. 1973, U.S. Dist. Ct. (so. dist.) N.Y. 1973, U.S. Ct. Appeals (2d cir.) 1973, Tex. 1976, U.S. Supreme Ct. 1977, U.S. Dist. Ct. (so. dist.)

Tex. 1978, U.S. Ct. Appeals (5th and 11th cirs.) 1982. Assoc. Winthrop, Stimson, Putnam & Roberts, N.Y.C., 1972-76; ptnr. Moore & Peterson, Dallas, 1976-89; mng. ptnr. Moore and Peterson, Dallas, 1980-88; ptnr. Johnson & Gibbs, Dallas, 1989-92; sr. ptnr. Weil, Gotshal & Manges, Dallas, N.Y.C., 1992—; chmn. Internat. Corp. Practice Group, 1997—, mem. mgmt. com. 1997—; adj. prof. law So. Meth. U., Dallas, 1977-78. Lectr. in field. Mem. fin. com. St. Rita Ch., Dallas, 1983-88, Our Lady of Lake Ch., Rockwall, Tex., 1987—; mem. Ch. of the Resurrection; bd. dirs. Make-A-Wish Found. Metro N.Y., 1998—. Mem. ABA, Tex. Bar Assn., Dallas Bar Assn., Assn. of Bar of City of N.Y. Roman Catholic. Avocations: skiing, golf, literature. General corporate, Securities, Mergers and acquisitions. Home: 133 Grandview Ave Rye NY 10580-2030

**ROBERTSON, ALEXANDER, IV**, lawyer; b. L.A., Dec. 27, 1959; s. Alex Jr. and Stephanie (Searles) R.; children: Alexander V, Jessica Neal. BSBA, Pepperdine U., 1982, JD, 1986. Bar: Calif. 1986, U.S. Dist. Ct. (ctrl. dist.) Calif. 1986, U.S. Claims Ct. 1986, U.S. Ct. Appeals (9th cir.) 1988, U.S. Dist. Ct. (ea., no. and so. dists.) Calif. 1989; cert. technician 1st class, amateur radio operator; cert. state fire marshall in heavy rescue, Calif.; registered disaster svc. worker, Calif. Asst. gen. mgr. Alex Robertson Co., 1978-83; assoc. Acret & Perrochet, L.A., 1986-87; ptnr. Negele, Knopfler, Pierson & Robertson, Universal City, Calif., 1987-93; mng. ptnr. Knopfler & Robertson, Universal City, 1994—. Pres., bd. dirs. Calabasas Hills Cmty. Assn., 1989-90, sec., 1990-91; bd. dirs. Calabasas Park Homeowners Assn., 1990-92, v.p., 1991-92; asst. dir. Agoura Hills Disaster Response Team, mem. urban search rescue team, mem. mounted search and rescue team; mem. L.A. County Sheriff's Disaster Comms. Svc. Mem. ABA (forum on constrn. industry), Los Angeles County Bar, Beverly Hills Bar Assn., Cowboy Lawyers Assn., Assoc. Gen. Contractors Calif. (underground constrn. com.), Ventura County Bar Assn., Consumer Attys. of Calif., Consumer Attys. Assn. of L.A., Pepperdine Univ. Assocs. (alumni bd. 1987-90), San Fernando Valley Bar Assn., Bldg. Industry Assn., So. Calif. Contractors Assn., Engring. Contractors Assn., Community Assn. Inst., The Beavers. Avocations: equestrian, search and rescue, helicopter pilot. State civil litigation, Construction, Real property. Office: Knopfler & Robertson 21650 Oxnard St Ste 500 Woodland Hills CA 91367-4911

**ROBERTSON, DOUGLAS STUART**, lawyer; b. Portland, Oreg., Jan. 9, 1947; s. Stuart Neil and Mary Katherine (Gates) R.; m. Nan Reinhorn, Dec. 27, 1970; 1 child, Lauren Amanda. BS, Oreg. State U., 1969, MA in Bus. Adminstrn., 1970; JD U. Denver, 1973. Bar: Oreg. 1973, U.S. Dist. Ct. Oreg. 1974, U.S. Ct. Appeal (9th cir.) 1977, U.S. Supreme Ct. 1977. Staff atty. Multnomah County Bar Assn. Legal Aid, Portland, 1973-75; ptnr. Bouneff, Chally & Marshall, Portland, 1975-80; asst. gen. counsel Orbanco Fin. Services, Portland, 1980-83; v.p., gen. counsel Hyster Credit Corp., Portland, 1983-86; v.p., gen. counsel PacifiCorp Credit Inc., 1986-90; ptnr. Lane, Powell, Spears Lubersky, Portland, 1990-91; v.p., gen. counsel, sec., In Focus Systems, Inc., Wilsonville, Oreg., 1991-96, bd. dirs. Lightware, Inc., 1996—; chmn. bd., CEO Deschutes River Preserve, Inc., Portland, 1982—. Mem. editl. bd. Denver Jour. of Internat. Law and Policy, 1971. Served with U.S. Army 1968-70. Mem. ABA, Comml. Law League, Multnomah County Bar Assn., Am. Assn. of Equipment (lessor's law forum), Am. Corp. Counsel Assn. (bd. dirs., treas. N.W. chpt.). Republican. Club: Flyfisher's of Oreg., Oreg. Trout. Contracts commercial, General corporate, Intellectual property. Home: 29 Hillshire Dr Lake Oswego OR 97034-7375 Office: Lightware Inc 9875 SW Sunshine Ct Ste 200 Beaverton OR 97005-4178

**ROBERTSON, EDWARD D., JR.**, state supreme court justice; b. Durham, N.C., May 1, 1952; m. Renee Ann Beal; two children. BA, U. Mo., 1974, JD, 1977. Asst. atty. gen. Mo., 1978-79; assoc. mcpl. judge City of Belton, Mo., 1980-81; dep. atty. gen. City of Belton, 1981-85; justice Mo. Supreme Ct., Kansas City, 1985-98. Office: Mo Supreme Ct 101 High St Jefferson City MO 65102-0150*

**ROBERTSON, EDWIN DAVID**, lawyer; b. Roanoke, Va., July 5, 1946; s. Edwin Traylor and Norma Burns (Bowles) R.; m. Anne Littelle Ferratt, Sept. 7, 1968, 1 child, Thomas Therit. BA with honors, U. Va., 1968, LLB, 1971. Bar: N.Y. 1972, U.S. Ct. Appeals (2d cir.) 1972, U.S. Dist. Ct. (ea. and so. dists.) N.Y. 1973, U.S. Supreme Ct. 1975, U.S. Dist. Ct. (ea. dist.) Mich. 1986. Assoc. Cadwalader, Wickersham & Taft, N.Y.C., 1972-80, ptnr., 1980—. Bd. dirs. Early Music Found. N.Y.C., 1983—, chmn., 1993—; bd. dirs. Oratorio Soc. of N.Y.C., 1988—, sec., 1991—. 1st lt. USAF, 1971-72. Echols scholar. Mem. ABA, Fed. Bar Coun., N.Y. County Lawyers Assn. (chmn. bankruptcy com. 1983-87, chmn. fin. com., bd. dirs. 1985-88, 95—, investment com. 1992—, exec. com. 1996—), Assn. of Bar of City N.Y., Soc. Colonial Wars, Down Town Assn., Jefferson Soc., Echols Scholar, Order of the Coif, Phi Beta Kappa, Phi Kappa Psi. Republican. Episcopalian. Federal civil litigation, Securities, Libel. Home: 315 E 72nd St New York NY 10021-4625 Office: Cadwalader Wickersham & Taft 100 Maiden Ln New York NY 10038-4818

**ROBERTSON, HUGH DUFF**, lawyer; b. Grosse Pointe, Mich., Mar. 14, 1957; s. Hugh Robertson and Louise (Grey) Bollinger; m. Mercedes Corpus Dano, May 3, 1997. BBA in Fin., U. Wis., Whitewater, 1978; JD, Whittier Coll., 1982. Bar: Calif. 1983, U.S. Tax Ct. 1984. Pres., CEO, A. Morgan Maree Jr. & Assocs., Inc., L.A., 1979—. Mem. ABA (forum com. on entertainment 1982—), State Calif., L.A. County Bar Assn., Beverly Hills Bar Assn., Acad. TV Arts and Scis., Am. Film Inst., Phi Alpha Delta. Republican. Episcopalian. Avocations: sports, swimming, reading. Entertainment, Finance, Real property. Office: A Morgan Maree Jr & Assocs 4727 Wilshire Blvd Ste 600 Los Angeles CA 90010-3848

**ROBERTSON, J. MARTIN**, lawyer; b. Danville, Ill., Apr. 30, 1952; s. Calloway Middleton and Barbara (Holland) R. AB in Polit. Sci., Miami U., Oxford, Ohio, 1974; JD, U. Cin., 1978; postgrad., Ohio State U., 1978-79. Bar: Ohio 1978, U.S. Dist. Ct. (so. dist.) Ohio 1980, U.S. Dist. Ct. (no. dist.) Calif. 1984, Calif. 1989, U.S. Dist. Ct. (so. dist.) Calif. 1989, U.S. Dist. Ct. (ea. and ctrl. dists.) Calif. 1992, U.S. Ct. Appeals (9th cir.) 1992, U.S. Dist. Ct. (no. dist.) Tex. 1998, U.S. Ct. Appeals (5th cir.) 1998, Tex. 1999. Atty. Southeastern Ohio Legal Services, Chillicothe and Steubenville, 1979-80; asst. dist. counsel Dept. of the Army, C.E. Office of Counsel, Huntington, W.Va. and Jacksonville, Fla., 1980-83; asst. atty. gen. State of Ohio, Columbus, 1983-84; trial atty., sr. trial atty. Dept. of Navy Office of Gen. Counsel, Washington and San Francisco, 1984-92; mem. Ware & Freidenrich, Palo Alto, Calif., 1992-93, Gray Cary Ware & Freidenrich, Palo Alto, 1994-97, Gray, Cary, Ware & Freidenrich, San Francisco, 1997—. Recipient Spl. Svc. award Dept. of the Army, 1983, award for Excellance Dept of Navy, 1991. Mem. ABA (natural resources law sect.), Bar Assn. San Francisco (environment and water law sect.). Environmental, Federal civil litigation, Land use and zoning (including planning). Office: Gray Cary Ware & Friedenrich PO Box 77630 San Francisco CA 94107-0630

**ROBERTSON, JAMES**, judge; b. Cleve., May 18, 1938; s. Frederick Irving and Doris Mary (Byars) R.; m. Berit Selma Persson, Sept. 19, 1959; children: Stephen Irving, Catherine Anne, Peter Arvid. AB, Princeton U., 1959; LLB, George Washington U., 1965. Bar: D.C. 1966, U.S. Supreme Ct. 1969. Assoc. Wilmer, Cutler & Pickering, Washington, 1965-69, ptnr., 1973-94; U.S. dist. judge D.C., 1994—; chief counsel Lawyers Com. for Civil Rights Under Law, Jackson, Miss., 1969-70; dir. Lawyers Com. for Civil Rights Under Law, Washington, 1970-72, co-chmn., 1985-87; co-chmn. D.C. Lawyers Com. for Civil Rights Under Law, Washington, 1982-84; mem. com. on grievances U.S. Dist. Ct., 1988-92, vice chmn., 1989-92; bd. dirs. South Africa Legal Svcs. and Edn. Project, Inc., 1987—, pres., 1989-94; bd. dirs. D.C. Prisoners Legal Svcs., Inc., 1992-94. Editor in chief George Washington Law Rev., 1964-65. Lt. USN, 1959-64. Fellow Am. Coll. Trial Lawyers, Am. Bar Found.; mem. ABA, D.C. Bar (bd. govs. 1986-93, pres.-elect 1990-92, pres. 1991-92), Am. Law Inst. Home: 3318 N St NW Washington DC 20007-2807 Office: US Courthouse Rm 6315 333 Constitution Ave NW Washington DC 20001-2800

**ROBERTSON, JERRY D.**, lawyer; b. Port Clinton, Ohio, Dec. 16, 1948; s. Edgar N. and Delores E. (Brough) R.; m. Kathryn A. Behlmer, Aug. 1, 1970; children: Matthew, Adam. BS, Bowling Green State U., 1971; JD, U. Toledo, 1974. Bar: Ohio 1974, U.S. Ct. Mil. Appeals 1974, U.S. Dist. Ct. (no. dist.) Ohio 1977, U.S. Supreme Ct. 1980. Pvt. practice Oak Harbor, Ohio, 1977—; instr. real estate law Terra tech. Coll., Fremont, Ohio, 1978-82; asst. pros. atty. Ottawa County, Ohio, 1980-84; law dir. Village of Oak Harbor, Ohio, 1982-98; bd. dirs. Luther Home of Mercy, Williston, Ohio. Capt. U.S. Army, 1974-77. Decorated Meritorious Svc. medal. Mem. ABA, Nat. Network of Estate Planning Attys., Nat. Acad. Elder Law Attys., Ohio Bar Assn., Toledo Estate Planning Coun., Am. Legion. Lutheran. Estate planning, Probate, Estate taxation. Home: 520 E Water St Oak Harbor OH 43449-1535 Office: PO Box 26 132 W Water St Oak Harbor OH 43449-1332

**ROBERTSON, LINDA LOU**, law librarian; b. Columbus, Ind., Feb. 17, 1940; d. Bernard and Margaret V. (Christian) R. BS, Ball State U., 1962; MLS, Ind. U., 1975. Tchr. Lee County Sch. Bd., Ft. Myers, Fla., 1962-65, sch. libr., 1965-68; libr. Bartholomew County Pub. Libr., Columbus, 1968-70; libr. dir. Wabash Carnegie Pub. Libr., Wabash, Ind., 1970-86; libr. adminstr. State Libr. of Iowa, Des Moines, 1987-88, law libr., 1988—; adj. faculty Ind. U., South Bend, 1982-86. Newspaper columnist Dewey Doings, 1984-86. Pres. Ind. Library Assn., Indpls., 1983-84; life mem. bd. dirs. Honeywell Found., Wabash, 1982—; city coun. mem., Wabash, 1980-84; mem. City Planning Commn., Wabash, 1980-84; co-founder Wabash County Arts Coun., Wabash, 1980, Leadership Devel. Wabash Coun., Wabash, 1983, Wabash County Crime Stoppers, Wabash, 1984. Named Sagamore of the Wabash, Gov. of Ind., 1986. Mem. Am. Assn. Law Librs., Iowa Libr. Assn. Office: State Law Libr Des Moines IA 50319-0001

**ROBERTSON, PAUL JOSEPH**, lawyer, educator; b. Chgo., Dec. 31, 1963; s. Mary Ellen (Statom) R. BSBA in Mktg., Georgetown U., Washington, 1985; BA in Sociology, St. Leo (Fla.) Coll., 1988; MBA, U. Ill., 1992, JD, 1992. Bar: Ill. 1992, U.S. Dist. Ct. (ea. dist.) Ill. 1992, U.S. Ct. Appeals (7th cir.) 1992. Counsel Region V U.S. Dept. Health and Human Svcs., Chgo., 1992-93, staff atty. Social Security Adminstrn., 1993-94; sr. atty. Office Gen. Counsel U.S. Dept. Health and Human Svcs., Bethesda, Md., 1994—; lectr. NIH, Found. for Advanced Edn. in Scis., Bethesda, 1995—; mem. black employees fed. adv. com. NIH, 1994-97. Campaign aide, FEC compliance, com. to elect Carol Moseley-Braun for U.S. Senate, Chgo., 1992. 1st lt. USAF, 1985-88. Decorated Air Force Meritorious Medal; recipient Joseph W. Rickert Award for Cmty. Svc., Faculty of Law, U. Ill., 1992. Mem. ABA, Nat. Bar Assn., Chgo. Bar Assn., Am. Legion, Masons. AME Ch. Avocations: Lacrosse, basketball, travel, reading, wine tasting. Office: NIH Bldg 31 -50 Rm 2B Bethesda MD 20892-0001

**ROBERTSON, WILLIAM ABBOTT**, arbitrator, mediator; b. San Francisco, Apr. 7, 1947; s. William A. Jr. and Roxana D. Robertson; m. Abigail K. Robertson; children: Sara W., Clair S.; stepchildren: Craig Harner, Geoffrey Harner, Katie Harner. BA, U. Calif., Davis, 1969; JD, U. of the Pacific, Sacramento, 1980. Bar: Calif. 1980, U.S. Dsit. Ct. (no. and ea. dists.) 1981, U.S. Ct. Appeals (9th cir.) 1981. Atty. Rodeno & Robertson, Napa, Calif., 1984-94, Robertson Law Office, Napa, 1994-96; pvt. practice mediation and arbitration, 1995—; judge pro tem Napa Consol. Cts., 1982—; assigned arbitrator Napa and Solano County Superior Cts., 1984—. Avocations: ranching, quarter horses. Office: Robertson Mediation Office PO Box 555 Saint Helena CA 94574-5055

**ROBIN, KENNETH DAVID**, lawyer; b. Phila., Jan. 18, 1944; s. Leo Bernard R. and Ethel Einhorn; m. Joan Ellen Maller, Sept. 2, 1967; 1 child, Blake; m. Valerie J. Lewick, Dec. 13, 1981; children: Samantha, Camille. BA, UCLA, 1964, JD, 1967. Spl. antitrust counsel Ivansaman Capnat, San Francisco, 1976-78; pvt. practice San Francisco, 1978—. Sgt. U.S. Army, 1967-73. General civil litigation, Environmental, Antitrust. Office: 2204 Union St San Francisco CA 94123-3902

**ROBIN, THEODORE TYDINGS, JR.**, lawyer, engineer, consultant; b. New Orleans, Aug. 29, 1939; s. T.eodore Tydings and Hazel (Corbin) R.; m. Helen Jones, June 8, 1963; children: Corbin, Curry, Ted, Phil. BME, Ga. Inst. Tech., 1961, MS in N.E., 1963, PhD, 1967; LLB, Blackstone Sch. Law, 1979. Bar: Calif. 1980, U.S. Patent and Trademark Office 1982; registered profl. engr., Ala., Calif. Rsch. engr. Oak Ridge (Tenn.) Nat. Lab., 1967; asst. prof. radiology and physics Emory U., Atlanta, 1969-69; project engr. Atomic Internat. divsn. N.Am. Rockwell, Canoga park, Calif., 1970-72; engr. mgmt. engring. divsn. So. Co. Svcs., Birmingham, Ala., 1972-83, mgr. nuclear support and quality assurance, 1989-90, mgr. quality assurance and resources, 1991-92; mgr. Hatch Design Configuration, 1993-94; program mgr. pooled inventory mgmt. program So. Electric Internat., Birmingham, 1984-88, bd. dirs. polit. action com., 1985-87; dir. nuclear stds., radiation safety officer, sr. patent counsel, prin. nuclear engring Theragenics Corp., Atlanta, 1996—; bd. dirs. polit. action com., 1985-87. Mem. ABA, ASME (mem. nuclear quality assurance subcom. on stds. coordinating and radioactive waste 1991-99), Am. Assn. Physicists Medicine, Am. Nuclear Soc. (chmn. Birmingham sect. 1987-88, nuclear power plant stds. com. 1989-94), Ga. Tech. Alumni Assn. (trustee 1997-99), Rotary (pres. Shades Valley club 1987-88, chmn. dist. 6860 internat. youth exch. com. 1989-90, R.I. dist. gov. 6860 1994-95), Sigma Xi. Achievements include research on power plant performance and reliability and effect of coal quality, space radiation effects on human cells, boiling heat transfer, nuclear reactor safety, multi-utility contracting, reliability economics, benchmarking and total quality management; patent law. Nuclear power, Environmental, Patent. Home and Office: 4524 Pine Mountain Rd Birmingham AL 35213-1828

**ROBINER, DONALD MAXWELL**, federal official, lawyer; b. Detroit, Feb. 4, 1935; s. Max and Lucia (Chassman) R.; children: Steven Ralph, Lawrence Alan; m. Phyllis F. Goodman; children: Brian Roberts, Marc Roberts. BA, U. Mich., 1957; postgrad., Wayne State U., 1957-58; JD, Case Western Res. U., 1961. Bar: Ohio 1961, U.S. Supreme Ct. 1964, U.S. Ct. Appeals (6th cir.) 1965; bd. cert. civil trial adv. emeritus Nat. Bd. Trial Advocacy. Assoc. Metzenbaum, Gaines, Schwartz, Krupansky & Stern, Cleve., 1961-67; ptnr. Metzenbaum, Gaines, Krupansky, Finley & Stern, Cleve., 1967-72; v.p. Metzenbaum, Gaines, Finley & Stern Co., L.P.A., Cleve., 1972-77, Gaines, Stern, Schwarzwald & Robiner Co., Cleve., 1977-81; exec. v.p., sec. Schwarzwald, Robiner & Rock, Cleve., 1981-90; prin. Buckingham, Doolittle & Burroughs, Cleve., 1991-94; U.S. trustee Ohio and Mich. region 9 U.S. Dept. of Justice, 1994—; v.p., sec. Richard L. Bowen & Assocs., Inc., Cleve., 1969-94; acting judge Shaker Heights Mcpl. Ct., 1973; mem. Bd. Bar Examiners, State of Ohio, Columbus, 1974-79; life mem. 6th Cir. Jud. Conf.; mediator alt. dispute resolution panel U.S. Dist. Ct. (no. dist.) Ohio, 1993-94. Sec. Friends of Beachwood (Ohio) Libr., Inc., 1981-88, trustee, 1981-96. Recipient Cert. of Appreciation Ohio Supreme Ct., 1974-79, Appreciation award Am. Soc. of Appraisers 1975. Mem. Fed. Bar Assn., Am. Arbitration Assn. (Svc. award 1975), Ohio Coun. Sch. Bd. Attys. (exec. com. 1990-94), Jud. Conf. 8th Appellate Dist. Ohio (charter, life), KP. Fax: 216-522-4988. E-mail: donald.m.robiner@usdoj.gov. Home: 3094 Richmond Rd Beachwood OH 44122-3247 Office: US Dept Justice Office of US Trustee BP Tower 200 Public Sq Ste 203300 Cleveland OH 44114-2397

**ROBINETT, TIMOTHY DOUGLAS**, lawyer; b. Long Beach, Calif., Mar. 27, 1967; s. Clyde A. and Jeanne K. Robinett; m. Erica Sandra Behrens, June 7, 1997. BA, U. Calif., Berkeley, 1989; JD, Loyola U., 1993. Bar: Calif. 1993, U.S. Dist. Ct. (cen., so., no. and ea. dists.) Calif. 1993. Assoc. Manning, Leaver, Bruder & Berberich, L.A., 1993—. Mem. L.A. County Bar Assn. General civil litigation, Consumer commercial. Office: Manning Leaver Bruder & Berberich 5750 Wilshire Blvd Ste 655 Los Angeles CA 90036-3637

**ROBINETTE, CHRISTOPHER JOHN**, lawyer; b. Raleigh, N.C., June 22, 1971; s. Kim V. and Billie Kaye Robinette; m. Amanda Irene Lenz, Oct. 13, 1996. BA, Coll. William and Mary, 1993; JD, U. Va., 1996. Bar: Va. 1996, U.S. Dist. Ct. (we. dist.) Va. 1997, U.S. Ct. Appeals (4th cir.) 1997, U.S. Dist. Ct. (ea. dist.) Va. 1998. Assoc. Tremblay & Smith LLP, Charlottesville, Va., 1996—. Contbr. to profl. jours. Adv. bd. mem. Salvation Army, Charlottesville, Va., 1997—; mem. Recreational Facilities Authority, Albemarle County, Va., 1998—. Mem. Va. State Bar (young lawyers divsn., litigation sect.), Va. Trial Lawyers' Assn., Charlottesville-Albermarle Bar Assn. Avocations: reading, jogging, weight lifting, traveling. General civil litigation, Contracts commercial. Office: Tremblay & Smith LLP 105-109 E High St Charlottesville VA 22902

**ROBINOWITZ, CHARLES**, lawyer; b. White Plains, N.Y., Sept. 29, 1942; s. Seymour and Shirley (Horowitz) R.; m. Selene Bea Greenberg, June 17, 1973; children: Scott, Mark. BA, Cornell U., 1964; LLB, U. Va., 1968. Bar: Oreg. 1969, N.Y. 1969, U.S. Dist. Ct. (all dists.) Oreg. 1969, U.S. Ct. Appeals (9th cir.) 1973, U.S. Supreme Ct. 1974. Law clk. U.S. Dist. Ct., N.Y.C., 1968-69; assoc. Dusenbery, Martin et al, Portland, Oreg., 1969-71; pvt. practice law Portland, 1971—. Bd. dirs. Jewish Fedn. Portland, 1991-97; pres. Cornell Club Oreg., 1991-95, Temple Beth Israel, Portland, 1988-94; bd. dirs. Friends of Chamber Music, Portland, 1975-79. Mem. ABA, ATLA, Oreg. Trial Lawyers Assn., Oreg. State Bar Assn., Multnomah County Bar Assn. Avocations: running, coaching Little League and youth basketball. Personal injury, Workers' compensation, Admiralty. Office: 1211 SW 5th Ave Ste 2962 Portland OR 97204-3729

**ROBINS, RONALD ALBERT, JR.**, lawyer; b. Columbus, Ohio, Nov. 19, 1963; s. Ronald Albert and Barbara (Feibel) R.; m. Mary Wales Leslie, Nov. 29, 1967. BA, Duke U., 1985; JD, Harvard U., 1989. Jud. clk. Hon. Milton Pollack, N.Y.C., 1989-90; assoc. Davis Polk & Wardwell, N.Y.C., 1990-93; assoc. Vorys Sater Seymour & Pease, Columbus, 1993-96, ptnr., 1997—. Chmn. alumni bd. Columbus Acad., 1997-99; chmn. adv. bd. for Columbus, Duke U., 1998. Mem. Columbus Bar Assn. General corporate, Mergers and acquisitions, Securities. Office: Vorys Sater Seymour and Pease LLP 52 E Gay St Columbus OH 43215-3161

**ROBINSON, ADELBERT CARL**, lawyer, judge; b. Shawnee, Okla., Dec. 13, 1926; s. William H. and Mayme (Forston) R.; m. Paula Kay Settles, Apr. 16, 1988; children from previous marriage: William, James, Schuyler, Donald, David, Nancy, Lauri. Student, Okla. Bapt. U., 1944-47; JD, Okla. U., 1950. Bar: Okla. 1950. Pvt. practice Muskogee, Okla., 1956-97; with legal dept. Phillips Petroleum Co., 1950-51; adjuster U.S. Fidelity & Guaranty Co., 1951-54, atty., adjuster-in-charge, 1954-56; ptnr. Fite & Robinson, 1956-62, Fite, Robinson & Summers, 1963-70, Robinson & Summers, 1970-72, Robinson, Summers & Locke, 1972-76, Robinson, Locke & Gage, 1976-80, Robinson, Locke, Gage & Fite, 1980-83, Robinson, Locke, Gage, Fite & Williams, Muskogee, 1983-95, Robinson, Gage, Fite & Williams, Muskogee, 1995-97; police judge, City of Muskogee, 1963-64, mcpl. judge, 1964-70; prin. justice Temp. Divsn. 36 Okla. Ct. Appeals, 1981-84, spl. dist. judge, 1997—; pres., dir. Wall St. Bldg. Corp., 1969-78, Three Forks Devel. Corp., 1968-77, Rolo Leasing Inc., 1971-97, Suroya II Inc., 1977—; sec. Muskogee Tom's Inc., Blue Ridge Corp., Harborcliff Corp.; bd. dirs. First Bancshares of Muskogee Inc., first of Muskogee Corp., First City Bank, Tulsa; adv. dir. First Nat. Bank & Trust Co. of Muskogee; mng. ptnr. RLG Ritz, 1980-97; ptnr. First City Real Estate Partnership, 1985-94; del. to U.S./China Jt. Session on Trade, Investment and Econ. Law, Beijing, 1987. Chmn. Muskogee County (Okla.) Law Day, 1963, Muskogee Area Redevel. Authority, 1963, Muskogee County chpt. Am. Cancer Soc., 1956; pres., bd. dirs. United Way of Muskogee Inc., 1980-88, v.p., 1982, pres., 1983; bd. dirs. Muskogee Cmty. Concert Assn., Muskogee Tourist Info. Bur., 1964-68; bd. dirs., gen. counsel United Cerebral Palsy Eastern Okla., 1964-68; trustee Connors Devel. Found., Connors Coll., 1981-99, chmn., 1987-89; active Muskogee Housing Authority, 1992-95. With inf. AUS, 1945-46. Mem. ABA, Okla. Bar Assn. (chmn. uniform laws com. 1970-72, chmn. profl. coop. com. 1965-69, past regional chmn. grievance com.), Muskogee County Bar Assn. (pres. 1971, mem. exec. coun. 1971-74), Okla. Assn. Def. Counsel (dir.), Okla. Assn. Mcpl. Judges (dir.), Muskogee c. of C., Delta Theta Phi., Rotary (pres. 1971-72). Methodist. Banking, Estate planning, Real property. Home: 2408 Saint Andrews Ct Muskogee OK 74403-1657 Office: 530 Court St # 87 Muskogee OK 74401-6033

**ROBINSON, AUBREY EUGENE, JR.**, federal judge; b. Madison, N.J., Mar. 30, 1922; s. Aubrey Eugene and Mabel (Jackson) R.; m. Sara E. Payne, Dec. 31, 1946 (dec.); children: Paula Elaine Robinson Collins, Sheryl Louise; m. Doris A. Washington, Mar. 17, 1973. B.A., Cornell U., 1943, LL.B., 1947. Bar: N.Y. and D.C. 1948. Practice with law firms Washington, 1948-65; assoc. judge Juvenile Ct. D.C., 1965-66; assoc. judge U.S. Dist. Ct. D.C., 1966—, chief judge, 1982-92, now sr. judge; gen. counsel Am. Council Human Rights, 1953-55, dir., 1955; mem. D.C. Commrs.'s Com. Child Placement Regulations, 1954-62; adj. prof. Am. U., 1975-84. Mem. D.C. Pub. Welfare Adv. Council, 1963-65; mem. Washington Urban League Adoption Project, 1959; mem. membership steering com. Health and Welfare Council D.C., 1961-66, Jud. Council of USA, 1982-92; mem. budget steering com. Health and Welfare Council Nat. Capital Area, 1963-66; mem. exec. com. Interreligious Com. Race Relations, 1966-67; exec. com., bd. dirs. D.C. Citizens for Better Pub. Edn., 1964-66; trustee United Planning Orgn. D.C., 1963-66, Washington Ctr. Met. Studies, 1967-74, Cornell U., 1982-91; bd. dirs. Family and Child Services Washington, 1954-63, v.p., 1958-61; bd. dirs. Family Service Assn. Am., 1958-68, Washington Action for Youth, 1962-64, Barney Neighborhood Settlement House, 1962-64, Eugene and Agnes E. Meyer Found., 1969-85, Consortium Univs. Washington Met. Area, 1969-74, Fed. Jud. Ctr., 1978-82; mem. adv. council Cornell Law Sch., 1974-80. Served with AUS, 1943-46. Mem. ABA (mem. com. cts. and community 1972—, mem. adv. com. judges function 1970-72), Nat. Conf. Fed. Trial Judges (chmn. 1973). Office: US Dist Ct US Courthouse 3rd & Constitution Ave NW Washington DC 20001

**ROBINSON, BARBARA PAUL**, lawyer; b. Oct. 19, 1941; d. Leo and Pauline G. Paul; m. Charles Raskob Robinson, June 11, 1965; children: Charles Paul, Torrance Webster. AB magna cum laude, Bryn Mawr Coll., 1962; LLB, Yale U., 1965. Bar: N.Y. 1966, U.S. Dist. Ct. (so. and ea. dists.) N.Y. 1975, U.S. Tax Ct. 1972, U.S. Ct. Appeals (2d cir.) 1974. Assoc. Debevoise & Plimpton (formerly Debevoise, Plimpton, Lyons & Gates), N.Y.C., 1966-75, ptnr., 1976—; mem. adv. bd., lectr. Practicing Law Inst.; arbitrator Am. Arbitration Assn., 1987—, bd. dirs.; dir. Sch. Choice Scholarships Found., 1997—. Bd. editors Chase Jour., 1997—; contbr. articles to profl. jours. Mem. adv. coun., bd. visitors CUNY Law Sch., Queens, 1984-90; trustee Trinity Sch., 1982-86, pres., 1986-88; bd. dirs. Found. for Child Devel., 1989—, chmn., 1991—; mem. Coun. on Fgn. Rels.; bd. dirs. Catalyst, 1993—, Am. Judicature Soc., Fund Modern Cts., 1990—, Wave Hill, 1994—, Garden Conservancy, 1996—; trustee Lawyers Com. for Civil Rights Under Law, 1997—, The William Nelson Cromwell Found., 1993—; bd. dirs. Irish Legal Rsch. Found. Inc., 1996—, Citizens Union Found. Inc., 1996—. Recipient Laura Parsons Pratt award, 1996. Fellow Am. Coll. Trust and Estate Counsel, Am. Bar Found., N.Y. Bar Found.; mem. ABA, N.Y. State Bar Assn. (vice chmn. com. on trust adminstrn., trusts and estates law sect. 1977-81, ho. of dels. 1984-87, 90-92, mem. com. ann. award 1993-94), Assn. of Bar of City of N.Y. (chmn. com. on trusts, estates and surrogates cts. 1981-84, judiciary com. 1981-84, coun. on jud. adminstrn. 1982-84, chair nominating com. 1984-85, 99—, mem. exec. com. 1986-91, chair 1989-90, v.p. 1990-91, pres. 1994-96, chair com. on honors 1993-94, mem. com. on long-range planning 1991-94, co-chair coun. on childen 1997—), Assn. of Bar of City of N.Y. Fund Inc. (bd. dirs., pres.), Women's Forum, Yale Coun., Yale Law Sch. Assn. N.Y. (mem. devel. bd., exec. com. 1981-85, pres. 1988-93), Yale Club, Washington Club. Estate planning, Probate, Estate taxation. Office: Debevoise & Plimpton 875 3rd Ave Fl 23 New York NY 10022-6256

**ROBINSON, BERNARD LEO**, retired lawyer; b. Kalamazoo, Feb. 13, 1924; s. Louis Harvey and Sue Mary (Starr) R.; m. Betsy Nadell, May 30, 1947; children: Robert Bruce, Patricia Anne, Jean Carol. BS, U. Ill., 1947, MS, 1958; JD, U. N.Mex., 1973. Bar: N.Mex. 1973, U.S. Supreme Ct. 1976. Rsch. engr. Assn. Am. Railroads, 1947-49; instr. arch. Rensselaer Poly. Inst., 1949-51; commd. 2d lt. U.S. Army, 1945, advanced through grades to lt. col., 1965, ret., 1968; engr. Nuclear Def. Rsch. Corp., Albuquerque, 1968-71; lawyer Albuquerque, 1973-85, Silver City, N.Mex., 1985-89, Green Valley, Ariz., 1989-90, Sierra Vista, Ariz., 1990-91; pres. Robinson Fin. Svcs., Tucson, 1993-95. Dist. commr. Boy Scouts Am., 1960-62; vice chmn. Rep. Dist. Com., 1968-70. Decorated Air medal. Mem. ASCE, ABA, Ret. Officers Assn., DAV, Assn. U.S. Army, VFW. General corporate, Banking. Home: 11821 N Pyramid Point Dr Oro Valley AZ 85737-3726

**ROBINSON, BERT KRIS**, lawyer; b. Austin, Tex., Aug. 2, 1936; s. Larry P. and Rose (Hansen) R.; m. Jane S. Smith, Aug. 25, 1956; children: Mary, Kristine, Johanna. BBA, U. Tex., 1958; JD, La. State U., 1963. Bar: La. 1963, U.S. Dist. Ct. (ea., we. and mid. dists.) La. 1963, U.S. Ct. Appeals (5th cir.) 1964, U.S. Tax Ct. 1970, U.S. Supreme Ct. 1970. V.p. Larry Robinson Photo Co., Shreveport, La., 1958-60; law clk. to judge U.S. Dist. Ct. La., Baton Rouge, 1963-64; assoc. Breazeale, Sachse and Wilson, Baton Rouge, 1964-66; sr. ptnr. Wray, Robinson and Kracht, Baton Rouge, 1966-89; prin. Law Offices Bert K. Robinson, Baton Rouge, 1989—; adj. prof. La. State U.,

Baton Rouge, 1986—. Assoc. editor La. Law Rev., 1963; contbr. articles to profl. jours. Founding pres. Baton Rouge chpt. Fed. Bar Assn., 1969; mem. Sunrise Rotary Club, Baton Rouge, 1991. Mem. ABA, Am. Inns of Ct., La. State Bar Assn. (ho. of dels. 1974-77), Christian Legal Soc., Baton Rouge Bar Assn. (pres. 1978). Avocation: photography. Construction, Personal injury, General civil litigation. Home: 10357 Old Hammond Hwy Baton Rouge LA 70816-8262 Office: Law Offices Bert K Robinson 10481 Old Hammond Hwy Ste F Baton Rouge LA 70816-8275

**ROBINSON, CALVIN STANFORD,** lawyer; b. Kalispell, Mont., Mar. 31, 1920; s. Calvin Alton and Berta Ella (Green) R.; m. Nancy Hanna, Dec. 13, 1945; children: Terrill S., Calvin D., Robert B., Barbara E. BA, U. Mont., 1944; student, U. Wash., U. Calif; JD, U. Mich., 1949. Bar: Ill. 1949, Mont. 1949. Assoc. Rooks & Freeman, Chgo., 1949-50; ptnr. Murphy, Robinson, Heckathorn & Phillips and predecessors, Kalispell, Mont., 1950-97; of counsel Crowley, Haughey, Toole, Hansen & Dietrick, P.C., 1997—; dir. Semitool Inc., Kalispell, 1979—, Winter Sports Inc., Whitefish, Mont., 1984—; mem. Mont. Gov.'s Com. Bus. Corp. Laws, Gov.'s Revenue Estimating Coun., 1986-88. Mem. Mont. Environ. Quality Council; past vice chmn. Mont. Bd. Housing; past mem. Mont. Bd. Edn., Mont. U. Bd. Regents. Served to lt. USNR, 1942-46. Fellow Am. Coll. Trust and Estate Counsel; mem. ABA, Mont. Bar Assn., N.W. Mont. Bar Assn., Ill. Bar Assn., Mont. State C. of C. (bd. dirs. 1985-93, chmn. 1990-91). Episcopalian. Banking, General corporate, Estate planning. Home: 315 Crestview Rd Kalispell MT 59901-2606 Office: PO Box 759 431 1st Ave NW Kalispell MT 59901-3908

**ROBINSON, DAVID HOWARD,** lawyer; b. Hampton, Va., Nov. 24, 1948; s. Beranrd Harris and Phyllis (Canter) R.; m. Nina Jane Briscoe, Aug. 20, 1979. BA, Calif. State U., Northridge, 1970; JD, Cabrillo Pacific U., 1975. Bar: Calif. 1977, U.S. Dist. Ct. (so. dist.) Calif. 1977, U.S. Ct. Claims, 1979, U.S. Supreme Ct. 1980. Adminstr. Cabrillo Pacific U. Coll. Law, 1977; assoc. Gerald D. Egan, San Bernardino, Calif., 1977-78, Duke & Gerstel, San Diego, 1978-80, Rand, Day & Ziman, San Diego, 1980-81; pvt. practice, San Diego, 1981-88; ptnr. Robinson and Rubin, San Diego, 1988-95; dep. atty. gen. State of Calif., San Diego, 1995—. Mem. Foothills Bar Assn. (bd. dirs., past treas.). Office: 110 West A St San Diego CA 92101-3711

**ROBINSON, DAVID LEE,** lawyer; b. New Albany, Miss., May 15, 1957; s. Billy Bruce and Sarah (Hollingsworth) R.; Francesca Elizabeth Bouton, Aug. 28, 1987; children: Adam, Max. BA, U. Miss., 1979, JD, 1981. Staff atty. Miss. D.H.S., Greenville, 1981-83; pvt. practice Greenville, 1983-84, asst. pub. defender, 1985; asst. dist. atty. Cleveland, Miss., 1986-88, Oxford, Miss., 1988-95; assoc. Farese, Farese & Farese, Ashland, Miss., 1995—. Family and matrimonial, General civil litigation. Office: Farese Farese & Farese PO Box 98 Ashland MS 38603-0098

**ROBINSON, DERRICK JEFFREY,** lawyer; b. New Haven, Sept. 5, 1951; s. William Aron Robinson and Jean Eunice Monroe Johnson; m. Pamela Celestine Allen, Dec. 20, 1975; children: Naima, Marcus. BA, Howard U., Washington, 1974; JD, Antioch Sch. Law, Washington, 1978. Bar: N.Y. 1982, U.S. Dist. Ct. (ea. dist.) N.Y. 1984, U.S. Ct. Appeals (2nd cir.) 1991. Asst. county atty. Suffolk County Atty.'s Office, Hauppauge, N.Y., 1982-84, sr. asst., 1984-85, prin. asst. county atty., 1985—; counsel to health and safety bd. Suffolk County Govt., Hauppauge, 1988-90, Freedom of Information Law appeals officer, 1994—. Author newsletter of Suffolk County Anti-Bias Task Force, 1995. Pres. Martin Luther King Commn., Suffolk County, 1993-94, bd. dirs., 1989-95; counsel North Amityville (N.Y.) Cmty. Econ. Coun., 1989—. Recipient Vol. Recognition Program award Newsday, L.I., 1993, Pres.'s award Suffolk County Martin Luther King Commn., 1993. Avocations: racquetball, golf, community theatre production. Home: PO Box 148 Amityville NY 11701-0148 Office: Suffolk County Attorneys Of Bldg 158 North Complex Veterans Memorial Hwy Hauppauge NY 11788

**ROBINSON, EDWARD NORWOOD,** lawyer; b. Roseboro, N.C., June 18, 1925; s. Edward Croswell and Lolita (Underwood) R.; m.Pauline L. Gray, Mar. 20, 1952; children: Edward Norwood Jr., James Gray, Michael Lindsay, Mark Alvin. BS in Engring., U.S. Mil. Acad., 1945; JD, Duke U., 1952. Atty. Robinson & Lawing, Winston-Salem, N.C.; N.C. civilian aide to Sec. of Army; appointed to 5th Dist. Acad. Selection Bd.; mem. ethics com. Bowman Gray Sch. Medicine; bd. visitors Duke U. Sch. Law, Wake Forest U. Sch. Law, Duke Divinity Sch.; lectr. in field. Co-editor Duke Law Jour. Past pres. Winston-Salem Rotary Club; past campaign chmn. United Way; past pres. C. of C.; past pres. local chpt. ARC; past dir. Winston-Salem Housing Found.; mem. Centenary United Meth. Ch., Winston-Salem, tchr. Chapel class, past chmn. bd. stewards; past chmn. Winston-Salem Dist. United Meth. Ch., Ch. Ext.; past dir., campaign chmn. Triad United Meth. Home. With U.S. Army. Recipient Charles L. Rhyne award Duke U. Law Alumni, 1997. Fellow Am. Coll. Trial Lawyers; mem. ABA (antitrust and litigation sects.), U.S. 4th Cir. Jud. Conf. (life), N.C. Bar Assn. (past dir.), Forsyth County Bar Assn. (past pres.), Pvt. Adjudication Ctr. Duke U. (past chmn. bd.), U.S. Mil. Acad. Assn. Grads. (bd. trustees), Order of the Coif, Joseph Branch Inns of Ct., Am. Inns of Ct. Avocations: golf, travel. Office: Robinson and Lawing LLP 370 Knollwood St Ste 600 Winston Salem NC 27103-1815

**ROBINSON, EDWARD T., III,** lawyer; b. Glen Cove, N.Y., May 23, 1932; s. Edward Jr. and Helen (Rahilly) R.; m. Lynn Simmons; children: Edward IV, Wendy, Christopher, Jeffrey, Lesley, Michael. AB, Holy Cross Coll., 1954; JD, Georgetown U., 1960. Bar: N.Y. 1961, U.S. Ct. Appeals (2d cir.) 1966. Counsel Royal-Globe Ins. Co., Mineola, N.Y., 1960-64; pvt. practice, Oyster Bay, N.Y., 1964-70, 91-94, 96—; ptnr. Robinson & Cincotta, Oyster Bay, 1970-85, Robinson & Lynch, Oyster Bay, 1985-91, Robinson, Bermingham & Donegan, Oyster Bay, 1994-96; mem. adv. bd. Chgo. Title Ins. Co., N.Y.C., 1982—, Fleet Bank, 1989-95, United Cerebral Palsy, 1980—; mem. Nassau County Commn. on Govt. Revision, 1993—; mem. County Exec. Blue Ribbon Panel on Criminal Justice; mem. exec. coun. N.Y. State Conf. Bar Leaders, 1986-90; counsel Oyster Bay-East Norwich Ctrl. Sch. Dist., 1966—; mem. N.Y. State grievance com. 10th Jud. Dist., 1995-99; mem. La Romana C.C., Dominican Republic, 1997. Mem. Nassau County Traffic and Parking Violations Bur.; pres. Holy Cross Coll. Club, L.I., 1989-90; trustee Nassau County coun. Boy Scouts Am.; chmn. Forget-Me-Not Ball, United Cerebral Palsy. Recipient Community Svc. award Nassau County coun. Boy Scouts Am.; named Man of Yr. United Cerebral Palsy, Nassau County, 1979. Mem. N.Y. State Bar Assn. (del., v.p. 1992-95, mem. ho. of dels. 1995—), Nassau County Bar Assn. (pres. 1986-87), C. of C. (pres. 1976-79), Meadowbrook Golf Club. Republican. Roman Catholic. Avocations: golf, tennis, jazz music. Real property, Probate, State civil litigation. Home: 60 Calvin Ave Syosset NY 11791-2106 Office: 34 Audrey Ave Unit 3 Oyster Bay NY 11771-1595

**ROBINSON, G. CRAIG,** lawyer; b. Ellinwood, Kans., July 17, 1954; s. Glenn I. and E. Jeanne (Underwood) R.; m. Dena R. Dombaugh, July 12, 1981; children: Blake A., Whitney G. BS, Kans. State U., 1976; JD, Washburn U., 1979. Bar: Kans. 1979, U.S. Dist. Ct. Kans. 1979, U.S. Mil. Ct. Appeals 1983, U.S. Supreme Ct. 1990. Pvt. practice Wichita, Kans., 1979—. Mem. Kans. State Lottery Commn. Democrat. Avocation: golf. Family and matrimonial, Criminal, General practice. Office: 330 N Main St Wichita KS 67202-1597

**ROBINSON, IRWIN JAY,** lawyer; b. Bay City, Mich., Oct. 8, 1928; s. Robert R. and Anne (Kaplan) R.; m. Janet Binder, July 7, 1957; children: Elizabeth Binder Schubiner, Jonathan Meyer, Eve Kimberly Wiener. AB, U. Mich., 1950; JD, Columbia U., 1953. Bar: N.Y. 1956. Assoc. Breed Abbott & Morgan, N.Y.C., 1955-58; asst. to ptnrs. Dreyfus & Co., N.Y.C., 1958-59; assoc. Greenbaum Wolff & Ernst, N.Y.C., 1959-65; ptnr. Greenbaum Wolff & Ernst, 1966-76; sr. ptnr. Rosenman & Colin, N.Y.C., 1976-90; of counsel Pryor, Cashman, Sherman & Flynn, 1990-92; sr. ptnr. Phillips, Nizer, Benjamin, Krim & Ballon, N.Y.C., 1992—; treas. Saarsteel, Inc., Whitestone, N.Y., 1970—. Bd. dirs. Henry St. Settlement, N.Y.C., 1960-85, Jewish Cmty. Ctr. Assn. N.Am., N.Y.C., 1967-94, mem. adv. bd., 1998—; bd. dirs. Heart Rsch. Found., 1989-94, pres., 1991-93. Mem. ABA, N.Y. State Bar Assn., Assn. Bar City of N.Y., Internat. Bar Assn., Thai-Am. C. of C. (founder, bd. dirs. 1992-95, pres. 1992-95), Vietnam-Am. C. of C. (founder, bd. dirs. 1992-95, pres. 1992-95), Philippine-Am. C. of C. (bd. dirs. 1960-98), Sunningdale Country Club, The Desert Mountain Club. Jewish. Banking, General corporate, Real property. Home: 4622 Grosvenor Ave Riverdale NY 10471-3305 Office: Phillips Nizer Benjamin Krim & Ballon 29th Flr 666 5th Ave New York NY 10103-0001

**ROBINSON, JAMES KENNETH,** federal official; b. Grand Rapids, Mich., Nov. 27, 1943; s. Kenneth and Marguerite (Anderson) R.; m. Marietta Sebree; children: Steven James, Renee Elizabeth. BA with honors, Mich. State U., 1965; JD magna cum laude, Wayne State U., 1968. Bar: Mich. 1968, U.S. Dist. Ct. (ea. and we. dists) Mich. 1969, U.S. Ct. Appeals (6th cir.) 1969, U.S. Supreme Ct. 1977. Law clk. to judge U.S. Ct. Appeals (6th cir.), 1968-69; assoc. Miller, Canfield, Paddock & Stone, Detroit, 1969-71; from assoc. to ptnr. Honigman Miller Schwartz and Cohn, Detroit, 1972-77, ptnr., 1981-93, chmn. litigation dept.; U.S. atty. Ea. Dist. Mich., 1977-80; adj. prof. Wayne State U. Law Sch., Detroit, 1973-84, dean, prof., 1993-98; asst. atty. gen. criminal divsn. U.S. Dept. Justice, Washington, 1998—; adj. prof. Detroit Coll. Law, 1970-73; mem. evidence test drafting com.-multistate bar exam Nat. Conf. Bar Examiners, 1975—; mem. adv. com. on evidence rules Jud. Conf. U.S., 1993-98; chmn. com. on rules of evidence Mich. Supreme Ct., 1975-78; lectr. Mich. Jud. Inst., 1977-98, Mich. Inst. CLE. Author: (with others) Introducing Evidence-A Practical Guide for Michigan Lawyers, 1988, Scope of Discovery, 1986, Michigan Court Rules Practice-Evidence, 1996, Courtroom Handbook on Michigan Evidence, 1997; contbg. author Emerging Problems Under the Federal Rules of Evidence, 3d edit., 1998; contbr. articles to profl. jours.; editor in chief Wayne Law Rev., 1967-68. Chmn. Gov.'s Commn. on Future Higher Edn. in Mich., 1983-84; pres. State Bar of Mich., 1990-91, commr. 1980-81, 83-91. Recipient Disting. Alumni award Wayne State U. Law Sch., 1979, 1986. Fellow Am. Bar Found., Mich. Bar Found., Am. Coll. Trial Lawyers, Internat. Soc. Barristers, Am. Acad. of Appellate Lawyers; mem. ABA (litigation and criminal justice sects., lectr.), Fed. Bar Assn. (dir. 1975-81), Detroit Bar Assn. (bd. dirs. 1975-81), Nat. Assn. Former U.S. Attys. (pres. 1984-85), Am. Law Inst., 6th Cir. Jud. Conf., Wayne U. Law Alumni Assn. (pres. 1975-76), Detroit Athletic Club, Detroit Yacht Club. Office: US Dept Justice Asst Atty Gen Criminal Divs 10th & Constitution NW Washington DC 20530-0001

**ROBINSON, JEAN MARIE,** lawyer; b. Milw.; d. Alonzo and Theresa (Payne) R. BA, Marquette U., 1982; JD, U. Wis., 1985. Bar: Wis., 1985, U.S. Dist. Ct. (we. dist.) Wis., 1985. CEO United Meth. Devel. Fund Investment Fund, N.Y.C., 1986-88; CFO Gen. Bd. of Ch. and Soc., Washington, 1988-90; gen. counsel Goodwill Industries Corp., Bethesda, Md., 1990—. Recipient Am. Jurisprudence award Lawyers Coop. Pub. Co., 1984. Mem. ABA (charitable contbns., probate and trust coms.), Am. Corp. Counsel Assn. (membership, tax, corp., labor and fin. coms.), Nat. Bar Assn., Am. Corp. Counsel Assn., Phi Alpha Delta (v.p. 1984-85). Methodist. Avocations: chess, tennis, photography. General corporate, Labor, Corporate taxation. Home: 9303 Elk Horn Rd Lorton VA 22079-3302 Office: Goodwill Industries Corp 9200 Wisconsin Ave Bethesda MD 20814-3896

**ROBINSON, JOHN KELLY,** lawyer; b. Oak Ridge, Tenn., May 28, 1964; s. James Norris and Charlotte Rhett (Lea) R.; m. Kathleen Marie Brandner, Mar. 9, 1991; children: John Norris, Margaret Lea. BSME, Rensselaer Poly. Inst., 1986; JD, George Washington U., 1994. Bar: N.Y. Assoc. Sullivan & Cromwell, N.Y.C., 1994—. Lt. USN, 1986-91. General corporate, Mergers and acquisitions, Securities. Office: Sullivan & Cromwell 125 Broad St Fl 28 New York NY 10004-2489

**ROBINSON, JOHN VICTOR,** lawyer; b. Harare, Zimbabwe, July 9, 1958; s. Denis Antony Beck and Elizabeth Jill R. BA, Rhodes U., Grahamstown, South Africa, 1983; MA, Oxford (Eng.) U., 1985; JD, U. Richmond (Va.), 1986. Bar: Va. Assoc. atty. Hunton & Williams, Richmond, Va., 1986-89, McSweeney, Burtch & Crump, Richmond, 1989-93, Cantor, Arkema & Edmonds, P.C., Richmond, 1993-97; pvt. practice Richmond, 1997—; past mem. regional com. Nat. Trial Competition, Richmond; apptd. adminstrv. hearing officer Va. Supreme Ct.; adj. asst. prof. Law U. Richmond Sch. Law. Rhodes scholar Oxford U., 1983-85. Mem. ABA, Va. Bar Assn., Bar Assn. City of Richmond. General corporate, General civil litigation, Intellectual property. Office: Koger Ctr Randolph Bldg 1500 Forest Ave Ste 222 Richmond VA 23229-5104

**ROBINSON, JOHN WILLIAM, IV,** lawyer; b. Atlanta, Apr. 29, 1950; s. J. William III and Elizabeth (Smith) R.; m. Ellen Showalter, Dec. 28, 1976; children: William, Anna. BA with honors, Washington & Lee U., 1972; JD, U. Ga., 1975. Bar: Fla., Ga., U.S. Dist. Ct. (no., so. and mid. dists.) Fla., U.S. Ct. Mil. Appeals, U.S. Ct. Appeals (5th and 11th cirs.), U.S. Supreme Ct.; cert. civil trial and bus. litigation lawyer, Fla., Nat. Bd. Trial Advocacy. Trial atty. Nat. Labor Rels. Bd., New Orleans, 1975-76; trial def. counsel 8th infantry U.S. Army, Mainz, Germany, 1977-78, trial counsel 8th infantry, 1979; law clerk, commr. Ct. Mil. Review, Washington, 1980; atty. Fowler, White, Gillen, Boggs, Villareal & Banker, P.A., Tampa, Fla., 1980—, head labor and employment law dept., 1993—, dir., 1998—; mem. faculty U. Md., 1977-79; arbitrator U.S. Dist. Ct. (mid. dist.) Fla. Editor-in-chief: Employment & Labor Relations Law, 1991-95; editor: Developing Labor Law, 1982—, Model Jury Instructions for Employment Litigation, 1994—; editor: Employment Litigation Handbook, 1998. Chmn. Tampa Bay Internat. Trade Coun., 1990-91, Rough Riders Dist. Boy Scouts Am., 1990, Drug Free Workplace Task Force, Greater Tampa C. of C., 1996. Capt. U.S. Army, 1976-80. Named one of Best Lawyers in Am. for labor and employment law. Mem. ABA (divsn. dir. 1996—, chmn. employment and labor rels. com. 1993-96, litigation sect.), Fla. Bar Assn. (chmn. labor and employment law sect. 1992-93), Wash. & Lee U. Bd. (pres. nat. alumni bd. 1990-91, trustee 1995—), Rotary (pres. Tampa Bay chpt.), Am. Inn of Ct. (pres., dir. and barrister). Avocations: tennis, history. Labor, Pension, profit-sharing, and employee benefits, General civil litigation. Office: Fowler White Gillen Boggs Villareal & Banker PA 501 E Kennedy Blvd Tampa FL 33602-5237

**ROBINSON, KENNETH PATRICK,** lawyer, electronics company executive; b. Hackensack, N.J., Dec. 12, 1933; s. William Casper and Margaret Agnes (McGuire) R.; m. Catherine Esther Lund, Aug. 26, 1961; children: James, Susan. BS in Elec. Engring., Rutgers U., 1955; JD, NYU, 1962. Bar: N.Y. 1962, U.S. Ct. Appeals (fed. cir.) 1990. With Hazeltine Corp., Greenlawn, N.Y., 1955-88 , patent counsel, 1966-69, gen. counsel, 1969-88, sec., 1971-88 , v.p., 1984-88 ; v.p. Hazeltine Rsch. Inc., Chgo., 1966-88, of counsel Brumbaugh, Graves, Donohue & Raymond, N.Y.C., 1989-92; prin. Kenneth P. Robinson, Huntington, N.Y., 1992—; dir. Hazeltine Ltd., London, 1973-80; dir. Imlac Corp., Needham, Mass., 1978-83. Served to 1st lt. USAF, 1955-57. Mem. ABA, IEEE, Am. Intellectual Law Assn., Licensing Execs. Soc. Roman Catholic. Patent, Trademark and copyright, Technology. Home: 137 Darrow Ln Greenlawn NY 11740-2923 Office: 474 New York Ave Huntington NY 11743-3542

**ROBINSON, KIMBERLY MARIE,** lawyer; b. St. Louis, Aug. 26, 1968. BS, Ctrl. Mo. State U., 1989; JD summa cum laude, Thurgood Marshall Sch. Law, Houston, 1993. Bar: Tex. 1993, U.S. Ct. Appeals (5th cir.) 1997, U.S. Ct. Appeals (9th cir.) 1998, U.S. Dist. Ct. (ea. and no. dist.) Tex. 1995, U.S. Dist. Ct. (so. and we. dist.) Tex. 1996. Briefing atty. 5th Dist. Ct. Appeals, Dallas, 1993-94; assoc. Gardere & Wynne, LLP, Dallas, 1994—. Bd. trustees St. Philip's Sch. and Cmty. Ctr., Dallas, 1995—, St. Philip's sch. and Cmty. Ctr. Nieghborhood Devel. Corp., 1997—; mem. Jr. League of Dallas, 1997—. Thurgood Marshall Sch. of Law scholar, 1990-93. Mem. State Bar of tex. (bar jour. com. 1996—), J.L. Turner Legal Assn., Dallas Bar Assn., Dallas Assn. Young Lawyers (dir. 1995-97). Appellate, General civil litigation. Office: Gardere & Wynne LLP 1601 Elm St Ste 3000 Dallas TX 75201-4761

**ROBINSON, MARIETTA S.,** lawyer. BA, U. Mich., 1973; JD, UCLA, 1978. Bar: Calif. 1978, Mich. 1979, U.S. Dist. Ct. (ea. dist.) Mich. 1979, U.S. Ct. Appeals (6th cir.) 1983, U.S. Supreme Ct. 1989. Data processing mktg. rep. IBM Corp., Flint, Mich., 1973-75; assoc. The Bank of Bermuda Legal Dept., Hamilton, 1978-79; from assoc. to ptnr. Dickinson, Wright, Moon, VanDusen & Freeman, Detroit, 1979-94; ptnr. Sommers, Schwartz, Silver & Schwartz, P.C., Southfield, Mich., 1985-89; owner Law Offices of Marietta S. Robinson, Detroit, 1989—; adj. prof. U. Detroit Sch. of Law, 1982-83, Wayne State U., Detroit, 1983-84; lectr. in field. Contbr. articles to profl. jours. Trustee Dalkon Shield Claimants Trust, 1989-97; appointee Gov. James Blanchard, State of Mich. Bldg. Authority, 1985-89, State Bar Mich./Mich. State Med. Soc. Coalition, 1993—. Listed in Best Lawyers in Am., 1999. Fellow ABA, Internat. Soc. Barristers, Mich. State Bar Found.; mem. State Bar Mich., State Bar Calif., ATLA, Mich. Trial Lawyers Assn., Women Lawyers Mich., Detroit Bar Assn., Oakland Bar Assn., U.S. Ct. Appeals (6th cir.) Jud. Conf. (life). Office: 1500 Buhl Bldg Detroit MI 48226-3602

**ROBINSON, MARY LOU,** federal judge; b. Dodge City, Kans., Aug. 25, 1926; d. Gerald J. and Frances Strueber; m. A.J. Robinson, Aug. 28, 1949; children: Rebecca Aynn Gruhlkey, Diana Ceil, Matthew Douglas. B.A., U. Tex., 1948, LL.B., 1950. Bar: Tex. 1949. Ptnr. Robinson & Robinson, Amarillo, 1950-55; judge County Ct. at Law, Potter County, Tex., 1955-59, (108th Dist. Ct.), Amarillo, 1961-73; assoc. justice Ct. of Civil Appeals for 7th Supreme Jud. Dist. of Tex., Amarillo, 1973-77; chief justice Ct. of Civil Appeals for 7th Supreme Jud. Dist. of Tex., 1977-79; U.S. dist. judge No. Dist. Tex., Amarillo, 1979—. Named Woman of Year Tex. Fedn. Bus. and Profl. Women, 1973. Mem. Nat. Assn. Women Lawyers, ABA, Tex. Bar Assn., Amarillo Bar Assn., Delta Kappa Gamma. Presbyterian. Office: US Dist Ct Rm 226 205 E 5th Ave # F13248 Amarillo TX 79101-1559

**ROBINSON, MICHAEL ALLEN,** lawyer; b. N.Y.C., Oct. 5, 1947. BA cum laude, Albany State Coll., 1972; JD, U. Denver, 1989. Bar: Colo. 1989, U.S. Ct. Appeals (10th cir.) 1993, U.S. Dist. Ct. Colo. 1990. Ptnr. Gubbels & Robinson, Castle Rock, Colo., 1991—. Bd. dirs. Cantril House Assistance, 1994; active Castle Rock Budget Commn., 1994—; chmn. Castle Rock Bd. Adjustment, 1994-96. With USN, 1966-70. Mem. Colo. Bar Assn., Douglas Bar Assn. (v.p., Atty. of Yr. 1992), Castle Rock C. of C. (bd. dirs. 1995—), VFW (post comdr. Castle Rock 1991-92). Democrat. Federal civil litigation, Criminal, State civil litigation. Home: 413 Wilcox St Ste 101 Castle Rock CO 80104-2477 Office: Gubbels & Robinson 210 5th St Castle Rock CO 80104-2406

**ROBINSON, NEIL CIBLEY, JR.,** lawyer; b. Columbia, S.C., Oct. 25, 1942; s. Neil C. and Ernestine (Carns) R.; m. Judith Ann Hunter, Sept. 4, 1971 (div. Nov. 1979); 1 child, Hunter Leigh; m. Vicki Elizabeth Kornahrens, Mar. 2, 1985; children: Neil C. III, Taylor Elizabeth. BS in Indsl. Mgmt., Clemson U., 1966; JD, U. S.C., 1973. Bar: S.C. 1974, U.S. Ct. Appeals (4th cir.) 1974, U.S. Dist. Ct. S.C. 1976. Asst. to dean U. S.C. Law Sch., Columbia, 1973-74; law clk. to judge Charles E. Jr. Simons Jr. U.S. Dist. Ct. S.C., Aiken, 1974-76; assoc. Grimball & Cabaniss, Charleston, S.C., 1976-78; ptnr. Grimball, Cabaniss, Vaughan & Robinson, Charleston, 1978-84; ptnr., pres. Robinson, Wall & Hastie, P.A., Charleston, 1984-91; ptnr., mem. exec. com. Nexsen, Pruet, Jacobs, Pollard & Robinson, Charleston, 1991—; permanent mem. 4th Cir. Jud. Conf., 1982—; pres. Coastal Properties Inst., Charleston, 1981—. Bd. dirs. Southeastern Wildlife Exposition, Charleston, 1987—, pres. 1994—, Charleston Maritime Festival, 1993—, pres. 1994-98, Parklands Found. of Charleston County; pres. S.C. Tourism Coun., Columbia, 1991—; co-founder, chmn. Charleston Planning Project Pub. Edn. Cpl. USMCR, 1960-66. Recipient Order of Palmetto, Gov. David Beasley, S.C., 1996. Mem. ABA, Urban Land Inst. (recreational devel. coun.), S.C. Bar Assn., Fed. Bar Assn., S.C. Def. Trial Lawyers Assn., Hibernian Soc. (mem. mgmt. com. 1984—, sec. 1998—), Kiawah Club, Haig Point Club, Country Club of Charleston, Phi Delta Phi. Presbyterian. Avocations: golf, hunting. Real property, Land use and zoning (including planning), Environmental. Home: PO Box 121 Charleston SC 29402-0121 Office: Nexsen Pruet Jacobs Pollard & Robinson 200 Meeting St Ste 301 Charleston SC 29401-3156

**ROBINSON, NICHOLAS ADAMS,** lawyer, law educator; b. N.Y.C., Jan. 20, 1945; s. Albert Lewis and Agnes Claflin (Adams) R.; m. Shelley Miner, Jan. 5, 1969; children: Cynthia M., Lucy A. BA cum laude, Brown U., 1967; JD cum laude, Columbia U., 1970. Bar: N.Y. 1971, U.S. Dist. Ct. (so. and ea. dists.) N.Y. 1972, U.S. Supreme Ct. 1974, U.S. Ct. Appeals (2d and 7th cirs.) 1972. Law clk. to U.S. dist. judge, so. dist. N.Y., 1970-72; assoc. Marshall, Bratter, Greene, Allison & Tucker, N.Y.C., 1972-78, counsel, 1978-82; assoc. prof. law Pace U. Sch. Law, White Plains, N.Y., 1978-81, prof., 1981—, dir. Ctr. for Environ. Legal Studies, 1982—; counsel Winer, Neuburger & Sive, N.Y.C., 1982-83; dep. commr., gen. counsel N.Y. State Dept. Environ. Conservation, Albany, 1983-85; counsel Sive, Paget & Reisel, 1985-92, Sidley & Austin, N.Y., London, 1992-96; legal adv. Internat. Union Conservation of Nature and Natural Resources, 1996—; del. U.S.A. environ. law meetings with USSR, 1974-92; chmn. Environ. Adv. Bd. to Gov. Mario Cuomo, 1985-94. Consulting editor Environ Law, 1996—; contbr. articles to profl. jours. Nat. bd. dirs. UN Assn. of U.S.A., 1966-76, 79-84, U.S. Com. for UNICEF, 1970-80, World Environment Ctr., 1981—, chmn., 1993—; bd. dirs. Westchester County Soil and Water Conservation Dist., 1976-83; chmn. N.Y. State Freshwater Wetlands Appeals Bd., 1976-83; mem. bd. edn. Union Free Sch. Dist. of Tarrytown, 1981-83, 85. Recipient N.Y. State Gov.'s Citation for Hist. Preservation, 1983, Eliz Haub prize in Environ. Law Free U. Brussels, 1992. Fellow Am. Bar Found.; mem. Internat. Council Environ. Law (gov. 1993—), Internat. Union Conservation of Nature and Natural Resouces (legal adv.), Commn. Environ. Law (chair 1997—), Am. Soc. Internat. Law, ABA, ALI, N.Y. State Bar Assn. (chmn. environ. law sect. 1979-80, environ. law award 1981), Assn. Bar City N.Y. (chmn. environ. law com. 1977-78, mem. internat. law com. 1985-88, internat. environ. law com. 1990-92, russian law com. 1992-95), Westchester County Bar Assn., Sierra Club (nat. bd. dirs. 1979-83), Phi Beta Kappa. Democrat. Unitarian. Home: 258 Kelbourne Ave Sleepy Hollow NY 10591-1322 Office: Pace U Sch Law 78 N Broadway White Plains NY 10603-3710

**ROBINSON, PATRICIA SNYDER,** lawyer; b. Hoboken, N.J., Dec. 5, 1952; d. Anthony James and Agnes Loretta (Riordan) Snyder; m. Daniel Lewis Robinson, Aug. 27, 1978. BA summa cum laude, Montclair State U., 1975; MSc, Rutgers U., 1980; JD, Rutgers U., Newark, N.J., 1986. Bar: N.J. 1986, U.S. Dist. Ct. N.J. 1986, D.C. 1992, U.S. Ct. Appeals (3d cir.) 1992. Grad. asst. Rutgers U., New Brunswick, N.J., 1975-77; chemist AT&T Bell Labs., Murray Hill, N.J., 1977-80; mgr. AT&T, Bedminster, N.J., 1980-87; assoc. Norris, McLaughlin & Marcus, Somerville, N.J., 1987; assoc. Collier, Jacob & Mills, Somerset, N.J., 1987-92, ptnr., 1993—. Contbr. articles to profl. jours. Mem. ABA, N.J. State Bar Assn., D.C. Bar Assn., Somerset County Bar Assn., N.Y. Acad. Sci., Phi Kappa Phi. Labor, Civil rights, General civil litigation. Office: Collier Jacob & Mills 580 Howard Ave Ste A Somerset NJ 08873-1167

**ROBINSON, RANDAL D.,** lawyer; b. Newark, Ohio, Apr. 2, 1949; s. Paul Alden and Bonnie J. C. R.; m. C. Brittney Copeland, Oct. 1, 1993; children: Brandon M., Frances M. BA, Denison U., 1971; JD, Capital U., 1975. Bar: Ohio 1975, U.S. Dist. Ct. (so. dist.) Ohio 1983, U.S. Ct. Appeals (6th cir.). Assoc. Harris, Lias & Strip, Columbus, Ohio, 1975-79; ptnr. Burman & Robinson, Columbus, 1979—; instr. bus. law Columbus (Ohio) Tech. Inst., 1983-84; instr., lectr. Franklin County Trial Lawyers Assn., 1998. Mem. ABA, Am. Arbitration Assn., Nat. Panel Arbitrators, Ohio State Bar Assn., Columbus Bar Assn. (lectr. family law legal assts. program 1980-82), Comml. Law League Am., Austin Healey Club N. Am., Inc. (bd. dirs., gen. counsel 1976—). Consumer commercial, Contracts commercial. Office: Burman & Robinson 601 S High St Fl 2 Columbus OH 43215-5680

**ROBINSON, RICHARD RUSSELL,** lawyer; b. Cedar Falls, Iowa, July 3, 1925; s. George Clarence and Juanita Louise (Thiede) R.; m. Carolyn Elizabeth Sage, Sept. 5, 1954 (dec. 1988); children: Timothy Todd, Elizabeth Ann, Edward William; m. Bette Hill Bullen, Dec. 27, 1994. AB, Harvard U., 1949; MA, U. Chgo., 1950; LLB, U. Wis., 1956. Bar: Wis. 1956, U.S. Dist. Ct. (ea. dist.) Wis. 1956, U.S. Ct. Appeals (7th cir.) 1957, U.S. Supreme Ct. 1964, U.S. Dist. Ct. (we. dist.) Wis. 1982. Law clk. Fed. Dist. Ct. Milw., 1956-58; ptnr. Godfrey, Trump & Hayes, Milw., 1970-90; ptnr. Godfrey, Braun & Frazier, 1997. Served with AUS, 1943-46. Decorated Combat Infantryman's Badge. Mem. State Bar Wis., Milw. Bar Assn., Am. Judicature Soc., Rotary, Masons. Methodist. State civil litigation, Federal civil litigation. Home: 10012 N Franklin Ct Mequon WI 53092-5457 Office: Godfrey Braun & Frazier 735 N Water St Fl 16 Milwaukee WI 53202-4100

**ROBINSON, RICHARD S.,** lawyer, musician, composer; b. N.Y.C., Jan. 23, 1956; s. Gerald and Leila June Robinson; m. Frances E. Morgen, Nov. 10, 1990. BA cum laude, U. Pa., 1978; JD, Seton Hall U., 1994. Bar: N.J. 1994, N.Y. 1995. Assoc. A.J. Fusco, Jr., P.A., Passaic, N.J., 1994-96, Ravin

Sarasohn, Roseland, N.J., 1997—. Composer, performer musical composition and guitar CD; contbr. articles to profl. jours. Registration checker Com. of Seventy, Phila., 1976. Recipient 2d prize Nathan Burken Meml. Competition, ASCAP/SHU, 1993. Mem. ABA, N.Y. State Bar Assn. (intellectual property sect., entertainment law sect.). Entertainment, Intellectual property, General civil litigation. Office: Ravin Sarasohn 103 Eisenhower Pkwy Roseland NJ 07068-1029

**ROBINSON, RICHARD SPENCER, II,** judge; b. Lincoln, Nebr., Sept. 13, 1950; s. Richard Spencer Robinson and Dorothy Maybelle Follett; m. Adrianne Louise Désirée van der Vlis, June 20, 1986; children: Dustin Michael, Erik David, Marlies Christien. BA, Brigham Young U., 1978, JD, 1982. Bar: Utah 1982, U.S. Dist. Ct. Utah, Nev. 1983, U.S. Dist. Ct. Nev. Law clk. Clark County Dist. Attys. Office, Las Vegas, Nev., 1982-83; asst. city pros. atty. West Valley City (Utah) Attys. Office, 1983-88; adminstrv. law judge Utah Dept. Corrections, Murray, 1988—; class '82 rep. J. Reuben Clark Law Sch. Alumni Bd., Salt Lake City, 1991-96. Cpl. USMC, 1970-72. Mem. Ch. of Jesus Christ of Latter-day Saints. Avocations: computers, skiing, music. Office: Utah Dept Corrections 6100 Fashion Blvd Murray UT 84107-7378

**ROBINSON, ROBIN WICKS,** lawyer; b. Roanoke Rapids, N.C., June 5, 1961; d. Wallace Wayne and Rozelle Royall Wicks; m. James Hendry Robinson, Jr., Nov. 7, 1992; 1 child, James Hendry Robinson III. BA in Politics (hon.), Converse Coll., Spartanburg, S.C., 1982; JD, U. N.C., Chapel Hill, 1985. Bar: N.C. 1986; 5th Jud. Dist. 1986, U.S. Dist. Ct. (ea. dist.) 1987; U.S. Dist. Ct. (we. dist.) 1997, 5th Jud. Dist. Arbitrator 1993, Superior Ct. Cert. Mediator, N.C., Dispute Resolution Commn, 1996. Assoc. atty. Ryals, Jackson & Mills, Wilmington, N.C., 1986-90; ptnr. Pennington & Wicks, Wilmington, N.C., 1990-93; pres, profl. corp. Ryals, Robinson & Saffo P.C., Wilmington, N.C., 1993—; ethics com. N.C. State Bar, Raleigh, N.C., 1990-93; exec. com. New Hanover County Bar Assn., Wilmington, 1994-97. Bd. mem. Cape Fear Mus. Assocs., Inc., Wilmington, N.C., 1991— (v.p. 1994-97, pres. 1997—); bd. mem., counsel Wilmington Symphony Orchestra, Inc., Wilmington, N.C., 1991—; commn. mem. USS N.C. Battleship Commn., Wilmington, N.C., 1989-93; mem. Bd. Deacons First Presbyn. Ch., Wilmington, N.C., 1996—, Chancel Choir, 1988—. Recipient Women of Achievement New Hanover Commn. for Women, Wilmington, N.C., 1997, Trustee Merit Scholarship Converse Coll., Spartanburg, S.C., 1978-82; named Mortar Bd. Converse Coll., Spartanburg, S.C., 1981—, Crescent Converse Coll., Spartanburg, S.C., 1979-80. Mem. Am. Bar Assn., N.C. Bar Assn., N.C. Acad. Trial Lawyers, New Hanover County Bar Assn., Phi Delta Phi, Phi Sigma Iota, Pi Gamma Mu. Republican. Presbyterian. Avocations: travel, piano, choral, swimming, tennis, sailing. Home: 1940 Hawthorne Rd Wilmington NC 28403-5329 Office: Ryals Robinson & Saffo PC 701 Market St Wilmington NC 28401-4646

**ROBINSON, SHAWN MICHAEL,** lawyer; b. Lynnwood, Calif., Apr. 5, 1964; s. Raymond Richard and Eileen Catherine (Cherry) R. BA in Mgmt. Sci., U. Calif., San Diego, 1987; JD, Western State U., 1992. Bar: Calif. 1993, U.S. Dist. Ct. (so. dist.) Calif. 1993; cert. contract rep. NFLPA. Claims rep. Aetna Life and Casualty, San Diego, 1987-94; assoc. Chapin, Fleming and Winet, San Diego, 1994-95, Campbell, Wolfenzon, Souhrada and Volk, San Diego, 1995-99; with Program Beta, San Diego, 1999—. Democrat. Roman Catholic. Avocations: football, basketball, tennis, racquetball, weightlifting. General civil litigation, Personal injury, Sports. Office: Program Beta 11545 W Bernardo Ct Ste 207 San Diego CA 92127-1631

**ROBINSON, STACEY MUKAI,** lawyer, associate; b. Honolulu, Apr. 8, 1969; d. Stanley Yukiyoshi and Elaine Tsuruko Mukai; m. John Henry Robinson, Mar. 9, 1996. BA cum laude, Williams Coll., 1991; JD, U. Va., 1995. Bar: Hawaii 1996, U.S. Dist. Ct. Hawaii 1996, U.S. Ct. Appeals (9th cir.) 1996. Assoc. McCorriston, Miho, Miller, Mukai, Honolulu, 1996—. Mem. ABA, Hawaii State Bar Assn. Federal civil litigation, General civil litigation, Insurance. Office: McCorriston Miho Miller Mukai 500 Ala Moana Blvd Ste 5-400 Honolulu HI 96813-4989

**ROBINSON, STEPHEN C.,** lawyer. BA, Cornell U., 1975, JD, 1978. U.S. dist. atty. dist. Conn. Dept. Justice, 1998—. Office: PO Box 1824 New Haven CT 06508-1824*

**ROBINSON, SUE L(EWIS),** federal judge; b. 1952. BA with highest honors, U. Del., 1974; JD, U. Pa., 1978. Assoc. Potter, Anderson & Corron, Wilmington, Del., 1978-83; asst. U.S. atty. U.S. Attys. Office, 1983-88; U.S. magistrate judge U.S. Dist. Ct. (Del. dist.), 1988-91, dist. judge, 1991—. Mem. Del. State Bar Assn. (sec. 1986-87). Office: US Dist Ct J Caleb Boggs Fed Bldg 844 N King St Lockbox 31 Wilmington DE 19801-3519

**ROBINSON, THEODORE CURTIS, JR.,** lawyer; b. Chgo., Jan. 22, 1916; s. Theodore Curtis and Edna Alice (Willard) R.; m. Marynel Werner, Dec. 28, 1940; children: Theodore Curtis III, Peter S. BA, Western Res. U., 1938, LLB, 1940. Bar: Ohio 1940, U.S. Dist. Ct. (no. dist.) Ohio 1946, U.S. Ct. Appeals (8th cir.) 1948, U.S. Dist. Ct. (we. dist.) Wis. 1950, U.S. Dist. Ct. (we. dist.) N.Y. 1950, U.S. Ct. Appeals (6th cir.) 1950, Ill. 1957, U.S. Dist. Ct. (no. dist.) Ill. 1957, U.S. Ct. Appeals (7th cir.) 1964, U.S. Supreme Ct. 1972. Assoc. Davis & Young, Cleve., 1940; law clk. no. dist. ea. divsn. U.S. Dist. Ct., Cleve., 1940-42; assoc. Leckie, McCreary, et al, Cleve., 1945-52; ptnr. McCreary, Hinslea & Ray, Cleve., 1953-57, McCreary, Hinslea, Ray & Robinson, Chgo., 1957-90; counsel Ray, Robinson, Hannin & Carle, Chgo., 1990-91; counsel Ray, Robinson, Carle, Davies & Snyder, Chgo., 1991-98, ret., 1998; mem. exec. com. Maritime Law Assn. of U.S., N.Y.C., 1981-83; pres. Propellor Club of U.S., Chgo., 1966-67; sec., treas. Internat. Shipmasters Assn., Chgo., 1958-91. Contbr. articles to profl. law reviews. Lt. USCG, 1943-45. Fellow Am. Coll. Trial Lawyers; mem. ABA, Chgo. Bar Assn. (com. chmn. 1973), Internat. Assn. Def. Counsel, Order of Coif, Traffic Club Chgo. (dir. 1986, 87), Whitehall Club (N.Y.), Nat. Eagle Scout Assn. Republican. Avocations: gardening, golf, reading. Admiralty. Office: Ray Robinson Carle Davies & Snyder 850 W Jackson Blvd Ste 310 Chicago IL 60607-3025

**ROBINSON, TIMOTHY STEPHEN,** lawyer; b. Kilgore, Tex., Dec. 31, 1958; s. Eddie Max and Mittie Cleo Robinson; m. Anisa Jane Laurence, May 20, 1978; children: Aaron Caleb, Alexandra Grace. BA in Econs., Austin Coll., Sherman, Tex., 1984; JD, Baylor U., 1987. Bar: Tex. 1987, Okla. 1997; cert. in personal injury Tex. Bd. Legal Specialization. Atty., litigation assocs. Ramey & Flock, Tyler, Tex., 1987-88, Fulbright & Jaworski, Dallas, 1988-91; ptnr. Robinson Carmody, Dallas, 1991-94, Robinson & Schwab, Plano, Tex., 1994—. Mem. ATLA, Tex. Bar Assn., Okla. Bar Assn. Personal injury. Office: Robinson & Schwab LLP 101 E Park Blvd Ste 769 Plano TX 75074-8820

**ROBINSON, TONI,** lawyer, educator; b. New Rochelle, N.Y.; d. Benjamin Mag and Eugenie (Lee) R.; m. Michael P. Plouf, Feb. 3, 1968. BA, Sarah Lawrence Coll., 1972; JD, Columbia U., 1976; LLM in Taxation, NYU, 1985. Bar: N.Y. 1977, U.S. Dist. Ct. (so. dist.) N.Y. 1977, U.S. Tax Ct. 1987. Assoc. Roberts & Holland, N.Y.C., 1976-79, Battle, Fowler, Jaffin & Kheel, N.Y.C., 1979-82; asst. prof. law U. Bridgeport, Conn., 1982-85, assoc. prof., 1985-88, prof., 1988-93, dir. tax clinic, 1982—; prof. law, dir. Tax Clinic Quinnipiac Coll., Hamden, Conn., 1993—; tax adviser Conn. Small Bus. Adv. Svc., Bridgeport, 1987-92, The Laurel Shelter; asst. sec. UN Expert Group on Tax Treaties, N.Y.C., 1978-79, dep. sec., 1979-82; legal adviser Internat. Percy Grainger Soc., White Plains, N.Y., 1985-91; presenter, author study materials continuing legal edn. programs; vis. prof. law Coll. of William and Mary, Williamsburg, Va., 1989-90. Contbr. articles on taxes to profl. publs. Founding bd. dirs. Laurel Shelter, Inc. Mem. ATLA, ABA (tax sect.), Assn. Bar City N.Y., Conn. Women's Bar Assn., Phi Delta Phi. Democrat. Mem. Soc. of Friends. Avocations: sailing, horses. Office: Quinnipiac Coll Sch Law 275 Mt Carmel Ave Hamden CT 06518-1961

**ROBINSON, VIANEI LOPEZ,** lawyer; b. Houston, Mar. 6, 1969; d. David Tiburcio and Romelia Gloria (Guerra) Lopez; m. Noel Keith Robinson, Jr., Apr. 16, 1994. AB in Psychology cum laude, Princeton U., 1988; JD, U. Tex., 1991. Bar: Tex. 1991; mediator's cert. Assoc. Bracewell & Patterson LLP, Houston, 1991-94, Wagstaff Law Firm, Abilene, Tex., 1994-97; owner Robinson Law Firm, Abilene, 1997—. Contbr. articles to profl. jours., chpts. to School Law in Texas, A Practical Guide, 1996, Texas Employment Law, 1998. Bd. dirs. Abilene Philharm., Noah Project Women's Shelter, Abilene C. of C., Abilene Indsl. Found., Ctr. for Contemporary Arts, Abilene, Day Nursery of Abilene; mem. Abilene Bd. of Adjustment. Presdl. scholar, Nat. Merit scholar, Nat. Hispanic scholar, 1985, Vinson & Elkins scholar U. Tex. Sch. Law, Austin, 1988-91. Fellow Tex. Bar Found.; mem. ABA (labor and employment law planning bd.), NSBA/TASB Coun. of Sch. Attys., State Bar Tex. (coun. mem. sect. of labor and employment law, various coms.), Coll. of the State Bar of Tex., Tex. Young Lawyers Assn. (bd. dirs. 1994-97), Abilene Bar Assn. (bd. dirs. 1999—), Abilene Young Lawyers Assn., Big Country Soc. for Human Resource Mgmt. (pres. 1999). Avocations: theater and dance, fine art, food and wine. Fax: 915-677-6044. Labor, Education and schools, Health. Home: 2410 Wyndham Ct Abilene TX 79606-4370 Office: Robinson Law Firm First Nat Bank Tower 400 Pine St Ste 1070 Abilene TX 79601-5173

**ROBINSON, WARREN A. (RIP ROBINSON),** lawyer; b. Denver, Mar. 23, 1957; s. William A. and Mary Jane Robinson; m. Janice M. Koerwer, Aug. 18, 1979; children: John William, Robert Joseph, Matthew Laurence, Sarah Elizabeth. BA, Seton Hall U., 1979; JD, U. Denver, 1982. Bar: Colo. 1982, U.S. Dist. Ct. Colo. 1982, U.S. Ct. Appeals (10th cir.) 1984. Assoc. Greengard, Blackman & Senter, Denver, 1982-83; assoc., ptnr. Silver & Hayes, P.C., Denver, 1983-89; ptnr. Silver, Robinson & Barrick, P.C., Denver, 1989-91; shareholder Robinson & Schuyler, P.C., Denver, 1991—. Mem. Colo. Bar Assn., Arapahoe County Bar Assn. Democrat. Christian. Avocations: sports, stained glass, coaching children. General civil litigation, Personal injury, Family and matrimonial. Office: Robinson & Schuyler PC 1624 Market St Ste 206 Denver CO 80202-1518

**ROBINSON, WILKES COLEMAN,** retired federal judge; b. Anniston, Ala., Sept. 30, 1925; s. Walter Wade and Catherine Elizabeth (Coleman) R.; m. Julia Von Poellnitz Rowan, June 24, 1955; children: Randolph C., Peyton H., Thomas Wilkes Coleman. AB, U. Ala., 1948; JD, U. Va., 1951. Bar: Ala. 1951, Va. 1962, Mo. 1966, Kans. 1983. Assoc. Bibb & Hemphill, Anniston, Ala., 1951-54; city recorder City of Anniston, 1953-55; judge Juvenile and Domestic Relations Ct. of Calhoun County, Ala., 1954-56; atty. legal dept. GM&O R.R., Mobile, Ala., 1956-58; commerce counsel, asst. gen. atty. Seaboard Air Line R.R., Richmond, Va., 1958-66; chief commerce counsel Monsanto Co., St. Louis, 1966-70; gen. counsel, v.p. Marion Labs., Inc., Kansas City, Mo., 1970-79; pres. Gulf and Gt. Plains Legal Found., Kansas City, Mo., 1980-85; also bd. dirs. Gulf and Gt. Plains Legal Found., Kansas City; atty. Howard, Needles, Tammen & Bergendoff, Kansas City, 1985-86; also bd. dirs.; v.p. S.R. Fin. Group, Inc., Overland Park, Kans., 1986-87; judge U.S. Ct. Fed. Claims, Washington, 1987-97, sr. judge, 1997—. Bd. govs. Kansas City Philharmonic Orch., 1975-77. Served with USNR, 1943-44. Mem. Indian Bayou Golf Club, Rotary, Masons, Phi Beta Kappa (past treas. Kansas City, Mo. chpt.), Phi Eta Sigma, Phi Alpha Theta, Kappa Alpha. Episcopalian. Home: 12 Weekewachee Cir Destin FL 32541-4426 Office: US Ct Fed Claims US Cts Bldg 717 Madison Pl NW Washington DC 20005-1011

**ROBINSON, WILLARD MONTELLOUS, JR.,** lawyer, retired commonwealth attorney; b. Greensville, Va., June 8, 1935; s. Willard Montellous and Rosa Randolf (Taylor) R.; m. Patricia Ames Ashby, June 28, 1958; children—Willard Montellous III, Melissa Ashby. B.A., U. Richmond, 1957, J.D., 1961. Bar: Va. 1961, U.S. Dist. Ct. Va. 1969. Assoc., Wallerstein & Goode, Richmond, Va., 1961; asst. commonwealth atty. Commonwealth of Va., Newport News, 1962-68, commonwealth atty., 1969-90. Mem. Va. Commonwealth Attys. Assn. (pres. 1974-75) , Nat. Dist. Attys. Assn. (v.p. 1981-82), Va. State Bar (chmn. criminal law sect. 1980-81). Methodist. Office: 11101 Warwick Blvd Newport News VA 23601-2396

**ROBINSON, WILLIAM C.,** lawyer; b. Charlotte, N.C., Aug. 30, 1965; s. William G. and Theo Robinson; m. Stacy Evans, Aug. 22, 1992; children: William C., Braxton. Grad., Davidson Coll., 1987; JD, U. N.C., 1990. Bar: N.C. 1990. Assoc. Golding Meeking, Charlotte, 1990-93; with Colombo & Robinson, Charlotte, 1993-96; trial atty. Cranfill, Sumner & Hartzog, Charlotte, 1996—. Mem. B.C. Bar Assn., N.C. Assn. Def. Attys., Mecklenburg County Bar Assn. Republican. Avocations: sports, reading. Personal injury, Insurance, Construction. Home: 3205 Sunny Ln Charlotte NC 28209 Office: Cranfill Sumner & Hartzog Hillsborough Pl PO Box 27808 Raleigh NC 27611-7808

**ROBINSON, ZELIG,** lawyer; b. Balt., July 7, 1934; s. Morton Matthew and Mary (Ackerman) R.; m. Karen Ann Bergstrom (div. Oct. 1987); children: John, Christopher, Kristin; m. Linda Portner Strangmann, Dec. 23, 1987. BA, Johns Hopkins U., 1954; LLB, Harvard U., 1957. Bar: Md. 1958. Legis. analyst Md. House of Dels., Annapolis, 1958; tech. asst. IRS, Washington, 1958-60; pvt. practice Balt., 1960-62; assoc. gen. counsel commerce com. U.S. Ho. of Reps., Washington, 1962-64; assoc. Weinberg & Green, Balt., 1964-66; special legal cons. commerce com. U.S. Ho. of Reps., Washington, 1966-68; pvt. practice Balt., 1966-72; mem. Gordon, Feinblatt, Rothman, Hoffberger & Hollander, LLC, 1972—; bd. dirs. Durapak Mfg. Co., Balt., Vac Pac, Inc., Balt., Universal Die Casting Co., Inc., Saline, Mich.; chmn. Md. Pub. Broadcasting, 1991-95; mem. Gov's. Commn. to revise Md. Code, Annapolis, 1968-89. Contbr. articles to profl. jours. Bd. dirs., v.p./sec. Gov.'s Mansion Found., Annapolis, Md.; v.p. bd. dirs. Md. Cmtys. and Citizens Fund, Chestertown, Md.; sec. bd. dirs. William Donald Schaefer Civic Fund; bd. dirs. Md. Arts Pl., Balt.; mem. Found. for Md. Pub. Broadcasting; bd. dirs., pres. Celebrate 2000, Inc., 1998—, bd. dirs., Baltimore Efficiency and Econ. Found., 1999—. With U.S. Army, 1958. Mem. ABA, Md. State Bar Assn. (laws com., internat. law com.). Democrat. Mergers and acquisitions, Private international, General corporate. Office: Gordon Feinblatt Rothman Hoffberger & Hollander LLC 233 E Redwood St Baltimore MD 21202-3332

**ROBISON, JOHN S.,** lawyer; b. Davenport, Iowa, Feb. 2, 1952; s. Dean Cooke and Helen Harvey R.; m. Laura Louise Davis, Oct. 8, 1977; children: Mary Era, Peter William, Julia Rose. BA in Econs., U. Mich., 1974; JD, U. Ill., Champaign, 1978. Bar: Wis., U.S. Tax Ct. Assoc. Warner, Norcross & Judd, Grand Rapids, Mich., 1978-81, Foley & Lardner, Madison, Wis., 1981-85; ptnr. Boardman, Suhr, Curry & Field LLP, Madison, 1985—. Dir. United Way Dane County, Madison, 1988-94, chmn. bd. dirs., 1991; dir. Madison Cmty. Found., 1993—. Mem. State Bar Wis. (dir. tax sect. 1996—). Avocations: exercise, golfing, reading. General corporate, Taxation, general, Health. Home: 5764 N Hill Ct Madison WI 53711-5299 Office: Boardman Suhr Curry & Field 1 S Pinckney St Fl 4 Madison WI 53703-2892

**ROBISON, WILLIAM ROBERT,** lawyer; b. Memphis, May 5, 1947; s. Andrew Cliffe and Elfrieda (Barnes) R. AB, Boston U., 1970; JD, Northeastern U., 1974. Bar: Mass. 1974, D.C. 1975, U.S. Dist. Ct. Mass. 1975, U.S. Ct. Appeals (1st cir.) 1975, U.S. Dist. Ct. Conn. 1977, U.S. Supreme Ct. 1977, Calif. 1978, U.S. Dist. Ct. (cen. dist.) Calif. 1979, U.S. Ct. Appeals (9th cir.) 1979. Assoc. Meyers, Goldstein, et al, Boston, 1975-76, Cooley, Shrair, et al, Springfield, Mass., 1976-78, Hertzberg, et al, Los Angeles, 1978-79, Marcus & Lewi, Santa Monica, Calif., 1980-81; sole practice Santa Monica, 1981—; lectr. Northeastern U., Boston, 1975-76; judge pro-tem., Mcpl. Ct., Los Angeles, 1984—, Los Angeles Superior Ct., 1987—. Co-author: Commercial Transactions, 1976. Bd. dirs. Boston Legal Asst. Project, 1972-75, Action for Boston Community Devel., Inc., 1971-75. Mem. ABA, Los Angeles County Bar Assn., Santa Monica Bar Assn. (Cert. of Appreciation 1987). Democrat. Unitarian. State civil litigation, Construction, Real property. Home and Office: 2546 Amherst Ave Los Angeles CA 90064-2712

**ROBRENO, EDUARDO C.,** federal judge; b. 1945. BA, Westfield State Coll., 1967; MA, U. Mass., 1969; JD, Rutgers U., 1978. With antitrust divsn. U.S. Dept Justice, Phila., 1978-81; ptnr. Meltzer & Schiffrin, Phila., 1981-86, Fox, Rothschild, O'Brien & Frankel, Phila., 1987-92; judge U.S. Dist. Ct. for Ea. Dist. Pa., Phila., 1992—; mem. Jud. Conf. Com. on Bankruptcy Rules. Fellow Am. Law Inst. Office: US Courthouse Rm 3810 Philadelphia PA 19106

**ROBSON, DOUGLAS SPEARS,** lawyer; b. Balt., Jan. 25, 1967; s. Martin C. Robson and Susan Robson Eck; m. Anne Marie Schreiber, July 27, 1991; children: Meghan, Brendan, Kevin. BA, Ind. U., 1989; JD, DePaul U., 1992. Bar: Ill., 1992, U.S. Dist. Ct. (no. dist.) Ill. 1993. Assoc. Wolfe & Polovin, Chgo., 1992-95; assoc. Hickey, Driscoll, Kurfirst, Patterson & Melia, Chgo., 1995-98, ptnr., 1999—. Mem. Chgo. Bar Assn. (mem. corp. and bus. law com., probate and trust law com.), Ill. State Bar Assn. General corporate, Estate planning, Real property. Home: 2609 Oriole Trl Long Beach IN 46360-1651 Office: Hickey Driscoll Kurfirst Patterson & Melia 77 W Washington St Ste 800 Chicago IL 60602-2804

**ROCAN, JACQUELYNE MARIE,** lawyer; b. Toronto, Ont., Can., Oct. 27, 1966; came to U.S. 1967; d. Lucien Joseph and Elsie Katherine (Schoepper) R. BS in Polit. Sci., U. Tulsa, 1987, JD, 1990. Bar: Okla. 1990, U.S. Dist. Ct. (no. dist.) Okla. 1990. Atty./adviser Fed. Energy Regulatory Commn., Washington, 1990-92; assoc. Akin, Gump, Strauss, Hauer & Feld, Houston, 1992—. Svc. group coord. high sch. youth group, Blessed Sacrament Ch., Alexandria, Va., 1991-92, St. Anne's Ch., Houston, Tex., 1992—; mem. drive Mus. of Fine Arts, Houston, 1992. Mem. ABA (chair., 1993—, vice-chair, 1992-93, exec. com. 1991-92, law student outreach com., young lawyers div., exec. com. 1992-93, natural resources, energy and environ. law com., young lawyers div., vice-chair Natural Gas Mktg. and Transp. com., 1993—, Gold Key award law student div. 1990, Silver Key award law student div. 1989), NAFE, Okla. Bar Assn. (legal intern com.), Fed. Bar Assn. (energy, environ. and natural resources sect.), Nat. Assn. Women Lawyers (Outstanding Grad. award 1990), Fed. Energy Bar Assn. (legis. and regulatory reform comm., nat. gas certificate and authorization comm.), Phi Alpha Delta. Republican. Roman Catholic. Avocations: painting, drawing, music. FERC practice. Office: Akin Gump Strauss Hauer & Feld 1900 Pennzoil Pl South Twr 711 Louisiana St Houston TX 77002-2716

**ROCHE, JOHN J.,** bank executive, lawyer. BS, Manhattan Coll., 1957; LLB, Harvard U., 1963. Assoc., then ptnr. Shearman & Sterling, 1963-89; exec. v.p. Citicorp/Citibank, N.A., N.Y.C., 1989-98; co-gen. counsel Citigroup, N.Y.C., 1998—. Office: Citigroup 153 E 53rd St Fl 23 New York NY 10022-4611*

**ROCHE, ROBERT JOSEPH,** lawyer; b. Seattle, Jan. 6, 1961; s. Wilbur Lawrence and Nadine (Mc Millen) R. BA, Cath. U. of Am., 1984; JD, U. Wash., 1988. Bar: Wash. 1990, U.S. Dist. Ct. (we. dist.) Wash. 1991, U.S. Ct. Appeals (9th cir.) 1997. Divsn. dir. Am. Heart Assn., Seattle, 1984-85; advance person Booth Gardner Gubernatorial campaign, Seattle, 1988; jud. clk. State of Wash. Ct. Appeals, Seattle, 1988-90; ptnr. Bullivant Houser Bailey, Seattle, 1998—. Pres. Agenda Northwest, Seattle, 1995; campaign chmn. United Way, Seattle, 1993—. Mem. Wash. State Bar Assn., King County Bar Assn., Cath. U. Alumni Assn. (pres. Pacific N.W. chpt. 1990—). Appellate, General civil litigation, Product liability. Office: Bullivant Houser Bailey 1601 5th Ave Ste 2400 Seattle WA 98101-3622

**ROCHE, THOMAS GARRETT,** lawyer; b. Pitts., Oct. 22, 1953; s. Gerald Dennis and Marian Alice (McGraw) R.; m. Carolyn Lee Berkey, Aug. 13, 1983. B.A., W.Va. U., 1976; J.D., Western State U. Coll. Law, 1979. Bar: Calif. 1982, U.S. Dist. Ct. (so. and cen. dists.) Calif. 1982. Asst. law librarian Nat. U. Sch. Law, San Diego, 1980-84; sole practice, San Diego, 1982—. Recipient Corpus Juris Secundum award Bancroft-Whitney Pub. Co., 1976-77. Mem. ABA, Calif. State Bar Assn., San Diego Trial Lawyers Assn., Delta Theta Phi (treas. 1977-78, Wm. H. Thomas Nat. Oral Advocacy award 1977). Federal civil litigation, State civil litigation, Criminal.

**ROCHELLE, DUDLEY CECILE,** lawyer; b. Franklinton, La., Sept. 10, 1950; s. James Cecil and Mildred Grace (Stennis) R. BA in Polit. Sci., La. State U., 1972; JD, Yale U., 1975. Bar: Ga. 1976, U.S. Dist. Ct. (no. dist.) Ga. 1976, U.S. Ct. Appeals (5th cir.) 1976, U.S. Tax Ct.; cert. arbitrator and mediator. Vista atty. Atlanta Legal Aid Soc., 1975-76; law clk. to Hon. Joel J. Fryer Fulton County Superior Ct., Atlanta, 1976-77; trial atty. U.S. Dept. Labor, Atlanta, 1977-82; assoc. Hendrick Spanos & Phillips PC, Atlanta, 1982-88, shareholder (ptnr.), 1988-94; shareholder (ptnr.) Spanos & Rochelle, P.C., Atlanta, 1994-97; shareholder Littler Mendelson, P.C., Atlanta, 1997—. Bd. dirs. Ga. Pub. Policy Found., 1996—, Midtown Alliance, Atlanta, 1982-92; mem. adv. bd. Coverdell Leadership Inst., Atlanta, 1996—. Mem. State Bar Ga. (mem. labor sect.), Atlanta Bar Assn. (mem. labor/employment sect., chairperson alt. dispute resolution com. 1986-92, mem. bench and bar com. 1986-87), Christian Legal Soc., Federalist Soc., Yale Club Ga. (bd. dirs. 1982-86). Republican. Avocations: outdoor activity, scuba diving, music. Labor, Federal civil litigation, Alternative dispute resolution. Home: 2745 Brook Grove Ct Atlanta GA 30339-5329 Office: Littler Mendelson PC Ste 1100 3348 Peachtree St NE Atlanta GA 30326-1008

**ROCHKIND, LOUIS PHILIPP,** lawyer; b. Miami, Fla., June 25, 1948; s. Reuben and Sarah R.; m. Rosalind H. Rochkind, July 4, 1971. BA in Psychology cum laude, U. Mich., 1970, JD cum laude, 1974. Bar: Mich. 1974, U.S. Dist. Ct. (e. dist.) Mich. 1974. Ptnr. Jaffe, Raitt, Heuer & Weiss, Detroit, 1974—; adj. prof. law Wayne St. U. Law Sch.; lectr. various profl. assns. and orgns. Assoc. editor U. Mich. Law Rev.; contbr. articles to profl. jours. publs. Mem. Am. Coll. Bankruptcy Lawyers, Detroit Bar Assn. (local rules in bankruptcy subcom. creditor-debtor law sect. 1980—), Phi Kappa Phi. Bankruptcy, Contracts commercial, Consumer commercial. Office: Jaffe Raitt Heuer & Weiss One Woodward Ave Ste 2400 Detroit MI 48226

**ROCHLIN, DAVIS SAMUEL,** lawyer; b. June 25, 1962; m. Pamela Finney. BS in Speech, Northwestern U., 1984; JD, U. Minn., 1990. Bar: Minn. 1990, U.S. Dist. Ct. Minn. 1996. Pvt. practice Mpls., 1990—. Mem. Minn. Bar Assn., Hennepin County Bar Assn. Contracts commercial, General civil litigation. Office: 600 Highway 169 S Ste 1025 Minneapolis MN 55426-1266

**ROCK, HAROLD L.,** lawyer; b. Sioux City, Iowa, Mar. 13, 1932; s. Harold L. and Helen J. (Gormally) R.; m. Marilyn Beth Clark Rock, Dec. 28, 1954; children: Michael, Susan, John, Patrick, Michele, Thomas. BS, Creighton U., 1954, JD, 1959. Bar: Nebr., N.Y., Minn., Mont., Wyo. Law clk. to judge U.S. Ct. Appeals 8th Circuit, Omaha, 1959-60, Fitzgerald Hamer Brown & Leahy, Omaha, 1960-65; ptnr. Kutak Rock, Omaha, 1965—; chmn. Nebr. Bd. Bar Examiners, 1989-96; bd. dirs. Mid City Bank, Omaha. Bd. dirs. Douglas County Hist. Soc., 1992—, Nat. Equal Justice Libr., 1995—, Nebr. Nebr. Humanities Coun., 1996—. Served to 1st lt. U.S. Army, 1954-56. Recipient Alumni Achievement award Creighton U., 1995. Mem. ABA (ho. of dels. 1970-96, bd. govs. 1992-95), Nebr. Bar Assn. (ho. of dels., bd. dirs. 1985—, pres. 1988, Nebr. Bar found. bd. dirs., 1982—), Omaha Bar Assn. (pres. 1972-73), Omaha Legal Aid Soc. (pres. 1969-72), Nebr. State Bd. Pub. Accts. (bd. dirs. 1981-85). Roman Catholic. Securities, General corporate, Constitutional. Office: Kutak Rock The Omaha Bldg 1650 Farnam St Ste A Omaha NE 68102-2186

**ROCKETT, D. JOE,** lawyer; b. Cushing, Okla., May 3, 1942; s. Gordon Richard and Hazel Peggy (Rigsby) R.; m. Mary Montgomery, Aug. 31, 1963; children: David Montgomery, Ann Morley. BA, U. Okla., 1964, JD, 1967. Bar: Okla. 1967, U.S. Dist. Ct. (we. dist.) Okla. 1968. Assoc. Kerr, Davis, Irvine & Burbage, Oklahoma City, 1967-69; assoc. Andrews Davis Legg Bixler Milsten & Price, Oklahoma City, 1969-73, mem., 1973—, also bd. dirs., pres., 1986-90, 96—; securities law advisor Oil Investment Inst., Washington, 1984-87. Bd. dirs. Myriad Gardens Conservatory, Oklahoma City, 1987—, chmn., 1991-92. Mem. ABA (fed. regulation of securities and partnership coms. of bus. law sect. 1984), Okla. Bar Assn. (securities liaison com. 1983, chmn. bus. assocs. sect. 1985, securities adminstr.'s select com. 1986—). Avocations: sailing, fishing, skiing. Securities, Mergers and acquisitions, General corporate. Office: Andrews Davis Legg Bixler Milsten & Price 500 W Main St Ste 500 Oklahoma City OK 73102-2275

**ROCKEY, ARLAINE,** lawyer; b. Parma, Ohio, Apr. 18, 1962; d. Arthur G. and Elaine D. R. BA, U. N.C., 1984; JD, U. Miami, 1989. Bar: Fla. 1989, N.C. 1991, D.C. 1992. Atty. Legal Svcs. of Gtr. Miami, Fla., 1989-91; assoc. Rockey & Collias, Charlotte, N.C., 1991-93, Legal Svcs. of So. Piedmont, Charlotte, 1993-99. Author: Ocean Court, 1999. Mem. ACLU (bd. dirs. N.C. chpt. 1994—), Assn. Reform of N.C. Marital Rape Laws (founder, co-chair 1991-93), N.C. Assn. Women Attys. (bd. dirs., edn. chair

1994). Avocations: music, travel. Family and matrimonial, Juvenile, Civil rights. Office: 4736 Sharon Rd Ste W-125 Charlotte NC 28210

**ROCKLEN, KATHY HELLENBRAND,** lawyer, banker; b. N.Y.C., June 30, 1951. BA, Barnard Coll., 1973; JD magna cum laude, New England Sch. Law, 1977. Bar: N.Y. 1978, U.S. Dist. Ct. (so. and ea. dists.) N.Y. 1982, U.S. Dist. Ct. (no. dist.) Calif. 1985. Interpretive counsel N.Y. Stock Exchange, N.Y.C.; 1st v.p. E.F. Hutton & Co. Inc., N.Y.C.; v.p., gen. counsel and sec. S.G Warburg (U.S.A.) Inc., N.Y.C.; counsel Rogers & Wells, N.Y.C; pvt. practice N.Y.C. Mem. exec. com. lawyers divsn. Am. Friends Hebrew U. Mem. N.Y. State Bar Assn., N.Y. Women's Bar Assn., Assn. Bar City N.Y. (exec. com., chmn. drugs and law com., chmn. fed. legis. com., securities law com., sec. 2d century com., sex and law com., young lawyers'com., corp. law com.). General corporate, Securities, Banking. Office: Law Office 515 Madison Ave New York NY 10022-5403

**ROCKOWITZ, NOAH EZRA,** lawyer; b. N.Y.C., Apr. 11, 1949; s. Murray and Anna Rae (Cohen) R.; m. Julie Rachel Levitan, Dec. 24, 1978; children—Shira Aviva, Leora Civia, Dahlia Yaffa. B.A., Queens Coll., 1969; J.D., Fordham U., 1973. Bar: N.Y. 1974, U.S. Dist. Ct. (so. and ea. dists.) N.Y. 1974, U.S. Ct. Appeals (2d cir.) 1974. Tchr., chmn. social studies dept. Intermediate Sch. 74, Queens, N.Y., 1969-73; atty. Cahill Gordon & Reindel, N.Y.C., 1973-78; corp. sec., asst. gen. counsel Belco Petroleum Corp., N.Y.C., 1978-85; v.p. and gen. counsel Hudson Gen. Corp., Great Neck, N.Y., 1985-98, sr. v.p., 1998—; trustee, mem. exec. com., chmn. bd. edn. The Solomon Schechter Sch. Westchester; trustee Beth El Synagogue of New Rochelle. Mem. ABA, Am. Soc. Corp. Secs., N.Y. State Bar Assn., Assn. of Bar of City of N.Y., Am. Corp. Counsel Assn., Phi Beta Kappa. General corporate, Contracts commercial, Securities. Office: Hudson Gen Corp 111 Great Neck Rd PO Box 355 Great Neck NY 11022-0355

**ROCKWOOD, LINDA LEE,** lawyer; b. Cedar Rapids, Iowa, July 25, 1950; d. Robert Walter and Dorothy Jean (Rehberg) Sorensen; children: Holly Lynn, Christian Douglas. BA, U. Denver, 1972; JD, U. Tex., 1984. Bar: Colo. 1984, U.S. Dist. Ct. Colo., U.S. Ct. Appeals (10th cir.). Econ. and consumer research analyst May Dept. Stores, St. Louis, 1973-75; asst. dir. Ctr. for Study Am. Bus., Washington U., St. Louis, 1975-77; mgr. Mid-Columbia Symphony, Richland, Wash., 1978-79; assoc. Holland & Hart, Denver, 1984-88; shareholder, dir. Parcel, Mauro & Spaanstra, Denver, 1988-98, pres., 1996-98; ptnr. Faegre & Benson, Denver, 1998—. Author: New Mines From Old Environmental Considerations in Remining and Reprocessing of Waste Materials, 1991, The Alcan Decisions: Causation Through the Back Door, 1993, RCRA Demystified: The Professional's Guide to Hazardous Waste Law, 1996. Bd. dirs. Colo. Hazardous Waste Mgmt. Soc., 1986, 89-91, pres., 1987-88. Mem. ABA (vice chmn. environ. values com. adminstrv. law sect. 1986-91, hard minerals com. natural resources law sect. 1987-90), Colo. Bar Assn. (exec. coun. environ. law sect. 1987-90), Order of Coif, Phi Beta Kappa. Presbyterian. E-mail: lrockwoo@faegre.com. Environmental, Administrative and regulatory. Office: Faegre & Benson LLP 2500 Republic Plaza 370 17th St Ste 2400 Denver CO 80202-5665

**ROCUANT, PAUL A.,** lawyer; b. Bridgeport, Conn., Oct. 18, 1967; s. Ramiro A. and Nadejda R.; m. Kathleen M. Kearney, May 14, 1994; 1 child, Rebecca Marue. BA, U. Conn., 1990; JD, U. New Eng., 1993. Bar: Fla. 1993, Mass. 1993, U.S. Supreme Ct. 1998. Assoc. Bass & Chernoff, Naples, Fla., 1993-95; atty. pvt. practice, Naples, Fla., 1995—; dir. Sparks Entertainment, Inc., Naples. Family and matrimonial, Personal injury. Office: 1100 5th Ave S Ste 409 Naples FL 34102-6419

**RODA, JOSEPH FRANCIS,** lawyer; b. Lancaster, Pa., June 22, 1949; s. Frank Edward and Mary Virginia (Reeder) R.; m. Dianne M. Nast, Aug. 23, 1980; children: Michael, Daniel, Joseph, Joshua, Anastasia. AB, Harvard Coll., 1971; JD, U. Pa., 1974. Bar: Pa. 1974, U.S. Dist. Ct. (ea. dist.) Pa. 1975, U.S. Dist. Ct. (mid. dist.) Pa. 1981, U.S. Ct. Appeals (3d cir.) 1981, U.S. Supreme Ct. 1982. Law clk. to judge U.S. Dist. Ct. (ea. dist.) Pa., Phila., 1974-75; assoc. Kohn, Savette, Marion & Graf, P.C., Phila., 1975-80; pvt. practice Lancaster, 1980—. Mem. ABA, ATLA, Am. Coll. Trial Lawyers, Pa. Trial Lawyers Assn. (bd. dels.), Pa. Bar Assn., Lancaster Country Club, Hamilton Club (Lancaster). Avocations: sports, piano. General civil litigation, Insurance, Personal injury. Home: 1059 Sylvan Rd Lancaster PA 17601-1923 Office: 801 Estelle Dr Lancaster PA 17601-2130

**RODDENBERRY, STEPHEN KEITH,** lawyer; b. Aguadilla, P.R., Sept. 20, 1948; s. Harry H. and Gladys (Davis) R.; m. Bonnie Lindquist, June 26, 1948; children—Thomas D., David A., Samuel C. A.B., Harvard U., 1970, J.D., 1973. Bar: Fla. 1974, N.Y. 1974. Assoc. firm Davis Polk & Wardwell, N.Y.C., 1973-78, McConnell Valdes & Kelley, Miami, Fla., 1978-83, Holland & Knight, Miami, 1984-88, Akerman, Senterfitt & Eidson, Miami, 1988—. Mem. Fla. Bar (chmn. corp. sect. 1984—). General corporate, Securities, Banking. Home: 14140 SW 69th Ave Miami FL 33158-1316 Office: Akerman Senterfitt & Eidson 1 SE 3rd Ave Miami FL 33131-1700

**RODEFER, JEFFREY ROBERT,** lawyer, prosecutor; b. Santa Fe, Mar. 29, 1963; s. Robert Jacob and Joanne D. (Thomas) R. BS, U. Nev., 1985; JD, Willamette U., 1988, cert. dispute resolution, 1988. Bar: Calif. 1990, Nev. 1990, U.S. Dist. Ct. Nev. 1990, U.S. Dist. Ct. (ea. dist.) Calif. 1990, U.S. Ct. Appeals (9th cir.) 1990, Colo. 1991, Oreg. 1997, U.S. Supreme Ct. 1997; cert. arbitrator, Nev. Legal intern Willamette U. Legal Aid Clinic, Salem, Oreg., 1987-88; legal rschr. transp. divsn. Nev. Atty. Gen. Office, Carson City, 1989-90, dep. atty. gen. taxation divsn., 1990-93, dep. atty. gen. gaming divsn., 1993-99, sr. dep. atty. gen. gaming divsn., 1999—. Author: Nevada Property Tax Manual, 1993, Nevada Gaming Law Index, 1999; contbr. articles to Nev. Lawyer. Contbg. mem. U. Nev. Coll. Bus. Adminstrn. and Athletic Dept., Reno, 1992, Willamette U. Coll. Law, Ann. Law Fund, Salem, 1992; active Nat. Parks and Recreation Assn., Washington, 1991; mem. First Christian Ch. Mem. Internat. Assn. Gaming Attys., U. Nev. Coll. Bus. Alumni Assn., Am. Inns of Ct. (Bruce R. Thompson chpt.), State Bar Nev. (functional equivalency com. 1993—), Phi Delta Phi. Republican. Fax: (775) 687-1287; e-mail: jrodefer@govmail.state.nv.us. Office: Nev Atty Gen Office 1000 E William St Ste 209 Carson City NV 89701-3117

**RODEHEFFER, BRENDA FRANKLIN,** lawyer; b. Jeffersonville, Ind., Nov. 26, 1950; d. Robert Glynn and Norma Jean (Campbell) Franklin; m. Mark Allen Rodeheffer, Aug. 5, 1978; children: James Allen, Robert John, Laura Marie. BA, Ind. U., 1972, JD cum laude, 1979. Bar: Ind. 1979, U.S. Dist. Ct. (so. dist.) Ind. 1979, U.S. Ct. Appeals (7th and fed. cirs.) 1992. Sr. trial counsel, dep. atty. gen. Ind. Office Atty. Gen., Indpls., 1979-92; assoc. Haskin & Assocs., Indpls., 1992-94; ptnr. Monday Rodeheffer Jones & Albright, Indpls., 1994—; presenter, mem. faculty Ind. CLE Forum, Indpls., 1996. Bd. dirs., trustee Friends Ednl. Trust, Indpls., 1994—; chmn. Potowatomi svc. unit Girl Scouts U.S.A., Indpls., 1996-97; presiding clk. 1st Friends Meeting, Indpls., 1998—. Mem. ABA, FBA, Nat. Employment Lawyers Assn., Ind. Employment Lawyers Assn. Mem. Soc. of Friends. Avocations: running, biking, school and church volunteer work. Civil rights, Labor. Home: 3424 E 67th Ct Indianapolis IN 46220-3796 Office: Monday Rodeheffer Jones & Albright 1915 Broad Ripple Ave Indianapolis IN 46220-2327

**RODEMEYER, MICHAEL LEONARD, JR.,** lawyer; b. Balt., May 25, 1950; s. Michael Leonard and Claire Isabel (Gunther) R.; m. Dorrit Carolyn Green, June 7, 1975; children: Justin, Christopher. AB, Princeton U., 1972; JD, Harvard U., 1975. Bar: Md. 1977, D.C. 1980, U.S. Ct. Appeals (10th cir.) 1980. Atty. Fed. Trade Commn., Washington, 1976-81, atty. advisor, 1981-84; counsel Subcom. on Natural Resources, Agr. Rsch. & Environ., Washington, 1984-88; staff dir., counsel U.S. Ho. of Reps., Washington, 1988-90, house com. on sci., chief dem. counsel, 1990-98; asst. dir. for environment White House Office of Sci. and Tech. Policy, Washington, 1998—. Democrat. Avocations: computing, bicycling. Home: 6000 Harvard Ave Glen Echo MD 20812-1114 Office: Office Sci & Tech Policy 443 Oeob Washington DC 20502-0001

**RODENBERG-ROBERTS, MARY PATRICIA,** advocacy services administrator, lawyer; b. New Ulm, Minn., July 13, 1963; d. Richard Theodore and Patricia Rae (Malone) Rodenberg; m. Richard Lee Roberts, Oct. 28, 1989; 9 children. BS in Corrections, Law Enforcement, Mankato State U., 1985; JD, Hamline U., 1989. Bar: Wis. 1991. Shift supr. Reentry Svcs., Inc., St. Paul, 1986-87; coord. REM Lyndale, Inc., Mpls., 1987-89; dir. advocacy REM Minn., Inc., Edina, 1989—; case mgr. REM Consulting and Svcs., Edina, 1991—. Mem. ABA, Am. Assn. Mental Retardation, Minn. Social Svcs. Assn., Minn. Brain Injury Assn. (bd. dirs. 1996—), Wis. Bar Assn., Assn. Residential Resources Minn. Republican. Lutheran. Avocations: reading, sewing, crafts, dog training.

**RODENBURG, CLIFTON GLENN,** lawyer; b. Jamestown, N.D., Apr. 5, 1949; s. Clarence and Dorothy Irene (Peterman) R.; m. Donna Michele Stockman, Mar. 1, 1980. B.S., N.D. State U., 1971; J.D., U. N.D., 1974; M.L.I.R., Mich. State U., 1976. Bar: N.D. 1974, U.S. Dist. Ct. (N.D.) 1974, U.S. Ct. Appeals (8th cir.) 1974, Minn. 1980, U.S. Supreme Ct. 1980, S.D. 1983, Nebr. 1984, U.S. Dist. Ct. (Minn.) 1984, U.S. Dist. Ct. (Nebr.) 1984, Wis. 1985, U.S. Dist. Ct. Wis. 1985, Mont. 1986, U.S. Dist. Ct. (Mont.) 1986. Ptnr., Johnson & Rodenburg, Fargo, N.D., 1976—; pres., gen. counsel Rodenburg Group, Inc., Fargo, 1980—. Contbg. editor: The Developing Labor Law, 1976-80; drafter N.D. garnishment statutes, 1982. Mem. Acad. Comml. and Bankruptcy Law Specialists. Consumer commercial, Contracts commercial, Labor.

**RODENBURG, JOHN A.,** lawyer; b. Council Bluffs, Iowa, Aug. 17, 1961; s. Lyle A. Rodenburg and Ruth M. (Fitch) Thomas; m. Mary J. Caughlan, June 29, 1985; children: Zachary L., Wesley J., Emma P. BSBA, Creighton U., 1983, JD, 1988. Law clk. Rodenburg Law Offices, P.C., Council Bluffs, 1984-88, pvt. practice, 1988—. Cubmaster Boy Scouts Am., Council Bluffs, 1995—. Mem. Iowa State Bar Assn., Pottawattamie County Bar Assn. Probate, Family and matrimonial, Labor. Home: 207 Langstrom St Council Blfs IA 51503-4932 Office: Rodenburg Law Offices 100 Park Ave Council Blfs IA 51503-4330

**RODERER, DAVID WILLIAM,** lawyer; b. Dayton, Dec. 25, 1945; s. Lawrence C. and Viola K. Roderer; m. Nancy Chewning Koch, Dec. 27, 1967; children: David Lawrence, Anne Mary. Student, U. Louvain, Belgium, 1969-70; BA, U. Dayton, 1970; JD, George Washington U., 1974. Bar: D.C. 1975, N.Y. 1986, U.S. Supreme Ct. 1994. Staff atty. U.S. Treasury, Comptroller of Currency, Washington, 1975-79, legis. counsel, 1979-83; dir. legis. Fannie Mae, Washington, 1983-86; ptnr. Jones Day Reavis & Pogue, N.Y.C. and Washington, 1987-93, Winston & Strawn, N.Y.C. and Washington, 1993-96; of counsel Goodwin Procter & Hoar, Washington, 1996—. Contbr. articles to profl. jours. With USN, 1963-66. Mem. ABA (co-chair banking com. adminstrv. law 1998—), Fed. Bar Assn. (exec. coun., banking com. 1998—). Roman Catholic. Avocations: reading, travel. Banking, Administrative and regulatory. Home: 3608 Norton Pl NW Washington DC 20016-3170 Office: Goodwin Procter & Hoar 1717 Pennsylvania Ave NW Washington DC 20006-4614

**RODES, LEONARD ANTHONY,** lawyer; b. Lynn, Mass., June 13, 1957; s. Anthony Louis Rodes and Demetra Papuchis; m. Deborah Rose Black, June 22, 1985; children: Antonia Black Rodes, Katherine Palmer Rodes. BA, Princeton U., 1979; JD, Boston U., 1983. Bar: N.Y. 1984, U.S. Dist. Ct. (so. dist.) N.Y. 1984, U.S. Ct. Appeals (3d cir.) 1997, U.S. Ct. Appeals (4th cir.) 1998, U.S. Dist. Ct. (ea. dist.) N.Y. 1997/. Assoc. Grutman Miller Greenspoon & Hendler, N.Y.C., 1983-86, Kronish Lieb Weiner & Hellman, N.Y.C., 1986-88, Rosenman & Colin, N.Y.C., 1988-92; ptnr. Trachtenberg & Rodes, N.Y.C., 1992—. General civil litigation. Office: Trachtenberg & Rodes LLP 545 5th Ave Rm 620 New York NY 10017-3620

**RODGERS, FREDERIC BARKER,** judge; b. Albany, N.Y., Sept. 29, 1940; s. Prentice Johnson and Jane (Weed) R.; m. Valerie McNaughton, Oct. 8, 1988; 1 child: Gabriel Moore. AB, Amherst Coll., 1963; JD, Union U., 1966. Bar: N.Y. 1966, U.S. Ct. Mil. Appeals 1968, Colo. 1972, U.S. Supreme Ct. 1974, U.S. Ct. Appeals (10th cir.) 1981. Chief dep. dist. atty., Denver, 1972-73; commr. Denver Juvenile Ct., 1973-79; mem. Mulligan Reeves Teasley & Joyce, P.C., Denver, 1979-80; pres. Frederic B. Rodgers, P.C., Breckenridge, Colo., 1980-89; ptnr. McNaughton & Rodgers, Central City, Colo., 1989-91; county ct. judge County of Gilpin, 1987—; presiding mcpl. judge cities of Breckenridge, Blue River, Black Hawk, Central City, Edgewater, Empire, Idaho Springs, Silver Plume and Westminster, Colo., 1978-96; chmn. com. on mcpl. ct. rules of procedure Colo. Supreme Ct., 1984—; mem. gen. faculty Nat. Jud. Coll. U. Nev., Reno, 1990—, elected to faculty coun., 1993— (chair 1999). Author: (with Dilweg, Fretz, Murphy and Wicker) Modern Judicial Ethics, 1992; contbr. articles to profl. jours. Mem. Colo. Commn. on Children, 1982-85, Colo. Youth Devel. Coun., 1989-98, Colo. Family Peace Task Force, 1994-96.Served with JAGC, U.S. Army, 1967-72; to maj. USAR, 1972-88. Decorated Bronze Star with oak leaf cluster, Air medal. Recipient Outstanding County Judge award Colo. 17th Judicial Dist. Victim Adv. Coalition, 1991; Spl. Community Service award Colo. Am. Legion, 1979. Fellow Am. Bar Found., Colo. Bar Found. (life); mem. ABA (jud. div. exec. coun. 1989—, vice-chair 1996-97, chair-elect 1997, chair 1998-99, mem. House of Dels. 1993—), Colo. Bar Assn. (bd. govs. 1986-88, 90-92, 93-99), Continental Divide Bar Assn., Denver Bar Assn. (bd. trustees 1979-82), First Jud. Dist. Bar Assn., Nat. Conf. Spl. Ct. Judges (chmn. 1989-90), Colo. County Judges Assn. (pres. 1995-96), Colo. Mcpl. Judges Assn. (pres. 1986-87), Colo. Trial Judges Coun. (v.p. 1994-95, sec. 1996-97), Denver Law Club (pres. 1981-82), Colo. Women's Bar Assn., Am. Judicature Soc., Nat. Coun. Juvenile and Family Ct. Judges, Univ. Club (Denver), Arlberg Club (Winter Park), Marines Meml. Club (San Francisco), Westminster Rotary Club (Paul Harris fellow 1996). Episcopalian. Office: Gilpin County Justice Ctr Central City CO 80427-0398

**RODGERS, JAMES DANIEL,** judge; b. Ft. Worth, July 31, 1956; s. James Henry and Ruth Eileen R.; m. Jill Ann Lippert, Nov. 7, 1981; children: JamesMatthew, Caitlin Diana. BA, Baylor U., 1978, JD, 1981. Assoc. Quisenberry & Sputlak, Ft. Worth, 1981-86; atty. pvt. practice, Ft. Worth, 1986-96; mcpl. ct. judge City of Ft. Worth, 1996—. Mem. exec. bd. Bapt. Gen. Conv., Tex., 1996—. Mem. Family Bar Assn., Optimists Club. Avocations: youth activities, reading. Office: 1000 Throclmovtch Fort Worth TX 76102

**RODGERS, KAREN SAMPSON,** lawyer; b. Meridian, Miss.; d. Grover Hale Sr. and Ever Lee Sampson; m. Thomas James Rodgers, Mar. 26, 1998. BS, Ala. A&M U., 1990; JD, U. Ala. Bar: Ala. 1996, U.S. Dist. Ct. (no., mid. and so. dists.) Ala. 1996. Adv. Ala. Disability Advocacy Program, Tuscaloosa, 1992-95; assoc. McPhillips, Shinbaum & Gill LLP, Montgomery, Ala., 1995—. With U.S. Army, 1986-94. Mem. Ala. Trial Lawyers Assn., Montgomery County Bar Assn., Toastmasters. Avocations: missionary work, reading, shopping, creating clothing styles, praying. Labor. Home: 2700 Endicott Dr Montgomery AL 36116-3215 Office: McPhillips Shinbaum & Gil 516 S Perry St Montgomery AL 36104-4631

**RODGERS, RICHARD M.,** management consultant, lawyer; b. Bklyn., Aug. 29, 1941; s. Lincoln and Dorothy (Zimmerman) R.; m. Sharan Raye Kaufman, Nov. 16, 1969; children: Jennifer Lynn, Suzanne Bari. BA, Adelphi U., 1963; MS, MBA in Indsl. Mgmt., Poly Inst. N.Y., 1973; JD, Bklyn. Law Sch., 1979. Bar: N.Y. 1980, Fla. 1980, U.S. Dist. Ct. (so. and ea. dists.) N.Y. 1980, U.S. Tax Ct. 1981, Pa. 1987, U.S. Dist. Ct. (ea. dist.) Pa. 1988, U.S. Supreme Ct. 1992. Mgr. N.Y. Tel., N.Y.C., 1967-71; v.p., dir. ops. ITT Comm. Sys., Hartford, Conn., 1971-74; supervising sys. analyst N.Y. State Office of Ct. Adminstrn., N.Y.C., 1974-80; dir. contracts adminstrn. Alta Tech., Inc., Stamford, Conn., 1981-84; cons. The Rodgers Group, Valley Stream, N.Y., 1984—; prof. bus. adminstrn. Adelphia U., Garden City, N.Y., 1985—. 1st lt. U.S. Army, 1963-66. N.Y. State Bd. Regents scholar, 1979. Mem. ABA, N.Y. State Bar Assn., Fla. Bar Assn., Pa. Bar Assn., Montgomery County Bar Assn., Masons, Shriners. Republican. Jewish. Office: 210 Wooded Ln Ambler PA 19002-2429

**RODGERS, STEPHEN JOHN,** lawyer, consultant; b. Phila., July 10, 1943; s. Harry Edward Rodgers and Antoinette Julia (Battaglini) Muckenfuss; m. Roberta Elaine Rhine, Sept. 21, 1974; children: Abigail Elizabeth, Rebecca Elizabeth. MD, Hahnemann U., 1969; JD, Widener U., 1989. Bar: Pa. 1990, N.J. 1990; med. lic., Pa., Del., N.J. Pvt. practice in family practice and emergency medicine Del. Pain Clinic, Wilmington, 1975-89, asst. dir., 1989-92; pvt. practice as medicolegal cons. Wilmington, 1992—; mem. Med. Assistance and Health Svcs. Adv. Bd., N.J., 1996-98; chair Task Force on Ind. Med. Exam., Dept. Labor and Industry, Commonwealth of Pa., 1996-98. Comdr. USN, 1968-75; capt. USNR, 1975—. Fellow Am. Acad. Family Physicians, Am. Acad. Disability Evaluating Physicians, Am. Acad. Emergency Medicine, Am. Coll. Legal Medicine; mem. Aerospace Med. Assn., Pa. Bar Assn. (health care com. 1991—), Del. Acad. Medicine, N.J. Acad. Family Physicians (ho. of dels. 1989, 90, 91), Vietnam Vets. of Am. Republican. Roman Catholic. Avocations: equestrian, pro bono veterans and disability advocate. Health. Home: PO Box 54 Alloway NJ 08001-0054 Office: Ste 30 1701 Augustine Wilmington DE 19803

**RODMAN, LEROY ELI,** lawyer; b. N.Y.C., Feb. 22, 1914; s. Morris and Sadie (Specter) R.; m. Toby Chertcoff, Mar. 14, 1943; children: John Stephen, Lawrence Bernard. AB, CCNY, 1933; J.D. (James Kent scholar), Columbia, 1936. Bar: N.Y. 1937. Practiced in N.Y.C., 1937-43, 46—; law sec. to U.S. dist. judge Bklyn., 1936; law asst. Am. Law Inst., N.Y.C., 1937; chief food enforcement unit N.Y. Regional Office, OPA, 1942-43; mem. firm Lawrence R. Condon, N.Y.C., 1937-42; ptnr. Joseph & Rodman, N.Y.C., 1946-53; sr. ptnr. Rodman, Maurer & Dansker, N.Y.C., 1964-73, Carro, Spanbock, Londin, Rodman & Fass, N.Y.C., 1973-78, Rodman & Rodman, N.Y.C., 1978-89, Teitelbaum, Hiller, Rodman, Paden & Hibsher, P.C., N.Y.C., 1990-96; of counsel Morrison, Cohen, Singer & Weinstein LLP, N.Y.C., 1996—; sec. Ameribrom, Inc. Editorial bd.: Columbia Law Rev, 1934-36; Contbr. articles to legal jours. Bd. dirs. Manhattan coun. Boy Scouts Am., v.p., 1961-68, pres., 1972-75; exec. bd. Greater N.Y. coun. Capt. JAGD AUS, 1943-46. Recipient Certs. Svc., Silver Beaver award Boy Scouts Am., 1962, Eagle Scout. Fellow Am. Coll. Trust and Estate Counsel; mem. ABA, N.Y. County Lawyers Assn., Assn. of Bar of City of N.Y., Judge Adv. Assn., Phi Beta Kappa. Jewish (trustee, v.p. synagogue, pres. brotherhood 1958-60). Clubs: Univ. (N.Y.C.); Metropolis Country (White Plains, N.Y.) (sec. 1976-77, 80-82, v.p. 1977-78, bd. govs. 1976-82). Probate, General corporate, Estate taxation. Home: 535 E 86th St New York NY 10028-7533 Office: 750 Lexington Ave New York NY 10022-1200

**RODOVICH, ANDREW PAUL,** magistrate; b. Hammond, Ind., Feb. 24, 1948; s. Andrew H. and Julia (Makar) R.; m. Gail Linda Patrick, May 27, 1972; children: Caroline Anja, Mary Katherine, James Patrick. BA, Valparaiso (Ind.) U., 1970, JD, 1973. Bar: Ind. Ptnr. Hand, Muenich & Rodovich, Hammond, 1973-78; chief dep. prosecutor Lake County Prosecutor's Office, Crown Point, Ind., 1979-82; U.S. magistrate U.S. Dist. Ct., Hammond, 1982—; referee Hammond City Ct., 1978; adj. prof. Valparaiso Law Sch., 1985—. Fellow Ind. Bar Found.; mem. Nat. Coun. U.S. Magistrates, Delta Theta Phi. Republican. Avocations: sports. Home: 7207 Baring Pky Hammond IN 46324-2218 Office: US Dist Ct 136 Federal Bldg Hammond IN 46320-1529

**RODOWSKY, LAWRENCE FRANCIS,** state judge; b. Balt., Nov. 10, 1930; s. Lawrence Anthony and Frances (Gardner) R.; m. Colby Fossett, Aug. 7, 1954; children: Laura Rodowsky Ramos, Alice Rodowsky-Seegers, Emily Rodowsky Savopoulos, Sarah Jones Rodowsky, Gregory, Katherine Rodowsky O'Connor. AB, Loyola Coll., Balt., 1952; LLB, U. Md., 1956. Bar: Md. 1956. Ct. crier, law clk. U.S. Dist. Ct. Md., 1954-56; asst. atty. gen. State of Md., 1960-61; assoc., ptnr. firm Frank, Bernstein, Conaway & Goldman, Balt., 1956-79; assoc. judge Ct. Appeals Md., Annapolis, 1980—; rules com. Ct. Appeals Md., 1969-80; lectr., asst. instr. U. Md. Law Sch., 1958-68, 87-91; reporter jud. dept. Md. Constl. Conv. Commn., 1966-67. Chmn. Gov. Md. Commn. Racing Reform, 1979. Fellow Am. Coll. Trial Lawyers; mem. Md. Bar Assn., Balt. Bar Assn. Roman Catholic. Home: 4306 Norwood Rd Baltimore MD 21218-1118 Office: Ct Appeals Md 620 C M Mitchell Jr CTHS Baltimore MD 21202

**RODRIGUES, DARYL ANTHONY,** lawyer; b. Hitchin, Eng., Dec. 22, 1962; came to the U.S., 1981; s. Noel L. F. and Helen I. Rodrigues; m. Lisa Kay Sem, Jan. 24, 1988; children: Garrison N., Hayden K. BA in Psychology, Seattle U., 1984, MA in Psychology, 1986; JD, Gonzaga U., 1994. Bar: Wash., U.S. Dist. Ct. (ea. and we. dists.) Wash. Staff atty., bailiff Benton/Franklin County Superior Cts., Kennewick, Wash., 1994-95; assoc. Contreras-Trejo & Trejo, Yakima, Wash., 1995; ptnr. Michaelsen Mix & Rodrigues, LLC, Spokane, Wash., 1996; pres., pvt. practice law Spokane, 1998—; bd. dirs. Samaritan Counseling Ctr., Spokane, Vol. Lawyers Program, Spokane. Recipient Hon. Mention award Spokane County Bar Assn., 1998. Presbyterian. Avocations: computers, interactive entertainment. Criminal, Family and matrimonial, Personal injury. Home: 1907 W Mansfield Ave Spokane WA 99205-4153 Office: 1410 W Dean Ave Spokane WA 99201-1920

**RODRIGUEZ, ANTONIO JOSE,** lawyer; b. New Orleans, Dec. 7, 1944; s. Anthony Joseph and Josephine Olga (Cox) R.; m. Virginia Anne Soignet, Aug. 23, 1969; children: Henry Jacob, Stephen Anthony. BS, U.S. Naval Acad., 1966; JD cum laude, Loyola U. of the South, New Orleans, 1973. Bar: La. 1973, U.S. Dist. Ct. (ea. dist.) La. 1973, U.S. Ct. Appeals (5th cir.) 1973, U.S. Dist. Ct. (mid. dist.) La. 1975, U.S. Dist. Ct. (we. dist.) La. 1977, U.S. Ct. Appeals (11th cir.) 1981, U.S. Supreme Ct. 1987, U.S. Dist. Ct. (so. dist.) Miss. 1991, U.S. Ct. Appeals (4th cir.) 1991, U.S. Ct. Appeals (1st cir.) 1997, U.S. Ct. Internat. Trade, 1991. Assoc. Phelps, Dunbar, Marks, Claverie & Sims, New Orleans, 1973-77; ptnr. Phelps Dunbar, New Orleans, 1977-92, Rice Fowler Rodriguez Kingsmill & Flint, LLP, New Orleans, 1992—; prof. law Tulane U., New Orleans, 1981—; mem. nat. rules of the road adv. coun. U.S. Dept. Transp., Washington, 1987-90, chmn. nat. navigation safety adv. coun., 1990-94; spkr. on admiralty and environ. Co-author: Admiralty-Limitation of Liability, 1981—, Admiralty-Law of Collision, 1990—; author: (chpt.) Benedict on Admiralty, 1995—; assoc. editor Loyola Law Rev., 1971-73; contbr. articles to profl. maritime and environ. jours. Bd. dirs. Greater New Orleans Coun. Navy League, 1988—, Propeller Club of New Orleans, 1997—. Lt. USN, 1966-70; capt. USNR, 1970-95. Decorated Navy Commendation medal; recipient Disting. Pub. Svc. award U.S. Dept. Transp., 1993. Fellow La. Bar Found.; mem. ABA, La. Bar Assn., La. State Law Inst., Maritime Law Assn. U.S. (proctor 1975—), New Orleans Bar Assn., Southeastern Admiralty Law Inst., Assn. Average Adjusters U.S., Assn. Average Adjusters U.K., Naval Res. Assn. (chpt. pres. 1982-84), U.S. Naval Acad. Alumni Assn. (chpt. pres. 1981-83), Bienville club, Phi Alpha Delta, Alpha Sigma Nu. Republican. Roman Catholic. Admiralty, Environmental, General civil litigation. Home: 4029 Mouton St Metairie LA 70002-1303 Office: Rice Fowler Rodriguez Kingsmill & Flint LLP 201 Saint Charles Ave Fl 36 New Orleans LA 70170-1000

**RODRIGUEZ, CARLOS AUGUSTO,** lawyer; b. Havana, Cuba, Sept. 1, 1954; came to U.S., 1960; s. Urbano and Estela (Cardenas) R.; m. Valerie Carr, May 27, 1989. BA magna cum laude, Furman U., 1977; JD, U. Fla., 1980. Bar: Fla. 1980, U.S. Ct. Appeals (5th cir.) 1981, U.S. Dist. Ct. (so. dist. and trial bar) Fla. 1984, U.S. Ct. Appeals (11th cir.) 1995; bd. cert. civil trial atty. Asst. pub. defender Broward County Pub. Defender's Office, Ft. Lauderdale, Fla., 1980-83, chief asst. pub. defender, 1983-85; assoc. Fazio, Dawson & DiSalvo, Ft. Lauderdale, Fla., 1985-87; sole practice Ft. Lauderdale, Fla., 1987—; assoc. prof. U. Miami Sch. Law, Miami, 1983-85; lectr. criminal procedure Nova Law Cen., Ft. Lauderdale, 1983-85, lectr. on law Broward Community Coll., Ft. Lauderdale, 1983-87; mem. Nuisance Abatement Bd., 1989—, chmn., 1996—; vice chmn. Marine ADv. Bd., 1990. Mem. Marine Adv. Bd., Broward, Fla., 1986-96; rep. Primary Rep. Port Everglades Commn., Broward, 1984. Mem. ABA, ATLA, Am. Bd. Trial Advocacy, Acad. Fla. Trial Lawyers, Broward County Bar Assn., Phi Beta Kappa. Republican. Roman Catholic. Avocations: scuba diving, fishing, water and snow skiing. fAX: 954-463-9492. Personal injury, Criminal, General civil litigation. Home: 2448 SE 12th St Pompano Beach FL 33062-7040 Office: 633 S Andrews Ave Ste 402 Fort Lauderdale FL 33301-2849

**RODRIGUEZ, JOSEPH H.,** federal judge; b. 1930; m. Barbara Marriner. AB, La Salle Coll., 1955; JD, Rutgers U., 1958. Assoc. Brown, Connery et al, Camden, N.J., 1959-82; pub. advocate, pub. defender State of N.J., 1982-85; judge U.S. Dist. Ct. N.J., Camden, 1985—, now sr. judge; instr. law Rutgers U., N.J., 1972-82, 93—; chmn. State Commn. Investigation, N.J., 1974-79. Chmn. State Bd. of Higher Edn., N.J., 1971-73. Mem. N.J. State Bar Assn. (pres. 1978-79). Office: US Dist Ct PO Box 886 Rm 6060 One John F Gerry Plz Camden NJ 08101-0886

**RODRIGUEZ, LOURDES A. DE LOS ANGELES,** lawyer; b. Havana, Cuba, Mar. 1, 1957; came to U.S., 1960; d. Oscar Armando and Romana Irene (Orfila) R. BA, U. Miami, 1976, JD, 1988. Bar: Fla. 1990, U.S. Dist.

Ct. (so. dist.) Fla. 1990. Appeals officer IRS, N.Y.C., 1982-85, Miami, Fla., 1985-87; legal intern to Hon. Kenneth L. Ryskamp, So. Dist. Fla., Miami, 1987; legal intern to Hon. Charlene Sorrentino U.S. Dist. Ct. (so. dist.) Fla., Miami, 1987; various law clerkships Miami, 1988-91; assoc. Law Office Miguel A. Suarez, Miami, 1990-91, Castro, Ramirez & Netsch, P.A., Miami, 1991; atty. Am. Immigration Lawyer's Assn. pro bono project Legal Svcs. Greater Miami, Inc., 1991-95; pvt. practice Coral Gables, Fla., 1995—; vol. guardian ad litem 11th Jud. Cir., Miami, 1987-91. Mem. Cath. Hispanic Ctr., Miami, 1985—; bd. dirs. Task Force Cuban Civic Orgns., Miami, 1990—; cons., instr. to families Cuban prisoners/detainees, Miami, 1990—. Recipient Recognition award IRS, 1985, 11th Jud. Cir., 1989. Mem. Fla. Assn. Women Lawyers, Latinas Ptnrs. for Health, Amnesty Internat., Jr. League of Greater Miami. Avocations: cycling, reading, classical and jazz music, travel. Immigration, naturalization, and customs, Civil rights. Office: 2801 Ponce De Leon Blvd Ste 810 Coral Gables FL 33134-6920

**RODRIGUEZ, MIQUEL,** prosecutor; b. San Jose, Calif.. BA in Econs., BA in Polit. Sci., Cornell U., 1983; JD, Harvard U., 1986. Bar: Pa. 1988, D.C. 1990, Calif. 1990, U.S. Dist. Ct. Wis., U.S. Dist. Ct. Pa., U.S. Dist. Ct. D.C., U.S. Dist. Ct. Ky., U.S. Dist. Ct. Mont., U.S. Dist. Ct. Hawaii, U.S. Dist. Ct. (so., no., ea., ctrl. dists.) Calif., U.S. Ct. Appeals (9th cir.). Law clk. to Hon. Diarmuid F. O'Scannlain U.S. Ct. Appeals 9th cir., 1986-87; trial atty. civil rights divsn. U.S. Dept. Justice, Washington, 1987-90; assoc. ind. counsel Office of Ind. Counsel Kenneth Starr, Washington, 1994-95; asst. U.S. atty. criminal and appellate divsns. Office of U.S. Atty., Sacramento, 1990-94; asst. U.S. atty. criminal divsn. ea. dist. Office of U.S. Atty., Sacramento, Calif., 1995—. Office: Office of US Atty Federal Courthouse Sacramento CA 95814

**RODRIGUEZ-DIAZ, JUAN E.,** lawyer; b. Ponce, P.R., Dec. 27, 1941; s. Juan and Auristela (Diaz-Alvarado) Rodriguez de Jesus; m. Sonia de Hostos-Anca, Aug. 10, 1966; children: Juan Eugenio, Jorge Eduardo, Ingrid Marie Rodriguez. BA, Yale U., 1963; LLB, Harvard U., 1966; LLM in Taxation, NYU, 1969. Bar: N.Y. 1968, P.R. 1970. Assoc. Baker & McKenzie, N.Y.C., 1966-68, McConnell, valdes, San Juan, P.R.; undersec. Dept. Treasury P.R., 1971-73; mem. Sweeting, Pons, golzalez & Rodriguez, 1973-81; pvt. practice San Juan, 1981-94, Totti & Rodriguez-Diaz, 1994—; bd. dir. Ochoa Indsl. Sales Corp., Ochoa Telecom, Inc., Industrias Vassallo, Inc. Bd. govs. Aqueduct and Sewer Authority P.R., 1979-84; mem. adv. com. collective bargaining negotiation of P.R. elec. Power Authority to Gov. P.R., 1977-78; bd. govs. P.R. coun. Boy Scouts Am., mem. transition com., 1984-85; mem. adminstrv. coun. Ballajá. Mem. ABA, N.Y. State Bar Assn., P.R. Bar Assn., AFDA Club, San Juan Yacht Club, Palmas de Mar Country Club. Taxation, general, Contracts commercial, General corporate. Home: Urbanizacion San Patricion Calle Fresno # 1 Guaynabo PR 00968-4601 Office: Suite 1200 416 Ave Ponce De Leon Hato Rey San Juan PR 00918-3418

**RODRIGUEZ-ORELLANA, MANUEL,** law educator; b. Rio Piedras, P.R., Mar. 7, 1948; s. Manuel Rodriguez-Ramos and Elena (Orellana-Ramos) Rodriguez; m. Maria Dolores Pizarro-Figueroa, Jan. 30, 1984; 1 child, Laura Elena Rodriguez-Pizarro. BA, Johns Hopkins U., 1970; MA, Brown U., 1972; JD, Boston Coll., 1975; LLM, Harvard U., 1983. Bar: P.R. 1975, U.S. Dist. Ct. P.R. 1976. Staff atty. P.R. Legal Svcs., Inc., San Juan, P.R., 1975-77, dir. consumer law div., 1977-79; dean students Inter-Am. U. Sch. Law, San Juan, P.R., 1979-80, asst. prof. law, 1980-83; assoc. prof. law Northeastern U. Sch. Law, Boston, 1983-89, prof. law, 1989-93; cons. Office Ind. Counsel-Prosecutor of Commonwealth P.R., San Juan, 1985, Office Minority Leader of P.R. Ind. Party, Senate P.R., San Juan, 1985—; vis. scholar Harvard Law Sch., Cambridge, Mass., 1988; electoral commr. Commonwealth P.R., 1989-95; pvt. practice in civil litigation, 1995—; vis. prof. Eugenio M. de Hostas Sch. Law, Mayaguez, P.R., 1995-96, Inter-Am. U., 1998-99, prof. law 1998—. Author: Después de Todo: Poemas de Noche y Circunstancia, 1982. Candidate for resident commr. from P.R. in U.S. Ho. of Reps., 1996. Mem. ABA, Colegio de Abogados de P.R. (bd. govs. 1977-78).

**ROE, CHARLES BARNETT,** lawyer; b. Tacoma, June 25, 1932; s. Charles Brown and Gladys Luvena (Harding) R.; m. Marilyn Marie Quam, July 31, 1954; children: Sharon Lynn De Groot, Jeannine Carole Roe Dellwo. AB, U. Puget Sound, 1953; postgrad. U. Calif., Berkeley, 1957-58; JD, U. Wash., 1960. Bar: Wash. 1960, U.S. Dist. Ct. (ea. and we. dists.) 1960, U.S. Ct. Appeals (9th cir.) 1963, U.S. Supreme Ct. 1963, U.S. Ct. Appeals (D.C. cir.) 1964. Asst. atty. gen. depts. natural resources, conservation, water resources and pollution control commn., State of Wash., Olympia, 1960-70, asst. dir. dept. water resources, 1967-69, sr. asst. atty. gen., 1970-90; of counsel Perkins Coie, Olympia, 1991—; chief counsel dept. ecology and nuclear waste, 1970-85, Nuclear Waste Bd., 1983-90; counsel natural resources com. Wash. Ho. of Reps., Olympia, 1970; adj. prof. Gonzaga U. Sch. Law, Spokane, 1973-76, U. Puget Sound Law Sch., 1985-90; contractor Nat. Water Commn., Washington, 1970-71. Rep., Western States Water Coun., Salt Lake City, 1970-90; sec. Olympia Audubon Soc., 1962-63; chmn. bd. mgrs. United Chs., Olympia, 1967-68. Served to 1st USAF, 1954-57. Mem. ABA (chmn. water resources com. natural resources sect. 1981-83), Wash. State Bar (chmn. environ. law sect. 1971-72), Washington Cts. Hist. Soc. (bd. dirs. 1998—), Mason, Rotary, Kappa Sigma, Phi Delta Phi. Mem. United Ch. of Christ. Home: 2400 Wedgewood Dr SE Olympia WA 98501-3841 Office: Perkins Coie 1110 Capitol Way S Ste 405 Olympia WA 98501-2251

**ROE, MICHAEL FLINN,** lawyer; b. Washington, Oct. 28, 1959; s. Jerrold M. Roe and Marilyn Theresa (Matacia) Benstead; m. Patricia Eileen Barrett, Aug. 23, 1987; children: Brendan, Caitrin. BA, U. Notre Dame, 1981; JD, U. San Diego, 1985. Bar: Calif. 1985, Ill. 1992. Asst. counsel, dir. GSI, Inc., Chgo., 1984-88; dep. prosecutor criminal divsn. San Diego, 1988-90; trial atty. Corboy & Demetrio, P.C., Chgo., 1991-96, S. E. Loggans & Assocs., P.C., 1997—; guest lectr. trial techniques John Marshall Law Sch., Chgo., 1994; instr. Near North Metro High Sch., Chgo., 1994. Mem. ATLA, Ill. Trial Lawyers Assn. (product liability com. 1994-95), Ill. State Bar Assn., Amnesty Internat., Ireland C. of C., Ireland Soc. Democrat. Roman Catholic. Avocations: coaching, golf, tennis, horsemanship. Federal civil litigation, General civil litigation, Product liability.

**ROE, RAMONA JERALDEAN,** lawyer, state official; b. Gassville, Ark., May 27, 1942; d. Roy A. and Wanda J. (Finley) R. B.A., U. Ark., 1964; J.D., U.Ark.-Little Rock, 1976. Bar: Ark. 1976, U.S. Dist. Ct. (ea. and we. dists.) Ark. 1979. Mng. ptnr. Roe & Hunt, Rogers, Ark., 1977-78; pvt. practice, Rogers, Ark., 1978-81, Little Rock, 1982-84, 90-92; assoc. Richardson & Richardson, Little Rock, 1981-82; dep. exec. dir. Ark. Workers' Compensation Commn., Little Rock, 1984-90; legis. atty. Ark. Code Revision Commn., Little Rock, 1992—. Contbr. articles to profl. jours. Recipient Am. Jurisprudence awards U. Ark. Sch. Law, 1971-72, Corpus Juris Secundum award, 1971, Hornbook award, 1971, Am. Judicature award, 1972. Mem. AAUW (treas. 1980), Bus. and Profl. Women (chpt. treas.-v.p. 1978-80), Delta Theta Phi (clk. of rolls 1973-74, tribune 1974-75), Mensa, Lambda Tau. Methodist. Office: Ark Code Revision Commn 1515 W 7th St Ste 204 Little Rock AR 72201-3936

**ROE, ROGER ROLLAND,** lawyer; b. Mpls., Dec. 31, 1947; s. Roger Rolland Roe; m. Paula Speltz, 1974; children: Elena, Madeline. BA, Grinnell Coll., 1970; JD, U. Minn., 1973. Bar: Minn. 1973, U.S. Dist. Ct. Minn. 1974, U.S. Ct. Appeals (8th cir.) 1977, U.S. Supreme Ct. 1978, Wis. 1988, U.S. Dist. Ct. Nebr. 1995, U.S. Dist. Ct. (ea. and we. dists.) Wis. Law clk. to Hon. Judge Amdahl Hennepin County Dist. Ct., Mpls., 1973-74; from assoc. to ptnr. Rider, Bennett, Egan & Arundel, Mpls., 1974-91; mng. ptnr. Yaeger, Jungbauer, Barczak & Roe, Ltd., Mpls., 1992—; mem. nat. panel arbitrators Am. Arbitration Assn.; judge trial practice class and moot ct. competitions law sch. U. Minn.; guest lectr. Minn. Continuing Legal Edn. courses. Fellow Internat. Soc. Barristers; mem. ATLA (guest lectr.), Am. Bd. Trial Advs. (diplomat, Mass. chpt. pres. 1996-97), Minn. Trial Lawyers Assn., Million Dollar Round Table. Avocations: golfing, downhill skiing. Personal injury, Product liability, General civil litigation. Office: Yaeger Jungbauer Barczak & Roe Ltd 701 4th Ave S Ste 1400 Minneapolis MN 55415-1816

**ROEDDER, WILLIAM CHAPMAN, JR.,** lawyer; b. St. Louis, June 21, 1946; s. William Chapman and Dorothy (Reifeiss) R.; m. Gwendolyn Arnold, Sept. 13, 1968; children: William Chapman, Barcley Shane. BS, U. Ala., 1968; JD cum laude, Cumberland U., 1972. Bar: Ala. Law clk. to chief justice Ala. Supreme Ct., Montgomery, 1972; ptnr. McDowell Knight Roedder & Sledge, L.L.C., Mobile, Ala., 1997—. Comments editor Cumberland-Samford Law Rev.; contbr. articles to legal publs. Mem. ABA (vice chair com. trial tactics, torts and ins. practice 1995-96), Ala. State Bar Assn., Mobile County Bar Assn. (past sec., past chmn. ethics com. 1988-90, grievance com. 1994-96), Fed. Ins. and Corp. Counsel (chmn. products liability sect. 1990-93, regional v.p. 1994-96, bd. dirs. 1996—, exec. com. 1997—, sec.-treas. 1999—), Ala. Def. Lawyers Assn., Curia Honoris, Order of Barristers, Def. Rsch. Inst., Phi Alpha Delta (pres. 1971-72). Aviation, General civil litigation, Contracts commercial. Home: 211 Levert Ave Mobile AL 36607-3219 Office: McDowell Knight Roedder & Sledge LLC PO Box 350 Mobile AL 36601-0350

**ROEHL, JERRALD J.,** lawyer; b. Austin, Tex., Dec. 6, 1945; s. Joseph E. and Jeanne Foster (Scott) R.; m. Nancy J. Meyers, Jan. 15, 1977; children: Daniel J., Katherine C., J. Ryan, J. Taylor. BA, U. N.Mex., 1968; JD, Washington and Lee U., 1971. Bar: N.Mex. 1972, U.S. Ct. Appeals (10th cir.) 1972, U.S. Supreme Ct. 1977. Practice of Law, Albuquerque, 1972—; pres. Roehl Law Firm P.C. and predecessors, Albuquerque, 1976—; lectr. to profl. groups; real estate developer, Albuquerque. Bd. dirs. Rehab. Ctr. of Albuquerque, 1974-78; mem. assocs. Presbyn. Hosp. Ctr., Albuquerque, 1974-82; incorporator, then treas. exec. com. Ctr. City Coun., 1991—. Recipient award of recognition State Bar N.Mex., 1975, 76, 77. Mem. ABA (award of achievement Young Lawyers div. 1975, council econs. of law practice sect. 1978-80, exec. council Young Lawyers div. 1979-81, fellow div. 1984—, council tort and ins. practice sect. 1981-83), N.Mex. Bar Assn. (pres. young lawyers sect. 1975-76), Albuquerque Bar Assn. (bd. dirs. 1976-79), N.Mex. Def. Lawyers Assn. (pres. 1983-84), Sigma Alpha Epsilon, Sigma Delta Chi, Phi Delta Phi. Roman Catholic. Clubs: Albuquerque Country, Albuquerque Petroleum. Bd. advs. ABA Jour., 1981-83; bd. editors Washington and Lee Law Rev., 1970-71. Insurance, Federal civil litigation, General corporate. Home: 4411 Constitution Ave NE Albuquerque NM 87110-5721 Office: Roehl Law Firm PC 300 Central Ave SW Albuquerque NM 87102-3298

**ROESER, RONALD O.,** lawyer, consultant; b. Berwyn, Ill., May 6, 1950; s. John O. and Mary Jean (Marsden) R.; m. Susan Marie Gill, July 22, 1972; children: Michelle Marie, Michael Franklin. BA, So. Ill. U., 1972; JD, DePaul U., 1975. Bar: Ill. 1975, U.S. Dist. Ct. (no. dist.) Ill. 1975, U.S.Tax. Ct. 1975, U.S. Ct. Appeals (7th cir.) 1975. Assoc. Imming & Faber, Elgin, Ill., 1975-77; ptnr. Imming, Faber & Roeser, Elgin, 1977-81, Imming & Roeser, Elgin, 1981-83, Roeser & Vucha, Elgin, 1983-84, Roeser, Vucha & Carbary, Elgin, 1984—. Mem. Fed. Trial Bar, Ill. Bar Assn., Kane County Bar Assn., Chgo. Bar Assn., Ill. Trial Lawyers Assn., Dundee Jaycees (treas., bd. dirs. 1975—, Outstanding Merit awards 1976, 78, 81), Lions. Republican. Roman Catholic. Avocations: history, reading, contact sports. Contracts commercial, General civil litigation. Home: 34w921 Duchesne Dr Dundee IL 60118-3101 Office: Roeser & Vucha 920 Davis Rd Elgin IL 60123-1390

**ROESLER, JOHN BRUCE,** lawyer; b. Portland, Oreg., Oct. 9, 1943; s. Bruce Emil and Charlotte Amanda (Naess) R.; m. Kathryne Elise Nilsen, Aug. 14, 1965; children: Paul, Mark, Nico. BA, U. Kans., 1966, JD, 1971. Bar: Mo. 1971, N.Mex. 1979, Colo. 1998, U.S. Dist. Ct. (we. dist.) Mo. 1971, U.S. Dist. Ct. N.Mex. 1979, U.S. Dist. Ct. Colo. 1998. U.S. Ct. Appeals (10th cir.) 1979, U.S. Ct. Appeals (5th cir.) 1988, U.S. Ct. Appeals (4th cir.) 1992, U.S. Supreme Ct. 1987. Assoc. Gage & Tucker, Kansas City, Mo., 1971-74; civil rights advocate State of N.Mex. Human Rights, Santa Fe, 1977-78; law clk. Hon. Edwin L. Felter N.Mex. Supreme Ct., Santa Fe, 1978-79; asst. dist. atty. Taos (N.Mex.) Dist. Atty.'s Office, 1979-80; asst. spl. pros. Santa Fe Dist. Atty.'s Office, 1980-82; pvt. practice Santa Fe, 1982-97; of counsel Roth, Van Amberg, Gross, Rogers & Ortiz, 1991-94; spl. asst. atty. gen. Colo. Atty. Gen's Office, 1997-99; of counsel Jones & Keller, Denver, 1999—; instr. John Marshall Law Sch., Chgo., summer 1974; spkr. civil rights and children's rights issues U. Miami Sch. Law, 1991, U. Miami Sch. Medicine, 1991. Author: (books) How To Find the Best Lawyers, In Harm's Way: Is Your Child Safe in School; mem. law rev. U. Kans. Sch. Law, 1970-71; contbr. articles to profl. jours. and treatise. Speaker convention Nat. Com. for the Prevention of Child Abuse, 1988, 89, 90. Mem. Colo. Trial Lawyers Assn., Colo. Bar Assn., Denver Bar Assn. Democrat. Roman Catholic. Avocation: downhill skiing, hiking, gardening. Education and schools, Civil rights, Federal civil litigation. Home: 2571 S Sherman St Denver CO 80210

**ROESSLER, P. DEE,** lawyer, former judge, educator; b. McKinney, Tex., Nov. 4, 1941; d. W.D. and Eunice Marie (Medcalf) Powell; m. George L. Roessler, Jr., Nov. 16, 1963 (div. Dec. 1977); children: Laura Diane, Trey. Student, Austin Coll., 1960-61, 62-64, Wayland Bapt. Coll., 1961-62; BA, U. West Fla., 1968; postgrad., East Tex. State U., 1975, U. Tex.-Dallas, 1977; JD, So. Meth. U., 1982. Bar: Tex. 1982, U.S. Dist. Ct. (ea. dist.) Tex. 1983, U.S. Dist. Ct. (no. dist.) Tex. 1983. Tchr. Van Alstyne Ind. Sch. Dist., Tex., 1968-69; social worker Dept. Social Svcs., Fayetteville, N.C., 1971-73, Dept. Human Svcs., Sherman and McKinney, 1973-79, 81; assoc. atty. Abernathy & Roeder, McKinney, 1982-85, Ronald W. Uselton, Sherman, 1985-86; prof., program coord. for real estate Collin County C.C., McKinney, 1986-87, prof. criminal justice, 1986-91, legal asst., 1986—; mcpl. judge City of Mckinney Mcpl. Ct., 1986-89; mem. Tex. State Bar Com. on Legal Assts., 1990-94, Tex. State Bar Com. on Child Abuse & Neglect, 1996—. Mem. Collin County Shelter for Battered Women, 1984-86, chmn., 1984-85; v.p. Collin County Child Welfare Bd., 1986, pres., 1987-88, 96-97, treas., 1989, mem., 1985-89, 94-98; Rep. jud. candidate Collin County, 1986; chmn. bd. Tri County Consortium Mental Health Mental Retardation, 1984-85; mem. Tex. Area 5 Health System Agy., 1979, Collin County Mental Health Adv. Bd., 1978-79; trustee Willow Park Hosp., HCA, 1987-88; chair Collin County Criminal Justice Sub-com., 1987-88; mem. Collin County Pub. Responsibility Com., 1991-96, chair, 1994-95; bd. dirs. Ct. Apptd. Spl. Advocates, 1991-95. Mem. Collin County Bar Assn., Plano Bar Assn. Baptist. Avocations: gardening, reading, writing, traveling. Family and matrimonial, Criminal, State civil litigation. Home: 5 Shadybrook Cir Melissa TX 75454-8912 Office: Collin County Community Coll 2200 W University Dr Mc Kinney TX 75070-2906

**ROETHE, JAMES NORTON,** lawyer; b. Milw., Jan. 27, 1942; s. Arthur Frantz and Bess Irma (Norton) R.; m. Nita May Dorris, July 15, 1967; children: Melissa Dorris, Sarah Rebecca. BBA, U. Wis.-Madison, 1964, JD, 1967. Bar: Wis. 1967, U.S. Dist. Ct. (we. dist.) Wis. 1967, Calif. 1968, U.S. Dist. Ct. (no. dist.) Calif. 1972, U.S. Ct. Claims 1975, U.S. Ct. Appeals (9th cir.) 1980, U.S. Dist. Ct. (ea. dist.) Calif. 1982, U.S. Dist. Ct. (cent. dist.) Calif. 1986, U.S. Ct. Appeals (4th cir.) 1988, U.S. Ct. Appeals (2nd cir.) 1989. Assoc., Pillsbury, Madison & Sutro, San Francisco, 1971-77, ptnr., 1978-92; sr. v.p., dir. litigation, Bank of Am., San Francisco, 1992-96, exec. v.p., 1996—, gen. counsel, 1996-98, dep. gen. counsel, 1998—; staff atty. Commn. on CIA Activities within U.S., Washington, 1975. Editor: Africa, 1967; editor-in-chief Wis. Law Rev., 1966-67. Bd. dirs. Orinda Assn. (Calif.), 1984-85, pres. 1986. Commr. City Orinda Planning Commn., 1988-94, chmn., 1990, 93; bd. dirs. Calif. Shakespeare Festival, 1993—; bd. visitors U. Wis. Law Sch., 1994—. Served to lt. USNR, 1967-71. Fellow Am. Bar Found.; mem. ABA, Wis. Bar Assn., Calif. Bar Assn., Bar Assn. San Francisco, Orinda Country Club, Phi Kappa Phi, Order of Coif. Republican. Federal civil litigation, General civil litigation, Public utilities. Home: 36 Fallen Leaf Ter Orinda CA 94563-1209 Office: Bank of Am Legal Dept 555 California St San Francisco CA 94104-1502

**ROETTGER, NORMAN CHARLES, JR.,** federal judge; b. Lucasville, Ohio, Nov. 3, 1930; s. Norman Charles and Emma Eleanora R.; children: Virginia, Peggy. BA, Ohio State U., 1952; LLB magna cum laude, Washington and Lee U., 1958. Bar: Ohio 1958, Fla. 1958. Assoc. Frost & Jacobs, Cin., 1958-59; assoc. firm Fleming, O'Bryan & Fleming, Ft. Lauderdale, Fla., 1959-63, ptnr., 1963-69, 71-72; dep. gen. counsel HUD, Washington, 1969-71; judge U.S. Dist. Ct. (so. dist.) Fla., Ft. Lauderdale, 1972-97, sr. judge, 1997—. Lt. (j.g.) USN, 1952-55; to capt. Res. 1972. Mem. ABA, Fed. Bar Assn., Fla. Bar Assn., Broward County Bar Assn., Am. Judicature Soc., Order of Coif, Masons, Coral Ridge Yacht Club, Omicron Delta Kappa, Kappa Delta Rho. Presbyterian. Clubs: Masons; Coral Ridge Yacht (Ft. Lauderdale). Office: US Dist Ct 299 E Broward Blvd Ste 205F Fort Lauderdale FL 33301-1902*

**ROETZEL, DANNY NILE,** lawyer; b. Hancock, Mich., July 6, 1952; s. J.D. and Deva Dale (Butler) R.; m. Zenobia Ann Kennedy, Sept. 30, 1973. BS, SUNY, 1980; MA, Ctrl. Mich. U., 1987; JD cum laude, St. Louis U., 1987, MA, 1989. Bar: Mo. 1987. Youth counselor Mo. Divsn. Youth Svcs., Jefferson City, 1973-77; juvenile parole officer Mo. Divsn. Youth Svcs., Kansas City, 1977-79; facility mgr. II Mo. Divsn. Youth Svcs., Jefferson City, 1979-84; spl. cons. to dean Sch. Bus. and Adminstrn. St. Louis U., 1984-87; law clk. to chief magistrate U.S. Dist. Ct. (ea. dist.) Mo., St. Louis, 1987-89; staff atty. U.S. Ct. Appeals (8th cir.), St. Louis, 1989-90; spl. asst. U.S. Atty. U.S. Dist. Ct. (ea. dist.) Va., 1990-91; trial atty. criminal enforcement sect. tax divsn. U.S. Dept. Justice, Washington, 1990, 91—; spl. asst. U.S. Atty. U.S. Dist. Ct. (so. dist.) Calif., 1992—. Active White County Young Dems., Searcy, Ark., 1970-71, Harding U. Young Dems., 1970-71; exec. officer North St. Louis County Young Dems., 1985-87. Mem. Mo. Bar Assn., Sigma Iota Epsilon, Phi Alpha Delta. Avocations: reading history, travel. Office: US Dept Justice Tax Divsn Criminal Enforcement Sect Tenth Constitution Ave NE Washington DC 20530-0001

**ROFF, ALAN LEE,** lawyer, consultant; b. Winfield, Kans., July 2, 1936; s. Roy Darlis and Mildred Marie (Goodaile) R.; m. Sonyia Ruth Anderson, Feb. 8, 1954; 1 child, Cynthia Lee Roff Edwards; m. Molly Gek Neo Tan, July 21, 1980. BA with honors and distinction, U. Kans., 1964, JD with distinction, 1966. Bar: Okla. 1967. Staff atty. Phillips Petroleum Co., Bartlesville, Okla., 1966-75, sr. atty., 1976-85, sr. counsel, 1986-94; cons. in Asia, 1995—. Mem. editl. bd. Kans. Law Rev., 1965-66. Precinct com. man Rep. Party, Lawrence, Kans., 1963-64; assoc. justice Kans. U. Chancery Club; mem. Kans. U. Young Reps. Elizabeth Reeder scholar U. Kans., 1965-66, Eldon Wallingford award, 1964-66. Mem. ABA, Okla. Bar Assn., Washington County Bar Assn., Phoenix Club (Bartlesville) (bd. dirs. 1985-86, gen. counsel 1986-91), Order of the Coif, Masons, Hon. Order Ky. Cols., Phi Alpha Delta, Pi Sigma Alpha. Mem. First Christian Ch. Avocation: travel. Private international, General corporate, Contracts commercial. Home and Office: 2247 Mountain Dr Bartlesville OK 74003-6954

**ROGAL, JAMES LONDON,** lawyer; b. Boston, Jan. 30, 1956; s. Paul Bruce and Sondra (London) R.; m. Sue Ellen Silva, Oct. 17, 1984 (div. May 1994); m. Stefanie Louise Bupett, May 28, 1994; children: Mary Elizabeth, Rachel Louise. BA in Govt., St. Lawrence U., 1978; JD, New England Sch. Law, 1983. Bar: Mass. 1983, U.S. Dist. Ct. Mass. 1984. Assoc. Plunkett & Plunkett, Salem, 1983-89, Brasman & Matuson, Boston, 1989-91, Serino, Ley, Young, et al, Boston, 1991-94; pvt. practice Salem, Mass., 1994-95; assoc. Straub & Meyers, Salem, 1995; pvt. practice, of counsel Bolick & Welch, Salem, 1995—; mem. appellate panel Com. Pub. Counsel Svc., Boston, 1986—. Mem. zoning bd. appeals Town of Topsfield, Mass., 1997. Mem. Mass. Bar Assn., Mass. Assn. Criminal Def. Lawyers. Avocation: sports. Appellate, General civil litigation, Real property. Office: Bolick & Welch 32 Church St Salem MA 01970-3737

**ROGE, BRET ALAN,** lawyer; b. Milw., Jan. 31, 1959; s. Albert Harland and Gloria May Roge; m. Jill Marie Munson, Aug. 23, 1997; 1 child, Seth Alan. BBA in Acctg. sum cum laude, U. Wis., Milw., 1981; JD cum laude, Marquette U., 1984. Bar: Wis. 1984. Tax mgr. Arthur Young & Co., Milw., 1984-89; ptnr. Michael Best & Friedrich LLP, Milw., 1989—. Contbr. chpts. to books. Bd. dirs. Next Act Theatre, Milw., 1996-98, Waukesha County Econ. Devel. Corp., Waukesha, Wis., 1998. Mem. ABA, AICPA, Wis. Inst. CPA, Mil. Bar Assn., Beta Gamma Sigma. Avocations: biking, skiing, golfing. Corporate taxation, Contracts commercial, Real property. Office: Michael Best & Friedrich 100 E Wisconsin Ave Milwaukee WI 53202-4107

**ROGERS, CHARLES MYERS,** lawyer; b. Monticello, Utah, Nov. 21, 1947; s. Milton David and Wanda (Myers) R.; m. Jean Evelyn Rankin, Dec. 12, 1970 (div. June 1983); m. Christine Theresa Sill, Apr. 14, 1984; children: Christopher Thales, Fiona Eleanor. BA in Philosophy, U. Mo., Kansas City, 1973; JD, U. Mo., 1976. Bar: Mo. 1976, U.S. Dist. Ct. (we. dist.) Mo. 1976, U.S. Supreme Ct. 1994, U.S. Ct. Appeals (8th cir.) 1997, U.S. Ct. Appeals (9th cir.) 1999. From asst. pub. defender to 1st asst. pub. defender Jackson County Pub. Defender's Office, Kansas City, Mo., 1976-89; regional defender Mo. State Pub. Defender Sys., Kansas City, 1989-94; staff atty. Mo. Capital Punishment Resource Ctr., Kansas City, 1994-95; shareholder Wyrsch Hobbs Mirakian & Lee, Kansas City, 1995—; sole practice law, Kansas City, 1982-86. Served in U.S. Army, 1968-70. Mem. ABA, Nat. Assn. Criminal Def. Lawyers, Mo. Bar Assn., Mo. Assn. Criminal Def. Lawyers (bd. dirs. 1988—, 1st. v.p. 1999—). Democrat. Avocations: cycling, oenology. Criminal. Home: 7434 Madison Ave Kansas City MO 64114-1506 Office: Wyrsch Hobbs et al 1101 Walnut St Ste 1300 Kansas City MO 64106-2181

**ROGERS, DANFORTH WILLIAM,** lawyer; b. Buffalo, May 13, 1937; s. William Silliman and Grace W. (Danforth) R.; m. Carol Robinson, Sept. 9, 1961; children: Danforth W.S., Ninon M. BA, Yale U., 1959; JD, Cornell U., 1962. Assoc. LeBeouf, Lamb & Leiby, N.Y.C., 1963-65; assoc. Palmer & Serles, N.Y.C., 1965-69, ptnr., 1970-78; ptnr. Gifford Woody Palmer & Serles, N.Y.C., 1978-85, Townlay & Updike, N.Y.C., 1985-95; atty. pvt. practice, N.Y.C., 1996—. Mem. ABA, N.Y. State Bar Assn., Am. Contact Bridge League, North River Power Squad., Sons Revolution N.Y. General corporate, Contracts commercial, Mergers and acquisitions. Home and Office: 13 E 9th St New York NY 10003-5910

**ROGERS, DARLA POLLMAN,** lawyer; b. 1952. BA, Wheaton Coll.; JD, U. S.D. Bar: S.D. 1979. Ptnr. Meyer & Rogers, Pierre, S.D. Mem. ABA, S.D. Bar Assn. (pres.). Office: Meyer & Rogers PO Box 1117 Pierre SD 57501-1117*

**ROGERS, DAVID JOHN,** lawyer; b. Lawrence, Mass., Aug. 13, 1960; s. James Martin and Eleanor Elizabeth (Jones) R. BA, Coll. William and Mary, 1982; JD, U. Pitts., 1988. Bar: N.H. 1988, Mass. 1989. Contract adminstr. Sanders Assocs., Inc., Nashua, N.H., 1983-85; assoc. Devine, Millimet, Stahl & Branch, Manchester, N.H., 1988-89; ptnr. Carpenito & Rogers, PA, Salem, N.H., 1989-90; asst. corp. counsel City of Nashua, 1991; pvt. practice Londonderry, N.H., 1991-98; atty. Landmark Title, Inc., Manchester, N.H., 1998—; mem. Worker's Compensation Appeals Bd., State of N.H., 1993—. Active Salem Youth Com., 1989-95; fin. com. West Congl. Ch., Haverhill, Mass., 1990-95. U. scholar U. Pitts., 1988. Mem. Mass. Bar Assn., N.H. Bar Assn., Young Lawyers Com. Republican. Avocations: golf, running, reading, community theater. Real property, Workers' compensation. Home: 20 Cindy Dr Hooksett NH 03106-2003

**ROGERS, GARTH WINFIELD,** lawyer; b. Fort Collins, Colo., Nov. 4, 1938; s. Harlan Winfield and Helen Marie (Orr) R.; m. Joanne Kathleen Rapp, June 16, 1962; children: Todd Winfield, Christopher Jay, Gregory Lynn, Clay Charles. BS, U. Colo., 1958, LLB, 1962. Bar: Colo. 1962; U.S. Dist. Ct. Colo. 1962. Law clk. to presiding justice U.S. Dist. Ct., Denver, 1962-63; assoc. Allen, Stover & Mitchell, Ft. Collins, 1963-68; ptnr. Allen, Rogers & Vahrenwald, Ft. Collins, 1968-97; ret., 1997. Articles editor Rocky Mountain Law Rev., 1961-62. Past bd. dirs. Salvation Army, Ft. Collins, Ft. Collins C. of C., United Way of Ft. Collins, Trinity Luth. Ch., Ft. Collins, others; bd. dirs. Poudre Sch. Dist. Bd. Edn. Mem. ABA, Colo. Bar Assn., Larimer County Bar Assn. Avocations: Nicaragua projects, participative sports, amateur writing, reading. Banking, Real property. Office: 215 W Oak St Ste 202 Fort Collins CO 80521-2734

**ROGERS, GEORGE CHRISTOPHER,** lawyer; b. Cin., Jan. 21, 1957; s. George H. Jr. and Mary F. Rogers; m. E. Debora Benchoam, 1984; children: Tamara, Iara. BA, Cornell U., 1979; MA, Georgetown U., 1981; JD, Columbia U., 1990. Bar: N.Y. 1991, D.C. 1998. Fgn. policy analyst Washington Office L.Am., 1980-87; atty. Coudert Bros., N.Y.C., 1990-91, Muñoz de Toro, Buenos Aires, 1991-96, Dickstein, Shapiro, Morin & Oshinsky, Washington, 1996-98, Inter-Am. Devel. Bank, Washington, 1999. Public international, Finance. Office: Inter Am Devel Bank 1300 New York Ave NW Washington DC 20577-0001

**ROGERS, GORDON KEITH, JR.,** lawyer; b. Nashville, Nov. 3, 1942; s. Gordon Keith Rogers and Josephine McKelvey; m. Mary Butler Lydick, June 17, 1972; 1 child, Gordon Kieth Rogers, III. BA, Vanderbilt U., 1964, JD, 1971. Bar: Ga. 1972, Supreme Ct. Ga. 1972, Tenn. 1975, Supreme Ct. Tenn. 1975, U.S. Tax Ct. 1976, U.S. Ct. Appeals (6th cir.) 1978, U.S. Supreme Ct. 1978. Atty. AT & T, Atlanta, 1972, So. Bell, Atlanta, 1973-74, Armstrong, Allen et. al., Memphis, 1974, Threlkeld & Howard, Memphis, 1975-84, McDonnell, Dyer, Wyatt, Tarrant & Comps, Memphis, 1984-96; ptnr. Scroggs & Rogers, Collierville, Tenn., 1997—. Lt. USNR, 1965-68. Mem. Collierville C. of C., Collierville Rotary. Avocations: architecture, music. Probate, Estate planning, Contracts commercial. Office: Scroggs & Rogers 110 E Mulberry St Ste 200 Collierville TN 38017-2675

**ROGERS, HARVEY DELANO,** lawyer; b. Krosniewice, Poland, Jan. 2, 1946; s. Bernard and Rose (Zaltztrager) R.; m. Maria Cimitiere, Dec. 22, 1978; children: Daniel, Randall, Rachel, Amanda. BA, CCNY, 1968, MA, 1970; JD, U. Miami, 1974. Bar: Fla. 1975, U.S. Dist. Ct. (no. and so. dists.) Fla. 1975, U.S. Ct. Appeals (5th cir.) 1975, U.S. Ct. Appeals (11 cir.) 1981, Supreme Ct. Fla. 1975, U.S. Supreme Ct.1980. Sole practice Miami, Fla., 1974—; arbitrator Am. Arbitration, Miami, 1975—. Fellow Fla. Criminal Defense Attys.; mem. ABA, Lawyers Title, Fla. Trial Lawyers Assn., Phi Alpha Delta. Avocations: history, sports, fishing. General practice, Criminal, State civil litigation. Home: 6401 SW 123rd Ter Miami FL 33156-5560

**ROGERS, JAMES DEVITT,** judge; b. Mpls., May 5, 1929; s. Harold Neil and Dorothy (Devitt) R.; m. Leanna Morrison, Oct. 19, 1968. AB, Dartmouth Coll., 1951; JD, U. Minn., 1954. Bar: Minn. 1954, U.S. Supreme Ct. 1983. Assoc. Johnson & Sands, Mpls., 1956-60; sole practice Mpls., 1960-62; judge Mpls. Municipal and Dist. Ct., 1959-91; mem. faculty Nat. Judicial Coll. Bd. dirs. Mpls. chpt. Am. Red Cross, chmn. service to mil. families and vets. com.; bd. dirs. Minn. Safety Council, St. Paul, 1988-91. Served to sgt. U.S. Army, 1954-56. Mem. ABA (chmn. nat. conf. spl. ct. judge, spl. com. housing and urban devel. law, traffic ct. program com., chmn. criminal justice sect., jud. adminstrn. div.), Nat. Jud. Coll. (bd. dirs.), Nat. Christmas Tree Grower's Assn. (pres. 1976-78), Mpls. Athletic Club. Congregational. Office: 14110 Prince Pl Minnetonka MN 55345-3027

**ROGERS, JAMES STEVEN,** lawyer; b. Seattle, Sept. 18, 1947; s. Fred and Frances Ruth (Teitelbaum) R.; m. Theresa M. Rosellini; children: Zoey, Sabina. BS, U. Wash., 1969; JD, U. Ariz., 1972. Bar: Wash. 1973; cert. civil trial advocate. With Law Office of Lembhard G. Howell, Seattle, 1974-75, Wolfstone Panchot & Bloch, Seattle, 1975-78, Franco, Asia, Bensussen Coe & Finegold, Seattle, 1978-81, Crane, Stamper, Dunham, Drury & Rogers, Seattle, 1981-86, Law Offices of James S. Rogers, Seattle, 1987—. Fellow Internat. Acad. Trial Lawyers; mem. ATLA (bd. govs. 1993—), Am. Bd. Trial Advocates, Wash. State Trial Lawyers Assn. (pres. 1991-92), Attys. Info. Exch. Group (bd. dirs. 1991—), Western Trial Lawyers Assn. (officer 1993—). Product liability, Personal injury. Office: 705 2nd Ave Ste 1601 Seattle WA 98104-1711

**ROGERS, JAMES THOMAS,** lawyer; b. Denver, Oct. 3, 1941; s. John Thomas and Elizabeth (Milligan) R. JD, U. Wis., 1966. Bar: Wis. 1966, U.S. Tax Ct. 1976, U.S. Ct. Claims, 1975, U.S. Ct. Customs and Patent Appeals, 1975, U.S. Supreme Ct. 1973. Chmn., Madison (Wis.) Legal Aid Soc., 1965-66; dist. atty. Lincoln County (Wis.), 1967, 69-73; spl. dist. atty. pro tem Oneida County (Wis.), 1972, Price County (Wis.), 1972-76, Lincoln County (Wis.), 1976-84; spl. city atty. City of Wausau (Wis.), 1973, 74, 77; ptnr. Rogers & Bremer, Merrill, Wis., 1973-89; prin. Rogers Criminal Law Offices, Merrill, 1989—. bd. dirs. Merrill Fed. Savings & Loan Assn., 1990—, Home Supply Co-Op., Wausau, 1995—. Chmn. Judiciary Com., N.E. Crime Control Commn., 1971-72. Chmn., Lincoln County Republican Com., 1971-73; pub. defender bd. State of Wis., 1988—, 2d vice chmn., 1989-93, 1st vice chmn., 1993—. Bd. dirs. Wis. Judicare, 1990-92. Mem. State Bar Wis. (spl. com. on prosecutorial improvements 1983-89, spl. com. to rev. criminal sanctions 1987-88, conv. and entertainment com. 1989-93), Lincoln County Bar Assn. (pres. 1969-70), Wis. Dist. Attys. Assn. (life), ABA (liaison drunk driving com. of criminal justice sect., vice chmn. asset and investment mgmt. com. sec. econs. of law practice, marriage and cohabitation com. family law sect., def. svcs. commn. criminal law sect., liaison criminal justice sect.), Nat. Assn. Criminal Def. Lawyers (state and local def. bar liaison com., ad hoc subcom. on property of DNA evidence), Assn. Trial Lawyers Am. (constl. challenge com. 1988-92), Wis. Acad. Trial Lawyers (chmn. constl. challenge com. 1988-91), bd. dirs. 1985-91), Tex. Trial Lawyers Assn., N.Y. State Trial Lawyers Assn., Wis. Assn. Criminal Def. Lawyers (sec. 1986-87, pres.-elect 1987-88, pres. 1988-89, bd. dirs. 1986—, liaison to ABA criminal justice sect.), Wausau Club. Criminal. Home: PO Box 438 1408 E 8th St Merrill WI 54452-1537 Office: Rogers Criminal Law Offices PO Box 438 Merrill WI 54452-0438

**ROGERS, JANNEA SUZANNE,** lawyer; b. Mobile, Ala., Oct. 31, 1962; d. Jimmie Otto and Shelbie Jean (Stiener) R. BS, Spring Hill Coll., 1986; JD, Cumberland Sch. Law, 1989. Bar: Fla. 1989, U.S. Dist. Ct. (no. and so. dists.) Ala., U.S. Dist. Ct. (ctrl. and so. dists.) Fla. Assoc. Clark Scott & Sullivan, Mobile, Ala. Recipient Moot Ct. Scholarship Cumberland Scholarship Com., 1989, Am. Jurisprudence award, 1988. Mem. ABA, Assn. Trial Lawyers Am., Dade County Bar Assn., Fla. Bar, Ala. Bar. Republican. Baptist. Avocations: scuba diving, water skiing, photography. Federal civil litigation, State civil litigation, Criminal. Office: Clark Scott & Sullivan 56 Saint Joseph St # 10th Mobile AL 36602-3418

**ROGERS, JEAN GREGORY,** retired lawyer; b. Panama City, Fla., Dec. 15, 1934; d. William Green and Jean (Balkom) Gregory. BA in English, Agnes Scott Coll., Decatur, Ga., 1956; LLB, U. Md., Balt., 1962. Bar: Md. Ct. Appeals, 1963, U.S. Supreme Ct., 1968, U.S. Dist. Ct., Md., 1968, U.S. Ct. Appeals (4th cir.), 1969, U.S. Ct. Appeals (5th cir.), 1985, U.S. Ct. Appeals (10th cir.), 1988. Asst. county solicitor Office of County Solicitor Balt. County, Towson, Md., 1963-68; sole practitioner pvt. practice, Towson, Md., 1963-68; asst. U.S. atty. Office of U.S. Atty. Dept. Justice, Balt., 1968-73; asst. regional counsel Fed. Hwy. Adminstrn., Balt., 1973-75; regional counsel Fed. Hwy. Adminstrn., Fort Worth, Tex., 1975-96, ret., 1996; mem.. project com. SP20-6, Nat. Coop. Hwy. Rsch. Program Nat. Rsch. Coun., Transp. Rsch. Bd., Washington, 1986-96; mem., Group Coun. on Legal Resources, Transp. Rsch. Bd., Washington, 1979-82. Recipient Superior Achievement award for superior handling of complex litigation, Fed. Hwy. Adminstr., 1980. Mem. ABA. Presbyterian. Home: 2709 Whispering Trail Cir Arlington TX 76013-3129

**ROGERS, JON H.,** lawyer; b. Salt Lake City, Sept. 7, 1966; s. Howard B. and Venice M. Rogers; m. Leslie Ella Ballif, Oct. 5, 1994; children: Ian Brent, Alexandra Elizabeth. BA, U. Utah, 1989; JD, Vanderbilt U., 1992. Bar: Utah 1993, U.S. Dist Ct. Utah 1993. Assoc. Paul D. Colton, P.C., Layton, Utah, 1993-94; lawyer pvt. practice, Salt Lake City, 1994—; judge pro tem Third Circuit Ct. Small Claims Divsn., Salt Lake City, Utah, 1994-96, Third Dist. Ct., Small Claims Divsn., 1997—. Recipient Madelyn S. Silver Meml. scholarship U. Utah, Salt Lake City, 1988, scholarship Vanderbilt U. Sch. of Law, Nashville, Tenn., 1989-92. Mem. Nat. Assn. Consumer Attys., Comml. Law League of Am., Utah Trial Lawyers Assn. Mem. LDS Ch. Avocations: martial arts, poetry, langs., reading. Consumer commercial, Contracts commercial, General civil litigation. Office: Jon H Rogers Atty Northgate Bus Ctr 803 N 300 W Ste N144 Salt Lake City UT 84103-1414

**ROGERS, JUDITH M.,** judge; b. Newark, Jan. 14, 1932; d. Meyer and Florence; m. Arthur Rogers, Aug. 4, 1951 (dec. Mar. 1988); children: Debra Davis, Steven, Alison; m. Howard J. Weiss, Apr. 18, 1997. BS in Bus. Adminstrn., U. Fla., 1952; JD, Ind. U., 1961. Pvt. practice lawyer North Little Rock, Ark., 1962-77; juvenile ct. judge Pulaski County Juvenile Justice Ctr., Little Rock, 1977-82; chancery and probate judge Little Rock, 1983-88; judge Ark. Ct. Appeals, Little Rock, 1989—; mem. com. on child support Ark. Supreme Ct., Little Rock; pres. Ark. Juvenile Judges Assn., Little Rock; chmn. Nat. Coun. Juvenile and Family Judges Com. on Abuse and Neglect, Reno, Nev.; spkr. in field. Sec., mem. Dem. Nat. Conv., Chgo., 1968; nat. v.p. Young Dems. Club Am., Washington, 1970; Ark. rep. steering com. Nat. Women's Polit. Caucus, Washington, 1980; bd. dirs. United Way, Salvation Army. Named Gail Pettus Pontz Outstanding Female Atty., U. Ark. Sch. Law, Little Rock, 1987, one of Ark. Top 100 Women, Ark. Bus. Pub. Group, Little Rock, 1996, 97, 98; First woman in Ark. elected to Appellate Ct., Little Rock, 1989. Fellow Ark. Bar Assn. (mem. revision com. Handbook of Domestic Relations, mem. appellate practice com. 1998); mem. Ark. Women's Leadership Forum, Ark. Jud. Coun. (fed. ct. liason com. 1998), Beta Gamma Sigma. Methodist. Avocations: swimming, reading, bridge, movies. Office: Ark Ct Appeals 625 Marshall St Ste 2100 Little Rock AR 72201-1075

**ROGERS, JUDITH W.,** federal judge; b. 1939. AB cum laude, Radcliffe Coll., 1961; LLB, Harvard U., 1964; LLM, U. Va., 1988; LLD (hon.), D.C. Sch. Law, 1992. Bar: D.C. 1965. Law clk. Juvenile Ct. D.C., 1964-65; asst. U.S. atty. D.C., 1965-68; trial atty. San Francisco Neighborhood Legal Assistance Found., 1968-69; atty. assoc. atty. gen.'s office U.S. Dept. Justice, 1969-71, atty. criminal divsn., 1969-71; gen. counsel Congl. Commn. on Organization of D.C. Govt., 1971-72; coordinator legis. program Office of Dep. Mayor D.C., 1972-74, spl. asst. to mayor for legis., 1974-79, corp. counsel, 1979-83; assoc. judge D.C. Ct. Appeals, 1983-88, chief judge, 1988-94; cir. judge U.S. Ct. Appeals-D.C. Cir., 1994—; mem. D.C. Law Revision Commn., 1979-83; mem. grievance com. U.S. Dist. Ct. D.C., 1982-83; mem. exec. com. Conf. Chief Justices, 1993-94. Bd. dirs. Wider Opportunities for Women, 1972-74; mem. vis. com. Harvard U. Sch. Law, 1984-90; trustee Radcliffe Coll., 1982-88. Recipient citation for work on D.C. Self-Govt. Act, 1973, Disting. Pub. Svc. award D.C. Govt., 1983, award Nat. Bar Assn., 1989; named Woman Lawyer of Yr., Women's Bar Assn. D.C., 1990. Fellow ABA; mem. D.C. Bar, Nat. Assn. Women Judges, Conf. Chief Justices (bd. dirs. 1988-94), Am. Law Inst., Phi Beta Kappa. Office: US Ct Appeals 333 Constitution Ave NW Washington DC 20001-2866*

**ROGERS, L. LAWTON, III,** lawyer; b. Mullins, S.C., Oct. 14, 1936; s. Leslie Lawton Jr. and Anne (Stackhouse) R.; m. Mary H. Rogers, May 29, 1959; children: Lyndsey R., L. Lawton IV. BSEE, U. S.C., 1959; JD, Georgetown U., 1967; LLM, George Washington U., 1972. Bar: Va., D.C., U.S. Ct. Appeals (2d, 3d, 4th, 5th, 6th, 7th, 8th, 9th, 11th, fed. and D.C. cirs.), U.S. Patent Office, U.S. Supreme Ct. Ptnr. Rogers & Kileen, Alexandria, Va., 1980—. Lt. (j.g.) USN, 1959-62. Mem. Va. Bar Assn. D.C. Bar Assn., Internat. Trademark Assn., Intellectual Property Lawyers Assn. Intellectual property, General civil litigation. Office: Rogers & Killeen 510 King St Alexandria VA 22314-3132

**ROGERS, LEE JASPER,** lawyer; b. Fort Monmouth, N.J., May 6, 1955; s. Peter and Ethel Mae (Williams) R.; m. Vanessa Walisha Yarbrough, Apr. 18, 1981 (div. Oct. 1988); 1 child, Stephanie Alexandria. Student, Drew U., 1975, Monmouth Coll., 1975; BA in History, Hampton Inst., 1977; JD, Howard U., 1980. Pvt. practice Red Bank, N.J., 1981-91, 95—; asst. dep. pub. defender Ocean County region, Toms River, N.J., 1991-92; mortgage loan officer Allied Fin. Svcs., Neptune, N.J., 1992-93, Mortgage Money Mart, Edison, N.J., 1993-94, Residential First, Inc., Shrewsbury, N.J., 1994-95, Fairmont Funding, Lakewood, N.J., 1995-96; pvt. practice Red Bank, N.J., 1995—; vol. counsel Pro Bono Legal Svcs., Red Bank, N.J., 1982-91; pres., chmn. bd. Jay-Mar Entertainment Enterprises, Inc., 1986—; mem. vocal group, Pizazz, 1996—. Author numerous poems; vocal singing group Pizazz, 1991-94, 96—, Nu Eara, 1992; vocalist Piyayz, 1996—. Pres., bd. dirs. Ct. Basie Learning Ctr., Red Bank, N.J.; chmn. Red Bank Republican Club, 1994-95. Mem. ABA, NAACP (exec. com. Red Bank chpt. 1983-88), Assn. Trial Lawyers Am., Elks (sec. ho. com. Bates lodge #220 1988-90, loyal knight 1990-91, esteemed loyal knight 1993-94, chmn. by-laws com. 1993-94, mem. house com.). Baptist. Real property, Entertainment, Banking. Home: 298 Shrewsbury Ave Apt 3 Red Bank NJ 07701-1319 *Mastery is achieved through the development of the spirit, and the resulting obtainment of bliss. We should all seek to be at one within ourselves and with the world around us. To do this, we must walk with God. Only then can we find true happiness! After all, if God is with us...what man can be against us.*

**ROGERS, LEONARD DAVID,** lawyer; b. Norton, Va., Oct. 13, 1962; s. Jack D. and Marylou (Sturgill) R.; m. Donna Geneva Salyers, Oct. 11, 1991. BA in History, U. Va., Wise, 1985; JD, U. Tenn., 1988. Bar: Va. 1988, U.S. Dist. Ct. (we. dist.) Va. 1989, U.S. Dist. Ct. (we. dist.) Va. 1989, U.S. Ct. Appeals (4th cir.) 1989, U.S. Bankruptcy Ct. 1989. Assoc. Mullins, Thomason & Harris, Norton, 1988-90; ptnr. Cline, Adkins, Cline & Rogers, Norton, 1990-95; pvt. practice, 1996—. Mem. Forward Wise County, 1989. Mem. ABA, Va. Bar Assn., Va. State Bar, Va. Trial Lawyers Assn., Wise County C. of C. Avocations: golf, mountain biking, travel. Pension, profit-sharing, and employee benefits, Real property, General civil litigation. Office: Leonard D Rogers PC PO Box 1097 Wise VA 24293-1097

**ROGERS, RANDALL LEE,** judge; b. Ft. Worth, May 2, 1949; s. Raymond Lee and Shirley G. R.; m. Lois Ruth Jackson; children: Angelique, Randall Jr., Rebel, Niki, Scott. BBA in Internat. Econs., Tex. Tech. U., 1971, JD, 1974. Bar: Tex. 1974, U.S. Dist. Ct. (ea. dist.) Tex., U.S. Ct. Appeals (5th and 11th cirs.). Assoc. Crumley, Murphy, Shrull, Ft. Worth, 1974-76; felony prosecutor McLennan County Dist. Atty., Waco, Tex., 1976-83, Smith County Dist. Atty., Tyler, Tex., 1983-87; judge Smith County Ct., Tyler, 1987, Smith County Ct. Law 2, Tyler, 1987—; instr. advanced juvenile law Jud. Coll. Tex., Austin, 1996. Mem. city coun. City of Forest Hill, Tex., 1975-76; treas. Youth Alternatives, Smith County, Tyler, Tex., 1990-97. Mem. Internat. Order Odd Fellows (noble, grand 1995). Republican. Methodist. Avocation: camping. Office: Smith County Ct Law 2 Smith County Courthouse Tyler TX 75702

**ROGERS, RICHARD DEAN,** federal judge; b. Oberlin, Kans., Dec. 29, 1921; s. William Clark and Evelyn May (Christian) R.; m. Helen Elizabeth Stewart, June 6, 1947; children—Letitia Ann, Cappi Christian, Richard Kurt. B.S., Kans. State U., 1943; J.D., Kans. U., 1947. Bar: Kans. 1947. Ptnr. firm Springer and Rogers (Attys.), Manhattan, Kans., 1947-58; instr. bus. law Kans. State U., 1948-52; partner firm Rogers, Stites & Hill, Manhattan, 1959-75; gen. counsel Kans. Farm Bur. & Service Cos., Manhattan, 1960-75; judge U.S. Dist. Ct., Topeka, Kans., 1975—. City commr., Manhattan, 1950-52, 60-64, mayor, 1952, 64, county atty., Riley County, Kans., 1954-58, state rep., 1964-68, state senator, 1968-75; pres. Kans. Senate, 1975. Served with USAAF, 1943-45. Decorated Air medal, Dfc. Mem. Kans., Am. bar assns., Beta Theta Pi. Republican. Presbyterian. Club: Masons. Office: US Dist Ct 444 SE Quincy St Topeka KS 66683

**ROGERS, RICHARD MICHAEL,** judge; b. Lorain, Ohio, Dec. 8, 1944; s. Paul M. and Lillie (Morris) R.; m. Sophia Lydia Wagner, Dec. 23, 1967; children: L. Danielle, David K., Marisa D., Matthew D. BA, Ohio No. U., 1966, JD, 1972. Bar: Ohio 1972, U.S. Dist. Ct. (no. dist.) Ohio 1973. Assoc. Martin, Hall & Rogers, Marion, Ohio, 1972-76; ptnr. Rogers & Rogers, Marion, 1976-81; asst. law dir., police prosecutor City of Marion, 1973-74; pub. defender, 1975; asst. county prosecutor Marion County, 1976-81; village solicitor La Rue, Ohio, 1976-81; judge Marion Mcpl. Ct., 1982-88, Common Pleas Ct., 1989—; mem. traffic rules rev. commn. Ohio Supreme Ct., 1989—; judge dist. competition Nat. Bicentennial Competition on Constitution and Bill of Rights, 1988, judge state competition, 1988—, judge nat. competition, 1989, 93, 95; instr. faculty Ohio Jud. Coll. Mem. Marion Active 20/40 Svc. Club, 1973-84, treas., 1976-80, bd. dirs., 1976-84, pres., 1980-81; chmn. bd. dirs., pres., co-founder Marion Area Driver Re-edn. Project, 1974-81; pres. Big Bros./Big Sisters Marion County, 1986-87, bd. dirs., 1984-88; mem. sch. bd. St. Mary's Elem. Sch., 1985-88, v.p., 1986, bd. dirs. Marion Cath. High Sch. Endowment Fund, 1986—, v.p., 1991—; mem. Marion Cath. Jr./Sr. High Sch. Bd., 1988-94, pres., 1990-91; mem. fellow in criminal justice steering com. Marion campus Ohio State U., 1996—; mem. paralegal adv. com. Marion Tech. Coll., 1994-96; trustee Ohio State Bar Found., 1997—. Served with U.S. Army, 1968-69. Mem. Ohio State Bar Assn. (modern ct. com. 1982-85, jud. adminstrn. and legal reform com. 1982-93, mem. legis. subcom. 1989-93, mem. coun. dels. 1991-93, mem. law and procedure com. 1993-95, bd. govs. 1996-99, chair govt. affairs com. 1998-99), Marion County Bar Assn. (pres. 1985-86), Ohio Jud. Conf. (gen. adminstrn. 1984-85, vice chair family matters video com. 1991—, chmn. subcom. legal matters video, civil law and procedure com. 1991-95, editl. bd. Ohio Jury Instrn. 1995—), Ohio Bar Coll., Marion County Law Libr. Assn. (trustee 1982—, pres. 1991-93), Ohio Common Pleas Judges Assn., Delta Theta Phi, Sigma Pi. Republican. Methodist. Avocations: golf, scuba diving. Home: 310 Edgefield Blvd Marion OH 43302-5802 Office: Common Pleas Ct Marion County Courthouse 100 N Main St Marion OH 43302-3030 *Notable cases include: Hines vs. Thermal-Gard of Ohio, Inc., 1998, applicability of home solicitation sales acts.*

**ROGERS, THEODORE OTTO, JR.,** lawyer; b. West Chester, Pa., Nov. 17, 1953; s. Theodore Otto and Gladys (Bond) R.; m. Hope Tyler Scott, Nov. 7, 1981; children: Helen Elliot, Theodore Scott, Robert Montgomery Bond. AB magna cum laude, Harvard U., 1976, JD cum laude, 1979. Bar: N.Y. 1980, U.S Ct. Appeals (2nd cir.) 1984, U.S. Dist. Ct. (so. and ea. dists.) N.Y. 1980, D.C. 1981, U.S. Ct. Claims, 1982, U.S. Supreme Ct. 1983, U.S. Ct. Appeals (6th and 10th cirs.) 1983, U.S. Ct. Appeals (1st cir.) 1984, U.S. Ct. Appeals (fed. cir.) 1986. From assoc. to ptnr. Sullivan & Cromwell, N.Y.C., 1979—. Co-author: Employment Litigation in New York, 1996. Mem. U.S. Presdl. Transition Team, 1980. Mem. N.Y. State Bar Assn. (co-chair individual rights and responsibilities com. labor and employment law sect.), Assn. of Bar of City of N.Y. (labor and employment law). Republican. Labor, Probate, General civil litigation. Home: 535 E 86th St New York NY 10028-7533 Office: Sullivan & Cromwell 125 Broad St Fl 28 New York NY 10004-2489

**ROGERS, THOMAS SYDNEY,** communications executive; b. New Rochelle, N.Y., Aug. 19, 1954; s. Sydney Michael Rogers Jr. and Alice (Meier) Steinhardt; m. Sylvia Texon, Oct. 9, 1983; children: Robert Samuel, Jessica Lauren, Jason Benjamin. BA, Wesleyan U., 1975; JD, Columbia U., 1979. Bar: N.Y. 1980, U.S. Dist. Ct. (so. and ea. dists.) N.Y. 1980, U.S. Ct. Appeals (D.C. cir.) 1981. Legis. aide to Congressman Richard Ottinger U.S. Ho. Reps., Washington, 1975-76, sr. counsel subcom. telecommunications, 1981-86; assoc. Lord, Day & Lord, N.Y.C., 1979-81; v.p. policy planning and bus. devel. Nat. Broadcasting Co., Inc., N.Y.C., 1987-88; pres. NBC Cable, 1988-89, NBC Cable & Bus. Devel., 1989—; exec. v.p. NBC, N.Y.C., 1992—; vice chmn. NBC Internet, 1999—; pres., CEO internat. coun. Nat. Acad. TV Arts and Scis., 1994-97, chmn., 1998—; co-chmn., bd. dirs. Arts and Entertainment Networks, Inc.; bd. dirs. Rainbow Programming, Inc., Save the Children Found.; lectr. in field. Named one of Outstanding Young Men in Am., 1985. Mem. N.Y. State Bar Assn., Internat. Radio and TV Soc. Office: NBC Inc 30 Rockefeller Plz Rm 5229 New York NY 10112-0002

**ROGERS, WILLIAM JOHN,** lawyer; b. Phila., Aug. 17, 1950; s. William John and Jean Marie (Dolan) R.; m. Mary K. Neff, July 29, 1978; children: Colin, Brian, Kevin. Diploma, Fairfield U., 1972; JD, Northwestern U., Chgo., 1975. Assoc. Wildman, Harrold, Allen & Dixon, Chgo., 1975-81, ptnr., 1981-90; ptnr. Bollinger, Ruberry & Garvey, Chgo., 1991—. Article editor: Jour. of Criminal Law and Criminology, Northwestern U., 1973-75. Fellow Am. Coll. Trial Lawyers, Am. Bd. Trial Advs., Soc. Trial Lawyers/Ill. Product liability, Personal injury, Construction. Home: 2229 Beechwood Ave Wilmette IL 60091-1507 Office: Bollinger Ruberry & Garvey 500 W Madison St Chicago IL 60661-2511

**ROGERS, WILLIAM PIERCE,** lawyer; b. Norfolk, N.Y., June 23, 1913; s. Harrison Alexander and Myra (Beswick) R.; m. Adele Langston, June 27, 1936; children: Dale, Anthony Wood, Jeffrey Langston, Douglas Langston. AB, Colgate U., 1934; LLB, Cornell, 1937. Bar: N.Y. 1937, D.C. 1950. Asst. dist. atty. N.Y. County, 1938-42, 46-47; chief counsel U.S. Senate War Investigating Com., 1947, chief counsel Truman Com., 1947-48; chief counsel U.S. Senate Investigations Sub-Com. Exec. Expenditures Com., 1948-50; mem. firm Dwight, Royall, Harris, Koegel & Caskey, N.Y.C. and Washington, 1950-53; dep. atty. gen. U.S., 1953-57, U.S. atty. gen., 1957-61; ptnr. firm Royall, Koegel, Rogers & Wells, 1961-69; U.S. sec. state, 1969-73; now sr. partner firm Rogers & Wells LLP, N.Y.C. and Washington., 1973—; U.S. rep. 20th Gen. Assembly, UN, 1967, UN Ad Hoc Com. on South Africa, 1967; mem. Pres.'s Commn. Law Enforcement and Adminstrn., 1965-67; appt. chmn. Presdl. Commn. to Investigate Space Shuttle Challenger Accident, 1986. Served to lt. comdr. USN, 1942-46. Recipient Medal of Freedom, 1973. Fellow Am. Bar Found.; mem. Bar Assn. City N.Y., Am., N.Y. State, Washington bar assns., Am. Law Inst., Burning Tree Club (Bethesda, Md.), Country Club (Bethesda), Sky Club (N.Y.C.), Racquet and Tennis Club (N.Y.C.), Chevy Chase (Md.), Metropolitan Club (Washington), Alibi Club (Washington), Links, Order of Coif, Sigma Chi, Delta Theta Phi. Office: Rogers & Wells LLP 200 Park Ave Fl 8E New York NY 10166-0800 also: Rogers & Wells LLP 607 14th St NW Washington DC 20005-2000

**ROGOFF, JEFFREY SCOTT,** lawyer; b. Manhasset, N.Y., May 11, 1968; s. Arnold Steven and Paula Rogoff. BA, Binghamton U., 1990; JD, NYU, 1993. Bar: N.J. 1993, U.S. Dist. Ct. N.J. 1993, U.S. Ct. Appeals (3d cir.) 1998, U.S. Dist. Ct. (so. and ea. dists.) N.Y. 1994. Law clk. Magistrate Judge Michael Dolinger U.S. Dist. Ct. (so. dist.) N.Y., N.Y.C., 1993-94; assoc. Kronish, Lieb, Weiner & Hellman, N.Y.C., 1994-95, Schindel, Farman & Lipsius LLP, N.Y.C., 1995—. Mem. Phi Beta Kappa. Jewish. General civil litigation, Insurance, Appellate. Home: 11 Furman Dr Wayne NJ 07470-5304 Office: Schindel Farman & Lipsius LLP 225 W 34th St New York NY 10122-0049

**ROHAN, BRIAN PATRICK,** lawyer; b. Bklyn., July 1, 1964; s. John Eamon and Janet Dee (Trebian) R.; m. Lori Lanahan, Aug. 18, 1990; children: Connor James, Taylor Kathleen. BS, SUNY, Plattsburgh, 1986; MBA, Union Coll., 1990; JD, Union U., 1990. Bar: N.Y. 1991, Mass. 1991, U.S. Dist. Ct. (no. dist.) N.Y. 1991. Atty. Waite & Assocs., P.C., Albany, N.Y., 1990-96; pvt. practice Brian P. Rohan Law Offices, Albany, 1996-99; atty. Dreyer Boyajian LLP, Albany, 1999—. Bd. dirs. Catholic Family & Cmty. Svcs., Albany, 1991-94. Mem. ATLA, N.Y. State Bar Assn., Albany County Bar Assn. General civil litigation, General corporate, Bankruptcy. Office: Dreyer Boyajian LLP 75 Columbia St Albany NY 12210

**ROHDE, BRUCE C.,** food company executive, lawyer; b. Sidney, Nebr., Dec. 17, 1948. BS, BA, Creighton U., 1971, JD cum laude, 1973. Bar: Nebr. 1974, U.S. Dist. Ct. Nebr. 1974, U.S. Tax Ct. 1975, U.S. Ct. Appeals (8th cir.) 1976, U.S. Ct. Appeals (5th cir.) 1979, U.S. Supreme Ct. 1980, U.S. Claims Ct. 1981, U.S. Ct. Appeals (D.C. cir.) 1982. Lawyer McGrath, North, Mullin & Kratz, Omaha, to 1996; pres., CEO Conagra Inc., Omaha, 1996—. Mem. ABA (corp., banking and bus law sect., taxation sect., antitrust law sect., litigation sect.), Assn. Trial Lawyers Am., Nebr. Assn. Trial Lawyers, Nebr. State Bar Assn., Nebr. Soc. CPAs, Omaha Bar Assn., Beta Gamma Sigma, Beta Alpha Psi. Address: ConAgra Inc 1 Central Park Plz Ste 1100 Omaha NE 68102-1680

**ROHLFING, FREDERICK W.,** lawyer; b. Honolulu, July 21, 1956; s. Frederick W. and Joah H. (Halford) R.; m. Deon K. Tsuya, July 17, 1982; children: Renate, Frederick, Markus, Marissa. BA, Dartmouth Coll., 1978; JD, U. Chgo., 1983. Bar: Hawaii. Assoc. Torkildsson Katz Jossen & Loden, Honolulu, 1983-84, La offices of James M. Sattler, Honolulu, 1985-90; assoc. Stubengerg & Durrett, Honolulu, 1990-93, ptnr., 1993-95; prin. Frederick, Rohlfing & Assoc., Honolulu, 1995-97; ptnr. Rohlfing & Stone, Honolulu, 1997—; chief minority atty. Hawaii Ho. of Reps., Honolulu, 1985, Hawaii State Senate, Honolulu, 1995. Trustee Hawaii Mission Children's Soc., Honolulu, 1997—; mem. adv. bd. LDS Social Svcs., Honolulu, 1997—. Mem. Hawaii State Bar Assn. Mem. LDS Ch. Office: Rohlfing & Stone Attys at Law 737 Bishop St Ste 1800 Honolulu HI 96813-3202

**ROHLFING, FREDERICK WILLIAM,** lawyer, travel executive, political consultant, retired judge; b. Honolulu, Nov. 2, 1928; s. Romayne Raymond and Kathryn (Coe) R.; m. Joan Halford, July 15, 1952 (div. Sept. 1982); children: Frederick W., Karl A., Brad (dec.); m. Patricia Ann Santos, Aug. 23, 1983. BA, Yale U., 1950; JD, George Washington U., 1955. Bar: Hawaii 1955, Am. Samoa 1978. Assoc. Moore, Torkildson & Rice, Honolulu, 1955-60; ptnr. Rohlfing, Nakamura & Low, Honolulu, 1963-68, Hughes, Steiner & Rohlfing, Honolulu, 1968-71, Rohlfing, Smith & Coates, Honolulu, 1981-84; sole practice Honolulu, 1960-63, 71-81, Maui County, 1988—; dep. corp. counsel County of Maui, Wailuku, Hawaii, 1984-87, corp. counsel, 1987-88; land and legal counsel Maui Open Space Trust, 1992-97, also bd. dirs.; pres. Rohlfing Cons. & Travel, Inc., 1985—; polit. cons., 1996, 98; magistrate judge U.S. Dist. Ct. Hawaii, 1991-96. Mem. Hawaii Ho. Reps., 1959-65, 80-84; Hawaii State Senate, 1966-75; U.S. alt. rep. So. Pacific Commn., Noumea, New Caledonia, 1975-77, 1982-84. Capt. USNR, 1951-87. Mem. Hawaii Bar Assn., Maui Country Club, Fed. Magistrate Judges Assn., Naval Intelligence Profls. Avocations: ocean swimming, golf. Land use and zoning (including planning), Legislative, Administrative and regulatory. Home and Office: RR 1 Box 398 Kekaulike Ave Kula HI 96790

**ROHNER, RALPH JOHN,** lawyer, educator, university dean; b. East Orange, N.J., Aug. 10, 1938. A.B., Cath. U. Am., 1960, J.D., 1963. Bar: Md. 1964. Teaching fellow Stanford (Calif.) U., 1963-64; atty. pub. health div. HEW, 1964-65; prof. law Cath. U. Am. Sch. Law, Washington, 1965—, acting dean, 1968-69, assoc. dean, 1969-71, dean, 1987-95; staff counsel consumer affairs subcom. U.S. Senate Banking Com., 1975-76; cons. Fed. Res. Bd., 1976-83, chmn. consumer adv. council, 1981; cons. FDIC, 1978-80; spl. counsel Consumer Bankers Assn., 1984—; cons. U.S. Regulatory Coun., 1979-80. Co-author: Consumer Law: Cases and Materials, 1979, 2d edit., 1991; co-author, editor The Law of Truth in Lending, 1984. Bd. dirs. Migrant Legal Action Program, Inc., Washington, Automobile Owners Action Coun., Washington, Credit Rsch. Ctr., Georgetown U., Am. Fin. Svcs. Assn. Edn. Found. Conf. on Consumer Fin. Law. Mem. ABA, Am. Law Inst., Coll. of Consumer Fin. Svcs. Lawyers. Home: 10909 Forestgate Pl Glenn Dale MD 20769-2047 Office: Cath U Sch Law 620 Michigan Ave NE Washington DC 20064-0001 *We learn from those we teach, we are inspired to write by those who read, and we should serve as examples to those who aspire.*

**ROHR, RICHARD DAVID,** lawyer; b. Toledo, Ohio, Aug. 31, 1926; s. Lewis Walter and Marie Janet (Pilliod) R.; m. Ann Casey, Aug. 25, 1951; children: Martha, Elizabeth, Matthew, Sarah, Margaret, Thomas. BA magna cum laude, Harvard U., 1950; JD, U. Mich., 1953. Bar: Mich. 1954, U.S. Dist. Ct. (so. dist.) Mich. 1954, U.S. Ct. Appeals (6th cir.) 1960, U.S. Supreme Ct. 1961. Assoc. Bodman, Longley & Dahling, L.L.P., Detroit, 1954-58, ptnr., 1958-75, mng. ptnr., 1975—; adj. prof. U. Mich., Ann Arbor, 1976-82. With U.S. Army, 1945-46. Mem. ABA, Detroit Bar Assn., Detroit Bar Assn. Found. (trustee, pres.), Mich. Bar Assn., Renaissance Club, Detroit Athletic Club, Order of Coif, Phi Beta Kappa. Roman Catholic. Banking, Finance, General corporate. Home: 441 Rivard Blvd Grosse Pointe MI 48230-1627 Office: Bodman Longley Dahling LLP 100 Renaissance Ctr Ste 34 Detroit MI 48243-1001

**ROHRER, GEORGE JOHN,** retired lawyer; b. Elmira, N.Y., Oct. 24, 1931; s. George J. and Lois (Hess) R.; m. Martha M. Jacobs, Jan. 6, 1952; children: Jacquelyn D. Berbusse, Michael A., John S. JD with distinction, Pacific Coast U., 1967. Bar: Calif. 1969, U.S. Dist. Ct. (ctrl. dist.) 1969. Incentive dir. Blue Chip Stamp Co., L.A., 1963-69; gen. ptnr. Songer, Leavell Rohrer, Bellflower, Calif., 1969-80; sr. ptnr. Rohrer & Holtz, Anaheim, Calif., 1980-94; ret., 1994; panel atty. Calif. Assn. of Realtors/State, Hotline, Calif. 1977—; Founder/Dir. Midcities Nat. Bank, Bellflower, 1981-90; trustee S.E. area Bar Assn., Norwalk, Calif., 1974-75. Pres. Bellflower Kiwanis Club, 1972-73; dir. Los Cerritos Y.M.C.A., Bellflower, 1977-78; vol. counsel Am. Radio Relay League, 1987-92. Mem. Orange County Bar Assn., Los Angeles County Bar Assn., Orange County Amicus (pro bono), Bellflower C. of C. (pres. 1975-76), Masons, Shriners. Republican. Avocations: amature radio, fishing, travel. Real property, Estate planning, Banking.

**ROHRER, REED BEAVER,** lawyer; b. Langley AFB, Va., June 15, 1954; s. Richard L. and Elaine (Beaver) R.; m. Penny J. Pylant, June 25, 1977; children: Christopher S., Jennifer R. BBA, U. Hawaii, 1977; JD, Pepperdine U., 1980; LLM in Taxation, U. San Diego, 1981. Bar: Hawaii 1981, U.S. Dist. Ct. Hawaii 1981, U.S. Tax Ct. 1981. Tax specialist Grant Thorton (Alexander Grant), Honolulu, 1981-83; assoc. Oliver, Cuskaden & Lee, Honolulu, 1983-85; corp. counsel Bishop Trust Co. Ltd., Honolulu, 1985-89; v.p., corp. counsel Wall St. Fin. Corp., Irvine, Calif., 1989-92; prin. Law Firm of Reed B. Rohrer, Honolulu, 1992-94; ptnr. Rottenger & Rohrer, Honolulu, 1994—; bd. dirs. Rohrer Investment Corp., Coz U.S.A., Inc., Pacific Mktg. & Investments, Inc.; speaker in field. Author: (with others) Wills and Trusts Formbook, 1987; contbr. articles to profl. jours. Mem. ABA, Hawaii Bar Assn. (chmn. tax sect. 1988, estate and gift tax com.). Republican. Avocations: flying, surfing, diving, sailing. General corporate, Probate, Pension, profit-sharing, and employee benefits. Home: 1433 Ohialoke St Honolulu HI 96821-1411 Office: Rottenger & Rohrer 841 Bishop St Ste 1710 Honolulu HI 96813-3916 also: 733 Bishop St Unit 19 Honolulu HI 96813-4019 also: 2-17-55 Akasaka, Minato-Ku, Tokyo 107, Japan

**ROHRMAN, DOUGLASS FREDERICK,** lawyer; b. Chgo., Aug. 10, 1941; s. Frederick Alvin and Velma Elizabeth (Birdwell) R.; m. Susan Vitullo; children: Kathryn Anne, Elizabeth Clelia, Alessandra Claire. AB, Duke U., 1963; JD, Northwestern U., 1966. Bar: Ill. 1966. Legal coord. Nat. Communicable Disease Center, Altanta, 1966-68; assoc. Keck, Mahin & Cate, Chgo., 1968-73, ptnr., 1973—, ptnr. Lord, Bissell and Brook, Chgo.; exec. v.p., dir. Kerogen Oil Co., 1967—; chmn. bd. visitors Nicholas Sch. of Environment Duke U., 1993—. Co-author: Commercial Liability Risk Management and Insurance, 2 vols., 1978, 86, Lenders Guide to Environmental Law: Risk and Liability, 1993; contbr. articles on law to profl. jours. Vice chmn., commr. Ill. Food and Drug Commn., 1970-72. Served as lt. USPHS, 1966-68. Mem. ABA, Chgo. Bar Assn. (chmn. com. on food and drug law 1972-73), 7th Circuit Bar Assn., Environ. Law Inst., Am. Soc. Law and Medicine, Selden Soc., Duke U. Alumni Assn., William Preston Few Assn. (mem. pres. coun.), Legal Club, Mich. Shores Club, Kenilworth Club, Wigmore Club. Democrat. Episcopalian. Environmental, Contracts commercial, Product liability. Home: 520 Brier St Kenilworth IL 60043-1064 Office: Lord Bissell & Brook 115 S La Salle St Ste 3200 Chicago IL 60603-3972

**ROLAND, RAYMOND WILLIAM,** lawyer, mediator, arbitrator; b. Ocala, Fla., Jan. 3, 1947; s. Raymond W. and Hazel (Dunn) R.; m. Jane Allen, Dec. 28, 1968; children: John Allen, Jason William. BA, Fla. State U., 1969, JD, 1972. Bar: Fla. 1972, U.S. Dist. Ct. (no. dist.) Fla. 1973, U.S. Dist. Ct. (mid. dist.) Fla. 1985, U.S. Ct. Appeals (5th cir.) 1974, U.S. Ct. Appeals (11th cir.) 1983, U.S. Supreme Ct. 1985; cert. civil trial lawyer; cert. cir. ct. mediator. Assoc. Keen, O'Kelley & Spitz, Tallahassee, 1972-74, ptnr., 1974-77; ptnr., v.p. McConnaughhay, Roland, Maida & Cherr, P.A., Tallahassee, 1978-97; owner, mediator Roland Mediation Svcs.; mem. Fla. Acad. of Profl. Mediators, Inc. Bd. dirs. So. Scholarship Found., Tallahassee, 1985-89, 98—, v.p. 1989. Mem. Internat. Assn. Def. Coun., Def. Rsch. Inst., Fla. Bar (mem. Selection and Tenure com.), Tallahassee Bar Assn. (treas. 1979), Kiwanis (life, lt. gov. 1984-85), Capital City Kiwanis Club (Kiwanian of Yr. 1978, pres. 1979), Fla. Kiwanis Found. (life fellow), Fla. Bapt. Theol. Coll. (bd. visitors). Republican. Baptist. Avocations: reading, hiking, camping, golf. General practice, Insurance, Personal injury. Home: 1179 Ox Bottom Rd Tallahassee FL 32312-3519

**ROLES, FORREST HANSBURY,** lawyer; b. Balt., Aug. 19, 1942; s. Forrest and Agnes (Campbell) R.; m. Emily Lynn McPhail, Feb. 25, 1967; children: Margaret Jean, Elizabeth Jane. BA, Davidson Coll., 1964; LLB, W.Va. U., 1967. Bar: U.S. Dist. Ct. (so. dist.) W.Va. 1967, U.S. Ct. Appelas (4th cir.) 1971, U.S. Supreme Ct. 1978. Assoc. Jackson & Kelley, Charleston, W.Va., 1967-72, ptnr., 1972-82; ptnr. Smith, Heenan & Althen, Charleston, 1983-97, Hennan, Althen & Roles, Charleston, 1997—. Bd. dirs. Concord Coll. Found., 1996—, Kanawha County Pub. Defender, Charleston, 1986—. Named among Best Lawyers in Am. Woodward/White, Inc., 1995-98. Republican. Labor. Home: 904 Bird Rd Charleston WV 25314-1401 Office: Box 2549 1380 1 Valley Sq Charleston WV 25329

**ROLFE, JOHN L.,** lawyer; b. Washington, Jan. 30, 1944. BS in Econs., U. Pa., 1966, JD, 1969; LLM in Taxation, Temple U., 1984. Bar: Pa. 1970, U.S. Dist. Ct. (ea. dist.) Pa. 1970, U.S. Ct. Appeals (4th cir.) 1970, U.S. Ct. Appeals (3d cir.) 1976, N.Y. 1977, U.S. Dist. Ct. (no. dist.) N.Y. 1977, U.S. Supreme Ct. 1977, U.S. Tax Ct. 1984, U.S. Claims Ct. 1984. Law clk. U.S. Ct. Appeals for 4th Cir., Richmond, Va., 1969-71; asst. defender Phila. Pub. Defender's Office, Phila., 1971-72; asst. atty. gen. Pa. Crime Commn., St. Davids, 1972-74; pvt. practice, Devon, Pa., 1974-92; shareholder, seminar presenter Rolfe & Rosenbaum, P.C., Devon, Pa., 1992—. Author: Affirmations Book for Sharing, 1990. Sec. St. Lawrence County Environ. Mgmt. Coun., Canton, N.Y., 1979-80. Avocations: badminton, karate, writing movie scripts. Estate planning, Estate taxation, Probate. Office: Rolf & Rosenbaum PC 988 Jefferies Bridge Rd West Chester PA 19382-2054

**ROLFES, JAMES WALTER, SR.,** lawyer; b. Providence, May 21, 1942; s. George Henry and Mary Helen (Clark) R.; m. Dorothy Patricia Robison, Sept. 10, 1966; children: John George, James Walter Jr. BS, U. Cin., 1975; JD, No. Ky. State Coll., 1975. Bar: Ohio 1975, U.S. Supreme Ct. 1985. Asst. sec. Eagle Savings and Loan, Cin., 1967-70; acct. Kings Island, Kings Mill, Ohio, 1970-73, Bode-Finn, Cin., 1973-76; asst. prosecutor Madison County, London, Ohio, 1976-79; acting mcpl. ct. judge Madison County, London, 1982-90; pvt. practice London, 1975—; tchr. Madison County Alcohol Diversion Program, London, 1982-90, Ohio Peace Officers Tng. Acad., London, 1976-79. Chmn. Madison County Heart Assn., London, 1977, Madison County Mental Health Adv. Bd., London, 1980-84; pres. Fairfield Youth Assn. Recipient Millard W. Mack scholarship U. Cin., 1970. Mem. Ohio Bar Assn., Madison County Bar Assn. (pres. 1986), London Merchants Assn., Inc. (chmn. 1983-86), Rotary, K.C. (grand knight 1985-87). Republican. Roman Catholic. General practice. Office: 17 S Main St PO Box 0024 London OH 43140-0024

**ROLINGER, MARK STEPHEN,** lawyer; b. Waterloo, Iowa, Oct. 16, 1965; s. Russell Richard and Jean Marie R.; m. Lisa Renae McFarlane, May 25, 1990; children: Abigail Renea, Allison Grace. BA in Acctg., Wartburg Coll., 1988; JD, U. Iowa, 1991. Bar: Iowa 1991. Assoc. Redfern, Mason, Dieter, Larsen & Moore, Cedar Falls, Iowa, 1991-94, ptnr., 1994—. Mem. ABA, Iowa Bar Assn. (real estate and trust sect. 1994—). Roman Catholic. Estate planning, Probate, Estate taxation. Office: Redfern Mason Dieter Larsen & Moore 415 Clay St Cedar Falls IA 50613-2837

**ROLL, DAVID LEE,** lawyer; b. Pontiac, Mich., May 1, 1940; s. Everett Edgar and Garnette (Houts) R.; m. Nancy E. Spindle, Aug. 17, 1963; children: Richard, Molly. BA cum laude, Amherst Coll., 1962; JD, U. Mich., 1964. Bar: Mich. 1965, U.S. Dist. Ct. (ea. dist.) Mich. 1965, U.S. Ct. Appeals (6th cir.) 1969, D.C. 1974, U.S. Dist. Ct. D.C. 1975, U.S. Supreme Ct. 1975, U.S. Ct. Appeals (4th cir.) 1976, U.S. Ct. Appeals (D.C. cir.) 1983, U.S. Ct. Appeals (3rd and 11th cirs.) 1985, U.S. Ct. Appeals (9th cir.) 1992, U.S. Ct. Appeals (fed. cir.) 1993. Assoc. Hill, Lewis, Detroit, 1965-70, ptnr., 1970-72; asst. dir. gen. litigation Bur. of Competition Fed. Trade Commn., Washington, 1972-75; ptnr. Steptoe & Johnson, Washington, 1975-93, chmn., 1993-98, chmn. antitrust practice group, 1999—. Mem. ABA (chair Robinson Patman Act com., antitrust sect. 1984-86, Clayton Act com., antitrust sect. 1986-88, Energy Litigation com., litigation sect. 1992-93, mem. task force on indsl. competitiveness 1987, coun., antitrust sect. 1988-91, author, editor antitrust sect.). Antitrust, Administrative and regulatory, Federal civil litigation. Office: 1330 Connecticut Ave NW Washington DC 20036-1704

**ROLL, JOHN MCCARTHY,** judge; b. Pitts., Feb. 8, 1947; s. Paul Herbert and Esther Marie (McCarthy) R.; m. Maureen O'Connor, Jan. 24, 1970; children: Robert McCarthy, Patrick Michael, Christopher John. B.A., U. Ariz., 1969, J.D., 1972, LLM U. Va., 1990. Bar: Ariz. 1972, U.S. Dist. Ct. Ariz. 1974, U.S. Ct. Appeals (9th cir.) 1980, U.S. Supreme Ct. 1977. Asst. pros. atty. City of Tucson, 1973; dep. county atty. Pima County (Ariz.), 1973-80; asst. U.S. atty. U.S. Atty.'s Office, Tucson, 1980-87; judge Ariz. Ct. Appeals, 1987-91, U.S. Dist. Ct. Ariz., 1991—; lectr. Nat. Coll. Dist. Attys. U. Houston, 1976-87; mem. criminal justice mental health standards project ABA, 1980-83, mem. com. model jury instrns. 9th circuit, 1994—, chair, 1998—, mem. panel workshop criminal law CEELI program, Moscow, 1997; mem. U.S. Jud. Conf. Adv. Com. Criminal Rules, 1997—. Contbr. to Trial Techniques Compendium, 1978, 82, 84, Merit Selection: The Arizona Experience, Arizona State Law Journal, 1991, The Rules Have Changed: Amendments to the Rules of Civil Procedure, Defense Law Journal, 1994, Ninth Circuit Judges' Benchbook on Pretrial Proceedings, 1998; co-author: Manual on Jury Trial Procedures, Office of Cir. Exec., 1998. Coach, Frontier Baseball Little League, Tucson, 1979-84; mem. parish coun. Sts. Peter and Paul Roman Catholic Ch., Tucson, 1983-91, chmn., 1986-91; mem. Roman Cath. Diocese of Tucson Sch. Bd., 1986-90. Recipient Disting. Faculty award Nat. Coll. Dist. Attys., U. Houston, 1979, Outstanding Alumnus award U. Ariz. Coll. Law, 1992. Mem. Fed. Judges Assn. Republican. Lodge: K.C. (adv. coun. 10441). Office: US Dist Ct 55 E Broadway Blvd Tucson AZ 85701-1719

**ROLLIN, KENNETH B.,** lawyer; b. Chgo., Apr. 1, 1966; s. Arthur S. and Sandra S. Rollin; m. Eileen Berg, Nov. 7, 1992; children: Jack, Scott. BA, Ind. U., 1988; JD, Northwestern U., 1991. Assoc. Hedlund & Hanley, Chgo., 1991-93, Holleb & Coff, Chgo., 1993-96; atty. Walgreen Co., Deerfield, Ill., 1996-97, sr. atty., 1997—. General civil litigation, Real property, General corporate. Office: Walgreen Co 200 Wilmot Rd Deerfield IL 60015-4616

**ROLLINS, GENE A.,** lawyer; b. Neuces County, Tex., Apr. 23, 1957; s. David J. and Connie (Chadburn) R.; m. Laura Spencer, Sept. 5, 1979; children: Joseph, Aimee, Larisa, J. David, Philip, Heather, Anne. BA, U. Md., 1984; MS, Boston U., 1985; JD cum laude, Widener U., 1988. Bar: Del. 1988. Law clk. Del. Power & Light, Wilmington, 1987-88; assoc. atty. Prickett, Jones, Elliott, Kristol & Schnee, Wilmington, 1988-90; counsel, asst. v.p. Am. Express Centurion Bank, Newark, 1990-93; counsel, compliance officer Bank N.Y., Newark, 1993-94; sole practice Claymont, Del., 1994—. Founder, pres. Young Reps. Del., Wilmington, 1986; mem. Rep. Forum, Wilmington, 1987; dir. United to Serve Am., Wilmington, 1988-92. Sgt. U.S. Army, 1980-86, Berlin. Mem. VFW, Am. Legion, People to People Internat. Mem. Ch. Latter Day Saints. Avocations: motor sports, racquetball, computers, poetry, collecting. Banking, Contracts commercial, General corporate. Office: 7801 Governor Printz Blvd Claymont DE 19703-2615

**ROLLINS, MICHAEL F.,** lawyer; b. Randolph, Vt., Jan. 5, 1953; s. Franklin D. and Eleanor F. Rollins; m. Lorraine Rasp, Sept. 1, 1978; children: Seana Kelly, Lesley Kendra. BS in Bus., U. Ariz., 1974, JD, 1978. Bar: Ariz. 1978, Calif. 1981, Mass. 1985, Colo. 1995, U.S. Ct. Appeals (9th cir.) 1978, U.S. Dist. Ct. Ariz. 1978, U.S. Dist. Ct. (so., ctrl. and no. dists.) 1981, Calif., U.S. Supreme Ct. 1988. Law clk. to Hon. Carl A. Muecke Chief Judge, U.S. Dist. Ct. Ariz., Phoenix, 1978-79; assoc. Craig, Greenfield, Irwin, Phoenix, 1979-80; assoc. Winston & Strawn, Phoenix, 1980-84, ptnr., 1984-86; trial specialist Law Office of Richard Grand, Tucson, 1986-88; officer Shultz & Rollins, Ltd., Tucson, 1988—. Chmn., mem. Ariz. Structural Pest Control Bd., Phoenix, 1980-85, Kino Cmty. Hosp. Bd., Tucson, 1996—; mem. Ariz. Agrl. Employment Rels. Bd., Phoenix, 1985-87; mem. Pima Health Care Sys. Commn. Mem. ATLA, Def. Rsch. Inst., Nat. Coll. Advocacy (advocate). Personal injury, Professional liability, General civil litigation. Office: Shultz & Rollins Ltd 4280 N Campbell Ave Ste 214 Tucson AZ 85718-6594

**ROLLISON, GERARDO ROY,** lawyer; b. Warren, Ohio, Feb. 2, 1954; s. Roy Allen and Lillian (Ricci) R.; m. Kathy Lynne Sackett, Sept. 23, 1988; children: Dana Nicolette, MacKenzie. BS in Natural Resources, Ohio State U., 1976; JD, U. Toledo, 1980. Bar: Ohio 1980, U.S. Dist. Ct. (no. dist.) Ohio. Atty. pvt. practice Columbus, Ohio, 1980-88; adj. prof. Ohio Dominican Coll., Columbus, 1987-88; assoc. counsel Toledo Hosp., 1988-91, gen. counsel, 1991-98; chair health care practice group of firm Cooper, Walinski & Cramer, Toledo, 1998—. Trustee Columbus Cardiology Rsch., 1987. Mem. Am. Health Lawyers Assn., Ohio Bar Assn. Democrat. Roman Catholic. Avocations: tennis, writing, teaching. Health, General corporate. Office: Cooper Walinski & Cramer 900 Adams Toledo OH 43603

**ROM, JUDITH R.,** lawyer; b. Czech Rep., May 20, 1954; came to U.S., 1975; BA, Columbia U., 1980; JD, Yeshiva U., 1985. Bar: N.Y. 1986, U.S. Dist. Ct. (so. dist.) N.Y. 1986. Assoc. Davis, Polk & Wardwell, N.Y.C., 1985-97; sr. v.p. Scudder Kemper Investments, N.Y.C., 1997—. Mem. N.Y. State Bar Assn., Bar Assn. City of N.Y. Finance, Pension, profit-sharing, and employee benefits, Estate planning. Office: Scudder Kemper Investments 345 Park Ave New York NY 10022-6000

**ROMANO, EDGAR NESS,** lawyer; b. N.Y.C., Mar. 21, 1969; s. Nessim J. and Jacqueline S. BA cum laude, Brandeis U., 1991; JD, The John Marshall Law Sch., 1995. Bar: N.Y. 1995. Assoc. Brecher, Fishman, Pasternack, Popish, N.Y.C., 1995—. Mem. Am. Trial Lawyers Assn. (N.Y. Chpt.), Jewish Lawyer's Guild, N.Y. State Bar Assn. Workers' compensation, Personal injury, General civil litigation. Office: Brecher Fishman Pasternack Popish et al 222 Broadway New York NY 10038-2510

**ROMANYAK, JAMES ANDREW,** lawyer; b. Chgo., July 21, 1944; s. James and Helen (Piorkowski) R. BA, U. Ill., 1966, JD, 1969. Bar: Ill. 1969, U.S. Dist. Ct. (no. dist.) Ill. 1972, U.S. Ct. Appeals (7th cir.) 1972, U.S. Supreme Ct. 1984. Staff atty. Chgo. Bar Assn., 1970-71; exec. sec. Young Lawyers sect., 1971-72; gen. atty. Chgo., Milw., St. Paul & Pacific R.R., Chgo., 1972-79; pvt. practice, Chgo., 1979—. Dem. candidate for U.S. Ho. of Reps. from 14th Dist. Ill., 1978. Mem. ABA, Ill. State Bar Assn., Chgo. Bar Assn., Nat. Assn. R.R. Trial Counsel. Democrat. Roman Catholic. Federal civil litigation, State civil litigation. Office: Luce Forward Hamilton Scripps LLP 180 N Lasalle St Ste 1125 Chicago IL 60601-2696

**ROMARY, PETER JOHN MICHAEL,** lawyer; b. Leeds, Eng.; came to U.S., 1992; s. John Gerald Robert and Joy (Linley) R.; m. Marcia Wiggs; 1 child, Elizabeth Grace. LLB, U. Reading, Eng., 1992; JD, U. N.C., 1994. Bar: N.C. 1994, D.C. 1996, U.S. Dist. Ct. (ea. dist.) N.C., U.S. Ct. Appeals (4th cir.) 1996, U.S. Supreme Ct. 1997. Law clk. Pethybridges Solicitors, Bodmin, Eng., 1988-92; assoc. Harrington, Edwards & Braddy LLP, Greenville, N.C., 1994-96; ptnr. Harrington, Braddy & Romary, LLp, Greenville, 1996—; adj. prof. U. N.C. Sch. Law, Chapel Hill, 1995; supervising atty. New Directions Domestic Violence Shelter, Greenville, 1996—. Mem. Greenville/Pitt County Home Builders Assn., Grenville, 1994—. Mem. ABA, N.C. Acad. Trial Lawyers, Million Dollar Advocates Forum (life), Masons. Democrat. Episcopalian. Avocations: running, reading, current affairs. Personal injury, State civil litigation, Criminal. Office: Harrington Braddy & Romary 211 W 14th St Ste B Greenville NC 27834-4081

**ROME, DONALD LEE,** lawyer; b. West Hartford, Conn., May 17, 1929; s. Herman Isaac and Juliette (Stern) R.; m. Sheila Ward, Apr. 20, 1958; children: Adam Ward, Lisa, Ethan Stern. SB, Trinity Coll., 1951; LLB, Harvard U., 1954. Bar: Conn. 1954, U.S. Dist. Ct. 1955, U.S. Cir. Ct. Appeals 1965, U.S. Supreme Ct. 1965. Assoc. Ribicoff and Kotkin, Hartford, Conn., 1954-58, ptnr., 1958-67; ptnr. Rosenberg, Rome, Barnett, Sattin & Santos and predecessor, Hartford, 1967-83; ptnr. Robinson & Cole, Hartford, 1983-97, sr. counsel, 1998—; mem. Conn. Gov.'s Study Commn. on Uniform Consumer Credit Code, 1969-70; chmn. Conn. bar adv. com. of attys. to make recommendations to U.S. Dist. Ct. for proposed changed of bankruptcy rules in dist. Conn., 1975-77; mem. Bankruptcy Merit Screening Com. for Dist. Ct., 1980-81; mem. adv. com. Conn. Law Revision commn. on article 2A for Uniform Comml. Code, 1987-89; mem. CPR Inst. for Dispute Resolution Panel of Disting. Neutrals and CPR Fin. Svcs. Panel of Disting. Neutrals; mem. panel of mediators for U.S. Dist. Ct. and U.S. Bankruptcy Ct., Hartford, Am. Arbitration Assn. Nat. Panel Comml. Arbitrators and Mediators; lectr. law U. Conn., 1965-74, 81-83; mem. faculty Sch. Banking of South, La. State U., 1982-84; lectr. continuing legal edn. on mediation adn arbitration, secured creditors' rights, comml. fin., bankruptcy and uniform comml. code, 1958—. Prin. author, editor: Business Workouts Manual, 1985, 1992; co-author: A Comparative Analysis and Study of the Uniform Consumer Credit Code in Relation to the Existing Consumer Credit Law in Connecticut, 1970; contbg. author: Connecticut Practice Book, 1978, Collier Bankruptcy Practice Guide, 1981, Asset-Based Financing: A Transactional Guide, 1984, Controllers Business Advisor, 1994; mem. bd. editors Jour. Bankruptcy Practice, 1991—; contbr. articles to profl. jours. in legal field. Past mem. bd. dirs. New Eng. region Am. Jewish Com., also Hartford chpt., Hebrew Home for Aged, Hartford; past mem. bd. trustees Temple Beth Israel, West Hartford. Mem. ABA (bus. dispute resolution com. chmn., bankruptcy com., uniform comml. code, and comml. fin. svcs. com., sect. on bus. law, mediation com., sect. on dispute resolution), Conn. Bar Assn. (chmn. sect. comml. law and bankruptcy 1977-80, exec. com. banking law sect. 1984-95, chmn. spl. com. scope and correlation 1983-84, exec. comm. 1996—, dispute resolution sect.), Hartford County Bar Assn., Conn. Bar Found., Assn. Comml. Fin. Attys. (pres. 1978-80), Am. Law Inst., Am. Coll. Comml. Fin. Lawyers (chmn. alt. dispute resolution com., bd. regents), Harvard Law Sch. Assn. Conn. (pres. 1970-71), Hartford Club, Masons (32 deg., trial commn. Conn. grand lodge 1970-82). Contracts commercial, Bankruptcy, Banking. Home: 46 Belknap Rd West Hartford CT 06117-2819 Office: Robinson & Cole 1 Commercial Plz Hartford CT 06103-3509 *We are told by Kipling that success and failure are "imposters." I have found this fundamental teaching to be most helpful in the practice of law and in life generally. Concentration on long-term relationships and basic values is so much more important than ephemeral successes and failures.*

**ROMERO, FRANCISCO LEANDRO,** lawyer, educator; b. Wheatland, Wyo., Dec. 13, 1968; s. Francis John and Nyla Jean Romero; m. Gerane Mae Schubert, Aug. 1, 1992; 1 child, Gabriela Evangelista. BA in Pub. Adminstrn., Mont. State U., 1991; JD, Vt. Law Sch., 1994. Bar: Wyo. 1994, U.S. Dist. Ct. Wyo. 1994, U.S. Ct. Appeals (10th cir.) 1998. Assoc. Pence and MacMillan, Laramie, Wyo., 1995-96, Law Office of Julie Nye Tiedeken, Cheyenne, Wyo., 1996-97; asst. atty. gen. Office of the Atty. Gen.—State of Wyo., Cheyenne, 1998—; adj. instr. Laramie County C.C., Cheyenne, 1995—; mem. trial practice skills group and core tng. group Office of the Atty. Gen., Cheyenne, 1998—. Editor: (lit. jour.) Hearsay, 1994. Mem. Cheyenne Young Profls., 1996-98; participant Leadership Laramie, 1996-97. Nat. Hispanic scholar, 1990-91. Mem. Wyo. Bar Assn. (bar survey com. 1998—, govtl. lawyers sect. 1998—), Laramie County Bar Assn., Big Sky Alumni Assn. (regional coord. 1996—), Cheyenne C. of C. Democrat. Avocations: percussionist, writer/poet, home brewer. Home: 3520 Luther Pl Cheyenne WY 82001-1749 Office: Office of the Atty Gen Herschler Bldg St Fl W Cheyenne WY 82002-0001

**ROMERO, FREDDIE JOSEPH,** lawyer; b. Roswell, N.Mex., July 23, 1956; s. Fred Fresquez and Beatriz Rose (Kimbrell) R.; m. Lorena Helen Hickman, Apr. 25, 1987. BA in Govt., N.Mex. State U., 1978; JD, U. N.Mex., 1981. Bar: N.Mex. 1981, U.S. Dist. Ct. N.Mex. 1982, U.S. Ct. Appeals (10th cir.) 1982. Asst. city atty. City of Albuquerque, Albuquerque, 1981-82; assoc. atty. Atwood, Malone, Mann and Turner, Roswell, 1982-87, ptnr., 1987-95; ptnr. Cusack, Jaramillo, Romero and Assoc., Roswell, 1995—. Bd. dirs. Counseling Assocs. Inc., Roswell, 1984-89, pres., 1989-90; bd. dirs. Chaves County Hist. Soc., Roswell, Roswell Hispano C. of C., 1993—. Mem. ABA, N.Mex. Trial Lawyers Assn., Chaves County Bar Assn., N.Mex. Def. Lawyers Assn., N.Mex. Hispanic Bar Assn., Am. Inns of Ct. (barrister, southeastern N.Mex. chpt.), Young Lawyers N.Mex. Assn. (dir. 1987-88), State Bar of N.Mex. (libr. com. 1988—, chmn. trial practice sect. 1992-93, bd. dirs. supreme ct. disciplinary bd. 1993—, chmn. trial practice sect. 1992-93). Democrat. Roman Catholic. Avocations: N.Mex. colonial and territorial hist. rsch., legal philosophy, Basketball. General civil litigation, Personal injury, Workers' compensation. Office: Cusack Jaramillo Romero and Assocs 123 W 4th St Roswell NM 88201-4709

**ROMERO, JEFF,** lawyer; b. Albuquerque, Dec. 5, 1945; s. Efrain and Marguerite Gloria (Gallegos) R.; m. Evangeline Trujillo, Nov. 24, 1989; children: David A., Michael J., Rebecca J. BA, Mich. State U., 1967; JD, U. N.Mex., 1971. Bar: N.Mex. 1971, U.S. Dist. Ct. N.Mex. 1971, U.S. Ct. Appeals (10th cir.) 1975, U.S. Supreme Ct. 1993. Lawyer sole practice Jeff Romero, Atty. at Law, Albuquerque, 1972-75, 84-96; lectr. in law U. N.Mex. Law Sch., Albuquerque, 1975-77; asst. dist. atty. 2d Jud. Dist. Atty., Albuquerque, 1975-81; spl. prosecutor Atty. Gen. of N.Mex., Santa Fe, 1981-83; dist. atty. 2d Jud. Dist. of N.Mex., 1997—; bd. dirs. Employment Law Sect.-State Bar, Albuquerque, 1991. Mem. N.Mex. Trial Lawyers Assn., Assn. Trial Lawyers Am., Albuquerque Bar Assn., State Bar of N.Mex. Democrat. Labor, General civil litigation, Personal injury. Office: Dist Atty 2d Judicial Dist 111 Union Square St SE Albuquerque NM 87102-3432

**ROMERO, VICTOR CARREON,** law educator; b. Manila, Philippines, Jan. 28, 1965. Student, U. Philippines, Quezon City, 1983-84; BA, Swarthmore (Pa.), 1987; JD, U. So. Calif., L.A., 1992. Bar. Calif. 1992, Mass. 1995. Assoc. Folger, Levin & Kahn, L.A., 1992-93; law clk. to U.S. Dist. Judge David Kenyon L.A., 1993-95; asst. prof. law Penn State Dickenson Sch. Law, Carlisle, Pa., 1995-98, assoc. prof. law, 1998—; com. mem. Assn. Am. Law Schs. Com. on Recruitment and Retention of Minority Law Tchrs., 1997—. Contbr. articles to profl. jours. V.p. Am. Civil Liberties Union So. Ctrl. Pa. Chpt., 1996—. Named Nat. Finalist Am. Soc. Writers on Legal Subjects, 1992. Mem. Pa. State U. Faculty Senate. E-mail:

VCR1@psu.edu. Office: Penn State Dickinson Sch Law 150 S College St Carlisle PA 17013-2861

**ROMINGER, M. KYLE,** lawyer; b. Indpls., Mar. 5, 1968; s. Roger Kyle and Phyllis Rae Rominger; m. Jennifer Lynn Gist, July 16, 1994. BS in Ecology, Ethology and Evolution, U. Ill., 1990; JD, U. Louisville, 1997. Bar: Ill. 1997, U.S. Dist. Ct. (ctrl. dist.) Ill. 1997. Intern Office of Gov., Office of Dept. of Transp., State of Ill., Springfield, 1989; rsch. asst. U. Ill., Champaign, 1989; project mgr. Ill. EPA, Springfield, 1991-94; assoc. Giffin, Winning, Cohen & Bodewes, Springfield, 1997-99; project mgr. Ill. EPA, Springfield, 1999—. Mem. ABA, Ill. Bar Assn., Sangamon County Bar Assn., Phi Theta Kappa. Administrative and regulatory, Environmental. Office: Ill EPA Bureau Land 1021 N Grand Ave E Springfield IL 62794-9276

**RONAN, JAMES MICHAEL, JR.,** lawyer; b. Long Branch, N.J., May 25, 1951; s. James Michael and Gloria Marie (Wells) R.; m. Rita Ann Azzolino, May 18, 1980; children: Maria, Laura, Regina. BA, U. Notre Dame, 1973; JD, Villanova U., 1976. Bar: N.Y. 1976, U.S. Dist. Ct. 1976, U.S. Ct. Appeals (3rd cir.) 1978. Atty., partner Giordano, Halleran, Ciesla, Middletown, NJ, 1979-89; law clerk Hon. Clarkson S. Fisher U.S. Dist. Ct. Judge, 1978-79; atty., partner Donington, Karcher, Tinton Falls, NJ, 1989-95; atty., sr. partner Ronan, Tuzzio, Giannone, Tinton Falls, NJ, 1995—; treas. Haydn Proctor Inn of Ct., Freehold, N.J., 1995—; adv. bd. Riverview Med. Ctr., Red Bank, N.J., 1992—; mem. Monmouth Med. Ctr. Ethics Com., Long Branch, N.J., 1992—; mem. Monmouth County Ethics Com., Freehold, N.J., 1989-92; mcpl. prosecutor, Shrewsbury (N.J.) Mcpl. Ct., 1993—. Contbr. articles to profl. jours. Chairperson Shrewsbury (N.J.) Recreation Com., 1989-94. Mem. N.J. Bar Assn., Monmouth County Bar Assn. Roman Catholic. General practice. Office: Ronan Tuzzio Giannone 4000 State Route 66 Neptune NJ 07753-7308

**RONAYNE, DONALD ANTHONY,** lawyer; b. N.Y.C., July 14, 1942; s. James A. and Mary F. R.; m. Diane M. Wallace (div. June, 1980); m. Carol Fordonski, Mar. 16, 1985. BA, Yale U., 1964; postgrad., U. Paris-Sorbonne, 1964-65; JD, Stanford U., 1968. Bar: Calif. 1968, Idaho 1972, Hawaii 1984, N.J. 1988, Md. 1996. Pvt. practice Oakland, Calif., 1968-72; ptnr. Rayborn, Rayborn, Ronayne & Richie, Twin Falls, Idaho, 1972-80; pvt. practice Twin Falls, 1980-83, Honolulu, 1983-87, Morristown, N.J., 1988-95, Stevensville, Md., 1996—. Avocations: skiing, skin diving. General civil litigation, Personal injury, Criminal. Office: 118 Margaret Dr Stevensville MD 21666-3652

**RONDEAU, CHARLES REINHARDT,** lawyer; b. Jefferson, La., Oct. 14, 1966; s. Clement Robert and Irmtraut Juliana Rondeau. BA, Columbia U., 1988; JD, Southwestern U., L.A., 1992; diploma in Advanced Internat. Legal Stud, McGeorge Sch. Law, 1993. Bar: Calif. 1993, N.Y., N.J., U.S. Dist. Ct. N.J., U.S. Dist. Ct. (so. and ea. dists.) N.Y., U.S. Dist. Ct. (cent. dist.) Calif., U.S. Ct. Appeals (3rd and 9th cirs.), U.S. Tax Ct. 1994. Visiting jurist Cabinet Berlioz et Cie, Paris, 1992-93; assoc. Stanley A. Teitler, P.C., N.Y.C., 1993-95; ptnr. Rondeau & Homampour, Beverly Hills, Calif., 1995—; Judge Pro Tem, Los Angeles County Mcpl. Ct., 1999—. Rsch. editor: Southwestern U. Law Rev., 1989-92. Mem. ABA, L.A. County Bar Assn., Beverly Hills Bar Assn. Avocations: jazz, show jumping, skiing, sailing. General civil litigation, Entertainment, Private international. Office: Rondeau & Homampour PLC 8383 Wilshire Blvd Ste 830 Beverly Hills CA 90211-2407

**RONDEPIERRE, EDMOND FRANCOIS,** insurance executive; b. N.Y.C., Jan. 15, 1930; s. Jules Gilbert and Margaret Murray (Moore) R.; m. M. Anne Lerch, July 5, 1952; children: Aimee S., Stephen C., Peter E., Anne W. BS, U.S. Mcht. Marine Acad., 1952; JD, Temple U., 1959. Bar: D.C. 1959, Conn. 1988, U.S. Supreme Ct. 1992. Third mate Nat. Bulk Carriers, 1952-53; field rep. Ins. Co. N.Am., Phila., 1955-59, br. mgr., 1959-61, asst. sec. underwriting, 1965-67, asst. gen. counsel, 1967-70, sr. v.p., gen. counsel, 1970-76; v.p., dep. chief legal affairs INA Corp., Phila., 1976-77; v.p., gen. counsel Gen. Reins. Corp., Stamford, Conn., 1977-79, sr. v.p., corp. sec., gen. counsel, 1979-94, sr. v.p., 1994-95; pres. ARIAS-US, 1994—; bd. dirs. Arias-US. Lt. USN, 1953-55. Mem. ABA, Conn. Bar Assn., D.C. Bar Assn., Inter-Am. Bar Assn., Soc. CPCU, Internat. Assn. Def. Counsel (past bd. dirs.), AIDA Reins. and Ins. Arbitration Soc. (dir., pres.), Stamford Yacht Club. Roman Catholic.

**RONDON, EDANIA CECILIA,** lawyer; b. Santiago, Cuba, Oct. 22, 1960; came to U.S., 1965; d. Edalio Marcelino and Ylia Nayda (Jacas) R.; m. Antonio Omar Maldonado, Sept. 5, 1987. BA, Syracuse U., 1982; JD, Boston U., 1985. Bar: N.J. 1985, U.S. Ct. Appeals (3d cir.) 1985. Assoc. Thomas A. Declemente, P.C., Union City, N.J., 1985-88; pub. defender City of Union City, 1985—; assoc. ins. def. James D. Butler, P.A., Jersey City, 1988-93; assoc. Edania C. Rondon, P.A., Union City, 1993—. Mem. ABA, Hudson County Bar Assn. Democrat. Roman Catholic. Home: 630 Slocum Ave Ridgefield NJ 07657-1837 Office: Edania C Rondon PA 3700 Bergenline Ave Ste 201 Union City NJ 07087-4847

**RONEY, JOHN HARVEY,** lawyer, consultant; b. L.A., June 12, 1932; s. Harvey and Mildred Puckett (Cargill) R.; m. Joan Ruth Allen, Dec. 27, 1954; children: Pam Roney Peterson, J. Harvey, Karen Louise Hanke, Cynthia Allen Harmon. Student, Pomona Coll., 1950-51; BA, Occidental Coll., 1954; LLB, UCLA, 1959. Bar: Calif. 1960, D.C. 1976. Assoc. O'Melveny & Myers, L.A., 1959-67, ptnr., 1967-94, of counsel, 1994—; gen. counsel Pa. Co., 1970-78, Baldwin United Corp., 1983-84; dir. Coldwell Banker & Co., 1969-81, Brentwood Savs. & Loan Assn., 1968-80; spl. advisor Rehab. of Mut. Benefit Life Ins. Co., 1991-94; cons., advisor to Rehab. of Confederation Life Ins. Co., 1994-95; mem. policy adv. bd. Calif. Ins. Commn., 1991-95. Served to 1st lt. USMCR, 1954-56. Mem. ABA, Calif. Bar Assn. (ins. law com. 1991-95, chmn. 1993-94), L.A. County Bar Assn., D.C. Bar Assn., N.Y. Coun. Fgn. Rels., Pacific Coun. on Internat. Policy, Conf. Ins. Counsel, Calif. Club, Sky Club (N.Y.), Gainey Ranch Golf Club (Scottsdale), L.A. Country Club. Republican. Insurance, General corporate, Bankruptcy. Home: The Strand Hermosa Beach CA 90254 Office: 400 S Hope St Ste 1600 Los Angeles CA 90071-2811

**RONEY, PAUL H(ITCH),** federal judge; b. Olney, Ill., Sept. 5, 1921; m. Sarah E. Eustis; children: Susan M., Paul Hitch Jr., Timothy Eustis. Student, St. Petersburg Jr. Coll., 1938-40; B.S. in Econs, U. Pa., 1942; LL.B., Harvard U., 1948; LL.D., Stetson U., 1977; LL.M., U. Va., 1984. Bar: N.Y. 1949, Fla. 1950. Assoc. Root, Ballantine, Harlan, Bushby & Palmer, N.Y.C., 1948-50; ptnr. Mann, Harrison, Roney, Mann & Masterson (and predecessors), St. Petersburg, Fla., 1950-57; pvt. practice law, 1957-63; ptnr. Roney & Beach, St. Petersburg, 1963-69, Roney, Ulmer, Woodworth & Jacobs, St. Petersburg, 1969-70; judge U.S. Ct. Appeals (5th cir.), St. Petersburg, 1970-81; judge U.S. Ct. Appeals (11th cir.), St. Petersburg, 1981-86, chief judge, 1986-89, sr. cir. judge, 1989—; mem. adv. com. on adminstrv. law judges U.S. CSC, 1976-77; pres. judge U.S. Fgn. Intelligence Surveillance Ct. of Rev., 1994—. With U.S. Army, 1942-46. Fellow Am. Bar Found.; mem. ABA (chmn. legal adv. com. Fair Trial-Free Press 1973-76, mem. task force on cts. and public 1973-76, jud. adminstrn. div., chmn. appellate judges conf. 1978-79, mem. Gavel Awards com. 1980-83), Am. Judicature Soc. (dir. 1972-76), Am. Law Inst., Fla. Bar, St. Petersburg Bar Assn. (pres. 1964-65), Nat. Jud. Coll. (faculty 1974, 75), Jud. Conf. U.S. (subcom. on jud. improvements 1978-84, exec com. 1986-89, com. to review circuit coun. conduct and disability orders 1991-93). Fax: 727-893-3851. Office: US Ct Appeals Barnett Tower One Progress Plz 200 Central Ave Saint Petersburg FL 33701-3326

**RONGEY, ROBERT WILLIAM, II,** lawyer; b. Granite City, Ill., Jan. 20, 1960; s. Robert William and Marilyn Louise Rongey; m. Ann Elizabeth Callis, Sept. 12, 1992 (div. Mar. 1998); 1 child, Caroline JoAnna. BA, So. Ill. U., 1986, JD, 1992. Bar: Ill. 1987, U.S. Dist. Ct. (so. dist.) Ill. 1988, U.S. Ct. Appeals (7th cir.) 1995. Atty. Dunham, Boman and Leskera, Belleville, Ill., 1986-96, Callis Law Firm, Granite City, 1996—. Mem. ABA, Ill. State Bar Assn., Tri-City Bar Assn., St. Clair County Bar Assn. (arbitrator 1992—), Madison County Bar Assn., Phi Alpha Delta. Democrat. Presbyterian. Avocations: golf, motorcycles, travel, sports. Office: Callis Law Firm 1326 Niedringhaus Ave Granite City IL 62040-4626

**RONZETTI, THOMAS A. TUCKER,** lawyer, law educator; b. Ft. Meade, Md., Oct. 15, 1964; s. Thomas Anthony and Anna Susan (Arcieri) R.; m. Nancy Ellen Dennebaum, June 23, 1990; children: Michael Hogan, Cara Grace, Emma Faith. BA in Econs., Duke U., 1987; JD, U. Miami, 1992. Bar: Fla. 1992, U.S. Dist. Ct. (so. dist.) Fla. 1993, U.S. Ct. Appeals (11th cir.) 1996, U.S. Supreme Ct. 1998. Law clk. Judge Edward B. Davis, Miami, Fla., 1992-93; assoc. Valdez-Fauli, Cobb, et al, Miami, 1993-94; asst. county atty. Dade County Atty., Miami, 1994—; instr. U. Miami Sch. Law, 1992—. Editor-in-chief U. Miami Law Rev., 1991-92; contbr. chpt. to book. Mem. ABA, Order of the Coif. Avocations: guitar, boating, fishing. Office: Dade County Atty 111 NW 1st St Ste 2810 Miami FL 33128-1930

**ROONEY, GEORGE WILLARD,** lawyer; b. Appleton, Wis., Nov. 16, 1915; s. Francis John and Margaret Ellen (O'Connell) R.; m. Doris I. Maxon, Sept. 20, 1941; children: Catherine Ann, Thomas Dudley, George Willard. BS, U. Wis., 1938; JD, Ohio State U., 1948. Bar: Ohio 1949, U.S. Supreme Ct. 1956, U.S. Ct. Appeals 1956. Assoc. Wise, Roetzel, Maxon, Kelly & Andress, Akron, Ohio, 1949-54; ptnr. Roetzel & Andress, and predecessor, Akron, 1954—; dir. Duracote Corp. Nat. bd. govs. ARC, 1972-78; trustee, mem. exec. bd. Summit County chpt. ARC, 1968, 1975—; v.p. Akron coun. Boy Scouts Am., 1975—; pres. Akron Automobile Assn., 1980-83, trustee, 1983—; chmn. bd. Akron Gen. Med. Ctr., 1981-86, trustee, mem. exec. com., 1986—; trustee Mobile Meals Found., Bluecoats, Inc. Maj. USAAF, 1942-46. Decorated D.F.C. with 2 oak leaf clusters, Air medal with 3 oak leaf clusters; recipient Disting. Community Svc. award Akron Labor Coun.; Disting. Svc. award Summit County chpt. ARC, 1978. Mem. ABA, Ohio Bar Assn. Akron Bar Assn. Am. Judicature Soc., Rotary (past pres.), Portage Country Club (past pres.), Cascade Club (past chmn., bd. govs.), KC. Republican. Roman Catholic. Avocations: golf, travel, gardening. Labor, General corporate. Home: 2863 Walnut Ridge Rd Akron OH 44333-2262 Office: Roetzel & Andress 222 S Main St Akron OH 44308-1533

**ROONEY, JOHN PHILIP,** law educator; b. Evanston, Ill., May 1, 1932; s. John McCaffery and Bernadette Marie (O'Brien) R.; m. Jean Marie Kliss, Feb. 16, 1974 (div. Oct. 1988); 1 child, Caitlin Mairin. BA, U. Ill, 1953; JD, Harvard U., 1958. Bar: Ill. 1958, Calif. 1961, Mich. 1975, U.S. Tax Ct. 1973. Assoc. lawyer Chapman & Cutler, Chgo., 1958-60, Wilson, Morton, San Mateo, Calif., 1961-63; pvt. practice San Francisco, 1963-74; prof. law Cooley Law Sch., Lansing, Mich., 1975—. Author: Selected Cases (Property), 1985; contbr. articles to profl. jours. Pres. San Francisco coun. Dem. Clubs, 1970. 1st lt. U.S. Army, 1953-55. Recipient Beattie Teaching award Cooley Law Sch. Grads., 1979, 90, 92. Mem. ABA (real estate fed. tax problems com., title ins. com.), Mich. Bar Title Stds. Com., Ingham County Bar Assn., Univ. Club. Democrat. Unitarian. Office: Cooley Law Sch 217 S Capitol Ave Lansing MI 48933-1586

**ROONEY, MICHAEL JAMES,** lawyer, educator; b. Bloomington, Ill., Dec. 18, 1947; s. James Patrick and Nellie Mae (Schaefer) R.; children: Dawn Suzanne, Donald Edward, Joseph Michael; m. Deborah Daily, Nov. 27, 1992. BEd, Ill. State U., 1971; JD, U. Ill., 1976. Bar: Ill. 1976, U.S. Ct. Appeals (7th cir.) 1978. Atty. Atty's. Title Guaranty Fund, Inc., Champaign, Ill., 1976-81, v.p., corp. counsel, 1981-83, exec. v.p., 1983-88, pres., 1988-91; bus. devel. dir. Penta Corp., Champaign, 1991-92; v.p., Dallas area mgr. Chgo. Title Ins. Co., 1993-98; v.p., Ariz. dist. mgr. ATI Title Agy., 1999—; bd. dirs. Ill. Inst. Continuing Legal Edn., Springfield, 1984-93, chmn., 1991-92; vis. asst. prof. Coll. Commerce, U. Ill., Champaign, 1982-87. Author: Searching Illinois Real Estate Titles, 1978, Attorney's Guide to Title Insurance, 1980, rev. edit., 1984; also articles. Pres. Mahomet (Ill.)-Seymour Boosters, 1983-84. Fellow Am. Bar Found. (life), Ill. Bar Found. (charter); mem. ABA (chmn. real property com. gen. practice sect. 1983-87, budget officer 1990-91, coun. mem. 1991-93, mem. commn. on non-lawyer practice 1991-95, real property probate and trust law), Ill. Bar Assn. (sec. real estate sect. coun. 1984-85, vice chmn. 1985-86, chmn. 1986-87, ins. program com. 1988-93, sec. 1989-90, vice chmn. 1990-91, chmn. 1991-92, protect pub. from unauthorized practice of law 1988-93), Internat. Right of Way Assn. (instr. 1983—), Champaign County Bar Assn., Chgo. Bar Assn., Am. Coll. Real Estate Lawyers, Greater Dallas Assn. Realtors (bd. dirs. 1998-99, Affiliate of Yr. 1997, chair Affiliate Forum 1998). Real property, General corporate. Home: 8821 E Cave Creek Rd Carefree AZ 85377

**ROONEY, SCOTT WILLIAM,** lawyer; b. Suffern, N.Y., Sept. 25, 1961; s. Joseph William and Shirley Dorothy (Morris) R.; m. Linda Marie Miencier, July 24, 1987; children: Brendan Kenneth, Katy Lynn. BA, U. Mich., Dearborn, 1984; JD, Detroit Coll., 1989. Bar: Mich. 1989, U.S. Dist. Ct. Mich. 1989. Assoc. Charfoos & Christensen, P.C., Detroit, 1989—; founder Inst. Injury Reduction, Washington, 1988—, SAFE-Consumer Rights Group, Washington, 1992—; atty. pro-bono activity Legal Aid Clinic, 1990—. Bd. dirs. Bouy 13 High Sch. Scholarship Found.; adv. com. Detroit Cath. Pastoral Alliance, 1994—; com. mem. S.E. Mich. Bus. Consortium Alliance, 1994—. Mem. Ctr. Automotive Safety, Mich. Trial Lawyers Assn., Am. Trial Lawyers Assn., Fed. Bar Assn. (atty. pro bono activity 1990—), Cath. Lawyers Assn., Irish Am. Lawyers Assn., Mich. Bar Assn., Detroit Athletic Club. Roman Catholic. Avocations: basketball, fitness. General civil litigation, Product liability, Securities. Office: Charfoos & Christensen PC 5510 Woodward Ave Detroit MI 48202-3804

**ROOSEVELT, JAMES, JR.,** federal agency administrator, lawyer; b. L.A., Nov. 9, 1945; s. James and Romelle (Schneider) R.; m. Ann M. Conlon, June 15, 1968; children: Kathy, Tracy, Maura. AB, Harvard U., 1968, JD, 1971. Bar. Mass. 1971, D.C. 1973, U.S. Ct. Appeals (D.C. cir.) 1973, U.S. Ct. Appeals (1st cir.) 1976, U.S. Supreme Ct. 1975. Assoc. Winthrop, Stimson, Putnam & Roberts, N.Y.C., 1971; assoc. Herrick & Smith, Boston, 1975-80, ptnr., 1981-86; ptnr. Nutter, McClennen & Fish, Boston, 1986-88, Choate, Hall & Stewart, Boston, 1988-98; assoc. commr. for retirement policy Social Security Adminstrn., Washington, 1998—. Mem. Dem. Nat. Com., Washington, 1980—, Dem. State Com., Boston, 1980—; trustee Emmanuel Coll., Boston, 1982-92, 95—; trustee Care Group, Inc., Boston, Mt. Auburn Hosp., Cambridge, Mass., 1984—, chmn., 1988-92. Lt. JAGC, USN, 1972-75. Mem. ABA, Boston Bar Assn., Mass. Bar Assn., Am. Health Lawyers Assn. (chmn. Mass. chpt. 1982-85, dir. 1996—), Am. Hosp. Assn. (trustee 1999—), Mass. Hosp. Assn. (trustee 1987-99, chmn. 1996-97), Harvard Club. Roman Catholic. Avocation: public policy. Office: Social Security Admin 500 E St SW Ste 850 Washington DC 20254-0001

**ROOT, CAROLE A.Z.,** lawyer, nurse; b. Worcester, Mass., July 2, 1942; d. Joseph J. and Frances (Jasionis) Zuma; m. David Root (div. Jan. 1985); children: Erica A., Benjamin P. Diploma, Mass. Gen. Hosp., Boston, 1963; BS in Biology, Emmanuel Coll., Boston, 1978; JD, Northeastern U., 1982. Staff nurse Mass. Gen. Hosp., Boston, 1964-66, 69-70; head nurse, supr. Emerson Hosp., Concord, Mass., 1972-79; sole practitioner Boston, 1982-92, Somerville, Mass., 1992-96, Everett, Mass., 1996—; pub. adminstr. Middlesex County, Cambridge, Mass. Mem., sec. Zoning Bd. Appeals, Bedford, Mass., 1984-88; chair Human Rels. Coun., Bedford, 1992-94; mem. affirmative action com. Town of Bedford, 1994-95; mem., bd. dirs. Civil War Roundtable of Greater Boston, 1995—. Mem. Boston Bar Assn. (mentor com. 1988-89). Avocations: sewing, reading, Celtics basketball. General corporate, General practice, Bankruptcy. Office: 449 Broadway Everett MA 02149-3646

**ROOT, GERALD EDWARD,** planning and operational support administrator; b. Gridley, Calif., May 5, 1948; s. Loris Leo Root and Mary Helen (Wheeler) Murrell; m. Tricia Ann Caywood, Feb. 13, 1982; children: Jason Alexander, Melinda Ann. AA in Bus., Yuba C.C., Marysville, Calif., 1968; BA in Psychology, Calif. State U., Sonoma, 1974; MA in Social Sci., Calif. State U., Chico, 1977; postgrad., U. San Francisco, 1998—. Gen. mgr. Do-It Leisure Therapeutic Recreation, Chico, 1977-79; CETA projects coord. City of Chico, 1980-81; exec. dir. Voluntary Action Ctr., Inc., South Lake Tahoe, Calif., 1981-83; devel. dir. Work Tng. Ctr., Inc., Chico, 1983-92; exec. dir. North Valley Rehab. Found., Chico, 1986-92; dir. planning and operational support Superior Ct. of Calif., County of Sacramento, 1992—; project mgr. Juvenile Detention Alternatives Initiative, 1992-98, Feather River Industries Vocat. Tng., 1991, Creative Learning Ctr. Constrn., 1988-89, Correctional Options-Drug Ct., 1994, Violence Prevention Resource Ctr., 1995-96, Communities That Care-Juvenile Delinquency Prevention Initiative, 1995, Securing the Health and Safety of Urban Children Initiative, 1995-97, Joint Cabinets Youth Work Group/Child Welfare League Am., 1996-97, Task Force on Fairness-The Juvenile Justice Initiative, 1994-97, SacraMentor, Inc., CA Wellness Found., 1994-95, Violent Injury Prevention Coalition/Calif. Dept. Health and Human Svcs., 1995—, Domestic Violence Coordinating Coun., Sacramento County, 1995-98, Multicultural Perspectives on Family Violence Conf., 1997—, Family Violence Summit, 1997, Ptnrs. in Protection Conf. 1997 Child Abuse Prevention Coun., The Drug Store, Calif. Nat. Guard drug demand reduction program, 1996, 97, disporportionate minority confinement rsch. com. Criminal Justice Cabinet, 1997-99, Court Cmty.-Focused Strategic Plan, 1998-99. Bd. dirs. Cmty. Action Agy., Butte County, Calif., 1990-92, ARC, Butte County, 1989-90, Sunrise Recreation and Park Dist., 1996—; mem. adv. bds. Butte C.C. Dist., 1987-92, Cmty. Svcs. Planning Coun., 1994-96. Grantee Annie E. Casey Found., USDA, U.S. Dept. Justice, Robert Wood Johnson Found., Calif. Office Criminal Justice Planning, U.S. Dept. Labor, Office Juvenile Justice and Delinquency Prevention, Sacramento Criminal Justice Cabinet, CA Wellness Found. Office: Supr Ct Calif County of Sacramento 720 9th St Sacramento CA 95814-1311

**ROOTENBERG, SHARYN MICHELE,** lawyer; b. Bklyn., Mar. 15, 1969; d. Jacob and Ruth Rootenberg. BA, SUNY, Albany, 1990; JD, Yeshiva U., 1995. Bar: N.Y. 1990, N.J. 1990, U.S. Ct. Appeals (2d cir.) 1997. Legis. aide N.Y. State Assembly, Albany and Bklyn., 1988-90; assoc. Herzfeld & Rubin, N.Y.C., summer 1993, Edmonds & Beier, N.Y.C., summer 1994; asst. corp. counsel N.Y.C. Corp. Counsel, Family Ct. Divsn., Bklyn., 1995-97, N.Y.C. Corp. Counsel, Appeals Divsn., N.Y.C., 1997—; mediator pilot pro bono project, ABA, 1994-96. Committeeperson Kings county Dem. Com., Bklyn., 1992-96. Mem. ABA, N.Y. State Bar Assn., Assn. of Bar of City of N.Y. (com. Muncpl. Affairs, Outstanding Asst. Corp. Counsel award 1999), N.Y. County Lawyers Assn. Office: NYC Corp Counsel Appeals Divsn 100 Church St Fl 6 New York NY 10007-2601

**ROPER, HARRY JOSEPH,** lawyer; b. Bridgeport, Conn., Apr. 15, 1940; s. Harold Joseph and Madeline (Sullivan) R.; m. Helen L. Marlborough, Oct. 1, 1976; children—Kendall, Timothy, Melissa, Elizabeth. B.E.E., Rensselaer Poly. Inst., 1962; LL.B., NYU, 1966. Bar: Ill. 1966, U.S. Dist. Ct. (no. dist.) Ill. 1966, U.S. Ct. Appeals (7th cir.) 1966, U.S. Ct. Appeals (fed. cir.) 1982. Assoc., Neuman, Williams, Anderson & Olson, Chgo., 1966-70, ptnr., 1970-90, Roper & Quigg, 1990—. Mem. ABA (chmn. intellectual properties com. litigation sect. 1982-85), Chgo. Bar Assn., Bar Assn. 7th Fed. Cir., Patent Law Assn. Chgo., Am. Patent Law Assn., Chgo. Council Lawyers. Club: Union League (Chgo.). Federal civil litigation, Patent, Trademark and copyright. Home: 611 W Fullerton Pky Chicago IL 60614-2613 Office: Roper & Quigg 200 S Michigan Ave Chicago IL 60604-2402

**RORTY, BRUCE VAIL,** lawyer; b. Orange, Calif., Apr. 1, 1957; s. Malcolm MacNaughten and Nancy Carruthers Vail R.; m. Denise A. Landau, Nov. 11, 1995; 1 child, Cynthia Vail. Student, Dartmouth Coll., 1979; BA, U. Calif., Santa Cruz, 1981; JD, U. San Diego, 1985. Bar: Calif. 1986, U.S. Dist. Ct. (ctrl. dist.) Calif. 1990, U.S. Dist. Ct. (so. dist.) Calif. 1996, U.S. Ct. Appeals (9th cir.) 1999. Assoc. Patterson, Ritner, Lockwood, Zanghi & Gartner, L.A., 1988-89, Ramsey, Harris & Bronstein, L.A., 1989-96, Wesierski & Zurek, Irvine, Calif., 1996—. Mem. Los Angeles County Bar Assn., Orange County Bar Assn. Republican. Episcopalian. Avocations: photography, mountaineering, skiing, surfing, California history. General civil litigation, Professional liability, Labor. Home: 3625 Palos Verdes Dr N Palos Verdes Peninsula CA 90274 Office: Wesierski & Zurek 1 Corporate Park Ste 200 Irvine CA 92606-5152

**ROSAMILIA, CHARLES R.,** lawyer, real estate investor; b. Renovo, Pa., Dec. 11, 1954; s. Charles R. and Martha R. (Thompson) R.; m. Bonnie R. Day, Jan. 28, 1978; children: Rocco, Thom, Andrew. BA in Philosophy, Lock Haven U., 1975; JD, Duquesne U., 1978. Bar: Pa. 1978, U.S. Dist. Ct. (mid. dist.) Pa. 1979. Ptnr. Lingle & Rosamilia, Lock Haven, Pa., 1978; sr. ptnr. Rosamilia, O'Connor & Salisbury, Lock Haven, 1980-87, Rosamilia & Brungard, Lock Haven, 1988—. Trustee Lock Haven U., 1986-92; pres. West Br. Soccer Club, Lock Haven, 1991-97. Mem. Clinton County Bar Assn. (treas. 1981-83, pres. 1994-95), Lions Club, Elks Club. Republican. Roman Catholic. Avocations: tennis, fishing, hunting, coaching soccer. Personal injury, Workers' compensation, Real property. Home: 104 W Main St Lock Haven PA 17745-1220 Office: Rosamilia & Brungard 241 W Main St Lock Haven PA 17745-1242

**ROSE, ALAN DOUGLAS,** lawyer; b. Flushing, N.Y., Dec. 22, 1945; s. William Allen and Josephine (Grohe) R.; m. Janet Louise Clift, Aug. 20, 1966; children: Alan Douglas Jr., Windsor, Ainsley, Vanessa, Hillary, Lacey. BA, Harvard U., 1967; MSc, London Sch. Econs., 1969; JD, U. Va., 1972. Bar: Mass. 1974, U.S. Dist. Ct. Mass. 1975, U.S. Ct. Claims 1983, U.S. Ct. Appeals (1st cir.) 1976, U.S. Ct. Appeals (fed. cir.) 1986, U.S. Supreme Ct. 1991. Law clk. to judge U.S. Dist. Ct. Mass., Boston, 1972-73; assoc. Choate Hall & Stewart, Boston, 1973-75; asst. U.S. Atty. Dept. Justice, Boston, 1975-80; ptnr. Nutter McClennen & Fish, Boston, 1980-95; mgr. litigation dept., 1991-93; ptnr. Rose & Assocs., Boston, 1995—; lectr. Law Sch. Harvard U., Cambridge, Mass., 1981-82; spl. asst. atty. gen. Commonwealth Mass., 1991-92; mem. U.S. Dist. Ct. Civil Justice Adv. Bd., 1995—. Mem. ABA, Boston Bar Assn. (vice chair joint bar com. on jud. appointments 1991-92), City Mission Soc. (chmn., bd. dirs.). Democrat. Mem. United Ch. Christ. Federal civil litigation, Criminal, Education and schools. Home: 50 Bristol Rd Wellesley MA 02481-2728 Office: Rose & Assocs One Boston Pl Boston MA 02108-4400

**ROSE, ALBERT SCHOENBURG,** lawyer, educator; b. Nov. 9, 1945; s. Albert Schoenburg Sr. and Karleen (Klein) R.; children: Claudia, Micah Daniel. BSBA, U. Ala., 1967; JD, Washington U., St. Louis, 1970; LLM in Taxation, George Washington U., 1974. Bar: Mo. 1970, U.S. Dist. Ct. (ea. dist.) Mo. 1970, U.S. Tax Ct. 1970, U.S. Ct. Mil. Appeals 1970, U.S. Supreme Ct. 1970. Ptnr. Shifrin & Treiman, St. Louis, 1974-88; ptnr., chmn. tax dept. Blackwell Sanders Peper Martin LLP, St. Louis, 1988—; adj. prof. law Washington U., 1979-98, Fontbonne Coll., 1993-96. Co-author: Missouri Taxation Law and Practice, 1986, supplement, 1989. Capt. U.S. Army, 1970-74, Korea. Mem. planning com., Mid-Am. Tax Conf.; mem. Tax Lawyers Club (pres.). Taxation, general, Estate planning, General corporate. Office: Blackwell Sanders Peper Martin LLP 720 Olive St Fl 24 Saint Louis MO 63101-2338

**ROSE, DANNY,** lawyer; b. Berea, Ky., Apr. 5, 1960; s. Rufus Mae and Aline R.; m. Lana Marie Combs, Oct., 1988; children: Aline Marie, Alexander Lanham. BA, Eastern Ky. U., 1982; JD, U. Louisville, 1985. Bar: Ky. 1985, U.S. Dist. Ct. (ea. dist.) Ky. 1986. Asst. pub. adv. Commonwealth of Ky., Hazard, 1986-88, commonwealth atty., 1991; pvt. practice Hazard, 1989—. Recipient Walker award Dept. of Pub. Adv., 1987. Mem. Perry County Bar Assn. (pres. 1996), Buckhorn Lion's Club. Alternative dispute resolution, General civil litigation, Criminal. Office: 482 Main St # 1061 Hazard KY 41701-1777

**ROSE, DAVID E.,** lawyer; b. Columbus, Ohio, Feb. 21, 1944; s. Harvey S. and Florence (McCoy) R.; m. Virginia Lorenzen, June 3, 1967; 1 child, Suzanne. BS, Ohio State U., 1966; JD Capital U., 1977. Bar: Ohio 1978, U.S. Dist. Ct. (no. dist.) Ohio 1982, U.S. Dist. Ct. (no. dist.) Tex. 1983, U.S. Supreme Ct. 1984, U.S. Ct. Appeals (5th, 6th, 7th, 8th cirs.) 1984, U.S. Dist. Ct. Nebr. 1984, U.S. Dist. Ct. (ea. and we. dists.) Wis. 1984. Mgr. prospecting O.M. Scott & Sons, Marysville, Ohio, 1967, regional sales mgr., 1969-71, mgr. retailer services, 1971-79; corp. atty. Na-Churs Plant Food Co., Marion, Ohio, 1979—, also dir. mktg., 1986—. Served to 1st lt. U.S. Army, 1967-69. Mem. ABA, Ohio State Bar Assn., Marion County Bar Assn., Assn. Trial Lawyers Am., Comml. Law League Am., Phi Alpha Delta. Home: 2125 Olde Sawmill Blvd Dublin OH 43016-9091 Office: Na-Churs Plant Food Co 421 Leader St Marion OH 43302-2296

**ROSE, DAVID L.,** lawyer; b. Ft. Monmouth, N.J., Feb. 18, 1955; s. Llewellyn Paterson and Bebe (Faulk) R.; m. Laura Marie Jarvis, Sept. 3, 1989; children: Allison Michelle, Jessica Morgan, Ashley Elizabeth. BA in Comm., U. Colo., 1980; JD, Ariz. State U., 1991. Bar: Ariz. 1991, U.S. Dist. Ct. Ariz. 1991, U.S. Ct. Appeals (9th cir.) 1993, U.S. Supreme Ct. 1997. Law clk. Bonn & Anderson, Phoenix, 1988-91, Maricopa County Superior Ct., Phoenix, 1990-91; lawyer Anderson, Brody, Levinson, Weiser &

Horwitz, Phoenix, 1991-92, Brandes, Lane & Joffe, Phoenix, 1992-93; pvt. practice Phoenix, 1993—; lawyer Rose & Hildebrand, P.C., 1997—; pvt. practice Phoenix, 1993—. Editor: Missive, 1992. Bd. dirs. Maricopa County Family Support Adv. Com., Phoenix; adv. coun. Washington Sch. Dist., Phoenix; mem. Ariz. State Legis., Domestic Rels. Reform Com., Phoenix. Mem. Maricopa County Bar Assn. (adv. family law com.), ABA (adv. family law sect.), Nat. Congress for Men (pres.), Father's for Equal Rights of Colo. (pres.). Avocations: aviation, computer systems. Family and matrimonial, General civil litigation, Criminal. Office: 1440 E Washington St Phoenix AZ 85034-1109

**ROSE, DONALD MCGREGOR,** retired lawyer; b. Cin., Feb. 6, 1933; s. John Kreimer and Helen (Morris) R.; m. Constance Ruth Lanner, Nov. 29, 1958; children: Barbara Rose Mead, Ann Rose Weston. AB in Econs., U. Cin., 1955; JD, Harvard U., 1958. Bar: Ohio 1958, U.S. Supreme Ct. 1962. Asst. legal officer USNR, Subic Bay, The Philippines, 1959-62; with Office of JAG USNR, The Pentagon, Va., 1962-63; assoc. Frost & Jacobs, LLP, Cin., 1963-70, ptnr., 1970-93, sr. ptnr., 1993-97, ret. ptnr., 1997; co-chmn. 6th Cir. Appellate Practice Inst., Cin., 1983, 90, mem. 6th Cir. adv. com., 1990-98, chmn. subcom. on rules, 1990-94, chmn., 1994-96. Trustee Friends of Cin. Pks., Inc., 1980-89, 93-98, pres. 1980-86; trustee Am. Music Scholarship Assn., Cin., 1985-88; pres. Social Health Assn. Greater Cin. Area Inc., 1969-72; co-chmn. Harvard Law Sch. Fund for So. Ohio, Cin., 1985-87; pres. Meth. Union, Cin., 1983-85; chmn. trustees Hyde Pk. Cmty. United Meth. Ch., Cin., 1974-76, chmn. coun. on ministries, 1979-81, chmn. adminstrv. bd., 1982-84, chmn. mem. canvass, 1985, chmn. staff parish rels. com., 1988-90, chmn. commn. missions, 1993-95; trustee Meth. Theol. Sch. Ohio, vice chmn. devel. com., 1990-94, sec. 1992-94, chmn. devel. com., 1994-98, vice chmn., 1998, chmn., 1999—. Lt. USNR, 1959-63. Mem. Cin. Bar Assn., Univ. Club (Cin.), Cin. Country Club. Republican. Avocations: sailing, golf. General civil litigation. Home: 8 Walsh Ln Cincinnati OH 45208-3435 summer home: 11 Blackstone Rd Boothbay Harbor ME 04538-1943

**ROSE, ELIHU ISAAC,** lawyer; b. Bklyn., Nov. 27, 1941; s. Aaron Henry and Frances (Klinger) R.; AB, Columbia U., 1963, MBA, 1965; JD, St. John's U., Bklyn., 1968; m. Gail Roberta Cohen, Aug. 22, 1964; children—Melissa Kaye, Heidi Jill. CPA, N.Y.; bar: N.Y. 1969. Sr. tax acct. Price Waterhouse & Co., N.Y.C., 1967-71; dir. taxes Exec. Monetary Mgmt., Inc., N.Y.C., 1971-79; pres. Elihu I. Rose, P.C., Lake Success, N.Y., 1979—. Mem. ABA, Am. Inst. CPAs, N.Y. State Bar Assn., N.Y. State Soc. CPAs, Bar Assn. Nassau County, Pension Coun. L.I. (pres. 1981). Estate planning, Estate taxation, Personal income taxation. Office: 1983 Marcus Ave Ste 129 New Hyde Park NY 11042-1016

**ROSE, JOEL ALAN,** legal consultant; b. Bklyn., Dec. 26, 1936; s. Edward Isadore and Adele R.; m. Isadora Fenig, Apr. 12, 1964; children: Susan, Terri. BS in Econs., NYU, 1958; MBA, Wharton Grad. Sch., U. Pa., 1960. Asst. purchasing agt. Maidenform Inc., N.Y.C., 1960-62; personnel dir. E.J. Korvette Inc., N.Y.C., 1962-66; mgmt. cons. Daniel J. Cantor & Co. Inc., Phila., 1966—, sr. v.p., 1987—; mgmt. cons. to legal profession; coord. Ann. Conf. on Law Firm Mgmt. and Econs. Author: Managing the Law Office; mem. adv. bd. Law Office Economics and Management, 1987; contbg. columnist N.Y. Law Jour., 1984—, Nat. Law Jour. Extra, 1996—, Phila. Legal Intelligencer, 1995, L.A. Daily Times, 1999—, Legal Times of Washington, 1998; also articles to profl. jours.; bd. editors Acctg. for Law Firms; editl. adv. bd. Corp. Counsel's Guide to Law Dept. Mgmt. With U.S. Army, 1960, Res., 1960-66. Fellow Coll. of Law Practice Mgmt.; mem. ABA (chmn. acquisition and mergers com., practice mgmt. sect., large law firm interest group), Inst. Mgmt. Cons., Am. Arbitration Assn. (nat. panel), Adminstrv. Mgmt. Soc. (past chpt. pres.), Am. Mgmt. Assn., Assn. Legal Adminstrs. Office: Joel A Rose & Assoc Inc PO Box 162 Cherry Hill NJ 08003-0162

**ROSE, JONATHAN CHAPMAN,** lawyer; b. Cleve., June 8, 1941; s. Horace Chapman and Katherine Virginia (Cast) R.; m. Susan Anne Porter, Jan. 26, 1980; 1 son, Benjamin Chapman. A.B., Yale U., 1963; LL.B. cum laude, Harvard U., 1967. Bar: Mass. 1968, D.C. 1972, U.S. Supreme Ct. 1976, Circuit Ct. Appeals 1977, Ohio 1978. Law clk. Justice R. Ammi Cutter, Mass. Supreme Jud. Ct., 1967-68; spl. asst. to U.S. pres., 1971-73; gen. counsel Council on Internat. Econ. Policy, 1973-74; assoc. dept. atty. gen. U.S. Dept. Justice, 1974-75; dept. asst. atty. gen. U.S. Dept. Justice (Antitrust Div.), 1975-77; asst. atty. gen. Office of Legal Policy, 1981-84; ptnr. firm Jones, Day, Reavis & Pogue, Washington, 1977-81, 84—. Prin. Ctr. for Excellence in Govt.; pres. Yale Daily News Found.; bd. govs. Yale Alumni Assn., 1996—. 1st lt. U.S. Army, 1969-71. Mem. ABA, D.C. Bar Assn., Mass. Bar Assn., Ohio Bar Assn., Fed. Bar Assn., Am. Law Inst. Republican. Episcopalian. Clubs: Met, Chevy Chase, Union, Yale, Harvard. Administrative and regulatory, Federal civil litigation, Environmental. Office: Jones Day Reavis & Pogue 51 Louisiana Ave NW Washington DC 20001-2113

**ROSE, KIM MATTHEW,** lawyer, educator; b. Gallipolis, Ohio, Mar. 21, 1956; s. Dave and Lois Ann R.; m. Pamela Carol Sims, Aug. 11, 1990. Student, USMA, 1974-76; BBA, Ohio U., 1977; JD, Capital U. Law, 1981; MBA, Ashland Coll., 1988. Bar: Ohio 1981, U.S. Dist. Ct. (so. dist.) Ohio 1981, U.S. Ct. Appeals (6th cir.) 1987, U.S. Supreme Ct. 1988. Asst. prosecutor Knox County Prosecutor, Mt. Vernon, Ohio, 1982-90; ptnr. Zeller, Ritter & Rose, Mt. Vernon, 1982—; adj. prof. Mt. Vernon Nazarene Coll., 1982—. Mem. Met. Housing Authority, Knox County, 1990—; mem. adv. bd. Salvation Army, Mt. Vernon, 1991—; mem. Boys Village Corp. Bd., Smithville, Ohio, 1991—. Maj. USAR, 1974-95. Mem. Ohio State Bar Assn. (mem. substance abuse lawyer's assistance com.), Knox County Bar Assn. (past pres.), Mt. Vernon Nazarene Coll. Found. (rec. sec. bd. 1995—), Masons. Avocations: flying, skiing, fishing, golfing, biking. General practice, Probate, General corporate. Home: 1413 Greenbrier Dr Mount Vernon OH 43050-9101 Office: Zeller Ritter & Rose 118 E Gambier St Mount Vernon OH 43050-3546

**ROSE, LAURA RAUCH,** lawyer; b. Rivera, Calif., Mar. 25, 1958; d. Roscoe Roland and Lola Jane (Swihart) Rauch; m. Gary G. Rose, Feb. 14, 1994. BS in Polit. Sci., Shepherd Coll., 1981; JD, W.Va., 1984. Bar: W.Va. 1984; bd. cert. in civil trial advocacy. Assoc. Lewis, Ciccarello, Masinter & Friedberg, Charleston, W.Va., 1984-85, Martin and Seibert, Martinsburg, W.Va., 1985-86, Askin, Pill, Scales and Burke, L.C., 1986-88; ptnr. Greenberg and Coltelli, Martinsburg, 1988-92, Law Offices of Laura Rose and Assocs., Martinsburg, 1992—. Legal editor mag. W.Va. Women, 1985; host Sta. WRNR radio show Legally Speaking. Bd. dirs. Legal Svcs. Plan W.Va., 1988-90; mem. adv. bd. Salvation Army, Martinsburg, Berkeley County Dep. Sheriff Civil Svc. Bd., 1991-92. Named one of Top 10 Women on the Move Tri-State Area, 1993, Ofcl. Belle Boyd B.C. Hist. Soc., 1995-96. Mem. NAFE, Assn. Trial Lawyers Am. (vice chairperson Aquatic Injury Safety Group), W.Va. Bar Assn. (com. mem., bd. dirs. young lawyers div.), W.Va. Trial Lawyers Assn. (bd. govs. 1988—, exec. com. 1990-92, pres. elect 1996), Berkeley County Bar Assn. (pres. 1990-91), Nat. Bd. Trial Advocacy (bd. dirs.), Order of Barristers, Martinsburg/Berkeley County C. of C. Democrat. General civil litigation, Workers' compensation, Personal injury. Office: Law Offices Laura Rose Asso 210 W Burke St Martinsburg WV 25401-3322

**ROSE, NORMAN,** retired lawyer, retired accountant; b. N.Y.C., July 7, 1923; s. Edward J. and Frances (Ludwig) R.; div.; children: Ellen, Michael; m. Judith Rose; stepchildren: Dwight, Audrey, Jason. BBA, CCNY, 1947; JD, N.Y. Law Sch., 1953. Bar: N.Y. 1954, U.S. Dist. Ct. (ea. dist.) N.Y. 1956, U.S. Tax Ct. 1956, U.S. Dist. Ct. (so. dist.) N.Y. 1960, U.S. Supreme Ct. 1961, U.S. Ct. Appeals (2d cir.) 1967, Fla. 1979. Pvt. practice N.Y.C., 1954-69, Ft. Lauderdale, Fla., 1979-91; ptnr. Dean, Falanga & Rose, Carle Pl., N.Y., 1979-81; referee Small Claims Ct., N.Y.C., 1959-69; arbitrator Accident Claims Tribunal, Am. Arbitration Assn., 1960-65; C.P.A., N.Y.C., 1951-57; lectr. in field. Author law note Liability of Golfer to Person Struck by Ball, 1959 (Hon. Mention 1960). Pres. Nassau South Shore Little League, Lawrence, N.Y., 1966-68; treas. 5 Towns Dem. Club, Woodmere, N.Y., 1966-67; chmn. United Fund, Village of Lawrence, 1967. Capt. USAF, 1943-45, ETO. Decorated DFC, Air medal with 5 oak leaf clusters, Silver Star, Purple Heart. Mem. ATLA (sustaining), Acad. Fla. Trial Lawyers (sustaining), N.Y. State Assn. Plaintiffs Trial Lawyers, N.Y. State Bar Assn., Fla. Bar, Nassau County Bar Assn. (chmn. med-legal com. 1975-77), Lawyer/Pilots Bar Assn., Pompano Beach Power Squadron, Masons, Shriners. Personal injury, Insurance, State civil litigation. Home: 3200 Port Royale Dr N Fort Lauderdale FL 33308-7809

**ROSE, RICHARD LOOMIS,** lawyer; b. Long Branch, N.J., Oct. 21, 1936; s. Charles Frederick Perrott and Jane Mary (Crotta) R.; m. Marian Frances Irons, Apr. 1, 1960; children: Linda, Cynthia, Bonnie. BA, Cornell U., 1958; JD, Washington and Lee U., 1963. Bar: N.Y. 1963, Conn. 1965, U.S. Dist. Ct. (so. dist.) N.Y. 1964, U.S. Dist. Ct. Conn. 1965, U.S. Ct. Appeals (2d cir.) 1965, U.S. Supreme Ct. 1970. Assoc. Cummings & Lockwood, Stamford, Conn., 1965-71; ptnr. Cummings & Lockwood, Stamford, 1971-91, Kleban & Samor, P.C., Southport, 1991-93; of counsel Whitman Breed Abbott & Morgan, Greenwich, Conn., 1993-95; prin. Roberts, Kambas, Rose & Bates, P.C., Stamford, Conn., 1995—; bd. dirs. and sec. Index Corp.; mem. adv. com. Conn. Banking Commr. on Conn. Securities Laws, 1982—; dir. Conn. World Trade Assn. Editor: Washington and Lee Law Rev. Chmn. Fgn. Trade Zone Com. to Mayor of City of Bridgeport, Conn., 1988-90; mem. fgn. trade awareness com. S.W. Area Industry and Commerce Assn., Task Force, 1987-88; bd. dirs. German Sch. of Conn., Inc. 1st lt. U.S. Army, 1958-60, Korea. Mem. ABA, Conn. Bar Assn. (exec. com. corp. sect.), Internat. Bar Assn., New Canaan Country Club, Campfire Club Am. (bd. govs.), Phi Delta Phi, Omicron Delta Kappa, Phi Delta Theta. Republican. Banking, Contracts commercial, Public international. Office: Roberts Kambas Rose & Bates PC PO Box 15630 1055 Washington Blvd Stamford CT 06901-2216

**ROSE, ROBERT E(DGAR),** state supreme court justice; b. Orange, N.J., Oct. 7, 1939. B.A., Juniata Coll., Huntingdon, Pa., 1961; LL.B., NYU, 1964. Bar: Nev. 1965. Dist. atty. Washoe County, 1971-75; lt. gov. State of Nev., 1975-79; judge Nev. Dist. Ct., 8th Jud. Dist., Las Vegas, 1986-88; justice Nev. Supreme Ct., Carson City, 1989—, chief justice, 1993-94, 99—. Office: Nev Supreme Ct Capitol Complex 201 S Carson St Carson City NV 89701-4702

**ROSE, ROBERT GORDON,** lawyer; b. Newark, June 25, 1943; s. Harry and Ann Shirley (Gordon) R.; m. Ellen Nadley Berkowitz, July 2, 1966; children: Lisa Pauline, Michael Allan. BA, SUNY, Buffalo, 1965; MA, Columbia U., 1969; JD, Seton Hall U., 1974. Bar: N.J. 1974, U.S. Dist. Ct. N.J. 1974, U.S. Ct. Appeals (3rd cir.) 1974, U.S. Ct. Appeals (2nd cir.) 1975. Law clk. to Hon. John J. Gibbons U.S. Ct. Appeals (3rd cir.), Newark, 1974-75; assoc. Pitney, Hardin, Kipp & Szuch, Morristown, N.J., 1975-80, ptnr., 1980—. Contbr. articles to profl. jours. Mem. ABA, N.J. Bar Assn., Morris County Bar Assn. (trustee 1989-90). Avocations: travel, philately. General civil litigation, Environmental, Construction. Office: Pitney Hardin Kipp & Szuch Park Ave at Morris County PO Box 1945 Morristown NJ 07962-1945

**ROSE, TODD ALAN,** lawyer; b. Merced, Calif., Oct. 26, 1962; s. William Arthur and Mary (Brooks) R.; m. Teresa Gail Suiter, June 1, 1991; children: Miranda Brooke, Savannah Leigh, Emily Jane. BS, Murray State U., 1988; JD, Vanderbilt U. Law Sch., 1991. Bar: Tenn. 1991, U.S. Dist. Ct. (we. dist.) Tenn. 1992. Asst. dist. atty. State of Tenn., Paris, 1994-97; mem. Burch, Porter & Johnson, P.L.L.C., Paris, 1997—. General civil litigation, Personal injury, Product liability. Office: Burch Porter & Johnson PLLC 107 W Blythe St Paris TN 38242-4150

**ROSE, WILLIAM SHEPARD, JR.,** lawyer; b. Columbia, S.C., Mar. 9, 1948; s. William Shepard and Meta Cantey (Boykin) R.; m. Frances John Hobbs, Aug. 11, 1973; children: Katherine Cummings, William Shepard, III, Whitaker Boykin. BA in English, U. South, 1970; JD, U. S.C., 1973; LLM in Taxation, Georgetown U., 1976. Bar: S.C. 1973, Ohio 1977, D.C. 1974, U.S. Dist. Ct. D.C. 1976, U.S. Tax Ct. 1976, U.S. Supreme Ct. 1976, U.S. Claims Ct. 1978, U.S. Ct. Appeals (10th cir., 5th cir., 4th cir.) 1987, U.S. Ct. Appeals (3d, 6th, 7th, 8th, 9th and 11th cirs.) 1988. Trial atty. Office of Chief Counsel IRS, Washington, 1973-77; assoc. Frost & Jacobs, Cin., 1977-80, McNair Law Firm, PA, Hilton Head Island, S.C., and Washington, 1980-83, ptnr., 1983-87, 89—; asst. atty. gen., tax div. U.S. Dept. of Justice, Washington, 1987-89; chmn. and dir. Sea Pines Montessori Sch., 1983-86, Hilton Head Broadcasting, 1983-87, Hilton Head Planned Parenthood, 1985-87, MBR Corp., Adwell Corp., Links Group Inc., Hilton Head Prep. Sch., 1986-87, 89-93, dir. Boys & Girls Club of Hilton Head Island, 1992—, Hilton Head Humane Soc., 1985. Contbr. articles to profl. jours. Asst. to chmn. of bus. fund raising Beaufort County United Way, Hilton Head Island, 1984; vice-chmn. Beaufort County Rep. Party, 1991-92, 93, chmn. 1992-93, vice chmn. 1993-95; mem. Beaufort County Transportation Com., 1994-95; commr. Sea Pines Pub. Svc. Dist., South Island Pub. Svc. Dist. Mem. ABA (past co-chmn. subcom. tax sect.), Am. Coll. Tax Counsel, Ohio Bar Assn., D.C. Bar Assn., S.C. Bar Assn., Beaufort County Bar Assn., Hilton Head Bar Assn. Republican. Episcopalian. Clubs: S.C. Yacht Club (bd. govs. 1989-94, exec. com. 1993-94, rear commodore 1993-94), Hilton Head Cotillion, Ducks Unltd., Caroliniana Ball. Taxation, general, General corporate. Home: 11 Jessamine Pl Hilton Head Island SC 29928-4255 Office: PO Drawer 7787 52 New Orleans Rd Ste 204 Hilton Head Island SC 29928-4780

**ROSE-ACKERMAN, SUSAN,** law and political economy educator; b. Mineola, N.Y., Apr. 23, 1942; d. R. William and Rosalie (Gould) Rose; m. Bruce A. Ackerman, May 29, 1967; children: Sybil, John. BA, Wellesley Coll., 1964; PhD, Yale U., 1970. Asst. prof. U. Pa., Phila, 1970-74; lectr. Yale U., New Haven, Conn., 1974-75, asst. prof., 1975-78, assoc. prof., 1978-82; prof. law and polit. economy Columbia U., N.Y.C., 1982-87, dir. Ctr. for Law and Econ. Studies, 1983-87; Ely prof. of law and polit. econ. Yale U., New Haven, 1987-92, Luce prof. jurisprudence law and polit. sci., 1992—; panelist Am. studies program Am. Coun. Learned Socs., 1987-90; review panelist, faculty Fulbright Commn., 1993-96; vis. rsch. fellow World Bank, 1995-96. Author: (with Ackerman, Sawyer and Henderson) Uncertain Search for Environmental Quality, 1974 (Henderson prize 1982); Corruption: A Study in Political Economy, 1978; (with E. James) The Nonprofit Enterprise in Market Economies, 1986; editor: The Economics of Nonprofit Institutions, 1986; (with J. Coffee and L. Lowenstein) Knights, Raiders, and Targets: The Impact of the Hostile Takeover, 1988, Rethinking the Progressive Agenda: The Reform of the American Regulatory State, 1992, Controlling Environmental Policy: The Limits of Public Law in Germany and the United States, 1995, Corruption and Government: Causes, Consequences and Reform, 1999; contbr. articles to profl. jours.; bd. editors: Jour. Law, Econs. and Orgn., 1984—, Internat. Rev. Law and Econs., 1986—, Jour. Policy Analysis and Mgmt., 1989—, Polit. Sci. Quar., 1988—. Guggenheim fellow 1991-92, Fulbright fellow, Free U. Berlin, 1991-92. Mem. Am. Law and Econs. Assn. (bd. dirs. 1993-96), Am. Econ. Assn. (mem. exec. com. 1990-93), Am. Polit. Sci. Assn., Assn. Am. Law Schs., Assn. Pub. Policy and Mgmt. (policy coun. 1984-88, treas. 1998—). Democrat. Office: Yale U Law Sch PO Box 208215 New Haven CT 06520-8215

**ROSELLI, RICHARD JOSEPH,** lawyer; b. Chgo., Mar. 2, 1954; s. H. Joseph and Dolores Roselli; m. Lisa McNelis; children: Nicholas Joseph, Christiana Elise, Alexandra Grace, Michaela Luciana, Anthony Santino. BA, Tulane U., 1976, JD, 1980. Bar: Fla. 1981, U.S. Dist. Ct. (so. dist.) Fla. 1981, U.S. Ct. Appeals (5th and 11th cirs.); bd. cert. civil trial lawyer. Assoc. Krupnick & Campbell, Ft. Lauderdale, Fla., 1981-84; ptnr. Krupnick Campbell, Malone, Roselli, Ft. Lauderdale, 1984-91, Krupnick Campbell Malone Roselli Buser Slama & Hancock P.A., Ft. Lauderdale, 1999—, Krupnick Campbell Malone Roselli Buser Slama Hancock McNelis Liberman & McKee P.A., Ft. Lauderdale, 1999—. Trustee Fla. Dem. Party, 1992-95. Mem. ATLA (pres.' coun. 1996-97), Am. Bd. Trial Advocates, Am. Soc. Law and Medicine, So. Trial Lawyers Assn. (founder), Acad. Fla. Trial Lawyers (bd. dirs. 1987—, exec. com. 1990-97, sec. 1993, treas. 1994, pres. elect. 1995, pres. 1996, chmn. Fla. lawyers action group-PAC 1996, Golden Eagle award, 1989, 1996, 98, Silver Eagle award, 1990, Crystal Eagle award 1995), Broward County Trial Lawyers (bd. dirs.), Trial Lawyers for Pub. Justice, Lawyer Pilots Bar Assn., St. Jude Catholic Ch. Personal injury, Product liability. Office: 700 SE 3rd Ave Fort Lauderdale FL 33316-1154

**ROSEMAN, CHARLES SANFORD,** lawyer; b. Jersey City, Feb. 26, 1945; s. Leon and Edith (Neidorf) R.; children: Rochelle Lynn, Loren Scott. BA, Calif. State U., 1968; JD, U. San Deigo, 1971. Bar: Calif. 1972, U.S. Dist. Ct. (so. dist.) Calif. 1972, U.S. Dist. Ct. (cen. dist.) Calif. 1975, U.S. Supreme Ct. 1980, U.S. Claim Ct. 1990. Assoc. Greer, Popko, Nickoloff & Miller, San Diego, 1972-73; ptnr. Roseman & Roseman, San Diego, 1973-78, Roseman & Small, San Diego, 1978-82, Frank, Roseman, Freedus & Mann, San Diego, 1982-86, Roseman and Mann, 1986-92; pvt. practice San Diego, 1992—; judge pro tem San Diego County Superior Ct., 1977—; also arbitrator, mediator. Bd. dirs. Glenn Aire Cmty. Devel. Assn., San Diego, 1972-73, Big Bros. San Diego County, 1973-81; bd. dirs. San Diego County Anti-Defamation League, 1981—; chmn. exec. com. 1984-85, assoc. nat. commr., 1991—; bd. dirs. San Diego County Legal Aid Soc., 1988-89, Tifereth Israel Synagogue, pres. 1982-84. Mem. ABA, Assn. Trial Lawyers Am., Consumer Attys. of Calif. (Recognition of Experience award 1984—), Calif. Bar Assn., Am. Arbitration Assn. (arbitrator, panel 1980—), San Diego Bar Assn., Consumer Attys. of San Diego (bd. dirs. 1982-84), U. San Diego Sch. Law Alumni Assn. (bd. dirs. 1972-73), B'nai B'rith (pres. 1978). Democrat. Fax: (619) 239-6411. E-mail: csrl@flash.net. State civil litigation, Insurance, Personal injury. Office: Law Offices Charles S Roseman & Assocs 170 Laurel St San Diego CA 92101-1419

**ROSEN, ERIC ALAN,** lawyer; b. N.Y.C.; s. Charels Emanuel and Lillian (Diamond) R.; m. Beth Ilene Gross, July 9, 1989. BA, Columbia U., 1982; JD, Calif. Western Sch. Law, San Diego, 1985. Bar: N.Y. 1986, U.S. Dist. Ct. (so. dist. and ea. dist.) N.Y. 1987. Assoc. Silverberg Stonehill & Goldsmith, N.Y.C., 1985-90, Squadron, Ellenoff, Plesent, Sheinfeld & Sorkin, N.Y.C., 1991-97. Contracts commercial, Bankruptcy, General civil litigation. Office: Abrahams Garfinkel & Rosen LLP 370 Lexington Ave Ste 802 New York NY 10017-6503

**ROSEN, GERALD ELLIS,** federal judge; b. Chandler, Ariz., Oct. 26, 1951; s. Stanley Rosen and Marjorie (Sherman) Cahn; m. Laurie DeMond; 1 child, Jacob DeMond. BA, Kalamazoo Coll., 1973; JD, George Washington U., 1979. Researchist Swedish Inst., Stockholm, 1973; legis. asst. U.S. Senator Robert P. Griffin, Washington, 1974-79; law clk. Seyfarth, Shaw, Fairweather & Gerardson, Wash., 1979; from assoc. to sr. ptnr. Miller, Canfield, Paddock and Stone, Detroit, 1979-90; judge U.S. Dist Ct. (ea. dist.) Mich., Detroit, 1990—; mem. Jud. Evaluation Com. (co-chmn. 1983-88), Detroit; adj. prof. law Wayne State U., 1992—, U. Detroit Law Sch., 1994—; mem. U.S. Jud. Conf. Com. on Criminal Law; lectr. CLE confs., others. Co-author: Federal Civil Trials and Evidence, 1999; contbr. articles to profl. jours. Rep. candidate for U.S. Congress, Mich., 1982; chmn. 17th Congl. Dist. REp. Com., 1983-85; mem. Mich. Criminal Justice Commn., 1985-87; mem. Birmingham Athletic Club. Fellow Kalamazoo Coll. (sr. 1972). Mem. Fed. Judges Assn. (bd. dirs.). Jewish. Office: US Courthouse 231 W Lafayette Blvd Rm 802 Detroit MI 48226-2707

**ROSEN, HOWARD ROBERT,** lawyer; b. Montreal, Que., Can., Apr. 15, 1960; came to U.S. 1967; s. Kelvin and Binnie Lynn (Michaels) R. ; m. Adrienne Joy Unger, Apr. 11, 1987. BA, Emory U., 1982; JD, U. Miami, 1985. Bar: Fla. 1985. Asst. state atty. Dade County State Atty. Office, Miami, Fla., 1985—. Avocations: travel, sports. Home: 17931 NW 9th Ct Pmbk Pines FL 33029-3114 Office: Dade County State Atty 1350 NW 12th Ave Miami FL 33136-2102

**ROSEN, JON HOWARD,** lawyer; b. Bklyn., May 20, 1943; s. Eli and Vera (Horowitz) R.; m. Georgeanne Evans, 1993; children from previous marriage, Jason Marc, Hope Terry. BA, Hobart Coll., 1965; JD, St. John's U., 1968; postgrad., CCNY, 1969-71. Bar: N.Y. 1969, Calif. 1975, Wash. 1977. Atty. FAA, N.Y.C., 1968-71; regional atty., contract adminstr. Air Line Pilots Assn., N.Y.C., Chgo., L.A., San Francisco, 1971-77; pvt. practice Seattle, 1977-80; ptnr. Frank and Rosen, Seattle, 1981-98, Frank Rosen Freed Garfinkel and Roberts LLP, Seattle, 1999—; instr. labor studies Shoreline C.C., 1978-90. Trustee Temple DeHirsch Sinai, 1992-98, v.p., 1998—. Fellow Coll. Labor and Employment Lawyers; mem. ABA (union co-chmn. com. on employee rights and responsibilities 1992-96, union co-chmn. regional inst. sub com., co-regional EEOC liaison), King County Bar Assn. (past chmn. aviation and space law sect., past chmn. Pacific Coast Labor and Employment Law Conf., past chmn. labor law sect.), Nat. Employment Lawyers Assn. (founding state chair, state steering com. 1990-95), Wash. State Trial Lawyers Assn. (past chair employment law com.). Administrative and regulatory, Labor, Civil rights. Office: Frank Rosen Freed Garfinkel & Roberts LLP 705 2nd Ave Ste 1200 Seattle WA 98104-1729

**ROSEN, MARTIN JAY,** lawyer; b. N.Y.C., Nov. 15, 1942; s. Herman S. and Ida (Ginsberg) R.; m. Bonnie C., Dec. 24, 1964; children: Scott F., Brian M. BA, Hobart Coll., 1964; LLB, NYU, 1967. Bar: N.Y. 1967, U.S. Supreme Ct. 1976. Law asst. Appellate Divsn. First Dept., N.Y.C., 1967-68; assoc. Battle, Fowler, Stokes & Kheel, N.Y.C., 1968-69; confdl. law sec. to justice Supreme Ct. Westchester County, N.Y., 1969-71; sole practice White Plains, N.Y., 1975—; lectr. in field. Past editor Domestic Law Rev.; contbr. articles to legal jours. Fellow Am. Acad. Matrimonial Lawyers; mem. ABA, N.Y. State Bar Assn., Westchester County Bar Assn. (past chmn. family law), Rockland County Bar Assn., White Plains Bar Assn. Family and matrimonial. Office: 175 Main St Suite 415 White Plains NY 10601

**ROSEN, MARVIN SHELBY,** lawyer; b. Detroit, Aug. 8, 1947; s. Joseph P. and Rachel K. (Kaplan) R.; m. Sandra Mira Levy, Nov. 22, 1970; children: Joseph H., Bradley J. BA, Columbia U., 1970, JD, MBA, 1973; B in Hebrew Lit., Jewish Theol. Sem., N.Y.C., 1970. Bar: Mich. 1974, Fla. 1984. Assoc. Honigman Miller Schwartz and Cohn, Detroit, 1974-78; ptnr. Honigman Miller Schwartz and Cohn, 1978-84; mng. ptnr. Honigman Miller Schwartz and Cohn, West Palm Beach, Fla., 1984-97; shareholder Ruden, McClosky, Smith, Schuster & Russell, P.A., West Palm Beach, 1997—. Contbr. articles to profl. jours. Mem. bd. overseers List Coll., N.Y.C.; v.p. Pres. Country Club, 1995-99, Jewish Fedn. Palm Beach County, 1992-99; pres. Jewish Cmty. Day Sch., 1987-88; founding chmn. Commn. for Jewish Edn., 1990—; pres.-elect Temple Emanu-El, Palm Beach, 1999—. Named one of Best Lawyers in Am., 1989—. Mem. Mich. State Bar (chmn. com. on mortgages, land contracts and related security devices real property sect. 1982-84), Detroit Bar Assn. (chmn. real property sect. 1982-83). E-mail: msr@ruden.com. Fax: 561-832-3036. Real property, Finance. Office: Ruden McClosky Smith Schuster & Russell PA 222 Lakeview Ave Ste 800 West Palm Beach FL 33401-6148

**ROSEN, MATTHEW A.,** lawyer; b. Phila., 1952. BA, Swarthmore Coll., 1973; JD cum laude, Boston U., 1976; LLM, NYU, 1979. Bar: Pa. 1976, N.Y. 1979. Sr. ptnr. Skadden, Arps, Slate, Meagher & Flom LLP, N.Y.C. Corporate taxation, Taxation, general, Personal income taxation. Office: Skadden Arps Slate Meagher & Flom LLP 919 3rd Ave New York NY 10022-3902

**ROSEN, PAUL MAYNARD,** lawyer; b. Queens, N.Y., Sept. 29, 1943; s. Lewis L. and Leanore (Frant) R.; m. Clare E. Rosenberg, June 17, 1967; children: Rebecca K., Chad D. BS, Rensselaer Poly. Inst., 1965; JD, Cornell U., 1968. Bar: N.Y. 1969, U.S. Supreme Ct. 1980, U.S. Dist. Ct. (so. and ea. dist.) N.Y. 1981. Asst. dist. atty. Westchester County, White Plains, N.Y., 1970-72; law sec. Westchester County Ct. Judge, White Plains, N.Y., 1972-74; ptnr. Natale & Rosen, Yonkers, N.Y., 1974-80; pvt. practice law Briarcliff, N.Y., 1980—; impartial hearing officer State Edn. Dept., 1986—. Town chmn. Ossining Rep. Party, 1982-94; v.p. congregation Sons of Israel, 1982-84. With U.S. Army, 1968-70. Paul Harris fellow Rotary, 1985. Mem. Ossining Bar Assn., Rotary (pres. 1984), Masons. Criminal, Education and schools, Real property. Home and Office: 130 Marlborough Rd Briarcliff Manor NY 10510-2013

**ROSEN, RICHARD DAVID,** lawyer; b. Pitts., June 24, 1940; s. Benjamin H. and Bertha B. (Broff) R.; m. Ellaine H. Heller, June 23, 1963; children: Deborah H. Fidel, Jaime M. Cohen. BA, Yale U., 1962; JD, Harvard U., 1965. Bar: Pa. 1966, Fla. 1979. Mgr. Bachrach, Sanderbeck & Co., Pitts., 1965-70; mng. ptnr. Grant Thornton, Pitts., 1970-76; chmn. tax dept. Baskin & Sears, Pitts., 1977-78; pres. Gas Transmission, Inc., Pitts., 1979-88; dir., shareholder Cohen & Grigsby, Pitts., 1989—; bd. dirs., pres. R & R Oil Corp., Pitts.; bd. dirs., sec. Comml. Data Svcs., Sim Computer Leasing Corp., Pitts., Direct Mail Svc., Inc. Contbr. articles to profl. jours. Mem. investment com., trustee Jewish Healthcare Found., 1995—. Fellow Am. Coll. Trust and Estate Counsel; mem. ABA, Pa. Bar Assn. (mem. estate planning com. 1996—, chmn. 1998—), United Jewish Fedn. Greater Pitts.

(chmn. profl. adv. com. 1997—), Concordia Club (dir. 1998), Green Oaks Country Club (dir. 1997—). Avocations: golf, tennis. Home: 1198 Beechwood Ct Pittsburgh PA 15206-4522 Office: Cohen & Grigsby PC 11 Stanwix St Ste 15 Pittsburgh PA 15222-1312

**ROSEN, RICHARD LEWIS,** lawyer, real estate developer; b. N.Y.C., Mar. 6, 1943; s. Morris and Lorraine (Levy) R.; m. Doris Ellen Bloom, Aug. 28, 1983. BA, Cornell U., 1965; JD, N.Y. Law Sch., 1968; cert., NYU Real Estate Inst., 1980. Bar: N.Y. 1968, U.S. Dist. Ct. (so. and ea. dists.) N.Y. 1972; lic. real estate broker. Pvt. practice N.Y.C., 1971-73; ptnr. Rosen, Wise, Felzen & Salomon, N.Y.C., 1973-79, Rosen & Felzen, N.Y.C., 1979-84, Rosen, Rudd, Kera, Graubard & Hollender, N.Y.C., 1985-88, Bell, Kalnick, Klee and Green, N.Y.C., 1989-90; shareholder Rosen, Einbinder & Dunn, P.C., N.Y.C., 1990—. Named Ea. States Lightweight Weightlifting Champion, 1968; N.Y. State Regents scholar. Mem. ABA (mem. Forum Com. on Franchising), Am. Assn. Franchises and Dealers (former chmn. legal steering com., chmn. fair franchising stds. com., chmn. alternate dispute resolution com., bd. dirs.), Franchise Lawyers Assn., Am. Franchise Assn., N.Y. State Bar Assn. (founding mem. franchise law com., chmn. mission statement com. of franchise law com.), Nat. Franchise Mediation Program (mem. steering com.), Assn. Bar City N.Y. (panel mem. com. on franchising, panel mem. com. on corp. law), Red Key Hon. Soc., Cornell U., Sphinx Head Hon. Soc., Cornell U., Spiked Shoe Soc., Cornell U., Ea. Intercollegiate Athletic Assn. (named Lightweight Football All Ea. Selection 1963, 64). Avocations: tennis, skiing, physical fitness, guitar, reading. General corporate, Real property, Franchising. Home: 1 Old Jericho Tpke Jericho NY 11753-1205 also: Lamb Ave Quogue NY 11959 Office: Rosen Einbinder & Dunn PC 641 Lexington Ave New York NY 10022-4503

**ROSEN, SANFORD JAY,** lawyer; b. N.Y.C., Dec. 19, 1937; s. Alexander Charles and Viola S. (Grad) R.; m. Catherine Picard, June 22, 1958; children: Caren E. Andrews, R. Durelle Schacter, Ian D., Melissa S. AB, Cornell U., 1959; LLB, Yale U., 1962. Bar: Conn. 1962, U.S. Supreme Ct. 1966, Calif. 1974. Law clk. to Hon. Simon E. Sobeloff U.S. Ct. Appeals, Balt., 1962-63; prof. sch. law U. Md., Balt., 1963-71; assoc. dir. Coun. on Legal Edn. Opportunity, Atlanta, 1969-70; vis. prof. law U. Tex., Austin, 1970-71; asst. legal dir. Nat. ACLU, N.Y.C., 1971-73; legal dir. Mex.-Am. Legal Def. Fund, San Francisco, 1973-75; ptnr. Rosen, Remcho & Henderson, San Francisco, 1976-80, Rosen & Remcho, San Francisco, 1980-82; prin. Law Offices of Sanford Jay Rosen, San Francisco, 1982-86; sr. ptnr. Rosen & Phillips, San Francisco, 1986-89; prin. Rosen & Assocs., San Francisco, 1990; sr. ptnr. Rosen, Bien & Asaro, San Francisco, 1991—; mem. Balt. Cmty. Rels. Commn., 1966-69; mem. com. Patuxent Instn., Md., 1967-69; ad hoc adminstrv. law judge Calif. Agrl. Labor Rels. Bd., San Francisco, 1975-80; interim monitor U.S. Dist. Ct. for no. dist. Calif., San Francisco, 1989, early neutral evaluator, 1987—, mediator, 1993—; judge pro tem San Francisco Superior Ct., 1991—; perm. atty. del. Jud. Conf. U.S. Ct. Appeal for 4th Cir.; atty. del. Jud. Conf. U.S. Ct. Appeals 9th cir., 1996-98. Contbr. articles to profl. jours. Mem. Com. on Adminstrn. of Criminal Justice, Balt., 1968; mem. adv. com. HEW, Washington, 1974-75. Mem. ABA, Assn. Trial Lawyers Am. (chair civil rights sect. 1993-94), D.C. Bar Assn., Calif. Bar Assn., Bar Assn. San Francisco. Avocations: reading, travel, movies. General civil litigation. Office: Rosen Bien & Asaro 155 Montgomery St Fl 8 San Francisco CA 94104-4113

**ROSEN, SIDNEY MARVIN,** lawyer; b. Detroit, June 27, 1939; s. Fred A. and Gertrude (Cole) R.; m. Babette Van Praag, July 3, 1971; children: Jordan, Aviva. BS, U. Ariz., 1961, JD, 1964. Bar: Ariz. 1964, U.S. Dist. Ct. Ariz. 1964, Calif. 1965, U.S. Dist. Ct. (so. dist.) Calif. 1965, U.S. Supreme Ct. 1971. Asst. atty. gen. State of Ariz., Phoenix, 1964-66, spl. asst. atty. gen., 1968-69; assoc. Kirkwood, Kaplan, Russin & Vechi, Bangkok and Saigon, Vietnam, 1967-68; ptnr. Rosen, Ocampo and Fontes, Phoenix, 1970—; co-founder, law instr. Ariz. Bar Rev. Course, 1965-73; prof. internat. law Am. Grad. Sch. of Internat. Mgmt., Phoenix, 1975-76; former gen. counsel Nat. Speakers Assn., 1973-85. Candidate Dem. nomination for atty. gen. State of Ariz., 1974, U.S. Congress, 1976; mem. Ariz.-Mex. Gov.'s Commn., 1974—, counsel commerce and industry sect., 1974—; chmn. campaign Bonds for Israel, Ariz., 1980-85. Baird scholar, University scholar; recipient Speaker Preview Auditions First Pl. award Internat. Platform Assn., 1969-70, Silver Bowl award, 1969-70. Mem. Ariz. Bar Assn. (internat. relations com.), Calif. Bar Assn., Maricopa County Bar Assn., World Assn. Lawyers, Nat. Speakers Assn. (founder, former gen. counsel 1973-85), World Affairs Council, Hospitality Internat. (host), FIABCI (law instr. Internat. Real Estate Fedn. 1985—, gen. counsel Ariz. chpt. 1985—), Ariz. World Trade Assn. (former bd. dirs.), Jaycees (treas. Ariz. chpt. 1969-70, ambassador to Philippine Islands 1969-70), Pan Am. Club of Ariz. (past pres.), Traveler's Century Club, Valley Forward Assn. (bd. dirs.), Phi Alpha Delta (pres. 1963-64). Democrat. Jewish. Lodge: Kiwanis. Avocations: stamp collecting, photography, world traveling, camping, scuba diving. Private international, Estate planning, General corporate. Home: 2233 N Alvarado Rd Phoenix AZ 85004-1415 Office: Rosen Ocampo & Fontes 4323 N 12th St Ste 104 Phoenix AZ 85014-4506

**ROSEN, STEPHEN LESLIE,** lawyer; b. St. Paul, Minn., Nov. 20, 1948. BA, Hamline U., 1970; JD, So. Tex. U., 1974. Bar: Fla. 1974, U.S. Dist. Ct. Fla. 1975, U.S. Supreme Ct. 1980. Atty. Marlow, Mitzel, Ortmayer, Tampa, Fla., 1974-76, Wagner, Cunningham, Tampa, 1976-79, Morris and Rosen, Tampa, 1980-92, Rosen and Osborne, PA, Tampa, 1992—. Author: Worker's Compensation, Florida Bar, 1975, Longshore and Harborworkers Law, Florida Bar, 1978. Mem. Fla. Bar Assn. (chmn. worker's compensation bd. cert. com. 1988-90, chmn. statewide judicial nominating com., 1990-93, chmn. worker's compensation sect. 1992, Bud Adams award 1991). Workers' compensation.

**ROSEN, WILLIAM WARREN,** lawyer; b. New Orleans, July 22, 1936; s. Warren Leucht and Erma (Stich) R.; m. Eddy Kahn, Nov. 26, 1965; children: Elizabeth K., Victoria A. BA, Tulane U., 1958, JD, 1964. Bar: La. 1964, U.S. Dist. Ct. (ea. dist.) La. 1965, U.S. Ct. Appeals (5th cir.) 1965, U.S. Supreme Ct. 1984, U.S. Dist. Ct. (mid. dist.) La. 1985, Colo. 1989. Assoc. Dodge & Friend, New Orleans, 1965-68, Law Office of J.R. Martzell, New Orleans, 1968-70; pvt. practice New Orleans, 1970-79, 89-90; ptnr. Lucas & Rosen (and predecessor firms), New Orleans, 1979-87, Herman, Herman, Katz & Cotlar, New Orleans, 1987-88, Rosen and Samuel, New Orleans, 1990-95; of counsel Rittenberg & Samuel, New Orleans, 1996-99; founder & dir. Litigation Consultation Svcs., New Orleans, 1996-99; ptnr. Rosen & Lundeen, L.L.P., New Orleans, 1999—; adj. prof. trial advocacy Law Sch. Tulane U., 1988—, mem. adv. com. paralegal studies program, 1977-86, instr. bus. orgns., 1978, instr. legal interviewing, 1980-81; mem. adv. com. Paralegal Inst. U. New Orleans, 1990—, instr. legal interviewing and investigations, 1986-87; lectr. legal and paralegal fields; lectr. real and demonstrative evidence Nat. Edn. Network, 1993. Author: (with others) Trial Techniques publ. La. Trial Lawyers Assn., 1981; columnist Briefly Speaking publ. New Orleans Bar Assn., 1993—. Mem. budget and planning com. Jewish Welfare Fedn., 1970-73; mem. adv. coun. on drug edn. La. Dept. Edn., 1973; mem. profl. adv. com. Jewish Endowment Found., 1982—; mem. exec. com. U.S. Olympic Com., La., 1982-84; bd. dirs. Planned Parenthood La., 1994—; pres. Dad's Club, Isidore Newman Sch., 1984-85, Uptown Flood Assn., 1982-85; bd. dirs. Jewish Children's Home Svc., 1973-76, Met. Crime Commn. New Orleans, 1976-82; spl. agt. Office Spl. Investigations USAF, 1958-61. Fellow, Inst. of Politics. Loyola U. Mem. ABA, ATLA (keyperson com. 1986-89, vice chmn. paralegal com. 1986-89, mem. family law adv. com. 1989-90, sec. family law sect. 1990-91, lectr. legal edn. 1979, 81, 83, 86, 88); mem. La. Bar Assn. (vice chmn. pub. rels. com. 1970-73, 88-89, past chmn. state youth drug abuse edn. program, vol. lawyers for arts 1986-96, chmn. sr. counsel com. 1995-96), Am. Arbitration Assn., Nat. Fedn. Paralegal Assn. (adv. coun. 1989—), Assn. Atty. Mediators (pres. La. chpt. 1995), Nat. Choice in Dying (legal adv. com. 1992-96), Nat. Edn. Network (lectr. legal edn. 1993), New Orleans Bar Assn. (CLE com. 1990-91, chmn. 1991-92, mem. alternative dispute resolution com. 1996—, panel moderator 1997), Inn of Ct. (master 1992—), Rotary Club New Orleans (bd. dirs. 1996-98, chmn. legal com. 1996—). Avocation: photography (included in Louisiana Photographers publ. Contemporary Arts Ctr. 1988). Fax: 504-523-3370. E-mail: LCSNO@aol.com. State civil litigation, Federal civil litigation, General practice. Office: Rosen & Lundeen LLP 210 Baronne St Ste 704 New Orleans LA 70112-1722

**ROSENBAUM, JAMES MICHAEL,** judge; b. Fort Snelling, Minn., Oct. 12, 1944; s. Sam. H. and Ilene D. (Bernstein) R.; m. Marilyn Brown, July 30, 1972; children: Alexandra, Victoria and Catherine (twins). BA, U. Minn., 1966, JD, 1969. Bar: Minn. 1969, Ill. 1970, U.S. Supreme Ct. 1979. VISTA staff atty. Leadership Council for Met. Open Communities, Chgo., 1969-72; assoc. Katz, Taube, Lange & Frommelt, Mpls., 1972-77; ptnr. Rosenbaum & Rosenbaum, Mpls., 1977-79, Gainsley, Squier & Korsh, Mpls., 1979-81; U.S. dist. atty. U.S. Dept. Justice, Mpls., 1981-85; judge U.S. Dist. Ct., Minn., 1985—; 8th cir. rep. Jud. Conf. U.S., 1997—; mem. Jud. Conf. U.S. Author booklet: Guide to Practice Civil Rights Housing, 1972; co-author: U.S. Courts Design Guide, 1991-96. Campaign chmn. People for Boschwitz, Minn., 1978, bd. vis. U. Minn. Law Sch. (pres. 1996-97). Mem. Fed. Bar Assn. (bd. dirs., pres. 1992-93, 8th cir. rep. Judicial Conf. of U.S. 1998—). Republican. Jewish. Office: US Courthouse 300 S 4th St Minneapolis MN 55415-1320

**ROSENBAUM, MARCIA F.,** lawyer; b. Binghamton, N.Y., Aug. 3, 1945; d. Arthur I. S. and Miriam r. BS, Temple U., 1967; MBA, 1981; MSS, Bryn Mawr Coll., 1969; JD cum laude, Widener U., 1986. Bar: Pa. 1986, U.S. Dist. Ct. N.J. 1986, U.S. Ct. Appeals (3rd cir.) 1988. Asst. dir. Dept. Social Work Hosp. U. Pa., Phila., 1969-79; ptnr. Perry, Fialkowski & Perry, Phila., 1986—. Grantee NIH, 1967-69. Mem. ABA, Pa. Bar Assn., N.J. Bar Assn., Phila. Bar Assn. Health, Personal injury, General civil litigation. Office: Perry Fialkowski & Perry 30 S 15th St Ste 1600 Philadelphia PA 19102-4807

**ROSENBAUM, MARTIN MICHAEL,** retired insurance company executive, lawyer; b. Aug. 8, 1923; came to U.S., 1939, naturalized, 1944; s. emil Elias and Pauline (Latte) R.; m. Hanna Lore Serog, July 6, 1952; children: Thomas F., Evelyn J. BS in Bus. Adminstrn., Boston U., 1948; JD, N.Y.U., 1952, LLM in Taxation, 1956. Bar: N.Y. 1953, U.S. Supreme Ct. 1968. With Chubb & Son Inc., 1948-88, tax cons., 1988—; with Chubb Corp., N.Y.C., 1967-88, v.p. tax dir., sr. tax counsel, 1972-88; v.p. taxes subs., sr. v.p. Chubb & Son Inc., N.Y.C., 1968-88, Fed. Ins. Co., N.Y.C., 1968-88, Vigilant Ins. Co., N.Y.C., 1979-88, Pacific Indemnity Co., N.Y.C., 1979-88; retired, 1998; former dir. Gan-Anglo Am. Ins. Co., 1981-88, ret. 1997; past bd. dirs., pres. subs. DHC Corp. 1982-88; bd. dirs. Alliance Assurance Co. Am., Sun Ins. Office of Am., Inc., The London Assurance of Am. Inc., The Sea Ins. Co. of Am., Marine Indemnity Ins. Co. of Am.; lectr. in taxation field. With AUS, 1943-46; ETO. Mem. ABA (past chmn. fgn. ins. subcom., past chmn. Non-Life Ins. Subcom.), Am. Ins. Assn. (past chmn. tax com.), Soc. Ins. Accts. (past chmn. tax com.). Jewish. Home and Office: Apt 205 724 12th St Wilmette IL 60091-2637

**ROSENBERG, A. IRVING,** lawyer; b. Newark, Aug. 4, 1921; s. Sam and Dora Rosenberg; m. Toby Kalb, Dec. 12, 1943; children: Jeffrey, Elliot. Stenographic ct. reporting cert., Ct. Reporting Sch., Newark, 1940; Law Degree, Rutgers U., Newark, 1948. Bar: N.J. 1948. Office staf U.S. Secret Svc. Treasury Dept., Newark and N.Y.C., 1940-42; pvt. practice law, 1948—; pres., dir. Psychic Studies Inst., Union, N.J., 1978—; lectr. in field. Author: Autobiography of the Unconscious, 1978; law rev. staff Rutgers Law Rev. Jour., 1941; contbr. articles to profl. jours. Comdr. Jewish War Vets. Post, Union, 1971-72; dir. C. of C., Union, 1975-85; chancellor comdr. Knights of Pythias, Union, 1985-86. With USN, 1942-45. Mem. ABA (sr., sr. divsn.), Internat. Soc. for the Study of Multiple Personality and Dissociation (also N.J. chpt.), Am. Soc. for Psychical Rsch. Avocations: tennis, boating, antique collecting, trance mediumship and hypnosis. E-mail: airvingrose@prodigy.net. General practice, Real property, Probate. Office: 1227 Morris Ave Union NJ 07083-3307

**ROSENBERG, BURTON STUART,** lawyer; b. New Haven, Nov. 15, 1949; s. Herbert T. and Frances Rosenberg; children: Mark Daniel, David Matthew, Jeffrey Barrett. BA, Lehigh U., 1971; JD, NYU, 1974. Bar: Conn. 1975, U.S. Dist. Ct. Conn. 1975, U.S. Ct. Appeals (2d cir.) 1982. Assoc. Law Office Norman Zolot, New Haven, 1974-79; atty. Gen. Telephone & Electronics, Stamford, Conn., 1980-82; ptnr. Zolot & Rosenberg, New Haven, Conn., 1983-98; corp. couns. Town of Hamden, CT, 1991-97; Asst. Corp. Couns., City of Stamford, CT, 1998—. Contbg. editor: The Developing Labor Law, 1979. Mem. ABA (labor law sect.), Conn. Bar Assn. (co-chmn. arbitration sect. 1982, labor and employment law sect.), Assn. Trial Lawyers Am. Democrat. Jewish. Labor, Pension, profit-sharing, and employee benefits, Federal civil litigation. Office: 888 Washington Blvd Stamford CT 06901-2902

**ROSENBERG, DAVID A.,** lawyer; b. Columbus, Ohio, Jan. 25, 1969. BTL, Ner Israel Rabbinical Coll., 1990; JD, U. Balt., 1994. Bar: Md. 1995, U.S. Dist. Ct. Md. 1995. Assoc. Robert N. Grossbart, PA, Balt., 1996—. Bankruptcy, Personal injury. Office: Robert N Grossnbart PA 1 N Charles St Ste 1902 Baltimore MD 21201-3727

**ROSENBERG, DAVID MICHAEL,** lawyer; b. Atlanta; s. Charles Michael and Patricia (Vinson) R.; 1 child, Michael. BA, U. N.C., 1985; JD, U. Ga., Athens, 1988. Bar: Ga. 1988. Jud. law clk. Blue Ridge, Ga., 1988-89; atty. Robert K. Ballew P.C., Blue Ridge, 1989-94; sole practice Blue Ridge, 1994—. Author: Crumbs and Crackers—A History of Atlanta Baseball—1865-1964, 1988. Mem. Ga. Bar Assn., Kiwanis Club. Avocations: tournament bridge, coordinating and coaching youth sports, dramatic arts. Family and matrimonial, Criminal, Personal injury. Office: PO Box 1372 Blue Ridge GA 30513-0024

**ROSENBERG, FLORENCE PESSAH,** lawyer; b. N.Y.C., Jan. 8, 1922; d. Morris A. Pessah and Fanny Cantor; m. June 1, 1985; children: Richard C., sherry A. Waldorf, Barret Craig. JD, St. John's Law, 1946. Bar: N.Y. 1946, Calif. 1961. Atty. Fed. Cts., L.A., 1961-65; assoc. Hirschberg, Goodman & King, L.A., 1966-68; atty. Crenshaw Legal Clinic, L.A., 1971-80; pvt. practice Encino, Calif., 1981-94, Calabasas, Calif., 1994—; atty. domestic violence, Van Nuys, Calif., 1986—. Mem. L.A. Bar Assn. (Vol. 1988), San Fernando Bar Assn. (Pro Bono for Domestic Violence 1997). Family and matrimonial. Home and Office: 3753 Calle Jazmin Calabasas CA 91302-3040

**ROSENBERG, GARY MARC,** lawyer; b. N.Y.C., June 4, 1950; s. David and Edna (Goldberg) R.; m. I. Denise Estes, July 3, 1971; children: Dena Elyse, Janna Beth, Adam Ilan. BA, Queens Coll., 1971; JD, Bklyn. Law Sch., 1974. Bar: N.Y. 1975, U.S. Dist. Ct. (so. dist.) N.Y. 1976, U.S. Supreme Ct. 1985. Pres. Rosenberg & Estis, P.C., N.Y.C., 1976—. State civil litigation, Landlord-tenant, Real property. Office: Rosenberg & Estis PC 733 3rd Ave New York NY 10017-3204

**ROSENBERG, JEROME ROY,** lawyer, accountant; b. N.Y.C., Oct. 5, 1926; s. Louis and May (Schack) R.; m. Julia Daniels, Apr. 21, 1968; children: Louise I., Daniel M. BS, NYU, 1949, JD, 1953, LLM in Taxation, 1972; postgrad., Oxford U., 1949. Bar: N.Y. 1956, U.S. Dist. Ct. (so. dist.) N.Y. 1985, U.S. Dist. Ct. (ea. dist.) N.Y. 1985, U.S. Claims Ct. 1977, U.S. Tax Ct. 1965, U.S. Supreme Ct. 1968. Acct. Apfel & Englander, CPAs, N.Y.C., 1950-52; with Abraham J. Bilorr, CPA, N.Y.C., 1952-54, Samuel Aronowitz & Co., CPAs, N.Y.C., 1955-57, David Berdon & Co., CPAs, N.Y.C., 1957-63; sole practice N.Y.C., 1964—; spl. tax counsel Jackson & Nash, N.Y.C., 1964-70, Seward & Kissel, N.Y.C., 1968—; lectr. NYU, 1972; co-foudner N.Y. Tax Study Group, Inc. Author: Managing Your Own Money, 1979; asst. tech. editor Jour. Taxation, 1964; mem. editl. bd. Practical Acct., 1968-85; sr. tech. editor Income Tax Workbook, 1970-75. Served with USAF, 1943-45. Mem. ABA, Assn. Bar City N.Y., AICPA, N.Y. Soc. CPAs (mem. exec. tax com. 1983-92, CPAs Disting. Svc. award 1993. Personal income taxation, State and local taxation, Probate. Home: 50 Park Ave New York NY 10016-3075

**ROSENBERG, JODI L.,** lawyer; b. Bklyn., July 23, 1968; m. Daniel H. Rosenberg. BA in Polit. Sci., U. Mich., 1990; JD, Boston U., 1993. Bar: N.J. 1993, U.S. Dist. Ct. N.J. 1993, N.Y. 1994, U.S. Dist. Ct. (so. dist.) N.Y. 1996. Assoc. Giordano, Halleran & Ciesla, Middletown, N.J., 1993-95, Greenbaum, Rowe, Smith, Ravin, Davis & Himmel, Woodbridge, N.J., 1995—. Labor, Workers' compensation. Office: Greenbaum Rowe Smith etal 99 Wood Ave S Woodbridge NJ 07095

**ROSENBERG, JONATHAN S.,** lawyer; b. Manhasset, N.Y., Mar. 16, 1967; s. Gary Rosenberg and Wilma J. Rifkin. BA, U. Pa., 1988; JD, Columbia U., 1992. Bar: N.Y., U.S. Dist. Ct. (ea. dist.) N.Y., U.S. Dist. Ct. (so. dist.) N.Y. Social worker The Children's Aid Soc., N.Y.C., 1988-89, dir. of pub. policy and advocacy, 1997-98; staff atty. The Legal Aid Soc. of Criminal Appeals Bur., N.Y.C., 1992-94; civil rights atty. U.S. Dept. Edn., N.Y.C., 1995-97, 98—; Pres. Baltictown, Inc., Bklyn., 1998—. Mem. Bar Assn. City of N.Y. Office: US Dept Edn Office of Civil Rights 75 Park Pl Fl 14 New York NY 10007-2146

**ROSENBERG, LAWRENCE DAVID,** lawyer; b. Abington, Pa., May 29, 1967; s. Robert Allen and Geraldine Bella (Tishler) R.; m. Deborah Topol, Apr. 5, 1997. BA, Cornell U., 1989; JD magna cum laude, U. Pa., 1992. Bar: Pa., U.S. Ct. Appeals (3d, 5th and D.C. cirs.), D.C. Law clk. to Hon. Jane R. Roth U.S. Ct. Appeals, Wilmington, Del., 1992-93; trial atty. U.S. Dept. Justice, Washington, 1993-98; assoc. Jones, Day, Reavis & Pague, Washington, 1998—. Fditor U. Pa. Law Rev., 1990-92. Recipient various awards in forensics and debate. Avocations: travel, tennis, bridge, golf, music. Office: Jones Day Reavis & Pague 1450 G St NW Washington DC 20005-2001

**ROSENBERG, MARC S.,** lawyer; b. N.Y.C., June 15, 1958; s. Marvin and Bette Rosenberg; m. Tina Rosenberg; children: Brett, James, Katherine. AB, Princeton U., 1980; JD, Harvard U., 1983. Assoc. Cravath Swaine & Moore, N.Y.C., 1985-90, ptnr., 1990—. Securities, Mergers and acquisitions, General corporate. Office: Cravath Swaine & Moore 825 8th Ave Fl 38 New York NY 10019-7475

**ROSENBERG, MAX D.,** lawyer; b. Grand Forks, N.D., Oct. 8, 1930; s. Samuel and Ethyl R.; m. Sarah Rosenberg, Oct. 8, 1965; children: Arthur, Etty, Dara. BSc, U. N.D., 1952, LLB, 1957. Bar: N.D., 1957, U.S. Dist. Ct., 1957, N.D. State Ct. (8th cir.), 1975, U.S. Supreme Ct., 1979. Pvt. practice Garrison, N.D., 1957, Bismarck, N.D., 1957—. With U.S. Army, 1952-54. Mem. Masons and Shrine. Republican. Jewish. Avocations: golf, exercise, volleyball. Consumer commercial, Bankruptcy, Contracts commercial. Office: 309 N Mandan St Bismarck ND 58501-3859

**ROSENBERG, MICHAEL,** lawyer; b. N.Y.C., Oct. 13, 1937; s. Walter and Eva (Bernstein) R.; m. Jacqueline Raymonde Combe, Apr. 29, 1966; children: Andrew James, Suzanne Jennifer. AB in Econs. with honors, Ind. U., 1959; LLB, Columbia U., 1962. Bar: N.Y. 1963, U.S. Dist. Ct. (so. and ea. dists.) N.Y. 1966, U.S. Ct. Appeals (2d cir.) 1975, U.S. Dist. Ct. (ea. dist. so. div.) Mich. 1989. From. dep. asst. atty. gen. to asst. atty. gen. N.Y. State Dept. Law, N.Y.C., 1963-66; assoc. Hellerstein, Rosier & Rembar, N.Y.C., 1966-73; assoc. gen. counsel Gen. Instrument Corp., N.Y.C., 1973-78; from assoc. gen. counsel to dep. gen. counsel U.S. Filter Corp., N.Y.C., 1978-82; v.p., gen. counsel, sec. Alfa-Laval Inc., Ft. Lee, N.J., 1982-88; counsel Becker Ross Stone De Stefano & Klein, N.Y.C., 1988-89; ptnr. Rosenberg & Rich, White Plains, N.Y., 1989-95, Quinn, Marantis & Rosenberg, LLP, White Plains, N.Y., 1995-97, Marantis, Rosenberg & van Nes, LLP, White Plains, 1997—. Mem. Zoning Bd. Appeals Town of North Castle, N.Y., 1995—. Mem. ABA, N.Y. State Bar Assn., Westchester County Bar Assn. General corporate, Contracts commercial, Real property. Office: Marantis Rosenberg & van Nes LLP 3 Barker Ave White Plains NY 10601-1509

**ROSENBERG, PAUL I.,** lawyer; b. Newark, N.J., Feb. 26, 1937. BS in Econs., U. Pa. Wharton Sch., 1959; MBA, NYU, 1964, JD, 1970, LLM, 1975. Bar: N.J. 1970, U.S. Dist. Ct. N.J. 1970, N.Y. 1982, U.S. Dist. Ct. N.Y. 1982, U.S. Tax Ct. 1983. Ptnr. Fox and Fox LLP, Livingston, 1974—. Contbr. articles to legal publs. Fellow Am. Coll. Trust and Estate Counsel (mem. nat. employee benefits in estate-planning, estate and gift tax com.); mem. ABA (coms. estate and gift tax 1976—, vice-chmn. lifetime gifts, real property, probate and trust law), Essex County Bar Assn., N.J. State Bar Assn. Probate, Corporate taxation, Estate taxation. Home: One Belgrade Terr West Orange NJ 07052 Office: Fox and Fox LLP 70 S Orange Ave Livingston NJ 07039-4994

**ROSENBERG, PETER DAVID,** lawyer, educator; b. N.Y.C., Aug. 2, 1942; s. Frederick and Martha (Grossman) R. BA, NYU, 1962, B in Chem. Engring., 1963; JD, N.Y. Law Sch., 1968; LLM, George Washington U., 1971. Bar: N.Y. 1970, U.S. Ct. Appeals (2d cir.) 1970, U.S. Dist. Ct. (so. and ea. dists.) N.Y. 1971, U.S. Supreme Ct. 1973, U.S. Dist Ct. (no. and we. dists.) N.Y. 1979, U.S. Ct. Appeals (D.C. cir.) 1982, U.S. Ct. Internat. Trade 1982, U.S. Ct. Mil. Appeals 1982, U.S. Ct. Appeals (fed. cir.) 1983; registered U.S. Patent and Trademark Office. Primary examiner U.S. Patent and Trademark Office, Washington, 1968-95; of counsel Harris Beach & Wilcox, Syracuse, N.Y., 1995—; adj. prof. law Syracuse U. Coll. Law. Recipient Silver Medal award U.S. Dept. Commerce, 1981. Mem. ABA (antitrust and intellectual property sects.). Author: Patent Law Fundamentals, 1975, 2d edit. 1980, rev. 1999, Patent Law Basics, 1999, rev. 1999; asst. editor Jour. Patent and Trademark Office Soc., 1968-95; contbr. articles to profl. jours. Home: PO Box 788 4916 Rte 11 Pierrepont Manor NY 13674

**ROSENBERG, ROBIN L.,** lawyer; b. West Palm Beach, Fla., Jan. 22, 1962; d. Marvin M. and Baylie R. Rosenberg; m. Michael M. McAuliffe, Dec. 14, 1993; 1 child, sydney Rosenberg McAuliffe. BA, Princeton U., 1983; MA, Duke U., 1989, JD, 1989. Bar: Fla. Law clk. to James C. Paine U.S. Dist. Ct. (so. dist.) Fla., West Palm Beach, 1989-90; atty. U.S. Dept. Justice, Washington, 1990-94; atty., asst. city atty. City of West Palm Beach, 1995-97; atty., ptnr. Holland & Knight LLP, 1997—. Chair Friends of Bob Graham Steering Com. for Palm Beach County, Fla., 1998. Mem. Exec. Women of the Palm Beaches. General civil litigation, Labor, Civil rights. Office: Holland & Knight LLP 625 N Flagler Dr Ste 700 West Palm Beach FL 33401-4027

**ROSENBERG, RUTH HELEN BORSUK,** lawyer; b. Plainfield, N.J., Feb. 23, 1935; d. Irwin and Pauline (Rudich) Borsuk; children—Joshua Cohen, Sarah, Rebecca, Daniel, Miriam, Tziporah, Isaac. A.B., Douglass Coll., 1956; J.D., U. Pa., 1963. Bar: Pa. 1964, N.Y. 1967, D.C. 1986, Md. 1987, Va. 1994, Mass. 1995, U.S. Ct. Appeals (3d cir.) 1969, U.S. Supreme Ct. 1969, U.S. Ct. Appeals (4th cir.) 1994. Law clk. Ct. Common Pleas, Phila., 1963-64; assoc. Blank, Rudenko, Klaus & Rome, Phila., 1964-67; atty. Office Corp. Counsel, City of Rochester, 1967-68; assoc. Nixon, Hargrave, Devans & Doyle, Washington, 1968-74, ptnr., 1975—; vice chairperson character and fitness com. Appellate divsn. 4th dept. 7th Jud. Dist. N.Y. Supreme Ct., 1976-80, mem. grievance com., 1981-84. Bd. dirs. Soc. Prevention Cruelty to Children, 1976-77, N.Y. Civil Liberties Union, 1972-85, v.p. 1976-85; bd. dirs. Jewish Home and Infirmary, 1978-83, pres., 1980-83; v.p. Jewish Fedn. Rochester, 1983, Yachad, Inc., Jewish Cmty. Housing Devel. Corp., 1990-94; bd. dirs. Jewish Cmty. Coun., Greater Washington, 1989-93, Leadership Washington, 1990-91, Libr. Theatre, 1994-97, Op. Understanding, D.C., 1994-95. Mem. ABA, D.C. Bar Assn., Md. Bar Assn., Va. Bar Assn., Phi Beta Kappa. Real property, Land use and zoning (including planning). Office: Nixon Peabody LLP 1 Thomas Cir NW Ste 700 Washington DC 20005-5802

**ROSENBERG, SUSAN,** lawyer; b. Bklyn., July 24, 1945; d. Harold and Kitty (Paris) Schildkraut; m. Neil David Rosenberg, June 10, 1967; children: Lonnie Stuart, Seth Ian. AB, Washington U., 1967; JD cum laude, Marquette U., 1983. Bar: Wis. 1983. Tchr. history Balt. City Pub. Schs., 1967-70; assoc. Samster, Aiken & Mawicke, S.C., Milw., 1983-88; ptnr. Aiken & Mawicke, S.C., Milw., 1988-90, Domnitz Mawicke Goisman & Rosenberg S.C., Milw., 1990—. Mem. Marquette U. Law Rev., 1981-83. Bd. dirs. Women to Women, Inc., Milw., 1984-86, Ctr. Pub. Representation, 1992-95. Thomas More scholar, 1981-83; Adolph I. Mandelker scholar, 1982-83. Mem. Wis. Acad. Trial Lawyers (bd. dirs. 1989—, treas. 1998-99), Assn. Women Lawyers (bd. dirs. 1994—), pres. 1995-96). Jewish. Office: Domnitz Mawicke Golsman & Rosenberg S C 1509 N Prospect Ave Milwaukee WI 53202-2323

**ROSENBERRY, WILLIAM KENNETH,** lawyer, educator; b. St. Louis, Aug. 14, 1946; s. William Hugh and Shirley Anne (Love) R.; m. Linda Lou Lang, Aug. 24, 1968 (div. 1985); children: Ashlie Anne, Allison Renee; m. Donna L. Pruitt; stepchildren: Corey David Pruitt, Lindsey Lee Pruitt. BBA, U. Tex., Arlington, 1967; JD, Baylor U., 1970. Bar: Tex.

1970, Colo. 1991, U.S. Dist. Ct. (no. dist.) Tex. 1971; bd. cert. specialist in comml. real estae law, residential real estae law, Tex. Assoc. Hinds & Chambers, Arlington, 1970-71; ptnr. Duke, Rosenberry, Duke & Jelinek, Arlington, 1971-76; pvt. practice, Arlington, 1976—; mem. faculty U. Tex., 1991—; bd. dirs. Equitable Bank, NA, Arlington, Equitable Bankshares, Dallas; gen. mgr. Triple R. Properties; escrow officer Am. Title Co., 1984—. Assoc. editor Baylor Law Rev., 1969. Pres. Pantego Christian Acad. Boosters, Arlington, 1990-92; mem. Arlington City Zoning Bd., 1989-92; bd. dirs. Baylor Bear Found. of Baylor U. Recipient oustanding part-time faculty teaching award dept. real estate and fin. U. Tex., 1992; named to Outstanding Young Men in Am., 1980. Mem. Arlington Bar Assn. (bd. dirs. 1987), Arlington Sportsmans Club, Baylor Bear Found. (dir.), Arlington Republican Club. Mem. Pantego Bible Ch. Avocations: fishing, hunting, jogging. Family and matrimonial, Real property, State civil litigation. Office: 3010 W Park Row Dr Arlington TX 76013-2048

**ROSENBLATT, ALBERT MARTIN,** judge; b. N.Y.C., Jan. 17, 1936; s. Isaac and Fannie (Dachs) R.; m. Julia Carlson, Aug. 23, 1970; 1 dau., Elizabeth. BA, U. Pa., 1957; LLB (JD), Harvard U., 1960. Bar: N.Y. 1961. Dist. atty. Dutchess County, N.Y., 1969-75, county judge, 1976-81; justice N.Y. State Supreme Ct., 1982-89, appellate div., 1989-98, N.Y. Ct. Appeals, 1999—, instrv. judge N.Y. State, 1987-89; vis. prof. Vaar Coll., 1993; mem. N.Y. State Fair Trial Free Press Conf., 1973-75; creator Dutchess County 1st consumer protection bur., 1973; instr. newly elected state supreme ct. judges and county judges; chmn., curriculum head tng. programs state dist. attys., asst. dist. attys., 1974, 75; presenter trial advocacy workshop Law Sch., Harvard U., 1998; instr. law tng. N.Y. State Police Acad., 1997; lectr. Nat. Dist. Attys. Assn., 1968-74; mem. vis. faculty trial advocacy worksop Harvard Law Sch., 1998. Bd. dirs. United Way Cmty. Chest, 1970; bd. dirs. Bardavon 1869 Opera House, Dutchess County Hist. Soc.; mem. adv. bd. Jewish Cmty. Ctr., 1987—. With USAR, 1960-66. Mem. N.Y. State Bar Assn. (named Outstanding Prosecutor 1974, Outstanding Jud. Svcs. award 1994), N.Y. State Dist. Attys. Assn. (pres. 1974, Frank S. Hogan award 1987, Jud. Svcs. award, 1994), Profl. Ski Instrs. Am. (cert. 1984—), Baker St. Irregulars Club (former assoc. editor Baker St. Jour.). Republican. Jewish. Mem. bd. editors N.Y. State Bar Jour., 1992—; contbr. to N.Y. State Bench Book for Trial Judges, 1986-87; contbr. articles on law to profl. jours. and popular mags. Home: 300 Freedom Rd Pleasant Valley NY 12569-5431 Office: Supreme Ct Chambers 10 Market St Poughkeepsie NY 12601-3228

**ROSENBLATT, HOWARD MARSHALL,** lawyer, underwriter; b. Jacksonville, Fla., May 4, 1947; s. Harry and Gertrude (Schulman) R.; m. Eve Darlene Ackerman, Feb. 22, 1976; children: Raphael Tzvi, Micah Jacob. BAE, U. Fla., 1969, JD, 1981. Bar: Fla. 1982; CLU, ChFC. Tchr. Duval County Bd. Pub. Instrn., Jacksonville, 1969-70; field underwriter Mut. Life Ins. Co. of N.Y., Gainesville, Fla., 1971—; registered rep. MONY Securities Corp., Gainesville, 1974—; pvt. practice law Gainesville, 1983—. Chmn. Alacuha County U.S. Constn. Bicentennial Commn., 1986-87; Dem. candidate for Fla. Ho. of Reps., 1988; bd. dirs. 8-FAWL, Alachua County divsn. Am. Cancer Soc., 1993—, Planned Parenthood North Ctrl. Fla., 1994— (treas. 1996-98); pres. Congregation B'nai Israel, 1993-95. Recipient Fred West Meml. award Fla. Jaycees, 1983. Fellow Life Underwriter Tng. Coun.; mem. ABA, The Fla. Bar (chmn. member benefits com. 1995—), 8th Jud. Cir. Bar Assn., Am. Judicature Soc., Fla. Assn. Life Underwriters (v.p. region IV 1987-91 chaplain, 1992-93), Gainesville Assn. Life Underwriters (pres. 1982-84, Agt. of Yr. 1974, 84, 87), Gainesville Estate Planning Coun. (pres. 1982-83), Million Dollar Round Table (life, membership communication com., found. knight), Am. Soc. Fin. Svc. Profls. (local pres. 1981, patron gold key soc.), Fla. Blue Key, B'nai B'rith (pres. Gainesville lodge H1368 1974-75, 76-77, Gainesville unit 1994-99). Democrat. Avocations: golf, teaching, reading, youth-related activities. Probate, Estate planning, Finance. Office: The Seagle Bldg 2830 NW 41st St Ste J Gainesville FL 32606-6667

**ROSENBLATT, PAUL GERHARDT,** judge. AB, U. Ariz., 1958, JD, 1963. Asst. atty. gen. State of Ariz., 1963-66; adminstrv. asst. to U.S. Rep., 1967-72; sole practice, Prescott, 1971-73; judge Yavapai County Superior Ct., Prescott, 1973-84; judge, U.S. Dist. Ct. Ariz., Phoenix, 1984—. Office: US Dist Ct 230 N 1st Ave Phoenix AZ 85025-0230

**ROSENBLATT, STEPHEN WOODBURN,** lawyer; b. Atlanta, Dec. 20, 1948; s. William F. and Nancy E. (Gosser) R.; m. Elisabeth M. Gernert, Mar. 22, 1975; children: Katherine, Emily, Nancy. BA, Vanderbilt U., 1970; JD with honors, U. Miss., 1975. Bar: U.S. Dist. Ct. (no. and so. dists.) Miss. 1975, U.S. Ct. Appeals (5th cir.) 1977. Mem. Butler, Snow, O'Mara, Stevens & Cannada, PLLC, Jackson, Miss., 1975—; pres. Miss. Young Lawyers Divsn., Jackson, 1984-85; mem. Miss. Bd. of Bar Commn., Jackson, 1983-86, Miss Bankruptcy Conf., 1994. Pres. Fellows Young Lawyer's Assn. Sect., 1994-95, Chmn. bd. deacons 1st Presbyn. Ch., Jackson, 1984, elder, 1986—, Chmn. bd., Jackson Prep. Sch., 1994-95. Served with U.S. Army, 1970-72. Mem. Miss. Bar Assn. (2d v.p. 1985-86), Hinds County Bar Assn., Miss. Bankruptcy Conf. (pres. 1994), Jackson Young Lawyers Assn. (pres. 1982), Jackson Vanderbilt Club (pres. 1979), Am. Bankruptcy Inst. Presbyterian. Avocations: golf, tennis, jogging, camping, skiing. E-mail: steve.rosenblatt@butlersnow.com. Bankruptcy, Contracts commercial, Alternative dispute resolution. Office: 17th Fl Deposit Guaranty Pl 210 E Capitol St Jackson MS 39201-2307

**ROSENBLOOM, NORMA FRISCH,** lawyer; b. N.Y.C., Dec. 2, 1925; d. Jacob Frisch and Anna (Fox) Frisch Schwartz; m. Philip Rosenbloom, Oct. 31, 1946; children: David, James, Eric. BA, New Sch. Social Rsch., 1951; JD, Rutgers U., Newark, 1979. Bar: N.J. 1979, N.Y. 1980. Mem. faculty, head dept. music Ranney Sch., Tinton Falls, N.J., 1962-74; chief law clk. Monmouth County (N.J.) Prosecutor's Office, 1979-80; assoc. Karasic & Karasic, P.C., Oakhurst, N.J., 1980-82; ptnr. Abrams, Gatta, Rosen & Rosenbloom, Ocean Twp., N.J., 1982-90, Abrams, Gatta, Rosen, Rosenbloom & Sevrin, P.C., 1990-92; of counsel Abrams, Gatta, Falvo & Sevrin, P.A., 1992—, Abrams Gatta Falvo LLP; asst. county counsel Monmouth County, 1987-88; mem. N.J. Supreme Ct. Family Part Practice Com., 1997-98. Sec., mem. exec. bd. Temple Beth Miriam, Elberon, N.J., 1969-74; mcpl. leader Monmouth Beach (N.J.) Dem. Com., 1973—; del. Dem. Nat. Conv., 1976; freeholder rep. to Monmouth County Cmty. Action Program, poverty program, 1975-76; bd. dirs. Cen. Jersey Regional Health Planning Bd., 1973-75; trustee search com. Brookdale C.c., Lincroft, N.J., 1984-85; trustee Planned Parenthood Monmouth County, 1981-88. Recipient award for cmty. involvement Asbury Park-Neptune Youth Coun., 1970. Fellow Am. Acad. Matrimonial Lawyers; mem. ABA, N.J. Women Lawyers Assn. (pres. 1994-95), N.J. State Bar Assn. (dispute resolution sec.), women Lawyers Monmouth County. Democrat. Jewish. Avocation: classical pianist. Family and matrimonial. Home: Channel Club Towers Monmouth Beach NJ 07750 Office: Abrams Gatta Falvo LLP 1127 Highway 35 Asbury Park NJ 07712-4070

**ROSENBLOOM, THOMAS ADAM,** lawyer; b. N.Y.C., Mar. 17, 1963; s. Robert I. and Pauline W. R.; m. Jessica E. Bussgang, Aug. 18, 1990; children: Raquel Jae, Alana Sofia. BA, U. Wis., 1985; JD, Boston U., 1988. Bar: N.Y. 1988, Mass. 1990. Assoc. Wormser, Killy, Galaf & Jacobs, White Plains, N.Y., 1988-89, O'Connor, Broude & Aronson, Waltham, Mass., 1989-96; ptnr. Epstein, Becker & Green, Boston, 1996—. Vol. tchr. Jr. Achievement, Boston, 1995-96; vol. Taft Sch./Harvard Bus. Sch., Boston, 1989-90. Mem. ABA, N.Y. State Bar Assn., Mass. Bar Assn. Avocations: basketball, exercise, theater, art, travel. General corporate, Mergers and acquisitions, Securities. Office: Epstein Becker & Green 27th Fl 75 State St Boston MA 02109-1807

**ROSENBLUM, EDWARD G.,** lawyer; b. Union City, N.J., Aug. 2, 1944; s. Milton and Frances (Nardi) R.; m. Charis Ann Schlatter, Dec. 1, 1971; children: Deborah, Michelle. BA, Rutgers U., 1966, JD, 1969. Bar: N.J. 1969. Ptnr. Rosenblum & Rosenblum, P.A., Jersey City, 1971-79, Secaucus, N.J., 1979-93; ptnr. Rosenblum Wolf & Lloyd, P.A., Secaucus, 1994—, Teaneck, 1998—; lectr. in field. Author: N.J. Lawyer, 1980, N.J. Municipalities, 1987. Active Hudson County chpt. Am. Cancer Soc., Hoboken, N.J., 1987—. Mem. N.J. State Bar Assn. (vice chmn. tax ct. rules com. taxation sect. 1984—, chmn. real property tax com. 1984—, vice chmn. taxation sect. 1987—, chmn.-elect 1987, chmn. 1988-89, Supreme Ct. com. on tax ct. 1982-92). Condemnation, State and local taxation. Office: 300 Frank Burr Blvd Teaneck NJ 07666

**ROSENBLUM, GLENN FREDRICK,** lawyer; b. Phila., Dec. 31, 1952; s. Edwin Irwin and Roberta (Brodsky) R.; m. Sherrie Joan Greenberg, Sept. 18, 1983; 1 child, Erica Rachel. BA, Temple U., 1973; JD, U. Pa., 1976. Bar: Pa. 1976, U.S. Dist. Ct. (ea. dist.) Pa. 1976, N.J. 1979, U.S. Dist. Ct. N.J. 1979, U.S. Ct. Appeals (3d cir.) 1986, U.S. Dist. Ct. (mid. dist.) Pa. 1987. Jud. law clk. Phila. Ct. Common Pleas, 1976-81; editor-in-chief Pa. Dist. and County Reports, Phila., 1981-83; ptnr. Korn, Kline & Kutner, Phila., 1983-91; assoc. Alan R. Kutner & Assocs., Bala Cynwyd, Pa., 1991-98, Montgomery, McCracken, Walker & Rhoads, Phila., 1998—; nat. lectr. Multistate Legal Studies, Phila., 1978-85; instr. C.C. Phila., 1981; seminar spkr. Greater Phila. Claims Assn., 1996. Opinion editor Pa. Law Jour., 1978-83. Committeeman Lower Merion Dem. Com., 1993—; area rep. Montgomery County Dem. Exec. Com., 1998—; mem. Lower-Merion-Narberth Dem. Exec. Com., 1998—. Mem. ABA, Phila. Bar Assn., Phi Beta Kappa, Pi Sigma Alpha. Jewish. Home: 559 Haverford Rd Wynnewood PA 19096-2512 Office: Montgomery McCracken Et Al 123 S Broad St Fl 24 Philadelphia PA 19109-1023

**ROSENBLUM, SCOTT S.,** lawyer; b. N.Y.C., Oct. 4, 1949; s. Harold Lewis and Greta Blossom (Lesher) R.; m. Barbara Anne Campbell, Oct. 29, 1977; children: Harold, Emma, Casey. AB summa cum laude, Dartmouth Coll., 1971; JD, U. Pa., 1974. Bar. U.S. Dist. Ct. (so. dist.) N.Y. 1975. From assoc. to ptnr. Stroock & Stroock & Lavan, N.Y.C., 1974-91; ptnr. Kramer, Levin, Naftalis & Frankel, N.Y.C., 1991-93, mng. ptnr., 1994—; N.Y. Adv. Bd. Mid. East Quarterly, Phila., 1994—; bd. dirs. Dovenmuehle Mortgage, Inc., Schaumburg, Ill, Greg Manning Auctions, Inc., West Caldwell, N.J., Temco Svc. Industries, Inc., N.Y.C. Co-author: Public Limited Partnerships and Roll-Ups, Securities Law Techniques, The Practitioner's Guide to Transactions and Litigation, 1995. Trustee Village of Saltaire, N.Y., 1993—. Mem. ABA (high tech. com. 1983-84), Assn. Bar City N.Y. (corps. com. 1991-94), Phi Beta Kappa. Avocation: sailing. General corporate, Securities, Mergers and acquisitions. Home: 19 Wildwood Cir Larchmont NY 10538-3426 Office: Kramer Levin Naftalis & Frankel 919 3rd Ave Rm 3802 New York NY 10022-3852

**ROSENBLUM, WILLIAM F., JR.,** lawyer; b. N.Y.C., May 11, 1935. AB cum laude, Princeton U., 1957; JD, Columbia U., 1960. Bar: N.Y. 1961, U.S. Dist. Ct. (so. dist.) N.Y. 1965. Gen. atty. Stanley Warner Corp., 1964-66; assoc. Leon, Weill & Mahony, 1967-70, Finley, Kumble, Wagner & Heine, 1970-74; pvt. practice, 1975; v.p. legal affairs Rep. Nat. Bank N.Y., 1976-82; v.p. legal affairs Rep. N.Y. Corp., 1982-86, sr. v.p., dep. gen. counsel, corp. sec., 1987—. Mem. N.Y. State Bar Assn. (mem. sect. bus. law, commodities regulation 1990—), Assn. of Bar of City of N.Y. (mem. futures regulations com. 1987-90). General corporate, Securities, Banking. Office: Republic NY Corp 452 Fifth Ave Fl 7 New York NY 10018-2706

**ROSENDAHL, PATRICIA MCGARVEY,** lawyer; b. Galveston, Tex., Sept. 1, 1952; d. James Ligon and Elvera (McCoy) McGarvey; m. Torben Erik Rosendahl, July 3, 1976; children—James, Erik, Alicia, Jennifer. AA, Palomar Coll., 1974; BA, U. Tex., 1975; postgrad. U. Houston Law Sch., 1984-87 ; assoc. McLeod, Alexander, Powel and Apffel. Cert. social worker. Med. social worker Tex. Dept. Health, Galveston, 1977-84; head articles editor Houston Jour. Internat. Law, 1986-87 . Mem. ABA, Fed. Bar Assn., State Bar Tex., Order of Barons, Admiralty Law Soc. (sec. 1985-86 ), Health Law Orgn., Phi Delta Phi, Phi Kappa Phi. Episcopalian. Avocations: travel, writing, reading.

**ROSENDAHL, ROGER WAYNE,** lawyer. B, U. So. Calif., 1965; JD, Georgetown U., 1969, LLM, 1971. Bar: N.Y. 1973, Calif. 1975. Ptnr. Cadwalader, Wickersham & Taft, N.Y.C.; asst. prof. law U. Frankfurt, Germany. Mng. editor Law and Policy in Internat. Bus. Mem. fgn. svc. adv. com. U.S. Trade Rep. Schulte zur Hausen fellow. Mem. ABA (past officer, coun.), Asia-Pacific Lawyers Assn. (v.p. 1984-89), Am. Arbitration Assn. (internat. panel). Finance, Private international, Public international. Office: Cadwalader Wickersham & Taft 100 Maiden Ln New York NY 10038-4818

**ROSENFELD, MARTIN JEROME,** executive recruiter, educator; b. Flint, Mich., Oct. 3, 1944; s. Israel Edward and Lillian Edith (Natchez) R.; m. Marcy Tucker Colman; 1 child, Joshua; stepchildren: Jessica Colman, Zachary Colman. BA, Mich. State U., 1968, MHA, 1978; MBA with high honors, Ind. No. U., 1979. Adminstr. Care Corp., Grand Rapids, Mich., 1969-70, Chandler Convalescent Ctr., Detroit, 1970-71, Grand Community Hosp., Detroit, 1971-73; exec. v.p., chief exec. officer Msgr. Clement Kern Hosp. Spl. Surgery, Warren, Mich., 1973-84; pres. M.J. Rosenfeld Assocs., 1984-85; COO Dickenson, Wright, Moon, Van Dusen & Freeman, 1985-88; chmn. Rosenfeld Assocs., 1989-91; pres. Sanford Rose Assocs., Detroit, 1991-97; acting COO New Ctr. Hosp., Detroit, 1995-96; pres., CEO, chmn. Rosenfeld & Co., Inc., 1998-99; CEO, chmn. Brookside Consulting Group, LLC, West Bloomfield, Mich., 1999—; instr. Marygrove Coll., 1975-80; assoc. prof. Mercy Coll., Detroit, 1978-80; mem. faculty Inst. on Continuing Legal Edn., Ann Arbor, Mich., Inst. Law Firm Mgmt., Ann Arbor; instr. Legal Tech '87, Chgo. Author papers in field. Mem. editl. bd. The Human-Size Hosp.; mem. panel of experts The Health Care News. V.p. Detroit chpt. Jewish Nat. Fund, 1978—; pres. Cranbrook Village Homeowners Assn., 1977; chmn. Community Hosps. of Southeastern Mich., 1981-84; mem. tech. work group Comprehensive Health Planning Coun. of Southeastern Mich., 1981-84; mem. fin. mgmt. com., mem. hosp. affairs bd. Greater Detroit Area Hosp. Coun., 1981-84; bd. dirs., com. chmn. Detroit Symphony Orch., 1984-90; bd. dirs., mem. fund raising com. Detroit Met. Orch., 1984-87. Mem. ABA, Assn. Legal Adminstrs., Am. Assn. Health Care Cons., Royal Soc. Health, Am. Podiatry Assn. (com. hosps. 1981-84), Warren C. of C. (com. chmn. 1975), Nat. Assn. Legal Search Cons., Nat. Assn. Pers. Svcs., Mich. Assn. Pers. Svcs., Sanford Rose Assocs. Dirs. Assn. (pres. 1993-95, treas. 1995-97). Office: Brookside Consulting Group LLC Ste PMB 358 6689 Orchard Lake Rd West Bloomfield MI 48322

**ROSENGREN, PAUL GREGORY,** lawyer; b. Oakland, Calif., Apr. 3, 1952; s. Jack Whitehead and Patricia Jean (Dorking) R.; m. Nikki Christine Ballard, Aug. 21, 1976. AB, Princeton U., 1974; MBA, JD, U. Calif., Berkeley, 1977. Bar: Calif. 1978, D.C. 1978, U.S. Ct. Appeals (5th cir.) 1979. Assoc. Covington & Burling, Washington, 1978; law clk. to justice U.S. Ct. Appeals (5th cir.), New Orleans and Baton Rouge, La., 1978-79; assoc. Gibson, Dunn & Crutcher, Washington, 1979-85; assoc. gen. counsel Fannie Mae, Washington, 1985-88, v.p., dep. gen. counsel, 1988—. Note and comment editor U. Calif. Law Rev., 1975-77. Mem. Huntington Met. Area Task Force, Fairfax County, Va., 1984-85; bd. dirs., pres. Heritage Hill Townhouses Assn., Alexandria, Va., 1980-82. Mem. ABA, D.C. Bar Assn., Calif. Bar Assn., Washington Met. Area Corp. Counsel Assn., Am. Corp. Counsel Assn. Avocations: theatre, travel, tennis, reading. Securities, Antitrust, General corporate. Office: Fannie Mae 3900 Wisconsin Ave NW Washington DC 20016-2892

**ROSENHOFFER, CHRIS,** lawyer; b. Cin., Apr. 19, 1913; s. Joseph and Barbara (Stitzel) R.; m. Alberta Arlene Jarvis, Dec. 28, 1935 (div. Apr. 1992); children: Chris Jr., Dennis P., Gary A., John J., Nancy A., Todd D. BS Commerce, Salmon P. Chase Coll. Commerce, Cin., 1948; JD, Salmon P. Chase Coll. Law, Cin., 1951. Bar: Ohio, 1951, U.S. Dist. Ct. (so. dist.) Ohio 1952. Acct., log buyer Al J. Boehm Walnut Co., Kenova, W.Va., 1938-44; acct. The Green Embry Co., Cin., 1948-51; judge Clermont County Ct., Batavia, Ohio, 1958-62, 67-86; pvt. practice law Batavia, 1951—; spl. counsel Atty. Gen. of Ohio, Batavia, 1963-64. Treas. Clermont County Rep. Club, Batavia, 1957-58; team mem. Citizens Amb. Program, Seattle, 1988, 93; mem. sch. bd. West Clermont Local Sch. Dist., Amelia, Ohio, 1958-74. With U.S. Army, 1944-46. Mem. Ohio Bar Assn., Ohio Acad. Trial Lawyers, Clermont County Bar Assn. (pres. 1962), Cin. Bar Assn., Am. Legion. Methodist. Avocations: fishing, hunting. General civil litigation, General practice, Probate. Office: 97 Main St Batavia OH 45103

**ROSENN, HAROLD,** lawyer; b. Plains, Pa., Nov. 4, 1917; s. Joseph and Jennie (Wohl) R.; m. Sallyanne Frank, Sept. 19, 1948; 1 child, Frank Scott. BA, U. Mich., 1939, JD, 1941; LLD (hon.), Coll. Misericordia, 1991. Bar: Pa. 1942, U.S. Supreme Ct. 1957. Ptnr. Rosenn & Rosenn, Wilkes Barre, Pa., 1948-54; ptnr. Rosenn, Jenkins & Greenwald, Wilkes Barre, 1954-87, of counsel, 1988—; mem. Pa. State Bd. Law Examiners, 1983-93, Pa. Gov.'s Justice Commn., 1968-73, Pa. Crime Commn., 1968-73, Fed. Jud. Nominating Com., Pa., 1977-79, Appellate Ct. Nominating Com., Pa., 1979-81; asst. dist. atty. Luzerne County, Pa., 1952-54. Chmn. ARC, Wilkes-Barre, 1958-60, life mem. bd.; pres. Pa. Coun. on Crime and Delinquency, Harrisburg, 1969-71; bd. dirs. Coll. Misericordia, Dallas, Pa., 1976-86, emeritus, 1986—, Hoyt Libr., Kingston, Pa., 1971-78, Nat. Coun. on Crime and Delinquency, N.Y.C., 1969-71; chmn. United Way Campaign of Wyoming Valley, 1975, chmn. of bd., 78-80; pres. Temple Israel of Wilkes Barre, 1972-74, chmn. bd. 1974-84, life mem. bd.; comdr. post 395 Am. Legion, Kingston, 1948; bd. dirs. Keystone State Games, 1982—, Jewish Fedn. Bd. of Greater Wilkes-Barre, 1994—, St. Vincent de Paul Soup Kitchen, 1987—. Capt. USAAF, 1942-45, ETO. Recipient Erasmus medal Dutch Govt., Disting. Svc. award in Trusteeship, Assn. Governing Bds. Univs. and Colls., 1990, Disting. Cmty. Svc. award Greater Wilkes-Barre Soc. Fellows Anti-Defamation League, 1991, Clara Barton honor award Wyoming Valley chpt. ARC, 1992, Lifetime Achievement award United Way of Wyoming Valley, 1992, Outstanding Vol. Fundraiser award Greater Pocono chpt. Nat. Soc. of Fundraising Execs. 1995; honoree Wyoming Valley Interfaith Coun., 1986; named Golden Key Vol. of Yr., United Way of Pa., 1989; inductee Jr. Achievement Hall of Fame for N.E. Pa., 1997. Mem. ABA, Pa. Bar Assn., Am. Judicature Soc., The Pa. Soc., B'nai B'rith (pres. Wilkes Barre 1952-53, Cmty. Svc. award 1976), U. Mich. Club N.E. Pa. (pres. 1946-76), Westmoreland Club (Wilkes-Barre), Huntsville Golf Club (Lehman, Pa.). Republican. Jewish. General corporate, Family and matrimonial, General practice.

**ROSENN, KEITH SAMUEL,** lawyer, educator; b. Wilkes-Barre, Pa., Dec. 9, 1938; s. Max and Tillie R. (Hershkowitz) R.; m. Nan Raker, June 21, 1960; 1 child, Eva; m. Silvia R. Rudge, Mar. 21, 1968; children: Jonathan, Marcia. AB, Amherst Coll., 1960; LLB, Yale U., 1963. Bar: Pa. 1964, U.S. Ct. Appeals (3rd cir.) 1979, Fla. 1981, U.S. Ct. Appeals (11th cir.) 1982. Law clk. to Judge Smith U.S. Ct. Appeals (2nd cir.), 1963-64; asst. prof. law Ohio State U. Coll. Law, 1965-68, assoc. prof., 1968-70, prof., 1970-79; project assoc. Ford Found., Rio de Janeiro, 1966-68; assoc. Escritorio Augusto Nobre, Rio de Janeiro, 1979-80; prof. law U. Miami, Fla., 1979—; project coord. Olin Fellowship Program Law and Econs. Ctr., U. Miami, Fla., 1980-81, assoc. dean Law Sch., 1982-83, dir. fgn. grad. law program, 1985—; cons. Hudson Inst., 1977, U.S. State Dept., 1981-82, World Bank, 1988-90; Fulbright lectr. Argentina, 1987, 88. Author: (with Karst) Law and Development in Latin America, 1975; Law and Inflation, 1982, Foreign Investment in Brazil, 1991; co-editor: A Panorama of Brazilian Law, 1992, Corruption and Political Reform in Brazil, 1999; advisor InterAm. Law Rev.; contbr. articles to law jours. Recipient Order of Democracy award Congress of Republic of Colombia, 1987, Lawyer of the Ams. award, 1989, Inter-Am. Jurisprudence prize, 1998; grantee Social Sci. Rsch. Coun., 1970, Dana Found., 1982. Mem. ABA, Am. Law Inst., Inter-Am. Bar Assn., Fla. Bar, Am. Soc. Comparative Law (bd. dirs.). Jewish. Office: U Miami Law Sch PO Box 248087 Coral Gables FL 33124-8087

**ROSENN, MAX,** federal judge; b. Plains, Pa., Feb. 4, 1910; s. Joseph and Jennie (Wohl) R.; m. Tillie R. Hershkowitz, Mar. 18, 1934; children: Keith S., Daniel Wohl. BA, Cornell U., 1929; LLB, U. Pa., 1932. Bar: Pa. 1932, U.S. Supreme Ct. 1955, Cts. of Philippines 1946. Gen. practice Wilkes-Barre, Pa., 1932-70; dir. Franklin Fed. Savs. & Loan, Wilkes-Barre, 1937-70, Wyoming Nat. Bank, Wilkes-Barre, 1958-70; spl. counsel Pa. Dept. Justice, 1939; asst. dist. atty. Luzerne County, 1942-44; also solicitor various mcpl. boroughs, ptnr. firm Rosenn & Rosenn, 1947-54, Rosenn, Jenkins & Greenwald, Wilkes-Barre, 1954-70; sec. pub. welfare Pa., 1966-67; judge U.S. Ct. Appeals (3d cir.), 1970-81, sr. judge, 1981—; former mem. criminal procedure rules com. Supreme Ct. Pa., 1958-85; mem. Pa. Commn. to Revise Pub. Employee Laws, 1968-69; Pa. chmn. com. children and youth White House Conf., 1968-70. Contbr. articles to legal publs. Mem. Pa. Bd. Pub. Welfare, 1963-66; chmn. Pa. Gov.'s Hosp. Study Commn., Pa. Gov.'s Coun. for Human Svcs., 1966-67; mem. exec. bd. Commonwealth of Pa., 1966-67; chmn. Commn. Met. Govt., 1957-58; pres. Property Owners Assn. Luzerne County, 1955-57; chmn. Pa. Human Rels. Commn., 1969-70, Legis. Task Force Structure for Human Svcs., 1970; alt. del. Rep. Nat. Conv., 1964; pres. Wyoming Valley Jewish Com., 1941-42; life trustee Wilkes-Barre Jewish Community Ctr.; chmn. Flood Recovery Task Force, 1972. Max Rosenn U.S. Courthouse dedicated, 1996. Fellow Am. Coll. Trial Lawyers, Internat. Acad. Trial Lawyers; mem. ABA, Pa. Bar Assn., Luzerne County Bar Assn., Am. Law Inst., Am. Soc. Law and Medicine (charter mem., former assoc. editor jour.), Am. Judicature Soc., B'nai B'rith (pres. dist. grand lodge 1947-48, life bd. govs., former chmn. bd. dirs. Anti-Defamation League Pa., W.Va. and Del. 1955-58, nat. commr. 1964—), Westmoreland Club, Masons (33d degree), Alpha Epsilon Pi. Jewish. Office: US Ct Appeals 229 Max Rosenn US Cthse 197 S Main St Wilkes Barre PA 18701-1500

**ROSENSAFT, LESTER JAY,** management consultant, lawyer, business executive; b. Leominster, Mass., Jan. 11, 1958; s. Melvin and Beatrice (Golombek) R.; m. Elizabeth Amanda Lahti, July 29, 1992; 1 child, Mia Elizabeth. BS in Econs., Wharton Sch., U. Pa., 1978; JD, Case Western Res. U., 1981, MBA, 1981; LLM in Corporate Law, NYU, 1983. Bar: Ohio 1981, U.S. dist. ct. (no. dist.) Ohio 1982, U.S. dist cts. (ea., we., no., so. dists.) N.Y. 1982. Practice corp. and comml. law, Ohio, 1981—, reorgn. law fed. cts. Ohio, N.Y., 1982—; mem. firm Hall, Rosensaft & Yen, Cleve. and Singapore, 1981—; with Cons. to Mgmt., Inc., Cleve., N.Y.C., Boston, Hong Kong, 1977—, v.p., 1977-80, pres. and chief exec. officer, 1980-83, chmn., 1983—; pres. and chief exec. officer Eljay Devel. Corp., 1985-86; chmn., chief exec. officer Logistix Ltd., 1987—; ptnr. Sanctuary Assocs., Boston, 1988—; exec. v.p., chief fin. officer Omni Teleproductions, Inc. Boston, 1988-89, also bd. dirs.; pres., chief exec. officer The Union Meat Co., East Hartford, Conn., 1989-90, also bd. dirs.; pres. Golub Enterprises II, Inc., 1989-90, also bd. dirs.; chief operating officer The CCC Fin. Orgn., Cleve., 1992-95; pres., chief operating officer Retiree Techs., Inc., Cleve. and N.Y.C., 1993-95, also bd. dirs.; pres., chief executive officer, bd. dirs. ASA Comm., Inc., N.Y.C., 1995—, bd. dirs. ASA Aquisition Corp., 1998—, also mem. Fin. and Strategic Planning com.; mem. com. ASA Mgmt. and Exec. Com, 1995—, ASA Investment Com., 1996-98; chmn. Chatham Fin., Cleveland, N.Y.C., 1995—; vice chmn. bd. Paramount Systems Design Group, Inc., N.Y.C., 1982—; v.p. corp. devel., mem. bd. dirs. Ameritec Corp., N.Y.C., 1983-85; v.p., chief fin. officer, mem. bd. dirs. Chipurnoi Inc., L.I. City, N.Y., 1983-85; v.p., chief fin. officer Kinnerton Industries, N.Y.C. and London, 1983-85; vice chmn., gen. counsel, mem. bd. dirs. GIOIA Couture, Inc., Akron, Ohio, 1984-86; dir. Honeybee Robotics Ltd., Taiwan and N.Y.C., Pelletier Brothers, Inc., 1986-88, Advanced Radiator Techs., Inc., Fitchburg, Mass., 1987-88; ednl. cons.; advisor indsl. devel. and strategic urbanism; cons. federally funded biomed. research projects; active Combined Jewish Philanthropies; participant 40th Anniversary II Pres.'s Mission, 1987; chmn. Region V Outreach Mission, 1988; vice chmn. Regional Campaign Leadership Mission, 1991; mem. Russian Resettlement Com., 1988-91, Major Gifts Gala Com., 1989; assoc. alumni trustee U. Pa., 1991—; active U. Pa. Secondary Com. of Cen. Mass., U. Pa. Bd. Govs., Cleve., 1992—. Co-author (with Melvin Rosensaft): Industrial Development Survey for City of Leominster, 1978. Contbr. articles to profl. jours. Mem. exec. adv. council Keene State Coll., 1984—. Recipient APEX Grand award 1999, ESMA Best of Show award 1999, ACE award, Silver and Gold Quill awards 1996-99. Mem. ABA, Assn. Corp. Growth Turnaround Mgmt. Assn., Greater Cleve. Bar Assn., Ohio State Bar Assn., Assn. Bar City N.Y., Assn. Trial Lawyers Am., Am. Mgmt. Assn., Am. Mktg. Assn. Wharton Club Cleve. (exec. com.), Wharton Club N.Y., U. Pa. Clubs Cleve., U. Pa. Club N.Y., Bankruptcy Lawyers Bar Assn., N.Y.C. Reorgn. Roundtable, Internat. Soc. Strategic Planning Cons., Soc. Profl. Mgmt. Cons., Inst. of Mgmt. Cons. (cert. mgmt. cons.), Coun. of Cons. Orgns., Coll. of Firm Prins., North Cen. Mass. C. of C. (indsl. devel. com. 1984—), Phi Alpha Delta (vice justice). Clubs: Mendham Racquet, Boca Beach, Boca Pointe Golf and Racquet, Boca West, Boca Raton Hotel and Club (Boca Raton, Fla.). Address: 9 Whispering Ivy Path Mendham NJ 07945 Office: 750 Lexington Ave New York NY 10022-1200

**ROSENSAFT, MENACHEM ZWI,** lawyer, author, foundation executive, community activist; b. Bergen-Belsen, Germany, May 1, 1948; came to U.S., 1958, naturalized, 1962; s. Josef and Hadassah (Bimko) R.; m. Jean Bloch, Jan. 13, 1974; 1 child, Joana Deborah. BA, MA, Johns Hopkins U., 1971; MA, Columbia U., 1975, JD, 1979. Bar: N.Y. 1980. Adj. lectr. dept. Jewish studies CCNY, 1972-74, professorial fellow, 1974-75; rsch. fellow Am. Law Inst., 1977-78; law clk. to judge U.S. Dist. Ct. (so. dist.) N.Y., N.Y.C., 1979-81; assoc. Proskauer, Rose, Goetz & Mendelsohn, N.Y.C., 1981-82, Kaye, Scholer, Fierman, Hays & Handler, N.Y.C., 1982-89; v.p., sr. assoc. counsel Chase Manhattan Bank, N.Y.C., 1989-93; spl. counsel Hahn & Hessen, N.Y.C., 1994-95; sr. internat. counsel Ronald S. Lauder Found., N.Y.C., 1995-97; exec. v.p. Jewish Renaissance Found., Inc., N.Y.C., 1996—. Author: Moshe Sharett, Statesman of Israel, 1966, Fragments, Past and Future (poetry), 1968, Not Backward to Belligerency, 1969; editor: Bergen Belsen Youth mag., 1965; book rev. editor Columbia Jour. Transnat. Law, 1978-79; co-editor (with Yehuda Bauer) Antisemitism: Threat to Western Civilization, 1988; contbg. editor: Reform Judaism, 1993—; contbr. to various publs. including N.Y. Times, Newsweek, N.Y. Post, L.A. Times, Phila. Inquirer, Miami Herald, Internat. Herald Tribune, Jerusalem Post, Liberation, Paris, Davar, Tel Aviv, El Diario, Santiago de Chile, Columbia Human Rights Law Rev., Jewish Social Studies, Leo Baeck Inst. Year Book XXI, Columbia Jour. Environ. Law, (with Michael I. Saltzman) Tax Planning Internat. Rev., Fellowship, Reform Judaism, United Synagogue Rev., Forward, Midstream, N.Y. Jewish Week, Jewish Telegraphic Agy. Bull. Chmn. Internat. Network Children Jewish Holocaust Survivors, 1981-84, founding chmn., 1984—; nat. pres. Labor Zionist Alliance, 1988-91; chmn. commn. human rights World Jewish Congress, 1986-91, chmn. exec. com. Am. sect., 1986-90; mem. Gen. Coun. World Zionist Orgn., 1987-92; mem. U.S. Holocaust Meml. Coun., 1994—, chmn. content com., 1994—, chmn. collections and acquisitions com., 1996—, chmn. task force on procedures for com. on conscience, 1996, mem. exec. com., 1996—; mem. N.Y.C. Holocaust Meml. Commn., 1982-96, chmn. collections com., 1987-89; bd. dirs., exec. com. Nat. Com. for Labor Israel, 1988-91, 95—; mem. Am. Zionist Tribunal, 1988-90, chmn., 1990; sec. Am. Zionist Fedn., 1990-93; bd. dirs. Am. Jewish Joint Distbn. Com., 1988-91, Mercaz, 1991-97; mem. nat. adv. bd. United Synagogue Conservative Judaism, 1995—, also chmn. United Synagogue delegation to Nat. Jewish Cmty. Rels. Adv. Coun., 1994-97; mem. exec. com. Nat. Jewish Cmty. Rels. Adv. Coun., 1994-97; mem. N.Y. County Dem. Com., 1981-85; organizer, leader demonstration against Pres. Reagan's visit to Bitburg Cemetery and Bergen-Belsen concentration camp, 1985; del. meeting on recognition of Israel between five Am. Jews and leaders of Palestine Liberation Orgn., Stockholm, 1988; mem. adv. coun. Park Ave. Synagogue, 1993-94, trustee, 1994—, sec., 1998—, chmn. Sherr Inst. Adult Jewish Studies, 1993—. Recipient Abraham Joshua Heschel Peace award, 1989, Parker Sch. recognition of achievement with honors in internat. and fgn. law, 1979; Harlan Fiske Stone scholar, 1977-79. Mem. ABA, Phi Beta Kappa. Federal civil litigation, Private international. Home: 179 E 70th St New York NY 10021-5109 Office: Jewish Renaissance Found 767 5th Ave Ste 4600 New York NY 10153-4699

**ROSENSTEIN, ROBERT BRYCE,** lawyer, financial advisor; b. Santa Monica, Calif., Feb. 26, 1954; s. Franklin Lee and Queen Esther (Shall) R.; children: Shaun Franklin, Jessica Laney, Madeline Frances. BA, Calif. State U., Northridge, 1976; JD, Southwestern U., 1979. Bar: Calif. 1979, U.S. Dist. Ct. (cen. and no. dists.) Calif. 1980, U.S. Tax Ct. 1981; registered environ. assessor. Service rep. Social Security Adminstrn., Los Angeles, 1974-77; tax cons. Am. Tax Assocs., Los Angeles, 1970-78, ptnr., 1978; prin., pres. Robert B. Rosenstein, PC, Los Angeles, 1979-84; ptnr. Rosenstein and Werlin, Los Angeles, 1984-87; pres. Robert Bryce Rosenstein Ltd., Temelula, 1987-99; chief fin. officer BSE Mgmt. Inc., Los Angeles, 1987-90, corp. counsel, 1987-92, sr. v.p. corp. devel., acquisitions, 1990-92; pres. Robert Bryce Rosenstien Corp., 1999—; bd. dirs. BSE Mgmt. Inc, Sirius Computer Corp., Spartan Computer, Unicomp, Inc., Diagnostic Engring. Inc.; pres. Will Find Inc., 1986-87; judge pro tem Three Lakes Jud. Dist., 1997—. Judge pro tem Riverside County, Calif., 1996—. Recipient Am. Jurisprudence award Bancroft Whitney; Order of Cheviler. Mem. ABA (taxation and environ. coms., vice chmn. gen. bus. sect. 1995), Assn. Trial Lawyers Am., L.A. Bar Assn. Republican. Jewish. Lodges: Masons, Ionic, Composite. Avocations: sports, reading, golf. General corporate, Personal income taxation, Public utilities. Office: 41877 Enterprise Cir N Ste 200 Temecula CA 92590-5628

**ROSENSTEIN, SHEILA KOVALESKI,** lawyer; b. Springfield, Mass., Sept. 18, 1946; d. Leopold P. and Helen Mary (Durnin) Kovaleski; m. Walter Rosenstein, June 2, 1970 (div. 1982); 1 child, Alexandra N.; m. William B. Barnes, Nov. 21, 1987. AB, Barnard Coll., 1968; JD, Columbia U., 1971. Bar: Conn. 1981, U.S. Dist. Ct. Conn. 1982. Assoc. Hurwitz & Sagarin, Milford, Conn., 1982-84; pvt. practice Fairfield, Conn., 1982-88; ptnr. Rosenstein and Barnes, Fairfield, 1988—. V.p. LWV, Fairfield, 1982-88. Mem. ABA, Conn. Bar Assn., Greater Bridgeport Bar Assn. Family and matrimonial, General civil litigation, General practice. Office: 1100 Kings Hwy Fairfield CT 06432-5400

**ROSENSTOCK, LOUIS ANTHONY, III,** lawyer; b. Petersburg, Va., July 27, 1941. BA, Washington and Lee U., 1963; JD, LLB, U. Richmond, 1966. Bar: Va. 1966. Judge 11th Jud. Dist., Petersburg, 1973-75; sole practice, 1975-98. Capt. JAGC, U.S. Army, 1966-71. Mem. ABA, Va. State Bar, Petersburg Bar Assn. (pres. 1984-85), Va. Trial Lawyers Assn. Government contracts and claims. Office: City of Petersburg City Hall Annex 103 W Tabb St Petersburg VA 23803-3211

**ROSENTHAL, ALAN D.,** lawyer; b. Dallas, Apr. 28, 1949; s. Harry and Esther P. (Moskowitz) R.; m. Sondra Elise Aron, May 19, 1985; children: Adam Caplan, Kenneth Caplan, Jennifer. BSEE, Princeton U., 1971; JD, U. Tex., 1974. Ptnr. Baker & Botts, Houston, 1974-92, Fish & Richardson, Houston, 1992-98, Rosenthal & Osha, Houston, 1998—. Avocations: fishing, cooking, travel. Patent, Trademark and copyright. Home: 6614 Wakeforest St Houston TX 77005-3956 Office: Rosenthal & Osha 700 Louisiana St Ste 4550 Houston TX 77002-2793

**ROSENTHAL, BRIAN DAVID,** lawyer; b. Glen Ridge, N.J., May 1, 1952; s. Charles and Dorothy H. (Stanger) R.; m. Joy N. Weisman, Aug. 11, 1974; children: Adam M., Elizabeth J., Alexander H. BA magna cum laude, U. Pa., Phila., 1974; JD, Georgetown U., Washington, 1977. Bar: Pa. 1977, U.S. Dist. Ct. (ea. dist.) Pa. 1983, U.S. Ct. Appeals (3rd cir.) 1984. Asst. dist. atty. Phila. Dist. Attys. Office, 1977-82; assoc. atty. Ominsky Joseph & Welsh PC, Phila., 1982-85; ptnr. Ominsky Welsh & Rosenthal PC, Phila., 1986-92; pres., founding ptnr. Rosenthal & Weisberg PC, Phila., 1992—; commr. Bd. Commrs., Lower Merion Township, Pa., 1994—; settlement master Phila. Ct. Common Pleas, 1993—. Author: Medical Malpractice in Pennsylvania, 1993, Insurance Litigation in Pennsylvania, 1993. Pres. Lower Merion Little League, 1991—; dir. baseball Kaiserman J.C.C., Penn Wynne, Pa., 1985; bd. dirs. Nat. Multiple Sclerosis Soc., Phila., 1979-84. Named Outstanding Vol. Kaiserman Jewish Cmty. Ctr., Penn Wynne, 1985, Outstanding Adult Vol. Lower Merion Little League, 1993. Mem. ABA (sects. on litigation, tort and ins. practice, criminal justice), Assn. Trial Lawyers Am., Pa. Trial Lawyers Assn., Pa. Bar Assn., Phila. Bar Assn. (coms. medico legal com., state judiciary com. 1993—), Phi Beta Kappa. Avocations: baseball, reading, travel, coaching. Professional liability, Personal injury, General civil litigation. Office: Rosenthal & Weisberg PC 2 Logan Sq Ste 1565 Philadelphia PA 19103-2730

**ROSENTHAL, HERBERT MARSHALL,** lawyer. BA, UCLA; JD, Hasting Coll. Law, U. Calif., San Francisco. Bar: Calif. 1962. Formerly exec. dir. State Bar Calif., San Francisco; pvt. practice Millbrae, Calif. Administrative and regulatory. Office: PO Box 507 Millbrae CA 94030-0507

**ROSENTHAL, ILENE GOLDSTEIN,** lawyer; b. New Haven, Aug. 27, 1952; d. Sidney Leon and Marian (Goodman) Goldstein; m. Steven Sigmund Rosenthal, Oct. 1, 1983; children: Alexandra M., Eliana D. BA, Wesleyan U., 1974; JD, Georgetown U., 1982. Bar: Calif. 1983, U.S. Dist. Ct. (cen. and no. dists.) Calif. 1983, D.C. 1985, U.S. Ct. Appeals (D.C. cir.) 1985, U.S. Dist. Ct. D.C. 1986. Law clk. to Hon. William P. Gray U.S. Dist. Ct. for Cen. Dist. Calif., L.A., 1982-83; assoc. Wyman, Bautzer, Rothman, Kuchel & Silbert, L.A., 1983-84; asst. U.S. Atty. D.C., Washington, 1985-88; minority gen. counsel House Gov. Ops. Com., Washington, 1989-91; gen. counsel, dir. litigation Software Publs. Assn., Washington, 1991-94; gen. counsel and v.p. for govt. affairs Lightspan Partnership, Inc., Washington, 1994-97; pres. New Image Media, LLC, Washington, 1997—; chair Everybody Wins! DC, 1995—; bd. dirs. Nat. Coalition for Tech. in Edn. and Tng., 1996—; v.p. bd. dirs. Aidan Montessori Sch., Washington; contbr. edit. Tech. & Learning, 1999—. Contbg. editor: Tech. and Learning Mag., 1999—. Chair Aidan Montessori Sch., Washington, 1998—. Computer, Intellectual property, Federal civil litigation. Office: 2619 Woodley Pl NW Ste 201 Washington DC 20008-1525

**ROSENTHAL, JAY P.,** lawyer; b. Port Chester, N.Y., Apr. 27, 1955; s. Jerome R. and Deborah A. (Levine) R.; m. Joyce A. Kornfeld, Mar. 16, 1986; children: Drew W., Brooke A. BA in Polit. Sci., SUNY, Binghamton, 1977; JD, St. John's U., Queens, N.Y., 1981. Bar: N.Y. 1982, N.J. 1982, D.C. 1987, Ariz. 1991. Clk., assoc. Robert S. Tobin, PC, N.Y.C., 1981-83, Herzfeld & Rubin, P.C., N.Y.C., 1983-87, Ecker, Loehn & Ecter, Yonkers, N.Y., 1987-89, Oxman, Geigner, Natale & Tolis, Hawthorne, N.Y., 1989-93, Jones, Skelton & Hochuli, P.C.C., Phoenix, 1993—; adj. prof. bus. law Mercy Coll., Yorktown, N.Y., 1989-91. Co-chmn. fine arts coun. Temple Chai, Phoenix, 1995-97. Mem. ABA, State Bar Ariz., N.Y. State Bar Assn., Ariz. Assn. Def. Counsel. General civil litigation, Personal injury, Civil rights. Office: Jones Skelton & Hechuli PPC 2901 N Central Ave Ste 800 Phoenix AZ 85012-2798

**ROSENTHAL, KATE,** lawyer, educator; b. Binghamton, N.Y., May 1, 1954; d. Charles Leopold and Ann Solis-Cohen R. BA in Political Sci., History, Earlham Coll., 1976; JD, Syracuse U., 1981. Bar: N.Y. 1982, U.S. Dist. Ct. (no. dist.) N.Y. 1982, U.S. Ct. Appeals (2nd cir.) 1991. Assoc. Alderman, Samuels, Jerry & Rossi, Syracuse, N.Y., 1981-83; pvt. practice Syracuse, N.Y., 1983—; adv. bd. Thompson Publishing, Rochester, N.Y. Adv. com. Medical Examiner Syracuse, 1990-94; mem. Gender Bias com. 5th Dist. Syracuse, 1990-92, Syracuse City Charter Review commn., 1990. Recipient Mover Shaker in Field of Law award Herald Jour. Newspaper, Syracuse, 1988. Mem. Nat. Conference Criminal Justice Act Panel Attorneys (no. dist. rep. 1995—), N.Y. State Assn. Criminal Defense Lawyers (v.p., bd. mem. 1993—) Syracuse Assn. Criminal Defense Lawyers (co-founder 1990—), N.Y. State Bar Assn. (fifth dist. rep. to exec. com. 1996—). Democrat. Jewish. Avocations: travel, snorkeling, photography. Criminal. Office: 500 108 W Jefferson St Syracuse NY 13202

**ROSENTHAL, KENNETH W.,** lawyer; b. Frankfurt, Fed. Republic Germany, Nov. 2, 1929; came to U.S., 1944; s. Ludwig and Florence (Koenigsberger) R.; m. Joan Finkelstein, Apr. 10, 1960; children: Jeffrey, David. BA, Syracuse U., 1951; LLB, U. Calif., San Francisco, 1958. Bar: Calif. 1959, U.S. Dist. Ct. (no. dist.) Calif. 1959, U.S. Ct. Appeals (9th cir.) 1959, U.S. Supreme Ct. 1972. Assoc. Jay A. Darwin, San Francisco, 1959-61; ptnr. Darwin, Rosenthal & Leff, San Francisco, 1961-69; pres. Rosenthal & Leff Inc., San Francisco, 1969-89; of counsel Molligan, Cox & Moyer, San Francisco, 1989-98; del. 9th Cir. Jud. Conf., 1986-89. Contbr. numerous articles to profl. jours. Mem. Nat. Bd. Trial Advocacy (cert.), Am. Bd. Trial Advs. (cert.), Calif. Bar. Assn. (legal specialization sect., civic trial advocacy com., mediator, arbitrator 1993—), San Francisco Bar Assn., San Francisco Trial Lawyers Assn. (bd. dirs. 1976-84, pres. 1984). Democrat. Jewish. Avocations: photography, walking. Admiralty, Alternative dispute resolution, Federal civil litigation. Office: Cox & Moyer 703 Market St San Francisco CA 94103-2102

**ROSENTHAL, LEE H.,** federal judge; b. Nov. 30, 1952; m. Gary L. Rosenthal; children: Rebecca, Hannah, Jessica, Rachel. BA in Philosophy with honors, U. Chgo., 1974, JD with honors, 1977. Bar: Tex. 1979. Law clk. to Hon. John R. Brown U.S. Ct. Appeals (5th cir.), 1977-78; assoc. Baker & Botts, 1978-86, ptnr., 1986-92; judge U.S. Dist. Ct. (so. dist.) Tex., 1992—; vis. com. Law Sch. U. Chgo., 1983-86, 94-97; mem. Fed. Jud. Conf. Adv. Com. for Fed. Rules of Civil Procedure, 1996—; chair 1999 Fifth Cir. Jud. Conf. Mem. bd. editors Manual for Complex Litigation, 1999—. Mem. devel. coun. Tex. Children's Hosp., 1988-92; pres. Epilepsy Assn. Houston/Gulf Coast, 1989-91; trustee Briarwood Sch. Endowment Found., 1991-92; bd. dirs. Epilepsy Found. Am., 1993-98. Fellow Tex. Bar Found.; Mem. ABA, Am. Law Inst. (consultative group for transnat. rules of civil procedure), Texas Bar Assn., Houston Bar Assn. Office: US Dist Ct US Courthouse Rm 11535 515 Rusk St Houston TX 77002-2600

**ROSENTHAL, MEYER L(OUIS),** lawyer; b. Wilkes-Barre, Pa., May 27, 1944; s. Samuel J. and Lottie G. (Goncher) R.; m. Susan M., Aug. 19, 1967; children: Norman, Bonnie. BA, Rutgers U., 1966, JD, 1969. Bar: N.J. 1969, U.S. Dist. Ct. N.J. 1969, Calif. 1975, U.S. Dist. Ct. (cen. dist.) Calif. 1981, U.S. Dist. Ct. (ea. dist.) N.Y. 1980, U.S. Dist. Ct. (so. dist.) N.Y. 1981, U.S. Ct. Appeals (9th cir.) 1981. Law sec. Hon. Leon Milmed N.J. Superior Ct., Newark, 1969-70; assoc. Kaufman & Kaufman, Elizabeth, N.J., 1970-76; ptnr. Trueger & Rosenthal, Morristown, N.J., 1976-82; atty. pvt. practice, Morristown, N.J., 1982—. Editor Rutgers Law Rev. Cub scout leader Morris Area Boy Scouts Am., Randolph, N.J., 1980; chmn. Morris City Human Rels. Commn., Morristown, 1992-95, chmn. emeritus, 1999. Recipient Cmty. Hero award Morris County Orgn. Hispanic Affairs, 1996. Mem. Comml. Law League Am., Calif. Bar Assn., N.J. Bar Assn., B'nai B'rith (bd. govs. 1975—, pres. dist. 3 1988-89, Internat. Young Leadership award 1982, Internat. Founders award 1985; nat. comm. anti-defamation league). State civil litigation, Contracts commercial, Real property. Office: 161 Washington St Morristown NJ 07960-3753

**ROSENTHAL, MICHAEL BRUCE,** lawyer; b. Buffalo, Aug. 16, 1955; s. Jack and Elaine Lois (Brill) R.; m. Tori Johnson; children: Lainey, Haley. BA, Colo. Coll., 1978; JD, U. Wyo., 1981. Bar: Wyo. 1983, U.S. Dist. Ct. Wyo. 1983, U.S. Ct. Appeals (10th cir.) 1986. Landman Mobil Coal Resources, Inc., Denver, 1981-84; pub. defender State of Wyo., Gillette, 1984-86; assoc. Hathaway, Speight, Kunz, Trautwein & Barrett, Cheyenne, Wyo., 1986-90; ptnr. Hathaway, Speight, Kunz, & Trautwein, Cheyenne, Wyo., 1990-94; Hathaway, Speight & Kunz, 1994—. Mem. DePaul Hosp. Health Care Task Force, Cheyenne, 1990-92; chmn. Cheyenne Bd. of Adjustment, 1989-90; pres. Cheyenne Symphony Orch., 1991-92, bd. dirs. 1986-94; bd. dirs. Wyo. chpt. Am. Cancer Soc., Cheyenne, 1990-92, Cheyenne Symphony Found., 1992—, pres., 1992-97; bd. dirs. Laramie County Cmty. Found., 1993—. Mem. ABA, Wyo. Bar Assn., ATLA, Wyo. Trial Lawyers Assn. (bd. dirs. 1988—, sec.-treas. 1993, pres.-elect 1993-94, pres. 1994-95), Laramie County Bar Assn. Republican. Avocations: cycling, tennis, squash, golf. Personal injury, Federal civil litigation, State civil litigation. Office: Hathaway Speight & Kunz PO Box 1208 Cheyenne WY 82003-1208

**ROSENTHAL, STEVEN SIEGMUND,** lawyer; b. Cleve., May 22, 1949; s. Fred Siegel and Natalie Josephine Rosenthal; m. Ilene Edwina Goldstein, Oct. 1, 1983; children: Alexandra M., Eliana D. AB, Dartmouth Coll., 1971; JD, Harvard U., 1974. Bar: Fla. 1974, D.C. 1975, U.S. Supreme Ct. 1978, Calif. 1983. Law clk. U.S. Ct. Appeals (D.C. cir.), 1974-75; assoc. Covington & Burling, Washington, 1975-80; assoc. Morrison & Foerster, Washington, 1980-81, ptnr., 1981-97; ptnr. Cooper, Carvin & Rosenthal, PLLC, Washington, 1998—; lawyer rep. Jud. Conf. D.C. Cir., 1981-83. Pres. Family and Child Services Washington, 1986-88, trustee, 1978—. Mem. ABA, Am. Law Inst., Phi Beta Kappa. Republican. Administrative and regulatory, Government contracts and claims, Federal civil litigation. Office: Cooper Carvin & Rosenthal PLLC 1500 K St NW Ste 200 Washington DC 20005-1264

**ROSENZWEIG, CHARLES LEONARD,** lawyer; b. N.Y.C., Apr. 12, 1952; s. William and Frieda (Dechner) R.; m. Rya R. Mehler, June 14, 1975; children: Jessica Sara, Erica Danielle. AB cum laude, Princeton U., 1974; JD, NYU, 1977. Bar: N.Y. 1978, U.S. Dist. Ct. (ea. and so. dists.) N.Y. 1978, U.S. Ct. Appeals (7th cir.) 1980, U.S. Ct. Internat. Trade 1981, U.S. Ct. Appeals (2d cir.) 1985. Assoc. Graubard, Moskovitz et al, N.Y.C., 1977-85; ptnr. Rand, Rosenzweig, Smith, Radley, Gordon & Burstein LLP, N.Y.C., 1987—; mem. panel of neutrals comml. divsn. Supreme Ct. State N.Y. Editor NYU Jour. Internat. Law. and Politics. Chmn. of bd. Jewish Cmty. Ctr., Harrison. Mem. ABA (internat. law sect.), N.Y. State Bar Assn. (co-chair internat. litigation com. 1995-98, mem. exec. com. comml. and fed. litigation sect.), Am. Arbitration Assn., NYU Alumni Assn. (chmn. jour. internat. law and politics alumni 1985-87), Princeton Club. Avocations: skiing, cycling, tennis, scuba diving. Private international, Federal civil litigation, General corporate. Home: 37 Franklin Rd Scarsdale NY 10583-7563 Office: Rand Rosenzweig et al 605 3rd Ave New York NY 10158-0180

**ROSENZWEIG, JANICE POPICK,** lawyer; b. Balt., Apr. 23, 1950; d. Bernard and Harlee Sedell (Senzer) Popick; m. Richard Michael Pearlstein, Aug. 5, 1972 (div. July 1977); 1 child, Rachel A.; m. Norman Rosenzweig, Sept. 25, 1983. BA in Psychology cum laude, Brandeis U., 1972; JD, U. Md., Balt., 1992. Bar: Md. 1992, U.S. Dist. Ct. Md. 1993. Program coord. N. Charles Found., Cambridge, Mass., 1976-78; tenant rels. coord. Equity Mgmt. Group, Boston, 1976-79; dir. planning, rsch., data processing The Parole Bd., State of Mass., Boston, 1978-80; program mgr. Chesapeak Physicians, P.A., Balt., 1980-81; regional sales mgr. Dart Med., Mason, Mich., 1982-83; profl. med. rep. Syntex Labs., Inc., Palo Alto, Calif., 1983-86; mktg. cons. Harford Physicians PPO and Healthfast, Inc., Balt., 1985-87; med. sales rep. G.D. Searle & Co., Chgo., 1987-89; lawyer, pvt. practice Brooklandville, Md., 1992—; sec., bd. dirs. State Med., Inc., Balt., 1990-94; bd. dirs. Leagl Aid Bur. Inc., 1995—. Co-editor (newspaper) The Raven, U. Md. Sch. of Law, 1989-91, editor, 1991-92 (2d pl. ABA Law Sch. Newspaper Contest non-polit. cartoon 1990); acting editor (newsletter) Mid-Atlantic Ethics Com., 1994-95; contbr. Bedford County Pa. Guide, 1987. Mem. Pleasant View Comty. Assn., Balt., 1984—; chair Brandeis U. area alumni admissions coun., Balt., 1986—. Mem. ABA, Balt. County Bar Assn., Balt. City Bar Assn. Health, Labor, Family and matrimonial. Office: PO Box 952 Brooklandville MD 21022-0952

**ROSENZWEIG, THEODORE B.,** lawyer; b. N.Y.C., Apr. 14, 1948; s. Joseph and Elsa Ruth (Davis) R.; m. Barbara Conviser, Jan. 23, 1977; 1 child, Brian Eliott. BA, NYU, 1969; JD, Fordham U., 1973. Bar: N.Y. 1974, U.S. Dist. Ct. (ea. dist.) N.Y. 1976, U.S. Dist. Ct. (so. dist.) N.Y. 1976, U.S. Ct. Appeals (2d cir.) 1977. Asst. dist. atty. Kings County Dist. Atty.'s Office, Bklyn., 1973-79, sr. trial atty. homicide bur., 1978-79; assoc. McAloon & Friedman, P.C., N.Y.C., 1979-82, ptnr., 1983—; mem. faculty Nat. Inst. for Trial Advocacy Program, Benjamin N. Cardozo Sch. of Law, N.Y.C., 1984—. Mem. N.Y. State Bar Assn. (trial lawyers sect.). Democrat. Jewish. State civil litigation, Personal injury. Home: 17 S Morris Ln Scarsdale NY 10583-6015 Office: McAloon & Friedman PC 116 John St New York NY 10038-3300

**ROSETTI, SCOTTY RESTER,** lawyer, business owner; b. Gulfport, Miss., Apr. 24, 1941; s. Scotty and Hazel (Rester) R.; married, Oct. 28, 1986; children: Ashley, Raegan, Lindsey, Aaron. BS, U. So. Miss., 1965; JD, U. Miss., Oxford, 1968. Bar: Miss. 1969, U.S. Dist. Ct. Miss. 1969, U.S. Supreme Ct. 1969. Pvt. practice Gulfport, 1968-78; Computech, Ltd. (formerly Gause Blvd. Moving-Storage) Gause Blvd. Moving-Storage, Slidell, La., 1978—. Home: 124 Reservation Dr Gulfport MS 39503-3044

**ROSINEK, JEFFREY,** judge; b. N.Y.C., Sept. 13, 1941; s. Isidore and Etta (Kramer) R.; m. Sandra Gwen Rosen, Aug. 7, 1977; 1 child, Ian David. B.A. in History, U. Miami, 1963, postgrad. in Polit. Sci., J.D., 1974. Bar: Fla., 1974. Tchr., Coral Gables (Fla.) High Sch., 1963-78; sole practice, Miami, Fla., 1974-76; assoc. Tendrich and Todd, Miami, 1976-77; ptnr. Todd, Rosinek & Blake, Miami, 1977-84, Rosinek and Blake, 1984-86; judge Dade County Court, Miami, 1986-89, 11th Jud. Cir., Fla., 1990—; instr. Boston U., 1975; mem. faculty Fla. Coll. Advanced Judicial Studies, 1992—; lectr., presenter in field. Contbr. articles to newspapers and profl. jours. Chmn. Miami Environ. Research Adv. Com., 1969-73; mem. Miami Beach Transportation commn., Nat. Bicentenial Competition on the constitution & Bill of Rights com., Dade County Youth Adv. Bd., 1973-75; bd. dirs. U. Miami Law Sch., treas. alumni, jud. dir.; past pres. Dade County Young Democrats; mem. Congl. Civilian Rev. Bd., 1975-90, chmn., 1976-78; bd. dirs., treas. Fla. Congl. Com., Legal Services Greater Miami; chmn. Dade County Adv. Coun. Close-Up Found.; Fla. chmn. Project Concern Internat.; internat. state chmn. Fla. Walk for Mankind, Project Concern, legal adv. com. Kiwanis, 1982-86; v.p. Beth David Congregation, 1982-86; bd. trustees Haven Ctr.; bd. dirs., treas., organizer South Miami-Kendall pro bono project Legal Service of Greater Miami, 1983-86; traffic review com. Dade County, 1987-92; bd. dirs. Fla. Law Related Edn., 1988—, Adv. Program, 1988—; mem. Miami-Dade County task force for homeless, 1992-94; active Dade Coalition for the Homeless, 1992—, Dade County Homeless Trust. 1993—, chmn. criminal justice com.; chmn. Beck Mus. of Judaica, 1988-89; ednl. dir. Temple Judea; jud. circuit rep. Dept. Corrections "Boot Camp" program, 1994—; 11th jud. circuit organizer, rep. Homeless Alt. Rehab. Tracking Program, 1994—, rep. Comprehensive Homeless Integration Program (CHIP), 1992-94, chair Fla. 1st Annual Edn. Seminar/Retreat, 1995, Eugene P. Spellman Am. Inn of Ct., 1996—, ABA Task Force Reduction of Litigation Cost and Delay, 1995—, South Fla. Super Bowl XXXIII Host Com.; 1st v.p. Coral Gables H.S. Parent-Tchrs.-Students Assn., 1995-96, pres., 1996-98. Recipient award Jewish Theol. Sem., 1978, Outstanding Law Student award, Merit award Profl. Law Enforcement Assn., Appreciation award Liberty City Christian Assn., Mem. ABA, Dade County Bar Assn., South Miami-Kendall Bar Assn. (past pres.), Coral Gables Bar Assn., Fla. Bar Assn. (jud. nominating procedures com., rules com. family law sect. 1984-87), Miami Beach Bar Assn. (bd. dirs.), Cuban Am. Bar Assn., Dade County Bar (criminal cts. com., 1994—), Chabad of South Dade (bd. dirs. 1999—), Dade Ptnrs., Fla. Conf. Crct. Ct. Judges (criminal justice com. 1995—), Wig and Robe (chancellor 1973-74), Bar and Gavel Soc., U. Miami Law Sch. Alumni Assn. (sec., treas. 1985-87, jud. dir. 1987—), Am. Judges Assn. (bd. govs. 1988-92, sec. 1992-93, 2d v.p. 1993-94, 1st v.p., 1994-95, pres.-elect 1995-96, pres. 1996-97, chair 32nd Annual Edn. Conf., Miami Beach, 1992; mem. Image of Judiciary Com, Domestic Violence Com., 1990-96; chair fed. state rels. com. 1994-96; exec. com. 1997; chair nominations com. 1997, edn. com. 1998—; chair 38th Annual Edn. Conf., Orlando, 1998; coord. Close-up Found. project, 1997—), Nat. Court Reporters Assn. (strategic com. 1993—). Clubs: Biscayne Bay Kiwanis (disting. past pres., lt. gov. Fla. Dist., Maj. Emphasis chmn., pres. 1994—, named Kiwanian of Yr., 1983-84), Key Internat. (counselor Fla. dist., past pres. 1980-81, pres. 1994-95, sec. 1995—, Key of Honor 1979, Key Club honoree 1984), Kiwanis Internat. (life mem.), Greater Miami C. of C. (Carrfour Housing Corp. for homeless, v.p. permanent housing 1996-98, pres. 1999—). Home: 535 Bird Rd Coral Gables FL 33146-1307 Office: 1351 NW 12th St Miami FL 33125-1644

**ROSKOVENSKY, VINCENT JOSEPH, II,** lawyer; b. Uniontown, Pa., Mar. 15, 1950; s. Vincent S. and Gertrude F. Roskovensky; m. Christine D. Bruni, July 16, 1977; 1 child, Vincent M. BA, U. Pitts., 1971; JD, Duquesne U., 1974. Bar: Pa. 1974, U.S. Dist. Ct. (we. dist.) Pa. 1975. Sole practice, Uniontown, 1974—; asst. dist. atty. Fayette County (Pa.), 1975-77; solicitor Smithfield Borough, Smithfield, Pa., 1980-88, Albert Gallatin Mcpl. Authority, Lake Lynn, Pa., 1980—; pres. Poca Coal Land Co., Uniontown. Treas., past pres. Fayette County Children and Youth Adv. Com., Uniontown; mem. exec. bd. Westmoreland-Fayette Coun., 1990—, v.p., 1998—; dist. chmn. Boy Scouts Am., 1994-98. Mem. Pa. Bar Assn., Fayette County Bar Assn., Assn. Trial Lawyers Am., ABA. Democrat. Roman Catholic. Club: Exchange. State civil litigation, General practice, Criminal. Home: Heritage Hills Rd Uniontown PA 15401 Office: 9 Court St Uniontown PA 15401-3501

**ROSKY, BURTON SEYMOUR,** lawyer; b. Chgo., May 28, 1927; s. David T. and Mary W. (Zelkin) R.; m. Leatrice J. Darrow, June 16, 1951; children: David Scott, Bruce Alan. Student, Ill. Inst. Tech., 1944-45; BS, UCLA, 1948; JD, Loyola U., L.A., 1953. Bar: Calif. 1954, U.S. Supreme Ct 1964, U.S. Tax Ct 1964; C.P.A., Calif. Auditor City of L.A., 1948- 51; with Beidner, Temkin & Ziskin (C.P.A.s), L.A., 1951-52; supervising auditor Army Audit Agy., 1952-53; practiced law L.A., Beverly Hills, 1954—; ptnr. Duskin & Rosky, 1972-82; s Rosky, Landau & Fox, 1982-93; ptnr. Rosky, Landau & Stahl, Beverly Hills, 1993; lectr. on tax and bus. problems; judge pro tem Beverly Hills Mcpl. Ct., L.A. Superior Ct.; mem. L.A. Mayor's Community Adv. Council. Contbr. profl. publs. Charter supporting mem. Los Angeles County Mus. Arts; contbg. mem. Assocs. of Smithsonian Instn.; charter mem. Air and Space Mus; mem. Am. Mus. Natural History, L.A. Zoo; supporting mem. L.A. Mus. Natural History; mem. exec. bd. So. Calif. coun. Nat. Fedn. Temple Brotherhoods, mem. nat. exec. bd.; mem. bd. govs. Loyola Sch. Law, L.A. With USNR, 1945-46. Walter Henry Cook fellow Loyola Law Sch. Bd. Govs. Fellow Jewish Chautauqua Soc. (life mem.); mem. Am. Arbitration Assn. (nat. panel arbitrators), Am. Assn. Attys.-CPAs (charter mem. pres. 1968), Calif. Assn. Attys.-CPAs (charter mem., pres. 1963), Calif. Soc. CPAs, Calif., Beverly Hills, Century City, Los Angeles County bar assns., Am. Judicature Soc., Chancellors Assocs. UCLA, Tau Delta Phi, Phi Alpha Delta.; mem. B'nai B'rith. Jewish (mem. exec. bd., pres. temple, pres. brotherhood). Club: Mason. General corporate,

Estate planning, Probate. Office: Rosky Landau & Stahl 8383 Wilshire Blvd Beverly Hills CA 90211-2410

**ROSMARIN, SUSAN GRESSER,** lawyer; b. Hackensack, N.J., May 25, 1954; d. Newton Hillel and Evelyn (Bialer) Gresser; m. Sam Rosmarin, June 19, 1983; children: Max Zachary, Lee Alexander. BA, Brandeis U., 1976; JD, Boston U., 1980; LLM in Corp. Law, NYU, 1986. Assoc. Banger & Weiss, N.Y.C., 1980-87; gen. counsel Commodore Environ. Svc., Secaucus, N.J., 1987-90; assoc. Carro Spanback/Castr & Cuiffo, N.Y.C., 1990-92, Thelen Marrin Johnson & Bridges, N.Y.C., 1992-93; gen. counsel UNESCO, Inc., Carlstadt, N.J., 1993-94; ptnr. Osborn, Rosmarin & Sesti, LLP, N.Y.C., 1994-97; counsel Stryker Tams & Dill, LLP, Newark, 1997—; gen. counsel Nat. Lead Assessment and Abatement Coun., Olney, Md., 1993—; instr. NYU Sch. Continuing Edn., N.Y.C., 1993—. Editor Environ. Compliance & Litig., 1996—; contbr. articles to profl. jours. Mem. ABA, N.J. Bar Assn. Environmental, General corporate, Toxic tort. Office: Stryker Tams & Dill LLP Two Penn Plz E Newark NJ 07105

**ROSNER, LEONARD ALLEN,** lawyer; b. N.Y.C., Apr. 13, 1967; s. Arnold and Betty (Zimmerman) R.; m. Rachel Stein, Nov. 19, 1994; 1 child, Andrew N. AB in Polit. Sci., Syracuse U., 1989, AB in Pub. Rels., 1989, JD cum laude, 1992. Bar: N.Y. 1993. Assoc. Law Office Stephen D. Rogoff Esq., Rochester, N.Y., 1992—. Fin. editor Syracuse Jour. Internat. Law and Commerce, 1991-92. Assigned coun. Monroe County Assigned Coun., Rochester, 1993-94. Mem. N.Y. Bar Assn., Monroe County Bar Assn. Avocations: golfing, reading, television sports, nautilus. General practice, Criminal, Family and matrimonial. Home: 150 Frenchwoods Cir Rochester NY 14618-5251 Office: 14 Franklin St Ste 900 Rochester NY 14604-1504

**ROSOFF, WILLIAM A.,** lawyer, executive; b. Phila., June 21, 1943; s. Herbert and Estelle (Finkel) R.; m. Beverly Rae Rifkin, Feb. 7, 1970; children: Catherine D., Andrew M. BS with honors, Temple U., 1964; LLB magna cum laude, U. Pa., 1967. Bar: Pa. 1968, U.S. Dist. Ct. (ea. dist.) Pa. 1968. Law clk. U.S. Ct. Appeals (3d cir.), 1967-68; instr. U. Pa. Law Sch., Phila., 1968-69; assoc. Wolf, Block, Schorr & Solis-Cohen, Phila., 1969-75, ptnr., 1975-96, chmn. exec. com., 1987-88; vice chmn. Advanta Corp., Spring House, Pa., 1996—; trustee RPS Realty Trust, 1990-96, Atlantic Realty Trust, 1996—; guest lectr. confs. and seminars on tax law; mem. tax adv. bd. Commerce Clearing House, 1983-94; mem. legal activities policy bd. Tax Analysts, 1978—; mem. Little, Brown Tax Adv. Bd., 1994-96; chmn. bd. dirs. RMH Telesvcs., Inc., 1997—. Editor U. Pa. Law Rev., 1965-67; mem. bd. contbg. editors and advisors Jour. Partnership Taxation, 1983—; author reports and papers on tax law. Bd. dirs., mem. com. on law and social action Phila. coun. Am. Jewish Congress. Fellow Am. Coll. Tax Counsel; mem. Am. Law Inst. (cons. taxation of partnerships 1976-78, assoc. reporter taxation of partnerships, 1978-82, mem. adv. group on fed. income tax project 1982—, cons. taxation of pass-through entities 1995—), Locust Club (dir.), Order of Coif, Beta Gamma Sigma, Beta Alpha Psi. Corporate taxation, Personal income taxation. Office: Advanta Corp Welsh and McKean Rd Spring House PA 19477

**ROSOFF, WILLIAM L.,** lawyer; b. N.Y.C., May 23, 1946. BA, Columbia U., 1968; MA, U. Calif., Berkeley, 1969, PhD, 1975; JD, Harvard U., 1978. Bar: N.Y. 1979. From assoc. to ptnr. Davis Polk & Wardwell, N.Y.C., 1978-98; sr. v.p., gen. counsel RJR Nabisco Holdings Corp., N.Y.C., 1998—; bd. dirs. Deltic Timber Corp. Mem. ABA. Mergers and acquisitions. Office: RJR Nabisco Holdings 1301 Ave of the Americas New York NY 10019*

**ROSS, CATHERINE JANE,** lawyer, social policy analyst; b. N.Y.C., Dec. 27, 1949; d. Alexander I. and Wilma (Saltzman) R.; m. Jonathan Rieder, Mar. 14, 1981. B.A., Yale Coll., 1971; Ph.D., Yale U., 1977, J.D., 1987. Post doctoral fellow/research assoc. Yale Bush Ctr. in Child Devel. and Social Policy, New Haven, 1977-79; asst. prof. Yale Child Study Ctr., New Haven, 1979-85; assoc. Paul, Weiss, Rifkind, Wharton & Garrison, 1987-94; asst. prof. history and edn. Boston Coll. Law Sch., 1994-96; assoc. prof. George Washington U. Law Sch., 1996—; mem. HHS Expert Working Group Adoption 2002;; cons. Adminstrn. for Children Youth and Families, HEW, 1979, Conn. Dept. Children and Youth Services, 1978-84, ednl. films and radio programs. Joint editor: Child Abuse: An Agenda for Action, 1980. Del., Conn. Task Force on Juvenile Justice, 1979-80; com. mem. Conn. Task Force on Foster Care, 1979-81. Mellon fellow Aspen Inst. for Humanistic Studies, 1983-84. Fellow Am. Bar Found.; mem. ABA (vice-chair working group on unmet legal needs of Am.'s Children and their families 1993-94, steering com. unmet legal needs of children 1993-94, chair 1994-97, co-chair, 1997—, mem. sect. litigation task force children); grantee Edna McConnell Clark Found., 1981-82, Herman and Amelia Ehrmann Found., 1979-82, Ford Found., 1980-82, John and Catherine MacArthur Found., 1981. Jewish. General civil litigation, Constitutional, Juvenile.

**ROSS, CHRISTOPHER THEODORE,** lawyer; b. Denver, Oct. 19, 1925; s. Michael Peter and Martha (Stickhausen) R.; m. Luise Maria Reile, June 11, 1952 (div.); children: Mark Alexander, Katherine Luise, Sonya Catherine (dec.). LLB, U. Buffalo, 1950; JD, SUNY, Buffalo, 1968. Bar: N.Y. 1961, U.S. Dist. Ct. (we. dist.) N.Y. 1952, U.S. Ct. Mil. Appeals 1953, U.S. Supreme Ct. 1970, U.S. Ct. Appeals (2d cir.) 1971. Assoc. Lutwak, Parrino & Maurin, Buffalo, 1959-63; atty. pvt. practice, Buffalo, 1963—. Pres. N.Y. State Assn. Bds. Visitors Dept. Mental Hygiene, 1874-78; pres. West Seneca (N.Y.) Devle. Ctr., 1968-70, 72-74; trustee Buffalo Boy's & Girls Clubs. With USN, 1943-46, 52-59; comdr. USNR, ret.; capt. N.Y. NAval Militia, ret. Mem. N.Y. Bar Assn., N.Y. State Assn. Criminal Def. Lawyers, Erie County Bar Assn., Erie County Trial Lawyers Assn., Lawyer-Pilots Assn., Naval Res. Assn. (v.p. legis., v.p. ret. persons), NAval order of U.S., U.S. Navy League, Royual Can. Mil. Inst. (bd. dirs. 1994-97, hon. officer, internat. affairs), Sovereign Mil. Order of Jerusalem, Naval Officers Assn. Can., Buffalo Athletic Club, Quiet Birdmen Club, Saints and Sinners Club, Silver Wings Club, Aero Club, Toronto Naval Club. Republican. Roman Catholic. Criminal, Personal injury, Aviation. Office: 715 Delaware Ave # 101 Buffalo NY 14209-2230

**ROSS, DAVID LEE,** lawyer; b. Orange, N.J., May 25, 1944; s. David S. and Beryl M. (Moorman) R.; children: Karen Elizabeth, Michael David McIver. BS, East Tenn. State U., 1965; JD, Washington & Lee U., 1969. Bar: Va. 1969. Gen. counsel Va. Tech. U., Blacksburg, 1973-77, Va. Commonwealth U., Richmond, 1977—; chmn. bd. dirs. Richmond Cmty. H.S. Found.; chmn. adv. bd. Richmond Cmty. Sch. Lt. cmdr. USN, 1969-73. Presbyterian. Education and schools, General civil litigation, Health. Home: 1215 Wilmington Ave Richmond VA 23227-4425 Office: Va Commonwealth Univ 1010 E Marshall St Richmond VA 23298-5033

**ROSS, DONALD HENRY,** lawyer; b. Modesto, Calif., Oct. 14, 1923; s. Guy Walden Ross and Dolly Mae Brewer; m. Ruth Lorene Kitching, May 13, 1946; children: Genie Ann Kuehne, Robin Mae. BS in Indsl. Mgmt., U. So. Calif., 1953; Ms in Internat. Affairs, George Washington U., 1965; JD, U. Pacific, 1982. Bar: Nev. 1982. Sgt. pilot RAF, 1941-42; commd. 2d. lt. USAF, 1942, advanced through grades to maj. gen., retired, 1974; atty. pvt. practice, Carson City, Nev., 1982—. Republican. Avocations: flying, old car restoration, shooting. Home and Office: 4350 Meadow Wood Rd Carson City NV 89703-9493

**ROSS, DONALD ROE,** federal judge; b. Orleans, Nebr., June 8, 1922; s. Roe M. and Leila H. (Reed) R.; m. Janice S. Cook, Aug. 29, 1943; children: Susan Jane, Sharon Kay, Rebecca Lynn, Joan Christine, Donald Dean. JD, U. Nebr., 1948, LLD (hon.), 1990. Bar: Nebr. bar 1948. Practice law Lexington, Nebr., 1948-53; mayor City of Lexington, 1953; assoc. Swarr, May, Royce, Smith, Andersen & Ross, 1956-70; U.S. atty. Dist. Nebr., 1953-56; gen. counsel Rep. party, Nebr., 1956-58; mem. Rep. Exec. Com. for Nebr., 1952-53; nat. com. mem. Rep. Nat. Com., 1958-70, vice chmn., 1965-70; sr. judge U.S. Ct. Appeals 8th cir., 1971—.

**ROSS, HAROLD ANTHONY,** lawyer; b. Kent, Ohio, June 2, 1931; s. Jules and Helen Assumpta (Ferrara) R.; m. Elaine Louise Hunt, July 1, 1961; children—Leslie Ann, Gregory Edward, Jonathan Harold. B.A. magna cum laude, Case Western Res. U., 1953; J.D., Harvard U., 1956. Bar: Ohio 1956. Assoc. Marshman, Hornbeck, Hollington, Steadman & McLaughlin, Cleve., 1961-64; pres. Ross & Kraushaar Co., Cleve., 1964—; gen. counsel Brotherhood of Locomotive Engrs., Cleve., 1966—. Trustee Citizens League Greater Cleve., 1969-75, 76-82, pres., 1981-82; active Charter Rev. Com. North Olmsted, 1970, 75. Served with AUS, 1956-58. Mem. ABA (co-chair rwy. and airline labor law sect. 1976-78), Ohio State Bar Assn., Cleve. Bar Assn., Phi Beta Kappa, Delta Sigma Rho, Omicron Delta Kappa. Roman Catholic. Labor. Office: 1548 Standard Bldg 1370 Ontario St Cleveland OH 44113-1701

**ROSS, HOWARD PHILIP,** lawyer; b. May 10, 1939; s. Bernard and Estelle (Maremont) R.; m. Loretta Teresa Benquil, 1962 (div.); children: Glen Joseph, Cynthia Ann; m. Jennifer Kay Shirley, 1984. BS, U. Ill., 1961; JD, Stetson Coll. Law, 1964. Bar: fla. 1964, U.S. Ct. Appeals (5th cir.) 1965, U.S. Supreme Ct. 1969, U.S. Ct. Appeals (11th cir.) 1981; cert. civil trial lawyer, bus. litigator. Assoc. Parker & Battaglia and predecessor firm, St. Petersburg, Fla., 1964-67; ptnr. Battablia, Ross, Hastings, Dicus & Andrews and predecessor, St. Petersburg, 1967-87; ptnr. Battaglia, Ross, Dicus & Wein, P.A., 1987—, pres., CEO, 1992—; lectr. Stetson Coll. Law, St. Petersburg, 1971-72, adj. prof., 1987. Author: Florida Corporations, 1979; co-author: Managing Discovery in Commercial and Business Litigation, 1993; contbr. articles to profl. jours. Hon. chair St. Petersburg br. Awards Banquet NAACP, 1995; bd. dirs. St. Petersburg Neighborhood Housing Svcs., Inc., 1996-97, Cmty. Alliance, 1997—. Recipient Woman's Svc. League Best Groomed award, 1979, Fla. Bar Merit citation, 1974, Cmty. Svc. award NAACP, 1998, Humanitarian award YMCA of Tampa Bay, 1999. Mem. ABA, Fla. Bar Assn. (chmn. civil trial certification com. 1993-94), St. Petersburg Bar Assn., St. Petersburg Area C. of C. (bd. govs. 1990-95, v.p. pub. affairs 1992-93, v.p. membership 1993-94, exec. com. 1992-95, counsel 1994-95, dean entrepreneurial acad. 1996—, Mem. of Yr. 1993-94), Citizen Rev. Com. City of St. Petersburg (chmn. subcom. 1992-94, co-chair 1994-97). Republican. Jewish. General civil litigation, General corporate, Contracts commercial. Office: Battaglia Ross Dicus & Wein PA PO Box 41100 980 Tyrone Blvd N Saint Petersburg FL 33710-6382

**ROSS, JAMES ULRIC,** lawyer, accountant, educator; b. Del Rio, Tex., Sept. 14, 1941; s. Stephen Mabrey and Beatrice Jessie (Hyslop) R.; m. Janet S. Calabro, Dec. 28, 1986; children: James Ulric Jr., Ashley Meredith. BA, U. Tex., 1963, JD, 1965. Bar: Tex. 1965, U.S. Tax Ct. 1969; CPA, Tex. Estate tax examiner IRS, Houston, 1965-66; tax acct. Holmes, Raquet, Harris & Shaw, San Antonio, 1966-67; pvt. practice law and acctg. Del Rio and San Antonio, Tex., 1968—; instr. St. Mary's U., San Antonio, 1973-75; assoc. prof. U. Tex., San Antonio, 1975-99, ret. Contbr. articles on U.S. and Internat. Estate Planning and Taxation to legal and profl. jours. Active Am. Cancer Soc., Residential Mgmt., Inc., Am. Heart Assn. Mem. ABA, Tex. Bar Assn., Tex. Soc. CPAs, San Antonion Bar Assn., San Antonio Estate Planners Coun. Probate, Corporate taxation, Personal income taxation. Home: 3047 Orchard Hl San Antonio TX 78230-3078 Office: 760 Tex Commerce Bank Bldg 7550 IH 10 W San Antonio TX 78229-5803

**ROSS, JULIA,** lawyer; b. N.Y.C., Oct. 28, 1940; 1 child, Jennifer. BA, San Francisco State Coll., 1964; MA, Calif. State U., 1971; MPH, U. Calif., Berkeley, 1972; JD, Golden Gate U., 1977. Bar: Calif. 1977, U.S. Dist. Ct. (no. dist.) Calif. 1977. Realtor Mason McDuffee, Berkeley, Calif., 1973-77; educator health Mission Mental Health Svcs., San Francisco, 1973; counselor, coord. teen clinics Planned Parenthood, San Francisco, 1969-71; judge pro tem Berkeley-Albany Mcpl. Ct., 1982—; atty. pvt. practice, Berkeley, 1977—. Contbr. articles to mags. Mem. Calif. State Bar Assn., Alameda County Bar Assn., Berkeley-Albany Bar Assn. (pres. 1991). Real property, Probate, Personal injury. Office: PMB 301 1442 Walnut St Berkeley CA 94709-1405

**ROSS, KENNETH L.,** lawyer; b. Orange, Tex., Dec. 2, 1944; s. Albert LeVergene Ross and Noreen Belle Welch; m. Lorinda Foltmer Ross, June 4, 1967 (div. 1976); 1 child, Ashley Nicole; m. Linda Cooper, May 27, 1978; children: Dixie Lee, Megan Mae. BA, Southeastern La. U., 1967; JD, La. State U., 1971. Bar: La. 1972, U.S. Dist. Ct. (ea. dist.) La. 1981, U.S. Supreme Ct. 1992, U.S. Dist. Ct. (mid. dist.) La. 1998. Ptnr. Seale Sledge & Ross, Hammond, La., 1972-79, Seale Macaluso Daigle & Ross, Hammond, 1979-96, Seale Daigle & Ross, Hammond, 1997—; bd. dirs. Ross & Wallace Paper Products, Inc., Hammond, One Mass. Ave. Corp., Washington; chmn. S.E. Region Airspace Conf. for Air Nat. Guard, Washington, 1996-98. Mem. Hammond Airport Bd., 1995; chmn. Leadership Tangipahoa, Hammond, 1996. Brig. gen. USAF Air Nat. Guard, 1969-98. Decorated DSM; recipient Leion of Merit State of La., 1998. Mem. Nat. Guard Assn. of the U.S. (exec. coun. 1992—, Disting. Svc. medal 1996), Nat. Guard Assn. of La. (pres. 1988), La. Dist. and State Bar Assn., La. Regional Airport Authority. Republican. Southern Baptist. Avocations: flying, boating, scuba diving. General civil litigation, General corporate, Probate. Home: 610 W Thomas St Hammond LA 70401-3164 Office: Seale Daigle & Ross APLC 200 N Cate St Hammond LA 70401-3301

**ROSS, MARK SAMUEL,** lawyer, educator, funeral director, writer; b. Newark, June 6, 1957; s. Herbert and Selma Ruth (Feldman) R.; m. Robin Liebman, May 19, 1984; children: Adam Micah, Danielle Leah. BA with honors, Rutgers U., 1979; JD, Benjamin Cardozo Law Sch., 1982; diploma, McAllister Inst. Funeral Svc., 1984. Bar: N.J. 1983, U.S. Dist. Ct. N.J. 1983, N.Y. 1989. V.p. Art/Craft Monuments-Shalom Memls., Union, N.J., 1980—; sec., treas., counsel Menorah Chapels at Milburn, Union, N.J., 1983—; funeral dir. Menorah Chapels at Millburn, Union, N.J., 1984—; atty. pvt. practice, Union, N.J., 1983—; counsel Com. for Consumer Protection, Union, 1985—; adj. prof. law Am. Acad.-McAllister Inst., N.Y.C., 1984-85; instr. Jewish law Emanu-El Religious Sch., Westfield, N.J., 1985. Author: (newspaper column) Through My Father's Eyes, 1995—. V.p. Temple Beth Am, Springfield, N.J., 1986-92, pres., 1992-94; counsel Found. Jewish Arts and Heritage, Inc., Union, 1986—. Named Man of Yr. Springfield B'nai B'rith, 1995; recipient Internat. Cmty. Svc. award, B'nai B'rith Internat., 1995. Mem. ABA, Assn. Trial Lawyers Am., Union County Bar Assn., B'nai B'rith (pres. 1980-83, Nat. Founders award 1982). Avocations: art, music, photography, golf. Probate, Administrative and regulatory, General practice. Office: 2950 Vauxhall Rd Vauxhall NJ 07088-1246 also: PO Box 641 Millburn NJ 07041-0641

**ROSS, MATTHEW,** lawyer; b. N.Y.C., Dec. 28, 1953; s. Harvey and Cecile (Shelsky) R.; m. Susan Ruth Goldfarb, Apr. 20, 1986; children: Melissa Danielle, Henry Max, Thomas Frank. BS in Econs., U. Pa., 1975; JD, U. Va., 1978. Bar: N.Y. 1979, U.S. Dist. Ct. (so. dist.) N.Y. 1979. Assoc. Cravath, Swaine & Moore, N.Y.C., 1978-84; prin., assoc. gen. counsel KPMG Peat Marwick LLP, N.Y.C., 1984-90; prin., deputy gen. counsel Deloitte & Touche LLP, N.Y.C, 1990—. Mem. ABA (corp. law sect.), N.Y. State Bar Assn. (corp. banking and bus. law sect.), Assn. of Bar of City of N.Y. (corp. law com.), Beta Gamma Sigma. Avocations: basketball, tennis, skiing, travel. General corporate, Securities, Professional liability. Home: 17 Carthage Ln Scarsdale NY 10583-7507 Office: Deloitte & Touche LLP 1633 Broadway New York NY 10019-6708

**ROSS, MICHAEL AARON,** lawyer; b. Newark, Sept. 15, 1941; s. Alexander Ash and Matilda (Blumenthal) R.; m. Leslie Gordon, June 26, 1976; children—Christopher Gordon, Alan Gordon. B.A., Franklin and Marshall Coll., 1963; J.D., Columbia U., 1966; M.S. in Econs., U. London, 1967. Bar: N.Y. 1968. Assoc., then ptnr. Shearman & Sterling, N.Y.C., 1967-93; dep. gen. Citigroup, N.Y.C., 1993—. Mem. ABA, Am. Law Inst., New York County Lawyers Assn., Assn. of Bar of City of N.Y., Conf. Bd., University Club. Banking, Finance. Office: Citigroup 153 E 53rd St New York NY 10043-0001

**ROSS, MICHAEL CHARLES,** lawyer. BA, U. Va., 1970, JD, 1977. Assoc. Latham & Watkins, 1977-85, ptnr., 1985-93; sr. v.p., gen. counsel, sec. Safeway Inc., Oakland, 1993—. Office: Safeway Inc 5918 Stoneridge Mall Rd Pleasanton CA 94588-3229*

**ROSS, MICHAEL FREDERICK,** magistrate, lawyer; b. Coral Gables, Fla., Sept. 20, 1950; s. George Thomas and Frances (Brown) Skaro. BA, Yale U., 1973; JD, U. Conn., 1979; MLS, So. Conn. State U., 1981. Bar: Conn. 1979, Fla. 1979, N.J. 1983, Mass. 1984, V.I. 1985, U.S. Dist. Ct. Conn. 1979, U.S. Dist. Ct. N.J. 1983, U.S. Dist. Ct. Vt. 1984, U.S. Dist. Ct. V.I. 1985, U.S. Ct. Claims 1980, U.S. Tax Ct. 1980, U.S. Ct. Customs and Patent Appeals 1980, U.S. Ct. Mil. Appeals 1980, U.S. Ct. Appeals (1st, 2d and D.C. cirs.) 1980, U.S. Ct. Appeals (5th, 9th and 11th cirs.) 1981, U.S. Ct. Appeals (Fed. cir.) 1982, U.S. Ct. Appeals (3d, 4th, 6th, 7th, 8th and 19th cirs.) 1983, Temp. Emergency Ct. Appeals 1985, Mashantucket Pequot Tribal Ct. 1995, U.S. Supreme Ct. 1982. Pvt. practice New Haven, Conn., 1979-82, Madison, Conn., 1985—; chief of adjudications Conn. Motor Vehicle Dept., Wethersfield, 1980-82; adminstrv. law judge State of Conn. Motor Vehicle Dept., Wethersfield, 1985—; asst. atty. gen. State of Conn., Hartford, 1982-84, Dept. of Law, St. Croix, V.I., 1984-85; magistrate Superior Ct. of Middlesex, New Haven and New London Counties, Conn., 1988—; mem. faculty Conn. Bar Assn. Acad. Profl. Devel. of Continuing Legal Edn., 1987, 91. Chmn. Madison Zoning Bd. Appeals, 1991-95. Mem. ABA, Am. Trial Lawyers Assn. (jud.), V.I. Bar Assn., Mensa, Conn. Def. Lawyers Assn., Conn. Magistrates Assn., Fence Club, Morys Assn. Club, Madison Men's Club. Democrat. Jewish. Home: PO Box 109 417 Fox Hollow Rd Woodstock CT 06281-1108 Office: 48 Mohawk Trl Guilford CT 06437-1107

**ROSS, OTHO BESCENT,** lawyer; b. Charlotte, N.C., July 23, 1951; s. Otho B. Jr. and Dorothy (Lowe) R. BS in Engring. magna cum laude with distinction, Duke U., 1974; JD, U. N.C., 1977. Bar: N.Y. 1978, U.S. Dist. Ct. (so. and ea. dists.) N.Y. 1978, U.S. Ct. Claims, 1987, U.S. Patent and Trademark Office, 1987. Sr. atty. Sony Corp. Am., Park Ridge, N.J., 1983-87; assoc. Stiefel, Gross and Kurland, N.Y.C., 1987-88; atty. IBM Corp., East Fishkill, N.Y., 1988-90; staff atty. IBM Corp., Purchase, N.Y., Stamford, Conn., Thornwood, N.Y., 1990-95; atty. AT&T Corp., Middletown, N.J., 1995-96; of counsel Reid & Priest LLP, N.Y., 1996-97; pvt. practice, 1997—. Rsch. editor N.C. Law Rev., 1976; spkr. Internet World Columbia, 1997, Internet World Mex. City, 1997; contbr. articles to Jour. Patent Office Soc., N.C. Law Rev., N.Y. Law Jour. Mem. ABA, Assn. of Bar of City of N.Y., Computer Law Assn., NYNMA, AIP Internet Soc. Contracts commercial, Computer, Patent. Office: 600 3rd Ave Fl 28 New York NY 10016-2001

**ROSS, RICHARD LEE,** lawyer; b. St. Louis, Feb. 26, 1928; s. Julius A. and Minnie B. (Blum) Razovsky; m. Marjorie N. Ross, Apr. 6, 1952; children: Maurice N., Julian E. AB, Washington U., St. Louis, 1948, JD, 1950. Bar: Mo. 1950, U.S. Dist. Ct. (8th cir.) 1950, U.S. Supreme Ct. 1970. V.p., sec. Banner Industries, Inc., St. Louis, 1950-62; ptnr. Slonim & Ross, St. Louis, 1962-77; pvt. practice St. Louis, 1978—; bd. dirs. NMR Inc. Contbr. articles to profl. jours. Recipient Outstanding Achievement in Labor Relations award, Automotive Workers of Am., St. Louis, 1967. Mem. ABA, Nat. Acad. Arbitrators (mem. various coms.), Mo. Bar Assn. (mem. various coms.), Met. Bar Assn. (mem. various coms.), Meadow Brook Country Club. (bd. dirs.), Shriners (unit pres.). Alternative dispute resolution, Labor, Securities. Home and Office: 451 Conway Meadows Dr Chesterfield MO 63017-9624

**ROSS, ROBERT A.,** lawyer; b. Bklyn., Nov. 27, 1958; s. Victor and Selma Ross; m. Bara Mayo, Sept. 1, 1990; children: Malina, Brielle, Hailey. Bachelor's degree, CCNY, 1980; JD, Hofstra Law Sch., 1983. Pvt. practice Kew Gardens, N.Y., 1983—; small claims arbitrator Queens Civil Ct., 1989—; village justice Oyster Bay Cove, N.Y., 1998—. Recipient Am. Jurist award Lawyers Coop. Pub., 1980. Mem. Queens Bar Assn. (family law com.). Family and matrimonial, Personal injury, General practice. Office: 12510 Queens Blvd Kew Gardens NY 11415-1519

**ROSS, ROGER SCOTT,** lawyer; b. Columbus, Ohio, Oct. 25, 1946; s. Donald William and Iris Louise (Smith) R.; m. Lynn Louise Patton, July 29, 1967; 1 child, Anastacia Lynn. Student, Ohio State U., 1964-66; BS in Laws, Western State U., Fullerton, Calif., 1983; JD, Western State U., 1985. Bar: Calif. 1985, U.S. Dist. Ct. (cen. dist.) Calif. 1985. Office mgr. Dial Fin. Co., Buena Park, Calif., 1970-78; asst. br. mgr., loan officer Calif. 1st Bank, Rolling Hills Estates, 1978-79; asst. v.p., loan officer Lloyds Bank, Monterey Park, Calif., 1979-85; pvt. practice law Tustin, Calif., 1985-86; ptnr. Anderson & Ross, El Toro, Calif., 1986-87; pvt. practice Orange, Calif., 1987-90, Bellflower, Calif., 1990-94, Anaheim, Calif., 1994—; atty., coach Constnl. Rights Found. of Orange County, 1987—. Mem. AAONMS, ABA, Calif. Bar Assn., L.A. County Bar Assn., Assn. Trial Lawyers Am., Orange County Trial Lawyers Assn., Calif. F&AM, Nat. Forensic Club, Rotary. Republican. Avocations: golf, sailing, tennis. Estate planning, Probate, Real property. Office: 421 N Brookhurst St Ste 126 Anaheim CA 92801-5618

**ROSS, WAYNE ANTHONY,** lawyer; b. Milw., Feb. 25, 1943; s. Ray E. and Lillian (Steiner) R.; m. Barbara L. Ross, June 22, 1968; children: Gregory, Brian, Timothy, Amy. BA, Marquette U., 1965, JD, 1968. Bar: Wis. 1968, Alaska 1969. Asst. atty. gen. State Alaska, 1968-69; trustee, standing master Superior Ct. Alaska, 1969-73; assoc. Edward J. Reasor & Assocs., Anchorage, 1973-77; prin. Wayne Anthony Ross & Assocs., 1977-83; ptnr. Ross, Gingras & Frenz, Anchorage and Cordova, Alaska, 1983-84, Ross & Gingras, Anchorage and Cordova, 1985; pres. Ross, Gingras and Miner, P.C., Anchorage, 1986-93; pres. Ross and Miner P.C., Anchorage, 1993—; former col. Alaska State Def. Force; pres. Tyone Mountain Syndicate, Inc. Alaska Rep. Nat. Committeeman, 1992-98; Republican candidate for Gov. of Alaska, 1998. Decorated knight comdr. Order of Polonia Restituta (Poland), knight Equestrian Order of the Holy Sepulchure of Jerusalem (Vatican). Mem. NRA (bd. dirs. 1980-92, 94—, benefactor), Alaska Bar Assn. (Stanley award), Anchorage Bar Assn., Alaska Gun Collectors Assn. (pres. emeritus), Ohio Gun Collectors Assn. (hon. life), Smith and Wesson Collectors Assn., 49th Territorial Guard Regiment (pres. 1987-94, 95-96), Alaska Territorial Cavalry (sec.1991-97), Mil. Vehicle Preservation Assn. (v.p. 1994-96), Alaska Peace Officers Assn. Roman Catholic. Family and matrimonial, Criminal, Personal injury. Home: PO Box 101522 Anchorage AK 99510-1522 Office: Ross & Miner 327 E Fireweed Ln Ste 201 Anchorage AK 99503-2110

**ROSS, WILLIAM JARBOE,** lawyer; b. Oklahoma City, May 9, 1930; s. Walter John and Bertha (Jarboe) R.; m. Mary Lillian Ryan, May 19, 1962; children: Rebecca Anne Roten, Robert Joseph, Molly Kathleen. BBA, U. Okla., 1952, LLB, 1954. Bar: Okla. 1954. Since practiced in Oklahoma City; asst. municipal counselor Oklahoma City, 1955-60; mem. firm Rainey, Ross, Rice & Binns, 1960—, ptnr., 1965-99; mem. admissions and grievences com. U.S. Dist. Ct. (we. dist.) Okla. Bd. visitors Coll. of Law U. Okla.; past pres. St. Anthony's Hosp. Found., Harn Homestead, Bizell Libr. Soc., U. Okla.; trustee Ethics and Excellence in Journalism Found., Inasmuch Found. Mem. Okla. Bar Assn., Okla. Heritage Assn. (vice chmn. edn. com.), The Newcomen Soc., Okla. City Golf and Country Club, Econ. Club, Rotary, Phi Alpha Delta, Beta Theta Pi, KC. General practice, Estate planning, Probate. Home: 6923 Avondale Ct Oklahoma City OK 73116-5008

**ROSS, WILLIAM ROBERT,** lawyer; b. Sundance, Wyo., Aug. 10, 1929; s. James Thomas and Kathryn Melvina (Ormsby) R.; m. Dorothy Evelyn Spencer, Mar. 19, 1951 (dec. July 1980); children: James Bradley, Keith Spencer, Rebecca Ann Ross Duncan; m. Kathleen Riggin Worthington, July 30, 1983. BS in Law, U. Nebr., 1958; LLB, U. Md., 1958. Bar: Wyo. 1958, Colo. 1967. Atty., spl. asst. to solicitor U.S. Dept. of Interior, Washington, 1958-61; atty. Am. Sugar Co., N.Y.C., 1961-64; internat. counsel Gates Rubber Co., Denver, 1964-69; pres. Wexco Internat. Corp., Denver, 1969-70; atty., shareholder Lohf & Barnhill, PC, Denver, 1970-87; pres., shareholder Lohf, Shaiman & Ross, PC, Denver, 1987-93; pvt. practice Littleton, Colo., 1993—; instr. Law Sch., U. Denver, 1967-73, instr. Bus. Sch., 1970-72. Contbr. articles to profl. law jours. With USAF, 1950-54. Mem. Wyo. State Bar, Colo. Bar Assn., Denver Bar Assn. General corporate, Private international, Legislative. Office: 9425 S Desert Willow Way Littleton CO 80126-5744

**ROSSEEL-JONES, MARY LOUISE,** lawyer; b. Detroit, Apr. 19, 1951; d. Rene Octave and Marie Ann (Metcko) Rosseel; m. Mark Christopher Jones, Mar. 16, 1985; 1 child, Kathleen Marie. BA in French with honors, U. Mich., 1973, MA in French, 1976; JD, U. Detroit, 1981. Bar: Mich. 1982, U.S. Ct. Appeals (6th cir.) 1982, U.S. Dist Ct. (ea. dist.) Mich. 1982, U.S. Dist. Ct. (we. dist.) Mich. 1983. Teaching asst. French U. Mich., Ann Arbor, 1974-76; law clk. Johnson, Auld & Valentine, Detroit, 1979-80; assoc. Monaghan, Campbell et al, Bloomfield Hills, Mich., 1981-82; lectr. law U. Clermont, Clermont-Ferrand, France, 1981-82; staff atty. Mich. Nat. Corp., Bloomfield Hills, 1983-85, Am. Motors Corp., Southfield, Mich., 1985-87;

staff counsel Chrysler Corp., Auburn Hills, Mich., 1987-98; freelance editor, writer, pvt. practice, 1998—. Editor: sequel One Life to Give. Republican. Roman Catholic. Avocations: classical pianist, interior design. Personal injury, General corporate, Insurance.

**ROSSEN, JORDAN**, lawyer; b. Detroit, June 13, 1934; s. Nathan Paul and Rebecca (Rizy) R.; m. Susan Friebert, Mar. 24, 1963 (div. June 1972); 1 child, Rebecca; m. M. Elizabeth Bunn, Jan. 3, 1981; children—N. Paul, Jordan David. B.A., U. Mich., 1956; J.D., Harvard U., 1959. Bar: Mich. 1960, U.S. Dist. Ct. (ea. dist.) Mich. 1960, U.S. Ct. Appeals (6th cir.) 1966, U.S. Ct. Appeals (7th cir.) 1974, U.S. Supreme Ct. 1966, N.Y. 1998. Assoc. Sullivan, Elmer, Eames & Moody, Detroit, 1960-62; assoc. Sugar & Schwartz, Detroit, 1962-64; asst. gen. counsel UAW, Detroit, 1964-74, assoc. gen. counsel, 1974-83, gen. counsel, 1983-98; of counsel Meyer, Suozzi, English and Klein, Mineola, N.Y., 1998—; vice pres. N.P. Rossen Agy., Inc., Detroit, 1960-83; gen. counsel Mich. Health & Social Security Research Inst., Inc., Detroit, 1965-83; dir. UAW Job Devel. & Tng. Corp., Detroit, 1984-90. Editor: Mich. Bar Labor Section Publication, 1961-64. Contbr. articles to profl. jours. Pres. Young Democrats, Mich., 1963-65; chmn. Americans for Democratic Action, Mich., 1966-68; chmn. Voter Registration Dem. Party, Mich., 1967. Recipient Human Rights award City of Detroit, 1978. Mem. ABA, Mich. Bar Assn., Nat. Bar Assn., Fed. Bar Assn., Wolverine Bar Assn., Women Lawyers Assn., Lawyers Guild. Jewish. Fax: 516-741-3259. Labor, Administrative and regulatory, Civil rights. Office: 1505 Kellum Pl Mineola NY 11501-4811

**ROSSI, EUGENE JOSEPH**, prosecutor, law educator; b. Middletown, Conn., July 24, 1956; s. Joseph Theodore and Alma Maria (Gerolami) R.; m. Diane Deaton, May 18, 1985; children: Leigh Taylor, William Deaton. BS cum laude, Fairfield (Conn.) U., 1978; JD, Am. U., 1982; LLM, Georgetown U., 1994. Bar: DC 1982, Conn. 1988.. Washington rep. Gov. Bill O'Neill, 1983-89; sr. trial atty. criminal sect. tax divsn. U.S. Justice Dept., Washington, 1989—; spl. asst. U.S. atty. Office of U.S. Atty., Alexandria, Va., 1997—. Roman Catholic. Avocations: basketball, running, writing. Home: 16 W Rosemont Ave Alexandria VA 22301-2624

**ROSSI, WILLIAM MATTHEW**, lawyer; b. Coldwater, Ohio, June 11, 1954; s. Hugh Dominic and Patricia Jean (Putts) R.; m. Constance Sue Streacker, July 21, 1973; children: Bryan Thomas, Lauren Michelle, Alexandria Marie. BA cum laude, Miami U., Oxford, Ohio, 1977; JD magna cum laude, U. Dayton, 1981. Bar: Ohio 1981, U.S. Dist. Ct. (so. dist.) Ohio 1982, U.S. Supreme Ct. 1986, U.S. Ct. Appeals (6th cir.) 1987, Fla. 1991, U.S. Dist. Ct. (so. and mid. dists.) Fla. 1992, U.S. Ct. Appeals (11th cir.) 1992. Assoc. Milliken & Fitton, Hamilton, Ohio, 1981-83; dep. law dir., chief city negotiator City of Middletown, Ohio, 1984-89; pvt. practice, 1989-92; assoc. Jackson, Lewis, Schnitzler and Krupman, Orlando, Fla., 1992-93; asst. county atty. Sarasota County, Fla., 1993—; bd. dirs. Columbia Inst. Bus., Middletown, 1977-78; lectr. Sawyer Coll., Dayton, 1982-83; small claims referee, 1984-92. Asst. coach Knothole Baseball, Middletown, 1981; bd. dirs. Butler County Mental Health Ctr., Hamilton, 1983-85, Summer Youth Theatre, Middletown, 1985-86; mem. bd. rev. Troop 20 Boy Scouts Am., 1986-87; mem. adv. bd. St. Joseph's Coll. Recipient Am. Jurisprudence award Lawyers Coop. Pub. Co., 1979, 81, Internat. Youth Achievement award Internat. Biog. Ctr. and Am. Biog. Inst., 1982. Mem. ABA, Fla. Bar Assn., Nat. Pub. Employer Labor Rels. Assn., Phi Beta Kappa, Phi Delta Phi (bd. dirs., historian 1979-80). Republican. Roman Catholic. Avocations: golf, travel, writing. Labor, State civil litigation. Home: 6215 Aventura Dr Sarasota FL 34241-9448

**ROSSO, CHRISTINE HEHMEYER**, lawyer; b. N.Y.C., Apr. 7, 1947; d. Alexander and Florence I. (Millar) Hehmeyer; m. David John Rosso, Mar. 18, 1978; children—Christine, Mark. BA, Pitzer Coll., 1969; JD, Northwestern U., 1972. Bar: Ill. 1972. Assoc., Isham, Lincoln & Beale, Chgo., 1972-78; participating ptnr. Chapman and Cutler, Chgo., 1978-83; chief charitable trusts and solicitations div. Office of Ill. Atty. Gen., Chgo., 1983-87; chief Consumer Protection Div., 1986; chief Antitrust Bur., 1989—. Pres. bd. dirs. Chgo. Hearing Soc., 1991-93, sec. 1994—; mem. women's bd. Goodman Theatre, Chgo., Alliance Francais, Chgo. Mem. ABA, Ill. State Bar Assn. (chmn. antitrust sect. coun. 1995-96), Chgo. Bar Assn. (vice chmn. pub. utility law com. 1979, chmn. 1980), Nat. Assn. State Charity Ofcls. (pres. 1987-88), Econ. Club of Chgo. Episcopalian. Home: 520 W Fullerton Pky Chicago IL 60614-5919 Office: Atty Gen Ill 100 W Randolph St Ste 12-204 Chicago IL 60601-3271

**ROSS-RAY, FRANCES ANN**, lawyer; b. Painesville, Ohio, June 17, 1959; d. Francis Kelly and Patsy Paige (Banks) Ross; m. Robert Joseph Ray, Aug. 13, 1983; children: Nicholas Ross, Robert Gordon, Francis Andrew. BS in Polit. Sci., U. Houston, 1986, JD, 1989. Bar: Pa. 1989, U.S. Dist. Ct. Pa. 1989. Atty. Buchanan Ingersoll, Pitts., 1989-92, Babst Calland Clements & Zomnir, Pitts., 1992—. Mem. ABA, Pa. Bar Assn. Alleghany County Bar Assn., Order of Coif. Environmental, Administrative and regulatory. Home: 9570 Saratoga Dr Pittsburgh PA 15237-6138 Office: Babst Calland Clements & Zomnir 2 Gateway Ctr Pittsburgh PA 15222-1425

**ROSTEK, NANCY ELIZABETH**, lawyer; b. Plainfield, N.J., June 13, 1970; d. Charles B. and JoAnne M. Longo; m. Thomas G. Rostek, Aug. 13, 1994. BS, Pa. State U., 1992; JD, Villanova U., 1995. Bar: Pa. 1995, N.J. 1996. Law clk. Hon. Rosemary Higgins Cass, Superior Ct. N.J., Newark, 1995-96, Hon. Dickinson R. Debevoise, U.S. Dist. Ct. for N.J., Newark, 1996-97; assoc. Klett Lieber Rooney & Schorling, Pitts., 1997—. Recipient Disting. Svc. award Villanova Law Rev., 1995. Mem. ABA, Pa. Bar Assn., Order of the Coif, Phi Kappa Phi, Potomac Appalachian Trail Club, Eberly Coll. Sci. Federal civil litigation, General civil litigation, State civil litigation. Office: Klett Lieber Rooney & Schorling One Oxford Ctr 40th Fl Pittsburgh PA 15219

**ROSZKOWSKI, STANLEY JULIAN**, retired federal judge; b. Boonville, N.Y., Jan. 27, 1923; s. Joseph and Anna (Christkowski) R.; m. Catherine Mary Claeys, June 19, 1948; children: Mark, Gregory, Dan, John. BS, U. Ill., 1949, JD, 1954. Bar: Ill. 1954. Sales mgr. Warren Petroleum Co., Rockford, Ill., 1954; ptnr. Roszkowski, Paddock, McGreevy & Johnson, Rockford, 1955-77; judge U.S. Dist. Ct. (we. dist.), Rockford, Ill., 1977-98; pres. First State Bank, Rockford, 1963-75; chmn. bd. First State Bank, 1977—; mediator-arbitrator JAMS/ENDISPUTE, Chgo., 1998—. Chmn. Fire and Police Commn., Rockford, 1967-74, commr., 1974—; chmn. Paul Simon Com., 1972; active Adlai Stevenson III campaign, 1968-71, Winnebago County Citizens for John F. Kennedy, 1962, Winnebago County Dem. Cen. Com., 1962-64; bd. dirs. Sch. of Hope, 1960—; mem. Ill. Capital Devel. Bd., 1974—. With USAAF, 1943-45. Decorated Air medal with 2 oak leaf clusters.; recipient Pulaski Nat. Heritage award Polish Am. Congress, Chgo., 1982. Mem. ABA, Ill. Bar Assn., Fla. Bar Assn., Winnebago County Bar Assn., Am. Coll. Trial Lawyers, Am. Judicature Soc., Assn. Trial Lawyers Am., Ill. Trial Lawyers Assns., Am. Arbitration Assn. (arbitrator), Fed. Judges Assn. (bd. dirs. 1988—).

**ROTCH, JAMES E.**, lawyer; b. Auburn, Ala., Mar. 26, 1945; s. Elroy B. and Martha (Ellisor) R.; m. Darlene Edwards; children: Jamison B., Susannah R., Amie L. Vaughn. BS, Auburn U., 1967, postgrad., 1967-68; JD, U. Va., 1971. Bar: Ala. 1971, U.S. Dist. Ct. (no. dist.) Ala. 1973. Rsch. asst. Office Instl. Rsch. Auburn (Ala.) U., 1967-68; clk. U.S. Judiciary System, Birmingham, Ala., 1971-72; assoc. Bradley Arant Rose & White LLP, Birmingham, 1971-76; ptnr. Bradley, Arant, Rose & White LLP, Birmingham, 1976—, administrv. ptnr., 1990-93; mem. adv. com. Bioelastics Rsch. Ltd., Birmingham, 1992—, Gov.'s Task Force on Biotechnology, Ala., 1993. Pres. adv. com. Birmingham Mus. Art, 1989-92; bd. dirs. Operation New Birmingham, 1990-91, 95—, co-chmn. cmty. affairs com., mem. exec. com.; Coalition for Better Edn., Birmingham, 1990—; active Boy Scouts Am.; bd. dirs. Birmingham Com. for Olympic Soccer, 1994-96, Ala. Sports Found., 1994-98, Entrepreneurial Ctr. Inc., 1996—; mem. adminstrv. bd. Canterbury United Meth. Ch., 1991-93. Capt. USAR, 1972-78. Mem. ALA, Auburn U. Bar Assn., Birmingham Bar Assn., Internat. Bar Assn., Ala. State Bar Assn., Leadership Birmingham, Leadership Ala., Auburn Coll. Liberal Arts (adv. coun.), U. Va. Alumni Assn., Newcomen Soc., Birmingham Area C. of C. (trustee 1992), Auburn U. Alumni Assn., Birmingham Venture Club (bd. dirs. 1990-94, v.p. 1991, pres. 1992-93), Country Club of Birmingham, Jockey Club, Summit Club (charter), Kiwanis (sec.). Methodist. Avocations: horses, bird hunting, cattle farming, golf. General corporate, Mergers and acquisitions, Securities. Office: Bradley Arant Rose & White LLP 2001 Park Pl Ste 1400 Birmingham AL 35203-2736

**ROTH, ALAN J.**, lawyer; b. Bklyn., Feb. 18, 1955; s. Benjamin and Naomi (Wisler) R. BA, Am. U., 1976; JD, N.Y.U., 1979. Bar: Conn. 1979, U.S. Dist. Ct. Conn. 1979, D.C. 1980, U.S. Ct. Appeals (D.C. cir.) 1980, U.S. Ct. Appeals (2d cir.) 1982, U.S. Supreme Ct. 1983. Law clk. to Hon. M. Joseph Blumenfeld U.S. Dist. Ct., Hartford, Conn., 1979-80; assoc. Tyler, Cooper & Alcorn, New Haven, Conn., 1980-84; counsel com. energy and commerce U.S. Ho. of Reps., Washington, 1985-92, chief counsel com. energy and commerce, 1992, staff dir., chief counsel, 1993-95, minority staff dir., chief coun. com. on commerce, 1995-97; ptnr. Bryan Cave LLP, 1997-98; pvt. practice Washington, 1998—; adj. professorial lectr. sch. pub. affairs Am. U., Washington, 1989-92. Democrat. Jewish. Office: 500 13th St NW Ste 700 Washington DC 20004-1103

**ROTH, BARBARA M.**, lawyer; b. Chgo., Aug. 19, 1951; d. Philip E. and Frieda (Favash-Oster) R.; m. Michael H. Canick, Apr. 9, 1989. BA, U. Ill., 1973; JD, DePaul U., 1978; LLM, NYU, 1997. Bar: Ill. 1978, N.Y. 1980, U.S. Dist. Ct. (no., so. and ea. dists.) N.Y., U.S. Dist. Ct. (ea. dist.) Wis. Assoc. Epstein, Becker & Green, N.Y.C., 1979-81; assoc. Townley & Updike, N.Y.C., 1981-87, ptnr., 1987-95; ptnr. Haythe & Curley, N.Y.C., 1995—, head labor and employment practice group, 1997—. Contbr. chpt. to book and articles to profl. jours. Mem. N.Y. State Bar Assn. (chair com. on individual rights, responsibilities 1986-89), Assn. Bar City of N.Y. (products liabliity com. 1988-91). Labor, General civil litigation, Product liability. Office: Haythe & Curley 237 Park Ave New York NY 10017-3140

**ROTH, EUGENE**, lawyer; b. Wilkes-Barre, Pa., June 28, 1935; s. Max and Rae (Klein) R.; m. Constance D. Smulyan, June 16, 1957; children: Joan Roth Kleinman, Steven P., Jeffrey H., Lawrence W. BS, Wilkes U., 1957; LLB, Pa. State U., 1960. Bar: Pa. 1960, U.S. Dist. Ct. (mid. dist.) Pa. 1961. Assoc. Rosenn, Jenkins & Greenwald, Walkes-Barre, 1960-64, ptnr., 1964—; mem. Northeastern Pa. Regional bd. 1st Union Bank; bd. dirs. RCN Corp., Commonwealth Telephone Enterprises, Inc.; chmn. Greater Wilkes-Barre Partnership, Inc., 1991-93. Trustee Wilkes U., 1979—, chmn. 1993-98; chmn. United Way of Wyoming Valley, 1983; chmn. annual campaign Osterhout Free Libr. Campaign, 1999; Northeastern Pa. regional bd. dirs. Pa. State Geiseinger-Wyoming Valley Hosp. Recipient Disting. Pennsylvanian award Phila. C. of C., 1980, Disting. Citizen award N.E. Pa. Boy Scouts Am., 1998; named Outstanding Vol. Fund Raiser Nat. Soc. Fund Raising Exec., 1993; Cmty. Svc. award B'nai B'rith, 1994. Mem. ABA, Pa. Bar Assn., Luzerne County Law and Libr. Assn., Wilkes-Barre C. of C. (chmn. 1980, vice com. for econ. growth), Wyo. Valley United Jewish Campaign (chmn. 1978 and 1993), B'nai B'rith. Republican. Jewish. Avocations: reading, community svc. Contracts commercial, General corporate, Mergers and acquisitions. Office: Rosenn Jenkins & Greenwald 15 S Franklin St Wilkes Barre PA 18711-0076

**ROTH, HADDEN WING**, lawyer; b. Oakland, Calif., Feb. 10, 1930; s. Mark and Jane (Haley) R.; m. Alice Becker, Aug., 1987; 1 child, Elizabeth Wing. AA, Coll. Marin, 1949; BA, U. Calif., Berkeley, 1951; JD, U. Calif., San Francisco, 1957. Bar: Calif. 1958, U.S. Dist. Ct. (no. dist.) Calif. 1958, U.S. Ct. Appeals (9th cir.) 1958, U.S. Supreme Ct. 1966. Pvt. practice San Rafael, 1970—; judge Marin County Mcpl. Ct., 1966-70; spl. cons. Marin Muni Water Dist., Corte Madera, Calif., County of Marin; atty. Bolinas Pub. Utility Dist., Ross Valley Fire Svc., Tiburon Fire Protection Dist., Town of Ross and San Anselmo, Calif.; hearing officer dist. hosps., 1981—; lectr. law Golden Gate Coll. Law, San Francisco, 1971-73. Chmn. Marin County prison task force, 1973; bd. dirs. Marin Gen. Hosp., 1964-66. Named Outstanding Citizen of Yr., Coll. Marin, 1972. Mem. ABA, Am. Trial Lawyers Assn., Calif. Bar Assn., Marin County Bar Assn., San Francisco Trial Lawyers Assn., Am. Assn. Ind. Investors, Assn. Bus. Trial Lawyers. Avocations: running, weights, reading. Alternative dispute resolution, Appellate, General civil litigation. Office: Hadden Roth Law Offices 1050 Northgate Dr San Rafael CA 94903-2526

**ROTH, JAMES ANTHONY**, lawyer; b. Kansas City, Dec. 24, 1968; s. Michael Gordon R. and Marie Kathleen (Anthony) Purkey. BA in Polit. Sci., Kans. State U., 1991; JD, Oklahoma City U., 1994. Bar: Kans. 1994, U.S. Dist. Ct. Kans. 1994, Okla. 1995, U.S. Dist. Ct. (we. dist.) Okla. 1995. Law clk. Hon. Joe Mark Elkouri, Oklahoma City, 1994-95; dep. commr., staff atty. Oklahoma County Dist. One, Oklahoma City, 1995-99; spl. counsel Oklahoma County, 1999—. Chmn. AIDS Legal Resource Project, Oklahoma City, 1995—. Mem. Nat. Assn. Civil County Attys. (sec. 1996-98, pres. 1998-99, bd. dirs. 1999), Okla. Bar Assn. (bd. dirs. 1995—), Kans. Bar Assn., ABA. Independent. Avocations: nature, gardening, politics, reading. Email: jimroth@oklahomacounty.org. Home: 2221 NW 54th St Oklahoma City OK 73112-7714 Office: Oklahoma County 320 Robert S Kerr Ave Ste 105 Oklahoma City OK 73102-3441

**ROTH, JANE RICHARDS**, federal judge; b. Philadelphia, Pa., June 16, 1935; d. Robert Henry Jr. and Harriett (Kellond) Richards; m. William V. Roth Jr., Oct. 9, 1965; children: William V. III, Katharine K. BA, Smith Coll., 1956; LLB, Harvard U., 1965; LLD (hon.), Widener U., 1986, U. Del., 1994. Bar: Del. 1965, U.S. Dist. Ct. Del. 1966, U.S. Ct. Appeals (3d cir.) 1974. Adminstrv. asst. various fgn. service posts U.S. State Dept., 1956-62; assoc. Richards, Layton & Finger, Wilmington, Del., 1965-73, ptnr., 1973-85; judge U.S. Dist. Ct. Del., Wilmington, 1985-91, U.S. Ct. Appeals (3d cir.), Wilmington, 1991—; adj. faculty Villanova U. Sch. Law. Hon. chmn. Del. chpt. Arthritis Found., Wilmington; bd. overseers Widener U. Sch. Law; bd. consultors Villanova U. Sch. Law; trustee Hist. Soc. Del. Recipient Nat. Vol. Service citation Athritis Found., 1982. Fellow Am. Bar Found.; mem. ABA, Fed. Judges Assn., Del. State Bar Assn. Republican. Episcopalian. Office: J Caleb Boggs Fed Bldg 844 King St Rm 5100 Wilmington DE 19801-3519*

**ROTH, MICHAEL JOHN**, lawyer; b. Alma, Mich., Apr. 20, 1969; s. William John and Marion Elizabeth Roth; m. Betty Jane Darling, July 27, 1991; children: Michael John, Emily Elizabeth. BA in History, U. Mich., 1991; JD, Valparaiso U., 1994. Bar: Mich. 1994, U.S. Dist. Ct. (we. dist.) 1994. Atty. Buchanan & Bos, Grand Rapids, Mich., 1994-95; aaty. Buchanan, Silver & Beckering, Grand Rapids, 1995-96, Law, Weathers & Richardson, P.C., Grand Rapids, 1996—. Assoc. editor Valparaiso U. Law Rev., 1993, exec. editor, 1994. Mem. coun. Mayflower Congl. Ch., Grand Rapids, 1997—; mem. Cmty. Action Coun., East Grand Rapids, Mich., 1998. Dean's scholar Valparaiso U., 1993. Mem. Blythefield Country Club, GRBA Young Lawyers Soc., U. of M. Club (adv. bd. 1998—), Inns. of Ct. Avocations: golf, football, basketball. General civil litigation, Criminal, Insurance. Office: Law Weathers & Richardson 333 Bridge St NW Ste 800 Grand Rapids MI 49504-5360

**ROTH, PAMELA SUSAN**, lawyer; b. N.Y.C., Nov. 23, 1961; d. Edward Abraham and Susan Violet (Castro) R. BS in Biology, Adelphi U., 1982, MBA, 1986; JD, Pace U., 1990. Bar: N.Y. 1991, U.S. Dist. Ct. (ea. and so. dists.) N.Y. 1991, U.S. Ct. Appeals (10th cir.) 1993, Colo. 1995, U.S. Dist. Ct. Colo. 1995, U.S. Supreme Ct. 1995. Asst. gen. counsel N.Y.C. Dept. Probation, Bklyn., 1990-91; asst. dist. atty. Kings County Dist. Atty., Bklyn., 1992-93; assoc. Law Firm of Portales & Assocs., Denver, 1993-95; pvt. practice N.Y.C., 1995—; gen. counsel Hispano Crypto-Jewish Rsch. Ctr., Denver, 1994—. Mem. ABA, Am. Soc. Internat. Law, Hispanic Nat. Bar Assn., Bklyn. Bar Assn., Internat. Assn. Jewish Lawyers and Jurists, Kings County Criminal Bar Assn. Avocations: aerobics, skiing, roller blading, gourmet cooking. Personal injury, State civil litigation, Criminal. Office: 26 Court St Ste 2003 Brooklyn NY 11242-1120 Address: 2361 E 71st St Brooklyn NY 11234-6511

**ROTH, PAUL NORMAN**, lawyer; b. N.Y.C., May 4, 1939; s. Sol and Florence (Glassman) R.; m. Ellen Joan Lipp, May 24, 1964; children: Stefanie H., Jessica A. AB, Harvard U., 1961, LLB, 1964. Bar: N.Y. 1966, U.S. Ct. Appeals (2d cir.) 1966, U.S. Dist. Ct. (so. and ea. dists.) N.Y. 1967, U.S. Supreme Ct. 1975. Assoc. Cleary, Gottlieb, Steen & Hamilton, N.Y.C., 1965-69; ptnr. Schulte Roth & Zabel, N.Y.C., 1969-. Trustee Ctrl. Synagogue, N.Y.C., 1987-95; bd. dirs. Citizens Com. for N.Y.C., 1999—. Fulbright fellow, Netherlands, 1965. Mem. ABA (com. on pvt. investment entities, vice chmn.), Nat. Assn. Securities Dealers (legal adv. bd. 1999—), Lawyers Alliance for N.Y. (bd. dirs. 1999—), N.Y. State Bar Assn., Assn. of Bar of City of N.Y. (com. on securities regulation 1982-85, chmn. 1989-92), Harvard Law Sch. Assn. N.Y. (trustee 1987-90, v.p. 1992-93), Century Country Club. Securities, General corporate, Mergers and acquisitions. Office: Schulte Roth & Zabel 900 3rd Ave Fl 19 New York NY 10022-4774

**ROTH, PHILLIP JOSEPH**, retired judge; b. Portland, Oreg., Feb. 29, 1920; s. Harry William and Minnie Alice (Segel) R.; m. Ida Lorraine Thomas, Feb. 22, 1957 (div. 1977); children: Phillip Joseph, David William; m. Allison Blake Ramsey, Feb. 14, 1978 (div. 1994). BA cum laude, U. Portland, 1943; JD, Lewis and Clark Coll., 1948. Bar: Oreg. 1948, U.S. Dist. Ct. Oreg. 1949, U.S. Ct. Appeals (9th cir.) 1959, U.S. Supreme Ct. 1962. Dep. atty. City of Portland, 1948-50; dep. dist. atty. Multnomah County, Portland, 1950-52; sole practice Portland, 1952-64; cir. judge Multnomah County State of Oreg., Portland, 1964-94, presiding cir. judge, 1970-71, 76-78; adj. prof. Lewis & Clark U. Law Sch., Portland, 1978-80, mem. standing com., 1972-90; mem. exec. com. Nat. Conf. State Trial Judges, 1980-91. Author: Sentencing: A View From the Bench, 1973; co-author: The Judicial Immunity Doctrine Today: Between the Bench and a Hard Place, 1984, The Brief Jour.; The Dangerous Erosion of Judicial Immunity, 1989. Mem. Oreg. Legislature, 1952-54; Rep. nominee for Congress, 1956; chmn. Oreg. Rep. Ctrl. Com., 1962-64; mem. adv. bd. Portland Salvation Army, 1976—; mem. bd. overseers Lewis and Clark Coll., 1972-90. Named Alumnus of Yr. U. Portland, 1963; named Alumnus of Yr. Lewis & Clark Law Sch., 1973. Fellow Am. Bar Found.; mem. ABA (chmn. jud. immunity com. jud. adminstrn. divsn. 1982-90, mem. commn. on standards jud. adminstrn. divsn. 1973-77, chmn. conf. state trial judges 1990-91, HBH Comm. on State Justice Initiatives 1994-98, chmn. jud. adminstrn. divsn. 1994-95), Oreg. Bar Assn. (bd. govs. 1961-64), Multnomah County Bar Assn. (pres. 1959), Am. Judicature Soc., Oreg. Cir. Judges Assn. (pres. 1988-89), U. Portland Alumni Assn. (pres. 1967), Lewis and Clark Coll. Alumni Assn. (pres. 1974-76, 80-81), Multnomah Law Libr. Assn. (bd. dirs.), City Club, Univ. Club, Masons, Shriners, Rotary, B'nai B'rith, Delta Theta Phi. Jewish. Home: 2495 SW 73rd Ave Portland OR 97225-3274

**ROTH, RANDALL W.**, lawyer; b. Ellinwood, Kans., May 14, 1948. BS summa cum laude, Regis Coll., 1970; LLM, U. Miami, 1975. Bar: Colo. 1975, Kans. 1980, Hawaii 1983. Of counsel Goodsill Anderson Quinn & Stifel, Honolulu; prof. law U. Hawaii, 1982—. Mem. ABA, Am. Coll. Trust and Estate Counsel, Hawaii State Bar Assn. (pres. 1999), Alpha Sigma Nu. E-mail: rroth@hawaii.edu. Taxation, general, Probate. Office: Goodsill Anderson Quinn & Stifel 1099 Alakea St Honolulu HI 96813-4511

**ROTHBAUM, SANDRA LAZARUS**, lawyer; b. Indpls., Aug. 29, 1944; d. Kiefer and Sara (Lisker) L.; m. Donald Alan Rothbaum, June 18, 1967; children: Daniel, Anne, Michael, Lia, Mark, Jonathan, Aaron, Jessica. BA cum laude, Harvard U., 1966; MA, U. Wis., 1967; JD summa cum laude, Ind. U., 1984. Bar: Ind. 1984, U.S. Dist. Ct. (no. and so. dists.) Ind. 1984. Assoc. Rubin & Levin, Indpls., 1984-87, Garelick, Cohen & Fishman, Indpls., 1987-88; pvt. practice Carmel, Ind., 1988-90; ptnr. Atlas & Rothbaum, Indpls., 1990-94, Cohen Garelick & Glazier, Indpls., 1994—. Co-pres., sec. Nat. Coun. Jewish Women, 1988-89; co-chmn. women's div. Jewish Fedn. Greater Indpls., 1989—. Recipient Am. Jurisprudence award, 1980, 81, 84, Wall St. Jour. award, 1984. Mem. ABA, Ind. Bar Assn., Indpls. Bar Assn., Harvard Club Ind. (v.p. 1989-91). General practice, Estate planning, Probate. Office: Cohen Garelick & Glazier 8888 Keystone Xing Ste 800 Indianapolis IN 46240-4616

**ROTHBERG, GLENDA FAY MORRIS**, lawyer; b. Rome, Ga., Aug. 7, 1946; d. Glenn Howell and Fay (Givens) Morris; m. Gerald Rothberg, June 18, 1970 (div. Jan. 1989); children: Laura, Abigail. AB, Randolph-Macon Woman's Coll., 1968; JD, Benjamin Cardozo Law Sch., 1985. Bar: N.Y. 1986, U.S. Dist. Ct. (so. and ea. dists.) N.Y. 1987, U.S. Supreme Ct. 1990. Law guardian juvenile rights divsn. Legal Aid Soc., N.Y.C., 1988-91; pvt. practice N.Y.C., 1992—; faculty dir. Inst. for not-for-profit Mgmt. Columbia Bus. Sch., N.Y.C., 1994-98. Vol. Manhattan Mediation Ctr., N.Y.C., 1996—. Fellow Am. Bar Found.; mem. ABA, Assn. of Bar of City of N.Y. (com. chair 1996—). Family and matrimonial, Juvenile. Office: 300 Park Ave New York NY 10022-7402

**ROTHENBERG, ADAM LEIGH**, lawyer; b. Chgo., Sept. 9, 1963; s. Philip Burton and Roberta Lynn (Keylin) R.; m. Christie Curry, Sept. 23, 1989; children: Alexa Leigh, Zachary Ryan. Student, Tulane U., 1981-83; BABA, U. Wash., 1987; JD cum laude, Seton Hall U., 1993. Bar: N.J. 1993, U.S. Dist. Ct. N.J. 1993. Law clk. Blume Vazquez Goldfaden Berkowitz & Donnelly, Newark, 1992-93; assoc. Levinson, Axelrod, Wheaton, Grayzel, Caulfield, et al, Edison, N.J., 1993—. Mem. ATLA, N.J. ATLA (bd. govs. 1996—), Middlesex County Bar Assn., Middlesex County Trial Lawyers, Essex County Bar Assn., N.J. State Bar Assn. Spkrs. Bur. (spkr. 1997—). Avocations: tennis, golf, sailing. General civil litigation, Product liability, Personal injury. Home: 2389 Channing Ave Westfield NJ 07090-4507 Office: Levinson Axelrod Wheaton Grayzel Caulfield Marcoulus & Dunn 2 Lincoln Ave Edison NJ 08837-3217

**ROTHENBERG, DAVID S.**, lawyer, financial consultant; b. Plattsburgh, N.Y., July 7, 1969; s. Robert H. and kathleen Rothenberg. BA magna cum laude, SUNY, Stony Brook, 1991; JD cum laude, Union U., 1994. Assoc. Barlett, Pontiff, Stewart & Rhodes, Glens Falls, N.Y., 1994-95, Block & Colucci, Latham, N.Y., 1995-96, Shanely, Sweeney, Reilley & Allen, Albany, 1996; fin. cons., staff atty. Ayco Co., Clifton Park, N.Y., 1997—. Mem. N.Y. State Bar Assn., Phi Beta Kappa. Avocations: basketball, golf. Home: Pine Ridge Apt #72 Clifton Park NY 12065 Office: The Ayco Co 855 Rte 140 PO Box 8029 Exec Woods Ste #120 Clifton Park NY 12065

**ROTHENBERG, ELLIOT CALVIN**, lawyer, writer; b. Mpls., Nov. 12, 1939; s. Sam S. and Claire Sylvia (Feller) R.; m. Sally Smalying; children: Sarah, Rebecca, Sam. BA summa cum laude, U. Minn., 1961; JD, Harvard U. (Fulbright fellow), 1964. Bar: Minn. 1966, U.S. Dist. Ct. Minn. 1966, D.C. 1968, U.S. Supreme Ct. 1972, N.Y. 1974, U.S. Ct. Appeals (2d cir.) 1974, U.S. Ct. Appeals (8th cir.) 1975. Assoc. project dir. Brookings Inst., Washington, 1966-67; fgn. svc. officer, legal advisor U.S. Dept. State, Washington, 1968-73; Am. Embassy, Saigon; U.S. Mission to the UN; nat. law dir. Anti-Defamation League, N.Y.C., 1973-74; legal dir. Minn. Pub. Interest Rsch. Group, Mpls., 1974-77; pvt. practice law Mpls., 1977—; adj. prof. William Mitchell Coll. Law, St. Paul, 1983—; faculty mem. several nat. comm. law and First Amendment seminars. Author: (with Zelman Cowen) Sir John Latham and Other Papers, 1965, The Taming of the Press: Cohen v. Cowles Media Co., 1999, The Taming of the Press, 1999; contbr. articles to profl. and scholarly jours. and books, newspapers, popular mags. State bd. dirs. YMCA Youth in Govt. Program, 1981-84; v.p. Twin Cities chpt. Am. Jewish Com., 1980-84; mem. Minn. Ho. of Reps., 1978-82, asst. floor leader (whip), 1981-82; pres., dir. North Star Legal Found., 1983—; legal affairs editor Pub. Rsch. Syndicated, 1986—; briefs and oral arguments published in full Landmark Briefs and Arguments of the Supreme Ct. of the U.S., Vol. 200, 1992; mem. citizens adv. com. Voyageurs Nat. Pk., 1979-81. Recipient Legis. Evaluation Assembly Legis. Excellence award, 1980, Vietnam Civilian Svc. medal U.S. Dept. State, 1970, North Star award U. Minn., 1961; Fulbright fellow, 1964-65. Mem. ABA, Minn. Bar Assn., Harvard Law Sch. Assn., Am. Legion, Mensa, Phi Beta Kappa. Jewish. General civil litigation, Communications, Constitutional. Home and Office: 3901 W 25th St Saint Louis Park MN 55416-3803

**ROTHERMEL, RICHARD ALLAN**, lawyer; b. Paterson, N.J., Feb. 9, 1950; s. Daniel Angstadt and Jean (Archer) R.; m. Donna Mollica, July 1, 1973 (div. 1977); m. Barbara Lehman, Oct. 11, 1980; children: Jonathan, Brian, Kara. AB, Kenyon Coll., 1972; JD, Catholic U., Washington, 1976. Bar: N.Y. 1977. Fed. program analyst U. Okla., Washington, 1973-76; assoc. Glickman & McAlevey, New City, N.Y., 1977-79, Harter & Rothermel, Oneonta, N.Y., 1979-82; sole practice Oneonta, 1982-96, 99—; pub. defender Otsego county Cooperstown, N.Y., 1982—; ptnr. Rothermel & Taylor, Oneonta, 1997-99. Bd. dirs. Oneonta (N.Y.) Jaycees, 1985-88, Planned Parenthood Assn. Delaware and Otsego Counties, 1997—, Oneonta Dollars for Scholars; vol. Am. Heart Assn., Oneonta, 1985-87; elder Presbyn. Ch. Mem. ABA, N.Y. State Bar Assn., N.Y. State Defenders Assn. (lectr.

1984), Nat. Assn. Criminal Def. Lawyers, N.Y. State Trial Lawyers Assn., N.Y. State Assn. Criminal Def. Lawyers, Otsego County Bar Assn. Republican. Avocations: golf, tennis. Criminal, Workers' compensation, Personal injury. Home: 105 West St Oneonta NY 13820-1741 Office: 48 Dietz St Ste E Oneonta NY 13820-1827

**ROTHMAN, BERNARD,** lawyer; b. N.Y.C., Aug. 11, 1932; s. Harry and Rebecca (Fritz) R.; m. Barbara Joan Schaeffer, Aug. 1953; children: Brian, Adam, Helene. BA cum laude, CCNY, 1953; LLB, NYU, 1959. Bar: N.Y. 1959, U.S. Dist. Ct. (ea. and so. dists.) N.Y. 1962, U.S. Ct. Appeals (2d cir.) 1965, U.S. Supreme Ct. 1966, U.S. Tax Ct. 1971. Assoc. Held, Telchin & Held, 1961-62; asst. U.S. atty. Dept. Justice, 1962-66; assoc. Edward Gettinger & Peter Gettinger, 1966-68; ptnr. Schwartz, Rothman & Abrams, P.C., 1968-78, Ferster, Bruckman, Wohl, Most & Rothman, LLP, N.Y.C., 1978-98, Shays Rothman & Heisler LLP, N.Y.C., 1999; acting judge Village of Larchmont, 1982-88, dep. Village atty., 1974-81, former arbitrator Civil Ct., N.Y.C., family disputes panel Am. Arbitration Assn.; guest lectr. domestic rels. and family law on radio and TV, also numerous legal and mental health orgns. Author: Loving and Leaving-Winning at the Business of Divorce, 1991; co-author: Family Law Syracuse Law Rev. of N.Y. Law, 1992, Leaving Home, Family Law Review, 1987; contbr. articles to profl. jours. Mem. exec. bd., past v.p. Westchester Putnam coun. Boy Scouts Am., 1975—; past mem. nat. coun., 1977-81; mem. adv. com. N.Y. State PEACE, 1994—; pres. Congregation B'nai Israel, 1961-63, B'nai Brith, Larchmont chpt., 1981-83. Recipient Silver Beaver award Boy Scouts Am., Wood Badge award. Fellow Am. Acad. Matrimonial Lawyers (bd. govs. N.Y. chpt. 1986-87, 91-93), Interdisciplinary Forum on Mental Health and Family Law (co-chair 1986-97); mem. ABA (family law sect.), N.Y. State Bar Assn. (exec. com. family law sect. 1982—, co-chmn. com. on mediation and arbitration 1982-88, 93—, com. on legis. 1978-88, com. on child custody 1985-88, com. alt. dispute resolution), Assn. of Bar of City of N.Y. (women in the cts. com. 1996-99), N.Y. State Magistrate Assn., Westchester Magistrate Assn., N.Y. Rd. Runners Club, Limousine & Track Club. Democrat. Family and matrimonial, State civil litigation. Office: Shays Rothman Heisler & LLP 276 5th Ave New York NY 10001-4509

**ROTHMAN, DAVID BILL,** lawyer; b. N.Y.C., Apr. 25, 1952; s. Julius and Lillian (Halpern) R.; m. Jeanne Marie Hickey, July 7, 1974; children: Jessica Suzanne, Gregory Kozak. BA, U. Fla., 1974, JD, 1977. Bar: Fla. 1977, U.S. Dist. Ct. (so. dist.) Fla. 1980, U.S. Ct. Appeals (5th cir.) 1980, U.S. Supreme Ct. 1981, U.S. Ct. Appeals (11th cir.) 1982, U.S. Dist. Ct. (ea. dist.) Ky. 1985, U.S. Dist. Ct. (mid. dist.) Fla. 1986; bd. cert. criminal trial law Fla. Bd. Asst. state atty. Dade County State Atty.'s Office, Miami, Fla., 1977-80; ptnr. Thornton Rothman, P.A., Miami, 1980—; adj. prof. U. Miami Sch. Law, 1995—; com. mem. Fla. Rules Criminal Procedures, 1990-93, metro Dade Ind. Rev. Panel, 1989-97, co-chmn., 1990-91, chmn., 1991-92, 95-97; panel mem. fee arbitration 11th Cir. Ct., 1994-96, co-chair, 1995-96; bd. govs. Fla. Bar, 1999—. Mem. ABA, Fla. Bar Assn. (bd. govs. 1999—), Dade County Bar Assn. (criminal ct. com. 1984—, chmn. 1987-90, bd. dirs. 1990-93, treas. 1993-94, sec. 1994-95, v.p. 1995-96, pres. 1997-98), Nat. Assn. Criminal Def. Lawyers, Fla. Assn. Criminal Def. Lawyers (bd. dirs. Miami chpt. 1991—, pres. Miami chpt. 1993-94, statewide sec. 1996-97, treas. 1997-98, v.p. 1998-99, pres.-elect 1999—). Democrat. Jewish. Avocations: running, racquetball, weightlifting, reading. Criminal. Home: 9951 SW 127th Ter Miami FL 33176-4833 Office: Thornton & Rothman PA 200 S Biscayne Blvd Ste 2690 Miami FL 33131-2310

**ROTHMAN, DENNIS MICHAEL,** lawyer; b. Flushing, N.Y., Aug. 7, 1953; s. Samuel and May Emilia Rothman; m. Shari Susan Silverman; children: Erica Blair, Cary James. BA, Yale U., 1974; JD, St. John's U., 1977. Bar: N.Y. 1978, N.J. 1997, U.S. Dist. Ct. (ea. and so. dists.) N.Y. 1978, U.S. Ct. Appeals (2d cir.) 1978, U.S. Dist. Ct. N.J. 1998, U.S. Tax Ct. 1984, U.S. Supreme Ct. 1998. Staff law clk. U.S. Ct. Appeals (2d cir.), N.Y.C., 1978-79; assoc. Lester Schwab Katz & Dwyer, N.Y.C., 1979-82; assoc. Wiener, Zuckerbrot, Weiss & Newman, N.Y.C., 1982-87, ptnr., 1988-90; ptnr. Lester Schwab Katz & Dwyer, N.Y.C., 1991—. Federal civil litigation, State civil litigation, Antitrust. Office: Lester Schwab Katz & Dwyer 120 Broadway Fl 38 New York NY 10271-0071

**ROTHMAN, FRANK,** lawyer, motion picture company executive; b. Los Angeles, Dec. 24, 1926; s. Leon and Rose (Gendel) R.; m. Mariana Richardson, Aug. 7, 1985; children: Steven, Robin, Susan. B.A., U. So. Calif., 1949, LL.B., 1951. Bar: Calif. 1952, D.C., U.S. Dist. Ct. (cen. dist.) Calif. 1951. Dep. city atty. City of Los Angeles, 1951-55; mem. law firm Wyman, Bautzer, Rothman, Kuchel & Silbert, Los Angeles, 1956-82; chmn. bd., chief exec. officer MGM-UA Entertainment Co., Culver City, Calif., 1982-86; ptnr. Skadden Arps Slate, L.A., 1986—. Bd. editors U. So. Calif. Law Rev., 1948. Served with USAAF, 1945-46. Fellow Am. Coll. Trial Lawyers; mem. L.A. Bar Assn., Calif. Bar Assn., Calif. Club. Democrat. FERC practice, General civil litigation. Home: 10555 Rocca Pl Los Angeles CA 90077-2904 Office: Skadden Arps Slate 300 S Grand Ave Bldg 3400 Los Angeles CA 90071-3109

**ROTHMAN, HOWARD JOEL,** lawyer; b. N.Y.C., July 10, 1945; s. Samuel and Avy (Avrutin) R.; m. Joan Andrea Solomon, July 2, 1967; children: Samantha, Rodney. BA, CCNY, 1967; JD, Bklyn. Law Sch., 1971; LLM, NYU, 1972. Bar: N.Y. 1972. From assoc. to ptnr. Marshall, Bratter, Greene, Allison & Tucker, N.Y.C., 1972-82; ptnr. Rosenman & Colin LLP, N.Y.C., 1982-97, Kramer, Levin, Naftalis & Frankel, N.Y.C., 1997—; mem. adv. panel Commr. Fin. of City of N.Y., 1981-83. Author profl. books and articles. Bd. dirs. Alliance Resident Theatres N.Y., 1989-96. Mem. ABA (corp. tax. com. 1977-87, income from real property com. 1980—), Internat. Bar Assn., N.Y. State Bar Assn. (exec. com. tax sect. 1999—, corps. com. 1979-87, partnerships com. 1979—, N.Y.C. tax matters com. 1977—, income from real property com. 1977—), Bur. Nat. Affairs (real estate jour. 1984—, tax mgmt. adv. bd. 1979—), Alliance Resident Theatres N.Y. (bd. dirs. 1989-96), Alliance for Young Artists and Writers (bd. dirs. 1994—), Poetry Soc. Am. (bd. dirs. 1996—). Corporate taxation, Taxation, general, State and local taxation.

**ROTHMAN, JESSE,** lawyer; b. N.Y.C.; s. Louis and Anna Rothman; m. Lillian Wolfe, Mar. 2, 1940; children: John L., Warren H., Anne. LLB, Bklyn. U., 1931. Bar: N.Y. 1935. Pvt. practice N.Y.C. Mem. Am. Acad. Matrimonial Lawyers. Family and matrimonial. Hom: 16 Doris Rd Mamaroneck NY 10543-1008

**ROTHMAN, MARIE HENDERSON,** law librarian; d. Jesse Robert and Martha (Miller) Henderson; m. Arthur Rothman, Aug. 28, 1958. AB with distinction and honors, U. Pa., 1956; MS with honors, Columbia U., 1964; MA, NYU, 1969. Head UN collections, gen. library NYU, 1963-67; govt. documents librarian Bklyn. Ctr. Library, L.I. U., 1967-72; exec. dir. N.Y. Ams. for Democratic Action, N.Y.C., 1973-74; legis. aide N.Y.C. Coun., 1975-79; exec. dir. East Midtown Community Coun., 1979-80; tech. svcs. asst. N.Y. Law Sch. Library, 1981-82; tech. svcs. librarian Weil, Gotshal & Manges, 1982-83; law librarian Fed. Res. Bank N.Y., 1984-86; sr. mng. lib. Matthew Bender & Co., Inc., N.Y.C., 1986—. Author: Citation Rules & Forms for United Nations Documents & Publications, 1971. Vice pres. Village Ind. Dems., N.Y.C., 1972-73; coordinator Manhattan Women's Polit. Caucus, N.Y.C., 1972-78. Mem. ABA, Am. Assn. Law Libraries, Spl. Libraries Assn., Phi Beta Kappa, Beta Phi Mu. Office: Matthew Bender & Co Inc 2 Park Ave New York NY 10016-5675

**ROTHMAN, MICHAEL JUDAH,** lawyer; b. Mpls., June 7, 1962; s. Harvey Michael and Elaine Louise (London) R.; m. Shari Latz, Aug. 1, 1993. BA, Carleton Coll., 1984; JD, U. Minn., 1988. Bar: Minn. 1988, U.S. Dist. Ct. Minn. 1988, Calif. 1993, U.S. Dist. Ct. (ctrl. dist.) Calif. 1993, U.S. Ct. Appeals (9th cir.) 1995, U.S. Supreme Ct. 1995. Law clk. to Hon. J. Gary Crippen Minn. Ct. of Appeals, St. Paul, 1988-89; adminstrv. asst. Minn. State Senate, 1989-92; atty. Rubenstein & Perry, L.A., 1993-95, Loeb & Loeb, L.A., 1995-96; assoc. Barger & Wolen, LLP, L.A., 1996—. Vol. atty. F.A.M.E. Ch. and Temple Isaiah Legal Project, L.A., 1994-96. Recipient Best Brief award Regional Internat. Moot Ct. Competition, Colo., 1988. Mem. ABA, Calif. Bar Assn., L.A. County Bar Assn. Democrat. Avocations: golf, running, reading. General civil litigation, Administrative and regulatory, Insurance. Office: Barger & Wolen 515 S Flower St Fl 34 Los Angeles CA 90071-2201

**ROTHSCHILD, DONALD PHILLIP,** lawyer, arbitrator; b. Dayton, Ohio, Mar. 31, 1927; s. Leo and Anne (Office) R.; m. Ruth Eckstein, July 7, 1950; children: Nancy Lee, Judy Lynn Hoffman, James Alex. AB, U. Mich., 1950; JD summa cum laude, U. Toledo, 1965; LLM, Harvard U., 1966. Bar: Ohio 1966, D.C. 1970, U.S. Supreme Ct. 1975, R.I. 1989. Teaching fellow Harvard U. Law Sch., Cambridge, Mass., 1965-66; instr. solicitor's office U.S. Dept. Labor, Washington, 1966-67; vis. prof. U. Mich. Law Sch., Ann Arbor, 1976; prof. law George Washington U. Nat. Law Ctr., Washington, 1966-89, emeritus, 1989; prof. law N.Y. Law Sch., 1989-96; dir. Consumer Protection Ctr., 1971—; dir. Inst. Law and Aging, Washington, 1973-89, Ctr. for Community Justice, Washington, 1974-88, Nat. Consumers League, Washington, 1981-87; v.p. Regulatory Alternatives Devel. Corp., Washington, 1982—; cons. Washington Met. Council Govt., 1979-82; mayoral appointee Adv. Com. on Consumer Protection, Washington, 1979-80; chmn. bd. dirs. D.C. Citizens Complaint Ctr., Washington, 1980; counsel Tillinghast, Collins & Graham, Providence, 1989-95, chair human resource group. Co-author: Consumer Protection Text and Materials, 1973; Collective Bargaining and Labor Arbitration, 1979; Fundamentals of Administrative Practice and Procedure, 1981. Contbr. numerous articles to profl. publs. Mem. Fed. Trade Commn. Adv. Council, Washington, 1970. Recipient Community Service award Television Acad., Washington, 1981. Mem. ABA, Nat. Assn. Coll. and Univ. Attys. (Brown U.), Nat. Acad. Arbitrators, Fed. Mediation and Conciliation Service, Am. Arbitration Assn., D.C. Bar Assn., Phi Kappa Phi. Jewish. Labor, Administrative and regulatory, Contracts commercial. Office: Shadow Farm Way Unit 4 Wakefield RI 02879-3631

**ROTHSCHILD, MARTIN JAY,** lawyer; b. Watertown, N.Y., May 19, 1953; s. Harold S. and Gloria Rothschild; m. Laurie Rothschild, Jan. 20, 1963; children: Ethan, Sara. BA, Syracuse U., 1975; JD, SUNY, Albany, 1978. Bar: N.Y. 1979, Fla. 1980, U.S. Dist. Ct. (no. dist.) N.Y. 1979. Ptnr. Tractenburg & Rothschild, Schenectady, N.Y.; pvt. practice Syracuse, 1989—; legal commentator Sta. WTVH Channel 5, Syracuse, WHEN-Radio, Syracuse, USA Radio. Mem. Assn. Trial Lawyers Am., N.Y. State Trial Lawyers, Onondaga County Bar Assn., ABA. Avocation: photography. Personal injury, Product liability. Office: 3216 Erie Blvd E Syracuse NY 13214-1204

**ROTHSCHILD, TOBY JAMES,** lawyer; b. Los Angeles, Sept. 1, 1944; s. Otto and Sylvia (Singer) R.; m. Elena L. Hyman, Aug. 6, 1967; children: Marnie, Dana. BA, San Francisco State U., 1966; JD, UCLA, 1969. Bar: Calif. 1970, U.S. Dist. Ct. (cen. dist.) Calif. 1970, U.S. Ct. Appeals (9th cir.) 1971, U.S. Supreme Ct. 1973. Staff atty. Los Angeles Neighborhood Legal Service, 1969-71; staff atty. Legal Aid Found., Long Beach, Calif., 1971-73, exec. dir., 1973—; chmn. State Bar Com. on Adminstrn. Justice, 1986-87, vice chmn. Conf. Dels., 1995-96. Author: Automobile Transactions, 1981; contbr. articles to profl. jours. Bd. dirs., vice chmn. Western Ctr. on Law and Poverty, 1973-88; v.p. Long Beach Jewish Community Ctr., 1983-88, pres. 1989-90. Recipient Lauren Miller Legal Svcs. award State Bar Calif, 1995. Mem. Am. Arbitration Assn., Long Beach Bar Assn. (pres. 1993), L.A. County Bar Assn. (bd. govs. 1997—). Consumer commercial, Landlord-tenant, Alternative dispute resolution. Office: Legal Aid Found of Long Beach 110 Pine Ave Ste 420 Long Beach CA 90802-4421

**ROTHSTADT, GARRY SIGMUND,** lawyer; b. Paterson, N.J., Dec. 2, 1958. BA, Rutgers Coll., 1980, JD, 1983. Bar: N.J. 1983, U.S. Dist. Ct. N.J. 1983. Jud. clk. Superior Ct. N.J., Paterson, 1983-84; assoc. Cole Geaney Yamne & Byrne, Paterson, 1984-88; ptnr. Chiocca Rothstadt & Sweeney, Wayne, 1988-89, Choicca & Rothstadt, Wayne, 1989-90, Bray Chiocca Rappaport & Rothstadt, LLC, Parsippany, N.J., 1990—. Mem. ABA, N.J. State Bar Assn., Passaic County Bar Assn. (sec. 1993-94, treas. 1994-95, v.p. 1995-96, pres.-elect 1996-97, pres. 1997—). State civil litigation, Contracts commercial, Construction. Office: Bray Chiocca et al Koll Exec Ctr 100 Misty Ln Parsippany NJ 07054-2710

**ROTHSTEIN, AMY LONE,** lawyer, mediator; b. N.Y.C., July 23, 1948; d. Nathaniel and Jane Rothstein; m. Peter Charles Salerno, Sept. 25, 1987. BA, Boston U., 1969; JD, NYU, 1972. Bar: N.Y. 1973, U.S. Dist. Ct. (so. and ea. dists.) N.Y. 1973, U.S. Ct. Appeals (2nd cir.) 1977. Litigation assoc. Weil Gotshal & Manges, N.Y.C., 1972-74; staff atty. The Legal Aid Soc., N.Y.C., 1974-84; asst. U.S. atty. U.S. Attys. Office So. Dist. N.Y., N.Y.C., 1984-88; asst. gen. counsel Gruntal & Co., Inc., N.Y.C., 1988-90; dep. bur. chief N.Y. State Atty. Gen.'s Office, N.Y.C., 1990-95; of counsel Doar Devorkin & Rieck, N.Y.C., 1997—; adj. faculty Bklyn. Law Sch., 1994-98; pro bono mediator So. and Ea. Dists. N.Y. Supreme Ct., N.Y.C., spl. master. MEm. N.Y. County Lawyers Assn., Assn. of the Bar of the City of N.Y. Alternative dispute resolution, Securities, Federal civil litigation. Home: 283 Hicks St Brooklyn NY 11201-4560 Office: Doar Devorkin & Rieck 233 Broadway Rm 1001 New York NY 10279-0173

**ROTHSTEIN, BARBARA JACOBS,** federal judge; b. Bklyn., Feb. 3, 1939; d. Solomon and Pauline Jacobs; m. Ted L. Rothstein, Dec. 28, 1968; 1 child, Daniel. B.A., Cornell U., 1960; LL.B., Harvard U., 1966. Bar: Mass. 1966, Wash. 1969, U.S. Ct. Appeals (9th cir.) 1977, U.S. Dist. Ct. (we. dist.) Wash. 1971, U.S. Supreme Ct. 1975. Pvt. practice law Boston, 1966-68; asst. atty. gen. State of Wash., 1968-77; judge Superior Ct., Seattle, 1977-80; judge Fed. Dist. Ct. Western Wash., Seattle, 1980—, chief judge, 1987-94; faculty Law Sch. U. Wash., 1975-77, Hastings Inst. Trial Advocacy, 1977, N.W. Inst. Trial Advocacy, 1979—; mem. state-fed. com. U.S. Jud. Conf., chair subcom. on health reform. Recipient Matrix Table Women of Yr. award Women in Communication, Judge of the Yr. award Fed. Bar Assn., 1989; King County Wash. Women Lawyers Vanguard Honor, 1995. Mem. ABA (jud. sect.), Am. Judicature Soc., Nat. Assn. Women Judges, Fellows of the Am. Bar, Wash. State Bar Assn., U.S. Jud. Conf. (state-fed. com., health reform subcom.), Phi Beta Kappa, Phi Kappa Phi. Office: US Dist Ct 705 US Courthouse 1010 5th Ave Ste 215 Seattle WA 98104-1189

**ROTHSTEIN, JONATHAN ALAN,** lawyer; b. Chgo., Aug. 13, 1955; s. David B. and Ruth M. Rothstein; m. Susan R. Gzesh, June 25, 1981; 1 child, Max David. AB, U. Chgo., 1976; JD, George Washington U., 1979. Bar: Ill. Supreme Ct. 1979, U.S. Dist. Ct. (No. Dist. Ill.) 1979, U.S. Ct. Appeals (7th cir.) 1992, U.S. Supreme Ct. 1994. Ptnr. Rothstein Adams & Rothstein, Chgo., 1981-84; hearing officer Ill. Labor Rels. Bd., Chgo., 1984-85; rep., gen. counsel Gen. Svc. Employees Union, Chgo., 1985-86; assoc. gen. counsel Chgo. Housing Authority, 1986-87, dir. dept. human resources, 1987-88, spl. asst. to chmn. of bd. dirs., 1988-89; ptnr. Gessler Hughes & Socol Ltd., Chgo., 1990—. Contbg. author: Civil Rights Litigation & Attorneys Fees Handbook, 1995, Civil Rights Litigation & Attorneys Handbook, 1996. Mem. Cook County Econ. Devel. Adv. Com., 1994-98. Recipient 18th Ann. Chgo. award Mex. Am. Legal Def. & Edn. Legal Svcs., 1998. General civil litigation, Civil rights, Labor. Office: Gessler Hughes & Socol Ltd 70 W Madison St Ste 2200 Chicago IL 60602-4253

**ROTI, THOMAS DAVID,** lawyer, food service executive; b. Evanston, Ill., Jan. 20, 1945; s. Sam N. and Theresa S. (Salerno) R.; m. Donna Sumichrast, July 22, 1972; children: Thomas S., Kyle D., Rebecca D., Gregory J. BS, Loyola U., Chgo., 1967, JD cum laude, 1970. Bar: Ill. 1970, U.S. Dist. Ct. (no. dist.) Ill. 1971, U.S. Ct. Appeals (7th cir.) 1971. Sr. law clk. to presiding justice U.S. Dist. Ct. No. Dist. Ill., 1971-72; assoc. Arnstein, Gluck & Lehr, Chgo., 1972-73, Boodell, Sears et al., Chgo., 1973-75; asst. gen. counsel Dominick's Finer Foods, Inc., Northlake, Ill., 1975-77, v.p., gen. counsel, 1977-97; mem. nat. conf. lawyers and econs. com. Food Mktg. Inst., Washington, 1987-97, legis. com. Ill. Retail Mchts. Assn., Chgo., 1987—; dir. NCCJ. Trustee Joint Civic Com. Italian Ams., Chgo., 1986—; mem. Chgo. Coun. EDU-CARE Scholarship Program, 1988. Maj. U.S. Army, 1967-83. Recipient Am. Jurisprudence award, 1970; Alumni Assn. award Loyola U., 1970. Mem. ABA, Ill. Bar Assn., Chgo. Bar Assn., Am. Corp. Counsel Assn., Chgo. Zool. Soc., Loyola Alumni Assn., Art Inst. Chgo., Phi Alpha Delta, Alpha Sigma Nu. Roman Catholic. General corporate, Computer, Contracts commercial. Home and Office: 5002 Sunset Ct Palatine IL 60067-9047

**ROTSTEIN, ANDREW DAVID,** lawyer; b. N.Y.C., June 13, 1950; s. Maurice Joseph and Selma (Sacks) R.; m. Regina Mary Anuzelli, Aug. 20, 1976 (div. Mar. 1983). BA, Columbia U., 1973, JD, 1994. Bar: N.Y. 1995, Mass. 1995. Polit. activist various locations, 1974-90; assoc. Sullivan & Cromwell, N.Y.C., 1994-98, Gibson, Dunn & Crutcher, N.Y.C., 1998—. Sr. editor Columbia Law Rev., 1992-94. Harlan Fiske Stone scholar Columbia U., 1992-94. Mem. ABA, Assn. of Bar of City of N.Y. Democrat. General civil litigation. Home: 11 Sterling Pl Apt 2F Brooklyn NY 11217-3273 Office: Gibson Dunn & Crutcher 200 Park Ave Fl 47 New York NY 10166-4799

**ROTTER, EMANUEL NORMAN,** lawyer; b. Milw., Jan. 11, 1928; s. Louis H. and Sarah (Manhoff) R.; m. Sandra Schulner, July 5, 1952 (dec. Sept. 1996); children: Margie S., Barbara A., Steven M. BBA, U. Wis., 1949; JD, Marquette U., 1952. Bar: Wis. 1952, U.S. Dist. Ct. (ea. dist.) Wis. 1952. Sole practice, Milw., 1952—; cert. guardian ad litern MBA, Wis., 1953-63; ct. commr. Milwaukee County (Wis.), 1982-95; active Jewish Nat. Fund, Milw., 1998—. Mem. ABA (gen. practice sect., sub-com. sole practitioners and small firms), Wis. Bar Assn., (pres. law sect., gen. practice sects.), Milwaukee County Bar Assn. (arbitration com., fee arbitration com., legis. com., probate, family, gen. corp. and bankruptcy/creditor's rights sects.), Milw. Bar Assn. Found., Am. Arbitration Assn. (panel), Nature Conservatory, Nat. Audubon Soc., U.S. Tennis Assn., Am. Assn. Ret. Persons, Zionist Orgn. Am., Am. Jewish Com. Jewish. Lodges: B'nai B'rith. Consumer commercial, Landlord-tenant, General practice. Office: 130 W Silver Spring Dr Milwaukee WI 53217-4707

**ROULEAU, MARK A.,** lawyer; b. Frankfurt, W. Germany; s. Franklin Pierce Rouleau and Margery Elizabeth MacLaughlin; m. Phensri Shanaratna; children: Emily Marker, Matthew Marker. BA in Polit. Sci., So. Ill. U., 1980, BA in Econs. with honors, 1980; JD, DePaul U., 1983. Bar: Ill.; U.S. Dist. Ct. (no. dist. Ill.). Assoc. Crosby & Lambert, Rockford, Ill., 1984-94; prin. Mark Rouleau & Assocs., Rockford, 1994—; presenter in field. Contbr. articles to profl. jours. Active Boy Scouts Am. Mem. ABA (del. 1992-94), Ill. State Bar Assn. (sec., vice-chmn. to chmn. 1992-94, 98—), Ill. Trial Lawyers Assn., Winnebago County Bar Assn. Personal injury, General civil litigation, Criminal. Office: Mark Rouleau & Assocs 5301 E State St Ste 215D Rockford IL 61108-2392

**ROUNSAVILLE, GUY, JR.,** lawyer; b. 1943. BA, Stanford U., 1965; JD, U. Calif., San Francisco, 1968. Bar: Calif. 1969. Atty. Wells Fargo, 1969-73, v.p., counsel, 1974-77, v.p., chief counsel, 1977-78, sr. v.p., chief counsel, sec., 1980-85, exec. v.p., chief counsel, sec., 1985-98; ptnr. Allen, Matkins, Leck, Gamble & Mallory, San Francisco, 1999—. General corporate, Banking. *

**ROUSE, GERALD EDWARD,** judge; b. Grand Island, Nebr., Jan. 19, 1944; s. Warren Duane and Mary Elizabeth (Weinerich) R.; m. Stephanie E. Egley, Aug. 31, 1968; 1 child, Suzanne E. BA, Hastings Coll., 1968; JD, U. Nebr., 1971. Bar: Nebr. 1971. Dep. county atty. Platte County Atty.'s Office, Columbus, Nebr., 1971; county judge 5th jud. dist. State of Nebr., Seward, 1971—; lead judge Nebr. Permanency Planning Task Force, 1984—. Mem. adv. bd. Transitional Living Ctr., Columbus, 1982—. Recipient Founder's Day award Epworth Village, 1990, Commrs. award for prevention of child abuse and neglect Dept. Health and Human Svcs. Denver, 1991. Mem. Nebr. Juvenile Justice Assn. (past pres., Pres. award 1989-90), Nat. Coun. Juvenile and Family Ct. Judges (trustee 1988-94, sec. 1994-95, treas. 1997, v.p. 1997—, pres. 1999-00), Nebr. State Bar Assn. (exec. com. family law sect. 1990—), Nebr. County Judges Assn. (chmn. juvenile svcs. com. 1990—). Avocations: tennis, bicycling. Office: Seward County Ct PO Box 37 Seward NE 68434-0037

**ROUSE, LEGRAND ARIAIL, II,** retired lawyer, educator; b. Spartanburg, S.C., June 11, 1933; s. LeGrand and Hilda Virginia (Ariail) R.; m. Patricia Adelle White, Aug. 23, 1958; children: LeGrand A. III, Laurie Adelle Rouse-Hazel, Daniel Morris. AB in History and Polit. Sci., Wofford Coll., 1954; LLB, U. S.C.; 1959, JD, 1970; MA in Govt., Am. U., 1969. Bar: S.C. 1959, U.S. Dist. Ct. S.C. 1959, U.S. Ct. Appeals (4th cir.) 1964, U.S. Supreme Ct. 1963. Sole practice, Spartanburg S.C., 1959-63, 68-69; assoc. counsel, jud. improvements subcom. U.S. Senate Judiciary Com., Washington, 1963; profl. staff mem. U.S. Senate P.O. and Civil Service Com., Washington, 1964-68; instructional specialist Office of Instructional TV, S.C. Dept. Edn., Columbia, 1970-73; social studies cons. curriculum devel. S.C. Dept. Edn., 1973-79; spl. asst. legal and legis. affairs to State Supt. Edn., Columbia, 1979-91; spl. asst. to sr. exec. asst. Policy, Rsch., and Leadership, Columbia, 1991; cons. S.C. Council for Social Studies, Columbia, 1973-78; dir. S.C. Council Econ. Edn., Columbia. Author: Government-Politics-Citizenship, tchr. lesson guide, 1971-72; creator, on-camera instr. Government-Politics-Citizenship TV series, 1970-72; project dir. econs. edn. kit for tchrs. grades 1-12: People, Production, Profits, 1977. Mem. S.C. Ho. of Reps., Columbia, 1961-64; alt. del. Nat. Democratic Conv., 1964. Served to 1st lt. USAR, 1955-57. Recipient Schoolmens' medal Freedoms Found. at Valley Forge, 1974. Mem. S.C. Bar Assn., S.C. State Employees' Assn. (pres. 1980-82), Masons, Nat. Sojourners (pres. chpt. 184). Methodist. Home: 1021 Milton Ln Columbia SC 29209-2321

**ROUSE, MICHAEL ADAMS,** lawyer; b. Omaha, May 3, 1957; s. James William and Beatrice Dorothy Rouse; m. Brenda Elizabeth Trumbauer, Apr. 26, 1997; 1 child, Emma Elizabeth. BA in Psychology, Creighton U., 1984, JD, 1990. Bar: Nebr., Mo., Kans. Assoc. co Baker, Sterchi, Cowden & Rice, Kansas City, Mo., 1990-92; mgr. loss prevention Mut. of Omaha Ins. Co., Omaha, 1992-93, counsel, 1993-95, assoc. counsel law divsn., fin. svcs. dept., 1995-96, contract adminstr., 1996-98; assoc. counsel, law dept. Guarantee Life Ins. Co., Omaha, 1998—. Contbr. articles to profl. jours. Mem. Omaha Jaycees. Republican. Roman Catholic. Avocations: piano, western horseback. Contracts commercial, Real property, General corporate. Office: Guarantee Life Ins Co 8801 Indian Hills Dr Omaha NE 68114-4059

**ROUSE, RANDALL LYLE,** lawyer; b. Lubbock, Tex., June 26, 1951; s. Robert L. and Elta (Carroll) R.; m. Judy S. Rouse, Aug. 16, 1975; children: Richard Layne, Jenness Dianne. BA, Tex. Tech., Lubbock, 1973, JD, 1975. Bar: U.S. Dist. Ct. (so. dist.) W.Va. 1978, U.S. Dist. Ct. (we. dist.) Tex. 1981, U.S. Dist. Ct. (no. dist.) Tex. 1994. Assoc. Miller & Miller, Amarillo, Tex., 1975-77, Revere Coal Co., Charleston, W.Va., 1977-78, John R. Mitchell, Charleston, 1978-80; ptnr. Shafer, Davis, Ashley, O'Leary & Stoker, Odessa, Tex., 1980—; mem. rules com western dist. Tex. BAnkruptcy Ct., Midland, 1996—. Chmn. bd. Crisis Pregnancy Ctr., Midland, 1996—; bd. dirs. Salvation Army, Odessa, 1990, West Tex. Lit. Coun., Odessa, 1987-90. Mem. ABA, State Bar Tex., State Bar W.Va., 5th Cir. Bar, Am. Bd. Trial Advocates, Rutherford Inst. Republican. Avocations: grief counseling and Christian ministry. Professional liability, Labor, Bankruptcy. Home: 5801 Stonecrest Midland TX 79707-9779 Office: 700 N Grant Ave Odessa TX 79761-4561

**ROUSE, ROBERT KELLY, JR.,** judge; b. Lexington, Ky.; s. Robert Kelly and Luane (Adams) R.; m. Donna R. Walker, Dec. 21, 1969; children: Kelly B., Erin E. AA, Daytona Beach (Fla.) C.C., 1966; BS, Fla. State U., 1968; JD, U. Fla., 1974. Bar: Fla. 1974. Ptnr. Regency Talent, Daytona Beach, 1968-69; supr. food divsn. Walt Disney Co., Anaheim, Calif., 1969-70; mgr. restaurants Walt Disney World Co., Orlando, Fla., 1970-71; asso., then ptnr. Smalbein, Eubank, Johnson, Rosier & Bussey, P.A., Daytona Beach, 1974-81; ptnr. Smith, Schoder, Rouse & Bouck, P.A., Daytona Beach, 1981-95; circuit judge State of Fla., Daytona Beach, 1995—; chief judge Seventh Jud. Cir., 1999—. With USAR, 1969-75. Mem. Am. Bd. Trial Advs., Volusia County Bar Assn. (pres. 1989-90), Volusia Civil Trial Attys. Assn. (pres. 1993-95). Office: Volusia County Courthouse Annex 125 E Orange Ave Ste 307 Daytona Beach FL 32114-4420

**ROUSH, EDWARD WESLEY, JR.,** lawyer; b. Clinton, Ind., Feb. 16, 1957; s. Edward Wesley and Sue Ann (Campbell) R.; m. Cathy Leigh Sarver, Sept. 10, 1983; children: Andrew Wesley, Caroline Elizabeth, Alexa Faith. BA in History, U. Tex., Dallas, 1980; JD, St. Mary's Law Sch., San Antonio, 1983. Bar: Tex., 1983. Pvt. practice Dallas, 1986-88; atty. Lynch Chappell Allday, Austin, Tex., 1983-84; v.p., gen. counsel The Bargo Group, Inc., Laredo, Tex., 1984-86; sr. atty. Malouf, Roush & Dickenson, Dallas, 1988-89; assoc. atty. Milgrim Thomajan & Lee, Dallas, 1989-90; sr. atty. Roush & Assocs., Dallas, 1990-93; chmn., chief exec. officer Continental Investment Corp., Atlanta, 1991, Blue Cactus Post, Dallas, 1994—, Ancarlex Entertainment, Dallas, 1995—; bd. dirs. Data Processing Security, Inc., Ft. Worth. Named one of Outstanding Young Men Am., 1985. Mem. Univ. Club Dallas. Republican. Home: 2400 Bridge View Ln Plano TX 75093-2547

**ROUSTAN, YVON DOMINIQUE,** lawyer, real estate broker; b. Managua, Nicaragua, June 22, 1944; came to U.S., 1962; s. Pierre Dominique and Concepcion (Reyes) R.; m. Estela Maria Fiol, Apr. 1, 1967; children: Estela, Pierre, Paul. BA, St. Mary's Coll., Winona, Minn., 1966; MBA, U. Chgo., 1969; JD, DePaul U., 1976. Bar: Ill. 1976, U.S. Supreme Ct. 1987. Chief chemist Bird and Son Inc., Chgo., 1967-69; mgr. Grasas S.A., Chinandega, Nicaragua, 1969-72; assoc. Vincent Lopez, Chgo., 1976-77; sole practice Chgo., 1977—. Mem. Chgo. Bar Assn., Coun. of Trial Lawyers. Lodge: Lions (Chgo.) (v.p. 1983, pres.). Avocations: computers, reading. Criminal, Real property, Personal injury. Office: 2911 N Cicero Ave Chicago IL 60641-5131

**ROUTH, JOHN WILLIAM,** lawyer; b. Knoxville, Tenn., Dec. 3, 1957; s. John C. and Mary (Parker) R.; m. Martha Carol Carter, Aug. 6, 1983; children: John Carter, Carol Ann. BA, U. Tenn., 1979, JD, 1983. Bar: Tenn. 1983, U.S. Dist. Ct. (ea. dist.) Tenn. 1983. Assoc. Francis W. Headman, Knoxville, 1983-87, Wm. R. Banks and Assocs., Knoxville, 1987-97; judicial commr. Knox County Gen. Sessions Ct., Knoxville, 1992-94; sole practice law Knoxville, 1997—. Bd. dirs. Cerebral Palsy Ctr. for Handicapped Adults, Knoxville, 1985-88; chmn. adminstv. bd. Emerald Ave. United Meth. Ch., Knoxville, 1988-90, 98—. Mem. Tenn. Bar Assn., Knoxville Bar Assn., Tenn. Assn. Criminal Def. Lawyers, City Salesman Club (v.p. 1988, sec. 1987, pres. 1998). Methodist. Personal injury, Criminal, General practice. Office: 4611 Old Broadway St Knoxville TN 37918-1784

**ROUX, KERMIT LOUIS, III,** lawyer; b. New Orleans, Aug. 24, 1969; s. Kermit Louis Jr. and Kathryn (Felt) R. BBA, So. Meth. U., 1991; JD, Tulane U., 1994. Bar: La. 1994, U.S. Dist. Ct. (ea., we., and mid. dists.) La. 1994. Atty. Lowe Stein Hoffman Allweiss & Hauver, New Orleans, 1994—; bd. dirs. Audubon Capital Corp., New Orleans, Paradigm Devel. Corp., New Orleans, Typhon Group, L.L.C. Mem. Federalist Soc., New Orleans, 1994—, Greater New Orleans Republicans, New Orleans, 1994—; pro bono liaison New Orleans Pro Bono Project, 1995—; mem. fin. com. Immaculate Conception Ch., New Orleans, 1996. Mem. ABA, Fed. Bar Assn., La. Bar Assn., New Orleans Bar Assn. Republican. Roman Catholic. Avocation: competitive shooting. Consumer commercial, General civil litigation, General corporate. Home: 5200 Purdue Dr Metairie LA 70003-1043 Office: 701 Poydras St Ste 3600 New Orleans LA 70139-7735

**ROVELL, MICHAEL JAY,** lawyer; b. Chgo., Mar. 30, 1949; s. Bernard and Charlotte (Schaefer) R.; m. Laurie Strauss, Sept. 2, 1979; children: Brandon, Kendall, Ryan. BA with honors, U. Ill., Chgo., 1969; JD with honors, U. Ill., 1972. Bar: Ill. 1972, U.S. Dist. Ct. (no. and so. dists.) Ill. 1972, U.S. Ct. Appeals (7th cir.) 1973, U.S. Ct. Appeals (8th cir.) 1981, U.S. Supreme Ct. 1983, U.S. Ct. Appeals (5th cir.) 1986, U.S. Ct. Appeals (1st cir.) 1990, U.S. Dist. Ct. P.R. 1992, U.S. Ct. Appeals (10th cir.) 1992, U.S. Ct. Appeals (3rd cir.) 1993, U.S. Ct. Appeals (2nd cir.) 1996, U.S. Ct. Appeals (9th cir.), 1997, Belgium 1997. Assoc. Jenner & Block, Chgo., 1972-78, ptnr., 1979-90; prin. Law Offices of Michael J. Rovell, Chgo., 1990—; dir. Cook County Spl. Bail Project, 1972-74; chief exec. officer, bd. dirs. Sunbelt Communications, Colorado Springs, Colo., 1976-78; of counsel Wampler, Buchanan & Breen, Miami, Troncoso & Becker, San Juan, P.R., Law Offices of Robert Bright, Oklahoma City and affiliate offices London, Paris, Brussels; bd. editors U. Ill. Law Forum, 1971-72. Bd. dirs. Steppenwolf Theatre, Chgo., 1979-81. Mem. ABA (coord. litigation seminar on electronic surveillance), Ill. Bar Assn., Hillcrest Country Club (Long Grove, Ill.). Avocations: golf, tennis, bowling. Federal civil litigation, Criminal, General civil litigation. Home: 1516 Christina Ln Lake Forest IL 60045-3848 Office: 20 N Clark St Ste 2450 Chicago IL 60602-5002

**ROVEN, JOHN DAVID,** lawyer; b. N.Y.C., Mar. 16, 1954; s. Philip MOrris and Joyce R.; m. Oct. 25, 1986 (div. July, 1992); children: Melanie, Julia. BA, Coker Coll., 1974; JD, U. S.C., 1981. Bar: S.C. 1981, U.S. Dist. Ct. S.C. 1981, Tex. 1986, U.S. Dist. Ct. (so. dist.) Tex. 1986, Nebr. 1988, U.S. Dist. Ct. (ea. dist.) Tex. 1994. Investigator, law clk. S.C. Atty Gen. Office, Columbia, 1977-81; law clk. U.S. Dist. Ct. S.C., Greenville, 1982-83; assoc. Ness, Motley, Loadholt, Richardson & Poole, PA, Charleston, S.C., 1984-85; ptnr. Jones & Granger, Houston, Tex., 1986-95; prin., founder Roven & Assocs., PC, Houston, 1995—; appointed liason counsel FELA Plaintiffs' Com., Asbestos Multi-Dist. Litigation U.S. Dist. Ct. (ea. dist.) Pa. Bd. dirs. Chrysalis Repertory Dance Co., Houston, 1991-94, mem. adv. bd. 1994-98. Recipient Alumnus of Yr. award Coker Coll., Hartsville, S.C., 1984; designated Approved Counsel, Brotherhood Maintenance of Way Employees, Washington, 1989. Fellow ATLA (railroad litigation sect. 1992-94), Acad. Rail Labor Attys. (chmn. occupational disease divsn. 1990-93, Advocate of Yr. 1992). Democrat. Avocations: horse breeding, tng., long distance running. Product liability, Toxic tort, Labor. Office: John Roven & Assocs PC 9575 Katy Fwy Ste 400 Houston TX 77024-1411

**ROVINE, ARTHUR WILLIAM,** lawyer; b. Phila., Apr. 29, 1937; s. George Isaac and Rosanna (Lipsitz) R.; m. Phyllis Ellen Hamburger, Apr. 7, 1963; children: Joshua, Deborah. AB, U. Pa., 1958; LLB, Harvard U., 1961; PhD, Columbia U., 1966. Bar: D.C. 1964, N.Y. 1984. Assoc. Curtis, Mallet-Prevost, Colt & Mosle, N.Y.C., 1964-66; asst. prof. Cornell U., Ithaca, N.Y., 1966-72; editor Digest of U.S. Practice in International Law U.S. Dept. State, Washington, 1972-75, asst. legal adviser, 1975-81; agt of U.S. Govt. to Iran-U.S. Claims Tribunal U.S. Dept. State, The Hague, Netherlands, 1981-83; of counsel Baker & McKenzie, N.Y.C., 1983-85, ptnr., then sr. ptnr., 1985—; adj. prof. law Georgetown U., Washington, 1977-81; vis. lectr. law Yale U., 1998. Author: The First Fifty Years: The Secretary-General in World Politics, 1920-1970, 1970; editor: Digest of U.S. Practice in International Law, 1973, 74; co-editor: The Case Law of the International Court of Justice, 1968, 1972, 1974, 1976; bd. editors Am. Jour. Internat. Law, 1977-87; also articles on internat. law. Mem. panel on settlement of transnat. bus. disputes, N.Y. panel Ctr. for Pub. Resources; chmn. law subcom. of internat. adv. coun. on profl. edn. Coun. on Internat. Ednl. Exch.; mem. Coun. on Fgn. Rels. Mem. ABA (chmn. internat. law sect. 1985-86, del. to Ho. of Dels. 1988-90), Am. Soc. Internat. Law (cert. of merit 1974, exec. coun. 1975-77, v.p. 1998-99, pres.-elect 1999—), U.S. Coun. for Internat. Bus. (arbitration com.), Am. Arbitration Assn. (panel of arbitrators), Assn. of Bar of City of N.Y. (coun. on internat. affairs). Private international, Federal civil litigation, Alternative dispute resolution. Home: 150 E 61st St New York NY 10021-8529 Office: Baker & McKenzie 805 3rd Ave New York NY 10022-7513

**ROVIRA, LUIS DARIO,** state supreme court justice; b. San Juan, P.R., Sept. 8, 1923; s. Peter S. and Mae (Morris) R.; m. Lois Ann Thau, June 25, 1966; children—Douglas, Merilyn. B.A., U. Colo., 1948, LL.B., 1950. Bar: Colo. 1950. Justice Colo. Supreme Ct., Denver, 1979-95, chief justice, 1990-95, ret., 1995; mem. Pres.'s Com. on Mental Retardation, 1970-71; chmn. State Health Facilities Council, 1967-76. Bd. dirs Children's Hosp.; trustee Temple Buell Found., Denver Found., Harry S. Truman Scholarship Found. With AUS, 1943-46. Mem. ABA, Colo. Bar Assn., Denver Bar Assn. (pres. 1970-71), Colo. Assn. Retarded Children (pres. 1968-70), Alpha Tau Omega, Phi Alpha Delta. Clubs: Athletic (Denver), Country (Denver). Home: 4810 E 6th Ave Denver CO 80220-5137

**ROVNER, ILANA KARA DIAMOND,** federal judge; b. Riga, Latvia, Aug. 21, 1938; came to U.S., 1939; d. Stanley and Ronny (Medalje) Diamond; m. Richard Nyles Rovner, Mar. 9, 1963; 1 child, Maxwell Rabson. AB, Bryn Mawr Coll., 1960; postgrad., U. London King's Coll., 1961, Georgetown U., 1961-63; JD, Ill. Inst. Tech., 1966; LittD (hon.), Rosary Coll., 1989, Mundelein Coll., 1989; DHL (hon.), Spertus Coll. of Judaica, 1992. Bar: Ill. 1972, U.S. Dist. Ct. (no. dist.) Ill. 1972, U.S. Ct. Appeals (7th cir.) 1977, U.S. Supreme Ct. 1981, Fed. Trial Bar (no. dist.) Ill. 1982. Jud. clk. U.S. Dist. Ct. (no. dist.) Ill., Chgo., 1972-73; asst. U.S. atty. U.S. Atty.'s Office, Chgo., 1973-77; dep. chief of pub. protection, 1975-76, chief pub. protection, 1976-77; dep. gov., legal counsel Gov. James R. Thompson, Chgo., 1977-84; dist. judge U.S. Dist. Ct. (no. dist.) Ill., Chgo., 1984-92; cir. judge U.S. Ct. Appeals (7th cir.), Chgo., 1992—. Trustee Bryn Mawr Coll., Pa., 1983-89; mem. bd. overseers Ill. Inst. Tech./Kent Coll. Law, 1983—; trustee Ill. Inst. Tech., 1989—; mem. adv. coun. Rush Ctr. for Sports Medicine, Chgo., 1991-96; bd. dirs. Rehab. Inst. Chgo., 1998—; civil justice reform act adv. com. for the 7th cir., Chgo., 1991-95; bd. vis. No. Ill. U. Coll. Law, 1992-94; vis. com. Northwestern U. Sch. Law, 1993—, U. Chgo. Law Sch., 1993-96, 7th cir. race and gender fairness com., 1993—, U.S. Ct. Appeals (7th cir.) fairness com., 1996—, 7th cir. gender study task force, 1995-96; chair Ill. state selection com., Rhodes Scholarship Trust, 1998. Recipient Spl. Commendation award U.S. Dept. Justice, 1975, Spl. Achievement award 1976, Ann. Nat. Law and Social Justice Leadership award League to Improve the Cmty., 1975, Ann. Guardian Police award, 1977, Profl. Achievement award Ill. Inst. Tech., 1986, Louis Dembitz Brandeis medal for Disting. Legal Svc. Brandeis U., 1993, 1st Woman award, Valparaiso U. Sch. Law, 1993, ORT Women's Am. Cmty. Svc. award, 1987-88, svc. award Spertus Coll. of Judaica, 1987, Ann. award Chgo. Found. for Women, 1990, Arabella Babb Mansfield award Nat. Assn. Women Lawyers, 1998, award Chgo. Attys. Coun. of Hadassah, 1999; named Today's Chgo. Woman of Yr., 1985, Woman of Achievement Chgo. Women's Club, 1986, others; Hebrew Immigrant Aid Soc. Chgo. 85th Anniversary honoree, 1996; named one of 15 Chgo. Women of the Century, Chgo. Sun-Times, 1999. Mem. ABA (judges adv. com. to standing com. on ethics and profl. responsibility 1997—), Fed. Bar Assn. (jud. selection com. Chgo. chpt. 1977-80, treas. Chgo. chpt. 1978-79, sec. Chgo. chpt. 1979-80, 2d v.p. Chgo. chpt. 1980-81, 1st v.p. Chgo. chpt. 1981-82, pres. Chgo. chpt. 1982-83, 2d v.p. 7th cir. 1983-84, v.p. 7th cir. 1984-85), Fed. Judges Assn., Nat. Assn. Women Judges, Women's Bar Assn. Ill. (ann. award 1989, 1st Myra Bradwell Woman of Achievement award 1994), Chgo. Bar Assn. (commendation def. of prisoners com. 1987), Chgo. Coun. Lawyers, Decalogue Soc. of Lawyers (citation of honor 1991, merit award 1997), Kappa Beta Pi, Phi Alpha Delta (hon.). Republican. Jewish. Office: 219 S Dearborn St Ste 2774 Chicago IL 60604-1803

**ROWAN, ROBERT ALLEN,** lawyer; b. New Orleans, Nov. 15, 1947; s. Robert Leroy and Mary Louise (Brockmeyer) R.; m. Gillian Halpenny, Aug. 11, 1974; children: Matthew, Christian, Megan. BA, U. Mo., 1970; JD, U. Mich., 1973. Bar: Hawaii 1973, U.S. Dist. Ct. Hawaii 1973, U.S. Claims Ct. 1974, U.S. Tax Ct. 1975, U.S. Ct. Appeals (9th cir.) 1975, U.S. Supreme Ct. 1978, U.S. Ct. Appeals (fed. cir.) 1985, D.C. 1985, Md. 1986, U.S. Dist. Ct. (ea. dist.) Va. 1989, U.S. Ct. Appeals (4th and 5th cirs.) 1989, U.S. Ct. Appeals (2d cir.) 1994, U.S. Dist. Ct. (so. and no. dists.) N.Y. 1996, U.S. Dist. Ct. (we. dist.) Wash. 1998, U.S. Dist. Ct. (no. dist.) Ill. 1998, U.S. Dist. Ct. Del. 1999. From assoc. to co-mng. ptnr. Cades, Schutte, Fleming & Wright, Honolulu, Washington, 1973-88; ptnr. Fleischman & Walsh, Washington, 1988; shareholder, dir., trustee, pension fund Nixon & Vanderhye, Arlington, Va., 1988—; Bd. dirs. Sports Therapy Svc., Inc., McLean, Va.; panelist Hawaii State Bar, Honolulu, 1980, 83; lectr. Construction Industry Mfrs. Assn., 1996. Commr. McLean Youth Inc. Basketball, 1990-92. Mem. Va. State Bar Assn., D.C. Bar., Md. Bar, Hawaii State Bar Assn. Avocations: coaching, kayaking, boating, bicycling. Federal civil litigation, Patent, Trademark and copyright. Office: Nixon & Vanderhye 1100 N Glebe Rd Ste 800 Arlington VA 22201-5791

**ROWDEN, MARCUS AUBREY,** lawyer, former government official; b. Detroit, Mar. 13, 1928; s. Louis and Gertrude (Lifsitz) Rosenzweig; m. Justine Leslie Bessman, July 21, 1950; children: Gwen, Stephanie. B.A. in Econs, U. Mich., Ann Arbor, 1950, J.D. with distinction, 1953. Bar: Mich. 1953, D.C. 1978. Trial atty. Dept. Justice, 1953-58; legal advisor U.S. Mission to European Communities, 1959-62; solicitor, assoc. gen. counsel, gen. counsel AEC, 1965-74; commr., chmn. U.S. NRC, Washington, 1975-77; 2tnr. Fried, Frank, Harris, Shriver and Jacobson, Washington, 1977—. Served with AUS, 1946-47. Decorated officer Order Legion of Honor Republic of France; Recipient Disting. Service award AEC, 1972. Mem. Am., Fed., Mich., D.C. bar assns., Internat. Nuclear Law Assn., Order of Coif. Home: 7937 Deepwell Dr Bethesda MD 20817-1927 Office: Fried Frank Harris Shriver and Jacobson 1001 Pennsylvania Ave NW Washington DC 20004-2505

**ROWE, DAVID WINFIELD,** lawyer; b. Chgo., Nov. 7, 1954; s. Bernard John and Gertrude Katherine (Johnson) R.; m. Martha Lynn Plott, June 12, 1977; children: Daniel, Peter. BA, Davidson Coll., 1976; PhD in Psychology, U. Tenn., 1981; JD, U. Mich., 1987. Bar: Colo. 1987, U.S. Dist. Ct. Colo. 1987, U.S. Ct. Appeals (10th cir.) 1987, Nebr. 1989, U.S. Dist. Ct. Nebr. 1989. Vis. asst. prof. Davidson (N.C.) Coll., 1981-82; mental health worker Peninsula Psychiat. Hosp., Louisville, 1982-84; asst. prof. dept. psychology U. Tenn., Knoxville, 1982-84; assoc. Gorsuch, Kirgis, Campbell, Walker & Grover, Denver, 1987-89; NIMH postdoctoral fellow in law and psychology U. Nebr., Lincoln, 1989-91; ptnr. Kinsey, Ridenour, Becker & Kistler, Lincoln, Nebr., 1991—; mem. interim study group on foster care Health and Human Svcs. com. Nebr. State Legislature, 1990-91; adj. prof. psychology U. Nebr., Lincoln, 1992-94; bd. dirs., treas. Lincoln Attention Ctr. for Youth; mem. Lincoln Mediation Ctr. Author: (with others) Dimensions of Child Advocacy: Advocating for the Child in Protection Proceedings, 1990, Children Under Three in Foster Care, 1991. Exec. com. Lancaster County Rep. Com., 1991-97, chmn., 1993-95; bd. dirs. Lincoln-Lancaster Mental Health Found., 1993—, v.p., 1995-96, pres., 1996-97; mem. Ctrl. Com. Nebr. Rep. Com., 1993-97; mem. exec. com. Nebr. Rep. Com., 1993-97; deacon Westminster Prebyn. Ch., 1996-99. Mem. ABA, Nebr. Bar Assn. (alternative dispute resolution com. 1990—), Kiwanis (pres. Lincoln 1997—). General civil litigation, Bankruptcy, Family and matrimonial. Office: Kinsey Ridenour Becker & Kistler 206 S 13th St Lincoln NE 68508-2040

**ROWE, ELIZABETH WEBB,** office administrator; b. Canton, Ohio, Dec. 2, 1957; d. Thomas Dudley Webb and Verity Elizabeth (Voight) O'Brien; m. David Lee Rowe, June 21, 1986; children: Schuyler Jourdan, Thomas Prentiss. AB in History, Mt. Holyoke Coll., 1979. Legal asst. Wilkie Farr & Gallagher, N.Y.C., 1979-82, legal asst. supr., 1983-88, adminstrv. asst., 1988-89; outreach dir. St. Bartholomew's Ch., 1989-93, dir. comm., 1991-93; paralegal mgr. Patterson, Belknap, Webb & Tyler LLP, N.Y.C., 1993-98; office mgr. Alpha N.Am., N.Y.C., 1998—; legal asst. Cmty. Law Offices, N.Y.C., 1980-82; clerical asst. 17th Precinct Police Detective, N.Y.C., 1981-82. Chair homeless shelter St. Bartholomew's Ch., N.Y.C., 1984-85; vol. Breakfast Feeding Program, 1983-92, mem. Comty. Ministry Coun., 1986-88, 93-96; mem. N.Y. Jr. League, 1979-94; Pres.'s Coun. Mt. Holyoke Coll., 1988-91; rep. Mt. Holyoke Coll. Alumnae Fund, 1986-89, 94—, class officer, 1989-94; bd. dirs. 509 E. 83d St. Corp., E. 67th St. Owners, Inc., Emma J. Adams Meml. Fund, Mid-Manhattan Ctr., Inc. Recipient Mary Lyon award Mt. Holyoke Coll., 1994. Home: 133 E 80th St Apt 2C New York NY 10021-0305 Office: Alpha N Am 109 E 50th St New York NY 10022-6804

**ROWE, JOHN R.,** lawyer; b. Glens Falls, N.Y., Feb. 6, 1943; s. Robert W. and Ruth R. R.; m. Gail H. Naylor, Feb. 8, 1964 (div. Feb. 1976); m. Judy Wyatt, May 8, 1993; children: Leslie Renk, John Jr., Jeffrey, Teresa. BA in Polit. Sci., U. Idaho, 1964; JD, George Washington U., 1967. Bar: Idaho, U.S. Dist. Ct. Idaho 1967, D.C. 1968. Dep. pros. atty. Ada County, Boise, 1968-70; pvt. practice Boise, 1971-72, 79-85; assoc. Moffatt, Thomas, Barrett & Blanton, Boise, 1972-75; ptnr. Tway & Rowe, Boise, 1975-76; counsel Idaho State Bar, 1977-78; dir. gov. rels. Rural Metro Corp., Scottsdale, Ariz., 1986-89; sr. atty. Am. W. Airlines, Phoenix, 1989-95; assoc. Hopkins, Roden, Crockett, Hansen & Hoopes, PLLC, Boise, 1996-99. Pres. Scottsdale Cmty. Theatre, 1991-94; sec. Ada County Indsl. Devel. Bd., Boise, 1997—. Mem. Idaho State Bar Profl. Conduct Bd., Rotary (sgt. of arms 1998—). Avocations: golfing, acting and directing film, video, theatre. Alternative dispute resolution, Contracts commercial, Entertainment. Office: Rowe Law Offices PLLC 1509 Tyrell Ln Ste D Boise ID 83706-4063

**ROWE, LARRY JORDAN,** lawyer; b. Boston, May 24, 1958; s. Benson and Marcia Rowe; m. Nancy Ellen Cardinal; children; Jonathan B., Elizabeth J. AB, Dartmouth Coll., 1980; MPP, Harvard U., 1984, JD, 1984. Bar: Mass. 1985, U.S. Dist. Ct. Mass. Assoc. Ropes & Gray, Boston, 1984-93, ptnr., 1993—. Mem. Sudbury (Mass.) Fin. Com., 1998—; pres. Hillel Found. New Eng., 1991-94, bd. dirs., 1986—. Mem. ABA, Mass. Bar Assn., Boston Bar Assn. General corporate, Securities, Non-profit and tax-exempt organizations. Home: 10 Spiller Cir Sudbury MA 01776-2681 Office: Ropes & Gray 1 International Pl Fl 4 Boston MA 02110-2624

**ROWLAND, MAUREEN L.,** lawyer; b. Hazleton, Pa., Oct. 7, 1963; d. Francis A. and Mary Jane Rowland; m. Bryan Keith Johnson, Aug. 3, 1985 (div. 1992); m. Christopher M. Streett, May 28, 1994. BA in History, U. Scranton, 1984; JD, U. Md., 1988. Bar: U.S. Ct. Appeals Md. Assoc. publs. dir. MICPEL, Balt., 1988-91; asst. pub. defender Office of Pub. Defender, Balt., 1991-97; assoc. litigation atty. Law Offices of Michael H. Burgoyne, Towson, Md., 1998—; truste MICPEL, Balt., 1991—; advisor Harford C.C., Bel Air, Md., 1997—. Editor Practice Manual for the Maryland Lawyer, 1992, 93, 94, 95, 96, 97, Practice in the District Court of Maryland--Criminal, 1993, 95, 97, Maryland D.W.I., 1998. Mem. City of Bel Air Bd. Appeals, 1998; advisor Rt. 1 Overlay Task Force, Bel Air, 1998. Recipient Cert. of Appreciation, People's Pro Bono Action Ctr., 1998. Mem. ABA (dist. 8 rep. young lawyers divsn. 1995-96), Md. State Bar Assn. (mem. Leadership Acad. 1996—, chairperson young lawyers sect. 1997-98). Roman Catholic. Avocations: dogs, skiing, reading. E-mail: mrowland@crosslink.net. Fax: 410-847-9689. Office: Law Office of Michael H Burgoyne 305 Washington Ave Ste 501 Towson MD 21204-4747

**ROWLAND, ROBERT ALEXANDER, III,** lawyer; b. McAllen, Tex., Apr. 27, 1943; s. Robert Alexander Jr. and Marguerite (Gerry) R.; m. Victoria Nalle, Apr. 2, 1977; children: Julia Marie, Emily Nalle. BS, Tex. A&M U., 1966; JD, George Washington U., 1972. Bar: Tex. 1972, U.S. Dist. Ct. (so. dist.) Tex. 1973, U.S. Ct. Appeals (5th cir.) 1973, U.S. Supreme Ct. 1976, U.S. Dist. Ct. (no. dist.) Tex. 1979, U.S. dist. Ct. (we. dist.)( Tex. 1982, U.S. Dist. Ct. (ea. dist.) Tex. 1983. Law clk. U.S. Ct. Appeals (5th cir.), Houston, 1973-74; assoc. Vinson & Elkins, Houston, 1975-81; ptnr. susman, Godfrey & McGowan, Houston, 1982-88; mng. dir. Johnson and Gibbs, Houston, 1988-91; ptnr. Hutcheson & Grundy, LLP, Houston, 1992-94; chmn., CEO Associated Counsel of Am., 1995—. Bd. dirs. The Vol. Ctr., Houston, 1975-84, pres., 1982-83; founding mem. bd. dirs. Tex. Accts. and Lawyers for Arts, 1979-92, pres., 1989-91; bd. dirs. Contemporary Art Mus. Houston, 1974-80, 91-94, Sarah Campbell Blaffer Gallery of Art U. Houston, 1989-94, Tex. Opera Theater, 1988-89, Houston parks Bd., 1993—, Nat. Recreation and Park Assn., 1992-95; mem. devel. coun. sch. liberal arts Tex. A&M U., 1992—; co-chair Mayor's Transition Com. on Parks of City of Houston, 1992-94. Capt. U.S. Army, 1966-69, Vietnam. Fellow Cultural Arts Coun. Houston, 1981-86. Fellow Houston Bar Found., Tex. Bar Found.; mem. Houston Bar Assn. (dir. 1979-88, sec. 1984-85, second v.p. 1985-86, chmn. law and the art com. 1984-85), State Bar Tex., Houston Young Lawyers Assn. (bd. dirs. 1975-79, pres. 1978-79), River Oaks Country Club, Coronado Club, Phi Delta Phi. Episcopalian. Federal civil litigation, State civil litigation. Home: PO Box 131149 Houston TX 77219-1149 Office: Associated Counsel Am Inc Ste 125 4605 Post Oak Pl Houston TX 77027-9744

**ROWLETT, ROBERT DUANE,** lawyer; b. Oceanside, Calif., June 13, 1962; s. Duane R. and Ann Margaret Lewis. BSME, U. Calif., Santa Barbara, 1985, MSME, 1987; JD, U. San Diego, 1995. Bar: Calif. 1995; registered profl. engr., Calif. Project engr. Bardex Corp., Goleta, Calif., 1985-87; sr. engr. Gen. Atomics, Inc., La Jolla, Calif., 1987-92; patent counsel 3D Systems, Inc., Valencia, Calif., 1995-96; patent atty. Howard, Rice, Nemerovski, et al, Pasadena, Calif., 1997—. Mem. Am. Intellectual Property Law Assn., Orange County Bar Assn. Democrat. Roman Catholic. Avocations: surfing, fishing. Intellectual property, Patent, Trademark and copyright. Office: Howard Rice Nemerovski et al 610 Newport Center Dr Ste 450 Newport Beach CA 92660-6435

**ROWLEY, GEORGE HARDY,** lawyer; b. Greenville, Pa., May 30, 1923; s. George H. and Susan Mossman (Templeton) R.; m. Rosamond Kahle, Sept. 23, 1950 (dec. July 1997). Student, Thiel Coll., 1941-42; BA, Yale U., 1947; JD, Harvard U., 1949. Bar: Pa. 1950, U.S. Supreme Ct. 1974. Asst. U.S. atty. Western Dist. Pa., 1950-52; of counsel Rowley, Wallace, Keck, Karson & St. John, Greenville, Pa., 1952—; mem. Greenville adv. bd. First Seneca Bank, Butler, Pa., dist. trial nominating commn., 1973-75. Sec. bd. trustees Greenville Hosp. Lt. (j.g.) USN, 1943-46. Fellow Am. Coll. Trial Lawyers; mem. ABA, Pa. Bar Assn., Mercer County Bar Assn., Def. Rsch. Inst., Iroquois Boating & Fishing Club, Greenville Country Club. Insurance, General civil litigation. Home: 157 Plum St Greenville PA 16125-1764 Office: Rowley Wallace Keck Karson & St John PO Box 510 Greenville PA 16125-0510

**ROWLEY, GLENN HARRY,** lawyer; b. Hyannis, Mass., May 16, 1948; s. Harold Frederick and Olive Nellie (Jones) R.; 1 child, Brewster Westgate. BBA, U. Mass., 1970; JD with cum laude, Western New Eng. Coll., 1980. Bar: Mass. 1980, U.S. Dist. Ct. Mass. 1981, U.S. Tax Ct. 1981; cert. elder law atty. Nat. Elder Law Found./ABA. Staff mem. Cape Cod Planning and Econ. Devel. Commn., Barnstable, Mass., 1975-76; staff, estate planning tax dept. Coopers and Lybrand, Springfield, Mass., 1980-81; legal assoc. Roberts and Farrell, West Chatham, Mass., 1982-84; ptnr. Roberts, Farrell & Rowley, West Chatham, 1984-97; pvt. practice, 1997—; cons. Local Citizen Scholarship Trusts, Harwich and Chatham, Mass., 1985—. Contbr.: (weekly news column) The Cape Codder, The Enterprise, The Register, others.; contbr. articles to profl. jours. Founding mem. Brewster (Mass.) Conservation Trust, 1984; past elected mem. Brewster Hist. Dist. Com., 1975; mem. adv. bd. The May Inst., The Cape Cod Writers Ctr., Inc. With USN, 1971-74, Iceland. Recipient Am. Jurisprudence awards Lawyers Co-op. Pub. Co., 1978, 79. Mem. Mass. Bar Assn., Ocean Edge Exec. Club, Profl. Writers of Cape Cod, Cape Cod Estate Planning Coun., Nat. Acad. Elder Law Attys., Phi Delta Phi. Avocations: travel, writing. Estate planning, Probate, Estate taxation. Home: Annaniases Knoll/Sheep Pond Brewster MA 02631 Office: The Marketplace PO Box 1489 26 George Ryder Rd S West Chatham MA 02669

**ROY, ARTHUR PUTNAM,** lawyer; b. Baton Rouge, Nov. 23, 1940; s. Chalmer John and Elizabeth Putnam (Richards) R.; m. Sara Hinrichsen, Mar. 16, 1963; children: Mary Louise Manchadi, Christine Elizabeth Roy Yoder, Sara Katherine Allex. BS, Iowa State U., 1962; JD, U. Colo., 1969. Bar: Colo., 1969, U.S. Dist. Ct. Colo., 1969, U.S. Ct. Appeals (10th cir.), 1972, U.S. Supreme Ct., 1973. Pvt. practice Ft. Collins, Colo., 1969-70; assoc. counsel State Bd. Agriculture, Ft. Collins, 1970-73; dep. dist. atty. Office of Dist. Atty., Greeley, Colo., 1973-74; pvt. practice Greeley, Colo., 1974-94; judge Colo. Ct. Appeals, Denver, 1994—. Capt. USAR, 1963-74, Vietnam, 1965-66. Mem. ABA, Colo. Bar Assn. (v.p. 1984-85), Weld County Bar Assn. (pres. 1983-84), Greeley Redeye Rotary Club (pres. 1989-90). Republican. Congregational. Home: 1924 19th Ave Greeley CO 80631-5210 Office: Colo Ct Appeals 2 E 14th Ave Denver CO 80203-2115

**ROY, CHRISTOPHER DENIS,** lawyer; b. Barre, Vt., Dec. 3, 1964; s. Denis Antoine and Helen Christine (Christiansen) R.; m. Lisa Anne Johnson, May 15, 1993. BA, Harvard U., 1986; JD, Cornell U., 1989. Bar: Vt. 1989, U.S. Dist. Ct. Vt. 1990, U.S. Ct. Appeals (2d cir.) 1991. Law clk. to Hon. Albert W. Coffin U.S. Dist. Ct. for Vt., Burlington, 1989-90; dir. Downs Rachlin & Martin, PLLC, Burlington, 1990—; treas., bd. dirs. Williston (Vt.) Elder Housing, Inc., 1994-96. Mem. Burlington Planning Commn., 1991-93; v.p. Burlington City Rep. Com., 1991-93; pres. Pinecrest Village Assn., Williston, 1994-96; sec., exec. com. Vt. Rep. Party, 1997—; fin. chair Chittenden County Rep. Com., 1997—; chair Williston Town Rep. Com., 1997—. Mem. ABA, Vt. Bar Assn., Chittenden County Bar Assn., Nat. Sch. Bd. Assn., Vt. Sch. Bd. Assn., Williston-Richmond Rotary Club. Roman Catholic. Avocations: skiing, homebrewing, politics, bicycling, ice hockey. Land use and zoning (including planning), General civil litigation, Education and schools. Office: Downs Rachlin & Martin PLLC PO Box 190 199 Main St Burlington VT 05402-0190

**ROY, ELSIJANE TRIMBLE,** federal judge; b. Lonoke, Ark., Apr. 2, 1916; d. Thomas Clark and Elsie Jane (Walls) Trimble; m. James M. Roy, Nov. 23, 1943; 1 son, James Morrison. JD, U. Ark., Fayetteville, 1939; LLD (hon.), U. Ark., Little Rock, 1978. Bar: Ark. 1939. Atty. Rose, Loughborough, Dobyns & House, Little Rock, 1940-41, Ark. Revenue Dept., Little Rock, 1941-42; mem. firm Reid, Evrard & Roy, Blytheville, Ark., 1945-54, Roy & Roy, Blytheville, 1954-63; law clk. Ark. Supreme Ct., Little Rock, 1963-65; assoc. justice Ark. Supreme Ct., 1975-77; U.S. dist. judge then sr. judge Ea. and We. Dists. Ark., Little Rock, 1977—; judge Pulaski County (Ark.) Cir. Ct., Little Rock, 1966; asst. atty. gen. Ark., Little Rock, 1967; sr. law clk. U.S. Dist. Ct., Little Rock and Ft. Smith, 1967-75; Mem. med. adv. com. U. Ark. Med. Center, 1952-54; Committeewoman Democratic Party 16th Jud. Dist., 1940-42; vice chmn. Ark. Dem. State Com., 1946-48; mem. chmn. com. Ark. Constnl. Commn., 1967-68. Recipient disting. alumnae citation U. Ark., 1978, Gayle Pettus Pontz award, 1986, Brooks Hays Meml. Christian Citizenship award, 1994; named Ark. woman of yr., Bus. and Profl. Women's Club, 1969, 76, outstanding appellate judge, Ark. Trial Lawyers Assn., 1976-77, Delta Theta Phi mem. of yr.

1989; named among top 100 women in Ark. bus., 1995; Paul Harris fellow Rotary Club Little Rock, 1992. Recipient disting. alumnae citation U. Ark., 1978, Gayle Pettus Pontz award, 1986, Brooks Hays Meml. Christian Citizenship award, 1994; named Ark. Woman of Yr., Bus. and Profl. Women's Club, 1969, 76, Outstanding Appellate Judge, Ark. Trial Lawyers Assn., 1976-77, Mem. of Yr., Delta Theta Phi, 1989; named among top 100 women in Ark. bus., 1995, Ark. Bus. Top 100 Women in Ark., 1995; Paul Harris fellow Rotary Little Rock, 1992. Office: US Dist Ct 600 W Capitol Ave Ste 423 Little Rock AR 72201-3326

**ROY, JAMES PARKERSON,** lawyer; b. Lafayette, La., Aug. 27, 1951; s. Joseph A. Roy II and Jewell (Parkerson) Lowe; m. Linda Ann Malin, Aug. 1975 (div. 1986); chidlren: John, James Jr., Christopher; m. Virginia R. Roy, 1990. BS, La. State U., 1973, JD, 1976; LLM, Georgetown U., 1977. Bar: La. 1976. Civil trial atty. Domengeaux, Wright & Roy, Lafayette, 1976—. Mem. ABA, Assn. Trial Lawyers Am., La. Trial Lawyers Assn. (pres. 1990-91), La. Bar Assn. Democrat. Episcopal. Avocations: hunting, boating, reading, travel. Admiralty, Personal injury, General civil litigation. Office: Domengeaux Wright & Roy 556 Jefferson St Ste 500 Lafayette LA 70501

**ROY, MATTHEW LANSING,** lawyer; b. Gainesville, Fla., May 5, 1968; s. Lansing John and JoAnn Ruth R.; m. Melinda Iresta Leaver, Aug. 15, 1993. BS in Acctg., Oral Roberts U., 1990; JD, U. Fla., 1993. Bar: S.C. 1994, Oreg. 1994. Atty. Drose, Davidson & Bennett, Greenville, S.C., 1993-94, Vick & Conroyd, Salem, Oreg., 1994—. Recipient Family Law Book award, U. Fla., 1993. Mem. ABA, New Lawyers Divsn. Oreg. State Bar Assn. (co-chair CLE com. 1996—). Republican. Avocations: hunting, fishing, skiing, golf, basketball. Personal injury, Workers' compensation, Product liability. Home: 1340 Roseway Ct SE Salem OR 97302-1818 Office: Vick & Conroyd 698 12th St SE Ste 200 Salem OR 97301-4010

**ROZAN, ALAIN,** lawyer; b. Cusset, France, Dec. 7, 1957; came to U.S., 1981; s. Jacques and Elaine R.; m. Elizabeth Armour, Mar. 5, 1985 (div. Dec. 1995); m. Kristine Hoff, Apr. 19, 1996. M of Bus. Law, Clermont-Ferrand Law Sch., France, 1979; JD, NYU, 1982. Bar: N.Y. 1985, U.S. Surpeme Ct. 1988. Assoc. Richard K. Bernstein Assocs., N.Y.C., 1982-89; founding ptnr. Rozan & Nilson, N.Y.C., 1989—. Mem. Voll. Lawyers for Arts. Democrat. Roman Catholic. Avocation: songwriting. Private international, Entertainment. Office: Rozan & Nilson 122 E 42d St New York NY 10168

**ROZANSKI, STANLEY HOWARD,** lawyer; b. N.Y.C., July 19, 1952; s. Israel and Frida (Huber) R.; m. Ilene Newman, Dec. 31, 1975; 1 child, Justin. BA, Hunter Coll., 1974; JD, San Fernando Coll. Law, 1977. Bar: Calif. 1978, U.S. Dist. Ct. (cen. dist.) Calif. 1978, U.S. Ct. Appeals (9th cir.) 1982. Ptnr. Rozanski & Friedland, L.A., 1980—, San Jose, Calif., 1983—, L.A., San Jose; judge pro tem L.A. County Cts., 1985—. Recipient Outstanding Contributions award State Bar Calif., 1985. Mem. Calif. Bar Assn., Assn. Trial Lawyers Am., Calif. Trial Lawyers Assn., L.A. Trial Lawyers Assn., ABA, L.A. County Bar Assn., Beverly Hills Bar Assn. Jewish. Avocations: skiing, swimming, golf. Criminal, Personal injury, Insurance. Office: Rozanski & Friedland 11601 Wilshire Blvd Ste 1480 Los Angeles CA 90025-1750

**ROZEL, SAMUEL JOSEPH,** lawyer; b. Louisville, Apr. 22, 1935; s. Sam and Anna (Sessmer) R.; m. Jeanne Frances Foulkes, July 3, 1965; children: Brooke Jane, John Samuel. BSL, U. Louisville, 1955, LLB, 1957; grad., Advanced Mgmt. Program, Harvard U., 1979. Bar: Ky. 1958, D.C. 1962, Minn. 1968, Ind. 1970, N.Y. 1983. Atty. FTC, Washington, 1962-67; antitrust counsel Honeywell, Inc., Mpls., 1967-69; atty. Magnavox Corp., Ft. Wayne, Ind., 1969-71, gen. counsel, 1971, v.p., 1972-75, sec., 1973-75; v.p. U.S. Philips Corp., N.Y.C., 1975-77, sr. v.p., 1977—; assoc. gen. counsel Philips Electronics N.Am. Corp., N.Y.C., sec. exec. mgmt. com., 1980—; v.p., sec., gen. counsel, dir. Phillips Electronics N.Am. Corp., N.Y.C., 1987-91, sr. v.p., sec., gen. counsel, mem. exec. com. bd. dirs., 1991—; bd. dirs. Philips Electronics N.Am. Corp., Philips Electronics N.Am. Region, Std. Communications Corp. Served to capt. JAGC, AUS, 1957-62. Mem. ABA, Fed. Bar Assn., Ky. Bar Assn., Ind. Bar Assn., N.Y. Bar Assn., Harvard Club (N.Y.C.), Met. Club (Washington). Home: 215 S Bald Hill Rd New Canaan CT 06840-2908 Office: Philips Electronics N Am 125 Park Ave New York NY 10017-5529

**ROZZELL, SCOTT ELLIS,** lawyer; b. Texarkana, Tex., Apr. 12, 1949; s. George M. and Dora Mae (Boyett) R.; m. Jackie Golden, June 1, 1996; children by previous marriage: Stacey Elizabeth, Kimberly Marie. BA, So. Meth. U., 1971; JD, U. Tex., 1975. Bar: Tex. 1975, U.S. Dist. Ct. (so. dist.) Tex. 1975, U.S. Dist. Ct. (no. dist.) Tex. 1977, U.S. Ct. Appeals (1st, 3d, 9th cirs.) 1977, U.S. Ct. Appeals (5th and D.C. cirs.) 1976. Assoc. Baker & Botts, Houston, 1975-82, ptnr., 1983—; mem. State of Tex. Aircraft Pooling Bd., 1997—; mem. devel. bd. U. of Tex. Health Sci. Ctr. Houston. Bd. dirs. Manned Space Flight Edn. Found., Inc., 1997—; vice chair Cancer Counseling Inc., Houston, 1991-92. Fellow Tex. Bar Found. (sustaining life), Houston Bar Found. (sustaining life, bd. dirs. 1991-93, chair 1993), Am. Bar Found.; mem. ABA, State Bar Tex. (bd. dirs. 1997—), Houston Bar Assn. (bd. dirs. 1991-95, pres. 1996-97), Fed. Energy Bar Assn., Houston Young Lawyers Assn. (bd. dirs. 1978-82, pres. 1983-84), Plaza Club (bd. dirs. 1995—). Republican. Presbyterian. Avocation: flying vintage airplanes. Public utilities, Administrative and regulatory. Home: 2740 Barbara Ln Houston TX 77005-3420 Office: Baker & Botts 3000 One Shell Plz 910 Louisiana St Ste 3000 Houston TX 77002-4991

**RUA, M. JANE,** lawyer; b. Crestline, Ohio, May 3, 1958; d. Stanley E. and Mildred Schneider; m. Ronald M. Rua, Mar. 15, 1991; 1 child, Alyson Elizabeth; stepchildren:; Robert, Ryan. BN, U. Toledo, 1980; JD, Ohio State U., 1986. Bar: Ohio 1986. Nurse U. Louisville Med. Ctr., 1980-82, Ohio State U. Hosp./Mercy Hosp., Columbus, 1982-86; lawyer Jeffries, Kube, Forrest & Monteleone Co., LPA, Cleve., 1986—. Mem. ATLA, Ohio Acad. Trial Lawyers, Lake County Bar Assn., Cleve. Bar Assn., Cleve. Acad. Trial Attys., Nat. Honor Soc., Sigma Theta Tau. Personal injury. Office: Jeffries Kube Forrest & Monteleone Co LPA 101 W Prospect Ave Ste 1650 Cleveland OH 44115-1093

**RUBACK, ALAN STEVEN,** lawyer; b. Bklyn., June 9, 1949; s. Isidore and Shirley Ruback; m. Carol Maselli, Jan. 24, 1976; children: Joshua, Jenna. BA, SUNY, Stony Brook, 1971; JD, New Eng. Sch. of Law, 1974. Bar: Mass. 1974, Fla. 1978, U.S. Dist. Ct. (5th dist.) Fla. 1978. Staff atty. Office of Hearings and Appeals Social Security Adminstrn., Raleigh, N.C., 1976-77, Miami, Fla., 1977-82, Ft. Lauderdale, Fla., 1982-83; ptnr. Connors Ruback & Koster P.A., Ft. Lauderdale, 1983-96; sole practice Ft. Lauderdale, 1996—. Mem. Nat. Orgn. Social Security Claimant's Reps. (sustaining), Mass. Bar Assn., Fla. Bar Assn., B'nai B'rith Justice League. Pension, profit-sharing, and employee benefits. Office: PO Box 1659 440 S Andrews Ave Fort Lauderdale FL 33301-2830

**RUBEL, ERIC A.,** lawyer; b. Hempstead, N.Y., July 12, 1960; s. Ralph and Josephine Rubel; m. Susan Rubel, Jan. 20, 1991; children: Alexaner, Molly. BA cum laude, Middlebury Coll., 1982; JD with highest honors, George Washington U., 1985. Law clk. to Hon. Jane Restani U.S. Ct. Internat. Trade, N.Y.C., 1985-86; gen. counsel U.S. Consumer Product Safety Commn., Washington, 1994-97; assoc. Arnold & Porter, Washington, 1986-94, ptnr., 1993-94, 97—. Mem. ABA (vice chair sect. adminstrv. law and regulatory practice 1997-98), Order of Coif. Federal civil litigation, Product liability, Administrative and regulatory. Office: Arnold and Porter 555 12th St NW Washington DC 20004-1206

**RUBEN, AUDREY H. ZWEIG,** lawyer, arbitrator, actress; b. Union City, N.J.; m. Robert J. Ruben; children: Pamela J. Ruben Golum, James B. BA, NYU, 1948; MA, Columbia U., 1953; JD, St. John's U., 1976. Bar: N.Y. 1977, U.S. Dist. Ct. (so. and ea. dists.) N.Y. 1977, U.S. Supreme Ct. 1982. Law intern Westchester Dist. Atty.'s Office, White Plains, N.Y., summer 1975, Westchester Legal Svcs., White Plains, 1976-77; assoc. Granik, Silverman, New City, N.Y., 1977-79, Pierro, Colangelo & Killea, Port Chester, N.Y., 1979-84; legal adminstr. Poloron Products, Harrison, N.Y., 1984-86; pvt. practice Rye, N.Y., 1986-90; arbitrator N.Y. State Office of Ct. Adminstrn., 1979-90, Am. Arbitration Assn., 1980—, Better Bus. Bur., 1980—, N.Y. Stock Exch., 1991—, Nat. Assn. Securities Dealers, 1991—, Pacific Stock Exch., 1993—; mediator Westchester Med. Ctr. Cluster-Westchester County, N.Y., 1984-90; law guardian Family Ct., Westchester County, 1979-84; guardian ad litem Surrogates Ct., Westchester, 1978-84. Theatre critic (newspaper) L.I. Herald; movie reviewer Saddleback Valley News; freelance children's book reviewer. Commr. Human Rights Commn., Rye, 1984-89, Rye Cable TV Commn., 1989-90; pres. LWV of Rye, 1971-73; bd. dirs. pub. rels. com. Community Media Orgns.; bd. dirs. Rye Youth Coun., 1974-80. Mem. ABA, Am. Arbitration Assn., N.Y. State Bar Assn., N.Y. Women's Bar Assn. (legis. and real property com.), Westchester County Bar Assn. (corp. law com.), Portchester/Rye Bar Assn., Internat. Fedn. Women Lawyers, Am. Judges Assn., Women in Law Depts., Columbia U. Club, Woman's Club (bd. dirs. 1966-90). Avocations: theatre, swimming, aerobics, skiing, dancing. Administrative and regulatory, Alternative dispute resolution. Home and Office: 21285 Amora Mission Viejo CA 92692-4930

**RUBENFELD, LEONARD,** lawyer; b. Peekskill, N.Y., May 7, 1912; s. Louis and Gussie Yormark R.; m. Amelia Kooperstein, Feb. 21, 1940; children: Sharon, Deborah. LLM, Fordham U., 1938. Bar: N.Y., U.S. Dist. Ct. (so. dist.) N.Y. Dist. atty. Westchester County Dist. Attys. Office. Staff sgt. U.S. Army, 1934-38. Republican. Jewish. Home: 1 Lakeview Dr Ph 4 Peekskill NY 10566-2236

**RUBENSTEIN, ALAN MORRIS,** district attorney; b. Phila., Mar. 13, 1946; s. Philip and Lilyian Ruth (Eveloff) R.; m. Marilynn Z. Rubenstein, Mar. 31, 1973; children: Samuel Alex, Justin Simon. BA in History, Temple U., 1967; JD, U. Toledo, 1970. Bar: Pa. 1971, U.S. Dist. Ct. (ea. dist.) Pa. 1971, U.S. Ct. Appeals (3d cir.) 1985, U.S. Supreme Ct. 1980. Pvt. practice Phila., 1970-73; asst. dist. atty. Bucks County Dist. Atty.'s Office, Doylestown, Pa., 1973-75, dep. dist. atty., 1975-79, chief dep. dist. atty., chief trials, 1979-83, 1st asst. dist. atty., 1983-86, dist. atty., 1986—; mem. law enforcement coordinating com. for ea. dist. Pa., U.S. Dept. Justice. Mem. drug task force adv. com. Office Atty. Gen., Commonwealth of Pa.; mem. Bucks County Prison Adv. Bd.; bd. dirs. Bucks County Hero Scholarship Fund; advisor, bd. dirs. for Southeastern Pa., Joe Frazier's Golden Gloves; judge Pa. Athletic Commn., Del. Boxing Commn., N.J. Athletic Control Bd. Recipient award for outstanding performance and svc. to cmty. Fraternal Order Police, Phila., 1987, Disting. Pub. Svc. award County and State Detectives Assn. Pa., 1989, award for outstanding svc. in field law enforcement Delaware Valley Assn. Profl. Police Ofcls., 1991, Law Enforcement commendation medal Valley Forge chpt. Nat. Soc. SAR, 1992, award in appreciation for svc. for drug and alcohol prevention through edn. Nat. Awareness Found., 1996, N.E. Cmty. Svc. award, 1996, Diamond Achievement award in social scis. Temple U. Coll. Arts and Scis., 1997. Mem. ATLA, Am. Coll. Pros. Attys., Assn. Govt. Attys. in Capital-Death Penalty Litigation, Am. Judicature Soc., Pa. Dist. Attys. Assn. (exec. com. 1985-97, sec.-treas. 1989-90, v.p. 1990-91, pres. 1991-92, Pa. Dist. Attys. Inst. (bd. dirs. 1986-97, pres. 1993-94, 96-97), Order Ky. Cols., Phi Alpha Delta. Republican. Jewish. Office: Bucks County Dist Atty's Office Main and Court Sts Doylestown PA 18901

**RUBENSTEIN, ANDREA FICHMAN,** lawyer; b. Hartford, Conn., Dec. 6, 1947; d. Milton and Sara (Bronstein) Fichman; m. James Arthur Rubenstein, Aug. 23, 1970; children: Daniel H.F., Rebecca C.F. BA, Wheaton Coll., 1969; JD, U. Minn., 1977. Bar: Minn. 1978, U.S. Dist. Ct. Minn. 1986, U.S. Ct. Appeals (8th cir.) 1995. Atty. Law Offices of Cooper et al, Mpls., 1978-80; assoc. atty. Arthur, Chapman & Michaelson, P.A., Mpls., 1980-83; atty., of counsel Hedin Law Office, Mpls., 1985—; pres., bd. dirs. Mpls. Legal Aid Soc., 1985—; pres., chair pers. com. Minn. Women's Fund, Mpls., 1995—. Dir. Alternatives for People with Autism, Brooklyn Park, Minn., 1981—; bd. dirs. Mpls. YWCA, 1983-89. Mem. Nat. Employment Lawyers Assn. (Mpls. chpt. 1993—), Hennepin County Bar Assn. (dist. ethics com. 1983-88, 90-97, 98—). Fax: 612-871-1312. Labor, Civil rights. Office: Hedin & Goldberg PA 2100 Stevens Ave S Minneapolis MN 55404-2533

**RUBENSTEIN, JAY D.,** lawyer, consultant; b. Paterson, N.J., Aug. 8, 1947; s. Julius and Sylvia D. (Krieger) R.; m. Gena I. Connolly Fischer, May 21, 1989. BA, Rutgers Coll., 1969; JD, Rutgers Sch. of Law, 1973. Bar: N.J. 1973, Idaho 1974; N.Y. 1983; U.S. Dist. Ct. N.J. 1973, U.S. Dist. Ct. Idaho 1974; U.S. Ct. Appeals (3rd cir.) 1982; U.S. Supreme Ct. 1982. Atty. VISTA Western Idaho Legal Aid Svcs., Caldwell, Idaho, 1973-74; atty. assoc. Rubenstein & Sherwood, Esqs., Totowa, N.J., 1975-81; atty. shareholder Stern Steiger Croland, P.A., Parmus, N.J., 1981-95; ptnr. Shapiro & Croland, Esqs., Hackensack, N.J., 1995—. Trustee and gen. counsel The Milton Schamach Found., Inc., N. Haledon, N.J., 1982—. Mem. ABA, N.J. State Bar Assn., Bergen County Bar Assn., Passaic County Bar Assn., Idaho State Bar Assn. Appellate, Family and matrimonial, Estate planning. Office: Shapiro & Croland Esqs 411 Hackensack Ave Hackensack NJ 07601-6328

**RUBENSTEIN, JOSHUA SETH,** lawyer; b. Bklyn., Aug. 5, 1954; s. Seth and Elaine (Freedman) R.; m. Marta Johnson: children: Mary-Jane, Kenan, Rebecca, Marlena. BA magna cum laude, Columbia U., 1976, JD, 1979. Bar: N.Y. 1980, N.J. 1980, U.S. Dist. Ct. (ea. dist.) N.Y. 1980, U.S. Dist. Ct. (so. dist.) N.Y. 1980, U.S. Dist. Ct. N.J. 1980, U.S. Tax Ct. 1986. Assoc. Fried, Frank, Harris, Shriver & Jacobson, N.Y.C., 1979-82; assoc. Rosenman & Colin LLP, N.Y.C., 1982-88, ptnr., 1988—, chmn., 1999—; mgmt. com. Rosenman & Colin, N.Y.C., 1994—, chmn. trusts & Estates dept., 1995—; adv. bd. TE/DEC Systems, Inc., Jour. N.Y. Taxation; lectr. in field; adv. com. on surrogate's cts. Office of Ct. Adminstrn., 1997—; adv. coun. Columbia Law Sch. Trusts, Wills and Estate Planning, 1997—. Contbr. articles to legal publs. dir., sec. Irvington Inst. Med. Rsch., 1991, treas., 1991-92, sec., 1992-93, co-pres., 1993-94, pres., 1994—; chmn. estates and trust splty. group, chmn. splty. group; task force, mem. exec. com. lawyers divsn. United Jewish Appeal-Fedn., 1989-99; mem. legis. com., devel. com., bd. governance com., Madeleine Borg com., chmn., mem. exec. com., 1994—; trustee Jewish Bd. Family and Children's Svcs., 1991—. Recipient James H. Fogelson award Lawyer's divsn. United Jewish Appeal-Fedn., 1993; named to Best Lawyers in N.Y., N.Y. Mag. Fellow Am. Coll. Trusts and Estate Counsel (state laws com.), N.Y. State Bar Found.; mem. ABA (real property and probate sect.), Internat. Acad. Estate and Trust Law (academician 1997—), Practising Law Inst. (estate adv. com., lectr. 1984—, Hadassah estate planning seminar faculty and adv. bd. 1993—), N.Y. State Bar Assn. (trust and estate law sect., treas. 1997-98, sec. 1998-99, incoming chair 1999—, lect. 1984—, vice chmn. legis. com. 1988, chmn. 1988-91, co-chmn. ad hoc com. to rev. proposals of EPTL adv. com. of N.Y. State 1991—, mem.-at-large exec. com. 1992-95, liaison to legis. policy com. 1995—, Pres.'s Pro Bono Svc. award 1991, Exec. Com. award, 1992, 95, 96, treas. 1997), N.J. Bar Assn. adv. com. rels. with legis. and exec. brs., real property and probate sect.), Assn. of Bar of City of N.Y, Phi Beta Kappa. Democrat. Jewish. Estate planning, Probate, Estate taxation. Office: Rosenman & Colin 575 Madison Ave Fl 26 New York NY 10022-2585

**RUBENSTEIN, SARAH WRIGHT,** lawyer; b. N.Y.C., Nov. 7, 1970; d. Richard Wright and Deborah Wing (Rodgers) R.; m. Robert Henry Dubinsky, May 29, 1994. BA, Amherst Coll., 1992; JD, U. Chgo., 1997. Bar: Mo. 1998, Ill. 1998. Environ. cons. Environ. Ops. Inc., St. Louis, 1992-94; assoc. Sonnenschein Nath & Rosenthal, St. Louis, 1997—. Bd. dirs. Young Friends of Mo. Botanical Garden, 1997—. Democrat. Jewish. Avocations: horseback ridng, competing. General civil litigation, Environmental. Home: 7429 Parkdale Ave Saint Louis MO 63105-2909 Office: Sonnenschein Nath & Rosenthal One Met Sq Ste #3000 Saint Louis MO 63102

**RUBEO, STEPHEN VINCENT,** lawyer; b. Yonkers, N.Y., May 21, 1963; s. Elio and Elide Rubeo. BS, Manhattan Coll., Bronx, N.Y., 1985; JD, Pace U., White Plains, N.Y., 1992. Bar: N.Y. 1993, Conn. 1993; cert. police officer, N.Y. Police officer New Rochelle (N.Y.) Police Dept., 1986-91; atty. in sole practice, Yonkers, 1993—; atty. Fraternal Order of Police, Pelham, N.Y., 1996-98. Mem. Fedn. of Police, N.Y. State Bar Assn., N.Y. Criminal Defenders, Yonkers Lawyers Assn. (exec. bd. 1998—). Avocations: martial arts instruction. Criminal, General practice, Real property. Office: 23 Mcgeory Ave Yonkers NY 10708-6618

**RUBIN, ALLAN AVROM,** lawyer, regulatory agency consultant; b. Chgo., Feb. 2, 1916; s. Sol and Sadie (Bloom) R.; m. Harriet Ann Schainis, June 24, 1941; children: Sally Ann Rubin Kovacs, Donald Bruce. AB, U. Mich., 1937, JD, 1939. Bar: Ill. 1939, U.S. Dist. Ct. (no. dist.) Ill. 1939, U.S. Dist. Ct. D.C., U.S. Supreme Ct., Order of Coif. Atty. Randolph Bohrer Law Firm, Chgo., 1939-41; atty., counsel FCC, Washington, 1941-43; chief counsel OPA, Washington, 1943-46; regional counsel OPA, Chgo., 1946-50; pvt. practice Chgo., 1950-52; gen. counsel, exec. v.p. U.S. Brewers Assn., Washington, 1952-82; govt. counsel G. Heileman Brewing Co., Washington, 1982-89; pres. Allan A. Rubin, P.C., Washington, 1982—; cons., WOC (Pro Bono), Fed. Emergency Mgmt. Agy., Washington, 1968—; mem. Nat. Def. Exec. Res., Washington, 1968—; dir. legal adv. com. Am. Nat. Metric Coun., 1975-82, chmn., 1979-81. Editor Mich. Law Rev., 1938-39. Mem. ABA, FBA, Ill. Bar Assn., Army and Navy Club, Internat. Club, Order of Coif, Nat. Lawyers Club, Officers Clubs of Mil. Dist. of Washington. Home and Office: 9111 Kittery Ln Bethesda MD 20817-2138

**RUBIN, BURTON JAY,** lawyer, editor; b. Bklyn., Jan. 23, 1946; s. Samuel and Sidell (Greenfield) R.; m. Janice Ann Edelstein, Feb. 17, 1974; 1 child, Jennifer Sidell. AB in Biology, Guilford Coll., Greensboro, N.C., 1966; JD, U. N.C., 1969. Bar: Va. 1971, U.S. Dist. Ct. (ea. dist.) Va. 1997, U.S. Ct. Customs and Patent Appeals 1975. Legal editor Labor Rels. Reporter, Bur. Nat. Affairs, Inc., Washington, 1970; asst. editor U.S. Law Week, 1970-74, asst. mng. editor Patent, Trademark and Copyright Jour., 1974-75, mng. editor U.S. Patents Quar., 1975-85; atty. Am. Soc. Travel Agts., 1985-87, gen. counsel, 1987—, pvt. practice, 1990—; cons. Roundhouse Sq. Psychiat. Ctr., Alexandria, Va. Mem. Fairfax County Water Authority, Va.; mem. Fairfax County Police-Citizens Adv. Coun., 1982-83, alt. mem., 1984-85; mem. West Springfield Police-Citizens Adv. Com., 1979-85, chmn., 1981; bd. dirs. Bur. Nat. Affairs, 1984-85; mem. Fairfax County Rep. Com., 1982-85. Mem. ABA, Am. Soc. Assn. Execs. (legal counsel 1996—, vice chmn. 1997-98, chmn. 1998-99). Contbr. articles to profl. jours. Office: Am Soc Travel Agts 1101 King St Alexandria VA 22314-2944

**RUBIN, E(RWIN) LEONARD,** lawyer; b. Chgo., Jan. 11, 1933; s. Samuel and Frances Birdie (Rabin) R.; m. Stephanie Siegel, Mar. 4, 1961 (div. Dec. 1981); children: Matthew, Suzanne; m. Audrey Gay Holzer, May 8, 1983; children: Margot, Bette. Student, U. Ill., Urbana, 1948-51; AB, U. Miami, 1956, JD, 1959. s. N.Y. 1960, Ill. 1962, U.S. Dist. Ct. (no. dist.) Ill. 1962, U.S. Ct. Appeals (7th cir.) 1990. Assoc. Hays, St. John A&H, N.Y.C., 1960-62, Devoe, Shadur, Mikva & P., Chgo., 1962-65; gen. counsel Playboy Enterprises, Inc., Chgo., 1965-78; ptnr. E. Leonard Rubin Law Offices, Chgo., 1978-81, Epton, Mullin & Druth Ltd., Chgo., 1981-86, Brinks, Hofer, Gilson & Lione, Chgo., 1986-96, Gordon & Glickson, LLC, Chgo., 1996—; adj. prof. U. Ill., John Marshall Law Sch. Pres. Lawyers for Creative Arts, Chgo., 1983-85; chmn. bd. dirs. Mus. Holography; bd. dirs. Wisdom Bridge Theatre, Chgo., 1983-85. Cpl. U.S. Army, 1953-5, ETO. Mem. ABA, Ill. Bar Assn., Chgo. Bar Assn. (bd. mgrs. 1983-85, chmn. various coms., dir. Christmas Spirits Satire Show 1965—), Union Internat. Des Avocats (pres. intellectual property commn.), Copyright Soc. Am. (trustee, pres. midwest chpt.). Jewish. Trademark and copyright, Entertainment, Libel. Home: 270 Sunset Dr Northfield IL 60093-1047 Office: Gordon & Glickson LLC 444 N Michigan Ave Ste 3600 Chicago IL 60611-3901

**RUBIN, HERBERT,** lawyer; b. Lisbon, Conn., June 4, 1918; s. Simon and Rose (Berko) R.; m. Rose Luttan, July 6, 1941; children: Barbara, Caroline, Donald. AB, CCNY, 1938; JD, NYU, 1942. Bar: N.Y. 1942, U.S. Dist. Ct. (so. and ea. dists.) N.Y. 1951, U.S. Supreme Ct. 1956, U.S. Ct. Appeals (2d, 3d, 4th, 6th, 9th, 10th, D.C. cirs.). Assoc. Newman & Bisco, 1942; mem. faculty NYU Law Sch., 1946-50, 57-62; prof. creditors' rights Rutgers U. Law Sch., 1949-57; pvt. practice, 1946-47, 50-56; ptnr. Atkin & Rubin, 1948-50; ptnr. Sereni, Herzfeld & Rubin, and successor Herzfeld & Rubin, N.Y.C., 1956—, sr. ptnr., 1968—; instr. mil. law, 1944-46; prof. constl. law LIU, 1963-68; trustee North Shore L.I. Jewish Hosp. Editor-in-chief NYU Law Rev., 1940-41; bd. editors N.Y. Law Jour., 1971—; contbr. articles to profl. jours. Mem. N.Y. State Banking Bd., 1975-85, N.Y. State Jud. Selection Com., 1975-83, Sen. Moynihan's Jud. Selection Com., 1982—, Sen. Schumer's Jud. Selection Com., 1999—, City Charter Revision Commn., 1998—. 1st lt. Signal Corps, AUS, 1942-46. Recipient award NCCJ, 1967, United Jewish Appeal, 1968, 97, Israel Bonds, 1973, NYU Law Assn. award 1987, Judge Weinfeld award, 1992. Fellow Am. Bar Found.; mem. ABA (mem. coun. N.Y. state), N.Y. State Bar Assn., Queens County Bar Assn. (pres. 1970), Assn. Bar City Of N.Y., Fed. Bar Coun., City Downtown Club, World Trade Ctr. Club. Mem. Liberal Party. Jewish. General corporate, Private international, General civil litigation. Office: Herzfeld & Rubin 40 Wall St Fl 54 New York NY 10005-2301

**RUBIN, HOWARD JEFFREY,** lawyer; b. Phila., Apr. 8, 1947; s. Martin C. and Natalie S. (Lerner) R.; m. Nan H. Foster, June 30, 1974; children: Jacob S., Leslie D. BA, Colgate U., 1969; JD, Columbia U., 1972. Bar: N.Y. 1973, U.S. Dist. Ct. (so. and ea. dists) N.Y. 1974, U.S. Ct. Appeals (2d cir.) 1975, U.S. Supreme Ct. 1985. Staff atty. N.Y.C. Dept. Consumer Affairs, 1972-73; co-dir. employment rights project, lectr. in law Sch. of Law Columbia U., N.Y.C., 1974-79; ptnr., chmn. litigation dept., mgmt. com. Davis & Gilbert, N.Y.C., 1979—. Co-author: Fair Employment Litigation, 1975, Fair Employment Litigation Manual, 1977, N.Y. State Department of Human Rights Litigation Manual, 1978, Employment Relationships: Law and Practice, 1998. Bd. dirs. U.J.A. Fedn. of N.Y., 1986-92, mem. Jewish Continuity Commn., 1997—; pres. Town & Village Synagogue, N.Y.C., 1990-92; chmn. Prozdor H.S., N.Y.C., 1994-97; mem. Bd. Jewish Edn., 1997—. Mem. ABA, Assn. of Bar of City of N.Y. Intellectual property, Federal civil litigation, Labor. Home: 1035 Park Ave New York NY 10028-0912 Office: Davis & Gilbert 1740 Broadway Fl 3 New York NY 10019-4379

**RUBIN, JANE LOCKHART GREGORY,** lawyer, foundation executive; b. Richmond, Va., May 27, 1944; d. Phillip Henry and Jane Ball (Lockhart) Gregory; m. Reed Rubin, Jan. 22, 1966; children: Lara Ross, Maia Ayers, Peter Lyon. BA, Vassar Coll., 1965; JD, Columbia U., 1975; LLM in Taxation, NYU, 1984. Bar: N.Y, 1976. Assoc. Coudert Brothers, N.Y.C., 1977-84; of counsel Lankenau, Kovner & Kurtz, N.Y.C., 1985-95; dir. Interamericas, N.Y.C., 1992—; bd. dirs., treas. Reed Found., N.Y.C., 1985—; mem. adv. bd. Vt. Studio Ctr., 1985—; mem. Mcpl. Archives Reference and Rsch. Adv. Bd., 1991-94; mem. N.Y.C. Commn. for Cultural Affairs, 1992-94; mem. profl. adv. coun. Lincoln Ctr. for the Performing Arts, 1994—; mem. bd. visitors Columbia Law Sch., 1994—. Author: intro. and catalog for exhibit Temple of Justice: The Appellate Division Court House; (with others) The Art World and the Law, 1987. Bd. dirs., vice chair Vol. Lawyers for the Arts; ; bd. govs. The John Carter Brown Libr. Harlan Fiske Stone scholar Columbia U. Sch. Law. Mem. ABA (sect. real property and probate law, sect. internat. law and practice), N.Y. Bar Assn., Union Internationale des Avocats, Assn. Bar City of N.Y. (com. on non-profit orgns. 1984—), Copyright Soc. of U.S.A. Non-profit and tax-exempt organizations, Estate planning, Trademark and copyright. Office: Inter Americas 162 E 78th St New York NY 10021-0406 Home: 135 Central Park W New York NY 10023-2413

**RUBIN, JEFFREY MARK,** lawyer, insurance company executive; b. N.Y.C., Apr. 26, 1956; s. Irwin S. and Tamara (Benenson) R.; m. Susan L. Rubin, Aug. 4, 1990; children: Leigh, Kate. BA in Polit. Sci., SUNY, Oneonta, 1978; JD, Cornell U., 1981. Bar: Ill. 1981. Assoc. Abramson & Fox, Chgo., 1981-84; from assoc. to ptnr. Phelan, Pope & John, Ltd., Chgo., 1984-96; of counsel Lovell White Durrant, Chgo., 1996-97; sr. v.p., sec., gen. counsel, bd. dirs. Internat. Ins. Co., Chgo., 1997—. Mem. ABA (chair corp. counsel com. 1995-96), Chgo. Bar Assn. (chair jud. evaluation com. 1995-96, bd. mgrs. 1997—), Law Club of Chgo., Abraham Marovitz Inn of Ct. Insurance, General corporate, General civil litigation. Office: Internat Ins Co 181 W Madison St Ste 2300 Chicago IL 60602-4513

**RUBIN, MICHAEL,** lawyer; b. Boston, July 19, 1952; m. Andrea L. Peterson, May 29, 1983; children: Peter, Eric, Emily. AB, Brandeis U., 1973; JD, Georgetown U., 1977. Bar: Calif. 1978, U.S. Dist. Ct. (no. dist.) Calif. 1978, U.S. Ct. Appeals (9th cir.) 1978, U.S. Ct. Appeals (5th, 7th, 10th cirs.) 1982, U.S. Supreme Ct. 1984, U.S. Ct. Appeals (D.C. cir.) 1984, U.S. Ct. Appeals (11th cir.) 1987. Teaching fellow Law Sch. Stanford (Calif.) U., 1977-78; law clerk to Hon. Charles B. Renfrew U.S. Dist. Ct. (no. dist.) Calif., San Francisco, 1978-79; law clerk to Hon. James R. Browning U.S. Ct. Appeals (9th cir.), San Francisco, 1979-80; law clerk to Hon. William J. Brennan, Jr. U.S. Supreme Ct., Washington, 1980-81; assoc. Altshuler &

Berzon, San Francisco, 1981-85, ptnr., 1985-89; ptnr. Altshuler, Berzon, Nussbaum, Berzon & Rubin, San Francisco, 1989—. Federal civil litigation, Labor, Civil rights. Office: Altshuler Berzon Nussbaum Berzon & Rubin 177 Post St Ste 300 San Francisco CA 94108-4700

**RUBIN, ROBERT SAMUEL,** lawyer; b. Cin., Apr. 25, 1954; s. Carl B. and Gloria (Weiland) R.; m. Virginia K. Carson, May 14, 1983; children: John C., Claire W., Elizabeth K. LLB, U. Wales, Aberystwyth, Eng., 1976; JD, U. Cin., 1979. Bar: Ohio 1979, U.S. Dist. Ct. (so. dist.) Ohio 1979. Assoc. Brown, Cummins & Brown, Cin., 1979-82; assoc. Porter, Wright, Morris & Arthur, Cin., 1982-88, partner, 1988-92; ptnr. Cohen Todd Kite & Stanford, Cin., 1992—; mem. arbitration rules com. U.S. Dist. Ct. (so. dist.) Ohio 1984, fed. mediation panel, 1990—. Mem. cmty. initiatives com., cert. com. United Way and Cmty. Chest, 1995—. Mem. Ohio Bar Assn. (banking law subcom.), Cin. Bar Assn., U. Cin. Coll. Law Alumni Assn. (trustee 1988-90), Univ. Club. Banking, Contracts commercial, Real property. Home: 3693 Kroger Ave Cincinnati OH 45226-1931 Office: Cohen Todd Kite & Stanford 525 Vine St Ste 1600 Cincinnati OH 45202-3176

**RUBINE, ROBERT SAMUEL,** lawyer; b. Rockaway, N.Y., Feb. 28, 1947; s. George and Beatrice (Simon) R.; m. Marilyn Goldberg Rubine, Aug. 15, 1970; children: Seth B., Marisa H. BA, Queens Coll., 1968; JD, Syracuse U., 1971. Bar: N.Y. 1972, Fla. 1975; U.S. Dist. Ct. (ea. and so. dists.) N.Y., 1976; U.S. Supreme Ct. 1976. Trial atty. Legal Aid Soc. Nassau County, Mineola, N.Y., 1971-77; atty. Reifman and Rubine, Jericho, N.Y., 1977-79; ptnr. Stein, Rubine and Stein, Mineola, 1979-94, Rubine and Rubine, Mineola, 1995—; adj. prof. C.W. Post Coll., Greenvale, N.Y., 1979-82. Author: (chpt.) Criminal and Civil Investigation Handbook, 1981. Dir. Legal Aid Soc. Nassau County, 1989—, pres., 1994-95, treas., 1996—. Mem. N.Y. State Bar Assn., N.Y. State Assn. Criminal Def. Lawyers, N.Y. State Defenders Assn., Nassau County Bar Assn. Avocation: golf. Criminal, Family and matrimonial, Personal injury. Home: 5 Woodland Rd Oyster Bay NY 11771-3910 Office: Rubine and Rubine PLLC 114 Old Country Rd Mineola NY 11501-4400

**RUBINO, VICTOR JOSEPH,** academic administrator, lawyer; b. N.Y.C., Dec. 25, 1940; s. Joseph V. and Olympia (Gayda) R.; 1 child, Victor Gayda. BA in Govt., Cornell U., 1962, LLB, 1965. Bar: N.Y. 1965, U.S. Dist. Ct. (so. dist.) N.Y. 1969. Staff atty. Westchester Legal Svcs., White Plains, N.Y., 1968-71; assoc. Squadron Ellenoff Plesent & Lehrer, N.Y.C., 1971; treas., program officer Council on Legal Edn., N.Y.C., 1971-79; assoc. dir. Practising Law Inst., N.Y.C., 1979-83, exec. dir., 1983—. Democratic candidate for N.Y. State Assembly, 1970; chmn. Rye (N.Y.) Human Rights Commn., 1975-76. Served to capt. U.S. Army, 1966-68. Mem. ABA, Assn. Bar City N.Y. Office: Practising Law Inst 810 7th Ave Fl 30 New York NY 10019-5818

**RUBINSTEIN, FREDERIC ARMAND,** lawyer; b. Antwerp, Belgium, Apr. 20, 1931; came to U.S., 1942; s. Samuel N. and Steffa (Warrenreich) R.; m. Susan August, Dec. 24, 1968; 1 child, Nicolas Eric August Rubinstein. BA, Cornell U., 1953, JD, 1955. Bar: N.Y. 1955. Assoc. Law Offices of I. Robert Feinberg, N.Y.C., 1955-60; assoc. Guggenheimer & Untermyer, N.Y.C., 1960-65, ptnr., 1965-85; ptnr. Kelley Drye & Warren LLP, N.Y.C., 1985—. Vice chmn. zoning & planning com. Local Community Bd. # 6, N.Y.C., 1980-86. Mem. ABA (bus. law sect., emerging growth ventures subcom., chmn. 1988-96), Cornell Club of N.Y. General corporate, Securities, Mergers and acquisitions. Office: Kelley Drye & Warren LLP 101 Park Ave New York NY 10178-0002

**RUBINSTEIN, KENNETH,** lawyer; b. Munich, Germany, Jan. 13, 1947; came to U.S., 1949; s. Jacob and Golda (Turk) R.; m. Shoshana Becker, June 30, 1968; children: Asher, Sharon, Elizabeth Joy. BBA with honors, CCNY, 1968; JD, NYU, 1979. Bar: N.Y. 1980, U.S. Dist. Ct. (so. and ea. dists.) N.Y. 1980, U.S. Supreme Ct. 1996, U.S. Ct. Appeals (2d cir.) 1997, U.S. Tax Ct. 1997. Assoc. Fried, Frank, Harris, Schriver & Jacobson, N.Y.C., 1979-82; pres. Edgemont Devel. Corp., Scarsdale, N.Y., 1983-89; pres., gen. counsel Daniel Equities Corp., White Plains, N.Y., 1989-91; atty. pvt. practice, N.Y.C., 1991—. Author: Municipal Labor Relations in New York, 1968; contbr. articles to profl. jours. Mem. ABA (probate and tax sect.), N.Y. State Bar Assn. (estate tax sect.), Assn. Bar of City of N.Y. Jewish. Avocations: music, photography, travel. Estate planning, Estate taxation. Office: 485 Madison Ave Fl 15 New York NY 10022-5803

**RUBRIGHT, JAMES ALFRED,** oil and gas company executive, lawyer; b. Phila., Dec. 17, 1946; s. James Alfred and Helen Lucille (Evans) R. (deceased); m. Mary Elizabeth Angelich, Dec. 30, 1988; children: Noah Michael, Benjamin James, Jaime Anne, Nathaniel Drew, James McCurdy, William Angelich. BA, Yale U., 1969; JD, U. Va., 1972. Bar: Ga. 1972. Ptnr. King & Spalding, Atlanta, 1972-94; sr. v.p., gen. counsel Sonat Inc., Birmingham, 1994-97; pres. So. Natural Gas Co. subs. Sonat Inc., Birmingham, 1997-98; exec. v.p. Sonat Inc., Birmingham, 1998—. Office: Sonat Inc 1900 5th Ave N Birmingham AL 35203-2610 also: Sonat Inc PO Box 2563 Birmingham AL 35202-2563

**RUCKER, DOUGLAS PENDLETON, JR.,** lawyer; b. Richmond, Va., Dec. 26, 1945; s. Douglas Pendleton and Margaret (Williams) R.; 1 child, Louise Meredith. BA, Hampden-Sydney Coll., 1968; JD, U. Va., 1972. Bar: Va. 1972, D.C. 1986, U.S. Dist. Ct. (ea. and we. dists.) Va. 1972, U.S. Ct. Appeals (4th cir.) 1982, U.S. Supreme Ct. 1982, U.S. Ct. Claims 1995. Assoc. Sands, Anderson, Marks & Miller, Richmond, Va., 1972-76; mem. Sands, Anderson, Marks & Miller, Richmond, 1977—. Active St. John's Episcopal Ch., mem. vestry, 1994-98, register, 1996, jr. warden, 1997, sr. warden, 1998; Lewis Ginter Bot. Garden; bd. dirs. Va. Ctr. for the Book Capital chpt. ARC; bd. dirs. James River Devel. Corp.; mem. adv. com. Richmond Renaissance. With Va. Army NG, 1968-74. Fellow Va. Law Found. (bd. dirs. 1998—), Va. Bar Assn. (constrn. law chmn. 1992, real estate and bus. law sects., exec. com. 1992-97, pres. 1996), Richmond Bar Assn. (real estate sect., bd. dirs. 1994-97), Bar Assn. D.C., Am. Arbitration Assn. (comml. securities and constrn. industry panels), Met. Richmond C. of C., Commonwealth Club, Country Club Va., Downtown Club. Real property, Construction, General corporate. Office: Sands Anderson Marks & Miller PO Box 1998 Richmond VA 23218-1998

**RUCKER, R.D.,** lawyer; b. Swifton, Ark., Jan. 14, 1950; s. Curtis and Demora (Tidwell) R. BA, U. Ark., 1971; MA, U. Iowa, 1972, PhD, 1981; JD, U. Tex., 1985. Bar: Tex. 1985, U.S. Dist. Ct. (no. dist.) Tex. 1988, U.S. Ct. Appeals (5th cir.) 1989. Asst. atty. gen. Atty. Gen.'s Office, Austin, Tex., 1985-86; asst. dist. atty. Dist. Atty.'s Office, Waco, Tex., 1986-87; 1st asst. pub. defender Pub. Defender's Office, Wichita Falls, Tex., 1987-88; atty. R.D. Rucker's Law Office, Dallas, 1988—. Author: Eros and the Sexual Revolution: Studies in the Psychology of the Human Mind, 1991, Drugs, Drug Addiction and Drug Dealing: The Origin and Nature of, and the Solution to, the American Drug Problem, 1991, Abraham Lincoln's Social and Political Thought, 1992, Jesus Christ and the Origin of Christianity, 1993, Marriage, Love, and the Family: An Investigation into the Role of the Black Woman in the African-American Family, 1998. Avocations: poetry, track, calisthenics. E-mail: RDRUCK@aol.com. Appellate, Criminal. Office: PO Box 226167 Dallas TX 75222-2167

**RUCKER, VALERIE LYNN,** legal assistant; b. Houston, Feb. 14, 1960; d. Eugene A. and Dorothy Mae (Hopper) Supple; m. Jerry O. Rucker Jr., Apr. 14, 1984; 1 child, Carrie Lynn. BS cum laude, U. Houston, 1996. Cert. legal asst. Legal asst. Yocel Alonso, P.C., Houston, 1981-82; coord. legal recruiting Childs, Fortenbach, Beck & Guyton, Houston, 1982-84; legal asst. Mirabal & Assoc., Houston, 1984-86, Eikenburg, Stiles George, Buchman & Leigh, Houston, 1986-92; night coord. Mayer, Brown & Platt, Houston, 1992-94; legal asst. Rosen & Newey, P.C., Houston, 1994-96, Ahmad & Zavitsanos, P.C., Houston, 1996—. Contbr. articles to profl. jours. Mem. State Bar Tex. (Legal Assts. div., speaker ann. meeting 1991), Houston Legal Assts. Assn. (chair ethics com. 1989-90, recording sec.-corr. sec. 1991-92), Psi Chi. Avocations: reading, computers, writing. Office: Ahmad & Zavitsanos PC 1221 McKinney St Ste 3460 Houston TX 77010-2009

**RUDD, DONNIE,** lawyer, educator; b. Winnie, Tex., Feb. 28, 1942; s. Eddie and Veta Mae (Bales) R.; m. Dianne Marks, Apr. 3, 1974; children—Lori, Cindy, Jack, Glory, Louisa, Donisa, Terisa, Donald. B.S. in Chem. Engring., Tex. A&M U., 1964; J.D., Chgo.-Kent Coll. Law, 1969. Bar: Ill., 1969, Can. Patent Office, 1968, U.S. Patent Office, 1967, U.S. Tax Ct., 1971, U.S. Dist. Ct. (no. dist.) Ill., 1969, U.S. Ct. Mil. Appeals, 1971, U.S. Ct. Appeals (7th cir.), 1971, U.S. Ct. Customs and Patent Appeals, 1971, U.S. Ct. Claims, 1973, U.S. Cts. Appeals (5th and 11th cirs.), 1981. Patent atty. Quaker Oats Co., 1965-72; dir. litigation U.S. Gypsum Co., 1972-75; sr. ptnr. Rudd & Assos., Schaumburg, Ill., 1975—; instr. condominium law Harper Coll., DuPage, Oakton Coll. Pres. Bd. Edn. Sch. Dist. 54, 1972-76; mem. Hoffman Estates (Ill.) Plan Commn., 1972-76. Named one of Five Most Outstanding Condominium Attys. in Am. Condominium Council, Chgo., 1983. Mem. ABA, Ill. State Bar Assn., NW Suburban Bar Assn., Lawyer-Pilots Bar Assn. Republican. Baptist. Author: The Everything Book on Condominiums, 1982, 1984 Amendments to the Illinois Condominium Act, 1984, The 100 Most Commonly Asked Questions About Condominiums, 1985; contbr. articles on condominium law to profl. jours. Real property, Federal civil litigation, State civil litigation. Office: 1030 W Higgins Rd Schaumburg IL 60195-3200

**RUDDY, FRANK,** lawyer, former ambassador; b. N.Y.C., Sept. 15, 1937; s. Francis Stephen and Teresa (O'Neil) R.; children: Neil, David, Stephen. AB, Holy Cross Coll., 1959; MA, NYU, 1962, LLM, 1967; LLB, Loyola U., New Orleans, 1965; PhD, Cambridge U., Eng., 1969. Bar: D.C., N.Y., Tex., U.S. Supreme Ct. Faculty Cambridge U., 1967-69; asst. gen. counsel USIA, Washington, 1969-72; sr. atty. Office of Telecomm. Policy, White House, Washington, 1972-73; dep. gen. counsel Exxon Corp., Houston, 1973-74, counsel, 1974-81; asst. adminstr. AID (with rank asst. sec. state) Dept. State, Washington, 1981-84; U.S. ambassador to Equatorial Guinea, 1984-88; gen. counsel U.S. Dept. Energy, Washington, 1988-89; v.p. Sierra Blanc Devel. Corp., Washington, 1989-92; pvt. practice Law Offices of Frank Ruddy, Washington, 1992-94; vis. scholar Johns Hopkins Sch. Advanced Internat. Studies, 1990-94; dep. chmn. UN Referendum for Western Sahara, 1994, Johnston, Rivkin & Foley, Washington, 1995-96, Rivlin & Taylor, et al, 1996-97; ptnr. Ruddy & Muir, Washington, 1998—. Author: International Law in the Enlightenment, 1975; editor: American International Law Cases (series), 1972—; editor in chief Internat. Lawyer, 1978-83; contbr. articles to legal jours. Bd. dirs. African Devel. Found., Washington, 1983-84. Served with USMCR, 1956-61. Mem. ABA (chmn. treaty compliance sect. 1991-93), Am. Soc. Internat. Law, Internat. Law Assn., Hague Acad. Internat. Law Alumni Assn., Oxford and Cambridge Club (London), Conservative Club, Internat. Club, Dacor House. Republican. Roman Catholic. Nuclear power, Environmental, Private international. Home: 5600 Western Ave Chevy Chase MD 20815-3406 Office: Ruddy and Muir 1825 I St NW Ste 400 Washington DC 20006-5415

**RUDDY, JAMES W.,** lawyer; b. 1949. AB, U. Mich., 1971; JD, Wayne State U., 1973. Bar: Wash. 1974, Mich. 1974. Assoc. gen. counsel Safeco Corp., 1984-89, v.p., gen. counsel, 1989—, now sr. v.p., gen. counsel. Antitrust, General corporate, Finance. Office: Safeco Corp Safeco Plz T 22 Seattle WA 98185-0001

**RUDE, BRIAN WILLIAM,** lawyer; b. Mpls., June 20, 1961; s. Kenneth M. and June A. Rude; m. Cathy A. Rude, Oct. 20, 1990; children: Lydia, William, Robert. BS in Bus., Ind. U., 1982, MBA, JD, 1985. Bar: Minn. 1986, U.S. Dist. Ct. Minn. 1987, U.S. Tax Ct. 1988. Assoc. Resnick & Bortsh, P.A., Mpls., 1987-88, Chestnut & Brook, P.A., Mpls., 1988-90; pvt. practice Brian W. Rude, Atty. at Law, Mpls., 1990—. Mem. Minn. State Bar Assn. (constrn. law sect., legis. subcom. 1994—), Hennepin County Bar Assn. (corp., tax, real property and debtor/creditor sect. 1987—). Construction, General corporate, Contracts commercial. Office: 3412 Skycroft Cir Minneapolis MN 55418-1719

**RUDEBUSCH, ALICE ANN,** lawyer; b. Milw., July 9, 1966; d. Leroy George and Maryann Grace (Carlson) Rudebusch; m. Todd William Nejedlo, May 25, 1991 (div. 1999). BA, Northwestern U., 1988; JD, U. Wis., 1991; Certificat De Langue, Université De Paris, 1986. Bar: Wis. 1991, U.S. Dist. Ct. (we. dist.) Wis. 1991, U.S. Dist. Ct. (ea. dist.) Wis. 1995, U.S. Dist. Ct. (no. dist.) Ill. 1995. Assoc. Hanson Gasiorkiewicz & Weber, S.C., Racine, Wis., 1991-96; ptnr. Hanson & Gasiorkiewicz, S.C., Racine, Wis., 1997—. Bd. dirs. YWCA, Racine, 1995—, sec., 1996-98, pres., 1999-2000; vol. Legal Action of Wis., Kenosha, 1996-97. Mem. State Bar Wis., Wis. Acad. Trial Lawyers, Racine County Bar Assn. General civil litigation, Personal injury, Workers' compensation. Office: Hanson & Gasiorkiewicz SC 2932 Northwestern Ave Racine WI 53404-2249

**RUDER, DAVID STURTEVANT,** lawyer, educator, government official; b. Wausau, Wis., May 25, 1929; s. George Louis and Josephine (Sturtevant) R.; m. Susan M. Small; children: Victoria Chesley, Julia Larson, David Sturtevant II, John Coulter; m stepchildren: Elizabeth Frankel, Rebecca Wilkinson. BA cum laude, Williams Coll., 1951; JD with honors, U. Wis., 1957. Bar: Wis. 1957, Ill. 1962. Of counsel Schiff Hardin & Waite, Chgo., 1971-76; assoc. Quarles & Brady, Milw., 1957-61; asst. prof. law Northwestern U., Chgo., 1961-63, assoc. prof., 1963-65, prof., 1965—, William W. Gurley meml. prof. of law, 1994—, assoc. dean Law Sch., 1965-66, dean Law Sch., 1977-85; chmn. Securities and Exch. Commn., Washington, 1987-89; ptnr. Baker & McKenzie, Chgo., 1990-94, sr. counsel, 1994—; cons. Am. Law Inst. Fed. Securities Code; planning dir. Corp. Counsel Inst., 1962-66, 76-77, com. mem., 1962-87, 90—; adv. bd. Ray Garrett Jr. Corp. and Securities Law Inst., 1980-87, 90—; vis. lectr. U. de Liege, 1967; vis. prof. law U. Pa., Phila., 1971; faculty Salzburg Seminar, 1976; mem. legal adv. com. bd. dirs. N.Y. Stock Exch., 1978-82; mem. com. profl. responsibility Ill. Supreme Ct., 1978-87; adv. bd. Securities Regulation Inst., 1978—, chmn., 1994-97; bd. govs. Nat. Assn. Securities Dealers, 1990-93, chmn. Legal Adv. Bd., 1993-96, Arbitration Policy Task Force, 1994-97; trustee Fin. Acctg. Found., 1996—; mem. Internat. Acctg. Stds. Com. Strategy Working Party, 1997—. Editor-in-chief: Williams Coll. Record, 1950-51, U. Wis. Law Rev, 1957; editor: Proc. Corp. Counsel Inst, 1962-66; contbr. articles to legal periodicals. 1st lt. AUS, 1951-54. Fellow Am. Bar Found.; mem., com. chmn. ABA (coun. sect. corp. banking and bus. law 1970-74), Chgo. Bar Assn., Wis. Bar Assn., Am. Law Inst., Order of Coif, Comml. Club of Chgo., Econ. Club of Chgo., Gargoyle Soc., Phi Beta Kappa, Phi Delta Pi, Zeta Psi. Home: 325 Orchard Ln Highland Park IL 60035-1939

**RUDER, LAWRENCE THEODORE,** lawyer; b. Chgo., July 20, 1954; s. Melvin and Phyllis R.; m. Diane F. Freeman, May 17, 1981; children: Dana, Michael, Alexis. BA, U. Ill., 1976; JD, John Marshall Law Sch., 1980. Bar: Ill., 1980. Sr. and founding ptnr. Ruder and Assocs., Chgo., 1980—. Bd. govs. legal com., chmn. bylaws com. Highland Park (Ill.) Cmty. House, 1995—; trustee dist. 112 Edn. Found., Highland Park, 1997—. Ruder scholarship: Hispanic Lawyers Scholarship Fund, 1998. Mem. Assn. Trial Lawyers Am. (mem. product liability sect. 1980—), Ill. Trial Lawyers Assn. (mem. product liability com. 1980—), Ill. State Bar Assn., Chgo. Bar Assn. Fax: 312-332-2750. E-mail: ltr@ruderlaw.com. Office: Ruder and Assocs 221 N Lasalle St Ste 707 Chicago IL 60601-1301

**RUDGE, HOWARD J.,** corporate lawyer. BA, BS, Bucknell U., 1958; JD, George Washington U. Nat. Law Ctr., 1964. Bar: D.C. 1964, Va. 1964. V.p., gen. counsel Conoco, Inc., 1988-90; sr. v.p., gen. counsel Conoco, Inc., Houston, 1990-94, Du Pont De Nemours & Co., Wilmington, Del., 1994—. General corporate. Office: DuPont De Nemours & Co 1007 Market St Wilmington DE 19801-1227*

**RUDINSKI, MICHAEL J.,** lawyer; b. Williamsport, Pa., Jan. 29, 1954; s. Edward Paul and Ruth Mary (Nittinger) R.; m. Mary M. Gardner, Jan. 22, 1993; children: Anthony, Jeffrey, Scott. A in Bus., Williamsport (Pa.) Area C.C., 1974; B in Psychology, Lycoming Coll., 1976; JD, Thomas M. Cooley Law Sch., 1982. Assoc. Campana and Campana, Williamsport, 1982-83; ptnr. Campana, Rudinski & Groulx, Williamsport, 1984-94; pvt. practice Williamsport, 1994—; solicitor Borough of DuBoistown, Pa., 1987-94. Bd. dirs. Newberry Little League, Williamsport, 1974-76, Little Mountaineer Little League, South Williamsport, Pa., 1983-90. Mem. Am. Trial Lawyers Assn., Nat. Assn. Criminal Def. Lawyers, Pa. Assn. Criminal Def. Lawyers. Avocations: jet skiing, golf, baseball, weight lifting. Criminal, Juvenile. Office: 339 1/2 Market St Williamsport PA 17701-6329

**RUDISILL, ROBERT MACK, JR.,** lawyer; b. Charlotte, N.C., Apr. 15, 1945; s. Robert Mack and Lucretia Rose (Hall) R.; m. Frances Barbara McMillan, Aug. 17, 1968 (div. June 1983); children: David Stuart, Michael Joseph; m. Deborah June Olive Baker, Oct. 28, 1989. Cert., U. Geneva, Switzerland, 1965; BA, U. Fla., Gainesville, 1967; cert., Hague Acad., Netherlands, 1969; JD, Duke U., 1970. Bar: Mich. 1970, U.S. Ct. Claims 1971, U.S. Supreme Ct. 1977, Fla. 1978. Assoc. Warner, Norcross & Judd, Grand Rapids, Mich., 1970-75; asst. counsel Mellon Bank, N.A., Pitts., 1975-76; dir. affiliate legal affairs Southeast Banking Corp., Miami, Fla., 1976-81; v.p., gen. counsel Sun Banks, Inc., Orlando, Fla., 1981-86; ptnr. Smith, Mackinnon, Mathews, Harris & Christiansen, Orlando, Fla., 1986-88, Foster & Kelly, Orlando, 1988-90; v.p. regulatory compliance Kirchman Corp., Orlando, 1990—; mem. adv. coun. Banking Law Inst., N.Y., 1984-90; co-founder So. Bank Counsel Group, Miami, 1979; co-founder, dir. Corp. Counsel Assn., Miami, 1978; instr. Am. Bankers Assn. Nat. Comml. Lending Sch., Norman, Okla., 1989-90, Sch. Banking of the South, Baton Rouge, 1984-86, Fla. Sch. Banking, Gainesville, 1980—; moderator Robert Morris Assocs. nat. workshops on comml. loan documentation, Phila., 1978-94; adj. prof. Valencia Community Coll., 1990-92. With USAFR, 1963-69. Mem. ABA, Fla. Bar Assn. (chmn. corp. counsel com. 1980-82, co-chmn. fin. instns. com. 1988-89), Grand Rapids C. of C. (chmn. urban mass transit com.), Mensa. Republican. Episcopalian. Avocations: sailing, underwater photography, playing guitar. Banking, Contracts commercial, Mergers and acquisitions. Office: Kirchman Corp 711 E Altamonte Dr Altamonte Springs FL 32701-4899

**RUDLIN, DAVID ALAN,** lawyer; b. Richmond, Va., Nov. 4, 1947; s. Herbert and Dorothy Jean (Durham) R.; m. Judith Bond Faulkner, Oct. 4, 1975; 1 child, Sara Elizabeth. BA with high distinction, U. Va., 1969, JD with honors, 1973. Bar: Va. 1973, U.S. Dist. Ct. (ea. dist.) Va. 1975, U.S. Ct. Appeals (4th cir.) 1975, U.S. Ct. Appeals (10th cir.) 1980, U.S. Ct. Appeals (2d cir.) 1983, U.S. Supreme Ct. 1979. Assoc. gen. counsel U.S. Commn. on Orgn. of Govt. for Conduct Fgn. Policy, Washington, 1973-75; assoc. Hunton & Williams, Richmond, 1975-82, ptnr., 1982—; adj. faculty civil litigation, appellate practice, libel litigation Duke Univ. Law Sch., Univ. Richmond, The Williams Sch. of Law, Washington and Lee Sch. of Law, William and Mary Sch. of Law, U. Va. Sch. of law; faculty mem. Boulder and S.E. Regional programs Nat. Inst. Trial Advocacy; vis. lectr. U. Va. Sch. Law, Charlottesville, 1980—. Author: (book chpts.) Toxic Torts: Litigation of Hazardous Substances Cases, 1983, 2d edit., 1992, Federal Litigation Guide, 1989, Corporate Counselor's Guide to Environmental Law, 1989, Sanctions: Rule 11 and Other Powers, 1992, Business and Commercial Litigation in Federal Courts, 1997, Corp. Counsel's Guide to ADR Techniques, 1999; contbr. articles to profl. jours. and mags., chpts. to books; mem. bd. editl. advisors The Environ. Counselor, Chesterland, Ohio, 1989—, The Toxics Law Reporter, Washington, 1988—. Alumni Metro Leadership Richmond, 1988-89. Mem. ABA (chmn. litig. sect. environ. litig. com. 1985-88, co-chmn. litig. sect. liaison with jud. com. 1988-91, vice-chmn. toxic and hazardous substances and environ. law com. tort and ins. practice sect. 1988-91, co-liaison to standing com. on environ. law from environ. litig. com. litig. sect. 1988-92, dir. div. IV litig. sect. 1991-95, litig. sect. co-chair programs subcom. first amendment and media litig. com. 1993—, mem. litig. sect. task force on specialization 1994—, co-chair litigation sect., 1997, numerous others), Am. Arbitration Assn. (Va. mediation panel 1996—), Va. Bar Assn. (chair joint com. on alt. dispute resolution with Va. State Bar 1991-97, exec. com. mem.), Richmond Bar Assn. (chmn. mem. com. 1988-91, mem. judiciary com. 1991-94, mem. continuing legal edn. com. 1994-96), Va. Assn. Def. Attys., CPR Inst. Dispute Resolution (products liability com. 1988, 97—, judge Ann. Awards in Alt. Dispute Resolution 1990—, mem. panels disting. neutrals Va. 1997—), Assn. Canadian Studies in U.S. (inaugural pres. 1999—). General civil litigation, Libel, Environmental. Office: Hunton & Williams Riverfront Pla E Tower 951 E Byrd St Ste 200 Richmond VA 23219-4074

**RUDLOFF, WILLIAM JOSEPH,** lawyer; b. Bonne Terre, Mo., Feb. 19, 1941; s. Leslie W. and Alta M. (Hogenmiller) R.; m. Rita Howton, Aug. 5, 1965; children: Daniel, Andrea, Leslie, Susan. AB, Western Ky. U., 1961; JD, Vanderbilt U., 1965. Bar: Ky. 1965, Tenn. 1965, U.S. Supreme Ct. 1975; Diplomate Am. Bd. Profl. Liability Attys.; cert. civil trial specialist Nat. Bd. Trial Advocacy. U.S. magistrate Western Dist. Ky., 1971-75. NDEA fellow U. Nebr. 1961-62, U. Ky. fellow. Fellow Ky. Bar Found. (charter life); mem. Am. Bd. Trial Advocates, Am. Counsel Assn., Def. Rsch. Inst., Ky. Def. Counsel, Trial Attys. Am., Am. Coll. Legal Medicine, Internat. Assn. Def. Counsel. State civil litigation, Federal civil litigation, Insurance. Home: 126 Broadway St Smiths Grove KY 42171-8258 Office: 553 E Main St Bowling Green KY 42101-2256

**RUDMAN, PAUL LEWIS,** state supreme court justice; b. Bangor, Maine, Mar. 26, 1935; s. Abraham Moses and Irene (Epstein) R.; m. Inez Lee Kolonel, Oct. 8, 1961; Andrew Isaac, Carole Sue. AB, Yale Coll., 1957; JD, George Washington U. Sch. Law, 1960. Bar: Maine 1960, D.C. 1960; U.S. Dist. Ct. Maine, 1961. Ptnr. Rudman & Winchell, Bangor, 1960-92; justice Maine Supreme Jud. Ct., Bangor, 1992—. Capt. Maine Air NG, 1960-66. Office: Maine Supreme Jud Ct State of Maine Judicial Ctr Bangor ME 04330*

**RUDNICK, ALAN A.,** management company executive, corporate lawyer; b. Cleve., 1947. BA, U. Chgo., 1969; JD, Case Western Res. U., 1973. Bar: Ohio 1973, Md. 1984, Va. 1988. With Chessie Systems, Inc., 1976-86, asst. treas., 1980-82, asst. v.p. taxation, 1982-84, asst. v.p., treas. taxation, 1984-85; gen. counsel CSX Corp., Richmond, Va., 1985-91, v.p., gen. counsel, corp. sec., 1991—. Mem. ABA, Ohio Bar Assn., Md. Bar Assn., Va. Bar Assn. Office: CSX Corp PO Box 85629 Richmond VA 23285-5629

**RUDNICK, HOLLY LYNN,** laywer; b. Wright-Patterson AFB, Ohio, Apr. 1, 1971; d. Terry I. and Jennifer C. Phillips; m. Phillip M. Rudnick, Mar. 16, 1996. BS in Physics, U. Tex., Dallas, 1993; JD, U. Tex., Austin, 1996. Bar: Tex. 1996, U.S. Patent and Trademark Office 1998. Assoc. Groover & Assocs., Dallas, 1996-97, Jenkens & Gilchrist, Dallas, 1997—. Mem. Am. Intellectual Property Law Assn., Dallas-Ft. Worth Intellectual Property Law Assn. Avocations: reading, movies. Patent, Intellectual property. Office: Jenkens & Gilchrist 1445 Ross Ave Ste 3200 Dallas TX 75202-2799

**RUDNICK, REBECCA SOPHIE,** lawyer, educator; b. Bakersfield, Calif., Nov. 26, 1952; d. Oscar and Sophie Mary (Loven) R.; m. Robert Anthoine, Dec. 2, 1990. BA, Willamette U., Salem, Oreg., 1974; JD, U. Tex., 1978; LLM, NYU, 1984. Bar: Tex. 1978, La. 1979, N.Y. 1980, Calif. 1980. Law clk. to Hon. Charles Schwartz, Jr. U.S. Dist. Ct., New Orleans, 1978-79; assoc. Winthrop, Stimson, Putnam & Roberts, N.Y.C., 1979-85; spl. counsel N.Y. Legis. Tax Study Commn., N.Y.C., 1983-84; asst. prof. law Ind. U., Bloomington, 1985-90; assoc. prof. Ind. U. Sch. Law, Bloomington, 1990-94; assoc. prof. law London Law Consortium, Eng., 1994; vis. assoc. prof. law U. Conn., Hartford, 1984-85; vis. asst. prof. law U. Tex., Austin, 1988; vis. assoc. prof. law U. N.C., Chapel Hill, 1991, Boston U., 1994-95, U. Pa., Phila., 1995-96; prof.-in-residence, IRS, 1991-92; vis. scholar NSW, Australia, 1994, U. Sydney, Australia, 1994; vis. prof. law Seattle U., 1996-97, Wayne State U., 1997, U. Ky., 1998, U. Houston, 1998, Tulane U., 1999, Northwestern Sch. Law, Lewis and Clark Coll., 1999—. Contbr. articles to profl. jours. Dir., gen. counsel Project GreenHope: Svcs. for Women, N.Y.C., 1980-83; advisor, tech. asst. Internat. Monetary Fund, Washington, 1994. Mem. ABA (tax sect. 1982—, sec. tax sect. passthrough entities task force 1986-88, subcom. chairs for incorps. and CLE/important devel. tax sect., 1989—, corp. tax com. 1989—, tax sect. task force on integration 1990—), Am. Assn. Law Schs. (editor tax sect. newsletter 1987—), Assn. Bar of City of N.Y. (admiralty com. 1982-85), Internat. Fiscal Assn., Internat. Bar Assn. Address: Northwestern Sch Law Lewis and Clark Coll 10015 SW Terwilliger Blvd Portland OR 97219

**RUDNICK, WILLIAM ALAN,** lawyer; b. Chgo., Apr. 22, 1964; s. Paul David and Hope Korshak Rudnick; m. Katherine Stuart Bergman, Apr. 13, 1991; children: Spencer Ford, William Stuart. BA, Tufts U., 1986; JD, Northwestern U., 1989; MBA, U. Chgo., 1997. Bar: Ill. 1989. Assoc. Rudnick & Wolfe, Chgo., 1989-96, ptnr., 1997—. Lead advance Dukakis for Pres., 1988; chmn. Perlee for State Rep., Chgo., 1992. Recipient Tomorrow's Leaders Today award Pub. Allies, Chgo., 1995, Hunger's Hope-Bd. Leadership award Second Harvest, 1998. Mem. ABA. Avocations: reading, skiing, exercising, cooking. hiking. Real property, General corporate, Mergers and acquisitions. Office: Rudnick & Wolfe 203 N Lasalle St Ste 1500 Chicago IL 60601-1293

**RUDO, SAUL E.,** tax lawyer; b. Balt., Aug. 2, 1958; m. Gail Rudo, June 12; children: Victor, Sarah. BS in Acctg., U. Ill., 1980; JD, Harvard U., 1983. Bar: Ill. 1983. Ptnr. Katten Muchin & Zavis, Chgo., 1983—; spkr. in field. Bd. dirs. Bernard Weinger Jewish Cmty. Ctr., Deerfield, Ill., 1997-99; Jewish Coun. for Youth Svcs., Chgo., 1992-96. Mem. Chgo. Bar Assn. (mem. partnership tax com., chmn. internat. tax com.), U. Ill. Commerce Alumni Assn. (bd. dirs. 1997-99). Taxation, general, Public international, Mergers and acquisitions. Home: 510 Susan Ln Deerfield IL 60015-3951 Office: Katten Muchin & Zavis 525 W Monroe St Ste 1600 Chicago IL 60661-3693

**RUDOLF, STEVEN GEORGE,** lawyer; b. Batesville, Ind., Oct. 9, 1964; s. George John and Rosemary A. Rudolf; m. Michele D. Bodi, May 12, 1990; children: Madison D., Briana N., Sydney D. BS in Bus. with distinction, Ind. U., 1986; JD cum laude, Boston U., 1989. Bar: Ill. 1989, U.S. Dist. Ct. (no. dist.) Ill. 1989, U.S. Ct. Appeals (7th cir.) 1992, Ind. 1996, U.S. Dist. Ct. (no. and so. dists.) Ind. 1996. Assoc. Vedder Price Kaufman & Kammholz, Chgo., 1989-95; assoc. Bose McKinney & Evans, Indpls., 1995-98, ptnr., 1998—. Author: Model Employee Policies for Indiana Employers, 1996, 98. Bd. dirs., sec. Cath. Social Svcs., Indpls., 1997—; organizing com. Star of Hope, Indpls., 1998—. Mem. Soc. Human Resource Mgmt., Human Resource Assn. Ctrl. Ind. Labor, Federal civil litigation. Office: Bose McKinney & Evans 135 N Pennsylvania St Indianapolis IN 46204-2400

**RUDOLPH, ANDREW J.,** lawyer; b. Camden, N.J., Jan. 16, 1957; s. Richard M. and Selma (Weiner) R.; m. Melinda Jean Pearlman, Dec. 21, 1980; children: Joshua Aaron, Julia Rose. BA cum laude, U. Pa., 1978, JD magna cum laude, 1982. Bar: Pa. 1982, U.S. Dist. Ct. (ea. dist.) Pa. 1982, U.S. Tax Ct. 1983. Assoc. Dechert Price & Rhoads, Phila., 1982-88; cons. Hewitt Assocs., Bedminster, N.J., 1989-90; ptnr. Wolf, Block, Schorr and Solis-Cohen, Phila., 1990-91, Ballard Spahr Andrews & Ingersoll, Phila., 1991-95, Pepper Hamilton LLP (and predecessor firm), Phila., 1996—; lectr. Temple U. Sch. Law, Phila., 1991—. Mem. ABA, Phila. Bar Assn., Order of Coif, Haddon Field Club. Democrat. Jewish. Pension, profit-sharing, and employee benefits, Taxation, general. Home: 667 Washington Ave Haddonfield NJ 08033-3435 Office: Pepper Hamilton LLP 3000 Two Logan Sq Philadelphia PA 19103-2799

**RUDOLPH, GEORGE COOPER,** lawyer; b. Butte, Mont., June 29, 1951. Student, Mont. Coll. Mineral, Sci. and Tech., 1969-71; BA in Psychology magna cum laude, U. S.C., 1973; JD, U. Calif., San Francisco, 1976. Bar: Calif. 1976, U.S. Dist. Ct. (cen. dist.) Calif. 1977, U.S. Dist. Ct. (no. dist.) Calif. 1977, U.S. Ct. Appeals (9th cir.) 1977, U.S. Dist. Ct. (so. dist.) Calif. 1983, U.S. Supreme Ct. 1985. Assoc. Fulop, Rolston, Burns & McKittrick, Beverly Hills and Newport Beach, Calif., 1976-81; assoc. Fulop & Hardee, Newport Beach, 1981-82, ptnr., 1982; ptnr. McKittrick, Jackson, DeMarco & Peckenpaugh, Newport Beach, 1983-87, The Rudloph Law Group, Costa Mesa, Calif., 1988-99; lectr. Calif. Continuing Edn. of The Bar, 1985-94, UCLA, U. Calif., Irvine, San Diego, Santa Barbara, 1985-89. Mem. ABA, Assn. Trial Lawyers Am., Orange County Bar Assn., Los Angeles County Bar Assn., Beverly Hills Bar Assn., B'nai B'rith. Democrat. Jewish. Federal civil litigation, State civil litigation, Insurance. Office: Buchalter Nemer Fields & Younger Ste 300 19100 Von Karman Irvine CA 92623-4635

**RUDWALL, DAVID FULLER,** lawyer; b. Evanston, Ill., May 7, 1953; s. John Charles and Nancy (Spoerri) R.; m. Barbara Ann Granzow, Dec. 17, 1983; children: Paul David, Rachel Ann, Jonathan Fuller. BS, George Peabody Coll. Tchrs., 1977; JD, Ohio State U., 1982. Bar: Ohio 1982, U.S. Dist. Ct. (so. dist.) Ohio 1982, U.S. Supreme Ct. 1986. Assoc. Bieser, Greer & Landis, Dayton, Ohio, 1982-89, Turner, Granzow & Hollenkamp, Dayton, Ohio, 1990-91; pvt. practice Dayton, Ohio, 1991—. Assoc. editor Ohio State Law Jour., 1981-82. Bd. dirs. Camp for Kids Who Can't, Dayton, 1989-91. Mem. ABA, Ohio State Bar Assn. (ins. and negligence law coms. 1986-88), Dayton Bar Assn., Ohio Acad. Trial Lawyers, Assn. Trial Lawyers Am., Carl D. Kessler Inn of Ct. General civil litigation, Personal injury, Professional liability. Office: 2090 W Alex Bell Rd Dayton OH 45459-1164

**RUDY, ELMER CLYDE,** lawyer; b. Elgin, Ill., Apr. 10, 1931; s. Elmer Carl and Bernice (Tobin) R.; m. Margaret L. Meyer, July 5, 1953; children: Lynne, Elizabeth, Paul, Charles, Leslie. BA, Beloit Coll., 1953; LLB, U. Mich., 1958. Bar: Ill. 1958, U.S. Dist. Ct. (no. dist.) Ill. 1959. Assoc. Williams, McCarthy & Kinley, Rockford, Ill., 1958-64; ptnr., mng. ptnr. Williams, McCarthy, Kinley, Rudy & Picha, Rockford, 1964-81; pres. Williams & McCarthy, P.C., Rockford, 1982-87, v.p., 1988—; pres. Norill, Inc., Rockford, 1984-91; chmn. bd. Wesley Willows, Inc., 1992-95. Pres. Rockford Mus. Assn., 1983-86, bd. dirs., 1972—; bd. dirs. Coun. of 100, Inc., Rockford, 1985-92. Cpl. U.S. Army, 1953-55. Mem. ABA, Ill. Bar Assn. (chmn. state taxation sect. coun. 1987-88), Winnebago County Bar Assn. (pres. 1980-81), Am. Judicature Soc., Rotary (dir. local club 1985-89). Republican. Roman Catholic. Avocations: sports, history reading. General corporate, Administrative and regulatory, State and local taxation. Home: 5024 Braewild Rd Rockford IL 61107-1610 Office: Williams & McCarthy PC PO Box 219 Rockford IL 61105-0219

**RUDY, JAMES FRANCIS XAVIER,** lawyer; b. N.Y.C., Feb. 1, 1954; s. Bertrand Robert and Margaret Eleanor (Campiglia) R.; m. Mary Elizabeth Haas, Aug. 17, 1978; children: Lauren Elizabeth, James F.X. Jr. BA, U. Ariz., 1976; JD, Fordham U., 1979. Bar: N.Y. 1980, N.J. 1981, U.S. Dist. Ct. (so. dist.) N.Y. 1980, U.S. Dist. Ct. N.J. 1981, U.S. Supreme Ct. 1985. Assoc. Briger & Assocs., N.Y.C., 1979-81, Katzenbach, Gildea & Rudner, Trenton, N.J., 1981-85; ptnr. Katzenbach, Gildea & Rudner, Lawrenceville, N.J., 1985-93; ptnr. Fox, Rothschild, O'Brien & Frankel, Lawrenceville, 1993—, chmn. health law group, 1994—; twp. atty. Ewing Twp., N.J., 1992-93, atty. Rent Control Bd., 1992-93, atty. Ethical Stds. Bd., 1992-93, atty. Condemnation Bd., 1992-93. Author: University of San Francisco Law Review, 1981. Legal counsel Ewing Rep. Club, 1991-93; mem. Washington Twp. Planning Bd., Robbinsville, N.J., 1993-98; wrestling coach Washington Twp. Recreation, Robbinsville, 1993—; dist. committeeperson Ewing Twp. Rep. Com., Ewing, 1990-92; mem. Washington Twp. Town Ctr. com. 1996—. Mem. ABA, N.Y. State Bar Assn., Nat. Health Lawyers Assn., Assn. of Bar City of N.Y., N.J. State Bar Assn. , Mercer County C. of C. (bus. com. 1993-94), Ewing Twp. Kiwanis Club (dir. 1994-95), Phi Beta Kappa, Phi Kappa Phi. Republican. Roman Catholic. Avocations: golf, home improvement, gardening, wrestling, rollerblading. Health, Mergers and acquisitions, General corporate. Home: 8 Barto Way Robbinsville NJ 08691-2422 Office: Fox Rothschild OBrien & Frankel 997 Lenox Dr Lawrenceville NJ 08648-2317

**RUESS, BRIAN KNIGHT,** lawyer; b. Hollywood, Calif., Jan. 16, 1965; s. Waldo and Conchita Sanchez Ruess; m. Natasha Karena Ellis, July 12, 1992; children: Adam Antonio, Tatiana Isabella. Student, Calif. Inst. Tech., 1983-84; BA in Biology, Reed Coll., 1987; JD, Lewis & Clark Coll., 1995. Bar: Oreg. 1995, U.S. Dist. Ct. Oreg. 1996. Law clk. Oreg. Dept. Justice, Salem, 1993; assoc. Lane Powell Spears Lubersky, Portland, Oreg., 1994-97, Martin, Bischoff, Templeton, Langslet & Hoffman LLP, Portland, 1997—. Contbr. chpt. to book. Mem. ABA, Am. Judicature Soc., Def. Rsch. and Trial Lawyers Assn., Oreg. Assn. Def. Counsel, Multnomah Bar Assn. Avocations: bicycle commuting, automobile enthusiast. Product liability, Personal injury, General civil litigation. Office: Martin Bischoff Templeton et al 900 Pioneer Tower 888 SW 5th Ave Portland OR 97204-2012

**RUF, H(AROLD) WILLIAM, JR.,** lawyer, corporation executive; b. Madison, Wis., July 1, 1934; s. Harold W. and Margaret (Dottridge) R.; m. Suzanne Williams, Aug. 25, 1962 (div. Jan. 1978); m. Jocelyn C. Ruf, Nov. 21, 1981; children: David W., Margaret E., Katharine S. BS, U. Wis., 1960, JD, 1962. Bar: Wis. 1962, Ohio 1963. Field atty. N.L.R.B., Cleve., 1962-65; counsel Oglebay Norton Co., Cleve., 1965-74, dir. indsl. rels., 1974-78, v.p., 1978-94; v.p. adminstrn. and legal affairs Oblebay Norton Co., Cleve., 1994-97. Trustee Shaker Lakes Nature Ctr., Cleve., 1986-93; pres. bd. trustees Moreland Ct. Condo. Assn. Clubs: Cleve. Skating, Cleve. Union. Labor. Home: 13515 Shaker Blvd Cleveland OH 44120-5602 Office: Oglebay Norton Co 1100 Superior Ave E Fl 20 Cleveland OH 44114-2598

**RUFE, CYNTHIA MARIE,** judge; b. Phila., Oct. 30, 1948; d. Lucien Russell and Antoinette Marie (Galizia) Favata; m. John J. Rufe, Jan. 2, 1999; children: Tiffany Marie, Meredith Anne. BA, Adelphi U., 1970; secondary edn. cert., Bloomsburg State Coll., 1972; JD, SUNY, Buffalo, 1977. Bar: Pa. 1977, U.S. Dist. Ct. (ea. dist.) Pa. 1983, U.S. Ct. Appeals (3d cir.) 1987, U.S. Supreme Ct. 1984. Tchr. Bristol (Pa.) Jr./Sr. H.S., 1970-72; law clk. Div. of Clains, State of N.Y., Buffalo, 1976; asst. pub. defender Bucks County, Doylestown, Pa., 1977-79, dep. pub. defender, 1979-81; pvt. practice Newtown, Pa., 1982-93; judge Ct. of Common Pleas, Bucks County, 1994—; mem. procedural rules com. Supreme Ct. of Pa. Appellate Ct., 1999—; solicitor Childred and Youth Agy., Bucks County, 1984-88; spkr., panelist on various law related issues, Bucks County, Phila. and Pa., 1977—; participant Conf. State Trial Judges, 1994—. Pres. bd. dirs. Preventive Rehab. Youth and Devel., Bristol, 1978-81; bd. dirs. Reaching-at-Problems Group Home, Chalfont, Pa., 1981-84, Three Arches, Inc., Falls Twp., Pa., 1985, Orgn. to Prevent Teenage Suicide, 1984-93, Youth Svcs., Inc., 1984-93, Today, Inc., 1987-93, Schofield Ford Bridge Reconstrn. Com., 1990-93. Recipient Trial Lawyer's award Erie County Bar Assn., 1977, Four Chaplains Legion of Honor, 1987. Mem. ABA, ATLA, Pa. Conf. Trial Judges Assn., Bucks County Bar Assn. (dir. 1983-85, chair criminal law sect. 1987-88, chair bench-bar com. 1988-89, chair membership com. 1983-85), Pa. Bar Assn., Pa. Trial Lawyers Assn., Pa. Coll. Criminal Def. Lawyers, Ill. State Bar Assn., Soroptimists (past pres.). Republican. Roman Catholic. Office: Judges Chambers Courthouse Doylestown PA 18901

**RUFFNER, CHARLES LOUIS,** lawyer; b. Cin., Nov. 7, 1936; s. Joseph H. and Edith (Solomon) R.; m. Mary Ann Kaufman, Jan. 30, 1966 (div. 1993); children: Robin Sue, David Robert; m. Nanette Diemer, Feb. 26, 1995. BSBA in Acctg., U. Fla., 1958; JD cum laude, U. Miami, 1964. Bar: Fla. 1964, U.S. Dist. Ct. (so. and mid. dists.) Fla. 1964, U.S. Ct. Appeals (5th cir.) 1964, U.S. Ct. Appeals (11th cir.) 1984, U.S. Claims Ct. 1966, U.S. Tax Ct. 1966, U.S. Supreme Ct. 1968. Cert. in taxation. Trial atty. tax div. Dept. Justice, Washington, 1964-67; pres. Forrest, Ruffner, Traum & Hagen, P.A., Miami, Fla., 1967-78; pres. Ruffner, Hagen & Rifkin, P.A., Miami, 1978-81; tax ptnr. Myers, Kenin, Levinson, Ruffner, Frank & Richards, Miami, 1982-84; pres. Charles L. Ruffner, P.A., 1984—; lectr. Fla. Internat. U., Miami. Author: A Practical Approach to Professional Corporations and Associations, 4 edits., 1970, (column) Tax Talk, Miami Law Rev.; editor: Miami Law Rev., 1963-64; contbr. numerous articles on taxation to law jours. Mem. ABA, Fed. Bar Assn., Fla. Bar (exec. council tax sect. 1967-92, 95—, amicus curiae in test case of validity profl. corps.), Dade County Bar Assn., South Fla. Tax Litigation Assn. (chmn. 1986—), Phi Alpha Delta, Phi Kappa Phi. E-mail: cruff7117@aol.com. Corporate taxation, Personal income taxation, State and local taxation. Office: Courvoisier Centre II 601 Brickell Key Dr Ste 507 Miami FL 33131-2652

**RUFIEN, PAUL CHARLES,** lawyer; b. Denver, Nov. 24, 1964; s. Charles Edgar and Medora Janet (McCormick) R. and Patricia Fagan; m. Darcy Lee McGraw, June 23, 1990; 1 child, Melanie René. BA in Polit. Econs., Colo. Coll., Colorado Springs, 1987; JD, Pepperdine U., 1990. Bar: Colo. 1990. Shareholder Collins & Cockrel, P.C., Denver, 1990—. Recipient Am. Jurisprudence award Bancroft/Whitney, 1988. Mem. ABA, Colo. Bar Assn., Local Govt. Com., Gaming, Sports and Entertainment Com. Avocation: sports. Condemnation, Government contracts and claims, Real property. Office: Collins & Cockrel PC 390 Union Blvd Ste 400 Denver CO 80228-1556

**RUGER, JAMES RICHARD,** lawyer, pharmacologist, pharmacist; b. Bklyn., July 12, 1952; s. Harold C. and Evelyn (Kartcher) R. BS in Pharmacy, St. John's U., Jamaica, N.Y., 1975, MLS, 1977, MS in Pharmacology, 1978, JD, 1983; PhD in Pharmacology, St. John's U., 1986. Bar: N.Y. 1984, U. S. Dist. Ct. (ea. and so. dists.) N.Y. 1984. Tchr. asst., fellow St. John's U., N.Y.C., 1975-77; pharmacist Mercy Hosp., Rockville Ctr., N.Y., 1977-78; coordinator drug info. svcs. Queen's Hosp., St. John's U., 1978-81; pharmacist Braddock Drugs, Bellerose, N.Y., 1981-83; ptnr. Rivkin, Radler, Dunne & Bayh, Uniondale, N.Y., 1986-90; sr. litigation counsel Sterling Drug Inc., N.Y.C., 1990—; asst. gen. counsel Sanofi, Inc., N.Y.C.; adj. asst. prof. St. John's U. 1990—; Author: Pharmacy Technical Manual, 1988; contbr. articles to profl. jours and legal/med. texts. Mem. ABA, N.Y. State Bar Assn., Am. Coll. Toxicology, N.Y. Acad. Sci., Am. Soc. Pharmacy Law. Environmental, Personal injury, Toxic tort. Office: Legal Dept 5th Fl 90 Park Ave New York NY 10016-1301

**RUGGERI, ROBERT EDWARD,** lawyer; b. N.Y.C., Sept. 16, 1952; s. Mario Philip and Margaret Gloria (Pascale) R.; m. Mary Beth Thackeray, June 6, 1981. BA, Union Coll., 1974; JD, Antioch U., 1980. Bar: D.C. 1981, N.Y. 1993, U.S. Dist. Ct. D.C. 1982, U.S. Ct. Internat. Trade 1982, U.S. Ct. Appeals (fed. and D.C. cirs.) 1982, U.S. Supreme Ct. 1984. Trainee Commn. European Communities, Brussels, Belgium, 1980-81; legal cons. Secretariat, OECD, Paris, France, 1981-82; assoc. Stewart & Stewart, Washington, 1982-83, Graham and James, Washington, 1984-85, Rogers & Wells, Washington, 1985-92; dep. dir. legal affairs N.Y. State Dept. Environ. Conservation, 1993-94; assoc. counsel SUNY System, Albany, 1994—; arbitrator NAFTA panels apptd. by U.S., Can., and Mex. govts., 1992—; adj. prof. Georgetown U. Law Ctr., 1988-92. Editor comments Antioch Law Jour., 1979-80. Fulbright scholar, 1980-81. Mem. ABA, D.C. Bar Assn., Washington Fgn. Law Soc. (sec., treas. 1985-87, bd. govs. 1987-88), Am. Soc. Internat. Law. Roman Catholic. Legislative. Home: 1846 Union St Niskayuna NY 12309-4502 Office: SUNY Office U Counsel Univ Plz Rm S315 Albany NY 12246-0001

**RUH, JOSEPH F., JR.,** lawyer; b. Aug. 23, 1954; m. Julia A. Garver R. BA in History & Polit. Sci., U. Rochester, 1976; JD, SUNY at Buffalo Law Sch., 1983. Bar: N.Y. 1983, U.S. Dist. Ct. (we. dist.) 1984. Naval officer U.S. Navy, 1976-80; law clk. U.S. Magistrate, Buffalo, N.Y., 1983-85; assoc. atty. Harris, Beach & Wilcox, Rochester, 1985-89; corp. counsel Computer Consoles, Inc., Rochester, 1989-91, Eastman Kodak Co., Rochester, 1991—; dir. Computer Law Assn., Washington, 1996—. Editor: The Internet and Business: A Lawyer's Guide to the Emerging Legal Issues, 1996. Lt. Cmdr. U.S. Navy, 1976-80. Office: Eastman Kodak Co 343 State St Rochester NY 14650-0001

**RUHM, THOMAS FRANCIS,** retired lawyer, investor; b. Bridgeport, Conn., June 8, 1935; s. Herman David and Martica (Sturges) R.; m. Michele Wood, Oct. 5, 1974; children: Wendy Sturges, Thomas Wood. BA, Yale U., 1957; JD, Havard U., 1962. Bar: N.Y. 1963, U.S. Dist. Ct. (so. and ea. dists.) N.Y. 1964, U.S. Ct. Appeals (2nd cir.) 1969. Assoc. Shearman & Sterling, N.Y.C., 1962-70; asst. gen. counsel Bessemer Securities Corp., N.Y.C., 1970-96, v.p., 1981-96; ret., 1996; chmn. legal aspects venture capital investing Practicing Law Inst., N.Y. and San Francisco, 1979-81; lectr. on venture capital NYU Grad. Sch., 1986-90; expert on fed. securities law, venture capital legal matters, investment tax policy, Fed. Res. monetary policy; frequent witness during 1980s fed. tax hearings. Contbg. author: Technology and Economic Policy, 1986; contbr. articles to profl. jours. Commr. upper divsn. Eastchester (N.Y.) Youth Soccer League, 1990-91, coach, 1985-91, dir. coaching 1995-96; sr. warden Christ Ch., Bronxville, N.Y., 1991-94; past v.p. and treas. Bronxville (N.Y.) Sch. PTA. Mem. Univ. Club, Bronxville Field Club, Quogue Field Club. Republican. General corporate, Securities, Finance.

**RUIZ, MICHELE ILENE,** lawyer; b. Washington, Nov. 3, 1969. BS, Cornell U., 1991; JD, U. Chgo., 1994. Bar: U.S. Dist. Ct. (no. dist.) Ill. 1994. Assoc. McDermott, Will & Emery, Chgo., 1994-96, Sidley & Austin, Chgo., 1996—. General corporate, Securities. Office: Sidley & Austin One First National Plaza Chicago IL 60603

**RUIZ, VANESSA,** state judge; b. San Jaun, P.R., Mar. 22, 1950; D. Fernando and Irma (Bosch) Ruiz-Suria; m. Eduardo Elejalde, Feb. 11, 1972 (div. Jan. 1982); children: Natalia, Alexia; m. David E. Birenbaum, Oct. 22, 1983; stepchildren: Tracy, Matthew. BA, Wellesley Coll., 1972; JD, Georgetown U., 1975. Bar: D.C. 1972, U.S. Supreme Ct. 1981. Assoc. Fried, Frank, Harris, Shrives & Kampelman, Washington, 1975-83; sr. mgr., counsel Sears World Trade Inc., Washington, 1983-94; assoc. judge D.C. Ct. of Appeals, 1994—; speaker in field. Mem. ABA, Inter-Am. Bar Assn. Office: Ct of Appeals 500 Indiana Ave NW Washington DC 20001-2131 also: Pepper Hamilton & Scheetz 1300 19th St NW Washington DC 20036-1609

**RUIZ-VALERA, PHOEBE LUCILE,** law librarian; b. Barranquilla, Colombia, Jan. 27, 1950; d. Ramon and Marion (Mehlman) Ruiz-Valera; m. Thomas Patrick Winkler, Mar. 27, 1981. BA cum laude, Westminster Coll., 1971; MLS, Rutgers U., 1974; MA, NYU, 1978. Libr. trainee Passaic (N.J.) Pub. Libr., 1973-74, reference libr., 1974; libr. assoc. cataloger NYU Law Libr., N.Y.C., 1974-79, asst. curator, cataloger, 1979-81; libr. III, cataloger Rutgers U. Libr., New Brunswick, N.J., 1981-82; chief cataloger Assn. Bar City N.Y., 1982-85, head tech. svcs., 1985-99; catalog libr. Cleary, Gottlieb, Steen and Hamilton, N.Y.C., 1999—. Mem. Am. Assn. Law Librs., Am. Translators Assn. (cert. translator English to Spanish), Law Libr. Assn. Greater N.Y., Reforma, Salalm. Democrat. Presbyterian. Office: 1 Liberty Plz Fl 43 New York NY 10006-1404

**RULE, CHARLES FREDERICK (RICK RULE),** lawyer; b. Nashville, Apr. 28, 1955; s. Frederick Charles and Mary Elizabeth (Malone) R.; m. Ellen Friedland, May 13, 1976. BA, Vanderbilt U., 1978; JD, U. Chgo., 1981. Bar: U.S. Ct. Appeals. (D.C. cir.) 1983. Law clk. U.S. Ct. Appeals (fed. cir.), Washington, 1981-82; spl. asst. to asst. atty. gen. Antitrust div. Dept. Justice, Washington, 1982-83, dep. asst. atty. gen. policy planning, 1984-85, acting asst. atty. gen., then dep. asst. atty. gen. regulatory affairs, 1985-86, asst. atty. gen., 1986-89; ptnr. Covington & Burling, Washington, 1989—; legal, econ. analyst Lexecon, Inc., Chgo., 1979-80. Mem. Bar of D.C. Ct. Appeals, Phi Beta Kappa, Phi Eta Sigma. Republican. Presbyterian. Office: Covington & Burling PO Box 7566 Rm 915B 1200 Pennsylvania Ave NW Washington DC 20004-2403

**RUMAGE, JOSEPH PAUL, JR.,** lawyer; b. New Orleans, Mar. 17, 1958; s. Joseph Paul and Nancy (Simms) R. BA in English, Northwestern U., 1979; JD, Tulane U., 1982. Bar: La. 1982, U.S. Ct. Appeals (5th cir.) 1986, U.S. Dist. Ct. (ea. dist.) La. 1983, U.S. Dist. Ct. (mid. dist.) La. 1991. Ptnr. McTernan, Parr & Rumage, New Orleans, 1982-88; prin. Paul Rumage, Atty. at Law, New Orleans, 1988—; bd. dirs. Windsor Fin. Group, Inc., New Orleans; spkr. in field. Bd. dirs. Mid-City Cmty. Housing Devel. Orgn., Inc., 1992—, pres., 1993—. Recipient Certs. of Appreciation, City of New Orleans, 1990, New Oreans Police Dept., 1990, Kiwanis, 1991. Fellow La. Bar Found.; mem. La. Bar Assn., Mid-City Neighborhood Orgn. (bd. dirs. 1988—, pres. 1991, 94). Bankruptcy, Personal injury, Contracts commercial. Office: Paul Rumage Atty at Law 404 S Jefferson Davis Pky New Orleans LA 70119-7126

**RUMAN, SAUL I.,** lawyer; b. Chgo., May 12, 1925; s. James A. and Pauline (Scharfer) R.; m. Beverlee Mahan, June 17; children: Loral Ruman Conrad, Melissa Ruman Stewart, Elizabeth Ruman Plumlee. BS, Ind. U., 1949, JD with distinction, 1952. Bar: Ind. 1952, U.S. Supreme Ct. 1963, U.S. Dist. Ct. Ind. 1952, U.S. Ct. Appeals (7th cir.) 1962. Pvt. practice, Hammond, Ind., 1952—; mng. ptnr. Ruman, Clements, Tobin & Holub, P.C., 1990; former lectr. bus. law Ind. U. N.W.; mem. faculty numerous insts. on law; mem. com. on rules of practice and procedure Supreme Ct. Ind., 1983-92, Ind. Jud. Nominating Commn., 1990; mem. Ind. Supreme Ct. character and fitness com., 1975—. Pres. Ind. U. Sch. Law Alumni Assn., 1972-73, bd. visitors, 1973—; bd. advisors N.W. Campus Ind. U., 1973-85, class rep., 1983; faculty Nat. Inst. Trial Advocacy, 1984-86. Trustee Ind. Legal Svcs. Fund, 1978, 84. Served with USN, 1942-45. Fellow Internat. Acad. Trial Lawyers (dir. 1980-86); mem. Ill. Trial Assn., Ind. Bar Assn. (chmn. trial lawyers sect. 1970-71), Ind. Trial Lawyers Assn. (emeritus dir., pres. 1980-81, lifetime achievement award 1997), Coll. Fellows, Assn. Trial Lawyers Am., Am. Bd. Trial Advocates, Order of Coif. Personal injury, Federal civil litigation, State civil litigation. Office: 5261 Hohman Ave Hammond IN 46320-1721

**RUMBAUGH, CHARLES EARL,** arbitrator, mediator, educator, lawyer, speaker; b. San Bernardino, Calif., Mar. 11, 1943; s. Max Elden and Gertrude Maude (Gulker) R.; m. Christina Carol Pinder, Mar. 2, 1968; children: Eckwood, Cynthia, Aaron, Heather. BS, UCLA, 1966; JD, Calif. Western Sch. Law, 1971; cert. in advanced mgmt., U. So. Calif., 1993. Bar: Calif. 1972, U.S. Dist. Ct. (cen. dist.) Calif. U.S. Ct. Appeals (9th cir.), U.S. Supreme Ct. Engr. Westinghouse Electric Corp., Balt., 1966-68; legal counsel Calif. Dept. of Corps., L.A., 1971-77; legal counsel Hughes Aircraft Co., L.A., 1977-84, asst. to corp. dir. contracts, 1984-89, asst. to corp. v.p. contracts, 1989-95; corp. dir. contracts/pricing Lear Astronics Corp., 1995-97; pres. Ctr. for Conflict Resolution, 1998-99; arbitrator, mediator, comml., govt. contracts, internat. law, franchise, securities, torts, personal injury, real estate and constrn. panels Am. Arbitration Assn., L.A. and San Francisco; mem. arbitration and mediation panels ArbitrationWorks (formerly Arbitration and Mediation Internat.), 1994—, Nat. Assn. Security Dealers, Franchise Arbitration & Mediation Inc., L.A. County Superior Ct., Santa Barbara County Superior Ct.; spkr. in field; mem. panel pvt. alt. dispute resolution neutrals U.S. Ct. Fed. Claims; mem. armed svcs. bd. of contract appeals panel of pvt. alt. dispute resolution neutrals, DLA panel of dispute neutrals, also settlement officer U.S. Dist. Ct. Mem. editl. bd. Nat. Contract Mgmt. Jour.; contbr. articles to profl. jours. Counselor Boy Scouts Am., L.A., 1976—; mem. City of Palos Verdes Estates (Calif.) Citizen's Planning Com., 1986-90; judge pro tem L.A. County Superior Ct., L.A., 1991—. Fellow Nat. Contract Mgmt. Assn. (founder, chmn. alt. dispute resolution com., cert. profl. contracts mgr., nat. bd. advisors, nat. v.p. southwestern region 1993-95, nat. dir. 1992-93, pres. L.A./South Bay chpt. 1991-92, Fellow of Yr. award 1994); mem. ABA (dispute resolution sect., forum on franchising, forum on constrn. industry, pub. contract law sect.), Nat. Assn. Purchasing Mgmt., Calif. Dispute Resolution Coun. (cons. to qualifications com. 1997-99), Nat. Def. Indsl. Assn. (vice-chmn. west coast legal subcom. 1994—), Fed. Bar Assn. (pres. Beverly Hills chpt. 1992-93), State Bar Calif. (franchise law com. 1992-95, Wiley W. Manual award 1992), LA County Bar Assn., South Bay Bar Assn., Soc. Profls. in Dispute Resolution (chmn. internat. sector com., past bd. dirs. L.A. chpt.), Aerospace Industries Assn. (chmn. procurement techniques com. 1987-88, 93-94), Christian Legal Soc. Avocations: camping, skiing, jogging, equestrian. Office: PO Box 2636 Rolling Hills Estates CA 90274-8636

**RUMMAGE, STEPHEN MICHAEL,** lawyer; b. Massillon, Ohio, Dec. 27, 1955; s. Robert Everett and Kathleen Patricia (Newman) R.; m. Elizabeth Anne Seivert, Mar. 24, 1979; children: Everett Martin, Carter Kevin. BA in History and English, Stanford U., 1977; JD, U. Calif., Berkeley, 1980. Bar: Wash. 1980, U.S. Dist. Ct. (we. dist.) 1980, U.S. Ct. Appeals (9th cir.) 1983, U.S. Supreme Ct. 1985. Assoc. Davis, Wright et al, Seattle, 1980-85; ptnr. Davis Wright Tremaine, Seattle, 1986—. Co-author: Employer's Guide to Strike Planning and Prevention, 1985. Mem. Wash. Athletic Club. Democrat. Roman Catholic. General civil litigation, Securities, Appellate. Office: Davis Wright Tremaine 1501 4th Ave Ste 2600 Seattle WA 98101-1688

**RUMMEL, EDGAR FERRAND,** retired lawyer; b. New Bern, N.C., June 29, 1929; s. Robert French and Reba Jeanette (Burgess) R.; m. Lillian Hildebrandt, Dec. 28, 1954. BA, Ohio State U., 1955; JD, DePaul U., 1965; LLB, U. London, Eng., 1973; LLM, George Washington U., 1978. Bar: U.S. Dist. Ct. D.C. 1967, U.S. Ct. Appeals (D.C. cir.) 1968, U.S. Supreme Ct. 1971, Md. 1980. Atty.-adviser Dept. Army, Washington, 1971-74, 78, counsel U.S. Army Real Estate Agy., Frankfurt, W.Ger., 1975-77, supervisory atty.-adviser, asst. div. chief Office of Chief of Engrs., Dept. Army, Washington, 1977-83; sr. atty. advisor Office of Judge Advocate Gen., Dept. Army, Washington, 1983-85, trial atty., 1987; spl. asst. U.S. Atty. Dist. Colo., 1985-87, ret. 1987; chmn. mineral leasing com. Dept. Def., 1981-84; mem. Oreg. Nat. Trial Adv. Council, 1983-84. With AUS, 1947-51. Mem. Md. State Bar Assn., Am. Soc. Legal History. Democrat. Episcopalian (vestryman 1981-84). Home: 7812 Adelphi Ct Hyattsville MD 20783-1848

**RUMPF, BRIAN E.,** lawyer; b. Sommerville, N.J., May 11, 1964; s. Howard A. and Marilyn M. Rumpf; m. Debra Hubert, Oct. 10, 1990; children: Justin Patrick, Kassidy Theresa. BA, The Cath. U. Am., Washington, 1986; JD, Washington & Lee U., 1989. Bar: N.J. 1989, Pa. 1989, U.S. Dist. Ct. N.J. 1989. Assoc. Hiering & Hoffman, Toms River, N.J., 1989-97; mng. ptnr. Brian E. Rumpf P.C., Little Egg Harbor, N.J., 1997—. Committeeperson Township of Little Egg Harbor, 1987—. Mem. ABA, N.J.

Bar Assn. General practice, Personal injury, General civil litigation. Home: 3 Genevieve Ct Little Egg Harbor Township NJ 08087 Office: 960 Radio Rd Little Egg Harbor Township NJ 08087

**RUMPF, PIERRE CAMERON,** lawyer; b. Boston, May 14, 1963; s. Robert-Michel and Catherine (Cameron) R. BS in Criminal Justice, Salem State Coll., 1987; JD, Mass. Sch. of Law, 1995. In-house counsel, bus. mgr. Recreational Dimensions, Beverly, Mass., 1990-97; asst. atty. gen. Mass. Atty. Gen.'s Office, Boston, 1993; pvt. practice Manchester, Mass., 1995-97; ptnr. Fritz & Rumpf, Manchester, 1998—. Chief of staff Randal Fritz for U.S. Congress, Manchester, 1998. With USAR, 1983-89. Mem. Mass. Bar Assn., Delta Theta Phi. Avocations: sailing, reading, weightlifting, snowboarding, chess. Contracts commercial, General practice, Landlord-tenant. Office: Fritz & Rumpf 24B Elm St Manchester MA 01944-1313

**RUNCO, WILLIAM JOSEPH,** judge; b. Detroit, Jan. 23, 1957; s. Joseph Tony and Rose Mary (Rossi) R.; m. Rhonda Lee Hyde, May 30, 1987; children: Erica, Gabriella, Joseph. BA in Econs., U. Mich., 1979, JD, 1981. Bar: Mich. 1983, U.S. Dist. Ct. (ea. dist.) Mich. 1984. Commr. Wayne County, Detroit, 1981-83; mem. Mich. Ho. Reps., Lansing, 1983-86, 89-91, minority whip, 1983-84; ptnr. Edick, Esper & Runco, Dearborn, Mich., 1985-88, Runco, Tyler & Xuereb, Dearborn, 1988-91; judge 19th Dist. Ct., 1991—; adj. lectr. U. Mich., Dearborn, 1991—; adj. lectr. Henry Ford C.C., 1996—. Mediator Wayne County Mediation Tribunal, Detroit, 1987-91; del. Rep. Nat. Conv., Detroit, 1980, New Orleans, 1988; mem. Electoral Coll., 1989; mem. citizens adv. com. U. Mich., Dearborn, 1987-89; mem. C.A.S.L. alumni affiliate bd. U. Mich., Dearborn, 1994-97. Mem. ABA, Dearborn Bar Assn., Mich. Dist. Judges Assn. (bd. dirs., pres.), Dearborn Pioneers, Mich. Jud. Conf. (bd. mem., vice-chairperson). Roman Catholic. Avocations: golf, aviation, ice hockey. Office: 19th Dist Ct 16077 Mi Ave Dearborn MI 48126-2999

**RUNDLETT, ELLSWORTH TURNER, III,** lawyer; b. Portland, Maine, Jan. 12, 1946; s. Ellsworth Turner II and Esther (Stevens) R.; m. Lisa Warren, Oct. 25, 1964 (div. June 1967); 1 child, Ellsworth Turner IV; m. Jamie Donnelly, June 7, 1982 (div. 1986); m. Marilyn DeJenzano, Aug. 17, 1994. AB cum laude, Bowdoin Coll., 1968; JD, U. Maine, 1973. Bar: Maine 1973, U.S. Dist. Ct. Maine 1973, U.S. Ct. Appeals (1st cir.) 1973; cert. civil trial specialist, Nat. Bd. Trial Advocacy; diplomate Nat. Coll. Advocacy. Bodwoin Coll. intern U.S. Senate, Washington, 1967; law clk. Superior Ct. Maine, Portland, 1972-73; asst. corp. counsel City of Portland, 1973-76; ptnr. Childs, Rundlett, Fifield & Childs, Portland, 1980—. Author: Maximizing Damages in Small Personal Injury Cases, 1991; contbr. legal articles to Maine Bus. Digest, 1978-84. Pres. Pine Tree Alcohol Treatment Ctr., Windham, Maine, 1978-80; trustee Portland Players, Inc., South Portland, Maine, 1977-84, pres., 1985-87. Mem. ATLA, Cumberland County Bar (trustee 1983-84, 86-87, v.p. 1988-90, pres. 1990), Maine Bar Assn. (bd. govs. 1991—), Maine Trial Lawyers Assn. (pres.-elect 1999—), U. Maine Law Alumni (bd. dirs. 1984-87, v.p. 1988, pres. 1989, bd. govs. 1991—), Cumberland Club, Portland Club (gov. 1983-86), Bowdoin Club of Portland (pres. 1978). Personal injury, General practice, State civil litigation. Office: Childs Rundlett & Fifield 257 Deering Ave Portland ME 04103-4858

**RUNES, KENNETH ALAN,** lawyer; b. Chicago Heights, Ill., Jan. 23, 1959; s. Eugene and Helen Lee (Hersh) R. BSW, U. Ill., 1981; JD, Northeastern U., 1991. Bar: Ill. 1991, U.S. Ct. Appeals (7th cir.) 1994, U.S. Dist. Ct. (no. dist.) Ill. 1997. Foster care case worker Ctrl. Bapt. Family Svcs., Chgo., 1981-84; family counselor Ctrl. Bapt. Family Svcs., Elgin, Ill., 1984-86; case worker Ill. Dept. Children and Family, DeKalb, Ill., 1986-88; assoc. Tucker, Pavesich & Assocs., Oak Lawn, Ill., 1991-94, Thill, Favaro, Buzek & Gorman, Ltd., Palatine, Ill., 1994—. Candidate for sch. bd. Sch. Dist. # 206, Chicago Heights, 1977. Mem. N.W. Suburban Bar Assn. Avocations: music, sports strategy games. State civil litigation, Family and matrimonial, General practice. Office: Thill Favaro Buzek and Gorman Ltd Ste 100 835 N Sterling Ave Palatine IL 60067-2246

**RUNFOLA, ROSS THOMAS,** lawyer, educator, writer, journalist, poet; b. Buffalo, Aug. 30, 1943; s. Joseph Paul and Isabelle Louise (Santi) R.; children: Jennifer, Ross Thomas; m. Nancy S. Cox, Aug. 10, 1993. BA summa cum laude, SUNY, Buffalo, 1965, MA, 1968, PhD, 1973, JD, 1981. Bar: N.Y. 1982. Prof. social scis. Medaille Coll., Buffalo, 1969—; asst. prof. SUNY, Buffalo, 1970-73; sports columnist Buffalo New Times, Buffalo, 1973-74; co-anchor Sta. WUTV, Buffalo, 1974; reporter Buffalo Courier Express, Buffalo, 1975-76; columnist Spree mag., Buffalo, 1979-82; legal asst. Erie County Pub. Adminstr., Buffalo, 1981; ptnr. Fiorella, Leiter & Runfola, Buffalo, 1982-86; spl. matrimonial counsel Matusick, Spadafora & Verrastro, Buffalo, 1986-87; ptnr. Siegel, Kelleher & Kahn, Buffalo, 1987—; dir. Matrimonial Mediation Ctr. Author: Jock: Sports and Male Identity, 1980; contbr. numerous articles to profl. jours.; chief film scriptwriter: Organized Sports: Are They Good for Young People, 1975. Active Mayor's Energy Task Force City of Buffalo, 1973, Attica Prison Task Force, N.Y., 1973, Western N.Y. Consortium on Higher Edn., 1974, Erie County (N.Y.) Task Force on Physical Edn. and Recreation for Meeting the needs of the Handicapped, 1974, Instl. Task Force Pvt. Colls. Western N.Y., 1974, Western N.Y. Higher Edn. Task Force, 1975, Legis. Adv. Com. N.Y. State Assembly, 1976, Children's Hosp. Adolescence Program, 1978, Western N.Y. Heart Assn., 1978, Southern Poverty Law Ctr., 1978—, Erie County Dem. Com., 1978—, Step Family Assn. Western N.Y., 1983—, Frontier Dem. Club, 1983—; mem. adv. com. United Way Buffalo, 1991—; bd. dirs. Monsignor Carr Inst., Just Buffalo Lit. Ctr., 1996. Named One of Ten Best Coll. Profs. Western N.Y. Buffalo News, 1987, Prof. of Yr. Medaille Coll., 1998; recipient 1st pl. award oral competition Greater Buffalo Poetry Slam, 1995, Social Svcs. award Nat. Conf. for Community and Justice, 1998. Mem. ABA, AAUP, N.Y. State Bar Assn., Erie County Bar Assn. (vice chmn. matrimonial and family law com. 1992—), N.Y. State United Tchrs., N.Y. State Coun. Divorce Mediation, Am. Acad. Family Mediators. Roman Catholic. Avocations: writing, reading, bicycling, cross country skiing. Family and matrimonial, Entertainment. Home: 96 Cleveland Ave Buffalo NY 14222-1610 Office: Siegel Kelleher & Kahn 420 Franklin St Buffalo NY 14202-1302 also: 18 Agassiz Cir Buffalo NY 14214-2601

**RUNFT, JOHN L.,** lawyer; b. Baker City, Oreg., Aug. 14, 1938; s. Donald Lorraine and Arrena Runft; m. Enid E. McConnell, Sept. 5, 1964; children: Linda Lorraine, Marnie Edwina, Karl Jonathan. BA, Albertson Coll., 1962; JD, U. Chgo., 1965. Bar: Idaho 1965, U.S. Dist. Ct. Idaho 1965, U.S. Ct. Appeals (9th cir.) 1970, U.S. Supreme Ct. 1977, U.S. Ct. Claims 1980, U.S. Ct. Appeals (fed. cir.) 1983. Assoc. Moffat, Thomas, B&B, Boise, Idaho, 1965-66; assoc., then jr. ptnr. Eberle, Berlin et al, Boise, 1967-74; ptnr. Runft & Longet Teig, Boise, 1974-82, Runft, Leroy et al, Boise, 1982-89; pvt. practice Boise, 1990—; pres., bd. dirs. Karlinmar Corp.; mng. mem. Karlinmar, LLC; bd. dirs. Tower Venture, LLC; officer, bd. dirs. Diatect Internat. Corp. Bd. dirs. Boise Philharm. Assn., 1966-93, pres.,1 980-81; bd. dirs., founder Idaho Cmty. Found., Boise, 1988-96; mem. Idaho Women's Commn., Boise, 1977-82; mem. Pres.' Ptnrs. Coll. Idaho, 1982-90; civilian aide to sec. Army of U.S., 1988-95. With U.S. Army, 1955-58. Nat. Honor scholar; recipient Svc. award Idaho Cmty. Found., 1995. Mem. ABA, Idaho State Bar Assn., Mountain States Legal Found. (chmn. bd. litigation, Svc. award 1995). Republican. Avocations: fishing, hiking, gardening, classical music, history. Contracts commercial, General corporate, General civil litigation. Office: 1020 W Main St Ste 305 Boise ID 83702-5745

**RUNGE, PATRICK RICHARD,** lawyer; b. Iowa City, Iowa, Oct. 25, 1969; s. Richard Gary and Sally Louise (Cozzolino) R. BSBA in Econs., U. Nebr., Omaha, 1991; JD, Creighton U., 1994. Bar: Nebr. 1994, U.S. Dist. Ct. Nebr. 1994. Prodn. editor U.N.O. Gateway, Omaha, 1990-91; graphic designer Omaha (Nebr.) Pub. Power Dist., 1991-97; intern U.S. Dist. Ct., Omaha, 1993; rsch. asst. Creighton U., Omaha, 1993; sr. cert. law student Creighton Legal Clinic, Omaha, 1994; atty. Runge Law Office, Omaha, 1994-95, Runge & Chase, Omaha, 1995—; pub. defender Winnebago Tribe of Nebr., 1996—. Disting. scholar Omaha (Nebr.) World-Herald, 1987-91; Merit scholar Creighton Law Sch., Omaha, 1991-94. Mem. Winnebago Bar Assn., Phi Delta Phi. Democrat. Lutheran. Family and matrimonial, Criminal, Constitutional. Office: Runge & Chase 7701 Pacific St Ste 323 Omaha NE 68114-5480

**RUNQUIST, LISA A.,** lawyer; b. Mpls., Sept. 22, 1952; d. Ralf E. and Violet R. BA, Hamline U., 1973; JD, U. Minn., 1976. Bar: Minn. 1977, Calif. 1978, U.S. Dist. Ct. (ctrl. dist.) Calif. 1985, U.S. Supreme Ct. 1995. Assoc. Caldwell & Toms, L.A., 1978-82; ptnr. Runquist & Flagg, L.A., 1982-85; pvt. practice Runquist & Assocs., L.A., 1985-99, Runquist & Zybach, L.A., 1999—; mem. adv. bd. Exempt Orgn. Tax Rev., 1990—, Calif. State U. L.A. Continuing Edn. Acctg. and Tax Program, 1995—. Mem. editorial bd. ABA Bus. Law Today, 1995—; contbr. articles to profl. jours. Mem. ABA (bus. law sect. coun. 1995—, com. on nonprofit corps. 1986—, chair 1991-95, subcom. current devels. in nonprofit corp. law 1989—, chair 1989-91, subcom. rels. orgns. 1989—, chair 1987-91, 95-98, subcom. legal guidebook for dirs. 1986—, ad hoc com. on info. tech., 1997—, chair 1997-98, co-chair, 1998—, sect. liaison to ABA tech. coun. 1997—, subcom. model nonprofit corp. act, partnerships and unincorp. bus. orgns. com. 1987—, state regulation of securities com. 1988—, tax law sect. exempt orgns. com. 1987—, subcom. religious orgns. 1989—, co-chair 1995-97, subcom. non (c) (3) orgns. 1997—, co-chair 1997—), Calif. Bar Assn. (bus. law sect., nonprofit and unincorp. orgns. com. 1985-92, 93-96, 97—, chair 1989-91), Christian Legal Soc., Ctr. Law and Religious Freedom, Christian Mgmt. Assn. (dir. 1983-89). Non-profit and tax-exempt organizations, General corporate, Securities. Office: 10618 Woodbridge St Toluca Lake CA 91602-2717

**RUNYAN, CHARLES ALAN,** lawyer; b. Ogbomosho, Nigeria, Oct. 25, 1951; parents Am. citizens; s. Farrell Edward and Elizabeth (Barnett) R.; m. Elizabeth Long, Apr. 1, 1984; children: Cameron Alan, Charles Alexander, Robert Taylor. Diplome d'etudes Francais, U. Poitiers, Tours, France, 1969; BA, U. S.C., 1973, JD cum laude, 1976. Bar: S.C. 1976, U.S. Dist. Ct. S.C. 1976, U.S. Ct. Appeals (4th cir.) 1976. Assoc. Glenn, Porter & Sullivan P.A., Columbia, S.C., 1977-79; ptnr. McNair Law Firm, 1979-87, Speights & Runyan, Hampton, S.C., 1987—; legal writing instr. U. S.C. Sch. of Law, 1975-76. Exec. editor S.C. Law Rev., 1975-76. Mem. ABA (forum com. on constrn. industry 1985—), S.C. Bar Assn., S.C. Trial Lawyers Assn., Assn. Trial Lawyers Am. Construction, General civil litigation, Personal injury. Office: Speights & Runyan 304 Lee Ave Hampton SC 29924-2023

**RUNYON, BRETT L.,** lawyer; b. Fresno, Calif., Oct. 20, 1959. AA, Fresno City Coll., 1981; BS, Calif. State U., Fresno, 1982; JD, San Joaquin Coll. Law, 1986. Bar: Calif. 1988, D.C., U.S. Dist. Ct. (ea. dist.), U.S. Ct. Appeals (Fed. cir.) 1998. Atty. Marderosian Oren & Paboojian and predecessor firm, Fresno, 1988—; Arbitrator Fresno County Superior Ct., Fresno County Farm Bur. Mem. ABA, ATLA, Fed. Bar Assn., No. Calif. Assn. Def. Counsel, Fresno County Bar Assn., Delta Theta Phi (meritorious svc. award 1986). Insurance, Product liability, Toxic tort. Office: Marderosian Oren & Paboojian 1260 Fulton Mall Fresno CA 93721-1916

**RUPERT, DONALD WILLIAM,** lawyer; b. Clearfield, Pa., Oct. 15, 1946; s. Donald Lee and Dorothy Mae (Bonsall) R.; m. Patricia A. Rupert, June 21, 1969. BS in Chemistry, Miami U., Ohio, 1968; JD, Washburn U., Topeka, 1976. Bar: Tex. 1976, Ill. 1978, U.S. Ct. Appeals (Fed. cir.) 1978, U.S. Dist. Ct. (so. dist.) Tex. 1977, U.S. Ct. Appeals (7th cir.) 1981, U.S. Dist. Ct. (no. dist.) Ill. 1979, U.S. Supreme Ct., 1992. Assoc. Arnold, White & Durkee, Houston, 1976-78, Kirkland & Ellis, Chgo., 1978-83, ptnr., 1983-86; ptnr. Neuman, Williams, Anderson & Olson, Chgo., 1986-90; founding ptnr. Roper & Quigg, 1990-93; ptnr. Keck, Mahin & Cate, Chgo., 1993-96; ptnr. Mayer, Brown & Platt, Chgo., 1996—; cons. USAF, Dayton, Ohio, 1974-81. Contbr. articles to profl. jours. Served to capt. USAF, 1968-74. Miami U. Undergrad. Rsch. fellow, 1967, Grad. Rsch. fellow, 1968. Mem. ABA, Am. Intellectual Property Law Assn., Tex. Bar Assn., Phi Kappa Phi. Democrat. Presbyterian. Federal civil litigation, Patent, Intellectual property. Home: 2519 Park Pl Evanston IL 60201-1315 Office: Mayer Brown & Platt 190 S La Salle St Ste 3100 Chicago IL 60603-3441

**RUPORT, SCOTT HENDRICKS,** lawyer; b. Nov. 22, 1949; s. Fred Hendricks and Juyne (Kennedy) R.; m. Linda Darlene Smith, Sept. 12, 1970; children: Brittany Lyle, Courtney Kennedy. BSBA, Bowling Green U., 1971; JD, U. Akron, 1974. Bar: Ohio 1974, Pa. 1984, U.S. Dist. Ct. (no. dist.) Ohio 1974, U.S. Ct. Appeals (6th cir.) 1975, U.S. Supreme Ct. 1978; cert. civil trial specialist Nat. Bd. Trial Advocacy. Assoc. Schwab, Sager, Growenburgh, Rothal, Fort, Skidmore & Nukes, Akron, Ohio, 1974-76, Skidmore & George Co. LPA, Akron, 1976-79, Skidmore, Ruport & Haskings, Akron, 1979-83; ptnr. Roderick, Myers & Linton, Akron, 1983-85, Ruport Co. LPA, Akron, 1985—; instr. real estate law U. Akron, 1976-77, adj. asst. prof. constrn. tech. Coll. Engring., 1983—. Capt. Fin. Corps. USAR, 1971-79. Mem. ABA, ATLA, Ohio Bar Assn., Ohio Acad. Trial Lawyers (chmn. civil and bus. litigation sect. 1989), Akron Bar Assn., Beta Gamma Sigma, Sigma Chi. Republican. Presbyterian. Federal civil litigation, Construction, State civil litigation. Office: Ruport Co LPA 1 Cascade Plz Fl 10 Akron OH 44308-1111

**RUPPE, ARTHUR MAXWELL,** lawyer; b. Boone, N.C., Dec. 15, 1928; s. Arthur Monroe and Floye (Robinson) R.; m. Ruth Marie Ledford; children: Ruth Carol, Sharon Marie, Arthur Maxwell Jr., Susan Lunette. *Wife, BA in Education, 1953, University of North Carolina at Chapel Hill. Daughter, Ruth Carol Gibson, BA in English, 1979, University of North Carolina at Wilmington is a Flight Attendant with U.S. Airways. Daughter, Sharon Marie Smith, BA in Education, 1982, University of North Carolina at Chapel Hill; JD from Campbell University College of Law, 1985, is an Attorney. Son, Max Jr., BA in Recreation/Political Science, 1985, University of North Carolina at Chapel Hill is a Real Estate Appraiser. Daughter, Susan Lunette Black, BS in Business Administration, Masters in Accounting, 1990, University of North Carolina at Chapel Hill is a CPA.* AA, Gardner Webb Coll., 1947; AB, U. N.C., 1950, JD, 1952. Bar: N.C. 1952, U.S. Dist. Ct. (ea. dist.) N.C. 1955, U.S. Ct. Mil. Appeals 1968; cert mediator. Asst. staff, judge advocate U.S. Army, Ft. Bragg, N.C., 1952-55; sole practice Fayetteville, N.C., 1955-98; mediator, 1997—. Served to 1st lt. U.S. Army, 1952-55. Mem. ABA, N.C. Bar Assn. (patron), 12 Jud. Dist Bar Assn., Cumberland County Bar Assn. (pres. 1982-83), K.P. Democrat. Baptist. Avocations: snow ski, tennis. Alternative dispute resolution. Home: 336 Summertime Rd Fayetteville NC 28303-4658

**RUPPERT, JOHN LAWRENCE,** lawyer; b. Chgo., Oct. 7, 1953; s. Merle Arvin and Loretta Marie (Ford) R.; m. Katharine Marie Tarbox, June 5, 1976. BA, Northwestern U., 1975; JD, U. Denver, 1978; LLM in Taxation, NYU, 1979. Bar: Colo. 1978, U.S. Dist. Ct. Colo. 1978, Ill. 1979, U.S. Tax Ct. 1981. Assoc. Kirkland & Ellis, Denver, 1979-84, ptnr., 1984-88; ptnr. Ballard, Spahr, Andrews & Ingersoll, Denver, 1988-96; shareholder Brownstein Hyatt Farber & Strickland, P.C., Denver, 1996—; lectr. U. Denver Coll. Law, fall 1984-92; adj. prof. law grad. tax program, 1993-94; sec. Capital Assocs., Inc., 1989-96, acting gen. counsel, 1989-90; sec. and spl. counsel to the bd. dirs. Bros. Gourmet Coffees, Inc., 1995—; asst. sec. Renaissance Cosmetics, Inc., 1996-98. Contbr. articles to profl. jours. Mem. ABA, Colo. Bar Assn. (mem. exec. coun. tax sect. 1985-89), Denver Bar Assn. Corporate taxation, Personal income taxation, Mergers and acquisitions. Office: Brownstein Hyatt Farber & Strickland PC 410 17th St Fl 22D Denver CO 80202-4402

**RUSCH, JONATHAN JAY,** lawyer; b. Nyack, N.Y., Oct. 16, 1952; s. Thaddeus David and Alice Marjorie (Lewis) R.; m. Doreen Evelyn Lacovara, Aug. 10, 1974; children: Rachel Madeline, Catherine Elizabeth. AB in Pub. Affairs with honors, Princeton U., 1974; MA, U. Va., 1978, JD, 1980. Bar: D.C. 1981, U.S. Dist. Ct. D.C. 1981, U.S. Ct. Appeals (D.C. cir.) 1981, U.S. Ct. Appeals (7th cir.) 1985, U.S. Ct. Appeals (9th cir.) 1990, U.S. Ct. Appeals (5th cir.) 1992, U.S. Supreme Ct. 1992. Assoc. Cleary, Gottlieb, Steen & Hamilton, Washington, 1980-83; spl. asst. to atty. gen. U.S. Dept. Justice, Washington, 1983-84; counsel Pres. Commn. on Organized Crime, Washington, 1984-86; acting dir., then dir. office of fin. enforcement U.S. Dept. Treasury, Washington, 1986-88; trial atty. fraud sect., criminal divsn. U.S. Dept. Justice, Washington, 1988-93, asst. spl. counsel House banking facility, 1992, sr. litigation counsel fraud sect., criminal divsn., 1993—, spl. counsel for fraud prevention, criminal divsn., 1998—; adj. prof. Georgetown U. Law Ctr., 1996—. Recipient Atty. Gen.'s Disting. Svc. award, 1995. Mem. ABA (coun. mem. adminstrv. law sect. 1990-93, chmn. criminal process com. 1987-90, 93-98, chmn. regulatory initiatives com. 1998—), Assn. Am. Law Schs., Tower Club. Home: 4600 Connecticut Ave NW Apt 207 Washington DC 20008-5702 Office: US Dept Justice 1400 New York Ave NE Washington DC 20002-1722

**RUSCHKY, ERIC WILLIAM,** prosecutor; b. Wareham, Mass., June 28, 1948; s. Harold William and Viola Emma R.; m. Mary Lenwood Dixon, Apr. 1, 1972; 1 child, Jane Spencer. BA, Wheaton (Ill.) Coll., 1970; JD, U. Va., 1973. Bar: Va 1973, S.C. 1974. Asst. U.S. atty. U.S. Dept. Justice, Columbia, S.C., 1974—. Active child support enforcement divsn. S.C. Dept. Social Svcs., Friends of Child Support.

**RUSH, FLETCHER GREY, JR.,** lawyer; b. Orlando, Fla., Dec. 28, 1917; s. Fletcher Grey and Elizabeth (Knox) R.; m. Lena Mae Willis, June 6, 1942; children: Patricia Rush White, Richard Fletcher. BSBA, JD with honors, U. Fla., 1942; LLD (hon.), Fla. So. Coll., 1975. Bar: Fla. 1942. Practice in Orlando, 1946—; pres. firm Rush, Marshall, Reber & Jones, P.A., 1957-91, of counsel, 1991—; Trustee Lawyers Title Guaranty Fund, 1953-65, chmn. bd., 1962-63, gen. counsel, 1968-90; v.p., dir., gen. counsel Orlando Fed. Savs. & Loan Assn., 1955-75; dir. Trust Co. Fla., 1974-82; mem. jud. nominating council Supreme Ct. Fla., 1972-73, jud. nominating commn., 1983-87. Contbr. articles to legal jours. Mem. Orlando Municipal Planning Bd., 1961-63; mem. Orlando Loch Haven Park Bd., 1973-81, vice chmn., 1978-81; bd. regents State Fla. Colls. and Univs., 1965; trustee Coll. Orlando, 1960-71, Fla. House, Inc., Washington, 1974-76, Fla. Supreme Ct. Hist. Soc., 1988-91; mem. president's council U. Fla., 1970—; v.p., exec. com. U. Fla. Found., 1973-75, bd. dirs., 1971-75; bd. dirs. Inst. for Study of Trial, Central Fla. U., 1978-80; mem. president's council Nat. Meth. Found., 1977-82. Served as officer F.A. AUS, 1942-46, ETO. Recipient Distinguished Service award Stetson U., 1967; Outstanding Alumnus award John Marshall Bar Assn. U. Fla. Coll. Law, 1971; Distinguished Alumnus award U. Fla., 1976. Fellow Am. Bar Found., Fla. Bar Found.; mem. ABA (ho. of dels. 1967-85, adv. bd. jour. 1968-71, chmn. standing com. on legislation 1973-75, on lawyers title guaranty funds 1979-83), Orange County (Fla.) Bar Assn. (pres. 1960-61), Fla. Bar (bd. govs. 1959-67, pres. 1966-67), Am. Judicature Soc. (dir. 1968—, exec. com. 1972, treas. 1973-75, v.p. 1975-77, pres. 1977-79), U. Fla. Law Center Assn. (trustee, exec. com., chmn. bd. trustees 1973-75), Blue Key (pres. Fla. 1941), Phi Kappa Phi, Alpha Tau Omega, Phi Delta Phi. Republican. Methodist (chmn. ch. adminstrv. bd. 1961-63, 75-76, trustee 1968-74, 77-80, trustee Fla. Conf., 1973-76). Clubs: Country, Univ. (Orlando) Orange County Old Timers (pres. 1986-87). Lodge: Kiwanis (pres. North Orlando club 1954). General corporate, Probate, Real property. Home: 1105 Edgewater Dr Orlando FL 32804-6311 Office: Rush Marshall Reber & Jones Magnolia Pl 5th Fl 109 E Church St Orlando FL 32801-3319

**RUSH, HENRI FRANCIS,** lawyer. BA, U. Minn., 1954; LLB, Georgetown U., 1963. Assoc. Donovan Leisure Newton & Irvine, N.Y.C.; atty. Office of Gen. Counsel Interstate Commerce Commn.; assoc. Swidler & Belnap, Washington; minority staff counsel U.S. Senate Com. on Commerce Sci. and Transp.; dep. fed. railroad adminstr. U.S. Dept. Transp.; sr. litig. atty. Interstate Commerce Commn., assoc. gen. counsel, dep. gen. counsel, gen. counsel; gen. counsel Surface Transp. Bd. Office: Surface Transp Bd 1925 K St NW Washington DC 20423-0001

**RUSHER, DERWOOD H., II,** lawyer; b. Roanoke, Va., Dec. 23, 1954; s. Derwood H. and Edith (McFadden) R.; m. Ashley Simmons, Aug. 15, 1987; children: Paige C, Peyton Clay, Amanda Shelby. BS, Va. Poly. Inst. and State U., 1977; JD, U. Richmond, 1980. Bar: Va. 1980, N.C. 1987, Ga. 1993, U.S. Dist. Ct. (mid. dist.) N.C. 1987, U.S. Dist Ct. (we. dist.) Va. 1987, U.S. Dist. Ct. (ea. dist.) Va. 1988, U.S. Ct. Appeals (4th cir.) 1980, U.S. Ct. Appeals (7th cir.) 1981, U.S. Ct. Appeals (3d, 5th, 6th, 8th, 9th, 10th, 11th, D.C., Fed. cirs.) 1987, U.S. Supreme Ct. 1987, U.S. Dist. Ct. Ariz. 1990, U.S. Dist. Ct. (no. dist.) Ga. 1993. Assoc. Street, Street, Street, Scott & Bowman, Grundy, Va., 1980-81; atty. Standard Oil Co., Chgo., 1981-84, Lexington, Ky., 1984-86; assoc. Womble, Carlyle, Sandridge & Rice, Winston-Salem, N.C., 1986-92; sr. atty. Rollins, Inc., Atlanta, 1992-95; counsel King & Spalding, Atlanta, 1996—. Mem. ABA, Phi Kappa Phi, Phi Delta Phi, Beta Gamma Sigma, Sigma Chi. Methodist. Product liability, Antitrust, Administrative and regulatory. Home: 1320 Northcliff Trace Roswell GA 30076-3274 Office: King & Spalding 191 Peachtree St Atlanta GA 30303-1763

**RUSHFORD, ROBERT HOWARD,** lawyer; b. Pitts., Jan. 18, 1962; s. Anthony J. Rushford and Alison Kresh; m. Carolyn J. Rushford, June 27, 1987; children: Nicholas H., James A. BA, U. Vt., 1984; JD summa cum laude, U. Pitts., 1988; LLM, Yale U., 1991. Bar: Vt. 1988, U.S. Dist. Ct. Vt. 1989. Law clk. Hon. Albert Coffrin, U.S. Dist. Ct. Vt., Burlington, 1988-89; assoc. Linton & Linton, Williston, Vt., 1989-96, Gravel and Shea, Burlington, 1996—. Bd. mem. Northern Vt. Home Builders Assn., Williston, 1997, chair legis. com. 1996—. Recipient David Stahl Meml. award U. Pitts., 1988. Mem. ABA, Vt. Bar Assn., Vt. Trial Lawyers Assn., Order of Coif. Avocations: running, skiing. Real property, Contracts commercial, Land use and zoning (including planning). Office: Gravel and Shea 76 Saint Paul St Burlington VT 05401-4470

**RUSMISEL, STEPHEN R.,** lawyer; b. N.Y.C., Jan. 27, 1946; s. R. Raymond and Esther Florence (Kutz) R.; m. Beirne Donaldson, Sept. 6, 1980 (div. Jan. 1984); 1 child, Margo Alexander; m. Melissa J. MacLeod, Aug. 24, 1985 (div. Oct. 1996); children: Benjamin William, Eric Scot Kunze, Erin Lea Kunze; m. Teresa R. Paterniti, June 28, 1997; 1 child, Sarah J. Lamendola. AB, Yale U., 1968; JD, U. Va., 1971. Bar: N.Y. 1972, U.S. Ct. Appeals (2d cir.) 1974, U.S. Dist. Ct. (so. dist.) N.Y. 1975. Assoc. Winthrop, Stimson, Putnam & Roberts, N.Y.C., 1971-80, ptnr., 1980—. Aux. officer Bedminster Twp. (N.J.) Police, 1976—. Mem. Practicing Law Inst., Am. Arbitration Assn. (arbitrator 1976—), Far Hills Polo Club (Annandale, N.J.), Ausable Club (St. Huberts, N.Y.), Essex Hunt Club (Peapack, N.J.), Phi Delta Phi. Republican. Avocations: polo, flying, carpentry, gardening, poetry. Mergers and acquisitions, Securities, General corporate. Home: Shadowline Farm Bedminster NJ 07921 Office: Winthrop Stimson Putnam & Roberts One Battery Park Plz New York NY 10004-1490

**RUSNAK, SUSAN E.,** lawyer; b. Erie, Pa., Apr. 9, 1968; d. Andrew John and Helen Rusnak. BA in Polit. Sci. summa cum laude, Edinboro U. Pa., 1990; JD, Case Western Res. U., 1993. Atty., project dir. ACLU Ohio, Cleve.; assoc. Denise Knecht & Assocs., Cleve., Dworken & Bernstein LPA, Cleve.; legis. chair Bus. and Profl. Women-Lake County. Author: AIDS and Civil Liberties Guide, 1994. Activist Human Rights Campaign Fund, Cleve., 1994; vol., tester Housing Advs., Inc., Cleve., 1995. Grantee Cleve. Found., 1993. Mem. Nat. Employment Lawyers Assn. Avocation: marathon running. Civil rights, Constitutional, Labor.

**RUSS, JAMES MATTHIAS,** lawyer; b. Duluth, Minn., Sept. 20, 1929; s. Matthias James and Agnes Margaret (Jerina) R.; m. Nanelle Davis, June 27, 1953; children: Tanya, Robin, Sarah, Claudia, Janine, Monica, Matthias James, Kateri. AB cum laude, Spring Hill Coll., 1955; JD, Georgetown U., 1957. Bar: D.C., 1957, Fla., 1958, U.S. Dist. Ct. (no., so. and mid. dists.) Fla., U.S. Ct. Appeals (5th and 11th cirs.), U.S. Supreme Ct.; cert. criminal trial lawyer 1987, criminal appellate lawyer 1992. County solicitor Orange County, Fla., 1961-65; lectr. criminal law and legal ethic. seminars. Contbr. articles to profl. jours. Trustee Orange County Legal Aid Soc.; chmn. The Chester Bedell Meml. Found., 1997-98. Recipient Tobias Simow Pro Bona Svc. award Fla. Supreme Ct., 1997. Master, Am. Inns of Ct.; Fellow Am. Coll. Trial Lawyers, Am. Bd. Criminal Lawyers; mem. ABA (criminal justice sect.-speedy trial com. 1976-77, com. on privacy 1982-83, def. function com. 1983-89, chmn. 1987-89), The Fla. Bar (chmn. criminal law com. 1964-65, 66-67, exec. coun. trial lawyers sect., 1967-68, mem. criminal law cert. com. 1988-91, recipient President's Pro Bono Svc. award, 9th jud. cir. 1993), Orange County Bar Assn. (exec. coun. 1967-70, sec. 1984-88), Nat. Assn. Criminal Def. Lawyers (2d v.p. 1992-93, 1st v.p. 1993-94, dir. 1984—, chmn. Lawyers' Assistance Strike Force 1987-89, Robert C. Heeney Meml. award 1988), Fla. Assn. Criminal Def. Lawyers (chmn. Lawyers' Assistance Strike Force 1988-89), Cen. Fla. Criminal Def. Lawyers Assn., Bd. Trial Advocacy (cert. 1982). Criminal, Appellate. Office: Tinker Bldg 18 W Pine St Orlando FL 32801-2697

**RUSSELL, C. EDWARD, JR.,** lawyer; b. Portsmouth, Va., Aug. 19, 1942. BA, Hampden-Sydney Coll., 1964; LLB, Washington & Lee U., 1967.

Bar: Va. 1967. Law clk. to Hon. John A. MacKenzie U.S. Dist. Ct. (ea. dist.) Va., 1967-68; atty. Kaufman & Canoles, Norfolk. Mem. ABA (bus. law sect., real property, probate and trust law sect.), Va. State Bar (bus. law sect., real property sect., health law sect.), Va. Bar Assn. (bus. law sect., real estate sect., chmn. young lawyers sect. 1977), Omicron Delta Kappa, Phi Alpha Delta. Office: PO Box 13368 Norfolk VA 23506-0368

**RUSSELL, CHARLES STEVENS,** state supreme court justice, educator; b. Richmond, Va., Feb. 23, 1926; s. Charles Herbert and Nita M. (Stevens) R.; m. Carolyn Elizabeth Abrams, Mar. 18, 1951; children: Charles Stevens Jr., David Tyler. B.A., U. Va., 1946, LL.B., 1948. Bar: Va. 1949, U.S. Dist. Ct. (ea. dist.) Va. 1952, U.S. Ct. Appeals (4th cir.) 1955, U.S. Supreme Ct. 1958. Assoc. Jesse, Phillips, Klinge & Kendrick, Arlington, Va., 1951-57, ptnr., 1957-60; ptnr. Phillips, Kendrick, Gearheart and Aylor, Arlington, 1960-67; judge 17th Jud. Ct. Va., Arlington, 1967-82; judge Supreme Ct. Va., Richmond, 1982-91, ret.; mem. jud. coun. Va., 1977-82; adj. prof. law George Mason U., Arlington, 1977-86, T.C. Williams Sch. Law U. Richmond, 1987-90; mem. exec. com. Va. State Bar, Richmond, 1964-67; mem. faculty Nat. Jud. Coll., Reno, 1980—, Appellate Judges Inst., NYU, 1986—. Mem. Adv. Com. on Youth, Arlington; mem. nat. council of trustees Freedoms Found., Valley Forge, Pa., 1986-91. Served to lt. comdr. USNR, 1944-51. Fellow Am. Bar Found.; mem. ABA, Arlington County Bar Assn., Va. Bar Assn., Richmond Bar Assn., Va. Trial Lawyers Assn., Am. Judicature Soc., Am. Law Inst. (adv. com. on complex litigation 1989-91). Episcopalian. Clubs: Downtown (Richmond), Fishing Bay Yacht. Home: 11 James Falls Dr Richmond VA 23221-3942 Office: Va Supreme Ct PO Box 1315 Richmond VA 23218-1315

**RUSSELL, DAN M., JR.,** federal judge; b. Magee, Miss., Mar. 15, 1913; s. Dan M. and Beulah (Watkins) R.; m. Dorothy Tudury, Dec. 27, 1942; children—Ronald Truett, Dorothy Dale, Richard Brian. B.A., U. Miss., 1935, LL.B., 1937. Bar: Miss. bar 1937. Practice in Gulfport and Bay St. Louis, Miss.; U.S. judge So. Dist. Miss., 1965—; now sr. judge. Lt. comdr. U.S. Naval Intelligence, 1941-45. Mem. Miss. Bar Assn., Hancock County Bar Assn., Hancock and Harrison Counties Bar Assn., Bay St. Louis Rotary Club (hon.), Gulfport Rotary Club (hon.), Am. Inns Ct. (hon. Russell-Blass-Walker chpt.), Federalist Soc. (adv. bd. Miss. chpt.), Hancock County C. of C., Tau Kappa Alpha, Scribblers. Club: Rotarian (pres. Bay St. Louis, Miss. 1946). Office: US Dist Ct PO Box 1930 Gulfport MS 39502-1930

**RUSSELL, DAVID L.,** federal judge; b. Sapulpa, Okla., July 7, 1942; s. Lynn and Florence E. (Brown) R.; m. Dana J. Wilson, Apr. 16, 1971; 1 child, Sarah Elizabeth. BS, Okla. Bapt. U., 1963; J.D., Okla. U., 1965. Bar: Okla. 1965. Asst. atty. gen. State of Okla., Oklahoma City, 1968-69, legal adviser to gov., 1969-70; legal adviser Senator Dewey Bartlett, Washington, 1973-75; U.S. atty. for Western dist. Okla. Dept. Justice, 1975-77, 81-82; ptnr. Benefield & Russell, Oklahoma City, 1977-81; chief judge U.S. Dist. Ct. (we. dist.) Okla., Oklahoma City, 1982—. Lt. comdr. JAGC, USN, 1965-68. Selected Outstanding Fed. Ct. Trial judge Okla. Trial Lawyers Assn., 1988. Mem. Okla. Bar Assn., Fed. Bar Assn. (pres. Oklahoma City chpt. 1981), Order of Coif (alumnus mem.). Republican. Methodist. Office: US Dist Ct 3309 US Courthouse 200 NW 4th St Rm 1210 Oklahoma City OK 73102-3092

**RUSSELL, DAVID WILLIAMS,** lawyer; b. Lockport, N.Y., Apr. 5, 1945; s. David Lawson and Jean Graves (Williams) R.; m. Frances Yung Chung Chen, May 23, 1970; children: Bayard Chen, Ming Rennick. AB, Dartmouth Coll., 1967, MBA, 1969; JD cum laude, Northwestern U., 1976. Bar: Ill. 1976, Ind. 1983. English tchr. Talledega (Ala.) Coll., summer 1967; math. tchr. Lyndon Inst., Lyndonville, Vt., 1967-68; asst. to pres. for planning Tougaloo (Miss.) Coll., 1969-71, bus. mgr., 1971-73; law clk. Montgomery, McCracken, Walker & Rhoads, Phila., summer 1975; with Winston & Strawn, Chgo., 1976-83; ptnr. Klineman, Rose, Wolf & Wallack, Indpls., 1983-87, Johnson, Smith, Pence, Densborn, Wright & Heath, Indpls., 1987-99, Bose McKinney & Evans, Indpls., 1999—; cons. Alfred P. Sloan Found., 1972-73; dir. Forum for Internat. Profl. Svcs., 1985—, sec., 1985-88, pres. 1988-89; U.S. Dept. Justice del. to U.S. China Joint Session on Trade, Investment & Econ. Law, Beijing, 1987; leader Ind. Products Trade Fair, Kawachinagano, Japan, 1996; lectr. Ind. law Ind. Gov.'s Trade Mission to Japan, 1986, internat. law Ind. Continuing Legal Edn. Forum, 1986-96, chmn., 1987, 89, 91; adj. prof. internat. bus. law Ind. U., 1993-95; bd. dirs. Ind. ASEAN Coun., Inc., 1988-93; nat. selection com. Woodrow Wilson Found. Adminstrv. Fellowship Program, 1973-76; vol. Lawyers for Creative Arts, Chgo., 1977-83; dir. World Trade Club of Ind., 1987-93, v.p., 1987-91, pres., 1991-92; dir. Ind. Swiss Found., 1991—, Writer's Ctr., Indpls., 1997—; dir. Ind. Soviet Trade Consortium, 1991-99, sec., 1991-92; v.p., bd. dirs. Ind. Sister Cities, 1988—; dir. Internat. Ctr. Indpls., 1988-92, v.p. 1988-89; Ind. dist. enrollment dir. Dartmouth Coll., 1990—; bd. dirs. Carmel Sister Cities, 1993—, v.p. 1995-96, pres. 1997-99; v.p., gen. coun. Lawrence Durrell Soc., 1993—; mem. bd. advisors Ctr. for Internat. Bus. Edn. and Rsch. Krannert Grad. Sch. Mgmt. Purdue U., 1995—; dir., v.p., gen. coun. Global Crossroads Found., Inc., 1995—. Woodrow Wilson Found. Adminstrv. fellow, 1969-72. Mem. ABA, ACLU, Ill. Bar Assn., Ind. Bar Assn. (vice chmn. internat. law sect., 1988-90, chmn. 1990-92, co-chmn. written publs. com. 1997—), Indpls. Bar Assn., Dartmouth Lawyers Assn., Indpls. Assn. Chinese Ams., Chinese Music Soc., Dartmouth Club of Ind. (sec. 1986-87, pres. 1987-88), Internat. Bar Assn., Zeta Psi. Presbyterian. General corporate, Real property, Private international. Home: 10926 Lakeview Dr Carmel IN 46033-3937 Office: Bose McKinney & Evans 2700 First Ind Plz 135 N Pennsylvania St Indianapolis IN 46204-2400

**RUSSELL, IRWIN EMANUEL,** lawyer; b. N.Y.C., Jan. 24, 1926; m. Suzanne Russell, Nov. 15, 1968. BS in Econs., U. Pa., 1947; JD, Harvard U., 1949. Bar: N.Y. 1949, Calif. 1971. Atty. office chief counsel Wage Stabilization Bd., Washington, 1951-53; pvt. practice N.Y.C., 1954-71; founder, chmn., dir. RAI Rsch. Corp., Hauppage, N.Y., 1954-91; exec. v.p., treas., dir. The Wolper Orgn., Inc., L.A., 1971-76; pvt. practice Beverly Hills, Calif., 1977—; dir. Walt Disney Co., Burbank, Calif., The Lipper Fund, Inc., N.Y.C. With USAAF, 1944-45. Entertainment, General corporate. Home: 10590 Wilshire Blvd Apt 1402 Los Angeles CA 90024-4563 Office: 9401 Wilshire Blvd Ste 760 Beverly Hills CA 90212-2933

**RUSSELL, JAMES FRANKLIN,** lawyer; b. Memphis, Mar. 21, 1945; s. Frank Hall and Helen (Brunson) R.; m. Marilyn Land, June 1, 1968 (div. May 1976); children: Mary Helen, Myles Edward; m. Linda Hatcher, July 9, 1977; 1 child, Maggie Abele. BA, Rhodes Coll., 1967; JD, Memphis State U., 1970. Bar: Tenn. 1971, U.S. Dist. Ct. (we. dist.) Tenn. 1971, U.S. Ct. Appeals (6th cir.) 1971, U.S. Dist. Ct. (no. dist.) Miss. 1976, U.S. Ct. Appeals (5th cir.) 1977, U.S. Ct. Appeals (8th cir.) 1987. Assoc. Nelson, Norvell, Wilson, McRae, Ivy & Sevier, Memphis, 1971-75; ptnr. Stanton, Russell & Challen, Memphis, 1975-78, Russell, Price, Weatherford & Warlick, Memphis, 1978-82, Price, Vance & Criss, Memphis, 1982-85, Apperson, Crump, Duzane & Maxwell, Memphis, 1985-97, 1985-97; cir. ct. judge Divsn. II 30th Jud. Dist., 1997—. V.p. mid-south chpt. Am. Red Cross, Memphis, 1992-94; treas. Epilepsy Found. West Tenn., Memphis, 1992-94. Mem. ABA, Nat. Assn. R.R. Trial Counsel, Internat. Assn. Def. Counsel, Tenn. Bar Assn., Tenn. Def. Lawyers Assn., Memphis Bar Assn. (pres. 1992). Episcopalian. Avocations: golf, snow skiing. Insurance, Transportation, Workers' compensation. Home: 1045 Reed Hooker N Eads TN 38028-6958 Office: Shelby County Courthouse 140 Adams Ave Memphis TN 38103-2000

**RUSSELL, JOHN ST. CLAIR, JR.,** lawyer; b. Albany, N.Y., Mar. 21, 1917; s. John St. Clair and Hazel (Barbiers) R.; m. Betty Kixmiller, Sept. 12, 1941; children: Patricia Russell, John St. Clair III (dec.), David K. AB cum laude, Dartmouth Coll., 1938; LLB, Yale U., 1941. Bar: N.Y. 1942, D.C. 1965. Mem. Hale Russell & Gray (and predecessors), N.Y.C., 1948-85; mem. Winthrop, Stimson, Putnam & Roberts, N.Y.C., 1985-90, sr. counsel, ret. ptnr., 1991—. Mem. Irvington (N.Y.) Zoning Bd. Appeals, 1955-89; chmn. Raoul Wallenberg Com. of U.S., 1985-90; exec. trustee Am.-Scandinavian Found.; mem. alumni coun. Dartmouth Coll., 1994-98. Maj. USMCR, OSS, 1942-46. Decorated Order of Vasa Sweden; recipient medal of merit Swedish Red Cross. Mem. ABA, Assn. Bar City N.Y., Dartmouth Club, Phi Beta Kappa, Phi Sigma Kappa. Office: Winthrop Stimson Putnam & Robert One Battery Park Pla New York NY 10004-1490

**RUSSELL, MAURICE LLOYD,** judge; b. Caldwell, Idaho, Aug. 6, 1950; s. Maurice Lloyd and Betty M. (Pledger) R.; m. Hilary Higginson, May 19, 1984. BA, U. Calif., Santa Cruz, 1972; MA, U. Calif., Santa Barbara, 1975; JD, UCLA, 1978. Bar: Oreg. 1978, U.S. Dist. Ct. Oreg. 1980. Gen. counsel Mid-Columbia Cmty. Action Coun., The Dalles, Oreg., 1978-79; assoc. Stephen H. Miller, Atty., Reedsport, Oreg., 1979-80; city atty., planner, asst. city m gr. City of Independence, Oreg., 1980-82; assoc. Chester Scott, P.C., Independence, Oreg., 1982-83; pres. M.L. Russell, P.C., Independence, Oreg., 1983-85; v.p., gen. counsel Citizens Savings & Loan Assn., Salem, Oreg., 1985-88; assoc. Churchill, Leonard et al, Salem, Oreg., 1988-93, Tarlow, Jordan & Schrader, Beaverton, Oreg., 1993-94; adminstrv. law judge State of Oreg. Dept. Transp., Salem, 1995—. Screenwriter, dir. (continuing legal edn. videotapes) Limits of Zealous Representation, 1995 (Inns of Ct. award 1995), Oregon Jury System, 1996, DUI—Recent Cases, 1996. Chair budget com. Chemeketa Cmty. Coll., Salem, 1996-97; pres., bd. dirs. Mid-Vlley Arts Coun., Salem, 1991-93, chmn. bd. dirs. Salem Pastoral Counselling Ctr., 1993-95. Mem. Oreg. State Bar Assn. (bd. mem. debtor-creditor sect. 1992-93, legis. subcom. 1990-92, 93-96), Masons (Master), Willamette Valley Am. Inns of Ct. Democrat. Episcopalian. Avocations: writing, flytying, fishing, blacksmithing, music. Office: Oregon Dept Transportation DMV 1905 Lana Ave NE Salem OR 97314-5000

**RUSSELL, MICHAEL JAMES,** lawyer; b. Northampton, Mass., May 19, 1958. Cert. in German, U. Vienna, 1979; BA summa cum laude, Gettysburg Coll., 1980; MA, JD, Vanderbilt U., 1984. Bar: Pa. 1984, D.C. 1985, U.S. Supreme Ct. 1995. Rsch. asst. Vanderbilt U., Nashville, 1982-84; legal intern U.S. State Dept., Washington, 1982; law clk. Stewart, Estes & Donnell, Nashville, 1983; atty. U.S. Dept. Agr., Washington, 1984-85; majority counsel subcom. on juvenile justice senate judiciary com. U.S. Senate, Washington, 1985-86, minority gen. counsel subcom. on constn., 1987, legis. dir. to Senator Arlen Specter, 1987-90; senate staff mem. Congrl. Crime Caucus, 1987-90; dep. dir. Nat. Inst. Justice U.S. Dept. Justice, Washington, 1990-93, acting dir., 1993-94; pres. Russell & Assocs., Washington, 1994-96; sr. pub. safety advisor Corp. Nat. Svc., Washington, 1994-96; dep. chief of staff to Senator Ben Nighthorse Campbell, 1996—. Editorial staff Vanderbilt Jour. Transnat. Law, Nashville, 1982-83, contbr., 1983, rsch. editor, 1983-84 (editor award 1984). Mem. senate staff club, 1985-90, Bush/Quayle Campaign's Crime Adv. Com., 1988, Friends of the Nat. Parks at Gettysburg, Pa., 1989-98; bd. fellows Gettysburg Coll., 1990—; vol. Nat. Constrn. Ctr., Phila., 1990; mem. Bush/Quayle Adminstrn. S.E.S. Assn., 1990-92; Eisenhower Leadership Prize Dinner Com., Eisenhower World Affairs Inst., 1992, 93, mem. com. to celebrate bicentennial of constn., Northampton, Mass., 1987; mem. Bush/Quayle Alumni Assn., 1993—. Recipient Voluntary Svc. award VA, Northampton, 1978, Trustees award Forbes Libr., Northampton, 1989, cert. of appreciation Correctional Edn. Assn., 1991, Phi Alpha Delta, 1989, Fed. Bur. Alcohol, Tobacco and Firearms, 1989, Gettysburg Coll. Career Svcs. Office, 1992, Young Alumni Achievement award Gettysburg Coll., 1992, Wasserstein Fellowship Harvard Law Sch. Office of Pub. Interest Adv., 1995-96. Mem. Am. Soc. Internat. Law, Pa. Soc. of Washington, Phi Beta Kappa, Psi Chi (jr. award 1979). Avocations: racquetball, politics, volunteer svc. Office: Office Senator Ben Nighthorse Campbell 380 Russell Senate Office Bldg Washington DC 20510-0001

**RUSSELL, PATRICK,** lawyer; b. Milw., Dec. 26, 1967; s. Michael H. and Susan K. Russell. BA, Marquette U., 1990; JD, U. Miami, 1993. Bar: Fla. 1994. Gen. counsel Insta-Check Sys., Inc., Miami, Fla., 1994-95; pvt. practice Miami, 1995—; adj. prof. Fla. Internat. U., North Miami, 1996. Mem. ABA, Fla. Bar Assn., Dade County Bar Assn. General civil litigation, Insurance, Consumer commercial. Office: Russell Law Offices 201 W Flagler St Miami FL 33130-1510

**RUSSELL, RICHARD LLOYD,** lawyer; b. Kokomo, Ind., Dec. 13, 1946; s. James E. and Doris R. R.; m. Cynthia L. Hamilton, May 29, 1999; children from previous marriage: Ryan, Rachel, Casey, Ryun. BA in Polit. Sci., Purdue U., 1970; JD, Ind. U., 1975. Bar: Ind. 1975. Chief dep. prosecutor Howard County, Kokomo, 1978-86; city atty. City of Kokomo, 1978-80; atty. Russell, McIntyre, Hilligoss & Welke, Kokomo, 1980—; chmn. bd. Kokomo Devel. Corp., 1996-98. Named Sagamore of Wabash, State Ind., 1991. Mem. Am. Trial Lawyers, Ind. Trial Lawyers (sustaining mem.), Ct. Appointed Spl. Adv. (bd. dirs. 1997—), Kokomo Howard County C. of C. (chmn. bd. 1997-98). Personal injury, State civil litigation, Family and matrimonial. Office: Russell McIntyre Hilligoss & Welke 116 N Main St Kokomo IN 46901-4625

**RUSSELL, ROBIE GEORGE,** lawyer; b. Moscow, Idaho, July 7, 1948; s. George Robie Russell and Jean Ray (Atkinson) O'Reilly; m. Nancy Kay Olson, May 31, 1975; children: George Robie, Erin Kay. BS in Polit. Sci., Pub. Adminstrn., U. Idaho, 1972, cert. in Pub. Adminstrn., 1974, JD, 1978. Bar: Idaho 1979, U.S. Dist. Ct. Idaho 1979, U.S. Ct. Claims 1980, U.s. Ct. Appeals (9th cir.) 1980, U.S. Tax Ct. 1981, U.S. Ct. Appeals (fed. cir.) 1985, U.S. Supreme Ct. 1985, Wash. 1991. Dep. atty. gen. State of Idaho, Boise, 1979-81, sr. dep. atty. gen., div. chief, 1981-86; regional adminstr. region 10 U.S. EPA, Alaska, Idaho, Oregon, Wash., 1986-90; pres. Environ. Property Mgmt., Inc., Bainbridge Island, Wash., 1991—; counsel Idaho Sec. of State, Boise, 1982-86. Contbg. author: Idaho Media Law Handbook, 1986; editor: Idaho Cities Mag., 1974-75, (newsletter) Local Govt. Legal News, 1981-86; contbr. articles to profl. jours. Pres., treas. Lincoln Day Assn., Boise, 1979-86; vice-chmn. Selective Svc. Bd., Boise, 1983-86; chmn., vice-chmn. Ada County Reps., Boise, 1984-86; chmn. Combined Fed. Campaign, 1988; mem. Puget Sound Fed. Exec. Bd., 1986-90; mem. Am. Ctr. Internat. Leadership, Soviet Union/Poland delegation, 1989. Named one of Outstanding Young Men in Am., 1980—. Mem. ABA, Idaho State Bar Assn., Wash. State Bar Assn., Boise Bar Assn., Nat. Inst. Mcpl. Law Officers, Assn. Idaho City Attys. (sec., treas. 1981-86, founder), Assn. Idaho Cities (advisor 1981—, Boyd Martin award 1985), Phi Alpha Delta, U. Idaho Alumni Assn. (bd. dirs. 1973-74), Sons and Daus. Idaho Pioneers, U. Idaho Vandal Boosters (Moscow, Idaho) (chpt. pres., bd. dirs. 1975—, nat. v.p. 1987-89, nat. pres. 1989-90, Vandal Booster of Yr. 1985). Republican. Club: U. Idaho Vandal Boosters (Moscow, Idaho) (chpt. pres., bd. dirs. 1975—, nat. v.p., 1987-89, nat. pres. 1989-90), Vandal Booster of Yr. 1985). Lodge: Elks. Avocations: stamp collecting, fishing, gardening, music, lit. Home: PO Box 10667 Bainbridge Island WA 98110 Office: Environ Property Mgmt Inc 2101 4th Ave Ste 700 Seattle WA 98121-2357

**RUSSELL, THOMAS B.,** judge; b. 1945. BA, Western Ky. U., 1967; JD, U. Ky., 1970. Ptnr. Whitlow, Roberts, Houston & Russell, Paducah, Ky., 1970-94; dist. judge U.S. Dist. Ct. (we. dist.) Ky., Paducah, 1994—. Mem. ABA, Ky. Bar Assn., Ky. Bar Found., Am. Bd. of Trial Advocates, Am. Bar Found., McCracken County Bar Assn., Am. Coll. of Trial Lawyers, Rotary. Methodist. Office: US Dist Ct W Ky Federal Bldg 501 Broadway St Paducah KY 42001-6856

**RUSSO, DONNA MARIE,** lawyer; b. Bklyn., Apr. 22, 1963; d. Frank Francis and Paulette Rita (Pagliaro) R. BA, Fordham U., 1984; JD, Hofstra U., 1986; M in Environ. Law, Vt. Law Sch., 1990. Bar: N.J. 1987, D.C. 1988, N.Y. 1996. Law clk. Staten Island (N.Y.) Dist. Atty., 1983-84, Law Offices of Donald V. Kane, Hempstead, N.Y., 1985-86, U.S. Dept. Health and Human Svcs., N.Y.C., 1985-86; assoc. Holzka, Donahue & Kuhn, Staten Island, 1986-88, Law Office of Philip J. Mattina, S.I., 1988-90, N.J. State Dept. Environ. Protection, Trenton, N.J., 1990-91, Cooper, Rose, & English, Summit and Rumson, N.J., 1991—. Mem. ABA, N.J. Bar Assn., N.Y. Bar Assn., D.C. Bar Assn., Essex County Inn of Ct. Insurance, Environmental.

**RUSSO, FRANK,** lawyer; b. Camden, N.J., Nov. 23, 1953; s. Frank Orlando Russo and Ruth Marie Zebedies; m. Colleen Marie Corr; 2 children. AA, Camden County C.C., 1974; BA, U. S. Fla., 1977; JD, Southwe. U., 1982; grad. Nat. Coll. DUI Def. program, Harvard U., 1997. Bar: Fla. 1985, Colo. 1992,. Cert. legal intern then pros. atty. Office State Atty., Clearwater, Fla., 1983-86; pvt. practice St. Petersburg, Fla., 1986—; pres. Meta Progress Inc.; guest lectr. U. S. Fla., St. Petersburg Jr. Coll.; treas. Cir. Ct. Jud. Campaign, 1996. Named Leading Am. Atty. Am. Rsch. Corp., 1998. Mem. Fla. Assn. Criminal Def. Lawyers, Pinellas County Bar Criminal Def. Lawyers Assn., St. Petersburg Bar Assn. Avocations: traveling, mountain biking. Criminal. Office: 11300 4th St N Ste 121 Saint Petersburg FL 33716-2939

**RUSSO, FRANK D.,** lawyer; b. L.A., June 4, 1951; s. Alphonse J. and Mary J. Russo; m. Toni A. Tullys, June 12,1988; 1 chlid, Alexander D. BA, Yale U., 1973; JD, U. Calif., Berkeley, 1976. Bar: Calif. 1976, U.S. Dist. Ct. (so. dist.) Calif. 1976; cert. specialist in workers' compensation, Calif. Adminstrv. asst. Calif. State Assembly, Sacramento, 1976-78; assoc. atty. Jewel & Leary, Oakland, Calif., 1978-82; ptnr. Jewel, Leary & Russo, Oakland, 1982-86; chief legal counsel Speaker of Calif. Assembly, Sacramento, 1987-88; ptnr. Smith, Wright & Peterson, Oakland, 1989-91; atty., sole practitioner Oakland, 1991-95; ptnr. Russo & Casetta, Oakland, 1996—; judge pro tem Workers' Compensation Appeals Bd., Sacramento, 1982; lectr. Contra Costa County AFL-CIO, 1985—. Contbg. mem. Pub. Opinion Quar., 1971-72, Indsl. Rels. Law Jour., 1965; contbr. articles to profl. jours. Chair United Dem. Campaign, Alameda county, 1984, 86, 88. Mem. Alameda County Bar Assn. (bd. govs. lawyer referral svc. 1992-96), Calif. Applicants Attys. Assn. (bd. govs. 1992—, pres. 1997-98), Alameda-Contra Costa County Trial Lawyers Assn. (bd. govs. 1991-93). Avocations: politics, hiking, music, gardening. Workers' compensation. Office: Russo & Casetta 492 9th St Ste 300 Oakland CA 94607-4055

**RUSSO, MICHAEL NATALE, JR.,** lawyer; b. Freeport, N.Y., July 4, 1963; s. Michael Natale Sr. and Patricia Mary R.; m. Elizabeth Murray, Nov. 19, 1988; children: Michael N. III, Connor S., Patrick L. BA in Internat. Affairs, Lafayette Coll., 1985; JD, Cath. U. Am., 1988. Bar: Md. 1988, D.C. 1990, U.S. Dist. Ct. Md. 1991. Law clk. Cir. Ct., Anne Arundel County, Annapolis, Md., 1988-89; assoc. Thieblot, Ryan, Martin & Ferguson, Balt., 1989-96; sr. assoc. Ferguson, Schetelich, Heffernan & Murdock, Balt., 1996-97; ptnr. Ferguson, Schetelich & Heffernan, Balt., 1997—. Mem. Md. State Bar Assn., Anne Arundel County Bar Assn., Bar Assn. Balt. General civil litigation, Contracts commercial, General corporate. Office: Ferguson Schetelich & Heffernan 1401 Nations Bank Ctr 100 S Charles St Baltimore MD 21201-2725

**RUSSO, RONALD JOHN,** lawyer; b. Tampa, Fla., July 14, 1949; s. Andrew and Lena (Genco) R.; 1 child, Taylor. BA, U. So. Fla., 1971; JD with honors, U. Fla., 1974, LLM in Taxation, 1975. Bar: Fla. 1974, U.S. Tax Ct. 1975. Assoc. Holland & Knight, Tampa, 1975-78; ptnr. Barnett, Bolt & Russo, Tampa, 1978-86, Glenn, Rasmussen, Fogarty, Merryday & Russo, Tampa, 1986-91; pvt. practice Tampa; instr. fed. tax rsch. U. Fla. Law Sch., Gainesville, 1974-75. Contbr. articles to legal jours. Mem. ABA, Fla. Bar, Hillsborough County Bar Assn. (treas. 1983-85, bd. dirs. 1985-89, chmn. exec. com. 1987-89, editor bull. 1988-89, pres.-elect 1989-90, pres. 1990-91, James M. McEwen Meml. award 1984), ABA House of Dels., Univ. Club. Republican. Roman Catholic. Family and matrimonial, Estate planning, Taxation, general. Home: 5149 W San Jose St Tampa FL 33629-6414 Office: 501 E Kennedy Blvd Ste 700 Tampa FL 33602-5200

**RUSSO, ROY R.,** lawyer; b. Utica, N.Y., July 26, 1936; s. Chester F. and Helen L. (Gacek) R.; m. Ann M. Obernesser, Sept. 19, 1959; children: Andrew F., Susan Elizabeth. BA, Columbia U., 1956; LLB cum laude, Syracuse U., 1959. Bar: N.Y. 1959, D.C. 1967, U.S. Supreme Ct. 1969. Pvt. practice law, Washington, 1959—; atty. FCC, Washington, 1959-66; ptnr. Cohn and Marks, Washington, 1966—; spl. counsel Nat. Cath. Conf. for Interracial Justice, Washington, 1984—. Mem. editl. adv. com. The Communications Act: A Legislative History of the Major Amendments 1934-96; mem. adv. bd. Pike and Fischer Comms. Regulation. Founding chmn. Commn. on Social Ministry, Richmond (Va.) Diocese, 1970-74; v.p., bd. dirs. St. Mary's Housing Corp., Annandale, Manassas, Fredericksburg, Ashburn, Va., 1971—; pres., bd. dirs. Caths. for Housing, Inc., 1979-84, Cath. Charities, Arlington (Va.) Diocese, 1980-84. With USAF, 1960-61. Recipient Alumni medal Alumni Fedn. Columbia U., 1994. Mem. ABA, Fed. Communications Bar Assn. (co-chair mass media practice com. 1988-91, nominations com. 1991-92), Computer Law Assn., Internat. Inst. Communications, John Jay Assocs., Soc. Columbia Grads., Columbia U. Club of Washington (sr. v.p. 1989-91, pres. 1991-95), Order of Coif, Phi Alpha Delta. Democrat. Club: Columbia Coll. (Washington) (mem. steering com. 1985—, chmn. Deans' Day program 1988—). Communications. Home: 6528 Bowie Dr Springfield VA 22150-1309 Office: Cohn and Marks 1920 N St NW Ste 300 Washington DC 20036-1622

**RUSSO, THOMAS ANTHONY,** lawyer; b. N.Y.C., Nov. 6, 1943; s. Lucio F. and Tina (Iarossi) R.: m. Nancy Felipe, June 18, 1966 (div. 1974); m. Janice Davis, June 10, 1977 (div. 1979); m. Marcy C. Appelbaum, June 16, 1985; children: Morgan Danielle and Alexa Anne (twins), Tyler James. BA, Fordham U., 1965; MBA, Cornell U., 1969, JD, 1969. Bar: N.Y., 1970, U.S. Ct. Appeals (2d cir.) 1971, U.S. Dist. Ct. (so. and ea. dists.) N.Y. 1971, U.S. Ct. Appeals (7th cir.) 1982. Staff atty. SEC, Washington, 1969-71; assoc. Cadwalader, Wickersham & Taft, N.Y.C., 1971-75; dir. div. trading and markets Commodity Futures Trading Commn., Washington, 1975-77; ptnr. Cadwalader, Wickersham & Taft, N.Y.C., 1977-92; mgmt. com., 1984-92; mng. dir., mem. op. com. Lehman Bros., N.Y.C., 1993—; vice chmn. bd. trustees Futures Industry Inst.; bd. dirs. Rev. Securities and Commodities Regulation, N.Y.C., Women's Interart Ctr.; trustee Inst. Internat. Edn., March of Dimes (nat. bd. dirs.). Author: Regulation of the Commodities Futures and Options Markets; co-author: Regulation of Brokers, Dealers and Securities Markets, Supplement Markets; editorial bd. mem. Internat. Jour. Regulatory Law and Practice; practitioner bd. advisors Stanford Jour. of Law.; mem. editl. bd. Futures and Derivatives Law Report. Mem. ABA (mem. futures regulations, exec. coun., adv. com. on fed. regulation of securities, past co-chmn. derivative instruments subcom. of com. on fed. regulation), Assn. of Bar of City of N.Y. (chmn. internat. law sub com. of the com. on commodities regulation 1984-85, chmn. com. commodities regulations 1981-82), D.C. Bar Assn. Securities, Banking, General corporate. Office: Lehman Bros Inc 200 Vesey St Fl 10 New York NY 10285-1000

**RUSSON, LEONARD H.,** state supreme court justice; b. Salt Lake City, May 15, 1933. JD, Utah Coll., 1962. Pvt. practice Salt Lake City, 1962-84; judge Utah Dist. Ct. (3d dist.), Utah Ct. Appeals; justice Utah Supreme Ct., Salt Lake City; vice chair Utah Bd. Dist. Ct. Judges; mem. Jud. Conduct Commn., Utah Supreme Ct. Adv. Com. on Code of Profl. Conduct. Office: Utah Supreme Ct PO Box 140210 450 S State St Salt Lake City UT 84114-0210*

**RUSSONIELLO, JOSEPH PASCAL,** lawyer; b. Jersey City, Oct. 12, 1941; s. Sabin G. and Justine B. (Terraciano) R.; m. Moira F. Ward, Aug. 29, 1969. B in Social Sci., Fairfield U., 1963; JD, NYU, 1966. Bar: N.J. 1967, Calif. 1969. Spl. agt. FBI, Washington, 1966-67; dep. dist. atty. City and County San Francisco (Calif.) Dist. Atty. Offices, 1969-75; assoc. Cooley Godward Castro Huddleson & Tatum, San Francisco, 1975-78; U.S. atty. U.S. Dept. Justice (no. dist.) Calif., San Francisco, 1982-90; ptnr. Cooley Godward L.L.P., San Francisco, 1978-82, 90—; pres., bd. dirs. San Francisco (Calif.) Law Sch., 1996—; analyst KTVU-Ch. 2, Oakland, Calif., 1994—. Pres. Northgate Cottages, Napa, Calif., 1988—; chmn. Catholics for Truth and Justice, San Francisco, 1991—; v.p. Mid-Pacific region Nat. Italian Am. Fedn., 1996—. Recipient Man of Yr. award NIAF, 1986; named Alumni of Yr.-Pub. Sector, NYU Law Sch., 1991. Fellow Am. Coll. Trial Lawyers; mem. Am. bd. Trial Lawyers (adv.), McFetridge Inn of Ct. (barrister). Republican. Avocations: tennis, golf, reading, playing the saxophone. Government contracts and claims, Criminal. Home: 2850 Jackson St San Francisco CA 94115-1146 Office: Cooley Godward LLP 1 Maritime Plz San Francisco CA 94111-3404

**RUSSOTTI, PHILIP ANTHONY,** lawyer; b. N.Y.C., Mar. 24, 1948; s. Philip Armond and Yolanda (Morelli) R.; m. Mary Wolfe, Jan. 20, 1973 (div. Mar., 1996); children: Thomas, Matthew, Peter; m. Kathleen Kettles, May 25, 1996. *Wife Kathleen, a registered nurse and attorney, is chairperson of the Association of the Bar of the City of New York's Committee on Alcohol and Substance Abuse. Son Tom graduates from Stanford University June 1999; son Matthew attends Wesleyan University and will study in Madrid 1999-2000; son Peter excels in classical languages, Latin and Greek, and baseball at St. Ann's High School, Brooklyn, New York. Grandparents emigrated from Sicily and Naples in early 1990's to New York City where they raised 7 children. Father Philip, 82, and mother Yolanda, 83, moved to New Jersey, where they raised their family, including sister Linda.* BA, Columbia U., 1970; JD, St. John's U., Queens, N.Y., 1973. Bar: N.Y. 1974, U.S. Dist. Ct. (so. dist.) N.Y. 1974, U.S. Dist. Ct. (ea. dist.) N.Y., 1980, U.S. Ct. Appeals (2nd cir.) 1982, U.S. Ct. Appeals (D.C. cir.)

1989, U.S. Ct. Internat. Trade 1986, U.S. Supreme Ct., 1997; bd. cert. civil trial atty. Nat. Bd. Trial Advocacy, 1997. Bur. chief, Supreme Ct. trial bur. asst. dist. atty. N.Y. County Dist. Atty.'s Office, N.Y.C., 1973-80; pvt. practice N.Y.C., 1980-84; partner Russotti & Barrison, N.Y.C., 1985-89, Wingate, Russotti & Shapiro, N.Y.C., 1990—; Lectr. in the field. *Phil is one of very few attorneys in New York who have successfully prosecuted and defended both criminal and civil cases in state and Federal courts over the past 25 years. Among his most significant cases was the acquittal of a youth who confessed on videotape to the rape and murder of an elderly woman, a crime he did not commit; he also obtained the largest verdict in the country for emotional damages to a woman who lost a baby at childbirth due to medical malpractice. Phil is certified by the national Board of Trial Advocacy as a Civil Trial specialist.* Gen. counsel Italian Am. Repertory Theatre, N.Y., 1985-90; mem. Prospect Park Alliance, Bklyn., 1996—. Recipient Am. Jurisprudence awards Bancroft Whitney & Lawyers Co-op, 1971, 73. Mem. ABA, ATLA, N.Y. State Bar Assn., N.Y. State Trial Lawyers Assn. Roman Catholic. Personal injury, Product liability, General civil litigation. Home: 433 Third St Brooklyn NY 11215 Office: Wingate Russotti Shapiro 420 Lexington Ave Rm 2750 New York NY 10170-2793

**RUST, ROBERT WARREN,** retired lawyer; b. Jamaica, N.Y., Aug. 16, 1928; s. Adolf Harry and Helen Margaret (Dauth) R.; m. Mary Ruth Duncan, Jan. 28, 1953 (dec. Aug. 1981); children: Benjamin, Lani, Debra, Bonnie, Randall, Wendy; m. Theresa Maria Nagymihaly, Dec. 18, 1982; 1 stepchild, Brandon. Student, St. Lawrence U., 1946-48; JD, U. Miami, Coral Gables, Fla., 1954; postgrad., Naval War Coll., 1975. Bar: Fla. 1954, U.S. Supreme Ct. 1960. Police officer City of Miami (Fla.) Police Dept., 1953-54; asst. auditor First Nat. Bank, Miami, 1954-56; assoc. Smathers, Thompson & Dyer, Miami, 1956-57; asst. U.S. atty. Dept. of Justice, Miami, 1957-61; assoc. Shutts & Bowen, Miami, 1961-63; chief asst. county solicitor Palm Beach County, West Palm Beach, Fla., 1963-66; state rep. Fla. Legislature, Palm Beach, Fla., Martin County, Fla., 1966-68; chief counsel House Crime Com., Tallahassee, Fla., 1968-69; U.S. atty. So. Dist. Fla., Miami, 1969-77; ptnr. Rust & Rust, Miami, 1977-89; ret., 1989,, 1989. Col. USMCR, 1947-88, Ret. Recipient award of merit for assisting in preventing assassination Pres. of U.S., Sec. of Treasury and Chief U.S. Secret Svc., 1964, Outstanding Legislator award St. Petersburg Times, 1967, Fla. lodge Fraternal Order Police, 1967, So. Fla. Law Enforcement Comty. award for Honesty, Integrity and Leadership as U.S. Atty., 1977, Outstanding Svc. award Nat. Exec. Bd. of Fed. Criminal Investigators, 1977, Outstanding Svc. award Secret Svc., 1977. Mem. NRA, Fla. Bar, Navy League, Marine Corps Res. Officers Assn. (pres. West Palm Beach chpt. 1964-65), Am. Legion, Mil. Order World Wars, Res. Officers Assn., Key Biscayne Yacht Club, Capitol Hill Club, Coconut Grove Sailing Club, Audobon Soc., Nat. Wildlife Fedn., Defenders of Wildlife, Rock Mt. Elk Found., Ducks Unlimited, Sierra Club, Rotary. Republican. Presbyterian. Avocations: sailing, shooting, skiing, dog sledding. Criminal, Estate planning, Estate taxation. Office: 1700 S Bayshore Ln Apt 2A Miami FL 33133-4041 Home: PO Box 7339 0251 Gold Nugget Dr Breckenridge CO 80424

**RUSTAD, JEANNINE,** lawyer; b. Keflavik, Iceland, Dec. 26, 1969; d. Gary L. and Angeline Rustad. BS in Fin., Bentley Coll., 1991; JD, Cath. U. Am., 1994. Bar: Va. 1995, U.S. Ct. Appeals (ea. dist.) Va. 1995, D.C. 1996, U.S. Bankruptcy Ct. (ea. dist.) Va. 1997. Assoc. Law Offices of George W. Campbell & Assocs., P.C., Arlington, Va., 1994-95, Greenstein, DeLorme & Luchs, P.C., Washington, 1995—. Mem. ABA (litigation sect., woman adv. com.), D.C. Bar Assn. (litigation sect.), D.C. Women's Bar Assn. (litigation sect.), Va. Bar Assn. Avocations: running, biking, photography. E-mail: jr@gdllaw.com. Fax: 202-452-1410; home fax: 703-527-1988. General civil litigation, Land use and zoning (including planning). Office: Greenstein DeLorme & Luchs PC 1620 L St NW Ste 900 Washington DC 20036-5613

**RUSTHOVEN, PETER JAMES,** lawyer; b. Indpls., Aug. 12, 1951; s. Richard and Henrietta (Iwema) R.; children from previous marriage: Julia Faith, David James; m. Linda C. Bennett, Dec. 28, 1987; children: Mark Bennett, Matthew Boyd. A.B. magna cum laude, Harvard U., 1973, J.D. magna cum laude, 1976. Bar: Ind., 1976. Assoc. Barnes, Hickam, Pantzer & Boyd, Indpls., 1976-81; assoc. counsel to Pres. of U.S. White House, Washington, 1981-85; of counsel Barnes & Thornburg, Indpls., 1985-86, ptnr., 1987—; counsel Presdl. Commn. on Space Shuttle Challenger Accident, 1986; spl. cons. U.S. Atty. Gen.'s Adv. Bd. on Missing Children, 1988; adj. fellow Hudson Inst., 1989-91, adj. sr. fellow, 1991—; sr. fellow Ind. Policy Rev. Found., 1991—; bd. advisors Indpls. Lawyers Chpt. Federalist Soc., 1993—, mem. nat. practitioners coun., 1995—. Contbr. monthly column The Am. Spectator mag., 1973-79; mem. bd. editors Harvard Law Rev., 1974-76, case editor, 1975-76; contbr. articles to nat. mags. Bd. dirs. Ednl. Choice Charitable Trust, 1994—, Legal Svcs. Orgn. Indpls., 1977-79; precinct committeeman Marion County Rep. Ctrl. Com., Indpls., 1978-81; state media dir. Ind. Reagan for Pres. Com., 1979-80, Ind. Reagan-Bush Com., 1980; speechwriter nat. Reagan for Pres. Campaign, 1980; mem. legal policy adv. bd. Washington Legal Found., 1989—; candidate for Rep nomination for U.S. Sen., Ind., 1998. Grantee Inst. Politics, Harvard U., 1972. Mem. Ind. Bar Assn., Indpls. Bar Assn., Phi Beta Kappa. Roman Catholic. Avocations: golf; contract bridge; baseball memorabilia. Office: Barnes & Thornburg 1313 Merchants Bank Bldg 11 S Meridian St Indianapolis IN 46204-3506

**RUTH, BRYCE CLINTON, JR.,** lawyer; b. Greenwood, Miss., Dec. 19, 1948; s. Bryce Clinton and Kathryn (Arant) R.; m. Martha M. Ruth; children: Lauren Elizabeth, Bryce Clinton III. BS, Delta State U., 1970; JD, Memphis State U., 1979. Bar: Tenn., 1979, U.S. Dist. Ct. (mid. dist.) Tenn. 1979, U.S. Ct. Mil. Appeals 1991, U.S. Ct. Appeals (6th cir.), 1994. Criminal investigation spl. agt. IRS, Memphis and Nashville, 1971-82; asst. dist. atty. Dist. Atty. Office, Gallatin, Tenn., 1982-89; asst. pub. defender Pub. Defender's Office, Gallatin, Tenn., 1989-90; pvt. practice White House, Tenn., 1989—; judge City of Cross Plains, Tenn., 1992—; juvenile ct. referee judge Robertson County, Tenn., 1995-98; mem. dist. investigating com. dist. VI Tenn. Bd. Law Examiners, 1989—; mem. child enforcement steering com. Asst. Dist. Atty. Office, 1983-84, chmn. legis. subcom., 1985; lectr. in field. Chmn. fin. com. White House First United Meth. Ch., 1983-88, trustee, 1988-90, chmn., 1990; trustee Vol. State Coll. Found., 1993—, chmn., 1998—; bd. dirs. Crime Stoppers of Sumner County, 1989-94; bd. dirs. White House Youth Soccer, 1992-93, coach, 1987-91; bd. dirs. White House Soccer Booster Club, 1996—, pres., 1998; bd. dirs. Sumner County CASA, 1992-93; coach Jr. Pro Football, 1980-85; video cameraman for football team White House H.S., 1991—; mem. Leadership Sumner, 1989; bd. dirs. White House Men's Club, 1981-83, 85-88, v.p., 1984, 88, pres., 1985. Maj. JAGC, USAR, 1983—. Recipient Disting. Expert award for pistol marksmanship U.S. Treasury, Disting. Svc. award City of White House. Mem. NRA, Tenn. Bar Assn. (del. 1993—, mem. family law code revision commn. 1996—), Sumner County Bar Assn. (chmn. domestic rels. com. 1984-85, v.p. 1998-99), White House Area C. of C. (bd. dirs. 1990-95, pres. 1993-94), United C. of C. of Sumner County (pres. 1995). Avocations: scuba diving, skiing, golf, hunting, pistol shooting. General civil litigation, Criminal, Family and matrimonial. Office: 3210 Hwy 31W PO Box 68 White House TN 37188-0068

**RUTH, HENRY SWARTLEY,** retired lawyer; b. Phila., Apr. 16, 1931; s. Henry Swartley and Lola Althouse (Zendt) R.; m. Christine Mallet-Prevost Polk, Dec. 4, 1955 (div. Oct. 1989); children: Laura Ruth-Davis, Diana, Tenley; m. Deborah Ruth Mathieu, Feb. 28, 1991. BA, Yale U., 1952; LLB, U. Pa., 1955. Bar: Pa. 1957, U.S. Dist. Ct. Pa. 1957, U.S. Ct. Appeals (3rd cir.) 1957, D.C. 1964, U.S. Dist. Ct. D.C. 1975, U.S. Supreme Ct. 1975, U.S. Ct. Appeals (4th cir.) 1978. Dep. spl. prosecutor, 1973-74, spl. prosecutor, 1974-75; chief criminal justice rsch. Urban Inst., Washington, 1975-76; gen. counsel UMWA Health and Retirement Funds, Washington, 1976-79; litigation ptnr. Shea & Gardner, Washington, 1979-81; chief litigation divsn. Saul, Ewing, Remick, & Saul, Phila., 1981-87; ethics and spl. litigation counsel Unisys Corp., Blue Bell, Pa., 1987-91; of counsel Crowell & Moring, Washington, 1991-94; ret., 1994; cons. Joint Legis. Com. on Crime, Trenton, N.J., 1967-68, Violence Commn., Washington, 1968, Nat. Legal Svcs. Orgn., Washington, 1975; ind. reviewer Office Sec. Treasury, Washington, 1993. Contbr. articles to profl. jours. With U.S. Army, 1955-57. Avocations: hiking, piano, golf. Home: 6251 N Camino Santa Valera Tucson AZ 85718

**RUTHERFORD, JAY K.,** lawyer; b. Seymour, Tex., Dec. 2, 1962; s. Jesse Boggs and Sharon Marlene Rutherford; m. Kay Ann Howell, June 25, 1983; children: Anne, Audrey, Ross. BS in Agrl. Econs., Tex. Tech. U., 1985; JD, U. Tex., 1988. Bar: Tex. 1988, U.S. Dist. Ct. (no. and ea. dists.) Tex., U.S. Ct. Appeals (5th cir.). Atty. Law, Snakard & Gambill, Ft. Worth, 1988-92, Jackson Walker LLP, Ft. Worth, 1992—. Bd. dirs. Jr. Achievement, Ft. Worth, 1996-98. Mem. ABA, State Bar Tex., Tex. Assn. Bus./C. of C. (chmn. 1995-98). Labor, Federal civil litigation, State civil litigation. Office: Jackson Walker LLP 301 Commerce St Ste 2400 Fort Worth TX 76102-4124

**RUTLAND, DAVID LEE,** lawyer; b. East Chicago, Ind., July 11, 1958; s. Marshall Edgar and Margaret (Powers) R.; m. Catherine Dorrian; children: Christopher, Michael, Steven, Brian. BS, Mt. St. Mary's Coll., 1980; JD, U. Md., 1983. Bar: Md. 1983, U.S. Dist. Ct. Md. 1984, D.C. 1985, U.S. Dist. Ct. D.C. 1985, U.S. Ct. Appeals (4th and D.C. cirs.) 1986, U.S. Supreme Ct. 1987, Va. 1993, U.S. Dist. Ct. (ea. dist.) Va. 1993. Law clk. to presiding judge Montgomery County (Md.) Cir. Ct., 1983-84; assoc. McCarthy, Wilson & Ethridge, Rockville, Md., 1984-85, Digges, Wharton & Levin, Annapolis, Md., 1985-89; ptnr. Wharton, Levin & Ehrmantraut, Annapolis, 1989-91, Wharton, Levin, Ehrmantraut, Klein & Nash, Annapolis, 1991—. Mem. ABA, Md. Bar Assn., D.C. Bar Assn., Md. Assn. Def. Trial Counsel, Def. Rsch. Inst., Am. Inns Ct., Va. State Bar Assn. General civil litigation, Product liability, Professional liability. Office: Wharton Levin & Ehrmantraut PO Box 551 104 West St Annapolis MD 21404-0551

**RUTLAND, JOHN DUDLEY,** lawyer; b. Austin, Tex., Jan. 4, 1931; s. Jesse Blake and Myrtle Estelle (Miller) R.; m. Eva Lou Smith, Jan. 1, 1953 (div.); 1 child, Joseph Blake; m. Beryl Ann Beebe, Apr. 25, 1985. B Bus., U. Tex., 1956; JD, U. Houston, 1961. Bar: Tex. 1961, U.S. Supreme Ct. 1971. With Gibraltar Savs. Assn., Houston, 1956-64, Southwestern Life Ins. Co., Dallas, 1964-67; sole practice, Beaumont, Tex., 1967—; cons. oil mktg. Mem. ABA, Fed. Bar, Tex. Bar Assn., Jefferson County Bar Assn., Port Arthur Bar Assn., Photog. Soc. Am. Episcopalian. Club: Beaumont Camera Club. Lodge: Rotary (past pres. West End, Beaumont). Administrative and regulatory, General corporate, Oil, gas, and mineral.

**RUTLEDGE, ROGER KEITH,** lawyer; b. Knoxville, Tenn., Dec. 27, 1946; s. Joseph P. and Jean Mae (Karnes) R.; m. Lily Mee Kin Hee, June 6, 1970; children: Amelia Leilani, Sarah Elizabeth. BA in History with honors, U. N.C., 1968; JD cum laude, Am. U., 1977. Bar: Tenn. 1977, U.S. Dist. Ct. (we. dist.) Tenn. 1978, U.S. Supreme Ct. 1982. Served in U.S. Peace Corps, Nepal, 1968-70; fgn. service officer U.S. Dept. State, Washington and Italy, 1971-76; ptnr. Rutledge & Rutledge, Memphis, 1977—; CEO Jabez Burns, Inc., 1998—; pres. Jabez Burns, Inc., 1998-99. Editor fiction Carolina Quar., 1967-68; assoc. editor Am. U. Law Rev., 1976-77. Mem. campaign com. Albert Gore Jr. U.S. Senate, Shelby County, 1984, for pres. campaign, 1988; bd. chmn. United Meth. Neighborhood Ctrs., Inc., 1992. Mem. ABA, Tenn. Bar Assn., Memphis Bar Assn. (editor Bar Forum 1986, asst. editor 1987). Democrat. Methodist. General practice, General corporate, General civil litigation. Office: Rutledge & Rutledge 1053 W Rex Rd Memphis TN 38119-3819 *Notable cases include: Fite vs. First Tenn. Prodns. Credit Assn., which involved age discrimination in employment, 1988; Capital Tool & Mfg. vs. Maschinenfabrik Herkules, which involved trade secret law and internat. injunction, 1988.*

**RUTTER, MARSHALL ANTHONY,** lawyer; b. Pottstown, Pa., Oct. 18, 1931; s. Carroll Lennox and Dorothy (Tagert) R.; m. Winifred Hitz, June 6, 1953 (div. 1970); m. Virginia Ann Hardy, Jan. 30, 1971 (div. 1992); children: Deborah Frances, Gregory Russell, Theodore Thomas; m. Terry Susan Knowles, Dec. 19, 1992. BA, Amherst (Mass.) Coll., 1954; JD, U. Pa., 1959. Bar: Calif 1960. Assoc. O'Melveny & Myers, Los Angeles, 1959-64; assoc. Flint & MacKay, Los Angeles, 1964-67, ptnr., 1967-72; ptnr. Rutter, Hobbs & Davidoff, Los Angeles, 1973—. Gov. The Music Ctr. of L.A. County, 1978-86, 89-92; bd. dirs. Music Ctr. Operating Co., 1992-96; bd. dirs. Chorus Am., Washington, 1987-96, pres., 1993-95; bd. dirs. L.A. Master Chorale Assn., 1964—, pres., 1980-92, chmn. 1992-96, vice chmn., 1996—; vestryman All Saints Ch., Beverly Hills, Calif., 1983-86, 88-90. Mem. ABA, Assn. Bus. Trial Lawyers (bd. dirs. 1980-82), L.A. County Bar Assn., Beverly Hills Bar Assn., Century City Bar Assn., English-Speaking Union (various offices L.A. chpt. 1963-91), L.A. Jr. C. of C. (bd. dirs. 1964-67). Democrat. Episcopalian. Avocations: classical and choral music, tennis, golf. Fax: 310-286-1728. E-mail: mar@rhdlaw.com. Federal civil litigation, Environmental, Family and matrimonial. Home: 1045 S Orange Grove Blvd Apt 10 Pasadena CA 91105-1795 Office: Rutter Hobbs & Davidoff Ste 2700 1900 Avenue Of The Stars Los Angeles CA 90067-4508

**RUTTER, ROBERT PAUL,** lawyer; b. Cleve., Apr. 25, 1954; s. Robert Skyles and Mary Jane (Glitz) R.; m. Kathy Alison Deliberato, Dec. 13, 1975; children; Robert, Joe, Kate, Anne. BS in Acctg., Ohio State U., 1975; JD, Case We. Res. U., 1979. Bar: Ohio, 1979; U.S. Dist. Ct. (no. dist.) Ohio 1993, D.C., 1995, U.S. Dist. Ct. (so. dist.) Ind. 1994, U.S. Dist. Ct. (no. dist.) Ind. 1995. Contbr. articles to profl. jours. Mem. Assn. Trial Lawyers Am., Ohio State Bar Assn., Ohio Acad. Trial Lawyers, Cleve. Acad. Trial Lawyers. Personal injury, Insurance. Home: 6591 Beechwood Dr Independence OH 44131-4635 Office: 4700 Rockside Rd Ste 650 Independence OH 44131-2151

**RUZOW, DANIEL ARTHUR,** lawyer; b. Bronx, N.Y., Apr. 27, 1951; s. Theodore Morton and Renee Rhoda Ruzow; m. Meris Francie Entin, June 16, 1974; children; Jenny, Benjamin. BA, Franklin & Marshall Coll., 1973; JD, Fordham U., 1976. Bar: N.Y. 1977, U.S. Ct. Appeals (2d cir.) 1977, U.S. Dist. Ct. (so. and ea. dists.) N.Y. 1977, U.S. Dist. Ct. (no. and we. dists.) N.Y. 1985. Assoc. Arum, Friedman & Katz, N.Y.C., 1976-79; asst. counsel N.Y. State Dept. Environ. Conservation, Albany, 1979-80, hearings counsel, 1980-84, asst. commr., commr.'s counsel, 1984-85; assoc. Whiteman, Osterman & Hanna, Albany, 1985-86, ptnr., 1986—, mng. ptnr., 1993—. Co-author: Environmental Impact Review in New York, 1999. Bioethics com. St. Margaret's House and Hosp. for Babies, Albany, 1984—. Mem. ABA, N.Y. State Bar Assn. (2d v.p. environ. law sect. 1999—, co-chmn. environ. impact assessment com. of environ. law 1983-97, mem. bd. of editors, editor environ. jour. 1984—), Assn. Bar City N.Y., Albany Bar Assn. Jewish. E-mail: dar@woh.com. Environmental, Administrative and regulatory, Land use and zoning (including planning). Home: 34 Via Da Vinci Clifton Park NY 12065-2907 Office: Whiteman Osterman & Hanna One Commerce Pla Albany NY 12260

**RYAN, BARRY THOMAS,** university administrator, lawyer; b. Palo Alto, Calif., Feb. 12, 1955. BA in History, Westmont Coll., Santa Barbara, Calif., 1977; PhD in History, U. Calif., Santa Barbara, 1987; JD, U. Calif., Berkeley, 1992. Bar: Calif. Asst. prof. history Westmont Coll., 1987-89; atty. Farella, Braun and Martel, San Francisco, 1992-93; asst. prof. history Northwestern Coll., Orange City, Iowa, 1993-94; prof. history Point Loma Nazarene U., San Diego, 1995-98, v.p., 1998—; vis. asst. prof. history U. Calif., Santa Barbara, 1987-89; adj. prof. law Thomas Jefferson Sch. Law, San Diego, 1996—; mem. bd. advisors Trinity Law Sch., Anaheim, Calif., 1998—; vice chmn. bd. trustees Tyndale Soc., Oxford (Eng.) U., 1998—. Office: Point Loma Nazarene U 3900 Lomaland Dr San Diego CA 92106-2899

**RYAN, D. JAY,** lawyer; b. N.Y.C., May 19, 1943; s. Dudley F. and Maud (Delaney) R.; m. Janeen L. Bausch, Aug. 12, 1979 (div. Jan. 1991); 1 child, Erin Delaney. AB in Am. Govt., Georgetown U., 1965; JD, U. Ariz., 1968. Bar: Ariz. 1968, U.S. Dist. Ct. Ariz. 1968, U.S. Ct. Appeals (9th cir.) 1972, U.S. Supreme Ct. 1972. Asst. atty. gen. Ariz. Atty. Gen.'s Office, Phoenix, 1970-72; sole practitioner Phoenix, 1968-70, 72-77; atty. Wilson, McConnell & Kahn, Phoenix, 1977-80; sole practitioner Phoenix, 1980—; mem. Ariz. State Bd. Accountancy, Phoenix, 1974-79. Bd. dirs. Ariz. Recreational Ctr. for the Handicapped, Phoenix, 1981—. Mem. State Bar Ariz. (adminstrv. law sect. 1975—, constrn. law sect. 1989—), Jaguar Club Ctrl. Ariz. (treas. 1996—). Republican. Roman Catholic. Avocations: weight lifting, jogging, water skiing, jet skiing. Administrative and regulatory, Construction, Personal injury. Office: 4150 W Northern Ave Phoenix AZ 85051-5765

**RYAN, DONALD SANFORD,** lawyer; b. Little Rock, July 9, 1934; s. John Fergus and Fay (Stuckey) R.; m. Joyce Scarbarough, Dec. 15, 1961; children: William, Thomas, Catherine. BA, Ark. Poly., 1957; JD, U Ark., 1960. Bar: Ark. 1960, Dist., Cir. Cts. Ark. 1960. Atty. Pope, Pratt & Schamburger, Little Rock, 1960-67; instr. Ark. Law Sch., Little Rock, 1965; atty. Dodds, Kidd, Ryan & Moore, Little Rock, 1967—. Fellow Am. Coll. Trial Lawyers; mem. ABA, Ark. Bar Assn., Ark. Trial Lawyers Assn. (pres. 1969-71), Assn. Trial Lawyers Am., Pulaski County Bar Assn.; assoc. Am. Bd. Trial Assocs. Methodist. General practice, Personal injury. Office: Dodds Kidd Ryan & Moore 313 W 2nd St Little Rock AR 72201-2409

**RYAN, GREGORY J.,** lawyer; b. N.Y.C., Apr. 23, 1957; s. John F. and Anne D. Ryan; m. Aimee R. Hoggard, Feb. 14, 1990; children: Jack, Grant, Annie. BA, Syracuse U., 1979; JD, Oklahoma City U., 1982. Bar: Okla. 1982, U.S. Dist. Ct. (we., no. and ea. dists.) Okla., U.S. Ct. Appeals (10th cir.), U.S. Supreme Ct. Asst. dist. atty. Oklahoma County Dist. Atty.'s Office, Oklahoma City, 1982-90; atty. Abowitz & Welch, P.C., Oklahoma City, 1990-94, Abel, Musser et al, Oklahoma City, 1994-96; atty., founding ptnr. DeYong, Ryan & Rischard P.A., Edmond, Okla., 1996—; guest lectr., judge appellate advocacy and trial practice classes Oklahoma City U. Sch. Law, 1988—. Mem. ATLA, Okla. Bar Assn., Oklahoma County Bar Assn., Edmond Bar Assn., Okla. Trial Lawyers Assn., Def. Rsch. Inst., Okla. Cath. Lawyers Guild, Edmond Tips Club, Am. Inn Ct., CV. Republican. Roman Catholic. Avocations: coaching Little League baseball, Cub Scouts, church activities and groups, golf. Personal injury, General civil litigation, Administrative and regulatory. Office: DeYong Ryan & Rischard PA 1320 E 9th St Ste 9 Edmond OK 73034-5772

**RYAN, HAROLD MARTIN,** judge; b. Detroit, Feb. 6, 1911; s. Martin and Ida Ryan; m. Lilliana Wargnier, Sept. 4, 1944; children: Kathleen, Nancy, Harold Jr., John, Theresa. Student, Mich. State U., 1930-31; JD, U. Detroit, 1935. Bar: Mich. 1935, U.S. Supreme Ct. 1935. Atty., 1935—; asst. pros. atty. Wayne County, Detroit, 1942-45; state senator Mich. 1st Dist., Lansing, 1948-61; U.S. congressman 14th Congrl. Dist. Mich., Washington, 1961-65; cir. ct. judge Wayne County, Detroit, 1978-85. With USAFR, 1961-66. Democrat. Roman Catholic. Avocations: golf, football, history. Home: 28601 Little Mack Ave Saint Clair Shores MI 48081-3012

**RYAN, J. RICHARD,** lawyer; b. N.Y.C., Oct. 23, 1929; s. Peter Leon and Mary Martha (Franklin) R.; m. Diana Louise Gambarelli, Nov. 6, 1954 (dec. Feb. 1988); children: Christopher, Claudia; m. Joan Frances Revelle, Jan. 21, 1995. BA, Georgetown U., 1951, JD, Fordham U., 1954. Bar: N.Y. 1956, U.S. Dist. Ct. (so. dist.) N.Y., 1957, U.S. Supreme Ct., 1987. Assoc. Engel, Judge, Miller, Sterling & Reddy, N.Y.C., 1956-63, ptnr., 1963-66; ptnr. Kantor, Shaw & Ryan, N.Y.C., 1966-71; ptnr. Ryan & Silberberg, N.Y.C., 1971-84, Ryan & Fogerty, 1984-88, Ryan, Botway, Reddy and Mesrop, 1988-90; sole practice, 1990—. Bd. dirs. Guiding Eyes for the Blind, Inc., pres., 1973-77, Am. Health Capital Ins. Co.; trustee Cooper Inst. for Advanced Studies in Medicine and Humanities. Mem. Bar Assn. City N.Y. (Young Lawyers Com. 1957-60), N.Y. State Bar Assn., ABA, The Soc. of the Friendly Sons of St. Patrick, Copyright Soc. Candidate for mayor, Pelham, N.Y., 1963. Served with AUS, 1954-56. Clubs: Pelham Country (past pres.), Union League, Winged Foot Golf Club. Entertainment, General corporate, Trademark and copyright. Office: 516 5th Ave New York NY 10036-7501

**RYAN, JAMES E.,** state attorney general; married; 6 children. BA in Polit. Sci., Ill. Benedictine Coll., 1968; JD, Ill. Inst. Tech., 1971. Bar: Ill. 1971. Asst. state's atty. criminal divsn. DuPage County State's Atty.'s Office, 1971-74, 1st. asst. state's atty., 1974-76; founder Ryan & Darrah; state's atty. DuPage County State's Atty.'s Office, 1984-94; atty. gen. State of Ill., 1994—. Recipient numerous awards from various orgns. including Nat. Assn. Counties, Alliance Against Intoxicated Motorists; named Lawyer of Yr. DuPage County Bar Assn., 1997. Mem. Ill. State's Attys. Assn. (pres.; Ezzard Charles award). Republican. Office: Office of Atty General 500 S 2nd St Springfield IL 62706-0001

**RYAN, JAMES FREDERICK,** lawyer, educator; b. Boston, Mar. 11, 1928; s. James Denvir and Harriet Chenery (Bonney) R.; m. Dorothea Elizabeth Dydek, Sept. 1, 1958. AB, Harvard U., 1949, LLB, 1952. Bar: Mass. 1952, U.S. Dist. Ct. Mass. 1959, U.S. Ct. Mil. Appeals 1957, U.S. Ct. Appeals (1st cir.) 1979, Supreme Ct. Republic of Korea, 1956, U.S. Supreme Ct. 1957. Teaching fellow in law Harvard U. Law Sch., 1956-57; pvt. practice, Boston, 1958—; lectr. Suffolk Law Sch., 1958—; atty. Mass. Crime Commn., 1963-64; asst. corp. counsel City of Boston, 1968-73. Pres. alumni council Roxbury Latin Sch., 1976-78. Served with JAG Corps, USAF, 1953-56, lt. col. USAFR. Recipient Wellington prize for disting. service Roxbury Latin Sch., 1970. Mem. ABA, Mass. Bar Assn., Boston Bar Assn., Harvard Club. Author: Massachusetts Bar Examination—Questions, Answers, Comments, 1973; contbr. articles to legal jours. State and local taxation.

**RYAN, JAMES JOSEPH,** lawyer; b. Cin., June 17, 1929; s. Robert J. and Marian (Hoffman) R.; m. Mary A. Noonan, Nov. 25, 1954; children: Kevin, Timothy, Nora, Daniel. AB, Xavier U., 1951, JD, U. Cin., 1954. Bar: Ohio 1954. Teaching assoc. Northwestern U., Chgo., 1954-55; ptnr. Dolle, O'Donnell & Cash, Cin., 1958-71, Taft, Stettinius & Hollister, Cin., 1971—; lectr. U. Cin. Coll. Law, 1960-65. Chmn. Health Planning Assn. Ohio River Valley, Cin., 1978-85; bd. dirs. Hamilton County Bd. of Mentally Retarded, 1968-80; trustee Resident Home for Mentally Retarded, 1980-97, St. Francis-St. George Hosp. Devel. Coun., 1989—. Mem. ABA, Ohio Bar Assn., Cin. Bar Assn. Republican. Roman Catholic. Clubs: Queen City, Western Hill. Avocations: reading, sports. Taxation, general, Corporate taxation, Estate planning. Home: 5316 Cleves Warsaw Pike Cincinnati OH 45238-3602 Office: 1800 Star Bank Ctr 425 Walnut St Cincinnati OH 45202-3923

**RYAN, JAMES LEO,** federal judge; b. Detroit, Mich., Nov. 19, 1932; s. Leo Francis and Irene Agnes R.; m. Mary Elizabeth Rogers, Oct. 12, 1957; children: Daniel P., James R., Colleen M. Hansen, Kathleen A. LLB, U. Detroit, 1956, BA, 1992; LLD (hon.), Madonna Coll., 1976, Detroit Coll. Law, 1978, Thomas M. Cooley Law Sch., Lansing, Mich., 1986, U. Detroit Sch. Law, 1986. Justice of peace Redford Twp., Mich., 1963-66; cir. judge 3d Jud. Circuit Mich., 1966-75; justice Mich. Supreme Ct., 1975-86; judge U.S. Ct. Appeals (6th cir.), 1986—; faculty U. Detroit Sch. Law, Nat. Jud. Coll., Reno, Am. Acad. Jud. Edn., Washington. Contbr. article to legal jour. Served with JAGC, USNR, 1957-60; to capt. JAGC, mil. judge Res., 1960-92, ret., 1992. Mem. Naval Res. Lawyers Assn., Nat. Conf. Appellate Ct. Judges, Fed. Judges Assn., State Bar Mich., Fed. Bar Assn., KC. Office: US Ct Appeals US Courthouse 231 W Lafayette Blvd Detroit MI 48226-2700

**RYAN, JOHN DUNCAN,** lawyer; b. Portland, Oreg., Dec. 20, 1920; s. Thomas Gough and Virgian Abigail (Hadley) R.; m. Florence A. Ryan, Jan. 30, 1970 (dec. 1987); m. Virginia Kane Wilson, June 15, 1996. BS, Fordham U., 1943; JD, Lewis & Clark Coll., Portland, 1950. Bar: Oreg. 1950. Private practice Portland, 1950—; adj. instr. Northwestern Sch. Law Lewis & Clark Coll., 1953-70. Author: (poems) Expressions, 1993, Expressions II, 1995. Sgt. Air Corps, U.S. Army, 1942-46, ETO. Recipient St. Thomas More award Catholic Lawyers for Social Justice, 1993. Mem. ABA (Oreg. delegate 1985-93, chmn. spl. com. on law & literacy 1991-93), Am. Coll. Trial Lawyers, Am. Trial Lawyers Assn., Oreg. State Bar (bd. govs. 1963-67), Oreg. Trial Lawyers Assn. (Trial Lawyer of Yr. 1993), Multnomah County Bar Assn. (Professionalism award 1997), Washington County Bar Assn. Admiralty, Federal civil litigation, General civil litigation. Home and Office: 1206 Circulo Aguilar Rio Rico AZ 85648-3355

**RYAN, JOHN WILLIAM,** lawyer; b. Watertown, S.D., Nov. 18, 1957. BA in Chemistry, Bucknell U., 1981; JD, Syracuse U., 1985; LLM in Patent and Trade Regulation, George Washington U., 1988. Bar: Pa. 1986, D.C. 1987, U.S. Ct. Appeals (fed. cir.) 1987, N.Y. 1991, U.S. Dist. Ct. (no., so. and ea. dists.) N.Y. 1991, U.S. Dist. Ct. (ea. dist.) Pa. 1992, U.S. Supreme Ct. 1993. Assoc. Morgan & Finnegan, N.Y.C., 1987-90, White & Case, N.Y.C., 1991-92; v.p., chief patent counsel IGEN, Inc., Rockville, Md., 1992-97; ptnr. Dorsey & Whitney LLP, Washington, 1997—; adj. prof. law Albany (N.Y.) Law Sch., 1990-92; trustee Grad. Tuition Scholarship, Albany (N.Y.) Med. Coll., 1990-91. Patent, Trademark and copyright, Intellectual property. Office: Dorsey & Whitney LLP Ste 300S 1001 Pennsylvania Ave NW Washington DC 20004-2505

**RYAN, JOSEPH,** lawyer; b. Seattle, Feb. 11, 1942; s. John Joseph and Jane (Wing) R.; m. Mary Katherine Gavin, Aug. 10, 1963; children: Michael Gavin, Kathleen Ann, Jennifer Jo. BA, U. Washington, 1964; JD, Columbia U., 1967. Bar: Calif. 1968, N.Y. 1983, D.C. 1983. Ptnr. O'Melveny & Myers, Los Angeles, 1976-94; exec. v.p., gen. counsel Marriott Internat., Inc., Washington, 1994—; sr. v.p., gen. counsel, bd. dirs. Ritz-Carlton Hotel Co., LLC, Atlanta, 1996—; tchr., lectr. N.Y. Law Jour. Author: Stating Your Case--How To Interview for a Job as a Lawyer, 1982, Take or Pay Contracts: Alive and Well in California, vol. 192, 1987, Current Investment Banking Activities in the United States, vol. 2, #15 M&A Report, 1988; co-author (with Lorin Fife) The Urban Lawyer, 1987; contbr. articles to law publs. Bd. dirs. Pasadena Playhouse, L.A., 1981-92, Planetary Soc., Pasadena, 1981, Westridge Sch., L.A., 1982-91, Natural History Mus. Los Angeles County, 1988-93. Capt. U.S. Army, 1968-70. Mem. ABA, N.Y. Bar Assn., D.C. Bar Assn., Calif. Bar Assn., Nat. Assn. Bond Lawyers (legis. com.). Republican. Roman Catholic. Avocations: running, biking, camping, hunting and fishing, boating. Mergers and acquisitions, Municipal (including bonds), Securities. Home: 10836 Alloway Dr Potomac MD 20854-1503 Office: Marriott Internat Inc Dept 52/923 10400 Fernwood Rd Dept 52 Washington DC 20058-0001

**RYAN, JOSEPH W., JR.,** lawyer; b. Phila., June 24, 1948; s. Joseph W. Sr. and Marie R. (Hillgrube) R.; m. Mary Pat Law, Sept. 11, 1971; children: Caitlin, Joseph W. III. BA, St. Joseph's U., Phila., 1970; MA, Villanova U., 1971; JD, U. Va., 1978. Bar: Ohio 1978, U.S. Supreme Ct. 1982. Ptnr. Porter, Wright, Morris & Arthur, Columbus, Ohio, 1978—; lectr. Sch. Dentistry Ohio State U., Columbus, 1982-89, Continuing Legal Edn. Inst., 1984—. Author: Use of Demonstrative Evidence, 1985; assoc. editor Litigation News, 1986—. Trustee Columbus Zool. Assn., 1980-90; bd. dirs. Columbus Speech and Hearing Ctr., 1988—, pres., 1995-96. Mem. ABA, Ohio State Bar Assn., Columbus Bar Assn., Internat. Assn. Def. Counsel, Am. Arbitration Assn. (panel of arbitrators). Republican. Roman Catholic. Public utilities, Insurance, General civil litigation. Office: Porter Wright Morris & Arthur 41 S High St Ste 30 Columbus OH 43215-6101

**RYAN, LEONARD EAMES,** judge; b. Albion, N.Y., July 8, 1930; s. Bernard and Harriet Earle (Fitts) R.; m. Ann Allen, June 18, 1973; 1 child, Thomas Eames Allen-Ryan. Grad., Kent Sch., 1948; AB, U. Pa., 1954; JD, NYU, 1962. Bar: D.C. 1963, N.Y. 1963, U.S. Ct. Appeals (D.C. cir.) 1963, U.S. Dist. Ct. (so. and ea. dists.) N.Y. 1965, U.S. Ct. Appeals (2nd cir.) 1966, U.S. Supreme Ct. 1967. Field engr. constrn. U.S. Steel Fairless Works, Morrisville, Pa., 1951-52; reporter Upper Darby (Pa.) News, 1954; newsman AP, Pitts., Phila., Harrisburg, N.Y.C., 1955-62; reporter, spl. writer on law N.Y. Times, 1962-63; info. adviser corp. hdqrs. IBM, N.Y.C., 1963; trial atty. firm Perrell, Nielsen & Stephens, N.Y.C., 1964-66; trial atty. civil rights div. Dept. Justice, Washington, 1966-68; asst. to dir. bus. affairs CBS News, N.Y.C., 1968; program officer Office Govt. and Law, Ford Found., N.Y.C., 1968-74; pvt. practice law, cons. pub. affairs, N.Y.C., 1974-91; v.p., sec. W. P. Carey & Co., Inc., N.Y.C., 1977-83; impartial hearing officer Edn. for All Handicapped Children Act of 1975, 1976-91; per diem adminstrv. law judge N.Y. State Agys., 1976-91; hearing examiner N.Y. State Family Ct., 1980-81; apptd. U.S. adminstv. law judge, 1991; adminstv. law judge Office Hearings and Appeals, San Rafael, Calif., 1991-93, Phila., 1993-94, N.Y.C., 1994—; arbitrator Small Claims Ct., N.Y.C., 1974-84; bd. dirs. Community Action for Legal Svcs. Inc., N.Y.C., 1971-77, vice-chmn., 1975-77; co-chmn. Citizens Com. to Save Legal Svcs., N.Y.C., 1975-76; bd. dirs. Lower East Side Svc. Ctr., N.Y.C., 1977-89. Author: (with Bernard Ryan Jr.) So You Want to Go Into Journalism, 1963; contbr. articles to profl. jours. Served with USAR, 1950-57. Mem. Am. Judicature Soc., Assn. of Bar of City of N.Y., N.Y. State Bar Assn., St. Elmo Club (Phila.), Heights Casino (Bklyn.). Home: 32 Orange St Brooklyn NY 11201-1634

**RYAN, LOUIS FARTHING,** lawyer; b. Richmond, Va., Mar. 18, 1947; s. Louis Anthony and Catherine Louise (Farthing) R.; m. Prudence Elwell Hartshorn, Sept. 5, 1970. BSE, Princeton U., 1969; JD, U. Va., 1973. Bar: Va. 1973. Mgmt. cons. Arthur Andersen & Co., Boston, 1969-70; assoc. firm Kaufman and Canoles, Norfolk, Va., 1973-77; sec. Landmark Communications, Inc., Norfolk, 1977—, v.p., gen. counsel, 1985-88, exec. v.p., gen. counsel, 1988—, exec. v.p. fin., 1995-96; sec. TeleCable Corp., Norfolk, 1984-85, v.p., gen. counsel, 1985-88., exec. v.p., gen. counsel, 1988-95. Bd. dirs. Feldman Chamber Music Soc., 1975-77, Jr. Achievement Tidewater, 1979-81, adv. coun., 1986—; bd. dirs., exec. com. Va. Symphony, 1979-89, pres., 1983-84; vol. United Way, 1975-88, chmn. campaign Norfolk divsn., 1988; mem. Norfolk Harborfest Com., 1979; mem. allocation com. Bus. Consortium for Arts Support, South Hampton Roads, 1987-95; chmn. auction Station WHRO-Pub. TV, 1987; bd. dirs., exec. com. Planning Coun., Norfolk, Va., 1988-93; bd. dirs. Leadership Hampton Rds., 1990—, chmn. budget com., 1993, chmn. bd., 1993-95, chmn. nominating com., 1997; mem. exec. adv. coun. Coll. Bus. and Pub. Adminstrn., Old Dominion U., 1990-96; mem. exec. steering com. Hampton Roads Black Achiever Program, 1990-92, mem. Forward Hampton Roads, 1990-91; mem. memberships com. Chrysler Mus., 1991, com. 101 of Future of Hampton Roads, Inc., 1992—; bd. dirs. Norfolk Assembly, 1991-95, Norfolk Festevents, 1994—. Mem. ABA, Va. Bar Assn., Va. State Bar (chmn. bus. law sect. 1980-81), Norfolk-Portsmouth Bar Assn., Am. Newspaper Pubs. Assn. (legal affairs com. 1986—), Hampton Roads C. of C. (bd. dirs. 1989-94, Norfolk divsn. 1990—, treas. 1994), Town Point Club, Norfolk Yacht and Country Club, Country Club Va. Episcopalian. Communications. Office: Landmark Communications Inc 150 W Brambleton Ave Norfolk VA 23510-2018

**RYAN, MARIANNE ELIZABETH,** lawyer; b. Ft. Knox, Ky., Nov. 15, 1964; d. John L. and Frances J. (McIntosh) R. BA, Trinity Coll., 1986; JD, Yale U., 1991. Bar: Ill. 1991, U.S. Dist. Ct. (no. dist.) Ill. 1991. Assoc. Pattishall, McAuliffe, Newbury, Hilliard & Geraldson, Chgo., 1991-93; internet editor Law Jour. EXTRA! The N.Y. Law Pub. Co., N.Y.C., 1994-95; rsch. scholar Nat. Ctr. for Philanthropy and the Law NYU Sch. Law, 1996—; adj. prof. trademark and copyright law John Marshall Law Sch., Chgo., 1993. Exec. editor Yale Jour. on Regulation. Mem. Assn. for Advancement of Computing in Edn., Computer Profls. for Social Responsibility, Internet Soc., N.Y. Acad. Scis., Phi Beta Kappa. Trademark and copyright, Computer, Intellectual property. Home: 379 Marcellus Rd Mineola NY 11501-1427

**RYAN, MARY FRANCES,** lawyer; b. Trenton, N.J., Nov. 17, 1967; d. John A. and Pauline M. Ryan; m. Edward C. Sweeney, Sept. 5, 1992. BA, U. Scranton, 1988; JD, U. Chgo., 1991. Bar: Pa. 1991. Law clk. hon. Franklin S. Van Antwerpen U.S. Dist. Ct. (ea. dist.) Pa., Easton, 1991-92; atty. Dechert Price & Rhoads, Phila., 1992—. Com. person Rep. Com. Chester County, Pa., 1996—; mem. exec. bd. Valley Forge Coun. Rep. Women, Chester County. Fax: 215-994-2222. E-mail: mfrances.ryan@dechert.com and mfryan@aol.com. Office: Dechert Price & Rhoads 4000 Bell Atlantic Tower 1717 Arch St Philadelphia PA 19103-2793

**RYAN, MILES FRANCIS, III,** lawyer; b. Washington, July 31, 1963; s. Miles Francis Jr. and Vernance Dolores (Beste) R. AB cum laude, Harvard U., 1986; JD, Columbia U., 1990. Bar: Pa. 1991, U.S. Ct. Fed. Claims 1995, U.S. Tax Ct. 1995, U.S. Ct. Appeals for Armed Forces 1995, U.S. Ct. Vets. Appeals 1995, U.S. Supreme Ct. 1995. Staff mem. U.S. Senator William Proxmire, Washington, 1980, 82, 83; intern U.S. Senator Tom Harkin, Washington, 1989; law clerk U.S. Dept. Commerce Office of Gen. Counsel's Honors Program, Washington, 1990-91, atty.-advisor, 1991-92; atty.-advisor U.S. Dept. Commerce Office Gen. Counsel's Office of Chief Counsel for Econ. Affairs, Washington, 1992-96; mem. U.S. Dept. Commerce Office of Gen. Counsel's Law Libr. Com., Washington, 1992, 93; key worker U.S. Dept. Commerce's Combined Fed. Campaign, Washington, 1992, 93. Mem. Harvard-Radcliffe Dem. Club, Cambridge, Mass., 1983-86; vol. Joe Kennedy for Congress Campaign, Cambridge, 1986, Don Mooers for Congress Campaign, Wheaton, Md., 1996; at-large mem., treas. Columbia U. Law Sch. Student Senate, N.Y.C., 1987-90, 89-90. Jaffin Pub. Interest and Student Funded Fellowship grantee Columbia U. Sch. Law, 1989, John Harvard scholar Harvard U., 1983-86; recipient Gold Medal award U.S. Dept. Commerce, 1995. Mem. ABA, FBA (D.C. chpt., bd. dirs., alt. nat. del., sec., pres.- elect, nat. coun. del., nat. membership com., younger lawyers divsn. bd. dirs., chair nat. admissions com.), Columbia U. Law Sch. Alumni Assn., Columbia U. Club, Harvard U. Club Washington, KC (local coun. co-comty. activities dir. 1982). Democrat. Roman Catholic. Avocations: reading historical, political and current affairs books and articles, attending public policy and historical lectures, visiting museums, attending the theater and concerts, travel. Home: 12502 Two Farm Dr Silver Spring MD 20904-2931

**RYAN, PATRICK M.,** prosecutor; m. Barbara K. Heinen; children: Michael, Jason, Megan. BA, U. Okla., 1967, JD, 1969. Bar: Okla., U.S. Dist. Ct. (we. and ea. dists.) Okla., U.S. Ct. Appeals (10th cir.), U.S. Ct. Mil. Appeals, U.S. Supreme Ct. Ptnr. Crowe & Dunlevy, Oklahoma City, 1974-81; pres., dir. Ryan, Geister & Whaley, Oklahoma City, 1982-95; U.S. atty. for western dist. Okla. Office of U.S. Atty., Oklahoma City, 1995—. Editor Okla. Law Rev. Trustee World Neighbors, 1994-97; active St. John the Bapt. Cath. Ch., Edmond, Okla. Served JAGC, USAF, 1969-74. Recipient Leadership award Okla. County Bar Assn., 1989. Fellow Okla. Bar Found. (v.p. 1978, 80), Am. Coll. Trial Lawyers (mem. Okla. state com. 1990—), Internat. Acad. Trial Lawyers; mem. ABA, Okla. Bar Assn. (gov. bd. govs. 1990-93, mem. young lawyers sect.), Order of Coif. Office: US Atty Office Western Dist 210 Park Ave Ste 400 Oklahoma City OK 73102-5628*

**RYAN, PATRICK NELSON,** lawyer; b. Indpls., Nov. 28, 1930; s. Thomas and Marie Linnie (Matthew) R.; m. Yvonne Winkler, Aug. 7, 1953; children: Geoffrey, Deborah Ryan Andrus, Valerie Ryan MacKay, Jill Anne Ryan, Matthew. BA, Butler U., 1953; JD, Ind. U., 1958. Bar: Ind. 1958, U.S. Dist. Ct. 1958, U.S. Supreme Ct. 1982. Practiced in Marion, Ind., 1958—; ptnr. Ryan, Welchons & Ryan, Marion; judge Ind. Trial Ct., Marion, 1968. Mem. sch. bd. Marion Pub. Schs., 1976-80. With U.S. Army, 1953-55. Mem. Am. Legion (dept. judge adv. 1994—), 40 and 8 (avocat 1971). Democrat. Baptist. Criminal, State civil litigation, Probate. Home: 2310 Lantern Ln Marion IN 46952-9249 Office: 112 S Boots St Marion IN 46952-3825

**RYAN, PHYLLIS PAULA,** lawyer; b. Cercemaggiore, Italy, Oct. 3, 1948; came to U.S. 1956; d. Giovanni Gesualdo and Giovannina Calabrese; m. Robert P. Ryan, Jan. 3, 1976 (div. July 1983); m. Donald J. Barberio, May 15, 1987. AS, SUNY, 1972; BA, U. Mass., 1978; JD, Western New Eng. Coll., 1981. Bar: Mass. 1981, Conn. 1987; RN, N.Y., Mass. Ptnr. Pellegrini & Seeley, Springfield, Mass., 1981—. Mem. bd. edn. Town of Suffield, Conn., 1995—. Mem. ATLA, Mass. Bar Assn., Mass. Acad. Trial Lawyers, Hampden County Bar Assn. General civil litigation, Personal injury. Home: 109 Thistledown Suffield CT 06078-1639 Office: Pellegrini & Seeley 1145 Main St Springfield MA 01103-2123

**RYAN, ROBERT COLLINS,** lawyer; b. Evanston, Ill., Sept. 15, 1953; s. Donald Thomas and Patricia J. (Collins) R.; m. Joanne Kay Holata, Nov. 5, 1983. BA in Econs., BS in Indsl. Engring. with high honors, U. Ill., 1976; JD, Northwestern U., 1979. Bar: Ill. 1979, U.S. Dist. Ct. (no. dist.) Ill. 1980, U.S. Ct. Appeals (Fed. cir.) 1982, U.S. Supreme Ct. 1984. Assoc., Allegretti, Newitt, Witcoff & McAndrews, Ltd., Chgo., 1979-83, ptnr. 1983-88; founding ptnr. McAndrews, Held & Malloy, Ltd., Chgo., 1988-96, of counsel, 1996—; chief legal and intellectual property officer, exec. v.p. StarGuide Digital Networks, Inc., Reno, 1996—; mem. Ian Burns & Assocs., P.C., Reno, 1998—; of counsel Pauley, Petersen, Kinne & Fejer, Hoffman Estates, Ill., 1998—; lectr. engring. law Northwestern U. Tech. Inst., Evanston, Ill., 1981-85, adj. prof. engring. law, 1985-90; lectr. patent law and appellate practice John Marshall Law Sch., 1991-93, adj. prof. patent law and appellate advocacy, 1993—; mem. faculty Nat. Jud. Coll., Reno, Nev., 1998—; mem. alumni bd. mech. and indsl. engring. dept. U. Ill., Urbana, 1996—. Exec. editor Northwestern Jour. Internat. Law & Bus., 1978-79; contbr. articles to profl. jours. Dir. Washoe Assn. Retarded Citizens, Reno, 1997—. James scholar U. Ill., 1976. Mem. ABA, Fed. Cir. Bar Assn., Intellectual Property Law Assn. Chgo., Licensing Execs. Soc., Tau Beta Pi, Phi Eta Sigma, Alpha Pi Mu, Phi Kappa Phi. Patent, Trademark and copyright, Computer. Home: 95 Rimfire Cir Reno NV 89509-2989 Office: StarGuide Digital Networks 300 E 2nd St Ste 1510 Reno NV 89501-1591

**RYAN, ROBERT DAVIS,** lawyer; b. Lynbrook, N.Y., Aug. 14, 1941; s. Thomas Francis and Agnes Frances (Davis) R.; m. Patricia Ellen Buckley, Aug. 19, 1972; children: John, Daniel, Carolyn. BBA, St. John's U., 1962; JD, Fordham U., 1972. Bar: N.Y. 1973, U.S. Dist. Ct. (so. and ea. dists.) N.Y. 1973, U.S. Ct. Appeals (2d cir.) 1975, U.S. Supreme Ct. 1984. Asst. dist. atty. Westchester County, White Plains, N.Y., 1972-77; assoc. Clark, Gagliardi & Miller, White Plains, 1977-82; ptnr. Rende, Ryan & Downes, White Plains, 1982—; adj. prof. law St. John's U., 1992-95, 99. Chmn. Cable TV Adv. Com., Lewisboro, N.Y., 1983-99. Mem. Assn. Trial Lawyers Am., N.Y. State Trial Lawyers Assn., Westchester County Bar Assn., N.Y. State Bar Assn. (continuing legal edn. com. trial lawyers sect.), No. Westchester Bar Assn. (bd. govs. 1987-92, pres. 1986-87), White Plains Bar Assn. Republican. Roman Catholic. General civil litigation, Personal injury, Product liability. Home: PO Box 113 Bedford NY 10506-0113 Office: Rende Ryan & Downes 202 Mamaroneck Ave Ste 600 White Plains NY 10601-5312

**RYAN, ROBERT JEFFERS,** lawyer; b. Evanston, Ill., Dec. 26, 1947. BBA in Fin., U. Notre Dame, 1970; JD, Loyola U., Chgo., 1973. Bar: Ill. 1973, U.S. Dist. Ct. (no. dist.) Ill. 1973. Pvt. practice Winnetka, Ill., 1979—. Probate, General corporate, General practice. Office: 560 Green Bay Rd Ste 303 Winnetka IL 60093-2242

**RYAN, THOMAS WILLIAM,** lawyer; b. Tulsa, Feb. 16, 1953; s. Dean Lawrence and Helen Ladeen (Steinkierchner) R.; m. Mary Ellen Poxon, Jan. 30, 1973; children: Matthew Alan, Jennifer Erin. BA, U. Houston, 1975, JD, 1978. Bar: Tex. 1978. Ptnr. Hart, Ryan & Pfeffer, Houston, 1978-80; contracts adminstr. Texaco Inc., Houston, 1980-85; asst. gen. counsel Total Minatome Corp., Houston, 1985-99; gen. counsel, corp. sec. Total Exploration Prodn. USA, Inc., Houston, 1999—. Coach youth sports YMCA, Houston, 1990. Mem. KC (adv. 1985-87), State Bar Tex. Avocations: golf, bowling. Oil, gas, and mineral, FERC practice, Labor. Office: Total Exploration Prodn USA Inc 909 Fannin St Ste 2200 Houston TX 77010-1025

**RYCE, DONALD THEODORE,** lawyer; b. New Orleans, Dec. 15, 1943; s. Donald Theodore and Martha (Herndon) R.; m. Claudine Dianne Walker, July 8, 1984; children: Ted, Martha, Jimmy. BA, U. Fla., 1966, JD, 1968. Bar: Fla. 1968, U.S. Dist. Ct. (so. dist.) Fla. 1972, U.S. Ct. Appeals (5th and 11th cirs.) 1973; approved arbitrator Broward County Sheriff's Office. Jud. law clk. Fla. Dist. Ct. Appeals (4th cir.), West Palm Beach, 1968-70; ptnr. Hogg, Allen, Ryce, Norton & Blue, Miami, Fla., 1970-89, Donald T. Ryce, P.A., Miami, 1989-96, Hogg, Ryce & Hudson, Miami, 1997—; co-chmn. liaison com. labor and employment sect. NLRB, Fla., 1990-92, mem. publs. com., 1990-91, exec. coun. labor and employment sect., 1994-98; apptd. missing children adv. bd. Fla. Dept. Law Enforcement, 1996—. Active Fla. Police Chiefs Edn. Rsch. Found.; dir. Jimmy Ryce Ctr. for Victims of Predatory Abduction. Named to Policeman Hall of Fame, 1996, Grand Knight of Order of Michael the Archangel; recipient Leadership award Fla. Police Chiefs Edn. Rsch. Found., 1993. Mem. ABA, Microcomputer Edn. for Employment of the Disabled (bus. adv. coun.), Winter Haven C. of C. (Cmty. Leadership award 1994), Miami Beach C. of C., Coral Gables C. of C., Miami Rotary. Episcopalian. Avocations: tennis, gourmet cooking. Fax: (305) 864-4161. E-mail: employerlawyer@netscape.net. Labor, General civil litigation. Office: 5151 Collins Ave Apt 1031 Miami Beach FL 33140-2716

**RYESKY, KENNETH H.,** lawyer; b. Phila., July 30, 1954; s. A. and Helene (Silbermann) R.; m. Tamara E. Weiss, Mar. 11, 1983; 1 child, H.Z. BBA, Temple U., 1977, JD, 1986; MBA, La Salle U., 1982. Bar: Pa. 1986, N.J. 1987, N.Y. 1988, U.S. Supreme Ct. 1996. Procurement specialist Def. Logistics Agy., Phila., 1979-87; atty. IRS, N.Y.C., 1987-91; pvt. practice East Northport, N.Y., 1991—; adj. asst. prof. Queens Coll./CUNY, Flushing, N.Y., 1993—. Co-author: Federal Government Intelligence Property Guide, 1995; contbr. articles to profl. jours. Jewish. Avocations: cooking, gardening, collecting. Fax: 516-266-3198. E-mail: 'khresq@sprintmail.com. Taxation, general, Consumer commercial. Office: PO Box 926 East Northport NY 11731-0529

**RYLAND, WALTER H.,** lawyer; b. Richmond, Va., Jan. 23, 1943; s. John William and Evelyn (Quillin) R.; m. Madelaine Aerni, July 10, 1976; children: Mark Vanley, Caroline Aerni. BA, Washington & Lee U., 1965, LLB, 1967. Chief dep. atty. gen. Office of the Atty. Gen. of Va., Richmond, 1978-82; ptnr. Williams, Mullen, Christian & Dobbins, Richmond, 1983—; Counselor, Va. Mus. Fine Arts, Richmond, 1983—; pres. J. Sargeant Reynolds Found., Richmond, 1990; legal adv., Southeastern Legal Found., Atlanta, Ga., 1989—. Co-editor: Racial Preferences in Government Contracting (Nat. Legal Ctr. for the Pub. Interest), 1993. Sec. bd. trustees Washington Internat. U. Va., 1989-91; bd. dirs. Coun. for Am. First Freedom, Richmond, 1988-92; pres. Theatre Va., Richmond, 1987-88; sec. Communication Disorders Found., Richmond, 1986-88, Cultural Art Ctr. and Glen Allen. Mem. ABA, Va. Bar Assn., Richmond Bar Assn. Constitutional, General corporate, Education and schools. Office: Williams Mullen Clark & Dobbins 2 James Ctr 1021 E Cary St Richmond VA 23219-4000

**RYLEY, ARTHUR CHARLES,** lawyer; b. Boston, Sept. 20, 1951; s. Arthur Charles and Margaret B. (Clancy) R.; m. Dianne Stoddard, June 11, 1972; children: Megan Elizabeth, John Stoddard. BA in Am. History, Hampshire Coll., 1977; JD cum laude, New Eng. Sch. Law, 1986. Bar: Mass., 1986, U.S. Dist. Ct. Mass., 1987, U.S. Ct. Appeals (1st cir.), 1987. Pvt. practice Barnstable, Mass., 1986—. Bd. trustees Cape Cod Acad., Osterville, Mass., 1996—. Mem. Mass. Bar Assn., Barnstable Bar Assn. Avocations: gardening, hiking, sailing. Criminal, Family and matrimonial, Juvenile. Office: 3291 Main St Barnstable MA 02630-1105

**RYMER, PAMELA ANN,** federal judge; b. Knoxville, Tenn., Jan. 6, 1941. AB, Vassar Coll., 1961; LLB, Stanford U., 1964; LLD (hon.), Pepperdine U., 1988. Bar: Calif. 1966, U.S. Ct. Appeals (9th cir.) 1966, U.S. Ct. Appeals (10th cir.), U.S. Supreme Ct. V.p. Rus Walton & Assoc., Los Altos, Calif., 1965-66; Assoc. Lillick McHose & Charles, L.A., 1966-75, ptnr., 1973-75; ptnr. Toy and Rymer, L.A., 1975-83; judge U.S. Dist. Ct. (cen. dist.) Calif., L.A., 1983-89, U.S. Ct. Appeals (9th cir.), L.A., 1989—; faculty The Nat. Jud. Coll., 1986-88; mem. com. summer ednl. programs Fed. Jud. Ctr., 1987-88, mem. com. appellate judge edn., 1996-99; chair exec. com. 9th Cir. Jud. Conf., 1990; mem. com. criminal law Jud. Conf. U.S., 1988-93, Ad Hoc com. gender-based violence, 1991-94, fed.-state jurisdiction com., 1993-96; mem. commn. on structural alternatives Fed. Cts. Appeals, 1997-98. Mem. editorial bd. The Judges' jour., 1989-91; contbr. articles to profl. jours. and newsletters. Mem. Calif. Postsecondary Edn. Commn., 1974-84, chmn., 1980-84; mem. L.A. Olympic Citizens Adv. Commn.; bd. visitors Stanford U. Law Sch., 1986-99, trustee, 1991—, chair, 1993-96, exec. com., chmn. bd. trustees com. acad. policy, planning and mgmt. and its ad. hoc. com. athletics., chmn. bd. visitors Sch. Law, 1987—; bd. visitors Pepperdine U. Law Sch., 1987—; mem. Edn. Commn. of States Task Force on State Policy and Ind. Higher Edn., 1987-89, Carnegie Commn. Task Force Sci. and Tech. Jud. and Regulatory Decisionmaking, 1990-93, Commn. Substance Abuse Coll. and Univ. Campuses, 1992-94, commn. substance abuse high schs. Ctr. Addiction and Substance Abube Columbia U.; bd. dirs. Constnl. Rights Found., 1985-97, Pacific Coun. Internat. Policy, 1995—, Calif. Higher Edn. Policy Ctr., 1992-97; Jud. Conf. U.S. Com. Fed.-State Jurisdiction, 1993, Com. Criminal Law, 1988-93, ad hoc comm. gender based violence, 1991-94; chair exec. com. 9th cir. jud. conf., 1990-94. Recipient Outstanding Trial Jurist award L.A. County Bar Assn., 1988; named David T. Lewis Disting. Jurist-in-Residence U. Utah, 1992. Mem. ABA (task force on civil justice reform 1991-93, mem. coord. com. agenda civil justice reform in Am. 1991), State Bar Calif. (antitrust and trade regulation sect., exec. com. 1990-92), L.A. County Bar Assn. (chmn. antitrust sect. 1981-82, mem. editl. bd. The Judges Jour. 1989-91, mem. com. professionalism 1988—, numerous other coms.), Assn. of Bus. Trial Lawyers (bd. govs. 1990-92), Stanford Alumni Assn., Stanford Law Soc. Soc. Calif., Vassar Club So. Calif. (past pres.). Office: US Ct Appeals 9th Cir US Court of Appeals Bldg 125 S Grand Ave Rm 600 Pasadena CA 91105-1621

**RYSKAMP, KENNETH LEE,** federal judge; b. 1932; m. Karyl Sonja Ryskamp; 1 child, Cara Leigh. AB, Calvin Coll., 1954; JD, U. Miami, 1956. Bar: Fla. 1956, Mich. 1957, U.S. Supreme Ct. 1970. Law clk. to presiding judge Fla. Ct. Appeals 3d Dist., 1957-59; pvt. practice Miami, Fla., 1959-61; ptnr. Goodwin, Ryskamp, Welcher & Carrier, Miami, 1961-84; mng. ptnr. Squire, Sanders & Dempsey, Miami, 1984-86; judge U.S. Dist. Ct. (so. dist.) Fla., Miami, 1986—. Office: US Dist Ct 701 Clematis St Rm 416 West Palm Beach FL 33401-5112

**SAARI, JOHN WILLIAM, JR.,** lawyer; b. Jersey City, Oct. 12, 1937; s. John William Sr. and Ina Marie (Bain) S.; m. Susan Jo Olson, Aug. 27, 1967 (div. June 1971); m. Marjorie Ann Palm, Nov. 16, 1973. Student, Duke U., 1955-58, U. N.C., 1962-63; JD with honors, Ill. Inst. Tech., Chgo., 1972. Bar: Ill. 1972, U.S. Dist. Ct. (no. dist.) Ill. 1972, Wis. 1980, U.S. Dist. Ct. (ea. and we. dists.) Wis. 1980, U.S. Ct. Appeals (7th cir.) 1972, U.S. Supreme Ct. 1997. Assoc. Yates, Goff, Gustafson & Been, Chgo., 1972-76, Hubbard, Hubbard, O'Brien & Hall, Chgo., 1976-78; atty. Ill. Bell Telephone Co., Chgo., 1978-79; assoc. Cirilli Law Office, Rhinelander, Wis., 1979-83; pvt. practice Rhinelander, 1983-90; ptnr. Mouw, Saari, Krueger, Paulson & Smith, Rhinelander, 1990—. Bd. dirs. Northwoods United Way, 1980-88, pres., 1983-84. With U.S. Army, 1958-61, ETO. Mem. ABA, Ill. Bar Assn., Wis. Bar Assn., Oneida-Vilas-Forest Bar Assn. (pres. 1996-97), Lions (pres. Sugarcamp 1983-84). Avocations: hunting, fishing, baseball, reading, golf. General civil litigation, Insurance, Personal injury. Home: 7279 Arbutus Dr Eagle River WI 54521-9249 Office: Mouw Saari Krueger Paulson Smith 8A W Davenport St Rhinelander WI 54501-3467

**SABADIE, FRANCISCA ALEJANDRA,** lawyer, interpreter, translator; b. New Orleans, July 7, 1947; d. Alfonso and Margaret Gibbons (Burke) S.; m. Robert Thomas Dwyer, Jan. 6, 1973. BA, Newton Coll., 1968; JD, Loyola U., 1975. Bar: N.Y. 1976, U.S. Dist. Ct. (so. and ea. dists.) N.Y. 1976, U.S. Ct. Appeals (2nd cir.) 1977. Clk. Sessions, Fishman, Rosenson, Snelling, Boisfontaine, New Orleans, 1973-75; assoc. Shearman-Sterling, N.Y.C. and Paris, 1975-84; real estate developer London, 1985-87; pvt. practice Scarsdale, N.Y., 1987—. Mem. pub. affairs com. Jr. League Ctrl. Westchester (N.Y.); freedom writer Amnesty Internat. Mem. Assn. Bar City of N.Y. (mem. entertainment com. 1998—). Roman Catholic. Avocations: music, cycling, cooking, reading, theatre. General civil litigation, Consumer commercial, Real property. Office: One Walworth Ave Scarsdale NY 10583-1417

**SABALJA, LORRAINE,** lawyer; b. Smithtown, N.Y., Mar. 14, 1969; d. Philip Anthony and Lorraine Agatha Sabalja. BBA, Loyola Coll., Balt., 1991; JD, Quinnipinc Coll., 1996. Bar: N.Y. 1997, Conn. 1997. Assoc. Law Office of Steven I. Hilsenrath, N.Y.C., 1997-98; asst. counsel Hadassah The Women's Zionist Orgn. Am., N.Y.C., 1998—. Mem. N.Y. State Bar Assn., Conn. Bar Assn., City Bar Assn. N.Y. Avocations: hiking, biking, running, tennis, horsemanship. Estate taxation, Non-profit and tax-exempt organizations, Probate. Home: 251 E 51st St New York NY 10022-6534 Office: Hadassah The Women's Zionist Orgn Am Inc 50 W 58th St New York NY 10019-2590

**SABERS, RICHARD WAYNE,** state supreme court justice; b. Salem, S.D., Feb. 12, 1938; s. Emil William and Elrena Veronica (Godfrey) S.; m. Colleen D. Kelley, Aug. 28, 1965 (dec. Feb., 1998); children: Steven Richard, Susan Michelle, Michael Kelley. BA in English, St. John's U., Collegeville, Minn., 1960; JD, U. S.D., 1966. Bar: S.D. 1966, U.S. Dist. Ct. S.D. 1966, U.S. Ct. Appeals (8th cir.) 1983. From assoc. to ptnr. Moore, Rasmussen, Sabers & Kading, Sioux Falls, S.D., 1966-86; justice Supreme Ct. S.D., Pierre and Sioux Falls, 1986—. Mem. editorial bd. U. S.D. Law Rev., 1965-66. State rep. March of Dimes, Bismarck, N.D., 1963; bd. dirs. St. Joseph Cathedral, Sioux Falls, 1971-86; trustee, bd. dirs. O'Gorman Found., Sioux Falls, 1978-86; active sch. bd. O'Gorman High Sch., Sioux Falls, 1985-86. Lt. U.S. Army, 1960-63. Named Outstanding Young Religious Leader, Jaycees, Sioux Falls, 1971. Mem. ABA, S.D. Bar Assn., Inst. Jud. Adminstrn., St. John's Alumni Assn. (pres. Sioux Falls chpt. 1975-91). Republican. Roman Catholic. Avocations: tennis, skiing, sailing, sports, wood carving. Home: 1409 E Cedar Ln Sioux Falls SD 57103-4514 Office: SD Supreme Ct 500 E Capitol Ave Pierre SD 57501-5070

**SABETTA, PAUL M.,** lawyer; b. New Haven, Apr. 20, 1949. BA in English, Providence Coll., 1971; JD, Northeastern U., 1974. Bar: Conn. 1974, U.S. Dist. Ct. Conn. 1975. Pvt. practice law New Haven, 1974—; title agt. Lawyers Title Ins. Corp., Middletown, Conn., 1985—, Am. Title Ins. Co., Hartford, Conn., 1990—. Mem. ABA, Conn. Trial Lawyers Assn. Avocations: golf, movies. General practice, Personal injury, Real property. Office: 216 Crown St Fl 5 New Haven CT 06510-2705

**SABEY, MARK L.,** lawyer; b. Urbana, Ill., Nov. 12, 1959; s. Burns Roy and Elaine (Bingham) S.; m. Lisa Blair, Nov. 27, 1985; children: Brian, David, Joshua, Matthew, Rachel, Daniel. BA in Am. Studies and Anthropology, Brigham Young U., 1983, JD cum laude, 1986. Bar: Colo. 1986, U.S. Dist. Ct. Colo. 1988, U.S. Supreme Ct. 1998. Jud. clk. Utah Supreme Ct., Salt Lake City, 1986-87; assoc. Saunders, Snyder, Ross & Dickson, P.C., Denver, 1987-88; ptnr. Sabey, Johns, Ordelheide & Smith, P.C., Denver, 1988-97; of counsel Kutak Rock, Denver, 1997—; dir. Power Glide Lang. Courses, Provo, 1997-98. Contbr. articles to profl. jours. Scoutmaster Boy Scouts Am., Englewood, Littleton, Colo., 1996-98, unit commr., 1995. Mem. ABA, Colo. Bar Assn. Labor, Appellate, Health. Office: Kutak Rock 717 17th St Ste 2900 Denver CO 80202-3329

**SABINO, WILLIAM,** lawyer, consultant; b. N.Y.C., Apr. 22, 1955; s. Albert Joseph and Mildred (Smoll) S. BA, CCNY, 1976; JD, U. N.C., 1979; LLM, Washington U., St. Louis, 1984. Bar: Ill. 1980, U.S. Tax Ct. 1984. Cons. tax. atty. Bloomfield, N.J., 1985—. Capt. U.S. Army, 1980-85. Mem. Phi Beta Kappa, Phi Alpha Theta. Republican. Avocations: sports, exercise, travel, reading, museums. Taxation, general. Home: 6B Byrne Ct Wayne NJ 07470-3633

**SABRA, STEVEN PETER,** lawyer; b. Fall River, Mass., Dec. 1, 1951; s. Peter B. and Eliza J. Sabra; m. Bernadette L. Brown, Sept. 24, 1977. BA in Polit. Sci., Fairfield U., 1973; JD, Duquesne U., 1976. Bar: Mass. 1977, U.S. Dist. Ct. Mass. 1977, U.S. Supreme Ct. 1985. Assoc. Law Offices of Richard N. LaSalle, Fall River, Mass., 1977-80; owner Law Offices of Steven P. Sabra, Somerset, Mass., 1980-87, Sabra Law Offices, Somerset, 1987-93, Law Offices Sabra & Aspden. P.A., Somerset, 1993—; arbitrator accident claims Am. Arbitration Assn., Boston, 1988—; mem. hearing com. Bd. Bar Overseers, Mass., 1988-93; mem. Southeastern Regional Com. of Jud. Nominating Coun., 1995—; corporator Fall River Five Cents Savs. Bank, 1987—; mem. Bd. of Bar Overseers, Mass., 1998—. Chmn., pres. Fall River Port Authority/Fall River Line Pier, Inc., 1992-95. Mem. ABA, ATLA, Mass. Bar Assn. (bd. delegates 1997—), Mass. Acad. Trial Attys., Bristol County Bar Assn. (pres. 1994-95), Fall River Bar Assn. (pres. 1985-87), Mass. Bar Found. Avocation: sports. Personal injury, Workers' compensation. Office: Law Offices Sabra & Aspden 1026 County St Somerset MA 02726-5138

**SACCO, RUDOLPH AUGUSTINE,** judge; b. Pittsfield, Mass., May 2, 1927; s. Domenico S. and Carmella (Pinyone) S.; m. Katherine M. Turschmann, June 21, 1953; children: Cami, Domenick, Carolyn, Robert, Judi, Catherine, Dianne Alycia, Rudolph A., Virginia. BS, Boston Coll., 1951; LLB, Suffolk U., 1956. Bar: Mass. 1957. Asst. atty. gen. Commonwealth of Mass.; commr. Dept. Pub. Utilities, Commonwealth of Mass.; judge, trial divsn. Probate and Family Ct. of Mass., 1973-97. Bd. dirs. Boy Scouts Am., United Cerebral Palsy, Big Sisters, Make A Wish, Italian Cultural Com. of Springfield. Served with USN, 1945-46. Mem. Mass. Bar Assn., Berkshire Bar Assn. (sec.), Am. Acad. Matrimonial Lawyers (bd. of mgrs.). Republican. Roman Catholic. Home: PO Box 2953 Pittsfield MA 01202-2953

**SACHER, STEVEN JAY,** lawyer; b. Cleve., Jan. 28, 1942; s. Albert N. and Cecil P. (Chessin) S.; m. Colleen Marie Gibbons, Nov. 28, 1970; children—Alexander Jerome, Barry Elizabeth, William Paul. BS, U. Wis., 1964; JD, U. Chgo., 1967. Bar: D.C. 1968. Assoc. solicitor Employee Retirement Income Security Act U.S. Dept. Labor, Washington, 1974-77; spl. counsel com. on labor and human resources U.S. Senate, Washington, 1977-79, gen. counsel, 1980-81; ptnr. Pepper, Hamilton & Scheetz, Washington, 1982-88; shareholder Johnson & Wortley, Washington, 1988-94; ptnr. Kilpatrick Stockton LLP, Washington, 1994—; adj. prof. law Georgetown U. Law Ctr., 1977; co-chair sr. editors Employee Benefits Law and Annual Supplements, Bur. Nat. Affairs, Washington, 1991—. Mem. adv. bd. BNA Pension and Benefits Reporter; mem. editorial bd. Benefits Law Jour., Jour. Pension Planning and Compliance, Jour. Taxation of Employee Benefits. Founding mem. ERISA Roundtable, Washington. Fellow Coll. Labor and Employment Lawyers. Mem. ABA (mgmt. co-chmn. com. on employee benefits, sect. on labor and employment law 1988-91, chmn. prohibited trans. subcom., com. on employee benefits, sect. on taxation 1986-91), D.C. Bar Assn. Pension, profit-sharing, and employee benefits, Labor, Legislative. Office: Kilpatrick Stockton LLP 700 13th St NW Ste 800 Washington DC 20005-3960

**SACHS, ERIC,** lawyer; b. New Hyde Park, N.Y., Aug. 3, 1959; s. Herbert Sachs and Sheila Kafka; m. Linda Kay, June 6, 1993; children: Taylor Michelle, Justin. BA, SUNY, Albany, 1981; JD, Bklyn. Law Sch., 1985. Bar: N.Y., U.S. Dist. Ct. (ea. dist.) N.Y., U.S. Dist. Ct. (so. dist.) N.Y., U.S. Supreme Ct. Asst. dist. attorney Bronx (N.Y.) County Dist. Attorney's Office, 1985-89; pvt. practice Bellmore, N.Y., 1989—; judiciary com. Bronx County Bar Assn., 1994—. Avocations: commercial pilot, scuba diving, skiing, swimming. Criminal, General practice, Personal injury. Office: 254 Pettit Ave Bellmore NY 11710-3629

**SACHS, HOWARD F(REDERIC),** federal judge; b. Kansas City, Mo., Sept. 13, 1925; s. Alex F. and Rose (Lyon) S.; m. Susanne Wilson, 1960; children: Alex Wilson, Adam Phinney. B.A. summa cum laude, Williams Coll., 1947; J.D., Harvard U., 1950. Bar: Mo. 1950. Law clk. U.S. Dist. Ct., Kansas City, Mo., 1950-51; pvt. practice law Phineas Rosenberg, Kansas City, 1951-56; with Spencer, Fane, Britt & Browne, 1956-79; U.S. dist. judge Western Dist. Mo., Kansas City, 1979—, chief dist. judge, 1990-92, now sr. judge. Contbr. articles to various publs.; contbr. chpt. to Mid-America's Promise, 1982. Mem. Kansas City Commn. Human Rels., 1967-73; chmn. Jewish Community Rels. Bur., 1968-71, Kansas City chpt. Am. Jewish Com., 1963-65; mem. exec. com. Nat. Jewish Community Rels. Adv. Coun., 1968-71; pres. Urban League Kansas City, 1957-58, Kansas City chpt. Am. Jewish Congress, 1974-77; co-chmn. Kansas City chpt. NCCJ, 1958-60; mem. Kansas City Sch. Dist. Desegregation Task Force, 1976-77; pres. Jackson County Young Democrats, 1959-60; treas. Kennedy-Johnson Club, Jackson County, 1960. Served with USNR, 1944-46. Mem. ABA, Mo. Bar, Kansas City Bar Assn., Am. Judicature Soc., Lawyers Assn. Kansas City, Dist. Judges Assn. (8th cir., pres. 1992-94), Phi Beta Kappa. Office: US Dist Ct US Courthouse 400 E 9th St Kansas City MO 64106-2607

**SACHS, RALPH GORDON,** lawyer, physician; b. Detroit, July 17, 1940. Student, U. Mich., 1957-58, Wayne State U., 1958-60, L.A. City Coll., 1960; DO, Kirksville Coll. Osteo. Med., 1965; JD, Detroit Coll. Law, 1973. Bar: Mich. 1973. Pvt. practice, Detroit, 1973—; physician Mich. Athletic Commn., Lansing, 1982—. Maj. U.S. Army, 1968-69. Mem. State Bar Mich. Jewish. Avocation: oil painting. Personal injury. Office: PO Box 10 Troy MI 48099-0010

**SACK, EDWARD J.,** lawyer; b. N.Y.C., Apr. 7, 1930. AB, Harvard U., 1951, LLB, 1954; LLM, NYU, 1959. Bar: N.Y. 1954, U.S. Dist. Ct. (so. dist.) N.Y. 1959, U.S. Ct. Appeals (4th cir.) 1975, U.S. Ct. Appeals (2nd cir.) 1979, U.S. Supreme Ct. 1982. Assoc. Simpson Thacher & Bartlett, N.Y.C., 1954-66; atty. Am. Electric Power Svc. Corp., N.Y.C., 1966-69; sr. atty. Consol. Edison Co., N.Y.C., 1969-79; gen. counsel Internat. Coun. Shopping Ctrs., N.Y.C., 1979—. Mem. Bar Assn. City of N.Y. Administrative and regulatory, Legislative. Office: 665 5th Ave New York NY 10022-5305

**SACK, ROBERT DAVID,** judge; b. Phila., Oct. 4, 1939; s. Eugene J. and Sylvia I. (Rivlin) S.; div.; children: Deborah Gail, Suzanne Michelle, David Rivlin; m. Anne K. Hilker, 1989. BA, U. Rochester, 1960; LLB, Columbia U., 1963. Bar: N.Y. 1963. Law clk. to judge Fed. Dist. Ct., Dist. of N.J., 1963-64; assoc. Patterson, Belknap & Webb, N.Y.C., 1964-70; ptnr. Patterson, Belknap, Webb & Tyler, N.Y.C., 1970-86, Gibson, Dunn & Crutcher, N.Y.C., 1986-98; sr. assoc. spl. counsel U.S. Ho. of Reps. Impeachment Inquiry, 1974; judge U.S. Ct. Appeals (2d cir.), 1998—; lectr. Practising Law Inst., 1973-97; adv. bd. Media Law Reporter. Author: Libel, Slander, and Related Problems, 1980, 2nd edit., 1994, CD-ROM edit., 1995, Sack on Defamation -- Libel, Slander, and Related Problems, 3d edit., 1999; co-author: Advertising and Commercial Speech, a First Amendment Guide, 1999; contbr. articles to profl. jours. Chmn. bd. dirs. Nat. Council on Crime and Delinquency, 1982-83; trustee Columbia seminars on media and society Columbia U. Sch. Journalism, 1985-92, N.Y.C. Commn. on Pub. Info. and Comm., 1995-98; v.p., dir. William F. Kerby and Robert S. Potter Fund; bd. visitors Sch. of Law, Columbia U., 1999—. Fellow Am. Bar Found.; mem. ABA (bd. govs. forum com. on comm. law 1980-88), N.Y. State Bar Assn., Assn. Bar City N.Y. (chmn. comm. law com. 1986-89). Office: US Cir Ct 2d Cir 40 Foley Sq New York NY 10007-1502

**SACK, SYLVAN HANAN,** lawyer; b. Phila., Dec. 26, 1932; s. Isadore F. and Mollye (Bellmore) S.; m. Ellen L. Foreman, Aug. 13, 1972; children: Reuben H., Sara I. M.S. in Bus. Adminstrn, Pa. State U., 1956; J.D., U. Balt., 1964. Bar: Md. 1964, U.S. Tax Ct. 1967, U.S. Supreme Ct. 1970; C.P.A., Md. Pvt. practice Balt., 1967—; assoc. counsel Safety First Club of Md., 1975-78, spl. counsel, 1979—; gov. Md. chpt. Retinitis Pigmentosa Found., 1974-75. Contbr. articles to profl. jours. Chmn. Indsl. Toxicology NIOSH Function, 1977, Occupational Disease Forum, 1979, OSHA and Diseases in Workplace Seminar, 1981. Mem. Fed. Bar Assn. (gov. chpt. 1968—, chmn. bd. govs. 1969-70, chmn. environ. law program 1984), ABA (chmn. subcom. sect. taxation 1972-75), Md. Bar Assn., Assn. Trial Lawyers Am.; mem. Md. Trial Lawyers Assn. (lectr. toxic torts 1983 conv.). Toxic tort, Personal injury, Environmental. Home: 27 Brightside Ave Baltimore MD 21208-4802 Office: 2404 Saint Paul St Baltimore MD 21218-5118

**SACKRIN, CINDY DAWN,** lawyer; b. Bklyn., Oct. 26, 1958; d. Jerome Neil and Lynne Rita (Smolowitz) Diamond; m. Alan D. Sackrin, Aug. 24, 1986; children: Adam, Nicole. BA, SUNY, Stony Brook, 1981; JD, U. Miami, 1984. Bar: Fla. 1985; bd. cert. in matrimonial and family law. Atty. Legal Aid Soc.-Dade County Bar Assn., Miami, Fla., 1985-92, Law Office of Bette Ellen Quiat, Miami, 1992-94, Franklin & Marbin, P.A., North Miami Beach, Fla., 1994-95; pvt. practice Law Offices of Cindy D. Sackrin, Hollywood, Fla., 1995—. Recipient Pro Bono award. Mem. Am. Inns. of Ct. (assoc.), Dade County Bar Assn., Broward County Bar Assn., Concerned Matrimonial Lawyers. Family and matrimonial. Office: Ste 200 2100 E Hallandale Beach Blvd Hallandale FL 33009-3770

**SACKS, DIANA L.,** lawyer; b. Chatham, Kent, Eng., May 15, 1938; d. Harold A. and Dorothy M. (Johnson) Lauder; divorced; children: Elizabeth Ann, Michael Thomas, Bruce Edward. BA, Franklin and Marshall U., Lancaster, Pa., 1979; JD, Temple U., 1982. Bar: Pa. 1986. Sec. Midland Bank Ltd., Bath, Eng., 1955-60; sec., adminstrv. asst. Dept. Cmty. Affairs, Harrisburg, Pa., 1977-79; staff atty. Gen. Assembly, Commonwealth of Pa., Harrisburg, 1985—. Mem. Pa. Bar Assn. (chair com. on the corrections sys., chair 1996-98), Dauphin County Bar Assn. Avocations: reading, gardening, travel. Office: Joint State Govt Commn Fin Bldg Rm G-16 Harrisburg PA 17111

**SACKS, KAREN GOLDFARB,** lawyer; b. N.Y.C., Nov. 22, 1966; s. Warren Edward and Linda Goldfarb; m. Eric Dylan Sacks, Aug. 30, 1998. BA, U. Mich., 1988; JD, NYU, 1991. Bar: N.Y. 1991. Assoc. Gordon Altman Butowsky Weitzen Shalov & Wein, N.Y.C., 1991-97; asst. gen. counsel Health Ins. Plan of Greater N.Y., N.Y.C., 1997—. Mem. ABA, N.Y. State Bar Assn., Assn. Bar City N.Y. (health law com.), Am. Health Lawyers Assn. Health, General corporate, Contracts commercial. Office: Health Ins Plan Greater NY 7 W 34th St New York NY 10001-8100

**SACKS, STEWART JONATHAN,** lawyer; b. Norfolk, Va., Feb. 8, 1957; s. Harold Howard and Annabel Lee (Glicksman) S.; m. Ellen Faye Abbey, June 5, 1988. Student, U. Edinburgh, 1976-77; BA, Coll. William and Mary, 1978; JD, U. Va., 1981. Bar: Va. 1981, U.S. Dist. Ct. (ea. dist.) Va. 1981. Assoc. Seawell, Dalton et al, Norfolk, 1981-82; ptnr. Kelley & Sacks, Norfolk, 1982-84, Faggert & Frieden, P.C. and predecessor Scanelli & Shapiro, Norfolk, 1984—; vis. instr. Old Dominion U., Norfolk, 1988. Div. chmn. United Jewish Fedn., Norfolk, 1985-87; regional bd. dirs. Anti-Defamation League, Norfolk, 1987—. Mem. Norfolk-Portsmouth Bar Assn. Avocations: surfing, reading, travel. Real property, General civil litigation, Construction. Home: 247 S Blake Rd Norfolk VA 23505-4405 Office: Faggert & Frieden PC 1600 Crestar Bank Bldg Norfolk VA 23510

**SADLER, LUTHER FULLER, JR.,** lawyer; b. Jacksonville, Fla., Apr. 10, 1942; s. Luther Fuller and Jane Grey (Lloyd) S.; children: Catherine Winchester, Anna Stephenson Lloyd. BA, Yale U., 1964, LLB, 1967. Bar: Fla. 1967. Ptnr. Mahoney, Hadlow, Chambers & Adams, Jacksonville, 1967-81, Commander, Legler, Werber, Dawes, Sadler & Howell, Jacksonville, 1982-91, Foley & Lardner, Jacksonville, 1991—; gen. counsel Jacksonville C. of C., 1987. Trustee Jacksonville Mus. of Contemporary Art, 1984-94, Episcopal Child Care and Devel. Ctrs., Inc., 1990-94. Lt. USNR, 1967-73. Mem. ABA, Fla. Bar Assn. (chmn. corp. banking and bus. law sect. 1979-80), Timuquana Country Club. Episcopalian. Banking, General corporate, Securities. Office: Foley & Lardner PO Box 240 200 N Laura St Jacksonville FL 32201-2040

**SADLER, RICHARD LAWRENCE,** lawyer, business executive; b. St. Louis, Nov. 1, 1944; s. Lawrence Fredrick and Mary Jane Sadler; m. Lynne Wangsgard, June 20, 1971; children: Jane W., Benjamin. BA in History, Carleton Coll., 1967; JD, Harvard U., 1974. Bar: Oreg., U.S. Dist. Ct. Oreg., U.S. Ct. Appeals, U.S. Supreme Ct. Ptnr. Copeland, Landye, Bennett & Wolf, Portland, Oreg., 1974—. Mem. Metro-TPHC Comn., Portland, 1997-98; mem. Mid Valley Initiatives, Salem, Oreg., 1998; chmn. Yamhill County Planning, McMinnville, Oreg., 1979-85. Avocations: farming, skiing, antique sports cars, jewelry making. Administrative and regulatory, General civil litigation, General corporate. Home: 20189 NE Trunk Rd Dundee OR 97115-9032 Office: Copeland Landye et al 3500 Wells Fargo Portland OR 97201

**SADLOCK, RICHARD ALAN,** lawyer; b. Paterson, N.J., Aug. 26, 1961; s. George Edward and Joan Theresa (Godleski) S.; m. Patricia Ellen Roth, Sept. 27, 1986; children: Joshua David, Tessa. BA, Gettysburg Coll., 1983; JD cum laude, Vt. Law Sch., 1986. Bar: Pa. 1986, U.S. Dist. Ct. (mid. dist.) Pa. 1987, U.S. Ct. Appeals (3rd cir.) 1991, U.S. Dist. Ct. (ea. dist.) Pa. 1993. Assoc. Angino & Rovner, P.C., Harrisburg, Pa., 1986—; mediator U.S. Dist. Ct. Middle Dist. Pa. Mem. Pa. Bar Assn., Dauphin County Bar Assn., Assn. Trial Lawyers Am., Pa. Trial Lawyers Assn. (speaker 1989—), Am. Arbitration Assn. (arbitrator for Ct. Common Pleas of Dauphin County). Roman Catholic. Avocations: tennis, golf, reading, weight lifting, collecting sports memorabilia. Personal injury, General civil litigation, State civil litigation. Office: Angino & Rovner PC 4503 N Front St Harrisburg PA 17110-1799

**SAEKS, ALLEN IRVING,** lawyer; b. Bemidji, Minn., July 14, 1932; m. Linda J. Levin; 1 child, Adam Charles. BS in Law, U. Minn., 1954, JD, 1956. Bar: Minn. 1956, U.S. Dist. Ct. Minn. 1956, U.S. Ct. Appeals (8th cir.) 1957, U.S. Ct. Appeals (fed. cir.) 1959, U.S. Supreme Ct. 1959, U.S. Ct. Appeals (11th cir.) 1997; cert. civil trial specialist. Asst. U.S. atty. Dept. Justice, St. Paul, 1956-57; assoc. Leonard Street and Deinard, Mpls., 1960-63, ptnr., 1964—; adj. prof. law U. Minn. Law Sch., 1960-65; chmn. Lawyer Trust Account Bd., Interest on Lawyers Trust Accounts, 1984-87. Chmn. Property Tax Com., 1986-87; bd. dirs. Citizens League, Mpls., 1984-87; pres. Jewish Cmty. Rels. Coun. of Minn. and the Dakotas, 1994-96. Served to 1st lt. JAGC, U.S. Army, 1957-60. Recipient City of Mpls. award, 1996. Fellow Am. Bar Found. (life); mem. Fund for the Legal Aid Soc. (chmn. 1997-98, Law Day Testimonial award 1996), Hennepin County Bar Assn. (pres. 1983-84), ABA (commn. on interest on lawyers trust accts. 1990-93), Minn. State Bar Assn., Order of Coif, Phi Delta Phi. Professional liability, Federal civil litigation, Probate. Office: Leonard Street and Deinard 150 S 5th St Ste 2300 Minneapolis MN 55402-4238

**SAENZ, L. ARNOLDO,** judge; b. Premont, Tex., Apr. 30, 1952; s. Leonel S. and Belia (Perez) S.; m. Gretchen Arlene Shoots, Apr. 25, 1987; children: Bryan Tinsley, Meagan, Brianna. BBA, Tex. A&I U., 1977. City sec. City of Premont, Tex., 1976-77; asst. county auditor Jim Wells County, Alice, Tex., 1978-89, county auditor, 1989-95, county judge, 1995—; chmn. Alice/Jim Wells County Econ. Devel. Bd., Alice, 1996-98; dir. I-69 Hwy. Alliance, 1996-98; treas. Coastal Bend Coun. Govts., Corpus Christi, Tex., 1997-98. Sec., treas. Real, Inc., Alice, 1994-98; chmn. Jim Wells County United Way, Alice, 1996-97. Avocations: photography, golfing. Office: Jim Wells County 200 N Almond St Alice TX 78332-4845

**SAETA, PHILIP MAX,** judge; b. L.A., Feb. 21, 1931; s. Maurice and Elizabeth (Jacobs) S.; m. Joanne Edith Hixson, Aug. 28, 1954; children: David, Peter, Sandra. AB, Stanford U., 1953, LLB, 1957. Bar: Calif. 1958, U.S. Dist. Ct. (cen. dist.) Calif. Assoc., ptnr. Beardsley, Hufstedler & Kemble, L.A., 1958-64; judge Mcpl. Ct., L.A., 1964-75; judge L.A. County Superior Ct., L.A., 1975-91, ret., 1991; pvt. judge, 1991—. With U.S. Army, 1953-55. Mem. ABA, Calif. Judges Assn. (Jefferson award 1987), L.A. County Bar Assn. Democrat. Jewish. Avocation: music.

**SAFFELS, DALE EMERSON,** federal judge; b. Moline, Kans., Aug. 13, 1921; s. Edwin Clayton and Lillian May (Cook) S.; m. Margaret Elaine Nieman, Apr. 2, 1976; children by previous marriage: Suzanne Saffels Gravitt, Deborah Saffels Godowns, James B.; stepchildren: Lynda Cowger Harris, Christopher Cowger. AB, Emporia State U., 1947; JD cum laude, LLB cum laude, Washburn U., 1949. Bar: Kans. 1949. Pvt. practice law Garden City, Kans., 1949-71, Topeka, 1971-75, Wichita, Kans., 1975-79; U.S. dist. judge Dist. of Kans., Topeka, 1979—; county atty. Finney County, Kans., 1951-55; chmn. bd. Fed. Home Loan Bank Topeka, 1978-79; mem. Jud. Conf. Com. on Fin. Disclosure, 1993-99. Mem. bd. govs. Sch. Law Washburn U., 1973-85; pres. Kans. Dem. Club, 1957; Dem. nominee Gov. of Kans., 1962; mem. Kans. Ho. of Reps., 1955-63, minority leader, 1961-63; mem. Kans. Corp. Commn., 1967-75, chmn., 1968-75; mem. Kans. Legis. Coun., 1957-63; Kans. rep. Interstate Oil Compact Commn., 1967-75, 1st vice chmn., 1971-72; pres. Midwest Assn. Regulatory Commn., 1972-73, Midwest Assn. R.R. and Utilities Commrs., 1972-73; trustee Emporia State U. Endowment Assn.; bd. dirs. Nat. Assn. Regulatory Utility Commrs., 1972-75. Maj. Signal Corps U.S. Army, 1942-46. Fellow Am. Bar Found., Kans. Bar Found.; mem. ABA, Kans. Bar Assn., Wichita Bar assn., Am. Judicature Soc., Delta Theta Phi. Lutheran. Fax: (785) 295-2809. Office: US Dist Ct 420 Federal Bldg 444 SE Quincy St Topeka KS 66683

**SAFI, DEBORAH CAVAZOS,** lawyer; b. Dallas, Feb. 8, 1953; d. Arnaldo Nelson and Ila Mae (Rinn) Cavazos; m. Hazim Jawad Safi, July 28, 1979; children: Jawad Joseph, Aminah Mae. BA, Baylor U., 1975, JD, 1977. Bar: Tex. 1977. Assoc. Andrews & Kurth, Houston, 1977-81; corp. atty. Transco Energy Co., Houston, 1981-83; of counsel Harman & Timby P.C. (formerly Anderson, Harrell & Timby P.C.), Houston, 1985-88, Bennett & Broocks, Houston, 1988-89; pvt. practice Houston, 1983-85, 89—. Mem. fund raising com. Children's Mus., Houston, 1986; co-leader Blue Bird/Camp Fire Girls, Waco, Tex., 1972-73, Tex. Bd. Legal Specialization, Real Estate Law Adv. Commn., 1988-89; vice chmn. combat hunger and homeless com. State Bar Tex., 1988-90. Named one of Outstanding Women of 1982, Transco Energy Co. and YWCA, Houston 1982. Fellow Tex. Bar Found., Houston Bar Found.; mem. ABA, Houston Bar Assn., Houston Young Lawyers Assn. (chmn. directory planning com. 1987-88, com. chair 1981-82, bd. dirs. 1982-84, treas. 1984-86, v.p. 1986-87, named Outstanding Com. Chmn. 1981-82, 87-88), Tex. Young Lawyers Assn. (bd. dirs. 1986-88, co-editor newsletter 1986-87, treas. 1988-89, mktg. and pub. rels. com. chmn. 1987-88), Tex. Bar Assn., Fed. Energy Bar Assn., Houston Bar Assn. (editorial bd. The Houston Lawyer 1988—), State Bar Tex. (vice chmn. Combat Hunger and Homeless com. 1988-90, mem. Bar Jour. com. 1989—), Hispanic Bar Assn. (bd. dirs. 1990-92), Delta Delta Delta, Phi Delta Phi. Oil, gas, and mineral.

**SAFON, DAVID MICHAEL,** lawyer; b. Boston, Sept. 6, 1962; s. Kenneth Norman and Barbara Safon; m. Lisa Eileen Spector, Aug. 28, 1988; children: Jennifer, Keith, Noah. BA in Econs. with honors, Coll. William and Mary, 1984; JD cum laude, Cornell U., 1987. Bar: N.Y. 1988, U.S. Dist. Ct. (so. and ea. dists.) N.Y. 1988. Assoc. Proskauer, Rose, Goetz & Mendelsohn, N.Y.C., 1987-89; assoc. Benetar, Bernstein, Schair & Stein, N.Y.C., 1989-96, ptnr., 1997—. Contbg. editor: (supplements) Age Discrimination, Employment Discrimination. Mem. ABA (com. on fed. labor stds. legis.), N.Y. State Bar Assn. (labor and employment law sect., com. on labor rels.), Assn. of Bar of City of N.Y., Phi Beta Kappa. Labor. Office: Benetar Bernstein Schair & Stein 330 Madison Ave Fl 39 New York NY 10017-5001

**SAFRAN, PERRY RENFROW,** lawyer, educator; b. Raleigh, N.C., Apr. 22, 1950; s. Stephen and Eleanor (Doak) S.; m. Susan Camille Morris, Aug. 20, 1977; children: Stephen Peterson, Jason Douglas, David Abram. BS with honors, N.C. State U., 1972; MBA, Wake Forest U., 1975; JD, Campbell U., 1981. Bar: N.C. 1981, U.S. Dist. Ct. (ea. dist.) N.C. 1981, U.S. Dist. Ct. (mid. dist.) N.C. 1984, U.S. Ct. Appeals (4th cir.) 1984. Constrn. engr. D.R. Allen & Son, Inc., Fayetteville, N.C., 1972-75, Sparrow Constrn., Raleigh, N.C., 1975-78; ptnr., co-founder Marshall & Safran, Raleigh, 1981-88; prin. Safran Law Offices, Raleigh, 1988—; lectr. Proof Mgmt. Cons., Richmond, Va., 1986—; engring. instr. N.C. State U., Raleigh, 1982—. Author: Construction Arbitration in North Carolina, 1982, Avoiding the Legal Pitfalls of Contracts, Collections, and Change Orders, 1986. Mem. Raleigh City Coun., 1985-87; vice-chmn. Raleigh Planning Commn., 1980-85. Mem. N.C. Bar Assn. (constrn. law sect., legisl. chmn. 1988), Raleigh-Durham-Chapel Hill Constrn. Law Roundtable (founder, chmn. 1982-88). Construction, Real property. Office: Safran Law Offices 120 S Boylan Ave Raleigh NC 27603-1802

**SAFT, STUART MARK,** lawyer; b. N.Y.C., Feb. 17, 1947; s. Stanley and Dorothy (Ligerman) S.; m. Stephanie C. Optekman, June 6, 1970; children: Bradley S., Gordon D. BA, Hofstra U., 1968; JD, Columbia U., 1971. Bar: N.Y. 1972, Fla. 1975, U.S. Dist. Ct. (so. dist.) N.Y. 1975, U.S. Supreme Ct. 1990. Asst. gen. counsel Joseph Bancroft & Son Co., N.Y.C., 1972-74; ptnr. Brauner, Baron, Rosenzwerz, Kligler & Sparber, N.Y.C., 1974-81, Powsner, Saft & Powsner, N.Y.C., 1981-84, Goldschmidt & Saft, N.Y.C., 1984-88; Wolf Haldenstein Adler Freeman & Herz, N.Y.C., 1988—; chmn., bd. dirs. Coun. of N.Y. Coops., N.Y.C., 1981—; chmn. bd. dirs., CEO Pvt. Industry Coun. of N.Y.C.; bd. dirs. Am. Women's Econ. Devel. Corp., Nat. Assn. Housing Coops., Nat. Coop. Bank; adj. asst. prof. NYU, Real Estate Inst. Author: Commercial Real Estate Forms, 3 vols., 1987, Commercial Real Estate Transactions, 1989, Commercial Real Estate Workouts, 1991, Real Estate Development: Strategies for a Changing Market, 1990, Commercial Real Estate Leasing, 1992, Real Estate Investor's Survival Guide, 1992, Commercial Real Estate Financing, 1993, Commercial Real Estate Forms, 2d edit., 5 vols., 1994, Commercial Real Estate Transactions, 2d edit., 1995, Commercial Real Estate Workouts, 2d edit., 1996; contbg. editor: The Real Estate Finance Jour., 1989—; contbr. articles to profl. jours. Served to capt. USAR, 1968-76. Mem. ABA, N.Y. Bar Assn., Fla. Bar Assn. Real property, General corporate. Office: Wolf Haldenstein Adler Freeman & Herz 270 Madison Ave New York NY 10016-0601

**SAGARIN, J. DANIEL,** lawyer; b. Bridgeport, Conn., Feb. 15, 1941; s. Philip H. Sagarin; m. Mary Demotses; children: Joshua, Mark, Raphael. BA magna cum laude, Lehigh U., 1962; JD, Yale U., 1965. Bar: Conn. 1965, U.S. Dist. Ct. Conn. 1965, Mass. 1966, U.S. Dist. Ct. Mass. 1966, U.S. Ctp Appeals (2d cir.) 1967, U.S. Supreme Ct. 1972, U.S. Claims Ct. Law clk. to Hon. Robert C. Zampano, U.S. Dist. Ct. for Conn., Hartford, 1965-66, asst. U.S. atty., 1967-70, spl. master spl. masters program, 1988—; ptnr. Hurwitz & Sagarin, LLC, Milford, Conn., 1970—; tutor Yale Law Sch., New Haven, 1965-66, lectr. trial practice, 1976-84. Fellow Am. Coll. Trial Lawyers (com. com.), Conn. Bar Found.; mem. ABA, ATLA, Conn. Bar Assn. (exec. com. criminal law sect. 1970—, mem. fed. practice com. 1985—), Conn. Trial Lawyers Assn. Federal civil litigation, State civil litigation, Securities. Home: 72 Vineyard Pl Guilford CT 06437-3237 Office: Hurwitz & Sagarin LLC 147 Broad St Milford CT 06460-4742

**SAGER, DANIEL IAN,** lawyer; b. Norristown, Pa., Sept. 2, 1966; s. Lawrence S. and Phyllis B. S.; m. Jennifer Lynn Spellman, Oct. 18,1 992; children: Joshua Ryan, Ethan Michael. BA, Clark U., 1988; JD, Villanova U., 1992. Bar: Pa. 1992, U.S. Dist. Ct. (ea. dist.) Pa. 1993. Assoc. Sager & Sager Assocs., Pottstown, Pa., 1992—. Bd. dirs. ARC, Pottstown, Pa., 1994—, Mercy & Truth Synagogue, Pottstown, 1995—. General practice, Bankruptcy, Family and matrimonial.

**SAGER, JONATHAN WARD,** lawyer; b. Syracuse, N.Y., Apr. 10, 1954; s. Roderick Cooper and Ruth (Ross) S.; m. Karen Wischerath, Oct. 26, 1979; children: Sarah Elizabeth, Rebecca Claire, William Ward, Charles Cooper. BA, Colgate U., 1975; JD, Washington and Lee U., 1978. Bar:

N.Y. 1979, U.S. Dist. Ct. (no. dist.) N.Y. 1979, Fla. 1980. Assoc. Williams, Micale & Wells, Syracuse, 1978-82, Edward W. Dietrich P.C., Syracuse, 1982-84; ptnr. Dietrich & Sager, Syracuse, 1984-85; assoc. counsel The Mut. Life Ins. Co. of N.Y., Syracuse, 1985-87, counsel, 1987-88, sr. counsel, 1988—. Counsel DeWitt Cmty. Ch. and DeWitt Cmty. Ch. Found., 1981-93; bd. dirs. MONY Fed. Credit Union, 1987-94, v.p., sec., pres.; bd. dirs. Am. Lung Assn., 1987—, pres., 1994-96, sec., 1997—; bd. dirs. Combined Health Appeal of Ctrl. N.Y., 1987-91. Mem. N.Y. State Bar Assn. (com. assn. ins. program), Fla. State Bar, Onondaga County Bar Assn. (grievance com., chmn. corp. counsel com. 1988-93), Am. Corp. Counsel Assn. Republican. Avocation: golf. Insurance, Labor, General corporate. Home: 5127 Shiraz Ln Fayetteville NY 13066-2578 Office: MONY Life Ins Co One MONY Plaza PO Box 4830 Syracuse NY 13221-4830

**SAGER, MADELINE DEAN,** lawyer; b. Turlock, Calif., Feb. 9, 1946; d. Paul Kenton and Jean Madeline (Ferguson) Dean; m. Gregory Warren Sager, June, 1970; children: Jeannette Carolyn, Robert Dean. BA, Sacramento State U., 1967; JD, U. Calif., Davis, 1970. Bar: Calif. 1971, U.S. Dist. Ct. (ea. dist.) Calif. 1971, U.S. Dist. Ct. (no. dist.) Calif. 1973. Atty. Blackmon, Isenberg, Moulds & Blicker, Sacramento, 1971-72, Redwood Legal Assistance, Ukiah, Calif., 1972-77, Sager & Sager, Ukiah, Willits, Calif., 1977-87, Leonard J. LaCasse, Ukiah, 1990—; dir. Law Libr. Bd., Ukiah, 1985. Sec. PTA, Calpella, Calif., 1989-90; mem. sch. site coun. Redwood Valley (Calif.) Mid. Sch., 1992-93; treas., dir. Ukiah Dolphin Swim, 1994-97; meet dir. Soroptimist Swim Meet, Ukiah, 1996. Mem. Mendocino County Bar Assn. (pres. 1986), Pacific Swimming (official 1995-98). Democrat. Presbyterian. Avocations: hiking, camping, music, travel. Insurance, Probate, Real property. Home: PO Box 72 Redwood Valley CA 95470-0072 Office: Leonard J LaCasse 119 S Main St Ukiah CA 95482-4919

**SAGER, STEVEN TRAVIS,** lawyer; b. Boston, June 3, 1957. AB, Allegheny Coll., 1979; JD cum laude, Western New Eng. Coll., 1986. Bar: Mass. 1986, N.Y. 1987, U.S. Dist. Ct. Mass. 1987, U.S. Ct. Appeals (1st cir.) 1987. Mem. staff Office of Marc Redlich, Boston, Mass., 1990—. Active Putterman Civic Assn., 1988-93, Brookline Civic Assn., 1988-93, Anti-Defamation League, Moot Ct., Friends of Beth Israel Hosp.; chmn. Young Profls. Com., 1988-90; bd. dirs. Newton Symphony Orch., v.p., 1992-93, pres., 1993-97. Mem. ABA (bus. law sect.), Mass. Bar Assn., N.Y. State Bar Assn., Boston Bar Assn., Smaller Bus. Assn. of New Eng., Metrowe St C. of C., Theta Chi. General corporate, Private international, General civil litigation. Office: Law Offices of Marc Redlich 3 Center Plz # 400 Boston MA 02108-2003

**SAHID, JOSEPH ROBERT,** lawyer; b. Paterson, N.J., Feb. 14, 1944; s. Joseph James and Helen (Vitale) S.; children: Annunziata, Joseph. BS, Rutgers U., 1965; LLB, U. Va., 1968. Bar: N.Y. 1973, U.S. Dist. Ct. N.Y., U.S. Ct. Appeals (2d and 3d cirs.), U.S. Supreme Ct. Staff mem. Nat. Commn. on Causes and Prevention of Violence, Washington, 1968-69; cons. Pres.'s Commn. on Campus Unrest, Washington, 1970; assoc. Cravath, Swaine & Moore, N.Y.C., 1972-77, ptnr., 1977-93, cons., 1994-97; ptnr. Barrack, Rodos & Bacine, N.Y.C., 1994-96; pvt. practice N.Y.C., 1996—. Author: Rights in Concord, 1969; co-author: Law and Order Reconsidered, 1969; contbr. articles to profl. jours. Lt. USCG, 1968-72. General civil litigation. Office: 18 E 50th St Fl 7 New York NY 10022-6817

**ST. ANTOINE, THEODORE JOSEPH,** law educator, arbitrator; b. St. Albans, Vt., May 29, 1929; s. Arthur Joseph and Mary Beatrice (Callery) S.; m. Elizabeth Lloyd Frier, Jan. 2, 1960; children: Arthur, Claire, Paul, Sara. AB, Fordham Coll., 1951; JD, U. Mich., 1954; postgrad., U. London, 1957-58. Bar: Mich. 1954, Ohio 1954, D.C. 1959. Assoc. Squire, Sanders & Dempsey, Cleve., 1954; assoc., ptnr. Woll, Mayer & St. Antoine, Washington, 1958-65; assoc. prof. law U. Mich. Law Sch., Ann Arbor, 1965-69, prof., 1969—, Degan prof., 1981-98, Degan prof. emeritus, 1998—, dean, 1971-78; pres. Nat. Resource Ctr. for Consumers of Legal Svcs., 1974-78; mem. Pub. Rev. Bd., UAW, 1973—; chmn. UAW-GM Legal Svcs. Plan, 1983-95; Mich. Gov.'s spl. counselor on workers' compensation, 1983-85; reporter Uniform Law Commrs., 1987-92; life mem. Clare Hall, Cambridge (Eng.) U. Co-author: (with R. Smith, L. Merrifield and C. Craver) Labor Relations Law: Cases and Materials, 4th edit., 1968, 10th edit., 1999; editor: The Common Law of the Workplace: The Views of Arbitrators, 1998; contbr. articles to profl. jours. 1st lt. JACG, U.S. Army, 1955-57. Fulbright grantee, London, 1957-58. Mem. ABA (past sec. labor law sect., coun. 1984-92), Am. Bar Found., State Bar Mich. (chmn. labor rels. law sect. 1979-80), Nat. Acad. Arbitrators (bd. govs. 1985-88, v.p. 1994-96, pres. 1999—), Internat. Soc. Labor Law and Social Security (U.S. br. exec. bd. 1983—, vice chmn. 1989-95), Indsl. Rels. Rsch. Assn., Coll. Labor and Employment Lawyers, Order of Coif (life). Democrat. Roman Catholic. Home: 1421 Roxbury Rd Ann Arbor MI 48104-4047 Office: U Mich Law Sch 625 S State St Ann Arbor MI 48109-1215

**ST. CLAIR, DONALD DAVID,** lawyer; b. Hammond, Ind., Dec. 30, 1932; s. Victor Peter and Wanda (Rubinska) Small; m. Sergine Anne Oliver, June 6, 1970 (dec. June 1974); m. Beverly Joyce Tipton, Dec. 28, 1987. BS, Ind. U., 1955, MS, 1963, EdD, 1967; JD, U. Toledo, 1992. Bar: Ohio 1992, U.S. Dist. Ct. (no. dist.) Ohio 1993, U.S. Supreme Ct. 1996. Assoc. prof. Western Ky. U. Coll. Edn., Bowling Green, 1967-68; assoc. prof. U. Toledo, 1968-77, prof., 1977-92; atty., ptnr. Garand, Bollinger, & St. Clair, Oregon, Ohio, 1992-97; pvt. practice Law Offices Donald D. St. Clair, Toledo, 1997—; mem. Ohio Coun. Mental Health Ctrs., Columbus, 1978-79; dir. honors programs U. Toledo. Author: (poetry) Daymarks and Beacons, 1983, Impressions from an Afternoon in a Paris Courtroom, 1998; contbr. articles to profl. jours. Organizer Students Toledo Organized for Peace, 1970-71; mem. Lucas County Dem. Party, 1990—. With U.S. Army, 1955-57. Mem. ABA, AAU (nat. bd. dirs. 1973-74), Ohio Bar Assn., Toledo Bar Assn., Ohio Acad. Trial Lawyers, Toledo Power Squadron (comdg. officer 1981), Bay View Yacht Club, Ohio Criminal Def. Lawyers Assn., Lucas County Bar Assn., Maumee Valley Criminal Def. Lawyers Assn., Ottawa County Bar Assn., Masons (32 degree), Shriners, Ancient Order Friars, Phi Alpha Delta. E-mail: STCLAIRLAW@IBM.NET. General practice, Personal injury, Criminal. Home: 3353 Christie Blvd Toledo OH 43606-2862 Office: 5415 Monroe St Toledo OH 43623-2800

**ST. CLAIRE, FRANK ARTHUR,** lawyer; b. Charlotte, N.C., June 16, 1949. BS, MIT, 1972; JD, NYU, 1975. Bar: Tex. 1975, U.S. Dist. Ct. (no. dist.) Tex. 1985; bd. cert. in comml. real estate law. Assoc. James H. Wallenstein, Dallas, 1975-78; v.p. Wallenstein & St. Claire, Dallas, 1978-81; pres. Frank A. St. Claire, P.C., Dallas, 1981-84; ptnr. St. Claire & Case, P.C., Dallas, 1984-88, pres., 1988-93; chmn. bd. Sunbelt Empire Title Co., Dallas, 1983-88; pres. St. Claire & Assocs., Dallas, 1993—; chmn. real estate section Godwin & Carlton, P.C., Dallas, 1994-96; ptnr., chmn. real estate sect. Strasburger & Price, L.L.P., Dallas, 1996—. Author: Texas Condominium Law, 1986; contbr. articles to profl. jours. Ofcl. del. Dallas to Baltic Legal Conf., Riga, Latvia, 1990. Mem. Am. Coll. Mortgage Attys. (chmn. pubs. com. 1998—, mem. programs com. 1998—), Tex. Bar Assn. (study of uniform condominium act com., legis. liaison com. 1981-85, vice chmn. 1981-82, chmn. 1982-85, chmn. condominium and coop. housing com. 1985-89, title ins. com., mem. coun. real estate, probate and trust coun. 1991-95, treas. 1996-97, sec., chair-elect 1997-98, chair 1998—), Dallas Bar Assn., Cmty. Assn. Inst. (bd. dirs. Dallas-Ft. Worth chpt. 1984-85, 87-89, pres.-elect 1989-90), Real Estate Fin. Exec. Assn. (asst. sec. 1996-97), Real Estate Coun., Am. Coll. Real Estate Lawyers (planning com. 1990-98, chmn. practice tech. com. 1993-96, mem. common interest ownership com. 1986-98, alternative dispute resolution com. 1993-95), Tex. Coll. Real Estate Attys. (chmn. projects com. 1991-92, bd. dirs. 1994—), Internat. Assn. of Attys. and Execs. in Corp. Real Estate (website com. 1997—). Episcopalian. Real property, Finance. Office: Nations Bank Plz 901 Main St Ste 4300 Dallas TX 75202-3714

**ST. PAUL, ALEXANDRA DE LA VERGNE,** lawyer; b. New Orleans, Apr. 12, 1955; d. Hugh De La Vergne and Laurie (Monte) St. P.; m. David K. Deitrich, Nov. 2, 1990. BS in Econs., U. Pa., 1977; JD, Loyola U., New Orleans, 1984. Bar: Fla. 1985, U.S. Dist. Ct. (ctrl. dist.) Fla. 1988, La. 1989; cert. cir. ct. mediator, Fla. Atty. Dye, Scott & Deitrich, P.A., Bradenton, Fla., 1985-89, Phelps, Dunbar, Marks, Claverie & Sims, New Orleans, 1989-90, Deitrich & St. Paul, P.A., Bradenton, 1990-98, Dye, Deitrich, Prather, Petruff & St. Paul, P.L., Bradenton, 1998—; dir. Sarasota-Manatee (Fla.) Lawyer Referral Svc., Inc., 1991-95, v.p., 1991-93, pres., 1993-95; dir. Gulf Coast Legal Svcs., Inc., 1991-95; mem. 12th Judicial Cir. pro bono com., 1993-94. Dir. Women's Resource Ctr. Manatee, 1994-95, v.p., 1995; bd. trustees Loyola U., Law Sch. vis. com., 1993-98; dir. Manatee Players, Inc., 1986-88, v.p., 1987-88; sec. Manatee County Head Start Adv. Coun., 1993-98, chmn., 1998-99; v.p. Tidy Island Condominium Assn., Inc., 1998-99. Recipient Tobias Simon Pro Bono Svc. award, Chief Justice of Fla. Supreme Ct., 1991. Mem. Fla. Bar Assn. (mem. grievance com. 1991-94, vice chair 1992-93, chair 1994-95; mem. family law, real property, and probate sects.), Manatee County Bar Asns. (dir. 1987-89, 90-91, treas. 1988-89; mem. family law, real property, and probate sects.), Fla. Assn. Women Lawyers (dir. Manatee County chpt. 1987-88, 91-98, 1st v.p. 1995-96, pres. 1992-93, 2d v.p. 1987-88), Bar Assn. Legal Aid Soc., Inc. (dir. 1991-94, v.p. 1992-93), Jr. League Manatee County, Inc. (dir. 1991-94, League atty. 1988-90, asst. treas. 1991-92, treas. 1992-93, chair pub. affairs com. 1993-94, nom. com. 1994-95), Leadership Manatee (class of 1993-94). Republican. Estate planning, Family and matrimonial, Real property. Office: Dye Deitrich Prather Petruff & St Paul PL 1111 3d Ave West Bradenton FL 34205

**SAKAI, PETER A.,** lawyer; b. McAllen, Tex., Oct. 21, 1954; s. Pete Y. and Rose Marie (Kawahata) S.; m. Raquel M. Dias, Mar. 10, 1982; children: George Y., Elizabeth K. BA, U. Tex., Austin, 1976, JD, 1979. Bar: Tex. 1979. Asst. dist. atty. County of Bexar, San Antonio, 1980-82; pvt. practice San Antonio, 1983-94; assoc. judge Bexar County Dist. Ct., San Antonio, 1994—; hearings arbitrator City of San Antonio, 1983-93; judge Mcpl. Ct., City of Elmendorf, Tex., 1985; juvenile assoc. judge 289th Dist. Ct., San Antonio, 1989-94; city atty. City of Leon Valley, Tex., 1986-90. Contbr. to profl. publs. Bd. dirs. Bexar County Juvenile Vols. in Probation, San Antonio, 1983-93; Japan Am. Soc. San Antonio, 1987-89, Cmty. Cultural Arts Orgn., San Antonio, 1987-92, Bexar County Local Devel. Corp., San Antonio, 1989-94. Mem. ABA, State Bar Tex., San Antonio Bar Assn. Avocation: sports. Office: Bexar County Courthouse 100 Dolorosa Rm 205 San Antonio TX 78205-3002

**SAKS, BORIS,** lawyer; b. USSR, Aug. 25, 1971; came to U.S., 1980; s. Michael and Lida Saks; m. Victoria R. Shlomovich, June 23, 1992; children: Abigail, Jacob Joel. AA, NYU, 1991, BS, 1993; JD, Yeshiva U., 1996. Bar: N.Y. 1997. Tax counsel N.Y.C. Dept. Fin., Bklyn., 1996-98; assoc. Goldberg Weprin & Ustin LLP, N.Y.C., 1998—.

**SALACUSE, JESWALD WILLIAM,** lawyer, educator; b. Niagara Falls, N.Y., Jan. 28, 1938; s. William L. and Bessie B. (Buzzelli) S.; m. Donna Booth, Oct. 1, 1966; children: William, Maria. Diploma U. Paris, 1959; AB, Hamilton Coll., 1960; JD, Harvard U., 1963. Bar: N.Y. 1965, Tex. 1980. Lectr. in law Ahmadu Bello U., Nigeria, 1963-65; assoc. Conboy, Hewitt, O'Brien & Boardman, N.Y.C., 1965-67; assoc. dir. African Law Ctr., Columbia U., 1967-68; prof., dir. Research Ctr., Nat. Sch. Adminstrn., Zaire, 1968-71; Middle East regional advisor on law and devel. Ford Found., Beirut, 1971-74, rep. in Sudan, 1974-77; vis. prof. U. Khartoum (Sudan), 1974-77; vis. scholar Harvard Law Sch., 1977-78; prof. law So. Meth. U., Dallas, 1978-80, dean, prof. law, 1980-86; dean, prof. internat. law The Fletcher Sch. Law and Diplomacy Tufts U., Medford, Mass., 1986-94; Henry J. Braker prof. comml. law Fletcher Sch. Law and Diplomacy Tufts U., 1994—; fellow Inst. Advanced Legal Studies, U. London, 1995; vis. prof. Ecole Nat. des Ponts et Chaussées, Paris, 1990—, Instituto de Empressa, Madrid, 1995—, U. Bristol Sch. Oriental and African Studies U. London, 1995—; cons. Ford Found., 1978-82, 93, U.S. Dept. State, 1978-80, U.N. Ctr. on Transnat. Corps., 1988—, Harvard Inst. Internat. Devel., 1990—, Asia Found., 1992, Harvard Law Sch./World Bank Laos Project, 1991-93; with Sri Lanka fin. sector project ISTI/USAID, 1993-94; lectr. Georgetown U. Internat. Law Inst., 1978-94, Universidad Panamericana, Mexico City, 1981; chmn. com. on Middle Eastern law Social Sci. Research Council, 1978-84; chmn. Coun. Internat. Exchange of Scholars, 1987-91; bd. dirs. Boston World Affairs Coun., 1988-95, Emerging Markets Income Funds. I & II, Inc., Global Ptnrs. Income Fund, Inc., Salomon Brothers Worldwide Income Fund, Inc., The Asia Tigers Fund, Inc., The India Fund. Inc., Emerging Markets Floating Rate Fund, Inc., Mcpl. Advantage Fund, Inc., Salomon Bros. High Income Funds I & II, Salomon Bros. 2008 Worldwide Dollar Govt. Term Trust; trustee Southwestern Legal Found., 1992—, Am. U. of Paris, 1993-97; pres. Internat. Third World Legal Studies Assn., 1987-91; chmn. Inst. Transnat. Arbitration, 1991-93; pres. Assn. Profl. Schs. Internat. Affairs, 1988-89. Author: (with Kasunmu) Nigerian Family Law, 1966, An Introduction to Law in French-Speaking Africa, vol. I, 1969, vol. II, 1976, (with Steng) International Business Planning, 1982; Making Global Deals-Negotiating in the International Marketplace, 1991, The Art of Advice, 1994, (video course) Negotiating in Today's World, 1995, contbr. articles to profl. jours. Mem. ABA, Dallas Bar Found. (trustee 1983-86), Coun. on Fgn. Rels., Am. Law Inst., Am. Soc. Internat. Law, Cosmos Club (Washington). E-mail: JSalacuse@Infonet.Tufts.edu. Home: 220 Stone Root Ln Concord MA 01742-4755 Office: Tufts U Fletcher Sch Law & Diplomacy Medford MA 02155

**SALAZAR, KENNETH L.,** state attorney general; b. Mar. 2, 1955; s. Henry and Emma Salazar; m. Hope Hernandez; children: Melinda, Andrea. BA in Polit. Sci., Colo. Coll., 1977, LLD (hon.), 1993; JD, U. Mich., 1981. Bar: Colo. 1981, U.S. Dist. Ct. Colo. 1981, U.S. Ct. Appeals (10th cir.) 1981. Farmer, rancher Conejos County, Colo.; law clk. Colo. Atty. Gen., summer 1979; assoc. Sherman & Howard, Denver, 1981-86; chief legal counsel Office of Gov., Denver, 1986-90; exec. dir. Colo. Dept. Natural Resources, Denver, 1990-94; dir. Parcel, Mauro & Spaanstra, Denver, 1994-99; atty. gen. State of Colo., 1999—; gov.'s rep. State Bd. Equalization, Denver, 1990. Chair Great Outdoors Colo., Denver, 1993-94, Rio Grande Compact Commn., 1995-97, Sangre de Cristo Land Grant Commn., 1993-95; mem. Colo. Water Conservation Bd., Denver, 1990-94; mem. City and County of Denver Ethics Panel, 1993; bd. dirs. Denver Cmty. Leadership Forum, 1988; gov.'s rep. State Bd. on Property Tax Equalization, 1987-91; del. Soviet-Am. Young Leadership Dialogue, 1984; bd. dirs. Servicios de la Raza HUD 202 Project, 1985-89, chair, 1986; mem. Am. Israel Friendship League, 1986-89. mem. adv. com. Colo. U. Las Sch. Natural Resources Law Ctr., 1989-92; mem. Western Water Policy Rev. Adv. Commn., 1995-97. Juan Tienda scholar. Mem. ABA, Colo. Bar Assn. (bd. govs. 1989-90, task force to assess the legal profession 1986), Denver Bar Assn. (2d v.p. 1989, chair policy-cmty. rels. subcoms. 1982-84), Hispanic Bar Assn. (ABA task force on opptys. for minorities in legal profession, bd. dirs. 1986-87), Am. Judicature Soc. Avocations: basketball, outdoor activities, politics. Home: 5140 Chase St Denver CO 80212-2828 Office: State Colo Dept of Law 1525 Sherman St Fl 5 Denver CO 80203-1700

**SALCH, STEVEN CHARLES,** lawyer; b. Palm Beach, Fla., Oct. 25, 1943; s. Charles Henry and Helen Louise (Alverson) S.; m. Mary Ann Prim, Oct. 7, 1967; children—Susan Elizabeth, Stuart Trenton. B.B.A., So. Meth. U., 1965, J.D., 1968. Bar: Tex. 1968, U.S. Tax Ct. 1969, U.S. Dist. Ct. (so. dist.) Tex. 1969, U.S. Dist. Ct. (ea. dist.) Tex. 1972, U.S. Ct. Appeals (5th cir.) 1969, U.S. Ct. Appeals (fed. cir.) 1982, U.S. Ct. Fed. Claims, 1982. Assoc. Fulbright & Jaworski, Houston, 1968-71, participating assoc., 1971-75, ptnr., 1975—. Co-author: Tax Practice Before the IRS, 1994; contbr. articles to legal jours. Pres. Tealwood Owners Assn., 1982-83, Meml. High Sch. PTA, 1985-86; mem. Tex. PTA (Hon. Life Member award 1986). Mem. ABA (coun. dir. 1985-88, vice chair tax sect. 1988-91, chair elect 1995-96, chair 1996-97), State Bar Tex., Houston Bar Assn., Fed. Bar Assn., Am. Law Inst., Nat. Tax Assn., Am. Coll. Tax Counsel, Internat. Fiscal Assn., Harris County Heritage Soc., Galveston Hist. Found., Smithsonian Assocs., Colonial Williamsburg Found., Am. Bar Found., Southwestern Legal Found., Houston Bar Found., Order of Coif, Beta Alpha Psi, Phi Eta Sigma, Phi Delta Phi. Presbyterian. Clubs: Lakeside Country, Houston Center, Galveston Country, Yacht,Pelican of Galveston, Galveston Artillery. Corporate taxation, Private international, Administrative and regulatory. Home: 342 Tamerlaine Dr Houston TX 77024-6147 Office: Fulbright & Jaworski 1301 Mckinney St Fl 51 Houston TX 77010-3031 *Set goals for yourself. Unless you know where you are and where you want to be in life, you will not be able to map a plan to accomplish your goals.*

**SALDANA, ADRIENNE L.,** lawyer; b. Houston, Jan. 23, 1969; d. Rudolph L. and Carolyn P. Saldana. BA in Lit. and Econs., Rice U., 1990; JD, Georgetown U., 1994. Bar: N.Y. 1995, Va. 1995, D.C. 1996, U.S. Dist. Ct. (so. and ea. dists.) N.Y. 1996, U.S. Dist. Ct. (ea. dist.) Mich. 1995. Assoc. O'Donnell, Schwartz & Anderson P.C., Washington, 1994-96, Spivak, Lipton, Watanabe, Spivak & Moss LLP, N.Y.C., 1996—. Contbr. articles to Georgetown Jour. Legal Ethics, The Record. Mem. ABA, N.Y. State Bar Assn., Assn. Bar City N.Y. (fed. legis. com.). Labor, Entertainment, Federal civil litigation. Home: 127 Riverside Dr New York NY 10024-3735 Office: 1700 Broadway New York NY 10019-5905

**SALDIN, THOMAS R.,** lawyer, consumer products company executive; b. 1946. BA, Carleton Coll., 1968; JD, Cin. Coll. Law, 1974. Law clk. to presiding justice U.S. Dist. Ct. (so. dist.) Ohio, 1974-76; assoc. Benjamin, Faulkner & Tepe & Sach, Cin., 1976-78; asst. gen. counsel Albertson's Inc., Boise, Idaho, 1978-81, v.p., gen. counsel, 1981-83, exec. v.p., adminstrv. gen. counsel, 1983—. Office: Albertson's Inc 250 E Parkcenter Blvd Boise ID 83706-3999*

**SALE, DAVID TODD,** lawyer; b. L.I., N.Y., July 3, 1968; s. Jon A. and Beth K. Sale. B Polit. Sci., Gettysburg Coll., 1990; JD, Nova Southeastern U., 1993. Bar: Fla. 1994, U.S. Dist. Ct. (so. dist.) Fla. 1994. Intern to spkr of house U.S. Ho. of Reps., Washington, 1988; asst. atty. gen. Fla. Atty. Gen.'s Office, Hollywood, 1994-95; asst. state atty. Broward County State Atty., Ft. Lauderdale, Fla., 1994-97; assoc. Law Office of Richard Leydig, Ft. Lauderdale, 1997—. Mem. Com. to Re-elect Atty. Gen. Butterworth, 1992, Com. to Re-elect Judge Gary Cowart, 1997. Mem. Broward County Bar Assn., Broward Assn. Criminal Def. Assn. Avocations: politics, history, basketball, golf, tennis. Criminal, Personal injury. Office: 107 SE 10th St Fort Lauderdale FL 33316-1023

**SALEH, DAVID JOHN,** lawyer; b. Buffalo, Apr. 24, 1953; s. Donald Thomas and Joan Barbara (Labaki) S.; m. Elizabeth Catherine Abdella, July 2, 1976; children: Anthony Donald, Amy Madeline, Anne Teresa, Andrew David. BA, SUNY, Buffalo, 1975, JD, 1978. Bar: N.Y. 1979, U.S. Dist. Ct. (we. dist.) N.Y. 1980. Assoc. Jeffrey D. Oshlag, Esq., Batavia, N.Y., 1978-82; ptnr. Oshlag & Saleh, Esqs., Batavia, 1982—; chief counsel, sec. Am. Real Time Svcs., Inc., N.Y.C., 1988-91; atty. Town of Stafford, N.Y., 1994—; prosecutor Village of Corfu, N.Y., 1997—; legal counsel City of Batavia Housing Authority, 1982—; atty. Village of Corfu, N.Y., 1981—, Pembroke Ctrl. Sch. Dist., 1985-90; chief counsel Intelligent Quotation Sys. Inc., Norwalk, Conn., 1987-93; prosecutor Town of Pembroke, 1988—; chief counsel, dir., treas. GB's Country Corners Inc., 1991-93; v.p., chief counsel Marine Ptnrs. Funding, Inc., 1994—; counsel Corfu Fire Dist., 1995—; prosecutor Village of Corfu, N.Y., 1997—; chief counsel Network & Comm. Group, Inc., 1997—; counsel Weston Info. Techs. Inc., others. Mem. staff Buffalo Law Rev., 1976-78. Mem. Pembroke Vol. Fire Dept., 1976-79, Corfu Vol. Fire Dept., 1979—; bd. dirs. Corfu Area Bus. Assn., 1986-87; del. Rep. Caucus; trustee Corfu Free Libr. Assn., 1991—, pres., 1993-96; bd. dirs. St. Jerome Hosp. Found., 1992-98, treas., 1994-98; treas. Genesee Mercy Healthcare Found., Inc., 1996-98. Mem. ABA, ATLA, N.Y. Defenders Assn., N.Y. State Bar Assn., Genesee County Bar Assn. (mem. jud. nominations com. for 8th jud. dist. N.Y., chmn. criminal def. com. 1995—), Erie County Bar Assn., N.Y. State Housing Renewal Ofcls., U. Buffalo Alumni Assn. (bd. dirs., v.p. fin. 1997-99, exec. v.p., pres.-elect 1999—), Lions. Republican. Roman Catholic. Criminal, General practice, General corporate. Home: 54 E Main St Corfu NY 14036-9601 Office: Oshlag & Saleh Esqs 432 E Main St Batavia NY 14020-2519

**SALEH, JOHN,** lawyer; b. O'Donnell, Tex., June 29, 1928; s. Nahum and Arslie S. BBA, U. Tex., 1950, JD with honors, 1952; cert. U.S. Army Judge Advocate Sch., U. Va., 1953. Bar: Tex. 1952, U.S. Ct. Mil. Appeals, 1953, U.S. Tax Ct. 1954, U.S. Dist. Ct. (no. dist.) Tex. 1956, U.S. Ct. Appeals (5th cir.) 1960, U.S. Supreme Ct. 1961, D.C. 1982. Pvt. practice Lamesa, Tex., 1954—. Mem. Order of the Coif, Phi Delta Phi. General civil litigation. Home: 605 Doak O'Donnell TX 79351 Office: 502 N 1st St Lamesa TX 79331-5406

**SALEM, ALBERT MCCALL, JR.,** lawyer; b. Washington, Apr. 3, 1939; s. Vivian (Zaytoun) S.; married; 4 children. AB, U. N.C., 1960, JD, 1963. Bar: N.C. 1963, Fla. 1965. Pvt. practice Tampa, Fla., 1966—. Served to capt. USAF, 1963-66. E-mail: albertsalemlaw@juno.com. State civil litigation, Estate planning, General practice. Office: 4600 W Kennedy Blvd PO Box 18607 Tampa FL 33679-8607

**SALES, JAMES BOHUS,** lawyer; b. Weimar, Tex., Aug. 24, 1934; s. Henry B. and Agnes Mary (Pesek) S.; m. Beuna M. Vornsand, June 3, 1956; children: Mark Keith, Debra Lynn, Travis James. BS, U. Tex., 1956, LLB with honors, 1960. Bar: Tex. 1960. Practiced in Houston, 1960—; sr. ptnr. Fulbright & Jaworski, 1960—, former head litig. dept., 1979-99. Author: Products Liability in Texas, 1985; co-author: Texas Torts and Remedies, 6 vols., 1986; assoc. editor Tex. Law Rev., 1960; editl. bd. Def. Law Jour.; contbr. articles to profl. jours. Trustee South Tex. Coll. Law, 1982-88, 90—, A.A. White Dispute Resolution Ctr., 1991-94; bd. dirs. Tex. Resource Ctr., 1990-97, Tex. Bar Hist. Found., 1990-99. 1st lt. USMCR, 1956-58. Named among Best Lawyers in Am., 1989-2000. Fellow Internat. Acad. Trial Lawyers, Am. Coll. Trial Lawyers (state chmn. 1993-96), Am. Bd. Trial Advocates, Am. Bar Found. (sustaining life, state chmn. 1993-98), Tex. Bar Found. (trustee 1991-95, vice-chmn. 1992-93, chmn. 1993-94, chair adv. bd. for planned giving 1994—, sustaining life mem.), Houston Bar Found. (sustaining life, chmn. bd. 1982-83); mem. ABA (ho. of dels. 1984—, mem. Commn. on IOLTA 1995-97), FBA, Internat. Assn. Def. Counsel, Nat. Conf. Bar Pres. (coun. 1989-92), So. Conf. Bar, So. Tex. Coll. Trial Advocacy (dir. 1983-87), State Bar Tex. (pres. 1988-89, bd. dirs. 1983-87, chmn. bd. 1985-86), Tex. Assn. Def. Counsel (v.p. 1977-79, 83-84), Tex. Law Rev. Assn. (bd. dirs. 1996—, pres. 1999—), Houston Bar Assn. (officer, bd. dirs. 1970-79, pres.-elect 1979-80, pres. 1980-81), Gulf Coast Legal Found. (bd. dirs. 1982-85), Bar Assn. 5th Fed. Cir., The Forum, Westlake Club (bd. govs. 1980-85), Inns of Ct. (bd. dirs. 1981-84), Order of Coif. Roman Catholic. State civil litigation, Federal civil litigation, Personal injury. Home: 10803 Oak Creek St Houston TX 77024-3016 Office: Fulbright & Jaworski 1301 Mckinney St Houston TX 77010-3031

**SALES, KENNETH L.,** lawyer; b. Louisville, Jan. 24, 1952; s. Raymond Lewis and Elise Lapp S.; 1 child, Savannah Lawren. B in Gen. Studies, U. Ky., 1973; JD, U. Louisville, 1975. Bar: U.S. Dist. Ct. (ea. and we. dists.) Ky., U.S. Ct. Appeals (6th cir.), Ky., U.S. Dist. Ct. (so. dist.) Ind., Ind., U.S. Tax Ct., U.S. Ct. Appeals (fed. cir.), U.S. Claims Ct., U.S. Supreme Ct., Pa. Lawyer Segal, Sales, Stewart, Cutler & Tillman, Louisville, 1976—; Bd. dirs. Paradigm Ins., Louisville, 1992—. Bd. dirs. Adv. Commn. Jefferson County Ct., Louisville, 1997—, Child Assault Prevention, Louisville, 1998; mem. adv. bd. Cystic Fibrosis Found., Louisville, 1993—; mem. Citizens Better Judges, Ky., 1988—. Mem. Am. Trial Lawyers Assn. (sustaining mem. 1993—). Democratic. Jewish. Avocations: snow skiing, tennis, electronics--audio, video, computer. General civil litigation, Personal injury, Product liability. Office: 325 W Main St Ste 2100 Louisville KY 40202-4251

**SALFI, DOMINICK JOSEPH,** lawyer; b. Phila., Aug. 29, 1937; s. Domenic and Madaline (Lombard) S.; m. Doris Gay Beard, Feb. 25, 1961 (div. Mar. 1984); children: Dea GAy Barrs, Joe, Dawn Ann Sccheuttet, Don C. BA, U. Fla., 1958, JD, 1961. Bar: Fla. 1961. Assoc. Law Offices of J. Russell Hoensby, Orlando, Fla., 1961-63; ptnr. Hoensby, Johnson, Yurko, Salfi, Orlando, 1963-66, Fishback, Davis, Dominick & Salfi, Orlando, 1966-70; state atty. 18th Jud. Cir., State of Fla., Sanford, 1967-69, cir. judge, 1970-87; pvt. practice Altamonte Springs, Fla., 1987—. Chmn. Seminole County (Fla.) Rep. Party, 1968-69; state committeeman State of Fla. Rep. Party, Seminole County, 1970. Avocations: computers, travel, softball. General practice, Contracts commercial, Labor. Home: 350 Markham Woods Rd Longwood FL 32779-2830 Office: 999 Douglas Ave Ste 3333 Altamonte Springs FL 32714-2063

**SALINGER, FRANK MAX,** lawyer; b. Landau, Isar, Germany, Dec. 4, 1951; s. Karl and Ingeborg F. (Herold) S.; m. Susan Ann Wagner, May 20, 1978. Student, Columbia Union Coll., Takoma Park, Md., 1969-72; JD, U. Balt., 1975. Bar: Md. 1975, U.S. Dist. Ct. Md. 1975, U.S. Ct. Appeals (4h cir.) 1978, U.S. Tax Ct. 1978, U.S. Ct. Mil. Appeals 1978, U.S. Ct. Appeals (5th cir.) 1982, U.S. Supreme Ct. 1983, U.S. Ct. Appeals (11th cir.) 1984, U.S. Ct. Appeals (9th cir.) 1986, D.C. 1986, U.S. Ct. Appeals (3d cir.) 1989. Pvt. practice Balt., 1975-77; counsel Md. State Senate, Annapolis, 1975-76; assoc. counsel Am. Fin. Corp., Silver Spring, Md., 1977-78; govt. rels.

counsel Truck Trailer Mfrs. Assn., Washington, 1978-80; v.p., gen. counsel, dir. govt. affairs Am. Fin. Svcs. Assocs., Washington, 1980-92; v.p. govt. rels. Advanta Corp., Wilmington, Del., 1992—. Co-author: (with Alvin O. Wiese and Robert E. McKew) A Guide to the Consumer Bankruptcy Code, 1989; (with Robert W. Green) State Regulations and Statutes on Consumer Credit, 1989, Federal Consumer Credit Regulations and Statutes, 1989. City councilman, Laurel, Md., 1976-78, zoning commr., 1976-78; chmn. Md. State Young Reps., 1977-78; bd. dirs. Am. Bankruptcy Inst., Washington, 1986-88. Mem. ABA (mem. com. on consumer fin. svcs., subcoms. on interest rate regulation and state regulation), Am. League Lobbyists (chair fin. svcs. sect. 1995-97), Federalist Soc. Law and Pub. Policy, Woodmore Country Club, Capitol Hill Club. Republican. Lutheran. Legislative, Banking, Consumer commercial. Office: Advanta Corp One Righter Pkwy Wilmington DE 19803

**SALISBURY, EUGENE W.,** lawyer, justice; b. Blasdell, N.Y., Mar. 20, 1933; s. W. Dean and Mary I. (Burns) S.; m. Joanne M. Salisbury, July 14, 1950; children: Mark, Ellen, Susan, David, Scott. BA in History and Govt. cum laude, U. Buffalo, 1959, JD cum laude, 1968. Bar: N.Y. 1960, D.C. 1973, U.S. Dist. Ct. (we. and no. dists.) 1961, U.S. Ct. Appeals (2d cir.) 1970, U.S. Ct. Appeals (D.C. cir.) 1973, U.S. Supreme Ct. 1973. Ptnr. Lipsitz, Green, Fahringer, Roll, Salisbury and Cambria, Buffalo, 1960—; justice Village of Blasdell, 1961—; lectr. N.Y. Office Ct. Adminstrn., N.Y.C., 1961—; mem. N.Y. State Commn. on Jud. Conduct, 1989—. Author: Manual for N.Y. Courts, 1973, Forms for N.Y. Courts, 1977. Capt. U.S. Army, 1948-54, Korea. Decorated Bronze Star, Purple Heart. Mem. ABA (del. spl. ct. sect. 1988—), D.C. Bar Assn., Erie County Bar Assn., N.Y. State Bar Assn., World Judges Assn., N.Y. State Magistrates Assn. (pres. 1973, Man of Yr. 1974), N.Y. State Jud. Conf., Upstate N.Y. Labor Adv. Council, 1995—. Labor, Pension, profit-sharing, and employee benefits. Office: Lipsitz Green Fahringer Roll Salisbury and Cambria 42 Delaware Ave Ste 300 Buffalo NY 14202-3857

**SALISCH, VICTORIA J.,** lawyer; b. Carmel, Calif., Dec. 20, 1942; d. Henry Earl Voltz and Thea M. (Rausch) Sanderson; m. Richard E. Salisch, Mar. 10, 1973 (dec. Dec. 1991); children: Shawn Giammattei, Kristen, Ryan. Student, Santa Rosa Jr. Coll., 1961-63, U. Calif., Davis, 1968; JD, U. of the Pacific, 1971. Bar: Calif. 1972. Staff atty. State of Calif. Employment Dept., Sacramento, 1971-72; dep. pub. defender Fresno County, Calif., 1972-75; pvt. practice Salisch & Salisch, Fresno, 1975-93, Lang, Richert & Patch, Fresno, 1993—; instr. bus. law Calif. State U., Fresno, 1975-77; prof. law San Joaquin Coll. of Law, Fresno, 1975-78; chairperson assessment appeals bd. Fresno County, 1984-87. Bd. dirs. Bldg. Industry Assn., Fresno, 1997. Mem. Fresno C. of C. (com. activities 1994-97), Rotary Club Fresno (com. chairperson 1992-97). Republican. Avocations: skiing, traveling, cooking. Office: Lang Richert & Patch 5200 N Palm Ave Fresno CA 93704-2287

**SALIT, GARY,** lawyer. Corp. counsel Bell Howell Co., Skokie, Ill. Office: Bell & Howell Company 5215 Old Orchard Rd Ste 1100 Skokie IL 60077-1076*

**SALITERMAN, RICHARD ARLEN,** lawyer, educator; b. Mpls., Aug. 3, 1946; s. Leonard Slitz and Dorothy (Sloan) S.; m. Laura Shrager, June 15, 1975; 1 child, Robert Warren. BA summa cum laude, U. Minn., 1968; JD, Columbia U., 1971; LLM, NYU, 1974. Bar: Minn. 1972, D.C. 1974. Mem. legal staff U.S. Senate Subcom. on Antitrust and Monopoly, 1971-72; acting dir., dep. dir. Compliance and Enforcement div. Fed. Energy Office, N.Y.C., 1974; mil. atty. Presdl. Clemency Bd., White House, Washington, 1975; sr. ptnr. Saliterman & Siefferman, Mpls., 1975—; adj. prof. law Hamline U., 1976-81. Author: Advising Minnesota Corporations and Other Business Organizations, 4 vols., 1975. Chmn. Hennepin County Bar Jour., 1985-87; trustee, sec. Hopkins Edn. Found.; trustee W. Harry Davis Found., 1990-96; pres. Twin Cities Coun.; nat. bd. dirs. Navy League U.S., 1997—. General corporate, General practice, State civil litigation.

**SALLAY, TIBOR,** lawyer; b. Arad, Romania, Nov. 30, 1922; came to U.S., 1951; s. William and Irene (Kunstler-Jellinek) S.; m. Viviane Najar, June 27, 1966; 1 child, Andrew. BS in Comml. Scis., Acad. High Commerce and Indsl. Studies, Bucharest, Romania, 1945; PhD in Econs., Bolyai U., Cluj, Romania, 1946; LLB, Faculty of Law, Bucharest, 1947; JD, NYU, 1954. Bar: N.Y. 1956. Assoc. Bennett, House & Couts, N.Y.C., 1954-56, Silver, Saperstein & Barnet, N.Y.C., 1956-58; pvt. practice N.Y.C., 1959—; gen. counsel TNT Transport Group Inc. subs. TNT Ltd., Redfern, NSW, Australia, 1974-96, TNT Post Group N.V., The Netherlands, 1997—. Mem. Assn. of Bar of City of N.Y. General corporate, General civil litigation, General practice. Office: Tibor Sallay PC 342 Madison Ave New York NY 10173-0002

**SALLEY, GEORGE HENRY, III,** lawyer; b. Miami, Fla., Oct. 9, 1954; s. George H. Salley and Audrey L. Stone; m. Jean Welch Salley, Dec. 28, 1979; children: Paul Ryan, Adam Keith. BS, Brigham Young U., 1977; JD, Pepperdine U., 1980. Bar: Colo. 1981, U.S. Dist. Ct. Colo. 1981. Pvt. practice Colorado Springs, Colo., 1981—. Personal injury, Criminal, Family and matrimonial. Office: 104 S Cascade Ave Ste 207 Colorado Springs CO 80903-5102

**SALMAN, ROBERT RONALD,** lawyer; b. N.Y., Dec. 26, 1939; s. Samuel L. and Lillian Gertrude (Sincoff) S.; m. Reva Carol Rappaport, June 16, 1963; children: Elyse D. Spiewak, Suzanne A. BA magna cum laude, Columbia Coll., 1961, LLB cum laude, 1964. Bar: N.Y. 1965, U.S. Supreme Ct. 1974, U.S. Ct. Appeals (2nd cir.) 1967, U.S. Ct. Appeals (3rd cir.) 1993, U.S. Ct. Appeals (11th cir.) 1985, U.S. Ct. Appeals (9th cir.) 1979, U.S. Dist. Ct. so. dist., ea. dist.) N.Y. 1969. Assoc. Proskauer, Rose, Goetz & Mendelsohn, N.Y.C., 1964-67; asst. corp. counsel Law Dept. N.Y., N.Y.C., 1967-69; assoc. Phillips, Nizer, N.Y.C., 1969-73; ptnr. Phillips, Nizer, Benjamin, Krim & Ballon, N.Y.C., 1973-87, Reavis & McGrath, N.Y.C., 1987-88, Carter, Ledyard & Milburn, N.Y.C., 1988-94, Phillips & Salman, N.Y.C., 1994-97, Phillips Salman & Stein, N.Y.C., 1997—; adj. prof. Seton Hall Law Sch., Newark, N.J., 1995-98. Contbr. articles to profl. jours. Pres., founder The Assn. for A Better N.J. Inc., 1991—; pres. Marlboro Jewish Ctr., 1982-84. Recipient NEGEV Builder award Israel Bonds, 1980, Award of Honor UJA Fedn., 1981. Mem. N.Y. State Bar Assn., ABA, Assn. Bar City of N.Y. Avocations: charitable and communal work, baseball, reading, writing. Antitrust, General civil litigation, Entertainment. Office: 111 Broadway New York NY 10006-1901

**SALMON, STEVEN BRETT,** lawyer; b. Kansas City, Mo., Jan. 11, 1967; s. Alfred Carmo and Sarah Jane Salmon. BBA, U Mo., 1988; JD, U. Tulsa, 1992. Bar: Mo. 1993, U.S. Dist. Ct. (wes. dist) Mo. 1993, Kans. 1994, U.S. Dist. Ct. Kans. 1994, U.S. Supreme Ct. 1997. Assoc. F.A. White Jr., Kansas City, Mo., 1993-94; ptnr. Fincham, Salmon & Peters, Kansas City, 1994—. Mem. Ind. Order Odd Fellows, Liberty Hills C.C. Criminal, Family and matrimonial, Personal injury. Office: Fincham Salmon & Peters 5440 N Oak Trfy Kansas City MO 64118-4605

**SALO, ANN SEXTON DISTLER,** lawyer; b. Indpls., Sept. 2, 1947; d. Harry W. and Ann (Malloy) Distler; m. Donald R. Salo, June 3, 1972 (div. Feb. 1983); 1 child, Eric V. Salo; m. Phillip G. Clark, May 5, 1990; children: Ann Potter Clark, Philip Gray Clark. BA, Purdue U., 1969; JD, George Washington U., 1972; LLM in Taxation, Emory U., 1976. Bar: Ga. 1973, U.S. Dist. Ct. (no. dist.) Ga. 1974. Assoc. Hansell & Post, Atlanta, 1972-78, mng. ptnr., 1978-89; ptnr. Grenwald and Salo, Atlanta, 1989-92, Long, Aldridge & Norman, Atlanta, 1992-95, Salo & Walker, Atlanta, 1995—; adj. prof. law Emory U., 1983-86; mem. fin. planning adv. bd. Warren Gorham & Lamont, 1988—. Author: Estate Planning, 1988. Bd. dirs. Auditory Edn. Ctr., Atlanta, 1987-93, 98—; pres. Planned Parenthood of Atlanta, 1984-86; pres. Atlanta Humane Soc., 1990-93. Fellow Am. Coll. Trust and Estate Counsel; mem. Atlanta Estate Planning Coun., Atlanta Tax Forum. Estate planning, Probate. Office: Salo & Walker 2968 Lookout Pl NE Atlanta GA 30305-3272

**SALOMAN, MARK ANDREW,** lawyer; b. North Brunswick, N.J., Sept. 12, 1967; s. Josef Goldner and Susan (Lind) S.; m. Laurie Jill Greenwald, Mar. 14, 1993. BA in Am. Studies summa cum laude, Brandeis U., 1989; JD, U. Pa., 1992. Bar: N.J. 1992, U.S. Dist. Ct. N.J. 1992, N.Y. 1993, Pa. 1994, U.S. Ct. Appeals (3d cir.) 1995, U.S. Dist. Ct. (so. and ea. dists.) N.Y. 1997. Jud. law clk. Superior Ct. N.J., New Brunswick, 1992-93; assoc. Gebhardt & Kiefer, Clinton, N.J., 1993-96, Norris, McLaughlin & Marcus, Somerville, N.J., 1996-97, Grota, Glassman & Hoffman, Roseland, N.J., 1997—. Mem. ABA, N.J. Bar Assn., Am. Inn of Ct. (barrister 1997). Republican. Jewish. Avocations: alpine skiing, cross training. General civil litigation, Federal civil litigation, Insurance. Home: 66 Summit Dr Basking Ridge NJ 07920-1962 Office: Grotta Glassman et al 75 Livingston Ave Roseland NJ 07068-3701

**SALOMON, DARRELL JOSEPH,** lawyer; b. San Francisco, Feb. 16, 1939; s. Joseph and Rosalie Rita (Pool) S.; m. Christine Mariscal, Apr. 25, 1992; 1 child, Camilla Lind. Student Georgetown U., 1957-59; BS, U. San Francisco, 1964, JD, 1966. Bar: Calif. 1970, U.S. Dist. Ct. (ctrl. and no. dists.) Calif. 1970, U.S. Supreme Ct. 1971. Assoc., Offices of Joseph L. Alioto, San Francisco, 1970, 73., 1972; dep. city atty. City of San Francisco, 1972; assoc. Salomon & Costello, 1981; ptnr. Hill, Farrer & Burrill, L.A., 1984-87, Arter & Hadden, L.A., 1987-94; assoc. Keck, Mahin & Cate, San Francisco, 1994-96; chmn. Commerce Law Group A Profl. Corp., 1996—; lectr. law Santa Clara U. Mem. Human Rights Commn. City and County of San Francisco, 1975, mem., past pres. Civil Svc. Commn., San Francisco, 1976-84; trustee San Francisco War Meml. and Performing Arts Ctr., 1984-88; bd. dirs. L.A. Symphony Master Chorale, 1985-87, Marin Symphony Assn., 1995-97. D'alton-Power scholar Georgetown U., 1957; recipient Disting. Svc. citation United Negro Coll. Fund, 1975. Mem. ABA, Consumer Attys. of Calif. (bd. govs. 1977), Soc. Calif. Pioneers, L.A. Bar Assn., Chit Chat Club, San Francisco Lawyers Club. Fax: 415 421-6484. Antitrust, Intellectual property. Office: Commerce Law Group 3 Embarcadero Ctr Ste 1160 San Francisco CA 94111-4044

**SALOMON, SHEILA M.,** lawyer; b. Knoxville, Jan. 31, 1954; d. David M. and Sylvia K. Faulkner; m. Gary D. Salomon, Sept. 28, 1980. Student, Trinity Coll., Hartford, Conn., 1972-74; BA, Amherst Coll., 1976; JD, Boston U., 1980. Bar: Mass. 1980, Md. 1986, D.C. 1990, N.Y. 1991, Calif. 1993, U.S. Ct. Appeals (1st cir.) 1980, U.S. Dist. Ct. Mass. 1980, U.S. Dist. Ct. Md. 1986, U.S. Dist. Ct. (ea. dist.) N.Y. 1991, U.S. Dist. Ct. (no. dist.) Calif. 1993, U.S. Dist. Ct. (ctrl. dist.) Calif. 1998, U.S. Ct. Appeals (9th cir.) 1993. Asst. gen. counsel Mass. Dept. Pub. Welfare, Boston, 1981-85; asst. atty. gen. Md. Atty. Gen.'s Office, Balt., 1985-89; assoc. White & Case, N.Y.C., 1989-92, Michel & Manning, Walnut Creek, Calif., 1993-96, Sarrail Lynch & Hall, San Francisco, 1996—. General civil litigation, Insurance, Product liability. Office: Sarrail Lynch and Hall 44 Montgomery St San Francisco CA 94104-4602

**SALOOM, KALISTE JOSEPH, JR.,** lawyer, retired judge; b. Lafayette, La., May 15, 1918; s. Kaliste and Asma Ann (Boustany) S.; m. Yvonne Adelle Nassar, Oct. 19, 1958; children: Kaliste III, Douglas James, Leanne Isabelle, Gregory John. BA with high distinction, U. Southwestern La., 1939; JD, Tulane U., 1942. Bar: La. 1942. Atty. City of Lafayette (La.), 1948-52; judge City and Juvenile Ct., Lafayette, 1952-93, ret., 1993; judge pro tempore La. Ct. Appeal 3d Cir., 1992; of counsel Saloom & Saloom, Lafayette, La., 1993—; tech. adviser Jud. Adminstrn. of Traffic Cts.; mem. jud. coun. La. Supreme Ct., 1960-64; bd. dirs. Nat. Ctr. for State Cts., Williamsburg, Va., 1978-84, adv. coun., 1984—, mem. assocs. com., 1986— (Disting. Svc. award Trial Judge on State Level 1988); mem. Nat. Hwy. Traffic Safety Adminstrn. Adv. Com., U.S. Dept. Transp., 1977-80, Nat. Com. on Uniform Traffic Laws, 1986; expert panel Drunk Driving Protection Act U.S. Congress, 1989-91. With U.S. Army, 1942-45. mem. editorial bd. Tulane Law Rev., 1941; contbr. articles to profl. jours. Recipient Civic Cup, City of Lafayette, 1965, Pub. Svc. award U.S. Dept. Transp., 1980, Disting. Jurist award Miss. State U. Pre-Law Soc., 1987, Disting. Svc. award Nat. Ctr. for State Cts., 1988, Disting. La. Jurist award La. State Bar Found., 1992. Mem. ABA (Benjamin Flaschner award 1981, vice chair JAD com. on traffic ct. program 1989-99), Am. Judges Assn. (William H. Burnett award 1982), Nat. Coun. Juvenile Ct. Judges, La. City Judges Assn. (past pres.), La. Juvenile Ct. Judges Assn. (past pres.), Am. Judicature Soc. (panel drafting La. children's code 1989-91), Order of Coif, Equestrian Order of Holy Sepulchre (knight comdr.), Oakbourne Country Club, Rotary (Paul Harris fellow), KC. Democrat. Roman Catholic. Juvenile, State civil litigation, Transportation. Home: 502 Marguerite Blvd Lafayette LA 70503-3138 Office: 211 W Main St Lafayette LA 70501-6843

**SALOW, CYNTHIA LOUISE,** legal assistant, paralegal, poet; b. Manchester, Iowa, Jan. 2, 1955; d. Clarence John Salow and Iris Marcheta (Grigg) McElmeel; children: Lea Ament, Jason Halfhill, Jessie, Annie. Legal sec. diploma, Kirkwood C.C., Cedar Rapids, Iowa, 1982. Paralegal, legal asst. Tom Riley Law Firm, LLC, Cedar Rapids, 1982-97; litigation sec. Lombardo & Gilles, Salinas, Calif., 1997-98; legal asst. Horan Lloyd Law Offices, Monterey, Calif., 1997—; chmn. adv. bd. Kirkwood C.C., 1987-91. Author: Angel Poetry, 1995, Love and War in the American Home, 1997; contbr. poetry to lit. publs. Co-suptr. Sunday sch. Immanuel Luth. Ch., Earlville, Iowa, 1990-92, 94-97; supt. ch. sch. St. Timothy Luth. Ch., Monterey, Calif., 1997—. Avocations: study of angels, photography, writing poetry, snow skiing, hiking. Office: Horan Lloyd Law Offices 499 Van Buren St Monterey CA 93940-2623

**SALPIETRO, FRANK GUGLIOTTA,** lawyer; b. Raccuia, Italy, May 3, 1962; came to U.S., 1964; s. Vincent G. and Tina A. Salpietro; m. Janice Marie Golacinski, Aug. 8, 1987; children: Vincent, Francesco, Nicholas, Isabella. BA in Polit. Sci., Emory U., 1983; JD magna cum laude, U. Pitts., 1986. Bar: Pa. 1986. Ptnr. Meyer, Unkovic & Scott LLP, Pitts., 1986—. Mem. ABA, Pa. Bar Assn., Allegheny County Bar Assn., Rivers Club (Pitts.), Italian Sons and Daus. Am., Lions, Moose, Order of Coif, Mensa, Phi Beta Kappa. Roman Catholic. E-mail: fgs@muslaw.com. General civil litigation, Computer, Insurance. Office: Meyer Unkovic & Scott LLP 1300 Oliver Bldg Pittsburgh PA 15222

**SALSBURY, MICHAEL,** lawyer; b. 1949. BA, Dartmouth Coll.; JD, U. Va. Bar: D.C. 1975. Gen. counsel MCI Comms. Corp., Washington. General civil litigation, Criminal, Communications. Office: MCI Comms Corp 1801 Pennsylvania Ave NW Washington DC 20006-3606*

**SALTER, ANDREW H.,** lawyer; b. Boston, Mar. 29, 1955; s. Paul V. and Marjorie (Kimball) S.; m. Michele A. Gammer, Feb. 14, 1989; children: Alexander, Hannah. BA magna cum laude, Harvard U., 1977; JD, Georgetown U., 1981. Bar: Wash., U.S. Dist. Ct. (we. dist.) Wash., U.S. Dist. (ea. dist.) Wash., U.S. Ct. Appeals (9th cir.). Atty., ptnr. MacDonald, Hoague & Bayless, Seattle, 1981-89; ptnr. Miller Nash, Seattle, 1989—. Environmental, General civil litigation. Office: Miller Nash 601 Union St Ste 4400 Seattle WA 98101-2352

**SALTIEL, DAVID M.,** lawyer; b. Boston; s. Abraham M. and Anna L. S.; m. Rhoda B., Sept. 3, 1961; 1 child, Marjorie. BA, U. Mass., 1959; JD, Harvard U., 1962. Bar: Mass., U.S. Dist. Ct. Mass., U.S. Supreme Ct. Atty. Nutter, McClennan & Fish, Boston, 1962-89, Posternak, Blankstein & Lund, Boston, 1989—. Landlord-tenant, Real property, General corporate. Home: 95 Cynthia Rd Newton MA 02459-2836 Office: Posternak Blankstein & Lund 100 Charles River Plz Fl 9 Boston MA 02114-2794

**SALTMAN, STUART IVAN,** lawyer; b. Holyoke, Mass., Mar. 16, 1940; s. Abraham and Syd Eva (Schultz) S.; m. Sandra Lee, Sept. 19, 1964; children: Jason, Michael, Laura. BS in Polit. Sci., U. Mass., 1961; JD, Case Western Res. U., 1964. Bar: Mass. 1965, Ohio 1965, Pa. 1975. Assoc. gen. counsel Internat. Chem. Workers, Akron, Ohio, 1965; assoc. Metzenbaum, Gaines, Krupansky, Finley & Stern, Cleve., 1965-67; staff U.S. Dept. Labor, Cleve., 1967-69; staff NLRB, Cleve., 1969-70; regional atty. EEOC, Cleve., Phila. and Washington, 1970-75; chief labor counsel Westinghouse Electric Corp., Pitts., 1975-88, chmn. labor law sect. Grigsby, Gaca & Davies, Pitts., 1988-90; asst. gen. counsel Asea Brown Boveri Power T & D Inc., Windsor, Conn., 1990—. Recipient Excellence Hon. award in labor law Case Western Res. U. 1965. Mem. ABA, Allegheny County Bar Assn. (chmn. 1986-88). Club: Masons (Holyoke). Labor. Home: 23 Ivy Ln Windsor CT 06095-4736 Office: 2000 Day Hill Rd Windsor CT 06095-1565

**SALTMARSH, SARA ELIZABETH,** lawyer; b. Jacksonville, Fla., Nov. 15, 1956; d. Ernest Olmstead and Anne (Frankenberg) S. Student, Randolph-Macon Woman's Coll., 1974-76; BA in English with honors magna cum laude, Fla. State U., 1978; postgrad., Iowa State U., 1980-81; JD, U. Tex., 1986. Bar: Tex. 1987; cert. family law. Assoc. Ausley & Slaikeu, P.C., Austin, Tex., 1987-90, Law Offices of Edwin J. Terry, Jr., Austin, 1990-92; pvt. practice law Austin, 1992—; mem. security com. Travis County Commr.'s Ct., 1991-93. Editor: Reference Guide to Travis County Practice, 1991, 92, 93, 95, 96, 97. Bd. dirs. Faith Home for Children with AIDS, 1997-98. Givens Disting. scholar, 1974, Lyndon Baines Johnson Meml. scholar, 1976; recipient Am. Jur. award Wills and Estates, 1986, Marital Relations and Divorce, 1986. Fellow Tex. Bar Found., Austin Young Lawyer's Assn. Found.; mem. ABA, ATLA, Am. Inns of Ct. (barrister), Coll. State Bar Tex., Pro Bono Coll. State Bar Tex., Tex. Acad. Family Law Specialists, Tex. Exes, Travis County Bar Assn. (sec.-treas. family law sect. 1989-90, v.p. 1990-91, pres. 1991-92, bd. dirs. 1991-92, chair mentor program com. 1993-94, 96-98), Williamson County Bar Assn., Austin Young Lawyers Assn. (co-chmn. It's the Law com. 1990-91), Travis County Women Lawyers Assn., Tex. Ctr. Legal Ethics Professionalism, Austin Mus. Art, Fla. State U. Alumni Assn. (life), Sierra Club, Phi Beta Kappa, Lambda Iota Tau. Democrat. Avocations: dance, skiing, bicycling, water sports, basketry. Family and matrimonial, Alternative dispute resolution, Appellate. Office: 812 San Antonio St Suite 511 Austin TX 78701

**SALTZBURG, STEPHEN ALLAN,** law educator, consultant; b. Phila., Sept. 10, 1945; s. Jack Leonard and Mildrid (Osgood) Adelman; m. Susan Lee, March 10, 1990; children: Mark Winston, Lisa Marie, Diane Elizabeth, David Lee Mussehl. AB, Dickinson Coll., 1967; JD, U. Pa., 1970. Bar: Calif. 1971, D.C. 1972, Va. 1976. Law clk. U.S. Dist. Ct. (no. dist.) Calif., San Francisco, 1970-71, U.S. Supreme Ct., 1971-72; asst. prof. law sch. U. Va., Charlottesville, 1972-74, assoc. prof., 1974-77, prof., 1977-87, Class of 1962 prof., 1987-90; Howrey prof. trial advocacy, litigation and profl. responsibility George Washington U. Sch. Law, Washington, 1990—; reporter Alaska Rules of Evidence, 1976-77, Alaska Civil Jury Instrns., 1979-81, Adv. Com. on Rules of Criminal Procedure, 1984-89, Va. Rules on Evidence, 1984-85, Civil Justice Act Adv. Group, U.S. Dist. Ct. D.C., 1992-93, chmn., 1994—; dep. asst. atty. gen. criminal divsn. U.S. Dept. Justice, 1988-89; mem. adv. com. on Fed. Rules of Criminal Procedure, 1989-95, on Fed. Rules of Evidence, 1992-95; mediator dispute resolution program U.S. Ct. Appeals, 1993—. Author: American Criminal Procedure, 5th edit., 1996, Criminal Law: Cases and Materials, 1994, Evidence: The Objection Method, 1997, Federal Rules of Evidence Manual, 7th edit., 1998, Federal Rules of Evidence Trial Book, 1998, A Modern Approach to Evidence, 2d edit., 1982, Evidence in America, 1987, Military Rules of Evidence Manual, 4th edit., 1997, Basic Criminal Procedure, 1994, 2d edit., 1997, Military Evidentiary Foundations, 1994, Trying Cases to Win: Anatomy of a Trial, 1999. Mem. ABA (chmn. com. on trial advocacy criminal justice sect. 1992-96, task force on Ind. Counsel Act litig. sect. 1997-99, co-chmn. task force on civil trial stds. litig. sect. 1996-97), Am. Law Inst. Office: George Washington U Law Sch 720 20th St NW Washington DC 20006-4306

**SALVADOR, VERNON WILLIAM,** lawyer; b. Corcoran, Calif., May 25, 1941; s. Antonio Rocha Salvador and Adelaida Rosa Garcia; m. Marilyn Catherine Plevel, Dec. 20, 1964 (div. Feb. 1986); m. Elizabeth Jean Church, Feb. 14, 1998. BA, U. Calif., Berkeley, 1963; JD, U. Calif., San Francisco, 1966. BarL Calif. 1971, U.S. Ct. Appeals (9th cir.) 1971, N.M. 1980, U.S. Dist. Ct. N.M. 1980, U.S. Ct. Appeals (10th cir.) 1989, U.S. Supreme Ct. 1989. Atty. Legal Aide Soc., Oakland, Calif., 1970-75, Albuquerque, N.Mex., 1979-80; academic researcher Agores, Portugal, 1976-78; pvt. practice Albuquerque, 1981—. Photographer: (book) Festas Agoreanas, 1979; contbr. articles to profl. jours. Avocations: photography, history, philosophy. Civil rights, Constitutional. Office: 201 12th St Albuquerque NM 87102

**SALVADORE, GUIDO RICHARD,** lawyer; b. Norton, Mass., Oct. 14, 1927; s. Michele Salvadore and Maria Grazia Costantino; m. Barbara Ann Camparone, Oct. 25, 1958; children: Peter, Richard, Susan, Stephen, Marisa. AB, Brown U., 1951; LLB, Harvard U., 1954. Bar: R.I. 1954, U.S. Dist. Ct. R.I. 1955, U.S. Ct. Appeals (1st cir.) 1996. Atty. Salvadore & Salvadore, Providence, R.I.; ptnr. Higgins, Cavanaugh & Cooney, 1960-90; dir., pres. Great Am. Nursing Ctrs., Inc., Warwick, R.I., 1969-90. Dir., v.p. R.I. Grand Opera Co., Providence, 1985—. With USN, 1946-48. Mem. ABA, R.I. Bar Assn., Univ. Club, Metacomet Country Club. Republican. Roman Catholic. Avocations: golfing, basketball, dancing, reading. Contracts commercial, General corporate, Estate planning. Home: 38 Sunset Dr East Greenwich RI 02818-1915 Office: Salvadore & Salvadore 50 Kennedy Plz Providence RI 02903-2393

**SALVADORE, MAL ANDREW,** lawyer; b. Providence, Feb. 19, 1957; s. Amleto Ugo and Anne Salvadore; m. Donna Ann Salvadore, Oct. 16, 1983; children: Nicholas, Vanessa. BA, Brown U., 1979; MBA, Boston Coll., 1983, JD, 1983. Bar: R.I., Fla., U.S. Dist. Ct. R.I., U.S. Ct. Appeals (1st cir.). Assoc. Coffey McGovern & Noel, Providence, 1985-87; prin. Sondler Salvadore, Providence, 1987-98, Mal A. Salvadore, Ltd., Providence, 1998—. Recipient citation R.I. Supreme Ct., 1989. Mem. Aurora Civic Assn., Justinian Law Soc. Municipal (including bonds), Real property, Bankruptcy. Office: 400 Reservoir Ave Ste 3G Providence RI 02907-3553

**SALVAN, SHERWOOD ALLEN,** lawyer; b. N.Y.C., Dec. 2, 1942; s. Harry and Marie Ann (Deramo) S. BBA, St. Francis Coll., N.Y.C.; MBA, Pace U.; JD, NYU, postgrad. Bar: N.Y. 1969, U.S. Ct. Appeals (2d dist.) 1971, U.S. Dist. Cts. (so. and ea. dist.) N.Y. 1971, U.S. Cir. Ct. (2d cir.) 1972, U.S. Supreme Ct. 1980, D.C. 1981. Tax specialist Haskins & Sells, N.Y.C., 1969-71; sole practice N.Y.C., 1972—; mem. cen. screening com. first dept. N.Y. Appellate Div., 1977-82; spl. master N.Y. County Supreme Ct., 1977-85; arbitrator Am. Arbitration Assn., 1976-89, N.Y. County and Bronx County Civil Cts., 1976-89; adminstrv. law judge Environ. Control Bd. City of N.Y., 1975-77. Contbr. articles to profl. jours. V.p. N.Y. County Dem. Club, 1980—; jud. del. N.Y. County dems., 1983—. Mem. N.Y. County Lawyers Assn. (chairperson com. word processing 1978-86), Am. Judge Assn., NY Law Sch. Alumni Assn. (bd. dirs. 1984—). E-mail: woodmanlaw@aol.com. General practice, State civil litigation, Personal injury. Home: 526 E 83rd St New York NY 10028-7249

**SALVATORE, DAVID ANTHONY,** lawyer; b. Providence, Sept. 13, 1965. BA, Boston Coll., 1987; JD, Sufolk U., 1990. Asst. city solicotor City of Providence, 1991—; atty. pvt. practice, Providence, 1997—. Dir. Elmwood Neighborhood Svcs., Providence, 1992-97. Avocation: sailing. General civil litigation, General practice, Land use and zoning (including planning). Office: 156 Walnut Ave Norwood MA 02062-2015

**SALVATY, BENJAMIN BENEDICT,** lawyer; b. Chgo., Dec. 22, 1940; s. Benjamin Benedict and Marion Therese (Ryan) S.; m. Patircia Louise Recor, Aug. 29, 1964; children: Paul Benedict, Kathleen Anne. BBA, U. Notre Dame, 1962; JD, U. So. Calif., 1965. Bar: Calif. 1966, U.S. Dist. Ct. (no., cen., ea. and so. dists.) Calif., U.S. Ct. Appeals (9th cir.), U.S. Tax Ct., U.S. Supreme Ct. Sr. trial atty. Calif. Dept. Transp., 1966-79; gen. atty. The Atchison, Topeka and Santa Fe Railway Co., 1980-89; sr. ptnr. Hill, Farrer & Burrill, Los Angeles, 1990—. Mem. ABA (litigation sect. urban, state and local govt. law com. on condemnation, zoning and planning com.), Am. Bd. Trial Advs., Am. Judicature Soc., Internat. Right Way Assn., Irish Am. Bar Assn. (bd. dirs. 1985—, treas. 1991, sec. 1992, v.p. 1992-93, pres. 1993-94), Italian Am. Lawyers Assn., State Trial Attys. Assn. (pres. 1975-79), Calif. State Bar (chmn. condemnation com. 1987-88, vice chmn. 1986-87), Pasadena Bar Assn., L.A. County Bar Assn. (condemnation and land valuation com.). Fax: (213) 624-4840. Condemnation, Land use and zoning (including planning). Office: Hill Farrer & Burrill LLP One California Plz 37th Fl 300 S Grand Ave Los Angeles CA 90071-3109

**SALVO, JOSEPH ALDO,** lawyer; b. N.Y.C., Feb. 20, 1933; s. Charles A. and Marietta (Mancuso) S.; m. Joan Del Vecchio, May 30, 1959; children: Joseph C., John, Joanne. BBA, St. John's U., 1960, LLB, 1962. Bar: N.Y. 1962, U.S. Dist. Ct. (ea. and so. dists.) N.Y., U.S. Supreme Ct. Spl. agt. U.S. Treasury Dept.; pvt. practice Douglaston, N.Y., 1962—; counsel Italian Charities Am., Inc., Elmhurst, N.Y., 1975—. With U.S. Army, 1954-56. Mem. Queens County Bar Assn. (chmn. law office mgmt. com. 1983—),

Columbian Lawyers Assn. (pres. 1978-79), Nat. Itlaian Am. Bar Assn. Democrat. Roman Catholic. Avocations: music, sports, arts. General practice, Probate, Real property. Home: 1333 137th St College Point NY 11356-2006 Office: 42-24 Douglaston Pky Douglaston NY 11363-1528

**SALWEN, JOAN C.,** lawyer; b. N.Y.C., June 29, 1951; d. Sidney and Ruth (Starr) Salwen; m. Alan S. Zaitz, Oct. 18, 1980; children: Jacob, Jessica Sidney, Maxwell Abraham, Francesca Nadine. AB cum laude, Syracuse U., 1973; JD, U. Pa., 1976. Bar: N.Y. 1977. Assoc. Louis E. Cherico, White Plains, N.Y., 1977-80, Joel Martin Aurnou, White Plains, 1980-82; sole practice, Hartsdale, N.Y., 1983-84, Scarsdale, N.Y., 1984—. panel mem. Law Guardian panel 2nd Judicial Dist., N.Y. Mem. White Plains Bar Assn. (pres. 1991—), N.Y. State Bar Assn., White Plains Bar Assn. (bd. dirs. 1982-93, sec. 1988-89, treas. 1989-90), Westchester County Bar Assn. (bd. dirs. lawyer referral svc. 1983-84), Pi Sigma Alpha. Family and matrimonial, Juvenile, General practice. Home and Office: 15 Dickel Rd Scarsdale NY 10583-2117

**SALYER, DAVID RONALD,** lawyer; b. Barquisimeto, Lara, Venezuela, Jan. 28, 1959; came to U.S., 1976; s. Arthur George and Veda Mae (Baskett) S.; m. Faith Olivia Gibson, Aug. 11, 1990; children: Katherine Anne, Christian Michael. BA, William Jennings Bryan Coll., Dayton, Tenn., 1981; JD, U. Dayton (Ohio), 1990. Bar: Ohio 1991, U.S. Dist. Ct. (so. dist.) Ohio 1991. Constrn. laborer I.S.M.S., Inc., Beavercreek, Ohio, 1981-87; legal intern Nat. Legal Ctr., Indpls., 1989-90; atty. Roderer, Zimmers, Harker, Leppla, Dayton, Ohio, 1991-93; assoc. E.S. Gallon & Assocs., L.P.A., Dayton, 1993—. Contbr. articles to profl. jours. V.p., bd. dirs. Brazilian Evangel. Assn., Medway, Ohio, 1995—; awana Faircreek Ch., Fairborn, Ohio, 1992—, mem. bd. elders, 1998—. Mem. ATLA, Ohio State Bar Assn., Ohio Trial Lawyers Assn., Dayton Bar Assn. (mem. Understanding Healthcare Profession com. 1996—). Avocations: sports, guitar, stamp collecting. Personal injury, Product liability. Office: E S Gallon & Assocs LPA 40 W 4th St Ste 1100 Dayton OH 45402-1874

**SALZMAN, GARY SCOTT,** lawyer; b. Portchester, N.Y., May 26, 1963; s. David Stuart and Francine (Selenow) S.; m. Suzanne Sansone, Apr. 2, 1990. BBA, U. Miami, 1985, JD, 1988. Bar: Fla. 1988, U.S. Dist. Ct. (so. dist.) 1989, Colo. 1991, U.S. Dist. Ct. (mid. dist.) Fla. 1992, U.S. Ct. Appeals (11th cir.) 1992, U.S. Supreme Ct. 1992; cert. arbitrator and mediator; cert. in bus. litigation, Fla. Assoc. Robinson & Greenberg, PA, Coral Gables, Fla., 1988-89, Buchbinder & Elegant, PA, Miami, Fla., 1989, Mishan, Sloto, Hoffman and Greenberg, PA, Miami, 1989-91, Dempsey & Assocs., Winter Park, Fla., 1991-92; pvt. practice, Orlando and Winter Park, Fla., 1992-95; ptnr. Marlowe, Appleton, Weatherford & Salzman, Winter Park, 1996-98, Brown, Ward & Salzman, P.A., Orlando, 1998—; comml., employment and fin. arbitration panelist Am. Arbitration Assn. Mem. ABA, Fla. Bar Assn. (com. rels. with Inst. CPAs 1992-93, bus. litig. com. 1995—), Bus. Exec. Network, Orange County Bar Assn. Fax: 407-425-9596. E=mail: gssalzman@bwvslaw.com. Real property, Finance. Office: 111 N Orange Ave Ste 875 Orlando FL 32801-2346

**SALZMAN, STANLEY P.,** lawyer; b. N.Y.C., Jan. 30, 1931; s. George D. and Fanny M. (Pugach) S.; m. Leona Schames, June 18, 1958 (dec. Nov. 1967); m. Marilyn J. Bzura, Feb. 3, 1974; children: Ira J., Mark B., Debra G., Jeffrey M. David, Steven B. David. BA, Bklyn. Coll., 1952; JD, Bklyn. Law Sch., 1955. Bar: N.Y. 1956, U.S. Dist. Ct. (so. and ea. dists.) N.Y. 1960, U.S. Supreme Ct. 1964, U.S. Ct. Appeals (2d cir.) 1966. Assoc. Otterbourg, Steindler, Houston & Rosen, N.Y.C., 1957; ptnr. Venitt, Adler & Salzman, N.Y.C., 1958-66, Friesner & Salzman, LLP, Great Neck, N.Y., 1966—; bd. dirs. Colora Printing Inks Inc., Linden, N.J. Consumer commercial, State civil litigation. Office: Friesner & Salzman LLP 11 Grace Ave PO Box 220700 Great Neck NY 11022-0700

**SAM, DAVID,** federal judge; b. Hobart, Ind., Aug. 12, 1933; s. Andrew and Flora (Toma) S.; m. Betty Jean Brennan, Feb. 1, 1957; children: Betty Jean, David Dwight, Daniel Scott, Tamara Lynn, Pamela Rae, Daryl Paul, Angie, Sheyla. BS, Brigham Young U., 1957; JD, Utah U., 1960. Bar: Utah 1960, U.S. Dist. Ct. Utah 1966. Sole practice and ptnr. Duchesne, Utah, 1963-76; dist. judge State of Utah, 1976-85; judge U.S. Dist. Ct. Utah, Salt Lake City, 1985-97; chief judge U.S. Dist. Ct., Salt Lake City, Utah, 1997; atty. City of Duchesne, 1963-72; Duchesne County atty., 1966-72; commr. Duchesne, 1972-74; mem. adv. com. Codes of Conduct of Jud. Conf. U.S., 1987-91, Jud. Coun. of 10th Cir., 1991-93; mem. U.S. Del. to Romania, Aug. 1991. Chmn. Jud. Nomination Com. for Cir. Ct. Judge, Provo, Utah, 1983; bd. dirs. Water Resources, Salt Lake City, 1973-76. Served to capt. JAGC, USAF, 1961-63. Mem. Utah Bar Assn., Am. Judicature Soc., Supreme Ct. Hist. Soc., Am. Inns of Ct. VII (counselor 1986-89), A. Sherman Christensen Am. Inn of Ct. I (counselor 1989-98), Utah Jud. Conf. (chmn. 1982), Utah Dist. Judges Assn. (pres. 1982-83), Order of Coif (hon. Brigham Young U. chpt.). Mem. LDS Ch. Avocations: beekeeping, reading, sports, cooking chinese food. Office: US Dist Ct 148 US Courthouse 350 S Main St Ste 150 Salt Lake City UT 84101-2180

**SAMAD-SALAMEH, ALIA FAHMI,** lawyer; b. Chgo.; d. Fahmi Nimer Samad and Nifouz Saleem; m. Asad Salameh Sharmoug, July 16, 1987; children: Basil, Janine. BA, U. Ill., Chgo., 1986; postgrad., Golden Gate U., 1994; JD, U. Calif., San Francisco, 1996. Bar: Calif. 1996, U.S. Dist. Ct. (no. dist.) Calif. 1996, U.S. Ct. Appeals (9th cir.) 1996. Assoc. Schachter Kristoff Orenstein & Berkowitz, San Francisco, 1996—; chairperson Bay Area Arab Am. Atty.'s Forum, San Francisco. Mem. San Francisco Bar Assn. (exec. com. labor and employment sect.). Avocation: reading. E-mail: afs@skob.com. Labor, Civil rights, General civil litigation. Home: 953 Newman Dr South San Francisco CA 94080-1110 Office: Schachter Kristoff Orenstein & Berkowitz 505 Montgomery St Fl 14 San Francisco CA 94111-2552

**SAMALIN, EDWIN,** lawyer, educator; b. Sept. 19, 1935; s. Harry Louis and Sydell (Fisher) S.; m. children: David Seth, Andrew Evan, Jonathan Daniel; m. Carol M. Berardi, 1997. BS, U. R.I., 1957; JD, N.Y. Law Sch., 1962. Bar: N.Y. 1963, U.S. Supreme Ct. 1976. Tax atty. Electric Bond & Share Co., N.Y.C., 1963; ptnr. Samalin & Sklaver, Yorktown Heights, N.Y., 1969-78; pvt. practice Yorktown Heights, 1971-99; pres. Samalin & Bock, P.C., Yorktown Heights, 1984-98; adj. prof. Mercy Coll., Dobbs Ferry, N.Y., 1974-99; commodity cons. Murlas Commodities, Yorktown Heights, 1982-85; ptnr. Patterson (N.Y.) Realty Assn., 1983-99; pres. Sammark Realty Corp., Westchester, N.Y., 1984-92, Old Smoke House Realty Corp., 1987-92, Atty.'s Asset Mgmt. Corp., Registered Investment Advisors, 1992-99; Dem. candidate for County Legislature, 1973. Capt. U.S. Army, 1957-59. Mem. N.Y. State Bar Assn., Westchester County Bar Assn. (dir., former chair atty. client dispute com.), Yorktown Bar Assn. (pres. 1982, Man of Yr. 1983), Am. Arbitration Assn. (arbitrator 1974-99), Phi Delta Phi. Personal injury, State civil litigation, Real property. *Died July 8, 1999.*

**SAMANOWITZ, RONALD ARTHUR,** lawyer; b. N.Y.C., June 1, 1944; s. Sam and Thelma (Levin) S.; m. Ann Frieda Weisman, Dec. 18, 1971; 1 child, Samuel. BBA, CUNY, 1965; JD, Bklyn. Law Sch., 1967. Bar: N.Y. 1968, U.S. Dist. Ct. (ea. and so. dists.) N.Y. 1974, U.S. Supreme Ct. 1991. Ptnr. Krakower, Samanowitz & Goldman, N.Y.C., 1968-86, Resnicoff, Samanowitz, Endzweig & Brawer, Great Neck, N.Y., 1986-90, Samanowitz & Endzweig, Great Neck, N.Y., 1990—. Pres. Greater Fresh Meadows Civic Assn., Flushing, N.Y., 1984-85, award for Civic Svc. 1985, Flower Hill Civic Assn., 1992. Mem. N.Y. State Trial Lawyers Assn. (gov. L.I. divsn.), Brandeis Lawyers Assn. (sec. 1985), Queens Bar Assn. (family law com.), Nassau Bar Assn. (plaintiff roundtable 1988—), Great Neck Lawyers Assn. (past pres., chmn. bd.). Avocation: marathon running. General civil litigation, Family and matrimonial, Real property. Office: Samanowitz & Endzweig 98 Cuttermill Rd Great Neck NY 11021-3006

**SAMAY, Z. LANCE,** lawyer; b. Janoshaza, Hungary, Jan. 2, 1944. BA, Rutgers U., 1967; JD, Seton Hall U., 1970. Bar: N.J. 1970, U.S. Ct. Appeals (3rd cir.) 1974, U.S. Supreme Ct. 1976. Law sec. appellate divsn. Superior Ct., N.J., 1970-71; asst. U.S. atty. Dist. N.J., 1971-76; chief environ. protection divsn. Office of U.S. Atty. Fed. Dist., N.J., 1972-74; chief civil divsn., 1974-76; now pres. Z. Lance Samay, P.C., Morristown, N.J.; adj. prof. environ. law Seton Hall U. Sch. Law, 1973, 74, 76; trial instr. Atty. Gen.'s Advocacy Inst., 1975, 76; vice chmn. consumer affairs com. Fed. Exec. Bd., 1973-74, chmn. human resources com., 1974-75, chmn. relations with academia com., 1975-76. Co-founder, notes and rewrite editor Seton Hall Law Rev., 1969-70; case notes editor Seton Hall Law Jour., 1969. Recipient U.S. Atty. Gen.'s spl. commendation for outstanding svc., 1973, U.S. Dept. Justice spl. achievement award for sustained superior performance, 1972, 76. Mem. U.S. Atty.'s Alumni Assn., Seton Hall Law Alumni Assn. (adv. com. to dean 1971-72, trustee 1975-80, treas. 1975-76, pres. 1976-79, mem. dean's search com. for Seton Hall Law Ctr. 1977-78), Mountain Lakes Club (bd. govs., pres. 1989-91). General practice, Federal civil litigation, State civil litigation. Office: 1 Washington St Morristown NJ 07960-3933

**SAMET, DEE-DEE,** lawyer; b. Greensboro, N.C., Sept. 18, 1940. BA, U. Ariz., 1962, JD, 1963. Bar: Ariz. 1964. Ptnr. Samet & Gage, P.C., Tucson; arbitrator U.S. Dist. Ct. Ariz., Gender Equality Task Force, 1993; judge pro tem Pima County Superior Ct., 1985—; Ninth Cir. Lawyer rep., 1990-93; mem. Jud. Performance Rev. Commn., 1996—. Mem. State Bar Ariz. (1st v.p., family law sect., workers compensation sect., trial law sect., co-chair worker's compensation sect. 1988-89, gender bias task force, bd. govs. 1994-97, pres.-elect, pres.), Nat. Panel Arbitrators, Am. Arbitration Assn. (com. on exams., supreme ct. state Ariz. 1984-91), Pima County Bar Assn., Nat. Assn. Coun. for Children, Ariz. Assn. Coun. for Children, So. Ariz. Women Lawyers Assn. (bd. dirs. 1990, pres. 1994-95), Nat. Orgn. Social Security Claimants' Reps. Workers' compensation, Personal injury, Family and matrimonial. Office: Samet & Gage PC 717 N 6th Ave Tucson AZ 85705-8304*

**SAMINSKY, ROBERT L.,** lawyer; b. N.Y.C., Nov. 4, 1947; s. Hyman L. and Beatrice (Shatzkin) S.; m. Nancy Ann Epstein, Jan. 23, 1971; 1 son, Heath. BBA, Hofstra U., 1969; MS, CUNY, 1971; JD, St. John's U., Jamaica, N.Y., 1975. Bar: N.Y. 1976. Trial atty. criminal div. N.Y.C. Legal Aid Soc., 1976-77; assoc. Fischer Bros., N.Y.C., 1977-78; ptnr. Brecher, Fishman, Feit, Heller, Rubin, & Tannenbaum, P.C., Hauppauge, 1978—; guest lectr. Suffolk County Acad. of Law, 1989; lectr. N.Y. State Chiropractic Soc., 1992—. Mem. med. authorizations com. N.Y. Worker's Compensation Bd., 1989—. Editor John's Law Sch. Labor Law Jour., 1974. Assoc. Urban Tchr. Corps, N.Y.C., 1970. Mem. Suffolk County Bar Assn., N.Y. State Workers Compensation Bar Assn., N.Y. County Bar Assn., N.Y. State Bar Assn. , N.Y. State Trial Lawyers Assn. (community lecturer program 1989—) Labor Law Soc. (v.p. St. Johns Law Sch. chpt. 1974), Lions, Phi Delta Phi. Workers' compensation, Personal injury, Administrative and regulatory. Home: 24 Eva Ln Plainview NY 11803-3015 Office: Brecher Fishman Feit Heller Rubin & Tannenbaum 1455 Veterans Hwy Hauppauge NY 11788-4836

**SAMOLE, MYRON MICHAEL,** lawyer, management consultant; b. Chgo., Nov. 29, 1943; s. Harry Lionel and Bess Miriam (Siegel) S.; m. Sandra Rita Port, Feb. 2, 1967; children—Stacey Ann, Karen Lynn, Rena Mara, David Aaron. Student U. Ill., 1962-65; J.D., DePaul U., 1967; postgrad. John Marshall Lawyers Inst., 1967-69. Bar: Ill. 1967, U.S. Dist. Ct. (no. dist.) Ill. 1968, U.S. Dist. Ct. (so. dist.) Fla. 1989, U.S. Ct. Appeals (7th cir.) 1968, Fla. 1981. Pvt. practice, Chgo., 1967-79, Miami, Fla., 1981—; chmn. bd. Fidelity Electronics and subs., Miami, 1969-83; pres. Fidelity Hearing Instruments, Miami, 1984-86, Samole Enterprises, Inc., Miami, 1986—, Fla. Citrus Tower, Inc., Clermont, 1986—; bd. dirs. Enterprise Bank Fla., Miami, 1985-89, The Sports Collection, Inc., Miami, 1987-94; Bd. dirs. South Dade Greater Miami Jewish Fedn., Young Israel of Kendall, Anshe Emes Congregation. Jewish Vocat. Service scholar U. Ill., Champaign, 1962-65. Mem. ABA, Chgo. Bar Assn., Ill. State Bar Assn., Fla. Bar Assn., Kendall Bar Assn., Dade County Bar Assn., Ill. Trial Lawyers Assn., Miami C. of C., Phi Alpha Delta. Democrat. Lodges: Masons, Shriners. Family and matrimonial, General practice, General corporate. Office: Samole & Berger PA 9700 S Dixie Hwy Ste 1030 Miami FL 33156-2865

**SAMOTIN, NANCY,** lawyer, singer; b. N.Y.C., May 19, 1960; d. Julius and Mildred (Moser) S. BA, Binghamton U., 1981; JD, Hofstra Law Sch., 1984. Bar: N.Y. 1985, N.J. 1985. Ct. atty. OCA State of N.Y., N.Y.C., 1988-91, jud. hearing examiner Family Ct., 1991—. Mem. ABA, N.Y. County Lawyers Assn. Jewish.

**SAMOUR, CARLOS A.,** lawyer; b. San Miguel, El Salvador, Apr. 14, 1966; came to U.S., 1979; s. Carlos A. and Lilliam E. (Batarse) S. BA, Colo. U., 1987; JD, Denver U., 1990. Bar: Colo., 1990; U.S. Dist. Ct.; U.S. Ct. Appeals (10th cir.). Clk. Tenth Cir. Ct. Appeals, Denver; assoc. Holland & Hart, Denver; mem. Colo. Bd. Law Examiners. Recipient Order of St. Ives, U. Denver Law Sch., 1990. Mem. ABA, ATLA , Colo. Bar Assn., Denver Bar Assn., Hispanic Bar Assn., Colo. Trial Lawyers Assn. (minority caucus rep.). Avocations: argument/debate, sports. Personal injury, Product liability, General civil litigation. Office: Holland & Hart 555 17th St Ste 2900 Denver CO 80202-3979

**SAMPSON, DAVID SYNNOTT,** lawyer; b. Troy, N.Y., Oct. 2, 1942; s. Stephen Hastings and Ruth (Hall) S.; m. Arlene Mernit, July 1, 1967; children: Christopher Hastings, Jamie Everett. B.A., St. Lawrence U., 1965; J.D., Albany Law Sch., 1973. Bar: N.Y. 1975, D.C. 1977, U.S. Ct. Appeals (D.C. cir.) 1977. Reporter Troy Record, 1965-67; newsman AP, 1967-70; spl. asst. N.Y. State Dept. Environ. Cons., Albany, 1972-74; panel dir. Com. on Critical Choices for Ams., N.Y.C., 1974-75; chief legis. asst. U.S. Rep. H. J. Heinz, Washington, 1975-77; assoc. Boasberg, Hewes, Finkelstein & Klores, Troy, 1977-79; exec. dir. Am. Land Forum, Washington, 1978-79, Hudson River Valley Assn., Troy and Cold Spring, N.Y., 1987-89, Hudson River Valley Greenway Coun., Albany, 1989—; ptnr. Pattison, Sampson, Ginsberg & Griffin, Troy, N.Y., 1979-87. Pres. Samaritan Hosp. Found., 1985-87; bd. dirs. Samaritan Hosp., Troy, 1985-88, St. Gregorys Sch., Loudonville, N.Y., 1982-87, Troy Pub. Libr. Found., 1991—, Scenic Hudson, Poughkeepsie, N.Y., 1982-92, 93—; mem. adv. bd. Preservation League N.Y., Albany, 1989-89; mem. N.Y. State Freshwater Wetlands Appeals Bd., 1980-94, chmn., 1984-94; active U.S./UK Countryside Stewardship Exch., Eng., 1989; founder Czech-Hudson Greenway Project, 1992; bd. dirs. Hudson River Found., 1997—. Contbr. book revs., articles to profl. jours. Mem. Am. Conservation Assn. (bd. dirs. 1987—), N.Y. Pks. and Conservation Assn. (founding dir. 1986-94), N.Y. State Bar Assn. (chmn. hist. preservation com. 1980-85, exec. com. 1985—, chmn. environ. law sect. 1990-91), Bar Assn. City of N.Y. Recipient Greenway award DuPont Corp., 1994, Env. Alumni award, Albany Law Sch., 1997. Avocation: bicycling. Environmental.

**SAMPSON, JOHN DAVID,** lawyer; b. Lackawanna, N.Y., Feb. 20, 1955; s. Hugh Albert and May (Davidson) Henderson S.; m. Carol Jasen, July 29, 1978; children: Rachel Henderson, Matthew David. BA, Canisius Coll., Buffalo, 1977; JD, Union U., Albany, N.Y., 1982. Bar: N.Y. 1983, Pa. 1998, U.S. Dist. Ct. (we. dist.) N.Y. 1998, U.S. Dist. Ct. (no. dist.) N.Y. 1996. Assoc. Damon & Morey, Buffalo, 1982-87, Lippes Silverstein Mathias & Wexler, Buffalo, 1987-88; ptnr. Walsh & Sampson, P.C., Buffalo, 1988-93, Jasen, Jasen & Sampson P.C., Buffalo, 1993-99, Underberg & Kessler LLP, Buffalo, 1999—. Paul Harris fellow, 1997. Mem. ABA, N.Y. State Bar Assn., Erie County Bar Assn., Def. Rsch. Inst., Rotary of East Aurora (dir. 1993—, pres. 1995-96). Wesleyan Methodist. Avocations: golf, skiing, cycling. Personal injury, State civil litigation, Federal civil litigation. Home: 44 Elmwood Ave East Aurora NY 14052-2610 Office: Underberg & Kessler LLP 1100 Main Place Tower # 620 Buffalo NY 14202-3711

**SAMPSON, WILLIAM ROTH,** lawyer; b. Teaneck, N.J., Dec. 11, 1946; s. James and Amelia (Roth) S.; 1 child, Lara; m. Drucilla Jean Mort, Apr. 23, 1988; stepchildren: Andy, Seth. BA with honors in History, U. Kans., 1968, JD, 1971. Bar: Kans. 1971, U.S. Dist. Ct. Kans. 1971, U.S. Ct. Appeals (10th cir.) 1982, U.S. Ct. Claims 1985, U.S. Ct. Appeals (8th cir.) 1992. Assoc. Turner & Balloun, Gt. Bend, Kans., 1971; ptnr. Foulston & Siefkin, Wichita, Kans., 1975-86, Shook, Hardy & Bacon, Overland Park, Kans., 1987—; presenter legal edn. seminars and confs.; adj. prof. advanced litig. U. Kans., 1994; mem. faculty trial tactics inst. Emory U. Sch. Law, 1994, 95, 96, 97; lectr. area law schs. Author: Kansas Trial Handbook, 1997; mem. Kans. Law Rev., 1969-71, editor, 1970-71; contbr. articles to legal jours. Chmn. stewardship com. Univ. Friends Ch., Wichita, 1984-86; bd. dirs. Friends U. Retirement Corp., Wichita, 1985-87; chmn. capital fund drives Trinity Luth. Ch., Lawrence, Kans., 1990-93, mem. ch. coun., 1990-92; bd. dirs. Lied Ctr. of Kans., 1994-97. Lt. USNR, 1971-75. Fellow Am. Bar Found., Kans. Bar Found. (chmn. Kans. coll. advocacy 1986, long-range planning, CLE com. 1987-88); mem. ABA, Douglas County Bar Assn., Johnson County Bar Assn. (bench-bar com. 1989-99, Boss of Yr. award 1990), Wichita Bar Assn. (bd. dirs. 1985-86), Am. Bd. Trial Advs. (pres. Kans. chpt. 1990-91, nat. bd. mem. 1990-91), Internat. Assn. Def. Coun. (faculty mem. trial acad. 1994), Def. Rsch. Inst. (Kans. state rep. 1990-97, nat. bd. mem. 1998—, Exceptional Performance citation 1990, Outstanding State Rep. 1991, 92, 94), Kans. Assn. Def. Counsel (pres. 1989-90, legis. coun. 1991, 93, William H. Kahrs Disting. Achievement award 1994), Kans. U. Law Soc. (bd. govs. 1993-96), Am. Inn Ct. (Judge Hugh Means chpt., Master of Bench), Lawrence Country Club, Order of Coif, Delta Sigma Rho, Phi Alpha Theta, Omicron Delta Kappa. Republican. Lutheran. Avocations: jogging, golf, snow skiing, travel, reading. Federal civil litigation, Intellectual property, Product liability. Office: Shook Hardy & Bacon 9401 Indian Creek Pky Overland Park KS 66210-2005

**SAMSON, MARTIN HARRIS,** lawyer; b. Bklyn., Feb. 19, 1956; m. Eve Irene Klein, Aug. 17, 1986; children: Justin, Evan. BA magna cum laude, Duke U., 1978; JD, UCLA, 1981. Bar: Calif. 1982, N.Y. 1983. Atty. Shea & Gould, N.Y.C., 1982-90; ptnr. Phillips, Nizer, Benjamin, Krim & Ballon, LLP, N.Y.C., 1990—. Contbr. numerous articles to N.Y. Law Jour., Internet Newsletter; author The Internet Library of Law. Mem. N.Y. State Bar Assn., Calif. Bar Assn., N.Y. New Media Assn. General civil litigation, Computer. Office: Phillips Nizer 666 5th Ave Rm 2403 New York NY 10103-2402

**SAMUEL, RALPH DAVID,** lawyer; b. Augusta, Ga., May 8, 1945; s. Ralph and Louise Elizabeth (Wurreschke) S.; m. Lynn Christel Malmgren, June 12, 1971; children: Lynn Britt, Ralph Erik. AB, Dartmouth Coll., 1967; JD, Dickinson Sch. of Law, 1972. Bar: Pa. 1972, U.S. Dist. Ct. (ea. dist.) Pa. 1972, U.S. Ct. Appeals (3d cir.) 1973, U.S. Supreme Ct. 1976. Law clk. to hon. judge John P. Fullam U.S. Dist. Ct. (ea. dist.) Pa., Phila., 1972-74; assoc. MacCoy, Evans & Lewis., Phila., 1974-76; ptnr. Samuel and Ballard, P.C., Phila., 1976-98; pres., CEO Ralph D. Samuel & Co., P.C., Phila., 1998—; established Samuel Poetry Fellow Dartmouth Coll., Hanover, N.H., 1994. Contbr. articles to profl. jours., poetry to pubis. Trustee The George Sch., Newtown, Pa., 1983-90; chmn. bd. dirs. Stapeley in Germantown, 1985-90; chmn. budget com. Phila. Yearly Meeting of Friends, 1991-93; bd. dirs., mem. fin. com. Phila. Ranger Corps., 1992-94; pres. Cedar Park Neighbors, Phila., 1975-78, West Mt. Airy Neighbors, Phila., 1981-82. Mem. Pa. Soc., Athenaeum of Phila., Germantown Cricket Club, Sunday Breakfast Club. Mem. Soc. of Friends. Avocations: music, writing, squash, tennis. Personal injury, General civil litigation, Product liability. Office: 225 S 15th St Ste 1776 Philadelphia PA 19102-3908

**SAMUEL, RAPHAEL,** lawyer; b. N.Y.C., Oct. 11, 1946; s. Sam and Sarah R. (Hollenberg) S. BS in Math. magna cum laude, L.I. U., 1968; JD, NYU, 1971. Bar: N.Y. 1972, U.S. Dist. Ct. (so. and ea. dists.) N.Y. 1973, U.S. Ct. Appeals (2d cir.) 1973. Staff atty. N.Y.C. Housing Authority, 1972-78, asst. chief litigation, 1978-83, chief research, opinions and spl. assignments, 1983-87, asst. gen. counse. for spl. projects, 1987-93, assoc. gen. counsel for regulatory affairs, 1993—. Sec. Waterside Tenants Assn., N.Y.C., 1976-78; pres. 130 Water St. Tenants Assn., N.Y.C., 1978-80; sec. 50 8th Ave. Tenants Corp., Bklyn., 1980-83. Served with USNG, 1969-75. Mem. ABA, N.Y. State Bar Assn., Fed. Bar Coun., N.Y. County Lawyers Assn., Nat. Assn. Housing Redevel. Ofcls. Avocations: computer databases, opera, sporting events. Office: NYC Housing Authority 75 Park Pl Rm 11031 New York NY 10007-2146

**SAMUELIAN, THOMAS JOHN,** lawyer; b. Flushing, N.Y., Apr. 10, 1956; s. Samuel V. and Beatrice Virginia S. BA, MA, U. Pa., 1978, PhD, 1981; JD, Harvard Law Sch., 1991. Bar: N.Y. 1991, N.J. 1991, D.C. 1993, U.S. Supreme Ct. 1995. Asst. prof. Columbia U., N.Y.C., 1983-84; instr. U. Pa., Phila., 1979-88, asst. dir. Ctr. Soviet and East European Studies, 1985-88; clk. Ea. Dist. Pa., Phila., 1991-92; assoc. Morgan, Lewis & Bockius, Washington, 1992-94, Steptoe & Johnson, Washington, 1994-98; mng. atty. Steptoe & Johnson, Almaty, Kazakstan, 1995-96; dep. dir. Steptoe & Johnson, Moscow, 1996-98; mng. atty. Arlex Internat. Ltd., Yerevan, Armenia, 1998—; mem. adv. bd. IDR Assocs., Washington, 1996-97. Author: A Course in Modern Western Armenian, 1989, Armenian Dictionary in Transliteration, 1993. Bd. dirs. Americans for Clinton/Gore, Washington, 1996, Armenian Nat. Edn. Com., N.Y.C., 1984-87. Fellow Beinecke Found, 1977-79, Internat. Rsch. and Exchs. Bd., 1979. Mem. ABA (bd. govs. 1992-97, chmn. 1994). Mem. Armenian Apostolic Ch. Avocations: classical music, translation. Office: Arlex Internat Ltd, 15 Grigor Lusavovich St, Yerevah Armenia

**SAMUELS, DONALD L.,** lawyer; b. Washington, May 8, 1961; s. Jack Donald Samuels and Francis Diane (Katcher) Yeoman; m. Linda Marie Tveidt, Aug. 17, 1986. AB, Brown U., 1983; JD, Columbia U., 1986. Bar: Calif. 1986, U.S. Dist. Ct. (cen., no., ea. and so. dists.) Calif. 1988, U.S. Ct. Appeals (9th cir.) 1989, Colo. 1996, U.S. Ct. Appeals (7th cir.) 1996, U.S. Dist. Ct. Colo. 1997, U.S. Ct. Appeals (10th cir.) 1997, Tex. 1998. Law clk. L.A., 1986-87; assoc. Sidley & Austin, L.A., 1987-94, ptnr., 1994-95; ptnr. Samuels & Samuels, L.A., 1995-97; officer, dir., shareholder Ireland & Stapleton, Denver, 1997—. Mem. ABA, Los Angeles County Bar Assn., Phi Beta Kappa. Federal civil litigation, State civil litigation, Trademark and copyright. Home: 9931 E Progress Cir Greenwood Village CO 80111 Office: Ireland & Stapleton 1675 Broadway Ste 2600 Denver CO 80202-4685

**SAMUELS, JANET LEE,** lawyer; b. Pitts., July 18, 1953; d. Emerson and Jeanne (Kalish) S.; m. David Arthur Kalow, June 18, 1978; children: Margaret Emily Samuels-Kalow, Jacob Richard Samuels-Kalow, Benjamin Charles Samuels-Kalow. BA with honors, Beloit Coll., 1974; JD, NYU, 1977. Bar: N.Y. 1978, D.C. 1980. Staff atty. SCM Corp., N.Y.C., 1977-80, corp. atty., 1980-83, sr. corp. atty., 1983-85, assoc. gen. counsel Allied Paper div., 1983-86, corp. counsel, 1986, Holtzmann, Wise & Shepard, 1986-88. Mem. N.Y. State Bar Assn., Mortar Board, Phi Beta Kappa. General corporate, Securities, Contracts commercial.

**SAMUELS, JOEL GREGORY,** lawyer; b. L.A., Nov. 6, 1959; s. Melvin Howard and Charlotte Samuels; m. Marie Gfeller, Aug. 24, 1984 (div. Mar. 1998); children: Matthew, Michael, Alexander. AB in Pub. and Internat. Affairs, Princeton U., 1981; JD, Stanford U., 1984. Bar: Calif. 1984, U.S. Dist. Ct. (ctrl. dist.) Calif. 1985, U.S. Dist. Ct. (no. dist.) Calif. 1984, U.S. Ct. Appeals (9th cir.) 1985. Law clk. Hon. James R. Browning, Chief Judge U.S. Ct. Appeals (9th cir.), San Francisco, 1984-85; ptnr. Sidley & Austin, L.A., 1985—. Author: Federal Appellate Practice Guide: 9th Circuit, 1994; contbr. articles to profl. jours. Mem. Order of the Coif, Phi Beta Kappa. Republican. Jewish. Avocations: golf, travel, reading, mystery novels, opera. Bankruptcy, Federal civil litigation, Contracts commercial. Office: Sidley & Austin 555 W 5th St Ste 4000 Los Angeles CA 90013-3000

**SAMUELSON, DOUGLAS ALLEN,** lawyer; b. Ashland, Wis., Dec. 10, 1957; s. Roger Wayne and Audrey Ann S.; m. Judith Marie Sundstrom, Aug. 7, 1982; children: Rebecca Lynn, Matthew Allen. BS, U. Wis., 1980; JD, U. Houston, 1983. Bar: Tex. 1983; bd. cert. civil trial law 1997. Rsch. atty. Tex. Ct. Appeals, Houston, 1983-85; assoc. Reynolds, Allen & Cook, Houston, 1985-88; assoc., ptnr. Keck, Mahin & Cate, Houston, 1988-93; ptnr. Fleming & Samuelson, P.C., Houston, 1993-95, Keck, Mahin & Cate, Houston, 1995-96; prin. Samuelson & Assocs., Houston, 1997—. Dir., v.p. Pineloch Cmty. Assn., Houston, 1995-96. General civil litigation, Professional liability, Personal injury. Home: 14623 Underwood Creek Way Houston TX 77062-2147 Office: Samuelson & Associates PC 1001 Texas St Ste 440 Houston TX 77002-3130

**SAMUELSON, KENNETH LEE,** lawyer; b. Natrona Heights, Pa., Aug. 22, 1946; s. Sam and Frances Bernice (Robbins) S.; m. Marlene Ina Rabinowitz, Jan. 1, 1980; children: Heather, Cheryl. BA magna cum laude, U. Pitts., 1968; JD, U. Mich., 1971. Bar: Md. 1972, D.C. 1980, U.S. Dist. Ct. (trial bar) Md. 1984. Assoc. Weinberg & Green, Balt., 1971-73, Dickerson, Nice, Sokol & Horn, Balt., 1973; asst. atty. gen. State of Md., 1973-77; pvt. practice Balt., 1978; ptnr. Linowes and Blocher, Silver Spring (Md.), Washington, 1979-93, Semmes, Bowen & Semmes, Washington, D.C., and Balt., 1993-95; Wilkes, Artis, Hedrick & Lane, Chartered, Washington, D.C., and Md., 1995—; spkr. in field of telecomms. and fin. Author in field. Bd. dirs. D.C. Assn. for Retarded Citizens, Inc., 1986—; bd. govs. Wash. Bldg. Congress, 1998—. Mem. ABA (chmn. com. sect. real property, probate and trust law 1993—, moderator programs comml. leases 1987, 88, 89, 90, 91, 92, 94, 96, 97, 98), Am. Coll. Real Estate Lawyers (moderator, spkr. programs on telecomms. and financing 1998, 99), D.C. Bar (mem. comml. real estate com., chmn. legal opinions project and spkr. programs on real estate 1987, 89, 90), Md. State Bar Assn. (real property, planning and zoning sect., chmn. environ. subcom. legal opinions project 1987-89, litigation sect. 1982-84, chmn. comml. trans. com.), Md. Inst. Continuing Profl. Edn. Lawyers (spkr.), Am. Arbitration Assn. (arbitrator and mediator), Washington D.C. Assn of Realtors, Inc. (moderator program on comml. leasing 1992, program on letters of intent 1996), Nat. Assn. of Corp. Real Estate Execs. (spkr. program on telecomms. transactions 1997), Civil Code Drafting Com. of the Russian Legis. (spkr. programs on leasing 1994, 95), Apt. and Office Bldg. Assn. Met. Washington (moderator of programs and spkr. 1989, 92), East Coast Builders Conf. (moderator program on Asian financing 1990), Internat. Coun. Shopping Ctrs. (organized, co-faculty program "univ." 1988, NAFTA 1992, condemnations 1994, high tech. effects 1998, com. chmn. 1998—), Montgomery County Bar Assn. (jud. selections com. 1988-90), Phi Beta Kappa, Lambda Alpha. Real property, Contracts commercial, Municipal (including bonds). Office: Wilkes Artis Hedrick & Lane 1666 K St NW Ste 1100 Washington DC 20006-2897

**SAMUELSON, PAMELA,** law educator; b. Seattle, Aug. 4, 1948; d. Peter David and Margaret Susanne (Green) S.; m. Robert J. Glushko, May 7, 1988; 1 child, Robert M. BA in History, U. Hawaii, 1971, MA in Polit. Sci., 1972; JD, Yale U., 1976. Bar: N.Y. 1977, U.S. Dist. Ct. (so. dist.) N.Y. 1977. Rsch. assoc. Vera Inst. of Justice, N.Y.C., 1976-77; assoc. Willkie Farr & Gallagher, N.Y.C., 1977-81; prin. investigator Software Engring. Inst., Pitts., 1985-86; asst. prof. Law Sch. U. Pitts., 1981-84, assoc. prof. Law Sch., 1984-87, prof. Law Sch., 1987-96; prof. law and info. mgmt. U. Calif. Berkeley Law Sch., 1996—; vis. prof. Emory Law Sch., Atlanta, 1989-90. Contbr. articles to profl. jours. Bd. dirs. ACLU Greater Pitts., 1983-88. John D. and Catherine T. MacArthur Found. fellow, 1997. Mem. ABA (sci. and tech. sect.), Am. Intellectual Property Law Assn. (subcom. chair 1988-89), Assn. Am. Law Schs. (intellectual property sect. 1989). Democrat. Avocations: gardening, reading. Office: U Calif Berkeley Sch Law 341 North Berkeley CA 94720*

**SANBORN, VON ERIC,** lawyer; b. Manchester, N.H., Jan. 19, 1968; s. Duane and Esther (Rush) S.; m. Lisa Kim, Sept. 28, 1996. BA, Boston U., 1991; JD, Albany Law Sch., 1995; LLM in Taxation, Villanova U., 1996. Bar: N.Y. 1997, U.S. Tax Ct 1998. Internat. tax cons. Ernst & Young, Phila., 1997-98; tax assoc. Sheehan, Phinney, Bass & Green, Manchester, N.H., 1998—. Mem. ABA, N.Y. State Bar Assn., Internat. Fiscal Assn. Avocation: bicycling. Corporate taxation. Office: Sheehan Phinney Bass & Green PO Box 3701 1000 Elm St Manchester NH 03105-3701

**SANCHEZ, MANUEL,** lawyer; b. Mexico City, Mex., July 6, 1968; came to U.S., 1997; s. Manuel S. and Carmen Alvarez; m. Gina Paola Pavon, Aug. 30, 1997. JD, Escuela Libre de Derecho, Mex., 1992; LLM, U. Aberdeen, Scotland, 1996. Law clk. Estrada, Gonzalez & Ovanda, Mex., 1987-90; assoc. Gallastegui & Lazano, Mex., 1990-93; dep. dir. Min. of Commerce, Mex., 1993-94, dir., 1994-95; deputy dir. Min. of Fin., Mex., 1996-97; assoc. internat. law Gardere, Wynne, Sewell & Riggs, Houston, 1997—; prof. U. PanAm., Mex., 1987—. Roman Catholic. Avocations: cycling, sailing. Private international, Environmental, General corporate. Office: Gardere Wynne Sewell & Riggs 1000 Louisiana St Ste 3400 Houston TX 77002-5000

**SANCHEZ, WALTER MARSHALL,** lawyer; b. Lake Charles, La., July 3, 1959; s. John Augustine Sanchez and Louise Page Dugas Meyer; m. Frances E. Morgan, Oct. 18, 1986; children: Clare, Madeline, Kate, John. BS, La. State U., Baton Rouge, 1981, JD, 1984. Bar: La. 1984, U.S. Supreme Ct. 1984; bd. cert. family law specialist, La. Bd. of Legal Specialization. Assoc. Godwin, Painter, Roddy, Lorensi & Watson, Lake Charles, 1985-86; ptnr. Godwin, Roddy, Lorenzi Watson & Sanchez, Lake Charles, 1986-90, Lorenzi, Sanchez & Rosteet, L.L.P., Lake Charles, 1990—; vice chmn. La. Indigent Defender Bd., New Orleans, 1994-96; chmn. 14th Jud. Dist. Indigent Defender Bd., Lake Charles, 1987-96; mem. faculty trial advocacy tng. program La. State U. Law Ctr., 1993—; mem. Joint Legis. Com. for Study Indigent Def. Sys., 1996-97; mem. spl. com. to study reinstatement facult in divorce La. State Law Inst., 1998-99. Mem. La. Assn. Criminal Def. Attys. (bd. dirs. 1990—, pres. 1997-98), Am. Mensa, Order of St. Charles. Democrat. Roman Catholic. Criminal, Family and matrimonial, Personal injury. Office: Lorenzi Sanchez & Rosteet LLP PO Box 3305 Lake Charles LA 70602-3305

**SAND, LEONARD B.,** federal judge; b. N.Y.C., May 24, 1928. B.S., NYU, 1947; LL.B., Harvard, 1951. Bar: N.Y. 1953, U.S. Supreme Ct. 1956, D.C. 1969. Clk. to dist. ct. judge N.Y., 1952-53; asst. U.S. atty. So. Dist. N.Y., 1953-54; asst. to U.S. Solictor Gen., 1956-59; mem. firm Robinson, Silverman, Pearce, Aronsohn Sand and Berman, N.Y.C., 1960-78; judge U.S. Dist. Ct. So. Dist. N.Y., 1978—, now sr. judge; adj. prof. law NYU. Note editor: Harvard Law Rev, 1950-51. Del. N.Y. State Constl. Conv., 1967; v.p., treas. Legal Aid Soc. Fellow Am. Coll. Trial Lawyers; mem. ABA, Assn. Bar City N.Y. (v.p.), N.Y. State Bar Assn., Fed. Bar Coun. Office: US Dist Ct US Courthouse 500 Pearl St New York NY 10007-1316

**SAND, THOMAS CHARLES,** lawyer; b. Portland, Oreg., June 4, 1952; s. Harold Eugene and Marian Anette (Thomas) S.; m. Rhonda Diane Laycoe, June 15, 1974; children: Kendall, Taylor, Justin. Student, Centro des Artes y Lenguas, Cuernavaca, Mex., 1972; BA in English, U. Oreg., 1974; JD, Lewis and Clark Coll., 1977. Bar: Oreg. 1977, U.S. Dist. Ct. Oreg. 1977, U.S. Ct. Appeals (9th cir.) 1984. Assoc. Miller, Nash, Wiener, Hager & Carlsen, Portland, 1977-84, ptnr., 1984—; mem. Oreg. State Bar Com. on Professionalism, 1989, chmn., 1990; dir. young lawyers divsn. Multnomah County Bar Assn., 1980; spl. asst. atty. gen. Wasco County 1983 Gen. Election; speaker in field. Contbr. articles to legal jours. Mem. U.S. Dist. Ct. of Oreg. Hist. Soc., 1990—; bd. dirs. Portland Area coun. Camp Fire, Inc., 1978-90,pres., 1984-86; bd. dirs. Oreg. Indoor Invitational Track Meet, Inc., 1982-84. Recipient Boss of the Yr. award Portland Legal Secs. Assn., 1989. Mem. ABA (securities litigation com., subcom. on broker-dealer litigation), Oreg. Bar Assn., Multnomah Bar Assn. (bd. dirs. task force on structure and orgn. 1989, chmn. com. on professionalism 1988, nominating com. 1986, participating atty. in N.E. legal clin. Vol Lawyers project, award of merit for svc. to profession 1988), Securities Industry Assn. (compliance and legal divsn.), Northwestern Sch. of Law, Lewis and Clark Coll. Alumni Assn. (bd. dirs. 1992, pres. 1997), Valley Comm. Presbyterian Ch., Multnomah Athletic Club, Portland Golf Club. Avocations: golf, guitar, camping, river rafting, children's sports. Securities, General civil litigation. Office: Miller Nash Wiener Hager & Carlsen 111 SW 5th Ave Ste 3500 Portland OR 97204-3699

**SANDBACK, WILLIAM ARTHUR,** lawyer; b. N.Y.C., Aug. 2, 1945; s. William A. and Gertrude E. (Ryan) S.; married; children: Lauren, Adam. BA, Villanova U., 1967; postgrad. in English, L.I. U., 1968; JD, N.Y. Law Sch., 1971; LLM in Labor Law, NYU, 1974. Bar: N.Y. 1972, Fla. 1973, U.S. Dist. Ct. (ea. and so. dists.) N.Y. 1973. Fin. planner Aims Group, N.Y.C., 1971-72; asst. dist. atty. Nassau County, N.Y., 1972-73; law sec. to presiding justice Nassau County Ct., 1973-77; ptnr. Sandback, Birnbaum & Michelen, Mineola, N.Y., 1977—. Committeeman Nassau County Rep. Com., 1979-86. Mem. ABA, Nassau County Bar Assn. (com. mem.), Lions (pres. 1983-84). Roman Catholic. Avocation: golf. Criminal, Labor, State civil litigation. Office: Sandback Birnbaum Michelen 200 Old Country Rd Mineola NY 11501-4235 also: 2 Penn Plz Rm 1996 New York NY 10121-1999

**SANDBERG, JOHN STEVEN,** lawyer; b. Mpls., Sept. 1, 1948; s. Donald and Margery Susan (Knudsen) S.; m. Cynthia A. Tucker, July 17, 1982; children: Jennifer, Adam, Luke, Abigail. AB with honors, U. Mo., Columbia, 1970, JD cum laude, 1972. Bar: Mo., Ill., U.S. Ct. Appeals (7th and 8th cirs.), U.S. Dist. Ct. (ea. and we. dists.) Mo., U.S. Dist. Ct. (so. and ctrl. dists.) Ill., U.S. Dist. Ct. (we. dist.) Ky. Ptnr. Coburn, Croft & Putzell, St. Louis, 1972-79, Sandberg, Phoenix & von Gontard, St. Louis, 1979—. Author (books) Damages Deskbook, 1988, Missouri Product Liability Law, 1988. Pres. SAFE KIDS, St. Louis, 1989-96. Mem. Am. Bd. Trial Advocates. Admiralty, Personal injury, Federal civil litigation. Office: Sandberg Phoenix & von Gontard One City Ctr Fl 15 Saint Louis MO 63101-1883

**SANDENAW, THOMAS ARTHUR, JR.,** lawyer; b. Harlowton, Mont., Mar. 17, 1936; s. Thomas A. Sr. S.; m. Colleen A. Andrews, June 3, 1956 (div. May 1981); children: Cheryl Lea, Kevin K., Dana Scott; m. Deborah Rose Hammel, Sept. 26, 1981. BS, Mont. State U., 1958; JD, U. N.Mex., 1967. Bar: N.Mex. 1967, U.S. Dist. Ct. N.Mex. 1968, U.S. Ct. Appeals (10th cir.) 1968. Atty. Wilkinson, Durrett & Conway, Alamogordo, N.Mex., 1968-69, Spence & Sandenaw, Alamogordo, N.Mex., 1969-71, Shipley, Durrett, Conway & Sandenaw, Alamogordo, N.Mex., 1971-77; judge 12th jud. dist. Lincoln and Otero Counties, Alamogordo, N.Mex., 1978-79; atty. Overstreet & Sandenaw, Alamogordo, N.Mex., 1979-82; ptnr. Weinbrenner, Richards, Paulowsky, Sandenaw & Ramirez, Las Cruces, N.Mex., 1982-92; pvt. practice Las Cruces, N.Mex., 1992—. Dir. St. Lukes Health Care, Las Cruces, 1992—, Mesilla Valley Hospice, Las Cruces, 1992-95. Mem. ABA (econs. of law practice, litigation), Am. Bd. Trial Advocates, Am. Bd. Profl. Liability Attys. (diplomat 1993—), Nat. Bd. Trial Advocacy (cert. civil trial practice 1989), State Bar N.Mex. (chmn. pub. rels. com. 1967-68, bd. mem. family law sect. 1983-86, chmn. trial practice sect. 1987-88, bd. dirs. 1990—), N.Mex. Def. Lawyers Assn. (sec. 1984-85, v.p. 1985-86, pres. 1987-88, bd. dirs. 1983—, chmn. Amicus Curie com. 1991-96), N.Mex. Sr. Lawyers Div., N.Mex. Bench and Bar Com., Dona Ana County Bar Assn., Assn. Def. Trial Attorneys (exec. coun. 1996—), Rotary (past pres. Rio Grande chpt.), Am. Inn of Courts. Republican. Lutheran. Avocations: skiing, sailing, woodworking. Civil rights, General civil litigation, Insurance. Office: Sandenaw Carrillo & Piazza PC 2951 N Roadrunner Pkwy # A Las Cruces NM 88011-0814

**SANDERS, ALAN MARK,** lawyer; b. Patchogue, N.Y., Mar. 3, 1954; children: Adam, Brian.; BA in Polit. Sci. and Psychology, Am. U., 1976; JD, DePaul U., 1978; postgrad., NYU, 1979. Bar: N.Y. 1980, U.S. Dist. Ct. (ea. and so. dists.) N.Y. 1980. Jud. law sec. to Justice Emanuel Haber Queens, N.Y., 1979-80; jud. law sec. to Justice Nat Hentel Queens, 1980-81; house counsel Reliance Ins. Co., N.Y.C., 1981-83; ptnr. Malone, Tauber & Sohn, Freeport, N.Y., 1988—; lectr. in field of personal injury law. Mem. DePaul Coll. of Law Law Rev., 1978. Mem. N.Y. State Trial Lawyers Assn., Nassau County Bar Assn., Brandeis Assn. (bd. dirs. 1980—). Personal injury, State civil litigation.

**SANDERS, AMY STEWART,** lawyer; b. Claude, Tex., Jan. 31, 1965; d. Samuel Boyd and Joanne (Atkinson) Stewart; m. Gary D. Sanders, Apr. 11, 1992. BA in Polit. Sci., Tex. Tech. U., 1987, JD, 1990. Law clk. 8th dist. Ct. Appeals, El Paso, Tex., 1990-91; assoc. Mounce & Galatzan, El Paso, 1991-93, Scott & Hulse, El Paso, 1993—. Bd. dirs. Bienvivir Sr. Health Svcs., El Paso, 1993—; tutor Help One Student to Succeed, El Paso, 1993-97. Mem. El Paso Young Lawyers Assn. (Outstanding Young Lawyer 1997, pres. 1998-99), El Paso Women's Bar Assn. (sec. 1997), El Paso Estate Planning Coun. (bd. dirs. 1993), Tex. Young Lawyers Assn. (bd. dirs. 1997—, Outstanding Dir. 1999). Democrat. Methodist. Avocations: reading, scuba diving, cooking. Probate, Estate planning, Estate taxation. Office: Scott & Hulse 201 E Main Dr Ste 1100 El Paso TX 79901-1340

**SANDERS, BOBBY LEE,** lawyer; b. Ben Wheeler, Tex., Jan. 12, 1935; s. Levi Franklin and Veta Lee (Bigony) S.; m. Elsie Jean Beard, May 29, 1954; children: Samuel Franklin, Cynthia Lee. BS, East Tex. State U., 1956; MS, Fla. State U., 1958, PhD, 1962; JD, So. Methodist U., 1977. Bar: Tex. 1976. From asst. prof. to prof. Tex. Christian U., Ft. Worth, 1962-77; ptnr. Sanders & Sanders, Canton, Tex., 1977-86; pvt. practice, 1977—. Bd. dirs. Mental Health/Mental Retardation Regional Ctr. East Tex., Tyler, 1978-94; mem. Van Zandt County Libr. Adv. Bd., Canton, 1987-91; pres. Van Zandt County Assn. Retarded Citizens, Canton, 1979-81. Mem. Tex. State Bar Assn., Coll. State Bar of Tex., Van Zandt County Bar Assn. (pres. 1987-89). Democrat. Methodist. Avocations: golf, computers. Personal injury, Estate planning, General practice. Home and Office: PO Box 416 Canton TX 75103-0416

**SANDERS, DALE R.,** lawyer; b. N.Y.C., Feb. 1, 1946; m. Jo-Ann Sanders, Dec. 25, 1967; 1 child. Bar: Fla. 1970, Wyo. 1991, U.S. Dist. Ct. (so. dist.) Fla. 1971, U.S. Tax Ct. 1972. Atty. Kirsch & Druck, P.A., Ft. Lauderdale, Fla., 1970-71, Kirsch, Digiulian, Druck et al, Ft. Lauderdale, Fla., 1971-72, Digiulian, Spellacy, Lyons, Ft. Lauderdale, Fla., 1972-77, Lyons & Sanders, Chartered, Ft. Lauderdale, Fla., 1977—. With USAR, 1969-75. Mem. Fla. Bar (bd. govs. 1991-95), Broward City Bar (pres. 1990), Broward City Trial Lawyers (pres. 1980). Family and matrimonial. Office: Lyons and Sanders Chartered 600 NE 3rd Ave Fort Lauderdale FL 33304-2618

**SANDERS, DAVID LAWRENCE,** lawyer; b. Columbus, Miss., June 4, 1946; s. William Lee and Winifred Sargent S.; m. Mona Estelle Parker Sanders, Aug. 21, 1971; children: William Parker, Robert Lawrence. BS, U. S. Sewanee, Tenn., 1969; JD, U. Miss., Oxford, 1971. U.S. Dist. Ct. (no. and so. dists.) 1971, U.S. Ct. Appeals (5th cir.) 1977. Bd. dirs. Miss. Def. Lawyers Assn., Jackson, 1986-89; gov. appt. Miss. Constnl. Study Commn., Jackson, 1986-87; mem. Paralegal Cert. Study Com., Jackson, Miss., 1993; atty. Mitchell McNutt Threadgill, Smith & Sams, Columbus, Miss., 1993—; bd. dirs. Columbus-Lowndes Econ. Devel. Assn., 1992-98; mem. Commn. on Cmty. Excellence, Columbus, Miss., 1987-88; bd., pres. Chamber of Commerce, Columbus, Miss., 1993—; adv. bd. Deposit Guaranty Nat. Bank, Columbus, Miss., 1996—; mem. Moot Ct. Bd., 1971. Bd., pres. Columbus.MUW Symphony, Columbus, Miss., 1984-89, United Way of Lowndes County, Columbus, Miss., 1992-95; exec. com. Pushmataha Area Coun., Columbus, Miss., 1992—. Republican. Episcopalean. Avocations: boating, tennis, golf, bridge. General practice, Consumer commercial, Construction. Home: 1315 4th Ave N Columbus MS 39701-4943 Office: Mitchell McNutt Threadgill Smith & Sams 215 5th St N Columbus MS 39701-4523

**SANDERS, DENNIS CARL,** lawyer; b. Oct. 20, 1947; s. Doyle Vance and Renee Camilla Sanders; m. Frances Kay O'Neal; children: Shane, Reid. BA, Mercer U., 1969, JD, 1972. Bar: Ga 1972. Asst. dist. atty. Toombs Jud. Cir., Thomson, Ga., 1973-81, chief asst. dist. atty., 1981-84, dist. atty., 1984—; mem. commn. children and cts. State Bar Ga.; mem. gender bias commn. Supreme Ct. Ga. Play-by-play sports announcer Sta. WTHO-AM-FM, 1977—; author: The Art of Cross Examination, 1982, The Art of Prosecuting Murder Cases, 1982, The Use of Demonstrative Evidence in Trials, 1983. 1st lt. U.S. Army, 1970. Named Outstanding Young Men of Am., 1980. Mem. Nat. Coll. Dist. Attys. (lectr.), Dist. Atty.'s Assn. Ga. (pres. 1973—, Asst. Dist. Atty. of the Yr. 1981), Prosecuting Atty.'s Ga. (chmn. 1989-92), Toombs Cir. Bar Assn. (pres. 1973—), Masons, Bulldog Booster Club (pres. 1977—). Fax: 706-595-8616. E-mail: dsanders@thomson.net.

**SANDERS, DOUGLAS WARNER, JR.,** lawyer, municipal judge; b. Oklahoma City, Jan. 13, 1958; s. Douglas Warner Sr. and Jane (Livermore) S.; m. Brenda Gail Cox, Apr. 20, 1990; children: Douglas Warner III, Noel Layne, Jonathan Scott, Stephanie Marie. BS, Okla. State U., 1980; JD, Oklahoma City U., 1983. Bar: Okla., U.S. Dist. Ct. (ea., no. and we. dists.) Okla., U.S. Dist. Ct. (we. dist.) Ark. Assoc. Stipe Law Firm, Oklahoma City, 1983-85; ptnr. Sanders, Sanders & Sullivan, Poteau, Okla., 1985—; mcpl. judge City of Poteau, 1994—, City of Spiro, Okla., 1994—, Town of Shady Point, Okla., 1994—; city atty. Town of Wister, Okla., 1994—. Mem. ABA, Okla. Bar Assn. (bd. govs. 1992-94, v.p. 1997, pres. 1999, Pres.'s award 1997), LeFlore County Bar Assn. (Pres.'s award 1997). Democrat. Methodist. Avocation: golf. General practice. Home: 200 Crest Dr Poteau OK 74953-2104 Office: Sanders Sanders & Sullivan 104 S Church St Poteau OK 74953-3344

**SANDERS, EDWIN PERRY BARTLEY,** judge; b. Madisonville, Ky., July 12, 1940; s. Virgil Perry and Eunice Jane (Denton) S.; m. Kathryn Walker, Jan. 28, 1967; children—Christopher Charles, Carroll Denton. B.S. in Bus., Stetson U., 1965, J.D., 1968. Bar: Fla. Ptnr. Ford, Wren and Sanders, 1968-69; mem. Landis, Graham, French, Husfeld and Ford, P.A., DeLand, Fla., 1970-83; prof. real estate Stetson U. Sch. Bus. Adminstrn., 1980-83; judge 7th Jud. Cir. Ct., Volusia County, Fla., 1983—. Served with U.S. Army. Mem. Fla. Bar Assn., Volusia County Bar Assn. Democrat. Episcopalian. Clubs: Lake Beresford Yacht, Rotary (DeLand). Home: 340 Washington Oaks Dr Deland FL 32720-2760 Office: Volusia County Jail Bldg 130 W New York Ave Rm 104 Deland FL 32720-5416 also: PO Box 611 Deland FL 32721-0611

**SANDERS, HAROLD BAREFOOT, JR.,** federal judge; b. Dallas, Tex., Feb. 5, 1925; s. Harold Barefoot and May Elizabeth (Forrester) S.; m. Jan Scurlock, June 6, 1952; children—Janet Lea, Martha Kay, Mary Frances, Harold Barefoot III. BA, U. Tex., 1949, LLB, 1950. Bar: Tex. bar 1950. U.S. atty. No. Dist. Tex., 1961-65; asst. dep. atty. gen. U.S., 1965-66; asst. atty. gen., 1966-67; legis. counsel to President U.S., 1967-69; partner firm Clark, West, Keller, Sanders & Butler, Dallas, 1969-79; U.S. dist. judge for No. Dist. Tex., Dallas, 1979—, chief judge, 1989-95. Mem. Tex. Ho. of Reps., 1952-58; Dem. nominee U.S. Senate, 1972. Lt. (j.g.) USNR, World War II. Mem. ABA (chmn. nat. conf. fed. trial judges 1988-89), Fed. Bar Assn. (Disting. Svc. award Dallas 1964), Dallas Bar Assn., State Bar Tex. (jud. conf. U.S. 1989-92, jud. panel on multidistrict litigation 1992—), Blue Key, Phi Delta Phi, Phi Delta Theta. Methodist. Office: US Courthouse 1100 Commerce St Ste 15 Dallas TX 75242-1016

**SANDERS, L. GRAY,** lawyer; b. Tampa, Fla., June 12, 1963; s. Lowell L. and Alice Sanders; m. Catherine Smith, Nov. 19, 1994. BA, Washington & Lee U., 1985; JD, U. Fla., 1989. Bar: Fla. 1990, U.S. Dist. Ct. (mid. dist.) Fla. 1990, U.S. Ct. Appeals (11th cir.) 1990, U.S. Ct. Claims 1995, U.S. Supreme Ct. 1998. Assoc. Butler & Burnette, Tampa, 1990-92; assoc. Barbas, Weed, Morgan & Wheeley, Tampa, 1992-98, ptnr., 1998—; asst. city atty. City of Tampa, 1992—. Bd. fellows U. Tampa, 1998. Episcopalian. Workers' compensation, General civil litigation. Office: Barbas Weed Morgan & Wheeley 1802 W Cleveland St Tampa FL 33606-1852

**SANDERS, MICHAEL EDWARD,** lawyer; b. Hot Springs, Ark., Apr. 15, 1958; s. Doyle Edward and Kathryn Inez Sanders; m. Bethel S. Blosser; children: Mandy, Lecie, Michael. BS in Bus. Adminstrn., U. Ark., Monticello, 1992; JD, Stanford U., 1995. Bar: Calif. 1995, Ark. 1997. Assoc. Gibson, Dunn & Crutcher, Irvine, Calif., 1995-97, Smith, Brennan & Dickerson, Irvine, 1997-98; ptnr. Michael E. Sanders, Atty. at Law, Hot Springs, 1998—. General civil litigation, General practice, Labor. Office: 1424 Airport Rd Ste A2 Hot Springs National Park AR 71913-7994

**SANDERS, RICHARD BROWNING,** state supreme court justice; b. Tacoma, Wash.; m. Kathleen Sanders; children: Amy, Brien, Laura. BA, U. Wash., 1966, JD, 1969. Assoc. Murray, Scott, McGavick & Graves, Tacoma, Wash., 1969, Caplinger & Munn, Seattle, 1971; hearing examiner State Wash., Olympia, 1970; pvt. practice Wash., 1971-95; justice Wash. Supreme Ct., Olympia, 1995—; lectr. in field. Contbr. articles to profl. jours. Office: Supreme Court of Washington Temple of Justice PO Box 40929 Olympia WA 98504-0929

**SANDERS-COCHRAN, RACHEL DEANNA,** lawyer; b. Heflin, Ala., Aug. 4, 1962; m. Gregory D. Cochran, Nov. 4, 1994; children: William G., S. Sanders. BS magna cum laude, Auburn U., 1988; JD cum laude, Samford U., 1991. Bar: Ala. 1991, U.S. Dist. Ct. (mid. dist.) Ala. 1991, U.S. Dist. Ct. (no. and so. dist.) Ala. 1994, U.S. Ct. Appeals (11th cir.) 1994. Atty. Capell, Howard, Knabe & Cobbs, Montgomery, Ala., 1991-94, Pierce, Carr, Alford, Mobile, Ala., 1994-96, Carr, Alford, Clausen, Mobile, 1996, Rushton, Stakely, Johnston & Garrett, Montgomery, 1997—. Mem. ABA, Def. Rsch. Inst., Ala. Bar Assn. (mem. exec. com. young lawyers divsn.), Ala. Def. Lawyers Assn. Appellate, Federal civil litigation, Consumer commercial. Office: Rushton Stakely Johnston & Garrett 184 Commerce St Montgomery AL 36104-2538

**SANDERSON, CYNTHIA ELLEN,** lawyer; b. Mayfield, Ky., Jan. 19, 1957; d. Molton H. and Mary Lou Sanderson; 1 child, Keaton Osborne. BA, U. Ky., 1977; JD, No. Ky. U., 1981. Bar: Ky. 1981, U.S. Dist. Ct. (we. dist.) Ky., 1983, U.S. Ct. Appeals (6th cir.), 1987. Asst. pub. adv. Commonwealth of Ky., Prestonburg and Paducah, 1981-83; assoc. J.W. Owens, Paducah, 1983-84; ptnr. Sanderson & Scent, Paducah, 1992-97; pvt. practice, Paducah, 1984-92, 97—; domestic rels. and master commr. McCracken County, Paducah, 1989-92; mem. Ky. Child Support Guidelines Commn., 1997—. Co-author: Children's Rights Handbook, 1992; author: Child Support in Kentucky, 1997. Exec. dir. Child Watch, Paducah, 1984-85; mem. com. Boy Scouts Am., Paducah, 1998. Recipient Young Career Woman for S.W. Region Ky., Bus. and Profl. Women, 1986. Mem. Ky. Bar Assn. (spkr. 1998), McCracken County Bar Assn. (pres.-elect 1998), NAACP. Avocations: artist, rollerblading. Family and matrimonial. Office: 830 Jefferson St Paducah KY 42001-6820

**SANDERSON, DOUGLAS JAY,** lawyer; b. Boston, Apr. 21, 1953; s. Warren and Edith S. Sanderson; m. Audrey S. Goldstein, June 6, 1982; children: Scott M.G., Phoebe H.G. BA, Trinity Coll., Hartford, Conn., 1974; JD, George Washington U., 1977. Bar: Va. 1977, D.C. 1978, U.S. Dist. Ct. (ea. dist.) Va. 1978, U.S. Ct. Appeals (4th cir.) 1978. Assoc. Bettius, Rosenberger & Carter, P.C., Fairfax, Va., 1977-82; ptnr. Bettius & Sanderson, P.C. and predecessor firms, Fairfax, 1982-86; prin. Miles & Stockbridge P.C., Fairfax, 1986-95; br. head Miles & Stockbridge, Fairfax, 1989-91; co-owner McCandlish & Lillard, P.C., Fairfax, 1995—; trustee Cambridge Ctr. Behavioral Studies, Cambridge, 1981-90. Editor: Consumer Protection Reporting Svc., 1976-77. Bd. dirs. Legal Svcs. No. Va., Inc., 1991-97, pres., 1993-95. Mem. ABA, Va. Bar Assn., Fairfax Bar Assn., Ctrl. Fairfax C. of C. (bd. dirs. 1988-93). Avocations: sports, reading. Real property, Contracts commercial, Family and matrimonial. Office: McCandlish & Lillard 11350 Random Hills Rd Ste 500 Fairfax VA 22030-6044

**SANDLER, DAVID BRUCE,** lawyer; b. Newark, June 27, 1952; s. Maurice David and Leona E. S.; m. Debbie Dargavel, Oct. 6, 1995; children: Shannon, Nick, Corin, Rory. BS, U. Pa., 1974; JD, U. Louisville, 1980. Labr rels. supr. B.f. Goodrich, Louisville, 1975-77; mgr. labor rels. Am. Standard, Louisville, 1977-80; ptnr. Westfall, Talbott & Woods, Louisville, 1981-97; atty. Greenebaum, Doll & McDonald, Louisville, 1997—. Co-author: (chpt.) Kentucky Statutes Affecting Labor and Employment, 1992. Asst. gen. coun. Goodwill Ky., Louisville, 1984-86. Mem. ABA, Ky. Bar Assn., Louisville Bar Assn. Republican. Avocations: triathlons, backgammon, music. Labor, General civil litigation, Administrative and regulatory. Office: Greenebaum Doll & McDonald 3300 National City Tower Louisville KY 40202

**SANDLER, MICHAEL DAVID,** lawyer; b. Los Angeles, Feb. 27, 1946. AB, Stanford U., 1967; JD, Yale U., 1972. Bar: Calif. 1973, D.C. 1973, Wash. 1985. Assoc. Steptoe & Johnson, Washington, 1972-75, 77-79, ptnr., 1980-85; spl. asst. to legal adviser Dept. of State, Washington, 1975-77; ptnr. Foster, Pepper & Shefelman, Seattle, 1985-97, Sandler Ahern & McConaughy PLLC, Seattle, 1997—; adj. prof. law Georgetown U., Washington, 1979, 81-82, U. Wash., Seattle, 1985-92. Vol. Peace Corps, Ethiopia and Ghana, 1968-70. Mem. ABA (chair 1995-96 sect. internat. law and practice). Antitrust, Private international, General civil litigation. Office: Sandler Ahern & McConaughy PLLC 1200 5th Ave Ste 1900 Seattle WA 98101-3135

**SANDLER, ROSS,** law educator; b. Milw., Jan. 31, 1939; s. Theodore T. and Laurette (Simons) S.; m. Alice R. Mintzer, Sept. 15, 1968; children: Josephine, Jenny, Dorothy. AB, Dartmouth Coll., 1961; LLB, NYU, 1965. Bar: N.Y. 1965, Fla. 1965. Assoc. atty. Cahill Gordon Reindel & Ohl, N.Y.C., 1965-68; asst. U.S. atty. So. Dist. N.Y., 1968-72; assoc. atty. Trubin Sillcocks Edelman & Knapp, N.Y.C., 1972-75; sr. staff atty. Natural Resources Def. Coun., N.Y.C., 1975-81, 83-86; spl. advisor to mayor City of N.Y., 1981-82; exec. dir. Hudson River Found., N.Y.C., 1983-86; commr. N.Y.C. Dept. Transp., 1986-90; ptnr. Jones Day Reavis & Pogue, N.Y.C., 1991-93; law prof. N.Y. Law Sch., 1993—, dir. Ctr. for N.Y.C. law, 1993—; pres. N.Y. Legis. Svc., 1998—; mem. N.Y.C. Procurement Policy Bd., 1994—; vis. lectr. Yale Law Sch., New Haven, 1977; adj. prof. law NYU Law Sch., 1976-94; chair, mem. N.Y.C. Taxi and Limousine Commn., 1980-90. Co-author: A New Direction in Transit, 1978; columnist Environ. Mag., 1976-80; editor: (jour.) City Law; contbr. book chpt., op-ed columns, articles to profl. jours.; lectr. environ. law, spkr. confs. Trustee Woods Hole (Mass.) Rsch. Ctr., 1983—; mem. exec. com. Hudson River Found., 1986-96; mem. adv. coun. Ctr. Biodiversity and Conservation Am. Mus. Nat. History,

1996—. Recipient Pub. Interest award NYU Law Alumni, 1987, Louis J. Lefkowitz award Fordham Law Sch. Urban Law Jour., 1989, Lifetime Achievement award N.Y. State Bar Assn., 1998. Mem. City Club of N.Y. (chair 1992-93, trustee). Office: NY Law Sch 57 Worth St New York NY 10013-2959

**SANDMAN, DAN D.,** lawyer. BA, Ohio State U., 1970, JD, 1973. Bar: Ohio 1973, Pa. 1995. Gen. counsel, sec. Marathon Oil Co., 1986-92, USX Corp., Pitts., 1992—. General corporate, Environmental. Office: USX Corp 600 Grant St Ste 6172 Pittsburgh PA 15219-2805*

**SANDMAN, IRVIN W(ILLIS),** lawyer; b. Seattle, Mar. 19, 1954. BA summa cum laude, U. Wash., 1976; JD, UCLA, 1980. Bar: U.S. Dist. Ct. (we. and ea. dists.) Wash. 1980. Prin. Graham & Dunn, Seattle, 1980—. Staff mem. UCLA Law Review. Mem. ABA (vice chair hospitality law com. 1996—), Acad. Hospitality Attys. (charter), Wash. State Hotel and Motel Assn. (govtl. affairs key contact), Wash. State Bar Assn. (chmn. creditor/debtor sect. 1988-90, editor newsletter 1984—, speaker continuing legal edn.). Bankruptcy, Contracts commercial. Office: Graham & Dunn 1420 5th Ave Fl 33 Seattle WA 98101-4087

**SANDOR, LAWRENCE PAUL,** lawyer; b. N.Y.C., Apr. 18, 1962; s. Frank Maurice and Deanna (Camac) S.; m. Leslie Ann Benton, Jan. 2, 1988 (div.); 1 child, Tanner Ochs. BSBA, Boston U., 1983; JD, Emory U., 1986. Bar: Calif. 1987, Ga. 1990, N.Y. 1996, D.C. 1998. Assoc. Greco & Traficante, San Diego, 1987-90, Mack & Bernstein, Atlanta, 1990-92; pvt. practice San Diego, 1992-94; counsel Lew Lieberbaum & Co., Inc., Garden City, N.Y., 1995-97; assoc. McGuire Woods Battle & Boothe, Washington, 1997—; adj. prof. bus. law Grossmont Coll., San Diego, 1994. Mem. ABA, State Bar Calif., State Bar Ga., State Bar N.Y., D.C. Bar. Securities, Federal civil litigation. Office: McGuire Woods et al 1050 Connecticut Ave NW Washington DC 20036-5317

**SANDOZ, WILLIAM CHARLES,** lawyer; b. Opelousas, La., Aug. 23, 1928; s. Lawrence Broussard and Cecelia (Boagni) S.; m. Jane Simmons, Apr. 29, 1950; children: Yvonne Marie, William Simmons, Charles Jeffrey. Student, La. State U., 1945-47, U. Southwestern La., 1945-47; JD, La. State U., 1950. Bar: La. 1950, U.S. Dist. Ct. (we. dist.) 1950, U.S. Dist. Ct. (ea. dist.) La. 1972, U.S. Dist. ct. (mid. dist.) La. 1972, U.S. Ct. Appeals (5th cir.) 1963. Pvt. practice Opelousas, 1950-54, 83-87; ptnr. Sandoz & Sandoz, Opelousas, 1954-60, Sandoz, Sandoz & Schiff, Opelousas, 1960-83, Law Offices William C. Sandoz and W. Simmons Sandoz, Opelousas, 1983—; also Alexandria, Baton Rouge, Houma, Lafayette, Lake Charles, Monroe, New Orleans, and Shreveport; bd. dirs. Church Point (La.) Bank & Trust Co.; lectr. profl. assns. Mem. La. Law Rev., 1948. Named to Hall of Fame, La. State U. Law Sch., 1987. Mem. ABA, La. Bar Assn., St. Landry Parish Bar Assn., Assn. Trial Lawyers Am., La. Trial Lawyers Assn., Nat. Assn. Bankruptcy Trustees, Am. Bankruptcy Inst., Comml. Law League Am., KC (rec. sec. Opelousas 1950-52) Elks, Order of Coif, Delta Kappa Epsilon, Phi Delta Phi. Republican. Roman Catholic. Bankruptcy, Consumer commercial, Personal injury. Office: Sandoz & Sandoz 435 S Union St Opelousas LA 70570-6119

**SANDS, DARRY GENE,** lawyer; b. Charleston, Ark., Jan. 4, 1947; s. Anthony Wayne and Marjorie (Elkins) S.; m. Charlotte Moore, Dec. 28, 1968; 1 child, Spencer Justin. BS, U. Ark., 1969; JD, U. Kans., 1974. Bar: Mo. 1974, U.S. Dist. Ct. (we. dist.) Mo. 1974. Dir. Dicus, Davis, Sands & Collins, P.C., Kansas City, Mo., 1991—; spkr. in field. Contbr. articles to profl. jours. Mem. ABA, Nat. Assn. Coll. and Univ. Attys., Mo. Bar, Kansas City Met. Bar Assn. (chmn., past chair coll. and univ. law com., local govt. com.), Order of Coif, Lake Quivira Country Club. Democrat. Labor, General civil litigation, Education and schools. Home: 5341 Canterbury Rd Shawnee Mission KS 66205-2612 Office: Dicus Davis Sands & Collins PC 1930 City Center Sq 1100 Main St Kansas City MO 64105-2105

**SANDS, MICHAEL ARTHUR,** lawyer; b. Santa Barbara, Calif., June 11, 1971; s. Herbert Clark and Dayle Carole Sands; m. Melissa Kay St. Pierre, Mar. 23, 1996.; BA in Polit. Economy, Tulane U., 1992; JD, Santa Clara U., 1995. Bar: Calif. 1995, U.S. Dist. Ct. (no. dist.) Calif. 1995, U.S. Cir. Ct. (9th cir.) 1995. Assoc. Fenwick & West LLP, Palo Alto, Calif., 1995—. Mem. Assn. Bus. Trial Lawyers, Order Barristers. Republican. Avocations: golf, wine collecting, cooking, reading. Intellectual property, Federal civil litigation, State civil litigation. Office: Fenwick & West LLP Ste 700 Two Palo Alto Sq Palo Alto CA 94306

**SANDS, VELMA AHDA,** lawyer; d. John T. and Thelma Jane (Davis) Carlisle. BS, Calif. State U., Dominguez Hills, 1976; JD, Southwestern U., 1985. CPA. Cons. Peat Marwick Main, L.A., 1980-81; v.p. Security Pacific Bank, L.A., 1981-86; contr. L.A. Investors, 1986; mgr. IRC div. FN Realty Svcs., Pasadena, Calif., 1986-88; mgr. fin. reporting Luz Internat. Ltd., L.A., 1988-89; pvt. practice law L.A., 1990—; temporary judge L.A. Mcpl. Ct., 1996—; instr. Fame Entrepreneurial Tng. Program. Participant career day programs for local high schs.; mem. United We Stand. Nat. Assn. Black Women Lawyers scholar, 1982. Mem. ABA, NAFE, Bd. Black Women Lawyers (bd. dirs.), Nat. Assn. Bank Women (chair ways and means com. of scholarship fund 1986, scholar 1984), Am. Bridge Assn., L.A. County Bar Assn., Langston Bar Assn. (v.p. 1998), L.A. Bench and Bar Affiliates (scholarship com., meeting host, scholar 1983), Phi Alpha Delta. Bankruptcy, Personal injury, Administrative and regulatory. Home and Office: 3435 Wilshire Blvd Ste 2700 Los Angeles CA 90010-2013 Address: PO Box 38 Lawndale CA 90260-0038

**SANDS, W. LOUIS,** federal judge; b. 1949. BA, Mercer U., 1971, JD, 1974. Chief legal asst. to dist. atty. Macon Jud. Cir., 1974, asst. dist. atty., 1975-78; asst. U.S. atty. U.S. Dist. Ct. (mid. dist.) Ga., 1978-87; with Mathis, Sands, Jordan & Adams, Macon, 1987-91; judge superior ct. Macon Jud. Cir., 1991-93; dist. judge U.S. Dist. Ct. (mid. dist.) Ga., Albany, 1994—; ptnr. Investors Ltd., 1984-91; mem. task force substance abuse Ga. Supreme Ct., 1991—, mem. com. gender equality, 1993—; bd. dirs. Bank Corp. Ga./1st South Bank, N.A. Organist/min. music, officer Steward Chapel AME Ch., 1976—; active Cmty. Found. Ga., Inc.; mem. 30th anniversary planning com. Mercer U., mem. bd. visitors Walter F. George sch. law, 1994—; v.p. Ga. Commn. Family Violence, 1992—; bd. dirs. Macon Symphony, 1992—. 2d lt. Signal Corps, U.S. Army, 1971, res. Acad. scholar Mercer U.; grad. Leadership Macon, 1985, Leadership Ga., 1986. Mem. ABA, Am. Judicature Soc., State Bar Ga. (mem. bench and bar com. 1991—), Macon Bar Assn. (pres. 1991-92), Coun. Superior Ct. Judges (mem. bench and bar com. 1991—), Walter F. George Sch. Law Alumni Assn. (bd. dirs.), Scabbard and Blade Mil. Honor Soc., Alpha Phi Alpha, Sigma Pi Phi, Homosophian Club. Office: US Dist Ct PO Box 1705 345 W Broad Ave Albany GA 31701-2568

**SANDSTROM, DALE VERNON,** state supreme court judge; b. Grand Forks, N.D., Mar. 9, 1950; s. Ellis Vernon and Hilde Geneva (Williams) S.; m. Gail Hagerty, Mar. 27, 1993; children: Carrie, Anne; 1 stepchild, Jack. BA, N.D. State U., 1972; JD, U. N.D., 1975. Bar: N.D. 1975, U.S. Dist. Ct. N.D. 1975, U.S. Ct. Appeals (8th cir.) 1976. Asst. atty. gen., chief consumer fraud and antitrust div. State of N.D., Bismarck, 1975-81, securities commr., 1981-83, pub. svc. commr., 1983-92, pres. commn., 1987-91, justice Supreme Ct., 1992—; chair N.D. Commn. on Cameras in the Courtroom, 1993—, Joint Procedure Com., 1996—; mem. exec. com. N.D. Jud. Conf., 1995—, chair-elect, 1997—; mem. Gov.'s Com. on Security and Privacy, Bismarck, 1975-76, Gov.'s Com. on Refugees, Bismarck, 1976; chmn. Gov's Com. on Comml. Air Transp., Bismarck, 1983-84. Mem. platform com. N.D. Reps., 1972, 76, exec. com., 1972-73, 85-88, dist. chmn., 1981-82; former chmn. bd. deacons Luth. Ch.; mem. ch. coun., exec. com., chmn. legal and constl. rev. com. Evang. Luth Ch. Am., 1993—; mem. exec. bd. dirs., No. Lights Coun., dist. chair Boy Scouts Am., 1998—. Named Disting. Eagle Scout, Boy Scouts Am., 1997. Mem. ABA, N.D. Bar Assn., Big Muddy Bar Assn., Nat. Assn. Regulatory Utility Commrs. (electricity com.), N.A. Assn. Securities Adminstrs., Order of De Molay (grand master 1994-95, mem. Internat. Supreme coun., Legion of Honor award), Nat. Eagle Scouts Assn. (regent for life), Shriners, Elks, Eagles, Masons (33d degree, chmn. grand youth com. 1979-87, Youth Leadership award 1986). Office: State ND Supreme Court Bismarck ND 58505

**SANDY, ROBERT EDWARD, JR.,** lawyer; b. Libertyville, Ill., Feb. 16, 1943; s. Robert Edward and Elizabeth Ann (Carroll) S.; m. Joan Mary Phillips, Apr. 19, 1969; children: Mary Rosanne Phillips-Sandy, John Robert Phillips-Sandy. AB, Harvard U., 1965; JD, U. Chgo., 1968. Bar: Mass. 1969, Maine 1972, U.S. Dist. Ct. Mass. 1970, U.S. Dist. Ct. Maine 1972, U.S. Ct. Appeals (1st cir.) 1994, U.S. Supreme Ct. 1980. Atty. Boston Redevel. Authority, 1969-72; ptnr. Sandy and Sandy, Waterville, Maine, 1972-83, Sherman and Sandy, Waterville, 1983-87; sr. ptnr. Sherman & Sandy, Waterville, 1987—. Mem. Waterville Bar Assn., Maine Bar Assn., Maine Trial Lawyers Assn., ABA. Avocations: boating, skiing, community theater, Maine Internat. Film Festival. General practice, Family and matrimonial, Criminal. Home: 19 Greenwood Park Waterville ME 04901-4316 Office: Sherman & Sandy 74 Silver St Waterville ME 04901-6524

**SANDZA, ELIZABETH BARRY,** lawyer; b. Duluth, Minn., Aug. 26, 1951; d. Thomas Gerald and Marguerite Mary (Collins) Barry; m. Richard William Sandza, Feb. 14, 1976; children: Anne Elizabeth, Allison Barry, Richard William, Mary Molly Rose. BS, U. Minn., 1973; MA, Northwestern U., 1974; JD, Temple U., 1979. Bar: Del. 1979, Calif. 1981, Md. 1988, D.C. 1988, U.S. Dist. Ct. Del., U.S. Dist. Ct. (so. dist.) N.Y., U.S. Dist. Ct. (no. and ctrl. dists.) Calif., U.S. Dist. Ct. D.C., U.S. Ct. Appeals (9th cir.). Dep. atty. gen. Del. Dept. Justice, Wilmington, 1979-81; assoc. atty. Gordon & Rees, San Francisco, 1981-86; assoc. atty. LeBoeuf Lamb Greene & MacRae, Washington, 1986-89, ptnr., 1989—; formerly gen. counsel Discovery Creek Children's Mus., Washington. Past pres. Intown Play Group, Inc., Washington, 1990-94. Mem. Fedn. Ins. and Corp. Counsel, Def. Rsch. Inst. Democrat. Roman Catholic. Office: LeBoeuf Lamb Greene & MacRae 1875 Connecticut Ave NW Washington DC 20009-5728

**SANETTI, STEPHEN LOUIS,** lawyer; b. Flushing, N.Y., June 25, 1949; s. Alfred Julius Sanetti and Yolanda Marie (DiGioia) Boyes; m. Carole Leighton Koller, Sept. 21, 1974; children: Christopher Edward, Dana Harrison. B.A. in History with honors, Va. Mil. Inst., 1971; J.D., Washington and Lee U., 1974. Bar: Conn. 1975, U.S. Ct. Mil. Appeals 1975, U.S. Dist. Ct. Conn. 1978, U.S. Ct. Appeals (2d cir.) 1979, U.S. Supreme Ct. 1980. Litigation atty. Marsh, Day & Calhoun, Bridgeport, Conn., 1978-80; gen. counsel Sturm, Ruger & Co., Southport, Conn., 1980—, v.p., 1993—, also bd. dirs., 1998—; dir. Product Liability Adv. Coun. Tech. advisor Assn. Firearm and Toolmark Examiners; chmn. legis. & legal affairs com. Sporting Arms & Ammunition Mfrs. Inst. Served to capt., chief criminal law 1st Cavalry Div. Staff Judge Advocate, U.S. Army, 1975-78. Mem. Am. Acad Forensic Sci., Def. Rsch. Inst. Republican. Roman Catholic. General corporate, General civil litigation, Product liability. Office: Sturm Ruger & Co Inc 1 Lacey Pl Southport CT 06490-1241

**SANFILIPPO, JON WALTER,** lawyer; b. Milw., Nov. 10, 1950; s. Joseph Salvator and Jeanne Catherine (Lisinski) S.; m. Pamela Joy Jaeger, July 8, 1972; children: Kerri, Jessica, Jennifer. AS, U. Wis., West Bend, 1972; BS, U. Wis., Milw., 1974, MS, 1978; JD, Marquette U., 1988; postgrad., Nat. Jud. Coll., 1996. Bar: Wis. 1988, U.S. Dist. Ct. (ea. dist.) Wis. 1988, U.S. Dist. Ct. (we. dist.) Wis. 1989, U.S. Ct. Appeals (7th cir.) 1988, U.S. Supreme Ct. 1994; cert. elem. tchr., ednl. adminstr., Wis. Collection agt. West Bend Co., 1970-72; educator, athletic dir., coach St. Francis Cabrini, West Bend, 1974-77; clk. of cir. ct. Washington County, West Bend, 1976-89; ptnr. Schowalter, Edwards & Sanfilippo, S.C., West Bend, 1989-94; sch. prin.K-8 Campbellsport (Wis.) Sch. Dist., 1994-95; chief dep. clk. Cir. Ct. Milw. County, Milw., 1995—; acting clk. Cir. Ct. Milw. County, 1997-98; jud. ct. commr. Milw. County, 1997—; judo tchr. City of West Bend, 1967—; phys. edn. instr., judo coach U. Wis., West Bend, 1992—; fellow ct. exec. devel. program Inst. Ct. Mgmt. Nat. Ctr. State Cts., 1999. Author: Judo for the Physical Educator, 1981, Proper Falling for Education Classes, 1981. Mem. sch. bd. West Bend Sch. Dist., 1979-80; dist. chmn. Wis. Clk. of Cts. Assn., 1976-79, mem. exec. com., 1976-82, 97-98, mem. legis. com., 1982-84, 97-98. Recipient cert. study internat. and Chinese law East Chinese Inst. Politics & Law, Willamette U. Law Sch., Shanghai, People's Republic China, 1988, Black Belt 6th Degree U.S. Judo Assn., 1995, Black Belt 3d Degree Universal Tae Kwon Do Assn., 1988. Mem. ABA, Nat. Jud. Coll., Nat. Assn. for Ct. Adminstrn., Wis. Bar Assn. (bench/bar com. 1986-88, 97—), Milw. Bar Assn. (cts. com. 1995—, criminal bench/bar com. 1997—, family bench/bar coun. 1997—), Washington County Bar Assn., U. Wis.-Washington County Found. Inc. (bd. dirs. 1993-94), Assn. Wis. Sch. Adminstrs., Justinian Soc., Rotary (bd. dirs. West Bend Sunrise Club 1990-91, Paul Harris fellow). Roman Catholic. Avocations: Tai Kwon Do, Tai Chi, Judo, photography, model railroading. Office: Milw County Ct House 901 N 9th St Ste 104 Milwaukee WI 53233-1425

**SANG, PETER BENNETT,** lawyer; b. N.Y.C., July 28, 1941; m. Penelope M. Keenan, Aug. 24, 1996. BA in Econs., Bucknell U., 1962; LLB, Boston U., 1965, LLM in Taxation, 1967. Bar: Mass. 1965, U.S. Ct. Claims 1970, U.S. Tax Ct. 1970, Maine 1971. Tax acct. Coopers & Lybrand, Boston, 1965-68; assoc. Gadsby & Hannah, Boston, 1968-71; pvt. practice Portland, Maine, 1971-99, Trenton, Maine, 1999—. Commr. Maine Lottery, Augusta, 1973-77. Mem. Maine Bar Assn. (chmn. IRS tax liaison com. 1984—). Personal income taxation, Corporate taxation, Estate taxation. Office: RR 1 Box 262C Ellsworth ME 04605-9722

**SANGER, HERBERT SHELTON, JR.,** lawyer, former government official; b. Oak Hill, W.Va., Aug. 6, 1936; s. Herbert Shelton and Ethel Dean (Layne) S.; m. Rita Adele Baumgartner, Aug. 20, 1958; children: Charles, Carole, Warren, George. A.B. in English and Polit. Sci, Concord Coll., Athens, W.Va., 1958; LL.B., W.Va. U., Morgantown, 1961. Bar: W.Va. 1961, U.S. Supreme Ct. 1976, U.S. Ct. Appeals 5th and 6th cirs. 1973, 10th cir. 1978, 11th cir. 1981, 4th cir. 1982, U.S. Dist. Ct. (ea. dist.) Tenn. 1987, Tenn. 1988. Lifetime del. 6th Cir. Jud. Conf.; staff atty. Office of Gen. Counsel, TVA, Knoxville, 1961-69, asst. gen. counsel power, 1969-72; assoc. gen. counsel litigation and power Office of Gen. Counsel, TVA, 1972-73, dep. gen. counsel, 1973-75, gen. counsel, 1975-86; ptnr. Wagner, Myers & Sanger, P.C., Knoxville, 1986—; asst. prof. law U. Tenn.; Arthur B. Hodges prof. law W.Va. U.; chmn. bd. dirs. TVA Retirement System, 1975-86, Paribas Concorde Trust, Ltd., Regal Cinemas, Inc. Bd. dirs. East Tenn. Found., Knoxville Symphony Soc., pres., 1997—. Recipient Lawyers Coop award, 1961, Lawyers Title Ins. Co. award, 1961. Mem. ABA, Fed. Bar Assn., W.Va. Bar Assn., Tenn. Bar Assn., Am. Corp. Counsel Assn. (bd. dirs. 1982-87), Knoxville Symphony Soc. (bd. dirs.). Baptist. General corporate, Federal civil litigation, Public utilities. Home: 5100 Malibu Dr Knoxville TN 37918-4513 Office: Wagner Myers & Sanger PC PO Box 1308 1801 Plaza Tower Knoxville TN 37901-1308

**SANGERMAN, JAY J.,** lawyer, rabbi; b. Chgo., Mar. 7, 1944; s. Alfred and Helen (Eisenberg) S.; m. Barbara Lee Weiss, July 12, 1981. BA in Philosophy, U. Ill., 1968; BHL, MHL, Hebrew Union Coll., Cin., 1971; JD cum laude, Yeshiva U., N.Y.C., 1987. Bar: N.Y. 1988, N.J. 1990, Fla. 1990. Rabbi Etz Chaim Congregation, Lombard, Ill., 1968-73, Temple Sholom, New Milford, Conn., 1973-74, Beth Sholom, Bklyn., 1975-81, Union Temple, Bklyn., 1981-83; assoc. Fried, Frank, Harris, Shriver & Jacobson, N.Y.C., 1987-90; sole practitioner N.Y.C., 1990—; instr. in estate planning for the elder protection N.Y. Univ. Sch. Continuing Edn., 1997—. Alexander fellow Cardozo Sch. Law, 1986. Mem. N.Y. State Bar Assn. (chair elder law practice and ethics com. of elder law sect. 1991-97), Assn. of the Bar of the City of N.Y. (bioethics com., legal problems of aging com.), Nat. Acad. of Elder Law Attys. Union of Am. Hebrew Congregation's Commn. on Aging. Probate, Estate planning, Administrative and regulatory. Home: 171 E 84th St New York NY 10028-2000 Office: 60 E 42nd St Rm 650 New York NY 10165-0699

**SANISLO, PAUL STEVE,** lawyer; b. Cleve., Feb. 8, 1927; s. Paul and Bertha (Kasa) S.; m. Mary Ellen P. Conroy, May 7, 1949; 1 child, Susan J. B.A., Baldwin-Wallace Coll., 1948; J.D., Cleve. State U., 1961. Bar: Ohio 1961, U.S. Dist. Ct. (no. dist.) Ohio 1964. Order clk. Am. Agrl. Chem. Co., Cleve., 1948-52; safety engr. Park Drop Forge Co., Cleve., 1952-62, personnel mgr., 1954-62; assoc. then ptnr. Spohn & Sanislo, L.P.A., Cleve., 1962-81, pres., 1981-86; ptnr., pres. Sanislo, Bacevice & Assocs. LPA, Cleve., 1987—; spl. counsel Atty. Gen. Ohio, 1971; arbitrator Am. Arbitration Assn., 1972-78. Mem. Cleve. City Council, 1964-67; trustee Cleve.-Marshall Law Sch., 1962-63; trustee Cleve.-Marshall Ednl. Found., 1963-68 , pres., 1980-83; mem. Solon City Bd. Edn., Ohio, 1972-83, pres., 1974-83; chmn. Solon Charter Rev. Commn., 1971; past mem., organizer, legal adv. Solon Drug Abuse Ctr.; mem. Cuyahoga County Democratic Exec. Com.; ward leader 29th Ward Dem. Club, 1965-71, also past pres.; trustee Solon Dem. Ward Club, 1972-75. Recipient Disting. Service award City of Solon, 1984, Solon Bd. Edn., 1984, Solon Edn. Assn., 1984. Mem. Bar Assn. Greater Cleve. (Merit Service award 1978-79; chmn. workers compensation sect. 1975-96 ), Ohio Bar Assn., Cuyahoga County Bar Assn., Assn. Trial Lawyers Am., Cleve.-Marshall Law Sch. Alumni Assn. (pres. 1968-69), Hungarian Bus. and Tradesmen's Club (pres. 1967-68), Cleve. Assn. Compensation Attys. (pres. 1973-76). Democrat. Roman Catholic. Club: Aurora Country (v.p. 1983-87) (Ohio). Lodge: KC. Avocations: golf; travel. Workers' compensation, General practice, Personal injury. Office: 710 Standard Bldg Cleveland OH 44113

**SANNA, RICHARD JEFFREY,** lawyer; b. N.Y.C., July 20, 1949; s. Francis and Ann (Bryant) S.; m. Rosemarie A. Lagnena, Nov. 21, 1971; children: John, Kristin, Michele, Elisabeth. BA, St. Johns U., Jamaica, N.Y., 1971; JD, Del. Law Sch., 1975. Bar: N.Y. 1977, U.S. Dist. Ct. (so. dist.) N.Y. 1978, U.S. Dist. Ct. (ea. dist.) N.Y. 1979, U.S. Ct. Appeals (2d cir.) 1979, U.S. Supreme Ct. 1980. Assoc. McKay, King, Castricone & Piazza, Queens, N.Y., 1978-80; sr. ptnr. Sarisohn, Sarisohn, Thierman, Carner & LeBow, Commack, N.Y., 1980-82; ptnr. Migliore, Sanna & Infranco P.C., Commack, 1982-85; sole practice Hauppauge and Commack, N.Y., 1985; sr. counsel Eagle Funding, Natl., Jericho, N.Y., 1990—. mem. adv. council St. Martins of Tours Ch., Bethpage, N.Y., 1983—; atty. Bethpage Civic Assn., 1985—. Mem. N.Y. State Bar Assn., Suffolk County Bar Assn. (chmn. fee dispute com. 1984-86, recipient I.U.J.H. F.D. Roosevelt award for meritorious svc. AFL-CIO, 1992), Assn. Trial Lawyers Am., N.Y. Trial Lawyers Assn., Columbian Lawyers Assn. Republican. Roman Catholic. Lodge: K.C. Real property, Personal injury, General practice. Home: 91 Sycamore Ave Bethpage NY 11714-2226

**SANNER, ROYCE NORMAN,** lawyer; b. Lancaster, Minn., Mar. 9, 1931; s. Oscar N. and Clara Sanner; m. Janice L. Sterne, Dec. 27, 1972; children—Michelle Joy, Craig Allen. BS, Moorhead State U., 1953; LLB cum laude, U. Minn., 1961. Bar: Minn. 1961, U.S. Dist. Ct. Minn. 1961, U.S. Supreme Ct. 1981. Tchr. English Karlstad (Minn.) High Sch., 1955-57; counsel IDS Life Ins. Co., Mpls., 1961-68; v.p., gen. counsel IDS Life Ins. Co., 1969-72, exec. v.p., gen. counsel, 1972-77; dir. corp. devel. Am. Express Fin. Advisors, Mpls., 1968-69, v.p., gen. counsel, 1975-78, v.p., 1978-80, v.p., gen. counsel, 1980-82; v.p law Northwestern Nat. Life Ins. Co., Mpls., 1982-83, sr. v.p., gen. counsel, sec., 1983-96; sr. v.p., gen. counsel, sec. ReliaStar Fin. Corp. (formerly known as NWNL Cos., Inc.), Mpls., 1988-96; of counsel Maslon Edelman Borman & Brand, Mpls., 1996—; bd. dirs. Fairview Univ. Med. Ctr., Friendship Ventures, Inc., Fraser Cmty. Svcs.; chair bd. dirs. Fairview Hosp. and Healthcare Svcs. Served with U.S. Army, 1953-55. Mem. ABA, Minn. Bar Assn., Hennepin County Bar Assn., Fed. Bar Assn., Assn. of Life Ins. Counsel, Minn. Corp. Counsel Assn., Mpls. Club, Rotary. General corporate, Insurance, Securities. Home: 734 Widsten Cir Wayzata MN 55391-1784 Office: Maslon Edelman Borman & Brand 3300 Norwest Ctr 90 S 7th St Ste 3300 Minneapolis MN 55402-4140

**SANO, KAZUHIKO,** lawyer; b. Syracuse, N.Y., Aug. 19, 1965; s. Tuguo and Hiroko S.; m. Jeannine Yoo, Jan. 16, 1995. AB, Stanford U., 1987. Bar: Calif. 1994, Ill. 1994, U.S. Ct. Appeals (9th cir.) 1997, U.S. Ct. Appeals (7th cir.) 1995, U.S. Dist. Ct. (all dists.) Calif. 1997, U.S. Dist. Ct. (no. dist.) Ill. 1995. Law clk. Hon. Stanley Mosk Calif. Supreme Ct., San Francisco, 1993-94; assoc. Skadden Arps Slate Meagher & Flom, Chgo., 1994-97, Jackson, Tufts, Cole & Black, L.L.P., San Francisco, 1997-99, Stein & Lubin L.L.P., San Francisco, 1999—. Mem. ABA, San Francisco Bar Assn. Avocations: running, volleyball, reading, restaurants. Office: Transamerica Pyramid 600 Montgomery St Fl 14 San Francisco CA 94111-2702

**SANOBA, GREGORY A.,** lawyer; b. Media, Pa., Aug. 7, 1967. BS, U. Fla., 1989; JD, Washburn U., 1992. Bar: Fla. 1992. Assoc. Lucas & Brown P.A., Tampa, Fla., 1992-94, Ben Hardin Jr., P.A., Lakeland, Fla., 1995-96; ptnr. Sanoba & Sanoba, P.A., Lakeland, 1997—. Mem. Polk County Trial Lawyers Assn., Lakeland Bar Assn., Lakeland Assn. Realtors, Polk County Builders Assn. Real property, General civil litigation. Office: Sanoba & Sanoba PA 101 W Main St Ste 170 Lakeland FL 33815-1534

**SANSEVERINO, RAYMOND ANTHONY,** lawyer; b. Bklyn., Feb. 16, 1947; s. Raphael and Alice Ann (Camerano) S.; m. Karen Marie Mooney, Aug. 24, 1968 (dec. 1980); children: Deirdre Ann, Stacy Lee; m. Victoria Vent, June 6, 1982 (div. 1995). AB in English Lit., Franklin & Marshall Coll., 1968; JD cum laude, Fordham U., 1972. Bar: N.Y. 1973, U.S. Dist. Ct. (so. dist. and ea. dist.) N.Y. 1973, U.S. Ct. Appeals (2d cir.) 1974, U.S. Supreme Ct. 1986. Assoc. Rogers & Wells, N.Y.C., 1972-75, Corbin & Gordon, N.Y.C., 1975-77; ptnr. Corbin Silverman & Sanseverino LLP, N.Y.C., 1978—, mng. ptnr., 1985—. Contbr. articles to profl. jours.; articles editor Fordham Law Rev., 1971-72. Recipient West Pub. Co. prize, 1972. Mem. ABA, Assn. Bar City of N.Y., N.Y. State Bar Assn., Twin Oaks Swim and Tennis Club (bd. dirs. 1981—, pres. 1993—). Republican. Roman Catholic. Real property, Landlord-tenant. Office: Corbin Silverman Et Al 805 3d Ave New York NY 10022-7513

**SANTA MARIA, DIANA,** lawyer; b. Havana, Cuba, Dec. 9, 1959; Came to the U.S., 1961; d. Oscar Beaudois and Maria Teresita (Zimmermann) S.M.; m. Brian K. Sidella, May 25, 1984; children: Nickolas A., Alexander C. BA, U. Miami, 1981, JD, 1984. Bar: Fla., 1985, U.S. Dist. Ct. (so. dist.) Fla. Atty. assoc. Law Offices of Sheldon J. Schlesinger, Ft. Lauderdale, 1985-90; founding atty., ptnr., owner Law Offices of Diana Santa Maria, P.A., Ft. Lauderdale, 1991—; lectr. in field. Recipient Best Brief award Robert Orseck Meml. Moot Court Competition, 1983. Mem. Assn. Trial Lawyers Am., Acad. Fla. Trial Lawyers, Broward County Trial Lawyers Assn. Avocations: playing piano, reading. Personal injury, State civil litigation, Product liability. Office: 4801 S University Dr Fort Lauderdale FL 33328-3839

**SANTA MARIA, PHILIP JOSEPH, III,** lawyer; b. Ft. Lauderdale, Fla., Oct. 10, 1945; s. Philip Joseph Jr. and Margaret Elizabeth (Hillard) S.; m. Gail Suzanne Claussen, Aug. 23, 1969; children: Todd, Carly. AB, Gettysburg (Pa.) Coll., 1967; JD, Am. U., 1970. Bar: Md. 1970, U.S. Ct. Mil. Appeals 1971, U.S. Supreme Ct. 1975, D.C. 1976, Calif. 1976, U.S. Dist. Ct. Md. 1977, U.S. Ct. Appeals (4th cir.) 1977. Assoc. Simpson & Simpson, Rockville, Md., 1974-75; sole practice Gaithersburg, Md., 1975-79; ptnr. Haight, Rosfeld, Noble & Santa Maria, Gaithersburg, 1980-81, Santa Maria & Weiss, Chartered, Gaithersburg, 1981—. Mem. editorial bd. Am. U. Law Rev., 1969; author pamphlet What To Do. Mem. Standby Selective Service Local Bd. 69, Montgomery County, Md., 1981-83, Standby Selective Service Bd. of Appeals, Md., 1983-92, Met. Wash. YMCA Trustee's Coun., 1990-93. Served to capt. USAF, 1970-74. Named one of Outstanding Young Men in Am., 1971. Mem. ABA, Calif. Bar Assn., D.C. Bar Assn., Montgomery County Bar Assn., Md. Trial Lawyers Assn. Clubs: Montgomery Soccer, Inc. (league commr. 1985); Gaithersburg Tennis Assn. (pres. 1976); Snowbird Youth Ski (Md.) (pres. 1975-76). Personal injury, State civil litigation. Home: 10319 Royal Woods Ct Gaithersburg MD 20886-1027 Office: Santa Maria & Weiss Chartered 18522 Office Park Dr Gaithersburg MD 20886-0585

**SANTANA, JESSE ISAIAS,** lawyer; b. Marysville, Calif., June 26, 1963; s. Jose and Maria Santana; m. Sandra Curiel, Jan. 11, 1997. BA, Calif. State U., Chico, 1984; JD, U. San Francisco, 1987; LLM, Georgetown U., 1988. Bar: Calif. 1987, U.S. Dist. Ct. (no. dist.) 1988, D.C. 1989; U.S. Dist. Ct. (ea. dist.) 1995. Assoc. atty. Crosby Heafey Roach & May, Oakland, Calif., 1988-92, 94-95; dep. dist. atty. Fresno (Calif.) County Dist. Atty.'s Office, 1993-94; ptnr. Law Office of Beauchamp & Santana, Yuba City, Calif., 1995—. General civil litigation, Criminal, Personal injury. Office: Beauchamp & Santana 500 2nd St Yuba City CA 95991-5021

**SANTANA, ROBERT RAFAEL,** lawyer; b. Bklyn., Apr. 22, 1961; s. Carlos Roberto and Hilda Eva (Cabrera) S.; children: Robert Jr., Alexis. BBA, Fordham U., 1985; JD, NYU, 1990. Bar: N.Y. 1992, U.S. Dist. Ct. (ea. dist.) 1992, U.S. Dist. Ct. (so. dist.) 1993. Police officer N.Y.C. Police Dept., 1981-93, sgt., 1993-94; assoc. Morales & Silva, P.C., N.Y.C., 1992-94, ptnr., 1995-96; ptnr. Morales & Assocs., 1996-97, pvt. practice, 1997—. Mem.

ABA, N.Y. State Bar Assn., N.Y. County Lawyers Assn., Puerto Rican Bar Assn., Hispanic Nat. Bar Assn. Democrat. Roman Catholic. Avocations: basketball, football, baseball, travel, reading. General civil litigation, Bankruptcy, Family and matrimonial. Office: 11 Park Pl Rm 617 New York NY 10007-2801

**SANTAPIETRO, LISA,** lawyer; b. Newark, Oct. 21, 1969; d. John Joseph and Linda. BA, NYU, 1991; JD, Seton Hall U., 1994. Bar: N.J., Pa., U.S. Dist. Ct. N.J. Jud. law clk. Superior Ct. N.J., Newark, 1994-95; atty. Riker, Danzig, Scherer, Hyland & Peretti, Morristown, N.J., 1995—; Cert. Family Mediator. Vol. domestic violence crisis response team Morris County Prosecutors Office, N.J. Family and matrimonial. Office: Riker Danzig et al Headquarters Plz 1 Speedwell Ave Ste 2 Morristown NJ 07960-6823

**SANTO, RONALD JOSEPH,** lawyer; b. Detroit, Jan. 11, 1940; s. Joseph P. and Mary L. (Benzi) Angelosanto; m. Donna L. Macidoni, May 15, 1965; children: Michael, Donielle, Jason. AB, U. Detroit, 1962; JD, U. Mich., 1965. Bar: Mich., U.S. Ct. Appeals (6th cir.). Ptnr. Dykema, Gossett PLLC, Detroit, 1965—; chmn. bd. Bon Secours Hosp., Grosse Pointe, Mich., 1984. Contbr. articles to profl. jours. Civil rights, Labor. Office: Dykema Gossett PLLC 400 Renaissance Ctr Detroit MI 48243-1607

**SANTOLA, DANIEL RALPH,** lawyer; b. Syracuse, N.Y., Oct. 25, 1949; s. Dan D. and Sophie Irene (Podszebka) S.; m. Kathleen Elaine Beach, Aug. 21, 1971; children: Daniel, Jonathan. BA, SUNY, Buffalo, 1971; JD, Union U., Albany, N.Y., 1974. Bar: N.Y. 1975, U.S. Dist. Ct. (no. dist.) N.Y. 1975, U.S. Dist. Ct. Vt. 1986, U.S. Dist. Ct. (we. dist.) N.Y. 1992, U.S. Dist. Ct. (so., ea. dist.) N.Y., 1993. Assoc. Martin Brickman, Esq., Albany, N.Y., 1974-75; assoc. prof. Rensselaer Poly. Inst., Troy, N.Y., 1976-77, dir. law mgmt. program, 1976-77; assoc. Morris J. Bloomberg, Esq., Albany, 1978-81; ptnr. Bloomberg & Santola, Esq., Albany, 1982-87, Powers and Santola, Albany, 1987—; asst. town atty. Town of Bethlehem, Delmar, N.Y., 1978—. Author: (with others) Products Liability Practice Guide, Medical Equipment, 1988, N.Y. Negligence Guide, Construction Accidents, 1989, Compensating the Catastrophically Injured, 1990, Using SPECT Scans to Show Head Injuries. Mem. N.Y. State Bar Assn. (ho. of dels. 1995—), N.Y. State Trial Lawyers Assn. (past pres. capitol dist. affiliate, bd. dirs. 1988—), Albany County Bar Assn. (pres. 1997), Am. Bd. Trial Advs., N.Y. State Trial Lawyers Inst. (dir. decisions seminar 1984—), Capital Dist. Trial Lawyers Assn. (pres. 1985). Republican. Roman Catholic. Avocations: golf, snowboarding, scuba diving. Personal injury, Product liability. Office: Powers and Santola Esq 39 N Pearl St Ste 6 Albany NY 12207-2779

**SANTONI, CYNTHIA LEE,** lawyer; b. Galesburg, Ill.; d. Mark Dean and Cleo Berniece Vancil; m. David Wayne Santoni, July 30, 1988 (div. Mar. 1998); children: Mark Vincent, Joseph David, Nicholas Dean. BS, George Mason U., 1980; JD, George Mason U. Sch. Law, 1983. Assoc. Law Office R. Harrison Pledger, McLean, Va., 1983-90; ptnr. Pledger & Santoni, McLean, Va., 1990-96; atty., prin. Miles & Stockbridge, McLean, Va., 1996—. Charter mem. St. Judes Children's Rsch. Hosp., Annandale, Va., 1992—; mem. Fairfax (Va.) Bar Assn. com. professionalism. Mem. Va. Bar Assn., Va. Assn. Def. Attys., Def. Rsch. Inst., ABA Torts, Ins. Practice. Democrat. Avocations: soccer, hockey, fund raising. Personal injury. Office: Miles & Stockbridge 1751 Pinnacle Dr Ste 500 Mc Lean VA 22102-3833

**SANTOPIETRO, ALBERT ROBERT,** lawyer; b. Providence, R.I., Oct. 18, 1948; s. Alfred and Marie (Epifanio) S.; m. Linda Stuart, 1994; children: Hope, Spencer, Anna. BA, Brown U., 1969; JD, U. Va., 1972. Bar: R.I. 1973, Mass. 1997, U.S. Dist. Ct. R.I. 1973, Ill. 1974, Conn. 1983, Mass. 1997. Atty. Met. Life Ins. Co., Oak Brook, Ill., 1974-75, Seligman Group, N.Y.C., 1975-76; atty. Mut. Benefit Life Ins. Co., Newark, 1976-78, asst. counsel, 1978-81; atty. Aetna Life and Casualty, Hartford, Conn., 1981-82, counsel, 1982—; assoc. counsel Conn. Mut. Life Ins. Co., Hartford, 1991-95, counsel, 1995—; 2d v.p. & assoc. gen. coun. Mass Mutual. Finance, Real property. Home: 142 Pond Brook Rd Huntington MA 01050-9620 Office: Mass Mutual 1295 State St Springfield MA 01111-0002

**SANTORO, FRANK ANTHONY,** lawyer; b. Plainfield, N.J., Dec. 14, 1941; s. Frank V. and Nancy M. (Scavuzzo) S.; m. Patricia Ferrante, Oct. 10, 1964; children—Frank, Jennifer. B.S. in Chemistry, Seton Hall U., 1963, J.D., 1970. Patent atty. Exxon Corp., Linden, N.J., 1970-73; sole practice, South Plainfield, N.J., 1973—; atty. Planning Bd. Borough South Plainfield, 1971-73; mcpl. prosecutor Borough South Plainfield, 1972. Councilman Borough South Plainfield, 1977-79, mcpl. atty., 1985-93; mcpl. chmn. South Plainfield Republican Orgn., 1981-84. Mem. Middlesex County Bar Assn., UNICO Nat. Roman Catholic. General practice, Probate, Real property. Office: 129 S Plainfield Ave PO Box 272 South Plainfield NJ 07080-0272

**SANTORO, THOMAS MEAD,** lawyer; b. Glens Falls, N.Y., Feb. 16, 1946; m. Corinne Collins, Mar. 27, 1981. AB, Colgate U., 1967; JD, Union U., Albany, N.Y., 1972. Bar: N.Y., Fla., U.S. Dist. Ct. (no., so., ea. and we. dists.) N.Y., U.S. Dist. Ct. (so. dist.) Fla., U.S. Ct. Appeals (2d and 11th cirs.), U.S. Supreme Ct. Atty. Legal Aid, N.Y.C., 1972-73, Cmty. Legal Rights Found., Inc., Albany, N.Y., 1973-74; asst. atty. gen. N.Y. State Dept. Law, Albany, 1974-76; asst. counsel SUNY, Albany, 1976-79; assoc. Bouck, Holloway & Kiernan, Albany, 1979-81; dep. univ. counsel Cornell U., Ithaca, N.Y., 1981-97; gen. counsel Fla. Internat. U., Miami, 1997—. Contbr. chpt. to book. Trustee Albany Law Sch. of Union U., 1992—. Mem. N.Y. State Bar Assn., Fla. Bar Assn., Dade County Bar Assn., Nat. Assn. Coll. and Univ. Attys. Avocations: boating, skiing, bicycling. Email: santoro@fiu.edu. General civil litigation, Education and schools, Labor. Home: 4161 Malaga Ave Coconut Grove FL 33133-6324 Office: 11200 SW 8th St Miami FL 33199-0001

**SANTOS, HERBERT JOSEPH, JR.,** lawyer; b. Reno, Feb. 17, 1963; s. Herbert Joseph Sr. and Jeanette Dorothy (Olivera) S.; m. Kimberly Ellen Saylors, Mar. 8, 1986; children: Herbert Joseph III, Jarred Adam, Hannah McKenzie. BA in Sociology, U. Nev., Las Vegas, 1985; JD, U. of the Pacific, 1991. Bar: Nev. 1991, Calif. 1992, U.S. Dist. Ct. Nev. 1992, U.S. Supreme Ct. 1999. Head social worker Cmty. Welfare, Inc., Reno, 1986-87; inspector Nev. Athletic Commn., Reno, 1986-87; sr. legal rsch. asst. County Sacramento, Calif., 1987-91; assoc. Law Offices of Terry A. Friedman, Ltd., Reno, 1991-98; owner The Law Firm of Herb Santos Jr., 1999—; mem. State Bar Law Office Mgmt. and Procedures Com., 1996-98; chair election canvassing com. Nev. Bd. Govs, access to justice com., 1998, temp. apptd. jud. selection com. Author (instrn. manual) ORR, County of Sacramento Bankruptcy Forms and Procedures Manual with Practice Pointers, 1990; editor: The Writ, 1997-98; appeared in: (films) Kingpin, Father's Day, (TV miniseries) The Last Don, The Cheater's Partner in Mafia!, Body and Soul, Diamonds. Mem. Cmty. Coalition, Reno, 1986-87; mentor U. Nev., Reno, 1993—. Recipient Am. Jurisprudence award, 1991,. Mem. ABA (young lawyers divsn., del. for State of Nev. 1996, 97, 98, 99), ATLA, Nev. Trial Lawyers Assn., State Bar Nev. (exec. coun. mem. young lawyers sect. 1993—, pres. young lawyers sect. 1996-97, com. chair Ask-a-Lawyer young lawyers sect. 1994—. chair pub. com. 1996-97, Pro-Bono award 1997, apptd. alternate dispute resolution sect.-long range planning 1998), Washoe County Bar Assn. (exec. coun., sgt.-at-arms 1997-98, treas. 1998-99, sec. 1999—, Bar Leader award 1998), Am. Inns of Ct. (Hon. Bruce Thompson chpt. 1995-97). Republican. Roman Catholic. Avocations: family, boxing, basketball, golf. State civil litigation, Personal injury, Workers' compensation. Office: The Law Firm of Herb Santos Jr Liberty Ctr 350 S Center St Ste 350 Reno NV 89501-2113

**SAPIENZA, CHARLES PAT, JR.,** lawyer; b. New Castle, Pa., July 12, 1963; s. Charles Pat Sr. and Joyce Elaine (Pacelli) S.; m. Maria Ann Viggiano, June 22, 1985; children: Charles Pat III, Alaina Marie, Rachel Lynn, Adrianne Elise. BA, Westminster Coll., 1985; JD, U. Akron, 1989. Bar: Pa. 1989, U.S. Dist. Ct. (we. dist.) Pa. 1989, U.S. Ct. Appeals (3d cir.) 1995. Law clk. to Hon. Ralph D. Pratt, Lawrence County Ct. Common Pleas, New Castle, Pa., 1986; law clk. Luxenberg, Garbett & Kelly, Ellwood City, Pa., 1986-89, assoc. atty., 1989-94; ptnr. Luxenberg, Garbett, Kelly & Sapienza, New Castle, 1994—; solicitor New Castle Airport Auth., 1991—, New Castle Red Hurricane Club, 1991—; with Pa. Bar Inst. worker's compensation sect. Mem. ABA, ATLA, Pa. Bar Assn. (del. young lawyers divsn. Zone 10), Pa. Trial Lawyers Assn., Lawrence County Bar Assn. (trustee). Democrat. Roman Catholic. Avocations: golf, skiing, hunting. Personal injury, Workers' compensation, Product liability. Office: Luxenberg Garbett Kelly & Sapienza PC 101 S Mercer St New Castle PA 16101-3849

**SAPIN, CRAIG P.,** lawyer; b. L.A., Aug. 5, 1956; s. Sandy Sapin and Carol (Sapin) Gold; m. Carolyn Marie Clark, June 28, 1982; children: Stephanie, Patrick. BA in Econs., U. Calif., San Diego, 1978; JD, UCLA, 1981. Bar: Calif. 1981; cert. in taxation. From assoc. to ptnr. Procopio, Cory, Hargreaves & Savitch, San Diego, 1981—. Bd. dirs. Help Disabled War Vets., San Diego, 1995—. Mem. ABA, State Bar Calif., San Diego County Bar Assn. Taxation, general, Mergers and acquisitions, Personal income taxation. Office: Procopio Cory Hargreaves & Savitch 530 B St Ste 2100 San Diego CA 92101-4496

**SAPP, JOHN RAYMOND,** lawyer; b. Lawrence, Kans., June 18, 1944; s. Raymond Olen and Amy (Kerr) S.; m. Linda Lee Tebbe, July 3, 1965; children: Jeffrey, Jennifer, John. BA, U. Kans., 1966; JD, Duke U., 1969. Bar: Wis. 1969, U.S. Dist. Ct. (ea. dist.) Wis. 1969, U.S. Ct. Appeals (7th cir.) 1974, U.S. Ct. Appeals (4th cir.) 1984, U.S. Supreme Ct. 1974. Assoc. Michael, Best & Friedrich, Milw., 1969-76, ptnr., 1976-90, mng. ptnr., 1990—; dir. Roadrunner Freight Systems, Milw., 1992—. Bd. dirs. Milw. Symphony, 1981-95, mem. exec. com., 1993—; bd. dirs. Boy Scouts Am., Milw., 1986—, pres. 1990; mem. Milw. Arts Bd., 1990, Greater Milw. Com.; bd. dirs. Zool. Soc., 1992-95, Hexmundi, 1997—, mem. exec. com., 1997—. Avocations: golf, curling, print collecting. Labor.

**SAPP, SUSAN KUBERT,** lawyer; b. Lincoln, Nebr., June 12, 1965; d. Wayne William and Carole Grace (Burt) Kubert; m. Willie Leon Sapp, Mar. 26, 1988; children: Joshua A., Jared R. BS in Criminal Justice, U. Nebr., Lincoln, 1986, JD, 1989. Bar: Nebr. 1989; U.S. Dist. Ct.; Am. Acad. Adoption Lawyers, 1991; cert. fed. ct. mediator Fed. Ct. Dist. of Nebr., Lincoln, 1996—. Lawyer, ptnr. Cline Williams law Firm, Lincoln, Nebr., 1989—; adjunct prof. UNL Coll. Law, Lincoln, Nebr., 1992—. Contbr. articles to profl. jours. Southern Baptist. Education and schools, General civil litigation, Labor. Office: Cline Williams Wright Johnson & Oldfatner 233 S 13th St 1900 US Bank Bldg Lincoln NE 68508

**SAPP, WALTER WILLIAM,** lawyer, energy company executive; b. Linton, Ind., Apr. 21, 1930; s. Walter J. and Nona (Stalcup) S.; m. Eva Kaschner, July 10, 1957 (dec.); children: Karen Elisabeth, Christoph Walter. AB magna cum laude, Harvard, 1951; JD summa cum laude, Ind. U., 1957. Bar: Ind. 1957, N.Y. 1959, Colo. 1966, U.S. Supreme Ct. 1972, Tex. 1977. Pvt. practice N.Y.C., 1957-60, 63-66; practice in Paris, France, 1960-63, Colorado Springs, 1966-76; assoc. atty. Cahill, Gordon, Reindel & Ohl, Paris, 1960-63, N.Y.C., 1957-60, 63-65; partner Cahill, Gordon, Reindel & Ohl, 1966; gen. counsel Colo. Interstate Corp., 1966-76, v.p., 1968-76, sec., 1971-76, sr. v.p., dir., exec. com., 1973-75, exec. v.p., 1975-76; v.p. Coastal States Gas Corp., 1973-76; sr. v.p., gen. counsel Tenneco, Inc., Houston, 1976-92, sec., 1984-86; pvt. practice Houston, 1992—; Editor-in-chief Ind. U. Law Jour., 1956-57. Trustee Houston Ballet, 1982-85, Awty Internat. Sch., 1989-98, 99—, vice-chmn., 1994-97, pres. 1997-98; bd. dirs. Harris County Met. Transit Authority, 1982-84, Houston Internat. Protocol Alliance, 1992-94, Houston Symphony, 1989—, v.p., 1991-94; adv. bd. Inst. for Internat. Edn. S.W. region, 1987—, chmn., 1992-94, Internat. and Comparative Law Ctr. Southwestern Legal Found., 1976-92. Lt. USNR, 1951-54. Mem. ABA, N.Y. State Bar Assn., Tex. Bar Assn., Assn. Bar City of N.Y., Houston Bar Assn., Order of the Coif, French-Am. C. of C. (bd. dirs. 1987-92), Alliance Francaise Houston (bd. dirs. 1989—, v.p. 1991-94, 98—). Mem. United Ch. of Christ. General corporate, Private international, Securities. Office: 2108 Quenby St Houston TX 77005-1506

**SARASOHN, PETER RADIN,** lawyer; b. N.Y.C., Sept. 19, 1944; s. Alvin Norman and Vivian (Radin) S.; m. Patricia A. La Rose, June 15, 1969; children: Amy Sarasohn Spurr, Anne, Adam. JD, Boston U., 1973; BA, U. Mich., 1996. Bar: N.J. 1973, N.Y. 1985. Vol. Peace Corps, Thailand, 1966-68; asst. U.S. atty. U.S. Atty.'s Office, Newark, 1973-77, chief bank fraud divsn., 1976-77; with Ravin Sarasohn Cook Baumgarten Fisch & Rosen, Roseland, N.J., 1978—. Mem. ABA, N.J. Bar Assn. Bankruptcy, General civil litigation, Labor. Office: Ravin Sarasohn Cook Baumgarten Fisch & Rosen 103 Eisenhower Pkwy Roseland NJ 07068-1029

**SARAUSKAS, PAUL JUSTAS,** lawyer; b. Ill., Nov. 5, 1965; s. Justas and Rasa S. (Gadliauskas) S. BA, U. Ill., 1987; JD, John Marshall Law Sch., 1990. Bar: Ill., 1990, U.S. Dist. Ct. (no. dist.) Ill., 1991, U.S. Ct. Appeals (7th cir.), 1996. Law clerk Hon. Thomas Hoffman, Hon. Stephen Schiller Cir. Ct. Cook County, Chgo., 1990-91; atty. Stellato & Schumacher, Chgo., 1991-92, Querrey & Harrow, Chgo., 1993-97, O'Hagan, Smith & Amundson, Chgo., 1997—; arbitrator Cir. Ct. Cook County, Chgo., 1997, Cir. Ct. DuPage County, 1997. Pro bono atty. criminal defendants Appellate Ct. Ill., Chgo., 1997. Recipient 2d pl. award Nat. Tax Moot Ct. Comp., Buffalo. 1990. Mem. Ill. Bar Assn., Chgo. Bar Assn., Baltic Bar Assn., Appellate Lawyers Assn. Avocations: dog breeding and showing, languages, gardening, music, art. Appellate, Insurance, General civil litigation. Home: 2825 Grissom Ct Woodridge IL 60517-1940 Office: O Hagan Smith & Amundsen 150 N Michigan Ave Ste 3300 Chicago IL 60601-7586

**SARFAN, EDWARD I.,** lawyer; b. Newport News, Va., Sept. 19, 1960; s. Mayer A. and Dorene Z. Sarfan; m. Jody N. Sarfan; children: Sydney, Matthew. BA, Va. Tech., 1983; JD, Coll. William and Mary, 1986. Bar: Va. 1986, U.S. Dist. Ct. Va. 1986, U.S. Ct. Appeals (4th dist.) 1986. Assoc. Sarfan & Nachman, Newport News, 1986-90, ptnr., 1990—. Bd. dirs., mem. archtl. com. Colonial Acres Home Owners Assn., Hampton, Va., 1992—; pres.-elect Jewish Fedn. of Va. Peninsula, Newport News, 1998—, bd. dirs., 1992—. Recipient Young Leadership award Jewish Fedn. Va. Peninsula, 1998; named to Outstanding Young Men of Am., 1998. Mem. Newport News Bar Assn., Va. Trial Lawyers Assn. Avocations: fishing, scuba, sports. Criminal, State civil litigation, Personal injury. Home: 37 Sarfan Dr Hampton VA 23664-1759 Office: Sarfan & Nachman Newport News VA 23608

**SARGENT, JAMES CUNNINGHAM,** lawyer; b. New Haven, Feb. 26, 1916; s. Murray and Mary Hale (Cunningham) S.; m. Rebecca Porteous Jackson, Jan. 23, 1943; children: Stephen Denny, James Cunningham, Felicity Hale, Sarah Blanchard. Grad., Taft Sch., 1935; B.A., U. Va., 1938, LL.B., 1940. Bar: N.Y. 1940, D.C. 1961. With Clarke & Baldwin, N.Y.C., 1940-41; trial atty. Consol. Edison Co. of N.Y., 1941-51; asst. atty. gen., elections fraud bur. State of N.Y., 1948; law asst. appellate div. N.Y. Supreme Ct., 1951-54; asso. atty. Spence & Hotchkiss, N.Y.C., 1954-55; regional adminstr. SEC, N.Y.C., 1955-56; mem. SEC, 1956-60; asst. gen. counsel CIT Finance Corp., N.Y.C., 1960-64; mem. Whitman & Ransom (and predecessors), 1964-94; guest lectr. corporate securities U. Va. Law Sch., 1958-60, Practicing Law Inst., 1962—. Served from pvt. to capt. USAAF, 1942-46. Mem. St. Andrews Soc., Bar Assn. City N.Y., N.Y. County Lawyers Assn., ABA, Fed. Bar Assn., Fed. Bar Coun., Va. Bar Assn. (hon.), U. Va. Law Sch. Alumni Assn. (pres.), Order of Coif, Sky Club, Univ. Club (N.Y.C.), Church Club (N.Y.C.), Downtown Assn. (N.Y.C.), Capitol Hill Club (Washington), Army-Navy Club (Washington), Farmington Country Club, Phi Delta Phi. Episcopalian. General corporate, Securities. Home: 409 Altamont Cir Charlottesvle VA 22902-4617 Office: Gunsel Opton Handler Gottlieb Feiler & Katz 52 Vanderbilt Ave New York NY 10017-3808

**SARGENT, MARK A.,** dean, law educator. Dean Sch. Law Villanova U., 1997—. Office: Villanova U Sch Law 800 Lancaster Ave Villanova PA 19085-1603*

**SARGUS, EDMUND A., JR.,** judge; b. Wheeling, W.Va., July 2, 1953; s. Edmund A. Sr. and Ann Elizabeth (Kearney) S.; m. Jennifer L. Smart, Jan. 7, 1978; children: Edmund C., Christopher A. AB with honors, Brown U., 1975; JD, Case Western Res. U., 1978. Bar: Ohio 1978, U.S. Dist. Ct. (so. dist.) Ohio 1979, U.S. Dist. Ct. (no. dist.) Ohio 1981, U.S. Ct. Appeals (6th cir.) 1985, U.S. Dist. Ct. (no. dist.) W.Va. 1988, U.S. Ct. Appeals (4th cir.) 1988. Assoc. Cinque, Banker, Linch & White, Bellaire, Ohio, 1978-79, Stanley C. Burech, St. Clairsville, Ohio, 1980-82; ptnr. Burech & Sargus, St. Clairsville, 1983-93; U.S. Atty. Dept. of Justice, Columbus, Ohio, 1993-96; dist. judge U.S. Dist. Ct. (so. dist.) Ohio, Columbus, 1996—; spl. counsel Ohio Atty. Gen., Columbus, 1979-93; treas. Coalition for Dem. Values, Washington, 1990-93. Solicitor Village of Powhattan Point, Ohio, 1979-93; councilman City of St. Clairsville, 1987-91. Mem. ABA, Ohio Bar Assn. Democrat. Roman Catholic. Office: US Dist Ct 85 Marconi Blvd Columbus OH 43215-2823

**SARIS, PATTI BARBARA,** federal judge; b. 1951. BA magna cum laude, Radcliffe Coll., 1973; JD cum laude, Harvard U., 1976. Law clerk to Hon. Robert Braucher Mass. Supreme Judicial Ct., 1976-77; atty. Foley Hoag & Eliot, Boston, 1977-79; staff counsel U.S. Senate Judiciary Com., 1979-81; atty. Berman Dittmar & Engel, Boston, 1981-82; chief civil divsn. U.S. Atty.'s Office, 1984-86; U.S. magistrate judge U.S. Dist. Ct. Mass., 1986-89; assoc. justice Mass. Superior Ct., 1989-94; dist. judge U.S. Dist. Ct. Mass., 1994—; mem. com. on civil rules Supreme Jud. Ct. Comments editor civil rights Civil Liberties Law Rev. Bd. trustees Beth Israel Hosp.; active Wexner Heritage Found. Nat. Merit scholar, 1969; recipient award Mothers of Murdered Children, 1993. Mem. Nat. Assn. Women Judges, Am. Jewish Com., Women's Bar Assn. (bd. dirs. 1982-86), Mass. Bar Assn., Mass. Assn. Women Judges, Boston Bar Assn., Boston Inns Ct., Phi Beta Kappa. Office: US Courthouse Courthouse Way Ste 6130 Boston MA 02210

**SARKAR, NEIL STEVEN,** lawyer; b. Cin., June 27, 1971; s. Nibar K. and Rose Allene (Lieberman) S. BA with gen. honors, U. Chgo., 1993; post-grad., U. Cin., 1994; JD, Case Western Res. U., 1997. Bar: Ohio 1997, U.S. Dist. Ct. (no. dist.) Ohio 1998. Asst. Pauline Warfield Lewis Ctr., Cin., 1991; intern CBS News, Inc., N.Y.C., 1992, Legal Aid Soc. Cin., 1994; atty. McCray, Muzilla, Smith, Meyers & Betleski Co., LPA, Elyria, Ohio, 1997—. Staff editor Jour. Internat. Law, Cleve., 1993-95; author newsletter articles. Vol. Cin. Freestore/Foodbank, 1993-94. Mem. Ohio Bar Assn., Lorain County Bar Assn., Cleve. Bar Assn. (alternative dispute resolution com. 1998, com. on homeless 1998, law related edn. com. 1998, minority outreach com. 1998), Pi Kappa Alpha (chmn. cmty. svc. 1991). Labor, General corporate. Home: 12520 Arliss Dr Apt 10 Lakewood OH 44107-2148 Office: McCray Muzilla et al 940 Lorain Blvd Elyria OH 44035-2820

**SARKISIAN, ALAN HERBERT,** lawyer; b. Inglewood, Calif., Apr. 22, 1955; s. Herbert and Ann (Doramjian) S. BA in Polit. Sci., UCLA, 1977; JD, U. So. Calif., L.A., 1980. Bar: Calif. 1980, U.S. Dist. Ct. (cen. dist.) Calif. 1980, U.S. Ct. Appeals (9th cir.) 1980, U.S. Dist. Ct. (no., so. and ea. dists.) Calif. 1982. Assoc. Norby & Brodeur, Torrance, Calif., 1981-82; pvt. practice Torrance, 1982-84; assoc. Rezac & Stroud, L.A., 1984-85, Howard Hom & Assocs., L.A., 1985-88, Law Offices of Charles L. Grotts, L.A., 1988-89; pvt. practice L.A., Torrance, 1989—; personal injury arbitrator L.A. Superior Ct., 1991—. Mem. L.A. County Bar Assn. (immigration sect. 1985-88), Armenian Bar Assn. Republican. Mem. Christian Ch. Avocations: writing, stock market, sports. General corporate, Immigration, naturalization, and customs, Personal injury. Office: 3440 Torrance Blvd Ste 104 Torrance CA 90503-5805

**SARNACKI, MICHAEL THOMAS,** lawyer; b. Springfield, Mass., Nov. 13, 1965; s. Robert Michael and Jean Elizabeth S.; m. Kimberly Lynn King, Sept. 9, 1995; children: John Michael, Katherine Margaret. BA, U. Mass., Amherst, 1988; JD, We. New Eng. Coll. Law, 1992. Bar: Mass. 1992, U.S. Dist. Ct. Mass. 1994. Ptnr. Chartier, Ogan, Brady, Lukakis, Shute & Emm, Holyoke, Mass., 1992—. Mem. ABA, Mass. Bar Assn., Hampden County Bar Assn., Springfield Rugby Football Club (dir. 1994—), Elks, Am. Whitewater. Avocations: whitewater kayaking, rugby, running. Personal injury, General civil litigation, Construction. Office: 850 High St Holyoke MA 01040-3767

**SARNER, HARVEY,** lawyer; b. N.Y.C., Feb. 13, 1934; s. Michael and Lillian (Greenblatt) S.; m. Lorisanne C. Jelle, June 9, 1956; children: Kyra, Surah. BS, U. Minn., 1958, LLB, 1959. Atty., advisor Fed. Communications Commn., Washington, 1959-61; assoc. ho. counsel Am. Dental Assn., Chgo., 1961-71; atty. Sarner and Assocs., Chgo., 1971-87. Author: Dental Jurisprudence, 1968, Herman Wouk Checklist, 1994; editor SAA Dr.'s newsletter, 1972-87. Bd. dirs. Jewish Found. for Christian Rescuers, 1985—, Temple Isiah, Palm Springs, 1994—. With USN, 1951-55. Recipient Polish Pres. medal Polish Govt., 1994, Humanitarian award Am. Soc. Oral Surgeons, San Diego, 1993. Jewish. Avocations: book and antiquities collecting. Home: 701 W Panorama Rd Palm Springs CA 92262-2743

**SARNER, RICHARD ALAN,** lawyer; b. Stamford, Conn., Aug. 6, 1955; s. George and Patricia (Sloman) S.; m. Sharyn Frank, Apr. 5, 1986; children: Bryan, Lauren. BA, Dartmouth Coll., 1977; JD, Hofstra U., 1980. Bar: N.Y. 1982, U.S. Dist. Ct. (so. and ea. dists.) N.Y. 1982, U.S. Ct. Appeals (2d cir.) 1985, U.S. Dist. Ct. (no. dist.) N.Y. 1989, Conn. 1990, U.S. Dist. Ct. Conn. 1991, U.S. Supreme Ct. 1991. Assoc. Shea & Gould, N.Y.C., 1980-82, D'Amato & Lynch, N.Y.C., 1982-84, Lowenthal, Landau, Fischer & Ziegler, P.C., N.Y.C., 1984-90; sole practice Stamford, Conn., 1990—. Bd. dirs. The Stamford Mus. and Nature Ctr., 1993—; trustee King & Low-Heywood Thomas Sch., 1994—. Mem. ABA, N.Y. State Bar Assn., Conn. Bar Assn., Stamford/Norwalk Regional Bar Assn., Nat. Network Estate Planning Attys. Democrat. Estate planning, Estate taxation, Probate. Home: 122 Frost Pond Rd Stamford CT 06903-3031 Office: 184 Atlantic St Stamford CT 06901-3518

**SARNEY, SAUL RICHARD,** lawyer; b. Bklyn., Dec. 6, 1948; s. Albert Abraham and Edna (Goldstein) S. BA, Binghamton U., 1970; JD, U. Denver, 1973. Founding ptnr./shareholder Sarney, Trattler & Waitkus, PC, Denver, 1974-93; ptnr. Pelz & Sarney P.C., Denver, 1993-96; ptnr., shareholder Sarney & Pierson, PC, Denver, 1996—; guest lectr. Aurora (Co.) C.C., 1992—; seminar spkr. Profl. Edn. Syss., Inc., various seminars, programs & classes, 1976—. Past pres., bd. dirs. Diana Price Fish Found., Denver, 1993—; cornerstone ptnr. Colo. AIDS Project, Denver, 1993—. Mem. ATLA (ins., motor vehicle, profl. negligence and r.r. law sects.), Colo. Bar Assn. (chmn. interprofl. com., legal fee arbitration com.), Colo. Trial Lawyers Assn., Nebr. Trial Lawyers Assn., Denver Bar Assn. Avocations: film, cycling, scuba diving, wine, travel. Personal injury, Insurance, Professional liability. Office: Sarney & Pierson PC 950 S Cherry St Ste 918 Denver CO 80246-2666

**SARNO, MARIA ERLINDA,** lawyer, scientist; b. Manila, Philippines, July 26, 1944. BS in Chemistry magna cum laude, U. Santo Tomas, Philippines, 1967; MS in Chemistry summa cum laude, Calif. State U., Long Beach, 1975; JD cum laude, Western State U., 1993. Bar: Calif. 1994, U.S. Patent Office, 1993. Instr. U. Santo Tomas, Philippines, 1967-68; sr. chemist, analytical rsch. and quality assurance Rachelle Labs., Long Beach, Calif., 1969-74; teaching/rsch. asst. Calif. State U., Long beach, 1971-73; mgr. in charge of radioisotope section Curtis Nuclear Lab., L.A., 1974; assoc. chemist, asst. to dir. quality control Nichols Inst., San Pedro, Calif., 1974-75; mgr. rsch. and devel. Baxter Healthcare, Hyland, Calif., 1975-91; legal coord. sci. affairs Immunotherapy div. Baxter Biotech, Irvine, Calif., 1991-93, mgr. regulatory affairs, 1994-95; pvt. law practice, 1994—. *Maria Sarno posesses over 20 years of technical, managerial, industrial and academic experience. She is currently merging personal experience as a patentee with the law practice in Intellectual Property.* Editorial bd: (tech. editor) Western State U. Law Review; Contbr. articles to profl. jours.; patentee in field. Mem. ABA, Orange County Bar Assn., Los Angeles County Bar Assn., Am. Chem. Soc., Am. Intellectual Property Law Assn., Phi Kappa Phi, Phi Delta Gamma. Patent, Estate planning, General practice. Home: 12541 Kenobi Ct Cerritos CA 90703-7756

**SARNOFF, MARC DAVID,** lawyer; b. Bklyn., Dec. 28, 1959; s. Joel Sarnoff and Alaine (Katz) Stagnitta. BA, U. Tampa, 1981; JD, Loyola U., New Orleans, 1984; postgrad., Tulane U., 1985. Bar: La. 1985, Fla. 1986, U.S. Dist. Ct. (so. dist.) Fla. 1986, D.C. 1987. Assoc. Herman, Herman, Katz & Coller, New Orleans, 1984-85; asst. prosecutor Orleans Parish Dist. Atty. Office, New Orleans, 1985-86; assoc. Christenberry & D'Antoni, New Orleans, 1986-87, Law Offices of Howard D. Dillman, Miami, Fla., 1987-91; ptnr. Goldman, Moore and Sarnoff, Miami, 1991-92, Sarnoff & Bayer, Miami, 1992—. Capt. U. Tampa Swimming Team, 1978. Mem. Million Dollar Advs. Forum, Phi Delta Theta (v.p. 1980, 81). E-mail: sarnoff@ix.net.com.com. Personal injury, Admiralty, Civil rights. Home: 3197 Virginia St Miami FL 33133-4545 Office: Sarnoff & Bayer 3197 Virginia St Miami FL 33133-4545

**SAROFEEN, MICHAEL JOSEPH,** lawyer; b. Auburn, N.Y., July 15, 1953; s. John J. and Gloria A. (LaHood) S.; m. Geraldine M. Maneri, June 9, 1955; children: Shaena, Michaela, Christian. BS, Syracuse U., 1977, JD, 1980. Ptnr. Hiscock & Barclay, Syracuse, N.Y., 1980-95; ptnr., chair estate and tax dept. Devorsetz, Stinziano, Gilberti, Heintz & Smith P.C., Syracuse, 1995—; bd. advisors Syracuse U. Tax Inst. Pres. Children's Coun. of Ctrl. N.Y., Syracuse, 1983-92. Mem. N.Y. Bar Assn., Estate Planning Coun. Ctrl. N.Y. Corporate taxation, Estate planning, General corporate. Home: 4444 Stephanie Dr Manlius NY 13104-9391

**SAROKIN, H. LEE,** retired federal judge; b. Perth Amboy, N.J., Nov. 25, 1928; s. Samuel O. and Reebe (Weinblatt) S.; m. Marjorie Lang, Apr. 23, 1971; children: James Todd, Jeffrey Scott, Abby Jane. A.B., Dartmouth Coll., 1950; J.D., Harvard U., 1953. Bar: N.J. 1954. Assoc. Lasser, Lasser, Sarokin & Hochman, Newark, 1955-58; partner Lasser, Lasser, Sarokin & Hochman, 1958-79; asst. county counsel Union County, N.J., 1959-65; U.S. dist. judge Dist. of N.J., Newark, 1979-94; judge U.S. Ct. Appeals (3d cir.), Newark, 1994-96. Fellow Am. Bar Assn.; mem. Am. Law Inst.; Mem. N.J. Bar Assn., Essex County Bar Assn., Fed. Bar Assn.

**SARROUF, CAMILLE F.,** lawyer; b. North Adams, Mass., Apr. 23, 1933; m. Joyce Rahal Sarrouf; children: Camille F. Jr., Leza Marie, Thomas Kahlil, John Rahal. AB, Bowdoin Coll., 1955; LLB, U. Tex., 1960; LHD, New Eng. Sch. Law, 1980. Bar: Tex. 1960, Mass. 1961, U.S. Dist. Ct. Vt. 1961, U.S. Dist. Ct. Mass. 1962, U.S. Supreme Ct. 1980. Spl. asst. atty. gen. Commonwealth of Mass., Boston, 1961-62, spl. asst. dist. atty. Middlesex County, 1975, mem. jud. nominating commn., 1980-84; ptnr. Sarrouf, Tarricone & Flemming, Boston; adj. prof. law New Eng. Sch. Law, 1974-93; lectr., trial demonstrator CLE, law schs. and bar assns., pres. Mass. State Bar Assn. Chmn., bd. dirs. St. Jude Children's Rsch. Hosp., Memphis, 1988-90, 91-92, chmn., bd. govs., 1994-96; nat. dir. Kahlil Gibran Found., 1990-94; gen. counsel Diocese of Newton for the Melkite Caths. of the U.S., 1966—; mem. Grtr. Boston chpt. Arab-Am.-Jewish Dialogue Com., 1991-96. Recipient Papal Insigne, Pro Ecclesia et Pontifice, Pope Paul VI, 1975, Cross of Jerusalem, Patriach Maximos V. Hakin, 1983, Disting. Svc. award Nicholas G. Beram Vets. Assn., 1990; endowment honoree Camille F. Sarrouf scholarship Social Law Libr. Mass., 1990, Disting. Alumni award Wilbraham-Monson Acad., 1996, Am. ORT Jurisprudence award, 1994. Fellow Am. Bar Found., Am. Coll. Trial Lawyers (state chair for Mass. 1991-93, regent 1998), Mass. Bar Found., Roscoe Pound Found., Internat. Acad. Trial Lawyers; mem. ATLA (bd. govs. 1982-86), Mass. Acad. Trial Attys. (pres. 1986-88), Mass. Bar Assn. (treas. 1995, v.p. 1996, pres.-elect 1997, pres. 1998), Mass. Commn. Jud. Conduct, Am. Bd. Trial Advocates (advocate 1989), Am. Arabic Benevolent Assn. (founder, clk.). Office: Sarrouf Tarricone & Flemming 95 Commercial Wharf Boston MA 02110-3816

**SARROUF, CAMILLE FRANCIS, JR.,** lawyer; b. Boston, July 23, 1962; s. Camille Francis and Joyce Rahal Sarrouf; m. Sherri Laffey, Oct. 14, 1995; children: Stephen Francis, Elizabeth Grace. BS magna cum laude, Northeastern U., 1989; JD, Suffolk U., 1992. Bar: Mass. 1993, U.S. Dist. Ct. Mass. 1994. Atty. Sarrouf, Tarricone & Flemming, Boston, 1993, 95—; asst. dist. atty. Middlesex County Dist. Attys. Office, Cambridge, Mass., 1993-95. Head coach Belmont (Mass.) Youth Hockey, 1992—. Republican. Roman Catholic. Personal injury, General civil litigation, Aviation. Office: Sarrouf Tarricone & Flemming 95 Commercial Wharf Boston MA 02110-3816

**SARTAIN, JAMES EDWARD,** lawyer; b. Ft. Worth, Feb. 9, 1941; s. James F. and May Belle (Boaz) S.; m. Barbara Hardy, Aug. 17, 1962; 1 child, Bethany Sartain Hughes. BA, Tex. A&M U., 1963; LLB, Baylor U., 1966. Bar: Tex. 1966, U.S. Ct. Mil. Appeals, 1971, U.S. Dist. Ct. (no. dist.) Tex. 1974. Staff atty. Dept. Justice, Washington, 1970-72; staff atty. to U.S. Sen. William L. Scott Fairfax, Va., 1972; pvt. practice Ft. Worth, 1973—; sec. Penrose Lumber Co., Abilene, Tex., 1987—, Esprit Comm. Corp., Austin, Tex.; sec. Emerald Restoration, Inc., Abilene, Tex.; sec. Esprit Comm. Corp., Austin, Tex. Bd. dirs. Ft. Worth Boys Club, 1980-89, Oakwood Cemetery, Ft. Worth, 1979-84. Capt. arty. U.S. Army, Vietnam. Fellow Coll. State Bar Tex.; Mem. ABA, Abilene Bar Assn., Baylor Law Alumni Assn., Masons, Petroleum Club, Phi Delta Phi. Republican. Presbyterian. Consumer commercial, Contracts commercial, General corporate. Office: 6112 Mccart Ave Ste 201 Fort Worth TX 76133-3380 also: PO Box 450 Abilene TX 79604-0450

**SARTORE, JOHN THORNTON,** lawyer; b. N.Y.C., Nov. 5, 1946; s. Frank Jean and Mary Olive (Wacaser) S.; m. Sally Ann Coppersmith, Feb. 28, 1973; children: Michael, David, Delmy, Jenny. BA, Yale U., 1968; JD, Columbia U., 1971. Bar: Vt. 1972, U.S. Dist. Ct. Vt. 1972, U.S. Ct. Appeals (2d cir.) 1978, N.Y. 1989, U.S. Dist. Ct. (no. dist.) N.Y. 1992. Assoc. Paul, Frank & Collins, Inc., Burlington, Vt., 1971-74, mem., 1974—, pres., CEO, 1994—. Mem. ABA, Am. Coll. Trial Lawyers, Am. Bd. Trial Advocates, Vt. Bar Assn., N.Y. State Bar Assn., Chittenden County Bar Assn., New Eng. Legal Found. (dir.). General civil litigation, Insurance, Personal injury. Office: Paul Frank & Collins Inc One Church St Burlington VT 05402-1307

**SARZIN, EVAN,** lawyer, author; b. N.Y.C., Feb. 11, 1953; s. Clyde J. and Helen M. Sarzin; m. Melissa Cohen, May 20, 1984. BA, U. Pa., 1975; JD, U. Miami, 1978. Bar: N.Y. 1979, Fla. 1979, Pa. 1995. Assoc. Zalman & Schnurman, N.Y.C., 1978-84, ptnr., 1984-90; pvt. practice, N.Y.C., 1990—; pub. Gerard & Sarzin Pub., 1991—, Thelonious Monk 1991, Art of Jazz Trumpet 1992, Scat!, 1997. Author: Hard Bop, 1992. Avocations: sailing, music, racquet sports, history. General practice, Real property. Office: 11 Hanover Sq Fl 15 New York NY 10005-2819

**SASAKI, LARALYN MARIE,** project director, lawyer; b. Napoleon, Ohio, Dec. 8, 1963; d. Lawrence M. and Bonnie (Townsend) S. BS in Journalism, Ohio U., 1986; JD, U. Mich., 1991. Bar: Ohio 1991, U.S. Dist. Ct. Ohio 1993. Journalist The Wall Street Jour., Cleve., 1985, The L.A. Times, Washington, 1986, The Cin. Enquirer, 1987-88; jud. clk. Columbus, Ohio, 1991-93; assoc. Bricker & Eckler, Columbus, 1993-97; dir. Ohio Cts. Futures Commn. Supreme Ct. of Ohio, Columbus, 1997—. Vol. ARC. Mem. ABA, Asian Am. Bar Assn., Ohio State Bar Assn. Home and Office: 1280 City Park Ave Columbus OH 43206-3612

**SASSER, JONATHAN DREW,** lawyer; b. Monroe, N.C., Mar. 1, 1956; s. Herman Wallace and Faith Belzora (Harrington) S.; m. Debra A. Smith, Feb. 22, 1994. BA with honors, U. N.C., 1978, JD with honors, 1981. Bar: N.C. 1981, N.Y. 1983, U.S. Dist. Ct. (so. and ea. dists.) N.Y. 1983, U.S. Dist. Ct. (no. dist.) Tex. 1983, U.S. Dist. Ct. (ea. dist.) N.C. 1986, U.S. Ct. Appeals (4th cir.) 1987, U.S. Dist. Ct. (mid. dist.) N.C. 1987, U.S. Supreme Ct. 1988. Law clk. to assoc. justice N.C. Supreme Ct., Raleigh, N.C., 1981-82; assoc. Paul, Weiss, Rifkind, Wharton & Garrison, N.Y.C., 1982-86, Moore & Van Allen and predecessor firm Powe, Porter & Alphin P.A., Durham, N.C., 1986-89; ptnr. Moore & Van Allen, Raleigh, 1990—. Editor: Cellar Door, 1977-78. Dem. precinct chmn., Chapel Hill, N.C., 1976-82. John Motley Morehead Found. fellow, Chapel Hill, 1978; John Motley Morehead Found. scholar, Chapel Hill, 1974. Mem. ABA, N.C. State Bar Assn., N.C. Bar Assn., N.Y. State Bar Assn. Baptist. Avocations: running, triathlons, mountain climbing. Federal civil litigation, State civil litigation, Civil rights. Home: 311 Calvin Rd Raleigh NC 27605-1707 Office: Moore & Van Allen 1 Hannover Sq Ste 1700 Raleigh NC 27601-1761

**SASSOON, ANDRE GABRIEL,** lawyer; b. Cairo, Apr. 13, 1936; came to U.S., 1959; s. Gabriel and Sarine (Tawil) S.; m. Barbara Dee Freedman, Aug. 15, 1965; children: Daniel, Gabriel, Sarina. GCE, Oxford & Cambridge, England, 1953; JD, Villanova U., 1969; LLM, Harvard U., 1970. Bar: Pa. 1969, N.Y. 1970. Product mgr. Rohm & Haas Co., Phila., 1960-66; law clk. Dist. Atty.'s Office, Phila., 1968; assoc. Weil, Gotshal & Manges, N.Y.C., 1970-73; pvt. practice N.Y.C., 1973—; dir. elem. Youth in Distress, N.Y.C., 1982—; v.p., dir. internat. Anti-Drug Abuse Found., N.Y.C., 1987—; v.p., dir., mem. exec. com. Hebrew Immigrant Aid Soc., N.Y.C., 1977—; internat. sec., gov. bd. internat. govs. World Sephardi Fedn., N.Y.C., 1988—; co-pres., chmn., U.S. com., dir. internat. Jewish Com. for Sephardi '92, N.Y.C., 1989—; mem. N.Y. State Christopher Columbus Quincetenary Commn., Statewide Outreach Com., 1991—. Editor Villanova Law Rev.; contbr. articles to profl. jours. With USAR, 1960-66. Recipient Israel Trade award Govt. of Israel, 1985. Mem. ABA, Am. Arbitration Assn. (panel mem. 1971—), Am. Soc. Internat. Law, Order of the Coif, 0840 Internat. Pvt., 0860 Internat. Pub. Private international, Public international. Home: 888 Park Ave New York NY 10021-0235 Office: 600 Madison Ave New York NY 10022-1615

**SASTOW, GARY SAUL,** lawyer; b. Johannesburg, South Africa, Mar. 24, 1965; s. Ralph and Sarah Deborah (Isserow) Sasto; m. Elisa Dawn Engel, Aug. 5, 1990; children: Dahniel, Tamara. JD, N.Y. Law Sch., 1991. Bar: N.Y. 1992, U.S. Dist. Ct. (so. and ea. dists.) N.Y. 1992. Atty. Cooperman Levitt Winikoff Lester & Newman, PC, N.Y.C., 1996—, Menaker & Herrmann, N.Y.C., 1991-96. Mem. ABA, N.Y. State Bar Assn., Bar Assn. City N.Y., N.Y. County Lawyers Assn. Health, General corporate, General practice. Office: Cooperman Levitt Winikoff Lester & Newman PC 800 3rd Ave New York NY 10022-7604

**SATER, NAZLI G.,** lawyer; b. Alexandria, Egypt, Nov. 3, 1961; d. M. Mounir and Elweya K. Gazayerli; 1 child, Nayla. BA, Oakland U., 1982; JD, Wayne State U., 1985. Jud. rsch. atty. 6th Jud. Cir. Ct., Pontiac, Mich., 1986-88; assoc. Schefman & Miller PC, Birmingham, Mich., 1986-88, Moll, Deserkey & Beyer, 1990; shareholder Hyman and Lippitt PC, Birmingham, 1991—. Mem. State Bar Mich., Oakland County Bar Assn. (family law sect.). Family and matrimonial. Office: Hyman & Lippitt PC 185 Oakland Ave Ste 300 Birmingham MI 48009-3481

**SATINSKY, BARNETT,** lawyer; b. Phila., June 17, 1947; s. Alex and Florence (Talsky) S.; m. Fredda Andrea Wagner, June 17, 1973; children: Meagen, Sara Beth, Jonathan. AB, Brown U., 1969; JD, Villanova U., 1972. Bar: Pa. 1972, U.S. Dist. Ct. (ea. dist) Pa. 1975, U.S. Dist. Ct. (mid. dist.) Pa. 1975, U.S. Ct. Appeals (3d cir.) 1981. Law clk. Phila. Ct. Common Pleas, 1972-73; dep. atty. gen. Pa. Dept. Justice, Harrisburg, 1973-75; 1st asst. counsel Pa. Pub. Utility Commn., Harrisburg, 1975-77, chief counsel, 1977; assoc. Fox, Rothschild, O'Brien & Frankel, LLP, Phila., 1978-81; ptnr. Fox, Rothschild, O'Brien & Frankel, Phila., 1981—. Children Svcs. Rev. com., United Way Southeast Pa., 1984-86; bd. dirs. ACLU, Harrisburg, 1973-74, Voyage House, Inc., 1994-96. Mem. ABA (pub. utility, labor and employment law sects., employee benefits com. 1984—), Pa. Bar Assn. (labor rels., pub. utility law sects. 1980—, pub. utility law com., governing coun. 1991-93), Phila. Bar Assn. (labor law com. 1980—, chmn. pub. utility law com. 1988-91), Nat. Assn. Coll. and Univ. Attys., Nat. Assn. Regulatory Commrs. (staff subcom. law 1977), Soc. for Human Resource Mgmt., Tau Epsilon Law Soc. Democrat. Jewish. Labor, Public utilities, Civil rights. Office: Fox Rothschild O'Brien & Frankel LLP 2000 Market St Philadelphia PA 19103-3231

**SATO, GLENN KENJI,** lawyer; b. Honolulu, Jan. 6, 1952; s. Nihei and Katherine (Miwa) S.; m. Donna Mae Shiroma, Apr. 4, 1980 (dec. Aug. 1985); m. Nan Sun Oh, Mar. 27, 1987 (dec. Nov. 1997); children: Gavan, Allison, Garrett. BBA, U. Hawaii, 1975; JD, U. Calif., San Francisco, 1977. Bar: Hawaii 1978, U.S. Dist. Ct. Hawaii, 1978, U.S. Ct. Claims 1990. Assoc. Fujiyama, Duffy & Fujiyama, Honolulu, 1978-80, 83-87, ptnr., 1987-95; stockholder Law Offices of Glenn K. Sato, Honolulu, 1980-82; pres. ISL Svcs., Inc., Honolulu, 1983; ptnr. Sato & Thomas, Honolulu, 1995-98; pvt. practice Honolulu, 1998—; vice chmn. Pattern Jury Instrn. Com., State of Hawaii, Honolulu, 1993. *In twenty years of practicing trial law, Mr. Sato has tried many multi-million dollar cases. In 1990 and 1991, he tried two cases for six months and won both cases.* Treas. Polit. Action Com., Honolulu, 1993. mem. Platform Assn., Beta Gamma Sigma. Avocations: golf, hunting, target shooting, surfing. General civil litigation, Consumer commercial, Contracts commercial. Office: 1001 Bishop St Ste 770 Honolulu HI 96813-3429

**SATOLA, JAMES WILLIAM,** lawyer; b. Cleve., Aug. 26, 1961; s. William John and Catherine Ann (Recek) S. BS in Zoology, Ohio State U., 1984; JD, Case Western Reserve U., 1989. Bar: Ohio 1989, U.S. Dist. Ct. (no. dist.) Ohio 1990, D.C. 1991, U.S. Ct. Appeals (6th cir.) 1992, U.S. Supreme Ct. 1993, U.S. Dist. Ct. Ariz. 1997. Med. rsch. asst. I U. Hosps. of Cleve., 1985-86; law clk to judge John M. Manos U.S. Dist. Ct. (no. dist.) Ohio, Cleve., 1989-91; assoc. Squire, Sanders & Dempsey, Cleve., 1991—. Articles editor Case Western Reserve Law Rev., Cleve., 1988-89. Mem. Celebrezze Inn of Ct., Fed. Bar Assn. (sec., bd. dirs. no. dist. Ohio chpt.). Republican. Avocations: art, music, golf, landscaping. General civil litigation, Condemnation, Federal civil litigation. Home: 2608 Dysart Rd Cleveland Hts OH 44118-4409 Office: Squire Sanders & Dempsey LLP 4900 Key Tower 127 Public Sq Cleveland OH 44114-1216

**SATOVSKY, STACEY YAEL,** lawyer; b. Huntington, N.Y., Nov. 10, 1970; d. Gerald and Mili Finger; m. Jonathan Matthew Satovsky, May 26, 1996. AB, U. Mich., 1992; JD, Fordham U., 1995. Bar: N.Y. 1996. Assoc. Skadden, Arps, Slate, Meagher & Fion, N.Y.C., 1995-97; atty. Instinet Corp., N.Y.C., 1997—. Mem. Order of Coif. Contracts commercial, General corporate. Home: 257 Central Park W Apt 3D New York NY 10024-4108 Office: Instinet Corp 875 3rd Ave New York NY 10022-6225

**SATRAN, EDWARD SAUL,** lawyer; b. Bklyn., May 28, 1941; s. Abraham and Miriam Satran; m. Diane Chatlinoff, Mar. 27, 1965; children: Scott (dec. Mar. 1987), Robert. BBA, CCNY, 1962; JD, Columbia U., 1965. Bar: N.Y. 1995. Atty. trainee MABSTOA (NYCTA), N.Y.C., 1965-66; prin. app ct. atty. App Term 2nd Dept., N.Y.C., 1996—. Pres. Jud. Unit Local 101 Civil Svc. Employees Assn., N.Y.C., 1985—, Young Israel Oceanside, N.Y., 1987-89. Republican. Jewish. Avocations: tennis, high school basketball referee. Home: 44 Irma Dr Oceanside NY 11572-5717

**SATTER, RAYMOND NATHAN,** judge; b. Denver, Oct. 19, 1948; s. Charles Herbert and Muriel Vera (Tuller); m. Suzanne Elizabeth Ehlers, May 28, 1977. BA, U. Denver, 1970; JD, Cath. U., 1973. Bar: Colo. 1973, U.S. Dist. Ct. Colo. 1973, U.S. Ct. Appeals (10th cir.) 1973, U.S. Supreme Ct. 1976, U.S. Tax Ct. 1981. Assoc. Wallace, Armatas & Hahn, Denver, 1973-75; ptnr. Tallmadge, Wallace & Hahn, Denver, 1975-77; pvt. practice Denver, 1978-87; Denver County judge, 1987—; gen. counsel Satter Dist., Denver, 1977-78; assoc. mcpl. judge City of Englewood, Colo., 1985-86; mem. Colo. Supreme Ct. Com. on Civil Rules. Pres. Young Artists Orch. Denver, 1985-87; sec. Denver Symphony Assn., 1985-86. Mem. Colo. Bar Assn. (ethics com.), Denver Bar Assn. (bd. trustees 1998—, Jud. Excellence award 1992, 95). Avocations: sailing, opera, classical music, fishing, bridge. Office: Denver County Ct 108 City & County Bldg 1437 Bannock St Denver CO 80202-5337

**SATTERLEE, TERRY JEAN,** lawyer; b. Kansas City, Mo., Aug. 28, 1948; d. Charles Woodbury and Francis Jean (Shriver) S.; m. William W. Rice, Jan. 9, 1982; children: Cassandra Jean Rice, Mary Shannon Rice. BA, Kans. U., 1970; JD, U. Mo., 1974. Bar: Mo. 1974. Lawyer Arthur Benson Assocs., Kansas City, Mo., 1974-77, Freilich & Leitner, Kansas City, 1977-78, U.S. Environ. Protection Agy., Kansas City, 1978-83; of counsel Lathrop & Norquist, Kansas City, 1985-87, ptnr., 1987—, mem. exec. com., 1997-98. Contbr. articles to profl. jours. Chmn. Bd. Zoning Adjustment, Kansas City, 1983-87, Mo. State Pks Adv. Bd., 1997; Kansas City Hazardous Materials com; campaign com. Jackson County Exec; steering com. COMPASS Met. Planning, Kansas City, 1990-93. Mem. Mo. Bar Assn. (chair environ. com. 1990-93), Kansas City Bar Assn. (environ. com. chmn. 1986-90), Mo. C. of C. (natural resource coun. 1990-96, bd. dirs. 1997—), Kansas City C. of C. (environ. com. chmn. 1992), Women's Pub. Svc. Network. Democrat. Episcopalian. Environmental, Real property, Administrative and regulatory. Office: Lathrop & Gage 2345 Grand Blvd Ste 2500 Kansas City MO 64108-2603

**SATTERWHITE, HARRY VINCENT,** lawyer, writer; b. Columbus, Miss., Jan. 15, 1963; s. Gordon Andrew and Rosalyn Kathleen (Moore) S.; m. Aline Jackson Martin, Dec. 12, 1987; children: Harry Vincent Jr., Jackson Martin. BA, U. Ala., Tuscaloosa, 1985, MA, 1991, JD, 1994. Bar: Ala. 1994, Fla. 1997, Miss. 1997, U.S. Dist. Ct. (so. and no. dists.) Ala. 1994, U.S. Dist. Ct. (no., mid. and so. dists.) Fla. 1997, U.S. Dist. Ct. (no. and so. dists.) Miss. 1997, U.S. Ct. Appeals (11th cir.) 1994, U.S. Ct. Appeals (5th cir.) 1997, U.S. Supreme Ct. 1998. Reporter, photographer Foley (Ala.) Onlooker, 1985-86, Tuscaloosa News, 1986-91; assoc. Gillion, Brooks and Hamby, P.C., Mobile, Ala., 1994-96, Brooks and Hamby, P.C., Mobile, 1996-98, Janecky Newell, P.C., Mobile, 1998—. Author: Alabama's Open Meetings Law, 1991. Mem. Kappa Tau Alpha. Roman Catholic. Avocations: writing, photography, golf. General civil litigation, Insurance, Franchising. Office: Janecky Newell PC AmSouth Bank Bldg 107 Saint Francis St Ste 3300 Mobile AL 36602-3334

**SATURLEY, ELLEN MCLAUGHLIN,** lawyer; b. Boston, Sept. 4, 1955; d. George A. Jr. and Elizabeth L. McLaughlin; m. William C. Saturley, Oct. 29, 1978; children: Kathryn K., Jessica E. BA, Dartmouth Coll., 1977; JD, Boston Coll., 1980. Bar: N.H. 1980, Mass. Assoc. Hamblett & Kerrigan, P.A., Nashua, N.H., 1980-85; dir. Hamblett & Kerrigan, P.A., 1985-87, Deasy & Dwyer, P.A., 1988-96; of counsel McLaughlin Bros., L.L.P., Boston, 1997—. Bd. dirs. Cmty. Hospice Greater Nashua, Home Health & Hospice Care, Nashua. Mem. ABA (membership chair young lawyers divsn.), N.H. Bar Assn. (chair new lawyers com.). General civil litigation, Condemnation, Professional liability. Office: McLaughlin Bros LLP 28 State St Fl 31 Boston MA 02109-1775

**SAUER, ELISABETH RUTH,** lawyer; b. Charleston, W.Va., July 27, 1948; d. Gordon Chenoweth and Mary Louise (Steinhilber) S. B.A., Northwestern U., 1970; J.D., U. Mo., 1975. Bar: Mo. 1975. Assoc. Campbell, Erickson, Cottingham, Morgan & Gibson, Kansas City, Mo., 1975-80, ptnr., 1980-88; ptnr. Lashly Baer & Hamel, P.C., 1989-91; of counsel Swanson, Midgley, Gangwere, Clark & Kitchin, 1991-93; mem., owner Elisabeth R. Sauer, P.C., Kansas City, 1994—. Bd. dirs. Kansas City Met. Regional Com. on Status of Women, 1976-78; trustee UMKC Conservatory for Music. Mem. ABA, Mo. Bar Assn., Kansas City Bar Assn., Assn. Women Lawyers of Greater Kansas City, Nat. Women's Law Ctr., Internat. Assn. Ins. Receivers, Rockhill Tennis-Kenwood Club. General civil litigation, Insurance, Alternative dispute resolution. Office: 802 Broadway St Fl 2D Kansas City MO 64105-1507

**SAUERS, WILLIAM DALE,** lawyer, playwright; b. Santa Cruz, Calif., June 18, 1926; s. Myrl Melvin and Helen (Fightmaster) S.; m. Barbara Gean Cole, May 9, 1945; children: Kathleen McCarty, Deborah Nelson, Susan Reeves. AB, Fresno State U., 1949; JD, Stanford U., 1952. Bar: Calif. 1953, U.S. Dist. Ct. (no. dist.) Calif. 1953, U.S. Ct. Appeals (9th cir.) 1953, U.S. Supreme Ct. 1964. Asst. sec. State Bar of Calif., San Francisco, 1952-55; dep. dist. atty. County of Santa Clara, San Jose, Calif., 1955-58; ptnr. Finch, Sauers et al., Palo Alto, Calif., 1958-88; pvt. practice law Palo Alto, Calif., 1988—. Playwright: A Rainbow on Mt. Olympus, 1993, Did Not I Dance with You?, 1994, A Fork in the Road, 1995, What'll We Do With Mama, 1996. Sec. Urban Coaliton of Palo Alto, 1969-72; chmn. ARC chpt. Palo Alto, Calif., 1973-76, Family Svc. Assn., 1973-76, Sr. Coun. Affiliates, Palo Alto, 1981-85; chmn. bd. trustees Menlo Coll., Atherton, Calif., 1984-88;, dir. Oreg. Shakespeare estival, Ashland, 1989-95; pres. San Jose Repertory Theatre, 1989-91; chmn. San Francisco Shakespeare Festival, 1994-98. Mem. ABA, Calif. State Bar Assn., Phi Delta Phi. Republican. Episcopalian. Avocations: skiing, tennis, golf, fly fishing, back packing. General corporate, Mergers and acquisitions, Real property. Office: Hamilton Dolton & Sauers Ste 104 90 Middlefield Rd Menlo Park CA 94025-3510

**SAUFER, ISAAC AARON,** lawyer; b. Bronx, N.Y., June 16, 1953; s. Solomon and Beatrice (Kanofsky) S.; m. Debra Edith Goldberg, June 26, 1977; children: Suzanne, Nancy, Scott, Daniel, Jonathan. BA, Yeshiva U., N.Y.C., 1975; JD, Bklyn. Law Sch., 1978; LLM in Taxation, NYU, 1982. Bar: N.Y. 1979, N.J. 1986, Fla. 1986, Conn. 1987. Summer intern N.Y. County Dist. Attys. Office, N.Y.C., 1976; legal editor Prentice-Hall, Inc., Englewood Cliffs, N.Y., 1979-80; assoc. Kurzman Karelsen & Frank, LLP, N.Y.C., 1980-85, ptnr., 1986—; adj. assoc. prof. NYU Sch. Continuing and Profl. Studies, N.Y.C., 1988—; lectr. seminars, 1991, 93, 95, 97. Co-author: (N.Y. real property forms) Bergerman & Roth, 1986-87. Estate planning, Probate, Estate taxation. Office: Kurzman Karelsen & Frank LLP 230 Park Ave Rm 2300 New York NY 10169-0061

**SAUFLEY, LEIGH INGALLS,** state supreme court justice; m. William Saufley; 2 children. Grad., Maine Sch. Law. Pvt. practice Ellsworth; asst. counsel U.S. VA; asst., then dep. atty. gen. Maine, 1981-90; justice Maine Supreme Jud. Ct., 1997—. Office: Cumberland County Courthouse PO Box 368 142 Federal St Portland ME 04112-0368*

**SAUL, IRVING ISAAC,** lawyer; b. Washington, Pa., July 9, 1929; s. Israel Jacob and Jennie (Green) S.; m. Lita Brown, Dec. 29, 1950; children: Joanne Ilene, Sandra Lynn. BA, Washington and Jefferson Coll., 1949; LLB, U. Pitts., 1952; postgrad. Georgetown U., 1949, Ohio State U., 1951. Bar: Ohio 1952, U.S. Supreme Ct. 1961, U.S. Ct. Appeals (6th cir.) 1966, U.S. Ct. Appeals (7th cir.) 1978, U.S. Ct. Appeals (4th cir.) 1978, U.S. Ct. Appeals (fed. cir.) 1991, U.S. Dist. Ct. (so. dist.) Ohio 1954, U.S. Dist. Ct. (no. dist.) Ohio 1967, U.S. Dist. Ct. (ea. dist.) Wis. 1973. Pvt. practice, Dayton, Ohio, 1952—; cons. in antitrust litigation; bd. advs. Fed. Civil Practice Abstracts, 1986-88, Ohio Dist. Ct. Rev., 1988—; adj. prof. complex litigation Sch. of Law U. Dayton; lectr. in field. James Gillespie Blaine scholar, 1948. Mem. Ohio Bar Assn. (chmn. fed. cts. and practice com. 1977-79, chmn. pvt. enforcement com. 1979-92, bd. govs. antitrust sect. 1982-94), Dayton Bar Assn. (chmn. fed. ct. practice com. 1976-77, 78-80, chmn. com. on judiciary 1987-88), Am. Judicature Soc., Phi Beta Kappa. Jewish. Lodge: Masons (Shriner). Contbr. articles to profl. jours. Antitrust, Federal civil litigation, State civil litigation. Office: 113 Bethpolamy Ct Dayton OH 45415-2512

**SAUNDERS, BRYAN LESLIE,** lawyer; b. Newport News, Va., Apr. 18, 1945; s. Raymond Hayes and Lois Mae (Pair) S.; divorced; children: Kelly Brooke, Justin Lee; m. Anne Mason Dunbar, July 15, 1995. BS, East Tenn. State U., 1967; JD, U. Tenn., 1973. Bar: Va. 1973, U.S. Dist. Ct. (ea. dist.) Va. 1973, U.S. Ct. Appeals (4th cir.) 1991. Lawyer Cogdill & Assocs., Newport News, Va., 1973-76; pvt. practice Newport News, 1976—; commr. in chancery Cir. Ct. of Newport News, 1990-97. Sgt. U.S. Army, 1968-71. Decorated Bronze star, 1971; recipient Outstanding Svc. to Law Enforcement Newport News and Police Dept., 1986. Mem. Va. Bar Assn., Nat. Assn. Criminal Def. Lawyers, Va. Coll. Criminal Def. Attys., Pi Kappa Phi, Pi Gamma Mu. Avocations: chess, bridge, bowling. Criminal, Juvenile, General practice. Office: 728 Thimble Shoals Blvd Ste C Newport News VA 23606-4546

**SAUNDERS, GEORGE LAWTON, JR.,** lawyer; b. Mulga, Ala., Nov. 8, 1931; s. George Lawton and Ethel Estell (York) S.; children: Kenneth, Ralph, Victoria; m. Terry M. Rose. B.A., U. Ala., 1956; J.D., U. Chgo., 1959. Bar: Ill. 1960. Law clk. to chief judge U.S. Ct. Appeals (5th cir.), Montgomery, Ala., 1959-60; law clk to Justice Hugo L. Black U.S. Supreme Ct., Washington, 1960-62; assoc. Sidley & Austin, Chgo., 1962-67, ptnr., 1967-90; founding ptnr. Saunders & Monroe, Chgo., 1990—. With USAF, 1951-54. Fellow Am. Coll. Trial Lawyers; mem. ABA, Ill. State Bar Assn., Chgo. Bar Assn., Order of Coif, Chgo. Club, Tavern Club, Point-O'Woods Club, Quadrangle Club, Law Club, Legal Club, Phi Beta Kappa. Democrat. Baptist. General practice, Antitrust, Administrative and regulatory. Home: 179 E Lake Shore Dr Chicago IL 60611-1306 Office: Saunders & Monroe 1600 NBC Tower 455 N Cityfront Plaza Dr Chicago IL 60611-5314

**SAUNDERS, JEFFREY N.,** lawyer; b. Indpls., Aug. 23, 1959; s. Norman Collier and Margaret (Harvey) S.; m. Karol Kimpston, July 6, 1991; children: Andrew, Robert, Nathan. BA, Gustavus Adolphus Coll., 1981; JD, U. Minn., 1985. Bar: Minn. 1981. Assoc. Winthrop & Weinstine, P.A., St. Paul, 1985-90; devel. dir. Boy Scouts Am., St. Paul, 1990-92; shareholder Henson & Efron, P.A., Mpls., 1992-98; ptnr. Lindquist & Vennum, PLLP, Mpls., 1998—; bd. dirs. Medbasics, Inc., Kansas City, Kans., Transview Corp., Mpls. Bd. dirs. Edina Rotary Found., 1997—; vol., endowment com. Boy Scouts Am., St. Paul, 1992—. Mem. Edina-Morningside Rotary Club. Episcopalian. Avocations: golf, sailing, skiing. Mergers and acquisitions, Securities, Finance. Home: 4614 Bruce Ave Edina MN 55424-1123 Office: Lindquist & Vennum PLLP 4200 IDS Center Minneapolis MN 55402

**SAUNDERS, JENNIFER KAY,** lawyer; b. Columbus, Ohio, Oct. 25, 1958; d. Julio A. and Jean E. Ayulo; m. Matthew J. Saunders, May 17, 1986; children: Katie Jean, Duke William. AA, Marymount Coll.; BS, Calif. State U., Long Beach; JD, Southwestern U., 1984. Bar: Calif. 1985. Ptnr. Haight, Brown & Bonesteel, Santa Monica, Calif., 1984—. Professional liability. Office: Haight Brown & Bonesteel PO Box 680 Santa Monica CA 90406-0680

**SAUNDERS, LONNA JEANNE,** lawyer, newscaster, talk show host; b. Cleve.; d. Jack Glenn and Lillian Frances (Newman) Slaby. Student, Dartmouth Coll.; AB in Polit. Sci. with hons., Vassar Coll.; JD, Northwestern U., 1981; cert. advanced study in Mass Media, Stanford U., 1992. Bar: Ill. 1981. News dir., morning news anchor Sta. WKBK-AM, Keene, N.H., 1974-75; reporter Sta. KDKA-AM, Pitts., 1975; pub. affairs dir., news anchor Sta. WJW-AM, Cleve., 1975-76; helicopter traffic reporter WERE-AM Radio, Cleve., 1976-77; morning news anchor Sta. WBBG-AM, Cleve., 1978; talk host, news anchor Sta. WIND-AM, Chgo., 1978-82; atty. Arvey, Hodes, Costello & Burman, Chgo., 1981-82; host, "The Stock Market Observer", news anchor WCIU-TV, Chgo., 1982-85; staff atty. Better Govt. Assn., Chgo., 1983-84; news anchor, reporter Sta. WBMX-FM, Chgo., 1984-86; pvt. practice, Chgo., 1985—; news anchor Sta. WKQX-FM, Chgo., 1987; instr. Columbia Coll., Chgo., 1987-90; guest talk host Sta. WMCA, N.Y.C., 1983, Sta. WMAQ, Chgo., 1988, Sta. WLS, Chgo., 1989, Sta. WWWE, Cleve., 1989, Sta. KVI, Seattle, 1994, WCBM-AM, Balt., 1996, WRC-AM, Wash., D.C., 1997; host, prodr. The Lively Arts, Cablevision Chgo., 1986; talk show host The Lonna Saunders Show, Sta. KIRO-AM, Seattle, 1995-96; news anchor, WTOP-AM Radio, Washington, D.C., 1996-97; talk host, "Today and Tomorrow show", WMAL-AM radio, Washington, D.C., 1997, freelance reporter, CBS Radio Network, N.Y.C., 1995—; writer, General Media, N.Y.C., 1996—; atty. Lawyers for Creative Arts, Chgo., 1985-91. Columnist Chgo. Life mag., 1986—; editl. bd. Jour. Criminal Law and Criminology, 1979-81; contbr. articles to profl. jours.; creator pub. affairs program WBBM-AM, Chgo., 1985. Recipient Akron Press Club award for best pub. affairs presentation, 1978; grantee Scripps Howard Found., 1978-81; AFTRA George Heller Meml. scholar, 1980-81. Fellow Am. Bar Found.; mem. ABA (mem. exec. coms. Lawyers and the Arts, Law and Media 1986-92, chmn. exec. com. Law and Media 1990-91, 91-92, Young Lawyers divsn. liaison to Forum Com. on Communications Law 1991-93, Commn. for Partnership Programs 1993-94, regional divsn. chair Forum on Communications Law 1995-96). Roman Catholic. Avocations: theater, piano, baseball. Entertainment, Libel.

**SAUNDERS, MARK A.,** lawyer; b. N.Y.C., July 9, 1946; s. Phillip George and Florence (Schell) S.; m. Paula Squillante, Sept. 2, 1972; children: David Prescott, Christina Joy. BA cum laude, Fordham U., 1968; JD, U. Va.-Charlottesville, 1972. Bar: N.Y. 1973, U.S. Dist. Ct. (so. dist.) N.Y. 1973, U.S. Ct. Appeals (2d cir.) 1974, U.S. Ct. Appeals (D.C. Cir.) 1987, U.S. Supreme Ct., 1987. Ptnr. Holland & Knight, N.Y.C.; counsel to corp. fin. and mergers acquisition depts. Morgan Stanley & Co. Inc., 1975-80; mem. fac. Internat. Law Inst., Washington, 1985—; mem. comparative law delegation to govt. of People's Rep. of China, 1986; gen. counsel Softstrip Internat. Ltd. subs. Eastman Kodak Co., 1987. Author: American Depositary Receipts: An Introduction to U.S. Capital Markets For Foreign Companies, 1993, Fordham Internat. Law Jour., 1993; mng. bd. editors: Va. Jour. Internat. Law, 1971-72; cons. editor China Banking & Finance, 1988-92; mem. adv. bd. The Southwestern Legal Found. Recipient Jervey Fellowship in Fgn. and Comparative Law, Columbia U. Parker Sch. Internat. Law, 1972. Fellow Am. Coll. Investment Counsel; mem. ABA (coms. fed. securities, regulation & internat. securities matters & foreign investment in the U.S.), Assn. of Bar of City of N.Y., Internat. Bar Assn., Legatus (pres. N.Y.C. chpt.), Phi Beta Kappa. Roman Catholic. Securities, General corporate, Private international. Home: 3 Nutmeg Dr Greenwich CT 06831-3211 Office: Holland & Knight 195 Broadway New York NY 10007-3100

**SAUNDERS, PAMELA RUTH,** lawyer, mediator; b. Portsmouth, Va., Sept. 22, 1955; d. Jerald Allen and Rose Ann (Russell) S.; m. Thomas F. Selleys, Jr., 1995. BA, U. Minn., 1977; JD cum laude, William Mitchell Coll. Law, 1981. Bar: Minn., 1981. Assoc. Dorsey and Whitney, Mpls., 1981-87; pvt. practice St. Paul, 1988-89, Mpls., 1989-90; atty. U.S. Dept. Vet. Affairs, Mpls., 1990—; bd. dirs. Rock Lake Mfg., Inc. Mem. Legal Advice Clinics, Ltd., Mpls., 1982-90; mediator Minn. Human Rights Dept. Project. Recipient Am. Jurisprudence awards, 1978, 80; named "Hot" Atty. of Yr., VA, 1995, Friend of Social Work, 1996; recipient Hammer award 1996, Partnership award 1997. Mem. ABA, Minn. State Bar Assn., Am. Health Lawyers Assn., Hennepin County Bar Assn. Democrat. Avocations: swimming, reading, computers. Health, Alternative dispute resolution, Labor. Office: US Dept Vet Affairs Va Med Ctr 1 Veterans Dr Minneapolis MN 55417

**SAUNDERS, RICHARD R.,** lawyer; b. Washington, May 15, 1951; s. Richard R. and Audrey H. Saunders; m. E. Dianne Saunders, Sept. 11, 1976; children: Tyler R., Daniel H., Jesse H. BA, Princeton U., 1973; JD, U. Richmond, 1976. Assoc. Kuykendall, Whiting, Costello & Hanes, Leesburg, Va., 1976-82; ptnr. Hanes, Sevila, Saunders & McCahill, Leesburg, 1982-86, Sevila, Saunders & McCahill, Leesburg, 1986-98, Sevila, Saunders, Huddleston & White, Leesburg, 1998—; mem. ethics com. Va. State Bar, 1985-87; pres. Loudoun County Bar Assn., Leesburg, 1988. Mem. Va. Trial Lawyers Assn. General civil litigation, Family and matrimonial. Office: Sevila Saunders Huddleston & White PC 30 N King St Leesburg VA 20176-2818

**SAUNDERS, ROBERT M.,** lawyer; b. N.Y.C., July 31, 1959; s. Herbert L. and Loretta (Tymon) S.; m. Cheryl D. Lambek, Nov. 6, 1988; children: David, Dana. BA, SUNY, Buffalo, 1980; JD, U. Chgo., 1983. Bar: N.Y. 1984, U.S. Dist. Ct. (so. and ea. dist.) N.Y. 1988. Assoc. LeBoeuf, Lamb, Leiby & MacRae, N.Y.C., 1983-86, Brown & Wood, N.Y.C., 1986-88; assoc. Willkie Farr & Gallagher, N.Y.C., 1988-92, spl. counsel, 1993—. Bankruptcy. Office: Willkie Farr & Gallagher One Citicorp Ctr 787 7th Ave Lbby 2 New York NY 10019-6018

**SAUNDERS, TERRY ROSE,** lawyer; b. Phila., July 13, 1942; d. Morton M. and Esther (Hauptman) Rose; m. George Lawton Saunders Jr., Sept. 21, 1975. BA, Barnard Coll., 1964; JD, NYU, 1973. Bar: D.C. 1973, Ill. 1976, U.S. Dist. Ct. (no. dist.) Ill. 1976, U.S. Ct. Appeals (7th cir.) 1976, U.S. Supreme Ct. 1983. Assoc. Williams & Connolly, Washington, 1973-75; assoc. Jenner & Block, Chgo., 1975-80, ptnr., 1981-86; ptnr. Susman, Saunders & Buehler, Chgo., 1987-94; pvt. practice Law Offices of Terry Rose Saunders, Chgo., 1995—. Author: (with others) Securities Fraud: Litigating Under Rule 10b-5, 1989. Recipient Robert B. McKay award NYU Sch. Law. Mem. ABA (co-chair class actions and derivative suits com. sect. litigation 1992-95, task force on merit selection of judges), Ill. State Bar Assn., Chgo. Bar Assn., NYU Alumni Assn. (bd. dirs. 1985—), Order of Coif, Union League Club. Federal civil litigation, General civil litigation. Office: 30 N La Salle St Chicago IL 60602-2590

**SAUNTRY, SUSAN SCHAEFER,** lawyer; b. Bangor, Maine, May 7, 1943; d. William Joseph and Emily Joan (Guenter) Schaefer; m. John Philip Sauntry, Jr., Aug. 18, 1968 (div. Jan. 1998); 1 child, Mary Katherine. BS in Fgn. Svc., Georgetown U., 1965, JD, 1975. Bar: D.C. 1975, U.S. Dist. Ct. D.C. 1975, U.S. Ct. Appeals (D.C. cir.) 1975, (4th cir.) 1977, (6th cir.) 1978, (10th cir.) 1983, U.S. Supreme Ct. 1983. Congl. relations asst. OEO, Washington, 1966-68; program analyst EEO Com., Washington, 1968-70, U.S. Dept. Army, Okinawa, 1970-72; assoc. Morgan, Lewis & Bockius, Washington, 1975-83, ptnr., 1983-94; of counsel Howe, Anderson & Steyer, PC, Washington, 1994—. Co-author: Employee Dismissal Law: Forms and Procedures, 1986; contbr. articles to profl. jours. Mem. ABA, D.C. Bar Assn., D.C. Women's Bar Assn., Nat. Assn. Women Bus. Owners, AAUW, Phi Beta Kappa, Pi Sigma Alpha. Democrat. Labor. Office: Ste 1050 1747 Pennsylvania Ave NW Washington DC 20006-4604

**SAUVEY, DAVID R.,** lawyer; b. Algoma, Wis., Oct. 14, 1954; s. Raymond Norbert Sauvey and Joan F. Smits; m. Marian Weilert, Aug. 7, 1976; children: Gretchen, Peter, Carl, Philip. BA, Rockhurst Coll., 1976; JD, U. Mo., Kansas City, 1980. Bar: Mo. 1980, U.S. Dist. Ct. (we. dist.) Mo. 1980, Wis. 1984, U.S. Dist. Ct. (ea. dist.) Wis. 1984, Ind. 1993, U.S. Dist. Ct. (so. dist.) Ind. 1993, U.S. Ct. Appeals (8th cir.) 1997. Assoc. Smith, Gill, Fisher & Butts, Kansas City, 1980-82, Leon G. Kusnetsky, P.C., Kansas City, 1983; ptnr. Condon & Sauvey, Green Bay, Wis., 1984-86; litig. counsel Schneider Nat., Inc., Green Bay, 1986-92; ptnr. Kightlinger & Gray, Evansville, Ind., 1993—. Chmn. Bd. Zoning Appeals, Allouez, Wis., 1986-93. Mem. Transp. Lawyers Assn., Def. Rsch. Inst., Trucking Industry Def. Assn. (founder, pres. 1993—, Founder's award 1997), Def. Trial Counsel Ind. (chmn. transp. law com.), Ind. Motor Truck Assn., Alpha Phi Omega. Avocations: golfing, reading, music, bicycling, football. Transportation, General civil litigation, Labor. Office: Kightlinger & Gray 19 NW 4th St Ste 400 Evansville IN 47708-1795

**SAVAGE, JAMES CATHEY, III,** lawyer; b. Nashville, June 26, 1947; s. James C. Jr. and Mary (Estes) S.; m. Annette Egan, Aug. 5, 1975 (div.); children: Sean Patrick, Catriona Sarah; m. Clara Parra, Nov. 25, 1986; children: James C. IV, Anthony Joseph. BS, Austin Peay St. U., 1968; JD, Memphis State U., 1973; MS in Criminal Justice, Troy State U., 1977; LLM, John Marshall Law Sch., 1978, Georgetown U., 1981; Diploma of Program Mgmt., Def. Sys. Mgmt. Coll., 1997; LLD (hon.), North Tenn. Bible Inst., 1981. Bar: Tenn. 1973, U.S. Supreme Ct. 1977, D.C. 1981, Md. 1982; cert. tchr. Commd. 1st lt. U.S. Army, 1973, advanced through grades to lt. col, 1988; enlisted ranger and edn. dir. U.S. Army, Vietnam, 1969-70; ins. adjuster Tenn. Co., Molloy & Leary, Bituminious Casualty, 1971-73; judge adv. U.S. Army, Ga., Germany, 1973-77; vets. and contracts atty. V.A. Gen. Counsel, Washington, 1978-82; fgn. mil. sales atty. USAF Electronic Systems Ctr., Hanscom AFB, Mass., 1983-86; chief counsel U.S. Army Materials Tech. Lab, Watertown, Mass., 1986-92, U.S. Army Rsch. Lab, Watertown, Mass., 1992-95; sr. atty. Soldier Sys. Command, Natick, Mass., 1995-98; civilian mem. Army Acquisition Corps, 1995—; army reserve asst. counsel Defense Contract Mgmt., Boston, 1992-97; ret. Soldier Biol. and Chem. Command, 1998; chief gen. and labor law U.S. Army Soldiers Biol. Chem. Command, Natick, 1998—; adj. prof. City Colls. Chgo., Troy State U., Phillips Coll., John Marshall Law Sch., Middlesex, C.C., U. of Andes, 1974-92. Weekly show host Assembly (BCAT-TV), Burlington, Mass., 1989-93; contbr. articles to profl. jours. Bd. dirs. Metro West Habitat for Humanity, 1997-98; dep. dir. Internat. Rescue Com./Army Res. Project Resettlement for Refugees, Washington, 1980-82; canvasser Am. Heart Assn., Burlington, 1989-92; lay min. Christian Chs., 1974—; chmn. bd. deacons, mem. pastor/parish, pers., parish counsel and nomination coms. Burlington Congl. Ch., 1986-95, 1st Congl. Ch., Natick, 1995—, missions com., 1997—; mem. Christian Legal Soc., 1980—, Inst. Religion and Democracy, 1980—; corp. mem. United Ch. Bd. World Ministries, 1993—, recording sec., 1996—; active Christian Mil. Fellowship, 1984—; comdr., exec. officer New Eng. Selective Svc. Sys., 1986-92; officer Christian Fellowship, 1988—; mem. Cultural Coun. and Cable TV Adv. Bd., Town of Burlington; mem. Cable TV Adv. Bd., Town of Natick; mem. adv. bd. Hanscom Fed. Credit Union, 1999; lt. col. civil air patrol CAP Group I Mass., 1988-93. Decorated Bronze Star and 25 other mil. medals; named Mass. Citizen of Yr. Am. Legion, 1985; recipient Exceptional Profl. award, 1985, Excellence in Govt. and Outstanding Cmty. Svc. awards, Boston, 1987, 92, Fed. Exec. Bd., mil., edn. and cmty. svc. recognition resolution Mass. Ho. of Reps., 1992, Sustained Superior Performance award USG, 1983-99. Mem. FBA (nat. chmn. internat. procurement com. 1985-88, vice-chmn. 1979-90, past pres. Mass. chpt. 1985-86, nat. del., Disting. Svc. award), Assn. U.S. Army, New Eng. Chpt. Judge Advocates Assn. (pres./v.p. 1983-86), Res. Officers Assn. (nat. judge adv. 1993-94, state pres. 1993-94, pres.-elect 1992-93, state v.p. for Army 1990-92, state judge adv. 1985-86, pres. William Tudor and N.E. Civil Affairs chpts. 1984-89, Nat. Disting. Svc. awards), Nat. Civil Affairs Assn. (Nat. Disting. Svc. award), DAV (life, Honor Guard Burlington chpt. 113 1985-93), Natick VFW (life, state judge adv. and sr. vice comdr.-All Am. Post 1982-83), Natick AMVETS (life, post comdr.and state judge adv. 1982-83), Natick Am. Legion (PUFL 1979—), United Am. Vets. Mass. (adjutant), 75th Ranger Regiment Assn. (life, nat. dir. 1987-90), Combat Infantryman's Assn. (life mem.), Vietnam Vets. Am. (life, sec. D.C. chpt. 1980), Phi Delta Kappa (treas. Harvard U. chpt. 1990-92), Phi Alpha Delta. Avocations: computers, guitar and trumpet playing. Home: 15 Lake Shore Rd Natick MA 01760-2007 Office: US Army Soldier Biol and Chem Command Kansas St Legal Office Natick MA 01760-5035

**SAVAGE, JOHN WILLIAM,** lawyer; b. Seattle, Oct. 11, 1951; s. Stanley and Jennie Sabina (Siggstedt) S.; m. Rebecca Lee Abraham, Oct. 1, 1983; children: Bennett William, James Oliver. Student, Lewis and Clark Coll., 1969-71, JD Northwestern Sch. Law, 1977; BA, U. Wash., 1973. Bar: Oreg. 1977, U.S. Dist. Ct. Oreg. 1977, U.S. Ct. Appeals (9th cir.) 1977, U.S. Supreme Ct. Pvt. practice law Portland, Oreg., 1977-79; ptnr. Bailey, Olstad, Rieke, Geil & Savage, P.C., Portland, 1979-80; ptnr., shareholder Rieke, Geil & Savage, P.C., Portland, 1980-95; shareholder Rieke & Savage, P.C., Portland, 1995—. Mem. Oreg. Literacy Inc., Portland, 1979-85; mem. standing com. City Club, Portland, 1984-88, chmn. law and pub. safety standing com. 1986-87. Mem. ABA (chairperson young lawyers sect. Nat. Cmty. Law Week 1983-84, inmate grievance com. 1984-88), Assn. Trial Lawyers Am., Trial Lawyers for Pub. Justice, Oreg. Trial Lawyers Assn., Oreg. Bar Assn. (def. of indigent accused com. 1985-89), Oreg. Criminal Def. Lawyers Assn. (bd. dirs. 1984-86), Multnomah Bar Assn. (v.p. young lawyers sect. 1980, pres.-elect 1981, pres. 1982, Disting. Svc. award, bd. dirs. 1989-92, task force chair 1992-93, jud. selection com. 1998-99, Award of Merit 1994). Personal injury, Professional liability, General civil litigation. Home: 397 Furnace St Lake Oswego OR 97034-3957 Office: Rieke & Savage PC 140 SW Yamhill St Portland OR 97204-3007

**SAVAGE, KAY WEBB,** lawyer, health center administrator, accountant; b. Piedmont, Ala., Mar. 30, 1942; d. Robert Benjamin and Ellon Marie (Posey) Webb; m. Perry Lauren Savage, Nov. 18, 1961; children: Perry Lauren Jr., Shannon Hunter. BS in Secondary Edn., Jacksonville State Coll., Ala., 1963, AB, 1964; BS, Birmingham-So. Coll., 1987; JD, U. Ala., 1989. Bar: Ala. 1989; CPA, Ala.; cert. secondary tchr., Ala. Tchr. English, Hokes Bluff High Sch., Gadsden, Ala., 1963-64; tchr. sci. and math. McArthur Sch., Birmingham, Ala., 1964-68; tchr. sci. Mountain Brook Jr. High Sch., Birmingham, 1968-69; acct. Robert Resha, CPA, Birmingham, 1984-86; pvt. practice acctg. Birmingham, 1986—, pvt. practice law, 1989—; adminstr. Ala. Orthopaedic and Spine Ctr., Birmingham, 1987—; pres. Aleco, Inc., Birmingham, 1990—, Savage Enterprises, Birmingham, 1985—; bd. dirs. Assoc. Agys. Am., Coastal Bend Oil & Gas Co., Piedmont Ednl. Trust. Pres., sec. Snowcrest Condominium Assn., Snowshoe, W.Va., 1984-88; mem. exec. bd. Rep. Congl. Leadership Coun., Washington, 1988—; mem. Senatorial Trust, Washington, 1989, Presdl. Roundtable, Washington, 1989—, Piedmont Schs. Found., Birmingham Olympic Com., 1990—, Birmingham So. Coll. Arts Coun., 1992—, also gala advisor; v.p. United Cerebral Palsy, mem. multiple sclerosis class, 1995; sponsor U.S. Olympic Team; bd. dis. Piedmont Schs. Found., mem. scholarship com.; del. 1st Moscow Conf. on Law and Econ. Coop.; mem. exec. com. Com. for Fair Cts., 1994—; legis. chmn. Jefferson County Med. Alliance, 1994—, Ala. Med. Alliance, 1995; bd. dirs. End Meml. Found., 1994—. Fulbright fellow, 1964; recipient (5) Am. Jurisprudence awards. Mem. AAUW, Ala. Bar Assn., Ala. Soc. CPAs, Birmingham Bar Assn., Med. Group Mgmt. Assn., Bones Orthopedic Mng. Group, Attys. at Law and CPA U.S.A., Am. Soc. Law and Medicine, Pilot Lawyers Assn., Assn. Agys. Am. (bd. advisors), Coastal Ben Oil and Gas (bd. dirs.), Exec. Women Internat., C. of C. (bd. dirs. 1994—), Ninety Nines, Rotary Club Internat. (dir.), Sigma Delta Kappa (svc. award 1989), Sigma Kappa Delta, Sigma Tau Delta, Pi Gamma Mu. Avocations: flying, scuba diving, snow skiing, whitewater paddling, travel. General corporate, Taxation, general, Personal income taxation. Home: 3815 River View Cir Birmingham AL 35243-4801 Office: 52 Med Park East Dr Ste 115 Birmingham AL 35243

**SAVAGE, TIMOTHY JOSEPH,** lawyer; b. Phila., Mar. 24, 1946; s. Norbert J. and Edna M. (Mawson) S.; m. Linda S. Siegle, June 22, 1968; children: Timothy J., Daniel J., Christian S. BA, Assumption Coll., 1968; JD, Temple U., 1972. Bar: Pa. 1971, U.S. Dist. Ct. (ea. dist.) Pa. 1971, U.S. Supreme Ct. 1980, U.S. Ct. Appeals (2d and 3d cirs.) 1981, U.S. Dist. Ct. N.J. 1985, N.J. 1985, U.S. Tax Ct. 1985. Assoc. MacCoy, Evans & Lewis, Phila., 1971-74; ptnr. Savage and Ciccione, Phila., 1976-77; atty. examiner Pa. Liquor Control Bd., Harrisburg, 1976—; pvt. practice Phila., 1977—. Mem. Phila. Democratic County Exec. Com., 1976—; leader 23d ward Dem. Exec. Com., 1976—; vice chmn. Frankford Econ. Revitalization Com., 1976-80; bd. mgrs. Met. Boys Club Am.; sec., bd. dirs. N.E. Community for Mental Health/Mental Retardation, 1978-82; chmn. bldg. and fin. com. St. Joachim Roman Catholic Ch.; counselor N.E. Boys and Girls Club. Mem. ABA, Assn. Trial Lawyers Am., Pa. Bar Assn., Pa. Trial Lawyers Assn., Phila. Trial Lawyers Assn., Union League Phila. Avocations: boating, fishing. Federal civil litigation, State civil litigation, Criminal. Office: 5030 Oxford Ave Philadelphia PA 19124-2520

**SAVELKOUL, DONALD CHARLES,** retired lawyer; b. Mpls., July 29, 1917; s. Theodore Charles and Edith (Lindgren) S.; m. Mary Joan Holland, May 17, 1941; children: Jeffrey Charles, Jean Marie, Edward Joseph. BA magna cum laude, U. Minn., 1939; JD cum laude, William Mitchell Coll. Law, 1951. Bar: Minn. 1951, U.S. Dist. Ct. Minn. 1952, U.S. Ct. Appeals (8th cir.) 1960, U.S. Supreme Ct. 1971. Adminstrv. work various U.S. govt. depts., including Commerce, War, Labor, Wage Stblzn. Bd., 1940-51; mcpl. judge Fridley, Minn., 1952-53; pvt. practice law Mpls., St. Paul, Fridley, 1951-96, ret., 1997; chmn. bd. Fridley State Bank, 1962-95, Blaine State Bank, 1972-98; pres. Banrein, Inc., 1962-95, Blaine Bldg. Corp., 1972-98, Babbscha Co., 1962-95; mem. faculty William Mitchell Coll. Law, 1952-59, corp. mem., 1956—; sec. Fridley Recreation and Svc. Co., 1955-97; mem. Minn. Legislature, 1967-69. Mem. Gov.'s Com. Workers Compensation, 1965-67, Gov.'s Adv. Coun. on Employment Security, 1957-60, 62-63; gen. counsel Minn. AFL-CIO Fedn. Labor, 1952-71. 1st lt. AUS, 1943-46. Decorated Bronze Star; recipient Disting. Alumni award Coll. Liberal Arts U. Minn., 1995, Outstanding Alumnus award William Mitchell Coll. Law Alumni/ae Assn., 1997. Mem. ABA, Minn. Bar Assn. (chmn. 1957-58, bd. dirs. 1958-62, 68-69, labor law sect.), Hennepin County Bar Assn., Justice William Mitchell Soc., Am. Legion, U. Minn. Pres.'s Club, Phi Beta Kappa. Roman Catholic. Banking, General corporate. Office: 916 Moore Lake Dr W Fridley MN 55432-5148

**SAVELKOUL, DONALD WAYNE,** lawyer; b. Albert Lea, Minn., Aug. 26, 1967; s. Henry Jerome and Margaret Anne (Sykes) S.; m. Julie Clair Gutknecht, July 9, 1994; children: Sarah Marie, Hannah Clare. BS, St. John's U., Collegeville, Minn., 1990; JD, U. Minn., 1993. Bar: Minn. 1993, U.S. Dist. Ct. Minn. 1993, U.S. Dist. Ct. Iowa 1996. Clerk Lammer, Eckberg, Wolff & Vierling, P.A., Stillwater, Minn., 1992-93; atty., shareholder Peterson, Savelkoul, Schlichting & Davies, Ltd., Albert Lea, Minn., 1993—; prof. Riverland C.C., Albert Lea, Minn., 1994—. Bd. dirs. Albert Lea Cmty. Child Care Ctr., 1996—; com. mem. Albert Lea Hockey Assn., 1994—, Ducks Unlimited, 1995—. Recipient Outstanding Young Adult Albert Lea C. of C., 1986. Mem. ABA (civil litig. sec.), Freeborn County Bar Assn. (pres. 1998), Minn. State Bar (civil litig. sec.), Minn. Trial Lawyers Assn., Freeborn County C. of C. (housing and agr. coms. 1996—). Roman Catholic. Avocations: hockey, hunting, water skiing, downhill skiing. General civil litigation, Criminal, General corporate. Office: Peterson Savelkoul Schlichting & Davies Ltd 211 S Newton Ave Albert Lea MN 56007-2563

**SAVELL, POLLY CAROLYN,** lawyer; b. N.Y.C., Oct. 24, 1960; d. Joel Morton and Elsie Rhea (Crane) S. BA, U. Md., 1982; diploma, Internat. Comp. Law Inst., Paris, 1983; JD, NYU, 1985. Bar: N.Y. 1986. Assoc. corp. and entertainment divsn. Battle Fowler, N.Y.C., 1986-87; atty. Columbia Pictures Entertainment Inc., N.Y.C., 1987-89; counsel Turner Broadcasting Sys. Inc., Atlanta, 1989-91; sole practice Atlanta, 1991-93; asst. gen. counsel MCI WorldCom Inc., N.Y.C., 1993—. Mem. ABA, Fed. Comm. Bar Assn., Am. Corp. Counsel Assn., Assn. of Bar of City of N.Y. (telecom. law com.). Democrat. Methodist. Private international, Contracts commercial, Communications. Office: MCI WorldCom Inc 380 Madison Ave New York NY 10017-2513

**SAVICKAS, STEPHEN ANTHONY,** lawyer; b. Grand Rapids, Mich., June 22, 1958; s. Chester Julius Savickas and Anna Kowaleski. AAS, Ferris State U., 1979, AA, 1979, BS, 1981; JD, Cooley Law Sch., 1990. Bar: Mich., U.S. Supreme Ct., U.S. Dist. Ct. (we. dist.) Mich. Head graphics dept. Monroe County Libr., Monroe, Mich., 1982-84; head printing dept. Kent County Libr., Grand Rapids, Mich., 1985-87; law clk. U.S. Justice Dept., Grand Rapids, 1988-90; dep. prosecutor Branch County Prosecutor's Office, Coldwater, Mich., 1991-92; trial atty. Grand Rapids, 1993—. Pres. North End Neighborhood Assn., Grand Rapids, 1996-98. Mem. Elks, Theta Alpha Sigma (publicity chair 1980). Roman Catholic. Avocation: golf. Criminal, Personal injury, Civil rights. Office: 2456 Plainfield Ave NE Grand Rapids MI 49505-3875

**SAVILLE, DERRIC JAMES,** lawyer; b. Ft. Madison, Iowa, Oct. 2, 1964; s. Jacob Abraham and Brenda K. (Lawrence) S.; m. Jeannene Irene Abbott, Mar. 21, 1987. BS, U. Iowa, 1987; M of Studies in Law, JD cum laude, Vt. Law Sch., 1991. Bar: Minn. 1991, U.S. Dist. Ct. Minn. 1995, Upper Sioux Comty. Tribal Ct. 1996. Atty. Saville Law Office, Mpls., 1991—; chair subcom. Dist. Planning Adv. Commn. #279, Maple Grove, Minn., 1994-96. Articles editor Ferae Naturae, 1991. State del. Reform Party, Maple Grove, 1996; chair mental health adv. bd. Hennepin County Commitment Def. Project, 1998—. Mem. Minn. Head Injury Assn. (bd. dirs. 1995-96), Brain Injury Assn. Minn. (bd. dirs., chair-elect 1996—). Reform. Avocations: fishing, hiking, orienteering. Personal injury, Real property, Environmental. Home: 10835 101st Pl N Maple Grove MN 55369-3419 Office: Saville Law Office 10835 101st Pl N Maple Grove MN 55369-3419

**SAVILLE, ROYCE BLAIR,** lawyer; b. Cumberland, Md., Aug. 5, 1948; s. E. Blair and Audrey (Cosner) S.; m. Sharon Ann Brinkman, Apr. 3, 1981; children: Melissa Ann, Lauren Ashley, Meagan Elizabeth, Philip Clarke. BA, W.Va. U., 1970, JD, 1974. Bar: W.Va. 1974, U.S. Dist. Ct. (so. and no. dists.) W.Va. 1974. Assoc. William J. Oates, Jr. Atty. at Law, Romney, W.Va., 1974-75; ptnr. Oates & Saville Attys. at Law, Romney, 1975-78; pvt. practice Romney, 1978-99; mng. ptnr. Saville and Davis, PLLC, 1999—; pres. Potomac Land Co., 1975—; mental hygiene commr. Hampshire County, Romney, 1976—; mcpl. judge City of Romney, 1980-90. Mem. Hampshire County Devel. Authority, Romney, Hampshire County Farm Bur., Nat. Trust for Hist. Preservation; dir. Potomac Highlands Travel Coun., Elkins, W.Va., 1984-88; mem. adv. bd. Peterkin Conf. Ctr. of Renewal, Romney, 1988-90; del. W.Va. Dem. Conv., Charleston, 1984; vestryman St. Stephen's Episcopal Ch., Romney, 1984-86. Mem. ABA, ATLA, NRA (life), W.Va. Bar Assn., South Br. Valley Bar Assn. (pres. 1996-97), W.Va. Trial Lawyers Assn., Waterfowl U.S.A. (life), N.Am. Hunting Club (life), McNeill's Rangers Sons Confederate Vets. (judge adv.), W.VA. Law Sch. Assn. (life), W.Va. U. Alumni Assn. (life), Masons, Phi Alpha Delta (life), Rotary (Paul Harris fellow). Democrat. Episcopalian. Avocations: gun collecting, antique collecting, local history. Real property, State civil litigation, General practice. Home: Liberty Hall 276 E Main St Romney WV 26757-1821 also: Mill Island Moorefield WV 26836 Office: 95 W Main St PO Box 2000 Romney WV 26757-2000

**SAVILLE, YVONNE TAKVORIAN,** lawyer; b. Wilmington, Del., Mar. 5, 1970; d. Kenneth Bedros and Victoria Takvorian; m. Erik L. Saville, Oct. 14, 1995. BA, U. Del., 1992; JD, Widener U., 1995. Bar: Del. 1995, U.S. Dist. Ct. Del. 1996. Assoc. atty. Michael Weiss, P.A., Wilmington, 1995—. Recipient 1st Pl. Happy Endings Fiction Writing award Del. State Bar Assn., 1997, 2d Pl. award, 1998. Mem. ABA, Am. Trial Lawyers Assn., Del. Bar Assn., Del. Trial Lawyers Assn. (co-founder, chair new lawyers com.). Avocations: piano, football. Personal injury, Workers' compensation, General civil litigation. Home: 901 8th St Brighton Village Newark DE 19711 Office: Michael Weiss PA PO Box 370 Wilmington DE 19899-0370

**SAVITSKY, THOMAS ROBERT,** lawyer; b. Pa., Sept. 12, 1952; s. Stanley George and Adele (Kaleda) S.; m. Deborah Ann Sokirka, Jan. 13, 1973; children: Thomas Jason, Raina Alexandra. BS in Biology, Villanova U., 1974; MS in Microbiology, Temple U., 1978; JD, Widener U., 1983. Bar: U.S. Patent and Trademark Office, 1984, Mich. 1985, Tenn. 1988, U.S. Dist. Ct. (ea. dist.) Mich. 1985, U.S. Ct. Appeals (fed. cir.) 1991; cert. quality engr. Am. Soc. for Quality Control, 1981. Microbiologist Warner-Lambert Co., 1978-81; lab. supr. Betz Labs., Trevose, Pa., 1982-84; patent atty. The Dow Chem. Co., Midland, Mich., 1984-87, Eastman Chem. Co., Kingsport, Tenn., 1987-89; sr. patent atty. Eastman Chem. Co., Kingsport, 1989-91, licensing and bus. devel. mgr., 1991-92; asst. counsel Bristol-Myers Squibb Co., Princeton, N.J., 1992—. Mem. ABA, AAAS, Am. Intellectual Property Law Assn., Am. Soc. for Microbiology. Roman Catholic. Intellectual property, Patent. Home: 31 Academy Ct Pennington NJ 08534-2829 Office: Bristol-Myers Squibb Co PO Box 4000 Princeton NJ 08543-4000

**SAVITT, SUSAN SCHENKEL,** lawyer; b. Bklyn., Aug. 21, 1943; d. Edward Charles and Sylvia (Dlugatch) S.; m. Harvey Savitt, July 2, 1969 (div. 1978); children: Andrew Todd, Daniel Cory. BA magna cum laude, Pa. State U., 1964; JD, Columbia U., 1968. Bar: N.Y. 1968, U.S. Dist. Ct. (so. and ea. dists.) N.Y. 1973, U.S. Tax Ct. 1973, U.S. Ct. Appeals (2d cir.) 1981, U.S. Supreme Ct. 1980, U.S. Dist. Ct. (we. dist.) N.Y. 1996. Atty. Nassau County Legal Svcs., Freeport, N.Y., 1973-74; asst. corp. counsel City of Yonkers, 1977-78; from assoc. to ptnr. Epstein, Becker & Green, P.C.,

N.Y.C., 1978-94; ptnr. Winston & Strawn, N.Y.C., 1994—; adj. prof. Elizabeth Seton Coll., Yonkers, 1982-83; mem. NYU exec. coun. Met. Ctr. for Ednl. Rsch. Devel. and Tng., 1987-90; mediator Vol. Mediation Panel, U.S. Dist. Ct. (so. dist.) N.Y., 1997—, U.S. Dist. Ct. (ea. dist.) N.Y., 1999—. Mem. Hastings-on-Hudson (N.Y.) Sch. Bd., 1984-93, v.p., 1986, 87-88, pres., 1989-90, 92-93; bd. dirs. Associated Blind, 1993-95, Search for Change, 1996—, sec., 1998—; bd. dirs. Pa. State Profl. Women's Network of N.Y., 1996—, pres., 1998—. Mem. ABA (internat. law sect., litigation and labor law sect.), N.Y. State Bar Assn. (labor law sect., comml. litigation sect.), Women's Bar Assn., Fed. Bar Coun., Pa. State Alumni Club (v.p. Westchester County 1985-87), Phi Beta Kappa, Alpha Kappa Delta, Phi Gamma Mu, Pi Kappa Phi. Labor, Federal civil litigation, Alternative dispute resolution. Office: Winston & Strawn 200 Park Ave Rm 4100 New York NY 10166-4401

**SAVITZ, DAVID BARRY,** lawyer; b. Wilkes-Barre, Pa., June 6, 1943; s. Sam and Isabelle (Weber) S.; 1 child, Curtis; m. Robin Kash, Dec. 13, 1987; 2 children: Rachel Childs and Kristin Childs. BA, Pa. State U., State Coll., 1965; JD, U. Colo., Boulder, 1968. Bar: Colo. 1968, U.S. Dist. Ct. Colo. 1969, U.S. Ct. Appeals (10th cir.) 1973, U. S. Supreme Ct. 1978. Pvt. practice Denver, 1968—; instr./lectr. Denver Police Dept., 1976,77; lectr. Colo. Criminal Def. Bar, Denver, 1979,82, instr. 1988-90, 93, APA, Dallas, 1985; instr./judge Univ. Denver Law School, 1986-90. Contbr. articles to profl. jours. Bd. dirs. Kempe Children's Found., Denver, 1992-93, chmn. speaker's bur., 1992-93; active Survivors' United Network Legal Task Force, Denver, 1992. Recipient David Caul Mem. award Internat. Soc. Study Multiple Personality and Dissociation, 1991. Mem. ABA, Nat. Assn. Criminal Def. Lawyers, Am. Trial Lawyers Assn., Colo Criminal Def. Bar, Colo. Trial Lawyers Assn., Colo. Bar Assn. Avocations: jogging, biking. Criminal, General civil litigation. Home: 22434 Anasazi Way Golden CO 80401-8067 Office: 950 S Cherry St Ste 600 Denver CO 80246-2665

**SAVONA, MICHAEL JOSEPH,** lawyer; b. Wayne, Mich., Dec. 29, 1971; s. Francis J. and Karen A. (Partches) S. BA, Calif. U., 1993; JD, Am. U., 1996. Bar: Pa. 1996, U.S. Dist. Ct. (we. dist.) Pa. 1996, U.S. Ct. Appeals (3d cir.) 1997. Assoc. atty. Melenyzer & Assocs., Charleroi, Pa., 1996-97; mng. ptnr. Melenyzer, Stiffler & Savona, L.L.P., Charleroi, Pa., 1998—; bd. dirs. Ctr. in the Woods., Calif., Pa., 1998—. Exec. editor Am. U. Jour. Internat. Law and Policy, 1995-96. Mem. ABA, Assn. Trial Lawyer's Am., Pa. Bar Assn., Pa. Trial Lawyer's Assn., Order Son's Italy Am., St. Dominic Men's Club, Order Barristers. Democrat. Roman Catholic. Office: Melenyzer Stiffler & Savona 411 Washington Ave Charleroi PA 15022-1531

**SAWDEI, MILAN A.,** lawyer; b. Bakersfield, Calif., Aug. 23, 1946. BA, U. Calif., Long Beach, 1969; JD, W.S.U., 1975. Bar: Calif. 1975, U.S. Dist. Ct. (ctrl. dist.) Calif. 1975. House counsel Sanyo Electric, Inc., 1975-77; assoc. counsel Brown Co. (Gulf & Western), 1978-80; divsn. counsel Petrolane, Inc., 1980-83; sr. counsel Bergen Brunswig Corp., Orange, Calif., 1983-90, v.p., chief legal officer, 1990-92, exec. v.p., chief legal officer, sec., 1992—. Mem. ABA, Am. Corp. Counsel Assn., Am. Soc. Corp. Secs., L.A. County Bar Assn. General corporate, Real property, Finance. Office: Bergen Brunswig Corp 4000 W Metropolitan Dr Orange CA 92868-3598

**SAWICKI, MYRON,** lawyer; b. Elizabeth, N.J., Sept. 15, 1954; s. Wasyl and Elizabeth (Zoppa) S. AA, Santa Monica Coll., 1976; BS, Calif. State U.-Long Beach, 1978; JD, Southwestern U., 1980. Bar: Calif. 1980, U.S. Ct. Appeals (9th cir.) 1981, U.S. Dist. Ct. (cen. dist.) Calif. 1981. Spl. investigator William J. Burns, Internat. Detective Agy., Los Angeles, 1977-78; sole practice law, Los Angeles, 1981-83; dep. dist. atty. Mendocino County, Ukiah, Calif., 1983—. Mem. Calif. Dist. Atty. Assn., Nat. Dist. Atty. Assn. Home: PO Box 1095 Ukiah CA 95482-1095 Office: Mendocino County Dist Atty Courthouse Ukiah CA 95482

**SAWICKI, STEPHEN CRAIG,** lawyer, mediator; b. Chgo., July 28, 1950; s. Stephen Martin and Helen Jenny Sawicki; m. Mary Kim Gardner, Nov. 19, 1989; children: Stephen, Sara, Adam. BA, U. South Fla., 1973; JD, Samford U., 1977. Bar: Fla. 1977, U.S. Dist. Ct. (mid. dist.) Fla. 1977, U.S. Ct. Appeals (11th cir.) 1983. Banker First Fed. Savs. & Loan, Sarasota, Fla., 1972-73, Sun Bank, Orlando, Fla., 1973-74; ptnr. Hendry, Stoner, Sawicki & Brown, Orlando, Fla., 1977—; mem. panel mediators Fla. Dept. Bus. Regulation, 1990—, Fla. Dept. Ins., 1990—, Manville Personal Injury Settlement Trust, 1990—. Fellow Am. Coll. Civil Trial Mediators (exec. dir. 1996—). Avocations: music, tennis, hiking, sailing, architecture. Alternative dispute resolution, General civil litigation, Personal injury. Office: Hendry Stoner Sawicki and Brown 200 E Robinson St Ste 500 Orlando FL 32801-1956

**SAWICKI, ZBIGNIEW PETER,** lawyer; b. Hohenfels, Germany, Apr. 13, 1949; came to U.S., 1951; s. Witold and Marianna (Tukiendorf) S.; m. Katheryn Marie Loman, Aug. 19, 1972; children: James, Jeffrey, Jessica, Jason. BSChemE, Purdue U., 1972; MBA, Coll. St. Thomas, St. Paul, 1977; JD, Hamline U., 1980. Bar: Minn. 1980, U.S. Dist. Ct. Minn. 1981, U.S. Ct. Appeals (8th cir.) 1981, U.S. Patent and Trademark Office 1981, U.S. Ct. Appeals (fed. cir.) 1982, Can. Patent Office 1994, Can. Trademark Office 1995. Process engr. 3-M Co., St. Paul, 1973-75; process engring. supr. Conwed Corp., St. Paul, 1975-77; shareholder, bd. dirs. Kinney & Lange, Mpls., 1980—. Bd. dirs. Orono (Minn.) Hockey Boosters, 1992—. With USAF, 1970-72. Mem. ABA, Am. Intellectual Property Assn., Internat. Trademark Assn., Minn. Intellectual Property Assn. (past treas.), Am. Legion. Intellectual property, Patent, Trademark and copyright. Home: 4510 N Shore Dr Mound MN 55364-9602 Office: Kinney & Lange 312 S 3d St Minneapolis MN 55415-1624

**SAWYER, H(AROLD) MURRAY, JR.,** lawyer; b. Niagara Falls, N.Y., Jan. 10, 1946; s. Harold Murray and Susan (Imbrie) S.; m. Ann Randolph Gawthrop; children: Ann Sawyer Chilton, Amy Greenwood, Harold Murray III. BA, U. N.C., 1968; JD, Vanderbilt U., 1971. Bar: Del. 1971, U.S. Dist. Ct. Del. 1972, U.S. Ct. Appeals (3d cir.) 1972, U.S. Supreme Ct. 1979, Pa. 1981. Assoc. Richards, Layton & Finger, Wilmington, Del., 1971-72; dep. atty. gen. criminal div. State of Del., Wilmington, 1972-73; ptnr. Berg, Komissaroff & Sawyer, Wilmington, 1973-77; founding ptnr. Sawyer Akin & Herron, Wilmington, 1978—; pres. Registered Agents Ltd., Wilmington, 1978—, Am. Incorporators Ltd., Wilmington, 1985—; mem. bd. profl. responsibility Del. Supreme Ct., Wilmington, 1983-96. Contbr. articles to profl. jours. Trustee The Pilot Sch., Wilmington, 1980—; mem. New Castle County Coun., Wilmington, 1980-82, Del. Health Facilities Authority, 1983-92. Mem. ABA, Del. Bar Assn., Rotary (bd. dirs. Wilmington 1992-97, pres. 1995-96), Club Wilmington. Republican. Episcopalian. Avocations: golf, travel, reading. Real property, Estate planning, Probate. Office: Sawyer Akin & Herron 1220 N Market St PO Box 25047 Wilmington DE 19899-5047

**SAWYER, LEONARD SYLVESTER,** lawyer; b. Lincoln, N.H., June 14, 1925; s. Howard Symmes and Rose Veronica (Eagan) S.; m. Caroline Eldora Smith, Sept. 7, 1960; children: Edward M., Charles L. BA, U. N.H., 1947; LLB, Boston U., 1950. Bar: N.H. 1950. Ptnr. Edes & Sawyer, Woodsville, N.H., 1954-56; pvt. practice Plymouth, N.H., 1956-94; ret., 1994; justice Plymouth Dist. Ct., 1965-85. Selectman Town of Plymouth, 1963-65; moderator Plymouth Water and Sewer Dist., 1971—; del. N.H. Constl. Conv., 1984. Served with U.S. Army, 1950-54. Mem. N.H. Bar Assn., Am. Judicature Soc., Lions (past pres. Plymouth chpt.), Grange (master, treas.). Democrat. Roman Catholic. Avocations: hiking, swimming, reading. Real property, Probate, Family and matrimonial. Home: 13 Cummings St Plymouth NH 03264-1106

**SAXL, RICHARD HILDRETH,** lawyer; b. Boston, June 3, 1948; s. Erwin Joseph and Lucretia (Hildreth) S. BA, U. Pa., 1970; JD, Rutgers U., Camden, N.J., 1975. Bar: Conn. 1976, U.S. Dist. Ct. Conn. 1976, U.S. Ct. Appeals (2d cir.) 1977. Assoc. Jerry Davidoff, Westport, Conn., 1976-78; ptnr. Davidoff & Saxl, Westport, 1979-94; pvt. practice law offices Richard H. Saxl, Westport, 1994—; town atty. Fairfield, Conn., 1997—; v.p., trustee Landmark Learning, Inc., 1997—. Mem. Fairfield Town Plan and Zoning Commn., 1981-93, chmn., 1991-93; chair Fairfield Land Acquisition com., 1997; bd. dirs. Conn. Renaissance, Inc., Norwalk, 1979-82, pres., 1981-82; mem. Fairfield Charter Revision Commn., 1984-85, 92; Fairfield town atty., 1997—. Recipient Svc. award Conn. Fedn. Planning and Zoning Agys., 1993, cert. of commendation Conn. Jud. Dept., 1985-87. Mem. Conn. Bar Assn., Westport Bar Assn., Pequot Yacht Club. Democrat. Avocations: squash, sailing. Estate planning, Probate, Real property. Home: 753 Sasco Hill Rd Fairfield CT 06430-6376 Office: 321 Riverside Ave Westport CT 06880-4810

**SAXON, JOHN DAVID,** lawyer, policy analyst, educator; b. Anniston, Ala., July 21, 1950; s. J.Z. and Sarah Elizabeth (Steadham) S.; m. Elizabeth Lord, Mar. 10, 1973. BA with honors, U. Ala., 1972, JD, 1977; grad. Exec. Program Stanford U., 1986; MA, U. N.C., 1973. Bar: Ala. 1977, U.S. Dist. Ct. (no. dist.) Ala. 1977, U.S. Supreme Ct. 1983, U.S. Dist. Ct. (mid. dist.) Ala. 1989, U.S. Dist. Ct. (so. dist.) Ala. 1990, U.S. Ct. Appeals (11th cir.) 1990, U.S. Ct. Appeals (5th cir.) 1992. Adminstrv. asst. to acting chief exec. officer U. Ala.-University, 1976-77; assoc. Sirote, Permutt, Friend, Friedman, Held & Apolinsky, P.A., Birmingham, Ala., 1977-78; spl. asst. to Vice Pres. U.S., Washington, 1978-79; counsel subcom. on jurisprudence and govt. rels. Com. on Judiciary, U.S. Senate, Washington, 1979-80, counsel Select Com. on Ethics, 1980-83; dir. corp. issues RCA, Washington, 1983-86; Washington rep., Gen. Electric Co., 1986-87; assoc. counsel U.S. Senate Select com. on secret mil. assistance to Iran and the Nicaraguan Opposition, 1987-88; spl. counsel U.S. Senate Armed Svcs. com., 1988; counsel, Johnston, Barton, Proctor, Swedlaw & Naff, Birmingham, 1988-90; atty. Gathings & Davis, Birmingham, 1990-92; ptnr. Cooper, Mitch, Crawford, Kuykendall & Whatley, 1992-95; pres. and prin. John D. Saxon, P.C., 1995—; adj. instr. polit. communication U. Md., 1982-83; instr. speech communication U. Ala.-University, 1973; instr. speech communication and mgmt. Brewer Jr. Coll., Tuscaloosa, 1975-77; adj. instr. civil litigation Samford U., Birmingham, 1977-78; adj. prof. Washington Coll. Law The Am. U., 1988; adj. prof. adminstrn. law U. Ala., Birmingham, 1998; vis. scholar The Hastings Ctr., 1983; mem. Am. Observer Delegation, Kettering Found., U.S.-China Task Force, 1986; bd. dirs. White House Fellows Found., 1981-84 , pres., 1983-84; mem. bd. advisers Center for Publ. Law and Service, U. Ala. Sch. Law, 1976-83; bd. trustees Farrah Law Soc., 1988-94, vice-chmn., 1990-92, chmn., 1992-94; bd. dirs., exec. com. U. Ala. Law Found., vice chmn., 1996-98, chmn. 1998—; mem. Pres.'s Commn. White House Fellowships, 1983-84, 93—; mem. Washington Local Devel. Corp, 1986-88; chmn. Ala. Clinton for Pres. Campaign, 1992, 96; mem. platform com. Dem. Nat. Conv., 1992, del., 1996; treas. Ala. Dem. Party, 1995-99; mem. Fed. Appointments Patronage Com., 1997—; mem. policy adv. com. The Coalition for Excellence in Edn., chmn., 1991-92; dir. The A+ Rsch. Found.; mem. bd. advisors N.E. Ala. Devel. Forum, 1992—, Nat. Governing Bd. Common Cause, 1992-95; treas Common Cause Ala., 1998—, Leadership Birmingham Class of 1993-94; mem. pres. adv. coun. Birmingham So. Coll., 1993—; mem. adminstrv. bd. First United Meth. Ch., 1994-97; co-pres. Birmingham Boys Choir Found., 1994-96; asst. scoutmaster Troop 57 Boy Scouts of Am.; pres. Southside Baseball, 1995-97; adv. com. The Blackburn Inst., U. Ala.; bd. dir. Miles Coll. Ctr. for Cmty. Econ. Devel., 1995—. Served to 2d lt. U.S. Army, 1974, capt. Res. White House Fellow, 1978-79; named Disting. Mil. Grad., U. Ala., 1972, Outstanding Alumnus in Speech Communication, 1988. Mem. ABA (spl. com. litigation sect.), Ala. Bar Assn., Birmingham Bar Assn. (chmn. profl. ethics com. 1991-92, mem. grievance com. 1992—, co-chmn. 1995-96, chmn. 1997-98, bd. dirs., solo practitioner small firm sect. 1997—, chmn. budget com. 1999), Ala. Trial Lawyers Assn. (bd. govs. 1990-94, exec. com. 1994—), White House Fellows Assn. (pres. 1983-84), Kiwanis Club (Birmingham), Scabbard and Blade, The Order of Barristers, Bench and Bar (Outstanding Sr. award 1977), Downtown Dem. Club (pres. 1992-93), Jasons, Omicron Delta Kappa, Omicron Delta Epsilon, Phi Alpha Theta, Pi Sigma Alpha. Methodist. Contbr. articles to newspapers and legal publs., chpts. to books. Federal civil litigation, Labor, State civil litigation.

**SAXTON, WILLIAM MARVIN,** lawyer; b. Joplin, Mo., Feb. 14, 1927; s. Clyde Marvin and Lea Ann (Farnan) S.; m. Helen Grace Klinefelter, June 1, 1974; children: Sherry Lynn, Patricia Ann Painter, William Daniel, Michael Lawrence. A.B., U. Mich., 1949, J.D., 1952. Bar: Mich. Mem. firm Love, Snyder & Lewis, Detroit, 1952-53; mem. firm Butzel, Long, Detroit, 1953—, dir., chmn., CEO, 1989-96, dir. emeritus, 1997—; lectr. Inst. Continuing Legal Edn.; sec., bd. dirs. Fritz Broadcasting, Inc., 1983-97; mem. mediation tribunal hearing panel for 3d Jud. Dist. Mich., 1989—, 6th Jud. Dist., 1994—. Trustee Detroit Music Hall Ctr. Soc. for the Performing Arts, 1984-99; trustee Hist. Soc. U.S. Dist. Ct. (ea. dist.) Mich., 1992-95, pres., 1993-95. Recipient Distinguished award Mich. Road Builders Assn., 1987. Master of Bench Emeritus Am. Inn of Court; fellow Am. Coll. Trial Lawyers, Am. Bar Found., Am. Coll. Labor and Employment Lawyers, Mich. Bar Found.; mem. ABA, FBA, Detroit Bar Assn. (dir. 1974-79, Goodnow Pres.'s award 1996), Mich. Bar Assn. (atty. discipline panel, Disting. Svc. award 1998), Detroit Indsl. Rels. Rsch. Assn. (treas. 1980—, v.p. 1982, pres. 1984-85), Mich. Young Lawyers (pres. 1954-55), Am. Law Inst., Indsl. Rels. Rsch. Assn. Am. Arbitration Assn., U.S. 6th Cir. Ct. Appeals (life, mem. jud. conf., mem. bicentennial com.), Am. Inn Ct., Cooley Club, Renaissance Club, Detroit Golf Club (dir. 1983-89), Detroit Athletic Club. Federal civil litigation, Labor, State civil litigation. Office: Butzel Long 150 W Jefferson Ave Ste 900 Detroit MI 48226-4416

**SAYAD, PAMELA MIRIAM,** lawyer; b. San Francisco, Apr. 13, 1949; d. Samuel Daniel and Charlotte (Yonan) S.; A.B. in Polit. Sci., U. Calif.-Berkeley, 1970; J.D., U. Notre Dame Sch. Law, 1973; Bar: D.C. 1974, U.S. Dist. Ct. D.C. 1974, Mass. 1980, U.S Dist Ct. (no. dist.) Calif. 1981, Calif. 1982, U.S. Dist. Ct. (no. dist.) Calif., 1981, U.S. Ct. Appeals (9th cir.) 1981, U.S. Dist. Ct. D.C. 1974, U.S. Ct. Appeals (D.C. cir.) 1974, U.S. Dist. Ct. Mass. 1980, U.S. Dist. Ct. (ea. dist.) Calif. 1986. Atty. U.S. HEW, Washington, 1973-74; atty. solicitor's office Div. Indian Affairs, U.S. Dept. Interior, Washington, 1974-77; asst. U.S. atty. for D.C., Washington, 1977-80; assoc. Swartz & Swartz, Boston, 1980-81; assoc. Archer, Rosenak & Hanson, San Francisco, 1981-82, Bourhis, Lawless & Harvey, San Francisco, 1982-83; ptnr. Sayad & Trigero, San Francisco, 1983—; bd. of trustees Calif. Indian Legal Services, 1984—; bd. dirs. Found. Study Electorial Reform, U. Calif. Med. Ctr., 1990—. Author: (with others) Criminal Practice Inst. Manual, 1980; Litigating for Profit, 1983; also articles. Mem. ABA, Assn. Trial Lawyers Am., Calif. Trial Lawyers Assn., Bar Assn. San Francisco, Calif. Women Lawyers, San Francisco Trial Lawyers Assn., Gamma Phi Beta. Democrat. Presbyterian. Federal civil litigation, State civil litigation, Personal injury. Office: Sayad & Trigero 35 Avila Rd San Mateo CA 94402-2813

**SAYAS, CONRADO JOE,** lawyer; b. Silang, Cavite, Philippines, July 15, 1958; came to U.S., 1985; s. Conrado Ambalada and Eulalia (Ancanan) S.; m. Anna Reyes Santos, Oct. 17, 1987; children: Clare Anne, Christopher. BA, U. Philippines, 1978, LLB, 1982; LLM, Georgetown U., 1990. Bar: Philippines 1983, Calif. 1985, U.S. Dist. Ct. (cen. dist.) Calif. 1985, U.S. Ct. Appeals (9th cir.) 1985. Litigation atty. Angara, Concepcion, Regala, Philippines, 1984-85, Lauchengco, Mendoza & Sayas, L.A., 1985-86, Nelsen, Tang, Thompson, Pegue & Thornton, L.A., 1987-89, Alexander, Millner & McGee, L.A., 1990-91; sole practitioner L.A., 1991—. Mem. ATLA, Calif. Trial Lawyers Assn., L.A. Trial Lawyers Assn. Roman Catholic. Avocations: tennis, swimming, travel, reading, movies. Personal injury, General civil litigation, Product liability. Office: 3701 Wilshire Blvd Ste 416 Los Angeles CA 90010-2811

**SAYER, DARELL LEE,** lawyer; b. Vincennes, Ind., Sept. 3, 1952; s. D.G. and Nancy (Hawkins) S.; m. Nancy Sayer. BA, Ind. U., 1974; JD, Coll. of William & Mary, 1977. Asst. atty. Commonwealth of Va., Portsmouth, 1977-82; ptnr. Ferrell, Backus, Sayer and Nicolo, Portsmouth, 1982—. Mem. bd. Zoning Appeals, Portsmouth. Mem. Va. State Bar Assn. (bd. govs. criminal law sect., spl. justice, commr. in chancery), Portsmouth Bar Assn. (past pres.). Family and matrimonial, Criminal, Personal injury. Office: Ferrell Backus Sayer & Nicolo 309 County St Portsmouth VA 23704-3701

**SAYLER, ROBERT NELSON,** lawyer; b. Kansas City, Mo., June 1, 1940; s. John William and Roberta (Nelson) S.; m. Martha Leith, Aug. 1962; children: Christina, Bentley. BA, Stanford U., 1962; JD, Harvard U., 1965. Bar: U.S. Dist. Ct. D.C. 1966, U.S. Ct. Appeals (D.C. cir.) 1966, U.S. Supreme Ct. 1971, D.C. 1972, U.S. Ct. Appeals (2d cir.) 1977. From assoc. to ptnr. Covington & Burling, Washington, 1965—. V.p. Neighborhood Legal Services, Washington, 1980-82; pres. Legal Aid Soc., Washington, 1983-84. Fellow Am. Bar Found., Am. Coll. Trial Lawyers; mem. ABA (dir. programs, program chmn. 1981, 85, coun., chmn. litigation sect., mem. standing com. on fed. judiciary). Democrat. Federal civil litigation, General corporate, Insurance. Office: Covington & Burling PO Box 7566 1201 Pennsylvania Ave NW Washington DC 20004-2401

**SAYLES, CATHY A.,** lawyer; b. Kansas City, Mo., Sept. 8, 1960; d. Harold Richard and June A. Sayles. BA, U. Kans., 1982, JD, 1985. Bar: Kans. 1985, U.S. Dist. Ct. Kans. 1985, U.S. Ct. Appeals (8th and 10th cirs.) 1985. Assoc. Shamberg, Johnson, Bergman & Goldman, Overland Park, Kans., 1985-86, Couch & Pierce, Overland Park, 1986-89; sr. atty. for litigation Koch Industries, Inc., Wichita, Kans., 1989-95; legal cons., Kansas City, Mo., 1995-97; gen. counsel Ferrellgas, Inc., Liberty, Mo., 1997—. Mem. Phi Beta Kappa. General corporate, General civil litigation, Labor. Office: Ferrellgas Inc One Liberty Pla Liberty MO 64068

**SAYLOR, CHARLES HORACE,** lawyer; b. Bethlehem, Pa., Jan. 6, 1950; s. Howard James and Florence M. (Glasser) S.; m. Martha Louise Weaver, July 10, 1971; children: Amy Louise, Matthew Charles. BA, Pa. State U., 1971; JD, Dickinson Sch. Law, 1974. Bar: Pa. 1974, U.S. Dist. Ct. (mid. dist.) Pa. 1979. Law clk. Northumberland County Ct. Common Pleas, Sunbury, Pa., 1974-76; assoc. Wiest & Wiest, Sunbury, 1976-79; ptnr. Wiest, Wiest & Saylor, Sunbury, 1979-85, Wiest, Wiest, Saylor & Muolo, Sunbury, 1985-97, Wiest, Saylor, Muolo, Noon and Swinehart, Sunbury, 1998—; solicitor Twp. of Rush, Pa., 1979—, Twp. of Point, Pa., 1983—, County of Northumberland, 1993-95; instr. Pa. State U., Schuylkill Haven, 1986. Asst. editor Dickinson Law Rev., 1973, Northumberland (Pa.) Legal Jour., 1987—. Trustee Northumberland County Law Libr., 1986—, Priestley-Forsyth Meml. Libr., Northumberland, 1988-93, v.p., 1990-93; coach Am. Youth Soccer Assn., Northumberland, 1988-90; mem. com. YMCA, Sunbury, 1987—, bd. dirs., 1991—, pres. of bd. dirs., 1997—, chmn. sustaining campaign, 1992; asst. coach Girls Track and Field, Shikellamy H.S., 1992-93. Mem. Pa. Bar Assn., Northumberland County Bar Assn. (sec.-treas. 1985—), Pa. Trial Lawyers Assn. Republican. Roman Catholic. Avocations: running, golf. Personal injury, General civil litigation. Home: 233 Honey Locust Ln Northumberland PA 17857-9679 Office: Wiest Saylor Muolo Noon & Swinehart 240244 Market St Sunbury PA 17801-2526

**SAYLOR, THOMAS G.,** state supreme court justice; b. Meyersdale, Pa., Dec. 14, 1946. BA in Govt., U. Va., 1969; JD, Columbia U., 1972. Pvt. practice, 1972-82, 87-93; 1st asst. dist. atty. Somerset County, 1973-76; dir. Pa. Bur. Consumer Protection, 1982-83; 1st dep. atty. gen. Commonwealth of Pa., 1983-87; elected judge Superior Ct. Pa., 1993; elected justice Supreme Ct. Pa., 1997—. Contbr. articles to legal publications. Bd. dirs. Humane Soc. Harrisburg Area; bd. overseers Widener U. Sch. Law. Mem. ABA, Pa. Bar Assn., Cumberland County Bar Assn., Dauphin County Bar Assn., Appellate Judges Conf. Office: Fulton Bldg 16th Fl 200 N 3d St Harrisburg PA 17101*

**SAYRE, FLOYD MCKINLEY, III,** lawyer; b. Salisbury, N.C., June 10, 1962; s. Floyd M. Jr. and Ruth Ellen Sayre; m. Susie Conley, apr. 23, 1988; children: Grace Leigh, Thomas W., Floyd M. IV. BSBA, W.Va. U., 1983, MBA, 1997; JD, U. Ark., 1986. Assoc. Sayre & Sayre, Beckley, W.Va., 1986-89; city atty. City of Beckley, 1989-96; assoc. File Payne Scheret & File, Beckley, 1996—; atty. Town of Sophia, W.Va., 1997—; assoc. mcpl. judge City of Beckley, 1998—. Mem. W.Va. State Ethic Commn., Charleston, 1996-98. Mem. ABA, Raleigh County Bar Assn. (sec.-treas. 1986), W.Va. State Bar Assn. Democrat. Real property, General civil litigation, General practice. Home: 215 W Locust Dr Beckley WV 25801-3317 Office: Filie Payne Scheret File 130 Main St Beckley WV 25801-4611

**SAYRE, JOHN MARSHALL,** lawyer, former government official; b. Boulder, Colo., Nov. 9, 1921; s. Henry Marshall and Lulu M. (Cooper) S.; m. Jean Miller, Aug. 22, 1943; children: Henry M., Charles Franklin, John Marshall Jr., Ann Elizabeth Sayre Taggart (dec.). BA, U. Colo., 1943, JD, 1948. Bar: Colo. 1948, U.S. Dist. Ct. Colo. 1952, U.S. Ct. Appeals (10th cir.) 1964. Law clk. trust dept. Denver Nat. Bank, 1948-49; asst. cashier, trust officer Nat. State Bank of Boulder, 1949-50; ptnr. Ryan, Sayre, Martin, Brotzman, Boulder, 1950-66, Davis, Graham & Stubbs, Denver, 1966-89, of counsel Davis, Graham & Stubbs, 1993—; asst. sec. of the Interior for Water and Sci., 1989-93. Bd. dirs. Boulder Sch. Dist. 3, 1951-57; city atty. City of Boulder, 1952-55; gen. counsel Colo. Mcpl. League, 1956-63; prin. counsel No. Colo. Water Conservancy Dist. and mcpl. subdist., 1964-87, spl. counsel, 1987, bd. dirs. dist., 1960-64; former legal counsel Colo. Assn. Commerce and Industry. Lt. (j.g.) USNR, 1943-46, ret. Decorated Purple Heart. Fellow Am. Bar. Found. (life), Colo. Bar Found. (life); mem. ABA, Colo. Bar Assn., Boulder County Bar Assn. (pres. 1959), Denver Bar Assn., Nat. Water Resources Assn. (Colo. dir. 1980-89, 93-95, pres. 1984-86), Denver Country Club, Univ. Club, Mile High Club, Phi Beta Kappa, Phi Gamma Delta, Phi Delta Phi. Republican. Episcopalian. Real property, Environmental. Home: 355 Ivanhoe St Denver CO 80220-5841 Office: Davis Graham & Stubbs PO Box 185 Denver CO 80201-0185

**SAYRE, MATT MELVIN MATHIAS,** lawyer; b. Seattle, Sept. 5, 1934; s. Melvin Edward and Ethyl Elizabeth (Mathias) S.; m. Sheri Teagle, Oct. 21, 1956; children: Jeffrey Mathias, Steven Michael, David Matthew. BA, U. Wash., 1956; JD, Gonzaga U., 1964. Bar: Wash. 1964, D.C. 1981, U.S. Dist. Ct. (we. dist.) Wash. 1964, U.S. Ct. Appeals (9th cir.) 1972, U.S. Supreme Ct. 1980. Law clk. Justice Robert T. Hunter, Olympia, Wash., 1964-65; asst. counsel Pacific Car & Foundry Co., Renton, Wash., 1965-66; ptnr. Mullavey, Hageman, Treece & Sayre, Seattle, 1966-69, McBride & Sayre, 1969-71; sole practice Seattle, 1971-94; sr. ptnr. Sayre Law Offices, 1994—; judge pro tem King County Superior Ct., 1973-83, 89—; trustee King County Bar Found., 1985-88, 92-98. Bd. visitors Seattle Univ. Sch. Law, 1991—. Served to 1st lt. USAFR, 1957-60. Recipient Pro Bono Svc. award, 1988. Mem. ABA (Nat. Conf. Bar Pres.), Wash. Bar Assn. (spl. dist. counsel 1982-88, editorial adv. bd. 1986-89, chair Bac-Pac 1991-94, chair pub. rels. com. 1992-93), King County Bar Assn. (treas. 1982-85, trustee 1985-88, bench-bar delay reduction task force 1987-89, 2d v.p. 1988-89, 1st v.p. 1989-90, pres. 1990-91, Geisness award 1997), South King County Bar Assn., Wash. Trial Lawyers Assn., Beta Theta Pi, Phi Delta Phi. Clubs: Wash. Athletic, Seattle Yacht Club, Useless Bay Golf and Country, Lions. General practice, Probate, State civil litigation. Office: Boren & Jefferson Bldg 1016 Jefferson St Seattle WA 98104-2435

**SAYRE, RICHARD LAYTON,** lawyer; b. Spokane, Wash., May 21, 1953; s. Charles Layton and Elizabeth Jane (Ward) S.; m. Karen Linda Sayre, Mar. 8, 1979; children: Wendi Sue Stoken, Tracey Lynn Turner. BA, U. Wash., 1976; JD, Gonzaga U., 1979. Bar: Wash. 1979, U.S. Dist. Ct. (ea. and we. dist.) Wash. 1979, U.S. Ct. Appeals (9th cir.) 1986; cert. elder law atty. Nat. Elder Law Found. Deputy prosecuting atty. Spokane County, Spokane, 1979-84; shareholder Underwood, Campbell, Brock & Cerutti, Spokane, 1984-92, Sayre & Sayre P.S., Spokane, 1992—; pres. Nat. Acad. Elder Law Attys., Washington, 1995-96. Potentate, trustee El Katif Shrine Temple, Spokane, 1997; bd. govs. Shriner's Hosp. for Children, Spokane, 1993-96; exec. officer Order of DeMolay, Washington, 1993—, active mem. internat. supreme coun. Order DeMolay. Recipient Pro Bono award Spokane County Bar Assn., 1991, Recognition of Achievement & Contribution award Lutheran Social Svcs. of Washington, Idaho, 1992, 97, Achievement award Spokane Sexual Assault Ctr., 1997. Mem. Nat. Acad. Elder Law Attys., Spokane Estate Planning Coun. Democrat. Episcopal. Avocations: sailing, skiing. Estate planning, Probate, Elder. Office: Sayre & Sayre 111 W Cataldo Ave Ste 210 Spokane WA 99201-3203

**SCACCHETTI, DAVID J.,** lawyer; b. Newark, July 13, 1956; s. Edmond and Evelyn Scacchetti; m. Marcia Ellen Gessiness, Aug. 31, 1985; children: Gabriella Elise, Olivia Beth. BA in Polit. Sci. with honors, U. Cin., 1978, JD, 1981. Bar: Ohio 1982, U.S. Dist. Ct. (so. dist.) Ohio 1982, U.S. Dist. Ct. (ea. dist.) Ky. 1986, U.S. Dist. Ct. Ariz. 1997. Atty. Edward J. Utz, Esq., Cin., 1982; sole practitioner Cin., 1982-98; atty. Scacchetti & Scacchetti, Cin., 1998—. Mem. ATLA, Nat. Assn. Criminal Def. Lawyers, Greater Cin. Criminal Def. Lawyer Assn., Ohio Acad. Trial Lawyers, Ham. County Trial Lawyers Assn., Phi Beta Kappa. Avocations: writing, tennis, Tribal art, guitar, travel. Criminal, Personal injury, General civil litigation. Office: Scacchetti & Scacchetti 601 Main St 3d Fl Cincinnati OH 45202

**SCAFETTA, JOSEPH, JR.,** lawyer; b. Chester, Pa., May 10, 1947; s. Giuseppe and Mary (Koslosky) S.; m. Teresa M. Talierco, July 4, 1986. BS in Aero. Engring., Pa. State U., 1969; JD, U. Pitts., 1972; M in Patent Law, Georgetown U., 1973; MBA, George Washington U., 1983. Bar: Pa. 1972, U.S. Patent and Trademark Office 1973, D.C. 1978, Va. 1979, U.S. Supreme Ct. 1980, U.S. Ct. Appeals (fed. cir.) 1982. Legal rschr. Arent, Fox, Kintner, Plotkin et al, Washington, 1973; law clk. to presiding judge U.S. Dist. Ct. S.C., Columbia, 1973-74; assoc. Colton & Stone, Arlington, Va., 1975-77, Craig & Antonelli, Washington, 1977-78, Wigman & Cohen, Arlington, 1978-83, Wenderoth, Lind & Ponack, Washington, 1983-86, Cushman, Darby & Cushman, Washington, 1986-87; counsel Russell, Georges & Breneman, Arlington, 1987-91, Young & Thompson, Arlington, 1991-96; pvt. practice Arlington, 1996—; voting mem. Nat. Commn. for Social Justice, 1995-97. Author: Book Review Copyright Handbook, 1979, The Constitutionality/Unconstitutionality of the Patent Infringement Statute, 1979, (with others) Patents on Microorganisms, 1980; editor: An Intellectual Property Law Primer, 1975; contbr. articles to profl. jours. Mem. Consumer Affairs Commn., Alexandria, Va., 1985-87; charter mem. Christopher Columbus Quincentenary Jubilee Com., 1990-93; chair Va. chpt. Commn. for Social Justice, 1987—; mem. Fairfax County Dem. Com., Falls Church, 1987-89; parliamentarian City Dem. Com., Alexandria, 1985-87. Recipient Robert C. Watson award Am. Patent Law Assn., 1975. Mem. ABA, Am. Arbitration Assn. (mem. comml. panel), Va. Bar Assn., Am. Intellectual Property Law Assn. (mem. pub. info. com. 1983—), D.C. Bar Assn., Patent and Trademark Office Soc., Avanti Italiani (pres. Alexandria chpt. 1981-83), Sons of Italy, Grand Lodge Va. (state pres. 1993-95). Patent, Trademark and copyright. Office: 1755 Jeff Davis Hwy Ste 400 Arlington VA 22202-3530

**SCALES, CINDA L.,** lawyer; b. Martinsburg, W.Va., Mar. 31, 1956; d. Lawrence E. and Evelyn M. (Armbrester) Fink; m. Michael L. Scales; children: Stephanie, Lawren, Michelle. JD, U. Md., 1989; MBA, Shippensburg U., 1982, M in Psychology, 1985. Bar: W.Va., Md. Assoc. Askin, Pill, Scales & Burke, Martinsburg, W.Va., 1989-93; pvt. practice law Martinsburg, 1993-95, 97—; ptnr. Mills & Scales, Martinsburg, 1995-97; prof. Shepherd Coll., Sheperdstown, W.Va., 1984—. Mem. ABA, NOW, Eastern Panhandle Family Law Bar Assn. (v.p. 1996—), Berkeley County Bar Assn. (treas. 1994-96, sec. 1996—). Family and matrimonial, Personal injury, Bankruptcy. Office: 112 E King St Martinsburg WV 25401-4206

**SCALES, CLARENCE RAY,** lawyer; b. Morton, Miss., Aug. 23, 1922; s. Felix Augustus and Zola (DuBose) S.; m. Lura Evelyn Lee, Aug. 20, 1948; children: Clarence Ray Jr., Linda Alcott, Philip Lee. LLB, U. Miss., 1949, JD, 1968. Miss. 1949. Ptnr. Scales & Scales, P.A., Jackson, Miss., 1949—. Democrat. Baptist. General civil litigation, Criminal, Personal injury. Home: 1022 Northpointe Dr Jackson MS 39211-2917 Office: 414 S State St Ste 201 Jackson MS 39201-5021

**SCALES-TRENT, JUDY,** law educator; b. Winston-Salem, N.C., Oct. 1, 1940; d. William Johnson Jr. and Viola (Scales) Trent; 1 child, Jason Benjamin Ellis. BA, Oberlin Coll., 1962; MA, Middlebury Coll., 1967; JD, Northwestern U., 1973. Bar: D.C., N.Y. Staff atty. EEOC, Washington, 1973-76, spl. asst. to commr., 1977-79, spl. asst. to gen. counsel, 1979-80, appellate atty., 1980-84; prof. Buffalo Law Sch. SUNY, 1984—; chair pres.' panel for rev. of affirmative action procedures SUNY, Buffalo, 1989-93. Author: Notes of a White Black Women: Race, Color, Community, 1995; contbr. articles, revs., essays to profl. publs. Trustee Ujima Theater Co., Buffalo, 1989-92; bd. visitors Roswell Park Cancer Inst., Buffalo, 1991-96. Mem. Nat. Women and the Law Assn. (bd. dirs. 1987-91), Soc. Am. Law Tchrs. (bd. govs. 1992-95), Am. Assn. Law Schs. (chair com. on recruitment and retention of minority law tchrs. 1993-94), Urban League (adv. bd. 1994-97). Office: SUNY Buffalo Law Sch O'Brian Hall Buffalo NY 14260

**SCALETTA, PHILLIP JASPER,** lawyer, educator; b. Sioux City, Iowa, Aug. 20, 1925; s. Phillip and Louise (Pelmulder) S.; m. Helen M. Beedle; children: Phillip R., Cheryl D. Kesler. BS, Morningside Coll., Sioux City, Iowa, 1948; JD, U. Iowa, 1950. Bar: Iowa 1950, U.S. Dist. Ct. Iowa 1950, Ind. 1966, U.S. Supreme Ct. 1968. Ptnr. McKnight and Scaletta, Sioux City, 1950-51; field rep. Farmers Ins. Group, Sioux City, 1951-54, sr. liability examiner, Aurora, Ill., 1954-60; br. claims mgr., Ft. Wayne, Ind., 1960-66; prof. law Purdue U., West Lafayette, Ind., 1966—; dir. profl. masters programs of the Krannet Grad. Sch. of Mgmt. Purdue U., 1987-90; of counsel with Mayfield & Brooks Attys. at Law, 1967—; arbitrator Panel of Arbitrators Am. Arbitration Assn. Co-author: Business Law and Regulatory Environments, 5th edit., 1996, Business Law Workbook, 5th edit., 1996, Foundations of Business Law and Legal Environment, 1986, 4th edit., 1997, Student Workbook and Study Guide, 1986, 4th edit., 1997; contbr. numerous articles to profl. jours. Mem. Ind. Gov's Commn. Individual Privacy, 1975. Recipient Best Tchr. of Yr. award Standard Oil Ind. Found., 1972, Outstanding Tchr. award Purdue U. Alumni Assn., 1974, Most Effective Tchr. award Krannert Grad. Sch. Mgmt. Purdue U., 1991. Mem. Am. Bus. Law Assn. (pres., Sr. Faculty Excellence award 1989), Tippecanoe County Bar Assn., Tri State Bus Law Assn. (past pres.), Midwest Bus. Adminstrn. Assn., Beta Gamma Sigma (bd. govs.). Office: Purdue U 511 Krannert Bldg West Lafayette IN 47907

**SCALETTA, PHILLIP RALPH, III,** lawyer; b. Iowa City, Iowa, Dec. 18, 1949; s. Phillip Jasper and Helen M. (Beedle) S.; m. Karen Lynn Scaletta, May 13, 1973; children: Phillip, Anthony, Alexander. BSIM, Purdue U., 1972, MS, 1972; JD, Ind. U., 1975. Bar: Ind. 1975, U.S. Dist. Ct. Ind. 1975, Ill. 1993. Assoc. Ice Miller Donadio & Ryan, Indpls., 1975-81, ptnr., 1981—. Contbr. articles to profl. jours. Chmn. Ind. Continuing Legal Edn. Found., Indpls., 1989; mem. Environ. Quality Control Water Com., 1988-98. Mem. Ind. Bar Assn., Indpls. Bar Assn., Def. Rsch. Inst., Internat. Assn. Def. Counsel, Gyro Club Indpls. (v.p. 1992-93, pres. 1993-94, bd. dirs. 1990—). Avocations: golf, skiing, tennis. Environmental, General civil litigation. Home: 7256 Tuliptree Trl Indianapolis IN 46256-2136 Office: Ice Miller Donadio & Ryan 1 American Sq Indianapolis IN 46282-0001

**SCALIA, ANTONIN,** United States supreme court justice; b. Trenton, N.J., Mar. 11, 1936; s. S. Eugene and Catherine Louise (Panaro) S.; m. Maureen McCarthy, Sept. 10, 1960; children—Ann Forrest, Eugene, John Francis, Catherine Elisabeth, Mary Clare, Paul David, Matthew, Christopher James, Margaret Jane. A.B., Georgetown U., 1957; student, U. Fribourg, Switzerland, 1955-56; LL.B., Harvard, 1960. Bar: Ohio 1962, Va. 1970. Assoc. Jones Day Cockley & Reavis, Cleve., 1961-67; assoc. prof. U. Va. Law Sch., 1967-70; prof. law U. Va., 1970-74; gen. counsel Office Telecommunications Policy, Exec. Office of Pres., 1971-72; chmn. Adminstrv. Conf. U.S., Washington, 1972-74; asst. atty. gen. U.S. Office Legal Counsel, Justice Dept., 1974-77; vis. prof. Georgetown Law Center, 1977, Stanford Law Sch., 1980-81; vis. scholar Am. Enterprise Inst., 1977; prof. law U. Chgo., 1977-82; judge U.S. Ct. Appeals (D.C. cir.), 1982-86; justice U.S. Supreme Ct., Washington, 1986—. Editor: Regulation mag, 1979-82. Sheldon fellow Harvard U., 1960-61. Office: US Supreme Ct Supreme Ct Bldg 1 1st St NE Washington DC 20543-0001

**SCALISE-QUBROSI, CELESTE,** lawyer; b. San Antonio, May 15, 1959; d. Robert and Edna (King) Scalise; m. James S. Boyd Jr., Oct. 6, 1984 (div. Dec. 1988); m. Marshall Bruce Lloyd, May 13, 1989 (div. July 1995); m. Khalil Qubrosi, Feb. 16, 1997. BA, U. Tex., San Antonio, 1979; JD, Tex. Tech U., 1983. Bar: Tex. 1984, U.S. Ct. Appeals (5th cir.) 1984, U.S. Dist. Ct. (so. dist.) Tex. 1985, U.S. Dist. Ct. (no. dist.) Tex. 1990, U.S. Dist. Ct. (we. dist.) Tex. 1991, U.S. Dist Ct. (ea. dist.) Tex. 1992. Field ops. asst. Bur. of Census U.S. Dept. of Commerce, San Antonio, 1980; title examiner, law clk. Lubbock (Tex.) Abstract & Title Co., 1982-83; assoc. Bonilla & Berlanga, Corpus Christi, Tex., 1983-89; sr. assoc. Heard, Goggan, Blair & Williams, San Antonio, 1989-90; assoc. Denton & McKamie, San Antonio, 1990, Joe Weiss and Assocs., San Antonio, 1990; field litigation office Cigna litigation atty. Law Offices of Sean P. Martinez, San Antonio, 1990-97; pres. Fountain Rorm, Inc.; of counsel Aaron & Quirk, San Antonio, 1997-99, Law Office of Scalise-Qubrosi, 1999—; mem. adv. group Camino Real Health Systems Agy., Inc., San Antonio, 1978-80. Mem. substance abuse adv. com. Planned Parenthood Bd., Corpus Christi, 1983-85; vice chair Nueces County Mental Health/Mental Retardation Substance Abuse Com., San Antonio, 1987-89; mem. vestry Trinity Episcopal Ch. Mem. Tex. Bar Assn. (govt. lawyers sect., ins. def.), San Antonio Bar Assn., U. Tex. at San Antonio Alumni Assn., Delta Theta Phi. Episcopalian. Avocations: photography, reading, gem and minerals collector. Pension, profit-sharing, and employee benefits, Insurance. Home: 2130 W Gramercy Pl San Antonio TX 78201-4822 Office: Law Offices Scalise - Qubrosi 105 Furr Dr San Antonio TX 78201-4412

**SCANLAN, KEVIN J.,** lawyer; b. L.A., Mar. 28, 1970; s. James Thomas and Helen Marie Scanlan; m. Katie Scanlan, July 8, 1995. BA in Bus. Adminstrn., Carroll Coll., Helena, Mont., 1992; JD cum laude, Seattle U., 1996. Bar: Idaho, 1996, U.S. Dist. Ct. Idaho 1996. Atty. Hall, Farley, Oberrecht & Blanton, P.A., Boise, Idaho, 1996—. Editor Seattle Law Rev., 1994-96. Bd. dirs. Ronald McDonald House, Boise, 1997—. Mem. ABA, Idaho State Bar Assn. Roman Catholic. Avocations: fly fishing, skiing. Professional liability, General civil litigation, Intellectual property. Office: Hall Farley et al 702 W Idaho St Ste 700 Boise ID 83702-8908

**SCANLON, VERA MARY,** lawyer; b. Bklyn., June 23, 1968; d. Dennis P. and Alice (Keelty) S. AB, Columbia U., 1990; JD, Yale U., 1995. Bar: N.Y., N.J., U.S. Dist. Ct. (ea. and so. dists.) N.Y., U.S. Dist. Ct. N.J. Assoc. Hughes Hubbard & Reed LLP, N.Y.C., 1995-98; clk. to Hon. D. Dominguez U.S. Dist. Ct. Dist. P.R., San Juan, 1998; clk. to Hon. F. Block U.S. Dist. Ct. (ea. dist.) N.Y., Bklyn., 1998—. Mem. ABA, Assn. Bar City N.Y., Alumni Assn. Jesuit Vol. Corps South, Marymount Sch. Alumni Assn. Avocations: watercolor, Irish literature. Home: 224 89th St Brooklyn NY 11209-5612

**SCARBARY, OTIS LEE,** lawyer; b. Macon, Ga., Feb. 4, 1952; s. Otis Thomas Jr. and Shirley (Tucker) S.; m. Donna Lynne Hughes, June 11, 1981; 1 child, Amanda Leigh. BA, Mercer U., 1974, JD, 1977. Bar: Ga., U.S. Dist. Ct. (mid. dist.) Ga. 1977, U.S. Ct. Appeals (11th cir.) 1981. Pvt. practice Macon, 1977-83; asst. solicitor Bibb County, Office of Solicitor, Macon, 1983-96, solicitor-gen., 1996—. Mem. Ga. Assn. of Solicitors-Gen. (exec. bd. 1997—), Macon Bar Assn., State Bar of Ga. (govt. atty. involvement com.), Lions (exec. bd. Macon Evening Club 1997-99), Order of Police. Democrat. Avocations: jogging, diving, reading. Home: 110 Fredricksted Pl Macon GA 31204-1463 Office: Office of Solicitor-Gen Bibb County Cthouse Rm #504 Macon GA 31201

**SCARFONE, JOHN A.,** lawyer; b. Bronx, N.Y., Oct. 6, 1951; s. Pasquale and Anna Scarfone; m. Janet Starr, May 16, 1982; 1 child, Victoria G. BA in Psychology, CUNY, 1973; M in Healthcare Adminstrn., L.I. U., 1976; JD, St. John's U., 1990. Various positions Lenox Hill Hosp., N.Y.C., 1969-79, asst. v.p., 1979-84, v.p., 1984-88; v.p. ops. St. Clare's Hosp., N.Y.C., 1989-90, v., gen. counsel, 1991-97; assoc. Hirsch & Britt, Garden City, N.Y., 1998—. Mem. Am. Coll. Healthcare Execs. (diplomate). Democrat. Health, General corporate. Office: Hirsch & Britt 1225 Franklin Ave Ste 470 Garden City NY 11530-1693

**SCARINGI, MICHAEL JOSEPH,** lawyer, consultant; b. Seattle, May 9, 1944; m. Suzan Jean Allyn, Sept. 9, 1967; children: Anthony, Marco. AA, Highline Coll., Seattle, 1965; BA, Seattle U., 1967, MA, 1970; grad. law clerkship, Wash. State Bar Assn., 1987. Bar: Wash. 1989, U.S. Dist. Ct. (we. dist.) Wash. 1989. Cons. Wash. State Dept. Trans., Seattle, 1970—; atty. pvt. practice, Seattle, 1989—. Real property, General practice, Estate planning. Home: PO Box 670 Mercer Island WA 98040-0670 Office: 1299 156th Ave NE Ste 120 Bellevue WA 98007-7562

**SCARLETT, RANDALL H.,** lawyer; b. Athens, Ohio, July 12, 1957; s. John Donald and Sherry (Richards) S.; m. Mary Anne Scarlett, Sept. 21, 1991; children: Randall Alexander, Christina Marie. BA, San Francisco State U., 1982; JD, Golden Gate U., 1985. Bar: Calif. 1988, U.S. Dist. Ct. (no. dist.) Calif. 1985, U.S. Dist. Ct. (ea. dist.) Calif. 1988, U.S. Dist. Ct. (so. and ctrl. dists.) Calif. 1995, U.S. Ct. Appeals (9th cir.) 1995, U.S. Supreme Ct. 1995. Ptnr. Belli, Belli, Brown, Monzione, Fabbro & Zakaria, San Francisco, 1989-93, Brown, Monzione, Fabbro, Zakaria & Scarlett, San Francisco, 1993-96, Brown, Fabbro & Scarlett, San Francisco, 1996—; lectr. Mem. ATLA (sustaining, com. Traumatic Brain Injury Litigation Group), Consumer Attys. Calif. (sustaining), San Francisco Lawyers Assn., Bar Assn. San Francisco,. Avocations: golfing, scuba diving. General civil litigation, Personal injury, Environmental. Office: Brown Fabbro & Scarlett 425 Battery St Ste 400 San Francisco CA 94111-3210

**SCARMINACH, CHARLES ANTHONY,** lawyer; b. Syracuse, N.Y., Feb. 19, 1944; s. John Louis and Lucy (Egnoto) S.; children: John, Catherine, Karen, Charles, Robert. MA, U. Buffalo, 1965; JD, Syracuse U., 1968. Bar: N.Y. 1968, S.C. 1974. Gen. counsel Sea Pines Co., Hilton Head Island, S.C., 1973-78; sole practice Hilton Head Island, 1978-83; ptnr. Novit & Scarminach, P.A., Hilton Head Island, 1983-93, Novit Scarminach & Williams P.A., Hilton Head Island, 1993—; bd. dirs. Nations Bank, Hilton Head Island. Chmn. bd. Sea Pines Montessori Sch., Hilton Head Island, 1979-83; bd. dirs. Hilton Head Preparatory Sch., 1984-93, chmn. bd. trustees 1986-93. Maj. U.S. Army, 1968-73. Mem. ABA, S.C. Bar Assn., N.Y. State Bar Assn., Hilton Head Island C. of C. (bd. dirs. 1996-99), Sea Pines Club. Democrat. Roman Catholic. General corporate, General practice, Real property. Home: 10 Wood Duck Ct Hilton Head Island SC 29928-3010 Office: Novit Scarminach & Williams PA PO Box 14 Hilton Head Island SC 29938-0014

**SCAROLA, SUSAN MARGARET,** lawyer; b. Elizabeth, N.J., Mar. 19, 1948; d. Anthony and Ruth (Cohen) S. BA cum laude, Thiel Coll., 1970; JD, Rutgers-State of U. of N.J., 1976. Bar: N.J. 1976, N.Y. 1985, Fla. 1993; cert. criminal trial atty., matrimonial law atty. Law sec. to Judge Triarsi, Superior Ct. of N.J., Elizabeth, 1976-77; asst. prosecutor Union County Prosecutor's Office, Elizabeth, 1997-88; non-equity ptnr. Lomurro Davison Eastman & Munoz, Freehold, N.J., 1988-97; ptnr. Newman Scarola & Assoc., Old Bridge, N.J., 1997—; judge Mcpl. Ct., Twp. of Old Bridge, 1999. Trustee Legal Aid Soc. of Monmouth County, 1992, sec., 1998—; committeewoman Old Bridge Dem. Com., 1995-99. Named Women of Yr. Women Lawyers in Monmouth County, 1994. Mem. Monmouth Bar Assn. (chair family law com. 1995-97), N.J. Bar Assn., Fla. Bar Assn. Family and matrimonial. Office: Newman Scarola & Assocs 64 W Main St Freehold NJ 07728-2142

**SCARZAFAVA, JOHN FRANCIS,** lawyer; b. Oneonta, N.Y., Apr. 4, 1947; s. Francis R. and Nettie (Hotalen) S.; m. Nettie Jean Chambers; children: Robert Francis, Angela Duina, Amber Atkinson, Amy Raye Atkinson. BA, St. Bonaventure U., 1973; JD, St. Mary's U., San Antonio, 1975. Bar: Tex. 1975, U.S. Ct. Appeals (5th cir.) 1976, U.S. Dist. Ct. (we. dist.) Tex. 1978, U.S. Supreme Ct. 1979, N.Y. 1981, U.S. Dist. Ct. (no. dist.) N.Y. 1982. Assoc. Gochman & Weir, San Antonio, 1975-77, ptnr., 1977-78; ptnr. Scarzafava & Davis, San Antonio, 1978-82; prinicpal Scarzafava Law Office, Oneonta, 1982—; instr. various Nat. Coll. of Adv., 1979—; lectr. in field. Contbr. numerous articles to profl. law jours. Bd. dirs. St. Bonaventure U. Nat. Alumni 1982-90, pres. 1988-90; bd. trustees St. Bonaventure U. 1988-90; bd. dirs. A.O. Fox Hosp., 1998—. Named Alumnus of Yr. St. Bonaventure U., 1993. Mem. Assn. Trial Lawyers Am. (President's Club), Tex. Trial Lawyers Assn., N.Y. Trial Lawyers Assn. Roman Catholic. Personal injury, Federal civil litigation, State civil litigation. Home: 2 Ravine Pkwy Oneonta NY 13820-4618 Office: 48 Dietz St Ste C Oneonta NY 13820-1827

**SCATES, JENNIFER ANN,** lawyer; b. Midland, Tex., Sept. 5, 1957; d. Marion (Braquet) S.; m. Timothy John Hayles, Apr. 30, 1988; 1 child, Richard Maxwell Scates Hayles. BA, U. St. Thomas, 1980; JD, Oklahoma City U., 1985. Bar: Tex. 1986. Pvt. practice Houston, 1986-88, Austin, Tex., 1988—. Family and matrimonial. Office: 5750 Balcones Dr Ste 207 Austin TX 78731-4269

**SCENNA, MICHELE CARTON,** lawyer; b. Neptune, N.J., Nov. 14, 1969; d. John Charles and Joanne Kemp Carton; m. Derrick Andrew Scenna, Oct. 18, 1997. BA in History, Cath. U., 1992, JD, 1995. Bar: N.J. 1995, U.S. Dist. Ct. N.J. 1995. Law clk. Robert A. Coogan JSC Monmouth County Ct., Freehold, N.J., 1995-96; assoc. Lomurro Davison Eastman & Munoz, Freehold, 1996—. Recipient Am. Jurisprudence award in torts Am. Jurisprudence, 1993. Mem. Women Lawyers Monmouth County, Monmouth County Bar Assn. (young lawyer's divsn.), Jr. League Monmouth County. Roman Catholic. Family and matrimonial, General civil litigation, General practice. Home: 86 Secretariat Ct Eatontown NJ 07724-3843 Office: Lomurro Davison Eastman & Munoz 100 Willow Brook Rd Freehold NJ 07728-2879

**SCEPER, DUANE HAROLD,** lawyer; b. Norfolk, Va., Nov. 16, 1946; s. Robert George and Marion Eudora (Hynes) S.; m. Sharon Diane Cramer, July 4, 1981; stepchildren: Karin Stevenson, Diane Stevenson. BS in Law, Western State U., 1979, JD, 1980. Bar: Calif. 1982, U.S. Dist. Ct. (so. dist.) Calif. 1982. Field engr. Memorex/Tex. Instruments, San Diego, 1968-70; computer programmer San Diego, 1970-81; atty. Allied Ins. Group, San Diego, 1981-85; sole practice San Diego, 1985-87; ptnr. Paluso & Sceper, San Diego, 1987—; cons. computers 1980—; lectr. estate planning various orgns. Patentee in field. Active Com. to Elect King Golden to Congress, San Diego, 1978. Served with USAF, 1965-68. Recipient Am. Jurisprudence award, 1979. Mem. ABA, San Diego County Bar Assn., Assn. Trial Lawyers of Am., Calif. Trial Lawyers Assn., San Diego Trial Lawyers Assn., Am. Subrogation Attys., Assn. of Ins. Def. Counsel, So. Calif. Def. Counsel, Air Commando Assn. (life), Delta Theta Phi. Democrat. State civil litigation, Estate planning, Insurance. Home: 2641 Massachusetts Ave Lemon Grove CA 91945-3149 Office: Paluso & Sceper 707 Broadway Ste 1100 San Diego CA 92101-5322

**SCHAAB, ARNOLD J.,** lawyer; b. Newark, Dec. 26, 1939; s. Robert George and Pauline (Levine) S.; m. Marcia Stecker, 1964 (div. 1978); children: Emily Diana, Genevieve; m. Patricia Caesar, 1981 (div. 1996). BA, New Sch. Univ., 1962; LLB, Harvard U., 1965. Bar: N.Y. 1967, U.S. Dist. Ct. (so. and ea. dists.) N.Y. 1967. Assoc. Chadbourne & Parke, N.Y.C., 1966-69; ptnr. Anderson, Kill & Olick, N.Y.C., 1969-78; sr. ptnr. Pryor, Cashman, Sherman & Flynn L.L.P., N.Y.C., 1978—. Pres. Literacy Ptnrs., Inc.; mem. exec. com. Shaker Mus. and Libr., Old Chatham, N.Y.; mem. vis. com. Milano Grad. Sch. Mgmt. and Pub. Policy, New Sch. for Social Rsch. Fulbright scholar Law Faculty U. Paris, 1966. Fellow N.Y. Bar Found., Am. Bar Found.; mem. ABA (vice chair internat. fin. transactions com., forum com. on constrn. industry), N.Y. State Bar Assn. (chair internat. law and practice sect., chmn. spl. com. free trade in the Ams., ho. of dels., fin. com., long range planning com., by-laws com.), Assn. of Bar of City of N.Y., Computer Law Assn., Univ. Club (asst. treas., chmn. fin. com., chmn. audit com., mem. coun.), Doubles, Nat. Arts Club, Old Chatham Hunt Club. Private international, General corporate, Contracts commercial. Office: Pryor Cashman Sherman & Flynn 410 Park Ave Fl 10 New York NY 10022-4441

**SCHAAF, DOUGLAS ALLAN,** lawyer; b. Green Bay, Wis., Nov. 18, 1955; s. Carlton Otto and Fern (Brunette) S.; m. Kathlyn T. Bielke, Feb. 23, 1988. BBA magna cum laude in Internat. Bus., St. Norbert Coll., DePere, Wis., 1978; JD, U. Notre Dame, 1981. Bar: Ill. 1981, Calif. 1987. Assoc. McDermott, Will & Emery, Chgo., 1981-84, Skadden, Arps, Slate, Meagher & Flom, 1984-89; ptnr. Paul Hastings, Janofsky & Walker, L.A., 1989—; adj. faculty mem. John Marshall Law Sch., 1984-87. Atty. Chgo. Vol. Legal Services, 1984-87; bd. dirs. Orange County Alzheimer's Assn. Mem. Orange County Bar Assn. (chair tax sect. 1994-96). Corporate taxation, General corporate, Personal income taxation. Office: Paul Hastings Janofsky & Walker 695 Town Center Dr Ste 1700 Costa Mesa CA 92626-7191

**SCHABERG, JOHN IRVIN,** lawyer; b. St. Louis, Aug. 8, 1955; s. Irvin William Jr. and Hazel Mae (Matteson) S.; m. Denise Lynn Derickson, Sept. 26, 1981; children: Katherine Elizabeth, Caroline Marie, John Henry. BA, U. Tulsa, 1977; JD, U. Tex., 1980. Bar: Mo. 1980, Ill. 1981, U.S. Dist. Ct. (ea. dist.) Mo. 1981, U.S. Dist Ct. (no. dist.) Ill., U.S. Dist. Ct. (so. dist.) Ill. 1985. Assoc. Roberts & Heneghan, Inc., St. Louis, 1980-82, Hinshaw, Culbertson, Moelmann, Hoban & Fuller, Chgo., 1982-87; assoc., resident atty.-in-charge Hinshaw, Culbertson, Moelmann, Hoban & Fuller, Belleville, Ill., 1985-87; prin. Roberts, Perryman, Bomkamp & Meives, P.C., St. Louis, 1988—. Editor notes and comments Am. Jour. Criminal Law, 1978-80; contbr. articles to legal jours. Mem. ABA (torts and ins. practice sect., sect. litigation), Mo. Bar Assn., Ill. State Bar Assn., Bar Assn. Met. St. Louis, St. Clair County Bar Assn., Ill. Assn. Def. Trial Counsel, Mo. Orgn. Def. Lawyers. Roman Catholic. General civil litigation, Insurance, Communications. Office: Roberts Perryman Bomkamp & Meives PC 1 Mercantile Ctr Ste 2300 Saint Louis MO 63101-1612 also: 23 Public Sq Ste 402 Belleville IL 62220-1627

**SCHABES, ALAN ELLIOT,** lawyer; b. Cleve., Feb. 21, 1957; s. Herbert B. and Retha R. (Schuman) S.; m. Elissa Geduld, May 31, 1982; children: Dena, Shira, Eli. BSBA magna cum laude, Duquesne U., 1978; JD, Hofstra U., 1981. Bar: Ohio 1981, U.S. Dist. Ct. (no. dist.) Ohio 1981, U.S. Ct. Appeals (6th cir.) 1982. From assoc. to ptnr. Benesch, Friedlander, Coplan & Aronoff, Cleve., 1981—. Mem. Ohio Bar Assn., Cleve. Bar Assn. (licensure and certification subcom. of health law sect. 1988—, chair health law dept.), Nat. Health Lawyers Assn. (publs. com. 1990—). Avocations: reading, sports. Health, Administrative and regulatory, General corporate. Home: 2459 Brentwood Rd Beachwood OH 44122-1550 Office: Benesch Friedlander Coplan & Aronoff 2300 BP Tower 200 Public Sq Cleveland OH 44114-2378

**SCHACTER, STACEY JAY,** lawyer; b. Highland Park, Ill., Jan. 14, 1963; s. David and Harriet (Arkovitz) S.; m. Susan Lynn Campbell, June 20, 1988; children: Stacia Marie, Brianna Nicole. BS in Acctg., Econs., Miami U., Oxford, Ohio, 1985; JD, Ohio State U., 1988. Bar: Ohio 1989, U.S. Dist. Ct. (so. dist.) Ohio 1989, U.S. Bankruptcy Ct. 1989, U.S. Supreme Ct. 1992. Assoc. Dinsmore & Scohl, Cin., 1988-90; assoc. Harris, Harris Field Schacter & Bardach, Cin., 1990-99, of counsel, 1999—; v.p., gen. counsel EMCC, Inc., Pembroke, Mass., 1999—. Team walk com. March of Dimes, Cin., 1988-92; mem. Greater Cin. Venture Assn., 1990-92; pres.-elect, bd. dirs. Strategic Leadership Forum, 1997; mem. Duveneck com., mem. exec. com. Cin. Art Mus. Mem. Ohio Bar Assn., Cin. Bar Assn. (bankruptcy com. 1991—, spakers com., corp. securities law com.). Bankruptcy, Contracts commercial, Computer. Home: 82 Satuit Meadow Ln Norwell MA 02061 Office: EMCC Inc 33 Riverside Dr Pembroke MA 02359

**SCHADLE, WILLIAM JAMES,** lawyer; b. Dubuque, Iowa, Aug. 4, 1932; s. John Paul and Helen Bernadine (Hird) S.; m. Jane Louise Cameron, Nov. 20, 1972. BA, U. Iowa, 1959; JD, Drake U., Des Moines, 1984. Bar: Iowa 1984. Gen. counsel Hettinga Equipment, Inc., Des Moines, 1984-87; assoc. Thomas J. Reilly Law Firm, P.C., Des Moines, 1987-89; pvt. practice Des Moines, Iowa, 1989—. With USN, 1952-56. Mem. Iowa State Bar Assn. Personal injury, Family and matrimonial, General practice. Office: PO Box 35983 Des Moines IA 50315-0309

**SCHAEFER, ALAN CHARLES,** lawyer; b. Ft. Meade, Md., May 1, 1952; s. Martin and Gertrude (Foard) S.; m. Judith Ann Bard, June 15, 1974; 1 child, Alan Bard. BS in Polit. Sci., Ea. Ill. U., Charleston, 1973; JD with distinction, John Marshall Law Sch., 1985. Bar: Ill. 1985, U.S. Dist. Ct. (no. dist.) Ill. 1987, U.S. Ct. Appeals (7th cir.) 1989. Jud. clk. Ill. Appellate Ct., Chgo., 1985-87; assoc. Lord, Bissell & Brook, Chgo., 1987-91; prin. Schaefer & Schaefer, Hoffman Estates, Ill., 1991—. Assoc. editor John Marshall Law Rev., 1983-84. Mem. ABA, ISBA. Republican. Methodist. Avocations: photography, travel, writing. Environmental, Labor, General civil litigation. Home: 25835 N Oak Hill Rd Lk Barrington IL 60010-7023 Office: Schaefer & Schaefer 2300 Barrington Rd Ste 400 Hoffman Est IL 60195-2036

**SCHAEFER, DAVID ARNOLD,** lawyer; b. Cleve., May 3, 1948; s. Leonard and Maxine V. (Bassett) S.; m. Riki C. Freeman, Aug. 8, 1971; children—Kevin, Lindsey, Traci. BS, Miami U., Oxford, Ohio, 1970; MA, Northwestern U., 1971; JD, Case Western Res. U., 1974. Bar: Ohio 1974, U.S. Dist. Ct. (no. dist.) Ohio 1974, U.S. Ct. Appeals (6th cir.) 1978, U.S. Supreme Ct. 1978. Ptnr. Guren, Merritt et al, 1980-84, Benesch, Friedlander et al, Cleve., 1984-93; McCarthy, Lebit, Crystal & Haiman, Cleve., 1993—; Author: Deposition Strategy, 1981, 2d edit., 1984; contbr. articles to profl. publs. Soccer coach Ohio Amateur Youth Soccer League, Cleve., 1980-81, 84. Mem. ABA, Internat. Assn. Def. Counsel, Fed. Bar Assn. (pres. elect 1991-92, pres. 1992-93), Nat. Inst. Trial Advocacy (faculty), 8th Dist. Jud. Conf. (life). General civil litigation, Product liability. Office: McCarthy Lebit Crystal & Haiman 1800 Midland Bldg 101 W Prospect Ave Ste 1800 Cleveland OH 44115-1027

**SCHAEFFER, HERBERT D.,** lawyer; b. St. Louis, Aug. 6, 1934; m. Sara M. Senter, July 30, 1961; children: Alan, Mark, Scott. BA, JD, Washington U., 1959. Bar: Mo., Ala., U.S. Ct. Mil. Appeals, U.S. Supreme Ct. Atty. U.S. Dept. Health, Washington, 1964-65; pvt. practice law St. Louis, 1965—. Capt. USAF, 1961-64. Personal injury.

**SCHAEFFER, MATTHEW THOMAS,** lawyer; b. Troy, Ohio, July 28, 1970; s. Robert K. and Kathy L. Schaeffer. BA in Polit. Sci., Ohio State U., 1993; JD cum laude, Capital U., 1996. Bar: Ohio 1996, U.S. Dist. Ct. (so. and no. dists.) Ohio 1997. Legal extern Ohio Atty. Gen., Columbus, Ohio, 1994; mng. editor Capital Law Rev., Columbus, 1995-96; assoc. Luper, Sheriff & Neidenthal, Columbus, 1997—. Co-author: Bankruptcy Law and Procedure in Ohio, 1998. Lectr. Street Law, Columbus, 1994; tutor Read-to-Me, Columbus, 1994. J. Andrew Fulker Meml. scholar, 1995. Mem. Columbus Bar Assn. (bankruptcy com. mem. 1997—, professionalism com. mem. 1998—). Bankruptcy, General civil litigation, Contracts commercial. Home: 10 E Deshler Ave Apt 7 Columbus OH 43206-3450 Office: Luper Sheriff & Neidenthal 50 W Broad St Ste 1200 Columbus OH 43215-5907

**SCHAFER, GERARD THOMAS ROGER,** lawyer; b. Pitts., Mar. 20, 1956; s. Francis John Schafer and Lucille L. Davis; m. Marie Teres Paulick, Dec. 18, 1982; children: Michael, Brett, Rachael, Matthew. BS, Pa. State U., 1978; JD magna cum laude, U. Pitts., 1982. Bar: Pa. 1982, Va. 1984; U.S. Dist. Ct. (ea. dist.) Pa. 1982, U.S. Dist. Ct. (ea. dist.) Va. 1984. Assoc. Tucker Arensberg P.C., Pitts., 1982-84, Clark & Stant, P.C., Virginia Beach, 1984-85; asst. atty. Office of the Commonwealth's Atty., Virginia Beach, 1985-88; assoc. John W. Brown, P.C., Chesapeake, Va., 1988; sole practice law Virginia Beach, 1989-95; ptnr. Schafer, Russo & Martin (formerly Schafer & Russo), Virginia Beach, 1996—. Mem. Va. Trial Lawyers Assn., Allegheny County Bar Assn. (award 1982), Order of the Coif. Avocations: sports, music. Personal injury, Criminal. Office: Schafer Russo & Martin 4455 South Blvd Ste 310 Virginia Beach VA 23452-1159

**SCHAFER, STEVEN HARRIS,** lawyer; b. Woonsocket, R.I., Apr. 19, 1954. BA in Econs. magna cum laude, U. Mass., 1976; JD, Boston Coll., 1979. Bar: Conn. 1979, U.S. Dist. Ct. Conn. 1979, Mass. 1980, U.S. Dist. Ct. Mass. 1981, U.S. Ct. Appeals (1st cir.) 1981. Assoc. O'Brien, Shafner et al, Groton, Conn., 1979-81, Parker, Coulter, Daley & White, Boston, 1981-84, Meehan, Boyle & Cohen, Boston, 1985; sole practice Boston, 1985—. Mem. ABA, Mass. Bar Assn., Mass. Bar Found., Mass. Acad. Trial Attorneys (pres. 1998-99), Boston Bar Assn., Assn. Trial Lawyers Am. (bd. govs. 1994-97), Phi Kappa Phi. Personal injury, Product liability, Professional liability. Home: 5 Powisset St Dover MA 02030-1602 Office: 10 High St Ste 820 Boston MA 02110-1605

**SCHAFF, MICHAEL FREDERICK,** lawyer; b. Queens, N.Y., Nov. 14, 1957; s. Raymond and Norma S.; m. Robin Barbara Rose, Mar. 17, 1985; children: Rachel Lindsay, Aaron Jacob. BA, Rutgers Coll., New Brunswick, N.J., 1979; MBA, CUNY, 1982; JD, N.Y. Law Sch., N.Y.C., 1982; LLM, Boston U., 1983. Bar: N.Y. and N.J. 1982, Md. 1983, U.S. Dist. Ct. N.J. 1983, U.S. Dist. Ct. Md. 1983, U.S. Tax Ct. 1983. Assoc. Ober, Kaler, Grimes & Shriver, Balt., 1983-84, Greenberg, Dauber & Epstein, Newark, 1984-86; assoc. Wilentz, Goldman & Spitzer, Woodbridge, N.J., 1986-91, ptnr., 1991—; mem. N.J. Legislative Com. for the Study of Pain Mgmt. Masters Rsch. fellow, Bernard M. Baruch Coll., 1980. Mem. Am. Health Lawyers Assn. (vice chmn. physician's orgn. com. 1997—, newsletter editor 1997—, editor newsletter 1997—), N.J. Bar Assn. (chair computer related law com. 1991-93, dir. health and hosp. law sect. 1996—, vice chair 1997-98, chair elect 1998—, chair 1999—), Middlesex County Bar Assn. (chair health and hosp. law com. 1995—), Med. Group Mgmt. Assn., N.J. Med. Group Mgmt. Assn., N.J. Venture Club, Omicron Delta Epsilon. General corporate, Health, Computer. Office: Wilentz Goldman & Spitzer Woodbridge Ctr Dr Ste 901 Woodbridge NJ 07095-1146

**SCHAFFER, DEAN AARON,** lawyer; b. Lincoln, Nebr., May 17, 1962; s. Edward E. and Sally J. (Schlieter) S.; m. Nancy E. Strieter, Dec. 27, 1986; children: Samantha E., Shannon J. BA, Baylor U., 1984; JD, U. Tex., 1988. Bar: Tex. 1988, U.S. Dist. Ct. (we. dist.) Tex. 1994, U.S. Supreme Ct. 1998. Briefing atty. Tex. Ct. Appeals (3rd cir.), Austin, Tex., 1988-89; assoc. Fulbright & Jaworski L.L.P., Austin, 1989-92, participating assoc., 1993-98; chief consumer protection divsn. Office of Atty. Gen. State of Tex., Austin, 1999—; guest lectr. Sch. Law U. Tex., Austin, 1990—; presenter on liability issues in managed care, 1995—. Contbr. articles to profl. publs. Vol. atty. Vol. Legal Svcs. Ctrl. Tex., Austin, 1991—; bd. dirs. Interfaith Care Alliance, Austin, 1996—, Redeemer Luth. Ch., Austin, 1996—. Recipient Project award of Achievement, young lawyers divsn. ABA, Austin, 1994, Tex. Young Lawyers Assn., 1994, Cert. of merit In-Sch. Scouting Program, Austin, 1996. Fellow Austin Young Lawyers Assn. (pres., bd. dirs.); mem. Travis County Bar Assn. (mem. coun. litigation sect. 1996—, bd. dirs., mem. exec. com.),. Health, Insurance, General civil litigation. Home: 7606 Long Point Dr Austin TX 78731-1218 Office: Fulbright & Jaworski LLP 600 Congress Ave Ste 2400 Austin TX 78701-3271

**SCHAFFER, SETH ANDREW,** lawyer; b. Bklyn., Jan. 7, 1942; m. Karen (Kiki) Cohn, Dec. 1, 1968; children: Amanda, Julia, James. BA in Econs. magna cum laude, Harvard U., 1963, LLB cum laude, 1967; postgrad., Cambridge (Eng.) U., 1964. Bar: N.Y. 1970, U.S. Dist. Ct. (so. dist.) N.Y. 1973, U.S. Ct. Appeals (2nd cir.) 1973, U.S. Supreme Ct. 1980. Tchr. math. and econs. York (Pa.) Country Day Sch., 1967-68; assoc. dir. Vera Inst. Justice, 1969-72; asst. U.S. atty. U.S. Dist. Ct. (so. dist.) N.Y., 1972-75; chief counsel Moreland Act Commn. on Nursing Homes, N.Y.C., 1975-76; of counsel Stanley S. Arkin, P.C., Attys. at Law, 1976-77; v.p., gen. counsel, sec. of univ. NYU, N.Y.C., 1977-93, sr. v.p., gen. counsel, sec., 1993—; adj. prof. law NYU Sch. Law. Dir. Not for Profit Coordinating Com. N.Y., Nat. Ctr. Philanthropy and the Law, N.Y.C. Henry fellow Cambridge U., 1964. Mem. Nat. Assn. Coll. and Univ. Attys. (past pres.), Assn. of Bar of City of N.Y., Phi Beta Kappa. Education and schools, Health, Federal civil litigation. Home: 14 Washington Mews New York NY 10003-6608 Office: NYU 70 Washington Sq S New York NY 10012-1091

**SCHAFFNER, HOWARD,** lawyer; b. Chgo., Nov. 2, 1943; s. Irving and Frieda Schaffner; m. Gail Schaffner, July 14, 1970; children: Paula, Stacy. JD, John Marshall Law Sch., 1970. Asst. state's atty. Cook County States Atty.'s Office, Chgo., 1970-78; ptnr. Hofeld & Schaffner, Chgo., 1978—. Mem. Ill. Trial Lawyers Assn. (bd. mgrs. 1980—; author Cont. Legal Edn. 1980—, Ill. Inst. Cont. Legal Edn. 1980, 83, 86), Ill. State Bar Assn. Personal injury. Office: Hofeld & Schaffner 30 N Lasalle St Ste 3120 Chicago IL 60602-2576

**SCHAFRICK, FREDERICK CRAIG,** lawyer; b. Detroit, Sept. 20, 1948; s. Rudolph Henry and Patricia Eleanor (Zemer) S.; m. Sharon Lee Halpin, May 23, 1981; children: Michael Nile, Nathaniel Henry. AB, U. Mich., 1970, JD, 1973. Bar: D.C. 1973, U.S. Ct. Appeals (D.C. cir.) 1975, U.S. Supreme Ct. 1977. Law clk. U.S. Ct. Appeals (2d cir.), N.Y.C., 1973-74; assoc., then ptnr. Shea & Gardner, Washington, 1974—. Adminstrv. editor Mich. Law Rev., 1973. Mem. ABA, Order of Coif, Phi Beta Kappa. Democrat. Presbyterian. Aviation, Appellate, Administrative and regulatory. Home: 5416 Nebraska Ave NW Washington DC 20015-1350 Office: Shea & Gardner Ste 800 1800 Massachusetts Ave NW Washington DC 20036-1872

**SCHALK, ROBERT PARTRIDGE,** lawyer; b. Pueblo, Colo., June 20, 1931; s. Robert Louis and Elizabeth (Partridge) S.; m. Carolyn Ruthina Shoun, June 7, 1957; children: Steven Douglas, David Allen, Julie Dawn, Jeffrey Scott. BBA, U. Colo., 1953; JD, U. So. Calif., 1961; BBA, U. Colo., 1963. Bar: Calif. 1962; CPA, Calif., 1960; lic. real estate broker, Calif.; securities lic. Assoc. Millikan & Montgomery, L.A., 1961-63; tax lawyer L.H. Penney & Co., CPAs, San Francisco, 1963-67; pvt. practice law Santa Cruz, Calif., 1967—. Lt. USN, 1953-55. Corporate taxation, Taxation, general, Personal income taxation. Office: 550 Water St Santa Cruz CA 95060-4124

**SCHALL, ALVIN ANTHONY,** federal judge; b. N.Y.C., Apr. 4, 1944; s. Gordon William and Helen (Davis) S.; m. Sharon Frances LeBlanc, Apr. 25, 1970; children: Amanda Lanford, Anthony Davis. BA, Princeton U., 1966; JD, Tulane U., 1969. Bar: N.Y. 1970, U.S. Dist. Ct. (so. and ea. dists.) N.Y. 1973, U.S. Ct. Appeals (2d crct.) 1974, D.C. 1980, U.S. Dist. Ct. D.C. 1991, U.S. Ct. Appeals (D.C. crct.) 1991, U.S. Ct. Fed. Claims 1982, U.S. Ct. Appeals (fed. crct.) 1987, U.S. Supreme Ct. 1989. Assoc. Shearman & Sterling, N.Y.C., 1969-73; asst. U.S. atty. ea. dist. N.Y. Borough of Bklyn., 1973-78, chief appeals div., 1977-78; trial atty. civil div. U.S. Dept. Justice, Washington, 1978-87, sr. trial counsel, 1986-87, asst. to atty. gen., 1988-92; ptnr. Perlman & Ptnrs., Washington, 1987-88; judge U.S. Ct. Appeals (fed. crct.), Washington, 1992—. Office: 717 Madison Pl NW Washington DC 20439-0002

**SCHALL, RICHARD MILLER,** lawyer; b. N.Y.C., June 3, 1949; s. Edward William and Rhoda (Miller) S.; m. Marie Witwicki, Dec. 2, 1973; children: Benjamin, Michael. BA, Swarthmore Coll., 1971; MA, Rutgers U., New Brunswick, N.J., 1984; JD, NYU, 1987. Bar: Pa. 1987, N.J. 1987, U.S. Dist. Ct. N.J., 1988, U.S. Dist. Ct. (ea. dist.) Pa. 1988, U.S. Ct. Appeals (3d cir.) 1988. Jud. clk. U.S. Ct. Appeals for 3d Cir., Phila., 1987-88; shareholder, ptnr. Tomar, Simonoff, Adourian, O'Brien, Kaplan, Jacoby & Graziano, Cherry Hill, N.J., 1988—; adj. prof. Rutgers U. Sch. Law, Camden, N.J., 1990-95. Root-Tilden Snow scholar NYU, 1984-87. Mem. ATLA, N.J. Bar Assn., N.J. Employment Lawyers Assn. (exec. bd.). Avocations: cross-country skiing, hiking, biking. Labor, Civil rights. Home: 113 Flynn Ave Moorestown NJ 08057-1645 Office: Tomar Simonoff Et Al 20 Brace Rd Ste 100 Cherry Hill NJ 08034-2639

**SCHALLER, BARRY R.,** judge. BA, Yale Coll., 1960, JD, 1963. Bar: Conn. 1963, U.S. Dist. Ct. Conn. 1963, U.S. Ct. Appeals (2nd cir.) 1964, U.S. Supreme Ct. 1966. Ptnr. Bronson & Rice, Attys., New Haven, 1963-74; judge Ct. of Common Pleas, Cir. Ct., 1974-78, Superior Ct., State Conn., 1978-92, Appellate Ct., State Conn., 1992—; counsel to Ho. of Reps., 1969; mem. bd. pardons State of Conn., 1971-74, chair, 1973-74; mem. exec. com. Conn. Planning Com. on Criminal Adminstrn., 1972-74; chair Superior Ct. Benchbook Com., 1985-92; vis. lectr. Yale Coll., 1986, 88; clin. instr. evidence and trial practice Yale Law Sch., 1989—; lectr. W.Va. Magistrates Conf., 1990, Vt. Jud. Coll., 1992, Fla. Jud. Coll., 1993, 94, 96, 99, Ohio Jud. Coll., 1999; faculty Conn. Judges Inst., 1987-90; mem. Superior Ct. Jury Instrn. Com., 1989-92; mem. exec. com. Conn. Ctr. for Jud. Edn., 1989-92; active Superior Ct. Civil Case Mgmt. Task Force; mem. jud. evidence code drafting com. Author: A Vision of American Law: Judging Law, Literature, and the Stories We Tell, 1997; contbr. articles to profl. jours. Assoc. fellow Branford Coll.; adminstrv. co-sec. Yale Class of 1960; mem. adv. com. Fair Haven Mediation Bd., 19980-82; vestry mem., tchr. Trinity Ch., Branford, St. Andrew's Ch., Madison. Recipient book award Quinnipiac Law Sch., 1997; Guggenheim fellow Yale Law Sch., 1975-76, 84, 85-86. Fellow Conn. Bar Found. (charter life, fellows adv. com.); mem. ABA (CEELI adv.), Conn. Bar Assn., Hartford County Bar Assn., New Haven County Bar Assn., Conn. Judges Assn. (dir. 1990-92), Am. Judges Assn., Am. Judicature Soc., Am. Law Inst., Yale Law Sch. Assn. (exec. com. 1990-92), Am. Inns of Ct. (bencher 1989-90), Phi Delta Phi. Office: Appellate Ct State Conn 95 Washington St Hartford CT 06106-4406

**SCHALLERT, EDWIN GLENN,** lawyer; b. L.A., Aug. 7, 1952; s. William Joseph and Rosemarie Diane (Waggner) S. AB, Stanford U., 1974; JD, Harvard U., 1981, MPP, 1981. Bar: N.Y. 1974, U.S. Ct. Appeals (7th cir.) 1986, U.S. Ct. Appeals (2d cir.) 1989, U.S. Dist. Ct. (so. dist.) N.Y. 1975. Legis. aid to U.S. rep. Les Aspin Washington, 1975-78, law clk. to Hon. J. Skelly Wright, 1981-82, law clk. to Hon. Thurgood Marshall, 1982-83; assoc. Debevoise & Plimpton, N.Y.C., 1983-89, ptnr., 1989—. Mem. Internat. Inst. for Strategic Studies, Coun. Fgn. Rels. (term mem. 1983-88), Phi Beta Kappa. Democrat. Avocation: tennis. General civil litigation, Securities, Bankruptcy. Office: Debevoise & Plimpton 875 3d Ave New York NY 10022-6225

**SCHANES, CHRISTINE ELISE,** lawyer; b. Jersey City, Apr. 9, 1948; d. Steven Eli and Christine (Marra) S.; m. Ron Taylor; children: Christine Elizabeth, Patrick Steven. BA, U. San Diego, 1970; JD, Am. U., 1973; PhD, U. Notre Dame, 1975. Bar: calif. 1973, U.S. Dist. Ct. (cen., no. and so. dists.) Calif. 1973. Dep. atty. gen. Calif. Dept. Justice, Los Angeles, 1975-78; sr. atty. Atlantic Richfield Co., Los Angeles, 1978-83; sole practice Santa Monica, Calif., 1983—. Co-dir. Children Helping Poor and Homeless People, 1987—. Recipient Outstanding Achievement award Urban League, 1969. Mem. Calif. Bar Assn. Public international, Contracts commercial, Civil rights. Office: CHPHP 2554 Lincoln Blvd Ste 522 Venice CA 90291-5082

**SCHAPIRO, MARY,** federal agency administrator, lawyer; b. N.Y.C., June 19, 1955; d. Robert D. and Susan (Hall) S.; m. Charles A. Cadwell, Dec. 13, 1980. BA, Franklin and Marshall Coll., 1977; JD, George Washington U., 1980. Bar: D.C. 1980. Trial atty., 1980-81; counsel to chmn. Commodity Futures Trading Commn., 1981-84; gen. counsel Futures Industry Assn., 1984-88; commr. SEC, Washington, 1988-94; chmn. Commodity Futures Trading Commn. (CFTC), Washington, 1994-96; pres. Nat. Assn. Securities Regulation, Inc., Washington, 1996—. Office: Nat Assn Securities Regulation Inc 1735 K St NW Washington DC 20006-1516

**SCHAR, STEPHEN L.,** lawyer; b. Chgo., Oct. 19, 1945; s. Sidney and Lillian (Lieberman) S.; m. Jessica S. Feit, Aug. 17, 1980; children: Scott Andrew, Elizabeth Loren. BA, U. Chgo., 1967; JD, DePaul U., 1970. Bar: Ill. 1970, U.S. Dist. Ct. (no. dist.) Ill. 1970. Assoc. Aaron, Aaron, Schimberg & Hess, Chgo., 1970-77, ptnr., 1977-80; ptnr. Aaron, Schimberg, Hess, Rusnak, Deutsch & Gilbert, Chgo., 1980-84, Aaron, Schimberg, Hess & Gilbert, Chgo., 1984, Aaron, Schimberg & Hess, Chgo., 1984, D'Ancona & Pflaum, Chgo., 1985-98; mem. D'Ancona & Pflaum LLC, Chgo., 1999—; instr. estate planning Loyola U., Chgo., 1978-79. Bd. dirs. Jewish Children's Bur. Chgo., 1982—, pres., 1996-98; pres. Faulkner Condominium Assn., Chgo., 1980-82, Carl Sandburg Village Homeowners Assn., Chgo., 1981-82. Mem. Ill. Bar Assn., Chgo. Bar Assn. (pres. probate practice divsn. III 1979), Chgo. Estate Planning Coun. Estate planning, Probate, Estate taxation. Home: 2155 Tanglewood Ct Highland Park IL 60035-4231 Office: D'Ancona & Pflaum LLC 111 E Wacker Dr Ste 2800 Chicago IL 60601-4200

**SCHARF, MICHAEL PAUL,** law educator; b. Pitts., Apr. 25, 1963; s. Harry and Joan (Seder) S.; m. Trina Elizabeth Smith, May 9, 1988; 1 child, Garrett Michael. AB, Duke U., 1985, JD, 1988. Bar: D.C. 1989. Jud. clk. U.S. Ct. Appeals (11th cir.), Jacksonville, Fla., 1988-89; atty.-adviser Office Legal Adviser, U.S. Dept. State, Washington, 1989-93; assoc. prof. law New England Sch. of Law, Boston, 1993—; mem. U.S. Del. to 46th and 47th Sessions of UN Gen. Assembly, U.S. Del. to 49th Session of UN Human Rights Commn.; adj. prof. Georgetown U. Law Ctr., Washington, 1992; chmn. bd. dirs. Internat. Model UN Assn. Inc. N.Y.C., 1984-88; mng. dir. Pub. Internat. Law and Policy Gorup, 1995—; dir. New Eng. Ctr. for Internat. Law and Policy, 1996—; expert commentator Ct. TV, 1996. Author: An Insider's Guide to the International Criminal Tribunal for the Former Yugoslavia, 1995, International Criminal Law: Cases and Materials, 1996, Balkan Justice: The Story Behind the First International War Crimes Trial Since Nuremberg, 1997. Mem. ABA (U.S. Govt. rep. blue ribbon task force on internat. criminal ct. 1991-93), D.C. Bar (chmn. steering com. internat. law sect. 1991-93), Internat. Law Assn. (exec. com. Am. br. 1996—), Order of Coif, U.N. Assn. Greater Boston (bd. dirs. 1993—). Avocations: skiing, sailing, tennis, softball. Home: 21 Leonard Rd Framingham MA 01701-4915 Office: New England Sch of Law 154 Stuart St Boston MA 02116-5616

**SCHARF, ROBERT LEE,** retired lawyer; b. May 13, 1920; s. Charles A. and Ethel Virginia (McNabb) S.; m. Jacqueline B. Scharf, Nov. 2, 1940; children: Bonnie Scharf Heald, Mary Ellen Pinero, Robert L. Jr. JD, Loyola U., 1948. Bar: Ill. 1949, Calif. 1972; lifetime teaching credential Calif. C.C. With FBI, 1940-73; dep. city atty. City of L.A., 1973-84; atty. Mitsui Mfrs. Bank, L.A., 1984-85; ret., 1985; part-time emeritus pro-bono atty. Mental Health Advocacy Office, L.A.; former L.A. County arbitrator; former pro-tem judge Small Claims Ct. 2d lt. U.S. Army, 1944-46. Mem. L.A. County Bar Assn., San Fernando Valley Bar Assn., Soc. Former FBI Agts. Mem. L.A. County Bar Assn., San Fernando Valley Bar Assn., Soc. Former FBI Agts. Pension, profit-sharing, and employee benefits.

**SCHAUER, FREDERICK FRANKLIN,** law educator; b. Newark, Jan. 15, 1946; s. John Adolph and Clara (Balayti) S.; m. Margery Clare Stone, Aug. 25, 1968 (div. June, 1982); m. Virginia Jo Wise, May 25, 1985. AB, Dartmouth Coll., 1967, MBA, 1968; JD, Harvard U., 1972. Bar: Mass. 1972, U.S. Supreme Ct. 1976. Assoc. Fine & Ambrogne, Boston, 1972-74; asst. prof. law W.Va. U., Morgantown, 1974-76, assoc. prof., 1976-78; assoc. prof. Coll. William and Mary, Williamsburg, Va., 1978-80, Cutler prof., 1980-83; prof. of law U. Mich., Ann Arbor, 1983-90; Frank Stanton prof. of 1st Amendment Kennedy Sch. of Govt., Harvard U., Cambridge, Mass., 1990—, acad. dean, 1997—; vis. scholar, mem. faculty law Wolfson Coll. Cambridge (Eng.) U., 1977-78; vis. prof. Law Sch., U. Chgo., 1990; vis. fellow Australian Nat. U., 1993, 98; William Morton Disting. Sr. fellow in humanities Dartmouth Coll., 1991; vis. prof. law Harvard Law Sch., 1996, 97; Ewald Disting. vis. prof. law U. Va., 1996, vis. prof. govt. Dartmouth Coll., 1997; acad. dean, Frank Stanton prof. first amendment Kennedy Sch. Govt. Harvard U., Cambridge, 1997—. Author: The Law of Obscenity, 1976, Free Speech: A Philosophical Enquiry, 1982 (ABA cert. merit 1983), Supplements to Gunther Constitutional Law, 1983-96, Playing by the Rules: A Philosophical Examination of Rule Based Decision-Making in Law and Life, 1991, The First Amendment: A Reader, 1992, 2d edit., 1995, The Philosophy of Law, 1995; editor: Legal Theory, 1995; contbr. articles to profl. jours. Mem. Atty. Gen.'s Commn. on Pornography, 1985-86. Served with Mass. Army N.G., 1970-71. NEH fellow, summer 1980. Fellow Am. Acad. Arts and Scis.; mem. Am. Philos. Assn., Am. Soc. for Polit. and Legal Philosophy (v.p. 1996—), Assn. Am. Law Schs. (chmn. sect. constl. law 1984-86). Office: Kennedy Sch of Govt Harvard U Cambridge MA 02138

**SCHAUER, TONE TERJESEN,** lawyer; b. Arendal, Norway, Jan. 1, 1941; came to U.S., 1958; d. Haakon and Signe (Andersen) Terjesen; children from previous marriage: Randi Vargas, Shawn Wilson, Kristina Schauer; m. John Richilano; 1 child, Jamie. BA, Colo. State U., 1969, M in French Lit., 1971; JD, U. Colo., 1977. Bar: Colo. 1977, U.S. Ct. Appeals (10th cir.) 1977. Dep. pub. defender State of Colo., Denver, 1977-83; pvt. practice Boulder, Colo., 1983-90, Denver, 1990—. Mem. ABA, Colo. Bar Assn., Denver Bar Assn. Democrat. Avocations: skiing, sailing, hiking, reading, knitting. Criminal, Family and matrimonial, Probate. Home: 356 Marion St Denver CO 80218-3928 Office: 150 E 10th Ave Denver CO 80203-2740

**SCHAUF, CAROLYN JANE,** lawyer; b. Visalia, Calif., Sept. 30, 1946; d. William Powell and Mildred (Hudiburgh) Gateley; m. Jack Eldon Schuaf, Apr. 24, 1971; children: Christie, Jeffrey. JD, Western State Coll. Law, Fullerton, Calif., 1985. Bar: Calif. 1986. Pvt. practice, Downey, Calif., 1986—. Mem. SE Bar Assn., Los Angeles County Bar Assn. Probate, Bankruptcy, Family and matrimonial. Office: 8301 Florence Ave Downey CA 90240-3936

**SCHAUMBERG, TOM MICHAEL,** lawyer; b. Amsterdam, The Netherlands, May 29, 1938; came to U.S., 1947; s. Ernest and Pollo Gertrude Schaumberg; m. Gail A. Greenberg, Aug. 25, 1963 (div.); children: Steven James, Lisa Jill, Erica Beth. BA, Yale U., 1960; LLB, Harvard U., 1963; postgrad., U. Frankfurt, Germany, 1964. Bar: Ohio 1964, D.C. 1968, U.S. Supreme Ct. 1972, Md. 1975, U.S. Ct. Appeals (fed. cir.) 1979. Atty. U.S. Fed. Trade Commn., Washington, 1964-67; assoc., ptnr. Gadsby & Hannah, Washington, 1968-74; ptnr. Rollinson & Schaumberg, Washington, 1974-78, Plaia & Schaumberg, Washington, 1978-86, Howrey & Simon, Washington, 1987-88; sr. ptnr. Adduci, Mastriani & Schaumberg, Washington, 1989—; panelist U.S.-Can. Free-Trade Agreement, Washington, 1990-95. Contbr. articles to profl. periodicals. Mem. Dupont Cir. Citizens Assn., Washington, 1988—. Mem. Internat. Trade Commn. Trial Lawyers Assn. (pres. 1984-85, exec. com. 1987—). Private international, General civil litigation, Intellectual property. Office: Adduci Mastriani & Schaumberg 1200 17th St NW Fl 5 Washington DC 20036-3006

**SCHECHTER, DONALD ROBERT,** lawyer; b. N.Y.C., Feb. 24, 1946; s. Joseph and Katherine (Beer) S.; m. Roberta Sharon Horowitz, July 3, 1968; children: Elizabeth Anne, Sarah Marilyn. BA, Queens Coll., 1967; JD, Bklyn Law Sch., 1971. Asst. dist. atty. Queens County, Kew Gardens, N.Y., 1971-73; asst. atty. gen. organized crime task force City of N.Y., 1973-74; sole practice Forest Hills, N.Y., 1974—; legal counsel Centro Civico Colombiano, Jackson Heights, N.Y., 1978—, Fedn. of Merchants and Profls. of Queens, Spanish Orgn., Jackson Heights, 1978—; hearing officer Family Ct., Queens County, Jamaica, N.Y., 1977; consumer counsel Civil Ct., Queens County, 1980. Mem. ABA, N.Y. State Bar Assn., Queens County Bar Assn. (chmn. lawyer placement), Nassau County Bar Assn., Audobon Soc., Sierra Club. Democrat. Jewish. Clubs: Glass Soc. Corvette, N.Y. Mets Dream Week. Lodge: KP. Avocations: antique automobiles, baseball, history, antiques. Entertainment, Criminal, General practice. Office: 80-02 Kew Gardens Rd Ste 1040 Kew Gardens NY 11415-3600

**SCHECHTER, HOWARD,** lawyer; b. N.Y.C., Feb. 11, 1952. BA, NYU, 1972, JD, 1975. Bar: N.Y., U.S. Dist. Ct. (ea. and so. dists.) N.Y., U.S. Ct. Appeals (2d cir.). Assoc. Schekter, Aber & Hecht, N.Y.C., 1975-79, Schekter, Aber & Rishty, N.Y.C., 1979-81; atty. pvt. practice, N.Y.C., 1983-86; ptnr. Schechter, Aber, Rishty, Goldstein & Schechter, P.C., N.Y.C., 1981-83; pvt. practice Law Offices of Howard Schechter, N.Y.C., 1983-86; atty. Blodnick, Pomeranz, N.Y.C., 1986-87; ptnr. Schechter & Brucker, N.Y.C., 1987—; lectr. NYU Sch. Continuing Edn. Real Estate Profl. Programs, 1996—. Contbr. articles to profl. jours. Bd. dirs. N.Y. State Assn. Renewal and Housing Ofcls., Inc., 1979-84, parliamentarian, 1984-89; pres. Roslyn Hilltop Ednl. Found., Inc., 1994—. Mem. ABA, Nat. Assn. Housing Coops., N.Y. State Bar Assn., Coun. N.Y. Coops., Fedn. N.Y. Housing Coops., Assn. of Bar of City of N.Y.C., Phi Beta Kappa. Real property, State civil litigation, Landlord-tenant. Office: Schechter & Brucker 350 5th Ave Ste 4510 New York NY 10118-4585

**SCHECK, FRANK FOETISCH,** retired lawyer; b. Albuquerque, Apr. 9, 1923; s. Frank Henry and Ethel Jane (Garrett) S.; m. Jane Leonore Rembowski, Aug. 17, 1946; children: Christopher G., Jennifer J., Carl P. BS, Calif. Inst. Tech., 1948; LLB, Columbia U., 1951. Bar: N.Y. 1951, U.S. Dist. Ct. (so. dist.) N.Y. 1953, U.S. Ct. Appeals (2d cir.) 1959, U.S. Supreme Ct. 1959, U.S. Ct. Appeals (7th cir.) 1966, U.S. Ct. Appeals (D.C. and Fed. cirs.) 1983. Assoc. Pennie, Edmonds, Morton, Barrows & Taylor, N.Y.C., 1951-60; ptnr., Pennie, Edmonds, Morton, Taylor & Adams, N.Y.C., 1961-69; sr. ptnr. Pennie & Edmonds, 1970-91; retired, Pennie & Edmonds, 1991. With U.S. Army, 1942-45. Decorated Purple Heart. Mem. N.Y. Patent Law Assn. (dir. 1982-85, v.p. 1987-89, pres. elect 1989-90, pres. 1990-91). Conservative. Presbyterian. Patent, Federal civil litigation. Home: 5 Linden Gate Ln Newport RI 02840-3334

**SCHECTER, BENJAMIN SETH,** lawyer; b. Lexington, Ky., June 11, 1971. BA in English, SUNY, Geneseo, 1993; JD, U. Louisville, 1996. Bar: Supreme Ct. Ky. 1996, U.S. Dist. Ct. (we. dist.) Ky. 1997. Assoc. Pike Legal Group, Shepardsville, Ky., 1996-97, Pedley Zielke Gordinier Olt & Pence, PLLC, Louisville, 1997—; moot ct. negotiations team U. Louisville, 1996. Editor-in-chief Brandeis Brief Legal Mag., 1994-96; editor Jour. Law & Edn., 1994-96. Bd. atty. Camelot Empowerment Assn., Louisville, 1998. Mem. ABA, Ky. Bar Assn., Louisville Bar Assn. General civil litigation, Condemnation, Construction. Office: Pedley Zielke Gordinier Olt & Pence 1150 Starks Bldg 455 S 4th Ave Louisville KY 40202-2593

**SCHEER, MARK JEFFREY,** lawyer; b. N.Y.C., Jan. 6, 1962; s. Morton Herbert and Joan Sylvia (Weiss) S.; m. Sheryl Lynn Weinberg, Oct. 24, 1987; children: Matthew Jordan, Danielle Nicole, Lindsay Gayle. BS in Acctg., U. Fla., 1983, M in Acctg., 1984, JD, 1987. Bar: Fla. 1987, U.S. Tax Ct. 1988, U.S. Dist. Ct. (so. dist.) Fla. 1991. Ptnr. Gunster, Yoakley, Valdes-Fauli & Stewart, P.A., Miami, Fla., 1987—. Mem. ABA, AICPA, Fla. Bar Assn., Fla. Isnt. CPAs. Jewish. Corporate taxation, Estate planning, Bankruptcy. Office: 2 S Biscayne Blvd Miami FL 33131-1806

**SCHEFFLER, STUART JAY,** lawyer; b. Phila., Oct. 9, 1950; s. Walter and Fritzy (Salkoff) S.; m. Barbara Jane Green, July 3, 1975. BA cum laude, Pa. State U., 1972, MPA, 1973; JD, Temple U., 1980. Bar: Pa. 1980, U.S. Dist. Ct. (ea. dist.) Pa. 1981, U.S. Ct. Appeals (3d cir.) 1983, U.S. Supreme Ct. 1986. Tchr. Sch. Dist. of Phila., 1974-75; claims authorizer Social Security Adminstrn., HEW, Phila., 1975-76, equal opportunity specialist Office of Civil Rights, 1976-77; paraprofessional Law Offices of Ronald A. Bell., Bala

Cynwyd, Pa., 1978-80; assoc. Law Office of Robert B. Mozenter, Phila., 1980-81, Gekoski & Bogdanoff, Phila., 1981-82; ptnr. Rubin & Scheffler, Phila., 1982-84; sole practice, Phila., 1984-94; of counsel Solomon, Berschler, Warren & Schatz, P.C., Norristown, Pa., 1994—. Councilman Bakers Bay Condominium Assn., Phila., 1982; bd. dirs. Key West Coun. on the Arts, 1999—. Fellow Acad. of Advocacy, mem. ABA (tort and ins. practice, sports and entertainment, civil litigation sects.), Pa. Bar Assn. (legis. liaison, medico-legal coms.), Phila. Bar Assn., Am. Trial Lawyers Assn., Phila. Trial Lawyers Assn., Pa. Trial Lawyers Assn., Drug Info. Assn., Internat. Platform Assn., Phi Beta Kappa, Delta Sigma Rho, Tau Kappa Alpha, Zeta Beta Tau. Democrat. Club: Hartikvah Basketball Assn. (Phila.) (v.p. 1974—). Personal injury, State civil litigation, Insurance. Office: 522 Swede St Norristown PA 19401-4834

**SCHEIBER, HARRY N.**, law educator; b. N.Y.C., 1935. BA, Columbia U., 1955; MA, Cornell U., 1957, PhD, 1961; MA (hon.), Dartmouth Coll., 1965, D.Jur.Hon. Uppsala U. (Sweden), 1998,. instr. to assoc. prof. history Dartmouth Coll., 1960-68, prof., 1968-71; prof. Am. history U. Calif., San Diego, 1971-80; prof. law Boalt Hall, U. Calif., Berkeley, 1980—, chmn. jurisprudence and social policy program, 1982-84, 90-93, assoc. dean, 1990-93, 96-99; The Stefan Riesenfeld Prof., 1991—; vice chair Univ. Academic Senate, 1993-94. chair, 1994-95; Fulbright disting. sr. lectr., Australia, 1983, marine affairs coord. Calif. Sea Grant Coll. Program, 1989—; vis. rsch. prof. Law Inst. U. Uppsala, Sweden, 1995, hon. prof. DiTella U., Buenos Aires, 1998—. Chmn. Littleton Griswold Prize Legal History, 1985-88; pres. N.H. Civil Liberties Union, 1969-70; chmn. Project '87 Task Force on Pub. Programs, Washington, 1982-85; dir. Berkeley Seminar on Federalism, 1986-95; cons. judiciary study U.S. Adv. Commn. Intergovernmental Rels., 1985-88; dir. NEH Inst. on Constitutionalism, U. Calif., Berkeley, 1986-87, 88-91. Recipient Sea Grant Colls. award, 1981-83, 84-85, 86—; fellow Ctr. Advanced Study in Behavioral Scis., Stanford Calif., 1967, 71; Guggenheim fellow, 1971, 88; Rockefeller Found. humanities fellow, 1979, NEH fellow, 1985-86; NSF grantee, 1979, 80, 88-89; Fellow U. Calif. Humanities Rsch. Inst., 1989. Mem. Am. Hist. Assn., Orgn. Am. Historians, Agrl. History Soc. (pres. 1978), Econ. History Assn. (trustee 1978-80), Law and Soc. Assn. (trustee 1979-81, 1996-99), Am. Soc. Legal History (dir. 1982-86, 90-93, 96-99), Nat. Assessment History and Citizenship Edn. (chmn. nat. acad. bd. 1986-87), Marine Affairs and Policy Assn. (bd. dirs. 1991-96), Ocean Governance Study Group (steering com. 1991—), Internat. Coun. Environ. Law. Author numerous books including: (with L. Friedman) American Law and the Constitutional Order, 1978, 2d edit. 1988, The State and Freedom of Contract, 1998; contbr. articles to law revs.and social sci. jours., 1963—. Office: U Calif Berkeley Law Sch Boalt Hall Berkeley CA 94720-2150

**SCHEICH, JOHN F.**, lawyer; b. Bklyn., Aug. 6, 1942; s. Frank A. and Dorothy (O'Hara) S. BA, St. John's U., N.Y.C., 1963, JD, 1966; postgrad., John Marshall Law Sch., Chgo., 1968. Bar: N.Y. 1967, U.S. Ct. Internat. Trade Admission 1969, U.S. Dist. Ct. (ea. and so. dists.) N.Y. 1971, U.S. Ct. Appeals (2nd cir.) 1971, U.S. Supreme Ct. 1975, Pa. 1980. Spl. agt. FBI, U.S. Dept. Justice, Washington, 1966-69; asst. dist. atty. Queens County, Kew Gardens, N.Y., 1969-72; pvt. practice, Richmond Hill, N.Y., 1970-76, 79-91; ptnr. Raia & Scheich, P.C., Richmond Hill, 1976-79; sr. ptnr. Scheich & Goldsmith, P.C., Richmond Hill, Hicksville, N.Y., 1991-95, Scheich, Goldsmith & Dreishpoon, P.C, Richmond Hill, Hicksville, 1996—; mortgage settlement atty. GMAC, N.Y., 1996—; lectr. estate planning Nat. Bus. Inst., 1994; mem. assigned counsel panel for indigent defendants in major felony and murder cases 9th and 11th jud. dists. N.Y. State Supreme Ct., Queens County, 1972-94; lectr. Lawyers in the Classroom, 1979-91; chmn. arbitration panel Civil Ct. City of N.Y., 1981-90; bd. dirs. Ra-Li Brokerage Corp., v.p., 1975—; adv. bd. 1st Am. Title Ins. Co. Am., 1995—, mortage settlement atty. for Gen. Motors Acceptance Corp. N.Y. state, 1996—. Editor: Conashaugh Courier, 1989-92; mem. editorial bd., 1988-92; contbg. columnist, 1981-89. Mem. Com. for Beautification of East Norwich, Nassau County, L.I., N.Y., 1983—, bd. dirs., 1993-96, pres. 1996—; mem. Holy Name Soc. of Our Lady of Perpetual Help Ch., 1963—, sec., 1965-67, v.p., 1969-71, pres., 1971-73; bd. dirs. Conashaugh Lakes Cmty. Assn., Milford, Pa., 1981-90, organizing mem. Conashaugh Lakes Lot Owners interim com., 1977-81, sec. 1981-82, v.p. 1982-84, pres. 1984-86, past pres. 1986-88; mem. St. Edward the Confessor Sch. Bd., Syosset, N.Y., 1986-90; parish coun. Our Lady of Perpetual Help Roman Cath. Ch., 1976-82, pres. 1978-80, fin. com., adv. to pastor, 1970-82, chmn. fin. com., 1979-82; bd. dirs. Northslope II Homeowners Assn., Shawnee-on-Delaware, Pa., 1988-90, 92-94; mem. East Norwich Rep. Club, 1982—, bd. dirs. 1984-87, 93—, v.p. 1987-89, pres. 1989-93; nat. trust and estate assoc. Meml. Sloane Kettering Cancer Ctr., N.Y.C., 1994—; active Internat. Wine Ctr., 1985-96, St. Edward the Confessor Ch., Syosset, 1982—, St. Vincent Ch., Dingman Hills, Pa., 1977—, St. Dominic's Ch., Oyster Bay, N.Y., 1982— (apptd. pastor's adv. coun. on estate planning,1998, mem. Legacy Soc. 1998), Lincoln Ctr. Performing Arts, Inc., 1985—, Nat. Rep. Senatorial Com., 1988—, Bravo Soc., 1994—, Concern for Dying, 1984—, Sea Cliff Chamber Players, 1992-99; mem. Nassau County Rep. Com., Town of Oyster Bay, 1993—, St. John Vianney Roman Cath. Ch., St. Petersburg Beach, Fla., 1994—, Non-Resident Fellow, James Beard Found., NYC, 1995—, Performing Arts Ctr. Pinellas County, St. Petersburg, 1994—, Rep. Nat. Senate Adv. Coun., 1997—, Rep. Nat. Com. Chmn.'s Honor Roll, 1997 (cert. Achievement 1998), Pact, Inc. Ruth Eckerd Hall-Richard B. Baumgardner Ctr. for Performing Arts, Clearwater, Fla., 1995—; chmn. tri-centennial celebration com. Village of East Norwich, 1996-97; mem. Fransiscan Ctr. Guild, Tampa, Fla., 1996—, Tilles Ctr. Performing Arts, Inc., Long Island U., Brookville, N.Y., 1997—, adv. coun. estate planning St. Dominic's Ch., 1998, St. Dominic's Legacy Soc., 1998. Recipient J. Edgar Hoover award, 1967, award of appreciation, Civil Trial Inst., St. John's U. Sch. of Law, 1991, 95, Disting. Svc. award, 1992, cert. of appreciaiton Conashaugh Lakes Cmty. Assn., 1990, Dist. Svc. award Kiwanis Club, 1992, Cert. of Merit for Disting. Svc. award Nassau County Exec. Hon. Thomas Gulotta, 1989, Presdl. Order of Merit award Pres. George Bush, 1991, Order of Merit award Nat. Rep. Senatorial Com., 1994, Cert. Achievement, Rep. Nat. Com., 1998; named one of Best Trial Lawyers in the U.S., Town and Country Mag., 1985; non-resident fellow James Beard Found., N.Y.C., 1995—. Mem. ABA (cert. of appreciation Am. Bar Endowment 1992), ATLA, Pa. StaBar Assn., N.Y. State Bar Assn., Queens County Bar Assn., Nassau County Bar Assn., N.Y. State Trial Lawyers Assn., Ciminal Cts. Bar Assn., Internat. Platform Assn., John Marshall Lawyers Assn. (bd. dirs. 1992—, pres. 1992-97, treas. 1997—), Soc. Former Spl. Agts. of FBI, N.Y. State Assn. Criminal Def. Lawyers, St. John's Coll. Alumni Assn., Asst. Dist. Attys. Assn. Queens County, St. John's U. Sch. of Law Alumni Assn., St. John's Prep. Sch. Alumni Assn., Friends of the Arts of Nassau County, Inc., Cath. Lawyers Guild of Queens County, N.Y., KC, Brookhaven Wine Lovers Soc., East Norwich Civic Assn., Sun Island Assn., Phi Alpha Delta. Avocation: collecting fine wines. General practice, Personal injury, Probate. Home: 170 Sugar Toms Ln East Norwich NY 11732-1153 Office: Scheich Goldsmith & Dreishpoon PC 10342 Lefferts Blvd South Richmond Hill NY 11419-2012 also: 109 Newbridge Rd Hicksville NY 11801-3908 also: 3901 Conashaugh Trl Box 4042 Conashaugh Lakes Milford PA 18337

**SCHEIMAN, EUGENE R.**, lawyer; b. Bklyn., July 15, 1943. BA, L.I. U., 1966; JD cum laude, Bklyn. Law Sch., 1969. Bar: N.Y. 1970, U.S. Dist. Ct. (so. and ea. dists.) N.Y. 1971, U.S. Ct. Appeals (1st cir.) 1972, U.S. Ct. Appeals (5th cir.) 1973, U.S. Ct. Appeals (4th cir.) 1974, U.S. Supreme Ct. 1976, U.S. Ct. Appeals (2nd cir.) 1977, U.S. Ct. Appeals (fed. cir.), U.S. Ct. Appeals (11th cir.) 1989, U.S. Ct. Appeals (3rd cir.) 1990. Mem. Baer Marks & Upham, N.Y.C. Rsch. editor Bklyn. Law Rev., 1968, editor-in-chief, 1969. Mem. ABA (sect. on individual rights and responsibilities), N.Y. State Bar Assn., Assn. Bar. City of N.Y. (mem. com. comm. and media law, com. on profl. discipline), Philonomic Honor Soc. Criminal, Professional liability, Libel. Office: Baer Marks & Upham 805 3rd Ave Fl 19 New York NY 10022-7598

**SCHEIN, JULIA RUTH**, law librarian, consultant; b. Phila., Oct. 28, 1958; d. Lawrence and Rose Schein; m. Timothy O'Donnell Harrington, Aug. 17, 1985; children: Timothy Sean, Megan S. BA, Emory U., 1980, MLS, 1986. Cataloger, ref. libr. Powell, Goldstein, Fraser & Murphy, Atlanta, 1986-89, head libr., 1989-96; dir. libr. svcs. The Cadence Group, Atlanta, 1996-97, dir. rsch., 1997—. Treas. PTA, Anne E. West Elem. Sch., 1995-97. Mem. Am. Assn. Law Librs., Assn. Ind. Info. Providers, Spl. Librs. Assn. (chair membership com. Ga. chpt. 1996-98), Atlanta Law Librs. Assn. (pres./v.p. 1993-95, treas. 1988-89). Office: The Cadence Group 1095 Zonolite Rd NE Atlanta GA 30306-2003

**SCHEINER, HOWARD**, judge; b. Bklyn., Apr. 25, 1960; s. Jack and Lenore Barbara Scheiner; m. Patricia Ann Sullivan, Mar. 31, 1995; children: Aaron Benjamin, Hannah Gabrielle, Kallee Sullivan, Patrick Sullivan. AA, Broward C.C., Ft. Lauderdale, Fla., 1980; 9BA, Fla. Atlantic U., 1983; JD with honors, Fla. State U., 1985. Bar: Fla. 1986, U.S. Ct. Appeals (11th cir.) 1986, U.S. Dist. Ct. (so. dist.) Fla. 1987, U.S. Dist. Ct. (mid. dist.) Fla. 1988. Law clk. to Judge Nesbitt, 3d Dist. Ct. Appeals, Miami, Fla., 1986-87; assoc. Fuller, Johnson & Farrell, P.A., Tallahassee, 1987-89, Bobo, Spicer & Ciotoli, P.A., West Palm Beach, Fla., 1989-91, Miller, Kagan & Chait, P.A., Deerfield Beach, Fla., 1991; ptnr. Langer, Scheiner & Thorne, P.A., West Palm Beach, 1991-95; judge Office Chief Judge Workers' Compensation, State of Fla., West Palm Beach, 1995—. Mem. adv. bd. St. Mary's Hosp., West Palm Beach, Fla., 1994-95; bd. dirs. Boys and Girls Club Palm Beach County, 1997—. Mem. Fla. Bar (workers' compensation rules com. 1999—), Conf. Judges Compensation Claims (pres.-elect 1998-99, pres. 1999—). Jewish. Avocations: computers, antique book collecting, magic. Office: Fla Office Judge 5405 Okeechobee Blvd West Palm Beach FL 33417-4543

**SCHEINHOLTZ, LEONARD LOUIS**, lawyer; b. Pitts., June 2, 1927; s. Bernard A. and Marie (Getzel) S.; m. Joan R. Libenson, Aug. 16, 1953; children: Stuart, Nancy, Barry. BA, U. Pa., 1948, MA, 1949; LLB, Columbia U., 1953. Bar: Pa. 1954, U.S. Ct. Appeals (3d cir.) 1959, U.S. Ct. Appeals (6th cir.) 1968, U.S. Supreme Ct. 1972, U.S. Ct. Appeals (4th cir.) 1973, U.S. Ct. Appeals (5th cir.) 1981, U.S. Ct. Appeals (11th cir.) 1991, U.S. Ct. Appeals (2d cir.) 1993. Assoc. Reed, Smith, Shaw & McClay, Pitts., 1953-62, spl. ptnr., 1962-64, gen. ptnr., 1964-97, head labor dept., 1980-86; dir. Am. Arbitration Assn., N.Y.C., 1980-96. Author: Exemption Under the Anti-Trust Laws for Joint Employer Activity, 1982, The Arbitrator as Judge and Jury: Another Look at Statutory Law in Arbitration, 1985. Vice chmn. Pa. AAA Fedn., Harrisburg, 1982-85 ; chmn. W. Pa. AAA Motor Club, 1979-82; trustee Montefiore Hosp., Pitts., 1976-79; bd. dirs. United Jewish Fedn. Pitts., 1997—. Served with USN, 1945-46. Mem. ABA, Pa. Bar Assn., Allegheny County Bar Assn. Republican. Jewish. Labor, Pension, profit-sharing, and employee benefits. Home: 746 Pinoak Rd Pittsburgh PA 15243-1153 Office: Reed Smith Shaw & McClay Mellon Sq 435 6th Ave Pittsburgh PA 15219-1886

**SCHELER, BRAD ERIC**, lawyer; b. Bklyn., Oct. 11, 1953; s. Bernard and Rita Regina (Miller) S.; m. Amy Ruth Frolick, Mar. 30, 1980; children: Ali M., Maddie H., Zoey B. BA magna cum laude, Lehigh U., 1974; JD, Hofstra U., 1977. Bar: N.Y. 1978, U.S. Dist. Ct. (so. and ea. dists.) N.Y. 1978. Assoc. Weil, Gotshal & Manges, N.Y.C., 1977-81; sr. ptnr., chmn. bankruptcy and restructuring practice Fried, Frank, Harris, Shriver & Jacobson, N.Y.C., 1981—. Rsch. editor Hofstra U. Law Rev., 1975-77. Treas., bus. mgr. Trustees of Gramercy Park, N.Y.C., 1979-87. Fellow Am. Coll. Bankruptcy; mem. ABA (bus. bankruptcy com. corp. banking and bus. law sect., creditors' righ ts com. litig. sect.), N.Y. State Bar Assn., Assn. Bar City of N.Y. (com. on bankruptcy and corp. reorgn. 1991-94), Sigma Alpha Mu (v.p. 1973). Jewish. Bankruptcy, Contracts commercial, Finance. Home: 94 Larchmont Ave Larchmont NY 10538-3723 Office: Fried Frank Harris 1 New York Plz Fl 22 New York NY 10004-1980

**SCHELL, GEORGE AARON**, lawyer; b. Waco, Tex., May 11, 1939; s. George Alvin and Jessie Lee S.; m. Anne, 1960 (div. 1973); 1 child, Michael. BA, Baylor U., 1961, MA, 1963; JD, Loyola U., 1977; MS, Calif. State U., 1990. Bar: Calif. Prof. speech, comm. & debate Loyola Marymount U., L.A., 1963-77; pub. defender Plumas County, Quincy, Calif., 1978-80; deputy city atty. City of L.A., 1977-78, 81—. Office: LA City Atty 14410 Sylvan St Ste 106 Van Nuys CA 91401-2647

**SCHELL, JAMES MICHAEL**, lawyer; b. Yakima, Wash., 1949. BA cum laude, Yale U., 1972; JD, Columbia U., 1976. Bar: N.Y. 1977. Mem. Skadden, Arps, Slate, Meagher & Flom, N.Y.C. Office: Skadden Arps Slate Meagher & Flom 919 3rd Ave New York NY 10022-3902

**SCHELL, NORKA M.**, lawyer, consultant; b. Feira Santana, Bahia, Brazil, May 28, 1958; d. Agostino A. and Maria do Carmo Silva. BA, Coll. San Anthonio, Feira Santana, 1976; JD, Faculdde de Dirito, Gao.Valodares, 1984; LLM in Internt. Law, Golden Gate U., San Francisco, 1988. Paralegal Sindicato dos Metalungico, Ipatinga, 1983-84; atty. N.M. Da Silva Law Office, Ridgewood, N.J., 1989-95; pvt. practice N.M. Da Silva Law Office, Short Hills, N.J., 1995—. Mem. ATLA, San Francisco Bar Assn., N.Y. Bar Assn., Assn. Bar City N.Y. Avocations: sports, photography, travel, languages and music. Public international, Alternative dispute resolution, Franchising. Office: 87 Woodland Rd Short Hills NJ 07078-2420

**SCHELL, RICHARD A.**, federal judge; b. 1950. BA, So. Meth. U., 1972, JD, 1975. Bar: Tex. 1975. Asst. dist. atty. Collin County, Tex., 1976; mem. firm Boyd, Veigel & Gay, 1977-81; judge County Ct. Law Collin County, 1982-86, 219th Jud. Dist. Ct. Tex., 1986-88, U.S. Dist Ct. (ea. dist.) Tex., Beaumont, 1988—; instr. rsch. methods and legal writing So. Meth. U., 1975-76. Mem. State Bar Tex. Office: US Dist Ct PO Box 1470 Beaumont TX 77704-1470

**SCHENDEL, WILLIAM BURNETT**, lawyer; b. 1948. BA, Swarthmore Coll., 1970; JD, Boston U., 1970. Bar: Alaska 1974; U.S. Dist Ct. (4th dist.) Ak. Ptnr. Schendel & Callahan, Fairbanks, Alaska, 1981—; pres. Alaska Bar Assn. Mem. ABA, Alaska Bar Assn. Labor, Civil rights. Office: Schendel & Callahan 613 Cushman St Ste 200 Fairbanks AK 99701-4655

**SCHENING, JUDITH ANNE**, lawyer; b. Ottawa, Ont., Can., Apr. 14, 1961; came to U.S., 1965; d. Albert and Barbara Anne Schening. BA, U. Houston, 1984; JD, No. Ill. U., 1987. Bar: Tex. 1987, Ill. 1988. Briefing atty. U.S. Dist. Ct., Dallas, 1987-89; atty. Fulbright & Jaworski LLP, Dallas, 1989—. Mem. ABA. General civil litigation, Product liability. Office: Fulbright & Jaworski LLP 2200 Ross Ave Ste 2800 Dallas TX 75201-2784

**SCHENK, ERICH LEHNER**, lawyer; b. Houston, Sept. 2, 1970; s. Norman Otto and Carolee (Bauer) S. BS in Bus. and Econs., Trinity U., 1992; JD, So. Tex. U., 1996. Bar: Tex. 1996. Assoc. Tekell, Book, Matthews & Limmer, Houston, 1996—. Mem. ABA, Tex. Bar Assn., Houston Bar Assn., Houston Young Lawyers Assn. Avocations: fishing, hunting, reading. E-mail: eschenk@tbml.com. Home: 2800 Jeanetta St Apt 2001 Houston TX 77063-4039 Office: Tekell Book Matthews & Limmer 1221 Mckinney St Ste 4300 Houston TX 77010-2015

**SCHENKLER, BERNARD**, lawyer; b. Trani, Italy, Aug. 25, 1948; s. Wolf and Nettie Schenkler; m. Ellen Haberman, Sept. 25, 1977; children: Alan, Sarah. BA, U. Pa., 1970; JD, Columbia U., 1973; diploma in mcpl. law, Rutgers U., 1991. Bar: N.Y. 1974, N.J. 1977, D.C. 1979, U.S. Ct. Appeals (2d cir.) 1975, U.S. Dist. Ct. (so. and ea. dists.) N.Y. 1975, U.S. Tax Ct. 1978, U.S. Ct. Mil. Appeals 1978, U.S. Ct. Appeals (3rd cir.), U.S. Dist. Ct. (no. and we. dists.) N.Y. 1980, U.S. Ct. Claims 1985, U.S. Ct. Internat. Trade 1985, U.S. Ct. Appeals (fed. cir.) 1990, U.S. Ct. Appeals (D.C. cir.) 1990, U.S. Ct. Appeals (4th cir.) 1991, U.S. Ct. Vets. Appeals 1990, U.S. Supreme Ct. 1980. Atty bus. law unit N.Y.C. Human Resources Adminstrn., 1973-76, exec. asst. to gen. counsel, 1977; assoc. Ravin, Sarasohn, Cook, Baumgarten & Fisch, West Orange, N.J., 1978-85; ptnr. Ravin, Sarasohn, Cook, Baumgarten, Fisch & Rosen, Roseland, N.J., 1986—. Author: Bankruptcy Aspects of Municipal Real Estate Taxation, 1991, Death and Bankruptcy, How the Probate and Bankruptcy Processes Interact, 1994, Close Encounters With the Bankruptcy Code, 1997. Mem. Randolph Twp. (N.J.) Bd. of Ethics, 1978-80. Mem. ABA, N.Y. State Bar Assn., N.J. State Bar Assn., Essex County Bar Assn., D.C. Bar. Jewish. Club: White Meadow Temple Men's Club (Rockaway, N.J.). Avocations: karate (brown belt), golf, astronomy. Bankruptcy, Contracts commercial, State civil litigation. Office: Ravin Sarasohn Cook Baumgarten Fisch & Rosen 103 Eisenhower Pkwy Ste 13 Roseland NJ 07068-1072

**SCHEPPS, VICTORIA HAYWARD**, lawyer; b. Brockton, Mass., June 11, 1956; d. William George and Lucy Victoria (Mitcheroney) Hayward; m. Frank Schepps, Sept. 18, 1982; children: Frank IV, Lucia. BA, Suffolk U., 1977; JD, U. San Diego, 1981. Instr., Northeastern U., Boston, 1981-83; assoc. Hoffman & Hoffman, Boston, 1983-85, Mark J. Gladstone, P.C., 1985-87; Doktor, Hirschberg & Schepps, 1987-88, Schepps & Reilly, 1988-90; pvt. practice Law Office of Victoria Hayward Schepps, Stoughton, Mass., 1990—. Mem. Mass. Conveyancing Assn., Mass. Assn. Bank Counsel, Inc. Democrat. Roman Catholic. Real property. Office: 6 Cabot Pl Ste 9 Stoughton MA 02072-4625

**SCHER, HOWARD DENNIS**, lawyer; b. Ft. Monmouth, N.J., Apr. 23, 1945; s. George Scher and Rita (Eitches) Zar; children: Seth Micah, Eli David. BA, Brandeis U., 1967; JD, Rutgers U., 1971. Bar: Pa. 1971, U.S. Dist. Ct. (ea. dist.) Pa. 1971, U.S. Ct. Appeals (3rd cir.) 1971, U.S. Supreme Ct. 1975. Asst. city solicitor City of Phila., 1971-73; assoc. Goodis, Greenfield, Henry & Edelstein, Phila., 1973-77; assoc. Montgomery, McCracken, Walker & Rhoads, Phila., 1977-80, ptnr., 1980—. Trustee Fedn. of Jewish Agys. of Greater Phila., 1994—; dir. Akiba Hebrew Acad., Merion, Pa., 1996-98; mem. pres.'s coun. Brandeis U.; pres. Jewish Employment and Vocat. Svcs., 1998—; exec. com. Com. of Seventy. Fellow Am. Coll. Trial Lawyers; mem. ABA, Pa. Bar Assn., Phila. Bar Assn., Brandeis U. Alumni Assn. (v.p. 1983-87). Federal civil litigation, State civil litigation. Home: 2222 Locust St Philadelphia PA 19103-5511 Office: Montgomery McCracken Walker & Rhoads 123 S Broad St Fl 24 Philadelphia PA 19109-1099

**SCHERF, JOHN GEORGE, IV**, lawyer; b. Tuscaloosa, Ala., Oct. 12, 1962; s. John G. III and Roberta Cannon (Timmons) S.; m. Lorie Lankford, Feb. 12, 1994; 1 child, Austin Tyler. AA, Okaloosa Walton Jr. Coll., Niceville, Fla., 1983; BA in Psychology, U. West Fla., 1987; JD, Samford U., 1991. Bar: Ala. 1992, U.S. Dist. Ct. (no. dist.) Ala. 1994, U.S. Dist. Ct. (mid. dist.) Ala. 1997, U.S. Dist. Ct. (so. dist.) Ala., 1999. Clk., assoc. Taylor & Taylor, Birmingham, Ala., 1992-93; assoc. Frank S. Buck, P.C., Birmingham, 1993-95; pvt. practice Birmingham, 1995—. Mem. ATLA, Ala. Bar Assn., Ala. Trial Lawyers Assn., Birmingham Bar Assn. Democrat. Methodist. Personal injury, Insurance, General civil litigation. Home: 1324 Springs Ave Birmingham AL 35242-4862 Office: Scherf Davis & Gedgoudas 2122 1st Ave N Birmingham AL 35203-4202

**SCHERKER, ELLIOT H.**, lawyer; b. N.Y.C., Jan. 7, 1952; s. Leo and Dorothy S.; m. Karen M. Gottlieb, Jan. 27, 1985; children: Emily, Amanda. BA, U. Miami, 1972, JD, 1975. Cert. in appellate practice Fla. Bar, 1995. Asst. pub. defender Dade County Pub. Defender, Miami, 1975-92; assoc. Greenberg Traurig, P.A., Miami, 1992-94, shareholder, 1995—; mem. appellate rules com. Fla. Bar, 1996—. Co-author: (bar pub.) Fla. Appellate Manual, 1988—; contbr. article to Stetson Law Rev. Counsel Hope Ctr., Miami, 1998—. Recipient Defender Svcs. award Nat. Legal Aid and Defender Assn., 1984. Mem. ABA, Fla. Bar Assn., Dade County Bar Assn. Democrat. Appellate, General civil litigation, Land use and zoning (including planning). Office: Greenberg Traurig PA 1221 Brickell Ave Miami FL 33131-3224

**SCHERMER, BETH**, lawyer; b. St. Louis, Sept. 23, 1955; d. J. Leonard and Thelma Schermer; m. Samuel G. Coppersmith, Aug. 28, 1983; children: Sarah, Ben, Louis. BS, Yale U., 1977; JD, Harvard U., 1980. Bar: Ariz. 1980. Atty., ptnr. Lewis & Roca, Phoenix, 1980-98; ptnr. Coppersmith Gordon Schermer Owens & Nelson, Phoenix, 1998—. Co-author: Arizona Hospital and Healthcare Association Compliance Guide, 1998; editor: AAHA Managed Care Handbook, 1993. Bd. dirs. Ctrl. Ariz. Shelter Svcs., Phoenix, 1995—; bd. dirs. Friends of Phoenix Pub. Libr., 1989-95, pres., 1994. Mem. Am. Health Lawyers Assn. (bd. dirs. 1997—, pres.-elect), Am. Acad. Health Care Attys. (bd. dirs. 1992-97). Health, General corporate, Administrative and regulatory. Office: Coppersmith Gordon et al 2633 E Indian School Rd Ste 300 Phoenix AZ 85016-6765

**SCHERMER, JUDITH KAHN**, lawyer; b. N.Y.C., Feb. 28, 1949; d. Robert and Barbara Kahn; m. Daniel Woodrough Schermer; 1 child, Sarah Nicole. BA, U. Chgo., 1971; JD, William Mitchell Coll. Law, 1987. Bar: Minn. 1987, U.S. Dist. Ct. Minn. 1987. Advt. and promotion specialist U. Chgo. Press, 1971-75; systems analyst Allstate Ins. Co., Northbrook, Ill., 1975-78, Lutheran Brotherhood, Mpls., 1980-83; polit. aide Mpls. City Coun., 1986-87; ptnr. Schermer & Schermer, Mpls., 1987—. Assoc chair 5th Congl. dist., state exec. com. Dem. Farm Labor Party; bd. dirs. Minn. Consumer Alliance. Mem. ATLA, Minn. Trial Lawyers Assn. (bd. govs., chair legis. com.), Minn. State Bar Assn., Minn. Women Lawyers, Nat. Employment Law Assn., Minn. Consumer Alliance (bd. dirs.). General civil litigation, Labor, Civil rights. Home: 4624 Washburn Ave S Minneapolis MN 55410-1846 Office: Schermer and Schermer Lumber Exch Bldg 10 S 5th St Ste 700 Minneapolis MN 55402-1033

**SCHERR, STEPHANIE LYNN**, lawyer; b. Poughkeepsie, N.Y., Aug. 10, 1968; d. Allan Lee and Marsha (Kahn) S. BA, Georgetown U., 1990, JD, 1995, MBA, 1995. Bar: N.Y. 1996. Assoc. LeBoeuf, Lamb, Greene & MacRae, N.Y.C., 1995-98, Morrison & Foerster LLP, N.Y.C., 1998—. General corporate, Securities. Office: Morrison & Foerster Rm 203 1290 Avenue Of The Americas Fl 41 New York NY 10104-0050

**SCHERZER, MARK P.**, lawyer; b. Bronx, N.Y., Apr. 24, 1951; s. Felix and Sylvia (Warman) S. BA, Haverford Coll., 1973; MA in Anthropology, U. Chgo., 1975; JD, Yale U., 1978. Bar: N.Y. 1979, U.S. Dist. Ct. (so. dist.) N.Y. 1979, U.S. Dist. Ct. (ea. dist.) N.Y. 1980, U.S. Ct. Appeals (6th cir.) 1985, U.S. Ct. Appeals (2d cir.) 1996. Assoc. Botein, Hays, Sklar & Herzberg, N.Y.C., 1978-80; pvt. practice N.Y.C., 1980-84, 90—; ptnr. Scherzer & Palella, N.Y.C., 1984-90; legis. counsel New Yorkers for Accessible Health Coverage, N.Y.C., 1994-99. Contbr. to books on law. Mem. healthcare and ins. steering com. NEA, Washington, 1996-97; mem. nat. adv. bd. Artists health Ins. Resource Ctr., N.Y.C., 1997-98. Mem. Lesbian and Gay Law Assn. of Greater N.Y. (Cmty. svc. award 1992). Democrat. Jewish. Health, Insurance. Office: 5 Beekman St Rm 213 New York NY 10038-2206

**SCHEU, WILLIAM E.**, lawyer; b. Jacksonville, Fla., Jan. 3, 1946; s. William E. and Sara Lee (Bates) S.; m. Margaret Corbin, July 8, 1967; children: Margaret Ann, Mary Lee, Sara. BA in History, U. South, 1967; JD, U. Fla., 1970. Bar: Fla. 1970, U.S. Dist. Ct. (mid. dist.) Fla. 1971. Atty. Ulmer, Murchison, Ashby & Tayler, Jacksonville, Fla., 1970-96, Rogers, Towers, Bailey, Jones & Gay, Jacksonville, Fla., 1997—. Past pres. Jacksonville Cmty. Coun., Inc., Jacksonville Area Legal Aid, Inc., Willing Hands, Inc., Vis. Nurses Assn. North Fla., Inc., Citizens Two-Term Limit, Inc. Mem. Advocates for Better Jacksonville, Meninak Club (life), NAACP. Republican. Presbyterian. Real property. Office: Rogers Towers Bailey Jones & Gay 1301 Riverplace Blvd Ste 1500 Jacksonville FL 32207-1811

**SCHEVE, THOMAS JOHN**, assistant prosecutor; b. Cin.. BA in English Lit., Xavier U., 1972; MA in English Lit., U. Cin., 1975; JD, No. Ky. U., 1978. Pub. defender Hamilton County Pub. Defender's Office, Cin., 1978-81; tax atty. The Kroger Co., Cin., 1981-84; asst. prosecuting atty. Hamilton County Prosecutor's Office, Cin., 1984—. Contbr. articles to profl. jours. Office: Hamilton County Prosecutor 230 E 9th St Ste 400 Cincinnati OH 45202-2174

**SCHIAVENZA, JAMES MICHAEL**, lawyer; b. Berkeley, Calif., Oct. 11, 1949; s. John Thomas and Bernice A. Schiavenza; m. Ellen Mary Schiavenza, June 30, 1990; 1 child, Kathleen Anne. BS, Santa Clara U., 1971, JD, 1974. Bar: Calif. 1974, U.S. Dist. Ct. (no. dist.) Calif. 1974, U.S. Ct. Appeals (9th cir.) 1974, U.S. Dist. Ct. (ea. dist.) Calif. 1980, U.S. Supreme Ct. 1980, U.S. Dist. Ct. (so. dist.) Calif. 1985. Dep. atty. gen. Office of the State Atty. Gen., Sacramento, 1975-85, 86—; ptnr. Campagne & Schiavenza, Fresno, Calif., 1985-86; prof. law Lincoln Law Sch. of Sacramento, 1986—; adj. prof. law U. Calif.-Davis, 1988-94. Named Litigator of the Yr., Office of the State Atty. Gen., 1991, Prof. of the Yr., Lincoln Law Sch. of Sacramento, 1992, 97. Mem. state Bar of Calif., Santa Clara U. Alumni Assn. (Sacramento chpt. treas. 1987-97, pres. 1998—). Democrat. Roman Catholic. Avocations: golf, philately. Office: Office of the Attorney General PO Box 944255 Sacramento CA 94244-2550

**SCHIAVO, PASCO LOUIS**, lawyer; b. Hazleton, Pa., June 21, 1937; s. Louis and Josephine (Cortese) S., B.A., Lafayette Coll., 1958; J.D., U. Pa.,

1962. Bar: Pa. 1962, U.S. Dist. Ct. (mid. dist.) Pa. 1965, U.S. Supreme Ct. 1970, U.S. Ct. Appeals (3d cir.) 1972. Assoc. Laputka, Bayless, Ecker & Cohn, Hazleton, 1963-65; asst. dist. atty. Luzerne County, Wilkes-Barre, Pa., 1963-65; pvt. practice, Hazleton, 1965—; mem. disciplinary bd. Supreme Ct. Pa., Harrisburg, 1977-83. Contbr. articles to profl. jours. Pres. Luzerne County Commn. Econ. Opportunity, Wilkes-Barre, 1966-68. Mem. ABA, Pa. Bar Assn., Luzerne County Bar Assn., Pa. Trial Lawyers Assn., Assn. Trial Lawyers Am., Am. Judicature Soc., Nat. Bd. Trial Advocacy (diplomate, cert. civil trial advocate). Personal injury, State civil litigation, General practice. Office: 21 E Broad St Hazleton PA 18201-6520

**SCHIESEL, STEVEN,** lawyer; b. N.Y.C.; s. Estelle Schiesel; m. Elaine Leddomado, May 15, 1988. BA cum laude, Columbia U., 1989; JD, Fordham U., 1992. Bar: N.Y. 1993, Conn. 1992, U.S. Dist. Ct. (so. dist.) N.Y. 1993. Assoc. Newman Schlau Fitch & Lane, N.Y.C., 1992-94; ptnr. Pecoraro & Schiesel, N.Y.C., 1994—. Mem. staff Fordham Internat. Law Jour., 1991. Mem. ATLA, Am. Coll. Legal Medicine (assoc.), Million Dollar Advocates Forum (life), Mensa, Intertel. Personal injury, Insurance, General civil litigation. Office: Pecoraro & Schiesel 1 Whitehall St New York NY 10004-2109

**SCHIESSWOHL, CYNTHIA RAE SCHLEGEL,** lawyer; b. Colorado Springs, Colo., July 7, 1955; d. Leslie H. and Maime (Kascak) Schlegel; m. Scott Jay Schiesswohl, Aug. 6, 1977; children: Leslie Michelle, Kristen Elizabeth. BA cum laude, So. Meth. U., 1976; JD, U. Colo., 1978; post-grad., U. Denver, 1984. Bar: Colo. 1979, Wyo. 1986, Ind. 1988, U.S. Dist. Ct. Colo. 1979, U.S. Ct. Appeals (10th cir.) 1984, family mediator, 1992, civil mediator 1994. Rsch. clk. City Atty.'s Office, Colorado Springs, Colo., 1976; investigator Pub. Defender's Office, Colorado Springs, 1976; dep. dist. atty. 4th Jud. Dist. Colo., 1979-81; pvt. practice law Grand Junction, Colo., 1981-82, Denver, 1983-84; assoc. Law Offices of John G. Salmon P.C., 1984-85; pvt. practice Laramie, Wyo., 1985-88, Indpls., 1988-90; of counsel Rund & Wunsch, Indpls., 1990—; guest lectr. Pikes Peak C.C., 1980; adj. prof. polit. sci. and speech Butler U., Indpls., 1993—, spl. asst. to dean for pre-law, 1993-95, asst. dean for pre-profl. svcs., 1995—. Advisor Explorer Law Post Boy Scouts Am., 1980-81; vol. Girl Scouts Am., 1993-94; ex officio mem. ch. devel. com. Ctrl. Rocky Mt. region Christian Ch. (Disciples of Christ), 1986-88; mem. evangelism commn. United Meth. Ch., 1987-88, fin. com. youth and music depts., 1979-81, lay del. Rocky Mountain Ann. Conf., 1986-87, academic tutor youth programs, 1989—, Sunday sch. tchr., 1995—; mem. ch. and soc. com. Meridian St. United Meth. Ch., 1989-93, mem. refugee resettlement com., 1990-93; pres. (hon.) United Meth. Women, 1996—, mem. ch. choir, mem. sch. tchr., 1997—; hearing officer Wyo. Dept. Edn., 1987-88; vol. Project Motivation, Dallas, 1974; chairperson Wyo. Med. Rev. Panel, 1987; lectr. Ind. Pastor's Conf., Rethinking Prisons Conf., 1990, Econ. Edn. for clergy Conf., 1991; bd. dirs. Art Ctr. and Art Assn. Henry County, 1997—; trustee New Castle Cmty. Sch. Corp., 1998—, sec., 1999—. Named U. scholar So. Meth. U., 1973. Mem. ABA (internat. law com.), Ind. State Bar Assn., Wyo State Bar, Colo. Bar Assn. (ethics com. 1984-85, long range planning com. 1985-88, chairperson 1986-87), Am. Immigration Lawyers Assn. (sec. Ind. chpt. 1991-92, 93-94, chpt. vice chair 1992-93, asylum liaison 1990-99, chpt. chair 1994-95, bd. govs. 1994-95) Indpls. Bar Assn. (internat. law sect. ethics com. 1990-93), Midwest Assn. Pre-Law Advisors, Nat. Assn. Advisors for Health Professions, Ind. Sch. Bd. Assn. (awards com. 1999—), Pi Sigma Alpha, Alpha Lambda Delta, Alpha Delta Pi. Republican. General practice, Immigration, naturalization, and customs, Religion. Office: 933 Bundy Ave New Castle IN 47362-5278

**SCHIFFBAUER, WILLIAM G.,** lawyer; b. Columbia, S.C., Feb. 17, 1954; s. John R. and Jean A. Schiffbauer; m. Sarah L. Powers; children: J. William, Elisabeth, James Benjamin. BS, U. Nebr., 1976; JD, Creighton U., 1979; LLM, George Washington U., 1987. Bar: Nebr. 1979, U.S. Dist. Ct. Nebr. 1979, U.S. Ct. Claims 1982, U.S. Tax Ct. 1982, D.C. 1988. Counsel U.S. Senator J.J. Exon, Washington, 1979-85; ptnr. Groom & Nordberg, Washington, 1985-97, Schiffbauer Law Firm, Washington, 1997—. Mem. ABA, Nebr. Bar Assn., D.C. Bar Assn., Environ. Law Inst., Nat. Health Lawyers Assn., Omicron Delta Kappa. Democrat. Roman Catholic. Legislative, Environmental, Health. Office: 1155 Connecticut Ave NW Ste 420 Washington DC 20036-4306

**SCHIFFER, LARRY PHILIP,** lawyer; b. N.Y.C.; s. Jerry and Alma Schiffer; m. Gail Beverly Wachtelkonig, Aug. 19, 1978; children: Jessica, Jamie. BA magna cum laude, CUNY, Bklyn., 1976; JD, Union U., 1979. Bar: N.Y. 1980, U.S. Dist. Ct. (so. and ea. dists.) N.Y. 1980. Law asst. N.Y. Supreme Ct.-Appellate Divsn., Bklyn., 1979-81; assoc. Werner, Kennedy & Evench, N.Y.C., 1982-89; ptnr. Werner & Kennedy, N.Y.C., 1989-99, LeBoeuf, Lamb, Greene & MacRae, LLP, N.Y.C., 1999—; moderator N.Y. Ins. Law Forum, Counsel Connect; spkr. in field. Mem. editl. bd. Andrews Internat. Reinsurance Dispute Reporter, 1996—; contbr. articles to profl. jours. Bd. mem. Mill Brook Civic Assn., Valley Stream, N.Y. Mem. ABA (mem. tort and ins. practice sect., chmn. excess surplus lines and reins. com. 1994-95, editor ESLR com. newsletter 1991-93, vice chair, webmaster, listserv moderator 1997—, coord. regional meetings, mem. CLE bd. 1998—, chair tech. com. 1997-99, comms. coordinating group com. 1997-99, chair-elect electronic media coordinating group 1998-99, mem. litigation sect.), Assn. of Bar of City of N.Y. (com. on med. malpractice 1991-97), N.Y. State Bar Assn. (chair. com. assn. ins. programs, mem. comml. and fed. litigation sect., mem. torts, ins. and compensation law sect.). Fax: 212-424-8500. E-mail: lschiffe@llgm.com and lpschiffer@yahoo.com. Insurance, General civil litigation, Alternative dispute resolution. Home: 77 Rushfield Ln Valley Stream NY 11581-2320 Office: LeBoeuf Lamb et al 125 W 55th St New York NY 10019-5369

**SCHIFTER, RICHARD,** lawyer, government official; b. Vienna, Austria, July 31, 1923; came to U.S., 1938; s. Paul and Balbina (Blass) S.; m. Lilo Krueger, July 3, 1948; children: Judith, Deborah, Richard P., Barbara, Karen. BS in Social Sci. summa cum laude, CCNY, 1943; LLB, Yale U., 1951; DHL (hon.), Hebrew Union Coll., 1992. Bar: Conn. 1951, D.C. 1952, U.S. Supreme Ct. 1954, Md., 1958. Assoc. Fried, Frank, Harris, Shriver & Jacobson, Washington, 1951-57, ptnr., 1957-84; dep. U.S. rep. with rank of ambassador UN Security Council, N.Y.C., 1984-85; asst. sec. of state for human rights and humanitarian affairs Dept. State, Washington, 1985-92; U.S. rep. UN Human Rights Commn., Geneva, 1983-86, 93; spl. asst. to pres., counselor Nat. Security Coun., Washington, 1993-97, spl. adviser to Sec. of State, 1997—; head U.S. del. Conf. on Security and Cooperation in Europe Experts Meeting on Human Rights, Ottawa, Ont., Can., 1985, Dem. Insts., Oslo, 1991; bd. dirs. U.S. Inst. Peace, 1986-92; mem. Congl. Commn. on Security and Cooperation in Europe, 1986-92. V.p., pres. Md. Bd. Edn., Balt., 1959-79; chmn. Md. Gov.'s Commn. on Funding Edn. of Handicapped Children, 1975-77, Md. Values Edn. Commn., 1979-83, Montgomery County Dem. Cen. Com., Md., 1966-70; del. Dem. Nat. Conv., 1968; bd. govs., chmn. Nat. Adv. Com., Am. Jewish Com., 1992-93. With U.S. Army, 1943-46, ETO. Recipient Disting. Svc. award Sec. of State, 1992. Mem. Phi Beta Kappa. Democrat. Jewish. Home: 6907 Crail Dr Bethesda MD 20817-4723 Office: US Dept of State Office Of Advisor Sec State Washington DC 20520-0001

**SCHILD, RAYMOND DOUGLAS,** lawyer; b. Chgo., Dec. 20, 1952; s. Stanley Martin and Cassoundra Lee (McArdle) S.; m. Ellen Arthea Carstensen, Oct. 24, 1987; children: Brian Christopher, Melissa Nicole. Student, U.S. Mil. Acad., 1970; BA summa cum laude, De Paul U., 1974, JD magna cum laude, 1982; M in Life Scis., Order of Essenes, 1996. Bar: Ill. 1982, U.S. Dist. Ct. (no. dist.) Ill. 1982, U.S. Ct. Appeals (7th cir.) 1982, Idaho 1989, U.S. Dist. Ct. Idaho 1989, U.S. Ct. Appeals (9th cir.) 1989, U.S. Supreme Ct. 1990. Assoc. Clausen, Miller, Gorman, Caffrey & Witous, Chgo., 1982-84; law clk. to chief judge law divsn. Cir. Ct. Cook County, Chgo., 1984-85; assoc. John G. Phillips & Assocs., Chgo., 1985-87, Martin, Chapman, Park & Burkett, Boise, Idaho, 1988-89; pvt. practice Boise, 1989-90; pres. Martin, Chapman, Schild & Lassaw, Chartered, Boise, 1990-96; dir., v.p. Behavioral Mgmt. Ctrs.; v.p. Am. Mgmt., Inc.; bd. dirs. Image Concepts Internat., Inc., Boise; lectr. on legal edn. ICLE and NBI, 1993-98. Co-host legal radio talk show KFXD, 1994; legal columnist Idaho Bus. Rev., 1988-96. Mem. adv. bd. Alliance for the Mentally Ill, Boise, 1991—, Parents and Youth Against Drug Abuse, Boise, 1991-92; fair housing adminstr. Sauk Village (Ill.) Govt., 1987-88; instr. Ada County Youth Ct., Boise, 1992—. Schmitt fellow DePaul U., 1974; recipient award of merit Chgo. Law Coalition, 1987. Mem. ATLA, Idaho Trial Lawyers' Assn., Ill. State Bar Assn., Idaho State Bar Assn., Boise Estate Planning Counsel, Shriners (temple atty. 1994—, liaison Crippled Children's Hosp.), Masons (jr. steward 1992). Avocations: tennis, trombone, writing, music. General civil litigation, General corporate, Probate.

**SCHILDT, STEVEN JOSEPH,** lawyer; b. Cleve., May 24, 1968; s. James M. and Lillian F. Schildt. BA, Princeton U., 1991; JD, Temple U., 1996. Bar: Pa. 1996, U.S. Dist. Ct. (ea. dist.) 1996, N.J. 1996. Staff cons. Arthur Andersen, N.Y.C., 1991-93; assoc. McKissock and Hoffman, Phila., 1996—; mem. Def. Rsch. Inst., Chgo., 1996—, Pa. Def. Inst., Phila., 1996—. Named Nat. All-Star U.S. Rugby Assn., 1988. Mem. ABA, Pa. Bar Assn., Phila. Bar Assn., Princeton Football Assn. Avocations: running, racquet sports. General civil litigation, Insurance, Professional liability. Home: 2200 Ben Franklin Pkwy Apt W206 Philadelphia PA 19130-3624 Office: Mckissock and Hoffman 1700 Market St Fl 30 Philadelphia PA 19103-3913

**SCHILKEN, BRUCE A.,** lawyer; b. Rochester, Minn., Mar. 20, 1941; s.David A. and Florence A. Schilken; m. Marianne Marriott, June 24, 1961; children: Patrick A., Michael C. BS, Regis U., Denver, 1963; JD, U. Denver, 1965. Tax mgr. Touche Ross & Co. CPAs, Denver, 1965-74; ptnr. Tague, Goss, Schilken & Beem PC, Denver, 1974-80; owner, ptnr. Schilken & Kautt P.C., Denver, 1980—. Contbr. articles to Colo. Lawyer. Mem. Colo. Bar Assn., Arapahoe County Bar Assn. (bd. dirs. 1985-87), Colo. Soc. CPAs, Red Rocks Country Club. Avocations: golf, travel, camping. Estate planning, General corporate, Probate. Office: Schilken & Kautt PC 925 W Kenyon Ave Ste 1 Englewood CO 80110-3471

**SCHILLER, DONALD CHARLES,** lawyer; b. Chgo., Dec. 8, 1942; s. Sidney S. and Edith (Lastick) S.; m. Eileen Fagin, June 14, 1964; children—Eric, Jonathan. Student, Lake Forest Coll., 1960-63; J.D., DePaul U., 1966. Bar: Ill. 1966, U.S. Dist. Ct. (no. dist.) Ill. 1966, U.S. Supreme Ct. 1972. Ptnr. Schiller, DuCanto & Fleck (formerly Schiller & Schiller and Schiller & DuCanto), Chgo., 1966—; chair domestic rels. adv. com. Cir. Ct. Cook County, 1993—, exec. com., 1986-93; speaker profl. confs. Contbr. chpts. and articles to profl. publs. Mem. steering com. on juvenile ct. watching, LWV, 1980-81. Recipient Maurice Weigle award Chgo. Bar Found., 1978, Disting. Alumni award, DePaul U., 1988, various certs. of appreciation profl. groups: named One of Am.'s Best Divorce Lawyers, Town and Country, 1985, 98, The Nat. Law Jour., 1987, The Best Lawyers in Am., 1987, 89, 91, 93, 97, One of Chgo's. Best Div. Lawyers, Crain's Chgo. Bus., 1981, Today Chgo. Woman, 1985, Inside Chgo. mag., 1988. Fellow Am. Bar Found., Am. Acad. Matrimonial Lawyers (chair continuing legal edn. 1993-94); mem. ABA (bd. govs. 1994-97, chmn. family law sect. 1985-86, Ill. State del. 1980-84, mem. Ho. of Dels. 1984—, editor-in-chief Family Law Newsletter 1977-79; mem. editorial bd., assoc. editor Family Adv. Mag. 1979-84, speaker at confs. and meetings), Ill. Bar Assn. (pres. 1988-89, chmn. family law sect. 1976-77, editor Family Law Bull. 1976-77, bd. govs. 1977-83, treas. 1981-84, v.p. 1984-86, chmn. various coms., lectr., incorporator Ill. State Bar Assn. Risk Retention Group, Inc. 1988), Chgo. Bar Assn., Am. Coll. Family Law Trial Lawyers (diplomate). Family and matrimonial. Office: Schiller DuCanto & Fleck 200 N La Salle St Ste 2700 Chicago IL 60601-1099

**SCHILLING, EDWIN CARLYLE, III,** lawyer; b. Baton Rouge, Apr. 5, 1943; s. Edwin Carlyle and Ann (LeTarde) S.; m. Lanell Holder, Dec. 18, 1964; children: Joel, Daniel. BA in Physics/Math., Baylor U., 1966; JD, La. State U., 1969. Bar: La. 1969, Colo. 1989, Alaska 1990, U.S. Supreme Ct. 1982, U.S. Ct. Mil. Appeals 1981, U.S. Tax Ct. 1982, U.S. Ct. Appeals (Fed. cir.) 1982. Commd. USAF, 1969-89, advanced through grades to lt. col.; assoc. prof. law USAF Acad., Colo., 1972-76; staff judge advocate Kunsan AB, Korea, 1976-77, Myrtle Beach (S.C.) AFB, 1977-80; dir. USAF Legal Assistance Program, Washington, 1980-83; with Air War Coll., 1983-84; staff judge advocate Elemdorf AFB, Alaska, 1984-87; asst. staff judge advocate Air Force Acctg. and Fin. Ctr., Lowry AFB, Colo., 1987-89; pvt. practice law Aurora, Colo., 1989—. Co-author book: Survival Manual for Women in Divorce, 1990, Survival Manual for Men in Divorce; co-author video tape/manual: How to Successfully Manage Military Divorce, 1990. Sec. Eastridge Civic Assn., Aurora, 1988—; bd. dirs. Consumer Credit Counseling Svc., Anchorage, 1985-87, Myrtle Beach Fed. Credit Union, 1978-81. Mem. ABA (exec. mem. fed. procedures and legislation com.), La. Bar Assn., Colo. Bar Assn., Alaska Bar Assn. Republican. Presbyterian. Avocations: photography, fishing, hiking, camping, amateur radio. Family and matrimonial, Military. Office: 2767 S Parker Rd Ste 230 Aurora CO 80014-2701

**SCHILLING, JOHN RUSSELL,** lawyer, retail executive; b. Huntington Park, Calif., Nov. 27, 1942; s. Alice S.; m. Susan Foster, Aug. 25, 1962 (div. Jan. 1976); children: Jennifer Susan, Lisa Ann, John Payton; m. Caroline Schilling, Aug. 20, 1976 (div. Dec. 1985); 1 child, Brice David; m. Sabrina Celeste August,, Aug. 21, 1993; children: Elissia Jeanne, Chanel Marie, Chloe Celeste. BA, U. Calif., Santa Barbara, 1964; JD, UCLA, 1967. Bar: Calif. 1968. Chief rsch. atty., 4th Dist., Div. II Ct. Appeals, San Bernardino, Calif., 1967-69; pvt. practice Orange County, Calif., 1969—; lectr. in field. Trustee Santa Ana (Calif.) Unified Sch. Dist., 1971-75. Fellow Am. Acad. Matrimonial Lawyers (v.p. 1985—); mem. Calif. State Bar Assn., Orange County Bar Assn. (sect. treas. 1984—), Robert A. Banyard Inn of Ct. (master bencher 1996—), ABA (sect. child custody com. 1968—). Family and matrimonial. Office: 4675 Macarthur Ct Ste 590 Newport Beach CA 92660-8800

**SCHILLING, LAURA K.,** lawyer; b. N.Y.C., Oct. 25, 1968; d. Donald and Annette Schilling. BBA, Emory U., 1990; JD, Ga. State U., 1996. Bar: Ga. 1996, D.C. 1996, Fla. 1997; CPA, Ga. Acct. Habif Arogetti & Wayne, Atlanta, 1990-92; fin. staff Equitable Real Estate, Atlanta, 1992-93; pvt. practice law Atlanta, 1996—; fin. planner Creative Fin. Group, Atlanta, 1997—. Bd. dirs. Boys and Girls Club, Atlanta, 1997. Estate planning, Probate, General corporate. Office: Creative Fin Group 53 Perimeter Ctr E Ste 450 Atlanta GA 30346-2286

**SCHIMMERLING, THOMAS EMILE,** lawyer; b. N.Y.C., July 21, 1952; s. Alfred Israel and Anne (Fleischmann) S.; 1 child, Kristyn Anne. BA, Hartwick Coll., 1974; JD, Syracuse U., 1976. Bar: N.Y. 1977, Fla. 1979, U.S. Supreme Ct. 1980. Br. counsel SBA, Jacksonville, Fla., 1977-78; owner, prin. Schimmerling Law Offices, Delhi, Oneonta, Binghamton, N.Y., 1978—; chief defender Delaware County, N.Y., 1988—; adj. prof. SUNY, Delhi, 1991-92. Author: Guide to Divorce & Custody Cases, 1994, Your Rights if Injured, 1996. Chmn. Delaware County Dem. Com., Delhi, 1980-85; mem. town coun. Town of Middletown, Margaretville, N.Y., 1974-78, town atty., 1979-81. Mem. ABA (assoc. editor family law litig. 1995-97), ATLA (chair family law sect. 1996-97), N.Y. State Bar Assn. (lectr. negligence law issues 1996-97), N.Y. State Trial Lawyers Assn., N.Y. State Bar Assn., Fleischmann C. of C. (pres. 1979-81), Delaware County C. of C. (exec. com. 1991-93). Democrat. Jewish. Avocations: skiing, hiking, music, boating, stamp collecting. Family and matrimonial, Personal injury, State civil litigation. Home: Grimm Rd Meridale NY 13806 Office: 98 Main St Delhi NY 13753-1220

**SCHINDLER, RONALD IRVIN,** lawyer; b. Port Angeles, Wash.; s. William I. and F. Colleen (Jenson) S.; m. Helena Onggo, June 7, 1988; children: Alexander Ong Yong Hui, Andrew Ong Yong Hsin. BA, Idaho State U., 1990; JD, U. Denver, 1993, LLM, 1998. Bar: Colo. 1994, Idaho 1996, U.S. Dist. Ct. Idaho 1996. Geologist Exploration Methods, Englewood, Colo., 1990; intern Sen. Tim Wirth, Denver, 1992; law clk. Cyprus Amax Minerals Co., Engelwood, 1992-94; atty. Bradley Campbell Carney & Madson, Golden, Colo., 1994-95; shareholder, v.p. Root & Schindler, Denver, 1995—; presenter in field. Contbr. articles to profl. jours.; editor: Colo. Water Ct. Reporter, 1991, 92. Mem. ABA, SME, Geol. Soc. Am., Colo. Bar Assn., Idaho Bar Assn., Denver Bar Assn., Rocky Mountain Assn. Mineral Landmen (pres.), Rocky Mountain Mineral Law Found. (pubs. com. 1996—). Republican. Mem. LDS Ch. Avocations: music, horsemanship. Natural resources, Environmental, Intellectual property. Office: Root & Schindler 410 17th St Ste 460 Denver CO 80202-4455

**SCHINDLER, STEVEN ROY,** lawyer; b. N.Y.C., May 21, 1958; s. Jack J. and Gloria Schindler; m. Susan M. Kath, June 14, 1987; children: Alexandra, Emma. BA, Oberlin Coll., 1980; JD, Fordham U., 1985. Bar: N.Y. 1986, U.S. Dist. Ct. (so. and ea. dists.) N.Y. 1986, U.S. Dist. Ct. (no. dist.) N.Y. 1987, U.S. Ct. Appeals (2d cir.) 1996, U.S. Supreme Ct. 1996. Assoc. Burns, Summit, Rovins & Feldesman, N.Y.C., 1985-87, Winthrop, Stimson, Putnam & Roberts, N.Y.C., 1987-96; founding ptnr. Schindler Cohen & Hochman LLP, N.Y.C., 1997—. Mem. ABA, Internat. Bar Assn., Assn. Bar City N.Y. Avocations: tennis, hiking, history. General civil litigation, Alternative dispute resolution. Office: Schindler Cohen & Hochman LLP One Liberty Pla 35th Fl New York NY 10006-1404

**SCHIRA, DIANA RAE,** lawyer; b. Wausau, WI, Apr. 27, 1964; d. Ray Vernes and Alice LaVerne (Hasl) Deckelman; m. Jeffery David Schira, June 20, 1992; children: Rae Hannah, Hazel Marie, Iris Lydia. BA, U. Wis., Madison, 1986; JD, Marquette U., Milw., 1989. Bar: Wis. 1989, U.S. Dist. Ct. (ea. and we. dists.) Wis. 1989. Pvt. practice Schira Law Firm, S.C., Mosinee, Wis., 1989—. Mem. ABA, Phi Delta Phi. Democrat. Personal injury, Family and matrimonial, General civil litigation. Office: Schira Law Firm SC PO Box 266 1116 Western Ave Mosinee WI 54455-1535

**SCHIZAS, JENNIFER ANNE,** law association administrator; b. Grand Island, Nebr., Aug. 18, 1959; d. John Delano and Jacqueline May (Pieper) S. BJ, U. Nebr., 1982. Rschr. U.S. Senator Carl T. Curtis, Washington, 1978; pub. rels. dir. Nebr. Solar Office, Lincoln, 1979; reporter Sta. WOWT-TV, Omaha, 1980-83; bur. chief Sta. KHAS-TV, Hastings, Nebr., 1983-84; divsn. dir. March of Dimes, Lincoln, 1986-90; exec. dir. Lincoln Arts Coun., 1990-92, Nebr. Food Industry Assn., Lincoln, 1992-93; dir. comm. Nebr. Bar Assn., Lincoln, 1993—; mem. editor's exch. adv. bd. West Pub. CO., Eagan, Minn., 1995. Mem. Am. Soc. Assn. Execs., Nat. Assn. Bar Execs. (pub. rels. cons. 1995), Nebr. Soc. Assn. Execs. Sertoma Club (v.p.). Democrat. Greek Orthodox. Avocations: running, painting, antique collecting and refinishing. E-mail: jschizas@nebar.com. Home: 621 S 30th St Lincoln NE 68510-1427 Office: Nebr Bar Assn 635 S 14th St Lincoln NE 68508-2700

**SCHIZER, ZEVIE BARUCH,** lawyer; b. Bklyn., Dec. 19, 1928; s. David and Bertha (Rudavsky) S.; m. Hazel Gerber, Aug. 23, 1962; children: Deborah Gail, Miriam Anne, David Michael. BA magna cum laude, NYU, 1950; JD, Yale U., 1953. Bar: N.Y. 1954, U.S. Dist. Ct. (so. and ea. dist.) N.Y. 1959, U.S. Ct. Appeals (2d cir.) 1959, U.S. Supreme Ct. 1959. Assoc. Guzik & Boukstein, N.Y.C., 1953-54; teaching fellow NYU Sch. Law, 1954-55; assoc. Philips, Nizer, Benjamin & Krim, N.Y.C., 1955-56, Aranow, Brodsky, Einhorn & Dann, N.Y.C., 1956-57; asst. counsel jud. inquiry Appellate Divsn. 2nd Dept., Bklyn., 1957-62; assoc. Hays, Porter, Spanier & Curtis, N.Y.C., 1963-68, ptnr., 1968-85; sec. United Aircraft Products, Inc., Dayton, Ohio, 1970-83; ptnr. Schizer & Schizer, N.Y.C., 1985—. Trustee Bklyn. Pub. Libr., 1966—, pres. 1985-88, N.Y. Young Dem. Club, N.Y.C., 1960-61; trustee East Midwood Jewish Ctr., Bklyn., 1991—. Mem. N.Y. County Lawyers Assn. (mem. profl. ethics com., mem. com. on profl. discipline), Phi Beta Kappa. Democrat. Jewish. General corporate, Securities, Probate. Home: 1134 E 23rd St Brooklyn NY 11210-4519 Office: Schizer & Schizer 3 New York Plz New York NY 10004-2442

**SCHLACKS, STEPHEN MARK,** lawyer, educator; b. Pittsburg, Kans., Oct. 13, 1955. BA, Austin Coll., Sherman, Tex., 1978; MBA, U. Dallas, 1982; JD, Baylor U., 1986. Bar: Tex. 1987, U.S. Dist. Ct. (so. dist.) Tex. 1987, (no., ea. and we. dists.) Tex. 1988, U.S. Ct. Appeals (5th cir.) 1987, (8th cir.) 1989, U.S. Supreme Ct. 1990. In mgmt. Johnson & Johnson Products, Inc., Sherman, 1978-84; assoc. atty. Wetzel & Assocs., The Woodlands, Tex., 1986-92; ptnr. Hope, Causey & Schlacks, P.C., Conroe, Tex., 1992-96, Law Office of Stephen M. Schlacks, The Woodlands, Tex., 1996—; adj. faculty North Harris County C.C., Houston, 1990—. Leon Jaworski scholar, 1984, Harcourt Brace Jovanovich scholar, 1986. Mem. Fed. Bar Assn., Montgomery County Bar Assn., Tex. Assn. Def. Counsel, Sigma Iota Epsilon, Pi Gamma Mu. Republican. Presbyterian. General civil litigation, Insurance. Home: 66 Racing Cloud Ct The Woodlands TX 77381-5203 Office: 2202 Timberloch Pl Ste 110 The Woodlands TX 77380-1163

**SCHLANG, DAVID,** real estate executive, lawyer; b. N.Y.C., May 2, 1912; s. Alexander and Blanche (Cohen) S.; m. Arlene Roth, May 9, 1948. LLB, NYU, 1933. Bar: N.Y. 1935, U.S. Dist. Ct. (so. dist.) N.Y. 1940. Individual practice law, 1935-42; sec. Schlang Bros. & Co., Inc., N.Y.C., 1945—. Trustee Brookdale Hosp., Bklyn., 1980—, vice chmn., 1983—; bd. dirs., vice chmn. Samuel Schulman Inst. Nursing and Rehab. of Brookdale Hosp., 1973—, sec. bd. dirs., 1976—; vice chmn. Linroc Nursing Home, 1993—; dir. Legion Meml. Sq., Inc., 1983—; founding mem. U.S. Congl. Adv. Bd.; mem. U.S. Def. Com. Served with AUS, 1942-45. Decorated Croix de Guerre with palm (France); recipient Conspicious Svc. award State of N.Y., 1965. Mem. ABA, Criminal Investigation Div. Agts. Assn., N.Y. State Bar Assn., N.Y. County Lawyers Assn., Real Estate Bd. N.Y., N.Y. State Assn. Realtors and Appraisers, Internat. Orgn. Real Estate Appraisers, Nat. Assn. Real Estate Appraisers, U.S. Senatorial Club, Met. Club. Home: 737 Park Ave New York NY 10021-4256 Office: 67 Wall St New York NY 10005-3101

**SCHLEGELMILCH, JOHN PAUL,** lawyer; b. Bklyn., Nov. 8, 1966; s. William and Paula S.; m. Sandra Mae Pickens, April 23, 1995; children: H. Tyler, Austin Carter. BA, U. Nev., 1988; JD, Willamette U., 1991, certificate in dispute resolution, 1991. Bar: Nev. 1991. Assoc. Vargas & Bartlett, Reno, Nev., 1991; deputy dist. attorney Lyon County, Yerington, Nev., 1991-95, chief deputy dist. attorney, 1995—; chmn. Rural Seat Nev. Probono Project Nev. State Bar bd. govs., Carson City, 1993-96; rural dir. Young Lawyer Section Nev. State Bar, Yerington, 1992-95; adj. prof. Nat. Judicial Coll., Reno, 1998. Soccer coach Yerington High Sch., 1998; exec. com. Washoe County Republican Party, Reno, 1986-88. Recipient Nev. Probono award Nev. Supreme Ct., 1997. mem. Nat. Dist. Attorney Assn. (Nev. chpt.), Masonic Lodge. Office: Lyon County District Attorney 31 S Main St Yerington NV 89447-2595

**SCHLEI, NORBERT ANTHONY,** lawyer; b. Dayton, Ohio, June 14, 1929; s. William Frank and Norma (Lindsley) S.; m. Jane Moore, Aug. 26, 1950 (div. 1963); children: Anne C. Buczynski, William K., Andrew M.; m. Barbara Lindemann, Mar. 7, 1965 (div. 1981); children: Bradford L., Graham L. (dec. 1995), Norbert L. (dec. 1996), Blake Lindsley, Elizabeth Eldridge; m. Joan Masson, Dec. 29, 1995. BA, Ohio State U., 1950; LLB magna cum laude, Yale U., 1956. Bar: Ohio 1956, Calif. 1958, D.C. 1963, U.S. Supreme Ct. 1963. Law clk. to Justice Harlan U.S. Supreme Ct., 1956-57; assoc. atty. O'Melveny & Myers, L.A., 1957-59; ptnr. Greenberg, Shafton & Schlei, L.A., 1959-62; asst. atty. gen. U.S. Dept. Justice, Washington, 1962-66; ptnr. Munger, Tolles, Hills & Rickershauser, 1968-70, Kane, Shulman & Schlei, Washington, 1968-70; ptnr.-in-charge Hughes Hubbard & Reed, L.A., 1972-89; pres., CEO Kahala Capital Corp., Santa Monica, Calif., 1983—; spl. counsel Clinicorp Inc., L.A., 1991-93. Author: (with M.S. McDougal and others) Studies in World Public Order, 1961 (Am. Soc. Internat. Law ann. book award); State Regulation of Corporate Financial Practices, 1962; editor-in-chief Yale Law Jour., 1955-56. Dem. nominee for Calif. Assembly, 1962, for sec. of state Calif., 1966. Mem. State Bar Calif., Riviera Country Club (Pacific Palisades, Calif.). Avocations: tennis, golf, skiing, sailing. Federal civil litigation, General corporate, Private international.

**SCHLEICHER, ESTELLE ANN,** lawyer; b. Buffalo, Sept. 28, 1947; d. Martin Edward and Peggy (Lewin) S. BA, SUNY-Brockport, 1969; JD, U. Pacific, 1979. Research asst. SRI Internat., Menlo Park, Calif., 1969-72; clk. Wallace J. Smith Inc., Sacramento 1976-78; assoc., 1980-81; pvt. practice, Sacramento, 1981—; judge pro tem Sacramento County Small Claims Ct.; instr., Pacific Coll. Legal Careers, Sacramento, 1982-85. Bd. dirs. Sacramento County Law Library Found. Judge, coach high sch. Law-related Ednl. Conf., Sacramento, 1982—. Soroptimist scholar, 1978; McGeorge scholar, 1977-79. Mem. ABA, Calif. State Bar Assn. (com. on appellate cts. 1986—, sec., hist. com. 1987—), Sacramento County Bar Assn. (dir. small law practice sect. 1986—), Assn. Trial Lawyers Am., Calif. Trial Lawyers Assn. (assoc. editor CTLA Forum), Capitol City Trial Lawyers Assn. (dir. 1986-87, appellate editor Litigator 1989—), McGeorge Sch. Law Alumni Assn. (bd. dirs. 1987-89, sec. 1988, 1st v.p. 1989—). Jewish. State civil litigation, Federal civil litigation, Criminal. Office: 2201 21st St Sacramento CA 95818-1709

**SCHLEIFER, REBECCA ANN,** lawyer, public health advocate; b. Boston, Nov. 11, 1961; d. Maxwell Joseph and Esther (Marks) Schleifer. AB, Harvard U./Radcliffe Coll., 1984; MPH, U. Calif., Berkeley, 1990, JD, 1993. Bar: Calif., Fla., Wash., U.S. Dist. Ct. (so., mid. and no. dists.) Fla., U.S. Dist. Ct. (we. dist.) Wash. Paralegal, environ. protection divsn. Atty. Gen.'s Office, Boston, 1988-89; rsch. asst. U. Calif., Berkeley, 1989, 91, instr., 1989, 92; law clk. to Judge Frank Coffin U.S. Ct. Appeals, Portland, Maine, 1993-94; atty., health advocate Evergreen legal Svcs., Sunnyside, Wash., 1994-95; staff atty. Migrant Farm Worker Justice Project, Belle Glade, Fla., 1996—. Contbr. articles to profl. jours.; presenter in field. Tchr. citizenship classes United Farm Workers, Sunnyside, 1995; Hebrew sch. tchr. Beth Ha'am Synagogue, Portland, 1993-94; outreach worker Homeless Outreach Project, Berkeley Cmty. Law Ctr., 1989-93; bar/bat mitzvah tutor, West Palm Beach, Fla., 1997—. Genevieve McInerney fellow, 1988-89. Mem. APHA. Jewish. Avocations: swimming, reading, hiking. Office: Migrant Farm Worker Justice Project PO Box 2110 Belle Glade FL 33430-7110

**SCHLEIMER, KAREN BETH,** lawyer; b. Bklyn., July 26, 1948; d. Irving G. and Irene (Bober) S.; 1 child, Kimberly Gail. BA, U. Pa., 1970. Bar: N.Y. 1977, U.S. Dist. Ct. (ea. and so. dists.) N.Y. 1977, U.S. Supreme Ct. 1981; cert. N.Y. State Office Econ. Devel. With Cravath, Swaine & Moore, N.Y.C., 1979-80; assoc. Finley Kumble et al., N.Y.C., 1981-84, Weil, Gotshal & Manges, N.Y.C., 1984—; pvt. practice N.Y.C., 1984—. Author: N.Y. Real Estate, 1984. Mem. Zoning Bd. Appeals, Mt. Kisco, 1983—, master plan revision com. 1998-99; Dem. dist. leader, Mt. Kisco, 1984-89. Mem. ABA. Avocations: canoeing, skiing. E-mail: relawnyc@aol.com. Fax: 212-245-2480. Real property, Banking, General corporate. Office: 250 W 57th St Ste 2017 New York NY 10107-2099

**SCHLENGER, ROBERT PURNELL,** lawyer; b. Balt., Mar. 1, 1932; s. Leo Brennen and Martha (Thompson) S.; m. Gretchen Lausch, Oct. 4, 1958; children: Robert Jr., Carl B., Paul T. BS, U. Va., 1953; LLB, U. Md., 1964. Bar: Md., U.S. Dist. Ct. Md., U.S. Ct. Appeals (4th cir.), U.S. Supreme Ct. Indsl. rels. asst. Bethlehem Steel, Sparrows Point, Md., 1957-62; indsl. rels. assoc. Bendix Radio, Baltimore County, Md., 1962-64, Lord, Whip, Coughlan & Green, Balt., 1964—; ptnr., stockholder Lord & Whip, P.A., Balt., 1964—; pres. Lacross Hall of Fame, Balt., 1970-97. Bd. dirs. U.S. Lacrosse, Balt., 1997—; lacrosse ref. N.C.A.A., 1957-84. Lt. USN, 1953-56. Avocation: improvement and working for the Internat. Lacrosse Fedn. Product liability, Federal civil litigation. Office: 29 Windemere Pkwy Phoenix MD 21131-2423 Office: Lord & Whip PA 120 W Fayette St Fl 8 Baltimore MD 21201-3741

**SCHLESINGER, HARVEY ERWIN,** judge; b. June 4, 1940. BA, The Citadel, 1962; JD, U. Richmond, 1965. Bar: Va. 1965, Fla. 1965, U.S. Supreme Ct. 1968. Corp. counsel Seabord Coast Line R.R. Co., Jacksonville, Fla., 1968-70; chief asst. U.S. atty. Mid. Dist. Fla., Jacksonville, 1970-75, U.S. magistrage judge, 1975-91, U.S. Dist. judge, 1991—; adj. prof. U. N. Fla., 1984-91; mem. adv. com. on Fed. Rules of Criminal Procedure to U.S. Supreme Ct., 1986-93; mem. Jud. Conf. Adv. Com. on Adminstrn. of Magistrate Judges Sys., 1996—, chmn., 1998—; chmn. U.S. Dist. Ct. Forms Task Force, Washington, 1983—, Jud. Ct. Ad hoc Com. on Long Range Planning, 1998—, Jud. Conf. Jud. Officers Resources Working Group, 1998—; chmn. 11th Cir. Dist. Judges Assn., 1991—, sec.-treas. 1996- 97, v.p. 1997-98, pres.-elect. 1999—. Bd. dirs. Pine Castle Ctr. for Mentally Retarded, Jacksonville, 1970-87, pres., 1972-74, chmn. bd. dirs., 1973-74; trustee Pine Castle Found., 1972-76; trustee Congregation Ahavath Chesed, Jacksonville, 1970—, v.p., 1975-80, pres., 1980-82; v.p. S.E. Coun. Union Am. Hebrew Congregations, 1984-88; asst. commr. for exploring N. Fla. Coun. Boy Scouts Am., 1983-86, exec. com., 1986-98, adv. bd., 1998—; mem. Boy Scouts Am. Nat. Jewish Com. on Scouting, Irving, Tex., 1986-93; mem. Fla. Sesquicentennial Commn., 1995-96; trustee River Garden Home for Aged, 1982—, sec., 1985—; co-chmn. bd. govs. Jacksonville chpt. NCCJ, 1983—, presiding co-chmn. 1984-89, nat. bd. trustees, N.Y.C., 1986-93. Capt. JAGC U.S. Army, 1965-68. Recipient Silver Beaver award Boy Scouts Am., 1986, George Washington Medal Honor, Freedoms Found., Valley Forge, Pa., 1987, Silver Medallion Humanitarian award NCCJ, 1992. Mem. ABA (fed. rules of evidence and criminal procedure com. 1979-98, Nat. Conf. Spl. Ct. Judges, 1975-90, conf. newsletter editor, 1988-90, Nat. Conf. Fed. Trial Judges, 1990—, chmn. legislation com., 1996-97, Flascher award 1989), Va. Bar Assn., Fla. Bar Assn., Fed. Judges Assn., Jacksonville Bar Assn., Fed. Bar Assn. (pres. Jacksonville chpt. 1974, 75, 81-82), Am. Judicature Soc., Chester Bedell Am. Inns of Ct. (pres. 1992-96), Rotary (Paul Harris fellow, pres. S. Jacksonville club), Masons (past master, past venerable master, knights comdr. of Ct. Honour, Scottish Rite bodies), Shrine. Office: 311 W Monroe St PO Box 1740 Jacksonville FL 32201-1740

**SCHLESINGER, SANFORD JOEL,** lawyer; b. N.Y.C., Feb. 8, 1943; s. Irving and Ruth (Rubin) S.; children: Merideth, Jarrod, Alexandra; m. Suzanne Beth Mangold, 1994; 1 stepchild, Mariel Mangold. BS in Govt. with hons., Columbia U., 1963; JD, Fordham U., 1966. Bar: N.Y. 1966, U.S. Dist. Ct. (so. and ea. dists.) N.Y. 1967, U.S. Ct. Appeals (2d cir.) 1968, U.S. Ct. Internat. Trade 1969, U.S. Tax Ct. 1993, U.S. Supreme Ct. 1978. Assoc. Frankenthaler & Kohn, N.Y.C., 1966-67; asst. atty. gen. trusts and estates bur. charitable found. div. State of N.Y., N.Y.C., 1967-69; ptnr. Rose & Schlesinger, N.Y.C., 1969-81, Goldshmidt, Oshatz, Powsner & Saft, N.Y.C., 1981-85; ptnr., head trusts and estates dept. Shea & Gould, N.Y.C., 1985-93; ptnr., head wills and estates dept. Kaye, Scholer, Fierman, Hays & Handler LLP, N.Y.C., 1993—; ptnr. co-chair family owned bus. practice group Kaye, Scholer, Fierman, Hays & Handler, N.Y.C., 1993—; adj. faculty Columbia U. Sch. Law, 1989-94; adj. prof. N.Y. Law Sch., 1978—; adj. prof. grad. program in estate planning U. Miami Sch. Law, 1995—; mem. estate planning adv. com. Practising Law Inst., 1990—; bd. advisors and contbrs. Jour. of S Corp. Taxation, 1989-96; lectr. in field; condr. workshops in field. Author: Estate Planning for the Elderly Client, 1984, Planning for the Elderly or Incapacitated Client, 1993; columnist, mem. editl. bd. Estate Planning mag., 1995—; contbr. articles to profl. jours. Mem. adv. bd. Inst. Fed. Taxation NYU, 1988-96, chmn., 1993-94; mem. legis adv. com. Scarsdale (N.Y.) Sch. Bd., 1981-83, mem. nominating com., 1979-82; pres. dist. 17 N.Y.C. Cmty. Sch. Bd., 1970-71; mem. fin. and estate planning adv. bd. Commerce Clearing House, 1988—; mem. adv. bd. Tax Hotline, 1997—. Fellow Am. Coll. Trust and Estate Counsel; mem. ABA (chmn. social security and other govt. entitlements com. 1990-91, chmn. probate and trust com.-estate planning, drafting charitable giving coms., 1992-94), Internat. Acad. Estate & Trust Law (Academician 1992—), Nat. Acad. Elder Law Attys., Bklyn. Bar Assn., Assn. of Bar of City of N.Y., N.Y. State Bar Assn. (treas. trusts and estates sect. 1991-92, sec. trusts and estates sect. 1992-93, chmn. trusts and estates sect. 1994-95, chmn. exec. com. 1st jud. dist. 1987-91, jour. bd. editors 1995—). Avocations: baseball, writing. Estate planning, Probate, Estate taxation. Office: Kaye Scholer Fierman Hays & Handler 425 Park Ave New York NY 10022-3506

**SCHLEUSNER, CLIFFORD EDWARD,** lawyer; b. Saco, Mont., Feb. 15, 1918; s. Otto H. and Mary Schleusner. Tchrs. cert., No. Mont. Coll., 1939-40, 40-41; BA, U. Mont., 1951, LLB, JD, 1951. Bar: Mont. 1951, U.S. Ct. Appeals (9th cir.) 1965, U.S. Supreme Ct. 1965. Pvt. practice law Billings, Mont., 1951—; asst. U.S. atty. U.S. Attys. Office, Billings, 1961-69; dep. county atty. Yellowstone County Attys. Office, Billings, 1970-75. Staff sgt. USAF, 1941-46, WWII. Mem. Billings Heights Kiwanis (pres. 1981-82). General practice, Real property, Probate. Home: 436 Crow Ln Billings MT 59105-1700 Office: 926 Main St Ste 9 Billings MT 59105-3359

**SCHLINKER, JOHN CRANDALL,** lawyer; b. Flint, Mich., Mar. 27, 1962; s. Clarence Herman and Eleanor Faye Schlinker; m. Stepheni Willis, Apr. 20, 1996. BA, Western Mich. U., 1986; JD, U. Notre Dame, 1989. Bar: Mich. 1989, U.S. Dist. Ct. (we. dist.) Mich. 1989, U.S. Dist. Ct. (ea. dist.) Mich. 1990, U.S. Ct. Claims 1992, U.S. Ct. Appeals (6th cir.) 1995. Atty. Foster Swift Collins & Smith, Lansing, Mich., 1996—. Labor, General civil litigation, Civil rights. Office: Foster Swift Collins & Smith 313 S Washington Sq Lansing MI 48933-2172

**SCHLITT, LYN M.,** lawyer. Gen. counsel Internat. Trade Commn., Washington, 1978—. Office: Internat Trade Commn 500 E St NW Washington DC 20436-0003

**SCHLOSS, JOHN P.,** lawyer; b. Cleve., Oct. 22, 1961; s. Charles M. and Margaret Jane Schloss. BA, Haverford Coll., 1984; JD, Case Western Res. U., 1989. Bar: Ohio 1989. Jud. law clk. Eight Dist. Ct. of Appeals of Ohio, Cleve., 1989-92; corp. atty. Figgie Internat. Inc., Willoughby, Ohio, 1993—. Trustee Lyric Opera Cleve., Ohio, 1990-96; fundraiser Univ. Sch. Alumni Assn. Mem. ABA, Ohio State Bar Assn. Avocations: platform tennis, tennis, golf, basketball. Aviation, Personal injury, Landlord-tenant. Office: Schloss & Glickman LLC 1140 Leader Bldg Cleveland OH 44114

**SCHLUETER, DAVID ARNOLD,** law educator; b. Sioux City, Iowa, Apr. 29, 1946; s. Arnold E. and Helen A. (Dettmann) S.; m. Linda L. Boston, Apr. 22, 1972; children: Jennifer, Jonathan. BA, Tex. A&M U., 1969; JD, Baylor U., 1971; LLM, U. Va., 1981. Bar: Tex. 1971, Dec. 1973, U.S. Ct. Mil. Appeals 1972, U.S. Supreme Ct. 1976. Legal counsel U.S. Supreme Ct., Washington, 1981-83; assoc. dean St. Mary's U., San Antonio, 1984-89, prof. law, 1986—; reporter Fed. Adv. Com. on Criminal Rules, 1988—; chmn. JAG adv. coun., 1974-75. Author: Military Criminal Justice: Practice and Procedure, 1982, 4th edit., 1996; (with others) Military Rules of Evidence Manual, 1981, 4th edit., 1997, Texas Rules of Evidence Manual, 1983, 5th edit., 1998, Texas Evidentiary Foundations, 1992, 2d edit., 1998, Military Evidentiary Foundations, 1994, Military Criminal Procedure Forms, 1997, Federal Evidence Tactics, 1997; editor-in-chief: Emerging Problems Under the Federal Rules of Evidence, 3d edit., 1998; contbr. articles to legal publs. Maj. JAGC, U.S. Army, 1972-81. Fellow Am. Law Inst., Tex. Bar Found. (life), Am. Bar Found. (life); mem. ABA (vice-chmn. criminal justice sect. coun. 1991-94, vice-chmn. com. on criminal justice and mil. 1983-84, chmn. standing com. on mil. law 1991-92, mem. standing com. on armed forces law, chmn. editl. adv. bd., Criminal Justice Mag., 1989-91), Tex. Bar Assn. Republican. Lutheran. Office: St Marys U Sch Law 1 Camino Santa Maria St San Antonio TX 78228-8500

**SCHLUETER, JAMES WILLIAM,** lawyer; b. Cin., June 5, 1947; s. Franklin Charles and Kathryn Elizabeth (Moore) S.; m. Diane Marilynn Vickery Schlueter, Apr. 7, 1977. BA, U. Cin., 1970; JD, Chase Coll. Law, Ky., 1974. Bar: Ohio 1974, U.S. Dist. Ct. (so. dist.) 1974, U.S. Supreme Ct. 1978. Ct. constable Common Pleas Ct. Hamilton County, Cin., 1970-74; atty. pvt. practice, Cin., 1975-93, West Union, Ohio, 1993—; magistrate Common Pleas Ct. Adams County, West Union, Ohio, 1996—. Contbr. articles to profl. jours. Mem. Adams County Bar Assn., Cin. Bar Assn. Home: 505 Walt Allsgood Rd West Union OH 45693-9419 Office: Common Pleas Court PO Box 305 West Union OH 45693-0305

**SCHLUETER, LINDA LEE,** law educator; b. L.A., May 12, 1947; d. Dick G. Dulgarian and Lucille J. Boston; m. David A. Schlueter, Apr. 22, 1972; children: Jennifer, Jonathan. BA, U. So. Calif., 1969; JD, Baylor U., 1971. Bar: D.C. 1973, U.S. Supreme Ct. 1976, Ct. Mil. Appeals, 1990, Tex. 1997. Govt. rels. specialist hdqrs. U.S. Postal Svc., Washington, 1973-75; staff atty. Rsch. Group, Inc., Charlottesville, Va., 1979-81; pvt. practice Washington, 1981-83; asst. prof. law Sch. Law St. Mary's U., San Antonio, 1983-87, assoc. prof., 1987-90, prof., 1990-94; presenter law Tex. Women Scholars Program, Austin, 1986, 87; bd. dirs Inst. for Comparative and Internat. Legal Rsch. Author: Punitive Damages, 1981-89, 3rd edit., 1995, ann. suppls., Legal Research Guide: Patterns and Practice, 1986, 3rd edit., 1996; editor Cmty. Property Jour. , 1986-88, Cmty. Property Alert, 1989-90; assoc. editor Modern Legal Sys. Cyclopedia, 20 vols., 1990, ann. suppls. Mem. ABA, Bexar County Women's Bar Assn., San Antonio Conservation Soc., Order of Barristers, Phi Alpha Delta. Republican. Lutheran.

**SCHLUSSER, ROBERT ELMER,** lawyer; b. Harrisburg, Pa., Aug. 24, 1942; s. Elmer Charles and Mildred Gladys (Brown) S.; m. Margaret Murray Steiniger, June 10, 1966 (div. Dec. 1980); children: Adam, Jason, Hannah; m. Joanna Reiver, July 16, 1982; children: Amelia, Daniel. BA in econs. cum laude, Dickinson Coll., 1964; JD, Dickinson Sch. Law, 1967; LLM in taxation, George Washington U., 1969. Bar: Pa. 1967, Del. 1971, N.Mex. 1993, U.S. Dist. Ct. (mid. dist.) Pa. 1968, U.S. Dist. Ct. Del. 1972, U.S. Ct. Appeals (3rd cir.) 1973, U.S. Ct. Appeals, 1991, U.S. Supreme Ct. 1973. U.S. Ct. Fed. Claims, 1970. Dir. Murdoch & Walsh P.A., Wilmington, Del., 1969-82; ptnr. Schlusser & Reiver, Wilmington, Del., 1982-87, Schlusser, Reiver, Hughes & Sisk, Wilmington, Del., 1988-94; dir. Schlusser & Reiver P.A., Wilmington, 1995—; speaker at numerous confs., seminars. Probate, State civil litigation, Estate taxation. Office: Schlusser & Reiver 1700 W 14th St Wilmington DE 19806-4058

**SCHMALL, STEVEN TODD,** lawyer; b. Chgo.. BA, Washington U., St. Louis, 1982, JD, 1986. Bar: Ill. 1987, U.S. Dist. Ct. (no. dist.) Ill. 1987, U.S. Ct. Appeal s(7th cir.) 1988, U.S. Dist. Ct. (cen. dist.) Ill. 1989. Asst. atty. gen. Ill. Atty. Gen. Office, Chgo., 1987-92; atty. pvt. practice, Chgo., 1992—. Construction, General civil litigation, General practice. Office: Law Offices of Jeffery M Leving Ltd 19 S Lasalle St Ste 450 Chicago IL 60603-1490

**SCHMELZ, BRENDA LEA,** legal assistant; b. Washington, Mo., June 13, 1958; d. Edward G. and Wilma D. (Hektor) R.; m. Jan M. Schmelz, Oct. 7, 1978; children: Edward L., Brent T. Secretarial sci. cert. with honors, East Ctrl. Coll., Union, Mo., 1977. Sec., paralegal Mittendorf & Mittendorf, Union, 1976-83, Eckelkamp, Eckelkamp, Wood & Kuenzel, Washington, 1983—; mem. legal secretarial adv. bd. East Ctrl. Coll., 1978, chmn., 1987; mem. legal secretarial adv. bd. State Fair C.C., 1995. Mem. Nat. Assn. Legal Secs. (mem. certifying bd. 1997—, chmn. 1998—, Jett award 1999), Mo. Assn. Legal Secs. (pres. 1994-96, pres-elect 1992-94, v.p. 1986, 89-91, sec. 1984-86, 89-90, dir. pub. rels. 1987-89, Legal Sec. of Yr. 1987), Franklin County Legal Secs. (pres. 1989-92, Legal Sec. of Yr. 1986, 95), Union of Women Today, Phi Beta Kappa. Republican. Roman Catholic. Home: 1792 Oak Parc Union MO 63084-3607 Office: Eckelkamp Eckelkamp Wood & Kuenzel Bank of Washington Bldg Main & Oak Washington MO 63084

**SCHMERTZ, ERIC JOSEPH,** lawyer, educator; b. N.Y.C., Dec. 24, 1925; married; 4 children. A.B., Union Coll., 1948, LL.D. (hon.), 1978; cert., Alliance Francaise, Paris, 1948; J.D., NYU, 1954. Bar: N.Y. 1955. Internat. rep. Am. Fedn. State, County and Mcpl. Employees, AFL-CIO, N.Y.C., 1950-52; asst. v.p., dir. labor tribunals Am. Arbitration Assn., N.Y.C., 1952-57, 59-60; indsl. relations dir. Metal Textile Corp. subs. Gen. Cable Corp., Roselle, N.J., 1957-59; exec. dir. N.Y. State Bd. Mediation, 1960-62, corp. dir., 1962-68; labor-mgmt. arbitrator N.Y.C., 1962—; mem. faculty Hofstra U. Sch. Bus., 1962-70; prof. Hofstra U. Sch. Law, 1970—, Edward F. Carlough disting. prof. labor law, 1981-98, dean Sch. Law, 1982-89; disting. prof. emeritus of law, 1998—; of counsel Rivkin, Radler, Kremer, 1989—; commr. labor rels. City of N.Y., 1990-91; scholar-in-residence Pace U. Sch. Law, 1998—; 1st Beckley lectr. in bus. U. Vt., 1981; bd. dirs. Wilshire Oil Co.; mem. N.Y. State Pub. Employment Rels. Bd., 1991—; cons. and lectr. in field. Co-author: (with R.L. Greenman) Personnel Administration and the Law, 1978; contbr. chpts. to books, articles to profl. jours., to profl. law confs., seminars and workshops. Mem. numerous civic orgns. Served to lt. USN, 1943-46. Recipient Testimonial award Southeast Republican Club, 1969; Alexander Hamilton award Rep. Law Students Assn.; Eric J. Schmertz Disting. Professorship Pub. Law and Pub. Svc. established Hofstra Law Sch., 1993. Mem. Nat. Acad. Arbitrators, Am. Arbitration Assn. (law com., Whitney North Seymour Sr. medal 1984), Fed. Mediation and Conciliation Svc., N.Y. Mediation Bd., N.J. Mediation Bd., N.J. Pub. Employment Rels. Bd., Hofstra U. Club, Princeton Club. Office: 275 Madison Ave New York NY 10016-1101

**SCHMID, FRANCES M.,** law librarian, lawyer, nurse; b. Chgo., May 12, 1954; d. Edward Michael and Frances Mary (Schrieber) Schmid; m. James Allen Shepard, Mar. 2, 1972 (div. Sept. 1985); 1 child, Jeremiah Brian. BSN, Tex. Christian U., 1977; postgrad., St. Mary's Coll., 1984-85; MLS, Tex. Women's U., 1987; JD, St. Mary's Sch. Law, 1991. RN, Tex. Nurses aide Masonic Home for Aged Masons, Arlington, Tex., 1972-75; asst. dir. nurses Metroplex Nursing Home, Grand Prairie, Tex., 1977-78; nurse cons. Jewell Enterprises/Stonebrook Properties, Arlington, 1978-86; law librarian Jackson, Walker, Winstead, Cantwell & Miller, Dallas, 1987-89, St. Mary's Law Libr. and Univ. Libr., Dallas, 1989-93; law librarian, assoc. Dean & Howell, Dallas, 1993-94, McKenna & Cuneo, Dallas, 1994—. Author: Feminist Jurisprudence: Emerging From Plato's Cave-A Research Guide, 1996. Mem. Am. Assn. Law Libraries (Scholarship award, 1988), Tex. State Bar Assn. (health care sect., woman sect.), Dallas Assn. Law Libraries. Republican. Methodist. Avocations: parenting, writing, reading. Home: 2414 Winewood St Arlington TX 76013-3332 Office: McKenna & Cuneo 5700 Bank One Ctr 1717 Main Dallas TX 75201

**SCHMID, JOHN HENRY, JR.,** lawyer; b. Erie, Pa., May 11, 1944; s. John Henry Sr. and Margery (St. Lawrence) S.; m. Carol Christine Imig, July 1, 1967; children: Christine Catherine, Heidi Imig. BA, Beloit Coll., 1966; JD, U. Wis., 1969. Bar: Wis. 1969, U.S. Dist. Ct. (we. dist.) Wis. 1969, U.S. Ct. Appeals (7th cir.) 1993, U.S. Supreme Ct. 1993. Sr. ptnr. Axley Brynelson, Madison, Wis., 1969—. Emergency med. technician Village of Maple Bluff, Madison, 1977-84, trustee, 1985-89. Mem. Assn. Def. Trial Attys., Civil Trial Counsel Wis. Avocations: fishing, golf, travel. Insurance, Workers' compensation, General civil litigation. Home: 802 Farwell Dr Madison WI 53704-6034 Office: Axley Brynelson 2 E Mifflin St Madison WI 53703-2889

**SCHMIDT, AMY K.,** lawyer; b. Tulsa, June 24, 1965; m. John P. Schmidt, Sept. 1990. BS in Acctg., Oral Roberts U., 1987; JD, U. Tulsa, 1990. Bar: Ill. 1991, U.S. Dist. Ct. (ctrl. dist.) Ill. Assoc. Sgro & LaMarca, Springfield, Ill., 1991-95; ptnr. Stratton, Stone, Kopec & Sturm, Springfield, 1995—. Mem. Sangamon County Bar Assn. (sec.), Sangamon County Young Lawyers (pres. 1997), Am. Inns of Ct. (barrister Lincoln Douglas chpt. 1998—). Methodist. Family and matrimonial. Home: 1620 S Bates Ave Springfield IL 62704-3350 Office: Stratton Stone Kopec Et Al 725 S 4th St Springfield IL 62703-2218

**SCHMIDT, CHARLES EDWARD,** lawyer; b. N.Y.C., Oct. 6, 1951; s. Donald J. and Yanina S. (Giera) S.; children: John Charles, Michael Joseph. AB cum laude, Boston Coll., 1972; JD, Fordham U., 1975; Bar: N.Y. 1976, U.S. Supreme Ct. 1982. Law clk. Lilly Sullivan & Purcell, P.C., N.Y.C., 1973-76, assoc., 1976-84; assoc. Donovan Maloof Walsh & Kennedy, N.Y.C., 1984-86; ptnr. Kennedy & Lillis, N.Y.C., 1986-93, Kennedy Lillis Schmidt & English, 1993—. Mem. ABA, N.Y. State Bar Assn., Maritime Law Assn. (carriage of goods com. 1987—), Assn. Average Adjusters U.S. (assoc.). Roman Catholic. Admiralty, Insurance, Federal civil litigation. Home: 30-2607 Newport Pkwy Jersey City NJ 07310-1572 Office: Kennedy Lillis Schmidt & English 100 Maiden Ln New York NY 10038-4818

**SCHMIDT, DANIEL EDWARD, IV,** lawyer; b. N.Y.C., Dec. 17, 1946; s. Daniel Edward III and Mary (Mannion) S.; m. Gail Kennedy, Sept. 5, 1980; children: Kathryn Kennedy, Michael Kennedy. BA, St. Lawrence U., 1971; postgrad., New Sch., 1972; JD, St. John's U., 1975. Bar: N.Y. 1976; cert. arbitrator. From asst. counsel to assoc. gen. counsel Prudential Property & Casualty, Holmdel, N.J., 1975-81, assoc. gen. counsel, divsn. head, 1981-82; v.p., assoc. gen. counsel, asst. sec. Prudential Reins Co., Newark, 1982-84; dir., v.p., gen. counsel, corp. sec. Scor U.S. Group, N.Y.C., 1984-86, dir., sr. v.p., gen. counsel, corp. sec., 1986-89; dir., exec. com., sr. v.p., gen. counsel, corp. sec. Sorema N.A. Group, N.Y.C., 1989-94, dir., exec. com., exec. v.p., group gen. counsel, 1995-99; dir. exec. com., group exec. v.p., chief legal officer Sorema N.A. Group, N.Y.C., The Netherlands, 1999—; dep. gen. mgr., gen. counsel, corp. sec. Sorema Internat. Holding, N.V., Groupama, The Netherlands, 1993-96; with U.S Counsel, Groupama, 1996—; pvt. practice reins. arbitrator, umpire, Little Silver, N.J., 1987—; reins. lectr., 1986—; bd. dirs. ARIAS (U.S.), N.Y.C., (alt.) Brokers & Reinsurance Markets Assn. Mem. editl. bd. Arias- U.S. Quar. Bd. dirs., exec. com. ARC, Monmouth County, Shrewsbury, N.J., 1981-84; presiding judge Ecclesiastical Trial Ct., Episcopal Diocese of N.J. With U.S. Army, 1967-70. Mem. ABA, Am. Arbitration Assn. (panel comml. arbitrators), N.Y. Bar Assn., Assn. Internat. Droit des Assureurs (U.S. chpt.), Bamm Hollow Country Club, Desert Mountain Club. Episcopalian. Avocations: cycling, golf, tennis, skiing. General corporate, Insurance, Securities. Home: 628 Little Silver Point Rd Little Silver NJ 07739-1737 Office: Sorema NA Group 199 Water St Fl 20 New York NY 10038-3526

**SCHMIDT, EDWARD CRAIG,** lawyer; b. Pitts., Nov. 26, 1947; s. Harold Robert and Bernice (Williams) S.; m. Elizabeth Lowry Rial, Aug. 18, 1973; children: Harold Robert II, Robert Rial. BA, U. Mich., 1969; JD, U. Pitts., 1972. Bar: Pa. 1972, U.S. Dist. Ct. (we. dist.) Pa. 1972, U.S. Ct. Appeals (3d. cir.) 1972, U.S. Ct. Appeals (D.C. cir.) 1975, U.S. Supreme Ct. 1981, U.S. Ct. Appeals (9th cir.) 1982, U.S. Ct. Appeals (4th cir.) 1982, U.S. Ct. Appeals (6th cir.) 1987, U.S. Ct. Appeals (11th cir.) 1990, U.S. Ct. Appeals (2d cir.) 1992, U.S. Ct. Appeals (4th cir.) 1994. Assoc. Rose, Schmidt, Hasley & Di Salle, Pitts., 1972-77, ptnr., 1977-90, Jones, Day Reavis & Pogue, Pitts.; mem. adv. com. Superior Ct. Pa., 1978-80; NITA instr. Duquesne U., 1998—. Co-editor; Antitrust Discovery Handbook-Supplement, 1982; asst. editor: Antitrust Discovery Handbook, 1980; contbr. articles to profl. jours. Bd. dirs. Urban League, Pitts., 1974-77, NITA instr., Duyuesne U., 1998. 99. Mem. Supreme Ct. Hist. Soc., Pa. Bar Assn., D.C. Bar Assn., Allegheny County Bar Assn. (pub. rels. com. coun. civil litigation sect. 1977-80), Internat. Acad. Trial Lawyers, Acad. Trial Lawyers Allegheny County (bd. govs. 1985-87), U. Pitts. Law Alumni Assn. (bd. govs. 1980), Western Res. Acad. Alumni Assn. (trustee 1998—). Clubs: Rolling Rock (Ligonier, Pa.), Duquesne (Pitts.), Longue Vue (Pitts.). Republican. Antitrust, Personal injury, Federal civil litigation. Home: 159 Washington St Pittsburgh PA 15218-1351 Office: Jones Day Reavis & Pogue One Mellon Bank Ctr 31st Fl 500 Grant St Pittsburgh PA 15219-2502

**SCHMIDT, JOHN H.,** legal consultant; b. Louisville, Ky.; s. Henry A. and Mary J. S.; m. Kara M., Aug. 11, 1995. BA, U. Ky., 1989, MBA, 1995, JD, 1995. Bar: Ky. 1998. Ops. mgr. KD & Steele, Inc., Cin., 1995-96; v.p. mfg. Cox Cabinet Co., Inc., Campbellsville, Ky., 1996-98; cons. Summit Group, Cin., 1998—. Avocations: woodworking, remodeling, reading. Home: 2080 Glade Ln Lexington KY 40513-1604

**SCHMIDT, JOHN H., JR.,** lawyer; b. Irvington, N.J., June 10, 1952; s. Helen V. (Hupalo) S.; m. Colleen M. Rafferty, June 15, 1974; children: Alexander, Kevin, Kelly Anne. BA in Econs., Rutgers Coll., 1973; JD, Seton Hall U., 1977. Bar: N.J. 1977, U.S. Dist. Ct. N.J. 1977, U.S. Ct. Appeals (3d cir.) 1979, U.S. Supreme Ct. 1985; cert. civil trial atty., N.J. Assoc. Lindabury, McCormick & Estabrook, Westfield, N.J., 1977-85; ptnr. Lindabury, McCormick & Estabrook, Westfield, 1985—. Bd. dirs. Vis. Homemakers Ea. Union County, Westfield, 1978-88, Cancer Community Adv. Bd. Elizabeth (N.J.) Med. Ctr., 1986—; pres. bd. dirs. Westfield YMCA, 1985-89; trustee Chemocare, Inc., 1995—. Mem. ABA, Assn. Trial Lawyers Am., N.J. Bar Assn., Union County Bar Assn., Westfield Jaycees (pres. 1980-81), Westfield Soccer Assn. Roman Catholic. General civil litigation, Labor. Office: Lindabury McCormick & Estabrook 184 Elm St PO Box 2369 Westfield NJ 07091-2369

**SCHMIDT, JOSEPH W.,** lawyer; b. Jeffersontown, Ky., July 6, 1946; s. A.W. and Olivia Ann (Hohl) S.; m. Angela Petchara Apiradee, Dec. 20, 1969; children: Narissa Ann, Suriya Christine. BA in Psychology, Bellarmine Coll., 1969; AB in Commerce, U. Md., Bangkok, 1972; JD, Columbia U., 1975. Bar: N.Y. 1976. Law clk. to presiding judge U.S. Dist. Ct. (so. dist.), N.Y., 1975-76; assoc. Breed, Abbott & Morgan, N.Y.C., 1976-83, ptnr., 1983-93; ptnr. Whitman Breed Abbott & Morgan, 1993-96, Coudert Bros., N.Y.C., 1996—. Adminstrv. editor Columbia Jour. of Law and Social Problems, 1974-75. Woodrow Wilson fellow, 1968; Harlan Fiske Stone scholar, 1975. Mem. ABA, Assn. of Bar of the City of N.Y., N.Y. Bar Assn., Am. Coll. Investment Counsel. Avocations: skiing, reading. Finance, General corporate, Mergers and acquisitions. Office: Coudert Bros 1114 Avenue Of The Americas New York NY 10036-7703

**SCHMIDT, KATHLEEN MARIE,** lawyer; b. Des Moines, June 17, 1953; d. Raymond Driscoll and Hazel Isabelle (Rogers) Poage; m. Dean Everett Johnson, Dec. 21, 1974 (div. Nov. 1983); children: Aaron Dean, Gina Marie; m. Ronald Robert Schmidt, Feb. 7, 1987. BS in Home Econs., U. Nebr., 1974; JD, Creighton U., 1987. Bar: Nebr. 1987, U.S. Dist. Ct. Nebr. 1987, U.S. Ct. Appeals (8th cir.) 1989, U.S. Supreme Ct. 1991. Apprentice printer, journeyman Rochester (Minn.) Post Bull., 1978-82; dir. customer info. Cornhusker Pub. Power Dist., Columbus, Nebr., 1982-83; artist Pamida, Omaha, 1983; offset artist Cornhusker Motor Club, Omaha, 1983-84; assoc. Lindahl O. Johnson Law Office, Omaha, 1987-88; pvt. practice Omaha, 1988-90; ptnr. Emery, Penke, Blazek & Schmidt, Omaha, 1990-91; pvt. practice, Omaha, 1992—; atty. in condemnation procs. Douglas County Bd. Appraisers, Omaha, 1988-99; presenter Nebr. Sch. Bd. Assn., 1991, 92. Mem. Millard Sch. Bd., Omaha, 1989-96, treas. 1991, 92; mem. strategic planning com. Millard Sch. Dist., 1990; mem. Omaha Mayor's Master Plan

Com., 1991-94. Named hon. mem. Anderson Mid. Sch., Omaha, 1991; recipient Award of Achievement, Nebr. Sch. Bd. Assn., 1991, 94. Mem. Nebr. Bar Assn., Omaha Bar Assn. (spkrs. bur. 1992—), Nat. Sch. Bd. Assn. (del. federal rels. network 1991-96, cert. recognition 1991). Republican. Lutheran. Family and matrimonial, Personal injury, Probate. Home: 10008 S 173d Cir Omaha NE 68136 Office: 399 N 117th St Ste 305 Omaha NE 68154-2562

**SCHMIDT, L(AIL) WILLIAM, JR.,** lawyer; b. Thomas, Okla., Nov. 22, 1936; s. Lail William and Violet Kathleen (Kuper) S.; m. Diana Gail (div. May 1986); children: Kimberly Ann, Andrea Michelle; m. Marilyn Sue, Aug. 11, 1990; stepchildren: Leland Darrell Mosby, Jr., Crystal Rachelle Mosby. BA in Psychology, U. Colo., 1959; JD, U. Mich., 1962. Bar: Colo. 1962, U.S. Dist. Ct. Colo. 1964, U.S. Tax Ct. 1971, U.S. Ct. Appeals (10th cir.) 1964. Ptnr. Holland & Hart, Denver, 1962-77, Schmidt, Elrod & Wills, Denver, 1977-85, Moye, Giles, O'Keefe, Vermeire & Gorrell, Denver, 1985-90; of counsel Hill, Held, Metzger, Lofgren & Peele, Dallas, 1989—; pvt. practice law Denver, 1990—; lectr. profl. orgns. Author: How To Live-and Die-with Colorado Probate, 1985, A Practical Guide to the Revocable Living Trust, 1990; contbr. articles to legal jours. Pres. Luth. Med. Ctr. Found., Wheat Ridge, Colo., 1985-89; pres. Rocky Mountain Prison and Drug Found., Denver, 1986—; bd. dirs. Luth. Hosp., Wheat Ridge, 1988-92, Bonfils Blood Ctr. Found., 1995—, Planned Giving Adv. Group of Nat. Jewish Hosp., Denver, 1996-98, St. Joseph Hosp. Found., 1999—; planned giving advisor Aspen Valley Med. Found., 1997—; mktg. and gifts adv. com. The Denver Found., 1998—. Fellow Am. Coll. Trust and Estate Counsel (Colo. chmn. 1981-86); mem. ABA, Am. Judicature Soc., Rocky Mtn. Estate Planning Coun. (founder, pres. 1970-71), Greater Denver Tax Counsel Assn., Am. Soc. Magicians, Denver Athletic Club, Phi Delta Phi. Republican. Baptist. Avocation: magic. Estate planning, Probate, Estate taxation. Office: 1050 17th St Ste 1700 Denver CO 80265-2077 also: Law Offices of Robert L Bolick Ltd 6060 Elton Ave Ste A Las Vegas NV 89107-0100

**SCHMIDT, PAUL JOEL,** lawyer; b. Milw., Nov. 25, 1961; s. Joel Schmidt and Mary Bierlein. BA, Colo. Coll., 1985; postgrad., U. Mich., 1986-88; JD, U. Colo., 1992. Bar: Colo. 1992, U.S. Dist. Ct. Colo. 1993. Assoc. Crane, Leake, Casey et al, Durango, Colo., 1993-95; dep. dist. atty. 6th Jud. Dist., Durango, 1995—. Actor Project A Jacky Chan H.K., 1983. Regional coord. Access Fund, Four Corners, 1993-95. Chinese Studies fellow U. Mich., 1987-88. Avocations: mountaineering, rock climbing, hiking, mountain-biking, skiing. Office: Office Dist Atty 1060 E 2d Ave Durango CO 81301

**SCHMIDT, RICHARD MARTEN, JR.,** lawyer; b. Winfield, Kans., Aug. 2, 1924; s. Richard M. and Ida (Marten) S.; m. Ann Downing, Jan. 2, 1948; children—Eric, Gregory, Rolf (dec.), Heidi. A.B., U. Denver, 1945, J.D., 1948. Bar: Colo. bar 1948, D.C. bar 1968. Dep. dist. atty. City and County of Denver, 1949-50; mem. firm McComb, Zarlengo, Mott & Schmidt, Denver, 1950-54; ptnr. Schmidt & Van Cise (and predecessor), Denver, 1954-65; 65; gen. counsel USIA, 1965-68; of counsel Cohn and Marks, Washington, 1969—; counsel spl. agrl. investigating subcom. Counsel Am. Soc. Newspaper Editors, 1968—; mem. Gov.'s Coun. Local Govt., Colo., 1963-64; chmn. Mayor's Jud. Adv. Com., Denver, 1963-64, Gov.'s Supreme Ct. Nominating Com., 1964-65; mem. Gov.'s Oil Shale Adv. Com., 1963-65, Colo. Commn. on Higher Edn., 1965; mem. bd. Nat. Press Found., 1993—. Trustee U. Denver. Mem. ABA (chmn. standing com. on assn. comms. 1969-73, chmn. forum com. on comms. 1979-81, co-chmn. nat. conf. lawyers and reps. of media 1984-89, mem. commn. on lawyer advt. 1964-68), Colo. Bar Assn. (gov.), Denver Bar Assn. (pres. 1963-64), D.C. Bar Assn., Cosmos Club (Washington). Episcopalian. Communications, Libel, Civil rights. Home: 115 5th St SE Washington DC 20003-1123 Office: Cohn and Marks 1920 N St NW Ste 300 Washington DC 20036-1622

**SCHMIDT, STEPHANIE,** legal assistant; d. Richard Stephan and Maria Eugenia (Luna) S. BA, U. Dallas, 1995. Cashier La Madeleine, Houston, 1996; adminstrv. asst. Interim Personnel, Houston, 1996; substitute tchr. Spring Branch ISD, Houston, 1996; sect. clerk Fulbright & Jaworski LLP, Houston, 1996-97, legal asst., 1997; legal clerk Fulbright & Jaworski LLP, Dallas, 1997—. Vol. Alzheimer's clinic Baylor Rsch. Ctr., Houston, 1996-97, Mus. Fine Arts, Houston, 1997—. Mem. Am. Psychiat. Assn. (grad. affiliate). Avocations: cooking, photography, reading, gardening.

**SCHMIDT, THOMAS BERNARD, III,** lawyer; b. Harrisburg, Pa., Mar. 12, 1946; s. Thomas B. and Regina K. Schmidt; m. Donna L. Fisher, Apr. 29, 1989; children: Nicholas B., Nathaniel T. BA with honors, Boston Coll., 1968; JD, Dickinson Sch. of Law, 1974. Bar: U.S. Supreme Ct. 1980, U.S. Ct. Appeals (3d. cir.) 1980, U.S. Dist. Ct. Md., Penn., 1974. Tchr. Carlisle (Pa.) Sch. Dist., 1968-71; adminstrv. asst. Atty. Gen. of Pa., Harrisburg, 1971-74; atty. Pepper Hamilton LLP, Harrisburg, 1974-82, ptnr., 1982—; bd. dirs. Harristown Devel. Corp., Harrisburg Hotel Corp.; adj. faculty Dickinson Sch. Law, Carlisle, 1988—. Bd. dirs. Ctr. Legal Edn. Advocacy & Def., Phila., 1994—. General civil litigation, Product liability, Administrative and regulatory. Office: Pepper Hamilton LLP 200 One Keystone Plz Harrisburg PA 17101

**SCHMIDT, WAYNE WALTER,** legal association executive; b. St. Louis, Feb. 8, 1941; s. Warren W. and Geneva N. (Walker) S.; children: Andrew M., Nancy K. Diploma in English and Comparative Law, City of London Coll., 1963; BA, U. N.Mex., 1964; JD, Oklahoma City U., 1966; LLM, Northwestern U., 1974. Bar: N.Mex. 1966, Ill. 1968, D.C. 1970, N.Y. 1982. Dir. police legal advisor program Northwestern U., 1968-70; counsel Internat. Assn. Chiefs of Police, 1970-73; exec. dir. Am. for Effective Law Enforcement, Inc., Chgo., 1973—; pres. Pub. Safety Pers. Rsch. Inst., 1974—, Govt. Employment Rsch. Inst., Inc., 1986-89, Lauterbrunnen Properties, 1990-93; dir. Comprehensive Ensurers Market Syndicate, Inc., 1984-91, 93-94, Capital Exch. Mgmt., Inc., 1988-91; cons. Uniform Code of Criminal Procedure. Co-author: Legal Aspects of Criminal Evidence, 1978, Introduction to Criminal Evidence, 1982; editor Fire and Police Personnel Reporter, 1975—, Pub. Employment Health Law and Benefits, 1986-89, Fire and Police Annual Case Digest, 1984—. Served with U.S. Army, 1966-67. Mem. ABA (liaison to criminal justice council 1973—), Internat. Assn. Chiefs of Police (vice chair legis. com. 1988—). E-mail: aele@aol.com. Office: 5519 N Cumberland Ave Ste 1008 Chicago IL 60656-1480

**SCHMIDT, WILLIAM ARTHUR, JR.,** lawyer; b. Cleve., Oct. 2, 1939; s. William Arthur and Caroline (Jäger) S.; m. Gerilyn Pearl Smith, Sept. 30, 1967; children: Deborah, Dawn, Jennifer. BSBA, Kent State U., 1962; JD, Cleve. State U., 1968. Bar: Ohio 1968, Ill. 1990. Contract specialist NASA-Lewis, Cleve., 1962-66, procurement analyst, 1967-68; atty. Def. Logistics Agy., Alexandria, Va., 1968-73; assoc. counsel Naval Sea Sys. Command, Arlington, Va., 1973-75; procurement policy analyst Energy R & D Adminstrn., Germantown, Md., 1975-76; sr. atty. U.S. Dept. Energy, Germantown, 1976-78; counsel spl. projects U.S. Dept. Energy, Oak Ridge, Tenn., 1978-83; judge Agr. Bd. Contract Appeals, Washington, 1983-87; judge Bd. Contract Appeals HUD, Washington, 1987; chief legal counsel Fermilab, Batavia, Ill., 1987-92; gen. counsel Univ. Rsch. Assn., Inc., Washington, 1992—. Co-author: (NASA handbook) R & D Business Practices, 1968. Mem. Fed. Bar Assn. (past pres. East Tenn. 1978-83, 25 Yr. Svc. award 1994), Ill. Bar Assn., Bd. Contract Appeals Judges Assn. (dir.-sec. 1986-88), Sr. Execs. Assn., Delta Theta Phi (dist. chancellor 1978-83), Sigma Chi. Republican. Lutheran. Avocations: classic cars, Civil War history. Government contracts and claims, General corporate, Non-profit and tax-exempt organizations. Home: 7209 Bloomsbury Ln Spotsylvania VA 22553-1944 Office: Univ Rsch Assn Inc 1111 19th St NW Ste 400 Washington DC 20036-3627

**SCHMITT, DAVID JON,** lawyer; b. Dubuque, Iowa, June 27, 1963; s. Donald Raymond and Janet Rose S.; m. Wendy Sue Vaile, May 23, 1992; children: Michael, John. BBA, U. Iowa, 1985; JD cum laude, Creighton U., 1989. Bar: Nebr. 1989, Iowa 1995. Judicial law clk U.S. Dist. Ct. Nebr., Omaha, 1989-91; adj. faculty Creighton U., 1990-93; assoc. Kennedy, Holland, DeLacy & Svoboda, 1991-98; ptnr. Lamson, Dugan & Murray, Omaha, 1999—. Mem. ABA, Nebr. Bar Assn., Omaha Bar Assn., Iowa State Bar Assn., Nat. Lawyers Assn., Defense Counsel Assn. of Nebr. General civil litigation, Insurance, Personal injury. Office: Lamson Dugan & Murray 10306 Regency Parkway Dr Omaha NE 68114-3708

**SCHMITT, JOHN PATRICK,** lawyer; b. Hempstead, N.Y., Oct. 23, 1956; s. William Jude and Janet Patricia (Hurley) S.; m. Sylvia Yvonne Picard, Mar. 10, 1979; children: Emily, Patrick, Daniel, Peter. AB, Georgetown U., 1977; JD, Fordham U., 1980. Bar: N.Y. 1981. Assoc. Lord Day & Lord, N.Y.C., 1980-82; assoc. Patterson, Belknap, Webb & Tyler LLP, N.Y.C., 1983-88, ptnr., 1989—. Mem. ABA, N.Y. State Bar Assn., Assn. of Bar of City of N.Y. Democrat. Roman Catholic. General corporate, Finance, Entertainment. Office: Patterson Belknap Webb & Tyler 1133 Avenue Of The Americas New York NY 10036-6710

**SCHMITT, WILLIAM ALLEN,** lawyer; b. Louisville, Aug. 29, 1909; s. Michael Joseph and Naoma Katherine Schmitt; m. Dorothy S. Turner, June 12, 1936 (dec. Feb. 1998); 1 child, Selene S. Kaelin. Grad., U. Louisville, 1933. Bar: Ky. 1936, U.S. Dist. Ct. (we. dist.) Ky. 1936, N.C. 1997. Assoc. atty. Schmitt & Schmitt, Louisville, 1936-60; judge Jefferson County Probate Ct., Louisville, 1962-70; alcohol beverage control adminstr. Jefferson County Govt., Louisville, 1962-70; law ptnr. Schmitt & Sandmann, Louisville, 1968-74; pvt. practice law Louisville, 1974—. Author: Kentucky Probate, 1980, 2nd edit., 1997; contbr. articles to profl. jours. Election poll judge various gen. elections, Louisville; active Muir Chapel United Meth. Ch.; pres. Wildwood Country Club, 1964, Legal Aid Soc., Louisville, 1968. Lt. USN, 1944-46. Inductee Ky. Tennis Hall of Fame, 1995. Mem. ABA, ATLA, Am. Arbitration Assn. (arbitration panelist 1983—, cert. mediator 1985—), Nat. Assn. Securities Dealers (arbitration panelist 1990—, cert. mediator 1994—), Am. Coll. Trust and Estate Counsel (state chmn. 1978-83), Ky. Bar Assn. (life, spkr. at seminars and convs. 1960-80, pres. 1970-71, chmn. probate com. 1974-79), N.C. State Bar Assn., N.C. State Bar, Fla. Acad. Cert. Mediators, Louisville Bar Assn. (spkr. at seminars 1960-80, pres. 1966, chmn. probate com. 1974-79, various meritorious svc. awards 1966-75). Avocation: tennis. Estate planning, Probate, Personal injury. Home: 109 Sagewood Rd Jamestown NC 27282-9489 Office: PO Box 42 Jamestown NC 27282-0042 Office: 500 Ky Home Life Bldg 239 S 5th St Louisville KY 40202-3213

**SCHMOLL, HARRY F., JR.,** lawyer, educator; b. Somers Point, N.J., Jan. 20, 1939; s. Harry F. Sr. and Margaret E. S.; m. Rita L. Miescier, Aug. 29, 1977. BS, Rider Coll., 1960; JD, Temple U., 1967. Bar: Pa., D.C. 1969, N.J. 1975. With claims dept. Social Security Adminstrn., Phila., 1960-67; staff atty. Pa. State U., State College, 1968-69; instr. criminal justice Pa. State U., University Park, 1969-74; regional dir. Pa. Crime Commn., State College, 1969-70; campaign aide U.S. Senator Scott Hugh, Harrisburg, Pa., 1970; pvt. practice law State College, 1970-74, Manahawkin, N.J., 1975-96; assoc. prof. criminal justice, bus. law Burlington County Coll., Pemberton, N.J., 1974-92; prof., 1992—, pres. elect edn. assn., 1992-93, 96-97, pres. edn. assn., 1993-94, 97-98; judge mcpl. ct., Stafford Twp., 1982-85. Author: New Jersey Criminal Law Workbook, 1976, 2nd edit., 1979, Absecon Diary of Margie Roth, 1933-37, 1999. Former gen.counsel german Heritage Coun. N.J., Inc.; mem. Barnegat Twp. Rent Control Bd., 1991, Barnegat Twp. Zoning Bd., 1994; mem. fund distbn. com. United Way of Burlington County, N.J., 1987—; trustee H.B. Smith Indsl. Village Conservacny, 1988—; mem. Stafford Twp. Com., 1979-81; dep. mayor, 1979. Mem. Pa. Bar assn., N.J. Bar Assn., German-Am. Club So. Ocean County (past pres.), Tri-State Jazz Soc., Pheasant Run Homeowners Assn. (trustee). Probate, Personal injury, General practice. Office: 72 Peppergrass Dr S Mount Laurel NJ 08054-6926

**SCHMUDDE, LEE GENE,** corporate lawyer; b. Harvey, Ill., Apr. 13, 1950; s. Kenneth H. and Jean E. (Alexander) S.; m. Mariann Verscharen, June 25, 1976; 1 child, Leighanne K. BA summa cum laude, Cornell Coll., Mount Vernon, Iowa, 1972; JD, Duke U., 1975. Bar: Fla. 1975, U.S. Dist. Ct. (ctrl. dist.) Fla. 1975. Law clk. to Chief Judge Joseph P. McNulty 2d Dist. Ct. Appeals, Lakeland, Fla., 1975-76; atty. Peterson, Myers, Lake Wales, Fla., 1976-78; v.p. legal and environ. affairs Walt Disney World Co., Orlando, Fla.; lectr. ABA, Fla. Bar, Orange County Bar Assn., Def. Lawyers Assn. Contbr. articles to Fla. Bar Jour. Bd. dirs., treas. Fla. Symphony Orch., Orlando, 1997; bd. dirs. Children's Home Soc., 1981-85; mem. adv. bd. Jr. Achievement, 1995—; chmn. Fla. Self-Ins. Guaranty ASsn., 1985, 93, bd. dirs., 1985—. Mem. Fla. Bar Assn. (lectr.), Am. Zoo and Aquarium Assn., U.S. C. of C. (Outstanding Young Man of Am. 1975), Fla. Assn. Self-Insurers (bd. dirs. 1984-85), Phi Beta Kappa. Avocations: tennis, basketball, sport fishing. Administrative and regulatory, General corporate, Environmental. Office: Walt Disney World Co PO Box 10 000 Lake Buena Vista FL 32830-1000

**SCHMULTS, EDWARD CHARLES,** lawyer, corporate and philanthropic administrator; b. Paterson, N.J., Feb. 6, 1931; s. Edward M. and Mildred (Moore) S.; m. Diane E. Beers, Apr. 23, 1960; children: Alison C., Edward M., Robert C. BS, Yale U., 1953; JD, Harvard U., 1958. Bar: N.Y. 1959, D.C. 1974. Assoc. White & Case, N.Y.C., 1958-65, ptnr., 1965-73, 77-81; gen. counsel Treasury Dept., Washington, 1973-74; undersec. Treasury Dept., 1974-75; dep. counsel to Pres. U.S., 1975-76; dep. atty. gen. of U.S. Dept. Justice, Washington, 1981-84; sr. v.p. external rels., gen. counsel GTE Corp., Stamford, Conn., 1984-94; lectr. securities laws. Bd. dirs. GreenPoint Fin. Corp., Germany Fund, Ctrl. European Equity Fund, Deutsche Profolios/Deutsche Funds, Inc.; chmn. bd. trustees Edna McConnell Clark Found. 2d. lt. USMC, 1953-55, 1st lt.; capt. USMCR. Mem. Am. Bar Assn., Assn. Bar City N.Y., Adminstrv. Conf. U.S. (council 1977-84), Sakonnet Golf Club, Met. Club.

**SCHNACK, HAROLD CLIFFORD,** lawyer; b. Honolulu, Sept. 27, 1918; s. Ferdinand J. H. and Mary (Pearson) S.; m. Gayle Hemingway Jepson, Mar. 22, 1947; children: Jerrald Jay, Georgina Schnack Hankinson, Roberta Schnack Poulin, Michael Clifford. BA, Stanford, 1940, LLB, 1947. Bar: Hawaii, 1947. Dep. prosecutor City and County Honolulu, 1947-48; gen. practice with father F. Schnack, 1948-60; pvt. practice, Honolulu, 1960-86; pres. Harcliff Corp., 1961—, Schnack Indsl. Corp., 1969-73, Instant Printers, Inc., 1971-81, Koa Corp., 1964—, Nutmeg Corp., 1963-89, Global Answer System, Inc., 1972-78. Pres. Goodwill Industries of Honolulu, 1971-72. Mem. ABA, Hawaii Bar Assn., Internat. Platform Soc., Nat. Fedn. Ind. Bus. Coun. of 100, Outrigger Canoe Club, Pacific Club, Phi Alpha Delta, Alpha Sigma Phi. Office: 817 A Cedar St PO Box 3077 Honolulu HI 96802-3077

**SCHNEBLE, ALFRED WILLIAM, III,** lawyer; b. Dayton, Ohio, Nov. 4, 1956; s. A. William and Marijane (Spitler) S. BS, Marquette U., 1978; JD, Ohio No. U., 1981. Bar: Ohio 1981, Fla. 1983. Staff atty. James W. Knisley Co., Dayton, 1981-83; pvt. practice Dayton, 1983-85; prin. Alfred W. Schneble III Co. LPA, Dayton, 1986—. Mem. ABA, Ohio Bar Assn., Fla. Bar Assn., Dayton Bar Assn. Republican. Roman Catholic. State civil litigation, General corporate, Personal injury. Office: 111 W 1st St Ste 1000 Dayton OH 45402-1106

**SCHNEE, CARL,** prosecutor. Bar: Del. 1962. Asst. pub. defender, 1965-69; former sr. ptnr. Prickett, Jones, Elliot, Kristol and Schnee; U.S. atty. Del. dist. U.S. Dept. Justice. Mem. Del. Bar. Office: Ste 110 1201 Market St Wilmington DE 19801*

**SCHNEIDER, ARTHUR,** lawyer, educator; b. N.Y.C., July 13, 1947; s. Arthur and Edythe Schneider; m. Marianne S. Schneider, June 27, 1975. BA, U. Md., 1972; JD, Antioch Sch. Law, 1975. Bar: Md., D.C. Ptnr., prin. Day & Schneider, P.A., Hagerstown, Md., 1979—; adj. prof. Frostburg (Md.) State U., 1990-98. Bd. dirs. YMCA, Hagerstown, 1993-97. With USAF, 1966-70. Mem. Md. State Bar Assn. (bd. dirs. 1997-98, exec. com. 1997-98), Antipfan Exch. Club (pres. 1982). Democrat. Avocations: golf, reading. Personal injury, Workers' compensation, Family and matrimonial. Office: Day & Schneider PA 920 W Washington PO Box 889 Hagerstown MD 21741-0889

**SCHNEIDER, DANIEL MAX,** law educator; b. Cin., Sept. 13, 1948; s. Meyer R.and Berenice R. (Hecht) S.; children: Anna, Claire. AB, Washington U., St. Louis, 1970; JD, U. Cin., 1973; LLM, NYU, 1976. Bar: Ohio 1973, N.Y. 1978, Ill. 1992. Law clk. to presiding judge U.S. Dist. Ct. (so. dist.) Ohio, Columbus, Ohio, 1973-75; assoc. LeBoeuf, Lamb, Leiby & MacRae, N.Y.C., 1977-81, Murphey, Young & Smith, Columbus, 1981-84; prof. No. Ill. U., DeKalb, 1984—; vis. prof. Washington U. Sch. Law, 1988, U. Wis. Law Sch., 1996. Author: Taxation of Dividends and Corporate Distributions, 1995; co-author: Federal Tax Aspects of Corporate Reorganizations, 1988; contbr. articles to profl. jours. Yale U. Law Sch. research fellow, 1976-77. Mem. Am. Law Inst. Office: No Ill Univ Coll Law De Kalb IL 60115

**SCHNEIDER, DAVID MILLER,** lawyer; b. Cleve., July 27, 1937; s. Earl Philip and Margaret (Miller) S.; children: Philip M., Elizabeth Dale. B.A., Yale U., 1959; LL.B., Harvard U., 1962. Assoc. Baker & Hostetler, Cleve., 1962-72, ptnr., 1972-89; chief legal officer Progressive Casualty Ins. Co., Cleve., 1989—; sec. The Progressive Corp., Cleve., 1989—. Trustee Alcoholism Svcs. of Cleve., 1977—, pres., 1980-82, chmn., 1982-84; v.p. Ctr. for Human Svcs., Cleve., 1980-83; trustee Cleve. chpt. NCCJ, 1986—. Mem. ABA, Ohio Bar Assn., Bar Assn. Cleve., Union Club, Tavern Club, Hunt Club, Town Club (Jamestown, N.Y.), Ojibway Club (Pointe au Baril, Ont., Can.). Republican. Episcopalian. General corporate, Insurance, General practice. Home: 2767 Belgrave Rd Cleveland OH 44124-4601 Office: The Progressive Corp 6300 Wilson Mills Rd Cleveland OH 44143-2109

**SCHNEIDER, ELAINE CAROL,** lawyer, researcher, writer; b. Mpls., Aug. 28, 1957; d. Allan William and Deborah G. Schneider; m. William Mack Olivé, Oct. 10, 1987 (div. July 1996); 1 child, Vanessa Inez Olivè. BA, U. Minn., 1979; JD, William Mitchell Coll. Law, St. Paul, 1982. Bar: N.Mex. 1984, Minn. 1998. Assoc. Settles, Kalamarides & Assocs., Anchorage, 1982, Dickson, Evans & Esch, Anchorage, 1982; legal rschr. John Hanson, Anchorage, 1983; legal rschr., Anchorage, 1983; account rep. Westlaw Svcs., Inc., Albuquerque, 1984; sales rep. Westlaw Svcs., Inc., New Orleans, 1985-86; libr. sales rep. West Pub. Co., Spokane, Wash., 1986-88; reference atty. West Pub. Co., St. Paul, 1988-97, product mgr., 1997-98; pvt. practice immigration legal svcs. Minn.; pro bono atty. Minn. Advocates for Human Rights, Mpls.; mem. ethics adv. bd. N.Mex. Bar, Albuquerque, 1984-85. Author: Substantive Judicial Law Outline of Habeas Corpus, 1984, What They Don't Teach You in the Bar Review Course, 1991; mem. law rev. staff William Mitchell Coll. Law, 1980-81. Pro bono individual atty. Immigration and Naturalization law Minn. Advocates for Human Rights, Refugee and Immigrant Project. Recipient Vol. Pro Bono Atty. award, 15th Ann. Minn. Advocates for Human Rifhts, 1999. Mem. Phi Beta Kappa. Avocations: ventriloquism, skiing, swimming, travel, languages. Immigration, naturalization, and customs. Office: Minn Advocates For Human Rights Flour Exchange Bldg 310 4th Ave S Ste 1000 Minneapolis MN 55415-1016 also: 701 4th Ave S Ste 500 Minneapolis MN 55415-1810

**SCHNEIDER, HAROLD LAWRENCE,** lawyer; b. N.Y.C., June 24, 1942; s. Milton and Florence (Haimowitz) S.; m. Sandra Berkowitz, Aug. 3, 1974; children: Mara Susan, Douglas Howard. BS, CCNY, 1964; JD, Fordham U., 1967; LLM, NYU, 1968. Bar: N.Y. 1967. Ptnr. Kirkpatrick & Lockhart LLP, N.Y.C.; lectr. continuing legal edn. programs and bus. seminars. Editor Fordham Law Rev., 1967; contbr. articles to profl. jours. Mem. ABA, N.Y. State Bar Assn., N.Y.C. Bar Assn. Jewish. Avocations: sports memorabilia, reading, music, antiquing. Mergers and acquisitions, General corporate, Securities. Home: 305 E 86th St Apt 4J New York NY 10028-4702 Office: Kirkpatrick & Lockhart LLP Ste 4500 1251 Avenue Of The Americas New York NY 10020-1190

**SCHNEIDER, JOHN THOMAS,** prosecutor. Atty. U.S. Dept. Justice, Fargo, N.D., 1993—. Office: US Attys Office PO Box 2505 # P Fargo ND 58108-2505

**SCHNEIDER, KAREN BUSH,** lawyer, educator; b. Lansing, Mich., Mar. 17, 1951; d. Gerard Joseph and Emily Virginia (Szoka) Bush; m. Lawrence Patrick Schneider, May 8, 1976; 1 child, Emily Margaret. BA magna cum laude, U. Notre Dame, 1973, JD, 1976. Bar: Mich. 1976, U.S. Dist. Ct. (we. dist.) Mich. 1976, U.S. Dist. Ct. (ea. dist.) Mich. 1981. From assoc. to ptnr. Foster, Swift, Collins & Smith P.C., Lansing, 1976-88; ptnr. White, Przybylowicz, Schneider & Baird P.C., Okemos, Mich., 1988—, pres., 1994-97; adj. prof. Thomas M. Cooley Law Sch., Lansing, 1985—, vis. prof., 1988-89; mem. jud. qualifications com. State Bar Mich., 1987-91; arbitrator, Mich. Employment Rels. Commn., 1990—. Contbr. legal briefs to profl jours. Fellow Mich. State Bar Found.; mem. ABA, Am. Arbitration Assn. (labor arbitrator 1985—), Ingham County Bar Assn. (bd. dirs., sec. 1982-83, pubs. com. 1983-85, chmn. pubs. com. 1984-85), Am. Lung Assn. Mich. (bd. dirs. 1985-89, chmn. pers. com. 1986-89), Assn. of Career Women, U. Notre Dame Alumni Assn. of Lansing (sec. 1979-80, pres. 1980-81, pub. rels. officer 1981-82, v.p. 1983-85), Capital Area Humane Soc. (bd. dirs. 1984-90, corr. sec. 1984, rec. sec. 1985, fundraising chmn. 1985-90, pres. 1986), State Bar of Mich. (continuing edn. com. 1997—, Biennial Diana award for profl. and cmty. svc. 1999). Roman Catholic. Avocations: fitness swimming, gourmet cooking. E-mail: Kschneider@wpsbpc.com. Labor, Civil rights. Home: 16717 Thorngate Rd East Lansing MI 48823-9772 Office: White Przybylowicz Schneider & Baird PC 2300 Jolly Oak Rd Okemos MI 48864-3546

**SCHNEIDER, LAZ LEVKOFF,** lawyer; b. Columbia, S.C., Mar. 15, 1939; s. Philip L. and Dorothy Harriet (Levkoff) S.; m. Ellen Linda Shiffrin, Dec. 12, 1968; 1 child, David Allen. BA, Yale U., 1961, LLB, 1964; LLM, NYU, 1965. Bar: D.C. 1965, N.Y. 1965, Fla. 1970. Assoc. Fulton, Walter & Duncombe, N.Y.C., 1965-67, Roseman, Colin Kaye Petschek Freund & Emil, N.Y.C., 1967-69, Kronish, Lieb, Weiner, Shainswit & Hellman, N.Y.C., 1969-70; ptnr. Ruden Barnett McClosky & Schuster, Ft. Lauderdale, Fla., 1980-86, Sherr, Tiballi, Fayne & Schneider, Ft. Lauderdale, 1987-91, Berger, Davis & Singerman, P.A., Ft. Lauderdale, 1991—; pvt. practice Ft. Lauderdale, 1980-86; bd. dirs. Ocean Biochem. Inc. Grad. editor Tax Law Rev., 1964-65. Exec. com. Fla. regional bd. Anti Defamation League, 1972—. Mem. Fla. Bar Assn., Broward Cunty Bar Assn. (chmn. sect. corp. bus. and banking law 1978-80), Yale Club (pres. 1977-79). Jewish. General corporate, Securities. Office: 100 NE 3rd Ave Fort Lauderdale FL 33301-1176

**SCHNEIDER, MAHLON C.,** lawyer; b. 1939. BA, U. Minn., 1962, law degree, 1964. Bar: Minn. 1965. Atty. Green Giant Co., 1980; atty. Pillsbury, 1980-84, v.p., gen. counsel foods divsn., 1984-89; corp. atty. Geo. A. Hormel & Co., Austin, Minn., 1989-90, v.p., gen. counsel, 1990—. Contracts commercial, Product liability. Office: Hormel Foods Corp 1 Hormel Pl Austin MN 55912-3680

**SCHNEIDER, PAM HORVITZ,** lawyer; b. Cleve., Nov. 29, 1951; m. Milton S. Schneider, June 30, 1973; 1 child, Sarah Anne. BA, U. Pa., 1973; JD, Columbia U., 1976. Bar: N.Y. 1977, Pa. 1979. Assoc. White & Case, N.Y.C., 1976-78; assoc. Drinker Biddle & Reath, Phila., 1978-84, ptnr., 1984—. Contbr. articles to profl. jours. Fellow Am. Coll. Trust and Estate Counsel (regent); mem. ABA (past chair, real property probate and trust law sect.), Internat. Acad. Estate and Trust Law (academician). Estate planning, Estate taxation, Probate. Office: Drinker Biddle & Reath 1345 Chestnut St Ste 1300 Philadelphia PA 19107-3496

**SCHNEIDER, PATRICIA J.,** court reporter; b. Beaver Dam, Wis., Mar. 2, 1958; d. George P. and Margaret Ella Marie (Seidensticker) S. AD, Madison Area Tech. Coll., 1978. Registered diplomate reporter. Freelance ct. reporter Wilson & Assocs., Louisville, 1978-79, Curtin, Schneider & Lawrey, Louisville, 1979-96, Louisville, 1996—. Bd. dirs. Louisville Luth. Home, 1985, 88; sec. Concordia Luth. Ch., Louisville, 1982—. Mem. Nat. Ct. Reporters Assn., Ky. Ct. Reporters Assn. (pres. 1985-87, bd. dirs. 1996-99), Phi Kappa Phi. Democrat. Lutheran. Avocations: reading, golf.

**SCHNEIDER, RICHARD GRAHAM,** lawyer; b. Bryn Mawr, Pa., Aug. 2, 1930; s. Vincent Bernard and Marion Scott (Graham) S.; m. Margaret Peter Fritz, Feb. 15, 1958; children: Margaret W., Richard Graham, John F. BA, Yale U., 1952; JD, U. Pa., 1957. Bar: Pa. 1958. Assoc. Dechert Price & Rhoads, Phila., 1957-66; ptnr. Dechert Price & Rhoads, 1966-95; of counsel, 1995—. Case editor U. Pa. Law Rev., 1956-57. Trustee Baldwin Sch., Bryn Mawr, 1971-79; trustee Episcopal Acad., Merion, Pa., 1976-83. 1st lt. USAF, 1952-54, PTO. Mem. ABA, Pa. Bar Assn., Phila. Bar Assn., Order of Coif, Merion Cricket Club, Merion Golf Club (sec. 1997—), Yale Club (pres. 1966-68). Republican. Presbyterian. Antitrust, General civil litigation. Office: Dechert Price & Rhoads 4000 Bell Atlantic Tower 1717 Arch St Ste 3 Philadelphia PA 19103-2793

**SCHNEIDER, ROBERT E., II,** lawyer; b. 1939. BS, Purdue U., 1962; JD, Ind. U., 1966. Bar: Ind. 1966. Trust officer Ind. Nat. Bank, 1969-74, legal counsel, 1974-79; sr. v.p., gen. counsel, sec. INB Fin. Corp., Indpls., 1979-93, NBD Bank N.A., Indpls., 1993—; now sr. v.p., gen. counsel Bank One Corp., Chgo. General corporate. Office: Bank One Corp One 1st National Plz Chicago IL 60670

**SCHNEIDER, THOMAS PAUL,** prosecutor; b. June 5, 1947; s. Milton and Gloria (Bocaner) S.; m. Susan G. Stein, May 31, 1987; children: Rachel Jenny, Daniel Joshua. BA with honors, U. Wis., 1972, JD, 1972. U.S. atty. U.S. Dept. Justice, Milw., 1993—. Mem. Wis. Bar Assn., Milw. Bar Assn. Democrat. Jewish. Office: US Attys Office 517 E Wisconsin Ave Rm 530 Milwaukee WI 53202-4580

**SCHNELLER, JOHN, IV,** lawyer; b. Metairie, La., June 26, 1966; s. John III and Sylvia Marie (Johns) S.; m. Patricia Lee Richard, Sept. 30, 1995. BS in Econs., U. Pa., 1988; JD, U. Ill., 1991; LLM in Taxation, NYU, 1992. Bar: La. 1992, Tex. 1993, U.S. Tax Ct. 1993. Assoc. Guarisco, Weiler & Cordes, New Orleans, 1992-93, Schlanger, Mills, Mayer & Grossberg, LLP, Houston, 1993-95, Chamberlain, Hrdlicka, White, Williams & Martin, 1995-97, Haynes & Boone, Houston, 1997-98, Schlanger Mills Mayer & Grossberg LLP, Houston, 1998—. Mem. ABA, Tex. Bar Assn., La. State Bar Assn., Houston Young Lawyers Assn. Avocations: golf, fishing, reading, computers, travel. Taxation, general, General corporate, Mergers and acquisitions. Home: 5874 Sugar Hill Dr Houston TX 77057-2004

**SCHOBER, THOMAS GREGORY,** lawyer; b. Waukesha, Wis., Aug. 17, 1948; s. Theodore Michael and Rosalie (Blando) S.; m. Patricia Ann Farrell, Jan. 17, 1981; children: Wendy, Sara, Sarah, Sonya, Christy, Marc. BS, Marquette U., 1970, JD, 1972. Bar: Wis. 1973, U.S. Dist. Ct. (ea. and we. dists.) Wis. 1973, U.S. Tax Ct. 1976. Mng. ptnr., atty. Schober & Radtke, S.C., New Berlin, Wis., 1973-96, Schober & Schober, S.C., New Berlin, Wis., 1996—; prof. acctg. U. Wis., Waukesha, 1975-77; prof. law Marquette Law Sch., Milw., 1977-81; mem. adv. bd. Luth. Social Svcs., Milw., 1983-86; bd. dirs. Stepping Stones Child Devel. Ctr., New Berlin. Airport commr. Waukesha County Airport Commn., 1991—. With Wis. N.G., 1970-76. Republican. Lutheran. Avocation: pilot. General corporate, Mergers and acquisitions, Real property. Office: Schober and Schober SC 16845 W Cleveland Ave New Berlin WI 53151-3532

**SCHOCHET, IRA A.,** lawyer; b. Bklyn., Mar. 6, 1956; s. Sol and Lillian Schochet; m. Randi Parks, May 9, 1992; children: Paul Aaron, Nathaniel Lewis. BA, SUNY, Binghamton, 1977; JD, Duke U., 1981. Atty. Gruntal Fin. Corp., N.Y.C., 1982-84; assoc. Hendler & Murray, N.Y.C., 1985-86; assoc. Goodkind Labaton Rudoff & Sucharow, N.Y.C., 1986-90, ptnr., 1991—. Mem. N.Y. Bar Assn. (exec. com. fed. comml. litigation sect., chmn. class action com. 1997—). Federal civil litigation, Securities. Office: Goodkind Labaton Rudoff & Sucharow LLP 100 Park Ave New York NY 10017-5516

**SCHOCHOR, JONATHAN,** lawyer; b. Suffern, N.Y., Sept. 9, 1946; s. Abraham and Betty (Hechtor) S.; m. Joan Elaine Brown, May 31, 1970; children: Lauren Aimee, Daniel Ross. BA, Pa. State U., 1968; JD, Am. U., 1971. Bar: D.C. 1971, U.S. Dist. Ct. D.C. 1971, U.S. Ct. Appeals (D.C. cir.) 1971, Md. 1974, U.S. Dist. Ct. Md. 1974, U.S. Ct. Appeals (4th cir.) 1974, U.S. Supreme Ct. 1986. Assoc., McKenna, Wilkinson & Kittner, Washington, 1970-74; assoc. Ellin & Baker, Balt., 1974-84; ptnr. Schochor, Federico & Staton, Balt., 1984—; lectr. in law; expert witness to state legis. Assoc. editor-in-chief American U. Law Rev., 1970-71. Mem. ABA, Assn. Trial Lawyers Am. (state del. 1991, state gov. 1992-95), Am. Bd. Trial Advocates (membership com. 1994—), Am. Bd. Trial Advocates, Am. Judicature Soc., Md. State Bar Assn. (spl. com. on health claims arbitration 1983), Md. Trial Lawyers Assn. (bd. govs. 1986-87, mem. legis. com., 1985-88, chmn. legis. com. 1986-87, sec. 1987-88, exec. com. 1987-92, v.p. 1987-88, pres.-elect 1989, pres. 1990-91), Balt. City Bar Assn. (legis. com. 1986-87, spl. com. on tort reform 1986, medicolegal com. 1989-90, circuit ct. for Balt. City task force-civil document mgmt. system 1994-95), Bar Assn. D.C., Internat. Platform Assn., Phi Alpha Delta. Personal injury, Federal civil litigation, State civil litigation. Office: Schochor Federico & Staton PA 1211 Saint Paul St Baltimore MD 21202-2783

**SCHOCK, ROBERT CHRISTOPHER,** lawyer; b. New Rochelle, N.Y., Apr. 12, 1948; s. Carl Frederick and Elizabeth Woodbury (Slocomb) S. BA cum laude, Wake Forest U., 1970; JD, U. Tenn., 1973. Bar: Tenn. 1974, Ga. 1978, U.S. Dist. Ct. (no. dist.) Ga. 1978, U.S. Ct. Appeals (5th cir.) 1978, U.S. Ct. Appeals (11th cir.) 1982. Gen. atty. U.S. Dept. Justice Immigration Svc., Atlanta, 1974-80; sole practitioner Atlanta, 1980—. Contbr.: Immigration Law, 1996. Mem. Am. Immigration Lawyers Assn. (Atlanta chpt. treas. 1992-93, sec. 1993-94, INS liaison chair 1995-96), Phi Alpha Theta. Presbyterian. Avocations: exercise, travel, gardening. Immigration, naturalization, and customs, Private international, Public international. Office: 235 Peachtree St NE Ste 400 Atlanta GA 30303-1400

**SCHODER, WENDELL LOUIS,** lawyer; b. Battle Creek, Mich., July 11, 1926; s. Harold Maurice and Hildred Angeline (Baird) S.; m. Helen Marie Bauman, Feb. 3, 1951; children—Patrice Schoder Emmerson, Robert, Gerald, Martha Schoder Terry, Mary, David. Student Georgetown U., 1946-47; J.D., U. Detroit, 1951. Bar: Mich. 1951, U.S. Dist. Ct. (we. dist.) Mich. 1953. Sole practice, Battle Creek, 1951-64; cir. ct. commr. Calhoun County, Marshall, Mich., 1954-60, asst. pros. atty., 1960-64, probate judge, 1965-84; of counsel Holmes, Mumford, Schubel, Norlander & Macfarlane, Battle Creek, 1984-88 ; instr. law Kellogg Community Coll., Battle Creek, 1974-79; lectr. in field. Contbr. in field. Apptd. Mich. Mental Health Adv. Council, Lansing, 1975-77; chmn. Mich. Mental Health Research, Lansing, 1975-77; pres. Goodwill Industries/Family Services, Battle Creek, 1969-70. Served with U.S. Army, 1944-46. Recipient Mental Health Services award VA, 1981, Commendation Chief Atty. VA, 1984; Snyder-Kok award Mental Health Assn. for Mich., 1983. Mem. Mich. Bar Assn. (chmn. probate and estate planning council 1987-88), Calhoun County Bar Assn. (pres. 1963-64), Mich. Assn. Probate Judges. Republican. Roman Catholic. Club: Exchange (pres. 1973-74) (Battle Creek). Lodges: K.C. (4 degree). Probate. Home and Office: 251 Martha Dr Battle Creek MI 49015-3805

**SCHOEMANN, RUDOLPH ROBERT,** lawyer; b. Chgo., Nov. 2, 1930; s. Rudolph and Anna Elise (Claus) S.; m. Florence Margaret Olivier, May 17, 1952 (div.); children—Peggy Ann Schoemann Salathe, Rudolph Robert III, Richard Randolph (dec.), Rodney Ryan; m. Marie Louise Gandolfo Webb, Dec. 2, 1983. Student, Wabash Coll., Crawfordsville, Ind., 1946-47; B.C.S., Loyola U. of South, New Orleans, 1959, LLB, 1952, JD, 1968; B.A., Tulane U., 1966, LL.M. in Admiralty Law, 1981, LL.M. in Internat. Law, 1989; postgrad. U. New Orleans, 1981-82. Bar: La. 1952, U.S. Supreme Ct. 1959, U.S. Ct. Appeals (5th cir.) 1952, U.S. Ct. Appeals (11th cir.) 1981, U.S. Ct. Appeals (D.C. cir.) 1982, U.S. Dist. Ct. Md. 1957, U.S. Dist. Ct. (ea. dist.) La. 1952, U.S. Dist. Ct. (we. dist.) La. 1960, U.S. Dist. Ct. (mid. dist.) La. 1952, U.S. Ct. Mil. Appeals, 1953, U.S. Ct. Customs and Patent Appeals 1953, U.S. Ct. Claims 1953. Assoc. James J. Morrison, New Orleans, 1952-54; ptnr. Smith & Schoemann, New Orleans, 1955-60, Schoemann & Gomes, 1961-63, Schoemann, Gomes, Ducote & Collins, 1963-67, Schoemann, Gomes & Ducote, 1968-74, Rudolph R. Schoemann, 1974-77, Schoemann & Golden, 1978-79, Schoemann, Swaim, Morrison & Cockfield, 1979-80, Schoemann & Assocs., 1980—(all New Orleans). Served with La. N.G., 1949-52, to 1st lt. JAGC, U.S. Army, 1952-53; capt. Res. ret. Mem. ABA, La. Bar Assn., New Orleans Bar Assn., La. Def. Assn., New Orleans Def. Assn., Def. Research Inst., Soc. Naval Architects and Marine Engrs., Fed. Bar Assn. Democrat. Lutheran. Insurance, Admiralty, Personal injury. Address: 3670 Gentilly Blvd New Orleans LA 70122-4910

**SCHOEN, STEVAN JAY,** lawyer; b. N.Y.C., May 19, 1944; s. Al and Ann (Spevack) S.; m. Cynthia Lukens; children: Andrew Adams, Anna Kim. BS, U. Pa., 1966; JD, Cornell U., 1969; MPhil in Internat. Law, Cambridge U. (Eng.), 1980. Bar: N.Mex. 1970, N.Y. 1970, U.S. Supreme Ct. 1076, U.S. Tax Ct. 1973, U.S. Ct. Internat. Trade 1982. Nat. dir. Vista law recruitment U.S. OEO, Washington, 1970-71; atty. Legal Aid Soc. of Albuquerque, 1971-73; chief atty., spl. asst. atty. gen. N.Mex. Dept. Health and Social Svcs., Albuquerque, 1973-77; ptnr. Brennan, Schoen & Eisenstadt, 1979-88, Stevan J. Schoen P.A., 1989; probate judge Sandoval County, 1990-98; arbitrator NYSE; mem. N.Mex. Supreme Ct. Appellate Rules Com., 1982-92; chmn. rules com. Com. on Fgn. Legal Cons., 1993, N.Mex. Supreme Ct. Com., Probate Ct. Rules and Forms, Jud. Edn. Planning com.; mem. Children's Code Rules Com., 1976-78. Mem. Mayor's Albuquerque Abd. Com. on Fgn. Trade Zone, 1992-94; v.p. Placitas Vol. Fir Dept., 1974-86; bd. edn. Bernalillo Pub. Sch. Dist., 1996-97. Recipient Cert. for Outstanding Svc. to Judiciary, N.Mex. Supreme Ct., 1982, Outstanding Svc. award N. Mex. Supreme Ct., 1992, Cert. of Appreciation, N.Mex. Sec. of State, 1980, Pro Bono Pub. Svc. award, 1989, Cert. of Recognition Legal Aid, 1994, award Las Placitas Assn., 1996, Outstanding Pub. Svc. N.Mex State Senate, 1998. Mem. Am. Judges Assn., Nat. Coll. Probate Judges, State Bar N.Mex. (past chmn. real property, probate and trust sect. 1989, Outstanding Contbn. award 1989, task force on regulation of advt. 1990-91, past chmn. appellate practice sect. 1991, past chmn. internat. law sect. 1991-92, commn. on professionalism 1992-95, organizing com. U.S.-Mex. law inst. 1992), N.Mex. Probate Judges Assn. (chmn. 1993-99, award 1998, N.Mex. state bar bench and bar rels. com. 1998—), Oxford-Cambridge Soc. N.Mex. (sec.), M.Mex. Assn. Counties (adv. bd. 1995-99). Fax: 505-888-2806. Private international, Probate, Real property. Home: 14 Rainbow Valley Rd Placitas NM 87043-8801 Office: 4316 Carlisle Blvd NE Ste A Albuquerque NM 87107-4829

**SCHOENE, KATHLEEN SNYDER,** lawyer; b. Glen Ridge, N.J., July 24, 1953; d. John Kent and Margaret Ann (Bronder) Snyder. BA, Grinnell Coll., 1974; MS, So. Conn. State Coll., 1976; JD, Washington U., St. Louis, 1982. Bar: Mo. 1982, U.S. Dist. Ct. (we. and ea. dists.) Mo. 1982, Ill. 1983. Head libr. Mo. Hist. Soc., St. Louis, 1976-79; assoc. Peper, Martin, Jensen, Maichel & Hetlage, St. Louis, 1982-88, ptnr., 1989-98; ptnr. Armstrong Teasdale LLP, St. Louis, 1998—; bd. dirs. Legal Svcs. of Eastern Mo. Author: (with others) Missouri Corporation Law and Practice, 1985, Missouri Business Organizations, 1998; contbr. articles to profl. jours. Trustee Grinnell (Iowa) Coll., ex officio voting mem., 1991-93; bd. dirs. Jr. League St. Louis, 1995-96, Leadership Ctr. Greater St. Louis, 1995-96, FOCUS St. Louis, 1996—, mem. exec. com., 1997-99; active St. Louis Forum, 1997—, Herbert Hoover Boys and Girls Club, St. Louis, 1999—. Mem. ABA, Nat. Conf. Bar Founds. (trustee 1996—, pres. elect 1997-98, pres. 1998-99), Nat. Health Lawyers Assn., Nat. Assn. Bond Lawyers, The Mo. Bar (bd. govs. 1997-99), Ill. State Bar Assn., Bar Assn. Met. St. Louis (treas. 1991-92, sec. 1992-93, v.p. 1993-94, pres.-elect 1994-95, pres. 1995-96, chairperson small bus. com. 1987-88, mem. exec. com. 1988-96, chairperson bus. law sect. 1988-89, mem. exec. com. young lawyers sect. 1988-90), St. Louis Bar Found. (bd. dirs. 1994—, v.p. 1995-96, pres. 1996-98). General corporate, Securities, Health. Home: 7824 Cornell Ave Saint Louis MO 63130-3701 Office: Armstrong Teasdale One Metropolitan Sq Saint Louis MO 63102

**SCHOENFELD, BARBARA BRAUN,** lawyer; b. Phila., Apr. 17, 1953; d. Irving Leon Braun and Virginia (Parker) Sand; m. Larry Jay Schoenfeld, June 29, 1975; children: Alexander, Gordon, Max. BA cum laude, U. Pa., 1974, M in City Planning, Social Work, 1977; JD, Boston U., 1982. Bar: R.I. 1982, U.S. Dist. Ct. R.I. 1982. Assoc. planner Del. Valley Hosp. Council, Phila., 1978-79; summer assoc. Tillinghast, Collins & Graham, Providence, 1980, 81; assoc. Edwards & Angell, Providence, 1982-86, Ropes & Gray, Providence, 1986-92; dep. treas., gen. counsel State of R.I., 1993-99; mktg. mgr. Brown Bros. Harriman & Co., Boston, 1999—. Chmn., bd. dirs. Com. Women's Health Concerns, Phila., 1978-79; bd. dirs. Jewish Family Svc., Providence, 1982-88, Jewish Fedn. of R.I., 1989-91; assoc. treas. Jewish Cmty. Ctr. of R.I.; bd. of assocs. Alumni Trustees U. Pa.; chmn. admissions com. U. Pa. Alumni Club, Providence, 1982-95; trustee The Wheeler Sch., 1994—. Mem. ABA, R.I. Bar Assn., Ledgemont Country Club (Seekonk, Mass.). Democrat. Jewish. Avocations: skiing, travel, French. Contracts commercial, General corporate, Finance. Office: Brown Bros Harriman & Co 40 Water St Boston MA 02109-3661

**SCHOENFELD, MICHAEL P.,** lawyer; b. Bronx, N.Y., Oct. 17, 1935; s. Jack and Anne S.; B.S. in Acctg., N.Y.U., 1955; LL.B., LL.D., Fordham U., 1958; m. Helen Schorr, Apr. 3, 1960; children—Daniel, Steven, Tracy. Admitted to N.Y. bar, 1959, U.S. Supreme Ct., 1963; atty. Am. Home Assurance Co., N.Y.C., 1958-62; ptnr. firm Schoenfeld & Schoenfeld, Melville, 1959—; v.p. Interstate Brokerage Corp., 1965-84, pres., 1984—; ptnr. Melville Realty Co., 1977—; legal adv. various bus. orgns. Vice pres., trustee Temple Beth David, Commack, N.Y., 1972-75; chmn. Community Action Com. of Dix Hills and Commack, 1970-72, Dix Hills Planning Bd., 1972-74; treas. Dix Hills Republican Club, 1976-80; mem. Huntington (N.Y.) Zoning Bd. Appeals, 1980-91, chmn., 1986-89. Recipient United Jerusalem award Israel Bond Drive, 1977; City of Hope Service award; George Bacon award Fordham Law Sch. Mem. N.Y. State Bar Assn., Suffolk County Bar Assn. Insurance, Personal injury, Product liability. Home: 14 Clayton Dr Dix Hills NY 11746-5517 Office: 999 Walt Whitman Rd Melville NY 11747-3007

**SCHOENFELD, STEVEN RUSSELL,** lawyer; b. N.Y.C., July 21, 1965; s. Michael and Helen Schoenfeld; m. Gayle Ann Morris, Sept. 6, 1992; 1 child, Zachary Austin. AB summa cum laude, Princeton U., 1987; JD, NYU, 1990. Assoc. Haythe and Curley, N.Y.C., 1990-98, ptnr., 1999—. Contbr. articles to profl. jours. General civil litigation, Contracts commercial. Office: Haythe & Curley 237 Park Ave New York NY 10017-3140

**SCHOEPPEL, JAMES,** lawyer; b. Murphysboro, Ill., Apr. 18, 1952; s. John and Ethelmae Schoeppel; m. Kay Kenney, Jan. 31, 1981; 1 child, Chacey. BS in Acctg., Okla. State U., 1974; JD, Okla. U., 1978. CPA, Okla. Ptnr. Curtis, McCue, Schoeppel & Hallren, Fairview, Okla., 1978-92; pvt. practice law Fairview, 1992—. Com. chair Major County Econ. Devel., Fairview, 1998; bd. dirs. Major County Emergency Med. Svc., Fairview, 1998. Mem. Okla. Bar Assn., Major County Bar Assn. (pres. 1978-92), Okla. Soc. CPAs, Fairview C. of C., Fairview Rotary (sec. 1984-85, pres. 1985-86, 99—, v.p. 1986-87). Republican. Methodist. Avocations: flying, boating, snooker, reading, construction. Nuclear power, Real property, Estate planning. Home: HC 60 Box 9 Fairview OK 73737-9505 Office: PO Box 190 Fairview OK 73737-0190

**SCHOFIELD, ANTHONY WAYNE,** judge; b. Farmington, N.Mex., Mar. 5, 1949; s. Aldred Edward and Margueriete (Knudsen) S.; m. Rebecca Ann Rosecrans, May 11, 1971; children: Josie, Matthew Paul, Peter Christian, Addie, Joshua James, M. Thomas, Jacob L., Daniel Z. BA, Brigham Young U., 1973, JD, 1976. Bar: Utah 1976, U.S. Dist. Ct. Utah 1976, U.S. Ct. Appeals (7th and 10th cirs.) 1977. Law clk. to hon. judge A. Sherman Christansen U.S. Dist. Ct. Utah, Salt Lake City, 1976-77; assoc. Ferenz, Bramhall, Williams & Gruskin, Agana, Guam, 1977-79; pvt. practice American Fork, Utah, 1979-80; assoc. Jardine, Linebaugh, Brown & Dunn, Salt Lake City, 1980-81; mem., dir. Ray, Quinney & Nebeker, Provo, Utah; judge 4th Jud. Dist. Ct., Provo, Utah, 1993—. Bishop Mormon Ch., American Fork, 1985-88; commr. American Fork City Planning Commn., 1980-85; trustee American Fork Hosp., 1984-93. Mem. Cen. Utah Bar Assn. (pres. 1987, 91). Avocations: photography, music. Office: 125 N 100 W Provo UT 84601-2849

**SCHOLL, DAVID ALLEN,** federal judge; b. Bethlehem, Pa., Aug. 20, 1944; s. George Raymond and Beatrice Roberta (Weaver) S.; m. Cynthia Ann Schuler Vetere, June, 1966 (div. 1972); m. Portia Elizabeth White, May 26, 1973; children: Tracy, Xavier; 1 stepchild, Sierra Milan. AB, Franklin & Marshall Coll., 1966; JD, Villanova U., 1969. Bar: Pa. 1969, U.S. Dist. Ct. (ea. dist.) 1970, U.S. Ct. Appeals (3d cir.) 1971, U.S. Tax Ct. 1975, U.S. Supreme Ct. 1975. Staff atty. Community Legal Services, Inc., Phila., 1969-73, 77-80; exec. dir. Delaware County Legal Assistance Assn., Chester, Pa., 1973-76; mng. atty. Lehigh Valley Legal Services, Bethelehem, Allentown, Pa., 1980-86; judge U.S. Bankruptcy Ct., Phila., 1986-94, chief judge, 1994-99. Bd. dirs. Phila. Vols. for Indigent Program, 1988-94, Consumer Bankruptcy Assistance Project, 1992-98. Recipient Joseph Harris award Ba'Hais of Lehigh Valley, Bethelehem, 1984, Vol. of Yr. award Temple LEAP Program, 1997. Mem. Pa. Bar Assn. (chairperson consumer law commn., 1983-86), Northampton County Bar Assn. Avocations: baseball, rock music. Office: 900 Market St Ste 201 Philadelphia PA 19107

**SCHOLLANDER, WENDELL LESLIE, JR.,** lawyer; b. Ocala, Fla., May 17, 1943; 1 son, Wendell Leslie III. BS, U. Pa., 1966, MBA, 1968; postgrad., Stetson U., 1969-70; JD, Duke U., 1972. Bar: N.C. 1977, Tenn. 1972, Fla. 1987. With Container Corp. Am., Fernandina, Fla., 1968-69; assoc. Miller, Martin, Chattanooga, 1972-75; asst. counsel R.J. Reynolds Industries, Inc., 1975-78, assoc. counsel, 1978-79, sr. assoc. counsel, 1979-82, sr. counsel, 1982-85; gen. counsel RJR Archer, Inc., Winston-Salem, N.C., 1979-85; of counsel Finger, Parker & Avram, Winston-Salem, 1985-87; ptnr. Schollander, Winston-Salem, 1987—; gen. counsel Splty. Tobacco Council, 1985-87. Mem. ABA, N.C. Bar Assn., Forsyth County Bar Assn., Mensa, SAR, Phi Delta Phi, Kappa Sigma. Presbyterian. General corporate, Bankruptcy, Franchising. Office: 2000 W 1st St Ste 509 Winston Salem NC 27104-4225

**SCHOLTZ, KENNETH P.,** lawyer; b. L.A., Mar. 24, 1938; s. Walter and Sylvia (Flax) S.; m. Marion G. Bloom, Nov. 12, 1966; children: Matthew M., Brian A., Wendy D. BS, Calif. Inst. Tech., 1960; LLB, U. Calif., Berkeley, 1963. Dep. atty. gen. Calif. Atty. Gen., L.A., 1964-68; atty. Joseph Lucas Enterprises, London, 1969-70; sole practitioner L.A., 1970; assoc. Berrien & Moore, Gardena and Torrance, Calif., 1971-73; sole practitioner Beverly Hills, Calif., 1973-79; ptnr. Quan, Cohen et al, L.A., 1979-98; settlement officer Ct. of Appeal, L.A., 1996—. Pres. L.A. Gifted Children's Assn., 1975-76; bd. dirs. L.A. Alzheimers Assn., 1994—. Ford Found. fellow, 1963-64. Mem. Red Ribbon Squares (pres. 1985-86), Santa Monica Oceanaires. Avocations: dancing, music, hiking. Alternative dispute resolution, Appellate, General civil litigation. Office: Quan Cohen et al 777 S Figueroa St Ste 3615 Los Angeles CA 90017-5832

**SCHON, ALAN WALLACE,** lawyer, actor; b. Mpls., Nov. 27, 1946; s. Hubert Adelbert and Jennie (Jamieson) S.; m. Linda Kay Long, June 14, 1969; 1 child, Cynthia Anne. BA, U. Minn., 1969; JD, William and Mary Coll., 1973; grad. Command & Gen. Staff Coll., U.S. Army, 1984. Bar: Minn. 1973, U.S. Dist. Ct. Minn., Alaska 1986, U.S. Dist. Ct. Alaska, U.S. Ct. Appeals (9th cir.) 1988, Va. 1995. Prin. Schon Law Office, Fairbanks, Alaska, 1986-94; owner, pub. Nordland Pub. Co., Hampton, Va., 1991-94; dep. city atty. mcpl. bonds, environ. law, pub.-pvt. econ. devel. funding environ. law City of Hampton, Va., 1994-99; nationwide environ. group mgr. Delphi Info. Network, Gen. Videotex Corp., Cambridge, Mass., 1991-94; ind. assoc. Pre-Paid Legal Svcs. Inc., 1999—. Author, pub. EnvironLaw, 1991-94; editor William and Mary Law Rev., 1970-73; performer Va. Opera, Norfolk, 1995-96, Va. Mus. Theater, Virginia Beach, 1997-98; film actor The Jackal, 1996, Quest: Flight 427, 1996; prin.ses performer in 6 cable shows Discovery Channel; screenwriter: Operation Desert Fire, 1997, Operation Firestorm, 1998. Dir. Alaska State Fair, Fairbanks, 1987-91, Fairbanks Light Opera Theater, Fairbanks, 1991-94; dir., sec. Riding for Am., Inc., 1993-97; dir. Interior Alaska Econ. Devel. Ctr., 1993-94. Maj. U.S. Army, 1974-86. Mem. Fairbanks C. of C. (chmn. environ. concerns com. 1992-94). Avocations: outdoor sports, arts. Home and Office: 13 Keeton Ct Hampton VA 23666-2271

**SCHONFELD, JOEL,** lawyer; b. N.Y.C., Jan. 12, 1935; s. Samuel P. and Ruth (Rottenberg) S.; m. Lori M. Dean, 1967; children: Robert, Chelsea. BA, Adelphi U., 1956; LLB, JD, Bklyn. Law Sch., 1959. Bar: N.Y. 1960. Ptnr. Schonfeld & Weinstein LLP, N.Y.C., 1995—. Trustee Adelphi U., Garden City, N.Y., 1963-68; bd. dirs. Gift of Life, Inc., Manhasset, N.Y., 1995-97, sec., 1996-97, v.p., 1998—. Paul Harris fellow, 1995, 97. Mem. Nassau County Bar Assn., Kings County Bar Assn., L.I. Yacht Club (Babylon, N.Y.), Rotary (sec. Bklyn. 1995, treas. 1997). Securities. Home: 82 Dune Rd Island Park NY 11550 Office: Schonfeld & Weinstein LLP 63 Wall St New York NY 10005-3001

**SCHOOLER, STEVEN JAMES,** lawyer; b. Pullman, Wash., Apr. 30, 1955; s. Arnold and Iris S.; m. Marsha Mae Mansfield, June 9, 1955; 1 child, Sarah. BA in Econs., George Washington U., 1973; JD, U. Mich., 1981. Bar: Wis. 1981, U.S. Dist. Ct. (ea. and we. dists.) Wis. 1981, U.S. Ct. Appeals (7th cir.) 1981. Atty. Axley Brynelson, Madison, Wis., 1981-89, Lawton & Cates, S.C., Madison, 1989—; chair, chair elect individual rights sect. Wis. State, Madison, 1994-96; pres., bd. dirs. Ctr. Pub. Representation, Madison, 1998—. Co-author: Law of Damages, 1988, Wisconsin Civil Procedures Before Trial, 1996; co-editor: Wisconsin Civil Forms Manual, 1995. Mem. adminstrv. coun. First United Meth. Ch., pres., 1993-96; bd. dirs. U. Wis. Madison Campus Ministries, sec., 1986-87; bd. dirs. Transitional Housing, Inc., Madison, 1991—. Mem. Order of Coif, Phi Beta Kappa. General civil litigation, Civil rights, Personal injury. Office: Lawton & Cates SC 214 W Mifflin St Madison WI 53703-2594

**SCHOOLEY, ELIZABETH WALTER,** lawyer; b. Phila., Dec. 21, 1958; d. William J. Jr. and Judith (Walter) S. BA, Chatham Coll., Pitts., 1980; JD, U. Pitts., 1989. Bar: Pa. 1989. Jud. clk. to Hon. John M. Clean McKean County, Pa., 1989-90; assoc. Begler, Kowall & Ombres, Pitts., 1991-94, Edward J. Feinstein, Pitts., 1994-95, Begler Kowall, Pitts., 1994-95, Frank, Bails, Murcko & Toal, Pitts., 1995—; vol. atty. Neighborhood Legal Svcs., Pitts., 1995—, Pro Se Motions Project, Pitts., 1998—. Mem. Pa. Bar Assn., Allegheny County Bar Assn. Democrat. Family and matrimonial, General civil litigation, Civil rights. Office: Frank Bails Murcko & Toal Gulf Tower 33d Fl 707 Grant St Pittsburgh PA 15219-1908

**SCHOONHOVEN, RAY JAMES,** retired lawyer; b. Elgin, Ill., May 24, 1921; s. Ray Covey and Rosina Madeline (Schram) (White) S.; m. Marie Theresa Dunn, Dec. 11, 1943; children: Marie Kathleen, Ray James, Jr., Pamela Suzanne, John Philip, Rose Lynn. B.S.C., U. Notre Dame, 1943; J.D., Northwestern U., 1948. Bar: Ill. 1949, U.S. Supreme Ct. 1954, D.C. 1973, U.S. Ct. Mil. Appeals 1954. Assoc. Seyfarth, Shaw Fairweather & Geraldson, Chgo., 1949-57, ptnr., 1957-92; ret.; chief rulings and ops. br. Wage Stabilization Bd. Region VII, Chgo., 1951-52. Book rev. editor: Ill. Law Rev., 1948. Served to lt.comdr. USNR, 1942-62. Mem. ABA, Ill. State Bar Assn., Chgo. Bar Assn., D.C. Bar Assn., Chgo. Athletic Assn., Univ. Club. Chgo., Fed. Bar Assn., Order of Coif. Republican. Roman Catholic. Labor, Administrative and regulatory. Home: 6636 N Ponchartrain Blvd Chicago IL 60646-1428 Office: Seyfarth Shaw Fairweather & Geraldson 55 E Monroe St Ste 4200 Chicago IL 60603-5863 *I work hard to preserve our free enterprise system and, hopefully, to make such contribution to our society that it is better for my having been a part of it.*

**SCHOONMAKER, SAMUEL VAIL, III,** lawyer; b. Newburgh, N.Y., Sept. 1, 1935; s. Samuel V. Jr. and Catherine (Wilson) S.; m. Carolyn Peters, Sept. 18, 1965; children: Samuel V. IV, Frederick P. BA magna cum laude, Yale U., 1958, JD, 1961. Bar: Conn. 1961, U.S. Dist. Ct. Conn. 1961, U.S. Dist. Ct. (so. and ea. dist.) N.Y. 1964, U.S. Ct. Appeals (2d cir.) 1964, U.S. Supreme Ct. 1965. Assoc. Cummings & Lockwood, Stamford, Conn., 1961-70, co-mng. ptnr., 1987-90, mng. ptnr., 1990-94, chmn. exec. com., 1987-96; founder, pres. Schoonmaker George & Colin, P.C., Greenwich, Conn., 1996—; state trial referee Conn. Superior Ct., 1989; pres. Schoonmaker Family Assn., New Paltz, N.Y., 1975-77. Sr. topical editor Conn. Bar Jour., 1977-81; mem. editl. bd. Fairshare and Am. Jour. Family Law, 1992—; contbr. articles to profl. jours. Chmn. Conn. Child Support Commn., 1984-86; mem. Conn. Family Support Com., 1986-90; mem. Darien (Conn.) Rep. Town Com., 1974-76, rep. town meeting, 1990-98; pres. Youth Tennis Found. New Eng., Needham, Mass., 1975-77; pres. New Eng. Lawn Tennis Assn., 1977-79 (Man of Yr. award 1979); trustee Huguenot Hist. Soc., 1999—. Fellow Am. Acad. Matrimonial Lawyers Conn. (bd. mgrs., Disting. Svc. award 1988), Internat. Acad. Matrimonial Lawyers, Am. Bar Found.; mem. ABA (chmn. family law sect. 1982-83), Conn. Bar Assn. (chmn. family law sect. 1971-74), Conn. Bus. and Industry Assn. (bd. dirs. 1993-98), S.W. Conn. Bus. and Industry Assn. (bd. dirs. 1990-97), Pub. Defenders Assn. (chmn.), Wee Burn Country Club (Darien, Conn., asst. sec.), Yale Club (N.Y.C.), Phi Beta Kappa. Avocation: tennis, platform tennis. Family and matrimonial. Home: 231 Old Kings Hwy S Darien CT 06820-5931 Office: Schoonmaker George & Colin PC PO Box 5059 5 Edgewood Ave Greenwich CT 06831-5059

**SCHOOR, MICHAEL MERCIER,** lawyer, lobbyist; b. Chgo., Feb. 24, 1942; s. Richard Carl and Ethel (Mercier) S.; m. JoLen Marty, Oct. 7, 1961; children: Mark, Marty, Gretchen, William. BA, U. N.Mex., 1969; JD, Georgetown U., 1972. Bar: N.Mex. 1972, D.C. 1973, U.S. Supreme Ct. 1975, U.S. Ct. Claims 1974, U.S. Dist. Ct. D.C. 1974, U.S. Ct. Appeals (10th cir.) 1974. Legis. asst. ADA, Washington, 1970-72; exec. U.S. C. of C., Washington, 1973-75; assoc. counsel U.S. Ho. of Reps., Washington, 1977; dir. legis. and govt. affairs Nat. Soc. Profl. Engrs., Washington, 1977-82; pres.

Schoor & Ptnrs., P.C., Washington and Dallas, 1982—; dir. Tex. Pub. Policy Found., Internat., Am. Assn. Clin. Nutritionists; chmn. bd. dirs. Clin. Nutritionists Cert. Bd., Renown Holding Co., Inc., various engring. firms. Counsel various polit. orgns.; coach youth soccer. Recipient Outstanding Svc. award N.Mex. Chiropractic Assn. 1975, Nat. Soc. Profl. Engrs., 1982. Mem. N.Mex. Bar Assn., D.C. Bar Assn. Republican. Roman Catholic. Legislative, Private international, Administrative and regulatory.

**SCHOPPMANN, MICHAEL JOSEPH,** lawyer; b. N.Y.C., May 17, 1960; s. Fred Richard and Dorothy Ann (Wood) S.; m. Marlene Elizabeth Macbeth, Nov. 21, 1987; children: Michael, Steven. BS, St. John's U., 1982; JD, Seton Hall U., 1985. Bar: N.J. 1985, U.S. Dist. Ct. N.J. 1986, U.S. Supreme Ct. 1992, D.C. 1993, N.Y. 1994. Assoc. Baker Garber Duffy & Baker, Hoboken, N.J., 1985-87; counsel Johnstone Skok Loughlin & Lane, Westfield, N.J., 1987-90; prin. Kern Augustine Conroy & Schoppmann, Bridgewater, N.J., 1990—. Author, editor: (text) Basic Health Law, 1993; author: New Legal Threats in Managed Care, New Criminals for the Millenium?. Mem. ATLA, N.J. Bar Assn. (chmn. adminstrv. law sect. 1994-98), N.Y. State Bar Assn., D.C. Bar Assn., Somerset County Bar Assn. E-mail: www.drlaw.com., schoppmann@drlaw.com. Health, Administrative and regulatory. Office: Kern Augustine Conroy & Schoppmann 1120 Us Highway 22 Ste 8 Bridgewater NJ 08807-2972

**SCHOR, LAURENCE,** lawyer; b. Bklyn., May 3, 1942; s. Julius and Ruth (Zackowitz) S.; m. Susan Leslie Gurevitz, Dec. 26, 1965; children: Meredith Nan, Joseph Sanford, Wendy Claire, Samuel Julius. BBA, So. Meth. U., 1963; JD, U. Tex., 1966; LLM, George Washington U., 1972. Bar: Tex. 1966, D.C. 1970, Md. 1993.; U.S. Ct. Appeals (D.C., 4th, 5th, 11th cirs.). Atty. NASA, Huntsville, Ala., 1966-68; asst. gen. counsel NASA support U.S. Army C.E., Washington, 1968-70; assoc. Sellers, Connor & Cuneo, Washington, 1970-73; from assoc. to ptnr. Max E. Greenberg, Trayman, Cantor, Reiss & Blasky, Washington, 1974-80; ptnr. Schnader, Harrison, Segal & Lewis, Washington, 1981-91, ptnr.-in-charge, 1986-88; mem. Miller & Chevalier, Washington, 1991-93; ptnr. Smith, Somerville & Case, LLC, Washington, 1993-96, McManus, Schor, Asburn &Darden, LLP, Washington, 1997—; lectr. George Washington U., others. Author: The Right to Stop Work, 1991; (manual) Delays, Suspensions and Accelerations, Workplace Safety and Health in the 1990's, 1992, Claims Against Bonding Companys, Construction Contractors' Handbook of Business and Law, 1992; author, editor 50 State Lien and Bond Laws, 1993-99; contbr. chpt. Construction Law. Founder, pres. Manor Lake Civic Assn., Montgomery County, 1969-71; precinct chmn. Montgomery County Dems., 1972-76; mem. D.C. City Coun. Procurement Reform Task Force, 1995-96. Mem. ABA (chmn. region III pub. contracts sect., 1982-88, constrn. com. 1986-90, sect. budget and fin. 1990-95), D.C. Bar Assn. (chmn. divsn. 10 govt. contracts and litigation, 1981-85), Fed. Bar Assn., Am. Coll. Constrn. Lawyers (founder, bd. dirs., treas. 1996—), Phi Alpha Delta (pres. T.C. Clark chpt. 1965-66). Jewish. Avocations: reading, travel. Government contracts and claims, Federal civil litigation, Construction. Home: 7021 Mountain Gate Dr Bethesda MD 20817-3913 Office: McManus Schor Asmar & Darden LLP 1301 Connecticut Ave NW Fl 6 Washington DC 20036-1815

**SCHOR, SUZI,** lawyer, psychologist; b. Chgo., Feb. 1, 1947; d. Samuel S. and Dorothy Helen (Hineline); 1 child, Kate. BSBA, Ind. U., 1964; MBA Mktg., Northwestern U., 1967, JD, 1970; PhD in Fine Arts (hon.), U. Nev., PhD in Clin. Psychology, 1989. Bar: Ill., 1971. Pvt. practice L.A., 1971-80; v.p. legal affairs Little Gypzy Mgmt., Inc., Beverly Hills, Calif., 1980—; mem. Pres.'s Coun. on Alcoholism. Author: 13th Step to Death, 1995; contbg. author Wine and Dine Mag.; contbr. articles to profl. jours. Bd. dirs. Nat. Ctr. for Hyperactive Children, L.A., 1989-91, sec. Rainbow Guild Cancer Charity, L.A., 1985-89, ind. cons. Jewish Legal Aid, L.A., 1988—; campaign coord. advisor Dem. Nat. Campaign, L.A., 1990, 94; donor mem. L.A. Coun. on World Affairs. Recipient Poet of Yr. award Nat. Libr. and Assn. of Poetry, 1995, 98. Mem. ABA (criminal justice com. 1994), AAUW, NAADAC, CAADAC, L.A. Breakfast Club (chmn. entertainment 1988-90), Rotary, Mensa. Jewish. Avocations: singing, skiing, writing. Entertainment, Criminal, General civil litigation.

**SCHORLING, WILLIAM HARRISON,** lawyer; b. Ann Arbor, Mich., Jan. 7, 1949; s. Otis William Schorling and Ruthann (Bales) Schorling Moorehead; m. Lynne Ann Newcomb, June 1, 1974; children: Katherine Pearce, Ann Oury, John Roberts. BA cum laude, Denison U., 1971; JD cum laude, U. Mich., 1975. Bar: Pa. 1975, U.S. Ct. Appeals (3d cir.) 1977, N.J., 1998. Ptnr. Eckert, Seamans, Cherin & Mellott, Pitts., 1984-89, Klett Lieber Rooney & Schorling, P.C., Pitts., 1989—; lectr. Pa. Bar Inst., Harrisburg, 1983—, Comml. Law League, N.Y.C., 1984—, Profl. Edn. Systems, Inc., Eau Claire, Wis., 1986—, Southwest Legal Found., Dallas, 1994—; founders' coun. Comml. Fin. Assn. Edn. Found., 1991—; bd. dirs. Consumer Bankruptcy Assistance Project, 1995—. Contbr. articles to profl. jours. Trustee Pa. Acad. Fine Arts. Fellow Am. Coll. Bankruptcy, Am. Bar Found.; mem. ABA (chmn. bus. bankruptcy com., lectr. 1988—), Am. Banker Inst. (lectr. 1994—), Phila. Bar Assn. (lectr. 1996—), E. Dist. Bankruptcy Conf., Pa. Bar Assn. (lectr. 1983—), Allegheny County Bar Assn. (chmn. bankruptcy and comml. law sect. 1991), The Com. of Seventy (vice chair), Longue Vue Club, Duquesne Club, Pyramid Club, Pa. Soc., Bedens Brook Club. Presbyterian. Bankruptcy, Contracts commercial. Home: 12 Scudder Ct Pennington NJ 08534-2325 Office: Klett Lieber Rooney & Schorling 2 Logan Sq Fl 12 Philadelphia PA 19103-2707

**SCHORR, BRIAN LEWIS,** lawyer, business executive; b. N.Y.C., Oct. 5, 1958; s. Philip I. and Hannah Schorr; m. Amy B. Horowitz, Aug. 19, 1984; 2 children. BA magna cum laude, MA, Wesleyan U., Middletown, Conn., 1979; JD, NYU, 1982. Bar: N.Y. 1983, D.C. 1985, U.S. Supreme Ct. 1988. Assoc. Paul, Weiss, Rifkind, Wharton & Garrison, N.Y.C., 1982-90, ptnr., 1991-94; exec. v.p., gen. counsel Triarc Cos., Inc., N.Y.C., 1994—; mem. bd. advisors Jour. Ltd. Liability Cos., 1994-98; lectr. CLE programs. Author: Schorr on New York Limited Liability Companies and Partnerships, 1994; contbr. articles to legal jours. Vice pres. Bronx (N.Y.) H.S. Sci. Endowment Fund, Inc. Mem. ABA, N.Y. State Bar Assn., Assn. Bar City N.Y. (chmn. com. on corp. law 1993-96, co-chmn. joint drafting com. N.Y. ltd. liability co. law), Tri Bar Opinion Com., Bronx H.S. Sci. Alumni Assn. (trustee). General corporate, Mergers and acquisitions, Finance. Office: Triarc Cos Inc 280 Park Ave New York NY 10017-1216

**SCHOTT, CLIFFORD JOSEPH,** lawyer; b. Newark, N.J., July 28, 1926; s. Clifford J. and Sally V. (Donnelly) S.; m. Nancybelle MacDonnell, July 22, 1951; children: Christylee, Clifford, Sally, Steven, Craig. Student, Upsala U., 1949-51; grad., U. Miami, 1952, JD, 1954. Bar: Fla. 1955, U.S. Dist. Ct. (so. dist.) Fla. 1956, U.S. Ct. Appeals (5th cir.) 1959, U.S. Ct. Appeals (11th cir.) 1981, U.S. Tax Ct. 1973, Fla. RR and Pub. Utilities Commn. 1963, U.S. Supreme Ct. 1968. Assoc. Holladay & Swann, Miami, Fla., 1955-56; ptnr. Hastings, Thomas & Sheppard, Miami, 1956-57; asst. gen. counsel Dade County Port Auth., Miami, 1957-60; atty., negotiator Eastern Airlines, Inc., Miami, 1960-63; assoc. Carver, Langston & Massey, Lakeland, Fla., 1963-66; ptnr. Wendel & Schott, Lakeland, 1966-68; pvt. practice Lakeland, 1968-83; sr. ptnr. Schott & Dale, P.A., Lakeland, 1983-89; pvt. practice Lakeland, Fla., 1989—; mcpl. judge City of Lakeland, 1967-68; asst. county solicitor County of Polk, Bartow, Fla., 1967-69. Pres., Polk County Assn. Retarded Children, Lakeland, 1966-67, com. chmn., 1967; counsel Ch. of the Resurrection, Lakeland; bd. dirs. St. Joseph's Sch., Lakeland, 1973. With USAAF, 1944-46, ETO. Mem. ABA, ATLA, Fla. Bar Assn., Lakeland Bar Assn., Polk County Trial Lawyers Assn. (adv. com. 1983—), Fla. Def. Lawyers Assn. (bd. dirs. 1985—), 10th Judicial Cir. Bar, Lakeland C. of C. (aviation adv. com.), Am. Legion (judge adv. 1978), Rotary (pres. 1969-70), KC (dep. grand knight 1973), Phi Alpha Delta. Republican. Roman Catholic. Avocations: tennis, fishing, squash, travel, reading. Federal civil litigation, General civil litigation, Personal injury. Home: 111 Florida Shores Blvd Daytona Beach Shores FL 32118-5629 Office: 908 S Florida Ave Lakeland FL 33803-1177

**SCHOWALTER, DEBORAH,** arbitrator, mediator; b. Milw., Feb. 12, 1948; d. Gilbert T. and Valerie H. (Krapfel-Kann) S. BA with honors, San Diego State U., 1970; postgrad., UCLA, 1972; JD, U. San Diego, 1975. Bar: Calif. 1975, U.S. Dist. Ct. (so. dist.) Calif. 1975. Pvt. practice San Diego, 1975-81; commr. L.A. Superior Ct., 1981-84; adj. prof. U. Md., Rimini, Italy, 1984-87; interpreter/housing officer USAF, Rimini, 1986-87; chief purchasing and contracting U.S. Army SETAF, Vicenza, Italy, 1992; spl. prof. John Marshall Law Sch., Atlanta, 1995-97; dispute resolver, pres. Problem Solvers, Atlanta and San Diego, 1995—; adj. prof. U. San Diego Sch. Law, 1979-80; journalist, photographer, artist, 1988—; lectr. in field. Contbr. articles to profl. publs. Elected ofcl. Organized Nieghbors of Edgewood, Atlanta, 1997-98; bd. dirs. Mid-City Cmty. Clinic, San Diego, 1979-81. NEH fellow. Mem. Club Boccacio (Italian). Avocations: photography, painting, French horn, gardening, remodelling houses. Office: Problem Solvers 215 Marion Pl NE Atlanta GA 30307-2729 Also: 1218 W Thorn St San Diego CA 92103-5334

**SCHRADER, ALFRED EUGENE,** lawyer; b. Nov. 1, 1953; s. Louis Clement and Helen Mae (Eberz) S.; m. Debra Susanne Britt-Garrett, Aug. 12, 1997. BA in Polit. Sci. magna cum laude, Kent State U., 1975; JD, Ohio State U., 1978. Bar: Ohio 1978, U.S. Dist. Ct. (no. dist.) Ohio 1978, U.S. Ct. Appeals (6th cir.) 1985, U.S. Supreme Ct. 1985. Dep. clk. Summit County Clk. of Cts., Akron, 1972-74; pvt. practice law Akron, 1978—; spl. counsel Bath Twp., Ohio, 1980-92, 95-98; spkr. Akron Bar Assn. Akron Univ. Sch. CLE Seminars. Trustee Springfield Twp., Ohio, 1973—, pres., 1975, 79, 82, 88, 90, 95-96; v.p. Springfield-Akron Joint Econ. Devel. Dist., 1995-97, pres., 1997—; mem. adv. com. Cmty. Devel. Block, Summit County, 1985-97, Twinsburg Twp. tax abatement counsel, 1994—, Summit County Annexation Com., 1981-85; mem. Summit County Jail Study Commn., 1983, 84; mem. adv. bd. Springfield Schs., 1975; acting law dir. City of Streetsboro, Portage County, Ohio, 1997. Mem. ATLA, Akron Bar Assn. (v.p. legis. com. 1981-82, v.p. local govt. sect. 1992-93, chair local govt. sect. 1993-95), Ohio Acad. Trial Lawyers, Ohio Bar Assn., Summit County Twp. Assn. (exec. com. 1983—), Ohio Twp. Assn., Risk Mgmt. Authority (bd. dirs. 1996—, sec. 1997—), Nat. Assn. Town and Twp. Attys. (bd. dirs. Ohio chpt. 1986, sec. 1987-93, v.p. 1993-97). Democrat. Roman Catholic. Fax: 330 762 2255. Fax: 330 762 2255. Personal injury, Land use and zoning (including planning), Municipal (including bonds). Home: 3344 Brunk Rd Akron OH 44312-3710 Office: Schrader Romanoski and Grant 441 Wolf Ledges Pkwy Ste 400 Akron OH 44311-1039

**SCHRADER, ROBERT GEORGE,** lawyer; b. White Plains, N.Y., Apr. 28, 1961; s. George Louis and Florence Rose (Smith) S.; m. Virginia Alexander Kurtz, Apr. 20, 1991; children: Robert George, Jr., De Grasse Alexandra. BA in Microbiology, Fla. Atlantic U., 1983; diploma, U. San Diego Paris Inst. for Comparative Law, 1986; JD cum laude, Nova U., 1987. Bar: Fla. 1987, U.S. Dist. Ct. (so. dist.) Fla. 1987, U.S. Ct. Intrenat. Trade 1988. Jud. intern to honorable Norman C. Roettger Jr. U.S. Dist. Ct. (so. dist.) Fla., Ft. Lauderdale, 1986; assoc. Sandler, Travis & Rosenberg, P.A., Miami, Fla., 1987-92; ptnr. Schrader & Zhang, P.A., North Miami, Fla., 1992-94, Sandler, Travis & Rosenberg P.A., 1994-95; of counsel Ruden, McClosky, Smith, Schuster & Russel, P.A., 1995-99; adjunct prof. Fla. Internat. U., 1994—; of counsel Robert G. Schrader, P.A., 1999—; pres. L'Auberge, Inc., 1999—; adj. prof. law internat. trade regulation Nova Southeastern U. Law Sch., 1997—; pres. L'Auberge, Inc. Editor jour. Customs and Trade Update, 1988-95; editor newsletter N.B.W.C.A., 1988-95; monthly columnist Internat. and Customs Law, Fla. Shipper Mag.; contbr. articles to profl. jours.; panel mem. TV program Immigration and Beyond, 1992. Mem. Bus. Vols. for the Arts, Miami, 1990-93; vol. of yr., mem. adv. bd. Camillus House, Miami, 1991-95; bd. dirs., legal counsel Inner City Childrens Dance Co., Miami, 1991-92; com. person Broward Rep. Exec. Com. Recipient UP and Comer award Price Waterhouse/South Fla. Mag., 1994; Fla. Atlantic U. faculty scholar, 1983, Goodwin scholar, 1984-86. Episcopalian. Avocations: gourmet chef, Shaolin kung fu, cycling, scuba diving, gardening. Private international, Immigration, naturalization, and customs. Office: Ruden McClosky 200 E Broward Blvd Fort Lauderdale FL 33301-1963

**SCHRAMM, PAUL HOWARD,** lawyer; b. St. Louis, Oct. 6, 1933; s. Benjamin Jacob and Frieda Sylvia (Goruch) S.; m. Sue-Ann Batson; children: Scott Lyon, Dean Andrew, Thomas Edward, Jeremy Arthur Savran. AB, U. Mo., 1955, JD, 1958. Bar: Mo. 1958, U.S. Dist. Ct. (ea. dist.) Mo. 1963, U.S. Ct. Appeals (8th cir.) 1967, U.S. Tax Ct. 1970, U.S. Supreme Ct. 1972, U.S. Dist. Ct. (ea. dist.) Wis., 1988. Ptnr. Schramm & Schramm, St. Louis, 1959-61, Schramm & Morganstern, St. Louis, 1970-76, Schramm, Pines & Marshall, St. Louis, 1977-79, Schramm, Newman, Pines & Freyman, St. Louis, 1979-82, Schramm, Pines & Spewak, St. Louis, 1983-85, Schramm & Pines, L.L.C., St. Louis, 1985—; pros. atty. City of Ellisville, Mo., 1973-77; judge Ellisville mcpl. div. St. Louis County Cir. Ct., 1977-83; teaching faculty trial advocacy Harvard Law Sch., 1991. Mem. Bar Assn. Met. St. Louis (exec. com. 1976-77, chmn. county sect. 1976-77), St. Louis County Bar Assn. (chmn. lawyers reference service 1971, cir. ct. jud. com. 1970), Phi Delta Phi. Club: University (St. Louis). Avocations: music, sports, reading. General civil litigation, General corporate, Family and matrimonial. Home: 7507 Byron Pl Saint Louis MO 63105-2703 Office: Schramm & Pines LLC 231 S Bemiston Ave Ste 950 Saint Louis MO 63105-1965

**SCHRAUFF, CHRISTOPHER WESLEY,** lawyer; b. Houston, July 18, 1968; m. Paula Leigh Barnes. BA, U. Tex., 1992, JD, 1996. Bar: Tex. 1996. V.p., counsel FIC Ins. Group, Austin, Tex., 1996—. Avocation: guitar. Real property, General corporate, Insurance. Office: FIC Ins Group 701 Brazos St Ste 1400 Austin TX 78701-3232

**SCHRECK, ROBERT J.,** lawyer; b. Buffalo, Jan. 5, 1956; s. Frank Joseph and Rachel Ann (Catalano) S.; m. Pamela Sheehan, Aug. 13, 1983; children: Robert F., Michael F. BA, SUNY at Buffalo, 1977, JD, 1981. Bar: N.Y. State 1982, U.S. Dist. Ct. (we. dist.) N.Y. 1982, U.S. Supreme Ct. 1987. Asst. dist. atty. Erie County Dist. Atty.'s Office, Buffalo, 1981-84; ptnr. Mattar & D'Agostino, Buffalo, 1984—; lectr. Better Bus. Bur., Buffalo, 1986—; chmn. rev. com. Erie County Assigned Coun., Buffalo, 1995—. Committeeman Erie County Rep. com., Buffalo, 1989—; vice chmn. Erie County Coordinating Coun. on Children & Families, Buffalo, 1991-94; dir. Am. Heart Assn., Western N.Y., 1996—, St. Joseph's Collegiate Instn., Buffalo, 1997, Buffalo Diocese Vicariate, Western N.Y., 1997; councilman St. Benedict's Cath. Ch. Parish Counsel, Buffalo, 1996—; coach Ctrl. Amherst (N.Y.) Little League, 1996—; pres. Ronald McDonald House, Buffalo, 1997-98. Recipient Connelly Trial Technique award U. Buffalo, 1981. Mem. ABA, N.Y. State Bar Assn., Erie County Bar Assn., Judges & Police Execs. Conf. of Erie County, Nat. Assn. of Watch and Clock Collectors, Brookfield Country Club, West Side Rowing Club, Western N.Y. Cert. Football Ofcls. Assn. (parliamentarian 1989—). Republican. Roman Catholic. Avocation: high sch. football ofcl. Libel, Criminal, Family and matrimonial. Home: 105 Audubon Dr Snyder NY 14226-4078 Office: Mattar & D'Agostino 17 Court St Ste 600 Buffalo NY 14202-3294

**SCHRECKENGAST, WILLIAM OWEN,** lawyer; b. Greenwood, Ind., Oct. 14, 1926; s. Vernon Edward and Marthena O. (Mullinix) S.; m. Helen Margaret Sheppard, Nov. 11, 1949 (div.); children: Pamela, Sandra, James, John; m. Virginia Thompson, Mar. 14, 1990. LLB, Ind. U., 1956. Bar: Ind. 1956, U.S. Ct. Appeals (7th cir.) 1956, U.S. Dist. Ct. (so. dist.) Ind. 1956, U.S. Supreme Ct. 1967. Ptnr. Kitley, Pontius & Schreckengast, Beech Grove, Ind., 1957-59, Kitley & Schreckengast, Beech Grove, 1959-63, 78-82, Kitley, Schreckengast & Davis, Beech Grove, 1963-78, Schreckengast & Lovern, Indpls., 1982-88, Schreckengast Lovern & Helm, Indpls., 1988—. Chmn. Ind. campaign John Walsh for Sec. of State, Indls., 1958; chmn. ward Beech Grove Dems., 1958-60. Served to 1st sgt. U.S. Army, 1944-46, PTO. Mem. ABA, Ind. Bar Assn. (bd. mgrs. 1973-74, pres. citation 1974, pres. trial lawyer sect. 1977-78), Ind. Def. Lawyers Assn. (diplomat), Am. Judicature Soc., Nat. Inst. Trial Advocacy (teaching faculty 1980-85), Platform Soc. Republican. Club: Hillview Country (Franklin, Ind.). Lodge: Masons. Avocations: golf, flying. State civil litigation, Insurance, Personal injury. Home: 8026 Singleton St Indianapolis IN 46227-2568 Office: Schreckengast Lovern & Helm 8007 S Meridian St Ste 1 Indianapolis IN 46217-2901

**SCHREFFLER, NEIL FRANKLIN,** lawyer; b. Danville, Pa., June 24, 1947; s. Franklin Harold and Lera Emma (Sheddy) S.; children: Elizabeth Ann Dollinger, Sept. 12, 1992; children: Gabrielle Freia, Franklin Henry. BBA, The Coll. of Ins., N.Y.C., 1970; JD, Syracuse U., 1973. Bar: N.Y. 1974, U.S. Dist. Ct. (ea. and so. dists.) N.Y. 1975, U.S. Dist. Ct. (no. dist.) 1992. Atty. Mony, N.Y.C., 1973-74; assoc. Lanzone & Assocs., N.Y.C., 1974-77, Lester Schwab Katz & Dwyer, N.Y.C., 1977, Lipsig Sullivan & Liapakis, N.Y.C., 1977-79, Fuchsberg & Fuchsberg, N.Y.C., 1979-81; pvt. practice N.Y.C., 1981-88; ptnr. Schreffler & Gitlin, N.Y.C., 1988—; advocate Nat. Coll. Advocacy, Washington, 1996—; mem. Million Dollar Advocates Forum, 1995—; sec. Small Law Firm Mgmt. Com.-City Bar, N.Y.C., 1996—. Assoc. editor: Syracuse Law Rev., 1972. Mem. ATLA (sustaining, mem. M Club 1996—, sec. small office practice sect., editor sect. newsletter, mem. ATLA-PAC task force, mem. pub. edn. com.), Nat. Employment Lawyers Assn., N.Y. State Trial Lawyers Assn. (dir., sustaining mem. 1997—, membership com.), N.Y. County Lawyers Assn. (Supreme Ct. com., labor rels. and employment law com.), Rockland County Bar Assn., Trial Lawyers for Pub. Justice, N.Y. Athletic Club (sec. law com. 1995-97). Democrat. Avocations: opera, tennis, fly fishing, skiing. Personal injury, Labor. Home: 35 Rome Ave Apt 1B Bedford Hills NY 10507-2342 Office: Schreffler & Gitlin 67 Broad St New York NY 10004-2415

**SCHREIBER, ALAN HICKMAN,** lawyer; b. Muncie, Ind., Apr. 4, 1944; s. Ephriam and Clarrisa (Hickman) S.; m. Phyllis Jean Chamberlain, Dec. 22, 1972; children—Jennifer Aline, Brett Justin. Student DePauw U., 1962-64; B.S. in Bus., Ind. U., 1966, J.D., 1969. Bar: Fla. 1971, U.S. Dist. Ct. (so. dist.) Fla. Asst., State Atty.'s Office, Ft. Lauderdale, Fla., 1971-76; pub. defender 17th Jud. Circuit, Ft. Lauderdale, 1976—; cons. Fla. Bar News on Criminal Law, 1982; lobbyist for indigent funding, Fla., 1980—; apptd. to Supreme Ct. Com. on Racial and Ethic Bias; co-chair Chiles-MacKay task force on criminal justice. Contbr. articles to profl. jours. Mem. Dem. Exec. Com., Ft. Lauderdale, 1980; mem. Plantation Dem. Club, 1983; campaign chmn. Goldstein for Atty. Gen. Fla., 1982. Named Young Dem. of Yr., Broward County Young Dems., 1980; Man of Yr., Jewish War Vets., 1982; recipient B'nai B'rith Pub. Servant award, 1990. Mem. Fla. Bar Assn., Broward County Bar Assn., ABA, Nat. Legal Aid Defenders Assn., Phi Alpha Delta. Criminal. Home: 885 Orchid Dr Fort Lauderdale FL 33317-1221 Office: 201 SE 6th St Fort Lauderdale FL 33301-3303

**SCHREIBER, CHARLES JOSEPH, JR.,** lawyer; b. Sacramento, Jan. 22, 1959; s. Charles Joseph Schreiber and Carol Anne Brotz. BA, U. Fla., 1981, MA, 1983, JD, 1988. Bar: Fla. 1990, U.S. Dist. Ct. (no., mid. and so. dists.) Fla., U.S. Dist. Ct. (we. dist.) Tex., 11th Cir. Ct. Appeals, 5th Cir. Ct. Appeals, U.S. Supreme Ct. Sr. jud. rsch. assoc. 1st dist. 1st. Dist. Ct. Appeal, Tallahassee, Fla., 1989-91; assoc. Smith, Hulsey & Busey, Jacksonville, Fla., 1991-93, Bateman & Graham, P.A., Tallahassee, 1993-97; assoc. Bateman & Harden, Tallahassee, 1997-98, ptnr., 1998; contract ptnr. Foley & Lardner, Tallahassee, 1998—; dir. Jacksonville Area Legal Aid, Inc., 1992-93. Active Tallahassee 25, 1997-98, 2d Harvest Food Bank, 1998; mem. Leadership Tallahassee Class XVII. Mem. ABA, Fed. Bar Assn. E-mail: cschreiber@foleylaw.com. Federal civil litigation, General civil litigation, State civil litigation. Office: Foley & Lardner 300 E Park Ave Tallahassee FL 32301-1514

**SCHREIBER, JEFFREY,** lawyer; b. Newark, Feb. 15, 1966; s. Melvin Samuel and Rita S.; m. Marsha Shluker, May 6, 1991; children: Leora L., Aviva M., Miriam A. BS cum laude, Yeshiva U., 1987; JD, NYU, 1990. Bar: N.J. 1990, U.S. Dist. Ct. N.J. 1990, N.Y. 1991, U.S. Dist. Ct. N.Y. 1991, U.S. Cir. Ct. (2d cir.) 1994. Assoc. Fried, Frank et al, N.Y.C., 1990-98; pvt. practice N.Y.C. and Brunswick, N.J., 1998—. Mem. Am. Bar Assn., N.Y. State Bar Assn., N.J. State Bar Assn. General civil litigation. Office: 2 G Aver Ct East Brunswick NJ 08816

**SCHREIBER, JOHN T.,** lawyer; b. N.Y.C., Mar. 30, 1960; s. Toby Schreiber and Morley Ann (Perrish) Clark; m. Theresa Ann Sawyer, Aug. 11, 1984; children: Zoe Cassandra Bloch Schreiber, Alana Nichole Perrish Schreiber. BA Politics, Brandeis U., 1982; JD, Santa Clara U., 1986. Bar: Calif. 1987, U.S. Dist. Ct. (no. dist.) Calif. 1987, U.S. Dist. Ct. (ea. dist.) Calif. 1990, U.S. Ct. Appeals (9th cir.) 1989. Assoc. Law Offices of Wm. D. McHugh, San Jose, Calif., 1987-88, Hallgrimson, McNichols, McCann & Inderbitzen, Pleasanton, Calif., 1989-92; pvt. practice Walnut Creek, Calif., 1993—; bd. dirs. East Bay Depot for Creative Re-use, Oakland. Field coord. Cen. Contra Costa County, Tom Bradley Campaign for Govs., Concord, Calif., 1982, Clinton-Gore Campaign, Walnut Creek, Calif., 1992; mem. Ask-A-Lawyer Program Contra Costa Legal Svcs. Found., Richmond, Calif., 1992—; co-chair Clinton-Gore Contra Costa County, 1996. Mem. ABA, Contra Costa Bar Assn. (program dir. appellate sect. 1993-95, pres. appellate sect. 1995-96), MCLE com. 1995—), Bar Assn. San Francisco (appellate sect. 1993—), Santa Clara Bar Assn., Am. Israeli Polit. Action Com. Avocations: reading, golf, softball, movies, exercising. General civil litigation. Office: 961 Ygnacio Valley Rd Walnut Creek CA 94596-3825

**SCHREIBER, KURT GILBERT,** lawyer; b. Milw., Aug. 22, 1946; s. Raymond R. and Mildred L. (Kleist) S.; m. Nelda Beth Van Buren, May 3, 1974; children—Katharine Anne, Matthew Edward. A.B. in Econs., Cornell U., 1968; J.D., U. Mich., 1971. Bar: Wis. 1971, Tex. 1979, Tenn. 1997. Internat. atty. Tenneco Internat. Holdings Co., London, 1974-78; atty. Tenneco Inc., Houston, 1978-80; 2d v.p., asst. gen. counsel Am. Gen. Corp., Houston, 1980-83, v.p., gen. counsel, 1983-84, sr. v.p., gen. counsel, 1984-93, sr. v.p., corp. sec., 1993-94; pvt. practice Houston, 1994-96; exec. v.p., gen. counsel Direct Gen. Corp., Nashville, 1996-98, pres., 1998—. Fellow Tex. Bar Found.; mem. ABA, Wis. Bar Assn., Tex. Bar Assn., Tenn. Bar Assn., Cumberland Club. General corporate, Private international. Home: 524 Turtle Creek Dr Brentwood TN 37027-5617

**SCHREIBER, SIDNEY M.,** retired state supreme court justice; b. N.Y.C., Nov. 18, 1914; s. Nathan and Estelle (Goldstein) S.; m. Ruth Burr, Dec. 22, 1940; 1 child, Florence. BA summa cum laude, Yale U., 1936, LLB, 1939. Bar: N.J. 1940, U.S. Dist. Ct. N.J. 1940, U.S. Dist. Ct. D.C. 1939, U.S. Ct. Appeals D.C. 1939. Atty. U.S. R.R. Retirement Bd., Washington, 1940, SEC, Phila.; ptnr., atty. McKeown & Schreiber, Newark, Scheiber, Lancaster & Demos, Newark; judge Superior Ct., State of N.J., Jersey City and Elizabeth, 1972-75; assoc. jsutice Supreme Ct., State of N.J., Newark and Trenton, 1975-84; of counsel Riker, Danzig, Scherer, Hyland & Perretti LLP, Morristown, N.J., 1984—. Editor Yale Law Jour., 1938-39; Contbr. articles to legal jours. Mem. Union County (N.J.) Park Commn. 1st lt. Army of U.S. Recipient William J. Brennan award Fed. Bar Assn. N.J., 1984; named Man of Yr., Anti-Defamation League, 1998. Mem. ABA, Union County Bar Assn., Phi Beta Kappa. Office: Riker Danzig et al One Speedwell Ave Morristown NJ 07962

**SCHREIER, KAREN ELIZABETH,** prosecutor. U.S. atty. U.S. Dept. Justice, Sioux Falls, S.D., 1993—. Office: US Attys Office 230 Phillips Ave Sioux Falls SD 57104

**SCHRIER-POLAK, CAROL,** lawyer. BA, Brandeis U., 1967; postgrad., Wayne State U., 1967-68; MSW, SUNY, Buffalo, 1969; JD, Temple U., 1977. Bar: Va. 1983, Pa. 1977. Assoc. planner rsch. and planning divsn. Cmty. Coun. Atlanta, 1969-72, project coord. child care planning project, 1972-73; exec. dir. Coun. for Children, Inc., Atlanta, 1972-74, Support Ctr. for Child Advocates Inc., Phila., 1977-83; legal cons. ABA/Nat. Resource Ctr. for Child Advocacy and Protection, Washington, 1983-84; sole practitioner Alexandria, Va., 1984-88; ptnr. Bean, Kinney & Korman, P.C., Arlington, Va., 1988—, 1990; presenter in field; mediator, 1994—; faculty Va. State Bar; mem. child support quadrenneal rev. panel Commonwealth of Va. Co-editor: Making Financial Decisions when Divorce Occurs: A Virginia Guide, 1993; editor legal manuals; contbr. articles to profl. jours. Bd. dirs. Legal Svcs. No. Va., 1991-97; bd. dirs. Mental Health Assn. No. Va., 1989-92. Fellow Am. Acad. Matrimonial Lawyers; mem. ABA, D.C. Bar Assn., Va. Bar Assn., Fairfax Bar Assn. (bd. dirs. 1993—, sec. 1995-96, pres. 1997-98). Office: Bean Kinney & Korman 2000 14th St N Ste 100 Arlington VA 22201-2552

**SCHRIMP, ROGER MARTIN,** lawyer; b. Stockton, Calif., May 26, 1941; s. Clarence and Mary Helen (Martin) S; m. Delsie Louise Canapa, July 7, 1963; children: Angela and Christine. AA with honors, Stockton C.C., 1961; AB with honors, U. Calif., Berkeley, 1963, JD, 1966; LLM, U. Pacific, 1982. Bar: Calif. 1966, U.S. Dist. Ct. (no., ctrl., and ea. dist.) Calif. 1967, U.S. Tax Ct. 1978, U.S. Supreme Ct. 1978, U.S. Claims Ct. 1981. Ptnr. Law Offices of Stockton & Schrimp, Modesto, Calif., 1966-86; private practice Law Offices of Roger M. Schrimp, Modesto, 1986-90; ptnr. Law Offices of Damrell, Nelson, Schrimp, Pallios & Ladine, Modesto, 1990—; bd. gov.s Calif. C.C., pres., chmn. econ. Devel. and vocat. edn. com., 1996—; founder, chmn. bd. Oak Valley Cmty. Bank, Oakdale, Calif. 1991—; chair Joint Adv. com. Vocational Edn., Calif. Bd. Edn.; mem. Calif. State U. Joint Standing com. Yosemite area council bd. Boy Scouts Am., 1967—, nat. council, 1986-93, council pres., 1986-87, exec. bd. mem., 1967—, western region bd. mem., 1990-98, area III v.p., 1990-95, area III pres. 1995—, western region exec. bd. 1995—; exec. com. Oak Valley Dist. Cmty. Hosp. Found., 1976-94, bd. trustees, 1970-94; chmn. Oakdale Airport Commn., 1974-88, commn. mem. 1970-88; bd. trustees Oakdale Elem. Sch. Dist., 1972-80; bd. dir. Am. Cancer Soc., Stanislaus/Tuolumne Br., 1967-80, pres., 1970-71; vice-chmn. culture commn. City of Modesto, 1989-93, mem., 1986-93; mem. Calif. Postsecondary Edn. Commn. (western region v.p. finance 1998—). Mem. ABA (com. agr., taxation section), State Bar Calif., Assn. Trial Lawyers Am., Calif. Trial Lawyers Assn., Stanislaus County Bar Assn. (pres. 1993-94), Am. Judicature Soc., Northern Calif. Assn. Def. Counsel, Def. Rsch. Inst., Lawyers-Pilot Assn., Oakdale Rotary Club (pres. 1980-81), Medesto Lions "500" Club (pres. 1973-74), Rancheros Visitadores, El Viage de Portola, Oakdale Shrine Club (pres. 1975), Oakdale Dinner Club (pres. 1970-71), Calif. Cattlemen's Assn. (bd. dir. 1994-97), San Joaquin/Stanislaus Cattlemen's Assn., Knights Ferry Lodge #112, Morning Star Lodge #68, McHenry Mansion Found., McHenry Mus. Found., Modesto Shrine Club, Internat. Order St. Hubertus, Univ. Calif. Alumni, Million Doallar Advocates Forum, Univ. Calif. Berkeley Boalt Hall Alumni Assn. (bd. dir. 1994—), Airplane Owners and Pilots Assn., Oakdale Sportsmen's Club. Republican. State civil litigation, Taxation, general. Office: Damrell Nelson Schrimp Pallios & Ladine 1610 I St Fl 5 Modesto CA 95354-1122

**SCHRODER, JACK SPALDING, JR.,** lawyer; b. Atlanta, July 10, 1948; s. Jack Spalding Sr. and Van (Spalding) S.; m. Karen Keyworth, Sept. 1, 1973; children: Jack Spalding III, James Edward. BA, Emory U., 1970; JD, U. Ga., 1973. Bar: Ga. 1973, U.S. Dist. Ct. (no. dist.) Ga. 1973, U.S. Ct. Appeals (5th cir.) 1973, U.S. Ct. Appeals (11th cir.) 1982. Assoc. Alston & Bird, Atlanta, 1973-78, ptnr., 1978—. Author: Credentialing: Strategies for a Changing Environment/BNA's Health Law and Business Series, 1996; co-editor, contbg. author: Georgia Hospital Law manual, 1979, 84,92. Bd. dirs. Rsch. Atlanta, 1996—, pres., 1999; participant Leadership Ga., Atlanta, 1986. United Way (chmn. legal divsn.), Atlanta, 1980. Mem. ABA (vice chmn. medicine and law com. 1989-90), Am. Health Lawyers Assn. (bd. dirs. 1994-99, chmn. med. staff and physician rels. com. 1991-94), Ga. Acad. Healthcare Attys. (pres. 1981-82), State Bar Ga. (bd. govs. 1987-89), Atlanta Coun. Younger Lawyers (pres. 1977-78), Atlanta Bar Assn. (pres. 1982-83), Atlanta Bar Found. (pres. 1991-95). Health. Office: Alston & Bird 1 Atlantic Ctr 1201 W Peachtree St NW Atlanta GA 30309-3424

**SCHROEDER, DOUGLAS JAY,** lawyer; b. Detroit, Apr. 19, 1947; s. Oliver and Jean Schroeder; m. Stephanie Schroeder; children: Alex, Nicholas. BA in Bus., Mich. State U., 1971; JD, U. Detroit, 1975. Bar: Mich. 1975. Law clk. to Hon. Norman R. Barnard Oakland County Probate Ct., Pontiac, Mich., 1971-73; law clk. to Hon. Farrell E. Roberts Oakland County Cir. Ct., Pontiac, 1973-75; ptnr. Dean & Fulkerson, Troy, Mich., 1975-81, 81-87; atty. Gase, Williams & Schroeder, Troy, 1987—. Mem. South Oakland County Bar Assn., Troy Rotary Club (pres. 1985). Avocations: golf, sailing. General practice, Criminal, General civil litigation. Office: Gase Williams & Schroeder 292 Town Center Dr Troy MI 48084-1774

**SCHROEDER, EDWARD JAMES,** lawyer; b. Abilene, Tex., June 29, 1947; s. Edward and Alice (Dufour) S. BA, McMurry Coll., 1970; MA, Hardin-Simmons U., 1973; postgrad., U. Louvain, Belgium, 1973; JD, St. Mary's U., San Antonio, 1979. Bar: Tex. 1979, U.S. Dist. Ct. (no. dist.) Tex. 1980, U.S. Ct. Appeals (5th cir.) 1981, U.S. Dist. Ct. (we. dist.) Tex. 1981, U.S. Tax Ct. 1997. Assoc. Trueheart McMillan, San Antonio, 1979-80, Westbrook & Goldston, San Antonio, 1980-81; ptnr. Westbrook Schroeder, San Antonio, 1981-83; pvt. practice San Antonio, 1983—. Pres. Kidney Found., San Antonio, 1983-85. Mem. San Antonio Bar Assn., Club Giraud, Friends of the McNay. General civil litigation, General practice, Estate planning.

**SCHROEDER, ERIC PETER,** lawyer; b. Floral Park, N.Y., July 20, 1970; s. Fredric G. and Linda M. Schroeder. BA, Duke U., 1992; JD, Vanderbilt U., 1996. Bar: Ga. 1997, U.S. Dist. Ct. (no. dist.) Ga. 1997, U.S. Ct. Appeals (11th cir.) 1998. Law clk. Hon. William C. O'Kelley, U.S. Dist. Ct. (no. dist.) Ga., Atlanta, 1996-97; atty. Powell, Goldstein, Frazer & Murphy, Atlanta, 1997—. Articles editor Vanderbilt Law Rev., 1995-96. Active Boys and Girls Club of Am., Atlanta, 1998; vol. Ga. Vol. Lawyers for the Arts, Atlanta, 1998; lawyer Anti-Defamation League, Atlanta, 1998. Mem. Atlanta Bar Assn., U.S. Copyright Soc., Order of Coif. Constitutional, Trademark and copyright, Libel. Home: 658 Park Dr NE Atlanta GA 30306-3614 Office: Powell Goldstein Frazer & Murphy 191 Peachtree St Atlanta GA 30303

**SCHROEDER, GERALD FRANK,** state supreme court justice; b. Boise, Idaho, Sept. 13, 1939; s. Frank Frederick and Josephine Ivy (Lucas) S.; m. Carole Ann McKenna, 1967; children: Karl Casteel, Erich Frank. BA magna cum laude, Coll. of Idaho (now Albertson Coll. of Idaho), 1961; JD, Harvard U., 1964. Bar: Idaho 1965. Assoc. Moffatt, Thomas, Barrett & Blanton, Boise, 1965-66; pvt. practice Boise, 1966-67; asst. U.S. atty. Dept. Justice, Boise, 1967-69; judge Ada County Probate Ct., Boise, 1969-71; magistrate State of Idaho, Boise, 1971-75; dist. judge U.S. Dist. Ct. (4th dist.) Idaho, 1975-95; justice Idaho Supreme Ct., 1995—; instr. Boise Bar Rev., 1973—; adj. faculty law Boise State U., 1986-95; former mem. Gov. Coun. on Crime and Delinquency. Author: Idaho Probate Procedure, 1971; (novel) Triangle of the Sons-Phenomena, 1983; contbr. chpt. to history text. Bd. dirs. Boise Philharm. Assn., 1978-81; adminstrv. and dist. judge 4th dist. State of Idaho, 1985-95. Toll fellow Nat. Coun. State Govt., 1990. Mem. Idaho Bar Assn., Boise Racquet and Swim Club (pres. bd. dirs. 1991-93).

**SCHROEDER, JAMES WHITE,** lawyer; b. Elmhurst, Ill., Apr. 19, 1936; s. Paul W. and Thelma C. (White) S.; m. Patricia N. Scott, Aug. 18, 1962; children: Scott W., Jamie C. BA, Princeton U., 1958; JD, Harvard U., 1964. Bar: Colo. 1964, U.S. Dist. Ct. Colo. 1964, U.S. Ct. Appeals (10th cir.) 1965, U.S. Supreme Ct. 1972, U.S. Dist. Ct. D.C. 1973, U.S. Ct. Appeals (D.C. cir.) 1974, U.S. Ct. Appeals (8th cir.) 1977, U.S. Ct. Appeals (3d cir.) 1981, U.S. Claims Ct. 1983, U.S. Ct. Appeals (fed. cir.) 1983. Ptnr., Moseley, Wells & Schroeder, Denver, 1965-72, Kaplan, Russin & Vecchi, Washington, 1973-92; counsel Whitman & Ransom, Washington, 1992-93; dep. under sec. USDA, 1993—; arbitrator Am. Arbitration Assn. Active Ams. for Democratic Action, Smithsonian Instn., Denver Symphony Orch., Denver Art Mus. Lt., USNR, 1958-64. Am. Field Service scholar, 1953; NROTC scholar, 1954. Mem. ABA, Fed. Bar Assn., Denver Bar Assn., Colo. Bar Assn., D.C. Bar Assn., Cap and Gown Club, Lincoln's Inn Club, City Club Denver (pres. 1972), Princeton Club Washington (pres. 1982-84). Democrat. Home: 4102 Lester Ct Alexandria VA 22311-1121

**SCHROEDER, LEILA OBIER,** retired law educator; b. Plaquemine, La., July 11, 1925; d. William Prentiss and Daisy Lavinia (Mays) Obier; divorced; 1 child, James Michael Cutshaw; m. Martin Charles Schroeder Jr., Sept. 19, 1969. BA, Newcomb Coll., 1946; MSW, La. State U., 1953, JD, 1965. Bar: La. 1965. Exec. dir. Evangeline Area Guidance Ctr. La. Dept. Hosps., Lafayette, 1955-57; dir. social services dept. East La. State Hosp. La. Dept. Hosps., Jackson, 1957-60; cons. psychiat. social work La. Dept. Hosps., Baton Rouge, 1960-61; research assoc. La. State U., Baton Rouge, 1965-68, asst. prof., 1968-73, assoc. prof., 1973-80, prof., 1980-96; ret., 1996. Author: The Legal Environment of Social Work, 1982, The Legal Environment of Social Work, 1995; contbr. articles to profl. jours. Fellow Am. Orthopsychiat. Assn.; mem. ABA, Nat. Assn. Social Workers, Acad. Cert. Social Workers, La. State Bar Assn., Baton Rouge Bar Assn. Home: 4336 Oxford Ave Baton Rouge LA 70808-4651

**SCHROEDER, MARY MURPHY,** federal judge; b. Boulder, Colo., Dec. 4, 1940; d. Richard and Theresa (Kahn) Murphy; m. Milton R. Schroeder, Oct. 15, 1965; children: Caroline Theresa, Katherine Emily. B.A., Swarthmore Coll., 1962; J.D., U. Chgo., 1965. Bar: Ill. 1966, D.C. 1966, Ariz. 1970. Trial atty. Dept. Justice, Washington, 1965-69; law clk. Hon. Jesse Udall, Ariz. Supreme Ct., 1970; mem. firm Lewis and Roca, Phoenix, 1971-75; judge Ariz. Ct. Appeals, Phoenix, 1975-79, U.S. Ct. Appeals (9th cir.), Phoenix, 1979—; vis. instr. Ariz. State U. Coll. Law, 1976, 77, 78. Contbr. articles to profl. jours. Mem. ABA, Nat. Assn. Women Judges (pres. 1998-99), Ariz. Bar Assn., Fed. Bar Assn., Am. Law Inst. (coun. mem.), Am. Judicature Soc., Nat. Assn. Women Judges (pres. 1998-99), Soroptimists. Office: US Ct Appeals 9th Cir 6421 Courthouse-Fed Bldg 230 N 1st Ave Phoenix AZ 85025-0230

**SCHROEDER, MARY PATRICIA,** lawyer; b. St. Louis, Feb. 16, 1951; d. Raymond Anthony and Mary Alice Bruntrager; m. Stanley Gerard Schroeder, Sept. 30, 1977; children: Mary Kathleen, David Alexander. BA, St. Louis U., 1973; JD, St. Mary's U. San Antonio, 1978. Bar: Mo. 1979, U.S. Dist. Ct. (ea. dist.) Mo. 1979, U.S. Ct. Appeals (8th cir.). Asst. cir. atty. Cir. Attys. Office, St. Louis, 1980-82; ptnr. Bruntrager & Billings, St. Louis, 1983—. Co-author: Mo. Trial Handbook, 1998. Coach Cath. Youth Coun., St. Louis, 1984—. Mem. Mo. Assn. Trial Attys. (legis. lobbying 1996—), Women Lawyers Assn. (chair fundraising 1995—), Lawyer's Assn. St. Louis (sustaining mem.). Avocations: golfing, tennis, reading. Appellate, Personal injury, Probate. Office: Bruntrager & Billings 1015 Locust St Ste 820 Saint Louis MO 63101-1323

**SCHROEDER, MATTHEW A.,** lawyer; b. Washington, Aug. 4, 1960; s. Anthony C. and Georgia R. S.; m. Jane Curtman, June 12, 1990; 2 children. BSBA, St. Louis U., 1983, JD cum laude, 1996. Bar: Mo., U.S. Dist. Ct. (ea. dist.) Mo. Ins. agt. Unin Ins., Union, Mo., 1983-88; acct. exec. McDonnell Ins., Inc., Memphis, 1988-93; assoc. Vincent & Hoven, Union, 1996-98; ptnr. Hansen Stierberger, Union, 1998—. St. Louis U. fellow, 1993-96. Mem. ABA, Met. St. Louis Bar Assn., Lions (dir. 1998—). Avocations: golf, fishing, camping, biking. General practice, Estate planning, Real property. Home: PO Box 84 Union MO 63084-0084 Office: PO Box 112 80 N Oak St Union MO 63084-1626

**SCHROEDER, MERRIE JO,** law librarian; b. Detroit, Dec. 4, 1950; d. Albert Elmer Warren and Betty Jane (Kyser) Warren-Smith; m. Patrick Paul McNally, June 15, 1974 (div. June 30, 1990); 1 child, Sean Paul; m. Theodore Robert Schroeder, Jan. 2, 1996. BA in Elem. Edn., Mich. State U., 1972; MA in Libr. Media, U. Colo., Denver, 1990. Elem. sch. tchr. Fraser (Mich.) Pub. Schs., 1972-75; circulation clk. Adams County (Colo.) Libr., 1975-76; sub. tchr. Jefferson County Sch. Dist., Lakewood, Colo., 1976-77; health scis. libr. tech. St. Anthony Hosps., Denver, 1977-84; tech. svcs. libr. Holland & Hart, Denver, 1984-88, mgr. libr. and file svc., 1988—; mem. adv. bd. West Pub. Co., Eagan, Minn., 1995—. Author: (chpt.) Winning with Computers, 1991. Recipient Excellence in Pvt. Law Librarianship award West Pub. Co., 1996. Mem. Am. Assn. Law Librs., Colo. Assn. Law Librs. (editor jour./newsletter 1992-95). Home: 2576 Vivian St Lakewood CO 80215-1059 Office: Holland and Hart 555 17th St Ste 2900 Denver CO 80202-3979

**SCHROEDER, MICHELE,** lawyer; b. Bklyn., Jan. 31, 1964; d. Angelo Dominic and Dolores Traboscia; m. Francis Xavier Schroeder, Sept. 21, 1996. BA in Environ. Studies, Binghamton U., 1986; JD, U. Vt., 1989. Bar: N.Y. 1990, Conn. 1990, U.S. Ct. Appeals (2d cir.), U.S. Dist. Ct. (ea. and so. dists.) N.Y. Assoc. Mott, Williams & Lee, Washington, 1989-91, Congdon & Flaherty, Garden City, N.Y., 1991-94; risk mgmt. exec. & environ. counsel Zurich Am. Ins. Co., N.Y.C., 1994—. Home: 55 Woodland Ave Rockville Centre NY 11570-6015 Office: Zurich Am Ins Co 1 Liberty Plz Fl 53D New York NY 10006-1404

**SCHROEDER, WILLIAM WAYNE,** lawyer; b. Appleton, Wis., Mar. 17, 1953; s. Donald Wayne and Mary Enneking S.; m. Wendy Hadwen, June 25, 1977; children: John Henry, Susan Hadwen. BA, Middlebury Coll., 1975; MBA, U. Calif., Berkeley, 1977; JD, Cornell U., 1980. Bar: Vt. 1981, U.S. Dist. Ct. Vt. 1981, Calif. 1983, U.S. Dist. Ct. (no. dist.) Calif. 1983, U.S. Tax Ct. 1987. Lawyer Downs, Rachlin & Martin, Burlington, Vt., 1981-83, 84—, Pillsbury Madison & Sutro, San Francisco, 1983-84; state chair Am. Coll. Mortgage Attys., 1995—. Chair Charlotte (Vt.) Planning Commn., 1995-96. Real property, Environmental, Corporate taxation. Office: Downs Rachlin & Martin PO Box 190 Burlington VT 05402-0190

**SCHROER, GENE ELDON,** lawyer; b. Randolph, Kans., Aug. 29, 1927; s. Harry Edward and Florence Lillian (Schwartz) S.; m. Edith Grace Kintner, Apr. 7, 1956 (div.); children: Kenneth G., Rebecca J., Sonya J., Connie J.; m. Anne Oliver; 1 child, Edward G. AB, Washburn U., 1957, LLB, 1957. Bar: Kans. 1957, U.S. Dist. Ct. Kans. 1957, U.S. Ct. Appeals (10th cir.) 1970, U.S. Supreme Ct. 1983. Pvt. practice Topeka, 1957-68; ptnr. Schroer, Rice, P.A., Topeka, 1968—, pres., 1970—, also bd. dirs. Contbr. articles to profl. jours. and chpts. to books. Supr. Shawnee County Soil Conservation Dist., Topeka, 1968-84. With U.S. Army, 1951-53. Mem. ABA, Kans. Bar Assn., Assn. Trial Lawyers Am. (gov. 1976-79, seminar lectr. 1973—, chmn. tort sect. 1974-75, instr. Nat. Coll. Adv. 1978, 81-88), Kans. Trial Lawyers Assn. (gov. 1972—, seminar lectr. 1974—, pres. 1974-75), Trial Lawyers for Pub. Justice (bd. dirs.), Nat. Bd. Trial Advocacy (sustaining founder), N.Y. Acad. Sci., Am. Bd. Trial Advs. (sec., treas. Kans. chpt. 1990-91, pres. 1991-92), Am. Bd. Profl. Liability Attys., Civil Justice Found. (founding sponsor), Trial Lawyers for Pub. Justice (bd. dirs. 1982-96). Democrat. Methodist. Personal injury, Federal civil litigation, State civil litigation. Office: Schroer Rice PA 115 SE 7th St Topeka KS 66603-3901

**SCHROM, GERARD KILLARD,** lawyer; b. N.Y.C., July 18, 1947; s. Erwin Randolph and Catherine Teresa (O'Keeffe) S.; m. Georgia Lee Marshall, Jan. 18, 1986. BS, Pa. State U., 1969; postgrad., Princeton U., 1973-75, Cambridge U., 1982; JD, Widener U., 1983. Bar: Pa., 1983, N.J. 1984. English tchr. Wakefield High Sch., Arlington, Va., 1969-70, Hunterdon Cen. High Sch., Flemington, N.J., 1972-76; pres. Schrom Contrn. Co., Sandwich, Mass., 1976-78; chmn. English dept. Garnet Valley High Sch., Concordville, Pa., 1979-89; pvt. practice Schrom & Ratasiewicz, Media, Pa., 1983—; arbitrator Am. Arbitration Assn. Editor features Del. Law Forum, 1982-83; author to legal articles. V.p., sec. Garnet Valley Edn. Assn., 1980-82. Recipient Am. Jurisprudence award, 1981, Fed. Bar Assn. award, 1983; Freedoms Found. scholar, 1982. Mem. ABA, NEA, Pa. Bar Assn. (scholar 1988), N.J. Bar Assn., Del. County Bar Assn., Am. Trial Lawyers Assn., Am. Judicature Soc., Pa. Edn. Assn., Moot Ct. Honor Soc., Princeton Club, Pa. State Club, Phi Alpha Delta, Sigma Alpha Epsilon. Home: 809 Eaton Rd Drexel Hill PA 19026-1524 Office: Schrom & Ratasiewicz 112 N Plum St Media PA 19063-2830

**SCHROPP, JAMES HOWARD,** lawyer; b. Lebanon, Pa., June 20, 1943; s. Howard J. and Maud E. (Parker) S.; m. Jo Ann Simpson, Sept. 4, 1965; children: James A., John C., Jeffrey M., Jeremy M. BA, U. Richmond, 1965; JD, Georgetown U., 1973. Bar: D.C. 1973, U.S. Supreme Ct. 1980. Asst. gen. counsel SEC, Washington, 1973-79; ptnr. Fried, Frank, Harris, Shriver & Jacobson, Washington, 1979—; adj. prof. Georgetown U., Washington, 1982-86; mem. faculty Na.t Inst. for Trial Advocacy. Mem. ABA (discovery com. litigation sect. 1984-86, tender offer litigation subcom. corp. banking and bus. law sect. 1985-86, task force on broker-dealer compliance supervisory procedures 1987-89). Securities, General corporate, Federal civil litigation. Office: Fried Frank Harris Shriver & Jacobson 1001 Pennsylvania Ave NW Washington DC 20004-2505

**SCHROTH, PETER W(ILLIAM),** lawyer, management and law educator; b. Camden, N.J., July 24, 1946; s. Walter and Patricia Anne (Page) S.; children: Laura Salome Erickson-Schroth, Julia James. AB, Shimer Coll., 1966; JD, U. Chgo., 1969; M in Comparative Law, U.Chgo., 1971; SJD, U. Mich., 1979; postgrad., U. Freiburg, Fed. Republic Germany, Faculté Internationale pour l'Enseignement de Droit Comparé; MBA, Rensselaer Poly. Inst., 1988. Bar: Ill. 1969, N.Y. 1979, Conn. 1985, Mass. 1990; solicitor Supreme Ct. England and Wales 1995. Asst. prof. So. Meth. U., 1973-77; fellow in law and humanities Harvard U., 1976-77, vis. scholar, 1980-81; assoc. prof. N.Y. Law Sch., 1977-81; prof. law Hamline U., St. Paul, 1981-83; dep. gen. counsel Equator Bank Ltd., 1984-87; v.p., dep. gen. counsel Equator Holdings Ltd., 1987-94, v.p., gen. counsel, 1994—; adj. prof. law U. Conn., 1985-86, Western New Eng. Coll., 1988—, adj. prof. of mgmt. Rensselaer Poly. Inst., 1988-98, prof. 1999—. Author: Foreign Investment in the United States, 2d edit., 1977; (with Stiefel) Products Liability: European Proposals and American Experience, 1981, Doing Business in Sub-Saharan Africa, 1991; bd. editors Am. Jour. Comparative Law, 1981-84, 91—, Conn. Bar Jour., N.Y. Internat. Law Rev., Jour. Bus. in Developing Nations; contbr. articles to profl. jours. Mem. ABA (editor in chief ABA Environ. Law Symposium 1980-82), Am. Soc. Comparative Law (bd. dirs. 1978-84, 91—), Am. Fgn. Law Assn., Internat. Bar Assn., Internat. Law Assn. (com. multinat. banking), Acad. Internat. Bus., Conn. Civil Liberties Union (bd. dirs. 1985-92), Environ. Law Inst. (assoc.), Columbia U. Peace Seminar (assoc.), Hartford Club (bd. govs. 1995-98), Am. Corp. Counsel Assn. (pres. Conn. chpt.), Conn. Bar Assn. (chair sect. of internat. law). Banking, Private international. Office: HSBC Equator (USA) Inc 45 Glastonbury Blvd Glastonbury CT 06033-4411

**SCHUBER, WILLIAM PATRICK,** lawyer; b. Teaneck, N.J., Apr. 15, 1947; s. William A. and Mary E. (Cleary) S. BA, Fordham U., 1969, JD, 1972. Bar: N.J. 1972, U.S. Supreme Ct. 1976. Assoc. Contant, Contant, Schuber, Scherby & Atkins, Hackensack, N.J., 1972-79, ptnr., 1979—; adj. prof. Montclair State Coll., 1983—. Mem. Bergen Country Housing Devel. Authority; councilman Borough of Bogota, 1972-79, mayor, 1979-84; mem. N.J. Gen. Assembly, 1981-90; Bergen Country Exec., 1990—. Capt. USAR, 1969-83. Mem. ATLA, N.J. Bar Assn., Bergen County Bar Assn., Rotary. Republican. Roman Catholic. State civil litigation, Probate, Real property. Home: 1042 Wildwood Rd Oradell NJ 07649-1332 Office: Office the County Exec Admin Bldg Court Plz S 21 Main St Rm 300E Hackensack NJ 07601-7021

**SCHUCK, CARL JOSEPH,** lawyer; b. Phila., Nov. 21, 1915; s. Joseph and Christina (Schadl) S.; m. Mary Elizabeth Box, June 7, 1941; children: Mary Ann (dec.), John, James, Catherine, Christopher. BS, St. Mary's Coll., 1937; postgrad., U. So. Calif., 1937-38; JD, Georgetown U., 1941. Bar: D.C. 1940, Calif. 1943, U.S. Supreme Ct. 1952. Atty. Dept. Justice, Washington, 1940-42, Alien Property Custodian, San Francisco, 1942-44, Overton, Lyman & Prince, L.A., 1944-47; mem. firm Overton, Lyman & Prince, L.A., 1947-79; profl. corp. mem. firm Overton, Lyman & Prince, L.A., 1979-85; lectr. Practising Law Inst., 1973; Del. 9th Cir. Jud. Conf., 1963-80, chmn. lawyer-dels. com., 1972, mem. exec. com., 1976-80, chmn. exec. com., 1977-78, mem. sr. adv. bd., 1989-95; mem. disciplinary bd. State Bar Calif., 1970-71. Fellow Am. Coll. Trial Lawyers (chmn. com. on complex litigation 1979-81, regent 1981-85), L.A. County Bar Assn. (trustee 1974-76), Phi Alpha Delta. Club: Chancery (pres. 1984-85). Antitrust, Federal civil litigation, State civil litigation. Home and Office: 16916 Hierba Dr Apt 254 San Diego CA 92128-2679

**SCHUCK, EDWIN GEORGE, JR.,** lawyer. BS cum laude, Columbia U., 1967, MBA, 1970, JD cum laude, 1970. Bar: N.Y. 1971, Calif. 1980, U.S. Tax Ct., U.S. Ct. Fed. Claims, U.S. Supreme Ct. With Sullivan & Cromwell, N.Y.C., 1970-76; with Donovan Leisure Newton & Irvine, N.Y.C. and L.A., 1976-80, ptnr., 1980-83; ptnr. Sidley & Austin, L.A., 1983-87, Munger, Tolles & Olson, L.A., 1987-95; atty. pvt. practice, L.A., 1996—; adj. prof. U. San Diego, 1987; lectr. in field. Contbr. articles to profl. jours. Pres. Bradbury Estates Assn., 1991-92, 94-96, Bradbury Cmty. Svcs. Dist., 1996; mem. Bradbury City Coun., 1996; mayor City of Bradbury, 1998. Mem. Calif. State Bar (taxation sect. vice chair, mem. exec. com. 1987-89, chair corp. tax com. 1992-93, chair 2d ann. meeting Calif. Tax Bar 1992), N.Y. State Bar Assn. (com. reorgn. corp. taxation, partnerships & U.S. tax problems of fgn. persons), L.A. County Bar Assn. (chair taxation sect. 1988-89, chair income tax com. 1985-87, chair corp. tax com. 1994-95), Internat. Fiscal Assn., Internat. Bar Assn. (spkr., presenter), Assn. Tax Counsel. Office: 626 Wilshire Blvd Ste 900 Los Angeles CA 90017-2922

**SCHUDER, RAYMOND FRANCIS,** lawyer; b. Wickford, R.I., Dec. 27, 1926; s. Rollie Milton and Selma (Ball) S.; AB, Emory U., 1949, JD, 1951; m. Betty Jo Williams, Mar. 14, 1948; children: Gregg Williams, Glen Arva. Bar: Ga. 1951. With Trust Co., Ga., Atlanta, 1951-54; assoc. firm Wheeler, Robinson & Thurmond, Gainesville, Ga., 1954-59; pvt. practice law, Gainesville, 1959-70, 76-96; ptnr. Schuder & Brown, Gainesville, 1971-76; Mcpl. ct. judge, Gainesville, 1956-60, 73-75, Magistrate ct. judge, 1985—. Supr. Upper Chattahoochee Soil and Water Conservation Dist., 1971-74; chief exec. officer, bd. dirs. Charles Thompson Estes Found., Inc., Gainesville. Cpl. USMCR, 1944-50; 1st lt. USAR, ret. Mem. State Bar Ga. (gov. 1966-70), Gainesville-Northeastern (pres. 1969-70) Bar Assn., Am. Legion, V.F.W., Elks. Methodist. Home: 2224 Riverside Dr Gainesville GA 30501-1232

**SCHUESSLER, CINDY SANDLIN,** lawyer, judge; b. Florence, Ala., Feb. 19, 1951; d. James Harold Sr. and Sarah Nell Sandlin; m. John M. Schuessler, May 14, 1971; 1 child, Christopher Warren. BA, U. North Ala., 1975; JD, Cumberland Sch. Law, 1978. Bar: Ala. 1978, U.S. Dist. Ct. (no. dist.) Ala. 1978. Assoc. Engel, Hairston, Birmingham, Ala., 1978-79, Peck & Slusher, Florence, 1980-83; ptnr. Schuessler & Sandlin, Florence, 1983—; instr. Faulkner U., Florence, 1985-88; mcpl. prosecutor, Town of Killen, Ala., 1983-94, city atty., 1989—; mcpl. judge Town of Rogersville, Ala., 1988—. Pres. Harlan Sch. PTA, Florence, 1988-90; chmn. bd. trustees Highland Bapt. Ch., Florence, 1989—; mem. grant com. United Way, florence, 1989-91. Mem. Ala. State Bar Assn., Ala. Mcpl. Judges Assn. (pres. 1992-93), Lauderdale County Bar Assn., Phi Kappa Phi, Phi Alpha Delta. Avocations: travel, swimming, reading. Family and matrimonial, General practice, Probate. Office: Schuessler & Sandlin 225 W Alabama St Florence AL 35630-5515

**SCHUETTE, CHARLES A.,** lawyer; b. Columbus, Ind., Feb. 24, 1942. BBA, U. Okla., 1964, JD, 1967. Bar: Okla. 1967, Fla. 1970, U.S. Supreme Ct. 1979, U.S. Dist. Ct. (so. dist.) Fla. 1982, U.S. Dist. Ct. (mid. dist.) Fla. 1982. Chmn., CEO Akerman, Senterfitt & Eidson P.A. Fellow Am. Bar Found.; mem. ABA, Fla. Bar, Okla. Bar Assn., Dade County Bar Assn. Real property, Contracts commercial, Public international. Office: Akerman Senterfitt & Eidson PA 1 SE 3d Ave 28th Fl Miami FL 33131-1700

**SCHULER, ALISON KAY,** lawyer; b. West Point, N.Y., Oct. 1, 1948; d. Richard Hamilton and Irma (Sanken) S.; m. Lyman Gage Sandy, Mar. 30, 1974; 1 child, Theodore. AB cum laude, Radcliffe Coll., 1969; JD, Harvard U., 1972. Bar: Va. 1973, D.C. 1974, N.Mex. 1975. Assoc. Hunton & Williams, Richmond, Va., 1972-75; asst. U.S. atty. U.S. Atty.'s Office, Albuquerque, 1975-78; adj. prof. law U. N.Mex., 1983-85, 90, 98—; ptnr. Sutin, Thayer & Browne, Albuquerque, 1978-85, Montgomery & Andrews, P.A., Albuquerque, 1985-88; sole practice Albuquerque, 1988—. Bd. dirs. Am. Diabetes Assn., Albuquerque, 1980-85, chmn. bd. dirs., 1984-85; bd. dirs. June Music Festival, 1980-95, pres., 1983-85, 93-94; bd. dirs. Albuquerque Conservation Trust, 1986-90, N.Mex. Osteo. Found., 1993-96; chairperson Albuquerque Com. Fgn. Rels., 1984-85; mem. N.Mex. Internat. Trade and Investment Coun., Inc., 1986—; mem. coun. St. Lukes Luth. Ch., 1976-80, 82-84, 91-96, v.p., 1978-80, 82-84, pres., 1994-95, chartered org. rep. troop 444, Boy Scouts Am., 1997—, mem. nominating com., mem.-at-large dist. com. Sandia dist., 1998—, dist. vice chmn., 1999—. Mem. Fed. Bar Assn. (coord.), ABA, Va. Bar Assn., N.Mex. Bar Assn. (chmn. corp., banking and bus. law 1982-83, bd. dirs. internat. and immigration law sect. 1987-95, chmn. 1993-94), Harvard U. Alumni Assn. (mem. fund campaign, regional dir. 1984-86, v.p. 1986-89, chmn. clubs com. 1985-88, chmn. communications com. 1988-91), Radcliffe Coll. Alumnae Assn. Bd. Mgmt. (regional dir. 1984-87, chmn. comms. com. 1988-91), Harvard-Radcliffe Club (pres. 1980-84). Securities, General corporate, Private international. Home: 632 Cougar Loop NE Albuquerque NM 87122-1808 Office: 4300 San Mateo Blvd NE Ste B380 Albuquerque NM 87110-8401

**SCHULER, WALTER E.,** lawyer; b. Memphis, Tenn., Sept. 8, 1962; s. James D. and Clare A. Schuler. BBA magna cum laude, U. Memphis, 1993; JD cum laude with cert. in health law with hons., St. Louis U., 1996. Bar: Tenn. 1996, U.S. Dist. Ct. (Western Dist.) Tenn. 1996, U.S. Ct. Appeals (6th cir.), 1998. Assoc. The Bogatin Law Firm, PLC, Memphis, Tenn., 1996—. Contbr. articles to profl. jours., chpt. to book. Sgt. (E-5), U.S. Army, 1985-90, staff sgt. (E-6) USAR, 1990-93. Recipient Commendation Medal-1st Oak Leaf Cluster, U.S. Army, 1989, Army Achievement Medal-2nd Oak Leaf Cluster, 1989, Nat. Def. Svc. Med., 1992. Mem. Am. Health Lawyers Assn., ABA, Tenn. Bar Assn., Memphis Bar Assn. Health, General corporate, General civil litigation. Office: Bogatin Law Firm PLC Ste 300 International Place Dr Memphis TN 38120

**SCHULHOFER, STEPHEN JOSEPH,** law educator, consultant; b. N.Y.C., Aug. 20, 1942; s. Joseph and Myrelle S.; m. Laurie Wohl, May 28, 1975; children: Samuel, Jonah. AB, Princeton U., 1964; LLB, Harvard U., 1967. Bar: D.C. 1968, U.S. Dist. Ct. (ea. dist.) Pa. 1973, U.S. Supreme Ct. 1973. Law clk. U.S. Supreme Ct., Washington, 1967-69; assoc. Coudert

Freres, Paris, 1969-72; prof. law U. Pa., Phila., 1972-86; prof. U. Chgo., 1986—. speedy trial reporter U.S. Dist. Ct., Wilmington, Del., 1975-80; cons. U.S. EPA, Washington, 1977-78, U.S. Sentencing Commn., Washington, 1987-94. Author: Unwanted Sex: The Culture of Intimidation and the Failure of Law, 1998; Prosecutorial Discretion and Federal Sentencing Reform, 1979. Editor: Criminal Law and its Processes, 1983, 89, 95; contbr. articles to profl. jours. Trustee, Community Legal Services, Inc., Phila., 1981-86. Walter Meyer grantee Am. Bar Found., 1984. Mem. ACLU (Ill. bd. dirs. 1993-97), Law and Soc. Assn. Office: U Chgo Law Sch 1111 E 60th St Chicago IL 60637-2776

**SCHULING, MARK RICHARD,** lawyer; b. Furstenfeldbruk, Germany, June 6, 1955; came to U.S., 1957; s. Richard Charles and Dorraine Faye S.; m. Eliza Jane Ovrom, Sept. 4, 1982; children: Charles Mark, Matthew Arthur. BA in Social Scis., Drake U., 1976, JD, 1980. Bar: U.S. Dist. Ct. (no. and so. dists.) Iowa 1982, U.S. Ct. Appeals (8th cir.) 1983; CPA, Iowa. Asst. atty. gen. Atty. Gen. State Iowa, Des Moines, 1980-84; assoc. Brick, Gentry Law Firm, Des Moines, 1984-87; prin. Brick, Gentry, Bowers, Swartz, Stoltze, Schuling & Levis, PC, Des Moines, 1987—. Dir. Des Moines Sch. Dist., 1996—; exchange dir. Friendship Force Des Moines. Mem. Iowa State Bar Assn., Polk County Bar Assn., Iowa Soc. CPA's, Greater Des Moines C. of C. (dir. 1996—), Order of Barristers. Democrat. Congregationalist. Avocations: biking, hiking, reading, golfing. Taxation, general, State and local taxation, Probate. Home: 500 Glenview Dr Des Moines IA 50312-2526 Office: Brick Gentry Bowers Swartz Stoltze Schuling & Levis PC 550 39th St Ste 200 Des Moines IA 50312-3529

**SCHULMAN, ROBERT S.,** lawyer; b. N.Y.C., July 9, 1941; s. Donald Benedict and Edythe (Smythe) S.; m. Susan Jan Von Helbig, Sept. 18, 1974; children: Elizabeth Jane, Jennifer Lynn. BA, Rutgers Univ, New Brunswick, 1963; JD cum laude, Rutgers Univ, Newark, 1966. Bar: N.J. 1967, Calif. 1976, U.S. Dist. Ct. N.J. 1967, U.S. Supreme Ct. 1970, U.S. Dist. Cts. (ctrl., no., so., ea., dists.) Calif. 1976, U.S. Ct. Appeals (9th cir.) Calif. 1976. With Pitney, Hardin & Kipp, Newark, N.J., 1966-74; dept. atty. gen. Office of N.J. Atty. Gen., Trenton, N.J., 1974-75; assoc. Cox, Castle & Nicholson, L.A., 1976-80; ptnr. Zobrist, Garner & Garrett, L.A., 1980-83, Stephens, Berg, Lasater & Schulman, L.A., 1984-91, Crosby, Heafey, Roach & May, L.A., 1991—; atty. Bd. of Edn., Fairview, N.J., 1972, Bd. of Adjustment, Fairview, N.J., 1971-73. Contbr. articles to profl. jours. dir. Deafwest Theatre, L.A., Calif., 1991-97. Mem. State Bar of Calif., San Gabriel Country Club, Calif. Club. Republican. Congregationalist. General civil litigation, Insurance. Home: 4229 Mesa Vista Dr La Canada Flintridge CA 91011-3825 Office: Crosby Heafey Roach & May 700 S Flower St Los Angeles CA 90017-4101

**SCHULMAN, STEVEN GARY,** lawyer; b. Gloversville, N.Y., June 10, 1951; s. Jacob and Selma Pearl (Shapiro) S. BA, Williams Coll., 1973; MA, Tufts U., 1975, MALD, 1976; JD, U. Chgo., 1980. Bar: N.Y. 1981, D.C. 1981, U.S. Dist. Ct. (so. dist.) N.Y. 1981. Law clk. to Hon. Robert L. Kunzig U.S. Ct. Claims, Washington, 1980-81; with Milberg Weiss Bershad Hynes & Lerach, LLP, N.Y.C., ptnr. Mem. ABA, ATLA, N.Y. State Bar Assn., D.C. Bar Assn., Assn. of Bar of City of N.Y. Federal civil litigation, Securities.

**SCHULNER, KEITH ALAN,** lawyer, business owner; b. Burbank, Calif., Aug. 4, 1966; s. Lawrence Mayor and Diane Bebe (Goldstein) S.; m. Debbie Dennison, July 28, 1991; 1 child, Eliana. BA, UCLA, 1989; JD, Loyola U., 1992. Bar: Calif. Owner Law Offices of Keith A. Schulner & Assocs., Camarillo, Calif., 1997—, lawyer mgr., 1992—; pub. defender L.A. County Pub. Defender's Office, Van Nuys, Calif., 1992; mentor Loyola U. Law Sch., 1997—. Mem. task force com. Jewish Fedn. Coun., 1997—; chairperson Havurah com. Temple Adat Elohim, 1997-98, brotherhood pres.; mentor, entertainment chairperson Fulfillment Fund, 1995—. Mem. Calif. State Bar Assn. (mediator, arbitrator 1997—), Calif. County Bar Assn. (mediator, arbitrator 1997—), Jerome H. Berenson Inns of Ct., Camarillo C. of C., Sigma Phi Epsilon. Personal injury, Alternative dispute resolution, Civil rights. Office: 360 Mobil Ave Camarillo CA 93010-6325

**SCHULT, THOMAS P.,** lawyer; b. Great Falls, Mont., Sept. 12, 1954; s. Peter Henry and Louise (de Russy) S.; m. Margo C. Soulé, Sept. 18, 1982. BS in Russian History, U. Va., 1976, JD, 1979. Bar: U.S. Dist. Ct. (we. dist.) Mo. 1979, U.S. Ct. Appeals (10th cir.) 1983, U.S. Ct. Appeals (7th, 8th and 11th cirs.) 1984, U.S. Ct. Appeals (5th cir.) 1985, U.S. Supreme Ct. 1987, U.S. Ct. Appeals (9th cir.) 1988. Ptnr. Lathrop Koontz & Norquist, Kansas City, Mo., 1979-89, Bryan Cave, Kansas City, 1989-94; Stinson, Mag & Fizzell, Kansas City, 1994—. Committeeman Jackson County Reps., Kansas City, 1984—. Mem. ABA (products liability com.), Products Liability Adv. Coun., Mo. Bar Assn. (lectr. continuing legal edn.), Fedn. of Ins. and Corporate Counsel, Def. Rsch. Inst. Episcopalian. Federal civil litigation, State civil litigation. Office: Stinson Mag & Fizzell 1201 Walnut St Ste 2800 Kansas City MO 64106-2117

**SCHULTE, BRUCE JOHN,** lawyer; b. Burlington, Iowa, June 27, 1953; s. James Andrew and Julia Germaine (Van Dale) S.; m. Mary E. Guest, July 1984 (div. Feb. 1995); children: James, John. BA in Am. Studies, U. Notre Dame, 1975; JD, U. Iowa, 1978. Bar: Iowa 1978, U.S. Dist. Ct. (so. dist.) Iowa 1979, U.S. Ct. Appeals (8th cir.) 1982, Minn. 1988, U.S. Dist. Ct. Minn. 1988, Ill. 1989. Law clk. Justice K. David Harris Supreme Ct. Iowa, Des Moines, 1978-79; ptnr. Dailey, Ruther, Bauer, Schulte & Hahn, Burlington, Iowa, 1979-87; atty. Bennett, Ingvaldson & McInerny, Mpls., 1988; gen. counsel Blackwood Corp., St. Paul, 1988-89; publs. editor Nat. Inst. for Trial Advocacy-U. Notre Dame, Ind., 1989-91; asst. dean pub. affairs Chgo. (Ill.) Kent Coll. Law, 1991-94; dep. dir. assoc. rels. West Pub., Eagan, Minn., 1995-97; dir. mktg., v.p. acad. consulting Performance Comm. Group, Chgo., 1997—; key person com. ATLA, 1984-88; mem. commn. on jud. dists. Supreme Ct. Iowa, 1987-88; publs. com. Nat. Law Firm Mktg. Assn., 1993-94. Author: Persuasive Expert Testimony, 1990, Laser Disc Technology in the Courtroom, 1990; editor: Cases and Materials on Evidence, 1991, Modern State and Federal Evidence, 1991, Problems and Cases for Legal Writing, 1991. Mem. state ctrl. com. Iowa Dem. party, 1984-88; devel. com. Frances Xavier Ward Sch., Chgo., 1993—; mem. cmty. task force Chgo. (Ill.) Downtown Circulator Project, 1994-96; v.p. pub. affairs U. Notre Dame Alumni Class of 1975. Notre Dame scholar U. Notre Dame, Ind., 1971-72; recipient Spectra award Internat. Assn. Bus. Communicators, 1993, Silver Trumpet, Publicity Club Chgo., 1994. Mem. ABA (mem. tech. com. lawyers conf. jud. adminstrn. divsn. 1995—), Ill. Bar Assn. (mem. standing com. legal edn. and admission to bar 1993-97), Chgo. Bar Assn. (mem. law office tech. com. 1995-97), Assn. Am. Law Schs., Chgo. Pub. Rels. Forum (treas. 1997), Notre Dame Club Chgo. (co-chair Hesburgh Forum com. 1993-98, trustee 1995-98, sec. 1997-98), Nat. Soc. Fundraising Profls. (cert. fundraising profl., Midwest conf. steering com. 1997—), Execs. Club of Chgo. Avocations: sailing, choir, gardening. State civil litigation. Office: 312 W Randolph St Chicago IL 60606-1721

**SCHULTE, JEFFREY LEWIS,** lawyer; b. N.Y.C., July 24, 1949; s. Irving and Ruth (Stein) S.; m. Elizabeth Ewan Kaiser, Aug. 13, 1977; children: Andrew Riggs, Ian Garretson, Elizabeth Alexandra. BA, Williams Coll., 1971; postgrad., Harvard U., 1971-72; JD, Yale U., 1976. Bar: Pa. 1978, Ga. 1993. Law clk. to hon. John J. Gibbons U.S. Ct. Appeals (3d cir.), Newark, 1976-77; assoc. Schnader, Harrison, Segal & Lewis, Phila., 1977-84, ptnr., 1985-92; founding ptnr. Schnader, Harrison, Segal & Lewis, Atlanta, 1992-98, exec. com., 1994-98; ptnr. Morris, Manning & Martin, Atlanta, 1998—; nat. steering com. lawyers com. to end "Pay-to-Play." Contbr. articles to profl. jours. Trustee Ga. Shakespeare Festival; bd. dirs. North Ardmore (Pa.) Civic Assn., pres., 1990; bd. dirs. Main Line YMCA, chmn., 1989-91. Mem. ABA, Pa. Bar Assn., State Bar Ga., Phila. Bar Assn., Atlanta Bar Assn. (chmn. comm. and media rels. com.), Atlanta Venture Forum, Bus. and Tech. Alliance, Yale Club of Ga. (bd. dirs. 1996-99), Williams Club Atlanta, Merion Cricket Club, Weekapaug Yacht Club (R.I.), Weekapaug Tennis Club, Phi Beta Kappa. Securities, Mergers and acquisitions, Finance. Office: Morris Manning & Martin 1600 Atlanta Financial Center 3343 Peachtree Rd NE Ste 1600 Atlanta GA 30326-1044

**SCHULTE, STEPHEN JOHN,** lawyer, educator; b. N.Y.C., July 7, 1938; s. John and Marjorie (Fried) S.; m. Patricia Walker, June 6, 1962 (div.); children: Susan Jean, Jeffrey David, Elizabeth Ann; m. Margaret Van Doren Cook, Mar. 12, 1975. BA, Brown U., 1960; JD, Columbia U., 1963. Bar: N.Y. 1964. Assoc. Lowenstein, Pitcher, Hochkiss & Parr, N.Y.C., 1963-66, Fried, Frank, Harris, Shriver & Jacobson, N.Y.C., 1966-69; founding ptnr. Schulte Roth & Zabel, N.Y.C., 1969—; adj. prof. law Benjamin N. Cardozo Law Sch., 1992—, vice chmn., bd. dirs., 1995—; adj. prof. law Fordham U., 1992—; lectr. securities law field; panelist various forums. Life trustee Choate Rosemary Hall Sch., Wallingford, Conn., 1982—, chmn. investment and fin. com., 1984-85, chmn. devel. com., 1985-86, chmn. nominating com., 1986-89, chmn. bd. trustees, 1990-95. Mem. ABA, N.Y. State Bar Assn. (com. on securities regulation), Assn. of Bar of City of N.Y. (chmn. com. on securities regulation), Norfolk Country Club. General corporate, Securities. Office: Schulte Roth & Zabel 900 3rd Ave Fl 19 New York NY 10022-4774

**SCHULTESS, LEROY KENNETH,** lawyer, consultant; b. Garrett, Ind., May 7, 1907; s. George Mathias and Elizabeth (Lehmbeck) S.; m. Sarah Mildred Atwater, Apr. 28, 1942. AB, Mich. U., 1929; JD, Northwestern U., 1932. Bar: Ind. 1933. Practice law, LaGrange, Ind.; pres. Creek Chub Bait Co., Garrett, Lure, Inc., Garrett; hon. dir. Farmers State Bank, LaGrange. Recipient Meritorious awards Farmers State Bank, VFW, Boy Scouts Am., Am. Lung Assn. Mem. U. Mich. Alumni Assn., LaGrange C. of C., ABA, Ind. Bar Assn. (Golden Anniversary award), LaGrange County Bar Assn. (Outstanding and Dedicated Svc. awards), Sigma Chi, Phi Delta Phi, Rotary (LaGrange) (pres. 1956-7), LaGrange Country. Lodges: Shriners, Masons. Banking, General corporate, Criminal. Home: 414 W Michigan St Lagrange IN 46761-1710 Office: Farmers State Bank Bldg 220 S Detroit St Lagrange IN 46761-1808

**SCHULTZ, DENNIS BERNARD,** lawyer; b. Detroit, Oct. 15, 1946; s. Bernard George and Madeline Laverne (Riffenberg) S.; m. Andi Lynn Leslie, Apr. 18, 1967; 1 child, Karanne Anne. BS, Wayne State U., 1970; JD, Mich. State U., 1977. Bar: Mich. 1977, U.S. Dist. Ct. (ea. and we. dist.) Mich., U.S. Ct. Appeals (6th cir.), U.S. Dist. Ct. (we. dist.) Pa. V.p. Barkay Bldg. Co., Ferndale, Mich., to 1976; law clk. Hon. George N. Bashara, Mich. Ct. Appeals, Detroit, 1977; shareholder Butzel Long, Detroit, 1978—. Editor Detroit Coll. Law Rev., 1977. Detroit Coll. Law Alumni Assn. scholar, 1976, Mich. Consolidated Gas Co. scholar, 1977. Mem. Detroit Bar Assn., Mich. Bar Assn. Republican. Roman Catholic. Avocations: boating, biking, golf. Construction, Contracts commercial, General civil litigation.

**SCHULTZ, G. ROBERT,** lawyer; b. Detroit, Apr. 25, 1934; s. George R. and J. Leone (Spencer) S.; m. Elizabeth Anne Burnett, Aug. 17, 1957; children: Suzanne McAree, Sarah Ovitt, Bruce, Robert, Katherine Brenner, Stephen. BA, U. Mich., 1958; JD, Stetson Coll. Law, 1967. Bar: Fla. 1967, U.S. Dist. Ct. (no., so. and mid. dists.), Fla. 1970, U.S. Supreme Ct. 1970; cert. family mediator. Pvt. practice St. Petersburg, Fla., 1967—. With U.S. Army, 1954-56. Fellow Am. Acad. Matrimonial Lawyers; mem. ABA (family law sect.), Fla. Bar Assn. (bd. cert. marital and family law). Family and matrimonial. Office: 1216 66th St N Saint Petersburg FL 33710-6226

**SCHULTZ, LOUIS WILLIAM,** judge; b. Deep River, Iowa, Mar. 24, 1927; s. M. Louis and Esther Louise (Behrens) S.; m. D. Jean Stephen, Nov. 6, 1949; children: Marcia, Mark, Paul. Student, Central Coll., Pella, Iowa, 1944-45, 46-47; LLB, Drake U., Des Moines, 1949. Bar: Iowa. Claims supr. Iowa Farm Mut. Ins. Co., Des Moines, 1949-55; partner firm Harned, Schultz & McMeen, Marengo, Iowa, 1955-71; judge Iowa Dist. Ct. (6th dist.), 1971-80; justice Iowa Supreme Ct., 1980-93; county atty. Iowa County, 1960-68; ret., 1993. Served with USNR, 1945-46. Mem. Am. Bar Assn., Iowa Bar Assn. (bd. govs.), Iowa Judges Assn. (pres.).

**SCHULTZ, RICHARD ALLEN,** lawyer, farmer; b. Emporia, Kans., Jan. 3, 1939; s. Ebur Samuel and Opal Mae (Porter) S.; m. Esther Marie Strafuss, May 8, 1971; children—William Allen, Bryan Lee. BS in Indsl. Mgmt., U. Kans., 1961; JD, Washburn U. of Topeka, 1970. Bar: Kans. 1971. Sole practice, Topeka, 1970—; dep. dir. Kans. Govs. Com. Criminal Adminstrn., 1971-73; asst. jud. adminstr. Kans. Supreme Ct., 1973-76; ct. adminstr. 3d Jud. Dist., Kans., 1976-83; dep. sec. Dept. Corrections State of Kans., Topeka, 1983-88; pvt. practice law, 1988—. Exec. bd. Topeka YMCA; dist. officer Jayhawk Area council Boy Scouts Am., Nat. Eagle Scout Assn.; dir. Kans. Vets. Found., Inc. Lt. USN, 1961-67. Decorated Navy Commendation award; recipient Topeka Bar Assn. Liberty Bell award, 1983. Mem. Topeka Bar Assn., Kans. Bar Assn., ABA, Nat. Trial Ct. Adminstrs., Knife and Fork Club, KU Williams Fund Outland Club, Am. Legion, Vietnam Vets. Am., Phi Alpha Delta, Alpha Tau Omega. Democrat. Methodist. Criminal, General practice. Office: 3109 SW Stone Ave Topeka KS 66614-2821

**SCHULZ, BRADLEY NICHOLAS,** lawyer; b. Staten Island, N.Y., July 1, 1959; s. George Robert Jr. and Mary Jane (Fazakerley) S. BA, Wake Forest U., 1981; JD, N.Y. Law Sch., 1984. Bar: N.Y. 1985, N.C. 1985, N.J. 1985, U.S. Dist. Ct. (ea. dist. ) N.C. 1985, U.S. Dist. Ct. (so. dist.) N.Y. 1985. Assoc. Mast, Tew, Armstrong & Morris, P.A., Smithfield, N.C., 1984-85; ptnr. Mast, Schulz Mast Mills & Stem, P.A., Smithfield, 1986-97, mng. ptnr., 1998—. Chmn. Young Republicans, Johnston County, Smithfield, 1988. Hankins scholar Wake Forest U., 1977-81, N.Y. Law Sch. scholar, 1981-84. Mem. ABA, N.C. Bar Assn., N.Y. Bar Assn., N.J. Bar Assn., N.C. Acad. Trial Lawyers, Johnston County Bar Assn., Theta Chi Fraternity. Republican. Episcopalian. Avocations: yachting, sailing, skiing. E-mail: Brad@mastschulz.com. General civil litigation, Insurance, Personal injury. Home: 102 Pheasant Run Clayton NC 27520-8301 Office: Mast Schulz Mast Mills & Stem PA PO Box 119 Smithfield NC 27577-0119

**SCHULZ, PAUL JOHN,** lawyer; b. Newark, May 9, 1954; s. Arthur Charles and Martha Ida (S.; m. Peggy Jane Hills, July 25, 1992; children: Amie, Heather, Lillie. BS, SUNY, Binghamton, 1976; JD cum laude, SUNY, Buffalo, 1981. Bar: N.Y. 1982. Assoc. Law Office Richard C. Southard, Lockport, N.Y., 1981-83, Albraht, Maguire, Heffern & Gregg, Buffalo, 1983-85, Lippes, Silverstein, Mathias & Wexler, Buffalo, 1985-91, 1991—. Chair bd. trustees Clarence (N.Y.) United Meth. Ch., 1994—. Avocations: golf, hiking, fishing. General corporate, Mergers and acquisitions, Pension, profit-sharing, and employee benefits. Office: Lippes Silverstein Mathias & Wexler 700 Guaranty Bldg Buffalo NY 14202

**SCHULZ, PETER JON,** lawyer; b. Milw., Feb. 27, 1967. BA cum laude, St. Olaf Coll., 1989; JD, Calif. Western U., 1993. Bar: Calif. 1993, U.S. Dist. Ct. (so. dist.) Calif. 1994, U.S. Dist. Ct. (ctrl. dist.) Calif. 1994. Assoc. Belsky & Assocs., San Diego, 1993-94; assoc. Greco & Traficante, San Diego, 1994-98, ptnr., 1999—. Mem. ATLA, San Diego County Bar Assn., Consumer Attys. San Diego, San Diego Barristers Club (pres. 1998). State civil litigation, Federal civil litigation, Insurance. Office: Greco & Traficante 350 W Ash St Ste 850 San Diego CA 92101-3494

**SCHULZE, ERIC WILLIAM,** lawyer, legal publications editor, publisher; b. Libertyville, Ill., July 8, 1952; s. Robert Carl and Barbara (Mayo) S. BA, U. Tex., 1973, JD, 1977. Bar: Tex. 1977, U.S. Dist. Ct. (we. dist.) Tex. 1987, U.S. Ct. Appeals (5th cir.) 1987, U.S. Dist. Ct. (ea. and so. dists.) Tex. 1988, U.S. Dist. Ct. (no. dist.) Tex. 1989, U.S. Supreme Ct. 1989; bd. cert. civil appellate law Tex. Bd. Legal Specialization, 1990—. Rsch. asst. U. Tex., Austin, 1978; legis. aide Tex. Ho. of Reps., Austin, 1979-81; editor Tex. Sch. Law News, Austin, 1982-85; assoc. Hairston, Walsh & Anderson, Austin, 1986-87; ptnr. Walsh, Anderson, Brown, Schulze & Aldridge, Austin, 1988—, mng. ptnr., 1993—; editor Tex. Sch. Adminstrs. Legal Digest, Austin, 1986-92, co-pub., 1991—, mng. editor, 1992—. Editor: (legal reference books) Texas Education Code Annotated, 1982-85; editl. adv. com. West's Edn. Law Reporter, 1996—. Del. Tex. State Democratic Conv., 1982, Travis County Dem. Conv., 1982, 84, 86. Recipient Merit award for pubs. Internat. Assn. Bus. Communicators-Austin br., 1983, Merit award for authorship Coll. of State Bar Tex., 1992. Mem. Fed. Bar Assn., Am. Bar Assn., Tex. Bar Assn., Travis County Bar Assn., Bar Assn. of 5th Cir., Defense Rsch. Inst., Nat. Council Sch. Attys., Tex. Council Sch. Attys., Edn. Law Assn., Toastmasters (pres. Capital City chpt. 1995). Education and schools, Civil rights, Appellate. Home: 3416 Mount Bonnell Cir Austin TX 78731-5745 Office: Walsh Anderson Brown Schulze & Aldridge PO Box 2156 Austin TX 78768-2156

**SCHUMACHER, BARRY LEE,** lawyer; b. Akron, Ohio, May 19, 1952; s. Lee Richard and Jane (Barry) S.; m. Judy Martha Sedlak, Dec. 7, 1974; children: John Barry, Jennifer Martha, Christopher James, Megan Marie, Molly Cate, Michael Jeffrey. BS in Biology, Allegheny Coll., 1974; JD, U. Denver, 1979, LLM in Taxation, 1980. Bar: Colo. 1979, U.S. Dist. Ct. Colo. 1979, U.S. Tax Ct. 1980, U.S. Ct. Appeals (10th cir.) 1982, U.S. Ct. Claims 1985. Law clk. to judge U.S. Dept. Interior, Denver, 1978; assoc. Oates, Austin, McGrath & Jordan, Aspen, Colo., 1980-82; ptnr. Wright & Schumacher, Aspen, 1982-88; pvt. practice B. Lee Schumacher, Aspen, 1988—; instr. law Colo. Mountain Coll., Aspen, 1985; dir. SetSung, Ltd., Basalt, Colo., 1996—. Editor Denver Law Jour., 1977-79, Denver Tax Law Jour., 1979-80. Sec., bd. trustees Aspen Country Day Sch., 1990-96; pres., bd. trustees Aspen Country Day Sch., 1997—. Mem. ABA, Denver Bar Assn., Pitkin County Bar Assn., Fraternal Order of Elks, Phi Alpha Delta. Republican. Corporate taxation, Real property, General practice. Home: 115 Glen Eagles Dr Aspen CO 81611-3302

**SCHUMACHER, DAWN KRISTI ANN,** lawyer; b. Harbor Beach, Mich., Nov. 27, 1960; d. Eugene Elmer Pyrek and Janice Karen Langley; m. Tad Richard Schumacher, Aug. 19, 1990; 1 child, Jakob Christopher. BS, No. Mich. U., 1982; JD, Thomas M. Cooley Law Sch., 1985. Bar: Mich. 1985. Asst. city atty. City of Gaylord, Mich., 1985-86, City of Troy, Mich., 1990-95; chief asst. prosecutor Otsego County, Gaylord, 1986-90, Sanilac County, Sanovsky, Mich., 1995-96; pvt. practice Harbor Beach, Mich., 1996—; guest spkr. Mich. Mcpl. League, 1992—. Nat. Oratory scholar Thomas M. Cooley Law Sch., 1982. Roman Catholic. Avocations: painting, reading, hiking, cross-country skiing, bicycling. Criminal, Probate, Real property. Office: 240 State St Harbor Beach MI 48441-1205

**SCHUMACHER, PAUL MAYNARD,** lawyer; b. Columbus, Nebr., Apr. 4, 1951; s. Maynard Mathew and Rita Bell (Jarosz) S.; m. Michele Suzanne Gassé, June 26, 1976; children: Nicole Suzanne, Kristen Paulette. AA, Platte Coll., 1971; BS, Fort Hays U., 1973; JD, Georgetown U., 1976. Bar: Fla. 1976, Nebr. 1977, U.S. Dist. Ct. Nebr. 1977. Mem. staff U.S. Senate, Washington, 1974-76; sole practice Miami, Fla. and Columbus, 1976—; v.p. Community Lottery Systems, Inc., Columbus, 1990-92, pres., 1992—; v.p. Megavision Corp., Columbus, 1976—. Treas. prin. Rep. campaign com. U.S. Senate Candidate, Lincoln, Nebr., 1978-79; atty. Platte County, Columbus, 1979-87; chmn. Platte county Reps., 1988-94; mem. Nebr. Rep. State Ctrl. Com., 1994-96; CEO Lotto Nebr., 1992—; bd. dirs., CEO Cmty. Internet Sys., Inc., 1995—. Mem. Nebr. Bar Assn., Fla. Bar Assn., Platte County Bar Assn. (pres. 1992-93), Internat. Platform Assn., N.Am. Gaming Regulators Assn. (internat. gaming com.), Rotary, Elks. Roman Catholic. Avocation: physics. Home: 6255 Meyer Rd Columbus NE 68601-8044 Office: PO Box 122 Columbus NE 68602-0122

**SCHUMACHER, SCOTT ALAN,** lawyer; b. Seattle, Dec. 3, 1962; s. Paul Roen and Doris (Hoffman) S.; m. Moira Ellen Carlson, July 5, 1986; children: Claire Evelyn, Paul Joseph. BA, Loyola Marymount U., L.A., 1986; JD, U. Puget Sound, 1990; LLM in Taxation, NYU, 1991. Bar: Wash. 1991. Atty. advisor U.S. Tax Ct., Washington, 1991-92; trial atty. tax divsn. U.S. Dept. Justice, Washington, 1992-96; atty. Chicoine & Hallett, Seattle, 1996—. Mem. ABA, Wash. State Bar Assn., Wash. Assn. Criminal Def. Lawyers. Taxation, general, Federal civil litigation, Criminal. Office: Chicoine & Hallett PS 1011 Western Ave Ste 803 Seattle WA 98104-1096

**SCHUPP, ANASTASIA LUKA,** lawyer; b. Chgo.; d. Joseph Anthony and Anastasia Maria (Romel) Luka; m. William Schupp, Apr. 20, 1968 (div. June 1994); 1 child, William Joseph. BS in Social Sci., Loyola U., 1966, JD, 1977; MA, U. Mich., 1968; jagellonian, U. Sum., Poland, 1993. Bar: Ill. 1982, U.S. Supreme Ct. 1994. Law libr. Seyfarth, Shaw, Fairweather & Geraldson, Chgo., 1979-82; ptnr. Flader & Haces, Chgo., 1982-85; assocl. Hyatt Legal Svcs., Chgo., 1985-86; pvt. practice Chgo., 1986—; lectr. Chgo. Bd. Realtors, 1988-89, Robert Morris Coll., Orland Park, Ill., 1993, East West U., Chgo., 1993, Montay Coll., Chgo., 1994-95, academic coun., 1994-95. Editor: An Ethnic Christmas, 1982; (newsletter) The Overture, 1980-81; contbr. articles to profl. jours. Vol. Chgo. Vol. Legal Svcs., 1991—; arbitrator Chgo. Archdiocese, 1994—; atty. coord. Com. to Elect Richard J. Owens for Judge, Chgo., 1993-94. Recipient Honorable Mention Polish Arts Club, 1996. Mem. Womens Bar aSsn. Ill. (chair com. 1984, 94), Chgo. Bar Assn., Advs. Soc. (historian 1985-87), Coalition of Polish Am. Women (parliamentarian), First Cath. Scouak Ladies Assn., Royal Horticultural Soc. Democrat. Roman Catholic. Avocations: art, writing, gardening. Probate, Real property, Family and matrimonial. Home and Office: 360 W Shore Trl Sparta NJ 07871-1404

**SCHUSTER, E. ELAINE,** lawyer; b. Oklahoma City, June 8, 1936; d. John Otto and Eula Delone (Campbell) Schuster. AB, Sweet Briar Coll., 1958; MA in Econs. and Fin., U. Okla., 1961, JD, 1968. Bar: Okla. 1968, U.S. Dist. Ct. (we. dist.) Okla. 1969, U.S. Ct. Appeals (10th cir.) 1976, U.S. Dist. Ct. (no. dist.) Okla. 1981, U.S. Dist. Ct. (ea. dist.) Okla. 1991. Prof. econs. Southeastern State U., Durant, Okla., 1961-65; assoc. Whitten & Whitten, Oklahoma City, 1968-71; asst. dist. atty. Oklahoma County, 7th Dist., 1972-78; ptnr. Jones, Schuster & Flaugher, Oklahoma City, 1978-82; prin., E. Elaine Schuster, P.C., Oklahoma City, 1982—; lectr. in field. Contbr. articles to profl. jours. Mem. Oklahoma County Bd. Adjustment, 1978-97, chmn., 1984-97; citizen mem. profl. liaison com. City of Oklahoma City, 1980—; mem. Bd. Edn., Metro Area Vocat. Tech. Sch. Dist., 1982—, Oklahoma City, pres., 1984-85, 91-92, 92-93, 98-99, 99—; mem. ch. bd. University Pl. Christian Ch., 1982-86, 89-92, elder, 1989-92, trustee, 1992; bd. overseers Sweet Briar Coll., 1986-90. GE grantee U. Va., 1963; named Outstanding Bus. Woman. of Okla. Town Club of Bus. and Profl. Women, 1986, Hon. All State Sch. Bd., Oklahoma State Sch. Bds. Assn., 1999. Mem. Okla. Bar Assn. (del. 1996-97, alt. del. 1998-99), Oklahoma County Bar Assn. (bench and bar com. 1994-95, long range planning com. 1995-97), Okla. Trial Lawyers Assn. (bd. dirs. 1996-99), AAUW (br. pres. 1978-80, Okla. div. bd. 1969-75, 81-83, 85-87, Polished Diamond award S.W. cen. region 1987), Kappa Beta Pi, Delta Kappa Gamma (hon.). Avocations: hiking, photography, travel. Probate, General civil litigation, General corporate. Office: Heritage Law Ctr 515 NW 13th St Oklahoma City OK 73103-2203

**SCHUSTER, PHILIP FREDERICK, II,** lawyer, writer; b. Denver, Aug. 26, 1945; s. Philip Frederick and Ruth Elizabeth (Robar) S.; m. Barbara Lynn Nordquist, June 7, 1975; children: Philip Christian, Matthew Dale. BA, U. Wash., 1967; JD, Willamette U., 1972. Bar: Oreg. 1972, U.S. Dist. Ct. Oreg. 1974, U.S. Ct. Appeals (9th cir.) 1986, U.S. Supreme Ct. 1986. Dep. dist. atty. Multnomah County, Portland, Oreg., 1972; title examiner Pioneer Nat. Title Co., Portland, 1973-74; assoc. Buss, Leichner et al, Portland, 1975-76; from assoc. to ptnr. Kitson & Bond, Portland, 1976-77; pvt. practice Portland, 1977-95; ptnr. Dierking and Schuster, Portland, 1996—; arbitrator Multnomah County Arbitration Program, 1985—; student mentor Portland Pub. Schs., 1988—. Author: The Indian Water Slide; contbg. author OSB CLE Publ., Family Law; contbr. articles to profl. jours. Organizer Legal Aid Svcs. for Community Clinics, Salem, Oreg. and Seattle, 1969-73; Dem. committeeman, Seattle, 1965-70; judge Oreg. State Bar and Classroom Law Project, H.S. Mock Trial Competition, 1988—. Mem. ABA, ATLA, NAACP (exec. bd. Portland, Oreg. chpt. 1979-98), ACLU, Multnomah Bar Assn. (Vol. Lawyers Project), Internat. Platform Assn., Alpha Phi Alpha. Avocations: river drifting, camping, swimming, walking, writing. Personal injury, Workers' compensation, Real property. Office: 1500 NE Irving St Ste 540 Portland OR 97232-4209 *Hard work and perseverence are the keys to accomplishing any goal. Protecting and nurturing our children and our environment are life's most noble goals. Success is the pursuit of these goals.*

**SCHUSTER, ROBERT PARKS,** lawyer; b. St. Louis, Oct. 25, 1945; s. William Thomas Schuster and Carolyn Cornforth (Daugherty) Hathaway; 1 child, Susan Michele. AB, Yale U., 1967; JD with honors, U. of Wyo., 1970; LLM, Harvard U., 1971. Bar: Wyo. 1971, U.S. Ct. Appeals (10th cir.) 1979, U.S. Supreme Ct. 1984, Utah 1990. Dep. county atty. County of Natrona, Casper, Wyo., 1971-73; pvt. practice law, Casper, 1973-76; assoc. Spence & Moriarty, Casper, 1976-78; ptnr. Spence, Moriarty & Schuster, Jackson, Wyo., 1978—. Trustee U. Wyo., 1985-89; Wyo. Dem. nominee for U.S. House of Reps., 1994; polit. columnist Casper Star Tribune, 1987-94. Ford Found. Urban Law fellow, 1970-71; pres. United Way of Natrona County, 1974; bd. dirs. Dancers Workshop, 1981-83; chair Wyo. selection com.

Rhodes Scholarship, 1989-98; mem. bd. visitors Coll. Arts and Scis., U. Wyo., 1991—; mem. Dem. Nat. Com., 1992—; chair Wyo. Public Policy Forum, 1992-98; mem. Wind River Reservation Econ. Adv. Coun., 1998-99. Mem. ABA, ATLA, Wyo. Trial Lawyers Assn. Federal civil litigation, State civil litigation. Home: PO Box 548 Jackson WY 83001-0548 Office: Spence Moriarity & Schuster 15 S Jackson St Jackson WY 83001

**SCHUSTER, STEVEN VINCENT,** lawyer; b. Englewood, N.J., Mar. 27, 1952; s. Vincent Theodore and Elaine (Danis) S. BA, Gettysburg Coll., 1974; JD, U. Richmond, 1977. Bar: Va. 1977, N.J. 1977, U.S. Dist. Ct. N.J. 1977. Assoc. firm Bruce K. Byers, Esquire, Ridgewood, N.J., 1977-78, Margolis & Gordon, Union, N.J., 1978-80, R.J. Inglima, P.A., Paramus, N.J., 1980-83; sole practice, Cresskill, N.J., 1983—; corp. counsel Agfa Corp., Ridgefield Park, N.J., 1983-89, atty. zoning bd. Borough of Dumont, 1983—; trustee Bergen County Task Force Crimes Against Children Inc., Agfa Gevaert Rex, White Plains, N.Y., 1983-85, corp. counsel, 1983-84; dir. Metacomet Inc.; commr. Bergen County Tax Bd., 1987—. Mem. county com. Bergen County Rep. Orgn., N.J., 1978-82, 85—; aide to state senator Gerald Cardinale, Cresskill, 1979—; councilman Borough of Cresskill, 1982-84; prosecutor Borough of Cresskill, 1986—. Recipient Presdl. Achievement award, Washington, 1981. Mem. ABA, N.J. Bar Assn., Va. Bar Assn., Bergen County Bar Assn. Roman Catholic. General corporate, Legislative. Address: 170 Palisade Ave Cresskill NJ 07626-2261 Office: 65B W Madison Ave Dumont NJ 07628-2908

**SCHUTT, WALTER EUGENE,** lawyer; b. Cleve., July 27, 1917; s. Erle Minchin and Elizabeth (Eastman) S.; A.B., Miami U., Oxford, Ohio, 1939; J.D., U. Cin., 1948; m. Dorothy Louise Gilbert, Apr. 18, 1942; children: Gretchen Sue, Stephen David, Elizabeth Ann, Robert Barclay. Admitted to Ohio bar, 1948, U.S. Dist. Ct. (so. dist.) Ohio 1953, U.S. Supreme Ct. bar, 1962, U.S. Tax Ct. 1983, U.S. Ct. Appeals (6th cir.) 1986. Practiced in Wilmington, Ohio, 1948—; city solicitor, Wilmington, 1950-53. Mem. Wilmington Bd. Edn., 1958-65; chmn. Clinton County chpt. ARC, 1951-53; Wilmington chmn. Cin. Symphony Orch. Area Artists Series, 1969-71; trustee Wilmington Coll., 1962-74, sec., 1966-74; trustee Quaker Hill Found., Richmond, Ind., 1970-75, Friends Fellowship Community, Inc., 1986-93; rep. U.S. preparations com. 6th Internat. Assembly World Council of Chs., 1982. Served to 1st lt. USAAF, 1943-46. Decorated D.F.C.; recipient Disting. Service award Wilmington Jr. C. of C., 1953. Mem. Am. Bar Assn. (arms control and disarmament com. 1977-80), Ohio State Bar Assn., Clinton County Bar Assn. (past pres.), World Peace Through Law Ctr. Mem. Soc. of Friends (presiding clk. Friends United Meeting 1978-81, rep. to bd. Nat. Council Chs. of Christ 1985-96; presiding clk. Friends com. on. nat. legis. 1984-87). Club: Rotary. General practice, Probate, Non-profit and tax-exempt organizations. Home: 81 Columbus St Wilmington OH 45177-1801 Office: Thorne Bldg 36 1/2 N South St Wilmington OH 45177-2361

**SCHUUR, ROBERT GEORGE,** lawyer; b. Kalamazoo, Dec. 5, 1931; s. George Garrett and Louise Margaret (DeVries) S.; m. Susan Elizabeth White, Sept. 28, 1968; children—Arah Louise Adele, Jeremiah Donald Garrett. A.B., U. Mich., 1953, LL.B., 1955. Bar: Mich. 1955, N.Y. 1956. Assoc. Reid & Priest, N.Y.C., 1955-65, ptnr., 1966—. Served with USN, 1956-58. Mem. ABA, N.Y. State Bar Assn., Assn. of Bar of City of N.Y., Phi Beta Kappa. Club: University (N.Y.C.). General corporate, Public utilities, Securities. Home: 163 E 82nd St New York NY 10028-1856 Office: Reid & Priest 40 W 57th St Fl 28 New York NY 10019-4097

**SCHUYLER, DANIEL MERRICK,** lawyer, educator; b. Oconomowoc, Wis., July 26, 1912; s. Daniel J. and Fannie Sybil (Moorhouse) S.; m. Claribel Seaman, June 15, 1935; children: Daniel M. Jr., Sheila Gordon. AB summa cum laude, Dartmouth Coll., 1934; JD, Northwestern U., 1937. Bar: Ill. 1937, U.S. Supreme Ct. 1942, Wis. 1943. Tchr. constl. history Chgo. Latin Sch., 1935-37; assoc. Schuyler & Hennessy (attys.), 1937-42, ptnr., 1946-48; ptnr. Schuyler, Richert & Stough, 1948-58, Schuyler, Stough & Morris, Chgo., 1958-76, Schuyler, Ballard & Cowen, 1976-83; ptnr. Schuyler, Roche & Zwirner, P.C., 1983-96, of counsel, 1996—; treas., sec. and controller B-W Superchargers, Inc. div. Borg-Warner Corp., Milw., 1942-46; lectr. trusts, real property, future interests Northwestern U. Sch. Law, 1946-50, asso. prof. law, 1950-52, prof., 1952-80, prof. emeritus, 1980—. Author: (with Homer F. Carey) Illinois Law of Future Interests, 1941; supplements, 1947, 54; (with William M. McGovern, Jr.) Illinois Trust and Will Manual, 1970; supplements, 1972, 74, 76, 77, 79, 80, 81, 82, 83, 84; contbr. to profl. jours. Rep. nominee for judge Cook County Cir. Ct., 1958; bd. dirs., life mem. United Cerebral Palsy Greater Chgo., Lawrence Hall Youth Svcs. Fellow Am. Bar Found.; mem. ABA (past mem. ho. of dels., past chmn. sect. real property, probate and trust law), Chgo. Estate Planning Coun. (past pres., Dist. Svc. award 1977), Am. Coll. Trust and Estate Counsel (past pres.), Chgo. Bar Assn. (past chmn. coms. on trust law and post-admission edn., past bd. mgrs.), Ill. Bar Assn. (past chmn. real estate and legal edn. sects., past bd. govs.), Wis. Bar Assn., Legal Club, Law Club, Univ. Club, Order of Coif, Phi Beta Kappa, Phi Kappa Psi. Estate planning, Health, General practice. Home: 909 W Foster Ave Apt 244 Chicago IL 60640-2510 Office: Schuyler Roche & Zwirner PC 130 E Randolph St Ste 3800 Chicago IL 60601-6317

**SCHUYLER, ROB RENE,** lawyer; b. Larchmont, N.Y., Aug. 13, 1932; s. William and Margaret S.; children: Marc Philip, Clifford Robert, Paul Frederick. Student, U. Paris, 1950-52; Bachelors, U. So. Calif., 1955; JD, U. Mich., 1958. Bar: Calif. 1958, U.S. Dist. Ct. 1958, U.S. Supreme Ct. 1962. Dep. city atty. L.A. City Atty.'s Office, 1959-62; ptnr. Maury & Schuyler, L.A., 1962-65; pvt. practice, L.A., 1965-73; ptnr. Mihaly, Schuyler & Mitchell (formerly Mihaly, Schuyler & Burton), L.A., 1973—. Mem. L.A. County Bar Assn. (chmn. internat. law sect. 1972-73), Wilshire Bar Assn. (pres. 1970). Republican. Fax: 310-284-7982. E-mail: robr-schuyler@earthlink.net. General corporate, General civil litigation, Estate planning. Office: Mihaly Schuyler & Mitchell 1888 Century Park E Ste 1500 Los Angeles CA 90067-1719

**SCHWAB, CAROL ANN,** law educator; b. Washington, Mo., Mar. 2, 1953; d. Calvin George and Edith Emma (Starke) Schermann; m. Steven Joseph Schwab, May 31, 1975. BA, Southeast Mo. State U., 1975; JD, U. Mo., 1978; LLM, Washington U., St. Louis, 1985. Bar: Mo. 1979, N.C. 1986. Law clk. to presiding justice U.S. Dist. Ct. (we. dist.), Kansas City, Mo., 1979-82; assoc. Bryan, Cave, McPheeters & McRoberts, St. Louis, 1982-84, Smith, Anderson, Blount, Dorsett, Mitchell & Jernigan, Raleigh, N.C., 1985-87; assoc. prof., resource mgmt. specialist N.C. Coop. Extension Svc., N.C. State U., Raleigh, 1988—, dept. ext. leader, 1997—; instr. legal writing St. Louis U. Sch. Law, 1984. Contbr. articles to profl. jours. Bd. dirs., co-chair fin. com. N.C. chpt. Nat. Com. for Prevention of Child Abuse, 1988-90, pres.-elect, 1990; mem. bd. assocs. N.C. Child Advocacy Inst., 1990-93; mem. Children's Summit Steering Com., 1993. Recipient John S. Divilbiss award U. Mo., 1977. Mem. N.C. Bar Assn. (editor The Will and Way quar. publ. 1990-91, sec. estate planning and fiduciary law sect. 1991-92, coun. mem. 1996-99, mem. comm. adv. com. 1991—, mem. tech. adv. com. 1995-98, mem. elder law com. 1996, sec. elder law sect. 1996—, mem. coun. 1996—, editor Elder Law Quarterly 1996-98, vice chair 1998-99, chair 1999—), Mo. Bar Assn. Republican. Roman Catholic. Office: NC State U PO Box 7605 Raleigh NC 27695-0001

**SCHWAB, HAROLD LEE,** lawyer; b. N.Y.C., Feb. 5, 1932; s. Harold Walter and Beatrice (Braverman) S.; m. Rowena Vivian Strauss, June 12, 1953; children: Andrew, Lisa, James. BA, Harvard Coll., 1953, LLB, Boston Coll., 1956. Bar: N.Y. 1957, U.S. Ct. Mil. Appeals 1958, U.S. Dist. Cts. (so. and ea. dist.) N.Y. 1967, U.S. Ct. Appeals (2d cir.) 1971, U.S. Supreme Ct. 1971, U.S. Dist. Ct. (no. dist.) N.Y. 1974, U.S. Ct. Appeals (D.C. cir.) 1986, U.S. Dist. Ct. (we. dist.) N.Y. 1988, U.S. Ct. Appeals (11th cir.) 1988, U.S. Ct. Appeals (5th cir.) 1991. Vice pres. H.W. Schwab Textile Corp., N.Y.C., 1959-60; assoc. Emile Z. Berman & A. Harold Frost, N.Y.C., 1960-67, ptnr., 1967-74; sr. ptnr. Lester Schwab Katz & Dwyer, N.Y.C., 1974—; lectr. N.Y. State Bar Assn., N.Y. County Lawyers Assn. Served to lt. col. USAFR. Fellow Internat. Acad. Trial Lawyers; mem. ABA, ASTM, Soc. Automotive Engrs., Assn. for Advancement of Automotive Medicine, Product Liability Adv. Council, N.Y. State Bar Assn. (chmn. trial lawyers sect. 1980-81), Am. Bd. Trial Advs. (pres. N.Y. chpt. 1982-83), Fedn. Ins. and Corp. Counsel (v.p. 1979-80), Assn. of Bar of City of N.Y. N.Y. County Lawyers Assn., N.Y. State Trial Lawyers Assn., Def. Assn. N.Y., Harvard Club of N.Y., Downtown Assn. Contbr. articles to legal jours.; editor Trial Lawyers Sect. Newsletter-N.Y. State Bar Assn., 1981-84; mem. editl. bd. Jour. Products and Toxics Liability, 1976-96. State civil litigation, Federal civil litigation, Product liability. Home: 205 Beach 142 St Neponsit NY 11694 Office: Lester Schwab Katz & Dwyer 120 Broadway Fl 38 New York NY 10271-0071

**SCHWAB, HOWARD JOEL,** judge; b. Charleston, W.Va., Feb. 13, 1943; s. Joseph Simon and Gertrude (Hadas) S.; m. Michelle Roberts, July 4, 1970; children: Joshua Raphael, Bethany Alexis. BA in History with honors, UCLA, 1964, JD, 1967. Bar: Calif. 1968, U.S. Dist. Ct. (cen. dist.) Calif. 1968, U.S. Ct. Appeals (9th cir.) 1970, U.S. Supreme Ct. 1972. Clk. legal adminstrn. Litton Industries, L.A., 1967-68; dep. city atty. L.A., 1968-69; dep. atty. gen. State of Calif., L.A., 1969-84; judge Mcpl. Ct. L.A. Jud. Dist., 1984-85; judge Superior Ct. Superior Ct. L.A. County, L.A., 1985—; mem. faculty Berkeley (Calif.) Judicial Coll., 1987—. Contbr. articles to profl. jours. Recipient CDAA William E. James award Calif. Dist. Atty.'s Assn., 1981. Mem. San Fernando Valley Bar Assn., Inn. of Ct., Phi Alpha Delta. Democrat. Jewish. Avocations: history, book collecting. Office: LA Superior Ct 900 3rd St San Fernando CA 91340-2935

**SCHWAB, NELSON, JR.,** lawyer; b. Cin., July 19, 1918; s. Nelson Sr. and Frances Marie (Carlile) S.; m. Elizabeth Bakhaus (div.); m. Sylvia Lambert; children: Nelson III, Richard O. BA, Yale U., 1940; LLB, Harvard U., 1943. Bar: Ohio 1947. Ptnr. Graydon Head & Ritchey, Cin., 1947-95; sr. counsel, 1995—; bd. dirs. Rotex, Inc., Ralph J. Stolle co., Security Rug Cleaning Co., Yoder Die Casting Corp. Grants Review Com. The Greater Cin. Found.; mem. Cin. Pub. Schs. Degration Task Force; former chmn. bd. Vol. Lawyers for the Poor Found.; trustee Cin. Scholarship Found., FISC; adv. bd. Cin. Playhouse in the Park; ; past mem., sec. Cin. Bus. Com., 1977-88, mm. Schs. Task Force; past mem. Cin. City Mgr.'s Working Rev. Com. 2000 Plan, chmn. Reconstituted 2000 Plan Rev. Com., 1990; pres. Greater Cin. C. of C., 1973; chmn. Greater Cin. Ednl. TV, 1965-70, hon. trustee; chmn. Cincinnati and Hamilton County Am. Red Cross, 1955-57, hon. trustee; incorporator United Appeal, 1955; mem. Cin. Sch. Bd., 1959-64. Honoree Greater Cin. Region NCCJ, 1990; Great Living Cincinnatian Grater Cin. C. of C., 1991. Mem. 6th Cir. Jud. Conf., Cin. Country Club (past bd. dirs., sec.), Commonwealth Club (past pres.), Comml. Club, Recess Club (past pres.), Gyro Club (past pres.), Queen City Club, Queen City Optimists (past pres.), Cin. Yale Club (past pres.), Lincoln's Inn Soc., Delta Kappa Epsilon. Estate planning, General corporate, General practice. Home: 2470 W Rookwood Ct Cincinnati OH 45208-3321 Office: Graydon Head & Ritchey 511 Walnut St # 53D Cincinnati OH 45202-3115

**SCHWAB, TERRANCE W.,** lawyer; b. Pitts., May 19, 1940; m. Eileen Caulfield, Jan. 4, 1969; children: Matthew Caulfield, Catherine Grimley, Claire Gillespie. BA magna cum laude, Harvard U., 1962; LLB cum laude, Columbia U., 1966. Assoc. Milbank, Tweed, Hadley & McCloy, N.Y.C., 1966-70; assoc. Kelley, Drye & Warren, N.Y.C., 1970-74, ptnr., 1975-96; sr. v.p., gen. counsel global fin. and investment banking The Sanwa Bank Ltd., N.Y.C., 1996—; lectr. various profl. orgns. Assoc. editor: Law Practice of Alexander Hamilton, 1964-1980; contbr. articles to profl. jours. Trustee, sec. Caramoor Ctr. for Music and Arts, Katonah, N.Y., 1971—; trustee Sch. of Convent of Sacred Heart, N.Y.C., 1987—, chmn., 1990-93. Mem. ABA, N.Y. State Bar Assn., Assn. of Bar of City of N.Y., Harvard Club. Banking, Contracts commercial, Private international. Office: The Sanwa Bank Ltd 55 E 52nd St Fl 24 New York NY 10022-5907

**SCHWAB, WILLIAM G.,** lawyer; b. Phila., Jan. 16, 1951; s. Carl J. and Caroline A. Schwab; m. Joyce A. Hunt; children: William, Kathryn, Brian. BS, Temple U., 1973, JD, 1976. Bar: Pa. 1976, U.S. Dist. Ct. (mid. dist.) Pa. 1981, U.S. Ct. Appeals (3rd cir.), U.S. Supreme Ct.; bd. cert. Am. Bd. Cert. in Bus. and Consumer Bankruptcy. Atty. Legal Svcs. Northeastern Pa., Lehighton, 1976-78; pvt. practice law Lehighton, 1978—, pvt. practice trustee, 1993—; bd. dirs. Pencor Svcs., Inc., Palmerton, Pa. Designer (websites) U.S. Bankrupty Ct. for Mid. Dist. Pa., 1996, Carbon County Bar Assn., 1997. Pres. United Way Carbon County, Lehighton, 1989-90; dist. chmn. Boy Scouts Am. Minsi Traks Coun., Allentown, Pa., 1992-93; treas. Blue Mountain Little League, Lehighton, 1993-98. Named Businessperson of Yr., Pa. Future Bus. Leaders Am., 1991. Mem. Am. Bankruptcy inst., Nat. Assn. Bankruptcy Trustees, Carbon County Bar Assn. (chancellor 1998). Republican. Avocation: web design. Bankruptcy, Real property, General corporate. Office: 811 Blakeslee Boulevard Dr E Lehighton PA 18235-8712

**SCHWABE, GEORGE BLAINE, III,** lawyer; b. Tulsa, Oct. 10, 1947; s. George Blaine Jr. and Marguerite Irene (Williams) S.; m. Jann Lee Schoonover, July 28, 1972; 1 child, George Blaine IV. BBA, U. Okla., 1970, JD, 1974. Bar: U.S. Ct. Appeals (10th cir.) 1974, Okla. 1974, U.S. Dist. Ct. (we. dist.) Okla. 1974, U.S. Dist. Ct. (no. dist.) Okla. 1985, U.S. Dist. Ct. (ea. dist.) 1998, U.S. Supreme Ct. 1991. From assoc. to ptnr. Crowe & Dunlevy, Oklahoma City, 1974-82; ptnr., dir. Mock, Schwabe, Waldo, Elder, Reeves & Bryant, Oklahoma City, 1982-96; shareholder, dir. Gable Gotwals Mock Schwabe, Oklahoma City, 1996-98; member Mock, Schwabe, Waldo, Elder, Reeves & Bryant, 1998—; adj. prof. law Oklahome City U.; lectr. in field. Capt. USAR. Fellow Am. Coll. Bankruptcy; mem. ABA (bus. bankruptcy com. sect. bus. law), Okla. Bar Assn., Bankruptcy and Reorganization Sect. (pres. 1987-88, bd. dirs. 1985—), Okla. City Golf & Country Club, Rotary. Republican. Mem. Christian Ch. (Disciples of Christ). Avocations: golf, snow and water skiing, tennis, travel. Contracts commercial, Consumer commercial, Bankruptcy. Office: Mock Schwabe et al 2 Leadership Sq 14th Fl 211 N Robinson Ave Oklahoma City OK 73102-7109

**SCHWABE, JOHN BENNETT, II,** lawyer; b. Columbia, Mo., June 14, 1946; s. Leonard Wesley and Hazel Fern (Crouch) S. A.B., U. Mo.-Columbia, 1967, J.D., 1970. Bar: Mo. 1970, U.S. Dist. Ct. (we. dist.) Mo. 1970, U.S. Ct. Mil. Appeals 1971, U.S. Supreme Ct. 1973; ordained minister John Schwabe Ministries. Owner, prin. John B. Schwabe, II Law Firm, Columbia, 1974—, St. Louis, 1984-96. Trustee, lay leader, mem. adminstrv. bd. Wilkes Blvd. United Meth. Ch., 1974-79, chmn. pastor-parish relations com., 1984-85 ; mem. Friends of Music, Columbia, 1979—, bd. dirs., 1979-81; bd. dirs. Mo. Symphony Soc., 1984-85; ordained min., founder John Schwabe Ministries. Capt. JAGC, USAF, 1970-74. Mem. ABA, Boone County Bar Assn. (sec. 1977-79), Bar Assn. Met. St. Louis, Mo. Assn. Trial Attys., Personal Injury Lawyers Assn., Lawyers Assn. St. Louis, Columbia C. of C., Am. Legion, Phi Delta Phi. Methodist. Personal injury, State civil litigation, Workers' compensation. Office: John B Schwabe II Law Firm Schwabe Bldg 2 E Walnut St Columbia MO 65203-4163

**SCHWALLIE, DANIEL PHILLIP,** legal consultant; b. Canton, Ohio, Mar. 9, 1955; s. Paul C. and Margaret Kailey (Livingston) S.; children: Halden Reid, Kailey Justine. BA magna cum laude, Kalamazoo Coll., 1977; MA, U. Iowa, 1982, PhD, 1984; JD cum laude, Case Western Res. U., 1991. Bar: Ohio 1991. Asst. prof. econs. Case Western Res. U., Cleve., 1984-91; assoc. Thompson, Hine & Flory, Cleve., 1991-93; cons. Hewitt Assocs. LLC, Lincolnshire, Ill., 1993-95, Independence, Ohio, 1995—; cons. to law firms, Cleveland Heights, Ohio, 1989-90; grant proposal reviewer NSF, Washington, 1987-88. Author: The Impact of Intergovernmental Grants on the Aggregate Public Sector, 1989; articles referee Oxford (Eng.) Econ. Papers, 1988, Pub. Fin. Quar., New Orleans, 1988-91; contbr. articles to profl. jours. Recipient Am. Jurisprudence award Lawyers Coop. Pub. Co. and Bancroft-Whitney Co., 1987. Mem. ABA, Phi Eta Sigma, Omicron Delta Epsilon, Beta Gamma Sigma. Avocations: photography, gourmet cooking, jogging, dogs. Office: Hewitt Assocs LLC Crown Centre 5005 Rockside Rd Independence OH 44131-2194

**SCHWAMM, VIRGINIA ANN,** lawyer; b. Oak Ridge, Tenn., July 7, 1957; d. O.E. III and Elizabeth Helton Schow; m. Justin M. Schwamm Sr., Mar. 27, 1982. BS, U. Tenn., 1978, JD, 1990. Bar: Tenn. 1990, U.S. Dist. Ct. (ea. dist.) Tenn. 1991, U.S. Ct. Appeals (6th cir.) 1991. Assoc. Bernstein, Stair & McAdams, Knoxville, Tenn., 1990-93; ptnr. Towle & Schwamm, Knoxville, 1993-98, Schwamm, Albiston & Higgins, Knoxville, 1998—. Bd. dirs. Planned Parenthood East Tenn., Knoxville, 1978-91, pres. bd. dirs., 1985-86; bd. dirs. Big Bros./Big Sisters, 1983, Second Harvest Food Bank, 1990-96, treas., 1991; bd. govs. Knoxville Mus. Art, 1998—. Mem. Tenn. Bar Assn. (ho. dels. 1996—, chair family law sect. 1997-98, award of merit 1997, family law code commn.). Family and matrimonial, Juvenile, General civil litigation. Office: Schwamm Albiston & Higgins 9724 Kingston Pike Ste 1200 Knoxville TN 37922-6917

**SCHWARCZ, SUSAN KOLODNY,** lawyer; b. N.Y.C., Feb. 4, 1954; d. Armand and Elaine (Witkin) Kolodny; m. Steven L. Schwarcz, Aug. 24, 1975; children: Daniel, Rebekah. BA cum laude, Barnard Coll., 1975; postgrad. in social work, Columbia U., 1975-76; JD, Yeshiva U., 1979. Bar: N.Y. 1980, N.C. 1997. Pleadings atty. U.S. Fidelity & Guaranty Co., N.Y.C., 1980-81; pvt. practice Great Neck, N.Y., 1981-85, Scarsdale, N.Y., 1985—, Chapel Hill, N.C., 1997—. Mem. Friends Eldridge Street Synagogue, N.Y.C., 1982—; mem. polit. action com. Jewish Action Com., N.Y.C., 1986—; mem. Commn. on Chapel Hill Pub. Arts Commn., 1998—. Mem. Westchester County Bar Assn. (family law com. 1985-97), Westchester Law Guardians Assn., N.C. Bar Assn., Orange County Bar Assn., Sierra Club. Avocations: travel, Asian philosophy and antiques. Office: 109 Boxwood Pl Chapel Hill NC 27514-6503

**SCHWARTZ, ALLEN G.,** federal judge; b. Bklyn., Aug. 23, 1934; s. Herbert and Florence (Safier) S.; m. Joan Ruth Teitel, Jan. 17, 1965; children: David Aaron, Rachel Ann, Deborah Eve. BBA, CCNY, 1955; LLB, U. Pa., 1958. Bar: N.Y. 1958. Asst. dist. atty. Office of Dist. Atty., N.Y. County, 1959-62; assoc. firm Paskus Gordon & Hyman, N.Y.C., 1962-65; ptnr. firm Koch Lankenau Schwartz & Kovner, N.Y.C., 1965-69, Dornbush Mensch Mandelstam & Schwartz, N.Y.C., 1969-75; mem. Schwartz & Schreiber, P.C., N.Y.C., 1975-77; corp. counsel City of N.Y., 1978-81; mem. Schwartz Klink & Schreiber, P.C., 1982-87; ptnr. Proskauer Rose Goetz & Mendelsohn, N.Y.C., 1987-94; judge U.S. Dist. Ct. (so. dist.) N.Y., N.Y.C., 1994—; mem. ex officio N.Y.C. Bd. Ethics, 1978-81; pro bono sports commr. City of N.Y., 1982-83. Research editor: U. Pa. Law Rev, 1957-58. Recipient Award of Achievement, Sch. Bus. Alumni, Soc. of the City Coll., 1981, Hogan-Morganthau Assocs. award, 1980, Corp. Coun. ann. award, 1995, Frank S. Hogan Assocs. award, 1995. Office: US Courthouse 500 Pearl St Rm 1350 New York NY 10007-1316

**SCHWARTZ, ANDREA B.,** lawyer; b. Bklyn., July 6, 1962; d. Larry and Rhea Schwartz. BA, Rutgers Coll., 1984, MS, 1986; JD cum laude, Seton Hall U., 1993. Bar: N.J., Pa., N.Y. Ct. Appeals, U.S. Dist. Ct. N.J., U.S. Dist. Ct. (so. and ea. dists.) N.Y., U.S. Ct. Appeals (3d cir.), U.S. Supreme Ct. Editor, market researcher R.H. Bruskin Assocs., New Brunswick, N.J., 1982-84; group leader, water safety instr. Raquette Lake (N.Y.) Girls Camp, 1984, 85 summers; spl. projects asst. State of N.J. dept. Environ. Protection, Trenton, N.J., Jan. 1986 to June 1986; water safety instr. Point O'Pines Camp for Girls, Prast Lake, N.Y., 1986 summer; campus recreation specialist Rutgers U., New Brunswick, N.J., 1984-86; parks and recreation dir. Twp. of Aberdeen, N.J., 1986-93; jud. intern Hon. John W. Bessell U.S. Dist. Ct. N.J., Newark, 1991 summer; law clk. to Hon. Gloria M. Burns U.S. Bankruptcy Ct., Camden, N.J., 1993-95; litig. assoc. Lowenstein Sandler PC, Roseland, N.J., 1995—; mem. adv. com. on recreation City of New Brunswick, N.J., 1987. Assoc. editor: Traps for the Unwary - A Primer for NJ Lawyers on the Pitfalls to Avoid in Everyday Practice, 1997. Trustee Vol. Ctr. for Greater Essex County, 1997—. Alan V. Lowenstein Pub. Interest fellow Lowenstein Sandler PC and Essex-Newark Legal Svcs., 1996-97. Mem. Essex County Bar Assn. (chair continuing legal edn. com. 1997—, Young Lawyer Achievement award 1998). Avocations: piano, movies. Federal civil litigation, State civil litigation, Contracts commercial. Office: Lowenstein Sandler PC 65 Livingston Ave Ste 2 Roseland NJ 07068-1791

**SCHWARTZ, ARTHUR Z.,** lawyer; b. N.Y.C., Feb. 11, 1953; s. Herman and Roselind (Grant) S.; m. Claire Basescu, Dec. 28, 1985; children: Jacob, Rebecca. BA, Columbia Coll., 1974; JD, Hofstra U., 1978. Bar: Pa. 1978, N.Y. 1979. Ptnr. Hall, Clifton & Schwartz, N.Y.C., 1979-84, Clifton & Schwartz, N.Y.C., 1984-89, Lewis, Greenwald & Kennedy, N.Y.C., 1989-95, Kennedy, Schwartz & Cure, N.Y.C., 1995—; gen. counsel Utility Workers Union, Washington, 1990-92, Amalgamated NE Regional Bd., N.Y.C., 1994—. Mem. exec. com. Village Ind. Democrats, 1989—; chair West Village Alliance for Parks, 1994—; leader Dem. Party Dist. Greenwich Village, N.Y.C., 1995—; mem. exec. com. Hudson River Park Alliance, N.Y.C., 1997—; waterfront chair Cmty. Bd. Manhattan, 1998—. Mem. Assn. Union Democracy (bd. dirs. 1985—). Jewish. Avocation: coaching little league. Home: 269 W 11th St New York NY 10014-2493 Office: Kennedy Schwartz & Cure 113 University Pl New York NY 10003-4527

**SCHWARTZ, BARRY FREDRIC,** lawyer, diversified holding company executive; b. Phila., Apr. 16, 1949; s. Albert and Evelyn (Strauss) S.; m. Sherry L. Handsman, Mar. 21, 1985; children: Fanny Rose, Abraham David. AB cum laude, Kenyon Coll., 1970; JD, Georgetown U., 1974. Bar: Pa. 1974, Ill. 1974, N.Y. 1992, U.S. Dist. Ct. (ea. dist.) Pa. 1974, U.S. Dist. Ct. (no. dist.) Ill. 1975, U.S. Dist. Ct. (so. dist.) N.Y. 1992, U.S. Ct. Appeals (7th cir.) 1977, U.S. Ct. Appeals (3d cir.) 1978, U.S. Ct. Appeals (4th cir.) 1979, U.S. Ct. Appeals (6th cir.) 1981, U.S. Supreme Ct. 1981, N.Y. 1992. Assoc. Sachnoff, Schrager, Jones & Weaver, Chgo., 1974-76; ptnr. Wolf, Block, Schorr & Solis-Cohen, Phila., 1976-89; exec. v.p. gen. counsel MacAndrews & Forbes Holdings, Inc., N.Y.C., 1989—. Securities, Federal civil litigation, Mergers and acquisitions. Home: 143 Park Ave Greenwich CT 06830-4849 Office: MacAndrews & Forbes Holdings Inc 35 E 62nd St New York NY 10021-8016

**SCHWARTZ, BARRY STEVEN,** lawyer; b. Bklyn., Mar. 12, 1950; s. Joseph and Helen (Lipkin) S.; m. Sherry Licht Cooper, Feb. 18, 1984; 1 child, Jennifer. BA, NYU, 1972; JD, Cath. U. Am., 1975. Bar: N.Y. 1976, U.S. Dist. Ct. (so. dist.) 1976, N.J. 1979, U.S. Ct. Appeals (2d cir.) 1988. Assoc. Seavey, Fingerit & Vogel, N.Y.C., 1976-81; pvt. practice law N.Y.C., 1980—; of counsel Seavey, Vogel & Oziel, LLP, N.Y.C., 1982-97, Seavey, Vogel & Oziel, N.Y.C., 1998—; atty. West New York (N.J.) Rent Control Board, 1984-86. Assoc. editor Cath. U. Law Rev., 1974-75. Mem. ABA, N.Y. State Bar Assn., Masons (master Audubon-Gotham club 1986). Avocations: music, reading, travel, computers. Real property, Landlord-tenant, General civil litigation. Home: 6 Corn Mill Ct Saddle River NJ 07458-1232 Office: 119 W 57th St New York NY 10019-2303

**SCHWARTZ, BERNARD JULIAN,** lawyer; b. Edmonton, Alberta, Can., July 29, 1960; came to U.S., 1982; s. Sol and Anne (Motkovich) S. BA, U. Alberta, 1981; JD, McGeorge Sch. Law, 1986. Bar: U.S. Supreme Ct. 1991. Atty. Ropers, Majeski, San Francisco, 1987-88, Riverside County Pub. Defenders, Riverside, Calif., 1988-89; pvt. practice Riverside, 1990—. Coach Riverside County H.S. Mock Trial Team, 1990, 96, 97. Mem. Calif. Attys. Criminal Justice, Calif. Pub. Defenders Assn., Riverside County Bar Assn. Criminal. Home: 6157 Hillary Ct Riverside CA 92506-2139

**SCHWARTZ, BRENDA KEEN,** lawyer; b. Ft. Smith, Ark., Dec. 5, 1949; d. James Pritchard and Era Erline (Jones) Denniston; m. Dean Edward Keen, June 23, 1973 (dec. June 1990); 1 child, Duncan Denniston Keen; m. Sylvan Schwartz, Jr., Apr. 26, 1992. BA, U. Houston, 1972, JD magna cum laude, 1975. Bar: Tex. 1975, U.S. Dist. Ct. (so. dist.) Tex. 1975. Assoc. Haynes & Fullenweider, P.L.C., Houston, 1975-79, v.p., ptnr., 1979-87; ptnr., officer Wallis & Keen, P.C., Houston, 1988-92; prin. Brenda Keen Schwartz P.C., Houston, 1992—. Contbr. articles to legal publs. Fellow Am. Acad. Matrimonial Lawyers (pres. Tex. chpt. 1996-97), Tex. Acad. Family Law Specialists (bd. dirs., newsletter editor 1997-99), Tex. Bar Found., Houston Bar Found.; mem. State Bar Tex. (family law coun. 1989-93). Roman Catholic. Family and matrimonial, Alternative dispute resolution. Office: 1800 Bering Dr Ste 690 Houston TX 77057-3158

**SCHWARTZ, CAROL VIVIAN,** lawyer; b. Newark, Apr. 5, 1952; d. A. Harold and Helen (Schwartz) S.; m. Robert L. Sills, June 9, 1985. BA, Tufts U., 1974; JD, Columbia U., 1977. Law clk. to presiding justice U.S. Dist. Ct. N.Y., N.Y.C., 1978-79; assoc. DeLevoise & Plimpton, N.Y.C., 1979-81; assoc. counsel Am. Express Co., N.Y.C., sr. counsel, now group counsel. Mem. ABA. Avocation: sailing. General corporate, Private international. Home: 520 E 86th St # 11A New York NY 10028-7534 Office: Am Express Co Am Express Tower 200 Vesey St New York NY 10285-1000*

**SCHWARTZ, CHARLES, JR.,** federal judge; b. New Orleans, Aug. 20, 1922; s. Charles and Sophie (Hess) S.; m. Patricia May, Aug. 31, 1950;

children: Priscilla May, John Putney. BA, Tulane U., 1943, JD, 1947. Bar: La. 1947. Ptnr. Guste, Barnett & Little, 1947-70; practiced in New Orleans, until 1976; ptnr. firm Little, Schwartz & Dussom, 1970-76; dist. counsel Gulf Coast dist. U.S. Maritime Adminstrn., 1953-62; judge U.S. Dist. Ct. (ea. dist.) La., New Orleans, 1976-91, sr. judge, 1991—; Mem. Fgn. Itelligence Surveillance Ct., 1992-98; prof. Tulane U. Law Sch., 1977—; lectr. continuing law insts., 1974-75; mem. Jud. Conf. Com. U.S. on implementation of jury system, 1981-85; mem. permanent adv. bd. Tulane Admiralty Law Inst., 1984—. Bd. editors Tulane Law Rev. Pres. New Orleans unit Am. Cancer Soc., 1956-57; v.p., chmn. budget com. United Fund Greater New Orleans Area, 1959-61, trustee, 1953-65; bd. dirs. Cancer Assn. Greater New Orleans, 1958—, pres., 1958-59, 72-73; bd. dirs. United Cancer Council, 1963-85, pres., 1971-73; mem. com. on grants to agencies Community Chest, 1965-87; men's adv. com. League Women Voters, 1966-68; chmn. com. admissions of program devel. and coordination com. United Way Greater New Orleans, 1974-77; mem. comml. panel Am. Arbitration Assn., 1974-76; bd. dirs. Willow Wood Home, 1979-85, 1989-92; bd. mgrs. Touro Infirmary, 1992—; trustee Metairie Park Country Day Sch., 1977-83; mem. La. Republican Central Com., 1961-76; mem. Orleans Parish Rep. Exec. Com., 1960-75, chmn., 1964-75; mem. Jefferson Parish Rep. Exec. Com., 1975-76; del. Rep. Nat. Conv., 1960, 64, 68; mem. nat. budget and consultation com. United Community Funds and Coun. of Am., 1961; bd. dirs. Community Svcs. Coun., 1971-73. Served to 2d lt. AUS, 1943-46; maj. U.S. Army Res.; ret. Mem. La. Bar Assn. New Orleans Bar Assn. (legis. com. 1970-75), Fed. Bar Assn., Fgn. Rels. Assn. New Orleans (bd. dirs. 1957-61), 5th Cir. Dist. Judges Assn. (pres. 1984-85), Lakewood Country Club (bd. dirs. 1967-68, pres. 1975-77). Office: US Dist Ct C-317 US Courthouse 500 Camp St New Orleans LA 70130-3313

**SCHWARTZ, CHARLES WALTER,** lawyer; b. Brenham, Tex., Dec. 27, 1953; s. Walter C. and Annie (Kuehn) S.; m. Kay Anne Kern, Sept. 24, 1996. BS, U. Tex., 1975, MA, 1980, JD, 1977; LLM, Harvard U., 1980. Bar: Tex. 1977; bd. cert. civil appellate law Tex. Bd. Legal Specialization. Law clk. U.S. Ct. Appeals (5th cir.), Austin, Tex., 1977-79; assoc. Vinson & Elkins L.L.P., Houston, 1980-86, ptnr., 1986—. Contbr. articles to law revs. Fellow Coll. of State Bar of Tex.; mem. ABA, Tex. Bar Assn. (former chmn. grievance com. 1993-99), Tex. Bar Found., Houston Bar Found., Houston Bar Assn., Am. Law Inst., Tex. Law Rev. Assn., Bar Assn. of 5th Cir. Mem. Tex. Bar Assn. (chmn. grievance com. 1993-99). Federal civil litigation, Antitrust, Securities. Home: 2825 Albans Rd Houston TX 77005-2309 Office: Vinson & Elkins LLP 2300 First City Tower 1001 Fannin St Ste 3300 Houston TX 77002-6706

**SCHWARTZ, DANIEL LEONARD,** lawyer; b. Livingston, N.J., May 5, 1968; s. Edward and Harriet Mae S.; m. Virginia H. Schwartz, Oct. 2, 1993; 1 child, Kayleigh Byers. BS, Syracuse U., 1990; JD cum laude, Am. U., 1993. Bar: Nev. 1993, N.J. 1994, Pa. 1994, U.S. Dist. Ct. Nev. 1993. Atty. Bernstein & Assocs., Las Vegas, Nev., 1993; dep. Nev. Atty. for Injured Workers, Las Vegas, 1994; atty. Gugino Law Firm, Las Vegas, 1994-97; ptnr. Gugino & Schwartz, Las Vegas, 1997—. Workers' compensation, Labor, Personal injury. Office: Gugino & Schwartz 1701 W Charleston Blvd Ste 500 Las Vegas NV 89102-2309

**SCHWARTZ, EDWARD ARTHUR,** lawyer; b. Boston, Sept. 27, 1937; s. Abe and Sophie (Gottheim) S.; m. Sheila Kauffman, Apr. 5, 1997; children: Eric Allen, Jeffrey Michael. AB, Oberlin Coll., 1959; LLB, Boston Coll., 1962; postgrad., Am. U., 1958-59, Northeastern U., 1970; postgrad. exec. program, Stanford U., 1979. Bar: Conn. 1962, Mass. 1965. Legal intern Office Atty. Gen. Commonwealth of Mass., 1961; assoc. Schatz & Schatz, Hartford, Conn., 1962-65, Cohn, Reimer & Pollack, Boston, 1965-67; v.p., gen. coun., sec. Digital Equipment Corp., Maynard, Mass., 1967-88; pres. New Eng. Legal Found., Boston, 1990-98, also bd. dirs.; vis. prof. law Boston Coll., 1986, adj. prof., 1987-89; also bd. dirs.; bd. dirs. SatelLife Corp.; bd. advisors Buffalo Hill Hist. Ctr. Editor Boston Coll. Indsl. and Comml. Law Rev, 1960-62, Ann. Survey Mass. Law, 1960-62. Chair, bd. trustees Rural Land Found. Mem. ABA, Mass. Bar Assn., Boston Bar Assn. General corporate. Home: 62 Todd Pond Rd Lincoln MA 01773-3808

**SCHWARTZ, EDWARD J.,** federal judge; b. 1912. Judge Mcpl. Ct. and Superior Ct., San Diego; judge U.S. Dist. Ct. for So. Dist. Calif., former chief judge, now sr. judge. Office: US Dist Ct 4134 US Courthouse 940 Front St San Diego CA 92101-8994

**SCHWARTZ, EDWARD LESTER,** retired lawyer; b. N.Y.C., July 13, 1910; s. Alexander and Serene (Brown) S.; m. Edna B. Smith, July 31, 1941; 1 child, Andrea Helen Saiet. BA, CCNY, 1931; JD, Harvard U., 1934. Bar: N.Y. 1935, Mass. 1939. Pvt. practice N.Y.C., 1935-39, Boston, 1939—; ret.; pat lectr. law Boston U., Northeastern U., Suffolk U., New Eng. Law Inst., Mass. Continuing Legal Edn. Inst.; asst. atty. gen. State of Mass., 1970-75; commr. Nat. Conf. Commrs. on Uniform Laws (life); chmn. spl. com. Uniform Securities Act, spl. com. Landlord/Tenant Relationship Act; Mass. commr. Interstate Coop., 1949-74. Author: Lease Drafting in Massachusetts, 1961; contbr. articles to profl. jours. Mem. ABA, Am. Law Inst. (life), Am. Judicature Soc., Boston Bar Assn., Mass. Bar Assn. (lectr.), Scribes, New Eng. Law Inst. (exec. com.), Mass. Continuing Legal Edn. (bd. dirs.). Probate, Real property. Home: 17 Ledgewood Rd Weston MA 02493-1423

**SCHWARTZ, ESTAR ALMA,** lawyer; b. Bklyn., June 29, 1950; d. Henry Israel and Elaine Florence (Scheiner) Sutel; m. Lawrence Gerald Schwartz, June 28, 1976 (div. Dec. 1977); 1 child, Joshua (dec.). JD, N.Y.U., 1980. owner Estaris Paralegal Svc., Flushing, N.Y., 1992—. Mgr., ptnr. Scheiner, Scheiner, DeVito & Wytte, N.Y.C., 1966-81; fed. govt., social security fraud specialist DHHS, OI, OIG, SSFIS, N.Y.C., 1982-83; pensions Todtman, Epstein, et al, N.Y.C., 1983-85; office mgr., sec. Sills, Beck, Cummis, N.Y.C., 1985-86; office mgr., bookkeeper Philip, Birnbaum & Assocs., N.Y.C., 1986-87; office mgr., sec. Stanley Posses, Esq., Queens, N.Y., 1989-90. Democrat. Jewish. Avocations: needlepoint, horseback riding, tennis, bowling, writing children's stories. Personal injury, Product liability, Pension, profit-sharing, and employee benefits. Home and Office: 67-20 Parsons Blvd Apt 2A Flushing NY 11365-2960

**SCHWARTZ, HOWARD J.,** lawyer; b. N.Y.C., July 17, 1946; s. Joseph and Fay S.; m. Kathryn Brancati; children: Hania, Bethany, Christopher. BA, Muhlenberg Coll., 1968; JD, NYU, 1972. Atty. Rabinowitz, Boudin & Standard, N.Y.C., 1973-74, Legal Aid Soc., N.Y.C., 1974-77; ptnr. Schwartz & Sands, N.Y.C., 1977-79, Robinson, Perlman & Kirschner, N.Y.C., 1979-86, Davis & Gilbert, N.Y.C., 1986-92; prin. Porzio, Bromberg & Newman, Morristown, N.J., 1993—. Contbr. articles to profl. jours. Coach Montville Recreation Dept., N.J., 1993—. Mem. ABA, N.Y. State Bar Assn., N.J. State Bar Assn., Internat. Assn. Defense Counsel, Inns of Ct. Avocations: skiing, tennis. Entertainment, Intellectual property, Trademark and copyright. Office: Porzio Bromberg & Newman 163 Madison Ave Morristown NJ 07960-7324

**SCHWARTZ, IRWIN H.,** lawyer; b. Bklyn., Mar. 25, 1948; s. Julius and Sylvia (Holzman) S.; m. Barbara T. Granett, July 3, 1971; 1 child, Matthew Lane. BA, Bklyn. Coll., 1968; JD, Stanford U., 1971. Bar: Calif. 1972, Washington 1972, U.S. Ct. Appeals (9th cir.) 1972, U.S. Supreme Ct. 1977. Asst. U.S. atty. U.S. Dist. Ct. (we. dist.) Wash., Seattle, 1972-74, exec. asst. U.S. atty., 1974-75, fed. pub. defender, 1975-81; pvt. practice Seattle, 1981—. Mem. ABA (criminal justice sect. coun. 1991-94), Nat. Assn. Criminal Def. Lawyers (v.p. 1999—), Wash. Athletic Club (Seattle). Avocations: photography, woodworking. Federal civil litigation, Criminal. Office: 710 Cherry St Seattle WA 98104-1925

**SCHWARTZ, JAMES EVAN,** lawyer; b. N.Y.C., June 16, 1956; s. Louis and Elaine Florence (Friedman) S.; m. Susan Lea Cohen, Nov. 18, 1989; children: Jessica, Deborah, Andrew. BA, U. Pa., 1978; JD, Duke U., 1981. Bar: N.Y. 1982, U.S. Dist. Ct. (so. and ea. dists.) N.Y. 1987. Assoc. Bell, Kalnick, Beckman, Klee & Green, N.Y.C., 1981-83, Goldschmidt, Fredericks & Oshatz, N.Y.C., 1983-84, Jarblum, Solomon & Fornari, P.C., N.Y.C., 1984-86, Liebman, Adolf & Charme, P.C., N.Y.C., 1986-87, Carb, Luria, Cook & Kufeld, N.Y.C., 1987-95; ptnr. Carb, Luria, Glassner, Cook & Kufeld, N.Y.C., 1995—; arbitrator Civil Ct. of City of N.Y. Mem. ABA, Assn. of Bar of City of N.Y. Democrat. Jewish. Avocations: skiing, running, tennis, numismatics. General civil litigation, Real property, Contracts commercial. Home: 16 Carriage House Ln Mamaroneck NY 10543-1004 Office: Carb Luria Cook & Kufeld LLP 521 5th Ave New York NY 10017-4640

**SCHWARTZ, JEFFREY SCOTT,** lawyer; b. N.Y.C., Aug. 2, 1959; s. Philip Harold and Carolyn Annette (Stern) S.; m. Lynette Pam Vigdor, Dec. 23, 1984; children: Michelle Renee, Joel Benjamin. BA, SUNY, Oneonta, 1981; JD, Western State U. Coll. Law, San Diego, 1984. Bar: Calif. 1987, U.S. Dist. Ct. (so. dist.) Calif. 1987, U.S. Supreme Ct. 1997, D.C. 1998. Legal asst. Law Office William O'Connell, San Diego, 1983-87, assoc., 1987-88; pvt. practice, San Diego, 1988—; chmn. legal clinic San Diego State U., San Diego City Coll., San Diego County Bar Assn., 1987—, vice chmn. Pub. Info. and Rels. com., 1991. Mem. ABA, State Bar Calif. (advisor gen. practice sect., author Criminal Justice Jour. 1983), San Diego County Bar Assn. (chmn. call for action 1989, 91—), ATLA, Calif. Trial Lawyers Assn., San Diego Trial Lawyers Assn., Delta Theta Phi (supreme ct. justice 1987—, Percy J. Power award 1987, Wiley W. Manuel award for legal svcs. 1990). Democrat. Jewish. Personal injury, General civil litigation, General practice. Office: 501 W Broadway Ste 1700 San Diego CA 92101-3595

**SCHWARTZ, JOHN ROBERT,** judge; b. Rochester, N.Y., July 9, 1944; s. Adam J. and Grace M. (Locke) S.; m. Linda Pedley, Nov. 28, 1970; children: Jonathan, Jennifer. BSBA, John Carroll U., 1966; JD, Albany Law Sch., 1969. Bar: N.Y. 1970, U.S. Dist. Ct. (we. dist.) N.Y. 1970. Assoc. Fix, Spindelman, Turk & Himlein, Rochester, 1970-73, ptnr., 1974-83; counsel N.Y. State Senate, Albany, 1970-73; judge State of N.Y., Rochester, 1983—; supervising judge Rochester City Ct., 1992—; town atty. Town of Ogden, N.Y., 1972-74. Bd. dirs. Sch. of the Holy Childhood, Rochester, 1976—, Ctr. for Dispute Settlement, Rochester, 1987—, Camp Stella Maris, Livonia, N.Y., 1987—. Mem. Monroe County Bar Assn. (bd. dirs. 1986—). Office: Rochester City Ct Hall Of Justice Rochester NY 14614

**SCHWARTZ, KENNETH JEFFREY,** lawyer; b. N.Y.C., Oct. 24, 1966; s. Ira and Phyllis S. BA, Washington U., 1988; JD, U. Miami, 1991. Bar: Fla. 1992, U.S. Dist. Ct. (so. and mid. dists.) Fla. 1997. Assoc. Law Offices of Craig Z. Sherar, Coral Gables, Fla., 1992-93; sole practice law South Miami, Fla., 1993-96; ptnr. Osherow & Schwartz, Boca Raton, Fla., 1996-98; sole practice law Boca Raton, 1998—. Mem. ABA, ATLA, Acad. Trial Lawyers Fla. Avocations: golf, fishing. Intellectual property, Transportation, Real property. Office: 4800 N Federal Hwy Ste 201B Boca Raton FL 33431-3408

**SCHWARTZ, LEONARD,** lawyer; b. Bklyn., May 12, 1954; s. Harry and Betty (Krull) S.; m. Barbara Greenberg, Oct. 22, 1977; children: Jason, Rebecca, Ariele. BA magna cum laude, Bklyn. Coll., 1974; JD, Bklyn. Law Sch., 1977. Bar: N.Y. 1978, U.S. Dist. Ct. (so. and ea. dists.) N.Y. 1978, U.S. Supreme Ct. 1991. Assoc. John Anthony Bonina & Assocs., Bklyn., 1977-80, Law Firm John J. Feeley, N.Y.C., 1980, Fuchsberg & Fuchsberg, N.Y.C., 1980-83; ptnr. Oliveri & Schwartz P.C., N.Y.C., 1983—; panelist Med. Malpractice Mediation Panel N.Y., Kings, Richmond Counties, 1985—. Mem. ATLA, Am. Arbitration Assn. (panelist 1985—), N.Y. State Bar Assn., N.Y. State Trial Lawyers Assn (bd. dirs. 1993—), N.Y. County Lawyers Assn. (com. mcpl. liability 1992—). Personal injury, State civil litigation. Office: Oliveri & Schwartz PC 30 Vesey St 4th Fl New York NY 10007-2914

**SCHWARTZ, LEONARD JAY,** lawyer; b. San Antonio, Sept. 23, 1943; s. Oscar S. and Ethel (Eastman) S.; m. Sandra E. Eichelbaum, July 4, 1965; 1 child, Michele Fay. BBA, U. Tex., 1965, JD, 1968. Bar: Tex. 1968, Ohio 1971, U.S. Supreme Ct. 1971, U.S. Dist. Ct. (no., ea., wes. and so. dists.) Tex., U.S. Dist. Cts. (no. and so. dists.) Ohio, U.S. Dist. Ct. Nebr., U.S. Ct. Appeals (5th, 6th, 7th and 11th cirs.). Assoc. Roberts & Holland, N.Y.C., 1968-70; ptnr. Rigely, Schwartz & Fagan, San Antonio, 1970-71; staff counsel ACLU of Ohio, Columbus, 1971-74; ptnr. Schwartz & Fishman, Columbus, Ohio, 1974-79; elections counsel to sec. of state State of Ohio, Columbus, 1979-80; ptnr. Waterman & Schwartz and successor firms, Austin, Tex., 1981-85; shareholder, mng. dir. Schwartz & Eichelbaum, P.C., Austin, 1985—; gen. counsel various sch. dists.; adj. prof. law U. Tex. Sch. Law, Austin; labor and employment law cons. and sch. law Tex. Assn. Sch. Adminstrs; condr. workshops in field. *As lead counsel, Leonard successfully argued Jett v. Dallas Independent School District before the United States Supreme Court in 1989. This case is a reversediscrimination benchmark win for public institutions. Leonard has argued and won a case before federal and state appellate courts for over 100 cases. A few of the numerous appellate cases won by Leonard are: Salinas v. Central Education Agency, 706 S.W. 2d 991; Sterzing v. Ft. Bend Independent School District, 376 F. Supp. 657, modified on other grounds, 496 F. 2d 92; and Minarcini v. Strongsville City School District, 541 F. 2d 577, 582.* Contbr. articles to profl. jours. Mem. chancellor's coun. U. Tex. Sys.; mem. U. Tex. Pres.'s Assocs., Littlefield Soc., Sch. of Law Keeton Fellows. Recipient Outstanding Teaching Quiz Master award U. Tex. Sch. Law, 1968. Mem. ABA, Tex. Bar Assn., Bar Assn. 5th Cir., Fed. Bar Assn., Phi Delta Phi. Democrat. Jewish. Labor, Federal civil litigation, Administrative and regulatory. Office: Schwartz & Eichelbaum PC One Commodore Plz 800 Brazos St Ste 870 Austin TX 78701-2507

**SCHWARTZ, MARTIN A.,** lawyer; b. Bklyn., June 18, 1942; s. Sam and Julia A. Schwartz; m. Elaine Schwartz, Nov. 2, 1968; children: Dennis Z., Deborah C., Alison. BA, Bklyn. Coll., 1964; LLB, NYU, 1967, LLM, 1968. Atty. Botein Hayes Sklar & Herzberg, N.Y.C., 1967-71, Proskauer Rose Goetz & Mendelsohn, N.Y.C., 1971-80, Fieldstone Oliver Sumberg & Mondre, Miami, 1980-81; ptnr. Rubin Baum Levin Constant Friedman & Bilzin, Miami, 1982-98, Bilzin Sumberg Dunn Price & Ayelrod, LLP, Miami, 1998—. Pres. David Posnack Jewish Cmty. Ctr., Davie, Fla., 1997, bd. dirs., 1986—. Real property, Contracts commercial. Office: Bilzin Sumberg Dunn Price & Ayelrod LLP 200 S Biscayne Blvd Ste 2500 Miami FL 33131-2336

**SCHWARTZ, MILTON LEWIS,** federal judge; b. Oakland, Calif., Jan. 20, 1920; s. Colman and Selma (Lavenson) S.; m. Barbara Ann Moore, May 15, 1942; children: Dirk L., Tracy Ann, Damon M., Brooke. A.B., U. Calif. at Berkeley, 1941, J.D., 1948. Bar: Calif. bar 1949. Rsch. asst. 3d Dist. Ct. Appeal, Sacramento, 1948; dep. dist. atty., 1949-51; practice in Sacramento, 1951-79; partner McDonough, Holland, Schwartz & Allen, 1953-79; U.S. dist. judge Eastern Dist. Calif., U.S. Dist. Ct., Calif., 1979-90, sr. judge, 1990—; prof. law McGeorge Coll. Law, Sacramento, 1952-55; mem. Com. Bar Examiners Calif., 1971-75. Pres. Bd. Edn. Sacramento City Sch. Dist., 1961; v.p. Calif. Bd. Edn., 1967-68; trustee Sutterville Heights Sch. Dist. Served to maj. 40th Inf. Divsn. AUS, 1942-46, PTO. Named Sacramento County Judge of Yr., 1990; Milton L. Schwartz Am. Inn of Court named in his honor, Davis, Calif. Fellow Am. Coll. Trial Lawyers; mem. State Bar Calif., Am. Bar Assn., Am. Bd. Trial Advocates, Anthony M. Kennedy Am. Inn of Ct. (pres. 1988-90, pres. emeritus 1990—). Office: US Dist Ct 1060 US Courthouse 650 Capitol Mall Sacramento CA 95814-4708

**SCHWARTZ, MURRAY LOUIS,** lawyer, educator, academic administrator; b. Phila., Oct. 27, 1920; s. Harry and Isabelle (Friedman) S.; m. Audrey James, Feb. 12, 1950; children: Deborah, Jonathan, Daniel. BS, Pa. State U., 1942; LLB, U. Pa., 1949; LLD (hon.), Lewis and Clark Coll., 1977. Bar: Pa. 1950, U.S. Ct. Appeals (D.C. cir.) 1950, U.S. Supreme Ct. 1954. Chemist Standard Oil Ind., Whiting, 1942-44; law clk. Fred M. Vinson, Chief Justice U.S, 1949-51; assoc. firm Shea, Greenman, Gardner & McConnaughey, Washington, 1951-53; spl. asst. to U.S. atty. gen. Office Solicitor Gen., 1953-54; 1st dept. city solicitor City Phila., 1954-56; assoc. firm Dilworth, Paxson, Kalish & Green, Phila., 1956-58; prof. law Law Sch., UCLA, 1958-91, dean, 1969-75; David G. Price and Dallas P. Price prof. of law UCLA, 1988-89, exec. vice chancellor, 1988-91; vice chancellor academic affairs U. Calif., Santa Barbara, 1991-92, interim sr. v.p. acad. affairs, 1992-93; chmn. exec. com., bd. dirs. Social Sci. Rsch. Coun., 1981-85; bd. dirs. Mattel, Inc. Author: (with K.L. Karst and A.J. Schwartz) The Evolution of Law in the Barrios of Caracas, 1973, Law and the American Future, 1976, Lawyers and the Legal Profession, 2d edit. 1985; contbr. articles to profl. jours. Served to lt. (j.g.) USNR, 1944-46. Home: 1339 Marinette Rd Pacific Palisades CA 90272-2626

**SCHWARTZ, MURRAY MERLE,** federal judge; b. 1931. BS, Wharton Sch. U. Pa., 1952; LLB, U. Pa., 1955; LLM, U. Va., 1982. Part-time referee in bankruptcy Dist. of Del., 1969-74; judge U.S. Dist. Ct. Del., 1974-85, chief judge, 1985-89, sr. judge, 1989—. Author: The Exercise of Supervisory Power by the Third Circuit Court of Appeals, 1982. Mem. Del. State Bar Assn., Am. Judicature Soc. Office: US Dist Ct Lockbox 44 844 N King St Ste 18 Wilmington DE 19801-3570

**SCHWARTZ, PHILIP,** lawyer; b. N.Y.C., June 7, 1930; s. Louis and Kate (Brodsky) S.; m. Iris M. Ballin, Nov. 28, 1953 (div. 1979); children: David, Elyse, Donna; m. Monique W. Wagner, July 26, 1982 (div. 1991); m. Carol J. Pruett, Aug. 14, 1992. BA, George Washington U., 1952, JD, 1959; LLM in Taxation, Georgetown U., 1961; postgrad. U. Paris, London Sch. Econs., Harvard U. Bar: Va. 1959, D.C. 1966, U.S. Tax Ct., 1966, U.S. Ct. Appeals (D.C. cir.) 1966, U.S. Ct. Mil. Appeals 1966, U.S. Supreme Ct. 1966, U.S. Ct Appeals (4th cir.) 1982, U.S. Ct. Internat. Trade, 1988, N.Am. Coun. London Ct. Internat. Arbitration, 1988. Sr. intelligence analyst Nat. Security Agy., Washington, 1952-54, 56-63; assoc. Varoutsos, Koutoulakos & Arthur, Arlington, Va., 1963-67; ptnr. Schwartz & Ellis, Ltd., Arlington, 1968—; instr. No. Va. Life Underwriters Tng. Council, 1974, No. Va. Paralegal Inst., Arlington, 1976; moot ct. judge George Washington U., Washington, Georgetown U., Washington, Jessup Internat. Law Competition; commr. Chancery Arlington Cir. Ct., judge Pro Tempo; speaker in field. Mem. Arlington County Bd. Zoning Appeals, 1972-85, Arlington County Coun. Human Relations, 1973; bd. dirs. Jewish Community Ctr. Greater Washington, 1975. Served with M.I., U.S. Army, 1954-56. Contbr. articles to profl. jours. Master Bench Am. Inns of Ct.; fellow Internat. Acad. Matrimonial Lawyers (pres. 1996—), Am. Acad. Matrimonial Lawyers (bd. govs., v.p.); mem. ABA (chmn. family law sect. com. internat. laws 1983-86, chmn. internat. law sect. com. enforcement fgn. judgments), Am. Coll. Divorce Trial Lawyers (diplomate), Internat. Bar Assn. (chmn. family law div. 1988-92, governing coun. gen. practice sect., liaison officer to IMF), Va. Trial Lawyers Assn. (instr. 1984), Assn. Trial Lawyers Am. (vice chmn. internat. practice sect.), Va. State Bar (bd. govs. internat. law sect., liaison to ABA internat. law sect., spl. com/ reducing litigation delay and costs), Calif. Bar Assn. (internat. law sect.), N.Y. State Bar Assn. (internat. law, family law sect.), D.C. Bar (internat. law, family law sect.), Arlington County Bar Assn. (cts. com., legis. com., jud. selection com.), Brit. Inst. Internat. and Comparative Law, Am. Soc. Internat. Law, World Assn. Lawyers, Union Internationale des Avocats, Inter-Am. Bar Assn., Internat. Soc. Family Law, Solicitors Family Law Assn., Soc. English and Am. Lawyers, Am. Fgn. Law Assn., Internat. Law Assn., Asia-Pacific Lawyers Assn., Arlington Jaycees, Kiwanis, Phi Epsilon Pi, Delta Phi Epsilon, Phi Delta Phi. Family and matrimonial, Private international, General corporate. Office: Schwartz & Ellis Ltd 6950 Fairfax Dr Arlington VA 22213-1012

**SCHWARTZ, RENEE GERSTLER,** lawyer; b. Bklyn., June 18, 1933; d. Samuel and Lillian (Neulander) Gerstler; m. Alfred L. Schwartz, July 30, 1955; children—Carolyn Susan, Deborah Jane. A.B., Bklyn. Coll., 1953; LL.B., Columbia U., 1955. Bar: N.Y. 1956, U.S. Dist. Ct. (so. and ea. dists.) N.Y. 1956, U.S. Ct. Appeals (2d cir.) 1956, U.S. Dist. Ct. D.C. 1983, U.S. Supreme Ct. 1986. Assoc. Botein, Hays & Sklar, N.Y.C., 1955-64, ptnr., 1965-89, Kronish, Lieb, Weiner & Hellman, N.Y.C., 1990—. Bd. dirs. New Land Found., N.Y.C., 1965—. Mem. Bar Assn. City N.Y. Family and matrimonial, Public utilities, Libel. Home: 115 Central Park W New York NY 10023-4153 Office: Kronish Lieb Weiner & Hellman 1114 Avenue Of The Americas New York NY 10036-7703

**SCHWARTZ, RICHARD ANTHONY,** lawyer; b. Fremont, Ohio, July 15, 1948; s. Richard Aloysios and Mary Elizabeth Schwartz; d. Sandra Marie Griffin, Apr. 16, 1971; children: Jennifer, Richard, Dean, Julie, Christian. BA, U. Toledo, 1970; JD, Ohio State U., 1977. Bar: Ohio 1978, U.S. Dist. Ct. (so. dist.) Ohio 1978. Lawyer Smith & Schnacke, Dayton, Ohio, 1978-85; lawyer, shareholder Coolidge, Wall, Womsley & Lombard, Dayton, 1985—. Asst. treas. Sealy for Congress Com., Dayton, 1980. Mem. Dayton Bar Assn. (chmn. bus. law com. 1991-93), Rotary Club Dayton (sec. of found. 1990-94, pres. of found. 1995). Mergers and acquisitions, Securities, General corporate. Office: Coolidge Wall Womsley & Lombard 33 W 1st St Ste 600 Dayton OH 45402-1289

**SCHWARTZ, ROBERT H.,** lawyer; b. Detroit, Apr. 7, 1948; s. Earl M. and Betty (Kert) S.; m. Linda, June 13, 1971. BA, Wayne State U., 1969, JD, 1972. Bar: Mich. 1972, U.S. Dist. Ct. Mich. 1972, U.S. Tax Ct. 1980, U.S. Ct. Appeals, U.S. Supreme Ct., U.S. Ct. Appeals. Assoc. Garan, Lucow, Miller, Detroit, 1972-73; sole practice Southfield, Mich., 1973-75, 80-84; atty. Barr & Schwartz, Southfield, Mich., 1975-77; ptnr. Gourwitz, Barr & Schwartz, Southfield, Mich., 1977-80; with Raymond & Prokop P.C., Southfield, Mich., 1984—, pres., mng. ptnr., 1997—. Pres., Jewish Nat. Fund Metro. Detroit, 1997—. Mem. Mich. Bar Assn. (mem. comml. litigation), Mich. Health Care Lawyers (pres. 1985), Oakland County Bar Assn., Healthcare Fin. Mgmt. Assn. (co-chair law com.), Am. Health Lawyers Assn., Med. Group Mgmt. Assn. Avocations: photography, baseball. Health, State civil litigation, General corporate. Office: Raymond & Prokop PC 2000 Town Ctr Ste 2400 Southfield MI 48075-1315

**SCHWARTZ, ROBERT IRWIN,** lawyer; b. Pitts., Oct. 26, 1952; s. Howard Bernard and Birdie Helen Schwartz. BS, U. Pitts., 1976; JD, So. Calif. Inst. Law, 1979. Pvt. practice Ventura, Calif., 1980-86; ptnr. Scwartz & Powell, Ventura, 1986—. Pres. Ventura County Barrister, 1983-84. Mem. ABA, Ventura County Bar Assn., Ventura County Criminal Def. Assn. (v.p. 1984-85, Richard Erwin award 1998). Criminal. Office: Schwartz & Powell 6633 Telephone Rd Ste 150 Ventura CA 93003-0713

**SCHWARTZ, ROGER ALAN,** judge; b. N.Y.C., May 2, 1945; s. George Martin Ronald and Claire Marie (Dorsch) S.; m. Carmela Patricia Gillan, Sept. 29, 1979; 1 child, Julia Claire. BA, Muhlenberg Coll., 1967; JD, Temple U., 1973, M in Labor Law, 1976, MPA, 1979; disting. grad., U.S. Army Command and Gen. Staff Coll.; MA in History summa cum laude, U. Scranton, 1997; postgrad. studies, Marywood U., 1997—. Bar: Pa. 1973, N.Y. 1982, D.C. 1976, U.S. Dist. Ct. (ea. dist.) Pa. 1973, U.S. Ct. Appeals (3d cir.) 1976, U.S. Mil. Appeals 1981, U.S. Ct. Appeals (Fed cir.) 1986, U.S. Supreme Ct, 1976. Personnel mgmt. specialist CSC, Phila., 1973-74, asst. appeals officer, 1974-78; sr. adminstrv. judge U.S. Merit Systems Protection Bd., Phila., 1979-89; adminstrv. law judge Social Security Adminstrn., Wilkes-Barre, Pa., 1989—; arbitrator Phila. Ct. Common Pleas, 1973-89; asst. prof. Inst. for Paralegal Tng., Phila., 1976-77. With U.S. Army, 1968-70, Vietnam, Persian Gulf War, 1990; col. JAGC Res. Decorated Bronze Star, Purple Heart, Nat. Svc. medal with svc. star, Meritorious Svc. medal with one oak leaf cluster, Meritorious Achievement medal with 1 oak leaf cluster, Army Commendation medal with 4 oak leaf clusters. Mem. ABA, Phila. Bar Assn., Am. Judicature Soc., Am. Arbitration Assn., Res. Officers Assn. (Pa. state sec. 1996-97), Rotary (bd. dirs. Wilkes Barre chpt.). Avocations: piano, computers, billiards. Office: Social Security Adminstrn Office Hearings & Appeals 7 N Wilkes Barre Blvd Wilkes Barre PA 18702-5241

**SCHWARTZ, STEPHEN JAY,** lawyer; b. Portland, Maine, Sept. 6, 1960; s. Jack Leonard and Sara Belle (Modes) S.; m. Susan Greenspun, Oct. 25, 1987; children: Leonard Samuel, Andrew Joseph, Jack Edward. BA with distinction, U. Maine, 1982; JD, Santa Clara U., 1985. Bar: Maine 1985, U.S. Dist. Ct. Maine 1985. Asst. dist. atty. Prosecutorial Dist. No. 1 York County, Alfred, Maine, 1986-87; ptnr. Schwartz & Schwartz, P.A., Portland, Maine, 1987—; mem. criminal rules adv. com. Maine Supreme Jud. Ct., 1991—. Comments editor Santa Clara Law Rev., 1985; editor Maine Defender, 1992-95; mem. editl. adv. com. Maine Bar Jour., 1990—. Pres. Jewish Fedn. and Cmty. Coun. of So. Maine, Portland, 1994-96. Recipient Richard D. Aronson Young Leadership award Jewish Fedn. and Cmty. of So. Maine, 1994. Mem. ABA, ATLA, Maine State Bar Assn. (chmn. criminal law sect. 1991-92, mem. jud. evaluation com.), Cumberland Bar Assn., Maine Trial Lawyers Assn., Nat. Assn. Criminal Def. Lawyers, Maine Assn. Criminal Def. Lawyers (founder, 1st pres. 1992-93), Pi Sigma Alpha, Sigma Phi Epsilon. Personal injury, Probate, Criminal. Office: Schwartz & Schwartz PA 482 Congress St PO Box 15337 Portland ME 04112-5337

**SCHWARTZ, THEODORE FRANK,** lawyer; b. Clayton, Mo., Aug. 14, 1935; s. Ben and Mary (Roufa) S.; m. Barbara Jean Rader, Aug. 30, 1959; children: Michael D., Kenneth R. JD, Washington U., St. Louis, 1962.

Bar: Mo. 1967, D.C. 1972, Calif. 1974, N.Y. 1981, Fla. 1994; U.S. Dist. Ct. (ea. dist.) Mo. 1962, U.S. Ct. Appeals (8th cir.) 1963, U.S. Dist. Ct. (so. dist.) Ind. 1968, U.S. Dist. Ct. (so. dist.) Tex. 1971, U.S. Ct. Appeals (5th cir.) 1971, U.S. Ct. (cen. dist.) Calif. 1978, U.S. Ct. Appeals (7th cir.) 1979, U.S. Ct. Appeals (2d, 10th and 11th cirs.) 1980, U.S. Ct. Appeals (9th cir.) 1981, U.S. Supreme Ct. 1981. Assoc. Charles M. Shaw, Clayton, 1962-64; ptnr. Ackerman, Schiller & Schwartz, Clayton, 1964-74; sole practice Clayton, 1975—. Mem. ABA, Assn. Trial Lawyer Am., Mo. Assn. Trial Lawyers, Am. Judicature Soc., Nat. Assn. Criminal Def. Lawyers. Antitrust, Federal civil litigation, State civil litigation. Home: 597 Purdue Ave Saint Louis MO 63130-4136 Office: 130 S Bemiston Ave Ste 700 Clayton MO 63105-1928

**SCHWARTZ, WILLIAM,** lawyer, educator; b. Providence, May 6, 1933; s. Morris Victor and Martha (Glassman) S.; m. Bernice Konigsberg, Jan. 13, 1957; children: Alan Gershon, Robin Libby. AA, Boston U., 1952, JD magna cum laude, 1955, MA, 1960; postgrad., Harvard Law Sch., 1955-56; LHD (hon.), Hebrew Coll., 1996, Yeshiva U., 1998. Bar: D.C. 1956, Mass. 1962, N.Y. 1989. Prof. law Boston U., 1955-91, Fletcher prof. law, 1968-70, Roscoe Pound prof. law, 1970-73, dean Sch. of Law, 1980-88, dir. Ctr. for Estate Planning, 1988-91; univ. prof. Yeshiva U., N.Y.C., 1991—; of counsel Swartz & Swartz, 1973-80; v.p. for acad. affairs, chief acad. officer Yeshiva U., N.Y.C., 1993-98; counsel Cadwalader, Wickersham and Taft, N.Y.C., Washington, Charlotte, London, 1988—; mem. faculty Frances Glessner Lee Inst., Harvard Med. Sch., Nat. Coll. Probate Judges, 1970, 77, 78, 79, 88; gen. dir. Assn. Trial Lawyers Am., 1968-73; reporter New Eng. Trial Judges Conf., 1965-67; participant Nat. Met. Cts. Conf., 1968; dir. Mass. Probate Study, 1976—; chmn. spl. com. on police procedures City of Boston, 1989, 91; bd. dirs. UST Corp., chmn. of co., 1993-94, chmn. bd. dirs., 1996—; bd. dirs. Viacom Inc., Viacom Internat. Inc.; mem. adv. com. WCI Steel, Inc.; mem. legal adv. bd. N.Y. Stock Exch. Author: Future Interests and Estate Planning, 1965, 77, 81, 86, Comparative Negligence, 1970, A Products Liability Primer, 1970, Civil Trial Practice Manual, 1972, New Vistas in Litigation, 1973, Massachusetts Pleading and Practice, 7 vols., 1974-80, Estate Planning and Living Trusts, 1990, The Convention Method: The Unused Amending Superhighway, 1995, Jewish Law and Contemporary Dilemmas and Problems, 1997, Does Time Heal All Wrongs?, 1999, others; note editor: Boston U. Law Rev., 1954-55; property editor: Annual Survey of Mass. Law, 1960—; contbr. articles to legal jours. Bd. dirs. Kerry Found.; trustee Hebrew Coll., 1975—, Salve Regina Univ.; rep. Office Public Info., UN, 1968-73; chmn. legal adv. panel Nat. Commn. Med. Malpractice, 1972-73; examiner of titles Commonwealth of Mass., 1964—; spl. counsel Mass. Bay Transp. Authority, 1979; trustee Yeshiva U.; pres. Fifth Ave. Synagogue, N.Y.C., 1997—. Recipient Homer Albers award Boston U., 1955, John Ordronaux prize, 1955; Disting. Service award Religious Zionists Am., 1977; William W. Treat award; William O. Douglas award. Fellow Am. Coll. Probate Counsel; mem. ABA, Am. Law Inst., Mass. Bar Assn. (chmn. task force tort liability), N.Y. State Bar Assn., Assn. Bar City N.Y., Nat. Coll. Probate Judges (hon. mem.), Phi Beta Kappa. Office: 100 Maiden Ln New York NY 10038-4818 *I have been guided by the maxim: "Ideals are like stars. You cannot touch them with your hands, but like the seafaring man, if you choose them as your guide and follow them, you will reach your destiny."*

**SCHWARTZBERG, HUGH JOEL,** lawyer, corporate executive, educator; b. Chgo., Feb. 17, 1933; s. Ralph M. and Celia (Kaplan) S.; m. Joanne Gilbert, July 7, 1956; children: Steven J., Susan Jennifer. BA cum laude, Harvard Coll., 1953; JD, Yale U., 1956. Bar: Conn. 1956, Ill. 1957. Assoc. Lederer, Livingston, Kahn & Adsit, Chgo., 1957-62; assoc. Marks, Marks & Kaplan, Chgo., 1962-67, ptnr., 1967-79; ptnr. Schwartzberg, Barnett & Schwartzberg, Chgo., 1970-75, Schwartzberg, Barnett & Cohen, Chgo., 1975—; pres. Arizi Corp., Green Valley, Ariz., 1972-73, BMDC Warehouse Inc., Buffalo, 1975—; adj. prof. Medill Grad. Sch. Journalism, Northwestern U., Evanston, Ill., 1976, 78; ptnr Ledgecrest Village, New Britain, Conn., 1975-86, SFS Lambert, Hyde Park Apts., Bath, Maine, 1975-88, Delaware Park Apts., Buffalo, 1972-86, High Wall, Highland Park, Ill., 1975—; chmn. bd. Zytek Mfg., Inc., Manila, 1987-96; bd. pubs. New Am. Writing, Chgo., 1993—. Chmn. Ill. State adv. com. to U.S. Civil Rights Commn., 1985-92, commr., 1985—; bd. dirs. Fund for Open Soc., Phila.; chmn. exec. com., 1996; bd. dirs. Home Health Svc. of Chgo., North, 1974-88; mem. Cook County (Ill.) Sheriff's Adv. Com., 1972-86; trustee Modern Poetry Assn.; pub. Poetry Mag., Chgo., 1980—, sec. 1997-98; chmn. com. in internat. affairs, pub. affairs com. Jewish United Fund, Chgo., 1980-83; co-chmn. emergency task force on Indo-Chinese refugees, 1978-80; bd. dirs. Jewish Edn., 1973-76, 1987-90; U.S. sponsor Project S. Africa, 1985-94; sec. Raoul Wallenberg com., Chgo.. Recipient testimonial Joint Youth Devel. Com., 1967, citation of merit, WAIT Radio, Chgo., 1974. Fellow Ill. Bar Found. (charter); mem. ABA (regional atty. sect. on indvidual rights and responsibilities 1985-86), Chgo. Bar Assn. (chmn. com. civil rights 1979-80), Tau Epsilon Rho (nat. historian 1988, nat. scholar 1990, pres. 1992—, Schwartzberg Scholarship Found.), Harvard Club, Yale Club, Chgo. Lit. Club, Soc. of Clubs, Union League Civic and Arts Found. (gen. counsel 1990-95, sec. 1995-96, v.p. 1996—, pres. 1998-99), Union League Club (bd. dirs. 1997—, chmn. pub. affairs com. 1999—), Chaine des Rotisseurs (commandeur), B'nai B'rith (pres. dist. 6, 1986-88, internat. bd. 1982—, sr. internat. v.p., 1992-96, co-pres. world ctr. 1996-98, Appreciation award Anti Defamation League 1975, Torch of Freedom award 1988). Avocations: poetry, photography. State civil litigation, Real property, Probate. Home: 853 W Fullerton Ave Chicago IL 60614-2412 Office: Schwartzberg Barnett & Cohen 55 W Monroe St Ste 2400 Chicago IL 60603-5040

**SCHWARTZBERG, PAUL DAVID,** lawyer; b. N.Y.C., July 25, 1959; s. Melvin and Zelda Zara (Jacobs) S.; m. Ellen Beth Fassler; children: Joanne Lynn, Marc. BA, Hampshire Coll., 1982; JD cum laude, Vt. Law Sch., 1987. Bar: Vt. 1988, N.Y. 1988. Pres. Environ. Law Found., Inv., N.Y., 1987—; environ. atty. Town of Patterson, N.Y., 1990-93; real estate specialist N.Y.C. Dept. Environ. Protection, 1993—; spl. environ. atty. Town of New Paltz, 1996; facilty assoc. Lincoln Inst. Land Policy, Cambridge, Mass., 1990-93; admissions assoc. Hampshire Coll., Amherst, Mass., 1989—; student advisor SUNY, Empire State Coll., White Plains, N.Y., 1990-94; presenter in field. Producer radio program Let's Talk Trash, 1989-90 (2 AP Broadcasters award 1990); mem. Vt. Law Rev., 1985. Sec.-treas. Putnam Arts Coun., Mahopac, N.Y., 1988-89; campaign advance Walter F. Mondale Presdl. Campaign, 1984, Hart Presdl. Campaign, 1984, Peter Shapiro Govtl. Campaign, N.J., 1985, Sen. Patrick Leahy Campaign, Vt., 1986. Mem. Am. Planning Assn. (Meritorious Svc. award for pub. participation 1991). Avocations: skiing, photography, bicycling. Office: NYC Dep Rte 28A Shokan NY 12481

**SCHWARTZEL, CHARLES BOONE,** lawyer; b. Louisville, Jan. 4, 1950; s. Charles Joseph and Rosemary Jane (Redens) S.; m. Rose Marie Carlisi, June 20, 1980; children: Sally Ann, Charles Gerard. BA, Vanderbilt U., 1972; JD, U. Tex., 1975. Bar: Tex. 1975. Atty. Vinson & Elkins L.L.P., Houston, 1975-98, ptnr., 1983-98; pvt. practice Houston, 1998—. Contbr. articles to profl. jours. Councilman City of West University Place, Tex., 1985-89; vol. Trees For Houston, 1985—. Fellow Am. Coll. Trust and Estate Counsel; mem. ABA (chmn. real property, probate and trust law sect. com. on creditors' rights in estates and trusts 1989-93), Tex. Bar Assn. Roman Catholic. Probate, Estate planning, Estate taxation. Office: Attorney at Law 1010 Lamar St Ste 1520 Houston TX 77002-6315

**SCHWARTZMAN, ANDREW JAY,** lawyer; b. N.Y.C., Oct. 4, 1946; s. Joel Jay and Theresa (Greenhauff) S.; m. Linda Lazarus, June 8, 1986. AB, U. Pa., 1968, JD, 1971. Bar: N.Y. 1972, D.C. 1974, Temporary Emergency Ct. Appeals 1977, U.S. Dist. Ct. D.C. 1978, U.S. Ct. Appeals (D.C. cir.) 1981, U.S. Ct. Appeals (2d cir.) 1987, U.S. Ct. Appeals (4th, 7th, 8th, 9th cirs.) 1991, U.S. Supreme Ct. 1980. Staff cousnel United Ch. of Christ Office of Comm., N.Y.C., 1971-74; atty. adviser Fed. Energy Office, Washington, 1974-77; sr. atty. adviser U.S. Dept. Energy, Washington, 1977-78; bd. dirs. Safe Energy Comms. Coun., pres. bd. dirs., 1989—; dir. Media Access Project, Washington, 1978-96, pres., CEO, 1996—; mem. adv. panel Study on Comms. Systems for an Info. Age, Office of Tech. Assessment; mem. adv. bd. Ctr. for Democracy and Tech., 1996—, Office Tech. Assessment; lectr. Fairleigh Dickinson U., 1972-73; bd. dirs. Telecommunications Research Action Ctr.; mem. comms. coun. forum Aspen Inst. on Comms. and Soc., 1992—; mem. bd. dirs. Min. Media and Telecomms. Conf., 1994—. Contbg. author: Les Brown's Dictionary of Television, 3d edit., Ency. of the Consumer Movement, 1997; contbr. articles to legal jours. Recipient Everett Parker award United Ch. of Christ, 1994. Mem. ABA, Fed. Comms. Bar Assn., U. Pa. Alumni Assn. Home: 3624 Military Rd NW Washington DC 20015-1724 Office: Media Access Project 1707 L St NW Ste 400 Washington DC 20036-4213

**SCHWARTZMAN, JAMES CHARLES,** lawyer; b. Kearney, Nebr., Apr. 17, 1945; s. Bernard and Estelle (Lubin) S.; m. Nancy Miriam Hankin, June 26, 1967; children: Kimberly Hankin, Kamian Hankin. B.A., Washington U., St. Louis, 1967; J.D. cum laude, Villanova U., 1972. Bar: Pa. 1972, U.S. Dist. Ct. (ea. dist.) Pa. 1973, U.S. Ct. Appeals (3d cir.) 1973, U.S. Supreme Ct. 1979, U.S. Tax Ct. 1979, U.S. Ct. Claims 1979. Law clk. U.S. Dist. Ct. (ea. dist.) Pa., Phila., 1972-73, U.S. Supreme Ct. Pa.; asst. U.S. atty. U.S. Dept. Justice, Phila., 1973-77; sr. ptnr. Schwartzman & Hepps, P.C., Phila., 1977-92; Schwartzman & Assocs., 1993—; mem. Disciplinary Bd., Supreme Ct. Pa., 1983-89, vice chmn., 1985-86, chmn., 1986-88; dir. Bank & Trust Co. of Old York Rd., Willow Grove, Pa., 1983-92; bd. dirs. Southeastern Pa. Trans. Authorty, 1992—, Blue Cross of Phila., 1993—; mem. Phila. Spl. Trial Ct. Nominating Commn., 1987-95. Contbr. article to Villanova Law Rev., 1972, mem. editorial staff, 1971-72. Mem. Pa. Bar Assn., Phila. Bar Assn., Pa. Trial Lawyers Assn., Phila. Trial Lawyers Assn., Continuing Legal Edn. Bd. (vice chmn. 1992-95, chmn. 1996—), Order of Coif. Federal civil litigation, Criminal, Personal injury.

**SCHWARZ, CARL A., JR.,** lawyer; b. N.Y.C., Apr. 27, 1936; s. Carl A. and Genevieve C. Byrne; m. Maryellen McG., Apr. 30, 1966; children: Peter Thomas, Elizabeth Anne. BS, Fordham U., 1957, JD, 1960. Bar: N.Y. 1960, U.S. Dist. Ct. (so., ea., we. and D.C. dists.) N.Y. 1960, U.S. Ct. Appeals (2d cir.) 1960. Ptnr. Schwarz & DeMarco, Garden City, N.Y.; chmn., bd. trustees N.Y. Sch. Interior Design. Trustee Cath. Charities; Capt. USAF, 1961-65. Mem. Manhasset Bay Yacht Club (rear commodore), Order of Malta. Roman Catholic. Labor, Pension, profit-sharing, and employee benefits. Office: Schwarz & DeMarco LLP 1225 Franklin Ave Garden City NY 11530-1691

**SCHWARZ, FREDERICK AUGUST OTTO, JR.,** lawyer; b. N.Y.C., Apr. 20, 1935; s. Frederick August Otto and Mary Delafield (DuBois) S.; m. Marian Ladd, June 19, 1959; children: Frederick August Otto III, Adair L., Eliza Ladd; m. Frederica Perera, May 11, 1996. BA in History magna cum laude, Harvard Coll., 1957, LLB magna cum laude, 1960; LLD (hon.), N.Y. Law Sch., 1987, CUNY, 1993. Bar: N.Y. 1961, U.S. Dist. Ct. (so. dist.) N.Y. 1963, U.S. Ct. Appeals (2nd cir.) 1978, U.S. Ct. Appeals (9th cir.) 1972, U.S. Ct. Appeals (10th cir.) 1973, U.S. Supreme Ct. 1973. Law clk. to chief judge J. Edward Lumbard U.S. Ct. of Appeals, 2d Circuit, 1960-61; asst. commr. for law revision Govt. of No. Nigeria, 1961-62; assoc. firm Cravath, Swaine & Moore, N.Y.C., 1963-68; ptnr. Cravath, Swaine & Moore, 1969-75, 1976-81, 87—; chmn. N.Y.C. Charter Revision Commn., 1989; corp. counsel City of N.Y., 1982-86; chief counsel Senate Select Com. on Intelligence, 1975-76; speaker in the field. Author: Nigeria: The Tribes, The Nation, or the Race, 1966; Editor Harvard Law Sch. Law Review. Contbr. articles to profl. jours. Chmn. Fund for the City of N.Y., 1977-81, 87—; pres. Vera Inst. Justice, 1978-81, chmn. 1987—; mem. bd. overseers Harvard U., 1977-83; mem. Com. to Visit Harvard Coll., N.Y.-N.J. Citizens Commn. on AIDS; trustee Experiment in Internat. Living, 1965-82; bd. dirs. NAACP Legal Def. Fund. Constl. Edn. Found., Manhattan Bowery Corp., 1970-81, Lawyers for the Public Interest, 1976-81, FAO Schwarz, 1970-85; chair leadership N.Y. Adv. Coun., 1989—; trustee Nat. Resources Def. Coun., 1987-92, chmn., 1992—, Legal Action Center, 1973-81, N.Y.C. Criminal Justice Agy., 1977-81, Town Sch., 1972-80, Am. Com. on Africa, 1965-79, Milton Acad., 1960's, Vera Inst. of Justice, Atlantic Found., NAACP Legal Def. Fund, Constitutional Edn. Dound., William Nelson Cromwell Found. Recipient Liberty award Lambda Legal Def. and Edn. Fund, 1987, The Louis Lefkowitz award Fordham Urban Law Jour. 1990, Civic Leadership award Citizens Union City of N.Y., 1990, The Whitney North Seymour Pub. Svc. award Fed. Bar Coun., 1991.. Fellow N.Y. Bar Found.; mem. ABA, Assn. of Bar of City of N.Y. (mem. exec. com. 1986-90, coun. on criminal justice, chmn. juvenile justice com. 1980-81, chmn. nominating com. 1983, Cardozo lectr. 1991), Am. Law Inst., Harvard Law Sch. Assn. of N.Y.C. (pres. 1983-84), N.Y. State Bar Assn., N.Y.C. Bar Assn. General civil litigation. Office: Cravath Swaine & Moore 825 8th Ave Fl 38 New York NY 10019-7475

**SCHWARZ, KENT LOUIS,** lawyer; b. Ft. Sill, Okla., July 3, 1967; s. Louis Anthony and Jeane J. Schwarz. BS in Acctg., Wake Forest U., 1989; JD with distinction, Emory U., 1994; LLM in Taxation, NYU, 1995. Bar: N.Y. 1995, N.J. 1995; CPA, N.C. Clk. for Hon. Carleton Powell, U.S. Tax Ct., Washington, 1995-97; assoc. Graham Curtin & Sheridan, P.A., Morristown, N.J., 1997—. Mem. ABA. Avocations: basketball, windsurfing, reading. Taxation, general, General corporate. Office: Graham Curtin & Sheridan 4 Headquarters Pla Morristown NJ 07962-1991

**SCHWARZ, MICHAEL,** lawyer; b. Brookline, Mass., Oct. 19, 1952; s. Jules Lewis and Estelle (Kosberg) S.; m. Rebecca Handy; 1 child, Patrick Joshua Charles. BA magna cum laude, U. No. Colo., 1975; postgrad., U. N.Mex., 1977, JD, 1980; reader in Negligence Law, Oxford U., 1978; diploma in Legal Studies, Cambridge U., 1981. Bar: N.Mex. 1980, U.S. Dist. Ct. N.Mex. 1980, U.S. Ct. Appeals (10th, D.C., and Fed. cirs.) 1982, U.S. Ct. Internat. Trade, 1982, U.S. Tax Ct. 1982, N.Y. 1987, U.S. Supreme Ct. 1983. Vol. VISTA, Albuquerque, 1975-77; rsch. fellow N.Mex. Legal Support Project, Albuquerque, 1978-79; supr. law Cambridge (Eng.) U., 1980-81; law clk. to chief justice Supreme Ct. N.Mex., Santa Fe, 1981-82; pvt. practice Santa Fe, 1982—; spl. pros. City of Santa Fe, 1985, spl. asst. atty. gen., 1986-88; mem. editl. adv. com. Social Security Reporting Svc., 1983-95. Author: New Mexico Appellate Manual, 1990, 2d edit., 1996; contbr. articles to profl. jours. Vice dir. Colo. Pub. Interest Rsch. Group, 1974; scoutmaster Great S.W. Area coun. Boy Scouts Am., 1977-79; mem. N.Mex. Acupuncture Lic. Bd., 1983. Recipient Cert. of Appreciation Cambridge U., 1981, Nathan Burke Meml. award, 1980, N.Mex. Supreme Ct. Cert. Recognition, 1992, 93, 95. Mem. ABA (litig. com. on profl. responsibility, litig. com. on pretrial practice and discovery, 10th cir. editor 1998), ATLA, Am. Arbitration Assn., Bar Assn. U.S. Dist. Ct. Dist. N.Mex., State Bar N.Y., N.Mex. State Bar (bd. dirs. employment law sect. 1990-96, family law sect. 1998—), N.Y. Bar Assn., First Jud. Dist. Bar Assn. (treas. 1987-88, sec. 1988-89, v.p. 1989-90, pres. 1990-91, local rules com. 1989-92), U.S. Dist. Ct. N.Mex. (local civil rules com. 1997-99), N.Mex. Supreme Ct. (standing com. on profl. conduct 1990—, chmn. 1998—), Am. Inns of Ct. N.Mex. (barrister), Nat. Employment Lawyers Assn. (nat. chpt., N.Mex. chpt.), Defenders of Wildlife, Amnesty Internat., Internat. Wolf Ctr. Federal civil litigation, State civil litigation, Civil rights. Home and Office: PO Box 1656 Santa Fe NM 87504-1656

**SCHWARZ, PAUL WINSTON,** judge; b. Sacramento, Sept. 24, 1948; s. Egon Ferdinand and Louise (Fulcher) S.; m. Virginia Adams, July 12, 1987; children: Austin Winston, Julie Adams. BA in Philosophy, Calif. State U., San Jose, 1971; JD, Santa Clara U., 1974. Bar: Pa. 1975, U.S. Supreme Ct. 1978, D.C. Ct. Appeals 1987, Va. 1992. Commd. 2d. lt. U.S. Army, 1971, advanced through grades to lt. col., 1992; corp. counsel Oracle Corp., Bethesda, Md., 1992-93; sec., v.p. and corp. counsel Oracle Complex Systems Corp., Arlington, Va., 1992-93; counsel McAleese & Associates, P.C., Washington, DC, 1993-94; apptd. U.S. adminstrv. law judge, 1994. Author: A Roadmap into the World of Federal Contracts, 1989. Decorated Legion of Merit, U.S. Army Gen. Staff Badge award. Mem. ABA (chmn. com. on pub. contract law gen. practice sect. 1991, vice-chmn. judiciary com. 1995), Army and Navy Country Club, Army and Navy Club Washington D.C., Nat. Soc. SAR. Episcopalian. Avocations: swimming, pistol. Home: 5336 Sugar Hill Dr Houston TX 77056-2028

**SCHWARZ, STEPHEN GEORGE,** lawyer; b. Babylon, N.Y., Feb. 13, 1956; s. Fred George and Evelyn Elsie Schwarz; m. Katherine Anne KaKretz, July 18, 1982 (div. Dec. 1993); children: Timothy, Allyson; m. Patricia Jean Tanacea, Apr. 1, 1995; 1 child, Jessica. BS in Biology, U. Albany, 1978; JD in Law, Union U., Albany, N.Y., 1981. Bar: N.Y. 1982, U.S. Dist. Ct. (we. dist.) N.Y. 1982, U.S. Ct. Appeals (2d cir.) 1987, U.S. Dist. Ct. N.Y. (no. dist.) 1990, U.S. Supreme Ct. 1990. Assoc. Harris Beach & Wilcox, Rochester, N.Y., 1981-83; jud. law clk. U.S. Dist. Ct. N.Y., Rochester, 1983-84; assoc. Faraci & Lange LLP, Rochester, 1984-89, ptnr., 1989-92, mng. ptnr., 1992—. V.p. Family Resource Ctrs. Rochester, 1992-95, pres., 1995-97. Mem. Am. Bd. Trial Advocates, N.Y. State Bar Assn., N.Y. State Trial Lawyers Assn. (pres. Genesee Valley chpt. 1997—), Monroe County Bar Assn. (trustee 1992-94). Avocations: skiing, hiking, climbing. E-mail: sschwarz@faraci.com. General civil litigation, Personal injury, Product liability. Office: Faraci & Lange LLP 400 Crossroads Blvd Rochester NY 14614

**SCHWARZER, WILLIAM W,** federal judge; b. Berlin, Apr. 30, 1925; came to U.S., 1938, naturalized, 1944; s. John F. and Edith M. (Daniel) S.; m. Anne Halbersleben, Feb. 2, 1951; children: Jane Elizabeth, Andrew William. AB cum laude, U. So. Calif., 1948; LLB cum laude, Harvard U., 1951. Bar: Calif. 1953, U.S. Supreme Ct. 1967. Teaching fellow Harvard U. Law Sch., 1951-52; asso. firm McCutchen, Doyle, Brown & Enersen, San Francisco, 1952-60; ptnr. McCutchen, Doyle, Brown & Enersen, 1960-76; judge U.S. Dist. Ct (no. dist.) Calif., San Francisco, 1976—; dir. Fed. Jud. Ctr., Washington, 1990-95; sr. counsel Pres.'s Commn. on CIA Activities Within the U.S., 1975; chmn. U.S. Jud. Conf. Com. Fed.-State Jurisdiction, 1987-90; mem. faculty Nat. Inst. Trial Advocacy, Fed. Jud. Ctr., All-ABA, U.S.-Can. Legal Exch., 1987, Anglo-U.S. Jud. Exch., 1994-95, Salzburg Seminar on Am. Studies; disting. prof. Hastings Coll. Law U. Calif. Author: Managing Antitrust and Other Complex Litigation, 1982, Civil Discovery and Manadatory Disclosure, 1994, Federal Civil Procedure Before Trial, 1994; contbr. articles to legal publs., aviation jours. Trustee World Affairs Coun. No. Calif., 1961-88; chmn. bd. trustees Marin Country Day Sch., 1963-66; mem. Marin County Aviation Commn., 1969-76; mem. vis. com. Harvard Law Sch., 1981-86. Served with Intelligence, U.S. Army, 1943-46. Fellow Am. Coll. Trial Lawyers (S. Gates award 1992), Am. Bar Found.; mem. ABA (Meador Rosenberg award 1995), Am. Law Inst., San Francisco Bar Assn., State Bar Calif., Coun. Fgn. Rels. Office: 450 Golden Gate Ave San Francisco CA 94102-3661

**SCHWEGLER, LAWRENCE M.,** deputy district attorney; b. Lackawanna, N.Y., July 21, 1950; s. Clayton W. and Marjorie I. Schwegler; m. Jamie L. Ketchner, July 12, 1980; 1 child, James C. BA, SUNY, Buffalo, 1974; MS in Edn., St. Bonaventure U., 1976; CAS, SUNY, Oswego, 1983; JD, U. Toledo, 1985. Bar: W.Va. 1986, Ohio 1986, Pa. 1986, N.Y. 1987, U.S. Dist. Ct. (so. dist.) W.Va. 1986, U.S. Dist. Ct. (so. dist.) Ohio 1986, U.S. Dist. Ct. (we. dist.) 1987. Atty. in pvt. practice, New Martinsville, W.Va., 1986-87, Woodsfield, Ohio, 1986-87; asst. dist. atty. Erie County Dist. Atty.'s Office, Buffalo, 1987-91, bur. chief-narcotics, 1991-95, bur. chief County Ct., 1995-96, bur. chief City Ct., 1996-97, dep. dist. atty. for prosecution, 1997—; mem. faculty Nat. Coll. Dist. Attys., 1998—, Erie County Ctrl. Police Svcs., Buffalo, 1998—. Mem. ABA. Office: Erie County Dist Atty Ofc 25 Delaware Ave Buffalo NY 14202-3903

**SCHWEIGERT, JACK F.,** lawyer; b. July 26, 1947; s. Charles Arthur and Alma Mae S.; m. Valerie Bavero, 1981; children: Carly, Scott. BS in Econs., U. Gannon, 1969; JD, U. Akron, 1974. Bar: Hawaii 1975, U.S. Ct. Appeals (9th cir.) 1975, U.S. Ct. Appeals (4th cir.), U.S. Claims Ct. 1977, Ct. Internat. Trade, Customs Ct. Pvt. practice Honolulu, 1975—. Co-author: Medical Malpractice, 1986; appeared in numerous TV, newspaper, mag. stories. Past pres. and dir. Pauoa Cmty. Assn.; republican Mayoral candidate, Honolulu, 1980, libertarian Mayoral candidate, Honolulu, 1992. With U.S. Army, 1969-71. Mem. Hawaii State Bar Assn., Hawaii Assn. Criminal Def. Lawyers, Honolulu Lions Club (immediate past pres., dir. 1990—, Melvin Jones award 1997-98), Phi Alpha Delta. Republican. Fax: 808-533-7490. Civil rights, Criminal. Office: The Lawyers Bldg 550 Halekauwila St Ste 309 Honolulu HI 96813-5035

**SCHWEIKART, DEBORA ELLEN,** lawyer; b. Belfonte, Pa., Apr. 14, 1971; d. Kenneth Earl and Catherine Joyce (Seaman) S. BA in Russian Lang. and Lit., U. Pitts., 1992, JD, 1996. Bar: Pa. Rsch. asst. U. Pitts. Sch. Law, 1994-96, teaching asst., 1994-95; teaching asst. Pa. Govs. Sch. Internat. Studies, Pitts., 1994-96; atty. Peterson Cons., Pitts., 1997; jud. clk. N.Mex. Ct. Appeals, 1997-99. Contbr. articles to profl. publs. Scholar Internat. Christian Youth Exch., Ronde, Denmark, 1989, Am. Coun. Tchrs. Russian, 1992, Internat. Women's Club, 1992, U. Pitts., 1996; Emery Means Findley, Jr. Grad. fellowship, 1999. Mem. Dona Anna County Bar Assn. (treas. 1998), Am. Inns of Ct., Kappa Alpha Theta (house dir. 1996-97). Avocations: photography, horseback riding. Home: 3333 Majestic Rdg Apt C302 Las Cruces NM 88011-4687 Office: 201 W Picacho Ave Ste C Las Cruces NM 88005-1833

**SCHWEITZER, MELVIN L.,** commissioner, lawyer; b. N.Y.C., Oct. 27, 1944. BA, NYU, 1966; JD, Fordham U., 1969. Bar: N.Y. 1969. Atty. Rogers & Wells, N.Y.C.; commr. The Port Authority of N.Y. and N.J., 1993—; assoc. Rogers & Wells, N.Y.C., 1969-74, ptnr., 1975-98, of counsel, 1998—; mem. Gov. Commn. on N.Y. Fin. Svcs.Industry, 1989—. Counsel, law chmn. N.Y. State Dem. Com., 1974-85. Mem. Assn. Bar City N.Y., Phi Sigma Alpha. Office: Rogers & Wells 200 Park Ave Fl 8E New York NY 10166-0800

**SCHWELB, FRANK ERNEST,** judge; b. Prague, Czechoslovakia, June 24, 1932; came to U.S., 1947; s. Egon and Caroline (Redisch) S.; m. Taffy Wurzburg, Apr. 9, 1988. BA, Yale U., 1949-53; LLB, Harvard U., 1958. Bar: N.Y. Ct. Appeals 1958, U.S. Dist. Ct. (so. and ea. dists.) N.Y. 1960, U.S. Ct. Appeals (2d cir.) 1961, U.S. Supreme Ct. 1965, U.S. Ct. Appeals (4th cir.) 1968, D.C., D.C. Ct. Appeals, U.S. Dist. Ct. D.C. 1972. Assoc. Mudge, Stern, Baldwin & Todd, N.Y.C., 1958-62; trial atty. Civil Rights Div. U.S. Dept. Justice, Washington, 1962-69, chief eastern sect., 1969, chief housing sect., 1969-79, spl. counsel for litigation, 1979; spl. counsel rev. panel on new drug regulation HEW, Washington, 1976-77; assoc. judge Superior Ct. D.C., Washington, 1979-88, D.C. Ct. Appeals, Washington, 1988—; instr. various legal edn. activities. Contbr. articles to profl. jours. With U.S. Army, 1955-57. Recipient Younger Fed. Lawyer award, Fed. Bar Assn., 1967. Mem. Bar Assn. D.C., World Peace Through Law Ctr., World Assn. Judges, Nat. Lawyers Club, Czechoslovak-Am. orgns. Avocations: tennis, table tennis, sports, Gilbert and Sullivan operettas, Shakespeare. Home: 4879 Potomac Ave NW Washington DC 20007-1539 Office: DC Ct Appeals 500 Indiana Ave NW Washington DC 20001-2138

**SCHWEMM, ROBERT G.,** dean, law educator. Practice law Sidley & Austin; chief trial counsel Leadership Counsel for Met. Open Cmtys., Chgo.; tchr. U. Ky., Lexington, 1975—, acting dean, prof. law, 1998—; scholar-in-residence Housing and Civil Enforcement sect. U.S. Justice Dept.'s Civil Rights Divsn.; apptd. Fed. Res. Bd.'s Consumer Advisor Coun., 1998—. Author: (treatise) Housing Discrimination: Law and Litigation; contbr. articles to law revs. and jours. Office: U Ky Coll Law Lexington KY 40506-0048*

**SCHWENDIMAN, DAVE J.,** prosecutor. Asst. U.S. atty. State of Utah, Salt Lake City. Office: US Atty's Office 185 S St Ste 400 Salt Lake City UT 84103-4139*

**SCHWENKE, ROGER DEAN,** lawyer; b. Washington, Oct. 18, 1944; s. Clarence Raymond and Virginia Ruth (Gould) S.; m. Carol Lynne Flenniken, Nov. 29, 1980; 1 child: Matthew Robert; stepchildren: Tracy L. Wolf Dickey, Mary M. Wolf. BA, Ohio State U., 1966; JD with honors, U. Fla., 1969. Bar: Fla. 1970. Instr. Coll. Law U. Fla., Gainesville, 1969-70; assoc. Carlton, Fields, Ward, Emmanuel, Smith & Cutler P.A., Tampa, Fla., 1970-74; ptnr. Carlton, Fields, Ward, Emmanuel, Smith & Cutler P.A., 1975—; adminstr., dept. head Real Estate, Environ. and Land Use Dept., 1978—; adj. prof. Coll. Law, Stetson U., St. Petersburg, Fla., 1979-80; mem. faculty U. Miami Coll. of Law Master of Law's in Real Estate Devel. Program, 1994-96. Author chpt. in Environmental Regulation and Litigation in Florida, 1987, chpt. in Florida Real Property Complex Transactions, 1997; contbr. articles to profl. jours; chpt. to book. Mem. diocesan coun. Episc. Diocese SW Fla., 1978-86, mem. standing com., 1989-92, chief judge Eccles. Ct., 1996—. Recipient Gertrude Brick Law Rev. prize U. Fla., 1969. Fellow Am. Coll. Real Estate Lawyers (bd. govs. 1985-88), Am. Law Inst.; mem. ABA (standing com. on environ. law 1980—, coun. real property sect. 1988-95), Fla. Bar Assn., Air & Waste Mgmt. Assn., Order of Coif, Greater Tampa C. of C. (chmn. environ. coun. 1980-81), Tampa Club. Democrat. Fax: 813-229-4133. Contracts commercial, Environmental, Real property. Office: Carlton Fields PO Box 3239 Tampa FL 33601-3239

**SCHWINN, STEVEN DAVID,** lawyer, mediator; b. Dayton, Ohio, Sept. 15, 1969; s. David Ronald and Marilyn Esther (Durst) S.; m. Sandra Gutek, May 26, 1995. BA, Mich. State U., 1992; JD, The Am. U., 1995, postgrad., 1993—. Bar: Mich. 1995. Asst. gen. counsel Peace Corps, Washington, 1995—; adj. prof. law Am. U., 1996—; mediator D.C. Superior Ct., 1996—. Vol. lawyer Washington Legal Clinic for Homeless, 1995—. Home: 11204 Edson Park Pl # 8 North Bethesda MD 20852

**SCIALABBA, DAMIAN ANGELO,** lawyer; b. Bklyn., May 16, 1963; s. Dominick Anthony and Elmerinda Gilda (Caccavo) S.; m. Brenda Jean Carpenter, Apr. 24, 1993; children: Dominick Antonio, Emily Marion. BS, Ursinus Coll., 1984; JD, St. Johns U., 1987. Bar: N.J. 1987, U.S. Dist. Ct. N.J. 1987, NY 1988. Law clk. to Hon. Jared Honigfeld and Hon. B. Thomas Leahey N.J. Superior Ct. (Essex County), Newark, 1987-88; assoc. Sellar, Richardson, Stuart & Chisholm, Roseland, NJ, 1988-91, Mongello & Marshall, P.A., South Plainfield, NJ, 1991-96; ptnr. Mongello, Marshall & Scialabba, LLC, South Plainfield, NJ, 1996—. Judge Voice of Democracy competition VFW, N.J., 1995. Mem. ATLA, N.J. State Bar Assn., N.Y. State Bar Assn., Middlesex County Bar Assn., Phi Delta Phi, Psi Chi, Pi Gamma Nu, Alpha Phi Omega. General practice, Personal injury, Criminal. Office: Mongello Marshall & Scialabba LLC 1550 Park Ave Ste E South Plainfield NJ 07080-5592

**SCIALABBA, DONALD JOSEPH,** lawyer; b. N.Y.C., Aug. 4, 1950; s. Angelo Joseph and Sarah Scialabba; m. Lorraine Anne Capizzi, June 20, 1976; children: Christopher, Daniel, Laura. BS in Econs., CCNY, 1973; JD, Seton Hall U., 1980. Bar: N.Y. 1981, U.S. Dist. Ct. (ea. and so. dists.) N.Y. 1982, U.S. Ct. Appeals (2d cir.) 1994. Assoc. Costello & Shea, N.Y.C., 1981-88; ptnr. Costello Shea & Gaffney, N.Y.C., 1989—. Mem. N.Y. County Lawyers Assn. Avocations: golf, woodworking, photography. Personal injury, Product liability, Appellate. Office: Costello Shea & Gaffney 1 Battery Park Plz Fl 3 New York NY 10004-1488

**SCIANNA, RUSSELL WILLIAM,** lawyer, educator; b. Reading, Pa., Sept. 26, 1956; s. Russell Joseph and Marjorie Louise (Wilson) S.; m. Joanne Frances Melcher, June 24, 1978; children: Russell Jr., Christopher, Elizabeth, Nicholas. BS in Fgn. Service, Georgetown U., 1978; JD, Boston U., 1981; MBA, Kutztown U., 1991. Bar: Pa. 1981, U.S. Dist. Ct. (ea. dist.) Pa. 1985. Tax acct. Ernst & Whinney, Reading, 1981-82; sole practice Reading, 1982-87; pres. Bulldog Assocs., Inc., 1987-92; assoc. atty. Forry, Ullman, Ullman, & Ferry, PC, 1992-94; pvt. practice, 1994—; lectr. bus. law and acctg. Penn State U., Reading, 1982-85; lectr. bus. Reading Area C.C., 1990-93; solicitor Reading Zoning Hearing Bd. and Civil Svc. Bds., 1994—; pres. Reading Optical Co., Inc., 1982-84; asst. pub. defender, asst. dist. atty. Berks County, Reading, 1985. Mem. Reading Zoning Hearing Bd., 1982-86; trustee Reading Area Community Coll., 1985-86; bd. dirs. Reading Cen. Br. YMCA, 1982-85. Mem. Pa. Bar Assn., Berks County Bar Assn., Rotary-West Reading/Wyomissing. Avocations: golf, backgammon. General practice, General corporate, Taxation, general. Office: PO Box 7622 225 Kenhorst Blvd Reading PA 19607-1535

**SCIBILIA, JOSEPH LOGAN,** lawyer; b. Mineola, N.Y., Nov. 23, 1965. JD, St. John's U., Jamaica, N.Y., 1991. Bar: Conn. 1991, N.Y. 1992, Ga. 1998. Atty. Milgrim Thamajan & Lee P.C., N.Y.C., 1991-93, Hebb & Gitlin P.C., Hartford, Conn., 1994-97, Sutherland Asbill & Brennan LLP, Atlanta, 1997—. Banking, General corporate, Finance. Office: Sutherland Asbill & Brennan 999 Peachtree St NE Ste 2300 Atlanta GA 30309-3996

**SCIOCCHETTI, NANCY,** lawyer; b. Schenectady, N.Y., May 20, 1962; d. Andrew Sr. and Lina (DeLeonardis) S.; m. Scott K. Townsend, Dec. 8, 1990 (div. Nov. 1997); 1 child, Emma. BA cum laude, Siena Coll., 1983; JD, Albany U., 1986. Bar: N.Y. 1987, U.S. Dist. Ct. (no. dist.) N.Y. 1987. Assoc. Sherrin & Glasel LLP, Albany, N.Y., 1987-91, ptnr., 1991—. Recipient Disting. Svc. award Legal Aid Soc. Northeastern N.Y., 1992. Mem. Jr. League of Albany (grants chair 1998—, parliamentarian 1999—), Italian Am. Bar Assn. (bd. dirs. 1998—). Avocations: travel, reading, entertaining. Health. Office: Sherrin & Glasel LLP 74 N Pearl St Ste 4 Albany NY 12207-2708

**SCIOCCHETTI, PAUL VINCENT,** lawyer; b. Schenectady, N.Y, Mar. 1, 1961; s. Augusto Julius and Josephine (DeLeonardis) S. BA, Siena Coll., 1983; JD, Pace U., 1986. Bar: N.Y. 1987, U.S. Dist. Ct. (no. dist.) N.Y. Assoc. Parisi, DeLorenzo, Gordon, Pasquariello & Weiskopf, P.C., Schenectady, 1986-87, Capasso Burns & Massaroni, Schenectady, 1987-90; pvt. practice, 1990-94; of counsel Donald Zee, P.C., Albany, 1995-97; pvt. practice, 1997—; mem. panel arbitrators Am. Arbitration Assn., Syracuse, N.Y., 1987—, Schenectady County Arbitration Commn., 1987—; mem. Ctrl. Park Music Stage Task Force, 1999. Bd. dirs. Hispanic Cmty. Coalition, Electric City Music Festival, Inc., 1990-94, Boys and Girls Club Am., 1993-94; chmn. Com. for Preservation of Schnectady County Parks (Adopt-a-Park), 1990-95; Mayfair com. Residential Opportunities, Inc., 1996-97. Mem. ATLA, N.Y. State Trial Lawyers Assn., N.Y. State Bar Assn. (entertainment, arts and sports law sect. exec. com. 1991—), Schenectady County Bar Assn., Pace U. Alumni Assn. (chmn. Capital Dist. chpt. 1988-89), Nat. Italian Am. Found. (founder, co-chair greater capital dist./upstate N.Y. chpt.), N.Y. State Assn. (small law firm task force 1996). Roman Catholic. Contracts commercial, Real property, Transportation. Home: 2033 Rosedale Way Schenectady NY 12303-4842 Office: 201 Nott Ter Schenectady NY 12307-1025

**SCIONTI, MICHAEL JOSEPH,** lawyer; b. Tampa, Fla., Oct. 2, 1968; s. Morris Michael and Susan Mary S. BS, Fla. State U., 1990; JD, Tex. A&m U., 1996. Bar: Fla. 1996, Ga. 1997, U.S. Dist. Ct. (mid. dist.) Fla. 1997, U.S. Ct. Appeals (11th cir.) 1997. Asst. atty. gen. Atty. Gens. Office, Tampa, Fla., 1996-98; asst. state atty. State Attys. Office, Tampa, Fla., 1998—. Mem. Hillsborough County Bar Assn. (criminal law divsn. 1997-98), Optimists Club (bd. dirs. 1998). Democrat. Roman Catholic. Office: Office of State Atty County Courthouse Annex 801 E Twiggs St Tampa FL 33602

**SCIPIONE, RICHARD STEPHEN,** insurance company executive, lawyer; b. Newton, Mass., Aug. 27, 1937; s. Charles John and Alice (Scotto) S.; m. Lois Mugford, Aug. 29, 1964; children: Jeffrey Charles, Douglas Loring. BA, Harvard U., 1959; LLB, Boston U., 1962. Bar: Mass. 1962. Atty. John Hancock Mut. Life Ins. Co., Boston, 1965-69, asst. counsel, 1969-74, assoc. counsel, 1975-79, sr. assoc. counsel, 1980-82, 2d v.p., counsel, 1982-84, v.p., gen. solicitor, 1984-85, sr. v.p. and gen. solicitor, 1986-87, gen. counsel, 1987—; bd. dirs. New England Legal Found., John Hancock Advisers/Distbrs.; trustee John Hancock Mutual Funds. Served to capt. U.S. Army, 1962-65. Mem. ABA (dir. New Eng. Coun.), Assn. Life Ins. Counsel (gov. 1994-98), Chatham Yacht Club, South Shore Country Club. Office: John Hancock Mut Life Ins Co Box 111 John Hancock Pl Boston MA 02117

**SCIRICA, ANTHONY JOSEPH,** federal judge; b. Norristown, Pa., Dec. 16, 1940; s. A. Benjamin and Anna (Sclafani) S.; m. Susan Morgan, May 6, 1966; children—Benjamin, Sara. B.A., Wesleyan U., 1962; J.D., U. Mich., 1965; postgrad., Central U., Caracas, Venezuela, 1966. Bar: Pa., 1966, U.S. Dist. Ct. (ea. dist.) Pa., 1984, U.S. Ct. Appeals (3d cir.), 1987. Ptnr. McGrory, Scirica, Wentz & Fernandez, Norristown, Pa., 1966-80; asst. dist. atty. Montgomery County, Pa., 1967-69; mem. Pa. Ho. of Reps, Harrisburg, 1971-79; judge Montgomery County Ct. Common Pleas, Pa., 1980-84, U.S. Dist. Ct. (ea. dist.) Pa., Phila., 1984-87, U.S. Ct. Appeals (3d cir.), 1987—; chmn. Pa. Sentencing Commn., 1980-85. Fulbright scholar Central U., Caracas, Venezuela, 1966. Mem. Montgomery Bar Assn., Pa. Bar Assn., ABA. Roman Catholic. Office: US Courthouse 601 Market St Rm 22614 Philadelphia PA 19106-1715*

**SCOBEE, H. EVANS,** lawyer; b. Baton Rouge, Nov. 2, 1951; s. Hansen E. and Dorothy (Voorhies) S.; m. Meghan Brown. BA in English, La. State U., 1973, JD, 1975. Bar: La. 1975, U.S. Ct. Appeals (5th cir.) 1975. Ptnr. Durrett, Hardin, Baton Rouge, 1975-94, Chaffe McCall et al, Baton Rouge, 1994—. Health, General civil litigation, Product liability. Office: Chaffe McCall et al Ste 202 8550 United Plaza Blvd Baton Rouge LA 70809-2256

**SCOFIELD, DAVID WILLSON,** lawyer; b. Hartford, Conn., Oct. 17, 1957; s. Leslie Willson and Daphne Winifred (York) S. AB, Cornell U., 1979; JD, U. Utah, 1983. Bar: Utah 1983, U.S. Dist. Ct. Utah 1983, U.S. Dist. Ct. Ariz. 1993, U.S. Dist. Ct. Hawaii 1995, U.S. Ct. Appeals (10th cir.) 1990, U.S. Ct. Appeals (9th cir.) 1995, U.S. Supreme Ct. 1996, U.S. Ct. Claims, 1997. Assoc. Parsons & Crowther, Salt Lake City, 1983-87; assoc. Callister, Duncan & Nebeker, Salt Lake City, 1987-89, ptnr., 1989-92; founding ptnr. Parsons, Davies, Kinghorn & Peters, Salt Lake City, 1992-96, pres., 1996-97. Author: Trial Handbook for Utah Lawyers, 1994; mem. Utah Law Rev., 1981-83; contbr. articles to legal jours. Bd. dirs. Westminster Coll. Found., 1994-96, chmn. cultivation com., 1995-96. Named to Outstanding Young Men of Am., 1986. Mem. ABA, Assn. Trial Lawyers Am., Utah Trial Lawyers Assn., Salt Lake County Bar Assn., Zeta Psi. Congregationalist. Avocations: American history, writing, sports. Federal civil litigation, General civil litigation, General practice. Home: 2331 Scenic Dr Salt Lake City UT 84109-1432 Office: Parsons Davies Kinghorn & Peters 185 S State St Ste 700 Salt Lake City UT 84111-1550

**SCOFIELD, LOUIS M., JR.,** lawyer; b. Brownsville, Tex., Jan. 14, 1952; s. Louis M. and Betsy Lee (Aiken) S.; children: Christopher, Nicholas. BS in Geology with highest honors and high distinction, U. Mich., 1974; JD with honors, U. Tex., 1977. Bar: Tex. 1977, U.S. Dist. Ct. (ea. and so. dists.) Tex., U.S. Ct. Appeals (5th cir.) 1981, U.S. Supreme Ct. 1984. Ptnr. Mehaffy & Weber, Beaumont, Tex., 1982—; spkr. CNA Ins., Dallas, Jefferson County Ins. Adjusters, S.E. Tex. Ind. Ins. Agts., Gulf Ins. Co., Dallas, Employers Casualty Co., Beaumont, Tex. Employment Commn., Jefferson County Young Lawyers Assn., Jefferson County Bar Assn., South Tex. Coll. of Law, John Gray Inst., Lamar U., 1991, Tex. Assn. Def. Counsel, 1991; cert. arbitrator Nat. Panel of Consumer Arbitrators; arbitrator BBB; presenter Forest Park H.S., Martin Elem. Sch., St. Anne's Sch. Contbr. articles to profl. jours.; columnist Jefferson County Bar Jour. Patron Beaumont Heritage Soc., John J. French Mus.; bd. dirs. Beaumont Heritage Soc., 1983-84, mem. endowment fund com., 1988; chmn. lawyers divsn. United Appeals Campaign, 1984; grand patron Jr. League of Beaumont, 1989, 90. Fellow Tex. Bar Found., State Bar of Tex. (mentors com. 1995); mem. ABA (contbg. editor newsletter products, gen. liability and consumer law com., vice chmn. of com.), Assn. Def. Trial Attys. (Tex. state membership chmn., exec. coun. 1999-2002), Tex. Assn. Def. Counsel (dir. at large 1986-87, v.p. 1987-89, adminstrv. v.p. 1989-90, program chmn. San Diego 1989), Def. Rsch. Inst., Am. Judicature Soc., Jefferson County Bar Assn. (disaster relief project 1979, outstanding young lawyer's com. 1980), Beaumont Country Club, Tower Club of Beaumont, Phi Beta Kappa. Democrat. Episcopalian. Avocations: golf, reading, fishing. General civil litigation, Personal injury, Insurance. Home: 4790 Littlefield St Beaumont TX 77706-7748 Office: Mehaffy & Weber PO Box 16 Beaumont TX 77704-0016

**SCOGLAND, WILLIAM LEE,** lawyer; b. Moline, Ill., Apr. 2, 1949; s. Maurice William and Harriet Rebecca S.; m. Victoria Lynn Whitham, Oct. 9, 1976; 1 child, Thomas. BA magna cum laude, Augustana Coll., 1971; JD cum laude, Harvard U., 1975. Bar: Ill. 1975, U.S. Dist. Ct. (no. dist.) Ill. 1975. Assoc. Wildman, Harrold, Allen & Dixon, Chgo., 1975-77, Hughes Hubbard & Reed, Milw., 1977-81; from assoc. to ptnr. Jenner & Block, Chgo., 1981—. Author: Fiduciary Duty: What Does It Mean?, 1989; co-author Employee Benefits Law, 1987. Mem. Phi Beta Kappa, Omicron Delta Kappa. Republican. Pension, profit-sharing, and employee benefits, Mergers and acquisitions. Office: Jenner & Block 1 E Ibm Plz Fl 4000 Chicago IL 60611-7603

**SCOPTUR, PAUL JOSEPH,** lawyer, educator; b. Milw., Jan. 4, 1953; s. James Scoptur and Mary Louise Mente; m. Christina Marie Engel, Nov. 6, 1981; children: James, Katherine, Mark, Alexandra. BA, U. Wis., Milw., 1974; JD, Marquette U., 1978. Bar: Wis. 1978, U.S. Dist. Ct. (we. and ea. dists.) Wis. 1978. Atty. Aiken & Mawicke SC, Milw., 1978-90; ptnr. Aiken & Scoptur SC, Milw., 1990—; adj. prof. law Marquette U., Milw., 1997—; lectr. in field. Trustee Nat. Coll. Advocacy, Washington, 1993—. Avocations: coaching athletics, sports, educating attorneys. Personal injury, Professional liability, General civil litigation. Office: Aiken & Scoptur SC 260 E Highland Ave Fl 700 Milwaukee WI 53202-2567

**SCORSINE, JOHN MAGNUS,** lawyer; b. Rochester, N.Y., Dec. 3, 1957; s. Frank and Karin (Frennby) S.; m. Susan Nauss, May 31, 1980 (div.); m. Theresa A. Burke, Dec. 17, 1988; 1 child, Jennifer E. BS, Rochester Inst. Tech., 1980; JD, U. Wyo., 1984. Bar: Wyo. 1984, U.S. Dist. Ct. Wyo. 1984, U.S. Ct. Appeals (10th cir.) 1989, U.S. Army Ct. Criminal Appeals 1995. Part-time deputy sheriff Monroe County (N.Y.), 1978-80; police officer Casper (Wyo.) Police Dept., 1980-81; intern U.S. Atty. Office, Cheyenne, Wyo., 1983-84; pvt. practice Rock Springs, Wyo., 1984-85; ptnr. Scorsine and Flynn, Rock Springs, 1986; prin. Scorsine Law Office, Rock Springs, 1986-95; commr. Dist. and County Court, 1986-95; dep. chief of staff for mil. support Wyo. Nat. Guard, 1995—; ptnr. Sunset Advt., 1987-89; chmn. bd. dirs. Youth Home Inc., Rock Springs, 1987-88; treas. Sweetwater County Cmty. Corrections Bd., 1990-95; mem. Nat. Ski Patrol, 1976—, Wyo. Bd. of Parole, 1998—. Leader Medicine Bow Ski Patrol, Laramie, Wyo., 1983; legal advisor Rocky Mountain divsn. Nat. Ski Patrol, 1984; asst. patrol leader White Pine Ski Area, Pinedale, Wyo., 1986; avalanche advisor Jackson Hole Snow King Ski Patrol, 1987-96, avalanche instr. 1993—; sect. chief Teton sect. nat. Ski Patrol, 1991-94, mem. Eldore Ski Patrol, 1996—; mem. Sweetwater County Search and Rescue, 1989-95, tng. officer, 1993-95; mem. Sweetwater County Emergency Dive Team, 1990-95, mem. Sweetwater County Fire Dept., 1992-94, Reliance Vol. Fire Dept., 1994-95; lt.k, training officer Laramie Cmty. Fire Dist. #6 and Burns Ambulance Svc., 1995-98, treas./sec. bd. dirs. 1997-98, Am. N. Peary Land expdn., 1989; scoutmaster Boy Scouts Am., 1987-93, 96-98, 4H leader, 1997—; pres. Sweetwater County Vol. Fire Assn., 1993-94; mem. Laramie County Sch. Dist. #2 accreditation panel; dir. emergency svcs. Wyo. Civil Air Patrol, 1998—, comdr. Wyo. wing, 1999—. Maj. JAG, USAR , 1991—; bd. dirs., sec. Burns Cmty. Ambulance, 1997—. Recipient Yellow Merit star Nat. Ski Patrol, 1993, Fritch Volunteerism award, 1993, Armed Forces Outstanding Vol. Svc. medal. Mem. ABA, Wyo. State Bar, Wyo. Trial Lawyers Assn., Assn. Am. Trial Lawyers, Rock Springs C. of C., Res. Officers Assn. (nat. councilman 1993—, state pres. 1994), Rotary. Democrat. Lutheran. Avocations: rock climbing, backpacking, hunting, scuba, karate. General practice, Criminal, Appellate. Home: 1090 State Hwy 214 Burns WY 82093 Office: Wyo Nat Guard 5500 Bishop Blvd Cheyenne WY 82009-3320

**SCOTT, BETSY SUE,** lawyer; b. Chgo., July 3, 1951; d. Leo and Regina Mackta; m. Thomas Jefferson Scott Jr., Apr. 25, 1981; children: Elspeth Watts, Marghuerita Taylor, Thomas Jefferson Scott III. Cert. in French lang., U. Paris, 1971; BA, Hamilton Coll., 1972; JD, Cumberland Coll., 1976. Bar: Pa. 1976, N.Y. 1980, D.C. 1984. Trust adminstr. Mfrs. Hanover Trust, N.Y.C., 1976-78; assoc. Fink, Weinberger et al, N.Y.C., 1978-80; employee benefits officer 1st Va. Bank, Falls Church, 1982-83; mem. Hill, Betts & Nash, Washington, 1983-85; sole practice, litigation cons. Washington, 1985-86; employee benefits atty., Pension and Welfare Benefits Adminstrn. U.S. Dept. Labor, Washington, 1986-90; atty. Office Fgn. Assets Control, U.S. Treasury Dept., Washington, 1990—; translator French-English litigation, Washington, 1985—. Mem. Great Falls Womens Club, River Bend Golf and Country Club. Republican. Avocations: sailing, fencing, gardening. Office: US Treasury Dept Office Fgn Assets Control 1500 Pennsylvania Ave NW Washington DC 20220-0001

**SCOTT, BRIAN DAVID,** lawyer; b. Spokane, Wash., Sept. 30, 1946; s. Dick E. and Helene L. (Johnson) S.; m. Lynita G. Muzzall, Sept. 9, 1972; children: D. Alexander, Rachel E., S. Andrew. BA, U. Wash., 1968; JD, U. Wis., 1972. Bar: Wis. 1972, Wash. 1972, U.S. Dist. Ct. (we. dist.) Wash. 1972, U.S. Dist. Ct. (we. dist.) Wis. 1972. Asst. atty. gen. Wash. State Atty. Gen.'s Office, Seattle, 1972-74; assoc. Jackson, Ulvestad, Goodwin, Grutz, Seattle, 1974-81; ptnr. Goodwin, Grutz & Scott, Seattle, 1981-96, Grutz, Scott & Kinney, Seattle, 1996—. Mem. ATLA, Wash. Trial Lawyers Assn., Wash. Athletic Club. Democrat. Avocations: boating, skiing, travel. Personal injury, Product liability, Workers' compensation. Home: 158 Prospect St Seattle WA 98109-3750 Office: Grutz Scott & Kinney 600 University St Ste 1928 Seattle WA 98101-4178

**SCOTT, DAVID MATTHEW,** lawyer; b. Evanston, Ill., Aug. 26, 1972; s. David Allen and Barbra Marie Scott. BA, Ohio State U., 1994, JD, 1997. Bar: Ohio 1997, U.S. Dist. Ct. (so. dist.) Ohio 1997. R&D intern S.C. Johnson Wax, Racine, Wis., 1992-93; law clk. Franklin County Mcpl. Ct., Columbus, Ohio, 1995; law clk., atty. Luper, Sheriff & Neidenthal, L.P.A., Columbus, 1996—. Vol. George Bush for Pres., Columbus, 1992. Mem. Ohio State Bar Assn., Athletic Club Columbus, Minifield Village Golf Club. Avocations: golf, literature. General civil litigation, General corporate, Personal injury. Office: Luper Sheriff & Neidenthal LPA 50 W Broad St Ste 1200 Columbus OH 43215-5907

**SCOTT, DAVID RODICK,** lawyer, legal educator; b. Phila., Dec. 30, 1938; s. Ernest and Lydia Wister (tunis) S.; m. Ruth Erskine Wardle, Aug. 20, 1966; children: Cintra W., D. Rodman. AB magna cum laude, Harvard U., 1960, JD, 1965; MA, Cambridge U., 1962. Bar: Pa. 1966, D.C. 1977, U.S. Dist. Ct. (ea. dist.) Pa. 1966, U.S. Ct. Appeals (3rd cir.) 1966, U.S. Ct. Appeals (D.C. cir.) 1977, U.S. Supreme Ct. 1977. Law clk. to assoc. justice Supreme Ct. Pa., Phila., 1965-66; assoc. Pepper, Hamilton & Scheetz, Phila., 1966-69, 72-76; asst. dist. atty. City of Phila., 1970-72; sr. trial atty. criminal div. U.S. Dept. Justice, Washington, 1976-80; chief counsel, acting dir. Office Govt. Ethics, Washington, 1980-84; univ. counsel Rutgers U., New Brunswick, N.J., 1984—; acting dir. U.S. Office Govt. Ethics, 1982-83; tchr., lectr. in law Cath. U. Am., Washington, 1977-81, Inst. Paralegal Tng., Phila., 1970-74; instr. Faculty of Arts and Scis., Rutgers U.; lectr. in field. Contbr. chpts. to textbooks, articles to profl. jours. Trustee United Way Greater Mercer County, 1990—, Princeton Area Cmty. Found., Inc., 1991—; bd. mgrs. Episc. Acad., Merion, Pa., 1970-74. Keasbey Found. fellow, 1960-62. Mem ABA, Pa. Bar Assn., Nat. Assn. Coll. and Univ. Attys. (bd. dirs. 1993-96), Am. Friends Cambridge U. (head N.J. chpt. 1987-93). General corporate, Education and schools. Home: 255 Russell Rd Princeton NJ 08540-6733 Office: Rutgers U Office of Univ Counsel Winants Hall New Brunswick NJ 08901

**SCOTT, EDWARD ALOYSIUS,** lawyer; b. Chgo., July 25, 1923; s. Edward A. and Bride Winifred (Kelly) S.; m. Joan C. Boyter, Jan. 4, 1947; children: Edward III, Karen, Susan, Barbara, Deborah, Kevin, Terrence. BS, DePaul U., 1948, LLD, 1950. Bar: Ill. 1951. Pvt. practice law South Holland, Ill. Capt. USAF, 1941-45. Mem. Assn. Trial Lawyers Am., Celtic Legal Soc., Chgo. Bar Assn., Ill. Bar Assn., Trial Lawyers Club of Chgo., Phi Alpha Delta. Roman Catholic. Avocation: golf. General civil litigation, General practice, Personal injury. Office: 15330 Greenwood Rd South Holland IL 60473-1924

**SCOTT, G. JUDSON, JR.,** lawyer; b. Phila., Nov. 16, 1945; s. Gerald Judson and Jean Louise (Evans) S.; m. Ildiko Kalman, Mar. 21, 1971; children: Nathan Emory, Lauren Jean. AA, Foothill Jr. Coll., Los Altos, Calif., 1965; BA, U. Calif., Santa Barbara, 1968; JD cum laude, U. Santa Clara, 1975. Bar: Calif. 1975, U.S. Dist. Ct. (no. dist.) Calif. 1975, U.S. Ct. Appeals (9th cir.) 1975, U.S. Supreme Ct. 1981. Assoc. Feldman, Waldman & kline, San Francisco, 1975-76, Law Offices John Wynne Herron, San Francisco, 1976-80; of counsel firm Haines & Walker, Livermore, Calif., 1980; ptnr. Haines Walker & Scott, Livermore, 1980-84; officer, dir., shareholder firm Smith, Etnire, Polson and Scott, Pleasanton, Calif., 1984-88; pvt. practice, 1988—; judge pro tem Livermore-Pleasanton Mcpl. Ct., 1981-83; settlement commr. Alameda County Superior Ct., 1994—; lectr. Calif. Continuing Edn. of Bar. Contbg. author: Attorney's Guide to Restitution, 1976; editor: The Bottom Line, 1989-91. Pres. Walnut Creek Open Space Found., Calif., 1981-83. Rear adm. USNR, 1968—. Mem. ATLA (sustaining), Consumer Attys. Calif. (reviewer of pending Calif. legis.), Ea. Alameda County Bar Assn. (v.p. 1981-82), Calif. State Bar (mem. standing com. on lawyer referral svcs. 1985-88, mem. exec. com. law practice mgmt. sec. 1988-93, chairperson 1992-93), Alameda County Bar Assn. (chmn. law office econs. com. 1986-87, mem. jud. nomination evaluation com. 1996-97, bd. dirs. 1997-98, v.p. 1999, chairperson task force 1997), Alameda-Contra Costa County Trial Lawyers Assn., Livermore C. of C. (past chmn. growth study 1983), Pleasanton C. of C., Million Dollar Advs. Forum. Republican. Episcopalian. Personal injury, General civil litigation, Insurance. Office: 6140 Stoneridge Mall Rd Ste 125 Pleasanton CA 94588-3233

**SCOTT, GREGORY KELLAM,** state supreme court justice; b. San Francisco, July 30, 1943; s. Robert and Althea Delores Scott; m. Carolyn Weatherly, Apr. 10, 1971; children: Joshua Weatherly, Elijah Kellam. BS in Environ. Sci., Rutgers U., 1970, EdM in Urban Studies, 1971; JD cum laude, Ind. U., Indpls., 1977. Asst. dean resident instrn. Cook Coll. Rutgers U., 1972-75; trial atty. U.S. SEC, Denver, 1977-79; gen. counsel Blinder, Robinson & Co., Inc., Denver, 1979-80; asst. prof. coll. law U. Denver, 1980-85, assoc. prof., 1985-93, prof. emeritus, 1993—, chair bus. planning program, 1986-89, 92-93; justice Colo. Supreme Ct., Denver, 1993—; of counsel Moore, Smith & Bryant, Indpls., 1987-90; v.p., gen. counsel Comml. Energies, Inc., 1990-91; presenter in field. Author: (with others) Structuring Mergers and Acquisitions in Colorado, 1985, Airport Law and Regulation, 1991, Racism and Underclass in America, 1991; contbr. articles to profl. jours. Mem. ABA, Nat. Bar Assn., Nat. Assn. Securities Dealers, Inc., Nat. Arbitration Panel (arbitrator), Colo. Bar Found., Sam Cary Bar Assn., Am. Inn Ct. (founding mem. Judge Alfred A. Arraj inn). Avocations: golfing, reading, traveling. Office: Supreme Ct Colo Judicial Bldg 2 E 14th Ave Denver CO 80203-2115

**SCOTT, JOHN ROLAND,** lawyer, oil company executive; b. Wichita Falls, Tex, May 13, 1937; s. John and Margaret S.; m. Joan Carol Redding, Sept. 5, 1959; 1 child, John Howard. Llb, Baylor Sch. Law, Waco, Tex., 1962. Bar: Tex. 1962, Alaska 1970, Tex., 1965, U.S. Dist. Ct. (we. dist.), U.S. Dist. Ct. Alaska 1975. Assoc. litigation sect. Lynch & Chappell, Midland, Tex., 1962-65; regional atty. Atlantic Richfield Co., Midland, 1965-79; sr. atty. Anchorage, 1969-77, Dallas, 1977-80; v.p., assoc. gen. counsel Mitchell Energy & Devel. Corp., Houston, 1980-82; asst. gen. counsel Hunt Oil Co., Dallas, 1982-84, v.p., chief counsel, 1984-91, sr. v.p. gen. counsel, 1994—; bar examiner in Alaska, 1974-77;. Mem. State Bar Tex. (lectr.), Dallas Bar Assn., ABA, Phi Alpha Delta. Republican. Oil, gas, and mineral, General corporate, Private international. Office: Hunt Oil Co 1445 Ross Ave Ste 1800 Dallas TX 75202-2739

**SCOTT, JOSEPH MITCHELL, JR.,** lawyer, judge; b. Lexington, Ky., Sept. 1, 1946; s. Joseph Mitchell and Marjorie Louise (Rush) S.; m. Patricia Ann Thompson, Aug. 2, 1980; children: Rush Thomspon, Jane Mitchell. BBA in Acctg., U. Notre Dame, 1968; JD, U. Ky., 1971. Bar: Ky. 1971, U.S. Ct. Appeals (6th cir.) 1984. Ptnr. Stoll, Keenon & Park, Lexington, 1971-99; judge U.S. Bankruptcy Ct., Lexington, Ky., 1999—. 1st lt. U.S. Army, 1968-71. Bankruptcy, Contracts commercial, Banking. Office: PO Box 1111 Lexington KY 40588-1111

**SCOTT, KATHRYN FENDERSON,** lawyer; b. Augusta, Ga., June 6, 1970; d. Robert Thomas Fenderson and Christine (Cunningham) Cormier. BA, Eckerd Coll., St. Petersburg, Fla., 1992; JD, Stetson U., St. Petersburg, 1995. Bar: Fla. 1995, U.S. Dist. Ct. (mid. dist.) Fla. 1995, U.S. Ct. Appeals (11th cir.) 1997. Assoc. Govan, Burns & Jones, St. Petersburg, 1995-97; ptnr. Scott & Fenderson, St. Petersburg, 1997—; editl. bd. Paraclete, St. Petersburg Bar Assn., 1996—; mentor program Stetson U. Coll. Law, St. Petersburg, 1996—. Recipient Am. Jurisprudence award Lawyer's Coop. Pub., 1992. Mem. ABA, Assn. Trial Lawyers Am., Assn. Fla. Trial Lawyers, St. Petersburg Bar Assn., Clearwater Bar Assn. Fax: 727-321-4499. E-mail: itslegal@aol.com. Personal injury, Family and matrimonial, Criminal. Office: Scott and Fenderson 4554 Central Ave Ste L Saint Petersburg FL 33711-1046

**SCOTT, MARK ANTHONY,** lawyer; b. Charlottesville, Va., Feb. 4, 1956; s. James Russell Jr. and Mary Eliza S.; m. Joan Q. Scott, July 19, 1975; children, Darius, Byron. AS, Victor Valley Coll., 1978; BA, Calif. State U., Fresno, 1980; JD, Howard U., 1984. Bar: U.S. Dist. Ct. (no. dist.) Ga., U.S. Dist. Ct. (ea. dist.) Tenn. Assoc. counsel Provident Life and Accident Ins. Co., Chattanooga, 1984-87; pvt. practice Chattanooga, 1987-89, Atlanta, 1997—; ptnr. Taylor, Scott & McClary, Atlanta, 1989-91; asst. regional counsel U.S. Dept. Housing and Urban Devel., Atlanta, 1991-93; exec. dir. Nat. Funeral Dirs. and Morticians Assn., Atlanta, 1993-95; v.p. corp. devel. The Harrison-Ross Group, L.A., 1995-97. Sgt. USAF, 1975-78. Avocations: golfing, reading. Criminal. Office: 41 Marietta St NW Ste 410 Atlanta GA 30303-2819

**SCOTT, PETER BRYAN,** lawyer; b. St. Louis, Nov. 11, 1947; s. gilbert Franklin and Besse Jean (Fudge) S.; children: Lindsay W., Sarah W., Peter B. Jr. AB, Drury Coll., 1969; JD, Washington U., St. Louis, 1972, LLM, 1980. Bar: Mo. 1972, Colo. 1980; diplomate Ct. Practice Inst.; accredited estate planner. Pvt. practice St. Louis, 1972-80; assoc. McKie and Assocs., Denver, 1980-81; ptnr. Scott and Chesteen, P.C., Denver, 1981-84, Veto & Scott, Denver, 1984-92; pvt. practice Denver, 1992—; tchr. Denver Paralegal Inst., Red Rocks C.C. Mem. Evergreen Christian Ch., Disciples of Christ. Capt. USAR, 1971-79. Mem. ABA, Mo. Bar Assn., Colo. Bar Assn., 1st Jud. Dist. Bar Assn. Republican. General corporate, Estate planning, Probate. Home: 6305 W 6th Ave Unit C18 Lakewood CO 80214-2349 Office: 6595 W 14th Ave Denver CO 80214-1998

**SCOTT, ROBERT EDWIN,** dean, law educator; b. Nagpur, India, Feb. 25, 1944; came to U.S., 1955; s. Roland Waldeck and Carol (Culver) S.; m. Elizabeth (Loch) Shumaker, Aug. 14, 1965; children: Christina Elaine, Robert Adam. BA, Oberlin (Ohio) Coll., 1965; JD, Coll. of William and Mary, 1968; LLM, U. Mich., 1969, SJD, 1973. Bar: Va. 1968. From asst. to prof. Law Sch. Coll. of William and Mary, Williamsburg, Va., 1969-74; prof. law Sch. of Law U. Va., Charlottesville, 1974-82, Lewis F. Powell, Jr. prof. Sch. of Law, 1982—, dean and Arnold H. Leon prof., 1991—. Author: Commercial Transactions, 1982, 91, Sales Law and the Contracting Process, 1982, 91, Contract Law and Theory, 1988, 93, Payment Systems and Credit Instruments, 1996. Fellow Am. Bar Found.; mem. Va. Bar Assn. Democrat. Methodist. Home: 1109 Hilltop Rd Charlottesville VA 22903-1220 Office: U Va Sch of Law Charlottesville VA 22903

**SCOTT, ROBERT GENE,** lawyer; b. Montague, Mass., Aug. 29, 1951; s. Edwin Ray and Barbara Agnes (Painchaud) S.; m. Laura Beth Williams, May 27, 1978; children: Jason Robert, Amanda Marie, Leah Beth. BS, U. Notre Dame, 1973, MS, 1975; postgrad., U. Tex., 1975-76; JD, U. Notre Dame, 1980. Bar: Ind. 1980, U.S. Dist. Ct. (no. dist.) Ind. 1980, U.S. Patent Office 1980, Mo. 1981, U.S. Dist. Ct. (we. dist.) Mo. 1981, U.S. Ct. Appeals (11th cir.) 1986, U.S. Ct. Appeals (8th cir.) 1987, U.S. Ct. Appeals (10th cir.) 1987, Kans. 1989, U.S. Dist. Ct. Kans. 1989. Asst. women's basketball coach U. Notre Dame, Ind., 1977-80; assoc. atty. Oltsch, Knoblock & Hall, South Bend, Ind., 1980-81; atty. Swanson, Midgley et al, Kansas City, Mo., 1981-82; exec. adminstr. Coun. of Fleet Specialists, Shawnee Mission, Kans., 1982-83; atty. Levy and Craig, Kansas City, Mo., 1983-89, Turner, Vader & Koch, Chartered, 1989-93; pvt. practice, 1993-95; atty. Neill, Scott, Terrill & Embree, LLC, Lenexa, Kans., 1996—; mem. equilaw panel arbitrators Panel Arbitrators, U.S. Dist. Ct. (we. dist.) Mo. Precinct committeeman Johnson County Rep. Party, Kans., 1983-84. Mem. ABA, Ind. Bar Assn., Mo. Bar Assn., Kansas City Bar Assn., Kansas City Lawyers Assn., Kans. Bar Assn., Wyandotte County Bar Assn., Am. Arbitration Assn. (mem. panel of arbitrators, constrn. arbitrator adv. bd.), Nat. Assn. Security Dealers (panel arbitrators, complex litigation panel), Notre Dame Club of Kansas City (pres. 1985-86), S.W. United Soccer Club of Kans. (pres. 1994—), Heartland Soccer Assn. (v.p. 1997—). Republican. Roman Catholic. General civil litigation, Trademark and copyright, Workers' compensation. Office: 8730 Bourgade St Ste 101 Lenexa KS 66219-1428

**SCOTT, ROBERT WILLIAM,** mediator, lawyer, educator, consultant; b. Washington, June 29, 1952; s. Robert Vernon and Louise Wentz S.; m. Deborah Lynn French, June 4, 1977; children: Zachary D., Travis M. BS, Drexel U., 1974; JD, U. Balt., 1980; MS in Conflict Mgmt., George Mason U., 1990. Bar: Va. 1980, D.C. 1981, U.S. Dist. Ct. (ea. dist.) Va. 1982, U.S. Ct. Appeals (4th cir.) 1982; cert. gen. and family mediator. Analyst Planning Rsch. Corp. U.S. Dept. Justice, Washington, 1980-82, analyst Koba Assocs., Inc., 1982-85; pvt. practice Springfield, Va., 1985-93; mediator No. Va. Mediation Svc., Fairfax, Va., 1990—, mediation coord., 1993-94; exec. dir. Inst. Conflict Analysis and Resolution No. Va. Mediation Svc., George Mason U., Fairfax, Va., 1994—; panelist U.S. Dept. Justice Americans with Disabilities Act, A Mediation Program, 1998; fair housing conciliation panelist Va. Fair Housing Office, 1995; task force appointment Fairfax County Legal Assistance Task Force, 1995-97, Va. Commonwealth U., 1997-98; chair employee adv. com. Drug Enforcement Adminstrn./NADDIS contract employees, Washington, 1981-85; mediator evaluator Mediator Cert. Program Md. Com. on Dispute Resolution, 1996; mediator celebrant Fairfax County Cir. Ct., 1992-94. Mem. crisis intervention Alexandria (Va.) Hotline, 1989-91; bd.dirs. Newington Forest Cmty. Assn., Springfield, 1989-90. Named to Leadership Fairfax Class of 1999, 1998. Mem. D.C. Bar Assn., Va. State Bar (appointed mem. pub. rels. subcom. Va. State Bar/Va. Bar Assn. joint com. alt. dispute resolution 1997, appointed mem. cmty. mediation subcom. Va. State Bar/Va. Bar Assn. joint com. alt. dispute resolution 1998), Soc. Profls. Dispute Resolution, Va. Mediation Network. Office: No Va Mediation Svc Inst Conflict Analysis Resolution George Mason U 4D3 4260 Chain Bridge Rd Ste A2 Fairfax VA 22030-4297

**SCOTT, RONALD CHARLES,** lawyer; b. Greenville, S.C., Jan. 8, 1948; s. Robert Claude and Louise Helen (Tinsley) S.; m. Debra Whaley, Aug. 11, 1973; children: Robert Marion, Jordan Whaley, Carter Whaley. BBA cum laude, The Citadel, 1970; MBA, U. S.C., 1972, M in Acctg., JD, 1976. Bar: S.C. 1976, U.S. Dist. Ct. S.C. 1977, U.S. Tax Ct. 1977. Pres. Scott & Mathews P.A., Columbia, S.C., 1978-92, Scott Law Firm, P.A., Columbia, S.C., 1993—; pres. Heritage Title, Columbia, 1980—. Bd. of visitors, pres.'s adv. council Med. U. S.C.; past state pres. Nat. Soc. to Prevent Blindness, past state sec.; state fundraising chmn. Arthritis Found. Served to capt. (adj. gen. corps.) USAR, 1970-76. Named Outstanding Young Man of Columbia Jaycees, 1982; recipient State Dist. Svc. award U.S. Jaycees, 1982, Leadership S.C. award Office of the Gov., 1986; recipient Fellowship Regional Finalist award White House, 1984. Mem. ABA (past state rep., significant legis. com., real property com.), S.C. Bar Assn. (sec. subcom. model corp. act panel), Columbia C. of C. (com. of 100, Leadership Columbia award 1981), Summit Club, Palmetto Club (Columbia), DeBordieu Club (Georgetown, S.C.), Capital City Club. Administrative and regulatory, Health, Real property. Office: Scott & Scott Law Firm PA 1331 Laurel St # 2065 Columbia SC 29201-2513

**SCOTT, SARAH ALICE,** lawyer; b. Ames, Iowa, July 17, 1950; d. Duane Clarence and Elizabeth Ann (Clark) S.; m. Bruce Everett Cory, Jan. 18, 1976 (div. 1990); 1 child, Olivia A. BA cum laude, U. Kans., 1972; JD, U. Houston, 1978. Sole practice Houston, 1979-82; staff atty. D.C. 37 Mcpl. Employees Legal Svcs., N.Y.C., 1982-86; asst. corp. counsel law dept. City of N.Y., 1986-89, gen. counsel office of chief med. examiner, 1989—. Mem. Assn. Bar of City of N.Y. (sec. 1994-95, chair 1995-98). Office: Office of Chief Med Examiner 520 1st Ave New York NY 10016-6499

**SCOTT, THEODORE R.,** lawyer; b. Mount Vernon, Ill., Dec. 7, 1924; s. Theodore R. and Beulah (Flannigan) S.; children: Anne Laurence, Sarah Buckland, Daniel, Barbara Gomon. AB, U. Ill., 1947, JD, 1949. Bar: Ill. 1950. Law clk. to judge U.S. Ct. Appeals, 1949-51; pvt. practice Chgo., 1950—; assoc. Spaulding Glass, 1951-53, Loftus, Lucas & Hammand, 1953-58, Ooms, McDougall, Williams & Hersh, 1958-60; ptnr. McDougall, Hersh & Scott, Chgo., 1960-87; of counsel Jones, Day, Reavis & Pogue, 1987-97, Rockey, Milnamow & Katz, 1998—. 2nd lt. USAAF, 1943-45. Decorated Air medal. Fellow Am. Coll. Trial Lawyers; mem. ABA, Ill. Bar Assn., Chgo. Bar Assn., 7th Cir. Bar Assn. (past pres.), Legal Club Chgo., Law Club Chgo., Patent Law Assn. Chgo. (past pres.), Union League Club, Exmoor Country Club (Highland Park, Ill.), Phi Beta Kappa. Federal civil litigation, Patent, Trademark and copyright. Home: 1569 Woodvale Ave Deerfield IL 60015-2350

**SCOTT, THOMAS EMERSON, JR.,** prosecutor; b. Pittsburg, Penn., Apr. 27, 1948; s. Thomas Emerson Sr. and Marie (Ebel) S.; m. Ginger Claud, Mar. 1978 (div. Aug. 1980); m. Joyce Newman, Aug. 6, 1983. BA in Econs. cum laude, U. Miami, 1969, JD cum laude, 1972; LLM, U. Va., 1989. Bar: Fla. 1972, U.S. Dist. Ct. (so. dist.) Fla. 1972, U.S. Ct. Appeals (5th and 11th cirs.) 1972. Law clk. to cir. judge 11th jud. cir. ct., State of Fla., Dade County, 1970-71; assoc. Bradford, Williams, McKay, Kimbrell, Hamann & Jennings, P.A., Miami, Fla., 1972-76, mem. firm, 1977-79; assoc. Huebner, Shaw & Burrell, Ft. Lauderdale, Fla., 1976-77; cir. judge 11th jud. cir. State of Fla., Miami, 1979-84; ptnr. Kimbrell, Hamann, Jennings, Womack, Carlson & Kniskern P.A., Miami, 1984-85, Steel Hector & Davis, Miami, Fla., 1990—; judge U.S. Dist. Ct. (so. dist.) Fla., Miami, 1985-90; U.S. atty. U.S. Dist. Ct., Fla., 1997—; chmn. security com. U.S. Dist. Ct., so. dist. Fla.; instr. litigation skills U. Miami, Coral Gables, 1984-86; instr. Nita program U. Fla.; instr. trial advocacy program Nova U.; instr. profl. responsibility and product liability St. Thomas U. Contbr. articles to profl. jours. Served to 1st lt. USAR, 1969—. Mem. ABA (co-chmn. com. on discovery litigation sect.), Fla. Bar Assn. (chmn. standing com. on professionalism, past chmn. CLE trial advocacy program), Dade County Bar Assn. (Outstanding Jurist award Young Lawyers' sect.), U.S. Dist. Judges' Assn., Product Liability Adv. Coun. Found. Republican. Roman Catholic. Avocations: running, collectibles. Office: US Atty So Dist Fla 99 NE 4th St Miami FL 33132-2131*

**SCOTT-WARREN, DANESSIA MARIE,** lawyer; b. Buffalo, N.Y., June 2, 1968; d. Daniel and Mary Lou Scott; m. Christopher Morris Warren, June 26, 1993. BA, Canisius Coll., 1990; JD, U. Toledo, 1993. Bar: N.Y. Dir. legal dept. People Inc., Williamsville, N.Y., 1994—; trustee Mt. St. Joseph Acad., Buffalo, 1997—. Mem. ABA, N.Y. State Bar Assn., Erie County Bar Assn. Republican. Roman Catholic. Home: 170 Presidio Pl Williamsville NY 14221-3756

**SCOULAR, ROBERT FRANK,** lawyer; b. Del Norte, Colo., July 9, 1942; s. Duane William and Marie Josephine (Moloney) S.; m. Donna V. Scoular, June 3, 1967; children—Bryan T., Sean D., Bradley R. B.S. in Aero. Engring., St. Louis U., 1964, J.D., 1968. Bar: Mo. 1968, Colo. 1968, N.D. 1968, U.S. Supreme Ct. 1972, Calif. 1979. Law clk. to chief judge U.S. Ct. Appeals (8th cir.), 1968-69; ptnr. Bryan, Cave, McPheeters & McRoberts, St. Louis, 1969-89; mng. ptnr. Bryan, Cave, McPheeters & McRoberts, Los Angeles, 1979-84, exec. com., 1984-85, sect. leader tech., computer and intellectual property law, 1985-89; ptnr. Sonnenschein, Nath, Rosenthal, Chgo., 1990—; mng. ptnr. Sonnenschein, Nath, Rosenthal, L.A., 1990—, mem. policy and planning com., 1995—; co-leader intellectual property practice, 1990-98; dir. Mo. Lawyers Credit Union, 1978-79. Contbr. articles to profl. jours. Bd. dirs. St. Louis Bar Found., 1975-76, 79; bd. dirs. L.A. Area Coun. Boy Scouts Am.; league commr. Am. Youth Soccer Orgn.; mem. alumni coun. St. Louis U., 1979-82; hon. dean Dubourg Soc. Recipient Nat. Disting. Eagle Scout award. Mem. ABA (nat. dir. young lawyers div. 1977-78), Am. Judicature Soc., Bar Assn. Met. St. Louis (v.p. 1978-79, sec. 1979, chmn. young lawyers sect. 1975-76), Los Angeles County Bar Assn., Assn. Bus. Trial Lawyers, Calif. Bar. Assn., Mo. Bar (chmn. young lawyers sect. 1976-77, disting. svc. award), Computer Law Assn., Fed. Bar Assn., Dubourg Soc. (hon. dean). General civil litigation, Government contracts and claims, Intellectual property. Home: 1505 Lower Paseo La Cresta Palos Verdes Peninsula CA 90274 Office: Sonnenschein Nath & Rosenthal 601 S Figueroa St Ste 1500 Los Angeles CA 90017-5720

**SCOVILLE, LAURENCE MCCONWAY, JR.,** arbitrator, mediator; b. Brunswick, Ga., Sept. 24, 1936; s. Laurence McConway and Mary (Williams) S.; m. Lynn Bayne Johnston, Aug. 20, 1960; children: Evelyn Mary, Laurence M. III, Robert J. AB, Dartmouth Coll., 1958; LLB, U. Mich., 1961. Bar: Mich. 1961, U.S. Dist. Ct. (ea. and we. dists.) Mich. 1961, U.S. Ct. Appeals (6th cir.) 1972, U.S. Supreme Ct. 1986. Assoc. Clark, Klein & Beaumont, Detroit, 1961-68, ptnr., 1968-95, mem. exec. com., 1976-95, chmn., 1990-95; mem. Clark Hill PLC, Detroit, 1996-98, of counsel, 1998; bd. dirs. The Detroit Legal News, 1989—; chmn. rules com. U.S. Dist. Ct. (ea. dist.) Mich., Detroit, 1988-92. Author: Construction Litigation: Representing the Contractor, 1986, 91. Bd. dirs., exec. com. Detroit Econ. Growth Corp., 1990-98; bd. dirs. Stratford Festival Am., 1997—; bd. govs. Stratford Shakespearean Festival, 1996—; founder, chmn. Mich. Friends of the Stratford Festival, 1998—. Mem. Nat. Assn. Sec. Dealers (mediator, arbitrator), State Bar Mich., Dartmouth Lawyers Assn., CPR Inst. Dispute Resolution (panel of disting. neutrals), Am. Arbitration Assn. (mediator, nat. panel arbitrators, large complex case program), Am. Soc. Employers (bd. dirs. 1993-98), Dartmouth Lawyers Assn., Dartmouth Rowing Club (bd. stewards 1988—), Met. Affairs Coalition (bd. dirs. 1992-98, vice chmn. 1995-98 ), Econ. Club Detroit (sec. 1988-95, bd. dirs. 1994-99), Detroit Club (bd. dirs. 1989-94, pres. 1993-94), Country Club Detroit, Dataw Island Club. Avocations: family, hunting and fishing, theatre, golf, platform tennis. Email: larlyn@hay.net (summer), larlyn@isk.net (winter). Address (summer): RR2 Beach O'Pines Box 30, Grand Bend, ON Canada N0M 1TO Office: 24 Reeve Ct Saint Helena Island SC 29920-3018

**SCOWCROFT, JEROME CHILWELL,** lawyer; b. Pocatello, Idaho, May 17, 1947; s. Harold and Alberta Mary (Chilwell) S.; m. Corinne Gail Cox, Mar. 12, 1983; children: Jason Trevor, Brian Jonathan. BA, Stanford U., 1969; M in Research Psychology, U. Calif., San Diego, 1973; JD, Duke U., 1978. Bar: N.Y. 1980, Wash. 1986. Assoc. Haight, Gardner, Poor & Havens, N.Y.C., 1978-81, Schwabe, Williamson & Wyatt, Seattle, 1985—; editor, legal advisor Lamorte, Burns & Co., N.Y.C. and Greenwich, Conn., 1981-85; lectr. in admiralty law U. Wash., 1988-89, adj. prof., 1988—. Bd. advisors Maritime Adv. Svcs., Arbitration Award Digest, 1981—; contbg. editor U.S. Maritime Arbitration, Internat. Congress Comml. Arbitration, 1983—; case editor Jour. of Maritime Law and Commerce, 1987—; contbr. articles to profl. jours. With U.S. Army, 1970-72. Fellow HEW, 1975-76. Mem. ABA, Maritime Law Assn. U.S. (vice chmn. carriage of goods com. 1991—), Seattle World Trade Club, Propeller Club. Republican. Episcopalian. Avocations: math., photography, tennis, hiking. Admiralty, Contracts commercial, Private international. Home: 2524 Sahalee Dr E Redmond WA 98053-6357

**SCOWN, MICHAEL JOHN,** lawyer; b. Glen Ellyn, Ill., Apr. 19, 1959; s. William Floyd and June Althea (Goodrich) S.; m. Catherine Maria Sevilla, Oct. 10, 1992. AB in Polit. Sci., U. Calif., Berkeley, 1981; JD, U. San Francisco, 1985. Bar: Calif. 1985, U.S. Dist. Ct. (no. dist.) Calif. 1985, U.S. Ct. Appeals (9th cir.) 1985. Fgn. svc. officer U.S. Dept. State, 1985-88; assoc. Russin & Vecchi, San Francisco, 1988-92, ptnr., 1993-98; sr. atty. corp. bus. devel. Intel, Hong Kong, 1999—. Contbr. articles to profl. jours.; editor: U. San Francisco Law Rev., 1984-85. Chmn. bd. govs. Am. C. of C., Ho Chi Minh City, Vietnam, 1995-96, bd. govs., 1994-98. Mem. ABA, Olympic Club. Private international, General corporate, Finance. Office: Intel Semiconductor Ltd, 32/F 2 Pac Pl 88 Queensway, Hong Kong China

**SCREMIN, ANTHONY JAMES,** lawyer; b. Miami, Fla., June 20, 1941; s. Anthony Scremin and Rose Marie (Zullo) S.; m. Barbara Jean Thompson, Oct. 22, 1960 (div. July 1977); children: Julie Beth, Sylvia Ann, Ann Marie; m. Iliana Margarita Rodriguez, Mar. 17, 1979. BBA, U. Miami, 1966, JD, 1968. Bar: Fla. 1968, U.S. Dist. Ct. (so. dist.) Fla. 1969, U.S. Ct. Appeals (3d cir.) 1985, U.S. Ct. Appeals (9th cir.) 1986, U.S. Ct. Appeals (11th cir.) 1987. Assoc. Hawkesworth & Kay, Miami, 1968-69; assoc., trial asst. Steven, Demos, et al, Miami, 1969-70, Welch & Carroll, Miami, 1969-70; head trial atty. Metro Transit Authority, Miami, 1970-71; ptnr., trial atty. Abramson, Scremin et al, Miami, 1971-78; prin., head trial atty. Anthony J. Scremin P.A., Miami, 1978—. Served with USCG, 1959-60. Recipient Cert. of Merit, Bar and Gavel Legal Soc., U. Miami, 1968, Outstanding Service award Labor Law Soc., U. Miami, 1968. Mem. Am. Arbitration Assn., Acad. Trial Lawyers Am., N.Y. State Trial Lawyers Assn., Fla. Bar Assn., Assn. Fla. Trial Lawyers, Nat. Assn. Criminal Def. Lawyers, Nat. Italian-Am. Bar Assn., Phi Delta Phi. Democrat. Roman Catholic. Avocations: karate, weight-lifting, construction. Criminal, State civil litigation, Personal injury. Home: 12651 SW 20th Ter Miami FL 33175-1407 Office: 37 NE 26th St Miami FL 33137-4405

**SCRENOCK, PAUL STEVEN,** lawyer; b. Summerville, N.J., Mar. 29, 1952; s. Joseph John and Elsie (Neuman) S.; m. Malyn Niebling, June 21, 1975; children: David Paul, Rebecca Malyn, Ryan Paul. BA, U. Wis., 1974; JD, John Marshall Sch. Law, 1977. Bar: Wis. 1977, Ill. 1978, U.S. Dist. Ct. (we. dist.) Ill. 1978. Assoc. Screnock Law Office, Baraboo, Wis., 1977-79; pvt. practice Friendship and Westfield, Wis., 1979—, Adams, Wis., 1979—. Incorporator Damon A. Renner Scholarship Fund Inc., 1987; chartered sec. Adams County United Way Inc., 1988—; sec., bd. dirs. adv. bd. Villa Pines, Friendship, 1982—. Mem. ABA, Wis. Bar Assn., Tri-County Bar Assn., Adams County Jaycees (chartered pres. 1979). General practice, Probate, Real property. Office: 333 N Main St Adams WI 53910-9658

**SCRIGGINS, LARRY PALMER,** lawyer; b. Englewood, N.J., Nov. 27, 1936; s. Thomas Dalby and M. Patricia (Fowler) S.; m. Victoria Jackola, Feb. 17, 1979; children: Elizabeth J., Thomas P. AB, Middlebury Coll., 1958; JD, U. Chgo., 1961. Bar: Md. 1962. Law clk. to chief judge Md. Ct. Appeals, 1962; assoc. Piper & Marbury, L.L.P., Balt., 1962-69, ptnr., 1969-98, sr. counsel, 1999—, vice chmn., 1988-93, mem. exec. com., CFO, 1993-98; mem. legal adv. com. N.Y. Stock Exch., 1992-96; bd. dirs. USF & G Corp., 1979-98, Center Stage Assocs., 1979-89, Balt. Choral Arts Soc., 1979-96, Balt. Conv. Bur., 1982-95, YMCA of Greater Balt., 1987-94, Fund for Ednl. Excellence, 1990-98, chmn. bd. trustees, 1993-98; bd. dirs. Nat. Aquarium in Balt., bd. govs. 1987-93; bd. dirs. Balt. Symphony Orchestra, 1996—. Contbr. articles to profl. jours. Fellow Am. Bar Found.; mem. AICPA (planning com. 1989-92), Md. Bar Assn. (coun. 1976-78, chmn. 1977-78, chmn. com. on corp. laws 1981-84), ABA (sect. on bus. law coun. 1972-76, chair 1991-92, vice chair and editor-in-chief The Bus. Lawyer 1989-90, chmn. law and acctg. com. 1985-88, chmn. common corp. laws 1996—, chmn. ad hoc com. on ethics 2000 1999—), Internat. Bar Assn., Am. Judicature Soc., Am. Law Inst., Task Force on Fin. Instruments, Fin. Acctg. Stds. Bd. General corporate, Securities, Finance. Home: 13663 E Columbine Dr Scottsdale AZ 85259-3752 Office: Piper & Marbury LLP 36 S Charles St Baltimore MD 21201-3020

**SCRIVEN, JOHN G.,** lawyer, chemical company executive. Bar: Mich. 1993. Sr. staff counsel Dow Europe S.A., 1981-83; gen. counsel Dow Chem. Co., Midland, Mich., 1983-86, v.p., gen. counsel, 1986—, now v.p., gen. counsel, sec. Office: Dow Chem Co 2030 Dow Ctr Midland MI 48674-0001*

**SCRIVEN, WAYNE MARCUS,** lawyer; b. Sumter, S.C., Aug. 31, 1953; s. Philip Roosevelt and Sarah Ella (Pringle) S. BA in History Edn. cum laude, Va. Union U., 1975; JD, Golden Gate U. Sch. of Law, 1979. Bar: Va. 1980, U.S. Dist. Ct. (ea. dist.) Va. 1980, U.S. Ct. Appeals (4th cir.) 1980, S.C. 1982, U.S. Dist. Ct. S.C. 1982, U.S. Supreme Ct. 1984, Calif. 1987, U.S. Dist. Ct. (no. dist.) Calif. 1986, U.S. Ct. Appeals (9th cir.) 1986, D.C. 1993, U.S. Dist. Ct. D.C. 1994, U.S. Dist. Ct. Md. 1994, U.S. Ct. Appeals (fed. cir.) 1994, D.C. Directing atty. Petersburg (Va.) Legal Aid Soc., 1980-81; staff atty. Carolina Regional Legal Svcs. Corp., Florence, S.C., 1981-82; solo practice atty. Florence, S.C., 1982-85, Richmond, Va., 1985-86, San Francisco, 1986-93, Washington, 1993—; contract atty. Neighborhood Legal Asst. Program, Marion, S.C., 1982-83, pro bonocontract atty., 1983-85, Carolina Regional Legal Svcs. Corp., Florence, 1983-85, Bar Assn. of San Francisco, 1987-93; notary public, S.C., 1981-91, Va., 1986-91. Bd. dirs. Young Men's Christian Assn., Florence, 1982-83, Pee Dee Crisis Ctr., Florence, 1983-84, San Francisco Neighborhood Legal Asst. Program, 1992-93. Named one of Outstanding Young Men of Am., U.S. Jaycees, 1982; recipient Outstanding Lawyer in Pub. Svc., Bar Assn. San Francisco, 1988-91. Mem. ABA, Washington Bar Assn., Assn. Trial Lawyers of Am., U.S. Supreme Ct. Hist. Soc. Baptist. Avocations: fishing, guitar playing, nature trail walking. E-mail: Wayne-Marcus-Scriven@abanet.org. General practice, Labor, Personal injury. Office: Scriven & Assocs 1225 Eye St NW Ste 500 Washington DC 20005-3914

**SCRIVNER, THOMAS WILLIAM,** lawyer; b. Madison, Wis., Sept. 10, 1948; s. William H. and Jane (Gehrz) S.; m. Meredith Burke, Aug. 16, 1980; children: Allison, David. AB, Duke U., 1970, MAT, 1972; JD, U. Wis., 1977. Assoc. Michael, Best & Friedrich LLP, Milw., 1978-85, ptnr., 1985—. Mem. ABA, Wis. Bar Assn., Milw. Bar Assn. (labor sect.), Corp. Practice Inst. (pres. 1989-92). Episcopalian. Labor, Administrative and regulatory. Home: 4626 N Cramer St Milwaukee WI 53211-1203 Office: Michael Best & Friedrich LLP 100 E Wisconsin Ave Ste 3300 Milwaukee WI 53202-4108

**SCROGGS, LARRY KENNETH,** lawyer, state legislator; b. Beebe, Ark., Oct. 8, 1941; s. Kenneth Chalmers and Mildred Lorene (McDonald) S.; m. Mary Patricia Rushing, Aug. 25, 1967; children: Larry Kenneth Jr., James Kevin, Michael Kyle. BA, Harding U., 1963; JD, Vanderbilt U., 1971. Bar: Tenn. 1971, U.S. Dist. Ct. (we. dist.) Tenn. 1971, U.S. Ct. Appeals (8th cir.) 1982, U.S. Ct. Appeals (6th cir.) 1989, U.S. Supreme Ct. 1981. Assoc. Law Firm of Leo Bearman, Memphis, Tenn., 1971-72; assoc. Holt, Batchelor, Spicer, Memphis, 1972-76, ptnr., 1976-80; ptnr. Less & Scroggs, Memphis, 1980-92; pvt. practice, Germantown, Tenn., 1992-96; ptnr. Scroggs & Rogers, Collierville, Tenn., 1997—; mem. Tenn. Ho. of Reps., Nashville, 1997—; mcpl. ct. judge City of Germantown, 1980-86; atty. for County Trustee, Shelby County, Memphis, 1990—. Mem. campaign steering com. George Bush for Pres., Memphis, 1987-92; vol. Ed Bryant for Congress campaign, Memphis, 1994, Don Sundquist for Gov. campaign, Memphis, 1994. Lt. U.S. Navy, 1964-67, Vietnam. Mem. ABA, Tenn. Bar Assn., Memphis Bar Assn. (bd. dirs. 1990-91). Republican. Mem. Ch. of Christ. Avocations: photography, boating, tennis. Federal civil litigation, State civil litigation, Construction. Office: Scroggs & Rogers 110 E Mulberry St Ste 200 Collierville TN 38017-2675

**SCULLIN, FREDERICK JAMES, JR.,** federal judge; b. Syracuse, N.Y., Nov. 5, 1939; s. Frederick James and Cleora M. (Fellows) S.; m. Veronica Terek Sauro, Aug. 31, 1984; children: Mary Margaret, Kathleen Susan, Kellie Anne, Rebecca Rose; 1 stepchild, Angel Jenette Sauro. B.S. in Econs., Niagara U., 1961; LL.B., Syracuse U., 1964. Bar: N.Y. 1964, Fla. 1976, U.S. Dist. Ct. (no. dist.) N.Y. 1967, U.S. Supreme Ct. 1971. Assoc. Germain & Germain, Syracuse, 1967-68; asst. dist. atty. Onondaga County, Syracuse, 1968-71; asst. atty. gen. N.Y. State Organized Crime Task Force, 1971-78; dir. regional office N.Y. State Organized Crime Task Force, Albany, 1974-78; chief prosecutor, dir. Gov.'s Council on Organized Crime State of Fla., Tallahassee, 1978—; sole practice Syracuse, 1979-82, U.S. atty. for No. Dist. N.Y., 1982-92; judge U.S. Dist. Ct. (no. dist.) N.Y., 1992—. With U.S. Army, 1964-67, Vietnam; col. USAR. Decorated Air medal, Bronze Star; Cross of Gallantry (Vietnam). Mem. Am. Judicature Soc., Fla. Bar Assn., Fed. Bar Assn., Fed. Bar Coun., Onon City Bar Assn. Office: US Dist Ct US Courthouse 100 S Clinton St Syracuse NY 13261-6100

**SCULLION, KEVIN PETER,** lawyer; b. Chgo., June 9, 1952; s. Peter and Annette (Murphy) S. Student, Purdue U., 1970-72; B.A., Northwestern U., 1974; postgrad. Tulane U. Sch. Law, Grenoble, France, 1976; J.D., DePaul U., 1977, LLM in Taxation, 1986; M.B.A., U. Chgo., 1979; student, U. Edinburgh, Scotland, 1979. Bar: Ill. 1977, U.S. Dist. Ct. (no. dist.) Ill. 1977, Ind., 1978, Fla. 1978, U.S. Dist. Ct. (so. dist.) Ind. 1978, D.C. 1980, U.S. Dist. Ct. (ea. dist.) Mich., 1991, U.S. Dist. Ct. Ariz. 1992. C.P.A., Ill. In-house counsel Fin. Fed. Savs. & Loan Assn., Olympia Fields, Ill., 1977-79; assoc. firm Quinn, Jacobs & Barry, Chgo., 1979-83; tax mgr. Price Waterhouse, Chgo., 1983-86, sr. v.p. Graver, Reich & Co., Inc., Northfield, Ill., 1986-91; ltd. ptnr. Graver, Bokhof & Goodwin, Chgo., 1991—; bd. dirs. Oberg Internat., Inc., Arlington, Wash. Mem. ABA, Chgo. Bar Assn., Ill. State Bar Assn., Ind. State Bar Assn., Am. Inst. C.P.A.s, Ill. CPA Soc., Internat. Assn. Fin. Planners. Roman Catholic. Avocations: running, reading, travel. Probate, Corporate taxation, Personal income taxation. Home: 386 Muskegon Ave Calumet City IL 60409-2347

**SCULLY, ERIK VINCENT,** lawyer, accountant; b. Pitts., Mar. 24, 1957; s. Vincent C.A. and Gloria Dolores (Peterson) S.; m. Margaret Mary Scully, Sept. 10, 1982; children: Erik John, Ryan Frederick, Meghan Marie. BA, Syracuse U., 1979; JD, St. Louis U., 1982; postgrad., Duquesne U., Pitts., 1986. Bar: Pa. 1982, U.S. Tax Ct. 1983; CPA, Pa. Asst. bank officer Mark Twain Bankshares, Inc., St. Louis, 1980; law clk. Thomas, Mottaz & Eastman, Alton, Ill., 1981-82; with Mercer, Mercer, Carlin and Scully, Pitts., 1982-91; ptnr. Scully & Scully, Pitts., 1992-94, Scully & Scully, L.L.P., Pitts., 1995—. Mem. Pitts. Ctr. for the Arts, Soc. Sculptors of Pitts. Mem. Pa. Bar Assn., Allegheny County Bar Assn. (taxation sect.), Pa. Inst. CPAs (speakers bur. tax sect., com. on govt. rels.). Taxation, general, Probate, General civil litigation. Home: 10550 Grubbs Rd Wexford PA 15090-9424 Office: Scully & Scully LLP 2220 Koppers Bldg Pittsburgh PA 15219

**SCULLY, ROGER TEHAN,** lawyer; b. Washington, Jan. 10, 1948; s. James Henry and Marietta (Maguire) S.; m. Martha Anne Seebach, Dec. 29, 1979. BS, U. Md., 1977; JD, Cath. U., 1980. Bar: Md. 1980, D.C. 1981, U.S. Tax Ct. 1982, U.S. Supreme Ct. 1988. V.p. Bogley Related Cos., Rockville, Md., 1971-75; law clk. to presiding justice Superior Ct. of D.C., Washington, 1979-81; assoc. Lerch, Early & Roseman, Bethesda, Md., 1981-82; gen. counsel Laszlo N. Tauber, M.D. & Assocs., Bethesda, 1982-94, Jefferson Meml. Hosp., Alexandria, Va., 1982-94; spl. counsel Venable,

Baetjer, Howard & Civiletti, Washington, 1991-96; cons. in real estate Order of Friar Minor, N.Y.C., 1977—; lectr. Mortgage Bankers Assn., Washington, 1984—; bd. dirs. Nozzoli Constrn. Co., Washington; exec. com., spl. counsel to bd. dirs., bd. dirs. Chromachron Technology Corp., Toronto; bd. dirs. MusicWorks, N.Y.C.; vice chair Sayett Tech., Inc., Rochester, N.Y.; vice chair, bd. dirs., exec. com. MediaShow, Inc., Rochester. Author: (with Quarles & Howard) Summary Adjudication Dispositive Motions and Summary Trials, 1991. Mem. pres.'s coun. St. Bonaventure U., Olean, N.Y., 1995—, chmn. pres.'s coun., 1986-95; trustee Belmont Abbey Coll., Charlotte, N.C., 1993-95, Edmund Burke Sch., Washington, 1984—; bd. dirs. Nat. Children's Choir, Washington, 1980-94. Recipient First Order Affiliation Order of Friars Minor, 1985; named one of Outstanding Young Men in Am., 1982. Fellow D.C. Bar Assn.; mem. ABA, ATLA, FBA, Md. Bar Assn. (chmn. corp. counsel sect.), Am. Judicature Soc., Assn. Governing Bd. of Univs. and Colls., Am. Inns of Ct., Irish Legal Soc., Selden Soc., U.S. Jud. Conf. of 4th Cir. (permanent mem.), U.S. Jud. Conf. Fed. Cir. (del.), Jud. Conf. of D.C. (del.). Republican. Roman Catholic. Real property, Contracts commercial, Private international. Home: 10923 Wickshire Way North Bethesda MD 20852 Office: 5110 Ridgefield Rd Ste 108350 Bethesda MD 20816-3346

**SCULLY, THOMAS FRANCIS,** lawyer; b. Orange, N.J., Jan. 10, 1952. BA in English, Fairfield U., 1974; JD, U. Bridgeport, 1980. Bar: N.J., U.S. Dist. Ct., Supreme Ct. of N.J.; cert. criminal trial atty. Staff atty. N.J. Office Adminstrv. Law, Trenton, 1981-83; asst. coun. N.J. Sch. Bds. Assn., Trenton, 1983-84; assoc. Law Firm of Kenney & McManus, Red Bank, N.J., 1984-85; dep. pub. defender N.J. Office of Pub. Defender, Trenton, 1985—; co-chmn. Monmouth County Bar Assn., 1991-92, mem. criminal practice com. 1992-93. Co-Author: (book) Basic School Law, 2d edit. 1983. Roman Catholic. Home: 57 Dogwood Ln Fair Haven NJ 07704-3605 Office: Office of Pub Defender RH Justice Complex 25 Market St # N850 Trenton NJ 08611-2148

**SCURO, JOSEPH E., JR.,** lawyer; b. Jersey City, Mar. 28, 1948; s. Joseph E. and Phyllis (Amato) S.; m. Virginia Ruth Shaw. BA with honors, Manhattan Coll., 1970; JD, Ohio State U., 1972. Bar: Tex., Ohio, U.S. Dist. Cts., U.S. Ct. Appeals (5th and 10th cir.), U.S. Tax Ct., U.S. Mil. Appeals, U.S. Supreme Ct. Asst. atty. gen. Ohio, 1973-81; chief legal counsel Ohio State Hwy. Patrol, 1975-81; practice law, 1973—; of counsel Nicholas & Barrera, San Antonio and Dallas, 1982-90; counsel to San Antonio, Dallas and Grapevine Police Officers Assns, Combined Law Enforcement Assn. Tex., Alamo Heights Police Officers Assn., Tex. Mcpl. League; former legal adviser, spl. counsel to cities of San Marcos, New Braunfels, Balcones Heights, La Vernia, Poteet, Laredo, Odessa, Dilley, Hondo, Highland Park, Kyle, Universal City, Del Rio, Greenville, Galveston, Arlington, Austin and others; former spl. counsel on tng. San Antonio Police Dept.; former counsel to Bexar County Constable's Assn.; condr. seminars. Contbr. articles on police and law enforcement to profl. jours. Bd. dirs. Nat. Hispanic Arts Endowment. Served to capt. USAF, 1970-75. Fellow Southwestern Legal Found. (sec. 1986-91); mem. ABA, Tex. Bar Assn., Ohio Bar Assn., San Antonio Bar Assn., Columbus (Ohio) Bar Assn., Am. Trial Lawyers Assn., Police Exec. Research Forum, Internat. Assn. Chiefs of Police (legal officer sect.), Ams. for Effective Law Enforcement (bd. advs.), Southwestern Law Enforcement Inst. (bd. advs.), Internat. Soc. Law Enforcement and Criminal Justice Instrs., Fed. Criminal Investigators Assn. (hon.), Ohio Assn. Polygraph Examiners (hon.). Republican. Presbyterian. Criminal, Federal civil litigation, State civil litigation. Office: Main Place Station PO Box 50966 Dallas TX 75250-0966

**SCZUDLO, WALTER JOSEPH,** lawyer; b. Fairbanks, Alaska, May 28, 1953; s. Walter and Dolores J. Sczudlo; children: Lauren Hall, Elizabeth Fairbanks, Walter Christopher; m. Rebecca Grey Tucker, Mar. 8, 1996. AB, Middlebury Coll., 1975; JD, Golden Gate U., 1979; LLM, Georgetown U., 1987; postgrad., U. Calif., Santa Barbara, 1972, Tule U., 1971-72, Vt. Law Sch., 1976-77. Bar: Alaska 1979, Calif. 1980, D.C. 1986, U.S. Ct. Appeals (9th cir.) 1980, U.S. Ct. Appeals (D.C. cir.) 1986, U.S. Dist. Cts. (no., cen., ea. and so. dists.) Calif., U.S. Dist. Ct. Alaska, U.S. Ct. Claims, U.S. Tax Ct. Law clk. to presiding justice Alaska Supreme Ct., 1978-79; assoc. atty. Merdes, Schaible, Staley and Delisio, Anchorage, 1979-82; legis. dir., gen. counsel U.S. Senator Murkowski, Washington, 1982-84; sr. tax assoc. Schramm and Raddue, Santa Barbara, Calif., 1984-85; dir. congl. rels., counsel Natural Gas Supply Assn., Washington, 1985-88; Washington counsel Shell Oil Co., 1988-96; v.p., Washington counsel Intercontinental Energy Corp., 1996-99; gen. counsel, vice pres. pub. affairs and comms. Nat. Soc. Fund Raising Execs., Washington, 1999—; prin. ptnr. WEBK Broadcasting 105.3 FM, Killington, Vt., 1985—; dir. Sun's Edge, Inc., Santa Barbara, 1987—, Natural Gas Roundtable, Washington, 1987—. Author: (with other) Washington Legal Foundation, 1988. Com. chmn. Steve Cowper for Gov., Anchorage, 1982. Recipient Am. Jurisprudence award Bancroft-Whitney Pub. Co., 1978. Roman Catholic. Avocations: mountaineering, cross-country skiing, tennis. FERC practice, Legislative, Corporate taxation. Home: 6700 Loring Ct Bethesda MD 20817-3148 Office: NSFRE 1101 King St Ste 700 Alexandria VA 22314-2944

**SEABOLT, RICHARD L.,** lawyer; b. Chgo., Aug. 28, 1949. *Wife, Kathleen Hallissy, also graduated with a Juris Doctor from Hastings College of Law, University of California, in 1975, and was a deputy district attorney from 1975 to 1993. Sons Jack Seabolt and Will Seabolt are students at Wildwood Elementary School, Piedmont, California. Father, Lee Seabolt, before retirement was President and Chairman of Selz Seabolt Associates, a Chicago based public relations firm.* BGS with distinction, U. Mich., 1971; JD, U. Calif., Hastings, 1975. Bar: Calif. 1975. With Hancock, Rothert & Bunshoft, San Francisco, 1975—, ptnr., 1981—; pres. Def. Seminar Assocs., 1992—. *Hancock, Robert & Bunshoft has offices in San Francisco, Los Angles, Tahoe City, and London, England and focuses its practice on complex business and insurance litigation. Lead defense lawyer, representing certain Underwriters' at Lloyd's of London in an environmental insurance coverage trial between Aerojet-General Corporation and 54 insurers. After a ten month trial, the jury rendered a verdict for the defendants. The defense verdict in that case was featured in 1992 articles in California Law Business and the National Law Journal as among the largest cases tried to a defense verdict in California and in the United States for that year. In 1997 California Supreme Court Affirmed that verdict.* Frequent speaker and author profl. journs., pres. Defense Seminar Assoc., 1992, AAA Large Complex Case Panel-Construction (Arbitration). Mem. ABA, Am. Arbitration Assn.(large complex case panel, construction), State Bar Calif., Bar Assn. San Francisco. Fax: 415-955-2599. Appellate, General civil litigation, Contracts commercial. Office: Hancock Rothert & Bunshoft 4 Embarcadero Ctr San Francisco CA 94111-4106

**SEACREST, GARY LEE,** lawyer; b. Chambersburg, Pa., July 27, 1946; s. John Alton and Virginia (Robinson) S.; m. Constance Marie Zullinger, Feb. 21, 1970; children—Ryan John, Meredith Marie. B.S., Pa. State U., 1968; J.D. with distinction, Emory U., 1975. Bar: U.S. Dist. Ct. (no. dist.) Ga. 1975, U.S. Ct. Appeals (5th cir) 1978, U.S. Cir. Ct. Appeals (11th cir.) 1982, U.S. Dist. Ct. (mid. dist.) Ga. 1982, U.S. Dist. Ct. (so. dist.) Ga. 1983. Atty. IRS, Atlanta, 1975; assoc. Barwick, Bentley & Binford, Atlanta, 1976-78; ptnr. Barwick, Bentley, Karesh & Seacrest, and Bentley, Karesh, Seacrest, Labovitz & Campbell, Atlanta, 1978—; cons. ins. industry, Atlanta, 1980—; dir. several corps. Mem. German-Am. Relations Com., Berlin, 1971; bd. dirs. Glenridge Civic Assn., Atlanta, 1978; bd. dirs. Branches Civic Assn., Atlanta, 1980-81, pres., 1982. Served with U.S. Army, 1969-72. Mem. ABA, Ga. Bar Assn., Atlanta Bar Assn., Ga. Defense Lawyers Assn., Defense Research Inst., Kappa Delta Rho. Republican. Clubs: Lawyers of Atlanta, Cherokee Town and Country. Insurance, Federal civil litigation, State civil litigation. Home: 7390 Wildercliff Dr NW Atlanta GA 30328-1143

**SEAGLE, J. HAROLD,** lawyer; b. Marion, N.C., May 9, 1947; s. Rufus James and Alma Rhoda (McMahan) S.; m. Linda Jean Cranford, June 3, 1967; 1 child, James Mark. BA, U. N.C., 1973, JD, 1977. Bar: N.C. 1977; U.S. Dist. Ct. (ea., middle, we. dists.) N.C. 1977, 88, 92; U.S. Ct Appeals (4th cir.) 1982; U.S. Supreme Ct. 1982. Assoc. atty. Rountree & Newton, Wilmington, N.C., 1977-79; ptnr. Rountree & Seagle, L.L.P., Wilmington, N.C., 1979—; past pres. Fifth Jud. Dist. Bar. Speaker in field. Bd. trustees and bd. deacons Winter Park Baptist Ch.; past moderator Wilmington Baptist Assn.; bd. dirs. Rescue Mission of Cape Fear; past adv. Bd. Coastal Bioethics Network; past chmn. annual fund drive Am. Cancer Soc.; past sect. chmn. Cape Fear United Way, past co-chmn. grievance com. Mem. New Hanover County Bar Assn. (co-chair grievance com.), N.C. Bar Assn., N.C. State Bar, N.C. Acad. Trial Lawyers, N.C. Coll. of Advocacy, Southeastern Admiralty Law Inst. (officer), Maritime Law Assn. of U.S. (proctor), N.C. Bar Coun. of Pres., Wilmington Inns of Ct. (exec. com., master). Avocations: acoustic guitar, motorcycle racing. Admiralty, Federal civil litigation, Personal injury. Office: Rountree & Seagle LLP 2419 Market St Wilmington NC 28403-1135

**SEAMAN, CHARLES WILSON,** lawyer; b. Natchitoches, La., Mar. 8, 1946; s. George Benson and Edna Marie (Barrilleaux) S.; m. Twylla Corrine Eversull, Sept. 12, 1968; 1 child, James Scott. BS, Northwestern State U., 1969; JD, U. Miss., 1972. Bar: Miss. 1973, La. 1973, U.S. Dist. Ct. (we. dist.) La. 1981. Assoc. Long & Peters, Jena, La., 1973; pvt. practice Natchitoches, La., 1974, 1976—; ptnr. Kelly, Seaman & Ware, Natchitoches, 1975; atty. Vill. of Clarence, La.; bd. dirs. Kisatchie Legal Services, Natchitoches, 1983. Mem. Rep. Nat. Com. Named Senator, Law Sch. Student Body, U. Miss., 1972, sec., 1973; bd. dirs. Moot Ct. Bd., U. Miss., 1973. Mem. ABA, Miss. Bar Assn., La. Bar Assn., Assn. Trial Lawyers Am., Natchitoches Parish Bar Assn., Elks, BPOE. Roman Catholic. General civil litigation, Family and matrimonial, Personal injury. Office: 854 Washington St Natchitoches LA 71457-4728

**SEAMAN, PEGGY JEAN,** lawyer; b. New Orleans, Nov. 21, 1949; d. William David and Leah Catherine (Bourdet) Smith; m. Terry Noako Seaman, Dec. 22, 1970 (div.); children: Vanya Lianne, Ember Catherine. BA, Rutgers U., Camden, 1974; JD, N.Y. Law Sch., 1978. Bar: N.Y. 1978, Va. 1980, U.S. Dist. Ct. Va. 1980, U.S. Dist. Ct. (so. and ea. dists.) N.Y. 1978. Pvt. practice N.Y.C., 1978-79; gen. atty. Merit Systems Protection Bd., Office of Appeals, Washington, 1980-82; presiding ofcl., Washington regional office Merit Systems Protection Bd., Office of Appeals, Falls Church, Va., 1982-85; adminstrv. judge St. Louis regional office Merit Systems Protection Bd., Office of Appeals, 1985-87; atty. Office of Dep. Exec. dir. for Regional Ops., Washington, 1987-89; gen. atty. Office of Appeals Counsel, Washington, 1989-95; adminstrv. judge Denver Field Office Office of Appeals Counsel, 1995-99; adminstrv. judge Western Regional Office Office of Appeals Counsel, San Francisco, 1999—. Recipient Sustained Superior Performance awards Merit Systems Protection Bd., Spl. Act award, 1988, Chmn.'s honor award, 1991. Mem. ABA, Athenaeum Honor Soc., Mensa. Democrat. Home: 4305 Clement St San Francisco CA 94121-1441 Office: Western Regional Office 205 Montgomery St San Francisco CA 94104-2901

**SEAMAN, ROBERT E., III,** lawyer; b. Chgo., Apr. 2, 1947; s. Robert E. II and Rae June (Blair) S.; children: Kimberly Desiree, Charissa Alaine, Robert E. IV, Jason Robert. BA in Polit. Sci., The Citadel, 1969; JD, U. Va., 1972; postdoctoral, N.Y. Inst. Fin., 1975-77, Harvard U., 1979. Bar: N.Y. 1975, S.C. 1978, U.S. Dist. Ct. (so. dist.) N.Y. 1975, U.S. Tax Ct. 1980, U.S. Ct. Appeals (2nd cir.) 1975, U.S. Ct. Appeals (4th cir.) 1979, U.S. Supreme Ct. 1979, U.S. Ct. Mil. Appeals 1980. Assoc. Breed, Abbott & Morgan, N.Y.C., 1972-74; v.p.-legal, asst. sec. Paine, Webber, Jackson & Curtis Inc. and subs., N.Y.C., 1974-77, asst. to chmn. bd. PaineWebber Inc., 1974-77; assoc. gen. counsel Col. Life and Accident Ins. Co., Columbia, S.C., 1977-80; sole practice, 1980—; gen. counsel Jacom Computer Services, Inc., Northvale, N.J., 1977—; chmn. The dorchester Group, 1987—; bd. dirs., gen. counsel Internat. Chem. Cons., Ltd., 1983-88; pres. Titan Trading Co., Inc., Columbia, 1984-86, Comptel Data Sys., 1984—; chief exec. officer, pub. Up2Date Market Adv. Service, Columbia, 1985-87; chmn. bd., CEO Race Mktg. Assocs. Inc.; lectr. various ednl. instns. Co-author: How to Use the Relative Strength Index to Increase Trading Profits, 1986, Legal Issues in the Leasing Process, 1991; editor in chief: The Reading Guide and Virginia Law School Outline Series, 1971-72; sr. editor Va. Law Weekly, 1970-72; contbr. articles to profl. jours. Student senator S.C. Legislature, 1968-69; mem. coll. presdl. adv. com., state dir. Collegiate Counsel of UN, 1968-69; trustee Faith United Meth. Ch.; coord. phon-a-thon campaign Midlands S.C. youth div. YMCA, 1980-82; class chmn. Citadel Devel. Found., 1980; chpt. chmn., campaign adv. com. chmn., vice chmn. exec. com. Midlands chpt. March of Dimes, 1978-81; mem. task force Greater Columbia C. of C.; vice chmn. bd. KIDS North Jersey, 1990-94; founder, chmn. The Millennium Found., 1992—. Served capt. M.I., inf. U.S. Army, 1972 -77, Res., 1977-83. Robert R. McCormick scholar McCormick Found., and Chgo. Tribune, 1965-69, DuPont scholar U. Va., 1969-72; winner Estate Planning contest 1st Nat. Bank Chgo., 1971; recipient Leadership award Citadel Devel. Found., 1979-80, named Young Man of Yr., S.C. Greater Met. Area Jaycees, 1980; recipient Recognition award Nat. March of Dimes, 1981; named Knight Comdr., Grand Cross, Min. Fin. and Advocar Gen., Order St. John Knights of Malta. Mem. Assn. of Bar of City of N.Y., ABA (state regulation of securities com., subcom. on oil and gas, subcom. on regulation of equipment leasing, securities industry assn. compliance divsn. 1974-77), Am. Assn. Equipment Lessors, Info. Tech. Resellers Assn., NYSE, AMEX, Nat. Assn. Securities Dealers (registered rep.), Commodities Futures Trading Commn. (registered prin.), N.Y. Bar Assn., S.C. Bar Assn., Citadel Brigadier Club (bd. dirs.), Ill. Citadel Club (pres.), Knights of Malta (Knighted and designated Knight Comdr., Grand Cross, Minister of Fin. and Avocar Gen. Order of St. John), Pi Sigma Alpha; Clubs: Yale Club N.Y.C., Rockland Country Club, Com. of 100 Club, Met. Bus. Club, Palmetto Soc., Toastmasters (pres. Lexington chpt., ann. impromptu speech contest champion, Toastmaster of Yr. 1979). Contracts commercial, Securities, Finance. Office: 560 Route 303 Orangeburg NY 10962

**SEAMON, RICHARD HENRY,** law educator; b. Balt., Aug. 18, 1959; s. Henry William Jr. and Grace Marguerite (Reinemer) S.; m. Kathleen Linda Morotti, Aug. 22, 1982 (div. May 1989); m. Holly Vaughan Dawkins, May 25, 1996. BA, Johns Hopkins U., 1980, MA, 1981; JD, Duke U., 1986. Bar: Md. 1986, D.C. 1988, U.S. Ct. Appeals (D.C. cir.) 1987, U.S. Ct. of Appeals (4th cir.) 1990, U.S. Supreme Ct. 1991. Law clk. to Hon. Kenneth W. Starr U.S. Ct. Appeals (D.C. cir.), Washington, 1986-87; assoc. Covington & Burling, Washington, 1987-90; asst. to solicitor gen. U.S. Dept. Justice, Washington, 1990-96; asst. prof. law U. S.C., Columbia, 1996—. Mem. ABA, Order of Coif, Phi Beta Kappa. Office: U of SC Law Sch Main & Greene Sts Columbia SC 29208-0001

**SEAMONS, QUINTON FRANK,** lawyer; b. Idaho Falls, Idaho, Mar. 5, 1945; s. Eldon Monroe and Lois (Merrill) S.; m. Michele Geyer Seamons. BA cum laude with honors, Brigham Young U., 1968; JD, U. Utah, 1971. Bar: Utah 1971, D.C. 1976, Ill. 1977, U.S. Supreme Ct. 1975, U.S. Ct. Appeals (7th cir.) 1979, U.S. Dist. Ct. (no. dist.) Ill. 1978. Legis. asst. to Senator Wallace F. Bennett of Utah U.S. Senate, Washington, 1969-71; law clk. Utah Atty. Gen., Salt Lake City, 1970-71; staff atty. divsn. mkt. regulation, legal counsel SEC, Washington, 1971-76; ptnr. Wilson & McIlvaine, Chgo., 1976—; arbitrator NASD Proceedings; adj. prof. Chgo. Kent Coll. Law, 1996—. Asst. editor: The Summation: A Journal of Utah Law; Contbr. articles to profl. jours. Trustee Riverwoods Homeowners Assn., Ill., 1992, Ill. Cancer Coun., 1980-84; bd. dirs. Vol. Legal Svcs., Chgo., 1993; coach Northfield Park Dist., 1978-84. Hinckley scholar, U. Utah, 1969; recipient Outstanding Young Men of Am. award, 1970, Am. Jurisprudence award Bancroft-Whitney Co. and U. Utah, 1971. Mem. ATLA, ABA (bus. law sect., litigation sect.), Chgo. Bar Assn. (securities law com., corps. com., class actions com.), Blue Key, Phi Kappa Phi, Phi Alpha Delta, Phi Sigma Alpha. Avocations: sports memorabilia, reading and research of Civil War, Renaissance & Medieval history, book collecting, basketball, health club. General civil litigation, General corporate, Securities. Office: 3200 N Central Ave Ste 1000 Phoenix AZ 85012-2430

**SEAR, MOREY LEONARD,** federal judge, educator; b. New Orleans, Feb. 26, 1929; s. William and Yetty (Streiffer) S.; m. Lee Edrehi, May 26, 1951; children: William Sear II, Jane Lee. JD, Tulane U., 1950, LLD, 1999. Bar: La. 1950. Asst. dist. atty. Parish Orleans, 1952-55; individual practice law Stahl & Sear, New Orleans, 1955-71; spl. counsel New Orleans Aviation Bd., 1956-60; magistrate U.S. Dist. Ct. (ea. dist.) La., 1971-76, judge, 1976—, chief judge, 1992-99; judge Temp. Emergency Ct. of Appeals, 1982-87; adj. prof. Tulane U. Coll. Law; former chmn. com. on adminstrn. of bankruptcy sys., former chmn. adv. com. on bankruptcy rules, former mem. com. on adminstrn. of fed. magistrate sys. Jud. Conf. U.S.; former mem. Jud. Conf. of U.S. and Its Exec. Com.; former mem. cir. coun. 5th Cir. of U.S.; founding dir. River Oaks Pvt. Psychiat. Hosp., 1968. Pres. Congregation Temple Sinai, 1977-79; bd. govs. Tulane Med. Ctr., 1977—; former chmn. Tulane Med. Ctr. Hosp. and Clinic, 1980-85. Decorated grad. ofcl. Vasco Nunez de Balboa (Panama). Mem. ABA, La. Bar Assn., New Orleans Bar Assn., Order of Barristers, Order of the Coif (hon.). Office: US Dist Ct C-256 US Courthouse 500 Camp St New Orleans LA 70130-3313

**SEARLE, PETER J.,** lawyer; b. Summit, N.J., Nov. 6, 1959; s. Richard L. and Joan M. S.; m. Melissa A., Aug. 13, 1992; children: Keenan, Kevin, Kathryn. BA, Calif. State U., Fullerton, 1982; JD, Southwestern U. Sch. Law, 1986. Atty. Chase, Rotchford, Drukker & Bogust, L.A., 1986-96; v.p., claims mgr. CNA Comml. Ins., Brea, Calif., 1997—. Mem. ABA, Am. Def. Inst., Calif. Constrn. Defect Claims Mgrs. Assn. (chair 1997—). Office: CNA Ins 1800 E Imperial Hwy Ste 200 Brea CA 92821-6065

**SEARS, DOUGLAS WARREN,** lawyer; b. Newton, Mass., June 11, 1947; s. Douglas Hubbard and Anne (Thomas) S.; m. A. Suzanne Tuggle, Oct. 3, 1976; children: Rebecca Anne, Douglas Warren Jr. BA, Harvard Coll., 1969, MDiv, 1976; MEd, Boston State Coll., 1980; JD, Suffolk U., 1986. Bar: Mass. 1987, U.S. Dist. Ct. Mass., 1987, U.S. Ct. Appeals (1st cir.) 1987, U.S. Supreme Ct. 1996. Secondary sch. tchr. various schs., 1969-87; assoc. Peckham, Lobel, Casey, Prince & Tye, Boston, 1987-89, Allen Rodman, P.C., Malden, Mass., 1989-91; dep. dir. divsn. dispute resolution Dept. Indsl. Accidents, Boston, 1991—. Vis. min. Christ's Ch. Longwood, Brookline, Mass., 1986—; chmn. Rep. Town Com., Tewksbury, 1992—; mem. Tewksbury Hist. Commn., 1992—; sec. bd. trustees Tewksbury (Mass.) Hosp., 1993—; mem. Tewksbury Sch. Com., 1995—; mem. Govs. Adv. Com. on Chaplains in State Instns., Boston, 1996—; assoc. mem. Rep. State Com., Boston, 1996—. Mem. Tewksbury/Wilmington Elks (justice 1995—). Unitarian-Universalist. Avocation: gardening. Office: Dept Indsl Accidents 600 Washington St Boston MA 02111-1704

**SEARS, JOHN WINTHROP,** lawyer; b. Boston, Dec. 18, 1930; s. Richard Dudley and Frederica Fulton (Leser) S.; m. Catherine Coolidge, 1965 (div. 1970). AB magna cum laude, Harvard U., 1952, JD, 1959; MLitt, Oxford U., 1957. Bar: Mass. 1959, U.S. Dist. Ct. Mass. 1982. Rep. Brown Bros. Harriman, N.Y.C., 1959-63, Boston, 1963-66; mem. Mass. Ho. Reps., 1965-68; sheriff Suffolk County, Mass., 1968-69; chmn. Boston Fin. Commn., 1969-70, Met. Dist. Commn., 1970-75; councilor-at-large Boston City Coun., 1980-82; trustee Sears Office, Boston, 1975—. Contbr. articles to profl. jours. Apptd. bd. dirs. Fulbright Scholarship, 1991-93; trustee Christ's Ch., Longwood, Brookline, Mass., 1965—, Sears Trusts, Boston, 1975—; hon. trustee J. F. Kennedy Libr., 1991—; bd. dirs. Am. Mus. Textile Heritage, 1987-97, Shirley-Eustis Assoc., Environ. League, Mass., 1994-97; Rep. candidate Sec. State, Mass., 1978, Gov. of Mass., 1982; vice chmn. Ward 5 Rep. Com., 1965-69, 75-85; chmn. Rep. State Com., 1975-76, mem., 1980-85; del. Rep. Nat. Conv., 1968, 76, State Conv., 1966-92; mem. U.S. Electoral Coll., 1984; bd. dirs. United South End Settlements, 1966—, chmn., 1977-78. Lt. comdr. USNR, 1952-54, 61-62. Recipient Outstanding Pub. Servant award Mass. Legis. Assn., 1975; Rhodes scholar, 1955. Mem. Mass. Bar Assn., New Eng. Hist. and Geneal. Soc. (bd. dirs., councillor 1977-82), Mass. Hist. Soc., Handel and Haydn Soc. (gov. 1982-87), Signet Soc., Boston Atheneum, Tennis and Racquet Club, Somerset Club, The Country Club (Brookline), St. Botolph Club, Wednesday Evening Club of 1777, Thursday Evening Club of 1846 (pres. 1999), Spee Club (Cambridge chpt., pres., trustee), Phi Beta Kappa. Republican. Legislative, Probate. Home: 7 Acorn St Boston MA 02108-3501 *As the working years come to an end, some of us look for ways to teach, to help neighbors, especially those in need, to build up the beauty and excellence we may have encountered in our own lives, and do our best to pass them on to others.*

**SEARS, LEAH J.,** state supreme court justice; b. June 13, 1955; d. Thomas E. and Onnye J. Sears; married; children: Addison, Brennan. BA, Cornell U.; JD, Emory U.; M in Apellate Jud. Process, U. Va.; JD (hon.), Morehouse Coll., 1993. Judge City Ct. Atlanta; atty. Alston & Bird, Atlanta; trial judge Superior Ct. Fulton County; justice Supreme Ct. Ga., Atlanta, 1992—. Contbr. articles to profl. jours. Bd. dirs. Sadie G. Mays Nursing Home, Ga. chpt. Nat. Coun. Christians & Jews; mem. adv. bd. United Way Drug Abuse Action Ctr., Outdoor Activity Nature Ctr.; mem. Cornell U. Women's Coun.; mem. steering com. Ga. Women's History Month, Children's Def. Fund Black Cmty. Crusade Children; founder Battered Women's Project, Columbus, Ga. Recipient Outstanding Young Alumna award Emory U., One of 100 Most Influential Georgians Ga. Trend mag., Excellence in Pub. Svc. award Ga. Coalition Black Women, 1992, Outstanding Woman of Achievement YWCA Greater Atlanta, One of Under Forty & On the Fast Track, 1993. Mem. ABA (chair bd. elections), Nat. Assn. Women Judges, Ga. Bar Assn., Women's Forum Ga., Gate City Bar Assn., Atlanta Bar Assn. (past chair jud. sect.), Ga. Assn. Black Women Attys. (founder, pres.), Fourth Tuesday Group, Jack & Jill Am. (Atlanta chpt.), Links Inc. (Atlanta chpt.), Alpha Kappa Alpha. Office: Ga Supreme Ct 504 State Judicial Bldg Atlanta GA 30334-9007*

**SEARS, ROSS ALLEN, II,** lawyer; b. Bellaire, Tex., Oct. 29, 1964; s. Ross Allen and Gretchen Dorothy (Grabau) S.; m. Vickie Lynn Frank, Nov. 16, 1991; children: MacKenzie Alexis, Madison Avery Sears. BS in Psychology, U. Houston, 1988, JD, 1991. Bar: Tex., U.S. Dist. Ct. (so. dist.) Tex. Assoc. Hays, McConn, Rice & Pickering, Houston, 1991-94; ptnr. Williamson & Sears, LLP, Houston, 1994—. Mem. Big Bros. & Sisters, Houston, 1994; mem. steering com. Local Jud. Candidates, Houston, 1996—. Mem. ATLA, Tex. Bar Assn., Houston Bar Assn. (bench book com. 1995—), Houston Young Lawyers Assn. Methodist. Avocations: hunting, fishing, golfing, skiing, coin collecting. Personal injury, Labor, Professional liability. Office: Williamson & Sears LLP 300 Fannin St Ste 300 Houston TX 77002-2044

**SEARS, RUTH ANN,** lawyer; b. Kansas City, Mo., June 15, 1954; d. Robert Carl and Bessie Bryan (Nicholas) Henderson; m. Irwin Curtis Sears Jr., Aug. 6, 1977. BA, Cen. Meth. Coll., 1976; JD, U. Mo., 1979. Bar: Mo. 1980, Kans. 1980, Tex. 1998, U.S. Dist. Ct. Kans. 1980. Clk. to judge Mo. Supreme Ct., Jefferson City, 1979-80; atty. Southwestern Bell Telephone Co., Topeka, Kans., 1980-91; sr. atty. Southwestern Bell Telephone Co., St. Louis, 1991-97; gen. atty. Southwestern Bell Telephone Co., Dallas, 1998—. Mem. Mo. Bar Assn., Kans. Bar Assn. General corporate, Contracts commercial, Communications. Office: Southwestern Bell Telephone Co Rm 2900 One Bell Plz Dallas TX 75202

**SEARS, TERRY H.,** lawyer, educator; b. Corpus Christi, Tex., July 26, 1966; s. Ross Allen Sears and Gretchen Dorothy Grabau; m. Cherry Harmon, Aug. 18, 1984; children: Samantha, Trey. BS in Psychology cum laude, U. Houston, 1986-89, JD, 1993. Bar: Tex. 1993, U.S. Dist. Ct. (so. dist.) Tex. 1995. Assoc. Butler & Hailey, P.C., Houston, 1993—; adj. lectr. U. Houston Law Ctr., 1993—. Mem. ABA, Houston Bar Assn., Fort Bend Bar Assn. General civil litigation, State and local taxation, Real property. Office: Butler & Hailey PC 5718 Westheimer Rd Ste 1600 Houston TX 77057-5782

**SEAVE, PAUL L.,** prosecutor. AB in History, Princeton U., 1975; JD cum laude, U. Pa., 1979. Jud. clk. to Chief Justice Samuel J. Roberts Pa. Supreme Ct., 1979-80; litig. assoc. Ballard, Spahr, Andrews & Ingersoll, Phila., 1980-83; asst. U.S. atty., chief criminal complaints unit U.S. Attys. Office, L.A., 1983-87; assoc. Gibson, Dunn & Crutcher, Washington, 1988-89; chief Orange County br. U.S. Attys. Office, Santa Ana, Calif., 1989-93; first asst U.S. atty. U.S. Attys. Office, Sacramento, 1993-97; U.S. atty. U.S. Attys. Office Ea. Dist., Sacramento, 1997—; instr. Littleton Legal Writing; mem. FBA, 1991-93; adj. prof. Northwestern U. Sch. Law, L.A., 1986, Loyola Law Sch., L.A., 1992, McGeorge Sch. Law, Sacramento, 1996; spkr. in field. Editor: U. Pa. Law Rev.; contbr. articles to profl. jours. Vice chair, bd. dirs. Sacramento Jewish Cmty. Rels. Coun., 1994—. McConnell scholar Princeton U. Mem. ABA (co-chair white collar crime ethics subcom. 1992-93, bd. dirs. white collar crime subcom. 1992-95), Ea. Dist. Jud. Conf. (planning com. 1995, 96), Inns of Ct. Office: Office US Atty 501 I St Ste 10-100 Sacramento CA 95814-7300*

**SEAVER, ROBERT LESLIE,** retired law educator; b. Brockton, Mass., June 13, 1937; s. Russell Bradford and Lois (Marchant) S.; m. Marjorie V. Rote, Aug. 21, 1960 (div. 1974); children: Kimberly, Eric, Kristen; m.

Elizabeth A. Horwitz, May 22, 1984. AB cum laude, Tufts U., Medford, Mass., 1958; JD, U. Chgo., 1964. Bar: Ohio 1964, U.S. Ct. Appeals (6th cir.) 1964, U.S. Dist. Ct. (so. dist.) Ohio 1965. Assoc. Taft, Stettinius and Hollister, Cin., 1964-66; v.p., sec., gen. counsel IDI Mgmt. Inc., Cin., 1966-74; pvt. practice Cin., 1974-75; prof. law emeritus No. Ky. U. Salmon P. Chase Coll. Law, Highland Heights, 1975—; of counsel Cors & Bassett, Cin., 1993—; ret., 1999; cons. in field, 1975—. Author/editor: Ohio Corporation Law, 1988; contbr. chpts. to books. Advisor subcom. on pvt. corps of Ky. Commn. on Constl. Rev., 1987. With USMC, 1958-61. Recipient Justice Robert O. Lukowsky award of Excellence Chase Law Sch. Student Bar Assn., 1986. Mem. Ohio Bar Assn., Cin. Bar Assn., No. Ky. Bar Assn. Republican. Unitarian. Avocations: duplicate bridge, history. Home: 826 Woodscene Ct Cincinnati OH 45230-4334 Office: Northern Kentucky U Salmon Chase Coll Law Highland Heights KY 41099

**SEAWELL, DONALD RAY,** lawyer, publisher, arts center executive, producer; b. Jonesboro, N.C., Aug. 1, 1912; s. A.A.F. and Bertha (Smith) S.; m. Eugenia Rawls, Apr. 5, 1941; children: Brook Ashley, Donald Brockman. A.B., U. N.C., 1933, J.D., 1936, D.Litt., 1980; L.H.D., U. No. Colo., 1978. Bar: N.C. 1936, N.Y. 1947. With SEC, 1939-41, 45-47, Dept. Justice, 1942-43; chmn. bd., dir., pub., pres. Denver Post, 1966-81; chmn. bd., dir. Gravure West, L.A., 1966-81; dir. Swan Prodns., London; of counsel firm Bernstein, Seawell, Kove & Maltin, N.Y.C., 1979—; chmn. bd., chief exec. officer Denver Ctr. for Performing Arts, 1972—; ptnr. Bonfils-Seawell Enterprises, N.Y.C.; bd. vis. U. N.C. Chmn. bd. ANTA, 1965—; mem. theatre panel Nat. Coun. Arts, 1970-74; bd. govs. Royal Shakespeare Theatre, Eng.; trustee Am. Acad. Dramatic Arts, 1967—, Hofstra U., 1968-69, Cen. City Opera Assn., Denver Symphony; bd. dirs., chmn. exec. com. Air Force Acad. Found., Nat. Ints. Outdoor Drama, Walter Hampden Meml. Library, Hammond Mus.; pres. emeritus Helen G. Bonfils Found., 1997—, chmn. fin. com., 1997—, Denver Opera Found., 1997—; dir. Found. for Denver Ctr. for Performing Arts, Population Crisis Com., pres. 1982-91; bd. dirs. Family Health Internat., Found. for Internat. Family Health; bd. visitors N.C. Sch. Arts, 1992—. With U.S. Army, WW II. Recipient Am. Acad. Achievement award, 1980, Tony award for producing On Your Toes, 1983, Voice Research and Awareness award Voice Found., 1983. Mem. Bucks Club (London), Dutch Treat Club (N.Y.C.), Denver Country Club, Denver Club, Cherry Hills Country Club, Mile High Club (Denver), Garden of Gods Club (Colorado Springs, Colo.). Office: Denver Ctr for Performing Arts 1050 13th St Denver CO 80204-2157

**SEAWORTH, MARY ELLEN,** lawyer; b. Bismarck, N.D., Oct. 28, 1947; d. George H. and Margaret M. (Fortune) S.; m. Henry H. Howe, Dec. 4, 1976; children: Oren, Deborah, Tavia, Christopher. Student, Coll. St. Teresa, 1965-68; BA in Speech and Theatre, U. N.D., 1971, BS in Edn., 1973, JD, 1983. Bar: Minn. 1983, N.D. 1984, U.S. Dist. Ct. N.D. 1984. Ptnr. Howe and Seaworth, Grand Forks, N.D., 1983—; Instr. (part time) legal assistance program Northland Community Coll., Thief River Falls, Minn., 1988, 89. Editorial staff N.D. Law Review, 1982-83. Trustee Grand Forks Symphony, 1984-94; bd. dirs. Greater Grand Forks Community Theatre, 1983—, LWV, 1991—; mem. com. Gov.'s Commn. Children Adolescents at Risk, 1985-86; commr. for Commn. Uniform State Laws, 1985-95; Dem. com. person. Recipient Women Who Care award U. N.D. Women's Ctr., 1986; named one of Outstanding Young Women Am., 1984.. Mem. N.D. Bar Assn. (chmn. family law sect. 1988, 96, Minn. Bar Assn., Trial Lawyers Nat. & State, ABA (family law sect.), Am. Acad. Matrimonial Lawyers. Family and matrimonial, Personal injury, Criminal. Office: Howe and Seaworth Law Offices 421 Demers Ave Grand Forks ND 58201-4507

**SEAY, FRANK HOWELL,** federal judge; b. Shawnee, Okla., Sept. 5, 1938; s. Frank and Wilma Lynn Seay; m. Janet Gayle Seay, June 2, 1962; children: Trudy Alice, Laura Lynn. Student, So. Meth. U., 1956-57; B.A., U. Okla., 1960, LL.B., 1963. Bar: Okla. 1963. Atty. Seminole County, 1963-66; asst. dist. atty., 1967-68, assoc. dist. judge, 1968-74; judge Okla. Dist. Ct. 22, 1974-79; judge ea. dist. U.S. Dist. Ct., Okla., 1979—, chief judge; now dist. judge U.S. Dist. Ct. (ea. dist.) Okla. Mem. ABA, Okla. Bar Assn., Seminole County Bar Assn. Democrat. Clubs: Masons, Elks, Lions. Office: US Dist Ct PO Box 828 Muskogee OK 74402-0828

**SEBELIUS, KEITH GARY,** lawyer; b. Norton, Kans., Nov. 8, 1949; s. Keith George and Elizabeth Adeline (Roberts) S.; m. Kathleen Gilligan, Dec. 31, 1974; children: Edward Keith, John McCall. BA magna cum laude, Kans. State U., 1971; JD, Georgetown U., 1974. Bar: Kans. 1974, U.S. Dist. Ct. Kans. 1974, U.S. Ct. Appeals (10th cir.) 1977, U.S. Supreme Ct. 1977. Assoc. Eidson, Lewis, Porter & Haynes, Topeka, Kans., 1974-79, ptnr., 1979-89; ptnr. Davis, Wright, Unrein, Hummer & McCallister, Topeka, 1989-93; mng. ptnr. Wright, Henson, Somers, Sebelius, Clark & Baker, LLP, Topeka, 1993—; participant jud. conf. U.S. Ct. Appeals (10th cir.), 1987—. Contbr. chpt. to: Civil Rights Primer, 1982, Section 1983 Litigation, 1987. Pres., bd. dirs. Kans. Legal Svcs., Topeka, 1986-90, Sunflower State Games, Lawrence, Kans., 1992—; bd. dirs. Friends of the Zoo Topeka, 1993—, Everywoman's Resource Ctr., Topeka, 1997—. Mem. ABA, Kans. Bar Assn. (pres. employment law sect. 1989-90), Kans. Trial Lawyers Assn. (mem. bd. govs. 1986—). Avocations: scuba diving, tennis. Labor, Civil rights, Federal civil litigation. Home: 224 SW Greenwood Ave Topeka KS 66606-1228 Office: Wright Henson Somers Sebelius et al 100 SE 9th St Fl 2 Topeka KS 66612-1213

**SEBOK, ANTHONY JAMES,** lawyer, educator; b. Phila., Jan. 9, 1963; s. George and Marianne Sebok. BA, Cornell U., 1984; MPhil, U. Oxford, Eng., 1986; JD, Yale U., 1991; PhD, Princeton U., 1993. Bar: N.Y. 1991. Law clk. to Judge E. Cahn U.S. Dist. Ct., Phila., 1991-92; asst. prof. Bklyn. Law Sch., 1992-95, assoc. prof., 1995-97, prof., 1997—; vis. assoc. prof. Benjamin Cardozo Sch. Law, N.Y.C., 1997. Author: Legal Positivism in American Jurisprudence, 1998; co-editor: Philosophy of Law, Vols. 1-5, 1994. Bd. dirs. Latsky/Goldhuber Dance Co., N.Y.C., 1998—. Berlin Prize fellow Am. Acad. in Berlin, 1999. Mem. Am. Assn. for Polit. and Legal Philosophy. Office: Brooklyn Law Sch 250 Joralemon St Brooklyn NY 11201-3798

**SEBRIS, ROBERT, JR.,** lawyer; b. N.Y.C., May 20, 1950; s. Robert and Ruth (Kagis) S.; m. S. Lawson Hollweg, Sept. 8, 1973; children: Jared Matthew, Bryan Taylor. BS in Indsl. Labor Rels., Cornell U., 1972; JD, George Washington U., 1978. Bar: D.C. 1978, Wash. 1980. Labor rels. specialist Onondaga County Office labor rels., Syracuse, N.Y., 1973-74, U.S. Dept. Labor, Washington, 1972-75; labor rels. mgr. U.S. Treasury Dept., Washington, 1975-78; employee rels. mgr. Washington, 1978-80; assoc. Davis, Wright, Todd, Riese & Jones, Seattle, 1980-84; ptnr. Davis, Wright, Tremain, Bellevue, Wash., 1985-92; Sebris Busto, P.S., Bellvue, Wash., 1992—; expert witness T.E.A.M. Act Amendments NLRA U.S. Senate hearing, 1997. Co-Author: Employer's Guide to Strike Planning, 1985; contbr. articles to profl. jours. Mem. Bellevue C.C. Found., 1988-95, pres., 1995-96; chair employment law cert. program U. Wash. Law Sch., 1996-97. Mem. ABA (health law forum, labor and employment law sect., com. on employee rights), Wash. Bar Assn., D.C. Bar Assn., Seattle/King County Bar Assn. (chmn. labor law sect. 1991-92), Pacific Coast Labor Law Conf. (planning com. 1980-93, chmn. 1991-92), Am. Acad. Healthcare Attys., Soc. Human Resource Mgmt. Avocations: golf, soccer, coaching youth sports. Labor, Alternative dispute resolution. Home: 16301 Mink Rd NE Woodinville WA 98072-9463 Office: Sebris Busto PS 1500 Plz Ctr 10900 NE 8th St Bellevue WA 98004-4405

**SECOLA, CARL A., JR.,** lawyer; b. New Haven, Dec. 2, 1960; s. Carl A. and Marie R. Secola; m. Linda J. Diolosa, Sept. 10, 1988; children: Carl A. III, Caroline Fay. BA, Fairfield U., 1982; JD, Quinnipiac Coll. (formerly U. Bridgeport), 1985. Bar: Conn. 1985, U.S. Dist. Ct. Conn. 1986. Atty. Lynch, Traub, Keefe & Errante, P.C., New Haven, 1986-91; ptnr. Kinney & Secola, LLC, New Haven, 1991—; asst. town atty. Town of Hamden, Conn., 1991-97; lectr. in field; contbg. author seminars and pubs. Mem., chair planning sect. Planning and Zoning Com., Hamden, 1989-90; mem. Dem. Town Com., Hamden, 1988-98; local coord. for U.S. Sen. Christopher Dodd's 1992 Re-election campaign, Hamden, 1992. Recipient U. Bridgeport Sch. of Law Theodore I Koskoff Mock trial Team Disting. Alumni award, 1989. Mem. ATLA, Conn. Trial Lawyers Assn. (legis. com. 1990-91), Conn. Bar Assn., New Haven County Bar Assn. Roman Catholic. Avocations: photography, fishing, skiing, boating, coaching little league. Personal injury, State civil litigation, Federal civil litigation. Home: 3 Deer Hill Rd Hamden CT 06518-1018 Office: Kinney & Secola LLC 685 State St New Haven CT 06511-6509

**SECOLA, JOSEPH PAUL,** lawyer; b. Hartford, Conn., May 18, 1959; s. Pasquale Anthony and Anna Maria; m. Mary Alice Ipavich, June 20, 1982; children: Peter, Sharon, Mary Joy, Timothy, Paul, Andrew. BA in History, Fairfield U., 1981; JD, Oral Robert U., 1984. Bar: Conn. 1984, N.Y. 1985, U.S. Dist. Ct. Conn. 1985, Va. 1986, U.S. Dist. Ct. (so. dist.) N.Y. 1988, U.S. Ct. Appeals (2d cir.) 1989, U.S. Supreme Ct. 1990, U.S. Dist. Ct. (we. dist.) N.Y. 1996. Pvt. practice Brookfield, Conn., 1984—. Mem. bd. edn. City of Milford, Conn., 1989-90, Greater Danbury (Conn.) Cath. Elem. Schs., 1992-96. Mem. Nat. Employment Lawyers Assn., Am. Trial Lawyers Assn., Conn. Trial Lawyers Assn., Conn. Bar Assn., Conn. Employment Lawyers Assn., Litchfield County Bar Assn., Greater Danbury Bar Assn. Republican. Roman Catholic. Avocation: sports. E-mail: seco-la.law@snet.net. Fax: (203) 740-2355. Personal injury, General civil litigation, Appellate. Office: Ste 500 67 Federal Rd Bldg A Brookfield CT 06804-2538

**SECREST, JAMES SEATON, SR.,** lawyer; b. Middletown, Ky., Dec. 9, 1930; s. Elmer S. and Linney (Witherbee)S.; m. Mary Sue Corum, Sept. 2, 1950; children: James Seaton, Lynne Suzanne. J.D., U. Louisville, 1954. Bar: Ky. 1954. Ptnr. Goad & Secrest, Scottsville, Ky., 1955-62; solo practice Scottsville, Ky., 1962-77; ptnr. Secrest & Secrest, Scottsville, 1977—. City judge pro tem Scottsville, 1955-58; judge Allea County, 1958-61; city atty. Scottsville, 1962-66; atty. Allen County, 1966-89, dep. judge-exec., 1990-99; bd. dirs. Barren River Area Devel. Dist., 1970, mem. regional bd. ethics; mem. adv. bd. dirs. Starbank, Scottsville, 1998; bd. dirs. Commonwealth Health Corp. Mem. Scottsville C. of C. (pres. 1962), Ky. County Attorneys Assn. (pres. 1973), Ky. Assn. Counties (bd. dirs. 1985-86), ABA, Ky. Bar Assn. Republican. Methodist. Club: Rotary (pres. 1960). General practice, Probate, Real property. Home: 10055 New Glasgow Rd Scottsville KY 42164-9534 Office: Secrest & Secrest PO Box 35 210 W Main St Scottsville KY 42164-1123

**SECREST, RONALD DEAN,** lawyer; b. Kansas City, Mo., Nov. 13, 1951; s. William Francis and Corrine Elizabeth (Clarke) S. BS, Stanford U., 1974; JD, U. Va., 1977. Bar: Tex. 1979, U.S. Dist. Ct. (so. dist.) Tex. 1979, U.S. Ct. Appeals (5th cir.) 1980, U.S. Ct. Appeals (11th cir.) 1981, U.S. Dist. Ct. (no. dist.) Tex. 1986, U.S. Dist. Ct. (we. dist.) Tex. 1989, U.S. Ct. Appeals (10th cir.) 1989, U.S. Supreme Ct. 1990. Law clk. to presiding justice U.S. Ct. Appeals (5th cir.), Houston, 1977-78; ptnr. Fulbright & Jaworski, Houston, 1978-92, Beck, Redden & Secrest, Houston, 1992—. Fellow Tex. Bar Found., Houston Bar Found.; mem. ABA, Internat. Assn. Def. Counsel, Tex. Assn. Def. Counsel, Tex. Bar Assn., Houston Bar Assn. Federal civil litigation, State civil litigation, Environmental. Home: 430 Thamer Ln Houston TX 77024-6946 Office: Beck Redden & Secrest 1221 Mckinney St Ste 4500 Houston TX 77010-2029

**SEDERBAUM, ARTHUR DAVID,** lawyer; b. N.Y.C., Sept. 14, 1944; s. William and Harriet (Warschauer) S.; m. Francine Haba, Dec. 30, 1967 (div. Aug. 1982); children: Rebecca, David; m. Phyllis Padow, Jan. 18, 1986; 1 child, Elizabeth. AB cum laude, Columbia U., 1965, JD, 1968; LLM, NYU, 1972. BAr: N.Y. 1968, Fla. 1980, U.S. Dist. Ct. (so. and ea. dists.) N.Y. 1972. Assoc. Zissun Grundman Frome Rosenzweig & Orens, N.Y.C., 1968-70, Berlack, Israels & Liberman, N.Y.C., 1970-72, Rubin Baum Levin Constant & Friedman, N.Y.C., 1972-76; ptnr. Certilman, Hart, Balin, Buckley, Kremer & Hyman, N.Y.C., 1976-88, Olshan, Grundman, Frome, Rosenzweig & Orens, N.Y.C., 1988-92, Patterson, Belknap, Webb & Tyler, L.L.P., N.Y.C., 1992—; mem. adv. bd. Bur. Nat. Affairs Estates, Gifts and Trusts Jour.; mem. adv. bd. NYU Inst. Fed. Taxation, CCH Fin. and Estate Planning. Author: Setting Up and Executing Trusts, 1988; contbr. articles to Tax Mgmt. Estates, Titles and Trusts Jour. Recipient J.K. Lasser Tax prize NYU Inst. Fed. Taxation, 1968. Fellow Am. Coll. Trusts and Estates Coun.; mem. ABA, N.Y. State Bar Assn. (vice chmn. com. on estate planning trustes and estates law sect.), Assn. Bar City N.Y. (com. surrogates cts.), Practicing Law Inst. (chmn. income taxatin of estates and trusts program). Probate, Estate planning, Estate taxation. Home: 5 Pheasant Dr Armonk NY 10504-1321 Office: Patterson Belknap Webb & Tyler LLP 1133 Avenue Of The Americas New York NY 10036-6710

**SEDLAK, JOSEPH ANTHONY, III,** lawyer; b. Cleve., Feb. 22, 1952; s. Joseph Anthony Jr. and Winefred Veronica (Nantell) S.; m. Susan Ann Dill, Oct. 1, 1983; children: Joseph Anthony IV and John Warrior Sedlak (twins). BA, Ohio State U., 1974; JD, St. Mary's U., San Antonio, 1977. Bar: Tex. 1977, Colo. 1980, U.S. Dist. Ct. Colo. 1980, U.S. Ct. Appeals (10th cir.) 1980. Assoc. Law Offices of Grady L. Roberts, Piersall, Tex., 1977-80, LoBato, Bliedt & Bliedt, Lakewood, Colo., 1980-81, Vranesic & Visciano, Denver, 1981-85; pres. Sedlak & Vogel P.C., Denver, 1985-91, Sedlak & Assocs. P.C., Denver, 1991—. Mem. Colo. Bar Assn., Denver Bar Assn., Am. Trial Lawyers Asn., Denver Jud. Adminstrn. Com., Denver C. of C., Racquet World Club, Denver Petroleum Club. Roman Catholic. Avocations: skiing, golf, hunting. State civil litigation, Personal injury, Criminal. Office: 621 17th St Ste 2655 Denver CO 80293-2601

**SEDWICK, JOHN W.,** judge; b. Kittanning, Pa., Mar. 13, 1946; s. Jack D. and Marion (Hilton) S.; m. Deborah Brown, Aug. 22, 1966; children: Jack D. II, Whitney Marie. BA summa cum laude, Dartmouth Coll., 1968; JD cum laude, Harvard U., 1972. Bar: Alaska 1972, U.S. Dist. Ct. Alaska 1972, U.S. Ct. Appeals (9th cir.) 1973. Lawyer Burr, Pease and Kurtz, Anchorage, 1972-81, 1982-92; dir. div. lands State of Alaska, Anchorage, 1981-82; judge U.S. Dist. Ct. Alaska, Anchorage, 1992—. Mem. Commonwealth North, Anchorage, 1985; bd. dirs. South Addition Alaska R.R. Com., Anchorage, 1984. Sgt. USNG, 1969-72. Mem. ABA, Alaska Bar Assn. (chmn. environ. law sect. 1984, law examiners com. 1986-89, civil rules com. 1990-92, fee arbitration com. 1991-92). Episcopalian. Office: US Dist Ct Box 32 222 W 7th Ave Unit 4 Anchorage AK 99513-7564

**SEE, HAROLD FREND,** judge, law educator; b. Chgo., Ill., Nov. 7, 1943; s. Harold Frend and Corinne Louise (Rachau) S.; m. Brenda Jane Childs, Dec. 2, 1978; children: Callie Suzanne, Garrett Brittain; children by previous marriage: Mary Elisabeth, Eric Palmer. Student, U. Chgo., 1962-63; BA, Emporia State U., 1966; MS, Iowa State U., 1969; JD, U. Iowa, 1973. Bar: Ill. 1973, U.S. Dist. Ct. (no. dist.) Ill. 1973, Ala. 1981, U.S. Ct. Appeals (fed. cir.) 1991. Instr. econs. Iowa State U., Ames, 1967-69; asst. prof. econs. Ill. State U., Normal, 1969-70; assoc. Sydley & Austin, Chgo., 1973-76; assoc. prof. law U. Ala., Tuscaloosa, 1976-78, prof., 1978—; justice Supreme Ct. Ala., 1997—. Contbr. to books, also articles and book reviews. Mem. ABA, Ala. Bar Assn., Am. Econ. Assn., Am. Law and Econs. Assn., Soc. Profls. in Dispute Resolution, Am. Law Inst., Ala. Law Inst. Baptist. Office: U Ala Sch Law PO Box 870382 Tuscaloosa AL 35487-0001 also: Supreme Ct Ala 300 Dexter Ave Montgomery AL 36104-3741*

**SEEGER, RONALD L.,** lawyer; b. Prairie Farm, Wis., June 10, 1930; s. John M. and Mildred G. (Moen) S.; m. Theresa A. Seeger, Sept. 3, 1955; children: Mark, Scott, John, Lynn, Eric. BA, U. Wis., 1951; JD, U. Minn., 1956. Bar: Minn. 1956, U.S. Dist. Ct. 1957, U.S. Supreme Ct. 1983. Pres. Dunlap & Seeger (was Michaels, Seeger, Rosenblad & Arnold), Rochester, Minn., 1956—. Counsel, City of Rochester Charter Commn., 1962-74, chmn., 1971-72; pres. Legal Assistance of Olmsted County, 1973-76; bd. dirs., v.p. Legal Assistace Minn., 1972-74; chmn. Gamehaven area Boy Scout Found., 1974-76, trustee; dir. Minn. Lawyers Mutual. With U.S. Army, 1951-53, Korea. Fellow Am. Bar Found.; mem. ABA (ho. of dels. 1974-80, 92-96, bd. govs. 1991-95), Minn. State Bar Assn. (bd. govs. 1974-85, pres. 1983-84, Lifetime Svc. award 1997), Minn. Bar Found. (dir.), Minn. Legal Cert. Bd. (chmn. 1985-90). General practice, General corporate, Labor. Home: 524 9th Ave SW Rochester MN 55902-2910 Office: PO Box 549 Rochester MN 55903-0549

**SEEMILLER, SUSAN,** lawyer; b. Portland, Maine, June 22, 1959; d. Arthur W.K. Jr. and Elizabeth Ann Simmons; m. Daniel Seemiller, Aug. 5, 1989; children: David James, Ryan Daniel. AS, Westbrook Coll., 1979, BS, 1987; JD, Pepperdine U., 1990. Bar: Calif. 1990, U.S. Dist. Ct. (ctrl. dist.) Calif. 1990, U.S. Ct. Appeals (10th cir.) 1991, U.S. Ct. Appeals (9th cir.) 1993, U.S. Supreme Ct. 1998; cert. med. asst. Am. Assn. Med. Assts. Paralegal specialist Office of U.S. Atty., Portland, 1981-87; law clk. hon. Ruggero J. Aldisert U.S. Ct. Appeals Third Cir., Santa Barbara, Calif., 1990-92; ptnr. Nordman, Cormany, Hair & Compton, Oxnard, Calif., 1992—. Editor-in-chief Pepperdine Law Rev., 1989-90. Roman Catholic. Avocations: reading, needlework, aerobics. E-mail: sseemiller@nchc.com. Fax: 805-988-8387. Office: Nordman Cormany Hair & Compton 1000 Town Center Dr Fl 6 Oxnard CA 93030-1132

**SEERY, JAMES P., JR.,** lawyer; b. N.Y.C., July 30, 1962; m. Kathleen B. Seery; children: Grace, Maggie, Lucy, Seamus, Owen. BA, Colgate U., 1984; JD magna cum laude, NYU, 1990. Bar: N.Y., Conn., U.S. Dist. Ct. (so. dist.) N.Y., U.S. Dist. Ct. (no. dist.) N.Y., U.S. Dist. Ct. (ea. dist.) N.Y. Assoc. Cadeater, Wickensham & Taft, N.Y.C., 1989-95, Phillips, Nizer, Benjamin, Krim & Ballon, Garden City, N.Y., 1995—. Bankruptcy. Office: Phillips Nizer Benjamin Krim & Ballon 600 Old Country Rd Garden City NY 11530-2001

**SEGAL, DONALD E.,** lawyer; b. Houston, Nov. 13, 1947. BA with honors, Brandeis U., 1969; JD, Boston Coll., 1972. Bar: Mass. 1972, D.C. 1973, U.S. Supreme Ct. 1976, U.S. Dist. Ct. (D.C. dist.) 1976. Assoc. chief counsel FDA, Washington, 1979-91; ptnr. Baker & Hostetler, Washington, 1991-93, Akin, Gump, Strauss, Hauer & Feld, Washington, 1993—. Editor Law Review; mem. Law Rev. Boston Coll. Mem. Food and Drug Law Inst. Office: Akin Gump Ste 400 1333 New Hampshire Ave NW Washington DC 20036-1564

**SEGAL, GARY L.,** lawyer; b. Miami Beach, Fla., Dec. 30, 1954; m. Cathy A. Segal, May 29, 1977; children: Kenneth, Paula. BS, Boston U., 1972-76; JD, Cath. U., 1976-79. Bar: Md. 1979, D.C. 1981, U.S. Dist. Ct. D.C., U.S. Dist. Ct. Md., U.S. Ct. Appeals (4th cir.), U.S. Supreme Ct. Staff atty. Office Fed. Register, Washington, 1979-81; ptnr. Galfond & Segal, Rockville, Md., 1981-92; pvt. practice, Rockville, 1992—. Mem. Md. Bar Assn., D.C. Bar Assn., Montgomery County Bar Assn., Md. Trial Lawyers Assn. Personal injury, Criminal, Family and matrimonial. Office: 600 Jefferson Plz Ste 308 Rockville MD 20850

**SEGALL, JAMES ARNOLD,** lawyer; b. Columbus, Ohio, Aug. 19, 1956; s. Arthur and Greta Helene (Cohen) S.; m. Janice Faye Wiesen, Mar. 14, 1981; children: Gayle Helene, Aryn Michelle, Craig Lawrence. BA, Coll. of William and Mary, 1978; JD, Washington and Lee U., 1981. Bar: Va. 1981, U.S. Dist. Ct. (ea. dist.) Va. 1981. Assoc. Phelps & King P.C., Newport News, Va., 1981-84, Buxton & Lasris P.C., Yorktown, Va., 1984-85; sole practice Newport News, 1985-89; pres. James A. Segall & Assocs., 1990-91, James A. Segall & Assocs., P.C., 1991-92, Segall & Moody, Newport News, 1992-98; ptnr. Krinick, Segall, Moody & Lewis, Newport News, Va., 1998—; lectr. Hampton Roads Regional Acad. Criminal Justice, 1986-89. Bd. dirs. ct.-apptd. Spl. Adv. Program, Newport News, 1986-87, Hamton-Newport News Cmty. Svcs. Bd., 1993—, treas., 1995-96, 99—, vice-chair, 1996-97, chair 1997-99; participant coop. office edn. program Newport News Pub. Schs., 1987-90; lectr. vol. programs 7th Dist. Ct. Svc. Unit, 1986-89; active City Newport News Cable TV Adv. Commn., 1990-93, Newport News Dem. City Com., 1990-91; bd. dirs. Rodef Sholom Temple, 1992-94, United Jewish Comty., the Va. Peninsula, Inc., 1990—, chmn. spl. activities and fundraising com., 1990-91, chmn. bylaws com., 1992-93, 95—, campaign coun., 1995—, cmty. rels. coun., 1995-98, v.p. human svcs., 1998—. Mem. Newport News Bar Assn., Va. Trial Lawyers Assn., Va. Coll. Criminal Def., B'nai B'rith (pres. 1989-91), Ruritan (sec. 1985-87), Moose. Avocations: computers, history, philosophy. General corporate, Family and matrimonial, Personal injury. Home: 306 Dogwood Dr Newport News VA 23606-3728 Office: Krinick Segall Moody & Lewis 525 Oyster Point Rd Newport News VA 23602-6014

**SEGALL, NORMAN S.,** lawyer; b. Newark, Sept. 13, 1945; s. Martin M. and Dorothy A. (Shiffren) S.; m. Carolyn Page Harris, Sept. 26, 1970; 1 child, Ryan. BA, Mich. State U., 1968; JD, U. Miami, 1973. Bar: Fla. 1973, U.S. Dist. Ct. (so. dist.) Fla. 1973, U.S. Ct. Appeals (5th cir.) 1973, U.S. Ct. Appeals (2d cir.) 1974, U.S. Ct. Appeals (11th cir.) 1978, U.S. Supreme Ct. 1978. Assoc. High, Stack, Davis & Lazenby, Miami, Fla., 1973-76; ptnr. Shaw & Segall, Miami, 1977; pvt. practice Miami, 1978-81; ptnr. Segall & Gold, Miami, 1981-90, Bentata Hoet Zamora Segall Lacasa & Schere, Miami, 1991-92, Keith Mack LLP, Miami, 1992—; arbitration Am. Arbitration Assn., Miami, 1990-92. Hearing officer Dade County Sch. Bd., Miami, 1985—. Jewish. Avocations: computer, sports, roller hockey. E-mail: nss@keithmack.com. General civil litigation, Contracts commercial, Family and matrimonial. Home: 495 Campana Ave Miami FL 33156-4219 Office: Keith Mack LLP 200 S Biscayne Blvd Fl 20 Miami FL 33131-2310

**SEGEL, KAREN LYNN JOSEPH,** lawyer; b. Youngstown, Ohio, Jan. 15, 1947; d. Samuel Dennis and Helen Anita Joseph; m. Alvin Gerald Segel, June 9, 1968 (div. Sept. 1976); 1 child, Adam James. BA in Soviet and East European Studies, Boston U., 1968; JD, Southwestern U., 1975. Bar: Calif., 1996, U.S. Tax Ct., 1996, U.S. Dist. Ct. (cen. dist.) Calif., 1996, U.S. Ct. Appeals (9th cir.), 1997. Adminstrv. asst. Olds Brunel & Co., N.Y.C., 1968-69, U.S. Banknote Corp., N.Y.C., 1969-70; tax acct. S.N. Chilkov & Co. CPA's, Beverly Hills, Calif., 1971-74; intern Calif. Corps. Commr., 1975; tax. sr. Oppenheim Appel & Dixon CPA's, L.A., 1978, Fox, Westheimer & Co. CPA's, L.A., 1978, Zebrak, Levine & Mepos CPA's, L.A., 1979; ind. cons. acctg., taxation specialist Beverly Hills, 1980—; bd. dirs. World Wide Motion Pictures Corp., L.A.; law student mentor Southwestern U., 1996-99, tax moot ct. judge, 1997. Editorial adv. bd. Am. Biog. Inst. High sch. amb. to Europe People-to-People Orgn., 1963. Named 1991, 93 Woman of Yr., Am. Biog. Inst. Mem. Nat. Soc. Tax Profls., Nat. Assn. Tax Practitioners, Nat. Trust for Hist. Preservation, Calif. State Bar, Winterthur Guild, Women's Inner Circle of Achievement, Calif. Young Lawyers Assn., Beverly Hills Bar Assn., Santa Monica Bar Assn., Complex Litigation Inns of Ct., L.A. County Bar Assn, Beverly Hills Tinseltown Rose Soc. Avocations: collecting seashells, lhasa apso dog breeding, art, traveling, music. Taxation, general.

**SEGGIO-BALL, JOSEPHINE,** lawyer; b. Silver Creek, N.Y., Nov. 28, 1946; d. Mario Nicholas and Bridget Marie (Fasanello) S.; m. James David Ball, Sept. 2, 1974; children: Mario Nicholas, Bridget Roberts. BA, Daemen Coll., 1968; JD, SUNY at Buffalo, 1971. Bar: N.Y. 1972, U.S. Dist. Ct. (we. dist.) N.Y. 1982. Assoc. Di Pasquale & Pack, Buffalo, 1971-78; ptnr. Pack, Grashow, Palmer, Greenman, Hurley & Ball, Buffalo, 1978-80, Pack & Ball, Buffalo, 1980-81, Pack, Harkman, Ball & Huckabone, Buffalo, 1981-94, Pack, Hartman, Ball, Brody & Kinney, P.C., Buffalo, 1994-98, Hartman, Ball, Brody & Kinney, P.C., Buffalo, 1998—. Bd. trustees Immaculata Acad., 1989-92. Mem. Erie County Bar Assn. Democrat. Roman Catholic. Real property, Probate, Estate planning. Home: 9689 Versailles Rd Angola NY 14006-9519 Office: Hartman Ball Brody & Kinney PC 230 Brisbane Bldg Buffalo NY 14203-7504

**SEGLUND, BRUCE RICHARD,** lawyer; b. Lansing, Mich., June 3, 1950; s. Richard Oswald and Josephine Ann (Krause) S.; m. Connie Sue Roberts, June 19, 1970; children: Jennifer Lynne, Nicole Marie. BS, Mich. State U., 1973; JD, Thomas M. Cooley Law Sch., 1979. Bar: Mich. 1981, U.S. Dist. Ct. (ea. dist.) Mich. 1981. Assoc. Michael W. Reeds, P.C., Walled Lake, Mich., 1981-82; sole practice Walled Lake, 1982-85; ptnr. Mick and Seglund, Walled Lake, 1985-89, Connelly, Crowley, Groth and Seglund, Walled Lake, 1989—. Mem. ABA, Mich. Bar Assn. (mem. character and fitness com. dist. J 1990—), Oakland County Bar Assn. (lectr. 1984), Mich. Jaycees (pres. Walled Lake 1982-83, exellence award 1982-83, pres. of yr. 1982-83), Walled Lake C. of C. (bd. dirs. scholarship fund 1985-88). Roman Catholic. Lodge: KC (adv. 1982-94). Labor, Municipal (including bonds), General corporate. Home: 8618 Buffalo Dr Commerce Township MI 48382-3408 Office: Connelly Crowley Groth & Seglund 2410 S Commerce Rd Walled Lake MI 48390-2129

**SEGOR, JOSEPH CHARLES,** lawyer; b. N.Y.C., Dec. 23, 1935; s. Cecil and Leonora (Schorr) S.; m. Phyllis Ashman, Mar. 17m 1963 (div. Dec. 1980); children: Julie, Deborah; m. Dorothy Woolf, June 5, 1983. BBA, U. Miami (Fla.), 1957, JD, 1960. Bar: Fla. 1960, U.S. Ct. Appeals (5th cir.) 1968, U.S. Supreme Ct. 1974, U.S. Ct. Appeals (11th cir.) 1981, U.S. Ct. Appeals (9th cir.) 1985,. Assoc. Philip Heckerling Law Office, Miami, Fla., 1961, Theodore Nelson Law Office, Miami, Fla., 1961-64, Ungerleider & Segor, Miami Beach, 1964-65; asst. dir. Legal Svcs. of Greater Miami,

1966-67; dep. dir. Fla. Rural Legal Svcs., Miami, 1967-68, exec. dir., 1968-69; exec. dir. Migrant Svcs. Found., Miami, 1969-74; assoc. Kaplan, Dorsey, Sicking & Hessen, Miami, 1974-78; ptnr. Chonin & Segor, Miami, 1978-79; dir. apellate div. Pub. Defenders Office 11th Cir. Fla., Miami, 1979-81; pvt. practice, Miami, 1981—. Chmn. bd. dirs. Fla. Rural Legal Svcs., Lakeland, 1977, Legal Svcs. Greater Miami, 1979-80; pres. Centro Campasino Farm Worker Ctr., Inc., Homestead, Fla., 1987—; mem. Dade County Housing Fin. Authority, Miami, 1991-94; bd. dirs. Biscayne Sr. Housing, Inc., 1987—. Mem. Dade County Bar Assn., Kendall South Miami Bar Assn. Jewish. Appellate, State civil litigation, Workers' compensation. Office: 12815 SW 112th Ct Miami FL 33176-4431

**SEGRETI, ALBERT MARK, JR.,** lawyer; b. N.Y.C., Apr. 4, 1945; s. Albert Mark and Bessy Wynell Segreti; m. Peggy Ann Lahrmer, Dec. 10, 1977; children: Krista, Alison, Anthony. AB, Wittenberg U., 1967; JD cum laude, Ohio State U., 1970. Bar: Ohio 1970, U.S. Dist. Ct. (so. dist.) Ohio 1971, U.S. Ct. Mil. Appeals 1972, U.S. Dist. Ct. (no. dist.) Ohio 1973, U.S. Ct. Appeals (6th cir.) 1976, U.S. Supreme Ct. 1978. Atty. Porter, Stanley, Treffinger & Platt, Columbus, Ohio, 1970-72; asst. atty. gen. environ. law Ohio Atty. Gen., Columbus, 1972-74, Segreti & Tousey, Columbus, 1974-81; law prof. Cumberland Sch. Law, Samford U., Birmingham, Ala., 1981-84; atty. Bieser Greer & Landis, Dayton, Ohio, 1984-90, Young & Alexander, Dayton, 1990-96, Haffey & Segreti, Dayton, 1996—. Contbr. articles to profl. jours. 1st lt. USAR. Mem. ABA (litigation sect.), Ohio State Bar Assn. (fed. cts. and environ. law), Dayton Bar Assn. (environ. law com.). Avocations: soccer coaching, walking, tennis, bird watching. Personal injury, Environmental, General civil litigation. Office: Haffey & Segreti 2365 Lakeview Dr Ste D Dayton OH 45431-3639

**SEHAM, MARTIN CHARLES,** lawyer; b. Jersey City, June 30, 1932; s. Samuel and Libbie (Siegel) S.; m. Phoebe Williams, Apr. 18, 1955; children: Amy, Jenny, Lee, Lucy. BA summa cum laude, Amherst Coll., 1954; JD magna cum laude, Harvard U., 1957. Bar: N.Y. 1957, U.S. Dist. Ct. (ea. and so. dists.) N.Y. 1957, U.S. Supreme Ct. 1963, U.S. Ct. Appeals (D.C. cir.) 1969, U.S. Ct. Appeals (9th cir.) 1973, U.S. Ct. Appeals (5th cir.) 1989. Assoc. Chadbourne, Parke, Whiteside & Wolff, N.Y.C., 1957-60, Poletti & Freidin, Prashker, Feldman & Gartner, N.Y.C., 1960-63; ptnr. Kopple & Seham, N.Y.C., 1963-68, Surrey, Karasik, Morse & Seham, N.Y.C., 1968-79, Seham, Klein & Zelman, N.Y.C., 1979-94; gen. counsel Am. Maritime Assn., N.Y.C., 1979—, Owners Com. Elec. Rates, N.Y.C., 1963-93; chmn. N.Y.C. Pub. Utility Review Bd., 1979-82; bd. dirs. The Print Club of N.Y., Inc., Black Culinarian Alliance. Author: Federal Wage & Hour Laws, 1962, Chapter Railway Labor Act Kheel Book, 1984, From Jerusalem to Dallas: The Impact of Labor Markets on Airline Negotiations, 1988; editor: Harvard Law Rev., 1955. Mem. Bergen County (N.J.) Urban League, bd. dirs. 1985—, pres. housing and devel. Corp. 1982—; mem. Bergen County Energy Council, 1982-85. Mem. ABA (com. labor arbitration and collective bargaining, com. on ry. and airline labor law, pub. utilities sect., past chmn. Internat. Labor Law com.), N.Y. Bar Assn. (labor arbitration com.), Assn. of Bar of City of N.Y., Harvard Club (N.Y.C.), Phi Beta Kappa. Democrat. Labor, Public utilities. Office: Seham Seham Meltz & Petersen 380 Madison Ave Ste 17 New York NY 10017-2513

**SEHEULT, MALCOLM MCDONALD RICHARDSON,** lawyer; b. Port of Spain, Trinidad, July 18, 1949; s. Errol Andre and Laura (Laltoo) S.; m. Robin Lynn Montanye; children: Kristie, Julie, Laura, Aimée. BA in Sociology magna cum laude, U. Toronto, 1971, BEd, 1972, MA, 1973; LLB, U. Toronto, Ottawa, 1976; DJuris, Kensington U., 1988, PhD. Bar: Ontario, Can. 1978, N.Y. 1987; cert. tchr., Toronto, Can. Pvt. practice Toronto, 1978-85; assoc. Outerbridge, Barristers & Solicitors, Mississauga, Ont., Can., 1985-86, Don Brown, Mississauga, 1986—; cons.; lectr. numerous profl. and cmty. groups and orgns. Producer, editor Where Is Tomorrow?, 1969; editor Ottawa Law Rev.; also articles. Mem. Justice for Children, Vanier Inst. of Family, Ont. Sch. Tchrs. Fedn.; bd. dirs. North York Branson Hosp. Mem. ABA, N.Y. State Bar Assn., Can. Bar Assn., Assn. Trial Lawyers Am., Law Soc. Upper Can., Medico-Legal Soc., Lawyers Club, Can. Civil Liberties Union, Royal Soc. Arts (fellow 1979), Mensa Internat., Can. Sociology and Anthropology Assn., Nat. Directory Sociology of Edn. and Ednl. Sociology, Am. Philatelic Soc., Phi Kappa Phi. Avocations: music, car rally racing, volleyball, swimming, antique furniture restoration. Juvenile, Family and matrimonial. Home: PO Box 14397 Bradenton FL 34280

**SEIDEL, ARTHUR HARRIS,** lawyer; b. N.Y.C., May 25, 1923; s. Philip and Pearl (Geller) S.; m. Raquel Eliovich, Aug. 21, 1949; children: Stephen A., Paul B., Mary Beth Sharp. B.S., CCNY, 1942; A.M., U. Mich., 1943; J.D. with honors, George Washington U., 1949. Bar: D.C. 1949, Pa. 1956, N.Y. 1957. Atty. patent dept. Gulf Oil Corp., Washington and Pitts., 1947-52; individual practice law, 1952-64; sr. ptnr. firm Seidel & Gonda, 1964-68; sr. ptnr. firm Seidel, Gonda & Goldhammer (P.C.), Phila., 1968-72, pres., 1972-84; pres. Seidel, Gonda, Goldhammer & Abbott, P.C., 1984-88, Seidel, Gonda, Lavorgna & Monaco, 1988—; lectr. in Intellectual Property Temple U. Law Sch., 1973-86, Am. Law Inst. Editor: George Washington Law Rev, 1949; author: (with others) Trademark Practice, 2 vols, 1963, Monographs on Patent Law and Practice, 5th edit, 1993, Trademarks and Copyrights, 6th edit., 1992, Trade Secrets and Employment Agreements 3d edit, 1995; also articles. Mem. Adv. Com. for Restatement of Law of Unfair Competition. Mem. ABA, Am. Law Inst., Pa. Bar Assn., Phila. Bar Assn., Am. Intellectual Property Law Assn., Phila. Intellectual Property Law Assn., Order of Coif. Patent, Trademark and copyright. Home: 904 Centennial Rd Narberth PA 19072-1408 Office: Seidel Gonda Lavorgna & Monaco 2 Penn Center Plz Ste 1800 Philadelphia PA 19102-1721 *My entire professional career has been devoted to the question of innovation, patents for inventions, trademarks for new businesses and copyrights for new writings. I have seen the United States become the world's leader in technology and business.*

**SEIDEL, REBECCA SUZANNE,** lawyer; b. Pitts., Apr. 7, 1967. BA, U. Notre Dame, 1989; JD, U. Dayton, 1993. Bar: Mass. 1993, Washington 1995, U.S. Ct. Appeals (fed. cir.) 1997. Assoc. Gibson & Behrman PC, Burlington, Mass., 1995-97, Campbell, Campbell & Edwards, Boston, 1997—. Mem. Order of Barristers. General civil litigation, Product liability, Insurance. Office: Campbell Campbell & Edwards 1 Constitution Plz Boston MA 02129-2025

**SEIDEL, RICHARD STEPHEN,** lawyer; b. Phila., Jan. 3, 1965; s. Gary Leonard and Judith Lee Seidel; m. Jodi Helene Woodin, May 14, 1992; children: Hallie Alexa, Jamie Morgan. BA in Criminal Justice cum laude, Temple U., 1986, JD cum laude, 1989. Bar: N.J. 1989, Pa. 1989, U.S. Dist. Ct. (ea. dist.) Pa. 1989, U.S. Ct. Appeals (3rd cir.) 1990. Assoc. Mesirov, Gelman, Jaffe, Cramer & Jamieson, Phila., 1989-94, Daniels, Saltz, Mongoluzzi & Barrett, Phila., 1994-96, Bernstein, Silver & Agins, Phila., 1996-98; ptnr. Agins, Haaz & Seidel, LLP, Phila., 1998—; presenter in field. Contbr. articles to profl. jours. Fellow Acad. Advocacy Temple U. Sch. Law, Phila., 1997. Mem. ABA, ATLA (student trial advocacy competition judge), Phila. Trial Lawyers Assn. (bd. dirs. 1997—, bar elections com., young lawyers com., Musmanno com.), Pa. Bar Assn., Phila. Bar Assn. (state civil com., state civil sub-com. on the Phila. discovery ct., state civil sub-com. on ABA civil trial practice stds., state civil mentoring program, medico-legal com., young lawyers divsn. H.S. mock trial competition, young lawyers divsn. law firm liaison, legal line vol.), Phila. Bar Found. Avocations: golf, music, sports. Professional liability, Personal injury, Product liability. Office: Agins Haaz & Seidel LLP 1604 Locust St Fl 3 Philadelphia PA 19103-6305

**SEIDEL, SELVYN,** lawyer, educator; b. Long Branch, N.J., Nov. 6, 1942; s. Abraham and Anita (Stoller) S.; m. Deborah Lew, June 21, 1970; 1 child, Emily. BA, U. Chgo., 1964; JD, U. Calif., Berkeley, 1967; Diploma in Law, Oxford U., 1968. Bar: N.Y. 1970, U.S. Dist. Ct. (so. and ea. dists.) N.Y. 1970, D.C. Ct. Appeals, 1982. Ptnr. Latham & Watkins, N.Y.C., 1984—; adj. prof. Sch. Law, NYU, 1974-85; instr. Practicing Law Inst., 1980-81, 84. Bd. dirs. Citizen Scholarship Fund Am., 1995—. Mem. ABA, New York County Bar Assn., N.Y.C. Bar Assn. (mem. fed. cts. com. 1982-85, internat. law com. 1989-92, 95-96, art law com. 1997—), Boalt Hall Alumni Assn. (bd. dirs. 1980-82), Contbr. articles to profl. jours. Federal civil litigation, Private international. Office: Latham & Watkins 885 3rd Ave Fl 9 New York NY 10022-4874

**SEIDEN, ANDY,** lawyer, e-commerce business development executive; b. N.Y.C., Sept. 16, 1956; s. Stanley and Dorothy Rose. BS in Indsl. and Labor Rels., Cornell U., 1978; vis. student, Harvard Law Sch., 1980-81; JD, U. Calif., Berkeley, 1981. Bar: Calif. 1981, N.Y. 1993. Assoc. Donovan Leisure Newton & Irvine, L.A., 1981-85, Curtis Mallet-Prevost Colt & Mosle, N.Y.C., 1987-89, Pettit & Martin, San Francisco, 1989-91; pvt. practice San Francisco, 1991-93; ptnr. Whitehead & Porter, San Francisco, 1993-95; v.p. bus. devel. and bus. affairs, gen. counsel Big Top Prodns., San Francisco, 1995-96; v.p. bus. and legal affairs Walt Disney Feature Animation, Burbank, Calif., 1997-98; with Seiden & Assocs., L.A., 1998—. Bd. dirs. L.A. League of Conservation Voters, L.A., 1983-85. Mem. ABA (com. on negotiated acquisitions 1994-96), Phi Kappa Phi. Democrat. Avocations: world travel, skiing, cultural anthropology, computers. Intellectual property, Entertainment, Contracts commercial. Office: PO Box 36 14010 Captains Row Marina Dl Rey CA 90292-7389

**SEIDEN, STEVEN JAY,** lawyer; b. N.Y.C., June 21, 1960; s. Martin S. and Rita (Glazer) S.; m. Kathryn LaRussa, Sept. 30, 1984; children: Robert B., Daniel M., Michael J. BA, SUNY, Oneonta, 1981; JD, Hofstra U., 1984. Bar: N.Y. 1985, U.S. Dist. Ct. (ea. and so. dists.) N.Y. 1985, U.S. Supreme Ct. 1995, U.S. Ct. Appeals (fed. cir.) 1995, U.S. Ct. Fed. Claims 1995, U.S. Ct. Appeals for the Armed Forces, 1995. Assoc. Shapiro, Baines,Saasto & Shainwald, Mineola, N.Y., 1984-88; ptnr. Seiden & Kaufman, Carle Place, N.Y., 1988-93, 95—, Seiden, Kaufman, & Bosek, Carle Place, N.Y., 1993-95. Mem. ABA, N.Y. State Bar Assn., N.Y. State Trial Lawyers Assn., Assn. Trial Lawyers Am., Nassau County Bar Assn., L.I. Trial Lawyers Assn. (bd. dirs.), Civil Justice Found. (founding sponsor). Jewish. Personal injury. Office: Seiden & Kaufman 1 Old Country Rd Ste 114 Carle Place NY 11514-1821

**SEIDLER, B(ERNARD) ALAN,** lawyer; b. N.Y.C., Nov. 26, 1946; s. Aaron H. and Ethel T. (Berkowitz) S.; m. Lynne Aubrey, Jan. 21, 1978; children—Jacob A., Morgan H., Lily R. B.A., Colgate U., 1968; J.D., Seton Hall U., 1972. Bar: N.Y. 1973, U.S. Dist. Ct. (ea. and so. dists.) N.Y. 1975, U.S. Ct. Appeals (2d cir.) 1976, U.S. Supreme Ct. 1977, U.S. Ct. Appeals (3rd cir.) 1984. Staff atty. N.Y. Legal Aid Soc., N.Y.C., 1972-75; sole practice, N.Y.C. and Nyack, N.Y., 1975—. Mem. ATLA, Snedens Landing Tennis Assn. (Palisades, N.Y.). General civil litigation, Probate, Criminal. Office: 127 S Broadway Nyack NY 10960-4433

**SEIDLITZ, JOHN E.,** lawyer; b. Havre, Mont., Nov. 1, 1956; m. Pamela Jean, Dec. 27, 1986 (widowed Aug. 1983); children: Jeremy, Jeff. BA, U. Mont., 1978, JD, 1981. Bar: Mont., U.S. Dist. Ct. Mont. 1981. Atty. Seidlitz Law Office, Chester, Mont., 1981-82, Marble & Seidlitz, Chester, Mont., 1982-87, Regnier, Lewis & Boland, Great Falls, Mont., 1987-91, pvt. practice, Great Falls, Mont., 1991—. Mem. Cascade County Bar Assn., Mont. Trial Lawyers Assn., State Bar of Mont., Assn. Trial Lawyers Am., Lions Club, K.C. Democrat. Roman Catholic. Avocations: scuba diving, golf. General civil litigation, Personal injury, Workers' compensation. Office: PO Box 1581 Great Falls MT 59403-1581

**SEIDMAN, PHILLIP KENNETH,** lawyer; b. Bklyn., June 18, 1907; s. Louis and Fanny (Goldfarb) S.; m. Leone White, Oct. 7, 1944 (dec.). BS, Columbia U., 1927; JD, U. Memphis Law Sch., 1935; PhD in Humanities (hon.), Rhodes Coll., 1988; PhD in Pub. Svc. (hon.), Christian Brothers U., 1990. CPA; Bar: Tenn. 1936, U.S. Tax Ct. 1936, Tenn. Supreme Ct. 1936, U.S. Dist. Ct. Appeals 1950. Founding ptnr. Seidman & Seidman (now BDO/Seidman) Internat. CPAs, chmn. bd. dirs., 1971-73; dir. Internat. Protein Co., 1992; pres., mem. faculty Memphis Coll. Accountancy, 1947-60; ret., 1972; lectr. fed. tax law So. Law Sch., Memphis, 1940-41; lectr. acctg. and econ. Rhodes Coll., 1940, U. Tenn., Memphis, 1941-42, Am. Inst. Banking, Memphis, 1940-42, Memphis State U., 1972-75; co-chmn. adv. bd. Christian Bros. U. Sch. Bus.; adc Gov. Clement, 1963-67, Gov. Ellington, 1967-71; mem. chancellor's roundtable U. Tenn., Memphis, 1998. Co-author: The Man Who Likes Memphis, 1975, Seidman's Legislative History of Federal Income Tax Laws 1861-1953, Seidman's Legislative History of Excess Profits Tax Laws 1917-1946. Pres. Memphis Orchestral Soc., 1954-60, Memphis Symphony, 1955-60, Memphis Little Theatre, 1961-63, Memphis Goodwill Industries, 1965-67; v.p. Alzheimer's Day Care, Inc., 1984, treas. ADRDA, 1982-83; chmn. Crime Stoppers, 1981-83, City of Hope Endowment, 1985; bd. dirs. Memphis and Shelby County Community Chest, 1956-59, LeBonheur Children's Hosp., 1966-67, Memphis State U. Found., 1966-76, Memphis Civic Arts Ctr., 1965, Memphis Bicentennial Com., 1974-76, Am. Jewish Com. 1955-70, Epilepsy Found. W. Tenn., 1987, Future Memphis, Inc., 1974, Shelby County Com. Law Enforcement Consolidation, 1980, Salvation Army, 1940—, Sr. Citizens, Inc., 1961-73, Family Svc. of Memphis, 1959-67, Memphis Ballet Soc., 1962-65, Memphis Health and Welfare Coun., 1957, Tenn. Coun. Econ. Edn., 1976, Memphis State U. Coll. Bus., 1971-76, LeBonheur Children's Hosp. Found., 1975-77, Found. for Better Govt. in Tenn., 1968, Juvenile Ct., 1972, Memphis Open Air Theatre, 1959, 67—, Davieshire Libr., 1989, Sr. Svcs., 1991—, Church Health Ctr., 1992—, Mid-South Assn. for Retarded Children, 1955; bd. dirs. St. Joseph Hosp., 1968, chmn. fin. com., 1968-71; bd. dirs. Memphis Sesquicentennial, 1950, comptr.; bd. dirs. Memphis Opera Theatre, 1959, 67—, permanent hon. v.p.; founder, chmn. Crime Stoppers, 1974; bd. dirs. Memphis-Delta Cmty. Health Edn. Coun., treas., 1978; trustee Rhodes Coll. formerly Southwestern Coll. at Memphis, 1977-80, Memphis and Shelby County Hosp. Auth., 1974-77; active Brooks Fine Arts Found., Tenn. Performing Arts Found., Public Concern Found. (Washington). Lt. cmdr. USN, 1942-45. Disting. Professorship in Polit. Econ. named in his honor Rhodes Coll., 1990; recipient Disting. Svc. award Salvation Army, 1970, Appreciation award Memphis State U. Sch. of Bus., 1970, Merit award City of Memphis, 1970, Achievement award Memphis Bicentennial Commn., 1976, Americanism award Memphis Civitan, 1976, Outstanding Citizen of Yr. award, 1982, Disting. Svc. medal Rhodes Coll., 1986, Liberty Bell award Memphis and Shelby County Bar Assn., 1982, Sertoma Svc. to Mankind award, 1982, Active Living award Sr. Citizen's Svcs., 1987, Community Svc. award Rotary Club, 1989, Joint Resolution of Citizen Commendation Tenn. Senate, 1989, Svc. award, Alzheimer's Assn., 1993, Pres. award Carnival Memphis, 1994; named Outstanding Businessman of Yr. Memphis State U., 1974, Educator of Yr. Greater Memphis State, Inc., 1974, Citizen of Yr. Newspaper Guild of Memphis, 1975, Memphis and Shelby County Optimist, 1982, Tenn. Acct. Hall of Fame, 1993. Mem. AICPAs, ABA (fed. and estate gift taxes), Am. Acctg. Assn., Nat. Assn. CPA Examiners, Tenn. Soc. CPAs, Nat. Tax. Assn., Tenn. Bar Assn., Tenn. State Bd. Accountancy, Mid-South Controllers Assn., Acad. Acctg. Historians, Estate Planning Coun. Memphis, Memphis Coll. Accountancy, Mil. Order World Wars, VFW, Am. Legion, Soc. Commd. Officers, Econ. Club Memphis (founder). Office: One Commerce S Ste 2190 Memphis TN 38103

**SEIFERT, LUKE MICHAEL,** lawyer; b. Smyrna, Tenn., Apr. 8, 1957; s. Donald R. and Joan (Clemas) S.; m. Kathleen Louise Schaffer, Aug. 1, 1980; children: Joseph, Nicholas, Peter, Rachel. BA, Creighton U., 1979; JD, William Mitchell Sch. of Law, St. Paul, 1983. Bar: U.S. Dist. Ct. Minn., Minn. Page Minn. Ho. of Reps., St. Paul, 1980, com. adminstr., 1981-82; assoc. Holmen Law Office, St. Cloud, Minn., 1983-87; pvt. practice St. Cloud, 1987-98; assoc. Quinlivan Law Firm, 1998—. Mem. ABA, Minn. Bar Assn., Minn. Trial Lawyers Assn., Minn. Def. Lawyers Assn., Stearns Benton Bar Assn. (sec., treas. 1986-87, v.p. 1987-88, pres. 1988-89), K.C. (guard 1986-87, advocate 1987-90), Delta Theta Phi. Workers' compensation, Personal injury, Criminal. Home: 1305 W Oakes Dr Saint Cloud MN 56303-0741 Office: Quinlivan Hughes Law Firm 600 Norwest Ctr Saint Cloud MN 56303

**SEIFERT, STEPHEN WAYNE,** lawyer, performing arts executive; b. Washington, May 25, 1957; s. Arthur John and Frances E. (Smith) S. BA summa cum laude, Yale U., 1979; JD, Stanford U., 1982. Bar: Colo. 1982, U.S. Dist. Ct. Colo. 1982, U.S. Ct. Appeals (10th cir.) 1982, U.S. Ct. Appeals (5th cir.) 1987, U.S. Supreme Ct. 1988. Ptnr.. Fairfield and Woods P.C., Denver, 1982-98; mng. dir. Fairfield & Woods P.C., Denver, 1990-92, 95-96; chmn. bd. dirs. Opera Colo., Denver, 1989-92, exec. dir., 1997—. Author: Colorado Creditors' Remedies--Debtors' Relief, 1990; contbg. author: Colorado Methods of Practice; contbr. articles to profl. jours. Trustee Denver Pub. Libr. Friends Found., Yale-Harvard Regatta Com., Allied Arts Inc., Rocky Mt. Region Inst. Internat. Edn. Mem. Law Club Denver (v.p. 1992-93, pres. 1993-94), Univ. Club, Phi Beta Kappa. Bankruptcy, Contracts commercial, General civil litigation.

**SEIFERT, THOMAS LLOYD,** lawyer; b. Boston, June 6, 1940; s. Ralph Frederick and Hazel Bell (Harrington) S.; m. Ann Cecelia Berg, June 19, 1965. BS cum laude, Ind. U., 1962, JD cum laude, 1965. Bar: Ill. 1965, Ind. 1965, N.Y. 1979. Assoc. law firm Keck, Mahin & Cate, Chgo., 1965-67; atty. Essex Group, Inc., Ft. Wayne, Ind., 1967-70, Amoco Corp., Chgo., 1970-73; assoc. gen. counsel, asst. sec. Canteen Corp., Chgo., 1973-75; sec., gen. counsel The Marmon Group, Inc. (and predecessor cos.), Chgo., 1975-78; v.p., gen. counsel, sec. Hanson Industries, Inc., N.Y.C., 1978-82; sr. v.p. law, chief fin. officer Petrie Stores Corp., N.Y.C., 1982-83; mem. Finley, Kumble, Wagner, Heine, Underberg, Manley, Myerson & Casey, N.Y.C., 1983-87, Paul, Weiss, Rifkind, Wharton & Garrison, N.Y.C., 1987-91; gen. counsel, chief legal officer Sterling Grace Capital Mgmt., L.P. and affiliated cos., N.Y.C., 1991—. Note editor Ind. Law Jour., 1964-65. Named to Ind. Track and Cross Country Hall of Fame, 1993. Mem. ABA, N.Y. State Bar Assn., Order of Coif, The Creek, Beta Gamma Sigma. General corporate, Real property, Mergers and acquisitions. Home: Museum Tower 15 W 53d St Apt 31 E New York NY 10019-5401 Office: Sterling Grace Capital Mgmt 515 Madison Ave Ste 2000 New York NY 10022-5403

**SEIFF, ERIC A.,** lawyer; b. Mt. Vernon, N.Y., Apr. 25, 1933; s. Arthur N. and Mathilde (Cohen) S.; m. Sari Ginsburg, June 26, 1960 (div. Oct. 1983); children: Judith C., E. Kenneth, Dean A.; m. Meredith Feinman, Jan. 15, 1984; children: Abigail, Sarah. BA, Yale U., 1955; LLB, Columbia U., 1958. Bar: N.Y. 1958, U.S. Dist. Ct. (so. dist.) N.Y. 1960, U.S. Dist. Ct. (ea. dist.) N.Y. 1981, U.S. Ct. Appeals (2d cir.) 1965, U.S. Supreme Ct. 1967. Assoc. Bower and O'Connor, N.Y.C., 1959-60, Yellin, Kramer & Levy, N.Y.C., 1961; asst. dist. atty. N.Y.C. Dist. Atty.'s Office, 1962-67; asst. counsel Agy. for Internat. Devel., Washington, 1967-70; counsel Agy. for Internat. Devel., Rio de Janeiro, 1970-72; gen. counsel N.Y. State Divsn. Criminal Justice Svcs., 1972-74; dep. chief atty. Legal Aid Soc. Criminal Def., N.Y.C., 1974-75; first dep. commr. N.Y. State Investigation Commn., 1975-77; chmn. N.Y. State Investigation Commn., N.Y.C., 1977-79; ptnr. Seiff, Kretz & Maffeo (formerly Scoppetta & Seiff), N.Y.C., 1981—; spl. dist. atty. Bronx County, 1986-89; spl. asst. atty. gen. State of N.Y., Gov.'s Task Force Investigating Conduct of Attica Prosecutions, 1975. Bd. dirs. Legal Aid Soc., N.Y.C., 1994—; Prisoners' Legal Svcs., N.Y.C., 1989—, Lawyers Fund for Client Protection, N.Y., 1980—. Recipient Frank S. Hogan Meml. award Frank S. Hogan Assn., 1994. Mem. N.Y. Criminal Bar Assn. (bd. dirs. 1980—, past pres.). Criminal, General civil litigation, Family and matrimonial. Office: Seiff Kretz & Maffeo 645 Madison Ave New York NY 10022-1010

**SEIGEL, JAN KEARNEY,** lawyer; b. Bayonne, N.J., Feb. 7, 1947; s. Max and Margaret (Kearney) S.; m. Judy L. Mascuch, Aug. 29, 1971; children: Margaret, Emily, Jonas, Luke. BSBA, Georgetown U., 1968, JD, 1971; LLM in Taxation, NYU, 1974. Bar: N.J. 1971, D.C. 1972, Ga. 1972, U.S. Ct. Appeals (3d cir.) 1979, U.S. Supreme Ct. 1979. Law sec. to Hon. Theodore Rosenberg Superior Ct. of N.J., Paterson, 1971-72; asst. prosecutor Passaic County Pros.'s Office, Paterson, 1972-76; pvt. practice Ridgewood, 1976-98; sr. ptnr. Seigel & Mongiardo, P.C., Ridgewood, N.J., 1990—; mem. faculty William Paterson Coll., 1974-79; lectr. N.J. Inst. for Continuing Edn., 1981—, N.J. State Bar and various county bar assns. Recipient Police Hon. Legion award Police Chiefs Assn. of N.J., 1980. Mem. ABA (rep. of N.J. young lawyers divsn. 1980-82), N.J. State Bar Assn. (Young Lawyer of Yr. award 1983, bd. trustees 1978-79), Passaic County Bar Assn. (bd. trustees 1973-81), Bergen County Bar Assn. Personal injury, Criminal. Office: Seigel & Mongiardo 505 Goffle Rd Ridgewood NJ 07450-4027

**SEIGFREID, JAMES THOMAS,** lawyer; b. Kansas City, Mo., Nov. 5, 1931; s. Ira Jerome and Irene A. (Welling) S.; m. Donna Lee Olsen, Aug. 20, 1955; children: James T. Jr., Mark W., Stephen L., Susan Seigfreid Crowe. BA, U. Mo., 1953, JD, 1955. Bar: Mo. 1955, U.S. Dist. Ct. (we. dist.) Mo. 1957, U.S. Ct. Appeals (8th cir.) 1958, U.S. Ct. Appeals (10th cir.) 1972, U.S. Tax Ct. 1989. Atty. Dietrich Davis Burrell Dicus & Rowlands, Kansas City, 1957-74; atty., pres., mng. dir. Seigfreid Bingham Levy Selzer & Gee P.C., Kansas City, 1974—; sec., bd. dirs. Hunt Midwest Real Estate Devel., Kansas City, Hunt Midwest Enterprises, Kansas City Chiefs Football Club Inc., Chiefs' Children's Fund. 1st lt. JAGC, USAF, 1955-57. Recipient St. Thomas More award, 1968, Skill Integrity & Responsibility award Associated Gen. Contractors, Jefferson City, Mo., 1991. Mem. ABA, Mo. Bar Assn., Metro. Bar Assn., Mission Hills Country Club. Roman Catholic. Avocations: golf, travel, reading. General corporate, Entertainment, Estate planning. Office: Seigfreid Bingham Levy Selzer & Gee PC 911 Main St Ste 2800 Kansas City MO 64105-5301

**SEIGLER, MICHAEL EDWARD,** lawyer, librarian; b. Tallahassee, Oct. 14, 1948; s. Claude Milo and Roberta Bradford (Whitfield) S.; m. Janet Cummings, Feb. 19, 1971; children: Kelly Elizabeth, Megan Whitfield. AA, Lake Sumter C.C., 1968; BS, Fla. State U., 1970, MS, 1974; JD, Atlanta Law Sch., 1980. Bar: Ga. 1980, U.S. Ct. Appeals (5th cir.) 1980, U.S. Ct. Appeals (11th cir.) 1980, U.S. Tax Ct. 1985, U.S. Supreme Ct. 1985, Cert. tchr., libr. Tchr., Sumter Correctional Inst., Bushnell, Fla., 1970-73; asst. libr. dir. Leesburg Pub. Libr. (Fla.), 1974-75, libr. dir., 1975-77; libr. dir. Atlanta Law Sch., 1979-81; atty. Brooks & Brock, Marietta, Ga., 1981-83; libr. Port Charlotte Pub. Libr. (Fla.), 1983-84; assoc. Brooks & Brock, Marietta, Ga., 1985, Brock & Barr, Marietta, 1985-86; Brock & Clay, 1987; judge pro hoc vice State Ct. of Cobb County, 1986; pvt. practice, 1988—; asst. dir. Pine Mountain Regional Libr., 1988-95; libr. dir. Smyrna Pub. Libr. Contbr. articles to jours. Vol. worker ACLU, Atlanta, 1979; mem. Fla. State U. Libr. Com., Tallahassee, 1974, Children's Program Com., Port Charlotte, 1983, Port Charlotte Cultural Ctr. Adv. Com., 1984, Pine Mountain Arts Coun., past bd. dirs.; mem. Cobb County Dem. Exec. Com., 1986-87; exec. com. Cobb Christmas, 1986-87. Named Tchr. of Yr., Sumter Correctional Inst., 1973. Mem. Nat. Libr. Assn. (com. chmn. 1975-76), Fla. Libr. Assn. (caucus chmn. 1976-77), Ga. Libr. Assn. (mem. com. chmn. 1992—, sec. 1993-94, parliamentarian 1997, 1st v.p. 1999), Metro Atlanta Libr. Assn. (v.p. 1997, pres. 1998), Southeastern Libr. Assn. (mem. com. 1988—), ALA, ABA, Cobb County Bar Assn. (com mem.), Atlanta Law Sch. Alumni Assn. (treas. 1986-90), Fla. State U. Alumni Assn. (life), Ga. Libr. Video Assn. (pres. 1991-92), Mensa (sec 1987, 89, pres. Ga. chpt. 1988, trustee Mensa Edn. and Rsch. Found., Leadership Meriwether 1992, pres. 1993). Democrat. Episcopalian. Lodges: Masons (sr. steward Gate City Lodge 2), Scottish Rite. Condemnation, Insurance, Taxation, general. Home: 3023 Bay Berry Dr SW Marietta GA 30008-5674 Office: 100 Village Green Cir SE Smyrna GA 30080-3478

**SEILER, JAMES ELMER,** judge; b. LaCrosse, Wis., Sept. 2, 1946; s. Elmer Bernard and Margaret Theresa (Mader) S.; m. Sonia Gonzales, Feb. 9, 1968; children: Rebecca, Cristina. BA, U. Wis., LaCrosse, 1968; JD, U. Wis., 1973. Bar: Wis. 1973, Minn. 1981, U.S. Supreme Ct. 1985, Mo. 1986. Pvt. practice Balsam Lake, Wis., 1973-81; in-house counsel Farm Credit Banks, St. Paul, 1981-85; corp. counsel Hussmann Corp., St. Louis, 1985-94; adminstrv. law judge Social Security, Evansville, Ind., 1994-95, Office of Hearings and Appeals, Creve Coeur, Mo., 1995—; chief adminstrv. law judge Hearing Office, Creve Coeur, Mo., 1997—. Candidate Dist. Atty., Polk County, Wis., 1980. With U.S. Army, 1969-71. Avocations: soccer coach, swimming, water skiing, running. Home: 18 Harbor Point Ct Lake Saint Louis MO 63367-1336 Office: 11475 Olde Cabin Rd Saint Louis MO 63141-7130

**SEINFELD, LESTER,** lawyer; b. Chgo., Mar. 22, 1911; s. Sigmund and Celia (Neumann) S.; m. Sylvia M. Moises, Mar. 10, 1935; children: Deanne Rubinstein, Dennis G. LLB, U. Wash., 1935. Bar: U.S. Dist. Ct. (so. dist.) Wash., U.S. Supreme Ct. Assoc. Davies Pearson, P.C., Tacoma, Wash. State civil litigation, Contracts commercial, Probate. Office: Davies Pearson PC 920 S Fawcett Ave Tacoma WA 98402-5606

**SEITELMAN, MARK ELIAS,** lawyer; b. N.Y.C., Apr. 14, 1955; s. Leo Henry and Pearl (Elias) S. BA, Bklyn. Coll., 1976; JD, Bklyn. Law Sch., 1979. Bar: N.Y. 1980, U.S. Dist. Ct. (ea., so., and we. dists.) N.Y. 1980, U.S. Supreme Ct. 1990, U.S. Ct. Mil. Appeals, 1995. Law asst. Criminal Ct., Bklyn., 1979; law clk. to Hon. Justice Aaron D. Bernstein N.Y. Supreme Ct., Bklyn., 1980; assoc. Lester, Schwab, Katz & Dwyer, N.Y.C., 1981-87, Weg and Myers, 1987-88, Kroll & Tract, 1988-90; pvt. practice N.Y.C., 1990—.

Appeared on WABC TV Eyewitness News; interviewed by N.Y. Daily News, N.Y. Newsday. Mem. ABA, ATLA (sustaining mem. motor vehicle and small practice sect.), N.Y. State Bar Assn., N.Y. County Bar Assn. (ins. and supreme ct. coms.), N.Y. State Trial Lawyers Assn. (sustaining mem., bd. dirs., mem. spkrs. bur., conv. com., legis. com., contbg. editor Trial Lawyers Quar.), N.Y. State Trial Lawyers Inst. (CLE program chmn., lectr.), Bklyn. Bar Assn. (legis. com., employment law com.). Insurance, Product liability, Personal injury. Office: 233 Broadway Rm 901 New York NY 10279-0999

**SEITMAN, JOHN MICHAEL,** lawyer, arbitrator, mediator; b. Bloomington, Ill., Feb. 9, 1942. BS, U. Ill., 1964, JD, 1966. Bar: Calif., U.S. Dist. Ct. (so., cen., no. and ea. dists.) Calif., U.S. Ct. Appeals (9th cir.). Prin. Lindley, Lazar & Scales, San Diego, 1966-97; mediator, arbitrator, mem. Calif. adv. coun. for Large, Complex Case Panel, Am. Arbitration Assn.; lectr. in continuing legal edn. Bd. dirs. San Diego County Bar Found., 1983-89, treas., 1983-84, pres., 1988-89; del. to 9th Cir. Jud. Conf., 1986, 88. Fellow Am. Bar Found.; mem. ABA, State Bar Calif. (pres. 1991-92), San Diego County Bar Assn. (pres. 1986). General civil litigation, Consumer commercial, General practice. Office: PO Box 2156 Del Mar CA 92014-1456

**SEITTER, DAVID CHARLES,** lawyer; b. Omaha, Oct. 13, 1954; s. Robert Lee and Elizabeth (Frandzen) S.; m. Rebecca Lynn Hopper, Mar. 29, 1986. BA, Washburn U., 1976, JD, 1979. Bar: Kans. 1980, U.S. Dist. Ct. Kans. 1980, U.S. Ct. Appeals (10th cir.) 1980, Mo. 1985, U.S. Dist. Ct. Mo. 1996. Assoc. Wagner, Leek & Mullins, Roeland Park, Kans., 1979-85; ptnr. Perry & Hamill, Overland Park, Kans., 1985-89; ptnr. Levy & Craig, Overland Park, 1989-97, Kansas City, Mo., 1997—; bd. dirs. Alpha Point, Inc., Marrilac; lectr. seminars on bankruptcy litigation to various orgns., 1988; trustee panel U.S. Bankruptcy Ct. Kans., 1984—. Diplomat Children's Mercy Hosp. Mem. Kans. Bar Assn. (continuing legal edn. com., pres. bankruptcy and insolvency sect. 1998—), Eastern Kans. Bank Coun., Phi Kappa Phi, Sigma Phi Epsilon. Methodist. Mergers and acquisitions, Bankruptcy, General corporate. Home: 14606 W 83rd Pl Lenexa KS 66215-6111 Office: Levy & Craig 911 Main St Ste 2000 Kansas City MO 64105-5331

**SEITZ, PATRICIA ANN,** lawyer; b. Washington, DC, Sept. 2, 1946; d. Richard J. and Bettie Jean (Merrill) S.; m. Alan Graham Greer, Aug. 14, 1981. BA in History cum laude, Kans. State U., 1968; JD, Georgetown U., 1973. Bar: Fla. 1973, D.C. 1975, U.S. Dist. Ct. (no., mid., so. dists., trial bar) Fla., U.S. Ct. Appeals (5th and eleventh cir.), U.S. Supreme Ct. Reporter Dallas Times Herald, Washington, 1970-73; law clk. to Hon. Charles R. Rickey U.S. Dist. Ct., Washington, 1973-74; assoc. Steel, Hector & Davis, Miami, Fla., 1974-79, ptnr., 1980-96; dir. office legal counsel Office of Nat. Drug Control Policy, Exec. Office of Pres., Washington, 1996-97; judge U.S. Dist. Ct. (so. dist.) Fla., 1998—; adj. faculty U. Miami Law Sch., Coral Gables, Fla., 1984-88; faculty Nat. Inst. Trial Advocacy, Boulder, Colo., 1982, 83, 95, Chapel Hill, N.C., 1984, 87. Fla. region, 1989; lectr. in field. Contbr. numerous articles to law jours. Mem. Dade Munroe Mental Health Bd., Miami, 1982-84, United Way of Greater Miami comty. devel. com., 1984-87; chmn. family abuse task force United Way of Greater Miami, 1986; chmn. devel. com. Miami City Ballet, 1986-87, bd. dirs., 1986-90. Fellow Am. Bar Found., Am. Bd. Trial Advocacy, Internat. Soc. Barristers; mem. ABA (chmn. various coms. 1979-85, Ho. Dels. 1992-96), Am. Arbitration Assn. (nat. bd. dirs. 1995-97, complex case panel arbitrator), The Fla. Bar (bd. govs. young lawyer divsn. 1981-82, bd. govs. 1986-92, pres. 1993-94, bd. cert. civil trial), Fla. Assn. Women Lawyers, Dade County Bar Assn. (pub. interest law bank). Roman Catholic. Avocations: travel, art. Office: Fed Courthouse Square 301 N Miami Ave Fl 5 Miami FL 33128-7702

**SEKIYA, GERALD YOSHINORI,** lawyer; b. Honolulu, Aug. 28, 1942; s. Shoji and Yachiyo (Baba) S.; m. Fay Naomi Shioji, Aug. 7, 1965; children: Jan, Gregory, Derek. BSEE, U. Ill., 1965; JD, U. Calif., San Francisco, 1968. Bar: Calif. 1968, Hawaii 1969, U.S. Dist. Ct. Hawaii, U.S. Dist. Ct. (no. dist.) Calif. 1968, U.S. Ct. Appeals (9th cir.) 1968, U.S. Supreme Ct. 1987. Law clk. U.S. Dist. Ct. (no. dist.), San Francisco, 1968-70; assoc., ptnr. Pratt, Moore, Bortz & Case, Honolulu, 1970-73; ptnr. Cronin, Fried, Sekiya, Kekina & Fairbanks, Honolulu, 1973—; reader Calif. State Bar Exam Com., San Francisco, 1970; mem. Hawaii Supreme Ct. Civil Rules Com., Honolulu, 1984—; mem. Hawaii Supreme Ct. Family Ct. Rules Com., 1989—; commr. Hawaii Jud. Arbitration Com., 1985—, Jud. Conduct Com., 1993—, chmn., 1994—. Coach Hawaii Kai Community Activities, 1978-80; mgr. Manoa Youth League. Mem. Am. Bd. Trial Advocates (pres. 1996—), Am. Inns of Ct. IV, Hawaii Bar Assn. (dir. 1980-81, 85-86), Hawaii Trial lawyers Assn. (pres. 1979), Hawaii Acad. Plaintiff Attys. (pres. 1985), Am. Coll. Trial Lawyers, Order of Coif. General civil litigation, Personal injury. Office: Cronin Fried Sekiya Kekina & Fairbanks 841 Bishop St Ste 1900 Honolulu HI 96813-3962

**SEKULOW, JAY ALAN,** lawyer; b. 1956. BA, JD cum laude, Mercer U. Bar: Ga. 1980. Chief counsel Am. Ctr. for Law and Justice, Virginia Beach, 1990—, European Ctr. for Law and Justice, 1998—; adj. prof. law Regent U. Author: From Intimidation to Victory, 1990, Knowing Your Rights, 1993, Students Rights and the Public School, And Nothing But The Truth, 1996, Christian Rights in the Workplace, 1997. Office: Am Ctr for Law & Justice 1000 Regent University Dr Virginia Beach VA 23464-5037

**SELBY, MYRA CONSETTA,** state supreme court justice; b. Bay City, Mich., July 1, 1955; d. Ralph Irving and Archie Mae (Franklin) S.; m. Bruce Curry; 1 child, Lauren. BA with honors, Kalamazoo (Mich.) Coll., 1977; JD, U. Mich., 1980. Bar: D.C. 1980, Ind. 1983, U.S. Dist. Ct. (so. dist.) 1983, Ct. Appeals (D.C. cir.) 1984, U.S. Ct. Appeals (8th cir.) 1985. Assoc. Seyfarth, Shaw, Fairweather & Geraldson, Washington, 1980-83; ptnr. Ice, Miller, Donadio & Ryan, Indpls., 1983-93; dir. Ind. Healthcare Policy, 1993-94; assoc. justice Ind. Supreme Ct., 1995—. Bd. dirs. Alpha Nursing Home, Flanner House, Inpls. Ballet Theatre. Avocations: soccer, biking, reading, ballet. Office: Ind Supreme Ct 312 State House 200 W Washington St Indianapolis IN 46204-2732*

**SELCHICK, JEFFREY MARK,** arbitrator, judge; b. N.Y.C., July 22, 1951; s. Bernard and Irene Selchick; m. Cathy Lynn Persans, Jan. 26, 1974; children: Lauren Anne, Brian Bernard, Karen Ruth, Alyson Hope. BA, SUNY, Plattsburgh, 1971; JD, Union U., Albany, N.Y., 1975. Bar: N.Y. 1976, U.S. Dist. Ct. (no. dist.) N.Y. 1976, U.S. Supreme Ct. 1979. Asst. counsel SUNY, Albany, 1975-76; asst. counsel N.Y. State Gov.'s Office of Employee Rels., Albany, 1976-78, dep. counsel, dir. litigation, 1978-82; arbitrator Albany, 1982—; adj. prof. law Union U., Albany, 1989-92; instr. Cornell U., Ithaca, N.Y., 1982-85; cons. N.Y. State Labor-Mgmt. Inst., Albany, 1985—; judge Village of Menands, N.Y., 1986—. Mem. Am. Arbitration Assn., Nat. Acad. Arbitrators, N.Y. State Magistrate's Assn., N.Y. State Bar Assn. Avocations: jogging, competitive pistol shooting, writing. Home and Office: PO Box 11-280 Albany NY 12211-0280

**SELFRIDGE, GORDON PHILLIP,** lawyer; b. Phila., Nov. 1, 1949; s. William John and Jean (Dornsife) S.; m. Maureen Elizabeth Cullen, July 21, 1990; 1 child, William Cullen. BA cum laude, Wake Forest U., 1971; JD, U. Miami, 1974; LLM in Environ. Law, George Washington U., 1977. Bar: Fla. 1974, D.C. 1975, Tex. 1979. Staff atty. NOAA, Washington, 1974-77, Mobil Oil Corp., Dallas, 1977-81; sr. atty. Sunoco Energy Devel. Corp., Dallas, 1981-83; pvt. practice Dallas, 1983-85; chief dep. county atty. Palm Beach County Atty.'s Office, West Palm Beach, Fla., 1985—. Contbg. editor mag. Directions, 1973-74; author law rev. environ. Law, 1976. Mem. West Palm Beach Water Catchment Adv. Bd., 1988&; bd. dirs., v.p. Pioneer Lakes Homeowners Assn., West Palm Beach, 1990—. Mem. ABA, Fla. Bar Assn., Tex. Bar Assn., D.C. Bar Assn. Avocations: sports, theater, science. Home: 7281 Pioneer Lakes Cir West Palm Beach FL 33413-2254

**SELIGMAN, DELICE,** lawyer; b. Worcester, Mass.; m. Frederick Seligman. AB, Clark U., MA; JD, NYU, 1971. Bar: N.Y. 1972, U.S. Dist. Ct. (so. and ea. dists.) N.Y. 1973, U.S. Supreme Ct. 1979. Assoc. Legal Aid Soc. Nassau County, Mineola, N.Y., 1972-76; ptnr. Seligman, Stein & Abromowitz, Garden City, 1976-86, Seligman & Seligman, N.Y.C., N.Y., 1986—; legal counsel Contemporary Sculptors, Roslyn, N.Y., 1987-90, Artists Network Great Neck, N.Y., 1987-90, Woodstock Animal Rights Movement, Legal Action for Animals, Stop Graffiti Now, Inc.; pres. Wildlife Legal Action, Inc. Bd. dirs. For Our Children and Us, Hicksville, N.Y., 1985—. Mem. Nassau Women's Bar Assn. (pres. 1982-83), Bar Assn. Nassau County (chairperson arts com. 1984-85), Phi Alpha Delta. Art, Entertainment. Home: Runge Rd Shokan NY 12481 Office: 26 Broadway New York NY 10004-1703 also: Seligman & Seligman 70 Main St Kingston NY 12401-3802

**SELIGMAN, FREDERICK,** lawyer; b. Bklyn.; s. Martin and Florence (Alperin) S.; m. Delice Felice. AB, Clark U., 1957; JD, N.Y. Law Sch., 1972. Bar: N.Y. 1973, U.S. Dist. Ct. (so. and ea. dists.) N.Y. 1974, U.S. Tax Ct. 1974, U.S. Ct. Appeals (2d cir.) 1975, U.S. Supreme Ct. 1979. Atty. N.Y.C. (N.Y.) Police Dept., 1972-73; asst. dist. atty. N.Y. County, N.Y.C., 1973-79; pvt. practice N.Y.C., 1980-85; ptnr. Seligman & Seligman, N.Y.C., 1986—. Mem. N.Y.C. Criminal Bar Assn., N.Y. State Defenders Assn. Criminal, General practice. Home: Runge Rd Shokan NY 12481 Office: Seligman & Seligman 26 Broadway New York NY 10004-1703

**SELIGMAN, GUY JAIME,** lawyer; b. Miami, Fla., Sept. 20, 1959; s. Harold and June Seligman; m. Naomi Small, Jan. 7, 1990; children: Noah, Cole. BS in Bus., Nova Southeastern U., 1984, JD, 1986. Bar: Fla. 1988. Atty. Dade State Atty.'s Office, Miami, 1986; pub. defender Broward County Pub. Defender's Office, Ft. Lauderdale, Fla., 1987; atty. in pvt. practice Ft. Lauderdale, 1988—. Mem. ABA, Am. Trial Lawyers Assn., Broward Criminal Def. Bar Assn. (bd. dirs.), Fla. Masons (master). Avocations: pro bono representations of childrens issues and Native American issues. Criminal, Appellate. Office: 320 SE 9th St Fort Lauderdale FL 33316-1128

**SELIGMAN, JOEL,** dean; b. N.Y.C., Jan. 11, 1950; s. Selig Jacob and Muriel (Bienstock) S.; m. Friederike Felber, July 30, 1981; children: Andrea, Peter. AB magna cum laude, UCLA, 1971; JD, Harvard U., 1974. Bar: Calif. 1975. Atty., writer Corp. Accountability Rsch. Group, Washington, 1974-77; prof. law Northeastern U. Law Sch., 1977-83, George Washington U., 1983-86, U. Mich., Ann Arbor, 1986-95; dean law U. Ariz., Tucson, 1995-99; dean sch. law Washington U., St. Louis, 1999—; cons. Fed. Trade Commn., 1979-82, Dept. Transp., 1983, Office Tech. Assessment, 1988-89. Author (with others) Constitutionalizing the Corporation: The Case for the Federal Chartering of Giant Corporations, 1976, The High Citadel: The Influence of Harvard Law School, 1978, The Transformation of Wall Street: A History of the Securities and Exchange Commission and Modern Corporate Finance, 1982, The SEC and the Future of Finance, 1985, (multi-volume) Securities Regulation; contbr. articles to profl. jours. Mem. State Bar Calif., Am. Law Inst. (adv. com., advisor corp. governance project). Office: Wash U Sch Law CB 1120 1 Brookings Dr Saint Louis MO 63130-4862

**SELIGMANN, WILLIAM ROBERT,** lawyer, author; b. Davenport, Iowa, Oct. 10, 1956; s. William Albert and Barbara Joyce (Carmichael) S.; m. Carole Lee Francis; children: D Anna, Matthew. BA, U. Calif., Santa Barbara, 1979; JD, Santa Clara U., 1982. Bar: Calif. 1983, U.S. Dist. Ct. (no. dist.) Calif. 1983. Assoc. Office of J.R. Dempster, Cupertino, Calif., 1983-85; city atty. City of Campbell, Calif., 1985—; ptnr. Dempster, Seligmann & Raineri, Los Gatos, Calif., 1985—; judge pro tem, Santa Clara County, 1992—. Bd. dirs. Los Gatos C. of C. Mem. Santa Clara County Bar Assn. (civil practice com., judiciary com.). Avocations: cross country skiing, scuba diving, swimming, writing, Aikido. General civil litigation, Land use and zoning (including planning), Real property. Office: Dempster Seligmann & Raineri 455 Los Gatos Blvd Ste 208 Los Gatos CA 95032-5523

**SELKIRK, ALEXANDER MACDONALD, JR.,** lawyer; b. Jamaica, N.Y., Oct. 2, 1943; s. Alexander MacDonald and Anne (Roth) S.; m. Joanne Patrician Diskant, July 21, 1974; children: Marianne C., Victoria L. BA in Polit. Sci., St. Johns U., Jamaica, 1965; JD, N.Y. Law Sch., 1970; LLM in Trade Regulation, NYU, 1973. Bar: N.Y. 1971, U.S. Dist. Ct. (so. and ea. dists.) N.Y. 1972, U.S. Ct. Appeals (2d cir.) 1972, U.S. Supreme Ct. 1976, Fla. 1991. Sr. staff atty. Hartford Ins. Co., N.Y.C., 1971-74; assoc. Richard C. Mooney, Esq., Hempstead, N.Y., 1974-77; sr. trial atty. Home Ins. Co., Huntington Sta., N.Y., 1978-80; asst. county atty. Suffolk County, Hauppauge, N.Y., 1980-88; assoc. Garcia & Stallone Esqs., Melville, N.Y., 1988-90, CIGNA Ins. Co., Woodbury, N.Y., 1990-95; trial counsel Martin Fallon Mulle, Huntington, N.Y., 1995—; arbitrator Suffolk County Dist. Ct. 10th Jud. Dist., 1982—; instr. N.Y. State JAG's Sch., 1997—. Feature writer Ronkonkoma Rev., 1986—; contbr. articles to legal publs. Committeeman Suffolk Country Rep. Com., Ronkonkoma, N.Y., 1977—; del. 10th Jud. Dist. Conv. Suffolk County, 1981-84; v.p. Holbrook Rep. Club, 1979-81, pres., 1981-83; bd. dirs. Holbrook Youth Devel. Corp., 1985—; pilot legal officer Nassau sr. squadron CAP, 1978-84; counsel. Com. for A Drug Free Holbrook, 1988—. Maj. JACG, N.Y. Army N.G., 1983—. Mem. Am. Arbitration Assn. (comml. arbitrator), N.Y. State Bar Assn., Internat. Platform Assn., Suffolk Country Bar Assn., NYU Alumni Assn., Holbrook C. of C. (bd. dirs. 1981—, v.p. 1987-89, pres. 1984-91, 92-93), Gt. Neck (N.Y.) Sportsman's Club, KC (adv. 1981-84, 87—, trustee 1984-87), Lions (bd. dirs. 1985-86, v.p. 1986-87, pres. 1987-88). Roman Catholic. Home: 12 Glen Summer Rd Holbrook NY 11741-5006 Office: Martin Fallon Mulle 100 E Carver St Huntington NY 11743-3593

**SELLERS, BARBARA JACKSON,** federal judge; b. Richmond, Va., Oct. 3, 1940; m. Richard F. Sellers; children: Elizabeth M., Anne W., Catherine A. Attended, Baldwin-Wallace Coll., 1958-60; BA cum laude, Ohio State U., 1962; JD magna cum laude, Capital U. Law Sch., Columbus, Ohio, 1979. Bar: Ohio 1979, U.S. Dist. Ct. (so. dist.) Ohio 1981, U.S. Ct. Appeals (6th cir.), 1986. Jud. law clk. Hon. Robert J. Sidman, U.S. Bankruptcy Judge, Columbus, Ohio, 1979-81; assoc. Lasky & Semons, Columbus, 1981-82; jud. law clk. to Hon. Thomas M. Herbert, U.S. Bankrupcty Ct., Columbus, 1982-84; assoc. Baker & Hostetler, Columbus, 1984-86; U.S. bankruptcy judge So. Dist. Ohio, Columbus, 1986—; lectr. on bankruptcy univs., insts., assns. Recipient Am. Jurisprudence prize contracts and criminal law, 1975-76, evidence and property, 1976-77, Corpus Juris Secundum awards, 1975-76, 76-77. Mem. Columbus Bar Assn., Am. Bankruptcy Inst., Nat. Conf. Bankruptcy Judges, Order of Curia, Phi Beta Kappa. Office: US Bankruptcy Ct 170 N High St Columbus OH 43215-2403

**SELLERS, JILL SUZANNE,** lawyer; b. Baton Rouge, Oct. 24, 1967; d. Tommy Davis Sellers and Rhonda Lynn (Zimmerman) Ross. BA, La. State U., 1988; vis. student cum laude, Suffolk U. Sch. Law, 1991-92; JD, Franklin Pierce Law Ctr., 1992. Bar: Mass. 1993, U.S. Dist. Ct. 1993, U.S. Ct. Appeals (1st cir.) 1993. Summer assoc. Law Office of Robert Hernandez, Malden, Mass., 1990; vol. intern Disability Rights Ctr., Concord, N.H., 1990, N.H. Pub. Defender, Manchester, N.H., 1991, N.H. Appellate Defender, Concord, 1991; summer assoc. Law Office of David Bownes, Laconia, N.H., 1991; vol. legal asst. Com. for Pub. Counsel Svcs., Dedham, Mass., 1992; atty. Jill S. Sellers, Atty. at Law, Concord, 1994-95; atty., bar adv./pub. defender Middlesex Def. Attys., Inc., Concord, 1993-95; atty. Law Office of Robert S. Potters P.C., Boston, 1992-95; notary pub., Mass., 1994; pub. defender divsn. Com. for Pub. Counsel Svcs., 1995—. Vol./chair vols. Habitat for Humanity, Roxbury, Mass., 1994. Mem. ATLA (state gov. young lawyers sect. 1993-94, 94-95-96, liaison 1993-95-96, sec./treas. criminal law sect. 1993-94, 1st vice-chair criminal law sect. 1995-96, chair criminal law sect. 1996—, spkr. 1996, Pub. Svc. award 1994), Mass. Acad. Trial Attys. (exec. com. young lawyers sect. 1994-95), Mass. Assn. Criminal Def. Attys., Boston Bar Assn., Cen. Middlesex Bar Assn. Democrat. Avocations: gymnastics-coaching and participating, reading, cooking. Criminal, General practice, Personal injury. Office: Ste 408 One Salem Green Salem MA 01970 Address: 5D Nimitz Way Salem MA 01970-2747

**SELLERS, JOHN W.,** lawyer; b. San Diego, May 3, 1965; s. John W. and Patricia A. (Costello) S.; m. Bonnie A. Sellers, Oct. 17, 1987; children: Elliott M., Amelia K. BS summa cum laude, Ea. N.Mex. U., Portales, 1992; JD, Seton Hall U., 1995. Sys. analyst USAF, 1984-92; pres., exec. officer Enterprise N.J., Inc., Newark, 1993-94; rsch. asst. Seton Hall U., Newark, 1993-94; summer assoc. Edwards & Antholis, Morristown, N.J., 1994-95; atty. DynCorp, Reston, Va., 1995-98; trial atty. asset forfeiture and money laundering sect. U.S. Dept. of Justice, Washington, 1999—. Republican. Roman Catholic. Administrative and regulatory, Federal civil litigation, Criminal. Office: US Dept Justice Rm 10100 1400 New York Ave NW Washington DC 20005

**SELLERS, MARC KELLOGG,** lawyer; b. Santa Maria, Calif., Apr. 18, 1953; s. Robert Donald and Lois Maureen (Adams) S.; m. Jolie Anne Sullivan, Oct. 24, 1987; children: Morgan, Blaire. BS, U. Redlands, 1975; JD, Loyola U., 1978; LLM, Georgetown U., 1980. Bar: Calif. 1978, Oreg. 1979, U.S. Dist. Ct. Oreg., U.S. Dist. Ct. Calif., U.S. Ct. Appeals (9th cir.), U.S. Supreme Ct. Shareholder Schwabe, Williamson & Wyatt, Portland, Oreg., 1987—, assoc., 1990-96; dir. Beaverton (Oreg.) Rotary Found., 1997—. Mem. Beaverton Rotary (pres. 1998-99, Paul Harris fellow 1992, Rotarian of Yr. 1997). Avocations: karate, mountain climbing, kayaking, motorcycling. Taxation, general, Criminal, Environmental. Office: Schwabe Williamson and Wyatt 1800 Pacwest Ctr 1211 SW 5th Ave Ste 1600 Portland OR 97204-3795

**SELTZER, JEFFREY LLOYD,** investment banker; b. Bklyn., July 27, 1956; s. Bernard and Sue (Harris) S.; m. Ana Isabel Sifre, Sept. 2, 1985; children: Ian Alexander, Pamela Allison. BS in Econs. cum laude, U. Pa., 1978; JD, Georgetown U., 1981. Bar: N.Y. 1982. Assoc. Austrian, Lance & Stewart, N.Y.C., 1981-85; assoc. gen. counsel, asst. v.p. Shearson Lehman Bros., N.Y.C., 1986; mng. dir. Lehman Bros., N.Y.C., 1986-94; dep. chmn., mng. dir. CIBC Oppenheimer Corp., N.Y.C., 1994—; spl. prof. law Hofstra U., 1999—. Author: The U.S. Greeting Card Market, 1977, Starting and Organizing a Business, 1984, Swap Risk Management: A Primer, 1988, A View for the Top: The Role of the Board of Directors and Senior Management in the Derivatives Business, 1995, Financial Strategy Roundtable: Derivatives, 1995. Mem. Nat. Policy Forum, 1994-97; mem. securities industry coalition Bush-Quayle campaign, 1992; mem. U.S. Trade Adv. Com. on Svc. Industries, Washington, 1990-94; small bus. adv. coun. Rep. Nat. Com., Washington, 1984-90; nat. adv. coun. U.S. SBA, 1982-87; advisor Friends of Giuliani, N.Y.C., 1989, New Yorkers for Lew Lehrman, N.Y.C., 1981-82; policy analyst Reagan-Bush Com., Arlington, Va., 1980; dir. Nassau County Sports Commn., 1997—, mem. exec. com.; mem. fiscal mgmt. adv. bd. County of Nassau; adv. bd. Huntsman Program on Internat. Studies and Bus., U. Pa., 1997—; chmn. Class 1978 fundraising U. Pa., 1997—; vice chmn., trustee Inst. Internat. Bankers, 1999—. Recipient Disting. Alumnus award W. C. Mepham H.S., 1994. Mem. ABA, Re. Nat. Lawyers Assn., Federalist Soc., Ctr. for Study of Presidency, Securities Industry Assn. (chmn. swap and derivative products com. 1990-94). Home: 3 Yates Ln Jericho NY 11753-1418 Office: 425 Lexington Ave New York NY 10017-3903

**SELVIG, JETTIE PIERCE,** lawyer; b. Bee Branch, Ark., Dec. 16, 1932; d. Jefferson Davis Pierce and Ruba Ann Bivens; m. Rolf S. Selvig Sr., Jan. 27, 1962; children: Rolf S. Jr., Erik K., John L. LLB, U. Ark., 1954. Bar: Ark. 1953, Calif. 1961, U.S. Supreme Ct. 1969. Pvt. practice, 1961—. Bd. dirs. San Francisco Neighborhood Legal Assistance Found. Recipient Cert. of Honor, Bd. Suprs. of City and County of San Francisco, 1969, Countess of Pulaski Proclamation, Quorum Ct. of Pulaski County, 1969, Silver Bowl of Appreciation, Girl Scouts Am.; named Hidden Heroine, San Francisco Bay Girl Scout Coun., 1976. Mem. ABA, Nat. Assn. Women Lawyers (life, state del., assembly del., bus. mgr., treas., v.p., pres.-elect, pres. 1969-70, chairperson, mem. women in pub. svc. com. 1971-75), Calif. State Bar (disciplinary com. 1972-74), Calif. Applicants' Attys. Assn. (dir. No. Calif. chpt. 1974, v.p. 1975, pres. 1976, 77, sec. and pres.-elect statewide assn., pres. statewide assn. 1981-82, life mem.), Queen's Bench (asst. sec.-treas., dir. 1972, treas. 1973, mem. Law Day com., chmn. publicity com., v.p. 1974, pres. 1975, Lifetime Achievement award 1995), Queen's Bench Found. (pres. 1974-76), Bar Assn. San Francisco, Women's Equity Action League (treas. Calif. divsn. 1970-72, pres. Calif. divsn. 1973), Legal Aid Soc. San Francisco (bd. dirs. 1976), Lawyer's Club San Francisco (life), del. to state bar conv.). Democrat. Fax: 415-981-0176. E-mail: jettie@ricochet.net. Workers' compensation, Probate. Office: 465 California St Ste 718 San Francisco CA 94104-1818

**SELWOOD, PIERCE TAYLOR,** lawyer; b. Evanston, Ill., July 31, 1939; s. Pierce Wilson and Alice (Taylor) S.; m. Alexis Fuerbringer, June 8, 1964; children: Allison, Jonathan. AB, Princeton U., 1961; JD, Harvard U., 1964. Bar: Calif. 1965, U.S. Dist. Ct. (cen. dist. ) Calif. 1965, U.S. Dist. Ct. (no. dist.) Calif. 1966, U.S. Dist. Ct. (ea. dist. ) Calif. 1989, U.S. Ct. Appeals (9th cir.) 1970. Assoc. Sheppard, Mullin, Richter & Hampton, L.A., 1964-70, ptnr., 1971—, chmn. litigation dept., 1986-91; lectr. Calif. Continuing Edn. Bar, Berkley, 1970-84, Practicing Law Inst., N.Y.C., 1980s, ABA Nat. Inst., Chgo., 1986. Mem. ABA (chmn. various subcoms. 1984-89), Calif. Bar Assn., L.A. County Bar Assn., Assn. Bus. Trial Lawyers (bd. gov.s 1977-79), Jonathan Club (L.A.), Princeton Club So. Calif. (pres. 1970-72). Republican. Episcopalian. Avocations: tennis, hiking, camping, travel. Federal civil litigation, State civil litigation. Office: Sheppard Mullin Richter & Hampton 333 S Hope St Fl 48 Los Angeles CA 90071-1406

**SELYA, BRUCE MARSHALL,** federal judge; b. Providence, May 27, 1934; s. Herman C. and Betty (Brier) S.; children: Dawn Meredith Selya Sherman, Lori Ann. BA magna cum laude, Harvard U., 1955, JD magna cum laude, 1958. Bar: D.C. 1958, R.I. 1960. Law clk. U.S. Dist. Ct. R.I., Providence, 1958-60; assoc. Gunning & LaFazia, Providence, 1960-62; ptnr. Gunning, LaFazia, Gnys & Selya, Providence, 1963-74, Selya & Iannuccillo, Providence, 1974-82; judge U.S. Dist. Ct. R.I., Providence, 1982-86, U.S. Ct. Appeals (1st cir.), Providence, 1986—; judge Lincoln Probate Ct., R.I., 1965-72; mem. R.I. Jud. Council, 1964-72, sec., 1965-70, chmn., 1971-72; mem. Gov.'s Commn. on Crime and Adminstrn. Justice, 1967-69; del. Nat. Conf. on Revisions to Fed. Appellate Practice, 1968-82; mem. various spl. govtl. commns. and adv. groups. Chmn. bd. trustees Bryant Coll., Smithfield, R.I., 1986-92; bd. dirs. Lifespan Health Sys., chmn. bd. dirs., 1994—, mem. bd. trustees R.I. Hosp. subs. Recipient Louis Dembitz Brandeis medal for disting. legal svc. Brandeis U., 1988, Neil Houston award Justice Assistance of Am., 1992. Mem. ABA, FBA, Fed. Judges Assn., R.I. Bar Assn. (chmn. various coms.), R.I. Bar Found., U.S. Jud. Conf. (mem. com. on jud. br.), Am. Arbitration Assn., Am. Judicature Soc. (bd. dirs.). Jewish. Home: 224 George St Providence RI 02906-3115 Office: US Ct Appeals US Courthouse 1 Courthouse Way Ste 6710 Boston MA 02210

**SEMAYA, FRANCINE LEVITT,** lawyer; b. N.Y.C., Mar. 26, 1951; d. Julie and Ann (Tannenbaum) Levitt; m. Richard Semaya, Aug. 3, 1975; children: Stefanie Rachel, David Steven, Scott Brian. BA magna cum laude, Bklyn. Coll., 1973, MS magna cum laude, 1975; JD, N.Y. Law Sch., 1982. Bar: N.Y. 1983, U.S. Dist. Ct. (ea. and so. dists.) N.Y. 1983. Sr. legal analyst, atty. Am. Internat. Group, Inc., N.Y.C., 1977-83; assoc. counsel, asst. v.p. Beneficial Ins. Group, Inc. (formerly Benico, Inc.), Peapack, N.J., 1983-87; v.p., counsel Am. Centennial Ins. Co., Peapack, 1985-87; legal/reins. cons. Peapack, 1987; counsel reins. Integrity Ins. Co. in Liquidation, Paramus, N.J., 1988-91; ptnr. Werner & Kennedy, N.Y.C., 1991-99, Cozen and O'Connor, N.Y.C., 1999—; spkr. in field. Editor: Law and Practice of Insurance Insolvency Revisited, 1989; contbg. editor Reference Handbook Ins. Co. Insolvency, 3rd edit., 1993. Mem. ABA (sect. del. to ho. dels. 1998—, tort and ins. practice sect. coun. 1994-97, chmn. task force on ins. insolvency 1995—, chmn. professionalism com. 1997-98, chmn. pub. regulation of ins. law com. 1990-91, chair pub. rels. com. 1993-94, co-editor State Regulation Ins. 1991), N.Y. State Bar Assn., Practicing Law Inst. (ins. law adv. com. 1995—), Assn. Bar City N.Y. (ins. law com.), Fedn. Regulatory Counsel, Phi Beta Kappa. Avocations: reading, travel. Insurance, Banking, Administrative and regulatory. Office: Werner & Kennedy 1633 Broadway Ste 4601 New York NY 10019-6780

**SEMPLE, JAMES WILLIAM,** lawyer; b. Phila., Nov. 18, 1943; s. Calvin James and Marie (Robinson) S.; m. Ellen Burns, Nov. 26, 1966; children: Megan Semple Greenberg, Luke Robinson. AB, St. Josephs U., Phila., 1965; JD, Villanova U., 1974. Bar: Del. 1974, U.S. Dist. Ct. Del. 1974, D.C. 1975, U.S. Ct. Appeals (3d cir.) 1982, U.S. Tax Ct. 1996. Ptnr. Morris, James, Hitchens & Williams, Wilmington, 1983—; lectr. numerous seminars; mediator Superior Ct. Voluntary Mediation Program. Mem. ABA, Am. Bd. Trial Advs., Fedn. Ins. and Corp. Counsel, Am. Judicature Soc., Am. Soc. Law and Medicine, Assn. Internat. de Droit d'Assurance. General civil litigation, Contracts commercial, Insurance. Office: Morris James Hitchens & Williams PO Box 2306 Wilmington DE 19899-2306

**SENDROFF, MARK D.,** lawyer; b. N.Y.C., Feb. 3, 1951; s. Ira L. and Estelle (Robinson) S. B.A., Syracuse U., 1972; J.D., Temple U., 1975. Bar: N.Y. 1976. Assoc. Alan H. Bomser, P.C., N.Y.C., 1976-79, Gottlieb Schiff Ticktin, N.Y.C., 1979-96 . Recipient 1st prize Nathan Burkan Meml. Competition ASCAP, 1975. Entertainment. Home: 139 W 82nd St New York

NY 10024-5501 Office: Sendroff & Assocs PC 1500 Broadway New York NY 10036-4015

**SENFT, JOHN L.,** lawyer; b. York, Pa., Oct. 28, 1966; s. Lavere C. and Gloria L. S. BA, Duke U., 1988; JD, U. Va., 1991. Bar: Md. 1991, Pa. 1992, U.S. Dist. Ct. (ea. dist.) Pa., U.S. Dist. Ct. (middle dist.) Pa., U.S. Dist. Ct. (no. dist.) Md. Assoc. Whiteford, Taylor & Preston, Balt., 1991-95, Barley, Snyder, Senft & Cohen, York, Pa., 1995—. Bd. dirs. Martin Libr., York, Pa., 1997—. Labor, Workers' compensation, General civil litigation. Office: Barley Snyder Senft & Cohen 100 E Market St York PA 17401-1219

**SENGHOR, SHARON ALVENA WHITE,** lawyer; b. N.Y.C., Sept. 28, 1952; d. Erman and Bernice Adela (Garth) W.; m. Keith Calhoun-Senghor, June 23, 1984. B.A., Yale U., 1974; M.A., Columbia U., 1975; J.D., 1980. Bar: N.Y. 1981, U.S. Dist. Ct. S.D.N.Y. 1982, E.D.N.Y. 1982, D.C. 1988. Program dir. Internat. House, N.Y.C., 1975-77; research coordinator Nat. Inst. Advanced Studies, Washington, 1977; intern N.Y.C. Corp. Counsel, summer 1978; assoc. Steptoe & Johnson, Washington, summer 1979; asst. gen. counsel Smithsonian Instn., Washington, 1980-85, 87—; fgn. assoc., Rau Weinberger & Ptnr, Munich, Fed. Republic of West Germany, 1986. Editor: Columbia Human Rights Law Rev. Fgn. Fellow Rau Weinberger and Ptnr., Munich, 1986; Charles Evans Hughes fellow, 1979. Mem. D.C. Bar Assn. (chairperson art law com. 1984-85), ABA (mem. faculty), Yale Alumni (schs. com.). Democrat. Lutheran. Office: Office of Gen Counsel Smithsonian Instn 1000 Jefferson Dr SW Washington DC 20560

**SENGPIEHL, PAUL MARVIN,** lawyer, former state official; b. Stuart, Nebr., Oct. 10, 1937; s. Arthur Paul and Anne Marie (Andersen) S.; B.A., Wheaton (Ill.) Coll., 1959; M.A. in Pub. Adminstrn., Mich. State U., 1961; J.D., Ill. Inst. Tech.-Chgo. Kent Coll. Law, 1970; m. June S. Cline, June 29, 1963; children—Jeffrey D., Chrystal M. Bar: Ill. 1971, U.S. Supreme Ct. 1982. Adminstrv. asst. Chgo. Dept. Urban Renewal, 1962-65; supr. Ill. Municipal Retirement Fund, Chgo., 1966-71; mgmt. officer Ill. Dept. Local Govt. Affairs, Springfield, 1971-72, legal counsel, Chgo., 1972-73; spl. asst. atty. gen. Ill. Dept. Labor, Chgo., 1973-76; asst. atty. gen. Ct. of Claims div. Atty. Gen. of Ill., 1976-83; hearing referee Bd. Rev., Ill. Dept. Labor, 1983-84; local govt. law columnist Chgo. Daily Law Bull., 1975-84; instr. polit. sci. Judson Coll., Elgin, Ill., 1963. Republican candidate for Cook County Recorder of Deeds, 1984; dep. committeeman Oak Park Twp Rep. Orgn.; elected alt. del., served del. Rep. Nat. Conv., 1992, elected del. Rep., 1996; People's Choice candidate pres. Oak Park Village, 1993; elected Rep. committeeman Oak Park Twp., 1994—; elected del. Rep. Nat. Convention, 1996. Mem. Ill. Bar Assn. (local govt. law sect. council 1973-79, vice chmn. 1976-77, co-editor local govt. newsletter 1976-77, chmn. 1977-78, editor newsletter 1977-78, state tax sect. council 1979-82, 84-85), Chgo. Bar Assn. (local govt. com., chmn. legis. subcom. 1978-79, sec. 1979-80, vice chmn. 1980-81, chmn. 1981-82, state and mcpl. tax com.), John Ericsson Rep. League Ill. (state sec. 1983-85, 95—, sec. Cook County 1982-97, pres. 1997—), Oak Park-River Forest C. of C. (sm. bus. coun., 1991—). Baptist (vice chmn. deacons 1973-76, 79-80, moderator 1983-86, supt. Sunday sch. 1986-93). Home: 727 N Ridgeland Ave Oak Park IL 60302-1735

**SENN, LISA ROBINSON,** lawyer; b. Charlotte, N.C., Aug. 2, 1959; d. Robert Joseph and Mary Dixon (Alexander) R.; m. William Mark Senn, June 11, 1983; children: William Robinson Senn, Mary Alexander Senn. BA in History summa cum laude, Erskine Coll., 1981; JD, U. S.C., 1984. Bar: S.C. 1984. Atty. Office Atty. Gen. S.C., Columbia, 1984-86, 90; assoc. Anderson, Lowder & Strait, P.A., Columbia, 1990-91, Griffith & Wicker, Newberry, S.C., 1991-92; ptnr. Wicker & Senn, P.A., Newberry, 1992—; Trustee Erskine Coll., Due West, S.C., 1995-97. Contbr. articles to profl. jour. Mem. archtl. review bd. Newberry, 1996—, improvement coun. Boundary St. Sch., Newberry, 1996—. Mem. Newberry County Bar, S.C. Bar. Estate planning, Family and matrimonial, General practice. Office: Wicker & Senn PA PO Box 398 1309 Hunt St Newberry SC 29108-3035

**SENN, STEPHEN RUSSELL,** lawyer; b. Lakeland, Fla., Aug. 30, 1964; s. William Henry and Elizabeth Carol (Busick) S.; m. Leslie Anne Jamesson, Aug. 5, 1989; children: Kaylie Erin, Nathaniel Ethan. BS, Fla. State U., 1986, JD, 1989. Bar: Fla. 1989, U.S. Dist. Ct. (mid. dist.) Fla. 1989, U.S. Ct. Appeals (11th cir.) 1992, U.S. Dis. Ct. Fla. (so. dist.) 1993, U.S. Dist. Ct. (no. dist.) Fla. 1994, U.S. Ct. Appeals (10th cir.) 1997, U.S. Ct. Appeals (4th, 8th, and 9th cirs.) 1998. Jud. clk. mid. dist. U.S. Dist. Ct. Fla., Tampa, 1989-91; atty. Peterson & Myers P.A., Lakeland, Fla., 1991—. Bd. dirs. Fla. Rural Legal Svcs. Inc., Lakeland, 1998. Appellate, Federal civil litigation, Civil rights. Office: Peterson & Myers PA 100 E Main St Lakeland FL 33801-4655

**SENNET, CHARLES JOSEPH,** lawyer; b. Buffalo, Aug. 7, 1952; s. Saunders M. and Muriel S. (Rotenberg) S. AB magna cum laude, Cornell U., 1974; JD with high honors, George Washington U., 1979. Bar: Ill. 1979, U.S. Dist. Ct. (no. dist.) Ill. 1979, U.S. Ct. Appeals (7th cir.) 1982, U.S. Ct. Appeals (D.C. cir.) 1993. Assoc. Reuben & Proctor, Chgo., 1979-83; assoc. counsel Tribune Co., Chgo., 1984-91, sr. counsel, 1991—; adj. faculty Medill Sch. Journalism, Northwestern U., 1991—; co-chair Television Music Lic. Com., 1995—. Contbr. articles to profl. jours. Mem. ABA (spkr. 1984-88, 91-97, mem. gov. bd. Forum on Comms. Law 1995—), NATAS, Ill. Bar Assn. (chmn. media law com. 1989-91), Chgo. Bar Assn., Fed. Comms. Bar Assn. Entertainment, Libel, Communications. Office: Tribune Co 435 N Michigan Ave Chicago IL 60611-4066

**SENSENICH, ILA JEANNE,** judge; b. Pitts., Mar. 6, 1939; d. Louis E. and Evelyn Margaret S. BA, Westminster Coll., 1961; JD, Dickinson Sch. Law, 1964, JD (hon.), 1994. Bar: Pa. 1964. Assoc. Stewart, Belden, Sensenich and Harrington, Greensburg, Pa., 1964-70; asst. pub. defender Westmoreland (Pa.) County, 1970-71; U.S. magistrate judge We. Dist. Pa., Pitts., 1971—; adj. prof. law Duquesne U., 1982-87. Author: Compendium of the Law of Prisioner's Rights, 1979; contbr. articles to profl. jour. Trustee emeritus Dickinson Sch. Law. Vis. fellow Daniel & Florence Guggenheim program in criminal justice Yale Law Sch., 1976-77. Mem. ABA, Fed. Magistrate Judges Assn. (sec. 1979-81, 88-89, treas. 1989-90, 2d v.p. 1990-91, pres.-elect 1992-93, pres. 1993-94), Pa. Bar Assn., Allegheny County Bar Assn. (fed. ct. sect.), Nat. Assn. Women Judges, Westmoreland County Bar Assn., Allegheny County Bar Assn. (fed. sect., com. women in law), Womens Bar Assn. We. Pa., Am. Judicature Soc. Democrat. Presbyterian. Avocations: skiing, sailing, bicycling, classical music, cooking. Office: 518B US PO And Courthouse Pittsburgh PA 15219

**SENTELLE, DAVID BRYAN,** federal judge; b. Canton, N.C., Feb. 12, 1943; s. Horace Richard, Jr., and Maude (Ray) S.; m. Jane LaRue Oldham, June 19, 1965; children: Sharon Rene, Reagan Elaine, Rebecca Grace. AB, U. N.C., 1965, JD with honors, 1968. Bar: N.C. 1968, U.S. Dist. Ct. (we. dist.) N.C. 1969, U.S. Ct. Appeals (4th cir.) 1970. Assoc. Uzzell & Dumont, Asheville, N.C., 1968-70; asst. U.S. atty. City of Charlotte, N.C., 1970-74, dist. judge, 1974-77; ptnr. Tucker, Hicks, Sentelle, Moon & Hodge, P.A., Charlotte, 1977-85; judge U.S. Dist. Ct. (we. dist.) N.C., Charlotte, 1985-87, U.S. Ct. Appeals D.C., 1987—; adj. prof. Fla. State U. Coll. Law; presiding judge Spl. Divsn. for Appointment of Ind. Counsels, 1992—. Contbr. articles to profl. jours. Chmn. Mecklenburg County Rep. Com., 1978-80; chmn. N.C. State Rep. Conv., 1979-80. Dameron fellow, 1967. Mem. Mecklenburg County Bar Assn. Baptist. Lodges: Masons, Scottish Rite, Shriners. Office: US Court of Appeals 333 Constitution Ave NW Washington DC 20001-2866

**SENTER, LYONEL THOMAS, JR.,** federal judge; b. Fulton, Miss., July 30, 1933; s. L. T. and Eva Lee (Jetton) S.; married. B.S., U. So. Miss., 1956; LL.B., U. Miss., 1959. Bar: Miss. 1959. County pros. atty., 1960-64, U.S. commr., 1966-68; judge Miss. Circuit Ct., Circuit 1, 1968-80; judge U.S. Dist. Ct. (no. dist.) Miss., 1980-82, chief judge, 1982-98, sr. judge, 1998—. Mem. Miss. State Bar. Democrat. Office: US Dist Ct PO Box 925 Aberdeen MS 39730-0925

**SENTER, MARK SEYMOUR,** lawyer; b. New Orleans, Oct. 5, 1962; s. Robert Reid and Norma (Stucker) S.; m. Lori Ann Blanchard, Dec. 28, 1991; children: Mark S. Jr., Matthew Stephen. BS in Econs., Auburn U., 1985; JD, Tulane U., 1992. Bar: La. 1992, U.S. Dist. Ct. (ea. dist.) La. 1993, U.S. Ct. Appeals (5th cir.) 1998. Assoc. Holoway & Assocs., New Orleans, 1992-94, Degan & Blanchard, New Orleans, 1994-96, Reich Meeks & Treadaway, New Orleans, 1996—. Vol. New Orleans Hospice Assn., 1997—, St. Catherine's Ch. Men's Club, 1998—. Mem. Maritime Law Assn. (assoc.), Jefferson Bar Assn. Roman Catholic. Avocations: golf, running, swimming. Admiralty, General civil litigation, General corporate. Office: Reich Meeks & Treadaway 3850 N Causeway Blvd Ste 1830 Metairie LA 70002-8184

**SEQUEIRA, MANUEL ALEXANDRE, JR.,** lawyer; b. Oct. 31, 1931; came to U.S., 1946, naturalized, 1954; s. Manuel Alexandre and Cecilia Maria (Xavier) S.; m. Angela Maria Lopes, Feb. 15, 1958; children: Joseph, Michael, Peter, Robert. BA, U. Notre Dame, 1955, JD, 1956. Bar: N.Y. 1957, U.S. Dist. Ct. (so. and ea. dists.) N.Y. 1958, U.S. Ct. Appeals (2d cir.) 1967, U.S. Supreme Ct. 1971. Assoc. atty. Hill, Rivkins, Carey, Loesberg, O'Brien & Mulroy, N.Y.C., 1956-67; litigation house counsel Am. Internat. Group (Sequeira, Rienzo & Gillies), N.Y.C., 1967-82; pvt. practice Mahopac, N.Y., 1983—. Mem. Christian Legal Soc., Westchester Bar Assn. Roman Catholic. General practice, Personal injury, Real property. Office: PO Box 563 Mahopac NY 10541-0563

**SERBIN, RICHARD MARTIN,** lawyer; b. Pitts., Dec. 21, 1947; s. Bernard Serbin and Ella (Stone) Kublanov; m. Francie M. Buncher, June 2, 1974; children: Lawrence B., Haley E., Joshua H. BA, U. Pitts., 1970; JD, Duquense U., 1974. Bar: Pa. 1974, N.C. 1996, U.S. Dist. Ct. (mid. dist.) Pa. 1974, U.S. Dist. Ct. (we. dist.) Pa. 1980, U.S. Ct. Appeals (3d cir.) 1981, U.S. Supreme Ct. 1985; cert. Nat. Bd. Trial Advocacy (civil). Assoc. Barron & Zimmerman, Lewistown, Pa., 1974-77; ptnr. Mullen, Casanave, Carpenter & Serbin, Altoona, Pa., 1977-81, Levine, Reese & Serbin, Altoona, 1982-97, Reese, Serbin, Kovacs & Nypaver, Altoona, 1997—; asst. dist. atty. Juniata County, Mifflintown, Pa., 1976-77; instr. Pa. State U., Altoona, 1979-83, 89; adj. settlement judge for Western Dist. Ct., Pa. Bd. dirs. Jewish Fedn., Altoona, 1980-89, Temple Beth Israel, Altoona, 1983-86, Pleasant Valley Community Living, 1982-86, Big Brothers/Sisters of Blair County, 1987-95; mem. Big Brothers and Friends of Boys, 1978-80. Mem. ABA, ATLA, Pa. Trial Lawyers Assn. (bd. govs. 1988-90), Blair County Bar Assn., Million Dollar Advocates Forum. Democrat. Jewish. Avocations: tennis, skiing. Personal injury, State civil litigation, Federal civil litigation. Office: Reese Serbin Kovacs & Nypaver 85 Logan Blvd Altoona PA 16602-3123

**SERCHUK, IVAN,** lawyer; b. N.Y.C., Oct. 13, 1935; s. Israel and Freda (Davis) S.; children: Camille, Bruce Mead, Vance Foster. BA, Columbia U., 1957, LLB, 1960. Bar: N.Y. 1961, U.S. Dist. Ct. (so. dist.) N.Y. 1963, U.S. Ct. Appeals (2d cir.) 1964, U.S. Tax Ct. 1966. Law clk. to judge U.S. Dist. Ct. (so. dist.) N.Y., 1961-63; assoc. Kaye, Scholer, Fierman, Hays & Handler, 1963-68; dep. supt., counsel N.Y. State Banking Dept., N.Y.C. and Albany, 1968-71; mem. Berle & Berle, 1972-73; spl. counsel N.Y. State Senate Banks Com., 1972; mem. Serchuk & Zelermyer LLP, White Plains, 1976—; lectr. Practising Law Inst., 1968-71. Mem. Assn. of Bar of City of N.Y., N.Y. State Bar Assn. Banking, General corporate, Mergers and acquisitions. Home: Mead St Waccabuc NY 10597 Office: Serchuk & Zelermyer LLP 81 Main St White Plains NY 10601-1711

**SERGEY, JAMES ADAM,** lawyer, educator; b. Oak Park, Ill., Mar. 28, 1949; s. Adam Michael and Mary Katerina (Antonik) S.; m. Marcia JoAnne Erikson, May 22, 1982; 1 child, Micah James. AB, Wheaton Coll., 1971; JD, DePaul U., 1983. Bar: Ill. 1983, U.S. Dist. Ct. (no. dist.) Ill. 1983, U.S. Dist. Ct. (ctrl. dist.) Ill. 1988. Pres., art dealer James Adam Sergey Inc., Chgo., 1972-83; asst. prof. Law Ill. State U., Normal, 1987—, atty., 1983-88; atty., advisor U.S. Dept. Health & Human Svcs., Peoria, Ill., 1988—; arbitration chair Cook County Cir. Ct., Ill., 1991—; corp. counsel Ind. Living Ctr., Normal, 1985-89, Twin City Ballet Co., Normal, 1987-89, Home Sweet Home Rescue Mission, Bloomington, Ill., 1987-88. Staff mem. DePaul Law Rev. Deacon Bloomington Evang. Free Ch., 1985-87. Recipient Quality Step Increase award Regional Chief Judge, 1990, 92, 93. Mem. ABA, Fed. Bar Assn., Christian Legal Soc., Ill. State Bar Assn. Avocations: Illinois postal history, Lincoln history, fly fishing. Home: 509 E Monroe St Morton IL 61550-2230 Office: Office Hearings & Appeals 300 Hamilton Blvd Peoria IL 61602-1234

**SERNA, PATRICIO,** state supreme court justice; b. Reserve, N.Mex., Aug. 26, 1939; m. Eloise Serna; 1 stepchild, John Herrera; children: Elena Patricia, Anna Alicia. BSBA with honors, U. Albuquerque, 1962; JD, U. Denver, 1970; LLM, Harvard U., 1971; postgrad., Nat. Jud. Coll., 1985, 90, 92, 94. Bar: N.Mex., Colo., U.S. Dist. Ct. N.Mex. Probation and parole officer State of N.Mex., Santa Fe, Las Cruces, 1966-67; spl. asst. to commn. mem. Equal Opportunity Commn., Washington, 1971-75; asst. atty. gen. State of N.Mex., Santa Fe, 1975-79; pvt. practice Santa Fe, 1979-85; dist. judge First Jud. Dist., Santa Fe, 1985-96; supreme ct. justice N.Mex. Supreme Ct., Santa Fe, 1996—; adj. prof. law Georgetown U., Washington, 1973, Cath. U., Washington, 1974-75; faculty advisor Nat. Jud. Coll., Reno, 1987. Exhibited at N.Mex. Mus. Fine Arts, Gov.'s Gallery, Santa Fe. Active Citizens Organized for Real Edn., Santa Fe, No. N.Mex. Martin Luther King Jr. State Holiday Commn., Santa Fe; past bd. dirs. Santa Fe Group Homes Inc. With U.S. Army, 1963-65. Mem. N.Mex. Bar Assn., N.Mex. Hispanic Bar Assn., Nat. Hispanic Bar Assn., Nat. Coun. Juvenile and Family Ct. Judges, No. N.Mex. Am. Inns of Ct., Santa Fe Bar Assn., Elks, Fraternal Order of Eagles, Fraternal Order of Police, Phi Alpha Delta. Avocations: hiking, fishing, ping pong, chess, painting. Office: NMex Supreme Ct PO Box 848 Santa Fe NM 87504-0848

**SERNETT, RICHARD PATRICK,** lawyer; b. Mason City, Iowa, Sept. 8, 1938; s. Edward Frank and Loretta M. (Cavanaugh) S.; m. Janet Ellen Ward, Apr. 20, 1963; children: Susan Ellen, Thomas Ward, Stephen Edward, Katherine Anne. BBA, U. Iowa, 1960, JD, 1963. Bar: Iowa 1963, Ill. 1965, U.S. Dist. Ct. (no. dist.) Ill. 1965, U.S. Supreme Ct. 1971. House counsel, asst. sec. Scott, Foresman & Co., Glenview, Ill., 1963-70; sec., legal officer Scott, Foresman & Co., Glenview, 1970-80; v.p., law sec. SFN Cos., Inc., Glenview, 1980-83, sr. v.p., sec., gen. counsel, 1983-85, exec. v.p., gen. counsel, 1985-87; pvt. practice Northbrook, Ill., 1988-90; v.p., sec., gen. counsel Macmillan/McGraw-Hill Sch. Pub. Co., 1990-92; v.p. Bert Early Assoc., Chgo., 1992-93; ptnr. Sernett & Blake, Northfield, Ill., 1993-95; ret., 1995; mem. U.S. Dept. State Adv. Panel on Internat. Copyright, 1972-75. Chmn. bd. dirs. Iowa State U., Broadcasting Co., 1987-94. Mem. ABA (chmn. copyright div. 1972-73, com. on copyright legis. 1967-68, 69-70, com. on copyright office affairs 1966-67, 79-81, com. on program for revision copyright law 1971-72), Am. Intellectual Property Law Assn., Am. Soc. Corp. Secs., Ill. Bar Assn. (chmn. copyright com. 1971-72), Chgo. Bar Assn., Patent Law Assn. Chgo. (bbd. mgrs. 1979-82, chmn. copyright law com. 1972-73, 77-78), Copyright Soc. U.S.A. (trustee 1972-75, 77-80), North Shore Country Club (Glenview, Ill.), Wyndemere Country Club (Naples, Fla.), Met. Club Chgo. Trademark and copyright, General corporate, Mergers and acquisitions. Home: 2579 Fairford Ln Northbrook IL 60062-8101

**SEROTA, JAMES IAN,** lawyer; b. Chgo., Oct. 20, 1946; s. Louis Henry and Phyllis Estelle (Horner) S.; m. Susan Perlstadt, May 7, 1972; children: Daniel Louis, Jonathan Mark. AB, Washington U., St. Louis, 1968; JD cum laude, Northwestern U., 1971. Bar: Ill. 1971, U.S. Dist. Ct. (no. dist.) Ill. 1972, D.C. 1978, U.S. Supreme Ct. 1978, U.S. Ct. Appeals (D.C. cir.) 1978, U.S. Dist. Ct. (D.C. dist.), U.S. Ct. Claims 1980, N.Y. 1981, U.S. Dist. Ct. (so. and ea. dists.) N.Y. 1981, U.S. Ct. Appeals (2d cir.) 1983. Trial atty. Antitrust div. U.S. Dept. Justice, Washington, 1971-77; assoc. Bell, Boyd & Lloyd, Washington, 1977-81; ptnr. Werner, Kennedy & French, N.Y.C., 1982-85, Levitsky & Serota, 1985-86, Huber, Lawrence & Abell, N.Y.C., 1987-98, Vinson & Elkins, 1998—. Contbr. articles to profl. jours.; editor Law Rev. Northwestern U.; law bd., antitrust columnist CCH Power and Telecom Law jour. Recipient Spl. Achievement award U.S. Dept. Justice, 1976. Mem. ABA (chmn. ins. industry com. 1987-90, vice chair program com. 1990-91, chair annual mtg. program 1991-94, chair fuel & energy com. 1994-97, coun. 1997—), N.Y. State Bar Assn., Assn. of Bar of City of N.Y. (antitrust and trade regulation com. 1988-91), Fed. Bar Council. Antitrust, Federal civil litigation.

**SEROTA, SUSAN PERLSTADT,** lawyer; b. Chgo., Sept. 10, 1945; d. Sidney Morris and Mildred (Penn) Perlstadt; m. James Ian Serota, May 7, 1972; children: Daniel Louis, Jonathan Mark. AB, U. Mich., 1967; JD, NYU, 1971. Bar: Ill. 1971, D.C. 1972, N.Y. 1981, U.S. Dist. Ct. (no. dist.) Ill. 1971, U.S. Dist. Ct. (so. dist.) N.Y. 1981, U.S. Dist. Ct. (ea. dist.) N.Y. 1985, U.S. Ct. Claims 1972, U.S. Tax Ct. 1972, U.S. Ct. Appeals (D.C. cir.) 1972. Ptnr. Winthrop, Stimson, Putnam & Roberts, N.Y.C., 1982—; adj. prof. Sch. Law, Georgetown U., Washington, 1974-75; mem. faculty Practicing Law Inst., N.Y.C., 1983—. Editor: ERISA Fiduciary Law, 1995, Supplement, 1998; assoc. editor Exec. Compensation Jour., 1973-75; dep. editor Tax Mgmt., Estate and Gift Taxation and Exec. Compensation, 1973-75; mem. editl. adv. bd. Benefits Law Jour., 1988—, Tax Mgmt. Compensation Jour., 1993—; mem. bd. editor ERISA and Benefits Law Jour., 1992—; contbr. articles to profl. jours. Fellow Am. Coll. Tax Counsel; mem. ABA (chmn. joint com. employee benefits 1987-88, taxation sect. 1991-92, vice-chair taxation sect. 1999—), Internat. Pension and Employee Benefits Lawyers Assn. (co-chair 1993-95), N.Y. State Bar Assn. (exec. com. tax sect. 1988-92), Am. Bar Retirement Assn. (dir. 1994—, pres. 1999-2000). Democrat. Pension, profit-sharing, and employee benefits, Taxation, general, Mergers and acquisitions. Office: Winthrop Stimson Putnam & Roberts One Battery Park Pla New York NY 10004-1490

**SERRALTA, GEDETY NAYETS,** lawyer; b. Miami, Fla., Jan. 6, 1964; d. Cesar Augusto and Gladys (Lopez) S. BS, Fla. Internat. U., 1987; JD, U. Miami, 1990. Bar: Fla. 1990, U.S. Dist. Ct. (so. and mid. dists.) Fla. 1993, U.S. Ct. Appeals (11th cir.) 1995. Trial atty. U.S. Equal Employment Opportunity Commn., Miami, 1990-93, sr. trial atty., 1993—. TV/radio appearances include Dateline NBC, CNN, Good Morning America, BBC, Fox TV. Mem. ABA, ATLA, The Order of the Coif. Avocations: aerobics, rollerblading, gardening, water and snow skiing. Office: US Equal Employment Opportunity Commn One Biscayne Tower 2 S Biscayne Blvd Ste 2700 Miami FL 33131-1804

**SERRATA, LIDIA,** lawyer; b. Victoria, Tex., Oct. 14, 1947; d. John Gentry and Eulalia (Candelaria) S.; m. Al Ledesma, Aug. 5, 1978; children: John, Joseph. BA, Trinity U., 1970; MSW, U. Tex., 1976, JD, 1977. Bar: Tex., 1978. Asst. dist. atty. State of Tex., Victoria, 1977-79; lawyer, sole practice Victoria, 1975—; mem. Grievance Com. State Bar, Victoria, 1989—, Tex. Bar Admission Com., Victoria, 1989—. Mem. Mexican Am. Dems., Victoria, 1988—, Hospice, Victoria, 1988-90; bd. dirs. Austin Presbyn. Theol. Sem., Austin, 1988—. Named Outstanding Alumnus Presbyn. Pan Am. Sch., 1989. Mem. Tex. State Bar. Democrat. Presbyterian. Avocations: scuba diving. Family and matrimonial, Health, Criminal. Home: 603 Kelly Crick Rd Victoria TX 77904-1347 Office: Law Office Lidia Serrata 302 E Constitution St Victoria TX 77901-8141

**SERRETTE, CATHY HOLLENBERG,** lawyer; b. Scranton, Pa., Apr. 28, 1954; d. Herbert Saul and Lee (Weisberger) Hollenberg; m. Dennis Louis Serrette, July 27, 1985; children: Kyle Malcolm, Desmond Harold, Malcolm Mandela. BS summa cum laude, U. Pitts., 1975; JD, George Washington U., 1980; LLM in Internat. Legal Studies, Am. U., 1991. Bar: N.Y. 1980, D.C. 1986, Md. 1986, U.S. Dist. Ct. D.C. 1987. Assoc. Advs. for Children, N.Y.C., 1980-81; ptnr. Kresky, Sinawski & Hollenberg, N.Y.C., 1981-84; legis. dir. Congressman Savage, Washington, 1985-86; pvt. practice, Oxon Hill, Md., 1987—; v.p. Law Found. of Prince Georges County, Inc., 1996—; co-legal dir. ACLU, Prince Georges County chpt. Writer ABA Commn. on the Disabled, 1978-79. Co-chairperson edn. com. NAACP, Prince Georges County, Md., 1987-88; chairperson parent's adv. com. Apple Grove Elem. Sch., 1987-88; co-coord. 26th legis. dist. Prince Georges County Rainbow Coalition, 1988; bd. dirs. Prince Georges County chpt. ACLU, 1994—, Prince Georges County Law Found., 1995—, treas. Mem. Nat. Lawyers Guild (D.C. chpt. chair So. Africa com. exec. bd., pres. South African Women's Day com. 1988—), D.C. Bar Assn., Md. Bar Assn., Prince Georges County Bar Assn., Md. Women's Bar Assn., Phi Beta Kappa. Jewish. Avocations: skiing, horseback riding, swimming, tennis. Family and matrimonial, Criminal, General civil litigation. Home: 1809 Clayton Dr Oxon Hill MD 20745-3724 Office: Hollenberg Serrette & McDermott 6192 Oxon Hill Rd Ste 511 Oxon Hill MD 20745-3142

**SERRITELLA, JAMES ANTHONY,** lawyer; b. Chgo., July 8, 1942; s. Anthony and Angela (Deleonardis) S.; m. Ruby Ann Amoroso, Oct. 3, 1981. BA, SUNY-S.I., 1965, Pontifical Gregorian U., Rome, 1966; postgrad., DePaul U., 1966-67; MA, U. Chgo., 1968, JD, 1971. Bar: Ill. 1971, U.S. Dist. Ct. (no. and ea. dist.) Ill. 1971, U.S. Supreme Ct. 1976, U.S. Tax Ct. 1985, U.S. Ct. Appeals (fifth cir.) 1995, U.S. Ct. Appeals (sixth cir.) 1992, U.S. Ct. Appeals (seventh cir.) 1993, U.S. Ct. Appeals (ninth cir.) 1996. Ptnr. Kirkland & Ellis, Chgo., 1978; ptnr. Reuben & Proctor, Chgo., 1978-86, Mayer, Brown & Platt, Chgo., 1986-97, Burke, Warren, MacKay & Serritella, PC, Chgo., 1997—; lectr. in field. Contbr. articles to profl. jours. Exec. bd. govt. rels. com. United Way of Chgo., 1979-84; bd. dirs. Child Care Assn. Ill., 1975-79, Lyric Opera Guild, 1979-84; v.p. Comprehensive Community Svcs. of Met. Chgo., 1976-81; chmn. adv. bd. DePaul U. Coll. Law Ctr. Ch./State Studies, 1982—, dean's vis. com., 1982—; trustee Mundelein Coll., 1982-86, St. Xavier Coll., St. Mary of the Lake Sem., 1982-83, Sta. WTTW Chgo. Pub. TV, 1978-81, Loretto Hosp., 1989-91; mem. geriatrics/gerontology steering com. McGaw Med. Ctr. Northwestern U., 1981-82; adv. bd. N.Am. Coll., 1990-92; mem. Bus. Execs. for Econ. Justice, 1988-94, State wide citizens com. on Child Abuse and Neglect, 1988-94; bd. advisors Alzheimer's Ctr. Rush-Presbyn.-St. Luke's Med. Ctr., 1990—; cons. Union of Bulgarian Founds., 1992, Internat. Acad. for Freedom of Religion and Belief, Budapest, Hungary, 1992. Fellow Am. Bar Found.; mem. ABA, FBA, NCCJ (adv. com. on ch., state and taxation), Am. Assn. homes for Aging, Nat. Health Lawyers Assn., Ill. State Bar Assn. (bd. govs., spl. com. on jud. redistricting), Ill. Bar Found. (charter), Chgo. Bar Assn. (com. on evaluation of jud. candidates), Cath. Lawyers Guild (bd. govs.), Canon Law Soc. Am. (active mem.), Diocesan Attys. Assn. (exec. com.), Nat. Cath. Cemetery Conf., Cath. Health Assn., The Chgo. Club, Econ. Club, Tavern Club. E-mail: jserritella@burkelaw.com. General practice. Office: Burke Warren MacKay & Serritella PC IBM Plaza 22nd Fl 330 N Wabash Ave Chicago IL 60611-3607

**SERVIS, WILLIAM GEORGE,** lawyer; b. Rochester, N.Y., July 1, 1922; s. Harry Hall and Lois Ellen Servis; m. Valentine Agnes Reynouard, June 24, 1947; children: Ronald, Terry, Kim Powell. LLD, N.Y. Law Sch., 1957. Bar: N.Y., U.S. Dist. Ct. N.Y. Counsel Hon. John J. Conway, Rochester, 1958-60; asst. dist. atty. Dist. Atty.'s Office, Rochester, 1960-71; pvt. practice Rochester, 1971—; lectr. Police and Fire Acad., Rochester, 1960-71, Monroe County Magistrates Assn., 1966-70; counsel Western Monroe Hist. Soc., Brockport, N.Y., 1960-70, Clarkson Town, 1965-75, Spencerport Vol. Ambulance, Spencerport, N.Y., 1965-97. With USN, 1942-46. Mem. ABA, N.Y. State Bar Assn., Monroe County Bar Assn. Republican. Mem. United Ch. of Christ. Avocations: sailing, swimming. Criminal, General practice, Probate. Home: 60 Laurelcrest Dr Spencerport NY 14559-2304 Office: 36 W Main St Ste 705 Rochester NY 14614-1703

**SERVISS, DANIEL MARC,** lawyer; b. Phila., Jan. 27, 1972; s. Alan Roger Serviss and Andrea Bonnie Bartholomeo; m. Lisa Ann Lafer, Feb. 18, 1996. BA, George Washingtn U., 1993; JD, Seton Hall U., 1996. Bar: N.J. 1996, U.S. Dist. Ct. N.J. 1996. Assoc. Mandelbaum, Salsburg, Gold, Lazris, Discenza & Steinberg, West Orange, N.J., 1996—. Assoc. editor Seton Hall Law Rev., 1993-96; contbr. articles to profl. jours. Centineal scholar Seton Hall U. Sch. Law, Newark, 1993-96. Mem. ABA, ATLA, N.J. State Bar Assn., ECBA. Family and matrimonial, State civil litigation. Office: Mandelbaum Salsburg Gold 155 Prospect Ave West Orange NJ 07052-4204

**SESSIONS, JEFFERSON BEAUREGARD, III,** senator; b. Hybart, Ala., Dec. 24, 1946; s. Jefferson Beauregard and Abbie (Powe) S.; m. Mary Montgomery Blackshear, Aug. 9, 1969; children: Mary Abigail, Ruth Blackshear, Samuel Turner. B.A., Huntingdon Coll., Montgomery, Ala., 1969; J.D., U. Ala., 1973. Bar: Ala. 1973. Assoc. Guin, Bouldin & Porch, Russellville, Ala., 1973-75; asst. U.S. atty. U.S. Dept. Justice, Mobile, Ala., 1975-77, U.S. atty., 1981-93; assoc., ptnr. Stockman & Bedsole Attys., Mobile, Ala., 1977-81; ptnr. Stockman, Bedsole & Sessions, Mobile, 1993-94; atty. gen. State of Ala., 1996; U.S. senator from Ala., 1997—; mem. U.S. atty. gen.'s adv. com., 1987-89, vice chmn. 1989; mem. environment and pub. works com., judiciary com. Presdl. elector State of Ala., 1972; mem. bd. trustees, exec. com. Mobile Bay Area Partnership for Youth, 1981—; chmn. adminstrv. bd. Ashland Pl. United Meth. Ch., Mobile, 1982; 1st v.p. Mobile Lions Club, 1993-94. Capt. USAR, 1975-85. Recipient U.S. Atty. Gen's.

award for significant achievements in the war against drug trafficking U.S. Atty. Gen. William P. Barr, 1992. Mem. ABA, Ala. Bar Assn., Mobile Bar Assn. Home: 1119 Hillcrest Xing E Mobile AL 36695-4505 Office: 493 Senate Russell Office Bldg Washington DC 20510-0001

**SESSIONS, WILLIAM STEELE,** lawyer, former government official; b. Ft. Smith, Ark., May 27, 1930; s. Will Anderson and Edith A. (Steele) S.; m. Alice Lewis, Oct. 5, 1952; children: William Lewis, Mark Gregory, Peter Anderson, Sara Anne. BA, Baylor U., 1956, LLB, 1958; hon. degree, John C. Marshall Law Sch., St. Mary's U., 1989; LLD (hon.), Dickinson Coll., 1988, Flager Coll., 1990, Davis & Elkins Coll., 1992, McMurry U., 1997. Bar: Tex. 1959; U.S. Dist Ct. (Western Dist.) Tex.; Ct. Appeals (5th Cir.). Ptnr. McGregor & Sessions, Waco, Tex., 1959-61; assoc. Tirey, McLaughlin, Gorin & Tirey, Waco, 1961-63; ptnr. Haley, Fulbright, Winniford, Sessions & Bice, Waco, 1963-69; sect. chief, govt. ops sect. criminal divsn. U.S. Dept. Justice, Washington, 1969-71; U.S. atty. U.S. Dept Justice, U.S. Dist. Ct., (we. dist) San Antonio, 1971-74; dist judge U.S. Dist. Ct. (we. dist.) Tex., San Antonio, 1974-87, chief judge, 1980-87; dir. FBI, Washington, 1987-93; ptnr. Sessions & Sessions, San Antonio, 1995—; bd. dirs. Fed. Jud. Ctr., Washington, chmn. bench book com., 1981—; mem. Tex. Commn. on Judicial Efficiency, 1995, Tex. Commn. on a Representative Student Body, 1998. Contbr. articles to profl. jours. Mem. Dr. Martin Luther King Jr. Fed. Holicy Commn., 1991-93, 94-96, hon. bd. dirs., 1993-94. Lt. USAF, 1951-55; capt. USAFR. Recipient Rosewood Gavel award St. Mary's U. Sch. Law, San Antonio, 1982, Disting. Alumni award Baylor U., Golden Plate award Am. Acad. Achievement, 1988, Law Enforcement Leadership award Assn. Fed. Investigators, 1989, medal of honor DAR, 1989, Disting. Eagle Scout award Boy Scouts Am., 1990, Person of Yr. award Am. Soc. for Indsl. Security, 1990, Magna Charta award Baronial Order of Magna Charta, 1990; named Lawyer of Yr., Baylor Law Sch., 1988, Father of Yr., Nat. Fathers Day Com., 1988, Ellis Island Congl. Medal of Honor, 1992; inducted into Eagle Scout Hall of Fame, 1998. Fellow ABA (chmn. spl. com. on judicial independence 1997-98); mem. Jud. Conf. U.S. (com. on ct. adminstrn., chmn. jud. improvements subcom. 1983-85, ad hoc com. on automation to subcom. 1984-87, mem. ad hoc ct. reporter com. 1984-87), San Antonio Bar Assn. (bd. dirs. 1973-74), Fed. Bar Assn. (pres. San Antonio sect. 1974), Am. Judicature Soc. (exec. com. 1982-84), Dist. Judges Assn. of 5th Cir. (pres. 1982-83), State Bar of Tex. (chmn. com. to develop procedures for cert. state law questions to Supreme Ct. by Fed. Cts. 1983-85), Waco McLennan County Bar Assn. (pres. 1968), San Antonio Inns of Ct. (pres. 1986), William S. Sessions Inns of Ct. Republican. Methodist. Avocations: hiking, climbing, canoeing. E-mail: wss@sessionslaw.com. Office: Sessions & Sessions 112 E Pecan St Ste 29 San Antonio TX 78205-1516

**SESSLER, ALBERT LOUIS, JR.,** lawyer; b. Davenport, Iowa, May 28, 1925; s. Albert Louis Sr. and Eva Ames (Dedrick) S.; m. Irene Helen Seifert, Nov. 20, 1951; children: Curtis N., Scott A., Janice M.; m. Robin Helen Palmer, Mar. 23, 1976. BS in Mech. Engring., Iowa State U., 1950; JD with honors, George Washington U., 1954. Bar: D.C. 1954, U.S. Patent and Trademark Office 1955, U.S. Supreme Ct. 1972, U.S. Ct. Appeals (Fed. cir.) 1982. Asst. examiner U.S. Patent Office, Washington, 1951-54; patent atty. NCR Corp., Dayton, Ohio, 1955-94, div. patent counsel, 1981-84, group intellectual property counsel, 1984-86, assoc. chief, group counsel, 1986-88, sr. and group counsel, 1988-92, asst. chief counsel, 1992, sr. atty., 1992-94, ret. 1994. Mem. bd. zoning appeals, City of Kettering (Ohio), 1970—, Chmn., 1990, 94, 98, mem. zoning task force, 1979. With U.S. Army, 1943-46, to 2nd lt., 1951-53. Decorated Bronze Star, Combat Infantry badge. Mem. Am. Intellectual Property Law Assn., D.C. Bar Assn., Dayton Patent Law Assn. (past pres.), Order of Coif. Republican. Lutheran. Intellectual property, Trademark and copyright. Home: 533 Enid Ave Dayton OH 45429-5411

**SESSO, GEORGE,** lawyer; b. Mount Vernon, N.Y., June 28, 1943; m. Barbara F. Kirschner, July 31, 1966; children: Howard, Pamela. BS in Econs. and Fin., Seton Hall U., 1965, JD, 1974; MBA, Fairleigh Dickinson U., 1968. Bar: N.J., U.S. Dist. Ct. N.J. With Employers Ins. of Wausau, N.J., 1965-76; atty. Great Am. Ins. Co., Parsippany, N.J., 1976—. Mem. N.J. Def. Assn. (chmn. fin. and tech. com., spkr., pres.-elect). Contracts commercial, Insurance. Office: Great Am Ins Co 500 Lanidex Ctr Parsippany NJ 07054-2712

**SESTRIC, ANTHONY JAMES,** lawyer; b. St. Louis, June 27, 1940; s. Anton and Marie (Gasparovic) S.; student, Georgetown U., 1958-62; JD, Mo. U., 1965; m. Carol F. Bowman, Nov. 24, 1966; children: Laura Antonette, Holly Nicole, Michael Anthony. Bar: Mo. 1965, U.S. Ct. Appeals (8th cir.) 1965, U.S. Dist. Ct. Mo., 1966, U.S. Tax Ct. 1969, U.S. Supreme Ct. 1970, U.S. Ct. Appeals (7th cir.) 1984, U.S. Dist. Ct. (no. dist.) Tex. 1985, U.S. Claims Ct. 1986. U.S. Dist. Ct. Ill., 1994, Minn. 1996. Law clk. U.S. Dist. Ct., St. Louis, 1965-66; ptnr. firm Sestric, McGhee & Miller, St. Louis, 1966-77; spl. asst. to Mo. atty. gen., St. Louis, 1968; ptnr. Fordyce and Mayne, 1977-78, Sestric & Garvey, St. Louis, 1978-96, Sestric Law Firm, 1996—; hearing officer St. Louis Met. Police Dept.; active Fed. Jud. Selection Commn., 1993; gen. chmn. 22nd jud. cir. bar com., 1995; bd. dirs. St. Louis Reinvestment Corp. Contbr. articles to profl. jours. Mem. Fed. Judicial Selection Commn., 1993, mem. St. Louis Air Pollution Bd. Appeals and Varience Rev., 1966-73, chmn., 1968-73; mem. St. Louis Airport Commn., 1975-76; dist. vice chmn. Boy Scouts Am., 1970-76; bd. dirs. Full Achievement, Inc., 1970-77; bd. dirs. Legal Aid Soc. of St. Louis, 1976-77, Law Library Assn. St. Louis, 1976-78; v.p. bd. St. Elizabeth Acad., 1985-86; bd. dirs. Thomas Dunn Memls., 1995-98, St. Louis Reinvestment Corp., 1997—, Marquette Learning Ctr., 1995-98; mem. U.S. Judicial Selections Commn., 1993-94. Mem. ABA (state chmn. judiciary com. 1973-75, cir. chmn. com. condemnation, zoning and property use 1975-77, standing com. bar activities 1982-88), Nat. Conf. Bar Pres.'s (exec. coun. 1987-90), Mo. Bar (vice chmn. young lawyers sect. 1973-76, bd. govs. 1974-77, chair law practice mgmt. com., 1997-99), Bar Assn. Met. St. Louis (chmn. young lawyers sect. 1974-75, exec. com. 1974-83, 94-95, pres. 1981-82, bd. govs. 1995-98, chair survey com. 1999). Federal civil litigation, State civil litigation, Estate planning. Home: 3967 Holly Hills Blvd Saint Louis MO 63116-3135 Office: The Sestric Law Firm 801 N 2nd St Saint Louis MO 63102-2560

**SETRAKIAN, BERGE,** lawyer; b. Beirut, Lebanon, Apr. 14, 1949; came to U.S. 1976; s. Hemayak and Arminee S.; m. Vera L. Nazarian, Nov. 22, 1975; children: Ani, Lara. Diplome d'Etudes de Doctorat, U. Lyons, France, 1973; Diplome d'Etudes de Doctorat Droit Compare, F.I.E.D.C., Strasbourg, France, 1974; Licence en Droit Francais, U. St. Joseph, Beirut, 1972, Licence en Droit Libanais, 1972. Bar: Beirut 1972, N.Y. 1983. Assoc. Tyan & Setrakian, Beirut, 1972-76; ptnr. Whitman & Ransom, N.Y.C., 1976-93, Whitman, Breed, Abbott & Morgan, N.Y.C., 1993—; bd. dirs. Cedars Bank, Calif., 1987—, Bank Audi, U.S.A., 1991; fgn. law cons., N.Y., 1978. Bd. dirs., v.p., sec. Armenian Gen. Benevolent Union, N.Y.C., 1977—; pres. Worldwide Youth orgns., 1978—; bd. dirs. Armenian Assy. of Am., Washington, 1978-87; bd. dirs. Am. Task Force for Lebanon, 1988—; bd. dirs. Am. U. Armenia, 1992—. Mem. ABA, N.Y. Bar Assn., Beirut Bar Assn., U.K. Law Soc., Am. Fgn. Law Assn., Englewood Field Club. Private international, Contracts commercial, Banking. Office: Whitman Breed Abbott Morgan 200 Park Ave New York NY 10166-0005

**SETTLE, ERIC LAWRENCE,** lawyer; b. N.Y.C., July 28, 1961; s. Elliott Titus and Thelma (Radzvill) S.; m. Robin Marks, Aug. 23, 1986; children: Adam Harrison, Alexander Howard. AB cum laude, Colgate U., 1983; JD with honors, George Washington U., 1986. Bar: Pa. 1986, U.S. Dist. Ct. (ea. dist.) Pa. 1987, U.S. Dist. Ct. (mid. dist.) Pa. 1995, U.S. Ct. Appeals (3d cir.) 1992, U.S. Supreme Ct. 1995. Assoc. Wolf, Block, Schorr & Solis-Cohen, Phila., 1986-90, Fox, Rothschild, O'Brien & Frankel, Phila., 1990-95; dep. gen. counsel to gov. Commonwealth of Pa., 1995-97; regional gen. counsel Aetna U.S. Healthcare, Inc., Blue Bell, Pa., 1997—. Trustee Colgate U., Hamilton, N.Y., 1983-86, Bryn Mawr Rehab. Hosp., 1993-94; pres. Riverview Condominium Assn., Phila., 1991-93; counsel Craig Snyder for U.S. Congress, Phila., 1992. George Cobb fellow Colgate U., 1981, 82. Mem. ABA (young lawyers divsn., career issues com. 1992-93), Pa. Bar Assn. (exec. com. young lawyers divsn. 1992-93), Phila. Bar Assn. (young lawyers sect. exec. com. 1990-92, dir. bar edn. ctr. 1993-95, trustee Phila. Bar Found., 1994), Phi Alpha Delta (marshal 1984-85). Health, Administrative and regulatory. Home: 1148 N Woodbine Ave Narberth PA 19072-1245 Office: Aetna/US Healthcare Law Dept 980 Jolly Rd # U19A Blue Bell PA 19422-1904

**SETZLER, EDWARD ALLAN,** lawyer; b. Kansas City, Mo., Nov. 3, 1933; s. Edward A. and Margaret (Parshall) S.; m. Helga E. Friedemann, May 20, 1972; children: Christina, Ingrid, Kirstin. BA, U. Kans., 1955; JD, U. Wis., 1962. Bar: Mo. 1962, U.S. Tax Ct. 1962. Assoc. Spencer, Fane, Britt & Browne, Kansas City, 1962-67, ptnr., 1968—, mng. ptnr., 1974-77, 78-82, chmn. trust and estate sect., 1974-99; lectr. CLE programs U. Mo. and Kansas City Sch. Law, 1983-95; mem. Jackson County Probate Manual Com., 1988—; Mo. rep. to joint editl. bd. Uniform Probate Code, 1989—. Co-author: Missouri Estate Administration, 1984, supplements, 1985-99; co-author, co-editor, reviewer Missouri Estate Planning, 1986, supplements, 1987-99; contbg. editor: A Will Is Not The Way -- The Living Trust Alternative, 1988; contbg. editor: Understanding Living Trusts, 1990, expanded edit., 1998; bd. editors Wis. Law Rev., 1961-62. Amb., bd. govs., bd. dirs., chmn. found. com. Am. Royal, 1982—; mem. planning giving com., bus. coun. Nelson Atkins Mus. Art, 1984—; mem. deferred giving com. Children's Mercy Hosp., 1991—; mem. Kansas City Estate Planning Symposium Com., 1984-92, chmn., 1991. Fellow Am. Coll. Trust and Estate Counsel (state chmn. 1992-97, mem. state membership com. 1986—); mem. ABA, Mo. Bar Assn. (lectr., vice chmn. probate and estate planning com. 1994-97), Kansas City Met. Bar Assn. (lectr., chmn. probate and trust 1979, 92, vice chmn. 1983-85, 91, legis. rev. com. 1991-95), Estate Planning Soc. Kansas City (co-founder 1965, pres. 1983-84, dir. 1984-85, mem. social com. 1968—), Soc. Trust Practitioners, London, Order of Coif, Sigma Chi, Phi Delta Phi. Estate planning, Probate, Estate taxation. Office: Spencer Fane Britt & Browne 1000 Walnut St Ste 1400 Kansas City MO 64106-2140

**SEUFERT, CHRISTOPHER J.,** lawyer; b. East Bridgewater, Mass., Aug. 12, 1959; s. Lawrence D. and Pauline W. (Lussier) S.; children: Christopher J., Megan. BA, U. Mass., Dartmouth, 1981; JD, Suffolk U., Boston, 1984. Bar: N.H. 1985, Mass. 1985, N.C. 1995, U.S. Dist. Ct. (1st cir.) 1987, U.S. Dist. Ct. N.H. 1985, U.S. Dist. Ct. Mass. 1985, U.S. Supreme Ct. 1988. Atty. Seufert Profl. Assocs., Franklin, N.H., 1985—; bd. dirs. N.H. Redevel. Inc., Franklin. Served with USCG, 1979-85. Mem. Franklin KC, Andover Lions Club. Republican. Roman Catholic. Office: Seufert Profl Assocs 59 Central St Franklin NH 03235-1134

**SEVEY, JACK CHARLES,** lawyer; b. Sacramento, June 5, 1938; s. Cecil Alvin and Virginia Lutisha S.; m. Roberta Rae Rossi; children: Jack C. Sevey Jr., Jeffrey C. Sevey, Kristin M. Haugen, James C. Sevey, Kara M. Sevey. AA, Sacramento Jr. Coll., 1959; BA, U. Calif., Berkeley, 1961; LLB, U. San Francisco, 1964. Bar: U.S. Dist. Ct. (no. dist.) Calif. 1965. Assoc. O'Conner & Lewis, Sacramento, 1965-68; ptnr. O'Conner & Sevey, Sacramento, 1968-78, Gessford, Sevey & Alpar, Sacramento, 1978-83, Sevey & Alpar, Sacramento, 1983-90, Crow Law Firm Inc., Sacramento, 1990—. Named Adv. of Yr., Sacramento Consumer Attys., 1995. Fellow Am. Coll. Trial Lawyers; mem. Am. Bd. Trial Advs. Personal injury. Office: Crow Law Firm 700 E St Sacramento CA 95814-1209

**SEVIER, ERNEST YOULE,** lawyer; b. Sacramento, June 20, 1932; s. Ernest and Helen Faye (McDonald) S.; m. Constance McKenna, Apr. 12, 1969; children: Carolyn Stewart, Katherine Danielle. A.B., Stanford U., 1954, J.D., 1956. Bar: Calif. 1956, U.S. Supreme Ct. 1965. Asso. mem. firm Sedgwick, Detert, Moran & Arnold, San Francisco, 1958-62; mem. firm Severson & Werson, San Francisco, 1962—. Served with USAF, 1956-57. Fellow Am. Bar Found.; mem. ABA (chmn. tort and ins. practice sect. 1982-83, exec. coun. 1976-84, chmn. standing com. on assoc. comms. 1988-90, chmn. coord. com. on Outreach to Pub. 1989-90, chmn. standing com. on lawyers responsibility for client protection 1991-94, commn. on non-lawyer practice 1992-95), Calif. Bar Assn., Internat. Assn. Def. Counsel, Fedn. Ins. and Corp. Counsel. Office: Severson & Werson 1 Embarcadero Ctr Fl 26 San Francisco CA 94111-3715

**SEVILLA, CHARLES MARTIN,** lawyer, writer; b. San Jose, Calif., Feb. 6, 1945; s. Michael A. and Phyllis S.; m. Donna Ellen, Sept. 30, 1949. BA, San Jose State U., 1966; JD, U. Santa Clara, 1969; LLM, George Washington U., 1971. Bar: Calif., U.S. Dist. Ct. (no. dist.) Calif., U.S. Dist. Ct. (so. dist.) Calif., U.S. Ct. Appeals (9th cir.), D.C., U.S. Dist. Ct. D.C., U.S. Ct. Appeals (D.C. cir.), U.S. Supreme Ct. Pvt. practice Washington, 1971; staff atty. Urban Law Inst. VISTA Legal Svcs., Washington, 1971; trial atty. Fed. Defenders, San Diego, 1971-72, chief trial atty., 1972-76; chief asst. state pub. defender L.A. Pub. Defender, 1976-79, chief dep. state pub. defender, 1979-83; ptnr. Cleary & Sevilla, LLP, San Diego, 1983—; Mem. standard jury instructions com. Criminal CALJIC, 1976-83; mem. Govs. Interim Adv. Commn. on Camarillo State Hosp., 1976-77; mem. Chief Justice Bird's Com. on Publ. Rule, 1978. Author: Wilkes: His Life and Crimes, 1990, Wilkes on Trial, 1993; co-editor: Disorderly Conduct, 1987, Disorder in the Court, 1992; co-editor, cons. Calif. Criminal Def. Practice, 1982—; contbr. articles to profl. jours. Mem. Nat. Assn. Criminal Def. Attys., Am. Acad. Appellate Lawyers, Calif. Attys. for Criminal Justice (pres. 1979-80), San Diego Criminal Def. Bar Assn. (bd. dirs.), L.A. County Bar Assn. (mem. criminal justice exec. com. 1976-78), San Diego County Bar Assn. (chmn. fed. ct. com. 1974-75). Ninth Cir. Adv. Com. Rules Ct. and Internal Procedures, San Diego Criminal Def. Lawyer's Club (pres. 1988). Fax: 619-232-3711. E-mail: cleasev@mill.net. Criminal. Office: Cleary & Sevilla LLP 1010 2nd Ave Ste 1825 San Diego CA 92101-4912

**SEWARD, GEORGE CHESTER,** lawyer; b. Omaha, Aug. 4, 1910; s. George Francis and Ada Leona (Rugh) S.; m. Carroll Frances McKay, Dec. 12, 1936 (dec. 1991); children: Gordon Day, Patricia McKay (Mrs. Dryden G. Liddle), James Pickett, Deborah Carroll (Mrs. R. Thomas Coleman). BA, U. Va., 1933, LLB, 1936. Bar: Va. 1935, N.Y., Ky., D.C., U.S. Supreme Ct. Assoc. Shearman & Sterling, N.Y.C., 1936-53, Seward & Kissel, N.Y.C., 1953—; founder, hon. chmn. Internat. Capital Markets Group of Internat. Fedn. Accts., Fedn. Internat. des Bourses de Valeurs, Internat. Bar Assn.; dir. Witherbee Sherman Corp., 1964-66, pres. 1950; trustee Benson Iron Ore Trust, 1969-80. Author: Basic Corporate Practice, 1977, Seward and Related Families, 1994; co-author: Model Business Corporation Act Annotated, 1960, We Remember Carroll, 1992. Trustee Arts and Scis. Coun. U. Va., 1983-93, pres., 1991-93; trustee Edwin Gould Found. for Children, 1955-96, Nature Conservancy of Ea. L.I., 1969-80, N.Y. Geneal. and Biog. Soc. Named to Louisville Male H.S. Alumni Assn. Hall of Fame, 1991; named Ky. Col., 1993. Fellow Am. Bar Found. (chmn. model corp. acts com. 1956-65), N.Y. State Bar Found.; mem. Internat. Bar Assn. (hon. life pres., hon. pres., founder sect. on bus. law, lectr. series named in his honor, New Delhi 1988, Lisbon 1992, Budapest 1993, Geneva 1994), ABA (chmn. bus. law sect. 1958-59, chmn. sect. com. corp. laws 1952-58, chmn. sect. banking com. 1960-61, mem. ho. of dels. 1959-60, 63-74, mem. joint com. with Am. Law Inst. on continung legal edn. 1965-74), Athenaeum Lit. Assn. (Louisville), Downtown Assn. (N.Y.C.), Knickerbocker Club, N.Y. Yacht Club, Univ. Club (Chgo.), Met. Club (Washington), Bohemian Club (San Francisco), Shelter Island Yacht Club, Gardiner's Bay Country Club, Greencroft Club (Charlottesville, Va.), Cum Laude Soc., Raven Soc., Order of Coif, Phi Beta Kappa Assocs. (pres. 1969-75), Phi Beta Kappa, Theta Chi, Delta Sigma Rho. General corporate, Finance, Private international. Home: 48 Greenacres Ave Scarsdale NY 10583-1436 Office: Seward & Kissel One Battery Park Plz New York NY 10004 also: Internat Bar Assn, 271 Regent St, London W1R 7PA, England

**SEWARD, RICHARD BEVIN,** lawyer; b. Bartlesville, Okla., May 27, 1932; s. Fredrick W. and Kittie Lea (Hudson) S.; m. Loydell E. Nash, Aug. 1, 1954; children: Ann M., Elizabeth, Amy M. B.S., Okla. State U., 1954; postgrad., Tulsa U., 1959-62; J.D., So. Methodist U., 1971. Bar: Tex. 1968. Personnel mgr. Unit Rig and Equipment Co., Tulsa, 1958-62, Gifford-Hill Cos., Dallas, 1962-66; labor cons. Dallas, 1966-68; partner firm Stanfield & Seward, Dallas, 1978-83; sole practice law Farmersville, Tex., 1983—. Served with AUS, 1955-57. Mem. Order of Coif. State civil litigation, General corporate, General practice. Home and Office: 14340 County Road 550 Farmersville TX 75442-7034

**SEXTON, JOHN EDWARD,** lawyer, dean, law educator; b. Bklyn., Sept. 29, 1942; s. John Edward and Catherine (Humann) S.; m. Lisa Ellen Goldberg; children: Jed, Katherine. B.A., Fordham U., 1963, Ph.D., 1978; J.D., Harvard U., 1979. Bar: N.Y. 1981, U.S. Supreme Ct. 1984. Prof. religion St. Francis Coll., Bklyn., 1965-75; law clk. U.S. Ct. Appeals, Washington, 1979, 80; law clk. U.S. Supreme Ct., Washington, 1980-81; prof. law NYU, N.Y.C., 1981—, dean Law Sch., 1988—; dir. Washington Sq. Legal Services, N.Y.C., 1983—, Pub. Interest Law Found., N.Y.C., 1983-85. Author: A Managerial Model of the Supreme Court, 1985, Federal Jury Instructions-Civil, 1985, How Free Are We? A Study of the Constitution, 1985, Cases and Materials in Civil Procedure, 1988. Dir. Root-Tilden Scholarship Program, 1984-88; mem. Assn. of Am. Law Schs. (pres. 1997-98). Home: 29 Washington Sq W New York NY 10011-9180 Office: NYU Law Sch 40 Washington Sq S New York NY 10012-1099

**SEYBERT, JOANNA,** federal judge; b. Bklyn., Sept. 18, 1946; married; 1 child. BA, U. Cin., 1967; JD, St. John's U., 1971. Bar: N.Y. 1972, U.S. Dist. Ct. (ea. and so. dists.) N.Y. 1973, U.S. Ct. Appeals (2d cir.) 1973. Trial staff atty. Legal Aid Soc., N.Y.C., 1971-73; sr. staff atty. Legal Aid Soc., Mineola, N.Y., 1976-80; sr. trial atty. Fed. Defender Svc., Bklyn., 1973-75; bur. chief Nassau County Atty's Office, Mineola, 1980-87; judge Nassau County Dist. Ct., Hempstead, N.Y., 1987-92, Nassau County Ct., Mineola, 1992-94, U.S. Dist. Ct. (ea. dist.) N.Y., Uniondale, 1994—. Mem. Bar Assn. Nassau County, Nassau County Women's Bar Assn., Theodore Roosevelt Am. Inns of Ct., Fed. Judges Assn., Nassau Lawyer's Assn. (past pres.). Office: 2 Uniondale Ave Uniondale NY 11553-1259

**SEYMOUR, BARBARA LAVERNE,** lawyer; b. Columbia, S.C., July 9, 1953; d. Leroy Semon and Barbara Lucile (Youngblood) Seymour. BS, S.C. State Coll., 1975; JD, Georgetown U., 1979; MBA, Harvard U., 1985. Bar: S.C. 1979, Tex. 1984, U.S. Dist. Ct. (ea. dist.) Tex. 1983, U.S. Dist. Ct. (so. dist.) Tex. 1985, U.S. Tax Ct. 1986, U.S. Claims Ct. 1991. Tax atty. Texaco Inc., White Plains, N.Y., 1979-80, Houston, 1980-98; exec. asst. Office of the CFO-Gen. Counsel, Equilon Enterprises LLC, Houston, 1998-99, asst. sec., counsel, 1999—; mem. IRS Commr.'s Adv. Group, 1995-97; mem. Simplified Tax and Wage Reporting Sys. Working Group, 1994-97; loaned exec. for task force to audit Tex. Employment Commn. by Gov. of Tex., 1987-88. Troop leader Girl Scouts U.S., White Plains, 1979-80, asst. troop leader, Houston, 1981-82; bd. dirs. Sickle Cell Disease Rsch. Found. Tex., Houston, 1986-92, treas., 1986-88, pres., 1988-90, chair 25th anniversary gala, 1996; vol. allocation panel United Way of the Tex. Gulf Coast; bd. dirs. Found. for Main St., Sandra Organ Dance Co.; mem. Black Exec. Exch. program Nat. Urban League 1980—; bd. dirs., exec. com. Houston Area Urban League, 1995—, 3d v.p., 1998—, chair 1997 Equal Opportunity Day Dinner; bd. dirs., asst. treas. Sheila Jackson Lee for Congress, 1995-97. Named One of 50 Outstanding Young Leaders of the Future, Ebony Mag., 1983; recipient Disting. Bus. Alumnus award S.C. State Coll., 1991, Eagle award Nat. Eagle Leadership Inst., 1995; selected for Leadership Houston, Leadership Am., 1990; finalist Five Outstanding Young Houstonians award Jaycees, 1988, one of 10 Foremost Fashionables in Houston, Alpha Kappa Alpha, 1994. Mem. ABA (environ. tax com., employment tax com.), Houston Black Women Lawyers Assn. (sec. 1981-82, treas. 1982-83), Houston Bus. Forum (bd. dirs. 1983, 87-90, treas. 1988-89, sec. 1989-90), Nat. Bar Assn. (com. chmn. 1982-83), S.C. Bar Assn., Tex. Bar Assn., Harvard U. Bus. Sch. Black Alumni Assn. (historian 1985-86), Black Law Alumni Coun. of Georgetown U. Law Ctr., W.J. Durham Soc., The Links, Inc. (v.p. Houston chpt. 1996—, chair 1995 Cotillion), Alpha Kappa Alpha. Democrat. Roman Catholic. Corporate taxation, Pension, profit-sharing, and employee benefits, State and local taxation. Office: Equilon Enterprises LLC 1100 Louisiana St Ste 2200 Houston TX 77002-5215

**SEYMOUR, MARY FRANCES,** lawyer; b. Durand, Wis., Oct. 20, 1948; d. Marshall Willard and Alice Roberta (Smith) Thompson; m. Marshall Warren Seymour, June 6, 1970; 1 foster child, Nghia Pham. BS, U. Wis., LaCrosse, 1970; JD, William Mitchell Coll., 1979. Bar: Minn. 1979, U.S. Dist. Ct. Minn. 1979, U.S. Ct. Appeals (8th cir.) 1979, U.S. Supreme Ct. 1986. With Cochrane and Bresnahan, P.A., St. Paul, 1979-94, Loper & Seymour, P.A., 1994—. Mem. ABA, Minn. Bar Assn., Ramsey County Bar Assn. Federal civil litigation, General civil litigation, State civil litigation. Office: Loper & Seymour PA 24 4th St E Saint Paul MN 55101-1002

**SEYMOUR, SAMUEL WHITNEY,** lawyer; b. Hanover, N.H., 1957. AB, Dartmouth Coll., 1979; JD, Columbia U., 1982. Bar: N.Y. 1983. Asst. U.S. Atty. U.S. Dist. Ct. (so. dist.) N.Y., 1988-91; ptnr. Sullivan & Cromwell, N.Y.C., 1991—. Office: Sullivan & Cromwell 125 Broad St Fl 28 New York NY 10004-2489

**SEYMOUR, STEPHANIE KULP,** federal judge; b. Battle Creek, Mich., Oct. 16, 1940; d. Francis Bruce and Frances Cecelia (Bria) Kulp; m. R. Thomas Seymour, June 10, 1972; children: Bart, Bria, Sara, Anna. BA magna cum laude, Smith Coll., 1962; JD, Harvard U., 1965. Bar: Okla. 1965. Practice Boston, 1965-66, Tulsa, 1966-67, Houston, 1968-69; assoc. Doerner, Stuart, Saunders, Daniel & Anderson, Tulsa, 1971-75, ptnr., 1975-79; judge U.S. Ct. Appeals (10th cir.) Okla., Tulsa, 1979-96, now chief justice, 1996—; assoc. bar examiner Okla. Bar Assn., 1973-79; trustee Tulsa County Law Library, 1977-78; mem. U.S. Jud. Conf. Com. Defender Svcs., 1985-91, chmn., 1987-91. Mem. various task forces Tulsa Human Rights Commn., 1972-76, legal adv. panel Tulsa Task Force Battered Women, 1971-77. Mem. Am. Bar Assn., Okla. Bar Assn., Tulsa County Bar Assn., Phi Beta Kappa. Office: US Courthouse 333 W 4th St Ste 4-562 Tulsa OK 74103-3819*

**SFEKAS, JAMES STEPHEN,** judge; b. Racine, Wis., Aug. 25, 1918; m. Litsa Mesologites, Sept. 2, 1945; children—Stephen J., Carole, Constantine J. B.S. in Econs., Johns Hoplins Univ., 1939; J.D., U. Md., 1948. Asst. solicitor City of Balt., 1956-59; spl. atty. Office of State Atty. Gen., Balt., 1959-72, adminstrv. spl. atty., 1972-77; judge Dist. Ct. Baltimore County, Towson, Md., 1977-80, Circuit Ct. Baltimore County, Towson, 1980—; chmn. alternative sentencing com. Dist. Ct., Towson, 1978-80; chmn. continuing legal edn. com. Baltimore County, 1984—. Served to capt. U.S.Army, 1941-46, ETO. Conf. of Cir. Judges. Democrat. Greek Orthodox. Office: 401 Bosley Ave Baltimore MD 21204-4420

**SFEKAS, STEPHEN JAMES,** lawyer, educator; b. Balt., Feb. 12, 1947; s. James Stephen and Lee (Mesologites) S.; m. Joanne Lorraine Murphy, May 27, 1973; children: James Stephen, Andrew Edward Stephen, Christina Marie; m. Elizabeth Ruff, Nov. 1, 1997. BS in Fgn. Svc., Georgetown U., 1968, JD, 1973; MA, Yale U., 1972. Bar: Md. 1973, U.S. Dist. Ct. Md. 1974, U.S. Ct. Appeals (4th cir.) 1974. Law clk. U.S. Dist. Ct., Balt., 1973-74; assoc. firm Frank, Bernstein, Conaway & Goldman, Balt., 1974-75; asst. atty. gen. State of Md., Balt., 1975-81; assoc. firm Tydings & Rosenberg, Balt., 1981-82, ptnr., 1983-86; with firm Miles & Stockbridge, Balt., 1986-90; ptnr. Weinberg & Green, Balt., 1991-98; now Saul, Ewing, Weinberg & Green, LLP, Balt., 1998—; instr. legal writing C.C. Balt., 1976-79; instr. legal ethics Goucher Coll., Balt., 1979; adj. prof. adminstrv. law U. Md., Balt., 1981-93, health, 1993—, law sch. U. Balt., 1993—; pres.'s adv. com. U. Md., 1998—. Editor Georgetown Law Jour., 1972-73; contbr. articles to legal publs. Bd. dirs. Md. region NCCJ, 1981-89, co-chmn. Md. region, 1986-89; mem. Piraeus Sister City Com., City of Balt., 1983-89; mem. parish coun. Greek Orthodox Cathedral of Annunciation, Balt., 1981-84; mem. internat. com. Balt. region ARC, 1984-85; mem. adv. com. on bread for the world Dept. Ch. and Soc., Greek Orthodox Archdiocese North and S.Am., 1984—; pres. Greek Orthodox Counseling and Social Svcs. of Balt., 1984-88; bd. dirs. Orthodox Christian Laity, 1990—, Ctrl. Md. Ecumenical Coun., 1991—; mem. bylaw com. Girl Scouts Ctrl. Md., 1989-91, Md. Leadership Program, 1997. Danforth fellow, Woodrow Wilson fellow, WHO fellow, London, 1979. Fellow Md. Bar Found., Soc. for Values in Higher Edn.; mem. ABA (Grant Morris fellow 1979, forum com. on health law), Md. Bar Assn., Bar Assn. Balt. City, Am. Health Lawyers Assn., Am. Soc. Hosp. Attys. Democrat. Administrative and regulatory, Health, Federal civil litigation. Office: Saul Ewing Weinberg & Green 100 S Charles St Baltimore MD 21201-2725

**SHABAZ, JOHN C.,** federal judge; b. West Allis, Wis., June 25, 1931; s. Cyrus D. and Harriet T. Shabaz; children: Scott J., Jeffrey J., Emily D., John D. Student, U. Wis., 1949-53; LLB, Marquette U., 1957. Pvt. practice law West Allis, Wis., 1957-81; mem. Wis. Assembly, 1965-81; judge U.S. Dist. Ct. (we. dist.) Wis., 1981-96, chief judge, 1996—. With U.S. Army, 1954-64. Office: US Dist Ct PO Box 591 Madison WI 53701-0591

**SHACKELFORD, PATRICIA ANN,** lawyer; b. Wilmington, Ohio, Sept. 27, 1953; d. Edward E. and Natalie (McIntire) S.; m. John S. Wood, Aug. 14, 1993; 1 stepchild, John W. II. BA cum laude, Trinity U., 1974; JD cum laude, Baylor U., 1993. Bar: Tex., U.S. Dist. Ct. (ea. dist.) Tex. 1997, U.S. Dist. Ct. (we. dist.) Tex. 1997, U.S. Dist. Ct. (so. dist.) Tex. 1997, U.S. Dist. Ct. (no. dist.) Tex. 1997, U.S. Ct. Appeals (5th cir.) 1997, U.S. Supreme Ct. 1997, U.S. Ct. Appeals (10th cir.) 1998. Paralegal David L. Perry & Assocs., Corpus Christi, Tex., 1983-91; atty. Ct. Appeals for 13th Jud. Dist., Corpus Christi, 1993-95; assoc. Matthews & Branscomb, Corpus Christi, 1995; assoc. Perry & Haas, Corpus Christi, 1996, ptnr., 1997-98; ptnr. Edwards, Perry & Haas, Corpus Christi, 1998—. Mem. ABA, ATLA, Am. Health Lawyers Assn., Tex. Trial Lawyers Assn., State Bar Assn. Tex., Corpus Christi Bar Assn. (treas. 1998—). Appellate, General civil litigation, Health. Office: Edwards Perry & Haas 802 N Carancahua St Ste 2100 Corpus Christi TX 78470-0002

**SHACKLETON, RICHARD JAMES,** lawyer; b. Orange, N.J., May 24, 1933; s. S. Paul and Mildred W. (Welsh) S.; m. Katharine L. Richards, June 16, 1956; children: Katharine Margaret, Julia Anne, Forrest Maxwell. Student, Kalamazoo Coll., 1957; JD, Rutgers U., 1961. Bar: N.J. 1961, U.S. Dist. Ct. N.J. 1967, U.S. Dist. Ct. (ea. dist., Eastern NY, 1987, Southern NY, 1986, Western NY, 1997, Northern NY, 1997) N.Y. 1982, U.S. Ct. Appeals (3rd cir.) 1983, U.S. Ct. Appeals (4th cir.) 1986 , U.S. Supreme Ct., 1969, Fed. Bar Coun., NJ, 1988. Ltd. atty. Berry Whitson & Berry, 1961; practice Ship Bottom, N.J., 1961—; sr. ptnr. Shackleton, Hazeltine & Dasti, Ship Bottom, 1965-84, Shackleton, Hazeltine & Bishop, 1984—. Pres. Beach Haven Inlet Taxpayers Assn., 1958-68, Ocean County Vis. Homemakers Assn., 1966-72, Brodhead Watershed Assn., 1997-98; mem. hist. soc. U.S. Dist. Ct. N.J. Mem. ABA, Am. Judicature Soc., Fed. Bar Coun. N.Y., N.J. Bar Assn. (litigation sect., product liability com., tort and ins. sect.), N.Y. Bar Assn., Ocean County Bar Assn., Def. Rsch. Inst. (mem. med. device and products sect.), Ocean County Lawyers Club, Henryville Conservation Club (chmn. bd.), Henryville Flyfishers Club (pres.), The Anglers' Club Phila., Phila. Gun Club, Sandy Island Gun Club (life), NRA (life), Brodhead Protectice Assn. (bd. dirs.), Brodhead Watershed Assn. (bd. dirs., pres. 1997-98), Phila. Flyfishers., Ancient Inc. Order of the Beefeater. Federal civil litigation, State civil litigation, Product liability. Home: 5614 West Ave Beach Haven NJ 08008-1059 Office: 22d St at Long Beach Blvd Ship Bottom NJ 08008

**SHACTER, DAVID MERVYN,** lawyer; b. Toronto, Ont., Can., Jan. 17, 1941; s. Nathan and Tillie Anne (Schwartz) S. BA, U. Toronto, 1963; JD, Southwestern U., 1967. Bar: Calif. 1968, U.S. Ct. Appeals (9th cir.) 1969, U.S. Supreme Ct. 1982. Law clk., staff atty. Legal Aid Found., Long Beach, Calif., 1967-70; asst. city atty. City of Beverly Hills, Calif., 1970; ptnr. Shacter & Berg, Beverly Hills, 1971-83, Selwyn, Capalbo, Lowenthal & Shacter Profl. Law Corp., 1984—; del. State Bar Conf. Dels., 1976—; lectr. Calif. Continuing Edn. of Bar, 1977, 82, 83, 86; judge pro tem L.A. and Beverly Hills mcpl. cts.; arbitrator L.A. Superior Ct., 1983—, also judge pro tem; disciplinary examiner Calif. State Bar, 1986. Bd. dirs. and pres. Los Angeles Soc. Prevention Cruelty to Animals, 1979-89. Mem. Beverly Hills Bar Assn. (bd. govs. 1985—, editor-in-chief jour., sec. 1987-88, treas. 1988-89, v.p. 1989-90, pres.-elect 1990-91, pres. 1991-92), Beverly Hills Bar Found. (bd. govs. 1998—), Am. Arbitration Assn. (nat. panel arbitrators, NASD arbitration panel), City of Hope Med. Ctr. Aux., Wilshire C. of C. (bd. dirs., gen. counsel 1985-87). General civil litigation, Estate planning, Personal injury. Office: Selwyn Capalbo Lowenthal & Shacter Profl Law Corp 8383 Wilshire Blvd Ste 510 Beverly Hills CA 90211-2404

**SHADDIX, JAMES W.,** lawyer; b. 1946. BBA, U. Tex., 1968, JD, 1971. Bar: Tex. 1971. With U.S. Treasury-IRS, 1972-77; atty. in pvt. practice, 1977-79; asst. gen. counsel Pennzoil-Quaker Co., 1979-90; gen. counsel Pennzoil Co., 1990-98; gen. cousnel Pennzoil-Quaker Co., 1998—. General corporate, Labor, Oil, gas, and mineral. Office: Pennzoil-Quaker State Co PO Box 2967 Houston TX 77252-2967

**SHADDOCK, WILLIAM EDWARD, JR.,** lawyer; b. Lake Charles, La., Jan. 18, 1938; s. William Edward Shaddock and Edith (Burton) Plauche; m. Winifred Craig Gorham, Aug. 2, 1958; children: Stephen Gorham, Mary Craig, Nancy Edith. BS, La. State U., 1960, JD, 1963. Bar: La. 1963, U.S. Dist. Ct. (we. dist.) La. 1964, U.S. Supreme Ct. 1968, U.S. Ct. Appeals (5th cir.) 1981; cert. specialist in estate planning and adminstrn. La. Bd. Legal Specialization. Assoc. Plauche & Stockwell, Lake Charles, La., 1963-66; ptnr. Stockwell, Sievert, Viccellio, Clements & Shaddock, L.L.P., Lake Charles, 1966—. Fellow Am. Coll. Trusts and Estates Counsel (state chmn. 1994-99). Republican. Methodist. Avocations: fishing, hunting, photography. Probate, Estate planning, Oil, gas, and mineral. Office: Stockwell Sievert Viccellio Clements & Shaddock PO Box 2900 One Lakeside Plz 4th Fl Lake Charles LA 70602

**SHADOAN, WILLIAM LEWIS,** judge; b. Galesburg, Ill., July 12, 1931; s. William Parker and Hortense (Lewis) S.; m. Katherine E. Thomson, 1961; children—Ann-Wayne Harlan, Kate, Tom. BS, U. Ky., 1955; JD, U. Louisville, 1961. Bar: Ky. 1961, U.S. Dist. Ct. (we. dist.) Ky. 1961. City atty., Wickliffe, Ky., 1963; county atty. Ballard County, Ky., 1963-76; chief regional judge 1st cir. Wickliffe, Ky., 1983—. Chmn., Ballard County Democratic Party, 1963; trustee Methodist Ch., Wickliffe, 1961-84; adviser Selective Service, Paducah, Ky., 1968; chmn. Wickliffe C. of C., 1967-71; mem. exec. com. Ky. Hist. Soc., Frankfort; vice chmn. Ky. Cert. of Need and Licensure Bd., 1973-84. Named assoc. justice Ky. Supreme Ct., 1984. Served to capt. U.S. Army, 1955-59. Mem. Ky. Health Systems Assn. (vice chmn. 1976-82), ABA, Ky. Bar (Outstanding Judge 1997), Assn. Trial Lawyers Am., Ky. County Ofcls. Bd. (chmn. 1976-80), Miss. River Commn. (chmn. 1976-83), Ky. County Attys. Assn. (pres. 1966-77), First Dist. Bar Assn. (pres.). Lodges: Mason (Wickliffe, 32 degree); Shriners (Madisonville, Ky.); Order of Eastern Star, Elks. Home: RR 2 Wickliffe KY 42087-9804 Office: Ballard Courthouse 4th St Wickliffe KY 42087

**SHADUR, MILTON I.,** judge; b. St. Paul, June 25, 1924; s. Harris and Mary (Kaplan) S.; m. Eleanor Pilka, Mar. 30, 1946; children: Robert, Karen, Beth. B.S., U. Chgo., 1943, J.D. cum laude, 1949. Bar: Ill. 1949, U.S. Supreme Ct. 1957. Pvt. practice practice Chgo., 1949-80; assoc. Goldberg, Devoe & Brussell, 1949-51; ptnr. Shadur, Krupp & Miller and predecessor firms, 1951-80; judge U.S. Dist. Ct. (no. dist.) Ill., Chgo., 1980-92, sr. judge, 1992—; commr. Ill. Supreme Ct. Character and Fitness, 1961-72, chmn., 1971; gen. counsel Ill. Jud. Inquiry Bd., 1975-80; mem. adv. com. on evidence rules to Jud. Conf. of U.S., 1992—. Editor-in-chief: U. Chgo. Law Rev., 1948-49. Chmn. visiting com. U. Chgo. Law Sch., 1971-76, mem. vis. com., 1989-92; bd. dirs. Legal Assistance Found. Chgo., 1972-78; trustee Village of Glencoe, 1969-74, Ravinia Festival Assn., 1976-93, exec. com. 1983-93, vice chmn. 1989-93, life trustee, 1994—. Lt. (j.g.) USNR, 1943-46. Fellow Am. Bar Found.; mem. ABA (spl. com. on youth edn. for citizenship 1975-79), Ill. State Bar Assn. (joint com. on rules of jud. conduct 1974), Chgo. Bar Assn. (chmn. legis. com. 1963-65, jud. com. 1970-71, profl. ethics com. 1975-76, sec. 1967-69), Chgo. Council Lawyers, Order of Coif. Office: US Dist Ct 219 S Dearborn St Chicago IL 60604-1702

**SHADWICK, GERALD,** management educator; b. Emporia, Kans.; m. Jeannine Wedell, June 5, 1954; children: Jeffrey, Monte, Jay, Nancy. BS with honors, Kans. State U., 1954; JD with honors, George Washington U., 1967. Bar: Va. 1967, U.S. Supreme Ct. Legis. asst. Congressman Graham Purcell, Washington, 1963-66; adminstrv. asst. Senator Frank Carlson, Washington, 1967-68; pres. First Nat. Bank, Salina, Kans., 1969-86; chmn., pres., CEO Bank One, Greeley, Colo., 1986-96; Monfort exec. prof. mgmt. U. No. Colo., Greeley, 1996—; adv. bd. mem. GE Johnson Constrn. Inc., Colorado Springs, Colo., 1984—; bd. dirs. Benchmark Oil and Gas, Denver. Bd. mem. Cmty. Found., Greeley, 1995—; treas. Greeley Philharm. Orch., 1995—; trustee Aims C.C., Greeley, 1996—. Capt. USAF, 1954-58. Mem. Rotary Club (pres.-elect). Home: 1720 37th Ave Greeley CO 80634-2804 Office: U No Colo Coll Bus Adminstrn 17th St At 8th Ave Greeley CO 80639-0001

**SHAEV, DAVID,** lawyer; b. Bklyn., July 5, 1949; s. Joseph and Gladys Shaev; m. Victoria A. Shaev, June 20, 1981; children: Brian, Jason. BA, Ohio U., 1971; JD, U. Louisville, 1974. Bar: Ky. 1974, U.S. Dist. Ct. (we. dist.) Ky. 1974, N.Y. 1976, U.S. Dist. Ct. (ea. and so. dists.) N.Y. 1976. Atty. Law Office of A. Markowitz, N.Y.C., 1976-81; pvt. practice law N.Y.C., 1981—. Mem. Nat. Assn. Consumer Bankruptcy Atty., N.Y. Bar Assn. (legal referral svc., bankruptcy panel). Avocations: tennis, skiing, Little League baseball coach. Bankruptcy, Family and matrimonial, Securities. Office: 200 Madison Ave New York NY 10016-3903

**SHAEVSKY, MARK,** lawyer; b. Harbin, Manchuria, China, Dec. 2, 1935; came to U.S., 1938, naturalized, 1944; s. Tolio and Rae (Weinstein) S.; m. Lois Ann Levi, Aug. 2, 1964; children: Thomas Lyle, Lawrence Keith. Student, Wayne State U., 1952-53; BA with highest distinction, U. Mich., 1956, JD with highest distinction, 1959. Bar: Mich. 1959. Law clerk to presiding judge U.S. Dist. Ct., Detroit, 1960-61; assoc. Honigman Miller Schwartz & Cohn, Detroit, 1961-64; ptnr. Honigman, Miller, Schwartz & Cohn, Detroit, 1965-69, sr. ptnr., 1969—; instr. law Wayne State U. Law Sch., Detroit, 1961-64; comml. arbitrator Am. Arbitration Assn., Detroit; bd. dirs. Charter One Fin. Inc., Charter One Bank. Contbr. Wayne State U. Law Rev., U. Mich. Law Rev., 1957-59, asst. editor, 1958-59. Dir. Detroit Mens Orgn. of Rehab. through Tng., 1969-79; mem. exec. bd. Am. Jewish Com., Detroit, 1965-74; trustee Jewish Vocat. Svcs., Detroit, 1973-76; sec., dir. Am. Friends Hebrew Univ., Detroit, 1976-84; mem. capital needs com. Jewish Welfare Fedn., Detroit, 1986-97; trustee William Beaumont Hosp., 1997—. With U.S. Army, 1959-60. Burton Abstract fellow, 1959. Mem. ABA, Mich. Bar Assn., Franklin Hills Country Club, Detroit Athletic Club, Order of the Coif, Phi Beta Kappa. General corporate, Securities, Real property. Home: The Hills of Lone Pine 4750 N Chipping Gln Bloomfield Hills MI 48302-2390 Office: Honigman Miller Schwartz & Cohn 2290 First National Bldg Detroit MI 48226

**SHAFER, STUART ROBERT,** lawyer. BS, Temple U., 1970; MA in Curriculum Devel., Mich. State U., 1971; JD, St. Mary's U., 1974. Bar: Tex. 1975, Mich. 1975, U.S. Dist. Ct. (ea. and we. dists.) Mich. 1975, U.S. Ct. Appeals (6th cir.) 1975, U.S. Supreme Ct. 1975. Law clk. Legal Aid Assn. Bexar County, San Antonio, 1973-75; chief atty., priority prosecution unit Ingham County Prosecutor's Office, Lansing, Mich., 1975-87; ptnr. Reid and Reid Law Firm, Lansing, Mich., 1987-95; pres. Stuart R. Shafer, P.C., Lansing, Mich., 1995—; mem Capitol Area Substance Abuse Commn., 1982-88, chair, 1984-86; coord. program and cmty. resources East Lansing Child Abuse Task Force, 1984-87; adj. prof. Thomas M. Cooley Law Sch., 1989-94; faculty Nat. Bus. Inst., Inc., 1991. Fax: 517-487-1409. E-mail: stushafer@aol.com. Criminal, Family and matrimonial, General civil litigation. Office: Bus and Trade Ctr 200 N Washington Sq Lansing MI 48933-1320

**SHAFFER, DAVID JAMES,** lawyer; b. Springfield, Ohio, July 30, 1958; s. Frank James Shaffer and Martha Isabelle (Hardman) Matthews; m. Julie Renee Cohen, Oct. 8, 1995; children: Brynn Danielle, Jedediah Clay. BA, Wittenberg U., 1980; JD, Stanford U., 1983. Bar: Calif. 1984, U.S. Dist. Ct. (no. and ea. dists.) Calif. 1984, U.S. Ct. Appeals (9th cir.) 1984, U.S. Dist. Ct. (so. dist.) Calif. 1985, U.S. Dist. Ct. (we. dist.) Wash. 1986, D.C. 1988, U.S. Dist. Ct. D.C. 1988, U.S. Ct. Appeals (D.C. cir.) 1988, U.S. Dist. Ct. (no. dist.) Tex. 1991, U.S. Supreme Ct. 1993, Md. 1994, U.S. Dist. Ct. Md. 1997. Supr. field ops. U.S. Census Bur., Columbus, Ohio, 1980; legal intern Natural Resources Def. Coun., Inc., San Francisco, 1982-83; assoc. Gibson, Dunn & Crutcher, San Jose, Calif., 1983; law clk. to Judge Betty B. Fletcher, U.S. Ct. Appeals for 9th Cir., Seattle, 1983-84; assoc. Gibson, Dunn & Crutcher, San Jose, 1984-87, Arnold & Porter, Washington, 1987-92; ptnr. Semmes, Bowen & Semmes, Washington, 1992-94, Arter & Hadden, Washington, 1995—. Campaign mgr. Clark County Dem. Party, Springfield, 1978-80; organizer Citizens for Sensible County Planning, Fairfax, Va., 1989-94. Alumni scholar Wittenberg U., 1976. Mem. ABA, FBA (chmn. EEO com. 1992-94, individual rights and responsibilities 1994-95, co-chmn. alt. dispute resolution 1995-96, mem. governing bd. labor law and labor rels. sect., editor newsletter Labouring Oar, Outstanding Svc. award 1992), D.C. Bar Assn., Calif. Bar Assn., Order of Coif. Avocations: music, hiking, nature study. Labor, Civil rights, General civil litigation. Office: Arter & Hadden 1801 K St NW Ste 400K Washington DC 20006-1301

**SHAFFER, DONALD,** lawyer; b. Cleve., Oct. 6, 1928; s. Nathan and Ruth (Glaser) S.; m. Doris Freed, June 10, 1949; children: Nathan, Robert, David. BA, Bklyn. Coll., 1949; JD, NYU, 1991. Bar: N.Y. 1992, U.S. Dist. Ct. (so. dist.) N.Y. 1992. Cooperating atty. ACLU, N.Y.C., 1992—; legal dir. Nassau Civil Liberties Union, Mineola, N.Y., 1995—. Co-chair New Progressive Party of L.I., 1995—; mem. state com. Working Families Party, State of N.Y., 1998—. Civil rights. Office: ACLU 125 Broad St Fl 18 New York NY 10004-2427

**SHAFFER, RICHARD JAMES,** lawyer, former manufacturing company executive; b. Pe Ell, Wash., Jan. 26, 1931; s. Richard Humphrys and Laura Rose (Faas) S.; m. Donna M. Smith, May 13, 1956; children: Leslie Lauren Shaffer Litsinger, Stephanie Jane Athenton. B.A., U. Wash.; LL.B., Southwestern U. Bar: Calif. Vice pres., gen. counsel, sec. NI, Inc., Long Beach, Calif., 1974-89; gen. counsel Masco Bldg. Products Corp., Long Beach, 1985-89; pvt. practice, Huntington Beach, Calif., 1989—; mem. ltd. liability co. drafting com. and task force Calif. State Bar, 1992-94; lectr. on ltd. liability cos. Trustee Ocean View Sch. Dist., 1965-73, pres., 1966, 73; mem. fin. adv. com. Orange Coast Coll., 1966; mem. Long Beach Local Devel. Corp., 1978-89, Calif. Senate Commn. on Corp. Governance, Shareholders' Rights and Securities Transactions, 1986-97, chmn. drafting com. ltd. liability co. act for senate com., 1991-93; mem. City of Huntington Beach Pers. Commn., 1996-98; bd. dirs. Huntington Beach Libr. Patrons, 1996-98. Mem. ABA, Nat. Assn. Securities Dealers (bd. arbitrators), Calif. Bar Assn. (exec. com. corp. law dept. com. bus. sect. 1981-88), Orange County Bar Assn., Huntington Harbour Yacht Club, Wanderlust Skiers of Huntington Harbour. General corporate, Real property, Finance.

**SHAFFER, ROBERTA IVY,** law librarian; b. Oceanside, N.Y., Nov. 27, 1953; d. Joseph Ceicel and Gladys (Dellerson) S.; m. Robert Maman, Aug. 14, 1995. AB in Econs., Vassar Coll., 1973; M of Librarianship, Emory U., 1975; JD, Tulane U., 1980; cert. in arts mgmt., Am. U., 1987. Bar: Tex. 1982, U.S. Dist. Ct. (so. dist.) Tex., U.S. Ct. Appeals (5th cir.), U.S. Supreme Ct. Dir. legal communications U. Houston Law Ctr., 1980-84, assoc. dir. law and tech., 1982-84; spl. asst. to law libr. Libr. of Congress, Washington, 1984-87; Fulbright sr. researcher Tel Aviv Faculty Law, 1987-88; pvt. practice cons. Washington, 1988-89; dir. devel. Washington Project for the Arts, 1989; acting libr. dir. George Washington U. Law Ctr., Washington, 1990; asst. dean U. Washington, Seattle, 1990-91; dir. libr. svcs. Covington & Burling, Washington, 1991-99; dean Grad. Sch. Libr. and Info. Sci. U. Tex., Austin, 1999—; cons. Coca-Cola Co., Atlanta, 1975-76, Research Info. Service, Houston, 1982-84; edn. rep. Westlaw, St. Paul, 1982-83. Bd. dirs. Friends of Torpedo Facatory Arts Ctr. Mem. ABA, Am. Assn. Law Librs., Internat. Assn. Law Librs. (sec. 1992-95, v.p. 1995—). Avocation: swimming, archeology, jewelry design. E-mail: rshaffer@gslis.utexas.edu. Office: GLSIS Univ Tex Austin Rm 564 George I Sanchez Bldg Austin TX 78712-1276

**SHAFFER, WAYNE ALAN,** lawyer; b. Reno, Oct. 15, 1954; s. William V. and Shirley Joy (Perry) S.; m. Robin E. Sprung, Jan. 7, 1978. BA, U. Nev., 1977; JD magna cum laude, Calif. Western Sch. Law, 1981. Bar: Nev. 1981, U.S. Dist. Ct. Nev. 1981, Calif. 1982. Dep. dist. atty. Washoe County, Reno, 1981-82; assoc. Lionel, Sawyer & Collins, Reno, 1982-84, Law Office Eugene J. Wait Jr., Reno, 1985-89; ptnr. Wait & Shaffer, Reno, 1989—; instr. Old Coll. Sch. Law, Reno, 1982. Mem. ABA, Nev. Bar Assn., Calif. Bar Assn., Assn. Def. Counsel No. Nev., Assn. Def. Counsel No. Calif. Republican. General civil litigation, Product liability, Personal injury. Office: Wait & Shaffer 305 W Moana Ln Ste D Reno NV 89509-4924

**SHAFFERT, KURT,** lawyer, chemical engineer; b. Vienna, July 20, 1929; s. Rudolph nee Schafranik and Irma (Altar) S.; m. Judith Pytel, June 12, 1955; children: Elona Ruth, Robin Laurette. BChemE, CCNY, 1951; LLB cum laude, NYU, 1963. Bar: N.Y. 1963, D.C. 1965, U.S. Supreme Ct. 1967, U.S. Patent and Trademark Office 1964. Chem. engr. Diamond Alkali Co., Newark, 1951-54; process devel. engr. Am. Cyanamid Co., Stamford, Conn., 1957-59; patent liaison engr. Uniroyal Inc., 1959-63; assoc. Arthur, Dry & Kalish, N.Y.C., 1963-66, Office of Robert F. Conrad, Washington, 1966-69; sr. ptrn. Shaffert, Miller & Browne, Washington, 1970-74; sr. trial atty. intellectual property sect. Antitrust divsn. Dept. of Justice, Washington, 1974-85, professions and intellectual property sect., 1985-94, intellectual property guidelines task force, 1994, civil task force, 1994—. Mem. Bethesda-Chevy Chase Jewish Comm. Group, 1965, pres., 1973-74, v.p. 1972-73, treas. 1971-72; mem. Jewish Comm. Ctr. of Greater Wash., 1970-78, bd. dirs., 1973-78; provided tape recorded Holocaust recollections for Stephen Spielberg Holocaust Archive Survivors of the Shoa Visual History Found., 1998. With U.S. Army, 1955-56. Mem. ABA (antitrust sect., patent, trademark and copyright sect.), Profl. Assn. Antitrust Divsn. Dept. of Justice (pres. 1978-79), Bar Assn. D.C. (council del. 1972-74), D.C. Bar Assn.

**SHAHEEN, MICHAEL EDMUND, JR.,** lawyer, government official; b. Boston, Aug. 5, 1940; s. Michael Edmund and Dorothy Wallace (Cameron) S.; m. Polly Adair Dammann, Sept. 11, 1976; children: Michael Edmund, Timothy Andrew. B.A., Yale U., 1962; LL.B., Vanderbilt U., 1965. Bar: Tenn. 1968. Dir. ann. capital support fund, instr. physics Memphis Univ. Sch., 1965-66; law clk. Judge Robert M. McRae, Jr., Memphis, 1966-68; individual practice law Tenn., Miss., 1968-73; dep. chief voting and public accomodations sect. Dept. Justice, Washington, 1973-74, dep. chief fed. programs sect., civil rights div., 1974-75; counsel to Atty. Gen. for Intelligence, 1975; spl. adv. to atty. gen., counsel, dir. Office Profl. Responsibility, 1975-98; spl. counsel to commr. IRS, Washington, 1998—; chief spl. counsel Office of Spl. Rev. Office of Ind. Counsel, Washington, 1998—; chief counsel Commn. on Advancement of Fed. Law Enforcement, Washington, 1998—; mayor, Como, Miss., 1970-73; pres. Como Resources, Inc., 1971-72; mcpl. judge, Como, 1970-73; chmn. Como Indsl. Devel. Commn., 1970-73. Mem. Phi Delta Phi, Zeta Psi. Office: Internal Rev Svc 1111 Constitution Ave NW Washington DC 20224-0001

**SHAHROOZ SCAMPATO, FRED,** lawyer; b. N.Y.C., July 26, 1962; gen. legal counsel Frederick Rsch. Corp., Plainfield, N.J., 1998; s. James Joseph and Nina Scampato; m. Froozan Fallah, Sept. 7, 1985; 1 child, Theresa. BA in Polit. Sci., Drew U., 1984, MA in Polit. Sci., 1985; JD, U. Ill., 1991. Bar: N.J., Supreme Ct. N.J. Jud. law clk. Superior Ct. N.J., New Brunswick, 1991-92; ptnr. Law Offices of Eichen & Cahn, Edison, N.J., 1992-98; pvt. practice Westfield, N.J., 1998—. Contbr. articles to profl. jours. Legal advisor Am. Pro Se Assn., Plainfield, 1994-98; v.p. Village of Convent Station (N.J.) Condominium Assn., 1996-98; spkr. in field. Mem. N.J. State Bar Assn., Union County Bar Assn., Middlesex County Bar Assn., Freemasons. Avocations: reading, writing, music, tennis. E-mail: Helios1067@aol.com. Fax: 908-301-9790. Office: 201 South Ave E Westfield NJ 07090-1456

**SHAIKH-BAHAI, CARRIE ANNE,** lawyer; b. Springfield, Ill., Nov. 20, 1966; d. Connie June Ohare; m. Farhad Shaikh-Bahai, Aug. 3, 1991; 1 child, Chloe June. BA, U. Ill., 1990; JD, Fordham U., 1994, MBA, 1994. Bar: Conn. 1995, N.Y. 1996. Atty., asst. v.p. Chgo. Title Ins., N.Y.C., 1994—. Mem. N.Y. State Bar Assn., Assn. of Bar of City of N.Y. Real property. Office: Chgo Title Ins 28th Fl 1211 Ave of the Americas New York NY 10016

**SHAIKUN, MICHAEL GARY,** lawyer; b. Ky., Mar. 17, 1942; s. Leon J. and Cleo (Taub) S.; m. Phyllis Miriam Cohen, Aug. 21, 1964; children: Benjamin, Stephanie, Alissa. BS in Econs. with highest honors, U. Pa., 1963; JD, Harvard U., 1966. Bar: Ky. 1966, U.S. Dist. Ct. (we. dist.) Ky. 1966. Assoc. Greenebaum Doll & McDonald PLLC, Louisville, 1966-69; mem. Greenebaum Doll & McDonald PLLC, 1970—. Contbr. articles to profl. jours. Bd. dirs. Jewish Cmty. Fedn. Louisville, 1971—, past pres.; past chmn. Found. for Planned Giving, Jewish Cmty. Fedn., Louisville; bd. dirs., chmn. fin. devel. YMCA Safe Place Svcs., 1995—. Mem. ABA, Ky. Bar Assn., Louisville Bar Assn. Democrat. Jewish. Avocation: computers. Bankruptcy, Contracts commercial, Real property. Home: 5907 Burlington Ave Louisville KY 40222-6118 Office: Greenebaum Doll & McDonald PLLC 3300 National City Tower Louisville KY 40202

**SHALLENBERGER, GARVIN F.,** lawyer; b. Beloit, Wis., Jan. 7, 1921; s. Garvin D. and Grace (Hubbell) S.; m. Mary L., May 5, 1945; children: Diane, Dennis Clark. BA in Pre-law, U. Mont., 1942; JD, U. Calif., Berkeley, 1949; LLD (hon.), Western State U., Fullerton, Calif., 1988. Bar: Calif. 1949, U.S. Dist. Ct. (cent. dist.) Calif. 1949, U.S. Ct. Appeals (9th cir.) 1949, U.S. Supreme Ct. 1961, U.S. Dist. Ct. (no. and so. dists.) Calif. 1963. Of counsel Rutan & Tucker, Costa Mesa, Calif.; chmn. spl. adv. com. state bar legal svcs. program, 1979-89, pub. law ctr Orange County, 1979-90. Recipient distinguished svc. award Boalt Hall (U. Calif. Berkeley), Judge Learned Hand Human Rel. award Nat. Jewish Com., 1990, Outstanding Alumnus award, U. Mont., 1999. Fellow Am. Coll. Trial Lawyers; mem. Am. Bd. Trial Advs. (a founder and 1st sec.),Calif. Bar Assn. (bd. govs. 1975-76, pres. 1977-78; mem. com. on jud. nominees 1978-79, pres. 1980), mem. Orange County Bar Assn. (bd. dirs. 1970-71, pres. 1972, Franklin West award 1979). Democrat. Avocations: tennis, writing. General civil litigation. Office: Rutan & Tucker PO Box 1950 Costa Mesa CA 92628-1950

**SHALOWITZ, HOWARD A.,** lawyer; b. Chgo., June 23, 1961; s. Mervin and Aileen (Goldstein) S. BA, U. Pa., 1983; JD, Washington U., 1987. Bar: Mo. 1987, Ill. 1988, U.S. Dist. Ct. (ea. dist.) Mo. 1988, U.S. Ct. Appeals (8th cir.) 1991, U.S. Ct. Appeals (7th cir.) 1993, U.S. Supreme Ct. 1994. Pvt. practice St. Louis, 1987—; legis. asst. Office of U.S. Senator Howard Metzenbaum, Washington, 1987; rsch. analyst Ill. Law Enforcement Commn., Chgo., 1981; mem. faculty Ctrl. Agy. for Jewish Edn., 1989-98. Lead tenor Gilbert and Sullivan operettas, 1979-84. Cantor; pres. St. Louis Circle Jewish Music, 1993-96, bd. dirs., 1987—. Bessie Bodek Miller scholar U. Pa., Phila., 1981-82; Glendy Burke Oratory medal Tulane U., New Orleans, 1981. Mem. ABA, Mo. Bar, Bar Assn. Met. St. Louis (chmn. lawyer referral and info. svc. com., treas., mem. exec. bd. govs.), Cantors Assembly. General practice, General civil litigation, Criminal. Office: 7108 Northmoor Dr Saint Louis MO 63105-2108

**SHAMBAUGH, STEPHEN WARD,** lawyer; b. South Bend, Ind., Aug. 4, 1920; s. Marion Clyde and Anna Violet (Stephens) S.; m. Marilyn Louise Pyle (dec. 1993); children: Susan Wynne Shambaugh Hinkle (dec. 1998), Kathleen Louise Shambaugh Thompson. Student, San Jose State Tchrs. Coll., 1938-40, U. Ark., 1951; LLB, U. Tulsa, 1954. Bar: Okla. 1954, Colo. 1964. Mem. staff Reading & Bates, Inc., Tulsa, 1951-54; v.p., gen. mgr., legal counsel Reading & Bates Drilling Co. Ltd., Calgary, Alta., Can., 1954-61; sr. ptnr. Bowman, Shambaugh, Geissinger & Wright, Denver, 1964-81; sole practice Denver, 1981-97; now ret.; dir., fin. counsel various corps. Col. USAF ret. Mem. Colo. Bar Assn., Okla. Bar Assn., P-51 Mustang Pilots Assn., Masons, Elks, Phi Alpha Delta. Banking, General corporate, Oil, gas, and mineral.

**SHAMIS, EDWARD ANTHONY, JR.,** lawyer; b. Pensacola, Fla., Dec. 12, 1949; s. Edward Anthony Sr. and Mona Kathryn (McLauglin) S.; m. Elizabeth Handley, Jan. 24, 1971; children: Ashley Vera, Edward Anthony III. BS, La. State U., 1972, JD, 1974. Bar: La. 1974, U.S. Dist. Ct. (ea. dist.) La. 1975, U.S. Tax Ct. 1981, U.S. Ct. Appeals (5th cir.) 1982, U.S. Supreme Ct. 1983. Pvt. practice, Slidell, La., 1974—; spl. counsel to Slidell City Coun., 1984—. Bd. dirs. Pope John H.S., Slidell, 1988-90, Children's Wish Endowment Fund, Inc. (formerly Northshore Children's Endowment Fund) 1991—; mem., pres. St. Tammany Assn. for Children with Learning Disabilities, Slidell, 1976-81; chmn. Slidell Bd. Zoning Adjustments, 1976-81; past mem. Boys Club; mem. St. Tammany Parish Ethics Commn. Mem. ATLA, La. Bar Assn. (hos. of dels. 1985-86, 88-89, 89-90, 94-97), St. Tammany Bar Assn., Slidell Bar Assn. (pres. 1978-79), La. Trial Lawyers Assn. (pres.'s adv. coun. 1980-81, 84-85, 89-90, 95-96). Republican. Avocations: hunting, computers, fishing, boating. Federal civil litigation, State civil litigation, Personal injury. Home: 32809 Cc Rd Slidell LA 70460-3275 Office: 486 Brownswitch Rd Slidell LA 70458-1102

**SHAMPANIER, JUDITH MICHELE,** lawyer; b. N.Y.C., July 2, 1968; d. Allen Abraham and Myrna (Jacobs) S. BA, Columbia Coll., 1990, JD, 1993. Bar: N.Y. 1994, U.S. Dist. Ct. (so. and ea. dists.) N.Y. 1994. Assoc. Dewey Ballantine, N.Y.C., 1993-96, Esanu, Katsky, Korins & Siger, N.Y.C., 1996—. Columnist In Brief, 1996—. Mem. ABA, N.Y. State Bar Assn., N.Y. Women's Bar Assn., Assn. of Bar of City of N.Y. Avocations: ballroom dancing, cooking, reading. General civil litigation, Trademark and copyright. Office: Esanu Katsky Korins & Siger 605 3d Ave New York NY 10158

**SHANAHAN, THOMAS M.,** judge; b. Omaha, May 5, 1934; m. Jane Estelle Lodge, Aug. 4, 1956; children: Catherine Shanahan Trofholz, Thomas M. II, Mary Elizabeth, Timothy F. A.B. magna cum laude, U. Notre Dame, 1956; J.D., Georgetown U., 1959. Bar: Nebr., Wyo. Mem. McGinley, Lane, Mueller, Shanahan, O'Donnell & Merritt, Ogallala, Nebr.; assoc. justice Nebr. Supreme Ct., Lincoln, 1983-93; judge U.S. Dist. Ct. Nebr., Omaha, 1993—. Office: US Dist Ct 215 N 17th St PO Box 457 Omaha NE 68101-0457

**SHANE, PETER MILO,** law educator; b. Oceanside, N.Y., July 12, 1952; s. Albert and Ann (Semanoff) S.; m. Martha Elisabeth Chamallas, June 27, 1981; 1 child: Elisabeth Ann. AB, Harvard U., 1974; JD, Yale U., 1977. Bar: N.Y. 1978, U.S. Ct. Appeals (5th cir.) 1978, D.C. 1979, U.S. Ct. Appeals (8th cir.) 1983, U.S. Supreme Ct. 1984, Pa. 1995. Law clk. to judge U.S. Ct. Appeals (5th cir.), New Orleans, 1977-78; atty., advisor office of legal counsel U.S. Dept. Justice, Washington, 1978-81; asst. gen. counsel Office of Mgmt. and Budget, Washington, 1981; assoc. prof. law U. Iowa, Iowa City, 1981-85, prof., 1985-94; dean U. Pitts., 1994-98, prof., 1994—; adj. lectr. Am. U., Washington, D.C., 1979-80; vis. prof. law Duke U., Durham, N.C., 1986, Boston Coll., Newton, Mass., 1999, Villanova (Pa.) U., 1999; cons. U.S. Dept. Edn., Washington, D.C., 1980, MacArthur Justice Found., Chgo., 1987; active Adminstrv. Conf. U.S., 1991, pub. mem., 1995; cons. Nat. Commn. Jud. Discipline and Removal, 1992-93; cooperating atty. Iowa Civil Liberties Union, Des Moines, 1982-94, bd. dirs., 1987-89; active Coun. on Legal Edn. Opportunity, 1996—; reporter Civil Justice Adv. Group, U.S. Dist. Ct. (we. dist.) Pa. Author: (with H.H. Bruff) The Law of Presidential Power: Cases and Materials, 1988, (with J. Mashaw and R. Merrill) Administrative Law: The American Public Law System, 1992, (with H.H. Bruff) Separation of Powers Law, 1996. Mem. Dem. cen. com. Johnson County, Iowa, 1982-88. Recipient citation for outstanding svc. Pa. House of Reps., 1998; named Young Leader of Higher Edn., Am. Assn. Higher Edn., 1998; Old Gold Summer fellow U. Iowa, 1981-84, Mellon Found. fellow, 1982. Mem. ABA (coun. sect. adminstrv. law and regulatory practice 1993-96, chmn. com. on govt. orgn. and separation of powers 1987-91), Assn. Am. Law Schs. (chair adminstrv. law 1990, chair remedies 1992, chair law sch. deans 1997), Am. Law Inst. Jewish. Office: U Pitts Sch Law 3900 Forbes Ave Pittsburgh PA 15213

**SHANE, RICHARD J.,** lawyer; b. Chgo., Dec. 12, 1953; s. Lois Elaine Shane; m. Karen Rice, Sept. 16, 1979; children: Kelly, Eric, Caitlin. BA, U. Ill., Chgo., 1976; JD, No. Ill. U., 1980. Bar: N.Mex. 1980, U.S. Dist. Ct. N. Mex. 1980, U.S. Ct. Appeals (10th cir.) 1980. Atty. Dist. Atty.'s Office, Albuquerque, 1981-84; ptnr. Padilla, Riley & Shane, PA, Albuquerque, 1984-97, Riley, Shane & Hale, PA, Albuquerque, 1997—. Contbr. articles to profl. jours. Mem. Met. Parks and Adv. Bd., Albuquerque, 1995-98; founder Vineyard Estates Neighborhood Assn., pres. 1993-98. Recipient Outstanding Tchg. award N.Mex. State Bar-Lawyers With Class, 1995, Outstanding Individual award Vinyard Estates Neighborhood Assn., 1993, Honor Roll award, 1995. Avocations: managing youth baseball, biking, hiking. General civil litigation, Insurance. Office: Riley Shane & Hale PA Ste 200-n 4101 Indian School Rd NE Albuquerque NM 87110-3988

**SHANE, SUZANNE V.,** lawyer; b. Port Jefferson, N.Y., May 1, 1963; d. George William and Elizabeth Ann Voss; m. William Charles Shane, Sept. 17, 1988; 1 child, Alexander. BA, SUNY, Stony Brook, 1985; JD, N.Y. Law Sch., 1988. Bar: N.Y. 1989, U.S. Dist. Ct. (so. and ea. dists.) N.Y. 1993. Assoc. Dunnington, Bartholow & Miller, N.Y.C., 1988-90, Power, Weiss & Marks, N.Y.C., 1990-94, Twomey, Latham, Shea & Kelley, Riverhead, N.Y., 1994—. Mem. Three Village Hist. Soc., Setauket, N.Y., 1988—; bd. dirs. Suffolk County Girl Scouts, Commack, N.Y., 1996—, Emma S. Clark Meml. Libr., 1999—. Mem. N.Y. State Bar Assn., Suffolk County Bar Assn., Suffolk County Women's Bar Assn. Avocation: genealogy research. General civil litigation, Education and schools, General corporate. Office: Twomey Latham Shea & Kelley 33 W 2d St Riverhead NY 11901

**SHANER, CONSTANCE HOKE,** lawyer; b. Bryn Mawr, Pa., Oct. 25, 1955; d. James Wallace and Jacqueline Snyder (Hoke) S.; m. Paul Joseph Pfingst, Oct. 24, 1987. BA, U. Calif. Davis, 1977; JD, U. San Diego, 1980. Bar: Calif. 1980, U.S. Dist. Ct. (so. dist.) Calif. 1980. Assoc. Raureby, Shaner & Gibson, Carlsbad, Calif., 1981-97; pvt. practice Carlsbad, 1997—. Mem. Consumer Attys. San Diego, North San Diego County Bar Assn. Personal injury. Office: 2755 Jefferson St Ste 215 Carlsbad CA 92008-1715

**SHANER, LESLIE ANN,** lawyer; b. Lynchburg, Va., Oct. 1, 1948; d. George Leslie and Ruby Ann (Ward) S.; 1 child, Jennifer Ann; m. Harris Sol Levy, Mar. 15, 1992. BA, Randolph-Macon Women's Coll., 1989; JD, Washington & Lee U., 1992. Bar: U.S. Dist. Ct. (we. dist.) Va. 1993, U.S. Ct. Appeals (4th cir.) 1993. Assoc. Singleton & Deeds, Warm Springs, Va., 1992-94, O'Keefe & Spies, Lynchburg, Va., 1994-96; sole practitioner Lynchburg, 1996—; bd. dirs. Woman's Resource Ctr., Lynchburg, Va. Chmn. Ctrl. Shenandoah Disabilities Svcs. Bd., 1993-94; bd. dirs. Highland Med. Ctr., Inc., 1992-93, Valley Cmty. Svcs. Bd., 1993—. Recipient Nat. Collegiate Humanities award, Am. Jurisprudence award, Future Interests. Mem. ABA, Va. State Bar Assn., Va. Bar Assn., Va. Trial Lawyers Assn., Allegheny-Bath-Highland Bar Assn. (sec.-treas. 1993-94, chmn. social com. 1993-94), Lynchburg Bar Assn., The Federalists Soc. (sec.), Phi Delta Phi, Phi Beta Kappa, Omicron Delta Kappa (pres.), Eta Sigma Phi, Phi Alpha Phi. Avocations: reading, needlework, gardening, travel. General civil litigation, Family and matrimonial, General practice.

**SHANK, SUZANNE ADAMS,** lawyer; b. Kansas City, Mo., Nov. 13, 1946; d. Howard Howe and Bettie Ann (Winkler) Hettick; m. Martin Smoler, May 18, 1991. BJ, U. Mo., 1972; MPA in Health Adminstrn., U. Mo., Kansas City, 1982, JD, 1982. Bar: Mo. 1982, U.S. Dist. Ct. (we. dist.) Mo. 1982. Journalist U. Kans. Med. Ctr., Kansas City, 1972-73; asst. editor Am. Family Physician, Kansas City, Mo., 1973-75; exec. dir. Lambert Med. Clinic, Kansas City, Mo., 1975-80; assoc. Shughart, Thomson & Kilroy, Kansas City, 1982-85; v.p. GE/Employers Reins. Corp., Overland Park, Kans., 1985—. Mem. Friends of Zoo, Kansas City, Mo., 1981—, Menorah Med. Ctr. Aux., Kansas City, 1982—, Women's Vision Internat., Kansas City, Mo., 1999—. Mem. ABA, Mo. Bar Assn., Kansas City Bar Assn. (chmn. ins. law com.), Soc. Profl. Journalists, Soc. CPCU (rsch. com.), Com. to Protect Journalists, Kappa Tau alpha. Insurance, General corporate, Contracts commercial. Home: 2703 W 66th Ter Shawnee Mission KS 66208-1810 Office: Employers Reins Corp PO Box 2991 Shawnee Mission KS 66201-1391

**SHANK, WILLIAM O.,** lawyer; b. Hamilton, Ohio, Jan. 11, 1924; s. Horace Cooper and Bonnie (Winn) S.; m. Shirleen Allison, June 25, 1949; children—Allison Kay, Kristin Elizabeth. BA, Miami U., Oxford, O., 1947; JD, Yale, 1950. Bar: Ohio, Ill. bars, also U.S. Supreme Ct. bar. Pvt. practice Hamilton, Ohio, 1951-55, Chgo., 1955—; mem. firm Shank, Briede & Spoerl, 1951-55; assoc. Lord, Bissell & Brook, 1955-58; atty. Chemetron Corp., 1958-60, sr. atty., 1960-61, gen. atty., asst. sec., 1961-71, sec., gen. counsel, 1971-78; v.p., gen. counsel, sec. Walgreen Co., Deerfield, Ill., 1978-89; ptnr. Burditt & Radzius, Chartered, Chgo., 1989-98; exec. v.p. Internat. Bus. Resources, Inc., Chgo., 1993—; ptnr. Williams & Montgomery, Ltd., Chgo., 1998—; mem. bus. adv. coun. Miami U., Oxford, Ohio, 1975—; arbitrator 19th Jud. Cir., Ill., 1995—. Bd. dirs. Coun. for Cmty. Svcs. Met. Chgo., 1973-77; trustee Libr. Internat. Rels., 1971-78; bd. dirs. Chgo. Civic Fedn., 1984-89, Welgreen Drug Stores Hist. Found., 1990—; mem. Chgo. Crime Commn., 1985-89. 1st lt., pilot 8th Air Force, USAAF, World War II, ETO. Fellow Am. Bar Found. (life); mem. ABA (com. corp. gen. counsel), Ill. Bar Assn., Chgo. Bar Assn. (chmn. com. on corp. law depts. 1971-72, 89-90), Am. Soc. Corp. Secs. (pres. Chgo. regional group 1983-84, nat. bd. dirs. 1984-87), Yale U. Law Sch. Assn. (pres. Ill. Alumni, formerly exec. com. New Haven), Walgreen Alumni Assn. (pres. 1992-94), Legal Club (pres. 1979-80), Law Club, Univ. Club, Econ. Club, Yale Club of Chgo., Omicron Delta Kappa, Phi Delta Phi, Sigma Chi. General corporate, General civil litigation, Estate planning. Home: 755 S Shore Dr Crystal Lake IL 60014-5530 Office: Williams & Montgomery Ltd 20 N Wacker Dr Ste 2100 Chicago IL 60606

**SHANKS, C.A. DUDLEY,** lawyer; b. Louisville, Mar. 9, 1947; s. Pearce H. and Claire M. Shanks; m. Rita Shanks, June 9, 1973; 1 child, Pearce V. BA, U. Louisville, 1969, JD, 1972. Atty. Segal & Shanks, Louisville, 1978—. Insurance, Personal injury. Home: 327 Guthrie Grn Louisville KY 40202-1813

**SHANKS, HERSHEL,** editor, writer; b. Sharon, Pa., Mar. 8, 1930; s. Martin and Mildred (Freedman) S.; m. Judith Alexander Weil, Feb. 20, 1966; children: Elizabeth Jean, Julia Emily. BA, Haverford (Pa.) Coll., 1952; MA, Columbia, 1953; LLB, Harvard, 1956. Bar: D.C. 1956. Trial atty. Dept. Justice, 1956-59; pvt. practice Washington, 1959-88; ptnr. Glassie, Pewett, Beebe & Shanks, 1964-88; editor Bibl. Archaeology Rev., Washington, 1975—; pres. Bibl. Archaeology Soc., 1974—, Jewish Ednl. Ventures Inc., 1987—. Author: The Art and Craft of Judging, 1968, The City of David, 1973, Judaism in Stone, 1979, Jerusalem--An Archaeological Biography, 1995, The Mystery and Meaning of the Dead Sea Scolls, 1998, also articles; co-editor: Recent Archaeology in the Land of Israel, 1984; editor: Ancient Israel, A Short History, 1988, Christianity and Rabbinic Judaism, 1992, Understanding the Dead Sea Scrolls, 1992; editor Bible Rev., 1985—, Moment mag., 1987—, Archaeology Odyssey, 1998—. Mem. ABA, D.C. Bar Assn., Am. Schs. Oriental Rsch., Nat. Press Club, Phi Beta Kappa. Home: 5208 38th St NW Washington DC 20015-1812 Office: Bibl Archaeology Soc 4710 41st St NW Washington DC 20016-1700 *I try to take time to identify what is important in my life, to focus on that and ignore the rest when it conflicts. It takes conscious effort not to dissipate energy on activities and attitudes that don't matter in the big picture of my priorities. Free to concentrate on what I value most, I try to accomplish something each day in a regular, habitual way.*

**SHANLEY, ANTHONY JOHN,** lawyer; b. N.Y.C., June 13, 1943; s. John P. Shanley. BS, Syracuse U., 1965; MS, Cornell U., 1967; JD, Cornell Law Sch., 1976. Bar: Calif. 1976, U.S. Dist. Ct. (so. dist.) Calif. 1976. Dep. city atty. City of San Diego, 1977—. Republican. Roman Catholic. Avocations: sport fishing, old toy trains. Fax: (619) 533-5856. E-mail: ujs@sdcity.com. Office: Office of City Atty Ste 1100 1200 3d Ave San Diego CA 92101

**SHANMAN, JAMES ALAN,** lawyer; b. Cin., Aug. 1, 1942; s. Jerome D. and Mildred Louise (Bloch) S.; m. Marilyn Louise Glassman, June 11, 1972; 1 child, Ellen Joan. BS, U. Pa., 1963; JD, Yale U., 1966. Bar: N.Y. 1967, U.S. Ct. Mil. Appeals 1971, U.S. Supreme Ct. 1971, U.S. Ct. Appeals (2d cir.) 1972, U.S. Dist. Ct. (so. and ea. dists.) N.Y. 1972, U.S. Ct. Internat. Trade 1976, U.S. Ct. Appeals (fed. cir.) 1987, U.S. Dist. Ct. (ea. dist.) Mich. 1989, U.S. Ct. Appeals (7th cir.) 1999. Assoc. Cahill Gordon & Reindel, N.Y.C., 1971-74, Freeman, Meade, Wasserman, Sharfman & Schneider, N.Y.C., 1974-76; mem. firm Sharfman, Shanman, Poret & Siviglia, P.C., N.Y.C., 1976-95; ptnr. Camhy Karlinsky & Stein LLP, N.Y.C., 1995-96; mem. firm Sharfman, Siviglia, Poret, Kook, Ross & Shanman, P.C., N.Y.C., 1996-98; ptnr. Edwards & Angell, LLP, N.Y.C., 1998—; speaker on reins. law topics. Capt. USAF, 1966-71. Mem. ABA, N.Y. State Bar Assn., Assn. of Bar of City of N.Y. (com. ins. law 1985-88, 90-92, 98—, com. profl. liability ins. 1988-92, com. on assn. ins. plans 1989—), Am. Arbitration Assn. (comml. panel arbitrators 1980—). Federal civil litigation, State civil litigation, Insurance. Office: Edwards & Angell LLP 750 Lexington Ave New York NY 10022-1253

**SHANNAHAN, WILLIAM PAUL,** lawyer; b. Detroit, Mich., Nov. 21, 1934; s. William and Jean (Boyle) S.; m. Saracia L. Price, Sept. 24, 1983; children: MeglynAnne, Michael-Padraic. AB, U. Detroit, 1956; JD, Georgetown U., 1958. Bar: D.C. 1958, Mich. 1958, Calif. 1962. Ptnr. Higgs, Fletcher & Mack, La Jolla, Calif., 1967-81, Aylward, Kintz, et al.2, La Jolla, Calif., 1981-87, pvt. practice, La Jolla, Calif., 1987—. with U.S. Army, 1959-60. Democrat. Roman Catholic. Taxation, general, Probate. Office: 1200 Prospect St Ste 425 La Jolla CA 92037-3660

**SHANNON, JOE, JR.,** lawyer; b. Nov. 9, 1940; s. Joe and Juanita Elizabeth (Milliorn) S.; children: Kelley Jane, Joseph Patrick, Shelley Carol. BA, U. Tex., 1962, LLB, 1963. Bar: Tex. 1963, U.S. Supreme Ct. 1977, U.S. Dist. Ct. (no. dist.) Tex. 1970, U.S. Ct. Appeals (5th cir.) 1977, U.S. Dist. Ct. (we. dist.) 1998; cert. family law Tex. Bd. Legal Specialization, matrimonial arbitrator. Ptnr. Shannon & Shannon, Ft. Worth, 1963-72; adminstrv. asst. to spkr. Tex. Ho. of Reps., Austin, 1970; chief criminal div. Tarrant County Dist. Atty., Ft. Worth, 1972-78; pvt. practice Ft. Worth, 1978-99; ptnr. Snakard & Gambill, Ft. Worth, 1986-90; chief econ. crimes Tarrant County Dist. Atty., 1999—; adj. prof. Tex. Weslyan Sch. Law. Mem. Tex. Ho. of Reps., 1964-70. Fellow Tex. Bar Found., Am. Acad. Matrimonial Lawyers (cert.); mem. ABA, State Bar of Tex. (adv. com. family law, state bd. legal specialization, dist. grievance com. 1973-76, chmn. 1975-76, 95—, sec. 2d ct. appeals adv. com. 1995—), N. Tex. Family Law Specialists, Tarrant County Family Law Bar Assn. (pres. 1998), Phi Alpha Delta, Masons, Shriners. Family and matrimonial, Insurance, Alternative dispute resolution. Office: 1701 River Run Fort Worth TX 76107-6579 *Notable cases include: State vs. Cullen Davis, 1977, richest man to be tried for murder; State vs. Mutscher, bribery conspiracy trial of Tex. House Speaker and assocs.*

**SHANNON, JOHN SANFORD,** retired railway executive, lawyer; b. Tampa, Fla., Feb. 8, 1931; s. George Thomas and Ruth Evangeline (Garrett) S.; m. Elizabeth Howe, Sept. 22, 1962; children: Scott Howe, Elizabeth Garrett, Sandra Denison. AB, Roanoke Coll., 1952; JD, U. Va., 1955. Bar: Va. 1955. Assoc. Hunton Williams Gay Powell & Gibson, Richmond, Va., 1955-56; solicitor Norfolk & Western Ry., Roanoke, Va., 1956-60, asst. gen. solicitor, 1960-64, gen. atty., 1964-65, gen. solicitor, 1965-68, gen. counsel, 1968-69, v.p. law, 1969-80, sr. v.p. law, 1980-82; exec. v.p. law Norfolk (Va.) So. Corp., 1982-96, ret., 1996; bd. dirs. Norfolk So. Ry. Co., Pocahontas Land Corp., Va. Holding Corp., Norfolk and Western Ry. Co. Editor-in-chief: Va. Law Rev., 1954-55. Chancellor Episcopal Diocese Southwestern Va., 1974-82; pres. bd. trustees North Cross Sch., Roanoke, 1973-82; trustee, past chmn. exec. com. Roanoke Coll., Salem, Va.; bd. dirs. Legal Aid Soc., Roanoke Valley, 1969-80, pres., 1970-79; trustee Chrysler Mus., Norfolk, 1982-94, Norfolk Acad., 1987—. Mem. Va. Bar Assn., Norfolk and Portsmouth Bar Assn., Shenandoah Club, Roanoke Country Club, Norfolk Yacht and Country Club, Harbor Club, Order of Coif, Sigma Xi, Omicron Delta Kappa, Phi Delta Phi. Home: 7633 Argyle Ave Norfolk VA 23505-1701

**SHANNON, MALCOLM LLOYD, JR.,** lawyer; b. Phila., Jan. 27, 1946; s. Malcolm L. and Rosalia U. (Yanura) S.; m. Jeanne Marie Halle, Dec. 28, 1974; children: Travis Alan, Kate Meredith. BBA, U. N.Mex., 1968, JD, 1971. Bar: N.Mex. 1971, U.S. Supreme Ct. 1976, Tex. 1981, Colo. 1984, Calif. 1986. Counsel Gen. Atomics, 1991—; lectr. mining and pub. land law U. N.Mex. Adv. com. solar energy application Tech. Vocat. Inst. of Albuquerque Pub. Schs., 1976; judge N.Mex. State Sci. Fair 1978-80; mem. ednl. accountability com. Cherry Creek Sch. Dist., 1984-86; bd. dirs. Denver U./Pioneer Jr. Hockey Assn., 1991-94. Author publs. in field. Mem. ABA, Am. Corp. Counsel Assn. Republican. Roman Catholic. Oil, gas, and mineral, General corporate, Real property. Home: 6199 S Jamaica Ct Englewood CO 80111-5714 Office: 5000 S Quebec St Ste 600 Denver CO 80237-2705

**SHANSTROM, JACK D.,** federal judge; b. Hewitt, Minn., Nov. 30, 1932; s. Harold A. and Willian (Wendorf) S.; m. June 22, 1957; children: Scott S., Susan K. BA in Law, U. Mont., 1956, BS in Bus., 1957, LLB, 1957. Atty. Park County, Livingston, Mont., 1960-65; judge 6th Jud. Dist. Livingston, 1965-82; U.S. magistrate Billings, Mont., 1983-90, U.S. Dist. judge, 1990-96; chief judge U.S. Dist. Ct., Mont., 1996—. Capt. USAF, 1957-60. Office: US Dist Ct PO Box 985 Billings MT 59103-0985

**SHANTZ, DEBRA MALLONEE,** lawyer; b. Springfield, Mo., Aug. 12, 1963; d. Arnold Wayne and Jean Marie (Pyle) Mallonee; m. Joseph Benjamin Shantz, Dec. 26, 1987; children: Benjamin, Riley. BS, S.W. Mo. State U., 1984; JD, U. Mo., 1988. Ptnr. Farrington & Curtis, P.C., Springfield, 1988-95; corp. counsel John Q. Hammons Hotels, Springfield, 1995—. General corporate. Home: 3760 E Meadowmere Pl Springfield MO 65809-2020 Office: John Q Hammons Hotels Ste 900 300 S John Q Hammons Pkwy Springfield MO 65806-2596

**SHAPERO, BERTRAM MALCOLM,** lawyer; b. Detroit, May 30, 1933; s. Harold Marion and Esther (Balton) S.; m. Christina Alicia Miller, Feb. 26, 1972 (div. July 1989); children: Kenneth, Kricia. Student, U. Mich., 1951-54; LLB, U. Va., 1957, JD, 1970. Bar: Fla. 1982, U.S. Dist. Ct. (so. dist.) Fla. 1982, U.S. Tax Ct. 1980, U.S. Dist. Ct. (mid. dist.) Fla. 1999. Pvt. practice Detroit, 1969-76; owner Bertram Shapero Maintenance Co., Palm Beach, Fla., 1977-81; assoc. Law Offices of Philip Auerbach, Miami and Ft. Lauderdale, Fla., 1982; sole propr. Bertram Shapero, Atty. at Law, Palm Beach, Fla., 1983—. Pres., various offices Hist. Soc. Palm Beach County, 1985-90; gen. counsel, dir. Save a Pet Fla., Palm Beach, 1984—; rec. sec., gen. counsel M.C. Allen Found., West Palm Beach, 1996—; dir., sec., treas. Paws 2 Hold, Inc., 1998. With U.S. Army, 1957-58, Res., 1957-63. Mem. State Bar of Fla. (probate rules com. 1993—). Avocations: bicycling, humane societies, playing piano. State civil litigation, Contracts commercial, Probate. Office: 120 S Olive Ave Ste 301 West Palm Beach FL 33401-5532

**SHAPIRO, ALEENA RIEGER,** lawyer; b. Jaslo, Poland; m. Richard A. Shapiro; children: Randi, Deborah. JD, NYU, 1981, LLM in Taxation, 1985. Bar: N.Y. 1982, U.S. Dist. Ct. (so. and ea. dists.) N.Y. 1982, U.S. Tax Ct. 1982. Ptnr. Shapiro and Wender, L.L.P., 1997—; prin. Aleena R. Shapiro, Atty., N.Y.C., 1989-97; assoc. Willkie Farr & Gallagher, N.Y.C., 1981-84, Battle Fowler, N.Y.C., 1984-87, Patterson, Belknap Webb & Tyler, N.Y.C., 1987-89. Mem. ABA (tax sect.), N.Y. State Bar Assn. (tax sect.), Assn. of Bar of City of N.Y. Taxation, general, General corporate, Estate planning. Office: 230 Park Ave Fl 26 New York NY 10169-2699

**SHAPIRO, DAVID L.,** lawyer; b. Corsicana, Tex., May 19, 1936; s. Harry and Alice (Laibovitz) S. BA, U. Tex., 1967; JD, St. Mary's U., 1970. Bar: Tex. 1970, U.S. Dist. Ct. (we. dist.) Tex. 1972, U.S. Supreme Ct. 1975, U.S. Ct. Appeals (5th cir.) 1981. Assoc. Law Office Jim S. Phelps, Houston, 1971; pvt. practice Austin, 1972—; spl. counsel com. human resources Tex. Ho. Reps., Austin, 1973-74; counsel subcom. health svcs. Tex. Senate, Austin, 1983-87. With U.S. Army, 1959-61. Mem. State Bar Tex. (chmn. lawyer referral svc. com. 1980-82, adminstrn. of justice com. 1990-93, jury svc. com. 1998—, contbr. Media Law Handbook supplement 1986), Travis County Bar Assn. (sec.-treas. 1977-78, dir. 1979, pres. family law sect. 1980-81), Coll. of State Bar of Tex., Austin Criminal Def. Lawyers Assn., Travis County Bar Assn. Democrat. Avocations: automobiles, reading. General civil litigation, Criminal, Family and matrimonial. Home: 920 E 40th St #106 Austin TX 78751-4821 Office: 1200 San Antonio St Austin TX 78701-1834

**SHAPIRO, DOUGLAS BRUCE,** lawyer; b. N.Y.C., Nov. 4, 1954; s. Herbert and Barbara Shapiro; m. Jeannette Lynn Duane, May 31, 1986; children: Benjamin Max, Michael Jerome. AB with high distinction, U. Mich., 1983, JD cum laude, 1986. Bar: Mich. 1986. Law clk. to Justice James Brickley Mich. Supreme Ct., Lansing, 1986-89; asst. defender State Appellate Defender Office, Detroit, 1989-90; staff atty. Ctr. for Social Gerontology, Ann Arbor, Mich., 1990-91; atty., ptnr. Muth & Shapiro P.C., Ypsilanti, Mich., 1991—. Contbr. articles to profl. jours. Mem. exec. bd. Ann Arbor Dem. Party, 1990-92. Mem. ATLA, State Bar Mich., Mich. Trial Lawyers Assn., Washtenaw Trial Lawyers Assn. (pres. 1998—, bd. dirs. 1995-98). Personal injury, Product liability, Constitutional. Office: Muth & Shapiro 301 W Michigan Ave Ste 302 Ypsilanti MI 48197-5450

**SHAPIRO, EDWIN HENRY,** lawyer; b. Chgo., Mar. 12, 1938; s. Irving and Esther (Mikell) S.; m. Lesley Dahlin, Dec. 27, 1959; children: Craig, Cori. BS in Acctg., U. Ill., 1959; JD, Northwestern U., 1963. Bar: Ill. 1963, U.S. Dist. Ct. (no. dist.) Ill. 1970, U.S. Supreme Ct. 1979. Tax acct. Arthur Andersen & Co., Chgo., 1962-67; ptnr. Rosenfeld, Rotenberg, Hafron & Shapiro, Schaumburg, Ill., 1967—. Mem. ABA, Ill. Bar Assn., N.W. Suburban Bar Assn. (pres. 1985-86), Tau Epsilon Phi. Avocations: swimming, travel. E-mail: rrhs2@aol.com. Real property, State civil litigation. Office: 1111 N Plaza Dr Ste 570 Schaumburg IL 60173-4992

**SHAPIRO, EDWIN STANLEY,** lawyer, judge; b. Bklyn., Jan. 14, 1931; s. Harry I. and Ann (Safanie) S.; m. Sandra I. Bernstein, Sept. 15, 1957; children: James A., Sarah E. BA, Trinity Coll., Hartford, Conn., 1952; LLB, Harvard Law Sch., 1955. Bar: N.Y. 1956, U.S. Dist. Ct. (so. and ea. dist.) N.Y. 1956, U.S. Ct. Appeals 1957. Atty. Levin & Weintraub, N.Y.C., 1956-57; pvt. practice N.Y.C., 1957-59; ptnr. Smith, Shapiro & Scheier, N.Y.C., 1959-62, Basch, Seits & Shapiro, N.Y.C., 1970-74, Seits & Shapiro, N.Y.C., 1974-81; town justice Ossining, N.Y., 1980—; pvt. practice N.Y.C., 1981-95, Briarcliff Manor, N.Y., 1996—; lawyer Staten Island Open Lands Found., 1965-67. Mem. Assn. of Bar of City of N.Y. (com. on state cts. 1982-83, environ. law com. 1970-73, corrections com. 1996-98). General civil litigation, Probate.

**SHAPIRO, GEORGE HOWARD,** lawyer; b. St. Louis, Nov. 10, 1936; s. Isadore T. and Alice (Schucart) S.; m. Mary Kenney Leonard, 1977 (div. 1994); 1 child, Ellen. BA, Harvard U., 1958, LLB, 1961; postgrad., London Sch. Econs., 1961-62. Bar: Ga. 1960, D.C. 1963. Atty. U.S. Dept. Labor, Washington, 1962-63; assoc. Arent Fox Kintner Plotkin & Kahn, Washington, 1963-69, ptnr., 1970—. Co-author: 'Cable Speech' The Case for First Amendment Protection, 1983; editor: New Program Opportunities in the Electronic Media, 1983, Current Developments in CATV, 1981. With USAR, 1962-68. Frank Knox Meml. fellow Harvard U., 1961-62. Mem. D.C. Bar Assn., Fed. Communications Bar Assn. Democrat. Jewish. Avocation: skiing. Communications, Federal civil litigation, Constitutional. Home: 3249 Sutton Pl NW # D Washington DC 20016-3507 Office: Arent Fox Kintner Plotkin & Kahn 1050 Connecticut Ave NW Ste 500 Washington DC 20036-5339

**SHAPIRO, ISAAC,** lawyer; b. Tokyo, Jan. 5, 1931; s. Constantine and Lydia (Chernetzky) S.; m. Jacqueline M. Weiss, Sept. 16, 1956; children: Tobias, Alexandra, Natasha. AB, Columbia U., 1954, LLB, 1956, postgrad., 1956-57. Bar: N.Y. 1957, U.S. Supreme Ct. 1971, Paris 1991. Assoc. Milbank, Tweed, Hadley & McCloy, N.Y.C., 1956-65, ptnr., 1966-86; resident ptnr. Milbank, Tweed, Hadley & McCloy, Tokyo, 1977-79; ptnr. Skadden Arps Slate Meagher & Flom LLP, N.Y.C., 1986—; resident ptnr. Skadden Arps Slate Meagher & Flom, Hong Kong, 1989-90, Paris, 1990—; tchg. fellow comparative law NYU, 1959-61; lectr. Soviet law, 1961-67; adj. asst. prof. NYU, 1967-69, adj. assoc. prof., 1969-71, 74-75; adj. prof. and dir. Russian Legal Studies, Columbia Law School, 1999—; bd. dirs. Bank of Tokyo Mitsubishi Trust Co., N.Y.C., PRT Group, Inc., N.Y.C. Author: (with Hazard and Maggs) The Soviet Legal System, 1969; author: Japan: The Risen Sun (in Japanese), 1982; editor: The Middle East Crisis-Prospects for Peace, 1969; contbr. articles to profl. jours. Mem. Joint Com. U.S.-Japan Cultural and Ednl. Cooperation, Washington, 1972-78; mem. Japan-U.S. Friendship Commn., 1975-78; mem. svcs. policy adv. com. to U.S. Trade Rep., 1981-91; trustee Nat. Humanities Ctr., Triangle Park, N.C., 1976-89, Bank of Tokyo Mitsubishi Trust Co. Found., 1996—; trustee, v.p. Chamber Music Soc. Lincoln Ctr., 1980-86, Isamu Noguchi Zaidan, Japan, 1999—; trustee, pres. Isamu Noguchi Fedn., 1985—; trustee, chmn. Ise Cultural Fedn., 1984-90; bd. dirs. Bus. Coun. for Internat. Understanding, 1989-95, Nat. Com. for U.S.-China Rels., 1989-95, Asian Cultural Coun., 1980—. With U.S. Army, 1950-52. Fulbright scholar, 1956-57. Mem. ABA, N.Y. State Bar Assn., Assn. Bar City N.Y., Japan Soc. (pres. N.Y. 1970-77), Coun. Fgn. Rels. Private international. Office: Skadden Arps Slate Meagher & Flom LLP, 68 rue faubourg St Honore, 75008 Paris France

**SHAPIRO, JAMES EDWARD,** judge; b. Chgo., May 28, 1930; s. Ben Edward and Rose (Slate) S.; m. Rhea Kahn, Dec. 28, 1958; children—Jeffrey Scott, Steven Mark. B.S., U. Wis., 1951; J.D., Harvard U., 1954. Bar: Wis. 1956, U.S. Dist. Ct. (ea. dist.) Wis. 1956, U.S. Ct. Appeals (7th cir.) 1962, U.S. Supreme Ct. 1971. Sole practice, Milw., 1956-57; resident house counsel Nat. Presto Industries, Eau Claire, Wis., 1957-60; ptnr. Bratt & Shapiro, Milw., 1960-64; sole practice, Milw., 1964-74; ptnr. Frank, Hiller & Shapiro, Milw., 1974-82; judge U.S. Bankruptcy Ct., Milw., 1982—, chief judge, 1996—. Mem. Bayside Bd. Appeals, Wis., 1969-77; Milw. county ct. commr., 1969-78; dir. Milw. Legal Aid Soc., 1969-77. Served to 1st lt. U.S. Army, 1954-56. Mem. State Bar Assn. Wis. (chmn. bankruptcy, insolvency, creditors rights sect.), Milw. Bar Assn. (past chmn., past vice chmn. bankruptcy sect.). Jewish. Office: US Courthouse 140 Fed Bldg 517 E Wisconsin Ave Milwaukee WI 53202-4500

**SHAPIRO, MATHIEU JODE,** lawyer; b. Phila., Feb. 17, 1969; s. Irving Lawrence and Sharon Gertner S.; m. Jessica Sarah Singal, Aug. 18, 1996. BA, Amherst Coll., 1991; JD, Boston Coll., 1995. Bar: Pa. 1995, N.J. 1995, U. S. Dist. (ea. dist.) Pa., U.S. Dist. Ct. N.J., U.S. Ct. Appeals (3d cir.). Assoc. Obermayer, Rebmann, Maxwell & Hippel, Phila., 1995—. Bd. dirs. Friends Select Alumni Bd., Phila., 1996—. Mem. ABA, Pa. Bar Assn., Phila. Bar Assn. General civil litigation, Constitutional, Contracts commercial. Office: Obermayer Robmann Maxwell & Hippel 1617 J F K Blvd Ste 1900 Philadelphia PA 19103

**SHAPIRO, MICHAEL HENRY,** government executive; b. Bayonne, N.J., Sept. 23, 1948; s. William and Sophie (Slotkin) S. BS, Lehigh U., 1970; MS, Harvard U., 1972, PhD, 1976. Assoc. prof. Harvard U., Cambridge, Mass., 1976-82, analyst, 1980-81, br. chief, 1981-83, dir. econs. and tech. divsn., 1983-89; dep. asst. adminstr., air and radiation U.S. EPA, Washington, 1989-93, dir. office of solid waste, 1993—. Office: EPA # 5101 401 M St SW Washington DC 20460-0002

**SHAPIRO, NELSON HIRSH,** lawyer; b. Feb. 3, 1928; s. Arthur and Anna (Zenitz) S.; m. Helen Lenora Sykes, June 27, 1948; children: ronald Evan, Mitchell Wayne, Jeffrey Mark, Julie Beth. BEE, Johns Hopkins U., 1948; JD, George Washington U., 1952. Bar: D.C. 1952, Va. 1981. Patent examiner U.S. Patent Office, 1948-50; patent advisor U.S. Signal Corps, 1950-52; mem. Shapiro & Shapiro, Arlington, Va., 1952-98, Vorys, Sater, Seymour and Pease LLP, Washington, 1998—. Patentee; contbr. articles to legal publs. and Ency. of Patent Practice and Invention Mgmt., 1964. Mem. ABA, Am. Patent Law Assn., Bar Assn. D.C., Order of Coif, Tau Beta Pi. Patent, Trademark and copyright. Home: 7001 Old Cabin Ln Rockville MD 20852-4531 Office: Vorys Sater et al 1828 L St NW 11th Fl Washington DC 20036-5104

**SHAPIRO, NORMA SONDRA LEVY,** federal judge; b. Phila., July 27, 1928; d. Bert and Jane (Kotkin) Levy; m. Bernard Shapiro, Aug. 21, 1949; children: Finley, Neil, Aaron. BA in Polit. Theory with honors, U. Mich., 1948; JD magna cum laude, U. Pa., 1951. Bar: Pa. 1952, U.S. Supreme Ct. 1978. Law clk. to presiding justice Pa. Supreme Ct., 1951-52; instr. U. Pa. Law Sch., 1951-52, 55-56; assoc. Dechert Price & Rhoads, Phila., 1956-58, 67-73; ptnr. Dechert Price & Rhoads, 1973-78; judge U.S. Dist. Ct. (ea. dist.) Pa., 1978—; assoc. trustee U. Pa. Law Sch., 1978-93; former trustee Women's Law Project, Albert Einstein Med. Ctr.; v.p. Jewish Pub. Soc.; trustee Fedn. Jewish Agys., 1980-83; mem. lawyers adv. panel Pa. Gov.'s Commn. on Status of Women, 1974; legal adv. regional Coun. Child Psychiatry, bd. dirs. Women Judges' Fund for Justice. Guest editor: Shingle, 1972. Mem. Lower Merion County (Pa.) Bd. Sch. Dirs., 1968-77, pres., 1977, v.p., 1976; v.p. Jewish Community Relations Council of Greater Phila., 1975-77; chmn. legal affairs com., 1978; pres. Belmont Hills Home and Sch. Assn., Lower Merion Twp.; legis. chmn. Lower Merion Sch. Dist. Intersch. Council; mem. Task Force on Mental Health of Children and Youth of Pa.; treas., chmn. edn. com. Human Relations Council, Lower Merion; v.p., parliamentarian Nes Ami Penn Valley Congregation, Lower Merion Twp. Named Woman of Yr., Oxford Circle Jewish Community Center, 1979, Woman of Distinction, Golden Slipper Club, 1979; Gowen fellow, 1954-55; recipient Hannah G. Solomon award Nat. Coun. Jewish Women, 1992. Mem. Am. Law Inst., Am. Bar Found., ABA (ho. dels. 1990-96, coun./chmn. conf. fed. judges 1986-87, chmn. jud. divsn. 1996-97), Pa. Bar Assn. (ho. of dels. 1979-81), Phila. Bar Assn. (chmn. com. women's rights 1972, 74-75, chmn. bd. govs. 1977-78, chmn. pub. rels. com. 1978), Fed. Bar Assn. (Bill of Rights award 1991), Nat. Assn. Women Lawyers, Phila. Trial Lawyers Assn., Am. Judicature Soc., Phila., Nat. Assn. Women Judges, Fellowship Commn., Order of Coif (chpt. pres. 1973-75), Tau Epsilon Rho. Office: US Dist Courthouse Independence Mall West 601 Market St Rm 10614 Philadelphia PA 19106-1714*

**SHAPIRO, PHILIP ALAN,** lawyer; b. Chgo., May 14, 1940; s. Joe and Nettie (Costin) S.; m. Joyce Barbara Chapnick, May 29, 1966; children: David Ian, Russell Scott, Mindi Jennifer. AA, Wilson Coll., 1960; BS in Fin., So. Ill. U., 1965; MBA in Mktg. with distinction, San Diego State U., San Diego, 1977; JD, Western State U., 1985, Western State U., 1985. Bar: Calif. 1988. Spl. agt. U.S. Secret Svc., Washington, 1965-67, Chgo., 1967-77; mgr. divsn. sales Roche Labs. divsn. Hoffman-La Roche, Inc., Chgo.; account exec. Cellular Comm., Inc., San Diego, 1985; with Complete Comm., San Diego, 1983—; assoc. Law Office Jeffrey S. Schwartz, 1988-91; pvt. practice, 1991—; chair gen. and solo practice section State Bar of Calif.; editor law rev. Western State U. Coll. Law. editor law rev. Western State U. Coll. Law. Mem. Spreckes Elem. Sch. Adv. Bd., San Diego, 1976-77; mem. University City Town Coun., San Diego, 1977; pres. Congregation Beth El, La Jolla, Calif., 1976-79. With USMC, 1958-60. Recipient Award of Merit, U.S. Treasury Dept., 1965, Israel Solidarity award, 1977, U. of Judaism award, 1978, Wiley W. Manuel award State Bar Calif., 1990, 91. Mem. ABA (vice chmn. gen. practice sect.), Calif. Trial Lawyers Assn., San Diego County Bar Assn., San Diego Trial Lawyers Assn., State Bar Calif. (exec. com. gen. practice sect.), San Diego Bus. Referrals (pres. 1998-99). Fax: 858-483-4639. E-mail: pshaplaw@san.rr.com. Bankruptcy, General practice, Personal injury. Office: 225 Broadway Ste 1210 San Diego CA 92101-5028

**SHAPIRO, RICHARD ALLEN,** lawyer; b. Phila., Feb. 27, 1958; s. A. Morton and Sandra Shapiro; m. Judith L. Dickert, May 30, 1982; children: Sara, Sharon. BA in Politics, Brandeis U., 1980; JD, Rutgers U., 1983. Bar: N.J. 1983, Pa. 1983, U.S. Dist. Ct. N.J. 1983, U.S. Dist. Ct. (ea. dist.) Pa., 1984, U.S. Ct. Appeals (3rd cir.) 1985. Prin. Shapiro & Shapiro, P.C., Cherry Hill, N.J., 1983—; solicitor Camden County Coll., Blackwood, N.J., 1987—. Mem. Camden County Workforce Investment Bd., 1995—; bd. dirs. Jewish Nat. Fund So. N.J. Region, Cherry Hill, 1996—; chmn. Cherry Hill Dem. Party, 1991—; del. Dem. Nat. Conv., N.Y.C., 1992; vice chmn. Camden County Dem. Party, 1997—. General practice, General corporate, Construction. Office: Shapiro and Shapiro PC 1415 Route 70 E Ste 508 Cherry Hill NJ 08034-2238

**SHAPIRO, RICHARD MICHAEL,** lawyer; b. New Haven, Feb. 7, 1951; s. Robert and Pearl Edith (Glassman) S. BA, U. South Fla., 1978; JD, Southwestern U., 1980. Bar: Conn. 1981, Fla. 1981, U.S. Dist. Ct. (mid. dist.) Fla. 1981. Jud. intern to presiding judge U.S. Dist. Ct. for Conn., 1978; assoc. Mitzel, Mitzel and Feegel, Tampa, Fla., 1981; asst. pub. defender State of Fla., Bradenton, 1982; pres., prin. Shapiro Law Group, Bradenton, 1982—; frequent lectr. locally, nationally and at various law schs. Trustee F.L.A.G., 1998—. Fellow Roscoe Pound Found.; mem. ABA, ATLA (sustaining mem., bd. govs. 1997—, sci. and med. integrity com., 1994—), Am. Judicature Soc., Fla. Bar Assn. (jud. selection, nomination and tenure com. 1989—, exec. coun. trial practice sect. 1997—), Acad. Fla. Trial Lawyers (Eagle founder, publ. com. 1989—, membership com. 1992—, bd. dirs. 1992—. co-chmn. med. malpractice taskforce, 1996-97, exec. com., CLE com. chmn. 1996-97, Constl. Challenge com. ), So. Trial Lawyers Assn. (bd. govs. 1996—, sec. 1999—), Trial Lawyers for Pub. Justice (Fla. state coord. 1992-97). Democrat. Jewish. Avocations: tennis, volleyball, scuba diving, boating. Personal injury, General civil litigation. Office: Shapiro Law Group 1732 Manatee Ave W Bradenton FL 34205-5925

**SHAPIRO, ROBERT LESLIE,** lawyer; b. Plainfield, N.J., Sept. 2, 1942. BS in Fin., UCLA, 1965; JD, Loyola U., L.A., 1968. Bar: Calif. 1969, U.S. Ct. Appeals (9th cir.) 1972, U.S. Dist. Ct. (cen., no. & so. dists.) Calif. 1982. Dep. dist. atty. Office of Dist. Atty., L.A., 1969-72; sole practice L.A., 1972-87, 88—; of counsel Bushkin, Gaims, Gaines, Jonas, L.A., 1987-88; Christensen, White, Miller, Fink & Jacobs, L.A., 1988-95; ptnr. Christensen, Miller, Fink, Jacobs, Glaser, Weil & Shapiro, L.A., 1995—. Author: Search for Justice, 1996. Recipient Am. Jurisprudence award Bancroft Whitney, 1969. Mem. Nat. Assn. Criminal Def. Lawyers, Calif. Attys. for Criminal Justice, Trial Lawyers for Pub. Justice (founder 1982), Century City Bar Assn. (Best Criminal Def. Atty. 1993). Criminal, General civil litigation. Office: 2121 Avenue Of The Stars Fl 19 Los Angeles CA 90067-5010

**SHAPIRO, SANDRA,** lawyer; b. Providence, Oct. 17, 1944; d. Emil and Sarah (Cohen) S. AB magna cum laude, Bryn Mawr Coll., Pa., 1966; LLB magna cum laude, U. Pa., 1969. Bar: Mass. 1970, U.S. Dist. Ct. Mass. 1971, U.S. Ct. Appeals (1st cir.) 1972, U.S. Supreme Ct. 1980. Law clk. U.S. Ct. Appeals (1st cir.), Boston, 1969-70; assoc. Foley, Hoag & Eliot LLP, Boston, 1970-75, ptnr., 1976—; mem. bd. bar overseers Mass. Supreme Judicial Ct., 1988-92, mem. gender bias study com., 1986-89. Contbr. articles to profl. jours. Bd. dirs. Patriots' Trail coun. Girl Scouts U.S., 1994-97; mem. bd. overseers Boston Lyric Opera, 1993—, New England Conservatory of Music, 1995—, Celebrity Series of Boston, 1997—. Woodrow Wilson fellow, 1966. Mem. ABA (ethics, professionalism and pub. edn. com. 1994—), Women's Bar Assn. of Mass. (prs. 1985-86), New Eng. Women in Real Estate, Nat. Women's Law Ctr. Network, Mass. Bar Assn. (chmn. real property sect. coun., com. on profl. ethics), Boston Bar Assn. (mem. coun.), U. Pa. Law Sch. Alumni Assn. (bd. mgrs. 1990-94), Order of Coif, Boston Club. Real property, Land use and zoning (including planning), Contracts commercial. Office: Foley Hoag & Eliot LLP 1 Post Office Sq Boston MA 02109-2106

**SHAPIRO, STANLEY K.,** lawyer; b. Bklyn., Feb. 7, 1956; s. Solomon K. and Rebecca Shapiro; m. Ann Hirsch, Aug. 4, 1985; children: Zachary Solomon, Eliezer Kahane, Rose Mariasha Hirsch, Carrie Daniela Hirsch. BA magna cum laude, SUNY, Albany, 1977; JD cum laude, U. Mich., 1980. Bar: N.Y. 1981, U.S. Dist. Ct. (so. and ea. dists.) N.Y. 1981, U.S. Ct. Appeals (2d cir.) 1988. Assoc. Cahill Gordon & Reindel, N.Y.C., 1980-85; pvt. practice N.Y.C., 1985—; spl. asst. dist. atty. Dist. Atty.'s Office, N.Y. County, N.Y.C., 1982-83; trustee Yavne Jewish Theol. Sem. Mem. N.Y. County Lawyers Assn. General civil litigation, Personal injury, Federal civil litigation. Office: 299 Broadway Ste 1200 New York NY 10007-1901

**SHARE, RICHARD HUDSON,** lawyer; b. Mpls., Sept. 6, 1938; s. Jerome and Millicent S.; m. Carolee Martin, 1970; children: Mark Lowell, Gregory Martin, Jennifer Hillary, Ashley. BS, UCLA, 1960; JD, U. So. Calif., 1963. Bar: Calif. Sup. Ct. 1964, U.S. Dist. Ct. (cen. and so. dists.) Calif., U.S. Supreme Ct. 1974. Field agt. IRS, 1960-63; mem. law divsn., asst. sec. Avco Fin. Svcs., 1963-72; founder Frandzel and Share, L.A., 1972—; lectr. Nat. Bus. Inst. Mem. Calif. Bankers Assn., Cmty. Bankers of So. Calif., Rivera Tennis Club, Pacific Palisades. Consumer commercial, Contracts commercial, Banking. Office: 6500 Wilshire Blvd Fl 17 Los Angeles CA 90048-4920 also: 100 Pine St Fl 26 San Francisco CA 94111-5102

**SHARETT, ALAN RICHARD,** lawyer, environmental litigator, mediator and arbitrator, law educator; b. Hammond, Ind., Apr. 15, 1943; s. Henry S. and Frances (Givel) Smulevitz; children: Lauren Ruth, Charles Daniel; m. Cherie Ann Vick, Oct. 15, 1993. Student, Ind. U., 1962-65; JD, DePaul U., 1968; advanced postgrad. legal edn., U. Mich. and U. Chgo., 1970-71. Bar: Ind. 1969, N.Y. 1975, U. S. Ct. Appeals (2d cir.) 1975, U.S. Ct. Appeals (7th cir.) 1974, U.S. Supreme Ct. 1973. Affiliate World Peace Through Law Ctr., Washington, 1967-68, Affiliate, 1967-68; assoc. Call, Call, Borns and Theodoros, Gary, Ind., 1969-71; judge protem Gary City Ct., 1970-71; environ. dist. atty. 31st Jud. Cir., Lake County, Ind., 1971-75; counsel Dunes Nat. Lakeshore Group, Ind., 1971-75; mem. Cohan, Cohan and Smulevitz, 1971-75; town atty. Independence Hill, Ind., 1974-75; judge pro tem Superior Ct., Lake County, Ind., 1971-75; pvt. practice Flushing, N.Y., 1980-82, Miami Beach, Fla., 1988—; lead trial counsel, chmn. lawyers panel No. Ind. ACLU, 1969-71; liaison trial counsel Lake County and Ind. State Health Depts., and Atty. Gen., 1971-75; professorial dir. NYU Pub. Liability Inst., N.Y.C., 1975-76; speaker, guest lectr., adj. faculty ATLA, Purdue U., NYU, Ind. U., De Paul U., Valparaiso U., St. Joseph Coll., U. Miami; coll. paralegal instr., 1970-89; adj. faculty prof. constl. law Union Inst., Miami, Cin., 1990-92; adj. prof. environ. litigation and alternative dispute resolution Ward Stone Coll., Miami, 1994; guest prof. internat. environ. law Dept. Internat. and Comparative Law, U. Miami, 1992—; mem. adv. panel, seminar speaker on internat. environ. law Interam. Dialogue on Water Mgmt., 1993; speaker on environ. transactions and litigation, North Dade county Fla. Bar Assn., 1995—; seminar speaker on environ. politics, U. Miami Dept. Environ. Sci., 1995—; mem. Nat. Dist. Attys. Assn., 1972-75, mem. environ. protection com.; pres. ESI Group, Nat. Environ. Responsibility Cons. Inc. Editor-in-chief DePaul U. The Summons, 1967-68; mem. staff DePaul Law Rev., 1968; contbr. articles to profl. jours. Gen. counsel Marjory Stoneman Douglas Friends of Everglades, 1992-93; asst. atty. gen., chair fed. and constnl. practice litigation group N.Y. State, N.Y.C., 1976-78; mem. Coalition Fla. Save Our Everglades Program; diplomate, vice chancellor Law-Sci. Acad. Am., 1967. Recipient Honors award in forensic litigation Law-Sci. Acad. Am., 1967. Mem. ABA (nat. article editor law student divsn. 1967-68, nat. com. environ. litigation, com. fed. procedures, com. toxic torts, hazardous substances and environ. law, com. energy resources law, com. internat. environ. law, com. internat. litigation, environ. interest group, sect. natural resources, energy and environ. law, judge negotiation competition championship round., law student divsn., midyr. meeting 1995, sect. sci. and tech., biotech. com., environ. law and pub. heath com., standing com sci. evidence, spl. com. legal edn., nat. toxic and hazardous substances and environ. law com., sect. tort and ins. practice, corp. gen. counsel com., non-profit orgns. com., media law and defamation torts com., tort and hazardous substances and environ. law com.), AAAS (physics, math, astronomy) , Judicature Soc., Am. Arbitration Assn., Am. Soc. Tng. and Devel., Soc. Human Rource Mgmt., Assn. Bar City of N.Y., N.Y. County Lawyers Assn. (com. on fed. cts. 1977-82), ATLA (nat. coms. toxic, environ. and pharm. torts, environ. litigatin), Environ. Law Inst., Am. Immigration Lawyers Assn., Ill. State Bar Assn. (staff editor 1967-68), N.Y. State Bar Assn. (environ. law sect., family law sect.), Ind. State Bar Assn. (environ. law sect., internat. law sect., trial practice sect.), Nat. Fla. Assn. Environ. Profls., Greater Miami C. of C. (trustee 1993-94, com. environ. awareness, environ. econs., biomed. exch., planning and growth mgmt., internat. econ. devel., bus. and industry econs. devel., govtl. affairs, ins., internat. banking, Europe/Pacific), N.Y. Acad. Sci., Astron. Soc. of Pacific, Am. Acad. Poets, So. Cross Astron. Soc. Environmental, Labor, Health. Office: ESI Group Nat Environ Responsibility Cons Inc 14630 Bull Run Rd Ste 213 Miami Lakes FL 33014-2017

**SHARFMAN, STEPHEN,** lawyer; b. 1944. AB, George Washington U.; JD, Georgetown U. Bar: D.C. 1970. Gen. counsel Postal Rate Commn., Washington. Office: Office Gen Counsel 1333 H St NW Washington DC 20268-0001*

**SHARIFF, VIVIAN RODRIGUEZ,** lawyer, accountant; b. Riverdale, N.Y., Dec. 16, 1969; d. Felix and Maria Rodriguez; m. A.J. Shariff, Dec. 28, 1987. AA in Bus., Miami Dade C.C., Miami, Fla., 1989; B of Acctg., Fla. Internat. U., Miami, 1991, M of Acctg., 1992; JD, U. Miami, 1995. Bar: Fla.; CPA, Fla. Acct. Norman A. Eliot & Co., Miami, 1991-96; atty., acct. Managed Recovery Svcs. Corp., Miami, 1996-97; sole practitioner Miami, 1997—. Mem. ABA, AICPA, ATLA, Am. Assn. Atty.-CPAs, Fla. Inst. CPAs, Dade County Bar Assn., Fla. Bar. Republican. Roman Catholic. Avocation: science fiction. Taxation, general, Probate, Estate planning.

**SHARLOT, M. MICHAEL,** dean. BA, Antioch U., 1958; LLB, U. Pa., 1962. Dean, John Jeffers rsch. chair in law U. Tex. Sch. Law, Austin, Wright C. Morrow prof. law; vis. prof. law U. Calif., Berkeley. Co-author: (books) Courtroom Handbook on Texas Evidence, 4th edit., 1997, Criminal Law: Cases and Materials, 4th edit., 1996, Texas Practice Guide to the Texas Rules of Evidence, 2 vols., 2d edit., 1993. Mem. Am. Law Inst. Office: U Tex Sch Law 727 E Dean Keeton St Austin TX 78705*

**SHARP, ALLEN,** federal judge; b. Washington, D.C., Feb. 11, 1932; s. Robert Lee and Frances Louise (Williams) S.; children: Crystal Catholyn, Scarlet Frances. Student, Ind. State U., 1950-53; AB, George Washington U., 1954; JD, Ind. U., 1957; MA, Butler U., 1986. Bar: Ind. 1957. Practiced in Williamsport, 1957-68; judge Ct. of Appeals Ind., 1969-73, U.S. Dist. Ct. (no. dist.) Ind., South Bend, 1973—. Bd. advisers Milligan (Tenn.) Coll. Served to JAG USAFR. Mem. Ind. Judges Assn., Blue Key, Phi Delta Kappa, Pi Gamma Mu, Tau Kappa Alpha. Republican. Mem. Christian Ch. Club: Mason. Office: US Dist Ct 124 Fed Bldg 204 S Main St South Bend IN 46601-2122

**SHARP, GEORGE KENDALL,** federal judge; b. Chgo., Dec. 30, 1934; s. Edward S. and Florence S.; m. Mary Bray; children: Florence Kendall, Julia Manger. BA, Yale U., 1957; JD, U. Va., 1963. Bar: Fla. 1963. Atty. Sharp, Johnston & Brown, Vero Beach, Fla., 1963-78; pub. defender 19th Cir. Ct., Vero Beach, 1964-68; sch. bd. atty. Indian River County, Fla., 1968-78; Fla. circuit judge 19th Cir., 1978-83; judge U.S. Dist. Ct. (mid. dist.) Fla., Orlando, 1983—. Office: US Dist Ct 635 US Courthouse 80 N Hughey Ave Ste 218 Orlando FL 32801-2224

**SHARP, REX ARTHUR,** lawyer; b. Liberal, Kans., Jan. 1, 1960; s. Gene Hugh and Jo Ann (King) S.; m. Lori Renee Lewis, May 23, 1987; children: Lori Alexandra, Lewis Arthur, William Hugh. Student, U. Okla., 1978-79; AB in Econs. with honors & distinction, Stanford U., 1982; JD cum laude, U. Mich., 1985. Bar: Tex. 1985, Kans. 1985, Okla. 1986, Colo. 1988, U.S. Dist. Ct. (so. and no. dists.) Tex., U.S. Dist. Ct. (we. and no. dists.) Okla., U.S. Dist. Ct. Kans., U.S. Dist Ct. (we. dist.) Mo. , U.S. Ct. Appeals (10th cir.), U.S. Supreme Ct.; civil trial cert. N.B.T.A. Litigation assoc. Fulbright & Jaworski, Houston, 1985-87; assoc. Neubauer, Sharp, McQueen, Dreiling & Morain, Liberal, 1987-89; ptnr. McKinley, Sharp, McQueen, Dreiling, Morain & Tate, P.A., Liberal, 1989-97, Husch & Eppenberger, Kansas City, Mo., 1997—; asst. city atty. City of Liberal, 1988-93, city atty., 1993-97. Avocation: golf. General civil litigation, Insurance, Personal injury. Office: Husch & Eppenberger LLC 1200 Main St Ste 1700 Kansas City MO 64105-2100

**SHARP, ROBERT WEIMER,** lawyer; b. Cleve., Feb. 12, 1917; s. Isaac Walter and Ruth (Weimer) S.; m. Norine Wines, Nov. 13, 1948; children: Kathleen L. Sharp Samuel, Pamela J. Sharp Adamson, Janet E. Sharp Schoon, Andrea L. Sharp Bobak, Gail N. Sharp Henderson. A.B. magna cum laude, Oberlin Coll., 1939; LL.B., Harvard U., 1942. Bar: Ohio 1944. Practiced in Cleve; ptnr. Gallagher, Sharp, Fulton & Norman and predecessors, 1958-92; pres. Bulkley Bldg. Co., 1966-70. Trustee emeritus St. Luke's Hosp. Assn.; trustee emeritus, hon life mem. Ohio divsn. Am. Cancer Soc.; trustee emeritus Ohio East Area United Meth. Found., 1974—, sec., 1967-74, 83-86, pres., 1974-80. Mem. ABA, Ohio Bar Assn., Cleve. Bar Assn., Phi Beta Kappa. Republican. Methodist. Probate, Taxation, general. Home: 3090 Fairmount Blvd Cleveland OH 44118-4129 Office: Gallagher Sharp Fulton & Norman 7th Fl Bulkley Bldg Cleveland OH 44115

**SHARP, ROGER JAY,** lawyer; b. Kennewick, Wash., Dec. 24, 1955; m. Linda Berg, Feb. 21, 1978; children: Rachelle, Janae, Claire, Carol, Paul. BA in Polit. Sci., Brigham Young U., 1978; JD, U. Wash., 1981. Bar: Wash. 1981, Oreg. 1986. Assoc. Leavy, Schultz & Sweeney, Pasco, Wash., 1981-82; sole practice law Manchester, N.H., 1982-85, Vancouver, Wash., 1985—; bd. dirs. Direct Focus, Inc., Vancouver. Pres. sch. bd. Battle Ground (Wash.) Sch. Dist., 1997. Republican. Avocation: computers. Office: 1112 Daniels St Ste 100 Vancouver WA 98660-2954

**SHARP, STEFANIE TERESA,** lawyer; b. Reno, Nev., June 16, 1966; d. F. De Armond and Joyce Sharp. BA, U. Calif., San Diego, 1988; JD cum laude, U. San Francisco, 1992. Bar: Calif. 1993. Assoc. St. Claire, McFetridge, Griffen & Legernes, San Francisco, 1993-96, Wright, Robinson, Osthimer & Tatum, San Francisco, 1996—. Mem. ABA, Calif. State Bar Assn., San Francisco Bar Assn. Republican. Avocations: running, mountain bike riding, scuba diving, horseback, riding. General civil litigation, Contracts commercial, Consumer commercial. Office: Wright Robinson Osthimer & Tatum 44 Montgomery St Fl 18 San Francisco CA 94104-4602

**SHARPE, CALVIN WILLIAM,** law educator, arbitrator; b. Greensboro, N.C., Feb. 22, 1945; s. Ralph David and Mildred (Johnson) S.; m. Maya Annette Hall, Jan. 25, 1970 (div. Oct. 1975); 1 child, Kabral; m. Janice M. Jones, Apr. 13, 1978; children: Melanie, Stephanie. BA, Clark Coll., 1967; postgrad., Oberlin Coll., 1968; MA, Chgo. Theol. Sem., 1996; JD, Northwestern U., Chgo., 1974. Bar: Ill. 1974. Tchr. elem. sch. N.Y. Sch. System, Bklyn., 1968-69; dir. homework study ctr. Ocean Hill Brownsville, Bklyn., 1969; investigator Ill. Gov.'s Task Force on Cook County Property Tax, Chgo., 1972-73; law clk. to judge Hubert L. Will U.S. Dist. Ct. (no. dist.) Ill., Chgo., 1974-76; assoc. Cotton, Watt, Jones, King & Bowlus, Chgo., 1976-77; trial atty. NLRB, Winston-Salem, N.C., 1977-81; asst. prof. U. Va., 1981-84; assoc. prof. Case Western Res. U., Cleve., 1984-88, prof., 1988—, John Deaver Drinko-Bakert Hostetler prof. law, 1999—, acad. dean, 1991-92; mem. exec. bd. Pub. Sector Labor Rels. Assn., Ohio, 1986—; chmn. evidence sect. Assn. Am. Law Schs., 1987-88; mem. Am. Labor Law Project to Soviet Union and Western Europe-People to People, 1988; mem. Youth Svcs. Adv. Bd. of the Cuyahoga County Juvenile Ct., 1989-91; cons. So. African Commn. on conciliation, mediation and arbitration, 1998—. Co-author: Understanding Labor Law, 1999. Bd. trustees Cleve. Hearing and Speech Ctr., 1985-88, Garrett-Evang. Theol. Sem., 1999—; bd. dirs. Cleve. Pub. Radio, 1993-94. Mem. Soc. Profls. in Dispute Resolution, Internat. Soc. Labor Law and Social Security, Indsl. Rels. Rsch. Assn. (convener and first chair labor and employment law sect. 1995-97), Nat. Acad. Arbitrators. Office: Case Western Res U Law Sch 11075 East Blvd Cleveland OH 44106-5409

**SHARPE, JAMES SHELBY,** lawyer; b. Ft. Worth, Sept. 11, 1940; s. James Henry and Wanzel (Vanderbilt) S.; m. Martha Moudy Holland, June 9, 1962; children: Marthanne Freeman, Caren, Stephen. BA, U. Tex., 1962, JD, 1965. Bar: Tex. 1965, U.S. Dist. Ct. (no. dist.) Tex. 1966, U.S. Dist. Ct. (ea. dist.) Tex. 1993, U.S. Ct. Appeals (5th and 6th cirs.) 1982, U.S. Ct. Appeals (fed. cir.) 1983, U.S. Ct. Appeals (10th cir.) 1992, U.S. Supreme Ct. 1972. Briefing atty. for chief justice Supreme Ct. of Tex., Austin, 1965-66; ptnr. Brown, Herman, Scott, Dean & Miles, Ft. Worth, 1966-84, Gandy Michener Swindle Whitaker & Pratt, Ft. Worth, 1984-87; shareholder Sharpe & Tillman, Ft. Worth, 1988—; adj. prof. polit. sci. Tex. Christian U., Ft. Worth, 1969-79, Dallas Bapt. U., 1987, 1992-94; gen. counsel U.S.A. Radio Network, Internat. Christian Media, Denton Pub. Co. Pres. Ft. Worth-Tarrant County Jr. Bar, 1969-70, bd. dirs., 1968, sec., 1968, v.p., 1968-69; head marshal USA-USSR Track and Field Championships, Ft. Worth, USA-USSR Jr. Track and Field Championships, Austin, Tex., Relays, Austin, 1963—, NCAA Nat. Track and Field Championships, 1976, 80, 85, 92, 95, S.W. Conf. Indoor Track and Field Championships, 1987-96, Olympic Festival, San Antonio, 1993, Colorado Springs, 1995; 12 time head marshal S.W. Conf. Track and Field Championships, Big 12 Outdoor Conf. Track and Field Championship, 1997, 98, 99. USA/Mobil Track Championship, 1994, 95; USA Nat. Jr. Track Championship, 1994, 95, 98, 99, USA Track and Field Track Championship, 1997, Master's Nat. Track and Field Nat. Championship, 1996, 98. Mem. ABA, State Bar of Tex. (dist. 7-A grievance com. 1983-85, com. adminstrn. of justice 1985-92, com. on ct. rules 1992—, chmn. 1992-93, 93-94). Baptist. Constitutional, General civil litigation, Libel. Home: 8304 Crosswind Dr Fort Worth TX 76179-3003 Office: Sharpe & Tillman 500 Throckmorton St Ste 2706 Fort Worth TX 76102-3814

**SHARPE, ROBERT FRANCIS, JR.,** lawyer; b. Long Branch, N.J., Mar. 9, 1952; s. Robert Francis and Audrey Carolyn (Rembe) S.; m. Rebecca A. Gillan, Feb. 23, 1991; 1 child, Robert Francis III. BA, DePauw U., 1975; BSE, Purdue U., 1975; JD, Wake Forest U., 1978. Bar: N.C. 1978. Atty. Capital Synergistics Corp., Winston-Salem, N.C., 1977-80; asst. counsel R.J. Reynolds Industries, Winston-Salem, 1980-82, assoc. counsel, 1983-85, counsel, 1985-86; corp. and comml. counsel R.J. Reynolds Tobacco Co., Winston-Salem, 1986-87; sr. counsel, asst. sec. R.J. Reynolds Nabisco, Inc., Atlanta, 1987-88, asst. gen. counsel, asst sec., 1988-89, v.p., sec., asst. gen. counsel, 1989-98; sr. v.p. pub. affairs & gen. coun. PepsiCo, Inc., Purchase, N.Y., 1998—. Bd. dirs. Lewisville (N.C.) Fire Dept. Mem. ABA, N.C. Bar Assn., Forsyth County Bar Assn., Atlanta Bar Assn., Am. Corp. Counsel Assn. Republican. Episcopalian. Avocation: retriever training. Securities, Contracts commercial, General corporate. Office: PepsiCo Inc 700 Anderson Hill Rd Purchase NY 10577-1444

**SHATTUCK, CATHIE ANN,** lawyer, former government official; b. Salt Lake City, July 18, 1945; d. Robert Ashley S. and Lillian Culp (Shattuck). B.A., U. Nebr., 1967, J.D., 1970. Bar: Nebr. 1970, U.S. Dist. Ct. Nebr. 1970, Colo. 1971, U.S. Dist. Ct. Colo. 1971, U.S. Supreme Ct. 1974, U.S. Ct. Appeals (10th cir.) 1977, U.S. Dist. Ct. D.C. 1984, U.S. Ct. Appeals (D.C. cir.) 1984. V.p., gen. mgr. Shattuck Farms, Hastings, Nebr., 1967-70; asst. project dir. atty. Colo. Civil Rights Commn., Denver, 1970-72; trial atty. Equal Employment Opportunity Commn., Denver, 1973-77; vice chmn. Equal Employment Opportunity Commn., Washington, 1982-84; pvt. practice law Denver, 1977-81; mem. Fgn. Svc. Bd., Washington, 1982-84, Presdl. Personnel Task Force, Washington, 1982-84; ptnr. Epstein, Becker & Green, L.A. and Washington, 1984—; lectr. Colo. Continuing Legal Edn. Author: Employer's Guide to Controlling Sexual Harassment, 1992; mem. editorial bd. The Practical Litigator, 1988—. Bd. dirs. KGNU Pub. Radio, Boulder, Colo., 1979, Denver Exchange, 1980-81, YWCA Met. Denver, 1979-81. Recipient Nebr. Young Career Woman Bus. and Profl. Women, 1967; recipient Outstanding Nebraskan Daily Nebraskan, Lincoln, 1967. Fellow

Am. Coll. of Labor and Employment Lawyers; mem. ABA (mgmt. chair labor and employment law sect. com. on immigration law 1988-90, mgmt. chair com. on legis. devels. 1990-93), Nebr. Bar Assn., Colo. Bar Assn., Colo. Women's Bar Assn., D.C. Bar Assn., Nat. Women's Coalition, Delta Sigma Rho, Tau Kappa Alpha, Pi Sigma Alpha, Alpha Xi Delta, Denver Club. Civil rights, Juvenile, Administrative and regulatory.

**SHATTUCK, GARY G.,** lawyer; b. Nashua, N.H., Oct. 20, 1950; m. Katherine H. Catlin, 1972. BA, U. Colo., 1972; JD magna cum laude, Vt. Law Sch., 1987. Bar: Vt. 1987, U.S. Dist. Ct. Vt. 1987, U.S. Ct. Appeals (2d cir.) 1992. Dep. sheriff Boulder County Sheriff's Dept., Boulder, Colo., 1973-75; patrol comdr. Vt. State Police, Waterbury, 1975-87; litigation assoc. Reiber, Kenlan, Schweibert & Hall, P.C., Rutland, Vt., 1987-89; asst. atty. gen. Office of Atty. Gen., Montpelier, Vt., 1989-91; suprvising atty. Vt. Drug Task Force, Montpelier, 1989-91; asst. U.S. atty. Organized Crime Drug Enforcement Task Force, U.S. Dept. Justice, Burlington, Vt., 1991—; adj. prof. Castleton (Vt.) State Coll., 1997-98. Bd. dirs. Rutland Mental Health, 1991; citizen's adv. com. Rutland Solid Waste Dist., 1987; del. Nat. Assn. Asst. U.S. Attys., 1994-99; bd. dirs. Vt. Archeol. Soc., 1998. Recipient Atty. Gen. Janet Reno Spl. Achievement award, 1993. Mem. Lake Champlain Maritime Mus., Inst. Nautical Archaeology, Nat. Trust Historic Presvn. Office: Office of US Atty PO Box 570 Burlington VT 05402-0570

**SHAUGER, SUSAN JOYCE,** lawyer, educator; b. Pompton Plains, N.J., July 11, 1943; d. A. Harold Shauger and Marian E. (Velsor) Tomes. BA, Hope Coll., 1965; MA in Teaching, Oberlin Coll., 1967; JD, Western New Eng. Coll., Springfield, Mass., 1986; Cert. of Advanced Grad. Study, U. Mass., 1988. Bar: Mass. 1987. Tchr., prin. Buckland-Colrain-Shelburne Regional Sch. Dist., Shelburne Falls, Mass., 1970-86; sole practitioner Buckland, Mass., 1988—. Mem. Franklin County Bar Assn. Avocations: musician, outdoors activities. E-mail: sshauger@shaugerlaw.com. General practice, Real property, Criminal. Home: 29 Upper St Buckland MA 01338-9701

**SHAUGHNESSY, JAMES MICHAEL,** lawyer; born Feb. 1, 1945; s. James Gregory and Frieda Louise (Brosche) S.; m. Linda Ann Bonfiglio, Aug. 17, 1968; m. 2d, Kari Marie Thoring, Nov. 19, 1977; children—Brendan Michael, Megan Ann. B.A., Adelphi U., 1967; J.D., NYU, 1969. Bar: N.Y. 1970, Calif. 1977, U.S. Dist. Ct. (so. and ea. dists.) N.Y. 1971, U.S. Ct. Appeals (2d cir.) 1974, Calif. 1977, U.S. Dist. Ct. (so. dist.) Calif. 1977, U.S. Ct. Appeals (9th cir.) 1977, U.S. Ct. Appeals (5th cir.) 1983, U.S. Supreme Ct. 1979, U.S. Dist. Ct. (no. dist.) N.Y. 1982, N.J. 1983, U.S. Dist. Ct. N.J. 1983, U.S. Tax Ct. 1983, U.S. Dist. Ct. (we. dist.) N.Y. 1987. Assoc. Casey, Lane & Mittendorf, N.Y.C., 1969-76, ptnr., 1976-82; ptnr. Haythe & Curley, N.Y.C., 1982-87, Windels, Marx, Davies & Ives, N.Y.C., 1987—. Served with N.Y. N.G., 1969-70. Recipient Benjamin F. Butler award Sch. Law NYU, 1969. Mem. ABA, N.Y. State Bar Assn., Fed. Bar Council, Assn. Bar City of N.Y. Republican. Roman Catholic. State civil litigation, Federal civil litigation. Office: Windels Marx Davies & Ives 156 W 56th St Fl 23 New York NY 10019-3867

**SHAUGHNESSY, ROXANNE C.,** lawyer; b. Apr. 5, 1955. AA in Liberal Arts, Normandale Coll., 1983; BA in Sociology, Hamline U., 1989; JD, William Mitchell Coll. Law, 1992. Bar: Minn. 1992, U.S. Claims Ct. 1993. Assoc. Shaughnessy, Warren & Shaughnessy, P.A., Mpls., 1992-93, ptnr., 1993-97, pres., 1997—. Bd. dirs. Uppermidwest Golden Gloves, 1983-91; chief judge Uppermidwest Region, 1985-91; nat. amateur boxing judge USA Boxing and Golden Gloves, 1977—; profl. boxing judge, 1997—; mem. Internat. Boxing Coun., 1998—. Mem. ABA, Minn. State Bar Assn., Hennepin County Bar Assn., Minn. Trial Lawyers Assn., Assn. of Trial Lawyers of Am. Office: 450 Sheehan Corp Ctr 4500 Park Glen Rd Minneapolis MN 55416-4871

**SHAW, BARRY N.,** lawyer; b. Newark, July 31, 1940; s. Harry G. and Evelyn (Kruger) S.; m. Cheryl Lynn Rosen, Mar. 24, 1963; children: Jennifer B., Jonathan M. BS in Acctg., Rutgers U., 1962, LLB, 1965. Bar: Pa. 1966, Oreg. 1996, U.S. Dist. Ct. (ea. dist.) Pa. 1966, U.S. Dist. Ct. N.J. 1974, U.S. Dist. Ct. Oreg. 1997, U.S. Ct. Appeals (3d cir.) N.J. 1974, U.S. Supreme Ct. 1988; CPA, Pa. Acct. Coopers & Lybrand, Phila., 1965-68; corp. counsel Lincoln Bank, Phila., 1968-72, Waste Resources Corp., Phila., 1972-74; ptnr. Spivack, Dranoff & Shaw, Phila., 1974-75, Dranoff & Shaw, Phila., 1975-79, Jubanyik, Varbalow Tedesco Shaw & Shaffer, Cherry Hill, N.J., 1979-95, Dilworth, Paxson, Kalish & Kauffman (successor firm), Cherry Hill, N.J., 1995-97, Davis, Gilstrap, Hearn & Shaw PC, Ashland, Oreg., 1997—; lectr. in banking law. Author: Selected Decisions in Lender Liability Law, 1990, Environmental Lender Liability, 1992. Chmn. Shamong Twp. (N.J.) Planning Bd., 1990-93, Local Civic Assn.; active Shamong Twp. Com., 1993-97; mayor Shamong Twp., 1995; sec. Pinelands Mcpl. (Mayors') Coun., 1996-97. Mem. Oreg. State Bar, N.J. State Bar, Pa. State Bar, Jackson County Bar Assn., Rotary. Republican. Avocations: farming, dogs. Contracts commercial, General corporate, Finance. Home: 980 Kubli Rd Grants Pass OR 97527-8623 Office: Davis Gilstrap Hearn & Shaw PC 515 E Main St Ashland OR 97520-2113

**SHAW, CHARLES ALEXANDER,** judge; b. Jackson, Tenn., Dec. 31, 1944; s. Alvis and Sarah S.; m. Kathleen Ingram, Aug. 17, 1969; 1 child, Bryan Ingram. BA, Harris Stowe State Coll., 1966; MBA, U. Mo., 1971; JD, Cath. U. Am., 1974. Bar: D.C. 1975, Mo. 1975, U.S. Ct. Appeals (8th and D.C. cirs.) 1975, U.S. Dist. Ct. (ea. dist.) Mo. 1976, U.S. Ct. Appeals (6th and 7th cirs.) 1976. Tchr. St. Louis Pub. Schs., 1966-69, D.C. Pub. Schs., Washington, 1969-71; law clk. U.S. Dept. Justice, Washington, 1972-73; law clk. NLRB, Washington, 1973-74, atty., 1974-76; assoc. Lashly, Caruthers, Theis, Rava & Hamel, St. Louis, 1976-80, asst. U.S. atty., 1980-87; judge Mo. Cir. Ct., St. Louis, 1987-94, asst. presiding judge, 1993-94; judge U.S. Dist. Ct., St. Louis, 1994—; hearing officer Office of the Mayor, Washington, 1973-74; instr. U. Mo., St. Louis, 1980-81. State bd. dirs. United Negro Coll. Fund, St. Louis, 1979-83; trustee St. Louis Art Mus., 1979-82, 89-96; bd. dirs. Arts and Edn. Coun., 1992-96, Metro Golf Assn., Landmarks Assn., St. Louis, 1980-82. Danforth Found. fellow, 1978-79; Cath. U. Am. scholar, 1971-74. Mem. D.C. Bar Assn., Mo. Bar Assn., Mound City Bar Assn., Bar Assn. Metro. St. Louis, Harris-Stowe State Coll. Alumni Assn. (bd. dirs., Disting. Alumni 1988), Phi Alpha Delta (Svc. award 1973-74). Avocations: golf, tennis. Office: 1114 Market St Saint Louis MO 63101-2043

**SHAW, CHARLES FRANKLIN, III,** prosecutor, defender; b. Neptune, N.J., Feb. 17, 1947; s. Charles Franklin Shaw Jr. and Eleanor Elizabeth Goeckel; m. Nancy Hamel, Nov. 7, 1981; children: Charles IV, Richard. BA in History, Lafayette Coll., 1969; JD, Boston U., 1973. Bar: N.J. 1993, U.S. Dist. Ct. N.J. 1993, U.S. Ct. Appeals (3rd cir.) 1976, U.S. Supreme Ct. 1978. Asst. prosecutor Monmouth County Prosecutor's Office, Freehold, N.J., 1973-79; ptnr. Coogan, Pandolfe, Shaw & Rubino, Brielle, N.J., 1980-87, Pandolfe, Shaw, Rubino, Spring Lake, N.J., 1987—; prosecutor Twp. of Neptune, N.J., 1981-85, 87-89, 92-96, Allenhurst (N.J.) Borough, 1986—, Village of Loch Arbour, N.J., 1991-96; pub. defender Neptune City (N.J.) Borough, 1997—; trustee, former pres. Legal Aid Soc. Monmouth County, 1983—; trustee Ocan/Monmouth Legal Svcs., Toms River, N.J., 1986-93; investigator Dist. IX Ethics Com., Trenton, 1996—. County committeeman 17th Dist. Neptune Twp., 1991—. With U.S. Army Nat. Guard, 1969-75. Mem. Trial Lawyers N.J., N.J. State Bar Assn., South Monmouth Bar Assn., Monmouth County Bar Assn. (trustee 1996). Republican. Presbyterian. Home: 41 Toomin Dr Neptune NJ 07753-3008 Office: Pandolfe Shaw & Rubino 215 Morris Ave Spring Lake NJ 07762-1360

**SHAW, DONALD RAY,** lawyer; b. Hugo, Okla., Nov. 29, 1945; s. Jesse Vernon and Velma Lee (Atkinson) S.; m. Nelda Jan Finley, May 31, 1969; children: Britton, Taylor. BBA, U. Okla., 1968, JD, 1975. Bar: Okla. 1975, U.S. Dist. Ct. Okla. 1978, U.S. Ct. Appeals (10th cir.) 1980. Pvt. practice law Idabel, Okla., 1975-77, 87—; dist. atty. Dist. 17, Idabel, 1978-87. Sec., treas. McCurtain County Dem. Party, 1989-91. Lt. col. USAFR., 1969-95. Mem. ABA, Okla. Bar Assn., Okla. CPA's, Gideons (treas. 1980-86), Am. Legion (comdr. 1976-78, judge advocate 1978—), Res. Officers Assn. (life, v.p. Okla. chpt. 1989-91, pres. 1994-95), Lions (bd. dirs. 1985-86, 90-93). Democrat. Presbyterian. Lodges: Lions (bd. dirs. 1985-86), Elks. Estate planning, Family and matrimonial, General practice. Home: 1312 E Madison Idabel OK 74745-5716 Office: 8 NE 3rd St PO Box 957 Idabel OK 74745-0957

**SHAW, ELIZABETH ORR,** lawyer; b. Monona, Iowa, Oct. 2, 1923; d. Harold Topliff and Hazel (Kean) Orr; m. Donald Hardy Shaw, Aug. 16, 1946; children: Elizabeth Ann, Andrew Hardy, Anthony Orr. AB, Drake U., 1945; postgrad. U. Minn., 1945-46; JD, U. Iowa, 1948. Bar: Ill. 1949, Iowa 1956. Assoc. Lord Bissell & Brook, Chgo, 1949-52; pvt. practice law, Arlington Heights, Ill., 1952-56; ptnr. Wood & Shaw, Davenport, Iowa, 1968-72; mem. Iowa Ho. of Reps., Des Moines, 1967-72; mem. Iowa Senate, Des Moines, 1972-77; county atty. Scott County, Davenport, 1977-78; corp. atty. Deere & Co., Moline, Ill., 1979-89; pvt. practice, Davenport, 1990-98, ret., 1999. Mem. Scott County Bar Assn. (com. chmn. 1970-72), Iowa State Bar Assn. (chmn. family law com. 1970-76), Order of Coif, Phi Beta Kappa, Kappa Kappa Gamma, PEO. Republican. Mem. United Ch. Christ. Administrative and regulatory, General corporate, Environmental. Home and Office: 29 Hillcrest Ave Davenport IA 52803-3726

**SHAW, GEORGE WILLIAM,** lawyer; b. Rochester, N.Y., Dec. 19, 1924; s. Frank Clyde and Eleanor Louise (Watt) S.; m. Kathryn Foote, Oct. 30, 1945; children—G. William, Frank, Thomas, Brian. B.E. with honors, Yale U., 1945; LL.B., 1949. Bar: N.Y. 1950, U.S. Ct. Appeals (2d cir.) 1964, U.S. Supreme Ct. 1976. Assoc. Edward H. Cumpston, Rochester, 1949-56; ptnr. Cumpston & Shaw, Rochester, 1956-83; pres. Cumpston & Shaw, P.C., Rochester, 1983-92, of counsel, 1992—. Co-author: Some Thoughts on Trademarks for Gen. Practitioners. Mem. Penfield Zoning Bd. Appeals, N.Y., 1959-67; chmn. Penfield Planning Bd., 1967-72; mem. Penfield Historic Preservation Bd., 1975—. Mem. ABA, Monroe County Bar Assn., N.Y. State Bar Assn., Am. Intellectual Property Law Assn., Rochester Patent Law Assn. (pres. 1971-72), Tau Beta Pi, Phi Delta Phi. Republican. Episcopalian. Club: Hunt Hollow Ski (Naples, N.Y.). Lodge: Rotary. Trademark and copyright, Patent. Office: Cumpston & Shaw 850 Crossroads Building Rochester NY 14614-1377

**SHAW, JOHN MALACH,** federal judge; b. Beaumont, Tex., Nov. 14, 1931; s. John Virgil Shaw and Ethel (Malach) Newstadt; m. Glenda Ledoux, Nov. 10, 1970; children: John Lewis, Stacy Shaw Walpole. Student, Tulane U., 1949-50; B.S. with spl. attainments in Commerce, Washington and Lee U., 1953; LL.B., J.D., La. State U., 1956. Bar: La. 1956; U.S. Dist. Ct. (we. dist.) La. 1958, U.S. Ct. Appeals (5th cir.) 1966. Ptnr. firm Lewis and Lewis, Opelousas, La., 1958-79; U.S. dist. judge Western Dist. La., Opelousas, 1979—; chief judge Western Dist. La., Lafayette, 1991-96, sr. judge, 1996—; Govt. appeal agt. Local Bd. 60, La., 1965-72. Mem.: La. Law Rev, 1954-56; asso. editor, 1955-56; author articles, 1954-56. Served with U.S. Army, 1956-58. Recipient Presdl. cert. of appreciation for services as appeal agt. Mem. Fed. Judges Assn., Fifth Cir. Dist. Judges Assn. Democrat. Methodist. Office: US District Ct 705 Jefferson St Lafayette LA 70501-6936

**SHAW, L. EDWARD, JR.,** lawyer; b. Elmira, N.Y., July 30, 1944; s. L. Edward and Virginia Anne (O'Leary) S.; m. Irene Ryan; children—Christopher, Hope, Hillary, Julia, Rory. B.A. in Econs., Georgetown U., Washington, 1966; J.D., Yale U., New Haven, 1969. Bar: N.Y. 1969. Assoc. Milbank, Tweed, Hadley & McCloy, N.Y.C., 1969-77, ptnr., 1977-83; sr. v.p., gen. counsel Chase Manhattan Corp., N.Y.C., 1983-85, exec. v.p., gen. counsel, 1985-96; vice chmn., gen. counsel Natwest Markets, N.Y.C., 1996-97, pres., 1997-99; gen. counsel Aetna Inc., 1999—. Mem. Assn. Bar City N.Y., Winged Foot Golf Club, Phi Beta Kappa. Roman Catholic. Avocations: youth athletics; golf. Office: Aetna Inc 151 Farmington Ave Hartford CT 06156-0002

**SHAW, LEANDER JERRY, JR.,** state supreme court justice; b. Salem, Va., Sept. 6, 1930; s. Leander J. and Margaret S. BA, W.Va. State Coll., 1952, LLD (hon.), 1986; JD, Howard U., 1957; PhD (hon.) in Pub. Affairs, Fla. Internat. U., 1990; LLD (hon.), Nova Law Sch., 1991, Washington & Lee Law Sch., 1991. Asst. prof. law Fla. A&M U., 1957-60; sole practice Jacksonville, Fla., 1960-69, 72-74; asst. pub. defender Fla., 1965-69; asst. state's atty. Fla., 1969-72; judge Fla. Indsl. Relations Commn., 1974-79, Fla. Ct. Appeals (1st dist.), 1979-83; justice Fla. Supreme Ct., Tallahassee, 1983—, chief justice, 1990-92. Office: Fla Supreme Ct Supreme Ct Bldg Tallahassee FL 32399

**SHAW, LEE CHARLES,** lawyer; b. Red Wing, Minn., Feb. 17, 1913; s. Marvil Thomas and Bernice (Quinland) S.; m. Lorraine Schroeder, July 1, 1939; children—Lynda Lee, Robert, Candace Jean, Lee Charles. B.A., U. Chgo., 1936, J.D., 1938. Bar: Ill. 1938. Assoc. Pope & Ballard, Chgo., 1938-44, ptnr., 1944-45; founding ptnr. Seyfarth, Shaw, Fairweather & Geraldson, Chgo., 1945—; mem. arbitration svcs. adv. com. Fed. Mediation and Conciliation Svc. Contbr. articles on labor law to profl. jours. Mem. ABA, Chgo. Bar Assn. (bd. mgrs. 1956-57), U. Chgo. Alumni Assn., Tavern Club, Union League Club (Chgo.). Republican. Episcopalian. Labor, Pension, profit-sharing, and employee benefits. Home: Pacific Regent La Jolla 3890 Nobel Dr Apt 1702 San Diego CA 92122-5784

**SHAW, MARK HOWARD,** lawyer, business owner, entrepreneur; b. Albuquerque, Aug. 26, 1944; s. Brad Oliver and Barbara Rae (Mencke) S.; m. Ann Marie Brookreson, June 29, 1968 (div. 1976); adopted children: Daniel Paul, Kathleen Ann, Brian Andrew; m. Roslyn Jane Ashton, Oct. 9, 1976; children: Rebecca Rae, Amanda Leith. BA, U. N.Mex., 1967, JD, 1969. Bar, N.Mex. 1969. Law clk. to presiding justice N.Mex. Supreme Ct., Santa Fe, 1969-70; ptnr. Gallagher & Ruud, Albuquerque, 1970-74, Schmidt & Shaw, Albuquerque, 1974-75; sr. mem. Shaw, Thompson & Sullivan P.A., Albuquerque, 1975-82; chief exec. officer United Ch. Religious Sci. and Sci. Mind Publs., L.A., 1982-91; bus. owner, entrepreneur Santa Fe, N.Mex., 1991-94; mem. Coppler & Mannick, P.C., Santa Fe, N.Mex., 1994-98; pvt. practice Santa Fe, Albuquerque, 1998—. Trustee 1st Ch. Religious Sci., Albuquerque, 1974-77, pres. 1977; trustee Sandia Ch. Religious Sci., Albuquerque, 1980-82, pres. 1981-82; trustee United Ch. Religious Sci., Los Angeles, 1981-82, chmn. 1982; trustee Long Beach (Calif.) Ch. Religious Sci., 1983-86, chmn. 1983-86; chmn. Bernalillo County Bd. Ethics, Albuquerque, 1979-82, pres. Santa Fe Rape Crisis Ctr., 1997-99, pres., 1999—. Served as sgt. USMCR, 1961-69. Mem. N.Mex. Bar Assn. Avocation: sailing, fly fishing. General practice. Home: 2724 Puerto Bonito Santa Fe NM 87505-6534 Office: 4550 Eubank Blvd NE Albuquerque NM 87111-2565

**SHAW, MELVIN ROBERT,** lawyer; b. Bklyn., Nov. 23, 1948; s. Arthur and Pearl (Gutterman) S. BA in Polit. Sci., L.I. U., 1970; MPA, U. Ill., 1972; LetD, London Inst. Applied Rsch., 1973; LLD (hon.), Roman Coll., Rome, 1974; BS in Law, Western State U., 1984, JD, 1984; MA in Human Behavior, Nat. U., 1985; MS in Mgmt., NYU, 1988; LLM in Health Law, DePaul U., 1989; postgrad. Golden Gate U., 1989; PhD in Pub. Health, NYU, 1994. Bar: Ind. 1985, U.S. Dist. Ct. (no. and so. dist.) Ind. 1985, U.S. Dist. (no. dist.) Calif. 1985, U.S. Dist. Ct. (ea. dist.) Wis. 1985, U.S. Dist. Ct. Hawaii 1985, U.S. Ct. Appeals (3d, 5th, 7th, 9th, D.C., fed. cirs.) 1985, U.S. Ct. Internat. Trade 1985, U.S. Ct. Mil. Appeals 1985, U.S. Ct. Fed. Claims 1985, U.S. Tax Ct. 1985, U.S. Supreme Ct. 1988, U.S. Dist. Ct. (no. dist.) Ill. 1989, U.S. Ct. Appeals for Vets. Claims, 1990, U.S. Dist. Ct. (ea., so., and no. dists.) N.Y. 1992. Exec. asst. N.Y. State Senate, Albany, 1969-71; polit. cons. Kirson & Shaw, Ltd., N.Y.C., 1972-76; pres. Master Pubs., Inc., Chgo., 1976-80; lectr. Inst. for Internat. Affairs, Washington, 1978—; sr. ptnr. Littlejohn & Shaw Assocs., N.Y.C., Chgo., San Diego, 1980-85; pvt. practice, South Bend, Ind. and N.Y.C., 1985—; instr. law Calif. Community Colls., 1985—; dir. Hudson Industries, San Diego, Master Comm., N.Y.C., Inst. for Internat. Affairs, 1979—. Contbr. articles to profl. jours. Editor Internat. Relations Jour., 1982. Active Am. Jewish Com., Jewish Nat. Fund, Dem. Nat. Com.; chmn., bd. govs. Mental Health and Criminal Justice Policy Inst. of Am.; v.p. Shorefront Mental Health Bd. Mem. ABA, ACLU, FBA, Ind. State Bar Assn., N.Y. State Bar Assn., Chgo. Bar Assn., Am. Soc. Internat. Law, (chpt. pres. 1983-84), Assn. Trial Lawyers of Am., Am. Judicature Soc., Am. Arbitration Assn., Nat. Health Lawyers Assn., Am. Soc. Communications and Media Execs., Am. Soc. Law, Medicine and Ethics (active mem.), Nat. Assn. Mgmt. Execs., Amnesty Internat., Odd Fellows, B'nai B'rith, Delta Theta Phi. Democrat. Jewish. Criminal, Health, Administrative and regulatory. Office: 82 Wall St Ste 1105 New York NY 10005-3600

**SHAW, RAY,** lawyer; b. Leesburg, Fla., Aug. 6, 1947; s. James Albert and Geraldine N. S.; m. Mary Anne Hancock, Aug. 6, 1979; 1 child, Truett. BSBA in Econs. with honors, U. Fla., 1970, JD, 1972. Bar: Fla. 1972, U.S. Dist. Ct. (mid. dist.) Fla. 1976; cert. civil mediator Fla. Supreme Ct., Fed. Ct., U.S. Bankruptcy Ct. Asst. state atty. Fla. Ct. Appeals (5th cir.), Leesburg, 1972-73; asst. city atty. City Attys. Office, Daytona Beach, Fla., 1973-74; pvt. practice Sarasota, Fla., 1974-77, Spring Hill, Fla., 1980—; asst. pub. defender Fla. Ct. Appeals (5th cir.), Brooksville, Fla., 1977-80. Contbr. articles to profl. jours. Mem. Fla. Bar Assn. (mem. bus. law sect., mem. appellate sect., mem. real property, probate and trust sect., mem. trial lawyers sect.), Hernando County Bar Assn. (former liaison fed. ct. rules com.), Acad. Fla. Trial Lawyers (mem. appellate sect.), Fed. Arbitration Program (mid. dist.) Fla. (charter mem.), Greater Hernando C. of C., Rotary (charter mem., past pres. 1983). Republican. Baptist. Avocations: biking-hiking. Fax: 352-799-0927. E-mail: rshaw@innet.com. Appellate, Bankruptcy, Probate. Office: 2150 Mariner Blvd Spring Hill FL 34609-3859

**SHAW, REBECCA LYNN,** lawyer; b. Tampa, Fla., Aug. 31, 1970; d. Walter Cobb and Barbara Weber Shaw. BA, Fla. State U., 1991, JD, 1995. Bar: Fla. 1995, U.S. Dist. Ct. (mid. dist.) Fla. 1996. Atty. Harris, Barrett, Mann & Dew, St. Petersburg, Fla., 1995—. Bd. dirs. Louise Graham Regeneration Ctr., St. Petersburg, 1997—. Mem. St. Petersburg Bar Assn., Suncoast Tiger Bay Club. Lutheran. Office: Harris Barrett Mann & Dew 150 2nd Ave N Fl 15 Saint Petersburg FL 33701-3356

**SHAW, ROBERT BERNARD,** lawyer; b. Newark, Jan. 26, 1934; s. Nathan and Serena Shaw; m. Sydelle Mae Resnick, Feb. 8, 1958; children: Howard, Lisa, Michael. BS, NYU, 1955; JD, Bklyn. Law Sch., 1958. Bar: N.Y. 1959, U.S. Dist. Ct. (so. and ea. dists.) N.Y., 1960. Ptnr. Shaw & Meyer, N.Y.C., 1959-61; pvt. practice N.Y.C., 1961-70, 74—; ptnr. Shaw, Issler & Rosenberg, N.Y.C., 1970-74. Past pres. Past Capts. Assn. USCG Aux. Mem. N.Y. State Bar Assn., Nassau County Bar Assn., City of N.Y. Police Res. Assn. (bd. dirs. 1997—). General civil litigation, Family and matrimonial. Office: 630 3rd Ave New York NY 10017-6705

**SHAWE, MARK THACKERAY,** lawyer; b. Savannah, Ga., Aug. 3, 1955; s. Arthur T. and Julia C. Shawe; m. Ellen Marie Ragan. BBA in Fin., U. Ga., 1977, JD, 1980. Bar: Ga. 1980. Ptnr. Weiner, Shearouse, Weitz, Greenberg & Shawe, Savannah, Ga., 1980—. Participant Leadership Savannah, 1986-88; pres. Citivan, Savannah, 1989. Avocations: tennis, boating, golfing. Contracts commercial, Real property, Banking. Office: Weiner Shearouse et al 14 E State St Savannah GA 31401-3713

**SHAY, DAVID E.,** lawyer; b. Scranton, Pa., Nov. 9, 1962; s. Howard E. Jr. and Arlene (Pace) S.; m. Kimberly R. Grow, June 22, 1985; children: Daniel E., Andrew W., Matthew D. BS in Journalism, Kans. U., 1984, JD, 1988. Bar: Mo. 1988, U.S. Dist. Ct. (we. dist.) Mo. 1988, U.S. Ct. Appeals (5th and 8th cirs.) 1991. Reporter KDXE, Sulphur Springs, Tex., 1984, KTTR/KZNN, Inc., Rolla, Mo., 1984-85; shareholder Shughart, Thomson & Kilroy, P.C., Kansas City, Mo., 1988—. Contbr. articles to profl. publs., chpt. to Mo. Bar Deskbook, 1991, 97. Mem. The Christian Ch. of Greater Kansas City, ministerial ethics com., 1999—. Mem. ABA, Mo. Bar Assn. (chair environ. and energy law com. 1995-97), Lawyers Assn. Kansas City/Young Lawyers (bd. dirs. 1991-97, officer 1993-97, pres. 1996-97), Kansas City Met. Bar Assn., Lawyers Encouraging Acad. Performance (dir. 1996-97), Order of Coif, Phi Kappa Phi. Republican. Mem. Christian Ch. (Disciples of Christ). Environmental, Insurance, General civil litigation. Office: Shughart Thomson & Kilroy 120 W 12th St Ste 1500 Kansas City MO 64105-1929

**SHAY, MADELINE LEE BRUMMER,** lawyer; b. N.Y.C., June 26, 1948; divorced. BA in Biology, Case Western Reserve U., 1970; MS in Med. Microbiology, Ohio State U., 1972, JD with honors, 1981. Bar: Ohio 1981, U.S. Dist. Ct. (so. dist.) Ohio 1981, Ct. of Internat. Trade. Bacteriologist Brown Labs., Columbus, Ohio, 1972; microbiologist St. Anthony Hosp., Columbus, Ohio, 1973-78; counsel The Procter & Gamble Co., Cin., 1981-90; asst. divsn. counsel North Atlantic divsn. U.S. Army Corps Engrs., N.Y.C., 1992—. Trustee Terr. Guild, Cin., 1989-92. Mem. ABA, Am. Soc. Microbiology, Nat. Registry of Microbiologists (specialist) (SM). Home: 138A Poly Pl Apt 35 Brooklyn NY 11209-8484 Office: Ft Hamilton Mil Cmty 302 General Lee Ave Brooklyn NY 11209-8400

**SHAYS, RONA JOYCE,** lawyer; b. N.Y.C., July 16, 1928; d. Samuel and Beatrice (Fleischer) Eskin; children: Douglas, Sharon; m. Henry C. Shays, Sept. 15, 1974. Student, U. Mich., 1944-47; LLB, Bklyn. Law Sch., 1950; MA, Columbia U., 1968. Bar: N.Y. 1950, U.S. Dist. Ct. (so. and ea. dists) N.Y. 1952. Law clk., assoc. Arthur Bardack, Esquire, Bklyn., 1947-51; assoc. Legal Aid Soc., Mineola, N.Y., 1951-52; legal asst. Mut. Life Ins. Co., N.Y.C., 1959-63; assoc. Hays, Sklar & Herzberg, N.Y.C., 1963-68; from assoc. to ptnr. Mitchell Salem Fisher & Shays, N.Y.C., 1968-76; ptnr. Shersky, Kalman & Shays, N.Y.C., 1976-77, Rosenthal & Shays, N.Y.C., 1977-95, Shays Kemper, N.Y.C., 1995-99, Shays, Rothman & Heisler, LLP, N.Y.C., 1999—. Named Matrimonial Law Arbitrator, Am. Acad. Matrimonial Lawyers, 1992. Fellow Am. Acad. Matrimonial Lawyers (sec. N.Y. state chpt. 1975-82, 90-91, v.p. N.Y. state chpt. 1984-85, 89-90, chair admissions com. N.Y. state chpt. 1986-91, counsel N.Y. state chpt. 1992-93, nat. co-chair interdisciplinary rels. com. 1990-94), Internat. Acad. Matrimonial Lawyers; mem. Assn. Bar City of N.Y. (matrimonial law com. 1982-85, 86-89, 92-95), Nat. Forum on Mental Health and Family Law (co-chair 1990-93), N.Y. State Interdisciplinary Forum on Mental Health and Family Law (co-chair 1986—). Family and matrimonial. Office: Shays Rothman & Heisler LLP 276 5th Ave New York NY 10001-4509

**SHEA, DAVID MICHAEL,** state supreme court justice; b. Hartford, July 1, 1922; s. Michael Peter and Margaret (Agnes) S.; m. Rosemary Anne Sasseen, Apr. 28, 1956; children: Susan, Kathleen, Margaret, Rosemary, Christina, Michael, Maura, Julie. BA, Wesleyan U., 1944; LLB, Yale U., 1948. Bar: Conn. 1948. Assoc. Tunick & Ferris, Greenwich, Conn., 1948-49; assoc. Bailey & Wechsler, Hartford, 1949-57; ptnr. Bailey, Wechsler & Shea, Hartford, 1957-65; judge Conn. Superior Ct., Hartford, 1966-81; justice Conn. Supreme Ct., Hartford, 1981-92, state judge referee, 1992—. Served with U.S. Army, 1943-46. Democrat. Roman Catholic. Office: Conn Superior Ct 95 Washington St Hartford CT 06106-4406

**SHEA, EDWARD EMMETT,** lawyer, educator, author; b. Detroit, May 29, 1932; s. Edward Francis and Margaret Kathleen (Downey) S.; m. Ann Marie Conley, Aug. 28, 1957; children: Michael, Maura, Ellen. AB, U. Detroit, 1954; JD, U. Mich., 1957. Bar: Mich. 1957, Fla. 1959, N.Y. 1961. Assoc. Simpson Thacher & Bartlett, N.Y.C., 1960-63, Dykema, Wheat, Spencer, Detroit, 1963-69, Cadwalader Wickersham & Taft, N.Y.C., 1969-71; v.p., gen. counsel, chmn. Reichhold Chems., White Plains, N.Y., 1971-81; adj. prof. Pace U. Grad. Sch. Bus., N.Y.C., 1982—; counsel, ptnr. Windels, Marx, Davies & Ives, N.Y.C., 1982-84, ptnr., 1986—; sr. v.p., gen. counsel GAF Corp., 1984-86; sec. Peridot Chems., 1988—; lectr. N.Y. Inst. Fin., 1995—. Author: An Introduction to the U.S. Environmental Laws, 1995, The Lead Regulation Handbook, 1996, The McGraw-Hill Guidebook to Acquiring and Divesting Businesses, 1998; editor: The Acquisitions Yearbook, 1991-93; contbr. articles to profl. jours. Mem. adv. bd. N.Y. State Small Bus. Ctr. Program, 1988-93. 1st lt. JAGC, USAF, 1957-60. Mem. N.Y. Athletic Club, Chemist's Club. Finance, Environmental, Private international. Office: Windels Marx Davies & Ives 156 W 56th St Fl 23 New York NY 10019-3867

**SHEA, JEREMY CHARLES,** lawyer; b. Dodgeville, Wis., July 4, 1937; s. Francis Michael and Martha (Early) S.; m. Ann Lee Davies, Aug. 4, 1962; children: Jeffrey William, Jennifer Lee. BA, Northland Coll., 1959; LLB, JD, U. Wis., 1961; LLM, Harvard U., 1963. Bar: Wis. 1961, U.S. Dist. Ct. (we. dist.) Wis. 1961, Minn. 1963, U.S. Dist. Ct. Minn. 1963, U.S. Supreme Ct. 1965. Law clk. to presiding justice Wis. Supreme Ct., Madison, 1962; atty. Leonard Street & Deinard, Mpls., 1963-64, Ross & Stevens, S.C., Madison, 1964-91, Quarles & Brady, Madison, 1991—; lectr. Law Sch., U.Wis., Madison, 1972—, Wis. Continuing Legal Edn., Madison, 1970—; bd. dirs. Park Bank, Madison, Citizens State Bank of Clinton (Wis.), Montello (Wis.) State Bank, State Bank of Argyle (Wis.). Articles editor Wis. Law Rev., 1960-61; contbr. articles to profl. jours.; book reviewer St.

Louis Post-Dispatch, 1965—, Wis. Mag. History, 1970—. Mem. bd. visitors Emerson Coll., Boston, 1980-88; trustee Northland Coll., Ashland, Wis., 1979—; bd. dirs Madison Ballet Co., 1972-78, Big Bros. and Big Sisters Found.; chmn. atty. sect. United Way. Named one of Best Lawyers in Am. Woodward White, N.Y.C., 1989-93. Mem. ABA, State Bar Assn. Wis. (chmn. continuing legal edn. sect. and ins. com. 1961—, fin. com., bd. dirs. corp. and bus. law sect.), Minn. State Bar Assn., Madison Curling Club (pres. 1987-88), Madison Aquatic Club (pres. 1970-75), Order of Coif, Rotary, Madison Club. Republican. Presbyterian. Banking, General corporate, Real property. Home: 7304 Cedar Creek Trl Madison WI 53717-1503 Office: Quales & Brady PO Box 2113 Madison WI 53701-2113

**SHEA, JOSEPH WILLIAM, III,** lawyer; b. Cin., Jan. 3, 1947; s. Joseph W. Jr. and Gertrude Mary (Reardon) S.; m. Elaine N. Miller, May 29, 1971; children: J. Blane, Doyle Reardon, C. Lauer. BA, U. Cin., 1969; JD, No. Ky. U., 1974. Bar: Ohio 1974, Ky. 1999, U.S. Dist. Ct. Ohio 1974, U.S. Ct. Appeals (6th cir.) 1980, U.S. Supreme Ct. 1981. Prin. Shea & Assocs., Cin., 1974—; founder Lawriter Sys. Corp., Cin., 1983-93; mem. Ohio Supreme Ct. Bd. Bar Examiners, chair 1988-89. Author: Shea's Forms for Ohio Trial Practice, 1983, Shea Civil Practice, 1985; contbg. author: Personal Injury in Ohio, CLE Institute and Wrongful Death Manual, 1984, Civil Litigation in Ohio, CLE Institute, Wrongful Death in Ohio, 1986, Personal Injury Litigation, 1988; editor Ohio Verdict Reporter, vols. 1-210, 1976—; contbr. articles to profl. jours. Mem. Gov.'s Ins. Task Force, Columbus, 1985—; mem. Supreme Ct. Bd. Bar Examiners, 1982-89, chmn., 1988-89; diplomat Nat. Bd. Trial Advocacy, 1985—. Fellow Ohio Acad. Trial Lawyers (pres. 1981-83, editor mag. 1981), Internat. Soc. Barristers; mem. ATLA (del. nat. conv. 1983-85, bd. govs. 1985—), Am. Bd. Trial Advocacy (adv. 1989—, nat. rep. 1990—), Ky. Acad. Trial Lawyers, Ohio Bar Assn. (negligence law com.), Ky. Bar Assn., Cin. Bar Assn. (negligence law com.), Nat. Conf. Examiners (bd. examiners 1984-89, chmn.), Nat. Bd. Trial Advocacy (cert. trial specialist 1985—, nat. bd. dirs.). Roman Catholic. Avocations: sailing, snow skiing. Federal civil litigation, State civil litigation, General civil litigation. Home: 5955 Drake Rd Cincinnati OH 45243-3305 Office: Shea & Assocs 600 Flatiron Bldg 401 E Court St Cincinnati OH 45202-1355

**SHEA, MEGAN CARROLL,** lawyer; b. Lake Forest, Ill., Sept. 7, 1967; d. Barry Joseph and Barbara (Pehrson) C.; m. Timothy J. Shea II. Student, Middlebury Coll., Paris, 1987-88; BA in Philosophy, French Lit., Boston Coll., 1989, JD, 1992. Bar: Mass., 1993, Ill. 1994, D.C. 1995. Law clk. Middlesex County Probate & Family Ct., Cambridge, Mass., 1990-91; assoc. Powers & Hall, Boston, 1991; asst. dist. atty. Norfolk County, Mass., 1992; prin., owner Carroll Assocs., Counsel for the Arts, Boston, 1994—; bd. dirs. Carroll Internat. Corp., Des Plaines, Ill. Arts review writer various publs. Mem. Am. Ireland Fund, Boston, Chgo., 1985—, DAR, Chgo., 1985—, Phillips Acad. Alumni Coun., Andover, Mass., 1991-95; trustee Regency Pk. Condominiums, Brookline, Mass., 1989-91; sec. Phillips Acad. Alumni Class of 1985, Andover, 1989-95. Recipient Golden Key Nat. Honor Soc., Boston Coll., 1989, Order of the Cross and Crown, Scholar of the Coll., 1989. Mem. ABA, Arts and Media Law Assn. of Boston Coll. (pres., founder), Social Register, Woman's Athletic Club Chgo., Order of Malta Aux., Jr. Internat. Club Lauterbach (Germany), East Chop Beach Club, East Chop Yacht Club, East Chop Tennis Club, Phi Delta Phi. Republican. Roman Catholic. Avocations: classical ballet, choreography, scuba diving, flying (lic. pilot). Home: 24 Columbia St Wellesley MA 02481-1603 also: 55 Mayflower Rd Lake Forest IL 60045 Office: Carroll Assocs Two Park Plaza Boston MA 02116

**SHEA, MICHAEL PATRICK,** lawyer; b. St. Louis, Mo., May 11, 1951; s. Jerome Spencer and Dorothy Marie S.; m. Ann M., June 18, 1976; 3 children. BA in Polit. Sci., U. Mo., St. Louis, 1973; JD, U. Mo., Kansas City, 1975. Bar: Mo. 1976, U.S. Dist. Ct. (ea. dist.) Mo. 1976, U.S. Ct. Appeals (8th cir.) 1977. Assoc. Gerald Bamberger, St. Charles, Mo., 1976-80; ptnr. Bamberger & Shea, St. Charles, 1980-84, Shea & Kohl, St. Charles, 1984-92, Shea, Kohl & Alessi, St. Charles, 1992-96, Shea, Kohl, Alessi & O'Donnell, St. Charles, 1996—; vice-chair Bd. Adjustment, Bellefontaine Neighbors, Mo., 1982-86, St. Charles, 1988-92; asst. pros. atty. City St. Charles, 1989—; bd. dirs. Legal Svcs. Ea. Mo., Inc., St. Louis. Mem. ABA, Bar Assn. Met. St. Louis, Mo. Bar, 11th Jud. Cir. Bar Assn. (pres. 1981). Democrat. Roman Catholic. Family and matrimonial. Office: Shea Kohl Alessi & O'Donnell LC 400 N 5th St Ste 200 Saint Charles MO 63301-1800

**SHEAD, WILLIAM C.,** lawyer; b. Sulphur Branch, Tex., Mar. 23, 1927; m. Thalia Smith, Dec. 19, 1950; children—Suzie, Sheri, Ginny, Libby, Katie. B.S., U. Houston, 1952, LL.M., 1954; J.D., South Tex. Coll. Law, 1959. Bar: Tex. 1960. Chief scout Mid-Continent div. Tidewater Oil Co.; lectr. Downtown Sch., U. Houston; asst. city atty. City of Houston; sole practice, Houston, 1960-86; assoc. judge, State of Tex., 1986— . Candidate Tex. Ho. Reps., 1962. Mem. ABA, Am. Judicature Soc., Assn. Trial Lawyers Am., Harris County Criminal Def. Lawyers Assn., Houston Bar Assn. (prison prerelease com., jud. qualifications com.), Nat. Assn. Criminal Def. Lawyers, Pasadena Bar Assn., Tex. Criminal Def. Lawyers Assn., Tex. Trial Lawyers Assn. Lodges: Masons, Lions. General practice. Office: 2927 Broadway St Houston TX 77017-1705

**SHEAFFER, CINDY ELAINE,** lawyer; b. Mechanicsburg, Pa., July 5, 1958; d. Maynard Leroy and Ruth Geraldine (Walters) Sheaffer; 1 child, Matthew Thomas Priest; m. Dennis Anthony DeStadio, Aug. 5, 1995. Paralegal Cert., Harrisburg (Pa.) Area C.C., 1988; BS, Pa. State U., Harrisburg, 1990; JD, Dickinson Sch. Law, Carlisle, Pa., 1993. Bar: Pa. 1994. Legal sec. McNees, Wallace & Nurick, Harrisburg, 1988-90; law clk. Schmidt & Ronca, P.C., Harrisburg, 1991; cert. legal intern Family Law Clinic, Carlisle, 1992; law clk. The Underwriters' Group, Harrisburg, 1993; pvt. practice Enola, Pa., 1995—; atty./instr. Ctrl. Pa. Bus. Sch., Summerdale, 1993—; pro bono atty. Ctrl. Pa. Legal Svc., Harrisburg, 1994—. Atty. vol. Dauphin County Custody Clinic, Harrisburg, 1995—; bd. dirs. Ronny Powley Ctr. for Social Ministries, Enola, 1995. Mem. ABA, Pa. Bar Assn., Dauphin County Bar Assn. Avocation: watching son's sports. Family and matrimonial, Probate. Office: PO Box 267 806 Wertzville Rd Enola PA 17025-1833

**SHEAFFER, WILLIAM JAY,** lawyer; b. Carlisle, Pa., Jan. 18, 1948; s. Raymond Jay and Barbara Jean (Bell) S.; m. Carol Ann Madison, Jan. 5, 1974. BA cum laude, U. Cen. Fla., 1975; JD, Nova U., 1978. Bar: Fla. 1978, U.S. Dist. Ct. (mid. dist.) Fla. 1979, U.S. Dist. Ct. (so. and no. dists.) Fla. 1981, U.S. Ct. Appeals (5th and 11th cirs.) 1981, U.S. Supreme Ct. 1983. Atty. State of Fla., Orlando, 1978-79; pvt. practice, Orlando, 1979—; apptd. to merit selection panel to consider U.S. Magistrate Judge Applicants, 1995, 97, 99. Served to ensign class 4 USN, 1967-71. Mem. ABA, NACDL, Fla. Bar Assn. (cert. criminal trial specialist, vice chmn. 9th judicial cir. grievance com. 1997, 98), Orange County Bar Assn. (Guardian Ad Litem of Yr. 1994, award of excellence 1995), Fed. Bar Assns., Fla. Assn. Criminal Def. Lawyers Inc., Fed. Trial Lawyers Assn., Am. Inns of Ct. (ctrl. Fla. master), Tiger Bay Club, Citrus Club. Democrat. Avocations: boating, running, skiing, scuba diving, golf. Fax: 407-648-0683. Administrative and regulatory, Criminal. Office: 609 E Central Blvd Orlando FL 32801-2916

**SHEAHAN, JOSEPH D.,** lawyer; b. Rock Island, Ill., Oct. 25, 1946; s. Joseph L. and Muriel (Bogart) S.; m. Judith Richards, Nov. 26, 1965; children: Michelle Lynn, Jessica Michelle. B.A., Augustana Coll., Rock Island, Ill.; J.D., Washburn U., 1978; postgrad. Georgetown U., 1978-80; honor grad. U.S. Dept. Justice, Washington, 1980. Bar admittee: Kans., 1978, Ill., 1979. Law clk. U.S. Ct. Appeals for 10th Circuit, Denver, 1978; asso. McGehee, Boling & Whitmire, Ltd., Silvis, Ill., 1980-82; sole practice, East Moline, Ill., 1982—; owner Ill.-Iowa Claim Service, Davenport; city atty. City of Green Rock (Ill.), 1980—; village atty. Village of Carbon Cliff, 1984—. Served with U.S. Army, 1967-70; Vietnam. Mem. ABA, Ill. Bar Assn., Rock Island County Bar Assn., Upper Rock Island C. of C. (dir. 1980-82). Democrat. Contbr. articles to legal jours. State civil litigation, Personal injury.

**SHEAHAN, ROBERT EMMETT,** lawyer, consultant; b. Chgo., May 20, 1942; s. Robert Emmett and Lola Jean (Moore) S.; m. Pati Smith, Mar. 20, 1991. BA, Ill. Wesleyan U., 1964; JD, Duke U., 1967; MBA, U. Chgo., 1970. Bar: Ill. 1967, La. 1975, N.C. 1978. Vol. VISTA, N.Y.C., 1967-68; trial atty. NLRB, Milw. and New Orleans, 1970-75; ptnr. Jones, Walker, Waechter, Poitevent, Carrere & Denegre, New Orleans, 1975-78; pvt. practice, High Point, N.C., 1978—; bd. dirs. Inst. for Effective Mgmt., Bus. Publs. Inst. Author: Employees and Drug Abuse: An Employer's Handbook, 1994, The Encyclopedia of Drugs in the Workplace, Labor and Employment Law in North Carolina, 1991, Personnel and Employment Law in North Carolina, 1992, Desk Book of Labor and Employment Law for Healthcare Employers, 1995, North Carolina's Healthcare Employers' Desk Manual, 1995, North Carolina lawyers' Desk Book; contbg. author: The Developing Labor Law, 1975—; editor: The World of Personnel; contbg. editor: Employee Testing and the Law; contbr. periodic supplements N.C. Gen. Practice Deskbook, 1992—. Bd. dirs. High Point United Way, 1979-83; mem. congressional action com. High Point C. of C., chmn., 1991—, bd. dirs., 1996—. Mem. ABA, N.C. Bar Assn., High Point Bar Assn., Ill. Bar Assn., La. Bar Assn. Republican. Roman Catholic. Clubs: Sedgefield (N.C.) Country, String and Splinter (High Point), Bald Head (N.C.) Island Club. Labor. Home: 101 Bellwood Ct Jamestown NC 27282-9446 Office: Eastchester Office Ctr 603 Eastchester Dr Ste B High Point NC 27262-7647

**SHEAR, ANDREW CHARLES,** lawyer; b. N.Y.C., Nov. 18, 1967; s. David Arnold and Helen Miriam Shear; m. Lynne J. Lazarus, July 3, 1994. BA in Govt., Wesleyan U., 1989; JD magna cum laude, NYU, 1993. Bar: N.Y. 1994, U.S. Dist. Ct. (so. dist.) N.Y. 1996, U.S. Ct. Appeals (7th cir.) 1997, U.S. Ct. Appeals (9th cir.) 1997. Law clk. N.Y. State Supreme Ct., N.Y.C., 1993-94; staff atty. Legal Aid Soc. Criminal Def. Divsn., Bklyn., 1994-96; assoc. Dershowitz & Eiger, P.C., N.Y.C., 1996—. Mem. Order of the Coif. Criminal, Appellate. Office: Dershowitz & Eiger PC 350 5th Ave New York NY 10118-0110

**SHEARER, DEAN PAUL,** lawyer; b. Waco, Tex., Aug. 30, 1960; s. Clyde Paul and Elaine Shearer; m. Linda Hallene, May 22, 1982; children: Stephanie Ann, John Paul. Student, U. Houston, 1978-81; BS, U. Houston-Clear Lake, 1982; JD, South Tex. Coll. Law, Houston, 1989. Bar: Tex. 1989; bd. cert. in estate planning and probate. Atty. Babchick Cohen & Shearer P.C., Houston, 1989—; adj. prof. U. Houston-Clear lake 1991-97; instr. Exec. Devel. program U. Houston Coll. Bus. Adminstrn. 1997—. Trustee, v.p. Clear Lake City Cmty. Assn., 1992-94; asst. den leader Boy Scouts Am., Houston, 1995-96; team mgr. Bay Area Youth Sports, Houston, 1994-99; vol. Jr. Achievement, 1994, Habitat for Humanity, 1995, 97, YMCA, 1997, 99. Mem. Houston Bar Assn. (co-chair campaign for homeless com. 1998-99, chair speakers bur. 1999—, continuing legal edn. com. 1997-98), State Bar Tex., State Bar Coll. Roman Catholic. Avocations: motorcycling, boating, bicycling. Estate planning, Probate, Estate taxation. Home: 810 Heathgate Dr Houston TX 77062-2624 Office: Babchick Cohen & Shearer PC 4615 Post Oak Place Dr Ste 279 Houston TX 77027-9753

**SHEARIN, JAMES TIMOTHY,** lawyer; b. Fishersville, Va., Mar. 11, 1961; s. James Lewis and Jeanette (Hurst) S.; m. Ellen Sigrid Aho, Nov. 22, 1986. BA, U. Conn., 1983, JD, 1986. Bar: Conn. 1986, U.S. Dist. Ct. Conn. 1987. Law clk. to Judge Peter Dorsey U.S. Dist. Ct. Conn., Hartford, 1986-88; with Pullman & Comley, Bridgeport, Conn., 1988—; vice-chmn. Conn. Legal Svcs., Inc. Adminstrv. editor: Connecticut Law Review, 1985-86. Vice-chmn. U. Conn. Law Sch. Found., Inc. William F. Starr fellow, 1986. Mem. ABA, Conn. Bar Assn., Bridgeport Bar Assn. (v.p.). Democrat. Congregationalist. Avocations: sports, woodworking. Home: 81 Taunton Hill Rd Newtown CT 06470-1728

**SHEARIN, KATHRYN KAY,** lawyer, legal and humor writer; b. Norfolk, Va., Dec. 24, 1946; d. John Willis and Kathryn (Riecken) S.; m. James Charles Bray, June 1, 1969 (div. May 1973). BA, U. N.C., Greensboro, 1968; MA, Boston U., 1972; MS, N.C. State U., 1978; JD, Rutgers U., Newark, 1980; LLM in Taxation, Georgetown U., 1983. Bar: N.J. 1980, U.S. Dist. Ct. N.J. 1980, D.C. 1981, Md. 1982, U.S. Tax Ct. 1982, U.S. Supreme Ct. 1984, Del. 1986, U.S. Dist. Ct. Del. 1986, U.S. Cir. Ct. (3d cir.) 1987. Law clk. to magistrate U.S. Dist. Ct. N.J., Newark, 1978-79; prin. stat. State of N.J., Trenton, 1979-80; atty., adviser U.S. Dept. of Justice, Washington, 1982-83; editor tax law BNA Tax Mgmt., Washington, 1983-84; editor, pub. Common Law Revue CapriComp, Wilmington, Del., 1984-86; pvt. practice law, 1986—; trust counsel, v.p., corp. sec. E.F. Hutton Trust Co., Wilmington, 1984-86; mng. atty. Hyatt Legal Svcs., 1986; lectr. in field. Writer Del. Corp. Law Update, 1987—. Libertarian candidate for atty. gen., Del., 1990; of counsel African Union 1st Colored Meth. Protestant Ch., 1991—. Mem. Profl. Orgn. for Agents (founder, charter 1999). Libertarian. Civil rights, Estate taxation, Family and matrimonial. Home and office: 1301 Maple Ave Wilmington DE 19805-5036

**SHEARING, MIRIAM,** state supreme court justice; b. Waverly, N.Y., Feb. 24, 1935. BA, Cornell U., 1956; JD, Boston Coll., 1964. Bar: Calif. 1965, Nev. 1969. Justice of peace Las Vegas Justice Ct., 1977-81; judge Nev. Dist. Ct., 1983-92, chief judge, 1986; justice Nevada Supreme Ct., Carson City, 1993-97, chief justice, 1997—. Mem. ABA, Am. Judicature Soc., Nev. Judges Assn. (sec. 1978), Nev. Dist. Ct. Judges Assn. (sec. 1984-85, pres. 1986-87), State Bar Nev., State Bar Calif., Clark County Bar Assn. Democrat.

**SHEBLE, WALTER FRANKLIN,** retired lawyer; b. Chestnut Hill, Pa., Sept. 14, 1926; s. Franklin and Harriett Elizabeth (Smith) S.; m. Nancy Altemus, July 7, 1956; 3 children. AB, Princeton U., 1948; JD, George Washington U., 1952, LLM, 1953. Bar: U.S. Dist. Ct. D.C. 1952, U.S. Ct. Appeals D.C. 1952, U.S. Supreme Ct. 1953, U.S. Ct. Appeals Md. 1960. Assoc. Hudson & Creyke, Washington, 1953-56, H. William Tanaka, Washington, 1956-61, 63-66; cons. Office of Pres., Washington, 1961-63; spl. asst. to postmaster gen., U.S. rep. Univ. Postal Union, Bern, Switzerland, 1966-70; spl. asst. to gen. counsel Interam. Devel. Bank, Washington, 1970-88; trustee New Eng. Coll. Mem. bd. mgrs. Chevy Chase Village, 1985-89; pres. Parents Assn. Nat. Cathedral Sch., 1969-70, mem. governing bd. 1970. Mem. ABA (exec. coun. gen. practice sect. 1982-87), Bar Assn. D.C., Colonial Club, Barristers Club, Met. Club, Chevy Chase Club. Avocations: gardening, surf fishing. General practice, Public international, Legislative. Office: 7700 Old Georgetown Rd Ste 800 Bethesda MD 20814-6100

**SHECTER, HOWARD L.,** lawyer; b. Boston, May 13, 1943. AB, Harvard U., 1965; JD, U. Pa., 1968. Bar: Pa. 1968. Assoc. Morgan, Lewis & Bockius LLP, Phila., 1968-73; ptnr. Morgan, Lewis & Bockius LLP, N.Y.C., 1973—. Mergers and acquisitions, General corporate, Private international. Office: Morgan Lewis & Bockius LLP 101 Park Ave Fl 44 New York NY 10178-0060

**SHEDD, DENNIS W.,** federal judge; b. 1953. BA, Wofford Coll., 1975; JD, U. S.C., 1978; M of Laws, Georgetown U., 1980. Bar: S.C. Mem. staff U.S. Senator Strom Thurmond, 1978-88; chief counsel U.S. Senate Jud. Com., Washington, 1985-86; of counsel Bethea, Jordan & Griffin, Columbia, S.C., 1988-90; pvt. practice, 1989-90; judge U.S. Dist. Ct. S.C., Greenville, 1991—; adj. prof. U. S.C., 1989-90. Mem. S.C. Bar Assn., Richland County Bar Assn., Phi Beta Kappa. Office: US District Court 1845 Assembly St Ste 1 Columbia SC 29201-2431

**SHEEDY, KATHLEEN ANN,** lawyer; b. June 18, 1956; d. Patrick Thomas Sheedy and Margaret Pelkey Mulvaney; m. Mark Louis Pedriani, Sept. 25, 1982; children: Gabrielle, Katherine, Jennifer. BS in Bus. Adminstrn., Georgetown U., 1978; JD, Marquette U., 1981. Bar: Wis. 1981, Ill. 1981, U.S. Dist. Ct. (no. dist.) Ill. 1981, U.S. Dist. Ct. (ea. dist.) Wis. 1981. Assoc. Chapman & Cutler, Chgo., 1981-83; mgr. Peat Marwick, Paris, 1983-84; assoc. Quarles & Brady, Milw., 1984-86; sr. mgr. KPMG Peat Marwick, Paris, 1986-90; sr. atty. Kohler (Wis.) Co., 1991—. Real property, Contracts commercial, General corporate. Office: Kohler Co Legal Dept 444 Highland Dr Kohler WI 53044-1500

**SHEEHAN, EDWARD MICHAEL,** lawyer; b. Ft. Worth, Mar. 22, 1950; s. Dennis James Sheehan and Jean Margaret La Comb; m. Carol Sue Colvin, July 16, 1988; children: Meghan, Brian. AA, Santa Ana Jr. Coll., 1974; BA, Tex. Tech. U., 1976; JD, U. Tex., 1979. Bar: Tex., U.S. Dist. Ct. (no. and so. dists.) Tex., U.S. Ct. Appeals (5th cir.). Asst. criminal dist. atty. Tarrant County Dist. Atty.'s Office, Ft. Worth, 1979-81; pvt. practice Ft. Worth, 1981-82; asst. U.S. atty. no. dist. Office of U.S. Atty., Ft. Worth, 1982-84; atty. Cantey Hanger Goch Munn & Collins, Ft. Worth, 1984-85, Kelly Hart & Hallman, Ft. Worth, 1985-90, Thompson & Knight P.C., Ft. Worth, 1990—. Sgt. USMC, 1968-72, Vietnam. Avocation: U.S. history. General civil litigation, General corporate, Aviation. Office: Thompson & Knight PC 801 Cherry St Ste 1600 Fort Worth TX 76102-6816

**SHEEHAN, LARRY JOHN,** lawyer; b. N.Y.C., Apr. 14, 1955; s. James Albert and Hortense Rose (Carlo) S.; m. Sylvia Margaret Poschman, Apr. 30, 1978; children: Nicole, Kelly, Daniel. BA, St. John's U., 1978; JD, N.Y. Law Sch., 1983. Bar: N.Y. 1984, U.S. Dist. Ct. (so. and ea. dists.) N.Y. 1984. Asst. dist. atty. Bronx Dist. Atty., N.Y.C., 1984-89; atty. Alemany, Gonzalez, McLoone & Sheehan, Scarsdale, N.Y., 1989—; atty. N.Y.C. Assigned Counsel, N.Y.C., 1989—, Fed. Assigned Counsel Plan, So. Dist., N.Y., 1991—, Ea. Dist., N.Y., 1993—. Campaign mgr. Dem. Party, Yonkers, N.Y., 1989. Mem. N.Y. State Bar Assn., Bronx County Bar Assn., Westchester County Bar Assn., N.Y. State Criminal Trial Assn. Roman Catholic. Avocations: reading, brief writing, basketball, running. Criminal, Bankruptcy, General civil litigation. Home and Office: Alemany Gonzalez McLoone & Sheehan 111 Brook St Scarsdale NY 10583-5143

**SHEEHAN, ROBERT C.,** lawyer; b. N.Y.C., Oct. 12, 1944; s. John Edward and Mary Elizabeth (Trede) S.; m. Elizabeth Mary Mammen, Aug. 17, 1968; children: Elizabeth, Robert, William. BA, Boston Coll., 1966; LLB, Univ. Pa., Phila., 1969. Bar: N.Y. 1970. Ptnr. Skadden, Arps, Slate, Meagher & Flom LLP, N.Y.C., 1978—, exec. ptnr., 1994—. Banking, General corporate, Mergers and acquisitions. Office: Skadden Arps Slate Meagher Flom LLP 919 3rd Ave New York NY 10022-3902

**SHEELER, HARVA LEE,** law librarian; b. Miami, Fla., Feb. 10, 1934; d. Harry Hersh and Rose (Caplan) Young; m. Walter Leon Sheeler, Nov. 9, 1957 (dec. Sept. 1985); children: Charles Harold, Harva Katharine. BA, U. Maine, 1955; MS in LS, Cath. U. Am., 1972. Reference libr. Fairfax County Pub. Libr., Fairfax, Va., 1972-74, Virginiana collection libr., 1974-79; mgr. law libr. Jones Day Reavis & Pogue, Washington, 1979-94, coord. firm librs., 1994—. Contbg. author: Managing the Private Law Library, 1988. Sec., bull. editor Fairfax County Fedn. Citizens Assns., 1966-80. Recipient A. Heath Onthank award for svc. Fairfax County Bd. Suprs., 1978, Nat. Facts on File award ALA, 1980. Mem. Am. Assn. Law Librs. (sec.-treas. pvt. law libr.-spl. interest sect. 1989-91), Spl. Librs. Assn., Law Libr. Soc. Washington (pres. Pvt. law libr.-spl. interest sect. 1982-84), Beta Phi Mu. Home: 2326 Wheystone Ct Vienna VA 22182-5236 Office: Jones Day Reavis & Pogue 51 Lousiana Ave NW Washington DC 20001

**SHEETS, THOMAS WADE,** lawyer; b. Decatur, Ind., July 23, 1956; s. Lewis Lindberg and Mary Alice (Lee) Hoffman S. Student Purdue U., 1974-75; B.S. in Edn., Ind. U.-Fort Wayne, 1978; J.D., Valparaiso U., 1981. Bar: Ind. 1981, U.S. Dist. Ct. (so. dist.) Ind. 1981, U.S. Dist. Ct. (no. dist.) Ind. 1982. Sole practice, Decatur, Ind., 1981—; bailiff Rentner Senate, 1980-81; pub. defender, Decatur, 1981-82, 86—; dep. pros. atty. 26th Jud. Cir., Decatur, 1982-86. Chmn. bd. Adams County Red Cross, 1984; v.p. bd. dirs. Adams/Wells chpt. Big Bros./Big Sisters, 1984. Recipient Am. Jurisprudence award Lawyers Coop. Pub. Co., 1979. Mem. Ind. State Bar Assn., Adams County Bar Assn. (pres. 1985-86, 96-97). Delta Theta Phi. Democrat. Lutheran. Family and matrimonial, General practice, Criminal. Home: 159 N 2nd St Decatur IN 46733-1608 Office: PO Box 528 157 N 2d St Decatur IN 46733-0528

**SHEETZ, RALPH ALBERT,** lawyer; b. Dauphin County, Pa., June 13, 1908; s. Harry Wesley and MaNora (Enders) S.; m. Ruth Lorraine Bender, May 19, 1938; 1 son, Ralph Bert. PhB, Dickinson Coll., 1930; JD, U. Ala., 1933. Bar: Pa. 1934, U.S. Dist. Ct. (mid. dist.) Pa. 1944. Solicitor, East Pennsboro Twp., Pa., 1937-53, Peoples Bank of Enola (Pa.), 1935-75; atty. Lawyers Title Ins. Corp., Richmond, Va., 1956-94, Commonwealth Land Title Ins. Co., Phila., 1957-94; atty. Employees Loan Soc., 1966-76. Ofcl. Appeal Area no. 4, SSS, Pa., assoc. legal adviser to Draft Bd. No. 2, adviser to registrants to Local Bd. No. 55, Harrisburg, Pa., 1974-76; counselor Camp Kanestake, Huntingdon County, Pa., Methodist Ch.; treas., atty. Enola Boys Club, from 1950; pres. East Pennsboro Twp. PTA, 1951-52; atty. hon. mem. Citizens Fire Co. No. 1, Enola, 1951; apptd. bd. gov's. Am. Biog. Inst. Rsch. Assn.; del. arts and communications 15th Internat. Congress, Singapore, 16th Internat. Congress Willard Inter-Continental Hotel, Washington, 1989, 17th Internat. Congress Safari Park Hotel, Nairobi, Kenya, 1990, 18th Internat. Congress Harbour Castle Westin Hotel, Toronto, Can., 1991, 19th Internat. Congress St. John's Coll., Cambridge, Eng., 1992, 20th Internat. Congress, Cambridge, Mass., 1993, 21st Internat. Congress, Edinburgh, Scotland, 1994; sec., treas. West Shore Regional Coordinating Com., Cumberland County, 1956-66; mem. bd. adjustments East Pennsboro Twp., 1959, chmn., 1959, mem. planning commn, 1956-59, vice-chmn., mem. zoning commn., 1958, chmn., 1959; mem. East Pennsboro Twp. Republican Club, from 1936; dep. dir. gen. Internat. Biog. Ctr. for the Ams., 1989. Recipient numerous awards and honors from Pres. of U.S. for svc. to SSS; Order of the Silver Trowel, Council of Anointed Kings Commonwealth of Pa., Altoona, 1948. Mem. ABA, Dauphin Bar Assn. (social com. 1934-95), Cumberland County Bar Assn., Pa. Bar Assn., Tall Cedars of Lebanon (historian Tall Cedars Forest No. 43 1980-89, exec. com. 1980-89), Shriners, Masons (York cross of honor), K.T. (comdr. 1946). Family and matrimonial, General practice, Probate. Home and Office: 798 Valley St Enola PA 17025-1618

**SHEFFIELD, ALDEN DANIEL, JR.,** lawyer; b. St. Paul, Sept. 10, 1947; s. Alden Daniel Sheffield and Martha Terrel Yaeger; m. Pamela Roesner, Oct. 8, 1983; children: Charles Alden Sheffield, Elliot Alden Sheffield. BA, Colo. Coll., 1969; JD, U. Minn., 1974. Atty. Ryley Carlock & Applewhite, Phoenix, 1975-92; sole practice Colorado Springs, 1992—. With U.S. Army, 1970-72. General civil litigation, Condemnation, Real property. Home: 1624 Culebra Pl Colorado Springs CO 80907-7333 Office: 90 S Cascade Ave Ste 830 Colorado Springs CO 80903-1675

**SHEFFIELD, FRANK ELWYN,** lawyer; b. Tallahassee, Jan. 4, 1946; s. Byron Elmer and Essie Faustine (West) S.; m. Judith Elizabeth Powell, July 26, 1968 (div. July 1971); m. Janice Alicia Gentry, Feb. 22, 1975; stepchildren: Lorimer H. Blitch, Richard S. Noles; children: Brett Elwyn, Jennifer Alicia. BS in Mktg., Fla. State U., 1968, JD, 1972. Bar: Fla. 1972, U.S. Dist. Ct. (no. dist.) Fla. 1972, U.S. Ct. Appeals (5th cir.) 1975, U.S. Tax Ct. 1978. Sole practice Tallahassee, 1972, 73-78, 80—; assoc. Dye & Conner, Tallahassee, 1973; ptnr. Michaels, Sheffield, Perkins & Collins, Tallahassee, 1978-80; sole practice Tallahassee, 1980—. Mem. ABA, Fla. Bar Assn., Assn. Trial Lawyers Am., Acad. Fla. Trial Lawyers, Fla. Assn. Criminal Def. Lawyers, Delta Sigma Pi. Democrat. Mem. Assembly of God Ch. Avocations: woodworking, scuba diving, automobile restoration. Family and matrimonial, Criminal, General civil litigation. Home: 4028 Old Bainbridge Rd Tallahassee FL 32303-2110 Office: 906 Thomasville Rd Tallahassee FL 32303-6220

**SHEFFIELD, WALTER JERVIS,** lawyer; b. Petersburg, Va., Mar. 20, 1946; s. John Courtney and Betty Lou (Loftis) S.; m. Susan Jarrett Moore, May 4, 1968 (div. June 1980); children: John Courtney II, Walter Alexander; m. Christina Meredith Shipp, Jan. 23, 1982; 1 child, Margaret Ashbrooke. BA magna cum laude, Old Dominion U., 1971; JD, Emory U., 1973; LLM in taxation, NYU, 1974. Bar: Va. 1975, U.S. Dist. Ct. (ea. dist.) Va. 1975, U.S. Ct. Appeals (4th cir.) 1975, U.S. Ct. Claims 1975, U.S. Tax Ct. 1975, U.S. Supreme Ct. 1979. Asst. to Sec. of Commonwealth, Office of Gov. Commonwealth of Va., Richmond, 1974-75; assoc. Cox, Woodbridge, Smith, Scott & VanLear, Fredericksburg, Va., 1975-76; city atty. City of Fredericksburg, 1976-86; pres. Sheffield & Bricken, Fredericksburg, 1979-91; pvt. practice Walter J. Sheffield, Atty., 1976-79, 91—; chmn. Va. State Bd. Surface Mining Rev., 1989-93; vice mayor City of Fredericksburg, 1988-92, chmn. fin. com., 1988-92; chmn. Rappahannock regional jail bd., 1988-90; constrn. dispute arbitrator Am. Arbitration Assn., 1985—; commr. in chancery City of Fredericksburg; mem. legis. and effective govt. coms. Va. Mcpl. League. Bd. dirs. 7th Dist. Dem. Com., 1985-89; mem. State Dem. Ctrl. Com., 1985-89; legal counsel, dir. Fredericksburg Area Mus. and Cultural Ctr., Inc., 1988—, Mary Washington Hosp. Found., 1989-91; trustee, chmn. adminstrv. bd. Fredericksburg United Meth. Ch.; mem. com. on instl. relationships Va. Ann. Conf. United Meth. Ch.; pres. Fredericksburg Civil War Roundtable, 1996-97. 1st lt. Quartermaster Corps, U.S. Army, 1966-69. Recipient Disting. Svc. award Fredericksburg Jaycees, 1978. Mem. Fredericksburg Area Bar Assn. (pres. 1997), Fredericksburg Area C. of C., Va. Trial Lawyers Assn., Phi Alpha Theta, Phi Delta Phi (magister 1972-73). Club: Fredericksburg Country. Personal injury, Probate, Contracts commercial. Home: 1314 Sophia St Fredericksburg VA 22401-3742 Office: PO Box 7818 Fredericksburg VA 22404-7818

**SHEFTMAN, HOWARD STEPHEN,** lawyer; b. Columbia, S.C., May 20, 1949; s. Nathan and Rena Mae (Kantor) S.; children: Amanda Elaine, Emily Catherine. BS in Bus. Adminstrn., U. S.C., 1971, JD, 1974. Bar: S.C. 1974, U.S. Dist. Ct. 1975, U.S. Ct. Appeals (4th cir.) 1982. Assoc. Kirkland, Taylor & Wilson, West Columbia, S.C., 1974-75; ptnr. Sheftman, Oswald & Holland, West Columbia, 1975-77, Finkel & Altman, LLC, Columbia, 1977—. Mem. S.C. Bar Assn. (chmn. practice and procedure com. 1999—), S.C. Trial Lawyers Assn. (chmn. domestic rels. sect. 1982-83, bd. govs. 1987-93, 94-98), Richland Bar Assn., Met. Sertoma Club (pres. 1986-87). Jewish. Family and matrimonial, State civil litigation, Federal civil litigation. Office: Finkel & Altman LLC PO Box 1799 Columbia SC 29202-1799

**SHEHAN, WAYNE CHARLES,** lawyer; b. Miami, Fla., Nov. 25, 1944; s. Joseph L. Shehan and Louise A. Salloum; m. Sherrin M. Graham, May 21, 1981; children: Christopher, Kevin. BS, U. Detroit, 1966, JD, 1969. Bar: Mich. 1969. Prin. Wayne C. Shehan, P.C., St. Clair Shores, Mich., 1969—; prof. U. Detroit, 1969-70; mediator Macomb County Cir. Ct., Mt. Clemens, Mich., 1988—; lectr. People's Law Sch., St. Clair Shores, 1987—. Precinct del. Macomb County Rep. Party, St. Clair Shores, 1974-80. Mem. State Bar Mich., Macomb County Bar Assn. (speakers bur.), Macomb County Trial Lawyers Assn. Avocations: skiing, tennis, bicycling, platform tennis, ice hockey. General civil litigation, Criminal, Family and matrimonial. Office: 22420 Greater Mack Ave Saint Clair Shores MI 48080-2012

**SHEIKH, KEMAL A.,** lawyer; b. Aberdeen, Md., Jan. 14, 1956; s. Ramsey U. and Betty J. Nelson Sheikh. BA, Colby Coll., 1977; LLB magna cum laude, U. Edinburgh, Scotland, 1983; JD, U. Pa., 1985. Bar: N.Y. 1987. Assoc. Curtis, Mallet-Prevost Colt & Mosle, N.Y.C., 1985-97, spl. counsel, 1997—. Contracts commercial, Mergers and acquisitions, Private international. Office: Curtis Mallet-Prevost Colt & Mosle 101 Park Ave Fl 34 New York NY 10178-0061

**SHEILS, DENIS FRANCIS,** lawyer; b. Ridgewood, N.J., Apr. 7, 1961; s. Denis Francis and Anna Marie (Clifford) S.; m. Harriet A. Bonawitz, Sept. 17, 1988. BA, La Salle Coll., 1983; JD, Fordham U., 1986. Bar: N.Y. 1987, Pa. 1987, U.S. Dist. Ct. (ea. dist.) Pa. 1987, U.S. Ct. Appeals (3d cir.) 1987, U.S. Dist. Ct. (so. and ea. dists.) N.Y. 1992, U.S. Supreme Ct. 1994, U.S. Dist. Ct. (no. dist.) N.Y. 1997, U.S. Ct. Appeals (2d cir.) 1999. Assoc. Kohn, Swift & Graf, P.C., Phila., 1987-97, shareholder, 1997—. Active Lower Makefield Twp. Cable TV Adv. Bd. Mem. ABA, N.Y. State Bar Assn., Phila. Bar Assn. Roman Catholic. General civil litigation, Federal civil litigation, State civil litigation. Home: 2124 Ashley Rd Newtown PA 18940-3737 Office: Kohn Swift & Graf PC 2400 1 Reading Ctr 1101 Market St Ste 1170 Philadelphia PA 19107-2911

**SHEIMAN, RONALD LEE,** lawyer; b. Bridgeport, Conn., Apr. 26, 1948; s. Samuel Charles and Rita Doris (Feinberg) S.; m. Deborah Joy Lovitky, Oct. 16, 1971; children: Jill, Laura. BA, U. Mich., 1970; JD, U. Conn., 1973; LLM in Taxation, NYU, 1974. Bar: Conn. 1973, U.S. Ct. Appeals (2d cir.) 1975, U.S. Dist. Ct. Conn. 1975, U.S. Tax Ct. 1975, U.S. Supreme Ct. 1977, D.C. 1978, N.Y. 1981. Sr. tax atty. Office of Regional Counsel IRS, Phila., 1974-78; pvt. practice Westport, Conn., 1978—. Mdm. adv. bd. Early Childhood Resource and Info. Ctr., N.Y. Pub. Libr., N.Y.C., 1984. Mem. ABA, Fed. Bar Assn., Conn. Bar Assn., Westport Bar Assn. Estate taxation, Corporate taxation, Personal income taxation. Home: 128 Random Rd Fairfield CT 06432-1408 Office: 1804 Post Rd E Westport CT 06880-5607

**SHEIN, MICHAEL,** prosecutor; b. Bronx, N.Y., June 21, 1970; s. Stewart Neil Shein and Barbara Hope Blackman. BS in Polit. Sci., SUNY, Oneonta, 1992; JD, Nova Southeastern U., 1995. Asst. state atty. Broward County, Fla., 1995-96; pvt. practice law Ft. Lauderdale, Fla. Dir. Broward County Crime Commn., Hollywood, Fla., 1998; v.p. membership B'nai B'rith Justice Unit, Broward, Fla., 1998. Office: 200 SE 6th St Ste 501 Fort Lauderdale FL 33301-3424

**SHEINFELD, MYRON M.,** lawyer, educator; b. Mass., Mar. 18, 1930; s. Robert and Sadye (Rosenberg) S.; m. Christina Trzcinski, Mar. 30, 1985; children: Scott, Tom. BA, Tulane U., 1951; JD, U. Mich., 1954. Bar: Mich. 1954, Tex. 1956. Rschr. Legis. Rsch. Inst., U. Mich., 1954; asst. U. S. atty. So. Dist. Tex., 1958-60; law clk. U.S. Dist. Judge, 1960-61; ptnr. Strickland, Gordon & Sheinfeld, Houston, 1961-68; shareholder, of counsel Sheinfeld, Maley & Kay, P.C., Houston, 1968—; adj. prof. law U. Tex.; mem. Nat. Bankruptcy Conf.; chmn. Tex. Bankruptcy Adv. Commn.; bd. dirs. Nabors Industries, Third Ave. Value Fund, Inc. Bd. editors Practical Lawyer; contbr. articles to profl. jours. With JAG U.S. Army, 1955-58. Fellow Am. Coll. Bankruptcy (bd. dirs.); mem. State Bar Tex., Houston Ctr. Club (bd. dirs., v.p.), Petroleum Club, Phi Beta Kappa, Phi Sigma Alpha. Bankruptcy, Taxation, general, Mergers and acquisitions. Office: Sheinfeld Maley & Kay PC 1001 Fannin St Ste 3700 Houston TX 77002-6709

**SHELAR, RICHARD CLYDE,** lawyer; b. Youngstown, Ohio, Oct. 30, 1939; s. Clyde W. and Evelyn I. (Frifogle) S.; m. Virginia M. Shelar, Aug. 18, 1995. BA, Youngstown U., Ohio, 1964; JD, Akron U., Ohio, 1969. Bar: Ohio 1969, U.S. Dist. Ct. (no. dist.) Ohio 1971, U.S. Supreme Ct. 1973. Asst. city prosecutor City of Youngstown, Ohio, 1972-76; solicitor Village of Washingtonville, Ohio, 1970—; pvt. practice Leetonia, Ohio, 1972—; magistrate Columbiana County N.W. Area Ct., 1994-98. Mem. ABA, Ohio Bar Assn., Columbiana County Bar Assn., Mahoning County Bar Assn., Leetonia Masonic Lodge 401, Am. Radio Relay League, Antique Auto Club Am., NRA. Avocations: antique auto collecting, amateur radio sta. K8CCV. General practice, Probate, Criminal. Office: 710 Columbia St Leetonia OH 44431-1230

**SHELBY, JEROME,** lawyer; b. N.Y.C., Mar. 17, 1930; s. Morris and Rose Shelby; m. Adrian Austin, Nov. 24, 1957; children: Karen A. Anderson, P. Austin. AB, NYU, 1950; LLB, Harvard U., 1953. Bar: D.C. 1953, N.Y. 1954. Assoc. Cadwalader, Wickersham & Taft, N.Y.C., 1953-63, ptnr., 1963-92, of counsel, 1993—; dir. Marine Transport Corp.; exec. v.p., dir. Energy Transp. Corp., N.Y.C., 1973—; dir. Astro Tankers Ltd.; trustee Seamen's Ch. Inst. Trustee Montclair (N.J.) Pub. Libr., Ridgefield Found. Mem. Assn. Bar City N.Y., Montclair Golf Club, Palm Beach Polo Club (Fla.). Admiralty, Contracts commercial, Family and matrimonial. Home: 74 Highland Ave Montclair NJ 07042-1910 Office: Cadwalader Wickersham & Taft 100 Maiden Ln New York NY 10038-4818

**SHELDON, J. MICHAEL,** lawyer, educator; b. Mt. Carmel, Pa., Sept. 1, 1951; s. Lloyd Loomis and Helen Roberta (Sosnoski) S. AA, Harrisburg (Pa.) Community Coll., 1978; BS, Pa. State U., 1980; M in Journalism, Temple U., 1991; JD, Widener U. Sch. Law, 1996. News announcer Sta. WNUE-AM, Ft. Walton Beach, Fla., 1974-76, Sta. WFEC-AM, Harrisburg, 1977-78; announcer Sta. WCMB-AM, Wormleysburg, Pa., 1979-80; writer newspaper Pa. Beacon, Harrisburg, 1982-85; media specialist Commonwealth Media Svcs., Harrisburg, 1982-86; dir. communications Pa. Poultry Fedn., Harrisburg, 1986-89; news anchor Sta. WGAL-TV, Lancaster, Pa., 1989-90; dir. pub. rels. Profl. Ins. Agts. - Pa., Md., Del., Mechanicsburg, Pa., 1990-92; v.p. comm. and mktg. United Way of the Capital Region, Harrisburg, Pa., 1992-93, Widener U. Sch. of Law, 1994-96; pres. Open Mike Comm., Harrisburg, 1994—; mem. adj. faculty dept. journalism Temple U., 1992; mem. faculty dept. humanities Pa. State U., 1995-97, 99—. Contbg. author: Pa. 12th Annual Civil Litigation Update, Spoliation of Evidence: Why You Can't Have Your Cake and Eat it Too, 1999; contbg. editor: A Practical Guidebook to Massachusetts Aviation Law, 1999; Contbr. articles to profl. jours. Pub. rels. advisor Cen. Pa. Leukemia Soc., Harrisburg, 1989-90; media advisor Polit. Campaign, Hershey, Pa., 1990. With USAF, 1969-73. Mem. Vets. of Foreign War (life), Am. Legion, Chi Gamma Iota, Delta Tau Kappa. Republican. Roman Catholic. Avocations: motorcycles, music, electronics, martial arts. Office: 6059 Allentown Blvd Harrisburg PA 17112-2672

**SHELDON, MICHAEL RICHARD,** judge, law educator; b. Schenectady, NY, Apr. 6, 1949; S. Richard Charles and Evelyn Marie (Delisle) S.; m. Diane Mary Micklos, May 29, 1971; children: Graham Andrew, Conor Michael, Rowan Richard, Cameron Ashleigh. AB, PrincetonU, 1971; JD, Yale U, 1974; postgrad., Georgetown U., 1974-76. Bar: D.C. 1975, U.S. Dist. Ct. D.C. 1975, U.S. Ct. Appeals (D.C. cir.) 1975, U.S. Dist. Ct. (no. dist.) N.Y. 1976, Conn. 1976, U.S. Dist. Ct. Conn. 1976, U.S. Supreme Ct. 1978, U.S. Ct. Appeals (2d. cir.) 1987. Legal int. Georgetown U. Law Ctr, Washington, 1974-76; prof. law, dir. legal clin. U. Conn. Sch. Law, Hartford, CT, 1976-91; adj. prof. law, 1991—; judge Conn. Superior Ct., 1991—; vis. scholar Yale U., New Haven, CT, 1985-86; vis. prof. U. Aix-Marseille, 1986; Bd. dirs. Conn. Civil Liberties Union, Hartford, 1979-83, ednl. cons., Office of Chief Pub. Defender, Hartford, 1978-91. Contbg. author: Handbook on the Connecticut law of Evidence, 1982. Bd. dirs., Legal Aid Soc. of Hartford Cty., 1978-91. Sr. Fell. Am. Leadership Forum, 1989—. Mem. Conn. Bar Assn. (exec. com. sect. on human rights and responsibilities, exec. com. sect. on criminal justice 1978—), Cmty. Ptnrs. in Action (bd. dirs. 1993—, v.p. 1994-97), Amer. Inst. of Ct. Recipient Outstanding Fac. Mem. Awd. Student Bar Assn. U Conn. Sch. law, 1979, 82, Alva P. Loiselle Awd. Conn. Moot Ct. Bd., 1989, U. Conn. Sch. law Rev Awd., 1998. Mem. Dem. Town Com., Canton, Conn., 1988-91; mem. bd. fin., Canton, 1989-91; pres., Canton-Kuntsevo Exchange Com., Inc., 1990-92.

**SHELL, LOUIS CALVIN,** lawyer; b. Dinwiddie County, Va., Dec. 8, 1925; s. Roger LaFayette and Susie Ann (Hill) S.; m. Barbara Marie Pamplin, Aug. 5, 1950; children—Pamela Shell Baskervill, Patricia Shell Caulkins. B.A., U. Va., 1946, LL.B., 1947. Bar: Va. 1947. Sr. trial atty. Shell, Johnson, Andrews, Baskervill & Baskervill, Petersburg, Va. Chmn. Petersburg Electoral Bd., 1952, vice mayor city council, 1957-60; trustee Petersburg Dist. United Methodist Ch. Named Outstanding Young Man, Petersburg Jr. C. of C., 1956. Fellow Am. Coll. Trial Lawyers; mem. Petersburg Bar Assn., Va. State Bar (council 1972-75), Kiwanis. Personal injury, State civil litigation. Home: 10813 Lakeview Dr Petersburg VA 23805-7152 Office: Shell Johnson Andrews Baskervill & Baskervill PC PO Box 3090 Petersburg VA 23805-3090

**SHELLEY, SUSANNE MARY,** lawyer, mathematics educator; b. Vienna, Austria, Feb. 2, 1928; came to U.S., 1946; d. Joseph and Paula (Grunbaum) Langer; m. Robert E. Shelley, July 21, 1946; children: Frances S. MacCallum, Mark Robert. BA, Calif. State U., Sacramento, 1961, MA, 1963; JD, U. Pacific, 1980. Bar: Calif. 1980, U.S. Dist. Ct. (ea. dist.) Calif. 1980. Tchr. math. Johnson High Sch., Sacramento, 1961-65; prof. math. Sacramento City Coll., 1965-84; gen. counsel Los Rios Community Coll. Dist., Sacramento, 1984-94, Johnson, Schachter, & Collins, Sacramento, 1994—. Author 13 math. textbooks. Named Outstanding Educator, Sacramento City Coll., 1967. Mem. ABA, Calif. State Bar Assn., Sacramento County Bar Assn., Order of Coif. Republican. Roman Catholic. Labor, Government contracts and claims. Home: 28 Shoreline Cir Sacramento CA 95831-2112 Office: Johnson Schachter & Collins 2180 Harvard St Ste 560 Sacramento CA 95815-3326

**SHELNUTT, JOHN MARK,** lawyer; b. Gainesville, Ga., Jan. 19, 1963; s. Dumas Broughton and Georgia Texana (Ruff) S.; m. Leila Christine Ricketson, June 24, 1989; children: John Mark Jr., Sarah. AA, Emory U., 1983, BA, 1985, JD, 1988. Bar: Ga. 1988, U.S. Dist. Ct. (mid. dist.) Ga. 1994. Asst. dist. atty. Dist. Atty.-Dougherty Jud. Cir., Albany, Ga., 1988, Dist. Atty.-Chattahoochee Jud. Cir., Columbus, Ga., 1989-94; ptnr. Berry and Shelnutt, Columbus, 1994—. Mem. ABA, State Bar Ga., Columbus Bar Assn., Ga. Trial Lawyers Assn., Ga. Assn. Criminal Def. Lawyers. Methodist. Criminal, Personal injury, Family and matrimonial. Home: 7802 Harpers Ferry Rd Upatoi GA 31829-1831 Office: Berry & Shelnutt 1024 2nd Ave Columbus GA 31901-2406

**SHELTON, DOROTHY DIEHL REES,** lawyer; b. Manila, Sept. 16; came to U.S., 1945; d. William Walter John and Hedwig (Glienecke) Diehl; m. Charles W. Rees, Jr., June 15, 1957 (div. 1971); children: Jane Rees Stebbins, John B., Anne Rees Slack, David C.,; m. Thomas C. Shelton, Mar. 4, 1977 (dec.). BA in Music, Stanford Univ., 1957; JD, Western State Univ. Coll. Law, 1976. Bar: Calif. 1977, U.S. Dist. Ct. (so. dist.) Calif. 1977. Pvt. practice, San Diego, 1977—. Mem. ABA, Calif. State Bar, San Diego County Bar Assn., Consumer Attys. San Diego, Stanford U. Alumni Assn., Jr. League San Diego, Gt. Pyrenees Club Am., Dachshund Club Am., Nu Beta Epsilon. Avocations: gardening, reading, tennis, Great Pyrenees dogs. General civil litigation, Criminal, Personal injury. Office: 110 W C St Ste 812 San Diego CA 92101-3906

**SHELTON, RALPH CONRAD,** lawyer, consultant; b. Montebello, Calif., July 14, 1961; s. Ralph Conrad and Maggie S.; m. Cheryl Lynn Snyder, Aug. 1987 (div. June 1991); 1 child, Ralph Conrad III; m. Laurie Schiff, Jan. 18, 1992. BS in Law, Western State U., 1986, JD, 1987. Bar: Calif. 1987, U.S. Ct. Appeals (9th cir.) 1988. Assoc. Hite & Assocs., Santa Ana, Calif., 1988-91; v.p., gen. counsel Transco Cos., Long Beach, Calif., 1990-91; ptnr. Schiff & Shelton, Santa Ana, 1991—. Chmn. Internat. Feline Found., 1996—. Mem. Mason (master 1995). Republican. Avocations: magician, comedy writer. General civil litigation, Entertainment, Family and matrimonial. Office: 3 Hutton Centre Dr Ste 620 Santa Ana CA 92707-8704

**SHEN, MICHAEL,** lawyer; b. Nanking, Jiangsu, Peoples Republic of China, Aug. 15, 1948; came to U.S. 1951; s. James Cheng Yee and Grace (Pai) S.; m. Marina Manese (div.); m. Pamela Nan Bradford, Aug. 12, 1983; 1 child, Jessica Li. BA, U. Chgo., 1969; MA, U. Pa., 1970; JD, Rutgers U., 1979. Bar: U.S. Dist. Ct. N.J. 1979, N.Y. 1980, U.S. Dist. Ct. (so., no. and ea. dists.) N.Y. 1980, N.J. 1981, U.S. Ct. Appeals (2d cir.) 1987, U.S. Supreme Ct. 1988, U.S. Ct. Appeals (3rd cir.) 1996. Staff atty. Bedford Stuyvesant Legal Svcs., Bklyn., 1979-80, Com. for Interns and Residents, N.Y.C., 1980-81; ptnr. Shneyer & Shen, P.C., N.Y.C. 1981—; pres. bd. dirs. Asian Am. Legal Def. and Edn. Fund, N.Y.c.; of counsel 318 Restaurant Workers Union, N.Y.C., 1984—. *Michael Shen is an employment and civil rights lawyer with twenty years of experience. He serves on the boards of various civil rights organizations. He represents individuals, employees and groups in discrimination (race, sex, age, disability), wage, and whistleblower claims, as well as victims of police misconduct and other civil rights violations.* Bd. dirs. Nat. Asian Pacific Am. Legal Consortium, N.Y.C., Nat. Employment Law Project; past bd. dirs. N.Y. Civil Liberties Union, N.Y.C., 1987-98. Mem. Internat. Platform Assn., Nat. Employees Lawyers Assn., N.Y. State Bar Assn., N.Y. County Bar Assn., Nat. Lawyers Guild. Avocations: arts, reading. Civil rights, Labor, Workers' compensation. Office: Shneyer & Shen PC 2109 Broadway Ste 206 New York NY 10023-2106 also: 1085 Cambridge Rd Teaneck NJ 07666-1901

**SHENEFIELD, JOHN HALE,** lawyer; b. Toledo, Jan. 23, 1939; s. Hale Thurel and Norma (Bird) S.; m. Judy Simmons, June 16, 1984; children: Stephen Hale, Christopher Newcomb. AB, Harvard U., 1960, LLB, 1965. Bar: Va. 1966, D.C. 1966. Assoc. to ptnr. Hunton & Williams, Richmond, Va., 1965-71, 71-77; dep. asst. atty. gen. antitrust div. Dept. Justice, Washington, 1977; asst. atty. gen. Dept. Justice, 1977-79, assoc. atty. gen., 1979-81; ptnr. Milbank, Tweed, Hadley & McCloy, 1981-86; ptnr. Morgan, Lewis & Bockius, Washington, 1986—, chmn., 1995-98; assoc. prof. law U. Richmond, 1975; prof. law Georgetown Law Ctr., 1981-83; chmn. Nat. Commn. for Rev. Antitrust Law and Procedures, 1978-79. Co-author The Antitrust Laws - A Primer, 3d edit., 1998; contbr. articles on law to profl. jours. Sec. Va. Dem. Com., 1970-72, treas., 1976-77; chmn. Richmond Dem. Party, 1975-77; bd. govs. St. Albans Sch., 1983-90, 97—, chmn. 1988-90; mem. chpt. Washington Cathedral, 1988-98; pres. Nat. Cathedral Assn., 1993-96; chmn. Va. Racing Commn., 1989-97. 2d lt. U.S. Army, 1961-62; to capt. Res., 1965. Mem. ABA, Va. Bar Assn. Antitrust, Federal civil litigation. Home: 220 Carrwood Rd Great Falls VA 22066-3721 Office: Morgan Lewis & Bockius 1800 M St NW Ste 6 Washington DC 20036-5802

**SHENG, JACK TSE-LIANG,** law librarian; b. Hsiang Ying, Hunan, China, Nov. 15, 1929; m. Helen S. Sheng, Sept. 20, 1939; children: Paul, Henry. LLB, Soochow U., Taiwan, 1963; LLM, Yale U., 1966; MS, La. State U., 1967; JD, Wayne State U., 1969. Teaching asst. Soochow U. Law Sch., Taipei, Taiwan, 1963-64; librarian I and II, cataloger Detroit Pub. Library, 1967-70; head librarian, assoc. prof. Soochow U., 1970-72; asst. law librarian Ohio No. U., Ada, 1972-75; law librarian Duval County Law Library, Jacksonville, Fla., 1975—; editorial asst. Gale Research Co., Detroit, 1969; law library cons. Del. Law Sch., Wilmington, 1973, CSX Corp., Jacksonville, Fla., 1983-85; instr. Fla. Jr. Coll., Jacksonville, 1976-83. Author: Index to Chinese Legal Periodicals, 1963-70, 1972. Mem. Am. Assn. Law Libraries. Democrat. Home: 4080 Old Mill Cove Trl W Jacksonville FL 32277-1569 Office: Duval County Law Libr 330 E Bay St Jacksonville FL 32202-2921

**SHENKER, JOSEPH C.,** lawyer; b. N.Y.C., Nov. 6, 1956. BS in Acctg., CUNY, 1977; JD, Columbia U., 1980. Bar: N.Y. 1981, U.S. Dist. Ct. (ea. and so. dists.) N.Y 1981, U.S. Claims Ct. 1982, U.S. Tax Ct. 1982, U.S. Supreme Ct. 1988. Assoc. Sullivan & Cromwell, N.Y.C., 1980-86, ptnr., 1986—. Contbr. articles to profl. jours. Bd. dirs. Am. Friends of Yeshivat Kerem B'yavneh, Inc., Rabbinical Sem. of Am. Mem. ABA, N.Y. State Bar Assn., Assn. of Bar of City of N.Y. General corporate, Real property, Securities. Office: Sullivan & Cromwell 125 Broad St Fl 33 New York NY 10004-2400

**SHENKO, WILLIAM EDWARD, JR.,** lawyer; b. Sioux Falls, S.D., July 1, 1954; s. William Edward and Jeanette Elizabeth Shenko; m. Linda Mulford, Nov. 21, 1981. AA, Edison C.C., Ft. Myers, Fla., 1975; BA, U. South Fla., 1977; JD, Stetson U., 1980. Bar: Fla. 1980, U.S. Dist. Ct. (mid. dist.) Fla. 1980, U.S. Dist. Ct. (so. dist.) Fla. 1982. Legal intern Organized Crime Unit, 6th Cir., Clearwater, Fla., 1980; asst. state atty. 20th Cir. of Fla. Juvenile Divsn., Ft. Myers, 1980, Lee County Commrs., Ft. Myers, 1980, Felony Divsn., 20th Cir., Ft. Myers, 1981; assoc. Alderman and Gerald, Ft. Myers, 1981-85; assoc., ptnr. Echols Cotter & Shenko, Ft. Myers Beach, Fla., 1985-95; pres. William E. Shenko, Jr. P.A., Ft. Myers Beach, 1995—; counsel Ft. Myers Beach Bd. Realtors, 1984, 94, 95, 96, Iona Mcgregor Fire Dist., Ft. Myers, 1984—; spl. master City of Sanibel, Fla., 1995-96; pres. Pink Shell VV Condo Assn., Ft. Myers Beach, 1988-93. Founder Ft. Myers Beach Incorporation Com., 1993; mem. bd. rev. Eagle Scouts, Ft. Myers, 1994-97; bd. dirs. Ft. Myers Beach Voters Assn., 1994-96. Mem. Ft. Myers Beach Civic Assn., Marathon Yacht Club, Ft. Myers Beach Bd. Realtors, Bonita Springs Bd. Realtors. Republican. Roman Catholic. Avocation: sailing. Real property, Probate, Government contracts and claims. Office: 2801 Estero Blvd Ste C Fort Myers Beach FL 33931-3530

**SHEPARD, JULIAN LEIGH,** lawyer, humanitarian; b. St. Paul, Feb. 17, 1957; s. Frank and Beatrice (Getsug) S.; m. Jo Ellen Cartmell, Aug. 6, 1988. BS, Ind. U., 1980, JD, 1983; postgrad., Am. U., 1995—. Bar: Pa. 1985, Ind. 1984, D.C. 1987; U.S. Ct. Appeals (D.C. cir.) 1984; U.S. Dist. Ct. (so. dist.) Ind. 1984. Atty. Nat. Assn. Broadcasters, Washington, 1984-86, asst. gen. counsel, 1986-87; counselor at law Heron, Burchette, Ruckert & Rothwell, Washington, 1987-88; sr. policy adv. mass media Nat. Telecommunications & Info. Adminstrn./U.S. Dept. Commn., Washington, 1988-90; v.p., gen. counsel Assn. for Maximum Svc. TV, Inc., Washington, 1990-95; atty. Verner, Liipfert, Bernhard, McPherson & Hand, Washington, 1995—; mem. fed. spectrum planning and policy adv. com., U.S. Dept. Commerce, Washington, 1992—. *As a communications lawyer, he is dedicated to the development of global communications technology to foster individual freedom and world peace. In this regard, he has played a significant role in the formulation of U.S. communications policy and the use of the radio spectrum. Participation in major proceedings at the Federal Communications Commission involved the allocation of radio spectrum, the formulation of U.S. positions at the World Administrative Radio Conferences of the International Telecommunications Union, the development of the digital television service in the U.S., and the U.S. licensing of future generations of global fixed and mobile satellite communications networks.* Co-chmn. editorial adv. bd. Fed. Comms. Law Jour., Washington, 1992-94; contbr. articles to profl. jours. Bd. dirs. vis. Georgetown U. Inst. on Comparative Polit. and Econ. Systems, 1984-95; prin. Coun. for Excellence in Govt., Washington, 1990-. Fellow Bar Assn. D.C.; mem. ABA (law practice mgmt. sect. leadership activities bd. 1995-96), Fed. Comms. Bar Assn. (law jour. com. 1992—), Ind. State Bar Assn., Phi Delta Phi (Nat. Belfour scholar 1983). Avocations: visual arts, scuba diving, underwater photography, amateur radio and computer telecommunications, boating. Communications, Administrative and regulatory, Legislative. Home: 5843 Hilldon St Mc Lean VA 22101-3325

**SHEPARD, RANDALL TERRY,** state supreme court justice; b. Lafayette, Ind., Dec. 24, 1946; s. Richard Schilling and Dorothy Ione (Donlen) S.; m. Amy Wynne MacDonell, May 7, 1988; one child, Martha MacDonell. AB cum laude, Princeton U., 1969; JD, Yale U., 1972; LLM, U. Va., 1995; LLD (hon.), U. So. Ind., 1995. Bar: Ind. 1972, U.S. Dist. Ct. (so. dist.) Ind. 1972. Spl. asst. to under sec. U.S. Dept. Transp., Washington, 1972-74; exec. asst. to mayor City of Evansville, Ind., 1974-79; judge Vanderburgh Superior Ct., Evansville, 1980-85; assoc. justice Ind. Supreme Ct., Indpls., 1985-87, chief justice, 1987—; instr. U. Evansville, 1975-78, Indiana U., 1995, 99. Author: Preservation Rules and Regulations, 1980; contbr. articles to profl. publs. Bd. advisors Nat. Trust for Hist. Preservation, 1980-87, chmn. bd. advisors, 1983-85, trustee, 1987-96; dir. Hist. Landmarks Found. Ind., 1983—, chmn., 1989-92, hon. chmn., 1992—; chmn. State Student Assistance Commn. on Ind., 1981-85; chmn. Ind. Commn. on Bicentennial of U.S. Constn., 1986-91; vice chmn. Vanderburgh County Rep. Ctrl. Com., 1977-80. Recipient Friend of Media award Cardinal States chpt. Sigma Delta Chi, 1979, Disting. Svc. award Evansville Jaycees, 1982, Herbert Harley award Am. Judicature Soc., 1992. Mem. ABA (coun. mem. sect. on legal edn. 1991—, chair sect. on legal edn. 1997—, immediate past chair appellate judges conf. 1997-98), Ind. Bar Assn., Ind. Judges Assn., Princeton Club (N.Y.), Capitol Hill Club (Washington), Columbia Club (Indpls.). Republican. Methodist. Home: 3644 Totem Ln Indianapolis IN 46208-4171 Office: Ind Supreme Ct 304 State House Indianapolis IN 46204-2213

**SHEPHERD, JOHN FREDERIC,** lawyer; b. Oak Park, Ill., May 22, 1954; s. James Frederic Shepherd and Margaret Joanne (Crotchett) Woollen; children: Eliza Marion, Justine Catherine. AB magna cum laude, Dartmouth Coll., Hanover, N.H., 1976; JD, U. Denver, 1979. Bar: Colo. 1979, U.S. Dist. Ct. Colo. 1979, D.C. 1981, U.S. Dist. Ct. D.C. 1981, U.S. Ct. Appeals (10th cir.) 1981, U.S. Ct. Appeals (D.C. cir.) 1982, U.S. Ct. Appeals (9th cir.) 1990, U.S. Supreme Ct. 1984. Assoc. Holland & Hart, Denver, 1979-81; assoc. Holland & Hart, Washington, 1981-85, ptnr., 1985-87; ptnr. Holland & Hart, Denver, 1987—; natural resources disting. practitioner in residence U. Denver Coll. Law, 1998. Reporter Mineral Law Newsletter, 1985-92. Mem. 50 for Colo., Denver, 1989. Mem. ABA (chmn. pub. lands and land use com. 1991-93, mem. coun. for sect. of natural resources energy and environ. law 1993-96), Rocky Mountain Mineral Law Found. (mem. long-range planning com. 1988—, trustee 1993-95), Dartmouth Alumni Club (pres. Washington chpt. 1985-86, trustee Rocky Mt. chpt., 1998—), Denver Athletic Club. Avocations: flyfishing, basketball, running. Oil, gas, and mineral, Environmental, Natural resources. Home: 848 Monroe St Denver CO 80206-4013 Office: Holland & Hart 555 17th St Ste 3200 Denver CO 80202-3950

**SHEPHERD, JOHN MICHAEL,** lawyer; b. St. Louis, Aug. 1, 1955; s. John Calvin and Bernice Florence (Hines) S.; m. Deborah Tremaine Fenton, Oct. 10, 1981; children: Elizabeth White, Katherine Tremaine. BA, Stanford U., 1977; JD, U. Mich., 1980. Bar: Calif. 1981, D.C. 1991, U.S. Dist. Ct. (no. dist.) Calif. 1981. Assoc. McCutchen, Doyle, Brown & Enersen, San Francisco, 1980-82; spl. asst. to asst. atty. gen. U.S. Dept. Justice, Washington, 1982-84, dep. asst. atty gen., 1984-86; assoc. counsel to The President The White House, Washington, 1986-87; sr. dep. comptroller of the currency Dept. Treasury, Washington, 1987-91; spl. counsel Sullivan & Cromwell, N.Y.C., 1991-93, Washington, 1993; exec. v.p., gen. counsel Shawmut Nat. Corp., Boston, 1993-95; ptnr. Brobeck, Phleger & Harrison LLP, San Francisco, 1995—; chmn. fin. svcs. and insolvency group, 1996-97, mem. policy com., 1997—. Contbr. articles to profl. jours. Asst. dir. policy Reagan-Bush Presdl. Transition Team, Washington, 1980-81; bd. dirs. Reagan Dep. Asst. Secs., Washington, 1985-90; trustee New Eng. Aquarium, 1994-96. Named one of Outstanding Young Men Am., U.S. Jaycees, 1984; Wardack Research fellow Washington U., 1976. Mem. ABA (chmn. fin. markets and ins. com., antitrust law sect. 1992-95, mem. banking law com. 1983—, vice chair 1998—, chmn. bank holding co. acquisitions subcom. 1995-98, bus. law sect., standing com. on law and nat. security 1984-96), D.C. Bar Assn., New Eng. Legal Found. (bd. dirs. 1994-96), Pacific Coun. Internat. Policy, Chevy Chase Club, Univ. Club, Met. Club, Olympic Club.

Banking, Mergers and acquisitions, General corporate. Home: 2699 Filbert St San Francisco CA 94123-3215 Office: Brobeck Phleger & Harrison LLP 1 Market St San Francisco CA 94105-1420

**SHEPHERD, STEWART ROBERT,** lawyer; b. Chgo., Sept. 9, 1948; s. Stewart and LaVina Beatrice (Nereim) S.; m. Margaret Brownell Shoop, Aug. 14, 1970; children: Elizabeth Ashby, Megan Brownell, Blair Stewart. BA, Rockford Coll., 1970; JD, U. Chgo., 1973. Bar: Calif. 1973, U.S. Dist. Ct. (no. dist.) Calif. 1973, Ill. 1976, U.S. Dist. Ct. (no. dist.) Ill. 1976. Assoc. Heller, Ehrman, White & McAuliffe, San Francisco, 1973-75; assoc. Hopkins & Sutter, Chgo., 1975-79, ptnr., 1979-96; ptnr. Sidley & Austin, 1996—. Mem. ABA, Order of Coif, Phi Beta Kappa. Pension, profit-sharing, and employee benefits, Corporate taxation. Office: Sidley & Austin One First National Plz Chicago IL 60603

**SHEPPARD, THOMAS RICHARD,** lawyer; b. Pasadena, Calif., Aug. 8, 1934; s. James Carroll and Ruth Mary (Pashgian) S.; m. Arlene Clubb, June 23, 1956; children—Eileen Diana, Pamela Lynn, Thomas Richard. A.B., Stanford U., 1956; LL.B., Harvard U., 1961. Bar: Calif. bar 1962. Assoc. firm Sheppard, Mullin, Richter & Hampton, Los Angeles, 1961-66; ptnr. Sheppard, Mullin, Richter & Hampton, 1966—; dir. numerous small corps.; pres. Legal Aid Found. Los Angeles, 1973. Trustee Harold Lloyd Found., Los Angeles, 1971-87, Della Martin Found., 1979—. Served to lt. (j.g.) USN, 1956-58. Mem. Am. Bar Assn., State Bar Assn. Calif., Los Angeles County Bar Assn., Am. Law Inst., Am. Coll. Real Estate Lawyers, Beta Theta Pi. Club: Calif. (Los Angeles) (bd. dirs. 1985-87, sec. 1987). Real property, Corporate taxation, Personal income taxation. Home: 1680 Oak Grove Ave San Marino CA 91108-1109 Office: Sheppard Mullin Richter & Hampton 333 S Hope St Ste 4800 Los Angeles CA 90071-1406

**SHEPRO, DANIEL,** lawyer; b. Springfield, Mass., Apr. 24, 1942; children: William, Jonathan, Jeffrey. BS, Yeshiva U., 1964; LLB, Boston U., 1967; postgrad., U. Miami. Ptnr. Willinger, Shepro, Tower & Bucci, Bridgeport, Conn., 1969—. E-mail: dshepro@aol.com. General civil litigation. Office: Willinger Shepro 855 Main St Bridgeport CT 06604-4915

**SHER, MICHAEL LEE,** lawyer; b. N.Y.C., Oct. 20, 1938; s. David and Mae Phyllis (Tulin) S.; m. JoAnn Veronica Giffuni, Feb. 2, 1970 (div.). AB, Johns Hopkins U., 1961; JD, Fordham U., 1968. Bar: N.Y. 1969, D.C. 1974, U.S. Dist. Ct. (ea., no, so, we. dists.) N.Y., U.S. Cir. Ct. (fed. cir.), U.S. Cir. Ct. (2d cir.), U.S. Supreme Ct. Spl. asst. to dir. pub. affairs Peace Corps, Washington, 1964-65; dep. dir., acting dir. exec. secretariat OEO Office of the Pres., Washington, 1965-66; assoc. Phillips, Nizer, Benjamin, Krim & Ballon, N.Y.C., 1969-70; dir., exec. secretariat, spl. asst., spl. counsel, sec. mgmt. rev. com. N.Y.C. Health and Hosps. Corp., 1971-72; v.p. Wertheim Asst. Mgmt. Svcs., Inc., 1972-76; assoc. Finley, Kumble, Wagner, Heine, Underberg, Manley & Casey, N.Y.C., 1976-79; dep. chmn., exec. dir., spl. counsel State of N.Y. Mortgage Agy., N.Y.C., 1979-82; pvt. practice N.Y.C., 1982—; lect. Practising Law Inst., U. Nanjing, China; rapporteur Task Force on Internat. Legal Svcs.; founder UNCITRAL Internat. Moot Arbitration Competition, Willem C. Vis Internat. Comml. Arbitration Moot; judge internat. final rounds Jessup Internat. Moot Ct. Competition. Trustee Dalton Sch., N.Y.C., 1962-66, Endl. Alliance, N.Y.C., 1970-88, mem. exec. com., 1974-75; mem. Gov.'s Com. Scholastic Achievement, N.Y.C., 1976-86; aux. mem. housing adv. sounding bd. Young Pres.'s Orgn.; bd. dirs. United Neighborhood Houses of N.Y., N.Y.C., 1983-88; initiator, chmn. Ad Hoc Com. of the Am. Community of Higher Edn.; mem. Nat. Com. on U.S.-China Rels.; aux. mem. sounding bd. young pres's. orgn. Boys Choir of Harlem, 1990—, Fr. Flanagan's Boys Home Boys Town USA, 1990—. Mem. ABA (coord. liaisons internat. law sect., liaison with coun. of Bars of the European cmty., dispute resolution sect.), Am. Bar Assn. Fellows (life), D.C. Bar Assn., Assn. Bar City N.Y. (mem. coun. on internat. affairs, co-chair UN group, mem. and rapporteur task force on internat. legal svcs., mem. coun. on internat. affairs, mem. com. on aeronautics, chmn. sub-com. on econs., mem. spl. com. on lawyers in transition and sub-com. on lectrs. and cont. edn., various others), Canadian Bar Assn., Union Internat. des Avocats, Am. C. of C. in France. Contracts commercial, General corporate, Private international. Home: 166 E 61st St New York NY 10021-8509 also: Maitre Francoise, Poubeau-Calando, 27 bis, rue de l'Abreuvoir, F-92100 Boulogne France

**SHERA TAYLOR, DIANA MARIE,** judge, lawyer; b. El Paso, Tex.. Paralegal Cert., San Francisco State U., 1983, BA, 1986; JD, Golden Gate U., San Francisco, 1992. Bar: Calif. 1993, Oreg. 1995, U.S. Dist. Ct. (no. dist.) Calif. 1993. Atty. Berding & Weil, Alamo, Calif., 1993-95; sole practitioner St. Helens, Oreg., 1996—; judge Columbia City (Oreg.) Mcpl. Ct., 1996—; bd. dirs., treas. Columbia County Legal Aid, St. Helens, 1997—; mediator Multnomah County Small Claims, Portland, Oreg., 1998—. Author newsletter Legalese Demystified, 1997—. Bd. dirs. Columbia Cmty. Mental Health Agy., St. Helens, 1998—; mem. adv. com. Area Agy. on Aging, St. Helens, 1997—; legal advisor Women's Resource Ctr., St. Helens, 1996—. Mem. ABA, Oreg. Mcpl. Judges Assn., Nat. Judges Assn., Oreg. Women Lawyers, Kiwanis Internat. Office: PO Box 232 Saint Helens OR 97051-0232

**SHERBY, KATHLEEN REILLY,** lawyer; b. St. Louis, Apr. 5, 1947; d. John Victor and Florian Sylvia (Frederick) Reilly; m. James Wilson Sherby, May 17, 1975; children: Michael R.R., William J.R., David J.R. AB magna cum laude, St. Louis U., 1969, JD magna cum laude, 1976. Bar: Mo. 1976. Assoc. Bryan Cave, St. Louis, 1976-85; ptnr. Bryan Cave LLP, St. Louis, 1985—. Contbr. articles to profl. jours. Bd. dirs Jr. League, St. Louis, 1989-90, St. Louis Forum, 1992—, pres., 1995-97); chmn. Bequest and Gift Coun. of St. Louis U., 1997—; jr. warden Ch. of St. Michael and St. George, 1998—. Fellow Am. Coll. Trust and Estate Coun. (regent 1997—), Estate Planning Coun. of St. Louis (pres. 1986-87), Bar Assn. Met. St. Louis (chmn. probate sect. 1986-87), Mo. Bar Assn. (chmn. probate and trust com. 1996—, chmn. probate law revision subcom. 1988-96). Episcopalian. Estate planning, Estate taxation, Probate. Home: 47 Crestwood Dr Saint Louis MO 63105-3032 Office: Bryan Cave LLP 1 Metropolitan Sq Ste 3600 Saint Louis MO 63102-2733

**SHERER, SAMUEL AYERS,** lawyer, urban planning consultant; b. Warwick, N.Y., June 17, 1944; s. Ernest Thompson and Helen (Ayers) S.; m. Dewi Sudewinahidah, June 28, 1980. AB magna cum laude, Oberlin Coll., 1966; JD, Harvard U., 1970; M in City Planning, MIT, 1970. Bar: D.C. 1972, U.S. Supreme Ct. 1979. Atty., advisor HUD, Boston, 1970; sr. cons. McClaughry Assoc., Washington, 1970-71, 74-76; cons. Urban Inst., Washington, 1971-72; atty., urban planner IBRD Jakarta (Indonesia) Urban Devel. Study, 1972-74; atty., advisor Office Minority Bus. U.S. Dept. Commerce, Washington, 1976-77; ptnr. Topping & Sherer, Washington, 1977-90; pres. Sherer-Axelrod-Monacelli, Inc., Cambridge, Mass., 1978-99; prin. The Washington Team, Inc., 1992—; bd. dirs. EnviroClean Solutions, Inc., The Urban Agr. Network; rep. Internat. Devel. Law Inst., Washington, 1983-90; sr. fellow Climate Inst., 1988—; cons. in field. Co-author: Urban Land Use in Egypt, 1977; editor: Important Laws and Regulations Regarding Land, Housing and Urban Development in the Arab Republic of Egypt, 1977, Important Laws and Regulations Regarding Land, Housing and Urban Development in the Hashemite Kingdom of Jordan, 1981. Bd. dirs. MIT Enterprise Forum of Washington-Balt., 1980-82; mem. D.C. Rep. Cent. Com., 1984-88; mem. nat. governing bd. Ripon Soc., Washington, 1977-83. Urban Studies fellow HUD, 1969-70. Mem. ABA, D.C. Bar Assn., Am. Planning Assn., The Am. Soc. of Internat. Law, Asia Soc., Phi Beta Kappa. Avocations: tennis, reading. Environmental, Public international, Land use and zoning (including planning). Home: 4600 Connecticut Ave NW Apt 205 Washington DC 20008-5702 Office: 316 Pennsylvania Ave SE Ste 202 Washington DC 20003-1177

**SHERESKY, NORMAN M.,** lawyer; b. Detroit, June 22, 1928; s. Harry and Rose (Lieberman) S.; m. Elaine B. Lewis, Oct. 30, 1977; 1 child, from previous marriage, Brooke Hillary. A.B., Syracuse U., 1950; LL.B., Harvard U., 1953. Bar: N.Y. 1953. Assoc. Gold & Pollack, N.Y.C., 1954-60; sole practice, N.Y.C., 1960-72; ptnr. Sheresky & Kalman, N.Y.C., 1972-77; ptnr. Colton, Hartnick, Yamin & Sheresky, N.Y.C., 1977-93; ptnr. Baer, Marks & Upham, N.Y.C., 1993-95; ptnr. Sheresky, Aronson & Mayefsky, 1995—. adj. prof. matrimonial litigation N.Y. Law Sch., 1979-86; mem. judiciary com. N.Y.C. Bar Assn.; pres.-elect Am. Coll. Family Trial Lawyers. Mem. Internat. Acad. Matrimonial Lawyers (past treas., gov. N.Y. chpt.), Am. Acad. Matrimonial Lawyers (gov., past pres. N.Y. chpt., pres. elect.), N.Y. State Bar Assn., Assn. Trial Lawyers Am., Met. Trial Lawyers Assn., Internat. Acad. Matrimonial Lawyers (bd. govs. 1986—, com. to examine lawyer conduct in matrimonial actions 1992-95). Author: (with Marya Mannes) Uncoupling, 1972; On Trial, 1977; contbr. editor: Fairshare mag. Family and matrimonial. Office: Sheresky Aronson & Mayefsky LLP 750 Lexington Ave New York NY 10022-1200

**SHERIDAN, DANIEL JOSEPH,** lawyer; b. Holyoke, Mass., June 29, 1961; s. Philip J. and Elizabeth A. (Cauley) S.; m. Kimberly A. Miller, May 21, 1988. BBA with honors, U. Mass., 1983; JD with honors, Western New Eng. Coll., 1986. Bar: Mass. 1986, U.S. Dist. Ct. Mass. 1987, U.S. Ct. Appeals (1st cir.) 1988, U.S. Supreme Ct. 1992. Labor rels. cons. Sheridan & Assocs., Inc., Holyoke, 1979-95; assoc. Powers & Bowler, Holyoke, 1986-87; prin. Law Offices Daniel J. Sheridan, Holyoke, 1987-88; ptnr. Sheridan & Sheridan, South Hadley, Mass., 1988—; Sheridan and Assocs., Inc., 1988-95. Mem. Mass. Bar Assn., Hampden County Bar Assn., Hampshire County Bar Assn., John Boyle O'Reilly Club (Springfield, Mass.). Labor, Workers' compensation, Education and schools. Home: 296 Brainerd St South Hadley MA 01075-1702 Office: Sheridan & Sheridan 660 Newton St South Hadley MA 01075-2020

**SHERIDAN, PETER N.,** lawyer; b. N.Y.C., Feb. 27, 1944; s. Stephen S. and Beatrice (Zimmer) S.; 1 child, Elizabeth. BA, U. Vt., 1965; JD, Bklyn. Law Sch., 1968. Bar: N.Y. 1969, U.S. Ct. Mil. Appeals 1970, U.S. Dist. Ct. (ea. and so. dist.) N.Y. 1972, U.S. Ct. Appeals 1972, U.S. Supreme Ct. 1974. Assoc., Mendes & Mount, N.Y.C., 1971-74; asst. gen. counsel CIBA-GEIGY Corp., Ardsley, N.Y., 1974-88; ptnr. Sheridan, Ruskin & Weathers, N.Y.C., 1988—. Bd. editors: Leader's Product Liability Newsletter, 1982—; lectr. Contbr. articles to profl. jours. Bd. dirs. Concerned Com. for Indo-Chinese Relations, N.Y.C., 1980-81; regional bd. dirs. Cystic Fibrosis Found., Greater N.Y. region, 1982—. Served to capt. U.S. Army, 1969-71, Vietnam. Mem. ABA (vice chair products gen. liability and consumer law com., sect. of torts and ins. practice 1981—), Am. Corp. Counsel Assn. (chair indsl. def. library 1983—). General corporate, Product liability. Home: 610 Rosemere Ave Silver Spring MD 20904-3021 Office: Sheridan Ruskin & Weathers Ste 830 500 Fifth Ave New York NY 10110

**SHERK, GEORGE WILLIAM,** lawyer; b. Washington, Mo., June 23, 1949; s. George William Sr. and Lorraine Martha (Meyer) S. AA, St. Louis Community Coll., 1970; BA, Colo. State U., 1972, MA, 1974; JD, U. Denver, 1978. Bar: Am. Samoa 1978, Colo. 1979, U.S. Dist. Ct. Colo. 1979, U.S. Ct. Claims 1984, U.S. Supreme Ct. 1985. Cons. office of legis. counsel Govt. of Am. Samoa, Pago Pago, 1978-79; atty. advisor western area power adminstrn. U.S. Dept. Energy, Colo., 1979-80; pvt. practice law Denver, 1980-82; staff assoc. Nat. Conf. State Legis., Denver, 1980-82; spl. asst. office of water policy U.S. Dept. Interior, Washington, 1982-83; atty. land and natural resources div. U.S. Dept. Justice, Washington, 1984-90; of counsel Will & Muys, Washington, 1990-93; pvt. practice Alexandria, Va., 1993—; vis. scholar U. Wyo. Coll. Law, 1993; vis. prof. Ga. State U. Coll. Law, 1994-95, Ga. State U. Policy Rsch. Ctr., 1995-96; assoc. professorial lectr. George Washington U. Sch. Engring. and Applied Sci., Washington, 1997—; lectr. various colls. and univs.; mem. assoc. faculty Va. Inst. Marine Sci., Coll. of William and Mary, Gloucester Pt., Va., 1989-94. Author, co-author or editor numerous books and articles on water law and alternative energy law; book review editor Rivers: Studies in the Science, Environmental Policy and Law of Instream Flow, 1989—. Mem. ABA, ASCE, Water Environ. Fedn., State Bar Colo. Avocations: automobile racing and rallying, sports, reading, outdoor activites, sailing. Real property, Environmental, Federal civil litigation. Home and Office: 801 N Pitt St # 1708 Alexandria VA 22314-1765

**SHERMAN, DAVID ROBERT,** lawyer; b. N.Y.C., Oct. 15, 1952; s. Stanley Edward and Joan (Horowitz) S.; m. Jane Marie Ragas, May 4, 1974; children: Philip Benjamin, Matthew Arthur, Amelia Marie. BSBA, U. New Orleans, 1974; JD, Loyola U., New Orleans, 1977; LLM in Taxation, Boston U., 1978. Bar: La. 1974, U.S. Dist. Ct. (ea. dist.) La. 1974, U.S. Tax Ct. 1974, U.S. Ct. Appeals (5th cir.) 1974. Ptnr. Donelon, Donelon & Sherman, Metairie, La., 1978-82, Gauthier, Murphy, Sherman, McCabe & Chehardy, Kenner, La., 1982-88, Chehardy, Sherman, Ellis & Breslin, Metairie, 1989—; instr. advanced estate planning course Am. Coll. CLUs; instr. estate planning U. New Orleans; bd. dirs. U. New Orleans Fund, New Orleans Sports Found., Met. Coun. Lifelong Learning. Mem. ABA, La. Bar Assn. (tax specialization sect.), New Orleans Estate Planning Council, New Orleans Employee Benefit Planners Assn., Delta Theta Phi, Omicron Delta Kappa, Phi Kappa Theta. Republican. Jewish. Probate, Corporate taxation, Personal income taxation. Office: Chehardy Sherman Ellis & Breslin 1 Galleria Blvd Ste 1100 Metairie LA 70001-2033

**SHERMAN, EDWARD FRANCIS,** dean, law educator; b. El Paso, Tex., July 5, 1937; s. Raphael Eugene and Mary (Stedmon) S.; m. Alice Theresa hammer, FEb. 23, 1963; children: Edward F. Jr., Paul. BA, Georgetown U., 1959; MA, U. Tex., El Paso, 1962, 67; LLB, Harvard U., 1962, SJD, 1981. Bar: Tex. 1962, Ind. 1976. Aide to gov. Nev., state govt. fellow Carson City, 1962; law clk. judge U.S. Dist. Ct. (we. dist.), El Paso, Tex., 1963; ptnr. Mayfield, Broaddus & Perrenot, El Paso, 1963-65; tchg. fellow Law Sch. Harvard U., Cambridge, Mass., 1967-69; prof. Sch. Law Ind. U., Bloomington, 1969-77; Edward Clark Centennial prof. U. Tex., Austin, 1977-96; prof., dean Tulane U. Law Sch., 1996—; Fulbright prof. Trinity Coll., Dublin, 1973-74; vis. prof. Stanford Law Sch., 1977; counsel Tex. County Jail Litigation, 1978-85; bd. dirs., officer Travis County Dispute Resolution, 1993—; mem. arbitrtor panel, course dir. Internat. Ctrs. Arbitration. Co-author: The Military in American Society, 1979, Complex Litigation, 1985, 3d edit., 1998, Processes of Dispute Resolution, 1989, 2d edit., 1996, Civil Procedure: A Modern Approach, 1989, 2d edit., 1995, Rau & Sherman's Texas ADR and Arbitration Statues, 1994, 3d edit., 1999. Capt. U.S. Army, 1965-67, lt. col. Res., 1970-90. Fellow Tex. Bar Found.; mem. ABA (reporter civil justice improvements project 1993, offer of judgement task force 1995, com. on pro bono and pub. svc. 1997—), Am. Arbitration Assn. (arbitrator panel), AAUP (gen. counsel 1986-88), Am. Law Inst., Tex. State Bar Assn. (alternative dispute resolution com. 1985-96, chair pattern jury charge com. 1983-94, Evans award for excellence in dispute resolution 1998), Tex. Civil Liberties Union (gen. cousel 1985-91), La. Law Inst., La. State Bar (mem. bd. govs. 1997-99, com. codes of lawyer and jud. conduct 1999—); La. Bar Found. (jud. liason com. 1999—), Assn. Am. Law Schs. (chmn. Sect. Litigation 1999, com. on clin. legal edn. 1999—. Home: 21 Newcomb Blvd New Orleans LA 70118-5527 Office: Tulane Law Sch 6329 Freret St New Orleans LA 70118-6231

**SHERMAN, FREDERICK HOOD,** lawyer; b. Deming, N.Mex., Aug. 9, 1947; s. Benjamin and Helen (Hood) S.; m. Janie Carol Jontz, Oct. 23, 1973; children: Jerah Elizabeth, Frederick Jakub. BBA, Southern Meth. U., 1970, JD, 1972. Bar: Tex. 1972, N.Mex. 1973, U.S. Dist. Ct. N.Mex. 1973, U.S. Dist. Ct. (we. dist.) Tex. 1974, U.S. Supreme Ct. 1979; cert. mediator. Assoc. Sherman & Sherman, Deming, 1973-74, ptnr., 1974-78; prin. Sherman & Sherman P.C., Deming, 1978—; assoc. prof. Western N.Mex. U., Silver City, 1975-77; mem. specialization com. N.Mex. Supreme Ct., 1986-94; liaison N.Mex. Supreme Ct and Workers Compensation Bd., 1991-94; mem. jud. selection com. State Bar N.Mex., 1985-88, legal retreat com., 1986-88, co-chair, 1986-87, alternative dispute resolution com., 1980-91; owner Rio Mimbres Wine; apptd. guardian of assets State Fiscal Acctg. State N.Mex., 1992—; state coord. Nat. Bd. Trial Advocates for Bd. Cert. of Trial Specialist, 1994-98. Contbr. articles to profl. jours. Chmn. Luna County Planning Commn., Deming, 1976-78; apptd. visitor to U. N.Mex. Law Sch., 1983—; treas. Luna County Econ. Devel. PSS, 1987-88, also bd. dirs.; bd. dirs. Luna County Hosp., 1991-94; bd. mem. Deming Pub. Sch., 1991-94, pres., 1991-92, elected bd. mem. 1991-95; chmn. bd. dirs. Luna County Charitable Found., 1991—; hon. dir. Deming Art Coun., 1989—; pres. Luna County Sch. Bd., 1991-92; pres., chmn. of the bd. Sherman Family Charitable Found., 1991—; mem. N. Mex. High Sch. Task Force, 1993-94. Recipient Svc. award N.Mex. Bd. Legal Specialization, 1994. Mem. ATLA (Notably Large award 1983, 84, 85), N.Mex. Trial Lawyers Assn. (bd. dirs. 1986—, sec. 1989, 97, Amicus Curiae award, 1991), N.Mex. Bar Assn., State Bar N.Mex. (commr. 1978-86, com. on alt. dispute resolutions practice 1980-90, jud. selection com. 1985, com. for legal retreat 1989, Outstanding Svc. award, 1986, 94 and Dedication award 1986), Tex. Bar Assn., 6th Jud. Bar Assn., Am. Inns. of Ct. (master atty. 1995), Coll. State Bar Tex. (pro bono, 1995—), KC. Democrat. Roman Catholic. Avocations: skiing, investments, camping, farming, wine making. Personal injury, General civil litigation, Pension, profit-sharing, and employee benefits. Office: Sherman & Sherman PO Box 850 Deming NM 88031-0850

**SHERMAN, HAROLD,** lawyer; b. Newark, Oct. 19, 1921; s. Myron H. and Mollie (Zell) S.; m. Sylvia Selikowsky, Feb. 20, 1943; children: Ralph, Neal. AB, Bklyn. Coll., 1942; PhD, NYU, 1956; JD, Pace U., 1986. Bar: Conn. 1987, U.S. Dist. Ct. Conn. 1988. Physicist Premier Crystal Labs., N.Y.C., 1944-47, Schlumberger-Doll Rsch., Ridgefield, Conn., 1956-83; instr. physics St. Peter's Coll., Jersey City, 1949-51; rsch. assoc. NYU, 1952-56; pvt. practice Ridgefield, 1987—; cons. Teleco Oilfield Svcs., Meriden, Conn., 1985-92. Patentee (5) in field. Vol., Conn. Legal Svcs., 1988-97. Mem. Conn. Bar Assn., Am. Phys. Soc., Soc. Profl. Well Log Analysts, Sigma Xi. Avocations: gardening, photography. Juvenile, Probate, Contracts commercial. Home and Office: 24 Webster Rd Ridgefield CT 06877-4308

**SHERMAN, JONATHAN HENRY,** lawyer; b. Washington, Jan. 4, 1963; s. Gerald Howard and Lola (Kay) S. BA in History magna cum laude, U. Rochester, 1984; MA in History, Yale U., 1989; JD, Stanford U., 1991. Bar: N.Y. 1992, U.S. Dist. Ct. (so. dist.) N.Y. 1992, U.S. Supreme Ct. 1995, U.S. Dist. Ct. (ea. dist.) N.Y. 1996, U.S. Ct. Appeals (11th cir.) 1996, U.S. Dist. Ct. (we. dist.) N.Y. 1998. Assoc. Cahill Gordon & Reindel, N.Y.C., 1991—; lectr. Stanford U., Palo Alto, Calif., 1991, Yale Coll., New Haven, 1993; adj. assoc. prof. law Fordham Law Sch., N.Y.C., 1998—. Sponsor, mentor Student-Sponsor Partnership, N.Y.C., 1992-96; contbr. The Cornerstone Sch., Jersey City, 1994. Mem. ABA, N.Y. State Bar Assn. (media law com. 1997—), Phi Beta Kappa. Democrat. Avocations: writing, reading, cycling. General civil litigation, Constitutional, Libel. Home: 1700 19th St NW Apt 3 Washington DC 20009-1669 Office: Cahill Gordon & Reindel 80 Pine St Fl 17 New York NY 10005-1790

**SHERMAN, LAWRENCE JAY,** lawyer; b. Pitts., May 20, 1942; s. Ben E. and Leonora C. (Weill) S.; m. Iris Shapiro, Aug. 19, 1967; children: Rachel L., Jessica S. BA in Polit. Sci. with honors, U. Pitts., 1963; JD, U. Mich., 1966. Bar: D.C. 1967, Calif. 1967, Md. 1984, U.S. Dist. Ct. D.C., U.S. Dist. Ct. Md., U.S. Claims Ct., U.S. Ct. Appeals (D.C., 1st, 3rd, 4th, 5th and 6th cir.). Appellate atty. NLRB, Washington, 1966-69; assoc. Cohen & Berfield, Washington, 1969-70; exec. dir. Migrant Legal Action Program, Washington, 1970-75; assoc. Lichtman, Abeles, Anker & Nagle, P.C., Washington, 1975-77; private practice Washington, 1977-81; ptnr. Sherman & Ladidus, Washington, 1981-86; counsel Deso, Thomas, Spevack, Weitzman & Rost P.C., Washington, 1991—; adj. prof. George Meany Ctr. for Labor Studies, Silver Spring, Md. 1988—; prin. Mng. Human Resources For 21st Century, Washington, 1990—. Contbr. articles to profl. jours. Fellow Am. Bd. Trial Advocates; mem. ABA (labor and employment law sect., litig. sect.), D.C. Bar (labor and employment law sect., litig. sect., co-chmn. steering com., 1981-85, labor law sect. 1978-84, co-chmn. labor law sect. 1983-84, lawyers coord. com.), Met. Lawyers Assn., Md. Lawyers Assn., Nat. Employment Lawyers Assn. Democrat. Avocations: tennis, racquetball, running, travel and reading. Labor, Civil rights, General civil litigation. Office: Deso Thomas Spevack & Weitzman PC 1828 L St NW Ste 660 Washington DC 20036-5112

**SHERMAN, LESTER IVAN,** retired lawyer; b. Flagler, Colo., June 1, 1936; s. Lester B. and Helen E. S.; m. Lois E. Hafling, July 19, 1958 (div. Mar. 1986); children: Kathi, Scott, Brett; m. Kay A. Swanson, Dec. 21, 1993. Student Colo. State U., 1954-55; BSBA, U. Denver, 1958, JD, 1961. Bar: Colo. 1961, U.S. Dist. Ct. Colo. 1961. Pvt. practice, Denver, 1961-62; assoc. Harold C. Greager, Ft. Collins, Colo., 1962-65; pvt. practice, Durango, Colo., 1965-67, 79-81, 86-97; ret. 1997; ptnr. Hamilton, Sherman, Hamilton & Shand, P.C., Durango, 1967-78; ptnr. Sherman Rhodes & Wright, P.C., Durango, 1981-86; judge La Plata County (Colo.) Ct., 1966-76; cons. in field; mem. Colo. Commn. on Jud. Qualifications, 1974-76. Mem. La Plata County Bd. for Mentally Retarded and Seriously Handicapped, Inc., 1968-75, pres., 1970-73; bd. dirs. Colo. County Judges Assn., 1973-74. Mem. S.W. Colo. Bar (pres. 1969-70), Colo. Bar Assn. (gov. 1970-72, 74-76), ABA, Petroleum Club, Elks, Phi Delta Phi, Sigma Chi. Republican. General corporate, Estate planning, Real property. Home: 320 N Skylane Dr Durango CO 81301-6040

**SHERMAN, RICHARD ALLEN,** lawyer; b. Atlanta, Mar. 16, 1946; s. Robert Hiram and Olivia Mae (Latham) S.; m. Mary Margaret Sawyer, June 23, 1973 (div. June 1994); children: Richard A. Jr., Jill Mary, James Warren; m. Catherine Agnes Oakley, May 4, 1996. BA, Tulane U., 1968, JD, 1972. Bar: Fla. 1974, La. 1973, U.S. Ct. Appeals (5th cir.) 1978, U.S. Ct. Appeals (11th cir.) 1981, U.S. Supreme Ct. 1981. Ptnr., head appellate divsn. Wicker, Smith, Blomqvist, Davant, Tutan, O'Hara, McCoy et al, Miami, 1973-83; pvt. practice Ft. Lauderdale, Fla., 1983—, practice limited to handling appeals in Fla. Active Rep. Nat. Com. Mem. ABA (vice-chmn. U.S. Ct. Appeals 5th cir. com. 1981), Fla. Bar Assn. (appellate rules com. 1979-81), Dade County Bar Assn. (chmn. appellate cts. com. 1982-83), Mensa, Pres. Club, Lauderdale Yacht Club, Upper Keys Sailing Club (bd. dirs.). Avocations: yacht racing, boating, scuba diving, travel, theatre. Insurance, Product liability, Personal injury. Office: 1777 S Andrews Ave Ste 302 Fort Lauderdale FL 33316-2517

**SHERMAN, SANDRA BROWN,** lawyer; b. Galesburg, Ill., May 14, 1953; d. Charles Lewis and Lois Maria (Nelson) Brown; m. Robert Sherman, June 10, 1979; children: Michael Wesley, Stephen Averill, Alexander Joseph. B of Music Edn., Ind. U., 1975; JD, U. Ill., 1979, LLM, 1981. Bar: Ill. 1979, Tex. 1982, N.J. 1984, U.S. Tax Ct. 1988, N.Y. 1997. Instr. law U. Ill., Champaign, 1979-81; assoc. Law Offices of William E. Remy, San Antonio, 1984; assoc. Gutkin Miller Shapiro & Selesner, Millburn, N.J., 1985-88, ptnr., 1989-91; counsel Riker Danzig Scherer Hyland & Perretti, Morristown, N.J., 1991-95, ptnr., 1996—. Contbr. articles to profl. jours. Trustee, sec. Found. U. Medicine and Dentistry N.J., 1998—; trustee Jersey Ballared Women's Svc., 1999—. Scholar Ind. U., 1971-75, U. Ill., 1977-79. Mem. ABA (probate and trust law divsn.), N.J. Bar Assn., Estate Planning Coun. No. N.J., Estate Planning Coun. N.Y.C., Park Ave. Club. Avocation: music. Estate planning, Taxation, general, General corporate. Home: 15 Hawthorne Dr New Providence NJ 07974-1111 Office: Riker Danzig Scherer Hyland & Perretti Headquarters Plz 1 Speedwell Ave Morristown NJ 07960-6823

**SHERMAN, STEPHEN MICHAEL,** lawyer; b. N.Y.C., Dec. 9, 1946; s. Arthur and Marjorie Elizabeth Sherman; m. Sue Lynn Gould, Oct. 10, 1965 (div. Oct. 1983); children: Michael Aaron, Laura Elizabeth Sherman Getz; m. Kathryn Sue Davis, June 1, 1985. BA, Ind. U., 1968, JD, 1972. Bar: Ind. 1972, U.S. Dist. Ct. (so. dist.) Ind. 1972, U.S. Ct. Appeals (6th cir.) 1975. Clk. chief justice Ind. Supreme Ct., Indpls., 1972-73; dep. atty. gen. Ind. Atty. Gen., Indpls., 1973-74; pvt. practice law Indpls., 1974—; staff counsel Legis. Coun. Adminstrv. Rules, Indpls., 1978-79; pres. Marion County Juvenile Detention Ctr. Adv. Bd., Indpls., 1987—; chmn. bd. Omega Concepts, Inc., Indpls., 1993—. Recipient Dawson award Tabernacle Presbyn. Ch., Indpls., 1988. Mem. ABA, Ind. State Bar Assn., Indpls. Bar Assn. (mem. grievance com. 1978—, mem. legal awareness com. 1985—). Democrat. Avocations: grandchildren, RV camping, travel, spectator sports. General practice, Personal injury, Family and matrimonial. Home: 6021 Winnpeny Ln Indianapolis IN 46220-5252 Office: PO Box 20576 Indianapolis IN 46220-0576

**SHERMAN, VICTOR,** lawyer; b. Indpls., Aug. 28, 1951; s. Marshall and Sara Lee Sherman; m. Claudia Ann Cron, Oct. 8, 1988; children: Mark, Daniel, Miles, Oliver, Luke. BS, UCLA, 1962; LLB, U. Calif., Berkeley, 1965. Bar: Calif. 1966, Conn. 1996, U.S. Ct. Appeals (9th cir.) 1971, U.S. Supreme Ct. 1996. Ptnr. Nasatir, Sherman & Hirsch, L.A., 1970-83, Main St. Law Bldg., Santa Monica, Calif., 1984—; mng. ptnr. Sherman & Sherman, Santa Monica, 1984—; speaker, founder Advanced Criminal Law Seminar, Aspen, Colo., 1981—. Pvt. 1st class U.S. Army, 1960-67. Mem. Nat. Assn. Criminal Def. Lawyers (life). Office: Sherman & Sherman 2115 Main St Santa Monica CA 90405-2215

**SHERMAN, WILLIAM FARRAR,** lawyer, former state legislator; b. Little Rock, Sept. 12, 1937; s. Lincoln Farrar and Nancy (Lowe) S.; m. Carole Lynn Williams, Sept. 2, 1967; children—John, Anna, Lucy. B.A. in History, U. Ark.-Fayetteville, 1960; LL.B., U. Va., 1964. Bar: Ark., 1964, U.S. Supreme Ct., 1970. Assoc., Smith, Williams, Friday & Bowen, Little Rock, 1964-66; asst. U.S. atty. Ea. Dist. Ark., 1966-69; Ark. Securities Commr., Little Rock, 1969-71; partner Jacoway, Sherman & Pence, Little Rock, 1971—; mem. Ark. Ho. of Reps., 1974-84; spl. assoc. justice Supreme Ct., 1991; del. Constl. Conv. Ark., 1979. Served with U.S. Army, 1960-61, now brig. gen. U.S. Army ret. Mem. ABA, Ark. Bar Assn., Pulaski County Bar Assn., Ark. Bar Found, Ark. Trial Lawyers Assn. Democrat. Methodist. General practice, Legislative, Military. Office: 221 W 2nd St Little Rock AR 72201-2505

**SHERR, MORRIS MAX,** lawyer; b. Marysville, Calif., Oct. 3, 1930; s. Alfred and Alice Carrie (Peters) S.; m. Bobbie Gray, June 27, 1954; children: David, Rodney. BA, Calif. State U., 1952; JD, U. Calif.-San Francisco, 1956. Bar: Calif. 1956. Prin. elem. sch., Stanislaus County, Calif., 1952-54; instr. Golden Gate Coll., 1954-55; instr. Calif. State U.-San Francisco, 1955-56; asst. prof. Calif. State U.-Fresno, 1956-59; assoc. Thompson & Rose, CPAs, Fresno, Calif., 1959-61; ptnr. Blumberg, Sherr & Kerkorian, Fresno, Calif., 1961-84, Morris M. Sherr & Assocs., Fresno, 1984—. Mem. adv. council St. Agnes Hosp. Found., 1978-83; mem. bd. deacons Evang. Free Ch. of Fresno, 1992—, mem. fin. com., 1995—. Mem. Am. Inst. CPAs, Fresno Estate Planning Coun. (dir. 1977-79), Fresno County Bar, Christian Legal Soc., Calif. State Bar (cert. tax specialist). Baptist (chmn. trustees 1967-69, deacon 1969-73). Mem. Am. Baptist Chs. of West (moderator). Clubs: Elks, Masons, Shriners. Estate taxation, Taxation, general, Probate. Office: 6051 N Fresno St Ste 200 Fresno CA 93710-5280

**SHERRY, JOHN SEBASTIAN,** lawyer; b. Homestead, Pa., Apr. 18, 1946; s. Sebastian John and Margaret Josephine (Coyne) S.; m. Joan Carol Paulsen, Aug. 9, 1969; children: Brendan P., Michael S., Conor J. BA, U. Dayton, 1968; JD, Duquesne U., 1971. Bar: Pa. 1971, U.S. Dist. Ct. (we. dist.) Pa. 1971, U.S. Supreme Ct. 1975, U.S. Ct. Appeals (3d cir.) 1976, U.S. Tax Ct. 1977, U.S. Claims Ct. 1977, U.S. Ct. Mi. Appeals 1977, U.S. Ct. Internat. Trade 1977. Sole practice, Pitts., 1971—; mng. atty. The Travlers Ins. Co., Pitts., 1972-78; mng. trial atty. The CNA Ins. Cos., Pitts., 1978-88, sr. mgr. staff counsel, 1988-94, mng. trial atty., 1994-96, asst. v.p. claims litigation, 1996-98; pvt. practice Pitts., 1999—; lectr. Trial Advocacy Found., Pitts., 1984, Nat. Inst. for Trial Advocacy, 1997, 98. Assoc. opinion editor Pitts. Legal Jour., 1977-78, editor YLS newsletter, 1980. Chmn. Bd. Auditors, South Park, Pa., 1977-85. Fellow Acad. Trial Lawyers Allegheny County (bd. govs. 1997-98); mem. ABA, Acad. Trial Lawyers (bd. govs., 1992-98, civil procedural rules com., 1999), Allegheny County Bar Assn. (continuing legal edn. com. 1978—, coun . civil litigation sect. 1985-87, 92, treas. 1988, vice chmn. 1989, chmn. 1991, civil procedure rules com. 1999), Pa. Def. Inst., Pa. Bar Assn. (jud. selection and reform com. 1992-93), South Park C. of C. (prs. 1978), Rivers Club, Pine Lake Trout Club, South Park Club, Lions (treas. South Park club 1980-81). Democrat. Roman Catholic. Avocations: fishing, hunting, lit. Federal civil litigation, State civil litigation, Insurance. Home: 181 Vernon Dr Pittsburgh PA 15228-1112

**SHERZER, HARVEY GERALD,** lawyer; b. Phila., May 19, 1944; s. Leon and Rose (Levin) S.; m. Susan Bell, Mar. 28, 1971; children: Sheri Ann, David Lloyd. BA, Temple U., 1965; JD with honors, George Washington U., 1968. Bar: D.C. 1970, U.S. Ct. Appeals (D.C. cir.) 1970, U.S. Ct. Fed. Claims 1970, U.S. Ct. Appeals (fed. cir.) 1970, U.S. Supreme Ct. 1974. Law clk. to trial judges U.S. Ct. Fed. Claims, Washington, 1968-69; law clk. to chief judge U.S. Ct. Appeals for Fed. Cir., Washington, 1969-70; assoc. Sellers, Conner & Cuneo, Washington, 1970-75, ptnr., 1975-80; ptnr. McKenna, Conner & Cuneo, Washington, 1980-82, Pettit & Martin, Washington, 1982-85, Howrey & Simon, Washington, 1985—; adv. bd. The Govt. Contractor, 1996—. Author: (with others) A Complete Guide to the Department of Defense Voluntary Disclosure Program, 1996; contbr. articles to profl. jours. Government contracts and claims, Private international. Office: Howrey & Simon 1299 Pennsylvania Ave NW Ste 1 Washington DC 20004-2420

**SHESTACK, JEROME JOSEPH,** lawyer; b. Atlantic City, N.J., Feb. 11, 1925; s. Isidore and Olga (Shankman) S.; m. Marciarose Schleifer, Jan. 28, 1951; children: Jonathan Michael, Jennifer. AB, U. Pa., 1944; LLB, Harvard U., 1949; LLD (hon.), Dickinson Coll. Law, 1997. Bar: Ill. 1950, Pa. 1952. Teaching fellow Northwestern U. Law Sch., Chgo., 1949-50; asst. prof. law, faculty editor La. State Law Sch., Baton Rouge, 1950-52; dep. city solicitor City of Phila., 1952, 1st dep. solicitor, 1952-55; ptnr. Schnader, Harrison, Segal & Lewis, Phila. and Washington, 1956-91, Wolf, Block, Schorr & Solis-Cohen, Phila., 1991—; adj. prof. law U. Pa., 1956; U.S. amb. to UN Human Rights Commn., 1979-80; U.S. del. to ECOSOC, UN, 1980; sr. U.S. del. to Helsinki Accords Conf., 1979-80; mem. U.S. Commn. on Improving Effectiveness of UN, 1989—; chmn . Internat. League Human Rights, 1973—, U.S. del. to CSCE Conf., Moscow, 1991; founder, chmn. Lawyers Com. Internat. Human Rights, 1978-80, Jacob Blaustein Inst. Human Rights, 1988-92; mem. nat. adv. com. legal svcs. OEO, 1965-72; bd. dirs., exec. com. Laywers Com. Civil Rights; mem. coun. Holocaust Mus.. 1999—. Editor: (with others) Rights of Americans, 1971, Human Rights, 1979, International Human Rights, 1985, Bill of Rights: A Bicentennial View, 1991, Understanding Human Rights, 1992, Thomas Jefferson: Lawyer, 1993, Francis Scott Key, 1994, Abraham Lincoln, Circuit Lawyer, 1994, The Holocaust, 1997, Moral Foundations of Human Rights, 1997, The Philosophy of Human Rights, 1997, W.B. Yeats, Poet of Passionate Intensity, 1997. Mem. exec. com. Nat. Legal Aid and Defender Assn., 1970-80; trustee Eleanor and Franklin Roosevelt Inst., 1986—; bd. govs. Tel Aviv U., 1983—, Hebrew U., 1969—; v.p. Am. Jewish Com., 1984-89; chmn. bd. dirs. Am. Poetry Ctr., 1976-91; trustee Free Libr. Phila., vice chmn., 1989-96. With USNR, 1943-46. Rubin fellow Columbia U. Law Sch., 1984; hon. fellow U. Pa. Law Sch., 1980. Mem. ABA (ho. of dels. 1971-73, 77—, mem. jud. com. 1985-90, bd. govs. 1992-95, exec. com. 1994-95, counsellor 1999—, pres. elect 1996, pres. 1997-98, pres. ALI-ABA 1997-98), Internat. Bar Assn. (chmn. com. on human rights 1990-94), Am. Soc. Internat. Law (exec. com. 1993-95, counsellor 1999—, internat. com. jurists exec. com. 1998—), Am. Law Inst., Am. Arbitration Assn. (bd. dirs. 1999—), Am. Coll. Trial Lawyers, Am. Acad. Appellate Lawyers, Order of Coif., Am. Soc. Internat. Law, Nat. Conf. Bar Found. (bd. dirs. 1998—). Antitrust, Libel, Securities. Home: Parkway House 2201 Pennsylvania Ave Philadelphia PA 19130-3513 Office: Wolf Block Schorr & Solis-Cohen Packard Bldg 1650 Arch St Philadelphia PA 19103

**SHETLAR, JAMES R.,** lawyer; b. Girard, Kans., Oct. 27, 1946; s. John Allen and Mabel Lillian (Graves) S.; m. Marilyn Steincamp, Nov. 17, 1984. BBA, Pittsburg State U., 1969; JD, Washburn U., 1972. Assoc. Stuart D. Mitchelson Law Offices, Mission, Kans.; ptnr. Cleaver, Sullivan & Shetlar, Overland Park, Kans.; sole practice Overland Park, Kans. Founder Kans. City Quail Unltd.; state chmn. campaign fin., lobby and ethics reform UWSA of Kans., 1995-97. Served with U.S. Army, 1970-71. Mem. Kans. Bar Assn., Johnson County Bar Assn. (sec.), Am. Trial Lawyers Assn., Kans. Trial Lawyers Assn. (bd. govs. 1980—, state chmn. workers comp.). Democrat. Methodist. Avocations: hunting, rafting, fishing, coaching rugby. Workers' compensation, General civil litigation, Personal injury. Home: 12727 Mohawk Cir Leawood KS 66209-1718

**SHIAU, H. LIN,** lawyer; b. Keelung, Taiwan, Nov. 26, 1962; came to U.S., 1971; d. Chuen H. and Shinglien W. S.; m. Vincent Altamura, Sept. 17, 1989; children: Eric, Alaina. BA, Dartmouth Coll., 1985; JD, Stanford U., 1988. Bar: N.Y., D.C., N.C. Litig. assoc. Davis, Polk & Wardwell, N.Y.C., 1988-91; counsel Coopers & Lybrand LLP, N.Y.C., 1991-95; sr. counsel Paramount Pks. Inc., Charlotte, N.C., 1996-97, v.p., assoc. gen. counsel, 1997—. General corporate, Entertainment, General civil litigation. Office: Paramount Pks Inc 8720 Red Oak Blvd Ste 315 Charlotte NC 28217-3990

**SHIELDS, CRAIG M.,** lawyer; b. Oceanside, N.Y., Nov. 28, 1941; s. John Anderson and Lillian Ethel (Hagen) S.; m. Candia Atwater Shields, July 13, 1963 (div. 1985); children: Mark, Christopher, Evan; m. Norma Magor Peters, Apr. 25, 1998. Bar: N.Y. 1967, U.S. Dist. Ct. (so. and ea. dists.) N.Y. 1967, U.S. Ct. Appeals (2d cir.) 1967, U.S. Supreme Ct. 1976. Assoc. Clark, Carr & Ellis, N.Y.C., 1966-69; ptnr. Borden & Ball, N.Y.C., 1969-76, Sage, Gray, Todd & Sims, N.Y.C., 1976-80; counsel Conboy, Hewitt, O'Brien & Boardman, N.Y.C., 1980-83; ptnr. Collier, Cohen, Shields & Bock, N.Y.C., 1983-92, Quinn & Suhr, White Plains, N.Y., 1992-95; v.p., gen. counsel United Vanguard Homes, Inc., Glen Cove, N.Y., 1992—. Contbr. articles to profl. jours. Bd. dirs. Group House of Port Washington (N.Y.) Inc., 1973-85, Children's House, Inc., Mineola, N.Y., 1985-89, Resources for Program Devel., Inc., Port Washington, 1982—; pres. Port Washington Community Action Coun., 1968-69; committeeman Dem. Party, Port Washington, 1967-71. Mem. ABA, Assn. of Bar of City of New York, N.Y.State Bar Assn. Democrat. Methodist. General corporate, Securities. Home: 103 E 86th St Apt 7A New York NY 10028-1058 Office: United Vanguard Homes Inc 4 Cedar Swamp Rd Glen Cove NY 11542-3744

**SHIELY, GERALD LAWRENCE,** lawyer; b. Ft. Lee, Va., May 13, 1954; s. Thomas Paul and Diana (Wooden) S. BBA, U. Tex., 1978; JD, U. Houston, 1981. Bar: Tex. 1982. Sr. ptnr. Thornton & Summers, San Antonio, 1982—. Mem. ABA, Tex. Assn. Def. Counsel, Def. Rsch. Inst., San Antonio Bar Assn. Insurance, Product liability, Professional liability. Home: 108 Pin Oak Forest St San Antonio TX 78232-2002 Office: Thornton & Summers 10100 Reunion Pl Ste 300 San Antonio TX 78216-4186

**SHIENTAG, FLORENCE PERLOW,** lawyer; b. N.Y.C.; d. David and Ester (Germane) Perlow; m. Bernard L. Shientag, June 8, 1938. BS, NYU, 1940, LLB, 1933, JD, 1940. Bar: Fla. 1976, N.Y. Law aide Thomas E. Dewey, 1937; law sec. Mayor La Guardia, 1939-42; justice Domestic Relations Ct., 1941-42; mem. Tchrs. Retirement Bd., N.Y.C., 1942-46; asst. U.S. atty. So. dist. N.Y., 1943-53; cir. ct. mediator Fla. Supreme Ct., 1992; pvt. practice N.Y.C., 1960—, Palm Beach, Fla., 1976—; lectr. on internat. divorce; mem. Nat. Commn. on Wiretapping and Electronic Surveillance, 1973—, Task Force on Women in Cts., 1985-86. Contbr. articles to profl. jours. Candidate N.Y. State Senate, 1954; bd. dirs. UN Devel. Corp., 1972-95, Franklin and Eleanor Roosevelt Inst., 1985—; bd. dirs., assoc. treas. YM and YWHA; hon. commr. commerce, N.Y.C. Mem. ABA, Fed. Bar Assn. (exec. com.), Internat. Bar Assn., N.Y. Women's Bar Assn. (pres., dir., Life Time Achievement award 1994), N.Y. State Bar Assn., N.Y.C. Bar Assn. (chmn. law and art sect.), N.Y. County Lawyers Assn. (dir.), Nat. Assn. Women LAwyers (sec.). Constitutional, Criminal, Family and matrimonial. Home: 737 Park Ave New York NY 10021-4256 *Success is a product of self respect and hard work at what you do well.*

**SHIERS, FRANK ABRAM,** lawyer; b. Marlboro, Mass., Oct. 23, 1920; s. Frank and Sarah (Chalk) S.; m. Sylvia A. Broz, Mar. 27, 1954; children: Frank A., Jane Marie Shiers Bryce. BA, Western Wash. U., 1942; JD, U. Wash., 1949. Bar: Wash. 1949, U.S. Dist. Ct. (we. dist.) Wash. 1950, U.S. Supreme Ct. 1969. Pvt. practice law Port Orchard, Wash., since 1949; ptnr. Greenwood & Shiers, Port Orchard, since 1950; now sr. ptnr. Shiers, Chrey, Cox, Caulkins, Digiovanni & Zak LLP, Port Orchard. Mem. Kitsap County Estate Planning Coun. 0620. Mem. Wash. State Bar Assn. (com. on profl. legal svcs. to armed forces and fee arbitration bd.), Kitsap County Bar Assn., VFW, Am. Legion, Navy League (past pres. Bremerton coun.), Young Men's Bus. Club (past pres. Wash. chpt.), Elks (past exalted ruler lodge 1181). Avocations: hunting, fishing, literature. Probate, Family and matrimonial, General practice. Office: Shiers Chrey Cox Caulkins DiGiovanni & Zak LLP 600 Kitsap St Ste 202 Port Orchard WA 98366-5397

**SHIGETOMI, KEITH SHIGEO,** lawyer; b. Honolulu, Oct. 16, 1956; s. Samson Shigeru and Doris (Ogawa) S.; m. Ann Keiko Furutomo, Oct. 29, 1985; children: Samson Shigeru II, Marisa Mae. BSBA magna cum laude, Drake U., 1978; JD, U. Hawaii, 1983. Bar: Hawaii, 1983, U.S. Dist. Ct. Hawaii 1983, U.S. Ct. Appeals (9th cir.) 1986. Dep. pub. defender Office of Pub. Defender, Honolulu, 1983-88; pvt. practice Honolulu, 1988-90, 94—; ptnr. Shigetomi & Thompson, Honolulu, 1990-94; ind. grand jury counsel Cir. Ct., State of Hawaii, Honolulu, 1988-89. Finalist Three Outstanding Young Persons Hawaii Jaycees, 1994; named Criminal Def. Lawyer of Yr. Consumer Bus. Rev., 1996, 1997. Mem. Hawaii State Bar Assn., Nat. Asian Pacific Bar Assn., Beta Gamma Sigma, Beta Alpha Psi, Phi Eta Sigma. Criminal, Juvenile, Personal injury. Office: 711 Kapiolani Blvd Ste 1440 Honolulu HI 96813-5238

**SHIGLEY, KENNETH LOWELL,** lawyer; b. Ft. Payne, Ala., May 16, 1951; s. Robert Nelson and Evangeline (Hartley) S.; m. Sara Chisholm McArthur, July 30, 1983; children: Anne Barron, Kenneth L. Jr. BA, Furman U., 1973; JD, Emory U., 1977. Bar: Ga. 1977, U.S. Dist. Ct. (no. dist.) Ga. 1977, U.S. Ct. Appeals (11th cir.) 1981, U.S. Supreme Ct. 1985, U.S. Dist. Ct. (so. and mid. dists.) Ga. 1986; advocate Nat. Coll. Advocacy. Asst. dist. atty. Tallapoosa Jud. Cir., Douglasville, Ga., 1977-78; pvt. practice Douglasville, 1979-81; assoc. VanGerpen & Rice, Atlanta, 1981-85, ptnr., 1986-88; ptnr. Van Gerpen, Shigley & Hoffman, Atlanta, 1989-91, Shigley Law Firm, LLC, Atlanta, 1991—; moderator Ga. Tort & Ins. Law Forum, Counsel Connect, 1995-97. Elder Peachtree Presbyn. Ch., Atlanta. Mem. ABA (tort and ins. practice sect.), Am. Judicature Soc., Christian Legal Soc., Nat. Bd. Trial Advocacy (cert. civil trial advocate), Am. Inns Ct. (master), State Bar Ga. (bd. govs. 1999—, co-chairperson legal ethics com. young lawyers sect. 1987-88, mem. code of profl. responsibility com. 1986—, chair ins. law sect. 1994-95, chair ins. law inst. 1994, mem. svcs. commn. 1999—), Ga. Bar Found., Ga. Defense Lawyers Assn., Lawyers Club of Atlanta. Presbyterian. Avocation: family and church activities. Insurance, General civil litigation, Personal injury.

**SHIH, MICHAEL MING-YU,** lawyer; b. Stanford, Calif., May 23, 1966; s. Kwang K. and Marion C. Shih; m. Melissa S. Marks, Nov. 23, 1997. BS, Cornell U., 1988; MS, U. Ill., 1990; JD, Fordham U., 1994. Bar: N.Y. 1995, U.S. Dist. Ct. (so. and ea. dists.) N.Y. 1995. Assoc. Kaye, Scholer, Fierman, Hays & Handler, LLP, N.Y.C., 1994-97, Kalow, Springut & Bressler, N.Y.C., 1997-99, The Beanstalk Group, Inc., N.Y.C., 1999—. Merck & Co., Inc. Patent Dept. fellow, 1991. Mem. ABA, N.Y. State Bar Assn., N.Y. Intellectual Property Law Assn., Assn. Bar City N.Y. Intellectual property, Trademark and copyright, Contracts commercial. Office: The Beanstalk Group Inc 950 3rd Ave New York NY 10022-2705

**SHIHATA, IBRAHIM FAHMY IBRAHIM,** bank executive, lawyer; b. Damietta, Egypt, Aug. 19, 1937; s. Ibrahim and Neamat (El Ashmawy) S.; m. Samia S. Farid, June 18, 1967; children: Sharif, Yasmine, Nadia. LL.B., U. Cairo, 1957, diploma in pub. law and fin., 1958, diploma in pvt. law, 1959; S.J.D., Harvard U., 1964; LLD (hon.), U. Dundee, Scotland, 1995, U. Paris Panthéon, Sorbonne, France, 1996. Mem. Conseil d'Etat, UAR, 1957-60, Tech. Bur. of Pres., Egypt, 1959-60; from lectr. to assoc. prof. internat. law Ain-Shams U., Cairo, 1964-66, 70-72; legal adviser Kuwait Fund for Arab Econ. Devel., 1966-70, 72-76; dir. gen. OPEC Fund for Internat. Devel., Vienna, 1976-83; exec. dir. Internat. Fund for Agrl. Devel., Rome, 1977-83; sr. v.p., gen. counsel World Bank, Washington, 1983—; sec. gen. Internat. Ctr. Settlement of Investment Disputes, Washington, 1983—; chmn. bd. Internat. Devel. Law Inst., Rome, 1983—; bd. dirs. Internat. Fertilizer Devel. Ctr., Muscle Shoals, Ala., 1979-84, Vienna Devel. Inst.; mem. exec. com. Am. Soc. Internat. Law, Washington, 1984-87; adv. com. Rsch. Ctr. Internat. Law, Cambridge, Eng., 1985—; founding adv., bd. dirs. Inst. Transnat. Arbitration, Houston, 1986—; hon. fellow Inst. Advance Legal Studies, U. London. Author: The Power of the International Court to Determine Its Own Jurisdiction, 1965, International Air and Space Law, 1966, International Economic Joint Ventures, 1969, International Guarantee for Foreign Investments, 1971, Treatment of Foreign Investments in Egypt, 1972, Secure and Recognized Boundaries, 1974, The Arab Oil Embargo, 1975, The Other Face of OPEC, 1982, The OPEC Fund for International Development-The Formative Years, 1983, A Program for Tomorrow-Challenges and Prospects of the Egyptian Economy in a Changing World, 1987, MIGA and Foreign Investment, 1988, The European Bank for Reconstruction and Development, 1990, The World Bank and the Arab World, 1990, The World Bank and in a Changing World, vol. 1, 1991, Legal Treatment of Foreign Investment: The World Bank Guidelines, 1993, Towards Comprehensive Reforms, 1993, The World Bank Inspection Panel, 1994, 2d edit., rev. 1999, The World Bank in a Changing World, vol. 2, 1995, vol. 3, 1996, vol. 4, 1997, 2d edit., 1999, Complementary Reform: Essays on Legal, Judicial and Other Institutional Reform Supported by the World Bank, 1997; editor ICSID Rev.-Fgn. Investment Law Jour. Sr. v.p. IBRD, 1983—, v.p., 1983-98, gen. counsel, 1983-98. Decorated Grosses Silbernes Ehrenzeichen am Bande fuer Verdienste um die Republik Oesterreich (Australia), 1983; recipient Babcock prize, 1964, Kuwait prize for sci. progress in social scis., 1983. Mem. Am. Soc. Internat. Law, Institut de Droit Internat. (Geneva). Office: IBRD General Counsel 1818 H St NW Washington DC 20433-0001

**SHILLING, MONICA JILL,** lawyer; b. Kansas City, Kans., Dec. 17, 1969; d. David Randall Shilling and Shelia Jan Brown. BA in Creative Writing and French, U. Redlands, 1992; JD magna cum laude, Georgetown U., 1995. Bar: Calif., 1995. Assoc. Skadden, Arps, Slate, Meagher & Flom LLP, L.A., 1995—. Mem. ABA, Calif. Bar Assn., L.A. County Bar Assn., Order of the Coif, Phi Beta Kappa. General corporate, Mergers and acquisitions, Finance. Office: Skadden Arps Slate Meagher & Flom LLP 300 S Grand Ave Los Angeles CA 90071-3109

**SHIMPOCK, KATHY ELIZABETH,** lawyer, writer; b. Mooresville, N.C., July 20, 1952; d. Charles Walter and Minna Ethel (McLean) S.; m. David Edward Vieweg, Sept. 3, 1983 (div. Mar. 1997); children: Jessica Kim Vieweg, Jayme Elise Kyung Vieweg. BA, Colo. Coll., 1973; JD, U. Wyo., 1977; MLL, U. Denver, 1979; MBA, Ariz. State U., 1992. Bar: Ariz. 1977. Asst. librarian Stanford (Calif.) U. Coll. Law, 1979-82; law librarian, asst. prof. law U. Bridgeport (Conn.) Coll. Law, 1982-83; dir. Law Libr. Adminstrv. Svcs., Mountain View, Calif., 1983-85; exec. asst. to dean Ariz. State U. Coll. Law, Tempe, 1985-87; dir. Law Libr. Adminstrv. Svcs., Mesa, Ariz., 1987-95; dir. libr. svcs. Jennings, Strouss & Salmon, Phoenix, 1988-89; dir. rsch. svcs. O'Connor, Cavanagh et al, Phoenix, 1989-95; pres. Juris Rsch., Mesa, 1995-96; counsel Muchmore & Wallwork, Phoenix, 1995-98; pres. Juris Rsch., Tempe, 1998—; mem. adv. bd. West Pub. Co., St. Paul, 1991-94. Author: Business Research Handbook: Methods and Sources for Lawyers and Business Professionals, 1996—; co-author: Arizona Legal Research Guide, 1992; contbr. chpts. to books, articles to profl. jours.; bi-monthly columnist AzALL News, 1996-97, Legal Assistant Today, 1993-96; contbr. book revs. to Libr. Jour., Legal Info. Alert, 1993-98; editor Southwest Assn. Law Librs. Bull., 1990, Ariz. State U. Coll. Law Law Forum, 1986, Juris Rsch. E-line, 1999—. Rsch. atty. Comml. Law Project for the Ukraine, Phoenix, 1995-96. Mem. ABA (co-chair law practice mgmt. environ. divsn. 1996—), Am. Assn. Law Librs. (chair 1994-95), Ariz. Assn. Law Librs. (pres. 1996-97, pres.'s award 1997, Disting. Mem. award 1998), State Bar of Ariz. (chair 1996—, Cont. Legal Edn. award 1998). Democrat. Unity. Avocations: reading, yoga, painting, drawing. Environmental, Intellectual property, Labor. Office: Juris Rsch PO Box 2157 Tempe AZ 85280-2157

**SHIN, CHANG SHIK,** lawyer; b. Busan, Korea, Feb. 13, 1961; s. Young Chin and S. Kyong Ok. BA, UCLA, 1987; JD, U. Calif., 1991. Bar: Calif. 1993, U.S. Dist. Ct. (ctrl. and ea. dists.) Calif. 1996. Law clk. Dept. Justice, San Francisco Superior Ct., San Francisco, 1996; prof. Oakland Coll. of Law, 1997—; lead counsel, assoc. Law Offices of M.B. Petersen, Oakland, 1994-96; pvt. practice San Francisco, 1996—; corp. cons. Kova and KASE C. of C., Silicon Valley, Calif., 1996—. Mem. ABA, Bar Assn. of San Francisco ( com. mem. litigation, intellectual properties and employment law), Calif. State Bar Assn. Avocations: running, art, swimming. Federal civil litigation, Contracts commercial, Intellectual property. Office: 114 Sansome St Ste 540 San Francisco CA 94104-3812

**SHIN, HELEN,** lawyer; b. Pa., Sept. 1, 1965. AB, Harvard U., 1987; JD, U. Calif., Berkeley, 1990. Bar: N.Y. 1991, Calif. 1991, U.S. Dist. Ct. (so. dist.) N.Y. 1997. Assoc. Debevoise & Plimpton, N.Y.C., 1990-94, Howard, Smith & Levin, N.Y.C., 1994-97; assoc. gen. counsel Nine West Group, White Plains, N.Y., 1997—. General corporate, Finance, Private international. Office: Nine West Group Inc 1129 Westchester Ave White Plains NY 10604-3549

**SHINDLER, DONALD A.,** lawyer; b. New Orleans, Oct. 15, 1946; s. Alan and Isolene (Levy) S.; m. Laura Epstein, 1969; children: Jay, Susan. BSBA, Washington U., St. Louis, 1968; JD, Tulane U., 1971. Bar: La. 1971, U.S. Dist. Ct. (ea. dist.) La. 1971, U.S. Tax Ct. 1974, Ill. 1975, U.S. Dist. Ct. (no. dist.) Ill. 1975; CPA, La.; lic. real estate broker, Ill. Assoc. Pope, Ballard, Shepard & Fowle, Chgo., 1975-78; assoc. Rudnick & Wolfe, Chgo., 1978-81, ptnr., 1981—; gen. counsel Second harvest Nat. Food Bank Network, 1998—; seminar lectr. ABA, Chgo. Bar Assn., Ill. Inst. CLE, Profl. Edn. Sys., Inc., Internat. Assn. Corp. Real Estate Execs., Urban Land Inst., Am. Corp. Counsel Assn., Bldg. Owners and Mgrs. Assn., others. Contbr. articles on real estate to legal jours. Trustee Glencoe (Ill.) Pub. Libr., 1981-87, pres., 1986-87; alumni bd. govs. Washington U., 1992-93; mem. Glencoe Zoning Commn./Bd. Appeals, 1994—. Lt. JAGC, USNR, 1971-75. Mem. ABA, La. State Bar Assn., Chgo. Bar Assn. (com. chmn. 1979-80, 83-84, 90-94, 96—, editor land trust seminars 1984-96), Urban Land Inst. (mem. exec. com. Chgo. dist. coun.), Internat. Assn. Corp. Real Estate Execs. (pres. Chgo. chpt. 1997-98, dir. 1991—), Internat. Assn. Attys. and Execs. in Corp. Real Estate, Union League Club (chair real estate group 1993-96), Order of Coif, Beta Gamma Sigma, Omicron Delta Kappa. Real property, General corporate, Environmental. Office: Rudnick & Wolfe 203 N La Salle St Ste 1800 Chicago IL 60601-1210

**SHINDURLING, JON J.,** prosecutor; b. Idaho Falls, Idaho, Apr. 13, 1947; s. Boyd Thomas and Donna Marie (Fullmer) S.; m. Christine Moss, May 24, 1974; children: Melissa, Marianne, Amanda, Alison. BA in English, Ariz. State U., 1972; JD, U. Idaho, 1977. Bar: Idaho. Ptnr. May & May Law Offices, Twin Falls, Idaho, 1977-88, Wright Law Offices, Idaho Falls, 1990-93; field dir. Sch. of Urban and Wilderness Survival, Shoshone, Idaho, 1988-90; dep. prosecuting atty. Bonneville County, Idaho Falls, 1994—, chief dep., 1995—; mem. continuing legal edn. com. Idaho Law Found., Boise, 1985-88; mem. civil jury instns. com. Idaho Supreme Ct., Boise, 1987-89, 96—. Mem. coun. exec. bd. Boy Scouts Am.-Snake River Area, Twin Falls, 1979-90; bd. dirs. Magic Valley YFCA, Twin Falls, 1988-90, Idaho Falls Opera Theatre, 1993—. Mem. Idaho State Bar (mem. bar examination com. 1979-82, chmn. com. 1980-82, mem. fee disputes resolution com. 1991—). Mem. LDS Ch. Avocations: reading, fishing, scouting. Office: Office Prosecuting Atty Bonneville County 605 N Capital Ave Idaho Falls ID 83402-3582

**SHINEVAR, PETER O'NEIL,** lawyer; b. Jackson, Mich., Oct. 3, 1955; m. Karen Kay Coats, Aug. 25, 1979. AB with high distinction, U. Mich., 1977, JD summa cum laude, 1980, postgrad., 1978-81. Bar: D.C. 1982, N.Y. 1994. Law clk. U.S. Ct. Appeals (D.C. cir.), Washington, 1981-82; assoc. Bredhoff & Kaiser, Washington, 1982-88, ptnr., 1989-92; assoc. dir. rsch. The Segal Co., 1992-95; spl. counsel O'Melveny & Myers, LLP, 1995—. Mem. ABA (sec. labor and employment law employer benefits com., mgmt. co-chair, subcom. on reporting and disclosure, sec. taxation, employee benefits com.), Assn. Assn. of the Bar of the City of N.Y., Order of the Coif, Phi Beta Kappa. Democrat. Pension, profit-sharing, and employee benefits, Labor. Office: O'Melveny & Myers LLP 153 E 53rd St Fl 54 New York NY 10022-4611

**SHINKLE, JOHN THOMAS,** lawyer; b. Albany, N.Y., May 9, 1946; s. Robert Thomas and Margery Joan (Kneip) S.; m. Csilla Elizabeth Bekasy, Sept. 2, 1967; children: Reka, Ildiko. BA, Yale U., 1967; JD, Harvard U., 1970. Bar: D.C. 1971, U.S. Supreme Ct. 1974, N.Y. 1983. Law clk. U.S. Ct. Appeals for D.C. Circuit, Washington, 1970-71; assoc. Caplin & Drysdale, Washington, 1971-77, ptnr., 1977-80; assoc. dir. div. corp. fin. SEC, Washington, 1980-81, dep. gen. counsel, 1981-82; gen. counsel Salomon Bros. Inc., N.Y.C., 1982-94, v.p. 1982-87, dir. 1988-94, Asia Pacific legal & compliance dir., 1995; mng. dir. Salomon Bros., Hong Kong, 1996-97; mng. dir. Salomon Smith Barney, Hong Kong, 1997—. Contbr. articles to profl. jours. Mem. ABA, Assn. of Bar of City of N.Y., Securities Industry Assn. (fed. regulation com. chmn. 1989-91), Futures Industry Assn. (dir. 1989-97). Club: Downtown Athetic (N.Y.C.). General corporate, Private international, Securities. Home: 1906C Queen's Garden, 9 Old Peak Rd, Hong Kong Hong Kong Office: Salomon Smith Barney, 3 Exchange Sq Fl 20, Hong Kong Hong Kong

**SHINMOTO, VANESSA M.,** lawyer; b. L.A., June 27, 1970; d. Thomas Hideo and Liddy Rafaela (Rodriguez) S. BA, UCLA, 1992; JD, Loyola U., L.A., 1997. Asst. editor Together newsmag., L.A., 1989-91; office asst. Law Offices of Kenneth M. Sigelman, Santa Monica, Calif., 1991-92; pub. info. intern ACLU, San Francisco, 1992; mkt. systems analyst Litigation Svcs. Inc., Culver City, Calif., 1993-94; law clk. Women's Advocacy Project, Austin, Tex., 1995, 96; intern Barristers Domestic Violence Project, L.A.,

1994-95. Recipient Pub. Interest Law Found. (Loyola U.) scholarship, 1995, student award for exemplary pub. svc. Nat. Assn. Pub. Interest Law, 1995. Avocation: yoga.

**SHINN, CLINTON WESLEY,** lawyer; b. Haworth, Okla., Mar. 7, 1947; s. Clinton Elmo and Mary Lucille (Dowdy) S.; m. Catherine Borne; children: Laura Kathryn, Clinton Wesley, Timothy Daniel. BS, McNeese State U., 1969; JD, Tulane U., 1972; LLM, Harvard U., 1973. Bar: La. 1972, U.S. Dist. Ct. (ea. dist.) La. 1975, U.S. Dist. Ct. (we. dist.) La. 1980, U.S. Ct. Appeals (5th cir.) 1981, U.S. Ct. Appeals (11th cir.) 1982, U.S. Tax Ct. (1982). Asst. prof. law Tulane U., New Orleans, 1973-75; assoc. Stone, Pigman et al, New Orleans, 1975-78, ptnr., 1979-97; ptnr. Gill & Shinn, LLC, Covington, La., 1998—; asst. prof. law Appalachian Sch. Law, 1999—; faculty advisor, 1974-75, editor in chief Tulane Law Rev., 1971-72. Editor in chief Tulane Law Rev., 1971-72. Co-founder, bd. dirs. Childhood Cancer Families Network, 1987-90; co-founder Camp Challenge, 1988; team leader Campaign for Caring, Children's Hosp., New Orleans, 1989-91; bd. dirs. Christ Episcopal Sch., Covington, 1988-91, chmn. long-range planning, 1990-91, exec. com., 1989-91, chmn. legal com., 1989-91, chmn. admissions/ recruitment com., 1988-90, mem. headmaster search com., 1993; bd. dirs. Greater New Orleans YMCA, 1989-98, 99—, exec. com., 1991-98, asst. sec., 1994-95, sec., 1996-98, mem. fin. com., 1994-98, exec. dir. search com., 1996, 2d vice-chair, 1998; mem. Leadership Coun., 1997-98; active Indian Guides/ Princesses; bd. dirs. West St. Tammany YMCA, 1987-95, exec. com., 1988-95, bd. chmn., 1989-90, 92-93; bd. dirs. Christwood, 1992-99, bd. v.p., 1997—; bd. dirs. La. Air & Waste Mgmt. Assn., 1993-99; chmn. corp. rels. com., 1992-93, vice-chmn., 1996-97, chair, 1997-98, past chair, 1998-99. Co-recipient Pals of the Yr. award Greater New Orleans YMCA Indian Guides/ Princesses, 1987-88; named Vol. of Yr. West St. Tammany YMCA, 1990, 92. Fellow Am. Coll. Trust and Estate Counsel, La. Bar Found., Northshore Estate Planning Coun.; mem. ABA, Nat. Assn. Securities Dealers (bd. arbitrators), Nat. Wildlife Fedn. (life), La. Bar Assn., La. Forestry Assn., New Orleans Bar Assn. (mem. ho. of dels. 1999—), New Orleans Estate Planning Coun., Northshore Estate Planning Coun., Air and Waste Mgmt. Assn., Order of Coif, Nat. Commn. for Planning Giving (New Orleans chpt.). Avocations: backpacking, gardening. Probate, General corporate, Environmental. Home: PO Box 694 Grundy VA 24614 Office: Gill & Shinn LLC 109 Northpark Blvd Ste 201 Covington LA 70433-5080 *In all things be firm but fair.*

**SHINN, MICHAEL ROBERT,** lawyer; b. Salem, Oreg., June 25, 1947; s. William Robert and Miriam Jean (Becke) S. BA, Willamette U., 1969, JD, 1973. Bar: Oreg. 1973, U.S. Dist. Ct. Oreg. 1973, U.S. Ct. Appeals (9th cir.) 1973. Law clk. to judge U.S. Dist. Ct., Portland, Oreg., 1974-75; pvt. practice Portland, 1975—; lectr. Masters at Trial Oreg., We. Trial Lawyers Assn., Oreg. State Bar, Mont. State Bar, Oreg. Law Inst., Nat. Bus. Inst. Editor Trial Lawyer Quar., 1988; dir., editor, producer: (videotape) (with Gerry Spence) Spence in Trial, 1989-90; co-producer, dir.: (videotape) Spence in Trial, Series for Trial Lawyers; cons. NBC mini-series Dead By Sunset, 1995. Pres. W. Hills and Island Neighbors Assn., Portland, 1983-84; del. Citizen to Citizen Legal Amb. Dels. to China, 1988; mem., bd. dirs. adv. coun. Oreg. Hearing Rsch. Ctr., 1992; bd. dirs. Portland Civic Theater. Inducted Willamette U. Athletic Hall of Fame, 1998. Mem. Oreg. Trial Lawyers Assn., (pres. 1980-81, edn. dir. 1984-89, svc. award 1986, 87), Am. Inns. of Ct. (master barrister 1988). Avocations: writing, wind surfing, skiing, water skiing, tennis, rugby. Personal injury, Civil rights, General civil litigation. Office: 621 SW Morrison St Ste 1000 Portland OR 97205-3821

**SHIPLEY, DAVID ELLIOTT,** dean, lawyer; b. Urbana, Ill., Oct. 3, 1950; s. James Ross and Dorothy Jean (Elliott) S.; m. Virginia Florence Coleman, May 24, 1980; 1 child, Shannon C. BA, Oberlin Coll., 1972; JD, U. Chgo., 1975. Bar: R.I. 1975. Assoc. Tillinghast, Collins & Graham, Providence, 1975-77; asst. prof. U. S.C. Sch. Law, Columbia, 1977-81, assoc. prof., 1981-85, prof., 1985-90, assoc. dean, 1989-90; dean U. Miss. Sch. Law, University, 1990-93, U. Ky. Coll. Law, Lexington, 1993-98; dean Sch. Law U. Ga., Athens, 1998—; vis. prof. Coll. William and Mary, Williamsburg, Va., 1983-84, Ohio State U. Coll. Law, Columbus, 1986-87. Author: South Carolina Administrative Law, 1983, 2d edit., 1989; co-author Copyright Law, 1992. Pres. Shandon Neighborhood Assn., Columbia, 1988-90. Named Prof. of Yr., U. S.C. Sch. Law, 1990, faculty scholar, 1989-90. Mem. ABA, R.I. Bar Assn., S.C. Bar Assn. (assoc.). Methodist. Avocations: running, yardwork, gardening, reading. Home: 475 River Bottom Rd Athens GA 30606-6430 Office: U Ga Sch Law Athens GA 30602-6012

**SHIPLEY, ROBERT ALLEN,** lawyer; b. Chgo., May 3, 1953; s. William Walter and Bernice (Allen) S.; m. Denise L. Sark, Jan. 2, 1989; children: Allyson Paige, Remy Taylor. BA in History, U. Ill., 1975; JD, No. Ill. U., 1978. Bar: Ill. 1979, U.S. Dist. Ct. (no. dist.) Ill. 1979. Assoc. Sheldon Oliver Zisook, Ltd., Chgo., 1979-80, Copeland Finn & Fieri, Ltd., Chgo., 1980-81, Gerald M. Sachs, Ltd., Chgo., 1981-82, Baskin Server Berke & Weinstein, Chgo., 1982-89; ptnr., pres. Shipley & Assocs., Ltd., Chgo., 1989—; instr. Am. Inst. Paralegal Studies, Chgo., 1990-92; spkr. Casualty Adjusters Assn., 1995. Mem. ABA, Ill. State Bar Assn. (civil practice com. 1997—, past chair interprofl. coop. com.), Chgo. Bar Assn. Avocations: music, literature, basketball. General civil litigation, Insurance, Personal injury. Office: Shipley & Assocs Ltd 415 N Lasalle St Ste 300 Chicago IL 60610-4541

**SHIPP, DAN SHACKELFORD,** lawyer; b. Yazoo City, Miss., Jan. 6, 1946; s. Dan Hugh and Anora Nona (Shackelford) A.; m. Carolyn Julie Perry, Nov. 30, 1974; children: Perry Lee, Clay Alexander. AA, Holmes Jr. Coll., 1966; BA, Miss. State U., 1968; JD, U. Miss., 1971. Bar: Miss. 1971, U.S. Dist. Ct. (no. dist.) Miss. 1971, U.S. Dist. Ct. (so. dist.) Miss. 1976, Colo. 1986, U.S. Ct. Appeals (5th cir.) 1982, U.S. Ct. Appeals (10th cir.) 1986, U.S. Dist. Ct. Colo. 1986. Pvt. practice Yazoo City, Miss., 1974-83, Aspen, 1986—; speaker in field. Recipient Master Advocate Cert. award Nat. Inst. for Trial Advocacy, 1993. Mem. ABA, Colo. Trial Lawyers Assn. (bd. dirs. 1986-88), Assn. Trial Lawyers Am., Colo. Bar Assn., Toastmasters Internat. Maroon Creek Club. Avocations: hunting, archery, traveling. E-mail: grand@rof.net. Fax: 970-925-1599. Personal injury, General civil litigation, General practice. Office: 407 J AABC PO Box 8629 Aspen CO 81612-8629

**SHIPP, ROSE LEVADA,** lawyer; b. Jersey City, N.J., Sept. 24, 1934; d. Anthony and Joyce Waldean (Gilbert) DeGregorio; m. David Crenshaw Shipp, Sept. 11, 1954; children: David Anthony (dec.) Sallie Dean, Daniel Linwood. BA magna cum laude, U. Louisville, Ky., 1970, JD, 1972. Bar: Ky. 1973. Student intern U.S. Atty.'s Office, Louisville, 1971-72; solo practice, Louisville, 1973-76, Taylorsville, Ky., 1979-86; asst. Commonwealth's atty., Louisville, 1976-78. Mem. Young Reps. Am., Louisville, 1968-72; treas., v.p. Republican Attys. of Louisville, 1973-75; precinct capt., 1974-75; audio tester Head Start, Louisville, 1964-65; Pres., Woodcock Honor Soc., U. Louisville, 1973. Mem. Ky. Bar Assn. Home: 2781 Maple Rd Louisville KY 40205-1735 Office: Rose Levada Shipp Atty at Law PO Box 483 Main St 2781 Maple Rd Louisville KY 40205-1735

**SHIPPER, DAVID W.,** lawyer; b. N.Y.C., Oct. 30, 1958; s. Herbert K. and Judith S. (Sigall) S. BA, NYU, 1979; JD, N.Y. Law Sch., 1982. Bar: N.Y. 1983, N.J. 1983, Fla. 1984; U.S. Dist. Ct. N.J. 1983, U.S. Dist. Ct. (so. and ea. dists.) N.Y. 1983; U.S. Tax Ct. 1989. Pvt. practice N.Y.C., 1983—. Trustee N.Y. Law Sch., 1999—. Mem. ABA, N.Y. State Bar Assn., N.Y. Law Sch. Alumni Assn. (dir. 1983—, treas. 1991-95, v.p. 1995-99, pres. 1999—), Phi Delta Phi. Probate, Real property, Taxation, general. Home: 201 E 69th St New York NY 10021-5471 Office: 567 3d Ave New York NY 10016

**SHIPPEY, SANDRA LEE,** lawyer; b. Casper, Wyo., June 24, 1957; d. Virgil Carr and Doris Louise (Conklin) McClintock; m. Ojars Herberts Ozols, Sept. 2, 1978 (div.); children: Michael Ojars, Sara Ann, Brian Christopher; m. James Robert Shippey, Jan. 13, 1991; 1 child, Matthew James. BA with distinction, U. Colo., 1978; JD magna cum laude, Boston U., 1982. Bar: Colo. 1982, U.S. Dist. Ct. Colo. 1985. Assoc. Cohen, Brame & Smith, Denver, 1983-84, Parcel, Meyer, Schwartz, Ruttum & Mauro, Denver, 1984-85, Mayer, Brown & Platt, Denver, 1985-87; counsel western ops. GE Capital Corp., San Diego, 1987-94; assoc. Page, Polin, Busch & Boatwright, San Diego, 1994-95; v.p., gen. counsel First Comml. Corp., San Diego, 1995-96; legal counsel NextWave Telecom Inc., San Diego, 1996-98; of counsel Procopio, Cory, Hargreaves and Savitch, LLP, 1998—. Active Pop Warner football and cheerleading. Mem. Phi Beta Kappa, Phi Delta Phi. Republican. Mem. Ch. of Christ. Avocations: tennis, photography. Banking, General corporate, Finance. Home: 15839 Big Springs Way San Diego CA 92127 Office: Procopio Cory Et Al 530 B St Ste 2100 San Diego CA 92101-4496

**SHIRE, HAROLD RAYMOND,** law educator, author, scientist; b. Denver, Nov. 23, 1910; s. Samuel Newport and Rose Betty (Herman) S.; m. Cecilia Goldhaar, May 9, 1973; children: David, Darcy, Esti. MBA, Pepperdine U., 1972, LLD (hon.), 1975; JD, Southwestern U., L.A., 1974; M in Liberal Arts, U. So. Calif., 1977; PhD in Human Behavior, U.S. Internat. U., San Diego, 1980. Bar: Calif. 1937, U.S. Dist. Ct. (so. dist.) Calif. 1939, U.S. Supreme Ct. 1978. Dep. dist. atty. L.A. County, Calif., 1937-38; asst. U.S. atty. So. Dist. Calif., L.A. and San Diego, 1939-42; pvt. practice L.A., 1946-56; pres., chmn. bd. Gen. Connectors Corp., U.S. and Eng., 1956-73; prof. mgmt. and law Pepperdine U., Malibu, Calif., 1974-75, U.S. Internat. U., San Diego, 1980-83; dir. Bestobell Aviation, Eng., 1970-74. Author: Cha No Yu and Symbolic Interactionism: Method of Predicting Japanese Behavior, 1980, The Tea Ceremony, 1984. Patentee aerospace pneumatics; invented flexible connectors; designed, manufactured flexible integrity systems. Advisor U. S.C. Gerontology Andrus Ctr., pre-retirement tng., 1976-80; bd. dirs. Pepperdine U., 1974-80; nat. bd. govs. Union Orthodox Jewish Congregations Am., 1973—; mem. Rep. Nat. Com.; pres. Jewish Nat. Fund Legion of Honor, 1991—; mem. Presdl. Roundtable, Washington, 1989-97. With U.S. Army, 1942-46. Decorated chevalier du vieux moulin (France); companion Royal Aero. Soc. (U.K.); recipient Tea Name Grand Master Soshitsu Sen XV Urasenke Sch., Kyoto, Japan, 1976, Medal of Honor Jewish Nat. Fund, Legion of Honor, 1991, U.S. Senate Medal of Freedom. Mem. Am. Legion (svc. officer China #1 Shanghai), Calif. Symphony Soc. (pres. 1998—), Masons (32 degree, Hiram award 1994), Royal Arch, Shrine, Legion of Honor Jewish Nat. Fund (chmn. 1998). Achievements include design and manufacture of fluidic systems flexible integrity for Saturn IV and welding in Apollo XI landing on moon, 1969. Office: PO Box 1352 Beverly Hills CA 90213-1352

**SHIRK, JENNIFER CONN,** lawyer; b. Pensacola, Fla., Nov. 10, 1957; d. Kenneth Eugene and Peggy (Halleen) Conn; m. Gregory Allen Shirk, Nov. 9, 1991. AA, Coll. of Sequoias, Visalia, Calif., 1977; BA, U. Calif., Berkeley, 1980; JD, U. San Diego, 1986. Bar: Calif. Sole practitioner Visalia, 1986—. Bd. dirs. Family Svcs. of Tulare County, Visalia, 1996—, Tulare/Kings Legal Svcs., visalia, 1992-96, Ct. Apptd. Spl. Advocates, Visalia, 1989-91. Mem. Tulare County Bar Assn. (bd. dirs. 1998—), Soroptimist. Republican. Christian. Family and matrimonial, Juvenile, Professional liability. Office: 2929 W Main St Ste D Visalia CA 93291-5700

**SHIRTZ, JOSEPH FRANK,** lawyer, consultant; b. Yeadon, PA, June 26, 1959; s. Raymond Loren and Ann Gredel (Lutz) S.; m. Catherine Irene Enright, Sept. 6, 1987; children: Ryan, Erin. BSME, U. Ala., Tuscaloosa, 1981; JD, Villanova, 1984. Bar: Pa. 1984, N.Y. 1985, N.J. 1986, U.S. Dist. Ct. N.J. 1986, U.S. Patent Office 1985, U.S. Ct. Appeals (fed. cir.) 1986. Law clk. Ct. of Common Pleas, Norristown, Pa., 1983; assoc. Pennie & Edmonds, N.Y.C., 1984-87; patent atty. Johnson & Johnson, New Brunswick, N.J., 1987-94, supervisory atty., 1994-98; assoc. patent counsel Johnson & Johnson, New Brunswick, 1998—. Mem. N.J., N.Y. Intellectual Property Law Assn. Patent, Taxation, general. Office: Johnson & Johnson One Johnson & Johnson Plaza New Brunswick NJ 08933-0001

**SHKLAR, MICHAEL CHARLES,** lawyer; b. Boston, Sept. 28, 1960; s. Gerald and Judith (Nisse) S.; m. Carol Marie Stamatakis, Mar. 23, 1985; children: Rachel, Abraham. BA, Carleton Coll., 1982; JD, Case Western Res. U., 1985. Bar: N.H. 1985, U.S. Dist. Ct. N.H. 1985, U.S. Ct. Appeals 1990, U.S. Ct. Vet. Appeals 1990, U.S. Supreme Ct. 1992, U.S. Tax Ct. 1993. Assoc. Feeney & Kraeger, Newport, N.H., 1985, Elliott & Jasper, Newport, 1986-87; pvt. practice Newport, 1987—. Pres. bd. Orion House, Inc., Newport, 1986-95; bd. dirs. Women's Supportive Svcs., Claremont, N.H., 1987-94, gen. counsel, 1994—; mem. Goshen Lempster (N.H.) Sch. Bd., 1988-93, chair, 1990-91; moderator Lempster (N.H.) Sch. Dist., 1998—, Town of Lempster (N.H.) 1998—. Mem. ATLA, N.H. Bar Assn. (mem. fee dispute resolution com. 1988-90, bd. govs. 1992-94, Pro Bono Atty. of Yr. 1987, 89, 91, 92), Sullivan County Bar Assn. (sec.-treas. 1998-99), N.H. Trial Lawyers Assn. (bd. govs. 1994-96). Democrat. Avocations: reading, cooking. General practice, Juvenile, Bankruptcy. Home: Schrenk Rd Lempster NH 03606 Office: PO Box 297 Newport NH 03773-0297

**SHLACKMAN, MARA,** lawyer; b. Miami, June 5, 1968; d. Carl and Lenora Glick S. BA, U. Miami, 1990, JD, 1993. Bar: Fla., U.S. Dist. Ct. (so. and mid. dists.) Fla. 1996. Atty. Fla. Dept. Health & Rehab. Svcs., Miami, 1994; assoc. Montero, Finizio, Velasquez, Weissing & Reyes, P.A., Ft. Lauderdale, 1995—. Bd. dirs. Broward Young Dems., Ft. Lauderdale, 1998; sec. Broward UM Alumni Club, Ft. Lauderdale, 1997—; mem. Young Profls. for Mara House, Ft. Lauderdale, 1996—. Mem. Broward County Bar Assn. (publs. com. 1998—), Toastmasters (pres. 1997-98). Avocations: travel, jogging, reading, art exhibitions. Office: Montero Finizio et al 200 SE 9th St Fort Lauderdale FL 33316-1020

**SHMUKLER, STANFORD,** lawyer; b. Phila., June 16, 1930; s. Samuel and Tessye (Dounne) S.; m. Anita Golove, Mar. 21, 1951; children—Jodie Lynne Shmukler Girsh, Joel Mark, Steven David. B.S. in Econs., U. Pa., 1951, J.D., 1954. Bar: D.C. 1954, Pa. 1955; U.S. Ct. Appeals (2d cir.), 1959, U.S. Supreme Ct. 1959, U.S. Ct. Appeals (3d cir.), 1960, U.S. Ct. Claims, 1966, U.S. Tax Ct., 1966, U.S. Ct. Mil. Appeals 1966. Atty., U.S. Bur. Pub. Roads, 1954-55, cons., 1955-57; sole practice, Phila., 1955—; lectr. Temple U. Law Sch., 1975-78; mem., past sec., exec. dir. crminal procedural rules com. Pa. Supreme Ct., 1971-87; mem. lawyers adv. com. Ct. Appeals for 3d cir., 1977-80, selection com. Criminal Justice Act Panel, 1979-84; chmn. selection com. Phila. Bar Ct. Appointments, 1988-91. Bd. dirs. Ecumenical Halfway House, 1967-71; bd. mgrs. Alumni Assn. Ctrl. High Sch., Phila. Served to col. JAGC, USAR, from 1955 (ret.). Recipient Phila. Bar Assn. Criminal Justice Sect. award, 1977, Justice Thurgood Marshall award, 1992; Legion of Honor, Chapel of the Four Chaplains, 1983. Mem. ABA, Pa. Bar Assn., Phila. Bar Assn. (bd. govs. 1971-73, past chmn. criminal justice com. and mil. justice com.), Fed. Bar Assn. (chmn. criminal law com. adminstrn. justice sect., co-chmn. criminal law com. Phila. chpt., Leadership award Phila. 1991, 94), Pa. Assn. Criminal Def. Lawyers, Nat. Assn. Criminal Def. Lawyers. Democrat. Jewish. Lodges: Justice Lodge, B'nai B'rith. Contbr. articles to profl. jours. Criminal, Military, Family and matrimonial. Home: 1400 Melrose Ave Melrose Park PA 19027-3155 Office: Packard Bldg 24th Fl 111 S 15th St Philadelphia PA 19102-2625

**SHOAFF, THOMAS MITCHELL,** lawyer; b. Ft. Wayne, Ind., Aug. 21, 1941; s. John D. and Agnes H. (Hanna) S.; m. Eunice Swedberg, Feb. 7, 1970; children: Andrew, Nathaniel, Matthew-John. BA, Williams Coll., 1964; JD, Vanderbilt U., 1967. Bar: Ind. 1968. Assoc. Isham, Lincoln & Beale, Chgo., 1967-68; ptnr. Baker & Daniels, Ft. Wayne, Ind., 1968—; bd. dirs. Weaver Popcorn Co., Inc., Ft. Wayne, Dreibelbiss Title Co., Inc., Ft. Wayne, Am. Steel Investment Corp., Ft. Wayne. Bd. dirs. McMillen Found., Ft. Wayne, Wilson Found., Ft. Wayne. Mem. ABA, Allen County Bar Assn., Ind. State Bar Assn. Presbyterian. Avocations: golf, sailing. General corporate. Office: Baker & Daniels 111 E Wayne St Ste 800 Fort Wayne IN 46802-2603

**SHOCKEY, GARY LEE,** lawyer; b. Casper, Wyo., Sept. 25, 1950; s. Bernis L. and Shirley E. (Diehl) S.; m. Dona K. Galles, June 1, 1979; children: Amber, Jeremy, Kimberly. AB in Polit. Sci. and Sociology, Yale U., 1973; JD, U. Wyo., 1976. Bar: Wyo. 1976, U.S. Dist. Ct. Wyo. 1976, U.S. Ct. Appeals (10th cir.) 1984, U.S. Ct. Appeals (9th cir.) 1988, U.S. Claims Ct. 1989, U.S. Supreme Ct. 1989, U.S. Ct. Appeals (fed. cir.) 1993, U.S. Dist. Ct. Ariz. 1994. Pub. defender State of Wyo. and City of Casper, 1976-78; sole practice, Casper, 1976-79; assoc. Spence, Moriarity & Schuster, Casper and Jackson, Wyo., 1978-82, ptnr., Jackson, 1982—. Mem. ABA, Wyo. State Bar (continuing legal edn. com. 1984-85, law and legis. reform com. 1986-88), Assn. Trial Lawyers Am., Wyo. Trial Lawyer's Assn. (bd. dirs. 1984-90). Personal injury, State civil litigation, Federal civil litigation. Office: Spence Moriarty & Schuster PO Box 548 Jackson WY 83001-0548

**SHOEMAKER, BOBBY LYNN,** lawyer; b. Bay Springs, Miss., Jan. 1, 1952; s. Dewey O'Farrell and Doris Ann (Evans) S.; m. Lillous Faye Alexander, Jan. 1, 1971; children: Megan Leigh, Lillous An, Bobby Barr, Joanna Ophelia. BA in History and Polit. Sci., U. So. Miss., 1974; JD, U. Miss., 1977. Bar: Miss. 1977, U.S. Dist. Ct. (no. and so. dists.) Miss. 1977. Pvt. practice Bay Springs, 1977—; mem. adv. bd. First United Bank, Bay Springs, 1983-89; referee Jasper County Youth Ct., Bay Springs, 1984—, Jasper County Lunancy Ct., Bay Springs, 1984—. Mem. ABA, ATLA, Miss. Bar Assn., Miss. Trial Lawyers Assn., Miss. Prosecutors Assn. (bd. dirs. 1980-83), Bay Springs C. of C. (pres. 1984-85), Rotary (sec. Bay Springs 1977, v.p. 1978, pres. 1979). Methodist. Consumer commercial, General practice, Criminal. Office: 44 5th St # 258 Bay Springs MS 39422

**SHOEMAKER, DANIEL W.,** lawyer; b. Harrisburg, Pa., Mar. 20, 1931; s. Norville Eugene and Victoria S.; m. Eleanor Boggs, Apr. 9, 1955 (div. 1987); children: Daniel W., William B.; m. Suzanne Leapley, July 3, 1987. BS, Millersville U., Pa., 1952; JD, Washington U., D.C., 1956. Bar: D.C. 1956, U.S. Ct. Appeals (3rd cir.) 1956, Pa. 1957. Dist. atty. York County, Pa., 1962-65; pvt. practice law York, Pa., 1989—. Del. Pa. State Constl. Conv., 1976. With U.S. Army, 1949-52. Mem. York County Bar Assn. (pres. 1976), Pa. Bar Assn. (del. 978-88). Republican. Episcopalian. Avocations: fox hunting, farming, sailing. General practice, Family and matrimonial, General civil litigation. Home: 12711 Shoemaker Rd Taneytown MD 21787-1005

**SHOEN, LYNN RENÉE,** lawyer; b. Spokane, Wash., Jan. 4, 1952; d. George William and Verna Clara Shoen; 1 child, Cameron Scott Christopher. BA, U. Nev., 1974; JD, Calif. Western U., 1978. Intern Sen. Howard Cannon U.S. Senate, Washington, 1975; law clk. Nev. Supreme Ct., Carson City, Nev., 1978-79; dep. dist. atty. Clark County Dist. Atty.'s Office, Las Vegas, Nev., 1979-81; assoc. Cromer, Barker, Michaelson, Gillock & Rawlings, Las Vegas, Nev., 1981-83; pres. Lynn P. Shoen Chartered, Las Vegas, Nev., 1983—; Pres. Pro Bono Project, Las Vegas, 1995—, counselor's counsellor, 1985. Contbr. articles to profl. jours. Recipient Disting. Svc. award Pro Bono Project, 1996. Mem. Nev. State Bar Assn., Clark County Bar Assn., So. Nev. Assn. Women Attys. Democrat. Avocations: art, writing. Office: 801 S Rancho Dr Ste A1 Las Vegas NV 89106-3870

**SHOENBERGER, ALLEN EDWARD,** law educator; b. Waynesburg, Pa., Sept. 18, 1944; s. Allen Edward and Evelyn S.; m. Cynthia Grant (div. 1975); 1 child, Michael Grant; m. Caroline Orzac, Aug. 3, 1980; 1 child, Elisa Orzac. BA with honors, Swarthmore Coll., 1966; JD with honors, Columbia U., 1969; LLM, NYU, 1972. Bar: Ill. 1973, U.S. Dist. Ct. (no. dist.) Ill. 1973, U.S. Ct. Appeals (7th cir.) 1977, U.S. Supreme Ct. 1977. Vis. lectr. U. Nairobi, Kenya, 1969-71; fellow Internat. Legal Ctr., Nairobi, 1969-71; asst. prof. Loyola U., Chgo., 1972-77, assoc. prof., 1977-85, prof., 1985—, chmn. faculty coun., 1983—; cons. Adminstrv. Conf. U.S., Washington, 1988; mem. Ill. A.G. Task Force for Handicapped, 1982—; chmn. adv. bldg. com. Cir. Ct. of Cook County, Chgo., 1988-93. Editor Spina Bifida publ., 1985-93, East African Law Reports, 1969-71, Jour. Nat. Assn. Adminstrv. Law Judges, 1996—; contbr. articles to profl. publs. Mem. Ill. Spina Bifida Assn., Chgo., 1980-93; hearing officer Ill. Pollution Control Bd., 1974-97, U.S. Dept. Energy, Ill., 1984-89. Recipient various grants, including NIE, 1973; fellow Ford Found., 1972, NEH, 1987. Mem. ABA, Fed. Bar Assn., Chgo. Bar Assn. (chmn. adminstrv. law com. 1985-86). Office: Loyola Sch of Law 1 E Pearson St Chicago IL 60611-2055

**SHOFF, PATRICIA ANN,** lawyer; b. Colby, Kans., Sept. 27, 1948; d. Clarence O. and Clara C. (Ortbal) Shoff; m. Thomas E. Salsbery, Oct. 6, 1979; children: Emily Anne, Edward Philip. BA with honors, U. Iowa, 1970, JD with distinction, 1973. Bar: Iowa 1973, U.S Dist. Ct. (no. and so. dists.) Iowa 1974. Law clk. Supreme Ct. of Iowa, Des Moines, 1973-74; assoc. Thoma Schoenthal Davis, Hockenberg & Wine, Des Moines, 1974-79; ptnr., shareholder Davis, Brown, Koehn, Shors & Roberts, P.C., Des Moines, 1979—; vice chair bd. law examiners Iowa Supreme Ct., 1991-95. Sec. bd. dirs. Iowa's Children and Families, 1980-91, v.p. 1981-82, pres. 1982-83, Very Spl. Arts Iowa, 1988-93, sec. 1990, chair pers. com., 1990-92, pres. 1992, chair resource devel. com. 1992—; mem. Gov.'s Com. Child Abuse Prevention, 1982-92, chair 1987-92; co-chair fundraising com. Hospice of Ctrl. Iowa, 1983-85; pub. rels. com. mem. St. Augustin's Ch., 1986-87; exec. bd. Mid-Iowa Coun. Boy Scouts Am., 1988—, nominating com., 1989-91, Homestead bd. dirs., 1993, pres.-elect, 1994, pres., 1995. Mem. ABA (family law sect., labor, employment law sect.), AAUW (juvenile justice com. 1974-76), Iowa Law Sch. Found. (bd. dirs. 1992—), Iowa State Bar Assn. (young lawyers sect., family law com. 1979-81, membership com. 1979-81, chair legal aid com. 1981-85, labor and employment law com. 1991-92, bd. govs. 1995—others), Iowa Supreme Ct. Bd. Law Examiners (vice-chair 1991-95), Polk County Bar Assn. (treas. 1989-92, v.p. 1992-93, pres. elect 1993, pres. 1994, Merit award 1990), Womens Fedn. Lawyers, Greater Des Moines C. of C. Fedn. (bd. dirs. 1984-85, bur. econ. devel. com. 1985—, exec. call com. 1985—), Polk County Women Attys., Iowa Orgn. Women Attys., Greater Des Moines C. of C. Leadership Inst. (pres. bd. govs. 1984-85, alumni orgn. 1984—), Jr. League (adv. planning 1983-84, placement advisor 1986-87, grants com. 1988), Phi Delta Phi. Democrat. Roman Catholic. Workers' compensation, Family and matrimonial, Labor. Office: Davis Brown Koehn Shors & Roberts 2500 Fin Ctr 666 Walnut St Des Moines IA 50309-3904

**SHOLLENBERGER, ELIZABETH ANN,** lawyer; b. Alliance, Ohio, Mar. 26, 1956; d. Herbert Russell and Nancy Marie (Craven) S. AB, Princeton U., 1978; JD, Yale U., 1981. Bar: N.Y. 1982, U.S. Dist. Ct. (so. and ea. dists.) N.Y. 1983. Assoc. Rosenman, Colin, Freund, Lewis & Cohn, N.Y.C., 1981-83, Milberg, Weiss, Bershad, Specthrie & Lerach, N.Y.C., 1983-85; corp. atty. Hess, Segall, Guterman, Pelz, Steiner & Barovick, N.Y.C., 1985-86; faculty Law Sch. NYU, 1986-88; atty. housing unit Bronx Legal Svcs., N.Y.C., 1988—. Pres. Village Reform Dem. Club, N.Y.C., 1983-86; Dem. Dist. leader, Greenwich Village, 1986-95; mem. Cmty. Bd. 2, N.Y.C., 1986-95. Federal civil litigation, State civil litigation, Landlord-tenant. Home: 60 E 9th St Apt 533 New York NY 10003-6445

**SHOOB, MARVIN H.,** federal judge; b. Walterboro, S.C., Feb. 23, 1923; s. Michael Louis and Lena (Steinberg) S.; m. Janice Paradies, Nov. 14, 1949; children: Michael, Wendy. Student, Ga. Inst. Tech., Va. Mil. Inst., 1942-43, 46; J.D., U. Ga., 1948. Bar: Ga. 1948. Ptnr. Brown & Shoob, Atlanta, 1949-55; ptnr. Phillips, Johnson & Shoob, Atlanta, 1955-56, Shoob, McLain & Merritt, Atlanta, 1956-79; judge U.S. Dist. Ct., Atlanta, 1979-91, sr. judge, 1991—; chmn. Juvenile Ct. Com., 1964-70; mem. Ga. State Bar Grievance Tribunal, 1975-79; chmn. Ga. State Bar Fed. Legislation Com., 1977-79; guest lectr. Continuing Legal Edn., Athens, Ga., 1975-77. Chmn. 5th Dist. Democratic Exec. Com., 1974-76. Mem. Phi Eta Sigma, Phi Kappa Phi. Jewish. Office: US Dist Ct 1921 US Courthouse 75 Spring St SW Atlanta GA 30303-3309

**SHOOK, ANN JONES,** lawyer; b. Canton, Ohio, Apr. 18, 1925; d. William M. and Lura (Pontius) Jones; m. Gene E. Shook Sr., Nov. 30, 1956; children: Scott, William, Gene Edwin Jr. AB, Wittenberg U., 1947; LLB, William McKinley Law Sch., 1955. Bar: Ohio 1956, U.S. Dist. Ct. (no. dist.) Ohio 1961, U.S. Ct. Appeals (6th cir.) 1981. Cost acct. Hoover Co., North Canton, Ohio, 1947-51; asst. sec. Stark County Prosecutor's Office, Canton, Ohio, 1951-53; ins. adjuster Traveler's Ins. Co., Canton, 1953-56; ptnr. Shook & Shook, Toledo, 1958-62, North Olmsted, Ohio, 1962—. Mem. at large coun. Olmsted Community Ch., Olmsted Falls, Ohio, 1987-90; chmn. ways and means com. North Olmsted PTA, 1968; area chmn. United Way Appeal, North Olmsted, 1963; v.p. LWV, Toledo, 1960-62. Mem. Cleve. Bar Assn. Avocations: reading, boating, dancing, fitness. Estate planning, Probate, Personal income taxation.

**SHOOSTER, FRANK MALLORY,** lawyer; b. Chester, Pa., Feb. 22, 1954; s. Herman and Dorothy (Schluger) S. BA in Philosophy and Poli. Sci., Antioch Coll., 1977; postgrad., U. Chgo., 1978; JD, U. Miami, 1982. Bar: Fla. 1982, U.S. Dist. Ct. (so. dist.) Fla. 1984, U.S. Ct. Appeals (11th cir.) 1995, U.S. Dist. Ct. (mid. dist.) Fla. 1997, U.S. Dist. Ct. (cen. dist.) Ill. 1997; bd. cert. civil trial law Fla. Bar, 1992. Instr. philosophy Antioch Coll., Yellow Springs, Ohio, 1974; rsch. aide U.S. Libr. Congress, Washington, 1975-76; legis. aide select com. on small bus. U.S. Senate, Washington, 1975-76; legis. aide to Senators Thomas McIntyre and William D. Hathaway,

1976; now mng. ptnr. Frank Mallory Shooster P.A., Ft. Lauderdale; cert. mediator Fla. Supreme Ct., 1991. Guest columnist Miami Herald, 1988. Atty. conservation com. Audubon Soc. Broward County, FT. Lauderdale, 1983-85; at-large rep. Environ Leaders Coun., 1983-86. Mem. ABA, ACLU, Assn. Trial Lawyers Am., Acad. Fla. Trial Lawyers (jour. columnist 1991, 92), Broward County Trial Lawyers Assn. Democrat. Personal injury, General civil litigation, Civil rights. Office: 777 S State Road 7 Margate FL 33068-2803

**SHORE, HEATHER FIELD,** lawyer; b. Greenville, S.C., July 23, 1968; d. Kenneth M. Shore and Nelda C. Leon. BS in Mktg., U. Colo., 1990; JD, Loyola U., Chgo., 1996. Bar: Colo. 1996. Sales exec. WNOK FM 100, Columbia, S.C., 1991-93; extern judge Rebecca R. Pallmeyer Chgo., 1994, 95; atty. Kennedy & Christopher, P.C., Denver, 1996-97, Tilly & Graves, P.C., Denver, 1997—. Vol. Law Line Ch. 9, Denver, 1998—. Mem. ABA, Colo. Bar Assn., Denver Bar Assn., Def. Rsch. Inst. Product liability, General civil litigation, General corporate. Office: Tilly & Graves PC 1050 17th St Ste 2500 Denver CO 80265-2080

**SHORES, JANIE LEDLOW,** retired state supreme court justice; b. Georgiana, Ala., Apr. 30, 1932; d. John Wesley and Willie (Scott) Ledlow; m. James L. Shores, Jr., May 12, 1962; 1 child, Laura Scott. J.D., U. Ala., Tuscaloosa, 1959; AB, Samford U., 1968; LLM, U. Va., 1992. Bar: Ala. 1959. Pvt. practice Selma, 1959; mem. legal dept. Liberty Nat. Life Ins. Co., Birmingham, Ala., 1962-66; assoc. prof. law Cumberland Sch. Law, Samford U., Birmingham, 1966-74; assoc. justice Supreme Ct. Ala., 1975-99; legal adviser Ala. Constn. Revision Commn., 1973; mem. Nat. Adv. Coun. State Ct. Planning, 1976—. Contbr. articles to legal jours. Bd. dirs. State Justice Inst., 1995-98. Mem. Am. Bar Assn., Am. Judicature Soc., Farrah Order Jurisprudence. Democrat. Episcopalian. Office: Ala Supreme Ct Rm 520 Jefferson County Courthouse Birmingham AL 35263-0054

**SHORR, SCOTT ALDEN,** lawyer; b. N.Y.C., July 5, 1968; s. Ronald Philip and Jean Fishack Shorr. AB, Vassar Coll., 1990; JD, U. Calif., Berkeley, 1995. Bar: Oreg. 1996, U.S. Dist. Ct. Oreg. 1997, U.S. Ct. Appeals (9th cir.) 1998. Law clk. to Hon. Richard L. Unis Oreg. Supreme Ct., Salem, 1995-96; assoc. Stoll Stoll Berne Lokting & Shlachter, Portland, Oreg., 1996—. Contbr. articles to profl. jours. Pres. bd. dirs. Hands On Portland, 1998—. Mem. Oreg. Trial Lawyers Assn., Multnomah Bar Assn., Fed. Bar Assn. Democrat. Avocations: soccer, music, politics. Federal civil litigation, Appellate, Securities. Office: Stoll Stoll Berne Lokting & Shlachter 209 SW Oak St Ste 500 Portland OR 97204-2798

**SHORS, JOHN D.,** lawyer; b. Ft. Dodge, Iowa, July 21, 1937; s. George A. and Catherine (Shaw) S.; m. Patricia Ann Percival, Oct. 7, 1967; children: John, Tom, Matt, Luke. BSEE, Iowa State U., 1959; JD, U. Iowa, 1964. Bar: Iowa, U.S. Supreme Ct. Assoc. then shareholder Davis, Brown, Koehn, Shors & Roberts, P.C., Des Moines, 1964—. Co-author: Closely Held Corporations in Business and Estate Planning, 1982. Pres. Mercy Hosp. Found., Des Moines, 1981-84; chair Iowa State U. Found., Ames, 1989-92; bd. dirs. Mercy Housing, Denver, 1992—. Cpl. U.S. Army, 1960-61. Recipient Iowa State U. Alumni medal, YLS Merit award Iowa State Bar Assn. Mem. Iowa State Bar Assn. (pres. 1992) Iowa Women Profl. Corp. (Good Guy award 1987), Iowa Rsch. Coun. (bd. dirs. 1994—), Am. Judicature Soc. (bd. dirs. 1974-79), Polk County Bar Assn. (pres. 1986), Rotary (Des Moines chpt.), DM Club, Glenoaks C.C. Republican. Roman Catholic. Office: Davis Brown Koehn Shors & Roberts PC 666 Walnut St Ste 2500 Des Moines IA 50309-3904

**SHORT, DAVID CARLOS,** lawyer, educator; b. Harlan County, Ky., May 30, 1938; s. Carless and Fannie Elizabeth (Smith) S.; m. Teri Davis, Sept. 1, 1976; children—David C., Samuel James, Rachel Davis. B.A., U. Ky., 1964, J.D., 1966; M.Internat. and Comparative Law, Vrije U., Brussels, 1975. Bar: Ky. 1967, Tenn. 1981. atty., co-dir. N.E. Ky. Legal Services, Morehead, 1967-69; gen. counsel Ky. Dept. Health, Frankfort, 1969-71; legis. counsel Peace Corps Moen Trust Territory of Pacific Islands, 1971; asst. atty. gen., 1973-78; sr. atty. Appalachian Research and Def. Fund, Lexington, Ky., 1971-72; regional dir. Office of Surface Mining, U.S. Dept. Interior, Knoxville, Tenn., 1978-81; assoc. Stites, McElwain & Fowler, Frankfort, 1981-82; dir., assoc. prof. Mineral Law Ctr., U. Ky. Coll. Law, Lexington, 1983-93; assoc. prof. Ky., 1983-87; dir. Mineral Law Ctr., 1983-93; prof. 1987-93; dean, prof. of law No. Ky. U. Chase Coll. Law, 1993-99; lectr. in field; trustee Eastern Mineral Law Found., chmn. teaching com., 1985, exec. com. 1987-92, designated trustee and governing mem., 1995—. Served with U.S. Army, 1962-63. Designated Pres. Meritorius Exec. by Pres. Jimmy Carter, 1980. Mem. ABA (co-chmn. acad. affairs of coal subcom. of natural resources sect. 1985, chmn. coal subcom., sec. natural resource environ. law, 1989-92, vice chair, 1983-89), Ky. Bar Assn. (organizer, first chmn. sect. of natural resources law 1983-84), Tenn. Bar Assn. Methodist. Club: Masons. Author: Pollution Viewed as an International Crime: Facts and Fantasies, 1975; Abandoned Mine Reclamation: Its Mechanics and Its Problems, 1982; editor-in-chief Jour. Mineral Law and Policy, U. Ky. Coll. Law, 1984-93; mng. co-editor Kentucky Mineral Law, 1986. Contbr. articles to profl. jours. Home: 29 Rob Roy Ave Fort Thomas KY 41075-1146

**SHORT, EUGENE MAURICE, JR.,** lawyer, accountant; b. San Francisco, Sept. 4, 1932; s. Eugene Maurice and Emeline Inez (Cox) S.; m. Ann Page, Sept. 4, 1953 (div. 1962); children: Lawrence, David, Dale; m. Karol Fageros, Dec. 1, 1963 (dec. Apr. 1988); children: Kristin, Karri; m. Mary Marhoefer Lynch, Apr. 2, 1992. BBA, City Coll. San Francisco, 1952, U. Miami, Fla., 1954; JD, U. Miami, 1959. Bar: Fla. 1959, U.S. Ct. Mil. Appeals 1960, U.S. Supreme Ct. 1963, U.S. Ct. Appeals (5th and 11th cir.) 1967, U.S. Tax Ct. 1971. Assoc. Carey, Goodman, Terry, Dwyer & Austin, Miami, Fla., 1959-62; ptnr. Peters, Maxey, Short & Maxey, P.A., Coral Gables, Fla., 1963—. Capt., U.S. Army, 1954-63. Mem. ABA, Dade County Bar Assn., Coral Gables Bar Assn., SAR, Royal Palm Tennis Club (dir.), Surf Club, Phi Alpha Delta, Sigma Nu. Avocation: bridge. General corporate, Estate planning, Private international. Home: 7041 SW 92nd St Miami FL 33156-1614 Office: Peter Maxey Short & Maxey PA 3001 Ponce De Leon Blvd Miami FL 33134-6824

**SHORT, FORREST EDWIN,** lawyer; b. Ft. Scott, Kans., Aug. 3, 1928; s. Forrest Edwin Sr. and Laura Elizabeth Short; m. Sharon Lynn Miller, May 1, 1955; children: Stacey Lynn, Laurie Leigh. JD, U. Ala., Tuscaloosa, 1953. Bar: Kans. 1955, U.S. Dist. Ct. Kans. 1956, U.S. Dist. Ct. (so. dist.) Ala. 1953, U.S. Ct. Appeals (10th cir.) 1975, U.S. Supreme Ct. 1976. Sole practitioner Ft. Scott, 1954-66; ptnr. Short & Short, Ft. Scott, 1966-77, Short & Gentry, Ft. Scott, 1977-83, Short, Gentry & Bishop, Ft. Scott, 1983-93; pres. Short, Gentry & Bishop, P.A., Ft. Scott, 1993—. Contbr. articles to profl. jours. 1st lt. JAG, U.S. Army, 1953-54. Mem. ABA, Kans. Bar Assn., Bourbon County Bar Assn., Ft. Scott Rotary Club (pres. 1996-97). Republican. Methodist. Avocations: golf, gardening. Criminal, Personal injury, General civil litigation. Office: Short Gentry & Bishop PA 4th and Judson Fort Scott KS 66701

**SHORT, JOEL BRADLEY,** lawyer, consultant, software publisher; b. Birmingham, Ala., Dec. 27, 1941; s. Forrest Edwin and Laura Elizabeth (Bradley) S.; m. Georgianna Pohl, June 5, 1965 (div. Apr. 1973); m. Nancy Ann Harty, Dec. 17, 1977; children: Christopher Bradley, Matthew Douglas. BA, U. Colo., 1963, LLB, 1966, JD, 1968. Bar: Kans. 1966, U.S. Dist. Ct. Kans. 1966, U.S. Ct. Appeals (10th cir.) 1975, U.S. Supreme Ct. 1976. Ptnr. Short & Short, Attys., Fort Scott, Kans., 1966-77, Nugent & Short, Overland Park, Kans., 1977-83; pvt. practice J. Bradley Short & Assoc., Overland Park, Kans., 1983-91; ptnr. Short & Borth, Overland Park, Kans., 1991—; owner Bradley Software; mem. tech. adv. com. Kans. Jud. Coun., Topeka, 1991-95. Contbg. author: Practitioner's Guide to Kansas Family Law, 1997. 1st lt. U.S. Army, 1967-73. Fellow Am. Acad. Matrimonial Lawyers; mem. Johnson County Bar Assn. (ethics com. 1983-98, family law com. 1983—). Avocation: sailing. Family and matrimonial. Office: Short and Borth 32/1111 Corporate Woods 9225 Indian Creek Pky Overland Park KS 66210-2009

**SHORT, SKIP,** lawyer; b. N.Y.C., July 13, 1951; s. Albert Joseph and Gertrude B. (Johnson) S.; m. Linda Marie Short; children: Sabrina Shiva, Salim Albert, Anjelica Lynn. BA, Fordham Coll., 1972; JD, Georgetown U., 1975. Bar: N.Y. 1976, U.S. Dist. Ct. (ea. dist.) N.Y. 1976, U.S. Dist. Ct. (so. dist.) N.Y. 1978, D.C. 1979, U.S. Ct. Appeals (1st & D.C. cirs.) 1983, U.S. Supreme Ct. 1984. Assoc. Russakoff & Weiss, Bklyn., 1975-76; sole practice, N.Y.C., 1975-79; ptnr. Short & Billy, N.Y.C., 1979—; cons. ins. seminars, 1978—; arbitrator N.Y. Civil Ct., 1981-93; adminstrv. law judge N.Y. Environ. Control Bd., 1980-82; arbitrator comml., no-fault, internat. and uninsured motorist tribunals Am. Arbitration Assn., N.Y.C., 1981—, mem. law com., 1991-93, mem. arbitrator screening com., 1992—, panels membership and arbitration rules subcom., 1993—; arbitrator U.S. Dist. Ct. (ea. dist.) N.Y., 1986—; spl. master N.Y. Supreme Ct., 1988—, N.Y. Civil Ct., 1994—; speaker Am. Arbitration Tng. Seminar, 1991, 93, 94, N.Y. St. Bar Assn. Continuing Legal Edn. Project, 1992, N.Y. State Trial Lawyers Assn., 1996. Author: First Party Claims, 1979; co-author: First Party Claims Under the New York Comprehensive Automobile Reparations Act, 3d edit., 1984; contbg. author: New York Insurance Law Treatise, 1991. Spl. envoy Internat. Human Rights Found., 1986-87. Mem. N.Y. State Bar Assn. (speaker continuing legal edn. program), N.Y. County Lawyers Assn. (spl. Masters com.). Federal civil litigation, Insurance, Private international. Office: Short & Billy 217 Broadway New York NY 10007-2909

**SHORTRIDGE, DEBORAH GREEN,** lawyer; b. Balt., Sept. 5, 1952; d. Harry Joseph Green and Dorothy Marie (Eser) Diamond; children: Bretton, Dana. BA magna cum laude, U. Balt., 1980, JD summa cum laude, 1982. Bar: Md. 1982, U.S. Dist. Ct. Md. 1983, U.S. Ct. Appeals (4th cir.), D.C. 1987. Assoc. prof. U. Balt., 1982-83; assoc. Weinberg and Green, Balt., 1982-89, adminstrv. ptnr., 1989-93; in-house counsel Weinberg & Green LLC, Balt., 1993-97, exec. gen. mem., gen. counsel, 1997-98; gen. ptnr., ethics com. chair Saul, Ewing, Remick & Saul, LLP, 1998—; mem. U. Balt. law adv. coun., 1993—. Bd. dirs. AIDS Interfaith Residential Svcs., Balt., 1991—, pres. 1996-98; bd. govs. U. Balt. Alumni Assn., 1985-91 (H. Melbane Turner Svc. award 1991); mem. bd. govs. ACLU of Md., 1983-90. Recipient Law Faculty award U. Balt. Law Sch., 1982. Mem. ABA (Ctr. for Profl. Responsibility), Md. State Bar Assn. (pro bono sect.), Bar Assn. Balt. City. Professional liability, Insurance, Personal injury. Office: Saul Ewing Weinberg & Green 100 S Charles St Baltimore MD 21201-2725

**SHORTRIDGE, JUDY BETH,** lawyer; b. Johnson City, Tenn., Feb. 17, 1954; d. George Edd and Anna Louise (Salmon) Copenhaver; m. Michael L. Shortridge, July 27, 1984; children: Sarah Elizabeth, Alexander Blake. BA, Va. Poly. Inst. and State U., 1976; MEd, U. Va., 1982; JD, U. Tenn., 1989. Bar: Va. 1990, U.S. Dist. Ct. (we. dist.) Va. 1990, Ea. Dist. Tenn., 1995. Tchr. Stafford County (Va.) Sch. System, 1976-84, Wise County (Va.) Sch. System, 1984-86; ptnr. Shortridge & Shortridge, P.C., Norton, Va., 1990—. Recipient Am. Jurisprudence award U. Tenn., 1989. Mem. Va. Bar Assn. Administrative and regulatory, Insurance, Personal injury. Home: 340 Winterham Dr Abingdon VA 24211-3800 Office: Shortridge & Shortridge PC 18 7th St NW Ste 300 Norton VA 24273-1946

**SHORTRIDGE, MICHAEL L.,** lawyer; b. Grundy, Va., May 26, 1957; s. Leon and Mavis S.; m. Judy Beth Copenhaver, July 27, 1984. BA with distinction, U. Va., 1979, JD, 1982. Bar: Va. 1982, U.S. Dist. Ct. (we. dist.) Va. 1982, U.S. Ct. Appeals (4th cir.) 1984, U.S. Tax Ct. 1985, U.S. Supreme Ct. 1987, U.S. Dist. Ct. (ea. dist.) Tenn. 1995, Ky. 1996, U.S. Dist. Ct. (ea. dist.) Ky. 1996, U.S. Ct. Appeals (6th cir.) 1997. Assoc. Mullins, Winston, Keuling-Stout, Thomason & Harris, Norton, Va., 1982-84; sole practice Norton, 1984-89; ptnr. Shortridge & Shortridge PC, 1989—; adj. faculty Clinch Valley Coll., U. Va., 1996-97. Steering com. Appalachian Sch. Law, Grundy, Va. Mem. ATLA, Va. Bar Assn., Wise County Bar Assn. (pres. 1996), Va. Assn. Def. Attys., Va. Trial Lawyers Assn., Def. Rsch. Inst., Am. Bankruptcy Inst., Glenrockie Country Club (Abingdon, Va.). Federal civil litigation, Bankruptcy, Personal injury. Office: Shortridge & Shortridge PC 18 17th St NW Ste 300 Norton VA 24273-1946 Address: 340 Winterham Abingdon VA 24211-3800

**SHOTWELL, CHARLES BLAND,** lawyer, air force officer, educator; b. Tucson, Jan. 10, 1955; s. William Bedford and Pauline (Bainbridge) S.; m. Jeannene V. Brooks, Aug. 10, 1988. BA, U. Puget Sound, 1977, JD, 1980; LLM in Internat. Law, Am. U., 1991. Bar: Hawaii 1980, U.S. Dist. Ct. Hawaii 1980, U.S. Ct. Mil. Appeals 1981, D.C. 1989, U.S. Ct. Appeals D.C. 1989. Commd. 2d lt. USAF, 1980, advanced through grades to lt. col., 1994; chief civil law USAF, K.I. Sawyer AFB, Mich., 1980-83; mil. justice reviewer USAF, Sembach Air Base, Fed. Republic Germany, 1983-84, area def. counsel, 1984-85; desk officer Internat. Negotiations Div., USAF, Ramstein Air Base, Fed. Republic Germany, 1985-88; chief legis. sect., dir. internat. programs Pentagon, USAF, Washington, 1988-91; assoc. prof. USAF Acad., 1992-95; Europe affairs advisor Joint Chiefs Staff NATO, Washington, 1995-98; sr. mil. fellow Inst. Nat. Strategic Studies, Washington, 1998—; adj. instr. aviation law and ins. Embry-Riddle Aero. U., Ramstein Air Base, 1985-88; USAF Nat. Def. fellow Tufts U., 1991-92; internat. politico-mil. planner U.S. Joint Staff, 1995-98; sr. mil. fellow Inst. Nat. Strategic Studies, Nat. Def. U., 1998—. Newsletter editor; contbr. to profl. publs. Mem. ABA, Hawaii State Bar Assn., D.C. Bar Assn., Air Force Assn. Avocations: skiing, running. Home: 5746 Union Mill Rd Apt 470 Clifton VA 20124-1088 Office: Inst Nat Stretegic Studies Ft Mc Nair Washington DC 20319-0001

**SHOUSE, WILLIAM CHANDLER,** lawyer; b. Lexington, Ky., June 22, 1948; s. Weldon and Hallie Chandler S.; m. Donna Katherine Shouse, July 12, 1980; children: Lauren, Chandler. BA in Engring., U. N.C., 1970; JD, U. Louisville, 1973. Bar: Ky. 1973. Mem. Shouse & Burrus, Lexington, Ky., 1973-84; ptnr. Landrum & Shouse, Lexington, Ky., 1984—. Personal injury, Criminal. Office: Landrum & Shouse PO Box 951 Lexington KY 40588-0951

**SHPIECE, MICHAEL RONALD,** lawyer, educator; b. Detroit, Nov. 13, 1956; s. Harold Edwin and Rose Marie (Wheeler) S.; m. Tracy B. Schwartz; children: David E. Schwartz, Daniel E. Schwartz. PhB, Wayne State U., 1977; JD, U. Mich., 1984. Bar: Mich. 1985. Com. adminstr. Joint Legis. Com. on Aging, Lansing, Mich., 1979-81; policy analyst to commr. Mich. Ins. Bur., Lansing, 1981; legis. cons Cmty. Action Program Mich. UAW, Lansing, 1981-82; dep. dir. Mich. Dept. Licensing and Regulation, Lansing, 1983-85; assoc., ptnr. Honigman Miller Schwartz & Cohn, Detroit, 1985-93; adj. prof. law Wayne State U. Law Sch., Detroit, 1996—; of counsel Shapack, McCullough & Kanter, Bloomfield Hills, Mich., 1994-98; prin. Miller, Shpiece & Andrews, Southfield, Mich., 1998—; pres. Friends of Child Abuse Prevention, Southfield, Mich., 1994—; bd. dirs. chmn. Mich. Freedom of Info. Com., Detroit, 1996-98. Contbr. articles to profl. jours. Pres. and trustee Farmington (Mich.) Bd. Edn., 1975-83; chairperson Farmington Hills Ad Hoc Com. on Ethids, 1990-96. Mem. Am. Statis. Assn., Econ. Club Detroit, ABA (vice chair employee benefit com. torts and ins. practice sect. 1996—), Oakland County Bar Assn. Democrat. Jewish. Pension, profit-sharing, and employee benefits, Health, Insurance. Home: 39372 Plumbrook Dr Farmingtn Hls MI 48331-2976 Office: Miller Shpiece & Andrews PC 26211 Central Park Blvd Ste 500 Southfield MI 48076-4161

**SHREVE, GENE RUSSELL,** law educator; b. San Diego, Aug. 6, 1943; s. Ronald D. and Hazel (Shepherd) S.; m. Marguerite Russell, May 26, 1973. AB with honors, U. Okla., 1965; LLB Harvard U., 1968, LLM, 1975. Bar: Mass. 1969, Vt. 1981. Appellate atty. and state extradition hearing examiner Office of Mass. Atty. Gen., 1968-69; law clk. U.S. Dist. Ct., Dallas, 1969-70; staff and supervising atty. Boston Legal Assistance Project, 1970-73; assoc. prof. Vt. Law Sch., Royalton, 1975-81; vis. assoc. prof. George Washington U., Washington, 1981-83; assoc. prof. law N.Y. Law Sch., N.Y.C., 1983-84, prof., 1984-87; vis. prof. law Ind. U., Bloomington, 1986, prof., 1987-94, Ira C. Batman faculty fellow, 1988-89, Charles L. Whistler faculty fellow, 1992-93, also dir. grad. studies; Richard S. Melvin Prof. of law, 1994—. Author: A Conflict of Laws Anthology, 1997; co-author: Understanding Civil Procedure, 2nd edit., 1994; mem. editl. bd. Am. Jour. Comparative Law, 1994—, Jour. Legal Edn., 1998; contbr. numerous articles to legal jours. Mem. Am. Law Inst., Am. Soc. for Pol. & Legal Phil. Bd. Edn., Am. Jour. Corp. Law, Assn. Am. Law Schs. (civil procedure sect. chair 1997, conflict of laws sect. chair 1998). Democrat. Episcopalian. Office: Ind U Sch Law Bloomington IN 47405

**SHROYER, THOMAS JEROME,** lawyer; b. Morris, Minn., Mar. 18, 1952; s. Virgil Ernest and Muriel June (Hanson) S.; m. Nan Kenwood Sorensen, June 30, 1979; children: Eric Sorensen, Peter Thomas. BA in Polit. Sci., U. Minn., 1974, JD, 1977. Cert. civil trial specialist Minn. State Bar Assn. With Thoma, Schoenthal, Des Moines, 1977-78; assoc. Chadwick Johnson & Bridell, Bloom, Minn., 1978-80; shareholder Moss & Barnett, Mpls., 1980—. Author: Accountant Liability, 1991. Federal civil litigation, State civil litigation. Address: 90 S 7th St 4800 Norwest Ctr Minneapolis MN 55402-3903 *Notable cases include: Cooley vs. CBS, Inc., which achieved def. verdict for CBS, Inc. on a $1.2 million claim of pirating a video tape of a heavyweight boxing match; Hagert vs. Glickman, 520 F. Supp., D. Minn, 1981; which defended accts. in maj. securities and tax cases; Burns vs. Ersek, 591 F. Supp. 837 D. Minn., 1984, which successfully moved to limit the "tolling" effect of a putative class action.*

**SHTOFMAN, ROBERT SCOTT,** lawyer; b. Phila., May 8, 1958; s. David S. and Lynne (Lamonosoff) S. BA, LaSalle U., 1980, JD, 1983. Bar: Pa. 1985, N.J. 1987, Calif. 1988, U.S. Dist. Ct. (ctrl. dist.) Calif. 1988. Assoc. Law Office of Robert Wasserwald & Assocs., L.A., 1988-92; pvt. practice L.A., 1992—. Mem. ATLA, Calif. Trial Lawyers Assn., Consumer Attys. Assn. L.A., Million Dollar Advocates Forum, Phi Alpha Epsilon. Jewish. Fax: 818-609-1210. Federal civil litigation, Personal injury, Entertainment. Office: 18034 Ventura Blvd Ste 296 Encino CA 91316-3516

**SHUBB, WILLIAM BARNET,** judge; b. Oakland, Calif., May 28, 1938; s. Ben and Nellie Bernice (Fruechtenicht) S.; m. Sandra Ann Talarico, July 29, 1962; children: Alisa Marie, Carissa Ann, Victoria Ann. AB, U. Calif., Berkeley, 1960, JD, 1963. Bar: Calif., 1964, U.S. Ct. Internat. Trade 1981, U.S. Customs Ct. 1980, U.S. Ct. Appeals (9th cir.) 1964, U.S. Supreme Ct. 1972. Law clk. U.S. Dist. Ct., Sacramento, 1963-65; asst. U.S. atty., Sacramento, 1965-71; chief asst. U.S. atty. (ea. dist.) Calif., 1971-74; assoc. Diepenbrock, Wulff, Plant & Hannegan, Sacramento, 1974-77, ptnr., 1977-80, 81-90; U.S. atty. Eastern Dist. Calif., 1980-81; judge U.S. Dist. Ct. (ea. dist.) Calif., 1990-96, sr. judge, 1996—; chmn. com. drafting of local criminal rules U.S. Dist. Ct. (ea. dist.) Calif., 1974, mem. speedy trial planning com., 1974-80; lawyer rep. 9th Cir. U.S. Jud. Conf., 1975-78; mem. faculty Fed. Practice Inst., 1978-80; instr. McGeorge Sch. Law, U. Pacific, 1964-66. Mem. ABA, Fed. Bar Assn. (pres. Sacramento chpt. 1977), Calif. Bar Assn., Assn. Def. Counsel, Am. Bd. Trial Advs., Sacramento County Bar Council.

**SHUEY, JAMES FRANK,** lawyer; b. Shreveport, La., May 17, 1953; s. John Miller and Mary Abbie S.; m. Susan Elizabeth Harmon, Dec. 29, 1979 (div. Jan. 1995); children: Kate Harmon, Rachel Ferguson. AB, Duke U., 1975; JD, La. State U., 1980. Bar: La. 1980, Tex. 1994; U.S. Dist. Ct. (ea. and we. dists.) La. 1981, U.S. Dist. Ct. (mid. dist.) La. 1982; U.S. Supreme Ct. 1991. Law clk. La. Supreme Ct., New Orleans, 1980-81; assoc. to ptnr. Lemle Kelleher, New Orleans, 1981-94; ptnr. Frilot Partridge, New Orleans, 1995—. Admiralty, Product liability, Personal injury. Office: Frilot Partridge Kohnke et al 1100 Poydras St New Orleans LA 70163-1101

**SHUGHART, DONALD LOUIS,** lawyer; b. Kansas City, Mo., Aug. 12, 1926; s. Henry M. and Dora M. (O'Leary) S.; m. Mary I. Shughart, July 25, 1953; children: Susan C., Shughart Hosgett, Nancy J. Goede. AB, U. Mo., Columbia, 1949, JD, 1951. Bar: Mo. 1951, U.S. Dist. Ct. (we. dist.) Mo. 1951, U.S. Tax Ct. 1979. With Shughart, Thompson & Kilroy, P.C., Kansas City, Mo., 1951—; with K.C. Mack Sales & Svc. Inc.; mem. Mo. Motor Carriers Assn. Bd. dirs. Rockhurst Coll.; mem. adv. bd. St. Joseph Hosp. Served with AC, U.S. Army, 1944-47. Mem. Kansas City Bar Assn. (chmn. bus. orgns. com. 1990-91), Mo. Bar Assn. (chmn. corp. com. 1980-81, 82-83), Lawyers Assn. Kansas City, Am. Judicature Soc., Mo. Orgn. Def. Lawyers (pres. 1971-72), U. Mo. Law Soc., Phi Delta Phi, Sigma Chi. Republican. Roman Catholic. General corporate, Estate planning. Home: 1242 W 67th Ter Kansas City MO 64113-1941 Office: Shug Thom Kilroy 12 Wyandotte Pla 120 W 12th St Kansas City MO 64105-1917

**SHULAW, RICHARD A.,** lawyer; b. Bowling Green, Ohio, Oct. 14, 1934; s. Francis Marion and Mary Frances (Morehead) S. AA, Ferris State Coll., 1958; LLB, Detroit Coll. of Law, 1963, JD, 1968. Bar: Mich., U.S. Dist. Ct. (ea. and we. dists.) Mich., U.S. Ct. Appeals (6th cir.), U.S. Supreme Ct. Sole practice Owosso, Mich., 1963—; chief asst. pros. atty. Shiwassee County, Mich., 1971, cir. ct. commr., 1965-67; neutral mediator Emmett, Charlevoix and Shiawassee Counties. With U.S. Army, 1954-55. Fellow Mich. State Bar Found.; mem. ABA, ATLA, Mich. Bar Assn. (ins. sect., negligence sect., law sect.), State Bar Mich. (sec., treas., v.p., mem. various coms., elected twice to rep. assembly), Shiawassee County Bar Assn. (v.p.), Mich. Trial Lawyers Assn., Mich. Def. Trial Counsel Inc., Owosso Country Club, Elks, KC (4th degree), Moose, Delta Theta Phi (past pres.). Republican. Roman Catholic. Avocation: golf. Home: 815 W Oliver St Owosso MI 48867-2108

**SHULKIN, JEROME,** lawyer; b. Stanley, N.D., May 2, 1929; s. Max and Sophia (Harris) S.; m. Jane Pearl Israel, Dec. 30, 1956, 1 child, Shellie Jo. BA, U. Minn, 1951; LLB, U. Wash., 1956. Bar: Wash. 1956, Oreg. 1957, U.S. Dist. Ct. (we. dist.) Wash. 1956, U.S. Dist. Ct. (ea. dist.) Wash. 1959, U.S. Dist. Ct. Oreg. 1960, U.S. Ct. Appeals (9th cir.) 1958, U.S. Supreme Ct. 1963. Law clk. Wash. Supreme Ct., Olympia, 1956-57; assoc. Miracle, Treadwell & Pruzan, Seattle, 1957-61, ptnr., 1961-68; ptnr. Casey, Pruzan, Kovarik & Shulkin, Seattle, 1968-76; sr. ptnr. Shulkin, Hutton & Bucknell Inc., P.S., Seattle, 1976-93, Shulkin, Hutton Inc., PS, Seattle, 1993—. Contbr. to law rev. Col. JAG U.S. Army, 1952-54, USAR, 1954-81, ret. Fellow Am. Coll. Bankruptcy (bd. dirs.); mem. Am. Bankruptcy Inst. (bd. dirs.), Am. Bankruptcy Bd. of Certification (bd. dirs., v.p.), Wash. State Bar Assn. (lectr. 1975—), Oreg. State Bar Assn. Jewish. Avocation: classic automobiles. Bankruptcy, Contracts commercial, General corporate. Office: Shulkin Hutton Inc PS 425 Pike St Ste 600 Seattle WA 98101-4078

**SHULMAN, ALVIN DAVID,** lawyer; b. Chgo., July 1, 1930; s. Louis and Ruth Ann (Lederman) S.; m. Gertrude Levy, Aug. 7, 1960; 1 child, Susan Beth. BS in Metall. Engring., U. Ill., 1952; JD, Northwestern U., 1958. Bar: Ill. 1958. Ptnr. Marshall, O'Toole, Gerstein, Murray & Borun, Chgo., 1961—. With U.S. Army, 1952-54. Mem. ABA, Intellectual Property Law Assn. Chgo. Jewish. Patent, Trademark and copyright. Office: Marshall O'Toole Gerstein Murray & Borun 233 S Wacker Dr Ste 6300 Chicago IL 60606-6357

**SHULMAN, CORINNE EDWARDS LEWIS,** mediator; b. Lynbrook, N.Y., Apr. 21, 1926; d. Wilbur Nelson and Ruth Pearl (McKenzie) Edwards; m. Paul Kenneth Lewis, Aug. 22, 1950 (div. June 1964); children: Paul K., Kim, Kevin, Kyle; m. William J. Lederer, 1965 (div. 1975); m. Nathan Shulman. BA, Hood Coll., 1948; MEd, U. Vt., 1972. Actuarial trainee Equitable Life Assurance, N.Y.C., 1948-51; pub. Pearl Harbor Pennysaver, Honolulu, 1954-57, Honolulu Beacon, 1957-65; dir. counseling Champlain Coll., Burlington, Vt., 1970-77; exec. dir. Hawaii Health Net, Honolulu, 1977-79; counselor Green Pastures Health Ctr., Scituate, Mass., 1979-83; mediator Neighborhood Justice Ctr., Honolulu, 1987—. Fundraiser Youth-at-Risk, Boston, 1979-85, Hawaii Youth-at-Risk, Honolulu, 1987-92; mem. Gov.'s Commn. Status Women, Burlington, 1973-75. Mem. AAUW. Home: 44-315 Kaneoke Bay Dr Kaneohe HI 96744

**SHULMAN, FREDERIC M.,** lawyer; b. Rochester, N.Y., Mar. 30, 1954; s. Lawrence I. and Enid Shulman; m. Gale Gold Shulman, June 4, 1978; children: Anne, Jacqueline, Hayley. BA in Econs., Yeshiva U., 1976; JD, Columbia U., 1979. Bar: N.Y. 1980, U.S. Dist. Ct. (so. dist.) N.Y. 1980, D.C. 1985, N.J. 1989, U.S. Dist. Ct. N.J. 1989, U.S. Ct. Appeals (3d cir.) 1993. Assoc. Hale, Russell & Gray, N.Y.C., 1979-86; assoc. Moore, Berson, Lifflander, N.Y.C., 1986-87, ptnr., 1988-90; assoc. Beattie Padovano, Montvale, N.J., 1990-92, ptnr., 1993-94; prin. Price, Meese, Shulman & D'Armino, Woodcliff Lake, N.J., 1994—. General civil litigation, Contracts commercial. Office: Price Meese Shulman & D'Aminio 50 Tice Blvd Woodcliff Lake NJ 07675-7654

**SHULMAN, HARRY,** lawyer; b. Washington, Oct. 11, 1958; s. Stephen Neal and Sandra Still Shulman. BA, Dartmouth Coll., 1980; JD, U. Va., 1985. Project mgr. Holywell Corp., Washington, 1981-82; assoc. Holland & Hart, Denver, 1986-92, ptnr., 1992-95; ptnr. Holland & Hart, Aspen, Colo., 1995—. Land use and zoning (including planning), Product liability, Contracts commercial. Office: Holland & Hart 600 E Main St Aspen CO 81611-1953

**SHULMISTER, M(ORRIS) ROSS,** lawyer; b. Atlanta, Jan. 6, 1940; s. Morris and Kathryn Sybella (Baker) S.; m. Benita Vee Rosin, Dec. 16, 1974. BEE, U. Fla., 1962, JD, 1973. Bar: Fla. 1973, U.S. Dist. Ct. (so. dist.) Fla. 1974, U.S. Dist. Ct. (mid. dist.) Fla. 1985, U.S. Ct. Appeals (5th and 11th cirs.) 1981. Pvt. practice Broward County, Fla., 1963-98, Ft. Lauderdale, Fla., 1974-98, Pompano Beach, Fla., 1998—; spl. master for code enforcement, Pompano Beach, Fla., 1991-92. Mem. Broward County Consumer Protection Bd., 1983—, chmn., 1999—; chmn. Charter Review Bd., Pompano Beach, Fla., 1994-97; dir. South Pompano Civic Assn., 1989—, v.p., 1989, pres., 1992-98. Lt. col. USAF, 1964-70, ret., USAFR, 1970-93. Mem. ABA, Fla. Bar (mem. constrn. law subcom., civil trial cert. 1984), Broward County Bar Assn., Broward County Trial Lawyers Assn., Am. Arbitration Assn. (arbitrator). General civil litigation, Probate, Construction. Office: 590 SE 12th St Pompano Beach FL 33060-9409

**SHULTS, THOMAS DANIEL,** lawyer; b. Massena, N.Y., Apr. 18, 1955; s. Robert Daniel and Beverly Jean (Stowell) S.; m. Deborah Lynn Barmore, Nov. 17, 1979; children: Daniel, Timothy. BS, Fla. State U., 1977; JD, Washburn U., 1982. Bar: Fla. 1983, U.S. Dist. Ct. (mid. and so. dists.) Fla. 1984, U.S. Tax Ct. 1985, U.S. Ct. Appeals (11th cir.) 1985; cert. mediator Fla. Supreme Ct., mediator U.S. Dist. Ct. Asst. state atty. State of Fla. State's Atty. Office, Orlando, 1983-84; litigation assoc. Abel, Band, Brown, et al, Sarasota, Fla., 1984-87; ptnr. Shults & Pomeroy, P.A., Sarasota, 1988-94, Thomas D. Shults, P.A., Sarasota, 1995-96, Hogreve & Shults, Sarasota, 1997—; adj. prof. Manatee C.C., Bradenton, Fla., 1994-95; mem. individual rights com. Fla. Bar, 1987-88; chmn. pub. edn. com. Sarasota Bar, 1991-92; mem. counsel of attys. Am. Subcontractors Assn., Sarasota, 1990-97; pres. Mental Health Cmty. Ctrs. Inc. Contbr. articles to profl. publs. Capt. U.S. Army, 1977-86. Mem. Order of Barristers, Sarasota Inn of Ct. Avocations: photography, camera collecting, film making, film history. General civil litigation, Criminal, Condemnation. Office: Hogreve & Shults 3700 S Tamiami Trl # R90 Sarasota FL 34239-6015

**SHULTS-DAVIS, LOIS BUNTON,** lawyer; b. Elkton, Md., Sept. 29, 1957; d. Asa Grant Bunton and Carolyn Elizabeth Bunton Pate; m. David Reed Shults (Dec. 8, 1979 (div. Sept. 1990); children: Kenneth Grant, Joseph David, Lawrence Scott; m. Michael Howard Davis, June 14, 1992. BS, East Tenn. State U., 1977; JD, U. Tenn., 1980. Bar: Tenn. 1980, U.S. Dist. Ct. (ea. dist.) Tenn. 1985. Assoc. Jenkins & Jenkins, Knoxville, Tenn., 1980-82, R.O. Smith Law Offices, Erwin, Tenn., 1982-85; ptnr. Shults & Shults, Erwin, 1985—; gen. counsel Erwin Nat. Bank, 1985—. Bd. dirs. Unicoi County Heritage Mus., Erwin, 1986-87, Unicoi County Ambulance Authority, Erwin, 1990-91, YMCA, Erwin, 1991-94; pres. Unicoi Elem. PTO, 1994, Unicoi County Mid. Sch. PTA, 1997; Tenn. Young Lawyers mock trial competition coach, 1993, 95-98; Scales program vol., 1998. Recipient Contbn. to Edn. award Unicoi County Sch. Bd., 1994, 98. Mem. Female Attys. of Mountain Empire, DAR (regent 1990-92), Internat. Platform Speakers Assn. Republican. Methodist. Avocations: snow skiing, reading, travel, gardening, home improvement. Probate, Real property, Family and matrimonial. Home: RR 1 Box 258B Unicoi TN 37692-9748 Office: Shults & Shults 111 Gay St Erwin TN 37650-1227

**SHULTZ, JOHN DAVID,** lawyer; b. L.A., Oct. 9, 1939; s. Edward Patterson and Jane Elizabeth (Taylor) S.; m. Joanne Person, June 22, 1968; children: David Taylor, Steven Matthew. Student, Harvard Coll., 1960-61; BA, U. Ariz., 1964; JD, Boalt Hall, U. Calif., Berkeley, 1967. Bar: N.Y. 1968, Calif. 1978. Assoc. Cadwalader, Wickersham & Taft, N.Y.C., 1968-77; ptnr. Lawler, Felix & Hall, L.A., 1977-83, mem. exec. com., chmn. planning com., co-chmn. recruiting and hiring com.; ptnr. Morgan, Lewis & Bockius, L.A., 1983—, chmn. mgmt. com., mem. lateral entry com.; chmn. profl. evaluation com., chmn. bus. plan com., chmn. practice devel. com., chmn. recruiting com. Trustee St. Thomas Ch., N.Y.C., 1969-72, Shore Acres Point Corp., Mamaroneck, N.Y., 1975-77; mem. adv. bd. Internat. and Comparative Law Center, Southwestern Legal Found., 1981—; active Practicing Law Inst. Adv. Bd., Corp. and Securities Law, 1992—. Mem. ABA, Assn. Bar City N.Y., State Bar Calif., N.Y. State Bar Assn., Jonathan Club (L.A.), Phi Delta Phi, Sigma Chi. Episcopalian. General corporate, Mergers and acquisitions, Securities. Office: Morgan Lewis & Bockius LLP 300 S Grand Ave Ste 22 Los Angeles CA 90071-3109

**SHULTZ, SILAS HAROLD,** lawyer; b. Scribner, Nebr., Mar. 21, 1938; s. Harold Mohr and Arlene E. (Spath) S. BS, U. Pa., 1960; LLB, U. Ariz., 1966. Bar: Ariz. 1966, U.S. Supreme Ct. 1988, Colo. 1995; cert. specialist in personal injury and wrongful death, Ariz.; cert. civil trial specialist Nat. Bd. Trial Advocacy. Ptnr., dir. Fennemore, Craig, P.C., Phoenix, 1966-85; trial specialist Law Office of Richard Grand, Tucson, 1985-88; officer Shultz & Rollins, Ltd., Tucson, 1988—. 1st lt. U.S. Army Res., 1961-66. Mem. ATLA (Ariz. gov. 1994—), Am. Bd. Trial Advocates, Ariz. Trial Lawyers Assn. (bd. dirs. 1990—). Personal injury, Product liability. Office: Shultz & Rollins Ltd 4280 N Campbell Ave Ste 214 Tucson AZ 85718-6594

**SHUMAKER, HAROLD DENNIS,** lawyer; b. Richmond, Va., July 8, 1946; s. Milton and Virginia (Grossman) S.; m. Lucy Jane Light, May 23, 1969. BS, U. Ala., 1969; JD, New England Sch. Law, 1983. Bar: Pa. 1983, U.S. dist. Ct. (mid. dist.) Pa. 1988. From br. fin. mgr. to regional fin. mgr. Sperry Univac, Harrisburg, Pa., 1970-80; sr. project adminstr. IOCS, Inc., Waltham, Mass., 1980-83; assoc. Sponaugle & Sponaugle, P.C., Lancaster, Pa., 1983-84; pres., gen. counsel, dir. Horizon Technologies, Inc., Marietta, Pa., 1984—; sr. staff atty. Commodore Bus. Machines, Inc., West Chester, Pa., 1985-87; pvt. practice Marietta, Pa., 1987—. Pres. Marietta-Maytown East Donegal Bicentennial, 1974-76, Marietta Restoration Assn., 1976; chmn. Marietta Housing Hearing Bd., 1984—; chmn. Marietta Planning Commn., 1996—. With USNG, 1969-75. Mem. ABA, Pa. Bar Assn., Lancaster Bar Assn., Ctrl. Pa. U. Ala. Alumni Assn. (v.p. 1985-86, 95-96, pres. 1999—), Lions (pres. 1977, 89-90, 97-98, v.p. 1988-89, 93-97, bd. dirs. 1990—, Melvin Jones fellow for humanitarian work 1998). Democrat. Jewish. Real property, General corporate, Probate. Home and Office: 402 W Market St Marietta PA 17547-1205

**SHUMAN, JOSEPH DUFF,** lawyer; b. Pitts., Dec. 27, 1942; s. Joseph and Anna Jane (Phillips) D.; m. Ann Stewart McMillan, Nov. 9, 1969; children: David Stewart, Lauren Forbes. BA, Yale U., 1964; LLB, Harvard U., 1967. Bar: Pa. 1968, U.S. Dist. Ct. (we. dist.) Pa. 1968. Assoc. Thorp, Reed & Armstrong, Pitts., 1967-73, ptnr., 1974—, co-chmn., corp. and bus. law dept., 1990-94, chmn., 1994-97. Republican. Presbyterian. General corporate, Mergers and acquisitions, Securities. Office: Thorp Reed & Armstrong 1 Riverfront Ctr Ste 2 20 Stanwix St Pittsburgh PA 15222-4895

**SHUMAN-MOORE, ELIZABETH,** lawyer; b. Elgin, Ill., 1956; d. Nicholas R. and Marilyn J. Shuman; m. Stephen J. Moore, 1981. B in Social Work, U. Ill., 1978; JD cum laude, Ind. U., 1982; student, Nat. Inst. for Trial Advocacy, 1986. Bar: Ill., Dist. Cts. for the No. Dists. of Ill., Ind. Atty. Legal Assistance Fedn., Chgo., 1983; atty. and legal dir. Leadership Coun. for Met. Open Communities, Chgo., 1983-90; atty. and dir. project to combat bias violence Chgo. Lawyers' Com. for Civil Rights, 1990—; various positions Chgo. Coun. of Lawyers, 1985—; Cook County State's Atty. hate crime prosecution coun., Chgo., 1990—, task force on gay and lesbian issues, 1990—; bd. dir. Com. for Better Housing, 1986—, The Fund for Justice of the Chgo. Coun. of Lawyers, 1989—. Coeditor, co-author: Fund for Justice Chgo. Coun. of Lawyers, Chgo. Coun. of Lawyers and Legal Assistance Found., Inc., Tenant-Landlord Handbook, 1989; co-drafter amendments to the Ill. Human Rights Act, 1989; contbr. articles to profl. jours. Office: 100 N LaSalle St Ste 600 Chicago IL 60602-2403

**SHUMATE, ALEX,** lawyer; b. DeKalb, Miss., June 14, 1950; m. Sharon Louise Holley, Aug. 3, 1974; children: John Alexander, Aaron Michael. BA in Polit. Sci., Ohio Wesleyan U., 1972; JD, U. Akron, 1975. Bar: Ohio 1975, U.S. Dist. Ct. (no. and so. dists.) Ohio 1976, U.S. Supreme Ct. 1980. Asst. atty. gen. State of Ohio, Columbus, 1975-83; atty. Brownfield, Bally & Goodman, Columbus, 1983-85; chief counsel, dep. chief of staff Gov., State of Ohio, Columbus, 1985-88; mng. ptnr. Squire, Sanders & Dempsey L.L.P., Columbus, 1988—; bd. dirs. Bank One Corp., Chgo, Bank One, N.A., Columbus, Intimate Brands, Inc., Columbus, William Wrigley Jr. Co., Chgo. Bd. trustees Ohio State U., Ohio Wesleyan U., Columbus Mus. of Art; governing com. The Columbus Found.; 1st vice chmn. Columbus Urban League; bd. trustees, exec. com. BalletMet; bd. govs. Pub. Policy Com., United Way of Franklin County; exec. com. 29th Dist. Citizens Caucus, 1992 Commn., Christopher Columbus Quincentennial Jubilee Commn.; founding trustee Participation 2000, Berwick Civic Assn. Recipient Jewish Nat. Fund Tree of Life award 1996, Robert S. Crane Trusteeshp award Leadership Columbus, 1995, Spl. Achievement award NAACP, 1989, Disting. cmty. Svc. award Columbus Urban League, 1987, Cert. of Outstanding Achievement 116th Ohio Gen. Assembly 1985, Polit. Leadership award 29th Dist. Citizens Caucus, 1984, Outstanding Legal Cmty. Svc. award Captial U. Sch. of Law, 1982, Superior Achievement award United Negro Coll. Fund, 1982; named Outstanding Alumni U. Akron Law Sch., 1994, Disting. Alumnus Ohio Wesleyan U., 1992. Fellow Columbus Bar Assn. (governing bd., Cmty. Svc. award 1986), Ohio State Bar Assn. (coun. of dels.); mem. Lambda Boule, John Mercer Langston Bar Assn., Greater Columbus C. of C. (1st vice chair), The Capital Club (bd. govs.). Legislative. Office: Squire Sanders & Dempsey LLP 41 S High St Ste 1300 Columbus OH 43215-6197

**SHUMATE, ROGER EUGENE,** lawyer; b. Rock Springs, Wyo., Mar. 16, 1958; s. Bob Louis and Audrey Joan (Clark) S.; m. Angela Pelkey, Oct. 13, 1990; children: Alaina Grace, Benjamin Graham. BA with honors, U. Wyo., 1980, JD, 1985. Bar: Wyo. 1985, U.S. Dist. Ct. Wyo. 1985, U.S. Ct. Appeals (10th cir.) 1985. Reporter, editor Daily Rocket Miner, Rock Springs, Wyo., 1980-82; dir. Legal Rsch. Svcs., Laramie, Wyo., 1984-85; assoc. Murane & Bostwick, Casper, Wyo., 1985-90, ptnr., 1990-96, mem., 1997—. Wallace Biggs scholar, dept. journalism U. Wyo., 1980. Mem. ABA, Wyo. Bar Assn., Natrona County Bar Assn., Wyo. Assn. Def. Trial Counsel, Def. Rsch. Inst. Avocations: skiing, racquet sports. General civil litigation, Labor, Personal injury. Office: Murane & Bostwick 201 N Wolcott St Casper WY 82601-1922

**SHURE, ANDREW F.,** Lawyer; b. New Haven, Apr. 15, 1970; s. H. William and Pearl-ellen Shure; m. Debra Aliza Rosenthal, Sept. 1, 1996. BA, Brandeis U., 1992; JD, Boston U., 1995. Bar: Mass. 1995, Conn. 1996. Assoc. Heller, Levin, Seksay & Ouellette, P.C., Boston, 1995-98, Hickley, Allen & Snyder, Boston, 1998—. Mem. young leadership divsn. Combined Jewish Philanthropies, Boston, 1996—; mem. steering com. Israeli Independence Day Celebration, Boston, 1996—. Mem. Conn. Bar Assn., Mass. Bar Assn., Boston Bar Assn. Real property, Contracts commercial, General corporate. Office: Hinckley Allen & Snyder 28 State St Boston MA 02109-1775

**SHURN, PETER JOSEPH, III,** lawyer; b. Queens, N.Y., Aug. 30, 1946; s. Peter J. Jr. and Vivienne M. (Tagliarino) S.; m. Ingrid Kelbert; children: Steven Douglas, Vanessa Leigh, David Michael. BSEE magna cum laude, Poly. Inst. Bklyn., 1974; JD magna cum laude, New Eng. Sch. Law, 1977; LLM in Patent and Trade Regulation Law, George Washington U., 1981. Bar: N.C., 1977, Va., 1979, Tex., 1982. Research scientist GTE Labs., 1965-77; sole practice, Raleigh, N.C., 1977-78; asso. Burns, Doane, Swecker & Mathis, Alexandria, Va., 1978-80; tech. advisor to judge U.S. Ct. Appeals (fed. cir.), 1980-81; ptnr. Arnold, White & Durkee, Houston, 1981—; adj. prof. South Tex. Coll. Law, 1984-88; invited mem. nat. panel neutrals Am. Arbitration Assn., 1993—. With U.S. Army, 1966-68. Mem. ABA, Houston Bar Assn., Am. Patent Law Assn. (Robert C. Watson award 1981), Houston Patent Law Assn., Assn. Trial Lawyers Am., IEEE, Sigma Xi. Contbr. articles to profl. jours. Alternative dispute resolution, Federal civil litigation, Intellectual property. Office: Arnold White & Durkee 750 Bering Dr Houston TX 77057-2149 also: PO Box 4433 Houston TX 77210-4433

**SHURTLEFF, JOHN HOWARD,** lawyer; b. Wheaton, Ill., June 27, 1928; m. Joan Fagerburg, Oct. 17,1953; children: Karin, Robert Scot. BS in Chem. Engring., U. Ill., 1950; JD, DePaul, 1955. Bar: Ill. 1955, U.S. Patent Office, 1955, U.S. Dist. Ct. (no. dist.) Ill. 1965, U.S. Ct. Appeals (fed. cir.) 1965. Engr. Underwriters Labs., Chgo., 1950-51; assoc., ptnr. Marzall, Johnston, Cook & Root and succeeding firms., Chgo., 1954-78; prin. Law Offices of John H. Shurtleff, Chgo., 1978--. Pres. Riverside (Ill.) Community Fund, 1964-65; mem. S.W. Suburban Mental Health Assn., Lyons and Riverside Twp., 1966-70; Riverside Zoning Commn. and Bd. Appeals, 1969-96, Community Family Service and Mental Health Ctr., Lyons and RiversideTwp. (v.p. 1970-71, pres. 1971-73); trustee Riverside Pub. Libr., 1974-78. With U.S. Army, 1952-54. Mem. ABA, Am. Patent Law Assn. (chmn. com. for indsl. design protection 1988-89), Am. Chem. Soc., Chgo. Bar Assn., Patent Law Assn. Chgo., Internat. Brotherhood Magicians, Masons, Sigma Phi Delta. Republican. Methodist. Patent, Trademark and copyright, Intellectual property. Office: Law Offices John Shurtleff 140 S Dearborn St Chicago IL 60603-5202

**SHURTZ, STEVEN PARK,** lawyer, shareholder; b. Panquitch, Utah, Jan. 23, 1956; s. Doyle Park and Loree (Munson) S.; m. Jane Wanee Welch, Dec. 29, 1978; children: Thomas Park, Melissa Jane, Amy Marie, Timothy Evan, Stephanie Ann, Richard Steven, Kimberly Jane, Nathan Samuel. BS in Chem. Engring., U. Utah, 1980, JD, 1983. Bar: Ill. 1983, Utah 1997, U.S. Dist. Ct. (no. dist.) Ill. 1983, U.S. Dist. Ct. Utah 1997, U.S. Patent & Trademark Office 1984, U.S. Ct. Appeals (fed. cir.) 1989. Assoc. Brinks Hofer Gilson & Lione, Chgo., 1983-88, shareholder, 1989—. Mem. ABA, Am. Intellectual Property Law Assn., Chgo. Bar Assn. Mormon. Intellectual property. Home: 1040 W Austin Ln Palatine IL 60067-5802 Office: Brinks Hofer Gilson & Lione Ste 3600 455 N City Front Plaza Dr Chicago IL 60611

**SHUSTER, DAVID JONATHAN,** lawyer; b. Perth Amboy, N.J., Jan. 21, 1969. BS in Fin., Pa. State U., 1991; JD magna cum laude, U. Balt., 1994. Bar: Md. 1994, U.S. Dist. Ct. Md. 1995, D.C. 1997. Jud. law clk. to Hon. Arrie w. Davis, U.S. Ct. Spl. Appeals Md., Balt., 1995-96; assoc. Wright, Constable & Skeen LLP, Balt., 1996—. Contbr. articles to profl. jours. Vol. atty. Legal Svcs. to the Elderly Program, Balt., 1996—. Mem. Md. State Bar Assn., Bar Assn. Balt. City, D.C. Bar Assn., Md. Def. Counsel, Inc. General civil litigation, Insurance, Consumer commercial. Office: Wright Constable & Skeen LLP 100 N Charles St Fl 16 Baltimore MD 21201-3805

**SHUTT, NEKKI,** lawyer; b. Honolulu, Nov. 25, 1966; s. Jon R. and Rebecca K. (Stevenson) S. BA, U. S.C., 1988, JD, 1995. Bar: S.C., U.S. Dist. Ct. S.C. Assoc. Baker, Barwick, Ravenel & Bender, Columbia, S.C., 1995—. Bd. dirs. Victory Fund, Washington, 1995—, co-chair, 1997—. Mem. ABA, S.C. Bar Assn. General civil litigation, Constitutional, Pension, profit-sharing, and employee benefits.

**SHYLLON, PRINCE E.N.,** lawyer, law educator; b. Freetown, Sierra Leone, Nov. 3, 1943; came to the U.S.; s. Henry W.O. and Lois (Johnson) S.; m. Millicent Boutchway, June 8, 1974; children: Nicky H., Selwyn A. BA in Economics, Shaw U., 1972; JD Sch. of Law, N.C. Ctrl. U., Durham, 1975. Bar: N.C. 1977, U.S. Dist. Ct. (ea. dist.), 1978, U.S. Ct. of Appeals (4th cir.), 1978. Ptnr. Shabica, Shyllon & Shyllon, Raleigh, N.C., 1977-79, Shyllon, Shyllon & Ratliff, Raleigh, N.C., 1979-85; prof. Bus. Law and Ins. Saint Augustines Coll., Raleigh, N.C., 1975-91; ptnr. Shyllon & Shyllon, Raleigh, N.C., 1986—; university counsel St. Augustines Coll., 1992—. Mem. ABA, N.C. Acad. of Trial Lawyers. Personal injury, Real property, Workers' compensation. Home: 1101 Athens Dr Raleigh NC 27606-2420 Office: Shyllon & Shyllon 4002 Barrett Dr Raleigh NC 27609-6604

**SIBLEY, JAMES MALCOLM,** retired lawyer; b. Atlanta, Aug. 5, 1919; s. John Adams and Nettie Whitaker (Cone) S.; m. Karen Norris, Apr. 6, 1942; children: Karen Mariea, James Malcolm Jr., Jack Norris, Elsa Alexandria Victoria, Quintus Whitaker. A.B., Princeton U., 1941; student, Woodrow Wilson Sch. Law, 1942, Harvard Law Sch., 1945-46. Bar: Ga. 1942. Assoc. King & Spalding, Atlanta, 1942-47, ptnr., 1947-91; bd. dirs. Summit Industries, Inc.; exec. com., mem. pub. affairs com. Coca-Cola Co., 1979-91; chmn. exec. com. John H. Harland Co., 1963-91; chmn. exec. com., mem. compensation com. Trust Co. of Ga., 1975-92; mem. exec. com., mem. compensation com. SunTrust Banks, Inc., 1985-92. Trustee Joseph B. Whitehead Found., Lettie Pate Evans Found., A.G. Rhodes Home, Inc., Robert W. Woodruff Found., Inc. (formerly Trebor Found.), John H. and Wilhelmina D. Harland Charitable Found., Inc.; trustee emeritus Callaway Gardens Found, Emory U. With USAF, 1942-45. Mem. ABA, Ga. Bar Assn., Atlanta Bar Assn., Am. Coll. Probate Counsel, Am. Bar Found., Am. Law Inst. Episcopalian. Clubs: Piedmont Driving, Commerce. Banking, General corporate, Probate. Home: 63 Peachtree Cir NE Atlanta GA 30309-3556 also: King & Spalding 191 Peachtree St NE Atlanta GA 30303-1740

**SIBLEY, SAM B., JR.,** lawyer; b. Norfolk, Va., Jan. 20, 1946; s. Sam B. and Eloise Newton Sibley; m. Debra Lee Shipman, Oct. 25, 1986. BA, Augusta Coll., 1968; JD, Mercer U., 1972. Solicitor Richmond County Ct., Augusta, Ga., 1979-80; dist. atty. City of Augusta, 1981-88; pvt. practice Augusta. Criminal. Office: 448 Telfair St Augusta GA 30901-5811

**SICA, JOHN,** lawyer; b. Scranton, Pa., Jan. 23, 1962; s. John Anthony and Betty May (Sherbourne) S. BS, U. Md., Princess Anne, 1987; JD, No. Ill. U., 1989. Bar: Md. 1990. Mng. lawyer Sentinel Title Corp., Frederick, Md., 1989-90; pvt. practice Frederick, 1990—. Mem. Am. Agrl. Law Assn., Md. Bar Assn. (pub. svc. com.), Bar. Assn. Balt. City (young lawyers sect.), Md. Trial Lawyers Assn. Agriculture, Land use and zoning (including planning), General practice. Home: 329 S Jefferson St Frederick MD 21701-6206

**SICULAR, DAVID R.,** lawyer; b. N.Y.C., July 17, 1957; s. Arthur and Lilian (Weinberger) S.; m. Lilian S. Stern, Sept. 29, 1985; children: Jonathan, Sarah, Rebecca. AB, Harvard U., 1978, JD, 1983. Assoc. Paul, Weiss, Rifkind, Wharton & Garrison, N.Y.C., 1983-94, ptnr., 1995—. Mem. N.Y. State Bar Assn. (exec. com. tax sect. 1995—). Taxation, general, Corporate taxation. Office: Paul Weiss Rifkind Wharton & Garrison Rm 200 1285 Avenue Of The Americas Fl 23 New York NY 10019-6028

**SIDAMON-ERISTOFF, CONSTANTINE,** lawyer; b. N.Y.C., June 28, 1930; s. Simon C. and Anne Huntington (Tracy) Sidamon-E.; m. Anne Phipps, June 29, 1957; children: Simon, Elizabeth, Andrew. B.S.E. in Geol. Engring, Princeton U., 1952; LL.B., Columbia U., 1957. Clk., then assoc. firm Kelley Drye Newhall Maginnes & Warren, N.Y.C., 1957-64; individual practice law N.Y.C., 1964-65, 74-77; exec. asst. to Congressman John V. Lindsay, 1964-65; city coordinator Lindsay Mayoral Campaign, N.Y.C., 1965; asst. to mayor City of N.Y., 1966, commr. hwys., 1967-68, transp. adminstr., 1968-73; ptnr. Sidamon-Eristoff, Morrison, Warren, & Ecker, N.Y.C., 1978-83; counsel Morrison & de Roos, 1984-88; pvt. practice N.Y.C., 1988-89; regional adminstr. Region II EPA, N.Y.C., 1989-93; of counsel Patterson, Belknap, Webb & Tyler, N.Y.C., 1993—; mem. N.Y. State Met. Transp. Authority Bd., 1974-89; commr. N.Y. State Jud. Commn. on Minorities, 1987-91; mem. Gov.'s Coun. on Hudson River Valley Greenway, 1989; trustee United Mut. Savs. Bank, N.Y.C., 1979-82; trustee Phipps Houses, N.Y.C., 1974—, chmn. 1986—. Trustee Allaverdy Found., N.Y.C., 1962—, Am. Farm Sch., Thessaloniki, Greece, 1973-79, Carnegie Hall, N.Y.C., 1967-92, Millbrook (N.Y.) Sch., 1971-89, hon. trustee, 1989—, Orange County (N.Y.) Citizens Found., 1974-81, Am. the Beautiful Fund, Washington, 1985-97; bd. dirs. Caramoor Center for Music and Arts, Katonah, N.Y., 1961-80, Tolstoy Found., Inc., N.Y.C., 1975—, chmn., 1979-89, 94—, Boyce Thompson Inst. for Plant Rsch., Ithaca, N.Y., 1994—; mem. Orange County (N.Y.) Planning Bd., 1997—; bd. dirs., mem. exec. com. Mid-Hudson Pattern for Progress, Poughkeepsie, N.Y., 1975-89, chmn., 1981-85; bd. dirs. Coun. on Mcpl. Performance, N.Y.C., 1979-87, chmn., 1979-83, vice chmn., 1986, 87, N.Y. State Republican committeeman, 1980-89. Served to 1st lt. arty. AUS, 1952-54, Korea. Decorated Bronze Star; recipient Honor award Kings County chpt. N.Y. State Soc. Profl. Engrs., 1969, Honor award Greater N.Y. coun. Girl Scouts U.S., 1973, Board Leadership award Coun. Mcpl. Performance, 1984, Transp. Man of Yr. award Greater N.Y. March of Dimes, 1985, Award of Excellence Mid-Hudson Pattern for Progress, 1990, Honor award Nat. and N.Y. Parks and Conservation Assn., 1992, Bronze medal USEPA, 1993, Civic Leadership award (with wife) Citizens Union, 1997, Force for Nature award (with wife) Natural Resources Def. Coun., 1999. Mem. ABA, N.Y. State Bar Assn., Assn. of Bar of City of N.Y., N.Y. County Lawyers Assn., Kent Moot Ct., AIME, Phi Delta Phi, Delta Psi. Eastern Orthodox. Clubs: Century Assn. (N.Y.C.), Knickerbocker (N.Y.C.), Racquet and Tennis (N.Y.C.). Administrative and regulatory, Environmental, Land use and zoning (including planning). Office: Patterson Belknap Webb & Tyler LLP 1133 Avenue Of The Americas New York NY 10036-6710

**SIDES, JACK DAVIS, JR.,** lawyer; b. Dallas, Sept. 18, 1939; s. Jack Davis Sr. and Edith Eugenia (Lowrie) S.; m. Nancy Pauline Cantwell, July 22, 1967 (div. Sept. 1976); children: Mary Katharine, Jack Davis III; m. Laura Gail Miller, Aug. 2, 1979; children: Susan Ashley, Stacy Anne. BBA, U. Tex., 1962, JD with honors, 1963. Bar: Tex. 1963. Assoc. Jackson, Walker, et al, Dallas, 1963-67, White, McElroy, White, Sides & Rector, Dallas, 1968-78; sole practice Dallas, 1978—. Editor: U. Tex. Law Review, 1963. With USAFNG, 1963-69. Fellow Dallas Bar Found., Tex. Bar Found. (life); mem. ABA, Tex. Bar Assn. (grievance subcom. 1979-86), Dallas Bar Assn. (ethics com. 1973-77, jud. com. 1988—), Tex. Assn. Def. Counsel, Dallas Assn. Def. Counsel (sec. 1973-74). Republican. Methodist. Club: Brook Hollow Golf (Dallas). Avocations: reading, tennis, exercising. Federal civil litigation, State civil litigation. Office: 2301 Cedar Springs Rd Ste 350 Dallas TX 75201-7803

**SIDMAN, ROBERT JOHN,** lawyer; b. Cleve., Aug. 4, 1943; s. Charles Frances and Louise (Eckert) S.; m. Mary Mato, July 29, 1967; children: Christa Mary, Alicia Mary. BA, Benedictine Coll., 1965; JD, U. Notre Dame, 1968. Bar: Ohio 1968, U.S. Dist. Ct. (so. dist.) Ohio 1970, U.S. Ct. Appeals (6th cir.) 1971, U.S. Supreme Ct. 1971. Law clk. U.S. Dist. Ct. (so. dist.) Ohio, Columbus, 1968-70; assoc. Mayer, Tingley & Hurd, Columbus, 1970-75; judge Bankruptcy Ct. U.S. Dist. Ct. (so. dits.) Ohio, Columbus, 1975-82; ptnr. Vorys, Sater, Seymour & Pease, Columbus, 1982—; prof. Ohio State U. Law Sch., Columbus, 1984, 85, 86. Mem. Nat. Conf. Bankruptcy Judges (bd. dirs. 1981-82), Assn. Former Bankruptcy Judges (bd. dirs. 1983-89, treas. 1986-87, pres. 1988-89). Bankruptcy, Contracts commercial, Federal civil litigation. Office: Vorys Sater Seymour & Pease PO Box 1008 52 E Gay St Columbus OH 43215-3161

**SIDWELL, SUSAN VON BROCK,** lawyer; b. Elmhurst, Ill., Mar. 20, 1960; d. Robert Carl and Mary Louise (Boone) Von Brock; m. Ira Lee Sidwell, Aug. 31, 1985; children: Walter Von Brock, Sarah Grace, Michelle Lee. BS in Acctg., Auburn U., 1982; JD, Vanderbilt U., 1989. Bar: Tenn. Cost acct. So. Natural Gas Co., Birmingham, Ala., 1982-85; assoc. Harwell, Howard, Hyne, Gabbert, Nashville, 1989-95, ptnr., 1995—; mem. hearing com. Bd. Profl. Responsibility, Nashville, 1997—. Mem. CABLE, Nashville, 1993—. Mem. ABA, Lawyers Assn. for Women (com. mem. 1993-94), Tenn. Bar Assn., Nashville Bar Assn. Securities, Mergers and acquisitions, General corporate. Office: Harwell Howard Hyne Gabbert & Manner PC 1800 1st American Ctr Nashville TN 37238

**SIEBEL, BRIAN J.,** lawyer; b. Hammond, Ind., Nov. 4, 1956; s. Robert S. and Barbara C. (Winters) Howkinson; m. Linda A. Howell, May 24, 1992; 1 child, Elizabeth Deloris. BA, Western Wash. U., Bellingham, 1982; JD, Am. U., 1990. Bar: N.Y. 1991, U.S. Dist. Ct. (we. dist.) N.Y. 1991, DC 1992, U.S. Ct. Appeals 1993, U.S. Supreme Ct. 1996. Jud. law clk. to Hon. John T. Curtin U.S. Dist. Ct. (we. dist.) N.Y., Buffalo, 1990-92; assoc. Dickstein, Shapiro, Morin & O'Shinsky, Washington, 1992-96; staff atty. Ctr. to Prevent Handgun Violence, Washington, 1996—. Mem. ATLA. Personal injury, Product liability.

**SIEBENEICHER, S. AARON,** lawyer; b. Houston, June 7, 1969; s. Walter Ray and Beatrice Reid S.; m. Tracy L'Nelle McCann, Oct. 26, 1969; 1 child, Hannah Nicole. BS in Polit. Sci. cum laude, La. Coll., 1991; JD, Loyola U., New Orleans, 1994. Bar: La.; U.S. Ct. Appeals (5th cir.). Law clk. to presiding justice, Alexandria, La., 1994-95; assoc. Bolen, Erwin & Johnson, Alexandria, 1995-97; ptnr. Johnson, Parker, Siebeneicher and Tannehill, Pineville, La., 1997-98, Johnson and Siebeneicher, Pineville, 1998—; bd. dirs. Extra Mile, Pineville, La. Spl. Edn. Ctr., Alexandria. Mem. ABA, La. State Bar Assn., Masons, Inns of Ct., La. Claims Assn. Lutheran. Avocations: antique car collections, hunting, golf. Office: PO Box 648 Alexandria LA 71309-0648

**SIEBERT, WILLIAM ALAN,** lawyer; b. Royal Oak, Mich., Jan. 25, 1955; s. William Edward and Mary Elizabeth (Northrup) S. BA, Albion Coll., 1977; JD, U. Detroit, 1980. Bar: Mich. 1980, U.S. Dist. Ct. (ea. dist.) Mich. 1981, U.S. Dist. Ct. (we. dist.) Mich. 1995. Gen. counsel RARE Realty, Beaverton, Mich., 1983-85; sole practice Gladwin, Mich., 1985—. Exec. com. Gladwin County Reps., 1983-92; candidate for Gladwin County Prosecuting Atty., 1984, 88; treas. Saginaw Bay dist. United Meth. Ministry, 1988. Mem. Mich. Bar Assn. (real property sect. title ins. com. 1984—), Clare-Gladwin Trial Lawyers, Masons (v.p. Gladwin Temple Assn. 1988-92, worshipful master 1992), Albion Coll. Alumni Bd., Phi Alpha Delta (chpt. clk. 1980). Consumer commercial, Criminal, Real property.

**SIEDZIKOWSKI, HENRY FRANCIS,** lawyer; b. Chester, Pa., Dec. 27, 1953; s. Henry W. and Virginia (Szymanski) S. BA cum laude, Juniata Coll., 1975; JD magna cum laude, Villanova U., 1979. Bar: Pa. 1979, U.S. Dist. Ct. (ea. dist.) Pa. 1979, U.S. Ct. Appeals (3d cir.) 1979, U.S. Ct. Appeals (6th cir.) 1981, U.S. Dist. Ct. (we. dist.) Pa. 1986. Assoc. Dilworth, Paxson, Kalish & Kauffman, Phila., 1979-86; ptnr. Baskin Flaherty Elliott & Mannino P.C., Phila., 1986-90, Elliott Bray & Riley, Phila., 1990-92, Elliott, Vanaskie & Riley, 1992-94, Elliot, Reihner, Siedzikowski & Egan, 1994—; mem. hearing com. disciplinary bd. Supreme Ct. Pa., 1985-91. Mem. ABA (chmn. Lanham act subcom. of bus. torts com. of litigation sect. 1986—, rotating editor newsletter of antitrust sect. franchisee com.), Pa. Bar Assn., Phila. Bar Assn. (chmn. subcom. disciplinary rules for profl. responsibility com. 1984-90). Democrat. Roman Catholic. Federal civil litigation, Bankruptcy, Franchising. Office: Elliott Reihner et al 925 Harvest Dr Blue Bell PA 19422-1956

**SIEFKIN, SUSAN DEEBLE,** judge; b. Long Beach, Calif., June 12, 1943; d. Roy Edgar and Cora Elizabeth (Cotant) Deeble; m. Randolph R. Siefkin, Aug. 21, 1965; children: Nelson R., Kristen M. BA, U. Calif., Santa Barbara, 1965; MA, Rutgers U., 1966; JD, Humphreys Coll., Stockton, Calif., 1983; student, U. Bordeaux, France, 1963=64. Bar: Calif. 1983, U.S. Dist. Ct. (ea. and no. dists.) Calif. 1983. Intermittent instr. polit. sci. Modesto (Calif.) Jr. Coll., 1970-79; assoc., shareholder Law Offices Gianelli & Israels, Modesto, 1983-89; assoc., ptnr. Damrell, Nelson, Schrimp, Pallios & Ladine, Modesto, 1991-95; judge Stanislaus County Mclp. Ct., Modesto, 1995-98, Stanislaus County Superior Ct., Modesto, 1998—; vis. lectr. polit. sci. Calif. State U. Stanislaus, Turlock, 1977-79. Mem. Modesto City Coun., 1975-83. Named Outstanding Woman, Stanislaus County Commn. for Women, 1982. Mem. Stanislaus County Bar Assn. (pres. 1989), Calif. Women Lawyers (bd. dirs., bd. govs. 1993-95), Modesto Rotary Club. Avocations: quilting, antiques, travel. Office: Stanislaus County Superior Ct 1100 I St Modesto CA 95354-2325

**SIEGAL, JOEL DAVIS,** lawyer; b. Plainfield, N.J., Feb. 9, 1937; s. Samuel and Florence (Ravitz) S.; m. Ronny J. Greenwald, Oct. 16, 1972; children: Samuel Jesse, Evan Charles. BA in Polit. Sci., U. Pa., 1958; JD, Yale U., 1961; MA in Internat. Rels., U. Stockholm, 1963. Bar: N.J., 1962, N.Y., 1965; U.S. Dist. Ct. N.J., 1962, U.S. Ct. Appeals (3rd cir.), 1963, U.S. Supreme Ct., N.Y., 1969, U.S. Dist. Ct. (so. and ea. dist.) N.Y., 1975. Law clk. to Hon. Arthur S. Lane Newark, N.J., 1961-62; law clk. to Hon. Phillip Forman, 1963-64; assoc. Hellring Lindeman Goldstein & Siegal, Newark, 1967-70, ptnr., 1970—; commr. Nat. Conf. Commrs. on Uniform Laws, 1991-98; mem. U.S. Dist. Ct. Adv. Bd., Newark, 1991-92. Contbr. articles to profl. jours. Mcpl. chmn. Dem. Party, Borough of Alpine, N.J., 1983-86. Mem. ABA, N.J. Bar Assn., Essex County Bar Assn., Assn. Fed. Bar N.J. (nat. del. N.J. 1974, pres. 1990-92, adv. bd. 1993—), Harmonie Club of N.Y.C. Democrat. Jewish. General civil litigation, Family and matrimonial. Office: Hellring Lindeman Goldstein Siegal 1 Gateway Ctr Newark NJ 07102-5311

**SIEGAL, RONNY JO,** lawyer; b. N.Y.C., July 16, 1947; d. Irwin Daniel and Doris Rae (Lewin) Greenwald; m. Joel Davis Siegal, Oct. 14, 1972; children: Samuel, Evan. Ba, Syracuse U., 1968; JD, Fordham U., 1972. Bar: N.Y. 1973, U.S. Dist. Ct. (so. and ea. dist.) N.Y. 1974, N.J. 1978, U.S. Dist. Ct. N.J. 1978, U.S. Ct. Appeals (3d cir.) 1983, U.S. Supreme Ct. 1994. Asst. dist. atty. Bronx Dist. Atty.'s Office, 1972-77, dep. bur. chief appeals, 1976-77; ptnr. Hellring, Lindeman, Goldstein & Siegal, Newark, 1978—. Chair planning bd. Borough of Alpine, N.J., 1992—; mem. legalized gambling study commn., 1993—; vice chmn. Bd. Adjustment, 1986-86, sec., 1981-82, vice chmn., 1983-86; Dem. committeewoman, Alpine, 1983—. Mem. ABA, N.J. Bar Assn., Bergen County Bar Assn., Women in Fed. Practice in N.J., N.J. Women Lawyers Assn., Women Lawyers in Bergen, Assn. of Fed. Bar State N.J. (v.p. 1991—). Democrat. Jewish. Avocation: running. General civil litigation, Family and matrimonial. Office: Hellring Lindeman Goldstein & Siegal One Gateway Ctr Newark NJ 07102

**SIEGAN, BERNARD HERBERT,** lawyer, educator; b. Chgo., July 28, 1924; s. David and Jeannette S.; m. Sharon Goldberg, June 15, 1952 (dec. Feb. 1985); m. Shelley Zifferblatt, Nov. 19, 1995. AA, Herzl. Jr. Coll., Chgo., 1943, 46; Student, Roosevelt Coll., Chgo., 1946-47; J.D., U. Chgo., 1949. Bar: Ill. 1950. Practiced in Chgo.; partner firm Siegan & Karlin, 1952-73; pres., sec. various small corps. and gen. partner in partnerships engaged in real estate ownership and devel., 1955-70; weekly columnist Freedom newspaper chain, other papers, 1974-79; cons. law and econs. program U. Chgo. Law Sch., 1970-73; adj. prof. law U. San Diego Law Sch., 1973-74, Disting. prof., 1975—; adj. scholar Cato Inst., Washington, 1991—, Heritage Found., 1992—; cons. windfalls and wipeouts project HUD, 1973-74; cons. FTC, 1985-86, U.S. Justice Dept., dir. constl. bibliog. project, 1986-88; keynote speaker 5th Internat. Conf. on Urbanism, Porto Alegre, Brazil, 1989; nominated by Pres. Reagan to U.S. Ct. Appeals (9th cir.) Feb. 2, 1987, confirmation denied July 14, 1988 by party line vote Senate Judiciary Com. Author: Land Use Without Zoning, 1972, Spanish edit., 1995, Other People's Property, 1976, Economic Liberties and the Constitution, 1980, The Supreme Court's Constitution: An Inquiry Into Judicial Review and Its Impact on Society, 1987, Drafting a Constitution for a Nation or Republic Emerging into Freedom, 1992, 2d edit., 1994, Portuguese, Ukrainian, Polish and Spanish edits., 1993, Property and Freedom: The Constitution, Supreme Court and Land Use Regulation, 1997, Adapting a Constitution to Protect Freedom and Provide Abundance (in Bulgarian), 1998; editor: Planning without Prices, 1977, The Interaction of Economics and the Law, 1977, Regulation, Economics and the Law, 1979, Government, Regulation and the Economy, 1980. Mem. pres.-elect's Task Force on Housing, 1980-81; mem. Pres.'s Commn. on Housing, 1981-82; mem. Nat. Commn. on bicentannial of U.S. Constn., 1985-91; chmn. adv. com. Affordable Housing Conf., San Diego, 1985, Rights of Regulated Conf., Coronado, Calif., 1976; chmn. Conf. on the Taking Issue, 1976; mem. Houston Regional Urban Design Team, Study of Houston, 1990; mem. U.S. team Bulgarian Econ. Growth and Transition Project, 1990; mem. devel. bd. Mingei Internat. Mus. World Folk Art, 1981-84. Served with AUS, 1943-46. Research fellow law and econs. U. Chgo. Law Sch., 1968-69; Urban Land Inst. research fellow, 1976-86; recipient Leander J. Monks Meml. Fund award Inst. Humane Studies, 1972, George Washington medal Freedom Founds. at Valley Forge, 1981, Spl. award Liberal Inst. of Rio Grande do Sul, Porto Alegre, Brazil, 1989, Thorsnes award for outstanding legal scholarship, 1998; named Univ. Prof., U. San Diego, 1997-98. Home: 6005 Camino De La Costa La Jolla CA 92037-6519

**SIEGEL, ARTHUR BERNARD,** lawyer; b. Bklyn., Mar. 22, 1932; s. Abraham and Sarah (Hecht) S.; m. Miriam Ann Barck, Dec. 22, 1963; children: Hugh David, Susan Barck. BA, Syracuse U., 1954; M in Indsl. and Labor Relations, Cornell U., 1958; JD, Columbia U., 1971. Bar: Pa. 1972, U.S. Dist. (mid. dist.) Pa. 1979. Ptnr. Finan, Beecher, Wagner & Rose, P.A., Milford, Pa., 1972-79, Beecher, Wagner, Rose, Siegel & Klemeyer, Milford, 1979; pvt. practice Milford, 1979—; pub. defender Pike County (Pa.), Milford, 1980-82; solicitor Pa. twps., Blooming Grove and Greene, Pike County Office on Aging; solicitor Pike County Recorder of Deets and Register of Wills. Contbr. articles Pike County Dispatch. Treas. Pike County Rep. com., Milford, 1982-84. Served to 1st. lt. USAF, 1955-57, served to capt. USAFR, 1967. Mem. ABA, Pa. Bar Assn., Pike County Bar Assn., Columbia U. Law Sch. Alumni Assn., Pike County Legal Aid Soc. (founder 1979), Phi Beta Kappa, Phi Kappa Phi, Sigma Delta Chi. Jewish. Avocations: photography, music, collecting memorabilia, travel. Real property, Family and matrimonial. Home: Pine Acres Milford PA 18337 Office: PO Box 1154 Milford PA 18337-2154

**SIEGEL, BERNARD LOUIS,** lawyer; b. Pitts., Sept. 15, 1938; s. Ralph Robert and Frieda Sara (Stein) S.; m. Marcia Margolis, Sept. 3, 1961 (div. Aug. 1983); children: Jonathan, Sharon; m. Susan Erickson, Aug. 31, 1997. BA, Brandeis U., 1960; JD, Harvard U., 1963. Bar: Pa. 1964, U.S. Dist. Ct. (we. dist.) Pa. 1964, U.S. Dist. Ct. (ea. dist.) Pa. 1985, U.S. Ct. Appeals (3d cir.) 1985, U.S. Supreme Ct. 1985. Assoc. Silin, Eckert & Burke, Erie, Pa., 1963-66; ptnr. Silin, Eckert, Burke & Siegel, Erie, Pa., 1966-73; 1st asst. dist. atty. Erie County, 1972-76; dep. atty. gen. Pa. Dept. Justice, Phila., 1976-78; dep. dist. atty. Dist. Atty. of Phila., 1978-86; pvt. practice Phila., 1986—; adj. prof. La Salle U., Phila., 1986—; lectr. Fed. Law Enforcement Tng. Ctr., Glynco, Ga., 1986-97, Mercyhurst Coll., Erie, 1974-76, Nat. Coll. Dist. Attys., Houston, 1978-85; adj. prof. Temple U. law sch., 1995—; mem. criminal rules com. Pa. Supreme Ct., Phila., 1976-85; commr. Pa. Crime Commn., Harrisburg, 1976-79. Author: (with others) Pennsylvania Grand Jury Practice, 1983, By No Extraordinary Means, 1986. Mem. ABA, Nat. Assn. Criminal Def. Lawyers, Pa. Assn. Criminal Def. Lawyers (bd. dirs. 1988—), Pa. Bar Assn. (chmn. criminal law sect. 1988-91), Phila. Bar Assn. (chmn. criminal justice sect. 1990-91). Democrat. Jewish. Avocations: bicycling, reading, hiking. Criminal. Office: Packard Bldg 24th Fl 111 S 15th St Philadelphia PA 19102-2625

**SIEGEL, CHARLES,** lawyer, investment banking and brokerage executive; b. N.Y.C., June 6, 1944; s. Edward and Ann (Aronson) S.; m. Francine Marie Prioli, Sept. 26, 1970; children—David Aaron, Stefanie Joy. B.S. in Econs., U. Pa., 1965; J.D., Boston U., 1968. Bar: N.Y. 1969, U.S. Dist. Ct. (so. and ea. dists.) N.Y. 1976, U.S. Ct. Appeals (2nd cir.) 1975, U.S. Ct. Appeals (8th cir.) 1978, U.S. Supreme Ct. 1979. Asst. arbitration dir. N.Y. Stock Exchange, Inc., N.Y.C., 1968-72, arbitrator, 1979—; v.p., asst. sec., asst. legal counsel Blyth Eastman Dillon & Co. Inc., N.Y.C., 1972-80; sr. v.p., spl. counsel E.F. Hutton & Co. Inc., N.Y.C., 1980-86; assoc. dir. Bear, Stearns, & Co. Inc., N.Y.C., 1986-88; sr. v.p., sr. assoc. gen. counsel PaineWebber Inc., N.Y.C., 1988-94, Kelley Drye & Warren, N.Y.C., 1995-98; gen. counsel Fleet Securities, Inc., N.Y.C., 1998—; lectr. Securities Industry Assn., N.Y.C., 1985, 86. Mem. ABA. Securities, General corporate, Federal civil litigation. Office: Fleet Securities Inc 26 Broadway New York NY 10004-1703

**SIEGEL, HOWARD JEROME,** lawyer; b. Chgo., July 29, 1942; s. Leonard and Idele (Lehrner) S.; m. Diane L. Gerber; children: Sari D., Allison J., James G. BS, U. Ill., 1963; JD, Northwestern U., 1966. Bar: Ill. 1966, U.S. dist. Ct. (no. dist.) Ill. 1967. Assoc., Ancel, Stonesifer & Glink, Chgo., 1966-70; ptnr. Goldstine & Siegel, Summit, Ill., 1970-75; sole practice, Chgo., 1975-77; pres. Wexler, Siegel & Shaw, Ltd., Chgo., 1978-82; ptnr. Keck, Mahin & Cate, Chgo., 1982-95, Neal Gerber & Eisenberg, Chgo., 1995—; dir. various corps. Mem. ABA, Chgo. Bar Assn., Ill. Bar Assn., Internat. Council Shopping Ctrs., Urban Land Inst., Chgo. Real.Estate Bd. Clubs: Standard (Chgo.); Twin Orchard Country (Long Grove, Ill.). Real property, General corporate. Office: Neal Gerber & Eisenberg 2 N La Salle St Ste 2100 Chicago IL 60602-3882

**SIEGEL, JEFFREY NORTON,** lawyer; b. N.Y.C., Nov. 27, 1942; s. George Siegel and Rose (Friedman) Gerber; m. Judith Sharon Chused, June 11, 1966; children: Daniel, Linda. AB, Brown U., 1964; LLB, Harvard U., 1967. Bar: N.Y. 1968. Assoc., ptnr. Golenbock & Barell, N.Y.C., 1967-89; ptnr. Whitman & Ransom, N.Y.C., 1990-93, Shack & Siegel, P.C., N.Y.C., 1993—. Mem. bus. com. The Jewish Mus. Mem. ABA, Assn. Bar City N.Y. (com. securities regulation 1987-90, com. profl. responsibility 1979-84), Phi Beta Kappa. General corporate, Securities, Mergers and acquisitions. Home: 975 Park Ave New York NY 10028-0323 Office: Shack & Siegel PC 530 5th Ave New York NY 10036-5101

**SIEGEL, JEFFREY ROY,** lawyer; b. Stuttgart, Germany, Jan. 16, 1957; s. Herbert B. and Joan M. (Goodkin) S.; m. Marilyn E. Seipp Siegel, Aug. 5, 1990; 1 child, Kenneth George. BA in Politics, Princeton U., 1979; JD, U. San Francisco, 1983. Clk. Colo. Ct. Appeals, Denver, 1984-85; assoc. Gibbons, Lees and Schaefer, Walnut Creek, Calif., 1985; PTNR. Gill & Siegel PC, Agana, Guam, 1985-89; pvt. practice San Ramon, Calif., 1990—; cons. Whitestone Group, N.Y.C., 1994—. Mem. State Bar Calif., Colo. Bar Assn., Assn. Trial Lawyers Am., Calif. Trial Lawyers Assn. Democrat. Jewish. Avocations: pvt. pilot, actor. Personal injury, Civil rights, Estate planning. Office: 2817 Crow Canyon Rd Ste 203 San Ramon CA 94583-1639

**SIEGEL, MARK JORDAN,** lawyer; b. Dallas, Feb. 22, 1949; s. Jack H. and Zelda (Sikora) S. BS in Psychology, North Tex. State U., 1972; JD, South Tex. Coll. Law, 1977. Bar: Tex. 1977, U.S. Dist. Ct. (no. dist.) Tex, 1980, U.S. Ct. Appeals (11th and 5th cirs.) 1982, U.S. Supreme Ct. 1982. Pvt. practice, Dallas, 1977-87; mem. bd. dirs. Scotch Corp., Dallas. Sponser Civil Justice Found. Mem. N. Dallas 40. Named one of Outstanding Young Men Am., 1985, 86. Mem. Tex. Trial Lawyers Assn., Dallas Trial Lawyers Assn., Assn. Trial Lawyers Am., Nat. Bd. Trial Advocacy (cert. civil trial specialist), Tex. Bd. Legal Specialization (cert. civil trial law). Personal injury, State civil litigation. Office: 3607 Fairmount St Dallas TX 75219-4710

**SIEGEL, NANCY JANE,** lawyer, mediator; b. Lansing, Mich., Nov. 13, 1958; d. David and Louise Ruth (Kellermann) S.; m. Daniel Edward Holeman; children: Nathan, Julia. BA, Mich. State U., 1980; JD, U. Tulsa, 1983. Bar: Okla. Supreme Ct. 1984, U.S. Dist. Ct. (no. dist.) Okla. 1984, U.S. Dist. Ct. (ea. dist.) Okla. 1985, U.S. Dist. Ct. (we. dist.) Okla. 1986, U.S. Ct. Appeals (10th cir.) 1986, U.S. Supreme Ct. 1990. Lawyer, ptnr. Richards, Paul, Richards & Siegel, Tulsa, Okla., 1982-95; lawyer, of counsel Doerner, Saunders, Daniel & Anderson, Tulsa, 1995-98, Okla. Mediation/Arbitration Svc., Tulsa, 1999—; adj. settlement judge Tulsa County Dist. Ct.-Early Settlement Program, 1992—, Dist. Ct.-No. Dist. Okla., Tulsa, 1995—. Bd. dirs. Jewish Fedn., Tulsa, 1997—, Tulsa Interfaith Alliance, 1999—. Mem. Internat. Assn. Def. Counsel (membership com. 1997-98, 98—), No. Dist. Okla. (admissions and grievance com. 1997—), Am. Inns Ct. (barrister 1989-92, 96-99, exec. com. 1990-92, inn adminstr. 1990-92, membership com. 1990-92, barrister pupilage group liaison 1997-98). Fax: 918-585-1875. E-mail: nsiegel@usaserve.net and njsiegel@hotmail.com. Alternative dispute resolution. Office: Okla Mediation/Arbitration Svc 2021 S Lewis Ave Ste 301 Tulsa OK 74104-5707

**SIEGEL, SARAH ANN,** lawyer; b. Providence, Aug. 29, 1956. BA in History cum laude, Brandeis U., 1978; JD, Washington U., St. Louis, 1981. Bar: Mo. 1982, U.S. Dist. Ct. (ea. dist.) Mo. 1983. Assoc. atty. St. Louis, 1982-83; staff atty. Land Clearance for Redevel. Authority, St. Louis, 1983-85, gen. counsel, 1985-88; gen. counsel Econ. Devel. Corp., St. Louis, 1988-90, St. Louis Devel. Corp., 1990-91; spl. counsel for devel. City of St. Louis, 1991-92; assoc. Suelthaus & Walsh, P.C., St. Louis, 1992-95, prin., 1995-99; gen. counsel Dierbergs Mkts. Inc., St. Louis, 1999—. Pres. Central Reform Congregation, St. Louis, 1991-93, v.p., 1989-91, bd. dirs. 1987-89. Mem. ABA, Mo. Bar Assn. (vice chair com. on eminent domain 1990-91, steering com. 1987-89, 95-96), Women's Lawyer Assn. (bd. dirs. 1985-90, v.p. 1989-90), Am. Corp. Counsel Assn. Avocations: hiking, swimming. Municipal (including bonds), Real property, Land use and zoning (including planning).

**SIEGEL, STANLEY,** lawyer, educator; b. N.Y.C., Mar. 2, 1941; s. David Aaron and Rose (Minsky) S. B.S. summa cum laude, NYU, 1960; J.D. magna cum laude, Harvard U., 1963. Bar: N.Y. 1963, D.C. 1964, Mich. 1970, Calif. 1976; CPA, Md. Atty. Office Sec. of Air Force, 1963-66; asst. prof. law U. Mich., Ann Arbor, 1966-69, assoc. prof., 1969-71, prof., 1971-74; ptnr. Honigman, Miller, Schwartz & Cohn, Detroit, 1974-76; prof. law UCLA, 1976-86; prof. law NYU, 1986—, assoc. dean, 1987-89; vis. prof. Stanford Law Sch., 1973, Ctrl. European U., Budapest, 1993—, U. Konstanz, Germany, 1996, Tel Aviv U., 1998; fellow Max-Planck Inst., Hamburg, 1988; cons. reorgn. U.S. Postal Svc., 1969-71; exec. sec. Mich. Law Revision Commn., 1973; mem. bd. examiners AICPA, 1980-83; mem. editl. bd. Lexis Electronic Author's Press, 1996—. Author: (with Schulman and Moscow) Michigan Business Corporations, 1979, (with Conard and Knauss) Enterprise Organization, 4th edit., 1987, (with D. Siegel) Accounting and Financial Disclosure: A Guide to Basic Concepts, 1983, (with others) Swiss Company Law, 1996. Served to capt. USAF, 1963-66. Mem. ABA, D.C. Bar Assn., Calif. Bar Assn., Assn. of Bar of City of N.Y., Am. Law Inst., AICPA. Office: NYU Law Sch 40 Washington Sq S New York NY 10012-1099

**SIEGENDORF, ARDEN M.,** judge. BBA, U. Miami, 1960, JD, 1963. Diplomate Fla. Acad. Profl. Mediators. Asst. atty. gen. State of Fla., 1963-71; county ct. judge, 1971-81; commr. City of Miami, 1971; pvt. practice, 1981-89, mediator, arbitrator, 1989—; pres. Tallahassee Mediation Ctr., Inc., 1992—; spkr. in field. Contbr. articles to profl. jours. Fellow Am. Coll. Civil Trial Mediators; mem. Fla. Bar, Soc. for Profls. in Dispute Resolution, Tallahassee Bar Assn., Fla. Govtl. Bar Assn. (past v.p.), Imon Arrow Honor Soc., Phi Alpha Delta, Omicron Delta Kappa. Address: 902 N Gadsden St Ste A Tallahassee FL 32303-6388

**SIEH, FRANK OSBORNE,** lawyer; b. N.Y.C., June 5, 1944; s. Edwin Frank and Rosemary Sieh; m. Nancy Ellen Sieh, June 2, 1972; children: Kathleen Ann Pirtle, Nicole Elise. JD, U. Calif., Berkeley, 1970, AB, 1976. Bar: Calif. 1971. Dep. dist. atty. Ventura (Calif.) County Dist. Attys. Office, 1970-71; assoc. Kinkle, Rodiger, Graf, Dewberry and Sprigs, Ventura, 1971-74; ptnr. Everhart and Sieh, Ventura, 1974-80; pvt. practice Ventura, 1980-84; asst. county counsel Ventura County Counsel, 1984-86, litigation supr., 1986-96, chief asst. county counsel, 1996—; pres. Ventura County Trial Lawyers, 1980-81, Ventura County Bar Assn., 1984. Mem. Exec. Com. State Bar, Calif., 1984-86. Democrat. Avocation: sailing. E-mail: siehfos@earthlink.net. and fsieh@coconet.org. Fax: 805-654-2185. Office: Ventura County Counsel 800 S Victoria Ave # 1830 Ventura CA 93009-0001

**SIEKMAN, THOMAS CLEMENT,** lawyer; b. Somerville, Mass., Sept. 22, 1941; s. Aloysius C. and Estelle M. (Forte) S.; m. Claire Dorgan, Oct. 15, 1966; children: Michael T., James T., Amy K. BS in Engring., Merrimack Coll., 1963; JD, Villanova U., 1966. Bar: Mass. 1966, U.S. Dist. Ct. Mass. 1969. Patent atty. Bethlehem (Pa.) Steel, 1966-68, Mohawk Data Scis., Stoneham, Mass., 1968-72, Chittick, Thompson & Pfund, Boston, Mass., 1972-73; from patent atty. to v.p. and gen. counsel Digital Equipment Corp., Maynard, Mass., 1973-98; Sr. v.p., gen. coun., sec. Compaq Computer Corp., 1998—; bd. dirs., chmn. N.E. Legal Found. Trustee Mass. Taxpayers Found.; mem. New Eng. Legal Found. Mem. ABA, Internat. Bar Assn., Boston Bar Found. (trustee). Avocations: squash, skiing. Fax: 281-518-8209. Home: 111 S Castlegreen Cir The Woodlands TX 77381-6339 Office: Compaq Computer Corp PO Box 692000 Houston TX 77269-2000

**SIEMENS, TERRANCE LEE,** patent executive; b. Waterloo, Iowa, May 4, 1938; s. Curtis Wieben and Vera Mae (Heitman) S.; m. Caroline Camille Runge, 1958 (div. 1973); children: Emillee, Douglas, Lynn, William, Thomas; m. Suzanne Collins; 1 child, Mark Collins Gregory. BSME, Iowa State U., 1962; MS, U. Ill., 1972. Rsch. engr. Deere & Co., Moline, Ill., 1960-70; primary examiner U.S. Patent Office, Washington, 1973-86; pres. Siemens Patent Svcs., Fairfax, Va., 1987—; expert witness in field, 1993—. Served in U.S. Army, 1958-60. Mem. Lions (pres. Crystal City club 1990—). Office: Siemens Patent Svcs 4600 Duke St Ste 328 Alexandria VA 22304-2598

**SIEMER, MARTIN W.,** lawyer; b. Teutopolis, Ill., Aug. 11, 1967; s. Joseph B. and Hilda F. Siemer; m. Lisa J. Buhnerkempe, July 10, 1993; children: Edward M., Lauren L. BS in Secondary Edn., U. Ill., 1991; JD, St. Louis U., 1994. Bar: Ill. 1994, U.S. Dist. Ct. (so. dist.) Ill. 1998, U.S. Ct. Appeals (7th cir.) 1998. Lawyer Parker, Siemer, Austin, Resch & Fuhr, Effingham, Ill., 1994—. Mem. bd. edn. Teutopolis Cmty. Unit Sch. Dist., 1997—. Mem. KC (chmn. picnic), Lions. Avocations: family, travel, golf. Appellate, Estate planning, Probate. Office: Parker Siemer Austin Resch & Fuhr 307 N 3rd St Effingham IL 62401-3467

**SIEMON, CHARLES L.,** lawyer; b. Washington, July 27, 1945; s. Robert T. and Margaret (Waugh) S. BA, Emory U., 1967; JD, Fla. State U., 1974. Assoc. Ross, Hardies et al, Chgo., 1974-83; ptnr. Siemon, Larsen & Purdy, Chgo., 1983—. Co-author: The Zoning Game Revisted, 1975, Vested Rights, The Permit Explosion, 1976. Served to lt. USNR, 1969-72. Mem. ABA, Am. Planning Assn., Urban Land Inst. (assoc.). Real property, Condemnation. Home: 18 Treasure Rd Marathon FL 33050-2504 Office: Siemon & Larsen 433 Plaza Real Boca Raton FL 33432-3932

**SIEMON, JOYCE MARILYN,** lawyer, writer; b. Bridgeport, Conn., Dec. 4, 1944; d. George Lewis and Rita (Siegel) Nissenson; 1 child, Alyssa Karen; m. Vicnent A. De Martino, Jan. 14, 1996. BA in English, Carnegie Inst. Tech., 1966; JD with high honors, Fla. State U., 1980. Bar: Fla. Tech. writer Computer Sci. Rsch. Ctr. Carnegie Inst. Tech., Pitts., 1966-67; tchr. Leesville (La.) Jr. High Sch., 1967-68; mag. editor VanTrump, Ziegler and Shane, Pitts., 1969; news editor Pitts. Press, 1970; staff writer Dade County Pub. Safety Dept., Miami, 1971-75; reporter North Dade Jour., Miami, 1977; freelance writer, 1977—; instr. legal writing and rsch. Coll. Law Fla. State U., Tallahassee, 1979-80; intern Fla. Supreme Ct., 1980; law clk. Office Gen. Counsel Fla. Dept. Gen. Svcs., Tallahassee, 1980; assoc. Young, Stern & Tannenbaum, P.A., North Miami Beach, 1981, Greenber, Traurig, Askew, Hoffman, Lipoff, Quentel & Wolff, Miami, 1981-82, Hornsby & Whisenand, Miami, 1982-85; pvt. practice North Miami Beach, 1985-92, Boca Raton, Fla., 1992—. Author: employee manual, advtsg. brochures, newspaper articles and ads, book revs.; editor: Lawrenceville: A Shoret History, 1969; columnist Siemon Says North Dade Jour., 1977; contbr., editor articles to profl. jours. Mem. Dade County Coord. Network, 1983. Mem. ABA, Am. Judicature Soc., Am. Jewish Congress (v.p. S.E. region), Internat. Platform Assn., Fla. Bar Assn. (various coms.), Dade County Bar Assn., Order of the Coif, Kiwanis Internat., Phi Alpha Delta. Alternative dispute resolution, Appellate.

**SIENKO, LEONARD EDWARD JR.,** lawyer; b. Hancock, N.Y., Aug. 24, 1946; s. Leonard Edward and Louise Albina (Gaudor) S. BA, Boston Coll., 1968, JD, 1977; MDiv, Andover-Newton Theol., 1971. Bar: N.Y. 1978, U.S. Dist. Ct. (no. dist.) N.Y. 1980, U.S. Supreme Ct. 1982. Estate tax atty. Del. County N.Y. State Dept. Taxation & Fin., Delhi, 1983-93; ct. atty. trial part Del. County Ct., Delhi, N.Y., 1993—; town atty. Town of Hancock, 1990—. County chair Del. County Dem. Com., N.Y., 1987-93. Mem. Del. County Bar Assn. (pres. 1993-95), N.Y. State Bar Assn. (Ho. Dels. 1993-97, N.Y. Law Net com. 1995—, mem. President's Task Force on Electronic Comm. 1996—). Democrat. Mem. Unitarian Universalist Ch. Avocations: computers. Home: 29 W Main St Hancock NY 13783-1027 Office: PO Box 579 12 E Main St Hancock NY 13783-1126

**SIFTON, CHARLES PROCTOR,** federal judge; b. N.Y.C., Mar. 18, 1935; s. Paul F. and Claire G. S.; m. Susan Scott Rowland, May 20, 1986; children: Samuel, Tobias, John. A.B., Harvard U., 1957; LL.B., Columbia U., 1961. Bar: N.Y. 1961. Assoc. Cadwalader, Wickersham & Taft, 1961-62, 64-66; staff atty. U.S. Senate Fgn. Rels. Com., 1962-63; asst. U.S. atty. N.Y.C., 1966-69; ptnr. LeBoeuf, Lamb, Leiby and MacRae, N.Y.C., 1969-77; judge U.S. Dist. Ct. (ea. dist.) N.Y., Bklyn., 1977—, chief judge, 1995—. Mem. Bar Assn. City of N.Y. Office: US Dist Ct US Courthouse 225 Cadman Plz E Rm 244 Brooklyn NY 11201-1818

**SIGAL, MICHAEL STEPHEN,** lawyer; b. Chgo., July 9, 1942; s. Carl I. and Evelyn (Wallack) S.; m. Kass M. Flaherty, May 16, 1971; 1 child, Sarah Caroline. BS, U. Wis.-Madison, 1964; JD, U. Chgo., 1967. Bar: Ill. 1967, U.S. Dist. Ct. (no. dist.) Ill. 1967. Assoc. firm Sidley & Austin and predecessor firm, Chgo., 1967-73, ptnr., 1973—. Mem. U. Chgo. Law Rev., 1965. Bd. dirs. EMRE Diagnostic Services, Inc., affiliate Michael Reese Hosp., Chgo., 1982-91, The Mary Meyer Sch., Chgo., 1986-87. Mem. ABA, Chgo. Bar Assn., Law Club, Mid-Day Club (Chgo.), Mill Creek Hunt Club (bd. dirs. 1992—, Wadsworth, Ill.), Phi Beta Kappa, Phi Kappa Phi, Phi Eta Sigma. Jewish. General corporate, Securities. Home: 2180 Wilmot Rd Deerfield IL 60015-1556 Office: Sidley & Austin 1 First Natl Plz Chicago IL 60603-2003

**SIGETY, CHARLES EDWARD,** lawyer, family business consultant; b. N.Y.C., Oct. 10, 1922; s. Charles and Anna (Toth) S.; m. Katharine K. Snell, July 17, 1948; children: Charles, Katharine, Robert, Cornelius, Elizabeth. BS, Columbia U., 1944; MBA, Harvard U., 1947; LLB, Yale U., 1951; LHD (hon.), Cazenovia Coll., 1994. Bar: N.Y. 1952, D.C. 1958. With Bankers Trust Co., 1939-42; instr. adminstrv. engring. Pratt Inst., 1948; instr. econs. Yale U., 1948-50; vis. lectr. acctg. Sch. Gen. Studies Columbia U., N.Y.C., 1948-50, 52; rapporteur com. fed. taxation for U.S. coun. Internat. C. of C., 1952-53; asst. to com. fed. taxation Am. Inst. Accts., 1950-53; with Compton Advt. Agy., N.Y.C., 1954; vis. lectr. law Yale U., 1952; pvt. practice law N.Y.C., 1952-67; pres., dir. Video Vittles, Inc., N.Y.C., 1953-67; dep. commr. FHA, 1955-57; of counsel Javits and Javits, 1959-60; 1st asst. atty. gen. N.Y., 1958-59; dir., mem. exec. com. Gotham Bank, N.Y.C., 1961-63; dir. N.Y. State Housing Fin. Agy., 1962-63; chmn. Met. Ski Slopes, Inc., N.Y.C., 1962-65; pres., exec. adminstr. Florence Nightingale

Health Ctr., N.Y.C., 1965-85; dir. Schaerer AG, Wabern, Switzerland, 1982-88; chmn. Internat. Bioimmune Sys., Inc., Great Neck, N.Y., 1999—; professorial lectr. Sch. Architecture, Pratt Inst., N.Y.C., 1962-66; mem. Sigety Assocs., cons. in housing mortgage financing and urban renewal, 1957-67; ho. cons. Govt. of Peru, 1956; mem. missions to Hungary, Poland, Fed. Republic Germany, Malta, Czechoslovakia, Russia, Israel, Overseas Pvt. Investment Corp., 1990-92; owner, operator Peppermill Farms, Pipersville, Pa., 1956—. Bd. dirs., sec., v.p., treas. Nat. Coun. Health Ctrs., 1969-85; bd. dirs. Am.-Hungarian Found., 1974-76, Pritikin Rsch. Found., 1991—, Stratford Arms Condo Assn., 1992-93, Global Leadership Inst., 1993—; founding mem., bd. dirs., Natl. Assn. for Continence, 1952—, trustee Cazenovia (N.Y.) Coll., 1981—, Delaware Valley Coll. Sci. and Agr., Doylestown, Pa., 1998—; del. White House Conf. on Aging, 1971, White House Conf. on Mgmt. Tng. and Market Econs. Edn. in Ctrl. and Ea. Europe, 1991; bd. visitors Lander Coll., U. S.C., Greenwood, 1982-84; mem. fin. com. World Games, Santa Clara, 1981, London, 1985, Karlsruhe, 1989, The Hague, 1993, Confrerie des Chevaliers du Tastevin, Confrerie de la Chaine des Rotisseurs, Wine and Food Soc., Wednesday 10. Lt. (j.g.) Supply Corps, USNR, 1942-46. Recipient President's medal Cazenovia Coll., 1990, George Washington laureate Am. Hungarian Found., 1996; named Prin. for Day, Townsend Harris H.S. N.Y.C. Bd. Edn., 1997-99, Disting. Alumnus U.S. Navy Supply Corps Sch., Athens, Ga., 1998; Baker scholar Harvard U., 1947. Mem. DOCA (Defense Orientation Conf. Assn.), Nat. Assn. Continence (founding mem., bd. dirs. 1982—),. Presbyterian. Administrative and regulatory, Land use and zoning (including planning), Real property. Office: 7155 Old Easton Rd Box 156 Pipersville PA 18947-9701

**SIGHINOLFI, PAUL HENRY,** lawyer; b. Chicopee, Mass., Aug. 10, 1948; s. Henry E. and Anne T. (Veale) S.; m. Vickie Sidou, Sept. 17, 1977; children: Kaitlin M., Christopher P., Michael P. AB, St. Anselm's Coll., 1970; MA, Trinity Coll., 1973; M, Springfield Coll., 1974; JD, Catholic U., Washington, 1981. Bar: Maine 1981, U.S. Dist. Ct. Maine 1981. Ptnr. Rudman & Winchell Law Offices, Bangor, Maine, 1981—; lectr. Husson Coll., Bangor, Maine, 1994—. Co-author: Workers Compensation, Employers Guide, 1993; mem. editl. bd. No. New Eng. Law Pub., 1989—. Mem. ABa, Maine Trial Lawyers Assn. Roman Catholic. Avocations: water sports, snow skiing. Workers' compensation, Labor, Health. Home: 22 Sylvan Dr Brewer ME 04412-9628 Office: Rudman & Winchell 84 Harlow St Ste 1 Bangor ME 04401-4950

**SIGMOND, CAROL ANN,** lawyer; b. Phila., Jan. 9, 1951; d. Irwin and Mary Florence (Vollmer) S. BA, Grinnell Coll., 1972; JD, Cath. U., 1975. Bar: Va. 1975, D.C. 1980, Md. 1988, N.Y. 1990, U.S. Dist. Ct. (ea. dist.) Va. 1975, U.S. Dist. Ct. (so. and ea. dist.) N.Y. 1991, U.S. Ct. Appeals (4th cir.) 1976, U.S. Ct. Appeals (fed. cir.) 1987. Asst. gen. counsel Washington Met. Area Transit Authority, 1978-85; acting assoc. gen. counsel for appeals and gen. law, 1985-86; assoc. Patterson, Belknap, Webb & Tyler, Washington, 1986-89, Berman, Paley, Goldstein & Kannry, N.Y.C., 1991-93; prin. Law Offices of Carol A. Sigmond, N.Y.C., 1993-97; of counsel Pollack & Greene, LLP, N.Y.C., 1998—; Mem. Women's Nat. Dem. Club. Active Womens Nat. Dem. Club. Mem. ABA, D.C. Bar Assn., Arlington County Bar Assn., Va. State Bar Assn., Md. State Bar Assn. Democrat. Mem. LDS. Avocations: piano, bridge. General civil litigation, Construction. Office: Pollack & Greene LLP 757 3rd Ave New York NY 10017-2013

**SIGMOND, RICHARD BRIAN,** lawyer; b. Phila., Dec. 7, 1944; s. Joseph and Jean (Nissman) S.; children: Michael, Catherine, Alina; m. Susan Helen Peteraf, Dec. 24, 1984. BS, Phila. Coll. Textiles & Sci., 1966; JD, Temple U., 1969. Bar: Pa. 1969, U.S. Supreme Ct. 1973, U.S. Dist. Ct. (ea. dist.) Pa. 1975, U.S. Ct. Appeals (3d cir.) 1975, N.Y. 1982, D.C. 1995. Atty. Pub. Defender Assn., Phila., 1969-70; ptnr. Meranze, Katz, Spear & Wilderman, Phila., 1970-84; sr. ptnr. Spear, Wilderman, Sigmond, Borish & Endy, Phila., 1985-89, Sagot, Jennings & Sigmond, Phila., 1989—; gen. counsel Internat. Brotherhood Painters and Allied Trades, 1997—; chmn., bd. dirs. Gatehouse Phila., 1972-83; lectr. Pvt. Industry Coun., Phila., 1985—, labor studies div., Pa. State U., 1978-82, 85-86. Mem. ABA (labor law com., litigation com.), AFL-CIO (lawyers coordinating com.), Pa. Bar Assn. (labor law com.), Phila. Bar Assn. (labor com.), Phi Alpha Delta. Avocations: sailing, writing. Labor, Pension, profit-sharing, and employee benefits, Federal civil litigation. Office: Penn Mutual Towers 510 Walnut St Fl 16 Philadelphia PA 19106-3601

**SIGNORILE, VINCENT ANTHONY,** lawyer; b. Jersey City, Mar. 22, 1959; s. Ralph R. and Rita (DeRosa) S. BS, St. Peter's Coll., Jersey City, 1981; JD, Seton Hall U., 1985. Bar: N.J. 1985, Pa. 1985. Aide Jersey City Mcpl. Coun., 1980-81, Office of Mayor, City of Jersey City, 1981; law clk. Corp. Counsel Jersey City, 1981-85; law sec. Superior Ct. N.J. for Hudson County, Jersey City, 1985-86; assoc. atty. Jersey City, 1986-89; ptnr. Signorile & Saminski, Jersey City, 1989-97; atty. Jersey City Zoning Bd. Adjustment, 1994-97, Bayonne City Ethics Bd., 1995-97; judge Jersey City Mcpl. Ct., 1996—. Mem. Hudson County Dem. Com., 1977-81, Jersey City Environ. Com., 1989-93, Jersey City Planning Bd. Com., 1991-93, Jersey City Ins. Fund Com., 1989-93; co-chmn. Hudson County Columbus Parade, 1984-85; elected to Mcpl. Coun. Jersey City, 1989-93. Mem. ABA, N.J. Bar Assn., Pa. Bar Assn., Hudson County Bar Assn. (treas. Young Lawyer's Assn. 1987-88, scholar 1984-85), Assn. Trial Lawyers Am. Roman Catholic. General practice. Home: 1691 John F Kennedy Blvd Jersey City NJ 07305-1841 Office: Jersey City Municipal Ct 769 Montgomery St Jersey City NJ 07306-4603

**SIGUENZA, PETER CHARLES, JR.,** supreme court justice; b. July 1, 1951; s. Peter C. and Barbara L. (Bordallo) S.; m. Joleen Taitano Rios, Dec. 6, 1969; 1 child, Dawn. BA, Calif. State U., 1976; JD, U. of the Pacific, 1980. Bar: Calif. 1981, Guam 1981, U.S. Ct. Appeals (9th cir.), Commonwealth No. Marianas 1983. Pvt. practice Klemm, Blair & Barusch; staff atty. Guam Legal Svcs. Corp.; clk. Superior Ct. Guam; libr. Calif. Ct. Appeal; judge Superior Ct. Guam, Agana, 1984-96, 1996—; designated judge Dist. Ct. Guam, Supreme Ct. Federated States Micronesia; chair bd. trustees Father Duenas Meml. Sch., 1991; chair rules commn. Supreme Ct. Guam, 1993. Mem. ABA, Am. Judges Assn. Office: Supreme Ct of Guam Judiciary Bldg 120 W O'Brien Dr Agana GU 96910*

**SIKORA, TOMASZ JACEK,** lawyer; b. Wroclaw, Poland, July 2, 1965; s. Zenon Stefan and Bronislawa Sikora. BA, Harvard Coll., 1987; JD, U. Va., 1995. Bar: Tex. 1995. Ptnr. The Monitor Ltd., Warsaw, Poland, and Washington, 1991-92; assoc. Vinson & Elkins LLP, Houston, 1995—. Roman Catholic. Avocation: sailing. Private international, General civil litigation, Federal civil litigation. Office: Vinson & Elkins LLP 1001 Fannin 2300 First City Tower Houston TX 77002

**SILAK, CATHY R.,** state supreme court justice; b. Astoria, N.Y., May 25, 1950; d. Michael John and Rose Marie (Janor) S.; m. Nicholas G. Miller, Aug. 9, 1980; 3 children. BA, NYU, 1971; M in City Planning, Harvard U., 1973; JD, U. Calif., 1976. Bar: Calif. 1977, U.S. Dist. Ct. (no. dist.) Calif. 1977, D.C. 1979, U.S. Ct. Appeals (D.C. cir.) 1979, U.S. Dist. Ct. (so. dist.) N.Y. 1980, Idaho 1983, U.S. Dist. Ct. Idaho 1983, U.S. Ct. Appeals (2nd cir.) 1983, U.S. Ct. Appeals (9th cir.) 1985. Law clk. to Hon. William W. Schwarzer U.S. Dist. Ct. (no dist.), Calif., 1976-77; pvt. practice San Francisco, 1977-79, Washington, 1979-80; asst. U.S. atty. So. Dist. of N.Y., 1980-83; spl. asst. U.S. atty. Dist. of Idaho, 1983-84; pvt. practice Boise, Idaho, 1984-90; judge Idaho Ct. Appeals, 1990-93; justice Idaho Supreme Ct., Boise, 1993—; assoc. gen. counsel Morrison Knudsen Corp., 1989-90; mem. fairness com. Idaho Supreme Ct. and Gov.'s Task Force on Alternative Dispute Resolution; instr. and lectr. in field. Assoc. note and comment editor Calif. Law Rev., 1975-76. Land use planner Mass. Dept. Natural Resources, 1973; founder Idaho Coalition for Adult Literacy; bd. dirs. Literacy Lab., Inc.; mem. adv. bd. Boise State U. Legal Asst. Program. Recipient Jouce Stein award Boise YWCA, 1992, Women Helping Women award Soroptimist, Boise, 1993. Fellow Idaho Law Found (ann., lectr.); mem. ABA (nat. conf. state trial judges jud. adminstrn. divsn.), Nat. Assn. Women Judges, Idaho State Bar (corp./securities sect., instr.), Am. Law Inst., Fellows of the Am. Bar Found. Office: Idaho Supreme Ct Supreme Ct Bldg PO Box 83720 Boise ID 83720-3720

**SILBER, ALAN,** lawyer; b. Newark, Oct. 21, 1938; s. Charles and Hermine (Hahn) S.; m. Dana Slater, July 5, 1996; 1 child, Laramie. BA, Duke U., 1960; LLB, Columbia U., 1965. Bar: N.J. 1965, U.S. Supreme Ct. 1965, Calif. 1972, U.S. Dist. Ct. (no. dist.) Calif. 1972, U.S. Ct. Appeals (9th cir.) 1972, N.Y. 1982, U.S. Ct. Appeals (2d, 3d, 4th, 6th cirs.) 1982, U.S. Dist. Ct. N.J. 1982, U.S. Dist. Ct. Hawaii 1982, U.S. Dist. Ct. (so., ea., and no. dists.) N.Y. 1982. Ptnr. Podvey Sachs Catenaci & Silber, Newark, 1980-82, Silber & Rubin, N.Y.C., 1982-87, Hayden & Silber, Weehawken, N.J., 1988—; bd. advisors Drug Policy Found., Washington, 1987—, The Vol. Com. of Lawyers, N.Y.C., 1997. Mem. Assn. Criminal Def. Lawyers N.J. (pres. 1992-93, founding mem.), Nat. Assn. Criminal Def. Lawyers (regional coord., 3d cir. strike force 1993—). Democrat. Jewish. Avocation: running. Criminal, Appellate, General civil litigation. Home: 160 W 16th St New York NY 10011-6285 Office: Hayden & Silber 1500 Harbor Blvd Weehawken NJ 07087-6732

**SILBER, ALBERT J.,** lawyer; b. Detroit, Mar. 15, 1912; s. Ben Baruch Silber and Ida (Kogut) S.; m. Merry J. Kurtz, June 9, 1935; children: Michael D., Marc S., Julie E. BA, Wayne State U., 1930; JD magna cum laude, U. Mich., 1932. Bar: Mich. 1933, U.S. Dist. Ct. Mich. 1933. Sec., gen. counsel, dir. Barley Earhart Co., Portland, Mich., 1938, 2B Systems Inc., Sterling Heights, Mich., 1976-96; mng. ptnr. Venoy Palmer Ctr., Westland, Mich., 1958—, N. King Investment Co., Dearborn, Mich., 1979—. Del. World Jewish Congress, 1948; pres. Mich. Coun. Am. Jewish Congress, 1949. Inductee Mich. Jewish Sports Hall of Fame, 1993. Fellow The Order of Coif; mem. Am. Contract Bridge League (Gold Life master), Mich. Bridge Assn. (pres. 1953—), Tau Epsilon Rho (nat. pres. 1950-51). Avocation: playing bridge. General corporate, Probate, Real property. Office: Silber and Silber 21700 Northwestern Hwy Ste 900 Southfield MI 48075-4985

**SILBER, NORMAN JULES,** lawyer; b. Tampa, Fla., Apr. 18, 1945; s. Abe and Mildred (Hirsch) S.; m. Linda Geraldine Hirsch, June 10, 1979; 1 child, Michael Hirsch. BA, Tulane U., 1967, JD, 1969; postgrad. in bus. adminstrn. NYU, 1970-72. Bar: Fla. 1970, U.S. Dist. Ct. (so. dist. Fla.) 1975, U.S. Tax Ct. 1975, U.S. Ct. Appeals (5th cir.) 1975, U.S. Ct. Appeals (11th cir.) 1981. With legal dept. Fiduciary Trust Co. N.Y., N.Y.C., 1969-72, asst. trust officer, 1971-72; exec. v.p. I.R.E. Fin. Corp., Miami, Fla., 1972-76; mng. atty. Norman J. Silber, P.A., Miami, 1973-85; ptnr. McDermott, Will & Emery, 1985—. Mem. ABA, Fla. Bar (chmn. 11th jud. cir. grievance com. I 1982-84). Republican. Jewish. Real property, General corporate, General practice. Home: 1232 Palermo Ave Miami FL 33134-6327 Office: McDermott Will & Emery 201 S Biscayne Blvd Ste 2200 Miami FL 33131-4336

**SILBERGELD, ARTHUR F.,** lawyer; b. St. Louis, June 1, 1942; s. David and Sabina (Silbergeld) S.; m. Carol Ann Schwartz, may 1, 1970; children: Diana Lauren, Julia Kay. BA, U. Mich., 1968; M in City Planning, U. Pa., 1971; JD, Temple U., 1975. Bar: N.Y. 1976, Calif. 1978, D.C. 1983, U.S. Ct. Appeals (2nd cir.), U.S. Ct. Appeals (9th cir.), U.S. Ct. Appeals (D.C. cir.). Assoc. Vladeck, Elias, Vladeck & Lewis, N.Y.C., 1975-77; field atty. NLRB, L.A., 1977-78; ptnr., head employment law practice group McKenna, Conner & Cuneo, L.A., 1978-89; ptnr. Graham & James, L.A., 1990-96; labor ptnr. Sonnenschein Nath & Rosenthal, L.A., 1996-99; ptnr. Proskauer Rose LLP, L.A., 1999—; instr. extension divsn. UCLA, 1981-89. Author: Doing Business in California: An Employment Law Handbook, 2nd edit., 1997, Advising California Employers, 1990, 91, 93, 94, 95 supplements; contbr. articles to profl. jours. Founding mem. L.A. Mus. Contemporary Art; bd. dirs. Bay Cities unit Am. Cancer Soc., Calif., 1981-85, Jewish Family Svc., L.A., 1981-85, Leadership coun., So. Poverty Law Ctr., L.A., Child Devel. Ctr., 1998—, Leadership Task Force, Drs. Without Borders. Mem. L.A. County Bar Assn. (chair labor and employment law sect. 1999—), Mus. Modern Art (N.Y.C.), Art Inst. Chgo. Labor. Office: Proskauer Rose LLP 2049 Century Park E Fl 32 Los Angeles CA 90067-3101

**SILBERLING, STEPHEN PIERCE,** lawyer; b. Far Rockaway, N.Y., Feb. 14, 1950; s. Edwyn and Margaret Ann Silberling; 1 child, Beverly June. BA, Haverford Coll., 1971; MA, U. Toronto, Ont., Can., 1973; JD, Vanderbilt U., 1979. Bar: Tenn. 1979, U.S. Dist. Ct. (mid. dist.) Tenn. 1979, U.S. Dist. Ct. (we. dist.) Tenn. 1980, Mo. 1980, U.S. Ct. Appeals (6th and 8th cirs.) 1980, N.Y. 1985, U.S. Dist. Ct. (ea. dist.) N.Y. 1985, U.S. Supreme Ct. 1991. Co-author: (book) Shopping the Insiders Way, 1985. Taxation, general, Contracts commercial, General corporate. Office: Silberling & Silberling Fed Plz 300 Rabro Dr Hauppauge NY 11788-4256

**SILBERMAN, ALAN HARVEY,** lawyer; b. Chgo., Oct. 22, 1940; s. Milton J. and Mollie E. (Hymanson) S.; m. Margaret Judith Auslander, Nov. 17, 1968; children: Elena, Mark. BA with distinction, Northwestern U., 1961; LLB, Yale U., 1964. Bar: Ill., 1964, U.S. Dist. Ct. (no. dist.) Ill., 1966, U.S. Ct. Appeals (7th cir.) 1970, (5th and 9th cir.) 1977, (D.C. cir.) 1979, (4th cir.) 1980, (11th cir.) 1981, (3rd cir.) 1982, (8th and 10th cirs.) 1993, U.S. Supreme Ct. 1978. Law clk. U.S. Dist. Ct., Chgo., 1964-66; assoc. Sonnenschein Nath & Rosenthal, Chgo., 1964-71, ptnr., 1972—; mem. antitrust adv. bd. Bur. Nat. Affairs, Washington, 1985—; mem. Ill. Atty. Gen. Franchise Adv. Bd., 1996—. Contbr. articles to profl. jours. Bd. dirs., v.p., sec. Camp Ramah in Wisc., Inc., Chgo., 1966-86, pres., 1986-94; bd. dirs. Nat. Ramah Commn., Inc. of Jewish Theol. Sem. Am., N.Y.C., 1970—, v.p., 1986-94, pres., 1994—; mem. U.S. del. 33d World Zionist Congress, Jerusalem, 1997. Mem. ABA (chmn. antitrust sect. FTC com. 1981-83, chmn. nat. insts. 1983-85, mem. coun. antitrust sect. 1985-88, fin. officer, 1988-90, sect. del. ho. of dels. 1990-92, chmn.-elect 1992-93, chmn. 1993-94), Ill. Bar Assn. (chmn. antitrust sect. 1975-76), Northwestern U. 1851 Soc. (chair 1994-97). Antitrust. Home: 430 Oakdale Ave Glencoe IL 60022-2113 Office: Sonnenschein Nath 233 S Wacker Dr Ste 8000 Chicago IL 60606-6342

**SILBERMAN, CHARLOTTE SCHATZBERG,** retired lawyer, artist; b. N.Y.C., Oct. 15, 1918; d. Louis and Annie (Hammerman) Schatzberg; m. Bernard Silberman, Sept. 24, 1942 (dec. Mar. 1991); children: Adela Wagman, Margery Miller Moores. BA, Hunter Coll., 1938; LLB, JD, Bklyn. Law Sch., 1940; postgrad., SUNY, Albany, 1977-84, Fla. Atlantic U., 1984—. Bar: N.Y. 1941. Pvt. practice law N.Y.C., 1940-43, Albany, N.Y., 1947-57; atty. State N.Y., Albany, 1957-63; assoc. counsel SUNY, Albany, 1963-74, dir. paralegal studies, 1975-77. Works exhibited Soc. of Four Arts, 1990, Cornell Mus., Delray Beach, Fla., 1994, 95. Home: 7076 Huntington Ln Apt 401 Delray Beach FL 33446-2554

**SILBERMAN, CURT C.,** lawyer; b. Wuerzburg, Fed. Republic Germany; came to U.S., 1938, naturalized, 1944; s. Adolf and Ida (Rosenbusch) S.; m. Else Kleemann, 1935. Student, U. Berlin, U. Munich; JD summa cum laude, Wuerzburg U., 1931, Rutgers U., 1947; Dr.h.c., Middlebury Coll., 1997. Bar: N.J. 1948, U.S. Supreme Ct., 1957. Pvt. practice internat. pvt. law, Florham Park, N.J., 1948—; counsel to Arnold R. Kent, Florham Park; lectr. internat. pvt. law, 1954, 81, 82, 87, 91, 95; prin. guest lectr. at Univ.'s 400th anniversary U. Wuerzburg, 1982. Pres., Am. Fedn. Jews from Cen. Europe, N.Y., 1962-86, chmn. bd., 1986—; pres. Jewish Philanthropic Fund of 1933, Inc., N.Y., 1971-87, chmn. bd. 1987—; trustee Leo Baeck Inst., N.Y., 1962—, N.Y. Found. Nursing Homes, Inc.; hon. trustee Jewish Family Svc. of Metro-West, N.J.; co-chmn. Coun. Jews from Germany, 1974—; chmn. Rsch. Found. for Jewish Immigration Inc. N.Y.; bd. dir. Conf. on Jewish Material Claims Against Germany. Recipient Golden Doctoral Diploma U. Wuerzburg Law faculty, 1982, Festschrift dedicated to him by Am. Fedn. Jews from Cen. Europe in N.Y., 1969, recipient Pub. Svc. medal. Mem. N.J. Bar Assn. (chmn. com. comparative jurisprudence 1966-73, chmn. com. internat. trade 1974-78), Essex County Bar Assn., CCS, Am. Coun. on Germany, Internat. Biographical Dictionary of Cen. European Emigrés (adv. bd.) Contbr. articles to legal jours. Private international.

**SILBERMAN, LAURENCE HIRSCH,** federal judge; b. York, Pa., Oct. 12, 1935; s. William and Anna (Hirsch) S.; m. Rosalie G. Gaull, Apr. 28, 1957; children: Robert Stephen, Katherine DeBoer Balaban, Anne Gaull Otis. AB, Dartmouth Coll., 1957; LLB, Harvard U., 1961. Bar: Hawaii 1962, D.C. 1973. Assoc. Moore, Torkildson & Rice and Quinn & Moore, Honolulu, 1961-64; ptnr. Moore, Silberman & Schulze, Honolulu, 1964-67; atty. appellate divsn. gen. counsel's office NLRB, Washington, 1967-69; solicitor of labor U.S. Dept. Labor, Washington, 1969-70, undersec. labor, 1970-73; ptnr. Steptoe & Johnson, Washington, 1973-74; dep. atty. gen. U.S. Washington, 1974-75; amb. to Yugoslavia, 1975-77; mng. ptnr. Morrison & Foerster, Washington, 1978-79, 83-85; exec. v.p. Crocker Nat. Bank, San Francisco, 1979-83; judge U.S. Ct. Appeals (D.C. cir.), Washington, 1985—; lectr. labor law and legis. U. Hawaii, 1962-63; adj. prof. adminstrv. law Georgetown U., Washington, 1987-94, 97, 99, NYU, 1995, 96, Harvard, 1998; Pres.' spl. envoy on ILO affairs, 1976; mem. gen. adv. com. on Arms Control and Disarmament, 1981-85; mem. Def. Policy Bd., 1981-85; vice chmn. State Dept.'s Commn. on Security and Econ. Assistance, 1983-84. Bd. dirs. Com. on Present Danger, 1978-85, Inst. for Ednl. Affairs, 1981-85; vice chmn. adv. coun. on gen. govt. Rep. Nat. Com., 1977-80. With AUS, 1957-58. Am. Enterprise Inst. sr. fellow, 1977-78, vis. fellow 1978-85. Mem. U.S. Fgn. Intelligence Surveillance Act Ct. of Rev., Coun. on Fgn. Rels.

**SILBERMAN, MORRIS,** lawyer; b. Phila., Sept. 16, 1957; s. Louis and Regina S.; m. Nelly N. Khouzam, May 31, 1986. BA, Tulane U., 1979; JD, U. Fla., 1982. Bar: Fla., U.S. Dist. Ct. (mid. dist.) Fla., U.S. Ct. Appeals (11th cir.), U.S. Supreme Ct., U.S. Ct. Claims. Law clk. Hon. Herboth S. Ryder, 1982-84; atty. DeManio, Harrison & Assocs., 1984-86, Richards, Gilkey et al, 1986-88; pvt. practice Clearwater, Fla., 1988—. Mem. Fla. Bar (bd. govs. 1996—, chair budget com. and election reform com.), Clearwater Bar Assn. (pres. 1993-94). Avocations: cooking, reading, travel. E-mail: msilberman@ij.net. General civil litigation, Appellate, Contracts commercial. Office: 1230 S Myrtle Ave Ste 101 Clearwater FL 33756-3445

**SILECCHIA, LUCIA ANN,** law educator; b. Flushing, N.Y., June 3, 1967; d. Fred and Eleanor Silecchia. BA, Queens Coll./CUNY, 1987; JD, Yale U., 1990. Bar: Conn. 1990, N.Y. 1991, D.C. 1991, U.S. Supreme Ct. 1995. Litigation assoc. Rogers & Wells, N.Y.C., 1990-91; instr. lawyering skills program Cath. U. Law Sch., Washington, 1991-92, asst. dir. lawyering skills program, 1992-93, asst. prof. law, 1993-97, assoc. prof., 1997—; assoc. Environ. Law Inst., Washington, 1993—; mem. Legal Writing Inst., Seattle, 1992—. Contbr. articles to profl. jours. Recipient Mirror of Justice award Guild Cath. Lawyers, 1996. Mem. ABA, N.Y. State Bar Assn. (com. on legal edn. 1996—), D.C. Bar Assn., Nat. Italian Am. Bar Assn. Home: 4600 Connecticut Ave NW Washington DC 20008-5750 Office: Cath U Law Sch Faculty Offices Washington DC 20064-0001

**SILER, EUGENE EDWARD, JR.,** federal judge; b. Williamsburg, Ky., Oct. 19, 1936; s. Eugene Edward and Lowell (Jones) S.; m. Christy Dyanne Minnich, Oct. 18, 1969; children—Eugene Edward, Adam Troy. B.A. cum laude, Vanderbilt U., 1958; LL.B., U. Va., 1963; LL.M., Georgetown U., 1964. Bar: Ky. 1963, Va. 1963, D.C. 1963. Individual practice law Williamsburg, 1964-65; atty. Whitley County, Ky., 1965-70; U.S. atty. Eastern Dist. Ky., Lexington, 1970-75; judge U.S. Dist. Ct., Eastern and Western Dists., Ky., 1975-91; chief judge Eastern Dist., Ky., 1984-91; judge U.S. Ct. Appeals (6th cir.), 1991—. Campaign co-chmn. Congressman Tim L. Carter, 1966, 5th Congl. Dist.; campaign co-chmn. U.S. Senator J.S. Cooper, 1966; trustee Cumberland Coll., Williamsburg, 1965-73, 80-88; 1st v.p. Ky. Bapt. Convention, 1986-87; bd. dirs. Bapt. Healthcare Systems Inc., 1990—. Served with USN, 1958-60, with Res. 1960-83. E. Barrett Prettyman fellow, 1963-64; recipient medal Freedom's Found., 1968. Mem. FBA, Ky. Bar Assn. (Judge of Yr. award 1992), D.C. Bar Assn., Va. State Bar. Republican. Baptist. Home: PO Box 129 Williamsburg KY 40769-0129 Office: US Ct Appeals 1380 W 5th St Ste 200 London KY 40741-1615

**SILER, J. BERNARD,** lawyer, educator; b. Washington, Nov. 11, 1951; s. H. Bernard and Frances (Hickman) S.; children: Brandon A., Max J., Joshua B. BA, U. Dayton, 1972; JD, U. Cin., 1978. Bar: Ohoi, D.C., U.S. Army Ct. Criminal Appeals. Legal advisor U.S. Bd. Vets. Appeals, Washington, 1980-84; pros. atty. D.C. Corp. Counsel, Washington, 1984—; adj. prof. Montgomery Coll., Takoma Park, Md., 1992—; lectr. Am. history various colls., univs., civic assns., 1990—. Bd. dirs. Police and Firefighters Retirement Bd., Washington, 1985-88. Maj., U.S. Army, 1997, Germany. Mem. Nat. Bar Assn., Kappa Alpha Psi. Avocations: whitewater kayaking, hiking, Civil War reenactment. Home: 1207 Sheridan St NW Washington DC 20011-1103

**SILETS, HARVEY MARVIN,** lawyer; b. Chgo., Aug. 25, 1931; s. Joseph Lazarus and Sylvia (Dubner) S.; m. Elaine L. Gordon, June 25, 1961; children: Hayden Leigh, Jonathan Lazarus (dec.), Alexandra Rose. BS cum laude, DePaul U., 1952; JD (Frederick Leicke scholar), U. Mich., 1955. Bar: Ill. 1955, U.S. Dist. Ct. (no. dist.) Ill. 1955, N.Y. 1956, U.S. Tax Ct. 1957, U.S. Ct. Mil. Appeals 1957, U.S. Ct. Appeals (7th cir.) 1958, U.S. Supreme Ct. 1959, U.S. Ct. Appeals (6th cir.) 1965, U.S. Ct. Appeals (2d cir.) 1971, U.S. Ct. Appeals (5th cir.) 1972, U.S. Ct. Appeals (11th cir.). Assoc. Paul, Weiss, Rifkind, Wharton & Garrison, N.Y.C., 1955-56; asst. atty. U.S. Dist. Ct. (no. dist.) Ill., 1958-60; chief tax atty. U.S. atty. No. Dist. Ill., Chgo., 1960-62; ptnr. Harris, Burman & Silets, Chgo., 1962-79, Silets & Martin, Ltd., Chgo., 1979-92; asst. advance tng. program IRS, U. Mich., 1952-53; law lectr. advance fed. taxation John Marshall Law Sch., 1962-66; adj. prof. taxation Chgo.-Kent Coll. Law, 1985—; gen. counsel Nat. Treasury Employees Union, 1968-92; mem. adv. com. tax litigation U.S. Dept. Justice, 1979-82; mem. Tax Reform Com., State of Ill., 1982-83; mem. Speedy Trial Act Planning Group U.S. Dist. Ct. (no. dist.) Ill., 1976-79; mem. civil justice reform act adv. com. U.S. Dist. Ct. (no. dist.) Ill., 1991-94; lectr. in field. Contbr. articles to profl. jours. Trustee Latin Sch., Chgo., 1970-76; active Chgo. Crime Commn., 1975-93, Gov.'s Commn. Reform Tax Laws, Ill., 1982-83. With AUS, 1956-58. Fellow Am. Coll. Trial Lawyers (chmn. com. on fed. rules of criminal procedure 1982-91, fed. rules of evidence com. 1988-93, jud. com., fed. criminal procedures com., Upstate Ill. com. chmn. 1990-91), Am. Coll. Tax Counsel, Internat. Acad. Trial Lawyers; mem. ABA (active various coms.), Bar Assn. 7th Fed. Cir. (chmn. com. criminal law and procedure 1972-82, bd. govs. 1983-86, sec. 1986-88, v.p. 1989-90, pres. 1990-91), NACDL, FBA (bd. dirs. 1971—, pres. 1977-78, v.p. 1976-77, sec. 1975-76, treas. 1974-75, active various coms.), Chgo. Bar Assn. (tax com. 1958-66, com. devel. law 1966-72, 78—, com. fed. taxation 1968—, com. evaluation candidates 1978-80, exec. com. tax sect. 1994—), Am. Bd. Criminal Def. Lawyers, Decalogue Soc. Lawyers, Bar Assn. N.Y. City, Standard Club, Cliff Dwellers Club, Chgo. Club, Phi Alpha delta, Pi Gamma Mu. General corporate, Criminal, Taxation, general. Office: Katten Muchin & Zavis 525 W Monroe St Ste 1600 Chicago IL 60661-3693

**SILK, ALLEN M.,** lawyer; b. Pitts., Feb. 28, 1947; s. Phillip and Ann S.; m. Judy, Aug. 17, 1969; children: Alyson, Lauren. BS in Acctg., Pa. State U., 1969; JD cum laude, Villanova U. Law Sch., 1973; LLM, NYU Sch. Law, 1974. Bar: Pa. 1973, N.J. 1975. Assoc. Wolf, Block, Schor & Solis-Cohen, Phila., 1974-76; shareholder Stark & Stark, Lawrenceville, N.J., 1976—; founding ptnr. Rutgers Family Bus. Forum, Princeton, N.J. General corporate, Estate planning, Taxation, general. Office: Stark & Stark 993 Lenox Dr Ste 101 Lawrenceville NJ 08648-2389

**SILK, THOMAS,** lawyer; b. Beaver, Pa., Dec. 12, 1937; s. Thomas and Alice Genevieve (Beck) S.; m. Arlene Schlaifer, Sept., 1959 (div.); 1 child, Nicole Amory; m. Susan Clark, 1979 (div.); m. Suzanne Vinson, Mar. 1996. AB, U. Calif., Berkeley, 1959, LLB, 1963. Bar: Calif. 1964, U.S. Dist. Ct. (no. dist.) Calif. 1964, U.S. Ct. Appeals (D.C., 2-10th cirs.) 1966-68, U.S. Supreme Ct. 1967. Appellate atty. tax divsn. U.S. Dept. Justice, Washington, 1964-66, spl. asst. to asst. atty. gen. tax divsn., 1966-68; assoc. Brobeck, Phleger & Harrison, San Francisco, 1968-71; founder, pres. Silk, Adler & Colvin, San Francisco, 1972—; author, lectr. internat. philanthrophy, tax-exempt orgns., nonprofit corps., charitable estate planning. Editor: Philanthropy and Law in Asia. Trustee Jenifer Altman Found., U. San Francisco Inst. for Nonprofit and Orgn. Mgmt.. Corporate taxation, General corporate, Probate. Office: Silk Adler & Colvin 235 Montgomery St San Francisco CA 94104-2902

**SILKENAT, JAMES ROBERT,** lawyer; b. Salina, Kans., Aug. 2, 1947; s. Ernest E. and Mildred R. (Iman) S.; children: David Andrew, Katherine Anne. BA, Drury Coll., 1969; JD, U. Chgo., 1972; LLM, NYU, 1978. Bar: N.Y. 1973, D.C. 1980. Assoc. Cravath, Swaine & Moore, N.Y.C., 1972-80; counsel Internat. Fin. Corp., Washington, 1980-86; ptnr. Morgan, Lewis & Bockius, N.Y.C., 1986-89, Morrison & Foerster, N.Y.C., 1989-92, Winthrop, Stimson, Putnam & Roberts, N.Y.C., 1992—; chmn. Council N.Y. Law Assocs., 1978-79, Lawyers Com. Internat. Human Rights, 1978-80. Editor ABA Guide to Fng. Law Firms, Moscow Conf. on Law Bilateral Econ. Rels., ABA Guide to Internat. Bus. Negotiations; contbr. articles to profl.

jours. Capt. U.S. Army, 1972-73. Fellow NEH, 1977, U.S. Dept. State, 1981. Fellow Am. Bar Found.; mem. ABA (chmn. internat. law and practice sect. 1989-90, chmn. sect. officer's conf. 1990-92, mem. ho. of dels. 1989—, bd. govs. 1994-97). Private international, Finance, General corporate. Office: Winthrop Stimson Putnam & Roberts One Battery Park Plz New York NY 10004

**SILLER, STEPHEN I.,** lawyer; b. May 8, 1949; m. Helen Seewald, June 6, 1971. BA, Bklyn. Coll., 1970, JD cum laude, 1973; LLM, NYU, 1978. Bar: N.Y. 1974, U.S. Dist. Ct. (so. and ea. dists.) N.Y. 1974, U.S. Ct. Appeals (2d cir.) 1974. Assoc. Fried, Frank, Harris, Shriver & Jacobson, N.Y.C., 1973-78; assoc. Feit & Ahrens, N.Y.C., 1978-80, ptnr., 1981-87; founder, sr. ptnr. Siller Wilk LLP, N.Y.C., 1987—. Mem. ABA (partnership law com., negotiated acquisitions com.), Internat. Bar Assn., Assn. Bar City of N.Y. (transp. com. 1978—, U.S. in global economy com. 1996-97). General corporate, Mergers and acquisitions, Securities. Office: Siller Wilk LLP 747 3rd Ave Fl 38 New York NY 10017-2803

**SILLS, NANCY MINTZ,** lawyer; b. N.Y.C., Nov. 3, 1941; d. Samuel and Selma (Kahn) Mintz; m. Stephen J. Sills, Apr. 17, 1966; children: Eric Howard, Ronnie Lynne Sills Lindberg. BA, U. Wis., 1962; JD cum laude, Union U., 1976. Bar: N.Y. 1977, U.S. Dist. Ct. (no. dist.) N.Y. 1977, U.S. Tax Ct. 1984. Asst. editor fin. news Newsweek mag., N.Y.C., 1962-65; staff writer, reporter Forbes mag., N.Y.C., 1965; rsch. assoc. pub. rels. Ea. Airlines, N.Y.C., 1965-67; asst. editor Harper & Row, N.Y.C., 1968-69; freelance writer, editor N.Y.C., Albany, 1967-70; confidential law sec. N.Y. State Supreme Ct., Albany, 1976-79; assoc. Whiteman, Osterman & Hanna, Albany, 1979-81, Martin, Noonan, Hislop, Troue & Shudt, Albany, 1981-83; ptnr. Martin, Shudt, Wallace & Sills, Albany, 1984; of counsel Krolick and DeGraff, Albany, 1984-89; ptnr. Hodgson, Russ, Andrews, Woods & Goodyear, Albany, 1990-91; pvt. practice Albany, 1991—; of counsel Lemery & Reid, Albany and Glens Falls, N.Y., 1993-94; asst. counsel N.Y. State Senate, 1983-88; cons. The Ayco Corp., 1975; jud. screening com. Third Jud. Dept., 1997—. Editor: Reforming American Education, 1969, Up From Poverty, 1968; rschr.: The Negro Revolution in America, 1963; contbr. articles to mags. Bd. dirs. Jewish Philanthropies Endowment, 1983-86, United Jewish Fedn. N.E. N.Y. Endowment Fund, 1992-96, Daus. Sarah Found., 1994-97, Albany Jewish Cmty. Ctr., 1984-87; mem. Guilderland (N.Y.) Conservation Adv. Coun., 1993-96; mem. planned giving tech. adv. com. Albany Law Sch., Union U., 1991-95, chmn., 1992-95; mem. regional cabinet State of Israel Bonds Devel. Corp. for Israel, 1991-92. Mem. ABA, N.Y. State Bar Assn., Albany County Bar Assn., Warren County Bar Assn., N.Y. Criminal and Civil Cts. Bar Assn., Estate Planning Coun. Ea. N.Y., Aux. Albany County Med. Soc., Capital Dist. Trial Lawyers Assn., Capital Dist. Women's Bar Assn., Phi Beta Kappa, Sigma Epsilon Sigma. Republican. Estate planning, General practice, Probate. Home: 16 Hiawatha Dr Guilderland NY 12084-9526 Office: 126 State St Albany NY 12207-1637

**SILVER, ALAN IRVING,** lawyer; b. St. Paul, Sept. 17, 1949; s. Sherman J. Silver and Muriel (Bernstein) Braverman; m. Janice Lynn Gleekel, July 8, 1973; children: Stephen, Amy. BA cum laude, U. Minn., 1971, JD cum laude, 1975. Bar: Minn. 1975, U.S. Dist. Ct. Minn. 1975, U.S. Dist. Ct. (ea. dist.) Wis. 1975, U.S. Ct. Appeals 8th and 10th cirs.) 1975. Assoc. Doherty, Rumble & Butler, P.A., Mpls., 1975-80; ptnr. Doherty, Rumble & Butler, P.A., St. Paul, 1980-99, Bassford, Lockhart, Truesdell & Briggs, P.A., Mpls., 1999—; mem. 2d Jud. Dist. Ethics Com., St. Paul, 1985-88, 4th Jud. Dist. Ethics Com., Mpls., 1990-97. Author numerous continuing edn. seminar material. Vol. atty. Legal Assistance Ramsey County, St. Paul, 1975-82; mem. St. Louis Park (Minn.) Sch. Bd., 1993—, chair, 1995-97; mem. St. Louis Park Human Rights Commn., 1987-91; chmn. site mgmt. coun. Susan Lindgren Sch., St. Louis Park, 1986-93; bd. dirs. Jewish Cmty. Rels. Coun., Anti-Defamation League Minn. and Dakotas, 1987-93, 97—, treas., 1992-93. Mem. ABA, Minn. Bar Assn. (exec. bd. antitrust sect. 1984), Hennepin County Bar Assn. Avocations: running, guitar, reading. Antitrust, General civil litigation. Home: 4320 W 25th St Minneapolis MN 55416-3841 Office: Bassford Lockhart Truesdell & Briggs PA 3550 Multifoods Tower 30 S 6th St Minneapolis MN 55402

**SILVER, BARBARA OAKS,** lawyer; b. Phila., Sept. 17, 1934; d. Samuel and Sara R. Berger; m. Martin Oaks (div. 1967); 1 child, Robert; m. Edward W. Silver, May 28, 1967. BA, U. Pa., 1956; JD, Temple U., 1969. Bar: Pa. 1969. Assoc. Mason & Ringe, Phila., 1969-71, Ewing & Cohen, Phila., 1971-72; ptnr. Silver & Silver, Phila., 1972-91, Astor Weiss Kaplan & Rosenblum, Phila., 1991—; prof. corp. law Paralegal Inst., Phila., 1973-85; lectr., seminar leader Inst. Awareness, Phila., 1975-85; frequent lectr. on family law and estate planning throughout ea. U.S. Mem. Pa. Bar Assn., Phila. Bar Assn., Pa. Commn. on Women in the Profession, Phi Beta Kappa. Avocations: bridge, music, crossword puzzles. Office: Astor Weiss Kaplan Et Al The Bellevue Ste 600 Philadelphia PA 19103

**SILVER, BARRY MORRIS,** lawyer, lay preacher; b. Mt. Vernon, N.Y., Nov. 18, 1956; s. Samuel Manuel and Elaine Martha (Shapiro) S. BA, Fla. Atlantic U., 1979; JD, Nova U., 1983. Bar: Fla. 1983. Law clk. to presiding justice 4th Dist. Ct. Appeals, West Palm Beach, Fla., 1982-83; pvt. practice Boca Raton, 1983—, sole practice, 1986—; tchr. Hebrew and religion Temple Beth El, Boca Raton, 1979-84; tchr. bilingual edn. Palm Beach County Schs., Delray Beach, Fla., 1981-83; faculty Palm Beach Jr. Coll., Boca Raton, 1990—; atty. NOW, South Palm Beach County; mem. Fla. Ho. Reps., 1997-98. Vol. Haitian Refugee Ctr., Miami, 1982; active Temple Sinai. Mem. Fla. Bar Assn., Palm Beach County Bar Assn., Sierra. Democrat. Jewish. Avocations: languages, tennis, Frisbee, chess, backgammon. General civil litigation, Personal injury, Civil rights. Home: 6940 Town Harbour Blvd Apt 2423 Boca Raton FL 33433-4334 Office: 7777 Glades Rd Ste 308 Boca Raton FL 33434-4150

**SILVER, CAROL RUTH,** lawyer; b. Boston, Oct. 1, 1938; d. Nathan and Mildred S.; children: Steven Chao, Jefferson Chao Frensley; m. Stanley Mayerson, 1990 (div. 1994). BA, U. Chgo., 1960, JD, 1964. Bar: Calif. 1964, U.S. Supreme Ct. 1970, U.S. Dist. Ct. (so. dist.) La., U.S. Dist. Ct. (no. and cen. dists.) Calif. Dir. atty. Calif. Rural Legal Assistance, Delano, 1965-68; exec. dir. Berkeley (Calif.) Neighborhood Legal Svcs., 1968-71; tchr. Golden Gate Law Sch., San Francisco, 1970-73; legal counsel to sheriff City of San Francisco, 1972-75; elected ofcl. Bd. of Suprs., City and County of San Francisco, 1978-89; real estate broker McGuire Real Estate, San Francisco, 1985—; pvt. practice law San Francisco, 1978—; spl. counsel ABRH Cons., Washington, 1988-90; cons. Nat. Legal Aid & Defender Assn., Washington, 1968-75; del. to hn. dels. Calif. Bar, Sacramento, 1972-74. Contbr. articles to profl. jours.; bd. editors Tikun. Pres. Golden Gate Bridge Dist., San Francisco, 1988, San Francisco Bay Area Air Pollution Control Dist., 1987, Friends of San Francisco Inmates and Deps., 1982, Golden Gate Dem. Club, San Francisco, 1976; founder Chinese Am. Internat. Sch., San Francisco, bd. dirs., 1980—; pres., co-founder Every Child A Wanted Child, San Francisco, 1989—; bd. dirs. UN World Ctr., San Francisco, 1981—; chmn. bd. dirs. Jewish Ednl. Ctr., 1997—; candidate for U.S. Congress, 1996. Fellow Sch. Govt., Harvard U., 1973-74; recipient Cable Car award Tavern Guild, 1985, Award of Merit, Lawyers Constl. Def. Com., 1965. Mem. NOW, ACLU, Nat. Abortion Rights Action League. Jewish. Avocations: jogging, opera, family activities, travel. E-mail: myersflat@aol.com. Real property, Alternative dispute resolution, Estate planning.

**SILVER, MARVIN S.,** lawyer; b. Portland, Maine, Nov. 21, 1951; BS, Syracuse U., 1974; JD, Boston U., 1977, LLM, 1981. Bar: Mass. 1977, U.S. Dist. Ct. Mass. 1978, U.S. Tax Ct. 1983. Atty. Seder & Seder, Worcester, Mass., 1977-82; atty. Seder & Chandler, Worcester, 1983—. Bd. dirs. Jewish Community Ctr. of Worcester, Inc., Mass., 1982-84; mem. fin. com. Town of Shrewsbury, Mass. 1986-93, vice chmn., 1987-88, chmn., 1988-89; bd. dirs. Children's Friend Inc., 1990-99, bd. dirs., treas. Westborough Edn. Found., Inc., 1996—. Fellow Am. Coll. Trust and Estate Counsel; mem. Mass. Bar Assn. (chmn. estate planning com. tax sect. 1982-84, mem. tax sect. coun. 1983-86, mem. bus. law sect., probate law sect., taxation sect.), Worcester County Bar Assn. (co-chmn. tax law sect. 1981-84, 86-87, 97-98, bankruptcy and comml. law sect. 1987-88), Estate and Bus. Planning Coun. Worcester County (pres. 1990-91). Club: Exchange Club of Tri-Towns, Inc. (pres. 1984-85) (Shrewsbury). General corporate, Estate planning, Estate taxation. Office: Seder & Chandler 339 Main St Ste 300 Worcester MA 01608-1585

**SILVER, SIDNEY J.,** lawyer; b. Hartford, Conn., Mar. 30, 1934; s. Daniel B. and Sara F. Silver; m. Margaret Ann McKewen; children: Patricia, David, Lisa, Beth, Daniel. BS, Lehigh U., 1957, MBA, 1959; JD, Georgetown U., 1962. Bar: Va. 1962, D.C. 1963, U.S. Tax Ct. 1965, U.S. Ct. Appeals (D.C. cir.) 1965, U.S. Supreme Ct. 1996. Mng. ptnr. Silver, Freedman & Taff, Washington, 1972—. With U.S. Army, 1953-55. General corporate, Corporate taxation, Estate planning. Office: Silver Freedman & Taff 1100 New York Ave NW Ste 700E Washington DC 20005-3962

**SILVERBERG, JAMES LORIN,** lawyer; b. Rochester, N.Y., Aug. 25, 1955; s. David Morton and Marilyn (Landes) S.; m. Wandra Silverberg; 1 child, Leah Yue. BA (hon.), SUNY, 1977; JD, George Washington U., 1980. Law clk. U.S. Attys. Office, Washington, 1979; legal specialist U.S. Dept. Justice, Washington, 1980; dir. Vol. Lawyers Fortheads, Washington, 1980-82; ptnr. Silverberg & Assocs., Washington, 1982-84, Silverberg & Wade, Washington, 1984-92, Kaufman & Silverberg, Washington, 1992—; law prof. Am. U., Washington, 1996-97; mem. Am. Soc. Appraisers, Washington, 1998; law prof. Washington Coll. Law, 1996-97. Author: Encyclopedia of Legal Forms for Design Professionals, 1998, Legislative Status of Rights of Publicity, 1998. Recipient Svc. award Washington Area Lawyers For the Arts, 1996. Mem. Assn. Trial Lawyers Am., Copyright Soc. U.S.. Jewish. Avocations: historical restoration, art collector. Home: 1000 Fell St Apt 628 Baltimore MD 21231-3560 Office: Kaufman & Silverberg 918 16th St NW Ste 400 Washington DC 20006-2902

**SILVERBERG, JAY L.,** lawyer; b. N.Y., Oct. 1, 1961; s. Sheldon and Elissa (Nenner) S.; children: Jennifer, Rebecca. BA, Brandeis U., 1983; JD, Boston U., 1986. Bar: N.Y. 1987, N.J. 1987, U.S. Dist. Ct. (so. dist.) N.Y. 1990, U.S. Dist. Ct. (ea. dist.) N.Y. 1991. Assoc. McCarter & English, Newark, 1986-87, Proskauer Rose, N.Y.C., 1987-91; mem. Silverberg, Stonehill & Goldsmith, P.C., N.Y.C., 1991—; lectr. Nat. Assn. Credit Mgmt., Dallas, 1995, Columbia U. Sch. Bus., 1996. Editor: Annual Review of Banking Law, 1986. Paul J. Liacos scholar Boston U. Sch. Law, 1985, G. Joseph Tauro scholar, 1984. Mem. Manhattan Credit Club (pres. 1998). Bankruptcy, Contracts commercial, General corporate. Home: 1085 Warburton Ave Yonkers NY 10701-1051 Office: Silverberg Stonehill & Goldsmith PC 111 W 40th St Fl 33 New York NY 10018-2561

**SILVERBERG, MARK VICTOR,** lawyer, educator; b. Akron, Ohio, Sept. 26, 1957; s. Alvin Harold and Marilyn (Bierman) S.; m. Marsha Phyllis Mermelstein, Aug. 11, 1979; children: Samantha Michele, Marissa Jill. BS, Rider Coll., 1979; JD, Pace U., 1983. Bar: N.J. 1983, N.Y. 1984, U.S. Dist. Ct. (so. dist.) N.Y., U.S. Dist. Ct. N.J. Atty. Met. Life Ins. Co., N.Y.C., 1983-84; corp. counsel H & N Chem. Co., Totowa, N.J., 1984-85; pvt. practice East Brunswick, N.J., 1985-90; gen. coun. East Coast Title Ins., 1990-91; sr. v.p. New Century Mortgage Corp., 1991—; CEO M&M Propery Corp.; sec./treas. Century Mortgage Svcs., Inc.; prof. law Middlesex County Coll., Edison, N.J., 1985—, Mercer County Coll., Trenton, N.J., 1985—, Upsala Coll., East Orange, N.J., 1991—. Mem. ABA (real estate, probate and property law sect., corp. law sect.), N.Y. State Bar Assn., N.J. Bar Assn. (real estate, probate and property law sect., corp. law sect.), Middlesex County Bar Assn., Rotary. Republican. Jewish. Avocations: basketball, golf, hockey, woodworking, gardening. Real property, General corporate, Probate.

**SILVERBERG, STEVEN MARK,** lawyer; b. Bklyn., June 7, 1947; m. Arlene Leopold, July 4, 1971; 2 children. BA, Bklyn. Coll., 1969; JD, NYU, 1972. Bar: N.Y. 1973, U.S. Dist. Ct. (so. and ea. dists.) N.Y. 1974, U.S. Supreme Ct. 1976, U.S. Ct. Appeals (2nd cir.) 1978. Asst. dist. atty. Kings County Dist. Atty., Bklyn., 1972-75; dep. town. atty. Town of Greenburgh, N.Y., 1975-79; ptnr. Stowell, Kelly & Silverberg, White Plains, N.Y., 1979-83, Hoffman, Silverberg & Wachtell, Elmsford, N.Y., 1983-86, Hoffman, Silverberg, Wachtell & Koster, White Plains, N.Y., 1986-89; pvt. practice White Plains, 1989-92; ptnr. Kirkpatrick & Silverberg LLP, White Plains, 1993—; adj. assoc. prof. N.Y. Law Sch., 1990-93. Co-author: Wetlands and Coastal Zone Regulations and Compliance, 1993; contbr. to profl. publs. Counsel Greenburgh Housing Authority, 1979-84, Town of Mamaroneck, N.Y., 1984-96; bd. dirs. Temple Beth Torah, Upper Nyack, N.Y., 1977-89, pres. 1984-86, N.J. West Hudson Valley Region Union of Am. Hebrew Congregations, 1986-88. Mem. ABA, N.Y. State Bar Assn., Westchester County Bar Assn. (chair environtl. law com. 1997—). Real property, Environmental, General corporate. Office: Kirkpatrick & Silverberg 81 Main St Unit 110 White Plains NY 10601-1720

**SILVERMAN, ALAN HENRY,** lawyer; b. N.Y.C., Feb. 18, 1954; s. Melvin H. and Florence (Green) S.; m. Gretchen E. Freeman, May 25, 1986; children: Willa C.F., Gordon H.F. BA summa cum laude, Hamilton Coll., 1976; MBA, U. Pa., 1980, JD, 1980. Bar: N.Y. 1981, U.S. Dist. Ct. (so. and ea. dist.) N.Y. 1981, U.S. Ct. Internat. Trade 1981, D.C. 1986, U.S. Supreme Ct. 1990. Assoc. Hughes, Hubbard & Reed, N.Y.C., 1980-84; asst. counsel Newsweek, Inc., N.Y.C., 1984-86; v.p., gen. counsel, sec., dir. adminstrn. Cable One, Inc., Phoenix, 1986—. Contbr. articles to profl. jours. Mem. prevention adv. com. Gov. Pa. Justice Commn., 1975-79; bd. dirs. Lawyers' Alliance for N.Y., 1982-85, N.Y. Lawyers Pub. Interest, 1983-85, Nat. Assn. JD-MBA Profls., 1983-85, Bus. Vols. for Arts, Inc., Phoenix, 1989-93, Ariz. Vol. Lawyers for the Arts, Inc., 1994-97, First Amendment Coalition Ariz., Inc., 1991—; mem. Maricopa County Citizens Jud. Adv. Coun., 1990-93. Mem. ABA, Assn. of Bar of City of N.Y., D.C. Bar Assn., Phi Beta Kappa. Communications, Libel, Entertainment. Home: 5833 N 30th St Phoenix AZ 85016-2401 Office: Cable One Inc 1314 N 3d St Phoenix AZ 85004

**SILVERMAN, ARNOLD BARRY,** lawyer; b. Sept. 1, 1937; s. Frank and Lillian Lena (Linder) S.; m. Susan L. Levin, Aug. 7, 1960; children: Michael Eric, Lee Oren. B Engring. Sci., Johns Hopkins U., 1959; LLB cum laude, U. Pitts., 1962. Bar: U.S. Dist. Ct. (we. dist.) Pa. 1963, Pa. 1964, U.S. Patent and Trademark Office 1965, U.S. Supreme Ct. 1967, Can. Patent Office 1968, U.S. Ct. Claims 1975, U.S. Ct. Appeals (3d cir.) 1982, U.S. Ct. Appeals (fed. cir.) 1985. Patent atty. Alcoa, New Kensington, Pa., 1962-67, 68-74, sr. patent atty., 1972-76; ptnr. Price and Silverman, Pitts., 1967-68; v.p., gen. patent counsel Joy Mfg. Co., Pitts., 1976-80; ptnr. Murray Silverman & Keck, Pitts., 1980-81, Buell, Blenko, Ziesenheim & Beck, Pitts., 1984; ptnr. intellectual property dept. Eckert, Seamans, Cherin & Mellott, Pitts., 1984—, chmn., 1992—, chair info. tech. practice group, 1995-97; spl. asst. atty. gen. State of W.Va., 1985—; spl. counsel patents U. Pitts., 1975—; spkr. on patents, trademarks, copyright, computer law; nat. panel of arbiters Am. Arbitration Assn., 1987—. Contbr. articles to profl. jours. Mem. Churchill CSC (Pa.), 1967-90, chmn., 1975-90; mem. Pitts. law com. Anti-Defamation League, 1981—, regional adv. bd., 1982—, ch-chmn. Pitts. region ann. dinner, 1983, mem. chmn. by-laws com., 1983; bd. govs. Slippery Rock U. Found., 1985-91; Pitts. steering com. MIT Enterprise Forum, 1986-87. With U.S. Army, 1963-64. Recipient Am. Spirit Honor medal, Ft. Knox, 1963,. Mem. ABA, ASME, Allegheny County Bar Assn. (chmn. pub. rels. com. 1978-80, vice-chmn. intellectual property sect. 1981-83), Pitts. Patent Law Assn. (chmn. pub. rels. com., 1968-69, chmn. patent laws com., 1970-72, chmn. nominating com., 1973, chmn. legis. action com., 1972-75, bd. mgrs. 1974-88, newsletter editor 1974-88, sec.-treas. 1976-84, v.p. 1984-85, pres. 1985-86, pub. rels. com. 1994-95, program com. 1995-96), Am. Intellectual Property Law Assn. (membership com. 1985-88, mem. pub. rels. com. 1994—), U.S. Trademark Assn. (chmn. task force on advt. agys. 1981, membership com. 1987-89), D.C. Bar Assn., Pa. Bar Assn., Nat. Assn. Coll. and Univ. Attys., Am. Chem. Soc. (chemistry and the law sect.), Licensing Execs. Soc. (co-chmn. Pitts. chpt. 1994-96), Brit. Inst. Chartered Patent Agts. (fgn. mem.), Johns Hopkins U. Alumni Assn. (chmn. publicity com. 1963-66, exec. com. 1966-87, v.p. 1969-70, pres. 1971-72, nat. alumni coun. 1989-92), U. Pitts. Gen. Alumni Assn., U. Pitts. Law Alumni Assn. (bd. dirs. 1992-97, treas. 1997-98, v.p. 1998—), Robert Bruce Assn. Law Fellows (life), Golden Panthers, Stratford Cmty. Assn. (v.p. 1966-67, gov. 1966-70, pres. 1967-68), Mensa (fellow, lawyers in Mensa 1978—, nat. assoc. counsel patents and trademarks copyrights 1980-82, inventors' spl. interest group 1980-86), Intertel (treas. Pitts. Forum 1983—), Duquesne Club, Order of Coif, Tau Epsilon Rho, Psi Chi. Republican. Jewish. Patent, Trademark and copyright, Computer. Home: 2019 High Pointe Ct Murrysville PA 15668-8515 Office: 600 Grant St 44th Fl Pittsburgh PA 15219-2703 *Welcome challenge and perform all tasks with enthusiasm, in a moral manner and to the very best of your ability.*

**SILVERMAN, ARTHUR CHARLES,** lawyer; b. Lewiston, Maine, June 13, 1938; s. Louis A. and Frances Edith (Brownstone) S.; BS in Elec. Engring., BS in Indsl. Mgmt., MIT, 1961; JD, Columbia U., 1964; m. Donna Linda Zolov, June 18, 1961; children: Leonard Stephen, Daniel Edward. Bar: N.Y. 1965, U.S. Supreme Ct. 1971. Engr., engring. asst. Gen. Electric Co., Pittsfield, Mass. and Phila., 1958-62; assoc. Baer & Marks, N.Y.C., 1965-68; assoc. Golenbock and Barell, N.Y.C., 1968-72, ptnr., 1972-89; ptnr. Reid & Priest LLP, N.Y.C., 1989-98, dep. chair, 1996-98; ptnr. Thelen Reid & Priest LLP, N.Y.C., 1998—. Treas., trustee Ramaz Sch., 1977-84, vice chmn., 1984-85, 86-88, chmn., 1988-92, hon. chmn., 1992—; bd. govs. MIT Hillel Found., 1979-84; mem. Bd. Jewish Edn. of City of N.Y., 1981-84; mem. exec. com. Nat. Jewish Ctr. for Learning and Leadership, 1984-90. Mem. IEEE, ABA, NSPE, N.Y. State Bar Assn., Fed. Bar Council, Assn. Bar City N.Y., N.Y. Soc. Architects, Internat. Bar Assn., Inter-Pacific Bar Assn., Constrn. Mgmt. Inst., Constrn. Specifications Inst. Construction, Real property, General civil litigation. Home: 200 E 74th St New York NY 10021-3618 Office: Thelen Reid & Priest LLP 40 W 57th St New York NY 10019-4001

**SILVERMAN, BARRY G.,** federal judge; b. N.Y.C., Oct. 11, 1951. BA summa cum laude, Ariz. State U., 1973, JD, 1976. Bar: Ariz. 1976, U.S. Dist. Ct. Ariz. 1976, U.S. Ct. Appeals (9th cir.) 1976, U.S. Supreme Ct. 1980. Asst. city prosecutor Phoenix, 1976-77; dep. atty. Maricopa County, 1977-79; ct. commr., 1979-84, judge, 1984-95; judge Superior Ct. Ariz. Maricopa County, 1995; apptd. magistrate judge U.S. Dist. Ct. Ariz., 1995; justice U.S. Ct. Appeals 9th cir., 1998—; instr. constnl. law Coll. Law, Ariz. State U., spring, 1983, adj. prof. advanced criminal procedure, spring 1989; lectr. comty. property BAR/BRI Ariz. Bar Rev. Course, 1989—; mem. Ariz. Supreme Ct. Com. on Jud. Edn. and Tng., 1988—. Recipient Exel award Soc. Nat. Assn. Publs., 1992. Mem. ABA, State Bar Ariz., Maricopa County Bar Assn. (Henry Stevens award 1991). Avocation: magic. Office: 6412 US Courthouse 230 N 1st Ave Phoenix AZ 85025-0230*

**SILVERMAN, DAVID MALANOS,** lawyer; b. Chgo., May 19, 1950; s. Bernard and Alice (Kreisel) S.; m. Eleni Malanos, Nov. 13, 1975. Student, Miami U., Oxford, Ohio, 1968-70; BA, New Coll., Sarasota, Fla., 1973; MA, Northwestern U., Evanston, Ill., 1976; JD, Northwestern U., Chgo., 1980. Bar: D.C. 1980. Assoc. Cole, Raywid & Braverman, Washington, 1980-85; ptnr. Cole, Raywid & Braverman, 1986-87, sr. ptnr., 1988—. Mem. D.C. Bar Assn., Internat. Trademark Assn., Fed. Comms. Bar Assn. Communications, Trademark and copyright, Intellectual property. Office: Cole Raywid & Braverman 1919 Pennsylvania Ave NW Washington DC 20006-3458

**SILVERMAN, MELVIN J.,** lawyer; b. Norwich, Conn., Apr. 2, 1939; s. Morris and Anna (Moyel) S.; m. Beverly Silverman, Aug. 12, 1963; children: Jonathan, Jason, Joel. BA in Math., U. Conn., 1960, JD, 1963. Bar: Conn. 1963, N.J. 1964. Assoc. Nevas & Nevas, Westport, Conn., 1965-67, Lepofsky & Lepofsky, Norwalk, Conn., 1967-76; pvt. practice Norwalk, 1976—; lectr. land use, contracts, continuing edu. Norwalk Community Coll., 1987—; atty., trial referee Conn. Jud. Dept., Bridgeport and Stamford, 1986—; spl. counsel Town of Ridgefield, Conn., Town of Wilton, Town of New Canaan; panelist numerous seminars; mem. chief justice's adv. com. on appellate rules 1993—. Contbr. articles to profl. jours. Pres., trustee Friends of Norwalk Pub. Lib., 1973-75; mem. coun. City of Norwalk, 1977-78, Wilton Solid Waste Study Commn., 1979. 1st lt. U.S. Army, 1963-65. Mem. Conn. Bar Assn. (exec. com. planning and zoning sect.). Democrat. Avocations: gardening, reading, racquetball. Land use and zoning (including planning), Real property, State civil litigation. Office: 172 Deforest Rd Wilton CT 06897-1912

**SILVERMAN, PERRY RAYNARD,** lawyer, consultant; b. N.Y.C., Nov. 5, 1950; s. Harry and Mary Sheila (Diamond) S.; m. Ruth Klarin, Oct. 7, 1979; children: Aaron, Rachel. BA, SUNY, Albany, 1971; JD, Boston U., 1974; MA, Ohio State U., 1981. Bar: W.Va. 1997, N.Y. 1975, Ohio 1976, U.S. Dist. Ct. (so. dist.) Ohio 1977, U.S. Dist. Ct. (no. dist.) Ohio 1978, U.S. Ct. Claims 1977, U.S. Supreme Ct. 1978. Rsch. assoc. polimetrics lab. Ohio State U., Columbus, 1974-75, rsch. assoc. behavioral scis. lab., 1974-76; asst. atty. gen. Ohio Atty. Gen.'s Office, Columbus, 1976-84; prin. Perry R. Silverman Co., LPA, Columbus, 1984—; spl. counsel Atty. Gen. of Ohio, 1984-95, City of Cambridge, Ohio, 1993-96; of counsel Friedman, Domiano & Smith, Cleve., 1998—; adj. prof. Capital U., Columbus, 1978, 82; cons. Survey Rsch. Assocs., Columbus, 1975-77. Trustee, Congregation Beth Tikvah, Worthington, Ohio, 1992-94. Mem. ATLA, Ohio State Bar Assn., Columbus Bar Assn., Ohio Assn. Trial Lawyers, Nat. Assn. Retail Collection Attys. (v.p. 1995—), Comml. Law League Am., Healthcare Fin. Mgmt. Assn., Ctrl. Ohio Patient Account Mgrs. Assn., Am. Collectors Assn. General civil litigation, Consumer commercial, Personal injury. Office: Perry R Silverman Co LPA 8351 N High St Columbus OH 43235-1440

**SILVERMAN, STEVEN D.,** lawyer; b. N.Y.C., Dec. 4, 1947; s. Hyman A. and Phyllis (Helfand) S.; m. Freddye Lynn Kaufman, June 24, 1971; children: Matthew Craig, Zachary Neal. BA, Adelphi U., 1969; JD, U. Md., 1972. Bar: Md. 1972, U.S. Dist. Ct. Md. 1979, U.S. Ct. Appeals (4th cir.) 1979, U.S. Supreme Ct. 1978. Asst. state's atty. Baltimore County State's Atty.'s Office, Towson, Md., 1971-75; assoc. Friedman, Pachino & Friedman, Dundalk, Md., 1975-81; pvt. practice law Dundalk, 1981-85; ptnr. Rosolio & Silverman, Towson, 1985-96; pvt. practice law Owings Mills, Md., 1996—; seminar presenter, lectr. Am. Bus. Inst., Inc., Eau Claire, Wis., 1992-93. Bd. dirs. Md. Vol. Lawyers Svcs., Balt., 1995—, v.p., 1997—, pres. 1998, 99—, seminar presenter, lectr., 1996—; pres. Greengate Homeowners Assn., Balt., 1993—; founder Greengate Security Corp., Balt., 1994. Mem. Md. State Bar Assn., Baltimore County Bar Assn., Summit Country Club. Democrat. Jewish. Avocations: sports, movies, foreign travel. Family and matrimonial, General practice. Home: 6 Mandel Ct Baltimore MD 21209-1016 Office: 9505 Reisterstown Rd Owings Mills MD 21117-4451

**SILVERMAN, SUSAN JOY,** lawyer; b. N.Y.C., Sept. 11, 1954; d. Sidney G. and Belle Silverman; m. Mark F. Montalbano, Dec. 21, 1980; children: Victoria Jo, Zachary Lucas. BA, CCNY, 1975; JD, Temple U., 1978. Bar: Fla. 1981, U.S. Ct. Appeals (11th cir.), U.S. Supreme Ct. Assoc. Marlow, Shofi et al, Miami, Fla., 1981-84, Branning, Breslau et al, Sarasota, Fla., 1987-92; pvt. practice, Sarasota, 1992—. Pres. Gulf Gate Elem. Sch. PTA, Sarasota, 1995, 98. Mem. Fla. Bar Assn., Acad. Fla. Trial Lawyers, Sarasota County Bar Assn. Appellate. Office: 3400 S Tamiami Trl Fl 2D Sarasota FL 34239-6093

**SILVERMAN, THOMAS NELSON,** lawyer, educator; b. Mar. 22, 1944; s. Sidney A. and Phyllis (Helfant) S.; m. Nila Brookner, Aug. 17, 1986; children: Samuel B., Faren J. AB, U. Miami, 1968; JD, Duquesne U., 1971; LLM, Harvard U., 1972; LLM in Taxation, NYU, 1975. Bar: Pa. 1971, Fla. 1974, U.S. Tax Ct. 1975; cert. Tax Atty. Fla. Bar, 1985. Law clk. to Hon. Henry Ellenbogen Allegheny County Ct., Pitts., 1972-73; staff atty. Westinghouse Credit corp., Pitts., 1973-76; assoc., ptnr. DeSantis, Cook, Gaskill & Silverman, North Palm Beach, Fla., 1976-86; ptnr. Cohen, Cohen & Silverman, North Palm Beach, 1986-90; pres. Thomas N. Silverman, P.A., Palm Beach Gardens, Fla., 1990—; adj. prof. Fla. Atlantic U., Boca Raton, 1976—. Author: Estate Planning for the Florida Resident, 1998. Mem. Palm Beach County Bar Assn. (chair probate and guardianship com.). Administrative and regulatory, Estate taxation, Taxation, general. Office: 4400 Pga Blvd Ste 102 Palm Beach Gardens FL 33410-6554

**SILVERMINTZ, MICHAEL B.,** lawyer; b. Bklyn., May 5, 1965; s. Jacob and Hana Silvermintz; m. Randi Koppel, Aug. 18, 1988; children: Daniel, Lauren, Sophie. BS in Civil Engring., Columbia U., 1986; JD, Yeshiva U., 1989. Bar: N.Y. 1989, N.J. 1989, U.S. Dist. Ct. (ea. and so. dists) N.Y., U.S. Dist. Ct. N.J. Assoc. Deutsch & Spring, N.Y.C., 1991-92; ptnr. Newman & Silvermintz, N.Y.C., 1992-94; assoc. Altieri, Kishner, Miuccio & Frind, N.Y.C., 1994-96; surety claims dir. Am. Internat. Group, N.Y.C., 1996-97; gen. counsel York Hunter, Inc., N.Y.C., 1997—. Mem. Assn. Bar City N.Y. (mem. constrn. law com. 1997-98). Construction, General corporate, Real property. Office: York Hunter Inc 1372 Broadway New York NY 10018-6106

**SILVERS, JANE FINK,** lawyer; b. Columbus, Ohio, Mar. 7, 1961; d. Samuel William and Mildred (Branan) F. BSBA, Ohio State U., 1983; JD, U. Cincinnati, 1986. Bar: Ohio 1986, U.S. Dist. Ct. Ohio 1990, U.S. Tax Ct.

1991; CPA, Ohio. Tax cons. Grant Thornton Accts. & Cons., Cin., 1986-90; assoc. Kepley, Gilligan & Eyrich, Cin., 1990-95; mem. Drew & Ward, Cin., 1995—. Big Sister Big Bros./Big Sisters, Cin., 1988—; trustee Alcoholism Coun., Cin., 1995—. Mem. ABA, Ohio Bar Assn., Cin. Bar Assn., Ohio Soc. CPAs. Taxation, general, General corporate, Estate planning. Office: Drew & Ward 4th & Vine Twr Ste 2400 Cincinnati OH 45202

**SILVERS, MARCIA JEAN,** lawyer; b. Miami, Fla., Feb. 8, 1955; d. Louis Dean and Janet Copeland Silvers; m. Robert Franklin Dunlap, Oct. 22, 1983; children: Robert Tully Dunlap, Lauren Mary Dunlap. BA, Fla. Atlantic U., 1977; JD cum laude, U. Miami, 1981. Bar: Fla. 1981, U.S. Dist. Ct. (so. dist.) Fla., U.S. Ct. Appeals (6th, 9th and 11th cirs.), U.S. Supreme Ct. Assoc. Joseph Beeler, Esq., Miami, 1982-83, Roy Black, Esq., Miami, 1983-85, James Jay Hogan, Esq., Miami, 1985-88; ptnr. Dunlap & Silvers, P.A., Miami, 1988—. Mem. Nat. Assn. Criminal Def. Lawyers. Lutheran. Appellate, Criminal, General civil litigation. Office: Dunlap and Silvers PA 2601 S Bayshore Dr Ste 601 Miami FL 33133-5460

**SILVERSTEIN, FRED HOWARD,** lawyer; b. Chester, Pa., Nov. 4, 1951; s. Norman H. and Miriam R. (Rogol) S.; m. Denise Bleich; children: Allison Joy, Chad Michael. BA, U. Md., 1973; JD, U. Balt., 1975. Law clk. Ct. Appeals Md., Annapolis, 1975-76; assoc. Law Offices of Bernard Goldberg, Ellicott City, Md., 1976-82; asst. pub. defender Pub. Defender's Office, State of Md., Ellicott City, 1976-90; pvt. practice Ellicott City, 1982-94; mng. ptnr. Law Offices of Fred Howard Silverstein, Ellicott City, 1995—; head transition team Clk. of Ct., Ellicott City, 1992. Mem. Greengate Cmty. Assn., Balt., 1994. Mem. ABA, Md. State Bar Assn., Howard Bar Assn. (bd. dirs. 1988-92, sec.-treas. 1986-95, pres.-elect), D.C. Bar Assn., Harvard County Bar Assn. (pres. 1995-96), Omicron Delta Kappa, Alpha Kappa Delta, Pi Sigma Alpha. Avocations: basketball, exercise. Family and matrimonial, General corporate, State civil litigation. Home: 2109 Sugarcone Rd Baltimore MD 21209-1027 Office: Law Offices of F H Silverstein 8355 Court Ave Ellicott City MD 21043-4505

**SILVERSTEIN, HARLAN JAY,** lawyer; b. Bklyn., Nov. 3, 1961; s. Gershon and Edith S.; m. Deborah Ann Kaplan, Aug. 17, 1985. BS in Econs., U. Pa., 1982; JD cum laude, St. John's U., N.Y.C., 1985. Bar: N.Y. 1986, U.S. Supreme Ct. 1996, U.S. Dist. Ct. (ea. and so. dists.) N.Y., U.S. Cir. Ct. (2d cir.). Assoc. Kaye, Scholer, Fierman, Hays & Handler, N.Y.C., 1985-87; atty. Kauh, McClain, McGuire, N.Y.C., 1987—; spkr. in field. Bd. dirs. Tilden Midtown Dem. Club, N.Y.C., 1993—; mem. N.Y. County Dem. Com., N.Y.C., 1996-97. Mem. ABA, Supreme Ct. Hist. Soc., Assn. Bar City N.Y., Phi Delta Phi. Avocations: sports, politics. Labor. Office: Kauh, McClain & McGuire 950 3rd Ave New York NY 10022-2705

**SILVERSTEIN, ROBERT SELNICK,** lawyer; b. Englewood, N.J., July 8, 1956; s. William Bernard and Sylvia (Selnick) S.; m. Wanda Jean Olson, June 6, 1981; children: Joshua Olson, Erica Olson. BA magna cum laude, Brown U., 1978; JD, NYU, 1981. Bar: N.J. 1981. Assoc. Riker Danzig Scherer Hyland & Perretti, Morristown, N.J., 1981-86; v.p. corp. counsel Lincoln Property Co., Parsippany, N.J., 1986-91; gen. counsel, sr. v.p. SJP Properties, Parsippany, N.J., 1991—; bd. trustees, exec. com., sec. Ridewise of Raritan Valley, Somerville, N.J., 1991—; bd. dirs. McRides, Morristown, N.J., 1988—; chmn. access code com. Nat. Assn. Indsl. Office Parks, Edison, N.J., 1991—; mem. adv. com. N.J. Hwy. Access Code, N.J. Dept. Transp., Trenton, 1992—. Real property, Land use and zoning (including planning), Landlord-tenant. Office: SJP Properties 1 Upper Pond Rd Parsippany NJ 07054-1050

**SILVESTRI, PHILIP SALVATORE,** lawyer; b. San Francisco, Nov. 10, 1944; s. Philip and Olga (Difilipo) S.; m. Dianne Loveland, June 22, 1968; children: Lauren, Steven, Karin. BA, U. San Francisco, 1966, JD, 1969. Bar: Calif. 1969; cert. family law specialist State Bar Calif. Assoc. Goth, Dennis & Aaron, Redwood City, Calif., 1969-84; ptnr. Goth, Aaron & Silvestri, Redwood City, 1984-87, Goth & Silvestri, A.P.C., Redwood City, 1987—. With N.G., 1969-75. Republican. Avocations: weight training, running. Family and matrimonial, Personal injury. Office: Goth & Silvestri APC 1000 Marshall St Ste B Redwood City CA 94063-2027

**SIMANDLE, JEROME B.,** federal judge; b. Binghamton, N.Y., Apr. 29, 1949; s. Paul R. Sr. and Mary F. Simandle; married; children: Roy C., Liza Jane. BSE magna cum laude, Princeton U., 1971; JD, U. Pa., 1976; diploma in Social Scis., U. Stockholm, 1974-75. Bar: Pa. 1977, N.J. 1978. Law clk. to Hon. John F. Gerry U.S. Dist. Ct., N.J., 1976-78; asst. U.S. atty. Dist. N.J., 1978-83; U.S. magistrate judge U.S. Dist. Ct., N.J., 1983-92, judge, 1992—; mem. lawyers adv. com. U.S. Dist. Ct. N.J., 1984-95; ct. adminstrn. case mgmt. com. Jud. Conf. U.S., 1991-97; mem. CPR Inst. for Dispute Resolution Commn. on Ethics and Stds. in Alternative Dispute Resolution, 1996—. Internat. grad. fellow Rotary Found., 1974-75. Fellow Am. Bar Found.; mem. ABA, Fed. Judges Assn. (bd. dirs. 1997—), Camden County Bar Assn., Camden Inn of Ct. (master 1987—, program chmn. 1990-93, vice chmn. 1996—). Office: US Dist Ct US Courthouse One John F Gerry Plz Camden NJ 08101-0888

**SIMIEN, CLYDE RAY,** lawyer; b. Opelousas, La., Jan. 9, 1960; s. Vincent Jr. and Mercedes Simien; m. Margo St. Julien. BSBA, U. Southwestern La., 1982; postgrad., La. State U., 1985; JD, So. U. La., 1986. Bar: La. 1986. Counselor spl. svcs. dept. U. Southwestern La., 1982-84; law clerk Hon. Ron Gomez, House of Reps., La., 1984, Bur. Legis., Senate, La., 1984-85, L.D. Sledge, Atty.-at-law, 1985-86, Sixteenth Judicial Dist. Ct., 1986—; ptnr. Simien & Miniex, Attys.-at-law, Lafayette, La., 1987—; asst. adj. prof. criminal justice Coll. of Arts and Humanities, U. Southwestern La.; asst. dist. atty. Parishes of St. Martin, Iberia, and St. Mary. Mem. ABA, La. Trial Lawyers Assn., La. State Bar Assn., Am. Trial Lawyers Assn., La. Soc. Ind. Accountants, Nat. Soc. Pub. Accountants, Nat. Dist. Attys. Assn., U. Southwestern La. Debate Team, U. Southwestern La. Alumni Assn. Personal injury. Office: Simien & Miniex APLC 104 Rue Iberville Lafayette LA 70508-3250

**SIMKANICH, JOHN JOSEPH,** lawyer, engineer; b. Clairton, Pa., 1941. BSEE, Drexel Inst. Tech., 1964; MSEE, Purdue U., 1966; JD, George Washington U., 1972. Bar: U.S. Patent Office 1970, Pa. 1973, U.S. dist. Ct. (ea. dist.) Pa. 1977, U.S. Supreme Ct. 1977, U.S. Ct. Appeals (Fed. cir.) 1982, U.S. Ct. Appeals (3d cir.) 1992. Elec. engr. U.S. Steel Co., 1963-65; engr. Westinghouse Aerospace, Balt., 1966-69; sys. developer TRW Sys. Inc., Washington, 1969-70; patent atty. Burroughs Corp., Paoli, Pa., 1970-74, Johnson & Johnson, New Brunswick, N.J., 1974-77; pvt. practice intellectual property law Newtown, Pa., 1977—; adv. Soup, Inc., Washington, 1970-72; introduced to FTC truth-in-advt. law; presenter in field. Patentee in field; product developer and licensing. Mem. ABA, IEEE (sr.), Pa. Bar Assn., Bucks County Bar Assn., Fed. Cir Bar Assn., Phila. Intellectual Property Law Assn., Am. Intellectual Property Law Assn., Delta Theta Phi, Eta Kappa Nu. Roman Catholic. Republican. Patent, Computer, Trademark and copyright. Office: PO Box 671 Newtown PA 18940-0671

**SIMMONS, CHARLES BEDFORD, JR.,** lawyer; b. Greenville, S.C., Dec. 4, 1956; s. Charles Bedford and Mary Margaret (Mason) S.; children: Charles B. III, Elizabeth S., Mason W. AA magna cum laude, Spartanburg Meth. Coll., 1977; BS magna cum laude, E. Tenn. State U., 1979; JD, U. S.C., 1982. Bar: S.C. 1982, U.S. Dist. Ct. S.C. 1983, U.S. Ct. Appeals (4th cir.) 1986. Law clk. to presiding justice S.C. Cir. Ct., Greenville, 1982-83; with Carter Law Firm, Greenville, 1983-86; ptnr. Wilkins, Nelson, Kittredge & Simmons, Greenville, 1986-89; civil ct. judge Greenville, 1989—; mem. bench-bar com. S.C. Supreme Ct., 1992—. Mem. adv. com. paralegal program Greenville Tech. Coll., 1989—, chmn., 1990-91; mem. Friends of 200 Adv. Bd., 1991—. Named Big Brother of Yr., Big Bros.-Big Sisters, 1988; recipient Svc. to Manking award Rotary Club, 1989, Outstanding Young Disting. Svc. award Greenville Jaycees, 1990-91. Mem. S.C. Bar Assn. (young lawyer liason 1985—, named Outstanding Young Lawyer of Yr. 1989), Greenville Bar Assn., Assn. Trial Lawyers Am., S.C. Trial Lawyers Assn., Greenville Young Lawyers (pres. 1988—), Gamma Beta Phi, Pi Gamma Mu, Phi Delta Phi. Republican. Presbyterian. Clubs: Greenville City, Textile (v.p. 1985—), Revelers (Greenville). Home: 11 W Hillcrest Dr Greenville SC 29609-4615 Office: Ste 207 County Courthouse Greenville SC 29601

**SIMMONS, DAVID NORMAN,** lawyer; b. Denver, Aug. 29, 1957; s. David Lee and Janet Thelma (Meseroll) S.; m. Neri Alcocer Argáez, Mar. 15, 1986; 1 child, Chester Rolando. BA, U. Denver, 1980, JD, 1985. Bar: Colo. 1986, U.S. Dist. Colo. 1987, U.S. Ct. Appeals (10th cir.) 1993. Pvt. practice Denver, 1986—; hon. legal counsel Mex. Consulate Gen., Denver, 1987—. Bd. dirs. Justice Info. Ctr., Denver, 1997—, Mexican Cultural Ctr., Denver, 1992-95; elder Presbyn. Ch. U.S.A., Denver, 1986—; with Civil Air Patrol, Auxiliary USAF,1971—. Colo. Wing legal officer, 1992-96, nat. legal officer, 1998—. Mem. Colo. Bar Assn. (diversity com. 1997—), Denver Bar Assn., Am. Immigration Lawyers Assn. (exec. com. Colo. chpt. 1993-97, pres. 1996-97), Denver Law Club (asst. sec. 1997-98, co-sec. 1998-99, treas. 1999—). Democrat. Avocations: pilot, choral singing, bicycling. Immigration, naturalization, and customs. Office: 333 W Hampden Ave Ste 703 Englewood CO 80110-2337

**SIMMONS, HEBER SHERWOOD, III,** lawyer; b. Memphis, Oct. 25, 1961; s. Heber Sherwood Jr. and Jean Frazer Simmons; m. Kathryn Merrell, Aug. 6, 1988; children: Wood, Daniel, Luke. BBA, U. Miss., 1984, JD, 1989. Assoc. Watkins Ludlam & Stennis, Jackson, Miss., 1989-94; ptnr. Armstrong Allen, Jackson, 1994—; mem. tort reform task force ABA, Chgo., 1992-94. Co-author: Mississippi Products Liability, 1994; editor-in-chief Miss. Law Jour., 1988-89. Bd. mem. Am. Heart Assn., Jackson, 1992—. Mem. Jackson Rotary Club (divsn. dir. 1995-96). Republican. Episcopalian. Avocations: carpentry, diving, hunting. Health, Professional liability, Personal injury. Home: 235 N Castle Dr Madison MS 39110-9458 Office: Armstron Allen Ste 200 2525 Lakeward Dr Jackson MS 39216

**SIMMONS, JAMES CHARLES,** lawyer; b. N.Y.C., June 5, 1935; s. James Knight and Helen (Bielefeld) S.; m. Carolyn Ann Edwards, June 12, 1957; children: James M., Shawn M. Dzielawa. BSMetE, Lehigh U., 1957; JD, Duquesne U., 1965. Bar: Pa. 1965, U.S. Dist. Ct. (we. dist.) Pa. 1965, U.S. Ct. Appeals (3rd cir.) 1965, U.S. Ct. Appeals (fed. cir.) 1977. Metall. engr. Crucible Steel Co. Am., Midland, Pa., 1957-66; atty. Crucible Steel Co. Am., Pitts., 1966-67; contract adminstr. Nuclear Materials & Equipment Corp., Apollo, Pa., 1967-69; patent atty. Bausch & Lomb, Rochester, N.Y., 1969-94; asst. gen. patent counsel Air Products and Chem., Inc., Allentown, Pa., 1994-97; sr. atty. Ratner & Prestia, Valley Forge, Pa., 1994-97; ptnr. Ratner & Prestia, Allentown, 1997—. Mem. ABA, Am. Intellectual Property Law Assn. (sec. 1993-96), Pa. Bar Assn., Fed. Cir. Bar Assn., Phila. Intellectual Property Law Assn., Bar Assn. Lehigh County, Benjamin Franklin Am. Inn of Ct. Intellectual property, Patent, Trademark and copyright. Office: Ratner & Prestia 5100 W Tilghman St Ste 265 Allentown PA 18104-9141

**SIMMONS, JOHN G.,** lawyer; b. Logan, Utah, Apr. 16, 1959; s. Gary B. and Joy N. Simmons; m. Shauna R. Rose, Nov. 17, 1990. AA, Idaho State U., 1979; BS, Brigham Young U., 1980, JD, 1983; LLM in Taxation, U. San Diego, 1986. Bar: Idaho, Colo., Utah, U.S. Dist. Ct. Idaho, U.S. Ct. Appeals (9th cir.), U.S. Tax Ct., U.S. Supreme Ct. Pvt. practice law Idaho Falls, Idaho, 1984-87, 98—; assoc. Quane, Smith, Howard & Hall, Pocatello, Idaho, 1987-90; assoc./PLLC mem. Holden, Kidwell, Hahn & Crapo, Idaho Falls, 1990-98; spkr. in field. Contbr. articles to profl. jours. Pres. Ea. Idaho Estate Planning Coun., 1992-93; mem. CLE com. and program planner Idaho Law Found., 1994—. Pension, profit-sharing, and employee benefits, Taxation, general, General corporate. Office: 1274 S Woodruff Ave Idaho Falls ID 83404-5544

**SIMMONS, KAREN DENISE,** lawyer, prosecutor; b. Lakeland, Fla., Aug. 27, 1962; d. Julian Cecil Simmons and Betty Jo Wells. AA, St. Pete Jr. Coll., Clearwater, Fla., 1983; BS, Fla. State U., 1986; JD, Stetson U., 1989. Bar: Fla., 1989. Asst. state atty. State Attys. Office, LaBelle, Fla., 1989-94; asst. gen. counsel Ft. Dept. Law Enforcement, Tallahassee, 1994—. Mem. Fla. Govt. Bar. Office: Fla Dept Law Enforcement 2331 Phillips Rd Tallahassee FL 32308-5333

**SIMMONS, PETER,** law and urban planning educator; b. N.Y.C., July 19, 1931; s. Michael L. and Mary A. S.; m. Ruth J. Tanfield, Jan. 28, 1951; children: Sam, Lizzard. A.B., U. Calif., Berkeley, 1953, LL.B., 1956; postgrad. (Alvord fellow), U. Wis., 1956-58. Prof. SUNY, Buffalo, 1963-67; mem. faculty Ohio State U., 1967-75, U. Ill., 1972, Case Western Res. U., 1974-75; prof. law and urban planning Rutgers U. Coll. Law, Newark, 1975—, dean, 1975-93; university prof. Rutgers U., 1993—. Contbr. articles to profl. jours. Mem. Ohio Housing Commn., 1972-74; commr. Ohio Reclamation Rev. Bd., 1974-75; chmn. N.J. Criminal Disposition Commn., 1983-84; mem. N.J. Law Revision Commn., 1987—. Mem. Am. Planning Assn., Urban Land Inst., Am. Law Inst., AAUP (nat. council 1973-75). Office: Rutgers U Law Sch 15 Washington St Newark NJ 07102-3192

**SIMMONS, PETER LAWRENCE,** lawyer; b. N.Y.C., May 1, 1965; s. John Derek and Rosalind (Wellish) S. AB magna cum laude, Columbia U., 1985, JD, 1987. Bar: N.Y. 1987, U.S. Dist. Ct. (so. and ea. dists.) N.Y. 1988, U.S. Ct. Internat. Trade 1991, U.S. Spreme Ct. 1991, U.S. Ct. Appeals (2d cir.) 1992, U.S. Ct. Appeals (1st cir.) 1993. Law clk. to Hon. Lawrence W. Pierce U.S. Ct. Appeals (2d cir.), N.Y.C., 1987-88; assoc. Fried, Frank, Harris, Shriver & Jacobson, N.Y.C., 1988-94, ptnr., 1994—. Treas., sr. editor Columbia Law Rev., 1985-87. Harlan Fiske Stone scholar, 1985-87. Mem. ABA, Fed. Bar Coun., N.Y. Bar Assn., Assn. of Bar of City of N.Y. (profl. responsibility com. 1998—, civil rights com. 1989-92), Phi Beta Kappa. General civil litigation. Home: 203 E 72nd St Apt 20A New York NY 10021-4551 Office: Fried Frank Harris Shriver & Jacobson 1 New York Plz Fl 22 New York NY 10004-1980

**SIMMONS, ROBERT JACOB,** lawyer; b. Fresno, Calif., Dec. 7, 1947. JD, San Joaquin Coll. Law, 1985. Pvt. practice Clovis, Calif., 1986—. With U.S. Army, 1967-68. Personal injury, Contracts commercial. Office: 190 W Menlo Ave Clovis CA 93612-0238

**SIMMONS, SCOTT MICHAEL,** lawyer; b. Russelville, Ark., Dec. 17, 1966; s. James William and Sharon Kay (Yoder) S.; m. Dana Ruth Vineyard Simmons, June 4, 1988. BS, Ark. Tech. U., Russelville, 1989; JD, U. Ark., Fayetteville, 1992; LLM, U. Denver, 1995. Bar: Ark. 1992; U.S. Dist. Ct. (ea. and we. dist.) 1993. Asst. gen. counsel Cooper Comm. Inc., Bella Vista, Ark., 1992-94; assoc. Peel Law Firm PA, Russellville, Ark., 1995-97; ptnr. Peel & Simmons PA, Russellville, Ark., 1997—. Treas., bd. mem. River Valley United Way Inc., Russellville, Ark., 1998—; treas. Russellville Youth Baseball Assn., Inc., 1998—. Mem. Russellville C. of C., Russellville Noon Rotary Club, Pope County Bar Assn., ABA, Ark. Bar Assn. Methodist. Estate taxation, Probate, Sports. Office: Peel & Simmons PA 120 S Glenwood Ave Russellville AR 72801-4921

**SIMMONS, SHERWIN PALMER,** lawyer; b. Bowling Green, Ky., Jan. 19, 1931. AB, Columbia U., 1952, LLB, 1954, JD, 1969. Bar: Tenn. 1954, Fla. 1957. Assoc. Fowler, White, Collins, Gillen, Humkey & Trenam, Tampa, Fla., 1956-60; ptnr. Fowler, White, Collins, Gillen, Humkey & Trenam, Tampa, 1960-70, Trenam, Simmons, Kemker, Scharf & Barkin, Tampa, 1970-77; stockholder, pres. Trenam, Simmons, Kemker, Scharf, Barkin, Frye & O'Neill, PA, Tampa, 1977-94; ptnr., chair tax group Steel Hector & Davis, LLP, Miami, Fla., 1994—; atty. adv. U.S. Tax Ct., Washington, 1954-56, mem. nominating commn., 1978-81; mem. adv. group Commr. of IRS, 1978-79, 89-90, U.S. Dept. Justice, 1979-80; adj. prof. U. Miami, 1995—. Author: Federal Taxation of Life Insurance, 1966; bd. of advisors mag. The Tax Times, 1986-87; contbr. articles to legal jours. Trustee Hillsborough County Soc. Crippled Children & Adults, 1956-65, pres., 1960-61; treas., chmn. Hillsborough County Pub. Edn. Study Commn., 1965-66; mem. adv. bd. Salvation Army, 1959-62, 64-66, sec., 1960-61; chmn., bd. dirs. The Fla. Orch., 1987-89; founding trustee, pres. Am. Tax Policy Inst., 1996-99; trustee Tampa Bay Performing Arts Ctr., Inc., 1984-93, program adv. com., 1985-89, investment com., 1986-91. Fellow Am. Coll. Trust and Estate Counsel (bd. regents 1982-88), Am. Bar Found. (fellow 1969—, devel. com. 1992-94), Am. Coll. Tax Counsel (regent 1987-93, vice chmn. 1989-91, chmn. 1991-93); mem. ABA (vice chmn. adminstrn. taxation sect. 1972-75, chmn. 1975-76, ho. of dels. 1985-90, bd. govs. 1990-93, chmn. bd. govs. fin. com. 1992-93, chmn. commn. on multidisciplinary practice 1998—), Am. Bar Retirement Assn. (bd. dirs. 1984-90, v.p. 1987-88, pres. 1988-89), Am. Law Network (chmn. subcom. on continuing profl. edn. 1983—), FBA, Fla. Bar Assn. (chmn. taxation sect. 1964-65), Am. Judicature Soc., So. Fed. Tax Inst. (trustee, pres. 1974, chmn. 1975 trustee emeritus 1999—), Internat. Acad. Estate and Trust Law, Internat. Fiscal Assn., Am. Law Inst. (mem. coun. 1985—, exec. com. 1994-97, 99—, mem. com. 1997—, chmn. 1999—). Corporate taxation, Estate taxation, Taxation, general. Office: Steel Hector & Davis LLP 200 S Biscayne Blvd Ste 4100 Miami FL 33131-2310

**SIMMONS, STEPHEN JUDSON,** lawyer; b. Columbus, Ohio, Feb. 19, 1946; s. Samuel A. and Jane A. (McGrath) S.; m. Claire Maxine Schriber, Aug. 15, 1970; children—Darren, Judson. B.A., Ohio State U., 1968; J.D., U. Cin., 1972. Bar: Tex. 1982, Ohio 1973. Sr. law clk. U.S. Dist. Ct. (ea. dist.) Tenn., Knoxville, 1972-74; asst. atty. gen. Office of Atty. of Ohio, Columbus, 1974-75; assoc. McGrath & Shirey, Columbus, 1975; corp. counsel Wendys, Inc., Columbus, 1975-79; sr. v.p., gen. counsel Precision Tune, Inc., Beaumont, Tex., 1979-87, also dir.; sr. v.p. adminstrn., dir. Kwik-Kopy Corp., Cypress, Tex., 1988-90; v.p. Deli Mgmt., Inc., 1990-94; pvt. practice, Houston, 1994—. Bd. editors U. Cin. Law Rev., 1971-72. Mem. Tex. Bar Assn. Roman Catholic. Franchising, General corporate, Real property. Home: 13603 Balmore Cir Houston TX 77069-2703 Office: 3845 Fm 1960 Rd W Ste 250 Houston TX 77068-3548

**SIMMONS, TERRY ALLAN,** lawyer; b. Oroville, Calif., Apr. 12, 1946; s. Daniel and Jeanne Simmons. AB in Anthropology, U. Calif., Santa Cruz, 1968; MA in Geography, Simon Fraser U., 1974; PhD in Geography, U. Minn., 1979; JD, U. Calif., Berkeley, 1989. Bar: Nev. 1991, Calif. 1992. Lectr. geography Lakehead U., Thunder Bay, Ont., Can., 1974-75; mgr. B.C. Wildlife Fedn., Cloverdale, B.C., Can., 1980-81; project planning engr. B.C. Hydro and Power Authority, Vancouver, 1981-83; pres. Humboldt Rsch Assocs. Inc., Walnut Creek, Calif., 1983-87, Vancouver, B.C., 1983-87; pvt. practice Reno, Nev., 1991—; environtl. policy com., Reno, 1991—; adj. assoc. rsch. prof. Desert Rsch. Inst., Reno, 1996—. Editor: Sustainability of the Pacific Coast Forests, 1999. Pres. Nev. World Trade Coun., Reno, 1997—; chmn. City of Reno Environtl. Bd., 1993-96; mem. air pollution control hearing bd. Washoe County Dist. Health Dept., Reno, 1997—. Alternative dispute resolution, Environmental, Real property. Office: 403 Flint St Reno NV 89501-2007

**SIMMONS SCOTT, VANESSA ANN,** lawyer; b. Bronx, N.Y., Sept. 15, 1971; d. Chillie Ann Simmons; m. Quentin E. Scott, Oct. 3, 1998. BA, Duke U., 1993; JD, Vanderbilt U., 1997. Bar: Ala. 1997, U.S. Dist. Ct. (no. and mid. dists.) Ala. 1997, U.S. Ct. Appeals (11th cir.) 1997. Law clk. to Hon. Alfred Robbins, N.Y. Supreme Ct., Mineola, 1996; assoc. Lange, Simpson, Robinson & Somerville LLP, Birmingham, Ala., 1997—. Fundraiser big gifts campaign YMCA, Birmingham, 1997-98. Mem. ABA, Birmingham Bar Assn., Alpha Kappa Alpha. Pension, profit-sharing, and employee benefits, General civil litigation. Office: Lange Simpson Et Al 417 20th St N Ste 1700 Birmingham AL 35203-3217

**SIMMS, JOHN SETH,** lawyer; b. Clearwater, Fla., Sept. 19, 1966; s. John William and Joyce Jeanette (Morehead) S.;m. m. Christine Denise Janney (div.); 1 child, Joyce Christine. AA, St. Petersburg Jr. Coll., 1985; BA, U. South Fla., 1987; JD, Stetson U. Coll. Law, 1990. Bar: Fla. 1991, U.S. Dist. Ct. (mid. dist.) Fla. 1991, U.S. Claims Ct. 1991, U.S. Supreme Ct. 1991, U.S. Tax Ct. 1991, U.S. Ct. Mil. Appeals 1991. Atty. Bruce P. Young P.A., Clearwater, 1991-94; ptnr. Staack & Simms P.A., Clearwater, 1994—. Sec. Planning & Zoning Bd. Town of Bellair, Fla., 1991-94, com. mem. Bldg. Bd. Adjustment & Appeal, 1991—; lectr. Dads Assisting Dads, 1997; steering com. Gus Bilinakis for State House, Palm Harbor, Fla., 1998, Bruce Young for Judge, Clearwater, 1994. Mem. Clearwater Bar Assn. Republican. Avocations: tennis, Miami Hurricane football, comic books & memorabilia. Family and matrimonial, State civil litigation, Federal civil litigation. Office: Staack & Simms PA 121 N Osceola Ave Fl 2D Clearwater FL 33755-4039

**SIMMS, ROBERT D.,** state supreme court justice; b. Tulsa, Feb. 6, 1926; s. Matthew Scott and Bessie L. (Moore) S.; m. Patricia C., Feb. 16, 1950; 1 son, Robert D. Student, Milligan Coll., Phillips U.; LLB, U. Tulsa. Bar: Okla. 1950. Pvt. practice law Sand Springs, Okla., from 1950; asst. county atty. Tulsa County, 1953-54; chief prosecutor County Atty.'s Office, 1955-58, county atty., 1958-62; judge Okla. Dist. Ct., Dist. 14, 1962-71, Okla. Ct. Criminal Appeals, 1971-72; justice Okla. Supreme Ct., 1985-; mem. Okla. Crime Commn. Mem. Gov.'s Spl. Com. on Drug Abuse, 1970; sponsor and coach Pee-Wee Baseball. Served with USN, 1943-46. Mem. Tulsa County Bar Assn., Okla. Bar Assn. (chmn. dist. atty. sect. 1959). Office: Okla Supreme Ct State Capital Bldg Room 200 Oklahoma City OK 73105*

**SIMON, BARRY PHILIP,** lawyer, airline executive; b. Paterson, N.J., Nov. 22, 1942; s. Alfred Louis and Rhoda (Tapper) S.; m. Hinda Bookstaber, Feb. 9, 1964; children: Alan, John, Eric. BA, Princeton U., 1964; LLB, Yale U., 1967. Bar: N.Y. 1965, Tex. 1986. Assoc. atty. Hughes Hubbard & Reed, N.Y.C., 1967-69, Sullivan & Cromwell, N.Y.C., 1969-72, Shea & Gould, N.Y.C., 1972-73; v.p., gen. counsel Teleprompter Corp., N.Y.C., 1973-82; v.p., sec., gen. counsel Continental Airlines, L.A. and Houston, 1982-86; v.p. in-charge internat. div. Continental Airlines, Houston, 1987-90; sr. v.p. legal affairs, gen. counsel, sec. Continental Airlines, 1990-92; sr. v.p. Tex. Air Corp., 1986-87; sr. v.p. legal affairs, gen. counsel, sec. Ea. Airlines, Miami, 1987-90; exec. v.p., gen. counsel GAF Corp., Wayne, N.J., 1993-95; sr. v.p. for internat. ops. Continental Airlines, Houston, 1996—; bd. dirs. Amadeus Reservations Sys. Mem. copyright com. Nat. Cable TV Assn., Washington, 1974-76, mem. utilities com., 1973-82; bd. dirs. Houston Grand Opera, Inprint, Alley Theatre. Recipient Class of 1888 Lit. prize Princeton U., 1961. General corporate, Bankruptcy, Pension, profit-sharing, and employee benefits.

**SIMON, BRUCE W.,** lawyer; b. N.Y.C., Dec. 25, 1943; s. Herman O. Simon and Ursula M. (Prussman) Willis. BA, U. Mo., Kansas City, 1966, JD, 1969. Bar: Mo. 1970, U.S. Dist. Ct. Mo. 1970, U.S. Ct. Appeals (11th cir.) 1987, U.S. Ct. Appeals (8th cir.) 1988, U.S. Ct. Appeals (10th cir.) 1991, U.S. Tax Ct. 1991, U.S. Supreme Ct. 1991. Pres. Mo. Assn. Criminal Def. Lawyers, 1991-92. Office: Simon & Simon 801 Walnut St Kansas City MO 64106-1805

**SIMON, DAVID ROBERT,** lawyer; b. Newton, Mass., June 21, 1934; m. Myrna B. Kiner, June 28, 1959; children—Marianne, Geoffrey. A.B., Harvard U., 1956, LL.B., 1960. Bar: Mass. 1960, N.J. 1963, N.Y. 1980. Law sec. to judge U.S. Dist. Ct., Newark, 1961-63; assoc. Newark Law Firm, 1964-68; ptnr. Simon & Allen, Newark, 1968-86; ptnr. Kirsten, Simon, Friedman, Allen, Cherin & Linken, Newark, 1987-89; ptnr. Whitman & Ransom, Newark, 1989-93; sole practitioner, 1994—. Served with USAR, 1956-64. Mem. ABA, N.J. State Bar Assn., Essex County Bar Assn. Antitrust, Federal civil litigation, State civil litigation. Home: 875 Fifth Ave 11E New York NY 10021-4952 Office: One Riverfront Plz Newark NJ 07102

**SIMON, H(UEY) PAUL,** lawyer; b. Lafayette, La., Oct. 19, 1923; s. Jules and Ida (Rogére) S.; m. Carolyn Perkins, Aug. 6, 1949; 1 child, John Clark. B.S., U. Southwestern La., 1943; J.D., Tulane U., 1947. Bar: La. 1947; CPA, La. 1947. Pvt. practice New Orleans, 1947—; asst. prof. advanced acctg. and taxation U. Southwestern La., 1944-45; staff acct. Haskins & Sells (now Deloitte & Touche), New Orleans, 1945-53, prin., 1953-57; ptnr. Deutsch, Kerrigan & Stiles, 1957-79; sr. founding ptnr. Simon, Peragine, Smith & Redfearn, 1979—; mem. New Orleans Bd. Trade. Author: Community Property and Liability for Funeral Expenses of Deceased Spouse, 1946, Income Tax Deductibility of Attorney's Fees in Action in Boundary, 1946, Fair Labor Standards Act and Employee's Waiver of Liquidated Damages, 1946, Louisiana Income Tax Law, 1956, Changes Effected by the Louisiana Trust Code, 1965, Gifts to Minors and the Parent's Obligation of Support, 1968; co-author: Deductions—Business or Hobby, 1975, Role of Attorney in IRS Tax Return Examination, 1978; assoc. editor: The Louisiana CPA, 1956-60; mem. bd. editors Tulane Law Rev., 1945-46, adv. bd. editors, 1992—; estates, gifts and trusts editor The Tax Times, 1986-87. Bd. dirs., mem. fin. com. World Trade Ctr., 1985-86; mem. New Orleans Met. Crime Commn., Coun. for a Better La., New Orleans Met. Area Com., Bur. Govtl. Rsch., Pub. Affairs Rsch. Coun.; co-chmn. NYU Tax Conf., New Orleans, 1976; mem. dean's coun. Tulane U. Law Sch. Fellow Am. Coll. Tax Counsel; mem. ABA (com. ct. procedure tax sect. 1958—), AICPA, La. Bar Assn. (com. on legis. and adminstrv. practice 1966-70, bd. cert. tax atty.), New Orleans Bar Assn., Internat. Bar Assn. (com. on securities issues and trading 1970-88), Am. Judicature Soc., Soc. La. CPAs, New

Orleans Assn. Notaries, Tulane U. Alumni Assn., New Orleans C. of C. (coun. 1952-66), Tulane Tax Inst. (program com. 1960-96), Internat. House (bd. dirs. 1976-79, 82-85), Internat. Platform Assn., City Energy Club, Press Club, New Orleans Country Club, Phi Delta Phi (past pres. New Orleans chpt.), Sigma Pi Alpha. Roman Catholic. Estate planning, General corporate, Corporate taxation. Home: 6075 Canal Blvd New Orleans LA 70124-2936 Office: 30th Fl Energy Ctr New Orleans LA 70163 *Developing and maintaining consistency and constancy in feeling and showing genuine respect towards others nourish and stimulate an individual to become day by day a better person. Whether alone or in the presence of others, one who daily abides by the guidance and rules he would advocate to others invariably finds the greatest reward of all—true respect for one's self.*

**SIMON, JAMES LOWELL,** lawyer; b. Nov. 8, 1944; s. K. Lowell and Elizabeth Ann (Unholz) S.; m. RuthAnn Beck, July 4, 1997; children: Heather Lyn Small, Brandon James; stepchildren: Gary G. Mower, Richard M. Nazareth II, Juliet A. Nazareth. Student, U. Ill., 1962-63, JD with honors, 1975; BSEE magna cum laude, Bradley U., 1967. Bar: Fla. 1975, U.S. Dist. Ct. (mid. dist.) Fla. 1976, U.S. Ct. Appeals (11th cir.) 1981, U.S. Patent Office 1983. Engr. Pan Am. World Airways, Cape Kennedy, Fla., 1967-68; assoc. Akerman, Senterfitt & Eidson, Orlando, Fla., 1975-80; ptnr. Bogin, Munns, Munns & Simon, Orlando, 1980-87, Holland & Knight, LLP, 1987-99. With Seminole County Sch. Adv. Coun., Fla., 1981-88, chmn., 1982, 83; with Forest City Local Sch. Adv. Com., Altamonte Springs, Fla., 1981-84, Code Enforcement Bd., Altamonte Springs, 1983-84, Cen. Bus. Dist. Study com., Altamonte Springs, 1983-85, Rep. Coun. of '76, Seminole County, 1982-87; mem. Seminole County Libr. Adv. Bd., 1989-92, sec., 1990, pres., 1991, Seminole County Citizens for Quality Edn., 1990-92; mem. Seminole County Sch. Dist. Strategic Planning Com., 1991—, Leadership Orlando Alumni, 1992—; bd. dirs. Found. for Seminole County Pub. Schs., Inc., 1992-95, chmn., 1993-94; bd. dirs. Greater Seminole C. of C., 1993; active Lake Brantley H.S. Band Boosters, 1995—, Lake Brantley H.S. PTSA, 1995—, Chorus Boosters, 1997, Leadership Club-Heart of Fla. United Way, 1997; sponsor concerts Orlando Philharm. Orch. for Boys and Girls Clubs Cen. Fla., 1996-97; regional dir. region 5 Holocaust Remembrance Project, 1997—. Capt. USAF, 1968-72. Mem. ABA, Orange County Bar Assn. (jud. rels. com. 1982-83, fee arbitration com. 1983—), Greater Orlando C. of C., Seminole County Bar Assn. (sec. trial lawyers sect. 1993-94), U. Ill. Alumni Club Cen. Fla., Phi Kappa Phi, Tau Beta Pi, Sigma Tau, Eta Kappa Nu. Republican. General civil litigation, Construction, Trademark and copyright. Home: 120 Springside Ct Longwood FL 32779-4965

**SIMON, JOHN GERALD,** law educator; b. N.Y.C., Sept. 19, 1928; s. Robert Alfred and Madeleine (Marshall) S.; m. Claire Aloise Bising, June 14, 1958; 1 son, John Kirby (dec.). Grad., Ethical Culture Schs., 1946; AB, Harvard U., 1950; LLB, Yale U., 1953; LLD (hon.), Ind. U., 1989. Bar: N.Y. 1953. Asst. to gen. counsel Office Sec. Army, 1956-58; with firm Paul, Weiss, Rifkind, Wharton & Garrison, N.Y.C., 1958-62; mem. faculty Yale Law Sch., 1962—, prof. law, 1967-76, Augustus Lines prof. law, 1976—, dep. dean, 1985-90, acting dean, 1991; dir., co-chmn. program on non-profit orgns. Yale U., 1977-88. Author: (with Powers and Gunnemann) The Ethical Investor, 1972. Pres. Taconic Found., 1967—; trustee, sec. Potomac Inst., 1961-93; mem. grad. bd. Harvard Crimson, 1950—; chmn. bd. dirs. Coop. Assistance Fund, 1970-76, vice chmn., 1977—; mem. governing coun. Rockefeller Archives Ctr., 1982-86; trustee The Found. Ctr., 1983-92, Open Soc. Inst.-N.Y., 1996—. 1st lt. U.S. Army, 1953-5 6. Recipient Certificate of Achievement Dept. Army, 1956. Mem. Phi Beta Kappa. Office: Yale U Law Sch New Haven CT 06520

**SIMON, MICHAEL SCOTT,** lawyer; b. Bronx, N.Y., Feb. 9, 1954; s. Philip and Miriam C. (Feller) S.; m. Elayne Robin Baer, May 26, 1974; children: Joshua Seth, Sarah Emily, Rachel Melissa. BA, SUNY, Stony Brook, 1976; JD, Boston U., 1979. Bar: N.Y. 1980, U.S. Dist. Ct. (ea. and so. dists.) N.Y. 1980, U.S. Ct. Appeals (2d cir.) 1981, U.S. Tax Ct. 1983, U.S. Supreme Ct. 1983; Fla. 1987. Asst. corp. counsel N.Y.C. Law Dept., 1979-82; assoc. Tenzer, Greenblatt, Fallon & Kaplan, N.Y.C., 1982-88; ptnr. Tenzer, Greenblatt L.L.P., N.Y.C., 1989—. Mem. ABA, N.Y. State Bar Assn., Fla. Bar Assn., N.Y. County Lawyers Assn., Assn. Bar City N.Y., Pi Sigma Alpha. Avocations: travel, music. State civil litigation, Real property, Landlord-tenant. Home: 4 Talon Way Dix Hills NY 11746-6239 Office: Tenzer Greenblatt LLP 405 Lexington Ave New York NY 10174-0002

**SIMON, NANCY RUTH,** lawyer; b. Gary, Ind.. BSEE, Iowa State U., 1985; MBA, U. Dallas, 1988; JD, So. Meth. U., 1991. Bar: Tex. 1991, Calif. 1994; registered to practice before U.S. Patent and Trademark Office 1992; lic. real estate salesperson. Elec. engr. Tex. Instruments, Dallas, 1986-88; law clk. to pvt. law firms Dallas, 1989-91; law clk. U.S. Attys. Office, 1991; assoc. Felsman, Bradley, Gunter & Dillon, LLP, Ft. Worth, 1991-93; patent counsel Apple Computer, Inc., Cupertino, Calif., 1993—; realtor Coldwell Banker, San Jose, Calif, 1997-98. Co-author: Attorneys' Fees in IPL Cases; mem. So. Meth. U. Law Rev. Jour. of Air Law and Commerce, 1990-91. Mem. ABA, State Bar Tex., State Bar Calif., Nat. Assn. Realtors, Calif. Assn. Realtors, Peninsula West Valley Assn. Realtors, Mensa Iowa State U. Student Alumni Assn. (mem. career awareness com. 1984-85), Sigma Iota Epsilon, Zeta Tau Alpha (social chmn. 1982-83, house mgr. 1983-84, chmn. jud. bd. 1984-85), Phi Delta Phi. Avocations: reading, music, scuba diving. Patent, Intellectual property, Computer. Office: Apple Computer Inc 1 Infinite Loop Cupertino CA 95014-2084

**SIMON, ROBERT S.,** lawyer; b. Ft. Worth, July 3, 1946; s. Milton Sylvan Simon and Florence Esther Meltzer; divorced; children: Luke Alexander, William Boyd. BBA in Fin. with honors, U. Tex., 1967, JD, 1970; MBA, Tex. Christian U., 1976. Bar: Tex. 1970, U.S. Dist. Ct. (no. dist.) Tex. 1974, N. Mex. 1982, U.S. Dist. Ct. N. Mex. 1983. Staff atty. Tarrant County Legal Aid, Ft. Worth, 1972; corp. counsel Pier One Imports, Inc., Ft. Worth, 1972-81; pvt. practice Albuquerque, 1972—; corp. counsel Westland Devel. Co., Inc., Albuquerque, 1989—, Titan Techs., Inc., Albuquerque, 1998—. Contbr. articles to profl. jours. and mags. Mem. S. region citizen adv. coun. Albuquerque Pub. Schs., 1991-96, chmn., 1994-96; chmn. Older Adult Svc. and Info. Sys., Albuquerque, 1998. Avocations: gourmet cooking, collecting cowrie shells. General corporate, Real property, General civil litigation. Office: 401 Coors Blvd NW Albuquerque NM 87121-1455

**SIMON, SEYMOUR,** lawyer, former state supreme court justice; b. Chgo., Aug. 10, 1915; s. Ben and Gertrude (Rusky) S.; m. Roslyn Schultz Biel, May 26, 1954; children: John B., Nancy Simon Cooper, Anthony Biel. BS, Northwestern U., 1935, JD, 1938; LLD (hon.), John Marshall Law Sch., 1982, North Park Coll., 1986, Northwestern U., 1987. Bar: Ill. 1938. Spl. atty. Dept. Justice, 1938-42; practice law Chgo., 1946-74; judge Ill. Appellate Ct., Chgo., 1974-80; presiding justice Ill. Appellate Ct. (1st Dist., 3d Div.), 1977, 79; justice Ill. Supreme Ct., 1980-88; ptnr. Rudnick & Wolfe, Chgo., 1988—; former chmn. Ill. Low-Level Radioactive Waste Disposal Facility Siting Commn.; former dir. Nat. Gen. Corp., Bantam Books, Grosset & Dunlap, Inc., Gt. Am. Ins. Corp. Mem. Cook County Bd. Commrs., 1961-66, pres., 1962-66; pres. Cook County Forest Preserve Dist., 1962-66; mem. Pub. Bldg. Commn., City Chgo., 1962-67; Alderman 40th ward, Chgo., 1955-61, 67-74; Democratic ward committeeman, 1960-74; bd. dirs. Schwab Rehab. Hosp., 1961-71, Swedish Covenant Hosp., 1969-75. With USNR, 1942-45. Decorated Legion of Merit; recipient 9th Ann. Pub. Svc. award Tau Epsilon Rho, 1963, Hubert L. Will award Am. Vets. Com., 1983, award of merit Decalogue Soc. Lawyers, 1986, Judge Learned Hand award Am. Jewish Com., 1994, Frances Feinberg Meml. Crown award Associated Talmud Torahs of Chgo., 1995, Bill of Rights in Action award Constl. Rights Found., 1997; named to Sr. Citizen's Hall of Fame, City of Chgo., 1989, Hall of Fame Jewish Comty. Ctrs. Chgo., 1989, Laureate Lincoln Acad. Ill., 1997, Chgo. Coun. Lawyers and the Appleseed Fund Justice Commitment to Justice award, 1998. Mem. ABA, Ill. Bar Assn., Chgo. Bar Assn., Chgo. Hist. Soc., Decalogue Soc. Lawyers (Merit award 1986), Izaak Walton League, Chgo. Hort. Soc., Comml. Club Chgo., Std. Club, Variety Club, Order of Coif, Phi Beta Kappa, Phi Beta Kappa Assocs. Administrative and regulatory, Antitrust, General civil litigation. Home: 1555 N Astor St Chicago IL 60610-1673 Office: Rudnick & Wolfe 203 N La Salle St Ste 1800 Chicago IL 60601-1210

**SIMON, STEPHANIE EDEN,** lawyer; b. Royal Oak, Mich., Sept. 29, 1970; d. Mitchell and Lynn Simon. AB in Religious Studies, Polit. Sci. with honors, U. Mich., 1992; JD, Wayne State U., 1995. Bar: Mich. 1995, U.S. Dist. Ct. (we. dist.) Mich. 1995. Law clk. Greenbaum & Greenbaum, PC, Farmington Hills, Mich., 1994-95; atty. Gockerman, Wilson, Saylor & Hesslin, PC, Manistee, Mich., 1995—; judge Mich. H.S. Mock Trial Competitions, Ctr. for Civic Edn. through Law, Grand Rapids, Mich., 1996-97; spkr. in field. Mem. U. Mich. Club Manistee (bd. dirs. 1996—), Manistee Jaycees (dir. 1997-98, Officer of Month June 1997). Avocations: painting, reading, hiking, golf, gardening. General civil litigation, Municipal (including bonds), Family and matrimonial. Office: Gockerman Wilson Saylor & Hesslin PC 414 Water St Manistee MI 49660-1531

**SIMON, THELMA BROOK,** lawyer, educator; b. Chgo., Oct. 11, 1916; d. John and Ida (Goodman) Brook; m. Harold M. Simon, Apr. 21, 1940; children: Elliott, Justin. BA, U. Ill., 1937; JD, U. Chgo., 1940. Bar: Ill. 1940, U.S. Supreme Ct. 1959. Mem. Angerstein & Angerstein, Chgo., 1940-42; lawyer dept. pub. debt U.S. Dept. Treasury, Chgo., 1942-43; law clk to Hon. Bristow Ill. Supreme Ct., 1946-62; law clk. to Judge LaBuy U.S. Fed. Dist. Ct., Chgo., 1962-65; pvt. practice Chgo., 1966-67, 70-71; law clk. to Justice Solfisburg Ill. Supreme Ct., 1968-69; asst. solicitor U.S. Dept. Labor, Chgo., 1971-73; prof. law John Marshall Law Sch. Adminstrv. Law and Torts, Chgo., 1973-75; Coord. Learning in Retirement Class Northwestern U., Evanston, Ill., 1989. Editor, researcher for U.S. Dist. Ct.: Jury Instructions in Federal Criminal Cases, 1965. Trustee Village of Wilmette, Ill., 1961-69, chmn. judiciary com.; precinct capt. Dem. Party New Trier Twp., Wilmette, 1969-91. Named Senior Citizen of Yr., Village of Wilmette, 1994; U. Chgo. Law Sch. scholar, 1937-40. Mem. ABA, Women's Bar Assn. Ill. (sec. 1953, v.p. 1955, pres. 1956-57), Wilmette LWV (30 Yr. Mem. award 1992), Alumni Assn. U. Chgo. Law Sch. (chmn. 1980-81), Chgo. Bar Assn. (chmn. adminstrv. law com. 1980-82, 50 Yr. Mem. award 1992). Avocations: creative writing, piano, gardening. E-mail: HARMAWIL@AOL.COM. Administrative and regulatory, Appellate, Constitutional. Home: 3119 Wilmette Ave Wilmette IL 60091-2925

**SIMONDS, TIMOTHY RAY,** lawyer; b. Chattanooga, June 9, 1964; s. W. Ray and Patricia Ann (Brown) S.; m. Cynthia Dawn Rider, Dec. 4, 1993; children: Austin R. Ware, Ashley P. Malone. BS in Polit. Sci., U. Tenn., Chattanooga, 1986; JD, U. Tenn., Knoxville, 1989. Bar: Tenn. 1989, U.S. Dist. Ct. (ea. and mid. dists.) Tenn. 1989, U.S. Ct. Appeals (6th, 11th and fed. cirs.) 1989. Litigation atty. Baker, Donelson, Bearman & Caldwell, Chattanooga, 1989—. Contbr. articles to profl. publs. Election inspector Hamilton County, Tenn., 1994. Mem. ABA, ATLA, Tenn. Bar Assn., Chattanooga Bar Assn. (profl. ethics lectr. 1991-94, mem. com. 1994). Avocations: tennis, boating, book collecting, reading. General civil litigation, Insurance, Contracts commercial. Office: Baker Donelson Bearman 1800 Republic Ctr 633 Chestnut St Chattanooga TN 37450-4000

**SIMONE, JOSEPH R.,** lawyer; b. N.Y.C., Jan. 7, 1949; m. Virginia E. Simone, May 29, 1971; children: Jacquelyn, Robert. BA cum laude, Queens Coll., 1971; LLM in Taxation, NYU, 1977; JD cum laude, Fordham U., 1974. Bar: N.Y. 1975, U.S. Dist. Ct. (so. dist.) N.Y. 1975, U.S. Ct. Appeals (2d cir.) 1975. Ptnr. Patterson, Belknap, Webb & Tyler, N.Y.C., 1982-88, Schulte, Roth & Zabel, N.Y.C., 1988—; spl. prof. law Hofstra U. Sch. Law, 1998-99; of counsel Schulte, Roth and Zabel, New York, 1999—. Author: (textbooks) Pension Answer Book, 5th edit., 1990, Essential Facts: Pension and Profit-sharing Plans, 1999; editl. advisor Jour. of Pension Planning. Mem. Am. Arbitration Assn. (panel on multiemployer pension plans, employee benefits law adv. com, co-chair symposium employee benefits), Phi Beta Kappa. Pension, profit-sharing, and employee benefits. Office: Schulte Roth & Zabel 900 3rd Ave Fl 19 New York NY 10022-4774

**SIMONS, BARBARA M.,** lawyer; b. N.Y.C., Feb. 7, 1929; d. Samuel A. and Minnie (Mankes) Malitz; m. Morton L. Simons, Sept. 2, 1951; 1 child, Claudia. BA, U. Mich., 1950, JD, 1952. Bar: N.Y. 1953, U.S. Supreme Ct. 1963, U.S. Ct. Appeals (D.C. cir.) 1971, (5th cir.) 1992, (1st cir.) 1994. Ptnr. Simons & Simons, Washington, 1962—. Pres. Forest Hills Citizens Assn., Washington, 1998—; past pres. D.C. chpt. U. Mich. Alumnae, Washington. Alumnae scholar U. Mich., 1946-50. Mem. Washington Coun. Lawyers, Nat. Partnership Women & Families, Sierra Club, Nat. Symphony Orch. Assn., Phi Beta Kappa, Phi Kappa Phi, Alpha Lambda Delta. FERC practice, Public utilities, Administrative and regulatory. Office: Simons & Simons 5025 Linnean Ave NW Washington DC 20008-2042

**SIMONS, BARRY THOMAS,** lawyer; b. Lynn, Mass., Dec. 14, 1946; s. Emanuel Isador and Betty (Darish) S.; m. Laurie Jean Louder, May 5, 1985; children: Britton Eugene, Brett Jacob. BS in Govt., Am. Univ., 1968; JD, NYU, 1971. Bar: Calif. 1971, U.S. Dist. Ct. (ctrl. dist.) Calif. 1972, U.S. Ct. Appeals (9th cir.) 1972, U.S. Supreme Ct. 1978, U.S. Dist. Ct. (so. and no. dists.) Calif. 1979. Pvt. practice Laguna Beach, Calif., 1971—. Editor (law rev.) N.Y. Law Forum, 1971. Apptd. mem. gen. plan revision com. and local coastal task force City of Laguna Beach, 1980. Mem. Orange County Bar Assn. (bd. dirs. 1981), Newport/Harbor Bar Assn. (bd. dirs. 1979), South Orange County Bar Assn. (pres. 1986, bd. dirs. 1980-95), Calif. Attys. for Criminal Justice (chair misdemeanor com. 1995), Nat. Assn. Criminal Def. Attys., Nat. Coll. D.U.I. Def. (founding mem., regent), Assn. Calif. D.U.I. Defenders (bd. dirs.), Deuce Defenders Assn. Fax no.: (949)497-3971; e-mail: simonslaw@AOL.com. Criminal, Juvenile. Office: 260 Saint Anns Dr Laguna Beach CA 92651-2737

**SIMONS, BERNARD PHILIP,** lawyer; b. N.Y.C., Nov. 14, 1942; s. Harold J. and Lila (Orchant) S.; m. Eve C. Steinberg, Nov. 28, 1971; 1 child, Caroline A. BA, Rutgers U., 1964; JD, Hastings Coll. of Law, San Francisco, 1967. Ptnr. Gendel, Raskoff, Shapiro & Quittner, L.A., 1969-87, Sanders, Barnet, Goldman, Simons & Mosk, L.A., 1988—. Capt. U.S. Army, 1967-69, Vietnam. Decorated Bronze Star. Mem. ABA, Calif. Bar Assn., L.A. County Bar Assn. E-mail: bsimoms@sanbarlaw.com. Fax: (310) 553-2435. Federal civil litigation, General civil litigation. Office: Sanders Barnet Goldman Simons & Mosk # 850 1901 Avenue Of The Stars Los Angeles CA 90067-6078

**SIMONS, CHARLES EARL, JR.,** federal judge; b. Johnston, S.C., Aug. 17, 1916; s. Charles Earl Sr. and Frances (Rhoden) S.; m. Jean Knapp, Oct. 18, 1941 (dec. 1991); children: Charles Earl III, Paul Knapp, Richard Brewster, Jean Brewster Smith. AB, U. S.C., 1937, LLB cum laude, 1939. Bar: S.C. 1939. Ptnr. Lybrand & Simons, Aiken, S.C., 1939-50, Thurmond, Lybrand and Simons, Aiken, 1950-54, Lybrand, Simons & Rich, Aiken, 1950-54, 1961-64; mem. S.C. Ho. of Reps., 1942, 47-48, 61-64; mem. ways and means com., 1947-48, 61-64; judge U.S. Dist. Ct. S.C., Aiken, 1964—, chief judge, 1980-86; sr. status U.S. Dist. Ct., 1987—; mem. S.C. Constl. Revision Com., 1948, Bd. Discipline and Grievance, S.C. Bar, 1958-61, Ethics Adv. Panel, 1981-87; jud. rep. 4th cir. Jud. Conf. U.S., 1973-79; chmn. subcom. on fed. jurisdiction of Com. on Ct. Adminstrn., 1986-87. Mem. Chief Met. Dist. Judges Conf., 1980-89, chmn., 1986-89; bd. dirs. S.C. Athletic Hall of Fame; mem. Jud. Conf. Commn. on Jud. Br., 1988-92. With USN, World War II. Recipient Algernon Sidney Sullivan award, 1937, 64. Mem ABA, S.C. Bar Assn. (com. mem.), Am. Law Inst., Am. Legion, U. S.C. Alumni Assn. (past pres. 1964), S.C. Golf Assn., Aiken Bus. Men's Club (past pres.), Palmetto Golf Club (pres. 1994-97), Rotary. Baptist. Home: PO Box 2185 Aiken SC 29802-2185 Office: US Dist Ct SC Charles E Simons Jr Fed Courthouse PO Box 2185 Aiken SC 29802-2185

**SIMONS, RICHARD DUNCAN,** lawyer, retired judge; b. Niagara Falls, N.Y., Mar. 23, 1927; s. William Taylor and Sybil Irene (Swick) S.; m. Muriel (Penny) E. Genung, June 9, 1951 (dec. 1992); m. Esther (Esi) Turkington Tremblay, May 21, 1994; children: Ross T., Scott R., Kathryn E., Linda A. AB, Colgate U., 1949; LLB, U. Mich., 1952; LLD (hon.), Albany Law Sch., 1983. Bar: N.Y. 1952. Pvt. practice Rome, N.Y., 1952-63; asst. corp. counsel City of Rome, 1955-58, corp. counsel, 1960-63; justice 5th jud. dist. N.Y. Supreme Ct., 1964-83, assoc. justice appellate divsn. 3d dept., 1971-72, assoc. justice appellate divsn. 4th dept., 1973-82; assoc. judge N.Y. Ct. Appeals, 1983-96, acting chief judge, 1992-93; counsel McMahon, Grow & Getty, Rome, N.Y., 1997—; dir. N.Y. State Capital Defender Office, 1997—; chief appellate judge Oneida Indian Nation, 1997—; mem. Law Sch. Admission Svcs., Bar Passage Study Com. Editorial staff: N.Y. Pattern Jury Instructions, 1979-83. Chmn. Republican City Com., 1958-62; vice chmn. Oneida County Rep. Com., 1958-62; bd. mgrs. Rome Hosp. and Murphy Meml. Hosp., 1953. Served with USN, World War II. NEH fellow U. Va. Law Sch., 1979. Fellow Am. Bar Found., N.Y. State Bar Found. (chmn. 1997-98); mem. ABA, N.Y. State Bar Assn., Oneida County Bar Assn., Rome Bar Assn., Am. Law Inst., Inst. Jud. Adminstrn. Home: 6520 Pillmore Cir Rome NY 13440-7337 Office: McMahon Grow & Getty 301 N Washington St Ste 4 Rome NY 13440-5152

**SIMONS, WILLIAM W.,** lawyer, mediator, arbitrator; b. N.Y.C., Mar. 13, 1928; s. Abraham R. and Yetta (Lubow) S.; m. Marilyn Frankel, May 23, 1953; children: Amy Joan Abramovich, Richard Anderew Simons. BA, NYU, 1950, JD, 1954. Bar: N.Y. 1954, Mass. 1960, U.S. Dist. Ct. (so. dist.) N.Y. 1962, U.S. Dist. Ct. (no. dist.) N.Y. 1963, U.S. Dist. Ct. Mass. 1963. Assoc. Moses & Singer, N.Y.C., 1954-60, Albert Silverman, Pittsfield, Mass., 1960-62; ptnr. Simons, Cook & Shepard, Pittsfield, 1962-78; justice Superior Ct. Mass., Boston, 1978-93; of counsel Reder & Simons, Pittsfield, 1993—; asst. dist. atty. Western Dist. Mass., Pittsfield/Springfield, 1968-73. Sgt. U.S. Army, 1946-47, Korea. Mem. N.Y. State Bar Assn., Mass. Bar Assn., Berkshire County Bar Assn. (pres. 1971-72). Alternative dispute resolution, State civil litigation. Office: Simons & Assocs 74 North St Pittsfield MA 01201-5116

**SIMONSON, MICHAEL,** lawyer, judge; b. Franklin, N.J., Feb. 5, 1950; s. Robert and Eleanor (Weiss) S. BA, U. Ariz., 1973; JD, Southwestern U., Los Angeles, 1976; LLM in Taxation, Washington U., St. Louis, 1978. Bar: Ariz. 1977, U.S. Dist. Ct. Ariz. 1979, U.S. Tax Ct. 1978. Bailiff, law clk. Superior Ct. Maricopa County Div. 2, Phoenix, 1976-77; sole practice, Scottsdale, Ariz., 1978-79; ptnr. Simonson, Groh, & Lindteigen, Scottsdale, 1979-81, Simonson & Preston, Phoenix, 1984-86, Simonson, Preston & Arbetman, 1986-87, Simonson & Arbetman, 1987-89; judge pro tempore Mcpl. Ct., City of Phoenix, 1984—, City of Mesa, 1990—; judge pro tempore Maricopa County Superior Ct., 1991—; adj. prof. Ariz. State U Coll. Bus., Tempe, 1984—, Coll. for Fin. Planning, Denver, 1984—, Maricopa County Community Colls., 1984—, Western Internat. U., Phoenix, 1984—, Ottawa U., 1987—; prof. law Univ. Phoenix, 1985—, area chmn. legal studies, 1986-90, Keller Grad. Sch. Mgmt., 1990—. Mem. Maricopa County Foster Child Care Rev. Bd. No. 17, 1978-81; pres. Camelback Mountainview Estates Homeowners Assn., 1980-81, Congregation Tiphereth Israel, 1979-81; dir., sec. Fifth Ave Area Property Owners Assn., 1988-92. Co-author: Buying and Selling Closely Held Businesses in Arizona, 1986, 89, Commercial Real Estate Transactions, 1986. Fellow Ariz. Bar Found.; mem. ABA (taxation sect., various coms.), State Bar Ariz. (cert. specialist in tax law), Maricopa County Bar Assn., Cen. Ariz. Estate Planning Coun., Nucleus Club, Mensa, Shriner, Masons. Democrat. Jewish. Corporate taxation, Estate taxation, Personal income taxation. Office: 6925 E 5th Ave Ste O Scottsdale AZ 85251-3804

**SIMPSON, CAROL ANNE,** lawyer; b. Greenville, S.C., Dec. 27, 1957; d. Harold N. Simpson and Serepta A. (Partee) Wilson. BSBA, U. N.C., 1979; JD, George Mason U., 1994. Legal asst. IRS, Washington, 1993; atty. Stern, Graham & Klepfer, Greensboro, N.C., 1994-97. Mem. Guilford County Rep. Exec. Com., 1995—; bd. dirs. N.C. Right to Life, Greensboro, 1994—, Peak Performances, Inc., Greensboro, 1995-98. Mem. N.C. Assn. CPAs, N.C. Bar Assn., Greensboro Bar Assn., Guilford Inn of Ct. Avocations: reading, movies. Home: 6704 Buxton Ct Greensboro NC 27406-8814

**SIMPSON, CHARLES R., III,** judge; b. Cleve., July 8, 1945; s. Charles Ralph and Anne Marie (Rachel) S.; married; 3 children. BA, U. Louisville, 1967, JD, 1970. Bar: Ky. 1970, U.S. Dist. Ct. (we. dist.) Ky. 1971, U.S. Cir. Ct. (6th cir.) 1985. With Rubin, Trautwein & Mays, Louisville, 1971-75, Levin, Yussman & Simpson, Louisville, 1975-77; judge U.S. Dist. Ct. (we. dist.) Ky., Louisville, 1986—, now chief judge; pvt. practice Louisville, 1977-86; part-time staff counsel Jefferson County Judge/Exec., 1978-84; adminstr. Jefferson County Alcoholic Beverage Control, 1983-84; city clk. City of Rolling Fields, 1985-86. Roman Catholic. Office: We Dist Ct Ky 247 US Courthouse 601 W Broadway Louisville KY 40202-2238

**SIMPSON, CRAIG EVAN,** lawyer; b. Boston, Feb. 18, 1952; s. Kenneth Charles and Louise Caroline (Houston) S.; m. Nadine Anne Conti, May 2, 1981; children: Conor Logan, Hayley Louise. BA, Washington and Jefferson Coll., 1974; JD, Duquesne U., 1977. Bar: Pa. 1977, U.S. Dist. Cot. (we. dist.) Pa. 1977. Investigator disciplinary bd. Pa. Supreme Ct., Pitts., 1979-80; asst. dist. atty. trial div. Dist. Atty.'s Office Allegheny County, Pitts., 1980-81; asst. disciplinary counsel disciplinary bd. Pa. Supreme Ct., Pitts., 1981-86; ptnr. Lindner & Simpson, Pitts., 1986—; instr. paralegal dept. C.C. Allegheny County, Pitts., 1986; frequent lectr. on atty. and jud. ethics and disciplinary law. Mem. Monroeville Ethics Commn., 1990-92; head coach Monroeville Marlins Swim Team, 1980-87; treas. Citizens for a Cmty. Civic Ctr., Monroeville, 1982. Mem. Pa. Bar Assn., Allegheny County Bar Assn. (coun. sole and small firm practitioners sect. 1993-96), Nat. Orgn. Bar Counsel (assoc.), Assn. Profl. Responsibility Lawyers, Pa. Trial Lawyers Assn., Pa. Atty. Discipline Study Commn., Eastern Swim Assn. (pres. 1996—). Roman Catholic. Avocations: reading, youth sports, coaching baseball, soccer and swimming. Home: 217 Rush Valley Rd Monroeville PA 15146-4308 Office: Lindner & Simpson 429 4th Ave Ste 1802 Pittsburgh PA 15219-1505

**SIMPSON, CURTIS CHAPMAN, III,** lawyer; b. Leonia, N.J., Apr. 19, 1952; s. Curtis Chapman Simpson Jr. and Marguerite (Johnson) Host; m. Joy D.; children: Ashley Blake, Curtis Chapman. BA, George Washington U., 1977; JD, Calif. Western U., 1980. Bar: Calif. 1981, U.S. Dist. Ct. (cen. dist.) Calif. 1983, U.S. Ct. Claims 1991. Pres. Curtis C. Simpson, III, P.C., Santa Barbara, Calif., 1981-84; assoc. Schurmer & Drane, Santa Barbara, 1984-90; prin. Curtis Simpson Law Offices, Santa Barbara, Oxnard, Calif., 1991—; ct.-appointed arbitrator superior cts. Santa Barbara County, Ventura County, San Luis Obispo County, all Calif., 1991—; guest lectr. U. Calif., Santa Barbara, 1997. Contbr. to profl. jours. Co-chmn. youth group leader, coach Montecito YMCA, 1992, 97—; bd. dirs. Montecito Ednl. Found., 1993—; co-pres. Montecito Ednl. Found., 1994-97. Mem. Assn. Trial Lawyers Am., Consumer Attys. Calif. (cert. recognition 1991—), State Bar Calif., Santa Barbara County Bar Assn., Ventura County Bar Assn., Hon. Order Ky. Cols., Coral Casino Beach and Cabana Club. Episcopalian. Personal injury, Product liability. Office: Curtis Simpson Law Offices 120 E De La Guerra St Santa Barbara CA 93101-2226

**SIMPSON, DANIEL REID,** lawyer, mediator; b. Glen Alpine, N.C., Feb. 20, 1927; s. James R. and Margaret Ethel (Newton) S.; m. Mary Alice Leonard, Feb. 25, 1930; children: Mary Simpson Beyer, Ethel B. Simpson Todd, James R., II. BS, Wake Forest U., 1949, LLB, 1951. Bar: N.C. 1951, U.S. Dist. Ct. (we. dist.) N.C. 1951, U.S. Ct. Appeals (4th and 5th cirs.) 1980; cert. mediator. Dir. First Union Nat. Bank, Morganton, N.C. Mem. N.C. Ho. of Reps., 1959-65; mem. N.C. Senate, 1984-96; del. Rep. Nat. Conv., 1968, 76; mem. N.C. Rep. Exec. Com. Served with AUS, 1943-45, PTO. Recipient Guardian Small Bus. award Order of Longleaf Pine; named to NRA Legion of Honor. Mem. N.C. Bar Assn., Burke County Bar Assn., Masons. Baptist. General corporate, Franchising. Home: 2358 E Point Rd Nebo NC 28761-9694 Office: Simpson Aycock PA 204 E Mcdowell St Morganton NC 28655-3545 also: PO Box 1329 Morganton NC 28680-1329

**SIMPSON, JACQUELINE ANGELIA,** legal administrator; b. Battersea, Eng., Apr. 19, 1965; came to U.S., 1968; d. Headley Emmanuel and Paula Hermeone Simpson. BA, SUNY, Stony Brook, 1986; MLS, Rockefeller Coll., SUNY, Albany, 1988; Cert. in French/Can. Studies, U. Laval, Que., Can., 1986. In fgn. affairs area, libr. svcs. divsn., Congl. Rsch. Svc. Libr. of Congress, Washington, 1988-98; asst. libr. Squire, Sanders and Dempsey, Washington, 1988-90, assoc. libr., 1990-95; East Coast libr. Squire, Sanders and Dempsey, LLP, Washington, 1995-99, East Coast practice support mgr., 1999—. Named to Outstanding Young Women of Am.; Louise Giles Minority scholar; ALA grad. asst. Mem. Am. Assn. Law Librs., Law Librs. Soc. Washington. Avocations: church, reading, singing, dining at different restaurants. Office: Squire Sanders & Dempsey LLP 1201 Pennsylvania Ave NW Washington DC 20004-2401

**SIMPSON, JENNIFER LYNN,** lawyer; b. Seattle, Oct. 5, 1968; d. Robert R. and Beverly J. S.; m. Scott Alan Robertson, Mar. 16, 1996; 1 child, Katherine Amelia Jean Robertson. BA, U. Puget Sound, 1990; JD, Willamette U., 1993, cert. in dispute resolution, 1993. Bar: Wash. 1993, U.S. Dist. Ct. (we. dist.) Wash. 1994. Atty. Davies Pearson P.C., Tacoma, Wash., 1993-96, Ogden Murphy Wallace P.C., Seattle, 1996—. Co-author: Washington State Municipal Attorney's Ethics Deskbook, 1997. Vol. Nat. Abortion Rights Action League, Seattle, 1991, Salem, Oreg., 1991-93. Mem. DAR. Avocations: skiing, cooking, hiking, travel, scuba diving. Municipal (including bonds), Land use and zoning (including planning). Office: Ogden Murphy Wallace 1601 5th Ave Ste 2100 Seattle WA 98101-1686

**SIMPSON, JOHN M.,** lawyer; b. Ponca City, Okla., Sept. 26, 1950. AB, Harvard U., 1972; JD, Columbia U., 1978. Bar: D.C. 1979, N.C. 1988. Mem. Fulbright & Jaworski L.L.P., Washington. Office: Fulbright & Jaworski LLP Market Square 801 Pennsylvania Ave NW Washington DC 20004-2615

**SIMPSON, KATHRYN LEASE,** lawyer; b. Pitts., Apr. 21, 1947; d. Anthony Joseph Lease and Helen L. Lizik; m. Barry Michael Simpson, Sept. 6, 1968; children: Bradford Michael, Caroline Michele. Student, U. Md., 1965-66; BS, Pa. State U., 1969; MBA, U. Pitts., 1975, JD, 1978. Bar: Pa. 1978, U.S. Dist. Ct. (we. dist.) Pa. 1978, U.S. Ct. Appeals (3rd cir.) 1980, U.S. Supreme Ct. 1990, U.S. Dist. Ct. (no. dist.) Ohio 1997. Tchr. Gateway Sch Dist., Monroeville, Pa., 1969-75; asst. dist. atty. Allegheny County Dist. Atty.'s Office, Pitts., 1978-85; atty., shareholder Grogan, Graffam, McGinley & Lucchino, P.C., Pitts., 1985-99; shareholder Mette, Evans & Woodside, Harrisburg, Pa., 1999—. Chair Edgewood Borough Planning Commn., 1996-99, mem., 1990-96. Mem. Acad. of Trial Lawyers of Allegheny County, Pa. Bar Assn. (profl. liability com. 1988—, chair 1997—). Professional liability, General civil litigation. Office: Mette Evans & Woodside 3401 N Front St PO Box 5950 Harrisburg PA 17110-0950

**SIMPSON, LYLE LEE,** lawyer; b. Des Moines, Oct. 15, 1937; s. R. Clair and Martha B. (Accola) S.; m. Marcene Eliane Tesdell, Sept. 9, 1978. B.A., Drake U., 1960, J.D., 1963. Bar: Iowa 1963, U.S. Dist. Ct. (so. and no. dists.) Iowa 1963, U.S. Ct. Appeals, 1963; U.S. Supreme Ct. 1970, U.S. Tax Ct. 1963, U.S. Ct. Mil. Appeals 1972. Sole practice law, Des Moines, 1963; mem. firm Beving and Swanson, Des Moines, 1964-68; sr. ptnr. Peddicord, Simpson & Sutphin, Des Moines, 1968-83; pres. Dreher, Simpson & Jensen, P.C., 1984—; gen. counsel campaign com. Gov. Iowa, 1978-98. Chmn. bd. trustees Broadlawns Med. Ctr., 1974-80; mem. Iowa Inaugural Com., 1983, 87, 89, 91, 95; bd. dirs. YMCA Boys Camp, 1967-86; pres. First Unitarian Ch., 1958-70; bd. dirs. Home, Inc., 1981-85, Project H.E.L.P.E.R., 1983-87, Batten Found.; pres., bd dirs. Polk County Health Services, 1972-88; chmn. Iowa Health Facilities Coun., 1988-93; pres. Iowa Humanities Bd., 1988-94; treas. Iowa Health Found.; pres. Humanist Endowment Fund, 1980—; treas. Iowa Humanities Found., 1994—; pres. East High Alumni Found., 1992—. Served to capt. U.S. Army N.G., 1955-68, comdr., USNR, 1968-86. Recipient Oren E. Scott award, Class of 1915 award in liberal arts Drake U., 1960. Mem. ABA, Polk County Bar Assn., Iowa Bar Assn., Am. Arbitration Assn., Am. Humanist Assn. (pres. 1979-89), Prairie Club (pres. 1992), Morning Club (pres. 1965), Le Chevaliers de vin Club (pres. 1976-85), YMCA Heritage Club (pres.), Masons, Scottish Rite (Shriner, 33 degree), Rotary. Republican. Congregationalist. Contbr. articles to profl. jours. General corporate, Estate planning, Real property. Address: 1500 Hub Tower Des Moines IA 50309-3940

**SIMPSON, MARY KATHLEEN,** lawyer; b. Pomona, Calif., Aug. 2, 1952; d. Ernest Peter and Opal Petunia (Frederiksen) Hanks; m. Sidney Lawrence Simpson, Nov. 17, 1976 (div. Aug. 1980). BS in Chemistry, La Verne Coll., 1974; JD, U. Calif. Berkeley, 1980. Bar: Calif. 1980, D.C. 1982, U.S. Dist. Ct. (no. dist.) Calif. 1985, U.S. Ct. Appeals (6th cir.) 1986; cert. family law specialist Calif. State Bar Assn., 1993. Law clk. U.S. Ct. Appeals 6th Cir., Memphis, 1980-81; assoc. Howrey & Simon, Washington, 1981-82; counsel Enforcement divsn. SEC, Washington, 1982-84; assoc. Hogan & Hartson, Washington, 1984-85, McCutcheon, Doyle et al, San Jose, Calif., 1985; pvt. practice San Jose, 1986—. 2d v.p. Santa Clara Valley Audubon Soc., Cupertino, Calif., 1994—; chair conservation com.-south, chair rare plants-south Santa Clara chpt. Calif. Native Plant Soc., 1996-98, v.p. Calif. Native Plants Soc., 1999—. Recipient Am. Jurisprudence award for torts and civil procedure Bancroft-Whitney, 1978. Avocations: amateur naturalist, birding. Appellate, Family and matrimonial. Home: 640 Millich Dr # B San Jose CA 95117-3631 Office: 1550 The Alameda Ste 305 San Jose CA 95126-2304

**SIMPSON, MICHAEL WAYNE,** lawyer, educator; b. Oklahoma City, Mar. 9, 1959; s. Darrell Wayne and Mary Ellen (Cooley) S.; m. Taunya Lee Johnstun; children: Jeremy, Charity. BA, U. Okla., 1982; JD, Oklahoma City U., 1985. Bar: Kans. 1986, Mo. 1987, Okla. 1993. Assoc. Ed Schneeberger Chartered, Leavenworth, Kans., 1986-88, O'Keefe and Knopp, Leawood, Kans., 1988, Norton, White and Norton, Leavenworth, Kans., 1988-89, Pistotnik Law Offices, Merriam, Kans., 1989-91; ptnr. Bangs, Hursh and Simpson, Overland Park, Kans., 1991-92; pvt. practice, Moore, Okla., 1993—; mediator, Moore, 1992—. Contbr. articles to law revs. Mem. Kans. Bar Assn. (legis. com. 1987-93), Kans. Trial Lawyers Assn. (bd. govs. 1989-93, chmn. workers compensation legis. com. 1989-90, ann. conv. 1990—). Lodge: Kiwanis. Avocations: walking, investment education, softball, golf. Personal injury, Workers' compensation. Home and Office: 1317 N Lincoln Ave Oklahoma City OK 73160-6515

**SIMPSON, RUSSELL AVINGTON,** retired law firm administrator; b. Greybull, Wyo., June 19, 1935; s. William Avington and Margaret E. (Draper) S.; m. Margarita A. del Valle, Dec. 19, 1960; children—Margaret E., Robert A., Alexandra P., Christina M. B.S. with honors, U. Wyo., 1957; LL.B., Harvard U., 1965. Bar: Tex. 1965, Mass. 1966. Assoc. firm Bonilla, de Pena, Read & Bonilla, Corpus Christi, Tex., 1965-66; asst. dean, dir. admissions Harvard Law Sch., Cambridge, Mass., 1966-75, asst. dean, dir. fin. aid, 1972-78, asst. dean for fin. and gen. adminstrn., 1978-84; dir. adminstrn. firm Hill & Barlow, Boston, 1984-90, v.p., treas. The Architects Collaborative, Cambridge, 1991-92; chmn. devel. com. Law Sch. Data Assembly Service, 1969; pres. bd. dirs. Law Sch. Admissions Services, Newtown, Pa., 1979-80, bd. dirs., 1989-91. Mem. town meeting Town of Belmont (Mass.), 1975-96; mem. Belmont Sch. Com., 1977-83. Served to capt. USAF, 1957-62. Mem. Tex. Bar Assn., Law Sch. Admission Council (trustee 1968-70, 72-78, 81-82, chmn. services com. 1972-74, chmn. test devel. and research com. 1976-78), Grad. and Profl. Sch. Fin. Aid Council (founding), Phi Kappa Phi. Democrat. Club: Belmont Rotary (bd. dirs. 1978-80). Home: 49 Elizabeth Rd Belmont MA 02478-3819

**SIMPSON, RUSSELL GORDON,** lawyer, mayor, counselor to not-for-profit organizations; b. Springfield, Mass., May 22, 1927; s. Archer Roberts and Maude Ethel (Gordon) S.; m. Bickley S. Flower, Sept. 11, 1954; children: Barbara G., Elisabeth Pires-Fernandes, Helen Blair. BA, Yale U., 1951; JD, Boston U., 1956; postgrad., Parker Sch. Internat. Law, 1962. Bar: Mass. 1956, U.S. Dist. Ct. (fed. dist.) Mass. 1957, U.S. Ct. Appeals (2d cir.) 1958, U.S. Supreme Ct. 1980. Advt. mgr. Burden Bryant Co., Springfield, 1951-53; assoc. Goodwin, Procter & Hoar, Boston, 1956-64, ptnr., 1965-87, of counsel, 1987—; sr. advisor to pres. World Learning, Inc., Brattleboro, Vt., 1988-89, exec. v.p., 1989-90, sr. v.p., 1990-91, trustee, 1991—, exec. com., 1994—; trustee, mem. exec. com., Save the Children Fedn., Westport, Conn., 1995—; mem. exec. group Internat. Save the Children Alliance, Geneva, Switzerland and London, Eng., 1996—; dir., vice chmn., mem. exec. com., Cmty. Found. Palm Beach and Martin Counties, West Palm Beach, Fla., 1994—; counselor to not-for-profit orgns., 1991—. Author: The Lawyer's Basic Corporate Practice Manual, 1971, rev. edit., 1978, 84, 87. Mayor Jupiter Island, Fla., 1993—; hon. consul New Eng. of Bolivia, 1958-82, mem. spl. com. to revise Mass. Corrupt Practices Act, 1961-62. Named Outstanding Young Man of Greater Boston, 1963. Fellow Am. Bar Found., Mass. Bar Found.; mem. Mass. Bar Assn. (chmn. banking and bus. law sect. 1980-83, bd. dels., exec. com. 1983-87, v.p. 1985-87), ABA (corp. banking and bus. law sect., com. on law firms, co-chmn. com. on law firm governance, panel on corp. law edni. programs). Mergers and acquisitions, General corporate, Private international. Home: 101 Harbor Way PO Box 1106 Hobe Sound FL 33475-1106

**SIMPSON, SHANNON SMITH,** lawyer; b. Huntsville, Ala., Oct. 7, 1969; d. L. Cleveland Smith and Terry Donley; Derek Woodly Simpson, Sept. 6, 1997. BA cum laude, Birmingham-So. Coll., 1991; JD cum laude, U. Ala., 1995. Bar: Ala. 1995, U.S. Dist. Ct. (no. dist.) Ala. 1996, U.S. Ct. Appeals (11th cir.) 1997. Assoc. Wolfe, Jones & Boswell, Huntsville, Ala., 1995-97, Wilmer, Cates, Fohrell & Kelley, Huntsville, Ala., 1997—. Mem. Madison County Bar Assn., Young Lawyers Bar Assn. (sec. 1996-97), Am. Inns of Ct. (Huntsville-Madison County chpt.). Labor, Workers' compensation, Civil rights. Office: Wilmer Cates Fohrell & Kelley PA 100 Washington St NE Ste 302 Huntsville AL 35801-4851

**SIMPSON, STEVEN DREXELL,** lawyer; b. Sturgis, Mich., Sept. 20, 1953; s. Rex and Lorraine Simpson; m. Peggy Deibert, Apr. 28, 1979; children: Andrew Drexell, Christine Elizabeth, Marianne Tyner. BA, Hillsdale (Mich.) Coll., 1975; JD, Wake Forest U., 1978; LLM in Taxation, Georgetown U., 1981. Bar: Fla. 1978, D.C. 1980, N.C. 1984. Assoc. Bradford, Williams et al, Miami, Fla., 1978-80, Webster & Chamberlain, Washington, 1980-82, Fisher, Wayland et al, Washington, 1982-84, Maupin, Taylor & Ellis, P.A., Raleigh, N.C., 1984-98; ptnr. Law Offices of Steven D. Simpson P.A., 1998—. Author: Taxation of Broadcasters, 1984, Tax-Exempt Organizations: Organization, Operation and Reporting Requirements, 1999, Taxable Expenditures, 1999; contbr. articles to profl. jours. Mem. ABA (exemp orgns. com.). Republican. Methodist. Avocations: golf, running. Health, Non-profit and tax-exempt organizations, Corporate taxation. Home: 409 Hillandale Dr Raleigh NC 27609-7036 Office: Landmark Center II 4601 Six Forks Rd Ste 530 Raleigh NC 27609-5210

**SIMS, AUGUST CHARLES,** lawyer, policeman; b. Columbus, Ohio, Aug. 18, 1948; s. Carl Russell Sims and Catherine A. (Colson) Phillips; m. Kathleen Mary McGuire, Apr. 3, 1971; children: Patricia Deanne, Michael Russell. AS, Columbus Community Coll., 1977; BA, Park Coll., 1979; JD, Capital U., 1984. Bar: Ohio 1984, U.S. Dist. Ct. (so. dist.) Ohio 1987. Sgt. divsn. police City of Columbus, 1970—; pvt. practice Columbus, 1984—; instr. criminal justice Ohio Peace Officer Tng. Coun., London, Ohio, 1976—, Cen. Ohio Police Officer Tng. Acad., Reynoldsburg, 1987—. Committeeman Licking County Rep. Party, Harrison, Ohio, 1985; mem. Fraternal Order Police Lodge 9, Columbus, 1970—. Recipient recognition for contbn. to police tng. Ohio Ho. of Reps., Ohio Senate. Mem. ABA, Ohio State Bar Assn., Columbus Bar Assn., Masons. Lutheran. Avocations: golf, fishing, scuba diving, hunting. Probate, Education and schools. Home: 7010 Gale Rd SW Pataskala OH 43062-9529 Office: Columbus Ohio Divsn Police 120 Marconi Blvd Columbus OH 43215-2376

**SIMS, HUNTER W., JR.,** lawyer; b. Richmond, Va., Oct. 21, 1944. BS, U. Va., 1967; JD, U. Richmond, 1971. Bar: Va. 1971. Law clk. to Hon. Walter E. Hoffman U.S. Dist. Ct. (ea. dist.), Va., 1971-72; asst. U.S. atty. State of Va. (ea. dist.), 1972-75; ptnr. Kaufman & Canoles P.C., Norfolk, Va. Fellow Am. Coll. of Trial Lawyers; mem. ABA, Va. State Bar Com. on Lawyer Discipline (adv. com. on rules of ct. jud. coun. Va. 1998—), Va. Bar Assn. (bd. govs. construction law sect. 1982-85, bd. govs. antitrust sect. 1989-92, bd. dirs. 1990-92), Va. State Bar, Fed. Bar Assn., Va. Beach Bar Assn., Am. Inns of Ct., Norfolk/Portsmouth Bar Assn. (sec. 1981-86), Omicron Delta Kappa, Phi Delta Phi, McNeill Law Soc. Federal civil litigation, Criminal, Libel. Office: Kaufman & Canoles PC PO Box 3037 1 Commercial Place Norfolk VA 23514-3037

**SIMS, KAREN ANN,** public defender; b. St. Louis, May 21, 1957. BA in Comms. and Pub. Rels., William Jewell Coll., 1990; JD, Washburn U., 1994. Asst. pub. defender State Pub. Defender's Office, Liberty, Mo., 1995—. Mem. ABA, Kans. Bar, Mo. Bar Assn., Clay County Bar Assn. Avocations: photography, travel. Office: Clay County Pub Defender 234 W Shrader St Liberty MO 64068-2448

**SIMS, REBECCA LITTLETON,** lawyer; b. Macon, Ga., May 24, 1957; d. William Harvey and Carlan Patricia (Hammond) Littleton; m. Charles Neil Sims, Jr., Dec. 29, 1984; children: Charles Neil III, William Vickers, Caroline Greer. Student, Tex. A & M U., 1977, Baylor U., 1978, U. South, 1979; JD, Baylor U., 1981; BA in Polit. Sci. honors, U. South, 1979. Bar: Ga. 1983, U.S. Dist. Ct. (so. dist.) Ga. 1984, U.S. Dist. Ct. (no. dist.) Ga. 1985, U.S. Dist. Ct. (mid. dist.) Ga. 1992. Law clk. Waco, Tex., 1981, Waycross Jud. Cir., Waycross and Douglas, Ga., 1982-83; asst. dist. atty. Waycross cir. Dist. Atty.'s Office, Douglas, 1983-84; spl. asst. to atty. gen. Dept. Family and Children's Svcs., Coffee County, 1988-90; pvt. practice Douglas, 1985-92; state ct. solicitor Coffee County, Ga., 1989-96; in-house counsel Sims Funeral Home, 1997—. Mem. altar guild St. Andrew's Episcopal Ch., Douglas, 1983-90, vestryman, clk. of vestry, 1986-88; bd. dirs. Shelter for Abused Women, Waycross, 1986-87; trustee Diocese of Ga., U. South, Savannah, 1988-91; mem. First Meth. Ch., Douglas, Ga., 1991—, United Meth. Women Cir. # 8, 1991—; dir. Vacation Bible Sch., 1997, 98; legis. aid Charles Neil Sims, Jr., Ga. Ho. Reps., 1997—. Mem. State Bar Ga., Acad. Boosters Club (awards chmn.), Green Thumb Garden Club, Master Gardeners Assn., Beta Sigma Phi (pres. 1997-98). Avocations: gardening, reading, needlework, cooking, antiques. Criminal, Family and matrimonial, Probate. Office: PO Box 2352 Douglas GA 31534-2352

**SIMS, ROGER W.,** lawyer; b. Cleve., Aug. 3, 1950. BA with high honors, U. Fla., 1972, JD, 1974. Bar: Fla. 1975. Mem. Holland & Knight, Orlando, Fla. Mem. Moot Ct. U. Fla.; contbr. to profl mags and jours. Mem. ABA, Fla. Bar Assn. (chmn. environ., land use law sect. 1988-89), Phi Beta Kappa, Phi Kappa Phi, Omicron Delta Kappa, Phi Alpha Delta, Fla. Blue Key. Administrative and regulatory, Environmental. Office: Holland & Knight PO Box 1526 200 S Orange Ave Ste 2600 Orlando FL 32801-3449

**SIMS, VICTOR DWAYNE,** lawyer; b. Middletown, Ohio, Aug. 1, 1959; s. Gerald Clifton and Ethel Ree (Bruce) S. Student, Am. U., 1980; BA, Heidelberg Coll., 1981; JD, Howard U., 1987. Bar: Ohio, 1989; U.S. Dist. Ct. (so. dist.) Ohio, 1990. Congl. intern U.S. Congress, Washington, 1980; fundraiser Telecommunications Rsch. and Action Ctr., Washington, 1984; assoc. Leslie I. Gaines & Assoc., Cin., 1989-91; pvt. practice Sims and Assocs., Cin., 1991—; mng. atty. Leslie I. Gaines & Assoc., 1990—; ptnr. Sims and Asmah Law Firm. Author poetry. Mem. ABA, Ohio Bar Assn., Cin. Bar Assn. Avocations: writing, music, current events. General practice, Criminal, Family and matrimonial. Office: 655 Eden Park Dr Ste 100 Cincinnati OH 45202-6009

**SINCERBEAUX, ROBERT ABBOTT,** lawyer, preservationist, foundation executive; b. N.Y.C., July 22, 1913; s. Frank Huestis and Jessie Marian (Batterson) S.; m. Elizabeth Morley, Apr. 19, 1940; children—Richard M., Suzanne Sincerbeaux Brian, Charles M. B.A. cum laude, Princeton U., 1936; LL.B., Yale U., 1939. Bar: N.Y. 1940. Assoc. White & Case, N.Y.C., 1939-42, Simpson, Thacher & Bartlett, N.Y.C., 1942-43; assoc. Sincerbeaux & Shrewsbury, N.Y.C., 1946-52, ptnr., 1952-72, of counsel, 1972—. Pres., Eva Gebhard-Gourgaud Found., N.Y.C., 1959—, trustee, 1947—; mng. trustee Cecil Howard Charitable Trust, N.Y.C., 1968-93; hon. trustee Woodstock Hist. Soc., Vt., 1992—; trustee Woodstock Found., 1976-91, Preservation Trust Vt., 1980—; chmn. design rev. bd. Village of Woodstock, 1983-91, Upper Valley Cmty. Found., 1994—, Fund for Vt.'s Third Century, 1988-91. Served to lt. comdr. USNR, 1943-65. Recipient Preservation award Preservation Trust Vt., 1983, Honor award Nat. Trust for Historic Preservation, 1984, Thomas award Vt. Land Trust, 1991, 97. Fellow Met. Mus. Art (life); mem. Soc. Col. Wars. Episcopalian. Clubs: Woodstock Country, Hanover Country, Lakota, Round Table; Nassau (Princeton), Belleair Country (Fla), Hanover Country. Probate, Estate taxation. Home: 80 Lyme Rd Apt 1010 Hanover NH 03755-1236 Office: One The Green Woodstock VT 05091

**SINCLAIR, I.B.,** lawyer; b. Pitts., June 19, 1933; s. I.B. and Emily A. Sinclair; 1 child, Meredith Armstrong Sinclair. BA, Pa. State U., 1955; LLB, Dickinson U., 1958. Bar: Pa. 1959, U.S. Dist. Ct. (ea. dist.) Pa., U.S. Ct. Appeals (3d cir.), U.S. Supreme Ct. 1965. Pvt. practice matrimonial law Delaware County, State College, Pa., 1959-97. Mem. editl. staff Ad Absurdum, 1994-96; contbr. articles to profl. jours. Bd. dirs. Defenders of Wildlife, 1977-86, vice chair, 1984-86, mem. exec. com., 1979-82, 84-86; chmn. Wildlife Info. Ctr., Inc., 1986-89, mem. adv. bd., 1989-91; pres. Pa. Resources Coun., 1980-82, v.p., 1979-80, mem. exec. com., 1986-90, dir. emeritus, 1997—; mem. exec. com. Coalition for Scenic Beauty, 1986-88; bd. dirs. Concerned Area Residents for Preservation of Tinicum Marsh, 1978-80; treas. Com. for Dove Protection, 1975—; mem. exec. com. Pa. Coun. to Abolish the Penalty of Death, 1960-85; legal counsel Keystone Trails Assn., 1984-90, pres., 1990-94. Capt. USAR, 1959-67. Fellow Am. Acad. Matrimonial Lawyers (bd. examiners Pa. chpt. 1984-98, parliamentarian 1990-92, treas. 1992-93, sec. 1993-94, pres. 1997-98); mem. ACLU, Wilderness Soc., Pub. Citizen Inc., Western Pa. Conservancy, Friends of the Earth, League of Conservation Voters, Save the Redwoods League, No. Environ. Coun., Greenpeace Found., Pa. Bar Assn. (bd. govs. 1966-67, chmn. unauthorized practice com. 1972-75), Delaware County Bar Assn. (judge pro tem 1996-97), Eastern Packard Club, Studebaker Club, Classic Car Club Am., Pa. Prison Soc., Pa. State Alumni Assn. (life), Omicron Delta Kappa. Republican. Methodist. Avocations: history, hiking, cross country skiing, canoeing, conservation. Family and matrimonial. Home: 1471 N Allen St State College PA 16803-3012 Office: 7 College Ct 1535 N Atherton St State College PA 16803-3043

**SINCLAIR, JULIE MOORES WILLIAMS,** law librarian, consultant; b. Montgomery, Ala., May 2, 1954; d. Benjamin Buford and Marilyn Moores (Simpson) Williams; m. Winfield James Sinclair, Dec. 16, 1978. BA, U. of South, 1976; MLS, U. Ala., Tuscaloosa, 1977; JD, Washington U., St. Louis, 1987. Bar: Ala. 1989, U.S. Dist. Ct. (no. dist.) Ala. 1989. Serials libr. Ala. Dept. Archives and History, Montgomery, 1977; cataloguing libr. Ala. Pub. Libr. Svc., Montgomery, 1978; league libr. Ala. League Municipalities, Montgomery, 1978-84; asst. libr. Mo. Ct. Appeals, St. Louis, 1984-86, law clk., 1987-88; cons. Law Libr. Cons., Birmingham, Ala., 1988—. Contbr. numerous articles to profl. jours. Mem. Ala. Bar Assn., Ala. Libr. Assn., Am. Assn. Law Librs., Law Libr. Assn. Ala. (charter, v.p. 1992-93, pres. 1993-94), Ala. Fedn. Bus. and Profl. Women (pres. 1997-98), Order of Gownsmen, Phi Alpha Theta. Episcopalian. Avocations: travel and sightseeing, reading, attending theatre, especially Shakespeare. Office: Law Libr Cons 3045 Independence Dr Ste D Birmingham AL 35209-4170

**SINDERBRAND, DAVID I.,** lawyer; b. Atlantic City, June 14, 1961; s. Saul Albert and Joyce Rita Sinderbrand; m. Jennifer M. Sinderbrand, June 24, 1995. BA, Ithaca Coll., 1983; JD, Calif. Western Sch. Law, San Diego, 1987. Bar: N.J. 1988, U.S. Dist. Ct. N.J. 1988. Lawyer Horn, Goldberg et al, Atlantic City, 1988-90, Manchel, Lundy & Lessin, Phila., 1990-92, Westmoreland, Vesper et al, Atlantic City, 1992—. Mem. Atlantic County Bar Assn. Personal injury, Product liability, General civil litigation. Office: Westmoreland Vesper et al Bayport One Ste 500 West Atlantic City NJ 08232

**SINE, WESLEY FRANKLIN,** lawyer; b. Salt Lake City, Dec. 13, 1936; s. Ira F. and Dora Ann (Popp) S.; m. Barbara A. Belnap, June 6, 1958 (div. 1978); children: Barri Ann, Jeri Charlene, Wesley D., Anthony L.; m. Melva Carol Holmes, Dec. 30, 1978; children: Tammy Louise, Dorethea Ann, Christina Jean, Jared F., Katrina C., Joshua F., Kathryn M. JD, U. Utah, 1962. Bar: Utah 1962, U.S. Dist. Ct. Utah 1962, U.S. Ct. Appeals (10th cir.) 1962. Pvt. practice Salt Lake City; bd. dirs. Utah Hotel Motel Assn., Salt Lake City, 1963-79, pres. 1976; pres. Salt Lake Valley Inn, Salt Lake City, 1978, Utah Apt. Assn., 1977, Utah State Bowling Proprs., 1965, 83. Mem. Rep. Lincoln Day Club, Salt Lake City, 1985—. Mem. Kiwanis (pres. Salt Lake City chpt. 1985-86, dist adminstr. collegiate orgn. Utah Idaho dist. 1988—, lt. gov. div. 2 Utah 1989-90). Mormon. General corporate, Family and matrimonial, Personal injury. Home: 451 Northmont Way Salt Lake City UT 84103-3322

**SINGER, BERNARD ALAN,** lawyer; b. Miami, Fla., Jan. 29, 1946; s. Arthur and Diane D. Singer; divorced; chldren: Steven, Barbara Ann; m. Karen Joyce Singer, June 3, 1995. BSBA, Northeastern U., 1968; JD, U. Miami, 1977. Bar: Fla., U.S. Tax Ct. Assoc. Abrams Anton, Hollywood, Fla., 1982-88; pres. Bernard A. Singer, P.A., Hollywood, 1988—. Served with U.S. Army Rex., 1968-74. Mem. North Dade-South Broward Estate Planning Coun., Greater Ft. Lauderdale Tax Coun. Avocation: boating. Taxation, general, Estate planning, General corporate. Office: 4925A Sheridan St Hollywood FL 33021-2829

**SINGER, GERALD MICHAEL,** lawyer, educator, author, arbitrator and mediator; b. Mpls., Sept. 9, 1920; s. Charles and Rachael Caroline (Feldman) S.; m. Lillian Kaplan, July 10, 1944; children: Barbara Ellen, Alan Mark. JD, Loyola U., L.A., 1968. Bar: Calif. 1969, U.S. Dist. Ct. Calif. (so dist.) 1969, U.S. Ct. Appeals (9th cir.) 1969, U.S. Supreme Ct. 1972. Pres. Bigg of Calif., Inc., 1948-69; pvt. practice, Encino, Calif., 1969—; adj. prof. law Loyola U., 1975-85, 92; judge pro tem Calif. Superior Ct., 1973—, arbitrator, 1976—; judge pro tem Calif. Mcpl. Ct., 1973—; arbitrator, mediator, 1988—; sr. panel mem. AAA Comml. Arbitrators, L.A., Internat. Arbitration World Ct., The Hague; lectr. to various law schs., bar assns. and legal groups, 1976—; freelance writer newspapers. Author: How To Go Directly Into Solo Law Practice (Without Missing a Meal), 1976, rev. edit. as How To Go Directly Into Your Own Computerized Solo Law Practice Without Missing a Meal (Or a Byte), 1986, updated, 1989, rev. edit. as How To Go Directly Into, and Manage, Your Own Solo Law Practice (Without Missing a Meal), 1993, 168-page supplement, 1996-97. Mem. Com. To Elect Ricard Nixon, Com. to Reelect Richard Nixon, Com. to Elect and Reelect Ronald Reagan, L.A. Staff sgt. Signal Corps, U.S. Army and USAAF, 1942-46. Mem. Am. Arbitration Assn. (arbitrator 1973—). Republican. Avocations: golf, sailing, horseback riding, photography, videography. Entertainment, Federal civil litigation. Office: NPO 271 Box 555 38-180 Del Webb Blvd Palm Desert CA 92211

**SINGER, JEFFREY,** lawyer; b. Bklyn., Apr. 5, 1955; s. Stanley and May Singer; m. Carol Joan Gilbert, Nov. 23, 1991; 1 child, Tori Hannah; stepchildren: Matthew Hollander, Michael Hollander. BA, SUNY at Stony Brook, 1976; JD, Bklyn. Law Sch., 1979. Bar: N.Y. 1980, U.S. Dist. Ct. (so. dist. and ea. dist.) N.Y. 1980, U.S. Ct. Appeals (2d cir.) 1982, U.S. Supreme Ct. 1984. Law clk. Segan, Culhane, Nemerov & Geen P.C., N.Y.C., 1977-79, assoc., 1980-86, ptnr., 1986—. Mem. Am. Trial Lawyers Assn., N.Y. State Trial Lawyers, Assn. of Bar of City of N.Y. Avocations: scuba diving, golf, wine collecting. Personal injury, Product liability. Office: Segan Nemerov & Singer PC 112 Madison Ave Fl 6 New York NY 10016-7416

**SINGER, JOSEPH K.,** lawyer, mediator; b. N.Y.C., June 20, 1943; s. Benjamin and Edna Singer; m. Maria A. Singer, May 16, 1984; children: Dani, Jeffrey, Gary, Joseph. BS, Dowling Coll., Oakdale, N.Y., 1986; JD, Nova U., Ft. Lawderdale, Fla., 1988; LLM in Tax, U. Miami, 1989. Bar: Fla. 1989, U.S. Tax Ct. 1989, U.S. Dist. Ct. (so. dist.) Fla. 1989, U.S. Bankruptcy Ct. Atty., dist. counsel IRS, Miami, 1989-90; pvt. practice Plantation, Fla., 1990-98; ptnr. Singer & Singer Law Firm, Chartered, Plantation, 1998—. Avocation: computers. Taxation, general, Estate planning, Family and matrimonial. Office: Singer & Singer Law Firm Chartered 201 N University Dr Ste 114 Plantation FL 33324-2094

**SINGER, MICHAEL HOWARD,** lawyer; b. N.Y.C., Nov. 22, 1941; s. Jack and Etta (Appelbaum) S.; m. Saundra Jean Kupperman, June 1, 1962; children: Allison Jill, Pamela Faith. BS in Econs., U. Pa., 1962; JD, NYU, 1965, LLM in Taxation, 1968. Bar: N.Y. 1965, U.S. Ct. Claims 1968, U.S. Supreme Ct. 1969, U.S. Ct. Appeals (6th cir.) 1970, D.C. 1972, U.S. Tax Ct. 1972, Nev. 1973, U.S. Ct. Appeals (9th cir.) 1973. Law asst. Appellate Term Supreme Ct., N.Y.C., 1965-68; trial lawyer Ct. Claims Tax Div., Washington, 1968-72; tax lawyer Beckley, DeLanoy & Jemison, Las Vegas, 1972-74; ptnr. Oshins, Singer, Segal & Morris, Las Vegas, 1974-87; pvt. practice Las Vegas, 1987; ptnr. Michael H. Singer Ltd., Las Vegas, 1987-96, Singer, Brown, and Barringer, LLC, Las Vegas, 1996-99, Singer & Brown, 1999—; settlement judge Nev. Supreme Ct., 1997-99. Pres. Las Vegas chpt. NCCJ, 1980-82. Mem. ABA, ABI, Nev. Bar Assn., Las Vegas Country Club (bd. dirs. 1999—). Democrat. Jewish. Avocations: golf, tennis. Taxation, general, Contracts commercial, General corporate. Home: 4458 Los Reyes Ct Las Vegas NV 89121-5341 Office: Singer Brown and Barringer LLC 520 S 4th St Fl 2 Las Vegas NV 89101-6524 *Personal philosophy: A reasonable settlement is more economically beneficial for the client than protracted litigation of a great lawsuit.*

**SINGER, MYER R(ICHARD),** lawyer; b. Everett, Mass., Oct. 24, 1938; s. Nathan and Celia (Rudin) S.; m. Elaine Doris Ginesky, June 17, 1962; children: Andrew L., Stephen D., Jocelyn G. BSBA, Boston U., 1960, LLB, 1963. Bar: Mass. 1963, U.S. Ct. Appeals (1st cir.) 1963. Atty. Boston Legal Aid Soc., 1963-64; pvt. practice Dennis Port, Mass., 1965—; trustee, corporator, mem. bd. investment Cape Cod Five Cents Savs. Bank, Harwich Port, Mass.; faculty Mass. Continuing Legal Edn., Inc., 1985, 90-98;

program chmn. Real Estate Devel. Cape Cod Mass. Bar Inst., 1999. Co-author: Creation and Care of Condominiums, 1985, Everything You Need to Know About the Cape Cod Commission Act, 1990; speaker in field. Mem., clk. Yarmouth (Mass.) Zoning Bd. Appeals, 1980-86; pres. Dennis Yarmouth Band Parents, 1986-87; mem. adv. bd. Cape Mus. Fine Arts, Dennis, 1988-96; former pres. Legal Svcs. of Cape Cod and Island, Inc.; former trustee Cape Cod Synagogue; former bd. dir. Cape Cod and Island Chpt. of Mass. Heart Assn. Mem. ABA, Mass. Bar Assn. (chmn. bar assn. program real estate devel. Cape Cod 1999), Barnstable County Bar Assn. (mem. exec. com. 1999—). Avocations: boating, photography. Land use and zoning (including planning), Real property. Home: 238 Greenland Circle East Dennis MA 02641-1302 Office: PO Box 67 26 Upper County Rd Dennis Port MA 02639-1119

**SINGER, RANDY DARRELL,** lawyer; b. Meshoppen, Pa., Apr. 4, 1956; s. Darrell F. and Charlotte Mae (Clapper) S.; m. Rhonda Jo Pursifull, Aug. 5, 1978; children: Rosalyn Kay, Joshua Kane. BA, Houghton Coll., 1978; JD, William & Mary Coll., 1986. Bar: Va. 1986, U.S. Ct. Appeals (4th cir.) 1988, U.S. Dist. Ct. (ea. dist.) Va. 1986. Assoc. Willcox & Savage P.C., Norfolk, Va., 1986-92, ptnr., 1992-97; of counsel Willcox & Savage P.C., Norfolk, 1997—; exec. v.p. N.Am. Mission Bd., Alpharetta, Ga., 1997—; adj. prof. Regent U. Law Sch., Virginia Beach, Va., 1989—; lectr. Va. Law Found., 1992. Trustee Houghton (N.Y.) Acad., 1990—, Atlantic Shores Christian Sch., Virginia Beach, 1991—, Freedom Ministries, Inc., 1997—, Family Net Inc., 1998—. Mem. Va. State Bar, Va. Assn. Def. Attys. (lectr. 1992), Norfolk/Portsmouth Bar Assn., Def. Rsch. Inst. Baptist. Avocations: canoeing, running, camping. General civil litigation, Product liability, Constitutional. Home: 130 English Oak Ct Alpharetta GA 30005-8976 Office: NAm Mission Bd 4200 N Point Pkwy Alpharetta GA 30022-4174

**SINGERMAN, PAUL JOSEPH,** lawyer; b. Cleve., June 4, 1958; s. Gilbert and Gayle Singerman; m. Kimberly Ann Clark, Apr.30, 1980; children: Annie Elise, Shari Leigh, Scott Adam. BA, Case Western Res. U., 1980, JD, 1983. Bar: Ohio 1983. Assoc. Burke, Haber & Berick Co. L.P.A., Cleve., 1983-86; assoc. Berick, Pearlman & Mills Co. L.P.A., Cleve., 1986-89, prin., 1990—; pres., COO, Berick, Pearlman & Mills Co. L.P.A., Cleve., 1998—. Trustee Cleve. Nat. Air Show, 1993—; trustee, v.p. adminstrn. Temple Israel/Ner Tamid, Cleve., 1994—; mem. adv. bd. PDI Ground Support Sys., Cleve., 1996—. Banking, General corporate, Real property. Office: Berick Pearlman & Mills 1350 Eaton Ctr 1111 Superior Ave E Ste 1350 Cleveland OH 44114-2569

**SINGH, HARCHARAN,** law librarian; b. Lahore, Pakistan, Sept. 5, 1937; came to U.S., 1970; s. Surjan Singh and Ajit Kaur; m. Surinder Kaur, May 10, 1938; children: Amardeep K., Harbinder. BA, Punjab U., Chandigarh, India, 1957, LLB, 1959, diploma in libr. sci., 1962, MA in Polit. Sci., 1969; MLS, CUNY, Flushing, 1973. Head libr. dept. law Punjab U., Chandigar, 1964-70; acquisition and serials libr. New Sch. Social Rsch., N.Y.C., 1973-79; asst. head dept. serials SUNY, Stonybrook, 1979-82; acquisition and serials libr. Bklyn. Law Sch., 1989—. Home: 14 Botany Ln Stony Brook NY 11790-2520 Office: Bklyn Law Sch Libr 250 Jora Lemon St New York NY 11790

**SINGLETARY, ALVIN D.,** lawyer; b. New Orleans, Sept. 27, 1942; s. Alvin E. and Alice (Pastoret) S.; m. Judy Louise Singletary, Dec. 3, 1983; children: Kimberly Dawn, Shane David, Kelly Diane. B.A., La. State U., 1964; J.D., Loyola U., New Orleans, 1969. Bar: La. 1969, U.S. Dist. Ct. (ea. dist.) La. 1972, U.S. Ct. Appeals (5th cir.) 1972, U.S. Supreme Ct. 1978, U.S. Ct. Appeals (11th cir.) 1981, U.S. Ct. Internat. Trade 1981, U.S. Ct. Customs and Patent Appeals 1982. Instr. Delgado Coll., New Orleans, 1976-77; sole practice, Slidell, La., 1970—; spl. asst. dist. atty. 22d Judicial Dist. Ct. Parish of St. Tammany, State of La.; sec.-treas. St. Tammany Pub. Trust Fin. Authority, Slidell, 1978—; Councilman-at-large City of Slidell, 1978—, interim mayor, 1985; mem. Democratic State Central Com., 1978-82; mem. Rep. State Ctrl. Com. Dist. 76, La., 1996—; del. La. Constl. Conv., 1972-73; chmn. sustaining membership enrollment Cypress dist. Boy Scouts Am., 1989—; chmn. Together We Build Program First Baptist Ch. of Slidell, La.; treas. Slidell Centennial Commn.; bd. dirs. St. Tammany Coun. on Aging. Mem. Delta Theta Phi. Baptist. Lodge: Lions. General practice, State civil litigation, Probate. Office: PO Box 1158 Slidell LA 70459-1158

**SINGLETON, JAMES KEITH,** federal judge; b. Oakland, Calif., Jan. 27, 1939; s. James K. and Irene Elisabeth (Lilly) S.; m. Sandra Claire Hoskins, Oct. 15, 1966; children: Matthew David, Michael Keith. Student, U. Santa Clara, 1957-58; AB in Polit. Sci., U. Calif., Berkeley, 1961, LLB, 1964. Bar: Calif. 1965, Alaska, 1965. Assoc. Delaney Wiles Moore and Hayes, Anchorage, 1963, 65-68, Law Offices Roger Cremo, Anchorage, 1968-70; judge Alaska Superior Ct., Anchorage, 1970-80, Alaska Ct. Appeals, Anchorage, 1980-90; judge U.S. Dist. Ct. for Alaska, Anchorage, 1990-95, chief judge, 1995—; chmn. Alaska Local Boundary Commn., Anchorage, 1966-69. Chmn. 3d Dist. Rep. Com., Anchorage, 1969-70. Mem. ABA, Alaska Bar Assn., Phi Delta Phi, Tau Kappa Epsilon. Office: US Dist Ct 222 W 7th Ave Unit 41 Anchorage AK 99513-7504

**SINK, ROBERT C.,** lawyer; b. Racine, Wis., 1938. AB, Duke U., 1959, LLB, 1965. Bar: N.C. 1965. Ptnr. Robinson, Bradshaw & Hinson, P.A., Charlotte, N.C. Assoc. editor Duke Law Jour., 1964-65. Trustee Pub. Libr. Charlotte and Mecklenburg County, 1985-90, chmn.; bd. dirs. Mus. New South, 1991-97, chmn., 1996-97. Lt. USN, 1959-62, USNR. Mem. N.C. Bar Assn. (councilor 1988-96, v.p. 1997, pres.-elect 1997-98, pres. 1998—), Mecklenburg County Bar Assn. (pres. 1986-87), Order of Coif, Phi Beta Kappa. Construction, Real property, Government contracts and claims. Office: Robinson Bradshaw & Hinson PA 101 N Tryon St Ste 1900 Charlotte NC 28246-0103

**SINNOTT, JOHN PATRICK,** lawyer, educator; b. Bklyn., Aug. 17, 1931; s. John Patrick and Elizabeth Muriel (Zinkand) S.; m. Rose Marie Yuppa, May 30, 1959; children: James Alexander, Jessica Michelle. BS, U.S. Naval Acad., 1953; MS, USAF Inst. Tech., 1956; JD, No. Ky. U., 1960. Bar: Ohio 1961, N.Y. 1963, U.S. Patent Office 1963, N.J. 1970, U.S. Supreme Ct. 1977. Assoc. Brumbaugh, Graves, Donohue & Raymond, N.Y.C., 1961-63; patent atty. Bell Tel. Labs., Murray Hill, N.J., 1963-64, Schlumberger Ltd., N.Y.C., 1964-71; asst. chief patent counsel Babcock & Wilcox, N.Y.C., 1971-79; chief patent and trademark counsel Am. Std. Inc., N.Y.C., 1979-92; of counsel Morgan & Finnegan, N.Y.C., 1992—; adj. lectr. N.J. Inst. Tech., Newark, 1974-89; adj. prof. Seton Hall U. Sch. Law, Newark, 1989—. Author: World Patent Law and Practice, Vols. 2-2P, 1998, A Practical Guide to Document Authentication, 1998, Counterfeit Goods Suppression, 1998; contbr. articles to profl. jours. Bd. dirs. New Providence (N.J.) Cmty. Swimming Pool, 1970; mem. local Selective Svc. Bd., Plainfield, N.J., 1971. Capt. USAF, 1953-61, col. AUS (ret.), 199. Decorated Legion of Merit, others. Mem. Am. Arbitration Assn. (arbitrator, WIPO Arbitration and Mediation Ctr.), N.Y. Intellectual Property Law Assn. (bd. dirs. 1974-76), Squadron A Club, Cosmos. Republican. Roman Catholic. Patent, Trademark and copyright. Home: 2517 Rolling Rd Valdosta GA 31602-1244 Office: Morgan & Finnegan LLP 345 Park Ave Fl 22 New York NY 10154-0053

**SINNOTT, JOHN WILLIAM,** lawyer; b. St. Louis, Jan. 5, 1966; s. John and Joan Martha Sinnott. AB, Dartmouth Coll., 1988; JD, Tulane U., 1995. Bar: La. 1995, U.S. Ct. Appeals (5th cir.) 1995, U.S. Dist. Ct. (ea., mid., and we. dists.) La. 1995. Assoc. Phelps Dunbar, New Orleans, 1995-96, Montgomery, Barnett, Brown, Read, Hammond & Mintz, New Orleans, 1996—. Capt. USMC, 1988-92. Mem. ABA, La. State Bar Assn., Def. Rsch. Inst. Product liability, Insurance, Personal injury. Office: Montgomery Barnett Brown Read Hammond & Mintz 3200 Energy Centre 1100 Poydras St New Orleans LA 70163-1101

**SINOR, HOWARD EARL, JR.,** lawyer; b. New Orleans, Sept. 6, 1949; s. Howard E. and Beverly M. (Bourgeois) S.; m. Terran Ann Woodward, June 10, 1972; children: Sally, Vera Sue, Sarah, Sadie. BA with hons., U. New Orleans, 1971; JD cum laude, Harvard U., 1975. Bar: La. 1975, U.S. Supreme Ct. 1983, U.S. Ct. Appeals (5th and 11th cir.), U.S. Dist. Ct. (ea., middle, we.) Dist. La. Assoc. Jones, Walker, Waechter, Poitevent, Carrere & Denegre, New Orleans, 1975-80; ptnr. Jones, Walker, Waechter, Poitevent, Carrere & Denegre, 1980-98, Gordon, Arata, McCollam, Duplantis & Eagan, New Orleans, 1999—. Contbg. author: La. Appellate Practice Handbook, 1990, 93; editor: CLE Manual of Recent Developments, 1985, 2d edit., 1986; contbr. articles to profl. jours. Recipient Pres.'s award, La. State Bar Assn., 1987. Fellow La. Bar Found.; mem. ABA, FBA, New Orleans Bar Assn., La. State Bar Assn. (chmn. antitrust sect. 1987-89). Avocations: golf, hiking, cross-country skiing. Environmental, General civil litigation, Construction. Office: Gordon Arata et al 201 Saint Charles Ave Fl 40 New Orleans LA 70170-1000

**SIPORIN, SHELDON,** lawyer, consultant. Bachelor's, CUNY; JD, U. Calif. Bar: N.Y., U.S. Dist. Ct. (ea. and so. dist.) N.Y., U.S. Ct. Appeals (2d. cir.). Asst. counsel Ctr. for Law and Health Care Policy, N.Y.C., 1983; assoc. Morgan, Melhuish & Monaghan, N.Y.C., 1984; sole practice N.Y.C., 1985—; cons. ADP-UCM, N.Y.C., 1986; of counsel various law firms, N.Y.C., 1985—. Vol. atty. Office of Aging, Legal Aid Soc., N.Y.C., 1985, Vol. Lawyers for Arts, 1990; arbitrator Am. Arbitration Assn., N.Y.C., 1983-86, small claims Civil Ct., N.Y.C., 1985-86, Civil Ct. Arbitration Panel, N.Y. County; trustee Lawyers Sq. N.Y., 1985. Mem. ABA (citizenship edn. com. young lawyers div. 1986-87), Am. Judges Assn., Soc. Profls. in Dispute Resolution (assoc.), N.Y. State Bar Assn. (com. fed. constn., film and video com. 1988—), N.Y. County Lawyer's Assn. (com. on entertainment law 1988—, arbitration and conciliation com. 1990-91, com. on legal tech. 1996—), Assn. Computing Machinery, Bklyn. Bar Assn. (com. on arbitration 1994—, Assn. Ind. Video and Filmmakers, Phi Beta Kappa. General civil litigation, Constitutional, Entertainment.

**SIPOS, VICTOR ATILLA,** lawyer, associate; b. Beverly, Mass., Feb. 19, 1971. BA in Internat. Rels., Brigham Young U., 1995; JD, Columbia U., 1998. Bar: Ariz. 1998, U.S. Dist. Ct. Ariz. 1998. Mem. ABA, Maricopa County Bar Assn. Office: Brown & Bain 2901 N Central Ave Ste 2000 Phoenix AZ 85012-2788

**SIPPEL, WILLIAM LEROY,** lawyer; b. Fond du Lac, Wis., Aug. 14, 1948; s. Alfonse Aloysious and Virginia Laura (Weber) S.; m. Barbara Jean Brost, Aug. 23, 1970; children: Katharine Jean, David William. BA, U. Wis., JD. Bar: Wis. 1974, U.S. Dist. Ct. (we. dist.) Wis. 1974, Minn. 1981, U.S. Dist. Ct. Minn. 1981, U.S. Ct. Appeals (10th cir.) 1984, U.S. Ct. Appeals (8th cir.) 1985. Research assoc. dept. agrl. econs. U. Wis., Madison, 1974-75; counsel monopolies and comml. law subcom. Ho. Judiciary Com., Washington, 1975-80; spl. asst. to asst. gen. antitrust div. U.S. Dept. of Justice, Washington, 1980-81; from assoc. to ptnr. Doherty, Rumble & Butler, Mpls. and St. Paul, Minn., 1981-99; ptnr. Oppenheimer, Wolff & Donnelly, LLP, Mpls., 1999—; bd. dirs. World Trade Week, Music in the Park, Inc. Co-author: The Antitrust Health Care Handbook, 1988. Mem. program com. Minn. World Trade Assn., Mpls., St. Paul, 1985-86, bd. dirs., 1986, Minn.; dir. Music in the Park, Mpls.; dir. Person to Person Inc.; vice-chmn. antitrust mktg. orders com. Nat. Coun. Former Cooperatives, 1999—. With USAR, 1971-77. Mem. ABA (vice chmn. ins. industry com. 1990-91), Minn. Bar Assn. (co-chmn. antitrust sect. 1986-88, internat. law sect. coun. 1986-89, treas. 1989-90, sec. 1990-91, vice chmn. 1995-96, chmn. 1996-97), Minn. Med. Alley Assn. (co-chmn. internat. bus. com. 1990-95, Hennepin County Office Internat. Trade (bd. dirs. 1988-93), Phi Beta Kappa. Roman Catholic. Avocations: computers, reading. E-mail: bsippel@owdlaw.com. Antitrust, Private international, Federal civil litigation. Home: 2151 Commonwealth Ave Saint Paul MN 55108-1730 Office: Oppenheimer Wolff Donnelly LLP Plaza VII 45 S Seventh St Ste 3400 Minneapolis MN 55402-1609

**SIPPERLY, PETER C.,** lawyer; b. Houston, May 21, 1944; s. William and Marie Rose (Cassard) S.; children: Kristin Cassard, Geoffrey Provost. BS, Springfield (Mass.) Coll., 1969, MEd, 1972; JD, Western New Eng. Coll. Sch. Law, 1982. Bar: N.Y. 1983, U.S. Dist. Ct. (no. dist.) N.Y. 1983. Tchr. Ramapo Cen. Sch. Dist., Suffern, N.Y., 1969-71; assoc. dean Skidmore Coll., Saratoga Springs, N.Y., 1972-79; assoc. King, Murphy, Adang & Arpey, Saratoga Springs, 1982-85, Jones & Mills, Saratoga Springs, 1985-86; ptnr. Jones & Sipperly, Saratoga Springs, 1986-87, Ferrara, Jones & Sipperly, Saratoga Springs, 1987-91; asst. pub. defender Saratoga County, Saratoga Springs, 1988—. Editor-in-chief: Western New England Law Rev., 1981, case not author, 1980. Bd. dirs. Am. Cancer Soc., Saratoga Springs, 1986, Greenfield (N.Y.) Ski Ctr. Inc. Served to sgt. USMC, 1964-67. Mem. ATLA, N.Y. State Bar Assn., Saratoga County Bar Assn., Saratoga County C. of C. (bd. dirs.). Roman Catholic. Avocations: hunting, fly fishing, tennis, golf, physical fitness. Office: 28 Clinton St Ste 1 Saratoga Springs NY 12866-2192

**SIPPLES, KYLE C.,** lawyer; b. Middletown, Conn., Nov. 10, 1970; s. Peter M. Sipples and Francine Sampar. BA, U. Vt., 1992; JD, U. Conn., 1996. Bar: Vt. 1996. Staff atty. Office of Child Support, Barre, Vt., 1996-97; dep. state's atty. Office of Caledonia County State's Atty., St. Johnsbury, Vt., 1997—. Office: Caledonia County State's Atty 26 Main St Fed Bldg Saint Johnsbury VT 05819

**SIRES, NORMAN GRUBER, JR.,** lawyer; b. Charleston, S.C., Sept. 14, 1942; s. N. Gruber and Emily (Neese) S.; m. Ann Jackson, Oct. 3, 1964; children: N. Gruber III, David Brian. BS in Bus. Adminstrn., U. S.C., 1967, JD, 1971. Bar: S.C. 1971, U.S. Dist. Ct. S.C. 1974. Pvt. practice Seneca, S.C., 1971—; pub. defender Oconee County, S.C., 1972—; city atty. City of Clemson (S.C.), 1981-95; pres. Oconee County Bar, 1978; commr. S.C. Indigent Def. Commn., 1992—. Mem. House Dels., S.C. Bar Assn. With U.S. Army, 1963-66. Coxain USCGR, 1996. Mem. S.C. Bar Assn., Oconee County Bar Assn. Republican. Methodist. Criminal, Family and matrimonial, General practice. Office: Commons Sq 123 PO Box 1277 Seneca SC 29679-1277

**SIRO, RIK NEAL,** lawyer; b. Bklyn., Dec. 31, 1957; s. Jack N. and Beatrice Siro; m. Teresa A. Woody, Aug. 9; 1 child, Alexander Lewis. BA, U. Mo., 1979; JD, U. Calif., San Francisco, 1982. Bar: Mo., Calif., U.S. Dist. Ct. (we. dist.) Mo., U.S. Dist. Ct. (no. dist.) Calif., U.S. Ct. Appeals (7th, 8th, 9th, 10th cirs.). Assoc. Murphy, Pearson, Bradley & Feeney, San Francisco, Calif., 1982-84, Gage & Tucker, Kansas City, Mo., 1984-86; sr. ptnr. Blumer, Nally & Siro, Kansas City, 1986—. Bd. dirs., pres.-elect, pres. Big Bros., Big Sisters of Greater Kans. City, 1987—; bd. dirs. Mattie Rhodes Counseling and Art Ctr., Kansas City, chair Art of the Mask Fundraising, 1993—. Mem. ATLA, Mo. Assn. Trial Attys. (bd. govs.), Nat. Employment Lawyers Assn., Kansas City Met. Bar Assn. Avocations: Spanish, French, skiing, guitar, piano. Labor, General civil litigation, Personal injury. Home: 3654 Belleview Ave Kansas City MO 64111-3860 Office: Blumer Nally & Siro 1621 Baltimore Ave Kansas City MO 64108-1347

**SISE, ROBERT J.,** lawyer; b. Albany, N.Y., Jan. 15, 1926; s. Michael Joseph and Florence Cecelia Sise; m. Theresa A. Sise, Sept. 17, 1949; children: Michael, Robert, John, Thomas, Richard, Willliam, Timothy, Joseph, Bernard. JD, Union U., 1949. Bar: N.Y. Atty. N.Y. State Tax Commn. Montgomery County, Amsterdam, 1955-59, asst. county atty., 1959-60, judge children's ct. and family ct., 1961-73, judge ct. of claims, 1973-90, dep. chmn. adminstrv. judge, 1977-83, 85-90, chief adminstrv. judge, 1983-85; ptnr. Sise & Sise P.C., Amsterdam. With USN, 1944-46. Democrat. Roman Catholic. Avocation: golf. General civil litigation, Estate planning. Home: 275 Guy Park Ave Amsterdam NY 12010-2215 Office: Sise & Sise PC 47 Church St Amsterdam NY 12010-4408

**SISK, GREGORY CHARLES,** lawyer, educator; b. Des Moines, May 29, 1960; s. James Anderson and Roberta Jean (Thornburg) S.; m. Melinda Fay Gilchrist, June 14, 1981; 1 child, Caitlin Anne. Student, Western Mont. Coll., 1978; BA in Polit. Sci., Mont. State U., 1981; JD, U. Wash., 1984. Bar: Wash. 1985, Iowa 1992, U.S. Ct. Appeals (3d cir. and 9th cir.) 1986, U.S. Ct. Appeals (2d, 5th, 11th and D.C. cirs.) 1987, U.S. Ct. Appeals (4th, 8th and fed. cirs.) 1988, U.S. Ct. Appeals (1st cir.) 1989, U.S. Supreme Ct. 1988. Legis. asst. U.S. Senate, Washington, 1984-85; jud. clk. U.S. Ct. Appeals (9th cir.), Seattle, 1985-86; appellate staff atty. civil div. U.S. Dept. Justice, Washington, 1986-89; assoc. Karr, Tuttle & Campbell, Seattle, 1989-91; asst. prof. Drake U., Des Moines, Iowa, 1991-94, assoc. prof., 1994-97, prof., 1997—. Mem. ABA, Fed. Bar Assn., Christian Legal Soc., Order of Coif, Nat. Order of Barristers, Law and Soc. Assn., Am. Polit. Sci. Assn. Republican. Roman Catholic. General civil litigation. Office: Law Sch Drake U Des Moines IA 50311

**SISK, PAUL DOUGLAS,** court official, lawyer; b. Colorado Springs, Colo., Mar. 30, 1950; s. Charles Ray Sisk and Patricia Joann (Linville) Botzler; m. Patricia Rizzo, Aug. 8, 1981; children: Hannah Elizabeth, Francesca Abigail. AB, Brown U., 1972; JD, Temple U., 1979; MA in Govt. Adminstrn., U. Pa., 1989. Bar: Pa. 1979, U.S. Ct. Appeals (3d cir.) 1980, U.S. Supreme Ct. 1983, U.S. Dist. Ct. (ea. dist.) Pa. 1985. Atty. U.S. Ct. Appeals (3d cir.), Phila., 1979-80, supervising atty., 1980-81, sr. staff atty., 1981-93, clk., 1993—; lectr. U. Pa. Law Sch., 1989-95; reporter Joint Supreme Ct.-3d Cir. Death Penalty Task Force, 1989—. Acct., warden Episcopal Ch., Springfield, Pa., 1979-81; bd. dirs Springfield Pastoral Care Found., 1979-82; sr. warden, vestryman St. Giles Ch., Upper Darby, Pa., 1991-95. Mem. Com. Appellate Staff Attys. (exec. bd. 1986-88). Home: 409 Christian Dr Wallingford PA 19086-6912 Office: US Ct Appeals 3d Cir 601 Market St Philadelphia PA 19106-1713

**SISSEL, GEORGE ALLEN,** manufacturing executive; b. Chgo., July 30, 1936; s. William Worth and Hannah Ruth (Harlan) S.; m. Mary Ruth Runsvold, Oct. 5, 1968; children: Jenifer Ruth, Gregory Allen. B.S. in Elec. Engring., U. Colo., 1958; J.D. cum laude, U. Minn., 1966. Bar: Colo. 1966, Ind. 1973, U.S. Supreme Ct. 1981. Assoc. Sherman & Howard, Denver, 1966-70; with Ball Corp., Broomfield, Colo., 1970—; assoc. gen. counsel Ball Corp., 1974-78, gen. counsel, 1978-95, corp. sec., 1980-95, v.p., 1981-87, sr. v.p., 1987-95; acting pres., CEO Ball Corp., Muncie, 1994-95, pres., 1995-98, CEO, 1995—, chmn. bd., 1996—, also bd. dirs.; bd. advisors First Chgo. Equity Capital, 1995—; bd. dirs. First Merchants Corp. Assoc. editor: U. Minn. Law Rev., 1965-66. Served with USN, 1958-63. Mem. ABA, Can. Mfrs. Inst. (bd. dirs., chmn.), Nat. Assn. Mfrs. (bd. dirs.), Colo. Bar Assn., Colo. Assn. Commerce & Industry, Order of Coif, MIT Soc. Sr. Execs., (bd. govs. 1987-95), Sigma Chi, Sigma Tau, Eta Kappa Nu. Methodist. Lodge: Rotary. General corporate, Antitrust, Administrative and regulatory. Office: Ball Corp 10 Longs Peak Dr Broomfield CO 80021-2510

**SITES, JAMES PHILIP,** lawyer, consul; b. Detroit, Sept. 17, 1948; s. James Neil and Inger Marie (Krogh) S.; m. Barbara Teresa Mazurek, Apr. 9, 1978; children: Philip Erling, Teresa Elizabeth. Student, U. Oslo, Norway, 1968-69; BA, Haverford Coll., 1970; JD, Georgetown U., 1973, ML in Taxation, 1979. Bar: Md. 1973, D.C. 1974, U.S. Supreme Ct. 1978, Mont. 1984, U.S. Tax Ct. 1984, U.S. Dist. Ct. Mont. 1984, U.S. Ct. Appeals (9th cir.) 1988. Law clk. to judge James C. Morton, Jr. Ct. Spl. Appeals Md., Annapolis, 1974-75; law clk. to judge Orman W. Ketcham Superior Ct. D.C., Washington, 1975-76; gen. atty. U.S. Immigration & Naturalization Svc., Washington, 1976-77; trial atty. tax div. U.S. Dept. Justice, Washington, 1977-84; ptnr. Crowley, Haughey, Hanson, Toole & Dietrich, Billings, Mont., 1984—; consul for Govt. of Norway State of Mont., Billings, 1987—; instr. Norwegian Ea. Mont. Coll., 1987-88, Sons of Norway, 1989—, instr. polit. sci. Mont. State U., Billings, 1997—; v.p. Scandinavian Studies Found., 1989—; bd. dirs. Billings Com. on Fgn. Rels., 1988—; bd. dirs. Festival of Cultures; mem. Mont. Coun. for Internat. Visitors, The Norsemen's Fedn., Billings Conoco Citizens Adv. Coun. Chair local exec. bd. Mont. State U., Billings, 1993—. U. Oslo scholar, 1969; recipient Peace Rsch. award Haverford Coll., 1970; Knight 1st Class, Royal Norwegian Order of Merit. Mem. Md. State Bar Assn., Mont. State Bar (co-chmn. com. on income and property taxes 1987-91, chair tax and probate sect. 1991-92, chair tax litigation subcom. 1992—), D.C. Bar Assn., Am. Immigration Lawyers Assn., Norwegian-Am. C. of C., Billings C. of C. (bd. dirs. 1998—, vice chair pub. affairs coun.), Hilands Golf Club, Kenwood Golf and Country Club, Billings Stamp Club, Elks, Masons. Avocations: philately, sports card collecting, hiking, Nordic skiing. State and local taxation, Administrative and regulatory, Immigration, naturalization, and customs. Office: Crowley Haughey Hanson Toole & Dietrich Consulate for Norway 490 N 31st St Billings MT 59101-1256

**SITRICK, DAVID HOWARD,** lawyer; b. Chgo., Dec. 3, 1950; s. Jules Herman and Marcia Sitrick; children: Gregory, Suzanne, Arielle. BSEE, BS in Computer Sci., U. Ill., 1973; JD, So. Meth. U., 1980. Bar: U.S. Patent Office 1978, Tex. 1980, Ill. 1981. Engr. Ford Motor Co., 1972-74, Continental Can Corp., 1974-75, Tex. Instruments Co., Dallas, 1975-81; assoc. Fitch, Even, Tabin, Flannery & Welsh, Chgo., 1981-83; ptnr. Welsh & Katz, Ltd., Chgo., 1983-86; pvt. practice Skokie, Ill., 1986—; exec. v.p. J. Herman Sitrick Advt., Skokie, 1986—; ptnr. Sitrick & Sitrick, Chgo. and Skokie, 1988—; mem. faculty Patent Resource Group, Washington, 1985-87; lectr. Japan Patent Assn./Patent Resource Group, Byte Computer Show, Chgo., 1984, Internat. Copyright Soc. Japan, Tokyo, 1987, Kellogg Sch. Mgmt. Northwestern U., dir. patents, copyrights, licensing and tech. law Internat. Bus. Devel. Ctr. Northwestern U., adj. prof. of law, Northwestern U. Sch. of Law; sr. legal advisor MIT/ANVAR Strategic Tech. Alliance, Boston, 1991, participant Alliance '91 Forum, Tokyo, 1991, mem. planning com., lectr., 1991. Author: Electronics and Computer Protection Chip, Mask and Program Protection; patentee in field. Mem. ABA, Ill. Bar Assn., Tex. Bar Assn. Avocations: music, sports, computers. Computer, Patent, Biotechnology. Home: 820 Burchell Ave Highland Park IL 60035-1342 Office: 8340 Lincoln Ave Skokie IL 60077-2466

**SITTON, LARRY BRUCE,** lawyer; b. Hendersonville, N.C., Jan. 20, 1940; s. Hicks McRary and Della Mae (Pace) S.; m. Carroll Speight Roberts, Mar. 28, 1964; children: Robert Louis, Sara Randall, Michelle Lin. BA cum laude, Wake Forest U., 1961, LLB cum laude, 1964. Bar: N.C. 1967. Law clk. to Hon. Eugene A. Gordon U.S. Dist. Ct. N.C., Greensboro, 1966-67; assoc. Smith Moore Smith Schell & Hunter, Greensboro, 1967-72, ptnr., 1972-85; ptnr. Smith Helms Mulliss & Moore, Greensboro, 1986—. Trustee, elder, deacon 1st Presbyn. Ch., Greensboro, 1978—; mem. bd. visitors Wake Forest Law Sch., Winston-Salem, N.C., 1982—; trustee A&T State U., Greensboro, 1985—; bd. dirs. Greensboro Cerebral Palsey Assn., 1986-89. Capt. U.S. Army, 1964-66. Hankins scholar, 1957-61, Babcock scholar, 1961-64. Mem. ABA, N.C. Bar Assn. (chmn. practical tng. com. 1980-82, chmn. long range planning com. 1983-85, chmn. dispute resolution com. 1985-87, bd. govs. 1987-90, chmn. nominations com. 1988-89, exec. com. 1989-90, chmn. quality of life task force 1989-91), Greensboro Bar Assn., Jud. Conf. for U.S. Ct. Appeals (4th cir.). Democrat. Avocations: racquetball, skiing. Home: 400 Fisher Park Cir Apt C Greensboro NC 27401-1646 Office: Smith Helms Mulliss & Moore 300 N Greene St Ste 1400 Greensboro NC 27401-2171

**SITZES, MADELINE D'REE PENTON,** lawyer; b. Corpus Christi, Tex., Aug. 13, 1942; d. Hewitt Hillard and Jo Thelma Penton; m. Charlie C. Sitzes, Mar. 31, 1967 (div. Dec. 1975). Student, Fla. State U., 1960-62; BS magna cum laude, North Tex. State U., 1972; JD, U. Houston, 1980. Bar: Tex. 1980, U.S. Ct. Appeals (5th cir.), U.S. Dist. Ct. (so. and we. dists.) Tex. Flight attendant Delta Air Lines, Dallas, 1962-67, 73-76, supr., 1975-76; cattle rancher Paradise, Tex., 1967-75; substitute tchr. Bridgeport (Tex.) Ind. Sch. Dist., Tex.; pvt. practice law Madeline Sitzes Atty. Law, Houston, 1980—; pvt. pilot, glider pilot, 1963—; pvt. instrn. tennis, Bridgeport, Dallas, 1967-76. Mem. Steering com. and Fundraising Commn. Ann Richards for Gov., Bob Bullock for Lt. Gov., Katherine Whitmire for Mayor of Houston; vol. Denton State Sch. for Mentally Retarded, 1970-72; Dem. nominee for judge, 127th Dist. Ct., 1988; dir. The Lighthouse for the Blind, Houston, 1988—. Mem. State Bar Tex., Houston Bar Assn., Am. Trial Lawyers Assn., Tex. Trial Lawyers Assn., Tex. Mariners Cruising Assn., Houston Trial Lawyers Assn., Phi Delta Phi. Episcopalian. General civil litigation, Family and matrimonial, Personal injury. Office: PO Box 431742 Houston TX 77243-1742

**SIVERD, ROBERT JOSEPH,** lawyer; b. Newark, July 27, 1948; s. Clifford David and Elizabeth Ann (Klink) S.; m. Bonita Marie Shuluck, Jan. 8, 1972; children: Robert J. Jr., Veronica Leigh. AB in French, Georgetown U., 1970; JD, 1973; postgrad. LaSorbonne, Paris, 1969. Bar: N.Y. 1974, U.S. Dist. Ct. (so. and ea. dists.) N.Y. 1974, U.S. Ct. Appeals (2nd cir.) 1974, U.S. Supreme Ct. 1980, U.S. Dist. Ct. (ea. dist.) Pa. 1984, U.S. Ct. Appeals (3rd cir.) 1984, (6th cir.) 1985, Ohio 1991, Ky. 1992. Assoc. Donovan Leisure Newton & Irvine, N.Y.C., 1973-83; staff v.p., litigation counsel Am. Fin. Group, Inc., Greenwich, Conn., 1983-86, v.p. litigation counsel, 1986-87, v.p. assoc. gen. counsel, Cin., 1987-92; sr. v.p., gen. counsel and sec. Gen. Cable Corp., 1992-94, exec. v.p., gen. counsel and sec., 1994—. Mem. ABA, Cin. Bar Assn., Assn. of Bar of City of N.Y., Ky. Bar Assn. Republican. General corporate, Federal civil litigation, Antitrust. Office: Gen Cable Corp 4 Tesseneer Dr Newport KY 41076-9167

**SIVOLELLA, JOHN JOSEPH,** lawyer; b. Springfield, N.J., Jan. 12, 1964; s. William and Dolores Ann (Purdue) S.; m. Eileen Karen Haws, Aug. 8, 1992. BA with high honors, Rutgers Coll., 1987; MPA, Princeton U., 1991; JD, NYU, 1992. Bar: N.J. 1992, U.S. Dist. Ct. N.J. 1992. Intern U.S. Dept. of State, Tegucigalpa, Honduras, 1989, U.S. Atty.'s Office, Newark, 1990; rsch. asst. Dean Oscar Chase NYU Law Sch., N.Y.C., 1990, 91; summer assoc. Steptoe & Johnson, Washington, 1991; jud. clk. to Justice Stewart G. Pollock Supreme Ct. of N.J., Morristown, N.J., 1992-93; assoc. Wilentz, Goldman & Spitzer, Woodbridge, N.J., 1993; asst. counsel Gov. Christine Todd Whitman, Trenton, N.J., 1994—; mem. bd. of adjustment City of Summit, 1996-97. Editor Annual Survey of Am. Law, 1990-91. Named Henry Rutgers Scholar, Rutgers U., 1987; Garden State Grad. fellow N.J. Dept. Higher Edn., 1988. Mem. N.J. State Bar Assn., Princeton Grad. Alumni Assn., Rutgers Alumni Assn., NYU Law Alumni Assn., Phi Beta Kappa, Phi Alpha Theta, Phi Sigma Iota. Republican. Roman Catholic. Avocations: athletics, travel, Spanish. Home: 204 Woodland Ave Summit NJ 07901-1644 Office: Office of Counsel to Gov CN 001 Trenton NJ 08625

**SIX, FRED N.,** state supreme court justice; b. Independence, Mo., Apr. 20, 1929. AB, U. Kans., 1951, JD with honors, 1956; LLM in Judicial Process, U. Va., 1990. Bar: Kans. 1956. Asst. atty. gen. State of Kans., 1957-58; pvt. practice Lawrence, Kans., 1958-87; judge Kans. Ct. Appeals, 1987-88; justice Kans. Supreme Ct., Topeka, 1988—; editor-in-chief U. Kans. Law Review, 1955-56; lectr. on law Washburn U. Sch. Law, 1957-58, U. Kans., 1975-76. Served with USMC, 1951-53; USMCR, 1957-62. Recipient Disting. Alumnus award U. Kans. Sch. Law, 1994. Fellow Am. Bar Found. (chmn. Kans. chpt. 1983-87); mem. ABA (jud. adminstrn. divsn.), Am. Judicature Soc., Kans. Bar Assn., Kans. Bar Found., Kans. Law Soc. (pres. 1970-72), Kans. Inn of Ct. (pres. 1993-94), Order of Coif, Phi Delta Phi. Office: Kans Supreme Ct 374 Kansas JudICIAL Center 301 SW 10th Ave Topeka KS 66612-1502

**SJOSTROM, CRAIG DAVID,** lawyer; b. San Diego, May 27, 1964; s. David John and Mary Lue (Kelsey) S.; m. Elizabeth Ann Pittier, June 13, 1992. BA, Wash. State U., 1986; JD, U. Idaho, 1991. Bar: Wash. 1991, U.S. Dist. Ct. (we. dist.) Wash. 1993. Atty. Phillips, Krause & Brown, Aberdeen, Wash., 1992-94, Bitar, Morgan & Bitar, Hoquiam, Wash., 1994-96, Bailey, Duskin & Peiffle, Arlington, Wash., 1996-98; pvt. practice Mount Vernon, Wash., 1998—. Recipient Am. Jurisprudence award, 1988, 89. Mem. Lions Club. Avocations: fishing, hunting, reading, zymurgy. General civil litigation, Family and matrimonial, Real property. Office: 409 Main St Mount Vernon WA 98273-3837

**SKAAR, JAMES DOUGLAS,** lawyer; b. Geneva, Ill., May 25, 1954; s. Loren A. Skaar and Lillian R. Mork; m. Mary E. George; 1 child: Laura Elizabeth Skaar. BS, U. Wis., 1975; JD, John Marshall Law Sch., 1981. Assoc. atty. Ruddy, Myler, Ruddy & Fabian, Aurora, Ill., 1981-85; ptnr. Smith, Landmeier, Skaar & Elders, Geneva, 1985—. Mem. bd. dirs. CASA Kane County, Geneva, 1989-96 (chmn. bd. dirs. 1995-96). Mem. Kane County Bar Assn. Avocation: vol. legal svc. for CASA child welfare orgn. State civil litigation, Estate planning, Estate taxation. Office: Smith Landmeier Skaar & Elders 15 N 2nd St Geneva IL 60134-2224

**SKAGGS, KATHY CHERYL,** writer, consultant; b. Campbellsville, Ky., Mar. 21, 1956; d. Charles Wilson and Naida Frances (Beams) S.; m. Dorman Gibson, Oct. 25, 1974 (div. Feb. 1984); children: Jacob Lee, Nathan Louis; m. Russell Turner, Dec. 13, 1985 (div. Aug. 1989). BA, Western Ky. U., 1978; JD, NYU, 1981. With Legal Svcs. Mid. Tenn., Gallatin, 1981-89; dir. community programs Vanderbilt U. Ctr. for Health Svcs., Nashville, 1989-94; writer, cons. Maple, Ky., 1994—. Co-author: Understanding Economics for Local Organizing, 1985; editor: Tennessee Domestic Violence Bench Book, 1996, 98; author: Program Evaluation: A Training Curriculum for Community Organizations, 1996, Legal Advocacy for Battered Women, 1997, The MIHOW Way: A Training Curriculum for Home Visitors, 1998, (poetry) The Place I Come From, 1998; contbr. poetry to popular publs. Pres., founder Sumner County Coalition Against Domestic Violence, Gallatin, 1983-85; chairperson, founder Tenn. Task Force on Family Violence, Nashville, 1985-87; Tenn. rep. Nat. Coalition Agsinst Domestic Violence, Washington, 1985-86; founder Coalition in Def. of Battered Women, 1991-95. Named Outstanding Young Woman of Am., 1986; recipient Sui Juris award Tenn. Task Force Against Domestic Violence, 1992; Emerging Artist Support and Encouragement grantee, 1999. Avocation: Spanish.

**SKAGGS, SANFORD MERLE,** lawyer; b. Berkeley, Calif., Oct. 24, 1939; s. Sherman G. and Barbara Jewel (Stinson) S.; m. Sharon Ann Barnes, Sept. 3, 1976; children: Stephen, Paula Ferry, Barbara Gallagher, Darren Peterson. BA, U. Calif., Berkeley, 1961; JD, U. Calif., 1964. Bar: Calif. 1965. Atty. Pacific Gas and Electric Co., San Francisco, 1964-73; gen. counsel Pacific Gas Transmission Co., San Francisco, 1973-75; ptnr. Van Voorhis & Skaggs, Walnut Creek, Calif., 1975-85, McCutchen, Doyle, Brown & Enersen, San Francisco and Walnut Creek, 1985—; mem.Calif. Law Revision Commn., 1990—, chmn. 1993; dir. John Muir/Mt. Diablo Health Sys., 1996—. Councilman City of Walnut Creek, 1972-78, mayor 1974-75, 76-77; bd. dirs. East Bay Mcpl. Utility Dist., 1978-90, pres., 1982-90. Mem. Calif. State Bar Assn., Contra Costa County Bar Assn., Urban Land Inst., Lambda Alpha, Alpha Delta Phi, Phi Delta Phi. Republican. State civil litigation, Land use and zoning (including planning), Condemnation. Office: McCutchen Doyle Brown & Enersen 1331 N California Blvd Walnut Creek CA 94596-4537

**SKAL, DEBRA LYNN,** lawyer; b. Dayton, Ohio, Oct. 2, 1958; d. Lawrence and Anne Bernice (Cunix) S. BS with high distinction, Ind. U., 1986; JD, Duke U., 1989. Bar: Ga. 1989. Assoc. Powell, Goldstein, Frazer & Murphy, Atlanta, 1989-96. Exec. editor: Alaska Law Rev., 1987-89. Coun. mem. YES! Atlanta, 1990-98; founding mem. Teaching Tolerance So. Poverty Law Ctr., Montgomery, Ala., mem. leadership coun. Klanwatch; mem. Lupus Found. Am., Atlanta, 1992—, Sjogren's Found., Port Washington, N.Y., 1992—, Am. Diabetes Assn., 1996—, Arthritis Found., Atlanta, 1993—. Mem. State Bar Assn. Ga., Beta Gamma Sigma. Banking, Securities, Consumer commercial.

**SKALKA, DOUGLAS SCOTT,** lawyer; b. N.Y.C., Sept. 28, 1960; s. Philip and Margery Skalka; m. Susan Michelle Prince, MAy 12, 1985; children: Elizabeth, Rachel, Abigail. AB, Cornell U., 1982; JD, Boston U., 1985. Bar: Conn. 1985, N.Y. 1986, U.S. Dist. Ct. Conn. 1986, U.S. Dist. Ct. (so. and ea. dists.) N.Y. 1990; cert. in bus. bankruptcy. Assoc. atty. Whitman & Ransom, Greenwich, Conn., N.Y.C., 1985-93; ptnr. Whitman Breet Abbott & Morgan, Greenwich, Conn., N.Y.C., 1994-95; prin. Neubert, Pepe & Monteith, P.C., New Haven and Southport, Conn., 1995—; mem. adv. bd. CPA/Law Forum of Fairfield County, Southport, Conn., 1996—. Contbg. editor: Bankruptcy, 1997, 98; editor-in-chief Probate Law Jour., 1984-85. Mem. exec. com. Southwestern Regional Planning Agy., Norwalk, Conn., 1996—; mem. Southwestern Corridor Action Coun., Bridgeport, Conn., 1998—. Recipient Bernard E. Farr Estate Planning award Boston U., 1985, Paul Liacos scholar, 1984. Mem. Conn. Bar Assn. (exec. com. of comml. law and bankruptcy sect. 1994—), Stamford/Norwalk Regional Bar Assn. (co-chair bankruptcy com. 1994-96), Am. Bankruptcy Inst., Conn. Turnaround Mgmt. Assn. (bd. dirs. 1996—). Bankruptcy, Contracts commercial, Consumer commercial. Office: Neubert Pepe & Monteith PC 195 Church St New Haven CT 06510-2009

**SKARDA, LYNELL GRIFFITH,** lawyer, banker; b. Clovis, N.Mex., Aug. 28, 1915; s. Albert S. and Bertha V. (Taylor) S.; m. Kathryn Burns Skarda, Dec. 25, 1939; children—Jeffry J., Patricia Lyn, Katrina A., Gregory A.F. BS, U. Calif., Berkeley, 1937; JD, Washington & Lee U., 1941. Bar: N.Mex. 1941. Sole practice, Clovis, 1941—; chmn. bd. Citizens Bank of Clovis 1968—; mem. Uniform Jury Instrn. Com., 1963-83. Served to capt. JAG Corps, U.S. Army, World War II. Fellow Am. Coll. Trust and Estate Counsel; mem. ABA, N.Mex. Bar Assn., Am. Judicature Soc. General practice, Banking, Probate. Home: PO Box 400 Clovis NM 88102-0400 Office: Citizens Bank Bldg PO Box 400 Clovis NM 88101

**SKARE, ROBERT MARTIN,** lawyer; b. Jan. 13, 1930; s. Martin Samuel and Verna Adelle (Forseth) S.; m. Marilyn Hutchinson, Aug. 28, 1954; children: Randolph, Robertson, Rodger, Richard. Student, St. Olaf Coll., 1947-48; BS, U. Minn., 1951, JD, 1954. Bar: Minn. 1956. Assoc. Best and Flanagan, Mpls., 1956-60, ptnr., 1960-90, sr. ptnr., 1970-90, of counsel, 1990—; gen. counsel, v.p. Luth. Brotherhood Mut. Funds, Mpls., 1969-93; corporate mcpl. counsel City of Golden Valley (Minn.), 1963-88; dir. Norwest Bank Minn. Community Bd., N.A. Nat. trustee Am. Luth. Ch.; bd. dirs. Search Inst., Mpls, 1980-97, Vesper Soc. Group, San Francisco, 1985—, Son of Heaven, Inc., Seattle, 1987-91, Aspen Inst. Cmty. Forum, 1997—, Nat. Coun. Search Inst. Youth Initiative, 1998—; nat. pres. Lutheran Human Rels. Assn. Am., 1977-79. 1st lt. CIC, U.s. Army, 1954-56. Recipient Pres. award Luth. Human Rels. Assn. Am., 1979, Presdl. Awd., Search Inst., 1997. Mem. ABA, Minn. State Bar Assn., Hennepin County Bar Assn., U. Minn. Alumni Club (charter), Mpls. Club, Torske Klubben, Sigma Alpha Epsilon (Disting. Alumni Svc. award 1978). General corporate, Real property. Home: 780 Mountain Laurel Dr Aspen CO 81611-2344 Office: 4000 US Bank Pl Minneapolis MN 55402-4331

**SKARE, THOMAS M.,** defender; b. St. Paul, Aug. 19, 1952; s. Theodore L. and Jocelyn F. S.; m. Nancie E. Sherry, June 3, 1978; children: Ian T., Ethan M. BA with honors, Hamline U., 1977, JD, 1987. Bar: Minn. 1977, U.S. Dist. Ct. Minn. 1990, U.S. Ct. Appeals (8th cir.) 1997; cert. civil trial advocate Nat. Bd. Trial Advocacy, 1998. Assoc. Hamline Law Rev., St. Paul, 1986-87; law clerk 6th Judicial Dist., Duluth, Minn., 1987-88; pub. defender 6th Judicial Dist., Cloquet, Minn., 1998—; atty. Newby, Lingren & Skare, Ltd., Cloquet, 1988—; mediator, arbitrator Minn. Supreme Ct. Bd. dirs. United Way, Cloquet, 1998—; pres. Luth. Brotherhood Br. 8369, Cloquet, 1998—. Mem. Am. Arbitration Assn., Nat. Trial Lawyers Assn., Minn. Trial Lawyers Assn., Minn. Bar Assn., 11th Dist. Bar Assn. Democrat. Office: Newby Lingren & Skare Ltd PO Box 760 Cloquet MN 55720-0760

**SKARPETOWSKI, CAROL,** lawyer; b. Trenton, N.J., Dec. 26, 1958; d. Edward and Dorothy (McKeever) S. BA, cert. in criminal justice, Rutgers U., 1980; JD, Loyola U., New Orleans, 1983; postgrad., Nat. Criminal Def. Coll., summer 1986. Bar: La. 1984, N.J. 1984, U.S. Dist. Ct. (ea. dist.) La. 1984, U.S. Dist. Ct. N.J. 1984. Law clk. Orleans Indigent Def. Program, New Orleans, 1981-84, staff atty., 1984-89; pvt. practice, New Orleans, 1984-89; asst. dep. pub. defender State of N.J., Trenton, 1989-95, Flemington, 1995—; assoc. Richard J. Garrett, New Orleans, 1986-88; staff atty. Advocacy Ctr. for Elderly and Disabled, New Orleans, 1986-87, 88. Mem. ABA, Nat. Assn. Criminal Def. Lawyers, Huntendon Bar Assn. (ethics com.). Democrat. Roman Catholic. Avocations: photography, roller skating, music. Fax: (908) 782-9337. Home: 46 Locust Ave Trenton NJ 08610-2614 Office: Office Pub Defender 84 Park Ave Flemington NJ 08822-1174

**SKELTON, BYRON GEORGE,** federal judge; b. Florence, Tex., Sept. 1, 1905; s. Clarence Edgar and Avis (Bowmer) S.; m. Ruth Alice Thomas, Nov. 28, 1931; children: Sue, Sandra. Student, Baylor U., 1923-24; AB, U. Tex., 1927, MA, 1928, LLB, 1931. Bar: Tex. 1931, Circuit Ct. Appeals 1937, U.S. Supreme Ct. 1946, FCC 1950, Tax Ct. U.S 1952, U.S. Treasury Dept 1952, ICC 1953. Practice of law Temple, Tex., 1931-66; partner Saulsbury & Skelton, 1934-42, Saulsbury, Skelton, Everton, Bowmer & Courtney, 1944-55, Skelton, Bowmer & Courtney, 1955-66; judge U.S. Ct. Claims, Washington, 1966-77; sr. fed. judge U.S. Ct. Claims, 1977-82, U.S. Ct. Appeals (fed. cir.), Washington, 1982—; county atty., Bell County, Tex., 1934-38; spl. asst. U.S. amb. to Argentina, 1942-45; city atty., Temple, 1945-60; dir. First Nat. Bank of Temple. Dem. nat. committeeman for Tex., 1956-64; del. Dem. Nat. Conv., 1948, 56, 60, 64; del. Tex. Dem. Conv., 1946, 48, 50, 52, 54, 56, 58, 60, 62, 64, vice chmn., 1948, 58; chmn. Dem. Adv. Coun. of Tex., 1955-57; former pres. Temple YMCA; pres. Temple Indsl. Found., 1966. Appointed Ky. Col. and Adm. in Tex. Navy, 1959; recipient Legion of Honor DeMolay, 1980, Temple Outstanding Citizen award, 1984. Mem. ABA, State Bar Tex., Bell-Lampasas and Mills Counties Bar Assn. (past pres.), Am. Law Inst., Am. Judicature Soc., Temple C. of C. (past pres., dir.), Ex-Students' Assn. U. Tex. (past pres., mem. exec.coun.), Gen. Soc. Mayflower Descs., Masons (past worshipful master), Shriners, Kiwanis (past pres.), Phi Beta Kappa, Pi Sigma Alpha, Sigma Delta Pi, Delta Theta Phi. Democrat. Methodist. Home: 1101 Dakota Dr Temple TX 76504-4905 Office: US Ct Appeals 305 Fed Bldg Temple TX 76501

**SKELTON, MARK ALBERT,** lawyer; b. Kingsport, Tenn., Jan. 8, 1957; s. George Haskell and Mary Lucille (Berry) S.; m. Joanna Coffey, Sept. 8, 1979. BBA, U. Tenn., 1979, JD, 1982. Bar: Tenn. 1983, U.S. Dist. Ct. (ea. dist.) Tenn. 1984, U.S. Ct. Appeals (6th cir.) 1990, U.S. Supreme Ct. 1993. Sole practice Rogersville, Tenn., 1983—; city atty. City of Surgoinsville, Tenn., 1984-98. Bd. dirs., v.p. Rogersville Heritage Assn., 1985-89; bd. trustees Surgoinsville First United Meth. Ch., 1992-96; chmn. bd. dirs. Surgoinsville Med. Ctr., Inc., 1994-99. Mem. ABA, ATLA, Tenn. Bar Assn., Tenn. Trial Lawyers Assn., Hawkins County Bar Assn., Nat. Assn. Criminal Def. Lawyers, Tenn. Assn. Criminal Def. Lawyers, Nat. Orgn. Social Security Claimants Reps., Hawkins County C. of C., Phi Kappa Phi, Beta Gamma Sigma, Gamma Beta Phi, Pi Sigma Alpha. Methodist. General practice, Personal injury, Family and matrimonial. Home: 903 Main St Surgoinsville TN 37873-6057 Office: 121 S Depot St Rogersville TN 37857-3303

**SKIBELL, ARTHUR,** lawyer; b. Kouno, Lithuania, June 16, 1942; came to U.S., 1948; s. Sidney and Regina Skibell; children: Jason M., Adrienne N. BA, U. Tex., 1964, LLB, 1966. Bar: Tex. 1966, U.S. Dist. Ct. (we. and no. dists.), U.S. Ct. Appeals (5th cir.). Asst. atty. gen. Atty. Gen. Office, State of Tex., Austin, 1967-69; assoc. Spinuzzi & Girard, Dallas, 1969-71; v.p., gen. counsel Rodeway Inns of Am., Dallas, 1971-80; atty. Skibell & Skibell, Dallas, 1981-87; v.p. Bird & Skibell P.C., Dallas, 1988—; mcpl. judge City of Farmers Branch, Tex., 1984-90. Served with U.S. Army Rex., 1967-73. Mem. Tex. Bar Assn., Dallas Bar Assn. Avocations: tennis, reading, racquetball. Real property, Probate, General civil litigation. Office: Bird & Skibell PC 16812 Dallas Pkwy Dallas TX 75248-1919

**SKILLERN, FRANK FLETCHER,** law educator; b. Sept. 26, 1942; s. Will T. and Vera Catherine (Ryberg) S.; m. Susan Schlaefer, Sept. 3, 1966; children: Nathan Edward, Leah Catherine. AB, U. Chgo., 1964; JD, U. Denver, 1966; LLM, U. Mich., 1969. Bar: Colo. 1967, Tex. 1978. Pvt. practice law Denver, 1967; gen. atty. Maritime Adminstrn., Washington, 1967-68; asst. prof. law Ohio No. U., 1969-71; asst. prof. law Tex. Tech U., Lubbock, 1971-73, assoc. prof. law, 1973-75, prof. law, 1975—; vis. prof. U. Tex. Law Sch., summer 1979, U. Ark. Law Sch., 1979-80, U. Tulsa Coll. Law, 1981-82; cons. and speaker in field. Author: Environmental Protection: The Legal Framework, 1981, 2d edit. published as Environmental Protection Deskbook, 1995, Regulation of Water and Sewer Utilities, 1989, Texas Water Law, Vol. I, 1988, rev. edit., 1992, Vol. II, 1991; contbr. chpts. to Powell on Real Property, Zoning and Land Use Controls, others; author cong. procs. and numerous articles. Mem. ABA (mem. publs. com. Sect. Natural Resources Law 1984—, vice chair internat. environ. law com. Sect. Natural Resources Law 1987). Office: Tex Tech U Sch Law PO Box 40004 Lubbock TX 79409-0004

**SKILLING, RAYMOND INWOOD,** lawyer; b. Enniskillen, U.K., July 14, 1939; s. Dane and Elizabeth (Burleigh) S.; m. Alice Mae Welsh, Aug. 14, 1982; 1 child by previous marriage, Keith A. F. LLB, Queen's U., Belfast, U.K., 1961; JD, U. Chgo., 1962. Solicitor English Supreme Ct. 1966. Bar: Ill 1974. Assoc. Clifford-Turner (now Clifford Chance), London, 1963-69, ptnr., 1969-76; exec. v.p., chief counsel Aon Corp. (and predecessor cos.), Chgo., 1976—; bd. dirs. Aon Corp. (and predecessor cos.). Commonwealth fellow, U. Chgo., 1961-62, Bigelow teaching fellow U. Chgo. Law Sch., 1962-63; Fulbright scholar U.S. Ednl. Commn., London, 1961-63; recipient McKane medal Queen's U., Belfast, 1961. Mem. ABA, Ill. Bar Assn., Chgo. Bar Assn., The Casino Chgo., Chgo. Club, Econ. Club Chgo., Racquet Club Chgo., The Carlton Club London, The City of London Club. Office: Aon Corp 123 N Wacker Dr Chicago IL 60606-1700

**SKILTON, JOHN SINGLETON,** lawyer; b. Washington, Apr. 13, 1944; s. Robert Henry and Margaret (Neisser) S.; m. Carmen Fisher, Jan. 28, 1967; children: Laura Anne, Susan Elizabeth, Robert John. BA, U. Wis., 1966, JD, 1969. Bar: Wis. Supreme Ct. 1969, U.S. Dist. Ct. (ea. and we. dists.) Wis. 1969, U.S. Ct. Appeals (7th cir.) 1969, U.S. Supreme Ct. 1989. Law clk. 7th Cir. Ct. Appeals, Milw., 1969-70; assoc. Foley & Lardner, Milw., 1970-77; ptnr. Foley & Lardner, Madison, Wis., 1977—. Bd. visitors U. Wis. Law Sch., Madison, 1982-90, chmn., 1988-89; chair Wis. Fed. Nominating Commn., 1994; mem. Gov.'s Task Force on Bus. Ct., 1994-95. Fellow Am. Bar Found., Am. Coll. Trial Lawyers; mem. ABA (chmn. standing com. on delivery of legal svcs. 1996—), Am. Law Inst., Am. Acad. Appellate Lawyers, 7th Cir. Bar Assn. (pres. 1985-86, chmn. 7th cir. adv. com. on rules 1994—), State Bar Wis. (pres. 1995-96, Pres.'s award of excellence 1989, Sirykin award for publ svc. 1996), Western Dist. Wis. Bar Assn. (pres. 1992-93), Western Dist. Adv. Group (chmn. 1991), Wis. Law Found. (pres.-elect 1997-99), James E. Doyle Am. Inn of Ct. (coun. 1992-94), Am. Inns of Ct. Found. (trustee 1995-98), U. Wis. Law Alumni Assn. (bd. dirs. 1991-97, pres. 1993-95). Federal civil litigation, General civil litigation, Product liability. Home: 8 N Prospect Ave Madison WI 53705-3936 Office: Foley & Lardner 150 E Gilman St Madison WI 53703-1499

**SKINNER, GREGORY SALA,** lawyer; b. Ross, Calif., Jan. 23, 1954; s. Henry Elwood and Ethel (Sala) S.; m. Sara Jill Dickey, Sept. 25, 1982; children: Brandon Gregory, Henry George. BA in Econs., U. Calif., Berkeley, 1976; JD, U. Calif., San Francisco, 1979. Bar: Calif. 1980, Nev. 1981, U.S. Dist. Ct. Nev. 1982. Pvt. practice Incline Village, 1980-94; shareholder Skinner, Sutton & Watson, P.C., Incline Village, 1994—. Mem. Olympic Club (San Francisco), Zeta Psi Alumni (pres. 1976). General civil litigation, General corporate, Personal injury. Office: Skinner Sutton Watson & Rounds PO Box 3150 800 Southwood Blvd Ste 207 Incline Village NV 89451-9461

**SKINNER, MICHAEL DAVID,** lawyer; b. Shreveport, La., Jan. 5, 1950; s. Roger Gilman and Jerry Ann (Sneed) S.; m. Janet Louise Horaist, Jan. 7, 1978. J.D., La. State U., 1976. Bar: La. 1977, U.S. Dist. Ct. (we. dist.) La. 1978, U.S. Ct. Appeals (5th and 11th cirs.) 1978, U.S. Dist. Ct. (mid. dist.) La. 1982, U.S. Supreme Ct. 1982, U.S. Dist. Ct. (so. dist.) Tex. 1983. Sole practice, Lafayette, La., 1976-84; ptnr. Guilliot, Skinner & Everett, 1984-86, Goode, Skinner & Hawkland, 1986-93; U.S. atty. we. dist. La., 1993—. Mem. Downtown Lafayette Unltd., Lafayette, 1984; bd. dirs. Assn. Culturelle de la Louisiane, Lafayette, 1984. Mem. La. State Bar Assn. Democrat. General corporate, Real property, Criminal. Office: US Atty Dist West La US Courthouse 300 Fannin St Ste 3201 Shreveport LA 71101-3068

**SKINNER, WALTER JAY,** federal judge; b. Washington, Sept. 12, 1927; s. Frederick Snowden and Mary Waterman (Comstock) S.; m. Sylvia Henderson, Aug. 12, 1950; 4 children. A.B., Harvard, 1948; J.D., 1952. Bar: Mass. 1952, U.S. Dist. Ct. 1954. Assoc. firm Gaston, Snow, Rice & Boyd, Boston, 1952-57; pvt. practice law Scituate, Mass., 1957-63; asst. dist. atty. Plymouth County, 1957-63; town counsel Scituate, 1957-63; asst. atty. gen., chief Criminal Div., Commonwealth of Mass., 1963-65; mem. firm Wardwell, Allen, McLaughlin & Skinner, Boston, 1965-74; judge U.S. Dist. Ct. of Mass., 1974—; sr. status, 1992—. Bd. dirs. Douglas A. Thom Clinic, 1966-70. Mem. Mass. Bar Assn., Boston Bar Assn. Office: US Dist Ct 1 Courthouse Way Boston MA 02210-3002

**SKINNER, WILLIAM FRENCH COCHRAN, JR.,** lawyer; b. Richmond, Va., June 18, 1943; s. W. French and Emma Sue (Linkous) S.; m. Judy Bryant, Aug. 28, 1965; children: Chip, Carey. BS in Commerce, Washington & Lee U., 1965; JD, Emory U., 1968. Bar: Ga. 1967, U.S. Dist. Ct. (no. dist.) Ga. 1973, U.S. Supreme Ct. 1974, U.S. Ct. Appeals (11th cir.) 1981. Assoc. Rich, Bass, Kidd & Broome, Decatur, Ga., 1968, 71-74; ptnr. Rich, Bass, Kidd & Skinner, Decatur, 1974; pvt. practice Decatur, 1974—. Capt. U.S. Army, 1969-70, Vietnam. Mem. State Bar Ga., DeKalb Bar Assn., Inc. Episcopalian. Avocations: sports, family. State civil litigation, Family and matrimonial, Real property. Office: 315 W Ponce De Leon Ave Ste 956 Decatur GA 30030-2471

**SKIPPER, WALTER JOHN,** lawyer; b. Kenosha, Wis., Aug. 5, 1964; s. Walter J. Sr. and Marilyn A. Skipper; m. Irene P. Skipper, Oct. 6, 1996; 1 child, Jonathan Walter. BS in Acctg., Fin. and Econ., Marquette U., 1985; JD, U. Wis., 1990. Bar: Wis. 1990, Md. 1991. Assoc. Fried, Frank, Hanes, Shriver & Jacobson, Washington, 1990-92, Quarles & Brady, Milw., 1992—. Author: Wisconsin Handbook for Securities Attorneys, 1994—. Mem. fin. com., Elm Grove, Wis., 1998—. Mem. Inst. Cert. Mgmt. Accts., Order of Coif, Alpha Sigma Nu, Beta Gamma Sigma. Securities, Mergers and acquisitions, General corporate. Home: 545 Hi View Ct Elm Grove WI 53122-2405 Office: Quarles & Brady 411 E Wisconsin Ave Ste 2550 Milwaukee WI 53202-4497

**SKIRNICK, ROBERT ANDREW,** lawyer; b. Chgo., Apr. 23, 1938; s. Andrew and Stella (Sanders) S.; children: Rebecca, David; m. Maria Ann Castellano, Oct. 4, 1974; 1 child, Gabriella. BA, Roosevelt U., 1961; JD, U. Chgo., 1966. Bar: U.S. Dist. Ct. (no. dist.) Ill. 1966, U.S. Ct. Appeals (7th cir.) 1968, U.S. Supreme Ct. 1970, U.S. Ct. Appeals (5th and 9th cirs.) 1982, N.Y. 1982, U.S. Ct. Appeals (3rd cir.) 1983, U.S. Dist. Ct. (ea. dist.) Mich. 1988, (so. and ea. dists.) N.Y. 1989, U.S. Ct. Appeals (2nd cir.) 1990, U.S. Dist. Ct. (no. dist.) Calif. 1992, U.S. Ct. Appeals (11th Cir.) 1992, U.S. Dist. Ct. (so. dist.) Tex. 1992, U.S. Dist. Ct. Ariz. 1993. Atty. office gen. counsel honors program HEW, Washington, 1966-68; ptnr. Fortes, Eiger, Epstein & Skirnick, Chgo., 1975-77, Much, Shelist, Freed, Chgo., 1977-79, Wolf, Popper, Ross, Wolf & Jones, N.Y.C., 1979-87, Kaplan, Kilsheimer & Foley, N.Y.C., 1988-89, Wechsler, Skirnick, Harwood, Halebian & Feffer, N.Y.C., 1989-95, Lovell & Skirnick, LLP, N.Y.C., 1995-97, Meredith Cohen Greenfogel & Skirnick, P.C., N.Y.C., 1997—; instr. NYU, 1979-80; cons. Nat. Legal Aid and Def. Assn., Chgo., 1968-69; spl. asst. atty. gen. Ill. Atty Gen. Office, Chgo., 1972-73; spl. antitrust counsel State of Conn., 1976-77; mem. adv. bd. Small Bus. Legal Def. Commn., San Francisco, 1982—; lectr. Practicing Law Inst., N.Y.C., 1986-87; spl. master So. Dist. N.Y., 1988-91; ct. appted co-lead counsel NASDAQ market makers antitrust litigation, 1994—. Author: (with others) Federal Subject Matter Jurisdiction of U.S. District Courts, Federal Civil Practice, 1974, Antitrust Class Actions-Twenty Years Under Rule 23, 1986, The State Court Class Action-A Potpourri of Difference in the ABA Forum, Summer 1985; contbg. author: Multiparty Bargaining in Class Actions, Attorneys' Practice Guide to Negotiations, 2d edit., 1996; bd. editors Ill. Bar Antitrust Newsletter, 1969-73; topic and articles editor Jour. Forum Com. on Franchising, 1981-86. Atty. Office Gen. Counsel Honors Program, U.S. Dept. HEW, 1966-68; chmn. Ill. Legis. Com. Antitrust Section Ill. Bar., 1970-71; Topic and Articles Editor, Jour. Forum Com. on Franchising, 1981-86. Mem. ABA (co-chair securities law subcom., litigation sect. 1987, mem. com. on regulation of futures and derivative instruments, mem. forum com. on franchising), ATLA, Fed. Bar Coun. (mem. com. on second cir cts. 1983-86), N.Y. State Bar Assn. (mem. class action com.), N.Y. State Trial Lawyers Assn., Ill. Bar Assn. (chmn. antitrust sect. Ill. legis. com. 1970-71), Nat. Assn. for Pub. Interest Law Fellowships (mem. exec. com., mem. selection com., mem. investment and fin. com., bd. dirs. 1991-97, v.p. 1994-97, mem. budget com. 1998—, nomination and election coms. 1998—, bd. of dirs. 1997—), Nat. Assn. Pub. Interest Law (mem. fin. and investment com. 1998—, nomination and election com. 1998-99, chair, nominations and elections com., 1999—, bd. dirs. 1997—), Washington, Navy League of U.S. (N.Y. coun., mem. jour. com. 1995-97), Carlton Club, Plandome Country Club. Antitrust, Federal civil litigation, Securities. Office: Meredith Cohen Greenfogel & Skirnick 63 Wall St New York NY 10005-3001

**SKIVER, STEPHEN ALLEN,** lawyer, physician; b. Toledo, Ohio, Feb. 14, 1949; s. Arnold Leroy and Elizabeth Jane (Boyer) S.; m. Catherine Ann Reynolds, June 26, 1971; children: Tonia, Justin, Ryan, Laura, Elyssa. BS, Ohio U., 1971; MD, Med. Coll. Ohio, 1974; JD, U. Toledo, 1988. Bar: Ohio 1989, U.S. Dist. Ct. (no. dist.) Ohio 1991; Cert. Am. Bd. Internal Medicine. Physician Maumee, Ohio, 1977-89; clin. asst. prof. medicine Med. Coll. Ohio, Toledo, 1983-89; physician Toledo, 1989—; assoc. Jacobson, Maynard, Tuschman, Toledo, 1990-97; ptnr. Buckley, King & Bluso, Toledo, 1997—adr. Personal injury. Home: 30025 E River Rd Perrysburg OH 43551-3430 Office: Buckley King & Bluso 420 Madison Ave Ste 1100 Toledo OH 43604-1209

**SKLAMBERG, ROBERT JOSEPH,** lawyer; b. Chgo., June 7, 1956; s. Leonard Richard and Mona Nadine (Olswang) S. BS, U. Ill., 1978; JD, Ill. Inst. Tech., 1981. Bar: Ill. 1981, U.S. Dist. Ct. (no. dist.) Ill. 1981. Assoc. atty. Law Offices of Jon W. Knudson, Chgo., 1981-83; asst. atty. gen. Ill. Atty. Gen.'s Office, Chgo., 1983-87, div. chief, 1987—; lectr. in field of ct. of claims, practice and procedure, law enforcement officers and firemen compensation act, 1991—. Campaign worker Hartigan for Gov., Chgo., 1990;

precinct capt. Niles Twp. Reg. Dem. Orgn., Skokie, Ill., 1979-84; former mem. Chgo. Coun. Fgn. Rels. Mem. Phi Eta Sigma. Avocations: politics, history, government, documentaries, travel. Home: 1660 N La Salle Dr Apt 1911 Chicago IL 60614-6016 Office: Ill Atty Gens Office 100 W Randolph St Chicago IL 60601-3218

**SKLAR, STANLEY LAWRENCE,** judge; b. N.Y.C., Jan. 25, 1932; s. Julius and Rebecca (Skerker) S.; m. Margot Algase, Dec. 10, 1972; 1 child, Deborah. BA, Columbia U., 1953, LLB, 1956. Bar: N.Y. 1957, U.S. Supreme Ct. 1967. Assoc. Zipser & Levitt, N.Y.C., 1957-60, Wolf, Popper, Ross, Wolf & Jones, N.Y.C., 1960-64; assoc. Rubin, Baum, Levin, Constant & Friedman, N.Y.C., 1964-67, ptnr., 1967-76; judge N.Y.C. Civil Ct., 1977-78; acting justice N.Y. State Supreme Ct., N.Y.C., 1978-85, justice, 1986—. Author: Shoplifting: What You Need to Know About the Law, 1982; contbr. articles to profl. jours. Mem. Assn. of Bar of City of N.Y., Am. Judicature Soc., Inst. Jud. Adminstrn., Scribes. Office: NY Supreme Ct 60 Centre St Fl 1 New York NY 10007-1488

**SKLAR, WILFORD NATHANIELD,** lawyer, real estate broker; b. Salt Lake City, Dec. 13, 1916; s. Benjamin B. Sklar and Blanche Blau; married Jan. 16, 1945; children: Beth-Lynn, Teri Helene. BBA, U. Pitts., 1942; JD, Southwestern Sch. Law, 1960. Bar: Calif. 1960, U.S. Dist. Ct. Calif. 1962, U.S. Supreme Ct. 1965. Pvt. practice Riverside, Calif., 1960—. Co-pub. worker's compensation books. Mem. Riverside Family Svcs., 1965-85. Sgt. USAF, 1942-46. Mem. B'nai B'rith (Akiba dist. award 1970, 74). Democrat. Jewish-Hebrew. Avocations: golf, coin collecting, real estate investments. Personal injury, Workers' compensation, Family and matrimonial. Home and Office: 5904 Copperfield Ave Riverside CA 92506-4510

**SKLAR, WILLIAM PAUL,** lawyer, educator; b. N.Y.C., Sept. 10, 1958; s. Morris and Helen (Meyers) S.; m. Lori Ann Hodges, Jan. 5, 1985. BBA magna cum laude, U. Miami, 1977, JD, 1980. Bar: Fla. 1980, N.Y. 1986, U.S. Dist. Ct. (so. dist.) Fla. 1981, U.S. Tax Ct. 1980, U.S. Ct. Appeals (5th cir.) 1980, U.S. Ct. Appeals (11th cir.) 1981. Assoc. Wood, Cobb, Murphy & Craig, West Palm Beach, Fla., 1980-85; ptnr. Wood, Cobb, Murphy & Craig, West Palm Beach, 1985-88; ptnr. Foley & Lardner, West Palm Beach, 1989—, ptnr.-in-charge, 1995—; chmn. Fla. Real Estate Dept., 1991—; adj. prof. law Sch. Law, U. Miami, Coral Gables, Fla., 1980—; dir. Inst. on Condo. and Cluster Devels., Inst. on Real Property Law, 1986—. Co-author: Cases and Materials in Condominium and Cluster Developments, 1980; author, co-editor; Florida Real Estate Transactions, 1983; contbr. articles to profl. jours. Atty. adv. bd. Morse Geriatric Ctr., West Palm Beach, 1984-88. Mem. ABA (chmn. subcom. on condominium and coop. housing sect. gen. practice 1983-88), Fla. Bar (com. condominium and planned devels. 1980—, bd. cert. real estate lawyer 1994, exec. coun. mem. real property, probate and trust law sect. 1997—), Palm Beach County Bar Assn., Coll. Cmty. Assn. Lawyers, Phi Delta Phi, Pi Sigma Alpha. Republican. Avocations: travel, tennis. Real property, Land use and zoning (including planning). Home: 7238 Montrico Dr Boca Raton FL 33433-6930 Office: Foley & Lardner East Tower 777 S Flagler Dr Ste 202 West Palm Beach FL 33401-6161

**SKOGLUND, MARILYN,** state supreme court justice; b. Chgo., Aug. 28, 1946. BA, So. Ill. U., 1971; clerkship, 1977-81. Bar: Vt. 1981, U.S. Dist. Ct. Vt. 1981, U.S. Ct. Appeals (2d cir.) 1983. Asst. atty. gen. Civil Law Divsn., 1981-88, chief, 1988-93; chief Pub. Protection Divsn., 1993-94; judge Vt. Dist. Ct., 1994-97; assoc. justice Vt. Supreme Ct., 1997—. Office: Vt Supreme Ct 109 State St Montpelier VT 05609-0001*

**SKOK, PAUL JOSEPH,** lawyer; b. Tarrytown, N.Y., Nov. 3, 1947; s. Paul Joseph Skok and Anna S. (Ruscigno) Barlow. BS, Purdue U., 1970; MA, Ball State U., 1974; JD, U. Denver, 1984. Bar: Colo. 1985, U.S. Dist. Ct. Colo. 1985. Assoc. Skaalerud and Price, Denver, 1985-86, Law Office Paul Joseph Skok, Denver, 1986—; lectr. in law U. Denver, 1990. Author: Trial Attorney's Guide to Insurance Coverage and Bad Faith, 1994, supplement edit., 1995, 96. Bd. dirs. Higher Ground Youth Challenge, 1999—. Mem. ABA, Colo. Bar Assn., Denver Bar Assn., Assn. Trial Lawyers Am., Colo. Trial Lawyers Assn., Delta Tau Delta (chpt. advisor, alumni supr. U. Colo. 1977-83, 88). Roman Catholic. Avocations: snow skiing, bicycling, swimming, water skiing, hiking. Personal injury, Insurance, Criminal. Home: 7660 Knox Ct Westminster CO 80030-4540 Office: 303 E 17th Ave Ste 700 Denver CO 80203-1260

**SKOKOS, THEODORE C., JR.,** lawyer; b. Fayetteville, Ark., May 9, 1968; s. Theodore Campbell and Pamela (Fain) S. BSBA, U. Ark., Fayetteville, 1990; JD, U. Ark., Little Rock, 1995; LLM, U. Denver, 1996. Bar: Ark. 1995, Colo. 1997, U.S. Dist. Ct. Ark. 1996, U.S. Tax Ct. 1996. Assoc. atty. Jewell & Moser, P.A., Little Rock, 1996-98; prin. Skokos & Assocs., P.A., Little Rock, 1999—. Taxation, general, Estate planning, General corporate. Office: Skokos & Assocs PA 425 W Capitol Ave Ste 3200 Little Rock AR 72201-3469

**SKOLER, DANIEL LAWRENCE,** lawyer, judge, educator; b. Newark, Jan. 15, 1929; s. Arthur Emil and Marian June (Bardack) S.; m. Shirley Weiss, Sept. 20, 1953; children—Glen David, Michael James, Deborah. Student Rutgers U., 1945-47, U. Chgo., 1947-49; J.D. cum laude, Harvard U., 1952. Bar: N.Y. 1953, Ill. 1963, D.C. 1968. Assoc. Willkie Farr Gallagher Walton & Fitzgibbon, N.Y.C., 1955-59; staff atty. U.S. Industries, Inc., N.Y.C., 1959-61; asst. dir. Am. Judicature Soc., Chgo., 1961-62; exec. dir. Nat. Council Juvenile Ct. Judges, Chgo., 1962-65; dir. Commn. on Correctional Facilities and Services ABA, 1971-75, Commn. on Mentally Disabled, Washington, 1976-77; dir. public service activities ABA, 1977-80; dir. office law enforcement assistance Law Enforcement Assistance Adminstrn., Dept. Justice, Washington, 1965-71; vis. fellow Nat. Inst. Law Enforcement and Criminal Justice, 1975-76; chmn. Trademark and Appeal Bd., Dept. Commerce, Washington, 1982-84, dep. asst. commr. for Trademarks, 1984-86 ; dep. assoc. commr. Hearings and Appeals, Social Security Adminstrn., Washington, 1980-82; adj. prof. Georgetown U., George Washington U., American U., D.C. Law Sch., Washington & Lee Law Sch.; mem. Commn. on Accreditation for Corrections, 1974-78, chmn., 1976-77. Dir. Edn. and training Fed. Jud. Ctr., 1986-91. Fellow Nat. Acad. Public Adminstrn.; mem. ABA Commn. on Legal Problems of the Elderly, 1981-86; assoc. commr. hearings and appeals Social Security Adminstrn., 1991-95; bd. dir. ABA sect. Individual Rights & Responsibilities and Govt. Lawyers Divsn.; bd. dir. Nat. Ctr. on Children and the Law; mem. U.S. Adminstrv. Conf. Author: Organizing the Non System: Government Structuring of Criminal Justice Services, 1977. Home: 7036 Buxton Ter Bethesda MD 20817-4404 Office: Social Security Administration 5107 Leesburg Pike Ste 200 Falls Church VA 22041-3255

**SKOLLER, RONALD AARON,** corporate lawyer; b. Bklyn., Aug. 29, 1944; s. Samuel and Sylvia Skoller; m. Susan A. Skoller; children: Dara, Maggie. BA, L.I. U., 1966; JD, U. Tulsa, 1968. Bar: Okla. 1969, U.S. Dist. Ct. (no. dist.) Okla., U.S. Ct. Appeals (10th cir.), U.S. Supreme Ct. Pvt. practice Tulsa, Okla., 1968-76; corp. atty. Cities Svc. Co., Tulsa, Okla., 1981-82; corp. atty.-litigation Occidental Oil & Gas Corp., Tulsa, Okla., 1982-96; of counsel Gable & Gotwals, Tulsa, Okla., 1996-98; gen. counsel litigation TransTexas Gas Corp., Houston, 1998—; dir. EnergyOne Fed. Credit Union, Tulsa, 1984-97. Mem. ABA, Okla. Bar Assn., Tulsa County Bar Assn. Avocation: bicycling. General civil litigation, Antitrust, Natural resources. Office: TransTexas Gas Corp 1300 N Sam Houston Pkwy E Houston TX 77032-2932

**SKOLNICK, MALCOLM HARRIS,** biophysics researcher, educator, lawyer, mediator; b. Salt Lake City, Aug. 11, 1935; s. Max Cantor and Charlotte Sylvia (Letman) S.; m. Lois Marlene Ray, Sept. 1, 1959; children: Michael, David, Sara, Jonathan. BS in Physics (with honors), U. Utah, 1956; MS in Physics, Cornell U., 1959, PhD in Theoretical Nuclear Physics, 1963; JD, U. Houston, 1986. Diplomate Am. Bd. Forensic Examiners. Staff scientist Elem. Sci. Study, Watertown, Mass., 1962-63; mem. Inst. for Advanced Study, Princeton, N.J., 1963-64; instr. Physics Dept. MIT, Cambridge, Mass., 1964-65; staff scientist dir. Edn. Devel. Ctr., Watertown, 1965-67; assoc. prof. physics Physics Dept. SUNY, Stony Brook, 1967-70; assoc. prof. dir. comm. Health Sci. Ctr. SUNY, Stony Brook, 1968-71; prof. biophysics grad. sch. biomed. sci. U. Tex. Health Scis. Ctr., Houston, 1971-94, prof. biomedical comm., 1971-83, prof. health svcs. rsch., 1988-95, dir. neurophysiology rsch. ctr., 1985-91; dir office tec. mgmt. U. Tex. Health Sci. Ctr., Houston, 1991-96; prof. tech. and health law U. Tex. Sch. Pub. Health, Houston, 1994—; of counsel Wishner & Assocs., Houston; pres., CEO Cryogenic Solutions, Inc., 1999—; chmn. health care tech. study sect. Nat. Ctr. Health Svcs. Rsch. HHS, 1975-79; editorial assoc. Cts., Health Sci. and Law, Washington, 1989-93; bd. dirs. Biodyne, Inc.; chmn. sci. adv. bd. Cryogenic Solutions Inc.; sci. adv. bd. S.W. Health Tech. Found. Patentee in field; contbr. numerous articles to profl. jours. With USNR, 1953-61, hon. discharge. Recipient Silver Beaver award Boy Scouts Am., 1978; Ford Found scholar, U. Utah, 1952; rsch. grantee Nat. Inst. for Drug Abuse, Brown Fund, Houston Endowment. Mem. ABA, APHA, Soc. Neurosci., Licensing Exec. Soc., Am. Intellectual Property Law Assn., Tex. Tech. Transfer Assn. (bd. dirs.), Houston Intellectual Property Law Assn., Houston Soc. Engring. in Medicine and Biology (bd. dirs.), Am. Bd. Forensic Examiners, Soc. Accident Reconstrn., Tex. Empowerment Network (pres., bd. dirs.), Soc. Automotive Engrs., Soc. Bioengring., Tex. Assn. Accid Reconstruction Specialists, Sigma Xi. Office: Sch of Pub Health Rm 342W PO Box 20186 Houston TX 77225-0186

**SKOLNICK, S. HAROLD,** lawyer; b. Woonsocket, R.I., June 17, 1915; s. David and Elsie (Silberman) S.; m. Shirley Marshall. A.B. cum laude, Amherst Coll., 1936; J.D., Boston U., 1940. Bar: R.I. 1940, D.C. 1947, U.S. Supreme Ct. 1946, Fla. 1952, U.S. Dist. Ct. (so. dist.) Fla. 1953, U.S. Ct. Appeals (5th cir.) 1960, U.S. Ct. Appeals (11th cir.) 1981. Atty., Dept. War, Washington, 1940-42; asst. gen. counsel, asst. chief legal dept. Office Chief Ordnance, Dept. Army, Washington, 1947-50; assoc. Francis I. McCanna, Providence, 1951-52; ptnr. French & Skolnick, Miami, 1953-60; sole practice, Miami, 1961—. Served to lt. col. U.S. Army, 1942-47. Mem. ABA, R.I. Bar Assn., D.C. Bar Assn., Dade County Bar Assn., Am. Judicature Soc., Nat. Def. Indsl. Assn. (life), Estate Planning Coun. of Greater Miami, Mason, Shriners. Insurance, Probate. Home and Office: 6521 SW 122d St Miami FL 33156-5550

**SKOLROOD, ROBERT KENNETH,** lawyer; b. Stockton, Ill., May 17, 1928; s. Myron Clifford and Lola Mae (Lincicum) S.; m. Marilyn Jean Riegel, June 18, 1955; children: Cynthia, Mark, Kent, Richard. BA, Ohio Wesleyan U., 1952; JD, U. Chgo., 1957. Bar: Ill. 1957, Okla. 1981, D.C. 1987, U.S. Supreme Ct., 1982, Va. 1985, U.S. Dist. Ct. (no. dist.) Ill. 1959, U.S. Ct. Appeals (7th cir.) 1970, U.S. Dist. Ct. (no. dist.) Okla. 1982, U.S. Dist. Ct. Nebr. 1985, U.S. Dist. Ct. (so. dist.) Ala. 1986, U.S. Dist. Ct. (so. dist.) N.Y. 1986, U.S. Dist. Ct. (ea. and we. dists.) Va. 1986, U.S. Ct. Appeals (2nd, 4th, 6th, 7th, 8th 10th and 11th cirs.) 1986, U.S. Dist. Ct. D.C. 1987, Ptnr. Reno, Zahm, Folgate, Skolrood, Lindberg & Powell, Rockford, Ill., 1957-80; prof. O.W. Coburn Sch. Law, Oral Roberts U., Tulsa, 1980-81, gen. counsel, 1980-84; exec. dir., gen. counsel Nat. Legal Found., Virginia Beach, Va., 1984-95; with Law Firm of Scogins & Skolrood, Roanoke, Va., 1995—. Contbr. articles to legal jours.; lead counsel on several major constitutional cases. Pres., John Ericsson Rep. Club, 1964; trustee No. Ill. conf. United Meth. Ch., 1957-74, chmn., 1972-74; pres. Ill. Home and Aid Soc.; mem. Evangelical Free Ch. Served with U.S. Army, 1952-54, Korea. Fellow Am. Coll. Trial Lawyers; mem. Ill. Bar Assn., Okla. Bar Assn., Va., Bar Assn., Dist of Columbia Bar Assn, ATLA, Va. Trial Lawyers Assn., Tex. Trial Lawyers Assn., Ill. Trial Lawyers Assn., Okla. Trial Lawyers Assn., Christian Educators Assn. Internat. (bd. reference), Kappa Delta Pi, Pi Sigma Kappa. Civil rights, Federal civil litigation, Constitutional. Home: 5217 Dresden Ln Roanoke VA 24012-8576 Office: Scogins & Skolrood 3243 Electric Rd Ste 1A Roanoke VA 24018-6440

**SKONEY, LESA HARTLEY,** lawyer, accountant; b. Lafayette, Ind., Apr. 25, 1960; d. Charles Foster and Cornelia Ann (Moman) H. BS, U. S.C., 1982; JD, U. Pitts., 1985. Bar: Pa. 1985, Tenn. 1988; CPA, Tenn. Tax assoc. Price Waterhouse Co., Nashville, 1985-87; assoc. John W. Nelley, Jr., P.C., Nashville, 1987-91; jr. ptnr. Tune, Entrekin & White, P.C., Nashville, 1991—. Bd. dirs. Nashville Pro Bono, Inc. (treas. 1999—). Fellow Nahville Bar Found.; mem. AICPA, Tenn. Bar Assn., Nashville Bar Assn. (treas. 1997). Taxation, general, Estate planning, Probate. Office: Tune Entrekin & White First Am Ctr 315 Deaderick St Fl 21 Nashville TN 37238-0002

**SKOPIL, OTTO RICHARD, JR.,** federal judge; b. Portland, Oreg., June 3, 1919; s. Otto Richard and Freda Martha (Boetticher) S.; m. Janet Rae Lundy, July 27, 1956; children: Otto Richard III, Casey Robert, Shannon Ida, Molly Jo. BA in Econs., Willamette U., 1941, LLB, 1946, LLD (hon.), 1983. Bar: Oreg. 1946, IRS, U.S. Treasury Dept., U.S. Dist. Ct. Oreg., U.S. Ct. Appeals (9th cir.), U.S. Supreme Ct. 1946. Assoc. Skopil & Skopil, 1946-51; ptnr. Williams, Skopil, Miller & Beck (and predecessors), Salem, Oreg., 1951-72; judge U.S. Dist. Ct., Portland, 1972-79; chief judge U.S. Dist. Ct., 1976-79; judge U.S. Ct. Appeals (9th cir.), Portland, 1979—, now sr. judge; chmn. com. adminstrn. of fed. magistrate sys. U.S. Jud. Conf., 1980-86; co-founder Oreg. chpt. Am. Leadership Forum; chmn. 9th cir. Jud. Coun. Magistrates Adv. Com., 1988-91; chmn. U.S. Jud. Conf. Long Range Planning Com., 1990-95. Hi-Y adviser Salem YMCA, 1951-52; appeal agt. SSS, Marion County (Oreg.) Draft Bd., 1953-66; master of ceremonies 1st Gov.'s Prayer Breakfast for State Oreg., 1959; mem. citizens adv. com., City of Salem, 1970-71; chmn. Gov.'s Com. on Staffing Mental Instns., 1969-70; pres., bd. dirs. Marion County Tb and Health Assn., 1958-61; bd. dirs. Willamette Valley Camp Fire Girls, 1946-56, Internat. Christian Leadership, 1959, Fed. Jud. Ctr., 1979; trustee Willamette U., 1969-71; elder Mt. Park Ch., 1979-81. Served to lt. USNR, 1942-46. Recipient Oreg. Legal Citizen of Yr. award, 1986, Disting. Alumni award Willamette U. Sch. Law, 1988. Mem. ABA, Oreg. Bar Assn. (bd. govs.), Marion County Bar Assn., Am. Judicature Soc., Oreg. Assn. Def. Counsel (dir.), Def. Research Inst., Assn. Ins. Attys. U.S. and Can. (Oreg. rep. 1970), Internat. Soc. Barristers, Prayer Breakfast Movement (fellowship council). Clubs: Salem, Exchange (pres. 1947), Illahe Hills Country (pres., dir. 1964-67). Office: Senior Circuit Judge 827 US Courthouse 1000 SW 3rd Ave Portland OR 97204-2930

**SKORA, SUSAN SUNDMAN,** lawyer; b. Chgo., Jan. 5, 1947; d. Gordon Manley and Julia Walker (Firebaugh) Sundman; m. Alan Patrick Skora, May 1, 1977. AB, U. Ill., Chgo., 1970; JD, Ill. Inst. Tech., 1980. Bar: Ill. 1980, Mich. 1983, U.S. Dist. Ct. (we. dist.) Mich. 1983. Dir. Chgo. programs U. Ill. Found., 1973-79; asst. dir. bus. affairs U. of Ill., Chgo., 1980-81, exec. asst., exec. v.p., 1981-83; 2d v.p. Nat. Bank of Detroit, Grand Rapids, 1983-88; v.p., dept. head bus. devel. NBD Grand Rapids Bank, 1985-88; v.p., trust div. head, mem. exec. com. First Bank, Davenport, Iowa, 1988-91; v.p., trust Firstar Bank, Davenport, Iowa, 1992-97; asst. prof. dept. bus. adminstrn. Black Hawk Coll., 1992; v.p. trust Wells Fargo Bank, Davenport, 1998—. Author: Cuneen Linguist, 1975. Mem. Scott County Osteo. Physicians and Surgeons Aux., 1988-99, treas., 1989, 91-99, v.p., 1990; v.p. West Mich. U. Ill. Alumni Club, 1983-86; mem. Quad City Osteo. Found., 1988—, bequest and fin. com. mem., 1988-95, 97—, bd. dirs., 1992-95; lead gift com. mem. Davenport Mus. Art, 1988, endowment com. mem. St. Ambrose U., 1988, Quad City Arts, 1992-94; devel. and fin. com. CASI, 1998, bd. govs., 1992—, chair trustees com., 1994-98; bd. dirs. Cmty. Found. of the Great River Bend, 1992—, chair trustee com., 1996-98, chair major gifts com., 1998, 2d v.p. 1998; bd. dirs. Quad City Planned Giving Coun., 1998—; mem. capital campaign com. Luth. Social Svcs., 1994; mem. Quad City Estate Planning Coun., 1988—. Mem. Bank Adminstrn. Inst. , U. Ill. Alumni Assn. (various offices to sec. 1989-91, exec. c om. bd. dirs. 1985-91, nominating com. 1991), Quad City Employee Benefits Group (treas. 1993-95, 96—), Davenport C. of C. (mem. com. 1996-97), Davenport Country Club (fin. com. 1996—), Exec. Women's Golf League, Classic Ladies Investment Club, Pi Alpha Tau. Avocations: gardening, reading, golf, auctions. Banking, Estate planning, Probate. Home: 1139 Brookview Dr De Witt IA 52742-9290 Office: Wells Fargo Bank 203 W 3rd St Davenport IA 52801-1901

**SKOTYNSKY, WALTER JOHN,** lawyer; b. Youngstown, Ohio, June 28, 1946; s. Walter and Kathleen Marie (Adams) S.; m. Sandra Lee Wiebeck, July 17, 1971; 1 child, Nicholas James. BSME, U. Mich., 1971; JD, U. Toledo, 1976. Bar: Ohio 1976, Mich. 1979. Engr. Andersons, Toledo, 1965-68, Libbey-Owens-Ford, Toledo, 1971-73; sole practice Toledo, 1976—; instr. real estate law U. Toledo, U. Mich., Ann Arbor, Bowling Green (Ohio) State U., Davis Bus. Coll., Toledo, 1976-80. Mem. Mich. Bar Assn., Ohio Bar Assn., Toledo Bar Assn., Lucas County Bar Assn.. U. Mich. ALumni Toledo (pres. 1986—). Republican. Roman Catholic. Clubs: U. Mich. Alumni Toledo (pres. 1986—); Ukranian/Am. Citizens (Toledo). Family and matrimonial, General practice, Real property. Home: 4830 Oakridge Dr Toledo OH 43623-4010 Office: 1018 Adams St Toledo OH 43624-1507

**SKRETNY, WILLIAM MARION,** federal judge; b. Buffalo, Mar. 8, 1945; s. William S. and Rita E. (Wyroski) S.; m. Carol Ann Mergenhagen; children: Brian Alexander, Brooke Ann, Nina Clare. AB, Canisius Coll., 1966; JD, Howard U., 1969; LLM, Northwestern U., 1972. Bar: Ill. 1969, U.S. Dist. Ct. (no. dist) Ill. 1969, N.Y. 1972, U.S. Ct. Appeals (7th cir.) 1972, U.S. Dist. Ct. (we. dist.) N.Y. 1973, U.S. Ct. Appeals (2d cir.) 1976, U.S. Supreme Ct. 1980. Asst. U.S. atty. Office of U.S. Atty. No. Dist. Ill., Chgo., 1971-73; asst. U.S. atty. Office of U.S. Atty. We. Dist. N.Y., Buffalo, 1973-81, 1st asst., 1975-81; gen. ptnr. Duke, Holzman, Yaeger & Radlin, Buffalo, 1981-83; 1st dep. dist. atty. Office Dist. Atty Erie County, Buffalo, 1983-88; with Gross, Shuman, Brizdle and Gillfillan, PC, Buffalo, 1988, Cox, Barrell, Buffalo, 1989-90; judge U.S. Dist. Ct. (we. dist.) N.Y., Buffalo, 1990—; task force atty. tng. Office U.S. Atty Gen., 1978; spl. counsel U.S. Atty Gen.'s Advocacy Inst., 1979; staff atty. Office Spl. Prosecutor, Dept. Justice, Washington, 1980; faculty advisor Nat. Coll. D.A.s, Houston, 1987; jud. conf. com. on security, space and facilities, 1994. Bd. dirs. Sudden Infant Death Found. We. N.Y., 1979, Cerebral Palsy Foun. We. N.Y., 1985; chmn. major corps. divsn. Studio Arena Theatre, Buffalo, 1982; chmn. Polish Culture, Canisius Coll., 1985, trustee, 1989; pres. Canisius Coll. Alumni Assn., 1989; regional chmn. Cath. Charities Appeal, 1986-87. Named Citizen of Yr. Am Pol Eagle Newspaper, 1977, 90, Disting. Grad. Nat. Cath. Edn. Assn. Dept. Elem. Sch., 1991, Disting. Alumnus Canisius Coll., 1993; named to Hall of Fame Law Sch. Northwestern U. Mem. ABA, Fed. Bar Assn., Fed. Judges Assn., Western N.Y. Trial Lawyers Assn., Erie County Bar Assn., Chgo. Bar Assn., Thomas More Legal Soc. (pres. 1980), Di Gamma, Phi Alpha Delta. Republican. Roman Catholic. Office: US District Court 68 Court St Rm 507 Buffalo NY 14202-3405

**SKRINE, BRUCE E.,** lawyer. Sr. v.p., gen. counsel, sec. John Hancock Mutual Life Ins. Co., Boston, 1996-97, sr. v.p., dep. gen. counsel, 1997—. Office: John Hancock Mut Life Insur Co PO Box 111 Boston MA 02117-0111

**SKROPITS, AMY ELIZABETH,** lawyer; b. Mansfield, Ohio, Dec. 2, 1969; d. Glen Artis and Elizabeth May McLaughlin; m. Robert John Skropits, Aug. 17, 1996. AA, U. Toledo Cmty. and Tech Coll., 1990; BS, U. Toledo, 1992, JD, 1995. Bar: Ohio 1996. Assoc. Kennedy, Purdy, Hoeffel & Gernert, Bucyrus, Ohio, 1996-98, Starkey & Stoll, Ltd., Bucyrus, 1998—. Mem. Ohio State Bar Assn., Crawford County Bar Assn., Altrusa Internat. Real property, Juvenile, General practice. Office: Starkey & Stoll Ltd 114 S Walnut St Bucyrus OH 44820-2324

**SKULINA, THOMAS RAYMOND,** lawyer; b. Cleve., Sept. 14, 1933; s. John J. and Mary B. (Vesely) S. AB, John Carroll U., 1955; JD, Case Western Res. U., 1959, LLM, 1962. Bar: Ohio 1959, U.S. Supreme Ct. 1964, ICC 1965. Ptnr. Skulina & Stringer, Cleve., 1967-72, Riemer Oberdank & Skulina, Cleve., 1978-81, Skulina, Fillo, Walters & Negrelli, 1981-86, Skulina & McKeon, Cleve., 1986-90, Skulina & Hill, Cleve., 1990-97; atty. Penn Ctrl. Transp. Co., Cleve., 1960-65, asst. gen. atty., 1965-78, trial counsel, 1965-76; with Consol. Rail Corp., 1976-78; pvt. practice Cleve., 1997—; tchr. comml. law Practicing Law Inst., N.Y.C., 1970; practicing labor arbitrator Fed. Mediation and Conciliation Svc., 1990—; arbitrator Mcpl. Securities Rulemaking Bd., 1994-98, N.Y. Stock Exch., 1995—, NASD, 1996—; mediator NASD, 1997—, AAA Comml., 1997—; mediator vol. panel EEOC, 1997-99, contract panel, 1999—. Contbr. articles to legal jours. Income tax and fed. fund coord. City of Warrensville Heights, Ohio, 1970-77; spl. counsel City of North Olmstead, Ohio, 1971-75, spl. counsel to Ohio Atty. Gen., 1983-93, Cleve. Charter Rev. Commn., 1988; pres. Civil Svc. Commn., Cleve., 1977-86, referee, 1986—; fact-finder State Employees Rels. Bd., Ohio, 1986—. With U.S. Army, 1959. Mem. ABA (R.R. and motor carrier com. 1988-96, jr. chmn. 1989-96, alt. dispute resolution com. 1998—), FBA, Soc. Profls. in Dispute Resolution, Cleve. Bar Assn. (grievance com. 1987-93, 1998— chmn. 1997-98, trustee 1993-96, ADR com. 1997—), Ohio Bar Assn. (bd. govs. litigation sect. 1986-98, negligence law com. 1989-96, ethics and profl. responsibility com. 1990—, alt. dispute resolution com. 1996—), Am. Arbitration Assn. (practicing labor arbitrator 1987—), Nat. Assn. R.R. Trial Counsel, Internat. Assn. Law and Sci., Pub. Sector Labor Rels. Assn., Internat. Indsl. Rels. Rsch. Assn. Democrat. Roman Catholic. Federal civil litigation, Alternative dispute resolution, Transportation. Home: 3162 W 165th St Cleveland OH 44111-1016 Office: 24803 Detroit Rd Cleveland OH 44145-2547

**SKWARYK, ROBERT FRANCIS,** judge; b. Erie, Pa., Nov. 4, 1948; s. Frank and Gloria (Hinkle) S. BS, Pa. State U., 1973; JD, U. Kans., 1977. Bar: Pa. 1977, U.S. Dist. Ct. (we. dist.) Pa. 1977. Legal intern legal svcs. Clallum and Jefferson Counties, Port Angeles, Wash., 1977; assoc. Galbo, McNelis, Restifo & Held, Erie, 1977-80; instr. bus. law Behrend Coll. Pa. State U., Erie, 1978-80; appeals referee Commonwealth of Pa., Harrisburg and Pottsville, 1981, Pitts. and Erie, 1985-88; adminstrv. law judge Commonwealth of Pa., Allentown, 1988-96, Pitts., 1996—. Contbg. author ct. opinions Pa. Liquor Control Bd., 1988—. Mem. Behrend Coll. Soccer Alumni Assn., Erie, 1974-90. Sgt. USMC, 1967-70, lt. (j.g.) USN, 1981-85, lt. USNR, 1986-92, Saudi Arabia, lt. comdr. USNR, 1992-98, comdr., 1998—. Mem. ABA, Pa. State Bar Assn., Erie County Bar Assn., Pa. Conf. Adminstrv. Law Judges, First Marine Air Wing Assn., Pa. State U. Alumni Assn. Avocations: soccer, flying, orienteering. Home: 833 Greentree Rd Apt 2-6 Pittsburgh PA 15220-3418 Office: Commonwealth Pa Office Adminstrv Law Judge 875 Greentree Rd Pittsburgh PA 15220-3508

**SLABACH, STEPHEN HALL,** lawyer; b. Oklahoma City, Nov. 15, 1934; s. Carl Edward and Alvine A. (Woellner) S.; m. Elizabeth Havard Cartwright, Feb. 15, 1958; children: Elizabeth Slabach Schmit, Stephen Edward, William Cartwright. BSME, Northwestern U., 1957; postgrad. George Washington U. Sch. Law, 1957-59; LLB, Stanford U., 1961. Bar: Calif. 1962, U.S. Dist. Ct. (no. dist.) Calif. 1962, U.S. Ct. Appeals (9th cir.) 1973, U.S. Supreme Ct. 1976. Law clk. to judge Calif. First Dist. Ct. Appeal, San Francisco, 1961-62; assoc. Cooley, Crowley, Gather, Godward, Castro & Huddleson, San Francisco, 1962-65; assoc. Cushing, Cullinan, Hancock & Rothert, San Francisco, 1965-73, ptnr., 1973-75; sole practice, Burlingame, Calif., 1975-88, San Mateo, 88—; Legal aid vol. San Mateo County; trustee San Mateo County Law Libr. Com., 1993—, v.p. 1998—; pres. Pacific Locomotive Assn., 1988-90, gen. counsel, 1980—; bd. dirs. Notre Dame H.S., Belmont, Calif., 1976-84, pres., bd., 1981-82. Mem. State Bar Calif., ABA, Am. Judicature Soc., Kiwanis (Burlingame). Republican. Episcopalian. General civil litigation, Estate planning, General corporate. Office: 520 S El Camino Real Ste 700 San Mateo CA 94402-1720

**SLACK, MARK ROBERT,** lawyer; b. Amherst, Ohio, Aug. 17, 1957; s. Robert James and Lois Jean (Basl) S.; m. Diana Joan Thomas, Sept. 23, 1994. BA in Pub. Adminstrn. & History, Ohio No. U., 1979, JD, 1982. Bar: Ohio 1983, U.S. Dist. Ct. (no. dist.) Ohio 1983, U.S. Tax Ct. 1984, U.S. Ct. Appeals (6th cir.) 1984, U.S. Supreme Ct. 1986; cert. nat. and state Better Bus. Bur. arbitrator. Social worker Columbiana County Welfare Dept., Lisbon, Ohio, 1979-80; criminal intern Allen County Welfare Dept., Lima, Ohio, 1982; social security intern Blackhoff Area Legal Svcs., Lima, 1982; mem. staff for docket indexing sys. juvenile divsn. Columbiana County Common Pleas, 1983; asst. pub. defender Columbiana County Pub. Defender's Office, Lisbon, 1984; pvt. practice law Salem, Ohio, 1983—; regional counsel Northeast Ohio Legal Svcs., Lisbon, 1984—, Youngstown, Ohio, 1988-89. Active Columbiana County Big Bros., 1985-86. Recipient 1st place cooking award Salem News, 1986; named Outstanding Young Men Am., 1980-89, 92, 96. Mem. ABA, Ohio Bar Assn., Columbiana County Bar Assn. (grievence com. 1996-97, Recognition for Pro Bono Svc. 1995, 96, 97), Mahoning Valley Astron. Soc. (legal advisor 1985—), Salem Hist. Soc. (v.p., trustee, legal advisor 1985-87, trustee 1997—), Youngstown Outspoken Wheelman (legal advisor 1985-93, chmn. presdl. sports award 1986-93, Outstanding Svc. award 1986-93), Mayflower Descendents of Am., Descendents of the Soldiers of Valley Forge, Phi Alpha Delta. Avocations: long distance bicycling, astronomy, regional history, cooking, geneaology. Family and matrimonial, General practice, Criminal. Home: 370 W 9th St Salem OH 44460-1556 Office: PO Box 765 Salem OH 44460-0765

**SLADE, LYNN HEYER,** lawyer; b. Santa Fe, N.Mex., Jan. 29, 1948; m. Susan Zimmerman, 1 child, Benjamin, 1 child from a previous marriage, Jessica. BA in Econs., U. N.Mex., 1973, JD, 1976. Bar: N.Mex. 1976, U.S. Dist. Ct. N.Mex. 1976, U.S. Ct. Appeals (10th cir.) 1978, U.S. Ct. Appeals (D.C. cir.) 1984, U.S. Supreme Ct. 1984. Ptnr. Modrall, Sperling, Roehl, Harris & Sisk, PA, Albuquerque, 1976—; adj. prof. U. N.Mex. Sch. Law, Albuquerque, 1990. Editor N.Mex. Law Rev., 1975-76; contbr. articles to profl. jours. Trustee-at-large Rocky Mountain Min. L. Found., 1995-97. Fellow N.Mex. Bar Found.; mem. ABA (sect. of environ., energy and resources, membership officer 1998—, chair com. on Native Am. natural resources 1991-94, coun. mem. 1995-98, mem. sects. litigation, dispute resolution, internat. law, pub. utilities and comm., and transp. law), N.Mex. State Bar (bd. dirs. sect. of natural resources 1983-87, bd. dirs. Indian law sect. 1987-90). E-mail: lslade@modrall.com. Natural resources, Environmental, Native American. Home: 143 Olguin Rd Corrales NM 87048-6930 Office: Modrall Sperling Roehl Harris & Sisk PA 500 4th St NW Ste 1000 Albuquerque NM 87102-2186

**SLADE, THOMAS BOG, III,** lawyer; b. Balt., June 22, 1931; s. Thomas Bog Jr. and Blanche Evangeline (Hall) S.; m. Sunya Johanna Bowen, July 25, 1959 (div. 1976); children: Sunya Kirsten, DeWitt Bowen, Vivian Watson; m. Mary Stewart Bolton, Apr. 3, 1976. BA, U. Va., 1953, LLB, 1954. Bar: Fla. 1956, U.S. Supreme Ct. 1966. Assoc. Patterson, Freeman, Richardson & Watson, Jacksonville, Fla., 1956-61; ptnr. Freeman, Richardson, Watson, Slade, McCarthy & Kelly, Jacksonville, 1961-80; pvt. practice Jacksonville, 1980-81; ptnr. Foley & Lardner, Jacksonville, 1981-92, 99—. 1st lt., U.S. Army, 1954-56. Mem. Fla. Bar (bd. govs. 1966-69, pres. young lawyers sect. 1967-68), Duval County Jacksonville Legal Aid Assn. (pres. 1970), Fla Yacht Club, Univ. Club of Jacksonville. Municipal (including bonds), Securities, Finance. Office: Foley & Lardner 200 N Laura St Jacksonville FL 32202-3500

**SLADKUS, HARVEY IRA,** lawyer; b. Mar. 5, 1929; s. Samuel Harold and Charlotte Dorothy Sladkus; m. Harriet Marcia Barske, Nov. 26, 1967 (div.); children: Steven David, Jeffrey Brandon; m. Roberta Frances Pope, Oct. 24, 1986. AB, Syracuse U., 1950; JD, NYU, 1961. Bar: N.Y. 1962, Conn. 1981, U.S. Supreme Ct. 1967. Assoc. Morris Ploscowe, N.Y.C., 1961-66; pvt. practice N.Y.C., 1968-95; ptnr. Dweck & Sladkus and Feiden, Dweck & Sladkus, N.Y.C., 1968-95, Dweck & Sladkus, LLP, 1996; pvt. practice, 1997—; small claims arbitrator Civil Ct. City of N.Y., 1977—. Contbg. author: Practice Under New York's Matrimonial Law, 1971-79, It's the Law Suffolk Times; contbr. columnist It's The Law, Suffolk Times; editor-in-chief Family Law Practice, 1982; contbr. articles on family and matrimonial law to legal publs. 1st lt. U.S. Army, 1952-53, Korea. Decorated Bronze Star; recipient George Washington Honor medal Freedoms Found., Valley Forge, 1953. Mem. N.Y. State Bar Assn., Assn. Bar City N.Y., Conn. Bar Assn., Am. Acad. Matrimonial Lawyers, Internat. Acad. Matrimonial Lawyers, Am. Judges Assn., Am. Arbitration Assn. (nat. panel arbitrators). Jewish. Family and matrimonial, State civil litigation, Federal civil litigation. Office: 425 Park Ave New York NY 10022-3506 *Notable cases include: Burns vs. Burns, first to constitute a tenant in occupancy to subscribe to shares of an apt. corp. going coop.; Brown vs. Brown, case of first impression reclause in agreement of ex-wife living with another man.*

**SLAGLE, JAMES WILLIAM,** lawyer; b. Marion, Ohio, Nov. 8, 1955; s. Gene and Emily Frances (Weber) S.; m. Heidi Ann Schweinfurth, Feb. 12, 1983. BA in Polit. Sci., Ohio State U., 1977, JD, 1980. Bar: Ohio 1980, U.S. Dist. Ct. (no. dist.) Ohio 1982. Pvt. practice Marion, 1980-96; spl. counsel Ohio Atty. Gen., Cols, 1984—; pros. atty. Marion County, 1985—. Pres. Hardinge Area coun. Boy Scouts Am., 1991-93, v.p. coun., 1989-91, dist. chmn., 1986-87. Mem. Marion County Bar Assn., Ohio Pros. Attys. Assn. (pres. 1995). Democrat. Methodist. Criminal, Government contracts and claims. Home: 528 King Ave Marion OH 43302-5320 Office: Marion County Pros Atty 133 1/2 E Center St Marion OH 43302-3801

**SLANINGER, FRANK PAUL,** lawyer; b. Lake City, Iowa, Sept. 19, 1944; s. Paul Vincent and Loveda Laura (Peterson) S. B.A., Loras Coll., Dubuque, Iowa, 1966; J.D., Harvard U., 1969. Bar: Colo. 1970, U.S. dist. ct. Colo. 1970, U.S. Ct. Appeals (10th cir.) 1970, U.S. Supreme Ct. 1973. Assoc. Schwartz & Snyder, Denver, 1970-73; staff atty. SEC, Denver, 1973-75; estate planner Mfrs. Life Ins. Co., Denver, 1976; sole practice, Denver, 1977—; co-pres. Champagne, 1983-84; bd. dirs. AMC Cancer Research Ctr. fund raiser, 1983—. Active Am. Cancer Soc. Mem. ABA, Colo. Bar Assn., Denver Bar Assn., Sertoma, Schussbaumer Ski Club. Democrat. Roman Catholic. General practice, Personal injury, Real property. Office: 1776 S Jackson St Ste 800 Denver CO 80210-3807

**SLATER, CRAIG ALLYN,** lawyer; b. Elmira, N.Y., Dec. 22, 1955; s. Gary B. and Nancy S.; m. Deborah F. Slater, July 29, 1978; children: Emily, Kaylin, Jared. BA, SUNY, 1978, JD, 1981. Bar: N.Y.; U.S. Ct. Appeals (2nd cir.); U.S. Dist. Ct. (we., no. and so. dist.). Sr. litigation assoc. pvt. practice, 1981-88; asst. atty. gen. N.Y. State Atty. Gen. Office, 1988-91; dir. environ. practice group Saperton & Day PC, 1991-95; ptnr. Harter, Secrest & Emery, 1995—. Contbr. articles to profl. jours. Mem. Wrie County Indsl. Adv. Bd., 1993—, City of Buffalo Med. Waste Disposal Options Task Force, 1991—, Erie County Plastic/Recycling Task Force, 1989-91, City of Buffalo Pesticide Adv. Bd., 1989-91. Mem. Erie County Bar Assn. (chair 1994—), N.Y. State Bar Assn., Environ. Law Inst., Erie County C.C. Environmental. Office: Harter Secrest & Emery LLP 1 Marine Midland Ctr Buffalo NY 14203-2842

**SLATER, LOURDES MARIA,** lawyer; b. Mayagüez, P.R., Dec. 6, 1967; d. Salvador Fuentes Valentin and Maria M. López. BS in Fgn. Svc. cum laude, Georgetown U., 1989; JD, U. Pa., 1992. Bar: N.J. 1992, D.C. 1992, N.Y. 1993, U.S. Dist. Ct. (so., ea., we. and no. dists.) N.Y. 1997; cert. notary pub., N.Y. Law clk. for Hon. Amy P. Chambers and Richard S. Rebeck N.J. Superior Ct., New Brunswick, 1992-93; assoc. Adams Duque & Hazeltine, N.Y.C., 1993-94, Luce Forward Hamilton & Scripps, N.Y.C., 1994—. Pro bono lawyer N.Y.C. City Human Resources Dept., 1994, C-Plan Agy., N.Y.C., 1997—. Scholar Hispanic Bar Assn., 1990-91. Mem. Assn. Bar City N.Y. (libr. com. 1993-97, com. on security affairs, 1997—). Republican. Roman Catholic. Office: Luce Forward Hamilton Et Al 153 E 53rd St Fl D20 New York NY 10022-4611

**SLATTERY, JILL SHERIDAN,** lawyer; b. East Orange, N.J., Apr. 4, 1943; d. Sanford and Melba Edith (Clark) Sheridan; m. William C. Slattery, Sept. 25, 1965; children: William S., Meaghan J. BSN, U. Pa., 1965; MS, Boston U., 1967; JD cum laude, Seton Hall U., 1979. Bar: N.J. 1980, U.S. Dist. Ct. N.J. 1980, U.S. Ct. Appeals (3d cir.) 1980, N.Y. 1990. Asst. prof. Rutgers U., Newark, 1974-76; law clk. to judge Hon. Robert Muir Morris County, Morristown, N.J., 1979-80; ptnr. Nardino & Slattery, Montclair, N.J., 1980-83, Agostini, Copeland & Slattery, Verona, N.J., 1990-93, Agostini & Slattery, Verona, 1993—; pvt. practice Montclair, 1983-90; mem. faculty, lectr. at nursing colls., N.J., 1980—; chair Essex County Jud. Apointment Com., 1990—; chair V-C dist. ethics com. N.J. Supreme Ct., 1992-95. Author, editor textbook: Maternal Child Nutrition, 1979. Mem. Essex County Dem. Orgn., Millburn, N.J., 1976—; bd. dirs. Ctr. for Family Studies, Springfield, N.J., 1994—; bd. dirs., pres. Millburn-Short Hills Scholastic Boosters, 1987-94; mem. ethics com. The Hospice, Inc. Named Woman of Yr., Millburn-Short Hills Bus. and Profl. Women's Club, 1985. Mem. Am. Assn. Nurse Attys., N.J. State Bar Assn., Essex County Bar Assn. (trustee). Avocation: travel. General practice, Family and matrimonial. Office: Agostini & Slattery 25 Pompton Ave Verona NJ 07044-2934

**SLAUGHTER, FRANK L., JR.,** lawyer; b. Bristol, Tenn., Dec. 19, 1967; s. Frank L. and Mary Ann S. BSBA, U. Tenn., 1990; JD, Nashville Sch. Law, 1997. Bar: Tenn., U.S. Dist. Ct. (ea. dist.) Tenn. Jud. commr., magistrate Williamson County Gen. Sessions Ct., Franklin, Tenn., 1996-97; jud. law clk. Hon. Don R. Ash, Murfreesboro, Tenn., 1996-97; ptnr. Slaughter & Slaughter, Bristol, 1997—. Pres. Sullivan County Young Dems., Bristol, 1998; precinct chmn. Sullivan County Election Commn., Bristol, 1998. Mem. ABA, ATLA, Nat. Assn. Criminal Def. Lawyers, Tenn. Bar Assn., Tenn. Trial Lawyers Assn., Tenn. Assn. Criminal Def. Attys., Bristol Bar Assn. Avocations: boxing, golf, art, travel. Personal injury, Criminal, General practice. Home: 1270 Volunteer Pkwy Apt B23 Bristol TN 37620-4654 Office: 1241 Volunteer Pkwy Ste 408 Bristol TN 37620-4635

**SLAUGHTER, MARSHALL GLENN,** lawyer; b. Wauchula, Fla., Jan. 15, 1940; s. Glenn S. and Carrie Melissa (Shelfer) S.; children: Glenn Scott II, Todd Harvey. BBA, U. Fla., 1961; JD, Stetson U., 1979. Bar: Fla. 1979, U.S. Dist. Ct. (mid. dist.) Fla. 1980. Pres. Slaughter Motor Sales, Wauchula, 1965-77; assoc. McDaniel & Smith, Lakeland, Fla., 1979-80, Edmund & McDaniel, Bartow, Fla., 1980-84; sole practice Bartow, 1984-87, Lakeland, 1987-89, Winter Haven, Fla., 1989—. Served to Lt. USNR, 1961-65. Mem. Fla. Bar Assn. (evidence com. 1982-84, computer law com. 1984-86, family law rules com. 1984—, judicial evaluation com. 1985—), Criminal Def. Lawyers Assn., Polk County Trial Lawyers Assn., Elks. Baptist. Avocations: scuba diving, travel, sailing, computers. Family and matrimonial, Criminal, Juvenile. Home: 316 E Carlisle Rd Lakeland FL 33813-1611 Office: 170 E Haines Blvd # 1145 Lake Alfred FL 33850-2818

**SLAVIK, DONALD HARLAN,** lawyer; b. Milw., June 17, 1956; s. Donald Jean and Sally Ann (Croy) S.; m. Cynthia Sue Barfknecht, Jan 5, 1980. BS in Nuclear Engring., U. Wis., 1978, JD, 1981. Bar: Wis. 1981, U.S. Dist. Ct. (ea. and we. dists.) Wis. 1981. Mem. Habush, Habush, Davis & Rottier, Milw., 1981—; lectr. engring. extension U. Wis., Madison, 1985-95. Author: (with others) Anatomy of a Roof Crush Case, 1985, Seat Belt Handbook, 1987, Crashworthiness, 1989, 98; contbr. articles to profl. jours. Mem. Assn. Trial Lawyers Am. (co-chair exch. com. 1986-87, 91-93, chmn. computer law office tech. 1993-97), Wis. Bar Assn., Attys. Info. Exch. Group (bd. dirs., exec. com. 1987—, lectr. 1987—), Assn. for Advancement of Automotive Medicine (sci. program com. 1996—). Personal injury, Product liability. Office: Habush Habush Davis & Rottier Ste 2300 777 E Wisconsin Ave Milwaukee WI 53202-5381

**SLAVIN, EDWARD A., JR.,** lawyer, writer; b. Camden, N.J., Mar. 20, 1957; s. Edward A. and Mary Elizabeth (Donlon) S. BS, Georgetown U., 1983; JD, Memphis State U., 1986. Bar: Tenn. 1987, D.C. 1988, U.S. Dist. Ct. (6th cir.) 1991, U.S. Dist. Ct. (fed. cir.) 1993. Editor Appalachian Observer, Clinton, Tenn., 1981-83; law clk. Dan M. Norwood, Memphis, 1984-86; law clk. Chief Judge N. Litt Dept. Labor, Washington, 1986-88; counsel Occpl. Health Legal Rights Found., Washington, 1988-89; legal counsel Constnl. Rights, Govt. Accountability Project, 1989-93; pvt. practice Deerfield Beach, Fla., 1994—. Author: Jimmy Carter, 1989; contbr. articles to profl. jours. Mem. ABA (chair human and civil rights com. young lawyers divsn. 1989-91, liaison coun. individual rights and responsibilities sect. 1989-91, Silver Key award 1986), ATLA. Democrat. Labor, Civil rights, Toxic tort. Home and Office: 35 SE 8th Ter Deerfield Beach FL 33441-4030

**SLAVITT, BEN J.,** lawyer; b. Newark, Dec. 31, 1934; s. Arthur and Berdie (Goodman) S.; children—Lauri, Julie, Donna, John. B.A., Bucknell U., 1956; LL.B., U. Va., 1959. Bar: N.J. 1959, U.S. dist. ct. N.J. 1959, U.S. Supreme Ct. 1973. Ptnr., Slavitt & Cowen PA, and predecessors, Newark, 1959—. Served with U.S. Army, 1959-60. Mem. N.J. Bar Assn. Democrat. Jewish. General civil litigation, Family and matrimonial, Real property. Office: Slavitt & Cowen 17 Academy St Ste 415 Newark NJ 07102-2905

**SLAVITT, HOWARD ALAN,** lawyer; b. L.A., Aug. 20, 1961. BA summa cum laude, U. Calif., Berkeley, 1985; MA, U. So. Calif., 1989; JD magna cum laude, Harvard U., 1994. Litigation assoc. Heller, Ehrman, White & McAuliffe, San Francisco, 1994-96, Coblentz, Patch, Duffy & Bass, San Francisco, 1996—. Exec. editor: Harvard Civil Right Civil Liberties Law Rev. 1993-94; contbr. articles to profl. jours. Avocations: photography, hiking, travel. General civil litigation, Intellectual property. Office: Coblentz Patch Duffy & Bass LLP 222 Kearny St Fl 7 San Francisco CA 94108-4510

**SLAVITT, JOSHUA RYTMAN,** lawyer; b. N.Y.C., May 10, 1963; s. David R. and Lynn (Meyer) S.; m. Nadine Hollander, May 30, 1993; children: Samuel, Shoshana. BA in Philosophy and Econs., U. Pa., 1986; JD, Boston U., 1991. Bar: Pa. 1991, U.S. Dist. Ct. (ea. dist.) Pa. 1991, N.J. 1992, U.S. Dist. Ct. N.J. 1992, U.S. Ct. Appeals (3rd cir.) 1995, U.S. Patent and Trademark Office 1997. Assoc. Marks, Kent & O'Neill, Phila., 1991-92, Klehr, Harrison, Harvey, Branzburg & Ellers, Phila., 1992-95, Synnestvedt & Lechner, Phila., 1996—. Cabinet mem. Jewish Fedn. Greater Phila., 1994—. Mem. ABA (litigation and intellectual property sects.), Phila. Intellectual Property Law Assn., Entrepreneur's Forum Greater Phila., Benjamin Franklin Am. Inn of Ct. (barrister). Intellectual property, Patent, Trademark and copyright. Office: Synnestvedt & Lechner LLP 2600 Aramark Tower 1101 Market St Ste 2600 Philadelphia PA 19107-2950

**SLAYTON, JOHN HOWARD,** lawyer, trust company executive; b. Sparta, Wis., July 6, 1955; s. Rex Gordon and Elizabeth (Ward) S.; m. Judith Hughes. BA in Polit. Sci. with honors, Marquette U., 1977; JD with honors, George Washington U., 1980, MBA in Fin., 1982; LLM in Taxation, Georgetown U., 1986. Bar: D.C. 1981, U.S. Ct. Appeals (D.C. cir.) 1981, U.S. Dist. Ct. (D.C. dist.) 1981, Va. 1993. Assoc. Metzger, Shadyac & Schwarz, Washington, 1980-83, Pillsbury, Madison & Sutro, Washington, 1983-87, Leland & Assocs., Inc., Washington, 1987-95; pres., CEO The Trust Co. of the South, Burlington, N.C., 1996—; instr. real estate syndication, Arlington (Va.) County Continuing Edn./Realty Bd., 1982; cons., Washington, 1995-96. Contbr. articles to profl. jours. Mem. ABA (com. fed. regulation of securities), D.C. Bar Assn., Va. Bar Assn. Roman Catholic. General corporate, Securities, Corporate taxation. Home: 1930 W Lake Dr Burlington NC 27215-4840 Office: The Trust Co of the South 3041 S Church St Burlington NC 27215-5154

**SLEDGE, JAMES SCOTT,** judge; b. Gadsden, Ala., July 20, 1947; s. L. Lee and Kathryn (Privott) S.; m. Joan Nichols, Dec. 27, 1969; children: Joanna Scott, Dorothy Privott. BA, Auburn U., 1969; JD, U. Ala., 1974, postgrad., 1989. Bar: Ala. 1974, U.S. Ct. Appeals (5th cir.) 1975, U.S. Ct. Appeals (11th cir.) 1981. Ptnr. Inzer, Suttle, Swann & Stivender, P.A., Gadsden, 1975-91; judge U.S. Bankruptcy Ct. No. Dist. Ala., 1991—; chair-elect Nat. Conf. Fed. Judges, 1997—; instr. U. Ala., Gadsden, 1975-77, Gadsden State C.C., 1989-90. Lay min., vestryman Holy Comforter Episc. Ch., Gadsden, 1976—; exec. com. Ala. Coun. on the Arts, 1994—; incorporator Episc. Day Sch., Gadsden, 1976, Kyle Home for Devel. Disadvantaged, Gadsden, 1979; bd. dirs. Salvation Army, 1984-91, Etowah County Health Dept., 1975-91, Episc. Day Sch., 1992-96, Gadsden Symphony, 1993-96; mem. Ala. Dem. Exec. Com., 1990-91, Etowah County Dem. Exec. Com., 1984-91; founder Gadsden Cultural Arts Found., 1983, chmn., 1986-91. Capt. U.S. Army, 1969-71, Vietnam. Decorated Legion of Honor (Vietnam); recipient Gov.'s award for art Ala. Coun. of Arts, 1993. Mem. ABA (publs. chair jud. divsn. 1997—), Gadsden-Etowah C. of C. (gen. counsel, v.p., bd. dirs. 1986-93), Kiwanis (bd. dirs. 1981-84), Phi Kappa Phi, Phi Eta Sigma. Home: 435 Turrentine Ave Gadsden AL 35901-4059

**SLEDGE, L. D.,** lawyer; b. Shreveport, La., July 22, 1935; s. Lawrence Leon and Dorothy (Wimberly) S.; divorced; children: John, Shannon, Jake, Tom. BS, La. State U., 1957, LLB, 1960. Assoc. McDonald & Buchler, Metairie, La., 1963-67; pvt. practice Baton Rouge, 1967—. Capt. JAGC, U.S. Army, 1960-63. Mem. ABA, La. Bar Assn., Assn. Trial Lawyers Am., La. Trial Lawyers Assn. (gov. 1977). Democrat. Avocations: writing, reading, computers, Scientology, family. Personal injury, Admiralty, General civil litigation. Home: 2154 E Ramsey Dr Baton Rouge LA 70808-1646 Office: Jefferson Hwy Baton Rouge LA 70809

**SLEET, GREGORY M.,** lawyer. BA in Polit. Sci. cum laude, Hampton U., 1973; JD, Rutgers U., 1976. Dep. atty. gen. U.S. Dist. Ct., Del., U.S. atty., 1994—. Office: US Dist Ct Dist Del Lockbox 19 844 King St Ste 18 Wilmington DE 19801-3570

**SLEETH, DAVID THOMPSON,** lawyer, physician; b. Evanston, Ill., Aug. 27, 1957; m. Kathleen Lyle, Dec. 21, 1979 (div. 1987); children: Michael Alan, Kelli Michelle; m. Lori Denise Shaw, Dec. 17, 1988. BS, So. Meth. U., 1979; JD, St. Mary's U., San Antonio, 1984; MD, St. George's U., 1999. Bar: Tex. 1985, U.S. Dist. Ct. (no. dist.) Tex. 1985, U.S. Dist. Ct. (ea. and we. dists.) Tex. 1989. With Law Offices of Windle Turley, Dallas, 1985-86, Law Offices of Charles Caperton, Dallas, 1986-88; assoc. Law Offices of Daniel W. Lowe, Dallas, 1988-89, Shannon, Gracey, Ratliff & Miller, Ft. Worth, 1989-91; pvt. practice Dallas, Tex., 1991-94, Greenville, Tex., 1995—. Maj. USMCR, 1979-94. Mem. ABA, Tex. Bar Assn., Hunt County Bar Assn. Republican. Methodist. Avocations: flying, jogging, tennis. Personal injury. Home and Office: 3010 Oaklawn Dr Belton TX 76513-1035

**SLEIGHT, VIRGINIA MAE,** lawyer; b. Queensbury, N.Y., Mar. 10, 1932; d. Henry Jay and Helen Adelaide (Bennett) S. BA in Polit. Sci., Russell Sage Coll., 1962. Bar: N.Y. 1964, U.S. Dist. Ct. (no. dist.) N.Y. 1966, U.S. Surpeme Ct. 1981. Clk. of ct. & hearing reporter Warren County Family Ct., Queensbury, N.Y., 1954-71; law asst., reporter Warren County Ct., Queensbury, N.Y., 1971-75, 1st asst. dist. atty., 1975-94, coord. asst. dist. atty., 1994-96; atty. pvt. practice, Queensbury, N.Y., 1996—. Adminstrv. v.p. Mohican Coun., Boy Scouts Am., Glens Falls, N.Y., 1994-98, mem. exec. bd. Twin Rivers Coun., Albany, 1998—. Mem. AAUW, N.Y. Bar Assn., Warren County Bar Assn., Bus. & Profl. Women, Soc. Prevention Cruelty to Animals Upstate N.Y., Chapman Hist. Mus. Republican. Avocations: swimming, skiing. Probate, Real property. Home and office: 369 Aviation Rd Queensbury NY 12804-2915

**SLEIK, THOMAS SCOTT,** lawyer; b. La Crosse, Wis., Feb. 24, 1947; s. John Thomas and Marion Gladys (Johnson) S.; m. Judith Mattson, Aug. 24, 1968; children: Jennifer, Julia, Joanna. BS, Marquette U., 1969, JD, 1971. Bar: Wis. 1971, U.S. Dist. Ct. (we. dist.) Wis. 1971. Assoc. Hale Skemp Hanson Skemp & Sleik, La Crosse, 1971-74, ptnr., 1975—. State pres. Boy Scouts Am., 1981-83, bd. dirs. Gateway Area Coun., 1973—, pres., 1980-81; trustee La Crosse Pub. Libr., 1981—; chair Wis. Jud. Commn., 1998—; bd. dirs. Children's Mus. of LaCrosse, 1997—, Greater La Crosse Area United Way, 1985-92, campaign chmn., 1986, pres., 1987; mem. Sch. Dist. La Crosse Bd. Edn., 1973-77, v.p., 1977. Fellow Am. Acad. Matrimonial Lawyers; mem. ABA, ATLA, Wis. Acad. Trial Lawyers, State Bar Wis. (bd. govs. 1987-94, pres. 1992-93, speaker litigation sect. and family law seminars), La Crosse County Bar Assn., Wis. Jud. Commn. Roman Catholic. State civil litigation, Family and matrimonial, Labor. Home: 4082 Glenhaven Dr La Crosse WI 54601-7503 Office: Hale Skemp Hanson Skemp & Sleik 505 King St Ste 300 La Crosse WI 54601-4062

**SLEMMER, CARL WEBER, JR.,** retired lawyer; b. Camden, N.J., Mar. 28, 1923; s. Carl and Annette (Donner) S.; m. Renée Jeannette Kinsey, Oct. 11, 1952; children: Michael, John, Sandra. BS, Muhlenberg Coll., 1948; JD, Temple U., 1963. Bar: N.J. 1972, Pa. 1972, U.S. Dist. Ct. N.J. 1972, Fla. 1974. Various pers. positions RCA, Camden, 1950-55; mgr. labor rels. Allied Chem. Corp., Morristown, N.J., 1955-67; dir. employee rels. Exide Corp., Phila., 1967-82; pvt. practice Cherry Hill, N.J., 1982-83; dir. labor rels. Columbia U., N.Y.C., 1983-89; mgr. tax office H & R Block, Marlton, N.J., 1991-93; ret., 1993. Mem. labor coun. U. Pa., Phila., 1967-82. Lt. (j.g.) USN, 1943-46, PTO. Republican. Presbyterian. Avocations: tennis, reading, travel, legal research. Home: 432 Paul Dr Moorestown NJ 08057-2809

**SLEVIN, JOHN A.,** lawyer; b. Peoria, Ill., Sept. 26, 1935; s. J. Spalding and Lucille (Wagner) S.; m. Mary M. Hurst, July 6, 1957; children: Kathleen, John, Maureen, Kevin, Bridget, Brian, Meaghan, Moira. PhB, U. Notre Dame, 1957, JD, 1960. Bar: Ill. 1960, U.S. Dist. Ct. (no. dist., cent. dist. and so. dist.) Ill., U.S. Ct. Appeals (7th cir.) 1966. Assoc. Hershey & Bliss, Taylorville, Ill., 1960-62; ptnr. Koos & Slevin, Peoria, 1962-63; pvt. practice Peoria, 1963-66; ptnr. Vonachen, Lawless, Trager & Slevin, Peoria, 1966—. Bd. dirs. Notre Dame (Ind.) Alumni Assn., 1983-86; bd. dirs., treas. Peoria Cursillo, 1991-95; pres. Vis. Nurses Assn., Peoria, 1984-90. Mem. ABA, ATLA, Ill. Bar Assn., Ill. Trial Lawyers Assn., Nat. Bd. Trial Advocacy (cert. civil trial advocate), Abraham Lincoln Inns of Ct. (bd. dirs. 1990—). Avocations: golf, cooking. Personal injury, Federal civil litigation, State civil litigation. Office: Vonachen Lawless Trager & Slevin 456 Fulton St Ste 425 Peoria IL 61602-1240

**SLEVIN, PATRICK JEREMIAH,** paralegal; b. White Plains, N.Y., Dec. 25, 1968; s. Jeremiah James Slevin and Frances Maria (Fuller) Kott; m. Eileen Patricia Barrett, Jan. 25, 1992; children: Brendan Liam, Mary Catherine. Paralegal cert., Inst. for Paralegal Studies, 1994; student, Eckerd Coll., 1995-99. Custom protection officer Wackenhut Security, Tampa, Fla., 1992; paralegal asst. Hampp Schneikart, St. Petersburg, Fla., 1992-93; paralegal Harris Mann Dew, St. Petersburg, 1993-94, A&K Abrahamson & Kennedy, Clearwater, Fla., 1994, BBP Barol Bush & Sisco, Tampa, 1994-96, Butler Burnett & Pappas, Tampa, 1996-97; physician agt. Global Mktg. Resources, Dunedin, Fla., 1997-98; mayor City of Safety Harbor, Fla., 1996—; paralegal Murphy & Runyons PA, Clearwater, 1998—; mem. Cmty. Devel. Citizen Adv. Com., Safety Harbor, 1994-96; cons. in field. Fla. state coord. Conservative Polit. Action Conf., Washington, 1997-98; fundraiser Big Bros./Sisters, Tampa, 1996. With USAF 1988-91. Featured as govt. leader in Tampa Bay mag., 1997. Mem. Found. Fla. Future, Am. Legion. Republican. Roman Catholic. Avocations: weightlifting, running, reading, movies, golfing. Home: 44 Harbor Oaks Cir Safety Harbor FL 34695-2828 Office: City Hall 750 Main St Safety Harbor FL 34695-3553

**SLEWETT, ROBERT DAVID,** lawyer; b. N.Y.C., June 4, 1945; s. Nathan and Evelyn (Miller) S.; m. Sheila Faith Winkler, Jan. 27, 1973; children: Gregory, Danielle. BA in Pub. Affairs, George Washington U., 1967; JD, Cornell U., 1970. Bar: Fla. 1970. Mem. Smith and Mandler, Miami Beach, Fla., 1970-73; with Robert Slewett, Miami Beach, 1973-87; ptnr. Steinberg, Slewett & Yaffe, Miami Beach, 1987-98, Robert D. Slewett, P.A., Miami Beach, 1998—. Sec., gen. counsel Nat. Parkinson Found., Miami, Fla., 1993—; bd. dirs., legal counsel Boystown of Jerusalem Found. Am., N.Y.C., 1993—; mem. Dade County Estate Planning Coun., Heritage Soc. Miami Jewish Home and Hosp. Named one of Leading Fla. Attys. in Field of Trusts and Estates. Mem. Nat. Acad. Elder Lawyers, Fla. Bar Assn. (probate litigation com. 1990-94), Dade County Bar Assn., Estate Planning Coun. Dade County. Fax: 305-949-7960. Estate planning, Probate, Real property. Home: 2235 NE 204th St Miami Beach FL 33180-1311 Office: 17071 W Dixie Hwy N Miami Beach FL 33160-3765

**SLEZAK, EDWARD M.,** lawyer; b. N.Y.C., Aug. 18, 1968; s. Edward Haurel Slezak and Grace Elaine Merrell; m. Erica M.B. Slezak, Sept. 4, 1994. BS cum laude, Am. U., 1990; JD cum laude, St. John's U., Jamaica, N.Y., 1993. Intern U.S. Congress, Washington, 1991, Nassau County Dist. Atty., Mineola, N.Y., 1992, Parliament-U.K., London, 1992; assoc. Bernstein & Wasserman, LLP, N.Y.C., 1993-97, Parker, Chapin, Flattan & Klimpl, LLP, N.Y.C., 1997—; bd. dirs. Meister County Internat., Ltd., N.Y.C. Mem. Bar Assn. of the City of N.Y. Republican. Avocations: weight training/fitness, basketball, mountain biking, traveling, reading. Mergers and acquisitions, Securities, General corporate. Office: Parker Chapin Flattan & Klimpl LLP 1211 6th Ave Ste 1700 New York NY 10036-8735

**SLICKER, FREDERICK KENT,** lawyer; b. Tulsa, Aug. 21, 1943; s. James Floyd and Lucille Geneva (Nordling) S.; children: Laura, Kipp. BA, U. Kans., 1965, JD with highest distinction, 1968; LLM, Harvard U., 1973. Bar: Kans. 1968, U.S. Ct. Mil. Appeals 1968, Tex. 1973, U.S. Supreme Ct. 1972, Okla. 1980. Assoc. Jackson, Walker, Winstead, Cantwell & Miller, Dallas, 1973-76; assoc. Worsham, Forsythe & Sampels, 1977-80, ptnr., 1980; assoc. Hall, Estill, Hardwick, Gable, Collingsworth & Nelson, Tulsa, 1980-81, mem., 1982-86; ptnr. Baker, Hoster, McSpadden, Clark, Rasure & Slicker, Tulsa, 1986-91; pvt. practice, Tulsa, 1991-92; shareholder Sneed Lang Adams & Barnett, Tulsa, 1992-96; pvt. practice law Tulsa, 1996—; gen. counsel, founder Lexon, Inc.; v.p., gen. counsel Image Analysis, Inc., Centrex, Inc., NUBAR Enterprises, Inc. Author: A Practical Guide to Church Bond Financing, 1985. Vice chmn. bd. trustees, chmn. admnstrv. bd., chmn. fin. com., treas., exec. com., trustee 1st United Meth. Ch., Tulsa; mem. task force Tulsa area Promise Keeper. Capt. U.S. Army, 1965-72. Mem. ABA, Okla. Bar Assn., Order of Coif. Democrat. Avocation: coaching baseball. Fax: (918) 496-9024. E-mail: fredslicker@compuserve.com. Franchising, Securities, Mergers and acquisitions. Home: 1628 E 36th Ct Tulsa OK 74105-3218 Office: 8908 S Yale Ste 410 Tulsa OK 74137-3545

**SLIGER, HERBERT JACQUEMIN, JR.,** lawyer; b. Urbana, Ill., Nov. 21, 1948; s. Herbert Jacquemin and Marina (Mantia) S.; m. Sandra Ann Ratti, May 3, 1996; children: Lauren Christine, Matthew Ryan, Nicholas Adam, Claire Nicole, Adam Gregory. BS in Fin., U. Ill., 1970; JD, U. Ariz., 1974. Bar: Ariz. 1974, Ill. 1975, U.S. Supreme Ct. 1983, Okla. 1984, U.S. Ct. Appeals (7th cir.) 1980, U.S. Tax Ct. 1980; CPA, Okla. Lawyer Charles W. Phillips Law Offices, Harrisburg, Ill., 1974-75; trust counsel Magna Trust Co., F/K/A Millikin Nat. Bank, Decatur, Ill., 1976-80, First of America Trust Co., Springfield, Ill., 1980-83; mgr. employee benefits trust dept. First Interstate Bank of Okla., NA, Oklahoma City, 1983-89; v.p., pension counsel Star Bank, NA, Cin., Cin., 1989-90; asst. gen. counsel Bank One Ariz. Corp., Phoenix, 1990-95; asst. gen. counsel, nat. practice group head Banc One Corp., Columbus, Ohio, 1995-98; state gen. counsel for Ariz. and Utah Banc One Corp., Phoenix, 1996-97; sec. of bd. and cashier Bank One, Ariz. NA, 1996-97; sec. of bd. and statutory agt. Banc One Ariz. Corp., 1996-97; sec. bd. Bank One Trust Co. N.A., Columbus, 1996—; asst. gen. counsel, trust counsel group lead law dept. Bank One Corp., Chgo., 1999—; co-chmn. Nat. Conf. Lawyers and Corp. Fiduciaries, 1992-94. Contbr. articles to profl. jours. Mem. ABA (sect. bus. law, banking law com., trust and investment svcs. subcom. 1991—, sect. real property, probate and trust law 1974—, fiduciary income taxation subcom. 1994—, fiduciary environ. problems com. 1993—, section of taxation, employee benefits com. 1991—), State Bar of Ariz., Okla. Bar Assn., Am. Bankers Assn. (chmn. trust counsel com. 1992-94, mem. and head of fiduciary law dept. Nat./Grad. Trust Sch. Bd. of Faculty Advisors 1994-95, faculty mem. teaching "fiduciary duties under ERISA" Nat. Employee Benefit Trust Sch. 1994-96, spokesman Environ. Risk Task Force 1994-95, mem. trust and investment divsn. exec. com. 1992-94, mini-adv. bd. chairperson trusts and estates 1995—), Nat. Conf. Lawyers and Corp. Fiduciaries (co-chmn. 1992-94). Roman Catholic. Avocations: phys. fitness, original print collecting. Pension, profit-sharing, and employee benefits, Probate, Estate planning. Home: Unit 121 1747 E Northern Ave Phoenix AZ 85020-3985 Office: Bank One Corp 201 N Central Ave Fl 22 Phoenix AZ 85073-0073

**SLIPSKI, RONALD EDWARD,** lawyer, educator; b. Youngstown, Ohio, May 27, 1953; s. Margaret Alice (Seman) Reno; m. Geralyn Balchak, May 17, 1980; children: Jana Veronica, Marek Joseph, Lukas Balchak, Adrian Matthew. BA, Youngstown State U., 1975, MA, 1976; JD, U. Akron, 1979. Bar: Ohio 1979, U.S. Dist. Ct. (no. dist.) Ohio 1981, U.S. Ct. Appeals (6th cir.) 1985. Law clk. Ohio Ct. Appeals 7th Appellate Dist., Youngstown, 1980-81; sr. ptnr. Green, Haines, Sgambati, Murphy & Macala Co., LPA, Youngstown, 1981—; instr. mgmt. and history dept. Youngstown State U., 1980—. Mem. ABA, Nat. Orgn. Social Security Claimant's Reps, Ohio State Bar Assn., Mahoning County Bar Assn., Mahoning-Trumbull Counties Acad. Trial Lawyers, Ohio Acad. Trial Lawyers, Am. Soc. for Legal History, Phi Kappa Phi. Workers' compensation, Labor, General practice.

**SLIVKA, MICHAEL ANDREW,** lawyer; b. Ambridge, Pa., Jan. 14, 1955; s. Andrew and Veronica (Yanko) S. AB in Psychology, Cornell U., 1977; JD, U. Miami, 1980. Bar: Fla. 1980, U.S. Dist. Ct. (so. dist.) Fla. 1981, U.S. Ct. Appeals (5th cir.) 1981, U.S. Ct. Appeals (11th cir.) 1981, Colo. 1997. Pvt. practice, Ft. Lauderdale, Fla., 1990-99; pvt. prac. Colorado Spgs., CO, 1999—. Precinct capt., exec. com. Broward County Rep. Party, 1991-92; v.p. West Broward Rep. Club, 1991-92; sec. North Dade/South Broward Estate Planning Coun., 1991-92. Recipient Albert C. Murphy scholar Cornell U., 1973. Mem. Fla. Bar Assn. (young lawyers sect., mem. collection forms com. 1983-85, bicentennial com. 1987), Bankruptcy Bar Assn., Assn. for Objective Law, Weston Area Jaycees (past sec.). Republican. Avocations: Objectivist philosophy, weightlifting, motorcycling, gardening. Personal injury, General civil litigation, Bankruptcy. Home and Office: 33 Lincoln Ave Manitou Springs CO 80824

**SLOAME, STUART C.,** lawyer; b. N.Y.C., Dec. 17, 1939; s. Milton L. and Harriet (Cohen) S.; m. Ellen J. Seeherman, Apr. 5, 1981; 1 child, Joanna Lynn. AB, Columbia Coll., 1961, LLB, 1964; LLM, Bklyn. Law Sch., 1966. Bar: N.Y., D.C. Atty. Fried Frank Harris Shriver & Jacobson, N.Y.C., 1965-66, Kronish Lieb Shainswit Weiner & Hellman, N.Y.C., 1968-69; law asst. to bd. justices 1st dept. N.Y. State Supreme Ct., 1966-68; pvt. practice N.Y.C., 1968-76; ptnr. Hershcopf Sloame and Stevenson, N.Y.C., 1977-81; dep. asst. sec. HUD, 1981-85, dep. gen. counsel, 1985-89; pvt. practice Washington, 1990—. Contbr. articles to profl. jours. Bd. dirs. Jewish Social Svcs. Agy. Met. Washington, 1990-93, Am. Jewish Com., 1998—; chmn. Met. Rep. Club, 1972-74. Mem. ABA (past chmn. sub com. cmty. reinvestment act. forum on affordable houseing and cmty. devel. law, mem. bd. editors Jour. Affordable Housing and Cmty Devel. Law), D.C. Bar Assn., Assn. Bar of City of N.Y. (com. on civil ct. 1977-80, com. on state ct. 1972-75, mcpl. affairs com. 1965-68), Columbia Law Sch. Alumni Assn. Washington (v.p. 1988—). Avocations: tennis, skiing, sailing, domestic and foreign policy. Administrative and regulatory, Federal civil litigation, Civil rights. Office: 4508 28th St NW Washington DC 20008-1034

**SLOAN, F(RANK) BLAINE,** law educator; b. Geneva, Nebr., Jan. 3, 1920; s. Charles Porter and Lillian Josephine (Stiefer) S.; m. Patricia Sand, Sept. 2, 1944; children—DeAnne Sloan Riddle, Michael Blaine, Charles Porter. AB with high distinction, U. Nebr., 1942, LLB cum laude, 1946; LLM in Internat. Law, Columbia U., 1947. Bar: Nebr. 1946, N.Y. 1947. Asst. to spl. counsel Intergovtl. Com. for Refugees, 1947; mem. Office Legal Affairs UN Secretariat, N.Y.C., 1948-78; gen. counsel Relief and Works Agy. Palestine Refugees, Beirut, 1958-60; dir. gen. legal divsn., dep. to the legal counsel UN Legal Office, N.Y.C., 1966-78, rep. of Sec. Gen. to UN Commn. Internat. Trade Law, 1969-78, rep. to Legal Sub-com. on Outer Space, 1966-78; rep. UN Del. Vietnam Conf., Paris, 1973; rep. UN Conf. on Carriage of Goods by Sea Hamburg, 1978; prof. internat. law orgn. and water law Pace U., 1978-87, prof. emeritus, 1987—; law lectr. Blaine Sloan Internat., 1988—. Author: United Nations General Assembly Resolutions in Our Changing World, 1991; contbr. articles to legal jours. Cons. UN Office of Legal Affairs, 1983-84, UN Water Resources Br., 1983; supervisory com., Pace Peace Ctr.; legal advisor Korean Missions, 1951, 53, UNTSO, Jerusalem, 1952, UNEF I, Gaza, 1957-58; prin. sec.UN Commn. to investigate Sec.-Gen. Hammarskjold's crash, 1961-62. Navigator AC, U.S. Army, 1943-46. Decorated Air medal. Mem. Am. Soc. Internat. Law, Am. Acad. Polit. and Social Sci., Am. Arbitration Assn. (panel of arbitrators), Order of Coif, Phi Beta Kappa, Phi Alpha Delta (hon.). Republican. Roman Catholic. Home: HCR-68 Box 72 Foxwind-Forbes Park Fort Garland CO 81133 Office: 78 N Broadway White Plains NY 10603-3710

**SLOANE, MARC K.,** lawyer; b. Phila., May 4, 1957; s. Bernard Louis and Arlene Loupus S.; m. Nancy Lindberg, June 11, 1983; children: Jeremy Harrison, Emily Samantha. BA, U. Md., 1979; JD, Emory U., 1982. Staff atty. Hyatt Legal Svcs., Atlanta, 1983-84, mng. atty., 1985; regional ptnr. Hyatt Legal Svcs., Balt., 1985-86; assoc. Bernard J. Sevel, P.A., Balt., 1986-89, Niles, Barton & Wilmer, Balt., 1989-94; counsel Balt. Gas and Elec. Co., Balt., 1994—. Avocations: bicycling, canoeing, flying. General civil litigation. Office: Balt Gas Elec Co 39 W Lexington St Fl 20 Baltimore MD 21201-3940

**SLOANE, MARILYN AUSTERN,** lawyer; b. N.Y.C., June 29, 1944; d. Leo Ellis and Betty (Schlanger) Austern; m. Judd Sloane, May 7, 1966 (div. 1981); m. Stanley Lisman, July 7, 1990; 1 child, Craig. BA, U. Vt., 1965; LLB, Columbia U., 1968. Bar: N.Y. 1969; cert. CLU. Lawyer L.I. (N.Y.) Lighting Co., 1968-70, Community Legal Assistance Corp. and Nassau County Community Devel. Corp., Long Island, 1970-74, Mutual of Am., N.Y.C., 1974-90; chief counsel Shore & Reich Ltd., N.Y.C., 1990-95; pvt. practice, 1995—; v.p. Nat. Health Welfare Retirement Assn., N.Y.C.; sr. v.p. devel. fin. services corp. Mut. Am., N.Y.C., sr. v.p., assoc. gen. counsel. Fellow Life Mgmt. Inst.; mem. Soc. CLU's (exec. v.p. N.Y. chpt. 1988-89, pres. 1989-90). Republican. Jewish. Avocations: skiing, hiking, aerobics, reading, biking. Insurance, Non-profit and tax-exempt organizations, Pension, profit-sharing, and employee benefits. Office: 8 Shawnee Trail Harrison NY 10528-1812

**SLOMAN, MARVIN SHERK,** lawyer; b. Fort Worth, Apr. 17, 1925; s. Richard Jack and Lucy Janette (Sherk) S.; m. Margaret Jane Dinwiddie, Apr. 11, 1953; children: Lucy Carter, Richard Dinwiddie. BA, U. Tex., 1948; LLB with honors, 1950. Bar: Tex. 1950, N.Y. 1951. Assoc. Sullivan & Cromwell, N.Y.C., 1950-56, Carrington, Coleman & Blumenthal, Dallas, 1956-60; ptnr., 1960-97, sr. counsel, 1998—. General practice, General civil litigation, Appellate. Office: Carrington Coleman Sloman & Blumenthal 200 Crescent Ct Ste 1500 Dallas TX 75201-1848

**SLONE, CHARLES R.,** lawyer; b. Bay City, Tex., Sept. 4, 1932; s. Lanford McKinney and Gussie Marian Slone; m. Tommye Frances Clements, Mar. 20, 1954; children: Bruce Wayne, Brenda Dianne. BS, Tex. A&M Coll., College Station, 1953; LLB, U. Tex., 1959. Bar: Tex. 1959. Assoc. Peareson, Scherer & Roberts, Richmond, Tex., 1959-64; ptnr. Pearejon, Scherer & Roberts, Richmond, Tex., 1965-74, Scherer, Roberts, Slone & Gresham, Richmond, 1975-76, Scherer, Roberts, Slone, Gresham & Lytle, Richmond, 1977-81, Scherer, Roberts, Slone, Gresham, Lytle & Moore, Richmond, 1982-89; pvt. practice Richmond, 1990—; city atty., City of Sugar Land, Tex., 1959-85. Mem. sch. bd. Lamar Consol. Ind. Sch. Dist., Rosenberg, Tex., 1976-79. 1st lt. U.S. Army, 1953-55. Baptist. Avocation: photography. Probate, Consumer commercial, Real property. Office: 304 Jackson St Richmond TX 77469-3109

**SLOVITER, DOLORES KORMAN,** federal judge; b. Phila., Sept. 5, 1932; d. David and Tillie Korman; m. Henry A. Sloviter, Apr. 3, 1969; 1 dau., Vikki Amanda. AB in Econs. with distinction, Temple U., 1953, LHD (hon.), 1986; LLB magna cum laude, U. Pa., 1956; LLD (hon.), The Dickinson Sch. Law, 1984, U. Richmond, 1992; LL.D. (hon.), Widener U., 1994. Bar: Pa. 1957. Assoc., then ptnr. Dilworth, Paxson, Kalish, Kohn & Levy, Phila., 1956-69; mem. firm Harold E. Kohn (P.A.), Phila., 1969-72; assoc. prof., then prof. law Temple U. Law Sch., Phila., 1972-79; judge U.S. Ct. Appeals (3d cir.), Phila., 1979—, chief judge, 1991-98; mem. bd. overseers U. Pa. Law Sch., 1993-99; bd. dirs. Nat. Constitution Ctr., 1998—. Mem. S.E. region Pa. Gov.'s Conf. on Aging, 1976-79, Com. of 70, 1976-79; trustee Jewish Publ. Soc. Am., 1983-89; Jud. Conf. of U.S., 1991-98, U.S. com. Bicentennial Constn., 1987-90, com. on Rules of Practice and Procedure, 1990-93. Recipient Juliette Low medal Girl Scouts Greater Phila., Inc., 1990, Honor award Girls High Alumnae Assn., 1991, Jud. award Pa. Bar Assn., 1994, U. Pa. James Wilson award, 1996, Temple U. Cert. of Honor award, 1996; Disting. Fulbright scholar, Chile, 1990. Mem. ABA, Fed. Bar Assn., Fed. Judges Assn., Am. Law Inst., Nat. Assn. Women Judges, Am. Judicature Soc. (bd. dirs. 1990-95), Phila. Bar Assn. (gov. 1976-78, Sandra Day O'Connor award 1997), Order of Coif (pres. U. Pa. chpt. 1975-77), Phi Beta Kappa. Office: US Ct Appeals 18614 US Courthouse 601 Market St Philadelphia PA 19106-1713

**SMAGULA, JOHN WILLIAM,** lawyer; b. Waterbury, Conn., Nov. 17, 1970; s. John Clarence and Carmella Smagula. BA in Internat. Rels., Pomona Coll., 1992; JD, Washington U., St. Louis, 1995. Bar: P.R. 1995, U.S. Ct. Appeals (1st cir.) 1996, N.Y. 1998, N.H. 1998. Assoc. Totti & Rodriguez Diaz, San Juan, P.R., 1995-97, Paul, Weiss, N.Y.C., 1997—. Dir. St. Charles Borromeo Ch., N.Y.C., 1997—; mem. dist. com. Manhattan coun. Boy Scouts of Am., N.Y.C., 1997—. Roman Catholic. Avocation: proficient in Spanish and Mandarin Chinese. Contracts commercial, Securities, Immigration, naturalization, and customs. Home: 1 River Ct Apt 2610 Jersey City NJ 07310-2011 Office: Paul Weiss Rifkind Wharton & Garrison Rm 200 1285 Avenue Of The Americas New York NY 10019-6065

**SMALKIN, FREDERIC N.,** federal judge. BA, Johns Hopkins U., 1968; JD, U. Maryland, 1971. Atty. office of judge advocate gen. Dept. Army, 1972-74, asst. to gen. counsel, 1974-76; pvt. practice Monkton, Md., 1976; magistrate U.S. Dist. Ct. Md., Balt., 1976-86, judge, 1986—; lectr. comml. law U. Md., Balt., 1978—, SMH bar rev., Balt., 1985-86, 93-95, BRI/Modern Bar Rev. Course, Inc., Balt., 1980-81; panel spkr. on Utilization of Magistrates at the 1985 fourth cir., Jud. Conf. Capt. U.S. Army, 1968-76, lt. col. CAP (USAF Auxiliary). Mem. Fed. Bar Assn., Order of Coif, Phi Beta Kappa. Office: US Dist Ct 101 W Lombard St Ste 3A Baltimore MD 21201-2626

**SMALL, ALDEN THOMAS,** judge; b. Columbia, S.C., Oct. 4, 1943; s. Alden Killin and Shirley Edna (Eldridge) S.; m. Judy Jo Worley, June 25, 1966; children: Benjamin, Jane. AB, Duke U., 1965; JD, Wake Forest U., 1969. Bar: N.C. 1969. Asst. v.p. First Union Corp., Greensboro, N.C., 1969-72; assoc. dir., gen. counsel Cmty. Enterprise Devel. Corp. Alaska, Anchorage, 1972-73; v.p., assoc. gen. counsel First Union Corp., Raleigh, N.C., 1973-82; judge U.S. Bankruptcy Ct., N.C., 1982—, chief judge, 1992—; bd. govs. Nat. Conf. of Bankruptcy Judges, 1987-90; adj. prof. law Campbell U. Sch. Law, 1980-82; bd. dirs. Am. Bankruptcy Inst., 1989-95, Fed. Jud. Ctr., 1997—; sec. Nat. Conf. Bankruptcy Judges, 1998—, pres.-elect, 1999; chmn. Nat. Conf. Bankruptcy Judges Ednl. Endowment, 1993-94; mem. long range planning com. U.S. Judicial Conf., 1991-95, adv. com. bankruptcy rules, 1996—; mem. bd. Fed. Jud. Ctr., 1997—; mem. faculty Nat. Comml. Lending Sch., 1981-82; cons. Nat. Coalition for Bankruptcy Reform, 1981-82. Contbg. editor Norton Bankruptcy Law and Practice. Mem. ABA, Am. Bankers Assn. (bankruptcy task force 1980-82), N.C. Bankers Assn. (bank counsel com. 1980-82), N.C. Bar Assn. (bankruptcy coun.), Kappa Sigma, Phi Alpha Delta. Republican. Office: US Bankruptcy Ct PO Box 2747 Raleigh NC 27602-2747

**SMALL, CLARENCE MERILTON, JR.,** lawyer; b. Birmingham, Ala., July 24, 1934; s. Clarence Merilton and Elva (Roberts) S.; m. Jean Russell, Nov. 18, 1935; children—William Stephen, Elizabeth Ann, Laura Carol. B.S., Auburn U., 1956; LL.B., U. Ala., 1961. Assoc., pres. Rives & Peterson, Birmingham, Ala., 1961—. Served to 1st lt. arty., AUS, to capt. JAGC. Fellow Am. Bar Found., Internat. Acad. Trial Lawyers, Am. Coll. Trial Lawyers, Ala. Law Found.; mem. Birmingham Bar Assn. (pres. 1979), Ala. Def. Lawyers Assn., ABA (ho. of dels. 1984-86), Ala. Bar Assn. (pres. 1992-93), Internat. Assn. Defense Counsel. Office: 1700 Financial Ctr Birmingham AL 35203-4611

**SMALL, DANIEL PRIESTLEY,** lawyer, educator; b. Washington, Jan. 16, 1943; s. Priestley J. and Genevieve (Clayton) S.; m. Katherine Goudie, June 18, 1966 (div. 1988); children: John D., Karl G., Ross C. BS, Va. Commonwealth U., 1965; JD, Coll. William & Mary, 1975, M Laws & Taxation, 1996. Bar: Va. 1975, U.S. Dist. Ct. (ea. dist.) Va. 1975, U.S. Ct. Appeals (4th cir.) 1978, U.S. Ct. Claims 1978, U.S. Tax Ct. 1975. Assoc. atty. McNamara & Smith, Hampton, Va., 1975-76, Eliades, Nye, Gregory & Papcun, Hopewell, 1976-78, Harris, Tuck, Freasier & Johnson, Rich, Va., 1977-78; trust tax officer Bank of Va. Trust Co., Richmond, Va., 1979-80; atty. Daniel P. Small P.C., Richmond, Va., 1980—; assoc. prof. J. Sargeant Reynolds Cmty. Coll., Richmond, Va., 1980—; adminstrv. hearing officer, Supreme Ct. Va., Richmond, 1985—, pres., 1992-94. Author: Additional Problems Manual, 1993. Asst. scoutmaster Boy Scouts Am., Richmond, Va., 1989-92. With U.S. Army, 1966-67. Democrat. Presbyterian. Avocations: running, camping, hunting. Office: PO Box 31474 Richmond VA 23294-1474

**SMALL, JONATHAN ANDREW,** lawyer; b. N.Y.C., Dec. 26, 1942; s. Milton and Teresa Markell (Joseph) S.; m. Cornelia Mendenhall, June 8, 1969; children: Anne, Katherine. BA, Brown U., 1964; student, U. Paris, 1962-63; LLB, Harvard U., 1967; MA, Fletcher Sch. of Law and Diplomacy, 1968; LLM, NYU, 1974. Bar: N.Y. 1967. VISTA vol. Washington and Cambridge, Mass., 1968; law clk. to judge U.S. Ct. Appeals (2d cir.), 1968-69; assoc. Debevoise & Plimpton, N.Y.C., 1969-75, ptnr., 1976—; cons. Spl. Task Force on N.Y. State Taxation, 1976. Trustee Brearley Sch., 1985-95; bd. dirs. Nonprofit Coordinating Com. of N.Y., 1985—, Muscular Dystrophy Assn., 1986-88. Mem. ABA, N.Y. State Bar Assn. (chmn. tax sect. com. exempt orgns. 1980-82, co-chmn., 1995), Assn. Bar City N.Y., Nonprofit Forum, Phi Beta Kappa. Corporate taxation, Non-profit and tax-exempt organizations, Personal income taxation. Home: 60 E End Ave New York NY 10028-7907 Office: Debevoise & Plimpton 875 3rd Ave Fl 23 New York NY 10022-6256

**SMALL, JONATHAN ANDREW,** lawyer; b. Balt., June 30, 1959; s. Marvin Myron and Suzanne (Bierstock) S. AA, Foothill Jr. Coll., 1980; BS in Math. with honors, Calif. Poly. State U., 1983; JD, U. Santa Clara, 1986. Bar: Calif. 1987, U.S. Dist. Ct. (no. and so. dists.) Calif. 1987, U.S. Patent Office 1987, U.S. Ct. Appeals (fed. cir.) 1987. Patent atty. Townsend & Townsend, San Francisco, 1986-89; counsel Xerox Corp., Palo Alto, Calif., 1989-92, 97-99, assoc. gen. patent counsel, 1999—; assoc. Weil, Gotshal & Manges, Menlo Park, Calif., 1992-93; gen. counsel Komag Inc., Milpitas, Calif., 1993-97. Editor-in-chief Santa Clara Computer and High-Tech. Law Jour., 1985-86; contbr. articles to legal jours. Mem. ABA (chair intellectual property sect., elect. filing), Am. Intellectual Property Law Assn. Avocations: bicycle touring, kayaking. Intellectual property, Consumer commercial, Patent. Office: Xerox Palo Alto Rsch Ctr 3333 Coyote Hill Rd Palo Alto CA 94304-1314

**SMALL, MARK EUGENE,** lawyer; b. Kokomo, Ind., June 11, 1955; s. Glendon Levaughn and Margaret Elizabeth (Donat) S.; m. Linda Diane Frankovic, July 5, 1982 (div. May 1985); m. Sarah Elaine Dunlap, Aug. 2, 1991. BA, DePauw U., 1978; JD, Ind. U., Indpls., 1989. Bar: Ind. 1989, U.S. Dist. Ct. (no. and so. dists.) Ind. 1989, U.S. Ct. Appeals (7th and 9th cirs.) 1990, U.S. Supreme Ct. 1998. Clerical asst. Northwestern Sch. Law, Chgo., 1982-85; circulation supr. Krannert Libr./Purdue U., West Lafayette, Ind., 1985-86; sr. law clk. Wilson & Kehoe, Indpls., 1987-89; pvt. practice law Indpls., 1989—; assoc. faculty Ind. U.-Purdue U., Indpls., 1990-94, debate coach, 1990-94. Author of short stories and poem. Mem. ATLA, Ind. Trial Lawyers Assn., Nat. Multiple Sclerosis Soc. Appellate, Personal injury, Criminal. Office: 6100 N Keystone Ave Ste 603 Indianapolis IN 46220-2430

**SMALLWOOD, CARL DEMOUY,** lawyer; b. Salonika, Greece, June 15, 1956; came to U.S.; s. Osborn Tucker and Hazel A. (Demouy) S.; m. Connie Jane Harris, Jan. 28, 1989; children: Jocelyn, Nathaniel. BSc, Ohio State U., 1977, JD, 1980. Bar: Ohio 1980, U.S. Dist. Ct. (so. dist.) Ohio 1980. Assoc. Vorys, Sater, Seymour and Pease LLP, Columbus, Ohio, 1980-86; ptnr. Vorys, Sater, Seymour and Pease LLP, Columbus, 1986—. Mem. ABA, Ohio State Bar Assn. (coun. of dels. 1991—), Columbus Bar Assn. (bd. govs. 1994—, sec.-treas. 1998-99) Am. Judicature Soc., Black Law Alumni Soc. (pres. Columbus 1996—), Ohio State U. Coll. of Law Alumni Soc. (pres. 1997-98, Josephine Sitterle Failer award 1994), Ohio State U. Alumni Assn. (life). Lutheran. General civil litigation, Professional liability, Workers' compensation. Home: 4121 Edgehill Dr Columbus OH 43220-4510 Office: Vorys Sater Seymour & Pease LLP 52 E Gay St Columbus OH 43215-3161

**SMALLWOOD, JOHN DANIEL,** lawyer; b. Wilmington, Del., Nov. 21, 1968; s. Robert E. and Dorothy C. Smallwood; m. Sheila Havard, Mar. 9, 1996. BA, Miss. State U., Starkville, 1990; JD, Miss. Coll., Jackson, 1993. Bar: Miss. 1994. Assoc. Jimmy D. Shelton & Assoc., Tupelo, Miss., 1994-95; ptnr. Estes-Mask & Smallwood, Tupelo, 1995-98, Smallwood & Smallwood, Tupelo, 1998-99, Holmes & White, PLLC, Petal, Miss., 1999—. Mem. Miss. State U. Found. Planned Gifts Coun., 1998—; unit commr. Boy Scouts Am. exec. com., Lee County, Miss., 1995—; vol. Habitat for Humanity, 1995—. Mem. ABA, Miss. Bar Assn., Miss. Young Lawyers Assn., Lee County Young Lawyers Assn. (pres. 1997-98). Episcopalian. Avocations: backpacking, camping, canoeing, travel. Family and matrimonial, General civil litigation, General practice.

**SMEAD, BURTON ARMSTRONG, JR.,** retired lawyer; b. Denver, July 29, 1913; s. Burton Armstrong and Lola (Lewis) S.; m. Josephine McKittrick, May 27, 1943 children: Amanda Armstrong, Sydney Hall. BA, U. Denver, 1934, JD, 1950; grad., Pacific Coast Bank Trust Sch., 1955. With Norwest Bank Denver (formerly Denver Nat. Bank), 1934-78, trust officer, 1955-70, v.p., trust officer, 1970-78; of counsel Buchanan Neville & Stouffer, Lakewood, Colo., 1985-99. Author: History of the Twelfth Field Artillery Battalion in the European Theater of Operations, 1944-45, Captain Smead's Letters to Home, 1944-45; editor: Colorado Wills and Estates, 1965. Pres., trustee Stebbins Orphans Home Assn., resigned, 1998; chmn. bd. dirs. Colo. divsn. Am. Cancer Soc., 1961-68. Maj. U.S. Army, 1941-45, ETO. Decorated Bronze Star; Croix de Guerre (France). Mem. Colo. Bar Assn. (treas. 1970-88, chmn. probate and trust law sect. 1967-68, exec. coun., bd. govs. 1970-88, coun. bd. govs. 1970-88, hon. 1989—, award of merit 1979), Arapahoe Bar Assn., Denver Estate Planning Coun. (co-founder, pres. 1971-72), Univ. Club (Denver). Republican. Episcopalian. Estate planning, Estate taxation, Personal income taxation. Home and Office: 111 Emerson St Apt 1143 Denver CO 80218-3790

**SMEDINGHOFF, THOMAS J.,** lawyer; b. Chgo., July 15, 1951; s. John A. and Dorothy M.; m. Mary Beth Smedinghoff. BA in Math., Knox Coll., 1973; JD, U. Mich., 1978. Bar: Ill. 1978, U.S. Dist. Ct. (no. dist.) Ill. 1978. Assoc. McBride, Baker & Coles and predecessor McBride & Baker, Chgo., 1978-84, ptnr., 1985—; adj. prof. computer law John Marshall Law Sch., Chgo.; chair Ill. Commn. on Electronic Commerce and Crime, 1996—; mem. U.S. Del. to UN Commn. on Internat. Trade Law. Author Online Law, 1996. Mem. ABA (chair electronic commerce divsn. 1995—). Computer, Intellectual property, General corporate. Office: McBride Baker & Coles 500 W Madison St Fl 40 Chicago IL 60661-2511

**SMEGAL, THOMAS FRANK, JR.,** lawyer; b. Eveleth, Minn., June 15, 1935; s. Thomas Frank and Genevieve (Andreachi) S.; m. Susan Jane Stanton, May 28, 1966; children: Thomas Frank, Elizabeth Jane. BS in Chem. Engring., Mich. Technol. U., 1957; JD, George Washington U., 1961. Bar: Va. 1961, D.C. 1961, Calif. 1964, U.S. Supreme Ct. 1976. Patent examiner U.S. Patent Office, Washington, 1957-61; staff patent atty. Shell Devel. Co., San Francisco, 1962-65; patent atty. Townsend and Townsend, San Francisco, 1965-91, mng. ptnr., 1974-89; sr. ptnr. Graham and James, San Francisco, 1992-97; pres., ptnr. Knobbe, Martins, Olson & Bear, San Francisco, 1997—; mem. U.S. del. to Paris Conv. for Protection of Indsl. Property; mem. adv. com. Ct. of Appeals for Fed. Cir., 1992-96. Contbr. articles to profl. jours. Pres. bd. dirs. Legal Aid Soc. San Francisco, 1982-84, Youth Law Ctr., 1973-84; bd. dirs. Nat. Ctr. for Youth Law, 1978-84, San Francisco Lawyers Com. for Urban Affairs, 1972—, Legal Svcs. for Children, 1980-88; bd. dirs., presdl. nominee Legal Svcs. Corp., 1984-90, 93—. Capt. Chem. Corps, U.S. Army, 1961-62. Recipient St. Thomas More award, 1982. Mem. ABA (chmn. PTC sect. 1990-91, ho. of dels. 1988—, mem. standing com. Legal Aid and Indigent Defendants 1991-94, chair sect. officer conf. 1992-94, bd. govs. 1994-97, standing com. on Pro Bono and Pub. Svc. 1997—), Intellectual Property Law Assn. (chmn. nat. coun. 1989), Nat. Inventors Hall of Fame (pres. 1988), Calif. Bar Assn. (v.p. bd. dirs. 1986-87), Am. Patent Law Assn. (pres. 1986), Internat. Assn. Intellectual Property Lawyers (pres. 1995—), Bar Assn. San Francisco (pres. 1978), Patent Law Assn. San Francisco (pres. 1974), World Trade Club, Olympic Club, Golden Gate Breakfast Club, Claremont Club (Berkeley). Republican. Roman Catholic. Patent, Trademark and copyright. Office: Knobbe Martens Olson & Bear 275 Battery St Ste 1840 San Francisco CA 94111-3335

**SMIGLIANI, SUZANNE LOVELACE,** lawyer; b. Bangkok, Thailand, Sept. 29, 1968; (parents Am. citizens); came to U.S., 1970; d. Samuel Orbison Strong and Patricia Ann Lovelace; m. Paul William Smigliani, Sept. 4, 1994; 1 child, Paul James. BA in History, Art History, UCLA, 1990; JD, U. San Diego, 1994. Bar: Calif. 1994, U.S. Dist. Ct. (so. dist.) Calif. 1994, U.S. Dist. Ct. (ctrl. dist.) Calif. 1998. Assoc. Ault, Deuprey, Jones & Gorman, San Diego, 1995-97; attorney Maxie, Rheinheimer, Stephens & Vrevich, San Diego, 1997—. Vol. Rolling Readers, San Diego, 1995-96. Republican. Protestant. Mem. San Diego Defense Lawyers, San Diego Barristers Club (pres. 1997, bd. dirs. 1996-97). General civil litigation, Personal injury, Construction. Home: 5908 Eton Ct San Diego CA 92122-3203 Office: Maxie Rheinheimer Stephens & Vrevich 600 W Broadway Ste 900 San Diego CA 92101-3354

**SMILEY, CHARLES ADAM, JR.,** lawyer; b. Louisville, Ky., Jan. 26, 1943; s. Charles Adam and N. Matilda Smiley; m. Barbara A. Bailer, Oct. 24, 1964 (div. Aug. 1987); children: Charles A. III, Brooke; m. Bettina Kannegiesser, Aug. 27, 1988; children: Kier, Dieter-Alexander, Katarina. BS, U. Mich., 1964; JD, Bklyn. Law Sch., 1968. Bar: Ohio 1969, U.S. Patent Ct., 1970, N.Y. 1972, Calif. 1990. Patent atty. Proctor and Gamble, Cin., 1968-70; atty. CBS, N.Y.C., 1970-72; dir. legal and bus. affairs ABC Sports, N.Y.C., 1972-76, v.p. legal and bus. affairs, 1976-79; v.p., asst. to v.p. tv and theatrical bus. affairs ABC, L.A., 1979-82; pres. Charles Smiley Orgn., L.A., Munich, 1982-89; atty. Bowers Williams & Smiley, Dayton, Ohio, 1990-95; ptnr. Smiley, Suarez & Assoc., Dayton, 1995-96; pvt. practice Dayton, 1996—. Mem. Ohio Assn. of Criminal Def. Lawyers, Dayton Bar Assn. Civil rights, Criminal, Juvenile. Office: Charles Smiley & Assocs 118 W 1st St Dayton OH 45402-1101

**SMILEY, GUY IAN,** lawyer; b. N.Y.C., July 30, 1938; s. Edward and Minerva June (Silverman) S.; m. Constance Ann Rodbell, July 30, 1967; children: Erica, Andrew. BA, Cornell U., 1960; JD, Columbia U., 1963. Bar: N.Y 1964, U.S. Dist. Ct. (so. dist.) N.Y. 1965, U.S. Dist. Ct. (ea. dist.) N.Y. 1965, U.S. Ct. Appeals (2d cir.) 1967, U.S. Supreme Ct. 1970. Assoc. Law Offices of Harry H. Lipsig, N.Y.C., 1964-68; ptnr. Smiley, Schwartz & Captain, N.Y.C., 1968—; arbitrator Am. Arbitration Assn., N.Y. 1974—, Civil Ct. City of N.Y., 1974-80; co-chmn. Combined Jud. Screening Panel City of N.Y., 1983—. Contbr.: (book) The Lawyers Secretary, 1972. V.p., gen. counsel Westchester Emergency Communications Assn., White Plains, N.Y., 1979—; vol. counsel Am. Radio Relay League, 1983—. Served to lt. (JAGC) USN 1966-70. Mem. Assn. Trial Lawyers Am. (sustaining), N.Y. State Trial Lawyers Assn. (mem. legis. com., 1979-85, bd. dirs. 1982—, editor-in-chief newsletter, 1984—, dep. treas. 1986), Jewish Lawyers Guild (sec. 1984—). Avocations: amateur radio, tennis, skiing. Personal injury, State civil litigation, Federal civil litigation. Home: 425 E 58th St New York NY 10022-2300 Office: Smiley Schwartz & Captain 60 E 42nd St Rm 950 New York NY 10165-0950

**SMILLIE, DOUGLAS JAMES,** lawyer; b. Glen Ridge, N.J., Aug. 16, 1956; s. James and Nancy (Albright) S.; m. Nancy Marie McKenna, Jan. 27, 1990; children: Sara Grace, Jeffrey Douglas, Heather Patricia. BA in Polit. Sci. cum laude, Muhlenberg Coll., 1978; JD, Villanova U., 1982. Bar: Pa. 1982, U.S. Dist. Ct. (ea. dist.) Pa. 1982, U.S. Ct. Appeals (3d cir.) 1983, N.J. 1984, U.S. Dist. Ct. N.J. 1984, U.S. Dist. Ct. (mid. dist.) Pa. 1995. Assoc. Clark, Ladner, Fortenbaugh & Young, Phila., 1982-90, ptnr., 1991-96; shareholder, v.p., chair litigation sect. Fitzpatrick Lentz & Bubba, P.C., Center Valley, Pa., 1996—. Author: When Worlds Collide: The Impact of the Bankruptcy Stay on Environmental Clean-Up Litigation, 1989, The Absolute Priority Rule: Catch 22 for Reorganizing Closely-Held Businesses, 1992; editor (newsletter) Environ. Impact, 1985-96; contbr. articles to profl. jours. Mem. ABA (litigation sect.), Nat. Bus. Inst. (seminar spkr. 1991, 99), Am. Bankruptcy Inst. (seminar spkr. 1986), Turnaround Mgmt. Assn., Comml. Law League Am. (bankruptcy and insolvency sect., creditors rights sect.), Assn. Comml. Fin. Attys., Robert Morris Assocs. (seminar spkr. 1995), N.J. Bar Assn. (bankruptcy sect., environ. law sect.), Phila. Bar Assn. (Ea. Dist. Bankruptcy Conf.), Lehigh County Bar Assn. Avocation: Second City Troop Rugby Football Club. Bankruptcy, Environmental, Contracts commercial. Office: Fitzpatrick Lentz & Bubba PO Box 219 Saucon Valley Rd at Rt 309 Center Valley PA 18034-0219

**SMITH, ANNE ORSI,** lawyer; b. Upper Darby, Pa., July 2, 1962; d. John Francis Jr. and Anne Robinson (Nichols) O.; m. Fletcher Bodky Smith Jr., June 3, 1988; 1 child, Fletcher Bodky Smith III. BA, Colgate U., 1984; JD, U. Ark., 1988. Bar: Ark. 1988, U.S. Dist. Ct. Ark. (ea. and we. dists.) 1990. Law clk. Ark. Supreme Ct., Little Rock, 1988-89; staff atty. Office of the Prosecutor Coord., Little Rock, 1989-91; hearing officer Ark. Appeal Tribunal, Little Rock, 1991-93; pvt. practice Little Rock, 1993—. Mem. ABA, Ark. Trial Lawyers Assn. (chmn. domestic rels.com. 1997-98), Ark. Bar Assn. (mem. com. juvenile justice), Pulaski County Bar Assn., Ark. Assn. of Women Lawyers (pres. 1995-96, v.p. 1994-95, paliamentarian 1993-94). Avocations: genealogy, herbs. Juvenile, Family and matrimonial. Office: 620 W 3rd St Ste 212 Little Rock AR 72201-2223

**SMITH, ARTHUR B., JR.,** lawyer; b. Abilene, Tex., Sept. 11, 1944; s. Arthur B. and Florence B. (Baker) S.; children: Arthur C., Sarah R. BS, Cornell U., 1966; JD, U. Chgo., 1969. Bar: Ill. 1969, N.Y. 1976. Assoc. Vedder, Price, Kaufman & Kammholz, Chgo., 1969-74; asst. prof. labor law N.Y. State Sch. Indls. and Labor Rels., Cornell U., 1975-77; ptnr. Vedder, Price, Kaufman & Kammholz, Chgo., 1977-86; founding mem. Murphy, Smith & Polk, Chgo., 1986-98; shareholder Ogletree, Deakins, Murphy, Smith & Polk, P.C., Chgo., 1999—; guest. lectr. Northwestern U. Grad. Sch. Mgmt., 1979, Sch. Law, spring 1980; mem. hearing bd. Ill. Atty. Registration and Disciplinary Commn. Author: Employment Discrimination Law Cases and Materials, 4th edit., 1994, supplement, 1997, Construction Labor Relations, 19984, supplement, 1993; co-editor-in-chief: 1976 Annual Supplement to Morris, The Developing Labor Law, 1977; asst. editor: The Developing Labor Law, 3d edit., 1992; contbr. articles to profl. jours. Recipient award for highest degree of dedication and excellence in tchg. N.Y. State Sch. Indsl. and Labor Rels., Cornell U., 1977. Mem. ABA (co-chmn. com. on devel. law under Nat. Labor Rels. Act, Sect. Labor Rels. Law 1976-77), N.Y. State Bar Assn., Phi Eta Sigma, Phi Kappa Phi, Chgo. Athletic Assn., Monroe Club. Presbyterian. Labor, Administrative and regulatory, Federal civil litigation. Office: Ogletree Deakins et al 2 First National Plz Fl 25 Chicago IL 60603

**SMITH, ARTHUR LEE,** lawyer; b. Davenport, Iowa, Dec. 19, 1941; s. Harry Arthur Smith (dec.) and Ethel (Hoffman) Duerre; m. Georgia Mills, June 12, 1965 (dec. Jan. 1984); m. Jean Bowler, Aug. 4, 1984; children: Juliana, Christopher, Andrew. BA, Augustana Coll., Rock Island, Ill., 1964; MA, Am. U., 1968; JD, Washington U., St. Louis, 1971. Bar: Mo. 1971, D.C. 1983. Telegraph editor Davenport Morning Democrat, 1962-64; ptnr. Peper Martin Jensen Maichel & Hetlage, 1971-95, Husch & Eppenberger, St. Louis, 1995—; arbitrator Nat. Assn. Security Dealers, 1980—, Am. Arbitration Assn., 1980—. Columnist St. Louis Lawyer. Lt. USN, 1964-68. Mem. ABA, D.C. Bar Assn. (chmn. law practice mgmt. 1990-91), Fed. Energy Bar Assn., Mo. Bar Assn. (chair adminstrv. law com. 1995-97, vice-chair ins. programs com. 1981-83, vice-chair antitrust com. 1981-83), P. Buckley Moss Soc. (dir. 1994—), Bar Assn. Met. St. Louis (chmn. law mgmt. com. 1993—, chair internet com. 1996-97, Pres.'s award for Exceptional Svc. 1995), Order of Coif. Federal civil litigation, Public utilities, Securities. Home: 1320 Chesterfield Estate Dr Chesterfield MO 63005-4400 Office: Husch & Eppenberger 100 N Broadway Ste 1300 Saint Louis MO 63102-2789

**SMITH, BRAD EDWARD,** lawyer; b. Longview, Wash., Jan. 26, 1960; s. Ward H. and Shirley Ann (LaDow) S.; m. Carol Ann Christnacht, Oct. 19, 1991; children: Brandon James, Conor Joseph, Taylor Michael. BA in Polit. Sci., U. Wash., 1982, JD, 1986. Bar: Wash. 1986, U.S. Dist. Ct. (we. dist.) Wash. 1986, U.S. Dist. Ct. (ea. dist.) Wash. 1992. Lobbyist Ind. Bus. Assn., Bellevue, Wash., 1983; intern, assoc. Montgomery Purdue Blankinship & Austin, Seattle, 1985-88; assoc. Miles Way & Coyne, Olympia, Wash., 1988-91, Huppin Ewing Anderson & Paul, Spokane, Wash., 1991—; gen. counsel Spokane Housing Authority, 1994-96. Mem. Wash. State Def. Trial Attys., Def. Rsch. Inst., Spokane County Bar Assn. (trustee libr. bd. 1996-98). Avocations: golf, volleyball, cycling, scuba diving, reading. Insurance, General civil litigation, Landlord-tenant. Office: Huppin Ewing Anderson Paul 221 N Wall St Ste 500 Spokane WA 99201-0833

**SMITH, BRADLEY JASON,** lawyer, recreational facility owner; b. Fremont, Ohio, Oct. 19, 1969; s. Kenneth Roger and Jane Ellen (Mayle) S.; m. Josie Lynn Lehmann, Oct. 1, 1993; children: Adam Jason, Christian Kenneth. BSBA, Ohio State U., 1992; JD, U. Toledo, Ohio, 1995. Bar: Ohio 1996. Franchise owner Triple "A" Painters, Columbus, Ohio, 1990-92; co-owner, mgr. Fremont (Ohio) Raceway Pk., 1992—; pvt. practice Fremont, 1996-99; county commr. Sandusky (Ohio) County, 1999—. Councilman-at-Large Fremont City Coun., 1995-97; asst. city prosecutor, Fremont, 1997-98; trustee, treas. Fremont Sesquicentennial, 1996—; bd. dirs. St. Josephs's Ctrl. Cath. Sch. Visitors' Bd., Fremont, 1996—, Ct. Appointed Spl. Advocates, Sandusky County, Ohio, 1994-96; Sandusky county commr., 1999—. Sgt. U.S. Army N.G., 1987-95. Recipient commendations Ohio Ho. of Reps., Columbus, 1989-92. Mem. Ohio State Bar Assn., Army N.G. Enlisted Assn., Sandusky County Bar Assn. (chmn. Law Day 1997—), Ohio State U. Alumni Assn., St. Joseph's Ctrl. Cath. Sch. Alumni Assn., Elks. Republican. Roman Catholic. Avocations: motor sports, racing, travel. Home: 112 S Granville Blvd Fremont OH 43420-2770 Office: 100 N Arch St Fremont OH 43420-2451

**SMITH, BRIAN,** lawyer. V.p., gen. counsel The Southland Corp., Dallas, 1992-97, sr. v.p. gen. counsel, 1997—. Office: The Southland Corporation PO Box 711 2711 N Haskell Ave Ste B10 Dallas TX 75204-2946

**SMITH, BRIAN DAVID,** lawyer, educator; b. Fayetteville, Ark., Oct. 29, 1953; s. Samuel Charles and Janelle (McCaskill) S.; children: Garrett Walker, Brian Austin, Marshall David; m. Teri Hill Smith. JD, La. State U., 1977. Bar: La. 1978, U.S. Dist. Ct. (we. dist.) La. 1979, U.S. Tax Ct. 1980, U.S. Ct. Appeals (5th cir.) 1980, U.S. Supreme Ct. 1990, Tex. 1993. Law clk. to presiding justice 1st Jud. Cir. Ct. La., Shreveport, La., 1978-79; assoc. Nelson, Hammons & Johnson, Shreveport, 1979-84, Lunn, Irion, Johnson, Salley & Carlisle, Shreveport, 1984—; instr. legal asst. cirriculum La. State U., Shreveport, 1984-87. Bd. dirs. YMCA of Shreveport-Bossier City, 1996-98. Mem. La. Bar Assn., La. Assn. Def. Counsel, State Bar Tex., Mensa, Shreveport Country Club. Methodist. Avocations: golf, running, shooting. Personal injury, Insurance, Federal civil litigation. Home: 5706 Lake Side Dr Bossier City LA 71111 Office: Lunn Irion Johnson Salley & Carlisle PO Box 1534 Shreveport LA 71165-1534

**SMITH, BRIAN WILLIAM,** lawyer, former government official; b. N.Y.C., Feb. 3, 1947; s. William Francis and Dorothy Edwina (Vogel) S.; m. Donna Jean Holverson, Apr. 24, 1976; children: Mark Holverson, Lauren Elizabeth. BA, St. John's U., N.Y.C., 1968, JD, 1971; MS, Columbia U., 1981. Bar: N.Y. 1972, D.C. 1975, U.S. Dist. Ct. (ea. and so. dists.) N.Y. 1975, U.S. Supreme Ct. 1976, U.S. Dist. Ct. D.C. 1986. Atty. Am. Express Co., N.Y.C., 1970-73, CIT Fin. Corp., N.Y.C., 1973-74; assoc. counsel, mng. atty. Interbank Card Assn. (named changed to Master Card Internat., Inc.), N.Y.C., 1974-75, sr. v.p., corp. sec., gen. counsel, 1975-82; chief counsel Compt. of Currency, Washington, 1982-84; ptnr. Stroock & Stroock & Lavan, Washington, 1984-92, mng. ptnr., 1986-92; ptnr. Mayer, Brown & Platt, Washington and N.Y.C., 1992—; lectr. fin. industry. Editor: Bank Investment Products Deskbook, 1995. Capt., USAR, 1970-78. Mem. ABA, N.Y. State Bar Assn., D.C. Bar Assn., Assn. Bar City N.Y., Fed. Bar Assn., N.Y. Athletic Club, Met. Club N.Y. Banking, Antitrust, General corporate. Home: 35 W Lenox St Chevy Chase MD 20815-4208 Office: Mayer Brown & Platt 1909 K St NW Washington DC 20006

**SMITH, BRIAN WILLIAM,** lawyer; b. N.Y.C., May 2, 1957; s. Charles Imgrip and Suzanne Nazareth (O'Brien) S. BA, U. Buffalo, 1978; JD, Duke U., 1981. Bar: Conn.; U.S. Dist. Ct. Conn. Dir. Legal Assistance to Prisoners, Hartford, Conn., 1982-87; assoc. Bai, Pollack & Dunnigan, Bridgeport, Conn., 1987-91, McGrail, Carroll & Turney, New Haven, Conn., 1991—. Mem. Conn. Bar Assn., Conn. Def. Lawyers Assn., Conn. Trial Lawyers Assn. Avocations: acoustic stringed instruments, musical performance. General civil litigation. Office: Cotter Cotter & Sohon 500 Boston Post Rd Milford CT 06460-2529

**SMITH, BYRON OWEN,** retired lawyer; b. Mitchell, S.D., July 28, 1916; s. Frank B. and Elizabeth (Klosterman) S.; m. Jean Knox Harris, Dec. 20, 1938; children: Sheryl S. (Mrs. Kenneth P. King), Laird W. (dec.), Ryland R., Ford R. A.B., Stanford, 1937, J.D., 1940. Bar: Calif. 1940. Assoc. Stephens, Jones, Inch & LaFever, L.A., 1940-41; ptnr. Stephens, Jones, LaFever & Smith, L.A., 1945-77; ptnr. Adams, Duque & Hazeltine, L.A., 1977-95, of counsel, 1995-96; ret., 1996. Served to comdr. USNR, 1942-45, 51. Fellow Am. Coll. Trust and Estate Counsel; mem. Calif. State Club Assn. (dir., pres. 1974), So. Calif. Golf Assn. (Dir. 1966-71), Eldorado Country Club (sec., dir. 1970-72), Calif. Club, Phi Delta Phi, Alpha Delta Phi. Probate, Estate planning, Estate taxation. Home: 75-701 Camino De Plata Indian Wells CA 92210

**SMITH, CAROLE DIANNE,** lawyer, editor, writer, product developer; b. Seattle, June 12, 1945; d. Glaude Francis and Elaine Claire (Finkenstein) S.; m. Stephen Bruce Presser, June 18, 1968 (div. June 1987); children: David Carter, Elisabeth Catherine. AB cum laude, Harvard U., Radcliffe Coll., 1968; JD, Georgetown U., 1974. Bar: Pa. 1974. Law clk. Hon. Judith Jamison, Phila., 1974-75; assoc. Gratz, Tate, Spiegel, Ervin & Ruthrouff, Phila., 1975-76; freelance editor, writer Evanston, Ill., 1983-87; editor Ill. Inst. Tech., Chgo., 1987-88; mng. editor LawLetters, Inc., Chgo., 1988-89; editor ABA, Chgo., 1989-95; product devel. dir. Gt. Lakes divsn. Lawyers Coop. Pub., Deerfield, Ill., 1995-96; product devel. mgr. Midwest Market Ctr. West Group, Deerfield, Ill., 1996-97; mgr acquisitions, bus. and fin. group CCH, Inc., Riverwoods, Ill., 1997—. Author Jour. of Legal Medicine, 1975, Selling and the Law: Advertising and Promotion, 1987; (under pseudonym Sarah Toast) 68 children's books, 1994-99; editor The Brief, 1990-95, Criminal Justice, 1989-90, 92-95 (Gen. Excellence award Soc. Nat. Assn. Pubs. 1990, Feature Article award-bronze Soc. Nat. Assn. Pubs. 1994), Franchise Law Jour., 1995; editor-in-chief The Brief, ABA Tort and Ins. Practice Sect., 1998—; mem. editl. bd. The Brief, ABA Tort and Ins. Practice Sect., 1995-98. Dir. Radcliffe Club of Chgo., 1990-93; mem. parents council Latin Sch. Chgo., 1995-96. Mem. ABA, ATLA, Def. Rsch. Inst. Office: CCH Inc Bus and Fin Group 2700 Lake Cook Rd Riverwoods IL 60015-3867

**SMITH, CARRIE LYNETTE,** lawyer; b. Buffalo, Oct. 1, 1964; d. Terry D. and Janet M. (Wilson) S. BA, Colgate U., Hamilton, N.Y., 1986; JD, SUNY, Buffalo, 1989. Bar: N.Y. 1990. Assoc. Smith, Keller, Hayes & Miner, Buffalo, 1990-94; ptnr. Smith, Keller, Miner & O'Shea, Buffalo, 1994—. Mem. Women's Bar Assn. State N.Y. (local dir. 1991-93, dir. state bd. 1993-95), Erie County Bar Assn., Western N.Y. Trial Lawyers Assn. (treas. 1999). State civil litigation, Personal injury, Insurance. Office: Smith Keller Miner & O'Shea 69 Delaware Ave Rm 1212 Buffalo NY 14202-3801

**SMITH, CHARLES Z.,** state supreme court justice; b. Lakeland, Fla., Feb. 23, 1927; s. John R. and Eva (Love) S.; m. Eleanor Jane Martinez, Aug. 20, 1955; children: Carlos M., Michael O., Stephen P., Felica L. BS, Temple U., 1952; JD, U. Wash., 1955. Bar: Wash. 1955. Law clk. Wash. Supreme Ct., Olympia, 1955-56; dep. pros. atty., asst. chief criminal div. King County, Seattle, 1956-60; ptnr. Bianchi, Smith & Tobin, Seattle, 1960-61; spl. asst. to atty. gen. criminal div. U.S. Dept. Justice, Washington, 1961-64; judge criminal dept. Seattle Mcpl. Ct., 1965-66; judge Superior Ct. King County, 1966-73; former assoc. dean, prof. law U. Wash., 1973; now justice Wash. Supreme Ct., Olympia. Mem. adv. bd. NAACP, Seattle Urban League, Wash. State Literacy Coun., Boys Club, Wash. Citizens for Migrant Affairs, Medina Children's Svc., Children's Home Soc. Wash., Seattle Better Bus. Bur., Seattle Foundation, Seattle Symphony Orch., Seattle Opera Assn., Community Svc. Ctr. for Deaf and Hard of Hearing, Seattle U., Seattle Sexual Assault Ctr., Seattle Psychoanalytic Inst., The Little Sch., Linfield Coll., Japanese Am. Citizens League, Kawabe Meml. Hous, Puget Counseling Ctr, Am. Cancer Soc., Hutchinson Cancer Rsch. Ctr., Robert Chinn Found.; pres. Am. Bapt. Chs. U.S.A., 1976-77, lt. col. ret. USMCR. Mem. ABA, Am. Judicature Soc., Washington Bar Assn., Seattle-King County Bar Assn., Order of Coif., Phi Alpha Delta, Alpha Phi Alpha. Office: Wash Supreme Ct Temple of Justice PO Box 40929 Olympia WA 98504-0929

**SMITH, CLARK ROBINSON,** lawyer; b. Chgo., Feb. 17, 1938; s. Carlton Robinson and Theda Clark (Peters) S.; m. Trina Helen Hendershot, Jan. 20, 1962; children: Clark Carlton, Luke Owen. BS in Econs., U. Pa., 1961; LLB, U. Wis., 1965. Bar: Mass. 1966, U.S. Surpeme Ct. 1976, U.S. Dist. Ct. Mass. 1976, U.S. Tax Ct. 1976. From law clk. to assoc. Johnson Clapp Ives & King, Boston, 1965-67; pvt. practice Boston, 1972—; bd. dirs., acting chair Zoning Bd. Appeals, Wenham, Mass., 1982-94; bd. dirs. Menasha Corp., Neenah, Wis., Beverly (Mass.) Nat. Bank. Trustee Beverly Regional YMCA, 1984—; bd. dirs. North Country Sch., Lake Placid, N.Y., 1988-95, Menasha Corp. Found., Neenah, 1994; chmn. bd. Theda C. Smith Found., Neenah, 1980—, United Way Cen. North Shore, Beverly, 1993-94. Fellow Mass. Bar Found. (mem. com., county advisor 1990—); mem. ABA, Mass. Bar Assn., Boston Bar Assn. (coms., vol. civil case appts. 1976—), Boston Bar Found. (life, endowment advisor 1990—). Republican. Episcopalian. Avocations: golfing, tennis, skiing. Estate planning, Probate, Estate taxation. Home: 11 Dodges Row Wenham MA 01984-1601 Office: 101 Federal St Ste 1900 Boston MA 02110-1817

**SMITH, CRAIG BENNETT,** lawyer; b. Wilmington, Del., Oct. 16, 1943; s. Wilfred Winter and Louetta Beatrice (Bennett) S.; m. Charlotte Anne Boucheron, May 27, 1967; 1 child, Stuart Evan. BA in English, Carleton Coll., 1966; MA in Creative Writing, Syracuse U., 1969, JD summa cum laude, 1975. Bar: U.S. Dist. Ct. Del. 1975. Assoc. Morris, Nichols, Arsht & Tunnell, Wilmington, 1975-83; ptnr. Biggs & Battaglia, Wilmington, 1983-84, Lassen, Smith, Katzenstein & Furlow, Wilmington, 1984-91, Smith, Katzenstein & Furlow, L.L.P., Wilmington, 1992—; mem. adv. bd. Bur. Nat. Affairs Corp. Practices Series, Washington, 1988—. Co-author: State Limited Partnership Laws, 1987, Guide to the Takeover Law of Delaware, 1988, Limited Partnerships: Legal Aspects of Organization, Operation and Dissolution, 1992 (book chpts.) New York and Delaware Business Entities, 1997; mem. editorial bd. State Ltd. Partnership Laws-Prentice Hall Law & Bus., 1987—; sr. notes and comments editor Syracuse Law Rev., 1974-75; contbr. articles to profl. jours. Mem. Del. Gov's High Tech. Task Force, Wilmington, 1986, com. bus. & indsl. devel. cos. Del. Econ. Devel. Office, Wilmington, 1988. Named to Justinian Soc., 1974. Fellow ABA (litigation sect. 1985—, bus. law sect. 1975—); mem. Del. State Bar Assn. (corp. law sect. coun. 1987-90, 93—, com. Del. Revised Uniform Ltd. Partnership Act 1984—, chancery ct. fiduciary rules adv. com. 1986-89), Order of Coif. Republican. Avocations: classical guitar playing, sculpturing. General corporate, Securities, General civil litigation. Home: 318 Spalding Rd Wilmington DE 19803-2422 Office: Smith Katzenstein & Furlow LLP The Corporate Plaza 800 Delaware Ave Wilmington DE 19801-1322

**SMITH, D. ZANE,** public defender; b. West Hollywood, Calif., Mar. 16, 1951; s. Dale and Robin Smith. BA in Philosophy, U. Calif., Santa Cruz, 1974; JD, U. Idaho, 1978. Bar: Calif., Alaska. Ptnr. Collins & Smith, Merced, Calif., 1981; assoc. Schanen Law Firm, Wasilla, Alaska, 1981-83, Jacoby & Meyers, L.A., 1985; dep. pub. defender Riverside County, Riverside, Calif., 1986-88, Ventura County, Ventura, Calif., 1988—. Mem. Ventura County Master Chorale. Avocation: music. Home: 2568 Bolker Dr Port Hueneme CA 93041-1717 Office: Ventura County Pub Defender 800 S Victoria Ave Ventura CA 93009-0001

**SMITH, DANIEL LYNN,** lawyer; b. Ottawa, Kans., June 22, 1952; s. Daniel H. and Mary K. (Lynn) S.; m. Alana A. Windhorst, Aug. 15, 1981; children: Tricia, Lauran, Alexa. BA, U. Kans., 1973; JD, Duke U., 1976. Bar: Kans. 1976, U.S. Dist. Ct. Kans. 1976, U.S. Ct. Appeals (10th cir.) 1977, U.S. Tax Ct. 1977. Assoc. Bronston Law Offices, Overland Park, Kans., 1976-78; ptnr. Oliver, Smith & Oliver, Overland Park, 1978-80, Bronston and Smith, Overland Park, 1981-92, Ankerholz & Smith, Overland Park, Kans., 1992—; pvt. practice Westwood, Kans., 1980-81. Mem. Kans. Bar Assn., Kans. Trial Lawyers Assn. (bd. govs. 1981—), Civil War Roundtable Kansas City, Phi Beta Kappa. General civil litigation, Personal injury, Workers' compensation. Home: 10075 Goodman Dr Shawnee Mission KS 66212-3432 Office: Ankerholz & Smith 6900 College Blvd Overland Park KS 66211-1547

**SMITH, DANIEL TIMOTHY,** lawyer; b. Denver, July 20, 1948; s. Harold Kennedy and Dorothy (Gannon) S. BA, Duke U., 1970; JD, U. Denver, 1973. Bar: Colo. 1973, U.S. Dist. Ct. Colo. 1973, U.S. Ct. Appeals (10th cir.), U.S. Supreme Ct. 1979, U.S. Ct. Claims 1979. Dep. dist. atty. Denver Dist. Atty. Office, 1973-74; spl. asst. atty. gen. Colo. Atty. Gen.'s Office, Denver, 1973-74; asst. U.S. atty. Dist. of Colo., Denver, 1974-76; ptnr. Wiggins & Smith P.C., Denver, 1977-87; pvt. practice Denver, 1987—. Chmn. fundraising Am. Cancer Soc., Denver., 1992-93; mem. golf com. Am. Heart Assn., Denver, 1988—. Mem. ABA, Colo. Criminal Def. Bar (sec. 1979-81). Avocation: golf. Criminal, General civil litigation. Office: 1900 Grant St Ste 580 Denver CO 80203-4301

**SMITH, DAVID BROOKS,** federal judge; b. 1951. BA, Franklin and Marshall Coll., 1973; JD, Dickinson Sch. Law, 1976. Pvt. practice Jubelirer, Carothers, Krier, Halpern & Smith, Altoona, Pa., 1976-84; judge Ct. Common Pleas of Blair County, Pa., 1984-88, U.S. Dist. Ct. (we. dist.) Pa., Johnstown, 1988—; asst. dist. atty. Blair County, part-time, 1977-79, spl. prosecutor, 1981-83, dist. atty. part-time, 1983-84; instr. Pa. State U., Altoona campus, 1977—, St. Francis Coll., 1986—; adv. com. on criminal rules U.S. Jud. Conf., 1993-99. Trustee St. Francis Coll. Mem. Pa. Bar Assn., Am. Judicature Soc., Pa. Soc., Amen Corner, Blair County Game, Fish and Forestry Assn., Fed. Judges Assn. (bd. dirs. 1993-97), Inns of Ct., Allegheny County Bar Assn., Pi Gamma Mu. Office: US Courthouse 319 Washington St Ste 104 Johnstown PA 15901-1624

**SMITH, DAVID BURNELL,** lawyer; b. Charleston, W.Va., Apr. 8, 1941; s. Ernest Dayton and Nellie Dale (Tyler) S.; m. Rita J. Hughes, Sept. 25, 1967. BA, U. Charleston, 1967; JD, U. Balt., 1972; MJS, U. Nev., 1995. Bar: Colo. 1972, Md. 1972, U.S. Supreme Ct. 1980, Ariz. 1983, U.S. Dist. Ct. Md. 1972, U.S. Dist. Ct. Colo. 1972, U.S. Ct. Appeals (4th Cir.) 1972, U.S. Ct. Appeals (9th cir. 1972, U.S. Ct. Appeals (10th cir.) 1983. Sales rep. Gulf Oil, Washington, 1967-72; pvt. practice Littleton, Colo., 1972-83, Glendale, Ariz., 1983-86, Phoenix, 1986-88, Scottsdale, Ariz., 1988—; protempore judge Wickenburg Mcpl. Ct., 1986—; presiding judge Peoria (Ariz.) Mcpl. Ct., 1987-94, Cave Creek Mcpl. Ct., 1995-98. Appeared as actor in movie Dead Girls Don't Tango, 1990. V.p. South Jefferson County Reps., Lakewood, Colo., 1979, pres., 1990; candidate Dist. 6 for Congress; pres. Ariz. Rep. Assembly Dist. 28. Served with USCG, 1959-66. Mem. ATLA, Nat. Assn. Criminal Lawyers, Am. Judicature Soc., ABA (vice-chmn. family law 1983), Nat. Assn. Criminal Def. Attys., Ariz. Magistrates Assn., Colo. Bar Assn., Ariz. Bar Assn., Md. Bar Assn., Colo. Trial Lawyers Assn., Maricopa County Bar Assn., Scottsdale Bar Assn. (bd. dirs. 1996—), Masons, Shriners, Elks. State civil litigation, Personal injury, Criminal. Home: PO Box 5145 36418 N Wildflower Rd Carefree AZ 85377-5145 Office: 4310 N 75th St Scottsdale AZ 85251-3505

**SMITH, DAVID JAMES,** corporation executive. Asst. sec. Archer Daniels Midland, Decatur, Ill., 1988-97, asst. gen. counsel, 1995-97, v.p., sec. gen. counsel, 1997—. Office: Archer Daniels Midland Co 4666 Faries Pkwy Decatur IL 62526*

**SMITH, DEIRDRE O'MEARA,** lawyer; b. N.Y.C., June 2, 1946; d. Thomas Francis and Mary Veronica (Meehan) O'Meara; children: Thomas Brady Ahr, Andrew Travers Ahr; m. Gerald Monroe Smith, Aug. 15, 1992. BA cum laude, Trinity Coll., 1968; MEd, Va. Commonwealth U., 1976; JD, U. Mo., 1982. Bar: Mo. 1982, U.S. Dist. Ct. (we. dist.) Mo. 1982. Tchr. Prince George's County Schs., Md., 1968-70, St. Michael's Sch., Richmond, Va., 1976-78; staff lawyer Mo. Supreme Ct., Jefferson City, 1982-83; gen. counsel State of Mo. Detention Facilities Commn., Jefferson City, 1983, State of Mo. Jud. Fin. Commn., Jefferson City, 1983-85; clk. of the ct. Mo. Ct. Appeals Eastern Dist., St. Louis, 1985-98. Bd. dirs. Downtown St. Louis, 1994-95. Recipient Acad. Excellence award in environ. law U. Mo. Sch. Law, 1981; disting. fellow St. Louis Bar Found. Fellow Am. Bar Found., Mo. Bar Found.; mem. ABA (jud. divsn. lawyers conf., exec. com. 1997—), Nat. Conf. Bar Pres., Nat. Conf. Bar Founds., Mo. Bar Assn. (Mo. Client Security Security Trust Fund bd. dirs. 1991-95, chmn. 1995-96), St. Louis County Bar Assn., Lawyers Assn. St. Louis (Outstanding Svc. award 1998), Met. St. Louis Bar Assn. (exec. com. 1988-96, pres. 1994-95), St. Louis Bar Found. (bd. dirs. 1989-96, pres. 1995-96), St. Louis Women Lawyers Assn. (bd. dirs. 1989-94, pres. 1992-93), Am. Judicature Soc. (bd. dirs. 1990-94, bd. exec. com. 1993—, v.p. 1995-97, sec. 1997-99, treas. 1999—), Nat. Conf. Appellate Ct. Clks. (exec. com. 1990-92), Media Club St. Louis (bd. dirs.), Phi Delta Phi. Roman Catholic.

**SMITH, DENNIS JAY,** lawyer; b. Newark, Sept. 2, 1943; s. Sidney H. and Theresa K. Smith; m. Sandra Kotzen Smith, Jan. 25, 1944; children: Sheryl, Lori. BA, Brandeis U., 1961; JD, Boston Coll., 1968. Bar: N.J. 1968, U.S. Ct. Appeals (3d cir.) 1986. Sole proprietor East Orange, N.J., 1968-77, Millburn, N.J., 1977-83; ptnr. Clancy Callahan & Smith, Newark, N.J., 1983-87, Roseland, N.J., 1987—. Mem. Am. Bar Assn., N.J. State Bar Assn. (ethics com. 1998—), Essex County Bar Assn. (chmn. gen. practice com. 1995-96), Mental Health Assn. Essex County (bd. dirs. 1977-98, pres. 1980-82). State civil litigation, Contracts commercial, General practice. Office: Clancy Callahan & Smith 103 Eisenhower Pkwy Ste 10 Roseland NJ 07068-1090

**SMITH, DOUGLAS DEAN,** lawyer; b. Idaho Falls, Idaho, Apr. 16, 1952; s. Dean C. and Evelyn (Haws) S.; m. Rhonda Lee Rasmussen, June 20, 1974; children: Ryan Douglas, Bradley Dean, Rochelle Lee, Brittany Kaylyn, Jeffery Scott, Michael Douglas. AA, Ricks Coll., 1974; BA, Brigham Young U., 1976, JD, 1978. Bar: Oreg. 1979, U.S. Dist. Ct. Oreg. 1979, U.S. Ct. Appeals (9th cir.) 1982, U.S. Supreme Ct. 1990. Assoc. Lindsay, Hart, Neil & Weigler, Portland, Oreg., 1979-83, ptnr., 1984-90; pvt. practice, Tigard, Oreg., 1990—. Contbr. articles to legal publs. Mem. ABA (antitrust sect., mem. forum com. of franchising, bus. sect.), Oreg. State Bar Assn. (continuing legal edn. author 1985-98). Republican. Mem. LDS Ch. Franchising, General corporate, Contracts commercial. Home and Office: 15760 SW Bull Mountain Rd Portland OR 97224-1241

**SMITH, DWIGHT CHICHESTER, III,** lawyer; b. Ft. Meade, Md., June 24, 1955; s. Dwight Chichester Jr. and Rachel (Stryker) S.; m. Mindy L. Kotler, Aug. 18, 1985; children: Dwight C. IV, Cornelia R. BA, Yale U., 1977, JD, 1981. Bar: D.C. 1982, N.Y. 1982. Para-legal House Ethics Com., Washington, 1977-78; law clk. to Hon. Hugh Bownes U.S. Ct. Appeals (1st cir.), Concord, N.H., 1981-82; assoc. Kaye, Scholer, Fierman, Hays & Handler, Washington, 1982-84, Covington & Burling, Washington, 1984-90; dep. chief counsel for legal policy Office of Thrift Supervision, Dept. of Treasury, Washington, 1990-94, dep. chief counsel for bus. transactions, 1995-99; counsel Alston & Bird LLP, Washington, 1999—. Article and book rev. editor Yale Law jour., 1980-81; contbr. articles to profl. jours. Mem. Potomac Boat Club, City Tavern Club. Presbyterian. Avocation: rowing. Home: 1606 32nd St NW Washington DC 20007-2930 Office: Alston & Bird LLP North Bldg 11th Fl 601 Pennsylvania Ave NW Washington DC 20004-2601

**SMITH, EDWARD SAMUEL,** federal judge; b. Birmingham, Ala., Mar. 27, 1919; s. Joseph Daniel and Sarah Jane (Tatum) S.; m. Innes Adams Comer, May 5, 1942; children: Edward Samuel, Innes Smith Cameron Richards. Student, Ala. Poly. Inst., 1936-38; B.A., U. Va., 1941, J.D., 1947. Bar: Va. 1947, D.C. 1948, Md. 1953. Assoc., then ptnr. firm Blair, Korner, Doyle & Appel, Washington, 1947-54; ptnr. firm Blair, Korner, Doyle & Worth, 1954-61; gen. counsel Nat. Cath. Edn. Assn., 1958-61; chief trial sect., tax. div. Dept. Justice, 1961, asst. for civil trials, dep. asst. atty. gen., 1961-63; ptnr. firm, head tax dept. Piper & Marbury, Balt., 1963-78; mng. ptnr. Piper & Marbury, 1971-74; assoc. judge U.S. Ct. Claims, Washington, 1978-82; judge U.S. Ct. Appeals (Fed. Cir.), Washington, 1982-89, sr. circuit judge, 1989—; liaison atty. gen. to Lawyers Com. Civil Rights Under Law, 1963; adj. faculty Cumberland Sch. Law, Samford U., 1992—. Bd. dirs. Roland Park Civic League, Inc., Balt., 1977-78; pres., St. Andrew's Soc. Washington, 1956-58. Served to lt. USNR, 1941-46; to comdr. USNR, Ret. 1968. Mem. ABA (chmn. com. on tax litigation 1977-78), Fed. Bar Assn., Md. State Bar Assn. (chmn. sect. of taxation 1971-72), D.C. Bar Assn., Va. State Bar, Met. Club, Chevy Chase Club, Lawyers Club of Washington, Summit Club (Birmingham), Lambda Chi Alpha. Democrat. Episcopalian. Office: Hugo Black US Courthouse 1729 5th Ave N Birmingham AL 35203-2000 also: US Ct Appeals Fed Crct Nat Cts Bldg 717 Madison Pl NW Washington DC 20439-0002 *The second most important rule of life is that we should never become disillusioned with the Golden Rule when others do not follow it.**

**SMITH, EDWIN DUDLEY,** lawyer; b. N.Y.C., Oct. 4, 1936; s. Edwin Dudley Jr. and Mary Jane (Bannigan) S.; m. Joan Joyce Mortenson, June 29, 1963; children: Edwin Dudley V, Patrick Townshend. BA, U. Kans., 1960, JD, 1963. Bar: Kans. 1963, Mo. 1992, U.S. Dist. Ct. Kans. 1963, U.S. Ct. Appeals (10th cir.) 1967, U.S. Supreme Ct. 1972, U.S. Dist. Ct. (we. dist.) Mo., 1998. Assoc. Fisher Patterson Sayler & Summers, Topeka, 1963-66; ptnr. Fisher Patterson Sayler & Smith, L.L.P., Topeka, 1966—. Contbg. author: Pharmacy Law Annual, 1991. Chpt. advisor Tau Kappa Epsilon Frat., 1988-93; mem. adv. bd. Florence Crittenton Svcs., Topeka, 1988-91; chmn. legis. com. U.S. Swimming, 1986-90; chmn. Missouri Valley Swimming, 1987-89. Fellow Kans. Bar Found.; mem. ABA, Kans. Bar Assn. (bd. govs. 1986-92, Outstanding Svc. award 1978), Topeka Bar Assn., Johnson County Bar Assn., Kansas City Met. Bar Assn., Internat. Assn. Def. Counsel, Am. Judicature Soc. (bd. dirs. 1984-89), Am. Bd. Trial Adv. (pres. Kans. chpt. 1989-90), Kans. Assn. Def. Counsel, Def. Rsch. Inst., Am. Soc. Pharmacy Law. Avocation: photography. General civil litigation, Personal injury, Professional liability. Home: 4344 W 124th Ter Leawood KS 66209-2277 Office: Fisher Patterson Sayler & Smith LLP 210 UMB Bank Bldg 11050 Roe Ave Overland Park KS 66211-1217 also: Fisher Patterson Sayler & Smith LLP 3550 SW 5th St Topeka KS 66606-1998

**SMITH, EDWIN ERIC,** lawyer; b. Louisville, Sept. 29, 1946; s. Lester Henry and Nancy Joy (Heyman) S.; m. Katharine Case Thomson, Aug. 16, 1969; children: Benjamin Clark, George Lewis, Andrew Laurence. BA, Yale U., 1968; JD, Harvard Law Sch., 1974. Bar: Mass. 1974, U.S. Dist. Ct. Mass. 1974. Assoc. Bingham Dana LLP, Boston, 1974-81, ptnr., 1981—; lectr. in field; Mass. commr. on uniform state laws; mem. uniform comml. code articles 5 and 9 drafting com.; U.S. del. to receivables assignment working group UN Commn. on Internat. Trade Law. Lt. USNR, 1969-71. Recipient Achievement Medal USN, 1971. Mem. ABA (chmn. uniform comml. code com. bus. law sect. 1995-99, advisor to the permanent editl. bd. uniform comml. code 1999—), Am. Law Inst. (Uniform Comml. Code article 9 study com.), Am. Coll. Comml. Fin. Lawyers (bd. regents, treas.), Assn. Comml. Fin. Attys. Banking, Bankruptcy, Contracts commercial. Home: 4 Chiltern Rd Weston MA 02493-2714 Office: Bingham Dana LLP 150 Federal St Boston MA 02110-1713

**SMITH, ELEANOR VAN LAW,** paralegal; b. Richmond, Va., Aug. 11, 1964; d. William Preston Jr. and Priscilla Norris Smith. AS, U. S.C., Columbia, 1985, BA in Interdisciplinary Studies, 1986; Paralegal Cert., Nat. Ctr. Paralegal Tng., Atlanta, 1987. Sales assoc. Ship n' Shore, Columbia, 1984-85, The Ltd., Columbia, 1985-86; office asst. Universal Printing, Charleston, S.C., 1986-87; sales assoc. Evelyn Rubin, Charleston, 1987; paralegal First Union Nat. Bank, Atlanta, 1988-89, L.J. Hooker Devel., Atlanta, 1989-90; sr. paralegal La Salle Ptns. Mgmt. and Svcs. Inc., Atlanta, 1990—, La Salle Ptnrs. Mgmt. Svcs., Inc., Atlanta, 1999—. Participant Habitat for Humanity, Atlanta, 1993-95, Multiple Sclerosis Soc., Atlanta, 1994-95, Osteoporosis Soc., Atlanta, 1997, Ptnr. for Spl. Olympics, 1999. Mem. Internat. Collectors Soc., Carolina Merchandising Club (sec. 1985-86), Delta Delta Delta. Republican. Episcopalian. Avocations: travel, tennis, cooking, knitting, exercise. Home: 838 Preston Woods Trl Dunwoody GA 30338-5432 Office: Jones Lang La Salle 3600 Piedmont Rd NE Ste 600 Atlanta GA 30305-1416

**SMITH, EMORY CLARK,** lawyer, financial advisor; b. Denton, Tex., Nov. 2, 1910; s. James Willis and Julia (Miller) S.; 1 child, Cynthia Smith O'Brien. BA, U. North Tex., 1929; MA, U. Tex., 1933; JD, So. Meth. U., 1937; SJD, George Washington U., 1954. Bar: Tex. 1937, Okla. 1937, U.S. Supreme Ct. 1954, U.S. Ct. Mil. Appeals 1955, U.S. Ct. Claims 1956, U.S. Ct. Customs and Patent Appeals 1956. Pvt. practice Oklahoma City, 1937-42; commd. USN, 1942-72, advanced through grades to capt.; chief counsel USN Oceanographic Office U.S. Civil Svc., Washington, 1972-73; cons. anti-trust atty. Foster Assocs., Washington, 1973-84; pvt. practice Washington, 1994; ret., 1995; adj. prof. internat. law Am. U., Washington, 1977-84; energy cons. Foster Assocs., 1973-84; fin. advisor Friday Music Found., Washington, 1988-94; lectr. in field. Author: Law of the Sea, 1954; contbr. articles to profl. jours. Vestryman St. Alban's Ch., Washington, 1957-59, St. Paul's Within the Walls, Rome, 1967-68. Named Disting. Alumnus U. North Tex., 1972. Fellow N.Y. Explorers Club, Fed. Bar Assn., Inter-Am. Bar Assn. (natural resources com. chmn. 1973-76), Masons. Republican. Episcopalian. Avocation: farming. Office: 2118 49th St NW Washington DC 20007-1524

**SMITH, FERN M.,** judge; b. San Francisco, Nov. 7, 1933. AA, Foothill Coll., 1970; BA, Stanford U., 1972, JD, 1975. Bar: Calif. 1975. children: Susan Morgan, Julie. Assoc. firm Bronson, Bronson & McKinnon, San Francisco, 1975-81, ptnr., 1982-86; judge San Francisco County Superior Ct., 1986-88, U.S. Dist. Ct. for Northern Dist. Calif., 1988—; mem. U.S. Jud. Conf., Adv. Com. Rules of Evidence, 1993-96, chair, 1996—; mem. hiring, mgmt. and pers. coms., active recruiting various law schs. Contbr. articles to legal publ. Apptd. by Chief Justice Malcolm Lucas to the Calif. Jud. Coun.'s Adv. Task Force on Gender Bias in the Cts., 1987-89; bd. visitors Law Sch. Stanford U. Mem. ABA, Queen's Bench, Nat. Assn. Women Judges, Calif. Women Lawyers, Bar Assn. of San Francisco, Fed. Judges Assn., 9th Cir. Dist. Judges Assn., Am. Judicature Soc., Calif. State Fed. Judicial Coun., Phi Beta Kappa.

**SMITH, FRANK TUPPER,** lawyer; b. Englewood, N.J., May 21, 1929; s. Frank T. and Mary Elizabeth S.; m. Jill K. Jacobsen, Mar. 9, 1957; children—Delia, Lisa Noel, Kathryn. B.A., Columbia Coll., 1951, J.D., Columbia U., 1954, M.B.A., NYU, 1963; cert. estate planning and probate law specialist, Tex. Bar: N.Y. 1956, Calif. 1966, Tex. 1974, U.S. Supreme Ct. 1963. Assoc., Vaughn & Lyons, N.Y.C., 1956-60; assoc. Edward R. Peckerman, N.Y.C., 1960-63; v.p. Bank of Calif., San Francisco, 1963-69; assoc. Paul Hastings Janofsky & Walker, Los Angeles, 1969-72; v.p., trust officer Republic Nat. Bank, Dallas, 1972-74; ptnr. Smith, Miller & Carlton, Dallas, 1975-87; sr. ptnr. Frank Tupper Smith & Assocs. PC, 1987—; lectr. estate and tax planning U. Tex., Dallas, Dallas Community Coll. Dist. Bd. dirs. Am. Heart Assn., 1979-82, Tex. chmn. planned giving com. 1980-82, nat. chmn. planned giving com., 1983-86; bd. dirs., v.p. fund raising Brain/Behavior Ctr., 1992—; bd. dirs. Planned Living Assistance Network North Tex., Inc., 1996—. Served with AUS, 1954-56. Mem. Calif. State Bar Assn., Tex. State Bar Assn., Dallas Bar Assn., ABA. Clubs: Columbia University North Tex. (pres. 1980-86), University, Rush Creek Yacht (Dallas). Estate planning, Estate taxation, Probate. Home: 3975 High Summit Dr Dallas TX 75244-6623 Office: 3860 W Northwest Hwy Dallas TX 75220-5183

**SMITH, FRED DEMPSEY, JR.,** lawyer; b. Mt. Airy, N.C., June 2, 1947; s. Fred Dempsey and Agnes Maybelle (Smith) S.; children: Emily Hope, Jenny Noel, Davis Sheffney. BA, U. Richmond, 1969; JD, U. Va., 1972. Bar: Va. 1976, U.S. Dist. Ct. (we. dist.) Va. 1977, U.S. Ct. Appeals 1980, U.S. Supreme Ct. 1981, U.S. Dist. Ct. (ea. dist.) Va. 1987. Prosecutor Henry County Commonwealth's Atty's. Office, Martinsville, Va., 1972-77; pvt. practice law Martinsville, 1977, 80-82, 85-87, 89—; ptnr. Gendron, Kirby & Smith, Martinsville, 1977-80; pres. Hartley & Smith, P.C., Martinsville, 1983-85; ptnr. Minor & Smith, Richmond, Va., 1987-88; mem. civil trial adv. Nat. Bd. Trial Advocacy. Contbr. article and seminar materials to legal publs. Mem. Henry County Dem. Com., 1975-76, candidate Va. Gen. Assembly, 1977; active Piedmont Regional Mental Health & Mental Retardation, Martinsville, 1975-83. Capt. JAGC, USAR, 1972-77. Recipient Appreciationcert. Gov. Va., 1971. Mem. ABA, ATLA, Va. State Bar Assn., Va. Trial Lawyers Assn. (bd. govs. 1983-90, mem. continuing legal edn. com. 1986-87, publ. com. 1984-85, amicus curiae 1988-90, chmn. ann. conv. 1990), Richmond Trial Lawyers Assn. (prs. 1991), Martinsville and Henry County Bar Assn. (v.p., pres. 1986-87). Mem. Disciples of Christ. Avocations: choir, piano, swimming, jogging. Personal injury, General civil litigation. Office: Young Haskins et al PO Box 72 Martinsville VA 24114-0072

**SMITH, FREDERICK THEODORE,** lawyer, educator; b. Jersey City, Apr. 7, 1956; s. George Gilbert and Caroline (Jeter) S. BA, Harvard Coll., 1978; BA, MA, Oxford (Eng.) U., 1980; JD, Harvard U., 1985; MPA, J.F. Kennedy Sch., 1985. Bar: N.J. 1987, U.S. Dist. N.J. 1990, U.S. Supreme Ct. 1996. Summer assoc. Lowenstein, Sandler, Kohl, Fisher & Boylan, Newark, 1982, Manatt, Phelps, Rothenberg & Tunney, L.A., 1983; intern Office of N.J. Pub. Adv., spring 1985; summer assoc. Kaye, Scholer, Fierman, Hays & Handler, Washington, 1985; jud. clerkship to Hon. David Nelson Fed. Dist. Ct., Boston, 1985-86; assoc. Shearman & Sterling, N.Y.C., 1984, 86-87; assoc. McCarter & English, Newark, 1987-93, ptnr., 1993—; N.J. Bd. Law Examiners, 1990—; hearing officer Essex County, N.J., 1988-91; adj. prof. Seton Hall Law Sch., N.J., 1994—. Editor: New Jersey Law of Product Liability, 1994; mem. editl. bd. N.J. Lawyer, 1993-95. Bd. overseers Gov.'s Schs. N.J., 1994—; trustee St. Peter's Prep. Sch., Jersey City, 1993—; bd. dirs. Newark YMCA, 1996—. Recipient Rhodes scholarship Oxford U./Rhodes Trust, Eng., 1978-80, Earl Warren scholarship NAACP Legal Def. Fund, 1981. Mem. Harvard Club N.J. (exec. com. 1990—). Product liability, Toxic tort, Contracts commercial. Home: PO Box 1449 Newark NJ 07101-1449 Office: McCarter and English 4 Gateway Ctr Ste 1200 Newark NJ 07102-4096

**SMITH, GEORGE BUNDY,** state supreme court justice; b. New Orleans, Apr. 7, 1937; m. Alene L. Smith; children: George, Jr., Beth Beatrice. Cert. Polit. Studies, Institut d'Etudes Politiques, Paris, 1958; BA, Yale U., 1959, JD, 1962; MA in Polit. Sci., NYU, 1967, PhD, 1974. temp. judge Family Ct. N.Y. State, Crimal Ct. N.Y.C. Staff atty. NAACP, 1962-64; law sec. to Hon. Jawn Sandifer, 1964-67, law sec. to Hon., Edward Dudley, 1967-71, law sect. to Hon. Harold Stevens, 1972-74; adminstr. model cities City of N.Y., 1974-75; interim judge Civil Ct. N.Y.C., 1975-76, judge, 1976-79; judge N.Y. State Supreme Ct., 1980-86, assoc. justice appellate divsn., 1st dept., 1987-92; assoc. judge N.Y. State Ct. Appeals, 1992—; apptd. mem. N.Y. State Ethics Commn. Unified Ct. System; adj. prof. law Fordham U., 1981—. Author: (with Alene L. Smith) You Decide: Applying the Bill of Rights to Real Cases; contbr. articles to profl. jours. Trustee Grace Congl. Ch., Harlem, N.Y., Horace Mann-Barnard Sch., Bronx, N.Y.; bd. dirs. Harlem-Dowling Westside Ctr. for Children and Family Svcs., N.Y.C.; former alumni trustee Phillips Acad., Andover, Mass. Mem. Met. Black Bar Assn. (founding, former pres. Harlem Lawyers Assn., bd. dirs., chmn. 1984-88), Assn. of Bar of City of N.Y. (v.p. 1988-89), Judicial Friends, Network of Bar Leaders. Office: NY Court Appeals 29th Fl 61 Broadway Rm 2900 New York NY 10006-2802 also: Ct of Appeals Hall 20 Eagle St Albany NY 12207-1009*

**SMITH, GEORGE CURTIS,** judge; b. Columbus, Ohio, Aug. 8, 1935; s. George B. and Dorothy R. Smith; m. Barbara Jean Wood, July 10, 1963; children: Curtis, Geoffrey, Elizabeth Ann. BA, Ohio State U., 1957, JD, 1959. Bar: Ohio 1959, U.S. Dist. Ct. (so. dist.) Ohio 1987. Asst. city atty. City of Columbus, 1959-62; exec. asst. to Mayor of Columbus, 1962-63; asst. atty. gen. State of Ohio, 1964; chief counsel to pros. atty. Franklin County, Ohio, 1965-70; prof. atty. Franklin County, 1971-80; judge Franklin County Mcpl. Ct., Columbus, 1980-85, Franklin County Common Pleas Ct., 1985-87; mem. Ohio Bicentennial Com. 2003; mem. Ohio Supreme Ct. Coun. on Victims Rights, 1988-94; judge in residence Law Sch. U. Cin., 1993; chair Fed. Ct. Case Settlement Svc., 1997; faculty Ohio Jud. Coll., Litig. Practice Inst.; chmn. 1994, Fed. Bench-Bar Conf., 1995; lectr. ABA Anti-Trust Sec., 1995, 97; alumni spkr. law graduation Ohio State U., 1995; pres. Young Rep. Club, 1963; chmn. Perry Group, Put-in-Bay, 1999; exec. com. Franklin County Rep. Party, 1971-80. Elder Presbyn. Ch. Recipient Superior Jud. Svc. award Supreme Ct. Ohio; Resolution of Hon., Columbus Bldg. and Constrn. Trades Coun. Mem. ATLA, FBA, Ohio Pros. Attys. Assn. (pres., Ohio Pros. of Yr. Award of Hon. Leadership award), Columbus Bar Assn., Columbus Bar Found., Ohio Mcpl. Judges Assn. (v.p. 1983), Columbus Athletic Club (pres., dir.), Lawyers Club of Columbus (pres. 1975), Masons (33d degree), Shriners. Office: 85 Marconi Blvd Columbus OH 43215-2823

**SMITH, GEORGE JOSEPH,** legal assistant; b. Paterson, N.J., Jan. 31, 1951; s. Edward Alfred and Cecelia Angela (Darms) S.; m. Jean Ann Corry, Mar. 25, 1976 (div. Oct., 1981); m. Margaret Elizabeth Johnson, Dec. 2, 1988; children: Nolan, Jessica. Student, County Coll. of Morris, Dover, N.J., 1970-72; BA in Polit. Sci., Blackburn Coll., Carlinville, Ill., 1972-75. Legal asst. Willkie, Farr & Gallagher, N.Y.C., 1983-86, Sills, Cummis, Zuckerman et al., Newark, 1987-89, Kay, Collyer & Boose, N.Y.C., 1989-92, De Cotiis, Fitzpatrick & Gluck, Trenton, N.J., 1992—. Mem. Nat. Assn. Bond Lawyers. Home: 265 Danforth Ave Jersey City NJ 07305-1942 Office: De Cotiis Fitzpatrick & Gluck 50 W State St Trenton NJ 08608-1220

**SMITH, GLEE SIDNEY, JR.,** lawyer; b. Rozel, Kans., Apr. 29, 1921; s. Glee S. and Bernice M. (Augustine) S.; m. Geraldine B. Buhler, Dec. 14, 1943; children: Glee S., Stephen B., Susan K. AB, U. Kans., 1943, JD, 1947. Bar: Kans. 1947, U.S. Dist. Ct. 1951, U.S. Supreme Ct. 1973, U.S. Ct. Mil. Appeals 1988. Ptnr. Smith, Burnett & Larson, Larned, Kans., 1947—; of counsel Barber, Emerson et. al., Lawrence, Kans., 1992—. Kans. state senator, 1957-73, pres. Senate, 1965-73; mem. Kans. Bd. Regents, 1975-83, pres., 1976; bd. govs. Kans. U. Law Soc., 1967—; mem. Kans. Jud. Coun., 1963-65; county atty. Pawnee County, 1949-53; mem. bd. edn. Larned, 1951-63; Kans. commr. Nat. Conf. Commn. on Uniform State Laws, 1963—. Bd. dirs. Nat. Legal Svcs. Corp., 1975-79. Served to 1st lt. U.S. Army, 1943-45. Recipient Disting. Svc. award, U. Kans. Law Sch., 1976; Disting. Svc. citation U. Kans., 1984. Fellow Am. Coll. Probate Counsel, Am. Bar Found.; mem. ABA (bd. of govs. 1987-90, chmn. ops. com. 1989-90, exec. com. 1989-90, chmn. task force on solo and small firm practitioner 1990-91, chmn. com. on solo and small firm practitioners 1992-94, chmn. task force on applying fed. legis. to congress 1994-96), Kans. Bar Assn. (del. to ABA ho. of dels. 1982-92, bd. govs. 1982-92, leadership award 1973, medal of Distinction 1993), Southwest Kans. Bar Assn., Am. Judicature Soc. Republican. Presbyterian. Clubs: Kiwanis, Masons, Rotary. General practice, Probate, Estate taxation. Home: 115 E 9th St Apt 5 Larned KS 67550-2647 Home: 4313 Quail Pointe Rd Lawrence KS 66047-1966

**SMITH, GRANT B.,** lawyer; b. Durham, N.C., Oct. 18, 1961; s. J. Graham and Jean Botler S.; m. Holly Harnsberger, Aug. 25, 1990; children: Caroline Grace, Sarah Elizabeth. BBA, U. Ga., 1983, MBA, 1984, JD, 1987. Assoc. Dennis, Corry & Porter, Atlanta, 1987-94, ptnr., 1995—, mng. ptnr., 1996-97. Mem. ABA (vice chair comml. transp. litigation com. 1998—, newsletter editor 1998—), Ga. Defense Lawyers Assn. (dir. 1998—). Transportation, Federal civil litigation, State civil litigation. Home: 1186 Village Cv NE Atlanta GA 30319-5308 Office: Dennis Corry & Porter 950 E Paces Ferry Rd NE Atlanta GA 30326-1180

**SMITH, GREGORY DALE,** lawyer, judge; b. Knoxville, Feb. 1, 1963; s. James C. and Essie Pearl (Norman) S.; m. Cynthia Luckett, Oct. 15, 1988; children: Leora, Philip. BS, Middle Tenn. State U., 1985; JD, Cumberland Law Sch., 1988. Bar: Tenn., U.S. Supreme Ct., U.S. Ct. Appeals (fed. crct.), U.S. Ct. Mil. Appeals, U.S. Dist. Ct. (mid., ea. and we. dists.) Tenn., Army Ct. of Mil. Rev., U.S. Ct. Vet. Appeals. Mcpl. magistrate City of Birmingham, Ala., 1987-88; assoc. Marks, Marks & Shell, Clarksville, Tenn., 1988-89; juvenile referee Montgomery County Juvenile Ct., Clarksville, Tenn., 1992-95; assoc. Richardson & Richardson, Clarksville, Tenn., 1989-93; pvt. practice Clarksville, 1993—; adj. prof. Austin Peay State U., Clarksville, 1989—; lectr. in field; hearing officer Tenn. Bd. Profl., 1993—; mcpl. judge, Pleasant View, Tenn., 1997. Author: The TACDL Guide to Defending Juvenile Cases in Tennessee, 1993; co-author: Juvenile Courts in Tennessee, 1998; contbr. articles to profl. jours. Bd. dirs. United Way of Clarksville and Montgomery County, 1992—, Treehouse Daycare Ctr., 1991-95, sec., 1992, v.p., 1993, pres. 1994; Leadership Clarksville; participant UN conf. juvenile drug prevention, 1994. Named Internat. Man of the Yr. Internat. Biog. Ctr., Cambridge, Eng., 1992, Outstanding Young Alumnus, Middle Tenn. State U., 1999. Mem. ABA (juvenile justice com. nat. chmn. 1990-92, nat. vice chmn. litigation 1992-93), Tenn. Assn. Criminal Def. Lawyers (chmn. juvenile justice com. 1991-95, chmn. ethics com. 1995—), Montgomery County Young Lawyers (pres. 1991—), Tenn. Bar Assn. (assoc. gen. counsel), Tenn. Young Lawyers Conf. (bd. dirs. 1992-94). Democrat. General practice, Juvenile, Criminal. Office: 1 Public Sq Ste 321 Clarksville TN 37040-3463

**SMITH, GREGORY DEAN,** association administrator; b. Wadena, Minn., Dec. 20, 1969; s. Gary Dean and Rose Elaine Smith. BA, Hamline U., 1991; JD, Georgetown U., 1995. Paralegal U.S. Dept. Labor, Washington, 1990-93, U.S. Atty.'s Office, Washington, 1993-95; task force dir. Am. Legal Exch. Coun., Washington, 1995-97; dir. govt. rels. Internat. Franchise Assn., Washington, 1997-99; mng. dir. Am. Rd. Transp. Builders Assn., Washington, 1999—. Home: Apt 101 21 6th St NE Washington DC 20002-6051 Office: Am Rd and Transp Builders Assn 1010 Massachusetts Ave NW Washington DC 20001-5402

**SMITH, GREGORY MICHAEL,** lawyer; b. Chgo., Oct. 31, 1968; s. James Joseph and Joanne Darlene Smith; m. Patricia Ann Walsh, July 25, 1998. BSME, U. Colo., 1992; JD, John Marshall Law Sch., 1998. Bar: Ill. Sr. quality engr. Shure Bros. Inc., Evanston, Ill., 1992-98; assoc. Potter & Thorelli, Chgo., 1998, Freeborn & Peters, Chgo., 1998—. Mem. ABA, Ill. State Bar Assn., Chgo. Bar Assn., Justinian Soc. Lawyers, Seventh Circuit Bar Assn. Roman Catholic. E-mail: gsmith@freebornpeters.com. Intellectual property, Patent, Trademark and copyright. Home: 1147 Lillian Ln West Chicago IL 60185-5170 Office: Freeborn & Peters 311 S Wacker Dr Ste 3000 Chicago IL 60606-6679

**SMITH, GRETCHEN NICOLE,** lawyer; b. Evanston, Ill., Apr. 29, 1971; d. Francis Patrick and Geraldine Ann Smith. BA, U. Ariz., 1993; JD, George Washington U., 1996. Bar: Ariz. 1996, U.S. Dist. Ct. Ariz. 1996, D.C. 1999. Assoc. Snell & Wilmer, Phoenix, Ariz., 1996—. Articles editor: (jour.) The Environ. Lawyer, 1995-96. Recorder Ariz. Women's Town Hall, Phoenix, 1997. Mem. Ariz. Assn. Def. Counsel (v.p. young lawyers divsn. 1996-98, pres. young lawyers divsn. 1998-99). Republican. Roman Catholic. Avocations: soccer, hiking, running. Product liability, General civil litigation. Office: Snell & Wilmer 1 Arizona Ctr Phoenix AZ 85004

**SMITH, H(AROLD) LAWRENCE,** lawyer; b. Evergreen Park, Ill., June 27, 1932; s. Harold Lawrence and Lorna Catherine (White) S.; m. Madonna Jeanne Koehl, June 9, 1956 (div. 1968); children: Lawrence Kirby, Sandra Michele, Madonna Clare Galloway; m. Nancy Leigh Baum, May 2, 1970 (dec. 1983); m. Louise Fredericka Jeffrey, Nov. 2, 1984 (div. 1994); m. Marianne Lorraine Laug, Apr. 19, 1997. BS, U.S. Naval Acad., 1956; JD, John Marshall Law Sch., 1965. Bar: Ill. 1965, Mich. 1986,U.S. Dist. Ct. (no. dist.) Ill. 1965, U.S. Ct. Appeals (7th cir.) 1967, U.S. Ct. of Customs and Patent Appeals, 1976, U.S. Ct. Appeals (fed. cir.) 1982, U.S. Patent and Trademark Office 1968. Asst. prof. naval sci. U. Notre Dame, 1960-61; tech. asst. Langner, Parry, Card & Langner, Chgo., 1961-65, assoc., 1965-69; patent atty. Borg-Warner Corp., Chgo., 1970-74; sr. patent atty. Continental Can Co., Inc., Chgo. and Oak Brook, Ill., 1974-82, asst. gen. counsel, Stamford and Norwalk, Conn., 1982-86; ptnr. Varnum, Riddering, Schmidt & Howlett, Grand Rapids, Mich., 1986-96, counsel, 1996-97; ptnr. Rader, Fishman, Grauer & McGarry, Grand Rapids, Mich., 1997—; adj. prof. patent law Cooley Law Sch., 1991—. Served to lt. USN, 1956-61. Fellow Mich. State Bar Found.; mem. Intellectual Property Law Assn. Chgo., Chartered Inst. Patent Agts. (London), World Affairs Coun. of Western Mich. (dir. 1996—, treas. 1998—), Internat. Platform Assn., Peninsular Club. Patent, Antitrust, Trademark and copyright. Office: Rader Fishman Grauer & McGarry 171 Monroe Ave NW Ste 600 Grand Rapids MI 49503-2634

**SMITH, IVAN HERBERT,** lawyer, consultant; b. Downs, Kans., Jan. 9, 1921; s. Zebulan Herbert Smith and Carrie Lorina Williams; m. Wanda Dale Leatherman, June 4, 1943 (div. June 1968); children: Diana Dale Crouse, Debra Dawn Storment; m. Middie Moore, Jan. 30, 1970 (dec. Aug. 1997). BA, Hastings Coll., 1947; LLB, U. Ark., 1950, JD, 1954. Bar: Ark. 1950. State social svc. atty. Ark. Welfare Dept., Little Rock, 1952-62, dir. legal svcs., 1962-85; state info. officer 1st Nat. Pres. Uniform Reciprocal Support, Little Rock, 1953-85; spl. atty. gen. State of Ark. Author: (manual) Handbook on Statute Drafting, 1949, Procedure on Reciprocal Support, 1961. Tchr. men's Sunday sch. class, 1976-96. Served to col. Neb. N.G., 1940-81. em. Am. Legion (state oratorical chmn. 1986-96, post, dist. and state vice chmn . 1969-98), Masons (33d degree, worship master 1998), Order Ea. Star (worthy grand patron Ark. 1989). Methodist. Home: 1208 N Oaks Ln North Little Rock AR 72118-3355

**SMITH, J. EDWARD,** lawyer; b. Poughkeepsie, N.Y., Nov. 16, 1962; s. F. Houston and Gaille R. S.; m. Roberta Jill Kotz, May 19, 1990; children: Brittany, Travis, Tyler. BBA, U. Tex., 1984, MBA, 1985; JD, NYU, 1993. Tax assoc. Coopers & Lybrand, Austin, Tex., 1985-90; assoc. Cahill Gordon & Reindel, N.Y.C., 1993-97; sr. counsel corp. & fin. Allied Signal Corp., Morristown, N.J., 1997—. Securities, Finance, General corporate. Home: 19 Yuro Dr Edison NJ 08837-2754 Office: Allied Signal Corp 101 Columbia Rd Morristown NJ 07960-4658

**SMITH, JAMES ALBERT,** lawyer; b. Jackson, Mich., May 12, 1942; s. J. William and Mary Barbara (Browning) S.; m. Lucia S. Santini, Aug. 14, 1965; children: Matthew Browning, Aaron Michael, Rachel Elizabeth. BA, U. Mich., 1964, JD, 1967. Bar: Mich. 1968, U.S. Dist. Ct. (ea. dist.) Mich., U.S. Ct. Appeals (6th and D.C. cirs.), U.S. Supreme Ct. Assoc. Bodman, Longley & Dahling, Detroit, 1967-75, ptnr., 1975—; mem. panel Atty. Discipline Bd., Wayne County, Mich., 1987—; arbitrator Am. Arbitration Assn., 1975—; mem. Banking Commrs. com. on Contested Case Adminstrn., 1978. Mem. pro bono referral group Call For Action, Detroit, 1982—. Mem. ABA, State Bar Mich., Detroit Bar Assn., Detroit Athletic Club, Grosse Pointe Sail Club. Roman Catholic. Avocations: sailing, travel. Federal civil litigation, Insurance, Public utilities. Office: Bodman Longley & Dahling 100 Renaissance Ctr Ste 34 Detroit MI 48243-1001

**SMITH, JAMES BARRY,** lawyer; b. N.Y.C., Feb. 28, 1947; s. Irving and Vera (Donaghy) S.; m. Kathleen O'Connor, May 28, 1977; children: Jennifer, Kelly. BA in Econs., Colgate U., 1968; JD, Boston U., 1974. Assoc. McDermott, Will & Emery, Chgo., 1974-78; assoc. Ungaretti & Harris, Chgo., 1978-80, ptnr., 1980O, head real estate dept., 1988O. Lt. U.S. Navy, 1968-70. Mem. Chgo. Bar Assn., Chgo. Mortgage Atty. Assn. Avocations: sports, reading, travel. Real property. Office: Ungaretti & Harris 3500 Three First Nat Pla Chicago IL 60602

**SMITH, JAMES DWIGHT,** lawyer; b. Atlanta, Apr. 30, 1956; s. Roland James and Georgia (Higgins) S.; m. Celeste Carlton, Oct. 8, 1983; 1 child, Anna Marie. BS, Samford U., 1977; postgrad., U. Ala., 1977-79, JD, 1982. Bar: Ala. 1982, U.S. Dist. Ct. (no. dist.) Ala. 1983, U.S. Ct. Appeals (11th cir.) 1983, U.S. Supreme Ct. 1993. Assoc. Hubbard, Waldrop, Tanner & Degraffenried, Tuscaloosa, Ala., 1982-84; ptnr. Searcy and Smith, P.C., Tuscaloosa, 1984-86; pvt. practice Tuscaloosa, 1986-89; mng. ptnr. Smith and Ferguson, Tuscaloosa, 1989-91, Smith and Kelly, Tuscaloosa, 1991-93; pvt. practice Tuscaloosa, 1993—; mem. profl. adv. bd. Ala. Mental Health Tech. Orgn., Tuscaloosa, 1985-86, 89-91; adj. judge Moot Ct. program U. Ala., 1983—. Assoc. editor Law and Psychology Rev., 1981-82; editorial adv. bd. Cts., Health Sci. and the Law, 1989-91; contbr. articles to profl. jours. Advisor, zone chmn. adminstr. Circle K. Internat., 1987—; mem. Tuscaloosa County Dem. Exec. Com.; chmn. Tuscaloosa County Dem. Party, 1997—; chmn. County Dem. Exec. Com. Mem. ATLA, Ala. Trial Lawyers Assn., Tuscaloosa Trial Lawyers Assn., Ala. State Bar (pub. rels. com. 1989-96, indigent def. com. 1995—), Tuscaloosa County Bar Assn. (Law Day com. 1982-86, pub. rels. com. 1989-98, law libr. com. 1994-97, mediator 1997—), U. Ala. Alumni Assn., Kiwanis (local pres., lt. gov.), Univ. Club. Democrat. Presbyterian (elder). Avocations: sports, personal computers. Personal injury, General civil litigation, Criminal. Home: 1502 7th St Tuscaloosa AL 35401-1908 Office: 2820 7th St Tuscaloosa AL 35401-1808

**SMITH, JAMES W., JR.,** state supreme court justice; b. Louisville, Miss., Oct. 28, 1943. BS, U. So. Miss., 1965; JD, Jackson Sch. Law, 1972; MEd with honors, Miss. Coll., 1973. Bar: Miss. 1972, U.S. Dist. Ct. (no. and so. dists.) Miss. 1973, U.S. Ct. Appeals (5th cir.) 1974. Pvt. practice Pearl, 1972-78, Brandon, 1979-80; prosecuting atty. City of Pearl, 1973-80; dist. atty. 20th Jud. Dist., 1977-82; judge Rankin County, 1982-92; Supreme Ct. justice Cen. Dist., 1993—; instr. courtroom procedure and testifying Miss. Law Enforcement Tng. Acad., 1980-91. With U.S. Army, 1966-69. Named Wildlife Conservationist of Yr. Rankin County, 1988; recipient Outstanding Positive Role Model for Today's Youth award, 1991, Child Forever award Miss. Voices of Children and Youth, 1992, You've Made a Difference award, 1995, Alumnus of Yr. award Hinds C.C., 1996. Mem. VFW, Miss. State Bar Assn., Rankin County Bar Assn., Nat. Wildlife Fedn., Nat. Wild Turkey Fedn., Jackson Downtown Rotary Club. Office: Carroll Gartin Justice Bldg PO Box 117 Jackson MS 39205-0117

**SMITH, JAMES WALKER,** lawyer; b. S.I., N.Y., May 11, 1957; s. James Patrick and Ann Catherine (Sullivan) S.; m. Erin Patricia Murphy, Aug. 15, 1982; children: Patrick James, Daniel Timothy, Meghan Kathleen, James John. BA magna cum laude, Fordham U., 1979, JD, 1982; LLM, NYU, 1988. BAr: N.Y. 1983, N.J. 1984, Pa. 1993, U.S. Supreme Ct. 1994. Assoc. Mendes & Mount, N.Y.C., 1982, Costello Shea & Gaffney, N.Y.C., 1982-86; ptnr. Anderson Kill Olick & Oshinsky P.C., N.Y.C., 1986-96, Smith Abbot, LLP, N.Y.C., 1996—; arbitrator N.Y.C. (N.Y.) Civil Ct., 1987-89; faculty chairperson hosp law Fordham Law Sch., N.YC., 1989-93; mediator U.S. Dist. Ct. (so. dist.) N.Y., N.Y.C., 1992-96. Author: Hospital Liability, 1985—; editor-in-chief: New York Practice Guide, 1993-97; contbg. editor: Medical Malpractice Law and Strategy, 1993—; bd. editors Fordham Urban Law Jour., 1981-82. Mem. N.Y. County Lawyer's Assn. (com. on tort law 1993-95), Assn. of the Bar of the City of N.Y. (com. on tort law 1990-92, com. on state cts. 1994—). Roman Catholic. Avocations: golf, coaching youth basketball. Product liability, Professional liability, Insurance. Home: 15 Flagg Ct Staten Island NY 10304-1157 Office: Smith Abbot LLP 100 Maiden Ln New York NY 10038-4818

**SMITH, JEANETTE ELIZABETH,** lawyer; b. Pitts., Sept. 23, 1965; d. Suellen Dell. Internat. rels studies, Univ. de las Americas, Puebla, Mex., 1985, Long Island U., Urbina, Italy, 1986, Athens (Greece) Ctr., 1987; BA in Internat. Rels., Fla. Internat. U., 1989; legal studies, U. Singapore, 1991; JD, U. Miami, 1992; postgrad. in Legal Edn., U. West Indies, Kingston, 1998-99. Bar: Pa. 1992, Fla. 1993. Asst. dir. NASA So. Tech. Applications Ctr., Miami, Fla., 1987-88; exec. asst. Trade Fin. Corp., Coral Gables, Fla., 1989; legal intern Khattar Wong & Ptnrs., Singapore; dir. overseas ops. Trans World Trade and Mktg., Miami, 1991-95; atty., counselor-at-law Law Firm of Jeanette E. Smith, Coral Gables, 1933-96; cons. Centricity, Inc., Miami, 1997; mng. ptnr. Jeanette E. Smith & Assocs., P.A., Miami, 1996—; gen. mgr. Meditation Records, Bahamas and Miami, 1998—. Recipient Women's Inner Circle of Achievement award. Mem. ABA, Internat. Bar Assn., Am. Immigration Lawyer's Assn., Greater Miami C. of C., Haiti Com., Caribbean C. of C. and Industry (bd. dirs. 1995—), Asian-Am. C. of C., Phi Alpha Delta. Avocations: foreign languages, travel. Immigration, naturalization, and customs, Entertainment, Private international.

**SMITH, JEFFREY ALLEN,** lawyer; b. Cleve., Feb. 2, 1944; s. William R. and Esther Mae Smith; m. Ruth Ann Sweeton, June 10, 1967 (div. 1997; children: Amy Esther, Adam Minor. AB, Clark U., 1966; JD, Boston U., 1969; postgrad., U. So. Maine, 1996—. Bar: Maine 1971, U.S. Dist. Ct. Maine 1971, U.S. Supreme Ct. 1980. Clk. to judge Maine Probate Ct., 1970; assoc. Law Offices of Harold J. Shapiro, Gardiner, Maine, 1971-73; ptnr. Smith Stein Bernotavicz & Orbeton, Hallowell, Richmond & Bath and predecessor firms Smith & Stein, and Smith Stein & Bernotavicz, Hallowell, Richmond, Hallowell, Maine, 1973-85, mng. ptnr., 1980-84, Smith & Assoc. P.A., Hallowell, 1985—, assoc. Douglas F. Jennings, 1993-96, ret., 1996; instr. trusts and estates and legal writing Beal Bus. Coll., Brunswick, Maine, 1981-82. Mem., Monmouth (Maine) Planning Bd., 1978-85; cubmaster Pine Tree council Boy Scouts Am., 1982-85; Vista vol. Alaska Legal Services, 1969-70. Mem. ABA, Maine Bar Assn., Kennebec County Bar Assn., Assn. Trial Lawyers Am., Maine Trial Lawyers Assn. (bd. govs. 1986—), Maine Organic Farmers and Gardeners Assn., bd. trustees Theater at Monmouth, bd. dir. Monmouth Cmty. Players. Democrat. Methodist (lay leader 1978—). Author: Santa's Will, 1978, Santa's Codicil, 1979, Letter to Smith Stein & Bernotavicz From Santa, 1982, contbr. articles to publs. General civil litigation, General practice, Personal injury. Home: Blue Heron Farm Town F Rd Monmouth ME 04259 Office: PO Box 351 144 Water St Hallowell ME 04347-1315

**SMITH, JEFFREY CARLIN,** lawyer; b. Chgo., Aug. 1, 1951; s. Robert Frederick and Marjorie (Carlin) S.; m. Phyllis Stagias, Oct. 7, 1978; children: Alex, Carlin. BS, Lewis and Clark Coll., 1974; JD, U. Calif., San Francisco, 1978; MBA, Pepperdine U., 1989. Bar: Calif. 1979, Md. 1989, D.C. 1989. Assoc. Gibbons, Stoddard & Lepper, Walnut Creek, Calif., 1978-81, Hyde & Drath, San Francisco, 1981-85; sr. staff counsel Times Mirror Co., L.A., 1985-88, assoc. gen. counsel, 1993-94, v.p. planning and devel., 1994-97; gen. counsel Balt. Sun, 1989-93; sr. v.p. gen. counsel IXC Comm., Austin, Tex., 1997—; Dir. Md., Del., D.C. Press Assn., Balt., 1990-93. Author: (with others) Fair Housing Advertising, 1992, Handbook Fair Housing Compliance, 1993. Dir. Pre-Columbian Art Rsch. Inst., San Francisco, 1983—; trustee Robert Louis Stevenson Sch., 1982-85, 87-90. Mem. Am. Soc. Corp. Secs., St. Francis Yacht Club, Austin Country Club, Bohemian Club. General corporate, Communications, Mergers and acquisitions. Office: IXC Comm 1122 S Capital Of Texas Hwy Austin TX 78746-6426

**SMITH, JEFFREY MICHAEL,** lawyer; b. Mpls., July 9, 1947; s. Philip and Gertrude E. (Miller) S.; 1 son, Brandon Michael. Student, U. Malaya, 1967-68; BA cum laude, U. Minn., 1970, JD magna cum laude, 1973. Bar: Ga. 1973. Assoc. Powell, Goldstein, Frazier & Murphy, 1973-76; ptnr. Rogers & Hardin, 1976-79, Bondurant, Stephenson & Smith, 1979-85, Arnall, Golden & Gregory, 1985-92, Katz, Smith & Cohen, 1992-98; shareholder Greenberg Traurig, 1998—; vis. lectr. Duke U., 1976-77, 79-80, 89-93; adj. prof. Emory U., 1976-79, 81-82; lectr. Vanderbilt U., 1977-82. Co-author: Preventing Legal Malpractice, 1998, Legal Malpractice, 1998. Co-author: Preventing Legal Malpractice, 1999, Legal Malpractice, 1999. Bd. visitors Law Sch. U. Minn., 1976-82. Mem. ABA (vice-chmn. com. profl. liability 1980-82, mem. standing com. lawyers's profl. liability 1981-85, chmn. 1985-87, standing com. lawyer competency 1993-95), State Bar Ga. (chmn. profl. liability and ins. com. 1978-89, trustee Inst. Cont. Legal Edn. in Ga. 1979-80), Order of the Coif, Phi Beta Kappa. Professional liability, Entertainment. Home: 145 15th St NE Apt 811 Atlanta GA 30309-3559 Office: Greenberg Traurig Ivy Place 2d Fl 3423 Piedmont Rd NE Atlanta GA 30305-1754

**SMITH, JERE CREWS, JR.,** lawyer; b. Atlanta, Apr. 23, 1967; s. Jere Crews Sr. and Eugenia Price Smith; m. Kathleen Gayle Thornton, June 25, 1994. BS, Fla. State U., 1989; JD, Mercer U., 1992. Atty. Moore, Ingram, Johnson & Steele, LLP, Marietta, Ga., 1992—. Construction, Consumer commercial, Contracts commercial. Home: 3145 Crestmount Way NW Kennesaw GA 30152-4677 Office: Moore Ingram Johnson 192 Anderson St SW Marietta GA 30060-1902

**SMITH, JERRY EDWIN,** federal judge; b. Del Rio, Tex., Nov. 7, 1946; s. Lemuel Edwin and Ruth Irene (Henderson) S.; m. Mary Jane Blackburn, June 4, 1977; children: Clark, Ruth Ann, J.J. BA, Yale U., 1969, JD, 1972. Bar: Tex. 1972. Law clk. to judge U.S. Dist. Ct. (no. dist.) Tex., Lubbock, 1972-73; assoc. then ptnr. Fulbright & Jaworski, Houston, 1973-84; city atty. City of Houston, 1984-88; cir. judge U.S. Ct. Appeals (5th cir.), Houston, 1988—. Chmn. Harris County Rep. Party, Houston, 1977-78; committeeman State Rep. Exec. Com., Tex., 1976-88. Mem. State Bar Tex., Houston Bar Assn. Methodist. Office: US Ct Appeals US Courthouse 515 Rusk St Ste 12621 Houston TX 77002-2603*

**SMITH, JERRY LEON,** lawyer; b. Tulsa, Oct. 18, 1938; s. William Ernest and Von Ceil S.; m. Ann Clay, June 21, 1961; children: Grant, Reed. BA, U. Okla., 1960; LLB, Cornell U., 1963. Assoc. White & Case, N.Y.C., Brussels, 1964-71; from assoc. to ptnr. Fried, Frank, Harris et al, N.Y.C., London, 1971-99, ret., of counsel, 1999—. Fulbright scholar, U. Aix-en-Provence-Marseilles, France, 1963-64. Mem. ABA, Assn. Bar City of N.Y. Avocations: literature, theater, music, visual arts, food and wine. General corporate, Mergers and acquisitions, Finance. Office: Fried Frank et al, 4 Chiswell St, London EC1 4UP, England

**SMITH, JILL GALBREATH,** lawyer; b. Kansas City, Mo., Nov. 1, 1963; d. William Lawrence and Joyce (Webb) Galbreath; m. Tracy Neil Smith, Apr. 28, 1990; children: Collin Blakely, William Connor, Cooper Whitney. BA in Polit. Sci., U. Kans., 1986, JD, 1989. Bar: Mo. 1989, Kans. 1990, U.S. Dist. Ct. (we. dist.) Mo. 1989, U.S. Dist. Ct. Kans. 1990. Assoc. Brown, James & Rabbitt, Kansas City, 1989-90, Perry, Hamill & Fillmore, Overland Park, Kans., 1990-95; of counsel Spencer, Fane, Britt & Browne, LLP, Overland Park, Kans., 1995—. Sec., bd. dirs. Johnson County CASA, Olathe, Kans., 1995—; mem. Jr. League of Wyandotte and Johnson Counties, Kansas City, 1992—. Recipient 1st place award for svc. to pub. ABA, 1995. Mem. Kans. Bar Assn., Mo. Bar Assn., Johnson County Bar Assn. (sec., pres.-elect, pres. young lawyers sect. 1992-95, bd. dirs. 1994-95, 96—), Kansas City Met. Bar Assn. General civil litigation, Labor, Workers' compensation. Office: Spencer Fane Britt and Browne LLP 9401 Indian Creek Pkwy Ste 700 Overland Park KS 66210-2007

**SMITH, JOHN ANTHONY,** lawyer; b. Poughkeepsie, N.Y., Sept. 10, 1942; s. John Charles and Eunice C. (Hatfield) S.; m. Carol A. Bechtel; children: Jessica R., Michael Anthony. BS, Cornell U., 1964, JD, 1971. Bar: Alaska 1971, U.S. Dist. Ct. Alaska 1971, U.S. Ct. Appeals (9th cir.) 1971, U.S. Supreme Ct. 1978. Assoc. Kay, Miller, Libbey, Kelly, Christie & Fuld, 1971, ptnr., 1972-73; ptnr. Gruenberg, Willard & Smith, 1973-74; sole practice Anchorage, Alaska, 1974-77; ptnr. Smith & Taylor, 1978; ptnr. Smith, Taylor & Gruening, Anchorage, 1979, sr. ptnr., 1979-84; sr. ptrn. Smith, Robinson & Gruening, 1984-85; sr. ptnr. Smith, Robinson, Gruening & Brecht, 1985-86, Smith, Gruening, Brecht, Evans & Spietzfadden, 1986; commr. Commerce and Econ. Devel., State of Alaska, 1986-88; ptnr. Davis, Wright & Tremaine, 1989-92; of counsel Bliss & Riordan, 1993-94, Baker, Brattain and Huguelet; ptnr. Schmeltger, Aptaker & Shepard, 1994—; chmn. State Bond Com., State of Alaska, 1987-88; chmn. Alaska Housing Fin. Corp., 1987-88, Alaska Indsl. Devel. and Export Authority, 1987-88; chmn. Alaska Mcpl. Bond Bank 1988-91; chmn. Alaska Ctr. for Internat. Bus., 1987-92, dir. 1992—; adj. prof. U. Alaska Sch. Criminal Justice; bd. dirs. Alaska Bus. Monthly; bd. dir. Ctr. for Nat. Policy, OAS Young Am. Bus. FUnd; internat. bd. advisors Zamovance, 1996—; mem. working group Devel. of a Strategic Econ. Devel. Plan for Washington, 1997—; atty. Embassy of Honduras, St. Paul Island, Alaska. Columnist Anchorage Times; contbg. editor Alaska Jour. Commerce. Mem. exec. com. House-Senate Dem. Coun.; nominee U.S. Senate 1992, U.S. House, 1994; pres. Alaska Inst. Rsch. and Pub. Svc.; coord. U. Alaska Paralegal Program; chmn. Bus. Justice Com.; chmn. Gov.'s Bodily Injury Reparation Commn., 1979-80; mem. internat. rels. com. Nat. Olympics Com., 1986-93; mem. exec. com. Anchorage Organizing Com. for the Winter Olympics; bd. dirs., counsel Anchorage Olympic Devel. Com.; dir. Glacier Creek Acad. Served to lt. (j.g.) USN, 1964-67. Mem. Alaska Bar Assn. (chmn. specialization com.), ABA, Am. Judicature Soc., Am. Trial Lawyers Assn., Anchorage C. of C. Democrat. Quaker. Administrative and regulatory, Federal civil litigation, Private international. Address: 9289 Ivy Tree Ln Great Falls VA 22066-2206

**SMITH, JOHN FRANCIS, III,** lawyer; b. White Plains, N.Y., Sept. 24, 1941; s. John Francis and Mary Dake (Mairs) S.; m. Susan Brown; children: John, Stephen, Peter. AB, Princeton U., 1963; LLB, Yale U., 1970. Bar: Pa. 1970, U.S. Supreme Ct. 1985. Assoc. Dilworth, Paxson, Kalish & Kauffman, Phila., 1970-75, ptnr., 1975-86, sr. ptnr., 1986-91; sr. litigation ptnr. Reed Smith Shaw & McClay, Phila., 1991—, mem. exec. com., 1993—. Mem. exec. com. Employment Discrimination Referral Project, 1971-74; pres. Society Hill Civic Assn., 1975-76, Phila. Chamber Ensemble, 1977-80; bd. govs. Pa. Economy League (ea. divsn.), 1983—, sec. 1995-97; vice chair Health Care Task Force, 1993-96; bd. dirs. World Affairs Council Phila., 1983-87, chmn. program com., 1986-87; Burn Found., 1987-95; moderator Main Line Unitarian Ch., 1986-89; founder and pres. Found. for Individual Responsibility and Social Trust (FIRST), 1995—. Served to lt. (j.g.) USNR, 1963-67; Vietnam. Mem. ABA, Phila. Bar Assn., Yale Law Sch. Alumni Assn. (exec. com. 1982-88, sec. 1987-88), Princeton Club (Phila.). Federal civil litigation, Labor. Office: Reed Smith Shaw & McClay 2500 One Liberty Pl Philadelphia PA 19103

**SMITH, JOHN HOLDER, JR.,** lawyer; b. Tennille, Ga., Feb. 19, 1968; s. John Holder Sr. and Lucy Nell Smith. BA, Emory U., 1990; JD, U. Ga., 1993. Bar: Ga. 1993, U.S. Dist. Ct. (mid. dist.) Ga. 1994. Ptnr. Young, Thagard, Hoffman, Scott & Smith, Valdosta, Ga., 1993—. Active Lowndes County Rep. Party, Valdosta, 1994—. Mem. Valdosta Bar Assn., Valdosta Lawyers Club (pres.-elect). Insurance, Personal injury, Landlord-tenant. Office: Young Thagard et al 801 Northwood Park Dr Valdosta GA 31602-1393

**SMITH, JOHN JOSEPH,** lawyer; b. Connellsville, Pa., June 5, 1955; s. John Joseph and Sarah Catherine (White) S. BA, Pa. State U., 1977; JD, Duquesne U., 1981; LLM in Tax., Temple U., 1993. Bar: Pa. 1981, N.J. 1983. Judge advocate gen. U.S. Army, Ft. Dix, N.J., 1982-85; dep. atty. gen., asst. atty. gen. Divsn. Criminal Justice, Trenton, N.J., 1985—. Lt. col. USAR., 1985—. Home: 8 Vine Way Bordentown NJ 08505-2736 Office: Divsn Criminal Justice 25 Market St Trenton NJ 08611-2148

**SMITH, JOHN KERWIN,** lawyer; b. Oct. 18, 1926; 1 child, Cynthia. BA, Stanford U.; LLB, Hastings Coll. Law. Ptnr. Haley, Purchio, Sakai & Smith, Hayward, Calif.; bd. dirs. Berkeley Asphalt, Mission Valley Ready-Mix, Coliseum Found., Mission Valley Rock, Rowell Ranch Rodeo, Hastings Coll. Law (alumnus of yr. award 1989). Gen. ptnr. Oak Hills Apts., City Ctr. Commercial, Creekwood I and II Apts.; Road Parks commn. 1957; city coun. 1959-66, mayor 1966-70; chmn. Alameda County Mayors conf. 1968, revenue taxation com. League Calif. Cities, 1968; vice chmn. Oakland-Alameda County Coliseum; vol. Hastings 1066 Found. (pres., vol. svc. award 1990), Martin Kauffman 100 Club. Mem. ABA, Calif. Bar Assn., Alameda County Bar Assn., Am. Judicature Soc., Rotary. Probate, Real property. Office: Haley Purchio Sakai & Smith 22320 Foothill Blvd Ste 620 Hayward CA 94541-2700

**SMITH, JOHN MICHAEL,** lawyer; b. Summit, N.J., Sept. 23, 1959; s. Paul Harry and Mary (Konieczny) S. BA in Polit. Sci., Ursinus Coll., Collegeville, Pa., 1981; JD, Del. Law Sch., Wilmington, 1985; LLM in Environ. Law, George Washington U., Washington, 1995. Bar: Pa. 1985, U.S. Ct. Military Appeals 1986. Asst. staff judge adv. 4th Combat Support Group, Seymour Johnson AFB, N.C., 1986-87, 343d Combat Support Group, Eielson AFB, AK, 1987-88; area def. counsel USAF Judiciary, Eielson AFB, AK, 1988-90; asst. staff judge adv. Headquarters 7th Air Force, Osan AFB, Rep. of Korea, 1990-91; dep. staff judge adv. 438th Airlift Wing, McGuire AFB, N.J., 1991-94, Air Force Environ. Law & Litigation Divsn., Arlington, Va., 1995—; Mem. Pa. Bar Assn., 1985-88. Recipient Air Force Commendation medal USAF, 1987, 90, 91, Air Force Achievement medal USAF, 1992, Air Force Meritorious Svc. medal, 1995. Roman Catholic. Avocations: racquetball, computers, bicycling. Home: 1620 Pleasant Run Keller TX 76248-5381 Office: AFL/JACE 1501 Wilson Blvd Ste 629 Arlington VA 22209-2403

**SMITH, JOHN STANLEY,** lawyer, mediator; b. Albany, N.Y., Nov. 15, 1946; s. Robert Stanley Smith and Sylvia Rose Murgia Neary; m. Lourdes Umandap; children from previous marriage: Jon Jeffrey, James Michael, Brian Matthew, Melissa Marie. BA, St. Bernardine of Siena Coll., Loudonville, N.Y., 1968; JD, U. Balt., 1986. Bar: Md. 1986, U.S. Dist. Ct. Md. 1987, D.C. 1988. Commd. U.S. Army, 1968, advanced through grades to lt. col.; comdr. assault helicoptor platoon U.S. Army, Vietnam, 1970-71; comdr. A Btry 3d Bn. 38th Field Artillery U.S. Army, Ft. Sill, Okla., 1972-74; comdr. 132 Assault Support Helicopter Co. U.S. Army, Hunter Airfield, 1975, ops. officer 145th Aviation Bn., 1976-78; divsn. artillery aviation officer 25th Divsn. Artillery U.S. Army, Schofield Barracks, 1979-80; dep. dir. Directorate of Res. Forces, Ft. Meade, Md., 1981-82; dep. chief Unit Tng. Br. First U.S. Army, 1982-84; divsn. chief Concepts Analysis Agy., Bethesda, Md., 1984-87; exec. officer war plans Dept. of Army, Washington, 1987-90; ptnr. Dziennik & Smith, Glen Burnie, Balt., 1990-92; v.p., gen. counsel Academy Title Group, Glen Burnie, 1992-93; pvt. practice Glen Burnie, 1992—; owner Smith Mediation Svcs., Glen Burnie, 1992—; pres. Lorimar Title Corp., Glen Bunnie, 1995—. Author: Mid Range Forces Study 88-92, 1985, Mid Range Forces Study 90-94, 1986, Mid Range Forces Study 90-97, 1987. Bd. dirs. No. Anne Arundel County Rep. Club, 1994-95. Decorated Legion of Merit, Bronze Star, Air Medal, Purple Heart. Mem. ABA, Md. Bar Assn., Anne Arundel County Bar Assn., Balt. City Bar Assn., Acad. Family Mediators, No. Anne Arundel County C. of C. (pres. 1996), K.C. Roman Catholic. Avocations: running, bowling, basketball, hiking, camping. General practice, Personal injury, Real property. Office: 5 Crain Hwy N Glen Burnie MD 21061-3516

**SMITH, JOSEPH PHILIP,** lawyer; b. Jackson, Tenn., June 14, 1944; s. William Benjamin and Virginia Marie (Carey) S.; m. Deborah J. Smith, Dec. 22, 1972; 1 child, Virginia Louise. BA, U. Miss., 1967, JD, 1975; MEd, U. So. Miss., 1977; EdD, U. Memphis, 1998. Bar: Miss. 1975, Tex. 1979, Tenn. 1995, U.S. Dist. Ct. (no. dist.) Miss. 1975, U.S. Dist. Ct. (no. dist.) Tex. 1982, N.Mex. 1991, Colo. 1991, U.S. Dist. Ct. N.Mex. 1993, U.S. Dist. Ct. Colo. 1993, U.S. Ct. Appeals (10th cir.) 1993. Tchr. math. Marks (Miss.) Jr. H.S., 1971-73; tchr., then asst. prin. Biloxi (Miss.) City Schs., 1975-78; oil and gas landman Modling & Assocs., 1978-79; assoc., then ptnr. Byrnes, Myers, Adair, Campbell & Sinex, Houston, 1979-85; farmer Quitman County, Miss., 1988-90; pvt. practice Marks, Miss., Memphis, Raton, N.Mex., 1985—. Mem. Archdiocese of Santa Fe Sch. Bd., 1991-92. Capt. USAF, 1967-71. Mem. ABA, Colo. Bar Assn., Miss. Pub. Defender Assn. (treas. 1988-90), Rotary (pres., sec. Marks club 1985-90, mem. Raton club 1990-91). Republican. Roman Catholic. Education and schools, Civil rights, Oil, gas, and mineral. Home: 674 Saint Augustine Sq Memphis TN 38104-5054

**SMITH, JULES LOUIS,** lawyer; b. N.Y.C., Oct. 7, 1947; s. Henry Newman and Leonora (Fuerth) S.; m. Alexandra Remington Northrop, Feb. 15, 1986. BS, Syracuse U., 1969, JD, 1971. Bar: N.Y. 1972, U.S. Dist. Ct. (no. dist.) N.Y. 1972, U.S. Dist. Ct. (we. dist.) N.Y. 1973, U.S. Ct. Appeals (2d cir.) 1975, U.S. Supreme Ct. 1982. Assoc. Blitman and King LLP, Syracuse, N.Y., 1971-77, ptnr., 1977-88, resident ptnr., 1988—; lectr. to legal and profl. assns., confs., colls., 1980—, including AFL-CIO Union Lawyers Conf., 1991, ABA Labor and Employment Law, 1992, 25th Pacific Coast Labor Law Conf., 1992, ABA Satellite Seminar, 1992, N.Y. State Bar Assn. Labor and Employment Law Sect. Ann. Meeting, 1993; lectr. Inst. Indsl. Labor Rels.; mem. N.Y. State Bar Assn. Task Force on Adminstrv. Hearings, Albany, 1986—; bd. advisors LeMoyne Inst. Labor Rels., LeMoyne Coll., Syracuse Inst. Labor Rels.; mem. exec. bd. Greater. Mem. editorial bd. Syracuse Law Rev., 1970-71; contbr. articles to legal publs. Sec. Onondaga Neighborhood Legal Svcs., 1978, pres., 1979, v.p. bd. dirs., 1983-87; chair Prevention Ptnrs., 1994-97, pres. 1994-96; co-chair legal divsn. fund raising activities Syracuse Symphony Orch., 1985-86; bd. dirs. fundraising activities Am. Heart Assn., 1985-86; bd. dirs. Greater Rochester Fights Back, 1990-92, vice chair, 1992-93, chair, 1994; pres. Prevention Ptnrs., 1994-96; bd. dirs. United Way Greater Rochester, 1991—; v.p. Rochester Com. on Fgn. Rels., 1990-94. Fellow N.Y. Bar Found.; mem. ABA (union chmn. EEO com. labor and employment law sect. 1985-88, co-chairperson labor and employment law sect., mem. ad hoc com. to comment on EEO com. Ams. with Disabilities Act regulations, Coll. of Labor and Employment Lawyers award 1996), FBA, N.Y. State Bar Assn. (chmn. membership and fin. com. 1980-83, mem. spl. com. on specialization 1983-85, chmn. labor and employment law sect. 1984-85, mem. ho. dels. 1989-92), Onondaga County Bar Assn., Monroe County Bar Assn., N.Y. State Trial Lawyers Assn., Am. Trial Lawyers Assn., Fed. Bar Coun., Indsl. Rels. Rsch. Assn., Assn. Ctrl. N.Y. (co-founder, v.p. 1981), Justinian Honor Soc., Order of Coif. Democrat. Jewish. Avocations: skiing, running, cooking, reading. Labor, Federal civil litigation, General civil litigation. Office: Blitman and King LLP 16 Main St W Ste 207 Rochester NY 14614-1601

**SMITH, KENT ELLIOT,** lawyer; b. Blair, Nebr., Dec. 11, 1965; s. Richard Adams and Jacqueline Anne (Reeh) S.; m. Steffanie Anne Jordan, Aug. 10, 1991. B Accountancy, U. Miss., 1988, JD, 1991. Assoc. Langston, Langston, Michael & Bowen, Bonneville, Miss., 1991-92; ptnr. Balducci & Smith, Oxford, Miss., 1992-94, Webb, Sanders, Deaton, Balducci, Smith & Faulks, Oxford, 1994—. Mem. Miss. Bar Assn., Ala. Bar Assn., Tenn. Bar Assn., Am. Inns of Ct. (exec. com. 1994-95), Def. Rsch. Inst., Am. Trial Lawyers Assn., ABA. Avocations: golf, hunting, family outings. Criminal, Insurance, Personal injury. Office: Webb Sanders Deaton et al PO Box 148 2154 S Lamar Blvd Oxford MS 38655-5224

**SMITH, LARRY FRANCIS,** lawyer, internist; b. Lynchburg, Va., Dec. 8, 1949; s. Fred C. and Ruth Guill S. BS in Biology magna cum laude, Hampden-Sydney U., 1972; MD, U. Va., 1976; JD, Washington and CEE U., 1995. Bar: Tex., U.S. Dist. Ct. (ea. and we. dists.) Tex. Med. pvt. practice Appomattox, Va., 1979—; assoc. Morgan & Weisbrod, Dallas, 1995-97, sr. equity ptnr., 1998—; mem. bd. zoning appeals Appomatox Ct., Va., 1990-92, chmn. redistricting com., 1990. Fellow Am. Coll. Legal Medicine; mem. Phi Beta Kappa. Avocation: private pilot. Personal injury, Professional liability, Product liability. Office: Morgan & Weisbrod PO Box 821329 Dallas TX 75382-1329

**SMITH, LARRY MACK,** judge; b. Florence, Ala., Nov. 26, 1940; s. S.B. and Eula Mae (Carter) S.; m. Hilda Sue Trapp, Aug. 2, 1968; children: Janet Leah, Samantha Kathryn, Caroline Alyce. BS, U. North Ala., Florence, 1964; JD, Birmingham (Ala.) Sch. Law, 1975. Bar: Ala. 1979. Pvt. practice Florence, 1979-92; mcpl. ct. judge (part-time) Killen, Ala., 1980-92; mcpl. ct. judge (part-time) Florence, 1986-92, cir. ct. judge, 1992—. Mem. Dem. Exec. Com., Florence, 1988-92. With Ala. NG, 1965-68. Mem. Rotary. Office: Cir Ct J Ste 317 Lauderdale Co Courthouse Florence AL 35630

**SMITH, LAUREN ASHLEY,** lawyer, journalist, clergyman, physicist; b. Clinton, Iowa, Nov. 30, 1924; s. William Thomas Roy and Ethel (Cook) S.; m. Barbara Ann Mills, Aug. 22, 1947; children: Christopher A., Laura Nan Smith Pringle, William Thomas Roy II. BS, U. Minn., 1946, JD, 1949; postgrad., U. Chgo., 1943-49; MDiv, McCormick Theol. Sem., 1950; postgrad., U. Iowa, 1992. Bar: Colo. 1957, Iowa 1959, Ill. 1963, Minn. 1983, U.S. Supreme Ct. 1967; ordained to ministry Presbyn. Ch., 1950. Pastor Presbyn. Ch., Fredonia, Kans., 1950-52, Lamar, Colo., 1952-57; pastor Congl. Ch., Clinton, 1975-80; editor The Comml., Pine Bluff, Ark., 1957-58; ptnr. Schoenauer Smith & Fullerton ASP, Clinton, 1995—; CEO LASCO Pub. Group, Clinton, 1995—, Interlink for the Internet Generation; internat. conferee Stanley Found., Warrenton, Va., 1963-72; legal observer USSR, 1978; co-sponsor All India Renewable Energy Conf., Bangalore, 1981; law sch. conferee U. Minn., China, 1983; founder, CEO, Interlink for the Internet Generation. Author: (jurisprudence treatise) Forma Dat Esse Rel, 1975, (monograph) First Strike Option, 1983; co-author: India On to New Horizons, 1989; columnist Crow Call, 1968—; co-editor Press and News of

India, 1978-82; pub. Crow Call; pseudonym Christopher Crow, 1981—; editor Asian Econ. Cmty. Jour.; contbr. articles to religious publs. Minister-at-large Presbyn. Ch. U.S.A., Iowa, 1987—; bd. dirs. Iowa divsn. UN Assn. U.S.A., Iowa City, 1970-85; fellow Molecular Nanotechnology Foresight Inst., Palo Alto, Calif.; Franciscans United Nations Non Govt. Orgn.; assoc. Westar Inst. (The Jesus Seminar), Santa Rosa, Calif., 1997; active Quad City Estate Planning Coun. Mem. Iowa Bar Assn., Ill. Bar Assn., St. Andrews Soc., Clinton County Bar Assn. (pres. 1968, Best in Iowa citation), Clinton Ministerial Assn., Samaritan Health Systems Chaplain Corps. (pres.), Quad City Estate Planning Coun., Quaker Internat. Yokefellow, Nat. Network for New Spiritual Formation Presbyn. Ch. USA, Franciscans Internat., City Club of Quad Cities (bd. dirs.).

**SMITH, LAVENSKI R. (VENCE),** state supreme court justice; m. Trendle Smith; 2 children. JD, U. Ark., 1987. Pvt. practice Springdale, 1991-94; staff lawyer Ozark Legal Svcs., 1987-91. Bd. dirs. N.W. Ark. Christian Justice Ctr.; trainer Ptnrs. for Family Tng., 1993-96. Republican. Office: Ark Supreme Ct Justice Bldg 625 Marshall St Little Rock AR 72201*

**SMITH, LAWRENCE A.,** lawyer. BA, U. Bridgeport, 1969; JD, Bklyn. Law Sch., 1976. Bar: N.Y. 1976. Corp. counsel Grumman Allied Industries, 1980-83; sr. v.p. legal The Home Depot, Inc., Atlanta, 1987—. General corporate. Office: Home Depot Inc 2455 Paces Ferry Rd SE Atlanta GA 30339-4024*

**SMITH, LAWRENCE RONALD,** lawyer; b. Santa Monica, Calif., July 26, 1966; s. Lawrence Horton Camp and Joan Marie (Keating) S.; m. Constance Amanda Sullivan, Oct. 18, 1997. BA in Polit. Sci., UCLA, 1988; JD, Whittier Coll., 1993. Bar: Calif. Internal clk. U.S. Dist. Ct., L.A., 1992-93; assoc. Bonne, Bridges, Mueller, O'Keefe & Nichols, L.A., 1994-96; v.p., gen. counsel AZ3, Inc. d.b.a. B.C.B.G., Vernon, Calif., 1996—. Mem. Am. Corp. Coun. Assn. (chmn. So. Calif. small legal depts. com. 1996—, chmn. 1996—), Calif. State Bar Assn., Whittier Law Sch. Alumni (bd. dirs. 1994—). Avocations: golf, soccer. Mergers and acquisitions, Finance, General corporate. Office: AZ3 Inc dba BCBG 2761 Fruitland Ave Vernon CA 90058-3607

**SMITH, LEO EMMET,** lawyer; b. Chgo., Jan 6, 1927; s. Albert J. and Cecilia G. (Dwyer) S.; m. Rita Gleason, Apr. 14, 1956; children: Mary Cecilia, Gerianne, Kathleen, Leo A., Maureen. JD, DePaul U., 1950. Admitted to Ill. bar, 1950; assoc. with law firm also engaged in pvt. industry, 1950-54; asst. states atty. Cook County, Ill., 1954-57; asst. counsel Traffic Inst., Northwestern U., Evanston, Ill., 1957-60; asst. exec. sec. Comml. Law League Am., Chgo., 1960-61, exec. dir., 1961-83, editor Comml. Law Jour., 1961-89, editor emeritus, 1989—; assoc. Howe & Hutton, Ltd., Chgo., 1985—. Fellow Chgo. Bar Found. (life); mem. Chgo. Bar Assn. (chmn. libr. com. 1983, sec. sr. lawyers com. 1994-95), Am. Acad. Matrimonial Lawyers (exec. dir. 1982-84), World Assn. Lawyers (founding mem. 1975), Am. Soc. Assn. Execs., Assn. Forum, Assn. Econs. Coun., Friends of Northwestern Sta. (spokesperson 1984). Contbr. articles to legal jours. General practice. Home: 1104 S Knight Ave Park Ridge IL 60068-4447 Office: Howe & Hutton Ltd 20 N Wacker Dr Ste 4200 Chicago IL 60606-3191

**SMITH, LOREN ALLAN,** federal judge; b. Chgo., Ill., Dec. 22, 1944; m. Catherine Yore; children: Loren Jr., Adam (dec.). BA in Polit. Sci., Northwestern U., 1966, JD, 1969; LLD (hon.), John Marshall Law Sch., 1995, Capital U. Law Sch., 1996, Campbell U., 1997. Bar: Ill. 1970, U.S. Ct. Mil. Appeals 1973, U.S. Ct. Appeals (D.C. cir.) 1974, U.S. Supreme Ct. 1974, U.S. Ct. Claims, 1985, U.S. Ct. Appeals (fed. cir.) 1986, U.S. Ct. Fed. Claims. Host nightly radio talk show What's Best for America?, 1972; cons. Sidney & Austin, Chgo., 1972-73; gen. atty. FCC, 1973; asst. to spl. counsel to the pres. White House, Washington, 1973-74; spl. asst. U.S. Atty., D.C., 1974-75; chief counsel Reagan for Pres. campaigns, 1976, 80; prof. Del. Law Sch., 1976-84; dep. dir. Office Exec. Br. Mgmt. Presdl. Transition, 1980-81; chmn. Adminstrv. Conf. U.S., 1981-85; appointed judge U.S. Ct. Fed. Claims, Washington, 1985, designated chief judge, 1986—; prof. law Del. Law Sch., 1976-84; adj. prof. Internat. Law Sch., 1973-74, Georgetown U. Law Ctr., 1992—, Washing Coll. Law, Am. U., 1996, Columbus Sch. Law, Cath. U. Am., 1996—, George Mason U. Sch. Law, 1998—; past mem. Pres.'s Cabinet Coun. on Legal Policy, Pres.' Cabinet Coun. on Mgmt. and Adminstrn.; chmn. Coun. Ind. Regulatory Agys.; served as disting. jurist in residence U. Denver; Allen chair U. Richmond Sch. Law, 1995. Co-author: Black America and Organized Labor: A Fair Deal?, 1979; contbr. articles to profl. jours. Adv. bd. mem. WETA Pub. Radio Cmty. Adv. Bd. Recipient Presdl. medal Cath. U. Am. Law Sch., 1993, Romanian medal of Justice Romanian Min. of Justice, 1995, Ronald Reagan Pub. Svc. award Nat. Property Rights Conf., 1997. Mem. Bar Assn. D.C. (hon. mem., judicial honoree award 1997), Univ. Club (Washington, named club mem. of the yr. 1991, chmn. entertainment com., centennial com.). Republican. Jewish. *

**SMITH, LOUIS ADRIAN,** lawyer; b. Lansing, Mich., Apr. 22, 1939; s. John Paul and Marjorie (Christmas) S.; m. Karen Emens, Feb. 5, 1966; children: Timothy P., Patrick L., Elizabeth K. BA cum laude, Mich. State U., 1962; JD, U. Mich., 1965; LLD (hon.), Thomas M. Cooley Law Sch., 1980. Bar: Mich. 1974, U.S. Ct. Appeals 1972, U.S. Supreme Ct. 1971. Atty. Fowler & Smith, Lansing, 1965-67, Doyle & Smith, Lansing, 1968-74, Louis A. Smith, Atty., P.C., Traverse City, Mich., 1975-76, Smith & Johnson, Attys., P.C., Traverse City, Mich., 1982—; co-founder and bd. dirs. Thomas M. Cooley Law Sch., Lansing, Mich., 1972-94; bd. dirs. Empire Nat. Bank, Traverse City; mem. adv. coun. Univ. Notre Dame (Ind.) Law Sch., 1987—. Bd. trustees Interlochen (Mich.) Arts Acad., 1988; gov. appointee State Tenure Commn., 1997—. With U.S. Army, 1957-61. Fellow Mich. State Bar Found.; mem. ABA, Fed. Bar Assn., State Bar Mich., Assn. Trial Lawyers, D.C. Bar, Ingham County Bar Assn., Grand Traverse-Leelanau-Antrim County Bar, Am. Judicature Soc., Traverse City Golf and Country Club (pres. 1989), Crystal Downs Country Club, Tournament Players Club at Prestantia, Royal Dornach Scotland. General practice, Contracts commercial, Labor. Office: Smith & Johnson PO Box 705 Traverse City MI 49685-0705

**SMITH, MARK STEVEN,** lawyer; b. Cinn., Dec. 11, 1950; s. Roy and Burnetta (Rosenbaum) S.; m. Holly Sider, Oct. 10, 1981; children: Aaron, Jenna. BA, Ohio State U., 1972; JD, IIT, 1976. Bar: Ill. 1976, Ohio 1976, U.S. Ct. Appeals (7th cir.). Atty., ptnr. Engelman & Smith, Evanston and Skokie, Ill., 1976—. Mem. Am. Trial Lawyers Assn., Ill. State Bar Assn. (com. mem. alternate dispute resolution com. 1991-92), Chgo. Bar Assn. Democrat. Jewish. Personal injury, General civil litigation. Home: 704 Michigan Ave Evanston IL 60202-2512 Office: Engelman & Smith 1603 Orrington Ave Ste 750 Evanston IL 60201-3844

**SMITH, MAURY DRANE,** lawyer; b. Samson, Ala., Feb. 2, 1927; s. Abb Jackson and Rose Drane (Sellers) S.; m. Lucile West Martin, Aug. 15, 1953; children: Martha Smith Vandervoort, Sally Smith Legg, Maury D. Smith, Jr. BS, U. Ala., 1950, LLB, JD, 1952. Bar: Ala., 1952; U.S. Dist. Ct. (mid., no. and so. dists.) Ala. 1953; U.S. Ct. Appeals, 1957, U.S. Supreme Ct., 1957. Asst. atty. gen. State of Ala., Montgomery, 1952-55; asst. dist. atty. Montgomery County, 1955-63; ptnr. Balch & Bingham LLP, Montgomery, 1955—; chmn. lawyers adv. com. Mid. Dist. Ala., Montgomery, 1990—; mem. U.S. Ct. of Appeals 11th cir. adv. com. on rules, Montgomery, 1990—, U.S. Dist. Ct. Mid. Dist. civil justice reform act adv. com., Montgomery, 1991—. Pres. Montgomery Area United Way, Ala., 1987; mem. Leadership Montgomery, 1994. Fellow Am. Coll. Trial Lawyers, Am. Bar Found.; mem. Univ. Ala. System (bd. trustees 1991-97, trustee emeritus 1997—), Ala. Law Inst. (mem. coun.), ABA (mem. litigation sect.), Montgomery County Bar Assn. (pres. 1976), Montgomery Area C. of C. (pres. 1984), Ala. State Bar (chmn. jud. bldg. task force 1987-94). Avocations: farming, tennis. General civil litigation, Criminal, Family and matrimonial. Home: 2426 Midfield Dr Montgomery AL 36111-1529 Office: Balch & Bingham LLP PO Box 78 Montgomery AL 36101-0078

**SMITH, MICHAEL CORDON,** lawyer; b. Boise, July 30, 1954; s. Jay Myrven Jr. and Jena Vee (Cordon) S.; m. Candace Louise Langley, Dec. 10, 1977; children: Angela K., Nicole E., Jeremy L., Melanie D. BS with high honors, Brigham Young U., 1977; JD, UCLA, 1980. Assoc. Johnson & Poulson, L.A., 1980-87, ptnr., 1987-91; pvt. practice Torrance, Calif., 1992—; judge pro tem L.A. Mcpl. Ct., 1986-94, L.A. Superior Ct., 1991-95, ct. apptd. arbitrator, 1986-91. Mem. ATLA, Nat. Employment Lawyers Assn., Calif. Employment Lawyers Assn., L.A. County Bar Assn. (vice chair law office mgmt. sect. 1992-94, exec. com. 1985-95, state bar conv. del. 1995), Consumer Attys. Assn. L.A. Republican. Mem. LDS Ch. Avocations: genealogy, computers, audio-visual electronics. Personal injury, Labor. Office: 23133 Hawthorne Blvd Ste 300 Torrance CA 90505-3724

**SMITH, MORTON ALAN,** lawyer; b. N.Y.C., Mar. 13, 1931; s. David and Augusta S.; m. Nancy, July 2, 1954 (div. July 1974); children: Robynn, Jeffrey, Richard; m. Jane Saffir, June 10, 1979; children: Michael, Richard. BA, U. Fla., 1953; LLD with honors, U. N.C., 1956. Bar: N.Y. 1957, D.C. 1957. Spl. trial atty. Office Chief Counsel IRS, Phila., 1956-58; spl. asst. U.S. Atty. Dist. N.J., 1957; law clk. to judge U.S. Tax Ct., Washington, 1958-60; assoc. Kaye Scholer, N.Y.C., 1960-62, Saul Silverman, N.Y.C., 1962-67; sr. ptnr. Hall, Dickler, Lawler, Kent & Friedman, N.Y.C., 1967—; bd. dirs. Eden Park Health Corp., Albany, N.Y. Contbr. articles to profl. jours. V.p. Rye Brook (N.Y.) Bd. Edn., 1968-73; organizer incorporation Village of Rye Brook, 1982, now spl. counsel; bd. dirs. Herbert Birch Sch. for Exceptional Children, N.Y.C., Westchester County United Way, 1991; leadership chmn. United Way Campaign, Rye Brook, 1989-91; mem. Westchester County Housing Implementation Commn.; bd. dirs. Eden Park Health Svcs., Albany, N.Y., Bocairc Home Owners Assn., Boca Raton, Fla. Mem. ABA (tax sec.). Avocations: golf, skiing, tennis, gardening, reading. Taxation, general, Criminal. Office: Hall Dickler Lawler Kent & Friedman 909 3rd Ave New York NY 10022-4731

**SMITH, NEAL EDWARD,** congressman; b. Hedrick, Iowa, Mar. 23, 1920; s. James N. and Margaret M. (Walling) S.; m. Beatrix Havens, Mar. 23, 1946; children—Douglas, Sharon. Student, U. Mo., 1945-46, Syracuse U., 1946-47; LL.B., Drake U., 1950. Bar: Iowa 1950. Farmer Iowa, 1937—; sole practice Des Moines, 1950-58; atty. 50 sch. bds. in Iowa, 1951-58; asst. county atty. Polk County, Iowa, 1951; mem. 86th-103rd Congresses from 4th Dist., 1959—. Chmn. Polk County Bd. Social Welfare, 1954-56; pres. Young Democratic Clubs Am., 1953-55. Served with AUS, World War II. Decorated Air medal with 4 oak leaf clusters, Purple Heart. Mem. Am. Bar Assn., Farm Bur., Farmers Union, DAV. Clubs: Masons, Moose. Home: RR 1 Altoona IA 50009-9801 Office: Davis Brown Koehn Shors The Financial Ctr 666 Walnut St Ste 2500 Des Moines IA 50309-3904

**SMITH, NORMAN LESLIE,** lawyer; b. Springs, Transvaal, South Africa, Oct. 15, 1952; came to U.S., 1982; s. Jack and Penelope S.; m. Jillian Terri, Oct. 26, 1980; children: Danielle C., Carli Talya, Sharni Shira. B in Procurationes, U. South Africa, 1975. Bar: Calif. 1982, South Africa 1976. Assoc. Fluxman & Partners, Johannesburg, South Africa, 1974-76; attorney, partner Slomowitz, Dobie, Smith & Myburgh, Benoni, South Africa, 1976-82, Solomon Ward Seidenwurm & Smith, San Diego, 1982—; adv. bd. Boatracs, Inc., San Diego, 1997—, SVI Holdings, Inc., San Diego, 1997—. Active Army Officer Citizen Force, 1975-82, South Africa. Democrat. Jewish. Avocations: tennis, kayaking, skiing, scuba diving. Private international, Contracts commercial, Intellectual property. Office: Solomon Ward Seidenwurm & Smith 401 B St Ste 1200 San Diego CA 92101-4235

**SMITH, PATRICIA A.,** lawyer, author; b. Staten Island, N.Y., May 11, 1956. BA, Bklyn. Coll., 1978; JD, Bklyn. Law Sch., 1986. Bar: N.Y. 1987, U.S. Dist. Ct. (so. and ea. dists.) N.Y. 1988, U.S. Supreme Ct. 1991. Atty. City of N.Y., 1988-90; assoc. for an ins. def. firm, N.Y.C., 1990-96; ptnr. Smith Abbot, L.L.P., N.Y.C., 1996—. Co-author: The Preparation and Trial of Medical Malpractice Cases, 1990; contbr. articles to profl. jours. Mem. Women's Bar Assn. State N.Y. (pres. Staten Island chpt. 1989-90), N.Y. County Lawyers Assn. Democrat. Roman Catholic. Avocations: skiing, photography. Personal injury, Product liability.

**SMITH, PETER THOMAS,** lawyer; b. Red Wing, Minn., Feb. 9, 1946; s. Everell Adrian and Mary Ann (Tondl) S.; m. Sandra Jeanne Konieczny, Aug. 31, 1968; children: Alexander John, Nicole Marie. BS with honors, Loyola U., 1968; JD with honors, George Washington U., 1971. Bar: D.C. 1971, Ill. 1977; U.S. Ct. Appeals (D.C. cir.) 1974; U.S. Ct. Mil. Appeals 1972; U.S. Supreme Ct., 1980. Judge advocate USMC, Washington, 1971-74; assoc. atty. Keller & Heckman, Washington, 1974-77; pvt. practice Sycamore, Ill., 1977-79; ptnr. Minnihan & Smith, Sycamore, Ill., 1980-84; pvt. practice Sycamore, 1985-90; ptnr. Smith & Strauss, Sycamore, 1990—; City atty. City of Sycamore, 1990—. Treas. DeKalb County Reps., 1980; pres. Sycamore Kiwanis Club, 1990; chmn. Sycamore United Givers Fund, 1985; chmn. DeKalb County Unit, Am. Cancer Soc., 1992-96, St. Mary's Sch. Found., 1997—. Capt. USMCR, 1968-75. Mem. ABA, Ill. State Bar Assn., DeKalb County Bar Assn., Kane County Bar Assn. Republican. Roman Catholic. Avocations: golf, fishing, hunting, travel. General civil litigation, Estate planning, Real property. Office: Smith & Strauss 207 W State St Sycamore IL 60178-1418

**SMITH, PEYTON NOBLE,** lawyer; b. Austin, Tex., Feb. 19, 1964; s. Ralph Morgan and Bess (Noble) S.; m. Elizabeth Barrington Nance, June 23, 1990; children: Lincoln David. BBA in Mktg. and Fin., Baylor U., 1986, JD, 1989. Bar: Tex. 1990, U.S. Dist. Ct. (we. dist.) Tex., U.S. Dist. Ct. (so. dist.) Tex. Assoc. Small Craig & Werkenthin PC, Austin, 1989-94; ptnr. Law Office of Jeffrey Jones, Austin, 1994-96, Jackson & Walker, L.L.P., Austin, 1997—; cons. Rooster Andrews Sporting Goods, Austin, 1998, Werner's Stores, Inc., 1994—, Randall's Food Stores, Houston, 1995—. Author, seminar spkr., cons. handbook for employees, 1997-98. Chmn., trustee Hyde Park Bapt. Ch., Austin, 1997-98. Fellow Tex. Bar Found.; mem. Tex. Assn. Def. Counsel, Assn. Corp. Growth, Tex. Young Lawyers Assn. (pub. rels. com. 1996). Baptist. E-mail: psmith@jw.com. General civil litigation, Health, Personal injury. Office: Jackson Walker 100 Congress Ave Ste 1100 Austin TX 78701-4042

**SMITH, RALPH E.,** lawyer; b. Chgo., Sept. 1, 1931; s. Everett L. and Mabel A. Smith; m. Patricia Sommer, Jan. 16, 1954; children: Susan Smith Mea, Rebecca Smith Logan. BS, U.S. Merchant Marine Acad., 1953; JD, Loyola U. of the South, 1965. Bar: La. 1965, U.S. Dist. Ct. La. 1965, U.S. Ct. Appeals (5th cir.) 1967, U.S. Ct. Appeals (11th cirs.) 1981, U.S. Supreme Ct. 1982. Assoc. Deutsch, Kemigm & Stites, New Orleans, 1966-92; pvt. practice law New Orleans, 1992—; judge adv. Nat. Assn. Fleet Tug Sailors, New Orleans; nat. v.p. Gulf Region, Am. Merchant Marine Vets., Cape Coral, Fla.; pres. USS Huse Assn., New Orleans. Capt. USNR, ret. Decorated Nat. Def. medal, Navy Expeditionary medal, Merchant Marine-Korean Svc. medal. Mem. Nat. Sojourners, Inc. (pres. La. chpt. 1997-98), Heroes of 76 (comd. 1999—). Presbyterian. Avocation: cattle farming. Admiralty, Insurance, Federal civil litigation. Office: Rm 811 203 Carondelet St New Orleans LA 70130-3017

**SMITH, RALPH WESLEY, JR.,** federal judge; b. Ghent, N.Y., July 16, 1936; s. Ralph Wesley and Kathleen S. (Callahan) S.; m. Nancy Ann Fetzer, Dec. 30, 1961 (div. 1981); children: Mark Owen, Tara Denise, Todd Kendall; m. Barbara Anne Milian, Nov. 8, 1982; stepchildren: Kim Highter, Jeffrey Highter, Eric Highter. Student, Sorbonne, U. Paris, Paris, 1954-55; BA, Yale U., 1956; LLB, Albany Law Sch., 1966. Bar: N.Y. 1966, U.S. Dist. Ct. (no. dist.) N.Y. 1966. Assoc. Hinman, Straub Law Firm, Albany, N.Y., 1966-69; chief asst. dist. atty. Albany County, N.Y., 1969-73, dist. atty., 1974; regional dir. state nursing home investigation Asst. Atty. Gen., Albany, 1975-77; dir. State Organized Crime Task Force, 1978-82; U.S. magistrate judge U.S. Dist. Ct. (no. dist.) N.Y., Albany, 1982—; judge moot ct. Albany Law Sch., 1983—; lectr. N.Y. State Bar Assn., 1985—, Am. Inns of Ct., 1994-99. Capt. (ret.) USNR, 1957-82. Mem. Fed. Magistrate Judges Assn. (dir. 2d cir. 1992-99), Columbia County Bar Assn., Columbia County Magistrates Assn. Republican. Roman Catholic. Avocations: fishing, bicycling, skiing, sailing, camping. Home: 2375 State Route 66 Chatham NY 12037-1801 Office: US Dist Ct 445 Broadway Ste 314 Albany NY 12207-2925

**SMITH, RAYMOND CARROLL,** lawyer; b. Paris, Ark., Dec. 9, 1929; s. Truman Henry and Lula Grace Smith; m. Mary Elaine Banker, Dec. 29, 1953; children: Todd Kevin, Amy Beth, Sharon Kaye, Ryan Oliver. Student, U. Ark., 1948-51, BS, 1977, JD, 1980. Bar: Ark. 1980, U.S. Dist. Ct. (we. dist.) Ark. 1980, U.S. Ct. Appeals (8th cir.) 1986, U.S. Supreme Ct. 1986. Ptnr. Smith & Smith, Fayetteville, Ark., 1980-85; pres. Raymond C. Smith, P.A., Fayetteville, 1986—. Lt. col. USAF, 1951-77. Mem. ATLA, Ark. Trial Lawyers Assn., Washington County Bar Assn., Lions Club (past pres.), Trout Unltd. (regional v.p., trustee). Avocation: fly fishing. Personal injury, Probate, General civil litigation. Office: 70 N College Ave Ste 11 Fayetteville AR 72701-5337

**SMITH, REBECCA BEACH,** federal judge; b. 1949. BA, Coll. William and Mary, 1971; postgrad., U. Va., 1971-73; JD, Coll. William and Mary, 1979. Assoc. Wilcox & Savage, 1980-85; U.S. magistrate Ea. Dist. Va., 1985-89; dist. judge U.S. Dist. Ct. (ea. dist.) Va., Norfolk, 1989—; exec. editor Law Review, 1978-79. Active Chrysler Mus. Norfolk, Jean Outland Chrysler Libr. Assocs., Va. Opera Assn., Friends of the Zoo, Friends of Norfolk Pub. Libr., Ch. of the Good Shepherd. John Marshall Soc. fellow; recipient Acad. Achievement and Leadership award St. George Tucker Soc.; named one of Outstanding Women of Am., 1979. Mem. ABA, Va. State Bar Assn., Fed. Bar Assn. Supreme Ct. Hist. Soc., Fourth Cir. Judicial Conf., The Harbor Club, Order of Coif., Phi Beta Kappa. Office: US Dist Ct US Courthouse 600 Granby St Ste 358 Norfolk VA 23510-1915

**SMITH, RICHARD STANLEY, JR.,** lawyer; b. Hartford, Conn., Sept. 18, 1959; s. Richard Stanley and Jane (Leshure) S.; m. Jeanne Marie Galvin, Oct. 7, 1989; children: Richard Stanley III, Shelby Marie. BA, Duke U., 1981, JD, 1984. Bar: Conn. 1984. Assoc. Murtha, Cullina, Richter & Pinney, LLP, Hartford, 1984-90, ptnr., 1991—; chmn. Conn. Task Force on Bus. Trusts, 1994-97. Mem. dist. com. West Hartford Reps., 1996—. Mem. ABA, Conn. Bar Assn. (sec. bus. law sect. 1994-96, 97-98, vice chmn. bus. law sect. 1998—), Hartford County Bar Assn., Hartford Golf Club (bd. dirs. 1995-98). Avocations: golf, hockey, gardening. General corporate, Securities, Mergers and acquisitions. Home: 54 Glenwood Rd West Hartford CT 06107-1507 Office: Murtha Cullina et al CityPlace I 185 Asylum St Hartford CT 06103-3408

**SMITH, ROBERT BLAKEMAN,** lawyer; b. Mt. Vernon, N.Y., June 18, 1949; s. William Blakeman and Helen Theresa (Curley) S.; m. Laura Lindley Brock, July 17, 1987; children: Morgan Lindley, Justin Pierce. BS, Rensselaer Poly. Inst., 1971, ME, 1973; JD, Boston U., 1976. Bar: N.Y. 1977, U.S. Dist. Ct. (so. and ea. dists.) N.Y. 1977, U.S. Dist. Ct. (no. dist.) N.Y. 1981, U.S. Dist. Ct. Ariz. 1992, U.S. Patent and Trademark Office 1977, U.S. Ct. Appeals (7th cir.) 1979, U.S. Ct. Appeals (fed. cir.) 1982, U.S. Supreme Ct. 1981. Assoc. Brumbaugh, Graves, Donohue & Raymond, N.Y.C., 1976-84, ptnr., 1984-89; of counsel White & Case, N.Y.C., 1989—; lectr. IEEE, N.Y.C., 1983-88, Practising Law Inst., 1990-99. Trustee Delta Phi Found., Ithaca, N.Y., 1978-86, St. Elmo Found., Pearl River, N.Y., 1986—. Mem. N.Y. Intellectual Property Law Assn., Am. Intellectual Property Law Assn. Patent, Trademark and copyright. Home: 100 Riverside Dr New York NY 10024-4822 Office: White & Case Bldg Ll 1155 Avenue Of The Americas New York NY 10036-2787

**SMITH, ROBERT ELLIS,** lawyer, journalist; b. Providence, Sept. 6, 1940; s. Ronald Bancroft and Clarice (Evans) S.; m. Kathryn Ritter, Aug. 4, 1984; children: Mark O., David E., Benjamin E., Gregor E. BA, Harvard U., 1962; JD, Georgetown U., 1975. Bar: D.C. 1976, R.I. 1987. News reporter Detroit Free Press, 1962-65, Newsday, Garden City, N.Y., 1966-70; asst. dir. Office for Civil Rights HEW, Washington, 1970-73; pub. Privacy Jour., Washington and Providence, 1974—; pvt. practice law Washington and Block Island, R.I., 1978—; spl. asst. atty. gen. State of R.I., Providence, 1991-92; vice chair R.I. Coastal Resources Mgmt. Coun., 1996—; mem. D.C. Commn. Human Rights, 1983-85. Author: Privacy: How to Protect What's Left of It, 1979, Compilation of State and Federal Privacy Laws, 1976, 78, 81, 84, 88, 92, 97, Workrights, 1983, Celebrities and Privacy, 1985, The Law of Privacy Explained, 1993, Our Vanishing Privacy, 1993. Pres. Block Island Conservancy, 1990-94; arbitrator R.I. Superior Ct. With U.S. Army, 1963-65. Mem. ABA, R.I. Bar Assn., Harvard Club. Avocation: writer, arbitrator. Civil rights, Libel, Land use and zoning (including planning). Office: Privacy Jour PO Box 28577 Providence RI 02908-0577 also: PO Box 984 Block Island RI 02807-0984

**SMITH, ROBERT EVERETT,** lawyer; b. N.Y.C., Mar. 15, 1936; s. Arthur L. and Augusta (Cohen) S.; m. Emily Lucille Lehman, July 17, 1960; children: Amy, Karen, Victoria. BA, Dartmouth Coll., 1957; LLB, Harvard U., 1960. Bar: N.Y. 1960, U.S. Dist. Ct. (so. dist.) N.Y. 1962, U.S. Ct. Appeals (2d cir.) 1963, U.S. Supreme Ct. 1967, U.S. Dist. Ct. (ea. dist.) N.Y. 1969, U.S. Ct. Appeals (3d cir.) 1982, U.S. Ct. Appeals (9th cir.) 1988. Assoc. Paul, Weiss, Rifkind, Wharton & Garrison, N.Y.C., 1960-65; from assoc. to ptnr. Baar, Bennett & Fullen, N.Y.C., 1965-74; ptnr. Guggenheimer & Untermyer, N.Y.C., 1974-85; ptnr. Rosenman & Colin LLP, N.Y.C., 1985-98, chmn., 1994-97, counsel, 1998—. With U.S. Army, 1961-64. Mem. ABA, N.Y. State Bar Assn., Assn. of Bar of City of N.Y., Fed. Bar Coun., N.Y. County Lawyers Assn., Am. Arbitration Assn. (nat. panel arbitrators), The Am. Law Inst. Federal civil litigation, State civil litigation, General corporate. Office: Rosenman & Colin LLP 575 Madison Ave Fl 26 New York NY 10022-2585

**SMITH, ROBERT MICHAEL,** lawyer, mediator, arbitrator; b. Boston, Nov. 4, 1940; s. Sydney and Minnie (Appel) S.; m. Catherine Kersey, Apr. 14, 1981 (dec. 1983). AB cum laude, Harvard Coll., 1962; diploma, Centro de Estudos de Espanol, Barcelona, 1963; MA in Internat. Affairs, Columbia U., 1964, MS in Journalism with high honors, 1965; JD, Yale U., 1975. Bar: Calif., N.Y., D.C., U.S. Supreme Ct.; solicitor Supreme Ct. of Eng. and Wales. Intern in econ. devel. UN, Geneva, 1964; corr. Time Mag., N.Y.C., 1965-66, The N.Y. Times, Washington, 1968-72, 75-76; atty. Heller, Ehrman, White & McAuliffe, San Francisco, 1976-78; spl. asst. Office of Atty. Gen. of U.S., Washington, 1979-80; dir. Office Pub. Affairs U.S. Dept. Justice, Washington, 1979-80; mem. U.S. delegation U.S. v. Iran Internat. Ct. of Justice, The Hague, 1980; asst. U.S. atty. No. Dist. Calif., San Francisco, 1981-82; counsel, sr. counsel to sr. litigation counsel Bank of Am. NT & SA, San Francisco, 1982-86; pvt. practice law San Francisco, 1988-98; ptnr. Morgenstein & Jubelirer, San Francisco, 1997-98; lectr. FBI Acad., Quantico, Va., 1980, Internat. Bankers Assn. Calif., 1994, Calif. Bankers Assn., 1994, Cmty. Bankers No. Calif., 1994, 95; judge Golden Medallion Broadcast Media awards State Bar of Calif., 1985; judge pro tem Mcpl. Ct. City and County of San Francisco, 1989—; conciliator Peninsula Conflict Resolution Ctr.; panelist World Intellectual Property Orgn., Geneva; arbitrator internat. Commercial arbitration ctrs., Vancouver, Cairo, Singapore, Kuala Lumpur; CPR Panel of Disting. Neutrals; mem. panel Nat. Assn. for Dispute Resolution. Author: Alternative Dispute Resolution for Financial Institutions, 1995, revised, 1996, 97, 98; bd. editors Yale Law Jour., 1974-75; editor Litigation, jour. ABA litigation sect., 1978-81; mem. editl. adv. bd. Bancroft-Whitney, 1991-94; contbr. articles to profl. jours. Bd. dirs. Neighborhood Legal Assistance Found., San Francisco, 1985-87, Nob Hill Assn., San Francisco, 1985-93; bd. dirs., fin. com. St. Francis Found., San Francisco, 1993-94. 1st lt. inf., USAR, 1965-71. Recipient UPI Award for Newswriting, 1958; Harvard Coll. scholar, 1958-62, Fulbright scholar, 1962-63; Columbia U. Internat. fellow, 1964-65. Fellow Chartered Inst. Arbitrators (London); mem. ABA (corp. counsel com. 1986-96, alternative dispute resolution sect. 1994-98), Assn. Atty. Mediators (v.p. No. Calif. chpt. 1995), State Bar of Calif. (pub. affairs com. 1982-85, litigation sect. 1990-96), Bar Assn. of San Francisco (bench-bar media com. 1985-96, alternative dispute resolution com. 1994-98), Assn. Bus. Trial Lawyers No. Calif., Assn. of Former U.S. Attys. No. Dist. Calif., Am. Arbitration Assn. (mem. comml. arbitration panel, No. Calif. adv. coun., mediator Am. Arbitration Ctr. for Mediation), The Mediation Soc. (chmn. bd.), Profl. Atty. Mediators, Cmty. Bds. of San Francisco (conciliator), French-Am. C. of C., German-Am. C. of C. West U.S., Harvard Club of San Francisco (bd. dirs. 1986-94, pres. 1992-94), Yale Club of San Francisco (bd. dirs. 1989-94), Soc. Profls. in Dispute Resolution, Nat. Panel Mediators and Arbitrators, Columbia U. Alumni Club of No. Calif. (exec. com. 1978-92), Nat. Assn. Dispute Resolution (panelist). E-mail: rms@robertmsmith.com. Alternative dispute resolution, General civil litigation, Banking. Office: 1250 Washington St San Francisco CA 94108-1041

**SMITH, R(OBERT) MICHAEL,** lawyer; b. Cin., Nov. 25, 1951; s. Barney and Jean (Maloney) S.; m. Leslie Y. Straub. BA in Polit. Sci., U. Cin., 1982; JD, Ohio State U., 1985. Bar: Ohio 1985, U.S. Dist. Ct. (so. dist.) Ohio, U.S. Supreme Ct. Law clk. to Justice Holmes Ohio Supreme Ct., Columbus, 1985-89; sr. staff atty., referee, editor Ohio Ct. Claims, Columbus, 1989-94; instr. law Ohio State U., 1985—, instr. continuing edn. courses, 1990—.

Incorporator, trustee various non-profit orgns., Cin. and Columbus; pres. So. Bapt. Messianic Fellowship, 1994-97; 2d v.p. Ohio So. Bapt. Conv. Republican. Avocations: target shooting, writing, running. Home: 748 S Roosevelt Ave Bexley OH 43209-2541 Office: 4325 Kinloch Rd Louisville KY 40207-2853

**SMITH, RONALD CHARLES,** lawyer, educator; b. Chgo., Dec. 9, 1933; s. Riley C. Smith and Rita Elizabeth (Thompson) De Vito; m. Mary Ann Scherer, June 27, 1971; children: Michael Charles, Matthew James. BS, Loyola U., 1955, JD, 1965. Bar: Ill. 1965, U.S. Dist. Ct. (no. dist.) Ill., 1967, U.S. Ct. Appeals (7th cir.) 1977, U.S. Supreme Ct. 1992. Lectr. Loyola U., Chgo., 1955-56; clk. Justice John McCormick Ill. Appellate Ct. Cook County, Chgo., 1965-66; atty. law dept. Santa Fe RR, Chgo., 1966-68; faculty mem. John Marshall Law Sch., Chgo., 1968-69, prof., 1970—; del. Ill. Constitutional Conv., Springfield, 1969-70; spl. asst. state's atty. Cook County, 1975-76, 1979-80; spl. hearing officer Ill. Civil Svc. Commn., 1977-78;. Author: (trial books) ABA National Criminal Justice Trial Advocacy Competition, 1990—; contbr. articles on Ill. Constitution to profl. jours. Bd. dirs. Com. on Ill. Govt., Chgo., 1971-78, Ill. Bd. Ethics, 1974-77, Centrally Held Eagle Receivables Program, Inc., 1994—; chmn. Ind. Precinct Orgn., Chgo., 1973-74; mem. Gov.'s Transition Task Force, Ill., 1972-73; mem. Ill. Supreme Ct. Criminal Rules Com., 1992—; mem. Cook County Criminal Justice Coord. Com., 1992—; chair edn. com. Chgo. Sisters Internat. Program, Galway, Ireland. Lt. comdr. USNAF, 1958-62. Recipient Alumni scholarship Loyola Law Sch., Chgo., 1962-65./. Mem. ABA (criminal justic sect., dir. Nat. Criminal Justice Trial Advocacy Competition 1990—, vice chair publs. 1996-98, vice chair planning 1999—), Internat. Bar Assn., Internat. Assn. Prosecutors, Blue Key, Pi Gamma Mu, Alpha Sigma Rho. Criminal, Public international. Home: 5400 N Wayne Ave Chicago IL 60640-1305 Office: John Marshall Law Sch 315 S Plymouth Ct Chicago IL 60604-3968

**SMITH, RONALD EHLBERT,** lawyer, referral-based distributor, public speaker, writer and motivator, real estate developer; b. Atlanta, Apr. 30, 1947; s. Frank Marion and Frances Jane (Canida) S.; m. Annemarie Krumholz, Dec. 26, 1969; children: Michele, Erika, Damian. BME, Stetson U., 1970; postgrad., Hochschule Fuer Musik, Frankfurt, Fed. Republic Germany, 1971-74; Masters in German Lit., Germany & Middlebury Coll., 1975; JD, Nova U., 1981. Bar: Fla. 1982, U.S. Dist. Ct. (mid. dist.) Fla. 1983, U.S. Ct. Appeals (11th cir.) 1990, Ga. 1994, U.S. Dist. Ct. (no. dist.) Ga. 1994. Asst. state atty. 10th Jud. Cir. Ct., Bartow, Fla., 1982-85; pvt. practice Lakeland, Fla., 1985-94, Atlanta, 1994—; of counsel Mark Boychuk & Assocs., 1998—; rsch. asst. 10th Jud. Cir. Ct., Bartow, 1981-82; instr. Broward County C.C., Ft. Lauderdale, Fla., 1976-79, 91-94, pub. and pvt. schs., Broward County, Atlanta Schs., 1998, Offenbach, Germany, 1971-78; instr. Polk C.C. and Police Acad., Winter Haven, Fla., 1981-94; adj. prof. English, Ga. State U., 1996—; adj. prof. law DeKalb Coll., 1997—; reader ETS GMAT, 1997—; part-time police instr. Police Acad., Forsyth, Ga., 1996—; counselor Jr. Achievement, 1997—. Tchr., drama dir. Disciples I and II, United Meth. Ch., Lakeland, 1980-94, Glenn Meml. United Meth. Ch., Atlanta, 1994—; Billy Graham counseling supr., 1994—;promoter Promise Keepers, 1995—; spkr., promoter ProNet, 1996—; min. music Scott Blvd. Bapt. Ch., Decatur, Ga., 1998, Gideon Internat., 1999—. Freedom Bridge fellow German Acad. Exch. Svc., Mainz, 1974-75. Mem. ABA, Christian Legal Soc., Lakeland Bar Assn., Atlanta Bar Assn. Estate planning, General civil litigation, Education and schools.

**SMITH, RONALD R.,** lawyer, former assistant prosecuting attorney; b. Bellevue, Ohio, May 23, 1940; s. Paul S. and Gladys E. Smith; m. Katherine S. Tanner, Dec. 17, 1977; children: Blaire P., Douglas K. BA, Heidelberg Coll., 1963; student, Cuyahoga C.C., Cleve., 1967; JD, Cleve. Marshall Coll. Law, 1973. Bar: Ohio, Fla., U.S. Dist. Ct. (no. dist.) Ohio 1975. Farmer Republic, Ohio, 1954-60; restaurant mgr. Polar Bar Dairyland, Tiffin, Ohio, 1960-63, 72-75; ins. fraud investigator Rsch. Assocs., Inc., Cleve., 1966-68; claims supr. Allstate Ins. Co., Akron and Cleve., 1968-70; multiline claims supr. Hartford Ins. Co., Cleve., 1970-72; asst. prosecutor Erie County, Sandusky, Ohio, 1975-97; sole practitioner Bellevue, 1980—; instr. Ohio Pros. Attys. Assn., Columbus, 1988; instr., trainer Police, Children's Svcs., Sandusky, 1990-97; instr., lectr. Bowling Green State U., Huron, Ohio, 1995-98. Pres. Thompson Alumni Loan Fund, Inc., Bellevue, 1985—. Served with U.S. Army, 1963-66. Mem. ATLA, Fla. Bar Assn., Ohio Bar Assn., Erie County Bar Asn., Ohio Acad. Trial Lawyers, Masons, Scottish Rite, Bellevue Kiwanis Club (pres.), Bay Area Divers, Inc. (trustee). Democrat. Lutheran. Avocations: boating, water skiing, scuba diving, travel, farming and conservation. Personal injury, Family and matrimonial, General practice. Home: 4580 N County Road 27 Republic OH 44867-9720 Office: PO Box 34 Bellevue OH 44811-0034

**SMITH, R(ONALD) SCOTT,** lawyer; b. Washington, June 30, 1947; s. Joseph Peter Smith and Roberta Ann (Bailey) George; m. Cheryle Rae Coffman, Nov. 15, 1974 (div. July 1977); m. Gloria Jean Haralson, Nov. 30, 1985. BJ, U. Mo., 1970, JD, 1973. Bar: Mo. 1973, U.S. Dist. Ct. (we. dist.) Mo. 1973, U.S. Ct. Appeals (10th cir.) 1990, U.S. Ct. Appeals (8th cir.) 1992, U.S. Dist. Ct. (ea. dist.) Mo. 1996. Field dir. The Mo. Bar, Jefferson City, 1973-75; law clk. to judge Mo. Ct. Appeals (we. dist.), 1975-76; ptnr. Shirkey, Norton & Smith, Kansas City, 1976-77, Jackson & Sherman, P.C. and predecessors, Kansas City, 1977-84, Birmingham & Furry, Kansas City, 1984, Birmingham, Furry & Smith, 1985-92, Birmingham, Furry, Smith & Stubbs, 1992-95, Furry & Smith, Kansas City, 1996—. Author: (with others) Automobile Accident Handbook, 1984, rev., 1986, Vexatious Refusal and Bad Faith, 1990, Insurance Claims, 1993; editor: The Rights & Responsibilies of Citizenship in a Free Society, 1974, Due Process of Law, 1974, News Headnotes, 1976-84, Young Lawyer, 1977-80; mem. editorial bd. Mo. Bar Jour., 1978-81; (TV series) legal script advisor Lex Singularis, 1973-75; (multimedia) producer, author Freedoms Lost, 1976; producer, playwright (musical-comedy play) Silly ib Philly, 1987. Mem. ABA (mem. varius coms.), Mo. Bar Assn. (dist. 12 chmn. 1979—, mem. varius coms., Disting. Svc. award young lawyers sect. 1978, 79, 80), West Mo. Def. Lawyers Assn., Kansas City Met. Bar Assn. (pres. young lawyers sect. 1981-82, mem. various coms., Disting. Svc. award young lawyers sect. 1982, Leadership award st. sect. 1985, Dirst Ann. Pres. award sr. sect. 1987), Kansas City Claim Assn., Phi Delta Phi. Democrat. Roman Catholic. Fax: (816) 842-5600. E-mail: furrysmith@aol.com. General civil litigation, Personal injury, Product liability. Home: 3411 Shady Bend Dr Independence MO 64052-2816 Office: 1600 Bryant Bldg 1102 Grand Blvd Kansas City MO 64106-2316

**SMITH, ROY PHILIP,** judge; b. S.I., N.Y., Dec. 29, 1933; s. Philip Aloysius and Virginia (Collins) S.; m. Elizabeth Helen Wink, Jan. 23, 1965; children: Matthew P., Jean E. BA, St. Joseph's Coll., Yonkers, N.Y., 1956; JD, Fordham U., 1965. Bar: N.Y. Asst. reg. counsel FAA, N.Y.C., 1966-79; adminstrv. law judge U.S. Dept. Labor, Washington, 1979-83; adminstrv. appeals judge Benefits Rev. Bd., Washington, 1983—, chmn., chief adminstrv. appeals judge, 1988-90; adj. prof. aviation law Dowling Coll., Oakdale, N.Y., 1972-79; adj. prof. transp. law Adelphi U., Garden City, N.Y., 1975-79; vis. prof. Georgetown U. Law Sch., 1989—. With U.S. Army, 1957-59. Mem. Assn. of Bar of City of N.Y. (sec.-treas. aeronautics com. 1978-79), Fed. Adminstrv. Law Judges Conf. (treas. 1983-84, mem. exec. com. 1982-83), Internat. Platform Assn., Friendly Sons of St. Patrick, Edgemoor Club, Georgetown U. Libr. Assocs. Avocation: tennis. Home: 6700 Pawtucket Rd Bethesda MD 20817-4836 Office: Benefits Rev Bd 200 Constitution Ave NW Washington DC 20210-0001

**SMITH, SAMUEL STUART,** lawyer; b. Harrisburg, Pa., Nov. 18, 1936; s. Joseph and Fannie (Latt) S.; m. Susan Ruth Egert, Dec. 10, 1960; children: Jeffrey Alan, Gary Michael, Lauren Paige. BBA, U. Miami, 1958, JD, 1960. Bar: Fla. 1961, U.S. Dist. Ct. (so. dist.) Fla. 1960, U.S. Supreme Ct. 1960. Ptnr. Smith & Mandler, P.A., Miami Beach, Fla., 1960-87, Ruden, McClosky, Smith Schuster & Russell, Miami, Fla., 1987—; adj. faculty U. Miami Sch. of Law, bd. dirs., 1982—, chmn. 1985-86. Bd. dirs. WPBT-TV, Miami, Jewish Family Svc., Miami, Guardianship Program Dade County, Comprehensive Personal Care Inc. Capt. U.S. Army, 1960-61. Fellow Am. Bar Found., Am. Coll. Trust and Estate Counsel (regent 1996—), Fla. Acad. Trial Lawyers, Fla. Bar Found. (pres. 1989-90), coll. Law Practice Mgmt. (trustee 1993—); mem. ABA (chmn. law econs. sect. 1979-80, gov. 1985-87, sec. 1993-96), The Fla. Bar (bd. govs. 1974-82, pres. 1981-82), Miami Beach Bar Assn. (pres. 1971-72), Dean's Nat. Adv. Coun. (chair 1992-93), U. Miami Alumni Assn. (pres. 1989-90, adv. bd., chair 1992-93). Democrat. Avocations: tennis. Probate, State civil litigation. Office: Ruden McClosky Smith Schuster & Russell 701 Brickell Ave Ste 1900 Miami FL 33131-2834*

**SMITH, SELMA MOIDEL,** lawyer, composer; b. Warren, Ohio, Apr. 3, 1919; d. Louis and Mary (Oyer) Moidel; 1 child, Mark Lee. Student, UCLA, 1936-39, U. So. Calif. Law School, 1939-41; JD, Pacific Coast U., 1942. Bar: Calif. 1943, U.S. Dist. Ct. 1943, U.S. Supreme Ct. 1958. Gen. practice law; with Moidel, Moidel, Moidel & Smith; nat. bd. Med. Coll. Pa., 1953—, exec. bd., 1976-80, pres., 1980-82, chmn. past pres. com., 1990-92. Composer numerous works including Espressivo-Four Piano Pieces (orchestral premiere 1987, performance Nat. Mus. Women in the Arts 1989); author: A Century of Achievement: The National Association of Women Lawyers, 1998. Field dir. civilian adv. com. WAC, 1943. Decorated La Orden del Merito Juan Pablo Duarte (Dominican Republic). Mem. ABA Sr. Lawyers Divsn. (vice-chair editl. bd. Experience mag. 1997-99, chair 1999—, chair arts com. 1998-99, exec. coun. 1999—), State Bar Calif. (conf. com. on unauthorized practice of medicine 1964, Disting. Svc. award 1993), L.A. Bar Assn. (servicemens legal aid com. 1944-45, psychopathic ct. com., Outstanding Svc. award 1993), L.A. Lawyers Club (pub. defenders com.), Nat. Assn. Women Lawyers (chair com. unauthorized practice of law, social commn. UN, regional dir. western states, Hawaii 1949-51, jud. adminstrn. com. 1960, nat. chair world peace through law com. 1966-67, liaison to ABA Sr. Lawyers Divsn. 1996—, chair bd. elections 1997-98, centennial com. 1997-99), League of Ams. (dir.), Inter-Am. Bar Assn., So. Calif. Women Lawyers Assn. (pres. 1947-48), Women Lawyers Assn. L.A. (chair Law Day com. 1966, subject of oral hist. project 1986, hon. life mem.), Coun. Bar Assns. L.A. County (charter sec. 1950), Calif. Bus. Womens Coun. (dir. 1951), L.A. Bus. Womens Coun. (pres. 1952), Calif. Pres. Coun. (1st v.p.), Nat. Assn. Composers U.S.A. (dir. 1974-79, luncheon chair 1975), Nat. Fedn. Music Clubs (vice-chair Western region 1973-78), Calif. Fedn. Music Clubs (chair Am. Music 1971-75, conv. chair 1972), Docents L.A. Philharm. (v.p. 1973-83), chair Latin Am. cmty. rels., press and pub. rels. 1972-75, cons. coord. 1973-75), Assn. Learning in Retirement Orgns. in West (pres. 1993-94, exec. com. 1994-95, Disting. Svc. award 1995), Euterpe Opera Club (v.p. 1974-75, chair auditions 1972, chair awards 1973-75), ASCAP, Iota Tau Tau (dean L.A., supreme treas.), Plato Soc. of UCLA (Toga editor 1990-93, sec. 1991-92, chmn. colloquium com. 1992-93, discussion leader UCLA Constitution Bicentennial Project, 1985-87, moderator UCLA extension lecture series 1990, Exceptional Leadership award 1994). General practice. Home: 5272 Lindley Ave Encino CA 91316-3518

**SMITH, SHARON LOUISE,** lawyer, consultant; b. Williamsport, Pa., Apr. 21, 1949; d. Stuart Mallory and Phyllis Virginia (Hartzell) S. Student, Schiller Coll., Heidelberg, Fed. Republic Germany, 1969-70; AB, Grove City Coll., 1971; MA, Kent State U., 1973; JD, Temple U., 1978. Bar: Pa. 1978, U.S. Dist. Ct. (we. dist.) Pa. 1980, U.S. Ct. Appeals (3rd cir.) 1992. Assoc. Laurel Legal Services, Brookville, Pa., 1980-82; pvt. practice Brookville, 1982—; cons. Prothonotary, Brookville, 1984-86. Mem. multidisciplinary team for child abuse Jefferson County Child Welfare Dept., Brookville, 1985; bd. dirs. Clarion-Jefferson Community Action, Brookville, 1982, Clearfield-Jefferson Drug and Alcohol Commn., DuBois, Pa., 1983-84. Mem. Pa. Bar Assn., Law Alumnae Assn. Temple U. Presbyterian. Avocations: swimming, reading. Bankruptcy, Real property, Probate. Home: 172 Franklin Ave Brookville PA 15825-1164 Office: 173 Main St Brookville PA 15825-1233

**SMITH, SHEILA MARIE,** lawyer; b. Chgo.; d. Donald Thomas and Catherine Ellen (Mariga) Morrison; m. Melvin Smith, Nov. 11, 1989. BSEE, Purdue U., 1981; JD, U. Cin., 1995. Bar: Ohio 1995, U.S. Dist. Ct. (so. dist.) Ohio 1996, U.S. Ct. Appeals (6th cir.) 1996. Mfg. engr., 1981-92; atty. Freking & Betz, Cin., 1995—; spkr. in field. Named to Order of Coif U. Cin., 1995. Mem. ABA, Am. Trial Lawyers Assn., Nat. Employment Lawyers Assn., Ohio Employment Lawyers Assn., Cin. Employment Lawyers Assn., Ohio Bar Assn., Cin. Bar Assn. Avocations: golf, traveling, cooking. Labor, Civil rights, Federal civil litigation. Home: 1568 Georgetown Rd Loveland OH 45140-8035 Office: Freking & Betz 215 E 9th St Fl 5 Cincinnati OH 45202-2139

**SMITH, SIMEON CHRISTIE, III,** lawyer, judge; b. Alexandria, La., Feb. 4, 1941; s. Simeon Christie II and Margaret Ford (Ferguson) S.; m. Shirley Mae Pearce, Jan. 28, 1967; children: Simeon Christie IV, E. Pearce Smith. BA, La. State U., 1964; JD, Loyola U., New Orleans, 1967. Bar: La. 1967, U.S. Dist. Ct. (we. dist.) La. 1972, U.S. Ct. Appeals (5th cir.) 1972, U.S. Dist. Ct. (mid. dist.) La. 1973, U.S. Dist. Ct. (ea. dist.) La. 1976, U.S. Supreme Ct. 1976, U.S. Ct. Appeals (11th cir.) 1981. Assoc. Wood & Jackson, Leesville, La., 1967-69; ptnr. Jackson Smith, Leesville, 1969-75; sr. ptnr. Smith, Ford & Clark, Leesville, 1975-95, The Smith Law Firm, L.L.P., Leesville, 1996—; city judge, Leesville, 1978—. Mem. ATLA, Am. Judicature Soc., La. Trial Lawyers Assn. (mem. bd. govs. 1976-90), La. State Bar Assn. (mem. ho. of dels. 1975-79), 30th Jud. Dist. Bar Assn. (pres. 1974-76). Democrat. Methodist. Personal injury, Federal civil litigation, State civil litigation. Office: PO Drawer 1528 300 Courthouse St Leesville LA 71496-1528

**SMITH, SIMEON CHRISTIE, IV,** lawyer; b. Lake Charles, La., Oct. 21, 1969; s. Simeon Christie III and Shirley Mae (Pearce) S.; m. Christina A. Lord. BA, La. State U., 1992, JD, 1996. Bar: La. 1997, U.S. Dist. Ct. (we., ea. and mid. dists.) La. 1997, U.S. Ct. Appeals (5th cir.) 1997. Ptnr. The Smith Law Firm, L.L.P., Leesville, La., 1997—. Fellow Roscoe Pound Found.; mem. ATLA, Fed. Bar Assn., La. State Bar Assn., La.rial Lawyers Assn. (bd. gos. 1997—), 30th Jud. Cir. Bar Assn. (sec., treas. 1997). Roman Catholic. Personal injury, Appellate, Criminal. Office: PO Drawer 1528 300 Courthouse Leesville LA 71446-1528

**SMITH, SPENCER THOMAS,** lawyer; b. N.Y.C., May 3, 1943; s. Spencer H. and Marie K. (Walter) S.; m. Jenny Matilda Anderson, Aug. 15, 1965; children: S. Anders, J. Kirsten. B.M.E., Cooper Union Sch. Engring., 1965; JD, Am. U., 1968. Bar: N.Y. 1969, U.S. Dist. Ct. (ea. and so. dists.) N.Y. 1971, U.S. Ct. Appeals (fed. cir.) 1983. Assoc. Nolte & Nolte, N.Y.C., 1968-70, Nims, Halliday, Whitman, Howes, Collison & Isner, 1970-72; group patent and licensing counsel Litton Industries, Inc., Hartford, 1984-85; sole practice Hartford, 1984-85; sr. group patent atty. Emhart Copr., Farmington, Conn., 1985-89, Black & Decker Corp., Towson, Md., 1989-98; legal counsel Emhart Glass, Windsor, Conn., 1998. Author: Primarily Merely, 1973. Coach basketball program Farmington Valley YMCA, Simsbury, Conn., 1976-80, Simsbury Youth Soccer Assn., 1976-86. Mem. Licensing Execs. Soc., Greater Hartford C. of C. (mem. high tech. continuing edn. task force 1981-89). Republican. Methodist. Patent, Federal civil litigation, Trademark and copyright. Home: 53 Silver Brook Ln North Granby CT 06060-1111 Office: Emhart Glass Mfg Inc 123 Day Hill Rd Windsor CT 06095-1709

**SMITH, STEPHEN EDWARD,** lawyer; b. Boston, Aug. 5, 1950; s. Sydney and Minnie (Appel) S.; m. Eileen Beth O'Farrell, June 15, 1986; children: Nora, Bennett, Liliana. AB in Polit. Sci., Boston U., 1972; JD, Washington U., St. Louis, 1976. Bar: Ill. 1976, Mass. 1985, U.S. Dist. Ct. (no. dist.) Ill. 1977, U.S. Dist. Ct. (no. dist.) Ind. 1986, U.S. Dist. Ct. Mass. 1987, U.S. Dist. Ct. (ea. dist.) Wis. 1987, U.S. Ct. Appeals (7th cir.) 1981, U.S. Supreme Ct. 1998. Assoc., ptnr. Brown & Blumberg, Chgo., 1976-80; founding ptnr. Cantwell, Smith & Van Daele, Chgo., 1980-84; ptnr. Gottlieb & Schwartz, Chgo., 1984-85; of counsel Siemon, Larsen & Prudy, Chgo., 1985-90; solo pracititioner Chgo., 1990-94; assoc. prof. clin. practice Ill. Inst. Tech. Chgo.-Kent Coll. law, Chgo., 1994-95; of counsel Field & Golan, Chgo., 1995—; mediator Ctr. for Conflict Resolution, Chgo., 1992—; cmty. adv. coun. WBEZ, Chgo., 1985—; arbitrator NASD, Chgo., 1994—, Nat. Futures Assn.; mediator, arbitrator Duke U. Pvt. Adjudication Ctr. Author: Update, ADR for Financial Institutions, 1996, 97. Past. bd. dirs., past pres. Jane Addams Ctr., Hull House Assn., Chgo. Fellow Chartered Inst. Arbitrators; mem. Am. Arbitration Assn. (comml. and internat. panels), Maritime Law Assn. U.S., Chgo. Internat. Dispute Resolution Assn. (dir.), Internat. Ct. Arbitration, London Ct. Internat. Arbitration (panel of neutrals), London Ct. Arbitration (panel of neutrals), Univ. Club Chgo., Legal Club Chgo., Chgo. Lincoln Am. Inn. Ct., Internat. C. of C. (panel of neutrals). Private international, Federal civil litigation, General civil litigation. Office: Field & Golan 15th Floor Three First Nat Plz Chicago IL 60602

**SMITH, STEPHEN JAMES,** lawyer; b. Milw., Feb. 16, 1949; s. James Milon and Helen Kathryn Smith; m. Jerilyn Sue Jenson, Feb. 6, 1971; children: Justin Paul, Lindsay Jeane, Erika Helen. BA magna cum laude, Luther Coll., 1971; JD cum laude, Northwestern U., 1976. Bar: Wis. 1976. Auditor Arthur Andersen & Co., Chgo., 1971-73; ptnr. Hostak, Henzi & Bichler, Ltd. (formerly Thompson & Coates), Racine, Wis., 1976—; reporter taxation sect. Wis. State Bar; mem. adv. bd. and steering com. Sustainable Racine, Inc., 1997—. Bd. dirs. Goodwill Industries S.E. Wis., Racine, 1980-83, Goodwill Industries Milw., 1983—, Racine Area United Way, 1982-88, Taylor Home, 1985-91, 97—, pres., 1998—; bd. dirs. Racine Cmty. Found., 1991—, pres., 1997—. Mem. ABA, Wis. State Bar. Lutheran. General corporate, Personal income taxation, Estate taxation. Office: Hostak Henzl & Bichler SC 840 Lake Ave Racine WI 53403-1566

**SMITH, STEPHEN M.,** lawyer; b. Newport News, Va., July 1, 1948; s. Joseph and Marian (Sturman) S.; m. Dawn Lee Williams, Dec. 10, 1978; children: Ryan David, Miles Stephen. BA in Psychology, William & Mary, 1971, JD, 1974. Bar: Va. 1974, N.Y. 1975, D.C. 1975, U.S. Supreme Ct., U.S. Ct. Appeals (2d, D.C., 4th cirs.). Lawyer Rothblatt, Rothblatt, et al., N.Y.C., 1974-76, Joseph Smith Ltd., Hampton, Va., 1976-99; bd. dirs. Enrenfried Techs. Mem. com. Va. Beach Dems., 1990—. With USN, 1968-70. Mem. ATLA, Va. Trial Lawyers Assn. (bd. dirs. 1978—), Brain Injury Assn. Va. (bd. dirs. 1997—). Avocations: fishing, reading, boating, jogging, golf. Personal injury, Libel, Product liability. Office: Joseph Smith Ltd 2100 Kecoughtan Rd Hampton VA 23661-3215

**SMITH, STEVEN LEE,** judge; b. San Antonio, Apr. 19, 1952; s. Bill Lee and Maxine Rose (Williams) S.; m. Rebecca Ann Brimmer, Aug. 5, 1978;children: William Christopher, Laura Charlotte. B in Music Edn. magna cum laude, Abilene Christian U., 1974; JD, U. Tex., 1977. Bar: Tex. 1977. U.S. Dist. Ct. (so. dist.) Tex. 1979, U.S. Dist. Ct. (we. dist.) Tex. 1980; cert. civil trial lawyer, Tex. Bd. Legal Specialization. Assoc. Dillon & Giesenschlag, Bryan, Tex., 1977-80, ptnr., 1980-84; ptnr. Dillon, Lewis, Elmore & Smith, Bryan, 1985-88, Hoelscher, Lipsey, Elmore and Smith, College Station, Tex., 1988-94; asst. mcpl. judge City of College Station, 1988-91, presiding mcpl. judge, 1992-95; judge Brazos County Ct. at Law # 1, Bryan, 1995-98, 361st Dist. Ct., Bryan, 1999—; sec. Nat. Conf. Spl. Ct. Judges, 1999—. Mem. devel. bd. Abilene Christian U., 1982—, vis. com. Dept. Music, 1983-86; chmn. March of Dimes Brazos Valley Chpt., 1983-84; Leadership Brazos Devel. Program, Bryan/Coll. Sta. C. of C., 1984-85; pres. Meml. Student Ctr. Opera and Performing Arts Soc., College Station, 1985-86. Recipient Charles Plum Disting. Svc. award Tex. A&M U., 1986. Mem. ABA, Abilene Christian U. Alumni Bd., U. Tex. Law Sch. Alumni Assn. (dist. dir. 1986-89), U. Tex. Ex-Students Assn. Exec. Coun. (club rep. 1987-88), Optimists (pres. 1982-83). Mem. Ch. of Christ. Avocations: golf, flying. Home: 3840 Cedar Ridge Dr College Station TX 77845-6275 Office: 361st Dist Ct 300 E 26th St Ste 305 Bryan TX 77803-5361

**SMITH, STEVEN RAY,** law educator; b. Spirit Lake, Iowa, July 8, 1946; s. Byrnard L. and Dorothy V. (Fischbeck) S.; m. Lera Baker, June 15, 1975. BA, Buena Vista Coll., 1968; JD, U. Iowa, 1971, MA, 1971. Bar: Iowa 1971, Ky. 1987, Ohio 1992. From asst. to assoc. dean Sch. Law U. Louisville, 1974-81, acting dean, 1974-75, 76, prof. law, 1971-88, assoc. in medicine Med. Sch., 1983-88; dep. dir/ Assn. Am. Law Schs., 1987-88; dean, prof. law Cleve. State U., 1988-96; pres., dean and prof. Calif. Western Sch. of Law, 1996—. Author: Law, Behavior and Mental Health: Policy and Practice, 1987; contbr. chpts. to books, articles to profl. jours. Trustee U. Louisville, 1980-82, SCRIBES, 1993—; chmn. faculty adv. com. Ky. Coun. Higher Edn., 1981-82; pres. Ky. Congress of Senate Faculty Leaders, 1982-84; bd. trustees Am. Bd. Profl. Psychology, 1994—. Recipient Grawemeyer award Innovative Teaching. Metroversity Consortium, 1983, Pres. award Cleve.-Marshall Law Alumni Assn., 1995. Fellow Ohio State Bar Found.; mem. ABA (stds. rev. com. 1991-95, govt. rels. com. 1993-95, joint commn. ABA/Assn. Am. Law Schs. financing of legal edn. 1993-94, 97—, coun. sect. legal edn. and admission to the bar 1997—), APA (pub. mem. ethics com.), Am. Econs. Assn., Assn. Am. Law Schs. (chmn. librs. com., dep. dir. 1987-88, mem. accreditation com. 1993-96, chair accreditation com. 1994-96), Ohio State Bar Assn. (coun. of dels. 1992-96), Order of Coif, City Club of Cleve. (pres. 1994-95). Office: Calif Western Sch of Law Office of the Pres 225 Cedar St San Diego CA 92101-3046

**SMITH, TAD RANDOLPH,** lawyer; b. El Paso, Tex., July 20, 1928; s. Eugene Rufus and Dorothy (Derrick) S.; m. JoAnn Wilson, Aug. 24, 1949; children: Laura Borsch, Derrick, Cameron Ann Compton. LLB, U. Tex., 1951, BBA, 1952. Bar: Tex. 1951. Assoc. firm Kemp, Smith Duncan & Hammond P.C., El Paso, Tex., 1951-52; ptnr. Kemp, Smith Duncan & Hammond P.C., El Paso, 1952-81, CEO, 1975-95, shareholder, 1981-88; of counsel Kemp, Smith, Duncan & Hammond P.C., El Paso, 1999—; bd. dirs. El Paso Indsl. Devel. Corp. Active United Way of El Paso; chmn. El Paso County Reps., 1958-61, Tex. Rep. State Exec. Com., 1961-62; alt. del. Rep. Nat. Conv., 1952, 62, del. 1964, dir. El Paso Elec. Co., 1961-90, State Nat. Bank of El Paso, 1969-90, The Leavell Co., 1970-94; trustee Robert E. and Evelyn McKee Found., 1970-90, Property Trust of Am., 1971-91; mem. devel. bd. U. Tex., El Paso, 1973-81, v.p., 1975, chmn. 1976; dinner treas. Nat. Jewish Hosp. and Rsch. Ctr., 1977, chmn. 1978, presenter of honoree, 1985; bd. dirs. NCCJ 1965-76, chmn. 1965-78; bd. dirs. Southwestern Children's Home, El Paso, 1959-78; trustee Hervey Found., 1990-99, Lydia Patterson Inst., 1994-99. Named Outstanding Young Man, El Paso Jaycees; recipient Humanitarian award El Paso chpt. NCCJ, 1983; appointed Bd. of Fellows, U. Tex. El Paso, 1997—. Fellow Am. Bar Found., Tex. Bar Found.; mem. ABA, Tex. Bar Assn., El Paso Bar Assn. (pres. 1971-72), El Paso C. of C. (dir. 1979-82), Sigma Chi. Republican. Methodist. General corporate, Securities, Finance. Home: 5716 Mira Grande Dr El Paso TX 79912-2006 Office: Kemp Smith Duncan & Hammond 2000 Norwest Plz 221 N Kansas St Ste 1700 El Paso TX 79901-1401

**SMITH, TERRY J.,** lawyer; b. Detroit, Mar. 7, 1938; s. Russell A. and Anna M. (Chape) S.; m. Lorene M. Yocum, May 17, 1980. BA with high honors, Mich. State U., 1960; JD, U. Chgo., 1965. Bar: 1965, U.S. Supreme Ct. 1972. Mem. Deming & Smith, Grand Ledge, Mich., 1965-72; research assoc. to Chief Judge Protem, Mich. Ct. Appeals, 1965-67; mem. Smith & Smith, Grand Ledge, 1973-76; pres. Smith Bros. Law Office, P.C., Grand Ledge, 1976—; dir. Debt Relief Legal Clinic of Mich., P.C., 1981—; mem. Mich. State Boundries Commn., 1970—; Village Atty., Lake Odessa, Mich., 1974—, Mulliken, Mich., 1980—; city atty., Grand Ledge, 1977-92; Twp. Atty., Eaton Twp., Mich., 1981—; mem. adv. bd. Mich. Nat. Bank-Grand Ledge, 1991-96, Mich. Nat. Bank-Lansing, 1996—. Mem. Eaton County Social Services Bd., 1970-77; bd. dirs. Grand Ledge Area Community Chest, 1964-73, v.p., 1970-73; dir. Grand Ledge Opera House Authority, 1987—, chair, 1993-95, 96—. Recipient Book award W. Pub. Co., 1964, Mich. Vol. Leadership award, 1995. Mem. ABA, Eaton County Bar Assn. (pres. 1968-69), Grand Ledge Area C. of C. (dir. 1966-73, 80—, pres. 1967), Rotary Internat. Probate, Real property, Estate planning. Home: 221 E Scott St Grand Ledge MI 48837-1733 Office: 207 E Jefferson St PO Box 56 Grand Ledge MI 48837-0056

**SMITH, THOMAS SHORE,** lawyer; b. Rock Springs, Wyo., Dec. 7, 1924; s. Thomas and Anne E. (McTee) S.; m. Jacqueline Emily Krueger, May 25, 1952; children: Carolyn Jane, Karl Thomas, David Shore. BSBA, U. Wyo., 1950, JD, 1959. Bar: U.S. Dist. Ct. Wyo. 1960, U.S. Ct. Appeals (10th cir.) 1960, U.S. Tax Ct. 1969, U.S. Supreme Ct. 1971. Of counsel Smith, Stanfield & Scott, LLC, Laramie, Wyo., 1963-94, Brown, Nagel, Waters & Hiser, LLC, Laramie, 1994—; atty. City of Laramie, 1963-86; instr. mcpl. law U. Wyo., 1987; dir. budget and fin. Govt. of Am. Samoa, 1954-56. Bd. dirs. Bur. Land Mgmt., Rawlins, Wyo., 1984-89, chmn. bd. dirs., 1989; pres. Ivinson Hosp. Found., 1994-95; bd. dirs. U. Wyo. Found., 1991-99, pres., 1996-97, bd. dirs. Bank of Laramie, 1998—. Francis Warren scholar, 1958. Mem Wyo. Bar Assn. (pres. 1984-85), Albany County Bar Assn., Western States Bar Conf. (pres. 1985-86), Elks. Republican. Episcopalian. Avocation: golf. Probate, Real property. Office: Brown Nagel Waters & Hiser LLC PO Box 971 515 E Ivinson Ave Laramie WY 82070-3157

**SMITH, T.J.,** lawyer; b. Ironton, Ohio, May 6, 1964; s. Jack M. and Phyllis McBrayer Smith; m. Amy Ellis, Sept. 2, 1989; children: Chance William, Zayne Edward. BA in Pers. and Indsl. Rels., U. Ky., 1986; JD, U. Louisville, 1989. Bar: Ky., U.S. Dist. Ct. (ea., we. and so. dists.) Ky., U.S. Ct. Appeals (6th cir.). Law clk. Ky. Supreme Ct., Frankfort, 1989; prosecutor Jefferson County Atty., Louisville, 1990-94; pvt. practice law Rice and George, Louisville, 1990-94; mng. ptnr. DeCamillis and Smith, Louisville, 1994—; labor cons. Burke Group, Newport Beach, Calif. Mem. Ky. Bar Assn., U. Ky. Varsity Lettermans Club (dir./officer 1997—). Democrat. Avocations: thoroughbred ownership, golf, working with children. Personal injury, Criminal, Labor. Office: DeCamillis and Smith 150 S 3rd St Louisville KY 40202-1326

**SMITH, TREVOR A.,** lawyer; b. Louisville, Apr. 9, 1970; s. John Lee and Phyllis Thompson Smith. BA, Boston Coll., 1992; JD, Miss. Coll., 1995. Law clk. Ky. Supreme Ct., Frankfort, 1995-96; atty. Smith & Helman, Louisville, 1996—. Mem. ABA, Ky. Bar Assn., Louisville Bar Assn. Democrat. Avocations: motorcycles, travel, music. General corporate, Family and matrimonial. Home: 2021 Murray Ave Louisville KY 40205-1213 Office: Smith and Helman 2000 Citizen Plaza 500 W Jefferson St Louisville KY 40202-2823

**SMITH, VICKI LYNN,** lawyer; b. Lebanon, Ind., Sept. 15, 1949; d. Hamer Dean and Betty Joan (Hill) S.; m. Denis Wayne Sloan, Aug. 18, 1967 (div. Jan. 1971); 1 child, Christopher Wayne; m. John Robert Sloop, Jan. 13, 1982. BS in Psychology, Purdue U., 1975; MS in Psychology, Fla. State U., 1979, JD with honors, 1981. Bar: Fla. 1981, U.S. Dist. Ct. (mid. dist.) Fla. 1982. Grad. asst. Fla. State U., Tallahassee, 1975-77, psychometrist, 1976-77; law clk. tax dept. Office Atty. Gen., Tallahassee, 1979-80; intern Office Pub. Defender, Tallahassee, 1980; asst. state's atty. Orange County, Orlando, Fla., 1981-84; ptnr. Sloop & Smith, PA, Orlando, 1984-90; instr. Fla. Inst. for Legal Assts., Orlando, 1986-88; arbitrator U.S. Dist. Ct. (mid. dist.) Fla., 1987—; mem. Atty.'s Title Ins. Fund., spl. master, 1991—. Contbr. articles to profl. jours. Vol. Respond, 1985, Guardian Ad Litem, Habitat for Humanity; bd. dirs. Foxwood Cmty. Assn., 1988-89, Seminole County Friends of Abused Children, 1995—. Mem. ABA, Fla. Bar Assn. (real property com. 1985-87, corp. and banking com. 1986-87), Seminole County Bar Assn. (jud. poll com. 1987-88), Orange County Bar Assn. (legis. com. 1985-86, real property com. 1986-91, estate planning com. 1986-90), Cen. Fla. Safety Coun., Am. Bus. Women's Assn. (pres. Nu Vista chpt. 1985-86, 88-89, v.p. 1987-89, chmn. program com. 1988-89), Phi Delta Phi, Psi Chi, Alpha Kappa Delta. Avocations: bridge, golf. Bankruptcy, Probate, Real property. Office: PO Box 447 Sanford FL 32772-0447

**SMITH, WALTER S., JR.,** federal judge; b. Marlin, Tex., Oct. 26, 1940; s. Walter S. and Mary Elizabeth Smith; children—Debra Elizabeth, Susan Kay. BA, Baylor U., 1964, JD, 1966. Bar: Tex. Assoc. Dunnam & Dunnam, Waco, Tex., 1966-69; ptnr. Wallace & Smith, Waco, 1969-78, Haley & Fulbright, Waco, 1978-80; judge Tex. Dist. Ct., 1980-83; U.S. magistrate U.S. Dist. Ct. (we. dist.) Tex., 1983-84; judge U.S. Dist. Ct. (we. dist.) Tex., Waco, 1984—. Named Outstanding Young Lawyer of Yr., Waco-McLennan County Bar Assn., 1976. Office: US Dist Ct PO Box 1908 Waco TX 76703-1908

**SMITH, WAYNE LARUE,** lawyer, consultant; b. Marietta, Ohio, June 15, 1955; s. Benjamin LeCompte and Bettigene (Jerman) S. BS, Ariz. State U., 1980, MBA, 1987; JD, U. Ariz., 1986. Bar: Fla. 1994, D.C. 1998, U.S. Dist. Ct. (so. dist.) Fla. 1995. Pres. D,B&H Staffing Svcs., Phoenix, 1984-87; v.p. Alan LaRue & Assocs., Phoenix, 1987-88; pres. The Proview Group, Boca Raton, Fla., 1988-93; lawyer Morgan & Hendrick, Key West, Fla., 1993-99, The Smith Law Firm, Key West, Fla., 1999—; bd. dirs. Fla. Lawyers Assistance, Inc., Ft. Lauderdale. Pres. Stop AIDS Project of South Fla., Inc., West Palm Beach, 1988-91; bd. dirs., treas. Comprehensive AIDS Program of Palm Beach County, 1989-93; mem. adv. bd. The Red Barn Theatre, Key West, 1995-99, The Met. Musical Theatre Co., Phoenix, 1996-99; pres. The Experience, Inc., Santa Fe, 1990-95. Recipient New Mem. award, Excellence award Fla. Atlantic Builders Assn., 1989; Up and Comer awards Price Waterhouse/South Fla. Bus. Jour., 1991-92. Mem. ABA, Fla. Bar Assn. (computer law com. 1998-99), Monroe County Bar Assn. (pres. 1995-96), D.C. Bar Assn. Democrat. Banking, Contracts commercial, General civil litigation. Office: The Smith Law Firm 330 Whitehead St Key West FL 33040-6543

**SMITH, WAYNE RICHARD,** lawyer; b. Petoskey, Mich., Apr. 30, 1934; s. Wayne Anson and Frances Lynetta (Cooper) S.; m. Carrie J. Swanson, June 18, 1959; children: Stephen, Douglas (dec.), Rebecca. AB, U. Mich., 1956, JD, 1959. Bar: Mich. 1959. Asst. atty. gen. State of Mich., 1960-62; pros. atty. Emmet County (Mich.), 1963-68; dist. judge 90th Jud. Dist., Mich., 1969-72; sr. ptnr. Smith & Powers, Petoskey; city atty. City of Petoskey, 1976-98. Trustee North Central Mich. Coll., 1981-98, chmn., 1992-97; mem. No. Mich. Community Mental Health Bd., 1972-92, chmn., 1979-81. Mem. ABA, Am. Judicature Soc., Emmet-Charlevoix Bar Assn. (pres. 1967), State Bar Mich., Mich. State Bar Found. Presbyterian. Real property, Probate, Land use and zoning (including planning). Home: 3056 St Louis Club Rd Petoskey MI 49770-9702 Address: PO Box 636 618 Howard St Petoskey MI 49770-2724

**SMITH, WENDY HOPE,** lawyer; b. N.Y.C., Jan. 19, 1957; d. Morton and Doris Smith. A.B., Smith Coll., 1978; J.D., Boston U., 1981. Bar: N.J. 1981; U.S. Dist. Ct. 1981, U.S. Ct. Appeals (3d cir.), Supreme Ct. of U.S. Law sec. to judge Superior Ct. N.J., Bergen County, 1981-82; assoc. firm Sellar, Richardson, Stuart & Chisholm, Roseland, N.J., 1982-89, ptnr. 1989-97; ptnr. Sellar Richardson, P.C., 1997—; mem. adv. com. Inst. Continuing Legal Edn., 1983-91. Mem. ABA, Am. Arbitration Assn., N.J. Bar Assn., Bergen County Bar Assn., Essex County Bar Assn., Trial Attys. N.J., Mensa. Club: Smith Coll. Alumnae Assn. (fund rep. 1978-83). General civil litigation, Personal injury, Insurance. Home: 401 Hancock Ct Edgewater NJ 07020-1627 Office: Sellar Richardson PC 6 Becker Farm Rd Roseland NJ 07068-1735

**SMITH, WILLIAM LAFAYETTE, JR.,** lawyer; b. Wills Point, Tex., Nov. 27, 1948; s. William Lafayette and Hazel Estes (Adams) S.; m. Ann Boutwell, June 11, 1970 (dec. 1993); children: Jefferson, Ginger, Amanda, Marcie, Melissa, Winter, Flint, Shannon. BA cum laude, North Tex. State U., 1975; JD, So. Meth. U., 1978. Bar: Tex. 1978, U.S. Dist. Ct. (ea. dist.) Tex. 1983, U.S. Dist. Ct. (no. dist.) Tex. 1989, U.S. Dist. Ct. (we. dist.) Tex. 1990, U.S. Ct. Appeals (5th cir.) 1983, U.S. Supreme Ct. 1990; cert. civil trial lawyer. Pvt. practice Denton, Tex., 1978—. With USN, 1968-71. Mem. Tex. Trial Lawyers Assn. (med. negligence and polit. coms. 1990-91), Assn. Trial Lawyers Am. Democrat. Methodist. Avocations: fishing, aerobatic flying. General civil litigation, Personal injury, Professional liability. Office: RR 2 Box 32B Teague TX 75860-8695

**SMITH, WILLIE TESREAU, JR.,** retired judge, lawyer; b. Sumter, S.C., Jan. 17, 1920; s. Willie T. and Mary (Moore) S.; student Benedict Coll., 1937-40; AB, Johnson C. Smith U., 1947; LLB, S.C. State Coll., 1954, JD, 1976; m. Anna Marie Clark, June 9, 1955; 1 son, Willie Tesreau, III. Admitted to S.C. bar, 1954; began gen. practice, Greenville, 1954; past exec. dir. Legal Svcs. Agy. Greenville County, Inc.; state family ct. judge 13th Jud. Circuit S.C., 1977-91; ret. 1991. Past mem. adv. bd. Greenville Tech. Edn. Ctr. Adult Edn. Program and Para-Legal Program; mem. adv. bd. Greenville Tech. Coll. Found. Bd.; mem., past bd. visitors Presbyn. Coll., Clinton, S.C.; past bd. dirs. Greenville Urban League; past trustee Greenville County Sch. Dist.; past v.p. Peace Ctr. for Performing Arts. With AUS, 1942-45, USAF, 1949-52. Represented in Bell South African Am. History Calendar. Mem. Am., Nat. (jud. coun.), S.C., Greenville County bar assns., Southeastern Lawyers Assn., Nat. Coun. Juvenile and Family Ct. Judges, Am. Legion, Greater Greenville C. of C. (past dir.), Phillis Wheatley Assn. (dir.), NAACP, Omega Psi Phi, Delta Beta Boule, Sigma Pi Phi. Presbyterian (past chmn. bd. trustees Fairfield-McClelland Presbytery, past moderator Foothills Presbytery). Clubs: Masons, Shriners, Rotary. Home: 601 Jacobs Rd Greenville SC 29605-3318

**SMITHSON, DAVID MATTHEW,** lawyer; b. Chgo., Jan. 14, 1957; s. Paul Stanley and Barbara Jane (Sherman) S.; m. Susan Marie Bletcher, Aug. 11, 1984; 1 child, Rachel Carmella. BS, U. Oreg., 1980; JD, Boston Coll., 1984. Bar: Calif. 1985, Conn. 1997, U.S. Dist. Ct. (ctrl. dist.) Calif. 1985, U.S. Dist. Ct. (so. dist.) Calif. 1987. Atty. Parker & Stanbury, L.A., 1984-89, Shield & Smith, L.A., 1989-91, Hornberger & Criswell, L.A., 1991-93, Chapman & Glucksman, L.A., 1993-95, Cummins & White, L.A., 1995—. Avocations: tennis, golf, travel, museums. Environmental, Insurance, Construction. Office: Cummins & White LLP 2424 SE Bristol St Ste 300 Newport Beach CA 92660-0764

**SMITHSON, LOWELL LEE,** lawyer; b. Kansas City, Mo., Apr. 29, 1930; s. Spurgeon Lee and Lena Louise (Ruddy) S.; m. Rosemary Carol Leitz, Jan. 30, 1960 (div. Sept. 1985); m. Phyllis Galley Westover, June 8, 1986; children: Carol Maria Louise, Katherine Frances Lee. AB in Polit. Sci., U. Mo., 1952, JD, 1954. Bar: Mo. 1954, U.S. Dist. Ct. (we. dist.) Mo. 1955, U.S. Supreme Ct. 1986. Ptnr. Smithson & Smithson, Kansas City, 1956-59; assoc. Spencer, Fane, Britt & Browne, Kansas City, 1959-64, ptnr., 1964—; adj. prof. law U. Mo., Kansas City, 1982. Pres. Kansas City Mental Health Assn., 1963-65; mem. bd. pres. All Souls Unitarian Ch. Kansas City, 1965-67; chmn. com. select dean for law sch. U. Mo., 1983. Served with U.S. Army, 1954-56, Korea. Mem. Kansas City Bar Assn., Lawyers Assn. Kansas City, Assn. Trial Lawyers Am., Western Mo. Def. Lawyers Assn., Fed. Energy Bar Assn., Phi Beta Kappa, Phi Delta Phi. Democrat. Unitarian Ch. Avocations: skiing, reading, painting, swimming, canoeing. General civil litigation, Environmental, Condemnation. Home: 1215 W 65th St Kansas City MO 64113-1803 Office: Spencer Fane Britt & Browne 1000 Walnut 1400 Commerce Bank Bldg Kansas City MO 64106-2140

**SMITS, ANNMARIE P.,** lawyer; b. Kassel, Germany, Aug. 26, 1967; came to U.S., 1969; d. Joseph R. Palermo and Betty A. (Bezares) Schrage; m. C. Wouter Smits, Mar. 18, 1993. BA magna cum laude, William Paterson U., Wayne, N.J., 1989; JD, Touro Law Ctr., Huntington, N.Y., 1994. Bar: N.J. 1994, N.Y. 1995. Paralegal Williams Leiden, Miller & Otley, Wayne, 1988-89, Toys "R" Us, Paramus, N.J., 1989-90, Henry schein, Inc., Port Washington, N.Y., 1990-93, Law Office Jean Angell, N.Y.C., 1993-94; assoc. Bryan Cave LLP, N.Y.C., 1994-97, Pitney Hardin Kipp & Szuch, Florham Park, N.J., 1997—. Mem. ABA, N.Y. State Bar Assn., N.Y. County Bar Assn., N.J. Bar Assn., Morris County Bar Assn. Democrat. Roman Catholic. Avocations: travel, aerobics, reading, foreign languages. Home: 117 Harvest Ln Lincoln Park NJ 07035-2041

**SMOAK, EVAN LEWIS,** lawyer; b. Columbia, S.C., Jan. 30, 1967; s. Lewis E. and Phyllis Anderson. BA cum laude, U. S.C., 1989; JD, U. Va., 1992. Bar: Conn. 1992, N.Y. 1993, U.S. Dist. Ct. (so. and ea. dists.) N.Y. 1993. Actor S.C. Ednl. Television, Columbia, 1977-86; atty. Werner & Kennedy, N.Y.C., 1992-97, Barger & Wolen, N.Y.C., 1997—. Art auction co-chair Empire State Pride Agenda, N.Y.C., 1996, 97, 98. Recipient Thomas Moore Craig award U. S.C., 1989. Mem. ABA, Assn. Bar of City of N.Y., Phi Beta Kappa. Democrat. Federal civil litigation, State civil litigation, Alternative dispute resolution. Home: 445 W 23d St New York NY 10011 Office: Barger & Wolen 500 5th Ave Fl 46 New York NY 10110-4699

**SMOCK, C(AROLYN) DIANE,** lawyer; b. Dec. 18, 1953; m. Bradford W. Wyche; children: Charles, Jessica. AB in Polit. Sci. magna cum laude, U. Ga., 1974; JD, U. Va., 1979. Bar: S.C. 1980; cert. mediator Nat. Jud. Coll. Legal asst. Alston, Miller & Gaines, Atlanta, 1974-76; assoc. Riley & Riley, Greenville, S.C., 1980-82; ptnr. Yarborough, Moore & Smock, Greenville, 1982-88; pvt. practice, 1988-90; judge Greenville County Probate Ct., 1990-98, 99—; part-time faculty mem. Greenville County Mus. Sch. Art, 1989, Greenville Tech. Coll., 1979. Mem. Greenville TEC Adv. Bd., 1979-83; bd. dirs. Greenville YWCA, 1980-82, Met. Arts Coun., 1981-83, Greenville Urban League, 1981-88, 94—, Upstate Visual Arts, 1992-93, Hughes Acad. PTA, 1996-99, Greenville High Sch. PTA, 1999—; exec. com. Greenville County Dem. Women, 1982-84; mem. Com. for Partnership in Arts Leadership, 1989; bd. dirs. Greater Greenville C. of C., 1985, treas., 1987; mem. adv. bd. Fine Arts Ctr., 1988; pres. Greenville Profl. Women's Forum, 1985—; mem. Greenville Higher Edn. Ctr. Adv. Coun., 1990-94; mem. profl. bd. councilors St. Francis Women's Hosp., 1991-93; chair S.C. Family Rsch. Found., 1989-90; founder, bd. dirs. S.c. lawyers for Arts, 1980-90; mem. Leadership S.C., 1989; bd. dirs. S.C. Arts Commn., 1985-88; mem. State Water Law Rev. Com., 1982. Recipient award Furman Exec. Week, 1996, Leadership Inst. in Judicial Edn., 1996, Career Woman of Yr. award Zonta, 1984, Young Career Woman award Piedmont Region of S.C., 1982. Mem. Nat. Coll. Probate Judges (adv. com. on interstate guardianships 1997-98, nominating com. 1995-96), S.C. Probate Judges Assn. (pres. 1984-85), ABA (conf. spl. ct. judges 1991-99, co-chair lawyers and the arts commn. young lawyers divsn. 1985-86), S.C. Bar (exec. com. young lawyers divsn. 1984-88), Greenville County Bar (exec. com. 1982), Phi Beta Kappa, Phi Kappa Phi. Democrat. Methodist. Probate. Home and Office: 211 Pinckney St Greenville SC 29601 Office: Greenville County Probate Ct 301 University Rdg Ste 1200 Greenville SC 29601-3683

**SMOCK, JAMES F.,** retired lawyer; b. Brookings, S.D., May 11, 1940; s. George Edwark and Charlett Smock; m. Karen Smock (div. July 1968); m. Patricia Smock (div. Mar. 1983); children: James Franklin, Jared Anthony. BS, Ind. State U., 1962; JD, Ind. U., 1966. Bar: Ind. Atty. Nisenbaum & Brown, Indpls., 1966-71; staff corp. legal dept. J.C. Penney Co., N.Y.C., 1971-73; pvt. practice Smock Law Firm, Terre Haute, Ind., 1973-86, Indpls., 1986-97; pub. defender, Terre Haute, 1973-76, city atty., 1976-80; pres. Hulman Field Airport Bd., Terre Haute, 1978-82. Mem. Ind. State Bar Assn. Avocations: snow skiing, boating. Bankruptcy, General corporate, General civil litigation.

**SMOCK, TIMOTHY ROBERT,** lawyer; b. Richmond, Ind., June 24, 1951; s. Robert Martin and Thelma Elizabeth (Cozad) S.; m. Martha Carolene Middleton, Apr. 4, 1992; children: Andrew Zoller, Alison Pierce. BA, Wittenberg U., 1973; JD cum laude, Ind. U., 1977. Bar: Ind. 1977, Ariz. 1979, U.S. Dist. Ct. (so. dist.) Ind. 1977, U.S. Dist. Ct. Ariz. 1979, U.S. Ct. Apeals (7th cir.) 1977, U.S. Ct. Appeals (9th cir.) 1979. Jud. clk. Ct. of Appeals of Ind., Indpls., 1977-79; assoc. Lewis and Roca, Phoenix, 1979-82; assoc./shareholder Gallagher & Kennedy, Phoenix, 1982-89; ptnr. Scult, French, Zwillinger & Smock, Phoenix, 1989-94, Smock and Weinberger, Phoenix, 1994—; judge, pro tempore Maricopa County Superior Ct., Phoenix, 1989—; faculty, State Bar Course on Professionalism, Ariz. Supreme Ct./State Bar, Phoenix, 1992—; speaker, Continuing Legal Edn., Maricopa County and Ariz. State Bar, 1988—. Mem. ABA, Ariz. Bar Assn., Maricopa Bar Assn., Def. Rsch. Inst. General civil litigation, Insurance, Professional liability. Office: Smock and Weinberger 2700 N Central Ave Ste 1125 Phoenix AZ 85004-1174

**SMOKE, RICHARD EDWIN,** lawyer, investment adviser; b. Detroit, Sept. 16, 1945; s. Bruno Donald and Else Marie (Reinvaldt) S.; m. Evelyn Panagsagan Navarro, Jan. 24, 1986. BA, Kalamazoo (Mich.) Coll., 1967; JD, Wayne State U., 1970. Bar: Mich. 1970, Calif. 1975, U.S. Supreme Ct. 1980. Gen. counsel Grosse Ile (Mich.) Bridge Co., 1975-78, pres., 1980-83, v.p., 1989—; gen. counsel Campbell-Ewald Co., Warren, Mich., 1978-80; pvt. practice law, investment adviser Grand Rapids, Mich., 1985—; dir. Kent County Cmty. Mental Health, 1996; adj. faculty Davenport Coll., 1993-95; trustee Grand Rapids Charter Twp., 1991-96; commr. County of Kent, 1996—. Bd. dirs. World Affairs Coun. Western Mich., Grand Rapids, 1988-93, pres., 1991-92; mem. exec. com. Kent County Rep. Party, Grand Rapids, 1989-92, 95—; trustee Kalamazoo Coll., 1970-79. London-Sloan fellow, 1983. Mem. State Bar Mich., State Bar Calif., Investment Analysts Chgo., Peninsular Club. Investment, Finance.

**SMOLEV, TERENCE ELLIOT,** lawyer, educator; b. Bklyn., Oct. 5, 1944; s. Lawrence and Shirley (Lebowitz) S.; m. Sherry Gale Rosen, Nov. 24, 1968 (div.); children: Cindy, Scott; m. Phyllis C. Rudko, Oct. 8, 1995. BBA, Hofstra U., 1966; JD, American U., 1969; LLM, NYU, 1974. Bar: N.Y. 1970. Acct. Peat Marwick & Mitchell, N.Y.C., 1969-70; dir. deferred giving Hofstra U., Hempstead, N.Y., 1971-74; editor Panel Publishers, Greenvale, N.Y., 1970-71; ptnr. Naidich & Smolev, P.C., Bellmore, N.Y., 1972-92; mem. bd. trustees Hofstra U., 1992—; adj. prof. Hofstra U., Hempstead, N.Y., 1971—; dist. counsel North Merrick (N.Y.) UFSD, 1975-99. Author of book chpt. Mem. Nassau County, N.Y. Dem. Com., 1972-80, mem. judicial screening com., 1992—; mem. IRS Small Bus. Adv. Com., Washington D.C., 1975-77; bd. dirs. Arthritis Found. L.I., 1995-97, mem Israeli Bond Cabinet Long Island, 1996—. Recipient George M. Estabrook award Hofstra U., 1991, Alumni Achievement award Hofstra U., 1993, Cmty. Svc. award Hebrew Acad. Nassau County, 1997; named Senator of Yr., Hofstra U., 1985, Alumnus of Yr., 1996. Mem. ABA, N.Y. State Bar Assn., Nassau County Bar Assn., N.Y. State Assn. Sch. Attys. (pres. 1984), Hofstra U. Alumni Senate (pres. 1987-89), Hofstra U. Club (bd. dirs. 1981-95). Avocations: photography, golf. Corporate taxation, Estate planning, General corporate. Office: One Old Country Rd Carle Place NY 11514

**SMOLKER, GARY STEVEN,** lawyer; b. L.A., Nov. 5, 1945; s. Paul and Shayndy Charolette (Sirott) S.; m. Alice Graham; children: Terra, Judy, Leah. BS, U. Calif.-Berkeley, 1967; MS, Cornell U., 1968; JD cum laude, Loyola U., L.A., 1973. Bar: Calif. 1973, U.S. Dist. Ct. (cen. dist.) Calif. 1973, U.S. Tax Ct. 1973, U.S. Ct. Appeals (9th cir.) 1973, U.S. Supreme Ct. 1978, U.S. Dist. Ct. (so., ea. and no. dists.) Calif. 1981. Guest researcher Lawrence Radiation Lab., U. Calif., 1967; teaching fellow Sch. Chem. Engring., Cornell U.; mem. tech. staff Hughes Aircraft Co., Culver City, Calif., 1968-70; in advanced mktg. and tech. TRW, Redondo Beach, Calif., 1970-72; sole practice, Beverly Hills, Calif., 1973-89, L.A., 1989—; guest lectr. UCLA Extension, 1973-74, Loyola U. Law Sch., 1979; speaker, panelist in field; adv. Loyola U. Law Sch., 1973—. Contbr. articles to profl. jours.; inventor self-destruct aluminum tungstic oxide films, electrolytic anticorrompise process. Mem. Nat. Assn. Real Estate Editors, Calif. State Bar Assn., L.A. County Bar Assn., Beverly Hills Bar Assn. (sr. editor jour. 1978-79, contbg. editor jour. 1980-82, 86-90, editor-in-chief 1984-86, pub. Smolker Letter 1985—). Jewish. Lodge: B'nai B'rith (anti-defamation league). Real property, Finance, Construction. Office: 4720 Lincoln Blvd Ste 280 Marina Dl Rey CA 90292-6977

**SMOUSE, H(ERVEY) RUSSELL,** lawyer; b. Oakland, Md., Aug. 13, 1932; s. Hervey Reed and Vernie (Rush) S.; m. Creta M. Staley, June 15, 1955; children: Kristin Anne, Randall Forsyth, Gregory Russell. AB, Princeton U., 1955; LLB, U. Md., 1958. Bar: Md. 1958, U.S. Tax Ct. 1979, U.S. Ct. Appeals (4th cir.) 1960, U.S. Supreme Ct. 1974. Atty., Atty. Gen.'s Honors Program, Dept. Justice, Washington, 1958-60, asst. U.S. atty. Dist. Md., 1960-62; assoc. Pierson and Pierson, Balt., 1962-64; atty. B.&O. R.R., Balt., 1964-66; mem. Pierson and Pierson, 1966-69; mem. Clapp, Somerville, Black & Honemann, Balt., 1969-74; Law Offices H. Russell Smouse, 1974-81; mem. Melnicove, Kaufman, Weiner & Smouse, P.A., Balt., 1981-89, chair litigation, 1985-89, Whiteford, Taylor & Preston, Balt., 1989-93, chair, litigation dept., 1989-93; head gen. litigation Law Offices Peter G. Angelos, 1993—; gen. counsel Balt. Orioles, 1993—; v.p. Legal Aid Bur. Balt. City, 1972-73; bd. dirs. Md. Legal Svcs. Corp., 1987-93. Fellow Am. Coll. Trial Lawyers; mem. ABA, Md. State Bar Assn. (gov. 1981-83), Bar Assn. Balt. City (chmn. grievance com. 1969-70, chmn. judiciary com. and nominating com. 1980, mem. exec. com. 1969-70, 80, chmn. exec. com. lawyers' com. for ind. judiciary 1989-96), Nat. Assn. R.R. Trial Counsel (exec. com., v.p. ea. region 1986-92). Republican. Presbyterian. Federal civil litigation, State civil litigation, Criminal.

**SMYTH, GERARD A.,** lawyer, administrator; b. N.Y.C., June 29, 1945; s. Eugene J. and Theresa Smyth; m. Janice Anderson, Aug. 1, 1987; children: Gregg Smyth, Tricia Smyth, Lindsey Hall, Thomas Hall. BA, Fairfield U., 1967; JD, U. Conn., 1975. Bar: Conn. 1975. Asst. atty. gen. State of Conn., Hartford, 1975-76; asst. pub. defender Divsn. Pub. Defender Svcs., State of Conn., Hartford, 1976-85, chief of capital def. and trial svcs., 1985-91, dep. chief pub. defender, 1991-94, chief pub. defender, 1994—; em. Conn. Alcohol and Drug Policy Coun., Hartford, 1996—; mem. Gov.'s Task Force on Justice for Abused Children, Hartford, 1997—. Mem. Zoning Bd. Appeals, Town of Granby, Conn., chmn. charter revision com. Capt. USAF, 1968-73. Mem. Nat. Assn. Criminal Def. Lawyers, Conn. Criminal Def. Lawyers Assn., Conn. Bar Assn. (exec. com. criminal justice 1994—), Hartford County Bar ASsn., Nat. Legal Aid and Defender Assn. Office: Office of Chief Pub Defender 30 Trinity St Fl 4 Hartford CT 06106-1629

**SMYTH, JEFFREY A.,** lawyer; b. Seattle, June 23, 1949; s. Alan C. and Lewauna A. Smyth; m. Mary Johanna Smyth, Aug. 6, 1972 (div. Mar. 15, 1976); m. Betty Ann Smyth, Sept. 6, 1980; 1 child, Graham Alan. BA with honors, West Wash. U., 1971; JD with distinction, U. of Pacific, 1975. Bar: Wash., Alaska, Hawaii, N.C., U.S. Ct. Appeals (9th cir.), U.S. Ct. Appeals (5th cir.). Assoc. Gordon, Thomas, Honeywell, Tacoma, Wash., 1975-80, Weinrich, Gilmore & Adolph, Seattle, 1981-84; prin. Smyth Law Offices, Seattle, 1985-87; shareholder Adolph & Smyth P.S., Seattle, 1987-95; pvt. practice Smyth Law Offices, Seattle, 1995—; panel mediator Fed. Ct. Rule 39.1 Panel, Seattle, 1987—. Coach Mercer Island (Wash.) Boys and Girls Club, 1995, 96. Mem. Wash. State Bar Assn. (fee dispute arbitrator 1992—), Wash. Sttae Trial Lawyers Assn., Columbia Tower Club. Avocation: rare books. Federal civil litigation, General civil litigation, State civil litigation.

**SMYTH, PAUL BURTON,** lawyer; b. Phila., Aug. 15, 1949; s. Benjamin Burton and Florence Elizabeth (Tomlinson) S.; m. Denise Elaine Freeland, May 31, 1975. BA, Trinity Coll, Hartford, Conn., 1971; JD, Boston Coll., 1974. Bar: Conn. 1974, D.C. 1975, U.S. Dist. Ct. D.C., 1980, U.S. Supreme Ct., 1985. With Dept. Interior, 1974—, atty. Office of Hearings and Appeals, Arlington, Va., 1974-76, atty. Office of Solicitor, Washington, 1976-82, asst. solicitor for land use and realty, Washington, 1982-87; deputy assoc. solicitor for energy and resources, Washington, 1987-93, acting dir. Office of Hearings and Appeals, Arlington, 1993-94, dep. assoc. solicitor. for energy and resources, Washington, 1994-95, for land and water resources, 1995—; lectr. environ. law George Washington U. Law Sch., Washington, 1997—. Bd. dirs. EcoVoce, 1998—; trustee Rocky Mountain Mineral Law Found., 1999—. Editor: Federal Reclamation and Related Laws Annotated, Reclamation Reform Act Compilation, 1982-88; contbr. articles to legal publs. Mem. ABA (coun. 1991-94, budget officer 1994-98, sect. natural resources, energy and environ. law, exec. editor Nat. Resources and the Environ. 1989-91). Office: Office of Solicitor Dept Interior 18th And C Sts NW Washington DC 20240-0001

**SMYTHE, ANDREW CAMPBELL,** lawyer; b. Boston, July 25, 1952; s. William S. and Barbara J. Smythe; m. Leslie Smythe, Sept. 20, 1980; children: Gretchen, Steven. BA in History, U. Colo., 1974; JD, Gonzaga U., 1977. Bar: Wash. 1978. Assoc. Layman Mullin, Spokane, Wash., 1978-88; ptnr. Turner Stoeve, Spokane, 1988-94, Chase Hayes, Spokane, 1994—. Pres. Hambler PTA, Spokane, 1996-98. Mem. Wash. State Bar Assn. (state rules com. 1992-95). Insurance, Federal civil litigation, General civil litigation. Office: Paine Hamblin Coffin Brocke & Miller 717 W Sprague Ave Ste 1200 Spokane WA 99201-3919

**SMYTHE, PETER CHRISTIAN,** lawyer; b. Red Bank, N.J., Oct. 27, 1964; 1 child, Alexander Stephen. BA in Comm., Oral Roberts U., 1988; diploma, Rhema Bible Tng. Ctr., Broken Arrow, Okla., 1987; JD, Tex. Tech., 1993. Bar: Tex. Ptnr. Law Offices of Peter Christian Smythe, Arlington, Tex., Wills & Smythe, Dallas, The Smythe Law Firm, Arlington. Mem. Tex. Trial Lawyers. Personal injury, Professional liability, Product liability. Office: The Smythe Law Firm Ste 210 2261 Brookhollow Plaza Dr Arlington TX 76006-7430

**SNAID, LEON JEFFREY,** lawyer; b. Johannesburg, Transvaal, Republic of South Africa, Dec. 24, 1946; came to U.S., 1981; s. Mannie and Hene (Blume) S.; children: Jedd, Nicole. Diploma in Law, U. Witwatersrand, Johannesburg, 1969. Bar: Supreme Ct. Republic South Africa 1971, High Ct. of the Kingdom of Lethoso 1976, Calif. 1982, U.S. Dist. Ct. (so. and ctrl. dists.) Calif. 1982; cert. immigration law specialist, State Bar Calif. Bd. Legal Specialization. Assoc. Reeders, Teeger & Rosettenstein, Johannesburg, 1972; sole practice Johannesburg, 1973-76; ptnr. Snaid & Snaid, Johannesburg, 1976-81; sole practice San Diego, 1982—; lectr. legal edn. seminars, San Diego, 1984—. Author, pub. quar. newsletter Immigration and Internat. Law, The Newcomers Guide to Living in the U.S.A. Mem. ABA, Am. Immigration Lawyers Assn. (past chmn. continuing legal edn. San Diego chpt.), San Diego County Bar Assn. (past chmn. immigration com.). Lodge: Rotary. Immigration, naturalization, and customs, Private international. Home: 5060 Via Papel San Diego CA 92122-3923 Office: 6265 Greenwich Dr Ste 103 San Diego CA 92122-5916

**SNAVELY, GORDON ALDEN,** lawyer; b. Detroit, June 7, 1942; s. Gordon Edward and Rosemary Snavely; m. Mary Jo Snavely, May 14, 1942; children: Gordon Edward II, Robert Alden, Suzanne Desmond. B. Commerce and Fin., U. Detroit, 1964, JD, 1967. Bar: Mich. 1967. Pvt. practice Bloomfield, Mich. Mem. claims rev. com. Oakland County, Mich. Mem. Oakland County Bar Assn. Avocations: golf, tennis. Estate planning, Probate. Home: 3240 Pine Lake Rd Orchard Lake MI 48324-1951 Office: 74 W Long Lake Rd Ste 203 Bloomfield Hills MI 48304-2775

**SNEAD, KATHLEEN MARIE,** lawyer; b. Steubenville, Ohio, July 1, 1948; d. Donald Lee and Mary Alice (Hobright) O'Dell; m. John Jones Snead, Oct. 14, 1972; 1 child, Megan Marie. BA, Pa. State U., 1970; JD, U. Denver, 1979. Bar: Colo. 1979, U.S. Ct. Appeals (10th cir.) 1980, U.S. Supreme Ct. 1986. Field examiner NLRB, Pitts., 1970-72; freelance photographer Charleston, W.Va., 1973-74; labor relations examiner U.S. Dept. Labor, Denver, 1974-77, labor relations officer, 1978-79; staff atty. Denver & Rio Grande Western R.R., Denver, 1979-81, asst. gen. atty., 1981-84, gen. atty., 1984-92; gen. atty. Southern Pacific Lines, 1992-96, Union Pacific R.R., Denver, 1996-97; pvt. practice Golden, Colo., 1997—. Mem. ABA, Colo. Bar Assn. (adv. coun. environ. law sect.), Colo. Women's Bar Assn., Colo. R.R. Assn. (dir. 1982-84). Avocations: reading, swimming, biking, skating. Environmental, Labor, General civil litigation. Home: 233 S Devinney St Golden CO 80401-5316

**SNEED, JOSEPH TYREE, III,** federal judge; b. Calvert, Tex., July 21, 1920; s. Harold Marvin and Cara (Weber) S.; m. Madelon Juergens, Mar. 15, 1944 (dec. Dec. 1998); children—Clara Hall, Cara Carleton, Joseph Tyree IV. BBA, Southwestern U., 1941; LLB, U. Tex., Austin, 1947; SJD, Harvard, 1958. Bar: Tex. bar 1948. Instr. bus. law U. Tex., Austin, 1947; asst. prof. law U. Tex., 1947-51, asso. prof., 1951-54, prof., 1954-57, asst. dean, 1949-50; counsel Graves, Dougherty & Greenhill, Austin, 1954-56; prof. law Cornell U., 1957-62, Stanford Law Sch., 1962-71; dean Duke Law Sch., 1971-73; dep. atty. gen. U.S. justice dept., 1973; judge U.S. Ct. Appeals (9th cir.), San Francisco, 1973—, now sr. judge; Cons. estate and gift tax project Am. Law Inst., 1960-69. Author: The Configurations of Gross Income, 1967, Footprints on the Rocks of the Mountain, 1997; contbr. articles to profl. jours. Served with USAAF, 1942-46. Mem. ABA, State Bar Tex., Am. Law Inst., Order of Coif. Office: US Ct Appeals PO Box 193939 San Francisco CA 94119-3939

**SNEERINGER, STEPHEN GEDDES,** lawyer; b. Lancaster, Ohio, Mar. 27, 1949; s. Stanley Carlylle and Mary Eleanor (Fry) S.; m. Kristine Karen Serfling, Oct. 6, 1974; children: Mary Rhonda, Robyn Kathleen. BA magna cum laude, Denison U., 1971; JD, Washington U., 1974. Bar: Mo. 1974. Sr. v.p. A.G. Edwards & Sons Inc., St. Louis, 1974—; arbitrator N.Y. Stock Exchange, Nat. Assn. Securities Dealers, Nat. Futures Assn., Am. Arbitration Assn. Editor: Urban Law Ann., 1973-74; bd. editors Securities Arbitration Commentator. Am. Jurisprudence scholar, 1974. Mem. ABA (mem. dispute resolution sect., arbitration com.), Mo. Bar Assn., Securities Industries Assn. (chmn. arbitration com.), Futures Industries Assn., Nat. Assn. Securities Dealers (past mem. arbitration com.). Securities, State civil litigation, Federal civil litigation. Office: AG Edwards & Sons Inc 1 N Jefferson Ave Saint Louis MO 63103-2205

**SNEIRSON, MARILYN,** lawyer; b. Yonkers, N.Y., July 23, 1946. BA, Brandeis U., 1968; JD, Rutgers U., 1981. Bar: N.J. 1981, N.Y. 1989, U.S. Ct. Appeals (3d cir.) 1988, U.S. Supreme Ct. 1989. Law clerk Hon. Sylvia Pressler Superior Ct. N.J. Appellate, Hackensack, N.J., 1981-82; assoc. Pitney, Hardin, Kipp & Szuch, Morristown, N.J., 1982-84, Cole, Schotz et als, Hackensack, 1984-89; ptnr. Beattie, Padovano, Montvale, N.J., 1989-94; ptnr., prin. Price, Sneirson, Shulman & Meese, Woodcliff Lake, N.J., 1994—; commentator Court TV. contbr. articles to profl. jours. Committeewoman Dem. County Com., Ridgewood, N.J., 1980—. Mem. N.J. Bar Assn., Justice Pashman Am. Inns Court (master), Bergen County Bar Assn. Avocation: art. Labor, Federal civil litigation, State civil litigation. Office: Price Sneirson Shulman & Meese 50 Tice Blvd Ste 14 Woodcliff Lake NJ 07675-7658

**SNELL, BRUCE M., JR.,** state supreme court justice; b. Ida Grove, Iowa, Aug. 18, 1929; s. Bruce M. and Donna (Potter) S.; m. Anne Snell, Feb. 4, 1956; children: Rebecca, Brad. AB, Grinnell Coll., 1951; JD, U. Iowa, 1956. Bar: Iowa 1956, N.Y. 1958. Law clk. to presiding judge U.S. Dist. Ct. (no. dist.) Iowa, 1956-57; asst. atty. gen., 1961-65; judge Iowa Ct. Appeals, 1976-87; justice Iowa Supreme Ct., 1987—. Comments editor Iowa Law Rev. Mem. ABA, Iowa State Bar Assn., Am. Judicature Soc., Order of Coif. Methodist. Home: PO Box 192 Ida Grove IA 51445-0192 Office: Iowa Supreme Ct St Capitol Bldg Des Moines IA 50319-0001

**SNELL, LORI B.,** paralegal; b. L.A., Apr. 30, 1958; d. Melvil N. and Freda B. Snell. BA, UCLA, 1982, Paralegal Cert., 1983, JD, 1986. Corp. paralegal Cooper, Epstein & Hurewitz, Beverly Hills, Calif., 1989-93, Silverberg, Katz, Thompson & Braun, L.A., 1993-94; corp. transactional paralegal Unihealth, Burbank, Calif., 1994—; pres. Corp. Paralegal Svcs., Encino, Calif., 1989—.

**SNELLINGS, DANIEL BREARD,** lawyer; b. New Orleans, Jan. 11, 1960; s. Breard and Emilie (Locascio) S.; m. Lisa Snellings, Oct. 14, 1989; children: Cody, Brooke, Kali, Daniel Jr. BS, Trinity U., 1983; MBA, Loyola U., 1985; JD, Tulane U., 1989. Bar: La. 1990, Miss. 1991, U.S. Supreme Ct. 1996, U.S. Fed. Claims Ct. 1995. Pvt. practice New Orleans, La. Mem. ATLA, Miss. Trial Lawyers Assn., La. Trial Lawyers Assn., Miss. Bar Assn., La. Bar Assn., Pearl River County Bar Assn., St. Tammany Parish Bar Assn. Roman Catholic. Personal injury, Workers' compensation, Admiralty. Office: James Minge & Assocs 2600 Energy Ctr New Orleans LA 70163-2600 also: 503 W Canal St Picayune MS 39466-3914

**SNELLINGS, ROSS SCHLEY,** real estate broker, preservationist; b. Augusta, Ga., Dec. 28, 1963; s. William Ross and Elizabeth T. Snellings; m. Deborah Rushton, Dec. 1, 1995 (dec. Feb. 1996). AB, U. Ga., 1986, JD, 1990, postgrad., 1997—. Bar: Ga. 1991, U.S. Dist. Ct. (so. dist.) Ga. 1992, U.S. Ct. Appeals (11th cir.) 1995. Assoc. Nixon, Yow, Waller & Capers, Augusta, 1990-92, Warlick, Tritt & Stebbins, Augusta, 1992-95; CEO Sand Hills Land Co., Augusta, 1992—; broker Sand Hills Properties, Augusta, 1995—; mgr. TaxLien Holding Co. LLC, 1997—. bd. trustee Hist. Augusta, 1994—; chmn. Hist. Preservation Commn., Augusta, 1993-98. Mem. Gamma Sigma Delta, Sigma Pi Kappa. Episcopalian. Office: Sand Hills Properties 2503 Wrightsboro Rd Augusta GA 30904-5340

**SNIDER, KEVIN ANDREW,** lawyer, company executive; b. Oil City, Pa., Feb. 5, 1970; s. William H. and Charlotte E. Snider. BS in Bus. Adminstrn., So. Coll., 1992; GSSP in Polit. Consulting, George Washington U., 1995; JD, U. Memphis, 1996. Bar: Tenn. 1996. Pres. Andrew's Entertainment, Inc., Germantown, Tenn., 1995—; chief mgr. Snider & Horner, PLLC, Germantown, 1996—; legal cons. WREG News Channel 3, Memphis, 1997—. Mem. East Shelby County Bar Assn. (pres. 1998—), Germantown C. of C. (bd. mem. 1997—), Germantown Lions Club (bd. mem. 1996—), Germantown Kiwanis Club. Republican. Office: Snider & Horner PLLC 2298 S Germantown Rd Germantown TN 38138-5951

**SNIHUR, WILLIAM JOSEPH, JR.,** lawyer; b. Paterson, N.J., Mar. 7, 1959; s. William Joseph and Lynn (Aboyoun) S.; m. May Lydia Cain, Oct. 14, 1990; children: Ariel Rose, Alexander Charles. Student, Mt. St. Mary's Coll., L.A., 1978-79, UCLA, 1979; BBA, U. Miami, 1982, JD, 1985. Law intern U.S. Atty.'s Office, Miami, Fla., 1984-85; assoc. Litman, Muchnick, Wasserman & Hartman, Hollywood, Fla., 1986-91; ptnr. Cain & Snihur, North Miami Beach, Fla., 1992—; adj. prof. Barry U., Miami Shores, Fla., 1989—; adj. faculty Legal Career Inst., Ftl. Lauderdale, Fla., 1991. Mem. editl. bd. The Fla. Bar Jour. and News, 1990-94; co-editor: The Fla. Bar Jour., 1991; contbg. writer The Fla. Bar News, 1995. Mem. exec. com. Philharm. Orch. of Fla., Ft. Lauderdale, 1990-92, bd. govs., 1990-93, pres.'s coun., 1990-93, ann. fund campaign leadership, 1991-92, long range planning com., 1992; pres., founder Maestro Broward Philharm., Ft. Lauderdale, 1989-92, Maestro Dade Philharm., co-founder, dir. fin., 1989-90; steering com. WTMI/Philharm. Festival and Radiothon, 1990; bd. dirs. Vinnette Carroll Repertory Theatre, 1989-91; entourage mem. Broward Ctr. for Performing Arts, 1992-93. Recipient music scholarships Mt. St. Mary's Coll., Aspen Music Sch., Depaw U., honor scholarship U. Miami, Coral Gables, 1981, UCLA, 1979, others. Mem. ATLA (mem. com. 1990-91), The Fla. Bar (bus. law, gen. practice, real property, probate and trust law sects., benefits com. 1995—), Broward County Bar Assn. (United Way com. 1989-90, chmn. pub. com. 1991-93, editor Broward Barrister 1991-93, pro bono legal assistance Broward Lawyers Care), North Dade Bar (bd. dirs. 1993-95), Am. Inst. Wine and Food (bd. dirs. 1998—, editor Connoisseur 1999—). Avocations: music, theater, wine. General civil litigation, General corporate, Probate. Office: Cain & Snihur 1550 NE Miami Gardens Dr North Miami Beach FL 33179-4836

**SNIPES, DANIEL BRENT,** lawyer; b. Dublin, Ga., Aug. 20, 1970; s. John Bernard and Jennifer Joiner Snipes; m. Laura Nikole Crumpton, Aug. 19, 1995. BBA, U. Ga., 1992, JD, 1995. Bar: Ga. 1995, Ga. Supreme Ct. 1996, U.S. Dist. Ct. (so. dist.) Ga. 1996, U.S. Ct. Appeals (11th cir.) 1996, S.C. 1997, U.S. Dist. Ct. (no. dist.) Ga. 1998. Lawyer Franklin & Taulbee, Statesboro. Pres. Bulloch County Bar Assn., Statesboro, 1997; team leader United Way S.E. Ga., Statesboro, 1998. Mem. First City Club Savannah, Statesboro Rotary Club, Forest Heights Country Club. Methodist. Avocation: outdoors. Product liability, Personal injury, Federal civil litigation. Office: Franklin & Taulbee PO Box 327 12 Siebald St Statesboro GA 30459

**SNITOW, CHARLES,** lawyer; b. N.Y.C., Feb. 7, 1907; m. Virginia Levitt, Nov. 2, 1935; children: Ann Barr, Alan Mark. AB, Cornell U., 1928, JD, 1930. Ptnr. Pomerance & Snitow, N.Y.C., 1931—; pres. Nat. Hardward Show Inc., N.Y.C., 1945-70, World Hobby Exposition, Chgo., Phila., 1948-53, Charles Snitow Orgn., N.Y.C., 1950-79, Internat. Auto Show, N.Y.C., 1952-80, Nat. Fancy Food Conf. Show, N.Y.C., 1955-70, U.S. World Trade Fair Inc., N.Y.C., San Francisco, 1957-66, Internat. Photography & Travel Show Inc., N.Y.C., 1960-72, Consumer Electronics Show, N.Y.C., 1967-77, Snitow Show Consultants, Inc., N.Y.C., 1975—; cons. Soviet Expn. Sci. and Tech., N.Y.C., 1959, N.C. Internat. Fair, Charlotte, 1959, Brit. Expn., N.Y.C., 1960, Cahners Expn. Group divsn. Reed Exhbn. Cos., N.Y.C., 1970-87, Brazil Expo, N.Y., Chgo., L.A., Dallas, Atlanta, Miami, Fla., 1981, Greater N.Y. Internat. Auto Show, 1982—, East/Cen. Europe Trade Expo, N.Y., 1994. Contbr. articles to Cornell Law Quar. Bd. dirs. Bill of Rights Found., N.Y.C., 1980; mem. Met. Opera Chorus, Schola Cantorum, Collegiate Chorale. Recipient cert. of honor March of Dimes, Gold Key-Medal of Honor, City of N.Y., 1960-62, Gran Prix Am., France, 1965, Garcia Moreno medal Equador, 1966; named Knight, Order of Merit, Republic of Italy, 1963; named to Order Hon. Ky. Cols., La. Cols. Mem. Nat. Assn. Expn. Mgrs. (hon., Kings Glove award for excellence 1991), Latin Am. C. of C., Cornell Club, Savage Club, Phi Beta Kappa, Alpha Kappa Delta. Avocation: singing. Private international. Home: 81 Walworth Ave Scarsdale NY 10583-1140 Office: Snitow Show Cons Inc 4 Sniffen Ct New York NY 10016-3505

**SNODGRASS, TERESA MARIE,** public defender; b. Orange, Calif., July 24, 1953; d. Richard Harrison and Doris Marie Snodgrass; m. Robert Harold Bennett, Mar. 14, 1992; 1 child, Nicole Marie. BA, U. Calif., San Diego, 1975; postgrad., U. Cath., Louvain, Belgium, 1975-77, Calif. State U., Fullerton, 1981-82; JD, U. La Verne Coll. Law, 1988. Bar: Calif. 1988. Law clk., Calif. Correctional Peace Officers Assn., Rancho Cucamonga, Calif., 1988-89; dep. pub. defender State Calif., Office Pub. Defender of San Bernardino County, Rancho Cucamonga, 1989—. Mentor Cmty. Ptnrship for Youth Devel., 1997—. Me. State Bar Assn. Calif., U. La Verne Alumni Assn. (treas., bd. dirs. 1989—). Democrat. Avocations: golf, reading, swimming, baseball, movies. Office: Pub Defenders Office 8303 Haven Ave Rancho Cucamonga CA 91730-3848

**SNOW, GARY PAUL,** judge, lawyer; b. Biloxi, Miss., Sept. 3, 1943; s. David Paul and Marietta Snow; m. Linda Esther Fast, Apr. 25, 1965; children: Molly Melinda Snow Martin, Wendy Lynn Snow Wrigley, Lindsay Rebecca. BA, Okla. Christian U., Oklahoma City, 1965; MA, U. Okla., 1967, JD, 1971. Bar: Okla. 1972, U.S. Dist. Ct. (ea. dist.) Okla. 1973, U.S. Dist. Ct. (we. dist.) Okla. 1986, U.S. Ct. Appeals (10th cir.) 1976, U.S. Supreme Ct. 1978. Instr. in history U. Southwestern La., Lafayette, 1967-69; atty. Sandlin, Daugherty & Snow, Holdenville, Okla., 1972-74, Gary P. Snow Firm, Holdenville, 1974-83; mcpl. judge City of Holdenville, 1975-77; city atty. Town of Calvin, Okla., 1975-77; atty. Mattingly & Snow, Seminole, Okla., 1983—; mcpl. judge City of Seminole, 1994—; city atty. Town of Bowlegs, Okla., 1983-88; judge Ct. Appeals, Temporary Divsn. No. 126, Oklahoma City, 1982; mem. ad hoc com. on lawyer discipline Okla. Supreme Ct., 1986. Bd. dirs., officer Youth and Family Svcs., Wewoka, Okla., 1978-91; officer Hughes County Dem. Party, Holdenville, 1973-83; bd. dirs., officer regional council Girl Scouts Am., McAlester, Okla., 1976-80; league dir. Kiwanis Little League Basketball, Seminole, 1993-96. Mem. Seminole Kiwanis Club (bd. dirs., officer, Disting. Svc. award 1993). Mem. Ch. of Christ (elder). Avocations: reading, running, tennis. Home: 2705 Eastgate Dr Seminole OK 74868-2403 Office: Mattingly & Snow 215 E Oak Ave Seminole OK 74868-3441

**SNOW, ROBERT BRIAN,** lawyer, educator; b. Rochester, N.Y., Apr. 9, 1953; s. Warren Buffington and Betty (Thrash) S.; m. Laura Rudman, May 11, 1976 (div. Sept. 1981); m. Patricia M. Lindsay, April 29, 1984; children: Robert Kyle, Alyssa Lindsay. BA in Polit. Sci. and Communications, U. N.H., 1975; postgrad., Suffolk U., 1975-76; JD, Boston Coll., 1978. Bar: N.H. 1979, U.S. Dist. Ct. N.H. 1979, U.S. Supreme Ct. 1982, Mass. 1985, D.C. 1985, U.S. Ct. Appeals (1st, D.C. and Fed. cirs.) 1979/85, U.S. Ct. Claims 1985. Asst. supr. Dept. Atty. Gen., Boston, 1977-78; dir. crime prevention and pub. info. State Dept. of Safety, Concord, N.H., 1978-79; atty., adminstr. subcontracts Kollsman Inst. Co. div. Sun Chem. Corp., Merrimack, N.H., 1979-81; sole practice Nashua, N.H., 1982—; atty. contracts divs. youth and adult svcs. State Dept. Human Svcs., Concord, 1983-88; instr. faculty Hesser Coll., Manchester, N.H., 1983-86, U. N.H., 1986—, Rivier Coll., 1991-92; chmn. bd. dirs., legal counsel Mt. Hope Bd. of Edn., Nashua, N.H., 1983—; chmn. appellate div. State Dept. Employment, Concord, 1983-85; prosecutor p.t. Hudson (N.H.) Police Dept., 1985-86; chmn. Juvenile Parole Bd., 1987-88; counsel N.H. Supreme Ct. Commn. on Character and Fitness, 1990-93; judge Goffstown Dist. Ct., 1988-94; appointed justice Merrimack Dist. Ct., 1994-96. Author rules N.H. Motor Vehicle Title, 1979, N.H. Fire Code, 1979, N.H. Profl. Code of Conduct, 1984, N.H. D.E.S. Appellate Rules, 1986, N.H. Juvenile Parole Rules, 1988, Rules for Commn. on Character and Fitness. Candidate N.H. Reps., Concord, 1982; candidate State Senate, Merrimack, 1983; del. State Constl. Conv., Concord, 1983. Named one of Outstanding Young Men in Am., 1985, 86, 87. Mem. ABA, N.H. Bar Assn. (profl. code rev. com., criminal practice rev. com.), N.H. Trial Lawyers Assn., Assn. Trial Lawyers Am. (real estate standards rev. com.), N.H. Trial Lawyers Assn., So. N.H. Bus. and Indsl. Club, Merrimack C. of C. Republican. Clubs: Merrimack Exchange (chartered), Soc. N.H. Bus. and Industry. Avocations: football, softball, running, basketball, skiing. Criminal, General corporate, Personal injury. Home: 10 Merrmeeting Dr Merrimack NH 03054-2933 Office: 2 Wellman Ave Nashua NH 03064-1463

**SNOWBARGER, VINCE,** congressman; b. Kankakee, Ill., Sept. 16, 1949; s. Willis Edward and Wahnona Ruth (Horger) S.; m. Carolyn Ruth McMahon, Mar. 25, 1972; children: Jeffrey Edward, Matthew David. BA in History, So. Nazarene U., 1971; MA in Polit. Sci., U. Ill., 1974; JD, U. Kans., 1977. Bar: Kans. 1977, U.S. Dist. Ct. Kans. 1977, Mo. 1987. Instr. Mid-Am. Nazarene Coll., Olathe, Kans., 1973-76; ptnr. Haskin, Hinkle, Slater & Snowbarger, Olathe, 1977-84, Dietrich, Davis, Dicus et al, Olathe, 1984-88, Armstrong, Teasdale, Schafly & Davis, Overland Park, Kans., 1989-92; Holbrook, Heaven & Fay, P.C., Merriam, Kans., 1992-94; ptnr. Snowbarger & Veatch LLP, Olathe, Kans., 1994-96; mem. 105th Congress from 3rd Kans. dist., 1997-99. Mem. Kans. Legislature, Topeka, 1985-96; majority leader Ho. of Reps., 1993-96; mem. Olathe Planning Commn., 1982-84, Leadership Olalthe; divsn. chmn. United Way, Olathe, 1985-88, chmn. citizen rev. com., 1991-95. Mem. Olathe Area C. of C. (bd. dirs. 1984), Overland Park C. of C. Republican. Nazarene. Avocation: politics. Home: 1451 Orleans Dr Olathe KS 66062-5728

**SNOWDEN, BARRY HOWARD,** lawyer; b. Freer, Tex., Feb. 22, 1945; s. Arthur Ray and Ambanez (Paris) S.; ivorced, 1976; children: Philip, Stephen, Mitch, Haley, Amber. BA, Baylor U., 1967, JD, 1970. Bar: Tex. 1970, U.S. Dist. Ct. (so. dist.) Tex. 1970. Asst. dist. atty. 79th Jud. Dist., Tex., 1970-73; pvt. practice, 1970—; ptnr. Morris, Lendais, Hollrah & Snowden, Houston, 1977—. With USNG, 1968-69. Republican. Baptist. Avocations: wine collector, travel. Real property, Mergers and acquisitions, Private international. Home: 5436 Fm 723 Rd Richmond TX 77469-8706 Office: Morris Lendai Hollrah & Snowden 1980 Post Oak Blvd Ste 700 Houston TX 77056-3881

**SNOWE, ALAN MARTIN,** lawyer; b. Bklyn., May 24, 1935; s. Nat and Lillian Rose (Anixter) S.; m. Susan Goldman, May 30, 1958; children: Karen J., Linda. B Commerce, NYU, 1957; LLB, Bklyn. Law Sch., 1962. Bar: N.Y. 1962, U.S. Dist. Ct. (so. and ea. dists.) N.Y. 1965, U.S. Tax Ct. 1974, U.S. Supreme Ct. 1976. Ptnr. Wachtel & Snowe, Hicksville, N.Y., 1967-94; pvt. practice Hicksville, 1994-96; ptnr. Snowe & Goldman, Esq., Hicksville, 1996—; lectr. NYU Sch. Continuing Edn., N.Y.C., 1975-82, Hofstra U. Sch. Continuing Edn., Uniondale, N.Y., 1994-96; arbitrator Dist. Ct. Nassau County, Hempstead, N.Y., 1985—. Mem. N.Y. State Bar Assn., Nassau County Bar Assn. (chair lawyer referral com. 1991-93). Avocations: sports, reading. General practice, Real property, Probate. Office: 382 S Oyster Bay Rd Hicksville NY 11801-3529

**SNOWISS, ALVIN L.,** lawyer; b. Lock Haven, Pa., June 16, 1930; s. Benjamin and Lillian (Kalin) S.; m. Jean Yarnell, Mar. 16, 1973. BA, U. Pa., Phila., 1952, JD, 1955; hon. alumnus, Pa. State U., 1998. Bar: Pa. 1956, U.S. Dist. Ct. (mid. dist.) Pa. 1958, U.S. Supreme Ct. 1972. Pvt. practice Lock Haven, 1955-61; ptnr. Lugg & Snowiss, Lock Haven, 1961-74, Lugg, Snowiss, Steinberg & Faulkner, Lock Haven, 1974-86, Snowiss, Steinberg & Faulkner, LLP, Lock Haven, 1987—; solicitor Clinton County, Lock Haven, 1964-72. Chmn. bd. Lock Haven Hosp. Found., 1986-92; pres. Lock Haven Hosp., 1982-86; bd. govs. Clinton County Cmty. Found., Lock Haven, 1970-97; chmn. adv. bd. Palmer Mus. Art, State College; v.p. bd. trustees Ross Libr., Lock Haven, 1963-86; mem. exec. com. Pa. Rep. Com., Harrisburg, 1974-80; state committeeman Clinton County Rep. Com., Lock Haven, 1967-80. Fellow Am. Coll. Trust and Estate Counsel, Am. Bar Found., Pa. Bar Found. (founding, bd. dirs. 1984-95); mem. Pa. Bar Assn. (zone del. 1976-82, zone gov. 1983-86, treas. 1987-90), Clinton County Bar Assn. (pres. 1975-76), Kiwanis (pres. Lock Haven 1966-67). Republican. Avocations: art history, golf, historical research. Estate planning, Probate, Real property. Home: 414 W Main St Lock Haven PA 17745-1107 Office: 333 N Vesper St Lock Haven PA 17745-1342

**SNYDER, ARTHUR KRESS,** lawyer; b. L.A., Nov. 10, 1932; s. Arthur and Ella Ruth (Keck) S.; m. Mary Frances Neely, Mar. 5, 1953; children: Neely Arthur, Miles John; m. Michele Maggie Noval, May 14, 1973; 1 child, Erin-Marisol Michele; m. Delia Wu, Apr. 18, 1981. BA, Pepperdine U., 1953; JD, U. So. Calif., 1958; LLD, Union U., 1980. Bar: Calif. 1960, U.S. Supreme Ct. 1982. Sole practice L.A., 1960-67; founder, pres. Arthur K. Snyder Law Corp., L.A., 1981-94; pres. Snyder & Archuletta, Attys., L.A., 1994—; pres. Marisol Corp., real estate and fgn. trade, 1978—; pres. real estate holdings Keck Investment Properties, 1990—; past instr. L.A. City Schs. Mem. City Coun. L.A., 1967-85. Served to capt. USMC. Decorated La Tizona de El Cid Compeador (Spain), medal Legion of Honor (Mex.), Hwa Chao Zee You medal (Republic of China), numerous other commendations, medals, awards. Mem. ABA, ATLA, Los Angeles County Bar Assn., World Film Inst. (chmn. bd. dirs. 1997—), Am.-Vietnamese Cultural Exch. Assn. (pres. 1998—), Calif. Bar Assn., L.A. County Bar Assn., Am. Judicature Soc., Masons. Baptist. Administrative and regulatory, Real property, State civil litigation. Office: 1000 W Sunset Blvd Ste 200 Los Angeles CA 90012-2105

**SNYDER, BROCK ROBERT,** lawyer; b. Topeka, Sept. 18, 1935; s. Ralph and Helen (Fritze) S.; m. Carol Lee Cunningham, June 5, 1957 (div. Nov. 1976); children: Lori, Holli, Staci; m. Sheryl Anita Clarke, Apr. 1, 1985; children: Brock Robert II, Samantha. BS, U. Kans., 1957; JD, Washburn U., 1964. Bar: Kans. 1964. Ptnr. Eidson, Lewis, Porter & Haynes, Topeka, 1964-82; sole practice Topeka, 1982—; lectr. on sch. discipline and due process, 1975-80; pres. Kans. Legal Services, Topeka, 1977-80. Served to capt. USMC, 1957-61. Fellow Kans. Bar Assn. (chmn. legal assts. com. 1983-84); mem. ABA, Kans. Trial Lawyers Assn. (bd. govs.), Topeka Bar Assn., Topeka Legal Aid Soc. (pres. 1976-78). Republican. Lutheran. Avocation: scuba. Personal injury, General practice, General corporate. Office: 1401 SW Topeka Blvd Topeka KS 66612-1818

**SNYDER, DEBORAH ANN,** lawyer; b. Plainfield, N.J., Jan. 6, 1969; d. Mauro Anthony and Penelope Mary Russo; m. Brian J. Snyder, Aug. 25, 1995. BA, Lehigh U., 1991; JD, Seton Hall U., 1996. Bar: N.J. 1996, U.S. Dist. Ct. N.J. 1996. With pro bono svc. program Seton Hall Sch. Law, Newark, summer 1994; summer intern Chancery Divsn. Essex County, Newark, summer 1994; lawyer Norris, McLaughlin & Marcus, Somerville, N.J., 1996—. Mem. N.J. Bar Assn. General corporate. Home: 18 Colony Dr Summit NJ 07901-2460 Office: Norris McLaughlin & Marcus 721 Rte 202/206 Bridgewater NJ 08807-1760

**SNYDER, DONALD EDWARD, JR.,** lawyer; b. Rochester, N.Y., Dec. 25, 1956; s. Donald E. and Dorothy E. (Stanke) S.; m. Mary Ann Campany, Sept. 1, 1991; children: Christin N., Donald E. III. BS, Cornell U., 1979; JD cum laude, Tulane U., 1982. Bar: N.Y. 1983. Atty. Gallo & Iacovangelo, Rochester, N.Y., 1983-84, Sutton, DeLeeuw, Clark & Darcy, Rochester, N.Y., 1984-95, Creary & Creary Attys., Rochester, N.Y., 1995-98, Cummings, Dunckel & Campany, LLP, Lowville, N.Y., 1998—. Past pres. Pinnacle Luth. Ch. Mwm. N.Y. State Bar Assn., Lewis County Bar Assn., Monroe County Bar Assn., Phi Delta Phi. Republican. Avocations: music, travel, recreation. Real property, Banking, General corporate. Home: 7635 Collins St Lowville NY 13367-1110 Office: Cummings Dunckel & Co LLP 7557 State St Lowville NY 13367

**SNYDER, JEAN MACLEAN,** lawyer; b. Chgo., Jan. 26, 1942; d. Norman Fitzroy and Jessie (Burns) Maclean; m. Joel Martin Snyder, Sept. 4, 1964; children: Jacob Samuel, Noah Scot. BA, U. Chgo., 1963, JD, 1979. Bar: Ill. 1979, U.S. Dist. Ct. (no. dist.) Ill. 1979, U.S. Ct. Appeals (7th cir.) 1981. Ptnr. D'Ancona & Pflaum, Chgo., 1979-92; prin. Law Office of Jean Maclean Snyder, Chgo., 1993-97; trial counsel The MacArthur Justice Ctr. U. Chgo. Law Sch., 1997—. Contbr. articles to profl. publs. Mem. ABA (mem. coun. on litigation sect. 1989-92, editor-in-chief Litigation mag. 1987-88, co-chair First Amendment and media litigation com. 1995-96, co-chair the woman advocate com. 1996-98, co-chair sect. litigation task force on gender, racial and ethnic bias in the cts. 1998—, standing com. on strategic communications, 1996—), ACLU of Ill. (mem., bd. dirs. 1996—), Lawyers for the Creative Arts (mem., bd. dirs. 1995-97). General civil litigation, Entertainment, Intellectual property. Office: The MacArthur Justice Ctr Univ of Chgo Law Sch 1111 E 60th St Chicago IL 60637-2776

**SNYDER, JOHN GORVERS,** lawyer; b. Boston, June 20, 1960; s. Philip Francis and Sylvia (Gorvers) S.; m. Hinda Mala Simon, July 8, 1984; children: Monica Paige, Kimberly Blaine. BA, Johns Hopkins U., 1982; JD, Cornell U., 1987. Bar: Mass. 1988, U.S. Dist. Ct. Mass. 1989. Ptnr. banking law, bus. law and corp. law dept. Craig & Macauley P.C., Boston, 1995—, assoc. banking law, bus. law and corp. law dept., 1987-94; lectr. New England Coll. Fin., 1994—. Active Combined Jewish Philanthropies, Boston, 1991—, Anti-Defamation League, Boston, 1993-94. Mem. Mass. Bar Assn., Boston Bar Assn., Phillips Exeter Acad. Alumni Assn., Phi Alpha Delta Internat., Omicron Delta Kappa (Johns Hopkins U. chpt., pres. 1981-82), Delta Upsilon (Johns Hopkins U. chpt.). Avocations: golf, tennis. Contracts commercial, General corporate, Bankruptcy. Home: 7 Laurus Ln Newton Center MA 02459-3138 Office: Craig & Macauley PC Fed Res Plz 600 Atlantic Ave Ste 2900 Boston MA 02210-2215

**SNYDER, MARK ALLEN,** lawyer; b. Balt., Nov. 20, 1951; s. Hyman William Snyder and Rhea Belle Thiman; m. Nancy Virginia Salmon, Aug. 18, 1974; children: Erin Hayley, Meredith Ann. Pres., mng. ptnr. Cohen, Snyder, Eisenberg & Katzenberg, Balt., 1976—. Bd. trustees Fair Oaks Cmty. Assn., Severna Park, Md., 1995-97, Md. Inst. for Continuing Profl. Edn. of Lawyers, 1995-97. Mem. Md. State Bar Assn. (bd. govs. 1998—), Md. Trial Lawyers Assn. (bd. govs. 1994-96), Anne Arundel Bar Assn. (bd. dirs. 1994—, pres. 1997-98, Pres. award 1994), Md. Workers Compensation Ednl. Assn. (bd. govs. 1996—), U. Balt. Alumni Assn. (bd. trustees 1980-82). Democrat. Jewish. Avocations: SCUBA, golf, skiing. Workers' compensation, Personal injury, Criminal. Office: Cohen Snyder Eisenberg & Katzenberg 347 N Charles St Baltimore MD 21201-4307

**SNYDER, THOM,** lawyer; b. Glendale, Calif., Oct. 28, 1945; s. Walter and Jeanne (Mott) S.; m. Georgina Rae Totoian, Apr. 6, 1968; children: Chad Thomas, Seth Michael. BA, Calif. State U., Fresno, 1968; MA, Calif. State U., 1976; JD, San Joaquin Coll. of Law, 1982. Tchr. Riverdale (Calif.) Elem. Sch., 1968-70; tchr., adminstr. Am. Union Sch., Fresno, 1972-78; assoc. McInturff & Behrens, Hanford, Calif., 1983-85; ptnr. Behrens, Snyder & Romaine, Hanford, 1985—; adj. prof. Coll. of the Sequoias, Visalia, Calif., 1987-90. Pres., bd. dirs. Ctrl. Valley Regional Ctr., Fresno, 1987-93; pres. Assn. Regional Ctr. Agys., Sacramento, 1989-92; v.p., bd. dirs. Career Devel. Program, Escondido, Calif., 1994—; bd. dirs. Hanford YMCA, 1994—; sponsor, coach local youth sports, Hanford, 1986—. With U.S. Army, 1970-72. Named Tchr. of Yr. Coll. of Sequoias, 1989; recipient Svc. Appreciation award Ctrl. Valley Regional Ctr., 1992, 93. Mem. Kiwanis (v.p. Hanford club 1994—). Republican. Presbyterian. General corporate, State civil litigation, Juvenile. Home: 350 Trinity Cir Hanford CA 93230-1353 Office: Behrens Snyder & Romaine 522 N Redington St Hanford CA 93230-3833

**SNYDER, WILLARD BREIDENTHAL,** lawyer; b. Kansas City, Kans., Dec. 18, 1940; s. N.E. and Ruth (Breidenthal) S.; m. Lieselotte Dieringer, Nov. 10, 1970 (dec. Nov. 1975); 1 child, Rolf; m. T.J. Sewall, May 17, 1996. BA, U. Kans., 1962, JD, 1965; postgrad., Hague Acad. Internat. Law, The Netherlands, 1965-66, U. Dijon, France, 1966; grad., Command and Gen. Staff Coll., Ft. Leavenworth, Kans., 1977. Bar: Kans. 1965, Mo. 1986, U.S. Tax Ct. 1977, U.S. Ct. Mil. Appeals 1981, U.S. Dist. Ct. Kans. 1965, U.S. Supreme Ct. 1977. Atty. Kansas City, 1970-80, 85—; trust officer, corp. trust officer Security Nat. Bank., Kansas City, 1980-83, corp. sec., 1983-85; pres. Real Estate Corp. Inc., Leawood, Kans., 1984—; adv. dir. United Mo. Bank, 1985-90; dir., mem. trust and investment com. Blue Ridge Bank, 1991—; German Consul (H) for Kans., Western Mo., 1972—. Mem. Platte Woods (Mo.) City Coun., 1983-84; mem. exec. bd. dirs. regional coun. Boy Scouts Am.; bd. govs. Liberty Meml. Assn.; bd. dirs., nominations com. MacJannett Found., Talloires, France; pres. Breidenthal-Snyder Found.; trustee St. Mary Coll.; trustee, nominations com. Hoover Pres. Libr. Col. Kans. Army NG, ret.; col. USAR ret. Decorated Bundesverdienst Kreuz, 1982, BVK 1KL (Germany), 1992, Bundeswehr Kreuz (silver), 1987, Ge. Abn., Legion of Merit, Meritorious Svc. medal, Army commendation medal; KARNG medal of excellence; named to Hon. Order Ky. Cols., 1988; recipient Golden Honour badge German Vet. Orgn., Bavaria, 1988, Mil. Order of WW award, OCS Hall of Fame. Mem. Mo. Bar Assn., Kansas City Bar Assn., Kansas City Hosp. Attys., Mil. Order of World Wars (chpt. comdr. 1983-84, regional comdr. 1987-91, Patrick Henry award), Nat. Eagle Scout Assn., Blue Ridge Bankshares (dir.). Avocations: scuba, hunting, Notgeld collections, cartridge collection. General corporate, Public international, Non-profit and tax-exempt organizations. Office: 8014 State Line Rd Ste 203 Leawood KS 66208-3712

**SOBEL, JAY,** lawyer; b. Red Bank, N.J., Mar. 26, 1966. BS, BA, U. Md., 1989; JD cum laude, Boston U., 1993. Atty. Schatz, Schatz, Ribikoff & Kotkin, Hartford, Conn., 1993-95, Thacher Proffitt & Wood, N.Y.C., 1995-97, Skadden Arps Slate Meagher & Flom, N.Y.C., 1997—. Contracts commercial, Real property. Home: 405 E 56th St Apt 10C New York NY 10022-2422

**SOBEL, JONATHAN F.,** lawyer; b. Cleve., Dec. 27, 1954; s. Marvin H. and Mimi S.; m. Linda Miller, July 21, 1994. BA, Colgate U., 1976; JD, Duke U., 1979. Bar: Ohio, U.S. Dist. Ct. (no. dist.) Ohio, U.S. Ct. Appeals (6th cir.). Assoc. Kabat & Mielziner, Beachwood, Ohio, 1980-86; ptnr. Kabat, Mielziner & Sobel, Beachwood, Ohio, 1986—; assoc. prof. Notre Dame Coll., South Euclid, Ohio, 1995—. Mem. Phi Beta Kappa. Avocation: sailing. Contracts commercial, Personal injury, Probate. Office: Kabat Mielziner & Sobel 25550 Chagrin Blvd Ste 403 Beachwood OH 44122-4640

**SOBLE, MARK RICHARD,** lawyer; b. San Francisco, Dec. 25, 1964. BA with deptl. honors, Stanford U., 1985; JD, U. Mich., 1988. Bar: Calif. 1988, U.S. Dist. Ct. (cen. dist.) Calif. 1988, U.S. Dist. Ct. (ea. dist.) Calif. 1990. Law clk. to chief judge U.S. Dist. Ct. for S.D., Pierre, 1988-89; assoc. Lewis, D'Amato, Brisbois & Bisgaard, L.A., 1989-90; counsel enforcement div. Fair Polit. Practices Commn., Sacramento, 1990-96, sr. counsel, 1996—. Note editor U. Mich. Jour. Law Reform, 1987-88. Raymond K. Dykema scholar U. Mich. 1987. Mem. State Bar Calif., Sacramento County Bar Assn. (mng. editor Docket 1997, mem.-at-large bar coun. 1998—). Office: Fair Polit Practices Commn 428 J St Ste 700 Sacramento CA 95814-2331

**SOBOCINSKI, JOSEPH S.,** federal law enforcement agent; b. Pitts., Dec. 24, 1958; m. Helen Marie, Aug. 7, 1982; children: Stephen, Matthew, Thomas. BA in History, St. Francis Coll., Loretto, Pa., 1980; JD, U. Pitts., 1984. Spl. agent, FBI U.S. Dept. Justice, 1984—.

**SOCARRAS, MICHAEL PETER,** lawyer; b. Sagua La Grande, Cuba, Sept. 29, 1961; came to U.S., 1973; s. Pedro and Maria Coralia Socarras; m. Lisa Ann Barmann, June 28, 1990; children: Michael Peter Jr., Sophia Christina, Alexander Paul. Student, London Sch. Econs., 1981-82; BA, Brandeis U., 1983; JD, Yale U., 1986. Bar: D.C. 1987, Mo. 1997. Law clk. to Hon. James L. Buckley U.S. Ct. Appeals (D.C. cir.), Washington, 1986-87; spl. asst. civil rights divsn. U.S. Dept. of Justice, Washington, 1987-89; assoc. Covington and Burling, Washington, 1989-96; of counsel Shook, Hardy & Bacon, Kansas City, Mo., 1996-98, ptnr., 1999—; bd. dirs. Nat. Law Ctr. for Interam. Free Trade, Tucson, 1998—; vice chair internat. law com. Mo. Bar, Columbia, 1998—. Author: (book chpt.) International Incidents, 1988. Outside counsel Dole-Kemp '96, Washington, 1996; vol. Bush-Quayle '92, Washington, 1992, Reagan-Bush '80, Waltham, Mass., 1980. Republican. Roman Catholic. Private international, Product liability. Office: Shook Hardy & Bacon LLP 1200 Main St Ste 2100 Kansas City MO 64105-2118

**SODD, GLENN,** lawyer; b. Arlington, Tex., June 29, 1948; s. Ellis and Betty (Rankin) S.; m. Patricia Ailshie; children: Jason, Jody, Jourdan. JD, Baylor U., 1972. Bar: Tex. 1972. Pres. Dawson, Sodd & Beard, P.C., Corsicana, Tex., 1972—; owner, operator 500-cow grazing dairy, Kerens, Tex. Pres. Indsl. Found., Corsicana, 1985-96; chmn. Navarro County Retarded Citizens Assn., Corsicana, 1978; mem. Corsicana Ind. Sch. Dist., 1986-87; bible tchr. Grace Comty. Ch., Corsicana; owner, pres. The Refuge. Fellow Am. Coll. Trial Lawyers; mem. Corsicana C. of C. (pres. 1982, Inds. Man of Yr. 1996). Baptist. General civil litigation, Condemnation, Personal injury. Office: PO Box 837 121 N Main St Corsicana TX 75110-5214

**SODEN, PAUL ANTHONY,** lawyer; b. N.Y.C., Feb. 3, 1944; s. Leo J. and Mildred E. (Callahan) S.; m. Irene M. Davis, Aug. 3, 1968; children—Christina M., Paul A. A.B., Fordham U., 1965, J.D., 1968. Bar: N.Y. 1968. Assoc. Cahill, Gordon & Reindel, N.Y.C., 1968-74; corp. counsel Technicon Corp., Tarrytown, N.Y., 1974-76, asst. gen. counsel, asst. sec., 1976-78, sr. v.p., gen. counsel, sec., 1978-87; v.p., dir. internat. law Sterling Winthrop Inc., 1987-88; v.p., gen. counsel, sec. Sterling Drug Inc., 1988-95; sr. v.p., gen. counsel, sec. The Reader's Digest Assn., Inc., 1995—. Mem. Am. Bar Assn., N.Y. State Bar Assn, Fordham U. Board of Trustees, Advisory Board Whitehead Inst. Club: Scarsdale (N.Y.) Golf. General corporate, Antitrust, Contracts commercial. Office: Reader's Digest Rd Pleasantville NY 10570-7000

**SODEN, RICHARD ALLAN,** lawyer; b. Feb. 16, 1945; s. Hamilton David and Clara Elaine (Seale) S.; m. Marcia LaMonte Mitchell, June 7, 1969; children: Matthew Hamilton, Mark Mitchell. AB, Hamilton Coll., 1967; JD, Boston U., 1970. Bar: Mass. 1970. Law clk. to judge U.S. Ct. Appeals (6th cir.), 1970-71; assoc. firm Goodwin, Procter & Hoar LLP, Boston, 1971-79, ptnr., 1979—; instr. Law Sch. Boston Coll., Chestnut Hill, Mass., 1973-74. Mem. South End Project Area Com.; hon. dir. United South End Settlements, pres., 1977-79; chmn. Boston Mcpl. Rsch. Bur.; pres. Boston Minuteman coun. Boy Scouts Am.; trustee Judge Baker Children's Ctr., chmn., 1994-96, pres., 1992-94; trustee New Eng. Aquarium, Boston U.; bd. visitors Boston U. Goldman Sch. Grad. Dentistry; mem. bd. overseers WGBH; mem. Mass. Minority Bus. Devel. Commn.; mem. Adv. Task Force on Securities Regulation; mem. Adv. Com. on Legal Edn.; steering com. Lawyers Com. for Civil Rights under Law, chmn., 1992-94. Mem. ABA (chmn. standing com. on bar svcs. and activities), Nat. Bar Assn., Mass. Bar Assn. (past vice chmn. bus. law coun. 1990-91), Boston Bar Assn. (pres. 1994-95), Mass. Black Lawyers Assn. (pres. 1980-81). General corporate, Finance, Securities. Home: 42 Gray St Boston MA 02116-6210 Office: Goodwin Procter & Hoar LLP Exchange Pl Boston MA 02109-2803

**SODERLAND, DOUGLAS R.,** lawyer; b. Seattle, Apr. 6, 1960; s. Stanley C. and Mary E. (Sutherland) S.; m. Parcae Lea Morford, Sept. 15, 1984; children: Devin L., Morgan L. BA magna cum laude, Western Wash. U., 1982; JD cum laude, U. Puget Sound, 1986. Bar: Wash. 1986, U.S. Dist. (we. dist.) Wash. 1986, U.S. Dist. (ea. dist.) Wash. 1994. Assoc. Houger, Miller & Stein, Seattle, 1986-90, Wilson, Smith, Cochran & Dickerson, Seattle, 1990-93, Groshong & Thornton, Seattle, 1993-98; ptnr. Soderland Waechter PLLC, Seattle, 1999—. Contbg. author: Washington Motor Vehicle Accident Deskbook, 1994. Insurance, Transportation. Office: Soderland Waechter 701 5th Ave Ste 2130 Seattle WA 98104-7030

**SOFFAR, WILLIAM DOUGLAS,** lawyer; b. Houston, Sept. 8, 1944; s. Benjamin and Esther Goldy (Garfinkel) S.; m. Nancy Elise Axelrod, Mar. 29, 1969 (div. Sept. 1989); children: Pamela Beth, Stephanie Michelle, Jill Denise. BA, U. Houston, 1966, JD, 1969. Bar: Tex. 1969, U.S. Dist. Ct. (so. dist.) Tex. 1970, U.S. Ct. Appeals (5th cir.) 1974, U.S. Supreme Ct. 1974; cert. mediator in civil law and family law. Atty. examiner U.S. Interstate Commerce Commn., Washington, 1969-70; atty. Law Office of Adolph Uzick, Houston, 1970-72, Walsh & Soffar, Houston, 1972-73; lawyer, sole practice Law Offices of William D. Soffar, Houston, 1973-74; ptnr. Soffar & Levit, Houston, 1974—; family law and civil mediator, basic mediation and family mediation trainer Atty.-Mediator's Inst. Bd. dirs. Miller Theater Adv. Coun., Houston, 1985-90, Zina Garrison Found., Houston, 1989-91. Mem. Houston Bar Assn. (bd. dirs., family law sect. mem. 1989-90), Jewish Cmty. Ctr. (health club com. 1971—), Jewish Family Svc. (bd. dirs. 1970-71), Phi Delta Phi. Jewish. Avocations: travel, reading, raquetball. General practice, Family and matrimonial, Personal injury. Office: Soffar & Levit 6575 West Loop S Ste 630 Bellaire TX 77401-3604

**SOGG, WILTON SHERMAN,** lawyer; b. Cleve., May 28, 1935; s. Paul P. and Julia (Cahn) S.; m. Saralee Frances Krow, Aug. 12, 1962 (div. July 1975); 1 child, Stephanie; m. Linda Rocker Lehman, Dec. 22, 1979 (div. Dec. 1990); m. Nancy Rosenfield Walsh, June 2, 1991. AB, Dartmouth Coll., 1956; JD, Harvard U., 1959. Bar: Ohio 1960, D.C. 1970, Fla. 1970, U.S. Supreme Ct., N.Y. 1985, U.S. Tax Ct., 1961. Assoc. Gottfried, Ginsberg, Guren & Merritt, 1960-63, ptnr., 1963-70; ptnr. Guren, Merritt, Feibel, Sogg & Cohen, Cleve., 1970-84; of counsel Hahn, Loeser, Freedheim, Dean and Wellman, Cleve., 1984-85; ptnr. Hahn Loeser & Parks LLP, Cleve., 1986—; trustee, pres. Cleve. Jewish News; adj. prof. Cleve. State Law Sch., 1960—; lectr. Harvard U. Law Sch., 1978-80. Author: (with Howard M. Rossen) new and rev. vols. of Smith's Review Legal Gems series, 1969—; editor: Harvard Law Rev.; contbr. articles to profl. jours. Trustee Jewish Cmty. Fedn. of Cleve., 1966-72; bd. overseers Cleveland Marshall Coll. Law, Cleve. State U., 1969—, vis. com. Coll. Bus. Adminstrn., 1996—; dir. Project for Improving Delivery of Legal Svcs., Case Western Res. U. Law Sch., 1991—; mem. U.S. and State of Ohio Holocaust commns. Fulbright fellow U. London, 1959-60. Mem. Ohio Bar Assn., Fla. Bar Assn., D.C. Bar Assn., N.Y. State Bar Assn., Germany Philatelic Soc., Oakwood Club, Union Club, Chagrin Valley Hunt, Phi Beta Kappa. General corporate, Taxation, general, Estate planning. Home: PO Box 278 Gates Mills OH 44040-0278 Office: Hahn Loeser & Parks LLP 3300 BP America Bldg 200 Public Sq Ste 3300 Cleveland OH 44114-2303

**SOGNIER, JOHN WOODWARD,** retired judge; b. Savannah, Ga., Dec. 17, 1919; 03937564s. Joseph W. and Viola (Trott) S.; divorced; children: John Woodward Jr. Anne Sognier Murray; m. Loretto Boswell, Nov. 9, 1985. Legal edn., Catholic. U., 1941; LLM in Twx, Emory U., 1994. Bar: Ga. 1946, U.S. Dist. Ct. Ga. 1946, U.S. Ct. Appeals 1964. Ptnr. Kennedy & Sognier, Savannah, 1946-80; judge Ga. Ct. Appeals, Atlanta, 1980-92; ret., 1992; rep. Gen. Assembly Ga., Atlanta, 1955-56; registrar Chatham County, Savannah, 1957-60, county atty., 1960-68. Sr. warden Christ Ch., Savannah; chmn. Ga. State Bd. Bar Examiners, 1974-79; trustee Continuing Jud. Edn. Com. 1982-88. Lt. col. USAF, 1942-45, ETO, 1951-53. Decorated D.F.C. Fellow Am. Coll. Trial Lawyers, Am. Bar Found.; mem. ABA. Episcopalian.

**SOHN, LOUIS BRUNO,** lawyer, educator; b. Lwów, Poland, Mar. 1, 1914; came to U.S., 1939, naturalized, 1943; s. Joseph and Fryderyka (Hescheles) S.; m. Elizabeth Mayo. LLM, Diplomatic ScM, John Casimir U., 1935; LLM, Harvard U., 1940, SJD, 1958; LLD (hon.), Free U. Brussels (Flemish sect.), 1990. Asst. to Judge M. O. Hudson, 1941-48; John Harvey Gregory teaching fellow Harvard Law Sch., 1946-47, lectr. law, 1947-51, asst. prof. law, 1951-53, John Harvey Gregory lectr. in world orgn., 1951-81, prof. law, 1953-61, Bemis prof. internat. law, 1961-81; Woodruff prof. internat. law U. Ga., 1981-91; vis. Congl. prof. George Washignton U. Law Sch., 1991-92; Disting. rsch. prof. and dir. rsch. and studies Internat. Rule of Law Ctr., George Washington U. Law Sch., 1992—; disting. fellow Jennings Randolph program U.S. Inst. Peace, 1991-92; cons. U.S. ACDA, 1960-70, Office Internat. Security Affairs, Dept. Def., 1963-70; rsch. asst. joint project for internat. law of future ABA and Can. Bar Assn., 1943-44; asst. to del. Permanent Ct. Internat. Justice, San Francisco Conf. UN, 1945; exec. sec. legal subcom. on atomic energy Carnegie Endowment for Internat. Peace, 1946; asst. reporter on progressive devel. internat. law Am. and Canadian bar assns., 1947-48; cons. UN secretariat, 1948, 69, legal officer, 1950-51; counselor internat. law Dept. State, 1970-71; U.S. del. to UN Law of Sea Conf., 1974-82; U.S. del. head Athens Conf. on Settlement Internat. Disputes, 1984. Author: Cases on World Law, 1950, Cases on United Nations Law, 1956, 2d edit., 1967, (with G. Clark) World Peace Through World Law, 1958, 3d edit., 1966, Basic Documents of African Regional Organizations, 4 vols, 1971-72, (with T. Buergenthal) International Protection of Human Rights, 1973, (with K. Gustafson) The Law of the Sea in a Nutshell, 1984, International Organization and Integration: student edit. 1986, (with T. Buergenthal) The Movement of Persons Across Borders, 1992, Rights in Conflict: The United Nations v. South Africa, 1994 ; also articles on internat. legal subjects; editor devel. internat. law: Am. Bar Assn. Jour, 1947-50; editorial bd.: Am. Jour. Internat. Law, 1958—. Recipient World Peace Hero award World Federalists of Can., 1974, Grenville Clark award, 1984, William A. Owens award for creative rsch. in social and behavioral scis. U. Ga., 1985, Harry Leroy Jones award Washington Fgn. Law Soc., 1993, Internat. Human Rights award UN Assn. Nat. Capital Area, 1997. Mem. ABA (hon., co-rapporteur joint working group with Can. Bar Assn. on peaceful settlement of disputes 1976—, vice chmn. internat. law and practice sect. 1983-91, chmn. 1992-93, mem. coun. 1993-97, councillor 1997—, Leonard J. Theberge award 1992), Am. Soc. Internat. Law (mem. exec. coun. 1954-57, v.p. 1965-66, hon. v.p. 1980-87, 90—, pres. 1988-90, Manley O. Hudson medal 1996), World Parliament Assn. (legal advisor 1954-64), Internat. Law Assn. (v.p. Am. br.), Am. Law Inst. (assoc. reporter Fgn. Rels. Law 1978-87), Inst. Internat. Law (Geneva) (reporter on consensus in internat. law 1997), Fedn. Am. Scientists (vice chmn. 1963, mem. coun. 1964-65, 68-69), Commn. Study Orgn. Peace (chmn. 1986—). Home: 801 15th St S Apt 1504 Arlington VA 22202-5023 Office: George Washington U Law Sch 720 20th St NW Washington DC 20052-0001

**SOHNEN, HARVEY,** lawyer; b. Bklyn., June 20, 1947; s. Nathan M. and Shirley (Strauss) S.; m. Kathleen M. Meagher, Mar. 17, 1978; children: Eleanor, Julia. BA, Columbia U., 1968; MS in Math., MIT, 1969; JD, U. Calif., Berkeley, 1974. Bar: Calif. 1974, U.S. Dist. Ct. (no. dist.) Calif. 1974, U.S. Dist. Ct. (ea. dist.) Calif. 1975, U.S. Supreme Ct. 1981. Staff atty. Stanislaus Co. Legal Assistance, Modesto, Calif., 1975-76, Legal Aid for Alameda County, Oakland, Calif., 1977-82; assoc. Lerner & Veit, San Francisco, 1982-85; ptnr. Page & Sohnen, Walnut Creek, Calif., 1986-98; prin. Walnut Creek, 1998—. Mem. Am. Inns of Ct., Calif. Employment Lawyers Assn., Contra Costa Bar Assn. Contracts commercial, Labor, Personal injury. Office: 1850 Mt Diablo Blvd Ste 650 Walnut Creek CA 94596-4426

**SOIFER, AVIAM,** educator, former university dean; b. Worcester, Mass., Mar. 18, 1948; married; 2 children. BA cum laude, Yale U., 1969, MA in Urban Studies, 1972, JD, 1972. Bar: Conn. 1974, U.S. Dist. Ct. Conn. 1974, U.S. Supreme Ct. 1994. Law clk. to Judge Jon O. Newman U.S. Dist. Ct. Conn., 1972-73; asst. prof. U. Conn. Sch. Law, 1976-77, assoc. prof., 1977-78, prof., 1978-80; prof. Boston U. Sch. Law, 1980-93, 98—; dean Boston Coll. Law Sch., 1993-98; vis. prof. Boston U. Sch. Law, 1979-80. Contbr. numerous articles to profl. jours. Vice chair Supreme Jud. Ct. Mass. Task Force on Jud. Edn., 1996—; mem. steering com. 1st Cir. Task Force on Gender, Race and Ethnicity, 1995-99; bd. trustees New Eng. Med. Ctr., 1997—. Harvard Program in Law and Humanities fellow, 1976-77; Kellog Nat. fellow, 1981-84. Mem. ABA (commn. on coll. and univ. legal studies 1996—0. Civil rights. Office: Boston Coll Law Sch 885 Centre St Newton Center MA 02459-1154

**SOKOL, I. SCOTT,** political and fundraising executive; b. Birmingham, Ala., Mar. 10, 1956; s. Ralph L. and Marjorie Anne (Rubenstein) S.; m. Susan K. McKenna, June 12, 1987 (div. June 1993); 1 child, Allison Morgan. BA summa cum laude, Duke U., 1978, JD, 1982. Bar: Ala. 1983. Assoc. Johnston, Barton, Proctor, Swedlaw & Naff, P.A., Birmingham, 1982-83; dir. U.S. Sen. Alan Cranston (Dem.-Calif.), Birmingham and Washington, 1983-84; spl. asst. to sec. of state (now gov.) Don Siegelman Ala. Sec. of State's Office, Montgomery, 1984-85; dir. pub./cmty. rels. Fla. Nurses Assn., Orlando, 1986-88; dir. field ops. Congressman Buddy MacKay, Orlando, 1988; polit. dir. Sen. George Stuart, Orlando, 1988-90; dir. cmty. rels. Home Builders Assn. Mid-Fla., Maitland, 1990-92; devel. dir. Planned Parenthood of Greater Orlando, Inc., 1992-93; field coord., acting dir. Save Our Everglades, Orlando, 1993-94; The Everglades Found., Orlando and Islamorada, Fla., 1993-94; v.p. govt. rels. The Everidge Group, Winter Park, Fla., 1994-95; exec. dir. S.C. Dem. Party, Columbia, 1995-97; dir. devel. Fla. Audubon Soc., Winter Park, 1997-99; exec. dir. Ctrl. Fla. chpt. Juvenile Diabetes Found. Internat., Orlando, 1999—. Bd. dirs. Ctrl. Fla. Women's Emergency Network; committeeman Orange County (Fla.) Dem. Exec. Com.; mem. Orange Audubon Soc. Mem. Ctrl. Fla. Soc. Assn. Execs. (membership com.), Ala. Bar Assn., Duke U. Alumni Assn., Phi Beta Kappa, Pi Alpha Sigma. Home: 557 Mystic Wood St Casselberry FL 32707-5146

**SOKOL, LARRY NIDES,** lawyer, educator; b. Dayton, Ohio, Sept. 28, 1946; s. Boris Franklin and Kathryn (Konowitch) S.; m. Beverly Butler, Aug. 3, 1975; children: Addie Teller, Maxwell Philip. BA, U. Pa., 1968; JD, Case Western Res. U., 1971. Bar: Oreg. 1972, U.S. Dist Ct. Oreg. 1972, U.S. Ct. Appeals (9th cir.) 1973, U.S. Supreme Ct. 1980. Law clk. chief judge Oreg. Ct. Appeals, Salem, 1971-72; pvt. practice Portland, Oreg., 1972—; prof. law Lewis and Clark Law Sch., Portland; adj. prof. law sch. environ. litigation Lewis & Clark U., 1984—. Commr. planning City of Lake Oswego, Oreg., 1981-84. Sgt. USAR, 1968-74. Mem. Oreg. State Bar Assn. (chmn. litigation sect. 1983, disciplinary rev. bd. 1982-85), Oreg. Trial Lawyers Assn. Democrat. Jewish. Avocations: running, swimming, squash, model trains, scuba diving. Personal injury, Environmental. Office: 735 SW 1st Ave Portland OR 97204-3326

**SOKOL, RONALD MARK,** lawyer; b. Tulsa, Okla., July 25, 1943; s. Phillip and Patricia Maxine S.; m. Nancy I. Bailey, Dec. 19, 1965; children: Steven, Brian, Eric. BA, Washington U., St. Louis, 1965, JD, 1968. Bar: Mo. 1968, U.S. Dist. Ct. (we. dist.) Mo. 1968, U.S. Ct. Appeals (8th cir.) 1990. Staff atty. Mo. Ins. Commn., Jefferson City, Mo., 1968, Legal Aid and Def. Soc., Kansas City, Mo., 1969-70, Fed. Pub. Defender, Kansas City, Mo., 1971-72; 5th circuit pub. defender Mo. Pub. Defenders, St. Joseph, 1972-74; assoc. Kranitz & Kranitz, St. Joseph, 1974-76; pvt. practice, St. Joseph, 1976—. Mem. Mo. Assn. Trial Attys. (bd. dirs. 1992-93). Avocations: sailing, skiing, off-road driving. Fax: 816-364-4486. Product liability, Professional liability, General civil litigation. Home: 10512 NW 76th St Weatherby Lake MO 64152-1579 Office: 507 Francis St Ste 214 Saint Joseph MO 64501-1748

**SOKOLOV, RICHARD SAUL,** real estate company executive; b. Phila., Dec. 7, 1949; s. Morris and Estelle Rita (Steinberg) S.; m. Susan Barbara Saltzman, Aug. 13, 1972; children: Lisa, Anne, Kate. BA, Pa. State U., 1971; JD, Georgetown U., 1974. Assoc. Weinberg & Green, Balt., 1974-80, ptnr., 1980-82; v.p., gen. counsel The Edward J. DeBartolo Corp., Youngstown, Ohio, 1982-86, sr. v.p. devel., gen. coun., 1986-94; pres., CEO DeBartolo Realty Corp., Youngstown, Ohio, 1994-96; pres., COO Simon DeBartolo Group, Indpls., 1996-98; pres, COO Simon Property Group, Indpls., 1998—. Mem. investment com. Jewish Fedn., Youngstown, 1992—; trustee U. Wis.-Madison Ctr. for Urban Land Econs. Rsch., Youngstown/Mahoning Valley United Way. Mem. Internat. Coun. Shopping Ctrs. (trustee 1994—, chmn. 1998-99), Urban Land Inst. (assoc.). Office: Simon Property Group 115 W Washington St # 15-West Indianapolis IN 46204

**SOKOLOW, LLOYD BRUCE,** lawyer, psychotherapist; b. N.Y.C., Nov. 3, 1949; s. Edwin Jay and Harriet (Corman) S.; m. Christina Carol Smolinski, Jan. 27, 1979; children: Joshua, Jessica. BA, U. Buffalo, 1971, MS, 1974, JD, 1978, PhD, 1979. Bar: N.Y. 1979, U.S. Dist. Ct. (we. dist.) N.Y. 1979, U.S. Dist. Ct. (no. dist.) N.Y. 1982, Conn. 1985, U.S. Supreme Ct. 1985, U.S. Dist. Ct. Conn. 1986. Rsch. scientist Rsch. Inst. on Alcoholism, Buffalo, 1976-80; legal cons. N.Y. Gov.'s Task Force on Drinking and Driving, Albany, 1979-82; pvt. practice specializing in family, health, bankruptcy and Schenectady, N.Y., 1980—; counsel, exec. dir. Conifer Park, Scotia, N.Y., 1981-83; counsel, dir. substance abuse svcs. Inst. of Living, Hartford, Conn., 1984-86; founder, exec. dir. Lifestart Health Svcs., 1986—; atty. Town of Knox, N.Y., 1980-92. Bd. dirs. Schenectady Community Svc. Bd., 1982-89, pres. 1989; dir. addictions State of Md., 1988-89; mem. Surrogate Decision Making Commn., N.Y. Commn. on Quality of Care; counsel Apogee, Inc. Regent scholar NY State, 1967; Univ. fellow U. Buffalo, 1973, Baldy Law fellow, 1979. Mem. APA, ABA, N.Y. State Bar Assn., Albany County Bar Assn. Health, Family and matrimonial, Real property. Office: 1356 Union St Schenectady NY 12308-3018

**SOLAN, LAWRENCE MICHAEL,** lawyer; b. N.Y.C., May 7, 1952; s. Harold Allen and Shirley (Smith) S.; m. Anita Lois Rush, Mar. 27, 1982; children: Renata, David. BA, Brandeis U., 1974; PhD, U. Mass., 1978; JD, Harvard U., 1982. Bar: N.J. 1982, N.Y. 1984. Clk. to Justice Pollock Supreme Ct. N.J., Morristown, 1982-83; assoc. Orans, Elsen & Lupert, N.Y.C., 1983-89, ptnr., 1989-96; assoc. prof. law Bklyn. Law Sch., 1996—; vis. assoc. prof. Princeton U., 1999—. Author: The Language of Judges, 1993, Pronominal Reference, 1983. Mem. Assn. of Bar of City of N.Y., Phi Beta Kappa. Home: 163 Ralston Ave South Orange NJ 07079-2344 Office: Bklyn Law Sch 250 Joralemon St Brooklyn NY 11201-3700

**SOLANO, CARL ANTHONY,** lawyer; b. Pittston, Pa., Mar. 26, 1951; s. Nick D. and Catherine A. (Occhiato) S.; m. Nancy M. Solano, 1989; children: Melanie A., Carla Nicole. BS magna cum laude, U. Scranton, 1973; JD cum laude, Villanova U., 1976. Bar: Pa. 1976, U.S. Dist. Ct. (ea. dist.) Pa. 1978, U.S. Ct. Appeals (3rd cir.) 1980, U.S. Ct. Appeals (5th cir.) 1981, U.S. Supreme Ct. 1982, U.S. Ct. Appeals (9th cir.) 1986, U.S. Dist. Ct. (mid. dist.) Pa. 1988, U.S. Ct. Appeals (6th cir.) 1988, U.S. Ct. Appeals (Fed. cir.) 1989, U.S. Ct. Appeals (7th cir.) 1996. Law clerk Hon. Alfred L. Luongo U.S. Dist. Ct., Ea. Dist. Pa., Phila., 1976-78; assoc. Schnader, Harrison, Segal & Lewis, Phila., 1978-84, ptnr., 1985—. adj. prof. Villanova U. Sch. Law, 1999. Mem. ABA, Am. Law Inst., Pa. Bar Assn. (statutory law com. 1980-95), Phila. Bar Assn., St. Thomas More Soc., Justinian Soc., Order of Coif, Pi Gamma Mu. Roman Catholic. Appellate, Communications, Libel. Home: 5 Barrister Ct Haverford PA 19041-1137 Office: Schnader Harrison Segal & Lewis LLP 1600 Market St Ste 3600 Philadelphia PA 19103-7240

**SOLANO, HENRY L.,** federal agency official; m. Janine Solano; children: Mateo, Amalia, Guadalupe. BS in Mech. Engring., U. Denver; JD, U. Colo.; LLD (hon.), U. Denver. Asst. atty. gen. Human Resources Divsn. Colo. Dept. Law, 1977-82; asst. U.S. atty. Dist. Colo., 1982-87; U.S. atty. for Colo. U.S. Dept. Justice, Denver, 1994-98; solicitor U.S. Dept. Labor, Washington, DC, 1998—; exec. dir. Colo. Dept. Instns., 1987-91, Colo. Dept. Regulatory Agys., 1987; acting exec. dir. Colo. Dept. Corrections, 1989-90; chair Cabinet Coun. on Families and Children, 1990-91; mem. adv. com. U.S. Atty. Gen., 1994-95;lectr. in field. Bd. dirs. Nat. Latino Children's Inst. (first vice chair/chair elect), Mex.Am. Legal Def. Edn. Fund, Denver Housing Authority, Denver Women's Commn., Colo. Dept. Social Svcs., Colo. Transit Constrn. Authority, Regional Transit Dist. Office: US Dept Labor 200 Constitution Ave NW Washington DC 20210*

**SOLBERG, WAYNE O.,** lawyer; b. Aneta, N.D., Apr. 4, 1932; s. George and Olga M. (Hovde) S.; m. Patricia A. Lind, Aug. 26, 1950; children: Ronald W., Mary P., Daniel G., Rebecca A., Roberta J., Jennifer L. BS in Archtl. Engring., N.D. State U., 1957, MSCE, 1961; JD, U. N.D., 1966.

Bar: N.D. 1966, U.S. Dist. Ct. N.D. 1966, U.S. Ct. Appeals (8th cir.) 1976, U.S. Supreme Ct. 1983. Ptnr. Solberg, Stewart, Boulger & Miller, Fargo, N.D., 1966-94, Solberg, Stewart, Miller & Johnson, Fargo, N.D., 1994—. Col. USAF and Air Nat. Guard, 1953-86. Lutheran. Lodges: Masons, Shriners, Lions (v.p. 1986—). General practice, Aviation, Construction. Office: 3126 10th St N Fargo ND 58102-1335

**SOLET, MAXWELL DAVID,** lawyer; b. Washington, May 15, 1948; s. Leo and Pearl (Rose) S.; m. Joanne Marie Tolksdorf, Sept. 27, 1970; children: David Marc, Paul Jacob. AB, Harvard U., 1970, JD, 1974. Bar: Mass. 1974, U.S. Tax Ct. 1976, U.S. Ct. Claims 1976, U.S. Supreme Ct. 1976. Assoc. Gaston Snow & Ely Bartlett, Boston, 1974-79, Mintz, Levin, Cohn, Ferris, Glovsky & Popeo, P.C., Boston, 1979-82; ptnr. Mintz, Levin, Cohn, Ferris, Glovsky & Popeo, P.C., 1982—. Mem. ABA, Mass. Bar Assn., Boston Bar Assn. (chmn. tax sect. 1987-89), Nat. Assn. Bond Lawyers (mem. steering com. bond atty.'s workshop 1992-95). State and local taxation, Taxation, general. Home: 15 Berkeley St Cambridge MA 02138-3409 Office: Mintz Levin Cohn Ferris Glovsky & Popeo PC One Financial Ctr Boston MA 02111

**SOLIDAY, MATTHEW D.,** lawyer; b. Valparaiso, Ind., Apr. 10, 1967. BA in Psychology, Ind. U., 1959; JD, Valparaiso U., 1992. Bar: Ind., U.S. Ct. Appeals (7th cir.), U.S. Dist. Ct. (no. dist.) Ind. Assoc. Rice & Rice, Portage, Ind., 1992-95; dep. prosecutor Porter County Prosecutor's Office, Valparaiso, 1995-97; dep. pub. defender Porter County Pub. Defender's Office, Valparaiso, 1997—. Mem. Nat. Assn. Criminal Def. Lawyers. Office: 257 Indiana Ave Ste A Valparaiso IN 46383-5504

**SOLIS, JORGE ANTONIO,** federal judge; b. 1951. BA, McMurray Coll., 1973; JD, U. Tex., 1976. Clk. Indsl. Accident Bd., 1975-76; asst. criminal dist. atty. U.S. Attys. Office, 1976-81; with Moore & Holloway, 1981-82; criminal dist. atty. U.S. Attys. Office, 1983-87, spl. prosecutor narcotics task force, 1988; judge 350th Dist. Ct., 1989-91; fed. judge U.S. Dist. Ct. (no. dist.) Tex., 1991—. Bd. dirs. HRC Drug Abuse Treatment Ctr., Abilene, Tex., 1979—, pres. bd. dirs., 1982-83, Meals on Wheels, 1984—, Abilene (Tex.) Girls Home, 1985—; active Gov. Task Force on Drug Abuse, 1987—. Mem. State Bar Tex., Abilene Bar Assn. (past bd. dirs.), Abilene Young Lawyers Assn. (sec.-treas. 1977-78), Tex. Dist. and County Attys. Assn. Office: US Dist Ct 1100 Commerce St Ste 13b31 Dallas TX 75242-1027

**SOLKOFF, JEROME IRA,** lawyer, consultant, lecturer; b. Rochester, N.Y., Feb. 15, 1939; s. Samuel and Dorothy (Krovetz) S.; m. Doreen Hurwitz, Aug. 11, 1963; children: Scott Michael, Anne Lynn. BS, Sch. Indsl. and Labor Relations, Cornell U., 1961; JD, U. Buffalo, 1964. Bar: N.Y. 1965, Fla. 1974, U.S. Dist. Ct. (we. dist.) N.Y. 1965; cert. specialist Elder Law, Elder Law Found. Assoc. Nusbaum, Tarricone, Weltman, Bilgore & Silver, Rochester, N.Y., 1964-66, Mousaw, Vigdor, Reeves, Heilbronner & Kroll, Rochester, 1966-70; sr. mcpl. atty. Urban Renewal Agy., Rochester, 1970-73; sole practice, Rochester, 1970-73; chief legal counsel Arlen Realty Mgmt., Inc., Miami, Fla., 1973-75; assoc. Britton, Cohen, Kaufman, Benson & Schantz, Miami, 1975-76; chief legal counsel First Mortgage Investors, Miami Beach, Fla., 1976-79; ptnr. Cassel & Cassel, P.A., Miami, 1979-82; sole practice, Deerfield Beach, Fla., 1982—; lectr. on fgn. investment practices in U.S., Eng., 1981-88, Montreal, Que., Can., 1981, estate planning, 1982—, medicaid law and elder law, 1988—. Author: Fundamentals of Foreign Investing in American Real Estate and Businesses, 1981, Checklist of N.Y. Mortgage Foreclosure Procedures, 1970, History of Municipal Employee Unions, 1964, Practice Guide for Florida Elder Law, 1996. Bd dirs. Broward Homebound Program, 1990—, pres. 1998—; bd. dirs. Jewish Community Ctrs. of South Broward, Fla., 1979-90, NE Alzheimers Daycare Ctr., Inc., 1990-92, ; mem. exec. bd. dirs. Broward Alzheimers Assn., 1995—. Mem. ABA ( mem. sects. real property, trust and probate law), Fla. Bar Assn. (sects. real property, trust and probate law, vice chmn. com. on the elderly 1987-91, lectr. estate planning for the aging and disabled 1989—, founder, chmn. elder law sect. 1994-95, mem. elder law sect., chmn. ethics com. 1998—), Nat. Acad. Elder Law Attys., Elder Law Attys. Estate planning, Probate, Real property.

**SOLOMON, ANDREW P.,** lawyer; b. Newark, 1953. BA, Brown U., 1975; JD, Harvard U., 1984. Bar: N.Y. 1985. With firm Sullivan & Cromwell, N.Y.C. Corporate taxation, Taxation, general. Office: Sullivan & Cromwell 125 Broad St Fl 28 New York NY 10004-2489

**SOLOMON, CINDI ANNE,** lawyer; b. New Hartford, N.Y., Dec. 13, 1965; d. Dominick Vincent and Mary Sharon Loiacano; m. Kerry Dean Solomon, June 12, 1992; children: Brandon Taylor, Coleman Tyler. BA, Vanderbilt U., 1988; JD, U. S.C. Sch. Law, 1996. Bar: S.C. 1996. Sales rep. Warner-Lambert, Knoxville, Tenn., 1988-89, Prentice Hall, Balt., 1990-93; assoc. Ness, Motley, Ladholt, Richardson & Poole, Charleston, S.C., 1996—. Mem. ATLA, ABA, S.C. Women Lawyers Assn., Charleston Bar Assn., S.C. Trial Lawyers Assn. Avocations: tennis, golf, skiing, cooking, kayaking. Product liability, Toxic tort, Federal civil litigation. Office: Ness Motley Loadholt Richardson & Poole 151 Meeting St Charleston SC 29401-2207

**SOLOMON, MARK RAYMOND,** lawyer, educator; b. Pitts., Aug. 23, 1945; s. Louis Isadore and Fern Rhea (Josselson) S. BA, Ohio State U., 1967; MEd, Cleve. State U., 1971; JD with honors, George Washington U., 1973; LLM in Taxation, Georgetown U., 1976. Bar: Ohio, Mich., U.S. Tax Ct., U.S. Ct. Fed. Claims, U.S. Dist. (ea. dist.) Mich., U.S. Ct. Appeals (6th cir.). Tax law specialist corp. tax br. Nat. Office of IRS, 1973-75; assoc. Butzel, Long, Gust, Klein & Van Zile, Detroit, 1976-78; dir., v.p. Shatzman & Solomon, P.C., Southfield, Mich., 1978-81; prof., chmn. tax and bus. law dept., dir. MS in Taxation Program, Walsh Coll., Troy, Mich., 1981—; of counsel in tax matters Meyer, Kirk, Snyder and Safford, PLLC, Bloomfield Hills, Mich., 1981—; adj. prof. law U. Detroit, 1977-81. Editor: Cases and Materials on Consolidated Tax Returns, 1978, Cases and Materials on the Application of Legal Principles and Authorities to Federal Tax Law, 1990. Mem. Mich. Bar Assn., Kiwanis (bd. dirs.), Phi Eta Sigma. Avocation: bridge (life master). Taxation, general, Corporate taxation, Estate planning. Home: 2109 Golfview Dr Apt 102 Troy MI 48084-3926 Office: Meyer Kirk Snyder & Safford PLLC 100 W Long Lake Rd Ste 100 Bloomfield Hills MI 48304-2773 also: Walsh Coll 3838 Livernois Rd Troy MI 48083-5066

**SOLOMON, MARK S.,** lawyer; b. May 4, 1960; s. Maurice and June (Kelly) S.; m. Kathleen Wu; 1 child, Grant Solomon. BA, Franklin & Marshall Coll., 1982; JD, George Washington U., 1985. Bar: Tex. Assoc. Shank, Irwin, Conant, et al, Dallas, 1985-90, Johnson, Bromberg & Leeds, Dallas, 1990-92; ptnr. Arter & Hadden, Dallas, 1992—, mng. ptnr., 1997—; dir. Sage Energy Co., San Antonio. General corporate, Securities, Mergers and acquisitions. Office: Arter & Hadden 1717 Main St Ste 4100 Dallas TX 75201-7389

**SOLOMON, MICHAEL BRUCE,** lawyer; b. Chgo., Nov. 8, 1945; s. Arthur J. and Ruth H. (Halpert) S.; m. Tunny Jamri, Dec. 17, 1983. BA, U. Miami, Coral Gables, Fla., 1967, JD, 1970. Bar: Fla. 1970; U.S. Dist. Ct. (so. dist.) Fla. 1972; U.S. Ct. Appeals (5th cir.) 1989, U.S. Ct. Appeals (11th cir.) 1990. Assoc. Theodore M. Trushin P.A., Miami Beach, Fla., 1970-77; ptnr. Klein, Oshinsky & Solomon, Hallandale, Fla., 1978-87; pvt. practice North Miami, Fla., 1988—, 1998—; spl. asst., pub. defender, Dade County, Fla., 1972-78; ombudsman Dade County pub. defender's office, Miami, 1972. Contbr. article to profl. jour. Mem. ATLA, So. Dist. Fla. Trial Bar. General civil litigation, Insurance, Personal injury. Office: 11077 Biscayne Blvd Penthouse Miami FL 33161

**SOLOMON, ROBERT H.,** lawyer; b. Bklyn., Aug. 23, 1958; s. Murray and Mildred (Teger) S.; m. Felicia Irene Smith, June 30, 1985; children: Zachary, Alexander. BS in Econ cum laude, U. Pa., 1979; JD, Duke U., 1982. Bar: N.Y. 1983, U.S. Supreme Ct., U.S. Ct. Internat. Trade, U.S. Dist. Ct. (ea. & so. dists.) N.Y. Assoc. LeBeouf Lamb Leiby & MacRae, N.Y.C., 1982-84, Wofsey Certilman Haft et al, N.Y.C., 1984-87, Zimmer Victor Schwartz et al, N.Y.C., 1987-89; prin. Robert H. Solomon, Long Beach, N.Y., 1989—; arbitrator N.Y. Dist. Ct., Hempstead, 1989—. Trustee Long Beach Bdn. Edn., 1995; pres. Lido Home Civic Assn. David Siegal scholar Duke U., 1980-82, Regents scholar, 1980. Mem. ABA, N.Y. State Bar Assn., Bar Assn. of N.Y.C., Nassau County Bar Assn., Long Beach Lawyers Assn. (pres. 1995—), Wharton Club. Avocation: tennis. Contracts commercial, Finance, General civil litigation. Office: 24 E Park Ave Long Beach NY 11561-3504

**SOLOMON, RODNEY JEFF,** lawyer; b. Hamilton, Ohio, Apr. 14, 1949; s. Julius Franklin and Justine Paula (Rodney) S.; m. Nancy Griesemer, Oct. 17, 1976; children: Julia, Justin. BA, Amherst Coll., 1971; MPA, Harvard U., 1976, JD, 1979. Bar: Mass. 1979, D.C. 1979, U.S. Dist. Ct. Mass. 1988. Legis. asst. Office of sen. Robert Taft Jr., Washington, 1971-76; legal asst. Cambridge-Somerville Legal Svcs., Cambridge, Mass., 1977-78; cons. Mayor's Office Cmty. Devel., Chelsea, Mass., 1977-78; assoc. Caplar & Bok, Boston, 1978; spl. counsel Mass. Housing Fin. Agy., Boston, 1979-80; acting asst. adminstr. planning and redevel. Boston Housing Authority, 1980-81, spl. counsel to receiver, dir. spl. projects, 1980-83, from acting gen. counsel to gen. counsel, 1983-92; from dep. exec. dir. to acting exec. dir. Housing Authority City of Atlanta, 1992-94; dir. spl. actions Office Pub. and Indian Housing/U.S. Dept. HUD, Washingon, 1994-96, sr. dir. policy and legislation, 1996-99; dep. asst. sec. for policy, program and legis. initiatives U.S. Dept. HUD, Washington, 1999—; mem. staff distressed properties com. Coun. Large Pub. Housing Authorities, Washington, 1990-94; mem. Housing Working Group, Pres.'s Commn. on Model State Drug Laws, 1992. Author reports, legislation in field. Bd. dirs. Midnight Basketball League of Atlanta, Inc. Recipient Friend of Coun. of Large Pub. Housing Authorities award (nat. legis.), 1991, Proclamation by Mayor of City of Boston of "Rod Solomon Day", June 18, 1992; citations for svc. to Boston's Pub. Housing Residents, Mass. Senate and Ho. of Reps., 1992; recognition of assistance provided on Housing and Community Devel. Act of 1992, U.S. Senate Banking, Housing and Urban Affairs Com., 1992. Mem. Mass. Bar Assn., D.C. Bar. Office: US Dept Housing Urban Devel 451 7th St SW Washington DC 20410-0001

**SOLOWAY, DANIEL MARK,** lawyer; b. Buffalo, Jan. 21, 1959; s. Sol Murray and Shirley (Prashker) S.; m. Natalie Ann-Marie Chin, June 10, 1989; children: Rachel Ann, Rebecca Leigh. BA cum laude, SUNY, Buffalo, 1982; JD with honors, Fla. State U., 1985. Bar: Fla. 1985, U.S. Dist. Ct. (no. dist.) Fla. 1985, (mid. dist.) Fla. 1995, (so. dist.) Ala. 1986, U.S. Ct. Appeals (11th cir.) 1985, U.S. Supreme Ct. 1989; bd. cert. in civil trial law, Fla.; cert. Nat. Bd. Trial Advocacy, 1998, civil ct. mediator, 1999. Law clk. Circuit Judge, Tallahassee, 1983-84, Douglass, Davey, Cooper & Coppins, Tallahassee, 1984-85; ptnr. McKenzie & Soloway, Pensacola, Fla., 1985-98; pvt. practice Pensacola, 1998—. Author: Criminal Justice: An Analysis Toward Reform, 1981; contbr. articles to profl. jours.; editor Escambia-Santa Rosa Bar Assn. newsletter, 1989-90, Dry Shoes, Fla. Bar Jour., 1992. Profl. adv. bd. N.W. Fla. Epilepsy Soc., Pensacola, 1989—; speaker on AIDS, State of Fla. Dept. HRS, 1988—; active Escambia County Human Rels. Commn., 1996-98. Recipient Pro Bono Svc. award Escambia-Santa Rosa Bar, 1989-90, Pro Bono Svc. Pres.'s award Fla. Bar, 1990. Mem. Million Dollar Advocates Forum (diplomat), ABA, Assn. Trial Lawyers Am., Escambia-Santa Rosa Bar Assn. (editor newsletter 1989-90), Acad. Fla. Trial Lawyers (speaker 1993—), Nat. Orgn. Social Security Claimants Reps.. Democrat. Jewish. Avocation: writing. Civil rights, Personal injury, General civil litigation. Office: 810 Scenic Hwy Ste B Pensacola FL 32503

**SOMER, STANLEY JEROME,** lawyer; b. N.Y.C., Oct. 29, 1943; s. David Meyer and Rose (Bleifeld) S.; children: Penny Lynn, Andrew Michael; m. Batia Lebhar, Sept. 13, 1987. BBA in Acctg., Hofstra U., 1966; JD, New York Law Sch., 1969. Bar: N.Y. 1970, U.S. Dist. Ct. (ea. and so. dists.) N.Y. 1972, U.S. Tax Ct. 1983. Assoc. Halpin, Keough & St. John, N.Y.C., 1970-71, Bodenstein & Gumson, N.Y.C., 1971-73; counsel Heatherwood Comm., Hauppauge, N.Y., 1973-74; ptnr. Somer & Wand, P.C., Commack and Smithtown, N.Y., 1974-88, Somer, Wand & Farrell, Commack and Smithtown, 1989-90; sole practice Commack and Smithtown, 1990-98; ptnr. Somer & Heller LLP, Commack, 1999—; lectr. N.Y. Law Sch., N.Y.C., 1970-73, Income Property Cons., Huntington, N.Y., 1976-85. Commiteeman Suffolk Reps., East Northport, N.Y., 1978. Mem. N.Y. State Bar Assn., Suffolk Bar Assn., Comm. Assoc. Inst., L.I. Builders Inst. Lodge: Lions (pres. East Northport chpt. 1977-78). Landlord-tenant, Real property, General practice. Office: Somer & Heller LLP 2171 Jericho Tpke Ste 350 Commack NY 11725-2947

**SOMERS, CLIFFORD LOUIS,** lawyer; b. Portland, Maine, Dec. 27, 1940; s. Norman Louis and Adeline Wilhemina (Witzke) S.; m. Barbara Suzanne Berry, Aug. 1, 1961; children: Alan Mark, Penelope Lee. BA, U. Fla., Gainsville, 1965, JD, 1967. Bar: Fla. 1967, U.S. Ct. Mil. Appeals 1968, U.S. Dist. Ct. (mid. dist.) Fla. 1972; cert. civil trial lawyer, cert. mediator. Ptnr. Burton, Somers & Reynolds, Tampa, 1975-77, Miller, McKendree & Somers, Tampa, 1977-85, McKendree & Somers, Tampa, 1985-89, Somers and Morgan, Tampa, 1989-91, Somers and Assocs., Tampa, 1991-99, Barr, Murman, Tonelli, Herzfeld & Ruben, Tampa, 1999—; instr. law U. Fla., Gainesville, 1967; sec., treas. Chester H. Ferguson-Morris S. White Inn, Am. Inns of Ct. 1987-89, pres.-elect, 1989-90, pres. 1990-91; chmn. Fla. Bar civil procedure rules com., 1991-92. Contbr. article to profl. jours. With U.S. Army, 1961-64, Vietnam; capt. JAG, U.S. Army, 1968-72, mil. judge, 1971-72. Mem. Fla. Bar Assn., Def. Rsch. Inst. (chmn. 2nd dist. area west coast 1985-95), Am. Legion (comdr. Post 278, 1975), Brandon Vet.'s Post and Park (pres. 1985), Am. Bd. Trial Attys. (v.p. Tampa chpt. 1990-91). Avocations: writing, aerobics, weight lifting. State civil litigation, Insurance, Personal injury. Home: 6036 S Macdill Ave Apt 224 Tampa FL 33611-4461 Office: Somers and Assocs 3242 Henderson Blvd Ste 301 Tampa FL 33609-3056

**SOMERS, FRED LEONARD, JR.,** lawyer; b. Orange, N.J., July 5, 1936; A.B., U. Va., 1958, LL.B., 1961. Bar: Va. 1961, Mo. 1963, Ga. 1967, U.S. Tax Ct. 1971, U.S. Supreme Ct. 1978. Ptnr. Somers Firm, LLC and predecessors, Atlanta, 1970—. Mem. Citizens Adv. Park Com., DeKalb County, Ga., 1969, Citizens Bond Commn. DeKalb County, 1970; chmn. DeKalb County Charter Commn., 1970; vice chmn. DeKalb County Planning Commn., 1971-77; chmn., trustee Callanwolde Found., 1971-83; chmn. Oglethorpe Housing Devel. Authority, De Kalb County, 1974; bd. dirs., pres. Nat. Club Assn., 1982—. Author: The Written management Contract: Comfort for the Cub and the Manager, 1987, More About Private Club Buyouts, 1986, Sources of Revenue for Clubs, 1989, Creative Funding for Capital Needs, 1989, A Prolegomenon To a Right of Private Association, 1988, Model Bylaws for the Private Club, 1996, Model Club Rules, 1998, How to Effectively Select a Club Operating Entity, 1990, After Portland, What Next?, 1990, Golf Course Development, 1991, Model Golf Rules - A Guide for Clubs, 1998, Changing Your Operating Entity, 1992, Let's Go Equity!, 1992, Open or Closed Door?, 1994, Golf Course Liability and Exposures: A Primer For Private Clubs, 1995, Pivot or Perish, 1996, Grass vs. Members: Should Spikeless Shoes be Optional or Mandatory?, 1996. Mem. ABA, Atlanta Bar Assn. Real property, General corporate, Computer. Home: 1015 Oakpointe Pl Atlanta GA 30338-2621 Office: 2 Ravinia Dr Atlanta GA 30346-2104

**SOMMER, ALPHONSE ADAM, JR.,** lawyer; b. Portsmouth, Ohio, Apr. 7, 1924; s. A.A. and Adelaide (Orlett) S.; m. Storrow Cassin, June 13, 1951; children: Susan, Edward, Nancy. A.B., U. Notre Dame, 1948; LL.B., Harvard U., 1950; LL.D., Cleve. State U., 1976. Bar: Ohio 1951, D.C. 1976. Assoc. Calfee, Halter, Calfee, Griswold & Sommer, Cleve., 1950-60; ptnr. Calfee, Halter, Calfee, Griswold & Sommer, 1960-73; commr. SEC, 1973-76; ptnr. Morgan, Lewis & Bockius, Washington, 1979-94, counsel, 1994—; chmn. pub. oversight bd., AICPA. Contbr. articles to profl. jours. Chmn. pub. oversight bd. AICPA. Served with AUS, 1943-46. Administrative and regulatory, General corporate. Home: 7105 Heathwood Ct Bethesda MD 20817-2915 Office: Morgan Lewis & Bockius 1800 M St NW Ste 925 Washington DC 20036-5802

**SOMMER, JEFFREY ROBERT,** lawyer; b. Phila., Feb. 18, 1958; s. Joseph Robert and Janet Ann (Richards) S.; m. Lisa Marie Sievers, June 22, 1985; children: Matthew Jon, Alexander Carlton, Andrew Robert. BA, Lehigh U., 1979; JD, Widener U., 1982. Bar: Pa. 1982, U.S. Dist. Ct. (ea. dist.) Pa. 1982, U.S. Ct. Appeals (3d cir.) 1983. Law clk. Ct. of Common Pleas, Montgomery County, Pa., 1981-83; assoc. Norton A. Freedman P.C., Norristown, Pa., 1983-90; asst. pub. defender Ct. of Common Pleas, Norristown, 1982-90; ptnr. Buckley, Nagle, Gentry, McGuire & Morris, West Chester, Pa., 1990—; asst. editor Chester County Law Reporter, West Chester, 1991—. Bd. dirs. West Chester Area Day Care Ctr., 1991—, Alcohol and Drug Abuse Coun., Unionville, Pa., 1992—; mem. Mcpl. Svcs. Authority, West Whiteland Twp., 1988-89; vice chmn. Zoning Hearing Bd., Pocopson Twp., 1990—; active Chester County coun. Boy Scouts Am., 1990—. Mem. Pa. Bar Assn., Chester County Bar Assn., Lehigh U. Alumni Assn., Rotary, Masons. Republican. Presbyterian. Probate, General civil litigation, Municipal (including bonds). Home: 723 Isaac Taylor Dr West Chester PA 19382-7030 Office: Buckley Nagle Gentry McGuire & Morris 304 N High St West Chester PA 19380-2614

**SOMMER, MARK F.,** lawyer; b. Portsmouth, Ohio, Nov. 8, 1962; s. Ralph B. and Joan J. Sommer; m. Bridget Downey, Oct. 29, 1988; children: Victoria, Daniel, Thomas, Therese, Bernadette. BSBA, Xavier U., 1985; JD, U. Cin., 1988. Bar: Ky., U.S. Dist. Ct. (we. dist.) Ky. 1988, U.S. Tax Ct. 1988, U.S. Dist. Ct. (ea. dist.) Ky. 1989, U.S. Ct. Fed. Claims 1989, U.S. Ct. Appeals (6th cir.) 1989, U.S. Dist. Ct. (no. dist.) Ill. 1990; Supreme Ct. Ky., 1988; Supreme Ct. U.S., 1995. Assoc. Greenebaum Doll & McDonald, Louisville, 1988-94, mem., 1995—; presenter in field. Contbr. numerous articles to profl. jours. Recipient Am. Jurisprudence Advanced Tax award. Mem. ABA (mem. environ. taxes subcom., mem. sects. tax, mem. state and local taxation com.), Fed. Bar Assn. (mem. sect. of tax), Ky. Bar Assn. (mem. sects. of tax, sec. tax sect. 1994-95, vice chair tax sect. 1995—), Louisville Bar Assn. (mem. sects. tax and young lawyers, chair tax sect. 1995—), Louisville C. of C. (team capt. ann. membership drive 1992-93), Xavier U. Alumni Assn., Glen Oaks Country Club, Legal Aid Soc. Louisville (vol. lawyer program), Downtown Louisville Rotary Club. Fax: 502-587-3695. E-mail: mfs@gdm.com. Taxation, general, State and local taxation, Administrative and regulatory. Home: 8507 Running Spring Dr Louisville KY 40241-5515 Office: Greenebaum Doll & McDonald PLLC 3300 National City Tower 101 S 5th St Louisville KY 40202-3103

**SOMMER, ROBERT GEORGE,** retired airline pilot, lawyer; b. N.Y.C., July 4, 1928; s. Irvin Cecil and Rose June S.; m. Ann Penelope Goodwin, May 20, 1950 (div. Aug. 1963); children: Daniel M., Douglas J.; m. Mary Elizabeth Cheetham, June 24, 1971; children: Eric H., Jody Lee. LLB, U. Fla., 1950, JD, 1967; grad., U.S. Army Command Gen. Staff Coll., 1971, Indsl. Coll. of Armed Forces, 1978. Bar: Fla. 1950, U.S. Dist. Ct. (so. dist.) Fla. 1950, U.S. Ct. Claims 1963, U.S. Ct. Mil. Appeals 1963, U.S. Supreme Ct., 1963, U.S. Tax Ct. 1986; cert. circuit ct. mediator, Fla.; cert. flight instr. FAA. Real property officer Bur. Land Mgmt., Dept. Interior, Alaska, 1953-55; ptnr. Sommer, Frank & Weston, Miami, Fla., 1955-60; pvt. practice Miami and Ocala, Fla., 1960—; capt. Delta Air Lines, Miami and Ocala, 1960-88; owner Crescent-S Thoroughbred Farms. Col. USAR, 1984. Mem. Soc. Am. Mil. Engrs., Exptl. Aircraft Assn., Airline Pilots Assn., Res. Officers Assn. U.S., Quiet Birdmen (bd. govs. 1988-99), Elks, Masons, Shriners. Avocations: skiing, hunting, fishing. Real property, General corporate, Aviation. Home: PO Box 578 Anthony FL 32617-0578 Office: PO Box 2796 Ocala FL 34478-2796

**SOMMERFELD, DAVID WILLIAM,** lawyer, educator; b. Detroit, Jan. 21, 1942; s. Henry Anthony and Hilda (Diffley) S.; m. Anne Marlaine Toth, June 27, 1964; children: Catherine, David Jr., Michael, Caroline. BS, U. Detroit, 1963; JD, Detroit Coll., 1967. Trust officer Nat. Bank Detroit, 1963-68; tax supr. Ernst & Ernst, Detroit, 1968-73; ptnr. Monaghan, Campbell, LoPrete & McDonald, Detroit, 1973-77; prof. Detroit Coll., 1977-86; ptnr. Butzel Long, Detroit, 1987—; lectr. Ind. Soc. CPAs, Indpls., 1980-93, Ohio Soc. CPAs, Columbus, 1987, W.Va. Soc. CPAs, Charleston, 1983-86, 91. Editor Mich. Probate and Trust Law Jour., 1981-83. Fellow Am. Coll. of Trust and Estate Counsel; mem. Mich. Bar Assn., Detroit Bar Assn., Am. Inst. CPA's, Mich. Assn. CPA's, Forest Lake Country Club. Roman Catholic. Club: Detroit Athletic. Avocations: bowling, spectator sports, gardening. Estate planning, Estate taxation. Office: Butzel Long 32270 Telegraph Rd Ste 200 Bingham Farms MI 48025-2457

**SOMMERS, CONRAD HOYLE,** lawyer; b. Dallas, July 5, 1952; s. Conrad John and Latrelle (Dunaway) S.; m. Angela Sue Wells, Sept. 9, 1978; children—Jaime Lynn, Jessica Lee. B.A., U. Tex. Austin, 1973, J.D., 1975, LL.M., 1976. Bar: Tex. 1976, U.S. Supreme Ct. 1981, U.S. Ct. Appeals (5th cir.) 1977, U.S. Tax Ct. 1977, U.S. Ct. Mil. Aps. 1978, U.S. Dist. Ct. (no. dist.) Tex. 1977. Ptnr., Lee & Sommers, Dallas, 1976-77; ptnr., v.p. Lee, Sommers, & Parks, P.C., Dallas, 1977-78; sole practice, Dallas, 1978—. Mem. Tex. Criminal Def. Lawyers Assn., Dallas County Criminal Bar Assn. Republican. Lutheran. Criminal, Family and matrimonial, Probate. Office: 6440 N Central Expy Dallas TX 75206-4101

**SOMMERS, GEORGE R.,** lawyer; b. N.Y.C., Jan. 27, 1955. BA, U. So. Fla., 1975; JD, NYU, 1987. Bar: N.J. 1987, U.S. Dist. Ct. N.J. 1987, N.Y. 1988, U.S. Dist. Ct. (all dists.) N.Y. 1988, U.S. Ct. Appeals (3d cir.) 1988, U.S. Ct. Appeals (2d cir.) 1989, U.S. Supreme Ct. 1992. Assoc. Sullivan & Cromwell, N.Y.C., 1987-90; pvt. practice lawyer N.Y.C., 1990—; pres. Bill of Rights Found., N.Y.C., 1994—. Seidler scholar NYU Sch. Law, N.Y.C., 1985. Mem. Hoboken Bar Assn. (pres. 1994). Jewish. Avocations: sailing, chess. Civil rights, General civil litigation, Constitutional. Office: 67 Wall St Ste 2411 New York NY 10005-3101

**SOMSEN, HENRY NORTHROP,** retired lawyer; b. New Ulm, Minn., Aug. 12, 1909; s. Henry N. and Meta (Koch) S.; m. Anne Elizabeth Duncan, Sept. 12, 1936 (dec.); children: Pennell Anne, Stephen Duncan. BA, U. Minn., 1932, JD, 1934. Bar: Minn. 1934. Practice law New Ulm, 1934-85; ptnr. Somsen, Dempsey, Johnson & Somsen, 1934-40, Somen Dempsey & Somsen, 1940-46, Somsen & Somsen, 1946-55; sole practice, 1955-64; ptnr. Somsen Dempsey & Schade, 1971-85, of counsel, 1985—. Bd. editors U. Minn. Law Rev., 1932-33. Trustee Minn. State Parks Found., 1967-77; bd. dirs. Minn. Council State Parks, 1956—, pres., 1974-75; bd. dirs., pres. New Ulm Community Concert Assn., 1947-85; bd. dirs. Union Hosp., New Ulm, 1959-77, Highland Homes, Inc., 1970-79, New Ulm Meml. Found., 1958-79; bd. dirs. New Ulm Industries Inc., 1952-85, pres., 1968-77; bd. dirs. New Ulm Industries Found., Inc., 1953-85, pres., 1968-77; mem. City Charter Commns., 1940, 51, 66, pres., 1966. Served to capt. JAGC, AUS, 1943-46. Mem. ABA, Minn. Bar Assn., Am. Judicature Soc., Am. Arbitration Assn. (panel of arbitrators 1967-85), Mpls. Club, Masons, Rotary, Shriners. Episcopalian. Home: 211 2d St NW Apt 1907 Rochester MN 55901-3101

**SONBERG, MICHAEL ROBERT,** judge; b. Bklyn., Oct. 17, 1947; s. Harold R. and Betty (March) Lifton. AB, CUNY, 1968; JD, Harvard U., 1971. Bar: N.Y. 1972. Assoc. Weiss, Rosenthal, Heller & Schwartzman, N.Y.C., 1971-79, Moore, Berson, Lifflander & Mewhinney, N.Y.C., 1979-82; ptnr. Moore, Berson, Lifflander, Eisenberg & Mewhinney, N.Y.C., 1983-90; counsel Serchuk & Zelermyer, N.Y.C., 1991; judge N.Y.C. Civil Ct., 1991-95, N.Y.C. Criminal Ct., 1995—. Mem. Overseers' Com. to Visit Harvard Law Sch., 1978-83; bd. Dirs., chmn. com. on legis. Citizens Union of City of N.Y., 1978-91. Mem. ABA, N.Y. State Bar Assn., Assn. of Bar of City of N.Y. (chmn. com. on state cts. of superior jurisdiction, 1987-90, co-chmn. coun. on jud. adminstrn. 1993-96, sec., mem. exec. com. 1997—), Bronx County Bar assn., N.Y. County Lawyers Assn., Lesbian and Gay Law Assn. of Greater N.Y., Assn. of Lesbian and Gay Judges (pres. 1996—), Internat. Assn. of Lesbian and Gay Judges (sec. 1993—), Harvard Law Sch. Assn. (coun. 1995-99, exec. com. 1996-99). Office: Criminal Ct City NY 215 E 161st St Bronx NY 10451-3511

**SONDERBY, SUSAN PIERSON,** federal judge; b. Chgo., May 15, 1947; d. George W. and Shirley L. (Eckstrom) Pierson; m. James A. De Witt, June 14, 1975 (dec. 1978); m. Peter R. Sonderby, Apr. 7, 1990. AA, Joliet (Ill.) Jr. Coll., 1967; BA, U. Ill., 1969; JD, John Marshall Law Sch., 1973. Bar: Ill. 1973, U.S. Dist. Ct. (cen. and so. dists. ) Ill. 1978, U.S. Dist. Ct. (no. dist.) Ill. 1984, U.S. Ct. Appeals (7th Cir.) 1984. Assoc. O'Brien, Garrison, Berard, Kusta and De Witt, Joliet, 1973-75, ptnr., 1975-77; asst. atty. gen. consumer protection div., litigation sect. Office of the Atty. Gen., Chgo., 1977-78; asst. atty. gen., chief consumer protection div. Office of the Atty. Gen., Springfield, Ill., 1978-83; U.S. trustee for no. dist. Ill. Chgo., 1983-86; judge U.S. Bankruptcy Ct. (no. dist.) Ill., Chgo., 1986-98, chief judge, 1998—; adj. faculty De Paul U. Coll. Law, Chgo., 1986; spl. asst. atty. gen., 1972-78; past mem. U.S. Trustee adv. com., consumer adv. coun. Fed. Res. Bd.; past sec. of State Fraudulent I.D. com., Dept. of Ins. Task Force on Improper Claims Practices; chairperson personnel rev. bd., mem. task force race and gender bias U.S. Dist. Ct.; judicial conf. planning com. 7th Cir.

Judicial Conf.; mem. Civil Justice Reform Act Adv. Com. Mem. Fourth Presbyn. Ch., Art Inst. Chgo.; past mem. Westminster Presbyn. Ch., Chgo. Coun. of Fgn. Rels.; past bd. dirs. Land of Lincoln Coun. Girl Scouts U.S.; past mem. individual guarantors com. Goodman Theatre, Chgo.; past chmn. clubs and orgns. Sangamon County United Way Capital campaign; past bd. dirs., chmn. house rules com. and legal subcom. Lake Point Tower; past mem. Family Svc. Ctr., Aid to Retarded Citizens, Henson Robinson Zoo. Fellow Am. Coll. Bankruptcy; mem. Nat. Conf. Bankruptcy Judges (legis. outreach com.), Am. Bankruptcy Inst., Comml. Law League Am. (exec. coun. bankruptcy and insolvency sect., bankrupcty com., past vice chmn. U.S. Trustee Rev. com., edn. com.), 7th Cir. Bar Assn. (former treas.), Fed. Bar Assn. (hon. mem.), Law Club of Chgo., Legal Club of Chgo. (hon.), Nordic Law Club, John Marshall Law Sch. Alumni Assn. (bd. dirs.), Abraham Lincoln Marovitz Inn of Ct. (master, former pres.). Avocations: travel, flying, interior decorating. Office: US Bankruptcy Ct 219 S Dearborn St Ste 638 Chicago IL 60604-1702

**SONDOCK, RUBY KLESS,** retired judge; b. Houston, Apr. 26, 1926; d. Herman Lewis and Celia (Juran) Kless; m. Melvin Adolph Sondock, Apr. 22, 1944; children: Marcia Cohen, Sandra Marcus. AA, Cottey Coll., Nevada, Mo., 1944; BS, U. Houston, 1959, LLB, 1961. Bar: Tex. 1961, U.S. Supreme Ct. 1977. Pvt. practice, Houston, 1961-73, 89—; judge Harris County Ct. Domestic Rels. (312th Dist.), 1973-77, 234th Jud. Dist. Ct., Houston, 1977-82, 83-89; justice Tex. Supreme Ct., Austin, 1982; of counsel Weil Gotshal and Manges, 1989-93, Houston Ctr., 1993—. Mem. ABA, Tex. Bar Assn., Houston Bar Assn., Houston Assn. Women Lawyers, Order of Barons, Phi Theta Phi, Kappa Beta Pi, Phi Kappa Phi, Alpha Epsilon Pi. Office: 2650 Two Houston Ctr 909 Fannin Houston TX 77010

**SONEGO, IAN G.,** assistant attorney general; b. Louisville, May 27, 1954; s. Angelo and Zella Mae (Causey) S. BA in Polit. Sci. with high honors, U. Louisville, 1976, JD, 1979. Bar: Ky. 1979, U.S. Dist Ct. (ea. dist.) Ky. 1980, U.S. Dist. Ct. (we. dist.) Ky. 1989, U.S. Ct. Appeals (6th cir.) 1989, U.S. Supreme Ct. 1990. Asst. atty. Office Commonwealth's Atty. Pike County, Pikeville, Ky., 1980, sr. asst. atty., 1988-89; assoc. John Paul Runyon Law Firm, Pikeville, 1981-87; asst. atty. gen. Office Atty. Gen., Frankfort, Ky., 1989—; lectr. criminal law Ky. Bar Assn., Jenny Wiley Park, 1981, Ky. Prosecutors Confs., 1989, 93; mem. Atty. Gen.'s task force child sexual abuse, 1992-94, Nat. Conf. on Domestic Violence, 1996. Contbg. editor Ky. Prosecuter Newsletter, 1991—. Recipient Kessleman award U. Louisville, 1975, Bd. Trustee award 1979. Outstanding Prosecutor award Ky. Atty. Mem. Ky. Commonwealth's Attys. Assn. (hon., lectr. 1987, 90, chmn. com. ethics 1984-86, bd. dirs. 1983-85, Outstanding Svc. award 1985, Spl. award 1987). Office: Office Atty Gen Criminal Appellate Divsn 1024 Capital Center Dr Frankfort KY 40601-8204

**SONG ONG, ROXANNE KAY,** lawyer, judge; b. Phoenix, Apr. 24, 1953; d. Joe Henry and Sue (Tang) Song; m. Richard H. Ong, Nov. 25, 1978; children: Jocelyn, Bradley. BA, Ariz. State U., 1975; JD, U. Ariz., 1978. Bar: Ariz. 1979, U.S. Dist. Ct. Ariz. 1979, U.S. Ct. Appeals (9th cir.) 1986, U.S. Supreme Ct. 1992. Pvt. practice Phoenix, 1979, 85—; asst. city prosecutor Phoenix City Prosecutor's Office, 1979-82; asst. city prosecutor, asst. city atty. Scottsdale (Ariz.) City Atty.'s Office, 1982-85; pro tempore judge Scottsdale City Ct., 1986-89; assoc. city judge City of Scottsdale, 1989-91; mcpl. ct. judge City of Phoenix, 1991—; mem. Ariz. Supreme Ct.'s Commn. on Minorities, adv. com. on Judicial Ethics; vice chair of Ariz. Supreme Ct. Com. on Judicial Edn. and Tng. Former mem. community adv. bd. Sta. KAET-TV, Tempe, Ariz; mem. First Chinese Bapt. Ch., Scottsdale Leadership Class V, Valley Leadership Class XV; mem. exec. bd. Ariz. So. Bapt. Conv.; co-leader Ariz. Cactus Pine troop Girl Scouts/Brownies; former mem. parent adv. bd. Paradise Valley/Scottsdale YMCA; bd. dirs. Ariz. Bapt. Children's Svcs., Inst. Cultural Diversity; mem. commn. on minorities, adv. com. on jud. ethics, vice chair com. on jud. edn. and tng., Ariz. Supreme Ct. Mem. ABA, Maricopa County Bar Assn., Christian Legal Soc., Ariz. Women Lawyers Assn., Am. Judges Assn., Nat. Assn. Women Judges, Ariz. Magistrates Assn., Ariz. Cts. Assn., U. Ariz. Law Coll. Assn., Phi Delta Phi, Phi Kappa Phi, Alpha Lambda Delta, Kappa Delta Phi, Pi Lambda Theta. Republican. Avocations: music, sports. Criminal, Immigration, naturalization, and customs. Office: Phoenix Mcpl Ct Divsn 15 400 N 7th St Phoenix AZ 85006-3386

**SONNEMAN, JOSEPH ABRAM,** legal researcher, lawyer, mediator; b. Chgo., Apr. 22, 1944; s. Eric O. and Edith A. Sonneman. BS, U. Ill., 1968; MA, Claremont (Calif.) Grad. Sch., 1970, PhD, 1977; JD cum laude, Georgetown U., 1989. Bar: Alaska. Pres., owner Five Star Photos, Juneau, 1989, Pacific Mediation and Arb, Juneau, 1989, Alaska Legal Rsch., Juneau, 1989—; pvt. practice Juneau, 1990. Author: the Exxon Valdez Deals, 1992; co-author, co-editor Rights in Data, 1988. Nominee Alaska Dem. Party U.S. Senate, 1998; pres. Juneau World Affairs Coun., 1995-98, Juneau Arts and Humanities Coun., 1973. With U.S. Army, 1963-66. Mem. Alaska Bar Assn., Hawaii State Bar Assn. Jewish. Avocations: gardening, target shooting, bicycling, walking. General civil litigation, Criminal, Public international. Office: Alaska Legal Rsch 324 Willoughby Ave Juneau AK 99801-1723

**SONNEMAN, KARL WALTER,** lawyer; b. Winona, Minn., Apr. 12, 1949; s. Elgin Otto and Helen E. (Wadewitz) S.; m. Karin Frances Leonard, Sept. 1, 1984; children: James Arthur, Thomas Karl, Jane Helen. BA, Northwestern U., 1971; JD, George Washington U., 1974. Bar: Va. 1974, D.C. 1975, U.S. Ct. Appeals (D.C. cir.) 1975, Minn. 1977, U.S. Dist. Ct. D.C. 1981, U.S. Supreme Ct. 1982. Assoc. Ames Hill & Ames, Washington, 1974-76; spl. asst. atty. gen. Office Atty. Gen., St. Paul, 1977-80, 82-90; assoc. Pierson, Ball & Dowd, Washington, 1980-82; ptnr. Sonneman & Sonneman, P.A., Winona, Minn., 1990—; asst. pub. defender, 1992—; adj. assoc. prof. St. Mary's U. Minn., 1991—, Winona State U., 1992—; gen. counsel Pub. Utilities Commn., St. Paul, 1982-88. Dir. Young Dems. Club, Alexandria, Va., 1981; mem. Winona County Dem. Com., 1994-98; mem. new bldg. com. Winona Mid. Sch., 1997; chair bldg. fund chair Faith Luth. Ch., 1991, endowment com., 1992—, bldg. com., 1991-96, coun. 1997—; mem. City Dem. Com., Alexandria, 1982. Mem. D.C. Bar, Order of Coif, Exch. Club. Democrat. E-mail: sonneman@luminet.net. Fax: 507-454-8887. Office: Ste 202 111 Riverfront Winona MN 55987-3456

**SONNETT, ANTHONY EVAN,** lawyer; b. N.Y.C., Apr. 13, 1960; s. Carl Sonnett and Enid Barrie Hoberman. BA, Vassar Coll., 1982; JD, Hofstra U., 1985. Bar: N.Y. 1986, Calif. 1991. Assoc. Lester, Schwab, Katz & Dwyer, N.Y.C., 1985-88, Herrick, Feinstein, N.Y.C., 1988-89; ptnr. Lester, Schwab, Katz & Dwyer, N.Y.C., 1989-95; founding ptnr. Yukevich & Sonnett, L.A., 1995—. Product liability, General civil litigation. Office: Yukevich & Sonnett 601 S Figueroa St Los Angeles CA 90017-5704

**SONNIER, BRENT GERARD,** lawyer, music company executive; b. Sulphur, La., Oct. 23, 1957; s. Clifford Joseph and Dorothy Jane (Trumps) S.; m. Edwenna Elaine Lowden, Aug. 19, 1978; 1 child, Lindsay Rachelle. BS in Geology, U. Southwestern La., 1980; JD, Okla. City U., 1990; MS in Environ. Sci., U. Okla., 1995. Bar.: Okla. 1991, La. 1993, U.S. Dist. Ct. (ctrl. and we. dists.) La. 1996, U.S. Ct. Appeals (5th cir.) 1998, U.S. Dist. Ct. (ea. dist.) La. 1999. Petroleum geologist OXY USA Inc., Oklahoma City, 1980-90, advisor regulatory affairs, 1990-95; assoc. atty. Onebane Law Firm, Lafayette, La., 1996—; mem. citizens adv. com. Okla. Corp. Commn. Mem. Western Hts. Pub. Sch. Bd., Oklahoma City, 1991-95. Avocations: playing blues guitar, composing contemporary music. Home: 2105 W Port St Abbeville LA 70510-3481 Office: Onebane Law Firm 102 Versailles Blvd Ste 600 Lafayette LA 70501-6765

**SOOY, RICHARD R.,** lawyer; b. Redlands, Calif., Sept. 21, 1948; s. John B. and Margaret M. Sooy. BS, Ariz. State U., Tempe, 1970; JD, McGeorge Sch. Law, Sacramento, 1978. Bar: Calif. 1978, Nev. 1998, U.S. Dist. Ct. (ea. dist.) Calif. 1978, U.S. Dist. Ct. (ctrl. dist.) Calif. 1979, U.S. Dist. Ct. (so. dist.) Calif. 1981, U.S. Dist. Ct. Nev. 1998. Atty. Morris, Polich & Purdy, L.A. and San Diego, 1979-86; ptnr., shareholder Edwards, Sooy & Byron, San Diego, Newport Beach, also Las Vegas, 1986—. Mem. ATLA, San Diego County Bar Assn., Def. Rsch. Inst., Assn. So. Calif. Def. Counsel, San Diego Def. Lawyers (bd. dirs. 1990-92). Avocations: tennis, skiing, golf. General civil litigation, Construction, Professional liability. Office: Edwards Sooy & Byron 101 W Broadway Fl 9 San Diego CA 92101-8201

**SOPEL, GEORGE C.,** lawyer; b. N.Y.C., Nov. 16, 1969; s. Georges and Michele Sopel; m. Sarah Katherine Louise Gagan, June 1, 1998. BA, McGill U., 1991, LLB, BCL, 1995. Bar: Mass. 1995, N.Y. 1996, Que. 1996. Law clk., atty. Stikeman, Elliott, Montreal, 1992-97; lectr. faculty of law Eötvös Lorand U., Budapest, Hungary, 1994; atty. Hutchins, Wheeler & Dittmar, Boston, 1997—; bd. dirs. New Eng.-Can. Bus. Coun., Boston, 1998—. Contbg. author: Executive Employment Law, 1993, Executives and Managers: Their Rights and Duties, 1997. Avocation: participation in sports of all kinds. General corporate, Finance, Computer. Home: 17 Fayette St Boston MA 02116-5518 Office: Hutchins Wheeler & Dittmar 101 Federal St Boston MA 02110-1817

**SOPKO, THOMAS CLEMENT,** lawyer; b. Warren, Ohio, Mar. 21, 1945; s. Clement and Mary (Sroka) S.; m. Joyce Ann Deffenbaugh, Aug. 5, 1967; children: Amy L., Kathleen A. BS in History, Xavier U., 1967; JD, U. Notre Dame, 1970. Bar: Ind. 1970, U.S. Dist. Ct. (no. dist.) Ind. 1970, U.S. Dist. Ct. (so. dist.) Ind. Assoc. Edward Kalamaros and Assocs., South Bend, Ind., 1970-75; ptnr. Hardig & Sopko, South Bend, 1976-85; pvt. practice South Bend, 1986-91; ptnr. Sopko & Firth, South Bend, 1991—; dep. prosecutor County of St. Joseph, South Bend, 1976-79; town atty. Town of Osceola, Ind., 1975-82; gen. counsel Notre Dame Fed. Credit Union, 1986—, Holy Cross Coll., Notre Dame, 1989—, speaker for continuing legal edn. seminars on civil litigation, trial practice and procedure, family law and mediation matters. Chmn. profl. divsn. United Way St. Joseph County; bd. dirs. St. Joseph County Alcoholism Coun., South Bend; active Jud. Nominating Com., St. Joseph County, 1985-88; chmn. St. Anthony's Parish Coun., South Bend, 1991-93. Scholar U. Notre Dame Law Sch., 1967-70. Fellow Ind. Bar Assn. Found.; mem. St. Joseph County Bar Assn. (pres. 1994-95, bd. govs. 1990—, pres.-elect 1993-94, v.p. 1992-93, chmn. continuing legal edn. 1992-94), Ind. Trial Lawyers Assn. (dist. chmn. 1979-80), Assn. Trial Lawyers Am., ABA. Republican. Roman Catholic. Avocations: downhill skiing, tennis, golf, jogging. State civil litigation, Family and matrimonial, General practice. Office: Sopko & Firth 5th Fl Plaza Bldg 210 S Michigan St South Bend IN 46601-2094

**SORCE, DAVID SAMUEL,** lawyer; b. Rochester, N.Y., Feb. 20, 1954; s. James Salvatore and Domenica (Gligora) S. BA, St. Bonaventure, Olean, N.Y., 1976; JD, Syracuse U., 1980. Bar: N.Y. 1981, U.S. Dist. Ct. (we dist.) N.Y., 1984, U.S. Bankruptcy Ct. 1984, U.S. Supreme Ct. 1991. Assoc. Harter, Secrest & Emery, Rochester, 1984-92; assoc. gen. counsel Canandaigua Wine Co., 1992—. Cmty. svc. Meml. Art Gallery, Rochester, Rochester Mus. Sci. Ctr., Rochester Philharmonic Orch. Mem. Monroe County Bar Assn. (bus. coun. 1994—). Avocations: reading, racquetball. General corporate, Securities. Office: Canandaigua Wine Co Inc 116 Buffalo St Canandaigua NY 14424-1086

**SORENSEN, HARVEY R.,** lawyer; b. Chgo., Nov. 3, 1947; s. Harvey T. and Jean Louise (Cline) S.; m. Emily Smith, May 31, 1969 (div. May 1980); children: Abigail, Jeanne, Cornelia; m. Stephanie Sorensen, Dec. 31, 1980; 1 child, Tyler. BA, Beloit Coll., 1969; MSBA, Boston U., 1972; JD cum laude, Northwestern U., 1974. Bar: Wis. 1974, U.S. DISt. Ct. (ea. dist.) Wis. 1974, U.S. Dist. Ct. Kans., U.S. Tax Ct., 1975. Tax acct. Arthur, Young & Co., Chgo., 1974; assoc. Whyte & Hirschboeck, Milw., 1974-75; asst. adj. prof. Wichita (Kans.) State U. Sch. Bus., 1979; ptnr. Foulston & Siefkin, Wichita, 1975—. Trustee, vice chmn. Kans. Pub. Telecomm. Svc., 1978—, chmn., 1997—; chmn. Wichita Downtown Devel. Corp., 1996—; project bus. cons. Jr. Achievement, 1978-93; trustee Wichita Symphony Soc., 1986-96, Wichita Collegiate Sch., 1994—, Wichita Sedgewick County Hist. Mus., 1986-89, Wichita Arts Coun., 1979-82; commr. City of Eastborough, Kans., 1991-93; bd. cmty. advisors KMUW, 1981-82; treas. St. James Episcopal Ch. With U.S. Army, 1970-72. Fellow Am. Coll. Tax Counsel; mem. ABA, Wichita Bar Assn., Kans. Bar Assn. (past sect., v.p., pres. tax. sect. 1984-88), Attys. for Family Held Enterprises, Rotary. Republican. Episcopalian. Corporate taxation, Estate taxation, Taxation, general. Home: 13 Colonial Ct Wichita KS 67207-1056 Office: Foulston & Siefkin 700 Nations Bank Fin Ctr Wichita KS 67202-2207

**SORKIN, DAVID JAMES,** lawyer; b. N.Y.C., June 26, 1959. BA, Williams Coll., 1981; JD, Harvard U., 1984. Bar: N.Y. 1985. Law clk. judge Charles M. Merrill U.S. Ct. Appeals 9th Cir., San Francisco, 1984-85; assoc. Simpson Thacher & Bartlett, N.Y.C., 1985-92, ptnr., 1993—. General corporate, Mergers and acquisitions, Securities. Office: Simpson Thacher & Barlett 425 Lexington Ave Fl 15 New York NY 10017-3954

**SORRELL, WILLIAM H.,** state attorney general; b. Burlington, Vt., Mar. 9, 1947; s. Marshal Thomas and Esther Sorrell; m. Mary Alice McKenzie; children: McKenzie, Thomas. AB, U. Notre Dame, 1970; JD, Cornell U., 1974. Dep. state's atty. Chittenden County State of Vt., 1975-77, state's atty. Chittenden County, 1977-78, 89-92; ptnr. McNeil, Murray & Sorrell, 1978-89, sec. adminstrn., 1992-97; atty. gen. State of Vt., 1997—. Pres. United Cerebral Palsy Vt.; sec. Vt. Coalition Handicapped; bd. dirs. Winooski Valley Pk. Dist. Office: Office Atty Gen 109 State St Montpelier VT 05609-0001

**SORRELS, RANDALL OWEN,** lawyer; b. Va., Dec. 11, 1962; s. Charles Vernon and Marjorie Elaine (Jones) S.; m. Cheryl Ann Casas, June 29, 1985; children: Ashley Michelle, Stephanie Leigh, Darby Nicole, Garrett Ryan. BA in Polit. Sci.and Speech Comm. magna cum laude, Houston Bapt. U., 1984; JD magna cum laude, South Tex. Coll. Law, 1987. Bar: Tex. 1987, U.S. Dist. Ct. (so. dist.) Tex.; bd. cert. in civil trial law and personal injury trial law tex. Bd. Legal Specialization. Assoc. Fulbright & Jaworski, Houston, 1987-90; ptnr. Abraham, Watkins, Nichols, Sorrels, Matthews & Friend, Houston, 1990—. Co-author: Dram Shop and Social Host Liability, 1995. Fellow Houston Bar Found. (bd. trustees 1997—), Tex. Bar Found., Am. Bd. Trial Advocates; mem. ABA, ATLA, State Bar Tex. (bd. dirs. 1994-97, bd. advisor pattern jury charge comm. Vol. 1 1994-97, Vol. 4, 1995-97, chmn. profl. devel. com. 1996-97, vice chair legis. com. 1996-97), Tex. Trial Lawyers Assn. (sustaining life mem., bd. dirs.), Houston Bar Assn., Houston Trial Lawyers Assn. (bd. dirs., v.p., pres.-elect, chmn. CLE com. 1993—), Houston Young Lawyers Assn. (Outstanding Young Lawyer of Houston 1999), Tex. Young Lawyers Assn., Coll. of the State Bar of Tex., Assn. of Civil Trial and Appellate Specialists, Am. Inns of Ct., Million Dollar Adv. Forum. Insurance, Personal injury, Product liability. Home: 311 Terrace Dr Houston TX 77007-5046 Office: Abraham Watkins Nichols Sorrels Matthews & Friend 800 Commerce St Houston TX 77002-1776

**SORTLAND, PAUL ALLAN,** lawyer; b. Powers Lake, N.D., July 30, 1953; s. Allan Berdette and Eunice Elizabeth (Nystuen) S.; m. Carolyn Faye Anderson, June 23, 1979; children: Joseph Paul, Martha Marie, Nicholas John, Benjamin David. BA, St. Olaf Coll., 1975; JD, U. Minn., 1978. Bar: Minn. 1978, N.D. 1981, U.S. Dist. Ct. Minn. 1979, U.S. Dist. Ct. N.D. 1980, U.S. Ct. Appeals (8th cir.) 1987, U.S. Supreme Ct. 1991. Assoc. Alderson & Ondov, Austin, Minn., 1978-80, Qualley, Larson & Jones, Fargo, N.D., 1980-83; ptnr. Holand, Lochow & Sortland, Fargo, 1983-85; pres. Sortland Law Office, Fargo, 1985-88; ptnr. Messerli & Kramer, Mpls., 1988-92; Sortland Law Office, Mpls., 1993—; adj. prof. bus. law Moorhead State U., 1987. Mem. ATLA, N.D. Bar Assn., Minn. Bar Assn. (cert. civil trial specialist), Kiwanis, Million Dollar Advocates Forum, Gamma Eta Gamma. Lutheran. State civil litigation, Federal civil litigation, Personal injury. Home: 120 Quebec Ave S Minneapolis MN 55426-1509 Office: 33 S 6th St Ste 4100 Minneapolis MN 55402-3729

**SOSENSKY, STEVEN C.,** lawyer; b. New Haven, Conn.. BA in Polit. Sci., U. Conn., 1985; JD, We. New Eng. Sch. of Law, 1988. Bar: Conn., U.S. Dist. Ct. Conn. Summer assoc. Schatz, Schatz, Ribicoff & Kotkin, Hartford, Office of the Atty. Gen., Hartford; assoc. Joseloff & Joseloff, Wethersfield, Conn., 1989-90; pvt. practice New Haven, 1991—; cons. bus. transactions, complex civil litigation, bankruptcy, wills and trusts, collections, pub. utilities law, environ. regulation, New Haven. Mem. Conn. Bar Assn. General civil litigation, Contracts commercial, Bankruptcy. Office: 9 Trumbull St New Haven CT 06511-6372

**SOSOKOFF, DAVID,** lawyer; b. N.Y.C., Sept. 22, 1959; s. Sheldon A. and Nancy (Grant) S. BA, U. Pa., Phila., 1981, JD, 1985. Assoc. Shearman & Sterling, N.Y.C., 1985-96; asst. gen. counsel Deloitte & Touche LLP, N.Y.C., 1991—. Recipient Thurgood Marshall award Assn. Bar N.Y., 1998. Mem. ABA, Assn. Bar City of N.Y., N.Y. City Lawyers Assn., Fed. Cts. Commn. N.Y. City Lawyers Assn. Office: Deloitte & Touche LLP 1633 Broadway New York NY 10019-6708

**SOSSAMAN, WILLIAM LYNWOOD,** lawyer; b. High Point, N.C., May 30, 1947; s. Robert Allison and Elizabeth Bryce (Hethcox) S.; m. Sandra Clare Ward, June 9, 1973; children: Joana Leslie, David Lynwood. AB, Davidson Coll., 1969; JD, Vanderbilt U., 1972. Bar: Fla. 1972, U.S. Ct. Mil. Appeals 1973, U.S. Dist. Ct. (mid. dist.) Fla. 1977, Tenn. 1978, U.S. Dist. Ct. (we. dist.) Tenn. 1979, U.S. Dist. Ct. (no. dist.) Miss. 1979, U.S. Dist. Ct. (ea. and we. dists.) Ark, 1980, U.S. Dist. Ct. (mid. dist.) Tenn. 1985, U.S. Dist. Ct. (ea. dist.) Mich. 1988, U.S. Ct. Appeals (6th and 8th cirs.) 1989, U.S. Ct. Appeals (11th cir.) 1991. Mktg. resch. analyst First Tenn. Bank, Memphis, 1967-70; assoc. Alley, Rock & Dinkel, Tampa, Orlando and Miami, Fla., 1972-73, Rock & Brown, Orlando, 1976-77, Young & Perl, Memphis, 1978-88; ptnr. Allen, Scruggs, Sossaman, & Thompson, Memphis, 1988—; asst. county atty. Shelby County Govt., Memphis, 1978-79; asst. city atty. City of Memphis, 1978-79. Author: Preventing Lawsuits for Wrongful Termination, 1995. N.Am. regional sec. Project Ams., Davidson, N.C., 1967-69. Capt. U.S. Army, 1973-76. Named Hon. City Councilman City of Memphis, 1982. Mem. ABA (labor and employment sect., litigation sect., EEO com.), Fla. Bar (labor and employment law sect.), Mgmt. Counsel Roundtable (chmn. 1986-87), Def. Rsch. Inst. (employment law com.), Tenn. Bar Assn. (labor law sect.), Memphis Bar Assn., The Justice Network (bd. dirs. 1990-93). Presbyterian. Labor, Federal civil litigation. Home: 8411 Beaverwood Dr Germantown TN 38138-7641 Office: Allen Scruggs Sossaman & Thompson 813 Ridge Lake Blvd Ste 300 Memphis TN 38120-9410

**SOTAK, RONALD MICHAEL,** lawyer; b. Washington, July 21, 1967; s. Ronald Andrew Sotak and Mildred Jean Ferrara; m. Eileen Marie Hudson, Sept. 27, 1997; children; Sydney, Emily. BA cum laude, Salisbury State U., 1989; JD with honors, Drake U., 1992. Asst. county atty. Story County Attys. Office, Nevada, Iowa, 1992-96; asst. atty. gen. Iowa Atty. Gen., Des Moines, 1996-97; atty. Newbrough, Johnston, et al, Ames, Iowa, 1997—. Dir. Mainstream Living, Ames, 1998, Ctr. for Creative Justice, Ames, 1998. Recipient Purple Ribbon award Assault Care Ctr. Extending Shelter and Support, Ames, 1997. Mem. ABA, Iowa Bar Assn., Story County Bar Assn. (past pres.), Blackstone Inn of Ct. Avocations: golf, running, fitness. Personal injury, Criminal, General civil litigation. Office: Newbrough Johnston et al 612 Kellogg Ave Ames IA 50010-6230

**SOTOMAYOR, SONIA,** judge; b. N.Y.C., June 25, 1954; d. Juan Luis and Celina (Baez) S.; m. Kevin Edward Noonan, Aug. 14, 1976 (div. 1983). AB, Princeton (N.J.) U., 1976; JD, Yale U., 1979. Bar: N.Y. 1980, U.S. Dist. Ct. (ea. and so. dists.) N.Y. 1984. Asst. dist. atty. Office of Dist. Atty. County of N.Y., N.Y.C., 1979-84; assoc., ptnr. Pavia & Harcourt, N.Y.C., 1984-92; fed. judge U.S. Dist. Ct. (so. dist.) N.Y., N.Y.C., 1992-98; cir. judge U.S. Ct. Appeals (2nd Cir.), N.Y.C., 1998—. Editor Yale U. Law Rev., 1979. Bd. dirs. P.R. Legal Def. and Edn. Fund, N.Y.C., 1980-92, State of N.Y. Mortgage Agy., N.Y.C., 1987-92, N.Y.C. Campaign Fin. Bd., 1988-92; mem. State Adv. Panel on Inter-Group Rels., N.Y.C., 1990-91. Mem. Phi Beta Kappa. Office: US Courthouse 40 Foley Sq New York NY 10007-1502

**SOTORRIO, RENE ALBERTO,** lawyer; b. Havana, Cuba, Nov. 21, 1952; s. Rene and Hada Sotorrio; children: Mari Lourdes, Vanessa. BA, Northwestern U., Chgo., 1973; JD, Georgetown U., 1976. Bar: Fla. 1977, U.S. Dist. Ct. (so. dist.) Fla. 1979, N.J. 1979, U.S. Dist. Ct. N.J. 1979, U.S. Ct. Appeals (11th cir.) 1979, U.S. Dist. Ct. (so. and ea. dist.) N.Y. 1986, U.S. Ct. Appeals (5th cir.) 1988, U.S. Dist. Ct. (so. dist.) Tex. 1988, U.S. Ct. Appeals (7th and D.C. cir.), U.S. Supreme Ct. Instr. pilot ct. program Harvard Law Sch. Ctr. for Criminal Justice, Guatemala City, Guatemala, 1990; mem. Office of Pub. Defender, Jersey City, 1980-82, Miami, Fla., 1982-84; pvt. practice law Miami, 1984—. Mem. ABA, Fla. Bar Assn., Cuban-Am. Bar Assn., N.J. Criminal Def. Lawyers Assn., Tex. Criminal Def. Lawyers Assn., Nat. Criminal Def. Lawyers Assn., Am. Inn of Ct. (pres. 1990—), Inter-Am. Bar Assn. (Best Paper award). Criminal, Private international, Federal civil litigation. Office: 2600 S Douglas Rd Ste 600 Miami FL 33134-6100

**SOUDER, SUSAN,** lawyer; b. Washington, Sept. 20, 1956. BA, U. Md., 1978; JD, Georgetown U., 1981. Bar: Md. 1981. Trial atty. U.S. Dept. Justice, Washington, 1981-85; spl. asst. U.S. atty. Los Angeles, 1983; ptnr. Gordon, Feinblatt, Rothman, Balt., 1985-94, Ballard Spahr Andrews & Ingersoll, Balt., 1994-97; pvt. practice Balt., 1997—. Mem. ABA, Md. State Bar Assn., Balt. City Bar Assn., Women's Bar Assn. Personal income taxation, Federal civil litigation, State civil litigation.

**SOUKUP, CHRISTOPHER EARL,** lawyer; b. Detroit, July 1, 1948; s. Earl Herbert and Joyce Doreen (Whitney) S.; m. Vicki Suzanne Rosen, Sept. 16, 1979. BA, Ohio State U., 1970; JD, Case-Western Res. U., 1975. Bar: Ohio 1975, U.S. Dist. Ct. (no. dist.) Ohio 1979. Tax agt. Ohio Dept. Taxation, Columbus, 1970-71; legal asst. Arthur G. McKee & Co., Independence, Ohio, 1972-73; ptnr. Hendershott & Soukup, 1975-97; assoc. Ziegler, Metzger & Miller, LLP, Cleve., 1998—; arbitrator Cuyahoga County Ct. of Common Pleas, Cleve., 1979—. Served to capt. M.I., U.S. Army, 1970-71. Mem. Ohio Bar Assn., Greater Cleve. Bar Assn. Real property, Landlord-tenant, General practice. Home: 2705 Easthaven Dr Hudson OH 44236-1509 Office: Ziegler Metzger & Miller LLP 30100 Chagrin Blvd Ste 222 Pepper Pike OH 44124-5705

**SOULE, ROBERT GROVE,** lawyer; b. Boston, Jan. 12, 1958; s. Augustus W. and Mary R. Soule; m. Maura Kelley, Aug. 21, 1982; children: Courtney K., Katherine W., Zachary A. BA, Harvard U., 1979; JD, Suffolk U., 1983. Bar: Mass. 1983, U.S. Dist. Ct. Mass. 1983. Of counsel First Am. Title Ins. Co., Boston, 1982-85, asst. regional counsel, 1985-87; New Eng. states counsel Minn. Title Ins. Co., Boston, 1987-89; N.E. regional counsel Old Republic Title Ins. Co., Boston, 1989-93; mgr. nat. divsn. Lawyers Title Ins. Corp. (LandAmerica), Boston, 1993—. Contbr. articles to profl. jours., chpts. to books. Mem. Am. Land Title Assn., New Eng. Land Title Assn. (bd. dirs. 1996—, pres. 1999—), Mass. Conveyancers Assn. (title standards com. 1987—, exec. com. 1989-92), Mass. Bar Assn. Fax: (617) 619-4848. Real property. Office: LandAmerica One Washington Mall Boston MA 02108-2804

**SOUTER, DAVID HACKETT,** United States supreme court justice; b. Melrose, Mass., Sept. 17, 1939; s. Joseph Alexander and Helen Adams (Hackett) S. BA, Harvard U., 1961, LLB, 1966; Rhodes scholar, Oxford U., 1961-63, MA, 1989. Bar: N.H. Assoc. firm Orr & Reno, Concord, 1966-68; asst. atty. gen. N.H., 1968-71, dep. atty. gen., 1971-76, atty. gen., 1976-78; assoc. justice Superior Ct. N.H., 1978-83, N.H. Supreme Ct., 1983-90; judge U.S. Ct. Appeals (1st cir.) N.H., 1990; assoc. justice U.S. Supreme Ct., Washington, 1990—. Trustee Concord Hosp., 1973-85, pres. bd. trustees, 1978-84; bd. overseers Dartmouth Med. Sch., 1981-87. Mem. N.H. Bar Assn., N.H. Hist. Soc. (v.p. 1980-85, trustee 1976-85), Phi Beta Kappa. Republican. Episcopalian.

**SOUTER, SYDNEY SCULL,** lawyer; b. Trenton, N.J., June 17, 1931; s. Sydney H. and Josephine (Scull) S.; children: Gifford MacLeod, Julia Elizabeth, Matthew Thomas, Jeffrey James, Michael Andrew. BA, Yale U., 1954, JD, 1959. Bar: Conn. 1959, N.J. 1960. Assoc. Minton, Dinsmore & Bohlinger, Trenton, 1960-62, McCarthy, Bascik & Hicks, Princeton, N.J., 1963-64; ptnr. Baggit, Souter & Stonaker, Princeton, 1965-66; sr. ptnr. Souter, Scozzari & Steffens, Princeton, 1966-69, Souter & Kettell, Princeton, 1970-75, Souter & Steffens, Princeton, 1977-80, Souter & Selecky, Princeton, 1980-82, Souter & Morrow, Princeton, 1983-91, Souter and Voliva, Princeton, 1991—; bd. dirs. Ewing Bank & Trust Co. (counsel 1962-70); pres. The Hamilton Bank (counsel 1971-77). Mcpl. Judge Montgomery Twp., Somerset County, N.J., 1966-68, East Windsor Twp., Mercer County, N.J., 1971-73, Princeton Twp., Mercer County, 1981-89; asst. counsel County of Mercer, Trenton, 1990-91, dep. counsel, 1991-96; counsel Mercer County Park Commn., 1996—. Mem. ABA, N.J. State Bar Assn., Mercer County Bar Assn., Princeton Bar Assn., Rotary Club Princeton (pres. 1990-91), Kiwanis Club (pres. Princeton 1968). Republican. Presbyterian. General civil litigation, Real property, Administrative and regulatory. Office: Souter and Voliva 40 Nassau St Princeton NJ 08542-4522

**SOUTHERN, ROBERT ALLEN,** lawyer; b. Independence, Mo., July 17, 1930; s. James Allen and Josephine (Ragland) S.; m. Cynthia Agnes Drews, May 17, 1952; children: David D., William A., James M., Kathryn S. O'Brien. B.S. in Polit. Sci., Northwestern U., 1952, LL.B., 1954. Bar: Ill. 1955. Assoc. Mayer, Brown & Platt, Chgo., 1954-64, ptnr., 1965-96, mng. ptnr., 1978-91; mng. ptnr. Mayer, Brown & Platt, L.A., 1991-96; CEO So. Assocs., Gurnee, Ill., 1997—. Editor in chief Northwestern U. Law Rev., 1953-54. Trustee, v.p., gen. counsel LaRabida Children's Hosp. and Rsch. Ctr., Chgo., 1974-89; trustee Kenilworth (Ill.) Union Ch., 1980-88; pres. Joseph Sears Sch. Bd., 1977-79; trustee Rush-Presbyn.-St. Luke's Med. Ctr., 1983-91, life trustee, 1991—; bd. dirs. Boys and Girls Clubs Chgo., 1986-91; governing mem. Orchestral Assn. Chgo., 1988-93. With U.S. Army, 1955-57. Mem. ABA, Chgo. Bar Assn., Law Club Chgo., Legal Club Chgo., Order of Coif, Indian Hill Club, Chgo. Club. Banking, General corporate, Securities. Office: 7600 Bittersweet Dr Gurnee IL 60031-5110

**SOUTHGATE, (CHRISTINA) ADRIENNE GRAVES,** lawyer; b. Biloxi, Miss., Feb. 26, 1951; d. James Henry Jr. and Helen Alvera (Mataya) Graves; m. Theodore John Southgate, June 26, 1972 (div. 1997); children: Edward James Leyland, Colin Scott Christian. BA, Wellesley (Mass.) Coll., 1973; postgrad., Gordon-Conwell Theol. Sem., South Hamilton, Mass., 1973-75; JD, Wayne State U., 1978, postgrad. Bar: Mich. 1979, U.S. Ct. Appeals (6th cir.) 1980, U.S. Ct. Appeals (5th, 7th and 11th cirs.) 1982, U.S. Supreme Ct. 1982, U.S. Ct. Appeals (3d, 4th, 8th, 9th, 10th and D.C. cirs.) 1983, U.S. Ct. Appeals (1st, 2d and fed. cirs.) 1984, R.I. 1985, U.S. Ct. Mil. Appeals 1998. Law clk. to presiding justice Mich. Supreme Ct., Detroit, 1979-81; chief appellate counsel Charfoos, Christensen & Archer, P.C., Detroit, 1981-85; assoc. Carroll, Kelly & Murphy, Providence, 1985-87; asst. dir., chief legal counsel R.I. Dept. Environ. Mgmt., Providence, 1987-89; gen. counsel R.I. Pub. Utilities Commn., Providence, 1989—; adj. instr. legal writing Detroit Coll. Law, 1979-81; counsel exec. com. Emma Willard Sch., Troy, N.Y., 1985-90; cons. Jr. League of Providence, R.I., 1986-91; adj. prof. Vt. Law Sch., 1987-91. Contbr. articles to profl. jours. Vol. atty. R.I. Protection and Advocacy Services, Inc., Internat. Inst. R.I.; mem., chair fin. stewardship com. Episcopal Diocese R.I.; bd. dirs. alumnae fund and exec. coun. Emma Willard Sch.; bd. dirs. Big Sisters Assn. R.I., YMCA Greater Providence, South East New Eng. Cluster YMCAs; R.I. rep. east field com. YMCA U.S.A.; sr. warden St. Matthew's Epsic. Ch.; local coord. World Learning Inc. Internat. H.S. Program; active Leadership R.I.; mem. R.I. bd. govs. external com. telecomm., 1994-95. Mem. ABA (editorial bd. gen. practice sect. 1982-93, various coms.), R.I. Bar Assn. (specialization com. 1985-86, adminstrv. law com. 1991—, young lawyers clerkship com. 1985-94), Fed. Energy Bar Assn., Fed. Bar Assn., Nat. Assn. Women Lawyers, Am. Judicature Soc., R.I. Women's Bar Assn., R.I. Wellesley Club. Administrative and regulatory, Public utilities, FERC practice. Home: 22 Rosedale Ave Barrington RI 02806-1556 Office: R I Pub Utilities Comm 100 Orange St Providence RI 02903-2803

**SOUTHGATE, RICHARD W.,** lawyer; b. Chgo., May 6, 1929; m. Anna Fisher Hart, Aug. 25, 1951; children—Richard W., Sarah B., Rebecca W. C., John P. A.B. cum laude, Harvard U., 1951, LL.B. cum laude, 1954. Bar: Mass. 1954. Assoc. Covington & Burling, Washington, 1956-58; assoc., then ptnr., chmn. policy com. Ropes & Gray, Boston, 1958-94; vol. atty. Greater Boston Legal Svcs., 1995—; mem. Mass. Commn. on Anti-Takeover Laws; adj. prof. Northeastern U. Sch. Law, Boston, 1996-97. Author: (with Donald W. Glazer) Massachusetts Corporation Law and Practice, 1991. Moderator, Town of Manchester, Mass., 1976-94. Served as sgt. U.S. Army, 1954-56. Mem. Boston Bar Assn., ABA, Mass. Bar Assn. Clubs: Essex County, Somerset; Harvard (Boston). Home: 22 School St Manchester MA 01944-1336 Office: Greater Boston Legal Svcs 197 Friend St Boston MA 02114-1802

**SOUTTER, THOMAS DOUGLAS,** retired lawyer; b. N.Y.C., Nov. 1, 1934; s. Thomas G. and Hildreth H. (Callanan) S.; m. Virginia Hovenden; children: Alexander D., Christopher A., Hadley H. BA, U. Va., 1955, LL.B., 1962; postgrad., Advanced Mgmt. Program, Harvard U., 1980. Bar: N.Y. 1962, R.I. 1969. Atty. Breed, Abbott & Morgan, N.Y.C., 1962-68; with Textron Inc., Providence, 1968-95; gen. counsel Textron Inc., 1970-95, v.p., 1971-80, sr. v.p., 1980-85, exec. v.p., gen. counsel, 1985-95; cons., 1995-97; mem. adv. bd. Internat. and Comparative Law Ctr., 1975-95; mem. Assn. Gen. Counsel; bd. dirs. Avco Fin. Svcs., Inc., 1985-95, Paul Revere Corp. 1993-95; trustee New England Legal Found. Nat. chmn. ann. giving campaign U. Va. Law Sch., 1992-94; former trustee Providence Preservation Soc., Providence Performing Arts Ctr.; mem. U. Va. Arts and Scis. Alumni Coun.; mem. Narragansett coun. Boy Scouts Am. Lt. USNR, 1955-59. Mem. ABA, N.Y. State Bar Assn., R.I. Bar Assn., Internat. Bar Assn. General corporate, Antitrust, Private international. Office: 2 White Birch Ln Barrington RI 02806-4932

**SOVIE, SUSAN ANNE,** lawyer; b. Watertown, N.Y., Oct. 27, 1969; d. David Alan and Bonnie Lou (Pinkerton) S. BA, Hartwick Coll., Oneonta, N.Y., 1991; JD cum laude, Syracuse U., 1994. Bar: N.Y. 1994. Ptnr. Swartz Law Firm, P.C., Watertown, N.Y., 1994—; adviser Youth Ct., Watertown, 1997—; Jefferson County liaison Law Guardian Panel/4th Dept., Rochester, N.Y., 1996—. Recipient Michael J. Dillon Law Guardion award 1998. Mem. ABA, N.Y. State Bar Assn., Jefferson County Bar Assn. (co-chair Young Lawyers com. 1996—). Democrat. Roman Catholic. Avocations: hiking, reading, walking, travel. Family and matrimonial, Juvenile. Office: Swartz Law Firm PC 240 Washington St Watertown NY 13601-3300

**SPACE, THEODORE MAXWELL,** lawyer; b. Binghamton, N.Y., Apr. 3, 1938; s. Maxwell Evans and Dorothy Marie (Boone) S.; m. Susan Shultz, Aug. 18, 1962 (div. Apr. 1979); children: William Schuyler, Susanna; m. Martha Collins, Apr. 6, 1991. AB, Harvard U., 1960; LLB, Yale U., 1966. Bar: Conn., 1966, U.S. Dist. Ct. Conn. 1966, U.S. Supreme Ct. 1970, U.S. Tax Ct. 1989, U.S. Ct. Appeals (2nd cir.) 1967, U.S. Ct. Appeals (6th cir.) 1992, U.S. Ct. Appeals (11th cir.) 1994, U.S. Dist. Ct. (ea. dist.) Mich. 1997. Assoc. Shipman & Goodwin, LLP, Hartford, Conn., 1966-71, ptnr., 1971—, mng. ptnr., 1984-87, adminstv. ptnr., 1988-91. Mem. Bloomfield (Conn.) Bd. Edn., 1973-85, chmn., 1975-85; treas. Citizens Scholarship Found., Bloomfield, 1971-73, bd. dirs., 1973-91; mem. Bloomfield Human Rels. Commn., 1973-75; mem. Bloomfield Town Dem. Com., 1976-83; corporator Hartford Pub. Libr., 1976—; trustee Conn. Hist. Soc., 1997—, mem. libr. com., 1990—, chair, 1993—; chmn. fin. com., coun. mem. Unitarian Soc. Hartford, 1988-91. Lt. (j.g.) USN, 1960-63. Mem. ABA, Conn. Bar Assn. (mem. exec. com. adminstrv. law sect. 1980—), Hartford County Bar Assn., Am. Law Inst., Am. Health Lawyers Assn., Conn. Health Lawyers Assn., Swift's Inn, Hartford Club. Democrat. Unitarian Universalist. Avocations: reading, classical music. Administrative and regulatory, General civil litigation, Health. Home: 59 Prospect St Bloomfield CT 06002-3038 Office: Shipman & Goodwin LLP One American Row Hartford CT 06103-2833

**SPADE, ERIC F.,** lawyer; b. Ft. Lauderdale, Fla., Apr. 30, 1966; s. William R. Spade and Eva M. Abele; m. Benita Y. Pearson, May 31, 1997. BA, Am. U., 1989; JD magna cum laude, Cleve. State U., 1995. Bar: Ohio 1995, U.S. Ct. Appeals (10th cir.) 1995, U.S. Dist. Ct. (no. dist.) Ohio 1996, U.S. Ct. Appeals (3rd cir.) 1996. Law clk. hon. Monroe G. McKay U.S. Ct. Appeals 10th Cir., 1995-96; assoc. Porter, Wright, Morris & Arthur, Cleve., 1996—; adj. prof. Cleve.-Marshall Coll. Law, 1998—; trustee Towards Employment, Inc., Cleve., 1998—. Contbr. articles to profl. jours. Mem. Ohio State Bar Assn. (12th dist. del. coun. dels. 1997—). Fax: 216-443-9011. E-mail: espade@porterwright.com. Appellate, Federal civil litigation, General civil litigation. Office: Porter Wright Morris & Arthur 1700 Huntington Bldg 925 Euclid Ave Ste 1700 Cleveland OH 44115-1483

**SPADY, MARGARET VIDYA,** lawyer, nurse; b. Georgetown, Guyana, July 24, 1958; came to U.S., 1974; d. Frank R. and Ena I. (Bissember) Jacob; m. Richard Dean Spady, Feb. 27, 1990; children: Justin D., Conor, D., Rachael N. AS in Nursing, Loma Linda (Calif.) U., 1980; BS in Acctg., Loma Linda U., La Sierra, Calif., 1983; JD, Pepperdine U., 1989. Bar. Calif. 1989, U.S. Dist. Ct. (cen. dist.) Calif. 1989, U.S. Dist. Ct. (ea. dist.) Calif. 1995. Staff nurse, team leader Loma Linda U. Med. Ctr, 1980-89; assoc. Gibson, Dunn & Crutcher, Newport Beach, L.A., Calif., 1988 89-90; staff nurse Plumas Dist. Hosp., Quincy, Calif., 1990-92; dep. co. counsel II Co. of Plumas-Office of Co. Counsel, Quincy, 1992-96; summer law clk. Marchison & Cumming, L.A., 1987. Co. Bd. dirs. Plumas Comm. Clin., Quincy, 1991-94, Town Hall Theatre, Quincy, 1990-92. Recipient award for Excellence in Preparation for Trial Practice of the Law, Am. Bd. Trial Advocates, L.A., 1989, Am. Jurisprudence award, Malibu, 1986, 87. Mem. ABA. Republican. Seventh Day Adventist. Avocations: reading, writing, music, skiing, golf. Office: Office Co Counsel Plumas 520 Main St Quincy CA 95971-9364 Address: PO Box 327 Decatur IN 46733-0327

**SPAEDER, ROGER CAMPBELL,** lawyer; b. Cleve., Dec. 20, 1943; s. Ferd N. and Luceil (Campbell) S.; m. Frances DeSales Sutherland, Sept. 7, 1968; children: Michael, Matthew. BS, Bowling Green U., 1965; JD with honors, George Washington U., 1970. Bar: D.C. 1971, U.S. Dist. Ct. D.C. 1971, U.S. Ct. Appeals (D.C. cir.) 1971, U.S. Supreme Ct. 1976, U.S. Ct. Claims 1979, U.S. Dist. Ct. Md. 1984, U.S. Ct. Appeals (2d and 4th cirs.) 1985. Asst. U.S. atty. D.C., Washington, 1971-76; ptnr. Zuckerman, Spaeder, Goldstein, Taylor & Kolker, Washington, 1976—; faculty Atty. Gen. Advocacy Inst., 1974-76, Nat. Inst. Trial Adv., 1978-79; adj. faculty Georgetown U. Law Ctr., 1979-80, Am. U. Ctr. Adminstrn. Justice, 1976-79; lectr. D.C. Bar Continuing Legal Edn. Programs, 1980—. Recipient Spl. Achievement award Dept. Justice, 1971. Mem. ABA (co-chair com. on complex crimes litigation 1989-92, divsn. co-dir. sect. litigation 1992—), Bar Assn. D.C. (lectr. Criminal Practice Inst. 1977-80), D.C. Bar (com. criminal jury instrns. 1972, div. courts, lawyers, adminstrn. of justice, 1976-78; adv. com. continuing legal edn. 1986), Def. Rsch. Inst., Assn. Trial Lawyers Am., Assn. Plaintiffs' Trial Attys., Nat. Assn. Criminal Def. Lawyers, Omicron Delta Kappa. Contbr. articles to profl. jours. and chpts. to books. Federal civil litigation, Criminal. Home: 7624 Georgetown Pike Mc Lean VA 22102-1412 Office: Zuckerman Spaeder Goldstein Taylor & Kolker 1201 Connecticut Ave NW Fl 12 Washington DC 20036-2605

**SPAETH, NICHOLAS JOHN,** lawyer, former state attorney general; b. Mahnomen, Minn., Jan. 27, 1950. AB, Stanford U., 1972, JD, 1977; BA, Oxford U., Eng., 1974. Bar: Minn. 1979, U.S. Dist. Ct. (Minn.) 1979, U.S. Ct. Appeals (8th cir.) 1979, N.D. 1980, U.S. Dist. Ct. (N.D.) 1980, U.S. Supreme Ct. 1984. Law clk. U.S. Ct. Appeals (8th cir.), Fargo, N.D., 1977-78; law clk. to Justice Byron White U.S. Supreme Ct., Washington, 1978-79; pvt. practice, 1979-84; atty. gen. State of N.D., Bismarck, 1984-93; ptnr. Dorsey & Whitney, Fargo, 1993-99, Openheimer, Wolff & Donnelly, Mpls., CA, 1999—; adj. prof. law U. Minn., 1980-83. Rhodes scholar, 1972-74. Democrat. Roman Catholic. Criminal. Office: Oppenheimer Wolff & Donnelly 3400 Plaza VII 45 S 7th St Ste 3400 Minneapolis MN 55402-1609

**SPAHN, GARY JOSEPH,** lawyer; b. N.Y.C., July 23, 1949; s. Harry G. and Mary (Hopkins) S.; m. Lois Luttinger, Aug. 9, 1975; children: Gary J. Jr., Lori J. BA, L.I. U., 1971, MA, 1976; JD, U. Richmond, 1975. Bar: Va. 1975, U.S. Ct. Appeals (4th cir.) 1975, U.S. Supreme Ct. 1980. Law clk. to Hon. Judge Dortch U.S. Dist. Ct. (ea. dist.) Va., Richmond, 1975-77; from assoc. to ptnr. Mays & Valentine, Richmond, 1977—, now ptnr., chmn. products liability and ins. sect.; lectr. in field, 1980—; mem. judicial conf. U.S. Ct. Appeals (4th cir.). Co-author: Virginia Law of Products Liability, 1990. Pres. Southhampton Citizens Assn., Richmond, 1982-85; bd. dirs. Southhampton Recreation Assn., Richmond. 1983, Chesterfield County Crime Solvers, 1997—; mem. coun. Southside Montessori Sch., Richmond, 1983-85. With USAF, 1967-73. Mem. ABA (litigation and tort and ins. sects.), Internat. Assn. Def. Counsel, Am. Assn. Ins. Attys., Assoc. Def. Trial Attys., Def. Rsch. Inst., Va. Assn. Def. Attys., Va. Mfrs. Assn., Products Liability Adv. Counsel, Va. Power Boat (commodore). Avocations: boating, basketball, racquetball. Personal injury, Insurance, General civil litigation. Office: Mays & Valentine PO Box 1122 1111 E Main St Richmond VA 23219-3531

**SPAIN, H. DANIEL,** lawyer; b. Pasadena, Tex., Nov. 27, 1950; s. Harry Willard and Janet Lessie Spain; m. Glenna Dianne Brittain, Dec. 27, 1975; children: Summer, Sara. BBA in Fin., U. Tex., 1973; JD, U. Houston, 1976. Bar: Tex. 1977, U.S. Supreme Ct. 1981, Colo. 1992, U.S. Dist. Ct. (ea., so., we. and no. dists.) Tex., U.S. Dist. Ct. (ea. dist.) Okla., U.S. Ct. Appeals (5th cir.); bd. cert. civil trial law Nat. Bd. Trial Advs.; bd. cert. Tex. Bd. Legal Specialization. Asst. gen. atty. So. Pacific Transp., Houston, 1977-80; atty. Thompson & Spain, Houston, 1981-86, Womble & Spain, Houston, 1987-99, Spain & Hastings, Houston, 1999—. Fellow Houston Bar Found.; mem. Maritime Law Assn. U.S. (assoc.), Def. Rsch. Inst., Nat. Assn. R.R. Trial Counsel, Tex. Assn. R.R. Trial Counsel, State Bar Tex., Houston Bar Assn. Baptist. Avocations: church work, golf. Personal injury, Product liability, General civil litigation. Office: Spain & Hastings 909 Fannin St Ste 2350 Houston TX 77010-1027

**SPAIN, RICHARD COLBY,** lawyer; b. Evanston, Ill., Nov. 17, 1950; s. Richard Francis and Anne Louise (Brinckerhoff) S.; m. Nancy Lynn Mavec, Aug. 3, 1974; children: Catherine Day, Sarah Colby. BA cum laude, Lawrence U., 1972; JD, Case Western Reserve U., 1975; LLM in taxation, John Marshall Law Sch., 1985. Bar: Ohio 1975, Ill. 1982, U.S. Dist. Ct. (no. dist.) Ohio 1977, U.S. Dist. Ct. (no. dist.) Ill. 1982, Mass. 1996. Ptnr. Spain & Spain, Cleve., 1975-82, Whitted & Spain, PC, Chgo., 1985-89, Spain, Spain & Varnet PC, Chgo., Northborough, Mass., 1989—; assoc. Canel Whitted & Aronson, Chgo., 1982-85; dir., sec. Stone Perforating Co., Chgo., 1988—, Chgo. EDM, Inc., Chgo., Wheeling, Ill., 1994—. Contbr. articles to profl. jours. Vice-chmn. ARC Ill., 1993—, Cmty. Health Charities, 1997—; dir., pres. Hanover Condominium Assn., Chgo., 1992—; dir. Chgo. Youth Symphony Orch., 1983—. Mem. Chikaming Country Club (dir. 1992-94), The Winter Club Lake Forest, The Carlton Club (Chgo.). Estate planning, Probate, Estate taxation. Home: 1320 N State Pkwy Chicago IL 60610-2118 Office: Spain Spain & Varnet PC 33 N Dearborn St Ste 2220 Chicago IL 60602-3109

**SPAIN, THOMAS B.,** retired state supreme court justice. Justice Ky. Supreme Ct, Frankfort, 1991-95; ret., 1995; of counsel John C. Whitfield PSC. Office: John C Whitfield PSC PO Box 656 29 E Center St Madisonville KY 42431-2037

**SPALDING, CATHERINE,** lawyer; b. Lebanon, Ky.; d. Hugh Cassianus and Sarah Bernadette Spalding Hill. BS in Biology, Spalding U., Louisville, 1970; JD, U. Louisville, 1983. Bar: Ky., U.S. Ct. Appeals (6th cir.), Ct. Vets. Appeals, Fed. Dist. Ct. Pvt. practice law Louisville, 1983—; asst. county atty. Jefferson County, 1993—. Editor newsletter Ky. Bar Assn., Family Law; editor book supplement: Kentucky Family Law, 1990. Past bd. dirs. LWV, Portland Mus. Louisville. Mem. ABA, Ky. Bar Assn. (chairperson family law sect. 1990-91, spkr., moderator seminats), Louisville Bar Assn. (chairperson social security sect. 1992-93), AAUW (past bd. dirs.), DAR (past bd. dirs.) Optimist Club (past bd. dirs.). Avocations: snow skiing, sailing. Personal injury, Juvenile, Family and matrimonial. Home: PO Box 70415 Louisville KY 40270-0415

**SPALTEN, DAVID ELLIOT,** lawyer; b. N.Y.C., June 13, 1956; s. Robert and Elinor Ruth (Okie) S.; m. Sharon Lee Seigrist, Aug. 10, 1988; 1 child, Jonathan Grant. BA in Biology, Alfred U., 1978; JD, Emory U., 1983. Bar: Ga. 1983, N.Y. 1986, U.S. Dist. Ct. (no. dist.) Ga. 1983, U.S. Dist. Ct. (mid. dist.) 1985, U.S. Ct. Appeals 1987, U.S. Tax Ct. 1996. Assoc. Merritt & Tenney, LLP, Atlanta, 1986-92, ptnr., 1993—; vis. faculty Emory U. Trial Techniques Program, Atlanta, 1996—; spkr. civil litig. Emory U. Adult Edn. Program, Atlanta, 1993. Mem. ABA, State Bar Ga. (intellectual property, litigation sect.), N.Y. State Bar Assn. Presbyterian. Avocations: economics, current events, tennis. Professional liability, Federal civil litigation, Intellectual property. Office: Merritt & Tenney LLP Ste 500 200 Galleria Pkwy NW Atlanta GA 30339-3183

**SPANBOCK, MAURICE SAMUEL,** lawyer; b. N.Y.C., Jan. 6, 1924; s. Benjamin and Belle (Ward) S.; m. Marion Rita Heyman, Nov. 21, 1954; children: Jonathan H., Betsy W. BA, Columbia U., N.Y.C., 1944; LLB, Harvard U., 1950. Bar: N.Y. 1950. Assoc. Goldstone and Wolff, N.Y.C., 1950-52; ptnr. Carro and Spanbock (name changed to Carro, Spanbock, Kaster et al), N.Y.C., 1952-94; of counsel Kleinberg Kaplan Wolff & Cohen, N.Y.C., 1994—. Trustee Carnegie Coun. on Ethics and Internat. Affairs, N.Y.C., 1980-86, 93, chmn. bd., 1987-92; hon. pres. Lincoln Square Synagogue, N.Y.C.; sec. Ohr Torah Stone Instns. Israel. Cpl. AUS, 1943-46, ETO. Mem. ABA (chmn. com. on taxation, patent, trademark and copyright law sect. 1979-81), Assn. of Bar of City of N.Y. (com. on copyright 1965-67, art law com. 1977-80, 86-88), Fed. Bar Coun., Nat. Panel Arbitrators, Am. Abitration Assn., Practising Law Inst. (panel on copyrights, 1979). Jewish. Estate planning, General corporate, Entertainment. Home: 88 Central Park W New York NY 10023-5209 Office: Kleinberg Kaplan Wolff & Cohen 551 5th Ave Fl 18 New York NY 10176-1800

**SPANGLER, JOHN THOMAS,** lawyer; b. Superior, Mont., Mar. 28, 1953; s. Thomas G. and Catherine (Strasser) S.; m. Cynthia Marie Muller, Aug. 3, 1985; 1 child, Nicholas. BBA, U. Mont., 1977; JD, UCLA, 1983. Bar: Mont. 1984, U.S. Dist. Ct. Mont. 1984. Acct. Maier & Carney, Portland, Oreg., 1977-80; assoc. Worder, Thane & Haines, P.C., Missoula, Mont., 1984, Cummings Law Firm, Missoula, 1985-92; pvt. practice Missoula, 1984-85, 92—. Mem. ABA, State Bar Mont., Western Mont. Bar Assn. Roman Catholic. Estate planning, Probate, Estate taxation. Office: PO Box 8925 Missoula MT 59807-8925

**SPANN, JAMES J., JR.,** lawyer; b. Westfield, N.Y., July 8, 1955; s. James J., Sr. and Jean (Killmeyer) S.; m. June M. Miller, May 27, 1995. BA, SUNY, Fredonia, 1974; JD, Thomas M. Cooley Law Sch., 1984. Bar: N.Y. 1985, D.C. 1986. Assoc. Anthony J. Spann, P.C., Dunkirk, N.Y., 1985—; magistrate N.Y. State Magistrate, Westfield, 1987—; bd. dirs. Westfield (N.Y.) Counseling Svcs. Mem. N.Y. State Bar Assn., N.Y. State Trial Lawyers Assn., Chautauqua Bar Assn. Family and matrimonial, Personal injury. Office: Anthony J Spann PC 427 Central Ave Dunkirk NY 14048-2106

**SPARKMAN, STEVEN LEONARD,** lawyer; b. Sarasota, Fla., May 30, 1947; s. Simeon Clarence and Ursula (Wahlstrom) S.; m. Terry Jeanne Gibbs, Aug. 23, 1969; children: Joanna Jeanne, Kevin Leonard. BA, Fla. State U., 1969, JD, 1972. Bar: Fla. 1972, U.S. Dist. Ct. (mid. dist.) Fla. 1974, U.S. Ct. Appeals (5th cir.) 1975. Legal rsch. asst. Office Gen. Counsel, Fla. Dept. Revenue, Tallahassee, 1971; legis. intern com. on community affairs Fla. Ho. of Reps., Tallahassee, 1971-72; jud. rsch. aide Fla. 2d Dist. Ct. Appeals, Lakeland, 1972-73; asst. county atty. Hillsborough County, Tampa, Fla., 1973-75; assoc. Carlton, Fields, Ward, Emmanuel, Smith & Cutler, P.A., Tampa, 1975-80, sr. atty., 1980—; mem. Fla. State U. Coll. Law Bd. Visitors, 1994—. Sec., bd. dirs. Bapt. Towers Plant City, Inc., 1981-84; deacon 1st Bapt. Ch., Plant City, 1980—. 1st lt. USAFR, 1973. Mem. Fla. Bar Assn. (exec. coun. local govt. law sect. 1978-79), Hillsborough County Bar Assn., Tampa Kiwanis (bd. dirs. 1980-82, 96-98, Layman of Yr. 1984, 89), Tampa Kiwanis Found. (bd. dirs. 1997—). Democrat. Real property, Land use and zoning (including planning). Office: Carlton Fields Ward Emmanuel Smith & Cutler PA 777 S Harbour Island Blvd Tampa FL 33602-5729

**SPARKS, BILLY SCHLEY,** lawyer; b. Marshall, Mo., Oct. 1, 1923; s. John and Clarinda (Schley) S.; A.B., Harvard, 1945, LL.B., 1949; student Mass. Inst. Tech., 1943-44; m. Dorothy O. Stone, May 14, 1946; children: Stephen Stone, Susan Lee Sparks Raben Taylor, John David. Admitted to Mo. bar, 1949; partner Langworthy, Matz & Linde, Kansas City, Mo., 1949-62, firm Linde, Thomson, Fairchild Langworthy, Kohn & Van Dyke, 1962-91, ret., 1991. Mem. Mission (Kans.) Planning Council, 1954-63; mem. Kans. Civil Service Comm., 1975-90. Mem. dist. 110 Sch. Bd., 1964-69, pres., 1967-69; mem. Dist. 512 Sch. Bd., 1969-73, pres., 1971-72; del. Dem. Nat. Conv., 1964; candidate for representative 10th Dist., Kans., 1956, 3d district, 1962; treas. Johnson County (Kans.) Dem. Central com., 1958-64. Served to lt. USAAF, 1944-46. Mem. Kansas City C. of C. (legis. com. 1956-82), Am., Kansas City bar assns., Mo. Bar, Law Assn. Kansas City, Harvard Law Sch. Assn. Mo. (past dir.), Nat. Assn. Sch. Bds. (mem. legislative com. 1968-73), St. Andrews Soc. Mem. Christian Ch. (trustee). Clubs: Harvard (v.p. 1953-54), The Kansas City (Kansas City, Mo.); Milburn Golf and Country, American Legion. General practice, State civil litigation, Federal civil litigation. Home and Office: 8517 W 90th Ter Shawnee Mission KS 66212-3053

**SPARKS, DAVID THOMAS,** lawyer; b. Bowling Green, Ky., Dec. 17, 1968; s. Lee Thomas and Ann Louis S. BS, We. Ky., 1992; JD, U. Ky., 1995. Bar: Ky. 1995, U.S. Dist. Ct. (we. dist.) Ky. 1995, U.S. Dist. Ct. (ea. dist.) Ky. 1996. Assoc. atty. Bell, Orr, Ayers & Moore, Bowling Green, 1995—. Deacon First Christian Ch., Bowling Green, 1988-98, elder, 1998, mem. personnel com., 1998. Mem. ABA, Ky. Bar Assn., Bowling Green Warren County Bar Assn., Future Bus. Leaders Am., Phi Beta Lambda. Republican. Mem. Christian Ch. Avocations: basketball, softball, model railroading, marine aquarium, reading. Insurance, General civil litigation, Family and matrimonial. Home: 2512 Thompson Dr Bowling Green KY 42104-4375 Office: Bell Orr Ayers & Moore PO Box 738 Bowling Green KY 42102-0738

**SPARKS, KENNETH FRANKLIN,** lawyer; b. Anniston, Ala., Dec. 31, 1963; s. Guy and Gail Sparks; m. Margaret Reid Wellensiek, May 27, 1989; children: William, Samuel, Peter. BS, MIT, 1986; JD, U. Mich., 1989. Bar: D.C. 1992, Ill. 1997, U.S. Ct. Appeals (fed. cir.) 1993, U.S. Ct. Appeals (D.C. cir.) 1995, U.S. Ct. Appeals (6th cir.) 1995, U.S. Ct. Appeals (7th cir.) 1996, U.S. Dist. Ct. D.C. 1995, U.S. Dist. Ct. (no. dist.) Ill. 1996, U.S. Ct. Appeals (4th cir.) 1999. Jud. law clk. to judge Cornelia Kennedy U.S. Ct. Appeals (6th cir.), Detroit, 1989-90; assoc. Shea & Gardner, Washington, 1990-95; assoc. Matkov Salzman Madoff & Gunn, Chgo., 1995-97, ptnr., 1998—. Truman scholar Truman Found., 1984-88. Mem. Mich. Alumni Assn., MIT Club of Chgo., Order of Coif. Labor, Federal civil litigation, Toxic tort. Office: Matkov Salzman Madoff & Gunn Ste 2900 55 East Monroe St Chicago IL 60603-5709

**SPARKS, ROBERT RONOLD, JR.,** lawyer; b. Bklyn., Dec. 4, 1946; s. Robert Ronold Sr. and Marjorie Anne (Boehm) S. BA, Va. Mil. Inst., 1969; JD, U. Va., 1972. Bar: U.S. Dist. Ct. (D.C. cir.) 1979, U.S. Dist. Ct. (ea. dist.) Va. 1979, U.S. Ct. Appeals (2d cir.) 1986, U.S. Ct. Appeals (D.C. cir.) 1975, Va. 1972, U.S. Ct. Appeals (4th cir.) 1982, U.S. Ct. Mil. Appeals 1976, U.S. Tax Ct. 1978, U.S. Supreme Ct. 1981, U.S. Dist. Ct. Md. 1993. From assoc. to ptnr. Sedam & Herge, McLean, Va., 1977-85; ptnr. Herge, Sparks & Christopher, McLean, 1985—; mem. Bd. Regents James Monroe Law Office Mus. and Meml. Library, Fredericksburg, Va., 1983-86. Mem. Fairfax County Redevel. and Housing Authority, Fairfax, 1981-82; commr. Fairfax County Indsl. Devel. Authority, 1980-81, Fairfax County Planning Commn., 1983-89. Lt. USNR, 1972-77, Philippines. Mem. Va. Bar Assn., D.C. Bar Assn., Rotary (treas., bd. dirs. 1978-80). Roman Catholic. General civil litigation, Constitutional. Home: 6448 Spring Ter Falls Church VA 22042-3141 Office: Herge Sparks Christopher 6862 Elm St Ste 360 Mc Lean VA 22101-3862

**SPARKS, SAM,** federal judge; b. 1939. BA, U. Tex., 1961, LLB, 1963. Aide Rep. Homer Thornberry, 1963; law clk. to Hon. Homer Thornberry U.S. Dist. Ct. (we. dist.) Tex., 1963-65; assoc. to ptnr., shareholder Hardie, Grambling, Sims & Galatzan (and successor firms), El Paso, Tex., 1965-91; dist. judge U.S. Dist. Ct. (we. dist.) Tex., 1991—. Fellow Am. Coll. Trial Lawyers, Tex. Bar Found. (life); mem. Am. Bd. Trial Advocates (advocate), State Bar Tex. Office: US Dist Ct Judge 200 W 8th St Ste 100 Austin TX 78701-2333

**SPARKS, STEPHEN STONE,** lawyer; b. Kansas City, Mo., June 21, 1954; s. Billy Schley and Dorothy (Stone) S.; m. Martha Nelson, Oct. 19, 1979; children: Matthew Nelson, Adam Nelson. BA, New Coll. of U. of South Fla., 1976; JD with distinction, U. Mo., Kansas City, 1979. Bar: Mo. 1979, U.S. Dist. Ct. (we. dist.) Mo. 1979, U.S. Dist. Ct. Kans. 1998. Assoc. Linde, Thomson, Langworthy, Kohn & Van Dyke P.C., Kansas City, 1979-82, ptnr., 1982-91; ptnr. Smith, Gill, Fisler & Butts, Kansas City, 1991-95, Bryan Cave LLP, Kansas City, 1995—. Mem. ABA, Kansas City Bar Assn., Lawyers Assn. K.C. Mo., Nat. Assn. Bond Lawyers, Milburn Country Club, Shadow Glen Golf Club. Democrat. Avocation: golf. E-mail: SSparks@BryanCaveLLP.com. Municipal (including bonds), Real property, General corporate. Home: 10818 W 102nd St Overland Park KS 66214-2539 Office: Bryan Cave LLP 1200 Main St Fl 35 Kansas City MO 64105-2122

**SPARR, DANIEL BEATTIE,** federal judge; b. Denver, June 8, 1931; s. Daniel John and Mary Isabel (Beattie) S.; m. Virginia Sue Long Sparr, June 28, 1952; children: Stephen Glenwood, Douglas Lloyd, Michael Christopher. BSBA, U. Denver, 1952, JD, 1966. Bar: Colo. U.S. Dist. Ct. Assoc. White & Steele, Denver, 1966-70; atty. Mountain States Telephone & Telegraph Co., Denver, 1970-71; ptnr. White & Steele, Denver, 1971-74; atty. Wesley H. Doan, Lakewood, Colo., 1974-75; prin. Law Offices of Daniel B. Sparr, Denver, 1975-77; judge 2d dist. Colo. Dist. Ct., Denver, 1977-90; judge U.S. Dist. Ct. Colo., Denver, 1990—. Mem. Denver Bar Assn. (trustee 1975-78), Denver Paralegal Inst. (bd. advs. 1976-88), William E. Doyle's/Am. Inns of Ct., Am. Bd. Trial Advs., ABA, Colo. Bar Assn. Office: US Dist Ct 1929 Stout St Denver CO 80294-1929

**SPARROW, RUTH S.,** lawyer; b. Boston; d. Marvin and Dorothy Jane (Goldman) S. BA in Politics with honors, U. Calif., Santa Cruz, 1980; JD, NYU, 1987. Bar: Pa., 1987. Assoc. tax dept. Wolf Block Schorr and Solis-Cohen LLP, Phila., 1987-95, ptnr. tax dept., 1995—, vice chmn. Wolf Block Govt. Asst. & Affordable Housing Group. Articles editor NYU Rev. of Law and Social Change, 1986-87; contbg. editor Jour. Affordable Housing and Cmty. Devel. Law. Mem. adv. bd. LIHC (Low Income Housing Credit) Monthly Report. Mem. ABA (mem. tax sect. 1987—), Pa. Bar Assn. (mem. tax sect. 1987—), Phila. Bar Assn. (mem. tax sect. 1987—), U.S. Amateur Ballroom Dance Assn. (mem. non-profit legal coun. 1996—). Taxation, general. Office: Wolf Block Schorr and Solis-Cohen LLP 1650 Arch St Fl 22 Philadelphia PA 19103-2029

**SPATH, GREGG ANTHONY,** lawyer; b. New Rochelle, N.Y., Nov. 13, 1952; s. Richard Dennis and Renee (Turtletaub) S.; m. Lois Lang, Mar. 18, 1979; 1 child, Emma Lang. Student, Coll. William and Mary, 1970-72; BA in English, U. Rochester, 1974; JD, New Eng. Sch. Law, 1977; LLM in Trade Regulation, NYU, 1979. Bar: N.Y. 1978, U.S. Supreme Ct. 1984, Pa. 1990. Spl. legal cons. Western Electric Co., N.Y.C., 1978-81; atty. St. Regis Paper Co., N.Y.C., 1981-82; asst. gen. counsel, sec. patent com. United Machinists and Mfrs., Inc., N.Y.C., 1982-87; corp. counsel Adidas USA, Inc., Warren, N.J., 1987-88; exec. v.p., corp. counsel Hy-Art Industries, Inc., Kingston, Pa., 1988-90; sec., treas., gen. counsel Regency Mfg. Co., Inc., Wilkes-Barre, Pa., 1990-93, Renee Mfg. Co., Inc., Exeter, Pa., 1993-95; corp. counsel real estate Nextel Comm., Inc., Reston, Va., 1996—. Contbr. New Eng. Law Rev., 1976, tech. editor, 1976-77. Mem. ABA (sects. of antitrust, patent, trademark and copyright law, real estate probate and trust law, corp. banking and bus. law). Avocations: fundraising, sports, music, theatre, cinema. Intellectual property, Contracts commercial, Real property. Office: Nextel Comm Inc 2001 Edmund Halley Dr Reston VA 20191-3421

**SPATOLA, JO-ANNE BUCCINNA,** judge; b. N.Y.C., June 1, 1945; d. Nicholas Theodore and Catherine Buccinna; m. Joseph A. Spatola, Jan. 28, 1967; children: Michael J., Madeleine A. BA, U. Md., 1967; JD cum laude, Seton Hall U., 1977. Bar: N.J. 1977, U.S. Dist. Ct. N.J. 1977, U.S. Supreme Ct. 1985. Sch. tchr. G. Gardner Shugart Jr. H.S., Hillcrest Heights, Md., 1967-68; pvt. practice law Westfield, N.J., 1978-91; judge N.J. Superior Ct., Elizabeth, 1991—; lawyer Union County Bd. Social Svc., Elizabeth, N.J., 1984-88. Coun. woman Scotch Plains (N.J.) Twp. Coun., 1985-91, dep. mayor, 1989, mayor, 1990. Mem. N.J. Coun. Family Ct. Judges. Roman Catholic. Office: Union County Ct House 2 Broad St Elizabeth NJ 07201-2202

**SPATT, ARTHUR DONALD,** federal judge; b. 1925. Student, Ohio State U., 1943-44, 46-47; LLB, Bklyn. Law Sch., 1949. Assoc. Davidson & Davidson, N.Y.C., 1949, Lane, Winard, Robinson & Schorr, N.Y.C., 1950, Alfred S. Julien, N.Y.C., 1950-52, Florea & Florea, N.Y.C., 1953; pvt. practice N.Y.C., 1953-67, Spatt & Bauman, N.Y.C., 1967-78; justice 10th judicial cir. N.Y. State Supreme Ct., 1979-82; adminstrv. judge Nassau County, 1982-86; assoc. justice appellate div. Second Judicial Dept., 1986-89; dist. judge U.S. Dist. Ct. (ea. dist.) N.Y., Bklyn., 1989-90, Uniondale, N.Y., 1990—. Active Jewish War Vets. Mem. ABA, Assn. Supreme Ct. Justices State of N.Y., Bar Assn. Nassau County, Jewish Lawyers Assn. Nassau County, Bklyn. Law Rev. Assn., Long Beach Lawyers Assn., Theodore Roosevelt Am. Inn of Ct., Master of the Bench. Office: US Dist Ct 2 Uniondale Ave Uniondale NY 11553-1258

**SPATT, ROBERT EDWARD,** lawyer; b. Bklyn., Mar. 26, 1956; s. Milton E. and Blanche S. (Bakstansky) S.; m. Lisa B. Malkin, Aug. 11, 1979; 1 child, Mark Eric. AB, Brown U., 1977; JD magna cum laude, U. Mich., 1980. Bar: N.Y. 1981. Assoc. Simpson Thacher & Bartlett, N.Y.C., 1980-87, ptnr., 1987—. Mem. ABA, N.Y. State Bar Assn., City of N.Y. Bar Assn., Order of Coif, ACLU. Avocations: photography, boating, reading. General corporate, Securities, Mergers and acquisitions. Home: 286 West Trl Stamford CT 06903-2402 Office: Simpson Thacher & Bartlett 425 Lexington Ave Fl 15 New York NY 10017-3954

**SPEAKER, SUSAN JANE,** lawyer; b. Dallas, Dec. 25, 1946; d. William R. and Jane E. (Aldrich) Turner; m. David C. Speaker, Dec. 21, 1968; children: David Allen, Melissa. BA, U. Ark., 1970, JD, 1985. Bar: Okla. 1985, U.S. Dist. Ct. (no., ea. and we. dists.) Okla. 1985. Assoc. Hall, Estill, Hardwick, Gable, Golden & Nelson, P.C., Tulsa, 1985-91; atty. Resolution Trust Corp., 1991-92; shareholder Speaker & Matthews, P.C., 1992-96; atty. Comml. Fin. Svcs., Inc., Tulsa, 1996-99; dir. properties and concessions Dollar Rent A Car Systems, Inc., 1999—. Editor U. Ark. Law Rev., 1983-85. Mem. ABA, ATLA, Okla. Bar Assn., Tulsa Bar Assn., Tulsa Title and Probate Lawyers Assn., Phi Beta Kappa, Delta Theta Phi. General civil litigation, Federal civil litigation, State civil litigation.

**SPEAR, H(ENRY) DYKE N(EWCOME), JR.,** lawyer; b. New London, Conn., Feb. 26, 1935; s. Henry D. N. and Helene (Vining) S.; m. Karla A. Dalley, Sept. 9, 1995. BA, Trinity Coll., Hartford, Conn., 1958; JD, U. Conn., 1960. Bar: Conn. 1960. Pvt. practice matrimonial law Hartford, 1961—. Mem. Conn. Bar Assn., Hartford County Bar Assn. Republican. Methodist. Family and matrimonial. Office: 10 Trumbull St Hartford CT 06103-2404

**SPEAR, JAMES HODGES,** lawyer; b. Dallas, Aug. 19, 1952; s. H.C. and Ruth Mae (Womack) S. BS summa cum laude, Sam Houston State U., 1979; JD, South Tex. Coll., 1983. Bar: Tex. 1982, U.S. Dist. Ct. (no., so., ea. and we. dists.) Tex., U.S. Dist. Ct. (no. dist.) Calif., U.S. Ct. Appeals (5th and 9th cirs.), U.S. Supreme Ct. Assoc. Taylor, Hays, Price, McConn & Pickering, Houston, 1983-84, McDonald, Perussian & Cullom, San Francisco, 1984-86, Godwin, Carlton & Maxwell, Dallas, 1986-89; mem. firm Spear, Downs & Judin, Dallas, 1989—; advocate instr. Nat. Inst. Trial Advocacy. With U.S. Army, 1973-78. Fellow State Bar Tex.; mem. ABA, Bar Assn. San Francisco, Dallas Bar Assn., Tex. Assn. Def. Counsel, Def. Rsch. Inst., Order of Lytae, Order of Barristers (prs. bd. advocates 1980-83), Phi Delta Phi. Insurance, Personal injury, Military. Office: Spear Downs & Judin 501 Elm St Ste 200 Dallas TX 75202-3351

**SPEARS, LARRY JONELL,** lawyer; b. Webb, Miss., Jan. 10, 1953; s. John Spears and Lillian Belle Embrey; m. Treycè L. Gaston, Jan. 14, 1989;children: Lyndzè Rae, Joshua Lawrence. BS, U. Ill., 1976, JD, 1979; MS, So. Ill. U., 1990. Bar: Ill. 1980. Asst. atty gen. Ill. Atty. Gen.'s Office, Murphysboro, 1980-84; asst. pub. defender Jackson County Pub. Defender's Office, Murphysboro, 1985; lectr. Crime Study Ctr., Carbondale, Ill., 1985; sole practice Carbondale, 1985-86; asst. state's atty. Peoria (Ill.) State's Atty. Office, 1986-90, Sangamon County State's Atty. Office, Springfield, Ill., 1990-94; cons. Minority Contractors Assn., Carbondale, 1985; mem. Inmate Advocacy Group, Murphysboro, 1985-86; lectr. Sangamon State U., Springfield, 1990-96. Elijah P. Lovejoy scholar, 1972. Mem. Ill. State Bar Assn., McLean County Bar Assn., Adminstrn. of Justice Assn. (treas. 1984-85), Am. Soc. Criminology (discussant 1984-85), Midwest Criminal Justice Assn., Am. Judicature Soc., LWV, Sphinx Club (Carbondale), Phi Alpha Delta (treas. 1979), Alpha Phi Sigma. Republican. Baptist. Avocations: golf, fishing, songwriting, tennis, volleyball. Home: 1603 E Oakland Ave Bloomington IL 61701-5617 Office: Ill State U Student's Legal Svcs Normal IL 61761

**SPEARS, ROBERT FIELDS,** lawyer; b. Tulsa, Aug. 1, 1943; s. James Ward and Berneice (Fields) S.; m. Jacquelyn Castle, May 10, 1961; children: Jeff, Sally. BBA, Tex. Tech. U., 1965; JD, U. Tex., 1968. Bar: Tex. 1968. Assoc. Rain, Harrell, Emery, Young & Doke, Dallas, 1968-73, ptnr., 1974-87; ptnr. Locke Purnell Rain Harrell, Dallas, 1987-91; gen. counsel Fin. Industries Corp., Austin, Tex., 1991-96; gen. counsel, sec. Lone Star Technologies, Inc., Dallas, 1996—. Pres. Sr. Citizens of Greater Dallas, 1988. Mem. ABA, Tex. Bar Assn., Dallas Bar Assn., Dallas Country Club, Phi Delta Phi. Republican. Baptist. Avocation: tennis. General corporate, Securities, Mergers and acquisitions. Office: Lone Star Technologies Inc PO Box 803546 Dallas TX 75380-3546

**SPECKMAN, DAVID LEON,** lawyer; b. Painesville, Ohio, June 15, 1969; s. Robert L. and Gayle A. Speckman; m. Helena B. Wallentin, Apr. 15, 1995. BA, U. Wash., 1992; MBA, U. San Diego, 1995, JD, 1995. Bar: Calif. 1995, U.S. Dist. Ct. (so. dist.) Calif. 1996; CPA, Wash.; cert. real estate broker, Calif. CPA Moss Adams, Seattle, 1992; jud. intern San Diego Superior Ct., 1994; assoc. Law Office of Nicholas A. Boylan, San Diego, 1995-97; prin. Law Office of David L. Speckman, San Diego, 1997—. Pres. San Diego Sch. of Law Pro Bono Legal Advocates, 1992-94; v.p. San Diego Sch. of Law Moot Ct. Bd., 1995; founder HIV Legal Svcs. Program, San Diego, 1993. Mem. AICPA, ABA, Calif. State Bar assn., San Diego County Bar Assn., Consumer Attys. San Diego, Beta Gamma Sigma. Avocations: scuba diving, long-distance running, alpine skiing. State civil litigation, Contracts commercial, Professional liability. Office: Law Office of David L Speckman 432 F St Ste 508 San Diego CA 92101-6100

**SPECTER, RICHARD BRUCE,** lawyer; b. Phila., Sept. 6, 1952; s. Jacob E. and Marilyn B. (Kron) S.; m. Jill Ossenfort, May 30, 1981; children: Lauren Elizabeth, Lindsey Anne, Allison Lee. BA cum laude, Washington U., St. Louis, 1974; JD, George Washington U., 1977. Bar: Mo. 1977, U.S. Dist. Ct. (ea. and we. dists.) Mo. 1977, U.S. Ct. Appeals (8th cir.) 1977, Ill. 1978, Pa. 1978, U.S. Dist. Ct. (ea. dist.) Ill. 1979, U.S. Ct. Appeals (7th cir.) 1979, Calif. 1984, U.S. Dist. Ct. (cen. dist.) Calif. 1985, U.S. Ct. Appeals (9th cir.) 1986, U.S. Dist. Ct. (so. dist.) Calif. 1987, U.S. Dist. Ct. (no. dist.) Calif. 1988. Assoc. Coburn, Croft, Shepherd, Herzog & Putzell, St. Louis, 1977-79; ptnr. Herzog, Kral, Burroughs & Specter, St. Louis, 1979-82; exec. v.p. Uniqey Internat., Santa Ana, Calif., 1982-84; pvt. practice law L.A. and Irvine, Calif., 1984-87; ptnr. Corbett & Steelman, Irvine, 1987—; instr. Nat. Law Ctr. George Washington U. 1975. Mem. ABA, Ill. Bar Assn., Mo. Bar Assn., Pa. Bar Assn., Calif. Bar Assn. Jewish. State civil litigation, Entertainment, Sports. Home: 37 Bull Run Irvine CA 92620-2510 Office: Ste 200 18200 Von Karmen Ave Irvine CA 92612-1029

**SPECTOR, DAVID M.,** lawyer; b. Rock Island, Ill., Dec. 20, 1946; s. Louis and Ruth (Vinikour) S.; m. Laraine Fingold, Jan. 15, 1972; children: Rachel, Laurence. BA, Northwestern U., 1968; JD magna cum laude, U. Mich., 1971. Bar: Ill. 1971, U.S. Dist. Ct. (no. dist.) Ill. 1971, U.S. Ct. Appeals (7th cir.) 1977, U.S. Ct. Appeals (4th cir.) 1984, U.S. Dist. Ct. (cen. dist.) Ill. 1984. Clk. Ill. Supreme Ct., Chgo., 1971-72; ptnr., assoc. Isham, Lincoln & Beale, Chgo., 1972-87; ptnr. Mayer, Brown & Platt, Chgo., 198-97, Hopkins & Sutter, Chgo., 1997—; chmn. ABA Nat. Inst. on Ins. Co. Insolvency, Boston, 1986; co-chmn. ABA Nat. Inst. on Internat. Reins.: Collections and Insolvency, N.Y., 1988; chmn. ABA Nat. Inst. on Life Ins. Co. Insolvency, Chgo., 1993; spkr. in field. Editor: Law and Practice of Insurance Company Insolvency, 1986, Law and Practice of Life Insurer Insolvency, 1993; co-editor: Law and Practice of International Reinsurance Collections and Insolvency, 1988; contbr. articles to profl. jours. Mem. ABA (chair Nat. Inst. on Life Insurer Insolvency 1993), Chgo. Bar Assn., Legal Club of Chgo. Insurance, Federal civil litigation. Home: 2100 N Lincoln Park W Chicago IL 60614-4648 Office: Hopkins & Sutter Three First National Plz Chicago IL 60602-4205

**SPECTOR, MARTIN WOLF,** lawyer, business executive; b. Phila., 1938. BA, Pa. State U., 1959; JD, U. Pa., 1962. Bar: Pa. 1962. Judge U.S. Dist. Ct., until 1967; asst. gen. counsel ARA Services, Phila., assoc. gen. counsel, 1969-76, v.p., 1976-83, gen. counsel, 1983—, formerly sr. v.p.; exec. v.p. ARAMARK, Phila., 1985—. Served to lt. USN, 1953-56. Office: ARAMARK 1101 Market St Ste 45 Philadelphia PA 19107-2988

**SPECTOR, PHILLIP LOUIS,** lawyer; b. L.A., July 15, 1950; s. Everett L. Spector and Rebecca (Horn) Newman; m. Carole Sue Lebbin, May 11, 1980; children: Adam, David. Student, U. Birmingham, Eng., 1970-71; BA with highest honors, U. Calif., Santa Barbara, 1972; M in Pub. Policy, Harvard U., 1976, JD magna cum laude, 1976. Bar: Calif. 1976, D.C. 1978, U.S. Ct. Appeals (D.C. cir.) 1983, U.S. Supreme Ct. 1983, U.S. Dist. Ct. D.C. 1985. Law clk. U.S. Ct. Appeals (2d cir.), Brattleboro, Vt., 1976-77; law clk. to U.S. Supreme Ct., Washington, 1977-78; assoc. asst. to Pres. U.S., Washington, 1978-80; assoc. Verner, Liipfert, Bernhard & McPherson, Washington, 1980-83; ptnr. Goldberg & Spector, Washington, 1983-92, Paul, Weiss, Rifkind, Wharton & Garrison, Washington, 1992—; cons. U.S. exec. br. Close-Up Found., Alexandria, Va., 1980—. Co-author: Communications Law and Practice, 1995, Communications and Techology Alliances: Business and Legal Issues, 1996; mem. bd. editors Multimedia & Internet Strategist; contbr. articles to profl. jours. Mem. Coun. on Fgn. Rels., N.Y.C., 1980-85; moot ct. judge Nat. Assn. Attys. Gen., Washington, 1987—; adviser Dem. caucus U.S. Ho. Reps., Washington, 1981-83; speechwriter, podium prodr. Dem. Nat. Convs., N.Y.C., 1980, Phila., 1982, San Francisco, 1984, Atlanta, 1988, N.Y.C., 1992, Chgo., 1996. Recipient Disting. Achievement in Pub. Svc. Medal U. Calif., Santa Barbara, 1981, Close-Up Found. awards Via Satellite Mag., Vol. Recognition award Nat. Assn. Attys. Gen., 1993; named Leading Satellite Specialist in Washington, European Counsel, 1998. Mem. ABA (chair internat. comm. law com.), Fed. Communications Bar Assn., Bethesda Country Club, Wintergreen Ptnrs., Phi Beta Kappa. Jewish. Communications, Private international, Legislative. Office: Paul Weiss Rifkind Wharton & Garrison 1615 L St NW Ste 1300 Washington DC 20036-5694

**SPECTOR, ROSE,** state supreme court justice. BA, Columbia U.; JD, St. Mary's Sch. Law, 1965. Judge County Ct. at Law 5, 1975-80, 131st Dist. Ct., 1981-92; justice Tex. Supreme Ct., 1993-98; atty. Bickerstaff, Heath, Pollan, Kever & McDaniel, L.L.P., Austin, Tex., 1998—. Office: Bickerstaff Heath et al 1700 Frost Bank Plz 816 Congress Ave Austin TX 78701-2442

**SPEER, JOHN ELMER,** paralegal, reporter; b. Conrad, Mont., Mar. 19, 1956; s. Elmer Constant and Mildred Saphronia (LaBelle) S.; m. Sharron D. Knotts, May 23, 1982 (div. Mar. 1986); 1 child, Jeremy Keith; 1 foster child, Casey. Paralegal assoc., Coll. of Great Falls, Mont., 1994; BS in paralegal studies, U. of Great Falls, Mont., 1999. Bar: Mont. 1996; cert. scuba diver. Farmer Valier, Mont., 1956-73; janitor Shelby (Mont.) pub. schs., 1974-75; freelance news reporter Sta. KSEN, Shelby, 1980—, various TV stas., newspapers, Great Falls, 1980-90; office cleaner Parkdale Housing Authority, Great Falls, 1990-95; freelance paralegal, Great Falls, 1993—; law clk., paralegal Mont. State Dist. Judge Thomas McKittrick, Great Falls, 1993; rschr. line-up identification appeal binder to U.S. Supreme Ct., 1993; trial assistance atty. Chas. Joslyn, spring 1996. Contbr. victim-witness assistance program operating manual, 1992. Counselor and adv. Victim-Witness Assistance Svcs., Great Falls, 1991-93. Mem. Mont. Big Sky Paralegal Assn., Am. Counseling Assn., Brain Injury Assn. of Mont. (chpt. v.p. 1997). Jehovah's Witness. Avocations: hiking, fishing, cooking, travel, swimming. Address: PO Box 206 Great Falls MT 59403-0206

**SPELFOGEL, SCOTT DAVID,** lawyer; b. Boston, Nov. 27, 1960; s. Evan. J. and Beverly (Kolenberg) S. BS, Boston U., 1982; JD, Syracuse U., 1985; LLM, Boston U., 1990. Bar: Mass. 1985, N.Y. 1986, U.S. Dist. Ct. (no. dist.) N.Y. 1986, U.S. Dist. Ct. Mass. 1987; lic. real estate broker, Mass., 1987. Assoc. Jeffrey M. McCrone, P.C., Syracuse, N.Y., 1985-87, Tatarian Law Offices, Boston, 1987-88; asst. gen. counsel The Berkshire Group, Boston, 1988-90, v.p., asst. gen. counsel, 1990-96, v.p., gen. counsel, 1996, sr. v.p., gen. counsel, 1997—. Mem. ABA, Am. Corp. Counsel Assn., Boston Bar Assn., N.Y. Bar Assn., Mass. Bar Assn. General civil litigation, General corporate, Real property. Home: 27 Sentry Hill Rd Sharon MA 02067-1521 Office: The Berkshire Group 1 Beacon St Ste 1500 Boston MA 02108-3116

**SPELLMAN, THOMAS JOSEPH, JR.,** lawyer; b. Glen Cove, N.Y., Nov. 11, 1938; s. Thomas J. and Martha H. (Erwin) S.; m. Margaret Mary Barth, June 23, 1962; children: Thomas Joseph, Kevin M., Maura N. BS, Fordham U., 1960, JD, 1965. Bar: N.Y. 1966, U.S. Dist. Ct. (so. and ea. dist.) N.Y. 1968, U.S. Ct. Appeals (2nd cir.) 1980, U.S. Supreme Ct. 1981. Staff atty. Allstate Ins. Co., N.Y.C., 1966-69; trial atty. Hartford Ins. Co., Hauppauge, N.Y., 1969-71; ptnr. Wheller & Spellman, Farmingville, N.Y., 1971-76, Devitt Spellman Barrett Callahan Leyden & Kenney LLP and predecessors, Smithtown, N.Y., 1976—; mem. grievance com. 10th Jud. Dist., Westbury, N.Y., 1984-92. Capt. USAR, 1960-68. Fellow Am. Bar Found., N.Y. Bar Found; mem. Suffolk County Bar Assn. (bd. dirs., sec.-treas., v.p. 1982, pres. 1992-93), N.Y. State Bar Assn. (Ho. of Dels. 1989—, nominating com. 1992-93, v.p. 1996-98). Personal injury, Insurance, General civil litigation. Home: 8 Highwoods Ct Saint James NY 11780-9610 Office: Devitt Spellman et al 50 Route 111 Ste 314 Smithtown NY 11787-3700

**SPELTS, RICHARD JOHN,** lawyer; b. Yuma, Colo., July 29, 1939; s. Richard Clark and Barbara Eve (Pletcher) S.; children: Melinda, Meghan, Richard John Jr.; m. Gayle Merves, Nov. 14, 1992. BS cum laude, U. Colo., 1961, JD, 1964. Bar: Colo. 1964, U.S. Dist. Ct. Colo. 1964, U.S. Supreme Ct. 1968, U.S. Ct. Appeals (10th cir.) 1970, U.S. Dist. Ct. (ea. dist.) Mich. 1986. With Ford Motor Internat., Cologne, Germany, 1964-65; legis. counsel to U.S. Senator, 89th and 90th Congresses, 1967-68; minority counsel U.S. Senate Subcom., 90th and 91st Congresses, 1968-70; asst. U.S. atty., 1st asst. U.S. atty. Fed. Dist. of Colo., 1970-77; pvt. practice Denver, 1977-89; risk mgr. sheriff's dept. Jefferson County, Golden, Colo., 1990-91; owner Video Prodn. for Lawyers, 1991—. Selected for Leadership Denver, 1977; recipient cert. for outstanding contbns. in drug law enforcement U.S. Drug Enforcement Adminstrn., 1977, spl. commendation for criminal prosecution U.S. Dept. Justice, 1973, spl. commendation for civil prosecution U.S. Dept. Justice, 1976. Mem. Fed. Bar Assn. (chmn. govt. torts seminar 1980), Colo. Bar Assn. (bd. govs. 1976-78), Denver Bar Assn., Colo. Trial Lawyers Assn., Denver Law Club, Order of Coif. Republican. Methodist. Federal civil litigation, State civil litigation, Criminal. Home and Office: 9671 Brook Hill Ct Littleton CO 80124-5431

**SPENCE, CRAIG H.,** lawyer; b. El Paso, Tex., Jan. 17, 1932; s. William and Beulah B. S.; m. Mary Jean, Sept. 29, 1962; children: Craig Jr., Michael, Douglas. BS, U.S. Mil. Acad., 1954; MS, Ga. Tech., 1965; JD, St. Mary's U., 1977. Bar: Tex. 1977. With U.S. Army, 1954-75. Avocations: golf, sports, travel. Family and matrimonial, General practice, Personal injury. Office: 6515 Broadway St San Antonio TX 78209-4564

**SPENCE, GERALD LEONARD,** lawyer, writer; b. Laramie, Wyo., Jan. 8, 1929; s. Gerald M. and Esther Sophie (Pfleeger) S.; m. Anna Wilson, June 20, 1947; children: Kip, Kerry, Kent, Katy; m. LaNelle Hampton Peterson, Nov. 18, 1969. BSL, U. Wyo., 1949, LLB, 1952, LLD (hon.), 1990. Bar: Wyo. 1952, U.S. Ct. Claims 1952, U.S. Supreme Ct. 1982. Sole practice Riverton, Wyo., 1952-54; county and pros. atty. Fremont County, Wyo., 1954-62; ptnr. various law firms, Riverton and Casper, Wyo., 1962-78; sr. ptnr. Spence, Moriarity & Schuster, Jackson, Wyo., 1978—; lectr. legal orgns. and law schs. Author: (with others) Gunning for Justice, 1982, Of Murder and Madness, 1983, Trial by Fire, 1986, With Justice for None, 1989, From Freedom to Slavery, 1993, How To Argue and Win Every Time, 1995, The Making of a Country Lawyer, 1996, O.J.: The Last Word, 1997, Give Me Liberty, 1998. Mem. ABA, Wyo. Bar Assn., Wyo. Trial Lawyers Assn., Assn. Trial Lawyers Am., Nat. Assn. Criminal Def. Lawyers. Criminal, Personal injury, Product liability. Office: Spence Moriarity & Schuster PO Box 548 Jackson WY 83001-0548

**SPENCE, HELEN JEAN,** lawyer; b. Wiesbaden, Germany, July 13, 1965; d. Clarence L. and Brooke B. Bishop; m. Keith R. Spence, Nov. 28, 1992; 1 child, Michael Keith. BA, Radford U., 1987; JD, Washington & Lee U., 1990. Bar: Va. 1990, U.S. Dist. Ct. (we. dist.) Va. 1990, U.S. Ct. Appeals (4th cir.) 1990. Sec. Radford (Va.) U. Alumni Affairs, 1986-87; clk. Black, Menk, Nolen & Gaines, Staunton, Va., 1989-90; assoc. Gail Cook Devilbiss, Esq., Radford, 1990-91; pvt. practice Radford, 1991-92; ptnr. Beller & Spence, P.C., Christiansburg, Va., 1992—; qualified guardian ad litem, 1997—. Mem. ethics com. New River Valley Hospice, Christiansburg, 1996-98; bd. dirs. Futureworks, Christiansburg, 1995, Legal Aid Soc. New River Valley, Christiansburg,1992-95; publicity chair Christiansburg Presbyn. Ch., 1992. Radford U. Found. scholar, 1983. Mem. ABA, Va. State Bar, Montgomery-Floyd-Radford Bar Assn. (v.p. 1992). Republican. Labor, Juvenile, Estate planning. Office: Beller & Spence PC 114 N Franklin St Christiansburg VA 24073-2953

**SPENCE, HOWARD TEE DEVON,** judge, arbitrator, lawyer, consultant, insurance executive, government official; b. Corinth, Miss., Sept. 29, 1949; s. T. P. and Dorothy M.S.; m. Diane Earl Williams, Feb. 26, 1977 (div. June 1986); children: Derek, Tina, Steven. BA, Mich. State U., 1970, M in Criminal Justice Adminstrn., 1975, M in Labor-Indsl. Relations, 1981, MBA, 1983; JD, U. Mich., 1976, M in Pub. Adminstrn., 1977. Bar: Mich. 1976, U.S. Dist. Ct. (ea. dist.) Mich. 1976, U.S. Ct. Appeals (6th cir.) 1976, U.S. Supreme Ct. 1980, U.S. Dist. Ct. (we. dist.) Mich. 1986; cert. ins. examiner. Counselor State Prison of So. Mich., Jackson, 1971-76; personnel adminstr. Mich. Dept. Commerce, Lansing, 1976-77; asst. dir. Mich. Pub. Service Commn., Lansing, 1977-78; dep. ins. commr. Mich. Ins. Bur., Lansing, 1978-92; ptnr., cons. Spence & Assocs., Lansing, 1983—; adminstrv. law judge State of Mich., Lansing, 1992—; arbitrator U.S. Dist. Ct. (we. dist.) Mich., Grand Rapids, 1986, Mich. Employment Rels. Commn., 1992—; adj. law prof. Thomas M. Cooley Law Sch., Lansing, 1977-80; adj. instr. Nat. Jud. Coll., Reno, 1993—; presenter in field. Author short stories. Sec., v.p. Ingham County Housing Commn., Okemos, Mich., 1985-90; bd. dirs. Econ. Devel. Corp. City of Lansing, 1981-85. Mem. ABA (editor in chief NCALJ Newsletter, 1998—), Mich. Bar Assn. (legal edn. com.), Nat. Bar Assn., Assn. Black Judges Mich., Mich. Assn. Adminstrv. Law Judges (pres. 1998), Nat. Conf. Adminstrv. Law Judges, Wolverine Bar Assn., Black Lawyers Assn., Ins. Regulatory Examiners Soc. (bd. dirs., nat. pres. 1990-91), NAACP (life), Blue Key, Alpha Phi Alpha, Kappa Delta Lambda (pres., chmn. bd. dirs., adminstr. Project Alpha, Edn. Found. Inc.). Mem. Ch. of Christ. Club: Renaissance, Economic (Detroit). Avocations: tennis, racquetball, camping, dancing. Home: 1637 Willow Creek Dr Lansing MI 48917-9643

**SPENCE, STEVEN ALLEN,** lawyer, mediator; b. Urbana, Ill., Dec. 22, 1954; s. Milton Edwin and Mary Beth S.; children: Dustin Kyle, Shawn Philip, Mark Christopher. Student, U. Stasburg (France), 1975-76; BA, Purdue U., 1977; JD, Ind. U., 1980. Bar: Ind. 1980. Intern Magistrate Faulkner, Ind., 1978-79, Marion County Prosecutor, Indpls., 1979-80; assoc. Duvall Tabbert Lally & Newton, Indpls., 1980-81; deputy atty. gen. Ind. Attorney General's Ofc., Indpls., 1981-83; pub. defender Marion County Pub. Defender Agy., Indpls., 1985-89, 1992-96; ptnr. Arany & Spence, Indpls., 1989-90, Buehler & Spence, Indpls., 1990-92; pvt. practice Indpls., 1992—. Republican Precinct committeeman Republican party, Indpls., 1979-92; chmn. trustee United Methodist Ch., Indpls., 1996-98. Mem. ITLA, Ind. State Bar Assn., Ind. Assn. Mediators (pres. 1996-97), Indpls. Bar Assn., Kiwanis, Phi Beta Kappa. Republican. United Methodist. Alternative dispute resolution, Personal injury, Family and matrimonial. Home: 8412 Springview Dr Indianapolis IN 46260-2309 Office: 9000 Keystone Xing Ste 1000 Indianapolis IN 46240-2140

**SPENCE, W. ROSS,** lawyer; b. Houston, Mar. 7, 1960; s. William C. and Nancy N. Spence; m. Ette V. Spence, Mar. 27, 1993; children: Clay Walker, Francis Martin. BA, U. Va., 1982; JD, U. Tex., 1986. Bar: Tex., U.S. Dist. Ct. (so. and no. dists.) Tex., U.S. Ct. Appeals (5th cir.), U.S. Claims Ct. Assoc. Andrews & Kurth, Houston, 1986-93; ptnr. Crady Jewett & McCulley LLP, Houston, 1993—. Mem. Houston Bar Assn. (chair lit. sect.), Garland Walker Inn of Ct., Houston Bar Found. Republican. Presbyterian. Federal civil litigation, General civil litigation, State civil litigation. Home: 4582 Elm St Bellaire TX 77401-3718 Office: Crady Jewett McCulley LLP 909 Fannin St Houston TX 77010-1001

**SPENCER, ANTHONY GEORGE,** lawyer; b. Fredericksburg, Va., Sept. 24, 1958; s. Frederick John and Norma (Spector) S. BA, U. Va., 1980, JD, 1983. Bar: N.Y. 1984, Va. 1990, U.S. Dist. Ct. (ea. dist.) Va. 1991, U.S. Ct. Appeals 1991, U.S. Tax Ct. 1994. Atty. Cabell, Kennedy & French, N.Y.C., 1983-84, Webster & Sheffield, N.Y.C., 1984-86; sole practitioner N.Y.C., 1986-88; atty. Morchower, Luxton & Whaley, Richmond, Va., 1990—. Editor-in-chief Va. Tax Rev., 1982-83; contbr. articles to profl. jours. Appellate, Criminal, General civil litigation. Office: Morchower Luxton & Whaley Nine E Franklin St Richmond VA 23219

**SPENCER, BILLIE JANE,** lawyer; b. Caro, Mich., Sept. 16, 1949; d. William Norman and Jane Isabel (Putnam) S. AB in Econs., U. Miami, Coral Gables, Fla., 1971, LLM in Tax, 1980; JD, U. Fla., Gainesville, 1973; course cert. St. Catherine's Coll., Oxford U., 1973; grad. with highest distinction, Naval War Coll., Washington, 1988; cert. landscaping mgmt., Tidewater C.C., Chesapeake, Va., 1997. Bar: Fla., Calif. Assoc. Frates Floyd, et. al., Miami, Fla., 1973-74; commd. lt. (j.g.) USNR, 1974, advanced through grades to comdr., 1988; judge advocate USNR, Subic Bay, Pensacola, 1975-78; sole practice San Francisco, and Stuart, Fla., 1978-85; asst. staff judge advocate USNR, Lemoore, Calif., 1982-83; DOD liaison USNR, Washington, 1985-88; civilian atty. USN, Mechanicsburg, Pa., 1988-90; counsel Navy Pub. Works Ctr. USN, Norfolk, Va., 1990-93; asst. counsel Atlantic divsn. Naval Facilities Engring. Comd., USN, Norfolk, 1993-98; counsel Naval Engring. Field Activity Mediterranean, Naples, Italy, 1998—; instr. econs. Fla. Inst. Tech., Jensen Beach, 1984-85; litigation cons. Castle & Cooke, Inc., San Francisco, 1979-83; clk. Ehrlichmann Watergate Trial team, Washington, 1974; del. state conf. on small bus., 1982; adj. analyst 6th quadrennial rev. of military compensation, 1987-88. Avocations: cello, painting, reading, gardening.

**SPENCER, DAVID ERIC,** lawyer; b. N.Y.C., Oct. 14, 1941; s. Harold and Sara (Halpern) S.; m. Nadja de Mogalhaes, Jan. 14, 1976; 1 child, David Mogalhaes Spencer. BA, Harvard U., 1963, JD, 1968; LLM in Taxation, NYU, 1973. Bar: N.Y., 1968. Atty. Fried, Frank Harris Shriner Jacobson, N.Y.C., 1969-72, Citicorp-Citibank, N.Y.C., 1974-79; pvt. practice N.Y.C., 1979—. Author: Student Politics in Latin America, 1985; mem. editl. bd. Internat. Fin. Law Rev., 1985—, Jour. Internat. Taxation, 1990—; contbr. articles to profl. jours. Dir. v.p. Brazilian Am. C. of C., N.Y.C., 1980-98. Democrat. Banking, Corporate taxation, General corporate. Home: 860 United Nations Plz Apt 9E New York NY 10017-1815 Office: Ste 4019 866 United Nations Plz New York NY 10017-1822

**SPENCER, DAVID JAMES,** lawyer; b. Altadena, Calif., June 23, 1943; s. Dorcy James and Dorothy Estelle (Pingry) S.; m. Donna Rae Blair, Aug. 22, 1965; children: Daniel, Matthew. BA, Rocky Mountain Coll., 1965; JD, Yale U., 1968. Bar: Minn. 1968, U.S. Dist. Ct. Minn. 1968, U.S. Ct. Appeals (8th cir.) 1970. Mem. firm Briggs and Morgan, P.A., Mpls. and St. Paul, 1968—. Contbg. author 10 William Mitchell Law Rev., 1984; contbr. articles to profl. jours. Trustee Rocky Mountain Coll., Billings, Mont., 1980—; bd. dirs. Reentry Svcs., Inc., 1993—, River Valley Arts Coun., 1996—, Stillwater Area Arts Ctr. Alliance, 1998—, Homeward Bound, Inc.; pres., bd. dirs. St. Croix Friends of Arts, Stillwater, Minn., 1981-84; bd. dirs. Valley Chamber Chorale, Stillwater, 1989-92; v.p. Minn. Jaycees, St. Paul, 1974; elder Presbyn. Ch. Recipient Silver Key St. Paul Jaycees, 1974; Disting. Svc. award Rocky Mountain Coll., 1981, Outstanding Svc. award, 1988, Disting. Achievement award, 1992. Fellow Am. Coll. Real Estate Lawyers; mem. ABA, Minn. Bar Assn., Hennepin County Bar Assn., Stillwater Country Club, Mpls. Athletic Club, Stillwater Sunrise Rotary Club (bd. dirs. 1997-99). Presbyterian. Avocations: trout fishing, golf, singing. Real property, Landlord-tenant, Condemnation. Home: 9987 Arcola Ct N Stillwater MN 55082-9523 Office: Briggs & Morgan 2200 First Nat Bank Bldg 332 Minnesota St Ste W2200 Saint Paul MN 55101-1396

**SPENCER, JAMES R.,** federal judge; b. 1949. BA magna cum laude, Clark Coll., 1971; JD, Harvard U., 1974, MDiv, 1985. Staff atty. Atlanta Legal Aid Soc., 1974-75; asst. U.S. atty. Washington, 1978, U.S. Dist. Ct. (ea. dist.) Va., 1983; judge U.S. Dist. Ct. (ea. dist.) Va., Richmond, 1986—; adj. prof. law U. Va., 1987—. Capt. JAGC, U.S.Army, 1975-78, res. 1981-86. Mem. ABA, Nat. Bar Assn., State Bar Ga., D.C. Bar, Va. State Bar, Richmond Bar Assn., Washington Bar Assn., Old Dominion Bar Assn., Omega Psi Phi, Sigma Pi Phi. Office: US Courthouse 1000 E Main St Richmond VA 23219-3525*

**SPENCER, SCOTT W.,** lawyer; b. Dayton, Ohio, Oct. 17, 1956; s. Eugene Willis and Evelyn Lucille (Oehrtman) S.; m. Maria de Lourdes Lavilla, Dec. 29, 1983; children: Leah Teresa, Hannah Caitlin. BA, Capital U., 1979, JD, 1984. Bar: Ohio 1985, U.S. Dist. Ct. (so. dist.) Ohio 1985, U.S. Dist. Ct. (no. dist.) Ohio 1986, U.S. Ct. Appeals (6th cir.) 1986, U.S. Supreme Ct. 1990. Intern U.S. Senate Steering Com., Washington, 1979-80; press sec. Rep. Caucus Ohio Ho. of Reps., Columbus, 1980-82, counsel to chmn. elections, fin. instns. and ins. com., adminstrv. aide, 1982-85; assoc. Huffman, Landis, Weaks & Lopez, Troy, Ohio, 1985, Brownfield, Cramer & Lewis, Columbus, 1985-87; ptnr. Lewis & Spencer, Columbus, 1987-95; founding prin., pres. Scott W. Spencer Co., L.P.A., 1996—; trustee Columbus Amateur Athletic Assn., 1987—; gen. counsel Ohio Rep. Party, 1992-95. Mem. ABA, Nat. Soc. Profl. Ins. Investigators, Internat. Assn. Arson Investigators, Rep. Nat. Lawyers Assn. (bd. dirs. 1994—), Ohio Bar Assn., Columbus Bar Assn. (pres. professionalism and admissions coms. 1989—), Columbus Claims Assn., Jaycees (v.p. mgmt., membership 1996—). Lutheran. Avocations: football, skiing, autoracing, politics. Appellate, Federal civil litigation, General corporate. Home: 5770 Hallridge Cir Columbus OH 43232-6493

**SPERBER, DAVID SOL,** lawyer; b. July 28, 1939; m. Zoila Luz Martinez, Dec. 27, 1986; children: Toby, Elliot, Joshua, Mira, Natalie, Emily, Benjamin. AB in Polit. Sci., UCLA, 1961, JD, 1964. Bar: Calif. 1965, U.S. Dist. Ct. Calif. 1965, U.S. Ct. Appeals (9th cir.) 1966, U.S. Supreme Ct. 1973, U.S. Dist. Ct. (5th cir.) 1978. Dep. atty. gen. Atty. Gen.'s Office, State of Calif., 1964-68; pvt. practice Encino, Calif., 1968—. Mem. UCLA Law Rev. Mem. County Dem. Ctrl. Com., L.A., 1968-69; mem. parole aide program Jr. Barristers, 1972-73; trustee Hillel Hebrew Acad.; assoc. chmn. met. divsn. United Jewish Welfare Fund; chmn. legal com. Yeshiva U. Holocaust Ctr.; pres. bd. trustees Hear Ctr. Haynes scholar; named Man of Yr., CHABAD, 1986. Mem. Calif. Trial Lawyers Assn. (ins. com.), L.A. Trial Lawyers Assn., San Fernando Valley Criminal Bar Assn., L.A. County Bar Assn. (criminal law and procedure sect., real property sect.), Lawyers Club (spkrs. bur.). General civil litigation, Insurance. Office: 15910 Ventura Blvd Ste 1525 Encino CA 91436-2830

**SPERBER, JOSEPH JOHN, IV,** lawyer; b. Glen Cove, N.Y., June 3, 1968; s. Joseph J. III and Valerie Ann (Quandt) S. BSBA in Fin. and Internat. Mgmt., Georgetown U., 1990, JD, 1994. Bar: N.Y. 1995, U.S. Dist. Ct. (so. and ea. dists.) N.Y. 1996, U.S. Ct. Appeals (2d cir.) 1997, U.S. Supreme Ct. 1998. Asst. dist. atty. Office Dist. Atty. Bronx County, Bronx, N.Y., 1994-98; assoc. Kelley Drye & Warren LLP, N.Y.C., 1998—. Mem. ABA, N.Y. State Bar Assn., Assn. Bar City N.Y., Georgetown Club N.Y., N.Y. Athletic Club. Avocations: running, sailing, swimming, cycling. General civil litigation, Federal civil litigation, State civil litigation. Office: Kelley Drye & Warren LLP 101 Park Ave New York NY 10178-0002

**SPERLING, ALLAN GEORGE,** lawyer; b. N.Y.C., Dec. 10, 1942; s. Saul and Gertrude (Lober) S.; m. Susan Kelz, 1965 (div. 1999); children: Matthew Laurence, Stuart Kelz, Jane Kendra. Bar: N.Y. 1969, U.S. Ct. Appeals (2d cir.) 1975. Law clk. to presiding justice U.S. Dist Ct., New Haven, 1967-68; assoc. Cleary, Gottlieb, Steen & Hamilton, N.Y.C., 1968-75, ptnr., 1976—. Editor Yale Law Jour. Bd. dirs. Vol. Lawyers for the Arts, 1998—; chmn. bd. Merce Cunningham Dance Found., N.Y.C., 1992-98, vice-chmn., 1985-92; chmn. bd. Rye (N.Y.) Arts Ctr. Inc., 1985-88, bd. dirs., 1990-94; bd. chmn. Friends of the Neuberger Mus. of Art, Purchase, N.Y., 1997—, bd. dirs. Mem. ABA, N.Y. State Bar Assn., Order of Coif, Phi Beta Kappa. Securities, Finance, General corporate. Home: 154 Kirby Ln Rye NY 10580-4320 Office: Cleary Gottlieb Steen & Hamilton 1 Liberty Plz Fl 38 New York NY 10006-1470

**SPERLING, JOY HARMON,** lawyer; b. Bklyn., Mar. 25, 1961; d. Aaron and Lenore Harmon; m. Norman Jay Sperling, July 1, 1984; 1 child, Daniel Steven. BA cum laude, Rutgers U., 1983, JD, 1986. Bar: N.J. 1986, U.S. Dist. Ct N.J. 1986, U.S. Ct. Appeals (3d cir.) 1995, U.S. Dist. Ct. (so. dist.) N.Y. 1998. Clk. to Hon W.P. Diana, Assignment and Chancery Judge Superior Ct. of N.J., Somerville, N.J., 1986-87; assoc. Pitney, Hardin, Kipp & Szuch, Morristown, N.J., 1987-95, ptnr., 1996—. Mem. ABA, N.J. State Bar Assn., Phi Beta Kappa. General civil litigation, Consumer commercial. Home: 11 Argonne Farm Dr Bridgewater NJ 08807-1480 Office: Pitney Hardin Kipp & Szuch PO Box 1945 Morristown NJ 07962-1945

**SPERLING, MACK,** lawyer; b. N.Y.C., Sept. 23, 1958; s. Robert J. and Florence Edith (Goldstein) S.; m. Ruth Ellen Rubin, Jan. 17, 1987; children: Juliet, Madeline, Dashiell. BS cum laude, Union Coll., 1980; JD with honors, U. N.C., 1983. Bar: N.C. 1983, Md. 1996, U.S. Ct. Appeals (4th cir.) 1984, U.S. Supreme Ct. 1992. Law clk. to Hon. Frank W. Bullock Jr. U.S. Dist. Ct. (mid. dist.) N.C., Greensboro, 1983-84; assoc. Brooks, Pierce, McLendon, Humphrey & Leonard, L.L.P., Greensboro, 1984-89, ptnr., 1989—; instr. legal writing U. N.C.-Chapel Hill Law Sch., 1984-91. Mem. N.C. Gen. Statutes Commn., Raleigh, 1992-98; v.p. B'nai Shalom Synagogue, Inc., Greensboro, 1996-98. Mem. Order of Coif. General civil litigation, Labor, Trademark and copyright. Office: Brooks Pierce et al 230 N Elm St Ste 2000 Greensboro NC 27401-2414

**SPERO, C. MICHAEL,** lawyer; b. N.Y.C., Oct. 3, 1936; s. Carl Mony and Mildred (Wolfe) S.; m. Joan Edelman, Nov. 9, 1969; children: Jason, Ben. BA, Amherst Coll., 1958; LLB, Yale U., 1961. Bar: N.Y. 1961, Fla. 1976. Assoc. Hughes, Hubbard & Reed, N.Y.C., 1961-64, Stroock & Stroock & Lovan, N.Y.C., 1964-70; ptnr. Wien, Malkin & Bettey, N.Y.C., 1970-96, Salans, Hertzfeld, Heilbronn, Christy & Viener, N.Y.C., 1996—. Bd. dirs., past pres., advisor Stanley Isaacs Neighborhood Ctr., Lincoln Ctr., Amherst Coll., United Jewish Appeal-Fedn., N.Y.C., 1964—. With U.S. Army, 1962. Mem. Frenchman's Creek Golf Club. Estate planning, Probate, Estate taxation. Home: 1165 Park Ave New York NY 10128-1210 Office: Salans Hertzfeld Heilbronn Christy & Viener 620 5th Ave New York NY 10020-2402

**SPERO, KEITH ERWIN,** lawyer; b. Cleve., Aug. 21, 1933; s. Milton D. and Yetta (Silverstein) S.; m. Carol Kohn, July 4, 1957 (div. 1974); children: Alana, Scott, Susan; m. 2d, Karen Weaver, Dec. 28, 1975. BA, Western Res. U. 1954, LLB, 1956. Bar: Ohio 1956. Assoc. Sindell, Sindell & Bourne, Cleve., 1956-57, Sindell, Sindell, Bourne, Markus, Cleve., 1960-64; ptnr. Sindell, Sindell, Bourne, Markus, Stern & Spero, Cleve., 1964-74, Spero & Rosenfield, Cleve., 1974-76, Spero, Rosenfeld & Bourne, L.P.A., Cleve., 1977-79, Spero & Rosenfield Co. L.P.A., 1979—; tchr. bus. law U. Md. overseas div., Eng., 1958-59; lectr. Case-Western Res. U., 1965-69; instr.; nat. panel arbitrators Am. Arbitration Assn. Trustee Western Res. Hist. Soc., 1984—, exec. com., 1992—, v.p., chmn. libr. display and collections com., 1992-95, chmn. chmn. history mus. com., 1995—. 1st. lt. JAGC, USAF, 1957-60; capt. Res., 1960-70. Fellow Am. Acad. Matrimonial Lawyers; mem. ABA, Ohio Bar Assn., Cleve. Bar Assn., Cuyahoga County Bar Assn., Ohio Acad. Trial Lawyers (pres. 1970-71), Assn. Trial Lawyers Am. (state committeeman 1971-75, bd. govs. 1975-79, sec. family law litigation sect. 1975-76, vice-chmn. 1976-77, chmn. 1977-79), Am. Bd. Trial Advs., Order of Coif, Cleve. Racquet Club, Hawthorne Valley Country Club, Masons, Dugway Creek Yacht Club (commodore 1985-87), Phi Beta Kappa, Zeta Beta Tau, Tau Epsilon Rho. Jewish (trustee, v.p. congregation 1972-78). Author: The Spero Divorce Folio, 1966, Hospital Liability for Acts of Profellsional Negligence, 1979. State civil litigation, Personal injury, Family and matrimonial. Office: 440 Leader Bldg E 6th and Superior Cleveland OH 44114-1214

**SPERO, MORTON BERTRAM,** lawyer; b. N.Y.C., Dec. 6, 1920; s. Adolph and Julia (Strasburger) S.; m. Louise Thacker, May 1, 1943; children: Donald S., Carol S. Flynn. BA, U. Va., 1942, LLB, 1946. Bar: Va. 1946, U.S. Supreme Ct. 1961. Mem. legal staff NLRB, Washington, 1946-48; sole practice Petersburg, Va., 1948-70, 85—; sr. ptnr. Spero & Levinson, Petersburg, 1970-75, Spero & Diehl, Petersburg, 1975-85; chmn. The Community Bank, Petersburg, 1976-79, dir., 1976-91. Chmn. United Fund Drive, 1960, bd. dirs., 1999—; pres. Dist. IV Petersburg Coun. Social Welfare, Southside Sheltered Workshop, 1965, pres. Congregation B'rith Achim, 1973. Served to lt. USNR, 1943-45. Recipient Outstanding Mem. award Petersburg chpt. B'nai B'rith, 1966; Svc. to Law Enforcement award Petersburg Police Dept., 1965. Fellow Am. Acad. Matrimonial Lawyers; mem. Va. Bar Assn., Petersburg Bar Assn. (pres. 1981-82), Va. State Bar (coun. 1981-84, chmn. criminal law sect. 1972, chmn. family law sect. 1979, bd. dirs. litigation sect. 1983-86, Lifetime Achievement award for family law sect. 1995), Va. Trial Lawyers Assn. (v.p. 1972), Civitan Club (hon.), Rotary, Elks (exalted ruler 1968). Democrat. Jewish. Fax: 804-733-0157. State civil litigation, Family and matrimonial, Criminal. Home and Office: 9706 Bunker Ct Petersburg VA 23805-9125

**SPERRY, MARTIN JAY,** lawyer; b. Troy, N.Y., May 15, 1947; s. Raymond Leon and Selma (Jenkins) S.; m. Mary Jane Lee-Sperry, NOv. 25, 1993; children from a previous marriage: Jana, Douglas, Jill. BSBA, U. Fla., 1969, JD, 1971. Bar: Fla. 1972, U.S. Dist. Ct. (mid. dist.) Fla. 1972, U.S. Dist. Ct. (so. dist.) Fla. 1974, U.S. Supreme Ct. 1976, N.Y. 1983. Sr. law clk. to chief judge U.S. Dist. Ct. (mid. dist.) Fla., Orlando, 1972-74; ptnr. Carey, Dwyer, Cole, Selwood & Bernard, Ft. Lauderdale, Fla., 1974-78, Krathen & Sperry, Ft. Lauderdale, Fla., 1978-84, Selwood & Sperry, Ft. Lauderdale, Fla., 1984-85, Sperry, Shapiro & Kashi, Ft. Lauderdale, Fla., 1985—; mem. Fourth Dist. Ct. Appeals Judicial Nominating Commn. Contbg. author: Casebook of Florida Constitutional Law, 1971. Served as capt. U.S. Army Reserves, 1969-77. Mem. Acad. Fla. Trial Lawyers (diplomate), Assn. Trial Lawyers Am. (sustaining), N.Y. State Bar Assn., Fla. Bar Assn. (bd. cert. civil trial lawyer), Fed. Bar Assn., Nat. Bd. Trial Advs. (cert. civil trial adv.), Am. Bd. Trial Advocates, Am. Inns of Ct. Democrat. Jewish. Lodge: B'nai B'rith. Avocations: sports, traveling. Personal injury, State civil litigation, Insurance.

**SPETH, MARIA CRIMI,** lawyer; b. Bklyn., May 19, 1964; d. Salvatore Joseph and Emma J. (Bonavita) Crimi; m. Raymond Alan Speth, Ag. 25, 1985; children: Christopher Raymond, Nicole Vincenza. BA, Hofstra U., 1985, JD, 1988. Bar: N.Y. 1988, Ariz. 1989. Assoc. Furey & Furey, Uniondale, N.Y., 1989-90; assoc. Beus, Gilbert & Morrill, PLLC, Phoenix, 1990-97, ptnr., 1997—. Vol. atty. Sr. Citizens Law Project, Phoenix, 1993—, Vol. Lawyers Program, Phoenix, 1993—. Mem. Ariz. Women's Lawyers Assn., Bus. Network Internat. (pres. Horizon chpt. 1996-97), Exec. Women's Golf Assn. (charter, pres. Valley of Sun chpt. 1996—). Roman Catholic. Avocation: golf. Office: Beus Gilbert & Morrill PLLC 3200 N Central Ave Ste 1000 Phoenix AZ 85012-2430

**SPEVAK, ERIC SCOTT,** lawyer; b. Syracuse, N.Y., Feb. 28, 1959; s. Mannie and Sylvia Spevak. BA, Hobart Coll., 1981; JD, Villanova U., 1984. Bar: Pa. 1984, N.J. 1984. Assoc. Archer & Greiner, P.C., Haddenfield, N.J., 1984-86; ptnr. Gerstein, Cohen & Spevak, Haddenfield, N.J., 1986-90, Adinolfi & Spevak, P.A., Cherry Hill, N.J., 1990—; instr. Inst. for Continuing Legal Education, N.J., 1995—. Contbr. articles to profl. jours. Mem. N.J. State Family Law Assn., (exec. com. 1995), South Jersey Family Inns of Ct. (v.p. 1997—), Camden County Bar Assn. (trustee 1988-92, chmn. family law com. 1989-94, co-chair 1999). Avocations: soccer coach, baseball coach, basketball official. Family and matrimonial. Office: Adinolfi and Spevak PA 70 Tanner St Haddonfield NJ 08033

**SPEYER, DEBRA GAIL,** lawyer; b. N.Y.C., Jan. 8, 1959; d. Frank R. and Lynn (Lederer) S.; m. Bruce H. Levin, Mar. 30, 1986. BBA, Hofstra U., Hempstead, N.Y., 1980, JD, 1984, MBA, 1988. Bar: N.Y. 1986, Pa. 1986, Conn. 1986, Fla. 1988, D.C. 1988. Atty., v.p. Thomson McKinnon Securities, N.Y.C., 1984-87; pvt. practice North Miami, Fla., 1987-88; atty. Nat. Assn. Securities Dealers, Phila., 1988-90; pvt. practice Phila., 1990—; arbitrator NASD, Am. Stock Exch., N.Y. Stock Exch., Phila. Stock Exch.; lectr. Phila. Bar Assn., 1996, course planner; cons. Phila. Corp. for the Aging. Dir. Nat. Cong. Syn Youth, Merrick, N.Y., 1983-86; pres. A.F.S.I., 1988-90, bd. dirs., 1990—; bd. dirs. Heart to Heart, 1993—, Judicare Sr. Citizen Project, 1998—; pres. AMIT, 1994-98. Named One of Best Lawyers in Phila. Phila. Mag. Mem. ABA, N.Y. State Bar Assn., Conn. Bar Assn., Pa. Bar Assn., Phila. Bar Assn. (co-chair elder law com. 1997—), Am. Trial Lawyers Assn., D.C. Bar Assn., Fla. Bar Assn., Phi Alpha Delta (treas. 1982-83). Avocations: golf, art. Securities, Probate, Estate planning. Office: The Lendell Bldg 232 S 3rd St Philadelphia PA 19106-3811

**SPIEGEL, H. JAY,** lawyer; b. Cleve., July 7, 1952; s. Martin and Thea (Lange) S. BS, Cornell U., 1974; JD, George Mason U., 1981. Bar: Va. 1981, U.S. Patent Office 1982, U.S. Ct. Appeals (fed. cir.) 1982, U.S. Dist. Ct. (ea. dist.) Va. 1982, U.S. Supreme Ct. 1984, D.C. 1986. Primary and asst. examiner U.S. Patent and Trademark Office, Arlington, Va., 1974-82; assoc. Sherman & Shalloway, Alexandria, Va., 1982-88, of counsel, 1988; pvt. practice. Alexandria, 1988-96; pvt. practice, Mt. Vernon, Va., 1996—; owner, pres. Premium Products, Inc., Alexandria, 1984—, Jumpstart. Patentee sporting goods and jewelry; inventor Toe-Tal Tee football tee, PENTA five panel football. Mem. Am. Intellectual Property Law Assn., Licensing Execs. Soc. Avocations: boating, travel. Patent, Trademark and copyright, Entertainment. Office: H Jay Spiegel & Assocs PC PO Box 444 Mount Vernon VA 22121-0444

**SPIEGEL, HART HUNTER,** retired lawyer; b. Safford, Ariz, Aug. 30, 1918; s. Jacob B. and Margaret (Hunter) S.; m. Genevieve Willson, Feb. 12, 1946; children: John Willson, Claire Margaret Spiegel Brian, Jennifer Emily Spiegel Grellman. BA, Yale U., 1940, LLB, 1946. Bar: Calif. 1946, D.C. 1960. Assoc. Brobeck, Phleger & Harrison, San Francisco, 1947-55, ptnr., 1955-90; chief counsel IRS, Washington, 1959-61, mem. adv. group to commr., 1975. Served to lt. USMC, 1942-46, PTO. Mem. ABA (coun. mem. tax sect. 1966-68), Am. Law Inst., Bar Assn. San Francisco (pres. 1983), Pacific Union Club, Berkeley Tennis Club (pres. 1964-65). Corporate taxation, State and local taxation. Home: 3647 Washington St San Francisco CA 94118-1832 Office: Brobeck Phleger & Harrison 1 Market Pla Spear St Tower San Francisco CA 94105

**SPIEGEL, JAYSON LESLIE,** lawyer; b. N.Y.C., Mar. 1, 1959; s. Jack and Frieda Rhoda (Michaelson) S.; m. Deborah Marie Scott, Nov. 1, 1986; children: Kyle Reid, Alicia Jean. AB, Georgetown U., 1980; JD, U. Va., 1983; postgrad., USMC Command and Staff Coll., 1991, Army Comd. & Gen. Staff Coll., 1996. Bar: Md. 1984, D.C. 1985, U.S. Ct. Appeals (D.C. cir.) 1986, U.S. Ct. Mil. Appeals 1987, U.S. Ct. Appeals (4th cir.) 1987, U.S. Supreme Ct. 1988, U.S. Ct. Claims 1990. Law clk. to assoc. judge Md. Ct. Appeals, Balt., 1983-84; assoc. Jordan, Coyne, Savits & Lopata, Washington, 1985-91, ptnr., 1991-94; dep. asst. sec. U.S. Army, 1994—, acting asst. sec., 1997—; lectr. law and transfusion medicine NIH, 1989, 91-94. Contbr. articles to profl. jours. Mem. recreation adv. bd. Montgomery County, Md., 1989-93. With USAR, 1981—, Desert Shield/Desert Storm, 1990-91. Mem. ABA (young lawyers mem. com. on law and nat. security, vice chair internat. criminal law com. 1991-94), D.C. Bar Assn. (founder, chmn. com. on law and nat. security 1987-94, Com. Chmn. of Yr. 1988, 91), Md. Bar Assn., Am. Def. Preparedness Assn., Nat. Security Indsl. Assn., Res. Officers Assn. (life), Army and Navy Club. Avocations: running, tennis. Federal civil litigation, General civil litigation, Insurance.

**SPIEGEL, JERROLD BRUCE,** lawyer; b. N.Y.C., Apr. 11, 1949; s. Seymour S. and Estelle (Minsky) S.; m. Helene Susan Cohen, Mar. 3, 1972; children: Dana Sean, Amy Barrett, Evan Tyler. BS, Queens Coll., 1970; JD cum laude, NYU, 1973. Bar: N.Y. 1974. Assoc. Austrian, Lance & Stewart, N.Y.C., 1973-75, Gordon Hurwitz Butowsky Baker Weitzen & Shalov, N.Y.C., 1975-79; ptnr. Shapiro Spiegel Garfunkel & Driggin, N.Y.C., 1979-86, Frankfurt, Garbus, Klein & Selz P.C., N.Y.C., 1986—. Editor Ann. Survey Am. Law, 1972-73,. Mem. ABA (corp. law sect.), Order of the Coif, Omicron Delta Epsilon. General corporate, Computer, Intellectual property. Office: Frankfurt Garbus Klein & Selz PC 488 Madison Ave Fl 9 New York NY 10022-5754

**SPIEGEL, LINDA F.,** lawyer; b. Bronx, N.Y., Mar. 13, 1953; d. Rubin E. and Edna (Zucker) S.; m. Paul Duboff, June 12, 1983; 1 child, Joshua Michael. AB, Barnard Coll., Columbia U., 1974; JD, Boston U., 1978. Bar: N.J. 1978, U.S. Dist. Ct. N.J. 1978, N.Y. 1980, U.S. Dist. Ct. (so. and ea. dists.) N.Y. 1980, U.S. Supreme Ct. 1982. Tax editor Prentice Hall, Englewood, N.J., 1978; pvt. practice, Hackensack, N.J., 1978-83, 88—; assoc. Friedman, Carney & Wilson, Newark, 1983-84; pvt. practice New Milford, N.J., 1984-85; assoc. LaFianza and Strull, Hackensack, 1985-87, ptnr., 1987-88; instr. Inst. Legal Asst. and Paralegal Tng., Mahwah, N.J., 1978-81. Spkr. Boy Scouts Am., Bergen, N.J., 1980; mem. atty.-acct. divsn. United Jewish Cmty., River Edge, N.J., 1978—; trustee Women's Am. Orgn. Rehab. through Tng., 1987-88; chmn. Jean Robertson Women Lawyers Scholarship Found., Inc., 1987-94. Mem. ABA, Am. Arbitration Assn. (comml. and constrn. arbitrator 1989—), N.J. Women Lawyers Assn., N.J. State Bar Assn., Bergen County Bar Assn. (trustee 1989-94, editor-in-chief Bergen Barrister 1991-94), Women Lawyers in Bergen County (pres. 1987-89), B'nai Brith. Democrat. Avocations: theater, tennis, swimming, square and country dancing. General civil litigation, Family and matrimonial, Alternative dispute resolution. Office: 79 Main St Ste 1 Hackensack NJ 07601-7126 *Notable cases include: A.L. vs. P.A., 213 N.J. Super 391, 1986, cert. den 107, J.J. 110, 1987.*

**SPIEGEL, ROBERT ALAN,** lawyer; b. N.Y.C., Apr. 1, 1952; s. Benjamin and Pauline Spiegel. BA, CUNY, 1974; JD, NYU, 1977; MPA, Syracuse U., 1984. Bar: Pa. 1978, D.C. 1985. Exec. rep. Found. Press., Mineola, N.Y., 1978-81; budget analyst Metro Studies Syracuse, N.Y., 1982-83; policy analyst Nat. Conf. State Legislatures, Washington, 1983; from atty.-advisor mgmt., budget & fin. to intergovt. rels. HUD, Washington, 1984-87; from atty.-advisor procurement law to judgement claims GAO, Washington, 1987-96; atty.-advisor judgement claims FMS, Hyattsville, Md., 1996—; adj. asst. prof. urban studies CUNY, Flushing, 1981-82. Contbg. author: Middle-Class Blacks in a White Society, 1975, A State Legislator's Guide to Public Pensions, 2d edit., 1983, The President's National Urban Policy Report, 1986; editor: An Analytical Legislative History of the Medical Device Amendments of 1976, 1976. Mem. ABA, Pa. Bar Assn., Bar Assn. D.C. Jewish. Home: 1724 17th St NW Apt 41 Washington DC 20009-2428 Office: FMS 3700 E West Hwy Hyattsville MD 20782-2015

**SPIEGEL, ROBERT IRA,** lawyer; b. Chgo., Apr. 13, 1940; B.A., U. Mich., 1961; J.D., Northwestern U., 1965. Bar: Ill. 1965, U.S. Dist. Ct. (no. dist.) Ill. 1965, U.S. Ct. Appeals (7th cir.) 1969, U.S. Supreme Ct. 1971. Practice, Chgo., 1969—; labor arbitrator Am. Arbitration Assn., 1968—; contbr. to seminars on immigration law. Mem. Am. Immigration Lawyers Assn. (past pres. Chgo. chpt.), Chgo. Bar Assn. (past chmn. immigration law com.), Decalogue Soc. Lawyers. Immigration, naturalization, and customs. Office: 53 W Jackson Blvd Chicago IL 60604-3606

**SPIEGEL, S. ARTHUR,** federal judge; b. Cin., Oct. 24, 1920; s. Arthur Major and Hazel (Wise) S.; m. Louise Wachman, Oct. 31, 1945; children: Thomas, Arthur Major II, Andrew, Roger Daniel. BA, U. Cin., 1942, postgrad., 1949; LLB, Harvard U., 1948. Assoc. Kasfir & Chalfie, Cin., 1948-52; assoc. Benedict, Bartlett & Shepard, Cin., 1952-53, Gould & Gould, Cin., 1953-54; ptnr. Gould & Spiegel, Cin., 1954-59; assoc. Cohen, Baron, Druffel & Hogan, Cin., 1960; ptnr. Cohen, Todd, Kite & Spiegel, Cin., 1961-80; judge U.S. Dist Ct. Ohio, Cin., 1980—; sr. status, 1995—. Served to capt. USMC, 1942-46. Mem. ABA, FBA, Ohio Bar Assn., Cin. Bar Assn., Cin. Lawyers Club. Democrat. Jewish. Office: US Dist Ct 838 US Courthouse 5th Walnut St Cincinnati OH 45202

**SPIEGLEMAN, JOHN G.,** lawyer; b. Denver, Feb. 29, 1968; s. Donald E. and Rose M. Spiegleman. BA, Denison U., 1990; JD, U. Colo., 1995. Bar: Colo. Mng. JMB Retail Properties Co., Chgo., 1990-92; assoc. Isaacson, Rosenbaum, Woods & Levy, Denver, 1995—. Active Colo. Dem. Party, Denver, 1995—, Children's Hosp., Denver, 1995—. Real property, General corporate, Finance. Home: 629 S Vine St Denver CO 80209-4614 Office: 633 17th St Ste 2200 Denver CO 80202-3661

**SPIELBERG, JOSHUA MORRIS,** lawyer; b. Atlanta, July 31, 1955; s. Sol and Gisela (Meyer) S.; m. Anindita Banerji, May 31, 1977; children: Lela, Ben, Hannah. BA, Oberlin Coll., 1977; JD magna cum laude, U. Pa., 1981. Bar: Del. 1982, N.J. 1985, Pa. 1985, U.S. Ct. Appeals (3d cir.) 1984, U.S. Ct. Appeals (6th cir.) 1990, U.S. Supreme Ct. 1997. Law clk. to Judge Walter K. Stapleton U.S. Dist. Ct. Del., Wilmington, 1981-82; Reginald Heber Smith fellow Cmty. Legal Aid, Wilmington, 1982-84; atty., ptnr. Tomar, Simonof et al, Cherry Hill, N.J., 1984—; trustee Camden Regional Legal Svcs., 1993—; mem. trust adv. com. DI Asbestos Disease Trust, Media, Pa., 1993—; lectr. Rutgers Law Sch., Camden, 1993—. Contbr. articles to law jours. Mgr. Little League baseball Haddon Twp. Athletic Assn., Westmont, N.J., 1994—. Recipient Fordham Human Rights award U. Pa. Law Sch., 1981. Mem. ATLA, N.J. Bar Assn. Democrat. Jewish. Avocations: baseball, bicycling, hiking. Toxic tort, Personal injury, Appellate. Home: 337 Westmont Ave Westmont NJ 08108-3536 Office: Tomar Simonoff et al 20 Brace Rd Ste 100 Cherry Hill NJ 08034-2639

**SPIELMAN, BETHANY JUNE,** ethics educator, consultant; b. West Bend, Wis., Feb. 27, 1952; d. Gerhard Carl and June Rose Spielman; m. Keith William Miller, Aug.7, 1976; children: Eric, Noah. PhD, U. Iowa, 1983; MHA, Duke U., 1984; JD, U. Va., 1992. Bar: Va. 1992. Asst. to the provost Coll. William and Mary, Williamsburg, Va., 1987-89; instr. dept. internal medicine U. Va., Charlottesville, 1989-90; asst. prof. med. humanities So. Ill. U., Springfield, 1993-99; clin. ethics cons. Meml. Med. Ctr., Springfield, Ill., 1997—; dir. med. ethics program So. Ill. U. Sch. Medicine, Springfield, 1997—, assoc. prof. med. humanities, 1999—. Editor: Organ Donation: Legal, Ethical and Policy Issues, 1996; mem. editl. bd. BioLaw, 1995; contbr. articles to profl. jours. Mem. Ctrl. Ill. Palliative Care Initiative, Springfield, 1998; mem. human values and ethics com. Meml. Med. Ctr., Springfield, 1997; mem. Ct. Apptd. Advocates of Ill., Springfield, 1995. Recipient Charles J. Frankel award in Health Law, Am. Coll. Legal Medicine, 1992; Va. Found. for Humanities and Pub. Policy fellow, 1987. Mem. ABA, Va. Bar, Am. Soc. for Bioethics and Humanities, Am. Soc. Law, Medicine and Dthics. Avocations: scuba diving, vegetarian cooking. Office: So Ill U Dept Med Humanities PO Box 19230 Springfield IL 62794-9230

**SPIELMAN, KIM MORGAN,** lawyer, educator; b. Ft. Wayne, Ind., Jan. 1, 1953; s. George Homer and Mary Ruth (Steininger) S.; m. Susan Kay Altekruse, Apr. 15, 1972; children: Matthew Ryan, Nathan Daniel. BS, Ind. U., 1982, MPA, 1984; JD with distinction, Ohio No. U., 1986. Bar: Ind. 1987, U.S. Dist. Ct. (no. and so. dists.) Ind. 1987, U.S. Ct. Appeals (7th cir.) 1990. Officer Ft. Wayne Police Dept., 1975-84; assoc. Barnes & Thornburg, Ft. Wayne, 1986-91; assoc. prof. Ind. U., Ft. Wayne, 1988—; chief counsel Allen County Prosecutor's Office, Ft. Wayne, 1991-92; with Beers, Mallers, Backs & Salin, Ft. Wayne, 1992-95; gen. counsel Hercules Machinery Corp., Ft. Wayne, 1995-98; instr. Ft. Wayne Police Acad. Del. Ind. State Rep. Conv., Indpls., 1982, 84, 92, 94, 96, 98; bd. dirs. Jr. Achievement of No. Ind.; ward chmn. Mayor's Police/Cmty. Rels. Task Force; steering com. Ft. Wayne Grand Prix.; mem. Bd. Public Safety, City Ft. Wayne, Leadership Ft. Wayne; pres. Safety and Security Svcs., LLC; leadership Ft. Wayne; judge pro tem, Allen County Superior Ct. Mem. ABA, Ind. Bar Assn., Allen County Bar Assn., Greater Ft. Wayne C. of C. Republican. Lutheran. Home: 3222 Sudbury Pl Fort Wayne IN 46815-6224 Office: 116 W Columbia St Fort Wayne IN 46802-1702

**SPIERER, HOWARD,** lawyer; b. Bklyn., Feb. 25, 1957; s. Seymour and Barbara Rose S.; m. Dorry G. Bless, Feb. 11, 1989; 1 child, Orli Sam. BA, NYU, 1980; JD, SUNY, 1986. Bar: Pa. 1986, U.S. Dist. Ct. (ea. dist.) Pa. 1986, N.J. 1987, U.S. Dist. Ct. N.J. 1987, N.Y. 1989, U.S. Dist. Ct. (so. and ea. dists.) N.Y. 1990. Atty. Cohen & Shapiro, Phila., 1986-89, Weil, Gotshal & Manges, N.Y.C., 1989-95, AT&T Corp., Basking Ridge, N.J., 1995—. Author: (play) Still Waiting, 1993. Vice chmn. Doe Fund, N.Y.C., 1995-96; bd. dirs. Svcs. Underserviced, N.Y.C., 1996—. Mem. ABA (editor in chief Litigation News 1995-98). General civil litigation, Alternative dispute resolution, Communications. Home: 139 Mount Joy Rd Milford NJ 08848-1748 Office: AT&T Corp 150 Allen Rd Liberty Corner NJ 07938

**SPIES, FRANK STADLER,** lawyer; b. Adrian, Mich., Aug. 7, 1939; s. Charles F. and Lucille M. (Stadler) S.; m. Lynette K. Wells, July 25, 1964; children: Anne, Jane, Charles. BBA, U. Mich., 1961, LLB, 1964. Bar: Mich. 1964, U.S. Dist. Ct. (we. dist.) Mich. 1964, U.S. Ct. Appeals (6th cir.) 1971. Assoc. Schmidt, Smith, Howlett & Halliday, Grand Rapids, Mich., 1964-66; asst. city atty. City of Grand Rapids, 1966-69, U.S. Dept. Justice, Grand Rapids, 1969-77; U.S. atty. Western Dist. Mich., Grand Rapids, 1974-77; pvt. practice Grand Rapids, 1977-81, 84-97; assoc. Kaufman, Payton & Kallas, Grand Rapids, 1981-84, Bensinger, Cotant, Menkes & Aardema, Grand Rapids, 1997—; instr. bus. law Davenport Coll., Grand Rapids, 1967-68, Grand Valley State U., Grand Rapids, 1978-79. Recipient Dirs. Honor award U.S. Secret Svc., 1977. Mem. ABA, Grand Rapids Bar Assn., Nat. Assn. Former U.S. Attys., Grand Rapids East Rotary,. Republican. Presbyterian. E-mail: fspies@BCMA.net. Insurance, Personal injury, Product liability. Home: 2122 Tenway Dr SE Grand Rapids MI 49506-4526 Office: 983 Spaulding Ave SE Grand Rapids MI 49546-3700

**SPIES, LEON FRED,** lawyer; b. Blue Grass, Iowa, Oct. 8, 1950; s. Fred William and Alma Lois (Lineburg) S.; m. Janet Rae Peterson, July 15, 1979; children: Caitlin, Allison. BBA with distinction, U. Iowa, 1972, JD with distinction, 1975. Bar: Iowa 1975, U.S. Dist. Ct. (no. and so. dists.) Iowa 1975, U.S. Ct. Appeals 1975, U.S. Supreme Ct. 1987. Assoc. Heintz & Mellon, Iowa City, 1975-76; ptnr. Mellon & Spies, Iowa City, 1976—; magistrate jud. dept. State of Iowa, 1978-83; instr. trial advocacy U. Iowa Coll. Law, 1996—. Bd. chmn. Johnson County Red Cross, Iowa City, 1982-84; bd. dirs. Big Bros./ Big Sisters, Johnson County, Iowa, 1985-89. Fellow Iowa Acad. Trial Lawyers; mem. ABA, ATLA, Iowa Bar Assn., Assn. Trial Lawyers Iowa, Am. Judicature Soc., Am. Inns of Ct. (master, pres. Dean Mason Ladd Inn 1995-96). Democrat. Methodist. State civil litigation, Criminal, Personal injury. Home: 2349 Kent Ct NE Iowa City IA 52240-9633 Office: Mellon & Spies 102 S Clinton St Iowa City IA 52240-4024

**SPIESS, F. HARRY, JR.,** lawyer; b. Norristown, Pa., Mar. 17, 1943; s. F. Harry and Sara E. (Jenkins) S.; m. Merrily S. Brown, Aug. 22, 1964; children: Jill, Blake, Alexandra, Ryan. AB, Lafayette Coll., Easton, Pa., 1964; JD, Villanova U., 1968. Bar: Pa. 1968. Assoc. Greenwell Porter Smaltz Royal, Wayne, Pa., 1968-72, ptnr., 1972-95; ptnr. Davis Bennett Barr & Spiess, Wayne, 1995—. Mem. Radnor Twp. Meml. Day Parade Com., 1976—, pres., 1985; pres. Wayne Jaycees, 1972-73, Rotary Club of Wayne, 1976-77, bd. dirs., counsel Radnor Hist. Soc., 1993—; charter mem. Hist. Assn. Tobyhanna Twp., 1996—; chmn. Constellation Dist. Boy Scouts Am., 1997—. Mem. Delaware County Bar Assn. (sec. 1981, chmn. golf com. 1994—), Monroe County Bar Assn., Main Line Lawyers Forum (past pres.), St. Davids Golf Club (counsel, sec.-treas. 1995—). Avocations: golf, reading. General practice, Estate planning, Contracts commercial. Home: Lansdowne Ave Wayne PA 19087 Office: Davis Bennett Barr & Spiess PO Box 191 130 W Lancaster Wayne PA 19087

**SPIESS, GARY A.,** lawyer. BA, Dartmouth Coll., 1962; LLB, Harvard U., 1966. Bar: Mass. 1966. Assoc. atty. Bingham Dana & Gould, 1966-76; 1st v.p., dep. gen. counsel Bank of Boston, 1975-86, dep. gen. counsel, 1986-87, gen. counsel, cashier, 1987—. Mem. Boston Bar Assn. (past pres.). Office: care Boston Bar Assn 16 Beacon St Boston MA 02108-3707

**SPILLANE, DENNIS KEVIN,** lawyer; b. N.Y.C., Sept. 15, 1953; s. Denis Joseph and Mary Kate (Sullivan) S. BA magna cum laude, Manhattan Coll., 1974; JD, N.Y. Law Sch., 1978; MS in Taxation, Pace U., 1986, post-masters cert. in bus., 1992. Bar: N.Y. 1979, U.S. Dist. Ct. (ea. and so. dists.) N.Y. 1979, U.S. Tax Ct. 1986, D.C. 1988, U.S. Ct. Appeals (2d cir.) 1988, U.S. Supreme Ct. 1988, Conn. 1989. Asst. dist. atty. Borough of Bronx, N.Y.C., 1978-85; prin. atty. N.Y. State Tax Dept., N.Y.C., 1985-87; supervising atty. Office of Profl. Discipline, N.Y. State Edn. Dept., 1987—; prof. law and taxation Pace U., 1987—. Contbr. articles to profl. jours. Mem. Conn. Bar Assn, N.Y. State Bar Assn., D.C. Bar Assn. Democrat. Roman Catholic. Office: NY State Edn Dept One Park Ave 6th Fl New York NY 10016

**SPILLANE, JOHN MICHAEL,** lawyer; b. El Dorado, Ark., Aug. 11, 1956; s. Leo Jerome and Kathryn Francis (Grady) S.; m. Bernadette Marie Smid, Mar. 18, 1978; children: Jonathan, Dominic. BA, Creighton U., 1978; JD, U. Tex., 1981. Bar: Colo. 1981, U.S. Dist. Ct. Colo. 1981, U.S. Ct. Appeals (10th cir.) 1981. With Grant, McHendrie, Haines & Crouse, Denver, 1981-85, Welborn, Dufford, Brown & Tooley, Denver, 1985-86; ptnr. Deutsch & Sheldon, Englewood, Colo., 1986-91; mem. Deutsch, Spillane & Reutzel, P.C., Denver, 1991—. Bd. dirs. counsel Beaver Ranch Children's Camp, Conifer, Colo., 1983-92; bd. dirs. Pioneer Jr. Hockey Assn., 1994-96. Mem. ABA, Colo. Bar Assn., Denver Bar Assn., Kiwanis (dir. 1983-85, pres. 1985-86). Avocations: tennis, martial arts, golf. Land use and zoning (including planning), Real property, General civil litigation. Office: Deutsch Spillane & Reutzel PC 9145 E Kenyon Ave Ste 200 Denver CO 80237-1819 *Notable cases include: Alpert vs. Far West, Denver Dist. Ct., represented plaintiffs in lender liability action involving breach of a commitment to lend.*

**SPILLIAS, KENNETH GEORGE,** lawyer; b. Steubenville, Ohio, Nov. 8, 1949; s. George and Angeline (Bouyoucas) S.; m. Monica Mary Saumweber, May 10, 1975; children: Geoffrey David, Alicia Anne, Stephanie Marie. BA, Pa. State U., 1971; JD magna cum laude, U. Pitts., 1974. Bar: Pa. 1974, Fla. 1978, U.S. Supreme Ct. 1978, U.S. Ct. Appeals (2d, 3d, 4th, 5th, 6th cirs.) 1975, (11th cir.) 1981, U.S. Dist. Ct. (mid. dist.) Fla. 1979, U.S. Dist. Ct. (so. dist.) Fla. 1978; cert. cir. ct. mediator. Trial atty. U.S. Dept. Justice, Washington, 1974-76; asst. dist. atty. Dist. Atty. of Allegheny County, Pitts., 1976-78; asst. atty. gen. Fla. Dept. Legal Affairs, West Palm Beach, Fla., 1978-79; ptnr. Spillias & Mitchell, West Palm Beach, 1979-82, Considine & Spillias, West Palm Beach, 1982-83, Schneider, Maxwell, Spillias et al, West Palm Beach, 1984-86, Wolf, Block, Schorr et al, West Palm Beach, 1986-88, Shapiro & Bregman, West Palm Beach, 1988-91; of counsel Greenberg, Traurig et al, West Palm Beach, 1991; pvt. practice West Palm Beach, 1991-97; ptnr. Lewis, Longman & Walker, P.A., West Palm Beach, 1997—; instr. bus. law Coll. of the Palm Beaches, West Palm Beach, 1980-81; CLE lectr. Palm Beach County Bar Assn., 1983—. County commr. Bd. County Commrs., Palm Beach County, 1982-86; co-founder, mem. Children's Svcs. Coun., Palm Beach County, 1986-91; steering com. Fla. Atlantic U. Inst. of Govt., Boca Raton, 1983-94; bd. dirs. The Literacy Coalition of P.B.C., West Palm Beach, 1990—, health and human svcs. Fla. Dist. IX, 1995-98, Ctr. for Family Svc., West Palm Beach, 1992-96, Palm Beach County Coun. of Arts, 1987-1988, West Palm Beach Planning Bd., 1997—; mem. policy coun. Fla. Inst. Govt., Tallahassee, 1985-86; fund raising chmn. United Cerebral Palsey Telethon, West Palm Beach, 1984-85; judge Palm Beach Post Pathfinders Awards, 1992-98. Recipient Cmty. Svc. award Downtown Civitan Club, West Palm Beach, 1983, Man of the Day award United Cerebral Palsey, 1986, Spl. Honoree award Palm Beach County Child Advocacy Bd., 1986, Children's Trust award Exch. Club/Dick Webber Ctr. for Prevention Child Abuse, 1991, Up and Comers Award in Law, South Fla. Bus. Jour./Price Waterhouse, 1988, Achievement award Nat. Assn. Counties, 1986; named to Outstanding Young Men of Am., U.S. Jaycees, 1975, 84. Mem. ABA, Acad. Fla. Trial Laywers, Palm Beach County Bar Assn. (appellate practice com. 1990—), Am. Hellenic Ednl. Progressive Assn. (Fla. Bar appellate advocacy and city, county and local govt. sects.), Order of Coif. Avocations: sports, scuba diving, theater, reading, music. General civil litigation, Appellate, Municipal (including bonds). Home: 147 Gregory Rd West Palm Beach FL 33405-5029 Office: Ste 1000 1700 Palm Beach Lakes Blvd West Palm Beach FL 33401-2006

**SPINA, ANTHONY FERDINAND,** lawyer; b. Chgo., Aug. 15, 1937; s. John Dominic and Nancy Maria (Ponzio) S.; m. Anita Phyllis De Orio, Jan. 28, 1961; children: Nancy M. Spina Okal, John D., Catherine M. Spina Samatas, Maria J. Spina Samatas, Felicia M. BS in Social Sci., Loyola U., Chgo., 1959; JD, DePaul U., 1962. Bar: Ill. 1962. Assoc. Epton, Scott, McCarthy & Bohling, Chgo., 1962-64; pvt. practice Elmwood Park, Ill., 1964-71; pres. Anthony & Spina, PC, 1971-84, Spina, McGuire & Okal, PC, Elmwood Park, 1985—. Author Rosemont Village Ordinances, 1971, Elmwood Park Bldg. Code, 1975, Leyden Twp. Codified Ordinances, 1987. Atty. Leyden Twp., Ill., 1969=89, Village of Rosemont, Ill., 1971; counsel for Pres. and dir. Cook County Twp. Ofcls. Ill., 1975-96; counsel for exec. dir. Ill. State Assn. Twp. Ofcls., 1975-96; counsel Elmwood Park Village Bd., 1967-89, Norwood Park St. Lighting Dist., 1988—, various Cook County Twps. including DuPage, 1980-82, Maine, 1981-97, Norwood Park, 1982—, Wayne, 1982-84, Berwyn Twp., 1997—, Hanover Twp., 1997, Cook county Hwy. Commrs. Traffic Fine Litigation, 1974-96, Hanover Twp. Mental Health Bd., 1991—, Glen Edens Assn., 1994—, Berwyn Twp. Mental Health Bd., 1997—; active Elmwood Pak Bldg. Code Planning Commn. Bd. Appeals. Recipient Lacodaire medal, Deans Key Loyola U., Loyola U. Housing awards, 1965, 71, 76; Appreciation award Cook County Twp. Ofcls., av rating Martindale-Hubbel. Mem. ABA, Ill. Bar Assn., Chgo. Bar Assn., West Suburban Bar Assn. Cook County (past chmn. unauthorized practice law sect.), Am. Judicature Soc., Justinian Soc. Lawyers, Ill. State Twp. Attys. Assn. (past v.p., pres. 1982-86, dir. 1986—), Nat. Inst. Town and Twp. Attys. (past v.p., pres. 1993-95, Ill. del.), Montclare/Leyden C. of C., Edgebrook C. of C. (past bd. dirs.), Nat. Assn. Italian Am. Lawyers (exec. com. joint civic com. Chgo. chpt.), World Bocce Assn. (dir. 1994—), St. Rocco Soc. Simbario, KC (scribe, trustee, past grand knight, bldg. corp. dir. 1967—), Calabresi in Am. Orgn. (bd. dirs. 1990—), Fra Noi Ethnic Publ. (dir. 1995—), Blue Key, Delta Theta Phi, Tau Kappa Epsilon, Pi Gamma Mu. Roman Catholic. State civil litigation, General practice, Estate planning. Office: 7610 W North Ave Elmwood Park IL 60707-4100

**SPINDLER, GEORGE S.,** lawyer, oil industry executive. BCE, Ga. Inst. Tech., 1961; JD, DePaul U., 1966. Bar: Ill. 1966. Asst. gen. counsel, patents and licensing Amoco Corp., Chgo., 1979-81, gen. mgr. info. svcs., 1981-85, v.p. planning and adminstrn., 1985-87, assoc. gen. counsel, 1987-88, dep. gen. counsel, 1988-89, v.p., gen. counsel, 1989-92, sr. v.p., gen. counsel, 1992-95, sr. v.p. law and corporate affairs, 1995—. Office: Amoco Corp PO Box 2106C 200 E Randolph Dr Chicago IL 60601-7125

**SPINING, W. CARL,** lawyer; b. Bowling Green, Ky., Feb. 11, 1967; s. William Parker and Carol Artis Spining; m. Erin Claire Doyle, Aug. 5, 1989; children: Molly Maureen, Patrick Ryan, Mary Caitlin, Jack Dugan. BA, U. Tenn., 1989, JD, 1993. Bar: Tenn. 1993, U.S. Dist. Ct. (mid. dist.) Tenn. 1993. Staff counsel Tenn. Dept. Revenue, Nashville, 1993-94; atty. Ortale, Kelley, Herbert & Crawford, Nashville, 1994—. Mem. Nashville Bar Assn. Roman Catholic. General civil litigation, General corporate, Probate. Office: Ortale Kelley Herbert & Crawford 200 4th Ave N Fl 3 Nashville TN 37219-2114

**SPIOTTO, JAMES ERNEST,** lawyer; b. Chgo., Nov. 25, 1946; s. Michael Angelo and Vinnetta Catherine (Henninger) S.; m. Ann Elizabeth Humphreys, Dec. 23, 1972; children: Michael Thomas, Mary Catherine, Joan Elizabeth, Kathryn Ann. AB, St. Mary's of the Lake, 1968; JD, U. Chgo., 1972. Bar: Ill. 1972, U.S. Dist. Ct. (no. dist.) Ill. 1973, U.S. Ct. Appeals (3rd and 7th cir.) 1974, U.S. Supreme Ct. 1978, U.S. Ct. Appeals (9th cir.) 1984, U.S. Dist. Ct. (so. dist.) Calif. 1984. Exclusionary rule study-project dir. Law Enforcement Assistance Agy. Grant, Chgo., 1972; law clk. to presiding justice U.S. Dist. Ct., Chgo., 1972-74; assoc. Chapman and Cutler, Chgo., 1974-80, ptnr., 1980—; chmn. program on defaulted bonds and bankruptcy Practising Law Inst., 1982—, chmn program on troubled debt financing, 1987—. Author: Defaulted Securities, 1990; contbr. numerous articles to profl. jours. With USAR, 1969-75. Mem. Assn. Bond Lawyers, Law Club of City of Chgo., Union League, Econs. Club Chgo. Roman Catholic. Bankruptcy, Municipal (including bonds), Federal civil litigation. Office: Chapman and Cutler 111 W Monroe St Ste 1700 Chicago IL 60603-4006

**SPIRTOS, NICHOLAS GEORGE,** lawyer, financial company executive; b. Youngstown, Ohio, Mar. 19, 1950; s. George Nicholas Spirtos and Tulla (Palaologos) Waldron; m. Andrea Carel DeFrane, Aug. 19, 1979. BA in Physics, Philosophy, UCLA, 1969, MA in Biochemistry, 1974, JD, 1978. Bar: Calif., 1978; cert. rape crisis counselor, Calif. Intelligence analyst, 1969-72; dir. product devel. Adolph's Food Products, Burbank, Calif., 1972-73; asst. to pres. Eckel Research and Devel., San Fernando, Calif., 1973-74; dep. State Public Defender Los Angeles, 1977-82; pvt. practice Pacific Palisades, Calif., 1982-94, Palm Desert, Calif., 1994—; co-founder Tekni-Query Cons., 1990; appellate lawyer Calif. and U.S. Supreme Ct., 1982; exec. v.p. Gen. Counsel Compensation Strategies Group, Santa Ana, Calif., 1988-89; pro bono legal counsel Junipero Serra H.S., Gardena, Calif., 1987-88; cons. to U.S. Govt., 1982—; bd. dirs. Myelin Project, Washington, 1993-95. Patentee solubilization of Sodium CMC at room temperature, 1972. Founder, fund raiser Pacific Multiple Sclerosis Research Found., Beverly Hills, Calif., 1982—, coordinator with Reed Neurology Ctr. at UCLA; bd. dirs. John F. Kennedy Ctr. Performing Arts, Very Spl. Arts for Cachella Valley, 1996—. Westinghouse Sci. scholar, 1965; recipient Gregor Mendell award in genetics, 1962; named Jr. Engr. of Yr. Am. Assn. Aero. Engrs., 1963, Outstanding Speaker U. So. Calif., 1965. Mem. State Bar Calif., Am. Pen Women (assoc.), Internat. Platform Assn., Mensa. Greek Orthodox. Avocation: classic automobiles, hot rods, quantum mechanics. Constitutional, Criminal. Office: 44489 Town Center Way # D-404 Palm Desert CA 92260-2723

**SPITZ, HUGO MAX,** lawyer; b. Richmond, Va., Aug. 17, 1927, s. Jacob Gustav and Clara (Herzfeld) S.; m. Barbara Steinberg, June 22, 1952; children: Jack Gray, Jill Ann Levy, Sally Spitz. AA, U. Fla., 1948, BLaws, 1951, JD, 1967. Bar: Fla. 1951, S.C., 1955, U.S. Dist. Ct. (so. dist.) Fla. 1951, U.S. Dist. Ct. (ea. dist.) S.C. 1956, U.S. Ct. Appeals (4th cir.) 1957. Asst. atty. gen. State of Fla., Tallahassee, 1951; assoc. Williams, Salomon & Katz, Miami, Fla., 1951-54, Steinberg & Levkoff, Charleston, S.C., 1954-57; sr. ptnr. The Steinberg Law Firm, L.L.P., Charleston, 1957—; lectr. S.C. Trial Lawyers Assn., Columbia, 1958—, S.C. U. Sch. Law, Columbia, 1975, S.C. Bar Assn., 1955—. Assoc. mcpl. judge Charleston, 1972-74, mcpl. judge, 1974-76; commr. Charleston County Substance Abuse Commn., 1976-79; bd. govs. S.C. Patient's Compensation Fund, Columbia, 1978-97; adv. mem., atty. S.C. Legis. Coun. for Workers' Compensation; chmn. bd. dirs. Franklin C. Fetter Health Ctr., Charleston, 1977-78; mem. S.C. Appellate Def. Commn., 1985-86; founding sponsor Civil Justice Found., 1986—; bd. pres. Charleston Jewish Fedn., 1990-91, pres., 1991-92. Pres., Synagogue Emanu-El, 1969-71. With USN, 1945-46. Fellow S.C. Bar Assn., U. S.C. Ednl. Found; mem. ABA, Civil Justice Found., S.C. Law Inst., S.C. Trial Lawyers Assn. (founder and pres. 1985-86), S.C. Claimants' Attys. for Worker's Compensation (exec. com. 1986), S.C. Worker's Compensation Ednl. Assn. (bd. dirs. 1978-98), S.C. Law Inst., Am. Judicature Soc., Assn. Trial Lawyers Am. (mem. pres. council 1986-87), Nat. Rehab. Assn., Nat. Orgn. Social Security Claimants' Reps. S.C. Bar (chmn. trial and appellate sect. 1982-83; ho. of dels. 1984-85), So. Assn. Workmen's Compensation Adminstrs., Nat. Inst. for Trial Advocacy (con. chmn. 1985). Democrat. Clubs: Hebrew Benevolent Soc. (pres. 1974-75, life), Jewish Community Ctr. (Charleston, v.p. 1972-74), Hebrew Orphan Soc. (life), B'nai B'rith, Elks (life). Workers' compensation, Personal injury, State civil litigation. Home: 337 Confederate Cir Charleston SC 29407-7430 Office: PO Box 9 Charleston SC 29402-0009

**SPITZBERG, IRVING JOSEPH, JR.,** lawyer, corporate executive; b. Little Rock, Feb. 9, 1942; s. Irving Joseph and Marie Bettye (Seeman) S.; m. Roberta Frances Alprin, Aug. 21, 1966 (div. 1988); children—Edward Storm, David Adam; m. Virginia V. Thorndike, Dec. 24, 1988. B.A., Columbia U., 1964; B.Phil., Oxford U., 1966; J.D., Yale U., 1969. Bar: Calif. 1969, D.C. 1985, Va. 1995. Asst. prof. Pitzer Coll., Claremont, Calif., 1969-71; fellow Inst. Current World Affairs, N.Y.C., 1971-74; vis. lectr. Brown U., Providence, 1973; assoc prof. SUNY, Buffalo, 1974-80; dean of coll. SUNY, 1974-78; gen. sec. AAUP, Washington, 1980-84; exec. dir. Coun. for Liberal Learning of Assn. Am. Colls., Washington, 1985-89; pres. The Knowledge Co., Fairfax, Va., 1985—; ptnr. Spitzberg & Drew, Washington, 1990-92; of counsel Spirer & Goldberg, Washington, 1993—; coord. Alvan Ikoku Coll., Nigeria, 1979-80; cons. Bd. Adult Edn., Kenya, 1973-74, Philander Smith Coll., Little Rock, 1978-80; co-dir. nat. study on campus life for Carnegie Found. for Advancement Teaching, 1989-90. Author and editor: Exchange of Expertise, 1978, Universities and the New International Order, 1979, Universities and the International Exchange of Knowledge, 1980; author: Campus Programs on Leadership, 1986, Racial Politics in Little Rock, 1987; co-author: (with Berdahl and Moodie), Quality and Access in Higher Education, 1991, (with Virginia Thorndike) Creating Community on College Campuses, 1992. Founder Coalition for Ednl. Excellence, Western N.Y., 1978-80; founding mem. Alliance for Leadership Devel., Washington, 1985; counsel GASP, Pomona, Calif., 1969-71; Dem. Committeeman, Erie County, N.Y., 1978-80; founding pres. Internat. Found. for St. Catherine's Coll., Oxford, 1986-91; founder Coun. for Liberal Learning; mem. Ethical Culture Soc. Nat. winner Westinghouse Sci. Talent Search, 1960; Kellett scholar Trustees of Columbia U., 1964-66. Mem. Am. Immigration Lawyers Assn., Nat. Acad. Elder Law Attys., Assn. Study Higher Edn., Washington Ethical Soc., Columbia Club, Yale Club (Washington). Jewish. Avocations: kids, the InterNet. Immigration, naturalization, and customs, Estate planning, Probate. Office: The Knowledge Co 10301 Democracy Ln Ste 403 Fairfax VA 22030-2545

**SPITZER, ELIOT,** state attorney general; m. Silda Spitzer; 3 children. G-rad., Princeton U.; JD, Harvard U. Clk. U.S. Judge Robert W. Sweet; assoc. Paul, Weiss, Rifkind, Wharton & Garrison, Skadden Arps Slate Meagher & Flom; ptnr. Constantine & Ptnrs., N.Y.C.; asst. dist. atty. State of N.Y., Manhattan, 1986-92; atty. gen. State of N.Y., Albany, 1999—; analyst, commentator on nat. news programs including NBC's Today Show, CNN's Burden of Proof, CNBC, Court TV. Editor Harvard Law Rev.; contbr. articles in leading newspapers and legal jours. Founder Ctr. for Cmty. Interest; trustee Montifiore Med. Ctr. Office: State Attorney General's Office The Capitol Albany NY 12224-0341 also: 120 Broadway New York NY 10271-0002

**SPITZER, HUGH D.,** lawyer; b. Seattle, Feb. 14, 1949; s. George Frederick and Dorothy Lea (Davidson) S.; m. Ann Scales, Oct. 14, 1983; children: Johanna Spitzer, Claudia Spitzer, Jenny Spitzer. BA, Yale U., 1970; JD, U. Wash., 1974; LLM, U. Calif., 1982. Bar: Wash. 1974, U.S. Dist/ Ct. (ea. and we. dists.) Wash. 1975, U.S. Ct. Appeals (9th and D.C. cirs.) 1975, U.S. Supreme Ct. 1980. Program analyst N.Y.C. Health and Hosp. Corp., 1970-71; labor lawyer Hafer, Cassidy & Price, Seattle, 1974-76; legis. asst. Seattle City Coun., 1976-77; legal counsel to mayor City of Seattle, 1977-81; mcpl. bond lawyer Foster Pepper & Shefelman, PLLC, Seattle, 1982—; affiliated prof. sch. law U. Wash. Contbr. articles to profl. jours. Vice chair Puget Sound Water Quality Authority Wash. State, 1989-96; chair Seattle Law Income Housing Levy Oversight com., 1988-96. Mem. Nat. Assn. Bond Lawyers, Pub. Legal Edn. Working Group. Democrat. Avocations: hiking, skiing. E-mail: spith@foster.com. Municipal (including bonds). Office: Foster Pepper & Shefelman PLLC 1111 3rd Ave Bldg Ste3400 Seattle WA 98101-3292

**SPITZER, VLAD GERARD,** lawyer; b. Bucharest, Romania, Mar. 3, 1956; came to U.S., 1963; s. Adrian and Carole Spitzer; m. Denise J. Borenstein, July 9, 1989; 1 child, Max Oliver. BA with honors, NYU, 1978; JD, Yeshiva U., 1981. Bar: N.Y. 1988, Conn. 1995, U.S. Dist. Ct. (so. and ea. dists.) N.Y. 1988, U.S. Dist. Ct. Conn. 1996, U.S. Ct. Appeals (2d cir.) 1994, U.S. Supreme Ct. 1995. Asst. dist. atty. Dist. Atty.'s Office of King's County, Bklyn., 1981-83; ptnr. Goldbergh & Spitzer LLC, N.Y.C., 1988—; mem. adv. bd. Nat. Employee Rights Inst., Cin., 1997—; founding mem. Conn. Employee Rights Inst., Stamford, Conn., 1997; coop. atty. ACLU, N.Y. Civil Liberties Union; judge Wagner Nat. Lab. and Employment Law Moot Ct., N.Y. Law Sch., 1996, 97, 98. Belkin scholar, 1981. Mem. ATLA (labor and employment sect. 1996—), Assn. of the Bar of the City of N.Y., Nat. Employment Lawyers Assn., Conn. Bar Assn. (labor and employment sect. 1996—, employee benefits com. 1996—), Nat. Employee Rights Inst., Stamford-Norwalk Regional Bar Assn., Stamford Rotary Club. Labor, Civil rights, General practice. Office: Goldbergh & Spitzer LLC 100 Prospect St Stamford CT 06901-1696

**SPITZLI, DONALD HAWKES, JR.,** lawyer; b. Newark, Mar. 19, 1934; s. Donald Hawkes and Beatrice (Banister) S.; children: Donald Hawkes III, Peter Gilbert, Seth Armstrong. A.B., Dartmouth Coll., 1956; LL.B., U. Va., 1963. Bar: Va. 1963. Assoc. Willcox, Savage, Lawrence, Dickson & Spindle, Norfolk, Va., 1964-67, 68-70; ptnr. Willcox, Savage, Lawrence, Dickson & Spindle, Norfolk, 1971-77; atty. Eastman Kodak Co., Rochester, N.Y., 1967-68; pres. Marine Hydraulics Internat., Inc., Chesapeake, Va., 1978-80; sole practice Virginia Beach, Va., 1980—; owner Chieftain Motor Inn, Hanover, N.H., 1980-87. Comdr. USNR, 1956-70. Episcopalian. Family and matrimonial, General practice, Bankruptcy. Office: 281 Independence Blvd Ste 605 Virginia Beach VA 23462-2975

**SPIVACK, GERALD W.,** lawyer; b. Phila., Oct. 23, 1938; s. Aaron and Anna (Shupack) S.; m. Joan Weinstein, June 22, 1958; children: Stuart, Milton, Kenneth. BS, Temple U., 1959, JD, 1962, LLM in Trial Advocacy, 1994. Bar: Pa., NJ. Asst. to chief justice, asst. state ct. reporter, chief dep. ct. adminstr., examiner Supreme Ct. of Pa., Phila., 1962-84; assoc. Pepper Hamilton & Sheetz, Phila., 1964; v.p., gen. counsel Life & Health Ins. Co. Am., Phila., 1984-86; assoc. Garfinkle Corbman & Greenburg, Phila., 1986-88; sole practitioner Phila., 1988-99; ptnr. Apwich & Spivack, Phila., 1999—. Assoc. editor Temple Law Quar., 1961-62; contbr. articles to profl.jours. Bd. dirs. Beth Sholom Congregation, Elkins Park, Pa., 1979—. Mem. Phila. Bar Assn. (bd. govs. 1998—), Temple Law Alumni/ae Assn. (pres. 1984), Tau Epsilon Rho (bd. dirs. 1996—). Personal injury, General civil litigation, Product liability. Home: 8470 Limekiln Pike Apt 614 Wyncote PA 19095-2701 Office: 1500 Walnut St Ste 405 Philadelphia PA 19102-3503

**SPIVACK, GORDON BERNARD,** lawyer, lecturer; b. New Haven, June 15, 1929; s. Jacob and Sophie (Ocheretianski) S.; m. Dolores Olivia Traversano, Jan. 16, 1956; children—Michael David, Paul Stephen. B.S. with philosophic orations and honors with exceptional distinction, Yale U., 1950, LL.B. magna cum laude, 1955. Bar: Conn. 1955, U.S. Supreme Ct. 1962,

N.Y. 1970. Trial atty. antitrust div. Dept. Justice, Washington, 1955-60; asst. chief field ops. antitrust div. Dept. Justice, 1961-64, chief field ops. antitrust div., 1964-65, dir. ops. antitrust div., 1965-67; assoc. prof. law Yale U., New Haven, 1967-70; vis. lectr. Yale U., 1970-78; ptnr. Lord, Day & Lord, N.Y.C., 1970-86, Coudert Bros., N.Y.C., 1986—; speaker on antitrust law; mem. Pres.'s Nat. Commn. for Rev. Antitrust Law and Procedures, Washington, 1978-79. Contbr. numerous articles on antitrust law to profl. jours. Served with U.S. Army, 1950-52. Recipient Sustained Superior Performance award Dept. Justice, 1955-60. Fellow Am. Coll. Trial Lawyers; mem. ABA, N.Y. State Bar Assn., Bar Assn. City N.Y., Yale Club (N.Y.C.), Pine Orchard Yacht and Country Club (Conn.). Jewish. Avocation: detective stories. Antitrust. Home: 118 Townsend Ter East Haven CT 06512-3129 Office: Coudert Bros 1114 Avenue Of The Americas New York NY 10036-7703

**SPIVEY, STEPHEN DALE,** lawyer; b. Clermont, Fla., Feb. 6, 1952; s. Herbert Basil Spivey and Marguerite Nordmann; previous marriage: Catherine Monohan; m. Rosemary Rosser, Sept. 7, 1990; children: Erin Alissa, Austin William. BA, BS, U. Ctrl. Fla., 1978; JD, Stetson Law Sch., St. Petersburg, Fla., 1980. Bar: U.S. Dist. Ct. (mid. dist.) Fla. Stockbroker, mgr. Merrill Lynch, Orlando, 1980-85; owner, ptnr. Chilton Fin., Orlando, 1985-86; staff atty. 5th Jud. Cir. Ct., Ocala, Fla., 1987-92; cir. coord. U.S. Justice Dept., Ocala, 1992-94; pvt. practice law Ocala, 1994—. Coord., advisor Marion County Teen Ct., Ocala, 1993-94 (outstanding svc. award 1996), Marion County Drug Ct., 1996-97; pres. bd. dirs. Recovery House, Inc., Ocala, 1990—; v.p. bd. dirs. Marion-Citrus Mental Health, Ocala, 1995—. Recipient Lewis F. Powell award Am. Coll. Trial Lawyers, 1980, Chief Justice's Commendation for Exemplary Pub. Svc. Supreme Ct. Fla., 1998; outstanding svc. award HRS Dist. III Planning Coun., 1994. Mem. ABA, Fla. Bar Assn., Pub. Investors Arbitration Bar Assn., Elks. Republican. Avocations: hunting, fishing, scuba diving, underwater photography. Securities, Product liability, General civil litigation. Office: 230 NE 25th Ave Ste 200 Ocala FL 34470-7075

**SPIZZIRI, JOHN ANTHONY,** lawyer; b. Paterson, N.J., Sept. 2, 1934; s. Louis George and Carmella (Ianacone) S.; m. Alexandra Vitale, July 15, 1972; children: John A. Jr., Victoria Jean, Miriam. BS, Georgetown U., 1957, JD, 1960. Bar: N.J. 1961, U.S. Dist. Ct. N.J. 1961. Pvt. practice, Wyckoff, N.J., 1961—; pros. Ramsey (N.J.) Borough, 1964-77, Oakland (N.J.) Borough, 1969-83, Borough Upper Saddle River, N.J.; counsel Franklin Lakes Planning Bd., 1970—; atty. Borough of Elmwood Park (N.J.), 1981—; police prosecutor Township of Wyckoff, 1964-66; condemnation commr. Meadowlands Sports and Expn. Authority, presiding condemnation commr. Rte. 287; asst. counsel Bergen County (N.J.), 1970-71; judge Mcpl. Ct., Oakland, 1986; attorney Wyckoff Ambulance Corp., 1970—, Franklin Lakes Ambulance Corp., 1994—. Mem. N.J. Gen. Assembly, 1971-77, also minority whip and asst. minority leader; mem. Wyckoff Sewer Com., Wyckoff Planning Bd.; mayor Township of Wyckoff, 1969; past pres. Wyckoff Rep. League; past co-chmn. Wyckoff Heart Fund; past vice chmn. N.W. Bergen County fund drive Boy Scouts Am.; Rep. mem. Com to Study Expenditures of Casino Gambling Revenue; mem. bd. 36, SSS. Mem. ABA, N.J. Bar Assn., Bergen County Bar Assn., Nat. Wildlife Fedn., Allendale Field and Stream Assn., Wyckoff Vol. Ambulance Corps (hon.), Lawyers Club Bergen County (past pres.), Lions (past bd. dirs., pres. Wyckoff chpt. 1989-90). Roman Catholic. General practice, Land use and zoning (including planning). Office: 356 Franklin Ave Wyckoff NJ 07481-1909

**SPOGNARDI, MARK ANTHONY,** lawyer; b. Milw., Oct. 7, 1959; s. Julius Ceasar and Audrey Lee Spognardi; m. Inga Katarina Mader, Aug. 25, 1990. BA with honors, U. Iowa, 1980; JD, DePaul U., 1984. Bar: Ill. 1984, U.S. Dist. Ct. (no. dist.) Ill. 1984, U.S. Ct. Appeals (7th cir.) 1986. Staff counsel NLRB, Washington, 1984-86; field atty. NLRB, Chgo., 1986-88; atty. in pvt. practice Chgo., 1988-94; assoc. atty. McBride Baker & Coles, Chgo., 1995-96, ptnr., 1996—. Contbr. articles to profl. jours. Mansfield fellow Legal Aid Found., Chgo., 1983. Mem. ABA, N.Am. rucking Indsl. Rels. Assn. (bd. dirs. 1996—), Ill. Bar Assn. Labor, Pension, profit-sharing, and employee benefits, Federal civil litigation. Office: McBride Baker & Coles 500 W Madison St Chicago IL 60661-2511

**SPONSLER, THOMAS CLYDE,** lawyer; b. Highland Park, Ill., Aug. 4, 1944; s. Thomas Clyde and Signe Ruth (Gaines) S.; m. Virginia Marie Payne, Jan. 2, 1966; 1 child, Brian Andrew. Student, Calif. State U., Long Beach, 1962-65; BS, Willametter U., 1966, JD, 1967; LLM, U. London, 1974. Bar: Calif. 1968, Oreg. 1975. Law clk. Oreg. Legis. Counsel, Salem, 1966-67; trial atty. U.S. Dept. Justice, Washington, 1967-68; dir. litigation Legal Aid Found., Long Beach, 1968-71; assoc. Demler Perona Langer & Bergkvist, Long Beach, 1971-72; sr. assoc. Barnes Schag Johnson & Kennedy, Newport Beach, Calif., 1972-73; asst. prof. law U. of the Pacific, Sacramento, 1974-75; dir. edn. Oreg. State Bar, Portland, 1975-78; city atty. City of Gresham, Oreg., 1979-97; county counsel Multnomah County, 1997—. Author, mng. editor: Oregon Government Law, 1993, Nature of Local Government, 1991; contbr. articles to profl. jours. Mem. Internat. Mcpl. Law Assn. (com. chmn. 1983-87), Oreg. State Bar, Calif. State Bar Assn. Office: 1120 SW 5th Ave Ste 1530 Portland OR 97204-1914

**SPONSLER, THOMAS H.,** law educator, dean. BA magna cum laude, U. Toledo, 1964, JD summa cum laude, 1967; LLM, Yale U., 1968. Bar: Ohio 1967, La. 1973, Calif. 1988, N.Y. 1997. Prof. law Loyola Law Sch., New Orleans, 1968-89, dean, 1983-89; dir. staff attys. U.S. Ct. Appeals (9th cir.), 1989-91; counsel profl. liability sect. FDIC, 1991-95; dean, pres. Albany Law Sch., N.Y., 1995—; mem. New Orleans Civil Svc. Commn., 1981-87, chmn., 1987-89; cons. Gov. Roemer of La., 1988; commr. Uniform State Laws, La., 1987-89; mem. task force on lawyer tng. Fed. Legal Svcs. Corp., 1986-87; spkr. in field. Contbr. articles to profl. jours. Mem. La. State Bar Assn. (bd. govs. 1984-89). Office: Albany Law Sch 80 New Scotland Ave Albany NY 12208-3494

**SPOONER, JACK BERNARD,** lawyer; b. St. Louis, July 4, 1961; m. Margaret C. Spooner; children: Kendal, Peyton, Jack Jr. BS in Comm., S.E. Mo. State U., 1985; JD, St. Louis U., 1988. Bar: Mo. 1988, U.S. Dist. Ct. (ea. dist.) Mo. 1988, Ill. 1989; cert. civil trial adv. Nat. Bd. Trial Advocacy. Assoc. Lashly, Baer & Hamel, St. Louis, 1988-90, Wittner, Poger & Rosenblum, P.C., St. Louis, 1990-94; ptnr. Emert & Spooner, St. Louis, 1994-96; shareholder Wittner, Poger, Rosenblum Spewak & Maylack, St. Louis, 1996—. Federal civil litigation, State civil litigation, Personal injury. Office: Wittner Poger Spewak & Maylack PC 7700 Bonhomme Ave Ste 400 Saint Louis MO 63105-1924

**SPOONHOUR, JAMES MICHAEL,** lawyer; b. San Antonio, Mar. 24, 1946; s. Robert W. and Marie C. (Schulze) S.; m. Terri Walker; children: Taylor, Erin, Whitney, Michael. BA, U. Nebr., 1968, MA, 1970; JD, Georgetown U., 1974. Bar: Fla. 1974, U.S. Dist. Ct. (mid. dist.) Fla. 1974. Assoc. Lowndes, Piersol, Drosdick & Doster, Orlando, Fla., 1974-76; asst. prof. law Loyola U., New Orleans, 1976-77; ptnr. Lowndes, Drosdick, Doster, Kantor & Reed, P.A., Orlando, 1977—. Contbr. to profl. publs. Bd. dirs. Vis. Nurse Assn., Orlando, 1979-89; chmn. sch. bd. The First Acad., Orlando, 1986-89. With USAF, 1970-72. Mem. ABA, Assn. Trial Lawyers Am., Fla. Bar, Orange County Bar Assn. Republican. Condemnation, General civil litigation, State and local taxation. Office: Lowndes Drosdick Doster Kantor & Reed PA 215 N Eola Dr Orlando FL 32801-2095

**SPORE, RICHARD ROLAND, III,** lawyer, educator; b. Memphis, May 28, 1962; s. Richard R. Jr. and Melba (Cullum) S.; m. Patricia Ann Witherspoon, Aug. 15, 1987; 1 child, Caroline Dare. BA, U. of the South, 1984; JD, U. Va., 1987; MBA, Christian Bros. U., 1992. Bar: Tenn. 1987. Assoc. Burch, Porter & Johnson PLLC, Memphis, 1987-94; mem. Burch, Porter & Johnson, Memphis, 1995—; adj. prof. bus. law Christian Bros. U., Memphis, 1992-97. Author: The Partnering Paradigm: An Entrepreneur's Guide to Strategic Alliances, 1994, Business Organizations in Tennessee, 1995. Mem. Pro Bono Panel for Sr. Citizens, Memphis, 1987—; chmn. small bus. coun. Memphis Area C. of C., 1993; pres. Sewanee Club of Memphis, 1989. Recipient Disting. Svc. award Pro Bono Panel for Sr. Citizens, 1992. Mem. ABA, Tenn. Bar Assn. (chair sect. corp. and bus. law), Memphis Bar Assn. Republican. Methodist. General corporate, Contracts commercial, Health. Office: Burch Porter & Johnson 130 Court Ave Memphis TN 38103-2288

**SPORKIN, STANLEY,** federal judge; b. Phila., 1932; m. Judith Sally Imber, Sept. 30, 1955; children: Elizabeth Michael, Daniel Paul, Thomas Abraham. AB, Pa. State U., 1953; LLB, Yale U., 1957. Bar: Del. 1958, Pa. 1958, U.S. Dist. Ct. D.C. 1963, U.S. Supreme Ct. 1964, U.S. Ct. Appeals (2d cir.) 1975, U.S. Ct. Appeals (4th cir.) 1978. Law clk. to presiding justice U.S. Dist. Ct. Del., 1957-60; assoc. Haley Woolenberg & Bader, Washington, 1960-61; staff atty. spl. study securities markets U.S. SEC, Washington, 1961-63, atty., 1963, chief atty. enforcement br., 1963-66, chief enforcement atty., 1966, asst. dir., 1967, assoc. dir., 1968-72, dep. dir. div. trading and markets, 1972-73, dir. div. enforcement, 1973-81; gen. counsel CIA, Washington, 1981-86; judge U.S. Dist. Ct. D.C., Washington, 1985—; adj. prof. Antioch Law Sch., 1974-81, Howard U., 1981—; mem. exec. com. U. Calif. Securities Regulation Inst., 1977—. Contbr. articles to profl. jours. Recipient Nat. Civil Svc. League's Spl. Achievement award, 1976, Rockefeller Pub. Svc. award, 1978, Pres.' Disting. Fed. Civilian Svc. award, 1979, Pa. State U. Almunus of Yr. award, 1979, William O. Douglas award for lifetime achievement Assn. Securities and Exch. Commn. Alumni, 1994; honored by B'nai B'rith Hall of Fame; named Alumni Fellow Coll. Bus. Administrn. Pa. State U., 1990. Fellow Am. Bar Found.; mem. ABA, Fed. Bar Assn. (exec. council securities law sect. 1978—), Del. Bar Assn., Bar Assn. of D.C., Am. Law Inst., Am. Inst. CPA's, Fed. Legal Council, Adminstrv. Conf. of U.S., Phi Beta Kappa, Phi Kappa Phi. Office: US Dist Ct US Courthouse Rm 2428 333 Constitution Ave NW Washington DC 20001-2802

**SPORN, JUDITH BERYL,** lawyer; b. N.Y.C., Mar. 3, 1951; d. Milton and Helen Florence (Berman) Shapiro; m. Robert C. Sporn, May 22, 1977; 1 child, David Benjamin. BA magna cum laude, SUNY, Buffalo, 1973; postgrad., Columbia U., 1973-74; JD, Loyola U., L.A., 1979. Bar: N.Y. 1979, Conn. 1982. Atty. firm Cohen & Tucker, N.Y.C., 1980-82, Barst & Mukamal, L.A., 1982-85; sole practice Westport, Conn., 1985—. Vol. atty. Vol. Lawyers for the Arts, N.Y.C., 1980-82, Los Angeles County Bar Pro Bono Immigration Project, L.A., 1983-85; bd. dirs. Women's Crisis Ctr., Norwalk, Conn., 1986. Mem. Fed. Bar Assn., Westport Bar Assn., Fairfield Women's Bar Assn., Am. Immigration Lawyers Assn. Avocations: skiing, travel. Immigration, naturalization, and customs. Office: 125 Main St Westport CT 06880-3303

**SPOSITO, JAMES ANTHONY,** lawyer, consultant; b. Carbondale, Pa., Jan. 11, 1943; s. Anthony James and Hortense (Talarico) S.; m. Karen Mascelli, Nov. 25, 1966 (div. Nov. 1976); children: James A. Jr., Angela. BS in History, U. Scranton, 1964; MS, Marywood Coll., Scranton, 1969; JD, George Mason U., 1980; LLD, Strasburg (France) U., 1980. Bar: Pa. 1980, U.S. Dist. Ct. (mid. dist.) Pa. 1980, U.S. Ct. Appeals (3rd cir.) 1983; cert. tchr., Pa. Tchr. elem. and secondary schs., Pa., 1966-76; aide to Congressman Phil Sharp U.S. Ho. of Reps., Washington, 1977-78; pres. James A. Sposito & Assocs., Scranton, 1980—; pres. Spo-Jac Enterprises, Carbondale, 1964—; pres., owner, broker Sposito Realty Co., Carbondale, 1965—. Advisor 114th legis. dist. State Rep.'s Office, Pa., 1978—. Acting 2d lt. U.S. Army N.G., 1964-71. Mem. ATLA, Pa. Bar Assn., Pa. Trial Assn., Susquehanna County Bar Assn., Lackawanna Bar Assn., Thunderbird Investment Club (pres. 1966-70), Elkview Country Club. (sr. golf mem.). Roman Catholic. Avocations: golf, hunting, fishing. General civil litigation, Criminal, Family and matrimonial. Home: RR 1 Box 1155 Carbondale PA 18407-9016 Office: 547 Hickory St Scranton PA 18505-1322

**SPOTILA, JOHN T.,** lawyer; married; 1 child. BS in Langs., Georgetown U., 1968; JD, Yale U., 1971. Bar: N.J., Pa.; U.D. Ct. Appeals, U.S. Dist. Ct., U.S. Supreme Ct. Formerly atty. and small bus. owner; now gen. counsel SBA, Washington, to 1999; counsellor to the dep. dir. for mgmt., adminstrv. designate Office of Info. and Regulatory Affairs, OMB, Washington, 1999—. Capt. C.E., U.S. Army. Mem. Phi Beta Kappa. Office: OMB 305 Old Exec Office Bldg Washington DC 20503-0001

**SPRADER, BOBBIE S.,** lawyer; b. Bowling Green, Ohio, Sept. 9, 1969; d. Robert A. and Phyllis J. Morelan; m. Steven G. Sprader, Sept. 13, 1997. BSBA, Bowling Green State U., 1991; JD, Ohio State U., 1994. Bar: U.S. Supreme Ct. 1994, U.S. Dist. Ct. (so. dist.) 1995. Assoc. Jacobson, Maynard, Tuschman & Kelur, Columbus, Ohio, 1995-98, Bricker & Eckler LLP, Columbus, 1998—. Personal injury, Workers' compensation, General civil litigation. Office: Bricker & Eckler LLP 100 S 3rd St Columbus OH 43215-4291

**SPRAY, VANN ALLAN,** lawyer; b. Gadsden, Ala., Aug. 3, 1971; s. Larry Vann and Ruthie Gail Spray. BA, U. Ala., 1993, JD, 1996. Bar: Ala. 1996, U.S. Dist. Ct. (no. dist.) Ala. 1997, U.S. Ct. Appeals (11th cir.) 1999. Assoc. atty. Simmons, Branson and Assocs., Gadsden, 1997-98, Ford and Howard, P.C., Gadsden, 1998—. Bd. dirs. Big Bros./Big Sisters Ala., 1997—; mem. Gadsden Quarerback Club. Mem. Etowah County Bar Assn. (sec., treas. 1998), Ala. Def. Lawyers Assn., Def. Rsch. Inst. Federal civil litigation, State civil litigation, Insurance. Office: Ford and Howard PC 645 Walnut St Ste 5 Gadsden AL 35901-4173

**SPRIGGS, EVERETT LEE,** lawyer; b. Safford, Ariz., July 30, 1930; s. Claude E. and Evelyn (Lee) S.; m. Betty Medley, Aug. 22, 1953; children; Claudia Lynn Reynolds, Lee M., Scott B. BS, Ariz. State U., 1955; JD, U. Ariz., 1958. Bar: Calif. 1960, U.S. Supreme Ct. 1983. City atty. criminal dept. Los Angeles, 1960-61; mem. firm Kinkle & Rodiger, Riverside, Calif., 1961-64; pres. Kinkle, Rodiger & Spriggs (P.C.), Riverside, 1965—; chmn. bd. dirs. Riverside Nat. Bank. With AUS, 1951-52. Mem. ABA, Calif. Bar Assn., Riverside County Bar Assn., L.A. County Bar Assn., Def. Rsch. Inst., So. Calif. Def. Counsel (editorial staff 1970-71), Assn. Trial Lawyers Am., Riverside Downtown Assn., Am. Bd. Trial Advocates, Supreme Ct. Hist. Soc., Def. Orientation Conf. Assn. Personal injury. Home: 1456 Muirfield Rd Riverside CA 92506-5576 also: 1126 E Balboa Blvd Balboa CA 92661-1314 Office: Kinkle Rodiger & Spriggs 3333 14th St Riverside CA 92501-3809 also: 600 N Grand Ave Los Angeles CA 90012-2212 also: 837 N Ross St Santa Ana CA 92701-3419 also: 1620 5th Ave San Diego CA 92101-2747 also: 125 E De La Guerra St Santa Barbara CA 93101-2239

**SPRINGER, CHARLES EDWARD,** retired state supreme court chief justice; b. Reno, Feb. 20, 1928; s. Edwin and Rose Mary Cecelia (Kelly) S.; m. Jacqueline Sirkegian, Mar. 17, 1951; 1 dau., Kelli Ann. BA, U. Nev., Reno, 1950; LLB, Georgetown U., 1953; LLM, U. Va., 1984; student Grad. Program for Am. Judges, Oriel Coll., Oxford (Eng.), 1984. Bar: Nev. 1953, U.S. Dist. Ct. Nev. 1953, D.C. 1954, U.S. Supreme Ct. 1962. Pvt. practice law Reno, 1953-80; atty. gen. State of Nev., 1962, legis. legal adv. to gov., 1958-62; legis. bill drafter Nev. Legislature, 1955-57; mem. faculty Nat. Coll. Juvenile Justice, Reno, 1978—; juvenile master 2d Jud. Dist. Nev., 1973-80; justice Nev. Suprem Ct., Carson City, 1981—; vice-chief justice Nev. Supreme Ct., Carson City, 1987, chief justice, 1998—, ret., 1999; mem. Jud. Selection Commn., 1981, 98, Nev. Supreme Ct. Gender Bias Task Force, 1981—; trustee Nat. Coun. Juvenile and Family Ct. Judges, 1983—; mem. faculty McGeorge Sch. Law, U. Nev., Reno, 1982—; mem. Nev. Commn. for Women, 1991-95. With AUS, 1945-47. Recipient Outstanding Contbn. to Juvenile Justice award Nat. Coun. Juvenile and Family Ct. Judges, 1989, Midby-Byron Disting. Leadership award U. Nev., 1988. Mem. ABA, Am. Judicature Soc., Am. Trial Lawyers Assn., Phi Kappa Phi. Office: Nev Supreme Ct Capitol Complex 201 S Carson St Carson City NV 89701-4702

**SPRINGER, JEFFREY ALAN,** lawyer; b. Denver, Feb. 26, 1950; s. Stanley and Sylvia (Miner) S.; m. Amy Mandel, Nov. 11 1995; children: Cydney Erin, Samantha Libby, Jackson Stanley, Harrison Louis. AB, Princeton U., 1972; JD, U. Colo., 1975. Bar: Colo. 1975, U.S. Dist. Ct. Colo. 1975, U.S. Ct. Appeals (10th cir.) 1975, U.S. Supreme Ct. 1978, U.S. Ct. Appeals (8th cir.) 1986. Assoc. Gerash & Springer, Denver, 1975-79; sole practice Denver, 1979-81; pres. Springer and Steinberg, P.C., Denver, 1981—; mem. com. on mcpl. ct. rules Supreme Ct. Colo., 1985-86; mem. standing criminal justice act com. U.S. Dist. Ct., 1994-96. Mem. ABA, Assn. Trial Lawyers Am., Colo. Trial Lawyers Assn. (bd. dirs. 1988-90), Colo. Criminal Def. Bar (bd. dirs. 1985-86, 87-88, pres. 1988-89). Criminal, Personal injury. Office: 1600 Broadway Ste 1950 Denver CO 80202-4920

**SPRINGER, MARILEE J.,** lawyer; b. Spartansburg, Pa., Feb. 28, 1971; d. Lowell Jones and Phyllis Maxine Weidner; m. Brian E. Springer, June 13, 1992. BA, Purdue U., 1993; JD, Ind. U., Indpls., 1996. Bar: Ind. 1996, U.S. Dist. Ct. (so. dist.), U.S. Supreme Ct. Assoc. Ice Miller Donadio & Ryan, Indpls., 1996—. Note devel. editor Ind. Law Rev., 1994-95. Adv. bd., exec. com. mem. Ind. Child Care Fund, Inc., Indpls., 1996—. Cox Meml. fellow, 1995-96. Mem. ABA, Ind. Bar Assn. (fellow 1994-95), Indpls. Bar Assn., Golden Key, Phi Beta Kappa. Corporate taxation, Taxation, general, General corporate. Office: Ice Miller Donadio & Ryan 1 American Sq # 82001 Indianapolis IN 46282-0001

**SPRINGER, PAUL DAVID,** lawyer, motion picture company executive; b. N.Y.C., Apr. 27, 1942; s. William W. and Alma (Markowitz) S.; m. Mariann Frankfurt, Aug. 16, 1964; children: Robert, William. BA, U. Bridgeport, 1963; JD, Bklyn. Law Sch., 1967. Bar: N.Y. 1968, U.S. Dist. Ct. (so. and ea. dists.) N.Y. 1968, U.S. Ct. Appeals (2d cir.) 1970, U.S. Supreme Ct. 1973, Calif. 1989. Assoc. Johnson & Tannenbaum, N.Y.C., 1968-70; assoc. counsel Columbia Pictures, N.Y.C., 1970; assoc. counsel Paramount Pictures, N.Y.C., 1970-79, v.p., theatrical distbn. counsel, 1979-85, sr. v.p., chief resident counsel East Coast, 1985-87; sr. v.p., asst. gen. counsel Paramount Pictures, L.A., 1987—; Bar: N.Y. 1968, U.S. Dist. Ct. (so. and ea. dists.) N.Y. 1968, U.S. Ct. Appeals (2d cir.) 1970, U.S. Supreme Ct. 1973, Calif. 1989. Trustee West Cunningham Park Civic Assn., Fresh Meadows, N.Y., 1978—. Mem. ABA, Assn. of Bar of City of N.Y., L.A. Copyright Soc., Acad. Motion Picture Arts and Scis., Motion Picture Pioneers. Antitrust, General corporate, Federal civil litigation.

**SPRINGER, ROBERT P.,** lawyer, financial adviser; b. Bklyn., Nov. 5, 1928; s. Leo J. and Anna K. (Kasen) S.; student N.Y. U., 1945; B.A., U. Mich., 1948; J.D., Harvard U., 1951; m. Nesha E. Bass, Sept. 23, 1951; children—Nancy, Mark, Carrie, Stephen. Admitted to N.Y. bar, 1951, U.S. Ct. Mil. Appeals, 1952, Mass. bar, 1954, U.S. Supreme Ct., 1978; partner firm Silk & Springer, and successors, Boston, 1955-69; pres., gen. counsel Gt. No. Land Corp., Boston, 1969-72; partner firm Linsky, Springer & Finnegan, Boston, 1973-78; sr. partner Springer, Havey & Ziemian, 1978-82; sr. mem. Law Offices Robert P. Springer, Boston, 1982-89; pres. Devon Fin. Mgmt. Corp., 1982-84; chmn. bd. dirs. Space Sciences, Inc., Waltham, Mass., 1967-69; personal counsel to gov. Mass., 1956-60, 62-64; gen. partner KSG Realty Co., Boston, 1968-81. Bd. dirs. Mass. Bay Transp. Authority, 1964-69, Greater Framingham Jewish Family Service, 1985-89; mem. Jewish Big Bros./Big Sisters Assn. of Greater Boston, 1987-89, Natick (Mass.) Town Meeting, 1954-69, 73-74; vice chmn. trustee coun. Leonard Morse Hosp., Natick, 1978-89; trustee Temple Beth Am, 1985-89. Served with JAGC, U.S. Army, 1951-54. Home: PO Box 783 Sunapee NH 03782-0783 Office: 35 Fairway Dr PO Box 783 Sunapee NH 03782-0783

**SPRITZER, RALPH SIMON,** lawyer, educator; b. N.Y.C., Apr. 27, 1917; s. Harry and Stella (Theuman) S.; m. Lorraine Nelson, Dec. 23, 1950; children: Ronald, Pamela. B.S., Columbia U., 1937, LL.B., 1940. Bar: N.Y. bar 1941, U.S. Supreme Ct. bar 1950. Atty. Office Alien Property, Dept. Justice, 1946-51; anti-trust div. Dept. Justice, 1951-54, Office Solicitor Gen., 1954-61; gen. counsel FPC, 1961-62; 1st asst. to solicitor gen. U.S., 1962-68; prof. law U. Pa., Phila., 1968-86, Ariz. State U., Tempe, 1986—; gen. counsel AAUP, 1983-84; Adj. prof. law George Wasington U., 1967; cons. Adminstrv. Conf. U.S., Ford Found., Pa. Gov.'s Justice Commn. Served with AUS, 1941-46. Recipient Superior Service award Dept. Justice, 1960; Tom C. Clark award Fed. Bar. Assn., 1968. Mem. Am. Law Inst. Home: 1024 E Gemini Dr Tempe AZ 85283-3004 Office: Ariz State Univ Coll Law Tempe AZ 85287

**SPRIZZO, JOHN EMILIO,** federal judge; b. Bklyn., Dec. 23, 1934; s. Vincent James and Esther Nancy (Filosa) S.; children—Ann Esther, Johna Emily Sprizzo Bolka, Matthew John. BA summa cum laude, St. John's U., Jamaica, N.Y., 1956; LLB summa cum laude, St. John's U., 1959. Bar: N.Y. 1960. Atty. U.S. Dept. Justice, 1959-63; asst. U.S. atty. so. dist. N.Y. Dept. Justice, N.Y.C., 1963-68, chief appellate atty., 1965-66, asst. chief criminal div., 1966-68; assoc. prof. Fordham U. Law Sch., N.Y.C., 1968-72; ptnr. Curtis, Mallet-Prevost, N.Y.C., 1972-81; dist. judge U.S. Dist. Ct. (so. dist.) N.Y., N.Y.C., 1981—; cons. Nat. Com. for Reform of Criminal Laws, N.Y.C., 1971-72; mem. Knapp Commn., 1971-72; assoc. atty. Com. of Ct. on Judiciary, N.Y.C., 1971-72. Co-contbr. articles to profl. law revs. Mem. ABA, D.C. Bar Assn., Assn. of Bar of City of N.Y. Office: US Dist Ct US Courthouse Foley Sq New York NY 10007-1501

**SPROAT, CHRISTINE A.,** lawyer; b. Poughkeepsie, N.Y., Feb. 6, 1952; d. John and Jean (Hayes) Morabito; m. James P. Sproat, June 29, 1984; children: Ashley E., William C. AAS in Nursery Edn. cum laude, Dutchess C.C., Poughkeepsie, 1976; BS in Psychology, SUNY, New Paltz, 1978, postgrad., 1979-80; JD, Pace U., 1983. Bar: N.Y. 1984, U.S. Dist. Ct. (so. dist.) N.Y. 1996, U.S. Dist. Ct. (ea. dist.) N.Y. 1997. Atty. Michael Haggerty, Esq., Poughkeepsie, 1983-86; law clk. to Hon. Judith A. Hillery N.Y. Supreme Ct., Poughkeepsie, 1986-96; atty. Gellert & Cutler, P.C., Poughkeepsie, 1996—; adj. prof. law Marist Coll., Poughkeepsie, 1994-96. Editor, contbg. author Criminal Law Digest, 1987. Trustee Dutchess C.C., Poughkeepsie, 1997—; pres. Beekman Women's Rep. Club, 1998—; mem. Mid-Hudson Women's Club Network, Highland, N.Y., 1997—. Mem. N.Y. State Bar Assn., Mid=Hudson Women's Bar (pres. 1986-87, 99—), Dutchess County Bar Assn. (asst. treas. 1998-99, treas. 1999—). Republican. Roman Catholic. Avocations: gardening, hiking. State civil litigation, Municipal (including bonds), Personal injury. Office: Gellert & Cutler PC 75 Washington St Poughkeepsie NY 12601

**SPROUSE, JAMES MARSHALL,** retired federal judge; b. Williamson, W.Va., Dec. 3, 1923; s. James and Garnet (Lawson) S.; m. June Dolores Burt, Sept. 25, 1952; children: Tracy Sprouse Ferguson, Jeffrey Marshall, Andrew Michael, Sherry Lee Sprouse Shinholser, Shelly Lynn Sprouse Schneider. AB, St. Bonaventure (N.Y.) U., 1947; LLB, Columbia U., 1949; postgrad. in internat. law, U. Bordeaux, France, 1950. Bar: W.Va. 1949. Asst. atty. gen. State of W.Va., 1949; with CIA, 1952-57; pvt. practice W.Va., 1957-72, 75-79; justice W.Va. Supreme Ct. Appeals, 1972-75; judge U.S. Ct. Appeals (4th cir.), Lewisburg, W.Va., 1979-92, sr. cir. judge, 1992-95, ret., 1995; pvt. practice, 1995—. With AUS, 1942-45. Fulbright scholar. Mem. ABA, W.Va. State Bar, W.Va. Bar Assn., W.Va. Trial Lawyers Assn., Kanawha County Bar Assn., VFW, Am. Legion, Shriners, Aheppa. Democrat. Presbyterian. Office: PO Box 159 Union WV 24983-0159

**SPROVIERI, CONNIE R.,** lawyer; b. Chgo., May 20, 1957; d. Salvatore R. and Jacqueline T. (Amyotte) S.; m. John P. Barba, July 1, 1978 (div. Sept. 1996); children: Amy, Katherine; m. Harold R. Rodinsky, May 24, 1997; stepchildren: Alexandra Rodinsky, Susan Rodinsky. BA, Dominican U., 1979, MBA, 1989; JD, John Marshall Law Sch., 1990. BaR: Ill. 1990. Atty. pvt. practice, Naperville, Ill., 1990-91; asst. states atty. Cook County State's Atty. Office, Chgo., 1991—. Mem. Art Inst. Chgo., 1997—; complaint rev. com. Operation Push, Chgo., 1997—; vol. reader Elec. Reading for Blind, Chgo., 1997—; peer assistance counselor Lawyers Assistance Program, Chgo., 1997—; rep. com. Downers Grove Twp., Dupage County, Ill., 1996-97. Justinian Soc. Lawyers scholar, 1988, John Marshall Law Sch. Dean's scholar, 1987. Avocations: piano, needlework, physical fitness, theater, crossword puzzles. Office: Cook County States Atty Office 50 W Washington St Rm 500 Chicago IL 60602-1356

**SPROW, HOWARD THOMAS,** lawyer, educator; b. Atlantic City, Dec. 4, 1919; s. Howard Franklin and Elizabeth B. (Riley) S.; m. Mildred J. Fiske, July 22, 1945; children—Howard Hamilton, Mildred Elizabeth (Mrs. Wilson), Matthew Thomas. A.B. cum laude, Colgate U., 1942; J.D., Columbia, 1945; LLD (hon.), St. Lawrence U., 1987. Bar: N.Y. 1946. Assoc. Brown, Wood, Fuller, Caldwell & Ivey, N.Y.C., 1945-53; ptnr. Brown, Wood, Fuller, Caldwell & Ivey, 1954-70; gen. counsel, v.p. corporate and pub. affairs, sec. Merrill Lynch, Pierce, Fenner & Smith Inc., N.Y.C., 1970-77, Merrill Lynch & Co., Inc., 1973-77; ptnr. Rogers & Wells, N.Y.C., 1977-80; of counsel Rogers & Wells, 1980-87; prof. law Albany Law Sch., Union U., 1980-90, prof. emeritus, 1990—; of counsel Crane & Mackrell, Albany, 1990-92; sr. counsel Whiteman Osterman & Hanna, Albany, 1992—; adj. prof. law Fordham U., 1974-80; mem. adv. panel to Law Revision Commn. on Recodification N.Y. State Ins. Law, 1973-84, chmn., 1976-80; bd. dirs. Farm Family Holdings, Inc., Glenmont, N.Y. Mem. editorial bd. Columbia Law

Rev, 1944-45; editor: Financing in the International Capital Markets, 1982. Mem. N.Y. State Bar Assn. Home: 55 Marion Ave Albany NY 12203-1820 Office: Whiteman Osterman & Hanna One Commerce Plz Albany NY 12260

**SPROWL, CHARLES RIGGS,** lawyer; b. Lansing, Mich., Aug. 22, 1910; s. Charles Orr and Hazel (Allen) S.; m. Virginia Lee Graham, Jan. 15, 1938; children: Charles R., Robert A., Susan G., Sandra D. AB, U. Mich., 1932, JD, 1934. Bar: Ill. 1935. Pvt. practice, 1934—; of counsel Taylor, Miller, Sprowl, Hoffnagle & Merletti, 1986—; dir. Simmons Engrng. Corp., Petersen Aluminum Corp. Mem. Bd. Edn., New Trier Twp. High Sch., 1959-65, pres. 1962-65; mem. Glencoe Zoning Bd. Appeals, 1956-76, chmn., 1966-76; mem Glencoe Plan Commn., 1962-65; bd. dirs. Glencoe Pub. Libr., 1953-65, pres. 1955-56; trustee Highland Park Hosp., 1959-69; bd. dirs. Cradle Soc., 1968-92. Fellow Am. Coll. Trial Lawyers; mem. Chgo. Bar Assn. (bd. mgrs. 1949-51), Ill. Bar Assn., ABA, Juvenile Protective Assn. (dir. 1943-53), Northwestern U. Settlement (pres. 1963-70, dir.), Soc. Trial Lawyers, Law Club (pres. 1969-70), Legal Club (pres. 1953-54), Univ. Chgo. Club, Skokie Country Club, Delta Theta Phi, Alpha Chi Rho. Presbyterian. General corporate, Probate, Estate taxation. Home: 380 Green Bay Rd Apt 2A Winnetka IL 60093-4051 Office: 33 N La Salle St Chicago IL 60602-2607

**SPRUILL, KERRY LYNDON,** judge; b. Alexandria, La., Sept. 1, 1954; s. Dwain H. and Alaine Sayes Spruill; m. Laura Roy, Oct. 18, 1975; 1 child, William C. BA, Northwestern State U., 1976; JD, La. State U., 1978. Bar: La. 1979. Judge 12th Jud. Dist. Ct. Divsn. A, Marksville, La. Mem. La. State Bar Assn., Avoyelles Rotary Club, Marksville C. of C., Mansura C. of C. Office: 12th Jud Dist Ct Divsn A PO Box 105 Marksville LA 71351-0105

**SPRUNG, ARNOLD,** lawyer; b. N.Y.C., Apr. 18, 1926; s. David L. and Anna (Stork) S.; m. Audrey Ann Caire; children: Louise, John, Thomas, Doran, D'Wayne. AB, Darmuth Coll., 1947; JD, Columbia U., 1950. Bar: N.Y. 1950, U.S. Dist. Ct. (so. dist.) N.Y. 1950, U.S. Patent Office 1952, U.S. Dist. Ct. (we. dist.) N.Y. 1954, U.S. Ct. Appeals (2d cir.) 1958, U.S. Ct. Customs and Patent Appeals 1958, U.S. Dist. Ct. (ea. dist.) N.Y. 1962, U.S. Dist. Ct. (no. dist.) Tex. 1971, U.S. Supreme Ct. 1971, and others. Sr. ptnr. Sprung, Kramer, Schaefer & Briscoe, Westchester, N.Y., 1950—. Lt. USN, 1943-46, PTO. Mem. ABA, N.Y. Intellectual Property Assn. Avocations: skiing, wind surfing, racquetball, biking, tennis. E-mail: asprung@aol.com. Patent, Trademark and copyright, Intellectual property.

**SPRY, DONALD FRANCIS, II,** lawyer; b. Bethlehem, Pa., Nov. 17, 1947; s. Donald Francis and Carol Annette (Bolger) S.; m. Mary Frances, June 20, 1981; stepchildren: Michael Matlaga, Michelle Fehnel. BA, Moravian Coll., 1969; JD, U. Pitts., 1972. Bar: Pa. 1972, U.S. Dist. Ct. (ea. dist.) Pa. 1975. Assoc. Law Offices of Edmund P. Turtzo, Bangor, Pa., 1973-76; ptnr. Turtzo, Spry, Powlette & Sbrocchi, P.C., Bangor, 1976-83, Turtzo, Spry, Powlette, Sbrocchi & Faul, P.C., Bangor and Stroudsburg, Pa., 1983-90, Turtzo, Spry, Sbrocchi, Faul & LaBarre, P.C., Bangor & Stroudsburg, Pa., 1990—. Capt. USAR 1979-80. Mem. ABA (family law sect.), Pa. Bar Assn. (family law sect. edn. law com., zone del. Ho. of Dels.), Northampton County Bar Assn. (family law com.), North County Bar Assn. (pres.-elect 1989, pres. 1990), Pa. Sch. Bds. Assn., Nat Sch. Bds. Assn., ACLU, Edn. Law Assn., Pomfret Club. Republican. Methodist. Family and matrimonial, Education and schools. Office: Turtzo Spry Sbrocchi Faul & LaBarre PC 109 Broadway Bangor PA 18013-2505 also: 930 N 9th St Stroudsburg PA 18360-1208

**SPURGEON, EDWARD DUTCHER,** law educator; b. Newton, N.J., June 2, 1939; s. Dorsett Larew and Mary (Dutcher) S.; m. Carol Jean Forbes, June 17, 1963; children: Michael Larew, Stephen Edward. AB, Princeton U., 1961; LLB, Stanford U., 1964; LLM in Taxation, NYU, 1968. Bar: Calif. 1965. Assoc. atty. Stammer McKnight et al, Fresno, Calif., 1964-67; assoc. atty. Paul Hastings Janofsky and Walker, L.A., 1968-70, ptnr., 1971-80; prof. law U. Utah, Salt Lake City, 1980-90, Wm. H. Leary prof. law and policy, 1990-93, assoc. dean acad. affairs Coll. Law, 1982-83, dean Coll. Law, 1983-90; dean Sch. Law U. Ga., Athens, 1993-98, prof., 1993—; vis. prof. law Univ. Coll. London, fall 1990, Stanford U. Law Sch., spring 1991; ex-officio mem. Utah State Bar Commn., 1984-90. Co-author: Federal Taxation of Trusts, Grantors and Beneficiaries, 1st edit., 1978, 2d edit., 1989, 3d edit., 1997. Mem. Utah Gov.'s Task Force Officers and Dirs. Liability Ins., 1985-87, Utah Dist. Ct. Reorgn. Commn., 1986-87, Justice in 21st Century Commn., Utah, 1989-91; bd. visitors, exec. com. Stanford U. Law Sch., 1988-93; pres., dir. Albert and Elaine Borchard Found., 1983—; exec. dir. Ctr. on Law and Aging, 1998—; dir. Nat. Sr. Citizens Law Ctr., 1999—. Mem. ABA (Commn. on Legal Problems of the Elderly 1991-95, spl. advisor 1995—), Am. Bar Found. Office: U of Ga Law School Athens GA 30602

**SPURLING, DENNIS MICHAEL,** lawyer; b. Haverhill, Mass., July 20, 1945; s. Forrest Fairfield and Eleanor Gertrude (Kenney) S.; m. Susan Elizabeth Ellis, Oct. 18, 1969; children: Erin E., Daniel M. BBA, U. Mass., 1968; JD, Suffolk U., 1973. Bar: Mass. 1973, U.S. Ct. Mil. Appeals 1974. Atty. pvt. practice, Haverhill, Mass., 1973—. Trustee Haverhill YMCA, 1995—; dir. Haverhill Boy Scouts Am., 1980—; cmty. contrb. Haverhill C. of C., 1994; dir. Heart Fund, Haverhill, 1975-80; dir. No. Essex C.C. Found., 1995—. Mem. Haverhill Bar Assn. Avocations: hiking, backpacking. General corporate, Estate planning, Private international. Home: 8 Washington St Atkinson NH 03811-2544 Office: 86 Summer St Haverhill MA 01830-5837

**SPYROS, NICHOLAS L., JR.,** lawyer; b. N.Y.C., Nov. 27, 1961; s. Nicholas Leonidas and Elizabeth (Kennedy) S.; m. Elizabeth Wolfe, Feb. 18, 1989; children: Sarah, Paul. BS in Physics, Georgetown U., 1983, MBA, 1985, JD, 1994. Bar: N.C. 1995. Asst. v.p. Merrill Lynch & Co., N.Y.C., 1986-91; v.p. Global Plasma Sys./Plasmat Tech. Corp., Washington and Raleigh, N.C., 1996-97; assoc. Carr McClellan Ingersol Thompson & Horn, Burlingame, Calif., 1997—. Republican. Greek Orthodox. Avocation: scuba diving. General corporate, Intellectual property, Mergers and acquisitions. Office: Carr McClellan Ingersol Thompson & Horn 216 Park Rd Burlingame CA 94010-4200

**SQUIRE, WALTER CHARLES,** lawyer; b. N.Y.C., Aug. 5, 1945; s. Sidney and Helen (Friedman) S.; m. Sara Jane Abamson; children: Harrison, Russell, Zachary, Andrew. BA, Yale U., 1967; JD, Columbia U., 1971. Bar: N.Y. 1971, U.S. Dist. Ct. (so. and ea. dists.) N.Y. 1975, U.S. Ct. Appeals (2d cir.) 1974, U.S. Supreme Ct. 1977. Ptnr. Jones Hirsch Connors & Bull P.C., N.Y.C., 1986-98, Jacobson, Mermelstein & Squire, LLP, N.Y.C., 1998—. Bd. govs. Arthritis Found. N.Y., Inc., 1993-99; bd. dirs. MedicAlert Found., N.Y., 1990-99. Mem. ABA, N.Y. State Bar Assn., Assn. of Bar of City of N.Y., Internat. Bar Assn., Licensing Execs. Soc., Am. Arbitration Assn. (arbitrator 1975—, mediator 1993—), Am. Acad. Hosp. Attys., Risk Ins. Mgmt. Soc. (lectr. 1983, 84). General corporate, Insurance, Trademark and copyright. Office: Jacobson Mermelstein et al 52 Vanderbilt Ave New York NY 10017-3808

**SQUIRES, JEFFREY E.,** defender, lawyer; b. Bath, N.Y., Aug. 31, 1954; s. Raymond Campbell and Doris Wilcox Squires. BA, SUNY, Cortland, 1976; JD, Syracuse U., 1979. Bar: N.Y. 1980, U.S. Dist. Ct. (we. dist.) N.Y. 1980. Closing atty. Farm Credit of Western N.Y. ACA, Hornell, 1984—; town atty. Town of Bath, 1986—; pub. defender Steuben County, Bath, 1988—. Mem. Sons Am. Legion, Benevolent and Protective Order Elks. Republican. Episcopalian. Avocations: hunting, motorcycles. Home: 7920 Harrisburg Hollow Rd Bath NY 14810-8275 Office: 14 E Pulteney Sq Bath NY 14810

**SQUIRES, JOHN HENRY,** judge; b. Oct. 21, 1946; married; five children. AB cum laude, U. Ill., 1968, JD, 1971. Bar: Ill. 1971, U.S. Dist. Ct. (cen. dist.) Ill. 1972, U.S. Tax Ct. 1978. Assoc. Brown, Hay & Stephens, Springfield, Ill., 1971-76; ptnr. Brown, Hay & Stephens, Springfield, 1977-87; judge U.S. Bankruptcy Ct. No. Dist. Ill. ea. divsn., 1988—; trustee in bankruptcy, 1984-87; adj. prof. law John Marshall Law Sch., Chgo., 1994, DePaul U., Chgo., 1995-96; lectr. Sangamon County Bar Assn., Winnebago County Bar Assn., Chgo. Bar Assn., Ill. Inst. CLE, Comml. Law League Am., Ill. Credit Union League. Mem. Nat. Conf. Bankruptcy Judges, Am. Bankruptcy Inst., DuPage County Bar Assn., Fed. Bar Assn., Chgo.-Lincoln Am. Inn of Ct., Am. Bus. Club, Union League Club Chgo. Office: US Bankruptcy Ct No Dist Ill Ea Div 219 S Dearborn St #656 Chicago IL 60604-1702

**SQUIRES, VERNON PELLETT,** lawyer; b. Evanston, Ill., Mar. 22, 1964; s. Vernon Tuttle Squires and Merelyn Ruth (Pellett) McKnight; m. Cindy Lee Hanawalt, Dec. 31, 1995; 1 child, Courtney. BA in Polit. Sci., Williams Coll., 1986; JD cum laude, U. Minn., 1993. Bar: Ill. 1993, U.S. Dist. Ct. (no. dist.) Ill. 1993, Iowa 1995, U.S. Dist. Ct. (no. and so. dists.) Iowa 1995, U.S. Ct. Appeals (8th cir.) 1998. Reporter Moline (Ill.) Dispatch, 1987-89, Milw. Jour., 1989; acct. exec. Zigman, Joseph & Stephenson, Milw., 1989-90; assoc. Wildman, Harrold, Allen & Dixon, Chgo., 1993-95, Bradley & Riley, P.C., Cedar Rapids, Iowa, 1995—. Mem. Leadership for Five Seasons. Recipient Spot News and Pub. Svc. Reporting award Associated Press, 1988, Investigative Reporting award Ill. Press Assn., 1988. Mem. ABA, Iowa State Bar Assn., Linn County Bar Assn., Dean Mason Ladd Inn of Ct., Kiwanis Club Internat. Cedar Rapids. Avocations: swimming, golf, reading. General civil litigation, Trademark and copyright, Civil rights. Office: Bradley & Riley PC 100 1st St SW Cedar Rapids IA 52404-5701

**SQUIRES, WILLIAM RANDOLPH, III,** lawyer; b. Providence, Sept. 6, 1947; s. William Randolph and Mary Louise (Gress) S.; m. Elisabeth Dale McAnulty, June 23, 1984; children: Shannon, William R. IV, Mayre Elisabeth, James Robert. BA in Econs., Stanford U., 1969; JD, U. Tex., 1972. Bar: Wash. 1973, U.S. Dist. Ct. (we. dist.) Wash. 1973, U.S. Dist. Ct. (ea. dist.) Wash. 1976, U.S. Ct. Appeals (9th cir.) 1976, U.S. Supreme Ct. 1976, U.S. Claims Ct. 1982. Assoc. Oles, Morrison, Rinker, Stanislaw, & Ashbaugh, Seattle, 1973-78; ptnr., chmn. litig. group Davis Wright Tremaine, Seattle, 1978-97; mem. Summit Law Group, Seattle, 1997—. Fellow Am. Coll. Trial Lawyers; mem. ABA, Internat. Bar Assn., Wash. State Bar Assn., Seattle-King County Bar Assn., Wash. Athletic Club, Rainier Club (Seattle). Episcopalian. Construction, Federal civil litigation, Labor. Home: 5554 NE Penrith Rd Seattle WA 98105-2845 Office: Summit Law Group 1505 Westlake Ave N Ste 300 Seattle WA 98109-6211

**STAAB, DIANE D.,** lawyer. BA, CUNY Hunter Coll., 1977; JD, Yeshiva U., 1980. Bar: N.Y. 1981. Assoc. atty. Hall, McNicol, Hamilton & Clark, 1980-84, Patterson, Belknap, Webb & Tyler, 1984-87; v.p., gen. counsel Ariz. Chem. Co. subs. of Internation Paper Co., Panama City, Fla., 1987-98; v.p., gen. counsel, corp. ethics/environ. compliance officer Ariz. Chem., Panama City, 1998—. Mem. ABA (mem. bus. law sect. fed. ref. of securities com. 1988—, vice-chmn. com. on corp. & bus. legis. subcom. on corp. governance 1992-98), Assn. of the Bar of the City of N.Y. (mem. spl. com. on election law 1987-89, mem. corp. law com. 1989-92, sec. com. on corp. law dept. 1992-93). Office: Ariz Chem 1001 E Business Hwy 98 Panama City FL 32401

**STAAB, MICHAEL JOSEPH,** lawyer; b. Hays, Kans., Oct. 12, 1955; s. Robert Joseph and Beatrice Agnes (Schenk) S.; m. Kathy Lee Brock, Jan. 11, 1986; children: Colton Brock, Matthew Michael. BA magna cum laude, Ft. Hays State U., 1978; JD, Drake U., 1981; LLM in Health Law, DePaul U., 1993. Bar: Idaho 1981, U.S. Dist. Ct. Idaho 1981, Utah 1986, U.S. Dist. Ct. Utah 1986, Ill. 1990, U.S. Dist. Ct. (no. dist.) Ill. 1990. Assoc. Quane, Smith, Howard and Hull, Boise, Idaho, 1981-83, Meuleman & Miller, Boise, Idaho, 1983; pvt. practice Boise, Idaho, 1983-85; ptnr. Biele, Haslam & Hatch, Salt Lake City, 1985-89, Parsons, Behle & Latimer, Salt Lake City, 1989-90; assoc. Steinberg, Polacek & Goodman, Chgo., 1990-93, Ruff, Weldenaar and Reidy, Ltd., Chgo., 1994-96, Gardner, Carton and Douglas, Chgo., 1996—; mem. Chgo. adv. bd. Drake U., 1996—. Contbr. articles to legal publs. Bd. dirs. Winnetka Village Caucus, 1992-94, Big Bros./Big Sisters, Salt Lake City, 1985-89, Utah Head Injury Assn., Salt Lake City, 1988-90, Pediat. Brain Injury Assn., Salt Lake City, 1988-90. Mem. ABA, Ill. Bar Assn., Chgo. Bar Assn., Nat. Health Lawyers Assn., Nat. Order of Barristers, Order of Omega, K.C., Phi Kappa Phi, Phi Alpha Theta, Phi Eta Sigma. Roman Catholic. Avocations: bicycling, reading, basketball, baseball, antiques. Health. Home: 173 De Windt Rd Winnetka IL 60093-3708 Office: 321 N Clark St Chicago IL 60610-4714

**STABELL, EDWARD REIDAR, III,** lawyer; b. Marietta, Ga., Nov. 13, 1964; s. Edward Reidar II and Jane (Williams) S.; m. Robin Suzanne Hill, Mar. 13, 1966; 1 child, Lindsey Katherine. BA, U. Ga., 1988; MA, Valdosta State Coll., 1989; JD, Mercer U., 1992. Bar: Ga. 1992. Law clk. U.S. Atty., Macon, Ga., 1991-92; atty. Inglesby, Falligant, Horne, Courington & Nash, Savannah, Ga., 1992-94, Brennan, Harris & Rominger, Savannah, 1994—. Mem. Mercer Law Rev., 1990-92; contbr. articles to profl. jours. Mem. Ardsley Pk./Chatham Crescent Neighborhood Assn., Savannah, 1995—, chmn. park and tree com., 1998-99; Rockdale/DeKalb Counties coord. Roy Barnes for Gov., 1990. Recipient Award for Pub. Svc. U.S. Dept. Justice, 1992. Mem. ABA, Ga. State Bar Assn., Savannah Bar Assn., George Def. Lawyers Assn. General civil litigation, Insurance, Professional liability. Office: Brennan Harris & Rominger 2 E Bryan St PO Box 2784 Savannah GA 31402-2784

**STABLER, LEWIS VASTINE, JR.,** lawyer; b. Greenville, Ala., Nov. 5, 1936; s. Lewis Vastine and Dorothy Daisy Stabler; m. Monteray Scott, Sept. 5, 1958; children: Dorothy Monteray Scott, Andrew Vastine, Monteray Scott Smith, Margaret Langston. BA, Vanderbilt U., 1958; JD with distinction, U. Mich., 1961. Bar: Ala. 1961. Assoc. Cabaniss & Johnston, Birmingham, Ala., 1961-67; assoc. prof. law U. Ala., 1967-70; ptnr. Cabaniss, Johnston, Gardner, Dumas & O'Neal (and predecessor firms), Birmingham, 1970-91, Walston, Stabler, Wells, Anderson and Bains, Birmingham, 1991-97; pvt. practice, Birmingham, 1997—; Mem. com. of 100 Candler Sch. Theology, Emory U. Bd. editors: Mich. Law Rev, 1960-61. Fellow Am. Bar Found. (life); mem. Am. Law Inst., Ala. Law Inst. (mem. council, dir. 1968-70), ABA, Ala. Bar Assn., Birmingham Bar Assn., Am. Judicature Soc., Am. Assn. Railroad Trial Counsel, Order of Coif. Methodist (cert. lay speaker). Clubs: Country of Birmingham, Rotary. Federal civil litigation, State civil litigation, Antitrust. Home: 3538 Victoria Rd Birmingham AL 35223-1404 Office: PO Box 53-1161 Birmingham AL 35253-1161

**STACEY, JAMES ALLEN,** retired judge; b. Norwalk, Ohio, Dec. 26, 1925; s. James Calvin and Glenna (Cleveland) S.; m. Marlyn Frederick, Aug. 21, 1948; children—James A., Libbie M. Romigh, Lorrie Stacey Singler, David F., CamAllison Shenigo, Tricia Stacey Berger. Student Bucknell U., 1943-44, Ohio Wesleyan U., 1944, 46, 47, U. N.C., 1944-45; J.D., Cleveland-Marshall Law Sch., 1951. Bar: Ohio 1952, U.S. Dist. Ct. (no. dist.) Ohio 1955. Ptnr., McGory & Stacey, Sandusky, Ohio, 1954-56; assoc. Steinemann & Zeiher, Sandusky, 1956-60; ptnr. Work, Stacey & Moyer, 1960-67; judge Sandusky Mcpl. Ct., 1967-95; ret., 1995; mem. Ohio State Traffic Law Com., 1969-95, chmn., 1978-82. Mem., Erie-Ottawa Mental Health Bd., 1968-87; mem. Ex-Offenders for Help Bd., 1975-81; bd. dirs. Camp Fire Girls, 1956-60, L.E.A.D.S., 1984-86, Sandusky C. of C., 1984-86. Served with USNR, 1943-46. Mem. Ohio State Bar Assn., Ohio Mcpl. Judges Assn. (exec. bd. 1970-80), Am. Judicature Soc., Am. Judges Assn., Erie County Bar Assn., Amvets, Sandusky Exch. Club, Elks, Eagles Club, Italian-Am. Beneficial Club. Republican. Presbyterian. Home: 1407 Julianne Cir Sandusky OH 44870-7032

**STACEY, RICHARD WAYNE,** lawyer; b. Grand Junction, Colo., July 16, 1961; s. Donald Wayne and Roberta (Brawner) S.; m. Suzanne Nakao, Feb. 19, 1994; children: Kimberly, Nicole. BA in English Lit., Colo. Coll., 1983; JD, Boston Coll., Newton, Mass., 1987. Bar: Mass. 1987, U.S. Ct. Appeals (1st cir.) 1988, U.S. Dist. Ct. Mass. 1989, U.S. Ct. Appeals (9th cir.) 1991, Guam 1994, Hawaii 1995, U.S. Dist. Ct. Hawaii 1995. Jud. clk. N.H. Superior Ct., Concord, 1987-88; clk. McBride, Wheeler et al, Boston, 1988; asst. dist. atty. U.S. Dist. Ct. (ea. dist.) Mass., Salem, 1988-90; asst. atty. gen. Office Atty. Gen. Guam, Agana, 1990-95; spl. asst. U.S. atty., 1994-95; 1st asst. atty. gen. criminal divsn. Office Atty. Gen. Guam, Agana, 1993-94; dep. pros. aty. Dept. Pros. Atty., Honolulu, 1995—. Mem. Nat. Dist. Attys. Assn. Avocations: running, volleyball, surfing. Office: Dept Pros Atty 1060 Richards St Fl 10 Honolulu HI 96813-2920

**STACHOWSKI, MICHAEL JOSEPH,** lawyer, consultant; b. Buffalo, Feb. 27, 1947; s. Stanley Joseph and Pearl (Wojcik) S.; children: Lisa Ann, Evan Michael, Crystal Lee; m. Deborah Ann Jakubczak, Oct. 19, 1979. BA, Canisius Coll., 1970; JD, SUNY-Buffalo, 1973; cert. Hague Acad. Internat. Law, Netherlands, 1976. Bar: N.Y. 1974, U.S. Dist. Ct. (we. dist.) N.Y. 1974, U.S. Ct. Appeals (2d cir.) 1974. Atty. Sportservice, Inc., Buffalo, 1973-74; assoc. Siegel & McGee, Buffalo, 1974-75; confidential clk. 8th dist. N.Y. Supreme Ct., Buffalo, 1975-77; rsch. counsel N.Y. State Assembly, Albany, 1977-80; sole practice, Buffalo, 1976-86, dep. atty. Town of Cheektowaga, N.Y., 1986-98, spl. prosecutor, 1996-98, litigation town atty., 1998—; Michael J. Stachowski P.C., 1987—. Campaign mgr. various jud. candidates, Buffalo, 1977—; fund raiser Erie County Democrats, Buffalo, 1979—, vice chmn. 1988-97, chmn. jud. screening com., 1991—; bd. dirs. Buffalo Columbus Hosp., 1988-96, sec., 1991-92, treas., 1993-95, chmn. merger com. with Buffalo Gen.; bd. dirs. Buffalo Healthcare Corp.; mem. N.Y. State Dem. Com., 1988-96. Mem. ATLA, N.Y. State Bar Assn., Erie County Bar Assn., East Clinton Profl. Businessmen's Assn. (v.p. 1976—, pres. 1985). Roman Catholic. Family and matrimonial, State civil litigation, Personal injury. Home: 12 Beaverbrook Ct Depew NY 14043-4242 Office: 2025 Clinton St Buffalo NY 14206-3311

**STACK, BEATRIZ DE GREIFF,** lawyer; b. Medellin, Antioquia, Colombia, Feb. 3, 1939; came to U.S., 1967; d. Luis and Carolina (González) de Greiff; m. Norman L. Stack Jr., Dec. 18, 1972; children: Carolina M., Ingrid C. BS, Sch. Sacred Heart, Medellin, 1956; LLD, U. Pontificia Bolivariana, Medellin, 1961; cert. of attendance, Inst. Internat. Studies, Geneva, Switzerland, 1965; M in Comparative Law, George Washington U., 1974. Bar: Medellin 1963, Pa. 1983, Va. 1992. Trademarks examiner U.S. Patent and Trademark Office, Arlington, Va., 1977-78; legal researcher Land and Natural Resources div. U.S. Dept. Justice, Washington, 1980-86; legal officer Food and Agr. Orgn., UN, Rome, 1986-89; legal counsel Pan Am. Health Orgn. Staff Assn., Washington, 1989-92; pvt. practice Mc Lean, Va., 1992—; city judge Caldas, Antioquia, 1989-92; city atty. City of Medellin, 1963; head polit. sci. inst. Antioquia State U., Medellin, 1965; instr. in lang. Peace Corps Vols., Mex., 1968; asst. exec. sec. Interam. Commn. Women, OAS, Washington, 1970; stats. asst. Pan Am. Health Orgn., Washington; cons. Inst. Internat. Law and Econ. Devel., Washington, 1974; ct. interpreter U.S. Magistrate Ct. Alexandria, Va.; legal cons. Mozambique, 1992. Sec. Cath. Daus. Am., Arlington, 1985-86; pres. Colombian Cultural Forum, 1991-94. Mem. Alumna Spanish Sacred Heart (v.p. 1990). Democrat. Roman Catholic. Federal civil litigation, Estate planning, Labor.

**STACK, DANIEL,** lawyer, financial consultant; b. Bklyn., July 29, 1928; s. Charles and Gertrude (Heller) S.; m. Jane Marcia Gordon, Apr. 18, 1953; children: Joan, Gordon. BA cum laude, Bklyn. Coll., 1949; LLB, Columbia U., 1952; LLM, Georgetown U., 1955. Bar: N.Y. 1956. Project Adminstr. Am. Overseas Finance Corp., 1957-58; Asst. counsel ABC-TV, N.Y.C., 1959-60; gen. counsel IFC Securities Corp., N.Y.C., 1961-63; exec. asst. to sr. v.p. N.Y. Stock Exch., 1963-64; sec. pension com. Consol. Foods Corp., Chgo., 1967-69; v.p. legal Seaway Multi Corp. Ltd., Toronto, Ont., Can., 1969-72; v.p. mergers and acquisitions Acklands Ltd., Toronto, 1972-74; sr. v.p., sec., counsel Greenwich Savs. Bank, N.Y.C., 1978-81; sole practice, N.Y.C., 1982-85; ptnr. Brennen and Stack, N.Y.C., 1986-96; cons. venture capital, corp. fin., med. edn., health care, mining, and oil, N.Y.C., 1982—; pres. Bus. and Fin. Resources, Inc., 1982-84; adj. faculty NYU; officer and dir. various public cos.; bd. advisors, Sch. of Bus., St. John's Univ., chmn. sect. on mergers and acquisitions, North Amer. Soc. for Corp. Planning, lectr., guest speaker on mergers and acquisitions, Fac. of Mgmt. Studies, Univ. Toronto, 1974, State Univ. of New York at Buffalo, 1976; gen. counsel Greater N.Y. Safety Council, 1980—. Mem. Congl. mil. service acads. nominations com. and Civil Service intern selection com., 1978—; info. officer U.S. Naval Acad., 1972—. Served to lt. j.g. USNR, 1952-55, capt. Res. ret. 1983. Decorated Joint Service Commendation medal, 1981. Naval Order of US, 1984, N.Y. State Regents scholar, 1945-49. Mem. N.Y. State Bar Assn., N.Y. County Lawyer's Assn., chmn. , Law Com., Ramapo Republican Org., ABA. Republican. General corporate, Mergers and acquisitions, Securities. Home: 8 Linda Dr Suffern NY 10901-3004

**STACK, GERALD FRANCIS,** lawyer; b. Syracuse, N.Y., Feb. 9, 1953; s. Robert James and Rosemary (Murphy) S.; m. Barbara Jeanne Henry, Feb. 14, 1975; children: Moira, Bridget, Fiona. AAS in Acctg., SUNY, Morrisville, 1973; BS in Acctg., LeMoyne Coll., 1975; JD, Syracuse U., 1980; LLM in Taxation, U. Fla., 1981. Bar: N.Y. 1980, U.S. Tax Ct. 1981, U.S. Dist. Ct. (no. dist.) N.Y. 1981. Assoc. Hancock & Estabrook, Syracuse, 1981-85, ptnr., 1986—; adj. prof. Syracuse U. Coll. Law, 1990—; dir. Homebound Handicap Assn., Syracuse, McGraw (N.Y.) Box; sec. Liftech Handling, Inc., Syracuse, 1989—. Contbr. articles on tax subjects to profl. jours. Mem. ABA, N.Y. State Bar Assn., Onondaga County Bar Assn. Taxation, general, Corporate taxation, Estate taxation. Office: Hancock & Estabrook 1500 Mony Tower I Syracuse NY 13202

**STACK, JANE MARCIA,** lawyer; b. Bklyn., Aug. 11, 1928; m. Daniel Stack, Apr. 18, 1953; children: Joan, Gordon. Student, Ohio U., 1945-47; BA, NYU, 1949; JD, N.Y. Law Sch., 1983. Bar: N.Y., 1984; U.S. Dist. Ct. (ea. and so. dists.) N.Y. 1988. Assoc. Shannon, Flaherty, Purchase, N.Y., 1984-85, Schwall & Becker, New City, N.Y., 1985-87; pvt. practice Suffern, N.Y., 1987-90; sr. atty. N.Y. State Div. Human Rights, N.Y.C., 1990—. Vice-pres. Montebello (N.Y.) Civic Assn., 1988—. Republican. Administrative and regulatory, Civil rights, Labor. Home: 8 Linda Dr Suffern NY 10901-3004 Office: NY State Div Human Rights 55 W 125th St New York NY 10027-4516

**STACKABLE, FREDERICK LAWRENCE,** lawyer; b. Howell, Mich., Dec. 4, 1935; s. Lawrence Peter and Dorothea R. (Kiney) S. BA, Mich. State U., 1959; JD, Wayne State U., 1962. Bar: Mich. 1962, U.S. Dist. Ct. (ea. and we. dists.) Mich. 1964; U.S. Supreme Ct. 1968. Lawyer Ingham County Cir. Ct. Commnr.; v.p. Mich. Assn. Cir. Ct. Commrs., 1963, pres., 1967-70; 18th dist. rep. Ingham County Bd. Suprs.; mem. Com. on Mich. Law Revision Commn.; state rep. 58th House Dist., 1971, 72, 73, 74. County del. Rep. Party, Ingham County, Mich., 1969-70, state del., Mich., 1971-74; Lansing city atty., 1975. Recipient Disting. Alumni award Wayne State U. Sch. Law, Detroit, 1987. Mem. Mich. Bar Assn., Ingham County Bar Assn., Nat. Conf. Commrs. Uniform State Laws, Mich. Trail Riders Assn. (dir., past pres.), Mich. Internat. Snowmobile Assn., Sportsman's Alliance Mich., Cycle Conservation Club, Am. Judicature Soc. Avocations: horseback riding, snowmobiling, skiing, traveling. General civil litigation, Personal injury, Probate. Office: 300 N Grand Ave Lansing MI 48933-1286

**STACKHOUSE, JOHN E.H.,** judge; b. N.Y.C., Apr. 3, 1939; s. George B. Stackhouse and Adeline Harbour; m. Linda Starlin, June 22, 1965 (div. Jan. 1983); children: Daniel A.H., Laura Ruth; m. Joan L. Beranbaum, May 19, 1985; 1 child, Ross H.S. BA in English, The Citadel, 1960; LLB, St. Johns U., Bklyn., 1966. Bar: N.Y. 1970, U.S. Dist. Ct. (so. dist.) N.Y. 1973. Judge Supreme Ct. N.Y. County, N.Y.C. Office: Supreme Ct NY 111 Centre St New York NY 10013-4390

**STACKHOUSE, ROBERT CLINTON,** lawyer; b. Medford, N.J., Oct. 10, 1923; s. Daniel Clinton and Mary Haines Stackhouse; m. Louise Morton; children: Robert Clinton Jr., Mary Claire, Stephen Morton. BA, Coll. William and Mary, 1949, BCL, 1951. Bar: Va. 1951, U.S. Dist. Ct. (ea. dist.) Va., U.S. Ct. Appeals (4th cir.), U.S. Supreme Ct. Assoc. L.B. Fine & Assocs., Norfolk, Va., 1951-56; founding ptnr. Stackhouse, Smith & Nexsen, Norfolk, 1956—; chmn. bd., sec. to bd. dirs. Heritage Bank & Trust, Norfolk, 1976-93; sec. Ind. Banks Va., holding co., 1980-89. Tech. sgt. U.S. Army, 1943-46, ETO. Mem. ABA, Va. State Bar, Va. Bar Assn. (hon.), Va. Trial Lawyers Assn. (hon., founding mem.), Norfolk and Portsmouth Bar Assn. (pres. 1982-83). Republican. Presbyterian. Avocations: golf, painting, music. General corporate, Banking, Bankruptcy. Office: Stackhouse Smith & Nexsen 1600 1st Va Bank Tower 555 Main St Norfolk VA 23514

**STACY, BURTON E., JR.,** lawyer; b. Charlottesville, Va., Sept. 21, 1967; s. Burton E. and Shirley C. S.; m. Charlotte McCrary, Mar. 16, 1996. BA in Finance, S.W. Miss. State U., 1990; MBA, U. Ark., 1992; JD, So. Meth. U., 1994. Law clk. to Hon. Judge Nixon U.S. Bankruptcy Ct., Little Rock, 1994-95; assoc. Riggs, Abney et al, Tulsa, 1996-98, Connor & Winters, Fayetteville, Ark., 1998—. Mem. Am. Inns of Ct., Ark. Bar Assn., Okla. Bar Assn., Colo. Bar Assn. Meth. Bankruptcy, General civil litigation. Office: Conner & Winters 100 W Center St Ste 200 Fayetteville AR 72701-6081

**STACY, DON MATTHEW,** lawyer; b. Bluefield, W.Va., Dec. 7, 1954; s. Fred T. and Emma J. (Holey) S.; m. Nancy Jane Lusk, Mar. 20, 1982. BA in Econs., W.Va. U., 1975, JD, 1979. Bar: W.Va. Atty. United Mine Workers Am., Beckley, W.Va., 1979-81; ptnr. Stacy and Shunute Attys. at Law, Mt. Hope, W.Va., 1981-82; pvt. practice Beckley, 1982—; sec. Citizens So. Bank, Beckley, 1995—. Named one of Best Lawyers in Am., 1998, 99. Mem. ATLA, W.Va. State Bar Assn., Raleigh County Bar Assn., W.Va. Trial Lawyers Assn. Personal injury, Workers' compensation, Pension, profit-sharing, and employee benefits. Office: 301 Prince St Beckley WV 25801

**STACY, RICHARD A.,** judge; b. Eldorado, Ark., Mar. 7, 1942; s. Jack Leonard S. and Estelle (Mabry) Carrier; m. Karen Kay King, Aug. 20, 1961; children: Mark L., Andrea L. BA, U. Wyo., 1965, JD, 1967. Bar: Wyo. 1967, Colo. 1967, U.S. Supreme Ct. 1972. Revisor Wyo. Statute Revision Com., Cheyenne, 1967-69; asst. atty. gen. State of Wyo., 1969-72; asst. U.S. atty. Dept. Justice, Cheyenne, 1972-75; U.S. atty. Dis. Wyo., Cheyenne, 1981-94; adminstrv. law judge Office of Hearing & Appeals, San Jose, Calif., 1994-99, Denver, 1999—; mem. atty. gen.'s adv. com. of U.S. attys. Dept. Justice, 1981-84. Mem. Gov.'s Statewide Drug Alcohol Adv. Bd., 1988-94. Mem. ABA, Wyo. Bar Assn., Colo. State Bar, Santa Clara County Bar Assn. (hon., com. on bench, bar, media, police relationships 1995—). Republican. Episcopalian. Club: Kiwanis (charter pres. Wheatland 1977). Office: Hearings & Appeals 1244 Speer Blvd Ste 752 Denver CO 80204-3584

**STADLER, JAMES ROBERT,** lawyer; b. Anderson, S.C., June 1, 1964; s. Robert Edgar and Dorothy Ann (Rhoads) S.; m. Laura Ann Rankin, Oct. 28, 1989. AB summa cum laude, Albion (Mich.) Coll., 1986; JD cum laude, U. Notre Dame, South Bend, Ind., 1989. Bar: Mich. 1989, U.S. Dist. Ct. (we. dist.) Mich. 1989. Ptnr. Varnum, Riddering, Schmidt & Howlett LLP, Grand Rapids, Mich., 1989—. Contbr. articles to profl. jours. Pres. Grace Luth. Ch., 1992-96.; sec. IRRA West Mich. Mem. ABA, Mich. Bar Assn., Grand Rapids Bar Assn., Phi Beta Kappa. Avocation: travel. Labor, Workers' compensation. Office: Varnum Riddering Schmidt & Howlett LLP PO Box 352 Grand Rapids MI 49501-0352

**STADNICAR, JOSEPH WILLIAM,** lawyer; b. Corpus Christi, Tex., Oct. 30, 1963; s. Edward and Carrie Louise (Garris) S.; m. Susan Marie Bitzel, Apr. 25, 1992. BBA, John Carroll U., 1986; MBA, Ohio State U., 1989, JD, 1990. Bar: Ohio 1990. Assoc. Gerald E. Schlafman Co., Fairborn, Ohio, 1991-95; pvt. practice Beavercreek, Ohio, 1995-97; asst. prosecuting atty. City of Fairborn, 1990-95; prosecuting atty. City of Beavercreek, 1990—; assoc. Hammond & Stier Law Office, Beavercreek, 1996-98, ptnr. Hammond, Stier and Stadnicar, 1998—. Trustee, v.p. Greene County Domestic Violence Project, Inc., Xenia, Ohio, 1995—; trustee, pres. Am. Heart Assn., Greene County, Ohio, 1996—. Mem. ABA, Ohio Bar Assn., Greene County Bar Assn., Ohio Acad. Trial Lawyers, Rotary, Beavercreek C. of C. Avocations: fishing, camping. General civil litigation, Contracts commercial, Personal injury. Office: 3834 Dayton Xenia Rd Beavercreek OH 45432-2833

**STADTMUELLER, JOSEPH PETER,** federal judge; b. Oshkosh, Wis., Jan. 28, 1942; s. Joseph Francis and Irene Mary (Kilp) S.; m. Mary Ellen Brady, Sept. 5, 1970; children: Jeremy, Sarah. B.S. in Bus. Adminstrn., Marquette U., 1964, J.D., 1967. Bar: Wis. 1967, U.S. Supreme Ct. 1980. with Kluwin, Dunphy, Hankin and McNulty, 1968-69; asst. U.S. atty. Dept. Justice, Milw., 1969-74; 1st. asst. U.S. atty. Dept. Justice, 1974-75; with Stepke, Kossow, Trebon and Stadtmueller, Milw., 1975-76; asst. U.S. atty. Dept. Justice, 1977-78, dep. U.S. atty., 1978-81, U.S. atty., 1981-87; judge U.S. Dist. Ct. (ea. dist.) Wis., Milw., 1987—, chief judge, 1995—. Recipient Spl. Commendation award Atty. Gen. U.S., 1974, 80. Mem. ABA, State Bar Wis. (bd. govs. 1979-83, exec. com. 1982-83), Am. Law Inst., Fed. Judges Assn. (bd. dirs. 1995—), Univ. Club (Milw.). Republican. Roman Catholic. Club: University (Milw.). Office: 471 US Courthouse 517 E Wisconsin Ave Milwaukee WI 53202-4500

**STAELIN, EARL HUDSON,** lawyer; b. Toledo, Ohio, Apr. 24, 1940; s. Carl Gustav and Margaret E. (Hudson) S.; m. Carol Jane Keeney, Mar. 24, 1973 (div. 1995); 1 child, Vijay Hudson. BA, Yale U., 1962; LLB, U. Mich., 1966. Bar: Ohio 1966, U.S. Dist. Ct. (no dist.) Ohio 1967, Tex. 1982, U.S. Dist. Ct. (we. dist.) Tex. 1988, U.S. Dist. Ct. (no. dist.) Tex. 1991, U.S. Ct. Appeals (5th cir.) 1994, Colo. 1998. Assoc. atty. Marshall, Melhorn, Toledo, 1966-69; pvt. practice Toledo, 1969; lectr. law U. Toledo Coll. Law, 1971-72; staff atty. Toledo Legal Aid Soc., 1969-71, dir., 1971-76, sr. staff atty., 1977-81; pvt. practice cons. nutrition Austin, Tex., 1981; staff atty. City of Austin Law Dept., 1982-86; pvt. practice Law Ofcs. of Earl H. Staelin, Austin, 1986—. Contbr. articles to profl. jours. Pres. Toledo Coun. on World Affairs, 1971-76; chmn. Mayors' com to rewrite Housing Code, Toledo, 1976; co-organizer Conferences on Nutrition and Crime, Austin, 1982, San Antonio, 1983. Mem. ATLA, State Bar Tex., Tex. Trial Lawyers Assn., Capitol Area Trial Lawyers Assn. Democrat. Unitarian. Personal injury, Product liability, Insurance. Home: 1707 Cinnamon Path Apt A Austin TX 78704-4893 Office: 106 E 6th St Ste 635 Austin TX 78701-3638

**STAFFORD, SHANE LUDWIG,** lawyer; b. Camden, N.J., Mar. 10, 1955; s. Joseph and Victoria Stafford; m. Connie, Jan. 19, 1980; children: Courtney, Ashley and Shaun (twins). BS, Calif. State U., 1977; JD, Southwestern U., L.A., 1980; LLD, U. Miami, 1980. Bar: Fla. 1980, U.S. Dist. Ct. (so. dist.) Fla. 1981. Intern Ins. Co. North Am., Miami, Fla., 1980-81; assoc. Miami, Fla., 1981-83; ptnr. Varner & Stafford, Lake Worth, Fla., 1983-85, Varner, Stafford & Seaman, Lake Worth, 1985—. Mem. Assn. Trial Lawyers Am., Acad. Trial Lawyers Fla., Palm Beach County Bar Assn., Phi Delta Phi. Avocations: golf, family. Insurance, Personal injury, Non-profit and tax-exempt organizations. Office: Varner Stafford & Seaman 2328 10th Ave N Ste 2B Lake Worth FL 33461-6606

**STAFFORD, WILLIAM HENRY, JR.,** federal judge; b. Masury, Ohio, May 11, 1931; s. William Henry and Frieda Gertrude (Nau) S.; m. Nancy Marie Helman, July 11, 1959; children: William Henry, Donald Helman, David Harrold. B.S., Temple U., 1953, LL.B., 1956; J.D., 1968. Bar: Fla. 1961, U.S. Ct. Appeals (5th cir.) 1969, U.S. Supreme Ct. 1970. Assoc. firm Robinson & Roark, Pensacola, 1961-64; individual practice law Pensacola, 1964-67, state atty., 1967-69, U.S. atty., 1969-75; U.S. dist. judge U.S. Dist. Ct. for No. Dist. Fla., Tallahassee, 1975—, chief judge, 1981-93, sr. judge, 1996—; sr. judge Fgn. Intelligence Surveillance Ct., 1996—; instr. Pensacola Jr. Coll., 1964, 68; mem. judicial council U.S. Ct. Appeals (11th cir.), 1986-89; apptd. com. on intercircuit assignments, 1987-92, subcom. on fed. jurisdiction, 1983-87; adj. prof. Fla. State U. Coll. Law, 1992-97. Lt. (j.g.) USN, 1957-60. Mem. Fla. Bar (mem. numerous coms., bench/bar commn. 1991-92, bench/bar implementation commn. 1993), Dist. Judges Assn. 11th Cir. (pres. 1984-85), State Fed. Judicial Council Fla., Am. Inns of Ct., Tallahassee Bar Assn., Tallahassee Inn (founding pres. 1989-91), Masons (33d degree), Rotary, Sigma Phi Epsilon, Phi Delta Phi. Republican. Episcopalian. Office: US Dist Ct 110 E Park Ave Tallahassee FL 32301-7750

**STAG, MICHAEL GREGORY,** lawyer; b. Tachikawa, Japan, July 15, 1967; came to U.S., 1969; s. Richard Hopkins and Paulette (Tasca) S. BBA, Loyola U., New Orleans, 1990; MBA, Loyola U., 1994, JD, 1994. Bar: La. 1994, U.S. Dist. Ct. (ea. dist.) La., U.S. Dist. Ct. (mid. dist.) La. Law clk. Capitelli & Wicker, New Orleans, 1993-94; law clk. to Hon. Ronald Sholes Civil Dist. Ct., New Orleans, 1994-95; assoc. McQuaig & Solomon, New Orleans, 1995-96, Sacks & Smith, New Orleans, 1996—. General civil litigation, Environmental. Office: Sacks & Smith 365 Canal St # 2850 New Orleans LA 70130-1112

**STAGEBERG, ROGER V.,** lawyer. B of Math. with distinction, U. Minn., 1963, JD cum laude, 1966. Assoc. Mackall, Crounse & Moore, Mpls., 1966-70, ptnr., 1970-86; shareholder and officer Lommen, Nelson, Cole & Stageberg, P.A., Mpls., 1986—; co-chmn. joint legal svcs. funding com. Minn. Supreme Ct., 1995-96. Mem. U. Minn. Law Rev. Bd. dirs. Mpls. Legal Aid Soc., 1970—, treas., 1973, pres., 1977, dir. of fund, 1980—, chmn. of fund, 1998—; chmn. bd. trustees Colonial Ch. of Edina, 1975, chmn. congregation, 1976, pres. found., 1978; officer, trustee Mpls. Found, 1983-88. Mem. Minn. State Bar Assn. (numerous offices and coms., pres. 1994), Hennepin County Bar Assn. (chmn. securities law sect. 1979, chmn. attys. referral svc. com. 1980, sec. 1980, treas. 1981, pres. 1983), Order of Coif. General corporate, Securities, Mergers and acquisitions. Office: Lommen Nelson Cole & Stageberg PA 1800 IDS Center 80 S 8th St Minneapolis MN 55402-2100

**STAGG, CLYDE LAWRENCE,** lawyer; b. St. Petersburg, Fla., May 22, 1935; s. Milton Gurr and Clyda Montese (Lawrence) S.; m. Betsy Barron, Aug. 22, 1959; children: Sharon, Brian, Lauren, Stephen. BSJ, U. Fla., 1956, LLB, 1959. Bar: Fla. 1959, U.S. Dist. Ct. (mid. dist.) Fla. 1959, U.S. Ct. Appeals (5th cir.) 1969, U.S. Supreme Ct. 1971, U.S. Ct. Appeals (11th cir.) 1987. Assoc. Shackleford, Farrior, Tampa, Fla., 1959-60; assoc. solicitor Hillsborough County Solicitor's Office, Tampa, 1960-61; chief asst. state's atty. State's Atty.'s Office State Atty.'s Office, Tampa, 1963-64, asst. state's atty. State's Atty.'s Office, 1961-63; ptnr. Whitaker, Mann & Stagg, Tampa, Knight, Jones & Whitaker, Tampa, 1965-67, Holland & Knight, Tampa, 1968-74, 80-86, Stichter, Stagg, Hoyt, et al, Tampa, 1974-79, Stagg, Hardy, Ferguson, Murnaghan & Mathews P.A., Tampa, 1986-93, Akerman, Senterfitt & Eidson P.A., Tampa, 1993—; bd. dirs. Fla. Lawyers Mut. Ins. Co. Mem., sec. Hillsborough Area Regional Transit Authority, Tampa, 1979-85; mem., sec., vice chmn., chmn. Tampa Sports Authority, 1985-89; bd. dirs. United Way Greater Tampa, Inc., 1988-91; bd. dirs. Fla. Blood Svcs. Inc., Tampa, 1989—, chmn., 1994-95; spl. counsel to U.S. Senator Bob Graham, 1988; commr., nat. conf. of commrs. Uniform State Laws, 1997—. Mem. ABA, Am. Bar Found., Fla. Bar, Hillsborough County Bar Assn. (pres. 1970-71), Fla. Bar Found., Am. Bd. Trial Advocates, Greater Tampa C. of C. (bd. dirs. 1988-91), Am. Inn Ct. (master emeritus of bench). Alternative dispute resolution, Federal civil litigation, State civil litigation. Home: 3303 W San Nicholas St Tampa FL 33629-7034 Office: Akerman Senterfitt & Eidson PA PO Box 3273 Tampa FL 33601-3273

**STAGG, TOM,** federal judge; b. Shreveport, La., Jan. 19, 1923; s. Thomas Eaton and Beulah (Meyer) S.; m. Margaret Mary O'Brien, Aug. 21, 1946; children: Julie, Margaret Mary. B.A., La. State U., 1943, J.D., 1949. Bar: La. 1949. With firm Hargrove, Guyton, Van Hook & Hargrove, Shreveport, 1949-53; pvt. practice law Shreveport, 1953-58; sr. ptnr. firm Stagg, Cady & Beard, Shreveport, 1958-74; judge U.S. Dist. Ct. (we. dist.) La., 1974-84, 91-92, chief judge, 1984-90, sr. judge, 1992—; Pres. Abe Meyer Corp., 1960-74, Stagg Investments, Inc., 1964-74; mng. partner Pierremont Mall Shopping Center, 1963-74; v.p. King Hardware Co., 1955-74; Mem. Shreveport Airport Authority, 1967-73, chmn., 1970-73; chmn. Gov.'s Tidelands Adv. Council, 1969-70; del. La. Constl. Conv., 1973-74; chmn. rules com., com. on exec. dept.; mem. Gov.'s Adv. Com on Offshore Revenues, 1972-74. Active Republican party, 1950-74, del. convs., 1956, 60, 64, 68, 72; mem. Nat. Com. for La., 1964-72, mem. exec. com., 1964-68; Pres. Shreveport Jr. C. of C., 1955-56; v.p. La. Jr. C. of C., 1956-57. Served to capt., inf. AUS, 1943-46, ETO. Decorated Bronze Star, Purple Heart with oak leaf cluster. Mem. Am., La., Shreveport bar assns. Office: US Dist Ct 300 Fannin St Ste 4100 Shreveport LA 71101-3123

**STAGNER, ROBERT DEAN,** lawyer; b. Simi, Calif., May 23, 1950; s. Cecil William and Mary Jane (Davis) S.; children: Rebecca Lyn, Brenda Deann. BA in History and Polit. Sci., Pasadena Coll., 1972; JD, Western State U., Fullerton, Calif., 1977; student, Civil Engring Tech. Ctr. Degree Studies. Bar: Calif. 1977, U.S. Dist. Ct. (cen. dist.) Calif. 1979. Ptnr. Stagner & Gregg, Orange, Calif., 1978-86, sr. ptnr., 1994—; project mgr. Carolina Gold, Inc., Mex., 1991; officer, cons. Richard Walker Inc., Anaheim, Calif., 1976-86, sec. 1978-81, bd. dirs., Seafood Dimensions ACAL Corp.; gen. counsel Greater Am. Produce, Anaheim, 1978-84, acting pres. 1984; pres. Orion Constrn., Tustin, Calif., 1980-82; counsel Whittier Police Officers Assn., 1982-85; cons. ballistics Kraemer Industries, Anaheim, 1985—, Exodus One Mktg., Placentia, Calif., 1985—, A.W. Schnitger, Encinada, Mexico, 1985—; mem. Nat. Edn. Corp.; instr. Navigation & Coastal Piloting; cons. Gower Industries, Ltd., 1994; co-founder Aegis Security and Exec. Protection, 1996; gen. counsel Lunches, Etc., Inc.; dir., corp. sec. Gower Industries Internat., 1998. Trainer USN Sea Cadet Corps, El Toro, Calif., 1984-94; adult edn. Nazarene Ch., Chino, Calif., 1982-85, bd. dirs. Ont. Nazarene Ch.; lifetime dep. gov. Am. Biog. Inst. Rsch. Assn., 1989; founding mem. Am. Air Mus., Eng., 1997; co-founder Round Tree Inst. for Pub. Svc., 1997, Barnabas Found., 1997. Named one of Outstanding Young Men Am., 1981. Avocations: hunting, fishing, woodworking, scuba diving, sky diving. General practice, Private international, Labor. Office: 630 N Tustin St # 179 Orange CA 92867-7127

**STAHL, MADONNA,** retired judge; b. Robinson, Ill., Sept. 26, 1928; d. Lawrence Joy and Inez Lucille (Kennedy) S.; children: Khushro Ghandhi, Rustom Ghandhi, Behram Ghandhi. BS, U. Ill., 1950; JD, Albany Law Sch., 1973. Bar: N.Y. 1974, U.S. Dist. Ct. (no. dist.) N.Y. 1974, U.S. Ct. Appeals (2nd cir.) 1975, U.S. Supreme Ct. 1978. Atty. trainee N.Y. State Dept. Commerce, Albany, 1973-74; atty. Legal Aid Soc., Albany, 1974-76; ptnr. Powers, Stahl & Somers (and predecessor firms), 1976-89; part-time judge Albany City Ct., 1984-89, full-time judge, 1990-97; ret., 1997; mem. com. on character and fitness N.Y. State Supreme Ct. A.D. 3d Dept., Albany, 1980-86. Lobbyist Com. for Progressive Legislation, Schenectady, 1968-70. Mem. N.Y. State Bar Assn., Women's Bar Assn. State N.Y. (Capital dist. pres. 1983-84), Albany County Bar Assn. Democrat. Unitarian.

**STAHL, NORMAN H.,** federal judge; b. Manchester, N.H., 1931. BA, Tufts U., 1952; LLB, Harvard U., 1955. Law clk. to Hon. John V. Spalding Mass. Supreme Ct., 1955-56; assoc. Devine, Millimet, Stahl & Branch, Manchester, N.H., 1956-59, ptnr., 1959-90; dist. judge U.S. Dist. Ct. (N.H. dist.), 1990-92; cir. judge U.S. Ct. Appeals (1st cir.), Concord, N.H., 1992—. Del. to Rep. Nat. Conv., 1988. Mem. N.H. Bar Assn. Office: US Ct Appeals 55 Pleasant St Rm 406 Concord NH 03301-3938

**STAKER, ROBERT JACKSON,** federal judge; b. Kermit, W.Va., Feb. 14, 1925; s. Frederick George and Nada (Frazier) S.; m. Sue Blankenship Poore, July 16, 1955; 1 child, Donald Seth; 1 stepson, John Timothy Poore. Student, Marshall U., Huntington, W.Va., W.Va. U., Morgantown, U. Ky., Lexington; LL.B, W.Va. U., 1952. Bar: W.Va. 1952. Practiced in Williamson, 1952-68; judge Mingo County Circuit Ct., Williamson, 1969-79; U.S. dist. judge So. Dist. W.Va., Huntington, 1979-95, sr. U.S. dist. judge, 1995—. Served with USN, 1943-46. Democrat. Presbyterian.

**STALCUP, RANDY STEPHEN,** lawyer; b. Great Bend, Kans., Feb. 3, 1947; s. Lawrence Clark and Wanda Lee (Pundsack) S.; m. Clara Belle Coltrane, July 30, 1976; children: William, Stephen, Laurie, Bradley. BA in Polit. Sci., Wichita State U., Kans., 1969; JD, Washburn U. Sch. Law, Topeka, Kans., 1975. Bar: U.S. Dist. Ct. 1976, U.S. Ct. Appeals (10th cir.) 1978, Kans. County and juvenile ct. probate judge Stafford County, Kans., 1971-72; ptnr. Williamson & Stalcup, Wichita, Kans., 1975-83; pvt. practice Wellington, Kans., 1983-89; assoc. atty. Brian Tamara Pistotnik P.A., Wichita, Kans., 1989—. Mem. Am. Trial Lwyers Assn., Kans. Trial Lawyers Assn., Sedgwick County Bar Assn. Personal injury, Workers' compensation. Home: 1728 Tamarisk Cir Wichita KS 67230-7649 Office: 2831 E Central Ave Wichita KS 67214-4706

**STALEY, JOHN FREDRIC,** lawyer; b. Sidney, Ohio, Sept. 26, 1943; s. Harry Virgil and Fredericka May (McMillin) S.; m. Sue Ann Bolin, June 11, 1966; children—Ian McMillin, Erik Bolin. A.B. in History, Fresno State Coll., 1965; postgrad. in pub. adminstrn. Calif. State U.-Hayward, 1967-68; J.D., U. Calif. 1972. Bar: Calif. 1972. Ptnr. Staley, Jobson & Wetherell, Pleasanton, Calif., 1972—; lectr. Hastings Coll. Law, 1973-74; founding mem., Bank of Livermore (now U.S. Bank); bd. dirs. Photomatrix (NASOAQ PHR+); del. U.S.-China Joint Conf. on Law, Beijing, 1987. Mem. Livermore City Coun., 1975-82, vice mayor, 1978-82; bd. dirs. Alameda County Tng. and Employment Bd., Alameda-Contra Costa Emergency Med. Svcs. Agy., Valley Vol. Ctr. With M.I., U.S. Army, 1966-67. Fellow Am. Acad. Matrimonial Lawyers; mem. ABA, Calif. State Bar, Alameda Bar Assn., Amador Valley Bar Assn., Calif. Assn. Cert. Family Law Specialists (pres. 1988-89, Hall of Fame award, 1994), Lawyer Friends of Wine, Hastings Coll. of the Law Alumni Assn. (bd. dirs.). Family and matrimonial, Real property. Office: Staley Jobson & Wetherell 5776 Stoneridge Mall Rd Ste 310 Pleasanton CA 94588-2838

**STALEY, JOSEPH HARDIN, JR.,** lawyer; b. Tyler, Tex., May 23, 1937; s. Joseph Hardin and Mildred Lucille (Wilkerson) S.; m. Linda Luan Best, June 20, 1959; children: Joe H. III, Stefanie Staley Rice, LuAnne Staley Hobbs. BA, Yale U., 1959; LLB, U. Tex., 1964. Bar: Tex. 1964, U.S. Dist. Ct. (no. dist., so. dist., we. dist.) Tex., U.S. Ct. Appeals (5th cir.), U.S. Tax Ct., U.S. Supreme Ct. Assoc. Locke, Purnell, Boren, Laney & Neely, Dallas, 1964-68; minority counsel U.S. Senate Banking and Currency Com., Washington, 1968-70; ptnr. Locke Purnell Rain Harrell, Dallas, 1970—; mem. grievance com. State Bar Tex., Dalls, 1977-86, bd. dirs., Austin, 1983-86. Candidate U.S. Congress, 13th Dist. Tex., 1970; nat. adv. coun. U.S. Small Bus. Adminstrn., Washington, 1972-78; bd. dirs. Yale Club Dallas, 1972—, Dallas Soc. for Crippled Children, 1980-85, Dallas Area Red Cross, 1984—, FOCAS, 1985-89, Met. Dallas YMCA, 1986—; mem. Tex. Constitution Revision Com., Dallas, 1974; regent Midwestern State U., Wichita Falls, Tex., 1989—. Fellow Tex. Bar Found.; mem. Salesmanship Club Dallas, The Links, Dallas Country Club (bd. govs.). Republican. Methodist. Avocations: golf, fishing, hunting. Administrative and regulatory, Condemnation, Transportation. Home: 4445 Rheims Pl Dallas TX 75205-3626 Office: Locke Purnell Rain Harrell 2200 Ross Ave Ste 2200 Dallas TX 75201-6776

**STALF, DALE ANTHONY,** lawyer; b. Cin., Sept. 6, 1956; s. Donald George and Vivian Ann (Roell) S.; m. Mary Tamara Smith, June 16, 1979; children: Nicole, Taylor, Cameron, Logan. BSBA, Xavier U., 1978; JD, U. Cin., 1983. Bar: Ohio 1983, U.S. Mil. Appeals 1984, U.S. Dist. Ct. (so. dist.) Ohio 1988, U.S. Ct. Appeals (6th cir.) 1988. Trial counsel Bamberg Law Center 1st A.D., Bamberg, Germany, 1984-85; officer-in-charge Erlangen Legal Office, Erlangen, Germany, 1985-87; atty. advisor Office of Gen. Counsel, Dept. of Def., Pentagon, 1987-88; assoc. atty. Lindhorst & Dreidame, Cin., 1988-91, ptnr., 1992—. Capt. U.S. Army, 1978-88. Mem. ABA, Cin. Bar Assn. (professionalism com. 1994—), O'Bannon Creek Golf Club. Republican. Roman Catholic. Avocations: family, golf, finances. State civil litigation, Federal civil litigation, Personal injury. Home: 3357 Hammersmith Ln Cincinnati OH 45248-2874 Office: Lindhorst & Dreidame Co LPA 312 Walnut St Ste 2300 Cincinnati OH 45202-4091

**STALIONS, WILLIAM C.,** lawyer; b. Detroit, Dec. 19, 1951; s. Marvin Emerson and Mary Frances Stalions; m. Linda Stonebraker, Aug. 9, 1975; children: Brent W., Grant C. BS, U. Fla., 1976; JD, Nova Southeastern U., 1982. Bar: Fla. Assoc. atty. Britton, Cohen, Kaufman, Benson & Schantz, Ft. Lauderdale, Fla., 1982-83, Benson, Ray & May, Ft. Lauderdale, 1983-84; founding ptnr. Benson, Stalions & Moyle, Ft. Lauderdale, 1984-91; assoc. atty. Broad and Cassel, Ft. Lauderdale, 1991-92, Ellis, Spencer and Butler, Hollywood, Fla., 1997-98; sole practitioner Ft. Lauderdale, 1992—; adj. prof. Southeastern U. Law Sch., 1997—. Student editor Nova Law Jour., 1981-82. Bd. dirs. Sheridan House Family Ministries, 1995—. Served with U.S. Army, 1970-72, Korea. Mem. Fla. Bar Assn. (unlicensed practice of law com. 1995—), Nova Southeastern U. Law Sch. Alumni Assn. (pres. 1995-96). Bankruptcy, Consumer commercial, General civil litigation. Office: 2699 Stirling Rd Ste A201 Fort Lauderdale FL 33312-6583

**STALL, RICHARD JOHN,** lawyer; b. Covington, Ky., July 5, 1941. BS, Purdue U., Lafayette, Ind., 1963; JD, Stanford U., Calif., 1966. Bar: Calif., U.S. Supreme Ct., U.S. Dist. Ct. (ctrl. dist.), U.S. Ct. Appeals (9th cir.). Assoc. Lawler, Felis & Hall, L.A., 1966-70; ptnr. pvt. practice, L.A., 1971-93, Stall, Astor & Goldstein, L.A., 1994—. Contbg. author: Insurance Journal. Mem. Am. Arbitration Assn., ABA, Assn. Bus. Trial Lawyers, Beverly Hills Bar Assn., Calif. State Bar Assn., L.A. County Bar Assn., Nat. Assn. Railroad Trial Counsel, Santa Monica Bar Assn., Lion's Club, Sigma Chi. Office: Stall Astor & Goldstein 10507 W Pico Blvd # 200 Los Angeles CA 90064-2319

**STALLARD, WAYNE MINOR,** lawyer; b. Onaga, Kans., Aug. 23, 1927; s. Minor Regan and Lydia Faye (Randall) S.; BS, Kans. State Tchrs. Coll., Emporia, 1949; JD, Washburn U., 1952; m. Wanda Sue Bacon, Aug. 22, 1948; children: Deborah Sue, Carol Jean, Bruce Wayne (dec.). Bar: Kans. 1952. Pvt. practice, Onaga, 1952—; atty. Community Hosp. Dist. No. 1, Pottawatomie, Jackson and Nemaha Counties, Kans., 1955—; Pottawatomie County atty., 1955-59; city atty. Onaga, 1953-79; atty Unified School Dist. 322, Pottawatomie County, Kans., 1966-83; bd. dirs. North Central Kans. Guidance Ctr., Manhattan, 1974-78; lawyer 2d dist. jud. nominating commn., 1980—; atty. Rural Water Dist. No. 3, Pottawatomie County, Kans., 1974—, Rural Water Dist. No. 4, Pottawatomie County, 1995—; chmn. Pottawatomie County Econ. Devel. Com., 1986-92, atty., 1992—. Fund dir. chmn. Pottawatomie County chpt. Nat. Found. for Infantile Paralysis, 1953-54. Served from pvt. to sgt., 8th Army, AUS, 1946 to 47. Mem. ABA, Pottawatomie County, Kans. bar assns., Onaga C. of C., Am. Judicature Soc., City Attys. Assn. Kan. (dir. 1963-66), Masons, Shriners, Order Ea. Star, Gamma Mu, Kappa Delta Pi, Delta Theta Phi, Sigma Tau Gamma. Mem. United Ch. of Christ. Estate planning, Taxation, general, Real property. Home: 720 High St Onaga KS 66521 Office: 307 Leonard St Onaga KS 66521-9734

**STALLINGS, JOSEPH HENRY,** lawyer; b. New Bern, N.C., Jan. 9, 1950; s. Daniel Livingston and Evelyn Mae (Ricks) S.; m. Leigh Laurens Leonard, Mar. 3, 1990; children: John Daniel, Jordan Patrick, Emily Katherine, Mark Livingston. AB, U. N.C., 1972, JD, 1975. Bar: N.Y. 1976, U.S. Dist. Ct. (so. and ea. dists.) N.Y. 1976, U.S. Ct. Appeals (5th cir.) 1979, N.C. 1979, U.S. Dist. Ct. (ea. dist.) N.C. 1979, U.S. Tax Ct. 1981, U.S. Ct. Claims 1983, U.S. Ct. Appeals (4th cir.) 1985. Assoc. Mudge, Rose, Guthrie & Alexander, N.Y.C., 1976-77, Ford, Marrin, Esposito & Witmeyer, N.Y.C., 1977-79; owner Beaman, Kellum & Stallings, New Bern, N.C., 1979-87, Howard, Stallings, Story, Wyche, From & Hutson P.A., Raleigh, N.C., 1987—. Editor: N.C. Law Rev., 1975. Trustee U. N.C., 1971-72, bd. govs., 1991-95; chmn. adv. com. N.C. region U.S. SBA, Charlotte, 1988—; bd. dirs. N.C. Human Relations Commn., Raleigh, 1971-72. Named Morehead scholar U. N.C., 1968-72, fellow U. N.C., 1969-72. Mem. ABA, N.C. State Bar Assn., Craven County/Wake County Bar Assn., Order of Coif, Phi Beta Kappa. General civil litigation, General corporate. Home: 203 E Green Forest Dr Cary NC 27511-9438 Office: Howard Stallings Story et al 4000 Westchase Blvd Ste 400 Raleigh NC 27607-3944

**STALLINGS, RONALD DENIS,** lawyer; b. Evansville, Ind., Feb. 22, 1943; s. Denis and Gertrude (Tong) S.; m. Vicki Lee Chandler, Aug. 21, 1965; children: Courtnay, Claire, Ryan. B in Indsl. Engring., Ga. Inst. Tech., 1965; LLB, U. Va., 1968. Bar: Ga. 1968. Assoc. Powell, Goldstein, Frazer & Murphy LLP, Atlanta, 1968-75, ptnr., 1976—. Co-author: Georgia Corporate Forms, 1988. Mem. ABA, Ga. Bar Assn., Atlanta Bar Assn., Nat. Assn. Bond Lawyers, Phoenix Soc. Atlanta (trustee 1987-93). Roman Catholic. Municipal (including bonds), General corporate, Finance. Home: 4601 Polo Ln NW Atlanta GA 30339-5345 Office: Powell Goldstein Frazer & Murphy LLP 191 Peachtree St NE Fl 16 Atlanta GA 30303-1740

**STALNAKER, LANCE KUEBLER,** lawyer; b. Tampa, Fla., Jan. 2, 1948; s. Leo Jr. and June Esther Stalnaker. BS in Journalism, U. Fla., 1970, JD, 1973. Bar: Fla. 1973, U.S. Dist. Ct. (mid. dist.) Fla. 1974, U.S. Ct. Appeals (5th cir.) 1974, U.S. Ct. Appeals (11th cir.) 1981. Ptnr. Stalnaker & Stalnaker, Tampa, 1973-75; pvt. practice Tampa, 1975-83, 91—; staff atty. Legal Aid Bur. of Hillsborough County, Tampa, 1983-85, interim exec. dir., atty., 1985-86, exec. dir., atty., 1986-90; asst. cir. ct. commr. 13th Jud. Ct., Tampa, 1981-82. Pres. St. John's Luth. Ch., 1997—. Capt. U.S. Army Res. Mem. Hillsborough County Bar Assn. (family law sect.), Fla. Bar (family law sect.). Family and matrimonial, Probate. Office: 1319 W Fletcher Ave Tampa FL 33612-3310

**STAMATO, LINDA ANN LAUTENSCHLAEGER,** law educator, mediator; b. Newark, July 30, 1940; d. Frederick John and Kathryn (Tremel) Lautenschlaeger; m. Frank Stamato Jr., Aug. 12, 1961 (div. Sept. 1981); children: Nina, Elizabeth, Eve. BA in Polit. Sci. with honors, Rutgers U., 1962, MA in Labor Studies with high honors, 1977, LLD, 1985; MA in Am. Studies with high honors, Seton Hall U., 1968; postgrad., NYU, 1978-81. Cert. mediator, arbitrator. Dep. dir. Ctr. Negotiation Rutgers U., New Brunswick, N.J., 1983—; mediator Mediation Assocs., Morristown, N.J., 1990—; lectr. law, public policy negotiation Sch. Pub. Policy Rutgers U., New Brunswick, N.J., 1995—; lectr. law, dispute resolution Law Sch. Rutgers U., Newark, Camden, N.J., 1985, 88-94; Mem. N.J. State Supreme Ct. Com. Dispute Resolution, 1990-94. Editl. bd. Mediation Quarterly, 1989—; contbr. articles to profl. jours. Chmn. bd. govs. Rutgers U., 1981-84; dir. edn. LWV, N.J.; chmn. Ctr. Analysis & Pub. Issues, Princeton, N.J., 1996—; mem. N.J. State Bd. Higher Edn., Trenton, 1981-84, 95-96. Mem.

Soc. Profls. Dispute Resolution. Democrat. Roman Catholic. Avocations: piano, painting, hiking. Home: 13-19 Franklin Pl # 5C Morristown NJ 07960-5366 Office: Ctr Negotiation & Conflict Resolution 33 Livingston Ave New Brunswick NJ 08901-1900

**STAMBLER, OLGA,** lawyer; b. Kiev, Ukraine, Dec. 8, 1969; came to U.S., 1974; d. Alfred and Asia S.; m. Richard C. Koenigsberg, July 6, 1997. BA, Brandeis U., 1992; JD, Fordham U. Law Sch., 1995. Bar: N.Y. 1996, Ill. 1999. Assoc. Dewey Ballantine, N.Y.C., 1995-97, Gordon, Altman, Butowsky, Weitzer, Shalov & Wein, N.Y.C., 1997-98, Bell, Boyd & Lloyd, Chgo., 1998—. General corporate, Finance. Office: Bell Boyd & Lloyd 70 W Madison St Ste 3300 Chicago IL 60602-4284

**STAMBOULIDIS, GEORGE ALEXANDER,** lawyer; b. N.Y.C., Sept. 28, 1961. BA, SUNY, Stony Brook, 1982; JD, Temple U., 1985. Bar: N.Y. 1986, N.J. 1986; U.S. Dist. Ct. (ea. dist.) N.Y. 1990, U.S. Ct. Appeals (2d cir.) 1991. Law clk. to Hon. Judge Steven L. Lefelt State of N.J., Lawrenceville, 1985-86; fed. jud. law clk. to Hon. Judge Louis C. Bechtle U.S. Dist. Ct. (ea. dist.) Pa., Phila., 1986-88; special fed. prosecutor organized crime strike force U.S. Dept. Justice, Newark, 1988-90; fed. prosecutor organized crime sect. U.S. Atty.'s Office for Ea. Dist. N.Y., Bklyn., 1990-95; dep. chief Long Island divsn. U.S. Atty.'s Office for Ea. Dist. N.Y., Garden City, N.Y., 1995-98, chief Long Island divsn., 1998—. Mem. ABA, N.Y. State Bar Assn., N.Y. County Lawyer's Assn., N.J. Bar Assn., Am. Hellenic Progressive Assn., Phi Beta Kappa. Avocations: racquetball, basketball, fishing, chess, downhill and water skiing. Office: US Attys Office Ea Dist NY 1 Pierrepont Plz 15th Fl Brooklyn NY 11201-2781

**STAMM, CHARLES H.,** lawyer. Exec. v.p., gen. counsel Tchrs. Ins. & Annuity Assn., N.Y.C. Office: Tchrs Ins & Annuity Assn 730 3rd Ave New York NY 10017-3206

**STAMP, FREDERICK PFARR, JR.,** federal judge; b. Wheeling, W.Va., July 24, 1934; s. Frederick P. Sr. and Louise (Aul) S.; m. Joan A. Corson, Sept. 20, 1975; children: Frederick Andrew, Joan Elizabeth. BA, Washington and Lee U., 1956; LLB, U. Richmond, 1959. Bar: W.Va. 1959, Va. 1959, Pa. 1986, U.S. Supreme Ct. 1973, U.S. Ct. Appeals (4th cir.) 1962, U.S. Dist. Ct. (no. dist.) W.Va. 1960, U.S. Dist. Ct. (so. dist.) W.Va. 1975, U.S. Dist. Ct. (we. dist.) Pa., U.S. Tax Ct. 1973, W.Va. Supreme Ct. Appeals 1966, Va. Supreme Ct. Appeals 1959. Assoc., then ptnr. Schrader, Stamp, Byrd, Byrum & Companion and predecessor firms, Wheeling, 1960-90; judge U.S. Dist. Ct. (no. dist.) W.Va., Wheeling, 1990-94, apptd. chief judge, 1994—; mem. ho. of dels. W.Va. Legislature, Charleston, 1966-70. Mem. W.Va. Bd. Regents, Charleston, 1970-77; trustee Linsly Sch., Wheeling, 1977—, U. Richmond, 1997—. Fellow Am. Bar Found., Am. Coll. Trial Lawyers; mem. W.Va. Bar Assn. (pres. 1981-82), W.Va. Commn. on Uniform State Laws, Nat. Conf. Commrs. on Uniform State Laws.

**STAMPER, JOE ALLEN,** lawyer; b. Okemah, Okla., Jan. 30, 1914; s. Horace Allen and Ann (Stephens) S.; m. Johnnie Lee Bell, June 4, 1936; 1 child, Jane Allen (Mrs. Ernest F. Godlove). B.A., U. Okla., 1933, LL.B., 1935, J.D., 1970. Bar: Okla. bar 1935. Practice in Antlers, 1935-36, 46—; mem. firm Stamper, Burrage & Hadley, 1974—; atty. Pushmataha County, 1936-39; spl. justice Okla. Supreme Ct., 1948. Mem. Okla. Indsl. Commn., 1939-40; pres. Antlers Sch. Bd., 1956-67, Pushmataha Found., 1957—; mem. Okla. Bicentennial Com., 1971—; vice chmn. bd. U. Okla. Law Center, 1975-78; mgr. Okla. Democratic party, 1946, dist. chmn., 1946-50; alt. del. Dem. Nat. Conv., 1952. Served to col. AUS, 1935-46, E O. Decorated Bronze Star. Fellow Am. Bar Found., Am. Coll. Trial Lawyers, Am. Bd. Trial Advocates (advocate); mem. ABA (del. 1974-91, state del. 1975-86, mem. com. on law book pub. practices 1974-76, bd. govs. 1986-89, standing com. on fed. jud. improvement 1989-92), SAR, Okla. Bar Assn. (bd. govs. 1969-73, Pres.'s award 1977, 80, 93), Okla. Bar Found. (pres. 1977), Mil. Order World Wars, Pi Kappa Alpha. Baptist (deacon). Clubs: Petroleum (Oklahoma City). Lodges: Masons, Shriners, Lions. Federal civil litigation, State civil litigation, General practice. Home: 1000 NE 2nd St Antlers OK 74523-2822 Office: PO Box 100 112 N High St Antlers OK 74523-2250

**STAMPS, THOMAS PATY,** lawyer, consultant; b. Mineola, N.Y., May 10, 1952; s. George Moreland and Helen Leone (Paty) S.; children: Katherine Camilla, George Belk, Elizabeth Margaret, Carley Lynn; m. Diana Lynn Whittaker, Dec. 11, 1993. BA, U. Ill., 1973; postgrad., Emory U., 1975-76; JD, Wake Forest U., 1979. Bar: Ga. 1979, N.C. 1979. Pers. dir. Norman Jaspan, N.Y.C., 1973-74; assoc. Macey & Zusmann, Atlanta, 1979-81; prin. Zusmann, Small, Stamps & White PC, Atlanta, 1981-85; mem. Strategic Capital Am., L.L.C., 1998—; ptnr. Destin Enterprises, Atlanta, 1983-85. Author: Study of a Student, 1973, History of Coca-Cola, 1976; asst. editor Ga. Jour. So. Legal History, 1991-94. Chmn. Summer Law Inst., Atlanta, 1981-85; mem. Dem. Party Ga., Atlanta, 1983—; atty. Vol. Lawyers for Arts, Atlanta, 1981-94, Atlanta Vol. Lawyers Found.; panel mem. U.S. Bankruptcy Trustees No. Dist. Ga., 1982-92; mem. Bench and Bar Com., State Bar Ga., 1996—; active High Mus. Art, 1986—, Atlanta Hist. Soc., Atlanta Bot. Gardens, Atlanta Symphony Orch., Ga. Trust Hist. Preservation, Ind.; sec. Friends of Woodrow Wilson, 1988—, chmn. dinner, 1990—; trustee Ga. Legal History Found., 1989—. Named to Honorable Order of Ky. Colonels; recipient Svc. award Inst. Continuing Legal Edn., Athens, Ga., 1981, 86. Fellow Ga. Bar Found.; mem. Atlanta Bar Assn. (com. chmn. 1981-85), N.C. Bar Assn., Lawyers Club, Phi Alpha Delta (justice, Atlanta 1982-83, emeritus 1983). Bankruptcy, General civil litigation, Contracts commercial. Office: 7715 Jett Ferry Rd Atlanta GA 30350-5419

**STANDIFER, RICK M.,** lawyer; b. Paris, Tex., Apr. 1, 1959; s. John B. and Betty J. (Watson) S.; m. Tina Y. Roberts, Dec. 14, 1985; children: Bailee Hollen, Sabre Savannah. AA, Paris Jr. Coll., 1979; BA, U. Tex., 1981; JD, U. Houston, 1984. Bar: Tex. 1984, Okla. 1990. Mng. ptnr. Clifford, Standifer & McDowell, Paris, 1986—. Coll. scholar U. Tex., 1980. Mem. Lamar County Bar Assn. (pres. 1991-92), Am. Trial Lawyers Assn., Tex. Trial Lawyers Assn. Avocations: hunting, collecting Indian artifacts. Personal injury, Insurance, State civil litigation. Home: 2765 NE Loop 286 Paris TX 75460-3427 Office: Clifford Standifer & McDowell 2765 NE Loop 286 Paris TX 75460-3427

**STANDISH, WILLIAM LLOYD,** judge; b. Pitts., Feb. 16, 1930; s. William Lloyd and Eleanor (McCargo) S.; m. Marguerite Oliver, June 12, 1963; children: Baird M., N. Graham, James H., Constance S. Bar: Pa. 1957, U.S. Supreme Ct. 1967. Assoc. Reed, Smith, Shaw & McClay, Pitts., 1957-63, ptnr., 1963-80; judge Ct. Common Pleas of Allegheny County (Pa.), 1980-87; judge U.S. Dist. Ct., Pa. we. dist., 1987—; solicitor Edgeworth Borough Sch. Dist., 1963-66. Bd. dirs. Sewickley (Pa.) Community Ctr., 1981-83, Staunton Farm Found., mem, 1984—, trustee, 1984-92; corporator Sewickley Cemetery, 1971-87; trustee Mary and Alexander Laughlin Children's Ctr., 1972-90; trustee Leukemia Soc. Am., 1978-80, trustee western Pa. chpt., 1972-80, Western Pa. Sch. for the Deaf, YMCA of Sewickley, 1996—. Recipient Pres. award Leukemia Soc. Am., 1980. Mem. ABA, Pa. Bar Assn., Allegheny County Bar Assn., Am. Judicature Soc., Acad. Trial Lawyers Allegheny County (treas. 1977-78, bd. dirs. 1979-80), Am. Inn of Ct. (Pitts. chpt. 1993—). Office: US Dist Ct 605 US Post Office Ct House 700 Grant St Pittsburgh PA 15219-1906

**STANFIELD, JANET LOUISE,** lawyer; b. New London, Conn., Jan. 1, 1954; d. Joseph Alden and Dolores Ellen (Sletvold); m. Gerald M. Stanfield, Oct. 27, 1990; 1 child, Eric Gerald. BS, Pa. State U., 1976; JD, Calif. Southern Law Sch., 1988. Bar: Calif. 1988. Attorney Stanfield, Inc., San Bernardino, Calif., 1988-92. Insurance. Home: 229 Grandview Dr Redlands CA 92373-6841 Office: Stanfield Inc PO Box 745 Bryn Mawr CA 92318-0745

**STANHOPE, WILLIAM HENRY,** lawyer; b. Chillicothe, Ohio, Aug. 17, 1951; s. William Wallace and Elizabeth C. Stanhope; m. Kristen A. Keirsey, July 26, 1976; children: Liesel, Sally, Kaitlyn. BA, Duke U., 1973; JD, Northwestern U. Law Sch., 1976. Bar: Minn. Supreme Ct. 1976, U.S. Dist. Ct. Minn. 1976, U.S. Dist. Ct. Ga. 1979, Ga. Supreme Ct. 1979, Ga. Ct. Appeals 1979. Assoc. Robins, Kaplan, Miller & Ciresi, Mpls., Atlanta, 1976-82; ptnr. Robins, Kaplan, Miller & Ciresi, Atlanta, 1982-91, mng. ptnr. SE Regional Office, 1991—; instr. NITA, Raleigh, N.C., 1988, Emory U., Atlanta, 1990—. Contbr. articles to profl. jours. Mem. ABA, Assn. Trial Lawyers Am., Ga. State Bar Assn., Ga. Trial Lawyers Assn. Insurance, Federal civil litigation. Office: Robins Kaplan Miller & Ciresi 2600 One Atlantic Plz 950 E Paces Ferry Rd NE Atlanta GA 30326-1180

**STANKEE, GLEN ALLEN,** lawyer; b. Clinton, Iowa, Sept. 27, 1953; s. Glen Earl and Marilyn Jean (Clark) S.; m. Carol Ann Prowe, Feb. 19, 1984. BSBA, Drake U., 1975; MBA, Mich. State U., 1977; JD, U. Detroit, 1979; LLM in Taxation, U. Miami, 1983. Bar: Mich. 1980, U.S. Dist. Ct. (ea. dist.) Mich. 1980, U.S. Ct. Appeals (6th cir.) 1980, U.S. Tax Ct. 1980, Fla. 1981, U.S. Ct. Appeals (11th cir.) 1981, U.S. Dist. Ct. (so. dist.) Fla. 1982, U.S. Dist. Ct. (mid. dist.) 1984, U.S. Supreme Ct. 1987; CPA, Fla. Assoc. Raymond & Dillon P.C., Detroit, 1980-81; assoc. Raymond & Dillon P.C., West Palm Beach, Fla., 1981-85, prin., 1985-86; prin. Raymond & Dillon P.C., Ft. Lauderdale, Fla., 1987-93; ptnr. Ruden, McClosky, Smith, Schuster & Russell, P.A., Ft. Lauderdale, 1993—. Contbr. articles to profl. jours. Mem. ABA, Fed. Bar Assn., Fla. Bar Assn., Mich. Bar Assn., Am. Inst. CPA's, Fla. Inst. CPA's, Palm Beach County Bar Assn., South Fla. Republican. Avocation: golf. State and local taxation, Federal civil litigation, Corporate taxation. Office: Ruden McClosky Smith Schuster & Russell PA PO Box 1900 Fort Lauderdale FL 33302-1900

**STANKEWICH, PAUL JOSEPH,** lawyer; b. Meriden, Conn., Apr. 15, 1968; s. Joseph Paul and Linda Marie (D'Agostino) S. BA in Polit. Sci., U. Conn., 1989, BA in Econs., 1990, JD, 1993. Atty. Pfizer, Inc., Groton, Conn., 1993, pvt. practice, Storrs, Conn., 1993-95, Bergman, Horowitz & Reynolds, New Haven, Conn., 1995—. Assoc. editor Conn. Jour. Internat. Law, 1992-93. Recipient Hartford County Fed. Bar Assn., 1993. Mem. ABA, Conn. Bar Assn., New Haven Bar Assn. Avocations: collecting sports memorabilia, writing, hiking, travel. Contracts commercial, Real property, General corporate. Office: Bergman Horowitz & Reynolds 157 Church St PO Box 526 New Haven CT 06502

**STANLEY, ARTHUR JEHU, JR.,** retired federal judge; b. nr. Lincoln, Kans., Mar. 21, 1901; s. Arthur and Bessie (Anderson) S.; m. Ruth Willis, July 16, 1927; children: Mary Louise Stanley Andrews, Carolyn Stanley Lane, Constance Stanley Yunghans, Susan Stanley Hoffman. LL.B., Kansas City Sch. Law (U. Mo.), Kansas City, 1928. Bar: Kans. bar 1928. County atty. Wyandotte County, Kans., 1935-41; U.S. dist. judge Dist. of Kans., Leavenworth, 1958-71; chief judge Dist. of Kans., 1961-71, sr. U.S. dist. judge, 1971-96; mem. Jud. Conf. U.S., 1967-70, chmn. com. on operation jury system, 1973-78, mem. bicentennial com., 1975-78. Mem. Kans. Senate, 1941. Served with 7th U.S. Cav. Can. Army, World War I; with USN, 1921-25; Yangtze Patrol Force 1923-25; 9th Air Force USAAF, 1941-45; disch. to Inf. Res. as lt. col. Fellow Am. Bar Found.; mem. ABA, Kans. Bar Assn., Wyandotte County Bar Assn. (past pres.), Leavenworth County Bar Assn., Am. Judicature Soc., Kans. Hist. Soc. (pres. 1974-75), Am. Legion. Anglican. Home: 501 N Esplanade St Leavenworth KS 66048-2027 *My goal in life has been to have and deserve the affection of my family and the respect of my professional colleagues.*

**STANLEY, BRIAN JORDAN,** corporate lawyer; b. Duncan, Okla., Sept. 10, 1954; s. Elmer E. and Betty Sue Stanley; m. Ruth Anne Lynn Stanley, Apr. 6, 1979 (div. Mar. 1989); children: Lindsey Jordan, Brent Alan; m. Francine Michelle La Valle, Oct. 18, 1996. BA in Polit. Sci., U. Okla., 1979; JD with honors, Oklahoma City U., 1985. Bar: Okla. 1985, U.S. Dist. Ct. (we. dist.) Okla. 1985. Sports writer The Norman (Okla.) Transcript, 1979-80; oil and gas landman Milt McCullough, Oklahoma City, 1980-81; trust officer Liberty Nat. Bank & Trust, Oklahoma City, 1981-83; atty. Michael P. Rogalin, Oklahoma City, 1985-86, William H. Mattoon, Norman, 1986-87, Fed. Deposit Ins. Corp., Oklahoma City, 1987, Reed, Shadid & Pipes, Oklahoma City, 1987-88, Mosburg, Sears, Kunzman & Bollinger, Oklahoma City, 1988; v.p., corp. gen. counsel The Hefner Co., Inc., Oklahoma City, 1989—; bd. dirs. The Hefner Co., Inc.; trustee Dr. Brent Hisey Irrevocable Trust, Oklahoma City, 1998—. Contbr. articles to profl. jours. Mem. ABA, Okla. Bar Assn. Republican. Methodist. Avocations: golf, Italian language. Real property, Oil, gas, and mineral, General corporate. Office: The Hefner Co Inc PO Box 2177 Oklahoma City OK 73101-2177

**STANLEY, JAMES TROY,** lawyer; b. East Chicago, Ind., July 12, 1944; s. Troy John and Josephine Elizabeth Stanley; m. Maya Durnovo, May, 1967 (div. 1974); m. Beatrice Lynn Shaver, Aug. 13, 1988; children: Madigan Elizabeth, Troy James. BA, Boston U., 1966; MBA, U. Alaska, 1972; JD, U. Okla., 1975. Bar: Okla. 1975, Alaska 1976. Pres. Stanley Corp. P.C., Anchorage, 1984-96, Stanley & Schadt P.C., Anchorage, 1996—. Mem., chair Airport Commn., Anchorage, 1977-97. Capt. USAF 1966-72. Mem. Alaska Bar Assn. (chmn. real estate law sect. 1985-90, 92-99). Real property, General corporate, Land use and zoning (including planning). Office: Stanley & Schadt PC 2909 Arctic Blvd Ste 103 Anchorage AK 99503-3810

**STANLEY, SHERRY A.,** lawyer; b. Buffalo, N.Y., Oct. 17, 1955; d. Arthur A. and Irene S.; m. William C. Hearon, Mar. 27, 1987. BA, U. West Fla., 1975; JD, U. Fla., 1978. Bar: Fla. 1978. Assoc. Mahoney, Hadlow & Adams, Miami, Fla., 1978-80; ptnr. Steel, Hector & Davis, Miami, 1980-87, Weil, Gotshal & Manges, Miami, 1987-92; sr. counsel Barnett Banks, Inc., Miami, 1992-94; ptnr. Coll, Davidson, Carter, Smith, Salter & Barkett, P.A., Miami, Fla., 1994—. Mem. Fla. Bar, Order of Coif, Phi Theta Kappa. Republican. Roman Catholic. Banking, Contracts commercial, Real property. Office: 201 S Biscayne Blvd Ste 320 Miami FL 33131-4324

**STANLEY, WILLIAM MARTIN,** lawyer; b. Milton, Fla., July 21, 1967; s. William Martin Sr. and Diane (Davies) S.; m. Lorraine Haire, Dec. 17, 1994. BA, Hampden-Sydney Coll., 1989; JD, D.C. Sch. law, 1994. Bar: Va. 1994, U.S. Dist. Ct. (we. and ea. dists.) Va. 1995, U.S. Ct. Appeals (4th cir.), 1994. Assoc. atty. Davis & Assocs., Fairfax, Va., 1994-96, Cohen, Gettings, Dunham & Davis, Arlington, Va., 1996-98; ptnr. Davis & Stanley, LLC, Fairfax, 1998—; bd. dirs. The Paralegal Inst., Fairfax, 1991—, prof., 1991—; bd. dirs. Cambridge Sta. Assn., Fairfax, 1996—. Mem. Fairfax City Rep. Com., 1996—. Mem. ATLA, Va. Trial Lawyers Assn., Fed. Bar Assn., Va. State Bar Assn. Methodist. Avocations: golf, fishing. Criminal, General civil litigation, General practice. Office: Davis & Stanley LLC 9502A Lee Hwy Fairfax VA 22031-2303

**STANSELL, LELAND EDWIN, JR.,** lawyer, educator; b. Central, S.C., July 13, 1934; s. Leland Edwin and Hettie Katherine (Hollis) S.; children: James Leland, Susan. BS, Fla. So. Coll., 1957; LLB, U. Miami, Fla., 1961, JD, 1968. Bar: Fla. 1961; cert. civil mediator Fla. Supreme Ct. Assoc. Wicker & Smith, Miami, 1961-62, ptnr., 1962-75; pvt. practice Miami, 1975-98, Leland E. Stansell, Jr., P.A., 1995—; chmn. Appellate Jud. Nominating Com., Dade County (Fla.), 1983-87; mem. adv. com. Am. Arbitration Assn., 1975-90. Served with U.S. Army, 1957. Mem. ABA (ho. of dels. 1982-86), Fla. Bar (bd. govs. 1966-70, 70-80), Dade County Bar Assn. (dir. 1969-72, exec. com. 1974-75, pres. 1975-76), U. Miami Law Alumni Assn. (dir., officer, pres. 1968-69), Fla. Criminal Def. Attys. Assn. (treas. 1964-66), Am. Judicature Soc., Am. Bd. Trial Advs., Internat. Assn. Def. Counsel, Fedn. Ins. Counsel, Miami Beach Rod and Reel Club (pres.), Coral Reef Yacht Club, Bankers Club, Ocean Reef Yacht Club, Delta Theta Phi (pres. Miami alumni chpt. 1966, regional dir. 1968. General civil litigation, Insurance, Personal injury. Office: 19 W Flagler St Miami FL 33130-4400

**STANTON, GEORGE PATRICK, JR.,** lawyer; b. Fairmont, W.Va., Nov. 21, 1933; s. George Patrick and Wilma Roberta (Everson) S.; m. Shirley Jean Champ, Sept. 3, 1956; children—George Patrick, Edward Scott. B.S. in Bus. Adminstrn., Fairmont Coll., 1956; M.B.A. in Fin., U. Dayton, 1969; J.D., U. Balt., 1977. Bar: Md. 1978, U.S. Dist. Ct. Md. 1978, W.Va. 1979, U.S. Dist. Ct. (so. dist.) W.Va. 1979, U.S. Dist. Ct. (no. dist.) W.Va. 1980, U.S. Ct. Appeals (4th cir.) 1985. Auditor 1st Nat. Bank Fairmont, 1955-61; asst. cashier S.C. Nat. Bank, Columbia, 1961-64; sr. systems analyst Chase Manhattan Bank, N.Y.C., 1964-65; asst. v.p. Winters Nat. Bank, Dayton, Ohio, 1965-69, Md. Nat. Bank, Balt., 1969-74; v.p. Equitable Trust Co., Balt., 1974-79; gen. ptnr. Stanton & Stanton Attys. at Law, Fairmont, 1979—; staff sect. leader, mem. faculty Sch. for Bank Adminstrn. U. Wis.-Madison, 1978-89. Treas. Mountaineer Area council Boy Scouts Am., Fairmont, 1982-90; pres. Three Rivers Coal Festival, Inc., Fairmont, 1984-85, pres., 1985-86, bd. dirs. 1982-86; pres. Appalachian Coal Festival, 1985-86, bd. dirs. 1985—; mem. adv. bd. Inst. for Living, Fairmont, 1983-85; pres. Firemans' CSC, Fairmont, W.Va., 1992-96. Mem. ABA, ATLA, Comml. Law League Am., W.Va. Bar Assn. (Kaufman award 1997), Marion County Bar Assn., Md. Bar Assn., W.Va. Trial Lawyers Assn., Marion County C. of C. (bd. dirs. 1983—), Fairmont State Coll. Alumni Assn. (bd. dirs. 1982—, pres. 1992-94), Fairmont Field Club, Rotary, Masons. Consumer commercial, Personal injury, Real property. Home: 2 W Hills Dr Fairmont WV 26554-5015 Office: Stanton & Stanton PO Box 968 Ste 707 Fairmont WV 26555-0968

**STANTON, LOUIS LEE,** federal judge; b. N.Y.C., Oct. 1, 1927; s. Louis Lee and Helen Parsons (La Fétra) S.; m. Berit Eleonora Rask; children: L. Lee, Susan Helen Benedict, Gordon R., Fredrik S. BA, Yale U., 1950; JD, U. Va., 1955. Assoc. Davis Polk Wardwell Sunderland & Kiendl, N.Y.C., 1955-66; assoc. Carter, Ledyard & Milburn, N.Y.C., 1966-67, ptnr., 1967-85; sr. judge U.S. Dist. Ct. (so. dist.) N.Y., N.Y.C., 1985—. Served to 1st lt. USMCR, 1950-52. Fellow Am. Coll. Trial Lawyers, N.Y. Bar Found.; mem. Va. Bar Assn.

**STANTON, PATRICK MICHAEL,** lawyer; b. Phila., Sept. 8, 1947; s. Edward Joseph and Helen Marie (Coghlan) S.; m. Kathleen Ann Fama, Aug. 22, 1970; children: Cheryl Marie, Susan Elizabeth. BS in History, St. Joseph's U., 1969; JD, U. Va., 1972; MBA, Fairleigh Dickinson, 1984. Bar: Ohio 1972, U.S. Dist. Ct. (so. dist.) Ohio 1972, N.J. 1982, U.S. Dist. Ct. N.J. 1982, N.Y. 1984. Assoc. Taft, Stettinius & Hollister, Cin., 1972-80; labor counsel Union Camp Corp., Wayne, N.J., 1980-83; dir. labor relations, equal employment oppurtunity programs W.R. Grace & Co., N.Y.C., 1983-86; of counsel Shanley & Fisher, P.C., Morristown, N.J., 1986-89, ptnr., chmn. labor and employment group, 1989-95; mng. dir. Stanton, Hughes, Diana, Salsberg, Cerra & Mariani, Florham Park, N.J., 1995—; adj. prof. bus. law Fairleigh Dickinson Univ.; pres. Sidney Reitman employment law Am. Inn. Ct., 1997—. Pres., bd. dirs. N.Y. State Adv. Coun. on Employment Law, Inc., N.Y.C., 1985-86. DuPont scholar U. Va., 1970. Mem. ABA, N.J. State Bar Assn. (exec. com. labor employment law sect. 1989—, rec. sec. 1995-97, treas. 1997-99, 2d vice chair 1999—), Phi Alpha Theta, Delta Mu Delta. Roman Catholic. E-mail: pstanton@stantonhughes.com. Labor. Home: 292 Forest Ave Glen Ridge NJ 07028-1808 Office: Stanton Hughes Diana Salsberg Cerra & Mariani 30A Vreeland Rd Ste 340 Florham Park NJ 07932-1901

**STANTON, R. THOMAS,** lawyer; b. Moline, Ill., 1943. BA, Knox Coll., 1965; postgrad., Harvard U.; JD, Northwestern U., 1969. Bar: Ohio 1969, N.Y. 1982. Mng. ptnr. Squire Sanders & Dempsey, Cleve. Mem. Order of Coif. (chmn. mgmt. com.). Fax: 216-479-8780. Finance. Office: Squire Sanders & Dempsey 4900 Key Tower 127 Public Sq Ste 4900 Cleveland OH 44114-1304

**STANTON, ROGER D.,** lawyer; b. Waterville, Kans., Oct. 4, 1938; s. George W. and Helen V. (Peterson) S.; m. Judith L. Duncan, Jan. 27, 1962; children: Jeffrey B., Brady D., Todd A. AB, U. Kans., 1960, JD, 1963. Bar: Kans. 1963, U.S. Dist. Ct. Kans. 1963, U.S. Ct. Appeals (10th cir.) 1972, U.S. Supreme Ct. 1973. Assoc. Stanley, Schroeder, Weeks, Thomas & Lysaught, Kansas City, Kans., 1963-68; ptnr. Weeks, Thomas, Lysaught, Bingham & Johnston, Kansas City, 1968-72, Weeks, Thomas & Lysaught, 1969-80, also bd. dirs., chmn. exec. com., 1981-82, Stinson, Mag & Fizzell, 1983-96; chmn. products practice group, also bd. dirs., 1993-95; ptnr. Berkowitz, Feldmiller, Stanton, Brandt, Williams & Stueve, Prairie Village, Kans., 1997—. Active Boy Scouts Am., 1973-79; pres. YMCA Youth Football Club, 1980-82; co-chmn. Civil Justice Reform Act com. Dist. of Kans., 1991-95. Fellow Am. Coll. Trial Lawyers (state chmn. 1984-86); mem. Internat. Assn. Def. Counsel, Exec. cmte. 1994-99 East Kansas/West Miss. Cptr., Am. Bd. Trial Adv., Def. Rsch. Inst. (state co-chmn. 1979-90, Exceptional Performance award 1979), Kans. Bar Assn. (Pres.'s award 1982), Johnson County Bar Found. (pres., trustee), Chmn. Bench/Bar Cmte. of Johnson Co. Bar Assn., Kans. Assn. Def. Counsel (pres. 1977-78), Kans. Inn. Ct., U. Kans. Sch. Law Alumni Assn. (bd. dirs. 1972-75). Chmn. bd. editors Jour. Kans. Bar Assn., 1975-83; contbr. articles to legal jours. Federal civil litigation, Securities, Health. Office: Berkowitz Feldmiller Stanton Brandt Williams & Stueve 4121 W 83rd St Ste 227 Prairie Vlg KS 66208-5323

**STANTON, VICTORIA MEAD,** lawyer; b. Albany, N.Y., Feb. 19, 1960; d. Douglas Rhodell and Marjorie Lemka S.; m. R. Matthew Sweeney, Jan. 21, 1989. BA, U. Rochester, N.Y., 1982; JD, Albany (N.Y.) Law Sch., 1987; LLM in Taxation, N.Y.U. Sch. Law, 1990. Bar: N.Y. 1988. Assoc. Rogers & Wells, N.Y.C., 1987-89, McNamee, Lochner, Titus & Williams, Albany, N.Y., 1989-91; exec. v.p., gen. counsel, sec. Farm Family Ins. Co., Albany, N.Y., 1991—; first vice chair N.Y. Ins. Assn., Albany, N.Y., 1998—. Mem. Jr. League of Albany, 1990—. General corporate, Insurance. Office: Farm Family Ins Co PO Box 656 Albany NY 12201-0656

**STAPLE, IRWIN,** lawyer; b. Bklyn., Jan. 23, 1929; s. Morris and Grace (Derringer) S.; m. Roslyn Berman, June 15, 1952 (div. July 1970); m. Gloria Schreiber, Nov. 24, 1971; children: Bernice, Mark, Jaclyn, Anne, Vicki, Robin, Beth. BA, Long Island U., 1949; LLB, Bklyn. Law Sch., 1952. Bar: N.Y. 1952. Pvt. practice Bklyn., 1952-75, New Rochelle, N.Y., 1976—. Mem. New Rochelle Bar Assn. (sec. 1978-80, bd. dirs. 1980-90, v.p. 1990, pres. 1992-94), U.S. Power Squadron (comdr. 1981-82, dist. lt. 1986-90, staff comdr. 1990-92, dist. comdr. dist. 2 1999-2000), Halloween Yacht Club, Polaris Yacht Club (rear commodore 1978-79). Avocations: boating, travel. General practice, Family and matrimonial, General civil litigation. Office: PO Box 705 366 North Ave New Rochelle NY 10801-4110

**STAPLES, JOHN NORMAN, III,** lawyer; b. Durham, N.C., Aug. 1, 1946; s. Norman Appleton Staples and Elizabeth (Stewart-Richardson) Smith; m. Lila Banks James, May 18, 1968; children: Susan Banks, John William, James Nicholas. BA in English, Trinity Coll., 1968; JD, Pepperdine U., 1976. Bar: Calif. 1976. Former ptnr. Millard, Morris & Staples, Carmel; head of adv. svcs. West Coast Alex Brown Capital Adv. Trust Co., San Francisco, Calif. Bd. dirs. Monterey Peninsula United Way, 1980-83, Planned Parenthood Monterey County, 1986-90; chmn. bd. dirs. All Sts. Episcopal Day Sch., Carmel Valley, Calif., 1986-89; trustee Monterey Peninsula Mus. Art; trustee Calif. Assn. Ind. Schs., 1986-89. Capt. USMC, 1968-73, lt. col. USAFR, Ret. Mem. ABA, Monterey County Bar Assn., Calif. Bar Assn. Office: Alex Brown Adv Trust Co 101 California St Fl 46 San Francisco CA 94111-5802

**STAPLES, LYLE NEWTON,** lawyer; b. Radford, Va., Feb. 16, 1945; s. Lester Lyle and Velma Jean (King) S.; m. Christie Mercedes Carr, Feb. 1, 1971; children: Scott Andrew, John Randolph, Brian Matthew, Melissa Ann. BA, U. Md., 1967, JD, 1972; LLM in Taxation, Georgetown U., 1977. Bar: Md. 1973, U.S. Supreme Ct. 1978, U.S. Tax Ct. 1981, U.S. Dist. Ct. Md. 1981, U.S. Ct. Appeals (4th cir.) 1981. Tax law specialist IRS, Washington, 1972-77; assoc. Hessey & Hessey, Balt., 1978-82, Rosenstock, Burgee & Welty, Frederick, Md., 1982-84; sole practice, Hampstead, Md., 1984-91; mem. firm Johnson, Parker & Hess, Westminster, Md., 1991-96; pvt. practice, Westminster, 1996—; vis. asst. prof. Towson (Md.) State U., 1981-82. Treas., bd. dirs. Literacy Coun. of Carroll County, Inc., 1993-98. Served with U.S. Army, 1968-69, Vietnam. Mem. ABA, Md. Bar Assn., Carroll County C. of C. Democrat. Methodist. Taxation, general, Estate planning, General corporate. Home: 813 Clearview Ave Hampstead MD 21074-2325 Office: 56 W Main St Westminster MD 21157-4844

**STAPLETON, CAROLYN LOUISE,** lawyer, clergywoman; b. West Point, N.Y., July 19, 1947; d. Carl William and Louise Maxine (Starrett) S.; m. Andrew J. Weaver, Oct. 4, 1998. BA, Mich. State U., 1969; MTh, So. Meth. U., 1972, D Ministry, 1983; JD, U. Hawaii, 1987. Bar: Hawaii 1987, U.S. Dist. Ct. Hawaii; ordained deacon United Meth. Ch., 1971, ordained elder, 1973. Assoc. min. St. John's United Meth. Ch., Corpus Christi, Tex., 1972-74; Methodist campus min. Emory U., Atlanta, 1974-78; chaplain Punahou Sch., Honolulu, 1978-80; civilian contract chaplain Aliamanu Mil. Housing, Honolulu, 1981; dir. family ministries Naval Sta. Chapel, Pearl Harbor, Hawaii, 1983-84; law clerk Family Ct. (1st cir.) Hawaii, 1985, Supreme Ct. Federated States of Micronesia, 1986, Office Disciplinary Counsel, Hawaii Supreme Ct., 1986-87; dep. atty. gen. State of Hawaii, Honolulu, 1987-88, staff atty. labor appeals bd., 1988-89; exec. dir., legal counsel Ethics Commn.

City and County of Honolulu, 1989—; staff assoc. for social justice and spiritual concerns Hawaii Coun. Churchs., 1990-94; bd. dirs., sec. Spiritual Life Ctr., Honolulu, 1990-95; trustee 1st United Meth. Ch., Honolulu, 1986-95; mem. Hawaii dist. div. ch. and society United Meth. Ch., 1979-95; mem. various coms. Coun. on Govtl. Ethics Laws, 1995-99. Contbg. author: Called from Within: Early Women Lawyers of Hawaii, 1992; prodr. slide and tape show Womanriver Flowing On: Glimpses of Some Foremothers in the United Methodist Tradition, 1981; contbr. articles to religious jours. Bd. dirs., v.p. Hawaii Lawyers Care, Honolulu, 1990-99; bd. dirs. Advs. for Pub. Interest Law, Honolulu, 1986-89; del., com. mem. Hawaii Dem. Conv., 1984, 86, 88, 90, 92, 94, 96, 98; precinct treas. Honolulu Dem. Party, 1986—; mem. Neighborhood Bd. 5, Honolulu, 1983-89; co-founder, bd. dirs. Hawaii Women's Polit. Action League, Honolulu, 1982-85; bd. dirs. Friends Judiciary History Ctr., sec., 1991—; bd. dirs. Interfaith Network Against Domestic Violence, 1990-95. Named One of 10 Outstanding Young Women Am., Pres. of U.S., 1974; Laskey scholar women's div. bd. missions United Meth. Ch., 1971; rsch. grantee Women's Studies Coun., So. Meth. U., 1981. Mem. AAUW (bd. dirs., various state and br. offices 1979—), Phi Delta Phi (parliamentarian, historian 1985—), Alpha Delta Pi (chaplain, historian 1966—). Avocations: photography, needlework. Office: Ethics Commn City & County Honolulu 715 S King St Ste 211 Honolulu HI 96813-3021

**STAPLETON, JOHN OWEN,** lawyer; b. Montgomery, Ala., July 24, 1951; s. Max O. Stapleton and Margaret (Lois) Gardner; m. Andrea Carol White, Apr. 1973 (div. June 1975); 1 child, Stefanie Michele; m. Nancy Jean Corbett, Sept. 20, 1980; 1 child, Kellie Nichole. BS, U. Montevallo, 1976; JD, Samford U., 1980. Bar: Fla. 1981, U.S. Dist. Ct. (no. dist.) Fla. 1981, U.S. Ct. Appeals (11th cir.) 1982, U.S. Ct. Appeals (Fed. cir.) 1985, U.S. Dist. Ct. (mid. and so. dist.) Fla. 1993; bd. cert. in city, county and local govt. law, Fla. Assoc. Shimek & Sutherland P.A., Pensacola, Fla., 1981-83; sole practice Pensacola, 1984-91; asst. county atty. Escambia County, Fla., 1992-93; asst. county atty. labor and employment divsn. Broward County, Fla., 1993—; of counsel Jackson Lewis Schnitzler & Krupman, Orlando, Fla., 1999—. guardian ad litem program 1st Jud. Cir., 1984-88. Democrat. Avocations: fishing, woodworking, boardgaming, reading, World War II ETO info. Office: Office of County Atty Broward County Govt Ctr 115 S Andrews Ave Ste 423 Fort Lauderdale FL 33301

**STAPLETON, JOHN WARREN,** lawyer; b. Huntington, W.Va., June 20, 1956; s. Warren G. and Juanita Stapleton; m. Laura Stapleton, Oct. 18, 1997; 1 child, Andrew. BA, Marshall U., 1976; JD, W.Va. Law Sch., 1979. Bar: W.Va. 1979, U.S. Dist. Ct. (so. dist.) W.Va. 1979, Ky. 1987, U.S. Dist. Ct. (ea. dist.) Ky. 1990. Sr. ptnr. Stapleton Law Offices, Huntington, 1979—. Capt. USAR. Mem. W.Va. State Bar (technet com.), Ky. Acad. Trial Attys. Baptist. Personal injury, Family and matrimonial, Criminal. Office: Stapleton Law Offices 400 5th Ave Huntington WV 25701-1906

**STAPLETON, WALTER KING,** federal judge; b. Cuthbert, Ga., June 2, 1934; s. Theodore Newton and Elizabeth Grantland (King) S.; m. Georgianna Duross Stapleton; children: Russell K., Theodore N., Teryl J. B.A., Princeton, 1956; LL.B., Harvard, 1959; LL.M., U. Va., 1984. Bar: Del. Assoc. mem. firm Morris, Nichols, Arsht & Tunnell, Wilmington, Del., 1959-65; dep. atty. gen. State of Del., 1963; partner Morris, Nichols, Arsht & Tunnell, 1966-70; judge U.S. Dist. Ct. Del., Wilmington, 1970-85; chief judge U.S. Dist. Ct. Del., 1983-85; judge U.S. Ct. Appeals (3d cir.), 1985—; Dep. atty. gen., Del., 1964; mem. Jud. Conf. U.S., 1984-85. Bd. dirs. Am. Bapt. Chs., U.S.A., 1978. Baptist. Office: US Ct Appeals 844 N King St Wilmington DE 19801-3519

**STARCHER, LARRY VICTOR,** state supreme court chief justice; b. Rocksdale, W.Va., Sept. 25, 1942. AB cum laude, W.Va. U., 1964, JD, 1967. Bar: W.Va. 1967. Former judge and chief judge W.Va. Ct. (17th jud. cir.), 1977-96; now justice W.Va. Supreme Ct. Appeals, 1997—; pvt. practice, Morgantown, 1976—; dir. North Ctrl. W.Va. Legal Aid Soc., 1969-76; former instr. law, pub. adminstrn., and history W.Va. U.; contract adminstr. W.Va. U., 1966-67, asst. to v.p., 1967-69. Editor W.Va. Law Rev.; contbr. articles to profl. jours. Mem. City Coun. Morgantown, 1971-72; former mem. Young Dems. Fellow Harvard U., summer 1978. Mem. Am. Correctional Assn., W.Va. Jud. Assn., W.Va. State Bar, Monongalia County Bar Assn., Beta Theta Pi, Phi Delta Phi, Phi Alpha Theta, Pi Sigma Alpha. Avocations: carpentry, gardening, skiing. Office: Supreme Ct Appeals Capitol Complex Bldg One Rm E 307 Charleston WV 25305

**STARING, GRAYDON SHAW,** lawyer; b. Deansboro, N.Y., Apr. 9, 1923; s. William Luther and Eleanor Mary (Shaw) S.; m. Joyce Lydia Allum-Poon, Sept. 1, 1949; children: Diana Hilary Agnes, Christopher Paul Norman. AB, Hamilton Coll., 1947; JD, U. Calif., Berkeley, 1951. Bar: Calif. 1952, U.S. Supreme Ct. 1958. Atty. Office Gen. Counsel, Navy Dept., San Francisco, 1952-53; atty. admiralty and shipping sect. U.S. Dept. Justice, San Francisco, 1953-60; assoc. Lillick & Charles, San Francisco, 1960-64, ptnr., 1965-95, of counsel, 1995—; titulary mem. Internat. Maritime Com.; bd. dirs. Marine Exchange at San Francisco, 1984-88, pres. 1986-88; instr. pub. speaking Hamilton Coll., 1947-48; adj. prof. Hastings Coll. Law, 1996-97, Boalt Hall, U. Calif., 1999. Author: Law of Reinsurance, 1993; assoc. editor Am. Maritime Cases, 1966-92, editor, 1992—; contbr. articles to legal jours. Mem. San Francisco Lawyers Com. for Urban Affairs, 1972-90; bd. dirs. Legal Aid Soc., San Francisco, 1974-90, v.p., 1975-80, pres., 1980-82. With USN, 1943-46, comdr. USNR. Fellow Am. Bar Found., Am. Coll. Trial Lawyers; mem. ABA (chmn. maritime ins. com. 1975-76, mem. standing com. admiralty law 1976-82, 86-90, chmn. 1990, ho. dels. 1986-90), FBA (pres. San Francisco chpt. 1968), Bar Assn. San Francisco (sec. 1972, treas. 1973), Calif. Acad. Appellate Lawyers, Maritime Law Assn. U.S. (exec. com. 1977-88, v.p. 1980-84, pres. 1984-86), Brit. Ins. Law Assn., Brit.-Am. C. of C. (bd. dirs. 1987—), World Trade Club San Francisco, Tulane Admiralty Inst. (permanent adv. bd.), Assocs. Maritime Mus. Libr. (dir. 1990—, pres. 1992-94). Admiralty, Insurance, General civil litigation. Home: 195 San Anselmo Ave San Francisco CA 94127-1513 Office: 2 Embarcadero Ctr Ste 2600 San Francisco CA 94111-3900 *"How small, of all that human hearts endure,/That part which laws or kings can cause or cure!".*

**STARK, ALBERT MAXWELL,** lawyer; b. Trenton, N.J., May 3, 1939; m. Ellen Stark, Nov. 20, 1966; children: Jared, Rachel. BA, Darmouth Coll., Hanover, N.H., 1960; LLD, U. Pa., Phila., 1963. Bar: N.J. 1964. Asst. to gov. of N.J., 1964; asst. atty. City of Trenton, 1965-66; asst. prosecutor Mercer County, N.J., 1967-68. Host radio programs Lawline, WHWH, 1985-95, In the Pub. Interest, WIMG, 1996. Mem. ABA, N.J. Bar Assn., Mercer County Bar Assn., Mercer County C. of C. (Citizen of Yr. 1994), Rotary Internat. (Fred Harris fellow 1996). Avocations: writing, tennis, skiing. Office: Stark & Stark 993 Lenox Dr Ste 301 Lawrenceville NJ 08648-2316

**STARK, JEFFREY ROZELLE,** lawyer; b. Orange, Calif., Apr. 2, 1951; s. Harwood Milton and Jean Gladys (Rozelle) S.; m. Margaret Pagano, Feb. 23, 1991; children: Tyler Chase, Jennifer Rozelle. BA, UCLA, 1972; JD, Loyola U. Bar: Calif. 1976, U.S. Dist. Ct. Calif. 1976. Atty. Cadoo, Tretheway, McGinn & Morgan, Marina del Rey, Calif., 1976-80; pvt. practice Marina del Rey, 1980-89; atty. Stark & Rasak, Torrance, Calif., 1989-92, Stark, Rasak & Clarke, Torrance, 1992—; chmn. bd. dirs. Bay Harbor Hosp. and Harbor Health Sys., Harbor City, Calif. 1989-97; bd. dirs. Little Co. of Mary Hosp. Bd. dirs. Billy Barty Found., Burbank, Calif., 1990-95; founding mem. Wellness, Redondo Beach, Calif., 1990-95. Mem. Phi Beta Kappa. Family and matrimonial, Personal injury. Home: 52 Village Cir Manhattan Beach CA 90266-7222 Office: Stark Rasak & Clarke 20355 Hawthorne Blvd Torrance CA 90503-2401

**STARK, MICHAEL J.,** lawyer; b. Phila., Mar. 18, 1948; s. Samuel and Edith S.; children from previous marriage: Terra Rachael, Cedar Abraham; m. M.J. Grande, Aug. 27, 1988; children; Isaac Taylor, Laurel Rose. BA in Polit. Sci., U. Fla., 1970; JD, Georgetown U. Sch. Law, 1974. Bar: Alaska 1974, U.S. Dist. Ct. Alaska 1975, U.S. Ct. Appeals (7th cir.) 1980, U.S. Ct. Appeals (9th cir.) 1983, U.S. Supreme Ct. 1981. Asst. atty. gen. Alaska Dept. Law, Juneau, 1974—; chief counsel Alaska Dept. of Corrections, 1981—. Bd. dirs. Juneau Coop. Preschool, 1997-99; soccer coach Juneau Parks & Recreation, 1996—. Mem. Am. Correctional Assn. (legal issues com. 1983-86). Avocations: reading, volleyball, coaching soccer, hiking, cross country skiing. Office: Alaska Dept Law PO Box 110300 Juneau AK 99811-0300

**STARK, STEPHEN M.,** lawyer; b. Ft. Dodge, Iowa, Mar. 19, 1957; s. Maurice E. and Mary M. (Murray) S.; m. Pamela A. Hammer, Nov. 12, 1983; children: Allison, Andrew, Sarah, Rachel. BS, Iowa State U., 1979; JD, U. Iowa, 1983. Atty. Fleeson Gooing Coulson & Kitch, Wichita, Kans., 1983—. Author: (with others) Kansas Environmental Law Handbook, 1992, rev., 1996. Chmn. fin. coun. The Ch. of The Blessed Sacrament, Wichita, 1995—. Mem. ABA, Kans. Bar Assn., Wichita Bar Assn. Avocation: coaching girls and boys grade school basketball. Office: Fleeson Gooing Coulson & Kitch 125 N Market St Ste 1600 Wichita KS 67202-1716

**STARKE, HAROLD E., JR.,** lawyer; b. Richmond, Va., Aug. 1, 1944. BA, Randolph-Macon Coll., 1967; JD, U. Richmond, 1971; LLM in Taxation, NYU, 1973. Bar: Va. 1971, D.C. 1981. Mem. Mays & Valentine, LLP, Richmond. Assoc. editor U. Richmond Law Rev., 1970-71. Bd. trustees Randolph-Macon Coll., 1983-85, 95-97. Fellow Am. Coll. Tax Counsel; mem. ABA (taxation, bus. law, real property, probate and trust law sects), Va. State Bar (chmn. taxation sect. 1985-86), Va. Bar Assn. (com. on taxation), D.C. Bar, Richmond Bar Assn., Richmond Estate Planning Coun., Randolph-Macon Estate Planning Coun. (chmn. 1985—), McNeill Honor Soc., Phi Delta Phi. Taxation, general, General corporate, Estate planning. Office: Mays & Valentine LLP NationsBank Center PO Box 1122 Richmond VA 23218-1122

**STARKOFF, ALAN GARY,** lawyer; b. Cleve., May 31, 1950; s. Harvey Herbert Starkoff and Honey Beverly (Stein) Simmons; children—Brandon Mitchell, Brooke Erin; m. Kathleen Klingbiel, Jan. 9, 1982; 1 child, William K. B.S., Ohio State U., 1972; J.D., Cleve. State U., 1975. Bar: Ohio 1975, Fla. 1975, Pa. 1981, U.S. Dist. Ct. (no. dist.) Ohio 1975, U.S. Supreme Ct. 1979. Assoc. Starkoff & Gallagher, Cleve., 1975-78; ptnr. Starkoff & Starkoff, Cleve. 1978-84; prin. Gaines & Stern Co. L.P.A., Cleve., 1984-98; prin. Schuttenstein Zox and Dunn, Columbus, Ohio, 1999—; dir. Stanspec Corp., Cleve. 1981—. Councilman City of University Heights, Ohio, 1980-81; vice chmn. Charter Rev. Commn., University Heights, 1979; mem. Cuyahoga County Republican Orgn., Cleve. 1980-81. Mem. ABA, Columbus Bar Assn., Fla. Bar Assn., Ohio State Bar Assn., Pa. Bar Assn., Assn. Trial Lawyers Am., Cleve. Trial Lawyers Assn. State civil litigation, General corporate, Personal injury. Home: 4387 Tarrytown Ct New Albany OH 43054-9679 Office: Schottenstein Zox & Dunn 41 S High St Columbus OH 43215-6101

**STARNES, CYNTHIA,** law educator; b. Abilene, Tex., Mar. 23, 1948; d. Rufus Garland and Alicia Mary (Garcia) S. BS, Mich. State U., 1973; JD, Ind. U., Indpls., 1983; LLM, Columbia U., 1989. Bar: Ind. 1983, U.S. Ct. Appeals (7th cir.) 1983. Instr. legal rsch. Fla. State U. Coll. Law, Tallahassee, 1986-88; instr. CLEO Summer Inst., Knoxville, Tenn., 1988; prof. Legal Inst., The Nat. Jud. Coll., Reno, 1990-93; vis. prof. U. Denver Coll. Law, 1994-95, Wayne State U. Law Sch., Detroit, 1995-96; prof. Detroit Coll. Law, Mich. State U., East Lansing, 1989—; lectr. Nat. Judges Assn., 1991, 92; vis. prof. U. Mich. Law Sch., Ann Arbor, 1998. Contbr. articles to profl. jours. Mem. ABA. Office: Mich State U Detroit Coll Law Law Coll Bldg East Lansing MI 48224-1300

**STARNES, JAMES WRIGHT,** lawyer; b. East St. Louis, Ill., Apr. 3, 1933; s. James Adron and Nell (Short) S.; m. Helen Woods Mitchell, Mar. 29, 1958 (div. 1978); children: James Wright, Mitchell A., William B. II; m. Kathleen Israel, Jan. 26, 1985. Student St. Louis U., 1951-53; LLB, Washington U., St. Louis, 1957. Bar: Mo. 1957, Ill. 1957, Fla. 1992. Assoc. Stinson, Mag & Fizzell, Kansas City, Mo., 1957-60, ptnr., 1960-90; ptnr. Mid-Continent Properties Co., 1959-90, Fairview Investment Co., Kansas City, 1971-76, Monticello Land Co., 1973—, of counsel Yates, Mauck, Bohrer, Elliff, Croessmann & Wieland, P.C., Springfield, Mo., 1995—; sec. Packaging Products Corp., Mission, Kans., 1972-89; chmn., treas. Galerie of Naples (Fla.), Inc., 1990-92. Bd. dirs. Mo. Assn. Mental Health, 1968-69, Kansas City Assn. Mental Health, 1966-78, pres., 1969-70; bd. dirs. Heed, 1965-73, 78-82, pres., 1966-67, fin. chmn. 1967-68; bd. dirs. Kansas City Halfway House Found., exec. com., 1966-69, pres., 1966; bd. dirs. Joan Davis Sch. for Spl. Edn., 1972-88, v.p., 1972-73, 79-80, pres., 1980-82; bd. dirs. Sherwood Ctr. for Exceptional Child, 1977-79, v.p., 1978-79. Served with AUS, 1957. Mem. ABA, Mo. Bar, Fla. Bar, Springfield Bar Assn., Kansas City Bar Assn., Washington U. Law Alumni Assn. (bd. govs. 1990-92). Presbyterian (deacon). Mem. adv. bd. Washington U. Law Quar., 1957-90. Securities, Municipal (including bonds), Mergers and acquisitions. Home: 2657 E Wildwood Rd Springfield MO 65804-5271 Office: Yates Mauck Bohrer Elliff Croessmann & Wieland 3333 E Battlefield St Ste 1000 Springfield MO 65804-4048

**STARR, EPHRAIM,** lawyer; b. Denver, Feb. 6, 1971; s. Kenneth Lewis Starr and Jacquelin Starr-Bocian; m. Donna Phelps, June 6, 1963. BA in English and Physics cum laude, Amherst Coll., 1993; JD magna cum laude, Duke U., 1996. Assoc. Kirkland & Ellis, L.A., 1996-98; IP counsel Allied Signal, Inc., Torrance, Calif., 1998—. Mem. Fed. Cir. Bar Assn. Avocations: cycling, watercolor painting, roller blading. Office: Kirkland & Ellis 300 S Grand Ave Ste 3000 Los Angeles CA 90071-3140

**STARR, HAROLD PAGE,** lawyer; b. Phila., June 17, 1932; s. Isaac and Edith Nelson (Page) S.; m. Emily W. Churchman, Sept. 3, 1960; children: Elizabeth Twells, Edith Nelson, Harold Page Jr., Alice Churchman, Isaac Barclay. BS, Yale U., 1954; LLB, Harvard U., 1961. Bar: Pa. 1962. Assoc. Pepper, Hamilton & Scheetz, Phila., 1961-69, ptnr., 1970-81; pvt. practice Phila., 1982—. Lt. (j.g.) USNR, 1955-58. General corporate, Finance, Securities. Office: 8411 Stenton Ave Wyndmoor PA 19038-8445

**STARR, IRA M.,** lawyer; b. Jersey City, N.J., May 22, 1936; s. Hyman S. and Frances (Bauer) S.; m. Diane Steinberg, Dec. 24, 1961; children: Shari, Steven. AB, Rutgers U., 1957; LLB, U. Va., 1961. Bar: D.C. 1961, N.J. 1974. Tax law specialist IRS, Washington, 1961-62; sr. atty. advisor U.S. Securities and Exch. Com., Washington, 1962-66; dir. ops., gen. counsel H. Hentz and Co., Inc., N.Y.C., 1966-68, R. Gilder and Co., Inc., N.Y.C., 1968-70, Merkin and Co., Inc., N.Y.C., 1970-73; ptnr. Meltzer and Starr, Jersey City, N.J., 1974-81, Ruskin Meltzer Starr and Hoberman, Jersey City, 1981-83, Ruskin Kors Meltzer Rubin and Starr, Jersey City, 1983-93, Starr, Gern, Davison and Rubin, Roseland, N.J., 1993—; mem. adv. bd. First Jersey Nat. Bank, Jersey City, 1982-88; mem. Dist. Ethics Com., Jersey City, 1989-93; arbitrator NASD; mediator Am. Arbitration Assn. Trustee, pres. Temple B'nai Abraham, Livingston, N.J., 1974; trustee Vis. Homemakers Svc. Hudson County, Jersey City, 1977—; fin. sec., trustee Jewish Hosp. and Rehab. Ctr., Jersey City, 1981-87. Recipient U.S. Civil Svc. Sustained Performance award U.S., S.E.C., Washington, 1963. Mem. ABA, N.J. Bar Assn. Avocations: tennis, bridge, music. Securities, General corporate, Real property. Office: Starr Gern Davison Rubin PC 103 Eisenhower Pkwy Roseland NJ 07068-1029

**STARR, ISIDORE,** law educator; b. Bklyn., Nov. 24, 1911. BA, CCNY, 1932; MA, Columbia U., 1939; LLB, St. John's U., Jamaica, N.Y., 1936; JSD, Bklyn. Law Sch., 1942; PhD, New Sch. Social Rsch., 1957. Bar: N.Y. 1937. Tchr. N.Y.C. high schs., 1934-61; assoc. prof., prof. edn. Queens Coll., 1961-75, emeritus, 1975—; dir. Inst. on Law-Related Edn., Lincoln-Filene Ctr., Tufts U., 1963; dir. Law Studies Inst., N.Y.C., 1974; adv. on Our Living Bill of Rights Film Series (6 films) Encyclopedia Britannica Ednl. Corp.; mem. Ariz. Ctr. for Law-Related Edn.; cons. in field. Bd. dirs. Phi Alpha Delta Juvenile Justice Program, 1981—. 1st lt. U.S. Army, 1943-46. John Hay fellow, 1952-53. Recipient Outstanding Citizen award Philip Morris Cos., 1992. Mem. ABA (hon. chair adv. commn. on Youth Edn. for Citizenship, Isidore Starr award for Spl. Achievement in Law Studies, Leon Jaworski award 1989), Am. Judicature Soc., Am. Soc. for Legal History, Am. Legal Studies Assn., Nat. Coun. Social Studies (past pres.), Phi Beta Kappa, Phi Alpha Delta (cert. of appreciation 1981). Author: The Lost Generation of Prince Edward County, 1968, The Gideon Case, 1968, The Feiner Case, 1968, The Mapp Case, 1968, The Supreme Court and Contemporary Issues, 1968, Human Rights in the United States, 1969, The American Judicial System, 1972, The Idea of Libery, 1978, Justice: Due Process of Law, 1981; co-editor Living American Documents, 1971.. Address: 6043 E Harvard St Scottsdale AZ 85257-1917

**STARR, IVAR MILES,** lawyer; b. N.Y.C., Sept. 19, 1950; s. Charles S. Scholnicoff and Rosalie (Paletz) Starr. AA, Nassau Community Coll., 1970; BA, Queens Coll., 1972; JD, U. Miami, 1980. Bar: Fla. 1981, U.S. Dist. Ct. (so. dist.) Fla. 1981, N.Y. 1988. Rep. securities sales Aetna Variable Life Ins. Co., Garden City, N.Y., 1973-75; freelance real estate broker New Fairfield, Conn., 1973-79; assoc. Law Offices of Peter Lopez, Miami, Fla., 1981-82, Mills & London P.A., Miami, 1982; pvt. practice Miami, 1982—; lectr. Dade County (Fla.) Consumer Advs. Office, 1984-87; instr. paralegal courses Briarcliffe Coll., 1991. Candidate judge Dade County Ct., 1988. Recipient Outstanding Svc. award Miami Beach Bd. Realtors, 1986, 87, 88, 91, 92. Mem. N.Y. State Bar Assn., The Fla. Bar (vol. bar liaison com. 1993-96), Miami Beach Bar Assn. (bd. dirs. 1984—, treas. 1991, v.p. 1993, pres.-elect 1995, pres. 1996, immediate past pres. 1997), Fla. Coun. Bar Assn. Presidents, Miami Beach C. of C. (lectr. 1985-89), Better Bus. Bur. South Fla. (arbitrator 1984—, Cert. of Appreciation 1985), Queens Coll. Alumni in South Fla. (chmn. 1986-96), Internat. Toastmasters (so. divsn. gov. dist. 47 1993-94, Able Toastmaster Bronze 1992, Able Toastmaster Silver 1993, dist. 47 pub. rels. officer 1997-98, Dist. 47 Enthusiasm award 1993-94, Disting. Toastmaster 1994, Advanced Toastmaster gold and Competent Leader 1997, Advanced Toastmaster Silver and Advanced Leader 1999). Avocations: boating, swimming, music. State civil litigation, General practice, Real property. Home: 7705 Abbott Ave Apt 504 Miami FL 33141-2389 Office: 350 Lincoln Rd Ste 407 Miami FL 33139-3148

**STARR, KENNETH WINSTON,** lawyer; b. Vernon, Tex., July 21, 1946; s. W. D. and Vannie Maude (Trimble) S.; m. Alice Jean Mendell, Aug. 23, 1970; children: Randall Postley, Carolyn Marie, Cynthia Anne. B.A., George Washington U., 1968; M.A., Brown U., 1969; J.D., Duke U., 1973; LLD (hon.), Hampden Sydney Coll., Shenandoah U., Mitchell Coll. Law. Bar: Calif. 1973, D.C. 1979, Va. 1979. Law clk. to Judge David Dyer U.S. Ct. Appeals (5th cir.), Miami, Fla., 1973-74; assoc. Gibson, Dunn & Crutcher, Los Angeles, 1974-75; law clk. to Chief Justice Warren E. Burger, U.S. Supreme Ct., Washington, 1975-77; assoc., ptnr. Gibson, Dunn & Crutcher, Washington, 1977-81; counselor to atty gen. of U.S. Dept. Justice, Washington, 1981-83; judge U.S. Ct. Appeals (D.C. circuit), Washington, 1983-89; solicitor gen. Dept. Justice, Washington, 1989-93; ptnr. Kirkland & Ellis, Washington, 1993—; ind. counsel for Whitewater, 1994—. Contbr. articles to legal jours. Legal advisor CAB transition team office of pres.-elect, 1980-81, legal advisor SEC transition team, 1980-81; bd. adv. Duke Law Jour. Recipient Disting. Alumni awards George Washington U., Duke U.; recipient Atty. Gen.'s Award for Disting. Svc., 1993, Am. Values award U.S. Indsl. Coun. Ednl. Found., 1993. Fellow Am. Bar Found. (judicial fellows com., judicial conf. com. on bicentennial of U.S. constitution); mem. ABA, Am. Law Inst., Am. Judicature Soc., Inst. Jud. Adminstrn. (pres.), Supreme Ct. Hist. Soc., Calif. Bar Assn., D.C. Bar Assn., Va. Bar Assn., Order of Coif, Phi Delta Phi (Hughes chpt. Man of Yr. 1973).

**STARR, MARVIN BLAKE,** lawyer; b. N.Y.C., May 11, 1928; s. Harry and Roslyn (Lapidos) S.; m. Anita Reizen, Sept. 15, 1951 (div.); children: Karen, Eric, Valerie; m. K. Jill Best, Aug. 3, 1980. BA, UCLA, 1952; JD, U. Calif., Berkeley, 1955. Bar: Calif. 1959. Shareholder Miller, Starr & Regalia, Oakland and Walnut Creek, Calif., 1964—; mem. faculty Sch. Bus. U. Calif., Berkeley, 1968-90; adj. prof. John F. Kennedy Sch. Law, 1992; speaker profl. and civic meetings, confs. and convs. throughout the U.S. Co-author: (with Harry D. Miller) The Current Law of California Real Estate, 3 vols., 1965-67, 5 vols., 1975-77, 9 vols., 1990; founder Real Estate Tax Digest, 1980, editor, prin. author, 1980-88. Real property. Office: Miller Starr & Regalia 1331 N California Blvd Ste 700 Walnut Creek CA 94596-4537

**STARRETT, FREDERICK KENT,** lawyer; b. Lincoln, Nebr., May 23, 1947; s. Clyde Frederick and Helen Virginia (Meyers) S.; m. Linda Lee Jensen, Jan. 19, 1969; children: Courtney, Kathryn, Scott. BA, U. Nebr., 1969; JD, Creighton U., 1976. Bar: Nebr. 1976, Kans. 1977, U.S. Dist. Ct. Nebr. 1976, Mo. 1987, U.S. Dist. Ct. Kans. 1977, U.S. Ct. Appeals (8th and 10th cirs.) 1983, U.S. Supreme Ct. 1993. Pvt. practice law Great Bend, Kans., 1976-77, Topeka, 1977-86; ptnr. Miller, Bash & Starrett, P.C., Kansas City, Mo., 1986-90, Lathrop Norquist & Miller, 1990-91, Lathrop and Norquist, Overland Park, Kans., 1991-95, Lathrop & Gage L.C., Overland Park, Kans., 1996—. Lt (j.g.) USNR, 1969-72. Mem. ABA, Kans. Bar Assn. (pres. litigation sect. 1985-86), Am. Bd. Trial Advs. (pres. Kansas chpt. 1997), Def. Rsch. Inst., Inc. (state rep. Kans.), Mo. Orgn. Def. Lawyers, Civitan Club (pres. 1985-86, Disting. Pres. award 1985-86). Democrat. Presbyterian. Avocations: aviation, scuba diving. Federal civil litigation, State civil litigation, Personal injury. Office: Lathrop & Gage LC 1050/40 Corporate Woods 9401 Indian Creek Pkwy Overland Park KS 66210-2005

**STARRETT, KEITH,** lawyer; b. McComb, Miss., July 15, 1951; s. Melvin and Mary (Roberts) S.; m. Barbara O'Neal, Dec. 18, 1971; children: Josh, Whit, Leah Claire. BS, Miss. State U., 1972; JD, U. Miss., 1974. Bar: Miss. 1974, U.S. Dist. Ct. (no. and so. dists.) Miss. 1974. Ptnr. Statham, Watkins & Starrett, Magnolia, Miss., 1975-79; pvt. practice Magnolia, 1980-89, McComb, 1989-92; cir. judge 14th Cir. Dist., 1992—. Baptist. Avocations: backpacking, jogging, canoeing. General civil litigation, Admiralty, General practice. Office: 299 Apache Dr Mc Comb MS 39648-6307

**STARRS, ELIZABETH ANNE,** lawyer; b. Detroit, Jan. 1, 1954; d. John Richard and Mabel Angeline (Gilchrist) S. BA, U. Mich., 1975; JD, Suffolk U., 1980. Bar: Mass. 1980, Colo. 1997, U.S. Dist. Ct. Mass. 1980, U.S. Ct. Appeals (1st. cir.) 1980, Colo. 1983, U.S. Dist. Ct. Colo. 1983, U.S. Ct. Appeals (10th cir.) 1983. Assoc. Denner & Benjoya P.C., Boston, 1980-83; assoc. Kennedy & Christopher P.C., Denver, 1983-86, ptnr., 1986—, pres., mng. ptnr., 1994—; instr. bus. law Bay State C.C., Boston, 1981-82. Troop leader Girl Scouts U.S., Denver, 1984-85; pres. Colo. Women's Bar Assn. Found., 1992-94. Mem. ATLA, Colo. Bar Assn. (litigation coun. 1989-96, chair 1993-94, profl. liability chair 1991-93), Denver Bar Assn., Colo. Women's Bar Assn. (bd. dirs. 1984-85, v.p. 1989-90, U.S. Dist. Ct. Colo. com. conduct 1997—), Am. Bd. Trial Advocates, Def. Rsch. Inst. Roman Catholic. Federal civil litigation, State civil litigation, Professional liability. Office: Kennedy & Christopher PC 1660 Wynkoop St Ste 900 Denver CO 80202-1197

**STARRS, JAMES EDWARD,** law and forensics educator, consultant; b. Bklyn., July 30, 1930; s. George Thomas and Mildred Agatha (Dobbins) S.; m. Barbara Alice Smyth, Sept. 6, 1954; children: Mary Alice, Monica, James, Charles, Liam, Barbara, Siobhan, Gregory. BA, LLB, St. John's U., Bklyn., 1958; LLM, NYU, 1959. Bar: N.Y. 1958, D.C. 1966, U.S. Ct. Mil. Appeals 1959, U.S. Dist. Ct. (so. and ea. dists.) N.Y. 1960. Assoc. Lawless & Lynch, N.Y.C., 1958; tchg. fellow Rutgers U., Newark, 1959-60; asst. prof. law DePaul U., Chgo., 1960-64; assoc. prof. law George Washington U., Washington, 1964-67, prof. law, 1967—, prof. forensic scis., 1975—; cons. Nat. Commn. Reform Fed. Criminal Laws, Washington, 1968, Cellmark Diagnostics, Germantown, Md., 1987—, Time-Life Books, 1993; participant re-evaluation sci. evidence and trial of Bruno Richard Hauptmann for Lindbergh murder, 1983; participant reporting sci. re-analysis of firearms evidence in Sacco and Vanzetti trial, 1986; project dir. Alfred G. Packer Victims Exhumation Project, 1989, A Blaze of Bullets: A Sci. Investigation into the Deaths of Senator Huey Long and Dr. Carl Austin Weiss, 1991, Meriwether Lewis Exhumation Project, 1992—, Frank R. Olson Exhumation Project, 1994, Jesse W. James Exhumation Project, 1995, Samuel Washington-Harewood Excavations, 1999. Author: (with Moenssens and Inbau) Scientific Evidence in Criminal Cases, 1986; (with Moenssens, Inbau and Henderson) Scientific Evidence in Civil and Criminal Cases, 1995; editor: The Noiseless Tenor, 1982; co-editor: (review) Scientific Sleuthing, 1976—; mem. editl. bd. Jour. Forensic Sci., 1980-98, Encyclopedia of Forensic Sciences; contbr. articles to profl. jours. Sgt. U.S. Army, 1950-53, Korea. Recipient Vidocq Soc. award, 1993; Ford Found. fellow, 1963; vis. scholar in residence USMC, 1984. Fellow Am. Acad. Forensic Sci. (chmn. jurisprudence sect. 1984, 94, 95, bd. dirs. 1986-89, 98—, Jurisprudence Sect. award 1988, Disting. fellow 1996); mem. ABA (emeritus), Mid-Atlantic Assn. Forensic Sci., Assn. Trial Lawyers Am., Internat. Soc. Forensic Sci. (chmn. jurisprudence sect. 1988), Internat. Assn. for Identification (co-chmn. historic cases sect. 1998—). Roman Catholic. Home: 8602 Clydesdale Rd Springfield VA 22151-1301 Office: George Washington U Nat Law Ctr 720 20th St NW Washington DC 20006-4306

**STATHIS, NICHOLAS JOHN,** lawyer; b. Calchi, Greece, Feb. 27, 1924; s. John and Sylvia (Koutsonouris) S. Student, Columbia U., 1942-43, 44-48, AB, 1946, JD, 1948. Bar: N.Y. 1949. Assoc. James Maxwell Fassett, N.Y.C., 1948-50; asst. counsel to spl. com. to investigate organized crime U.S. Senate, Washington, 1951; trial atty. Fidelity & Casualty Co., N.Y.C., 1952; law sec. to Harold R. Medina Judge U.S. Ct. Appeals (2d cir.), N.Y.C., 1952-54; spl. dep. atty. gen. N.Y. State Election Frauds Bur., Dept. Law, 1956; assoc. Watson, Leavenworth, Kelton & Taggart, N.Y.C., 1954-60, ptnr., 1961-81; ptnr. Hopgood, Calimafde, Kalil, Blaustein & Judlowe, N.Y.C., 1981-84, Botein, Hays & Sklar, N.Y.C., 1984-89; of counsel White & Case, N.Y.C., 1989-93; corp. coun., dir. intellectual property Aphton Corp., N.Y.C., 1993—; lectr. Practising Law Inst., 1968-69. Contbr. articles to profl. jours. on trademarks. Pres., exec. dir., chmn., bd. dirs. Found. Classic Theatre and Acad., 1973—; bd. dirs. Concert Artists Guild, 1974-91, Pirandello Soc., 1976—, Bklyn. Philharm. Orch., 1986-91, Orpheon, Inc., 1986-98, Friends of Young Musicians, 1998—. With AUS, 1943-44. Mem. ABA, Assn. of Bar of City of N.Y., N.Y. State Bar Assn., Fed. Bar Coun., Am. Intellectual Property Law Assn., N.Y. Intellectual Property Law Assn. Democrat. Greek Orthodox. Federal civil litigation, Patent, Trademark and copyright. Home: 1885 John F Kennedy Blvd Jersey City NJ 07305-2113 Office: 515 Madison Ave Rm 725 New York NY 10022-5403

**STATKUS, JEROME FRANCIS,** lawyer; b. Hammond, Ind., June 13, 1942; s. Albert William and Helen Ann (Vaicunas) S.; children: Wesley Albert, Nicholas Jerome. BA, So. Ill. U., 1964; JD, U. Louisville, 1968; MA, U. Wyo., 1974. Bar: Wyo. 1971, U.S. Dist. Ct. Wyo. 1971, Wis. 1989, D.C. 1977, U.S. Ct. Claims 1973, U.S. Supreme Ct. 1974, U.S. Ct. Appeals (10th cir.) 1973, U.S. Ct. Appeals (7th cir.) 1992. Law clk. U.S. Dist. Ct., So. Dist. Ill., Peoria, 1968-69; asst. atty. gen. State of Wyo., Cheyenne, 1971-75; legis. asst. to U.S. Senator Clifford Hansen Washington, 1975-76; asst. U.S. atty. U.S. Dept. Justice, Dist. of Wyo., 1976-77; sole practice Cheyenne, 1978-79; assoc. Horisky, Bagley & Hickey, Cheyenne, 1979-81; ptnr. Rooney, Bagley, Hickey Evans & Statkus, Cheyenne, 1981-88; exec. dir. Wyo. State Bar, 1988-89; trustee Village of Germantown, Wis., 1991-93; office share Ladewig and Rechlicz, 1990-93; pvt. practice Douglas, Wyo., 1993-96; asst. pub. defender State of Wyo., Douglas, 1993-96. Pres. Ret. Sr. Vol. Program, Cheyenne, 1982-83; treas. Pathfinder (drug rehab.), Cheyenne, 1982-85; bar commr. 1st Jud. Dist., 1985-87; mem. Future Milw., 1991; chair Waukesha County Devel. Disability Adv. Coun., 1996—. Served with USNR, 1969-70. Mem. Wyo. Bar Assn., D.C. Bar Assn., Wis. State Bar Assn., Wyo. Trial Lawyers Assn. (bd. dirs. 1984-85), Wis. Vietnam Vets, KC, VFW. Republican. Roman Catholic. General practice, Criminal. Home: PO Box 14 Germantown WI 53022-0014 Office: W156N 11340 Pilgrim Rd Germantown WI 53022

**STAUBER, RONALD JOSEPH,** lawyer; b. Toledo, Nov., 8, 1940; s. Frederick I. and Anna R. (Kline) S.; m. Doreen Lynn Toll, Aug., 19, 1967 (div.); children—Brandon, Deborah. B.B.A., U. Toledo, 1962; J.D., Ohio State U., 1965. Bar: Calif. 1967; U.S. Dist. Ct. (cen. and ea. dists.) Calif. 1967, U.S. Supreme Ct. 1972. Corp. counsel, Div. Corps., Dept. Investments, State of Calif., Los Angeles, 1965-67; ptnr. Blacker & Stauber, Beverly Hills, Calif., 1967-77; ptnr. Ronald J. Stauber, Inc., Beverly Hills and Los Angeles, 1978-86, 88—; ptnr. Stauber & Gersh, Beverly Hills and Washington, 1986-87. Bd. dirs. Jewish Free Loan; bd. dirs. Pico Robertson Redevel. Assn., Cardex Corp., Paris Ry. Co. (Am.) Inc. Served in USNG. Mem. Beverly Hills Bar Assn. (corps. com., real estate com.), Los Angeles Bar Assn. (bus. and corp. sect., judge pro tem Mcpl. Ct.), ABA (corps., banking and bus. law sect.), Calif. State Bar Assn. (real property sect.). Democrat. Jewish. Real property, General corporate. Office: 1880 Century Park E Ste 300 Los Angeles CA 90067-1666

**STAUBITZ, ARTHUR FREDERICK,** lawyer, healthcare products company executive; b. Omaha, Nebr., Mar. 14, 1939; s. Herbert Frederick Staubitz and Barbara Eileen (Dallas) Alderson; m. Linda Medora Miller, Aug. 18, 1962; children: Michael, Melissa, Peter. AB cum laude, Wesleyan U., Middletown, Conn., 1961; JD cum laude, U. Pa., 1964. Bar: Ill. 1964, U.S. Dist. Ct. (no. dist.) Ill. 1964, U.S. Ct. Appeals (7th cir.) 1964, Pa. 1972. Assoc. Sidley & Austin, Chgo., 1964-71; sr. internat. atty., asst. gen. counsel, dir. Japanese ops. Sperry Univac, Blue Bell, Pa., 1971-78; from asst. to assoc. to dep. gen. counsel Baxter Internat. Inc., Deerfield, Ill., 1978-85, v.p., dep. gen. counsel, 1985-90; v.p. Baxter Diagnostics, 1990-91; sr. v.p., sec., gen. counsel Amgen, Inc., Thousand Oaks, Calif., 1991-92; v.p., gen. mgr. Ventures Group Baxter World Trade Corp., Deerfield, Ill., 1992-93; v.p., sec., gen. counsel Baxter Internat. Inc., Deerfield, Ill., 1993, sr. v.p., gen. counsel, 1993-97, sr. v.p. portfolio strategy, 1997-98. Mem. Planning Commn., Springfield Twp., Montgomery County, Pa., 1973-74, mem. Zoning Hearing Bd., 1974-78; bd. dirs. Twp. H.S. Dist. 113, Deerfield and Highland Park, Ill., 1983-91, pres., 1989-91; trustee Food and Drug Law Inst., 1991-92, 93-96, Carthage Coll., Kenosha, Wis., 1996—, exec. com., 1999—; bd. dirs. Music of the Baroque, 1994—, vice-chmn. Mem. ABA. Episcopalian. General corporate, Antitrust, Private international. Home: 232 Deerfield Rd Deerfield IL 60015-4412 Home (winter): 6181 N Paseo Valdear Tucson AZ 85750-1071

**STAUFFER, ERIC P.,** lawyer; b. Tucson, Feb. 1, 1948; s. Robert D. and Jeanne E. (Catlin) S.; m. Jane F. Snyder, Aug. 2, 1969; children: Curtis Austen, Marcus Elias, Laura Afton. BA, U. South Fla., 1969; JD, Yale U., 1972. Bar: Ariz. 1972, Maine 1974, D.C. 1979. Spl. asst. to gov., fed. state coord. State of Maine, 1973-75; Maine alt. to New England Regional Commn., 1973-75; gen. counsel Maine State Housing Auth., 1976-77; adminstrv. asst. to chmn. Dem. Nat. Com., 1977-78; mem. Preti, Flaherty, Beliveau Pachios & Haley, LLC, Portland, Maine, 1978—. Bd. dirs. Jr. Achievement Maine, Inc., 1995-98; pres. Goodwill Industries, Maine, 1981-82, bd. dirs., 1979-93, 99—. Mem. Nat. Health Lawyers Assn., Maine State Bar Assn., Ariz. State Bar, D.C. Bar, Maine Real Estate Devel. Assn. (bd. dirs. 1991—, Pub. Svc. award 1992). Contracts commercial, Computer, Mergers and acquisitions. Office: Preti Flaherty Beliveau Pachios & Haley LLC PO Box 9546 One City Ctr Portland ME 04112-9546

**STAUFFER, RONALD EUGENE,** lawyer; b. Hempstead, N.Y., Jan. 22, 1949; s. Hiram Eugene and Florence Marie (Hintz) S.; m. Vicki Lynn Hartman, June 12, 1973; children: Eric Alan, Craig Aaron, Darren Adam. SB, MIT, 1970; JD magna cum laude, Harvard U., 1973. Bar: D.C. 1973, U.S. Ct. Mil. Appeals 1976, U.S. Tax Ct. 1979. Ptnr. Hogan & Hartson, Washington, 1977-87, Sonnenschein Nath & Rosenthal, Washington, 1988—. Contbr. articles to profl. publs. Capt. U.S. Army, 1970-77. Mem. ABA (chair TIPS Employee Benefits Com. 1977—), D.C. Bar Assn., Tau Beta Pi, Sigma Gamma Tau. Avocations: running, water skiing. Pension, profit-sharing, and employee benefits, Corporate taxation. Home: 10207 Woodvale Pond Dr Fairfax Station VA 22039-1658 Office: Sonnenschein Nath & Rosenthal 1301 K St NW Ste 600 Washington DC 20005-3317

**STAUFFER, SCOTT WILLIAM,** lawyer, CPA; b. Oshkosh, Wis., Aug. 17, 1954; s. Robert Edward and Shirley Lydia (Wrasse) S.; m. Debralee Bowland, Nov. 14, 1987. BBA in Acctg., U. Wis., 1975; JD, U. Denver, 1979. Bar: Colo. 1979. Tax acct. Arthur Andersen & Co., Denver, 1979-82; tax mgr. Gary-Williams Oil, Englewood, Colo., 1982-85; pvt. practice Denver, Aurora, Colo., 1986—. Pres. Colo. Chorale, Denver, 1984-85, 92-93. Mem. ABA, AICPA, Colo. Bar Assn., Denver Bar Assn. (chmn. law office mgmt. com. 1993-95, intraprofl. com. 1997—), Colo. Soc. CPAs (chmn. fed. tax com. 1994-96, 99—), Petroleum Accts. Soc. Colo., Am. Assn. Atty.-CPAs. Lutheran. Avocations: golf, travel, reading, computer. Personal income taxation, Corporate taxation, General corporate. Home: 8147 W Frost Pl Littleton CO 80128-4325 Office: 2851 S Parker Rd Ste 720 Aurora CO 80014-2728

**STAVIS, ROGER LEE,** lawyer; b. N.Y.C., Nov. 5, 1958; s. Nathan Joshua and Francine (Green) S.; m. Randy Beth Bielsky, Nov. 22, 1987; 1 child, Allyson P. BA magna cum laude, CUNY, Queens, 1979; JD with honors, George Washington U., 1982. Bar: N.Y. 1983, U.S. Dist. Ct. (so. and ea. dists.) N.Y. 1983, U.S. Ct. Appeals (2d cir.) 1986, U.S. Supreme Ct. 1986, U.S. Ct. Mil. Appeals 1988, U.S. Ct. Appeals (4th cir.) 1991, U.S. Ct. Appeals (3d cir.) 1993. Asst. dist. atty., supervising appellate atty. Bronx County, N.Y., 1982-86; assoc. Litman, Asche, Lupkin and Gioiella, N.Y.C., 1986-88; ptnr. Kartagener and Stavis, N.Y.C., 1988-93; pvt. practice N.Y.C., 1993—. Author: (with others) Criminal Trial Advocacy, 1992, Criminal Defense Techniques, 1991. Regents scholar State of N.Y., 1975; recipient Profl. Achievement award George Washington U. Law Alumni Assn., 1995. Mem. ABA, N.Y. State Bar Assn., Assn. Bar City N.Y., N.Y. County Lawyers Assn. Democrat. Jewish. Avocations: golf, reading, antiques. Criminal, General civil litigation. Home: 19 Fernwood Rd Larchmont NY 10538-1704 Office: 233 Broadway Fl 38 New York NY 10279-3899

**STAVNICKY, MICHAEL ROSS,** lawyer; b. Cleve.; s. Lawrence Steven Sr. and Linda Rose Stavnicky; m. Jolie Ann Bell, Oct. 10, 1998. B of Comm. summa cum laude, Ohio U., 1991; JD cum laude, Cleve. U., 1994. Bar: Ohio 1994, U.S. Dist. Ct. (no. dist.) Ohio 1994. Assoc. Conway, Marken, Wyner, Kurant & Kern, Pepper Pike, Ohio, 1994—. Mem. ABA, Ohio Bar Assn., Cleve. Bar Assn., Chagrin Valley C. of C. General civil litigation, General corporate, State civil litigation. Office: Conway Marken Wyner Kurant & Kern 30195 Chagrin Blvd Ste 300 Cleveland OH 44124-5703

**STAVROS, PETER JAMES,** lawyer; b. N.Y.C., Sept. 16, 1966; s. James P. and Suzanne T. Stavros. BA in English, Duke U., 1988; grad. in creative writing, Harvard U., 1989; JD, U. Ky., 1995. Bar: Ky. 1995, U.S. Dist. Ct. (ea. and we. dists.) Ky. 1995, U.S. Ct. Appeals (6th cir.) 1995, U.S. Ct. Appeals (fed. cir.) 1996. Reporter AP, Louisville, 1990, Charleston, W.Va., 1990, Indpls., 1991; law clk. Supreme Ct. Ky., Frankfort, 1995-96; assoc. Brown, Todd & Heyburn, Louisville, 1996—. Articles editor Ky. Law Jour., 1995. Mem. ABA, Ky. Bar Assn., Louisville Bar Assn. Avocations: cycling, running, weight training. Patent, Intellectual property, Federal civil litigation. Office: Brown Todd & Heyburn PLLC 400 W Market St Fl 32D Louisville KY 40202-3346

**STAYIN, RANDOLPH JOHN,** lawyer; b. Cin., Oct. 30, 1942; s. Jack and Viola (Tomin) S.; children: Gregory S., Todd R., Elizabeth J. BA, Dartmouth Coll., 1964; JD, U. Cin., 1967. Bar: Ohio 1967, U.S. Dist. Ct. (so. dist.) Ohio 1968, U.S. Dist. Ct. D.C. 1977, U.S. Ct. Appeals (6th cir.) 1968, U.S. Ct. Appeals (fed. cir.) 1986, U.S. Supreme Ct. 1974, U.S. Ct. Appeals (D.C. cir.) 1976, U.S. Ct. Internat. Trade, 1985. Assoc. Frost & Jacobs, Cin., 1967-72; exec. asst., dir. of legislation U.S. Sen. Robert Taft, Jr., Washington, 1973-74, chief of staff, 1975-76; assoc. Taft, Stettinius & Hollister, Washington, 1977, ptnr., 1978-88; ptnr. Barnes & Thornburg, Washington, 1988—; mem. adv. coun. U.S. and FGN. Comml. Svc., U.S. Dept. Commerce. Chmn., mem. numerous coms., chmn., worker campaigns for local politicians Rep. Party state and local orgns.; mem. Citizens to Save WCET-TV, 1967-72, Fine Arts Fund, 1970-72, Cancer Soc., 1970-72; chmn. agy. rels. com. Hamilton County Mental Health and Mental Retardation Bd., 1969-71, vice chmn., 1971, chmn., 1971-72; v.p. Recreation Commn., City of Cin., 1970-72; mem. funds mgmt. com. Westwood 1st Presbyn. Ch., 1968, v.p., 1969, pres., 1970, trustee, 1970, elder, 1971-72; bd. dirs. Evans Mill Pond Owners Assn., v.p., 1986, pres., 1987; chmn. Washington Nat. Cathedral Fund Com., mem. devel. com. Mem. ABA (sect. on internat. law and practice, vice chmn. com. on nat. legislation 1977-79, internat. sect., anti-trust sect.), Am. Soc. Assn. Execs. (legal sect., internat. sect.), Internat. Bar Assn., D.C. Bar Assn. (com. on internat. law). Avocations: theater, tennis, skiing, travel, reading. Private international, Administrative and regulatory, Legislative. Office: Barnes & Thornburg 1401 I St NW Ste 800 Washington DC 20005-2225

**STEAD, CALVIN RUDI,** lawyer; b. Rochester, Minn., Mar. 13, 1947; s. John Jr. and Pauline G. Stead; m. Elizabeth Anne Winyard, Dec. 29, 1984; children: Christina Nicole, John Fredrick. AB, Humboldt State U., 1970; MS, U. Tex., San Antonio, 1979; JD, U. San Diego, 1986. Bar: Calif. 1987, U.S. Dist. Ct. (so. dist.) Calif., 1988, U.S. Dist. Ct. (no., cen. and ea. dists.) Calif. 1989. House painter, furniture builder Santa Rosa, Calif., 1970-75; air pollution chemist County of San Diego, 1980-82; nuclear chemist San Onofre Nuclear Station, San Clemente, Calif., 1982-88; assoc. Sulzner, Belsky & Hayden, San Diego, 1988, Haight, Brown & Bonesteel, Santa Monica, Calif., 1989; ptnr. Borton, Petrini & Conron, Bakersfield, Calif., 1989—. Editor (newsletter) Toxic Alert, 1992-97; contbr. articles to profl. jours. Pres., bd. dirs. Sonoma County Taxpayers, Santa Rosa, 1992-94; bd. dirs. Kern Tax, Bakersfield, 1997—, Project Clear Air, Bakersfield, 1990-92; mem. adv. bd. Kern Transp., Bakersfield, 1991-93. With USAF, 1975-78. Mem. Air Waste Mgmt. Assn., Petroleum Club, Bakersfield C. of C. (govt. rev. coun. 1992, 93, 97, 98), Rotary. Republican. Lutheran. Avocations: golf, fly fishing. Toxic tort, Construction, Insurance. Office: Borton Petrini & Conron LLP 1600 Truxtun Ave Bakersfield CA 93301-5111

**STEADMAN, JAMES ROBERT,** lawyer; b. Girard, Pa., Aug. 28, 1950; s. Robert Emmet and Ruth Harriet (Blair) S.; m. Alison Terry, June 16, 1973; children—Elizabeth, Kathryn, Anne. BA in Polit. Sci., Grove City Coll., 1972; JD, Dickinson Sch. Law, 1975. Bar: Pa. 1975, U.S. Dist. Ct. (we. dist.) Pa. 1976, U.S. Supreme Ct. 1981. Atty., advisor Small Bus. Adminstrn., Harrisburg, Pa. 1975-76; pvt. practice, Girard, 1976—; dir. Penn. Attys. Title Ins. Co., Erie. Councilman, Girard Borough, 1978-82; bd. dirs. Willcox Libr., Girard, 1982—, treas., 1982-86; bd. dirs. Battles Village Sr. Citizen Housing, Girard, 1981-84, Erie Philharm., 1998—. Probate, Real property, Family and matrimonial. Home: 205 Penn Ave Girard PA 16417-1543 Office: PO Box 87 24 Main St E Girard PA 16417-1703

**STEADMAN, JOHN MONTAGUE,** judge; b. Honolulu, Aug. 8, 1930; s. Alva Edgar and Martha (Cooke) S.; m. Alison Storer Lunt, Apr. 8, 1961; children—Catharine N., Juliette M., Eric C. Grad., Phillips Acad., Andover, Mass., 1948; BA summa cum laude, Yale U., 1952; LLB magna cum laude, Harvard U., 1955. Bar: D.C. 1955, Calif. 1956, U.S. Supreme Ct. 1964, Hawaii 1977. Assoc. Pillsbury, Madison & Sutro, San Francisco, 1956-63; atty. Dept. Justice, 1963-64; dep. under sec. army for internat. affairs, 1964-65; spl. asst. to sec. and dep. sec. def. Dept. Def., 1965-68; gen. counsel Dept. Air Force, 1968-70; vis. prof. law U. Pa. Law Sch., 1970-72; prof. law Georgetown U. Law Ctr., Washington, 1972-85, assoc. dean, 1979-84; assoc. judge D.C. Ct. Appeals, 1985—; instr. Lincoln Law Sch., San Francisco, 1961-62, San Francisco Law Sch., 1962-63; vis. prof. U. Mich. Sch. Law, 1976, U. Hawaii Sch. Law, 1977; of counsel firm Pillsbury, Madison & Sutro, Washington, 1979-85. Editor: Harvard Law Rev, 1953-55. Sinclair-Kennedy Traveling fellow, 1955-56. Mem. Am. Law Inst., Phi Beta Kappa, Delta Sigma Rho, Zeta Psi. Episcopalian. Home: 2960 Newark St NW Washington DC 20008-3338 Office: DC Ct Appeals 500 Indiana Ave NW Ste 2 Washington DC 20001-2138

**STEADMAN, RICHARD ANDERSON, JR.,** lawyer; b. Charleston, S.C., Sept. 17, 1954; s. Richard A. and Elizabeth (Barber) S.; m. Sarah Stokes, Aug. 5, 1978. BA, Wofford Coll., 1976; JD, U. S.C., 1981. Bar: S.C. 1981, U.S. Dist. Ct. S.C. 1982. Assoc. Willis Fuller, P.A., Charleston, 1981-82; sole practice, Charleston, 1982—; assoc. Lewis, Lewis, Bruce & Truslow, Charleston, 1982-86, Joye Law Firm, North Charleston, 1986-87, gen. counsel Charleston Naval Shipyard Fed. Credit Union, 1987-92; pvt. practice, Charleston, 1992—; adj. prof. Trident Tech. Coll., 1995—. Mem. ABA (credit union com.), S.C. Bar Assn. (publs. editor Real Estate Lawyer 1982-83, comml. law com.), S.C. Bankruptcy Law Assn., Charleston County Bar Assn. Bankruptcy, State civil litigation, Real property. Home: 3702 Colonel Vanderhorst Cir Mount Pleasant SC 29466-8040 Office: PO Box 60367 Charleston SC 29419-0367

**STEAKLEY, RODERIC G,** lawyer; b. Tuscaloosa, Ala., Oct. 26, 1949; s. L.J. and Avie (Snider) S; m. Linda Whitt, May 20, 1972; children: Laura Ashleigh, John Michael, David Andrew. BA, U. Ala., 1972, JD, 1976. Bar: Ala. 1976, U.S. Dist. Ct. (no. dist.) Ala. 1976, Tex. 1978, U.S. Dist. Ct. (no. dist.) Tex. 1978, Idaho 1979, U.S. Dist. Ct. (ea. dist.) Wis. 1979, U.S. Tax Ct. 1979, U.S. Ct. Appeals (5th cir.) 1980, U.S. Ct. Temp. Appeals 1982, U.S. Dist. Ct. (so. dist.) Ala. 1989, U.S. Ct. Appeals (11th cir.) 1990, U.S. Ct. Claims 1992, U.S. Supreme Ct. 1992. Commd. 1st lt. U.S. Army, 1975-81; law clk. to Hon. J. Foy Guin, Jr. U.S. Dist. Ct. (no. dist.) Ala., 1976-77; assoc. Shank, Irwin & Conant, Dallas, 1977-80, ptnr., 1981-87; shareholder Sirote & Permutt, P.C., Huntsville, Ala., 1987—; bd. dirs. Better Bus. Bureau North Ala., exec. com., legal counsel;. Bd. dirs. Madison County YMCA, legal counsel; mem. bd. deacons First Bapt. Ch., Dallas, dir. Sunday sch. program, tchr.; Sunday sch. tchr. Trinity Methodist Ch., Tuscaloosa; trustee Whitesburg Baptist Ch., Huntsville, mem. bd. deacons, sunday sch. tchr. Scholar Am. Coll. Trial Lawyers, Ala. Trial Lawyers Assn.; recipient Leadership award Litton Industries; named one of the Outstanding Young Men of Am. Jr. C. of C. Mem. ABA, Fed. Bar Assn., Ala. Bar Assn., Tex. Bar Assn., Huntsville/Madison County Leadership 2000, Madison County 4H (bd. dirs.), Kiwanis (chmn. various coms.), Omicron Delta Kappa. Federal civil litigation, Government contracts and claims, Franchising. Office: Sirote & Permutt PC 200 Clinton Ave W Ste 1000 Huntsville AL 35801-4934

**STEANS, PHILLIP MICHAEL,** lawyer; b. Oak Park, Ill., May 23, 1943; s. William B. and Evelyn A. (Leonetti) S.; m. Randi R. Solberg, Sept. 17, 1966; children: Erik, Joshua, Molly. BA summa cum laude, Ripon (Wis.) Coll., 1965; JD, U. Chgo., 1968. Bar: Wis. 1968, Ill. 1968, U.S. Dist. Ct. (we. dist.) Wis. 1968. Ptnr. Solberg & Steans, Menomonie, Wis., 1968-85; mng. ptnr. Steans, Skinner, Schofield & Higley, Menomonie, 1985-91; shareholder Bakke-Norman, S.C., Menomonie, 1991-94; pres. Phillip M. Steans, S.C., Menomonie, 1994—; dist. atty. Dunn County, Wis., Menomonie, 1969-74; asst. city atty. City of Menomonie, 1969-86; asst. family ct. commr. Dunn County, 1993. NCAA scholar, 1965. Mem. Nat. Bd. Trial Advocacy (mem. civil and criminal sects.). Avocations: racquetball, reading. Personal injury, Product liability, Criminal. Home: E5745 708th Ave Menomonie WI 54751-5515 Office: 393 Red Cedar St Ste 6 Menomonie WI 54751-2267

**STEARNS, FRANK WARREN,** lawyer; b. Washington, July 20, 1949; s. Robert Maynard and Ermyntrude (Vaiden) S.; m. Judith Anne Ketcheson, Sept. 7, 1974; children: Frank W. Jr., Brian S., Joe G. BA, Washington & Lee, 1971; JD with honors, George Washington U., 1974. Bar: Washington DC 1975, Va. 1980, U.S. Supreme Ct. 1980, U.S. Dist. Ct. DC 1975, U.S. Ct. Appeals (DC cir.) 1975, U.S. Ct. Appeals (4th cir.) 1985. Law clk. Superior Ct. D.C., Washington, 1974-75; asst. corp. counsel Office of the Corp. Counsel, Washington, 1975-79; asst. county atty. County Atty's Office, Fairfax County, Va., 1979-80; mng. ptnr. Wilkes, Artis, Hedrick & Lane, Fairfax, Va., 1984—; bd. dirs. No. Va. Bldg. Industry Assn., 1987-94; trustee Greater Washington Bd. Trade, 1987—; chmn. tech. adv. com. NVBIA, Loudoun, Va., 1986-90. Commr. Arlington County Econ. Devel. Commn., Arlington, Va., 1987-91; mem. Coun. for Excellence in Govt., Washington, 1989—. Mem. Barristers, Counsellors. Avocations: tennis, golf. Real property, Land use and zoning (including planning), Construction. Office: Wilkes Artis Hedrick & Lane 11320 Random Hills Rd Ste 600 Fairfax VA 22030-6001

**STEARNS, RICHARD GAYLORE,** judge; b. L.A., June 27, 1944; s. Gaylore Rhodes and Jeannetta Viola (Hofheinz) S.; m. Patricia Ann McElligott, Dec. 21, 1975. BA, Stanford U., 1968; MLitt, Oxford U., Eng., 1971; JD, Harvard U., 1976. Bar: Mass. Dep. campaign mgr. McGovern for Pres., Washington, 1970-72; spl. asst. U.S. Senate, Washington, 1972-73; asst. dist. atty. Norfolk County, Dedham, 1976-79, 80-82; del. dir. Kennedy for Pres., Washington, 1979-80; asst. U.S. atty. U.S. Dept. Justice, Boston, 1982-90; assoc. justice Superior Ct. Mass., Boston, 1990-94; U.S. dist. judge U.S. Dist. Ct. Mass., Boston, 1994—. Author: Massachusetts Criminal Law: A Prosecutor's Guide, 19th edit., 1999. Mem. jud. conf. com. on federal-state jurisdiction, mem. mass torts working group; trustee Vincent Meml. Hosp., Boston. Rhodes scholar, 1968. Mem. ABA, Mass. Bar Assn., Phi Beta Kappa. Office: US Courthouse 1 Courthouse Way Ste 7130 Boston MA 02210-3009

**STEARNS, SUSAN TRACEY,** lighting design company executive, lawyer; b. Seattle, Oct. 28, 1957; d. Arthur Thomas and Roberta Jane (Arrowood) S.; m. Ross Alan De Alessi, Aug. 11, 1990; 1 child, Chase Arthur. AA, Stephens Coll., 1977, BA, 1979; JD, U. Wash., Seattle, 1990. Bar: Calif. 1990, U.S. Ct. Appeals (9th cir.) 1990, U.S. Dist. Ct. (no. dist.) Calif 1990, U.S. Dist. Ct. (we. dist.) Wash. 1991, Wash. 1991. TV news prodr. KOMO, Seattle, 1980-86; atty. Brobeck, Phleger & Harrison, San Francisco, 1990-92; pres. Ross De Alessi Lighting Design, Seattle, 1993—. Author periodicals in field. Alumnae Assn. Coun. Stephens Coll., Columbia, Mo., 1995—. Named Nat. Order of Barristers U. Washington, Seattle, 1990. Mem. ABA (mem. state labor and employment law subcom.), Wash. State Bar Assn. (mem. bench-bar-press com.), State Bar Calif., King County Bar Assn., Bar Assn.San Francisco, Wash. Athletic Club. Avocations: travel, dance. Office: Ross De Alessi Lighting Design 2815 2nd Ave Ste 280 Seattle WA 98121-3217

**STEBBINS, HENRY BLANCHARD,** lawyer; b. Hartford, Conn., June 14, 1951; s. Herbert Bellows and Katherine (Reynolds) S.; m. Alison Finney, May 30, 1976; children: Duncan Finney, Martha Reynolds, H. Benjamin. BA cum laude, U. N.H., 1973; JD, Boston U., 1976. Bar: N.H. 1976, U.S. Dist. Ct. N.H. 1976. Assoc. Sheenan, Phinney, Bass & Green, Manchester, N.H., 1976-80, ptnr., 1980-97; mgmt. com. Sheenan, Phinney, Bass & Green, Manchester, 1994-97; sr. ptnr. Stebbins Lazos & Van Der Beken, Manchester, N.H., 1997—. Trustee Manchester Boys and Girls Club, 1983—; chmn. Vocat. Partnership Found., 1986-91; bd. dirs. Brookside Ch. Nursery Sch., 1984-90, Leadership N.H., 1994-95; bd. dirs. United Way Greater Manchester, 1986-95, chmn., 1990-92; mem. N.H. Rep. State com., N.H. Rep. Fin. Com., N.H. Legal Counsel, Dole for Pres. Campaign; mem. fin. com. George W. Bush Presdl. Campaign. Mem. ABA, N.H. Bar Assn., Manchester Bar Assn. (pres. 1982-83), Assn. Bank Holding Cos. (lawyers div. 1985-93), Rissa Club. Banking, Real property, Construction. Office: 66 Hanover St Manchester NH 03101-2230

**STEEG, MOISE S., JR.,** lawyer; b. New Orleans, July 25, 1916; s. Moise S. and Carrie (Gutmann) S.; m. Marion B., Sept. 14, 1943 (dec.); children: Barbara Steeg Midlo, Marion, Robert M.; m. Melba Law, Nov. 29, 1969. LLB, Tulane U., 1937. Bar: La. 1937, U.S. Dist. Ct. (ea. dist.) La. 1939, U.S. Ct. Appeals (5th cir.) 1946, U.S. Supreme Ct. 1950, U.S. Ct. Appeals (11th cir.) 1981. Practice, New Orleans, 1937—; assoc. Rittenberg & Rittenberg, 1937-38; sole practice, 1938-46; founder Gertler & Steeg, 1946-48, Steeg & Morrison, 1948-50, Marcus & Steeg, 1950-54, Steeg & Shushan, 1954-71; sr. ptnr. Steeg & O'Connor, 1972—. Bd. dirs. Loyola U., chmn., 1979—, mem. search com. for dean Coll. Law; chmn., founder New Orleans Hist. Dist. and Landmarks Com.; bd. dirs. chmn. bd. New Orleans Mus. Art, 1980; bd. overseers Hebrew Union Coll.; bd. dirs. Delgado Jr. Coll., New Orleans Symphony; founder, dir. New Orleans Ednl. and Rsch. Corp.; bd. dirs. Louise Davis Sch. for Retarded Children, Touro Infirmary, 1963-69; mem. Ochsner Found. Hosp. Bd., 1985—; bd. visitors Trinity Episcopal Sch., 1989—; organizer, sec. New Orleans Bus. Coun., 1986; pres. Temple Sinai, 1966-67; chmn. Anti-Defamation League, Jewish Community Ctr., chmn. Acquarium Drive, Acquarium of Ams.; local counsel Nat. Dem. Party, 1966. Served to capt. USAF, 1942-46. Recipient Brotherhood Award, NCCJ, 1980, Disting. Alumnus award Tulane Law Sch., 1991, Isidore Newman Sch., Svc. award Newcomb Coll. Soc., Cmty. Svc. award New Orleans Bar Assn. Mem. Paul Tulane Honor Soc. Real property, Contracts commercial, Probate. Home: One River Place 3 Poydras St New Orleans LA 70130-1665 Office: 201 Saint Charles Ave Ste 3201 New Orleans LA 70170-1032

**STEEL, JOHN DEATON,** lawyer; b. Durham, N.C., June 3, 1959; s. Charles Leighton III and Elizabeth (Deaton) S.; m. Allyson Andrews Watson, Mar. 11, 1989 (div. Oct. 1992); 1 child, Edward Andrews. BS with honors, U. N.C., 1981, JD, 1984. Bar: Ga., U.S. Dist. Ct. (no. and mid. dists.) Ga. Assoc. atty. Freeman & Hawkins, Atlanta, 1984-89, Frankel & Hardwick, Atlanta, 1989-92; ptnr. Blackwood Matthews & Steel, Atlanta, 1992—; designated trial counsel Brotherhood of Local Engrs., Cleve., 1995—. Mem. ATLA, Ga. Trial Lawyers Assn. Personal injury, General civil litigation, Product liability. Office: 462 E Paces Ferry Rd NE Atlanta GA 30305-3301

**STEELE, DWIGHT CLEVELAND,** lawyer; b. Alameda, Calif., Jan. 23, 1914; s. Isaac Celveland Steele and Mirah Dinsmore Jackson; m. Alberta Evelyn Hill, Oct. 19, 1940; children: Diane Smith, Marilyn Steele. AB, U. Calif., Berkeley, 1935, LLB, JSD, 1939. Bar: Calif. 1939. V.p., mgr. Distributors Assn. of San Francisco, 1941-46; pres. Hawaii Employers Coun., Honolulu, 1946-59; pres., gen. counsel Lumber and Mill Employers Assn., Oakland, Calif., 1961-76, League to Save Lake Tahoe, 1976-78, 89—; chmn. citizens adv. com. Bay Conservation and Devel. Co., San Francisco, 1997—; chmn. Citizens for Eastshore State Park, Calif., 1986—; v.p. Save San Francisco Bay Assn., Berkeley, 1988-91. Dir. Spirit of Stockholm Found., Nairobi, Kenya, 1975-89, Planning and Conservation Found., Sacramento, 1975-91, Eugene O'Neill Found., Walnut Creek, Calif., 1976-81, Tahoe Baikal Inst., 1991—; chmn. Heart Fund Drive, Hawaii, 1959; advisor Legis.

Land Use Task Force, Sacramento, 1975-77. Mem. ABA, Hawaii Bar Assn. Democrat. Avocations: skiing, travel. Labor, Environmental. Home: PO Box 696 Tahoe City CA 96145-0696 Office: 1212 Rossmoor Pkwy Walnut Creek CA 94595-2501

**STEELE, ELIZABETH MEYER,** lawyer; b. San Mateo, Calif., Jan. 12, 1952; d. Bailey Robert and Kathryn Steele (Horrigan) Meyer; 1 child, Steele Sternberg. BA, Kirkland Coll., 1974; JD, U. N.Mex., 1977. Counsel U.S. Dept. Energy, Los Alamos, N.Mex., 1977-78; law clk. to judge Howard C. Bratton U.S. Dist. Ct., Albuquerque, 1978-80; assoc. Davis, Graham & Stubbs, Denver, 1980-84, ptnr., 1985-87; v.p., gen. counsel Jones Internat., Ltd., Englewood, Colo., 1987—. Communications, General corporate. Office: Jones Internat Ltd 9697 E Mineral Ave Englewood CO 80112-3446

**STEELE, KEVIN EDWARD,** lawyer; b. Gary, Ind., Nov. 24, 1967; s. Charles Walter and Petra Agnes (Manning) S.; m. Laura Therese Gordon, Nov. 11, 1995. BA, U. Notre Dame, Ind., 1990; JD, Ind. U., 1993. Bar: Ind. 1993, U.S. Dist. Ct. (no. and so. dist.) Ind. 1993, U.S. Ct. Appeals (7th cir.) 1993. Assoc. Burke, Costanza & Cuppy LLP, Merrillville, Ind., 1993—. Atty. Southlake Network, Inc., Crown Point, Ind., 1995—. Mem. ABA, Ind. Bar Assn., Lake County Bar Assn. General civil litigation, Construction, Insurance. Office: Burke Costanza & Cuppy LLP 8585 Broadway Ste 600 Merrillville IN 46410-5661

**STEELE, MANDY R.,** lawyer; b. Bklyn., Nov. 21, 1957; d. Jerome and Barbara Rosenbaum; m. Eliot J. Steele, June 17, 1979; children: Rochelle, Brandon, Ryan. BS, Bklyn. Poly. Inst., 1978; JD, New Eng. Sch. Law, 1981. Bar: N.J., N.Y., U.S. Dist. Ct. N.J., U.S. Dist. Ct. (so. dist.) N.Y., U.S. Dist. Ct. (ea. dist.) N.Y., U.S. Ct. Appeals (3d cir.). Instr. U. Md., Weisbaden, Germany, 1984-88; sr. trial atty. Leahey & Johnson, N.Y.C., 1988-90, Voorhees & Acciauati, Morristown, N.J., 1990-91; pvt. practice East Brunswick, N.J., 1991—; del. to China, Internat. Women in Law; panel mem. cable T.V. show. Mem. ABA, N.J. Bar Assn., Middlesex County Bar Assn. (assoc.). Office: 385 Highway 18 East Brunswick NJ 08816-5703

**STEELE, REBECCA HARRISON,** lawyer, educator; b. Durham, N.C., Sept. 18, 1956; d. Thomas H. Harrison and Betty Harrison Liles; m. Thomas T. Steele, Dec. 13, 1986; children: Sarah Elizabeth, Miranda Katherine. BA, U. S. Fla., 1978; postgrad., Carnegie-Mellon U., 1979-81; JD magna cum laude, Stetson U., 1995. Bar: Fla., U. S. Ct. Appeals (11th cir.), U. S. Dist. Ct. (so., mid. and no. dists.) Fla. Free-lance stage dir., theater mgr. various theater, 1975-94; assoc. program dir. New Dramatists, N.Y.C., 1983-84; adj. prof. U. S. Fla., Tampa, 1987-88, U. Tampa, 1990-91; assoc. Shackleford, Farrior, Tampa, 1995-97, Holland & Knight, Tampa, 1997—; adj. prof. Stetson U. Coll. Law, St. Petersburg, Fla., 1998—. Articles editor Stetson Law Rev. Mem. ABA (labor and employment law, employee benefits com. 1997—), Tampa Bay Pension Coun., West Coast Employee Benefits Coun., Athena Soc., Fla. Bar Assn. (labor and employment law, chair employee benefits com.), Hillsborough Assn. of Women Lawyers (sec. bd. dirs.). Pension, profit-sharing, and employee benefits, Probate, Appellate. Office: Holland & Knight LLP 400 N Ashley Dr Ste 2300 Tampa FL 33602-4322

**STEELE, RODNEY REDFEARN,** judge; b. Selma, Ala., May 22, 1930; s. C. Parker and Miriam Lera (Redfearn) S.; m. Frances Marion Blair, Aug. 1, 1964; children: Marion Scott, Claudia Redfearn, Parker Blair. AB, U. Ala., 1950, MA, 1951; LLB, U. Mich., 1954. Bar: Ala. 1954, U.S. Dist. Ct. (mid. dist.) Ala. 1959, U.S. Ct. Appeals (5th cir., now 11th cir.) 1981. Law clk. Ala. Ct. Appeals, 1956-57; assoc. Knabe & Nachman, Montgomery, Ala., 1957-61; asst. U.S. atty. Dept. Justice, Montgomery, 1961-66; staff atty. So. Bell T&T Co., Atlanta, 1966-67; judge U.S. Bankruptcy Ct., Mid. dist. Ala., Montgomery, 1967—, chief judge, 1985-99. Served with U.S. Army, 1954-56, Korea. Mem. ABA, Ala. State Bar, Montgomery County Bar Assn. Democrat. Episcopalian. Home: 127 Magnolia Curve Montgomery AL 36106 Office: US Bankruptcy Ct PO Box 1248 1 Court Sq Montgomery AL 36102-1248

**STEELE, THOMAS LEE,** lawyer; b. Kearney, Nebr., Oct. 16, 1959; s. Clyde M. and L. Lorene S.; m. Sarah E. Owens, May 8, 1992; 1 child, Andrew. BA, U. Mo., 1984; JD, Creighton U., 1987. Bar: Nebr. 1987, Mo. 1988, Kans. 1989, U.S. Supreme Ct. 1993. Assoc. Gage, Tucker, Margolin & Kirwan, Kansas City, Mo., 1988-92; spl. counsel, assoc. Rupe & Girard, Wichita, Kans., 1992-96; gen. counsel Gen. Fin. Svcs., Inc., Wichita, 1995—; bd. dirs. The Inland Corp., Norwich, Kans. Precinct chmn. Wichita Rep. Com., 1996—; mem. exec. bd. Quivira coun. Boy Scouts Am., 1993—. Mem. ABA, Mo. Bar Assn., Kans. Bar Assn., Nebr. Bar Assn., Pi Omicron Sigma. Presbyn. General corporate, Real property, Labor. Home: 156 Belmont Pl Wichita KS 67208 Office: Gen Fin Svcs Inc 8441 E 32d St N Wichita KS 67226

**STEELE, THOMAS MCKNIGHT,** law librarian, law educator; b. Bartlesville, Okla., June 4, 1948; s. James Robert and Erma Blanche (McKnight) S.; m. Barbara Van Curen, Mar. 23, 1973 (div. 1985); children: James Robert, Ryan Thomas, David Christopher Joyce, Justin Daniel Joyce; m. Martha Bolling Swann, Apr. 1985 (div. 1990); m. LeAnn P. Joyce, Jan. 1995. BA in History, Okla. State U., 1969; MLS, U. Oreg., 1974; JD, U. Tex., 1977. Adminstrv. asst. Tarlton Law Libr. U. Tex., Austin, 1975-77; acting law librarian Underwood Law Libr. So. Meth. U., Dallas, 1977-78, asst. law librarian, 1978-79; assoc. prof. law, dir. Franklin Pierce Law Ctr., Concord, N.H., 1979-82; asst. prof., dir. U. Miss. Law Libr., University, 1982-85; assoc. prof., dir. Wake Forest U. Sch. Law Libr., Winston-Salem, N.C., 1985-91; prof., dir. Profl. Ctr. Libr. Wake Forest U., Winston-Salem, N.C., 1991; cons. in field; exec. dir. SCRIBES--Am. Soc. Writers on Legal Subjects, 1988-97. Editor (newsletter) Scrivener, 1986-88; mng. editor Scribes Jour. Legal Writing, 1989-91; editor Pub. Librs. and Pub. Laws, 1986-88; compiler bibliography IDEA, 1981-83, Jour. Air Law and Commerce, 1977-81; co-author: A Law Library Move: Planning Preparation and Execution, 1994. With U.S. Army. Mem. Am. Assn. Law Librs. Democrat. Baptist. Office: Wake Forest U Sch Law PO Box 7206 Winston Salem NC 27109-7206

**STEELE, TODD BENNETT,** lawyer; b. Brownwood, Tex., Mar. 31, 1967; s. Artie Ben and Cheri Suzanne (Bennett) S. BS in Criminal Justice, Tarleton State U., Stephenville, Tex., 1989; JD, Tex. Wesleyan U., Irving, 1994. Bar: Tex. 1994. Law clk. Jerry W. Hayes, Atty.-at-Law, Dallas, 1992-95; assoc. Bud Jones, Inc., Dallas, 1995; with Bryan Healer, Brownwood, Tex., 1995—. Mem. Assn. Trial Lawyers Am., Tex. Trial Lawyers Assn., State Bar of Tex. Avocation: hunting. General civil litigation, Criminal, Personal injury. Office: 208 E Anderson St Brownwood TX 76801-2903

**STEELE, TRACY LYNN,** lawyer; b. Washington, Sept. 23, 1970; d. John Scott and Wilma Thomas Steele; m. Christopher LeGrande Scileppi, Apr. 20, 1996 (div.). BA in Math. and Econs., Sweet Briar Coll., 1992; JD, Pa. State U., 1995. Bar: Va. 1995, D.C. 1999. Assoc. Walsh, Colucci, Stackhouse, Emrich & Lubeley, P.C., Arlington, Va., 1995-98, Rudnick & Wolfe, Washington, 1998—. Bd. dirs. Sweet Briar (Va.) Coll., 1992-95; trustee Dickinson Sch. Law, Carlisle, Pa., 1998—, alumni mentor, 1999—; active Friends Assisting the Nat. Symphony Orch., Washington, 1998; mem. alumni coun. Pa. State U., 1999—. Mem. ABA, Va. Bar Assn., Arlington County Bar Assn., Fairfax County Bar Assn., Dickinson Coll. Gen. Alumni Assn. (bd. dirs. 1998—), Dickinson Sch. Law Alumni Assn. (pres. Washington chpt. 1998—), Pa. State U. Gen. Alumni Assn. (bd. dirs. 1998—). Episcopalian. Avocations: skiing, rollerblading, reading, antique shopping, traveling. Office: Rudnick & Wolfe Penthouse 1201 New York Ave NW Ph 1300 Washington DC 20005-6162

**STEELMAN, FRANK (SITLEY),** lawyer; b. Watsonville, Calif., June 6, 1936; s. Frank S. Sr. and Blossom J. (Daugherty) S.; m. Diane Elaine Duke, June 27, 1960; children: Susan Butler, Robin Thurmond, Joan Bentley, David, Carol. BA, Baylor U., 1958, LLB, 1962. Spl. agt. IRS, Houston, 1962-64, atty. for estate tax, 1964-68; trust officer First City Nat. Bank, Houston, 1968-71; sr. v.p., trust officer First Bank & Trust, Bryan, Tex., 1971-73; assoc. Goode, Skrivanek & Steelman, College Station, Tex., 1973-74; pvt. practice Bryan, 1974—; vis. lectr. Tex. A&M U., College Station, 1974-75; mcpl. judge City of Bryan, 1986-88. Bd. dirs. Bryan Devel. Found., 1994-97; mem. Bryan Zoning Bd. Adjustments, 1992-94; pres. Brazos Valley Estate Planning Coun., 1973-74, Am. Heart Assn., 1975-76; deacon, mem. ch. choir, Sunday sch. tchr. So. Bapt. Ch.; v.p. bd. dirs. Bryan Bus. Coun., 1998-99. Mem. Rotary (bd. dirs. Bryan club 1973-74). Avocations: walking, golf. Bankruptcy, Family and matrimonial, Probate. Office: 1810 Greenfield Plz Bryan TX 77802-3492

**STEENLAND, DOUGLAS,** lawyer. Sr. v.p., gen. counsel, sec. Northwest Airlines Inc., St. Paul. Office: Northwest Airlines Inc 5101 Northwest Dr Saint Paul MN 55111-3027

**STEFANO, JOSEPH M.,** lawyer; b. Jersey City, Sept. 9, 1970; s. Christopher A. and Joan (Noren) S.; m. Nicole Nardini, May 28, 1994. BA, Rutgers U., 1992; JD, Cornell U., 1995. Bar: N.Y. 1995, N.J. 1995. Assoc. Seward & Kissel, N.Y.C., 1995—. Bd. dirs., mem. bike tour com. Inst. for Children with Cancer and Blood Disorders, New Brunswick, N.J., 1990—. Mem. ABA (comml. fin. svcs. com. 1995—, aircraft fin. subcom. 1997—), The Wings Club. Aviation, Contracts commercial, Finance. Office: Seward & Kissel One Battery Park Plz New York NY 10004

**STEFANON, ANTHONY,** lawyer; b. Bellefonte, Pa., Sept. 6, 1949; s. Severino and Dorothy (Albright) S.; m. Elizabeth Jo Windsor, Nov. 22, 1969; children: Dyon, Justin. BS in Aerospace Engring., Pa. State U., 1971; JD, Dickinson U., 1977. Bar: Pa. 1977, U.S. Dist. Ct. (mid. dist.) Pa. 1977, U.S. Ct. Appeals (3rd cir.) 1991. Assoc. Myers & Potteiger, Harrisburg, Pa., 1977-79; ptnr. Myers, Potteiger & Stefanon, Harrisburg, Pa., 1979-82; assoc. Thomas & Thomas, Harrisburg, Pa., 1982-85; ptnr. Stefanon & Lappas, Harrisburg, Pa., 1985-88; pvt. practice Harrisburg, Pa., 1988—. Mem. Assn. of Trial Lawyers of Am., Pa. Trial Lawyers Assn., Pa. Bar Assn., Dauphin County Bar Assn. Avocations: pvt. aircraft pilot, squash, soccer, auto restorations. General civil litigation, Personal injury, Product liability. Office: 407 N Front St Harrisburg PA 17101-1221

**STEFFEN, THOMAS LEE,** lawyer, former state supreme court justice; b. Tremonton, Utah, July 9, 1930; s. Conrad Richard and Jewel (McGuire) S.; m. LaVona Ericksen, Mar. 20, 1953; children—Elizabeth, Catherine, Conrad, John, Jennifer. Student, U. So. Calif., 1955-56; BS, U. Utah, 1957; JD with honors, George Washington U., 1964; LLM, U. Va., 1988. Bar: Nev. 1965, U.S. Dist. Ct. Nev. 1965, U.S. Tax Ct. 1966, U.S. Ct. Appeals 1967, U.S. Supreme Ct. 1977. Contracts negotiator U.S. Bur. Naval Weapons, Washington, 1961-64; private practice Las Vegas, 1965-82; justice Supreme Ct. Nev., Carson City, 1982-94, chief justice, 1995-97, ret., 1997, chmn. code of jud. conduct study com., 1991; of cousnel Hutchison & Steffen, Las Vegas, also Provo, Utah, 1997—; vice chmn. Nev. State Jud. Edn. Coun., 1983-84; chmn. Nev. State-Fed. Jud. Coun., 1986-91, mem., 1986-93. Mem. editorial staff George Washington U. Law Rev., 1963-64; contbr. articles to legal jours. Bd. dirs. So. Nev. chpt. NCCJ, 1974-75; mem. exec. bd. Boulder Dam Area coun. Boy Scouts Am., 1979-83; bd. visitors Brigham Young U., 1985-89. Recipient merit citation Utah State U., 1983. Mem. Nev. Bar Assn. (former chmn. So. Nev. med.-legal screening panel), Nev. Trial Lawyers Assn. (former dir.). Republican. Mem. LDS Ch. Avocations: reading, spectator sports. Office: Lakes Business Park 8831 W Sahara Ave Las Vegas NV 89117-5865 also: 481 E Normandy Dr Provo UT 84604-5963

**STEGER, WILLIAM MERRITT,** federal judge; b. Dallas, Aug. 22, 1920; s. Merritt and Lottie (Reese) S.; m. Ann Hollandsworth, Feb. 14, 1948; 1 son, Merritt Reed (dec.). Student, Baylor U., 1938-41; LL.B., So. Meth. U., 1950. Bar: Tex. 1951. Pvt. practice Longview, 1951-53; apptd. U.S. dist. atty. Eastern Dist. Tex., 1953-59; mem. firm Wilson, Miller, Spivey & Steger, Tyler, Tex., 1959-70; U.S. dist. judge Ea. Dist. Tex. U.S. Dist. Ct. (ea. dist.) Tex., Tyler, 1970—, sr. judge, 1988—. Republican candidate for gov. of Tex., 1960; for U.S. Ho. of Reps., 1962; mem. Tex. State Republican Exec. Com., 1966-69; chmn. Tex. State Republican Party, 1969-70. Pilot with ranks 2d lt. to capt. USAAF, 1942-47. Mem. ABA, State Bar Tex., Masons (32 degree, Shriner). Home: 801 Meadowcreek Dr Tyler TX 75703-3524 Office: US Courthouse PO Box 1109 Tyler TX 75710-1109

**STEIGER, SHELDON GERALD,** lawyer; b. Cleve., May 27, 1945; s. Max and Fannie (Axelrod) S.; m. Sally Blumental, Sept. 6, 1971; children: Jeremy M., Suzanna L., Melissa R. BA, Ohio State U., 1967; JD, Cleve. State U., 1971. Bar: Ohio 1972, U.S. Dist. Ct. (no. dist.) Ohio 1975. Asst. dir. law City of Cleve., 1973-74; assoc. Berger & Kirschenbaum, Cleve., 1974; pvt. practive, Cleve., 1975—. Mem. Ohio Bar Assn., Cleve. Bar Assn. Workers' compensation, Probate. Home: 4426 Silsby Rd University Ht OH 44118-3939 Office: 55 Public Sq Ste 2222 Cleveland OH 44113-1901

**STEIGMAN, MEREDITH LEE,** lawyer; b. Manhasset, N.Y., Dec. 11, 1972; d. Richard Norman and Eileen Cudrin; m. Richard Mark Steigman, Nov. 29, 1997. BA, Amherst Coll., 1994; JD, Hofstra U., 1997. Bar: N.Y. 1998. Assoc. Jackson, Lewis, Schnitzer & Krepman, N.Y.C., summer 1995, Winthrop, Stimson, Putnam & Roberts, N.Y.C., 1996—. Editor Hofstra U. Sch. Law Rev., 1996-97. Mem. N.Y. State Bar Assn., Assn. for the Bar of the City of N.Y. Avocations: tennis, photography, travel. Labor, Pension, profit-sharing, and employee benefits, Workers' compensation. Office: Winthrop Stimson Putnam & Roberts One Battery Port Plz New York NY 10004

**STEIN, ALLAN MARK,** lawyer; b. Montreal, Quebec, Can., Oct. 18, 1951; came to U.S., 1977; s. Boris and Beatrice (Fishman) S. B in Commerce, Sir George Williams, 1972; BA, Loyola, Montreal, 1973; B in Civil Law, McGill U., 1976, LLB, 1977; JD, Nova U., 1979. Bar: Fla. 1979, U.S. Dist. Ct. (so. dist.) Fla. 1979, U.S. Ct. Appeals (5th cir.) 1980, U.S. Ct. Appeals (11th cir.) 1983, U.S. Dist. Ct. Ariz. 1993. Assoc. Law Offices of Paul Landy Beiley, Miami, Fla., 1980, Heitner & Rosenfeld, Miami, 1980-85, Rosenfeld & Stein, Miami, 1985-90, Rosenfeld, Stein & Sugarman, Miami, 1990-94, Rosenfeld & Stein P.A., Miami, 1994—. Mem. North Dade Bar Assn. (bd. dirs. 1985-90). Republican. Jewish. Avocation: photography, HISTORY. Consumer commercial, Contracts commercial, Bankruptcy. Office: 18260 NE 19th Ave Ste 202 Miami FL 33162-1632

**STEIN, ARNOLD BRUCE,** lawyer; b. Chgo., Oct. 2, 1948; s. Oscar and Lillian (Cohen) S.; m. Gail Stein, June 11, 1972; children: Jennifer, Jeffrey. BA in History with high honors & distinction, U. Ill., 1970; JD, Northwestern U., 1975. Assoc. Whitcup & Fiala, Chgo., 1975-77; ptnr. Whitcup & Stein, Chgo., 1977-80, Whitcup, Horn & Stein, Chgo., 1980-81, Schiller, Du Canto & Fleck, Chgo., 1981—. Named in book The Best Lawyers in America, Neifeh and Smith (authors). Mem. ABA (exec. bd. family law trial sect.), Ill. State Bar Assn., Phi Beta Kappa. Family and matrimonial. Home: PO Box 2 Barrington IL 60011-0002 Office: Schiller Du Canto and Fleck 200 N La Salle St Ste 2700 Chicago IL 60601-1099

**STEIN, CHERYL DENISE,** lawyer; b. N.Y.C., Nov. 3, 1953; d. Arthur Earl and Joyce (Weitzman) S. BA magna cum laude, Yale U., 1974; postgrad., U. Chgo., 1974-75; JD, Yale U., 1977. Bar: D.C. 1978, U.S. Dist. Ct. D.C. 1983, U.S. Dist. Ct. Md. 1995, U.S. Ct. Appeals (D.C. cir.) 1988. Atty. advisor CAB, Washington, 1978-79; assoc. Cohn & Marks, Washington, 1979-82; pvt. practice Washington, 1982—. Vol. reader radio reading svc. for the blind Washington Ear, Silver Spring, Md., 1982-91; vol. tutor Friends of Tyler Sch., 1992-95, Habitat for Humanity, Washington, 1997—; pvt. vol. tutor, 1995-97. Mem. Nat. Assn. Criminal Def. Lawyers, D.C. Assn. Criminal Def. Lawyers. Democrat. Jewish. Avocations: horseback riding, gardening. Criminal, General civil litigation. Office: 705 8th St SE Ste 100 Washington DC 20003-2856

**STEIN, DANIEL ALAN,** public interest lawyer; b. Washington, Mar. 9, 1955; s. Edward Seymour and Ann Rose Stein; m. Sharon McCloe, Oct. 18, 1986; children: Claire, Corrieanne. BA, Ind. U., 1977; JD, Cath. U. Am., 1984. Bar: D.C. 1984, U.S. Dist. Ct. D.C. 1985, U.S. Ct. Appeals (D.C. cir.) 1987, U.S. Tax Ct. 1987. Profl. staff mem. select com. on narcotics abuse and control U.S. Ho. of Reps., Washington, 1977-81; pvt. practice Washington, 1984-89; exec. dir. Immigration Reform Law Inst., Washington, 1986-88, Fedn. for Am. Immigration Reform, Washington, 1982-86, 89—. mem. adv. bd. Social Contract periodical, Petosky, Mich., 1990—. Mem. Capitol Hill Club, Nat. Press Club. Republican. Avocations: trombone, American history, western civilization, jazz, antique books. Office: Fedn for Am Immigration Reform 1666 Connecticut Ave NW Ste 400 Washington DC 20009-1039

**STEIN, DANIEL JEREMIAH,** lawyer; b. N.Y.C., Oct. 26, 1946; s. Joseph Stein and Sadie Singer. BA, U. Wis., 1970, JD, 1982. Bar: Wis. 1982, U.S. Dist. Ct. Wis. 1982. Sole practice Madison, Wis., 1982—. Criminal.

**STEIN, ELEANOR BANKOFF,** judge; b. N.Y.C., Jan. 24, 1923; d. Jacob and Sarah (Rashkin) Bankoff; m. Frank S. Stein, May 27, 1947; children: Robert B., Joan Jenkins, William M. Student, Barnard Coll., 1940-42; BS in Econs., Columbia U., 1944; LLB, NYU, 1949; grad. Ind. Jud. Coll., 1986. Bar: N.Y. 1950, Ind. 1976, U.S. Supreme Ct. 1980. Atty. Hillis & Button, Kokomo, Ind., 1975-76, Paul Hillis, Kokomo, 1976-78, Bayliff, Harrigan, Kokomo, 1978-80; judge Howard County Ct., Kokomo, 1981-89; ret., 1989; co-juvenile referee Howard County Juvenile Ct., 1976-78. Mem. Republican Women's Assn. Kokomo, 1980—; bd. dirs. Howard County Legal Aid Soc., 1976-80; dir. Howard County Ct. Alcohol and Drug Svcs. Program, 1982-89; bd. advisors St. Joseph Hosp., Kokomo, 1979—; bd. dirs. Kokomo Human Rels. Commn., 1967-70, Howard County Children's Ctr., 1993—. Mem. law rev. bd. NYU Law Rev., 1947-48. Mem. Am. Judicature Soc., Ind. Jud. Assn., Nat. Assn. Women Judges, ABA (apptd. Ind. del. jud. adminstrn. div. 1987), Ind. Bar Assn., Howard County Bar Assn. Jewish. Clubs: Kokomo Country, Altrusa. Home: 3204 Tally Ho Dr Kokomo IN 46902-3985

**STEIN, GARY S.,** state supreme court justice; b. Newark, June 13, 1933; s. Morris J. and Mollie (Goldfarb) S.; married, July 1, 1956; children—Jill, Carrie, Michael, Terri, Jo; m. Et Tilchin, July 1, 1956. A.B., Duke U., 1954, LL.B. with distinction, 1956; D.H.L. (hon.), N.J. Inst. Tech., 1985. Bar: D.C. 1956, Ohio 1957, N.Y. 1958, N.J. 1963. Research asst. U.S. Senate AntiTrust and Monopoly Subcom., Washington, 1955; assoc. Kramer, Marx, Greenlee & Backus, N.Y.C., 1956-65; sole practice Paramus, N.J., 1966-72; ptnr. Stein & Kurland, Esquires, Paramus, N.J., 1972-82; dir. Gov.'s Office of Policy and Planning, Trenton, N.J., 1982-85; assoc. justice Supreme Ct. N.J., Hackensack, 1985—; mcpl. atty., Paramus, 1967-71; counsel N.J. Election Law Revision Commn., 1970; atty. Bd. Adjustment, Teaneck, N.J., 1973-82. Mem. editorial bd. Duke Law Jour., 1954-56, assoc. editor, 1955-56. Mem. Dist. Ethics Com. for Bergen County, N.J., 1977-80, chmn. 1981. Served with U.S. Army, 1957-58, 61-62. Mem. ABA, N.J. State Bar Assn. (com. on state legislation 1973-79, chmn. 1973-76, jud. selection com. 1976-81, Constl. amendment com. 1977-79, court modernization com. 1976-79), Bergen County Bar Assn., Order of Coif. Jewish. Avocation: tennis. Office: NJ Supreme Ct 25 Main St Hackensack NJ 07601-7015

**STEIN, JOHN C.,** lawyer; b. Flint, Mich., May 8, 1939; s. Joseph Aloyosius and Gertrude (Carlin) S.; m. Dorothea Ruel, Nov. 20, 1965; children: John Jr., Christian, Peter, Thea. BA, U. San Francisco, 1963; JD, U. Calif. Hastings, San Francisco, 1966; cert., Mil. Justice Sch., Newport, R.I., 1968. Bar: Calif. 1966, U.S. Dist. Ct. (no., ctrl. and so. dists.) Calif. 1969. Dep. city atty. City of San Francisco, Office of City Atty., 1969-71; with The Boccardo Law Firm, San Francisco, 1971-81; mng. ptnr. The Boccardo Law Firm, San Jose, Calif., 1981-99; judge pro tem San Francisco County Superior Ct., 1978—, Santa Clara County Superior Ct., 1981—; lectr. U. Santa Clara Law Sch., 1985—, Hastings Coll. of Law, U. C. San Francisco. Bd. dirs. Katherine Delmar Burke Sch. Girls, San Francisco, 1988-92, Planning Orgn. for The Richmond, San Francisco, 1985-88. Capt. USMC, 1966-69. Fellow Am. Coll. Trial Lawyers; mem. ATLA, Consumer Attys. of Calif., Am. Bd. Trial Advocates. Democrat. Roman Catholic. Avocations: golf, skiing, SCUBA diving. Personal injury. Office: Boccardo Law Firm 111 W Saint John St Ste 1100 San Jose CA 95113-1107

**STEIN, JULIE LYNNE,** lawyer; b. Rochester, N.Y., Nov. 9, 1970; d. Frank and JoAnn Stein. BA, U. Md., 1993; JD, Union U., Albany, N.Y., 1996. Bar: N.Y. 1997. Atty. Western Auto Supply Co., Kansas City, Mo., 1996-98, YKK Corp. Am., Marietta, Ga., 1999—. Mem. ABA, Am. Corp. Counsel Assn., N.Y. State Bar Assn. Antitrust, Contracts commercial, Advertising. Home: 1110 Windy Ridge Ln SE Atlanta GA 30339-2413 Office: YKK Corp America 1306 Cobb Industrial Dr Marietta GA 30066-6636

**STEIN, LAWRENCE A.,** lawyer; b. Balt., Mar. 18, 1965; s. Hersh and Ellen (Hart) S.; m. Diane Wells, June 23, 1991; children: Joshua A., Julie E. AB, U. Chgo., 1988; JD, No. Ill. U., 1993. Bar: Ill. 1993, U.S. Dist. Ct. (no. dist.) Ill. 1993, U.S. Ct. Appeals (7th cir.) 1993, Md. 1994, U.S. Dist. Ct. Md. 1994, U.S. Supreme Ct. 1997. Dir. Huck, Bouma, Martin, Jones & Bradshaw, Wheaton, Ill., 1993—; advisor Prairie State Legal Svcs., Carol Stream, Ill., 1993—. Commr. Glen Ellyn (Ill.) Architecture Review Commn., 1994-97. Recipient Am. jurisprudence award for excellence in appellate advocacy Lawyers Coop., 1991. Mem. ABA, Ill. Trial Lawyers Assn., DuPage County Bar Assn., Ill. State Bar Assn., Am. Inns Ct., Phi Delta Phi. Republican. Jewish. Banking, Appellate. Home: 69 Ott Ave Glen Ellyn IL 60137-5632 Office: Huck Bouma Martin Jones & Bradshaw 1755 S Naperville Rd # 200 Wheaton IL 60187-8132

**STEIN, MILTON MICHAEL,** lawyer; b. N.Y.C., Sept. 18, 1936; s. Isidore and Sadie (Lefkowitz) S.; m. Jacqueline Martin, June 17, 1962; children: April, Alicia. AB, Columbia U., 1958, LLB, 1961. Bar: N.Y. 1962, Pa. 1971, U.S. Supreme Ct. 1971. Asst. dist. atty. N.Y. County, 1962-67; sr. counsel Nat. Commn. for Reform of Fed. Criminal Law, Washington, 1967-70; asst. dist. atty., chief of appeals City of Phila., 1970-73; asst. dir. Nat. Wire Tapping Commn., Washington, 1973-75; dir. D.C. Law Revision, Washington, 1975-77; spl. asst. HUD, Washington, 1977-79; asst. gen. counsel U.S. Commodity Futures Trading Commn., Washington, 1979-83; v.p. N.Y. Futures Exch., N.Y.C., 1983-89, N.Y. Stock Exch., N.Y.C., 1989—. Mem. ABA, N.Y. State Bar Assn., Assn. of Bar of City of N.Y. Democrat. Jewish. Administrative and regulatory, Securities. Home: Hudson House PO Box 286 Ardsley On Hudson NY 10503-0286

**STEIN, RALPH MICHAEL,** law educator, lawyer, arbitrator, mediator, consultant; b. Far Rockaway, N.Y., July 14, 1943; s. Siegfried and Ruth (Spier) S.; m. Susan Heineman, Feb. 23, 1969 (div. Aug. 1982); m. Marla B. Rubin, Oct. 31, 1982; 1 child, Theodore Alan Rubin. BA, New Sch. Social Rsch., 1971; JD, Hofstra U., 1974. Assoc. Skadden, Arps, Slate, Meagher & Flom, N.Y.C., 1974-75; vis. prof. law Syracuse U., N.Y., 1975-76; prof. law Pace U. Sch. Law, White Plains, N.Y., 1976—; spl. counsel for med. malpractice legislation to lt. gov. N.Y. State, 1982-85; chief hearing officer Greenburgh Police Dept., N.Y., 1982-92; cons. to hosps., nursing schs., 1975—. Co-author: Comparative Negligence, 1984; also law rev. articles on legal history, constl. law, torts, criminal law, historic preservation. Contbg. editor Real Estate Law Jour., 1984-91. Producer, moderator TV show: You and the Law, 1971-74. Investigator U.S. Senate Subcom. on Constl. Rights, Washington, 1970-71; mem. legal com. Anti-Defamation League, Westchester County, N.Y., 1984—, Westchester chpt. ACLU, 1984—. Served to capt. U.S. Army, 1965-68. Pace U. grantee, 1979, 81-83, 85, 87-88, 91-93. Mem. Soc. Am. Law Profs., Am. Soc. Legal History, Am. Soc. Law and Medicine, Civil War Roundtable N.Y., Navy League of U.S., Am. Civil Liberties Union. Democrat. Avocations: books, Civil War, cooking, travel, classical music and opera. Office: Pace U Sch Law 78 N Broadway White Plains NY 10603-3710

**STEIN, RITA,** lawyer; b. N.Y.C., Dec. 13, 1927; d. Samuel and Rebecca Kamerow; m. Milton Stein, Aug. 31, 1947; children: Lance, Lisa, Scott. BA, CUNY, 1948; MS, Hofstra U., 1967; JD, N.Y. Law Sch., 1978. Bar: N.Y. 1979, Fla. 1980, U.S. Dist. Ct. (ea. and so. dists.) N.Y. 1979, U.S. Supreme Ct. 1982. Tchr. HILI, Far Rockaway, N.Y., 1948-52, East Williston (N.Y) Schs., 1963-69, Hewlett (N.Y.) Sch. Dist., 1970-72; tax preparer H&R Block, Herricks, N.Y., 1972-74; acct. N.Y. State Ins. Dept., N.Y.C., 1975; assoc. Nagler & Gilbert, Mineola, N.Y., 1978-79; pvt. practice, Mineola, 1980—. Author newsletter Reports on the Law, 1981-98. Chair Sr. Com., Roslyn, N.Y., 1996—. Mem. Women's Bar Assn. State N.Y. (bd. dirs.), Nassau County Bar Assn. (bd. dirs. 1987-89, chmn. lawyer referral 1985-87, lectr.), Nassau County Women's Bar Assn. (pres. 1987-88), Roslyn Country Club Civic Assn. (bd. dirs., pres. 1980), Glen Head Tennis Club (bd. dirs. 1994—). Avocations: tennis, scuba diving, bridge. General practice, Estate planning, Family and matrimonial. Office: 200 Old Country Rd Mineola NY 11501-4235

**STEIN, ROBERT ALLEN,** legal association executive, law educator; b. Mpls., Sept. 16, 1938; s. Lawrence E. and Agnes T. (Brynildson) S.; m. Sandra H. Stein; children: Linda Stein Routh, Laura Stein Conrad, Karin Stein O'Boyle. BS in Law, U. Minn., 1960, JD summa cum laude, 1961; LLD (hon.), Uppsala U., Sweden, 1993. Bar: Wis. 1961, Minn. 1967. Assoc. Foley, Sammond & Lardner, Milw., 1961-64; prof. U. Minn. Law Sch., Mpls., 1964—; assoc. dean U. Minn., 1976-77, v.p. adminstrn. and planning, 1978-80; dean U. Minn. Law Sch., 1979-94; faculty rep. men's intercollegiate athletics U. Minn., 1981-94; of counsel Mullin, Weinberg & Daly, PA, Mpls., 1970-80, Gray, Plant, Mooty, Mooty & Bennett, Mpls., 1980-94; exec. dir., COO ABA, Chgo., 1994—; vis. prof. UCLA, 1969-70, U. Chgo., 1975-76; commr. Uniform State Laws Commn. Minn., 1973—; v.p. Nat. Uniform Laws Com., 1991-93, exec. comm., 1991—, sec., 1997—; acad. fellow Am. Coll. Trusts and Estates Counsel, 1975—; vis. scholar Am. Bar Found., Chgo., 1975-76; trustee Gt. No. Iron Ore Properties, 1982—, Uniform Laws Found., 1992—; advisor Restatement of Law Second, Property, 1977—, Restatement of Law Trusts (Prudent Investor Rule), 1989-90, Restatement of Law Third, Trusts, 1993—; chmn. bd. dirs. Ednl. Credit Mgmt. Corp., 1993—; bd. dirs. Fiduciary Counselling Inc. Author: Stein on Probate, 1976, 3d edit., 1995, How to Study Law and Take Law Exams, 1996, Estate Planning Under the Tax Reform Act of 1976, 2d edit, 1978, In Pursuit of Excellence: A History of the University of Minnesota Law School, 1980, contbr. articles to profl. jours. Founding bd. dirs. Park Ridge Ctr., 1985-95; co-chair Gov.'s Task Force on Ctr. for Treatment of Torture Victims, 1985, bd. dirs., 1985-87. Fellow Am. Bar Found (bd. dirs. 1987-94), Am. Coll. Tax Counsel; mem. ABA (coun. sect. of legal edn. and admission to bar 1986-91, vice chairperson 1991-92, chair-elect 1992-93, chair 1993-94), Internat. Acad. Estate and Trust Law (academician), Am. Judicature Soc. (bd. dirs. 1984-88), Am. Law Inst. (coun. mem. 1987—, exec. com. 1993—), Minn. Bar Assn. (bd. govs. 1979-94, exec. coun., probate and trust law sect. 1973-77), Hennepin County Bar Assn. Home: 990 N Lake Shore Dr Apt 7A Chicago IL 60611-1342 Office: American Bar Assn 750 N Lake Shore Dr Chicago IL 60611-4497

**STEIN, SIDNEY H.,** judge; b. 1945. AB cum laude, Princeton U., 1967; JD, Yale U., 1972. Law clerk Hon. Stanley H. Fuld, N.Y., 1972-73; ptnr. Stein, Zauderer, Ellenhorn, Frischer & Sharp, 1981-95; dist. judge U.S. Dist. Ct. (so. dist.), N.Y., 1995—. Contbr. articles to profl. jours. Bd. dirs. Prisoner's Legal Svcs. of N.Y., N.Y. Lawyers for Pub. Interest, Yale Law Sch. Fund, exec. com. Yale Law Sch. Assn. Fellow Am. Bar Found., N.Y. Bar Found., mem. N.Y. State Bar Assn., Assn. Bar City of N.Y. Office: US Dist Ct 500 Pearl St New York NY 10007-1316

**STEIN, STEPHEN WILLIAM,** lawyer; b. N.Y.C., Apr. 12, 1937; s. Melvin S. and Cornelia (Jacobowitz) S.; m. Judith N., Jan. 22, 1966. AB, Princeton U., 1959; LLB, Columbia U., 1962; LLM, NYU, 1963. Bar: N.Y. 1962, Fla. 1962. Assoc. White & Case, N.Y.C., 1963-67; atty. advisor U.S. Agy. Internat. Devel., Washington, 1967-69; regional legal advisor Mission to India U.S. Agy. Internat. Devel., New Delhi, 1969-71; asst. gen. counsel U.S. Agy. Internat. Devel., Washington, 1971-73; assoc. ptnr. Delson & Gordon, N.Y.C., 1973-87; ptnr. Kelley Drye & Warren, N.Y.C., 1987—; mem. U.S. exec. com. Indonesian Trade, Tourism & Investment Promotion Program, 1990-92; mem. U.S.-Indonesia Trade & Investment Adv. Com., 1989-92; vis. instr. internat. Devel. Law Inst., 1993; lectr. Internat. Law Inst., Washington, 1984, 85; spkr. in field. Mem. ABA (mem. sect. internat. law, co-chair African law com. 1999—), Internat. Bar Assn. (mem. sect. energy resources law, sect. bus. law, mem. various coms.), Assn. Bar of City of N.Y. (mem. com. project fin. 1997—, mem. com. Asian affairs 1992—, former mem. others), Am. Indonesian C. of C. (bd. dirs. 1986—, pres. 1989-96). Finance, Private international, Oil, gas, and mineral. Home: 320 Central Park W New York NY 10025-7659 Office: Kelley Drye & Warren 101 Park Ave Fl 30 New York NY 10178-0062

**STEIN, TRACY A.,** lawyer; b. Milw., Feb. 2, 1967; d. Bernard S. and Judith V. (Edelstein) S.; m. Marco V. Masotti, Aug. 31, 1996; children: Michela Stein Masotti, Alexander Stein Masotti. BA in Philosophy, U. Wis., 1988; JD, U. Va., 1992. Bar: N.Y., Conn., U.S. Dist. Ct. (so. and ea. dists.) N.Y., U.S. Dist. Ct. Conn. Atty. South Africa's Truth and Reconciliation Commn., Johannesburg, 1997; assoc. atty. Law Firm of LeBoeuf, Lamb, Greene & MacRae, N.Y.C., 1992—. Mem. ABA (labor and employment com.), Assn. Bar City N.Y., N.Y. State Bar Assn. (comml. and fed. litigation sect.). Labor, General civil litigation. Office: LeBoeuf Lamb Greene & MacRae 125 W 55th St New York NY 10019-5369

**STEINBACH, HAROLD I.,** lawyer; b. Bronx, N.Y., Aug. 31, 1956; s. Aaron and Phyllis (Feldfeber) S.; m. Beryl Joy Schwartz, Mar. 14, 1982; children: Sarah Brandl, Rachel Beth, Avi Michael. BA, SUNY, Binghamton, 1978; JD, NYU, 1981. Bar: N.Y. 1982, N.J. 1983, U.S. Dist. Ct. (so. dist.) N.Y. 1982. Assoc. Flemming, Zulack & Williamson, N.Y.C., 1981-83, Kleinberg, Kaplan, Wolff & Cohen, P.C., N.Y.C., 1983—. Trustee Jewish Braille Inst. Am., Inc., 1992—. Mem. N.Y. State Bar Assn. (bus. law and property law sects.), Phi Beta Kappa. Jewish. General corporate, Real property. Home: 665 Ogden Ave Teaneck NJ 07666-2203 Office: Kleinberg Kaplan Et Al 551 5th Ave New York NY 10176-0001

**STEINBAUM, ROBERT S.,** publisher, lawyer; b. Englewood, N.J., Oct. 13, 1951; s. Paul S. and Esther R. (Rosenberg) S.; m. Rosemary Konner, May 26, 1982; children: Marshall, Elliot. BA, Yale U., 1973; JD, Georgetown U., 1976. Bar: D.C. 1976, N.J. 1980, N.Y. 1982. Atty. Cole & Groner P.C., Washington, 1976-79; asst. U.S. atty. U.S. Atty.'s Office, Newark, 1979-84; atty. Scarpone & Edelson, Newark, 1984-87; publ. N.J. Law Jour., Newark, 1987—; trustee N.J. Jewish News, Whippany, 1990-95, 96—. Trustee Blood Ctr. N.J., East Orange, N.J., 1987-93, Leadership N.J., 1990, 98—, Leadership Newark, 1997—. Office: NJ Law Jour PO Box 20081 238 Mulberry St Newark NJ 07102-3528

**STEINBERG, HOWARD ELI,** lawyer, holding company executive, public official; b. N.Y.C., Nov. 19, 1944; s. Herman and Anne Rudel (Sinnreich) S.; m. Judith Ann Schucart, Jan. 28, 1968; children: Henry Robert, Kathryn Jill. AB, U. Pa., 1965; JD, Georgetown U., 1969. Bar: N.Y. 1970, U.S. Dist. Ct. (so. and ea. dists.) N.Y. 1973, U.S. Ct. Appeals (2d cir.) 1976. Assoc. Dewey, Ballantine, Bushby, Palmer & Wood, N.Y.C., 1969-76, ptnr., 1977-83; exec. v.p., gen. counsel, corp. sec. Reliance Group Holdings Inc., N.Y.C., 1983—; chmn. N.Y. State Thruway Authority, 1996-99; dep. chmn. L.I. Power Authority, 1999—. Editor case notes: Georgetown Law Jour., 1968-69. Bd. dir. Puerto Rican Legal Def. and Edn. Fund. Inc., 1993-95, Sheltering Arms Childrens Svc., 1997—; mem. N.Y. State Hudson River Heritage Coun.; bd. regents Georgetown U., 1999—; bd. overseers U. Pa. Sch. Arts and Scis., 1989—. Capt. JAGC, USAR, 1972-74. Mem. ABA, N.Y. State Bar Assn., Assn. of Bar of City of N.Y. (com. on securities regulation 1984-87, com. on corp. law 1987-90, com. on fed. legis. 1990-93, chair ad hoc com. on Senate Confirmation Process 1991-92), Univ. Club. Jewish. General corporate, Securities. Office: Reliance Group Holdings Inc 55 E 52nd St Fl 29 New York NY 10055-0190

**STEINBERG, JACK,** lawyer; b. Seattle, Jan. 6, 1915; s. Solomon Reuben and Mary (Rashall) S.; widower; children: Roosevelt, Mary Ann Steinberg Shulman, Quentin. BA, U. Wash., 1936, JD, 1938. Bar: Wash. 1938, U.S. Dist. Ct. (we. dist.) Wash. 1938, U.S. Ct. Appeals (9th cir.) 1938. Ptnr. Steinberg & Steinberg, Seattle, 1938—. Former editor and pub. The Washington Examiner; contbr. numerous articles to legal jours. Judge pro tem Seattle Mcpl. Ct., Seattle, 1952; past pres. Emanuel Congregation, Seattle, Seattle chpt. Zionist Orgn. Am. Recipient Scrolls of Honor award (3) The State of Israel. Mem. Assn. Trial Lawyers Am., Am. Judicature Soc., Wash. Bar Assn., Wash. Assn. Trial Lawyers, Seattle-King County Bar Assn. Jewish Orthodox. Avocation: outdoor activities. Contracts commercial, Family and matrimonial, General practice. Office: Steinberg & Steinberg 1210 Vance Bldg Seattle WA 98101

**STEINBERG, JEFFREY MARC,** lawyer, accountant; b. Newark, July 30, 1956; s. Marvin E. and Barbara (Nebret) S.; m. Melanie B. Grabowski, May 22, 1983; 1 child, Jonathan. BSBA, Boston U., 1978; MBA, Fairleigh Dickinson U., 1980; JD, N.Y. Law Sch., 1984. Bar: N.J. 1985, N.Y. 1988. Assoc. Jaffe & Schlesinger, Springfield, N.J., 1987-92; sole practitioner real estate and bankruptcy law, Springfield, 1992—. Real property, Bankruptcy, General corporate. Home: 9 Alder Ln Basking Ridge NJ 07920-3708 Office: 32 Commerce St Springfield NJ 07081-3004

**STEINBERG, JONATHAN ROBERT,** judge; b. Phila., Jan. 3, 1939; s. Sigmund Hopkins and Hortense B. (Gottlieb) S.; m. Rochelle Helene Schwartz, May 30, 1963; children: Andrew Joshua, Amy Judith. BA, Cornell U., 1960; LLB cum laude, U. Pa., 1963. Bar: D.C. 1963, U.S. Ct. Appeals (D.C. cir.) 1964. Law clk. to judge U.S. Ct. Appeals (D.C. cir.), 1963-64; atty. advisor, then dep. gen. counsel Peace Corps, Washington, 1964-69; com. on labor and pub. welfare, counsel subcom. on vets. affairs, U.S. Senate, 1969-71, counsel subcom. on R.R. retirement, 1971-73, counsel spl. subcom. on human resources, 1972-77, chief counsel com. on vets. affairs, 1977-81, minority chief counsel and staff dir. com. on vets. affairs, U.S. Senate, 1981-87, chief counsel and staff dir. com. on vets. affairs, 1987-90; assoc. judge U.S. Ct. of Appeals for Vets. Claims, 1990—. Contbr. to legal jours. Bd. dirs. Bethany West Recreation Assn., Bethany Beach, Del., 1973-84, 86-90. Mem. ABA, D.C. Bar Assn., Order of Coif. Democrat. Jewish. Home: 11204 Hawhill End Potomac MD 20854-2039 Office: US Ct of Appeals for Vets Claims 625 Indiana Ave NW Ste 900 Washington DC 20004-2917

**STEINBERG, MARTY,** lawyer; b. Balt., May 13, 1945. BS cum laude in Pharmacy, U. Pitts., 1968; JD cum laude, Ohio State U., 1971. Bar: Ohio 1971, Fla. 1974; U.S. Supreme Ct. 1981; Registered Pharmacist Ohio 1968. Atty. U.S. Dept. Justice, Washington, 1972-78, atty. in charge N.Y. regional offices, 1978-79; chief counsel, permanent subcommittee on investigations U.S. Senate, Washington, 1979-82; ptnr. Holland & Knight, Miami, Fla.; mng. ptnr. Hunton & Wilson, Miami, 1999—; inst. Canisius Coll. Buffalo, N.Y. 1978-79, SUNY Buffalo 1978-79, Am. U. Washington D.C. 1980-81. Contbr. to profl. jours. Bd. dirs. Miami Citizens Against Crime 1984—. Recipient Am. Jurisprudence award. Mem. ABA, Fla. Bar Assn., Ohio State Bar Assn., Am. Pharm. Assn., Am. Assn. Corp. Counsel, Am. Law Inst. (chmn. civic justice adv. com.). Office: Hunton & Wilson Law Firm Miami Ctr 201 S Biscayne Blvd Miami FL 33131-4332

**STEINBERG, SYLVAN JULIAN,** lawyer; b. New Iberia, La., July 25, 1933; s. Emanuel and Myrtle (Weil) S.; m. Judith Ann Benson, Sept. 7, 1959; children: Jeanne Wyn, Susan Beth, Jonathan Michael. BBA with honors, Tulane U., 1955, JD with honors, 1957. Bar: La. 1957, U.S. Dist. Ct. (ea. dist.) La. 1958, U.S. Supreme Ct. 1963, U.S. Ct. Appeals (5th cir.) 1976, U.S. Ct. Appeals (11th cir.) 1981, U.S. Dist. Ct. (mid. dist.) La. 1984, U.S. Dist. Ct. (we. dist.) 1989. Assoc. Weinstein and Bronfin, New Orleans, 1958-62; ptnr. Bronfin & Heller, New Orleans, 1962—; gen. adv. bd. cont. legal edn. Tulane Law Sch. Mem. editorial staff Tulane U. Law Rev., 1955-57, book rev. editor, 1957, mem. bd. adv. editors. Mem., former pres. bd. advisors B'nai B'rith Hillel Found. of Tulane U., Loyola U. and U. New Orleans; past pres. Tikvat Shalom Synagogue, New Orleans; cmty. rels. com., past trustee New Orleans Jewish Welfare Fedn., budget com.; former mem. New Orleans regional adv. bd. Anti-Defamation League; former mem. tech. adv. com. regional econ. devel. Regional Planning Commn.; past bd. dirs. Jewish Family and Children's Svc.; profl. adv. com. Jewish Endowment Found.; past chmn. bd. commrs. Cmty. Improvement Agy. for City of New Orleans; bd. dirs. New Orleans Redevel. Authority, 1994-95; former v.p. B'nai B'rith State of La. Maj. JAGC, U.S. Army, and USAR, 1957-66. Mem. ABA, New Orleans Bar Assn. (chmn. gen. practice com. 1986 mem. continuing legal edn. com., chmn. legis. com.), Fed. Bar Assn. (Fed. Ct. Bench bar liaison com.), La. Bar Assn. (mem. task force selection, election judges 1988), La. Assn. Def. Counsel, New Orleans C. of C. (mem. com. on housing), Masons, B'nai B'rith (v.p.). General civil litigation, Contracts commercial, Health. Home: 2710 Chestnut St New Orleans LA 70130-5731 Office: Bronfin & Heller 650 Poydras St Ste 2500 New Orleans LA 70130-6103

**STEINBERG, TERESA SHERWOOD,** paralegal, legal administrator; b. Valdosta, Ga., May 30, 1950; d. J.C. and Irma Lou (Williams) Sherwood; m. James Miller Steinberg, Apr. 18, 1970; children: James Jr., William Sherwood. Cert. legal asst., Valdosta State U., 1989. Legal sec., paralegal Dover, Sherwood, & Shelton, Valdosta, 1986-90; indigent def. adminstr. Lowndes County Bd. Commrs., Valdosta, 1990—; mem. juvenile justice com. Ga. Indigent Def., Atlanta, 1996-97. Mem., past officer, chmn. Valdosta Jr. Svc. League, 1979—; mem. Class of 1998 Leadership Lowndes; mem. exec. bd. LAMP; bd. dirs. Wesley Found. Valdosta State U. Mem. Nat. Paralegal Assn., South Ga. Assn. Legal Assts. (edn. chmn. 1989—), Valdosta-Lowndes County C. of C. Methodist. Avocations: gardening, cooking, sewing, designing. Office: Lowndes County Indigent Def Office Lowndes County Courthouse 108 E Central Ave Valdosta GA 31601-5507

**STEINBERGER, JEFFREY WAYNE,** lawyer, consultant; b. Bronx, N.Y., Nov. 27, 1947; s. Martin and Shirley (Blumen) S.; m. Marlene Zimmelman, Apr. 28, 1976 (div. June 1983); 1 child, Darren William. BS, Queens Coll., 1968; JD, U. Western Los Angeles, 1976. Sole practice, 1979—; owner Jeridean Industries, Los Angeles, 1968-75; mgr., artist Clout Agy., Beverly Hills, Calif., 1972-76; real estate broker Nat. Real Estate, Beverly Hills, 1974—; dist. atty. City of Los Angeles, 1976-77; cons. City of Hope, San Fernadino, Calif., 1979; judge pro tem Los Angeles Mcpl. Ct., 1984—. Producer, developer, host TV show Jeffs Law, 1979—. Developer, founder Coalition for Child Care, Beverly Hills, 1985. Served with USAR, 1969-70. Mem. Los Angeles Bar Assn., Beverly Hills Bar Assn., Assn. Trial Lawyers Am., Calif. Trial Lawyers Assn., Beverly Hills Trial Lawyers Assn., Los Angeles Bd. of Realtors, Beverly Hills Bd. of Realtors, Mensa. Avocations: karate-do, scuba exploration, hatha yoga, triathalons. Personal injury, Criminal, Entertainment. Office: 8383 Wilshire Blvd Ste 1032 Beverly Hills CA 90211-2409

**STEINBERGER, RICHARD LYNN,** lawyer, corporate executive; b. Columbus, Ohio, Mar. 24, 1939; s. Harold V. and Dorothy Dolan (Dunn) S.; m. Nancy Sue Orewiler, Sept. 9, 1961; children: Amy, Mitchell. AB magna cum laude, Butler U., 1961; JD, Ohio State U., 1964. Bar: Ohio 1964, U.S. Supreme Ct. 1967. Assoc. Pickel, Schaeffer & Ebeling, Dayton, Ohio, 1964-74; co-founder, exec. v.p. Nord Resources Corp., Dayton, 1968-85, pres., 1985-88; vice chmn. Nord Resources Corp., Santa Rosa, Calif., 1988-93, Sierra Rutile, Ltd., 1982-93; CEO Titanium Minerals Mktg. Internat., 1993-97; pres., COO Conquistador Mines USA, Inc., St. Helena, Calif., 1997—. Natural resources.

**STEINBRECHER, ALAN K.,** lawyer; b. Grosse Pointe, Mich., Apr. 13, 1946; s. Charles Henry and Helen Ann (King) S.; m. Susan Triplett (div. Dec. 1980); m. Millie P. Smith, May 19, 1984; children: Gregory, Kathryn, Lucy. BA, U. N.C., Chapel Hill, 1968; JD, Duke U., 1977. Bar: Calif. 1977, U.S. Dist. Ct. (cen., no., and so. dists.) Calif. 1978, N.Y. Atty. Paul, Hastings, Janofsky & Walker, L.A., 1977-85, ptnr., 1985—. Maj. donors chair San Marino (Calif.) Schs. Found., 1998; pres. San Marino Little League, 1998-99. Capt. USN, 1968-89. Mem. L.A. County Bar Assn. (treas. litigation sect. 1998). Aviation, General civil litigation, Product liability. Home: 1296 Saint Albans Rd San Marino CA 91108-1856 Office: Paul Hastings Janofsky & Walker 23d Fl 555 S Flower St Fl 23D Los Angeles CA 90071-2300

**STEINDLER, WALTER G.,** retired lawyer; b. N.Y.C., Dec. 2, 1927; s. Mortimer B. and Ray (Feingold) S.; m. Carol A. Halpin, June 28, 1969; children: Michael, Morty, Melissa, Amy, Ellen. BA, Queens Coll., 1950; JD, NYU, 1953. Bar: N.Y. 1953, U.S. Supreme Ct. 1965, U.S. Dist. Ct. (ea. dist.) N.Y. 1972, U.S. Dist. Ct. (so. dist.) 1974, U.S. Ct. Appeals (2d cir.) 1974. Ptnr. Borden Skidell Fleck & Steindler, Jamaica, N.Y., 1955-62; pvt. practice law Babylon, N.Y., 1962-67; town atty. Town of Babylon, 1967-69; asst. county atty. Suffolk County, N.Y., 1970-71; ptnr. Sarisohn, Carner, Steindler, Lebow, Braun & Castrovinci, Commack, N.Y., 1976-93; ret., 1993; capt., judge adv. 2d area command N.Y. Guard, N.Y.C., 1965-70; guardian ad litem 20th Jud. Cir. Lee County, Fla., 1995-98. With U.S. Army, 1946-47. Mem. Free Sons Israel (pres. 1953), Masons. Family and matrimonial, State civil litigation. Office: 350 Veterans Memorial Hwy Commack NY 11725-4330

**STEINER, DAVID MILLER,** lawyer; b. Phoenix, Apr. 9, 1958; s. Paul Miller and Nan (Adamson) S. BA, Columbia U., 1980; MALD, Tufts U., 1985; JD, Cornell U., 1988; M of Internat. and Pub. Affairs, Columbia U., 1989; LLM in Taxation, NYU, 1993. Bar: N.Y. 1988. English tchr. Peace Corps, Tahoua, Niger, 1980-82; law clk. to Judge Jane Restani U.S. Ct. Internat. Trade, N.Y.C., 1989-91; law clk. to Judge Reynaldo Garza U.S. Ct. Appeals (5th cir.), Brownsville, Tex., 1991-92; assoc. Wasserman, Schneider and Babb, 1993-95; with N.Y.C. Law Dept. Office of the Corp. Counsel, 1995—. Mem. ABA, Assn. Bar City N.Y. (state and local tax com.), N.Y. County Lawyers Assn. (com. on taxation), Fgn. Policy Assn., Apollo Cir.-Met. Mus. Art, Univ. Club, Columbia Club. Avocations: ballroom dancing, backgammon, running. Home: 4 W 109th St Apt 2A New York NY 10025-2673 Office: NYC Law Dept Office of Corp Counsel 100 Church St New York NY 10007-2601

**STEINER, DIANE,** lawyer; b. Bridgeport, Conn., Feb. 1, 1939; d. Joseph and Augusta Popkin; m. Paul Bernstein, Dec. 24, 1960 (div.); children: David Bernstein, Stefanie Brown; m. Robert Steiner, Nov. 15, 1990. JD, Benjamin N Cardozo Sch. Law, N.Y.C., 1989. Bar: N.Y. 1989. Assoc. Phillips Nizer Benjamin Krim & Ballon, N.Y.C., 1989-96, Sheresky Aronson & Mayefesky, N.Y.C., 1996—. Contbg. author: The Money Club, 1997, 98. Fellow Am. Acad. Matrimonial Lawyers. Avocations: cooking, skiing, travelling. Family and matrimonial. Office: Sheresky Aronson & Mayefsky 750 Lexington Ave New York NY 10022-1200

**STEINER, GEOFFREY BLAKE,** lawyer; b. El Paso, Tex., Aug. 28, 1952; s. LeRoy Marshall Steiner and Rosemary (Thurman) Milligan; m. Maria del Rosario Serrano, Dec. 24, 1975 (div. Jan. 1988); children: Karen Alexandra, Xavier Oliver; m. Rosemarie Sylvia Erb, May 5, 1990; 1 child, Geoffrey Blake Jr. AB, Washington U., St. Louis, 1978; JD, Samford U., 1981. Bar: Fla. 1983, U.S. Dist. Ct. (mid. dist.) Fla. 1983, U.S. Ct. Appeals (11th cir.) 1985. Asst. pub. defender Office Pub. Defender, 13th Jud. Cir., Tampa, Fla., 1982-84; assoc. Hamilton & Douglas, P.A., Tampa, 1984-86, Mulholland and Anderson, Tampa, 1986-87, Limberopolous, Steiner & Cardillo, Tampa, 1987-89; pres. Geoffrey B. Steiner, P.A., Tampa, 1989—. Co-author: Florida Rules of Juvenile Procedure Annotated, 1982. Mem. Fla. Bar (bd. cert. civil trial lawyer Bd. of Specialization and Certification), Hillsborough County Bar Assn., Assn. Trial Lawyers Am., Acad. Fla. Trial Lawyers, Fla. Assn. Criminal Defense Lawyers, Hunter's Green Country Club, Masons (32d degree), Shriners, Delta Theta Phi, Beta Theta Pi. Methodist. Avocations: golf, tennis. Personal injury, General civil litigation, Criminal. Office: 2529 W Busch Blvd Ste 100 Tampa FL 33618-4546

**STEINER, HENRY JACOB,** law and human rights educator; b. Mt. Vernon, N.Y., 1930; s. Meier and Bluma (Henigson) S.; m. Pamela Pomerance, Aug. 1, 1982; stepchildren: Duff, Jacoba. BA magna cum laude, Harvard U., 1951, MA, 1955, LLB magna cum laude, 1955. Bar: N.Y. 1956, Mass. 1963. Law clk. to Hon. John M. Harlan, U.S. Supreme Ct., 1957-58; assoc. Sullivan and Cromwell, N.Y.C., 1958-62; asst. prof. sch. law Harvard U., Cambridge, Mass., 1962-65, prof., 1965—, Jeremiah Smith, Jr. prof. law, 1986—, founder, dir. law sch. Human Rights Program, 1984—; chair Human Rights Studies Com., Harvard U., 1994—; vis. prof. CEPED, Rio de Janeiro, Brazil, 1968-69; chair Adv. Com. U. Middle East project, 1998—; vis. prof. Yale U., New Haven, 1972-73, Stanford U., 1965; cons. AID, 1962-64, Ford Found., 1966-69. Co-author: (textbook) Transnational Legal Problems, 4th edit., 1994, Tort and Accident Law, 2d edit., 1989, International Human Rights in Context: Law, Politics, Morals, 1996; author: Moral Argument and Social Vision in the Courts, 1987, Diverse Partners: Non-Governmental Organizations in the Human Rights Movement, 1991; former devels. editor Harvard Law Rev.; contbr. articles to profl. jours. Office: Harvard U Law Sch Cambridge MA 02138

**STEINER, LINDA JO,** lawyer; b. Fairfield, Iowa, Sept. 7, 1958; d. Albert Burkley and Karen Jean Steiner; m. Anthony W. Lewis, May 25, 1985 (div. June 1995); children: Abigail, Morgan, Madeleine, Christopher; m. G. Kevin Keller, Aug. 8, 1998. BA in History, U. Wyo., 1980, JD, 1983. Assoc. Philip P. Whynott, Cheyenne, Wyo., 1984-87, Daniel G. Blythe, Cheyenne, 1987-95; ptnr. Rogers Blythe & Lewis, Cheyenne, 1996, Blythe & Steiner, Cheyenne, 1996—. Mem. Laramie County Bar Assn. (pres. 1993-94). Republican. Roman Catholic. Avocations: cross-country skiing, horses, golf. Family and matrimonial. Home: 10025 Buck Brush Rd Cheyenne WY 82009-8828 Office: 122 E 17th St Cheyenne WY 82001-4516

**STEINGASS, SUSAN,** lawyer; b. Cambridge, Mass., Dec. 18, 1941. BA, Denison U., 1963; MA with honors, Northwestern U., 1965; JD with honors, U. Wis., 1976. Bar: Wis. 1976, U.S. Dist. Ct. Wis. 1976. Law clk. Hon. Nathan S. Heffernan Wis. Supreme Ct., 1976-77; assoc. ptnr. Stafford, Rosenbaum, Reiser and Hansen, 1977-85; ptnr. Habush, Habush, Davis & Rottier, S.C., Madison, Wis., 1985—; judge Dane County Cir. Ct., 1985-93; lectr. civil procedure, environ. law, evidence, trial advocacy Law Sch., U. Wis., 1981—; instr. Nat. Inst. for Trial Advocacy, Nat. Jud. Coll., 1993—; Dane County cir. ct. judge, 1985-93. Note and comment editor Wis. Law Rev., 1974-76; co-editor: Wisconsin Civil Procedure Before Trial--The Wisconsin Rules of Evidence: A Courtroom Handbook. Chairperson Wis. Equal Justice Task Force, 1989-91. Named Wis. Trial Judge of Yr. Am. Bd. Trial Advocates, 1992. Mem. ABA, ATLA, Am. Law Inst., Wis. Bar Assn. (pres. 1998-99), Wis. Law Alumni Assn. (bd. dirs.), Wis. Acad. Trial Lawyers, Dane County Bar Assn., Order of the Coif. E-mail: ssteinga@habush.com. Personal injury. Office: Habush Habush Davis & Rottier SC 150 E Gilman St Ste 2000 Madison WI 53703-1441*

**STEINHARDT-CARTER, BARBARA J.,** lawyer; b. N.Y.C., Apr. 29, 1947; d. David and Janith Steinhardt; m. Richard T. Mayer, June 17, 1967 (div. Dec. 1973); m. Dale Everett Carter, Aug. 17, 1991; children: Jeremy, Rachel. BA, Columbia U., 1969; JD, U. Calif., Davis, 1976. Bar: Calif. Regional counsel Legal Svcs. No. Calif., Sacramento, 1978-82; staff counsel Calif. Office Adminstrv. Law, Sacramento, 1982-84, 89—; prin. cons. Calif. Assembly Office Rsch., Sacramento, 1984-89. Avocations: sailing, skiing, writing, internet exploration. Fax: 916-323-6826. E-mail: bscarter@oal.ca.gov. Office: Office of Adminstrv Law 555 Capitol Mall Ste 1290 Sacramento CA 95814-4602

**STEINHAUER, GILLIAN,** lawyer; b. Aylesbury, Bucks, Eng., Oct. 6, 1938; d. Eric Frederick and Maisie Kathleen (Yeates) Pearson; m. Bruce William Steinhauer, Jan. 2, 1960; children: Alison (Humphrey) Eric, John, Elspeth. AB cum laude, Bryn Mawr (Pa.) Coll., 1959; JD cum laude, U. Mich., 1976. Bar: Mich. 1976, Mass. 1992, Tenn. 1998, U.S. Dist. Ct. (ea. dist.) Mich. 1976, U.S. Ct. Appeals (6th cir.) 1982. From assoc. to sr. ptnr. Miller, Canfield, Paddock & Stone, Detroit, 1976-92; dir. Commonwealth of Mass. Workers' Compensation Litigation Unit, Boston, 1992—. Chancellor Cath. Ch. St. Paul, Detroit, 1976-83, 91; pres. bd. trustees Cath. Cmty. Svcs. Inc., 1989-92; bd. dirs. Spaulding for Children, 1991-92, Davenport House, 1992-96, chair 1995-96, mem. Vestry St. Michael's Ch., Marblehead, Mass., 1994-97. Mem. Mich. State Bar Found. (life), Fed. Jud. Conf. 6th Cir. (life). Home: 79 Morning Side Pl Memphis TN 38104-3037

**STEINHORN, IRWIN HARRY,** lawyer, educator, corporate executive; b. Dallas, Aug. 13, 1940; s. Raymond and Libby L. (Miller) S.; m. Linda Kay Shoshone, Nov. 30, 1968; 1 child, Leslie Robin. BBA, U. Tex., 1961, LLB, 1964. Bar: Tex. 1964, U.S. Dist. Ct. (no. dist.) Tex. 1965, Okla. 1970, U.S. Dist. Ct. (we. dist.) Okla. 1972. Assoc. Oster & Kaufman, Dallas, 1964-67; ptnr. Parness, McQuire & Lewis, Dallas, 1967-70; sr. v.p., gen. counsel LSB Industries, Inc., Oklahoma City, 1970-87; v.p., gen. counsel USPCI, Inc., Oklahoma City, 1987-88; ptnr. Hastie & Steinhorn, Oklahoma City, 1988-95; mem., officer, dir. Conner & Winters, Oklahoma City, 1995—; adj. prof. law Oklahoma City U. Sch. Law, 1979—; lectr. in field. Mem. adv. com. Okla. Securities Commn., 1986—. Served to capt. USAR, 1964-70. Mem. ABA, Tex. Bar Assn., Okla. Bar Assn. (bus. assn. sect., sec.ptreas. 1986-87, chmn. 1988-89), Com. to Revise Okla. Bus. Corp. Act, Oklahoma City Golf and Country Club, Rotary, Phi Alpha Delta. Republican. Jewish. General corporate, Securities, Environmental. Home: 6205 Avalon Ln Oklahoma City OK 73118-1001 Office: Conner & Winters One Leadership Sq 211 N Robinson Ave Ste 1700 Oklahoma City OK 73102-7136

**STEINMAN, JOAN ELLEN,** lawyer, educator; b. Bklyn., June 19, 1947; d. Jack and Edith Ruth (Shapiro) S.; m. Douglass Watts Cassel, Jr., June 1, 1974 (div. July 1986); children: Jennifer Lynn, Amanda Hilary. Student, U. Birmingham, Eng., 1968; AB with high distinction, U. Rochester, 1969; JD cum laude, Harvard U., 1973. Bar: Ill. 1973. Assoc. Schiff, Hardin & Waite, Chgo., 1973-77; asst. prof. law Chgo.-Kent Coll. Law Ill. Inst. Tech., 1977-

82, assoc. prof., 1982-86, prof., 1986-98, Disting. prof., 1998—, interim dean, 1990-91; cons. in atty. promotions Met. Dist. Greater Chgo., 1981, 85; mem. fed. cts. com. Chgo. Coun. Lawyers. Contbr. articles to law jours. Coop. atty. ACLU Ill., Chgo., 1974, Leadership Coun. for Met. Open Cmtys., Chgo., 1975, Better Govt. Assn., 1975; arbitrator Better Bus. Bur. Met. Chgo., 1987; appointee Better Bus. Bur. Met. Chgo., 1987; appointee bd. arbitrators Nat. Assn. Security Dealers, 1989-99; appointed to Ill. Gov.'s Grievence Panel, 1987; bd. dirs. Pro Bono Advocates, 1985-99. Recipient Julia Beveridge award Ill. Inst. Tech., 1996, Ralph L. Brill award Chgo. Kent Coll. Law, 1997; Norman and Edna Frehling scholar Chgo.-Kent Coll. Law, 1989-93. Mem. ABA, Am. Law Inst. (adviser Fed. Jud. Code Revision project 1996-99, complex litigation project 1990-93, restatement of the law, third, torts, products liability 1993), Soc. Am. Law Tchrs., Chgo. Coun. Lawyers, AAUW (legal advocacy network 1987-99), Chgo.-Lincoln Am. Inn. of Ct. (master 1991), Order of Coif, Phi Beta Kappa. Democrat. Jewish. Office: Chgo Kent Coll Law 565 W Adams St Chicago IL 60661-3613

**STEINMETZ, DONALD WALTER,** former state supreme court justice; b. Milw., Sept. 19, 1924. B.A., U. Wis., 1949, J.D., 1951. Bar: Wis. 1951. Individual practice law Milw., 1951-58, asst. city atty., 1958-60; 1st asst. dist. atty. County of Milw., 1960-65; spl. asst. atty. gen. State of Wis., 1965-66; judge Milw. County Ct., 1966-80; justice Wis. Supreme Ct., 1980-99; chmn. Wis. Bd. County Judges; sec.-treas. Wis. Bd. Criminal Ct. Judges; mem. State Adminstrv. Commn. Cts., Chief Judge Study Com., Study Com. for TV and Radio Coverage in Courtroom, Wis. Council on Criminal Justice. Mem. ABA, Wis. Bar Assn., Am. Judicature Soc. *

**STEINWALL, SUSAN DEBORAH,** lawyer; b. St. Paul, May 13, 1952. AB, Grinnell Coll., 1974; MA, U. Wis., 1981; JD, U. Minn., 1991. Bar: Minn. 1991, U.S. Dist. Ct. Minn. 1992; cert. real property law specialist Minn. State Bar Assn. 1998. Newspaper reporter various newspapers Oconomowoc, Janesville, Wis., Duluth, Minn., 1974-80; archivist U. Minn., U. Wis.-River Falls, State Hist. Soc. Wis., 1981-88; rsch. asst. Minn. Ho. of Reps., St. Paul, 1990-91; shareholder Fredrikson & Byron, P.A., Mpls., 1991—; instr. St. Mary's Coll. Grad. Ctr., Mpls., 1989, Met. State U., St. Paul, 1993. Co-author: MDLA Release Deskbook; contbr. articles to law jours. Environmental, Real property, Land use and zoning (including planning). Office: Fredrikson & Byron 1100 Internat Ctr 900 2d Ave S Minneapolis MN 55402-3397

**STELL, CAMILLE STUCKEY,** paralegal, educator; b. Smithfield, N.C., Mar. 6, 1962; d. Harvey L. Jr. and Priscella W. Stuckey; m. C. Robert Stell, Jr., Aug. 6, 1983. BA, Meredith Coll., Raleigh, N.C., 1984. Cert. legal asst. Litigation paralegal Young Moore Henderson & Alvis, Raleigh, 1984-94; risk mgmt. and claims paralegal Lawyers Mut. Liability Ins. Co. N.C., Cary, 1994—; paralegal educator Legal Assts. program Meredith Coll., Raleigh, 1988—. Mem. paralegal editl. bd. Legal Asst. Today mag., 1996—. Democrat. Baptist. Avocations: reading, writing. Office: Lawyers Mut Liability Ins 8000 Weston Pkwy Ste 340 Cary NC 27513-2123

**STELL, JOHN ELWIN, JR.,** lawyer; b. Atlanta, June 19, 1954; s. John E. and Juanita (Bush) S.; m. Juliet Genene Saunders, Dec. 29, 1979; children: Carrie Juanita, John E. III, Charles Stapler. BA summa cum laude, Mercer U., 1975; JD cum laude, U. Ga., 1978. Bar: Ga. 1978, U.S. Dist. Ct. (no. dist.) Ga. 1978, U.S. Ct. Appeals (5th cir.) 1978, U.S. Dist. Ct. (mid. dist.) Ga. 1981, U.S. Ct. Appeals (11th cir.) 1981. Ptnr. Russell, Stell, Smith & McLocklin, Winder, Ga., 1978—; chief judge City of Auburn (Ga.), 1990-93; bd. govs. Ga. State Bar, 1990. Trustee Project Adam, Winder, 1982-94; city atty., Winder, 1986—, Commerce, 1993—. Mem. ABA, Ga. Bar Assn., Piedmont BarAssn. (pres. 1983), Barrow County C. of C. (bd. dirs. 1985-88, pres. 1988), SAR, SCV. Baptist. Insurance, Real property, State civil litigation. Home: PO Box 1045 Winder GA 30680-1045

**STELL, JOSEPH,** lawyer; b. Evansville, Ind., June 20, 1916; s. David and Diane Gertrude S.; m. Maxine Louise Stahn, Sept. 22, 1943; children: Eric, Susan, Ronald. BA, U. Calif., Berkeley, 1937; LLB, U. So. Calif., 1941, postgrad. in taxation, 1946-92. Bar: Calif. 1941, U.S. Dist. Ct. (so. dist.) Calif. 1949, U.S. Ct. Appeals 1949. Sr. ptnr., sr. trial counsel Stell, Levine, Bookman & Weiss, L.A., 1946-92; pvt. practice L.A., 1992—. Capt. USN, 1943-46, PTO. Democrat. Jewish. Avocations: skiing, tennis, motorcycle touring, dancing. General civil litigation, Probate, Real property. Home and Office: 342 Georgian Rd La Canada Flintridge CA 91011-3519

**STELLATO, LOUIS EUGENE,** lawyer; b. 1950. BBA, U. Tex., 1972; JD, U. Pitts., 1977; LLM, Temple U., 1979. Bar: PA. 1977. With Touche Ross & Co., 1979-81; with tax dept. Sherwin-Williams Co., 1981-87; sr. corp. counsel The Sherwin-Williams Co., 1987-90, asst. secy. and corp. dir. of taxes, 1990-91, v.p., gen. counsel, sec., 1991—. General corporate. Office: Sherwin Williams Co 101 Prospect Ave NW Cleveland OH 44115-1075

**STELLMAN, L. MANDY,** lawyer; b. Toronto, Ont., Can., Aug. 22, 1922; came to U.S., 1946, naturalized, 1948; d. Abraham and Rose (Rubinoff) Mandlsohn; m. Samuel David Stellman, July 11, 1943; children—Steven D., Leslie Robert. B.Sc. summa cum laude, Ohio State U., Columbus, 1966; J.D., Marquette U., 1970. Bar: Wis. 1971. Tchr., Toronto Pub. Schs., 1943-46; recreation specialist, Toronto, 1942-46; educator, social worker Columbus (Ohio) Jewish Ctr., 1951-64; instr. U. Wis. Extension, Milw., 1970-76; sole practice, Milw., 1971—. Bd. dirs. Women's Crisis Line, Women's Coalition, Milw. Jewish Home for Aged. Recipient Disting. Alumni award Ohio State U., 1976; Hannah G. Solomon award Nat. Council Jewish Women, 1984. Mem. Assn. Trial Lawyers Am., Lawyers Assn. for Women, ABA, Milw. Bar Assn., Wis. Assn. Trial Lawyers, Wis. Assn. Criminal Def. Lawyers, Nat. Council Jewish Women (life), Women's Polit. Caucus, Common Cause, NOW (Milw. Woman of Yr. 1977). Jewish. Family and matrimonial, Criminal, Juvenile. Home: 1545 W Fairfield Ct Milwaukee WI 53209-3431 Office: 3111 W Wisconsin Ave Milwaukee WI 53208-3957

**STELTZLEN, JANELLE HICKS,** lawyer; b. Atlanta, Sept. 18, 1937; d. William Duard and Mary Evelyn (Embrey) Hicks; divorced; children: Gerald William III, Christa Diane. BS, Okla. State U., 1958; MS, Kans. State U., 1961; JD, U. Tulsa, 1981. Bar: Okla. 1981, U.S. Dist. Ct. (no., ea. and we. dists.) Okla. 1981, U.S. Tax Ct. 1982, U.S. Ct. Claims 1982, U.S. Ct. Appeals (10th cir.) 1983, U.S. Ct. Appeals (Fed. cir.) 1984, U.S. Supreme Ct. 1986; lic. real estate broker. Pvt. practice, Tulsa, 1981-97; 2d dep. legal Tulsa County Clk., 1997—; lectr. Coll. of DuPage, Glen Ellyn, Ill., 1976, Tulsa Jr. Coll., 1981-88; dietitian, Tulsa; res. dep. for Tulsa County Sheriff's Office. Christian counselor 1st United Meth. Ch., Tulsa, 1986—, coord. legal counseling ministry, 1985—, lay pastor, 1987—; mem. Tulsa County Bd. Equalization and Excise Tax Bd., 1989-90; mem. Leadership Tulsa XX, 1993—; recipient of Leadership Tulsa Paragon award, 1996; bd. dirs. Sister Cities Tulsa/San Luis Potosi, 1988—, South Peoria Neighborhood Connection Found., 1991—, pres., 1995-96; active Tulsa County Tax Oversight Com., 1994—, Tulsa Home Rule Charter Com., 1994—. Recipient Okla. Sr. Olympics medal. Mem. Okla. Bar Assn., Tulsa County Bar Assn., Vol. Lawyers Assn. (bd. dirs.), Am. Dietetic Assn., Tulsa Dist. Dietetic Assn., Kiwanis Internat., Mensa, DAR, Delta Zeta. Republican. Avocations: swimming, scuba diving, jogging, bicycling, reading, painting, needlework, photography. Family and matrimonial, Probate, Real property. Home: 6636 S Jamestown Pl Tulsa OK 74136-2615

**STELZENMULLER, CYRIL VAUGHN,** lawyer; b. Fairfield, Ala., Jan. 25, 1928; s. James Grey and Helen (Brennan) S.; m. Jeannette Faye Wood, Mar. 19, 1965; 1 child, James Wood. BA, Cornell U., 1950, LLB with distinction, 1952. Bar: Ala. 1952, U.S. Dist. Ct. (no. dist.) Ala. 1955, U.S. Ct. Appeals (5th cir.) 1955, U.S. Ct. Appeals (D.C. cir.) 1973, U.S. Ct. Appeals (6th cir.) 1975, U.S. Supreme Ct. 1980, U.S. Ct. Appeals (11th cir.) 1982. Law clk. to judge U.S. Ct. Appeals (5th cir.), New Orleans, 1954-55; assoc. Burr & Forman, Birmingham, Ala., 1955-64, ptnr., 1964—. Contbr. articles to law rev. Col. ANG. Mem. Order of Coif, Phi Beta Kappa. Avocation: stained glass. Labor, General civil litigation. Home: 3537 Victoria Rd Birmingham AL 35223-1403 Office: Burr & Forman LLP Ste 3000 Southtrust Tower Birmingham AL 35203-3204

**STEMPLER, MICHAEL,** lawyer; b. Bklyn., Aug. 9, 1946; s. Samuel and Arliene C. (Schneider) S.; children: Tammy, Ilyse, Valerie. BA, U. Rochester, 1968; JD, Washington Coll., 1973. Bar: Md. 1973, D.C. 1974, U.S. Supreme Ct. 1977. Asst. states atty. Montgomery County States Attys. Office, Rockville, Md., 1971-73; asst. pub. defender State of Md., Rockville, 1973-75; appellate atty. CAB, Washington, 1975-76; ptnr. Stempler & Siegel, Rockville, 1976-80; v.p., gen. counsel MacArthur Beverage, Inc., Washington, 1980-87; gen. counsel, chief oper. officer JBS, Inc., Silver Springs, Md., 1987—. With U.S. Army, 1969-71, Vietnam. General corporate, Labor, Government contracts and claims. Home: 4293 Embassy Park Dr NW Washington DC 20016-3605 Office: JBS Inc 8630 Fenton St Fl 12 Silver Spring MD 20910-3806

**STENBERG, DONALD B.,** state attorney general; b. David City, Nebr., Sept. 30, 1948; s. Eugene A. and Alice (Kasal) S.; m. Susan K. Hoegemeyer, June 9, 1971; children: Julie A., Donald B. Jr., Joseph L., Abby E. BA, U. Nebr., 1970; MBA, Harvard U., 1974, JD cum laude, 1974. Bar: Nebr. 1974, U.S. Dist. Ct. Nebr. 1974, U.S. Ct. Appeals (fed. cir.) 1984, U.S. Ct. Claims 1989, U.S. Ct. Appeals (8th cir.) 1989, U.S. Supreme Ct., 1991. Assoc. Barlow, Watson & Johnson, Lincoln, Nebr., 1974-75; ptnr. Stenberg and Stenberg, Lincoln, 1976-78; legal counsel Gov. of Nebr., Lincoln, 1979-82; sr. prin. Erickson & Sederstrom, Lincoln, 1983-85; pvt. practice law Lincoln, 1985-90; atty. gen. State of Nebr., Lincoln, 1991—. Mem. Phi Beta Kappa. Republican. Office: Office of Atty Gen 2115 State Capitol Lincoln NE 68509

**STEPANIAN, LEO MCELLIGOTT,** lawyer; b. Butler, Pa., Nov. 12, 1929; s. Steven A. and Edith Marion (McElligott) S.; m. Dec. 26, 1953 (div. 1980); children: Leo II, Leanne, Joshua, Jonathan. BA cum laude, Notre Dame, South Bend, Ind., 1952; LLB, Pitts. Law Sch., 1955; JD, 1968. Bar: Pa., 1958; U.S. Dist. Ct. (we. dist.) Pa., U.S. Ct. Appeals (3rd cir.), U.S. Supreme Ct. Washington. Sr. ptnr. Stepanian & Muscatello, Butler, Pa., 1958—; chmn. bd. trustees Slippery Rock U.; pres. Butler County Mental Health Assn.; dir. Pa. Mental Health Assn., Butler County Luth. Family Counseling Svc., Butler Area Hall of Fame, Butler Quarterback Club; divsn. chmn. Butler County United Way, WQED Fund, Cancer Crusade, Heart Fund; commr. Butler Bantam Baseball League. Editor, co-founder: Butler County Legal Journal, 1970—. Co-founder Pa. Bar Assn. Section of County Legal Jours.; bd. dirs. St. Fidelis Coll. With U.S. Army, 1955-58. Recipient U.S. News and World Report award; named Am. Legionaire of Yr., 1986. Mem. Butler Moose Lodge, Knights of Columbus, Dirken Ritzert Post of Am. Legion, Chicora VFW, Pa. Bar Assn. (professionalism com., jud. evaluation com.), Golden Tornado Found. (steering com.). Avocations: boating, travel, gardening, sports. State civil litigation, General practice, Personal injury. Office: Stepanian & Muscatello 228 S Main St Butler PA 16001-5930

**STEPANIAN, STEVEN ARVID, II,** lawyer, financial consultant; b. Charleroi Penn., Apr. 15, 1935; s. Steven A. and Edithmarion M. (McElligott) S.; m. Pamela S. Abbey, Feb. 15, 1979. AB magna cum laude, U. Pitts., 1957; LLB, Harvard U., 1963. Bar: Pa. 1964, U.S. Supreme Ct. 1967. Assoc. Reed Smith Shaw and McClay, 1963-69, ptnr., 1970-78; pvt. practice law, 1978—; ptnr., gen. counsel Marine Magnesium Co.; NFL Alumni, 1982-89. Maj. USAF, 1957-60, 68-69. Mem. ABA (chair sports law com.), Pa. Bar Assn. Democrat. Roman Catholic. Clubs: Duquesne, Univ. (past pres.), Nemacolin Encampment (Pitts.). Entertainment, General corporate, Real property. Home: Gateway Towers 123 Millstone Dr Pittsburgh PA 15238-1623 Office: Gateway Towers Ste 4-G 320 Fr Duquesne Blvd Pittsburgh PA 15222-1103

**STEPEK, MARK WILLIAM,** lawyer; b. Detroit, Dec. 17, 1960; m. Kathleen Ann Stepek, Sept. 9, 1998; children: Myles, Blake. BA, Wayne State U., 1984; JD, Detroit Coll. Law, 1987. Bar: Mich. 1987. Pvt. practice Mt. Clemens, Mich., 1987—. Mem. Mich. Bar Assn., Macomb County Bar Assn. Fax: 810-463-5373. Criminal, Family and matrimonial, State civil litigation. Office: 66 Market St Mount Clemens MI 48043-5637

**STEPHAN, KENNETH C.,** state supreme court justice; b. Omaha, Oct. 8, 1946; m. Sharon Ross, April 19, 1969; children: Alissa Potocnik, Karen Stephan, Charles Stephan. BA, U. Nebr., 1968, JD with high distinction, 1972. Bar: Nebr. Former pvt. practice atty., 1973-97; judge Nebr. Supreme Ct., Lincoln, 1997—. With U.S. Army, 1969-71. Mem. Nebr. State Bar Assn. (former chmn. young lawyers sect., former mem. ho. dels.), Lincoln Bar Assn. (former bd. trustees), Am. Coll. Trial Lawyers (jud. fellow). Office: Nebr Supreme Ct State Capitol Bldg Rm 2211 PO Box 98910 Lincoln NE 68509-8910

**STEPHEN, JOHN ERLE,** lawyer, consultant; b. Eagle Lake, Tex., Sept. 24, 1918; s. John Earnest and Vida Thrall (Klein) S.; m. Gloria Yzaguirre, May 16, 1942; children: Vida Leslie Stephen Renzi, John Lauro Kurt. JD, U. Tex., 1941; postgrad., Northwestern U., 1942, U.S. Naval Acad. Postgrad. Sch., Annapolis, 1944; cert. in internat. law, U.S. Naval War Coll., Newport, R.I., 1945; cert. in advanced internat. law, U.S. Naval War Coll., 1967. Bar: Tex. 1946, U.S. Ct. Appeals (D.C. cir.) 1949, U.S. Tax Ct. 1953, U.S. Supreme Ct. 1955, U.S. Dist. Ct. D.C. 1956, U.S. Ct. Appeals (2nd cir.) 1959, U.S. Ct. Appeals (7th cir.) 1964, U.S. Dist. Ct. (so. dist.) N.Y. 1964, U.S. Dist. Ct. (so. dist.) Fla. 1969, D.C. 1972, U.S. Dist. Ct. (no. dist.) Ill. 1974, U.S. Dist. Ct. (we. dist.) Wash. 1975, Mich. 1981, U.S. Dist. Ct. (we. dist.) Mich. 1981, U.S. Dist. Ct. (so. dist.) Tex. 1981. Gen. mgr., corp. counsel Sta. KOPY, Houston, 1946; gen. atty., exec. asst. to pres. Tex. Star Broadcasting Corp. and affiliated cos., Houston, 1947-50; ptnr. Hofheinz & Stephen, Houston, 1950-57; v.p., gen. counsel TV Broadcasting Co., Tex. Radio Corp., Gulf Coast Network, Houston, 1953-57; spl. counsel, exec. asst. Mayor, City of Houston, 1953-57; spl. counsel Houston C. of C., 1953-56; sr. v.p., gen. counsel Air Transp. Assn. Am., Washington, 1958-70; v.p., gen. counsel Amway Corp. and affiliated cos., Ada, Mich., 1971-82; counsellor, cons. Austin, Tex., 1983—; chief protocol City of Houston, 1953-56; advisor Consulates Gen. of Mex., San Antonio, Houston, New Orleans, Washington, 1956-66; atty. Gen. Creighton W. Abrams, Comdr. U.S. Military Assistance Command, Vietnam, Saigon/Washington, 1970-71; mem. adv. bd. Jour. of Air Law and Commerce, 1966-72; vis. lectr. Harvard Bus. Sch., Pacific Agribus. Conf., The Southwestern Legal Found., Inter-Am. Law Conf.; apptd. by Pres. legal advisor, del. U.S. Diplomatic Dels. to Internat. Treaty Confs., Paris, London, Rome, Tokyo, Madrid, Bermuda, Guadalajara, Dakar, 1961-71, Internat. Air-Rte. Dels. to U.K., France, Spain, Portugal, Belgium, The Netherlands, Japan, Rep. of Korea, Mex., Australia, Argentina, Soviet Union, and Brazil, 1960-70; legal advisor, del. U.S. dels. to United Nations Specialized Orgns., Montreal, Geneva, 1964-71; U.S. rep. Internat. Conf. on Aircraft Disturbance, London, 1967; hon. faculty mem. sch. of law, sch. of bus., U. Miami, 1968—; accredited corr. United Nations, Rep. and Dem. Nat. Convs. Author, editor in field. Comm. group chief Harris County/Houston Civil Def.; chmn. legal com. Nat. Aircraft Noise Abatement Coun.; mem. adv. bd. Houston Mus. Fine Arts, 1953-57; bd. dirs. Contemporary Arts Assn., 1952-57, Tex. Transp. Inst., 1964-72. Comdr. USNR, 1941-46, PTO and S.E. Asia, decorated Naval Unit Commendation, six battle stars; mem. staff Supreme Allied Command, NATO, 1954. Recipient Jesse L. Lasky award RKO Pictures-CBS, Hollywood, Calif., 1939, H.J. Lutcher Stark prize U. Tex., 1939, 40, Walter Mack award PepsiCo, U. Tex., 1941, Best U.S. Pub. Svc. Broadcasts award CCNY, 1946, First-FM (West) award Frequency Modulation Assn., Houston, 1947, Tex. State Network award mobile coverage Nat. Presdl. Convs., Phila., 1948, Trusonic Wireless Microphone award Acad. Motion Picture Arts & Scis., Beverly Hills, 1951, Frank White award, Mutual Broadcasting Sys., N.Y., 1953, C.R. Smith Aviation Devel. award, Am. Airlines, N.Y., 1955, KLM Royal Dutch Airlines award, Washington, 1956, Capt. Eddie Rickenbacker Air Transport Advancement award Eastern Air Lines, N.Y., 1956, Allied Rod & Gun Club Triple Crown trophy, Gander, Nfld., 1958, Iron Duke award No. Va. Lit. Soc., Arlington, 1962, President's Outstanding commendation, U.S. Naval War Coll., Newport, 1967, IBM Corp. Exec. Computer Concepts prize, San Jose, Calif., 1976, M.Y. ENTERPRISE award Peter Island, Brit. V.I., 1978, Glacier Bay award M.V. MALIBU Sitka, Alaska, 1980. Mem. ABA (past chmn., mem. coun. sect. pub. utility, comms. and transp. law, standing com. on aero. law), Am. Law Inst., World Peace Through Law Ctr. Geneva (past chmn. internat. aviation law com.), Fed. Bar Assn. (exec. com. transp. coun., comms. coun.), D.C. Bar, State Bar Tex. (50 Yr. Meritorious Practice award 1996), State Bar Mich., Fed. Comms. Bar Assn., Assn. ICC Practitioners, Am. Judicature Soc., Washington Fgn. Law Soc. (vis. lectr. 1967-68), Japanese Air Law Soc. (hon. mem. 1966—), Venezuelan Air and Space Law Soc. (hon.), SOVEDADE (hon., Caracas), Naval War Coll. Found., Internat. Club (Washington), Explorers (Washington), Houston Polo Club, Lakeshore Club (Chgo.), Nat. Aviation Club (Washington), Saddle and Cycle Club (Chgo.), Breakfast Club (Houston), Execs. Club (Houston), Order Ky. Cols., Ark. Travelers, Tex. Navy Adm., Flying Col., Phi Eta Sigma, Delta Sigma Rho (pres Tex. chap. 1940). Administrative and regulatory, Antitrust, Communications. Home: 6904 Ligustrum Cv Austin TX 78750-8352

**STEPHENS, ALBERT LEE, JR.,** federal judge; b. L.A., Feb. 14, 1913; m. Barbara, Sept. 29, 1939; 2 children. AB, U. So. Calif., 1936, LLB, 1938. Bar: Calif. 1939, U.S. Dist. Ct. Nev. 1939. Pvt. practice L.A., 1939-43, 46-59; judge Superior Ct., L.A., 1959-61; now sr. judge U.S. Dist. Ct. (ctrl. dist.) Calif.; mem. legal profession panel U. So. Calif. Law Sch., 1961-65; lectr. UCLA Law Sch., 1954-55; sponsor, chair Dist. Judges Seminar (9th cir.), 1964-66. Lt. USNR, 1943-46, WWII. Nominated for appt. in 1961 by Pres. Kennedy. Mem. ABA, Calif. Bar Assn., L.A. County Bar Assn., Am. Jud. Soc., Jud. Conf. U.s. (trial practice and technique com.), U.S. Dist. Judges Assn. 9th Cir., Maritime Law Assn., U.s. Lawyers Club L.A., Chancery Club (pres. 1959). Office: US Dist Ct 232 S June St Los Angeles CA 90004-1046

**STEPHENS, ANDREW RUSSELL,** lawyer; b. Jan. 10, 1957; s. Harold Stephens and Evelyn Sbarsky; m. Sandra J. Hecker, May 25, 1985. BA, SUNY, Binghamton, 1978; JD, Stanford U., 1992. Bar: Calif. 1992, D.C. 1994. Editor Bus. Pub. Inc., Washington, 1984-89; assoc. Dinkelspiel, Donovan & Reder, San Francisco, 1992-93; mgr. regulatory affairs Koch Industries, Washington, 1993-97, mgr. legal policy issues, 1997-99; sr. assoc. Marzulla and Marzulla, Washington, 1999—. sr. program officer Charles G. Koch Charitable Found., Washington, 1997-99, Claude R. Lmbe Charitable Found., Washington, 1997-99. Mem. Federalist Soc. Avocations: restoring and renovating old houses, woodworking, weightlifting, racquetball. Federal civil litigation, Constitutional, Environmental. Office: Marzulla and Marzulla 1350 Connecticut Ave NW Ste 410 Washington DC 20036-1737

**STEPHENS, BRUCE EDWARD,** lawyer; b. York, Nebr., Nov. 25, 1955; s. Edward Reed and Donna Mae (Baer) S.; m. Janette Ann Harms, Aug. 8, 1985 (div.). BS, U. Nebr., Lincoln-Omaha, 1978, JD, 1981. Bar: Nebr. 1981, U.S. Dist. Ct. Nebr. 1981. Estate planning specialist Fed. Land Bank, Omaha, 1984; sr. trust officer, v.p. York (Nebr.) State Bank & Trust Co., 1984-86; pvt. practice York, 1986—. Mem. York Vol. Fire Dept., 1987—; bd. dirs. Yorkshire Playhouse, 1986—, Crimestoppers, York, 1986—. Capt. JAGC, U.S. Army, 1981-84, now Res. Mem. Nebr. Bar Assn., Order of Barristers, Elks. Republican. Methodist. Avocations: acting, hunting, photography. General civil litigation, Probate, General practice. Office: PO Box 56 York NE 68467-0056

**STEPHENS, DELIA MARIE LUCKY,** lawyer; b. Temple, Tex., Aug. 2, 1939; d. James Richard and Mattie (Barfield) Lucky; m. Billy C. Stephens, 1962 (div. 1983); children: William Carl, James Kelley. BA, U. Mary Hardin-Baylor, 1961; JD, Thurgood Marshall Sch. Law, Houston, 1981. Bar: Tex. 1981, U.S. Dist. Ct. (so. dist.) Tex. 1981. Pvt. practice law Houston, 1981—. Writer feature stories The Jour. Newspapers, 1976-79. Elder, trustee Clear Lake Presbyn. Ch., Houston, 1985—; founding dir. East-West Cultural Inst., 1991—; bd. dirs. Palmer Drug Abuse Coun., 1986-90. Mem. AAUW, Tex. State Bar Assn., Houston Bar Assn., Houston Rose Soc., Am. Rose Soc., Houston Mus. Fine Arts, U. Mary Hardin-Baylor Alumni Assn. (nominating com. 1973), Coastal Bend Mary Hardin-Baylor Club (pres. 1972), Clear Lake Area C. of C., Houston Outdoor Nature Club. Democrat. Presbyn. Avocations: roses, swimming, golf, drama, music. General civil litigation, Bankruptcy, Personal injury. Home: 482 Lost Rock Dr Webster TX 77598-2608 Office: 17000 El Camino Real Ste 104 Houston TX 77058-2632

**STEPHENS, FERRIS W.,** lawyer; b. Birmingham, Ala., Aug. 22, 1955; s. William John and Mildred Ann (Ritchey) S. BA, U. Ala., Tuscaloosa, 1978; JD, Samford U., 1981; postgrad., Northwestern U., 1985. Bar: Ala. 1981, U.S. Dist. Ct. (no., mid. and so. dists.) Ala. 1982, U.S. Ct. Internat. Trade 1982, U.S. Ct. Customs and Patent Appeals 1982, U.S. Ct. Mil. Appeals 1982, U.S. Ct. Appeals (11th cir.) 1982. Law clk. to presiding justice Ala. Ct. Criminal Appeals, Montgomery, 1981-82; asst. atty. gen. State of Ala., Montgomery, 1982—; adminstrv. law judge State of Ala.; lectr. on welfare fraud investigation and prosecution U. Del.; instr. Huntington Coll., Montgomery, 1983-84; dir. welfare fraud State of Ala.; mem. State Jud. System Study Commn., 1986. Narrator (cable TV) Legal Education Program, 1982-84; news dir. Sta. WVSU, Birmingham, 1980-81. Mem. Election Reform Commn., 1979-82; bd. dirs. Elderly Abuse. Recipient Nathan Burkan award ASCAP, 1981. Mem. Am. Trial Lawyers Assn., Ala. Bar Assn. (lawyer pub. relations and media relations commn., legis. liaison com.), Dist. Attys. Assn., Young Lawyers Assn. Montgomery Jaycees (v.p. 1984, legal counsel 1983), Phi Delta Phi, Delta Chi. Roman Catholic. Avocations: basketball, tennis. Home: 704 Staffordshire Ln Birmingham AL 35226-3435 Office: Atty Gen's Office State House Montgomery AL 36130-0001

**STEPHENS, (HOLMAN) HAROLD,** lawyer; b. Enterprise, Ala., Nov. 29, 1954; s. Holman Harrison and Louise (Bass) S. BA, U. Ala., 1976, JD, 1980. Bar: Ala. 1980, U.S. Dist. Ct. (no. dist.) Ala. 1980, U.S. Ct. Appeals (11th cir.) 1981, U.S. Supreme Ct. 1994. Asst. U.S. atty. U.S. Dist. Ct. (no. dist.) Ala., Birmingham, 1980-82; assoc. Lanier, Shaver & Herring, Huntsville, Ala., 1982-84; ptnr. Lanier, Shaver & Herring, Huntsville, 1985-88, Lanier, Ford, Shaver & Payne PC, Huntsville, 1988-98, Bradley Arant Rose & White LLP, Huntsville, 1998—; lectr. U. Ala., Huntsville, 1982-86, So. Jr. Coll., Huntsville, 1984-86. Bd. dirs. Huntsville-Madison County Mental Health Ctr., 1983-89, 91-97, pres. 1987-88; bd. dirs. Big Bros./Big Sisters of N. Ala., Huntsville, 1983-87, Friends of Pub. Radio, Huntsville, 1984-86, Girls Inc., 1998—. Mem. ABA, Trial Attys. Am., Ala. Bar Assn. (chmn. litigation sect. 1998-99), Huntsville-Madison (Ala.) County bar Assn. (v.p. young lawyers div. 1986-87, pres. 1987-88). Baptist. Avocations: tennis, golf, hiking. Fax: 256-517-5200; email: hstephens@barw.com. Federal civil litigation, State civil litigation, Insurance. Home: 1502 Locust Cir SE Huntsville AL 35801-2005 Office: Bradley Arant Rose & White LLC 200 Clinton Ave W Ste 900 Huntsville AL 35801-4900

**STEPHENS, JAMES F.,** lawyer; b. Avilla, Ind., May 30, 1962; s. Fred A. and Brenda C. Stephens; m. Tammy A. Stephens, July 30, 1988; children: Gabriel S., Abigael A. BA, Anderson U., 1985; JD, Valparaiso U., 1988. Bar: Ind. 1989, U.S. Dist. Ct. (no. and so. dists.) Ind. Law clk. Noble County Cir. and Superior Cts., Albion, Ind., 1986-87; intern Valparaiso U. Legal Svcs., Gary, Ind., 1987-88; law clk. Emerick & Diggins P.C., Kendallville, Ind., 1988-89; assoc. Emerick & Diggins P.C., Kendallville, 1989-90; founding and mng. atty. Stephens Law Firm P.C., Avilla, 1990—. Contbr. articles to local newspapers. Trustee Kendallville Park Bd., 1988-91, Kendallville Pub. Libr., 1988-91; legal advisor Faith United Meth. Ch., Kendallville, 1998—. Mem. Ind. State Bar Assn. (family and juvenile law, bus. law, internat. law, labor and employment law, land use and zoning sects.), Am. Tae Kwon Do Assn. Avocations: martial arts, outdoor recreation, family oriented activities. General civil litigation, Contracts commercial, Family and matrimonial. Office: PO Box 727 719 E Albion St Avilla IN 46710-9691

**STEPHENS, JENNIFER SUE,** law librarian; b. Denton, Tex., June 5, 1964; d. Elvis Clay and Joyce (Perkins) S. BBA, U. North Tex., 1986; MLS, Tex. Woman's U., 1990. Clk. Voertmans, Inc., Denton, 1985-86, U. North Tex., Denton, 1986-87; student asst. libr. Tex. Woman's U., Denton, 1988-89, grad. asst. libr., 1989-90; law libr. Dresser Industries, Inc., Dallas, 1990—. Mem. Am. Assn. Law Librs., Dallas Assn. Law Librs. (chair tech. sect. 1993-95), Southwestern Assn. Law Librs. Independent. Methodist. Avocations: computers, books, music, woodwork, bicycling.

**STEPHENS, JERRY EDWARD,** law librarian; b. Dodge City, Kans., June 13, 1945; s. Carl Edward and Mona Grace (McCarty) S.; m. Karen Yvonne Woods, May 27, 1967; children: Shannon Lea, Amy Lyn, Adam Ryan. BA, U. Okla., 1967, MLS, 1968; JD, U. Kans., 1976. Bar: Kans. 1976, U.S. Dist. Ct. Kans. 1976. Libr. North Tex. State U., Denton, 1968-70; law libr. U. Kans. Law Sch., Lawrence, 1970-76; rsch. libr. Kans. Supreme Ct. Law Libr., Topeka, 1976-78; rsch. analyst Kans. Legis. Rsch. Dept., Topeka,

1978-82; sales rep. West Pub. Co., St. Paul, 1982-86; regional dir. Grolier Ednl. Corp., Danbury, Conn., 1986-89; law libr. U.S. Ct. Appeals (10th cir.), Oklahoma City, 1990—. Mem. Am. Assn. Law Librs., Spl. Librs. Assn. Democrat. Unitarian. Avocations: gardening, sailing, racquetball. Home: 1405 Rockwood Dr Edmond OK 73013-6011 Office: US Ct Appeals (10th cir) 2305 US Courthouse Oklahoma City OK 73102

**STEPHENS, LAWRENCE KEITH,** lawyer; b. Cleve., Aug. 7, 1959; s. Gary Baker and Emilie Mae (Abbott) S.; m. Sunee Del Smith, Jan. 9, 1982; children: Shannon Ruth, Sierra Del. BS cum laude, Tex. A&M U., 1981; JD, Santa Clara U., 1990. Bar: Calif. 1990, Tex. 1992, U.S. Patent Office, 1987. Sys. programmer IBM, Irving, Tex., 1981-83; rep. account mktg. IBM, Charlottesville, Va., 1983-86; patent agt. IBM, Santa Clara, Calif., 1987-90; corp. counsel IBM, White Plains, N.Y., 1990-91, Austin, Tex., 1991-92; dir. intellectual property Taligent, Cupertino, Calif., 1992-96; spl. counsel Cooley Godward, LLP, Palo Alto, Calif., 1996-97; dep. chief intellectual property Rockwell Internat. Corp., Costa Mesa, Calif., 1997-98; with Andersen Consulting, 1998; founding ptnr. Hickman, Stephens and Coleman, L.L.P., 1999—; bd. dirs. Hilltop Manor, Inc., San Jose, Calif., chmn. 1995-97; bd. dirs. FBC, San Jose. Patentee in field; contbr. articles to profl. jours. Deacon First Bapt. Ch., San Jose, 1989-97. Mem. Am. Intellectual Property Law Assn. (chair copyright internet 1995—). Avocations: golf, skiing, swimming, bridge, roller blading. Intellectual property, Mergers and acquisitions, Patent. Home: 13730 Beaumont Ave Saratoga CA 95070-4935

**STEPHENS, MARJORIE JOHNSEN,** lawyer; b. Dallas, Aug. 29, 1949; d. Joseph Cornelius Stephens and Marjorie Marie Johnsen; m. Andrew N. Meyercord, Dec. 27, 1971 (div. Oct. 1985); children: Andrew J., Ben, Lee. BA, Tufts U., Medford, Mass., 1971; JD, So. Meth. U., Dallas, 1974, LLM in Taxation, 1981. Bar: Tex. 1974; bd. cert. in estate planning and probate, 1981, 93. Assoc. litigation and taxation Akin Gump Strauss Hauer & Feld, Dallas, 1974-79; ptnr. estate planning and tax Meyercord, Stephens & Bartholow, Dallas, 1979-83; assoc. Copeland & Almquist, Dallas, 1984-86; head tax sect. Smith, Underwood & Hunter, Dallas, 1987-88, pvt. practice, 1988—; lectr. in field Tex. Soc. CPAs, Dallas Estate Planning Coun., Estate Planning Coun. North Tex. Contbr. articles to profl. publs. Mem. ABA, Tex. Bar Assn., Dallas Bar Assn. Estate planning, Taxation, general. Office: 5956 Sherry Ln Ste 1413 Dallas TX 75225-8025

**STEPHENS, MARLA JEAN,** lawyer; b. Milw., Mar. 1, 1952; m. Robert J. Dvorak. BA, U. Wis., 1978; JD, Marquette U., 1981. Bar: Wis. 1981, U.S. Dist. Ct. Wis. 1981. Asst. pub. defender Office Wis. Pub. Defender, Milw., 1981-94, 1st asst. pub. defender, 1994-96; dir. appellate divsn. Office Wis. Pub. Defender, Milw. and Madison, 1996—; mem. Wis. Jud. Coun., Madison, 1996—. Mem. NACDL, Assn. for Women Lawyers, State Bar Wis. (appellate practice bd. 1999—). Office: Office Wis Pub Defender Appellate Divsn 735 N Water St Ste 912 Milwaukee WI 53202-4105

**STEPHENS, PAULA CHRISTINE (POLLY),** arbitrator, consultant; b. St. Louis, July 17, 1932; d. Herbert and Irene Lovey (Caldwell) Kuenzel; m. John James Stephens, Aug. 27, 1957 (div. Feb. 1971); children: David A., Nancy S. BA in Sociology, U. Mich., 1955. Registered rep. NASD; lic. real estate salesperson, Ohio, Fla., in uniform securities NYSE, ASE. Fin. cons. trainer, fin. cons. Merrill Lynch, various locations, 1978-87; field strategy mgr., tng. mgr. Merrill Lynch, Princeton, N.J., 1987-89, Venice, Fla., 1989-91; litigation cons. Sarasota, Fla., 1991-95; arbitrator Fla. State's Atty. Gen., Tallahassee, 1996—; litigation cons. Stephens Reven & Assocs., Sarasota, 1995—; arbitrator Am. Arbitrator Assn., Miami and N.Y.C., 1992—, Nat. Assn. Securities Dealers, 1992—; cons. Women's Resource Ctr. Displaced Homemaker Program, 1989-91; water safety coor. ARC, Tuscaloosa, Ala., 1954; supplemental recreation activities overseas employee ARC, Korea, 1956-57. Bd. dirs. Women's Resource Ctr., 1978-79, 94-95. Mem. U.S. Coast Guard Aux. Republican. Avocations: bridge, travel, swimming, tennis, reading. Office: Stephens Reven & Assocs Paradise Plz Ste 142 Sarasota FL 34239

**STEPHENS, ROBERT F.,** state supreme court chief justice; b. Covington, Ky., Aug. 16, 1927. Student, Ind. U.; LL.B., U. Ky., 1951. Bar: Ky. 1951. Asst. atty. Fayette County, Ky., 1964-69; judge Fayette County, 1969-75; atty. gen. Ky. Frankfort, 1976-79; justice Supreme Ct. Ky., Frankfort, 1979-99, chief justice, 1982-99; sec. Ky. Justice Cabinet, Frankfort, 1999—; pres. Conf. of chief justices, 1992-93; chmn. Nat. Ctr. for State Ct., 1992-93. Staff: Ky. Law Jour. Bd. dirs. Nat. Assn. Counties, 1973-75; 1st pres. Ky. Assn. Counties; 1st chmn. Bluegrass Area Devel. Dist.; chmn. Ky. Heart Assn. Fund Drive, 1976-78. Served with USN, World War II. Named Outstanding Judge of Ky., Ky. Bar Assn., 1986, Outstanding County Judge, 1972; recipient Herbert Harley award Am. Judicature Soc; inducted into U. Ky. Coll. of Law Hall of Fame, 1996. Mem. Warren Burger Soc., Nat. Ctr. for State Cts., Order of Coif. Democrat. Office: Ky Justice Cabinet Bush Bldg 403 Wapping St Frankfort KY 40601 Office: Ky Justice Cabinet 403 Wapping St Frankfort KY 40601-2638

**STEPHENS, STEVEN SCOTT,** lawyer, educator; b. Washington, Aug. 19, 1957; s. Norval R. Stephens and Eileen White; m. Heidi M. Stephens, Aug. 1, 1987; children: Samantha Marie, Eric Robert. BA, U. Md., 1981; JD, U. Balt., 1984; LLM, George Washington U., 1986; MS, Johns Hopkins, 1992; MA, U. S. Fla., 1994; MA in Econ., U. Md., 1996; PhD in Fin., U. S. Fla., 1998. Bar: Md. 1985, D.C. 1986, Fla. 1988, U.S. Supreme Ct. 1993. Rsch. atty. U.S. Ct. Appeals, Balt., 1982-85; atty. Birrane, Harlan & Sharretts, Balt., 1985-88, Alpert, Josey & Grilli, Tampa, Fla., 1988-93; pvt. practice Tampa, 1993—; adj. prof. Stetson U. Coll. of Law, St. Petersburg, Fla., 1992—; vis. asst. prof. U. South Fla. Coll. Bus. Administrn., 1998—. Contbr. articles to profl. jours. Chmn. Fla. Statewide Nominating Commn. for Judges of Compensation Claims, 1995-96.

**STEPHENS, WILLIAM TAFT,** lawyer; b. Huntsville, Ala., Dec. 3, 1943; s. Roy Carl and Mary Frances (Taft) S. BS in Aero Engring., Auburn (Ala.) U., 1966; JD, Harvard U., 1969. Bar: Ala. 1969, N.Y. 1970, U. S. Ct. Appeals (2d cir.) 1970, U.S. Supreme Ct. 1972, U.S. Dist. Ct. (so. dist.) Ala. 1978, U.S. Dist. Ct. (no. dist.) Ala. 1983, U.S. Ct. Appeals (11th cir.) 1983, U.S. Ct. Appeals (Fed. cir.) 1984. Engr. trainee NASA/Marshall Spaceflight Ctr., Huntsville, Ala., 1963-65, 67; propulsion engr. Boeing Co., Huntsville, 1966; assoc. Kenyon & Kenyon, N.Y.C., 1969-70, Sullivan & Cromwell, N.Y.C., 1970-73; chief civil divsn. State of Ala. Atty Gen.'s Office, Montgomery, 1973-80; gen. counsel Retirement Systems of Ala., Montgomery, 1980-98, dep. dir., counsel, 1998—; spl. counsel Ala. Legis., 1976-77, 1983; mem. permanent Study Commn. of State Jud. System, 1977-80; adj. prof. Auburn U., Montgomery, 1979-81; mem. Auburn U. Rsch. Coun., 1997—, Auburn U. Coll. of Liberal Arts Dean's Coun., 1997—. Contbr. articles to profl. jours. Candidate for State Atty. Gen., 1978; mem. Auburn U. Engring. Coun., 1981—; coach Little League Baseball, Montgomery, 1979—; bd. dirs. Boys Clubs of Montgomery, 1985-82. Mem. Nat. Assn. Pub. Pension Attys. (exec. com. 1989-95. pres. 1993-95), Ala. Bar Assn., Montgomery County Bar Assn., Auburn U. Bar Assn. (treas. 1983—), Auburn U. Alumni Assn. Methodist. Home: 2662 The Mdws Montgomery AL 36116-1158 Office: Retirement Systems Ala Montgomery AL 36130-0001

**STEPHENS, WILLIAM THEODORE,** lawyer, business executive; b. Balt., Mar. 31, 1922; s. William A. and Mildred (Griffin) S.; m. Arlene Alice Lesti, June 2, 1958; children: William Theodore Jr., Renée Adena. Grad., Balt. City Coll., 1941; student, U. Md., 1946-47; AB, JD, George Washington U., 1950, postgrad., 1951. Bar: D.C. 1951, Md. 1950, Va. 1959. Assoc. J.L. Green, Washington, 1950-51; with J.M. Cooper, Washington, 1952-54; sr. ptnr. Stephens Law Firm, Washington, 1955—; gen. counsel Exotech, Inc., Gaithersburg, Md.; bd. dirs., prin. owner BARBCO, Inc., Va., Fairfax Raquet Club; gen. counsel various nat. corps. and assns. 1st lt. AUS, 1941-45. Mem. ABA (D.C. Bar Assn. sec. taxation 1959—, sec. corps, banking and bus. law 1960—), Bar Assn. D.C. (sec. taxation 1959-60), Md. Bar Assn., Va. Bar Assn., XVI Corps Assn. (pres. 1967), Commonwealth Club, Univ. Club, Capitol Hill Club, Army-Navy Country Club, Regency Sport and Health Club, Jockey Club, LaCosta Country Club, Racquet Club Internat., Kappa Alpha (preceptor, ct. of honor, James Ward Wood Province 1988-91), Delta Theta Phi. General corporate, Legislative, Administrative and regulatory. Home: 1800 Old Meadow Rd Mc Lean VA 22102-1819 also: PO Box 2569 Rancho Santa Fe CA 92067-2569 also: 881 Ocean Dr Key Biscayne FL 30000 Office: PO Box 1096 Mc Lean VA 22101-1096

**STEPHENSON, ALAN CLEMENTS,** lawyer; b. Wilmington, N.C., Nov. 7, 1944; s. Abram Clements and Ruth (Smith) S.; m. Sherri Jean Miller, Dec. 19, 1970; children: Edward Taylor, Anne Baldwin. AB in Hist., U. N.C., 1967; JD, U. Va., 1970. Bar: N.Y. 1971. Assoc. Cravath, Swaine & Moore, N.Y.C., 1970-78, ptnr., 1978-88; mng. dir. Wasserstein, Perella and Co. Inc., N.Y.C., 1988-92; ptnr. Cravath, Swaine & Moore, N.Y.C., 1992—; bd. dirs. Victim Svcs., Inc., N.Y.C.; mem. external adv. bd. undergrad. honors program U. N.C., 1998—. Morehead scholar John M. Moorehead Found., 1963. Mem. N.Y. State Bar Assn., Assn. of Bar of City of N.Y., The Brook Club, The Links Club, Tuxedo Club, Union Club, Phi Beta Kappa. General corporate, Securities. Home: 1107 5th Ave New York NY 10128-0145 Office: Cravath Swaine & Moore 825 8th Ave Fl 38 New York NY 10019-7475

**STEPHENSON, BARBERA WERTZ,** lawyer; b. Bryan, Ohio, Dec. 10, 1938; d. Emerson D. and Beryl B. (Barber) Wertz; m. Gerard J. Stephenson Jr., June 22, 1960; 1 child, Thomas. Student, Smith Coll., 1956-57; BSEE, MIT, 1961; JD, U. N.Mex., 1981. Bar: N.Mex. 1981. Electronic engr. Digital Equipment Corp., Maynard, Mass., 1960-66; logic analyst Librascope, Glendale, Calif., 1966; electronic engr. Md. Dept. of Def., Ft. Meade, 1966-68; mem. tech. staff Xerox Data Systems, Rockville, Md., 1968; pvt. practice cons., Silver Spring, Md., 1969-78; pvt. practice law, Albuquerque, 1981—. Author: Financing Your Home Purchase in New Mexico, 1992; patentee analog to digital converter, kitchen calculator. Mem. N.Mex. Bar Assn. General corporate, Real property, Trademark and copyright.

**STEPHENSON, CHARLES GAYLEY,** lawyer; b. San Francisco, May 18, 1935; s. John Towle and Elizabeth (Gayley) S.; m. Tracy Elizabeth Innes, Aug. 26, 1961; children: Gayley, Kate, Anthony. BA, U. Calif., Berkeley, 1957; LLB, Stanford U., 1963. Bar: Calif. 1964, U.S. Dist. Ct. (no. dist.) Calif. 1964, U.S. Ct. Appeals (9th cir.) 1964. Assoc., ptnr. Chickering & Gregory, San Francisco, 1963-73; ptnr. Jackson, Tufts, Cole & Black and predecessors, San Francisco, 1973—. 1st lt. U.S. Army, 1957-59. Fellow Am. Coll. Probate Counsel; mem. Internat. Acad. Trusts and Estates Lawyers, Lagunitas Country Club, Pacific Union Club. Democrat. Episcopalian. Avocations: sports, movies, piano. Estate planning, Probate, Estate taxation. Home: 240 32d Ave San Francisco CA 94121-1014 Office: Jackson Tufts Cole & Black 650 California St Ste 3130 San Francisco CA 94108-2699

**STEPHENSON, MARIA I. O'BYRNE,** lawyer; b. Cali, Valle, Colombia, Nov. 12, 1951; came to U.S., 1965; d. Alvaro and Maria Teresa (Malvehy) O'Byrne; m. John Edward Stephenson, May 31, 1975; children: Teresa Maria, Phillip David. BA, Tulane U., 1973; JD, U. Houston, 1975. Bar: Tex. 1975, La. 1976. Assoc. Grisbaum & Kleppner, Metairie, La., 1976-78; ptnr. Bryan, Nelson, Allen, Schroeder & Stephenson, New Orleans, 1978-86; of counsel Maria I. O'Byrne Stephenson, New Orleans, 1986-95, Stephenson Matthews & Chavarri LLC, New Orleans, 1996—. Active Pan Am. Commn., Baton Rouge, 1993-96; bd. dirs. Shared Housing, New Orleans, 1994—. Recipient Diploma Al Merito, Consulate of Mex., 1994, Tributo de Reconcimiento, Consulate of Colombia, 1999. Mem. La. Bar (bd. dirs. internat. law sect. 1993-94), La.-Mex. Trade Assn. (officer 1991-94), Hispanic Lawyers Assn. (officer 1981-97, pres. 1997). Roman Catholic. Avocations: trade, travel, golf, tennis. Office: Stephenson Matthews & Chavarri LLC 905 World Trade Ctr New Orleans LA 70130

**STEPHENSON, MASON WILLIAMS,** lawyer; b. Atlanta, May 29, 1946; s. Donald Grier and Katherine Mason (Williams) S.; m. Linda Frances Partee, June 13, 1970; children: Andrew Mason, Walter Martin. AB cum laude, Davidson Coll., 1968; JD, U. Chgo., 1971. Bar: Ga. 1971, U.S. Dist. Ct. (no. dist.) Ga. 1985. Assoc. Alston, Miller & Gaines, Atlanta, 1971-76, ptnr., 1976-77; ptnr. Trotter, Bondurant, Griffin, Miller & Hishon, Atlanta, 1977-82, Bondurant, Miller, Hishon & Stephenson, Atlanta, 1982-85, King & Spalding, Atlanta, 1985—. Mem. fin. com. Atlanta Olympic Organizing Com., 1988-90. Mem. ABA (real property, probate and trust sect.), Am. Coll. Real Estate Lawyers, State Bar Ga. (exec. com., real property law sect. 1989-97, chair intangible rec. tax com. 1994—), Atlanta Bar Assn. (chair real estate sect. 1981-82), Causeway Club, Capital City Club, Phi Beta Kappa, Phi Delta Phi. Avocations: sailing, skiing, jogging. Real property. Office: King & Spalding 191 Peachtree St NE Ste 40 Atlanta GA 30303-1763

**STEPHENSON, MICHAEL MURRAY,** lawyer; b. San Pedro, Calif., July 31, 1943; s. George Murray and Josephine Ann (Wathen) S. Student, U. Okla., 1961, 62, 65, 66; student Harbor Coll., 1962-63, Universidad Ibero-Americana, Mexico City, summer 1964; A.B., U. So. Calif., 1965; J.D., Southwestern U., 1970. Bar: Calif. 1971. Dep. dist. atty. Los Angeles County, 1971-74; ptnr. Stephenson & Stephenson, San Pedro, Calif., 1974—; legal advisor Los Angeles County Underwater Instrs. Assn.; dir. Los Angeles County Underwater Instrs. Assn.; staff instr. Los Angeles Underwater Instrs. Certification Progrm and Advanced Diving progrm. Bd. dirs. ARC, San Pedro, 1975-76; alt. mem. Los Angeles County Dem. Central Com. Recipient Outstanding Teaching award, 28th Underwater Instrs. Cert. Course, Los Angeles, 1980, LA. County Outstanding Underwater Instr., 1990. Mem. State Bar Calif., Los Angeles Trial Lawyers Assn., Am. Trial Lawyers Assn., ABA, Calif. Trial Lawyers Assn. (lectr. underwater instr. liability), Harbor Bar Assn. (pres.), S. Bay Bar Assn., Nat. Assn. Underwater Instrs., Elks, YMCA Underwater Instrs. Assn. Democrat. Roman Catholic. Contbr. articles to profl. jours. State civil litigation, Personal injury, Family and matrimonial. Office: 150 W 7th St Ste 120 San Pedro CA 90731-3341

**STEPHENSON, RICHARD ISMERT,** lawyer; b. Augusta, Kans., Oct. 13, 1937; s. Paul Noble and Dorothy May (Ismert) S.; m. Mary Lynn Bryden, July 2, 1967 (div. 1973); 1 child, Richard William; m. Linda Cox, Apr. 5, 1976. BA, U. Kans., 1958; JD, U. Mich., 1965. Bar: Kans. 1965, U.S. Dist. Ct. Kans. 1965, U.S. Ct. Appeals (10th cir.) 1965. Assoc. Fleeson, Gooing, Coulson & Kitch, Wichita, Kans., 1965-72, ptnr., 1973-95; gen. counsel RAGE Inc. and Affiliated Cos., Wichita, 1995—. Lt. (j.g.) USNR, 1959-62. Recipient Hilden Gibson award U. Kans., 1958. Mem. ABA (forum on franchising), Def. Rsch. Inst., Internat. Assn. Def. Counsel, Kans. Bar Assn., Wichita Bar Assn., Wichita Country Club, Flint Hills Nat. Golf Club, Pi Sigma Alpha, Beta Theta Pi. Avocations: golf, fishing. General corporate. Home: 9203 Killarney Wichita KS 67206-4027 Office: RAGE Inc 1313 N Webb Rd Ste 200 Wichita KS 67206-4077

**STEPHENSON, ROSCOE BOLAR, JR.,** state supreme court justice; b. Covington, Va., Feb. 22, 1922. A.B., Washington and Lee U., 1943, J.D., 1947, LL.D. (hon.), 1983. Bar: Va. 1947. Ptnr. Stephenson & Stephenson, Covington, 1947-52; commonwealth's atty. Alleghany County, Va., 1952-64; ptnr. Stephenson, Kostel, Watson, Carson and Snyder, Covington, 1964-73; judge 25th Jud. Cir. Ct. Commonwealth Va., Covington, 1973-81; justice Va. Supreme Ct., Richmond, 1981-97, sr. justice, 1997—. Recipient Covington Citizen of Yr. award, 1973; recipient Outstanding Alumni award Covington High Sch., 1973. Fellow Am. Coll. Trial Lawyers; mem. Va. State Bar (council 1969-73), Va. Bar Assn., Va. Trial Lawyers Assn., Order of Coif, Omicron Delta Kappa. Home: North Ridge Hot Springs VA 24445 Office: Va Supreme Ct 214 W Main St PO Box 198 Covington VA 24426-0198 also: Virginia Supreme Court Supreme Court Bldg 100 N 9th St Richmond VA 23219-2335

**STEPNER, DONALD LEON,** lawyer; b. Boston, Apr. 23, 1939; s. Neil and Sadie (Adelman) S.; m. Beth Klass, Aug. 14, 1965 (div. Dec. 1985); children: David, Jeff. AA, Wentworth Inst., Boston, 1958; BA, Ky. Wesleyan U., 1963; JD, U. Ky., 1966. Bar: Ky. 1966, U.S. Dist. Ct. Ky. 1966, U.S. Ct. Appeals (6th cir.) 1966, U.S. Supreme Ct. 1971. Assoc. Charles Adams, Covington, Ky., 1966-69; ptnr. Adams, Brooking, Stepner, Woltermann & Dusing, Covington, 1969—; pres. Ky. State Ethics Com. Bd. dirs. Boys Club. Recipient Human Rels. award NCCJ, 1986. Fellow Am. Coll. Trial Lawyers; mem. ABA, Ky. Bar Assn. (pres. 1999—), No. Ky. Bar Assn. (judiciary com., ethics and unauthorized procedure com.), Ky. Def. Rsch. Inst., Kenton County Bar Assn. (pres. 1973-74, Merit award 1973, Gavel award 1973), U.S. Soccer Fedn. (cert. referee), Ky. High Sch. Referees Assn., No. Ky. Soccer Assn. (ofcl. pres. 1980—). Avocations: golf, jogging, biking. General civil litigation, Insurance, Personal injury. Office: Adams Brooking Stepner Woltermann & Dusing 421 Garrard St Covington KY 41011-2562*

**STEPTOE, MARY LOU,** lawyer; b. Washington, July 15, 1949; d. Philip Pendleton and Irene (Hellen) S.; m. Peter E. Carson, Sept. 1986; children: Elizabeth Maud, Julia Grace. BA, Occidental Coll., 1971; JD, U. Va., 1974. Bar: Va., 1974, Supreme Ct., 1987, D.C. 1996. Staff atty., Bur. of Competition FTC, Washington, 1974-79, atty. advisor to commr., 1979-86, exec. asst. to chmn., 1988-89, assoc. dir., Bur. of Competition, 1989-90, dep. dir., 1990-92, acting dir., 1992-95, dep. dir., 1995-96; ptnr. Skadden Arps Slate Meagher & Flom LLP, Washington.

**STEREN, MARC NATHAN,** lawyer; b. Bethesda, Md., Mar. 17, 1970; s. Moises Naun and Perla Wurm Steren. BA, Johns Hopkins U., 1993; JD, U. Pa., 1996. Bar: Md. 1996, D.C. 1997, U.S. Dist. Ct. Md. 1998, U.S. Dist. Ct. 1998. Jud. clk. hon. Paul H. Weinstein Rockville, Md., 1996-97; assoc. Anderson & Quinn, Rockville, 1997—. Mem. ABA, Inns Ct. Avocations: sports, reading, Argentine cooking. Federal civil litigation, Insurance, General corporate. Office: Anderson & Quinn 25 Wood Ln Rockville MD 20850-2228

**STERLING, ERIC EDWARD,** lawyer, legal policy advocate; b. N.Y.C., Oct. 25, 1949; s. Bowen and Helen (Champnella) S.; m. June S. Beittel, Oct. 1996; 1 child, Maya Rebecca. BA, Haverford Coll., 1973; JD, Villanova (Pa.) U., 1976. Bar: Pa. 1976, U.S. Supreme Ct. 1980. Asst. pub. defender Del. County, Media, Pa., 1976-79; asst. counsel sub. on criminal justice U.S. Ho. Reps., Washington, 1979-81, counsel subcom. on crime, 1981-89; pres. The Criminal Justice Policy Found., Washington, 1989—; cons. Dem., Rep. and Libertarian Party orgns. and candidates, 1982—; cons. The Brookings Instn., 1990, Office of Pers. Mgmt., 1990, GAO, 1992, Nat. News Media, 1989—; lectr. Am. U. Sch. Pub. Affairs, Washington, 1984-86, U. Colo. Conf. on World Affairs, 1990—, others. Founder, dir. Nat. Drug Strategy Network, 1989—; mem. D.C. Mayor's Adv. Com. on Drug Abuse, 1990; mem. steering com. D.C. Safe Streets Project, 1990-91; bd. dirs. Families Against Mandatory Minimums Found., 1991—, Forfeiture Endangers Am. Rights, 1993-95, William Penn House, 1992-98; mem. Vol. Com. of Lawyers, 1995—. Recipient Cert. of Appreciation, U.S. Bur. Alcohol, Tobacco and Firearms, 1982, U.S. Postal Inspection Svc., 1988, Justice Gerald LeDain award for achievement in law Drug Policy Found., 1999. Mem. ABA (individual rights and responsibility sect.), APHA, Am. Soc. Criminology, Nat. Assn. Criminal Def. Lawyers. Mem. Soc. of Friends. Avocations: swimming, bicycling, hiking. Office: The Criminal Justice Policy Found 1225 Eye St NW Ste 500 Washington DC 20005-3914

**STERLING, MICHAEL ERWIN,** lawyer; b. Chgo., Feb. 3, 1944; s. Dave and Roselle (Yarowsky) Silverman; m. Alicia Ruth Hayes, June 10, 1966; children: Aaron, Isaac, Jacob. BSC, DePaul U., 1965, JD, 1967; LLM, NYU, 1970. Bar: Ill., 1967, N.Y., 1969, Wash., 1970, U.S. Tax Ct., 1969, U.S. Ct. Appeals (9th cir.), 1970, U.S. Supreme Ct., 1971. Tax atty. J.K. Lasser, N.Y.C., 1968-70; staff atty. Preston, Gates & Ellis, Seattle, 1970-72; tax counsel PACCAR, Inc., Bellevue, Wash., 1972-79; pvt. practice Bellevue and Issaquah, Wash., 1979—. Mem. AICPA, Wash. Bar Assn. (chmn. sect. taxation 1981-82, vice chmn. 1979-80), Tax Execs. Inst. (v.p. 1979-80). Republican. Estate planning, General corporate, Taxation, general. Office: 4411 186th Ave SE Issaquah WA 98027-9759

**STERLING, TIMOTHY F.,** lawyer; b. Michigan City, Ind., Nov. 7, 1968; s. Arthur D. and Marie E. Sterling. BS, MS, Ind. State U., 1991; JD, U. Tulsa, 1996. Bar: Okla. 1996, U.S. Dist. Ct. (no. dist.) Okla. 1996. Atty. Knowles, King & Taylor, P.C., Tulsa, 1996-98. Vol. John 3:16 Mission, Tulsa, 1998—. Mem. Def. Rsch. Inst., Christian Leagl Soc., Okla. Assn. Def. Counsel, Am. Inns Ct. Insurance, General civil litigation, Personal injury. Office: Knowles King & Taylor PC 603 Expressway Tower 2431 E 51st St Tulsa OK 74105-6036

**STERN, CARL LEONARD,** former news correspondent, federal official; b. N.Y.C., Aug. 7, 1937; s. Hugo and Frances (Taft) S.; m. Joy Elizabeth Nathan, Nov. 27, 1960; children: Lawrence, Theodore. A.B., Columbia U., 1958, M.S., 1959; J.D., Cleve. State U., 1966, J.D. (hon.), 1975; J.D. (hon.), New Eng. Coll. Law, 1977. Bar: Ohio 1966, D.C. 1968, U.S. Supreme Ct. 1969. Law corr. NBC News, Washington, 1967-93; dir. Office of Pub. Affairs U.S. Dept. Justice, Washington, 1993-96; Shapiro Prof. of Media and Pub. Affairs George Washington U., 1996—; lectr. Nat. Jud. Coll.; adj. prof. George Washington U., Stanford U. Editorial bd.: The Dist. Lawyer. Mem. Dept. Transp. Task Force on Assistance to Families in Aviation Disasters, 1997. Recipient Peabody award, 1974, Emmy award, 1974, Gavel award, 1969, 74, Headliner Club award, 1991, Edmond J. Randloph award U.S. Dept. Justice. Mem. ABA (vice chmn. criminal justice sect. com. on criminal justice and the media, gov., forum com. on communications law, working group intelligence requirements and criminal code reform, mem. standing com. on strategic comms.), AFTRA (nat. exec. bd. 1984-86, first v.p. Washington, Balt. chpt. 1985-87). Home: 2956 Davenport St NW Washington DC 20008-2165 Office: George Washington U 409C Academic Ctr 801 22nd St NW Washington DC 20037-2515

**STERN, DONALD KENNETH,** prosecutor. BA, Hobart Coll., 1966; JD, Georgetown U., 1969; LLM, U. Pa., 1973. Intern Dist. Atty.'s Office, Mineola, N.Y., 1967, Citizen's Adv. Ctr., Washington, 1968; staff atty. Defender Assn. Phila., Cmty. Legal Svcs., Phila., 1969-71; adj. prof. law, supervising atty. Boston Coll. Law Sch., Boston Coll. Legal Assistance Bur., 1971-73, asst. prof. law, dir. clin. programs, supervising atty., 1973-75; asst. atty. gen., dir. gen. clin. program, Mass. Atty. Gen.'s Office, Boston Coll. Law Sch., 1975-77, asst. prof. law, dir. atty. gen. clin. program, spl. asst. atty. gen., 1977-78, asst. atty. gen., dir. atty. gen. clin. program, 1978-79; chief govt. bur. Mass. Atty. Gen.'s Office, 1979-82; assoc. Hale and Dorr, Boston, 1982-85, jr. ptnr., 1985-87, sr. ptnr., 1987, 91-93, of counsel, 1990-91; chief legal counsel to Gov. Mass., 1987-90; U.S. atty. Dist. Mass., 1993—. Office: US Courthouse 1 Courthouse Way Ste 9200 Boston MA 02210-3011

**STERN, EDWARD MAYER,** lawyer, educator; b. Albany, N.Y., Feb. 18, 1946; s. William Barnet and Louise (Mayer) S.; m. Ann Swanson, Jan. 22, 1972; children: Jared William, Jordan Carl. BS in Civil Engring., Tufts U., 1968; JD, Boston U., 1972. Bar: Mass. 1972, U.S. Dist. Ct. Mass. 1973, U.S. Supreme Ct. 1980, N.Y. 1983. Environ. engr. Fed. Water Pollution Control Adminstrn., Needham Heights, Mass., 1968-69; civil engr. Anderson-Nichols Engring. Co., Boston, 1970; legal aid law student Multi-Service Ctr., South Boston, Mass., 1971-72; staff atty. Boston Legal Assistance Project, 1972-74; counsel Treatment Alternative to Street Crime-Juvenile, Boston, 1974-75; atty., project dir. Action Plan for Legal Services, Boston, 1976; lawyer in residence U. Mass., Boston, 1976-77; pvt. practice, Newton, Mass., 1976—; v.p., gen. counsel Triangle Devel. Corp., Newton Centre, Mass., 1987-89; pres. Mass. Funding Group Inc., 1988-97; asst. dean for pre-law advising Boston U., 1977—; vis. lectr. U. Mass., 1977—, lectr. continuing edn. Tufts-New Eng. Med. Ctr., Boston, 1973-75; bd. dirs. Pre-Law Advisors Nat. Coun., 1986-88; bd. visitors Walnut Hill Sch., 1995-97; adv. coun. Paralegal Studies Program, Boston U., 1994—. Author: (with Emily Soltanoff) The NAPLA Pre-Law Advisor's Guide, 1984, 2nd revised edit., 1987; co-author (with Gerald Wilson) Book of Law School Lists, 1997, 3d edit., 1999; contbr. legal articles to profl. publs. Mem. med. policy rev. com. Nat. Neurofibromatosis Found., Inc., 1987—; bd. dirs. Citizens for Juvenile Justice, 1997—. With USAR, 1968-69, res. 1968-74. Named Outstanding Participant, Nat. Coll. Juvenile Justice, 1975; recipient Merit award Boston Mayor's Office Youth Activities Commn., 1973, Pub. Svc. award Nat. Neurofibromatosis Found., Inc., 1990. Mem. ABA, Mass. Bar Assn., N.E. Assn. Pre-Law Advisors, Inc. (pres. 1987-88), Nat. Neurofibromatosis Found. (med. policy com. 1987—). Jewish. General practice, Juvenile, Real property. Home: 178 Nehoiden Rd Waban MA 02468-1344 Office: 60 Austin St Ste 210 Newton MA 02460-1857

**STERN, ELIZABETH ESPIN,** lawyer; b. Prince Georges County, Md., June 21, 1961; d. Cesar A. and M. Cecilia (Salvador) E.; m. Michael L. Stern, May 16, 1992; 1 child, Alexander. BA magna cum laude, U. Va., 1983, JD, 1986. Bar: Va. 1986, U.S. Dist. Ct. (ea. dist.) Va., D.C. 1988. Ptnr. comml. immigration Shaw, Pittman, Potts & Trowbridge, Washington, 1986—; moderator Counsel Connects Immigration Discussion Group. Mem.

editorial bd. Bus Law Inc., 1987—; editor-in-chief Free-Market Cuba Bus. Jour; contbg. writer Tech. Law Notes, 1987—, The Changing Workplace, 1991—. Past chair young lawyers sect. Vol. Bar Assn. D.C. Recipient Martin Preis award Vol. Bar Assn. D.C., 1992. Mem. NAFE, Am. Immigration Lawyers Assn., Va. Bar Assn., D.C. Bar Assn. (internat. sec. 1986—, del. to ABA, chair young lawyers sect. 1992-93, Young Lawyer of Yr. 1994), Immigration Tech. Assn. Am. Republican. Avocation: journalism. Labor, Immigration, naturalization, and customs. Home: 8529 Century Oak Ct Fairfax Station VA 22039-3343 Office: Shaw Pittman Potts & Trowbridge 2300 N St NW Fl 5 Washington DC 20037-1172

**STERN, GERALD MANN,** lawyer; b. Chgo., Apr. 5, 1937; s. Lloyd and Fannye (Wener) S.; m. Linda Stone, Dec. 20, 1969; children: Eric, Jesse, Maia. B.S. in Econs., U. Pa., 1958; LL.B. cum laude, Harvard, 1961. Bar: D.C. 1961, Calif. 1991, U.S. Supreme Ct. 1971. Trial atty. civil rights div. U.S. Dept. Justice, 1961-64; assoc. firm Arnold & Porter, Washington, 1964-68; ptnr. Arnold & Porter, 1969-76; founding ptnr. Rogovin, Stern & Huge, Washington, 1976-81; exec. v.p., sr. gen. counsel Occidental Petroleum Corp., Washington, 1981-82, L.A., 1982-92; spl. counsel fin. instn. fraud and health care fraud U.S. Dept. Justice, Washington, 1993-95; ind. legal cons. pvt. practice, Washington, 1995—; cons. Antitrust divsn. U.S. Dept. Justice, 1998—. Author: The Buffalo Creek Disaster, 1976; co-author: Southern Justice, 1965, Outside the Law, 1997. Trustee Facing History and Ourselves, 1996—. Mem. ABA. Home and office: 3322 Newark St NW Washington DC 20008-3330

**STERN, HERBERT JAY,** lawyer; b. N.Y.C., Nov. 8, 1936; s. Samuel and Sophie (Berkowitz) S.; children: Jason Andrew and Jordan Ezekiel (twins), Samuel Abraham, Sarah Kathrine. B.A., Hobart Coll., 1958; J.D. (Ford Found. scholar), U. Chgo., 1961; LL.D. (hon.), Seton Hall Law Sch., 1973, Hobart Coll., 1974; L.H.D. (hon.), Newark State Coll., 1973; D.C.L. (hon.), Bloomfield Coll., 1973; Litt.D. (hon.), Montclair State Coll., 1973. Bar: N.Y. 1961, N.J. 1971. Asst. dist. atty. New York County, 1962-65; trial atty. organized crime and racketeering sect. Dept. of Justice, 1965-69; chief asst. U.S. atty. Dist. of N.J., Newark, 1969-70; U.S. atty. Dist. of N.J., 1971-74, U.S. dist. judge, 1974-87; ptnr. Stern & Greenberg, Roseland, N.J., 1990—; mem. adv. com. U. Chgo. Law Sch. Author: Judgment in Berlin, 1984 (Valley Forge award Freedoms Found. 1984, Torch of Learning award Am. Friends of Hebrew U. 1987), Trying Cases to Win, Vol. I, 1991, Vol. II, 1992, Vol. III, 1993, Vol. IV, 1995; co-author: Trying Cases to Win, Anatomy of A Trial, 1999. Trustee Hobart and William Smith Colls. Named One of America's 10 Outstanding Young Men U.S. Jr. C. of C., 1971; Swartzer scholar U. Chgo. Law Sch., 1985; recipient Dean's Club award U. Akron Sch. Law, 1986, medal of excellence Hobart Coll., 1990, Citizen's award N.J. Acad. Medicine, 1997. Fellow ABA, Am. Law Inst. (Clarence Darrow award), Internat. Platform Assn.; mem. ABA, N.J. Bar Assn., Fed. Bar Assn. (past pres. Newark chpt., recipient William J. Brennan, Jr. award 1987), Essex County Bar Assn., Am. Judicature Soc., Phi Alpha Delta. Subject of book Tiger in the Court, 1973. Office: 75 Livingston Ave Roseland NJ 07068-3701

**STERN, JOHN JULES,** lawyer; b. Paterson, N.J., Apr. 15, 1955; s. Howard and Muriel (Lubowitt) S.; children: Julianne Lauren, David Charles. Student, Northwestern U., 1972-73; BA, Brandeis U., 1976; M in Pub. Adminstrn., U. So. Calif., 1979, JD, 1979. Bar: Calif. 1979, U.S. Dist. Ct. (cen. dist.) Calif. 1979, U.S. Ct. Appeals (9th cir.) 1979, N.J. 1980, U.S. Dist. Ct. N.J. 1980, U.S. Ct. Appeals (3d cir.) 1982, U.S. Supreme Ct. 1982, U.S. Ct. Claims. Law sec. to chancery judge N.J. Superior Ct., Paterson, 1979-80; assoc. Stern, Steiger, Croland, Tanenbaum & Schielke, Paramus, N.J., 1980-83, ptnr., 1983-95; atty. Planning Bd., Montvale, N.J., 1989-93, Borough of Montvale, 1993—; ptnr. Forman Stern P.C., Paramus, 1995-97; sr. ptnr. Stern Berenbroick, LLC, Paramus, N.J., 1997—. Contbr. articles to profl. jours. Mem. ABA (jud. adminstrn. div., antitrust div. 1979—), N.J. Bar Assn., Calif. Bar Assn., Trial Attys. N.J. (trustee 1987-89), N.Y. Acad. Scis., Passaic County Bar Assn. (chmn. equity jurisprudence com. 1984—, chmn. com. civil and constl. rights 1984—), Bergen County Bar Assn., Morris County Bar Assn., Am. Judicature Soc. Democrat. Jewish. Avocations: sailing, soccer, golf. State civil litigation, Federal civil litigation, Antitrust.

**STERN, LYNNE ROTHSCHILD,** mediator, arbitrator; b. New Orleans, Feb. 1, 1947; d. Arthur Maurice and Aline Loewenberg Rothschild; m. Maurice Mayer Stern, Aug. 12, 1973; children: Maury Stern, Walter Stern. BA, U. Mich., 1968; JD, Columbia U., 1971. Bar: La. 1971; U.S. Dist. Ct. (ea. dist.) La. 1971, U.S. Ct. Appeals (5th cir.) 1971. Law clk. U.S. Dist. Ct. (ea. dist.) La., New Orleans, 1971-72; ptnr. Nelson, Nelson, Garretson, Lombard & Stern, New Orleans, 1972-74; asst. prof. Loyola Law Sch., New Orleans, 1974-76; part-time assoc. Phelps, Dunbar, New Orleans, 1981-82; cons. various attys., New Orleans, 1982-93; contract mediator The Martin Group, New Orleans, 1993-95, ADRinc., Metairie, La., 1995—. Author: (newsletter) Conflict Management, 1997. Pres. Kingsley House, New Orleans, 1988-90, Garden Dist. Assn., New Orleans, 1996-97. Mem. ABA (chmn. mediation sub-com., litigation sect. 1995—, award 1998), Nat. Healthcare Lawyers Panel of Mediators, NASD Panel of Mediators, La. Bar Assn. (program co-chmn. ADR sect. 1998—), New Orleans Bar Assn. Democrat. Jewish. Avocations: tennis. Office: ADRinc 3813 N Causeway Blvd Ste 200 Metairie LA 70002-1724

**STERN, MARK ALAN,** lawyer; b. Detroit, May 29, 1959; s. Eliot Jay and Suzanne Lee S.; m. Gretchen Mary Boss, Oct. 13, 1984; children: Sarah Ann, Daniel Joseph. BBA magna cum laude, Western Mich. U., 1981; JD summa cum laude, Wayne State U., 1984. Bar: Mich. 1984, U.S. Dist. Ct. (ea. and we. dists.) Mich. 1985, U.S. Ct. Appeals (6th cir.) 1985. Ptnr. Honigman Miller Schwartz and Cohn, Detroit, 1984—. Mem. ABA, Oakland County Bar Assn., Detroit Bar Assn. General civil litigation. Office: Honigman Miller Schwartz and Cohn 2290 1st Nat Bldg Detroit MI 48226

**STERN, RALPH DAVID,** lawyer; b. Longview, Tex., June 20, 1943; children: Eric, Justin. AB, Bucknell U., 1963; JD, U. Chgo., 1966. Bar: D.C. 1967, Ill. 1967, Calif. 1970, U.S. Supreme Ct. 1970. Law clk. Ill. Appellate Ct., Chgo., 1966-67; assoc. Ressman & Tishler, Chgo., 1968-70; exec. asst. Orange County Bd. Suprs., Santa Ana, Calif., 1970-71; gen. counsel San Diego City Schs., 1971-83; ptnr. Whitmore, Kay & Stevens, Palo Alto, Calif., 1983-88, Stern & Keebler, San Mateo, Calif., 1988-90; gen. counsel Schs. Legal Counsel, Hayward, Calif., 1990—; chmn. Nat. Coun. Sch. Attys., 1982-83; pres. Leagal Aid Soc. San Diego, 1976-79, Nat. Orgn. on Legal Problems of Edn., 1981-82. Editor: Law and the School Principal, 1978; contbr. articles to profl. jours. Mem. exec. bd., county membership chair Boy Scouts Am., San Diego, 1979-81; vice chmn. Laurels for Leaders, San Diego, 1980-83; mem. ednl. adminstrn. adv. com. U. San Diego, 1981-86.; mem. adv. com. West's Ednl. Law Reporter, 1981-85. Named Outstanding Young Citizen, San Diego Jaycees, 1977. Office: Schs Legal Counsel 313 W Winton Ave Rm 372 Hayward CA 94544-1136

**STERN, ROBERT MASON,** lawyer; b. Balt., May 9, 1944; s. Albert L. and Margaret E. (Jones) S.; m. Joan E. Venezia, Sept. 4, 1971; 1 child, Ryan. Student, Am. U., 1965; BA, Pomona Coll., 1966; JD, Stanford U., 1969. Bar: Calif. 1970, U.S. Dist. Ct. (no. dist.) Calif. 1970. Teaching fellow Stanford (Calif.) Law Sch., 1969-70; counsel assembly elections com. Calif. State Legis., Sacramento, 1971-72; elections counsel Calif. Sec. of State's Office, Sacramento, 1973-74; gen. counsel Fair Polit. Practices Commn., Sacramento, 1975-83; co-dir., gen. counsel Calif. Commn. on Campaign Financing, L.A., 1983—; host cable TV program Polit. Potpourri, L.A., 1989-93; election night polit. commentator Sta. KSMC Channel 30, Santa Monica, Calif., 1988, 90, 92; host cable TV program Rodney King Beating Trial, L.A., 1992; cons. L.A. City Ethics Commn., 1990-97; adminstr. Coun. on Govtl. Ethics Laws, 1994—; expert witness in campaign fin. cases. Co-author: The New Gold Rush, 1985, Money and Politics in Local Elections, 1989, Democracy by Initiative: Shaping California's Fourth Branch of Government, 1992, The Price of Justice, 1995, Campaign Money on the Information Highway, 1998; contbr. articles to profl. jours. Co-author Polit. Reform Act-Proposition 9 state-wide initiative, Calif., 1974; French horn player Palisades Symphony. Recipient Annual Ethics award Coun. on Govtl. Ethics, Orlando, Fla., 1988, Good Govt. award Calif. Common Cause, 1982. Mem. Americans for Nonsmokers Rights (bd. dirs. 1986-97). Avocation: playing French horn. Home: 471 21st Pl Santa Monica CA 90402-3115 Office: Ctr for Governmental Studies 10951 W Pico Blvd # 120 Los Angeles CA 90064-2126

**STERN, SHIRLEY,** lawyer, author; b. Bklyn., Aug. 16, 1929; d. Bernard and Bessie (Tasgal) Gartenstein; m. Leonard W. Stern, Dec. 24, 1949; children: Erwin Samuel, Elana Debra, Gil Avram. BA, CUNY, 1950, MA, 1956; JD, St. John's U., 1982. Bar: N.Y. 1983. Freelance writer, New Hyde Park, N.Y., 1972—; sole practice, New Hyde Park, 1983—. Author: Exploring Jewish History, 1979; Exploring Jewish Wisdom, 1980; Exploring Jewish Holidays, 1981; Exploring the Prayerbook, 1982; Exploring the Torah, 1984. Mem. Nassau County Bar Assn. Democrat. Jewish. Office: 26 Birchwood Dr New Hyde Park NY 11040-3744

**STERN, WALTER WOLF, III,** lawyer; b. Cin., Mar. 25, 1946; s. Walter W. Jr. and Harriet Louise Stern; m. Judith M. Looker, Jan. 4, 1974; 1 child, Rachael Louise. BA, Carthage Coll., 1969; JD, Marquette U., 1974. Bar: Wis. 1974, U.S. Dist. Ct. (ea. and we. dists.) Wis. 1974, U.S. Ct. Appeals (7th cir.) 1981, U.S. Supreme Ct. 1983. Pvt. practice Kenosha, Wis., 1974-82, 85-91; sr. ptnr. Joling Rizzo Willems Stern & Burroughs, Kenosha, 1982-85; pvt. practice Union Grove, Wis., 1991—; lectr. criminal law Carthage Coll., Kenosha, Wis., 1976—. Educator, Domestic Violence Project, Kenosha, 1983-94; hearing examiner Gen. Relief, Kenosha, 1990-95. Fellow Am. Acad. Forensic Scis. Avocations: fishing, hunting, jogging, reading, creative writing. Labor, Workers' compensation, Family and matrimonial. Home: PO Box 64 Union Grove WI 53182-0064 Office: Atty at Law PO Box 64 Union Grove WI 53182-0064

**STERN, WOLF H.,** lawyer; b. Gelsenkirchen, Germany, May 28, 1923; came to the U.S., 1940; s. Morris and Johanna Stern; m. Ruth Bein, July 5, 1947 (div. Nov. 1981); children: Lawrence Alan, Douglas Wayne, William Rodney, Wendy Kleeb; m. Alban Ann Powell, June 20, 1982. AA, UCLA, 1942, BA, 1947; JD, LLB, U. So. Calif., L.A., 1950. Sr. ptnr. Stern & Goldstock, Newport Beach, 1950-88; pvt. practice law Newport Beach, 1988—; pres. Bellflower Investment Co., 1964—; vice chmn. adv. bd. Bellflower Nat. Bank, 1962-64; vice chmn. Cerritos Valley BAnk, 1974-80; chmn. Bellflower Savs. & Loan, 1977-85. Pres. Bellflower-Lakewood Jewish Comm. Ctr., 1952, Bellflower Coord. Coun., 1953, Bellflower Jaycees, 1956; bd. dirs. Orange County Protocol Found. Sgt. U.S. Army Signal Corps. Named Young Man of Yr., City of Bellflower, 1954. Mem. ATLA, ABA, Calif. State Bar Assn., Orange County Bar Assn., Newport Irvine Profl. Assn. (pres. 1985, 94), Newport C. of C., Performing Arts Frat. (v.p.), Lions Internat. Costa Mesa-Newport Harbor (dist. gov. 1965-66, past pres. Bellflower Club 1954, 58). Avocations: photography, travel. Home: 49 Southampton Ct Newport Beach CA 92660-4207 Office: 170 Newport Center Dr Ste 230 Newport Beach CA 92660-6914

**STERNSTEIN, ALLAN J.,** lawyer; b. Chgo., June 7, 1948; s. Milton and Celia (Kaganove) S.; m. Miriam A. Dolgin, July 12, 1970 (div. July 1981); children—Jeffery A., Amy R.; m. Beverly A. Cook, Feb. 8, 1986; children: Cheryl L., Julia S. B.S., U. Ill., 1970; M.S., U. Mich., 1972; J.D., Loyola U., 1977. Bar: Ill. 1977, U.S. Dist. Ct. (no. dist.) Ill. 1977, U.S. Dist. Ct. (no. dist.) Ohio 1977, U.S. Dist. Ct. (ea. dist) Mich. 1986, U.S. Dist. Ct. (we. dist.) Mich. 1990, U.S. Ct. Customs and Patent Appeals 1978, U.S. Ct. Appeals (7th cir.) 1979, U.S. Ct. Appeals (Fed. cir.) 1982. Patent agent Sunbeam Corp., Oak Brook, Ill., 1972-76; ptnr. Neuman, Williams, Anderson & Olson, Chgo., 1976-84; div. patent counsel Abbott Labs., North Chgo., Ill., 1984-87; ptnr. & COO Brinks Hofer Gilson & Lione, Chgo., 1987—; adj. prof. of law John Marshall Law Sch., 1989-90, DePaul Univ., 1990-92, Univ. Ill., 1992—; lectr. Nat. Sci. and Tech. Devel. Agy. Chunlangkon U., Bangkok, Thailand, 1994; arbitrator Cir. Ct. Cook County, Ill., 1996—. Co-author: Designing an Effective Intellectual Property Compliance Program; contbr. article to profl. jour. Legal advisor Legal Aid Soc., Chgo., 1974-76, Pub. Defender's Office, Chgo., 1974. Teaching fellow U. Mich., 1971-72; research grantee U. Mich., U.S. Air Force, 1971-72. Mem. ABA, Chgo. Bar Assn., Patent Law Assn. of Chgo. (com. chmn. 1982), Am. Intellectual Property Law Assn., Licensing Execs. Soc., Tau Beta Pi, Sigma Tau, Sigma Gamma Tau, Phi Eta Sigma. Jewish. Patent, Trademark and copyright, Federal civil litigation. Office: Brinks Hofer Gilson & Lione Ste 3600 455 N Cityfront Plaza Dr Chicago IL 60611-5599

**STERRETT, SAMUEL BLACK,** lawyer, former judge; b. Washington, Dec. 17, 1922; s. Henry Hatch Dent and Helen (Black) S.; m. Jeane McBride, Aug. 27, 1949; children: Samuel Black, Robin Dent, Douglas McBride. Student, St. Albans Sch., 1933-41; grad., U.S. Mcht. Marine Acad., 1945; BA, Amherst Coll., 1947; LLB, U. Va., 1950; LLM in Taxation, NYU, 1959. Bar: D.C. 1951, Va. 1950. Atty. Alvord & Alvord, Washington, 1950-56; trial atty. Office Regional Counsel, Internal Revenue Service, N.Y.C., 1956-60; ptnr. Sullivan, Shea & Kenney, Washington, 1960-68; municipal cons. to office vice pres. U.S., 1965-68; judge U.S. Tax Ct., 1968-88, chief judge, 1985-88; ptnr. Myerson, Kuhn & Sterrett, Washington, 1988-89; of counsel Vinson & Elkins, Washington, 1990—. Bd. mgrs. Chevy Chase Village, 1970-74, chmn., 1972-74; 1st v.p. bd. trustees, mem. exec. com. Washington Hosp. Center, 1969-79, chmn. bd. trustees, 1979-84, mem. bd. trustees, 1999—; chmn. bd. trustees Washington Healthcare Corp., 1982-87; chmn. bd. trustees Medlantic Healthcare Group, 1987-89; mem. audit com. Medstar Health, 1990—; mem. Washington Cathedral, 1973-81, 99—, mem. fin. com., 1998—, chmn., 1999—; mem. governing bd. St. Albans Sch., 1977-81; trustee Louise Home, 1979-89. Served with AUS, 1943; Served with U.S. Mcht. Marine, 1943-46. Fellow Am. Bar Found.; mem. ABA, D.C. Bar Assn., Am. Coll. Tax Counsel, Soc. of the Cincinnati, Coun. for Future, Am. Inns. of Ct., Chevy Chase Club (bd. govs. 1979-84, pres. 1984), Met. Club, Lawyers Club, Alibi Club, Alfalfa Club, Ch. of N.Y. Club, Beta Theta Pi. Episcopalian. Taxation, general. Office: Vinson & Elkins 1455 Pennsylvania Ave NW Fl 7 Washington DC 20004-1013

**STETTNER, PAMELA PANASITI,** lawyer; b. Calif., Mar. 28, 1948; 1 child, Natalie. BA in Philosophy, U. So. Calif., 1969, MA in Philosophy, 1971; JD, Southwestern U., 1977. Bar: Calif. Pvt. practice Glendora, Calif., 1977—. Family and matrimonial. Office: 1433 E Alosta Ave Glendora CA 91740-3747

**STEUER, RICHARD MARC,** lawyer; b. Bklyn., June 19, 1948; s. Harold and Gertrude (Vengar) S.; m. Audrey P. Forchheimer, Sept. 9, 1973; children: Hilary, Jeremy. BA, Hofstra U., 1970; JD, Columbia U., 1973. Bar: N.Y. 1974, U.S. Dist. Ct. (ea. and so. dists.) N.Y. 1974, U.S. Ct. Appeals (2d cir.) 1974, U.S. Supreme Ct. 1979, U.S. Dist. Ct. (no. dist.) N.Y. 1984, U.S. Dist. Ct. (we. dist.) N.Y. 1997, U.S. Ct. Appeals (3d cir.) 1987, U.S. Ct. Appeals (5th cir.) 1995. Ptnr. Kaye, Scholer, Fierman, Hays & Handler LLP, N.Y.C., 1973—, co-chair antitrust practice group, 1996—; adj. assoc. prof. law NYU, 1985; lectr. in field; neutral evaluator U.S. Dist. Ct. Ea. Dist., N.Y, 1994-96. Author: A Guide to Marketing Law: Law and Business Inc., 1986; contbr. articles to profl. jours. Fellow Am. Bar Found.; mem. ABA (lectr. 1978, 85, 89, 96, 97, 98, 99, editl. bd. antitrust devel. vol. 1984-86, chmn. monograph com. refusals to deal and exclusive distributorships 1983, others, vice-chmn. program com. 1988-91, chmn. spring meeting program com. 1991-92, Sherman Act sect. 1 com. 1991-93, coun. sect. antitrust law 1993-96, chmn. publs. com. 1996-98, editl. chmn. Antitrust mag. 1998—), Assn. Bar City N.Y. (antitrust and trade regulation, internat. trade, lectures and CLE coms., lectr. 1983-97, chmn. antitrust and trade regulation 1995-98). Antitrust, Trademark and copyright, General civil litigation. Office: Kaye Scholer Fierman Hays & Handler LLP 425 Park Ave New York NY 10022-3506

**STEVENS, BETSY L.,** lawyer, social worker; b. Rochester, N.Y., Nov. 3, 1952; d. Wayne Smith and Margaret Rude (Hunt) S.; m. Dale Francis Schneeberger, Jan. 1, 1972; children: Charity Ann, Jacob Ransom. BS summa cum laude, Utica (N.Y.) Coll., 1979; JD, Syracuse (N.Y.) U., 1983, MSW, 1997. Bar: N.Y. 1984. VISTA vol. Syracuse Area Interreligious Coun., 1983-84; legal advisor Refugee Resettlement Program, Syracuse, 1985-87; dep. county atty. Onondaga County, Syracuse, 1987—; pro bono legal counsel polit. asylum case Refugee Resettlement Agy., Syracuse, 1987—; trainee children 1st program Mental Health Assocs., Syracuse; youth group leader United Meth. Ch., Fayetteville, N.Y., 1979-85. Democrat. Avocations: reading, swimming, biking, yoga. Office: Onondaga County Law Dept 421 Montgomery St Syracuse NY 13202-2923

**STEVENS, C. DANIEL,** lawyer; b. Richmond, Va., Nov. 10, 1940; s. Charles Robert and Alice Dixon Stevens; m. Sarah M. St. Clair, Jan. 24, 1963; children: John David, Robert Mark. BA, U. Richmond, 1962, LLB, 1966. Bar: Va. 1966. Assoc. McCaul, Grigsby & Pearsall, Richmond, 1966-70; assoc. Christian & Barton LLP, Richmond, 1970-76, ptnr., 1976—. Trustee Children's Hosp., Richmond, 1998—. Fellow Am. Coll. Trust and Estate Counsel; mem. Va. State Bar. Baptist. Avocations: golf, travel. Estate planning, Probate, Estate taxation. Home: 8004 Cameron Rd Richmond VA 23229-8402 Office: Christian & Barton LLP 909 E Main St Ste 1200 Richmond VA 23219-3013

**STEVENS, C. GLENN,** judge; b. Rockford, Ill., Oct. 29, 1941; s. Robert W. and Mary Louise (Shaughnessy) S.; m. Suzanne Ruth Corkery, July 4, 1967; children: Robert W., Angela M. BS, St. Louis U., 1964, JD, 1966. Bar: Ill. 1966, Mo. 1966, U.S. Dist. Ct. (so. dist.) Ill. 1966, U.S. Dist. Ct. (ea. dist.) Ill. 1968. Law clk. to judge U.S. Dist. Ct. (so. dist.) Ill., Springfield, Ill., 1966-67; instr. St. Louis U., 1967-68; assoc. Pope & Driemeyer, Belleville, Ill., 1967-74; ptnr. Pope & Driemeyer, Belleville, 1974-77; judge State of Ill., Belleville, 1977—. Bd. editors St. Louis U. Law Rev., 1965-66. Arbitrator Am. Arbitration Assn., St. Clair County, Ill, 1970-77. With U.S. Army, 1958-66. Mem. Mo. Bar Assn., Ill. Judges Assn., Am. Judges Assn., Ill. State Bar Assn., St. Clair County Bar Assn., East St. Louis Bar Assn., Phi Delta Phi (pres. Murphy Inn 1965-66). Democrat. Roman Catholic. Avocations: antique cars, soccer coach. Office: Saint Clair County Courthouse Public Sq Belleville IL 62220

**STEVENS, CHARLES J.,** lawyer, former prosecutor. BA in English, Colgate U., 1979; JD, U. Calif., Berkeley, 1982. Assoc. Gibson, Dunn & Crutcher, L.A., 1982-84; ptnr. in charge Gibson, Dunn & Crutcher, Sacramento, 1987-93; asst. U.S. atty. Office U.S. Atty., L.A., 1984-87; U.S. atty. ea. dist. Calif. U.S. Dept. Justice, Sacramento, 1993-97; ptnr., lawyer Steven & O'Connell Law Office, Sacremento, 1997—; mem. Civil Justice Reform Act com. for ea. dist. Biden Com. of Ea. Dist., 1991—; panel spkr. and lectr. in field. Contbr. articles to profl. jours. Master Anthony M. Kennedy Am. Inn. of Ct.; mem. FBA (chair program com. Sacramento chpt. 1992-93), State Bar Calif. (bd. editors Criminal Law News 1991-93). Office: 400 Capitol Mall Ste 1400 Sacramento CA 95814-4498

**STEVENS, CLARK VALENTINE,** lawyer; b. Detroit, Nov. 28, 1933; s. Valentine W. and Florence Mary (Potrykus) S.; m. Kathleen Rose Tobosky, Sept. 1, 1956; children: Mark, Glenn. B.S. in Acctg., U. Detroit, 1958; J.D., Wayne State U., 1967. C.P.A., Mich.; bar: Mich. 1967. Auditor, City of Detroit, 1958-60, IRS, 1960-65; tax mgr. Ernst & Ernst, 1965-69; mem. firm Regan & Stevens, 1969—; sec., dir. Mich. Rivet Corp., Warren, 1974—; bd. dirs. Tuff Machine Co., Warren, Mich. Mem. Mich. Bar Assn., Mich. Assn. C.P.A.s. Republican. Roman Catholic. Club: Grosse Pointe Yacht. Corporate taxation, General corporate, Estate planning. Office: Stevens & Howe PLC 23409 Jefferson Ave Ste 104 Saint Clair Shores MI 48080-3449

**STEVENS, JOHN NICKLESS,** lawyer; b. Clinton, Ill., Nov. 2, 1953; s. Harry Ronald and Ruth (Nickless) S.; m. Nancy Jeanne Haroldson, July 30, 1977. AB, U. Ill., 1975, JD, 1978. Bar: Ill. 1978, U.S. Dist. Ct. (cen. dist.) Ill. 1979. Assoc. Arnold, Gesell and Schwulst, Bloomington, Ill., 1978-81; ptnr. Arnold, Gesell and Schwulst, Bloomington, 1981-83, John N. Stevens Law Offices, Bloomington, 1983—; trustee bankruptcy U.S. Dist. Ct. (cen. dist.) Ill., 1980-86. Mem. McLean County Regional Planning Commn., 1988-91; mem. McLean County Bd., 1989—, chmn. justice com., 1990-94, chmn. fin. com., 1994—; bd. dirs. McLean County unit Am. Cancer Soc., 1980—; dir. McLean County Hist. Soc. Mem. ABA, Ill. Bar Assn. (state assembly 1986—, mem. presdl. com. on jud. polls 1989-91, membership and bar activities com. 1996—), McLean County Bar Assn. (treas. 1979-80), Ill. Bankers Assn. (com. mem.), Lincoln Club McLean County (dir., pres. 1983-84), Bloomington Country Club, Ill. Shakespeare Soc. (pres. 1990—), Rotary (pres. 1989-90). Republican. Presbyterian. Avocations: running, hiking, golf. Fax: 309-827-3305. Probate, Banking, Real property. Office: 306 N Center St Bloomington IL 61701-3903

**STEVENS, JOHN PAUL,** United States supreme court justice; b. Chgo., Apr. 20, 1920; s. Ernest James and Elizabeth (Street) S.; m. Elizabeth Jane Sheeren, June 7, 1942; children: John Joseph, Kathryn Stevens Jedlicka, Elizabeth Jane Stevens Sesemann, Susan Roberta Stevens Mullen; m. Maryan Mulholland, Dec. 1979. A.B., U. Chgo., 1941; J.D. magna cum laude, Northwestern U., 1947. Bar: Ill. 1949. Practiced in Chgo.; law clk. to U.S. Supreme Ct. Justice Wiley Rutledge, 1947-48; assoc. firm Poppenhusen, Johnston, Thompson & Raymond, 1949-52; assoc. counsel sub-com. on study monopoly power, com. on judiciary U.S. Ho. of Reps., 1951; ptnr. firm Rothschild, Stevens, Barry & Myers, 1952-70; U.S. circuit judge, 1970-75; assoc. justice U.S. Supreme Ct., 1975—; lectr. anti-trust law Northwestern U. Sch. Law,, 1952-54, U. Chgo. Law Sch., 1955-58; mem. Atty. Gen.'s Nat. Com. to Study Anti-Trust Laws, 1953-55. Served with USNR, 1942-45. Decorated Bronze Star. Mem. Chgo. Bar Assn. (2d v.p. 1970), Am., Ill., Fed. bar assns., Am. Law Inst., Order of Coif, Phi Beta Kappa, Psi Upsilon, Phi Delta Phi. Office: US Supreme Ct Supreme Court Bldg One 1st St NE Washington DC 20543

**STEVENS, MARK A.,** lawyer, environmental engineer; b. Phila., July 30, 1949; s. Raymond P. and Gertrude Stevens; m. Veronica A. Gustaferri. BA, Brandeis U., 1971; MSc in Engring., Wash. State U., Pullman, 1976; JD, Temple U., 1987. Bar: Pa., N.J. Prof. assoc. U. Man., Winnipeg, Can., 1976-78; tech. cons. BCM Engrs., Plymouth Meeting, Pa., 1978-86; assoc. Cohen Shapiro, Phila., 1987-90, Ballar Spahr, Phila., 1990-93, Wilbraham, Lawler, Phila., 1993-95; ptnr. Langsam Stevens & Morris, Phila., 1995—. Mem. ABA (litigation sect.), Pa. Bar Assn., N.J. State Bar Assn., Phila. Bar Assn. Administrative and regulatory, Environmental, Real property. Office: 1616 Walnut St Ste 812 Philadelphia PA 19103-5308

**STEVENS, PAUL SCHOTT,** lawyer; b. New Orleans, Nov. 19, 1952; s. Miles Gordon and Rosemary Louise (Schott) S.; m. Joyce Lynn Pilz, Aug. 18, 1979; Paul Schott Jr., Alexander Holmes, Andrew Colby, Carl Bernard. BA magna cum laude, Yale U., 1974; JD, U. Va., 1978. Bar: D.C. 1979, U.S. Dist. Ct. D.C. 1979, U.S. Ct. Appeals (D.C. cir.) 1979, U.S. Ct. Appeals (fed. cir.) 1983, U.S. Supreme Ct. 1982. Assoc., prin. Dickstein, Shapiro & Morin, Washington, 1978-85, ptnr., 1989-93; dep. dir., gen. counsel Pres.'s Blue Ribbon Commn. on Def. Mgmt., Washington, 1985-86; legal adviser NSC, Washington, 1987, exec. sec., 1987-89; spl. asst. to Pres. for nat. security affairs The White House, Washington, 1987-89; exec. asst. to Sec. of Defense, Washington, 1989; sr. v.p., gen. counsel Investment Co. Inst., Washington, 1993-97; sr. v.p., gen. counsel Mut. Funds and Internat. Enterprise, Charles Schwab & Co., Inc., San Francisco, 1997—; lectr. law Washington Coll. Law, Am. U., Washington, 1980-83; trustee M.G. Stevens Corp., New Orleans, 1978—; mem. quality of markets com. NASDAQ Stock Market, Inc., 1997, mem. investment cos. com. NASD Regulation, Inc., 1999—; mem. adv. bd. Ctr. Banking & Fin. Svcs. Laws, Boston U., 1996—. Chmn. bd. dirs. Student Conservation Assn., Charlestown, N.H., 1986-87, bd. dirs., 1985-91, 94-96, sec., gen. counsel, 1991-93. Recipient medal for disting. pub. svc. Dept. Def., 1989; Bates fellow Yale U., 1973, Scholar of House, 1973-74; Rotary Internat. Found. grad. fellow, 1978, U.S.-Japan Leadership fellow Japan Soc., 1989-90, assoc. fellow Saybrook Coll., Yale U., 1993—. Mem. ABA (chmn. standing com. law and nat. security 1995-98), Fed. Bar Assn., D.c. Bar Assn., Internat. Bar Assn., Coun. Fgn. Rels., Met. Club, Yale Club, Elizabethan Club, Cosmos Club. Republican. Roman Catholic. Office: care Charles Schwab & Co Inc 655 15th St NW Ste 350 Washington DC 20005-5706 also: Charles Schwab and Co Inc 101 Montgomery St San Francisco CA 94104-4122

**STEVENS, RHEA CHRISTINA,** lawyer; b. Chgo., Dec. 25, 1964; d. Samuel Nowell and Rhea Mae (Lipham) S.; m. Peter Linzer, June 20, 1992; 1 child, Grayson Nowell. BS in Psychology, U. Houston, 1989; MEd, Cambridge Coll., 1987; JD, U. Houston, 1992. Bar: Tex. 1992. Instr., client liaison Hippocrates Health Inst., Boston, 1985-86; reorganization cons. Psychotechnics, Inc., Cary, Glenview, Ill., 1987-88; pvt. practice law Houston, 1992—; founder, owner Aristic Enterprises, 1995, breeder Great Danes, Anatolian Shepherds, Papillons and Dobermans for svc. orgns. and show-August Kennels, 1988—; canine behaviorist. Rep. mid-Am. chpt. ARC to Nat. Conv., 1980; bd. dirs., treas. Clark Rd. Found., Houston, 1990-92, Houston ACLU, 1990-92; counsellor Boston Area Rape Crisis Ctr.,

1986-87. Recipient cert. commendation ARC, 1979-80. Mem. State Bar Tex. (disability issues com. 1996—, Pro Bono Coll. 1995—). Avocations: training and exhibiting dogs, locksmithing, computer consulting. Contracts commercial, Estate planning, General practice.

**STEVENS, ROGER ROSS,** lawyer; b. N.Y.C., Nov. 7, 1951; s. Stanley and Miriam S.; m. Nina Iaria, July 17, 1977; 1 child, Alexis. Student, NYU, 1969-71; BBA cum laude, Pace U., 1974, JD, 1979. Bar: N.Y. 1980, U.S. Dist. Ct. (ea. and so. dists.) N.Y. 1980. Supt. John T. Brady & Co., New Rochelle, N.Y., 1970-72; office mgr. John T. Brady & Co., 1973-79, corp. counsel, 1980-84; pvt. practice New Rochelle, 1985-86; asst. gen. counsel George A. Fuller Co., N.Y.C., 1986-94; gen. counsel PMS Cons. Mgmt. Corp., New Rochelle, N.Y., 1994—. Elected mem. Representative Town Meeting, Greenwich, 1980-98. Mem. N.Y. State Bar Assn., Am. Arbitration Assn. (arbitrator). Avocations: trap shooting, off road trucking, tennis. Construction, General corporate, Government contracts and claims. Office: PMS Cons Mgmt Corp 92 North Ave New Rochelle NY 10801-7413

**STEVENS, SCOTT ENGLISH,** lawyer; b. Longview, Tex., Apr. 15, 1969; s. Alexander Calvit and Flo (Francis) S.; m. Elaine Godsey, Nov. 18, 1995. BA, Tex. Christian U., 1991; JD, South Tex. Coll. of Law, 1994. Bar: Tex. 1994; U.S. Dist. Ct. (no. dist. and ea. dist.) Tex., 1995, U.S. Ct. Appeals (5th cir.) 1998. Law clk. Ross & Matthews, Ft. Worth, Tex., 1989-91, Vinson & Elkins, Houston, 1992-94; assoc. Harbour, Smith, Harris & Merritt, Longview, Tex., 1994—. Bd. dirs. Towne Lake Assn., Longview, 1997—, pres. 1998; bd. dirs. TCU Young Alumni Assn., Longview, 1996-97; judge TEEN Ct., Longview, 1996; vol. AHA, Longview, 1996, lectr. Law Day, 1995-97. Mem. ABA, Tex. Bar Assn., Northeast Tex. Bar Assn., Gregg County Bar Assn. Republican. Episcopalian. Avocations: golf, running, hunting. General civil litigation, Insurance, Personal injury. Office: Harbour Smith Harris & Merritt 404 N Green St Longview TX 75601-6405

**STEVENS, THOMAS CHARLES,** lawyer; b. Auburn, N.Y., Oct. 17, 1949; s. Alice (Kerlin) S.; m. Christine Eleanor Brown, June 2, 1973; children: Erin, Leigh, Timothy. BA, SUNY, Albany, 1971; JD, Duke U., 1974. Bar: Ohio 1974. Mng. ptnr. Thompson, Hine & Flory, Cleve., 1991-96; sr. exec. v.p., gen. counsel and sec. KeyCorp., Cleve., 1996—. Trustee Greater Cleve. Growth Assn., 1993-96, Greater Cleve. Roundtable, 1993—, Playhouse Sq. Found., 1998—; active Leadership Cleve., 1992-93, Young Audiences, 1999—, 1999 United Way Campaign. Mem. ABA, Cleve. Bar Assn., Am. Soc. Corp. Secs. (treas. 1998—), Nisi Prius. Banking, General corporate, Securities. Office: KeyCorp 127 Public Sq Cleveland OH 44114-1306

**STEVENS, TIMOTHY TOWLES,** lawyer; b. Allentown, Pa., Aug. 9, 1963; s. J. Timothy and Anita Lousie S.; m. Christine Marie Narzisi, Apr. 27, 1996. BA, U. N.C., 1985; JD, Villanova U., 1990. Bar: Pa. 1990, U.S. Dist. Ct. (ea. dist.) Pa. 1990, N.J. 1991, U.S. Dist. Ct. (we. dist.) Pa. 1991, V.I. 1996, U.S. Ct. Appeals (3d cir.) 1996. Intern Pa. Superior Ct., Phila., 1989; assoc. Bryant, Barnes & Simpson, Christiansted, V.I., 1996-97; ptnr. Stevens & Johnson, Allentown, Pa., 1991-96, 97—. Mem. Explorers Club. Avocations: triathlons, scuba diving, sailing, marine archaeology. General civil litigation, Appellate. Home: 1946 Willings Ln Hellertown PA 18055-2821 Office: 740 Hamilton Mall Ste 1 Allentown PA 18101-2433

**STEVENS, TODD FREDERICK,** lawyer; b. Seattle, Aug. 10, 1962; s. Robert James and Marion Orton (James) S. BA, Seattle U., 1983; JD, U. San Diego, 1988. Bar: Calif. 1988, U.S. Dist. Ct. (so. dist.) Calif. 1988. Assoc. Keeney & Waite, San Diego, 1988-95; ptnr. Keeney, Waite & Stevens, San Diego, 1995—. Legal columnist The Communicator, 1997—. Fin. com. chair Dumanis for Judge, San Diego, 1994. Recipient Pro Bono Atty. of Yr. award San Diego Vol. Lawyers, 1992, Award of Merit San Diego Legal Aid Soc., 1993. Mem. State Bar Assn. of Calif. (Pres.'s award 1992), Welsh Inn of Ct. (barrister 1996—), San Diego County Bar Assn. (bd. dirs. 1996-98, pres. 1999). Democrat. General civil litigation. Office: 550 W C St Ste 1550 San Diego CA 92101-3545

**STEVENS, WILLIAM J.,** lawyer; b. Chgo., Jan. 26, 1940; s. Richard James and Jane (Collidge) S.; m. Peggy Hess, Sept. 17, 1960; children: Mark, David. BA, U. Chgo., 1962; JD, Chgo. Kent, 1966. Bar: Ill. 1966, Ind. 1983, U.S. Dist. Ct. (no. dist.) Ill. 1966, Mich. 1996. Assoc. Tenney & Bentley, Chgo., 1966-70; ptnr. Foss Schuman & Drake, Chgo., 1970-86; pvt. practice Chgo., 1986-98; assoc. Kopka Landau & Pinkus, Crown Point, Ind., 1998—. Contbg. author: Illinois Trial Guide, 1991. Fax: 219-794-1892. Criminal, Federal civil litigation, State civil litigation. Office: Kopka Landau & Pinkus 5240 Fountain Dr Ste E Crown Point IN 46307-1000

**STEVENSON, ADLAI EWING, III,** lawyer, former senator; b. Chgo., Oct. 10, 1930; s. Adlai Ewing and Ellen (Borden) S.; m. Nancy L. Anderson, June 25, 1955; children: Adlai Ewing IV, Lucy W., Katherine R., Warwick L. Grad., Milton Acad., 1948; A.B., Harvard U., 1952, LL.B., 1957. Bar: Ill. 1957, D.C. 1977. Law clk. Ill. Supreme Ct., 1957-58; assoc. Mayer, Brown & Platt, Chgo., 1958-66; ptnr. Mayer, Brown & Platt, 1966-67, 81-83, of counsel, 1983-91; treas. State of Ill., 1967-70; U.S. senator from Ill., 1970-81; chmn. SC&M Internat. Ltd., Chgo., 1991-95, pres., 1995-98, chmn. of bd., 1998—. Mem. Ill. Ho. of Reps., 1965-67; Dem. candidate for gov. of Ill., 1982, 86. Capt. USMCR, 1952-54. Private international. Office: 225 W Wacker Dr Chicago IL 60606-1224

**STEVENSON, JAMES RICHARD,** radiologist, lawyer; b. Ft. Dodge, Iowa, May 30, 1937; s. Lester Lawrence and Esther Irene (Johnson) S.; m. Sara Jean Hayman, Sept. 4, 1958; children: Bradford Allen, Tiffany Ann, Jill Renee, Trevor Ashley. BS, U. N.Mex., 1959; MD, U. Colo., 1963; JD, U. N.Mex. 1987. Diplomate Am. Bd. Radiology, Am. Bd. Nuclear Medicine, Am. Bd. Legal Medicine, 1989; Bar: N.Mex. 1987, U.S. Dist. Ct. N.Mex. 1988. Intern U.S. Gen. Hosp., Tripler, Honolulu, 1963-64; resident in radiology U.S. Gen. Hosp., Brook and San Antonio, Tex., 1964-67; radiologist, ptnr. Van Atta Labs., Albuquerque, 1970-88, Radiology Assocs. of Albuquerque, 1988—, pres., 1994-96; radiologist, ptnr. Civerolo, Hansen & Wolf, Albuquerque, 1988-89; adj. asst. prof. radiology U. N.Mex., 1970-71; pres. med. staff AT & SF Meml. Hosp., 1979-80, chief of staff, 1980-81, trustee, 1981-83. Author: District Attorney manual, 1987. Participant breast screening, Am. Cancer Soc., Albuquerque, 1987-88; dir. profl. divsn. United Way, Albuquerque, 1975. Maj. U.S. Army 1963-70, Vietnam; col. M.C. USAR, 1988—. Decorated Bronze Star. Allergy fellow, 1960. Med.-Legal Tort Scholar award, 1987. Fellow Am. Coll. Radiology (councilor 1980-86, mem. med. legal com. 1990-96), Am. Coll. Legal Medicine, Am. Coll. Nuclear Medicine, Radiology Assn. of Albuquerque; mem. AMA (Physicians' Recognition award 1969—), Am. Soc. Law & Medicine, Am. Arbitration Assn., Albbuquerque Bar Assn., Am. Coll. Nuclear Physicians (charter), Soc. Nuclear Medicine (v.p. Rocky Mountain chpt. 1975-76), Am. Inst. Ultrasound in Medicine, N.Am. Radiol. Soc. (chmn. med. legal com. 1992-95), N.Mex. Radiol. Soc. (pres. 1978-79), N.Mex. Med. Soc. (chmn. grievance com.), Albuquerque-Bernalillo County Med. Soc. (scholar 1959), Nat. Assn. Health Lawyers, ABA (antitrust sect. 1986—), N. Mex. State Bar, Albuquerque Bar Assn., Sigma Chi. Republican. Methodist. Club: Albuquerque Country. Lodges: Elks, Masons, Shriners. Home: 3333 Santa Clara Ave SE Albuquerque NM 87106-1530 Office: Medical Arts Imaging Ctr A-6 Med Arts Sq 801 Encino Pl NE Albuquerque NM 87102-2612

**STEVENSON, R.J. (RANDY STEVENSON),** lawyer; b. Omaha, Sept. 22, 1959; s. John W. and Lorraine M. (Smith) S.; m. Laura D. Caporale, Aug. 18, 1984; children: Elizabeth A., Samuel C. BSBA, U. Nebr., Omaha, 1982; JD, U. Nebr., Lincoln, 1985. Bar: Nebr. 1985, U.S. Dist. Ct. Nebr. 1985, Iowa, 1996. Assoc. Baird Holm Law Firm, Omaha, 1985-90, ptnr., 1991—. Chmn. bd. dirs. BBB, Omaha, 1996—. Mem. Nebr. State Bar Assn. (exec. com. labor and employment law sect. 1994—), Human Resources Assn. of the Midlands (legis. com. 1990—), Rotary (bd. dirs. 1995-98). Presbyterian. Avocations: golf, travel. Labor. Office: Baird Holm Law Firm 1500 Woodmen Tower Omaha NE 68102

**STEVENSON, ROBERT BRUCE,** lawyer; b. Detroit, Jan. 28, 1951; s. Allan M. and Rose A. (Ferriole) S.; m. Sharon A. Buslepp, Mar. 19, 1982; children: Ruth, Kate. BA with highest honors, Mich State U., 1973; JD, U. Mich., 1976. Bar: Mich. 1976. Assoc. Hill, Lewis, Adams, Goodrich & Taft, Detroit, 1976-82, ptnr., 1982-86; assoc. Rose, Schmidt, Chapman, Duff & Hasley, Ann Arbor, Mich., 1986-87; ptnr. Stevenson Keppelman Assocs., Ann Arbor, 1987—. Author: Incorporating the Small Business - A Systems Approach, 1983. Mem. State Bar Mich. (chmn. employment benefits com., tax sect. 1987-89). Avocation: skiing. Pension, profit-sharing, and employee benefits. Office: 444 S Main St Ann Arbor MI 48104-2304

**STEVENSON, ROBIN HOWARD,** lawyer; b. Marlborough, Mass., Nov. 9, 1961; s. Gerald Howard and Rosemary Pearl Stevenson; m. René Collette Cone, Dec. 19, 1987; children: Victoria Collette. BA, U. South Fla., 1986; JD, U. Fla., 1992. Bar: Fla. 1993, U.S. Dist. Ct. (mid. dist.) Fla. 1994. Asst. pub. defender Pub. Defender's Office 10th Jud. Cir./Fla., Sebring, 1994; assoc. Weaver and Assocs., Lake Wales, Fla., 1994-98; sole practitioner Bartow, Fla., 1998—. Capt. U.S. Army Res., 1991—. Mem. Polk County Trial Lawyers Assn., Polk County Criminal Def. Lawyers Assn., Rex Quality Corp. Homeowners Assn. (pres. 1995-98), Kiwanis Club. Methodist. Avocations: weightlifting, running, fishing, reading, coin collecting. General civil litigation, Criminal, Appellate. Office: 1640 N Park Ave Bartow FL 33830-3105

**STEWARD, JAMES BRIAN,** lawyer, pharmacist; b. Cleve., Mar. 25, 1946; s. Louis Fred and Helen Elaine (Goodwin) S.; m. Betty Kay Krans, Dec. 14, 1968; children: Christina Lynn, Brian Michael. BS in Pharmacy, Ferris State Coll., 1969; JD, U. Mich., 1973. Bar: Mich. 1973, U.S. Dist. Ct. (we. dist.) Mich. 1979, U.S. Cir. Ct. (6th Cir.) 1980, U.S. Supreme Ct. 1986. Pharmacist Revco Pharmacies, Grand Rapids, Mich., 1969-70, Coll. Pharmacy, Ypsilanti, Mich., 1970-73; assoc. Bridges & Collins, Negaunee, Mich., 1973-80; ptnr. Steward, Peterson, Sheridan & Nancarrow, Ishpeming, Mich., 1980-94, Steward & Sheridan, Ishpeming, 1995—. Mem., chmn. Negaunee Commn. on Aging, 1974-86; mem., chmn., sec. Marquette County Commn. on Aging, 1976-82; trustee, v.p., pres. Negaunee Bd. Edn., 1984-88, 91-95; mem., chmn., adv. bd. trustee Ishpeming Area Cmty. Fund, 1995—; mem. combined ad hoc com. Marquette County Commn. on Aging, 1996. Mem. Mich. Bar Assn., Marquette County Bar Assn. (sec.- treas., v.p., pres.), Am. Soc. for Pharmacy Law, Ishpeming Cross County Ski Club, Superiorland Cross Country Ski Club, Wawonowin Country Club, Phi Delta Chi, Rho Chi. Avocations: cross country ski racing, downhill and water skiing, running, biking, classic cars. General corporate, Probate, Real property. Office: 205 S Main St Ishpeming MI 49849-2018

**STEWART, C. GREGORY,** lawyer. Grad., Rutgers Coll., 1971; Masters, Rutgers U., 1981, JD, 1975. Bar: U.S. Supreme Ct., U.S. Ct. Appeals (3d cir.), U.S. Dist. Ct. N.J. Staff atty. Lawyer's Com. Civil Rights Under Law, Washington, 1982-84; dir. divsn. civil rights N.J. Dept. Law and Pub. Safety, 1990-95; gen. counsel Equal Employment Opportunity Commn., Washington, 1995—; adj. prof. Rutgers Sch. of Law.; instr. John Jay Coll., N.Y.C. Recipient Cmty. Svc. award N.J. Conf. NAACP, Equal Justice Medal Legal Svc. of N.J., Disting. Leadership award in Edn. N.J. Assn. Black Educators. N.J. State Bar Assn., Nat. Bar Assn., ABA. Office: EEOC 1801 L St NW Washington DC 20507-0001*

**STEWART, CARL E.,** federal judge; b. 1950. BA magna cum laude, Dillard U., 1971; JD, Loyola U., New Orleans, 1974. Atty. Piper & Brown, Shreveport, La., 1977-78; staff atty. La. Atty. Gen. Office, Shreveport, 1978-79; asst. U.S. atty. Office U.S. Atty. (we. dist.) La., Shreveport, 1979-83; prin. Stewart & Dixon, Shreveport, 1983-85; spl. asst. dist. atty., asst. prosecutor City of Shreveport, 1983-85; judge La. Dist. Ct., 1985-91, La. Ct. Appeals (2d cir.), 1991-94, U.S. Ct. Appeals (5th cir.), 1994—; adj. instr. dept. mgmt. and mktg. La. State U., Shreveport, 1982-85. Mem. chancellor's adv. bd. La. State U., Shreveport, 1983-89, chmn., 1988-89; mem. black achievers program steering com. YMCA, 1990; active NAACP, 1988—. Capt. JAGC, 1974-77, Tex. Mem. ABA, Nat. Bar Assn., Am. Inns. of Ct. (Harry Booth chpt. Shreveport), Black Lawyers Assn. Shreveport-Bossier, La. Conf. Ct. Appeal Judges, La. State Bar Assn. (bench/bar liaison com.), Omega Psi Phi (Rho Omega chpt.). Office: US Ct Appeals 5th Cir 300 Fannin St Ste 2299 Shreveport LA 71101-3124

**STEWART, CHARLES EVAN,** lawyer; b. N.Y.C., Mar. 4, 1952; s. Charles Thorp and Jenifer Jennings (Barbour) S.; m. Cathleen Bacich, June 26, 1982 (div. Nov. 1986); m. Patricia A. McGlothlin, Sept. 10, 1988; 1 child, Charlotte Jenifer. BA cum laude, Cornell U., 1974, JD, 1977. Bar: N.Y. 1978, U.S. Dist. Ct. (so. and ea. dists.) N.Y. 1978, U.S. Ct. Appeals (2d cir.) 1978, U.S. Ct. Appeals (D.C. and 7th cirs.) 1980, U.S. Ct. Appeals (3d, 9th and 5th cirs.) 1981, U.S. Supreme Ct. 1981, U.S. Ct. Appeals (10th cir.) 1982, U.S. Claims Ct. 1983, U.S. Ct. Appeals (6th cir.) 1986. Assoc. Donovan Leisure Newton & Irvine, N.Y.C., 1977-86; 1st v.p., assoc. gen. counsel E.F. Hutton and Co., Inc., N.Y.C., 1987-88; exec. v.p., gen. counsel Nikko Securities Co. Internat., N.Y.C., 1988—; spl. asst. dist. atty. N.Y. County, 1979-80; adj. prof. Fordham U. Law Sch., 1996—; arbitrator NYSE, NASD. Contbr. articles to legal jours. Trustee Cornell U., vice chmn. adv. coun. Coll. Arts and Scis., mem. adv. coun. Law Sch.; trustee Nat. YWCA, Am. Hist. Assn. Mem. Assn. Bar City N.Y. (young lawyers com. 1979-83, uniform laws com. 1984-86, corp. law dept. com. 1988-91, spl. com. on Asian affairs 1989-91, securities regulation com. 1996—), Fed. Bar Coun. (com. on 2d cir. cts. 1978-93, trustee 1996—), Am. Soc. Internat. Law, Securities Industry Assn. (fed. regulation com. 1990—, chmn. 1996-98, lit. com. 1994—), Westminster Sch. Alumni Assn. (exec. com.), Downtown Athletic Club, Univ. Club, Kennebunk River Club, Arundel Beach Club, Madison Beach Club, Chevy Chase Club. Republican. Episcopalian. General corporate, Securities, General civil litigation. Home: 122 E 82d St New York NY 10028-0822 Office: Nikko Securities Co Internat 79th Fl One World Trade Center New York NY 10048

**STEWART, CRAIG HENRY,** lawyer, consultant; b. Houma, La., Oct. 31, 1965; s. Jerry and Corine (Jackson) S.; m. Angela Marie Wilson, July 2, 1993; children: Michelle, Shanelle, Christina. AS in Law Enforcement, Grambling State U., 1985, BS in Criminal Justice, 1986; JD, So. U., Baton Rouge, 1995. Bar: La., U.S. Dist. Ct. (ea., mid. and we. dists.) La. 1998. Narcotics investigator Terrebonne Parish Sheriff's Office, Houma, 1988-92; atty. Block & LaBat, Thibodaux, La., 1995-97, Indigent Defender's Bd., Houma, 1997, Law Office of Craig H. Stewart, Houma, 1997-98; city prosecutor City of Houma, 1998—. Lt. USMC, 1986-90. Democrat. Baptist. Avocations: running, reading, weightlifting, golf, my children. Personal injury, Admiralty, Criminal. Home: 216 Evelyn Ave Houma LA 70363-5434 Office: 7833 Main St Houma LA 70360-4455

**STEWART, DAVID PENTLAND,** lawyer, educator; b. Milw., Dec. 24, 1943; s. James Pentland and Frederica (Stockwell) S.; children from previous marriage: Jason, Jonathan; m. Jennifer Kilmer, June 21, 1986; children: Daniel, Mary Elizabeth. AB, Princeton U., 1966; JD, MA, Yale U., 1971; LLM, N.Y.U., 1975. Bar: N.Y. 1972, U.S. Dist. Ct. (ea. and so. dists.) N.Y. 1973, U.S. Ct. Appeals (2d cir.) 1973, D.C. 1976. Assoc. Donovan, Leisure, Newton & Irvine, N.Y.C., 1971-76; atty. adviser, office of legal adviser U.S. Dept. State, Washington, 1976-82, asst. legal adviser, 1982—; adj. prof. law Georgetown U., Washington, 1984—, Am. U., Washington, 1985-86; vis. lectr. Sch. Law U. Va., 1993-96, Nat. Law Ctr., George Washington U., 1993—. Contbr. articles to profl. jours.; also editorial adv. bds. Mem. dean's adv. coun. internat. law Am. U., 1984-88. Served to maj. USAR, 1970-87. Mem. ABA, Fed. Bar Assn., Am. Soc. Internat. Law., Internat. Law Assn. (adv. coun. procedural aspects internat. law inst.). Office: US Dept State Office Legal Adviser Washington DC 20520-0001

**STEWART, DAVID ROBERT,** lawyer; b. Evanston, Ill., Apr. 18, 1960; s. Robert Henry and Frances Catherine S. AB, Harvard U., 1982; MS, Edinburgh U., Scotland, 1984; JD, U. Calif., Berkeley, 1986. Bar: Ill. 1986, U.S. Dist. Ct. (no. dist.) Ill. 1987, U.S. Ct. Appeals (3rd cir.) 1996. Ptnr. Sidley & Austin, Chgo., 1986—. Editor Calif. Law Rev., 1984-85, note and comment editor, 1985-86. Grad. fellow Rotary Found., 1984. Mem. ABA, Boalt Hall Alumni Assn. (bd. dirs. 1998—). Avocation: backpacking. Securities, Antitrust, Administrative and regulatory. Office: Sidley & Austin 875 3rd Ave Fl 14 New York NY 10022-6293

**STEWART, ELLEN ELIZABETH,** lawyer; b. Englewood, N.J., May 14, 1955; d. John Morrow and Joyce (Clark) Stewart; m. Donald Robert Vancil, Dec. 13, 1986. BA, U. Colo., Boulder, 1977; MS in Health Adminstrn., U. Colo., Denver, 1979; JD, U. Denver, 1984. Bar: Colo. 1984, U.S. Dist. Ct. Colo. 1984, U.S. Ct. Appeals (10th cir.) 1986. Corp. analyst PSL Healthcare Corp., Denver, 1979-84, assoc. gen. counsel, 1984-86; atty. Gorsuch Kirgis, Denver, 1986—, ptnr., 1990—; mem. faculty Univ. Coll., U. Denver, 1986—; hon. faculty U. Colo. Denver Health Adminstrn. Program, 1986—. Mem. editl. adv. bd. Assn. Regional Acctg. Firms, Norcross, Ga., 1990—, Healthcare Fin. Mgmt. Assn., Westchester, Ill., 1992—; contbr. articles to profl. jours. Bd. dirs. Qualife Wellness Cmty., Denver, 1996—, Med. Care and Rsch. Found., Denver, 1995—, Cancer League of Colo., Denver, 1993—. Fellow Healthcare Fin. Mgmt. Assn. (pres. Colo. chpt. 1992-93, medal of Honor 1997); mem. Colo. Bar Assn. (chair health law sect. 1995-96), Colo. Women's Forum in Health Advocacy (pres. 1989-90). Republican. Presbyterian. Avocations: gourmet cooking, decorating, art collecting, travel. Health. Office: Gorsuch Kirgis LLP 1515 Arapahoe St Denver CO 80202-3150

**STEWART, HARRY A.,** lawyer; b. Daytona Beach, Fla., Aug. 7, 1940. BSBA, U. Fla., 1966, JD, 1973. Bar: Fla. 1974, U.S. Dist. Ct. (mid. dist.) Fla. 1974, U.S. Dist. Ct. (so. dist.) Fla. 1976, U.S. Ct. Appeals (5th cir.) 1974, U.S. Ct. Appeals (11th cir.) 1981, U.S. Supreme Ct. 1980. County atty. Broward County, Fla., 1978-84, Orange County, Fla., 1984-91; ptnr. Akerman, Senterfitt & Eidson, P.A., Orlando, Fla.; pres. Fla. Assn. County Attys., 1981-82, 89-91. Mem. ABA (natural resources law sect.), The Fla. Bar (govt. law and environ. law sects., chmn. local govt. law sect. 1981-82). E-mail: hstewart@akerman.com. Real property, Finance, Land use and zoning (including planning). Office: Akerman Senterfitt & Eidson PA PO Box 231 255 S Orange Ave Orlando FL 32802-3445

**STEWART, HUGH W.,** lawyer; b. Chgo., Feb. 27, 1921; s. John Carnduff and Agnes Emerita S.; m. Jeannette A., June 10, 1944; children: Gregory (dec.), Mary Jo, Julie, Jane, Elizabeth, Paul, Andrew, Cecilia. Student, St. John's Coll. U. Oxford, 1962; JD, U. Ariz., 1950. Sole practice law Tucson, 1963—. Commr. Indsl. Commn. Ariz., 1969-75; bd. dirs. State Compensation Fund Ariz., 1996—; fin. com. Pima County Rep. Party, Tucson. Lt. col. USAF, 1942-63. Mem. Air Force Assn. (nat. bd. dirs. 1966-69, 71-74), Phi Delta Phi. Republican. Roman Catholic. Avocations: golf, hunting, fishing. General corporate, Probate, Personal injury. Office: 5363 E Pima St Ste 200 Tucson AZ 85712-3663

**STEWART, ISAAC DANIEL, JR.,** state supreme court justice; b. Salt Lake City, Nov. 21, 1932; s. Isaac Daniel and Orabelle (Iverson) S.; m. Elizabeth Bryan, Sept. 10, 1959; children: Elizabeth Ann, Shannon. BA with high honors, U. Utah, 1959, JD with high honors, 1962. Bar: Utah 1962, U.S. Dist. Ct. Utah 1962, U.S. Ct. Appeals (10th cir.) 1962, U.S. Ct. Appeals (4th cir.) 1963, U.S. Ct. Appeals (9th cir.) 1964, U.S. Ct. Appeals (8th cir.) 1965, U.S. Supreme Ct. 1965. Atty. antitrust divsn. Dept. Justice, Washington, 1962-65; asst. prof., then assoc. prof. U. Utah Coll. Law, 1965-70; ptnr. Jones, Waldo, Holbrook & McDonough, Salt Lake City, 1970-79; assoc. justice Utah Supreme Ct., 1979—, assoc. chief justice, 1986-88, 94-98, assoc. justice, 1999—; lectr. in field; mem. Utah Bd. Oil, Gas and Mining, 1976-78, chmn., 1977-78; Utah rep. Interstate Oil Compact Commn., 1977-78, exec. com. 1978-79; mem. adv. com. rules of procedure Utah Supreme Ct., 1983-87; chmn. com. on bar-press guidelines Utah Bar; mem. U. Utah search com., 1968-70; legal advisor, 1966-68. Editor-in-chief Utah Law Rev.; contbr. articles to legal jours. Chmn. subcom. on legal rights and responsibilities of youth Utah Gov's Com. on Youth, 1972; pres. Salt Lake chpt. Coun. Fgn. Rels., 1982; mem. Salt Lake City C. of C., 1974-79, mem. govtl. modernization com., 1976-78; missionary for Mormon Ch. in Fed. Republic Germany, 1953-56; bd. dirs. U. Utah Alumni Assn., 1986-89. Recipient Alumnus of Yr. award U. Utah Coll. Law, 1989. Mem. ABA, Utah Bar Assn. (com. on law and poverty 1967-69, com. on specialization 1977-78, pub. rels. com. 1968-69, chmn. com. on antitrust law 1977-78, com. on civil procedure reform 1968, mem. exec. com. bd. of appellate judges 1990—, liaison to supreme and adv. coms. evidence & profl. conduct 1986—, Appellate Judge of Yr. 1986), Salt Lake County Bar Assn., Am. Judicature Soc., Order of Coif, Phi Beta Kappa, Phi Kappa Phi, Sigma Chi (Significant Sig award 1987). Office: Utah Supreme Ct PO Box 140210 450 S State St Salt Lake City UT 84114-0210*

**STEWART, JAMES KEVIN,** judicial administrator, management technology consultant; b. Berkeley, Calif., Nov. 28, 1942; s. Berthold and Myrle (Minson) S.; m. Marise Rene Duff, Oct. 26, 1985; children: Daphne Brooks, Andrew MacLaren, James Kevin Spencer, Mary Elizabeth Ainsley. B.S., U. Oreg., 1964; M.P.A., Calif. State U.-Hayward, 1977; grad. cert., U. Va., 1978; grad., FBI Nat. Acad., 1978. Cmmdr. criminal investigation div. Oakland Police Dept., 1976-81; instr. San Jose (Calif.) State U., 1978-81; spl. asst. atty. gen. Dept. Justice, Washington, 1981-82; dir. Nat. Inst. Justice, Washington, 1982-90, Booz, Allen & Hamilton, Inc., McLean, Va., 1990—; guest lectr. U. Calif., Berkeley, Harvard, U.; steering com. global organized crime initiative Ctr. Strategic Internat. Studies, 1994; U.S. del. Couns. of Europe, Strasborg, France, 1984; advisor DOD/DOJ Ops. Other Than War and Law Enforcement, 1994; chmn. pun. safety conf. SPTE, 1992; advisor, chmn. Dept. Justice Nat. Conf. Law Enforcement Tech., 21st Century, Washington, 1993; bd. dirs. White House Fellows Found., 1990; mem. Internat. Law Enforcement Conf., Washington, 1995. Recipient O.W. Wilson award for outstanding contbns. to law enforcement, 1986, Ennis J. Olgiati award Nat. Assn. Pre-Trial Services Agys., 1987, Predl. citation AIA, 1987, Nat. Criminal Justice Service award Nat. Criminal Justice Assn., 1988, Outstanding Nat. Contbn. to Policing Spl. award Police Exec. Research Forum, 1988, August Vollmer award Am. Soc. Criminology, 1992; White House fellow, 1981-82. Mem. Internat. Assn. Chiefs of Police (dir. 1981-82), Police Mgmt. Assn. (founder, pres. 1979-81), White House Fellows Alumni, White House Fellows Found. (bd. dirs.), FBI Nat. Acad. Assn., Internat. Homicide Investigation Assn. (charter), Nat. Inst. Corrections (bd. dirs.), Soc. for Reform of Criminal Law (planning chmn. Police Powers and Citizens Rights Conf.), Coun. For Excellence In Govt. (prin.), Delta Upsilon. Republican. Episcopalian. Club: University (Washington). Home: 503 Roosevelt Blvd Apt A424 Falls Church VA 22044-3117 Office: Booz Allen & Hamilton Inc 8283 Greensboro Dr Ste 700 Mc Lean VA 22102-3838

**STEWART, JAMES MALCOLM,** lawyer; b. Aberdeen, Wash., May 8, 1915; s. Malcolm M. and Ethel Lucille (Hinman) S.; m. Dorothy Vera Giardi, Sept. 16, 1945; children: Barbara Jane, Robert Bruce, William James. BA, U. Wash., 1939, JD, 1941. Bar: Wash., 1941, U.S. Dist. Ct. (we. dist.) Wash., 1948, U.S. Supreme Ct., 1998. Dep. prosecuting atty. Grays Harbor County, Wash., 1945-48; pvt. practice Montesano, Wash., 1952-99. Pres., dir. Gray Harbor Coll. Found., Aberdeen, 1955-95; bd. dirs. St. Joseph Hosp., Aberdeen, 1972-87; organizer Gray Harbor Cmty. Found., Aberdeen, 1993; scout leader Boy Scouts Am. Lt. USNR, 1942-45, PTO, admirality officer, 1945-46, lt. comdr., 1950-52, Korea, ret. Decorated 16 Battle Stars, 2 Silver Stars, Gold Star. Mem. Am. Judicature Soc., Wash. State Bar Assn. (50 Yr. award, 1991), Gray Harbor Bar Assn. (pres. 1953), Aberdeen Pioneers Assn. (pres., dir. 1948-98), Lions (Melvin Jones award 1997), Elks, Sigma Nu, Phi Delta Phi. Republican. Episcopalian. Avocations: tree farming, hiking, horseback riding, tennis. General corporate, Estate planning, General practice. Home: 711 3rd St N # D Montesano WA 98563-1625

**STEWART, JEFFREY B.,** lawyer, commodity trading advisor; b. Chgo., Feb. 6, 1952; s. Bruce A. and Harriet B. Stewart. A.B. magna cum laude (Rufus Choate scholar), Dartmouth Coll., 1974; J.D., Emory U., 1978. Bar: Ga. 1978, U.S. Dist. Ct. (no. dist.) Ga., U.S. Ct. Appeals (5th and 11th dists.). Ptnr., chair corp. dept., Arnall Golden & Gregory, Atlanta, 1978—. Mem. editorial bd. Emory Law Jour., 1977-78. Mem. ABA, State Bar Ga. Mergers and acquisitions, Securities, Health. Home: 4110 Pine Heights Dr NE Atlanta GA 30324-2847 Office: Arnall Golden & Gregory 1201 W Peachtree St NW Ste 2800 Atlanta GA 30309-3450

**STEWART, JOSEPH GRIER,** lawyer; b. Tuscaloosa, Ala., July 24, 1941; s. Jesse Grier and Kyle Vann (Pruett) S.; m. Linda Louise Hogue, Mar. 2, 1963; children: Joseph Grier Jr., Robert Byars, James Vann. BS, U. Ala., Tuscaloosa, 1963, LLB, 1966. Bar: Ala. 1966, U.S. Dist. Ct. (no. dist.) Ala. 1968, U.S. Dist. Ct. (middle Dist.of Ala.), 1996, U.S. Tax Court. Ptnr. Burr & Forman LLP, Birmingham, Ala., 1968—. Mem. ABA, Ala. State Bar, Birmingham Bar Assn. (chmn. com. 1989-90), Ala. Law Inst., Kiwanis, Birmingham Tip Off Club (pres. 1988-89). Methodist. Avocation: tennis. General corporate, Contracts commercial, Mergers and acquisitions. Office:

Burr & Forman LLP 3100 S Trust Tower 420 20th St N Birmingham AL 35203-5200

**STEWART, JUDITH A.,** lawyer. U.S. atty. So. Dist. Ind., Indpls., 1993—. Office: US Attys Office US Courthouse 5th Fl 46 E Ohio St Ste 500 Indianapolis IN 46204-1986

**STEWART, KENNETH PARSONS,** lawyer; b. Salina, Kans., July 2, 1924; s. Everett Emerson and Irene Marguerite (Parsons) S.; m. Marjorie Fern Correll, Apr. 30, 1944; children: Gail Sue, Julie Kay Stewart Russell, Marti Irene. AB in Oriental Langs., U. Mich., 1948, JD, 1950. Bar: Kans. U.S. Dist. Ct. Kans. Assoc. Boyer, Hondros & Donaldson, Wichita, Kans., 1950-54; ptnr. Boyer, Hondros & Donaldson, Wichita, 1954-68; ptnr. Boyer, Donaldson & Stewart, Wichita, 1968-94, sr. ptnr., 1994—; exec. coun., dir. United Ch. of Christ, N.Y.C., 1967-75. Dir. United Way Sedgwick County, Wichita, 1968-75; charter mem., dir. Kans. Health Ethics, Wichita, 1994—; precinct committeeman Rep. Party Sedgwick County, Wichita, 1996—. Mem. Kans. Bar Assn. (chair mediation 1993), Wichita Bar Assn. (mediation com. 1990-96). Avocations: jogging, swimming, gardening, volunteering, church and non-profit organizations. General corporate, Probate, Non-profit and tax-exempt organizations. Home: 1441 Spring Dr Wichita KS 67208-2418 Office: 1030 1st Nat Bank Bldg 106 W Douglas Ave Ste 1030 Wichita KS 67202-3300

**STEWART, MARK STEVEN,** lawyer; b. Palestine, Tex., Jan. 1, 1950; s. Bruce F. and Diana Wilba (Franks) S.; divorced; children: Steven Andrew, Carlton Preston, Preston Holmes, Mackenzie Elizabeth; m. Jennifer Ann Barefield, July 18, 1987. B.A., U. Tex., 1971, J.D., 1975. Bar: Tex. 1975, U.S. Dist. Ct. (no. dist.) Tex. 1976; bd. cert. in personal injury, trial law, Tex. Bd. Legal Specialization, 1982. Assoc. McDonald, Sanders et al., Ft. Worth, 1975-78; ptnr. Kugle, Stewart, Dent & Frederick, Ft. Worth, 1978-89; Mark S. Stewart & Assocs., 199); bd. dirs. Tarrant County Trial Lawyers, Ft. Worth, 1984-88. Inc. Mem. Assn. Trial Lawyers Am., Tex. Trial Lawyers Assn., Tarrant County Bar Assn. Personal injury, Workers' compensation. Home: 5100 Crestline Rd Fort Worth TX 76107-3617 Office: 1300 Summit Ave Ste 700 Fort Worth TX 76102-4424

**STEWART, MELINDA JANE,** judge; b. Merced, Calif., Apr. 10, 1949; d. Donald Joel and Betty Yvonne (Santi) S.; m. Brice G. Wilbur, Aug. 1998; children from previous marriage: Alexa Marie, Julienne Rose, Robert Patrick; stepchildren: Michelle, Keith, Kelly, Kevin. BA, Stanford U., 1972; JD, Golden Gate Law Sch., 1975. Bar: Calif. 1975, U.S. Dist. Ct. (no. dist.) Calif. 1975. Dep. dist. atty. Santa Clara County Dist. Atty., San Jose, Calif., 1976-80; atty. Miller & Hinkle Law Offices, San Jose, 1980; pvt. practice Tondreau & Goodman, San Jose, 1980-83; referee Santa Clara County Superior Ct., San Jose, 1983-89, judge, 1989—; faculty Calif. Ctr. for Jud. Edn. and Rsch., 1983—. Bd. dirs. Eastfield Ming Quong Childrens Ctr., 1993-98, pro bono project of Santa Clara County, 1992-95, YWCA Kids Connection, 1993-95, Hillbrook Sch., 1993-98. Named Calif. State Bar Assn. Family Law Judge of Yr., 1995; recipient Henry B. Collada Meml. award, 1995. Mem. Calif. Judges Assn., Assn. Family and Conciliation Cts. (Calif. chpt. bd. dirs.). Avocations: swimming, tennis, skiing. Office: Superior Ct Santa Clara County 191 N 1st St San Jose CA 95113-1001

**STEWART, PAMELA L.,** lawyer; b. Bogalusa, La., Mar. 13, 1953; d. James Adrian and Patricia Lynn (Wood) Lloyd; m. Steven Bernard Stewart, Aug. 31, 1974 (div. July 1980); 1 child, Christopher. BA, U. New Orleans, 1986; JD, U. Houston, 1990. Intern La. Supreme Ct., New Orleans, 1984, Councilman Bryan Wagner, New Orleans, 1984-85; legal asst. Clann, Bell & Murphy, Houston, 1988-89, Tejas Gas Corp., Houston, 1989-90; atty. Law Offices of Pamela L. Stewart, Katy, Tex., 1991—. Bd. dirs. Alliance for Good Govt., New Orleans, 1983-84, Attention Deficit Hyperactivity Disorder Assn. Tex., 1989-90; vol. Houston Vol. Lawyers Program, Houston, 1992—; mem. Planned Giving Coun. Innsbruck scholar, U. New Orleans, 1985. Fellow Inst. Politics; mem. ABA, Am. Bankruptcy Inst., Tax Freedom Inst., Nat. Assn. Consumer Bankruptcy Attys., Nat. Assn. Elder Law Attys., Am. Networking Trust Planning Attys., Houston Bar Assn., Nat. Assn. of Chpt. 13 Trustees (assoc.), Katy Bar Assn. (3d v.p. 1997-98), Houston Assn. Debtors Attys. (pres. 1996-98), Am. Acad. Estate Planning Attys., Upper Kirby Dist. Optimist Club, Planned Giving Coun. Methodist. Avocations: music, cooking, swimming, politics. Estate planning, Probate, Personal income taxation. Home: 4735 Ingersoll St Houston TX 77027-6601 Office: 4735 Ingersoll St Houston TX 77027-6601

**STEWART, RICHARD BURLESON,** lawyer, educator; b. Cleve., Feb. 12, 1940; s. Richard Siegfreid and Ruth Dysert (Staten) S.; m. Alice Peck Fales, May 13, 1967; children: William, Paul, Elizabeth; m. Jane Laura Bloom, Sept. 20, 1992; 1 child, Emily. AB, Yale U., 1961; MA (Rhodes scholar), Oxford (Eng.) U., 1963; LLB, Harvard U., 1966; D (hon.), Erasmus U., Rotterdam, 1993. Bar: D.C. 1968, U.S. Supreme Ct 1971. Law clk. to Justice Potter Stewart, U.S. Supreme Ct., 1966-67; assoc. Covington & Burling, Washington, 1967-71; asst. prof. law Harvard U., 1971-75, prof., 1975-82, Byrne prof. adminstrv. law,, 1982-89, assoc. dean, 1984-86; asst. atty. gen. environment and natural resources div. Dept. Justice, Washington, 1989-91; prof. law NYU Law Sch., 1992-94, Emily Kempin prof. law, 1994—; of counsel Sidley & Austin, 1992—; spl. counsel U.S. Senate Watergate Com., 1974; vis. prof. law U. Calif., Berkeley Law Sch., 1979-80, U. Chgo. Law Sch., 1986-87, Georgetown U., 1991-92, European U. Inst., 1995. Author: (with J. Krier) Environmental Law and Policy, 1978, (with S. Breyer) Administrative Law and Regulation, 1979, 3d edit., 1990, (with E. Rehbinder) Integration Through Law: Environmental Protection Policy, 1985, paper edit., 1987; editor: (with R. Revesz) Analyzing Superfund: Economics, Science, and Law, 1995. Fellow Am. Acad. Arts and Scis.; mem. ABA, Am. Law Inst. Office: NYU Law Sch 40 Washington Sq S New York NY 10012-1099 Address: Sidley & Austin 875 3rd Ave New York NY 10022-6225

**STEWART, RICHARD WILLIAMS,** lawyer; b. Harrisburg, Pa., Aug. 21, 1948; s. Alexander H. and M. Winifred (Williams) S.; m. Mary A. Simmonds, June 7, 1975; 1 child, Anne W. AB cum laude, Franklin and Marshall Coll., 1970; JD, Duke U., 1973. Bar: Pa. 1973, U.S. Dist. Ct. (mid. dist.) Pa. 1975, U.S. Tax Ct. 1984. Assoc. Stone & Sajer, New Cumberland, Pa., 1973-77; ptnr. Stone, Sajer & Stewart, New Cumberland, 1977-87; ptnr. Johnson, Duffie, Stewart & Weidner, 1987—; v.p. Secured Land Transfers, Inc., Camp Hill, Pa., 1985—; solicitor West Shore Sch. Dist., Lemoyne, Pa., 1977-93, No. York County Sch. Dist., Dillsburg, Pa., 1984—, Camp Hill Sch. Dist., 1986—; v.p. Cedar Cliff Abstract Agy., 1980-87, Secured Land Transfers, Inc., Camp Hill, Pa., 1985—; solicitor Fairview Twp., 1987-98. Chmn. Cumberland County Rep. Com., 1981-84; mem. Rep. State Com. Pa., 1990—; solicitor Fairview Twp., York County, Pa., 1987-98. Mem. ABA, Pa. Bar Assn., Cumberland County Bar Assn., Pa. Trial Lawyers Assn., Assn. Trial Lawyers Am., Central Pa. Estate Planning Council (bd. dirs. 1983-85), Pa. Sch. Solicitors Assn. (pres. 1995). Presbyterian. Lodge: Rotary (bd. dirs. West Shore). Consumer commercial, Probate. Home: 1811 Warren St New Cumberland PA 17070-1148 Office: 301 Market St Lemoyne PA 17043-1628

**STEWART, ROBB P.,** lawyer; b. Quantico, Va., Mar. 26, 1957; s. Robb and Molly (Francey) S.; m. Kathy Bell, July 26, 1980; children: Cecelia Francey, William Robbie, Mary Claire Easton. BA with honors, U. Tex., 1979; JD with honors, So. Meth. U., 1982. Lawyer Locke Purnell Rain Harrell, Dallas, 1982—, shareholder, 1989—. Presbyterian. Real property, Landlord-tenant. Office: Locke Liddell & Sapp LLP 2200 Ross Ave Ste 2200 Dallas TX 75201-2748

**STEWART, ROBERT FORREST, JR.,** lawyer; b. Niagara Falls, N.Y., Oct. 25, 1943; s. Robert Forrest and Margaret Joanne (Mahoney) S.; m. Tara Campbell Mescal, Aug. 27, 1966; children: Jane Margaret, Laura Campbell, Rebecca Forrest. BS, Coll. Holy Cross, Worcester, Mass., 1965; JD, Georgetown U., 1968; LLM in Labor, Temple U., 1978. Bar: D.C. 1968, Del. 1969, Pa. 1976. Law clk. to presiding judge U.S. Dist. Ct. Del., Wilmington, 1968-69; judge adv. USAF, 1969-72; assoc. Morris, Nichols, Arsht & Tunnell, Wilmington, 1972-76; assoc. Obermayer, Rebmann, Maxwell & Hippel, Phila., 1976-80, ptnr., 1981-85; ptnr. Duane, Morris & Heckscher, Phila. and Wilmington, 1985-92, Dilworth Paxson LLP, Phila. and Wilmington, 1992—. Author: At-Will Termination in Pennsylvania, 1983, Emerging Employee Rights, 1984, At-Will Termination in New Jersey, 1985, Legal Issues of Managing Difficult Employees in Delaware, 1988, Personnel and Employment Law in Pennsylvania/New Jersey/Delaware, 1990, Sexual Harassment, 1993, Employer's Guide to Delaware and Federal Employee Relations Laws and Regulations, 1998. Chmn. Common Cause Del., Wilmington, 1974-75, 79-80, 97—; pub. mem. coun. Del. Assn. Profl. Engrs., Wilmington, 1981-90; pres. adv. bd. Cath. Charities, Diocese of Wilmington, 1976-90; bd. dirs., vice chmn. United Way Del., 1994-97; mem. N.E. regional coun. United Way Am., 1993-97; bd. dirs., first vice chair Assoc. United Ways, 1996-97, Del. Citizens Opposed to Death Penalty, 1993—, Bayard House, 1993-98, First State Project with Industry, Inc., 1997—; bd. dirs. Catholic Schs. Diocese of Wilmington, 1998—; mem. exec. com. Del. Employer Coun. 1998—; mem. adv. bd. Seton Villa, Siena Hall and Children's Home, 1992—. Named Vol. of Yr., United Way Del., 1984; recipient United Way Del. Fellowship award, 1993. Mem. ABA, ACLU (bd. dirs. Del. chpt. 1972-76, 92-95), Del. State Bar Assn., Pa. Bar Assn., Phila. Bar Assn., Associated Builders Contractors (co-chmn. govt. rels. legal rights com. Del. chpt. 1999—), Del. State C. of C. (labor advisor 1980—, chmn. com. employee rels. 1987—), Rodney Sq. Club, Du Pont Country Club, Holy Cross Varsity Club (bd. dirs. 1981—), Coun. Engring. and Sci. Specialty Bd. (pub. mem. 1991—). Democrat. Roman Catholic. Labor. Office: Dilworth Paxson LLP 3200 Mellon Bank Ctr 1735 Market St Philadelphia PA 19103-7501 also: Ste 500 First Federal Plaza Wilmington DE 19801

**STEWART, WESLEY HOLMGREEN,** judge, lawyer; b. Dallas, Aug. 19, 1948; s. Wesley Gilbert and Anges Margaret (Schmitz) S. BA in Philosophy and Polit. Sci., Benedictine Coll., 1974; postgrad., So. Meth. U., 1974-75, 78-80. Bar: Tex. 1980, U.S. Dist. Ct. (no. dist.) Tex. 1981, U.S. Ct. Appeals (5th cir.) 1992, U.S. Dist. Ct. (we. dist.) Tex. 1992. Asst. dist. atty. county of Collin, McKinney, Tex., 1982-83; pvt. practice law Dallas, 1983-84, Denton, Tex., 1985-86; mcpl. judge Plano (Tex.) County, 1984; asst. dist. aty. County of Denton, 1984-85; judge County Ct. #3, Denton, 1986, County Ct. #1, Denton, 1987-90; chair Denton County Juvenile Bd., 1988-90. Del. Rep. State Conv., Dallas, 1986, Houston, 1988, chair credentials com. Dist. 22 Conv., Denton, 1988—; v.p. Dallas Federalist Soc., 1990-92, bd. advisors, 1992—; congrl. caucas chmn. Rep. State Conv., 1988; mem. Human Svcs. Com., Denton, 1993-97, chair, 1996-97. Mem. Tex. Bar Assn. Jewish. Avocations: sports, computers, philosophy. Home: 3901 Accent Dr Apt 318 Dallas TX 75287-6783

**STICK, MICHAEL ALAN,** lawyer; b. Elizabeth City, N.C., June 2, 1954; s. David and Phyllis (Stapells) S.; m. Debra Joan Braselton, May 22, 1993. BA, Davidson Coll., 1976; JD, U. N.C., 1981. Bar: Ill. 1981, U.S. Dist. Ct. (no. dist.) Ill. 1982, U.S. Ct. Appeals (7th cir.) 1983, U.S. Ct. Appeals (8th cir.) 1986. Assoc. Jenner & Block, Chgo., 1981-84, Butler, Rubin, Newcomer, Saltarelli & Boyd, Chgo., 1984-87; ptnr. Butler, Rubin, Saltarelli & Boyd, Chgo., 1988—. Co-author: Environmental Law Handbook, 1988, Environmental Law in Illinois, 1993; mem. staff U. N.C. Law Rev., 1979-80. Chmn. spl. gifts divsn. United Way Crusade of Mercy, Chgo., 1993-94. Me. ABA, Chgo. Bar Assn. Democrat. Methodist. Avocations: travel, skiing, art. General civil litigation, Environmental. Home: 616 E Hickory St Hinsdale IL 60521-2413 Office: Butler Rubin Saltarelli & Boyd Three First Nat Pla # 1800 Chicago IL 60602

**STICKEL, FREDERICK GEORGE, III,** lawyer; b. Newark, Oct. 7, 1915; s. Frederick G. and Helen Muriel (Walker) S.; m. Elizabeth Tobin, Sept. 23, 1940; children: Fred G., Virginia H., Jane, Elizabeth Louise, Kathryn; m. 2d, Doris B. Asdal, May 19, 1979 (dec. Oct. 1992). A.B., Princeton U., 1937; J.D., Columbia U., 1940. Bar: N.J. 1941, U.S. Dist. Ct. N.J. 1941, U.S. Supreme Ct. 1952. Assoc., Stickel & Stickel, Newark, 1941-46; ptnr. Stickel Kain & Stickel, Newark, 1946-78; sr. ptnr. Stickel & Koenig, Cedar Grove, 1978-88, Stickel, Koenig & Sullivan, 1988—, mcpl. atty. Roseland, N.J., 1948-68, Verona, N.J., 1961-63, Cedar Grove, 1945-55; v.p. N.J. State, County and Mcpl. Study Commn., 1966—; counsel Bd. Edn., Cedargrove, 1945-91, City of Orange Redevel. Agy., 1977-92; gen. counsel N.J. State League of Municipalities, 1984—; judge Mcpl. Ct. of Roseland, 1985-88. Recipient Disting. Svc. award Nat. Inst. Mcpl. Attys., 1955; N.J. League of Municipalities, 1980. Mem. ABA, N.J. State Bar Assn., Essex County Bar Assn., West Essex Bar Assn., N.J. Inst. Mcpl. Attys., N.J. Assn. Sch. Bd. Attys., Nat. Assn. Sch. Bd. Attys., Am. Judicature Soc., Columbia Law Assn., Class of 1937 Princeton U. (v.p. 1982-87). Republican. Clubs: Nassau of Princeton (N.J.); Rotary of Cedar Grove (past pres. 1941); Masons (West Essex). Contbr. articles on law to profl. jours. Land use and zoning (including planning), Estate planning, General practice. Office: 571 Pompton Ave Cedar Grove NJ 07009-1720 Address: 18 Alpine Rd Towaco NJ 07082-1302

**STICKNEY, JOHN MOORE,** lawyer; b. Cleve., Apr. 8, 1926; s. Isaac Moore and Alicia Margaret (Burns) S.; m. Elfriede von Rebenstock, Oct. 4, 1958; children: Michaela B., Alicia J., Thomas M. AB, Western Res. U., 1948, LLB, 1951. Bar: Ohio 1952. Sole practice, Cleve., 1952-79; ptnr. Burgess, Steck, Andrews & Stickney, Cleve., 1979-88; of counsel Weston, Hurd, Fallon, Paisley & Howley, Cleve., 1988-90, sole practice, 1990—; pres. Scranton-Averell, Inc., Cleve., 1979—. Trustee Cleve. Music Sch. Settlement, 1967—, Salzedo Sch. Harp, Cleve., 1962—, Bishop Brown Fund, Cleve., 1981—, Flats Oxbow Assn., Lake Erie Sci. & Nature Ctr., 1996—, also pres., 1970-72; co-trustee Margaret & Edwin Griffiths Trusts, Cleve., 1968—. Served with USNR, 1945-46. Mem. ABA, Ohio State Bar Assn., Cleve. Bar Assn., Hermit Club (Cleve.), Rowfant Club (Cleve.). Republican. Episcopalian. Estate planning, Estate taxation, General corporate.

**STIEFEL, LINDA SHIELDS,** lawyer; b. Syracuse, N.Y., Nov. 14, 1948; d. Harold F. and Ellen (Brown) Shields; m. John L. Stiefel, Sept. 20, 1969; 1 child, John L. BS, Tusculum Coll., 1988; JD, Akron Sch. Law, 1991. Bar: Ohio 1992, D.C. 1993, N.Y. 1998, U.S. Dist. Ct. (no. dist.) Ohio 1993, U.S. Supreme Ct. 1997. Judicial law clk. Stark County Common Pleas, Canton, Ohio, 1991-94; pvt. practice Louisville, Ohio, 1992-97, Cape Vincent, N.Y., 1998—. Active Ohio Dem. Nat. Com., Columbus, Stark County Dem. Party, Canton, Ohio, 1991-97; trustee, mem. exec. com. Am. Handweaving Mus.; trustee Cape Vincent Village Green, Cape Vincent Planning Bd. Mem. ABA, NOW, Ohio Bar Assn., Stark County Bar Assn., N.Y. State Bar Assn., Jefferson County Bar Assn. Methodist. Family and matrimonial, Appellate, Probate. Home and Office: 596 West Broadway Cape Vincent NY 13618

**STIEGEL, MICHAEL ALLEN,** lawyer; b. Greenfield, Mass., Sept. 15, 1946; s. Sid James and Ida Eleanor (Solomon) S.; m. Marsha Palmer, Sept. 10, 1983. BA, U. Ariz., 1968; JD cum laude, Loyola U., Chgo., 1971. Bar: Ill. 1971, U.S. Dist. Ct. Ill. 1971, U.S. Ct. Appeals (7th cir.) 1971, U.S. Ct. Appeals (6th cir.) 1975, U.S. Supreme Ct. 1975, Wis. 1985, Fla. 1987. Law clk. to fed. judge U.S. Dist. Ct. Ill., Chgo., 1971-72; assoc. Arnstein & Lehr, Chgo., 1972-78, ptnr., 1978-82, equity ptnr., 1982—, dir. trial dept., 1985-87, mng. ptnr., 1985-98; ptnr. Michael Best & Friedrich, Chgo., 1998—; vice chmn. exec. com., 1987-98; adj. prof. law Northwestern U.; faculty Nat. Inst. Trial Advocacy Equity, La. State U. Trial Advocacy Program, 1995. Contbr. articles to profl. jours. Mem. fin. com. Lynn Martin for Senate, Ill., 1989-90. Recipient Cert. of Appreciation, Nat. Safety Coun., Chgo., 1987, Cert. of Distinction, Chgo. Bar Assn., 1975. Mem. ABA (sect. on litigation and labor and employment law, vice chmn. trial evidence com. litigation sect. 1990-91, co-chmn. trial evidence com. 1991-95, lawyers conf. standards for admissibility of technologically sophisticated evidence com., co-chair nat. CLE programs 1995-97, coun. 1997—, litigation sect. advisor, uniform laws commn., drafting com. on Model Punitive Damages Act), Ill. Bar Assn., Fla. Bar Assn., Wis. Bar Assn., Chgo. Social Clubs, East Bank Club. Avocations: sports, reading, horse racing syndications. General civil litigation, Labor, Product liability. Office: Michael Best & Friedrich 77 W Wacker Dr Ste 4300 Chicago IL 60601-1635

**STIEHL, WILLIAM D.,** federal judge; b. 1925; m. Celeste M. Sullivan; children: William D., Susan M. Student, U. N.C., 1943-45; LLB, St. Louis U., 1949. Pvt. practice, 1952-78; ptnrs. Stiehl & Hess, 1978-81; ptnr. Stiehl & Stiehl, 1982-86; judge, former chief judge U.S. District Court, (so. dist.) Ill., East Saint Louis, 1986—; spl. asst. atty. gen. State of Ill., 1970-73. Mem. bd. Belleville Twp. High Sch. and Jr. Coll., 1949-50, 54-56, pres., 1956-57, Clair County, Ill., county civil atty., 1956-60. Mem. Ill. State Bar Assn., St. Clair County Bar Assn. Office: US Dist Ct 750 Missouri Ave East Saint Louis IL 62201-2954

**STIER, CHARLES HERMAN, JR.,** lawyer; b. Dayton, Ohio, Nov. 26, 1950; s. Charles Herman and betty Jane Stier; m. Debra Jean Dekk, Jan. 10, 1981; children: Adam C., Christine A., Eric D. BA, Wright State U., 1973; JD, U. Dayton, 1977, MA, 1985. Bar: Ohio 1977, U.S. Dist. Ct. Ohio, U.S. Tax Ct. 1980. Assoc. Stier Law Office, Xenia, Ohio, 1977-85, Hammond & Stier, Beavercreek, Ohio, 1985—; ptnr. Hammond, Stier & Stadnicar, Beavercreek, 1987—; magistrate Green County Juvenile Ct., Xenia, 1980-90; spl. asst. pros. Greene County Pros. Office, Xenia, 1984—. Cmty. bd. mem. Med. Health Svcs., Dayton, 1982-85; bd. dirs. Green County YMCA, 1983—, pres. bd. dirs., 1998; bd. dirs. Beavercreek Soccer Assn., 1994—; mem. exec. com. Greene County Dem. Party, 1980-82. Mem. Ohio State Bar Assn., Green County Bar Assn. (chmn. 1997-98). Avocations: coaching youth sports, running. Real property, Estate planning, Probate. Home: 1971 N Springcrest Ct Beavercreek OH 45432-1882 Office: Hammond Stier & Stadnicar 3836 Dayton Xenia Rd Beavercreek OH 45432-2845

**STILES, DEBRA JEAN,** lawyer; b. St. Paul, Dec. 22, 1958; d. Robert O. and Ruth J. Qually; m. John S. Stiles, Oct. 16, 1993; children: Daniel, Lisa. BA, Hamline U., 1988, JD, 1991. Bar: Minn. 1992, U.S. Dist. Ct. Minn. 1995. Fin. worker Ramsey County Human Svcs., St. Paul, 1977-85; cert. student atty. St. Paul City Attys. Office, 1989, St. Paul Pub. Defenders Office, 1989-91; adj. prof. Inver Hills Coll., Inver Grove Heights, Minn., 1992-97; atty. Debra Stiles Atty. at Law, Maplewood, Minn., 1992—, Criminal Def. Svcs., St. Paul, 1992—; judge mock trial competitions Hamline Law Sch., St. Paul, 1992—. Mem. Nat. Assn. Criminal Def. Attys., Minn. Assn. Criminal Def. Attys., Minn. Bar Assn., Ramsey County Bar Assn. Criminal. Office: Debra J Stiles Atty at Law 2785 White Bear Ave N Ste 400 Maplewood MN 55109-1307

**STILES, MARY ANN,** lawyer, author, lobbyist; b. Tampa, Fla., Nov. 16, 1944; d. Ralph A. and Bonnie (Smith) S.; m. Barry Smith. AA, Hills Community Coll., 1973; BS, Fla. State U., 1975; JD, Antioch Sch. Law, 1978. Bar: Fla. 1978. Legis. analyst Fla. Ho. of Reps., Tallahassee, 1973-74, 74-75; intern U.S. Senate, Washington, 1977; v.p., gen. counsel Associated Industries Fla., Tallahassee, 1978-81, gen. counsel, 1981-84, spl. counsel, 1986—; assoc. Deschler, Reed & Crichfield, Boca Raton, Fla., 1980-81; founding ptnr. Stiles, Taylor, & Grace, P.A., Boca Raton, Fla., 1982—; shareholder, dir. Stiles, Taylor, & Grace, P.A., Tampa; gen. dounsel Associated Industries Ins. Co., Inc., 1996—, Associated Industries Fla., Inc., 1997—, Associated Industries Ins. Svcs., Inc., 1997—; shareholder, dir. Six Stars Devel. Co. of Fla., Inc. Platnum Bank; br. chair Employers 1st Trust, Inc.; shareholder, pres. 42nd St., The Bistro. Author: Workers' Copmensation Law Handbook, 1980-94 edit. Bd. dirs., sec. Hillsborough C.C. Found., Tampa, 1985-87, 94-96; bd. dirs. Hillsborough Area Regional Transit Authority, Tampa, 1986-89, Boys and Girls Club of Tampa, 1986—; The Spring, 1992-93, What's My Chance, 1992-94; mem. Gov.'s Oversite Bd. on Workers' Compensation, 1989-90, Workers Comp. Rules Com., Fla. Bar, 1990-95, Workers Comp. Exec. Counsel Fla. Bar, 1990-95Jud. Nominating Commn. for Workers' Compensation Cts., 1990-93, trustee Hillsborough Cmty. Coll., 1994-99, vice-chair, 1995-96, chair, 1996-97; bd. dirs. Seminole Boosters, Inc., Fla. State U., 1996—. Mem. ABA, Fla. Bar Assn., Hillsborough County Bar Assn., Hillsborough Assn. Women Lawyers, Fla. Assn. Women Lawyers, Fla. Women's Alliance, Hillsborough County Seminole Boosters (past pres.). Democrat. Baptist. Club: Tiger Bay (Tampa, past pres., sec.). Avocations: boating, reading. Administrative and regulatory, Workers' compensation, Insurance. Office: 315 S Plant Ave Tampa FL 33606-2325 also: 111 N Orange Ave Ste 850 Orlando FL 32801-2338 also: 317 N Calhoun St Tallahassee FL 32301-7605 also: PO Box 310397 Miami FL 33231-0397

**STILES, MICHAEL,** prosecutor. Atty. U.S. Dept. Justice, Phila., 1993—. Office: US Attys Office 615 Chestnut St Fl 1250 Philadelphia PA 19106-4404

**STILL, CHARLES HENRY,** lawyer; b. Lubbock, Tex., Sept. 22, 1942; s. Charles Alphonso and Henri Sue S.; m. Frances Eugenia Odell, Apr. 29, 1967; children: Charles Henry Jr., Kathryn Elizabeth. BBA in Acctg., Tex. Tech. U., 1965; JD with honors, U. Tex., 1968. Bar: Tex. 1968. Assoc. Fulbright & Jaworski, Houston, 1968-75, ptnr., 1975—, head corp. dept., 1984—, mem. exec. com., 1992—; speaker numerous confs. and meetings; bd. dirs. Oyo Geospace Corp. Comment editor Tex. Law Rev., 1967-68. Bd. dirs. Alley Theatre, Houston, 1980-81, St. Luke's Episcopal Hosp., Houston, 1991—; mem. vestry Christ Ch. Cathedral, Houston, 1981-84, sr. warden, 1983, chancellor, 1986—. Fellow Am. Bar Found., Tex. Bar Found., Houston Bar Found.; mem. ABA (bus. law sect. 1968—, corp. laws com. 1983-89, fed. regulation of securities com. 1976—, subcom. on proxy statements and tender offers 1979—, com. on legal opinions 1989—, adminstrv. law sect. 1981—), Am. Law Inst., State Bar Tex. (chmn. bus. law sect. 1984-85, mem. coun. 1982-86, chmn. securities law com. 1981-83, com. on corp. laws 1985—, legislation in pub. interest com. 1983-84), Forest Club, Petroleum Club, Houston Ctr. Club, Order of Coif, Phi Delta Phi, Phi Kappa Phi, Gamma Phi Beta, Beta Alpha Psi, Phi Delta Theta, Phi Eta Sigma. Avocations: jogging, reading, photography. General corporate, Mergers and acquisitions, Securities. Home: 3734 Locke Ln Houston TX 77027-4006 Office: Fulbright & Jaworski 1301 Mckinney St Ste 5100 Houston TX 77010-3031

**STILL, LISA STOTSBERY,** lawyer; b. North Kingstown, R.I., Dec. 4, 1960; d. Lawrence Edward Stotsbery and Clarice Ann Dudley; m. July, 1992. AA with honors, Pensacola Jr. Coll., 1979; BA with honors, U. West Fla., 1981; JD, U. Fla., 1985. Bar: Fla. 1986, U.S. Dist. Ct. (mid. dist.) Fla. 1986, U.S. Ct. Appeals (11th cir.) 1987, U.S. Tax Ct. 1987, U.S. Supreme Ct. 1993. Tax specialist Coopers & Lybrand, Miami, Fla., 1986, Jacksonville, Fla., 1986-87; pvt. practice Jacksonville, 1987; trial atty. SBA, Jacksonville, 1987—; spl. asst. U.S. atty. No. and Mid. Dists. Fla., 1990—. Mem. ABA (com. enforcement creditors rights and bankruptcy 1990), FBA (treas. Jacksonville chpt. 1990-92, v.p. membership 1993, v.p. programs 1994, pres.-elect 1995, pres. 1996, immediate past pres. 1997, nat. coun. 1996—, chpt. activity fund 1997), Fla. Bar (govt. lawyer com. 1990-91, voluntary bar liaison com. 1996-99, fed. practice com. 1998—, bus. law sect., issue editor Bankruptcy Casenotes 1996). Avocations: water skiing, fitness instruction, biking. Office: SBA 7825 Baymeadows Way Ste 100B Jacksonville FL 32256-7549

**STILLER, SHARON PAULA,** lawyer; b. Rochester, N.Y., Mar. 31, 1951; d. Alfred Stiller and Hilda (Silver) Ring; m. John F. Everett, Nov. 21, 1981 (div.); 1 child, Sierra Alexandra. BA General civil litigation, Labor. Office: Underberg & Kessler 1800 Chase Tower Rochester NY 14604

**STILLMAN, ELINOR HADLEY,** lawyer; b. Kansas City, Mo., Oct. 12, 1938; d. Hugh Gordon and Freda (Brooks) Hadley; m. Richard C. Stillman, June 25, 1965 (div. Apr. 1975). BA, U. Kans., 1960; MA, Yale U., 1961; JD, George Washington U., 1972. Bar: D.C. 1973, U.S. Ct. Appeals (10th cir.) 1975, U.S. Ct. Appeals (9th cir.) 1976, U.S. Ct. Appeals (2d cir.) 1976, U.S. Ct. Appeals (5th cir.) 1983, U.S. Ct. Appeals (4th cir.) 1985, U.S. Supreme Ct. 1976. Lectr. in English CUNY, 1963-65; asst. editor Stanford (Calif.) U. Press., 1967-69; law clk. to judge U.S. Dist. Ct. D.C., Washington, 1972-73; appellate atty. NLRB, Washington, 1973-78; asst. to solicitor gen. U.S. Dept. Justice, Washington, 1978-82; supr. appellate atty. NLRB, Washington, 1982-86, chief counsel to mem. bd., 1986-88, 94—, chief counsel to chmn. bd., 1988-94. Mem. ABA, D.C. Bar Assn., Order of Coif, Phi Beta Kappa. Democrat. Office: Nat Labor Rels Bd 1099 14th St NW Washington DC 20005-3419

**STINE, J(AMES) LARRY,** lawyer; b. Birmingham, Ala., Dec. 18, 1950; s. James O. and Helen M. Stine; m. Kathryn Stokely, June 10, 1972; children: Kathryn Anne DeLoach, Laura Elizabeth, Amanda Leigh Franklin. BS cum laude, U. Ga., 1972, JD cum laude, 1975. Bar: Ga., U.S. Dist. Ct. (no. dist.) Ga. 1975, U.S. Dist. Ct. (mid. dist.) Ga. 1997, U.S. Ct. Appeals (11th cir.) 1992, U.S. Ct. Appeals (6th cir.) 1998, U.S. Dist. Ct. (ea. and we. dists.) Ark. 1999. Trial atty. U.S. Dept. of Labor, Atlanta, 1975-82, regional counsel, 1982-89; atty. Thompson, Mann & Hudson, Atlanta, 1989-92; of counsel Wimberly & Lawson, Atlanta, 1992-95; prin. Wimberly Lawson Steckel, Atlanta, 1995—; bd. dirs. King's Bridge, Atlanta. Author: Wage and Hour Law: Compliance and Practice, 1995, Family and Medial Leave

Act, 1999. Mem. Decatur Kiwanis (pres. 1988-89). Labor. Office: Wimberly Lawson & Steckel Ste #400 3400 Peachtree Rd NE Atlanta GA 30326-1107

**STINE, MARGARET ELIZABETH,** lawyer; b. Hawarden, Iowa, Oct. 14, 1963; d. Joseph Theodore and Nathalie Joan Schiefen; m. Thomas Earl Stine, June 16, 1990; children: Mary Catherine, Abigail Rose. BA, Creighton U., 1986; MPA, U. S.D., 1989, JD, 1991. Bar: Nebr. 1992, U.S. Dist. Ct. Nebr. 1992, U.S. Ct. Appeals (8th cir.) 1995, U.S. Supreme Ct. 1997. Asst. to the city mgr. City of Vermillion, S.D., 1988-89; atty. Harding, Shultz & Downs, Lincoln, Nebr., 1991—; bd. dirs. Fresh Start Homes, Worknet. Contbr. articles to profl. jours. Bd. dirs. Wings, Omaha, 1996—; pres. Bicentennial Estates Neighborhood, Lincoln, 1996—. Mem. ABA, Nebr. State Bar Assn., Fed. Bar Assn., Maj. Employers Coun. Republican. Avocation: running. Labor, Federal civil litigation, General civil litigation. Office: Harding Shultz & Downs 121 S 13th St PO Box 82028 Lincoln NE 68501-2028

**STINN, MICHAEL EDMUND,** lawyer; b. Ft. Smith, Ark., Oct. 12, 1958; s. Edmund August Stinn and Barbara Jeanne Weber; m. Mary R. Stinn, Sept. 28, 1984; children: Mary Kate, Megan. BS in Bus. Adminstrn., Georgetown U., 1980; JD, Cleve. State U., 1984. Lawyer William J. Coyne Law Firm, Cleve., 1982-94, Seeley, Savidge and Ebert Co. LPA, Cleve., 1994—; bd. mem. Cleve. Schs. Spl. Olympics Adv. Bd., 1995—. Treas. Georgetown U. Alumni Club Cleve., 1985—. Mem. Cleve. Bar Assn. (litigation com.). Democrat. Roman Catholic. Avocation: golf. Home: 21146 Erie Rd Rocky River OH 44116-2130 Office: 800 Bank One Ctr 600 Superior Ave E Cleveland OH 44114-2611

**STINNETT, MARK ALLAN,** lawyer; b. Jackson, Miss., Sept. 15, 1955; s. Allan J. and Joan (Mouser) S.; m. Carol Fowler, Sept. 5, 1992; children: Michelle, Michael. BA in Polit. Sci. with honors, Tex. Tech U., 1977; JD with honors, U. Tex., 1980. Bar: Tex. 1980, U.S. Dist. Ct. (no. and ea. dists.) Tex. 1981, U.S. Ct. Appeals (5th cir.) 1993. Shareholder Cowles & Thompson, Dallas, 1980—. Mem. Philmont Ranch com. Boy Scouts Am. Mem. ABA, Am. Inns of Ct., Am. Coll. Legal Medicine, Am. Health Lawyers Assn., State Bar of Tex., Dallas Bar Assn., Tex. Assn. Def. Counsel, Dallas Assn. Def. Counsel, Def. Rsch. Inst., Nat. Fire Protection Assn., Inns Ct. (barrister Dallas chpt. 1988-91), Tex. Ctr. Legal Ethics and Professionalism, Nat. Eagle Scout Assn., Philmont Staff Assn. (pres. 1994-98). Avocations: backpacking, softball, military history. Personal injury, Product liability, General civil litigation. Home: 5541 Mallard Trce Frisco TX 75034-5058 Office: Cowles & Thompson 901 Main St Ste 4000 Dallas TX 75202-3793

**STINNETT, TERRANCE LLOYD,** lawyer; b. Oakland, Calif., July 22, 1940; s. Lloyd Monroe and Gertrude (Hyman) S. BS, Stanford U., 1962; JD magna cum laude, U. Santa Clara, 1969. Bar: Calif. 1970, U.S. Dist. Ct. (no. dist.) Calif. 1970, U.S. Dist. Ct. (ea. ctrl. and so. dists) Calif. 1975, U.S. Ct. Appeals (9th cir.) 1970, U.S. Supreme Ct. 1975. Law clk. to judge Calif. Ct. Appeals, San Francisco, 1969-70; assoc. Hyman, Rhodes & Aylward, Fremont, Calif., 1970-71, Glicksberg, Kushner & Goldberg, San Francisco, 1972-77; mem. Goldberg, Stinnett Meyers & Davis, San Francisco, 1977—; bd. dirs. Fremont Bancorp, Fremont Bank, vice-chmn. bd., 1998—. Mem. ABA, Bar Assn. San Francisco (chmn. bench bar liaison com. for U.S. Bankruptcy Ct., No. Dist. of Calif. 1997). Republican. Roman Catholic. Bankruptcy. Home: 131 Alamo Hills Ct Alamo CA 94507-2243 Office: Goldberg Stinnett Meyers & Davis 44 Montgomery St Ste 2900 San Francisco CA 94104-4803

**STIRLING, CLARK TILLMAN,** lawyer; b. Washington, July 4, 1956; s. Edwin Tillman and Genevieve (Ruffner) S.; m. Linda Poumirau, May 30, 1986; children: Stephen Tillman, Grace Elizabeth. BS, Vanderbilt U., 1979; JD, George Washington U., 1983. Bar: D.C. 1984, Alaska 1984, Calif. 1987. Clk. to Judge Cutler, State of Alaska, Palmer, 1983-84; asst. dist. atty. State of Alaska, Anchorage, 1984-87; assoc. Archbald & Spray, Santa Barbara, Calif., 1987-91; ptnr. Law Offices Kristofer Kallman, Santa Barbara, 1991-95; pvt. practice, Santa Barbara, 1996—. Bd. dirs. Childrens Creative Project, Santa Barbara, 1992-95; pres. bd. dirs. Transition House, Santa Barbara, 1993—; mem. centennial com. All Sts.-By-Sea, Santa Barbara, 1996—. Mem. Calif. Bar Assn., Alaska Bar Assn., D.C. Bar Assn., Santa Barbara County Bar Assn. (co-chmn. litigation sect. 1996-97, conf. of dels. 1998—), Santa Barbara Inns Ct., Soc. of Cincinnati. Republican. Avocations: writing, reading, tennis. Office: 2019-C State St Santa Barbara CA 93105-3553

**STIRTON, CHARLES PAUL,** lawyer; b. Cedar City, Utah, Mar. 24, 1950; s. John K. and Idonna G. (Gower) S. BS in Math., U. Ariz., 1972, BS in Chemistry, 1972, JD, 1975. Bar: Ariz. 1975, U.S. Dist. Ct. Ariz. 1975, U.S. Ct. Appeals (9th cir.) 1975. Assoc. Laber, Lovallo & Colarich, Tucson, 1975-77; ptnr. Lovallo & Stirton, Tucson, 1977-84; sole practice Tucson, 1984—. Contbr. articles to newspapers. Mem. Big Brothers Tucson, 1973-80, adv. bd. Tucson Fitness Marathon, 1984-85, adv. bd. Wellness Council Tucson, 1986. Mem. Ariz. Bar Assn., Pima County Bar Assn. (ethics com. 1982-87), Phi Beta Kappa, Order of Coif. Democrat. Roman Catholic. Avocations: running, hiking, skiing, swimming, biking. General corporate, Probate, Real property. Office: 1325 N Wilmot Rd Ste 310 Tucson AZ 85712-5168

**STITH, BEVERLY JEAN,** paralegal; b. Washington, Mar. 27, 1949. Assoc. Degree in Transp. Mgmt., LaSalle U., 1977; Environ. Sci. Diploma, Calif. State U., 1993, Thomas Edison State Coll., 1993; BS/MBA-Bus. Adminstrn., Chadwick U., 1995. Transp. asst. Interstate Commerce Commn., Indpls., 1977-79; paralegal specialist Interstate Commerce Commn., Washington, 1979-84; legal staff asst. Armed Svcs. Bd. of Contract Appeals, Falls Church, Va., 1987-89; paralegal specialist Mil. Sealift Command, Far East, Yokohama, Japan, 1989-94, Def. Fin. and Acctg. Svc. (former Spouse Divsn.), Cleve., 1994—. Author: Prevention of Sexual Harassment in the Workplace, 1992. Decorated Navy Unit Commendation Cert./Mil. Sealift Command, (Desert Shield/Desert Storm), Yokohoma; named to Women's Inner Circle of Achievement. Mem. Nat. Paralegal Assn., Nat. Environ. Health Assn., Internat. Platform Assn. Republican. Baptist. Avocations: golf, horseback riding, collecting antiques. Home: 5146 Arch St Maple Heights OH 44137-1506 Office: Def Fin Acctg Svc Code L 1240 E 9th St Cleveland OH 44199-2001

**STIVER, CHARLES ELLWOOD, JR.,** lawyer; b. Patuxent River NAS, Md., July 21, 1949; s. Charles Ellwood Sr. and Marvel Lenore (Dunning) S.; m. Mary Jo Sherman, Apr. 28, 1990; children: Charles Ellwood III, Christina Elizabeth. BA, Stanford U., 1971, JD, 1974; LLM in Taxation, NYU, 1975. Bar: Calif. 1975, N.Y. 1976, U.S. Ct. Appeals (3d cir.) 1977, U.S. Supreme Ct. 1978, U.S. Ct. Fed. Claims 1983, U.S. Tax. Ct. 1989, Fla. 1993. Assoc. Davis Polk & Wardell, N.Y.C., 1975-83, sr. atty., 1983-87; sr. atty. Milbank, Tweed, Hadley & McCloy, N.Y.C., 1987-92; of counsel Greenberg, Traurig, Hoffman, Lipoff, Rosen & Quentel, Miami, Fla., 1992-93, shareholder, 1993—; adj. prof. U. Miami Law Sch., 1996—. Mem. ABA, Fla. Bar Assn., N.Y. State Bar Assn. Corporate taxation, Taxation, general, Personal income taxation. Office: Greenberg Traurig PA 1221 Brickell Ave Miami FL 33131-3224

**STIX, SALLY ANN,** lawyer; b. Cin., Jan. 1, 1950; d. Charles Nathan and Marjory Ann (Hauenstein) S.; 1 child, Emily. BA, U. Wis., Madison, 1974; JD, Ill. Inst. Tech., Chgo., 1979. Bar: Ill. 1979, U.S. Supreme Ct. 1990, Wis. 1993. Pvt. practice Chgo., 1980-93, Madison, 1993—. Pres. Mazomanie (Wis.) Barracudas Swim Team, 1995-96, Tri-County Swim League, 1997. Mem. Nat. Employment Lawyers Assn., Nat. Lawyers Guild, State Bar Wis., Legal Assn. for Women, AFL-CIO Lawyers Coordinating Coun. Avocation: gardening. E-mail: sastix@aol.com. Labor, Pension, profit-sharing, and employee benefits, Civil rights. Office: 122 W Washington Ave Ste 740 Madison WI 53703-2723

**STOBERSKI, MICHAEL EDWARD,** lawyer; b. Troy, N.Y., Oct. 18, 1966; s. John S. and Winifred A. (Boland) S.; m. Holly S. Sedarat, Oct. 21, 1994. BA, U. San Diego, 1988, JD, 1991. Bar: Calif. 1991, Nev. 1992, U.S. Dist. Ct. (so. dist.) Calif. 1991, Nev. 1992, U.S. Ct. Appeals (9th cir.) 1992. Shareholder Rawlings, Olson, Cannon, Gormley & Desruisseaux, Las Vegas, Nev., 1991—; counsel Clark County Pro Bono Project, Las Vegas, 1992-96, named Rookie of Yr. 1992-93. Mem. ABA, Def. Rsch. Inst., Clark County Bar Assn. Avocations: golf, skiing, scuba diving. State civil litigation, Professional liability, Product liability. Office: Rawlings Olson Cannon Et Al 301 Clark Ave Ste 1000 Las Vegas NV 89101-6597

**STOCK, ALICE BETH,** lawyer; b. N.Y.C., Mar. 3, 1961. BA, Yale U., 1983; JD, Harvard U., 1986. Bar: N.Y. 1987, U.S. Dist. Ct. (so. and ea. dists.) N.Y., U.S. Ct. Appeals (2nd cir.), U.S. Ct. Appeals (4th cir.). Assoc. Proskauer, Rose, Goetz & Mendelsohn, N.Y.C., 1986-91, Whitman & Ransom, N.Y.C., 1991-93, Whitman Breed Abbott & Morgan, N.Y.C., 1993-95; of counsel Reid & Priest LLP, N.Y.C., 1995-97, ptnr., 1997-99; ptnr. Tuelen Reid & Priest LLP, N.Y.C., 1999—. Editor, author: Havard Civil Rights-Civil Liberties Law Rev., 1984-86. Mem. ABA (mem. employment law sect.), Am. Immigration Lawyers Assn., N.Y. State Bar Assn. (mem. employment law sect.), Corp. Bar Weschester, Fairfield Indsl. Rels. Rsch. Assn., Assn. of the Bar of the City of N.Y. (former sec., immigration and nationality law com. 1990-93, 96-98). Labor, Immigration, naturalization, and customs. Office: Tuelen Reid & Priest LLP 40 W 57th St Fl 28 New York NY 10019-4001

**STOCK, LAURI JANE,** lawyer; b. Passaic, N.J., June 11, 1957; d. John Patterson and Marie (Lisbona) S. BA, U. Fla., 1979; JD, U. San Diego, 1988. Bar: Calif. 1988, U.S. Dist. Ct. (so. dist.) Calif. 1988. Lt. U.S. Navy, San Diego, Calif., 1981-87; prosecutor City Atty. of San Diego, 1988-90; ptnr. Malowney, Chialtas & Bishop, San Diego, 1990-92; sole practioner Law Office of Lauri Stock, San Diego, 1992—. Bd. dirs. Tom Homann Law Assn., 1997—. Decorated Navy Commendation medal. Mem. San Diego Front Runners. Avocations: road racing, rock climbing, classical piano, reading. Office: Law Office of Lauri Stock 1010 2nd Ave Ste 1909 San Diego CA 92101-4910

**STOCKARD, JANET LOUISE,** lawyer; b. Beaumont, Tex., July 22, 1948; d. Louis and Louise (Land) S. B.S. with honors, U. Tex., 1970, J.D., 1973. Bar: Tex. 1973. Sole practice, Austin, Tex., 1973—. Vol. dep. registrar for voter registration, Lake Travis Elem. Sch.; supporter Women's Advocacy Project, Rape Crisis Center; mem. City of Austin Parks and Recreation Bd., 1977-79; adv. com. mem. Lake Travis, 1996-97. Named one of Most Noteworthy Austinites of Yr., Austin Homes and Gardens mag., 1983, Best Atty. '96, Austin Chronicle Readers. Mem. State Bar Tex. (charter mem. coll. 1983-84, sch. law sect.), Travis County Bar Assn., Austin Young Lawyers Assn., Travis County Women Trial Lawyers (founder 1982, pres. 1983), Travis County Women Lawyers Assn. (founder 1976-77, pres. 1977-78), Barton Hills Horseshoe Bend Neighborhood Assn., Austin C. of C., U. Tex. Ex-Students Assn., Nat. Assn. Women Lawyers, Travis County Democratic Women, NOW, Longhorn Assocs. (charter mem. for excellence in athletics 1983), Better Bus. Bur., Kappa Delta Pi, Pi Sigma Alpha. Roman Catholic. Criminal. Office: 1411 West Ave Austin TX 78701-1537

**STOCKBURGER, JEAN DAWSON,** lawyer; b. Scottsboro, Ala., Feb. 4, 1936; d. Joseph Mathis Scott and Mary Frances (Alley) Dawson; m. John Calvin Stockburger, Mar. 23, 1963; children: John Scott, Mary Staci, Christopher Sean. Student, Gulf Park Coll., 1954-55; BA, Auburn U., 1958; M in Social Work, Tulane U., 1962; JD, U. Ark., Little Rock, 1979. Bar: Ark. 1979, U.S. Dist. Ct. (ea. dist.) Ark. 1980. Assoc. Mitchell, Williams, Selig, Gates & Woodyard and predecessor, Little Rock, 1979-85, ptnr., 1985-94, of counsel, 1994—; bd. dirs., sec. Cen. Ark. Estate Planning Council, Little Rock, 1984-85, 2d v.p., 1985-86; pres. Cen. Ark. Estate Council, 1987-88. Assoc. editor U. Ark. Law Rev., 1978-79. Bd. dirs. Sr. Citizens Activities Today, Little Rock, 1983-88, treas., 1986-88; bd. dirs. Vol. Orgn. for Ctrl. Ark. Legal Svcs., 1986-91, sec., 1987-88, chmn., 1989-91, H.I.R.E. Inc., 1994—; sec. Little Rock Cmty. Mental Health Ctr., 1994-96, v.p., 1996—. Mem. ABA, Ark. Bar Assn. (chmn. probate and trust law sect. 1986-88), Pulaski County Bar Assn. (bd. dirs. 1994-97), Am. Coll. Trust and Estate Counsel. Democrat. Methodist. Estate planning, Probate. Office: Mitchell Williams Selig Gates & Woodyard 425 W Capitol Ave Ste 1800 Little Rock AR 72201-3525

**STOCKBURGER, SUSAN ZLOMKE,** lawyer; b. Kansas City, Kans., Nov. 21, 1950; d. Clayton Gerald and Lola (Fintel) Zlomke; children: Ingrid, Peter, Anya, Jesse, Ellen. BA, U. Tex., 1973; JD, Pace U., 1995. Bar: N.Y., N.J. Assoc. Barlet & Lambiase, Warnick, N.Y., 1994-97; asst. county atty. Orange County, Goshen, N.Y., 1997—. Mem. ABA, N.Y. State Bar Assn., Orange County Bar Assn., Orange-Sullivan Women's Bar Assn. Home: 157 Mason St Montgomery NY 12549-1119 Office: Orange County Dept Law Main St Goshen NY 10549

**STOCKMAR, TED P.,** lawyer; b. Denver, May 9, 1921; s. Theodore Paul and Elda Marie (Robinson) S.; m. Suzanne Louise Harl, Feb. 14, 1947; children: Stephen Harl, John Brian, Anne Baldwin Stockmar Upton. BS in Petroleum Engring., Colo. Sch. Mines, Golden, 1943; LLB, U. Denver, 1948. Bar: Colo. 1948. Ptnr. Holme Roberts & Owen Denver, 1951-91; of counsel, 1991—. Co-author: Law of Federal Oil and Gas Leases 1964, 1984; also articles. Trustee Colo. Sch. Mines, Golden, 1948-82, bd. pres., 1970-80. 1st lt. USAF, 1943-45. Mem. Denver Bar Assn., Colo. Bar Assn., Rocky Mountain Oil and Gas Assn. (dir., exec. com. 1982-93, chmn. legal com. 1986-88), Denver Country Club, Univ. Club, Law Club. Republican. Avocations: bird watching, reading, gardening. Banking, General corporate, Natural resources. Home: 2552 E Alameda Ave Apt 8 Denver CO 80209-3324 Office: Holme Roberts & Owen LLP 1700 Lincoln St Ste 4100 Denver CO 80203-4541

**STOCKMEYER, NORMAN OTTO, JR.,** law educator, consultant; b. Detroit, May 24, 1938; s. Norman O. and Lillian R. (Hitchman) S.; m. Marcia E. Rudman, Oct. 1, 1966; children: Claire, Kathleen, Mary Frances. AB, Oberlin Coll., 1960; JD, U. Mich., 1963. Bar: Mich. 1963, U.S. Ct. Appeals (6th cir.) 1964, U.S. Supreme Ct. 1974. Legis. grad. fellow Mich. State U., 1963; legal counsel Senate Judiciary Com., Mich. Legislature, 1964; law clk. Mich. Ct. Appeals, 1965, commr., 1966-68, research dir., 1969-76; assoc. prof. law Thomas M. Cooley Law Sch., 1977-78, prof., 1978—; vis. prof. Mercer U. Sch. Law, 1986, Calif. Western Sch. Law, 1993; lectr. Mich. Judicial Inst., 1995. Editor Mich. Law of Damages, 1989; contbr. numerous articles to state and nat. legal jours. Named one of 88 Greats Lansing State Jour., 1988. Fellow Am. Bar Found. (life); mem. ABA (chmn. Mich. membership 1972-73, lectr. Appellate Judges Conf. jud. seminars 1972-76, ho. del. 1988-92, editorial bd. Compleat Lawyer 1990—), Nat. Conf. Bar Founds. (trustee 1985-90, sec. 1988-89), Mich. State Bar Found. (pres. 1982-85, trustee 1971-92), State Bar Mich. (chmn. Young Lawyers sect. 1971-72, rep. assembly 1972-79, bd. commrs. 1985-93), Ingham County Bar Assn. (bd. dirs. 1981-85), Mich. Assn. Professions (bd. dirs. 1981-84, Profl. of Yr. 1988), Thomas M. Cooley Legal Authors Soc. (pres. 1982-83), Scribes (bd. dirs. 1994—), Delta Theta Phi (dean Christiancy Senate 1962; Outstanding Prof. 1984). Address: PO Box 13038 Lansing MI 48901-3038

**STOCKWELL, LANCE,** law educator; b. N.Y.C., Feb. 21, 1942; s. Eugene Lawrence Stockwell and Nelle (Dark) Stephens; children: David Christopher, Kelsey Dian; m. Susan Meschke, Mar. 10, 1962 (div. Mar. 28, 1994); m. Gail Provost, Dec. 16, 1996. BBA, Okla. U., 1965; MA, Okla. State U., 1996; JD, U. Tulsa, 1968. Bar: Okla. 1968, U.S. Dist. Ct. (no. dist.) Okla. 1968, U.S. Ct. Appeals (10th cir.) 1969, U.S. Ct. Appeals (9th cir.) 1972, U.S. Dist. Ct. (we. dist.) Okla. 1973, U.S. Dist. Ct. (ea. dist.) Okla. 1977, U.S. Supreme Ct. 1988, U.S. Ct. Appeals (fed. cir.) 1990, U.S. Ct. Appeals (8th cir.) 1993. Ptnr. Boesche McDermott & Eskridge, Tulsa, 1968-95; adj. prof. law U. Tulsa, 1994—; freelance lectr. Tulsa, 1996—; bd. dirs. ctr. on dispute resolution U. Tulsa, 1994—, developer, dep. dir. practical skills cert. program. Author: (seminar workbook) Persuasion: A Matter of Mastery, Not Mystery, 1996. Named Outstanding Adj. Prof., 1996, 97. Fellow Am. Coll. Trial Lawyers, Okla. Bar Found.; mem. Am. Soc. Trial Cons., Am. Arbitration Assn. (arbitrator 1992—), Okla. Bar Assn. Avocations: writing, sailing, skiing. Office: U Tulsa Coll Law 3120 E 4th Pl Tulsa OK 74104-2418

**STODDARD, GLENN MCDONALD,** lawyer; b. Washington, Feb. 18, 1958; s. Charles Hatch and Patricia (Coulter) S.; m. Sharon Lynn Stake, Aug. 22, 1981; children: Patrick M., Chloe F. BS, U. Wis., Stevens Point, 1980; MS, U. Wis., Madison, 1984, JD, 1994. Bar: Wis. 1995, U.S. Dist. Ct. (ea. and we. dists.) Wis. 1995. Assoc. code adminstr. Washburn County, Shell Lake, Wis., 1980-81; assoc. planner Manitowoc County, Wis., 1981-82; legis. aide Wis. Legis., Madison, 1983-85; asst. dir. Gov.'s Commn. on Agr., Madison, 1985; exec. dir. Wis. Land Cons. Assn., Madison, 1985-89; dir. govt. affairs Wis. Farmers Union, Chippewa Falls, 1989-92; law clk. U. Wis. Legal Asst. Program, Madison, summer 1993, Wis. Dept. Justice, Madison, summer 1994; ptnr./shareholder Garvey & Stoddard, S.C., Madison, 1995-99. Author: Essentials of Forestry, 4th edit., 1987. Chmn. Wis. Environ. Decade, Inc., Madison, 1991-92. Named Outstanding Citizen Adv., Ctr. for Pub. Rep., Madison, 1991. Mem. ATLA, ABA, State Bar Wis., Wis. Acad. Trial Lawyers. Avocations: outdoor recreation, karate, Tai Chi, reading. General civil litigation, Environmental, Labor. Office: Garvey & Stoddard SC 634 W Main St Ste 201 Madison WI 53703-2662

**STOEBUCK, WILLIAM BREES,** law educator; b. Wichita, Kans., Mar. 18, 1929; s. William Douglas and Donice Beth (Brees) S.; m. Mary Virginia Fields, Dec. 24, 1951; children: Elizabeth, Catherine, Caroline. B.A., Wichita State U., 1951; M.A., Ind. U., 1953; J.D., U. Wash., 1959; S.J.D., Harvard U., 1973. Bar: Wash. 1959, U.S. Supreme Ct. 1967. Pvt. practice, Seattle, 1959-64; asst. prof. law U. Denver, 1964-67; assoc. prof. U. Wash., Seattle, 1967-70, prof., 1970-95; Judson Falknor prof., 1995—; of counsel Karr, Tuttle, Campbell, Seattle, 1988—. Author: Washington Real Estate: Property Law, 1995, Washington Real Estate: Transactions, 1995, Basic Property Law, 1989, Law of Property, 1984, 2nd edit., 1993, Nontrespassory Takings, 1977, Contemporary Property, 1996; contbr. articles to legal jours. Bd. dirs. Cascade Symphony Orch., 1978-83, Forest Park Libr., 1975-80. Mem. Am. Coll. Real Estate Lawyers, Am. Coll. Mortgage Attys., Wash. State Bar Assn., Assn. Am. Law Schs., Order of Coif, Seattle Yacht Club. 1st lt. USAF, 1951-56. Home: 3515 NE 158th Pl Lk Forest Park WA 98155-6649 Office: U Wash Law Sch 1100 NE Campus Pkwy Seattle WA 98105-6605

**STOFFEL, KLAUS PETER,** lawyer; b. Evergreen Park, Ill., Dec. 9, 1957; s. Karl and Ursula (Beckmann) S.; m. Cathy B. Wolff, Apr. 9, 1983; children: Lindsey Brooke, Michael Scott, Cali Blake. BSME, Bradley U., 1980; JD, Seton Hall U., 1984. Bar: N.Y. 1985, U.S. Patent and Trademark Office 1984, U.S. Dist. Ct. (so. dist.) N.Y. 1985, N.J. 1985, U.S. Dist. Ct. N.J. 1985. Engr. Okonite Co., Ramsey, N.J., 1980-81; assoc. Striker, Striker & Stenby, N.Y.C., 1984-85, Brumbaugh, Graves, Donohue & Raymond, N.Y.C., 1985-87, Cooper & Dunham, N.Y.C., 1987-88, Toren, McGeady & Assoc., P.C., N.Y.C., 1988-93, Cohen, Pontani, Lieberman & Pavane, N.Y.C., 1993—. Mem. ABA. Avocation: golf. Patent, Trademark and copyright. Home: 41 Cornell Dr Livingston NJ 07039-5516 Office: Cohen Pontani Lieberman & Pavane 551 5th Ave Rm 1210 New York NY 10176-0091

**STOHR, DONALD J.,** federal judge; b. Sedalia, Mo., Mar. 9, 1934; s. Julius Leo and Margaret Elizabeth (McGaw) S.; m. Mary Ann Kuhlman, July 31, 1957 children: Elizabeth M., Anne M., Jane C., Sara M., Ellen R. BS, St. Louis U., 1956, JD, 1958. Bar: Mo. 1958, U.S. Dist. Ct. (ea. dist.) Mo. 1958, U.S. Ct. Appeals (8th cir.) 1966, U.S. Supreme Ct. 1969. Assoc. Hocker Goodwin & MacGreevy, St. Louis, 1958-63, 66-69; asst. counselor St. Louis County, 1963-65, counselor, 1965-66; U.S. atty. Ea. Dist. Mo., St. Louis, 1973-76; ptnr. Thompson & Mitchell, St. Louis, 1969-73, 76-92; judge U.S. Dist. Ct. (ea. dist.) Mo., St. Louis, 1992—. Mem. ABA, Mo. Bar Assn., Am. Judicature Soc., St. Louis Met. Bar Assn. Office: US Court & Custom House 1114 Market St Rm 813 Saint Louis MO 63101-2034

**STOKES, ARCH YOW,** lawyer, writer; b. Atlanta, Sept. 2, 1946; s. Mack B. and Rose Stokes; m. Maggie Mead; children: Jennifer Jean, Austin Christopher, Susannah Rose, Travis, Emmarose. BA, Emory U., 1967, JD, 1970. Bar: Ga. 1970, U.S. Dist. Ct. (no. dist.) Ga. 1970, U.S. Ct. Appeals (5th cir.) Ga. 1970, U.S. Ct. Mil. Appeals 1971, U.S. Ct. Appeals (9th cir.) Ga. 1980, (2d cir.) Ga. 1990, U.S. Supreme Ct. 1981, U.S. Dist. Ct. (no. dist.) Calif. 1981, U.S. Ct. Appeals (11th cir.) Calif. 1982, U.S. Ct. Appeals (7th cir.) Calif. 1986, U.S. Ct. Appeals (1st cir.) Calif. 1992, U.S. Ct. Appeals (8th cir.) Calif. 1991, U.S. Dist. Ct. (no. dist. ) N.Y. 1991, U.S. Dist. Ct. (ea. dist.) Mich. 1986. Ptnr. Stokes Lazarus & Carmichael, Atlanta, 1972-92; ptnr. Stokes & Murphy, Atlanta, 1992—, San Diego and Pitts., 1992—. Author: The Wage & Hour Handbook, 1978, The Equal Employment Opportunity Handbook, 1979, The Collective Bargaining Handbook, 1981. Mem. bd. visitors Emory Univ.; Ga. State Univ. student rels. com. Cecil B. Day Sch. of Hospitality Adminstrn. Capt. USMC, 1971-73. Recipient Hal Holbrook award Internat. Platform Assn., 1990. Mem. ABA, ATLA, Union Internat. des Avocats, Internat. Soc. Hospitality Cons., Confrérie de la Chaîne des Rôtisseurs, Am. Hotel and Motel Assn. Labor, General civil litigation. Office: Stokes & Murphy PO Box 87468 College Park GA 30337-0468

**STOKES, HARRY MCKINNEY,** lawyer; b. Pitts., Jan. 1, 1942; s. Harry Emory and Eurith Elizabeth (McKinney) S.; m. Patricia Mason, Oct. 7, 1973; 1 child, Andrea Elizabeth. BS, U. Pitts., 1971; MBA, Columbia U., 1986; JD, Pace U., White Plains, N.Y., 1990. Bar: Conn. 1990, N.Y. 1991, D.C. 1992, U.S. Dist. Ct. Conn. 1991, U.S. Dist. Ct. (ea. and so. dist.) N.Y. 1991, U.S. Dist. Ct. D.C. 1992, U.S. Ct. Appeals (2d cir.) 1992, U.S. Supreme Ct. 1995. With IBM, Armonk, N.Y., 1971-90; assoc. Wiggin & Dana, Stamford, Conn., 1990—. Contbr. articles to profl. jours. Bd. dirs. Youth Continuum, New Haven, Conn. Mem. ABA (litigation sect.), Conn. Bar Assn. (CLE teaching faculty), Assn. of Bar of City of N.Y. (del. to state bar assn.), Conn. Trial Lawyers Assn., C. of C., Delta Theta Phi. Avocation: equestrian sports. General civil litigation, Product liability, Equine. Home: 49 Raemont Rd Granite Spgs NY 10527-1113

**STOKES, JAMES CHRISTOPHER,** lawyer; b. Orange, N.J., Mar. 19, 1944; s. James Christopher and Margaret Mary (Groome) S.; m. Eileen Marie Brosnan, Sept. 7, 1968; children: Erin Margaret, Michael Colin, Courtney Dorothy. AB, Holy Cross Coll., 1966; JD, Boston Coll., 1975. Bar: Hawaii 1975, U.S. Ct. Appeals (1st and 9th cirs.) 1976, Mass. 1977, U.S. Ct. Internat. Trade 1988. Officer USMC, 1966-72; assoc. Carlsmith, Carlsmith, Wichman & Case, Honolulu, 1975-76, Bingham, Dana & Gould, Boston, 1976-82; ptnr. Bingham, Dana & Gould, London, 1980-84, Boston, 1982—. Contbr. articles to profl. jours. Active personnel bd. Town of Wellesley, Mass., 1984-89, chmn. bd., 1988-89, town moderator, 1992-97. Capt. USMC, 1966-72, Vietnam. Mem. Hawaii Bar Assn., Mass. Bar Assn., Internat. Bar Assn., Boston Bar Assn., Traveller's Club (London), Union Club (Boston), Wellesley Club (bd. dirs.), German-Am. Bus. Club (Boston) (bd. dirs.). Roman Catholic. General corporate, Finance, Private international. Office: Bingham Dana LLP 150 Federal St Boston MA 02110-1713

**STOKES, JAMES SEWELL,** lawyer; b. Englewood, N.J., Jan. 24, 1944; s. James Sewell III and Doris Mackey (Smith) S.; m. Esther Moger, Aug. 19, 1967; children: Jessica Neale, Elizabeth Sewell. BA, Davidson (N.C.) Coll., 1966; LLB, Yale U., 1969. Bar: Ga. 1969. Asst. to gen. counsel Office Gen. Counsel of the Army, Washington, 1969-72; assoc. Alston, Miller & Gaines, Atlanta, 1972-77; ptnr. Alston & Bird (previously Alston, Miller & Gaines), Atlanta, 1977—, chmn. environ. group, 1987-96, 98—, chmn. bus. devel. com., 1983-85, 93-94, 96—; mem. ptnr.'s com. Alston & Bird, Atlanta, 1995-98; chmn., 1998; speaker on environ. matters to various seminars and meetings; mem. Gov.'s Environ. Adv. Coun., 1991—, chmn., 1997-99; chmn. Gov.'s Conf. on Pollution Prevention and the Environment, 1997. Contbr. articles to profl. jours. Co-chmn. Spotlight on Ga. Artists V, 1986; mem. City of Atlanta Zoning Rev. Bd., 1978-85, chmn., 1984-85; bd. dirs. Brookwood Hills Civic Assn., 1975-77, pres., 1977; bd. dirs. Nexus Contemporary Arts Ctr., Atlanta, 1987-92, vice chmn. capital campaign, 1989, chmn. nominating com., 1988, chmn. fundraising com., 1987-88; bd. dirs. Butler St. YMCA N.W. br., 1973-75, Dynamo Swim Club, 1988-91, Arts Festival Atlanta, 1994-98; trustee Inst. Continuing Legal Edn., Athens, 1980-81, Trinity Sch., Atlanta, 1988, 97—, Charles Loridans Found., 1994—; mem. session Trinity Presbyn. Ch., 1986-89, 97—, clk. of session, 1988-89, chmn. cmty. concerns com., 1987-88, chmn. pers. com., 1989-90, 99—, chmn. assoc. pastor search com., 1991-92; bd. dirs. Park Pride, 1992; Ga. C. of C., bd. dirs. 1998—, chmn. environ. com., 1987-92, environ. legal counsel, 1981-87; mem. spl. program Leadership Atlanta, 1979-80, Leadership Ga., 1985; mem. Ga. bd. advisors Trust for Pub. Land, 1990-95. Capt. U.S. Army, 1969-72. Decorated D.S.M.; recipient Spl. award Atlanta chpt. AIA, 1988, Mayor Andrew Young, 1985. Mem. ABA (natural resources sect.), State Bar Ga. (chmn. environ. law sect. 1979-82), Atlanta Bar Assn., City of Atlanta Hist. Preservation (policy steering com. 1989), Ga. C. of C. (bd.

dirs. 1998—), Atlanta C. of C. (water resources task force 1982-87, solid waste task force 1989, air quality task force 1993-97, environ. affairs com. 1998—), Ga. Indsl. Developers Assn. (hazardous waste com. 1983-84), Phi Beta Kappa, Omicron Delta Kappa. Avocations: swimming, bird watching, community activities. Environmental, Land use and zoning (including planning). Home: 129 Palisades Rd NE Atlanta GA 30309-1532 Office: Alston & Bird One Atlantic Ctr 1201 W Peachtree St NW Ste 4200 Atlanta GA 30309-3424

**STOKES, JOELYNN TOWANDA,** lawyer; b. Balt., May 28, 1961; d. Leslie M. and Mildred S. S. BA, Vanderbilt U., 1983; JD, Hofstra U., 1986. Assoc. Kitch Saurbier Drutchas Wagner & Kenney, Detroit, 1986-88, Harvey, Kruse, Westen & Milan, Detroit, 1988-90; ptnr. Hyatt Legal Svcs., Livonia, Mich., 1990-93; prin. atty. J.T. Stokes & Assocs., Farmington Hills, Mich., 1993—; adj. prof. Detroit Coll. Law, 1996-97. Mem. Delta Sigma Theta. Family and matrimonial, Probate, General civil litigation. Office: J T Stokes & Assocs 29010 W 8 Mile Rd Farmngtn Hls MI 48336-5910

**STOKES, RON,** lawyer; b. Springfield, Mo., Dec. 2, 1950; s. Joe Alfred Stokes and MaryLee (Bennett) O'Rourke; m. Christine Monteleone, Nov. 9, 1986. BA, U. Ill., 1973; JD, St. John's U., Jamaica, N.Y., 1976. Bar: N.Y. 1977, U.S. Dist. Ct. (so. dist.) N.Y. 1987. Assoc. Francis J. Young, Hartsdale, N.Y., 1976-78; pvt. practice Rye Brook, N.Y., 1979-95, Yorktown, 1995—. Mem. N.Y. State Dem. Com., 1976-95, Westchester County Dem. Exec. Com., White Plains, N.Y., 1976-95; mem. bd. mgrs. Rye Ridge Condominium, 1989-95. Mem. Westchester County Bar Assn. (sec. criminal justice sect. 1989-91, chair 1991-92), Sierra Club, Adirondack Mountain Club. Lutheran. Avocations: hiking, mountain climbing, sailing. Criminal, Probate, State civil litigation. Home and Office: 3224 S Shelly St Mohegan Lake NY 10547-1908

**STOLL, NEAL RICHARD,** lawyer; b. Phila., Nov. 7, 1948; s. Mervin Stoll and Goldie Louise (Serody) Stoll Wilf; m. Linda G. Seligman, May 25, 1972; children: Meredith Anne, Alexis Blythe. BA in History with distinction, Pa. State U., 1970; JD, Fordham U., 1973. Bar: N.Y. 1974, U.S. Dist. Ct. (ea. dist.) N.Y. 1974, U.S. Ct. Appeals (2d cir.) 1974, U.S. Ct. Appeals (11th cir.) 1982, U.S. Dist. Ct. (ea. dist.) Mich. 1983, U.S. Dist. Ct. (so. dist.) N.Y. 1974, U.S. Supreme Ct. 1986. Assoc. Skadden, Arps, Slate, Meagher & Flom, LLP, N.Y.C., 1973-81, mem., 1981—; lectr. Practicing Law-Inst., N.Y.C. Author: (with others) Aquisitions Under the Hart Scott Rodino Antitrust Improvements Act, 1980; contbr. articles to profl. pubs. Mem. Assn. Bar City of N.Y. (mem. trade regulation com. 1983-85), ABA, N.Y. State Bar Assn. Democrat. Antitrust, Federal civil litigation. Office: Skadden Arps Slate 919 3rd Ave New York NY 10022-3902

**STOLL, RICHARD G(ILES),** lawyer; b. Phila., Oct. 2, 1946; s. Richard Giles and Mary Margaret (Zeigler) S.; m. Susan Jane Nicewonger, June 15, 1968; children: Richard Giles III, Christian Hayes. BA magna cum laude, Westminster Coll., 1968; JD, Georgetown U., 1971. Bar: D.C. 1971, U.S. Dist. Ct. D.C. 1971, U.S. Ct. Appeals D.C. 1971, U.S. Ct. Appeals (4th cir.) 1977. Assoc. Arent, Fox, Kintner, Plotkin & Kahn, Washington, 1971-73; atty. Office of Gen. Counsel EPA, Washington, 1973-77, asst. gen. counsel, 1977-81; dep. gen. counsel Chem. Mfrs. Assn., Washington, 1981-84; ptnr. Freedman, Levy, Kroll & Simonds, Washington, 1984—; instr. environ. law and policy U. Va., Charlottesville, 1981-90. Co-author: Handbook on Environmental Law, 1987, 88, 89, 91, Practical Guide to Environment Law, 1987; contbr. articles to profl. jours.; moderator, panelist legal ednl. TV broadcasts and tapes ABA and Am. Law Inst. Elder Georgetown Presbyn. Ch.; frequent panelist and moderator on environ. law TV programs. Served to capt., USAR, 1968-76. Recipient Alumni Achievement award Westminster Coll., 1998. Mem. ABA (sect. natural resources, energy and environ. law; chmn. water quality com. 1980-82, hazardous waste com. 1983-85, coun. mem. 1985-88, sect. chmn. 1990-91), Washington Golf and Country Club. Avocations: piano, golf, music composition. Environmental. Office: Freedman Levy Kroll & Simonds 1050 Connecticut Ave NW Ste 825 Washington DC 20036-5366

**STOLLER, DAVID ALLEN,** lawyer; b. Burlington, Iowa, Oct. 27, 1947; s. Richard L. and Marjorie E. (Thornton) S.; m. Nancy E. Leachman, July 14, 1973; children: Aaron J., Anne C., John D. BSBA, Drake U., 1970, JD, 1977. Bar: Iowa 1977, N.C., 1985, U.S. Dist. Ct. (so. dist.) Iowa 1978, U.S. Dist. Ct. (no. dist.) Iowa 1981, U.S. Ct. Appeals (8th cir.) 1981, U.S. Dist. Ct. (ea. dist.) N.C. 1985, U.S. Ct. Appeals (4th cir.) 1986; cert. mediator, N.C. Assoc. city atty. City of Des Moines, 1977-81; assoc. Connolly, O'Malley, Lillis, Hansen & Olson, Des Moines, 1981-85, Ward & Smith, New Bern, N.C., 1985-89; ptnr. Dunn, Dunn., Stoller & Pittman, New Bern, 1990—. Bd. dirs. Episcopal Found. Diocese East Carolina, v.p., 1996-98; bd. dirs. Thompson's Children's Home, Inc., Charlotte, N.C.; mem., pres. standing com. Episcopal Diocese of East Carolina; mem., v.p. City of New Bern Planning and Zoning Bd. Eagle Scout Boy Scouts Am., 1964. Mem. ABA (dispute resolution sects.), Def. Rsch. Inst., N.C. Bar Assn. (dispute resolution sect.), N.C. State Bar (councillor 1995—), 3rd Jud. Dist. Bar, Craven County Bar Assn., Soc. of Profls. in Dispute Resolution, New Bern Golf and Country Club. Avocations: coaching youth soccer, basketball, T-ball. General civil litigation, Construction, Alternative dispute resolution. Home: 2432 Tram Rd New Bern NC 28562-7370 Office: Dunn Dunn & Stoller 3230 Country Club Rd New Bern NC 28562-7304

**STOLMAN, MARC DANIEL,** lawyer; b. Santa Cruz, Calif., Aug. 31, 1957. BA, U. Calif. San Diego, 1979; JD, U. San Francisco, 1982. Bar: Calif. 1982, U.S. Dist. Ct. (no. dist.) Calif., U.S. Ct. Appeals (9th cir.), U.S. Supreme Ct. Atty. Tiburon, Calif., 1982—. Author: A Guide to Legal Rights for People with Disabilities, 1994; contbr. articles to profl. jours. Bd. dirs. northern Calif. chpt. Nat. Multiple Sclerosis Soc., 1993—, San Francisco chpt. United Cerebral Palsy Assn., 1993-95. Mem. Calif. State Bar Assn. (tchr. continuing legal edn. 1995, commendation 1983-89), Bar Assn. of San Francisco (chair disability rights law com. 1994-96), Marin County Bar Assn. (continuing legal edn. com. 1997-98). Real property. Office: 1550 Tiburon Blvd Ste B Tiburon CA 94920-2515

**STOLTZFUS, JAMES ALLEN,** lawyer; b. Ephrata, Pa., Apr. 23, 1967; s. Samuel H. and Mary Ellen Stoltzfus; m. Julie Ann Hubbard, June 13, 1998. BS in BA, Millersville U., 1991; JD, Temple U., 1995. Bar: Del. 1995. Corp. atty. Skadden Arps Slate Meagher & Flom LLP, Wilmington, Del., 1995—. Bd. dirs. First Call for Help, Inc., Wilmington, 1997—. With USAF, 1985-88. Mem. Del. State Bar. Avocations: soccer, guitar, travel. Mergers and acquisitions, Securities, General corporate. Office: Skadden Arps Slate Meagher & Flom One Rodney Sq Wilmington DE 19809

**STOMMA, PETER CHRISTOPHER,** lawyer; b. Milw., May 29, 1966; s. Thaddeus and Hedwig Wanda (Struszczyk) S. BSEE, Marquette U., 1988; JD, Drake U., 1991. Bar: Wis. 1991, U.S. Dist. Ct. (ea. and we. dists.) Wis. 1991, U.S. Ct. Appeals (fed. cir.) 1991, U.S. Patent and Trademark Office 1991. Sr. assoc. Andrus, Sceales, Starke and Sawall, Milw., 1991—. Vol. Discovery World, Milw., 1991-94, Lawyers' Hotline Wis., Madison, 1991—; mem. devel. com. Legal Aid Milw., 1991-93; recruiting rep. Drake U., Des Moines, Iowa, 1992-94. Mem. ABA, Am. Intellectual Property Law Assn., Wis. Intellectual Property Law Assn., St. Thomas More Lawyer's Soc., Marquette Minuteman Club, Marquette Tip Off Club. Patent, Trademark and copyright, Entertainment. Office: Andrus Sceales Starke and Sawall 100 E Wisconsin Ave Ste 1100 Milwaukee WI 53202-4178

**STONE, ANDREW GROVER,** lawyer; b. L.A., Oct. 2, 1942; s. Frank B. and Meryl (Pickering) S.; divorced; 1 child, John Blair. BA, Yale U., 1965; JD, U. Mich., 1969. Bar: D.C. 1970, U.S. Dist. Ct. D.C. 1970, U.S. Ct. Appeals (D.C. cir.) 1972, Mass. 1981. Assoc. Rogers & Wells, Washington, 1969-71; atty. Bur. Competition, FTC, Washington, 1971-80; antitrust counsel Digital Equipment Corp., Maynard, Mass., 1980-83, mgr. N.E. law group, 1983-86, mgr. headquarters sales law group, 1986-88; asst. general counsel U.S. (acting), 1987, 88; corp counsel Washington, 1988-90; corp. counsel, pub. sect. mktg. Digital Equipment Corp., 1990-91; corp. counsel Thinking Machines Corp., Cambridge, Mass., 1992-95; pvt. practice on-site legal svcs. Marblehead, Mass., 1995—. Corp. mem. Tenacre Country Day Sch., Wellesley, Mass., 1981-88. Mem. ABA (bus. law sect., sci. tech. sect., pub. contracts sect., vice-chmn. comml. products and svcs. com. 1983-84), Mass. Bar Assn. (internat. law steering com. 1993-94), Boston Bar Assn. (membership com. 1998—, chair corp. counsel com. 1995-98, gen. counsel forum 1995—), Licensing Execs. Soc., Am. Arbitration Assn. (comml. arbitrator), Am. Intellectual Property Law Assn., New Eng. Corp. Counsel Assn., Assn. Ind. Gen. Counsel. Computer, Government contracts and claims, Contracts commercial.

**STONE, BERTRAM ALLEN,** lawyer; b. Chgo., Nov. 14, 1915; s. David and Fannie (Abrams) S.; m. Idelle Shirley Kotz, Nov. 25, 1951; children—Robert A., Ronald W., Judith Stone Weiss. Student U. Ill.; LL.B., J.D., Chgo. Kent Coll. Law, 1938. Bar: Ill. 1938, U.S. Dist. Ct. (no. dist.) Ill. 1939, U.S. Dist. Ct. (no. dist.) Ind. 1989. Ptnr. Cherkas, Rosenberg & Stone, 1950-58, Cherkas, Stone & Pogrund, 1958-61, Stone, Pogrund & Korey, 1961-86, Stone, Pogrund, Korey and Spagat, 1986—; gen. counsel Chgo. Metal Finishers Inst., 1961-63, Twin Cities Assn. Metal Finishers, 1961-63, Fabric Salesmen's Club Chgo. Bd. overseers. IIT-Chgo.-Kent Coll. Law; sec. Ill. Water, Waste and Sewage Group; mem. Ill. small bus. environ. task force EPA, 1993-94. Served to maj. USAF, 1941-45. Recipient award of merit, award of spl. recognition Nat. Assn. Metal Finishers. Mem. Ill. State Bar Assn., Chgo. Bar Assn. IIT Chgo.-Kent Coll. Law Alumni Assn. (past pres.), B'nai B'rith, Alpha Epsilon Pi. Environmental, General corporate, Probate. Address: 221 N La Salle St Chicago IL 60601-1206

**STONE, DONALD P.,** lawyer; b. Ironwood, Mich., July 31, 1937; s. Paul Clarence and Ethel (Moore) S.; m. Barbara Ann Schneider, Nov. 24, 1962 (dec.); children: Kimberly Ann, Paul Christian, Sandra Jane; m. Stephanie L. Brooks, Jan. 31, 1997. BA, Tchrs. cert., U. Mich., 1959, JD, 1962. Bar: Mich. 1962, U.S. Dist. Ct. (we. dist.) Mich. 1963. Ptnr. Klute, Stone, Campbell & Schofield, Niles, Mich., 1963—. Mem. ABA, Mich. Bar Assn., Berrien County Bar Assn. (pres. 1973-74), Elks. Presbyterian. Probate. Office: Klute Stone & Campbell 223 N 4th St # 249 Niles MI 49120-2301

**STONE, EDWARD HERMAN,** lawyer; b. July 20, 1939; s. Sidney and Ruth Stone; m. Pamela G. Gray (dec. 1990); children: Andrew, Matthew; m. Elaine Ornitz, Dec. 22, 1995. BS in Acctg., U. Ill., 1961; JD, John Marshall Law Sch., 1967. Bar: Ill. 1967, Calif. 1970; cert. specialist Calif. probate, estate planning, and trust law. With IRS, 1963-71; assoc. Eilers, Baranger, Myers & Smith, 1971-72; pvt. practice Newport Beach, Calif., 1972—; mem. Davis, Samuelson, Goldberg & Blakely (formerly Cohen, Stokke & Davis), Santa Ana, Calif., 1984-88; pvt. practice Santa Ana, 1988-89; ptnr. Edward H. Stone A Law Corp., 1990—; instr. income and estate taxes Western States U. Sch. Law, 1971-72, mem. CEB Joint Adv. Com., Estating Planning subcom.; judge pro tem, jud. arbitrator Orange County Superior Ct.; moderator, spkr. on probate and trust litigation. Contbr. articles to profl. jours. Bd. dirs. Eastbluff Homeowners Comty. Assn., Newport Beach, 1980-82, pres., 1981-82; pres. Jewish Family Svcs. Orange County, 1975; v.p., bd. dirs. Orange County Jewish Fedn. of Orange County, 1985-88; bd. dirs. Heritage Points Orange County, 1992-95. Mem. Orange County Bar Assn. (vice-chmn. estate planning probate and trust law sect. 1976-77, chmn. sect. 1977-78, chairperson ADR com. 1996, instr. Probate Clinic 1980, spkr. in substansive law; dir. 1977-82, chmn. Profl. Ednl. Coun. 1980-82, past chmn. profl. edn. coun., chmn. Orange County Bar del. of real property and probate sect. for state bar conv. 1992—), Phi Alpha Delta (pres. alumni chpt. 1975-76). Probate, General corporate, Estate planning.

**STONE, F. L. PETER,** lawyer; b. Wilmington, Del., Feb. 24, 1935; s. Linton and Lorinda (Hamlin) S.; m. Therese Louise Hannon, Apr. 7, 1969; 1 child, Lisa Judith. AB, Dartmouth Coll., 1957; LLB, Harvard U., 1960. Bar: Del. Supreme Ct. 1960, U.S. Ct. Appeals (3d cir.) 1964, U.S. Supreme Ct. 1965, U.S. Ct. Appeals (fed. cir.) 1983. Assoc. Connolly, Bove & Lodge, Wilmington, 1960-64; dep. atty. gen. State of Del., Wilmington, 1965-66; atty. Del. Gen. Assembly, Dover, 1967-68; counsel Gov. Del., Dover, 1969; U.S. atty. Dist. of Del., Wilmington, 1969-72; ptnr. Connolly, Bove, Lodge, & Hutz, Wilmington, 1972-97; counsel Trzuskowski, Kipp, Kelleher & Pearce, Wilmington, 1997-98; dep. atty. gen., counsel to ins. dept. State of Del., 1998—; mem. Del. Agy. to Reduce Crime, 1969-72, Del. Organized Crime Commn., 1970-72, State Drug Abuse Coun., 1990-93, State Judicial Nominating Commn., 1991-93, State Coun. Corrections, 1992-99; co-founder, adj. prof. criminal justice progra, West Chester (Pa.) U., 1975-79; chmn. Gov.'s Harness Racing Investigation Com., 1977, Del. Jai Alai Commn., 1977-78, Del. Govs. Corrections Task Force, 1986-88. Contbr. articles to profl. jours. Chmn. UN Day, Del., 1989; Rep. candidate for atty. gen. Del., 1990, mem. Rep. exec. com., Wilmington region, 1991—; chmn. re-election campaign, Del. Ins. Commr., 1996; mem. Del. Gov.'s Task Force on Prison Security, 1994-95; trustee Leukemia Soc. Am., N.Y.C., 1972-74, Marywood Coll., Scranton, Pa., 1974-79, Ursuline Acad., Wilmington, 1974-80; bd. dirs. Boys & Girls Club Del., 1997—. Mem. Port of Wilmington Maritime Soc. (bd. dirs., chair 1998—), Wilmington Country Club, Lincoln Club Del. (pres. 1994), Wilmington Rotary (bd. dirs. 1995-97), Nat. Assn. Former U.S. Attys. (bd. dirs. 1995-98). Roman Catholic. Avocations: hiking/mountaineering, tennis, music. General civil litigation, General corporate. Office: Del Dept Ins PO Box 429 841 Silver Lake Blvd Dover DE 19904-2465 *My major accomplishment has been establishing and maintaining a close relationship with my family, first and foremost, regardless of what activities and accomplishments were pursued in my professional, political and community life.*

**STONE, GEOFFREY RICHARD,** law educator, lawyer; b. Nov. 20, 1946; s. Robert R. and Shirley (Weliky) S.; m. Nancy Spector, Oct. 8, 1977; children: Julie, Mollie. BS, U. Pa., 1968; JD, U. Chgo., 1971. Bar: N.Y. 1972. Law clk. to Hon. J.S. Kelly Wright U.S. Ct. Appeals (D.C. cir.), 1971-72; law clk. to Hon. William J. Brennan, Jr. U.S. Supreme Ct., 1972-73; asst. prof. U. Chgo., 1973-77, assoc. prof., 1977-79, prof., 1979-84, Harry Kalven Jr. disting. svc. prof., 1984-93, deal Law Sch., 1987-93, provost, 1994—. Author: Constitutional Law, 1986, 3d edit., 1996, The Bill of Rights in the Modern State, 1992, The First Amendment, 1999; editor The Supreme Ct. Rev., 1991—; contbr. articles to profl. jours. Bd. dirs. Ill. divsn. ACLU, 1978-84; bd. advisors Pub. Svc. Challenge, 1989; bd. govs. Argonne Nat. Lab., 1994—. Fellow AAAS; mem. Chgo. Coun. Lawyers (bd. govs. 1976-77), Assn. Am. Law Schs. (exec. com. 1990-93), Legal Aid Soc. (bd. dirs. 1988), Order of Coif. Office: U Chgo 5801 S Ellis Ave Chicago IL 60637-5418

**STONE, HOWARD LAWRENCE,** lawyer; b. Chgo., Sept. 16, 1941; s. Jerome Richard Stone and Ceale (Perlik) Stone Tandet; m. Susan L. Saltzman, June 2, 1963; children—Lauren, David. Student U. Ill., 1960-61; B.S.B.A., Roosevelt U., 1963; J.D., DePaul U., 1972. Bar: Ill. 1972, U.S. Dist. Ct. (no. dist.) Ill. 1972, U.S. Tax Ct. 1972, U.S. Supreme Ct. 1982; C.P.A., Ill. Agt. IRS, Chgo., 1964-72; spl. asst. U.S. atty. and chief fin. auditor and investigator No. Dist. Ill., Dept. Justice, Chgo., 1972-76; sr. ptnr. Stone, McGuire & Benjamin, Chgo., 1976—; now with Altshuler, Melvoin & Glasser. lectr. in taxation. Author: Defending the Federal Tax Case: What To Do When the IRS Steps In, 1978; Client Tax Fraud—A Practical Guide to Protecting Your Rights, 1984. Co-editor, co-author: Handling Criminal Tax Cases: A Lawyers Guide, 1982, 87; co-author: Federal Civil Tax Law, 1982, 88; co-author: Negotiating to Win, 1985. Bd. dirs. Israel Bonds, Chgo., 1982, U. Chgo.; chmn. U. Ill. Found. Fund for Gerontology Rsch., 1984—; bd. dirs. Gastro Intestinal Research Found. U. Chgo., 1978—. Mem. Chgo. Bar Assn., Ill. State Bar Assn., Fed. Bar Assn., ABA, Decalogue Soc. Lawyers, Am. Inst. C.P.A.s, Ill. C.P.A. Found., Am. Assn. Atty.-C.P.A.s, Ill. C.P.A. Soc. (resident lectr. in tax fraud 1976-84, 90, 91, chmn. Investment Advisers Act task force 1983-84, co-chair accts. liability annual conf.). Jewish. Lodges: B'nai B'rith, Shriners. Criminal, Personal income taxation, Health. Office: Altschuler Melvoin & Glasser 30 S Wacker Dr Ste 2600 Chicago IL 60606-7405

**STONE, JERI,** lawyer, association director; b. Dallas, Aug. 10, 1954; d. Harold Bryan and Jean Marie (Turnbough) S.; m. Lonnie Floyd Hollingsworth, Jr.; children: Lonnie Floyd Hollingsworth III and Allen Stone Hollingsworth (twins). BS, So. Meth. U., 1975; JD, U. Tex., 1977. Bar: Tex. 1978. Assoc. Law Offices L.H. Owen III, Austin, Tex., 1977-78; dir. legal dept. Tex. Classroom Tchr.'s Assn., Austin, 1978-82, assoc. exec. dir., gen. counsel, 1982-85, gen. counsel, exec. dir., 1985—; vol. counsel Leadership Am. Alumnae Assn. Bd., 1988—; bd. dirs. Discovery Hall. Author, editor: The Classroom Teacher's Legal Rights Handbook, 1982, rev. edit., 1985. Participant Leadership Tex., Austin, 1987, Leadership Am., Washington, 1988. Mem. ABA, Tex. Bar Assn., Travis County Bar Assn., Barton Creek Club, University Club. Republican. Episcopalian. Home: 504 Las Lomas Dr Austin TX 78746-4689 Office: Tex Classroom Tchrs Assn PO Box 1489 Austin TX 78767-1489

**STONE, MATTHEW PETER,** lawyer; b. L.A., Sept. 21, 1961. BA in English, UCLA, 1985; JD, Loyola U., L.A., 1988. Bar: Calif. 1989, Ga. 1992, U.S. Dist. Ct. (ctrl. dist.) Calif. 1989, U.S. Dist. Ct. (no., mid. and so. dists.) Ga. 1992. Litigation assoc. Seligmann, Slyngstad & Wright, L.A., 1988-90, Musick, Peeler & Garrett, L.A., 1990-92; asst. atty. gen. Ga. Dept. of Law, Atlanta, 1992-95; litig. assoc. Casey, Gilson & Williams P.C., Atlanta, 1995-98; ptnr. Freeman Mathis & Gary, L.L.P., Atlanta, 1998—. Chmn. Law Day and Liberty Bell com. younger lawyers sect. State Bar of Ga., 1993-96, co-chair Law Day com., 1995-96, mem. instrastate moot ct. com. younger lawyers sect., 1994—; panel judge Ga. Intrastate Moot Ct. Competition, 1994—, ABA Nat. Appellate Advocacy Competition, S.E. Regional, 1994; chmn. Parks Project Hands on Atlanta Day, 1994; vol. Hands on Atlanta Day, 1993, 95; mem. ethical action com. Univ. Synagogue, L.A., 1990-92; participant Bet Tzedek Legal Svcs., L.A., 1986; participant, vol. Income Tax Assistance, L.A., 1988. Avocations: fishing, automobiles, physical fitness. Federal civil litigation, State civil litigation, Transportation. Office: Freeman Mathis & Gary LLP 100 Galleria Pkwy SE Fl 16 Atlanta GA 30339-3179

**STONE, MICHEL LEON,** lawyer; b. Chgo., Mar. 18, 1949; s. John Clay and Leone Christiane Stone; m. Pamela Dru Sutton, Feb. 13, 1988; 1 child, Elizabeth Sutton. AB cum laude, Harvard U., 1971; JD, NYU, 1976. Bar: Fla., N.Y., U.S. Dist. Ct. (so. and ea. dist.) N.Y., U.S. Dist. Ct. (no. dist.) Fla., U.S. Ct. Appeals (5th and 11th cirs.), U.S. Ct. Appeals (fed. cir.). Intern Urquhart & Chapman, Panama City, Fla., 1973-74, Legal Aid Soc., Juvenile Divsn., N.Y.C., 1975-76; from intern to assoc. Thal & Youtt, N.Y.C., 1975-78; from assoc. to ptnr. Urquhart, Pittman, Stone & Faucheux, Panama City, 1978-85; atty., chief capital divsn. Office of Pub. Defender, 14th Jud. Cir., Panama City, 1982-92; ptnr. Stone & Sutton, P.A., Panama City, 1985—; mem. death penalty steering com. Fla. Pub. Defender Assn., Tallahassee, 1990-92; lectr. USN and Marine JAG Officers Death Penalty Seminar, Camp LeJeune, N.C., 1992, Fla. Pub. Defender Assn. Death Penalty Confs., Tampa, Fla., 1992, 93; mem. jud. nominating commn. 14th Jud. Cir. of Fla., 1992-94. Co-author: (chpts.) Florida Public Defender Association Death Penalty Manual, 1992, rev., 1993; editor-in-chief NYU Review of Law and Social Change, 1975-76. Mem. Assn. Trial Lawyers Am. Democrat. Achievements include featured on CBS-TV program, 48 Hours, 1993. Personal injury, Criminal, Civil rights. Office: Stone and Sutton PA 116 E 4th St Panama City FL 32401-3109

**STONE, PETER GEORGE,** lawyer, publishing company executive; b. N.Y.C., July 29, 1937; s. Leo and Anne S.; m. Rikke Linde, Dec. 26, 1974; children: Adam, Rachel. BS in Econs., U. Pa., 1959; JD, Columbia U., 1962. Bar: N.Y. 1963. Assoc. Ballon Stoll & Itzler, N.Y.C., 1963-65, Raphael, Searles & Vischi, N.Y.C., 1965-67; v.p., counsel Firedoor Corp. Am., N.Y.C., 1967-69; ptnr. Cahill, Stone & Driscoll, N.Y.C., 1969-75; v.p. human resources and law, gen. counsel Ottaway Newspapers, Inc., Campbell Hall, N.Y., 1975—; lectr., columnist on media law numerous univs. including Jud. Coll. U. Nev., Hartwick Coll., Bucknell U., U. N.C., Western Conn. State U., SUNY. Bd. dirs., trustee, treas. Daily Pennsylvanian Alumni Assn. With USAR, 1962-63. Mem. ABA (forum com. on comm. law), N.Y. State Bar Assn. (ct. and cmty., pub. events and edn., pub. info. through TV coms., com. media law), N.Y. Bar Found., N.Y. State Fair Trial Free Press Assn., Newspaper Assn. Am. (com. on employee rels., com. on legal affairs, del. 1st amendment congress, com. on pub. policy), Am. Arbitration Assn., Soc. Human Resource Mgmt., Media Human Resources Assn. (pres.), Penn Club. Libel, General corporate, Constitutional. Office: PO Box 401 Campbell Hall NY 10916-0401

**STONE, PETER ROBERT,** lawyer; b. Mojave, Calif., July 16, 1956; s. Carl and Dorothy (Haisfield) S.; m. Georgia B. Harris, Oct. 6, 1979. AA, Antelope Valley Coll., 1976; BA, U. Calif., Santa Barbara, 1986; postgrad., Calif. State U., Sacramento, 1987; JD, U. of Pacific, 1992. Bar: Calif. 1992, U.S. Dist. Ct. (ea. dist.) Calif. 1992, Colo. 1993, U.S. Ct. Appeals (9th cir.) 1996, U.S. Supreme Ct. 1996. Law clk. Sacramento Dist. Atty.'s Office, summer 1991; rsch. att. Yolo Superior, Woodland, Calif., 1991-92; pvt. practice law Sacramento, 1994—; arbitrator, pro tem Yolo Superior Ct., Woodland, 1995—, Sacramento Superior Ct. Mem. ABA, Sacramento County Bar Assn. (mem. ins. com. 1996—), Consumer Attys. Calif., Comml. Law League Am., Consumer Attys. Sacramento, Soc. Profls. in Dispute Resolution. Personal injury, Consumer commercial, Contracts commercial. Office: 5777 Madison Ave Ste 1199 Sacramento CA 95841-3314

**STONE, RALPH KENNY,** lawyer; b. Bainbridge, Ga., Aug. 7, 1952; s. Ralph Patrick and Joyce (Mitchell) S.; m. Julie Ann Waldren, Aug. 24, 1974; children: Laura Lee, Rebecca, Michael. BBA magna cum laude, U. Ga., 1974, JD cum laude, 1977. Bar: Ga. 1977, U.S. Dist. Ct. (so. dist.) Ga. 1977, U.S. Supreme Ct. 1980, U.S. Ct. Appeals (11th cir.) 1981. Staff acct. Price Waterhouse & Co., Columbia, S.C., 1974; assoc. Calhoun & Donaldson, Savannah, Ga., 1977; ptnr. Franklin & Stone, Statesboro, Ga., 1977-88, Edenfield, Stone & Cox, Statesboro, Ga., 1988-94; pres. R. Kenny Stone, P.C., 1994—; instr. taxation Ga. So. Coll., Stateboro, 1979-80. Sect. chmn. United Way S.E. Ga., campaign chmn., 1989, pres. 1991; charter pres. Leadership Bulloch, Inc., 1984; chmn. Bulloch County Dem. Com., 1984-90, Bulloch 2000 Com., 1986-88; alt. del. Dem. Nat. Conv., 1988; sec. Ga. Assn. Dem. County Chairs, 1985-89, pres. 1989-91; dist. chmn. Boy Scouts Am., 1985; pres. Forward Bulloch Inc., 1986; participant Leadership Ga., 1986; mem. Ga. Bd. Industry Trade & Tourism, 1991-96. Mem. ABA, State Bar Ga., Bulloch County Bar Assn. (pres. 1982-83), Statesboro-Bulloch C. of C. (pres. 1986, chmn. bd. dirs. 1987, chmn. devel. authority Bulloch County 1991—), Rotary (Statesboro), Optimist Club (pres. 1980-81, dist. lt. gov. 1981-82), Phi Kappa Phi, Beta Alpha Psi. Baptist. Bankruptcy, State civil litigation, General practice. Home: 319 Dogwood Trl Statesboro GA 30461-4253 Office: R Kenny Stone PC PO Box 681 Statesboro GA 30459-0681

**STONE, RANDOLPH NOEL,** law educator; b. Milw., Nov. 26, 1946; s. Fisher and Lee Della Stone; m. Cheryl M. Bradley; children: Sokoni, Rahman, Marisa, Lee Sukari. BA, U. Wis., Milw., 1972; JD, Madison, 1975. Bar: D.C., 1975, Wis. 1975, Ill. 1977. Staff atty. Criminal Def. Consortium of Cook County, Chgo., 1976-78; clin. fellow U. Chgo. Law Sch., 1977-80; ptnr. Stone & clark, Chgo., 1980-83; staff atty., dep. dir. Pub. Defender Svc. for D.C., Washington, 1983-88; pub. defender Cook County Pub. Defender's Office, Chgo., 1988-91; lectr. U. Chgo. Law Sch., 1990, clin. prof. law, dir. Mandel Legal Aid Clinic, 1991—; adj. prof. Ill. Inst. Tech. Chgo.-Kent Coll. Law Sch., 1991, bd. overseers, 1990; lectr. law Harvard U., 1991—; mem. Ill. Bd. Admissions to the Bar, 1994—; bd. dirs. The Sentencing Project, 1986—; instr. trial advocacy workshop Harvard Law Sch., 1985-89. Adv. bd. Neighborhood Defender Svc. (Harlem), N.Y.C. Reginald Heber Smith fellow Neighborhood Legal Svcs. Program, Washington, 1975-76. Mem. ABA (sect. criminal justice coun. 1989-95, chair 1993, commn. domestic violence 1994-97), Ill. State Bar Assn. (sect. criminal justice coun. 1989-92), Chgo. Bar Assn. (bd. dirs. 1990-92), Nat. Legal Aid and Defender Assn. (def. com. 1988-96). Office: U Chgo Law Sch Mandel Legal Aid Clinic 6020 S University Ave Chicago IL 60637-2704

**STONE, SAMUEL BECKNER,** lawyer; b. Martinsville, Va., Feb. 4, 1934; s. Paul Raymond and Mildred (Beckner) S.; m. Shirley Ann Gregory, June 18, 1955; children: Paul Gregory, Daniel Taylor. BSEE, Va. Polytech. Inst. & State U., 1955; JD, George Wash. U., 1960. Bar: Md. 1960, Calif. 1963, Patent and Trademark Office. Patent examiner, 1955-58; patent adv. Naval Ordinance Lab., Silver Spring, Md., 1958-59; assoc. Thomas & Crickenberger, Washington, 1959-61, Beckman Instruments Inc., Fullerton, Calif., 1961-65; assoc. Lyon & Lyon, L.A., 1965-72, ptnr., 1972; mng. ptnr. Lyon & Lyon, Costa Mesa, Calif., 1982—; judge Disneyland Com. Svc. Awards, Anaheim, Calif., 1987. Mem. Orange County Bar Assn. (bd. dirs. 1988-91, travel seminar chair 1986-92), Orange County Patent Law Assn. (pres. 1987, bd. exec. com. 1987-90), Calif. Bar Assn. (intellectual property sect. bd. 1987-90), Am. Arbitration Assn. (intellectual property panel neutral arbitrators), Am. Electronics Assn. (lawyers com. 1988—, co-chair 1996-97), Orange County Venture Group (dir. 1985—, pres. 1996-97), Rams Booster Club (dir. 1984-90), Pacific Club (mem. legal adv. com., chair 1989-92, bd. dirs. 1999—). Republican. Avocations: tennis, waterskiing, music. Patent,

Trademark and copyright, Intellectual property. Home: 1612 Antigua Way Newport Beach CA 92660-4344 Office: Lyon & Lyon 3200 Park Center Dr Ste 1200 Costa Mesa CA 92626-7108

**STONE, SAUL,** lawyer; b. New Orleans, Dec. 15, 1906; s. Lazard David and Laura (Singer) S.; m. Sara Berenson, Apr. 7, 1938; children—David L., Richard B., Harvey M., Carol R. Stone Wright. LL.B., Tulane U., 1929. Bar: La. 1929, U.S. Ct. Appeals (5th cir.) 1930, U.S. Supreme Ct. 1950. Asst. U.S. atty., Eastern Dist. La., 1933-37; founder, ptnr. Wisdom and Stone and successor firm, Stone, Pigman, Walther, Wittmann and Hutchinson, New Orleans, 1957—. Mem. New Orleans Bar Assn., La. Bar Assn., ABA, Am. Law Inst. Real property, Corporate taxation, Probate. Home: 3 Poydras St New Orleans LA 70130-1665

**STONE, STEVEN DAVID,** lawyer, consultant; b. N.Y.C., July 6, 1952; s. Harris Bobby and Ray (Masin) S. AB, Princeton U., 1974; JD, U. Richmond, 1977. Bar: Va. 1977, U.S. Dist. Ct. (ea. dist.) Va. 1977, U.S. Ct. Appeals (4th cir.) 1977. Legis. asst. Va. Senate, Richmond, 1975-76; assoc. McCandlish, Lillard, Church & Best, Fairfax, Va., 1977-79; assoc. Fried, Fried & Klewans, Springfield, Va., 1980-83, ptnr., 1983-86; prin. Steven David Stone, P.C., Springfield and Alexandria, Va., 1986—; legal counsel Va. Assn. Ind. Spa Owners, Springfield, 1984-86, Va. Optometric Assn., 1988—. Chmn. Lee Dist. Dem. Com., Fairfax County, 1981-85; sec., treas. Lee Dist. Assn. Civic Orgns., 1981—; bd. dirs. Jewish Cmty. Coun. Greater Washington; sec. Va. Bd. Rights of Disabled, Richmond, 1985-90; mem. com. of 100, Fairfax County, 1979—, pub. affairs com. Am.-Israel Orgn., gov.'s overall adv. com. on Needs of Handicapped Persons, 1981-85, Nat. Orgn. of Legal Problems in Edn.; bd. dirs. So. Fairfax Housing Coalition, 1988-89; mem. adv. bd. Va.-Israel, 1997—; bd. dirs. Washington Polit. Action Com. William DuBose Sheldon Meml. scholar. Mem. ABA, Assn. Trial Lawyers Am., Va. Bar Assn., Va. Trial Lawyers Assn., Fairfax Bar Assn. (lobbyist), Alexandria Bar Assn., Fairfax County C. of C. (chmn. legis. affairs com. 1980-81), Lee-Mt. Vernon C. of C. Democrat. Jewish. Club: Princeton (Washington). State civil litigation, Education and schools, Legislative. Office: 1004 Prince St Alexandria VA 22314-2933

**STONE, THOMAS KENDALL,** lawyer; b. Louisville, Dec. 15, 1956; s. Earle Victor and Mary Ann (French) S. BA, U. Ky., 1979; JD, U. Louisville, 1984. Bar: Ky., U.S. Dist. Ct. (we. dist.) Ky. Clk. U.S. Magistrate, Louisville, 1984-85; assoc. Boehl Stopher, Paducah, Ky., 1985; sole practice Louisville, 1985—. Mem. Louisville Bar Assn., Assn. Trial Lawyers Am., Ky. Bar Assn., ABA, Smithsonian Instn. Presbyterian. Avocations: gardening, boating, camping, hiking. Bankruptcy, Family and matrimonial, Probate. Office: 7982 New Lagrange Rd Ste 3 Louisville KY 40222-4718

**STONE, VICTOR J.,** law educator; b. Chgo., Mar. 11, 1921; s. Maurice Albert and Ida (Baskin) S.; m. Susan Abby Cane, July 14, 1951; children: Mary Jessica, Jennifer Abby, Andrew Hugh William. AB, Oberlin Coll., 1942; JD, Columbia U., 1948; LLD, Oberlin Coll., 1983. Bar: N.Y. 1949, Ill. 1950. Assoc. Columbia U., N.Y.C., 1948-49; assoc. Sonnenschein, Chgo., 1949-53; rsch. assoc. U. Chgo., 1953-55; asst. prof. law U. Ill., Champaign, 1955-57, assoc. prof. law, 1957-59, prof. law, 1959-91, prof. law emeritus, 1991—, assoc. v.p. acad. affairs, 1975-78; mem. jud. adv. coun. State Ill., 1959-61; mem. com. jury instrns. Ill. Supreme Ct., 1963-79, reporter, 1973-79; mem. Ill. State Appellate Defender Commn., 1973-83, vice-chmn., 1973-77, 79-83; bd. dirs. Champaign County Ct.-Apptd. Spl. Advocate Program, 1995—, pres., 1995-96, chmn., 1998—. Trustee Oberlin Coll., 1982-97; trustee AAUP Found., 1983-90. Lt. USNR, 1942-46. Ford Found. fellow, 1962-63. Fellow Ill. Bar Found. (charter 1986—); mem. ABA, CASA (bd. dirs. 1994-98, pres. 1998-99), Ill. Bar Assn. (chmn. individual rights and responsibilities 1971-72, mem. coun. civil practice and procedure 1978-82), Chgo. Bar Assn., AAUP (gen. counsel 1978-80, pres. 1982-84 , pres. Ill. conf. 1968-70, pres. Ill. chpt. 1964-65, mem. coun. 1982-90), ACLU (bd. dirs. Ill. div. 1986-96, exec. com. 1991-96), Am. Bar Found. (life 1986), State Univs. Annitants Assn. (pres. 1994-95, mem. state exec. com. 1995-97). Co-editor: Ill. Pattern Jury Instructions, 1965, 71, 77; Civil Liberties and Civil Rights, 1977. Office: U Ill Coll Law 504 E Pennsylvania Ave Champaign IL 61820-6909

**STONER, MICHAEL ALAN,** lawyer; b. Newport, R.I., Mar. 15, 1944; s. David S. and Beatrice (Newman) S.; m. Beverly C. Spence, Mar. 16, 1968 (div. Feb. 1979); children: Dustin Michael, David Field; m. Virginia Fuller, June 1, 1979. BA, Duke U., 1966; JD, Emory Law Sch., 1969. Bar: Ga. 1969. Assoc. Ray Cunningham, Decatur, Ga., 1969, Joe Salem, Atlanta, 1969; capt. U.S. Army, Ft. Knox, Ky., 1970-73; ptnr. Zagoria & Stoner, Atlanta, 1974-79; pvt. practice Atlanta, 1980—. Bd. dirs. Muscular Dystrophy Assn. No. Dist. Ga., 1975—; vol. fund raiser Sudden Infant Death Syndrome Found., Atlanta, Cystic Fibrosis Found., 1990—, Hemophilia Found. Ga., Major League Baseball Players Assn., 1992—. Named Ky. Col. Gov. of Ky., 1973. Avocations: tennis, basketball, baseball card and memorabilia collecting, specializing in Mickey Mantle, Ted Williams, and Joe DiMaggio. Family and matrimonial, Personal injury, General practice. Home: 375 Wyth Way NE Atlanta GA 30342-2021

**STONER, WAYNE LEE,** lawyer; b. Omaha, May 7, 1960; s. Harold D. and Carol J. Stoner; m. Barbara D. Dallis, Sept. 19, 1987 (div. Apr. 1994); 1 child, John P. BA, U. Denver, 1983; JD, U. Pa., 1986. Bar: Mass. 1986, U.S. Dist. Ct. Mass. 1987, U.S. Ct. Appeals (D.C. cir.) 1992, U.S. Dist. Ct. (we. dist.) Tex. 1998. Assoc. Hale and Dorr LLP, Boston, 1986-91, jr. ptnr., 1991-95, sr. ptnr., 1995—; judge Ames Moot Ct. Competition, Harvard Law Sch., 1995—, Giles Rich Moot Ct. Competition, Boston, 1995. Mem. Am. Intellectual Property Law Assn., Boston Patent Law Assn., Boston Bar Assn., Phi Beta Kappa. Republican. Avocation: art collecting. Federal civil litigation, Intellectual property, Patent. Office: 60 State St Boston MA 02109-1800

**STOOPS, DANIEL J.,** lawyer; b. Wichita, Kans., May 27, 1934; s. Elmer F. and Margaret J. (Pickrell) S.; m. Kathryn Ann Piepmeier, Aug. 28, 1954; children: Sharon, Janet. BA, Washburn U., 1956, JD, 1958. Bar: Kans. 1958, Ariz. 1959, U.S. Dist. Ct. Kans. 1958, U.S. Dist. Ct. Ariz. 1960, U.S. Ct. Appeals (9th cir.) 1975, U.S. Supreme Ct. 1971. Assoc. Wilson, Compton & Wilson, Flagstaff, Ariz., 1959-64; ptnr. Wilson, Compton & Stoops, Flagstaff, 1964-67, Mangum, Wall & Stoops, Flagstaff, 1967-77, Mangum, Wall, Stoops & Warden, Flagstaff, 1977. Editor Washburn Law Rev., 1958. Pres. Flagstaff Festival of the Arts, 1988-89, Flagstaff Sch. Bd., 1961-73, Ariz. Sch. Bd. Assn., 1971. Fellow Ariz. Bar Found., Am. Bar Found.; Am. Coll. Trial Lawyers (state chmn. 1984-85), Internat. Soc. Barristers; mem. Ariz. Bar Assn. (pres. 1980-81), Masons, Elks. Republican. Methodist. Avocations: golf, political and historical reading and research. General civil litigation, Insurance, Personal injury. Office: Mangum Wall Stoops & Warden 100 N Elden St Flagstaff AZ 86001-5295

**STORER, THOMAS PERRY,** lawyer; b. Washington, July 14, 1944; s. Morris Brewster and Gretchen Geuder (Schneider) S.; m. Julia Manganip Owek, Dec. 22, 1966; children: Lingbawan Frederick, Allinnawa Elizabeth, Gessingga Nathaniel. BA in Math., Harvard U., 1965, JD, 1979; MPA, Woodrow Wilson Sch. Pub. and Internat. Affairs, 1969. Bar: Mass. 1979, U.S. Dist. Ct. Mass. 1979. Program officer U.S. Peace Corps, Kuala Lumpur, Malaysia, 1969-72; analyst, unit chief Bur. of Budget State of Ill., Springfield, 1972-74; dep. dir. Ill. Dept. Pub. Aid, Springfield, 1974-76; cons. Mass. Medicaid Program, Boston, 1976-79; assoc. Goodwin, Procter & Hoar, Boston, 1979-87, ptnr., 1987—. Vol. U.S. Peace Corps, Bontoc, Mountain Prov., Philippines, 1965-67; elder Newton (Mass.) Presbyn. Ch., Mass., 1987-98. Mem. ABA, Mass. Bar Assn. Avocations: music, computers. General corporate, Intellectual property, Computer. Home: 22 Hobart Rd Newton Centre MA 02459-1313 Office: Goodwin Procter & Hoar LLP Exchange Pl Boston MA 02109-2803

**STOREY, LEE A.,** lawyer; b. Ypsilanti, Mich., Nov. 28, 1959; d. Henry Perry Herold and Elsie Lorraine (Long) Wolf; m. William Storey; children: Jason Michael, Jenifer Lorraine. Student, U. Mich., 1977-79; BA, UCLA, 1982, MA, 1984; JD, U. Calif., Berkeley, 1987. Bar: Ariz. 1988, U.S. Dist. Ct. 1990. Circulations mgr. Inst. Archaeology UCLA, 1980-84; rsch. asst. John Muir Inst., Napa, Calif., 1985, Am. Indian Resources Inst., Oakland, Calif., 1985; assoc. editor Ecology Law Quarterly U. Calif., Berkeley, 1985-86; assoc. Evans, Kitchel & Jenckes, Phoenix, 1987-89, Gallagher & Kennedy, Phoenix, 1989-90, Meyer, Hendricks, Victor, Osborn & Maledon, Phoenix, 1991-95; ptnr. Meyer Hendricks Bivens & Moyes P.A., 1995-99; prin. ptnr. Moyes Storey, Ltd., 1999—; guest lectr. water transfers Hydrological Soc. Symposium, Phoenix, 1989, environ. studies Ariz. State U., Tempe, 1990, water quality Soc. Mining Engrs., Denver, 1991, water transfers Wind River Assocs., Denver, 1991-92, Phoenix, 1992, Central Ariz. Project Utilization, Am. Water Resources Assn. Symposium, Tucson, 1992, Colo. River Basin Tribes, Coun. Energy Resource Tribes, Tucson, 1993, Indian Sovereignty, U.S. Dept. Interior, Bureau Reclamation, Phoenix, 1993; Indian Econ. Devel. Fed. Indian Bar Albuquerque, 1994, Water Rights, Ariz. Judicial Conf., Ariz. State Bar, Tucson, 1994, National Land Coun. sem., Water Rights, Rico Rico, Ariz., 1995; adj. prof. Indian water rights Sch. Law Ariz. State U., 1992, 97, mem. adv. com. on Indian law program Coll. of Law, 1999—. Co-author: Leasing Indian Water: Choices in Colorado River Basin, 1988; contbr. articles to profl. jours.; mem. Calif. Law Rev. U. Calif. Berkeley, 1985-87. Landlord tenant clinics Vols. Lawyers Program, Phoenix, 1988-89; mem. Ariz. Ctr. for Law-Related Edn., Ariz. Bar Found., Drug Awareness Program for Schs., 1990; chmn. bd. Ambs. for Change, 1996—. Scholar UCLA, 1980-84; recipient Am. Jurisprudence award Lawyers Coop., 1986. Mem. ABA, Ariz. State Bar Assn. (mem. com. on minorities and women in law 1993-97, chair-elect Indian law sect. 1997-98, chair 1998—, asst. editor Environ. and Natural Resources newsletter 1990-94, editor Indian law sect. Arrow newsletter 1996—), Ariz. Women Lawyers Assn., Maricopa County Bar Assn. Real property, Environmental, Native American. Office: Moyes Storey 3003 N Central Ave Ste 1250 Phoenix AZ 85012-2902

**STORM, ROBERT WARREN,** lawyer; b. Battle Creek, Mich., June 3, 1951; s. Robert Warren and Patricia Ellen Knight (Klinck) S. AB in History, William and Mary Coll., 1973, JD, 1989; MA in History, Duke U., 1977. Bar: Conn., 1989; ordained elder Collinsville (Conn.) Congl. Ch., 1997. Historian, archivist U.S. Govt., Washington and Austin, Tex., 1977-85; cons. in info. mgmt. Arlington, Williamsburg, Va., 1985-88; assoc. Robinson & Cole, Hartford, 1989-92; pvt. practice West Hartford, 1993—. Dir. The Children's Home, Cromwell, Conn., 1993-99, v.p. 1995-96; gubernatorial apptd. State Hist. Records Adv. Bd., Hartford, 1993-96; hon. advisor Ethiopian Comty. Ctr., Conn., 1996—; dir. Conn. Coalition of Mut. Assistance Assns., 1997—, v.p., 1998-99, treas., 1999—; dir. Lea's Found. for Leukemia Rsch., 1998—; dir. Lea's Found. for Leukemia Rsch., 1998—. Mem. ABA, Conn. Bar Assn., Soc. of Descendants of the Founders of Hartford, Mil. Order of Loyal Legion of U.S. (jr. vice comdr. Conn. 1999—). Avocations: reading, writing, music, nature, the fine arts. General practice, Estate planning, Private international. Office: 37 Crestwood Rd West Hartford CT 06107-3405

**STORMENT, HAROLD LLOYD,** lawyer; b. Frankfort, Ky., Jan. 12, 1957; s. H. Lloyd and Maxine S. BS, JD, U. Louisville, 1982. Bar: Ky. 1983, U.S. Dist. Ct. (we. dist.) Ky. 1983. Pvt. practice Louisville, 1983—. Family and matrimonial, Personal injury, Probate. Office: 500 Kentucky Home Life Bldg 239 S 5th St Louisville KY 40202-3213

**STORMS, CLIFFORD BEEKMAN,** lawyer; b. Mount Vernon, N.Y., July 18, 1932; s. Harold Beekman and Gene (Pertak) S.; m. Barbara H. Grave, 1955 (div. 1975); m. Valeria N. Parker, July 12, 1975; children: Catherine Storms Fischer, Clifford Beekman. BA magna cum laude, Amherst Coll., 1954; LLB, Yale U., 1957. Bar: N.Y. 1957. Assoc. Breed, Abbott & Morgan, N.Y.C., 1957-64; with CPC Internat., Inc., Englewood Cliffs, N.J., 1964-97, v.p. legal affairs, 1973-75, v.p., gen. counsel, 1975-88, sr. v.p., gen. counsel, 1988-97, atty. alternate dispute resolution, corp. dir., 1997—; pvt. practice Greenwich, Conn., 1997—; bd. dirs. Corn Products Internat., Inc., Atlantic Legal Found.; mem. Conn. Alternate Dispute Resolution panel Ctr. for Pub. Resources. Trustee emeritus Food and Drug Law Inst. Mem. ABA (com. of corp. gen. counsel), Am. Arbitration Assn. (panel arbitrators large complex case program), Assn. Gen. Counsel (pres. 1992-94), Assn. Bar City N.Y. (sec., com. on corp. law depts. 1979-81), Indian Harbor Yacht Club, Transp. Assn. of Greenwich, Yale Law Sch. Assn. (exec. com.), Phi Beta Kappa. General corporate, Alternative dispute resolution. Home: 19 Burying Hill Rd Greenwich CT 06831-2604 Office: Two Greenwich Plz Ste 100 Greenwich CT 06830

**STORROW, CHARLES FISKE,** lawyer; b. Houston, Mar. 14, 1957; S. Charles Henry Fiske and Margaret (Hubbard) S.; m. Melissa Cary, Aug. 22, 1981. BA, U. Maine, 1979; JD, Vt. Law Sch., 1982. Bar: Vt. 1982, U.S. Dist. Ct. Vt. 1983. Law clk. to sr. judge U.S. Ct. Appeals (2d cir.), N.Y.C., 1982-83; assoc. Paul, Frank & Collins, Inc., Burlington, Vt., 1983-88; ptnr. Kimbell & Storrow, Montpelier, Vt., 1989—. Mem. ABA, Vt. Bar Assn., Washington County Bar Assn. Avocation: fly fishing. Public utilities, Environmental, State civil litigation. Office: Kimbell & Storrow 26 State St Ste 14 Montpelier VT 05602-2943

**STORY, JAMES EDDLEMAN,** lawyer; b. Calvert City, Ky., June 7, 1928; s. William Arthur and Estella (Harper) S.; m. Barbara Owens, Oct. 11, 1953; children: Paul, Margaret, Virginia Lee, Sara Jane, Betty Ann, James Arthur. BS, Murray State Coll., 1952; JD, U. Louisville, 1958. Bar: Ky. 1958. Tchr. Jefferson County Bd. Edn., Louisville, 1954-58; assoc. prof. U. Ky. C.C., Paducah, 1958-64; county atty. Lyon County, Eddyville, Ky., 1962-74; pub. defender Lyon County, Princeton, Ky., 1974-82; pvt. practive Eddyville, 1974—; atty. Lake Barkley Project, U.S. Army Corp Engrs., Cadiz, Ky., 1960-62. With U.S. Army, 1946-48. Mem. ATLA, Ky. Trial Lawyers Assn., Ky. Assn. Criminal Def. Lawyers, Ky. Bar Assn., Sierra Club, Wilderness Club, Kentuckians for the Commonwealth, Am. Legion, Lions. Mem. Ch. of Christ. Avocations: tennis, swimming, hunting, water skiing, boxing. Federal civil litigation, Constitutional, Criminal. Office: PO Box 216 Eddyville KY 42038-0216

**STORY, MONTE ROBERT,** lawyer; b. Edmore, Mich., May 18, 1931; s. Charles and Helen R. (Brown) S.; m. Barbara Brooks, June 27, 1953; children: Julie Kay Story-Wood, Bret C. BA, Mich. State U., 1953; JD, Detroit Coll. Law, 1970. Bar: Mich. 1970, U.S. Tax Ct. 1971. Ptnr. Lyle D. Hepfer & Co., CPA's, Lansing, Mich., 1953-64, Danielson, Story, Lake & Schultz, Lansing, 1964-71; chmn. bd. dirs. Farhat & Story PC, East Lansing, Mich., 1971—. Capt. USAFR, 1954-66. Mem. ABA, Am. Inst. CPA's, Mich. Assn. CPA's, Mich. State Bar Assn., Ingham County Bar Assn. Republican. Lutheran. General corporate, Estate planning, Probate. Office: Farhat & Story PC 4572 S Hagadorn Rd Ste 300 East Lansing MI 48823-5385

**STOTLER, ALICEMARIE HUBER,** judge; b. Alhambra, Calif., May 29, 1942; d. James R. and Loretta M. Huber; m. James Allen Stotler, Sept. 11, 1971. BA, U. So. Calif., 1964, JD, 1967. Bar: Calif. 1967, U.S. Dist. Ct. (no. dist.) Calif. 1967, U.S. Dist. Ct. (cen. dist.) Calif. 1973, U.S. Supreme Ct. 1976; cert. criminal law specialist. Dep. Orange County Dist. Attys. Office, 1967-73; mem. Stotler & Stotler, Santa Ana, Calif., 1973-76, 83-84; judge Orange County Mcpl. Ct., 1976-78, Orange County Superior Ct., 1978-83, U.S. Dist. Ct. (cen. dist.) Calif., L.A., 1984—; assoc. dean Calif. Trial Judges Coll., 1982; lectr., panelist, numerous orgns.; standing com. on rules of practice and procedure U.S. Jud. Conf., 1991—, chair, 1993-98; mem. exec. com. 9th Cir. Jud. Conf., 1989-93, Fed. State Jud. Coun., 1989-98, jury com., 1990-92, planning com. for Nat. Conf. on Fed.-State Jud. Relationships, Orlando, 1991-92, planning com. for We. Regional Conf. on State-Fed. Jud. Relationships, Stevens, Wash., 1992-93; chair dist. ct. symposium and jury utilization Ctrl. Dist. Calif., 1985, chair atty. liaison, 1989-90, chair U.S. Constn. Bicentennial com., 1986-91, chair magistrate judge com., 1992-93; mem. State Adv. Group on Juvenile Justice and Delinquency Prevention, 1983-84, Bd. Legal Specializations Criminal Law Adv. Commn., 1983-84, victim/witness adv. com. Office Criminal Justice Planning, 1980-83, U. So. Calif. Bd. Councilors, 1993—; active team in tng. Leukemia Soc. Am., 1993, 95; legion lex bd. dirs. U. So. Calif. Sch. Law Support Group, 1981-83. Winner Hale Moot Ct. Competition, State of Calif., 1967; named Judge of Yr., Orange County Trial Lawyers Assn., 1978, Most Outstanding Judge, Orange County Bus. Litigation Sect., 1990; recipient Franklin G. West award Orange County Bar Assn., 1985. Mem. ABA (jud. adminstrn. divsn. and litigation sect. 1984—, nat. conf. fed. trial judges com. on legis. affairs 1990-91), Am. Law Inst., Am. Judicature Soc., Fed. Judges Assn. (bd. dirs. 1989-92), Nat. Assn. Women Judges, U.S. Supreme Ct. Hist. Soc., Ninth Cir. Dist. Judges Assn., Calif. Supreme Ct. Hist. Soc., Orange County Bar Assn. (mem. numerous com.s, Franklin G. West award 1984), Calif. Judges Assn. (mem. com. on jud. coll. 1978-80, com. on civil law and procedure 1980-82, Dean's coll. curriculum commn. 1981), Calif. Judges Found. Office: Ronald Reagan Fed Bldg and Courthouse 411 W 4th St Santa Ana CA 92701-4500

**STOTT, GARY DON,** judge; b. Sterling, Utah, Dec. 10, 1941; s. Benjamin Don and Jean Stott; m. Katherine Tueller, Jan. 3, 1964; children: Shauna Godfrey, Gregory, Lisa Mecham. BS, Brigham Young U., 1965; JD, U. Utah, 1968. Bar: Utah, Wyo. Assoc. Ivie & Young, Provo, Utah, 1968-73; sr. ptnr. Stott, Young & Wilson, Provo, 1973-78; sr. ptnr., shareholder Richards, Brandt, Miller & Nelson, Salt Lake City, 1979-96; state dist. ct. judge Utah Fourth Dist. Ct., Provo, 1997—. Served with Utah N.G., 1960-66. Mem. Utah Bar Assn., Wyo. Bar Assn., Riverside Country Club (Provo; pres. 1991), Brigham Young U. Nat. Cougar Club (pres. 1990). Avocations: fly fishing, golf, reading, racquetball, family camping activities. Office: Dist J 125 N 100 W Provo UT 84601-2849

**STOTTER, JAMES, II,** lawyer, legal consultant; b. Cleve., Oct. 12, 1929; s. Raymond H. and Janet H. (Stern) S.; m. Hollie McGlohn, Oct. 31, 1954; children: Raymond Judd, Hillary Margaret, James Robin, Cameron Elizabeth. BA, Yale Coll., 1951; LLB, Yale U., 1954; M in Law Studies, U. So. Calif., 1961. Bar: Calif., U.S. Supreme Ct., U.S. Ct. Mil. Appeals. Asst. U.S. atty. U.S. Dept. Justice, L.A., 1957-59, 73-89, asst. chief civil div., chief drug forfeiture unit, 1980-89; pvt. practice L.A., Beverly Hills, Calif., 1960-67; instr., adj. prof. law U.S. Atty. Gen.'s Advocacy Inst. Calif. Coll. Law, U. West L.A., 1970-87; judge pro tem Mcpl. and Small Claims Ct., L.A., 1970-88; atty. at law Cambria, Calif., 1989—. Guide hist. monument Hearst Castle, San Simeon, Calif., 1991; active civic and vol. orgns., Cambria and San Luis Obispo, Calif. Capt. USAF, 1954-57. Mem. Am. Arbitration Assn. (mediator/arbitrator 1970—). General civil litigation, Aviation, General practice. Home and Office: 1595 Cardiff Dr 2d Flr Cambria CA 93428-5703

**STOTTER, LAWRENCE HENRY,** lawyer; b. Cleve., Sept. 24, 1929; s. Oscar and Bertha (Lieb) S.; m. Ruth Rapoport, June 30, 1957; children: Daniel, Jennifer, Steven. BBA, Ohio State U., 1956, LLB, 1958, JD, 1967. Bar: Calif. 1960, U.S. Supreme Ct. 1973, U.S. Tax Ct. 1976. Pvt. practice San Francisco, 1963—; ptnr. Stotter and Coats, San Francisco, 1981-97; sole practitioner, 1997—; mem. faculty Nat. Judicial Coll.; mem. Calif. Family Law Adv. Commn., 1979-80. Editor in chief: Am. Bar Family Advocate mag, 1977-82; TV appearances on Phil Donahue Show, Good Morning America. Pres. Tamalpais Conservation Club, Marin County, Calif.; U.S. State Dept. del. Hague Conf. Pvt. Internat. Law, 1979-80; legal adv. White House Conf. on Families, 1980—. Served with AUS, 1950-53. Mem. ABA (past chmn. family law sect.), Am. Acad. Matrimonial Lawyers (past nat. v.p.), Calif. State Bar (past chmn. family law sect.), San Francisco Bar Assn. (past chmn. family law sect.), Calif. Trial Lawyers Assn. (past chmn. family law sect.). Family and matrimonial. Home: 2244 Vistazo St E Tiburon CA 94920-1970 Office: 1255 Columbus Ave # 200 San Francisco CA 94133-1326

**STOUCK, JERRY,** lawyer; b. Washington, Mar. 24, 1955; s. Alex and Eileen Marion (Tepper) S.; m. Mindy A. Buren, Feb. 18, 1984; children: Danielle, David, Rachel. BA magna cum laude, Wesleyan U., 1977; JD, NYU, 1980. Bar: U.S. Dist. Ct. D.C. 1981, U.S. Ct. Fed. Claims 1981, D.C. Ct. Appeals 1981, Md. Ct. Appeals 1983, U.S. Ct. Appeals (4th cir.) 1983, U.S. Dist. Ct. Md. 1985, U.S. Ct. Appeals (fed. cir.) 1992, U.S. Supreme Ct. 1993, U.S. Ct. Appeals (D.C. cir.) 1997. Law clk. to Hon. Pettine U.S. Dist. Ct. R.I., 1980-81; assoc. McKenna, Conner & Cuneo, Washington, 1981-83; assoc. Spriggs & Hollingsworth, Washington, 1983-84, 87-89, ptnr., 1989—; assoc. Shulman, Rogers, Gandel, Rockville, Md., 1984-87. Mem. Phi Beta Kappa. E-mail: jrstouck@spriggs.com. Government contracts and claims. Office: Spriggs & Hollingsworth 1350 I St NW Ste 900 Washington DC 20005-3399

**STOUDENMIRE, WILLIAM WARD,** lawyer; b. Charlotte, N.C., Apr. 8, 1944; s. Sterling F. and Betty Zane (Scott) S. BA in Polit. Sci., Furman U., 1966; JD, U. S.C., 1970; grad. Va. Theol. Sem., 1993. Bar: Ala. 1970, U.S. Dist. Ct. (so. dist.) Ala. 1970, U.S. Ct. Appeals (5th cir.) 1971, U.S. Supreme Ct. 1973, U.S. Tax Ct. 1982, U.S. Ct. Appeals (11th cir.) 1982, U.S. Ct. Appeals (D.C. cir.) 1982, D.C. 1982; ordained to ministry Episcopal Ch. as deacon, 1993, as priest, 1994. Assoc. Pillans, Reams, Tappan, Wood, Roberts & Vollmer, 1970-74; jr. ptnr., 1974-78; sr. ptnr. Reams, Wood, Vollmer, Killion & Brooks, 1978-82, pvt. practice, Mobile, Ala., 1982-89; legal rsch. asst. Select Com. on Crime, U.S. Ho. of Reps., 1969; mem. law day com. Ala. State Bar, 1975-78, chmn., 1978. Mem. Leadership Mobile Adv. Coun. on Govt., 1982; mem. transition adv. com. Ala. Gov.-Elect Guy Hunt, 1986; mem. Mobile County Rep. Exec. Com., 1976-90, vice chmn., 1976-81, chmn., 1979-86; mem. Ala. Rep. Exec. Com., 1979-86, platform com., 1976, 78, co-chmn., 1978, vice-chmn., 1985-89; bd. trustees Wilmer Hall Episc. Diocese Children's Home, 1987-90, sec., 1987, vice chmn., treas. 1988-90; sec. Diocese of Ctrl. Gulf Coast, 1994-99; deacon Holy Cross Episcopal Ch., 1993, asst. 1994; vicar St. Cyprians Episcopal Ch., 1994; rector St. Mary's Episcopal Ch., 1994—. Served with USCGR, 1966-72. Mem. Mobile Bar Assn. (law day com. 1974-78, chmn. 1977, del. young lawyers sect. ABA conv. 1976, 77), ABA (internat. sect. human rights subcom. 1975—, chmn. 1976-79). General practice. Home: 4300 W Francisco Rd Apt 30 Pensacola FL 32504-9076 Office: St Mary's Episc Ch 302 Oak St Milton FL 32570-6734

**STOUP, ARTHUR HARRY,** lawyer; b. Kansas City, Mo., Aug. 30, 1925; s. Isadore and Dorothy (Rankle) S.; m. Kathryn Jolliff, July 30, 1948; children: David C., Daniel P., Rebecca Ann, Deborah E. Student, Kansas City Jr. Coll., Mo. 1942-43; BA, U. Kansas City, 1950; JD, U. Mo., Kansas City, 1950. Bar: Mo. 1950, D.C. 1979. Pvt. practice law, Kansas City, 1950—; chmn. U.S. Merit Selection Com. for Western Dist. Mo., 1981. Chmn. com. to rev. continuing edn. U. Mo., 1978-79; mem. dean search com. U. Mo. Law Sch., Kansas City, 1994-95; trustee U. Mo.-Kansas City Law Found., 1972—, pres., 1979-82; trustee U. Kansas City, 1979—. With USNR, 1942-45. Recipieent Alumni Achievement award U. Mo., Kansas City, 1975, Law Found. Svc. award U. Mo.-Kansas City Law Found., 1987. Fellow Internat. Soc. Barristers (state mem. chmn.), Am. Bar Found. (life mem.); mem. ABA (ho. dels. 1976-80), Kansas City Met. Bar Assn. (pres. 1966-67, Dean of Trial Bar award 1991), Mo. Bar (bd. govs. 1967-76, v.p. 1972-73, pres. elect 1973-74, pres. 1974-75), Lawyers Assn. Kansas City Mo., Mo. Assn. Trial Attys. (sustaining), Assn. Trial Lawyers Am. (sustaining), So. Conf. Bar Pres.'s (life), Mobar Research Inc. (pres. 1978-86), Phi Alpha Delta Alumni (justice Kansas City area alumni 1955-56). Lodges: Optimists (pres. Ward Pkwy. 1961-62, lt. gov. Mo. dist. internat. 1963-64), Sertoma, B'nai B'rith. General civil litigation, Personal injury, Contracts commercial. Home: 9002 Western Hills Dr Kansas City MO 64114-3566 Office: 1710 Mercantile Tower 1101 Walnut St Kansas City MO 64106-2134

**STOUT, GREGORY STANSBURY,** lawyer; b. Berkeley, Calif., July 27, 1915; s. Verne A. and Ella (Moore) S.; m. Virginia Cordes, Apr. 23, 1948; 1 son, Frederick Gregory. A.B., U. Calif., 1937, LL.B., 1940. Bar: Calif. 1940. Practice law San Francisco, 1946-92; asst. dist. atty., 1947-52; mem. Penal Code Revision Commn. Calif.; chmn. com. State Bar Calif. Contbr. articles to profl. jours. Served to master sgt. AUS, 1942-45. Fellow Am. Coll. Trial Lawyers, Am. Bar Found.; mem. ABA, Fed. Bar Assn., Am. Bd. Trial Advocates, Nat. Assn. Criminal Def. Lawyers (sec. 1958-59, pres. 1962-63). Democrat. Episcopalian. Club: Bohemian. Federal civil litigation, State civil litigation, Criminal. *Died March 10, 1999.*

**STOUT, JAMES DUDLEY,** lawyer; b. Lawrence County, Ill., June 22, 1947; s. Donald K. and Myrtle Irene (Pullen) S.; m. Susan A. West, Jan. 3, 1976 (div. Feb. 1985); children: Lindsey Diane, Kristi Lynn. BA, So. Ill. U., 1969; JD, U. Ill., 1974. Bar: Tex. 1974, U.S. Dist. Ct. (so. dist.) Tex. 1974, Ill. 1978, U.S. Dist. Ct. (cen. dist.) Ill. 1979, U.S. Dist. Ct. (so. dist.) Ill. 1986. Sole practice Humble, Tex., 1974-78; assoc. Law office Robert W. Dodd, Champaign, Ill., 1978-79; ptnr. Dodd, Stout, Martinkus, et al, Champaign, 1979-81, Zimmerly, Gadau, Stout, Selin & Otto, Champaign, 1981-85, Correll and Stout, Bridgeport, Ill., 1985-86; sole practice Bridgeport, 1986—. Served with U.S. Army, 1969-71. Mem. Assn. Trial Lawyers Am., Ill. Bar Assn., Tex. Bar Assn., Rotary, Lions. Lodges: Elks, Shriners. Avocations: golf, tennis, reading. General practice, Federal civil litigation, Oil, gas, and mineral. Office: 324 N Main St Bridgeport IL 62417-1524

**STOUT, LOWELL,** lawyer; b. Tamaha, Okla., July 23, 1928; s. Charles W. and Rosetta (Easley) S.; m. Liliane Josue, Nov. 29, 1952; children: Georgianna, Mark Lowell. Student, Northeastern State Coll., Tahlequah, Okla., 1946-49, U. Okla., 1949-51; LLB, U. N.Mex., 1952. Bar: N.Mex. 1952. Ptnr. Easley, Quinn & Stout, Hobbs, N.Mex., 1954-58, Girand & Stout, Hobbs, 1958-60; pvt. practice Hobbs, 1960-80; ptnr. Stout & Stout, Hobbs, 1980—. Cpl. U.S. Army, 1952-54. Perenially listed in Best Lawyers in America. Fellow Am. Coll. Trial Lawyers; mem. Assn. Trial Lawyers Am., State Bar N.Mex., N.Mex. Trial Lawyers Assn., Lea County Bar Assn. Personal injury, Workers' compensation, General civil litigation. Home: 218 W Lea St Hobbs NM 88240-5110 Office: Stout & Stout PO Box 716 Hobbs NM 88241-0716

**STOVALL, CARLA JO,** state attorney general; b. Hardner, Kans., Mar. 18, 1957; d. Carl E. and Juanita Jo (Ford) S. BA, Pittsburg (Kans.) State U., 1979; JD, U. Kans., 1982. Bar: Kans. 1982, U.S. Dist. Ct. Kans. 1982. Pvt. practice, Pittsburg, 1982-85; atty. Crawford County, Pittsburg, 1984-88; gov. Kans. Parole Bd., Topeka, 1988-94; attorney general State of Kansas, Topeka, 1995—; lectr. law Pittsburg State U. 1982-84; pres. Gilston Internat. Mktg., Inc., 1988—. Bd. dirs., sec. Pittsburg Family YMCA, 1983-88. Mem. ABA, Kans. Bar Assn., Crawford County Bar Assn. (sec. 1984-85, v.p. 1985-86, pres. 1986-87), Kans. County and Dist. Attys. Assn., Nat. Coll. Dist. Attys., Pittsburg State U. Alumni Assn. (bd. dirs. 1983-88), Pittsburg Area C. of C. (bd. dirs. 1983-85, Leadership Pitts. 1984), Bus. and Profl. Women Assn. (Young Careerist 1984), Kans. Assn. Commerce and Industry (Leadership Kans. 1983), AAUW (bd. dirs. 1983-87). Republican. Methodist. Avocations: travel, photography, tennis. Home: 3561 SW Mission Ave Topeka KS 66614-3637 Office: Atty Gen Office Kansas Judicial Ctr 2nd Fl Topeka KS 66612*

**STOVER, JAY ELTON,** lawyer; b. Jasper, Ala., May 4, 1970; s. Crable Elton and Jackie Carrol Glenn S.; m. Kathryn Marie Jones, Aug. 7, 1993; children: Reagan Marie, Jack Dylan. BS, U. Ala., Birmingham, 1992; JD, Samford U., 1995. Bar: Ala., U.S. Dist. Ct. (mid. dist.) Ala., U.S. Dist. Ct. (no. dist.) Ala. Staff atty. to Hon. H. Maddox Ala. Supreme Ct., Montgomery, 1995-96; atty. Callis & Stover, Rainbow City, Ala., 1996—. Mem. Ala. State Bar Assn., Etowah County Bar Assn., Etowah Inns of Ct. Baptist. Personal injury, Appellate. Office: Callis & Stover 101 Church St Ste 100 Rainbow City AL 35906-6242

**STOVSKY, MICHAEL DAVID,** lawyer; b. Cleve., Mar. 10, 1964; s. Robert Leonard and Alyce Joan Stovsky; m. Jill Denise Simon, Oct. 31, 1993; children: Alexa, Matthew. BA, Northwestern U., 1986; JD, U. Pa., 1991. Bar: Ohio 1991. Atty. Kahn, Kleinman, Yanowitz & Arnson Co., LPA, Cleve., 1991-96, Ulmer & Berne LLP, Cleve., 1996—. Contbr. articles to profl. jours. Mem. steering com. Northwestern U. Dance Marathon for United Cerebral Palsy, Evanston, Ill., 1984-85. Zeta Beta Tau/Jack London scholar, Evanston, 1983. Mem. ABA (mem. bus. law sect. com. on the law of commerce in cyberspace 1996—, mem. planning com. and faculty Nat. Inst. on Representing High Tech. Cos. 1998), Cleve. Bar Assn. (chmn. securities inst. panel on electronic securities practice 1998, chmn. tech. com. 1998), Phi Delta Phi, Alpha Lambda Delta. Avocations: golf, skiing, squash, running. Fax: 216-621-7488. Computer, General corporate, Securities. Office: Ulmer & Berne LLP 1300 E 9th St Ste 900 Cleveland OH 44114-1583

**STOWE, CHARLES ROBINSON BEECHER,** management consultant, educator, lawyer; b. Seattle, July 18, 1949; s. David Beecher and Edith Beecher (Andrade) S.; m. Laura Everett, Mar. 9, 1985. BA, Vanderbilt U., 1971; MBA, U. Dallas, 1975; JD, U. Houston, 1982, U. Warsaw; PhD, Warsaw U., Poland, 1998; Bar: Tex. 1982, U.S. Dist. Ct. (so. dist.) Tex., 1984, U.S. Tax Ct., 1984. Account exec. Engleman Co., pub. rels. and advt., Dallas, 1974-75; instr. Richland Coll., Dallas, spring 1976; acct. Arthur Andersen & Co., Dallas, 1976-78; part-time pub. rels. cons.; dir. Productive Capital Corp.; gen. ptnr. Productive Capital Assocs., 1975-81; pres. Stowe & Co., mgmt. cons., Dallas, 1978—; from asst. to prof. dept. gen. bus. and fin. Coll. Bus. Adminstrn., Sam Houston State U., 1982—, dir. Office Free Enterprise and Entrepreneurship, 1982—, Office Internat. Programs, 1998—; adminstrv. intern, asst. to pres., spring 1985; summer fellow Tex. Coordinating Bd., 1988. Trustee, Stowe-Day Found., 1979-90; mem. nat. adv. bd. Young Am.'s Found., 1979—; vol. faculty State Bar Tex. Profl. Devl. Program, 1988—; vol., mediator Dispute Resolution Ctr. Montgomery County; mediator so. dist. U.S. Dist. Ct. Tex. 1993; team chief, U.S. Milit. liason Republic of Poland, 1994; pub. affairs officer George C. Marshall European Ctr. for Security Studies, 1997. With USNR, 1971-74; capt. Res. Recipient Freedoms Found. award, 1969, Navy Achievement medal, 1973, Gold Star, 1985, Def. Meritorious Svc. medal with oak leaf cluster, 1995, 97, Navy Meritorious Svc. award, 1996; Price-Babson fellow Entrepreneurship Symposium, 1991. Mem. ABA, Am. Arbitration Assn., State Bar Tex. (vol. faculty profl. devel. program 1988-90, vice chair profl. efficiency and econ. rsch. com. 1993, chair law offcie mgmt. com. 1993-94), Walker County Bar Assn. (pres. 1987-88), Pub. Rels. Soc. Am., Tex. Assn. Realtors, U.S. Navy League, Naval Res. Assn., Res. Officers Assn., Sigma Iota Epsilon. Club: Dallas Vanderbilt (pres. 1977-78). Author: Bankruptcy I Micro-Mash Inc., 1989, rev. edit. 1995, The Implications of Foreign Financial Institutions on Poland's Emerging Entrepreneurial Economy, 1999; co-author CPA review; editor Houston Jour. Internat. Law, 1981-82; contbr. articles to profl. jours. Office: PO Box 2144 Huntsville TX 77341-2144

**STOYKO, WILLIAM NELSON,** lawyer; b. Reading, Pa., Nov. 4, 1946; s. Max and Ruth Louise S.; m. Elizabeth Emily Cox, May 24, 1983; children: Greta Elizabeth, Kira Alexandra. AB in Polit. Sci., Albright Coll., 1968; JD, Georgetown U., 1973. Assoc. Miller & Murray, Reading, Pa., 1973-76, ptnr., 1976-80; assoc. legal counsel, asst. sec. Landmark Banking Corp., Ft. Lauderdale, Fla., 1980-83; sr. legal counsel, sr. v.p. Ctrl. Fidelity Banks, Inc., Richmond, Va., 1983-87, sec., 1987-97, corp. exec. officer, sr. corp. counsel, 1992-96, corp. exec. v.p., 1996-98; sr. v.p., dep. gen. counsel Wachovia Corp., Richmond, 1998—; gen. counsel Ctrl. Fidelity Nat. Bank, 1996—. Bd. dirs. Berks County Heart Assn., Reading, Pa., 1978-80, Richmond (Va.) Symphony Orch., 1992—. With USAR, 1969-75. Republican. Lutheran. Avocations: reading, painting. Office: Wachovia Bank NA PO Box 27602 1021 E Cary St Richmond VA 23219-4000

**STRADER, TIMOTHY RICHARDS,** lawyer; b. Portland, Oreg., Jan. 17, 1956; s. Charles J. and Carol Jane (Dwyer) S.; m. Lisa M.K. Bartholomew, May 21, 1988; children: Kelly Meehan, Erin Dwyer. BBA in Mgmt., U. Notre Dame, 1978; JD, Willamette U., Salem, Oreg., 1981; LLM in Taxation, U. Fla., Gainesville, 1982. Bar: Oreg. 1981. Assoc. McEwen, Hanna, Gisvold & Rankin, Portland, 1982-85, Bullivant, Houser, Bailey, Hanna, Portland, 1985-87, Hanna, Urbigkeit, Jensen, et al., Portland, 1987-88, Hanna, Murphy, Jensen, Holloway, Portland, 1988-89; mem. Hanna, Kerns & Strader, P.C., Portland, 1989—. Mem. editorial bd. State Bar Estate Planning Newsletter, 1987—. Mem. alumni bd. Jesuit H.S., Portland, 1982-94, trustee, 1993-99; bd. dirs. Valley Cath. Sch., Beaverton, 1989-95. Mem. ABA, Multnomah Bar Assn., Multnomah Athletic Club. Estate planning, Probate, Corporate taxation. Office: Hanna Kerns & Strader 1300 SW 6th Ave Ste 300 Portland OR 97201-3461

**STRADLEY, RICHARD LEE,** lawyer; b. Chula Vista, Calif. Sept. 10, 1951; s. George R. and Betty J. (Laughman) S.; m. Christine A. Crofts, Sept. 7, 1991. B.A., Coll. Santa Fe, 1972; J.D., U. Miss., 1975. Bar: Miss. 1975, Mont. 1982, U.S. Dist. Ct. (no. dist.) Miss. 1975, U.S. Dist. Ct. (so. dist.) Miss. 1981, U.S. Dist Ct. (we. dist.) Tenn. 1982, U.S. Dist. Ct. Mont. 1980, U.S. Tax Ct. 1981, U.S. Ct. Appeals (5th and 9th cirs.) 1980, U.S. Ct. Appeals (10th and 11th cirs.) 1981, U.S. Supreme Ct. 1981, U.S. Dist. Ct. (no. dist.) Tex. 1984, Oreg. 1985, U.S. Dist. Ct. Oreg. 1986, U.S. Dist. Ct. Nebr. 1986, Wyo. 1994. Sole practice, 1975—; staff atty. East Miss. Legal Services, Forest, 1979. Mem. Christian Legal Soc. Avocations: chess, computers, woodworking. Probate, Estate taxation, Federal civil litigation. Office: PO Box 2541 Cody WY 82414-2541

**STRAFF, DONNA EVELYN,** lawyer; b. Phila., Sept. 25, 1952. BA, George Washington U., 1974; JD, Cath. U., 1980. Bar: Washington, 1980, Calif. 1981. Asst. v.p. Bank AmeriLease, San Francisco, 1985-87; asst. gen. counsel Round Table Pizza, San Francisco, 1987-89, Computerland, Pleasanton, Calif., 1989-94; v.p., gen. counsel Computerland, Pleasanton, 1994-97; sr. ops. counsel Hexcel Corp., Pleasanton, 1997—. Mem. State Bar of Calif. (corp. law dept. sect., bus. law sect.). General corporate, Contracts commercial, Franchising. Office: Hexcel Corp 5794 W Las Positas Blvd Pleasanton CA 94588-4083

**STRAHAN, JEFFERY V.,** lawyer; b. Beeville, Tex., Apr. 4, 1960; s. Wendell Lee and Lillian Aline S.; m. Janet K., Dec. 21, 1986; children: Jeffery Jr., Julie, Justin, Jessica. BA, Tex. Tech. U., 1986; JD, St. Mary's U., 1989. Bar: Tex. 1989, N.Mex. 1992. Assoc. Kemp, Smith, Duncan & Hammond, El Paso, Tex., 1989-91; ptnr. Armstrong & Strahan, El Paso, 1991-95; pvt. practice El Paso, 1995—. Mem. State Bar Tex., El Paso Bar Assn. Avocations: music, computers, hunting, fishing. Labor, General civil litigation. Office: 521 Texas Ave El Paso TX 79901-1417

**STRAIN, JAMES ARTHUR,** lawyer; b. Alexandria, La., Oct. 11, 1944; s. William Joseph and Louise (Moore) S.; m. Cheryl Sue Williamson, Aug. 19, 1967; children: William Joseph, Gordon Richard, Elizabeth Parks. BS in Econs., Ind. U., 1966, JD, 1969. Bar: Ind. 1969, U.S. Dist. Ct. (so. dist.) Ind. 1969, U.S. Ct. Appeals (7th cir.) 1972, U.S. Supreme Ct. 1975, U.S. Ct. Appeals (5th cir.) 1978. Instr. Law Sch. Ind. U., Indpls., 1969-70; law clk. to Hon. John S. Hastings 7th Cir. Ct. Appeals, Chgo., 1970-71; assoc. Cahill, Gordon & Reindel, N.Y.C., 1971-72; law clk. to Hon. William H. Rehnquist U.S. Supreme Ct., Washington, 1972-73; assoc. Barnes, Hickam, Pantzer & Boyd, Indpls., 1973-75; ptnr. Barnes, Hickam, Pantzer & Boyd (name changed to Barnes & Thornburg), 1976-96, Sommer & Barnard, PC, Indpls., 1996—; adj. asst. prof. law Ind. U. Sch. Law, 1986-92. Mem., bd. dirs. The Penrod Soc., Indpls., 1976—, Indpls. Symphonic Choir, 1988-91, Festival Music Soc., Indpls., 1990-96. Mem. 7th Cir. Bar Assn. (meetings chmn. Ind. chpt. 1979-88, portraits 1988-89, bd. govs. 1989—, 1st v.p. 1995, pres. 1996). Avocations: photography, music. Mergers and acquisitions, Securities, General corporate. Office: Sommer & Barnard PC 4000 Bank One Tower 111 Monument Cir Ste 4000 Indianapolis IN 46204-5198

**STRAND, ARNELLE MARIE,** lawyer; b. N.Y.C., June 13, 1952; d. Arnold John and Yolanda Rose (Solla) Iannaccone; m. Larry Stephen Strand, Aug. 18, 1973 (div. Aug. 1992); children: Daniel Stephen, Michael Thomas. BA, Iona Coll., 1973; MS, Adelphi U., 1976; JD, Stetson Coll. Law, 1994. Bar: Fla. 1994. Tchr. spl. edn. Valley Stream (N.Y.) UFSD, 1973-74; med. asst. Columbia Presbyn. Med. Ctr., N.Y.C., 1974-76; adminstrn.-orthop. surgery Howard A. Kiernan, M.D., N.Y.C., 1976-91; rsch. asst. family law Stetson Coll. Law, St. Petersburg, Fla., 1993-94; tchr. adult edn. Plainedge Union Free Sch. Dist., North Massapequa, N.Y., 1974-76; assoc. Wilson, Wilson & Long, PA, Palm Harbor, Fla., 1994-98. Co-author: (yearly update) Florida Dissolution of Marriage, 1994-97. Band Booster mem. River Ridge H.S. Royal Knights Marching Band, New Port Richey, Fla., 1995—. Recipient Am. Juriprudence award Stetson Coll. Law, 1994. Mem. ABA (family law planning com. 1995—, sec. domestic violence com. 1998-99), Am. Inns of Ct.-West Pasco, Trial Lawyers Assn., Fla. Bar Assn., Clearwater Bar Assn. (bench/bar com. 1995—, pro bono legal svcs. 1994—), West Pasco Bar Assn., Canakaris Inns of Ct. (programs com. 1997—, exec. com. 1997—). Family and matrimonial, Probate, Alternative dispute resolution. Office: 7616 Massachusetts Ave New Port Richey FL 34653-3022

**STRAND, JOAN H.,** law educator; b. 1950. BA, George Washington U., JD, 1975. Bar: D.C. 1976. Prof. law Nat. Law Ctr. George Washington U., Washington. Mem. ABA, D.C. Bar Assn. (pres.-elect, sec. 1993-94, bd. govs., family law sect., pub. svc. activities com.), D.C. Bar Found. (Jerrold Scoutt prize 1997). Office: George Washington U Nat Law Ctr Washington DC 20052-0001*

**STRAND, MARION DELORES,** social service administrator; b. Kansas City, Mo., Dec. 19, 1927; d. Henry Franklin and Julia Twyman (Noland) Pugh; m. Robert Carmen Scipioni, Aug. 2, 1947 (dec. 1984); children: Mark, Brian, Roberta, Laura, Steven, Mary,Angela, Julie, Victor, Robert, Lawrence; m. Donald John Strand, Sept. 1, 1985. BA, U. Kans., 1948; MS, SUNY, Brockport, 1975. Counselor N.Y. Dept. Labor, Rochester, 1971-75, 77-79; regulatory adminstr. N.Y. Dept. Social Svcs., Rochester, 1976-77, 79-81; pres. Greater Rochester Svcs., Inc. (doing bus. as Scribes & Scripts), 1982—; founder Ctr. for Law Access and Document Preparation. Columnist, local newspaper. Active polit. campaigns for women candidates, 1981—; UN envoy Unitarian Ch., Rochester, 1988-92; fin. chair William Warfield Scholarship Com., Rochester, 1988-90; chair bd. govt. affairs Genesee Valley Arthritis Found., Rochester, 1988-90; mem. parade com. 95/75 Celebration of Monroe County, 1995; mem. Lyell Av. Revitalization Com.; Congl. candidate 28th Congl. Dist., N.Y., 1998; candidate 28th Congrl. Dist. N.Y., 1998. Mem. NOW (1st pres. Greater Rochester 1982-83, pres. child care com. Greater Rochester sect. 1987-88, current sec. and mem. local organizing com. 1998 Women's rights Conv. and Vision Summit, chair family issues task force), AAUW, Paralegals of Rochester, DAR, Greater Rochester C. of C. (legis. com., small bus. coun. 1987—, bd. dirs. women's coun. 1981-91, pres. 1989-90), Alliance Ind. Artists (treas.), Nat. Network Family Law Policy (organizing), Susan B. Anthony Rep. Women's Club (program com., 1st v.p. 1994, co-chair Greater Rochester Coalition for Choice 1994-95) Golden Girls Investment Club (founder), Phi Beta Kappa, Psi Chi. Avocations: tennis, golf, art, organ playing. Home and Office: Greater Rochester Svcs Inc 50 Hidden Valley Rd Rochester NY 14624-2301

**STRAND, ROGER GORDON,** federal judge; b. Peekskill, N.Y., Apr. 28, 1934; s. Ernest Gordon Strand and Lisabeth Laurine (Phin) Steinmetz; m. Joan Williams, Nov. 25, 1961. AB, Hamilton Coll., 1955; LLB, Cornell U., 1961; grad., Nat. Coll. State Trial Judges, 1968. Bar: Ariz. 1961, U.S. Dist. Ct. Ariz. 1961, U.S. Supreme Ct. 1980. Assoc. Fennemore, Craig, Allen & McClennen, Phoenix, 1961-67; judge Ariz. Superior Ct., Phoenix, 1967-85, U.S. Dist. Ct. Ariz., Phoenix, 1985—; assoc. presiding judge Ariz. Superior Ct., 1971-85; lectr. Nat. Jud. Coll., Reno, 1978-87; mem. jud. conf. U.S. com. on automation and tech. Past pres. cen. Ariz. chpt. Arthritis Found. Lt. USN, 1955-61. Mem. ABA, Ariz. Bar Assn., Maricopa County Bar Assn., Nat. Conf. Fed. Trial Judges, Phi Delta Phi, Aircraft Owners and Pilots Assn. Lodge: Rotary. Avocations: computer applications, golf, fishing. Home: 5825 N 3rd Ave Phoenix AZ 85013-1537 Office: US Dist Ct Courthouse and Fed Bldg 230 N 1st Ave Ste 3013 Phoenix AZ 85025-0067

**STRANDE, JEFFREY JAY,** lawyer; b. Milw., Apr. 25, 1961; s. Neale Elwood and Sheila Elizabeth S.; m. Christine Carol Schulist, Aug. 3, 1985; children: Jennifer Rose, Jonathan Thomas, Kaylee Grace. AS, U. Wis.-Washington County, West Bend, 1981; BA, U. Wis., Milw., 1983; JD, Marquette U., 1986. Bar: Wis. 1986, U.S. Dist. Ct. (we. and ea. dists.) Wis. 1986, U.S. Ct. Appeals (7th cir.) 1990. Atty. Terwilliger Law Firm, Wausau, Wis., 1986-98, Piehler & Strande, S.C., Wausau, 1998—. Avocations: walking, swimming, reading, remodeling. Workers' compensation, Insurance, Family and matrimonial. Office: Piehler & Strande SC 401 5th St Ste 443 Wausau WI 54403-5404

**STRASBAUGH, WAYNE RALPH,** lawyer; b. Lancaster, Pa., July 20, 1948; s. Wayne Veily and Jane Irene (Marzolf) S.; m. Carol Lynne Taylor, June 8, 1974; children: Susan, Wayne T., Elizabeth. AB, Bowdoin Coll., 1970; AM, Harvard U., 1971, PhD, 1976, JD, 1979. Bar: Ohio 1979, Pa. 1983, U.S. Tax Ct. 1980, U.S. Ct. Fed. Claims 1980, U.S. Ct. Appeals (fed. cir.) 1982, U.S. Dist. Ct. (no. dist.) Ohio 1979, U.S. Dist. Ct. (ea. dist.) Pa. 1983. Assoc. Jones Day Reavis & Pogue, Cleve., 1979-82, Morgan Lewis & Bockius, Phila., 1982-84; assoc. Ballard Spahr Andrews & Ingersoll, LLP, Phila., 1984-88, ptnr., 1988—. Mem. ABA (tax sect., chmn. com. 1992-94), Phila. Bar Assn. (tax sect., chmn. fed. tax com. 1992, coun. mem. 1995, sec.-treas. 1996, vice-chmn. 1997-98, chmn. 1999—). Episcopalian. Corporate taxation, Taxation, general, Mergers and acquisitions. Office: Ballard Spahr Andrews & Ingersoll LLP 1735 Market St Ste 5100 Philadelphia PA 19103-7599

**STRASER, RICHARD ALAN,** lawyer; b. Washington, Feb. 11, 1945; s. Woodward John and Nina Louise (Weaver) S.; m. Beverly Jean Brickhouse, May 9, 1981; 1 child, Whitney Marie. B.A., George Washington U., 1971; J.D., Wake Forest U., 1974. Bar: Pa. 1975, Va. 1977, U.S. Ct. Appeals (5th cir.) 1979, U.S. Supreme Ct. 1980. Mgmt. asst. NASA Hdqrs., Washington, 1972, 1973; primary trademark atty. U.S. Patent and Trademark Office, Crystal City, Arlington, Va., 1974—. Dep. dir. Herndon Community Chorus, Va., 1981-82. Served with U.S. Army 1963-64. Mem. Delta Phi Alpha, Phi Alpha Delta. Democrat. Roman Catholic. Office: US Patent and Trademark Office Dept Of Commerce Washington DC 20230-0001

**STRASSBERG, JONATHAN ELLIOT,** lawyer, real estate developer; b. Cleve., May 23, 1960; s. Joseph Meyer and Evelyn Beth (Dukoff) S. BS in Communications, Boston U., 1982; JD, Yeshiva U., N.Y.C., 1986. Bar: N.Y. 1987, Ill. 1990, N.J. 1991. Assoc. Werner, Kennedy & French, N.Y.C., 1986-90, Sidley & Austin, Chgo., 1990, Johnson & Colmar, Chgo., 1991; sole practitioner Hamilton, N.J., 1991—. Contbr. articles to profl. jours. Contracts commercial, Insurance, Real property. Address: PO Box 8056 Trenton NJ 08650-0056

**STRASSBERG, RICHARD MARK,** prosecutor; b. N.Y.C., July 17, 1963. BS in Econs., Cornell U., 1985; JD, Harvard U., 1988. Bar: N.Y. 1989, U.S. Dist. Ct. (so. and ea. dists.) N.Y. 1989, U.S. Ct. Appeals (2nd cir.) 1998. Law clk. hon. Robert J. Ward U.S. Dist. Ct. (so. dist.) N.Y., N.Y.C., 1988-90; litigation assoc. Lankler, Siffert & Wohl, N.Y.C., 1990-94; asst. U.S. atty. U.S. Attys. Office (so. dist.) N.Y., N.Y.C., 1994—; referee U.S. Dist. Ct. N.Y., N.Y.C., 1992; adj. prof. Bklyn. Law Sch., 1997-98. Recipient Nat. Prosecutorial award Fed. Law Enforcement Officers Assn., 1996. Office: US Attys Office So Dist NY 1 Saint Andrews Plz New York NY 10007-1781

**STRASSBURG, ROGER WILLIAM, JR.,** prosecutor; b. Medina, Ohio, Jan. 15, 1954; s. Roger William Sr. and Lois Hotuedt Strassburg; m. Joyce Stassburg, May 20, 1995. Degree in Arts, Cornell U., 1975; Degree in Law, Case Western Res. U., 1982. Bar: Ariz., Ohio. Trial lawyer Rortze & Andress, Akron, Ohio, 1982-90, Joonseph & Shaffer, Akron, 1990-96; asst. atty. gen. Ariz. Atty. Gen. Office, Phoenix, 1996—. Legis. asst. U.S. Congress, Washington, 1976-79. Office: Ariz Atty Gen 1275 W Washington St Phoenix AZ 85007-2926

**STRASSLER, MARC A.,** corporate lawyer. Gen. counsel Supermarkets Gen. Corp., Woodbridge, N.J., sr. v.p., gen. counsel. Office: Pathmark Stores Inc PO Box 5301 200 Milik St Carteret NJ 07008-1102

**STRATTON, EVELYN LUNDBERG,** state supreme court justice; b. Bangkok, Feb. 25, 1953; came to U.S., 1971 (parents Am. citizens); d. Elmer John and Corrine Sylvia (Henricksen) Sahlberg; children: Luke Andrew, Tyler John; m. Jack A. Lundberg; 2 children. Student, LeTourneau Coll., Longview, Tex., 1971-74; AA, U. Fla., 1973; BA, U. Akron, 1976; JD, Ohio State U., 1978. Bar: Ohio 1979, U.S. Dist. Ct. (so. dist.) Ohio 1979, U.S. Ct. Appeals (6th cir.) 1983. Assoc. Hamilton, Kramer, Myers & Cheek, Columbus, 1979-85; ptnr. Wesp, Osterkamp & Stratton, 1985-88; judge Franklin County Ct. Common Pleas, 1989-96; justice Ohio State Supreme Ct., 1996—; vis. prof. Nat. Jud. Coll., 1997—; spkr. legal seminars. Contbr. articles to profl. jours. Trustee Ohio affiliate Nat. Soc. to Prevent Blindness, 1989—, bd. dirs., trustee Columbus Coun. World Affairs, 1990-99, chmn. bd. dirs., 1999—; bd. dirs., trustee Dave Thomas Adoption Found., 1996—, ArChSafe Found., 1997—; mem. women's bd. Zephyrus League Cen. Ohio Lung Assn., 1989—; with Alliance Women Cmty. Corrections, 1993—. Recipient Gold Key award LeTourneau Coll., Gainesville, Fla., 1974, Svc. commendation Ohio Ho. of Reps., 1984, Scholar of Life award St. Joseph's Orphanage, 1998. Mem. ABA, Columbus Bar Assn. (bd. govs. 1984-88, 90—, lectr.), Ohio Bar Assn. (jud. adminstrv. and legal reform com., coun. dels. 1992-96, Ohio Cmty. Corrections Orgn. (trustee 1995—), Columbus Bar Found. (trustee 1986-91, officer, sec. 1986-87, v.p. 1987-88), Women Lawyers Franklin County, Phi Alpha Delta (pres. 1982-83). Office: Supreme Ct Ohio 30 E Broad St Fl 3 Columbus OH 43215-3414

**STRATTON, WALTER LOVE,** lawyer; b. Greenwich, Conn., Sept. 21, 1926; s. John McKee and June (Love) S.; children: John, Michael, Peter (dec.), Lucinda; m. DeAnna Weinheimer, Oct. 1, 1994. Student, Williams Coll., 1943; A.B., Yale U., 1948; LL.B., Harvard U., 1951. Bar: N.Y. 1952. Assoc. Casey, Lane & Mittendorf, N.Y.C., 1951-53; assoc. Donovan, Leisure, Newton & Irvine, N.Y.C., 1956-63; ptnr. Donovan, Leisure, Newton & Irvine, 1963-84, Gibson, Dunn & Crutcher, 1984-93; ptnr. Andrews & Kurth, N.Y.C., 1993-95, of counsel, 1996—; asst. U.S. atty. So. Dist. N.Y., N.Y.C., 1953-56; lectr. Practising Law Inst. Served with USNR, 1945-46. Fellow Am. Coll. Trial Lawyers; mem. ABA, Fed. Bar Coun., N.Y. State Bar Assn. Clubs: Indian Harbor Yacht, Colo. Arlberg, Yale (N.Y.C.). Federal civil litigation, General civil litigation, State civil litigation. Home: 434 Round Hill Rd Greenwich CT 06831-2639 Office: Andrews & Kurth 805 3rd Ave New York NY 10022-7513

**STRAUB, CHESTER JOHN,** judge; b. Bklyn., May 12, 1937; s. Chester and Ann (Majewski) S.; m. Patricia Morrissey, Aug. 22, 1959; children: Chester, Michael, Christopher, Robert. AB, St. Peter's Coll., 1958; JD, U. Va., 1961. Bar: N.Y. State 1962, U.S. Dist. Ct. (so. and ea. dists.) N.Y. 1963, U.S. Ct. Appeals (2d cir.) 1967, U.S. Supreme Ct. 1978. Assoc. Willkie Farr & Gallagher, N.Y.C., 1963-71; ptnr. Willkie Farr & Gallagher, 1971-98; mem. N.Y. State Assembly, 1967-72, N.Y. State Senate, 1973-75, Dem. Nat. Com., 1976-80; Judge U.S. Ct. Appeals (2nd cir.), 1998—; former mediator U.S. Dist. Ct. (so. dist.) N.Y. and neutral evaluator U.S. Dist. Ct. (ea. dist.) N.Y.; chmn. N.Y. State statewide jud. screening com., 1988-94, first dept. jud. screening com., 1983-94; mem. Senator Moynihan's jud. selection com., 1976-98. Mem. Cardinal's Com. of Laity for Cath. Charities N.Y.; trustee Lenox Hill Hosp., With U.S. Army, 1961-63. Mem. Am. Bar Assn., N.Y. State Bar Assn., Assn. of Bar of City of N.Y.C., Kosciuszko Found. Office: US Ct Appeals Second Circuit 500 Pearl St New York NY 10007

**STRAUS, DOUGLAS CHARLES,** lawyer; b. Berkeley, Calif., Sept. 29, 1955; s. Alan Edward and Janice Louise (Meagher) S. B.S., Northwestern U., 1977; J.D., Boalt Hall, U. Calif.-Berkeley, 1980. Bar: Calif. 1980. Sole practice, Richmond, Calif., 1981-88; of counsel Norris & Norris, Richmond, 1983-88, ptnr., 1988—; assoc. Pillsbury, Madison & Sutro, San Francisco, 1980-81. Bd. dirs. Richmond Unified Edn. Fund, 1983-94, v.p. 1985—. McBaine Moot Ct. winner, Boalt Hall, 1980; Nat. Novice Debate champion, Nat. Debate Tournament, Northwestern U., 1974. Mem. Contra Costa County Bar Assn., Calif. State Bar. Democrat. Lodge: Rotary (pres. Richmond club 1994-95). State civil litigation, Federal civil litigation, Contracts commercial. Office: Norris and Norris Hilltop Office Park 3260 Blume Dr Ste 400 Richmond CA 94806-5277

**STRAUSE, RANDALL SCOTT,** judge; b. Louisville, June 13, 1963; s. James L. and Charlotte Ray (Motherhead) S.; m. Rene Marie Ricci, Aug. 7, 1987; children: Randall Scott Jr., James Austin. BA, Ind. U., 1985; JD, U. Louisville, 1988. Bar: Ky. 1989, S.C. 1991, U.S. Dist. Ct. (ea. and we. dists.) Ky. 1992, U.S. Ct. Appeals (6th cir.) 1992. Atty. pvt. practice, Louisville, 1989-90; law clk. to Hon. Joseph M. Hood U.S. Dist. Ct. (ea. dist.) Ky., Pikeville, 1990-92; atty. Alagia, Day, Trautwein & Smith, Louisville, 1992-94; prin. asst. to commr. dept. medicaid svcs. Commonwealth of Ky., Frankfort, 1994-95, chief adminstrv. law judge cabinet health svcs., 1995-99; dir. Strategic Mktg., Inc., Louisville, 1995-96. Bd. dirs. Louisville Tennis Assn., 1996-99, Kentuckiana Children's Ctr., 1998—. Rsch. grantee Tort & Litigation, 1987. Mem. ABA, Am. Health Lawyers Assn., Assn. Trial Lawyers Am., Nat. Assn. Adminstrv. Law Judges, Nat. Assn. Hearing Ofcls. (bd. dirs.), Ky. Bar Assn., S.C. Bar Assn., Nat. Assn. Securities Dealers (arbitrator 1998—), Ky. Real Estate Commn., Louisville Bar Assn., Kappa Sigma, Delta Theta Phi, Omicron Delta Kappa, Order of Ky. Cols. Republican. Episcopalian. Avocation: tennis. Home: 10107 Falling Tree Way Louisville KY 40223-3736 Office: One Riverfront Plz Ste 1400 Louisville KY 40202

**STRAUSER, ROBERT WAYNE,** lawyer; b. Little Rock, Aug. 28, 1943; s. Christopher Columbus and Opal (Orr) S.; m. Atha Maxine Tubbs, June 26, 1971 (div. 1991); children: Robert Benjamin, Ann Kathleen; m. Terri D. Seales, Oct. 17, 1998. BA, Davidson (N.C.) Coll., 1965; postgrad., Vanderbilt U., Nashville, 1965-66; LLB, U. Tex., 1968. Bar: Tex. 1968, U.S. Ct. Mil. Appeals 1971. Staff atty. Tex. Legis. Coun., Austin, 1969-71; counsel Jud. Com., Tex. Ho. of Reps., Austin, 1971-73; chief counsel Jud. Com., Tex. Constl. Conv., Austin, 1974; exec. v.p. and legis. counsel Tex.

Assn. Taxpayers, Austin, 1974-85; assoc. Baker & Botts, Austin, 1985-87; ptnr. Baker & Botts, 1988—. Assoc. editor Tex. Internat. Law Jour., 1968. Mem. Tex. Ho. Speakers Econ. Devel. Com., Austin, 1986-87; assoc. dir. McDonald Obs. Bd. Visitors, 1988—; mem. adv. bd. Sch. of Social Work, U. Tex. Lyceum Assn., 1980-81, 84-88; mem. bd. dirs. Tex. Assn. Bus. and C. of C.; mem. Dean's Roundtable, U. Tex. Law Sch.; bd. dirs. Austin Symphony Orch. Soc., 1985—, v.p., 1993-94, nominating com., 1998. Capt. USNR, ret. Named Rising Star of Tex., Tex. Bus. Mag., 1983. Mem. State Bar of Tex. (coun. mem. tax sect.), Tex. Assn. Bus. and C. of C.s (bd. dirs. 1999), Travis County Bar Assn., Headliners Club (Austin). Legislative, Administrative and regulatory. Home: 3312 Gilbert St Austin TX 78703-2102 Office: Baker & Botts 1600 San Jacinto Blvd Austin TX 78701

**STRAUSS, GARY JOSEPH,** lawyer; b. N.Y.C., July 6, 1953; s. Stanley Vinson and Frieda (Fischoff) S. BA magna cum laude, City Coll. of N.Y., 1974; JD, NYU, 1977. Bar: N.Y. 1978, Fla. 1980. Assoc. Finley, Kumble, Wagner, Heine & Underberg, N.Y.C., 1977-79; ptnr. Phillips, Nizer, Benjamin, Krim & Ballon, N.Y.C., 1979-87, Gaston & Snow, N.Y.C., 1987-88; pvt. practice N.Y.C., 1988—. Mem. ABA (chmn. N.Y. com. current literature and real property law 1977), Fla. Bar Assn., N.Y. State Bar Assn. Real property. Home: 57 W 38th St Fl 9 New York NY 10018-5500

**STRAUSS, PETER L(ESTER),** law educator; b. N.Y.C., Feb. 26, 1940; s. Simon D. and Elaine Ruth (Mandle) S.; m. Joanna Burnstine, Oct. 1, 1964; children: Benjamin, Bethany. AB magna cum laude, Harvard U., 1961; LLB magna cum laude, Yale U., 1964. Bar: D.C. 1965, U.S. Supreme Ct., 1968. Law clk. U.S. Ct. Appeals D.C. Cir., 1964-65, U.S. Supreme Ct., 1965-66; lectr. Haile Selassie U. Sch. Law, Addis Ababa, Ethiopia, 1966-68; asst. to solicitor gen. Dept. Justice, Washington, 1968-71; assoc. prof. law Columbia U., 1971-74, prof., 1974—, Betts Prof., 1985—, vice dean, 1996; gen. counsel NRC, 1975-77, Adminstrv. Conf. U.S., 1984-95; Byrne vis. prof. Sch. Law Harvard U., Cambridge, Mass., 1994. Adv. bd. Lexis Electronic Author's Press, 1995—. Recipient John Marshall prize Dept. Justice, 1970, Disting. Svc. award NRC, 1977. Editor: Administrative Law Abstracts, 1997—. Mem. ABA (chair sect. adminstrv. law and regulatory practice 1992-93, Disting. Scholarship award 1988), Am. Law Inst. Author: (with Abba Paulos, translator) Fetha Negast: The Law of the Kings, 1968; (with others) Administrative Law Cases and Comments, 1995, supplement 1999; Introduction to Administrative Justice in the United States, 1989; (with Paul Verkuil) Administrative Law Problems, 1983; contbr. articles to law revs. Office: Columbia U Law Sch 435 W 116th St New York NY 10027-7201

**STRAUSS, PHILIP REED,** lawyer; b. Atlanta, June 19, 1968; s. Walter A. and Nancy Reed (Shirley) S. BA in Internat. Studies, Emory U., 1990; JD, Duke U., 1993. Bar: Ill. 1994, W.Va. 1996, N.Y. 1998, D.C. 1998, Mass. 1998; U.S. Dist. Ct. (no. dist.) Ill. 1994, U.S. Ct. Appeals (7th cir., 4th cir.) 1996, U.S. Dist. Ct. (so. dist.) W.Va. 1996, U.S. Ct. Appeals (3d cir.) 1997. Law clk. to Justice Allen T. Compton Alaska Supreme Ct., Anchorage, 1993-94; assoc. Jones, Day, Reavis & Pogue, Chgo., 1994-95, Hedlund Hanley & John, Chgo., 1995-96, Hill, Peterson, Carper, Bee & Deitzler, Charleston, W.Va., 1996-97, Shearman & Sterling, San Francisco, 1997—. Exec. editor Alaska Law Rev., 1991-93. Contracts commercial, Product liability, Personal injury. Home: 555 California St San Francisco CA 94104-1502

**STRAUSS, ROBERT DAVID,** lawyer; b. Cambridge, Mass., Oct. 20, 1951; s. Walter Adolf and Lilo (Teutsch) S.; m. Deborah Mackall, Feb. 15, 1986 (div. Dec. 1998); 1 child, Benjamin Walter. BA, Emory U., 1973, JD, 1976. Bar: Ga. 1976. Assoc. Gambrell & Russell, Atlanta, 1976-81; ptnr. Smith, Gambrell & Russell, Atlanta, 1981-89, Trotter Smith & Jacobs, Atlanta, 1989-92, Troutman Sanders, Atlanta, 1992—. Contbr. articles to profl. jours. Mem. ABA (chmn. leasing subcom. 1988-94, uniform comml. code com.), State Bar of Ga., Equipment Leasing Assn. Am. Finance, Contracts commercial, Aviation. Home: 1445 Monroe Dr NE Apt F28 Atlanta GA 30324-5361 Office: Troutman Sanders 5200 NationsBank Plz 600 Peachtree St NE Atlanta GA 30308-2265

**STRAUSS, STEVEN MARC,** lawyer; b. Cherry Point, N.C., Jan. 31, 1957; s. Matthew C. and Iris Lynn (Leeds) S.; m. Lise N. Wilson, Aug. 22, 1982; children: Naomi, Will. BA in Polit. Sci. and English Lit. magna cum laude, Claremont (Calif.) Mens Coll., 1978; JD, UCLA, 1981. Bar: Calif. 1981; U.S. Ct. Appeals (9th cir.); U.S. Supreme Ct. 1994. Ptnr. Procopio Cory Hargreaves & Savitch LLP, San Diego, 1981—. Mem. LJCC, San Diego, 1996—, Congregation Beth Israel, San Diego, 1981—. Named Outstanding Trial Lawyer San Diego Trial Lawyers Assn., 1995, 96, 50 People to Watch in 1996, San Diego Mag., 1996, Top 8 Business Litigators, San Diego Mag., 1997. Mem. Am. Inns of Ct. (barrister 1993-95, master 1996—). Democrat. Jewish. Avocations: golf, wine. Real property, Intellectual property, General corporate. Office: Procopio Cory Hargreaves & Savitch LLP 530 B St Ste 2100 San Diego CA 92101-4496

**STRAUSS, WILLIAM VICTOR,** lawyer; b. Cin., July 5, 1942; s. William Victor and Elsa (Lovitt) S.; m. Linda Leopold, Nov. 9, 1969; children: Nancy T., Katherine S. AB cum laude, Harvard U., 1964; JD, U. Pa., 1967. Bar: Ohio 1967. Pres. Strauss & Troy, Cin., 1969—; pres. Security Title and Guaranty Agy., Inc., Cin., 1982—. Trustee Cin. Psychoanalytic Inst., 1990—, Cin. Contemporary Arts Ctr., 1997—. Mem. ABA, Nat. Assn. Office and Indsl. Parks, Ohio State Bar Assn., Cin. Bar Assn., Nat. Leased Housing Assn., Cin. World Affairs Coun. Contracts commercial, Real property, Estate planning. Home: 40 Walnut Ave Wyoming OH 45215-4350 Office: Strauss & Troy Fed Res Bldg 150 E 4th St Fl 4 Cincinnati OH 45202-4018

**STRAW, LAWRENCE JOSEPH, JR.,** lawyer; b. Phila., Dec. 22, 1945; s. Lawrence Joseph and Margaret (Wise) S.; m. Linda Carol McClain, Jan. 27, 1973; 1 child, Stacie Victoria. AB, Boston Coll., 1967; JD, U. So. Calif., 1970. Bar: Calif. 1971, U.S. Dist. Ct. (cen. dist.) Calif. 1971, U.S. Supreme Ct. 1977, U.S. Dist. Ct. (ea. and no. dists.) Calif. 1983, U.S. Ct. Appeals (9th cir.) 1983, U.S. Dist. Ct. (so. dist.) Calif. 1992. Atty. Mobil Oil Corp., L.A., 1970-72; assoc. dir. exec. office of pres. Office Econ. Opportunity, Washington, 1973; atty. Mobil Oil Corp., L.A., 1974-82; ptnr. Smaltz & Neelley, L.A., 1982-85, Straw & Gilmartin, Santa Monica, Calif., 1985-97, Straw & Gough, L.A., 1997—; lectr. Calif. Air Resources Bd. Air Pollution Enforcement Symposium, 1983—. Contbg. author California Environmental Law and Land Use Practice; mem. editorial bd. Calif. Environ. Law Reporter. Mem. edn. appeal bd. U.S. Dept.Edn., Washington, 1986-90; candidate Calif. Atty. Gen., 1986; chmn. L.A. County Tax Assessor's Adv. Com., L.A., 1987-90. Mem. State Bar of Calif., Federalist Soc., Conservative Caucus Inc. (treas. 1975—), Calif. Yacht Club. Republican. Roman Catholic. Avocation: yacht racing. Environmental, Federal civil litigation, State civil litigation. Office: Straw & Gough 12304 Santa Monica Blvd Ste 300 Los Angeles CA 90025-2593

**STRAW-BOONE, MELANIE,** lawyer; b. Jefferson, Ind., June 29, 1968; d. William Stewart and Sharon Lee S.; m. Daniel K. Boone Jr., May 25, 1991. B of Secondary Edn., Ind. U., 1991; JD, U. Louisville, 1994. Bar: Ky. 1994, Ind. 1994, U.S. Dist. Ct. (so., ea. and we. dists.) Ky., U.S. Ct. Appeals (6th and 7th cirs.). With Landrum & Shouse, Louisville, 1994—. Mem. Women's Lawyers Assn. Jefferson County. Family and matrimonial, Insurance. Office: Landrum & Shouse 220 W Main St Ste 1900 Louisville KY 40202-1395

**STRAZZELLA, JAMES ANTHONY,** law educator, lawyer; b. Hanover, Pa., May 18, 1939; s. Anthony F. and Teresa Ann (D'Alonzo) S.; m. Judith A. Coppola, Oct. 9, 1965; children: Jill M., Steven A., Tracy Ann, Michael P. AB, Villanova U., 1961; JD, U. Pa., 1964. Bar: Pa. 1964, U.S. Dist. Ct. DC, 1965, U.S. Dist. Ct. ( ea. and mid. dist.) Pa. 1969, U.S. Ct. Appeals (3rd cir.) 1964, U.S. Ct. Appeals (DC cir.) 1965, U.S. Ct. Appeals (4th cir.) 1983, U.S. Supreme Ct. 1969. Law clk. to Hon. Samuel Roberts Pa. Supreme Ct., 1965-69; vice dean, asst. prof. law U. Pa., Phila., 1969-73; faculty Temple U., Phila., 1973—; James G. Schmidt chair in law, 1989—, acting dean, 1987-89; chief counsel Kent State investigation Pres.'s Commn. Campus Unrest, 1970; chmn. Atty. Gen.'s Taks Force on Fedr. of Criminal Law, 1997-99; mem., chmn. justice ops. Mayor's Criminal Justice Coordinating Commn., Phila., 1983-85; Pa. Joint Coun. Criminal Justice, 1979-82; mem. Com. to Study Pa.'s Unified Jud. Sys., 1980-82; Jud. Coun. Pa., 1972-82; chmn. criminal procedural rules com. Pa. Supreme Ct., 1972-85; mem. task force on prison overcrowding, 1983-85, rsch. adv. com., 1988, Pa. Commn. on Crime and Delinquency; chmn. U.S. Magistrate Judge Merit Selection Com., 1991, mem., 1989, 90, 91; co-chair Mayor's Transition Task Force on Pub. Safety, Phila., 1992; designate D.C. Com. on Adminstrn. of Justice Under Emergency Conditions, 1968; del. D.C. Jud. Conf., 1985, 95; reporter Task Force on Federalization Criminal Law, 1998-99. Contbr. articles to profl. jours. and books. Mem. adv. bd. dirs., past pres. A Better in Lower Merion; dir. Hist. Fire Mus., Phila., 1978—; bd. dirs. Lower Merion Hist. Soc., 1998—, dir. Neighborhood Civic Assn., Bala-Cynwyd, Pa., 1984-87; bd. dirs. Smith Meml. Playground in Fairmount Pk., 1997—, Coun. Legal Edn. Opportunity Bd., 1997. Recipient award for disting. tchg. Linback Found., 1983, Advancement of Justice award Atty. Gen., 1989, Disting. Pub. Svc. award Assn. State and County Detectives, 1989, Spl. Merit award Pa. Assn. Police Chiefs, 1989, significant contbn. to legal scholarship and edn. Beccaria award Phila. Bar Assn. and Nat. IAB Assn., 1995. Fellow Am. Bar Found.; mem. Am. Law Inst., ABA (faculty appellate judges' seminars 1977—, various coms., acad. advisor appellate judges edn. com. 1993—), FBA (Phila. crim. law com. adv. bd. 1988-93, chmn. nat. criminal law com. 1991-92), Pa. Bar Assn. (commn. profl. stds. 1981-84, chmn. criminal law sect. 1986-88, Spl. Merit award 1987), Phila. Bar Assn. (criminal justice sect., appellate cts. com.), Order of the Coif (exec. bd. U. Pa.), St. Thomas More Soc. (pres. 1985-86, past dir. Phila. area, St. Thomas More award 1996). Roman Catholic. Home and Office: 100 Maple Ave Bala Cynwyd PA 19004-3017 Office: Temple U Law Sch 1719 N Broad St Philadelphia PA 19122-6002

**STRECK, FREDERICK LOUIS, III,** lawyer; b. St. Louis, Nov. 6, 1960; s. Frederick Louis Jr. and Joan Kathrine (Faerber) S.; m. Michelle Renee Harding; children: Frederick IV, Robert Harding, Joseph Walter, Samuel Franklin. BBA, Tex. Christian U., 1983; JD, St. Mary's U., 1986. Bar: Tex. 1986, U.S. Dist. Ct. (no. dist.) Tex. 1987, U.S. Ct. Appeals (5th cir.) 1987; bd. cert. in personal injury trial law, civil trial advocacy; diplomate Am. Bd. of Trial Advocacy. Atty. Kugle, Stewart, Dent & Frederick, Ft. Worth, 1986-89, The Dent Law Firm, 1990—. State del. Dem. Party, Tex., 1988. Fellow Tex. State Bar Coll.; mem. ABA, ATLA,, Tex. Trial Lawyers Assn., Million Dollar Advocates Forum. Democrat. Roman Catholic. Avocations: wine collecting, golf, fishing, scuba diving. Fax: 817-332-5809. E-mail: fstreck3@yahoo.com. Personal injury, Workers' compensation, Federal civil litigation. Office: The Dent Law Firm 1120 Penn St Fort Worth TX 76102-3417

**STRECKER, DAVID EUGENE,** lawyer; b. Carthage, Mo., Nov. 29, 1950; s. Eugene Albert and Erma Freida (Wood) S.; m. Katherine Ann Pugh; children: Charles David, Carrie Christina. BA, Westminster Coll., 1972; JD, Cornell U., 1975, M in Indsl. Labor Rels., 1976. Bar: N.Y. 1976, U.S. Dist. Ct. (no. dist.) N.Y. 1976, Okla. 1981, U.S. Ct. Appeals (no. dist.) Okla. 1981, U.S. Ct. Appeals (10th cir.) 1982, U.S. Dist. Ct. (ea. dist.) Okla. 1984, U.S. Ct. Appeals (6th cir.) 1990, U.S. Supreme Ct. 1991. Assoc. Conner & Winters, Tulsa, 1980-85, ptnr., 1985-91; ptnr. Shipley, Inhofe & Strecker, Tulsa, 1991-95, Strecker & Assocs. P.C., Tulsa, 1995—; instr. paralegal program Tulsa Jr. Coll., 1985—, mem. adv. com., 1986-91; mem. Cornell Secondary Schs. Com., Tulsa, 1985—; adj. instr. labor rels. Okla. State U., 1995—; barrister Am. Inns of Ct. Bd. dirs., v.p. Tulsa Sr. Svcs., 1988-91; mem. pers. com. Philbrook Art Mus. Capt. JAGC, U.S. Army, 1976-80. Mem. ABA, Okla. Bar Assn. (chmn. labor sect. 1990-91), Tulsa County Bar Assn. (continuing legal edn. com. 1981—), Soc. for Human Resource Mgmt., Tulsa Area Human Resources Assn. (gen. counsel 1989—, v.p. 1994—), Kappa Alpha. Democrat. Episcopalian. Avocations: jogging, golf. Labor, Federal civil litigation, Workers' compensation. Home: 5112 E 107th St Tulsa OK 74137-7238 Office: Nations Bank Ctr 15 W 6th St Ste 1600 Tulsa OK 74119-5410

**STREET, ERICA CATHERINE,** lawyer; b. Lansing, Mich., July 5, 1958; d. Cassius English and Helen Joanna (Hoesman) S.; m. Robert John Pratte, Oct. 20, 1984; 1 child, Chelsea Nicole Pratte. BA, Hillsdale Coll., 1979; JD, U. Mich., 1981. Bar: Minn. 1982, U.S. Dist. Ct. Minn. 1982, U.S. Ct. Appeals (8th cir.) 1983. Assoc. Best & Flanagan, Mpls., 1981-85; sr. counsel Fingerhut Corp., Minnetonka, Minn., 1985-89; sr. counsel Target Stores, Mpls., 1989-97, asst. gen. counsel, 1997-99; pres. Dayton Hudson Brands Inc., Mpls., 1999—. Entertainment, Intellectual property, Trademark and copyright. Office: Dayton Hudson Brands Inc 33 S 6th St Minneapolis MN 55402-3601

**STREET, JAMES J.,** lawyer; b. St. Paul, Oct. 24, 1960; s. Willis F. and Barbara J. Street; m. Rachel Sibley, Aug. 29, 1985; children: Gabriel Sibley, Anna Grace Sibley. BA, Macalester Coll., 1983; JD, U. Denver, 1986. Bar: Minn., U.S. Dist. Ct. Minn. Staff atty. Legal Assistance of Denver, 1986-87, Queens Legal Svcs., L.I., N.Y., 1987-90; mng. atty. So. Minn. Regional Legal Svcs., St. Paul, 1990-95, supervising atty., 1995—. Presbyterian. Office: So Minn Regional Legal Svcs 46 4th St E Ste 300 Saint Paul MN 55101-1113

**STREET, WALTER SCOTT, III,** lawyer; b. Richmond, Va., May 20, 1944; s. Walter Scott Jr. and Margaret (Hoyt) S.; m. Virginia Mapes, Aug. 23, 1967; children: Walter Scott IV, Christopher F., Elizabeth M. BA, Hampden-Sydney Coll., 1965; LLB, U. Va., 1968. Bar: Va. 1968, U.S. Ct. Appeals (4th cir.) 1968, U.S. Dist Ct. (ea. dist.) Va. 1968, U.S. Supreme Ct. 1974. Assoc. atty. Bremner, Byrne & Baber, Richmond, Va., 1968-70; house coun. Blue Cross Va., Richmond, 1970-71; ptnr. Wood & Street, Richmond, 1971-80, Williams, Mullen, Christian & Dobbins, Richmond, 1980—; sec.-treas. Va. Bd. Bar Examiners, Richmond, 1972—; commr. in chancery Chesterfield Cir. Ct., Va., 1970—. Gen. counsel Va. divsn. Am. Cancer Soc., 1976—; trustee Hargrave Mil. Acad., Chatham, Va., 1988-92. Fellow Va. Law Found.; mem. ABA, Nat. Conf. Bar Examienrs (chmn. adminstrs. com. 1980-81), Richmond Bar Assn., Va. State Bar (bar coun. 1991—, chmn. com. on legal edn. and admission to the bar 1991-93, exec. com. 1994—, pres.-elect 1998-99), Country Club Va. General civil litigation, Insurance, Bankruptcy. Office: Williams Mullen Christian & Dobbins 2 James Center 1021 E Cary St Richmond VA 23219-4000

**STREIB, VICTOR LEE,** law educator, dean; b. Marion, Ind., Oct. 8, 1941; s. Albert Wolfe and Melba Janice Streib; m. Lynn C. Sametz, Mar. 29, 1978; children: Noah, Jessi. BS in Indsl. Engring., Auburn U., 1966; JD, Ind. U., Bloomington, 1970. Bar: Ind. 1970, U.S. Supreme Ct. 1987. Rsch. assoc., scientist Inst. Rsch. Pub. Safety Ind. U., Bloomington, 1970-72, asst. to assoc. prof. dept. forensic studies, 1972-78; assoc. prof. law New Eng. Sch. Law, Boston, 1978-80; prof., assoc. dean coll. of law Cleve. State U., 1980-96; dean, prof. law Ohio No. U., Ada, 1996—; vis. prof. law U. San Diego, 1983-84; vis. fellow Assn. Am. Law Schs., Washington, 1993-94, site evaluator, 1994—; mem. adv. bd. Ctr. Capital Punishment Studies U. Westminster, London, 1996—. Author: Juvenile Justice in America, 1978, Death Penalty for Juveniles, 1987; editor: Capital Punishment Anthology, 1993, Law Deanship Manual, 1993. Mem. ABA (site evaluator 1991—), North Ctrl. Assn. (cons. evaluator 1990—). Avocation: physical fitness. Criminal, Juvenile. Office: Ohio No U Coll Law 525 S Main St Ada OH 45810-6000

**STREICHER, JAMES FRANKLIN,** lawyer; b. Ashtabula, Ohio, Dec. 6, 1940; s. Carl Jacob and Helen Marie (Dugan) S.; m. Sandra JoAnn Jennings, May 22, 1940; children: Cheryl Ann, Gregory Scott, Kerry Marie. BA, Ohio State U., 1962; JD, Case Western Res. U., 1966. Bar: Ohio 1966, U.S. Dist. Ct. (no. dist.) Ohio 1966. Assoc. Calfee, Halter & Griswold, Cleve., 1966-71, ptnr., 1972—; bd. dirs. The Mariner Group Inc., Ft. Myers, Fla., Spectra-Tech Inc., Stamford, Conn., Cuyahoga Bolt & Screw, Cleve.; mem. Divsn. Securities Adv. Bd., State of Ohio; lectr. Case Western Res. U., Cleve. State U.; mem. pvt. sector com. John Carroll U.; trustee Western Rsch. Hist. Soc. Trustee Achievement Ctr. for Children, Western Reserve Hist. Soc. Mem. ABA, Fed. Bar Assn., Ohio State Bar Assn., Assn. for Corp. Growth, Ohio Venture Assn., Greater Cleve. Bar Assn. (founding chmn. corp., banking, bus. law sect.), Ohio State U. Alumni Assn., Case Western Res. U. Alumni Assn., Newcomen Soc., Bluecoats Club (Cleve.), Mayfield Country (bd. dirs. 1985-89), Tavern Club, Union Club, Hunting Valley Gun Club, Sand Ridge Golf Club, Rotary, Beta Theta Pi, Phi Delta Phi. Roman Catholic. Republican. FAX: 216-241-0816. E-mail: j.streich@calfee.com. Securities. Home: 50 Windrush Dr Chagrin Falls OH 44022-6841

**STREICKER, JAMES RICHARD,** lawyer; b. Chgo., Nov. 9, 1944; s. Seymour and De Vera (Wolfson) S.; m. Mary Stowell, Mar. 11, 1989; children: David, Sarah. AB, Miami U., 1966; JD, U. Ill., 1969. Bar: Ill. 1969, U.S. Dist. Ct. (no. dist.) Ill. 1970, U.S. Ct. Appeals (7th cir.) 1971, U.S. Supreme Ct. 1980, U.S. Dist. Ct. (ea. dist.) Wis., (no. dist.) Ind. 1986. Asst. atty. gen. State of Ill., 1970-71, asst. appellate def., 1971-75; dep. appellate def. First Dist. Ill., 1975; asst. U.S. atty. No. Dist. Ill., 1975-80; chief criminal receiving and appellate div. U.S. Attys. Office, Ill., 1979-80; ptnr. Cotsirilos, Stephenson, Tighe & Streicker, Chgo., 1980—; instr. Trial Adv. John Marshall Law Sch., 1979-80, U.S. Atty. Gens. Adv. Inst. 1978-80, Nat. Inst. for Trial Adv. 1981—; lectr. Ill. Inst. Continuing Legal Edn., Sentencing, New Techniques and Attitudes, 1986, Healthcare Fraud and Abuse Seminar, 1998, Fed. Bar Assn., 1990, Healthcare Fraud and Abuse Seminar, 1998. Mem. ABA, Nat. Assn. Criminal Def. Lawyers, Am. Coll. Trial Lawyers, Am. Bd. Criminal Lawyers, Ill. State Bar Assn., Chgo. Bar Assn. Criminal, General civil litigation, Antitrust.

**STREVER, KEVIN KIRK,** lawyer; b. Denver, July 4, 1960; s. Merle A. and Donna Jo (Ritchie) S.; m. Lauri Jean Rask, Apr. 1, 1989. BS in Polit. Sci. cum laude, So. Oreg. State Coll., 1982; JD, U. Oreg., 1985. Bar: Oreg. 1985, U.S. Dist. Ct. Oreg. 1986, U.S. Ct. Appeals (9th cir.) 1986. Musician, 1977-84; legal clk. E.F. Hutton & Co., N.Y.C., 1984; atty. Barton & Strever P.C., Newport, Oreg., 1985—; Author (book chpt.) Recovering for Psychological Injuries, 1990, chpt. 4, Torst (Oreg. CLE 1992), "Torts Arising From Sexual Misconduct. Author (book chpt.) Recovering for Psychological Injuries, 1990. Mem. Oreg. State Bar (pres. 1997-98, bd. govs. 1995-98), Oreg. Criminal Def. Lawyers Assn., Assn. Trial Lawyers Am., Oreg. Trial Lawyers Assn. (Pres.'s club 1989—), Lincoln County Bar Assn. (pres. 1989). Avocations: retired professional guitarist, scuba diving, vacuum tube amplification, electronics. Personal injury, Criminal. Home: 421 NW 13th St Newport OR 97365-2402 Office: Barton & Strever PC 214 SW Coast Hwy Newport OR 97365-4927*

**STRICKLAND, TOM,** prosecutor; married; three children. Bachelor's degree, La. State U., 1974; JD, U. Tex., 1977. Chief policy adv. to Gov. Dick Lamm, 1982-84; sr. ptnr. Brownstein, Hyatt, Farber, and Strickland; U.S. atty. Colo. dist. U.S. Dept. Justice. Dem. candidate U.S. Sen., 1996. Office: Ste 1200 1961 Stout St Denver CO 80294*

**STRICKLAND, WILTON L.,** lawyer; b. Ft. Myers, July 1, 1942; s. Lorenzo Strickland and Mary Voncille Singletary; m. Barbara Hathaway Lahna (div. July 1984); children: Amy Beth Strickland-Quattlebaum, Wilton Hathaway Strickland. BA, U. Fla., 1964; JD, Stetson U., 1969. Bar: Fla. 1969, U.S. Dist. Ct. (so. dist.) Fla. 1969, Trial Bar (so. dist.) Fla. 1983, U.S. Dist. Ct. (mid. dist.) Fla. 1988, U.S. Ct. Appeals (5th cir.) 1978, U.S. Ct. Appeals (11th cir.) 1981, U.S. Supreme Ct. 1977. Ptnr. Howell, Kirby, Montgomery et al, Ft. Lauderdale, Fla., 1969-73, Ferrero, Middlebrooks & Houston, Ft. Lauderdale, 1974-77, Ferrero, Middlebrooks & Strickland, Ft. Lauderdale, 1977-91, Strickland & Seidule, Ft. Lauderdale, 1991-98; pvt. practice Wilton L. Strickland, P.A., Ft. Lauderdale, 1998—. Chmn. bd. Hospice Care Broward County, Inc.; bd. dirs. Salvation Army Broward County; mem. Helping Abandoned and Dependent Youth. Mem. ABA, ATLA, Fla. Bar (mem. ethics com.), Acad. Fla. Trial Lawyers (dir. 1980-84), Broward County Trial Lawyers Assn. (past pres. 1981), Broward County Bar Assn., Am. Bd. Trial Advs. (founder Broward County chpt.), Million Dollar Advocates Forum, The Bar Register of Preaminent Lawyers, Phi Alpha Delta (former pres. Brewer chpt.). Democrat. Presbyterian. Avocations: winter skiing, reading, hiking, boating, white water rafting. Personal injury, Product liability, General civil litigation. Home: 2897 NE 25th St Fort Lauderdale FL 33305-1722 Office: # 303 1401 E Broward Blvd Ste 303 Fort Lauderdale FL 33301-2100

**STRICKLER, SCOTT MICHAEL,** lawyer; b. Miami Beach, Fla., May 24, 1961; s. Lawrence Jerome and Barbara Susan (Fogelman) S.; m. Joy Ann Kohler, June 24, 1995; 1 child, Megan Halle. BS in Journalism, U. Md., 1981, JD with honors, 1985. Bar: Md. 1985, D.C. 1987, U.S. Dist. Ct. Md. 1988. Jud. law clk. 5th Jud. Cir. of Md., Annapolis, 1985-86; assoc. Stephen E. Moss, P.A., Bethesda, Md., 1986-89; ptnr., v.p. Moss, Strickler & Weaver, P.A., Bethesda, 1990-94, Moss & Strickler, P.A., Bethesda, 1994; ptnr. Moss Strickler & Sachitano, P.A., Bethesda, 1995—. Coach, dir. Bowie (Md.) Boys and Girls Club, 1976-81; dir. Bowie Basketball Sch., Inc., 1978-82; basketball coach Peninsula Athletic League, Annapolis, 1985-86, Olney (Md.) Boys and Girls Club, 1987—, I-270 Sports Club, Gaithersburg, Md., 1991—, Sports Challenge Internat., Palm Harbor, Fla., 1993—. Mem. ABA, Md. State Bar Assn., Montgomery County Bar Assn. (chair family law sect. 1998-99), Inst. Sports Attys., Kappa Tau Alpha. Avocations: basketball coach, participatory athletics, memorabilia collection. Family and matrimonial, Personal injury, Probate. Home: 15117 Grey Pebble Dr Darnestown MD 20874-3238 Office: Moss Strickler & Sachitano 4550 Montgomery Ave Ste 700 Bethesda MD 20814-3304

**STRICKSTEIN, HERBERT JERRY,** lawyer; b. Detroit, Sept. 4, 1932; s. Samuel and Leah (Freedman) S.; m. Elaine Frances Cohen, Aug. 22, 1963; children: Jaynee Esther, Jill Rose. AA, UCLA, 1952; BS in Law, U. So. Calif., 1954, JD, 1956. Dep. judge adv. USAF, 1957-60; dep. city atty. L.A., 1960-61; assoc. Axelrad, Seville & Ross, 1961-65; ptnr. Iliff & Strickstein, 1965-72; pvt. practice Herbert J. Strickstein Law Corp., L.A., 1972—. Contbr. numerous articles to profl. jours. Commr. Small Craft Harbor Comm., Marina del Rey, Calif., 1983—. Mem. State Bar Calif. Assn. (real property sec.), Beverly Hills Bar Assn., El Caballero Country Club, Del Rey Yacht Club, Mission Hills Country Club. Avocations: racquetball, golf, tennis, sailing. Real property. Office: 2049 Century Park E Ste 1200 Los Angeles CA 90067-3114

**STRIMBU, VICTOR, JR.,** lawyer; b. New Philadelphia, Ohio, Nov. 25, 1932; s. Victor and Veda (Stancu) S.; m. Kathryn May Schrote, Apr. 9, 1955; children: Victor Paul, Michael, Julie, Sue. BA, Heidelberg Coll., 1954; postgrad. Western Res. U., 1956-57; JD, Columbia U., 1960. Bar: Ohio 1960, U.S. Supreme Ct. 1972. With Baker & Hostetler LLP, Cleve., 1960—, ptnr., 1970—. Bd. dirs. North Coast Health Ministry; mem. Bay Village (Ohio) Bd. Edn., 1976-84, pres., 1978-82; mem. indsl. rels. adv. com. Cleve. State U., 1979—, chmn., 1982, 1998; mem. Bay Village Planning Comm., 1967-69; life mem. Ohio PTA; mem. Greater Cleve. Growth Assn.; trustee New Cleve. Campaign, 1987—, North Coast Health Ministry, 1989—, Heidelberg Coll., 1996—; mem. indsl. rels. adv. com. Cleve. State U., 1979—, chmn., 1982, vice chmn., 1998. With AUS, 1955-56. Recipient Service award Cleve. State U., 1980. Mem. ABA, Ohio Bar Assn., Greater Cleve. Bar Assn., Ohio Newspaper Assn. (minority affairs com. 1987—), Ct. of Nisi Prius Club, Cleve. Athletic Club, The Club at Soc. Ctr. Republican. Presbyterian. Labor. Office: Baker & Hostetler LLP 3200 National City Ctr 1900 E 9th St Ste 3200 Cleveland OH 44114-3475

**STRINGER, EDWARD CHARLES,** state supreme court justice; b. St. Paul, Feb. 13, 1935; s. Philip and Anne (Driscoll) S.; m. Mary Lucille Lange, June 19, 1957 (div. Mar. 1991); children: Philip, Lucille, Charles, Carolyn; m. Virginia L. Ward, Sept. 10, 1993. BA, Amherst Coll., 1957; LLD, U. Minn., 1960. Bar: Minn. Ptnr. Stringer, Donnelly & Sharood, St. Paul, 1960-69, Briggs & Morgan, St. Paul, 1969-79; sr. v.p., gen. counsel Pillsbury Co., Mpls., 1980-82, exec. v.p., gen. counsel, 1982-83, exec. v.p., gen. counsel, chief adminstrv. officer, 1983-89; gen. counsel U.S. Dept. Edn., Washington, 1989-91; chief of staff Minn. Gov. Arne H. Carlson, 1992-94; assoc. justice Minn. Supreme Ct., St. Paul, 1994—. Mem. ABA, Minn. State Bar Assn., Ramsey County Bar Assn. (sec. 1977-80), Order of Coif, Mpls. Club. Congregationalist. Home: 712 Linwood Ave Saint Paul MN 55105-3513 Office: Minn Judicial Center 25 Constitution Ave Saint Paul MN 55155-1500*

**STRINGER, NANETTE SCHULZE,** lawyer; b. Stuttgart, Germany, May 29, 1952; came to U.S., 1952; d. Herbert Charles and Marie-Jeanne (Raphael) Schulze; m. James Cooper Stringer, Oct. 9, 1982; children: David, Sarah, Amy. BA, Harvard U., 1974; JD, Stanford U., 1978. Bar: Calif. 1978, U.S. Dist. Ct. (no. dist.) Calif. 1978. Atty. Keogh, Marer & Flicker, Palo Alto, Calif., 1979-81, Carr, McClellan, Burlingame, Calif., 1981-83, Lakin-Spears, Palo Alto, 1983-89, Law Ofc. of John Miller, Palo Alto, 1991-93; atty., owner Nanette S. Stringer, Atty. at Law, Palo Alto, 1993—. Sec., bd. mem. Palo Alto Little League, 1995—. Mem. Palo Alto Bar Assn.

(lawyer referral svc. com.), Calif. State Bar (cert specialist family law bd. specialization, 1994—). Roman Catholic. Avocations: masters' swimming, running, gardening. Family and matrimonial. Office: 375 Forest Ave Palo Alto CA 94301-2521

**STRINGER, RONALD E.,** lawyer, educator; b. N.Y.C., Feb. 23, 1934; s. Irving and Mary Stringer; m. Sandra Deutsch, Oct. 30, 1986; children from previous marriage: Scott, David. AB, CCNY, 1954; LLB, Bklyn. Law Sch., 1957, JD, 1968. Bar: N.Y. 1958, U.S. Dist. Ct. (so. and ea. dists.) N.Y., U.S. Supreme Ct. Law sect. to comptroller City of N.Y., 1971-73, counsel to mayor, 1974-77; counsel Balsam Felber & Goldfield, 1977—; asst. prof. John Jay Coll. Criminal Justice, N.Y.C., 1992-99; hon. consul Dominican Republic, N.Y.C., 1972-74. Recipient Svc. award Alianza Hispano-Am., 1975. Democrat. Probate, General civil litigation, Legislative. Office: Balsam Felber & Goldfield 99 Wall St New York NY 10005-4301

**STROBEL, MARTIN JACK,** lawyer, motor vehicle and industrial component manufacturing and distribution company executive; b. N.Y.C., July 4, 1940; s. Nathan and Clara (Sorgen) S.; m. Hadassah Orenstein, Aug. 15, 1965; children: Gil Michael, Karen Rachel. BA, Columbia U., 1962; JD, Cleve. Marshall Law Sch., 1966; completed advanced bus. mgmt. program, Harvard U., 1977. Bar: Ohio bar 1966. Counsel def. contract adminstrn. services region Def. Supply Agy., Cleve., 1966-68; with Dana Corp., Toledo, 1968—; gen. counsel Dana Corp., 1970—, dir. govt. relations, 1970-71, asst. sec., 1971—, v.p., 1976—, sec., 1982—. Mem. ABA, Fed. Bar Assn., Machinery and Allied Products Inst., Ohio Bar Assn., Toledo Bar Assn. General corporate. Office: Dana Corp PO Box 1000 Toledo OH 43697-1000

**STROBER, ERIC SAUL,** lawyer; b. Bklyn., July 30, 1970; s. Charles and Debora Strober. BA, Syracuse U., 1992; JD, Bklyn. Law Sch., 1995. Bar: N.Y. 1996, U.S. Dist. Ct. (ea. dist.) N.Y. 1996. Law clk. Kramer, Dillof, Tessel, Duffy & Moore, N.Y.C., 1994-95; atty. Callan, Regenstreich, Koster & Brady, N.Y.C., 1995-97, Parker, Chapin, Flattau & Klimpl, N.Y.C., 1997-99, Riukin, Radler & Kremer, N.Y.C. Mem. ABA, N.Y. State Bar Assn. Personal injury, Toxic tort, Product liability. Office: Parker Chapin Flattau & Klimpl LLP Ste 1700 1211 Avenue Of The Americas New York NY 10036-8735

**STRODE, JOSEPH ARLIN,** lawyer; b. DeWitt, Ark., Mar. 5, 1946; s. Thomas Joseph and Nora (Richardson) S.; m. Carolyn Taylor, Feb. 9, 1969; children: Tanya Briana, William Joseph. BSEE with honors, U. Ark., 1969; JD, So. Meth. U., 1972. Bar: Ark. 1972. Design engr. Tex. Instruments Inc., Dallas, 1969-70, patent agt., 1970-72; assoc. Bridges, Young, Matthews, Drake, Pine Bluff, Ark., 1972-74, ptnr., 1975—. Chmn. Pine Bluff Airport Commn., 1993; bd. dirs. United Way Jefferson County, Pine Bluff, 1975-77, campaign chmn., 1983, pres., 1986, exec. com., 1983-87; bd. dirs. Leadership Pine Bluff, 1983-85. Mem. ABA, Ark. Bar Assn., Jefferson County Bar Assn. (pres. 1995), Pine Bluff C. of C. (dir. 1981-84, 94-97), Ark. Wildlife Fed. (dir. 1979-81), Jefferson County Wildlife Assn. (dir. 1973-80, pres. 1974-76), Order of Coif, Tau Beta Pi, Eta Kappa Nu. Club: Kiwanis (lt. gov. Mo.-Ark. div. 1983-84, chmn. lt. govs. 1983-84). Contracts commercial, Banking, Intellectual property. Home: 7600 Jay Lynn Ln Pine Bluff AR 71603-9387 Office: 315 E 8th Ave Pine Bluff AR 71601-5005

**STROM, J. PRESTON, JR.,** lawyer; b. May 21, 1959; s. Grace and J.P. Sr. S.; m. Donna Savoca, Oct. 5, 1985; children: Margaret, Caroline. BA, U. S.C., 1981, JD, 1984. Bar: S.C. 1984, U.S. Dist. Ct. S.C., 1984, U.S. Ct. Appeals (4th cir.) 1984. Asst. solicitor 5th Jud. Cir., S.C., 1985-86; ptnr. Leventis, Strom & Wicker, 1986-88, Harpootlian & Strom, 1988-90, Bolt, Popowski, McCulloch & Strom, 1990-93; acting U.S. atty. Office U.S. Atty., S.C., 1993, U.S. atty., 1993-96; atty. Strom and Young, LLP, Columbia, S.C., 1996—; chmn. Law Enforcement Coord. Com.; chmn. juvenile justice and child support enforcement subcom. U.S. Dept. Justice; active Atty. Gen. Adv. Com. Mem. S.C. Bar, S.C. Trial Lawyers Assn., Richland County Bar Assn. (chmn. criminal law sect.). General civil litigation, Criminal. Office: Strom Young & Thurmond LLP 1201 Hampton St Ste 3A Columbia SC 29201-2865

**STROM, LYLE ELMER,** federal judge; b. Omaha, Nebr., Jan. 6, 1925; s. Elmer T. and Eda (Hanisch) S.; m. Regina Ann Kelly, July 31, 1950; children: Mary Bess, Susan Frances, Amy Claire, Cassie A., David Kelly, Margaret Mary, Bryan Thomas. Student, U. Nebr., 1946-47; AB, Creighton U., 1950, JD cum laude, 1953. Bar: Nebr. 1953. Assoc. Fitzgerald, Brown, Leahy, Strom, Schorr & Barmettler and predecessor firm, Omaha, 1953-60, ptnr., 1960-63, gen. trial ptnr., 1963-85; judge U.S. Dist. Ct. Nebr., Omaha, 1985-87, chief judge, 1987-94, sr. judge, 1995—; adj. prof. law Creighton U., 1959-95, clinical prof., 1996—; mem. com. pattern jury instrns. and practice and proc. Nebr. Supreme Ct., 1965-91; spl. legal counsel Omaha Charter Rev. Commn., 1973; chair gender fairness task force U.S. Ct. Appeals (8th cir.), 1993-97. Exec. com Covered Wagon Coun. Boy Scouts Am., 1953-57, bd. trustees and exec. com. Mid-Am. Coun., 1988—; chmn. bd. trustees Marian H.S., 1969-71; mem. pres. coun. Creighton U., 1990—. Ensign USNR and with U.S. Maritime Svc., 1943-46. Fellow Am. Coll. Trial Lawyers, Internat. Acad. Trial Lawyers; mem. Nebr. Bar Assn. (ho. of dels. 1978-81, exec. coun. 1981-87, pres. 1989-90), Nebr. Bar Found. (bd. trustees 1998—), Omaha Bar Assn. (pres. 1980-81), Am. Judicature Soc., Midwestern Assn. Amateur Athletic Union (pres. 1976-78), Rotary (pres. 1993-94), Alpha Sigma Nu (pres. alumni chpt. 1970-71). Republican. Roman Catholic. Office: US Dist Ct PO Box 607 Omaha NE 68101-0607

**STROM, MILTON GARY,** lawyer; b. Rochester, N.Y., Dec. 5, 1942; s. Harold and Dolly (Isaacson) S.; m. Barbara A. Simon, Jan. 18, 1975; children: Carolyn, Michael, Jonathan. BS in Econs., U. Pa., 1964; JD, Cornell U., 1967. Bar: N.Y. 1968, U.S. Dist. Ct. (we. dist.) N.Y. 1968, U.S. Ct. Claims 1969, U.S. Ct. Mil. Appeals 1969, U.S. Ct. Appeals ((D.C. cir.) 1970, U.S. Supreme Ct. 1972, U.S. Dist. Ct. (so. dist.) N.Y. 1975. Atty. SEC, Washington, 1968-71; assoc. Skadden, Arps, Slate, Meagher & Flom, N.Y.C., 1971-77, ptnr., 1977—. Served with USCGR, 1967-68. Mem. ABA, N.Y. State Bar Assn. (corp. law sect.), Assn. of Bar of City of N.Y. Republican. Jewish. Club: Beach Point, Marco Polo. Avocations: tennis, skiing. General corporate, Securities. Office: Skadden Arps Slate Meagher & Flom 919 3rd Ave New York NY 10022-3902

**STROMBERG, JEAN WILBUR GLEASON,** lawyer; b. St. Louis, Oct. 31, 1943; d. Ray Lyman and Martha (Bugbee) W.; m. Gerald Kermit Gleason, Aug. 28, 1966 (div. 1987); children: C. Blake, Peter Wilbur; m. Kurt Stromberg, Jan. 3, 1993; 1 child, Kristoffer Stromberg. BA, Wellesley Coll., 1965; LLB cum laude, Harvard U., 1968. Bar: Calif. 1969, D.C. 1978. Assoc. Brobeck, Phleger & Harrison, San Francisco, 1969-72; spl. counsel to dir. div. corp. fin. SEC, Washington, 1972-76, assoc. dir. div. investment mgmt., 1976-78; of counsel Fulbright & Jaworski, Washington, 1978-80, ptnr., 1980-96; dir. fin. instns. and market issues GAO, Washington, 1996-97; pvt. practice, Washington, 1997—; mem. adv. panel on legal issues GAO, NASD select com. on Nasdaq, 1994-96; trustee AARP Investment Program and AARP Scudder Mut. Funds, 1997—. Mem. ABA (chmn. subcom. on securities and banks, corp. laws com., bus. sect. 1982-93), D.C. Bar Assn. (chmn. steering com. bus. sect. 1982-84), FBA (chair exec. coun., securities com. 1993-95), Am. Bar Retirement Assn. (bd. dirs. 1986-90, 94-96), Phi Beta Kappa. General corporate, Securities. Home and Office: 3816 Military Rd NW Washington DC 20015-2704

**STROMME, GARY L.,** law librarian; b. Willmar, Minn., July 8, 1939; s. William A. and Edla A. (Soderberg) S.; m. Suzanne Readman, July 21, 1990. BA, Pacific Luth. U., 1965; BLS, U. B.C., Vancouver, Can., 1967; JD, U. Calif., San Francisco, 1973. Bar: Calif. 1973, U.S. Supreme Ct. 1977. Serials libr. U. Minn. St. Paul. Campus Libr., 1967-69; asst. libr. McCutchen, Doyle, Brown and Enerson, San Francisco, 1970-71; asst. libr. Graham & James, San Francisco, 1971-73, ind. contracting atty., 1973-74; law libr. Pacific Gas and Electric Co., San Francisco, 1974-95; cons., 1995—; lectr. in field. Author: An Introduction to the use of the Law Library, 1974, 76, Basic Legal Research Techniques, 1979. With USAF, 1959-63. Mem. ABA (chmn. libr. com. of sect. econs. of law practice 1978-82), Am. Assn. Law Librs. (chmn. com. on indexing of legal periodicals 1986-88), Western Pacific Assn. Law Librs., No. Calif. Assn. Law Librs., Pvt. Law Librs., Corp. Law Librs. Home: 6106 Ocean View Dr Oakland CA 94618-1841

**STRONE, MICHAEL JONATHAN,** lawyer; b. N.Y.C., Feb. 26, 1953; s. Bernard William and Judith Semem (Sogg) S.; m. Andrea Nan Acker, Jan. 27, 1979; children: Noah Gregory, Joshua Samuel. BA cum laude, Colby Coll., 1974; JD, Fordham Law Sch., 1978. Bar: N.J. 1978, N.Y. 1979, Conn. 1988, U.S. Ct. Appeals (2d and 3d cirs.) 1979, U.S. Dist. Ct. (so. and ea. dists.) N.Y. 1979, U.S. Dist. Ct. N.J. 1979). Assoc. Ratheim Hoffman et al, N.Y.C., 1978-80, Boetin Hays et al, N.Y.C., 1980-84; v.p., assoc. gen. counsel, asst. sec. GE Investment Corp., Stamford, Conn., 1984—; v.p., gen. counsel Gindoff Enterprises, 1985-90. Bd. dirs. N.Y. chpt. Juvenile Diabetes Found., N.Y.C., 1981-89, vice chmn., 1981-88; mem. fin. com. Juvenile Diabetes Found. Internat., 1981-86; asst. prin. bassist Westchester Symphony Orch., Scarsdale, N.Y., 1982—, pres., 1982-87, chmn. bd., 1982-90, exec. mng. dir., 1990-93; vice chmn. ann. dinner NCCJ, 1987; bd. dirs. Parkinson's Diseast Soc. Am., 1989-96, chmn. merger com., 1991-96; bd. dirs. Parkinson's Action Network, 1994-98; trustee Jewish Cmty. Ctr. of Harrison, 1996—, mem. ritual com., 1996—, chmn. alt. svcs. com., 1997—; chmn. co. United Way campaign, 1999. Mem. ABA (chmn. pension plan investments 1989-91, chmn. asset mgmt. 1992-94, 95-97, significant legis. coms. 1985-92, chmn. subcom. on joint ventures 1988-90), Am. Coll. Real Estate Lawyers (com. professionalism 1994—), The Corp. Bar Assn., Nat. Assn. Real Estate Investment Mgrs. (sr. legal officers adv. com. 1993—, ann. forum chair 1997), Colby Coll. Alumni Coun. (nominating com. 1994-97), Fordham Law Alumni Assn., The Internat. Netsuke Soc., Jewish Geneal. Soc. Republican. Real property, Pension, profit-sharing, and employee benefits, General corporate. Home: 10 Genesee Trail Harrison NY 10528-1802 Office: Gen Electric Investment Corp 3003 Summer St Stamford CT 06905-4316

**STRONG, CARTER,** lawyer; b. Bronxville, N.Y., July 17, 1947; s. Shirley Carter and Hélène Strong; m. Helen Anne Marvel, May 17, 1980; children: Winslow C., Hilary H. BA in History, Ithaca Coll., 1969; JD, U. Miami, 1972. Bar: Fla. 1972, D.C. 1973. Assoc. Arent, Fox, Kintner, Plotkin & Kahn, PLLC, Washington, 1972-80, ptnr., 1981—. Mem. Chevy Chase Club, Siasconset Casino Assn. Avocations: tennis, golf, reading, travel. Securities, Mergers and acquisitions, General corporate. Office: Arent Fox Kintner Plotkin & Kahn PLLC 1050 Connecticut Ave NW Washington DC 20036-5339

**STRONG, FRANKLIN WALLACE, JR.,** lawyer; b. Iowa City, Iowa, Oct. 26, 1949; s. Franklin Wallace and Rosemary (Nielsen) S.; m. Ann Grant Walter, Mar. 20, 1976 (div. Nov. 1997); 1 child: Franklin Wallace Strong III. AB, U. Mich., Ann Arbor, 1971; JD, U. Mich. Law Sch., Ann Arbor, 1974; MBA, U. Dallas, 1993. Bar: Iowa 1974, S.C. 1991, Tex. 1992. Judge advocate U.S. Navy, Washington, 1974-91; gen. counsel ProSearch Assocs., Inc., Fort Worth, 1993; staff atty. Office of Hearings & Appeals, Columbia, S.C., 1996—. Lt. Cmdr. U.S. Navy, 1974-91. Mem. Phi Delta Legal Fraternity. Military, Health, Pension, profit-sharing, and employee benefits. Office: Office Hearings & Appeals 1927 Thurmond Mall Ste 200 Columbia SC 29201-2375

**STRONG, GEORGE GORDON, JR.,** litigation and management consultant; b. Toledo, Apr. 19, 1947; s. George Gordon and Jean Boyd (McDougall) S.; m. Annsley Palmer Chapman, Nov. 30, 1974; children: George III, Courtney, Meredith, Alexis. BA, Yale U., 1969; MBA, Harvard U., 1971; JD, U. San Diego, 1974. Bar: Calif. 1974, U.S. Dist. Ct. (cen. dist.) Calif. 1974; CPA, Calif., Hawaii, cert. mgmt. cons. Contr. Vitredent Corp., Beverly Hills, Calif., 1974-76; sr. mgr. Price Waterhouse, L.A., 1976-82, ptnr., 1987-93, mng. ptnr. west region dispute analysis and corp. recovery, 1993-98, mem. policy bd., bd. dirs., 1995-98; combination bd., bd. ptnrs. and prins. Pricewaterhouse Coopers LLP, L.A., 1997—; bd. ptnrs., prin Pricewaterhouse Coopers LLP, L.A., Calif., 1998—; global oversight bd. Pricewaterhouse Coopers LLP, L.A., 1998—; exec. v.p., COO Internat. Customs Service, Long Beach, Calif., 1982-84; CFO Uniform Software Systems, Santa Monica, Calif., 1984-85; exec. v.p., COO Cipherlink Corp., 1986; pres. Woodleigh Lane, Inc., Flintridge, Calif., 1985-87. Treas. L.A. SPCA; bd. dirs. So. Calif. Humane Soc. Mem. ABA, AICPA, Calif. State Bar, Calif. Soc. CPAs, Andover Abbott Alumni Soc. Calif. (bd. dirs.), Inst. Mgmt. Cons., Harvard Bus. Sch. Alumni Assn. (bd. dirs. 1996—), Harvard Bus. Sch. Assn. So. Calif. (chmn. bd. trustees scholarship fund 1992—, pres. 1988-89, dir. 1996—), Harvard Club N.Y., Yale Club N.Y., Lincoln Club, Calif. Club, Jonathan Club, Flint Canyon Tennis Club, Olympic Club, Annandale Golf Club, Coral Beach and Tennis Club, Mid Ocean Golf Club, Royal Bermuda Yacht Club, Palm Valley Country Club, Valley Hunt Club. Republican. Presbyterian. Avocations: golf, tennis, bridge. Computer, Federal civil litigation, State civil litigation. Home: 5455 Castle Knoll Rd La Canada Flintridge CA 91011-1319 Office: 400 S Hope St Ste 2200 Los Angeles CA 90071-2823

**STRONG, STEPHEN ANDREW,** lawyer; b. Longview, Tex., June 13, 1960; s. Jack B. and Rose N. (Otts) S.; m. LeAnn Troop, Aug. 6, 1983; children: Mark Andrew, Lindsey Michelle. BBA, Baylor U., 1983, JD, 1984. Bar: Tex. 1984. Assoc. Boyd, Veigel & Hance, Dallas, 1984-87, Liddell, Sapp, Zivley, Hill & LaBoon, Dallas, 1987-90; v.p., sr. counsel AmWest Savs. Assn., Dallas, 1990-94; sr. v.p., sr. counsel 1st Am. Bank Tex., SSB, Bryan, 1994—; adv. dir. Briarcrest Ins. Agy., Inc., Bryan, Tex., 1991-97, SALSCO, Inc., Bryan, 1990-97; adv. Rutherford Inst., Dallas, 1991—. Co-author: Southern Methodist U.—Mortgages in Depth, 1991. Adv. dir. Internat. Crusades Found., Inc., Dallas, 1988—; chmn. policy com. Brazos Christian Sch., 1997-98; chmn. Carrollton (Tex.)/Farmers Br. Christian Network, 1990-94; bd. dirs., fin. chmn. Concerned Parents Tex., Inc., Dallas, 1991—; deacon, dir. Sunday schs., Ctrl. Baptist Bryan; chmn. Pub. Sch. Awareness com. Citizens for Excellence in Edn., 1992—. Mem. Tex. Bar Assn., Baylor Bear Found., Tex. Eagle Forum. Avocations: family, church, golf, tennis. Banking, Contracts commercial, Real property. Office: 1st Am Bank Tex SSB 2800 S Texas Ave Bryan TX 77802-5343

**STROTHER, JAY D.,** legal editor; b. Wichita, Kans., May 31, 1967; m. Cynthia L. Mehnert, Sept. 7, 1991; 1 child, Garrett. BA, U. Tulsa, 1989. Editor U.S. Jr. C. of C., Tulsa, 1990-93, Assn. Legal Adminstrs., Vernon Hills, Ill., 1993—; editor-in-chief Legal Mgmt. Mag. Author: ALA News. Mem. Am. Soc. Assn. Execs., Soc. Nat. Assn. Publs., Internat. Assn. Bus. Communicators (bd. dirs., suburban v.p. 1994-95), Am. Soc. Bus. Press Editors. Office: Assn Legal Adminstrs 175 E Hawthorn Pkwy Vernon Hills IL 60061-1463

**STROTHMAN, JOHN HENRY,** lawyer; b. Mpls., July 10, 1939; s. Maurice Henry and Anne Healy Strothman; m. Barbara Joan Palmen, Sept. 22, 1972; children: David, Peter. BA, Yale U., 1961; JD, U. Minn., 1964. Bar: Minn. 1964. Law clk. to chief justice Oscar Knutson Minn. Supreme Ct., 1964-65; sr. ptnr. Lindquist & Vennum, Mpls., 1965—; dir., cons. in field. General corporate, General civil litigation, Contracts commercial. Office: Lindquist & Vennum 4200 IDS Ctr Minneapolis MN 55402

**STROUD, ROBERT EDWARD,** lawyer; b. Chester, S.C., July 24, 1934; s. Coy Franklin and Leila (Caldwell) S.; m. Katherine C. Stroud, Apr. 8, 1961; children: Robert Gordon, Margaret Lathan. AB, Washington and Lee U., 1956, LLB, 1958. Bar: Va. 1959, U.S. Ct. Appeals (4th cir.) 1967, U.S. Tax Ct. 1959. Assoc. McGuire, Woods, Battle & Boothe LLP, Charlottesville, Va., 1959-64; ptnr. McGuire, Woods, Battle & Boothe, LLP, Charlottesville, Va., 1964—, mem. exec. com., 1978-89; lectr. math. Washington and Lee U., 1957-59; lectr. bus. tax Grad. Bus. Sch., U. Va., Charlottesville, 1969-87, lectr. corp. taxation law sch., 1985-91; lectr. to legal edn. insts., lectr. in corp. law Washington and Lee Law Sch., 1984. Co-author: Buying, Selling and Merging Businesses, 1975; editor-in-chief Washington and Lee Law Rev., 1959; editor: Advising Small Business Clients, Vol. 1, 1978, 4th edit., 1994, Vol. 2, 1980, 3d edit., 1990; contbr. articles to profl. jours. Pres. Charlottesville Housing Found., 1968-73; mem. mgmt. coun. Montreat Conf. Ct., N.C., 1974-77; trustee Presbyn. Found., 1972-73, Union Theol. Sem., Va., 1983-91; bd. dirs. Presbyn. Outlook Found., 1974—, pres., 1985-88; mem. governing coun. Presbyn. Synod of the Virginias, 1973-78, moderator of coun., 1977-78, moderator of Synod, 1977-78; trustee, v.p. Va. Tax Found., 1984-95; adv. bd. Westminster Orgn. Concert Series, 1989-93; bd. dirs. Shannon Found. for Excellence in Pub. Edn., Charlottesville, 1996—; adv. bd. Ashlawn-Highland Summer Festival, 1989—, pres., 1994—; gov. coun. Presbyn. Presbytery of the James, 1993-96, moderator of coun., 1995-96; moderator of presbytery, 1997. Capt. inf. U.S. Army, 1958, with res. 1958-70. Fellow Am. Bar Found., Va. Law Found.; mem. ABA, Va. State Bar, Va. Bar Assn., Nat. Tax Inst., Am. Judicature Soc., Washington and Lee Law Sch. Assn. (governing coun. 1974-80, pres. 1979-80), Redland Club, Bull and Bear Club, Phi Delta Sigma, Omicron Delta Kappa, Phi Delta Phi. Democrat. General corporate, Mergers and acquisitions, Corporate taxation. Home: 345 Terrell Ct Charlottesville VA 22901-2171 Office: McGuire Woods Battle & Boothe LLP PO Box 1288 Charlottesville VA 22902-1288

**STROUD, TED WILLIAM,** lawyer; b. Lansing, Mich., Nov. 13, 1952; s. Melvin E. and Ina C. Stroud; m. Cilinda M. Droste, Apr. 19, 1980; children: Stephanie M., Mark W. BS (hons.), Mich. State Univ., 1976; JD cum laude, Cooley Law Sch., 1979. Bar: Mich. 1979, U.S. Dist Ct. (ea. dist., we. dist.) Mich. 1980. Assoc. McNeal & Oade, East Lansing, Mich., 1979-83; ptnr. Oade & Stroud, East Lansing, Mich., 1983-89, Oade, Stroud & Kleiman, East Lansing, Mich., 1989—. General civil litigation, Personal injury, Land use and zoning (including planning). Office: Oade Stroud & Kleiman 200 Woodland Pass East Lansing MI 48823-2000

**STROUGO, ROBERT ISAAC,** lawyer; b. N.Y.C., May 23, 1943; s. Victor and Mary Strougo; m. Barbara Lieb, June 27, 1976; children: Debra, David. BA, CCNY, 1965; JD, N.Y. Law Sch., 1970. Bar: N.Y. 1971, U.S. Dist. Ct. (so. and ea. dists.) N.Y. 1975. Pvt. practice N.Y.C., 1971—; owner NYC Realty; also investment and fin. adviser; arbitrator Civil Ct. of N.Y. Active Rep. Nat. Com.; mem. Nat. Rep. Senatorial Com., Rep. Campaign Coun. Recipient certs. of recognition Nat. Rep. Congl. Com., 1982-84; honoree Eisenhower Commn. Rep. Nat. Com., 1997. Mem. ABA, Kings County Bar Assn., N.Y. State Legis. Com., Nat. Defenders Assn., N.Y. State Com. on Trial Cts., Bklyn. Bar Assn., Am. Judges Assn., Am. Arbitration Assn. (arbitrator civil ct., C.J.A. panel ea. dist.), Am. Registry of Arbitrators. General practice, Real property, Securities. Home: 305 E 86th St # 17ne New York NY 10028-4702 Office: 21 E 40th St Ste 1800 New York NY 10016-0501

**STROUP, STANLEY STEPHENSON,** lawyer, educator; b. Los Angeles, Mar. 7, 1944; s. Francis Edwin and Marjory (Weimer) S.; m. Sylvia Douglass, June 15, 1968; children—Stacie, Stephen, Sarah. A.B., U. Ill., 1966; J.D., U. Mich., 1969. Bar: Ill. 1969, Calif. 1981, Minn. 1984. Atty. First Nat. Bank Chgo., 1969-78, asst. gen. counsel, 1978-80, v.p., 1980; sr. v.p., chief legal officer Bank of Calif., San Francisco, 1980-84; sr. v.p., gen. counsel Norwest Corp., Mpls., 1984-93, exec. v.p., gen. counsel, 1993-98; exec. v.p., gen. counsel Wells Fargo & Co., San Francisco, 1998—; mem. adj. faculty Coll. Law, William Mitchell Coll., St. Paul, 1985-98; mem. Regulatory Affairs Coun., Bank Adminstrn. Inst., 1996—. Mem. ABA, Ill. Bar Assn., State Bar Calif., Minn. Bar Assn., The Fin. Svcs. Roundtable. Banking, Contracts commercial. Office: Wells Fargo & Co 633 Folsom St San Francisco CA 94107-3600

**STROYD, ARTHUR HEISTER,** lawyer; b. Pitts., Sept. 5, 1945; s. Anne (Griffiths) S.; m. Susan Fleming, July 21, 1973; 1 child, Elizabeth. AB, Kenyon Coll., 1967; JD, U. Pitts., 1972. Bar: Pa. 1972, U.S. Dist. Ct. (we. dist.) Pa. 1972, U.S. Ct. Appeals (3d cir.) 1972. Law clk. to judge U.S. Ct. Appeals (3d cir.), Phila., 1972-75; mng. ptnr. Allegheny region Reed, Smith, Shaw & McClay, Pitts., 1975—; mem. Nat. Adv. Council on Child Nutrition, U.S. Dept. Agriculture, 1984-85. Treas. Mt. Lebanon Zoning Hearing Bd., 1978-81; pres. bd. dirs. Mt. Lebanon Sch. dist., 1981-87; solicitor Allegheny County Rep. Com., 1988-95; pres. bd. dirs. Ctr. for Theatre Arts, Pitts., 1984-93; grad. Leadership Pitts., 1991-92; chair bd. dirs. Mt. Lebanon Hosp. Authority, 1993—; coun. U. Pitts. Cancer Inst., 1993—; mem. alumni coun. Kenyon Coll., 1996—. Lt. USNR, 1969-71. Mem. Pa. Bar Assn., Allegheny County Bar Assn. (chair civil litigation sect., mem. judiciary com.), Acad. Trial Lawyers (bd. govs.), Duquesne Club. Episcopalian. Avocations: skiing. Federal civil litigation, State civil litigation, Construction. Home: 17 Saint Clair Dr Pittsburgh PA 15228-1830 Office: Reed Smith Shaw & McClay 435 6th Ave Ste 2 Pittsburgh PA 15219-1886

**STRUBLE, MICHELLE LEIGH,** lawyer; b. Meridian, Miss., June 24, 1970; d. Philip Charles and Gayle Judith Struble. BS, Cornell U., 1992; JD, Seton Hall U., 1996. Bar: N.J. 1996, U.S. Dist. Ct. N.J. 1996, N.Y. 1998, U.S. Dist. Ct. (we. dist.) N.Y. 1999. Law clk. to Hon. Amos Saunders Superior Ct., Paterson, N.J., 1996-97; atty. Phillips, Lytle, Hitchcock, Blaine & Huber, LLP, Buffalo, N.Y., 1997-99, Williams, Caliri, Miller & Otley, Wayne, N.Y., 1997-99. Reunion chairperson Cornell Class 1992, Ithaca, N.Y., 1992—. Mem. ABA, N.J. State Bar Assn., N.Y. Bar Assn., Passaic County Bar Assn., Robert J. Clifford Am. Inn Ct. Roman Catholic. Avocations: reading, biking, watching sports, aerobics, Eastern philosophy. Banking, Contracts commercial, Intellectual property. Office: Phillips Lytle Hitchcock Blaine & Huber 3400 HSBC Center Buffalo NY 14203

**STRUIF, L. JAMES,** lawyer; b. Alton, Ill., Sept. 18, 1931; s. Leo John and Clara Lillie (Bauer) S.; m. Shirley Ann Spatz, Mar. 24, 1965; children: Scott B., Jamie Lynn, Susan Marie, Jeffrey James. BS, Northwestern U., 1953; JD, U. Ill., Champaign, 1960. Bar: Ill. 1960, U.S. Dist. Ct. (so. Dist.) Ill. 1960. Gen. counsel So. Ill. U., 1960-64; pvt. practice Struif Law Offices, Alton, Ill., 1964—; lectr. So. Ill. U., Edwardsville, 1960-65. Author: Guide to Law for Laymen, 1987, Field Guide to 150 Prairie Plants of S.W. Ill., 1989. Scoutmaster Boy Scouts Am., Alton, 1966-69; active civil rights worker, Miss., 1964; trustee The James and Anne Nelson Found. With USN, submarines 1953-57, Pacific. Recipient Chmns. award Madison County Urban League, 1989, Blazing Star award The Nature Inst., 1990. Mem. Assn. Trial Lawyers Am., Ill. Trial Lawyers Assn., Ill. Bar Assn. Democrat. Mem. United Ch. of Christ. Avocations: nature, gardening, science, piano. Personal injury, General practice. Office: The Struif Law Offices 2900 Adams Pkwy Alton IL 62002-4857

**STRUTHERS, MARGO S.,** lawyer. BA, Carleton Coll., 1972; JD cum laude, U. Minn., 1976. Atty., shareholder Moss & Barnett, P.A. and predecessor firms, Mpls., 1976-93; ptnr. Oppenheimer Wolff & Donnelly, LLP, Mpls., 1993—. Mem. Am. Health Lawyers Assn., Minn. State Bar Assn (bus. law sect., former chair nonprofit com., former chair and mem. governing coun. health law sect.). Health. Office: Oppenheimer Wolff & Donnelly LLP Plaza VII 45 S 7th St Ste 3400 Minneapolis MN 55402-1609

**STRUTIN, KENNARD REGAN,** lawyer, educator, legal information consultant; b. Bklyn., Dec. 1, 1961; s. Fred and Estelle (Brodzansky) S. BA summa cum laude, St. John's U., Jamaica, N.Y., 1981; JD, Temple U. Sch. Law, Phila., 1984; MLS, St. John's U., 1994. Bar: N.Y. 1986, U.S. Dist. Ct. (ea. and so. dists.) N.Y. 1990, U.S. Dist. Ct. (no. and we. dists.) N.Y. 1991, U.S. Ct. Appeals (2d cir.) 1990, U.S. Ct. Appeals (fed. cir.) 1991, U.S. Tax Ct. 1991, U.S. Ct. Mil. Appeals 1991, U.S. Supreme Ct. 1990. Atty. pvt. practice, West Hempstead, N.Y., 1986; trial atty. Nassau County Legal Aid Soc., Hempstead, N.Y., 1987-88, Orange County Legal Aid Soc., Goshen, N.Y., 1988-90; atty. pvt. practice, West Hempstead, N.Y., 1990-91; staff atty. N.Y. State Defenders Assn., Albany, N.Y., 1991-93; adj. asst. prof. St. John's U., Jamaica, N.Y., 1993-96; small claims tax assessment hearing officer Supreme Ct., Nassau, Suffolk, N.Y., 1993-96; law libr. Syracuse U. Coll. Law, 1996-98; legal info. cons., 1998—; spkr. lawyer in classroom Nassau County Bar Assn., Mineola, N.Y., 1987-94; spkr. pre-release program Correctional Facilities, Lower Hudson Valley, N.Y., 1989-94. Author: ALI-ABA's Checklist Manual on Representing Criminal Defendants, 1998; co-author: (computer-assisted, interactive instrnl. program) Legal Research Methodology; contbr. articles to profl. jours. Recipient Orange County Exec. Recognition award, 1990, 93, 2nd place winner libr. divsn. Donald Trautman Ctr. for Computer-Assisted Legal Instrn. Lesson Writing Competition, 1996-97. Mem. Beta Phi Mu.

**STRUTZ, WILLIAM A.,** lawyer; b. Bismarck, N.D., May 13, 1934; s. Alvin C. and Ina Vee (Minor) S.; m. Marilyn Seagly, Aug. 31, 1957; children: Heidi Jane Mitchell, Colin Christopher, Nathaniel Paul. Student, Drake U., 1952-53; BA, North Ctrl. Coll., 1956; postgrad., Washington and Lee U., 1956-57; JD, U. N.D., 1959. Bar: N.D. 1959, U.S. Dist. Ct. N.D. 1959, U.S. Ct. Appeals (8th cir.) 1961. Atty., pres. Fleck, Mather & Strutz, Ltd., Bismarck, N.D., 1959—; mem. grievance com. N.D. Supreme Ct., Bismarck, 1974-77, chmn. supreme ct. svcs. com., 1979—. Bd. dirs. Vets. Meml. Pub. Libr., Bismarck, Shiloh Christian Sch., Bismarck, 1978—; pres. student body North Ctrl. Coll., 1956. Recipient Herbert Harley award Am. Judicature Soc., 1991. Mem. ABA, Am. Bd. Trial Advs. (adv.), Lions Club. Methodist. Avocations: reading, rare book collecting, music, sports. General civil litigation, Insurance, Personal injury. Home: 1238 W Highland Acres Rd Bismarck ND 58501-1259 Office: Fleck Mather Strutz Ltd 400 E Broadway Ave Bismarck ND 58501-4038

**STRUVE, GUY MILLER,** lawyer; b. Wilmington, Del., Jan. 5, 1943; s. William Scott and Elizabeth Bliss (Miller) S.; m. Marcia Mayo Hill, Sept. 20, 1986; children: Andrew Hardenbrook, Catherine Tolstoy, Frank Leroy Hill, Guy Miller, Beverly Marcia Wise Hill (dec.), Elena Wise Struve-Hill. AB summa cum laude, Yale U., 1963; LLB magna cum laude, Harvard U., 1966. Bar: N.Y. 1967, D.C. 1986, U.S. Dist. Ct. (so. dist.) N.Y. 1970, U.S. Dist. Ct. (ea. dist.) N.Y. 1973, U.S. Dist. Ct. (no. dist.) Calif. 1979, U.S. Dist. Ct. D.C. 1987, U.S. Ct. Appeals (2d cir.) 1969, U.S. Ct. Appeals (D.C. cir.) 1973, U.S. Ct. Appeals (8th cir.) 1976, U.S. Ct. Appeals (9th cir.) 1979, U.S. Supreme Ct. 1971, U.S. Dist. Ct. (we. dist.) N.Y. 1991. Law clk. Hon. J. Edward Lumbard, Chief Judge United States Ct. Appeals for 2d Circuit, 1966-67; assoc. Davis Polk & Wardwell, N.Y.C., 1967-72, ptnr., 1973—; ptnr. Ind. Counsel's Office, 1987-94. Mem. ABA, N.Y. State Bar Assn., Assn. of Bar of City of N.Y. (chmn. com. antitrust and trade regulation, 1983-86, chmn. com. fed. cts. 1998—), Am. Law Inst. Antitrust, General civil litigation. Home: 116 E 63rd St New York NY 10021-7303 Office: Davis Polk & Wardwell 450 Lexington Ave New York NY 10017-3911

**STRYKER, STEVEN CHARLES,** lawyer; b. Omaha, Nebr., Oct. 26, 1944; s. James M. and Jean G. (Grannis) S.; m. Bryna Dee Litwin, Oct. 20, 1972; children: Ryan, Kevin, Gerrit, Courtney. BS, U. Iowa, 1967, JD with distinction, 1969; postgrad. studies, Northwestern U. Grad. Sch. Bus, 1969-70, DePaul U., 1971. Bar: Iowa 1969, Tex. 1986; CPA Ill., Iowa. Sr. tax acct. Arthur Young & Co., Chgo., 1969-72; fed. tax mgr. Massey Ferguson, Des Moines, 1972-74; fed., state tax mgr. FMC Corp., Chgo., 1974-78; gen. tax atty. Shell Oil Co., Houston, 1978-81, asst. gen. tax counsel, 1981-83, gen. mgr., 1983-86, v.p., gen. tax counsel, 1986—. Mem. ABA, AICPA, Tex. Bar Assn., Iowa Bar Assn., Ill. Soc. CPAs, Iowa Soc. CPAs, Tax Execs. Inst., Am. Petroleum Inst. Corporate taxation. Home: 2121 Kirby D # 124 Houston TX 77019 Office: Shell Oil Co 1 Shell Plz Ste 4570 Houston TX 77001

**STUART, ALICE MELISSA,** lawyer; b. N.Y.C., Apr. 7, 1957; d. John Marberger and Marjorie Louise (Browne) S. BA, Ohio State U., 1977; JD, U. Chgo., 1980; LLM, NYU, 1982. Bar: N.Y. 1981, Ohio 1982, N.Y. 1982, Fla. 1994, U.S. Dist. Ct. (so. dist.) Ohio, 1983, U.S. Dist. Ct. (so. and ea. dists.) N.Y. 1985. Assoc. Schwartz, Shapiro, Kelm & Warren, Columbus, Ohio, 1982-84, Paul, Weiss, Rifkind, Wharton & Garrison, N.Y.C., 1984-85, Kassel, Neuwirth & Geiger, N.Y.C., 1985-86, Phillips, Nizer, Benjamin, Krim & Ballon, N.Y.C., 1987-97; pvt. practice N.Y.C., 1997—; adj. prof. So. Coll., Orlando, Fla., 1997-98. Surrogate Speakers' Bur. Reagan-Bush Campaign, N.Y.C., 1984; mem. Lawyers for Bush-Quayle Campaign, N.Y.C., 1988. Mem. ABA, N.Y. State Bar Assn., Winston Churchill Meml. Library Soc., Jr. League, Phi Beta Kappa, Phi Kappa Phi, Alpha Lambda Delta. Republican. Finance, Securities, General corporate. Office: 12251 University Blvd Orlando FL 32817-2134

**STUART, GLEN R(AYMOND),** lawyer; b. Kimpese, Congo, Mar. 4, 1959; came to U.S., 1960; s. Charles H. and Jeannette B. (Spinney) S.; m. Susan K. Sharpless, May 26, 1984; children: Jennifer Jacqueline, David Charles, Andrew William. BA, Franklin and Marshall Coll., 1981; JD, U. Va., 1984. Bar: Pa. 1984, U.S. Dist. Ct. (ea. dist.) Pa. 1984, U.S. Dist. Ct. (mid. dist.) Pa. 1986, U.S. Ct. Appeals (3rd cir.) 1988, U.S. Supreme Ct. 1997. Ptnr. Morgan, Lewis & Bockius, LLP, Phila., 1984—. Mem. ABA, Pa. Bar Assn., Phila. Bar Assn., Order of Coif. Democrat. Baptist. Avocations: soccer, golf, softball, tennis, running. Fax: (215) 963-5299; e-mail: stua5883@mlb.com. Federal civil litigation, Environmental, Public utilities. Home: 21 Harvey Ln Malvern PA 19355-2907 Office: Morgan Lewis & Bockius LLP 1701 Market St Philadelphia PA 19103-2903

**STUART, MARY HURLEY,** lawyer; b. Carthage, N.Y., Dec. 27, 1953; d. John William and Marie (Caulfield) Hurley; m. Charles E. Stuart, Aug. 8, 1981; children: Colleen Marie, Melanie Jeanne. BA, U. Maine, 1976; JD, U. Denver, 1981. Bar: Colo., U.S. Dist. Ct. Colo., U.S. Ct. Appeals (10th cir.), U.S. Supreme Ct. Jud. law clk. U.S. Dist. Ct., Denver, 1981-82; assoc. Holme Roberts & Owen, Denver, 1982-88; mem. Downey Stuart & Knickrenn P.C., Englewood, Colo., 1988-90; spl. counsel Bender and Treece P.C., Denver, 1990-92; spl. counsel Holme Roberts & Owen LLP, Denver, 1993-95, ptnr., 1995—. Editor Denver law Jour., 1979-81; contbr. articles to profl. jours. Bd. dirs., sec. Littleton (Colo.) Pub. Schs. Found., 1994—. Mem. Colo. Bar Assn. (bd. govs. 1994-96, chair availability of legal svcs. com. 1996-98, chair Amicus com. 1998—), Arapahoe County Bar Assn. (bd. dirs., sec., treas., pres. 1995-96, Outstanding Young Lawyer 1993), Colo. Bar Found., Order St. Ives, Phi Beta Kappa. Labor, Federal civil litigation, State civil litigation. Office: Holme Roberts & Owen LLP 1700 Lincoln St Ste 4100 Denver CO 80203-4541

**STUART, MICHAEL GEORGE,** lawyer; b. N.Y.C., May 24, 1951; s. George Bernard and Diana (Porikos) s.; m. Kim Stuart; children: Jennifer, Katherine Nicholas. BBA, Pace U., 1973, JD, 1980. Bar: Oreg. 1981, U.S. Dist. Ct. Oreg. 1981, U.S. Tax Ct. 1981, U.S. Ct. Appeals (9th cir.) 1982, N.Y. 1987, U.S. Supreme Ct. 1988, Ill. 1990, U.S. Dist. Ct. (no. dist.) Ill. 1990; CPA, Vt., Ill. Acct. Cambridge Instrument Inc., Ossining, N.Y., 1973-76; fin. cons. Bronxville, N.Y., 1976-78; legal asst. Frank B. Hall & Co., Briarcliff Manor, N.Y., 1978-79; supr. tax specialist Coopers & Lybrand, Portland, Oreg., 1979-81; fed. tax specialist Tektronix, 1981-83; pvt. practice law Beaverton, Oreg., 1983-89; tax mgr. Smith, Batchelder & Rugg, Lebanon, N.H., 1989; atty. Pontikes, Porikos, Rodes & Economos, Chgo., 1989-91; pvt. practice Chgo., Ill., 1991—; com. mem. Atty. Realtors, Beaverton, 1986, pres. Letip Arlington Heights, 1997. Pres. Young Adult League, Portland, 1983-85; sec. Portland Parish Council, 1983, treas. 1984; mem. Greek Civic Club Oreg., Portland, 1982—; bd. dirs. N.W. Sub. Plan Coun., 1989—, N.W. Boy Scouts, 1994—. Mem. Oreg. State Bar Assn. (tax bus. sect., taxation com. 1988), Am. Hellenic Ednl. Progressive Assn., Nat. Norwalk Estate Planning Attys. Democrat. Greek Orthodox. Lodge: Masons. Avocations: guitar, backpacking, woodworking, racquetball. Taxation, general, Estate taxation.

**STUART, PAMELA BRUCE,** lawyer; b. N.Y.C., Feb. 13, 1949; d. J. Raymond and Marion Grace (Cotins) S. AB with distinction, Mt. Holyoke Coll., 1970; JD cum laude, U. Mich., 1973. Bar: N.Y. 1974, D.C. 1975, U.S. Dist. Ct. D.C. 1979, U.S. Ct. Appeals (D.C. cir.) 1980, U.S. Supreme Ct. 1980, U.S. Dist. Ct. Md. 1989, Md. 1992, Va. 1993, U.S. Ct. Appeals (4th cir.) 1993, Fla. 1994, U.S. Dist. Ct. (ea. dist.) Va. 1994, U.S. Dist. Ct. (no. dist.) N.Y. 1996, U.S. Dist. Ct. (so. dist.) Fla. 1998, U.S. Dist. Ct. (so. dist.) N.Y. 1999, U.S. Dist. Ct. (ea. dist.) N.Y. 1999. Trial atty., deputy asst. dir. Bur. of Consumer Protection, FTC, Washington, 1973-79; asst. U.S. atty. U.S. Atty's Office, Washington, 1979-85; sr. trial atty. Office of Internat. Affairs, U.S. Dept. Justice, Washington, 1985-87; atty. Ross, Dixon & Masback, Washington, 1987-89; mem. Lobel, Novins, Lamont & Flug, Washington, 1989-92; pvt. practice, Washington, 1992—; instr. Nat. Inst. for Trial Advocacy, Atty. Gen.'s Advocacy Inst., Legal Edn. Inst., Fed. Practice Inst.; mem. Jud. Conf. D.C., 1985-88, 91-98; assoc. mem. Consular Corps Washington; legal analyst CNN, MSNBC, other TV networks. Author: The Federal Trade Commission, 1991; contbr. articles to profl. jours. Bd. dirs. Anacostia Econ. Devel. Corp., 1993—, Anacostia Holding Co., Inc., Anacostia Mgmt. Co., Inc., 1997—. Mem. ABA (mem. internat. criminal law com., chmn., 1993-96, chmn. fed. crim rules subcom. white collar crime com. sect. criminal justice), Bar Assn. D.C. (bd. dirs. 1995—), Asst. U.S. Attys. Assn. D.C. (exec. coun. 1993-99, pres. 1998-99), Assn. Trial Lawyers Am., Women's Bar Assn. D.C., Fla. Bar (mem. exec. coun. real property probate and trust law sect. 1999—), Alumnae Assn. Mt. Holyoke Coll. (bd. dirs. 1986-89, 92-95, Alumnae medal of honor 1990), Edward Bennett Williams Inn of Ct. (master of bench), Fed. City Club (bd. govs. 1992—), Cosmos Club. Avocations: writing, interior design, investments. Private international, Federal civil litigation, Criminal. Home: 5115 Yuma St NW Washington DC 20016-4336 Office: 888 16th St NW Washington DC 20006-4103

**STUART, RAYMOND WALLACE,** lawyer; b. Chattanooga, Feb. 13, 1941; s. Raymond Newton and Mary Vance (Wallace) S.; m. Peggy Woodard, Dec. 19, 1965; children: Raymond Warren, Laura Wallace. BS in Physics, U. Cin., 1963, JD, 1972. Bar: Ohio 1972. Pvt. practice Cin., 1972-74; atty. USIA, Washington, 1975-89, dep. gen. counsel, 1989—. Exec. editor Univ. Cin. Law Review, 1971-72. Capt. U.S. Army Spl. Forces, 1963-69. Avocations: hunting, fishing, reading fiction, golf. Home: 9894 Becket Ct Fairfax VA 22032-2412 Office: USIA Office of Gen Counsel 301 4th St SW Washington DC 20547-0009

**STUART, WALTER BYNUM, IV,** lawyer; b. Grosse Tete, La., Nov. 23, 1946; s. Walter Bynum III and Rita (Kleinpeter) S.; m. Lettice Lee Binnings May 18, 1968; children: Courtney Lyon, Walter Burke V. Student Fordham U., 1964-65; BA, Tulane U., 1968, JD, 1973. Bar: La. 1973, U.S. Dist. Ct. (ea. and we. dists.) La. 1974, U.S. Tax Ct. 1974, U.S. Supreme Ct. 1981, U.S. Dist Ct. (so. dist.) Colo. 1987, U.S. Dist. Ct. (so. dist.) Tex. 1989. Ptnr. Stone, Pigman, Walther, Wittman and Hutchinson, New Orleans, 1973-78, Singer Hutner Levine Seeman and Stuart, New Orleans, 1978-81, Gordon, Arata, McCollam and Stuart, New Orleans, 1981-88, Vinson & Elkins, Houston, 1988—; instr. Tulane U. Law Sch., 1978-82; mem. faculty Banking Sch. of the South; bd. dirs. Inst. Politics; mem. adv. bd. City Atty.'s Office, New Orleans, 1978-79. Bd. dirs., gen. counsel Houston Grand Opera, 1992—. Mem. ABA, La. Bar Assn., Tex. Assn. Bank Counsel (pres. 1994-95), La. Bankers Assn. (chmn. bank counsel com.). Banking, Contracts commercial, Federal civil litigation. Office: Vinson & Elkins 2500 First City Tower 1001 Fannin St Ste 3300 Houston TX 77002-6706

**STUART, WILLIAM CORWIN,** federal judge; b. Knoxville, Iowa, Apr. 28, 1920; s. George Corwin and Edith (Abram) S.; m. Mary Elgin Cleaver, Oct. 20, 1946; children: William Corwin II, Robert Cullen, Melanie Rae, Valerie Jo. BA, State U. Iowa, 1941, JD, 1942. Bar: Iowa 1942. Pvt. practice Chariton, 1946-62, city atty., 1947-49; mem. Iowa Senate from, Lucas-Wayne Counties, 1951-61; justice Supreme Ct. Iowa, 1962-71; judge U.S. Dist. Ct., So. Dist. of Iowa, Des Moines, 1971-86, sr. judge, 1986—. With USNR, 1943-45. Recipient Outstanding Svc. award Iowa Acad. Trial lawyer, 1987, Iowa Trial Lawyers Assn., 1988, Spl. award Iowa State Bar Assn., 1987, Disting. Alumni, U. Iowa Coll. Law, 1987. Mem. ABA, Iowa Bar Assn., Am. Legion, All For Iowa, Order of Coif, Omicron Delta Kappa, Phi Kappa Psi, Phi Delta Phi. Presbyterian. Club: Mason (Shriner). Home: 216 S Grand St Chariton IA 50049-2139

**STUBER, JAMES ARTHUR,** lawyer; b. Warren, Ohio, July 17, 1948; s. Andrew Frederick and Betty Jane (Long) S.; m. Susan Lee Carpenter, Apr. 4, 1998. BA, U. Pa., 1970; MA, Columbia U., 1973; JD, Georgetown U., 1976. Bar: Fla. 1977, D.C. 1978, U.S. Dist. Ct. (D.C. dist.) 1979, U.S. Ct. Appeals (11th cir.) 1983. Legis. asst. U.S. Congressman Paul Rogers, Washington, 1972-78; assoc. Hogan & Hartson, Washington, 1979-82; ptnr. Sang & Stuber, Palm Beach, Fla., 1983-84; pvt. practice law Palm Beach, 1984-89; ptnr. Stuber & Finley, West Palm Beach, 1990-91; shareholder Carlton, Fields et al, West Palm Beach, 1992-93; pvt. practice law West Palm Beach, 1993—; mem. Federal Caribbean Basin Bus. Adv. Coun., Washington, 1985-89; internat. adv. bd. Nova U. Sch. Bus., Ft. Lauderdale, 1989-91. Dir. French-Am. Bus. Assn. of the Palm Beaches, 1998—. Mem. Internat. Bar Assn., Am. Immigration Lawyers Assn., The Fla. Bar Assn. (bd. cert. in immigration & naturalization 1995), Palm Beach County Bar Assn. (cultural & civic activities award 1988). Democrat. Episcopal. Avocations: sailing, travel. Immigration, naturalization, and customs, Private international, General corporate. Office: 777 S Flagler Dr Ste 800W West Palm Beach FL 33401-6163

**STUCKENSCHNEIDER, JAMES THEODORE, II,** lawyer; b. McAlister, Okla., June 21, 1948; s. James T. and Emma Gene (Gainey) S.; m. Dana W. Hodges, Sept. 17, 1983. BE, Memphis State U., 1970; JD, Cumberland Sch. Law, 1977. Bar: Ala. 1977, U.S. Dist. Ct. (no. dist.) Ala. 1977; cert. in consumer bankruptcy Am. Bandruptcy Bd. Personnel mgr. Cole Nat. Corp., Cleve., 1970-72; sales rep. Texaco Inc., Mobile, Ala., 1972-74; sole practice Birmingham, Ala., 1977—. Mem. AlaSight, Birmingham, 1981—. Named one of Outstanding Men of Am., U.S. Jaycees, 1971. Mem. ABA (family law sect.), Ala. Bar Assn. (charter, bankruptcy sect.), Birmingham Bar Assn. (charter, bankruptcy sect., sec. 1994-95, chmn. 1996-97), Comml. Law League Assn. (sustaining), Lions (sec., bd. dirs., pres. Inverness chpt. 1981—, Lion of the Yr. 1986, Internat. Leadership award 1986, Melvin Jones fellow 1990), Masons. Avocations: hunting, fishing. Bankruptcy, Family and matrimonial, Probate. Office: 817 Frank Nelson Bldg Birmingham AL 35203

**STUCKY, JEAN SEIBERT,** lawyer; b. Berkeley, Calif., Feb. 9, 1951; d. Edward Raymond and Frances Selma (Berg) S.; m. Scott Wallace Stucky, Aug. 18, 1973; children: Mary-Clare, Joseph. BA in Econs., Wellesley (Mass.) Coll., 1973; JD, Cornell U., 1978; MA in Econs., Trinity U., San Antonio, 1980; postgrad., George Washington U., Washington, 1991—. Bar: D.C. 1978. Atty.-advisor Adminstrv. Conf. U.S., Washington, 1978-79, Divsn. Advice, NLRB, Washington, 1979-94; contractor labor counsel U.S. Dept. Energy, Office Gen. Counsel, Washington, 1994—. Mem. Washington Cathedral Altar Guild, 1988—. Mem. D.C. Bar, Dames of Loyal Legion of U.S., Washington Wellesley Club (pres. 1992-94), Wellesley Coll. Alumnae Assn. (regional chmn. 1995-97). Republican. Episcopalian. Avocations: gardening, flower arranging. Home: 1104 Homeplace Ln Potomac MD 20854-1406 Office: US Dept Energy Office Gen Counsel 1000 Independence Ave SW Washington DC 20585-0001

**STUCKY, SCOTT WALLACE,** lawyer; b. Hutchinson, Kans., Jan. 11, 1948; s. Joe Edward and Emma Clara (Graber) S.; m. Jean Elsie Seibert, Aug. 18, 1973; children: Mary-Clare, Joseph. BA summa cum laude, Wichita State U., 1970; JD, Harvard U., 1973; MA, Trinity U., 1980; LLM with high honors, George Washington U., 1983; postgrad., Nat. War Coll., 1993. Bar: Kans. 1973, U.S. Dist. Ct. Kans. 1973, U.S. Ct. Appeals (10th cir.) 1973, U.S. Ct. Mil. Appeals 1974, U.S. Supreme Ct. 1976, D.C. 1979, U.S. Ct. Appeals (D.C. cir.) 1979. Assoc. Ginsburg, Feldman & Bress, Washington, 1978-82; chief docketing and svc. br. Nuclear Regulatory Commn., Washington, 1982-83, legis. counsel U.S. Air Force, 1983-96; gen. counsel sen. com. on armed svcs. Nuclear Regulatory Commn., 1996—; lectr. bus. law Maria Regina Coll., Syracuse, N.Y., 1977; congrl. fellow Office Senator John Warner, 1986; res. judge adv. USAF Res., Washington, 1982—; col. Appellate Mil. Judge, USAF Ct. Criminal Appeals, 1991-95, 97-98; sr. reservist USAF Judiciary, 1995-97, Air Res. Personnel Ctr., 1998-99, Air Force Legal Svcs. Agy., 1999—. Contbr. articles to profl. jours. Capt. USAF, 1973-78. Decorated Air Force Meritorious Svc. medal with two oak leaf cluster. Mem. Fed. Bar Assn., Judge Advs. Assn. (bd. dirs. 1984-88), Res. Officers Assn., Wichita State U. Alumni Assn. (pres. chpt. 1981-86, nat. bd. dirs. 1986-92), Adoption Svc. Info. Agy. (bd. dirs. 1998—), Army and Navy Club (Washington), Mil. Order of Loyal Legion U.S. (state comdr. and recorder 1984-92, nat. treas. 1987-89, nat. vice comdr. 1989-93, nat. comdr.-in-chief 1993-95), Sons of Union Vets Civil War (chpt. vice-comdr 1986-88), Phi Delta Phi, Phi Alpha Theta, Phi Kappa Phi, Omicron Delta Kappa, Sigma Phi Epsilon. Republican. Episcopalian. Home: 11004 Homeplace Ln Potomac MD 20854-1406 Office: Sen Armed Svcs Com 228 Senate Office Bldg Washington DC 20510-0001

**STUDNICKI, ADAM A.,** lawyer; b. Torrance, Calif., Jan. 9, 1968; s. Walter and Danuta S. BS summa cum laude, Arizona State U., 1988; JD cum laude, Harvard U., 1991. Atty. Gallagher & Kennedy, Phoenix, 1991—. Mem. ATLA, Ariz. Trial Lawyers Assn., Ariz. Assn. Defense Counsel, Harvard Club (Phoenix br.). Personal injury, Product liability. Home: PO Box 14321 Scottsdale AZ 85267-4321 Office: Gallagher & Kennedy 2600 N Central Ave Ste 1800 Phoenix AZ 85004-3099

**STUDWELL, ROBERTA FRANCES,** law librarian; b. Phoenix, Oct. 31, 1951; d. Minter Francis and Lois Marie (Clark) Orcutt; m. Christopher Leon Studwell, Aug. 16, 1972; 1 child, Stephanie Marie. BA, Ariz. State U., 1973; MLS, U. Wash., 1980; JD, U. Miami, Fla., 1989. English tchr. Phoenix Sch. Sys., 1974-76; libr. technician U. Idaho, Moscow, 1976-80, acting assoc. libr., 1981, head tech. svcs., 1980-82; reference libr. Paul Boley Law Libr., Portland, Oreg., 1982-85; head reference U. Miami Law Libr., 1985-89; assoc. dir. U. Colo. Law Libr., Boulder, 1989-93; assoc. dean Libr. & Info. Svcs. Thomas M. Cooley Law Sch., Lansing, Mich., 1993—; adv. bd. Colo. Libr. Pres. Group, Denver, 1991-94. Co-author: Bibliography of Law Related Oregon Documents, 1984; editor Briefs in Law Librarianship Series, 1996—; contbr. articles to profl. jours. Mem. Am. Assn. Law Librs. (adv. coun. chair Chgo. 1995-96), Colo. Assn. Law Librs. (v.p.-program chair 1991-92, pres. 1992-93), Mich. Assn. Law Librs., Am. Assn. Law Schs. Office: Thomas M Cooley Law Sch PO Box 13038 217 S Capitol Ave Lansing MI 48933-1503

**STUMBO, JANET LYNN,** state supreme court justice; b. Prestonsburg, Ky.; d. Charles and Doris Stanley S.; m. Ned Pillersdorf; children: Sarah, Nancee, Samantha. BA, Morehead State U., 1976; JD, U. Ky., 1980. Bar: Ky. 1980, W. Va. 1982. Staff atty. to Judge Harris S. Howard Ky. Ct. Appeals, 1980-82; asst. county atty. Floyd County, 1982-85; ptnr. Turner, Hall & Stumbo, P.S.C., 1982-88; prosecutor Floyd Dist. Ct. and Juvenile Ct.; ptnr. Stumbo, DeRossett & Pillersdorf, 1989; judge Ct. Appeals, Ky., 1989-93, Supreme Ct. of Ky., 1993—. Named to Morehead State U. Alumni Assn. Hall of Fame, 1990; recipient Justice award Ky. Women Advocates, 1991, Outstanding Just award Ky. Women Advocates, 1995, Bull's Eye award Women in State Govt. Network, 1995. Office: Ky Supreme Ct Capitol Bldg Rm 226 700 Capitol Ave Frankfort KY 40601-3410 also: 311 N Arnold Ave Ste 502 Prestonsburg KY 41653-1279*

**STUMP, T(OMMY) DOUGLAS,** lawyer, educator; b. Cushing, Okla., Jan. 7, 1957; s. Thomas Burl and Lindsey L. Stump; children: Kelli Jo and Matthew Douglas. BA in English, E. Ctrl. U., Ada, Okla., 1979; JD, Oklahoma City U., 1982. Bar: Okla. 1983, U.S. Dist. Ct. (we. dist.) Okla. 1983, U.S. Ct. Appeals (10th cir.) 1983, U.S. Dist. Ct. (ea. and no. dists.) Okla. 1986, U.S. Ct. Appeals (5th cir.) 1986, U.S. Supreme Ct. 1986. Founding atty. T. Douglas Stump & Assocs., Oklahoma City, 1990—; adj. prof. law Oklahoma City U.; lectr. various continuing legal edn. programs, immigration seminars, 1983-98. Author: Matrimonal Maladies and the Alien, 1983, General Information Concerning United States Immigration Laws, 1989, L-1 Intracompany Transfers, 1995, Employment Based Immigration Law, 1995. Bd. dirs. Lyric Theater, mem. exec. com., co-sponsor various prodns., 1992-95, Oklahoma City Econ. Roundtable, founder and provider Focus on Success Scholarship Fund, Drumright H.S., Oklahoma City, 1993—. Fellow Okla. Bar Found., mem. ABA (young lawyers divsn. del. 1988, 1989, exec. mem. young lawyers divsn. com. on immigration law), Am. Immigration Lawyers Assn. (Okla., Tex., N.M. chptrs., chmn. com. on nonimmigrant visas 1986-88, Oklahoma City sect. chmn. 1987-91, chmn. membership com. 1988-90, treas. 1991-92, vice chmn. 1992-93, chmn. legis. action com., Okla. City INS liaison 1995—, pres. Tex. chpt. 1998-99, sr. editor publs. com., no. border task force), Okla. Bar Assn. (treas. 1988, sec. 1989, mem. com. on legal specialization 1987-91, mem. spl. com. on Unauthorized Practice of Law 1988-90, mem. house counsel sect. 1988—, mem. com. on legal ethics 1990-92, com. on civil procedure 1991-94, mem. solo and small firm task force 1993—, bd. dirs. young lawyers divsn. 1986-90, dir. com. on alien/refugee assistance 1986-89, chmn. com. on alien/refugee assistance 1986-90, Outstanding Dir. award 1987), Oklahoma County Bar Assn (mem. fee grievance com. 1990-91), Oklahoma City U Law Sch. Alumni Assn. (bd. dirs. 1989-94, pres. 1992-94, Outstanding Law School Alumni award 1993). Republican. Immigration, naturalization, and customs. Office: 50 Penn Pl Ste 1320 Oklahoma City OK 73118

**STUMPF, HARRY CHARLES,** lawyer; b. New Orleans, May 1, 1944; s. John Frederick and Amy Ruth (Lynch) S.; m. Mary Frances Henricks, Aug. 27, 1966 (div. Dec. 3, 1992); children: Ashley Frances Stumpf Borges, Piper Lynch Stumpf Decareaux, Harry Charles Jr.; m. Cynthia Anne Torgersen, Dec. 14, 1996. BBA, Tulane U., 1967, JD, 1968. Bar: La. 1968, U.S. Dist. Ct. (ea. dist.) La. 1968, U.S. Ct. Appeals (5th cir.) 1968, U.S. Supreme Ct. 1995. Assoc./of counsel Knight, D'Angelo & Knight, Gretna, La., 1968-83; ptnr. Stumpf, Dugas, LeBlanc, Papale & Ripp, Gretna, La., 1983-97. Lector/commentator St. Anthony Ch., Gretna, 1970—; trustee La. Cystic Fibrosis, New Orleans, 1975-78. Recipient Outstanding Svc. award West Jefferson Levee Dist., 1994. Fellow La. Bar Found.; mem. Jefferson Bar Assn., Westbank Rotary (dir. 1970—), Semreh Club. Avocations: golf, boating, skiing, computers. Condemnation, Probate, Real property. Office: 901 Derbigny St Ste 200 Gretna LA 70053-6205

**STUNTEBECK, CLINTON A.,** lawyer; b. Hibbing, Minn., May 25, 1938; s. Robert F. and S. Mary (Conti) S.; m. Mary Joan Carmody, Nov. 23, 1963; children: Robin, M. Alison, Susan, John, William. BA in Psychology, U. Minn., 1960; LLB, U. Maine, 1968. Bar: Pa. 1969, U.S. Dist. Ct. (ea. dist.) Pa. 1969. Ptnr., chmn. corp. fin. and securities, mem. exec. com. Schnader, Harrison, Segal & Lewis, Phila., 1968—; bd. dirs. Markel Corp., Greater Phila. First Partnership for Econ. Devel.; lectr. corp. and securities law. Contbr. articles to profl. jours. Pres. Radnor (Pa.) Twp. Bd. Commn., 1981-83, 92—; bd. visitors U. Maine Sch. Law; trustee Cabrini Coll.; bd. dirs. Am. Heart Assn. Capt. USAF, 1960-68. Mem. ABA, Am. Law Inst., Pa. Bar Assn., Phila. Bar Assn., Securities Industry Assn. (law and compliance com.), U. Maine Law Alumni Assn. (pres. 1974-76), Union League Phila., Phila. Country Club, Sunday Breakfast Club, Corinthian Yacht Club. Avocations: sailing, skiing, golf, tennis. Finance, Securities, Mergers and acquisitions. Home: 371 Rose Glen Dr Wayne PA 19087-4410 Office: Schnader Harrison Segal 1600 Market St Ste 3600 Philadelphia PA 19103-7240

**STURM, WILLIAM CHARLES,** lawyer; b. Milw., Aug. 4, 1941; s. Charles William and Helen Ann (Niesen) S.; m. Kay F. Sturm, June 10, 1967; children: Patricia, Elizabeth, Katherine, William, Susan. B.S. in Bus. Adminstrn., Marquette U., 1963, J.D., 1966. Bar: Wis. 1966, U.S. Dist. Ct. (ea. dist.) Wis. 1966, U.S. Supreme Ct. 1980. Sole practice, Milw., 1966-78; ptnr. Rausch, Hamell, Ehrle & Sturm, S.C., Milw., 1978-81, Rausch, Hamell, Ehrle, Sturm & Blom, Milw., 1981-83, Rausch, Hamell, Ehrle & Sturm, 1983-95, Rausch, Hamell, Sturm & Israel S.C., 1995-98, Rausch, Sturm, Israel & Hornik, S.C., 1999—; asst. prof. Marquette U., 1982-91; lectr. U. Wis., Milw., 1991-97, sr. lectr. 1997—. Mem. adv. bd. Pallotine Order, 1985—. Recipient Editors award Wis. Med. Credit Assn., 1980. Mem. ABA, Wis. Bar Assn., Comml. Law League Am. (exec. council midwestern dist. 1981-83, 86-88, chmn. state membership com. 1981-88, nat. nominating council 1984-86, 1988-89, sec., 2d v.p. midwestern dist. 1989-90, 1st v.p. midwestern dist. 1990-91, chmn. 1991-92, nat. bd. govs. 1997—), Nat. Speakers Assn., Am. Bus. Law Assn., Midwest Bus. Law Assn. (sec. 1988-89, v.p. 1989-90, pres. 1990-91), Wis. Profl. Speakers Assn., Healthcare Fin. Mgmt. Assn., Beta Alpha Psi (faculty v.p. Psi chpt. 1985-88, Eta Theta chpt. 1992—), Midwest Bus. And Health Assn. (v.p. procs. 1987-88, v.p. program 1988-89, pres. 1989-90). Clubs: Westmoor Country (Milw.); Kiwanis (pres. 1979, lt. gov. div. 5, 1980) (Wauwatosa, Wis.). Contbr. articles to profl. jours. Consumer commercial, Bankruptcy. Office: 1233 N Mayfair Rd Milwaukee WI 53226-3255

**STURTZ, WILLIAM ROSENBERG,** retired judge; b. Albert Lea, Minn., Apr. 7, 1925; s. William and Gladys (Rosenberg) S.; m. Helen Hedwig Schlotter, July 23, 1949; children: William, Richard (dec.), Robert, John. LLB, U. Mich., 1948, JD, 1951. Atty. Sturtz, Peterson, Sturtz & Butler, Albert Lea, Minn., 1951-69; probate & juvenile judge Freeborn County, Albert Lea, 1969-72, county ct. judge, 1972-86; dist. judge State of Minn., Albert Lea, 1986-91; faculty Lea Coll., Albert Lea, 1967-71. Mem. Am. Contract Bridge League, Shriners, Masons, Rotary. Republican. Avocations: travel, duplicate bridge, golf, cooking, theatre (actor, director, playwright). Home: 209 Ridge Rd Albert Lea MN 56007-1442

**STUTZMAN, THOMAS CHASE, SR.,** lawyer; b. Portland, Oreg., Aug. 1, 1950; s. Leon H. and Mary L. (Chase) S.; BA with high honors, U. Calif., Santa Barbara, 1972; JD cum laude, Santa Clara U., 1975; m. Wendy Jeanne Craig, June 6, 1976; children: Sarah Ann, Thomas ChaseJr. Bar: Calif. 1976; cert. family law specialist. Pvt. practice, San Jose, Calif., 1976-79; pres., sec., CFO Thomas Chase Stutzman, P.C., San Jose, 1979—; legal counsel Cypress Human Resources, Inc., DMJ Pro Care, Inc., Sparacino's Foods, Tax Firm, Inc., United Charities, Marina Assocs. Inc., Midnight Fraction Mine Inc., D.A.M. Good Engring./Mfg., Inc., E.M.I. Oil Filtration Systems, Inc., China Villa, Inc., Creative Pacifica, Inc., Am. West Furniture Mfg., Inc., Advanfab Corp., Am. First Tech., Analog Engring., Inc., Excel-Law Video, Inc., First Am. Real Estate Financing Co., Hoffman Industries, Inc., Info. Scan Tech., Inc., PRD Construction Mgmt. Svcs., Unifed Homes, Inc., Marine Biogenic Pharm. USA, Inc., Miller Networks, Mi Pueblo Mt. View, Inc., others; instr. San Jose State U., 1977-78. Bd. dirs. Santa Cruz Campfire, 1978-80, Happy Hollow Park, 1978-80, 83-86, Pacific Neighbors, pres., 1991-92. Mem. Calif. Bar Assn., Santa Clara County Bar Assn. (chmn. environ.

law com. 1976-78, exec. com. family law, exec. com. fee arbitration com.), Assn. Cert. Law Specialist, San Jose Jaycees (Dir. of the Year 1976-77), Almaden Valley Rotary Club, Lions (dir. 1979-81, 2d v.p. 1982-83, 1st v.p. 1983-84, pres. 1984-85), Scottish Rite, Masons, Phi Beta Kappa. Congregationalist State civil litigation, Family and matrimonial, Real property. Office: 1625 The Alameda Ste 626 San Jose CA 95126-2207

**STYER, JANE M.,** computer consultant; b. Bethlehem, Pa., Apr. 14, 1957; d. LeRoy V. and Pauline M. (Diehl) S. Assoc in Gen. Edn., NCACC, 1977, Assoc in Applied Sci., 1979; BS in Computer Sci., St. Francis de Sales Coll., 1985, cert. profl. legal sec., 1986. PC technician A+ cert. 1997. Legal sec., asst. Lower Saucon Police Dept.; asst. to treas., bookkeeper Lehigh Valley Motor Club, Allentown, Pa.; real estate and probate paralegal, office mgr. various attys., Lehigh & Delaware Valleys, Pa., 1976-82; title ins. agt., owner, mgr. Abstractors' Svcs., Bingen, Pa., 1982—; quality control theory checker, tax preparer H & R Block, 1992—. Mem. NAFE, Nat. Assn. Legal Secs. (Continuing Legal Edn. Recognition award 1988), Lehigh-Northampton Counties (chmn. continuing legal edn. com. 1984-88, seminar chmn. 1985-88), Pa. Assn. Notaries, Single Sq. Dancers U.S.A. (nat. sec. 1986-87), Bachelors and Bachelorettes, Internat. (sec. Mid-Atlantic region 1980-84). Avocations: camping, square and round dancing, horseback riding. E-mail: JMStyer@juno.com. Office: Abstractors' Svcs 3228 Bingen Rd Bethlehem PA 18015-5707

**SUAREZ, EDDIE A.,** lawyer; b. Havana, Cuba, Jan. 25, 1960; came to U.S., 1971; BA, Fla. State U., Tallahassee, 1983, JD, 1987. Bar: Fla., U.S. Dist. Ct. (mid. dist.) Fla. Asst. state's atty., prosecutor 13th Jud. Dist., Tampa, Fla., 1987—; assoc. Lazzara and Paul, Tampa, 1991-97; mng. ptnr. Suarez & Wardell, Tampa, 1997—. Mem. Nat. Assn. Criminal Def. Lawyers (bd. dirs. trial lawyers sect. 1991—), Fla. Criminal Def. Lawyers Assn. (bd. dirs. 1991-95), Hillsborough County Bar Assn. (co-chmn. criminal law sect. 1997-98), Hillsburg County Assn. Criminal Def. Lawyers (past pres.). Avocations: reading, exercising. Criminal. Office: Suarez & Wardell 400 N Tampa St Ste 2950 Tampa FL 33602-4797

**SUBAK, JOHN THOMAS,** lawyer; b. Trebic, Czechoslovakia, Apr. 19, 1929; came to U.S., 1941, naturalized, 1946; s. William John and Gerda Maria (Subakova) S.; m. Mary Corcoran, June 4, 1955; children—Jane Kennedy, Kate, Thomas, Michael. BA summa cum laude, Yale U., 1950, LLB, 1956. Bar: Pa. 1956. From assoc. to ptnr. Dechert, Price & Rhoads, Phila., 1956-76, v.p., gen. counsel, dir., 1976-77; group v.p., gen. counsel, dir. Rohm and Haas Co., Phila., 1977-93; counsel Dechert Price & Rhoads, Phila., 1994—; bd. dirs. Newport Corp. Editor: The Bus. Lawyer, 1982-83. Bd. dirs. Am. Cancer Soc., 1982-95; trustee Smith Coll. Lt. (j.g.) USN, 1950-53. Mem. ABA (chmn. corp. and bus. law sect. 1984-85), Am. Law Inst. (coun. mem.), Defender Assn. of Phila. (v.p., bd. dirs. 1982-95), Merion Cricket Club, Lemon Bay Club. Democrat. Roman Catholic. General corporate. Office: Dechert Price & Rhoads 4000 Bell Atlantic Tower Philadelphia PA 19102-2793

**SUBIN, ELI HAROLD,** lawyer; b. Phila., June 25, 1935; s. Benjamin and Freda (Kalen) S.; m. Suzon Bette Rosenbluth, Oct. 21, 1962; children: Andrea Beth Craig, Ben William. BA, U. Pa., 1957; LLB, U. Miami, Coral Gables, Fla., 1961. Bar: Fla., 1961, U.S. Dist. Ct. (mid. dist.) Fla., 1961, U.S. Supreme Ct., 1964, U.S. Ct. Appeals (5th, 11th cirs.), 1966. Trial atty. antitrust divsn. U.S. Dept. Justice, Phila., 1962-63; rsch. aide Dist. Ct. Appeal (1st dist.) Fla., Tallahassee, 1963-64; atty. Roth Segal & Levine, Orlando, Fla., 1964-72, Subin Shams, et. al. P.A., Orlando, 1972-96; city atty. City of Orlando, 1980-82; atty. Maguire, Voorhis & Wells, P.A., Orlando, 1997-98, Holland & Knight LLP, Orlando, 1998—; referee Supreme Ct. Fla., Tallahassee, 1975; mem. Fla. Bd. Bar Examiners, 1982-97, chmn., 1986-87. Mem. exec. com. Seminole County Dems., Sanford, Fla., 1970-74; mem. jud. nominating com. 9th cir. Fla., 1976-79; dir. Fla. Bar Found., Orlando, 1992—. 1st lt. USAR, 1957-64. Mem. Am. Law Inst., Am. Bd. Trial Advs. (assoc.), Orange County Bar Assn. (dir. 1968-71). Jewish. General civil litigation, Antitrust. Office: Holland & Knight LLP PO Box 1526 Orlando FL 32802

**SUBIN, FLORENCE,** lawyer; b. N.Y.C., June 5, 1935; d. George and Beatrice (Rodam) Katroser; m. Bert W. Subin, June 6, 1953 (dec.); children: Glen D., Beth Subin Ambler. BA, Herbert H. Lehman Coll., 1972; JD magna cum laude, Bklyn. Law Sch., 1975. Bar: N.Y. 1976, U.S. Dist. Ct. (so. and ea. dists.) N.Y. 1976. Pvt. practice N.Y.C. and Scarsdale, N.Y., 1976—. Mem. Assn. Trial Lawyers City of N.Y. (bd. dirs. 1982-86), Met. Women's Bar Assn. (pres. 1979-81, bd. dirs. 1981—), Bronx Women's Bar Assn. (pres. 1983-85), Bklyn. Law Sch. Alumni Assn. (pres. 1992-94), Phi Beta Kappa. Personal injury, Probate. Office: 291 Broadway New York NY 10007-1814

**SUBJACK, JAMES PATRICK,** district attorney; b. Dunkirk, N.Y., Feb. 9, 1949; s. Leonard Edward and Josephine (Lupone) S.; m. Janel Marie Humm, Aug. 25, 1979; children: Michael James, Jeanne Marie. BA in History, Pa. State U., 1970; JD, U. Ill., 1973. Bar: Ill 1973, N.Y. 1975, U.S. Dist. Ct. (we. dist.) N.Y. 1980. Relocation dir. Dunkirk Urban Renewal Agy., 1974-76; asst. dist. atty. Chautauqua County Dist. Atty.'s Office, Mayville, N.Y., 1976-78; sole practitioner Jamestown, N.Y., 1979-93; asst. social svcs. atty. Chautauqua County Dept. Social svcs., Mayville, 1980-82; assoc. corp. counsel City of Jamestown, 1982-87, corp. counsel, 1992-93; dist. atty. County of Chautauqua, Mayville, 1993—. Baseball coach Jamestown City Recreation Com., 1988-93; co-chair Cmty. Crime Prevention Coalition, Jamestown; mem. Jamestown Sr. and Law Together, 1994—; mem. Chautauqua County Child Sexual Abuse Intervention Team, Jamestown, 1993—. Recipient Law Enforcement award N.Y. State Dept. Environ. Conservation, 1997, N.Y. State Humane Soc., 1998. Mem. N.Y. State Bar Assn. (mem. criminal justice exec. com. 1997—), Jamestown Bar Assn. (pres. 1990-91), No. Bar Assn. of Chautauqua County, N.Y. State Dist. Attys. Assn. (mem. exec. com. 1999—). Democrat. Roman Catholic. Avocations: golf, travel, reading. Office: Chautauqua County Dist Atty Gerace Office Bldg Mayville NY 14757

**SUDARKASA, MICHAEL ERIC MABOGUNJE,** lawyer, consultant; b. N.Y.C., Aug. 5, 1964; s. Akinlowan Mabogunje and Niara Gloria (Marshall) S.; m. Joyce Ann Johnson, Nov. 22, 1990; children: Jasmine Ayana Yetunde, Jonathan Michael, Maya Elisabeth, Marielle Iman. Exchange student, Howard U., 1983; BA in History with honors, U. Mich., 1985; JD, Harvard U., 1988; postgrad., U. San Diego, Paris, 1990. Bar: Fla. 1989, U.S. Ct. Appeals (D.C.) 1990. Tech. asst. African Devel. Bank, Abidjan, Ivory Coast, 1988-89; founder, cons. 21st Century Africa, Inc., Lincoln University, Pa., 1989; assoc. Steel Hector & Davis, Miami, Fla., 1990; pres. 21st Century Africa, Inc., Washington, 1990-97; dir. internat. trade and investment promotion svcs. Labat-Anderson, Inc., McLean, Va., 1997—; bd. dirs. Calvert New Africa, Africa News Online, Calvert New World Fund. Author: The African Business Handbook: A Practical Guide to Business Resources for U.S./Africa Trade and Investment, 1991-92, 93-94, 96-97. Mem. overseas devel. coun. Africa Roundtable. Named One of 30 Leaders of Future, Ebony mag., 1991; recipient Muhammad Kenyatta Young Alumni award Harvard Black Law Students Assn., 1992. Mem. ABA (chmn. African law com. 1995—), Internat. Bar Assn. Avocations: sports, reading, travel. Office: Labat-Anderson Inc 800 Westpark Dr Ste 400 Mc Lean VA 22102

**SUDARSHAN, ARVIND JEWETT,** lawyer, principal; b. Rochester, N.Y., Mar. 22, 1962; s. George and Lalita Sudarshan. AB, Harvard U., 1983; JD, U. Tex., Austin, 1986. Assoc. McGinnis, Lochridge & Kilgore, Austin, 1983-87, ptnr., 1988-92; prin. Arvind J. Sudarshan, Atty. at Law, Austin, 1992. Antitrust, Federal civil litigation, General civil litigation. Office: 1801 Lavaca St Ste 102 Austin TX 78701-1329

**SUDDATH, THOMAS HOWLE, JR.,** lawyer; b. Singapore, Aug. 9, 1956; came to U.S., 1957; s. Thomas Howle and Eileen (Hammond) S.; m. Karen Dorothy McDonnell, July 9, 1994. AB, Colby Coll., 1978; JD, Cath. U., 1982. Bar: Pa. 1982, Colo. 1985, U.S. Dist. Ct. (ea. dist.) Pa. 1984, U.S. Dist. Ct. Colo. 1985, U.S. Ct. Appeals (3d cir.) 1997. Law clk. to Judge William Ditter Jr. U.S. Dist. Ct. (ea. dist.) Pa., Phila., 1982-84; assoc. Davis, Graham & Stubbs, Denver, 1984-88; asst. U.S. atty. U.S. Atty.'s Office, Phila., 1988-96; assoc. Montgomery, McCracken, Walker & Rhoads, Phila., 1996-98, ptnr., 1998—; counsel Health Care Compliance Assn., Phila., 1996—. Editor-in-chief Cath. U. Law Rev., 1982. Recipient Dir.'s award U.S. Dept. Justice, 1990. Mem. Phila. Bar Assn., Army and Navy Club. Episcopalian. Avocations: skiing, reading, running, travel. Federal civil litigation, Criminal. Office: Montgomery McCracken et al 123 S Broad St Philadelphia PA 19109-1029

**SUDOL, WALTER EDWARD,** lawyer; b. Passaic, N.J., Jan. 13, 1942; s. Walter and Ann (Kopec) S.; m. June Ann Jancio, Oct. 14, 1967; children: Karen Ann, Alyson Anne. BA, Tulane U., 1963; JD, Seton Hall U., 1975. Bar: N.J. 1975, U.S. Dist. Ct. N.J. 1975, N.Y. 1985. Indsl. engr. Westinghouse Electric Co., Jersey City, 1969-72, indsl. relations mgr., 1972-75; atty., mgr. contracts Westinghouse Electric Co., Millburn, N.J., 1975-80; gen. counsel, sec. Internat. Computers Ltd., East Brunswick, N.J., 1980-81, Belco Pollution Control Corp., Parsippany, N.J., 1981-85; v.p., gen. counsel, sec. H-R Internat., Inc., Edison, N.J., 1985-94; assoc. counsel Louis Berger Internat., Inc., East Orange, N.J., 1997—; cons. constrn. claims Westinghouse Electric Co., Washington, 1977-79, Foster Wheeler Energy Corp., Livingston, N.J., 1983-84. Pres. St. Andrew's Parish Council, Clifton, N.J., 1980. Served to capt. USNR, 1963-91, Vietnam. Mem. ABA, N.J. Bar Assn., Passaic County Bar Assn., Nat. Constructors Assn. (chmn. gen. counsels com. 1985-86), Am. Legion, VFW. Republican. Roman Catholic. Lodge: Masons. Avocations: sailing, tennis. General corporate, General practice, Private international. Home: 67 Village Rd Clifton NJ 07013-3436

**SUESS, JEFFREY KARL,** lawyer; b. Carbondale, Ill., May 27, 1960; s. Raymond Karl and Maryloy (Ronat) S.; m. Karen Elizabeth Mason, Oct. 17, 1987; children: Matthew Karl, Alexandra Margret, Mason Robert, Caroline Cooper. BA in Polit. Sci., Washington U., St. Louis, 1982, JD, 1985. Bar: Mo. 1985, Ill. 1986. Assoc. Evans & Dixon, St. Louis, 1985-92, ptnr., 1993—. Contbr. chpts. to book: Civil Procedure: Missouri Bar CLE, 1988, 90, 94. Trustee First Presbyn. Ch., St. Louis, 1990-93, pres. bd. deacons, 1987-89; commr. University City (Mo.) Arts and Letters Commn., 1994—, treas. Mem. ABA, Mo. Orgn. Def. Lawyers, Mo. Bar Assn. (civil procedure com.), St. Louis County Bar Assn., Vol. Lawyers Assn., Sigma Chi (sec. 1980), Phi Delta Phi (pres. 1983-84). Avocations: golf, hockey, soccer, raising children. General civil litigation, Product liability, Personal injury. Office: Evans & Dixon 200 N Broadway Ste 1200 Saint Louis MO 63102-2749

**SUFFETY, HAMED WILLIAM, JR.,** lawyer, associate; b. Saginaw, Mich., Nov. 25, 1957; s. Hamed William and Dorothy Marie (Davy) S.; m. Patricia Ann Guerriero, Sept. 20, 1986; 1 child: Hamed William III. BA, U. Mich., 1979; JD, Thomas M. Cooley Law Sch., 1983. Bar: Mich. 1983. Assoc. friend of ct. Saginaw (Mich.) County Friend of the Ct., 1984—. Mem. Saginaw County Bar Assn., Mich. State Bar Assn. (family law sect.). Democrat. Roman Catholic. Avocations: golf, bowling, tennis, cycling. Family and matrimonial, Juvenile. Office: Saginaw County Friend of the Court 615 Court St Saginaw MI 48602-4250

**SUFLAS, STEVEN WILLIAM,** lawyer; b. Camden, N.J., Oct. 7, 1951; s. William V. and Dorothy (Stafre) S.; m. Rochelle B. Volin, Apr. 15, 1978; children: Allison, Rebecca, Whitney. BA, Davidson Coll., 1973; JD with honors, U. N.C., 1976. Bar: N.J. 1976, Pa. 1978, U.S. Dist. Ct. N.J., U.S. Ct. Appeals (3d cir.). Field atty. NLRB, Phila., 1976-80; assoc. Archer & Greiner P.C., Haddonfield, N.J., 1980-86, ptnr., 1986—. Fellow Coll. of Labor and Employment Lawyers; mem. ABA, Pa. Bar Assn., Phila. Bar Assn., N.J. Bar Assn. (exec. com. labor and employment law sect. 1985—, officer 1993—), Order of Coif, Omicron Delta Kappa. Labor. Office: Archer & Greiner PC 1 Centennial Sq Haddonfield NJ 08033-2328

**SUGARMAN, ROBERT P.,** lawyer; b. Passaic, N.J., Aug. 29, 1949; s. Meyer and Sylvia (Schwartz) S.; m. Louise Aufiero, June 29, 1980; children: Lauren, Jason. BA, Rutgers Coll., 1971; JD, Columbia U., 1975. Bar: N.Y. and N.J. 1976, U.S. Dist. Ct. (so. dist.) N.Y. 1976, U.S. Dist. Ct. (ea. dist.) N.Y. 1977, U.S. Ct. Appeals (2d cir.) 1992. Assoc. Paul, Weiss, Rifkind, Wharton & Garrison, N.Y.C., 1975-79; assoc. Milberg Weiss Bershad Hynes & Lerach, N.Y.C., 1979-82, ptnr., 1983—. Federal civil litigation, Securities, General civil litigation. Office: Milberg Weiss et al 1 Penn Plz Ste 4835 New York NY 10119-0002

**SUGDEN, SAMUEL M.,** lawyer; b. 1942. BA, Kenyon Coll., 1963; JD, Vanderbilt U., 1966. Head energy practice LeBoeuf, Lamb, Greene & MacRae, N.Y.C., chmn. Office: LeBoeuf Lamb Green & MacRae 125 E 55th St New York NY 10022-3502*

**SUGERMAN, KAREN BETH,** lawyer; b. Bklyn., Aug. 2, 1952; d. Lewis and Ceilia S.; divorced; children: Justin Gary, Jonathan Gary. BA with honors, Syracuse U., 1974; JD, U. Miami, 1977. Bar: Fla. Assoc. Heinfun & Rosenfeld, Miami, 1978-80; ptnr. Gary & Gary, Miami, 1981-89, Rosenfeld, Stein & Sugerman, Miami, 1990-94; pvt. practice Miami, 1994-96; ptnr. Sugerman & Scopinich, Miami, 1996—. Mem. exec. coun. south Fla. chpt. Comml. Law League, 1995. Mem. North Dade Bar Assn. (pres. 1996-97, pres.-elect 1993-98). Avocations: tennis, running, musical composition, piano. Family and matrimonial, Consumer commercial. Office: Sugerman & Scopinich PA 17071 W Dixie Hwy N Miami Beach FL 33160-3765

**SUGGS, MICHAEL EDWARD,** lawyer; b. Conway, S.C., Nov. 9, 1962; s. Edward and Rebecca S. BSBA, U. S.C., 1985, JD, 1992. Bar: S.C. 1992, U.S. Dist. Ct., S.C., 1995. Asst. pub. defender Def. Corp. Horry County, Conway, S.C., 1993—. Troop 847 com. Boy Scouts Am., Loris, S.C., 1985—; coun. City of Loris, 1994—, mayor pro-tem, 1998—. Recipient Eagle Scout award Boy Scouts Am., 1976. Mem. S.C. Assn. Criminal Def. Lawyers, Horry County Bar Assn., Loris C. of C. Methodist. Home: 4932 Circle Dr Loris SC 29569-3146 Office: Def Corp Horry County PO Box 1666 114 Laurel St Conway SC 29526-5134

**SUHR, PAUL AUGUSTINE,** lawyer; b. Sonwunri, Chonbuk, Korea, Jan. 20, 1940; came to U.S. 1966; s. Chong-ju and Oksuk (Pang) So; m. Angeline M. Kang Suhr; 1 child, Christopher. BA, Campbell Coll., Buies Creek, N.C., 1968; MA, U. N.C., Greensboro, 1970; MS, U. N.C., Chapel Hill, 1975; JD, N.C. Cen. U., 1988. Bar: N.C. 1989, U.S. Dist. Ct. (ea. and mid. dist.) N.C. 1989, U.S. Ct. Appeals D.C. 1990, U.S. Ct. Appeals (4th cir.) 1992. Bibliographer N.C. Div. of State Libr., Raleigh, 1975-78; dir. Pender County Pub. Libr., Burgaw, N.C., 1978-80; libr. Tob. Lit. Svc., N.C. State U., Raleigh, 1980-85; pvt. practice law Law Office of Paul A. Suhr, Raleigh & Fayetteville, 1989—. Author short stories and novelettes various lit. mags., jours. and revs. Mem. Human Resources and Human Rels. Adv. Commn., City of Raleigh, 1990-95, chmn., 1994-95. N.C. Humanities Com. grantee, 1979-80; recipient Presdl. award President of Korea, 1992. Mem. ABA, ATLA, N.C. Bar Assn., N.C. Trial Lawyers Assn., Wake County Bar Assn. (bd. dirs. 1996-97), D.C. Bar Assn. Democrat. Roman Catholic. Avocations: gardening, fishing, writing. Personal injury, Criminal, Immigration, naturalization, and customs. Office: 1110 Navaho Dr Ste 502 Raleigh NC 27609-7322

**SUHRHEINRICH, RICHARD FRED,** federal judge; b. 1936. BS, Wayne State U., 1960; JD cum laude, Detroit Coll. Law, 1963, LLM, 1992; LLM, U. Va., 1990. Bar: Mich. Assoc. Moll, Desenberg, Purdy, Glover & Bayer, 1963-67; asst. prosecutor Macomb County, 1967; ptnr. Rogensues, Richard & Suhrheinrich, 1967; assoc. Moll, Desenberg, Purdy, Glover & Bayer, 1967-68; ptnr. Kitch, Suhrheinrich, Saurbier & Drutchas, 1968-84; judge U.S. Dist. Ct. (ea. dist.) Mich., Detroit, 1984-90, U.S. Ct. Appeals (6th Cir.), Lansing, 1990—. Mem. State Bar Mich., Ingham County Bar Assn. Office: US Ct Appeals 6th Cir USPO & Fed Bldg 315 W Allegan St Rm 241 Lansing MI 48933-1514*

**SUKO, LONNY RAY,** judge; b. Spokane, Wash., Oct. 12, 1943; s. Ray R. and Leila B. (Snyder) S.; m. Marcia A. Michaelsen, Aug. 26, 1967; children: Jolynn R., David M. BA, Wash. State U., 1965; JD, U. Idaho, 1968. Bar: Wash. 1968, U.S. Dist. Ct. (ea. dist.) Wash. 1969, U.S. Dist. Ct. (we. dist.) Wash. 1978, U.S. Ct. Appeals (9th cir.) 1978. Law clk. U.S. Dist. Ct. Ea. Dist. Wash., 1968-69; assoc. Lyon, Beaulaurier & Aaron, Yakima, Wash., 1969-72; ptnr. Lyon, Beaulaurier, Weigand, Suko & Gustafson, Yakima, 1972-91, Lyon, Weigand, Suko & Gustafson, P.S., 1991-95; U.S. magistrate judge, Yakima, 1971-91, 95—. Mem. Phi Beta Kappa, Phi Kappa Phi. Office: PO Box 2726 Yakima WA 98907-2726

**SULGER, FRANCIS XAVIER,** lawyer; b. N.Y.C., Sept. 3, 1942; s. John J. and Regina (Slawkowska) S.; m. Helga Nelsen, July 23, 1968; children: Derek N., Justin D. BA, Fordham U., 1964; JD, Harvard U., 1967. Bar: N.Y. 1970, U.S. Dist. Ct. (so. dist.) N.Y. 1979. Atty. F.I. duPont & Co., N.Y.C., 1968-70; assoc. Townsend & Lewis, N.Y.C., 1970-73, Thacher Proffitt & Wood, N.Y.C., 1973-78; ptnr. Thacher Proffitt & Wood, 1978—. Trustee Wildcliff Mus., New Rochelle, N.Y., 1970-74; mem. U.S. Olympic Rowing Com., Colorado Springs, Colo., 1980-84. Mem. U.S. Rowing Assn. (bd. dirs. 1979-84), N.Y. Athletic Club (rowing chmn. 1979-95), Larchmont (N.Y.) Yacht Club. Avocations: rowing, collecting antiques, computers. Finance, Securities, General corporate. Home: 10 Meadow Ln Greenwich CT 06831-3709 Office: Thacher Proffitt & Wood 2 World Trade Ctr New York NY 10048-0203

**SULLIVAN, BARRY,** law educator; b. Newburyport, Mass., Jan. 11, 1949; s. George Arnold and Dorothy Bennett (Furbush) S.; m. Winnifred Mary Fallers, June 14, 1975; children: George Arnold, Lloyd Ashton. AB cum laude, Middlebury Coll., 1970; JD, U. Chgo., 1974. Bar: Mass. 1975, Ill. 1975, Va. 1995, U.S. Dist. Ct. (no. dist.) Ill. 1976, U.S. Ct. Appeals (7th cir.) 1976, U.S. Ct. Appeals (10th cir.) 1977, U.S. Supreme Ct. 1978, U.S. Ct. Appeals (11th cir.) 1986, U.S. Ct. Appeals (5th and 9th cirs.) 1987, U.S. Ct. Appeals (fed. cir.) 1993, U.S. Ct. Appeals (D.C. cir.) 1994, U.S. Ct. Appeals (4th cir.) 1997. Law clk. to judge John Minor Wisdom U.S. Ct. Appeals (5th cir.), New Orleans, 1974-75; assoc. Jenner & Block, Chgo., 1975-80; asst. to solicitor gen. of U.S. U.S. Dept. of Justice, Washington, 1980-81; ptnr. Jenner & Block, Chgo., 1981-94; dean, prof. law Washington and Lee U., Lexington, Va., 1994—, v.p., 1998—; spl. asst. atty. gen. State of Ill., 1989-90; lectr. in law Loyola U., Chgo., 1978-79; adj. prof. law Northwestern U., Chgo., 1990-92, 93-94, vis. prof., 1992-93; Jessica Swift Meml. lectr. in constnl. law Middlebury Coll., 1991. Assoc. editor U. Chgo. Law Rev., 1973-74; contbr. articles to profl. jours. Trustee Cath. Theol. Union at Chgo., 1993—; mem. vis. com. U. Chgo. Divinity Sch., 1987—. Yeats Soc. scholar, 1968; Woodrow Wilson fellow, Woodrow Wilson Found., 1970. Mem. ABA (chmn. coord. com. on AIDS 1988-94, mem. standing com. on amicus curiae briefs 1990-97, mem. coun. of sect. of individual rights and responsibilities 1993-98, mem. sect. of legal edn. com. on law sch. adminstrn. 1994-98), Va. Bar Assn., Va. State Bar (chair sect. on edn. of lawyers 1998—), Bar Assn. 7th Fed. Cir. (vice chmn. adminstrv. justice com. 1985-86), Am. Law Inst., Law Club Chgo., Phi Beta Kappa. Democrat. Roman Catholic. Home: 201 Jackson Ave Lexington VA 24450-2007 Office: Washington and Lee U Sch Law Sydney Lewis Hall Lexington VA 24450

**SULLIVAN, BRENDAN V., JR.,** lawyer; b. Providence, Mar. 11, 1942. AB, Georgetown U., 1964, JD, 1967. Bar: R.I. 1967, D.C. 1970, U.S. Dist. Ct. D.C. 1970, U.S. Ct. Appeals (D.C. cir.) 1970, U.S. Supreme Ct. 1972, U.S. Dist. Ct. Md. 1974, U.S. Ct. Appeals (4th cir.) 1981, U.S. Ct. Appeals (3d cir.) 1979, U.S. Ct. Appeals (6th cir.) 1991, U.S. Ct. Appeals (9th cir.) 1996, U.S. Ct. Fed. Claims 1998. Mem. Williams & Connolly, Washington; lectr. Practicing Law Inst., 1981—, Md. Inst. for Continuing Profl. Edn. of Lawyers, Inc., 1979—, D.C. Criminal Practice Inst., 1975-81. Author: Grand Jury Proceedings, 1981, Techniques for Dealing with Pending Criminal Charges or Criminal Investigations, 1983, White Collar Criminal Practice Grand Jury, 1985. Fellow Am. Coll. Trial Lawyers; mem. ABA, R.I. Bar Assn., D.C. Bar. Office: Williams & Connolly 725 12th St NW Washington DC 20005-5901

**SULLIVAN, BRIAN THOMAS,** lawyer, business executive, entrepreneur; b. New Haven, Sept. 26, 1959; s. Thomas Joseph and Patricia (Mulherin) S. BS in Mgmt., U.S. Coast Guard Acad., 1981; JD, Harvard U., 1989; MBA, Stanford U., 1995. Bar: Conn. 1989, N.Y. 1990; lic. U.S. Mch. Marine officer. Corp. legal counsel Carrier Corp., Syracuse, N.Y./Farmington, Conn., 1989-93; gen. mgr. Raimon Land Pub. Co. Ltd., Bangkok, Thailand, 1995-96; spl. projects officer Amax Plating, Inc., Elgin, Ill., 1997-98; pvt. investor Chgo., 1997—. Lt. U.S. Coast Guard, 1981-86. Recipient Coast Guard Achievement medal. Mem. ABA. Democrat. Roman Catholic. Avocations: running, basketball. Office: The Sullivan Cos Inc 919 W George St Apt 3E Chicago IL 60657-5030

**SULLIVAN, DANA LOUISE,** lawyer; b. Glen Ridge, N.J., Oct. 4, 1967; d. Arthur James Sullivan Jr. and Joan (Adams) Drukker; m. David Scott Schell, Aug. 17, 1996. BA, Princeton U., 1989; JD, NYU, 1993. Bar: Oreg. 1994, Calif. 1994, D.C. 1996. Law clk. to Hon. Malcolm F. Marsh U.S. Dist. Ct. Oreg., Portland, 1993-95; assoc. Bernabei & Katz, Washington, 1995-97, Hoevet, Snyder & Boise, P.C., Portland, 1997—. Mem. Oreg. State Bar Assn. (pub. svc. com. 1998—), Fed. Bar Assn. (young lawyers com. 1998—), Multnomah Bar Assn. (pub. svc. com. 1997—), Oreg. Trial Lawyers Assn. (bd. govs. 1998—). Democrat. Civil rights, Federal civil litigation, Labor. Home: 2408 NE 8th Ave Portland OR 97212-3861 Office: Hoevet Snyder & Boise PC 1000 SW Broadway Ste 1500 Portland OR 97205-3081

**SULLIVAN, E. THOMAS,** dean; b. Amboy, Ill., Dec. 4, 1948; s. Edward McDonald and Mary Lorraine (Murphy) S.; m. Susan A. Sullivan, Oct. 2, 1971. BA, Brake U., 1970; JD, Ind. U., Indpls., 1973. Bar: Ind. 1973, Fla. 1974, D.C. 1975, Mo. 1980. Law clk. to Judge Joe Eaton, U.S. Dist. Ct. for So. Dist. Fla., Miami, 1973-75; trial atty. U.S. Dept. Justice, Washington, 1975-77; sr. assoc. Donovan, Leisure, Newton & Irvine, Washington, 1977-79; prof. law U. Mo., Columbia, 1979-84; assoc. dean, prof. Washington U., St. Louis, 1984-89; dean U. Ariz. Coll. Law, Tucson, 1989-95; William S. Pattee prof. law, dean U. Minn. Law Sch., Mpls., 1995—. Fellow Am. Bar Found.; mem. Am. Law Inst., Am. Econ. Assn. Home: 180 Bank St SE Minneapolis MN 55414-1042 Office: U Minn Law Sch Minneapolis MN 55455*

**SULLIVAN, EDWARD LAWRENCE,** lawyer; b. Boston, May 8, 1955; s. Edward L. and Dorothy L. (Gregory) S.; m. Susan M. Griffin, Dec. 2, 1983; children: Erica A., Brittany M. BA in Polit. Sci., St. Anselm Coll., 1977; JD, St. Louis U., 1980. Bar: Mo. 1980, U.S. Dist. Ct. (we. dist.) Mo. 1980, Mass. 1981, Ill. 1981, D.C. 1986. Atty., Ill. divsn. Peabody Coal Co., Fairview Heights, 1980-85; legis. counsel Peabody Holding Co., Washington, 1985-88; dir., legal and pub. affairs, western divsn. Peabody Coal Co., Flagstaff, Ariz., 1988-90; sr. counsel Peabody Holding Co.o., St. Louis, 1990-94; gen. counsel Powder River Coal Co., Gillette, Wyo., 1994; gen. counsel, western region Peabody Holding Co., St. Louis, 1995—. Industry rep. royalty policy com. U.S. Dept. Interior, Washington, 1995—. Mem. Bar Assn. Met. St. Louis. Administrative and regulatory, Contracts commercial, Natural resources. Office: Peabody Holding Co Inc 701 Market St Ste 700 Saint Louis MO 63101-1895

**SULLIVAN, EDWARD MICHAEL,** lawyer; b. Boston, June 2, 1929; s. Edward M. and Isabelle C. (Cassidy) S. BA, Dartmouth Coll., 1949; LLB, Harvard Coll., 1952. Bar: N.Y. 1952, Mass. 1953. Assoc. Wickes, Riddell, et al, N.Y.C., 1952-55; asst. counsel Boston & Maine R.R., 1955-57; pvt. practice Boston, 1957—. Avocations: reading, travel, squash. Federal civil litigation, General civil litigation, Probate. Office: Edward M Sullivan 28 Exeter St Boston MA 02116-2841

**SULLIVAN, EUGENE RAYMOND,** federal judge; b. St. Louis, Aug. 2, 1941; s. Raymond Vincent and Rosemary (Kiely) S.; m. Lis Urup Johansen, June 18, 1966; children—Kim, Eugene II. BS, U.S. Mil. Acad., 1964; JD, Georgetown U., 1971. Bar: Mo. 1972, D.C. 1972. Law clk. to judge U.S. Ct. Appeals (8th cir.), St. Louis, 1971-72; assoc. Patton Boggs & Blow, Washington, 1972-74; asst. spl. counsel The White House, Washington, 1974; trial counsel U.S. Dept. of Justice, Washington, 1974-82; dep. gen. counsel U.S. Air Force, Washington, 1982-84; gen. counsel U.S. Air Force, 1984-86; gov. Wake Island, 1984-86; judge U.S. Ct. Appeals (Armed Forces), Washington, 1986-90, 95—, chief judge, 1990-95; mem. Fed. Commn. To Study Honor Code at West Point, 1989-90. Trustee U.S. Mil. Acad., 1989—. With US Army, 1964-69. Decorated Bronze Star, Air medal, airborne badge, ranger badge, others. Republican. Roman Catholic. Home: 6307 Massachusetts Ave Bethesda MD 20816-1139 Office: US Ct Appeals (Armed Forces) 450 E St NW Washington DC 20442-0001

**SULLIVAN, FRANK, JR.,** state supreme court justice; b. Mar. 21, 1950; s. Frank E. and Colette (Cleary) S.; m. Cheryl Gibson, June 14, 1972; children: Denis M., Douglas S., Thomas R. AB cum laude, Dartmouth Coll., 1972; JD magna cum laude, Ind. U., 1982. Bar: Ind. 1982. Mem. staff Office of U.S. Rep. John Brademas, 1974-79, dir. staff, 1975-78; with Barnes & Thornburg, Indpls., 1982-89; budget dir. State of Ind., 1989-92; exec. asst. Office of Gov. Evan Bayh, 1993; assoc. justice Ind. Supreme Ct., 1993—. Mem. ABA, Ind. State Bar Assn., Indpls. Bar Assn. Home: 6153 N Olney St Indianapolis IN 46220-5166 Office: State House Rm 321 Indianapolis IN 46204-2728

**SULLIVAN, FREDERICK LAWRENCE,** lawyer; b. Holyoke, Mass., Oct. 11, 1937; s. Frederick L. and Helen (Fitzgerald) S.; m. Judith Ann Boldvay, Feb. 13, 1965; children: Mark, Meghan. BS, Manhattan Coll., 1959; JD, Fordham U., 1965. Bar: N.Y. 1966, U.S. Dist. Ct. (ea. and so. dist.) N.Y. 1972, Mass. 1973, U.S. Dist. Ct. Mass. 1972, U.S. Ct. Appeals (2nd cir.) 1972. Labor atty. Allied Stores Corp., N.Y.C., 1965-69; assoc. Jackson, Lewis, Schnitzler & Krupman, N.Y.C., 1969-72, Marshall & Marshall, Springfield, Mass., 1972-76; ptnr. Sullivan & Hayes, Springfield, Mass., 1976—; cons. Employee Rels., Inc., Springfield, 1977—. Co-author book: Massachusetts Non-Profit Organizations, 1992; contbr. articles to profl. jours. Pres. bd. dirs. Children's Mus., Holyoke, Mass., 1988-92; bd. dirs. United Way, Holyoke, 1987-92, Springfield Symphony, 1989-94; pres., chmn. St. Patrick's Parade Com., Holyoke, 1985-92. Mem. ABA, Mass. Bar Assn. (employment law coun. rep.). Labor. Office: Sullivan & Hayes 1 Monarch Pl Ste 1200 Springfield MA 01144-1001

**SULLIVAN, JAMES JEROME,** lawyer, consultant; b. Fargo, N.D., Feb. 23, 1943; m. Roberta Jean Ranes, Nov. 8, 1980; children: Kristen, Jason, Eric, Amy. PhB, U. N.D., 1966, JD, 1970. Bar: N.D. 1970, Wash. 1982. Atty. Northwestern Nat. Life Ins. Co., Mpls., 1970-73; regional counsel Econ. Devel. Admin. of U.S. Dept. Commerce, Seattle, 1973-90; law pvt. practice Bellevue and Issaquah, Wash., 1986—. Editor, contbr. articles to numerous periodicals. Recipient numerous legal awards. Mem. ABA, Wash. State Bar Assn., Wash. State Trial Lawyers Assn. Avocations: skiing, sailing, fishing, hunting, chess, reading. General corporate, Real property, Estate planning. Address: 11110 NE 38th Pl Bellevue WA 98004-7653

**SULLIVAN, JOHN ARTHUR,** lawyer; b. Everett, Mass.; s. Arthur and Dorothy (Duncan) S.; m. Carolyn Marie Mulvee, Apr. 26, 1969; children: Brian, Jennifer, Jessica. AB, Stonehill Coll., 1961; LLB, Suffolk Law Sch., 1967. Bar: Mass. 1967, U.S. Dist. Ct. Mass. 1969. Assoc. atty. Lane & Lane, Braintree, Mass., 1969-72; sole practice Braintree, Mass., 1972-78; ptnr. Shannon & Sullivan, Quincy, Mass., 1978-80; magistrate, clk. Plymouth (Mass.) Dist. Ct., 1980—. Pres. Mass. Mental Health Adv. Bd., Plymouth, 1993—; bd. dirs. High Point Treatment Ctr., Plymouth, 1996—; pres. Marshfield (Mass.) Capital Budget Com., 1984-90; Marshfield Rep. Com., 1992&. Roman Catholic. Avocations: painting, baseball, fishing. Office: Plymouth Dist Ct 7 S Russell St Plymouth MA 02360-7999

**SULLIVAN, JOHN CORNELIUS, JR.,** lawyer; b. Erie, Pa., Oct. 23, 1927; s. John Cornelius and Catherine J. (Carney) S.; m. Helen E. Kennedy, Feb. 3, 1951; children: John III, Timi Ann, Michael, Elizabeth. BA in Econs., Allegheny Coll., 1953; LLB, Dickinson Sch. Law, 1959. Bar: Pa. 1960, U.S. Supreme Ct. 1976. Sales rep. IBM Corp., 1953-56; mem. firm Nissley, Clecker & Fearen, Harrisburg, Pa., 1959-63; ptnr. Nauman, Smith, Shissler & Hall, Harrisburg, 1964—; asst. city solicitor City of Harrisburg, 1964-68, city solicitor, 1968-70; gen. counsel Harrisburg Redevel. Authority, 1964-68, Harrisburg Mcpl. Authority, 1964-87; solicitor Silver-Spring Twp., 1970-81; dir. accounts and fin. City of Harrisburg, 1963; mem. Pa. House of Reps., 1963-64. Assoc. editor Dickinson Law Rev., 1958-59; editor Dauphin County Reporter, 1961-63. Chmn. bd. dirs. Harrisburg Pub. Library, 1965-73; bd. dirs., sec. Harrisburg Hosp.; bd. dirs. Harrisburg Hosp. Found., 1975-89. Mem. ABA, Pa. Bar Assn., Dauphin County Bar Assn. (past. dir.), The Pa. Soc. (N.Y.C.), Phi Gamma Delta. Libel, Contracts commercial, Estate planning. Home: 107 Sample Bridge Rd Mechanicsburg PA 17055-1940 Office: 200 N 3rd St Fl D18 Harrisburg PA 17101-1518

**SULLIVAN, JOHN THOMAS, JR.,** lawyer; b. Oswego, N.Y., Feb. 27, 1947; s. John Thomas Sr. and Dorothy (Dashner) S.; m. Charlotte McQueen, Oct. 21, 1972; children: Kathleen, Julie, Danielle, Elizabeth. BA in Polit. Sci., SUNY, Oswego, 19p68; JD, Syracuse U., 1975. Bar: N.Y. 1976, U.S. Dist. Ct. (no. dist.) N.Y. 1976. Prin. Sullivan & Metcalf, Oswego; mem. Oswego County Legislature, 1972-76; sch. dist. atty. Oswego City Sch. Dist., 1981-88; mayor City of Oswego, 1988-91; city atty. City of Fulton, N.Y., 1995-97; asst. city atty. City of Oswego, 1998—; chmn. Oswego City Charter Revision Commn., 1976-77, mem. Citizens Adv. Coun. Internat. Commn., 1991-93, mem. Great Lakes Mayors' Conf. Com., 1988-91, chmn. environ. affairs com. N.Y. State Conf. Mayors, 1989-90. Exec. co-chair N.Y. State Dem. Com., 1995-98; founding mem. N.Y. State Dem. Rural Conf., 1995; co-chmn. N.Y. State Del. to 1996 Dem. Nat. Conv., 1996; mem. Assn. State Dem. Chairs, 1995-98; mem. Dem. Nat. Com., 1976-79; del. 5th Judicial Dist. Conv. 1973-95, Dem. Nat. Conv., 1972; candidate N.Y. State Assembly 117th Dist. 1974; mem. Heritage Found. Oswego. Named Oswego County Dem. of Yr., 1981, 88; selected commencement spkr. SUNY Oswego, 1997, Sheldon Hall re-dedication ceremony, 1998, keynote spkr. fall freshman convocation, 1989; recipient cert. appreciation People of Montserrat, 1989, Chancellor and Mems. SUNY Bd. Trustees, 1994, Oswego Rotary Club. Mem. N.Y. State Bar Assn., Oswego County Bar Assn., N.Y. State Workers Compensation Bar., Ancient Order Hibernians, Elks. Democrat. Roman Catholic. Avocations: racquetball, golf, music. Home: 59 W 5th St Oswego NY 13126-1527 Office: Sullivan & Metcalf 94 E Bridge St Oswego NY 13126-2203

**SULLIVAN, KATHIE JEAN,** library director, researcher, writer; b. Burlington, Vt., Mar. 6, 1955; d. Eugenia Lucille (Hayes) S. BS in Edn., U. Vt., 1977; MLS, SUNY, Albany, 1986. Cert. secondary English tchr., Vt. Tchr. English, Fair Haven (Vt.) Union H.S., 1977-80, Middlebury (Vt.) Union H.S., 1981-82; unit sec. Med. Ctr. Hosp. Vt., Burlington, 1980-81; tchr. lang. arts Castleton (Vt.) Jr. H.S., 1982-84; adult edn. tutor Southwestern Vt. Adult Basic Edn., Rutland, 1984-85; libr. dir. McNamee, Lochner, Titus & Williams, P.C., Albany, 1986-99; libr. Downs, Rachlin & Martin P.L.L.C., Burlington, Vt., 1999—. Contbr. articles and book revs. to profl. jours. Mem. Am. Assn. Law Librs. (editor newsletter column 1993-96, coun. chmn. 1994-95, com. chmn. 1995-96, vice chair Pvt. Law Libr. Spl. Interest Sect. 1998-99), Spl. Librs. Assn., Law Librs. New Eng., Assn. Law Librs. Upstate N.Y. (pres. 1994-95). E-mail: ksullivan@drm.com. Office: Downs Rachlin & Martin PLLC 199 Main St PO Box 190 Burlington VT 05402-0190

**SULLIVAN, KATHLEEN M.,** law educator. BA, Cornell U., 1976, Oxford (Eng.) U., 1978; JD, Harvard U., 1981. Law clk. Hon. James L. Oakes U.S. Ct. Appeals (2d cir.), 1981-82; pvt. practice, 1982-84; asst. prof. Harvard U., Cambridge, Mass., 1984-89; prof. Harvard U., Cambridge, 1989-93; prof. Stanford (Calif.) U., 1993—, Paradise fellow, 1995-96, Stanley Morrison prof., 1996—, dean, 1999—; vis. prov. U. So. Calif. Law Ctr., 1991, Stanford U., 1992; lectr., commentator on constnl. law. Co-editor: (with Gerald Gunter) Constitutional Law, 13th edit. Named one of 50 Top Women Lawyers Nat. Law Jour., 1998; recipient John Bingham Hurlbut awrad for excellence in tchg. Stanford U., 1996. Fellow Am. Acad. Arts and Scis. Office: Stanford U Law Sch 559 Nathan Abbott Way Stanford CA 94305-8602*

**SULLIVAN, KEVIN PATRICK,** lawyer; b. Waterbury, Conn., June 9, 1953; s. John Holian Sullivan and Frances (McGrath) Coon; m. Peggy Hardy, June 13, 1975 (div. Jan. 1985); m. Jarnine Welker, Feb. 15, 1985; children: S. Craig Lemmon, Michael Scott Lemmon, Lindsay Michelle Lemmon. BS in Polit. Sci., BS in Police Sci. cum laude, Weber State Coll., 1979; JD, Pepperdine U., 1982. Bar: Utah 1982, U.S. Dist. Ct. Utah 1982, U.S. Ct. Appeals (10th cir.) 1986, U.S. Supreme Ct. 1986. Assoc. Farr, Kaufman & Hamilton, Ogden, Utah, 1982-87; ptnr. Farr, Kaufman, Hamilton, Sulivan, Gorman & Perkins, Ogden, 1987-91, Farr, Kaufman, Sullivan, Gorman & Perkins, Ogden, 1991—; judge pro tem Utah 2d Cir. Ct.; city prosecutor of South Ogden, 1990-92. Mem. Eccles Community Art Ctr., Victim's Rights Com. of 2d Jud. Dist. Mem. ABA (criminal justice sect., litigation sect., justice and edn. fund lawyers' coun.), ACLU, ATLA, Utah Bar Assn. (criminal law, young lawyer, litigation sects., unauthorized practice law com.), Utah Trial Lawyers Assn., Utah Assn. Criminal Def. Lawyers, Weber County Bar Assn. (criminal law sect., pres.-elect 1993, pres. 1994), Weber County Pub. Defenders Assn. (assoc. dir. 1987), Weber State Coll. Alumni Assn., Amicus Pepperdine, Elks, Kiwanis, Phi Kappa Phi. Mem. LDS Ch. Avocations: skiing, golf, tennis, fishing. Criminal, Personal injury, State civil litigation. Home: 2731 E 6425 S Ogden UT 84403-5461 Office: Farr Kaufman Sullivan Gorman & Perkins 205 26th St Ste 34 Ogden UT 84401-3119

**SULLIVAN, MARY ANNE,** lawyer, government official. BA in Philosophy summa cum laude, Fordham U., 1973; JD, Yale U., 1976. Law clk. to Hon. Walter K. Stapleton U.S. Dist. Ct., Wilmington, Del., 1976-77; assoc. Hogan & Hartson, Washington, 1977-84, ptnr., 1985-94; dep. gen. counsel Environ. and Civilian and Def. Nuclear Programs, U.S. Dept. Energy, Washington, 1994-98; gen. counsel U.S. Dept. Energy, Washington, 1998—; instr. Lawyers Com. for Civil Rights; spkr. in field. Contbr. articles to profl. jours. Active Dem. Party, 1982—; sr. domestic issues advisr Geraldine Ferraro in Mondale Campaign; with debate prep. team Senator Bentsen in Dukakis Campaign; counsel to Clinton Campaign and Clinton/Gore Transition Team, 1992. FAX: 202-586-1499. Home: 2837 Twenty-ninth Pl NW Washington DC 20008 Office: US Dept Energy Gen Counsel Rm 6A-245 1000 Independence Ave SW Washington DC 20585-0001*

**SULLIVAN, MICHAEL D.,** lawyer; b. Chgo., Feb. 16, 1940; s. John J. and Tillie (Babel) S.; m. Irene A. Brandt. BBA cum laude, U. Notre Dame, 1962, JD, 1965. Bar: Ill. 1965, U.S. Dist. Ct. (no. dist.) Ill. 1966, U.S. Ct. Appeals (7th cir.) 1966, U.S. Tax Ct. 1967. Law clk. to judge U.S. Ct. Appeals (7th cir.), Chgo., 1965-66; assoc. Jenner & Block, Chgo., 1967-73; gen. atty. CMC & Chgo., Milw. R.R., 1974-78; gen. solicitor, corp. trustee property Chgo., Milw. R.R., Chgo., 1978-85; gen. solicitor Soo Line R.R., Chgo., 1985-86; pvt. practice River Forest, Ill.; atty. The Sullivan Firm, Ltd., Rolling Meadows, 1985—; counsel, bd. dirs. various orgns., Chgo., 1980-85. Mem. ABA, Ill. Bar Assn., Chgo. Bar Assn., N.W. Suburban Bar Assn. General corporate, Transportation, Taxation, general. Home: 739 Park Ave River Forest IL 60305-1705 Office: The Sullivan Firm Ltd 2550 Golf Rd Rolling Meadows IL 60008-4051

**SULLIVAN, MICHAEL DAVID,** state supreme court justice; b. Hattiesburg, Miss., Dec. 2, 1938; s. Curran W. and Mittie (Chambers) S.; m. Catherine Ainsworth Carter; children: David Paul, Rachel Michel, Margaret Elizabeth, Sarah Catherine. BS, U. So. Miss., 1960; JD, Tulane U., 1966; LLM in Jud. Process, U. Va., 1988. Atty. Hattiesburg, Miss., 1967-75; chancellor Miss. Chancery Ct. Dist. 10, 1975-84; justice Miss. Supreme Ct., Jackson, 1984-. Office: Mississippi Supreme Court Carroll Gartin Bldg 450 High St Jackson MS 39201-1006*

**SULLIVAN, MICHELLE CORNEJO,** lawyer; b. St. Louis, June 29, 1958; m. Dennis Keith Sullivan, May 18, 1985. BS, U. Calif., Berkeley, 1980; JD, U. Santa Clara, 1983. Bar: Calif., 1984; U.S. Dist. Ct. (no. dist.) Calif., 1984, (so. dist.) Calif., 1985; cert. family law specialist. Legal dept. Four-Phase Computers, Cupertino, Calif., 1984; asst. dist. atty. San Benito County, Hollister, Calif., 1984-85; assoc. Walters & Ward, Rancho Bernardo, Calif., 1986-87, Law Offices of Rebecca Prater, Carlsbad, Calif., 1987-88; pvt. practice Escondido and San Diego, Calif. Escondido, Calif., 1988—. Pres. Women in Networking, San Diego, 1987; western horse show judge Calif. State Horseman's Assn., 1985; mem. adv. com. San Diego Regional Conf. on Women, trustee, 1993-95. Recipient Law Faculty scholar U. Santa Clara, 1982-83. Mem. ABA, State Bar Assn., San Diego County Bar Assn. (cert. specialist), Bar Assn. No. San Diego County (chair family law sect. 1996-98, cert. specialist), Escondido Rotary Main Club, Rancho Bernardo C. of C. (amb. 1986-87), San Diego Trial Lawyers Assn. (family law sect.), Lawyers Club (v.p. 1988-89). Avocations: western horseback riding, golf, sailing, scuba diving. Family and matrimonial, Estate planning, Alternative dispute resolution. Office: 16486 Bernardo Center Dr San Diego CA 92128-2518

**SULLIVAN, MORTIMER ALLEN, JR.,** lawyer; b. Buffalo, Sept. 19, 1930; s. Mortimer Allen Sr. and Gertrude (Hinkley) S.; m. Maryanne Calella, Nov. 20, 1965; children: Mark Allen, Michael John. BA, U. Buffalo, 1954. Bar: N.Y. 1964, U.S. Dist. Ct. (we. dist.) N.Y. 1966, U.S. Dist. Ct. (no. dist.) N.Y. 1967, U.S. Supreme Ct. 1970. Counsel liability claims Interstate Motor Freight System, Grand Rapids, Mich., 1964-82; v.p. J.P.M. Sullivan, Inc., Elmira, N.Y., 1959-67; govt. appeal agt. U.S. Selective Service System, 1967-71; dep. sci. div. Erie County (N.Y.) Sheriff's Office, 1971—, lt., 1986—. Inventor (with others) in field; creator, dir. video depiction JudiVision, 1969; composer High Flight, 1983. Chmn. com. on Constn. and Canons Episcopal Diocese of Western N.Y., 1975-96; bd. dirs. Erie County Law Enforcement Found., Inc., 1987—; bd. dirs. Orchard Park (N.Y.) Symphony Orch., 1975-97, v.p., 1977-79, 91-94. With USAF, 1954-57; spl. agt. Air Force Office of Spl. Investigations, 1972-87, col. res. ret. Decorated Legion of Merit. Mem. Erie County Bar Assn. (chmn. law and tech. com., 1970-81), Transp. Lawyers Assn., Kappa Alpha Soc. Republican. Clubs: Saturn (Buffalo); Wanakah (N.Y.) Country. Avocation: aviation. General practice. Home: 19 Knob Hill Rd Orchard Park NY 14127-3917 Office: 88 S Davis St PO Box 1003 Orchard Park NY 14127-8003

**SULLIVAN, PETER THOMAS, III,** lawyer; b. Jersey City, Aug. 6, 1950; s. Peter T. Jr. and Daisy (Stallard) S.; m. Brenda J. Stanley, July 1, 1972 (div. 1980); children: Patrick, Margaret McGaw-Sullivan. BA, So. Ill. U., 1972; JD, DePaul U., 1976. Bar: Ill. 1976, U.S. Dist. Ct. (no. dist.) Ill. 1976, U.S. Ct. Appeals (7th ci.) 1982. Assoc. Thomas, Kostantacos & Traum, Rockford, Ill., 1976-77; atty. Pub. Defender's Office, Rockford, Ill., 1977-82; ptnr. Sreenan, Cain & Sullivan, Rockford, Ill., 1982-89; pvt. practice Pete Sullivan & Assocs., Rockford, Ill., 1989—. Mem. Assn. Trial Lawyers Am., Ill. Bar Assn., Ill. Trial Lawyers Assn. Democrat. Roman Catholic. Personal injury, Workers' compensation, Product liability. Office: Pete Sullivan & Assoc PC 134 N Main St Rockford IL 61101-1102

**SULLIVAN, ROBERT EMMET, JR.,** lawyer; b. Detroit, Oct. 2, 1955; s. Robert Emmet Sr. and Gloria Marie (Lamb) S. BA in Polit. Sci. and Sociology, Wayne State U., 1977; M Urban Planning, U. Mich., 1979; JD, U. Detroit, 1983; postgrad., Oxford (Eng.) U., 1981. Bar: Mich. 1984, U.S. Dist. Ct. (we. dist.) Mich. 1984, U.S. Dist. Ct. (ea. dist. ) Mich. 1984, U.S. Ct. Appeals (6th cir.) 1984, U.S. Ct. Appeal (D.C. cir.) 1984, U.S. Tax Ct. 1984, D.C. 1985, U.S. Supreme Ct. 1987. Planning commr. City of Detroit, 1982-85; shareholder Sullivan, Ward, Bone, Tyler & Asher, P.C., Detroit, 1984—; bd. dirs. Internat. Inst. of Met. Detroit. Contbr. articles to profl. jours. Active St. Scholastica Parish Ch., North Rosedale Park Civic Assn., Detroit Hist. Soc. Moffitt scholar, 1982, 83. Mem. AIA, Detroit Bar Assn., Mich. Soc. Planning Ofcls., Am. Inst. Cert. Planners. Roman Catholic. Land use and zoning (including planning), General civil litigation, Constitutional. Home: 7464 Wilshire West Bloomfield MI 48322-2875 Office: Sullivan Ward Bone Tyler & Asher 25800 Northwestern Hwy Southfield MI 48075-1000

**SULLIVAN, ROBERT F.,** mediator, lawyer; b. Buffalo, Aug. 10, 1956; s. John J. and Anna M. (Leahy) S.; m. Joanne M. Luker, Aug. 1, 1987; 1 child: Jack. BA, SUNY, Plattsburgh, 1980; JD, Syracuse U., 1988. Bar: N.Y. 1989. Assoc. atty. Groben, Gilroy, Oster & Saunders, Utica, N.Y., 1989-93, Nodell, Jones & Kendall, Hamilton, N.Y., 1993-95; coord. mediation prog. New Justice Conflict Resolution Svcs., Madison County, N.Y., 1996—. Mem. N.Y. State Bar Assn., Madison County Bar Assn. Home: 67 Hamilton St Hamilton NY 13346-1328 Office: New Justice Conflict Resolution Svcs PO Box 365 Oneida NY 13421-0365

**SULLIVAN, TERRANCE CHARLES,** lawyer; b. Neptune, N.J., Mar. 23, 1950; s. John Joseph and Marilyn Anne (DiBlasi) S.; m. Kathy Lavonne Collett, June 21, 1980; children: Jennifer Collett, Michael Charles, Cynthia Grace, Philip Gregory. *Maternal grandparent, Adolph DiBlasi, left Italy and emigrated to the United States through the port of New York at Ellis Island in 1898. Grandparent, Mary Tina Bissett (Sullivan), emigrated through Ellis Island in 1887 from Aberdeen, Scotland. Both were subsequently wed to American citizens.* BA, U. Ga., 1972; JD, U. Va., 1975. Bar: Ga. 1975. Assoc. Swift, Currie, McGhee & Hiers, Atlanta, 1975-77; assoc., ptnr. Phillips, Hart & Mozley, Atlanta, 1977-82; sr. ptnr. Hart & Sullivan, P.C., Atlanta, 1982-89, Sullivan, Hall, Booth & Smith, P.C., Atlanta, 1989-98, Butler, Wooten, Overby, Fryhofer, Daughtery and Sullivan, Atlanta, 1998—; bd. dirs. Atlanta Coun. Younger Lawyers, 1975-77. Contbr. articles on legal edn. to profl. jours. Bd. dirs. Murphey Candler Little League, 1997—; ass( .mem. deans coun. U. Va. Law Sch., 1993—. Capt. USAF Res., 1972-80. Fellow Am. Coll. Trial Lawyers, Am. Bd. Trial Advocate's; mem. ABA, State Bar Ga., Atlanta Bar Assn., Nat. Inst. Trial Advocacy, Atlanta Inst. Trial Advocacy (co-dir. 1986-88), Atlanta Lawyers Club, Trial Lawyers Assn. Am. (conf. speaker 1988), U. Ga. Nat. Alumni Assn. (bd. dirs. 1998—), Dekalb Med. Ctr., Medallion Soc. Roman Catholic. Fax: (404) 321-1713. Personal injury, Insurance, Health. Home: 3986 Fernway Ct NE Atlanta GA 30319-1667 Office: Butler Wooten Overby Fryhofer Daughtery and Sullivan 2719 Buford Hwy Atlanta GA 30324

**SULLIVAN, TERRY,** lawyer; b. Chgo., Sept. 19, 1943; s. John Joseph and Tillie (Babel) S. BA, St. Joseph's Coll., 1965; JD, Loyola U., Chgo., 1968. Bar: Ill., N.Y., U.S. Ct. Appeals (7th cir.). State atty. Cook County, Chgo., 1969-81; pvt. practice Chgo. and Rolling Meadows, Ill., 1981—; legal analyst WGN-TV, Chgo., 1994—. Author: Killer Clown, 1983. Mem. Irish Fellowship Club (bd. dirs. 1998—). Avocations: baseball, golf, preservation. Labor, General civil litigation, Criminal. Office: 2550 Golf Rd Rolling Meadows IL 60008-4051 also: 1800 N Hudson Ave Chicago IL 60614-5202

**SULLIVAN, WARREN GERALD,** business executive, lawyer; b. Chgo., Sept. 8, 1923; s. Gerald Joseph and Marie (Fairrington) S.; m. Helen Ruth Young, Aug. 21, 1948 (div.); children: Janet M., Douglas W., William C.; m. Helen Louise Curtis. BA, U. Ill., Urbana, 1947; JD, Northwestern U., 1950. Bar: Ill. 1950, Conn. 1971, Mo. 1981, U.S. Dist. Ct. (no. dist.) Ill. 1953, U.S. Dist. Ct. Conn. 1974, U.S. Ct. Appeals (7th cir.) 1955, U.S. Ct. Appeals (DC cir.) 1964, U.S. Ct. Appeals (6th cir.) 1966, U.S. Ct. Appeals (2nd cir.) 1974, U.S. Supreme Ct. 1968. Atty Ill. Dept. Revenue, Chgo., 1950-52; from assoc. to ptnr. Naphin, Sullivan & Banta and predecessors, 1952-69; personnel Avco Corp., Greenwich, Conn., 1969-75; v.p. indsl. rels. Gen. Dynamics Corp., St. Louis, 1975-84; mgmt. cons., 1984—. Author: Contbr. Articles to Profl. Jours. Bd. dirs. YMCA Greater St. Louis. 1st lt., 1949-54. Fellow Col.. Labor and Employment Lawyers (emeritus); mem. ABA, Conn. Bar Assn., Chgo. Bar Assn. (past chmn. labor law com.), Mo. Bar Assn., Bellerive Country (Creve Coeur, Mo.), St. Louis (Clayton, Mo.), Delta Tau Delta, Phi Delta Phi. Labor. Office: 410 N Newstead Ave Apt 11S Saint Louis MO 63108-2641

**SULLIVAN, WILLIAM J.,** state supreme court justice. Justice Conn. Superior Ct., 1978-97; judge Conn. Appellate Ct., 1997-99; assoc. justice Conn. Supreme Ct., 1999—. Office: Conn Supreme Ct Supreme Ct Bldg 231 Capitol Ave Hartford CT 06106*

**SULLY, IRA BENNETT,** lawyer; b. Columbus, Ohio, June 3, 1947; s. Bernie and Helen Mildred (Koen) S.; m. Nancy Lee Pryor, Oct. 2, 1983. B.A. cum laude, Ohio State U., 1969, J.D. summa cum laude, 1974. Bar: Ohio 1974, U.S. Dist. Ct. (so. dist.) Ohio 1974. Assoc. Schottenstein, Garel, Swedlow & Zox, Columbus, 1974-78; atty. Borden Inc., Columbus, 1978-80; sole practice, Columbus, 1980—; instr. Real Estate Law Columbus Tech. Inst., 1983-88; title ins. agt. Sycamore Title Agy., Columbus, 1983—. Active Ohio Dem. Bldg. Com., 1995-98; commentator Sta. WOSU, Columbus, 1980; bd. trustees Ohio State U. Undergrad. Student Govt. Alumni Assn., 1997—. Treas. Leland for State Rep., Columbus, 1982, 84, Leland for City Atty., Columbus, 1985; asst. treas. Pamela Conrad for City Council, Columbus, 1979; bd. dirs. Research Franklin County Celeste for Gov., Columbus, 1978. Mem. Columbus Bar Assn., Ohio Bar Assn., ABA. Democrat. Jewish. Club: Agonis (Columbus). Avocations: running, coin collecting. Real property, Probate, Contracts commercial. Home: 200 Reinhard Ave Columbus OH 43206-2616 Office: 844 S Front St Columbus OH 43206-2543

**SULTAN, FREDERICK WILLIAM, IV,** lawyer; b. Houston, Jan. 8, 1971; s. Frederick William Sultan III and Brenda Gay Caffey Johnson. BA, Rice U., 1993; JD, U. Tex., 1996. Bar: Tex. 1996. Briefing atty. Ct. Appeals 3rd Dist. Tex., Austin, 1996-97; atty. Clark, Thomas & Winters, Austin, 1997—. Editor-in-chief Am. Jour. Criminal Law, 1995-96. General civil litigation, Appellate. Home: 1506 Wilshire Blvd Austin TX 78722-1130 Office: Clark Thomas & Winters 700 Lavaca St Ste 1200 Austin TX 78701-3102

**SULTAN, JAMES LEHMAN,** lawyer; b. New Haven, Oct. 10, 1953; s. Stanley Ezra Sultan and Florence Lehman Nichols; m. Rosemarie Cardillicchio, July 19, 1992; 1 child, Gabriel. BA, Yale U., 1974; JD, Harvard U., 1980. Bar: Mass. 1980, U.S. Dist. Ct. Mass. 1981, U.S. Ct. Appeals (1st cir.) 1981, U.S. Supreme Ct. 1989. Legis. asst. U.S. Rep. Robert F. Drinan, Washington, 1974-77; law clk. to William Wayne Justice U.S. Dist. Ct., Tyler, Tex., 1980-81; assoc. Silvergate, Shapiro & Gertner, Boston, 1981-82; pvt. practice Boston, 1982-86; ptnr. Rankin & Sultan, Boston, 1986—; lectr. profl. seminars, 1987—. Contbr. (book) Massachusetts Criminal Law, 1990. Mem. Nat. Assn. Criminal Def. Lawyers. Criminal. Office: Rankin & Sultan 1 Comml Wharf North Boston MA 02110

**SULTANIK, JEFFREY TED,** lawyer; b. N.Y.C., July 26, 1954; s. Solomon and Anna (Tiger) S.; m. Judith Ann Clyman, Nov. 14, 1981; children: Evan A., Sara A. BA cum laude, U. Pa., Phila., 1976; JD, Hofstra U., 1979. Bar: Pa. 1979, Fla. 1980, U.S. Dist. Ct. (ea. dist.) Pa., U.S. Ct. Appeals (3d cir.). Ptnr. Fox, Rothschild, O'Brien & Frankel, L.L.P., Lansdale, Pa., 1979-81; solicitor Upper Merion Sch. Dist., 1995—; solicitor Boyertown (Pa.) Area Sch. Dist., 1981—, Perkiomen Valley Sch. Dist., Rahns, Pa., 1983—, North Montco Vocat.-Tech. Sch., Lansdale, 1981—, Souderton (Pa.) Area Sch. Dist., 1989—, Wallingford-Swarthmore Sch. Dist., 1999—; spl. counsel Penn Delco Sch. Dist., Aston, Pa., Coun. Rock Sch. Dist., Newtown, Pa., 1998, Kennett Consolidated Sch. Dist., 1999—, Colonial Sch. Dist., 1996—; chair pers. com., mktg./admissions com., sec. bd. trustees Germantown Acad., Ft. Washington, Pa., 1991—; presenter Coun. Sch. Attys., Anaheim, Calif., 1997. Regular columnist Your School and the Law, 1992. Mem. Nat. Orgn. Legal Problems of Edn., Nat. Assn. Sch. and Coll. Attys., Pa. Sch. Bds. Assn., Inc. (continuing edn. in sch. law award 1990, sch. mgmt. in-svc. edn. award 1985), Pa. Assn. Sch. Bus. Ofcls. (cert. of appreciation 1991), Pa. Bar Assn. (labor and edn. sects.), Montgomery County Bar Assn. (mcpl. law com. 1983—), Lehigh U. Law Forums, Assn. Del. Valley Ind. Schs. Republican. Jewish. Avocations: automobiles, travel. E-mail: jsultanik@frof.com. Education and schools, Labor, Municipal (including bonds). Home: 2056 Spring Valley Rd Lansdale PA 19446-5114 Office: Fox Rothschild O'Brien & Frankel LLP 1250 S Broad St Ste 1000 Lansdale PA 19446-5343

**SULTON, ANNE THOMAS,** lawyer, criminologist; b. Racine, Wis., Oct. 24, 1952; d. William Henry and Esther (Phillips) Thomas; m. James E. Sulton Jr., Aug. 1, 1981; children: James E. III, William Francis, Patrice Amandla. BA in Psychology, Wash. State U., 1973; MA in Criminal Justice, SUNY, 1975; PhD in Criminal Justice, U. Md., 1984; JD, U. Wis., 1985. Bar: Wis. 1985, U.S. Dist. Ct. (we. dist.) Wis. 1985, Colo. 1993, U.S. Dist. Ct. Colo. 1994, U.S. Ct. Appeals (7th cir.) 1995, U.S. Ct. Appeals (10th cir.) 1996. Instr. criminal justice and criminology Spelman Coll., Atlanta, 1976-78; rsch. assoc. Nat. Orgn. Black Law Enforcement Execs., Balt., 1978-80; lectr. criminal justice and criminology Howard U., Washington, 1980-84; asst. prof. criminal justice U. Wis., Oshkosh, 1984-85; project dir. Police Found., Washington, 1985-87; pvt. practice law Madison, Wis., 1985—, Englewood, Colo., 1993—; dir. grad. criminal justice program U. Balt.; former instr. Atlanta U., Atlanta Fed. Penitentiary, Md. State Penitentiary, Balt. City Police Tng. Acad., Inst. Criminal Justice and Criminology, U. Md., Taycheeda Correctional Instn. for Women, Century 21 Sch. Real Estate; presenter, spkr., facilitator in field; numerous TV and radio appearances. Contbr. articles to various publs., poetry to books, mags. and newspapers. Bd. dirs. Washington Halfway Home for Women, 1983; pres. bd. dirs. Willard Thomas Scholarship Found., Inc., Racine, Wis., 1973—, South Madison Neighborhood Ctr., 1987-88; mem. allocations panel on un- and underemployment United Way Dane County, 1987-88; spokesperson Coalition African-Am. Orgns., Madison, 1987-88, legal counsel NAACP Madison chpt., 1989-90, Denver chpt., 1994—. Recipient cert. Atlanta Commr. Pub. Safety, 1977, Outsdanding Citizen award Fulton County Commr.'s Office, 1977, cert. of appreciation Atlanta Crime Analysis Team, 1978; named to Washington Park High Sch. Hall of Fame, 1986; recipient Spl. Friend award Atlanta Fed. Penitentiary Bd., NAACP, 1978. Mem. NAACP, ABA, Wis. Bar Assn., Nat. African-Am. Braintrust on Criminal

Justice and Criminology, Police Exec. Rsch. Forum. Avocation: flying small aircraft. Non-profit and tax-exempt organizations, Civil rights.

**SUMBLIN, ANNE STONE,** lawyer; b. Bay Minette, Ala., Nov. 14, 1960; d. Norborne Clarke and Patricia (Bartlett) Stone; m. Martin Anthony Sumblin, Nov. 16, 1996. BS in Acctg., U. Ala., 1983, JD, 1987. Bar: Ala. 1987. Law clk. to Hon. Sam C. Pointer, Jr., U.S. Dist. Ct. for No. Dist. Ala., 1987-88; Ptnr. Walston, Wells, Anderson & Bains, L.L.P., Birmingham, Ala., 1995—; bd. dirs. U. Ala. Sch. of Law Found., 1997—;. Mem. Ala. State Bar Assn. Home: 405 Hwy 52 Kinston AL 36453 Office: Walston Wells Anderson & Bains LLP PO Box 345 Kinston AL 36453-0345

**SUMIDA, GERALD AQUINAS,** lawyer; b. Hilo, Hawaii, June 19, 1944; s. Sadamy and Kimiyo (Miyahara) S. AB summa cum laude, Princeton U., 1966; JD, Yale U., 1969. Bar: Hawaii 1970, U.S. Dist. Ct. Hawaii 1970, U.S. Ct. Appeals (9th cir.) 1970, U.S. Supreme Ct. 1981. Rsch. assoc. Ctr. Internat. Studies, Princeton U., 1969; assoc. Carlsmith, Ball, Honolulu, 1970-76, ptnr., 1976—; mem. cameras in courtroom evaluation com. Hawaii Supreme Ct., 1984-86. Co-author: (with others) Legal, Instutional and Financial Aspects of An Inter-Island Electrical Transmission Cable, 1984, Alternative Approaches to the Legal, Instutional and Financial Aspects of Developing an Inter-Island, Electrical Transmission Cable System, 1986; editor Hawaii Bar News, 1972-73; contbr. chpts. to books. Mem. sci. and statis. com. Western Pacific Fishery Mgmt. Coun., 1979—; mem. study group on law of armed conflict and the law of the sea Comdr. in Chief Pacific, USN, 1979-82; chmn. Pacific and Asian Affairs Coun. Hawaii, 1991, pres., 1982-91, bd. givs., 1976-96; bd. govs. ARC, 1994—, mem. exec. com., 1996—, chmn. human resources com., 1996—, chmn. Hawaii chpt., 1983—, bd. dirs., 1983—, vice chmn., 1990—; chmn. Hawaii C. of C., 1997-98, bd. dirs., 1990-99; vice chmn. Honolulu Com. Fgn. Rels., 1983—; pres., dir., founding mem. Hawaii Ocean Law Assn., 1978—; mem. Hawaii Adv. Group for Lawof Sea Inst., 1977—; pres. Hawaii Inst. Continuing Legal Edn., 1979-83, dir., 1976-87; pres., founding mem. Hawaii Coun. Legal Edn. Youth, 1980-83, dir., 1983-88; chmn. Hawaii Commn. Yr. 2000, 1976-79; mem. Honolulu Cmty. Media Coun., 1976—, exec. com., 1976-84, legal coun., 1979-83; bd. dirs. Hawaii Imin Centennial Corp., 1983-90, Hawaii Pub. Radio, 1983-88, Legal Aid Soc. Hawaii, 1984; founding gov., exec. v.p., chmn. rules and procedures Ctr. Internat. Comml. Dispute Resolution, 1987—; exec. com. Pacific Aerospace Mus., 1991—; exec. com. Pacific Islands Assn., 1988—; exec. com. Asia-Pacific Ctr. Res. Internat. Bus. Disputes, 1991-95; mem. Coun. Asia-Pacific Dispute Rsch. Ctrs., 1991-95; bd. dirs. U.S. C. of C., 1998—; mem. Pacific Basin Fireman's Coun., 1993—; mem. mgmt. com. PBEC-U.S. Nat. Com., 1994—. Recipient cert. of appreciation Gov. of Hawaii, 1979, resolutions of appreciation Hawaii Senate and Ho. of Reps., 1979; grantee Japan Found., 1979. Mem. ABA, Hawaii Bar Assn. (pres. young lawyers sect. 1974, v.p. 1984), Japan-Hawaii Lawyers Assn., Am. Soc. Internat. Law, Internat. Bar Assn., Am. Judicature Soc., , Inter-Pacific Bar Assn., Internat. Law Assn., Yale Club (N.Y.C.), Plaza Club (Honolulu), Colonial Club (Princeton). Democrat. Administrative and regulatory, General corporate, Private international. Home: 1130 Wilder Ave Apt 1401 Honolulu HI 96822-2755 also: Carlsmith Ball 1001 Bishop Pacific Tower #2200 Honolulu HI 96813

**SUMIDA, KEVIN P.H.,** lawyer; b. Honolulu, Feb. 14, 1954; s. William H. and Dorothy A. (Iwamoto) S. BA in Philosphy, Case Western Res. U., 1976; JD, U. Pa., 1979. Bar: Hawaii 1979, U.S. Ct. Appeals (9th cir.) 1981. Assoc. Fong & Miho, Honolulu, 1979-81; law clk. to hon. judge Harold M. Fong U.S. Dist. Ct., Honolulu, 1981-82; assoc. Matsui & Chung, Honolulu, 1982-89; ptnr. Matsui Chung Sumida & Chang, Honolulu, 1989—. Bd. dirs., officer Farrington Alumni and Community Found., Honolulu, 1980—. Mem. ABA (litigation sect., tort and ins. practice sect.), Hawaii Bar Assn. Avocation: music. General civil litigation, Insurance, Personal injury. Office: Matsui Chung Sumida & Chang 737 Bishop St Ste 1490 Honolulu HI 96813-3205

**SUMMER, FRED A.,** lawyer; b. Columbus, Ohio, June 27, 1946; s. Joseph A. and Judith L. Summer; s. Sandra Erkis, Dec. 20, 1968; children: Samantha J., Joshua A., Jeremy. AB cum laude, Harvard U., 1968; JD magna cum laude, U. Mich., 1973. Bar: Ohio 1973. Assoc. Murphey, Young & Smith, Columbus, 1974-80, ptnr., 1980-88; ptnr. Squire, Sanders & Dempsey LLP, Columbus, 1988-94, of counsel, 1994—. Pres. Temple Israel, Columbus, 1991-93. Served with U.S. Army, 1968-70, Viet Nam. Mem. ABA, Ohio State Bar Assn., Columbus Bar Assn., Order of Coif. Avocations: reading, bike riding, photography, music. Securities, General corporate, Finance. Office: Squire Sanders & Dempsey 41 S High St Columbus OH 43215-6101

**SUMMERS, ALICIA LEHNES,** lawyer; b. Trenton, N.J., July 21, 1964; d. James Valentine and Alice Elizabeth Lehnes; m. Michael Eugene Summers, Nov. 26, 1994; children: Matthew Ryan, Nicholas Andrew. BA, Furman U., 1986; JD, Washington & Lee U., 1989. Bar: Va. 1989. Atty. Moshos & Byrd, Fairfax, Va., 1989-91, Trichilo, Bancroft et al, Fairfax, Va., 1991-96, David West & Assocs., Alexandria, Va., 1996—. Mem. Va. Assn. Def. Attys., Fairfax Bar Assn. Insurance, Personal injury. Office: David West & Assocs 5285 Shawnee Rd Ste 110 Alexandria VA 22312-2328

**SUMMERS, CLYDE WILSON,** law educator; b. Grass Range, Mont., Nov. 21, 1918; s. Carl Douglas and Anna Lois (Yontz) S.; m. Evelyn Marie Wahlgren, Aug. 30, 1947; children: Mark, Erica, Craig, Lisa. BS, U. Ill., 1939, JD, 1942, LLD, 1998; LLM, Columbia U., 1946, JSD, 1952; LL.D., U. Leuven, Belgium, 1967, U. Stockholm, 1978. Bar: N.Y. 1951. Mem. law faculty U. Toledo, 1942-49, U. Buffalo, 1949-56; prof. law Yale U., New Haven, Conn., 1956-66, Garver prof. law, 1966-75; Jefferson B. Fordham prof. law U. Pa., 1975-90, prof. emeritus, 1990—; Hearing examiner Conn. Commn. on Civil Rights, 1963-71. Co-author: Labor Cases and Material, 1968, 2d edit., 1982, Rights of Union Members, 1979, Legal Protection for the Individual Employee, 1989, 2d edit., 1995; co-editor: Labor Relations and the Law, 1953, Employment Relations and the Law, 1959, Comparative Labor Law Jour., 1984-97. Chmn. Gov.'s Com. on Improper Union Mgmt. Practices N.Y. State, 1957-58; chmn. Conn. Adv. Council on Unemployment Ins. and Employment Service, 1960-72; mem. Conn. Labor Relations Bd., 1966-70, Conn. Bd. Mediation and Arbitration, 1964-72. Guggenheim fellow, 1955-56; Ford fellow, 1963-64; German-Marshall fellow, 1977-78; NEH fellow, 1977-78, Fullbright fellow, 1984-85. Mem. Nat. Acad. Arbitrators, Am. Arbitration Assn. (nat. chmn.), Internat. Soc. Labor Law and Social Legislation. Congregationalist. Home: 753 N 26th St Philadelphia PA 19130-2429 Office: U Pa Sch Law 3400 Chestnut St Philadelphia PA 19104-6204

**SUMMERS, HARDY,** state supreme court justice; b. Muskogee, Okla., July 15, 1933; s. Cleon A. and Fern H. Summers; m. Marilyn, Mar. 16, 1963; children: Julia Clare, Andrew Murray. BA, U. Okla., 1955, LLB, 1957. Asst. county atty. Muskogee County, 1960-62; pvt. practice law Muskogee, 1962-76; dist. judge 15th dist. Okla. Dist. Ct., 1976-85; justice Okla. Supreme Ct., Oklahoma City, 1985-99, chief justice, 1999—. Sec. Muskogee County Election Bd., 1965-72. Capt. JAGC, USAF, 1957-62. Mem. ABA, Okla. Bar Assn., Okla. Jud. Conf. (pres. 1984). Avocations: outdoor sports, music. Office: Okla Supreme Ct State Capital Bldg Rm 242 Oklahoma City OK 73105

**SUMMERS, JAMES BRANSON,** lawyer; b. Memphis, Sept. 18, 1950; s. James Mouzon and Marie (Jackson) S.; m. Deborah Ann Lambert, May 8, 1981; children: James W., Sarah Elizabeth. Student, U. Va.; BS in Fin., U. Tenn., Knoxville, 1973; JD, Memphis State U., 1976. Bar: Tenn. 1976; cert. Rule 31 mediator, civil trial specialist. Assoc. Neely Green Fargarson Brooke, Memphis, 1976-85, ptnr., 1985—; cons. playground safety, Memphis, 1988—. Assoc. editor Memphis State U. Law Jour., 1974-76; author/editor newsletter Tenn. Commentary, 1989-93, Report From Counsel, 1994—. Mem. exec. bd. Chicasaw Coun. Boys Scouts Am. Mem. ABA, Am. Law Firm Assn.-Practice Groups (labor and employment products liability transp.), Tenn. Bar Assn., Memphis Bar Assn., Shelby County Bar Assn. (sec. bd. govs. 1978-79, chmn. press liaison com. 1979), Tenn. Trial Lawyers Assn., Tenn. Def. Lawyers Assn., Def. Rsch. Inst. (cert. rule 31 fed. ct. mediator, Tenn. Supreme Ct. approved mediator, Nat. Bd. of Trial Advocacy civil trial specialist), Rotary Club Internat., Delta Theta Phi. Mem. Disciples of Christ Ch. Avocations: travel, writing, golf, computers. E-mail: jsummers@neelygreen.com. General civil litigation, Labor, Product liability. Office: Neely Green Fargarson Brooke & Summers 65 Union Ave Ste 900 Memphis TN 38103-5128

**SUMMERS, PAUL,** state attorney general; b. Sioux Falls, S.D.. BS, Miss. State U.; JD, U. Tenn. Dist. atty. gen. 25th Jud. Dist., Nashville, 1982-90; judge Ct. of Criminal Appeals, Nashville, 1990-99; atty. gen. State of tenn., Nashville, 1999—; adj. prof. law U. Memphis; former adj. faculty Cumberland U.; pres. elect, Tenn. Dist. Atty.'s Gen. Conf.; lectr. in field. Former mem. Tenn. Sentencing Commn.; col. Tenn. Army N.S. With USAF. Mem. Tenn. Bar Assn. (former gov.), Tenn. Dist. Attys. Gen. Conf. (pres.), on Court of Criminal Appeals, 1990—. Avocations: racquetball, rollerblading, karate (black belt). Office: Office of the Attorney General 500 Charlotte Ave Nashville TN 37243-1401*

**SUMMERS, THOMAS CAREY,** lawyer; b. Frederick, Md., Feb. 9, 1956; s. Harold Thomas and Doris Jean (Culler) S.; m. Robin Ann Stalnaker, May 12, 1990; children: Kristin, Heather, Lindsay. BA, Dickinson Coll., 1978; JD, U. Balt., 1981. Bar: Md. 1981, U.S. Dist. Ct. Md. 1981, D.C. 1986. Assoc. Ellin & Baker, Balt., 1979-89, Peter G. Angelos, Balt., Md., 1989—; adj. prof. law U. Balt. Sch. of Law. Mem. ABA, Md. State Bar Assn., Md. Trial Lawyers Assn. Democrat. Lutheran. Avocation: golf. Personal injury, Professional liability, State civil litigation. Office: Law Offices of P G Angelos One Charles Ctr Baltimore MD 21201

**SUMMERS-POWELL, ALAN,** lawyer. BA, Yale Coll., 1985; JD, U. Pa., 1988. Bar: N.Y. 1989, N.J. 1989, U.S. Dist. Ct. (fed. dist.) N.J. 1989, D.C. 1990, Fla. 1993, U.S. Dist. Ct. (mid. dist.) Fla. 1996, U.S. Ct. Appeals (11th cir.) 1996, U.S. Tax Ct. 1997. Pvt. practice Palm Harbor, Fla.; chmn. David Leasing and Devel., Inc. Bankruptcy, Consumer commercial, Probate. Office: PO Box 6043 Palm Harbor FL 34684-0643

**SUMNER, JAMES DUPRE, JR.,** lawyer, educator; b. Spartanburg, S.C., Nov. 30, 1919; s. James DuPre and Frances Grace (Harris) S.; m. Evvie Lucille Beach, Apr. 1, 1945 (dec.); children: Chery Erline (Mrs. Horacek), James DuPre III; m. Doris Kaiser Malloy, Oct. 20, 1972; children: John L. Malloy III, Mary Margaret Malloy, Kenneth S. Malloy, James M. Malloy. AB, Wofford Coll., 1941, LLB, U. Va., 1949; LLM, Yale U., 1952, JSD, 1955. Bar: Va. 1948, Calif. 1957. Practice law Los Angeles, 1957—; instr. law U. S.C., 1949-52; assoc. prof. UCLA, 1952-55, prof., 1955—; distinguished vis. prof. Instituto Luigi Sturzo, Rome, 1959; vis. prof. U. Tex., 1962, U. So. Calif., 1971; lectr. Calif. Bar Rev. Co-author: An Anatomy of Legal Education; contbr. articles to profl. jours. Lt. col. inf. AUS, 1941-46, ETO. Decorated Silver Star, Purple Heart with oak leaf cluster. Mem. Calif. Bar Assn., Va. Bar Assn., Westwood Village Bar Assn. (pres.), Rotary (pres. Westwood Village chpt.), L.A. Country Club, Braemar Country Club, Bel Air Assn. (bd. dirs.), Westwood Village Sertoma Club (pres.), Marrakesh Golf Club, Sertoma (pres.). Republican. Methodist. Home: 10513 Rocca Pl Los Angeles CA 90077-2904

**SUMPTER, DENNIS RAY,** lawyer, construction company executive; b. Lake Charles, La., Apr. 26, 1948; s. Griffin Ray and Winnie Marie (Vincent) S.; m. Brenda Sue Waite, June 8, 1968; children: Leslie, Stephanie. JD, La. State U., 1975; BA in Government, McNeese U., 1981. U.S. Dist. Ct. (we. dist.) La., U.S. Ct. Appeals (5th cir.). Atty. Sumpter Law Offices, Sulphur, La., 1976—; mayor City of Sulphur, 1978-90; judge ad hoc Sulphur City Ct., 1980; mem. La. Commn. for Law Enforcement, Baton Rouge, 1985-86; constrn. co. exec., 1988-94. Pres. La. Mcpl. Assn., State of La., 1985-86, bd. dirs., 1980-90; vice chmn. bd. dirs. West Calcasieu Airport, Sulphur, 1986-92. SSgt. USAF, 1967-71, Vietnam. Mem. La. Bar Assn., La. Trial Lawyers, S.W. La. Bar Assn. (ethics com., 1978), S.W. La. Trial Lawyers, Nat. Coll. Advocacy Trial Advocate, La. High Sch. Rodeo Assn. (v.p., pres.). Real property, Personal injury, General corporate. Address: 2713 Maplewood Dr Sulphur LA 70663-6109

**SUN, RAYMOND CHI-CHUNG,** lawyer; b. Singapore, Nov. 1, 1963; came to U.S., 1977.; BS in Computer Sci., UCLA, 1985; JD, U. So. Calif., 1988. Bar: Calif. 1988, U.S. Ct. Appeals (9th cir.) 1988, U.S. Dist. Ct. (cen. dist.) Calif. 1989, U.S. Patent and Trademark Office 1992. Assoc. Spensley Horn Jubas and Lubitz, L.A., 1987-92; counsel Baxter Internat., 1992-95; prin. Sun & Ho, Tustin, Calif., 1995-98. Avocations: chess, golf, wine. Patent, Trademark and copyright, Computer. Office: Sun & Ho 12420 Woodhall Way Tustin CA 92782-1165

**SUNDAR, VIJENDRA,** lawyer educator; b. Nausori, Rewa, Fiji Islands, Oct. 27, 1940; came to U.S., 1966; s. Bisu R. and Pran Pati Sundar; m. Lynette Sue Schmid, June 13, 1987; children: Jesse Christopher Mikaele, Eric Lynn Kalani, Christina Elizabeth Ululani. BBA in Mktg., U. Hawaii, 1976; JD, Antioch U., 1979. Bar: U.S. Ct. Mil. Appeals 1983, Omaha Tribal Ct. 1983, U.S. Trust Ter. of Pacific 1983. Co-owner, mgr. Rewa Ice & Aerated Water Factory, Rewa Lodge & Cafe, Nausori, Fiji Islands, 1962-67; coord., instr. Pacific and Asia Linguistics Inst., Honolulu, 1968, Univ. Hawaii, Peace Corps Ctrs., 1968-98; paralegal Puget Sound Legal Asst. Found., Tacoma, Wash., 1975-76; atty., rschr. Inst. for Law and Rsch., Washington, 1980-81; atty. Legal Aid Soc., Inc., Omaha, 1982-84, Multnomah County Legal Aid Svcs., Inc., Portland, Oreg., 1984-85; instr. Platt Coll., Jefferson City, Mo., 1986-88; acting dir., vis. asst. prof. Columbia Coll., Columbia, Mo., 1989; acad. & legal cons., 1990-92; owner, operator, businessman Fairview Motel, Kemmerer, Wyo., 1996—. Town councillor Nausori (Fiji Islands) Town Coun., 1965-68; bd. dirs. Improvement Means People Allied for Change Together, Omaha, 1983-84; commn. mem. com. welfare of farm workers, 1985; parliamentarian, bd. dirs. Am. Indian Ctr., Omaha, 1983-84. Reginald Heber Smith Ctmty. Lawyer fellow Howard Univ., 1984-85. Mem. ABA. Avocations: swimming, fishing, traveling, cooking, acting. Address: PO Box 367 Kemmerer WY 83101-0367

**SUNDBY, CONNIE L.,** paralegal; b. Minot, N.D., Oct. 4, 1955; d. Christ and Geraldine Schatz; m. Ed Sundby, Oct. 26, 1974; children: Ty J., Cody L. Student, Nat. Coll., Rapid City, S.D., 1973-74. Legal asst. Winkjer Law Firm, Williston, N.D., 1974-93, Schmitz Law Firm, Williston, 1993-95, McGee Hankla Backes & Dobrovolny, P.C., Minot, N.D., 1995—. Bd. dirs. N.D. Legal Assts. Task Force, 1994-96. Mem. ATLA (Paralegal divsn.), Nat. Assn. Legal Assts. (cert. legal asst., Affiliates award 1998), Western Dakota Assn. Legal Assts. (pres. 1994-96). Lutheran. Avocations: riding motorcycles, gardening, cooking, rodeo. Home: 1615 11th St SW Minot ND 58701-6155 Office: McGee Hankla Backes & Dobrovolny 15 2d Ave SW #305 Minot ND 58702

**SUNDERMEYER, MICHAEL S.,** lawyer; b. Kansas City, Mo., Feb. 8, 1951; s. Edgar W. and Ruth (Shobe) S.; m. Susan Talarico; children: Kim Marie, Mark Shobe. BA, U. Kans., 1973; JD, U. Va., 1976. Bar: D.C., Md., Va., U.S. Dist. Ct. D.C., U.S. Dist. Ct. Md., U.S. Dist. Ct. (ea. dist.) Va., U.S. Ct. Appeals (D.C. cir.), U.S. Ct. Appeals (4th cir.), U.S. Ct. Appeals (5th cir.). Law clk. to Hon. John Minor Wisdom U.S. Ct. Appeals (5th cir.), New Orleans, 1976-77; law clk. to Hon. Harry A. Blackmun U.S. Supreme Ct., Washington, 1977-78; assoc. Williams & Connolly, Washington, 1978-84, ptnr., 1985—. Editor-in-chief Va. Law Rev., 1975-76. Mem. ABA. Administrative and regulatory, Federal civil litigation, Criminal. Office: Williams & Connolly 725 12th St NW Washington DC 20005-5901

**SUNDVALL, SHEILA A.,** lawyer; b. Cleve., Jan. 21, 1963. BA, U. Mich., 1985, JD, 1988. Bar: Ill. 1988, U.S. Dist. Ct. (no. dist.) Ill. 1988, U.S. Ct. Appeals (7th cir.) 1989. Jud. clk. judge Richard D. Cudahy U.S. Ct. Appeals 7th Cir., Chgo., 1988-89; assoc. Sidley & Austin, Chgo., 1989-96, ptnr., 1996—; lectr. in field. Mem. Legal Club Chgo., Phi Beta Kappa, Order of Coif. Aviation, General civil litigation, Product liability. Office: Sidley & Austin 1 First Natl Plz Chicago IL 60603-2003

**SUNG, LAWRENCE M.,** lawyer, educator; b. Montreal, Que., Oct. 18, 1965; s. Cheng-po Sung and Chiu-Mei Chung. BA in Biology, U. Pa., 1985; PhD in Microbiology, Uniformed Svcs. Health U., 1990; JD, Am. U., 1993. Bar. Pa. 1993, D.C. 1994, U.S. Patent Office 1994. Jud. clk. U.S. Ct. Appeals (fed. cir.), 1993-95; assoc. Foley & Lardner, Washington, 1995-98; of counsel Arter & Hadden, L.L.P., Washington, 1998—; lectr. Am. U. Coll. Law, Washington, 1995—; prof. law George Washington U., 1996—. Contbr. articles to law jours. and newspapers. Mem. ABA, Am. Intellectual Property Law Assn., Am. Soc. Microbiology. Fax: 202-857-0172. E-mail: LSung@arterhadden.com. Patent, Intellectual property, Federal civil litigation. Office: Arter & Hadden LLP 1801 K St NW Ste 400K Washington DC 20006-1301

**SUOJANEN, WAYNE WILLIAM,** lawyer; b. Salem, Oreg., July 5, 1950. BA, Northwestern U., 1972; SM, MIT, 1974, PhD, 1977; JD, U. Pa., 1980. Bar: Pa. 1980, Calif. 1997. Assoc. Pepper, Hamilton & Scheetz, Phila., 1980-84; assoc. Hoyle, Morris & Kerr, Phila., 1985-88, ptnr., 1988-97; assoc. Kasdan, Simonds, McIntyre, Epstein & Martin, Irvine, Calif., 1997—. Contbr. chpt. to textbook, 1990. Joseph Scanlon fellow MIT, 1974-75. Mem. ABA, Pa. Bar Assn., State Bar of Calif., Phila. Bar Assn., Orange County Bar Assn., Am. Concrete Inst., Indsl. Rels. Rsch. Assn. Construction, Toxic tort, Product liability. Home: 11 Morning Vw Irvine CA 92612-3716 Office: Kasdan Simonds Et Al 2600 Michelson Dr Fl 10 Irvine CA 92612-1550 *Notable cases include: two defense jury verdicts in asbestos-in-buildings trials; Concrete Railroad Cross Tie Litigation, 882 FS 482.*

**SUPINO, ANTHONY MARTIN,** lawyer; b. Weehawken, N.J., Oct. 1, 1962; s. Anthony Edward and Gloria (DeBari) S. BA, Rutgers U., 1984, postgrad., 1984-85, JD, 1988. Bar: N.J. 1988, U.S. Dist. Ct. N.J. 1988, N.Y. 1989, U.S. Dist. Ct. (so. dist.) N.Y. 1990, U.S. Ct. Appeals (3d cir.) 1991. Law sec. to the Hon. Marie L. Garibaldi Supreme Ct. of N.J., Jersey City, 1988-89; litigation assoc. Cravath, Swaine & Moore, N.Y.C., 1989-92; spl. litigation assoc. Chadbourne & Parke, N.Y.C., 1992-93; ptnr. Arkin, Schaffer & Supino, N.Y.C., 1994-96; pvt. practice Law Offices of Anthony M. Supino, N.Y.C., West Orange, N.J., 1996—. Community organizer Human Serve Fund, New Brunswick, N.J., 1984. Democrat. Avocations: coin collecting, sports, weightlifting. Criminal, Securities, Antitrust. Home: 95 Ashland Ave West Orange NJ 07052-5419 Office: Law Offices of Anthony M Supino 475 5th Ave New York NY 10017-6220

**SUPLEE, KATHERINE ANN,** lawyer; b. Newark, Oct. 4, 1950; d. Frank Edward and Mary Teresa (Green) S. BA, Mt. Holyoke Coll., 1972; postgrad., Eagleton Inst. Politics, 1972-73; JD, Seton Hall U., 1977. Bar: N.J. 1978, U.S. Dist. Ct. N.J. 1978, U.S. Supreme Ct. 1983, N.Y. 1984. Assoc. Williams & Flynn, Westfield, N.J., 1978-80, Suplee, Clooney & Co., Elizabeth, N.J., 1978—; atty. Union Twp. Planning Bd., Union, N.J., 1981; mem. trustee panel U.S. Trustee in Bankruptcy, Newark, 1982—; spl. counsel City of Elizabeth N.J., 1986-88; bd. dirs. Am. Elevator & Machine Corp., Long Island City, N.Y., Edison (N.J.) Hi Tech, Inc.; mem. adv. coun. Summit Bank, 1989—, St. Elizabeth Hosp., 1991—. Fund raiser N.J. Opera Co., 1973-77, Save African Endangered Species Inc., 1980-82, Kosciusko Found., 1983-85; counsel Summit chpt. Friends of Opera, 1979-84; mem. Polish Assistance Inc., 1983—; bd. dirs. Westminster Ballet Co., Elizabeth, 1984-85, Union County Legal Svcs. Corp., Elizabeth, 1984-86. Mem. ABA, N.J. Bar Assn., Union County Bar Assn. (del. gen. coun. 1984, trustee 1997—), N.J. Women Lawyers (bd. dirs. 1980-87, sec. 1986-87, treas. 1988), Comml. Law League, N.J. Women in Fed. Practice (bd. dirs. 1985—, treas. 1987-89, pres. 1995-97), Bath and Tennis Club (Spring Lake, N.J.), Spring Lake Golf Club, Phi Alpha Delta. Roman Catholic. Bankruptcy, Contracts commercial, General corporate. Office: 233 Morris Ave #c Union NJ 07083-7118

**SUPRUNOWICZ, MICHAEL ROBERT,** lawyer, educator; b. Schenectady, N.Y., Apr. 25, 1955; s. Richard and Lorraine Suprunowicz; m. Katherine Patricia Strange, June 9, 1979; children: Jessica Lynn, Krista Leigh, Michael Anthony. BS, SUNY, Albany, 1973-77, MBA, 1978; JD, Union U., 1981. Atty. Higgins Roberts Beyerl & Coan PC, Schenectady, 1981—; adj. prof. law SUNY, Albany, 1983—, Union Coll., Schenectady, 1993—, Albany Law Sch., 1993-97. Fellow Am. Coll. Trust and Estate Coun.; mem. ABA, N.Y. State Bar Assn. Estate planning, Probate, Estate taxation. Office: Higgins Roberts Beyerl & Coan PC 1430 Balltown Rd Schenectady NY 12309-4301

**SURKIN, DEAN LESLIE,** lawyer, educator; b. N.Y.C., June 24, 1952; s. Morton and Florence Elaine (Lubin) S.; m. Jacqueline C. Birnbaum, May 17, 1998. BA, U. Pa., 1973; JD, NYU, 1976, LLM, 1985. Bar: N.Y. 1976. Assoc. Sanford Schott, Huntington, N.Y., 1976-77; pvt. practice, Mineola, N.Y., 1977-80, N.Y.C., 1986-87; atty.-editor Prentice Hall, Paramus, N.J., 1980-81, Matthew Bender, N.Y.C., 1981-82, Rsch. Inst. Am., N.Y.C., 1993-85; ptnr. Surkin & Handlin, P.C., N.Y.C., 1987-98; tax mgr. Moore Stephens, 1997—; adj. prof. taxation Pace U. Sch. Bus., N.Y.C., 1984—, NYU Sch. Continuing Edn., N.Y.C., 1988—. Contbr. articles to legal jours. Mem. N.Y. State Bar Assn., Assn. Bar City N.Y. Democrat. Jewish. Avocations: classical piano, table tennis, running, racquetball. Taxation, general. Office: 331 Madison Ave 5th Fl New York NY 10017-5102

**SURRATT, JOHN RICHARD,** lawyer; b. Winston-Salem, N.C., Aug. 7, 1928; s. Wade Talmage and Julia (Efird) S.; m. Estella Eason, Dec. 2, 1961; children: Margaret Virginia, Estella Elizabeth, Susan Efird. BS In Commerce, U.N.C., 1948; JD, Duke U., 1951. Bar: N.C. 1951. Pvt. practice Winston-Salem, 1951—; judge mcpl. ct. Winston-Salem; lectr. law Wake Forest U., Winston-Salem, 1976-80. Mayor City of Winston-Salem 1961-63, chmn. city planning bd., 1972-78; sec., mem. Forsyth County Dem. Exec. Com., N.C.; mem. bar candidate com. N.C. Bd. Law Examiners. Served to capt. U.S. Army Reserve, 1951-53, Korea. Mem. ABA, N.C. Bar Assn., Forsyth County Bar Assn. (pres. 1984, exec. com. 1986). Club: Old Town, Twin City. Lodge: Rotary (pres. local chpt. 1983). General corporate, Probate, Estate taxation.

**SUSKIN, HOWARD STEVEN,** lawyer; b. Chgo., Aug. 9, 1959. BA, Northwestern U., 1980; JD, U. Mich., 1983. Bar: Ill. 1983, U.S. Dist. Ct. (no. dist.) Ill. 1983, U.S. Ct. Appeals (7th cir.) 1984, U.S. Ct. Appeals (6th cir.) 1987, U.S. Ct. Appeals (4th cir.) 1987; arbitrator Am. Arbitration Assn. Mem. staff Office Gen. Counsel, HEW, Chgo., 1978-80; mem. staff Ill. Atty. Gen. Office, Chgo., 1981; assoc. Jenner & Block, Chgo., 1983-90, ptnr., 1991—; arbitrator Chgo Bd. Options Exch., Cir. Ct. Cook County. Editor Mich. Law Rev., 1982-83; co-author Illinois Civil Litigation Guide. Mem. ABA (arbitrator), Nat. Assn. Securities Dealers, Nat. Futures Assn., N.Y. Stock Exch., Chgo. Bar Assn. (chmn., legis. liaison mem. securities law com. 1997-98), Phi Beta Kappa. General civil litigation, Securities. Office: Jenner & Block 1 E Ibm Plz Fl 4000 Chicago IL 60611-7603

**SUSKO, CAROL LYNNE,** lawyer, accountant; b. Washington, Dec. 5, 1955; d. Frank and Helen Louise (Davis) S. BS in Econs. and Acctg., George Mason U., 1979; JD, Cath. U., 1982; LLM in Taxation, Georgetown U., 1992. Bar: Pa. 1989, D.C. 1990; CPA, Va., Md. Tax acct. Reznick Fedder & Silverman, P.C., Bethesda, Md., 1984-85; sr. tax acct. Pannell Kerr Forster, Alexandria, Va., 1985; tax specialist Coopers & Lybrand, Washington, 1985-87; supervisory tax sr. Frank & Co., McLean, Va., 1987-88; mem. editl. staff Tax Notes Mag., Arlington, Va., 1989-90; mem. adj. faculty Am. U., Washington, 1989—; tax atty. Marriott Corp., Washington, 1993-94; sr. tax mgr. Host Marriott Inc., Washington, 1994-99, KPMG LLP, Arlington, 1999—. Mem. ABA, AICPAs, Va. Soc. CPAs, D.C. Soc. CPAs, D.C. Bar Assn., Women's Bar Assn. of D.C., Am. Assn. Atty.-CPAs. Corporate taxation, State and local taxation, Taxation, general. Office: KPMG LLP 2300 Clarendon Blvd Arlington VA 22201-3367

**SUSMAN, ALAN HOWARD,** lawyer; b. Buffalo, Apr. 7, 1945; m. Jo Ellen Fisher, Aug. 8, 1970; children: Stephanie, Jennifer. BA, Hobart Coll., 1967; JD, SUNY, Buffalo, 1970. Bar: N.Y. 1971, Ariz. 1973, U.S. Dist. Ct. Ariz. 1973, U.S. Ct. Appeals (9th cir.) 1973, U.S. Supreme Ct. 1978. Assoc. Brizdle & Hankin, Buffalo, 1971-72; appellate law clk. Ariz. Ct. Appeals, Phoenix, 1972-73; atty. Maricopa County Atty.'s Office, Phoenix, 1973-75; ptnr. Schwartz & Susman, P.A., Phoenix, 1975-81; asst. atty. gen. State of Ariz., Phoenix, 1981-84; ptnr. Storey & Ross, P.C., Phoenix, 1984-88, Jaburg & Wilk, Phoenix, 1988—; judge pro tem Superior Ct. State of Ariz., Phoenix, 1986—; instr. Phoenix Coll, 1982, 83. Bd. dirs. Phoenix Jewish Community Ctr., 1985-87. Mem. N.Y. Bar Assn., Assn. Trial Lawyers Am., Ariz. Trial Lawyers Assn., Ariz. Bar Assn. (exec. com. young lawyers sect. 1976-77), Maricopa County Bar Assn., Am. Arbitration Assn. (mem. panel arbitrators). Democrat. Avocations: golf, reading. General civil litigation, Construction, Contracts commercial. Office: Jaburg & Wilk PC 3200 N Central Ave Ste 2000 Phoenix AZ 85012-2440

**SUSMAN, MORTON LEE,** lawyer; b. Detroit, Aug. 6, 1934; s. Harry and Alma (Koslow) S.; m. Nina Meyers, May 1, 1958; 1 child, Mark Lee. BBA, So. Meth. U., 1956, JD, 1958. Bar: Tex. 1958, U.S. Dist. Ct. (so. dist.) Tex. 1961, U.S. Ct. Appeals (5th cir.) 1961, U.S. Supreme Ct. 1961, U.S. Ct. Appeals (11th cir.) 1981, D.C. 1988, U.S. Ct. Appeals (D.C. cir.) 1988, N.Y. 1990, Colo. 1996. Asst. U.S. atty., Houston, 1961-64, 1st asst. U.S. atty., 1965-66, U.S. atty., 1966-69; ptnr. Weil, Gotshal & Manges and predecessor firm Susman & Kessler, Houston, 1969-97. Lt. USNR, 1958-61. Fellow Am. Coll. Trial Lawyers, Tex. Bar Found.; mem. ABA, Fed. Bar Assn. (dir., Younger Fed. Lawyer award 1968), Tex. Bar Assn., Skyline Country Club (Tucson). Democrat. Jewish. Federal civil litigation, State civil litigation, Criminal. Home: 3238 Ella Lee Ln Houston TX 77019-5924 Office: Weil Gotshal & Manges 700 Louisiana St Ste 1600 Houston TX 77002-2784

**SUSMAN, ROBERT M(ARK),** lawyer; b. St. Louis, Jan. 15, 1951; s. Bernard and Lorraine (Abramson) S.; m. Shelby Zarick; children: Jane, Stephanie. BA, Ind. U., 1973; JD, St. Louis U., 1976. Bar: Mo. 1976, U.S. Dist. Ct. (ea. dist.) Mo. 1976, U.S. Supreme 1994. Ptnr. Goffstein, Raskas, Pomerantz, Kraus, Sherman, Ruthmeyer & Susman, St. Louis, 1976—. Mem. ATLA (basic course trial advocacy Nat. Coll. Advocacy 1983), Mo. Assn. Trial Attys., Lawyers Assn. St. Louis (pres. 1988-89), Met. Bar Assn. St. Louis. Personal injury, Workers' compensation, Insurance. Office: 7701 Clayton Rd Saint Louis MO 63117-1301

**SUSSE, SANDRA SLONE,** lawyer; b. Medford, Ma., June 1, 1943; d. James Robert and Georgie Coffin (Bradshaw) Slone; m. Peter Susse, May 10, 1969 (div. May 1993); 1 child, Toby. BA, U. Mass., 1981; JD, Vt. Law Sch., 1986. Bar: Mass. 1986, U.S. Dist. Ct. Mass. 1988, U.S. Ct. Appeals (1st cir.) 1995. Staff atty. Western Mass. Legal Svcs., Springfield, 1986—. Mem. ABA, Mass. Bar Assn., Women's Bar Assn. Mass. Avocations: hiking, German literature, film, skating. Address: Western Mass Legal Serv 127 State St #4thFl Springfield MA 01103-1905

**SUSSMAN, HOWARD S(IVIN),** lawyer; b. N.Y.C., Feb. 12, 1938; s. Joseph and Dora (Sivin) S. AB cum laude, Princeton U., 1958; LLB, Columbia U., 1962. Bar: N.Y. 1964, U.S. Dist. Ct. (so. and ea. dists.) N.Y. 1967, U.S. Ct. Appeals (2d cir.) 1967, U.S. Tax Ct. 1969, U.S. Dist. Ct. (no. dist.) N.Y. 1970, U.S. Supreme Ct. 1970, Tex. 1979, U.S. Dist. Ct. (so. dist.) Tex. 1982, U.S. Ct. Appeals (5th cir.) 1982. Assoc. Chadbourne, Parke, Whiteside & Wolff, N.Y.C., 1963-71; asst. U.S. atty. So. Dist. N.Y., 1971-77; assoc. prof. law U. Houston, 1977-82; of counsel Wood, Lucksinger & Epstein, Houston, 1982-83; sole practice N.Y.C., 1983-94; ptnr. Sussman Sollis Ebin Tweedy & Wood, N.Y.C., 1995—; instr. continuing legal edn. U. Houston, Nat. Inst. for Trial Advocacy. Editor Columbia U. Law Rev., 1960-62; contbr. articles to profl. jours. Harlan Fiske Stone scholar, 1959-61, Edvard Cassels Stiftelse vis. scholar, Stockholm, 1962-63; travelling fellow Parker Sch. Fgn. and Comparative Law Columbia U., 1962-63. Mem. ABA, Tex. Bar Assn., Houston Bar Assn., N.Y. State Bar Assn., Assn. of Bar of City of N.Y. (com. adminstrv. law 1974-76, profl. conf. 1979, com. fed. legis. 1984-87, com. criminal law 1987-90, lectr. & continuing edn. 1990-93, fgn. & corp. law 1993-96), Fed. Bar Council. Club: Princeton N.Y. Federal civil litigation, Criminal, General practice.

**SUSSMAN, MARK RICHARD,** lawyer; b. Bklyn., Feb. 4, 1952; s. Vincent E. and Rhoda (Urowsky) S.; m. Lisa Rosner, June 8, 1975; children: Corey, Randi, Samuel. BS in Civil Engring., Tufts U., 1974; JD, U. Pa., 1977. Bar: Pa. 1977, D.C. 1980, Conn. 1981. Trial atty. land and natural resources div. U.S. Dept. Justice, Washington, 1977-81; assoc. Murtha, Cullina, Richter & Pinney, Hartford, Conn., 1981-86, ptnr., 1987—; chmn. environ. dept. Murtha, Cullina, Richter & Pinney, Hartford, Conn., 1990—; gov.'s blue ribbon panel to evaluate environtl. permit programs, 1996. Chmn. conservation commn. Windsor, Conn., 1984—; mem. Conn. Hazardous Waste Mgmt. Service Recycling Task Force, 1986, Legis. Task Force on Environ. Permitting, 1992, Conn. State Implementation Plan Revision Adv. Com., 1984—. Mem. ABA (natural resources sect.), Am. Arbitration Assn. (Conn. region environ. adv. coun.), Conn. Bar Assn. (chmn. conservation and environ. quality sect. 1984-87, faculty continuing legal edn.), Conn. Bus. and Industry Assn. (steering com. environ. policies coun. 1990-93, 98—) Tau Beta Pi. Environmental, Federal civil litigation, State civil litigation. Home: 62 Timothy Ter Windsor CT 06095-1652 Office: Murtha Cullina Richter & Pinney City Pl 185 Asylum St Ste 29 Hartford CT 06103-3469 *Notable cases include: Mumford Cove Assn. v. Town of Groton, 786 F. 2d 530, 640 F. Supp 392, 647 F. Supp. 671, 1986, represented homeowners assn. in Clean Water Act citizen's suit to force municipality to relocate sewer discharge pipe; City of Shelton v. Commr. of Environ. Protection, 193 Conn. 506, 1984, represented the Conn. Resources Recovery Authority in obtaining and defending permits for a solid waste landfill, Conn. Coastal Fishermen's Assn. v. Remington Arms Co., Inc., 989 F 2d 1302 (2d cir. 1993), represented defendant in Clean Water Act & RCRA citizens suit which found, in part, that lead shot may be considered a hazardous waste subject to remediation under RCRA statutory definition of hazardous waste.*

**SUSSMAN, NANCY,** lawyer, nurse; b. N.Y.C., Feb. 18, 1951; d. Henry and Freda (Luber) S.; children: Michael, Ashleigh. BSN, Calif. State U., L.A., 1974; JD, Calif. Western U., 1982. Ptnr. Hayworth and Sussman, San Diego, 1983-92, pvt. practice, 1992—. Mem. ATLA, San Diego Trial Lawyers Assn., Consumer Attys. of San Diego. Personal injury, Professional liability. Office: Hayworth and Sussman 1901 1st Ave Ste 220 San Diego CA 92101-2382

**SUSSMAN, NEIL A.,** lawyer; b. N.Y.C., Jan. 26, 1956; s. Herbert and Ruth S.; m. Suzanne R. Thompson, Aug. 31, 1990; children: Annabelle, Franklin. BS in Econs., U. Pa., 1978; JD, U. Wash., 1982. Bar: Wash. 1982. Atty. pvt. practice, Seattle, 1982—. Mem. Wash. State Bar Assn., King County Bar Assn. Entertainment, Taxation, general, Trademark and copyright. Office: 10727 Interlake Ave N Seattle WA 98133-8907

**SUTER, BEN,** lawyer; b. Sacramento, Dec. 14, 1954; s. Alexander Frederick and Anne Ida (De Bergen) S.; m. Lizanne Bouchard, Dec. 23, 1979; children: Tycho Benjamin, Hadley Theadora, Miles Kepler, Rex Sebastian. BA in Philosophy, U. Calif., Santa Barbara, 1978; JD, U. Calif., San Francisco, 1982. Bar: Calif. 1982, U.S. Dist. Ct. (cen., ea., no. and so. dists.) Calif. 1982, Ariz. 1983, Hawaii 1984, U.S. Dist. Ct. Ariz. 1990, U.S. Supreme Ct. 1987. Assoc. Keesal, Young & Logan, San Francisco and Long Beach, Calif., 1982-87, ptnr., 1987—. Securities, Federal civil litigation, Real property. Office: Keesal Young & Logan 4 Embarcadero Ctr San Francisco CA 94111-4106

**SUTER, WILLIAM KENT,** federal court administrator, former army officer, lawyer; b. Portsmouth, Ohio, Aug. 24, 1937; s. William Chauncey Suter and Ruth Margaret Fritz; m. Margaret Jean Bogart, May 23, 1959; children: William B., Charles W. BA in Social Scis., Trinity U., San Antonio, 1959; LLB, Tulane U., 1962. Bar: La. 1962, U.S. Supreme Ct. 1967, D.C. 1988. Commd. 1st lt. U.S. Army, 1962, advanced through grades to maj. gen., 1985; comdt. JAG Sch., Charlottesville, Va., 1981-84; chief judge, U.S. Army Ct. Mil. Rev. and Comdr. Legal Svcs. Agy., Falls Church, Va., 1984-85; asst. JAG Dept. Army, Washington, 1985-91; ret. U.S. Army, 1991; clk. U.S. Supreme Ct., Washington, 1991—. Mem. FBA, Federalist Soc., Nat. Legal Ctr. for the Pub. Interest. Presbyterian. Home: 5917 Reservoir Heights Ave Alexandria VA 22311-1017 Office: US Supreme Ct 1 First St NE Washington DC 20543

**SUTHERLAND, JOHN EDWARD,** lawyer, educator; b. Bangor, Maine, Nov. 6, 1951; s. W. Ward and Joan (Hartery) S.; m. Jennifer Scott, June 25, 1988; 1 child, Amanda Hemenway. BA, Boston U., 1974; JD, New England Sch. Law, 1978. Bar: Mass. 1978, Maine 1980. Prin. Brickley Sears & Sorett, Boston, 1984—; adj. prof. bus. law Suffolk U., Boston, 1993—. Pres. Nichols House Mus., Beacon Hill, Boston, 1997—. Mem. Tennis & Racket Club (Boston). Unitarian. Avocations: tree farming, sailing. Office: Brickley Sears & Sorett 75 Federal St Fl 17 Boston MA 02110-1985

**SUTHERLAND, LAURA MICHELLE,** lawyer; b. Elgin, Ill., Oct. 19, 1965; m. Richard Michael Bogovich; children: Natasha Nicole Bogovich, Joshua Daniel Bogovich. BA, No. Ill. U., 1986; JD, U. Wis., 1989. Bar: Wis. 1989. Law clk. Wis. Dept. Justice, Madison, 1988-89, Wisc. Ct. Appeals, Madison, 1989-90; asst. atty. gen. Wis. Dept. Justice, Madison, 1980-98; assoc. Boardman, Suhr, Curry & Field, LLP, Madison, 1998—; tchg. asst. legal writing U. Wis. Law Sch., Madison. Articles editor Wis. Law Rev. Trustee, bd. dirs. Cmty. Housing and Svcs., Madison, 1995-99. Mem. ABA, Wis. State Bar Assn., Wis. Women Environ. Profls. Home: 3200 Oakridge Ave Madison WI 53704-5850 Office: Boardman Suhr Curry & Field 1 S Pinckney St Madison WI 53703-2892

**SUTHERLAND, SHIRLEY M.,** lawyer; b. Dallas, Aug. 4; d. Robert Mansel and Darthia J. (Bullen) Alldredge; m. Kennett Sutherland, July 11, 1976 (div. 1987); children: Travis Carson Mahan, Kristen Amanda. BA, SMU, 1983, JD, 1986. BAr: Tex. 1986, U.S. Dist. Ct. (no. dist.) Tex. 1987. Asst. dist. atty. Dist. Atty. Henry Wade, Dallas, 1986-88; trial atty. Law Offices of Windle Turley, Dallas, 1988-90; head of litigation Law Offices of William Dever, Dallas, 1990-94; pvt. practice Dallas, 1994—. Mem. Single Adult Coun. Lovers Ln., United Meth. Ch., Dallas, 1990—, TAC Assocs., Dallas, 1991—. Mem. ABA, Am. Trial Lawyers Assn., Tex. Trial Lawyers Assn. (assoc. dir. 1991—), Dallas Trial Lawyers Assn. (dir. 1991—). Avocation: tennis. Personal injury. Office: 8117 Preston Rd Ste 490 Dallas TX 75225-6336

**SUTHERLUND, DAVID ARVID,** lawyer; b. Stevens Point, Wis., July 20, 1929; s. Arvid E. and Georgia M. (Stickney) S. BA, U. Portland, 1952; JD, U. N.Mex., 1957; postgrad., U. Wis., 1957. Bar: D.C. 1957, U.S. Supreme Ct. 1961. Atty. ICC, Washington, 1957-58; counsel Am. Trucking Assn., Washington, 1958-62; assoc. and ptnr. Morgan, Lewis & Bockius, Washington and Phila., 1962-72; ptnr. Fulbright & Jaworski, Washington and Houston, 1975-83; sr. ptnr. Zwerling, Mark & Sutherlund, Washington and Alexandria, Va., 1987-91; spl. counsel LaRoe, Winn, Moerman & Donovan, Washington, 1983—; prin. Sutherlund & Assocs., Washington, 1989—; bd. dirs., gen. counsel Nat. Film Svc., 1962-75; mem. family div. panel Pub. Defender Svc. for D.C., 1972-76. Founder, chmn. bd. govs. Transp. Law Jour, 1969-74. Vice chmn. Nat. Capitol Area coun. Boy Scouts Am., 1975-78; mem. bd. regents U. Portland, 1985-91. Spl. agt. CIC, U.S. Army, 1952-54. Mem. ABA, Fed. Bar Assn., D.C. Bar Assn., Transp. Lawyers Assn., Am. Arbitration Assn. (nat. panel arbitrators 1970—), Am. Judicature Soc., Internat. Club (Washington), Primsoll Club (New Orleans), Balboa Bay Club (Newport Beach, Calif.). Transportation, Public international, General corporate. Office: PO Box 7440 Fort Myers FL 33911-7440

**SUTPHIN, WILLIAM TAYLOR,** lawyer; s. William Halstead and Catharine (Bonner) S.; m. Alissa L. Kramer, June 21, 1958. AB in History, Princeton U., 1957; LLB, U. Pa., 1960. Bar: N.J. 1960; U.S. Ct. Appeals (3d cir.) 1964, U.S. Supreme Ct. 1965. Assoc. Stryker, Tams & Dill, Newark, 1960-67, ptnr., 1967-73; sole practice Princeton, N.J., 1973—; coadj. faculty mem. Rutgers U. Govt. Svcs. Tng. Program, 1973—; assoc. counsel N.J. Planning Ofcls., 1975—. Mem. Princeton Twp. Planning Bd., 1967-72, Regional Planning Bd. Princeton, 1970-74; atty. Green Brook Twp. Planning Bd., 1972—, Millstone Twp. Bd. Adjustment, 1978-98, Del. Twp. Bd. Adjustment, 1982—, Princeton Borough Bd. Adjustment, 1983—; committeeman Twp. Princeton, 1973-75, police commr., 1974-75; treas. Youth Employment Svc. Princeton Inc., 1981-84. Served with U.S. Army, 1953-56, capt. JAGC Ret. Mem. N.J. Bar Assn. (chmn. ins. com. 1979-81), Princeton Bar Assn. (pres. 1981-82), N.J. Inst. Mcpl. Attys. Land use and zoning (including planning), Probate, General civil litigation. Home: 501 Jefferson Rd Princeton NJ 08540-3418 Office: 34 Chambers St Princeton NJ 08542-3700

**SUTTER, J. DOUGLAS,** lawyer; b. San Antonio, Tex., Oct. 4, 1953; s. John Sutter and Mary Jo Brown; m. Karen S. Sutter, Oct. 5, 1985; 1 child, Colin Michael. BA, U. Tex., 1975, JD, 1979. Pntr. Ross, Griggs & Harrison, Houston, 1979-92, Kelly, Sutter, Mount & Kendrick, P.C., Houston, 1992—. Mem. ABA, Tex. Bar Assn., Houston Bar Assn., Austin Bar Assn., Maritime Bar Assn. Roman Catholic. Avocations: jogging, coin collecting, gardening, water skiing. State civil litigation, Contracts commercial, Personal injury. Home: 10122 Shady River Dr Houston TX 77042-1236 Office: 1600 Smith St Ste 3700 Houston TX 77002-7345

**SUTTER, LAURENCE BRENER,** lawyer; b. N.Y.C., Feb. 5, 1944; s. Meyer and Beatrice Sutter; m. Betty A. Satterwhite, June 9, 1979. AB, Columbia Coll., 1965; JD, N.Y.U., 1976. Bar: N.Y. 1977, U.S. Dist. Ct. (so. and ea. dists.) N.Y. 1977. Assoc. Shea & Gould, N.Y.C., 1976-80, Meyer, Suozzi, English & Klein P.C., Mineola, N.Y., 1980-82; assoc. counsel publs. Gen. Media Internat., Inc., N.Y.C., 1982-96, sr. v.p., gen. counsel, 1997—. With N.Y. Army N.G., 1966-72. Mem. Assn. of Bar of City of N.Y. (mem. com. on civil rights 1986-89, mem. com. on comm. and media law 1989-92, mem. com. on copyright and lit. property 1994-97), First Amendment Lawyers Assn., Orient (N.Y.) Yacht Club (dir. 1997—). Democrat. Jewish. Avocations: music, sailing. Communications. Office: Gen Media Comm Inc 12th Fl 11 Penn Plz Fl 12 New York NY 10001-2006

**SUTTERFIELD, JAMES RAY,** lawyer. Bar: La. 1967, U.S. Dist. Ct. (ea. dist.) La. 1967, U.S. Ct. Appeals (5th cir.) 1967, U.S. Dist. Ct. (mid. dist.) La. 1971, D.C. 1977, U.S. Supreme Ct. 1977, U.S. Dist. Ct. (we. dist.) La. 1982, U.S. Dist. Ct. (ea. dist.) Tex. 1985, Tex. 1993. Assoc. Law Offices Walter F. Marcus, New Orleans, 1967; assoc. Huddleston & Davis, New Orleans, 1968-70, ptnr., 1970-72; ptnr. Sutterfield & Vickery, New Orleans, 1973-82, Carmouche, Gray & Hoffman, New Orleans, 1982-89; sr. dir. Hoffman Sutterfield Ensenat A.P.L.C., New Orleans, 1989-97; sr. ptnr. Sutterfield & Webb LLC, 1997—; faculty mem. 10th diving accident and hyperbaric oxygen treatment course Duke U.; del. Undersea and Hyperbaric Med. Soc. Nat. Oceanographic and Almospheric Adminstrn.; speaker legal seminars. Author: (with others) Commercial Damages, 1989; mem. bd. editors Hull Claims Analysis; contbr. articles to profl. jours. Mem. ABA (chmn. excess surplus lines and reins. com.), La. Bar Assn., 5th Cir. Bar Assn., D.C. Bar Assn., La. Assn. Def. Counsel, Internat. Assn. Def. Counsel (chmn. maritime and energy law com., class action and multiparty litigation com.), Maritime Law Assn. U.S. (chmn. marine product liability com.), Def. Rsch. Inst. E-mail: jsutterfield@swslaw.com. Insurance, Admiralty. Office: Sutterfield Webb & Smith 650 Poydras St Fl 27 New Orleans LA 70130-6101

**SUTTLE, DORWIN WALLACE,** federal judge; b. Knox County, Ind., July 16, 1906; s. William Sherman and Nancy Cordelia (Hungate) S.; m. Anne Elizabeth Barrett, Feb. 1, 1939 (dec.); children: Stephen Hungate, Nancy Joanna Suttle Walker (dec.); m. Lucile Cram Whitecotton, Aug. 21, 1956; stepchildren: Fred and Frank Whitecotton. JD, U. Tex., 1928. Bar: Tex., U.S. Supreme Ct. 1960. Practiced law Uvalde, Tex., 1928-64; U.S. dist. judge Western Dist. Tex., 1964—; now sr. judge. Democrat. Methodist. Fax: 210-472-6572. Office: US District Court 655 E Durango Blvd San Antonio TX 78206-1102

**SUTTLE, STEPHEN HUNGATE,** lawyer; b. Uvalde, Tex., Mar. 17, 1940; s. Dorwin Wallace and Ann Elizabeth (Barrett) S.; m. Rosemary Williams Davison, Aug. 3, 1963; children: Michael Barrett, David Paull, John Stewart. BA, Washington and Lee U., 1962; LLB, U. Tex., 1965. Bar: Tex. 1965, U.S. Dist. Ct. (no. and we. dists.) Tex. 1965, U.S. Ct. Appeals (5th cir.) 1967, U.S. Supreme Ct. 1970. Law clk. to Hon. Leo Brewster U.S. Dist. Ct. (no. dist.) Tex., Ft. Worth, 1965-67; ptnr. McMahon, Surovik, Suttle, Buhrmann, Hicks & Gill, P.C., Abilene, Tex., 1970—. Pres. Abilene Boys Clubs, Inc., 1975-76; bd. dirs. Abilene Cmty. Theater, 1979-80, Abilene Fine Arts Mus., 1977-78. Fellow Am. Coll. Trial Lawyers, Am. Bd. Trial Advocates, Tex. Bar Found.; mem. Tex. Assn. Def. Counsel, Defense Rsch. Inst., Tex. Young Lawyers Assn. (chmn. bd. dirs. 1976), Am. Judicature Soc. (bd. dirs. 1981-84), Abilene Bar Assn. (pres. 1987-88), Tex. Bar Assn. (mem. coms. various sects.), State Bar Tex. (dir. 1999—), ABA (chmn. young lawyers sect. award of merit 1976), Abilene Country Club. Democrat. Episcopalian. Federal civil litigation, State civil litigation. Home: 1405 Woodland Trl Abilene TX 79605-4705 Office: McMahon Surovik Suttle Buhrmann Hicks & Gill PC PO Box 3679 Abilene TX 79604-3679

**SUTTON, BRIAN DALE,** lawyer; b. Wichita Falls, Tex., Sept. 22, 1961; s. Emmett and Susan (Spindler) S.; m. Fern V. Jacobs. BS, Tex. A&M U., 1984; JD, St. Mary's U., 1987. Bar: Tex. 1987, U.S. Dist. Ct. (ea. dist.) Tex. 1988. Assoc. Weller, Wheelus & Green, Beaumont, Tex., 1987-89, Dryden, Grossheim & Sutton, LLP, Beaumont, 1987—. Bd. dirs. Humane Soc. S.E. Tex., Beaumont, 1991—, pres., 1993-94. Mem. ABA, Assn. Trial Lawyers Am., Tex. Trial Lawyers Assn., S.E. Trial Lawyers Assn., Tex. State Bar. Personal injury, Product liability. Office: Dryden Grossheim & Sutton 398 Pearl St Ste 915 Beaumont TX 77701-2422

**SUTTON, DEBRA J.,** lawyer; b. Ft. Belvoir, Va., Jan. 2, 1960; d. Lester and Elizabeth Jane Sutton. AS, Polk C.C., 1985; BA, U. South Fla., 1986; JD cum laude, Stetson U., 1989. Bar: Fla. 1989, U.S. Ct. Appeals (11th cir.) 1994, U.S. Supreme Ct. 1997; bd. cert. in appellate practice. Law clk. Peterson, Myers Law Firm, Lakeland, Fla., 1989; staff atty. Dist. Ct. Appeals (2d dist.) Fla., Lakeland, 1989-90; pvt. practice Bartow, Fla., 1990—; keynote spkr. Phi Theta Kappa, Winter Haven, Fla., 1991; instr. jud. process Fla. So. Coll., Lakeland, 1992-93. Author: (chpt.) Fla. Manual for Legal Secretaries. Vol. Guardian Ad Litem Polk County Office, 1993—. Mem. ABA, Fla. Bar (charter mem. appellate advocacy com. 1994—), Polk County Trial Lawyers. Polk County Criminal Def. Lawyers, Willson Am. Inn of Ct. (charter, adminstr. 1990—, editor newsletter 1996), Polk County Family Law Lawers (mem. com. revision adminstrn. pursuant to Fla. family law rules procedure 1997). Presbyterian. Avocations: photography, writing, traveling, teaching. Appellate, Family and matrimonial, General civil litigation. Office: 343 W Davidson St Ste 101 Bartow FL 33830-3765

**SUTTON, JOHN EWING,** judge; b. San Angelo, Oct. 7, 1950; s. John F. Jr. and Nancy (Ewing) S.; m. Jean Ann Schofield, July 2, 1977; 1 son, Joshua Ewing; 1 stepson, Michael Brandon Ducote. BBA, U. Tex., 1973, JD, 1976. Bar: Tex. 1976, U.S. Tax Ct. 1977, U.S. Ct. Claims 1977, U.S. Ct. Appeals (5th cir.) 1978, U.S. Dist. Ct. (we. dist.) Tex. 1979, U.S. Supreme Ct. 1980; CPA, Tex. With Daugherty, Kuperman & Golden, Austin, 1975-76; tax specialist Peat, Marwick, Mitchell & Co., CPAs, Dallas, 1976-77; ptnr. Shannon, Porter, Johnson, Sutton and Greendyke Attys. at Law, San Angelo, Tex., 1977-87; judge 119th Dist. Ct. of Tex., 1987—. Treas. Good Shepherd Episcopal Ch., San Angelo, 1979-81; co-chmn. profl. divsn. United Way, San Angelo, 1980-82; trustee Angelo State U. Found., 1987—, pres., 1988-91, 95-97, v.p., 1992-94, 98-99, sec.-treas., 1991-92. Mem. ABA, Tex. Bar Assn., Tom Green County Bar Assn. (sec.-treas. young lawyers 1977-78), AICPAs, Tex. Soc. CPAs (bd. dirs. 1980-87, pres. San Angelo chpt. 1980-81, mem. state exec. com. 1981-82, 86-87, state sec. 1986-87, chmn. profl. ethics com. 1985-86, Young CPA of Yr. 1984-85), Concho Valley Estate Planning Coun. (v.p. 1979-80, also dir.). Office: Tom Green County Courthouse San Angelo TX 76903

**SUTTON, JOHN F., JR.,** law educator, dean, lawyer; b. Alpine, Tex., Jan. 26, 1918; s. John F. and Pauline Irene (Elam) S.; m. Nancy Ewing, June 1, 1940; children: Joan Sutton Parr, John Ewing. J.D., U. Tex., 1941. Bar: Tex. 1941, U.S. Dist. Ct. (we. dist.) Tex. 1947, U.S. Ct. Appeals (5th cir.) 1951, U.S. Supreme Ct. 1960. Assoc. Brooks, Napier, Brown & Matthews, San Antonio, 1941-42; spl. agt. FBI, Washington, 1942-45; assoc. Matthews, Nowlin, Macfarlane & Barrett, San Antonio, 1945-48; ptnr. Kerr, Gayer & Sutton, San Angelo, Tex., 1948-50, Sutton, Steib & Barr, San Angelo, 1951-57; prof. U. Tex.-Austin, 1957-65, William Stamps Farish prof., 1965-84, A.W. Walker centennial chair, 1984—, dean Sch. Law, 1979-84. Editor: (with Wellborn) Materials on Evidence, 8th edit., 1996, (with Dzienkowski) Cases and Materials on Professional Responsibility of Lawyers, 1989, (with Schuwerk) Guideline to the Texas Disciplinary Rules of Professional Conduct, 1990; contbr. articles to profl. jours. Served to 1st lt. JAGC USAR, 1948-54. Fellow Am. Bar Found. (life), Tex. Bar Found. (life); mem. ABA (com. on ethics 1970-76), State Bar Tex. (com. on rules of profl. conduct, com. adminstrn. rules of evidence), Philos. Soc. Tex., Order of Coif, U. Tex. Club, Phi Delta Phi, San Angelo Country Club, River Club of San Angelo, North Austin Rotary (pres. 1969). Presbyterian. Home: 3830 Sunset Dr San Angelo TX 76904-5956 Office: U Tex Sch Law 727 E Dean Keeton St Austin TX 78705-3224

**SUTTON, JONATHAN MARK,** lawyer; b. Flint, Mich., Nov. 21, 1959; s. James Owen and Rachel Bernice (Pederson) S. Bachelor's Degree, Cntl. Mich. U., 1982; JD, U. Tulsa, 1992. Bar: Okla. 1992, U.S. Dist. Ct. (ea. and we. dists.) Okla. 1994, U.S. Ct. Appeals (10th cir.) 1994, U.S. Supreme Ct. 1997. corp. counsel United Parcel Svc., Atlanta, 1993. Guardian for disabled vets. VA, Tulsa, 1996—. Mem. ATLA, Okla. Bar Assn. Avocations: skiing, scuba diving, hunting, motorcycles. Family and matrimonial, Personal injury, Workers' compensation. Office: 4401 S Harvard Ave Tulsa OK 74135-2638

**SUTTON, PAMELA DRU,** lawyer; b. N.Y.C., Mar. 9, 1950; d. Marvin Laurence and Janet (Giblen) S.; m. Michel L. Stone, Feb. 13, 1988; 1 child, Elizabeth Sutton Stone. AB cum laude, Harvard U., 1972; JD, Bklyn. Law Sch., 1978. Bar: Fla., N.Y.; U.S. Dist. Ct. (no. dist.) Fla.; U.S. Tax Ct.; U.S. Ct. Appeals (11th cir.). Intern ACLU Children's Rights Project, N.Y.C., 1976-77; intern Criminal Divsn. Legal Aid Soc., Juvenile Divsn., N.Y.C., 1977-78; from intern to assoc. Greenfield & Baker, N.Y.C., 1977-78; staff atty. Legal Svcs. North Fla., Panama City, 1979-80; sole practice law Panama City, 1980-85; atty. Capital Divsn. Office of Pub. Defender, 14th Jud. Cir., Panama City, 1983-92; ptnr. Stone & Sutton, Panama City, 1985—; mem. death penalty steering com. Fla. Pub. Defender Assn., Tallahassee, 1990-92; lectr. U.S. Navy & Marine JAG Officers Death Penalty Seminar, Camp LeJeune, N.C., 1992, Fla. Pub. Defender Assn. Death Penalty Confs., Tampa, Fla., 1992, 93, Fla. Assn. Criminal Defense Lawyers, 1993, Holy Nativity Episcopal Sch., 1995. Author: Note, Bklyn. Law Review, 1977; assoc. editor Bklyn. Law Review, 1977-78; co-author: (chpts) Florida Public Defender Association Death Penalty Manual, 1992, rev. 1993; featured on CBS-TV: 48 Hours, 1993. Pres. Bay County chpt. NOW, Panama City, 1992-94, 96-97. Recipient Guardiau Ad Litem Atty. Pro Bono award State Florida, 1993. Mem. ATLA, Fla. Acad. Trial Lawyers, Bay County Bar Assn. (pres. 1985). Democrat. Personal injury, Criminal, Family and matrimonial. Office: Stone & Sutton 116 E 4th St Panama City FL 32401-3109

**SUTTON, PAUL EUGENE, II,** lawyer; b. Richmond, Va., July 25, 1943; s. Paul Eugene I and Martha Florence (Fernandez) S.; m. Marie Carmaechal Williams, Dec. 24, 1964; children: Donna Maria, Travis Alan. AS, Fla. Jr. Coll., 1973; BA, U. Richmond, 1975, JD, 1980. Bar: Va. 1980, U.S. Supreme Ct. 1989. Legis. asst. Va. State Senate, Richmond, 1974-75; assoc. Esposito & Armstrong, Richmond, 1980; atty. GE, Lynchburg, Va., 1980-82; pvt. practice Virginia Beach, Va., 1982-84; pvt. practice law Norfolk, Va., 1986—. With USN, 1961-72. Decorated Nat. Def. Medal. Mem. ABA, Va. Bar Assn., Norfolk-Portsmouth Bar Assn., Assn. Trial Lawyers, Va. Trial Lawyers Assn., Nat. Assn. Criminal Def. Lawyers, Lions (pres. Norfolk chpt. 1993—). Baptist. Criminal, Family and matrimonial, Personal injury. Home and Office: 125 Saint Pauls Blvd Ste 530 Norfolk VA 23510-2708 *Notable cases include: Newman vs. City of Norfolk, the waterside festival marketplace blue law case, 1982; Commonwealth vs. Smith, the Franklin County, Va. Bland prison cocaine conspiracy case, 1985; Commonwealth vs. Van Fossen, the Monument ave. Richmond arson case, 1985, Commonwealth vs. Michael J. Diehl, the religious family murder of adopted child case, 1987; Commonwealth vs. Alan J. Marcotte, defending alleged murderer of returning Desert Storm gulf war hero.*

**SUTTON, RICHARD STANSBURY,** lawyer; b. Middletown, Ohio, July 16, 1945; s. Robert Stansbury Sutton and Betty Magel Thrusher; m. Janet Marie Robinson, Jan. 2, 1967 (div. June 1980); children: R. Gregory, Matthew Robert; m. Dayna Gay Frame, Sept. 30, 1983. BA in Polit. Sci., Ohio Wesleyan U., 1967; JD, Cleve. State U., 1972. Bar: Ohio 1972, U.S. Dist. Ct. (so. dist.) Ohio 1972. Law clk. for hon. William K. Thomas U.S. Dist. Ct. (no. dist.) Ohio, Cleve., 1972; assoc. Smith & Schnacke, Dayton, Ohio, 1972-75; pvt. practice law Dayton, 1975-82; ptnr. Sutton, Overholser & Schaffer, Dayton, 1982—; legal advisor to city coun. Miamisburg and Germantown, Ohio, 1972-75; tax bd. mem. West Carrollton, Ohio, 1973. Mem. ABA, ATLA, Ohio Assn. Trial Lawyers, Ohio Bar Assn. (various coms.), Miami Valley Trial Lawyers Assn. Avocations: playing in musical groups, golfing, skiing. Personal injury, Workers' compensation. Office: Sutton Overholser & Schaffer Ste 1628 First National Plaza Dayton OH 45402

**SUTTON, SAMUEL J.,** lawyer, educator, engineer; b. Chgo., July 21, 1941; s. Samuel J. and Elaine (Blossom) S.; m. Anne V. Sutton, Aug. 28, 1965; children: Paige, Jean, Leah, Jepson. BA in History and Philosophy, U.

Ariz., 1964, BSEE, 1967; JD, George Washington U., 1969. Bar: Ariz. 1969, D.C. 1970, U.S. Ct. Appeals (fed. cir.) 1983. Patent atty. Gen. Electric Co., Washington, Phoenix, 1967-70; ptnr. Cahill, Sutton & Thomas, Phoenix, 1970-95, of counsel, 1995—; prof. law Ariz. State U., Tempe, 1975—; expert witness Fed. Dist. Cts., 1983—; trial cons. to numerous lawyers, 1972—; v.p. engring. Shintech, Inc., 1991—; arbitrator Am. Arbitration Assn., Phoenix, 1971—. Author: Patent Preparation, 1976, Intellectual Property, 1978, Art Law, 1988, Law, Science and Technology, 1991, Licensing Intangible Property, 1994, Commercial Torts, 1995, Patent Litigation, 1996; pub. sculptures installed at Tanner Sq., Phoenix, Tucson Art Inst., Mobil Corp., Mesa, Ariz., Cox Devel. Co., Tempe, Ariz., Downtown Phoenix, Desert Bot. Garden, Phoenix, Gateway Ctr., Phoenix, Sedona Sculpture Garden, Construct Gallery, Phoenix. Chmn. air pollution hearing bd. City of Phoenix, Maracopa County, 1970-85. Recipient Patent prize Patent Resources Group, 1979, Publ. award IEEE, 1967, Genematus award U. Ariz., 1964, Disting. Achievement award Ariz. State U., 1980, Construct Sculpture prize, 1989. Avocation: large scale steel sculpture. Patent, Trademark and copyright, Intellectual property. Office: Cahill Sutton & Thomas 2141 E Highland Ave Ste 155 Phoenix AZ 85016-4791

**SUTTON, WILLIAM DWIGHT,** lawyer; b. Butler, Pa., Oct. 22, 1916; s. James S. Sutton and Ada Elizabeth Emrick; m. Mary Ella Newsome, Dec. 4, 1943; children: Ann, Melissa. BA, Washington & Jefferson, 1938; JD, U. Mich., 1941. Bar: Pa. 1946, U.S. Ct. Appeals (3d cir.) 1946, U.S. Supreme Ct. 1946. Assoc. atty. Donovan, Leisure, Newton & Irvine, N.Y.C., 1941-42; ptnr. Thorp Reed & Armstrong, Pitts., 1952-90, sr. ptnr., 1991—. Major U.S. Army, 1942-46, PTO. Decorated Bronze Star, 1944. Mem. ABA, Pa. Bar Assn., Allegheny County Bar Assn. General corporate, Private international, Probate. Home: Chatham Tower Apt 16 E Pittsburgh PA 15219 Office: Thorp Reed & Armstrong 20 Stanwix St Ste 900 Pittsburgh PA 15222-4895

**SUZUKI, NORMAN HITOSHI,** lawyer; b. Honolulu, Dec. 5, 1935; s. Hajime and Mildred (Fujimoto) S.; m. Lois A. Tatsuguchi, Aug. 19, 1962; children: Grant T., Brandon A. BA, U. Mich., 1957; LLB, Harvard U., 1960. Bar: Hawaii 1960, U.S. Dist. Ct. Hawaii 1960, U.S. Ct. Appeals (9th cir.) 1962, U.S. Supreme Ct. 1974. Sole practice Honolulu, 1960—; pres. Suzuki & Lee, Attys., Honolulu, 1990-93, Suzuki & Goo, Attys., Honolulu, 1993—. Served to capt. USAR, 1960-66. Mem. ABA, Hawaii Bar Assn. General corporate, Legislative, Probate. Home: 3517 Kahawalu Dr Honolulu HI 96817-1029 Office: Suzuki & Goo 1188 Bishop St Century Sq Suite 1805 Honolulu HI 96813

**SVAB, STEPHEN,** lawyer; b. Cleve., Oct. 28, 1954; s. Bert and Elizabeth (Biro) S. BA in English, John Carroll U., 1976; MA in Journalism, Penn State U., 1978; JD in Law, Case Western Reserve U., 1982. Bar: Ohio 1983, U.S. Dist. Ct. (no. dist.) Ohio 1983. Segment producer Nightwatch CBS News, Washington, 1984-88; assignment editor USA Today On TV, Rossyln, Va., 1989; chief news media divsn. Office of Pub. Affairs FCC, Washington, 1990-94, sr. atty. video svcs. divsn. Mass Media Bur, 1994—. Mem. Young Benefactors of Smithsonian Instn., Washington, 1993, Women's Mus. of the Arts, Washington, 1994. Mem. ABA, Ohio State Bar Assn., Fed. Comm. Bar Assn., N.Y. Rd. Runners Club. Roman Catholic. Avocations: weight tng., biking, tennis, reading, marathon running. Office: FCC 445 12th St SW Washington DC 20554-0001

**SVALYA, PHILLIP GORDON,** lawyer; b. Ferndale, Mich., June 28, 1943; s. John Michael and Ann Marie (Peters) S.; m. Lois Faith Wallace, Aug. 15, 1969; children: Daniel Gordon, Karina Renee. BS, U.S. Naval Acad., Annapolis, Md., 1966; JD, U. Santa Clara, Calif., 1973. Bar: Calif. 1974, U.S. Dist. Ct. (no. dist.) Calif. 1974. Pvt. practice law Peter Daniels, Sunnyvale, Mountain View, Calif., 1975-81, Cupertino, Calif., 1981—, 1981—. Lt. USN, 1966-70, capt. USNR SEAL ret., 1970-91. Mem. ATLA, Calif. Bar Assn., Consumer Attys. of Calif., Santa Clara County Bar Assn., Sunnyvale/Cupertino Bar Assn., Underwater Demolition Team-SEAL Assn., Trial Lawyers for Pub. Justice Assn. Republican. Avocations: skiing, running. Personal injury, Product liability, Professional liability. Office: Phillip G Svalya Inc 10455 Torre Ave Cupertino CA 95014-3203

**SVENGALIS, KENDALL FRAYNE,** law librarian; b. Gary, Ind., May 16, 1947; s. Frank Anthony and Alvida Linnea (Matheus) S.; m. Deborah Kay Andrews, May 23, 1970; children: Hillary Linnea, Andrew Kendall. BA, Purdue U., 1970, MA, 1973; MLS, U. R.I., 1975. Reference librarian Roger Williams Coll., Bristol, R.I., 1975, Providence (R.I.) Coll., 1975-77; asst. law librarian R.I. State Law Library, Providence, 1976-82, state law librarian, 1982—; adj. prof. libr. and info. studies U. R.I., 1987—. Author: The Legal Information Buyer's Guide and Reference Manual, 1996 (Best Legal Reference Book of 1996), 97-98, 98-99; editor: The Criv Sheet, 1988-94; contbr. articles to profl. jours. Chmn. jud. branch United Way Com. R.I., 1980. Recipient AALL Joseph L. Andrews Bibliographical awd. Mem. Am. Assn Law Librs. (state, ct. and county libr. spl. interest sect., recipient Connie E. Bolden significant publ. award 1993, 99, bd. dirs. 1986-88, 96-99), Law Librs. New Eng. (treas. 1983-85, v.p. 1985-86, pres. 1986-87), Com. on Rels. with Info. Vendors (editor 1988-94), New Eng. Law Libr. Consortium (v.p. 1990-92, pres. 1992-94). Republican. Lutheran. Home: 17 Mosher Dr Barrington RI 02806-1909 Office: RI State Law Libr Frank Licht Jud Complex 250 Benefit St Providence RI 02903-2719

**SWAFFORD, CHRISTOPHER MATT,** lawyer; b. Wichita, Kans., May 5, 1969; s. John W. and Nancy E. Swafford; m. Lisa Fitzpatrick, May 25, 1991; children: Zachary Duncan, Alexander Ian. AD, Stanford U., 1990; JD, UCLA, 1993. Bar: Calif. 1993, Mo. 1996, Kans. 1997, U.S. Ct. Appeals (8th and 9th cirs.). Assoc. Morrison & Foerster LLP, L.A., 1993-94; jud. clk. U.S. Ct. of Appeals 9th cir., Seattle, 1994-95; assoc. Polsinelli, White, Vardeman & Shalton, P.C., Kansas City, 1996—; founder, chair Year 2000 Practice Group, Polsinelli, White, Vardeman & Shalton. Mem. ABA (chair subcom. on litigation of non-competition agreements 1996-97). Avocations: sailing, bicycling, writing fiction. Office: Polsinelli White Vardeman & Shalton 700 W 47th St Ste 1000 Kansas City MO 64112-1805

**SWAIN, LAURA TAYLOR,** judge; b. Bklyn., Nov. 21, 1958; d. Justus E. and Madeline V. (Allgood) Taylor; m. Andrew J. Swain, Oct. 12, 1991. AB, Harvard U., 1979, JD, 1982. Bar: Mass. 1982, N.Y. 1983, U.S. Dist. Ct. (so. and ea. dists.) N.Y. 1983. Law clk to chief judge U.S. Dist. Ct. (so. dist.) N.Y., 1982-83; assoc. Debevoise & Plimpton, N.Y.C., 1983-95, counsel, 1995-96; U.S. bankruptcy judge U.S. Bankruptcy Ct., Bklyn., 1996—; mem. N.Y. State Bd. Law Examiners, Albany, 1986-96; mem. multistate bar exam. com. Nat. Conf. Bar Examiners, 1987-99, mem. testing, R&D devel. com., 1990-94, mem. long range planning com., 1994-96; cons. N.Y. Profl. Edn. Project, 1995-96. Co-contbr. articles on employee benefits, employee stock ownership plans, acctg. and bankruptcy to profl. pubs.; contbg. author: New York Insurance Law, 1991. Trustee Diocese of N.Y. (Episcopal), 1991-92; mem. Dessoff Choirs, N.Y.C., 1984-92; bd. dirs. Episcopal Charities, Inc., 1996—, Coalition Consumer Bankruptcy Debtor Edn., 1998—. Mem. ABA, Assn. of Bar of City of N.Y., Met. Black Bar Assn., N.Y. State Bar Assn., Nat. Conf. Bankruptcy Judges, Nat. Assn. Women Judges. Episcopalian. Avocation: music. Pension, profit-sharing, and employee benefits, Federal civil litigation, Labor. Office: US Bankruptcy Ct Ea Dist NY 75 Clinton St Brooklyn NY 11201-4201

**SWAIN, PHILIP C., JR.,** lawyer, mechanical engineer; b. Akron, Ohio, Dec. 10, 1957; s. Philip C. Sr. and Shirley I. (Tessier) S.; m. Roseanne K. Vita, May 5, 1990; children: Kimberly A., Jennifer R. BA and BSME, Tufts U., 1981; JD, Northwestern U., 1984. Bar: Ill. 1984, Mass. 1985, D.C. 1988, Calif. 1990. Acting asst. dean Sch. of Law Northwestern U., Chgo., 1984; law clk. U.S. Ct. Appeals (federal cir.), Washington, 1985-86; from assoc. to ptnr. Kirkland & Ellis, Chicago and L.A., 1986-97; ptnr. Foley, Hoag & Eliot, Boston, 1997—; adj. prof. Suffolk U. Sch. Law, 1998—. Mem. Federal Cir. Bar Assn. (pres.-elect 1999—). Avocations: running, ice hockey. Patent, Trademark and copyright, General civil litigation. Home: 114 Pine Hill Ln Concord MA 01742-4414 Office: Foley Hoag & Eliot One Post Office Sq Boston MA 02109

**SWAN, GEORGE STEVEN,** law educator; b. St. Louis. BA, Ohio State U., 1970; JD, U. Notre Dame, 1974; LLM, U. Toronto, 1976, SJD, 1983. Bar: Ohio 1974, U.S. Dist. Ct. (so. dist.) Ohio 1975, U.S. Supreme Ct. 1987, U.S. Ct. Appeals (6th and 11th cirs.) 1993, U.S. Ct. Appeals (10th cir.) 1994, D.C. 1997, Ga. 1997, U.S. Dist. Ct. (no. dist.) Ga. 1997, Fla. 1997, Minn. 1998, Nebr. 1998, N.D. 1998, U.S. Ct. Appeals (7th cir.) 1998, Mass. 1999; ChFC, CLU, CFP; registered investment advisor. Sec. of state N.C., 1990; asst. atty. gen. State of Ohio, Columbus, 1974-75; jud. clk. Supreme Ct. Ohio, Columbus, 1976-78; asst. prof. Del. Law Sch., Wilmington, 1980-83, assoc. prof., 1983-84; prof. law St. Thomas U. Law Sch., Miami, Fla., 1984-88; jud. clk. U.S. Ct. Appeals (7th cir.), Chgo., 1988-89; assoc. prof. N.C. Agrl. & Tech. State U., Greensboro, 1989-96, 97—; vis. prof. John Marshall Law Sch., Atlanta, 1996-97. Contbr. articles to law jours. Mem. Ohio State Bar Assn., D.C. Bar, State Bar Ga., Fla. Bar, Mass. Bar Assn., Nebr. State Bar Assn., N.D. State Bar Assn., Soc. of Fin. Svc. Profls., Internat. Assn. for Fin. Planning, Am. Polit. Sci. Assn., Inst. CFPs. Office: N C Agrl and Tech State U Merrick Hall 1601 E Market St Greensboro NC 27411-0001

**SWANEY, THOMAS EDWARD,** lawyer; b. Detroit, Apr. 25, 1942; s. Robert Ernest and Mary Alice (Slinger) S.; m. Patricia Louise Nash, Sept. 9, 1967; children: Julia Bay, Mary Elizabeth, David Paul. AB, U. Mich., 1963, JD, 1967; postdoctoral, London Sch. Econs., 1967-68. Bar: Ill. 1968. From assoc. to ptnr. Sidley & Austin, Chgo., 1968—; bd. dirs. Corey Steel Co., Cicero, Ill., Gertrude B. Nielsen Child Care & Learning Ctr., Northbrook, Ill., Ward C. Rogers Found., Chgo. Trustee H. Earl Hoover Found., Glencoe, Ill., 1986—, RF Found., Chgo., 1992—; trustee, bd. pres. 1st Presbyn. Ch., Evanston, Ill., 1984-87, 96-98; bd. dirs. Lakeland Conservancy, Minocqua, Wis., 1987—. Mem. ABA, Ill. State Bar Assn., Chgo. Bar Assn., Legal Club Chgo. Estate planning, Probate, Estate taxation. Office: Sidley & Austin 1 First Natl Plz Chicago IL 60603-2003

**SWANK, DAMON RAYNARD,** lawyer; b. Boulder, Colo., Sept. 14, 1940; s. Raynard Coe and Ethel Louise (Mershon) S.; m. Susan M. Heigl, June 13, 1970; children: Stephen Carl, Lauren Marie. BA, Coll. of Wooster, 1962; JD, U. Calif., Berkeley, 1965. Bar: Calif. 1965, U.S. Dist. Ct. (no. dist.) Calif. 1965, U.S. Ct. Appeals (9th cir.) 1965, U.S. Dist. Ct. (cen. dist.) Calif. 1969, Minn. 1977. Dep. pub. defender Pub. Defender Office County of Los Angeles, L.A., 1965-84; pvt. practice Long Beach, Calif., 1984—. Mem. Long Beach Bar Assn. (bd. govs. 1993-94). Avocation: offshore sailing. Criminal, Juvenile. Office: 7 Chaparral Ln Rancho Palos Verdes CA 90275-5167

**SWANN, BARBARA,** lawyer; b. N.Y., Sept. 15, 1950; d. George Arthur. BA summa cum laude, Montclair State U., 1988; JD, Rutgers Law, 1992. Bar: N.J. 1992, D.C. 1994, N.Y. 1995, U.S. Dist. Ct. N.J. 1992, U.S. Ct. Appeals (3rd cir.) 1994, U.S. Dist. Ct. N.Y. 1996. Correspondent The Associate Press, Newark, N.J., 1974-80; reporter, bureau chief The Hudson Dispatch, Union City, N.J., 1973-80; editorial page editor The Paterson (N.J.) News, 1980-81; v.p., acct. supr. Gerald Freeman, Inc., Clifton, N.J., 1981-86; pres. LePore Assoc., Inc., West Caldwell, N.J., 1986-89; law clk. to Hon. Robert N. Wilentz N.J. Supreme Ct., 1992-93; law clk. to Hon. Leonard I. Garth U.S. Ct. Appeals (3rd cir.), 1993-94; assoc. Cahill, Gordon & Reindel, N.Y., 1994-97; liaison Republic of Ga., ABA Cen. and East European Law Initiative, 1997—. Editor-in-chief: Rutgers Computer & Technology Law Jour., 1991-92. Founding trustee Ctr. for Children's Advocacy, Riverdale, N.J. 1994—. Mem. ABA, Assn. of the Bar of the City of New York, N.J. State Bar Assn., N.Y. County Lawyers' Assn. Am. Inn of Ct., D.C. Bar Assn. Libel, Constitutional, General civil litigation. Office: ABA Cen/Ea Europ Law Inst, Tbilisi Georgia

**SWANSON, ARTHUR DEAN,** lawyer; b. Onida, S.D., Apr. 19, 1934; s. Obert W. and Mary I. (Barnum) S.; m. Paula Swanson, Aug. 22, 1965 (div. Feb. 1984); children: Shelby, Dean, Sherry; m. Ann Swanson, Aug. 21, 1989. BA, Wash. State U., 1956; JD, U. Wash., 1963. Bar: Wash. 1963. Dep. prosecutor King County, Seattle, 1964-65; ct. commr. Renton and Issaquah Dist. Cts., Wash., 1966-68; pvt. practice law Renton, Wash., 1965—; lectr. various orgns.; former counsel Wash. State Law Enforcement Assn., Wash. State Dep. Sheriff's Assn. Served with Fin. Corps, U.S. Army, 1956-58. Named one of Best Lawyers Am., 1991-92, 93-94, 95-96, 97-98. Fellow Am. Coll. Trial Lawyers; mem. Wash. State Bar Assn. (past sec. trial sect.), Seattle-King County Bar Assn. (bd. trustees 1977-80), Assn. Trial Lawyers Am., Wash. State Trial Lawyers Assn. (past pres.), Am. Bd. Trial Advs. (bd. dirs., pres. Wash. state chpt. 1995-96), Damage Attys. Roundtable (pres. 1998-99). Democrat. Avocation: tennis. Personal injury, Insurance, State civil litigation. Office: 4512 Talbot Rd S Renton WA 98055-6216

**SWANSON, BRADLEY DEAN,** lawyer; b. Litchfield, Minn., July 24, 1950; s. Kermit Jerome and Aileen Lois Swanson; m. Paulette Kay Frydenlund, June 22, 1974 (div. June 1980); 1 child, Lindsey E.; m. Joanie Ann Lundeen, Nov. 1, 1980; children: Briana, Javen. BA, Gustavus Adolphus Coll., 1973; JD, Hamline U., 1977. Bar: Minn. 1977. Pvt. practice Dassel, Minn., 1977-85; in-house counsel NorBanc Group, Inc., Pine River, Minn., 1985-88; ptnr. Lundrigan & Swanson, Pine River, 1988-98; pvt. practice Pine River, 1998—; family law mediator, Minn., 1995—. Pres. Pine River C. of C., 1986; bd. mem. First Luth Ch., Pine River, 1994. With USAF Nat. Guard, 1968-74. Mem. Minn. State Bar Assn., Ninth Jud. Dist. Bar Assn., Ctrl. Lakes Rotary Club (sec., v.p., pres. 1992—), Kinship Ptnrs. (adv. bd. 1995-98). Republican. Avocations: hunting, fishing, flying, golfing. Family and matrimonial, Probate, General practice. Home: 2732 22nd St SW Pine River MN 56474-7805 Office: First & Barday PO Box 398 Pine River MN 56474-0398

**SWANSON, GILLIAN LEE,** law librarian; b. Bozeman, Mont., Sept. 13, 1961; d. Garry Arthur and Betty Ellen (McIelwain) S.; m. Thomas Darryl Fox, June 23, 1990. BA in Philosophy, U. Calgary, Alta., Can., 1985; LLB, U. Western Ont., London, Ontario, Can., 1988. Bar: Ont. 1991. Student-at-law Daniel, Wilson (formerly Harris, Barr), St. Catharine's, Ont., 1989-90; law libr. Banc One Corp., Columbus, Ohio, 1993—. Mem. Law Soc. Upper Can. Avocations: legal reference for banking and commercial issues, and for Canadian and American immigration and refugee legal and social issues. Home: 100 E Henderson Rd Columbus OH 43214-2717 Office: Banc One Corp 100 E Broad St Ste 1 Columbus OH 43215-3696

**SWANSON, KELLY HANSEN,** lawyer; b. Middletown, Conn., Nov. 19, 1946; s. Carl Everett and Charlotte (Weston) S.; m. Carolyn McLaughlin, Aug. 24, 1976; children: Jennifer, Julie, Victoria. BA, U. Ill., 1971; JD, U. Ark., 1974. Bar: Ark. 1974, Nev. 1974, U.S. Dist. Ct. Nev. 1974, U.S. Ct. Appeals (9th cir.) 1974, U.S. Tax Ct. 1979. Atty., law clk. Clark County Pub. Defender, Las Vegas, Nev., 1974-76; pres. Kelly H. Swanson, Chartered, Las Vegas, 1976-; mem. med.-legal malpractice screening panel State of Nev., so. dist., 1993—; justice of the peace pro tem. Contbr. articles to legal jours. With USAF, 1964-68. Mem. ABA, ATLA, Nev. Trial Lawyers Assn. (bd. govs. 1993-95), State Bar Nev. (fee dispute com. 1977-86), Nat. Network Estate Planning Attys. Avocations: golf, football. Estate planning, Bankruptcy, Real property. Office: 1200 S Eastern Ave Las Vegas NV 89104-2005

**SWANSON, LESLIE MARTIN, JR.,** lawyer; b. Yakima, Wash., May 16, 1940; s. Leslie Martin and Eleanor Louise (Morris) S.; children: Mark, Carl, Todd. BA, Augustana Coll., Rock Island, Ill., 1961; MA, Claremont Grad. U., Calif., 1964; JD, U. Oreg., 1966. Bar: Oreg. 1966, U.S. Dist. Ct. Oreg. 1966, U.S. Ct. Appeals (9th cir.) 1969, U.S. Supreme Ct. 1978. Ptnr. Harrang, Swanson, Long & Watkinson, Eugene, Oreg., 1966-85; pres., shareholder Swanson & Walters, Eugene, 1985-92; pvt. practice Les Swanson Jr., Atty. at Law, Portland, Oreg., 1992—; assoc. prof. and adj. prof. law U. Oreg., Eugene. Mem. Oreg. State Bd. Higher Edn., 1989—, pres., 1994-96; mem. Oreg. Arts Commn., 1980-83; v.p. bd. visitors U. Oreg. Sch. Law, 1987-89. Mem. Lane County Bar Assn. (pres. 1983-84), Am. Law Inst. Personal injury, Product liability. Office: 808 SW 3rd Ave Ste 400 Portland OR 97204-2433

**SWANSON, PAUL G.,** lawyer; b. Milw.; s. Vernon A. and Jane T. Swanson; m. Jody L. Chenkasky, Sept. 13, 1986; children: Michael B., Alexander B. BBA, U. Wis., Oshkosh, 1977; JD, U. Wis., 1979. Bar: Wis. 1979; cert. bankruptcy specialist ABBC. Atty. Swanson Law Office, S.C., Oshkosh, 1979-85; ptnr. Swanson, Stienhilber, et al, Oshkosh, 1985-90, Steinhilber, Swanson, et al, Oshkosh, 1990—. Mem. ABA, Nat. Assn. Bankruptcy Trustees (bd. dirs. 1996—), Nat. Assn. Consumer Law League, State Bar Wis. (pres. young lawyers divsn. 1986, 87, bd. dirs. bd. govs. 1988-94, treas. 1990-91). Avocations: skiing, sailing, squash. Bankruptcy. Home: 5172 Island View Dr Oshkosh WI 54901-1356 Office: PO Box 617 377 Park Plz Oshkosh WI 54901-4825

**SWANSON, ROBERT LEE,** lawyer; b. Fond du Lac, Wis., July 15, 1942; s. Walfred S. and Edna F. (Kamp) S.; m. Mary Ruth Francis, Aug. 19, 1967; children: Leigh Alexandra, Mitchell Pearson. BS, U. Wis., 1964; JD, Valparaiso U., 1970; LLM, Boston U., 1979. Bar: Wis. 1970, U.S. Dist. Ct. (ea. dist.) Wis. 1970, U.S. Dist. Ct. (we. dist.) Wis. 1974, U.S. Tax Ct. 1981, U.S. Dist. Ct. (cen.) Ill. 1988, U.S. Ct. Appeals (7th cir.) 1999. Atty. Kasdorf, Dahl, Lewis & Swietlik, Milw., 1970-73; atty., ptnr. Wartman, Wartman & Swanson, Ashland, Wis., 1973-80; city atty. City of Ashland, Wis., 1976-80; atty., ptnr. DeMark, Kolbe & Brodek, Racine, Wis., 1980-95; ptnr. Hartig, Bjelajac, Swanson & Koenen, Racine, 1995-99; lectr. civil rights and discrimination laws, 1980—; lectr. bus. law Cardinal Strich U., 1996-99, U. Wis.-Parkside, 1997-99. Columnist (legal) Burlington Std. Press, 1991-95, Wis. Restaurant Assn. Mag., 1986. Vice comdr. USCG Aux. Bayfield (Wis.) Flotilla, 1975-81; v.p., bd. dirs. Meml. Med. Ctr., Ashland, 1975-80; chmn. Ashland County Rep. Party, 1976-79; vol. atty. ACLU Wis., 1975-90. 1st lt. U.S. Army, 1964-66. Named one of Outstanding Young Men of Am., Jaycees, 1978; recipient Disting. Achievement in Art and Sci. of Advocacy award Internat. Acad. Trial Lawyers, 1970. Mem. Racine County Bar Assn. (bd. dirs. 1986-89), Wis. Acad. Trial Lawyers, Def. Rsch. Inst., Am. Hockey Assn. U.S. (coach, referee 1983-90), Am. Legion. Avocations: softball, volleyball, hockey. E-mail: rswanson@brightok.net. General civil litigation, General practice, General corporate. Home: RR1 Box 478 Stroud OK 74079

**SWANSON, SHANE ERIC,** lawyer; b. Denver, Jan. 28, 1971; s. Dean Eugene and Margery Ann Swanson; m. Tammy Mosteller, Sept. 2, 1995. BA, U. S.C., 1992, JD, 1995. Bar: S.C., U.S. Dist. Ct. S.C. 1995. Assoc. Grimball L. Cabaniss, LLC, Charleston, S.C., 1995-97, Buist Moore Smythe and McGee, Charleston, 1997-99; corp. counsel Automated Trading Desk Inc., Charleston, 1999—; resource atty. YLD-Teen Ct., Charleston, 1996—. Assoc. editor Young Lawyers' Divsn. Bar Tub Publ., 1998. Instr. World Tae Kwon Do Assn., Charleston, 1995—. Mem. Phi Beta Kappa. Avocations: Tae Kwon Do (4th degree black belt), reading. General civil litigation, General practice, Securities. Office: Automated Trading desk Inc 389 Johnnie Dodds Blvd Mount Pleasant SC 29464-2950

**SWANSON, WALLACE MARTIN,** lawyer; b. Fergus Falls, Minn., Aug. 22, 1941; s. Marvin Walter and Mary Louise (Lindsey) S.; m. Susan Windsor Swanson; children: Kristen Lindsey, Eric Munger. B.A. with honors, U. Minn., 1962; LL.B. with honors, So. Methodist U., 1965. Bar: Tex. 1965. Since practiced in Dallas; assoc. Coke & Coke, Dallas, 1965-70; ptnr. firm Johnson & Swanson, Dallas, 1970-88; prin. Wallace M. Swanson, P.C., Dallas, 1988—; chmn., CEO Ace Cash Express Inc., Irving, Tex., 1987-88, State St. Capital Corp., 1990—. Served with USNR, 1960-65. Mem. Tex. Bar Found., State Bar Tex. (securities com. 1972-86, chmn. 1978-80, coun. bus. law sect. 1980-86), Crescent Club. Methodist. General corporate, Mergers and acquisitions, Real property. Address: 5811 Redwood Ct Dallas TX 75209-2439

**SWANSON, WARREN LLOYD,** lawyer; b. Chgo., Sept. 2, 1933; s. Martin W. and Esther Swanson; m. Rosalie Elaine Simpson, June 23, 1963; 1 son, Christopher; m. Kathryn Ann Jasperson, Oct. 16, 1979 (dec. Sept. 1986). BA, U. Chgo., 1953; JD, Northwestern U., 1957. Bar: Ill. 1957, U.S. Dist. Ct. (no. dist.) Ill, 1958, U.S. Ct. Appeals (7th cir.) 1959. Lectr., Northwestern U. Law Sch., 1958-59; ptnr. Stoffels & Swanson, Chgo., 1959-63; spl. asst. states atty. Cook County, Ill., 1960-62; sole practice, Chgo., 1963-80; ptnr. Swanson, Ross & Block, Chgo., 1980-84, Swanson & Brown, Palos Heights, Ill., 1984—; city atty. Palos Heights, Ill., 1959—, co-counsel City of Park Ridge, 1957-63. Pres., Easter Seal Soc. Met. Chgo., 1970-74; mem. Chgo. Crime Commn., 1963—; trustee Ill. State Hist. Preservation Agy., 1994—; mem., dir. Congl. liaison chmn. nat. com. Kennedy Ctr. for Performing Arts, Washington, 1994—; dir. Lawson House YMCA. Recipient John Howard Assn. Disting. Svc. award, 1961, 63. Mem. Chgo. Bar Assn., Ill. Bar Assn., ABA, Writers Guild Am., Cliff Dwellers Club (bd. dirs.), Chgo. Yacht Club. Head writer daytime serials As the World Turns, 1970-72, Somerset, 1973-75; co-writer daytime serials Another World, 1963-66, Love is a Many Splendored Thing, 1966-68, Edge of Night, 1968-70; author: Museums of Chicago, 1976, Recreation Guide to Chicago and Suburbs, 1980. Real property, Consumer commercial. Office: 12600 S Harlem Ave Ste 202 Palos Heights IL 60463-1428

**SWARNS, CHRISTINA ALLISON,** lawyer; b. Queens, N.Y., July 16, 1968; d. Joseph Henry and Lucille Agnes S. BA, Howard U., 1990; JD, U. Pa., 1993. Staff atty. criminal def. divsn. The Legal Aid Soc., N.Y.C., 1994-96; asst. fed. defender Capital Habeas Corpus Unit, Defender Assn. Phila., 1996—. Speaker Nat. Coalition to Abolish Death Penalty, St. Louis, 1998, Vera Inst. Justice, N.Y.C., 1998. Office: Defender Assn Phila Capital Habeas Corpus Unit 437 Chestnut St Ste 510 Philadelphia PA 19106-2414

**SWARTZ, CHARLES ROBERT,** lawyer; b. Norfolk, Va., Jan. 28, 1944. BA, U. Va., 1965; JD, U. Ga., 1968. Bar: Va. 1968. Ptnr. McGuire Woods Battle & Boothe L.L.P., Richmond, Va., 1969—. Fellow Am. Coll. Real Estate Lawyers; mem. Internat. Assn. Attys. and Execs. in Corp. Real Estate. E-mail: crswartz@mwbb.com. Real property. Office: McGuire Woods Battle & Boothe LLP 1 James Ctr 901 E Cary St Richmond VA 23219-4057

**SWARTZ, MARK LEE,** lawyer; b. Amesbury, Mass., May 17, 1954; s. Bernard Jerome and Evelyn Vivian Swartz. BS, U. Mass., 1976; JD, Case Western U., 1979. Bar: Mass. 1979, Ohio 1979, U.S. Dist. Ct. Mass. 1980, U.S. Ct. Appeals (1st cir.) 1980. Pub. defender Essex County, Mass., 1980-83; pvt. practice Amesbury, Mass., 1980—; atty. Amesbury Housing Rehab. Program, 1980-81, Merrimac Housing Authority, Merrimac, 1980-86, Amesbury Housing Authority, 1980-86. Mem. Mass. Bar Assn., Phi Beta Kappa, Phi Kappa Phi. Republican. Avocations: reading, dancing, travel, chess, walking. Probate, Real property, Consumer commercial. Home: PO Box 185 Amesbury MA 01913-0004 Office: 1 School St Amesbury MA 01913-2812

**SWARTZ, MELVIN JAY,** lawyer, author; b. Boston, July 21, 1930; s. Jack M. and Rose (Rosenberg) S.; children: Julianne, Jonathan Samuel. BA, Syracuse U., 1953; LLB, Boston U., 1957. Bar: N.Y. 1959, Ariz. 1961. Assoc. Alfred S. Julian, N.Y.C., 1957-59; ptnr. Finks & Swartz, Youngtown, Sun City, Phoenix, Ariz., 1961-70, Swartz & Jeckel, P.C., Sun City, Youngtown, Scottsdale, Ariz., 1971-82; exec. v.p. APPPRO, Inc., Scottsdale. Author: Don't Die Broke, A Guide to Secure Retirement, 1974, (book and cassettes) Keep What You Own, 1989, rev. edit., 1999, Retire Without Fear, 1995, How Can Yo Forget My Money, 1999, What To Do When Your Spouse Dies, 1999; columnist News-Sun, Sun City, 1979-83; author column Swartz on Aging. Bd. dirs. Valley of the Sun Sch. for Retarded Children, 1975-79. Mem. ABA, Ariz. Bar Assn., N.Y. Bar Assn., Maricopa County Bar Assn., Scottsdale Bar Assn., Ctrl. Ariz. Estate Planning Coun., Masons (Phoenix). Jewish. Probate, Estate taxation, Estate planning. Office: 6619 N Scottsdale Rd Scottsdale AZ 85250-4421

**SWAUGER, TERRY ALLEN,** lawyer; b. Warren, Ohio, Apr. 14, 1969; s. Byron M. and Dorothy Ellen Swauger; m. Kellee Marie O'Dell, Oct. 7, 1995; 1 child, Jillian Paige. BA, Ohio State U., 1992; JD, Capital U., 1995. Bar: Ohio 1995, U.S. Dist. Ct. (no. dist.) Ohio 1998. Assoc. Tackett Zapka & Leuchtag, Warren, Ohio, 1995-97, Law Offices of Dennis W. Tackett, Warren, 1997—. Baptist. Avocations: sports, golf, Bocce. General practice, Criminal, Personal injury. Home: 104 Wade Ave Niles OH 44446-1927 Office: Law Offices Dennis W Tackett 106 E Market St Ste 308 Warren OH 44481-1151

**SWEARER, WILLIAM BROOKS,** lawyer; b. Hays, Kans.. Grad., Princeton U., 1951; law degree, U. Kans., 1955. Bar: Kans. 1955. Pvt. practice Hutchinson, Kans., 1955—; ptnr. Martindell, Swearer & Shaffer, LLP, Hutchinson, 1955—; mem. Kans. Bd. Discipline for Attys., 1979-92, chmn., 1987-92. With U.S. Army, 1952-53, Korea. Mem. ABA (ho. of dels. 1995—), Am. Bar Found. (state chair 1998—), Kans. Bar Assn. (pres. 1992-93, various offices, mem. coms.), Kans. Assn. Sch. Attys. (pres. 1989-90),

Reno County Bar Assn. Education and schools, General corporate, Probate. Office: PO Box 1907 Hutchinson KS 67504-1907

**SWEDA, EDWARD LEON, JR.,** lawyer; b. Boston, Mass., Dec. 31, 1955; s. Edward Leon and Lucy (Daniszewski) S. BA, Boston Coll., 1977; JD, Suffolk Law Sch., Boston, 1980. Pvt. practice Boston, 1981—; lobbyist Group Against Smoking Pollution, Boston, 1980-93. Vol. Common Cause, Boston, 1977-83. Recipient Appreciation award, Am. Lung Assn. Mass., Boston, 1989. Democrat. Roman Catholic. Criminal, Legislative, Labor. Home: 172 Boston St Dorchester MA 02125-1142 Office: GASP Kenmore Sta PO Box 15463 Boston MA 02215-0008

**SWEENEY, ASHER WILLIAM,** state supreme court justice; b. Canfield, Ohio, Dec. 11, 1920; s. Walter William and Jessie Joan (Kidd) S.; m. Bertha M. Englert, May 21, 1945; children: Randall W., Ronald R., Garland A., Karen M. Student, Youngstown U., 1939-42; LL.B., Duke U., 1948. Bar: Ohio 1949. Practiced law Youngstown, Ohio, 1949-51; judge adv. gen. Dept. Def., Washington, 1951-65; chief Fed. Contracting Agy., Cin., 1965-68; corp. law, 1968-77; justice Ohio Supreme Ct., Columbus, 1977—. Democratic candidate for Sec. of State Ohio, 1958. Served with U.S. Army, 1942-46; col. Res. 1951-68. Decorated Legion of Merit, Bronze Star; named to Army Hall of Fame Ft. Benning, Ga., 1981. Mem. Ohio Bar Assn., Phi Delta Phi. Democrat. Home: 6690 Drake Rd Cincinnati OH 45243-2706 Office: Ohio Supreme Ct 30 E Broad St Fl 3D Columbus OH 43215-3414

**SWEENEY, CLAYTON ANTHONY, JR.,** lawyer; b. Pitts., Jan. 2, 1964; s. Clayton Anthony and Sally (Dimond) S. BA in Econs. with honors, McGill U., 1987; JD, U. Pitts., 1991. Bar: Pa. 1992, Del. 1995, U.S. Dist. Ct. Del. 1995, U.S. Dist. Ct. (we. dist.) Pa. 1991, U.S. Dist. Ct. (eas. dist.) Pa. 1997, U.S. Ct. Appeals (3d cir.) 1992. Assoc. Burns, White & Hickton, Pitts., 1991-92; law clk. Hon. Donald J. Lee U.S. Dist. Ct. (we. dist.) Pa., Pitts., 1992-94; assoc. Skadden, Arps, Slate, Meagher & Flom, Wilmington, Del., 1994-96; sole practitioner Phila., 1997—. Vol. atty. Vols. for the Indigent Program, Phila., 1997—, Del. Vol. Legal Svcs., Wilmington, 1995. Mem. Fed. Bar Assn. (criminal law com.), Phila. Bar Assn., Allegheny County Bar Assn., Del. State Bar Assn., Pa. Assn. Criminal Def. Lawyers. Republican. Avocations: guitar, dance. Criminal, Juvenile, Consumer commercial. Office: 1528 Walnut St Ste 815 Philadelphia PA 19102-3608

**SWEENEY, DEIDRE ANN,** lawyer; b. Hackensack, N.J., Mar. 17, 1953; d. Thomas Joseph and Robin (Thwaites) S. AB cum laude, Mt. Holyoke Coll., 1975; JD, Fordham U., 1978. Assoc. Curtis, Mallet-Prevost, Colt & Mosle, N.Y.C., 1978-84, Eaton & Van Winkle, N.Y.C., 1984-86; ptnr. Jacobs, Persinger & Parker, N.Y.C., 1986—; adj. instr. Adelphi U., N.Y.C., 1982-86. Class agt. Mt. Holyoke Coll. Alumni Fund, South Hadley, Mass., 1975-80; chmn. nominating com. Mt. Holyoke Class of 1975, 1990-94; mem. Archdiocese N.Y. Bequests and Planned Gifts Com., 1988-97. Mem. Assn. of Bar of City of N.Y. (uniform state laws com. 1982-85). Democrat. Roman Catholic. Probate, Estate planning, Estate taxation.

**SWEENEY, DENNIS JOSEPH,** judge; b. New London, Conn., Sept. 25, 1946; m. Judy K. Winchel, July 27, 1968; 1 child, Shawna Marie. BBA, Gonzaga U., 1968, JD, 1972; LLM, U. Va., 1995. Bar: Wash., U.S. Dist. Ct. (ea. dist.) Wash., U.S. Ct. Appeals (9th cir.), U.S. Tax Ct., U.S. Supreme Ct.; CPA, Wash. Acct. Roger Fruci & Assocs. CPAs, Spokane, Wash., 1969-71; public defender Spokane County Public Defenders Office, Spokane, 1971-72; ptnr. Leavy, Schultz & Sweeney P.S., Pasco, Wash., 1972-91; elected judge divsn. III Wash. State Ct. Appeals, Spokane, 1991, chief judge divsn. III, 1996-98, presiding chief judge, 1998-99; presenter seminars, lectr. in Continuing Legal Edn. Program, Wash., 1990—, lectr. at Wash. State Judicial Coll. Contbr. articles to law revs. and ednl. legal jours. Bd. dirs. Heritage Coll., Toppenish, Wash., Benton Franklin Legal Aid, 1972—; mem. jurisprudence com. Access to Justice Bd.; vol. Richland Repertory Theater, benefit sausagefest for Christ the King ch.; Lt. U.S. Army, 1972. Named Appellate Judge of Yr., Wash. State Trial Lawyers Assn. Fellow ACTC; mem. AICPA, Wash. Soc. CPAs, Am. Bd. Trial Advocates. E-mail: Dennis.Sweeney@courts.wa.gov (office), Dsween2150@aol.com (home). Office: Ct Appeals State of Wash PO Box 2159 Spokane WA 99210-2159

**SWEENEY, EILEEN PATRICIA,** lawyer; b. Evanston, Ill., Nov. 6, 1951; d. Howard J. and Kathleen P. Sweeney; m. Lawrence Andrew Johnston, Sept. 1, 1979; children: Edward, Matthew, Kathleen. BA, Northwestern U., Evanston, 1973; JD, Northwestern U., Chgo., 1976. Bar: Ill. 1976, D.C. 1980. Staff atty. Legal Assistance Found. Chgo., 1976-79, Nat. Sr. Citizens Law Ctr., Washington, 1980-91; dir. gov. affairs Children's Def. Fund, Washington, 1991-98; dir. state low income initiatives project Ctr. on Budget and Policy Priorities, Washington, 1998—; mem. SSI modernization panel Soc. Security Administrn., Balt., 1990-92; mem. tech. com. Earnings Sharing, Washington, 1985-88. Contbr. articles to profl. jours. Bd. dirs. Nat. Clearinghouse Legal Svcs., 1993—; mem. commn. legal problems of elderly ABA, Washington, 1990-91; mem. expert panel re-thinking disability policy, 1993-96. Recipient Reginald Heber Smith award Nat. Legal Aid and Def. Assn., Washington, 1985, Alumna Yr. Regina Dominican H.S., Wilmette, Ill., 1985. Mem. Nat. Acad. Soc. Ins. Roman Catholic. Avocations: family, reading, walking, sewing. Administrative and regulatory, Legislative. Office: Ctr Budget and Policy Priorities 820 1st St NE Ste 510 Washington DC 20002-4243

**SWEENEY, EMILY MARGARET,** prosecutor; b. Cleve., May 2, 1948; d. Mark Elliot and Neydra (Ginsburg) Mirsky; m. Patrick Anthony Sweeney, Dec. 30, 1983; 1 child, Margaret Anne. B.A., Case Western Res. U., 1970; J.D., Cleve. Marshall Coll. Law, 1981. Bar: Ohio 1981. Tchr. English, Cleve. Pub. Schs., 1970; plant mgr. Union Gospel Press Pub. Co., Cleve., 1971-73; publ. specialist Cleve. State U., 1973-82; asst. U.S. atty. Dept. Justice, Cleve., 1982—, now U.S. atty., Cleve., 1993—. Precinct committeeman, Woodmere, Ohio, 1978; mem. Atty. Gen.'s Adv. Com. of U.S. Attys., 1993-96, 98—, chmn. office mgmt. and budget subcom., 1993—, mem. asset forfeiture, civil issues, controlled substances and drug demand reducation, LECC/victim witness subcoms., 1993—; chmn. law enforcement coordinating com. No. Dist. Ohio, 1993—. Recipient Eddy award for graphic design, 1977; Spl. Achievement award U.S. Dept. Justice, 1985. Mem. Fed. Bar Assn. Democrat. Office: US Atty's Office 1800 Bank One Ctr 600 Superior Ave E Ste 1800 Cleveland OH 44114-2600

**SWEENEY, FRANCIS E.,** state supreme court justice; b. Jan. 26, 1934; married; 4 children. BSBA, Xavier U., 1956; JD, Cleve.-Marshall Law Sch., 1963. Profl. football player Ottawa Rough Riders, Ont., Can., 1956-58; mem. legal dept. Allstate Ins. Co., Cleve., 1958-63; asst. prosecuting atty. Cuyahoga County, Cleve., 1963-70; judge Cuyahoga County Ct. of Common Pleas, Cleve., 1970-88; judge (8th cir.) U.S. Ct. Appeals, Cleve., 1988-92; justice Ohio Supreme Ct., Columbus, 1992—. With U.S. Army, 1957-58. Recipient Legion of Honor award Xavier U., 1956, Outstanding Jud. Svc. award Ohio Supreme Ct., 1972-85, Alumnus of Yr. award Xavier U., 1977. Office: Ohio Supreme Ct 30 E Broad St Fl 3 Columbus OH 43266-0001*

**SWEENEY, JOHN FRANCIS,** lawyer; b. Washington, Nov. 26, 1946; s. Albert Eugene and Mildred (Mattimore) S.; m. Noreen Marie Castelli, Aug. 9, 1969; children—Matthew John, Laura Marie. B.S. in Math., Carnegie-Mellon U., 1968; J.D., Georgetown U., 1973. Bar: N.Y. 1974, U.S. Supreme Ct. 1980, U.C. Ct. Appeals (Fed. cir.) 1982, U.S. Ct. Appeals (2d cir.) 1975, U.S. Ct. Appeals (3d cir.) 1981, U.S. Dist. Ct. (so. dist.) N.Y. 1975, U.S. Dist. Ct. (ea. dist.) N.Y. 1984. Mathematician, U.S. Army Strategy and Tactics Analysis Group, Bethesda, Md., 1968-70; computer analyst U.S. Army Computer Systems Support and Evaln Command, Arlington, Va., 1970-73; assoc. Morgan & Finnegan and predecessor firm Morgan Finnegan Pine Foley & Lee, N.Y.C., 1973-81, ptnr., 1981—, mem. exec. com. 1983—. Author: (poems) Rhymes, 1984. Mem. ABA Assn. of Bar of City of N.Y. (mem. patent com. 1983—), N.Y. Patent, Trademark and Copyright Law Assn., Democrat. Roman Catholic. Club: Head of the Bay (Huntington Bay, N.Y.). Patent, Trademark and copyright, Federal civil litigation. Home: Tulipwood Llyod Ln Lloyd Neck NY 11743 Office: Morgan & Finnegan 345 Park Ave Fl 22 New York NY 10154-0053

**SWEENEY, JOHN J(OSEPH),** lawyer; b. N.Y.C., Dec. 28, 1924; s. John J. and Rose H. (Galligan) S.; m. Rita V. Colleran, Aug. 27, 1955; children: Jean Maria, John J., Peter F., Thomas P., Michael J., Roseanne. LLB, St. John's U., 1951, BA, 1952. Bar: N.Y., 1951. Vol. lawyer Felony Ct. Legal Aid Soc., N.Y.C., 1951-52; asst. gen. counsel U.S. Trucking Corp., N.Y.C., 1952-55; pvt. practice N.Y.C., 1955-83; editor. N.Y. State Tax Monitor, N.Y.C., 1983-84; mortgage real estate loan officer N.Y.C., 1985-90; tchr. DeWitt Clinton H.S., N.Y.C., 1990-92; pvt. practice Scarsdale, 1992—; spl. master Supreme Ct., N.Y. County; pre-trial master Civil Ct., N.Y. County; commr., referee, receiver and guardian ad litem Supreme and Surrogate's Ct.; arbitrator Am. Arbitration Assn., Civil Ct., N.Y. County, Better Bus. Bur.; arbitrator, mediator N.Y. State Mediation Bd.; litigator local, state, and fed. cts. Pres. Arthur Manor Assn., Scarsdale, 1970-73, Cath. Big Bros., N.Y.C., 1971-73; mem. nominating com. Village Trustee, Scarsdale, 1970-76, mem. nominating com. sch. bd., 1973-76; mem. Scarsdale Hist. Soc., 1980—. With U.S. Army, 1943-46. Decorated Silver star, two Bronze stars, two Purple Hearts and three Battle stars, Combat Infantry Badge. Mem. Guild Cath. Lawyers (pres. 1969-71), Scarsdale Antiques Running Club (pres. 1984-86). Democrat. Avocations: marathon running, tennis, platform tennis, softball, writing. Product liability, General civil litigation. Home and Office: 223 Boulevard Scarsdale NY 10583-5832

**SWEENEY, JOHN LAWRENCE,** lawyer; b. Staten Island, N.Y., Jan. 5, 1962; s. Lawrence Patrick and Lauretta (Kronen) S.; m. Karen Anne Hrebenak, Aug. 26, 1988; children: Conor, Lauren, Devin, Pearse. BA, Yale U., 1984; JD magna cum laude, Seton Hall U., 1990; LLM in Taxation, NYU, 1993. Bar: N.J. 1990, U.S. Dist. Ct. N.J. 1990, N.Y. 1991, U.S. Tax Ct. 1995. Assoc. Connell, Foley & Geiser, Roseland, N.J., 1990-92, Lampf, Lipkind, Prupis & Pettegrew, West Orange, N.J., 1992-93; atty. pvt. practice, Morristown, N.J., 1993—. Interview supr. Yale Alumni Schs. Com., 1991—; charter mem. Seton Hall Prep Hall of Fame Com., 1984-94. Mem. N.J. Bar Assn., N.Y. Bar Assn., Morris County Bar Assn., Yale Club Ctrl. N.J. (trustee 1991-94, 1997—, sec. 1997-99, pres. 1999—), New Providence Lions Club Internat. Estate planning, Probate, Taxation, general. Home: 14 Farm Cottage Rd Gladstone NJ 07934-2007 Office: 51 Dumont Pl Morristown NJ 07960-4125

**SWEENEY, KEVIN MICHAEL,** lawyer; b. Westfield, Mass., May 28, 1965; s. Lawrence Arthur and Maureen Theresa (Cavanaugh) S.; m. Karen Elizabeth Marsian, May 15, 1993. BA, U. Mass., 1987; D Law, U. Wis., 1990. Bar: Mass., Wis.; U.S. Dist. Ct. (we. dist.) Wis., U.S. Dist. Ct. Mass. Asst. v.p., counsel, asst. sec. Office Gen. Counsel and Office Corp. Sec. Mass. Mut. Life Ins. Co., Springfield, Mass., 1993—; counsel, asst. sec. and chief compliance officer Mass Mutual Internat., Inc., Springfield, 1996—; counsel, asst. sec. and chief compliance officer Mass Mutual Internat., Inc., Luxembourg, 1996—, also bd. dirs., 1996-98; counsel, asst. sec., chief compliance officer Mass Mutual Internat. Bermuda, Ltd., Hamilton, 1996—; counsel, asst. sec. MML Reinsurance Bermuda, Hamilton, 1996-97; corp. sec. Mass Mutual Found. for Hartford, Inc., Hartford, Conn., 1996—; asst. sec. Mass Mutual Holding Co., 1998—, C. M. Life Ins. Co., 1998—, MML Bay State Life Ins. Co., 1998—, Mass. Mutual Benefits Mgmt., Inc., 1998—; asst. clk. Mass Mutual Holding MSC, Inc., 1999—; assoc. Bulkley, Richardson and Gelinas, Springfield, 1990-93; rsch. asst. U. Wis., Madison, 1988-90; law clk. Wis. Dept. Justice, Madison, 1989; project asst. and law clk. Legal Assistance to Institutionalized Persons, Madison, 1988-89. Author: (paper) Restructuring Insurance Companies Through Mergers, Acquisitions and Other Affiliations, ABA Ann. Mktg., 1999; rsch. asst.: (book) Tournament of Lawyers, 1991. Legal counsel, bd. dirs., dir. fin. Mass. Hugh O'Brian Youth Leadership Found., Inc., Boston, 1991-93; atty. advisor Mass. Bar Assn. H.S. Mock Ct. Competition, Springfield, 1990-91; mem. Dem. Town Com., West Springfield, 1990-91. Tech. sgt. ANG, 1983-91. Mem. ABA (young lawyers divsn. in-house counsel com., planning bd. mem. 1994-96), Am. Soc. Corp. Secs., Mass. Bar Assn., State Bar Wis., Phi Kappa Phi. Democrat. Roman Catholic. Avocations: travel, reading, listening to music. Office: Mass Mut Life Ins Co 1295 State St Springfield MA 01111-0001

**SWEENEY, KEVIN MICHAEL,** lawyer; b. Washington, Nov. 20, 1956; s. Timothy Dennis and Naomi (Rosen) S.; m. Joanne Cranney, June 28, 1986. BA, Coll. of William and Mary, 1978; JD, George Washington U., 1981. Bar: D.C. 1982, U.S. Ct. Appeals (D.C., 3d and 5th cirs.) 1982, U.S. Ct. Appeals (7th cir.) 1984, U.S. Ct. Appeals (4th, 10th and 11th cirs.) 1986, U.S. Supreme Ct., 1989. Assoc. Grove, Jaskiewicz, Gilliam & Cobert, Washington, 1981-87, ptnr., 1988-90; ptnr. Katten Muchin & Zavis, 1990—. Polit. action dir. Arlington (Va.) Young Dems., 1984-86, treas. 1986-87, parliamentarian, 1987-88; task force mem. Commn. on Arlingtons Future, 1986. Mem. ABA, Fed. Energy Bar Assn. FERC practice, Administrative and regulatory.

**SWEENEY, NEAL JAMES,** lawyer; b. Paterson, N.J., Nov. 1, 1957; s. Bernard Thomas and Mary Agnes (Keneally) S.; m. Mary Elizabeth Finocchiaro, Oct. 27, 1984; children: Daniel Fulton, Clare Kenneally, Moira Ann. BA in History and Polit Sci., Rutgers U., 1979; JD, George Washington U., 1982. Bar: Ga. 1982, U.S. Dist. Ct. (no. dist.) Ga. 1982, U.S. Dist. Ct. (no. dist.) Tex. 1982, U.S. Claims Ct. 1984, U.S. Ct. Appeals (5th cir.) 1987. Assoc. Smith, Currie & Hancock, Atlanta, 1982-87, ptnr., 1988-98; pntr. Kilpatrick Stockton LLP, Atlanta, 1998—. Co-author: Construction Business Handbook, 1985, Holding Subcontractors to Their Bids, 1986, Subcontractor Default, 1987, The New AIA Design and Construction Documents, 1988, Proving and Pricing Claims, 1995, Fifty State Construction Lien and Bond Law, 1992, Who Pays For Defective Design?, 1997; editor: Construction Subcontracting, 1991, Common Sense Construction Law, 1997; editor Wiley Construction Law Update, 1992—; notes editor G.W.U.J. Internat. Law and Econs., 1981-82. Mem. ABA (pub. contract law sect., forum com. on constrn. industry), Atlanta Bar Assn., Am. Arbitration Assn. (panel of arbitrators), Water Environment Fedn. (editl. adv. bd. 1994-97). Roman Catholic. Construction, Government contracts and claims, Federal civil litigation. Home: 3834 Vermont Rd NE Atlanta GA 30319-1211 Office: Kilpatrick Stockton LLP 1100 Peachtree St NE Ste 2800 Atlanta GA 30309-4501

**SWEENEY, PAUL JOHN,** lawyer; b. Quincy, Mass., June 21, 1953; s. Arthur and Ardelle (Killory) S.; m. Valerie Ann Horton, Apr. 15, 1978; children: Falon, Siobhan. BA, U. Mass., 1979; JD, Suffolk U., 1984; LLM, MA in Tax Law, Boston U., 1988. Bar: Mass. 1984, U.S. Dist. Ct. Mass. 1984. Adminstrv. asst. to register of probate Norfolk County Probate Ct., Dedham, Mass., 1979-84, legal supr. fiduciary dept., 1984-88, asst. register of probate, 1984-88; ptnr. Moran & Sweeney, PC, LLC, Boston, 1989—. Lay leader Harbor United Meth. Ch., Scituate, Mass., 1996—. Mem. ATLA (family law sect.), Mass. Bar Assn., Boston Bar Assn. Republican. Avocations: sailing, cruising, clam digging, skiing, church activities. Family and matrimonial, Estate planning, Probate. Office: Moran & Sweeney PC LLC 153 Milk St Boston MA 02109-4809

**SWEENEY, ROBERT KEVIN,** lawyer; b. St. Louis, Dec. 26, 1959; s. Robert Vincent Sweeney and Kathleen Patricia (Rush) Rhymer; m. Donna Marie Anvender, Nov. 23, 1979; children: Allison Marie, Molly Clare. BS, So. Ill. U., 1987; JD, St. Louis U., 1990. Bar: Mo. 1990, U.S. Dist. Ct. (ea. and we. dists.) Mo. 1990, U.S. Ct. Appeals (5th cir. and 8th cir.) 1990. Assoc. Linde, Thomson, Kansas City, Mo., 1990-91, Craig & Craig, St. Louis, 1989-91, 91-93, Franz, Franz & Sweeney, St. Louis, 1993-95; ptnr. Spector, Sweeney & Wolfe, Kirkwood, Mo., 1995—. Dir. Interfaith Alliance, St. Louis, mem. presdl. trust fund Dem., Washington, 1991—. Mem. ABA, AFL-CIO, Am. Judicature Soc., Lawyers Coord, Com., ABA, Mo. Bar Assn., St. Louis Met. Bar Assn., Kansas City Met. Bar Assn., St. Louis County Bar Assn., Order of Woolsack, Alpha Sigma Nu, Phi Kappa Phi. Roman Catholic. Avocations: softball, volleyball, handball. Labor, Pension, profit-sharing, and employee benefits. Home: 1338 Libra Dr Arnold MO 63010-3009 Office: Spector & Sweeney 206 W Argonne Dr Kirkwood MO 63122-4235

**SWEENEY, THOMAS FREDERICK,** lawyer; b. Detroit, Feb. 10, 1943; s. Harold Eugene and Marion Genevieve (Lunz) S.; m. Susan Carol Horn, Dec. 27, 1968; children: Sarah Elizabeth, Neal Thomas. AB, U. Mich., 1965, JD, 1968. Bar: Mich. 1968, U.S. Dist. Ct. (ea. dist.) Mich, 1968, U.S. Tax Ct. 1979, U.S. Supreme Ct. 1985. Assoc. Fischer, Franklin, Ford, Simon & Hogg, Detroit, 1969-73, ptnr., 1974-85; ptnr. Houghton, Potter, Sweeney & Brenner, Detroit, 1986-95; mem. Clark Hill, Birmingham, Mich., 1995—. Contbr. articles to legal jours. Bd. dirs. Cmty. House Assn., 1990-98, pres. 1993-95; mem. Birmingham (Mich.) Charter Rev. Commn., 1977; trustee Baldwin Pub. Libr., Birmingham, 1981—. Mem. ABA, Oakland County Bar Assn. (chmn. taxation com. 1988-89), Detroit Bar Assn., Detroit Club, Forest Hills Swim Club (pres. 1985-87). Roman Catholic. Estate taxation, Probate, Taxation, general. Home: 1493 Buckingham Ave Birmingham MI 48009-5866 Office: Clark Hill 255 S Old Woodward Ave Ste 301 Birmingham MI 48009-6182

**SWEENY, WENDY PRESS,** lawyer; b. Coral Gables, Fla., June 24, 1960; d. Samuel and Carol Sue Press; m. Kermit P. Sweeny Jr., Sept. 3, 1989; 1 child, Briana Mikel. AA in Bus., Broward C.C., 1981; BA in Bus., U. South Fla., 1983; JD, Nova U., 1987. Fla. 1987, Wyo. 1988, U.S. Dist. Ct. Wyo. 1988. Assoc. Messenger & Jurovich, Thermopolis, Wyo., 1987-91; county prosecuting atty. Waskakie County, Worland, Wyo., 1991-95; pvt. practice Worland, 1995—. Mem. Girl Scouts USA. Mem. Bus. and Profl. Women's Assn. (pres. 1998). Avocation: rock climbing. Criminal, Family and matrimonial, General practice. Office: 1116 Robertson Ave Worland WY 82401-2826

**SWEET, JONATHAN JUSTIN,** lawyer, educator, writer; b. Denver, Feb. 14, 1957; s. Justin Sweet and Lesly Miller; m. Pamella Passaro, June 8, 1987; 1 child, Misha. BA, U. Calif., Berkeley, 1978; JD, U. San Francisco, 1985. Bar: Calif. 1986. Owner Law Offices of Jonathan J. Sweet, San Jose, Calif., 1992-99; prin. Bicknell & Sweet, Los Gatos, Calif., 1999—; adj. prof. law U. San Francisco Law Sch., 1994—; presenter seminars on litigation strategies and construction; expert witness and cons. on constrn. law and constrn. contract law. Author: (books) Avoiding or Minimizing Construction Litigation, 1993, Sweet on Construction Industry Contracts/Major AIA Documents, 1996; contbr. articles and supplements to publs. on constrn. law topics. Arbitrator, judge pro tem Santa Clara Superior Ct., 1991—. Mem. Calif. State Bar Assn. (mem. real property sect. and constrn. sub-sect.), Assn. Gen. Contractors of Calif. (legal adv. com.), Santa Clara County Bar Assn. Avocations: competitive fencing, golf, tennis. Construction, Real property, Insurance. Office: Bicknell & Sweet PO Box 536 Los Gatos CA 95031-0536

**SWEET, LOWELL ELWIN,** lawyer, writer; b. Flint, Mich., Aug. 10, 1931; s. Leslie E. and Donna Mabel (Latta) S.; m. Mary Ellen Ebben, Aug. 29, 1953; children: Lawrence Edward, Diane Marie, Sara Anne. BA in Psychology, Wayne State U., 1953; LLB, U. Wis., 1955. Bar: Wis. 1955, U.S. Dist. Ct. (ea. dist.) Wis. 1955, U.S. Dist. Ct. (no. dist.) Ill. 1958. Ptnr. Morrissy, Morrisy, Sweet & Race and predecessor firms, Elkhorn, Wis., 1957-70; ptnr., pres. Sweet & Reddy, Elkhorn, 1970—; instr. gen. practice sect. U. Wis. Law Sch., 1978, 79, 86, 90; lectr. real estate law Wis. Bar, Gateway Tech., Carthage Coll. Inst., 1974—. Author: Phased Condominiums for Matthew Bender, 1992; co-editor: Condominiuim Law Handbook, 1981, 93; mem. editl. bd. Workbook for Wis. Estate Planners, 1990. Mem. Walworth County Rep. com.; sect. Wis. Jt. Survey Commn. on Debt Mgmt. With CIC, U.S. Army, 1955-57. Named Outstanding Young Man of Am., Elkhorn Jaycees, 1966; recipient citation for svc. in drafting Wis. Condominium Law, Wis. Legislature, 1978. Fellow ABA; mem. Wis. Bar Assn. (gov. 1972-75, 91-93, 99—), Walworth County Bar Assn., Am. Judicature Soc., Assn. Trial Lawyers Am., The Best Lawyers in Am., Am. Coll. Real Estate Lawyers, Kiwanis, Lions, Moose, KC. Real property, Probate, General corporate. Home: 411 W Marshall St Elkhorn WI 53121-1624 Office: Sweet & Reddy SC 114 N Church St Elkhorn WI 53121-1202

**SWEET, ROBERT WORKMAN,** federal judge; b. Yonkers, N.Y., Oct. 15, 1922; s. James Allen and Delia (Workman) S.; m. Adele Hall, May 12, 1973; children by previous marriage—Robert, Deborah, Ames, Eliza. B.A., Yale U., 1944, LL.B., 1948. Bar: N.Y. 1949. Asso. firm Simpson, Thacher & Bartlett, 1948-53; asst. U.S. atty. So. Dist. N.Y., 1953-55; asso. firm Casey, Lane & Mittendorf, 1955-65, partner, 1957-65; counsel Interdepartmental Task Force on Youth and Juvenile Delinquency, 1958-78; dep. mayor City of N.Y., 1966-69; partner firm Skadden, Arps, Slate, Meagher & Flom, N.Y.C., 1970-77; mem. hearing office N.Y.C. Transit Authority, 1975-77; U.S. dist. judge So. Dist. N.Y., N.Y.C., 1978—; participant USIA Rule of Law Program in Albania, 1991; observer Albanian elections, 1992. Pres. Community Service Soc., 1961-78; trustee Sch. Mgmt. Urban Policy, 1970—, Taft Sch.; vestryman St. Georges Epis. Ch., 1958-63. Served to lt. (j.g.) USNR, 1943-46. Recipient Alumni citation of merit Taft Sch., 1985, various other awards, citations for service as dept mayor N.Y.C. Mem. ABA, Assn. of Bar of City of N.Y., N.Y. Law Inst., N.Y. County Lawyers Assn., State Bar Assn., Am. Legion (comdr. Willard Straight Post). Clubs: Quaker Hill Country, Century Assn., Merchants, Indian Harbor Yacht, Mid City Rep.

**SWEETLAND, HEATHER LEIGH,** judge; b. St. Paul, Oct. 11, 1952; d. Stephen Myers and Estelle Clara Sweetland; m. Steven Paul Coz, Apr. 14, 1984; 1 child, Benjamin. BS in Tchg., Mankato State Coll., 1974; JD, William Mitchell Coll. Law, 1982. Bar: Minn. 1982, U.S. Dist. Ct. Minn. 1982. Atty. Legal Aid Svc. N.E. Minn., Duluth, 1982; assoc. Eckman & Fillenworth, Ltd., Duluth, 1982-90; ptnr. Fillenworth & Sweetland, Duluth, 1990-96; judge St. Louis County Dist. Ct., Duluth, 1996—; asst. pub. defender 6th Jud. Dist., Duluth, 1982-96. Bd. dirs. YWCA, Duluth, 1983-88; mem. Foster Parents Adv. Bd., St. Louis County, 1984-89; mem. various bds. Trinity Luth. Ch., Duluth, 1985-96. Office: St Louis County Dist Ct 100 N 5th Ave W Duluth MN 55802-1202

**SWENSON, DIANE KAY,** lawyer; b. Sioux Falls, S.D., June 16, 1952; d. Clarence Donald and Mildred Ann (Meyer) S. BA magna cum laude, Augustana Coll., 1974; JD, Hamline U., 1981. Bar: Minn. 1981. Tchr. Malvern (Iowa) Pub. Schs., 1974-76, Rosemount Pub. Schs., Apple Valley, Minn., 1976-78; legis. asst. U.S. Sen. Larry Pressler, Washington, 1981-86; exec. v.p. Am. Tort Reform Assn., Washington, 1986—. V.p. Emmanual Luth. Ch., Bethesda, Md., 1997. Mem. ABA. Republican. Avocation: skiing. Home: 5704 Chapman Mill Dr Apt 160 Rockville MD 20852-5567 Office: Am Tort Reform Assn 1850 M St NW Washington DC 20036-5803

**SWERDLOFF, ILEEN POLLOCK,** lawyer; b. Bronx, N.Y., July 15, 1945; d. Seymour Pollock and Selma (Goldin) Feinstein; m. Mark Harris Swerdloff, Dec. 24, 1967; 1 child, Jonathan Edward. BA, SUNY, 1967; JD, Western New Eng. Sch. of Law, 1978. Bar: Conn. 1979, U.S. Dist. Ct. Conn. 1981, U.S. Supreme Ct. 1985. Mng. ptnr. Swerdloff & Swerdloff, West Hartford, Conn., 1980—. Sec. Chrysalis Ctr., Hartford, Conn., 1988-91, pres., 1991-92. Mem. Am. Bar Assn., Conn. Bar Assn., Hartford County Bar Assn., Hartford Assn. Women Attys. Jewish. Avocations: knitting, aerobics. Family and matrimonial, Consumer commercial, General practice. Home: 9 Beacon Heath Farmington CT 06032-1524 Office: Swerdloff & Swerdloff 61 S Main St West Hartford CT 06107-2486

**SWERDLOFF, MARK HARRIS,** lawyer; b. Buffalo, Sept. 7, 1945; s. John and Joan (Harris) S.; m. Ileen Pollock, Dec. 24, 1967; 1 child, Jonathan Edward. BA, SUNY, Buffalo, 1967; JD, U. Conn., 1975. Bar: Conn. 1975, U.S. Dist. Ct. Conn. 1975, U.S. Ct. Appeals (2d cir.) 1983, U.S. Supreme Ct. 1985, Fla. 1977. Assoc. Wilson, Asbel & Channin, Hartford, Conn., 1975-78; ptnr. Swerdloff & Swerdloff, West Hartford, Conn., 1978—; pres. Arpus Enterprises, Old Saybrook Conn., 1993—; trial fact finder Superior Ct., Hartford, 1990—; arbitrator Dispute Resolution Inst., Hartford, 1990—. Mem. ABA, Conn. Bar Assn., Conn. Trial Lawyers Assn. Democrat. Jewish. Avocations: photography, travel, cooking. General civil litigation, Personal injury, Family and matrimonial. Home: 9 Beacon Heath Farmington CT 06032-1524 Office: Swerdloff & Swerdloff 61 S Main St West Hartford CT 06107-2486

**SWERDZEWSKI, JOSEPH,** lawyer; b. Southampton, N.Y., Jan. 29, 1949; s. Frank and Rosella (Lapinski) S.; m. Natalie J. Conklin, Sept. 29, 1975 (div. Sept. 1991); children: Peter, Thomas, Matthew; m. Gayle Lela Swerdzewski, Feb. 26, 1994; stepchildren: Eric Soden, Jonathan Soden. BA, Coll. Holy Cross, Worcester, Mass., 1971; JD, Fordham U., 1974. Bar: N.Y. 1975, Colo. 1985. Law asst. Suffolk County, N.Y. County Execs. Office, Riverhead, N.Y., 1974-75; supervisory atty. Fed. Labor Rels. Authority, L.A., 1979-82; regional atty. Fed. Labor Rels. Authority, Denver, 1982-91, spl. coun. for gen. counsel, 1991-93; gen. counsel Fed. Labor Rels. Authority, Washington, 1993—; instr. Met. State Coll., Denver, 1985-93; cons. Griffith Assocs., Chgo., 1989-92. Apptd. by Pres. Clinton for a Senate Conformation. Capt. USAF, 1975-79, Lt. col. USAFR. Democrat. Fax:

202-482-6608. Office: Fed Labor Rels Authority 607 14th St NW Ste 210 Washington DC 20005-2000

**SWERLING, JACK BRUCE,** lawyer; b. N.Y.C., May 30, 1946; s. Benjamin Fidel and Jeanette (Fidler) S.; m. Erika Andrea Helfer, Jan. 17, 1970; children: Bryan, Stephanie. BA, Clemson U., 1968; JD, U. S.C., 1973. Bar: S.C. 1973, U.S. Dist. Ct. S.C. 1973, U.S. Ct. Appeals (4th cir.) 1974, U.S. Supreme Ct. 1978. Ptnr. Law Firm of Isadore Lourie, Columbia, S.C., 1973-83, Swerling, Harpootlian & McCulloch, Columbia, 1983-92; pvt. practice Columbia, 1992—; mem. Pre-Trial Intervention Adv. Com., 1980-82; mem. adv. com. Child Victim Ct. Notebook div. Pub. Safety Programs, 1987; mem. S.C. Bd. Law Examiners, 1987-92; adj. prof. U. S.C. Sch. Law, Columbia, 1986—; clin. prof. dept. Neuropsychiatry Sch. Medicine, 1988—; mem. S.C. Supreme Ct. com. on model criminal jury instructions, chmn. bule ribbon task force criminal docketing com.; mem. legal com. NORML. Author: South Carolina Criminal Trial Notebook, 1991; contbr. articles to profl. jours. Co-pres. Jewish Community Ctr., Columbia, 1977; bd. dirs. Rape Crisis Network, Columbia, 1985, Animal Protection League, Columbia, 1986. Recipient Am. Jurisprudence award Am. Jurisprudence Ency., 1973. Fellow Am. Coll. Trial Lawyers, Am. Acad. Appellate Lawyers, Am. Bd. Criminal Lawyers, S.C. Bar Found.; mem. ABA, ATLA, Am. Judicature Soc., Nat. Assn. Criminal Def. Lawyers, S.C. Trial Lawyers Assn. (chmn. criminal law sect. 1979-82), S.C. Bar Assn. (chmn. criminal law sect. 1985-86), Richland County Bar Assn. (chmn. criminal law sect. 1988-89). Democrat. Jewish. Avocation: photography. Criminal. Office: 1720 Main St Ste 301 Columbia SC 29201-2850

**SWETNAM, DANIEL RICHARD,** lawyer; b. Columbus, Ohio, Dec. 22, 1957; s. Joseph Neri and Audrey Marguerite (Mason) S.; m. Jeannette Deanna Dean, June 7, 1980; children: Jeremiah Daniel, Laura Janelle, Andrew Michael. BA, Ohio State U., 1979; JD, U. Cin., 1982. Bar: Ohio 1982, U.S. Dist. Ct. (so. dist.) Ohio 1982, U.S. Ct. Appeals (6th cir.) 1986, U.S. Supreme Ct. 1986. Assoc. Schwartz, Warren & Ramirez, Columbus, 1982-88, ptnr., 1989-96; prin. Schottenstein, Zox & Dunn, Columbus, 1997—. Deacon Grace Brethren Ch., Worthington, Ohio, 1989—; mem. Grace Brethren Christian Schs. Commn., 1993-98. Mem. ABA, Ohio State Bar Assn., Columbus Bar Assn., Comml. Law League Am., Order of Coif. Republican. Avocations: golf, tennis. Bankruptcy, General civil litigation. Home: 2178 Stowmont Ct Dublin OH 43016-9563 Office: Schottenstein Zox & Dunn 41 S High St Columbus OH 43215-6101

**SWIBEL, STEVEN WARREN,** lawyer; b. Chgo., July 18, 1946; s. Morris Howard and Gloria S.; m. Leslie S.; children: Deborah, Laura. BS, MIT, 1968; JD, Harvard U., 1971. Bar: Ill. 1971, U.S. Dist. Ct. (no. dist.) Ill. 1971, U.S. Tax Ct. 1973, U.S. Ct. Appeals (7th cir.) 1981. Assoc. Sonnenschein Carlin Nath & Rosenthal, Chgo., 1971-78, ptnr., 1978-84; ptnr. Rudnick & Wolfe, 1984-93, Schwartz, Cooper, Greenberger, Krauss Chartered, 1993—; adj. prof. taxation Ill. Inst. Tech. Kent Coll. Law, Chgo., 1989—; lectr. in field; contbr. articles to profl. jours. Ednl. counselor MIT, 1979—; bd. dirs. MIT Alumni Fund, 1992-95, Ragdale Found., 1987—, treas. 1987-92; bd. dirs. Kids In Danger, 1998—. Recipient Lobdell Disting. Svc. award MIT Alumni Assn., 1989. Mem. ABA (com. partnerships sect. taxation), Ill. Bar Assn., Chgo. Bar Assn. (fed. taxation com., exec. subcom. 1984—, chmn. subcom. on real estate and partnerships 1986-87, vice chmn. 1988-89, chmn. 1990), Met. Club, MIT Club (dir. Chgo. chpt. 1980-91, 96—, sec. 1980-87, pres. 1987-89), Sigma Xi, Tau Beta Pi, Eta Kappa Nu. Corporate taxation, General corporate, Personal income taxation. Office: Schwartz Cooper Greenberger & Krauss Chartered 180 N La Salle St Ste 2700 Chicago IL 60601-2757

**SWIDER, ROBERT ARTHUR,** lawyer; b. Hillside, N.J., Sept. 24, 1953; s. Arthur Alexander and Doris Ann S.; m. Catherine Mary Simmons, Oct. 14, 1984; 1 child, Cassidy Brooks. BA, Seton Hall U., 1975; JD, Lewis & Clark U., 1981. Bar: Oreg. 1981, U.S. Dist. Ct. Oreg. 1983, U.S. Ct. Appeal s(9th cir.) 1995, U.S. Supreme Ct. 1996. Law clk. Bonneville Power Adminstrn., Portland, 1980-81; attu. pvt. practice, Portland, 1982-83, 84—; assoc. Jackson & Vause, Portland, 1983-84. Co-author: (chpts.) Computer Law Manuel, 1998, editor, 1996. Mem. Oreg. State Bar Assn. (mem. computer law sect. 1989-93, 97—, chair 1993-94 ). Avocations: skiing, camping, rafting, basketball, photography. Personal injury, Computer, General civil litigation. Office: 621 SW Morrison St Ste 1410 Portland OR 97205-3817

**SWIDERSKI, ALEX MICHAEL,** lawyer; b. Duluth, Minn., July 19, 1947; s. Benjamin Frank and Helen Irene (Mikrut) S.; m. Debra Lou McKinney, June 3, 1989 (div. Apr. 22, 1993); m. Kathryn Anne Swiderski, Apr. 26, 1997. BA, Harvard U., 1969; JD, Northwestern U., Boston, 1977. Bar: Alaska 1977. Atty. Law Office of Lawrence Kulik, Anchorage, 1978-80, Alaska Pub. Defender Agy., Anchorage, 1981-89; atty. environ. sect. Alaska Atty. Gen. Office, Anchorage, 1993—, attorney oil spill litigation sect., 1990-93; bd. dirs. Great Land Trust, Anchorage, 1997—. Home: 3903 Arkansas Dr Anchorage AK 99517-2518 Office: Attorney Generals Office 1031 W 4th Ave Ste 200 Anchorage AK 99501-5903

**SWIEDLER, ALAN M.,** lawyer; b. N.Y.C., May 16, 1952. BA, NYU, 1973; JD, Hofstra U., 1976. Bar: N.Y. 1978, U.S. Dist. Ct. (so. and ea. dists.) N.Y. 1978, U.S. Ct. Appeals (2d cir.) 1980, U.S. Supreme Ct. 1988. Pvt. practice N.Y.C. Mem. Assn. Bar of City of N.Y. State civil litigation, Contracts commercial, General corporate. Office: 575 Lexington Ave New York NY 10022-6102

**SWIFT, JACK H.,** lawyer; b. L.A., Oct. 12, 1939; s. Herbert and Margaret (deMarris) S.; m. Catherine Ann Shawhan, June 18, 1960; children: Daniel Alden, Michael Lewis. BA, Georgetown U., 1961; JD, Western State U., 1995. Intern San Diego Pub. Defender, El Cajon, Calif., 1994-95; assoc. Dupree & Assocs., San Diego, 1995-96; atty. pvt. practice, Chula Vista, Calif., 1997—. Mem. South Bay Bar Assn., Maritime Law Assn. U.S. Republican. Roman Catholic. Avocations: hunting, fishing, boating. Admiralty, General civil litigation, Probate. Home and office: 1639 Mills St Chula Vista CA 91913-2016

**SWIFT, JOHN GOULDING,** lawyer; b. Lake Charles, La., Nov. 12, 1955; s. Goulding William Jr. and Betty Jane (Richardson) S.; m. Jan Lynette Whitehead. BS, La. State U., 1977, JD, 1980. Bar: La. 1980, U.S. Dist. Ct. (we. dist.) La. 1982, U.S. Ct. Appeals (5th cir.) 1983, U.S. Dist. Ct. (mid. dist.) La. 1985, U.S. Dist. Ct. (ea. dist.) Tex. 1986, U.S. Dist. Ct. (ea. dist.) La. 1986, U.S. Ct. Appeals (4th cir.) 1992, U.S. Supreme Ct. 1997. Law clk. to presiding justice U.S. Dist. Ct. (we. dist.) La., Lake Charles, 1980-81; assoc. Davidson, Meaux, Sonnier, McElligott & Swift, Lafayette, La., 1981-85, ptnr., 1985-89, sr. ptnr., 1990—. Mem. Gulf Coast Conservation Assn.; bd. dirs. Hidden Hills Cmty., Inc., 1987-93, pres., 1989-93; bd. dirs. Lafayette Parish unit Am. Cancer Soc., 1992—, pres., 1996-97, bd. dirs. La. divsn., 1995-96; youth dir., mem. adminstrv. bd. Meth. Ch., 1992-93, chair staff-parish rels. com., 1996, mem. adminstrv. bd., 1996, 98, 99, trustee, 1996-98, chair, 1998. Mem. ABA, La. Bar Assn. (ho. of dels. 1996—), La. Def. Counsel, La. Bar Found. (bd. dirs. 1997—), Assn. Def. Trial Attys., Lafayette Parish Bar Assn. (bd. dirs. 1988-95, pres. 1993-94), 15th Jud. Dist. Bar Assn. (pres. 1993-94), La. State U. Alumni Fedn., Ducks Unltd., Kiwanis (Acadiana chpt. 1989-95), Acadiana Inns of Ct. Republican. Avocations: running, fishing, hunting. General civil litigation, Insurance, Product liability. Home: 104 Hidden Hills Lake Arnaudville LA 70512-6429 Office: Davidson Meaux Sonnier McElligott & Swift 810 S Buchanan St Lafayette LA 70501-6882

**SWIFT, STEPHEN CHRISTOPHER,** lawyer; b. N.Y.C., Jan. 7, 1954; s. James Stephen and Rhoda Emma Jean (Howd) S. AA, Lansing C.C., 1980; BA, Mich. State U., 1983; JD, Wayne State U., 1988. Bar: Mich. 1988, Hawaii 1989, D.C. 1991, Va. 1995, Md. 1998, U.S. Dist. Ct. D.C., , U.S. Dist. Ct. Md., U.S. Dist. Ct. (ea. and we. dists.) Md., U.S. Dist. Ct. Hawaii, U.S. Ct. Fed. Claims, U.S. Bankruptcy Ct. (ea. and we. dists.) Va., U.S. Tax Ct., U.S. Ct. Appeals (fed., D.C., 4th, 9th cirs.), U.S. Supreme Ct.; registered patent atty. Pvt. practice Honolulu, 1989-94, Arlington, Va., 1995—. Mem. ABA, Fed. Bar Assn., Fed. Cir. Bar Assn., Am. Intellectual Property Law Assn. E-mail: scswift@erols.com. Fax: 703-418-1895. Intellectual property, Patent, Trademark and copyright. Office: 2231 Crystal Dr Ste 500 Arlington VA 22202-3722

**SWIFT, STEPHEN HYDE,** lawyer, property manage and developer; b. Milton, Mass., May 3, 1955; s. Stephen Hathaway and Caroline Cullers (Hyde) S.; m. Elizabeth Belle Hales, Apr. 25, 1981; children: Hales, Isabelle, Edith, Sterling, Clara. AA, Brigham Young U., 1975, BA, 1981; JD, St. Louis U., 1984. Bar: Colo. 1985, U.S. Dist. Ct. Colo. 1988. Missionary LDS Ch., 1975-77; pvt. practice, Colorado Springs, Colo., 1985—. Chmn. Rep. Caucus, Colorado Springs, 1986. Mem. ABA, ATLA, Colo. Bar Assn. (chmn. subcom. bankruptcy 1995—), El Paso County Bar Assn. Avocations: mountain biking, running, indoor soccer, coaching soccer. Bankruptcy, Family and matrimonial, Personal injury. Office: 733 E Costilla St Ste Aandb Colorado Springs CO 80903-3783

**SWIFT, STEPHEN JENSEN,** federal judge; b. Salt Lake City, Sept. 7, 1943; s. Edward A. and Maurine (Jensen) S.; m. Lorraine Burnell Facer, Aug. 4, 1972; children: Carter, Stephanie, Spencer, Meredith, Hunter. BS, Brigham Young U., 1967; JD, George Washington U., 1970. Trial atty. U.S. Dept. Justice, Washington, D.C., 1970-74; asst. U.S. atty. U.S. Atty.'s Office, San Francisco, 1974-77; v.p., sr. tax counsel Bank Am. N.T. & S.A., San Francisco, 1977-83; judge U.S. Tax Ct., Washington, 1983—; adj. prof. Golden Gate U., San Francisco, 1978-83, U. Balt., 1987—. Mem. ABA, Calif. Bar Assn., D.C. Bar Assn. Office: US Tax Ct 400 2nd St NW Washington DC 20217-0002

**SWIGGART, CAROLYN CLAY,** lawyer; b. Bloomington, Ill., Sept. 19, 1958. AB, Wellesley Coll., 1980; JD, U. Conn., 1983. Bar: Mass. 1983, Conn. 1985, U.S. Dist. Ct. Mass. 1985, U.S. Dist. Ct. Conn. 1986, U.S. Supreme Ct. 1989. With firm Rutkin & Oldham LLC, Westport and Greenwich, Conn. Dist. rep. Representative Town Meeting, Darien, Conn., 1990-94. Mem. Conn. Bar Assn. (co-chmn. Basic Practice Manual 1991-94, editor Basic Practice Manual 1986-91), Stamford Regional Bar Assn., Mass. Bar Assn., Tokeneke Club. Avocations: sailing, tennis. Probate, Family and matrimonial, General practice. Office: Rutkin & Oldham LLC 321 Riverside Ave Westport CT 06880-4810 Address: PO Box 941 Darien CT 06820-0941

**SWIHART, FRED JACOB,** lawyer; b. Park Rapids, Minn., Aug. 19, 1919; s. Fred and Elizabeth Pauline (Judnitsch) S.; m. Edna Lillian Jensen, Sept. 30, 1950; 1 child; Frederick Jay. BA, U. Nebr., 1949, JD, 1954; M in Russian Lang., Middlebury Coll., 1950; grad., U.S. Army Command and Staff Coll., 1965. Bar: Nebr. 1954, U.S. Dist. Ct. Nebr. 1954, U.S. Ct. Appeals (8th cir.) 1977, U.S. Supreme Ct. 1972. Claims atty. Chgo. & Eastern Ill. R.R., 1954-56; atty. Assn. Amer. R.R.s, Chgo., 1956-60; assoc. Wagener & Marx, Lincoln, Nebr., 1960-61; prosecutor City of Lincoln, 1961-68; sole practice Lincoln, 1968—. Editor Law for the Aviator, 1969-71. Served to lt. col. U.S. Army, 1943-46, ETO, Korea, ret. col., USAR, 1979. Fellow Nebr. State Bar Found.; mem. ABA, Nebr. Bar Assn., Fed. Bar Assn., Assn. Trial Lawyers Am., Am. Judicature Soc., Aircraft Owners and Pilots Assn. (legis. rep.), Nebr. Criminal Def. Attys. Assn., Nat. Assn. Criminal Def. Lawyers, Mercedes Benz Club Am., Nebr. Assn. Trial Attys., Nat. Assn. Uniformed Svcs., Res. Officers Assn., Nat. Assn. Legion of Honor, Internat. Footprint Assn., Am. Legion (adm. Nebr. Navy), Mason (knight comdr. of ct. of honor), Shriners, The Cabiri. Republican. Presbyterian. Avocations: collecting art, music, pistol competition. Personal injury, State civil litigation, Criminal. Home and Office: 1610 Susan Cir Lincoln NE 68506-1854

**SWING, CHRISTOPHER FREDERICK,** lawyer; b. Beech Grove, Ind., June 13, 1965; s. Thomas Jay and Jacqueline Sue Swing; m. Djuna Marie Mastroine, Nov. 13, 1987; children: Mackenna Marie, Peyton Thomas. BBA in Fin., Kent State U., 1987; JD, Case Western Res. U., 1991. Bar: Ohio 1991, U.S. Dist. Ct. (no. dist.) Ohio 1991, Fla. 1992, U.S. Ct. Appeals (6th cir.) 1996. Atty. Brouse & McDowell, Akron, Ohio, 1991—. Bd. dirs. Christmas in April, Summit County, Ohio, 1997-98; planning commn. mem. City Govt., Munroe Falls, Ohio, 1998. Mem. ABA, Ohio State Bar Assn., Fla. Bar Assn. General civil litigation, Land use and zoning (including planning). Home: 508 Willow Grove Dr Munroe Falls OH 44262-1411 Office: Browne & McDowell 500 First National Tower Akron OH 44308-1471

**SWIRE, JAMES BENNETT,** lawyer; b. Bklyn., July 10, 1942. AB, Princeton U., 1963; LLB, Harvard U., 1966. Bar: N.Y. 1967, D.C. 1976. Assoc. Rogers Hoge & Hills, N.Y.C., 1966-73; ptnr. Townley & Updike, N.Y.C., 1982-95, chmn. mgmt. com., 1990-95; ptnr. Dorsey & Whitney, LLP, N.Y.C., 1995—, office head, 1998—, mem. mgmt. com., 1999—; guest lectr. food and drug law Seton Hall Law Sch., 1977. Trustee Cancer Care, Inc., 1978—, v.p., 1982-86, chmn. exec. com., 1986-90, pres. 1990-95; chmn. Beth Issrael-St. Luke's Roosevelt Cancer Ctr., N.Y.C., 1999—. Mem. ABA, Assn. Bar City N.Y. (chmn. com. medicine and law 1977-80, sec. com. on trademarks and unfair competition 1985-88), N.Y. State Bar Assn., Internat. Trademark Assn. (assoc.). Trademark and copyright, Federal civil litigation, Intellectual property. Office: 250 Park Ave New York NY 10177-0001

**SWITZER, FREDERICK MICHAEL, III,** lawyer, mediator; b. St. Louis, Sept. 7, 1933; s. Frederick Michael Jr. and Viola Marie (Bardenheier) S.; m. Suzanne Elizabeth Reichardt, Aug. 28, 1970. BA cum laude, U. Notre Dame, 1956; JD, Washington U., 1959, LLM, 1972. Bar: Mo. 1959, U.S. Ct. Mil. Appeals 1960, U.S. Supreme Ct. 1962, U.S. Dist. Ct. (ea. dist.) Mo. 1993, U.S. Tax Ct. 1974, U.S. Ct. Appeals (8th cir.) 1978, U.S. Dist. Ct. (we. dist.) Mo. 1992, U.S. Ct. Appeals (4th cir.) 1994. Assoc. Switzer, Barnes & Toney, St. Louis, 1963-65, ptnr., 1965-75; ptnr. Fordyce & Mayne, St. Louis, 1975-87, Coburn Croft, St. Louis, 1987-92, Danna, McKitrick, P.C., St. Louis, 1992—; dir. Bardenheier Wine Co., St. Louis, 1983-85; instr. St. Louis Univ., 1971-72. Pres., dir. St. Louis Industry Adv. Group, 1971-90; dir. St. Louis Abbey Sch. Soc., 1975—; mem. employee benefits adv. com. City of Ladue (Mo.), 1980—, St. Louis Indsl. Rsch. Assn., 1991—; secr., dir. Citizens for Mo.'s Children, St. Louis, 1986-91; adv. bd. Am. Youth Found., St. Louis, 1989—. Capt. USNR, 1959-63. Recipient Mitchell award for playwriting, Univ. Notre Dame, 1959. Mem. ABA (labor employment section, equal employment opportunity law com., immigration law com., litig. section, gen. practice section), Assn. Atty. Mediators, Mo. Bar Assn. (labor law com., chmn. mil. law com. 1969-71, bar jour. com.), St. Louis Bar Assn. (labor law com.), Assn. Trial Lawyers Am., Strathalbyn Farms Club (past dir., past asst. secr.), Phi Delta Phi. Republican. Roman Catholic. Avocations: sailing, equestrian, tennis. Labor, General civil litigation, General practice. Office: Danna McKitrick PC 150 N Meramec Ave Fl 4 Saint Louis MO 63105-3779

**SWITZER, ROBERT EARL,** lawyer, educator, military law and criminal justice consultant; b. Buffalo, Nov. 24, 1929; s. Earl Alexander and Verne (Nowak) S.; m. Zylphia D. Casper, Nov. 29, 1992; children: Tracey Ann, Beth Ann. BA with distinction in History, Bethany (W.Va.) Coll., 1951; JD, U. Buffalo, 1956; postgrad. Nat. Jud. Coll., Reno, 1978. Bar: N.Y. 1958, U.S. Ct. Mil. Appeals, 1966, U.S. Supreme Ct. 1976. Estate planner M & T Trust Co., Buffalo, 1956-58; sole practice, Buffalo, 1959-65; asst. county atty. Erie County, Buffalo, 1962-65; commd. 2d lt. U.S. Marine Corps, 1951, advanced through grades to col., 1973; inf. officer, 1951-53; trial csl., def. csl., 1965-66, dep. staff judge adv., 1967-69; staff judge adv., 1969-70, 75-77; dir. Law Ctr., 1971-72; cir. mil. judge, 1973-74, 1978-81; ret., 1981; instr. law criminal justice dept. Coastal Carolina C.C., Jacksonville, N.C., 1981—, head dept. paralegal tech., instr., 1987—, chmn. tech. and pub. svc. div., 1989-90; mil. law cons., 1981—; chmn. bd. dirs., Jacksonville Community Penalties; lectr. on criminal law and trial advocacy, 1970—, v.p. faculty assembly, 1986-87; pres. Trabeth Corp., 1991—. Bd. dirs. Boys & Girls Club of Onslow County, United Way Onslow County, Coastal Carolina community Coll. Found. Inc.; dist. committeeman Erie County Rep. Com., 1960-65; del. 8th Jud. Dist. Nominating Conv., 1962-64; scoutmaster Boy Scouts Am., Quantico, Va., 1952-53, advisor Explorer scout post, Jacksonville, 1981-82. Decorated Navy Commendation medal; named Eagle Scout with gold palm Boy Scouts Am., 1947, Tchr. of the Year award N.C. State Bd. Community Colls., 1992. Mem. ABA, Fed. Bar Assn. (pres. Hawaii chpt. 1977-78), Assn. Trial Lawyers Am., N.C. Acad. Trial Lawyers, Internat. Platform Assn., Acad. Criminal Justice Scis., N.C. Criminal Justice Assn. (chmn. long-range planning com. 1986-89), So. Criminal Justice Assn., Nat. Assn. Legal Assts., N.C. Paralegal Assn., Ret. Officers Assn. (pres. 1993—), Rotary, Masons, Phi Kappa Tau (Phi Chapt.). Episcopalian. Office: Coastal Carolina Community Coll 444 Western Blvd Jacksonville NC 28546-6816 Address: 205 Aand Dollar Cv Sneads Ferry NC 28460-9114

**SWOPE, DENISE GRAINGER,** lawyer, educator; b. Columbia, S.C., Apr. 27, 1966; d. Thomas Dayton and Faye (Amerson) Grainger; m. William Koatsworth Swope, May 19, 1990. BA cum laude, U. S.C., 1986, JD, 1990. Bar: S.C. 1991. Asst. solicitor Charleston County (S.C.) Solicitor, 1991-92; pvt. practice Charleston, 1992—; instr. Inst. for Legal Edn., Columbia and Greenville, S.C., 1993—, Charleston So. U., 1994—. Atty., S.C. Bar Pro Bono Program, Columbia, 1991-95. U. S.C. Sch. Law Recruitment scholar, 1987, Outstanding Handicapped Law Student scholar, 1989. Mem. ABA, S.C. Bar Assn., Golden Key. Family and matrimonial, Criminal, Personal injury. Office: 1133 Hillside Dr # 2B Charleston SC 29407-6194

**SWOPE, RICHARD MCALLISTER,** retired lawyer; b. West Chester, Pa., Apr. 19, 1940; s. Charles Seigel and Edna McPherson (McAllister) S.; m. Karen Diane Glass, Aug. 24, 1963 (div. 1972). BS in Edn., Bucknell U., 1962; LLB cum laude, Washington and Lee U., 1968. Bar: Va. 1968. Shareholder Williams, Kelly & Greer, P.C., Norfolk, Va., 1973-98; ret., 1998; instr. Nat. Inst. Trial Advocacy, 1982-86. Mem. Virginia Beach Beautification Commn.; bd. dirs. Virginia Beach Orchestral Assn., 1982-88; v.p., bd. dirs. Swope Found., West Chester, Pa., 1961—; v.p. Swope Scholarship Found. Capt. USMC, 1962-65. Mem. Va. Assn. Def. Attys. (bd. dirs. 1975-78, 88-90), Va. State Bar Assn., Norfolk/Portsmouth Bar Assn., Virginia Beach Bar Assn., Virginia Beach C. of C., Rotary (pres. 1982, Paul Harris fellow). Avocation: golf. Civil rights, General civil litigation, Insurance. Home: 936 Poquoson Cir Virginia Beach VA 23452 Office: 936 Poquoson Cir Virginia Beach VA 23452-4646

**SWOPE, SCOTT PAUL,** lawyer; b. Trenton, Mich., Nov. 9, 1968. AA, St. Petersburg Jr. Coll., 1990; BS, U. South Fla., 1994; JD, U. Fla., 1997. Bar: Fla. 1997, U.S. Dist. Ct. (mid. dist.) Fla. 1997. Deputy sheriff Pinellas County Sheriff's Office, Largo, Fla., 1988-94; atty. Tew, Zinober, Barnes, Zimmet & Unice, Clearwater, Fla., 1997-98, Alan S. Gassman, P.A., Clearwater, Fla., 1998—. U. Fla. Coll. Law scholar, Gainesville, 1994-97. Mem. Acad. Fla. Trial Lawyers, Pinellas County Estate Planning Coun., Clearwater Bar Assn. General civil litigation, Probate, General corporate. Office: Alan S Gassman PA 1245 Court St Ste 102 Clearwater FL 33756-5856

**SWYERS, WALTER JOHN, JR.,** lawyer; b. Springfield, Mass., July 14, 1934; s. Walter John and Anne Gail Swyers; m. Jamie Elizabeth Wright, Oct. 8, 1970; children: John Timothy, Jennifer Brooke Elizabeth, Matthew Lindsey. BS in Commerce, U. Louisville, 1956, MBA, 1961, JD, 1971. Bar: Ky., Fla., U.S. Dist. Ct. (ea. and we. dists.) Ky., U.S. Ct. Appeals (6th cir.), U.S. Supreme Ct. Purchasing agt.-packaging Colgate Palmolive Co., Louisville, 1958-63; exec. dir. Printing Industry Trade Assn., Louisville, 1963-68; exec. asst. Jefferson County Fiscal Ct., Louisville, 1970-72; sole practitioner Louisville, 1972—. Mem. adv. bd. Salvation Army, 1985—; bd. dirs. Derby Festival Com., Louisville, 1965-68. Served with U.S. Army, 1956-58, Germany. Mem. Ky. Trial Lawyers Assn. Democrat. Presbyterian. General civil litigation, Construction, Real property. Home: 203 Council Rd Louisville KY 40207-1507 Office: 2100 National City Tower Louisville KY 40202

**SYAT, SCOTT MITCHELL,** lawyer; b. Boston, Aug. 16, 1968; s. Stephen Richard and Deborah S.; m. Shari Lynn Kaye, Oct. 4, 1998. BA, U. Mass., 1990; JD, New Eng. Sch. of Law, 1993. Bar: Mass. 1993, U.S. Dist. Ct. Mass. 1994. Mem. ABA, ATLA, Mass. Bar Assn., Mass. Acad. of Trial Attys., Mass. Criminal Defense Lawyers Assn. Personal injury, Criminal. Office: 1400 Hancock St Fl 8 Quincy MA 02169-5233

**SYKES, TRACY ALLAN,** lawyer; b. Waukesha, Wis., Apr. 27, 1961; s. George and Florence May (Fowler) S. BA in Econs. magna cum laude, U. Wis., Eau Claire, 1983; JD, Boston U., 1986. Bar: Mass. 1986, U.S. Ct. Appeals (1st cir.) 1986, U.S. Dist. Ct. Mass. 1986, Minn. 1988, U.S. Ct. Appeals (8th cir.) 1988, U.S. Dist. Ct. (ea. dist.) Wis. 1989, U.S. Dist. Ct. Minn. 1990, D.C. 1992. Assoc. Rubin & Rudman, Boston, 1986-88, Doherty, Rumble & Butler, Mpls., 1988-90, Robins, Kaplan, Miller & Ciresi, Mpla., 1990-92; ptnr. Robins, Kaplan, Miller & Ciresi, Mpls. and Boston, 1992—; mediator Crime and Justice Found., Boston, 1987-88. Author: Hiring, Firing and Managing, 1992, ADA...Employers' Perspective, 1993. Mem. ABA, ATLA, Minn. Bar Assn., Boston Bar Assn., D.C. Bar Assn. Avocations: golf, scuba diving, photography. Labor, General civil litigation, Intellectual property. Office: Robins Kaplan Miller Ciresi 222 Berkeley St Boston MA 02116-3748

**SYLVESTER, KATHRYN ROSE,** lawyer; b. Camden, N.J., Jan. 20, 1968; d. Frank Albert and Bergetta Anne Sylvester; m. William S. Palmieri. BA, Rosemont (Pa.) Coll., 1990; MS in Environ. Law, Vt. Law Sch., South Royalton, 1991, JD, 1994. Bar: Conn., U.S. Dist. Ct. Conn.; mem. Gaming Disputes Ct., Mohegan Tribe. Temp. asst. clk. Milford (Conn.) Superior Ct., 1994-97; assoc. Waller, Smith & Palmer, P.C., New London, Conn., 1997-98, Hunt, Leibert Chester & Jacobson, Hartford, Conn., 1998—. Mem. ABA, New Haven County Bar Assn. Avocations: blues music, travel, antiquarian books, antiques, cooking. Real property, Environmental, Landlord-tenant. Home: 352 Amity Rd Bethany CT 06524-3407 Office: Hunt Leibert Chester & Jacobson 94 Hungerford St Hartford CT 06106-4626

**SYMMES, WILLIAM DANIEL,** lawyer; b. Spokane, Wash., Sept. 10, 1938; s. William John and Sheila (Deacon) S.; m. Jayne Peters, June 20, 1959; children: Ashley, William. AB cum laude, Georgetown U., 1960; MBA, Columbia U., 1962; LLB, Stanford U., 1965. Bar: Calif. 1966, U.S. Ct. Appeals (9th cir.) 1966, Wash., 1968, U.S. Supreme Ct. 1982. Assoc. Burris & Lagerlof, L.A., 1965-68, Witherspoon, Kelley, Davenport & Toole, Spokane, 1968—; adj. prof. Gonzaga U., Spokane, 1971-77; part owner, officer, dir. Pacific Coast League AAA Spokane Indians, 1978-82, Las Vegas Stars, 1983-85. Bd. dirs. Greater Spokane Sports Assn., 1984—, Spokane Youth Sports Assn., 1985—, Focus 21, also others. Named Outstanding Young Man Yr. Spokane Jr. C. of C., 1969. Fellow Am. Coll. Trial Lawyers; mem. ABA, Am. Bd. Trial Advocates, Wash. State Bar Assn., Calif. Bar Assn., Spokane County Bar Assn. (chmn. jud. liaison com. 1982-84), Def. Rsch. Inst., Wash. Def. Lawyers Assn., Spokane C. of C., Focus 21, Empire Club, Spokane Club, Manito Golf and Country Club. Product liability, Insurance, General civil litigation. Home: 3606 S Eastgate Ct Spokane WA 99203-1411 Office: Witherspoon Kelley Davenport & Toole 1100 Nat Bank Bldg Spokane WA 99201

**SYNN, GORDON,** lawyer; b. Santa Monica, Calif., June 8, 1963; s. Kyung Chan and Esook S. BA, UCLA, 1986; JD, Harvard U., 1989. Bar: N.Y. 1990. Assoc. Debevoise & Plimpton, N.Y.C., 1989-93, Wilkie Farr & Gallagher, N.Y.C., 1993-95, Souadron Ellenoff, N.Y.C., 1995-97; gen. counsel, v.p. bus. affairs Fox L.Am., L.A., 1997—. Mem. N.Y.C. Bar Assn. Avocations: painting, writing, acting. Entertainment, General corporate, Intellectual property. Office: Fox Latin Am 11833 Mississippi Ave Los Angeles CA 90025-6114

**SYRASKI, TINA LOUISE,** lawyer; b. Buffalo, Apr. 13, 1963; d. Walter John and Rosemarie Syraski; m. Daniel Paul Nowicki, July 11, 1987; children: Michael Richard; 1 child from previous marriage, Brenda Danielle Nowicki. AA, Bryant and Stratton, Williamsville, N.Y., 1987; BS, SUNY, Buffalo, 1990, JD, 1993. Bar: N.Y. 1994. Sole practitioner Corfu, N.Y., 1994-97; staff atty. Lewis & Lewis, P.C., Buffalo, 1995-96; assoc. atty. Gregory A. Pope & Assocs., Lockport, N.Y., 1997—. In house vol. atty. Vol. Lawyers Project, Buffalo, 1994-97 vol. atty., 1997—. Named Mentor of Yr., Vol. Lawyers Project, 1997. Mem. Genesee County Bar Assn., Erie County Bar Assn. Family and matrimonial, Estate planning, Workers' compensation. Office: Gregory A Pope & Assocs 247 East Ave Lockport NY 14094-3825

**SYVERUD, KENT DOUGLAS,** dean; b. Rochester, N.Y., Oct. 23, 1956; s. Warren Lukken and Janet (Thatcher) S.l; m. Ruth Chi-Fen Chen, May 22, 1982; children: Steven, Brian, David. BSFS, Georgetown U., 1977; JD, U. Mich., 1981, MA, 1983. Bar: D.C. 1982, Mich. 1993. Law clk. to Judge Oberdorfer U.S. Dist. Ct. D.C., Washington, 1983-84; law clk. Justice O'Connor Supreme Ct. U.S., Washington, 1984-85; assoc. Wilmer, Cutler & Pickering, Washington, 1985-97; exec. sec. Mich. Law Revision Commn., Lansing, 1993-95; prof. U. Mich. Law Sch., Ann Arbor, 1987-97; dean,

Garner Anthony prof. Vanderbilt U. Law Sch., Nashville, 1997—; chair exec. com. Inst. for Continuing Legal Edn., Ann Arbor, 1995-97. Mem. Am. Law Inst., Law and Soc. Assn. Office: Vanderbilt Law Sch 21st Ave S Nashville TN 37240-0001*

**SZABO, ELIZABETH MARYANN,** lawyer; b. Passaic, N.J.; d. William Guy and Stasia (Siejwa) S. BA cum laude, Wilson Coll., 1976; JD, N.Y.U., 1986. Bar: N.J. 1988, U.S. Dist. Ct. N.J. 1988, Pa. 1988, N.Y. 1991, U.S. Dist. Ct. (ea. dist.) N.Y. 1991, U.S. Dist. Ct. (so. dist.) N.Y. 1991, U.S. Supreme Ct. 1994. Asst. dir. Multistate Legal Studies, N.Y.C., 1986-90; pvt. practice N.Y.C., 1991—; arbitrator Small Claims Ct., Civil Ct. City of N.Y., 1997—; columnist Immigration Law, Asenta Newspaper, 1997—, Weekly Bengalee, 1994-96, India Horizons, 1995. Fundraiser Campaign for Coun. Woman Jenny Lim, N.Y.C., 1997. Mem. Nat. Lawyers Guild (exec. com. 1996-98, sec. N.Y. chpt. 1996-98, lectr. immigration law), N.Y. County Lawyers Assn. (consumer bankruptcy com. 1994-98, immigration com. 1994-98, Pro Bono award 1994, 95), N.Y. State Bar Assn. (public interest com. 1995-97), Small Claims Arbitrators Assn., Fed. Bar Assn. Democrat. Episcopalian. Avocations: photography, poetry, painting, acting. Home: 401 Broadway Ste 1502 New York NY 10013-3005

**SZABO, VALERIE,** lawyer; b. Greenville, Mich., Mar. 6, 1956; d. Bernard and Shirley (Fine) S.; m. Glenn Goldenhorn, Sept. 27, 1987. BA, U. S.C., 1977; JD, George Mason U., 1980. Assoc. Ilona Ely Freedman, Alexandria, Va., 1981-83; pvt. practice Arlington, 1984-96; ptnr. Szabo & Angus, PLLC, Arlington, 1996—. Mem. ABA, ATLA, Va. Bar Assn., Va. Trial Lawyers Assn., Fairfax County Bar Assn., Arlington County Bar Assn., Delta Theta Phi. Democrat. Fax: 703-841-5404. Family and matrimonial. Office: Szabo & Angus PLLC 1313 Dolley Madison Blvd Mc Lean VA 22101-3926

**SZALLER, JAMES FRANCIS,** lawyer; b. Cleve., Jan. 22, 1945; s. Frank Paul and Ellen Grace (O'Malley) S.; m. Roberta Mae Curtin, Oct. 23, 1967 (div. Aug. 1975); m. Charlene Nancy Smith, Apr. 28, 1984. AA, Cuyahoga Community Coll., 1967; BA, Cleve. State U., 1970, JD cum laude, 1975. Bar: Ohio 1975, U.S. Dist. Ct. (no. dist.) Ohio 1975, U.S. Supreme Ct. 1982, U.S. Ct. Appeals (6th cir.) 1983, U.S. Ct. Appeals (4th cir.) 1986. Assoc. Metzenbaum, Gaines & Stern, Cleve., 1975-79; sr. ptnr. Brown & Szaller Co., L.P.A., Cleve., 1979—; lectr. law Cleve. State U., 1977-81. Mem. editorial bd. Cleve. State U. Law Rev., 1973-75.; contbr. articles to profl. jours. Mem. Ohio State Bar Assn., Greater Cleve. Bar Assn., Cleve. Acad. Trial Lawyers, Ohio Acad. Trial Lawyers, Assn. Trial Lawyers Am., Nat. Coll. Advocacy (advocate). Democrat. Roman Catholic. Avocations: gourmet cooking, automobile racing. General civil litigation, Personal injury. Office: Brown & Szaller Co LPA 14222 Madison Ave Cleveland OH 44107-4510

**SZANYI, KEVIN ANDREW,** lawyer; b. Buffalo, Jan. 7, 1960; s. Andrew John and Alice M. (Degenhart) S.; m. Lyn Barnes, Dec. 28, 1996; 1 child, Colin Joseph. BA, U. Dayton, 1982; JD, SUNY, Buffalo, 1985. Bar: N.Y. 1985. Assoc. Hodgson Russ Andrews Woods & Goodyear, Buffalo, 1985-92, ptnr., 1993-95; ptnr. Harris Beach & Wilcox, Buffalo, 1995-99, Webster Szanyi LLP, Buffalo, 1999—. Mem. Def. Rsch. Inst., Nat. Assn. R.R. Trial Counsel. Product liability, Toxic tort, Personal injury. Office: Webster Szanyi LLP 1400 Liberty Bldg Buffalo NY 14202

**SZAREK, MILTON LOUIS,** lawyer; b. Providence, Feb. 26, 1935; s. Louis Walter and Josephine Katherine (Kowal) S.; children—Anna Marie, Louisa Joe. A.A., R.I. Jr. Coll., 1968; B.A., U. R.I., 1970; J.D., Howard U., 1973. Bar: R.I. 1974, US. Dist. Ct. R.I. 1974, U.S. Supreme Ct. 1979. Sole practice, Coventry, R.I., 1974—; probate judge Town of Coventry, 1979-80. Moderator Washington Fire Dist., Coventry, 1975—; mem. sch. com. Coventry Sch. Com., 1974-78, chmn. sch. com., 1976-78. Served with U.S. Army, 1955-57. Mem. R.I. Bar Assn. Democrat. Roman Catholic. Lodge: Masons. Probate, Criminal, General practice. Office: 1320 Main St Coventry RI 02816-8462

**SZCZESNY, RONALD WILLIAM,** lawyer; b. Detroit, Nov. 26, 1940; s. Raymond Joseph and Sophie (Welc) S.; children: Timothy, Laurie, Kristen; m. Susan Joy Feragne, May 25, 1985. BA in Chemistry, Wayne State U., 1963, JD, 1972. Bar: Mich. 1975, U.S. Dist. Ct. (ea. dist.) Mich. 1975, U.S. Tax Ct. 1975, U.S. Supreme Ct. 1983, U.S. Ct. Appeals 1985. Rsch. chemist Wyandotte Chems., Mich., 1961-64; exptl. chemist Cadillac Motor Car Co., Detroit, 1964-66, gen. supr. material lab., 1966-69, materials engr., 1969-72; staff analysis engr. GM Co., Warren, Mich., 1972-77; assoc. Zeff and Zeff & Materna, Detroit, 1977-89, Stern Cohan and Stern, Southfield, Mich., 1989-97; pvt. practice Madison Heights, Mich., 1997—. Mem. ATLA, Mich. Trial Lawyers Assn., Detroit Bar Assn., Oakland County Bar Assn., Macomb County Bar Assn., Soc. Automotive Engrs., Advocates Bar Assn., Am. Acad. Forensic Scis., Internat. Assn. Arson Investigators, Mich. Assn. Arson Investigators, U. Mich. Pres.'s Club, Am. Soc. Safety Engrs., Nat. Assn. Fire Investigators, Nat. Fire Protection Assn. Democrat. Roman Catholic. Personal injury, Product liability, General civil litigation. Home: 27333 Spring Arbor Dr Southfield MI 48076-3543 Office: 28051 Dequindre Rd Madison Heights MI 48071-3001

**SZUCH, CLYDE ANDREW,** lawyer; b. Bluefield, W.Va., Nov. 22, 1930; s. Nicholas and Aranka (Rubin) S.; m. Rosalie Hirschman Wulfson, Sept. 5, 1954; children: Peter Alan, Richard Coleman. BA, Rutgers, 1952; LLB, Harvard U., 1955. Bar: N.J. 1955, U.S. Dist. Ct. N.J. 1955, U.S. Ct. Appeals (3rd cir.) 1958, U.S. Supreme Ct. 1962. Law clk. to assoc. justice William J. Brennan Jr. U.S. Supreme Ct., Washington, 1956-57; asst. U.S. atty. U.S. Atty. Office, Newark, 1957-58; assoc. Pitney, Hardin & Kipp, Newark, 1958-62; ptnr. Pitney, Hardin, Kipp & Szuch, Morristown, N.J., 1962—; mem. panel Ctr. for Pub. Resources, N.J.; bd. dirs. Vt. Rlwy. Inc., Clarendon & Pittsford R.R. Co., Burlington, Vt., Brennan Ctr. for Justice; panelist AAA Large Complex Cases. Gov. N.J. region Nat. Conf. for Comty. and Justice. Fellow Am. Bar Found.; mem. ABA, Am. Law Inst., N.J. State Bar Assn., Morris County Bar Assn., Essex County Bar Assn., Fed. Bar Assn. (N.J. chpt.), N.J. C. of C. (bd. dirs.), Nat. Legal Aid Defender Assn., Hist. Soc. U.S. Ct. Appeals for 3d Cir., Park Ave. Club. Federal civil litigation, General civil litigation, State civil litigation. Office: Pitney Hardin Kipp & Szuch PO Box 1945 Morristown NJ 07962-1945

**SZWALBENEST, BENEDYKT JAN,** lawyer; b. Poland, June 13, 1955; s. Sidney and Janina (Bleishtif) S.; m. Shelley Joy Leibel, Nov. 8, 1981. BBA, Temple U., 1978, JD, 1981. Law clk. Fed. Deposit Ins. Corp., Washington, 1980; law clk. to presiding justice U.S. Dist. Ct. (ea. dist.) Pa., Phila., 1980-81; staff atty., regulatory specialist Fidelcor, Inc. and Fidelity Bank, Phila., 1981-86; regulations specialist sr. regulatory staff Fed. Res. Bank of N.Y., N.Y.C., 1986-89; s.v.p. regulatory compliance, sec. Custodial Trust Co. subs. Bear Stearns, Princeton, 1990—; mng. dir. Bear Stearns & Co., Inc., 1998—. Author: Federal Bank Regulation, 1980. Mem. Commonwealth of Pa. Post-secondary Edn. Planning Commn., Harrisburg, 1977-79; trustee Pop Warners Little Scholars, Phila., 1981-86. Recipient E. Gerald Corrigan Pres.'s Award for Excellence, 1988. Mem. ABA (nat. sec., treas. law student div. 1980-81, Silver Key award 1980, Gold Key award 1981), Am. Judicature Soc., Am. Bankers Assn. (cert. compliance specialist, lectr. 1984—), Temple U. Sch. Bus. Alumni Assn. (sec. 1982-84, v.p. 1984-86, pres. 1986-88, bd. dirs. gen. alumni assn. 1986-88), Tau Epsilon Rho, Omicron Delta Epsilon. Avocations: baseball, tennis, skiing. Banking, Administrative and regulatory, Securities. Home: 1504 Brookfield Rd Yardley PA 19067-3930 Office: Custodial Trust Co 101 Carnegie Ctr Princeton NJ 08540-6231

**SZYMANSKI, DAVID J.,** judge; b. Detroit, June 12, 1954; s. Frank Stanley and Lillian (Mikula) S.; m. Jackie F. Szymanski, June 24, 1961; children: Nicole, Natalie, David. BA, U. Notre Dame, 1976; JD, Wayne State U., 1982. Bar: Mich. 1982, Fla. 1983, U.S. Dist. Ct. Tchr., ocach North Montgomery Schs., Crawfordsville, Ind., 1976-79, Detroit Pub. Schs., 1979-80; jud. asst. Mich. 48th Dist. Ct., West Bloomfield, 1980-82; assoc. atty. Lippitt, Lyons and Whiteford, Southfield, Mich., 1982-86, Clark, Hardy, Lowes, Pollard, Page, Birmingham, Mich., 1986-90; probate judge, chief judge pro tem Wayne County, Detroit, 1990—; mem. Wayne County Teen Pregnancy, Detroit, 1992—; mem. steering com. Polish Am. Citizens for Equity, Detroit, 1992—. Precinct del. Mich. Dem. Party, S.E. Mich., 1982-90. Roman Catholic. Avocations: hockey, snowboarding, windsurfing, gardening. Office: Wayne Probate Ct 2 Woodward Ave Rm 1303 Detroit MI 48226-3437

**TA, TAI VAN,** lawyer, researcher; b. Ninh Binh, Vietnam, Apr. 16, 1938; came to U.S., 1975; s. Duong Van and Loan thi (Pham) T.; m. Lien-Nhu Tran, Oct. 26, 1967; children: Becky, John, Khuong Virginia, Dora. LLB, U. Saigon, Vietnam, 1960; MA, U. Va., 1964, PhD, 1965; LLM, Harvard U., 1985. Bar: Mass. 1986, U.S. Dist. Ct. Mass. 1987. Prof. U. Saigon Law Sch., 1965-75, Nat. Sch. Adminstrn., 1965-75; ptnr. Tang thi Thanh Trai & Ta Van Tai, 1968-75; legal rschr. Reed Smith Shaw & McClay, Pitts., 1975; rsch. assoc. Harvard U. Law Sch., Cambridge, Mass., 1975—, adj. lectr., 1998—; pvt. practice, Brookline, Mass., 1986—; rsch. scholar NYU Law Sch., N.Y.C., 1990-94; cons. Milbank Tweed Hadley & McCloy, N.Y.C., 1979, Shearman & Sterling, N.Y.C., 1979, Paul Weiss Rifkind Wharton and Garrison, N.Y.C., 1989, 90. Co-author: The Laws of Southeast Asia, 1986, The Le Code: Law in Traditional Vietnam, 1987, Investment Law in Vietnam, 1990; author: Vietnamese Tradition of Human Rights, 1988; contbr. articles to profl. jours. V.p. Vietnamese Refugees Assn., Mass., 1976-79; advisor to Vietnamese community, Mass., 1989—. Fulbright scholar 1960-62; grantee Asia Found., 1972, Ford Found., 1975-76, Aspen Inst. 1993. Avocations: piano, swimming, foreign languages. Criminal, Private international, General practice. Home: 145 Naples Rd Brookline MA 02446-2548 Office: Harvard U Law Sch Pound 423 1563 Massachusetts Ave Cambridge MA 02138-2903

**TABATA, MARIE AIKO,** lawyer; b. Hoboken, N.J., June 26, 1968; d. Chiaki Tabata and Dori (Simone) Guthrie. BS in Biochemistry, La. State U., 1990; JD, Ill. Inst. Tech., Chgo., 1993. Bar: Ill., U.S. Dist. Ct. (no. dist.) Ill. Atty. Law Offices of Randall S. Goulding, Chgo., 1993-95; atty., ct. coord. Office of the Clk. of the Cir. Ct., Chgo., 1995—. Mem. Chgo. Bar Assn. (vice-chair 2d divsn. civil practice com. 1997—). Address: 3721 N Pine Grove Ave Apt 2-F Chicago IL 60613-4122

**TABER, KELLEY MORGAN,** lawyer; b. Oakland, Calif., Dec. 15, 1966; d. Lawrence Kirk and Donna (Christopherson) T.; m. Gary David Jakobs, Oct. 12, 1996. AB magna cum laude, Harvard U., 1988; JD, U. Calif., Davis, 1996. Bar: Calif. 1996, U.S. Dist. Ct. (no., ea. and ctrl. dists.) Calif. 1997, U.S. Ct. of Appeals (9th cir.) 1998. Environ. analyst EIP Assocs., Sacramento, Calif., 1989-90; land use analyst Remy & Thomas, Sacramento, 1990-91, River West Devel., Sacramento, 1991-92; environ. cons. Kelley Taber & Assocs., Sacramento, 1992-96; assoc. Landels, Ripley & Diamond, San Francisco, 1996-98, De Cuir & Somach, Sacramento, 1998—. Trustee Sacramento Country Day Sch., 1991-96; vol. tutor Mustard Seed Sch. for Homeless Children, Sacramento, 1991-93. Mem. Calif. State Bar (legis. rev. com. environ. law sect.), Assn. Environ. Profls. (v.p. Sacramento 1991-92, state bar environ. law sect. legis. rev. com.), Milton L. Schwartz Inn of Ct., Sacramento County Bar Assn. Avocations: hiking, backpacking, bicycling, cooking, volunteer work. E-mail: ktaber@decuirsomach.com. Environmental, Land use and zoning (including planning), Natural resources. Office: De Cuir & Somach 400 Capitol Mall Ste 1900 Sacramento CA 95814-4436

**TABERNILLA, ARMANDO ALEJANDRO,** lawyer; b. Palm Beach, Fla., Nov. 24, 1959; s. Francisco H. and Hilda M. (Molina) T.; m. Holly B. Susac, May 11, 1991; children: Christian A., Sofia F. BSE, Duke U., 1981; JD, U. Va., 1984. Assoc. Steel, Hector & Davis, Miami, 1984-90, ptnr., 1990-92; assoc. gen. counsel IVAX Corp., Miami, 1992-94, v.p., gen. counsel, 1994-96, sr. v.p., gen. counsel, 1996-98; v.p., gen. counsel Fla. Crystals Corp., Palm Beach, 1998—. Trustee Cuban Mus. of Ams., Miami, 1995-98; bd. visitors Fla. State U. Sch. Law, Tallahassee, 1995-98. Mem. ABA, Dade County Bar Assn., Phi Beta Kappa. Avocations: woodworking, golf, reading, art. General corporate, Securities, Mergers and acquisitions. Office: Fla Crystals Corp 340 Royal Poinciana Way Palm Beach FL 33480-4048

**TABIN, SEYMOUR,** lawyer; b. Chgo., May 6, 1918; s. Solomon and Lillian (Klingman) T.; m. Frances Greenfield, Oct. 26, 1940; 1 child, Lee Edward. BA, U. Chgo., 1938, D in Law cum laude, 1940. Bar: Ill. 1940, U.S. Dist. Ct. (no. dist.) Ill. 1940, U.S. Tax Ct. 1948, U.S. Supreme Ct. 1950. Ptnr. Froelich, Grossman, Teton & Tabin, Chgo., 1950-76; of counsel Gottlieb & Schwartz, Chgo., 1975-93; pvt. practice Highland Park, Ill., 1993—. Lt. USNR, 1942-45. Mem. Chgo. Bar Assn., Ill. Bar Assn., Order of Coif, Phi Beta Kappa. Republican. Jewish. Avocations: tennis, bridge, computers, travel, grandchildren. Banking, General corporate. Home and Office: 1148 S Lincoln Ave Highland Park IL 60035-4110

**TABLER, BRYAN G.,** lawyer; b. Louisville, Jan. 12, 1943; s. Norman Gardner and Sarah Marie (Grant) T.; m. Susan Y. Beidler, Dec. 28, 1968 (div. June 1987); children: Justin Elizabeth, Gillian Gardner; m. Karen Sue Strome, July 24, 1987. AB, Princeton U., 1969; JD, Yale U., 1972. Bar: Ind. 1972, U.S. Dist. Ct. (so. dist.) Ind. 1972, U.S. Dist. Ct. (no. dist.) Ind. 1976, U.S. Ct. Appeals (7th cir.) 1976, U.S. Supreme Ct. 1976. Assoc. Barnes & Thornburg, Indpls., 1972-79, ptnr., chmn. environ. law dept., 1979-94; v.p., gen. counsel, sec. IPALCO Enterprises, Inc., 1994—; sr. v.p., gen. coun., sec. Indpls. Power & Light Co., 1994—; mem. exec. com. Environ. Quality Control, Inc., Indpls., 1985—. Mem. Indpls. Mus. of Art, 1972—; bd. dirs. Indpls. Symphony Orch. 1st lt. U.S. Army, 1964-68, Vietnam. Mem. ABA, Ind. Bar Assn., Bar Assn. of the 7th Cir., Indpls. Bar Assn. Avocation: golf. Environmental, Federal civil litigation, General corporate. Home: 8932 Wickham Rd Indianapolis IN 46260-1644 Office: Indpls Power & Light Co One Monument PO Box 1595 Indianapolis IN 46206-1595

**TABOR, DARREN LEE,** judicial clerk; b. Chgo., Dec. 19, 1968; s. Gregory Randolph and Bobbie Darlene Tabor; m. Rebecca Jovene Pryzybien, Aug. 6, 1995. AA, Morraine Valley C.C., Palos Hills, Ill., 1990; BA, Loyola U., Chgo., 1992; JD, John Marshall Law Sch., 1995. Bar: N.Mex. 1995, Ill. 1998, U.S. Dist. Ct. (no. dist.) Ill. 1998. Jud. extern U.S. Dist. Ct. (no. dist.) Ill., Rockford, 1994; jud. clk. Supreme Ct. N.Mex., Santa Fe, 1995-97, Ill. Appellate Ct., Woodstock, 1997—. Recipient Corpus Juris Secundum awards West Pub., 1994; Dean's scholar John Marshall Law Sch., Chgo., 1993, Fred F. Herzog scholar John Marshall Law Sch., Chgo., 1994. Mem. ABA, Ill. State Bar Assn., Chgo. Bar Assn. Avocations: developing computer software, creating web sites, outdoor activities, dog training. Home: 2900 Bristol St Ste E204 Costa Mesa CA 92626-7908 Office: Ill Appellate Ct 2nd Dist 1700A S Eastwood Dr Woodstock IL 60098-4657

**TACHA, DEANELL REECE,** federal judge; b. Jan. 26, 1946. BA, U. Kans., 1968; JD, U. Mich., 1971. Spl. asst. to U.S. Sec. of Labor, Washington, 1971-72; assoc. Hogan & Hartson, Washington, 1973, Thomas J. Pitner, Concordia, Kans., 1973-74; dir. Douglas County Legal Aid Clinic, Lawrence, Kans., 1974-77; assoc. prof. law U. Kans., Lawrence, 1974-77, prof., 1977-85, assoc. dean, 1977-79, assoc. vice chancellor, 1979-81, vice chancellor, 1981-85; judge U.S. Ct. Appeals (10th cir.), Denver, 1985—; U.S. sentencing commr., 1994-98. Office: US Ct Appeals 10th Cir 4830 W 15th St Ste 100 Lawrence KS 66049-3885

**TACKITT, SYLVAN WRIGHT,** lawyer; b. Banta, Ind., June 12, 1909; s. Mitchell Albert Ward and Carrie Blanche (Stewart) T.; m. Elizabeth Estelle Stephenson, Sept. 6, 1934 (dec. Nov. 1970); children: Stephen Wright (dec.), Martha Anne Distler; m. Harriet Martin Cartmel, May 13, 1972 (dec. Dec. 1995); m. Edith Boyer Schuman, May 14, 1997. BS in Bus., Ind. U., 1931, LLB, 1933. Bar: Ind. 1931. Pvt. practice Bloomington, 1933—; prosecuting atty. Monroe County, Bloomington, Ind., 1942-46, county atty., 1964-65. Mem. 1st Christian Ch., Bloomington, 1934—; pres. YMCA, Bloomington, 1951-52; bd. dirs. Monroe County Pub. Libr., Monroe County Pub. Libr. Found.; govt. appeal agt. 1948-68. Recipient Sagamore of Wabash award Gov. of Ind., 1982. Fellow Lions (Melvin Jones fellow, pres. Bloomington chpt. 1947-48); mem. ABA, Ind. State Bar Assn. (bd. mgrs. 1970-72), Monroe County Bar Assn. (pres. 1960-61), Bloomington Country Club, Columbia Club (Indpls.), Masons, Sigma Alpha Epsilon. Republican. Avocations: golf, bridge, cryptograms, collecting marbles and orientalia. Estate planning, Probate. Home: 1304 E 2d St Bloomington IN 47401-5104 Office: 103 N College Ave Ste 203 Bloomington IN 47404-3947

**TACKOWIAK, BRUCE JOSEPH,** lawyer; b. Milw., July 10, 1956; s. Eugene Charles and Bernadine Tackowiak. BA in History and Polit. Sci., U. Wis., 1979; cert. emergency med. technician, Madison Area Tech. Coll., 1981; Diploma in Internat. and Comparative Law, Magdalen Coll., U. Oxford, Eng., 1986; JD, U. San Diego, 1988. Bar: Calif. 1990, Ill. 1991, U.S. Dist. Ct. (ctrl. and so. dists.) Calif. 1990, U.S. Ct. Appeals (9th cir.) 1990. Atty. LaFollette, Johnson, De Haas, Fesler & Ames, L.A., 1990-92, Hillsinger & Costanzo, L.A., 1992-93, Roxborough, Pomerance & Gallegos, LLP, L.A., 1993-97; prin. Law Offices of Bruce J. Tackowiak, L.A., 1997—; assoc. Am. Inns of Ct., 1992—. Sr./mng. editor U. San Diego Jour. Contemporary Legal Issues, 1987-88. Mem. ABA, ATLA, Calif. Bar Assn., Los Angeles County Bar Assn., Ill. Bar Assn., Chgo. Bar Assn., World Futurist Soc. (profl.). Avocations: team sports, running, tennis. General civil litigation, General corporate, Insurance. Office: 6500 Wilshire Blvd Ste 1600 Los Angeles CA 90048-4920

**TAFT, NATHANIEL BELMONT,** lawyer; b. Tarrytown, N.Y., Aug. 12, 1919; s. Louis Eugene and Etta Minnie (Spivak) Topp; m. Norma Rosalind Pike, May 22, 1943; children: Charles Eliot, Stephen Pike. BS in Econs., Fordham U., 1940; JD, Harvard U., 1948. Bar: N.Y. 1949. Asst. to gen. counsel N.Y. State Ins. Dept., Albany, 1948-50; law dept. N.Y. Life Ins. Co., N.Y.C., 1951-65, group dept., 1965-84, ret. as group v.p., 1984; sole practice law White Plains, N.Y., 1985—; chmn. group ins. com. Life Ins. Coun. N.Y., 1981-84; adviser Tex. State Bd. Ins., 1989-91; lectr., author on healthcare reform, 1992—. Contbr. articles to profl. jours.; author monographs on group ins. regulation. Chmn. White Plains Adult Edn. Coun., 1960-62; trustee Jewish Cmty. Ctr., White Plains, 1977-86, sec.-treas., 1980-84; bd. dirs. Westchester Philharm., 1991—, sec., 1993—, gen. counsel, 1998—; v.p., gen. counsel, 1999—. Mem. ABA, N.Y. State Bar Assn., Health Ins. Assn. Am. (chmn. N.Y. minimum standards com. 1981-83), Nat. Assn. Physicians (sec.-treas. 1991—), Health Reins. Assn. Conn. (sec. 1975-85), Harvard Club (N.Y.C.). Republican. Jewish. Avocations: golf, writing. Insurance, Administrative and regulatory, Pension, profit-sharing, and employee benefits. Home and Office: 16 Sparrow Cir White Plains NY 10605-4624

**TAIT, JOHN REID,** lawyer; b. Toledo, Apr. 7, 1946; s. Paul Reid and Lucy Richardson (Ruddew) T.; m. Christina Ruth Bjornstad, Mar. 12, 1972; children: Gretchen, Mary. BA, Columbia Coll., 1968; JD, Vanderbilt U., 1974. Bar: Idaho 1974, U.S. Dist. Ct. Idaho 1974, U.S. Ct. Appeals (9th cir.), U.S. Supreme Ct., Nez Perce Tribal Ct. Assoc. Keeton & Tait, Lewiston, Idaho, 1974-76, ptnr., 1976-86, 89—, Keeton, Tait & Petrie, 1986-88, Keeton & Tait, 1989—. Chmn. bd. No. Rockies Action Group, Helena, Mont., 1985-86, bd. dirs. 1981-88, Lewiston Hist. Preservation Commn., Idaho, 1975-94, chmn., 1988-94; bd. dirs. Idaho Legal Aid Svcs., Boise, 1975—, Idaho Housing Agy., Boise, 1984-91, St. Joseph Regional Med. Ctr. Found., Inc., 1989-94, Lewiston Ind. Found. for Edn., Inc., 1996—; Dem. precinct committeeman, 1976-86, state committeeman, 1977-94; co-chmn. Idaho state re-election com. John V. Evans, 1978; Idaho del. Nat. Dem. Conv., N.Y., 1980, mem. standing com. on credentials, N.Y., 1980, San Francisco, 1984; regional coord. Idaho State Dem. Party, 1996—; treas. Larry LaRocco for Congress, 1990, 92. With U.S. Army, 1968-71. Recipient Pro Bono Svc. award Idaho State Bar 1988, Community Recognition award Lewiston Intergovtl. Coun., 1992, Spl. Recognition award Idaho Legal Aid Svcs., Inc., 1993. Mem. ABA, ATLA, NACDL, Idaho Trial Lawyers Assn. (regional dir. 1976-77, 86-88, 96—), Clearwater Bar Assn. (sec. 1974-76, pres. 1984-86), Consumer Attys. Calif. Democrat. General practice, Workers' compensation, State civil litigation. Office: Keeton & Tait Box E 312 Miller St Lewiston ID 83501-1944

**TAKAHASHI, STEVEN SHIGERU,** lawyer; b. Seattle, Sept. 12, 1962; s. George Etsu and Toshiko Takahashi. BA in Society and Justice, U. Wash., 1985; JD, U. Oreg., 1989. Bar: Wash. 1989. Staff atty. Assoc. Counsel for the Accused, Seattle, 1989—. Avocations: bodybuilding, travel, cooking, investing, fine dining. Criminal. Home: 8403 S 120th St Seattle WA 98178-4519 Office: Assoc Counsel for Accused 110 Prefontaine Pl S Ste 200 Seattle WA 98104-2674

**TAKASHIMA, HIDEO,** lawyer, accountant; b. Kobe, Hyogo-Ken, Japan, Mar. 2, 1919; came to U.S., 1956; s. Yoshimitsu and Yoshie (Akagi) T.; m. Adrianna Elizabeth Selch Coe, Oct. 31, 1961 (div. Apr. 1984); children: James, George K., Oliver Sachio Hydon; m. Chizu Kojima, Mar. 14, 1986. Chartered acct., Kanagawa U., Yokohama, Japan, 1941; LLM in Criminal Law, Taihoku Imperial U., Japan, 1943; LLM in Bus. Law, Yale U., 1957; SJD in Antitrust Laws, N.Y. Law Sch., 1959; postgrad., Yale U., 1961-62. Bar: D.C. 1973, N.Y. 1990, U.S. Tax Ct. 1973, U.S. Ct. Appeals (D.C. cir.) 1973, N.J. 1974, U.S. Dist. Ct. N.J. 1974, U.S. Ct. Claims 1974, U.S. Ct. Appeals (3d cir.) 1977, U.S. Supreme Ct. 1977, U.S. Ct. Appeals (2d cir.) 1993. Lectr. criminology Yen Ping Coll., Taipei, Taiwan, 1946-47; mgr. Taiwan br. Warner Bros. F.N. Pix, Inc., Taipei, 1947-52; with labor union activities dept. FOA MSM/C, Am. Embassy, Taipei, 1953-54; tax editor Prentice-Hall, Inc., Englewood Cliffs, N.J., 1961-66; editor-in-chief Washington Publs., Inc., N.Y.C., 1966-69; tax atty., editor Am. Inst. CPAs, N.Y.C., 1971-72; pres., Charles Hideo Coe, P.A., Park Ridge, N.J., 1973—; corp. coun. DNP Am., Inc., 1973-90; dir. Coe & Coe, Inc., Park Ridge, N.J., 1973—; pvt. practice acctg., 1980—; gen. counsel Rissho Kosei Kai N.Y. Buddhist Ctr., Inc., 1990—. U.S. del. U.S./Japan Bilateral Session: A New Era in Legal and Econ. Relations, Tokyo, Aug.-Sept., 1988. People to People legal del. to European countries to assist U.S. immigration law legislation, 1979; People's Republic China and USSR, 1989; gen. coun. Rissho Kosei Kai N.Y. Buddhist Ctr., Inc., 1990—. Author: My Unsuspecting Formosa, 1944; editor-in-chief The Tax Barometer, 1966-69. Instr. Judo-Kendo New Milford (N.J.) Recreation Commn., 1963-69, Park Ridge Recreation Com., 1969-72, Pascack Valley Kendo Club, Park Ridge, 1969-71. Served as capt. Chinese Kuo-Min-Tang, Taipei, 1945. Yale Law Sch. fellow, 1956-57; N.Y. Law Sch. scholar, 1958, Prentice-Hall, Inc. scholar grad. div. NYU Sch. Law, 1961-63. Mem. Am. Immigration Lawyers Assn. (sec. N.J. chpt. 1978-83), Assn. Trial Lawyers Am., N.Y. State Bar Assn., Japanese Am. Assn. N.Y., Yale U. Law Sch. Alumni Assn., NYU Law Alumni Assn., Taihoku Imperial U. Law Sch. Alumin Assn., Kanagawa U. O.B. Judo Club. Republican. Club: Yale. General civil litigation, General corporate, Immigration, naturalization, and customs. Office: 3 Park Ave Park Ridge NJ 07656-1231

**TAKASUGI, ROBERT MITSUHIRO,** federal judge; b. Tacoma, Sept. 12, 1930; s. Hidesaburo and Kayo (Otsuki) T.; m. Dorothy O. Takasugi; children: Jon Robert, Lesli Mari. BS, UCLA, 1953; LLB, JD, U. So. Calif., 1959. Bar: Calif. bar 1960. Practiced law Los Angeles, 1960-73; judge East Los Angeles Municipal Ct., 1973-75, adminstrv. judge, 1974, presiding judge, 1975; judge Superior Ct., County of Los Angeles, 1975-76; U.S. dist. judge U.S. Dist. Ct. (cen. dist.) Calif., 1976—; nat. legal counsel Japanese Am. Citizens League; guest lectr. law seminars Harvard U. Law Sch. Careers Symposium; commencement spkr.; mem. Legion Lex U. So. Calif. Law Ctr.; chmn. Pub. Defs. Indigent Def. & Psychiat. Panel Com.; mem. Affirmative Action Com., Habeas Corpus-Death Penalty Com., Exec. Com., Jury Com., Settlement Rule Com., Adv. Com. on Codes of Conduct of the Jud. Conf. of the U.S., 1988-92, Code of Conduct of Judges. Mem. editorial bd. U. So. Calif. Law Rev., 1959; contbr. articles to profl. jours. Mem. Calif. adv. com. Western Regional Office, U.S. Commn. on Civil Rights; chmn. blue ribbon com. for selection of chancellor L.A. C.C. With U.S. Army, 1953-55. Harry J. Bauer scholar, 1959; recipient U.S. Mil. Man of Yr. award for Far East Theater U.S. Army, 1954, Jud. Excellence award Criminal Cts. Bar Assn., cert. of merit Japanese-Am. Bar Assn., Disting. Svc. award Asian Pacific Ctr. and Pacific Clinics, 1994, Freedom award Sertoma, 1995, Pub. Svc. award Asian Pacific Am. Legal Ctr. So. Calif., 1995, Trailblazer award So. Calif. region NAPABA, 1995, Spl. award Mex.-Am. Bar Assn., 1996, Spirit of Excellence award ABA, 1998; named Judge of Yr. Century City Bar Assn., 1995. Mem. U. So. Calif. Law Alumni Assn. (dir.). Office: US Dist Ct 312 N Spring St Los Angeles CA 90012-4701

**TALAFOUS, JOSEPH JOHN, SR.,** lawyer; b. N.Y.C., Sept. 6, 1929; s. Karol J. and Anna (Sulik) T.; m. Louise Lukac, June 18, 1955; children: Mary Lou, Joseph J. Jr., Caroline, Theresa. AB, Rutgers U., 1954; JD, Seton Hall U., 1959. Bar: N.J. 1959, U.S. Dist. Ct. N.J. 1959, U.S. Dist. Ct. (so. dist.) N.Y. 1959, U.S. Dist. Ct. (ea. dist.) N.Y. 1965, U.S. Supreme Ct. 1965, U.S. Ct. Internat. Trade 1982, N.Y. 1984. Sole practice (now Talafour & Talafour) Jersey City, 1959—; asst. prosecutor Hudson County, N.J., 1962-63; asst. corp. csl. City of Jersey City, 1965-72; judge Mcpl. Ct., Jersey City, 1974-77; commr. N.J. Gov.'s Commn. Internat. Trade. Pres., Slovak Am. Heritage Found., Inc., 1976—; v.p. Slovak League Am.; Slovak mem. Gov.'s Ethnic Coun. Served with U.S. Army, 1951-53, Korea. Mem. ABA, N.J. Bar Assn., N.Y. State Bar Assn., Assn. of Bar of City of N.Y., Hudson County Bar Assn., Hague Acad. Internat. Law. General practice, Real property, Probate. Office: 61 Sip Ave Jersey City NJ 07306-3106

**TALBERT, HUGH MATHIS,** lawyer; b. Kennett, Mo., Dec. 3, 1937; s. Clifford Roscoe and Katharyn (Hoy) T.; m. Carol Sullivan, June 1, 1962 (div. Feb. 1968); m. Carol Ann Frederick, July 18, 1973; children: Katharyn Hoy, William Hugh, Geoffrey Richard. AB, Washington U., St. Louis, 1959, LlB, 1962. Bar: Mo. 1962, U.S. Dist. Ct. (ea. dist.) Mo. 1965, Ill. 1965, U.S. Dist. Ct. (so. dist.) Ill. 1966, U.S. Ct. Appeals (7th cir.) 1971. Assoc. Strubinger, Tudor, Tombrink and Wion, St. Louis, 1962-65, Wiseman, Hallett, Mosele and Shaikewitz, Alton, Ill., 1965-67; ptnr. Chapman and Talbert, Granite City, Ill., 1967-73; pres. Talbert & Assocs., P.C., Alton, 1974—; asst. adj. prof. Trial Advocacy St. Louis U. Law Sch., 1992—. Mem. ABA, Assn. Trial Lawyers Am., Ill. State Bar Assn., Ill. Trial Lawyers Assn. (mem. bd. mgrs. 1978-87), The Mo. Bar Assn., Mo. Assn. Trial Lawyers, Madison County Bar Assn., Maritime Law Assn. of the U.S., Acad. of Rail Labor Attys., Million Dollar Advs. Forum. Democrat. Methodist. Avocations: landscaping, hiking and mountaineering, sailing. Personal injury, Admiralty, Product liability. Home: 1750 Liberty St Alton IL 62002-4514 Office: Talbert & Assocs PC PO Box 800 630 E Broadway Alton IL 62002-6308

**TALBOT, MARK MITCHELL,** prosecutor; b. McAllen, Tex., Nov. 12, 1959; s. Morgan K. and Jane M. Talbot; m. Laura Elaine Boyer, Nov. 23, 1996; children: Margaret Jane, Morgan Leslie. BA, Tex. Tech U., 1983; JD, Mich. State U., 1990. Bar: U.S. Dist. Ct. (so. dist.) Tex. 1991. Asst. dist. atty. Hidalgo County Dist. Atty.'s Office, Edinburgh, Tex., 1990—; judge McAllen (Tex.) Teen Ct., 1992—. Pres. Hidalgo County Young Lawyers, 1994-95; v.p. McAllan Citizen's League, 1998-99, pres., 1999—. Mem. Hidalgo County Bar Assn. (bd. dirs. 1998—). Episcopalian. Avocations: golf, water polo. Office: Hidalgo County Dist Atty 100 N Closuer Edinburg TX 78539

**TALBOTT, BEN JOHNSON, JR.,** lawyer; b. Louisville, May 2, 1940; s. Ben Johnson and Elizabeth (Farnsley) T.; m. Sandra Riehl, Oct. 19, 1963; children: Elizabeth, Betty, John, Ben, Sandra. AB magna cum laude, Xavier U., Cin., 1961; LLB, Harvard U., 1964. Bar: Ky. 1965, U.S. Ct. Appeals (6th cir.) 1967. Law clk. to presiding justice U.S. Dist. Ct. Ky., Louisville, 1964-65; assoc. Middleton, Reutlinger & Baird, Louisville, 1965-68, ptnr., 1968-80; ptnr. Westfall, Talbott & Woods, Louisville, 1980—; atty. Stitzel-Weller Distillery, 1970-72, Louisville Gen. Hosp., 1974-83, Louisville and Jefferson County Bd. Health, 1974-80, U. Louisville, Louisville, 1980—. Mem. adv. bd. Louisville 15, Sta. WKPC-TV, Bd. dirs., 1972-74, pres. 1974; past bd. dirs. U. Louisville Found., U. Louisville Med. Sch. Fund Orgn.; bd. dirs. Louisville Theatrical Assn., 1971—, pres., 1975-76, chmn., 1977-78; bd. dirs. Def. Enterprise Fund, 1994—; bd. dirs. Macauley Theatre, 1975, TARC Adv. Com., 1971, Jefferson County Capital Constrn. Com., 1971, Louisville Orch., 1976-86, pres., 1979-81; bd. trustees, trustee U. Louisville, 1970-79, sec., 1974, vice chmn., 1975, chmn. fin. com., 1976; bd. dirs. Ky. Ctr. for the Arts, 1983—, Louisville Lung Assn., 1974-75, treas., 1975; bd. dirs. Historic Homes Found., 1972-78, v.p. 1978, advisor, atty. 1978—. Named Outstanding Young Man of Louisville, Louisville Jaycees, 1976. Mem. ABA, Ky. Bar Assn. (chmn. 1989, Gen. Practice Session of the CLE), Louisville Bar Assn. (past mem. exec. com.), The Def. Rsch. and Trial Lawyers Assn., Harvard Law Sch. Assn. of Ky. (sec. 1965, pres. 1989—), Phi Kappa Phi. Avocations: golf, tennis, skiing. Personal injury, General civil litigation, General corporate. Home: 566 Blankenbaker Ln Louisville KY 40207-1167 Office: Westfall Talbott & Woods 501 S 2nd St Louisville KY 40202-1864

**TALESNICK, STANLEY,** lawyer; b. Indpls., June 4, 1927; s. Louis and Rose (Galerman) T.; m. Joan Goldstone, Mar. 16, 1952 (div. Feb. 1967); children: Jill Wilkins, Jane Talesnick, Kay Gilmore; m. Claudia Jean Ferrell, Nov. 28, 1969 (dec.). AB, Ind. U., 1948, LLB, 1950, JD, 1967. Bar: Ind. 1950, U.S. Dist. Ct. (no. and so. dists.) Ind. 1950, U.S. Dist. Ct. (ea. dist.) Wis. 1991, U.S. Ct. Appeals (7th cir.) 1961, U.S. Supreme Ct. 1980; cert. bus. bankruptcy law Am. Bd. Cert. Ptnr. Dulberger, Talesnick, Claycombe & Bagal, Indpls., 1952-57, Bagal & Talesnick, Indpls., 1957-67, Talesnick & Kleiman, Indpls., 1967-74, Dann Pecar Newman Talesnick & Kleiman, Indpls., 1974-94; bankruptcy and creditor's rights counsel Leagre, Chandler & Millard, Indpls., 1995—; asst. city atty. City of Indpls., 1959-67; instr. bus. law Butler U., Indpls., 1981-82. Chmn. Ind. bd. NCCj, 1974-76; v.p. Jewish Fedn. Greater Indpls., 1985-89, pres. 1989-91; bd. dirs. Coun. Jewish Fedns., 1986-90; treas. Indpls. Hebrew Congregation, 1967-70; v.p. Indpls. Hebrew congregation Found., 1992-96. With USN, 1945-46, USNR. Disting. fellow Ind. Bar Assn.; recipient Liebert I. Mossler Cmty. Svc. award outstanding & enduring vol. svcs. Jewish Fedn. Greater Indpls. Inc., 1997. Fellow Comml. Law Found.; mem. Ind. State Bar Assn. (ho. of dels. 1985—), Indpls. Bar Assn. (v.p. 1989-90, chmn. comml. and bankruptcy sect. 1985, bd. mgrs. 1994-96), Lawyers Assn. Indpls., Comml. Law League Am., Am. Bankruptcy Inst., B'nai Brith (local pres. 1957-58). Democrat. Jewish. Fax: (317) 808-3254. Bankruptcy, Contracts commercial, Banking. Home: 8342 Eagle Crest Ln Indianapolis IN 46234-9528 Office: Leagre Chandler & Millard 1400 1st Indiana Plz 135 N Pennsylvania St Indianapolis IN 46204-2400

**TALIAFERRO, BRUCE OWEN,** lawyer; b. Kansas City, Mo., Feb. 13, 1947; s. Paul Everett and Irene Winifred (Warden) T.; m. Gail Ann Niesen, Aug. 16, 1969; children—Tracy Ann, Patrick Andrew. B.A., U. Ark., 1969; J.D., U. Tulsa, 1971. Bar: Okla. 1972, U.S. Dist. Ct. (no. dist.) Okla. 1972, U.S. Ct. Appeals (10th cir.) 1975, U.S. Sup. Ct. 19. Assoc. Dennis J. Downing & Assocs., Tulsa, 1972-78; ptnr. Taliaferro, Malloy & Elder, Tulsa, 1979-84; sole practice, Tulsa, 1984—. Served to maj. USAFR, 1976-89 . Mem. ABA, Okla. Bar Assn., Tulsa County Bar Assn. (chmn. law day com. 1973), Am. Judicature Soc., Am. Soc. Law and Medicine, Okla. Assn. Def. Csl., Tulsa Claim Men Assn., Delta Theta Phi. Republican. Mem. Ch. of Christ. Club: Candlewood (Tulsa). Workers' compensation, Estate planning, Personal income taxation. Home: 7269 Oak Fairway Tulsa OK 74131-3457 Office: 2738 E 51st St Tulsa OK 74105-6231

**TALIAFERRO, HENRY BEAUFORD, JR.,** lawyer; b. Shawnee, Okla., Jan. 12, 1932; s. Henry Beauford Sr. and Laudys L. (Anthony) T.; m. Janet Stewart Myers, Nov. 23, 1955 (div. Feb. 1985); children: Sarah Stewart T. deLeon, Henry B. III, William N.; m. Patricia Ann Calloway, May 16, 1987. BA, U. Okla., 1954, JD, 1956. Bar: Okla. 1956, U.S. Supreme Ct. 1966, D.C. 1969, U.S. Claims Ct. 1970. Assoc. Monnet, Hayes & Bullis, Oklahoma CIty, 1956-59, ptnr., 1959-66; exec. dir. O.E.O. legal svcs. program Oklahoma County, 1966-67; dir. congl. rels., acting exec. dir. Pres.'s Nat. Adv. Commn. on Civil Disorders, Washington, 1967-68; assoc. solicitor for Indian Affairs Dept. of the Interior, Washington, 1968-69; pvt. practice law Washington, 1969-70; ptnr. Casey, Lane & Mittendorf, Washington, 1970-80; exec. v.p., gen. counsel The GHK Cos., Oklahoma City, 1980-83; of counsel Kerr, Irvine & Rhodes, Oklahoma City, 1987—; cons. O.E.O. Legal Svcs., 1966-67, Gas Pipeline Acquisitions & Mgmt., Oklahoma City, 1983-87; mem. Interstate Oil and Gas Compact Commn., 1980—, Okla. Commn. on Nat. Gas Policy, 1991—, Okla. Energy Resources Bd., 1994—, vice chair, 1996-97, chair, 1997—. Author: (with others) Report of Presidents National Advisory Commission on Civil Disorders, 1968; contbr. articles to profl. jours. Candidate 5th dist. U.S. Ho. of Reps., Okla., 1966; mem. planning commn. Fairfax County, Va., 1973, platform com. Dem. Nat. Conv., San Francisco, 1984. Mem. ABA, Okla. Bar Assn., D.C. Bar Assn., Met. Club (Washington), Oklahoma City Golf and Country Club. Democrat. Episcopalian. Avocations: fishing, golf. FERC practice, Environmental, Administrative and regulatory. Office: Kerr Irvine Rhodes & Ables 201 Robert S Kerr Ave Ste 600 Oklahoma City OK 73102-4267

**TALIEH, KOOROSH,** lawyer; b. Tehran, Oct. 9, 1960; came to U.S., 1976; s. Manouchehr Taliem and Mehrmah Tehrani. BA, Amherst Coll., 1983; JD, Georgetown U., 1988. Bar: D.C., Pa. Atty. Spriggs & Hollingsworth, Washington, 1988-93, Anderson, Kill & Olick, Washington, 1993—. Insurance. Office: Anderson Kill & Olick Ste 7500 2000 Pennsylvania Ave NW Washington DC 20006-1853

**TALLEY, GEORGE TYLER,** lawyer; b. Valdosta, Ga., Mar. 6, 1944; s. William Giles and Mary (McGlamry) T.; m. Polly Jane Tyson, June 2, 1963; children: George Tyler Jr., Gregory Tyson, Debra Lynn, Charles Scott. BS, U. S.C., 1965, JD, 1968. Bar: S.C. 1968, Ga. 1968, U.S. Dist. Ct. (mid. dist.) Ga. 1969, U.S. Ct. Appeals (11th cir.) 1994. Solicitor State Ct. Ga., Lowndes County, 1972-76; atty. City of Valdosta, 1976—. Mem. State Bar Ga. (chmn. workers compensation sect. 1993-94), Ga. Mcpl. Assn. Republican. Methodist. Avocations: golf, hunting, fishing. Office: Tillman McTier ColemanTalley et al 910 N Patterson St Valdosta GA 31601-4531

**TALLEY, MICHAEL FRANK,** lawyer; b. Chesterfield, S.C., Aug. 14, 1945; s. Frank and Rosena A. Talley; m. Dianne Wright, May 24, 1980; children: Michanna, Michael. BA, S.C. State U., 1966; MA, Howard U., 1971, JD, 1976. Bar: S.C. 1976, U.S. Dist. Ct. S.C. 1976, U.S. Ct. Appeals (4th cir.) 1976, U.S. Ct. Appeals (11th cir.) 1994. French instr. S.C. State U., Orangeburg, 1970-71, Tenn. State U., Nashville, 1971-73; staff atty. Presdl. Clemency Bd., White House, Washington, 1975; atty. Bishop Law Firm, Greenville, S.C., 1976-77, Talley, Green & Lewis, Greenville, 1977-87, Talley Law Firm, Greenville, 1987—; French lab. instr. Howard U., Washington, 1973-76. Bd. dirs. Legal Svcs. for Western S.C., Greenville, 1978-82. Earl Warren Legal fellowship NAACP Legal Def. Fund, 1973-76; recipient Cert. of Appreciation S.C. Bar Pro Bono Program, 1991. Mem. S.C. Bar Assn., Nat. Bar Assn., Greenville C. of C., Kappa Alpha Psi. Avocations: fishing, traveling, swimming, reading. Personal injury, Criminal, General practice. Home: 208 Boling Rd Greenville SC 29611-7604 Office: Talley Law Firm 206 Green Ave Greenville SC 29601-3436

**TALLEY, RICHARD BATES,** lawyer; b. Oklahoma City, Mar. 19, 1947; s. Olin Jack and Betty Lee (Bates) T.; m. Joan Walker, Sept. 15, 1992; children from a previous marriage: Richard Bates, Samuel Logan, Bradley Dale, Rachel Alexandra. BBA, Okla. U., 1969, JD, 1972. Bar: Okla. 1972, U.S. Dist. Ct. (we. dist.) Okla. 1972, U.S. Ct. Appeals ( 10th cir.) 1973, U.S. Dist. Ct. (no. dist.) Tex. 1987, U.S. Tax Ct. 1987.; CPA, Okla. Atty. Talley and Crowder, Norman, Okla., 1995; bd. dirs. Bacchus Enterprises, Inc., Norman, The Top of the Center, Inc. Mem. ABA, Okla. Bar Found., Okla. Bar Assn., Okla. Trial Lawyers Assn., Okla. Soc. CPAs, Cleve. County Bar Assn., Soc. CPAs. Democrat. Methodist. Avocations: clock collecting, motorcycling, golf, boating. General civil litigation, Contracts commercial, General corporate. Home: 1819 Joe Taylor Cir Norman OK 73072-6650 Office: Talley and Crowder 219 E Main St Norman OK 73069-1304

**TALLMAN, RICHARD C.,** lawyer; b. Oakland, Calif., Mar. 3, 1953; s. Kenneth A. and Jean M. (Kemppe) T.; m. Cynthia Ostolaza, Nov. 14, 1981. BSC, U. Santa Clara, 1975; JD, Northwestern U., 1978. Bar: Calif. 1978, Wash. 1979, U.S. Dist. Ct. (no. dist.) Calif. 1979, U.S. Dist. Ct. (we. dist.) Wash. 1979, U.S. Ct. Appeals (9th cir.) 1979, U.S. Dist. Ct. Hawaii 1986, U.S. Supreme Ct. 1997, U.S. Dist. Ct. (ea. dist.) Wash. 1998. Law clk to Hon. Morrell E. Sharp U.S. Dist. Ct. (we. dist.) Wash., Seattle, 1978-79; trial atty. U.S. Dept. Justice, Washington, 1979-80; asst. U.S. atty. U.S. Dist. Ct. (we. dist.) Wash., Seattle, 1980-83; ptnr. Schweppe, Krug & Tausend, PS, Seattle, 1983-89; mem. Bogle & Gates, PLLC, Seattle, 1990—; chmn. western dist. Wash. Lawyer Reps. to Ninth Cir. Jud. Conf., 1996-97. Instr. Nat. Park Svc. Seasonal Ranger Acad., Everett and Mt. Vernon, Wash., 1983-93; chmn. Edmonds C.C. Found., Lynnwood, Wash., 1990-92; gen. counsel Seattle-King County Crime Stoppers, 1987—; mem. exec. bd. Chief Seattle coun. Boy Scouts Am., 1997—. Mem. ABA, FBA (trustee 1992-93, v.p. 1994, pres. 1995), Seattle-King County Bar Assn., Rainier Club, Wash. Athletic Club. Avocations: hunting, hiking, fishing. Criminal, Government contracts and claims, Federal civil litigation. Office: Bogle & Gates Two Union Sq # 4700 1011 Western Ave Ste 803 Seattle WA 98104-1083

**TALMADGE, PHILIP ALBERT,** state supreme court justice, former state senator; b. Seattle, Apr. 23, 1952; s. Judson H., Jr., and Jeanne C. T.; m. Darlene L. Nelson, Sept. 6, 1970; children: Adam, Matthew, Jessica, Jonathan, Annemarie. BA magna cum laude with high honors in Polit. Sci., Yale U., 1973; JD, U. Wash., 1976. Bar: Wash. 1976. Assoc. Karr Tuttle Campbell, 1976-89; pres. Talmadge & Cutler, P.S., 1989-95; senator State of Wash., 1979-95; justice Supreme Ct. Wash., 1995—; chair Senate Judiciary Com., 1981, 83-87, Senate Health and Human Svcs. Com., 1992-95, Wash. Senate, 1978-94, ways and means com., children and family svc. com., edn. com. Fellow Am. Assn. Appellate Lawyers; mem. King County Bar Assn., Wash. State Bar Assn., Seattle-King County Bar Assn. Author: The Nixon Doctrine and the Reaction of Three Asian Nations, 1973; editor Law Rev., U. Wash., 1975-76; contbr. articles to profl. jours.*

**TALPALATSKY, SAM,** lawyer; b. Kishinev, Moldova, June 1963; came to U.S., 1975; BS in Computer Engring., Iowa State U., 1984; JD, Thomas Jefferson Sch. Law, 1993. Engr. Hewlett Packard, Omaha, 1985-87; tech. mgr. Waveter, San Diego, 1987-89; engr. Tektronix, San Diego, 1989-92, patent atty., 1992-94; patent atty. Directed Electronics, Vista, Calif., 1995—; adj. prof. Thomas Jefferson Sch. of Law, San Diego, 1996—. Mem. San Diego Intellectual Property Law Assn. (treas., bd. dirs. 1998). Intellectual property, Patent. Office: Directed Electronics Inc 2560 Progress St Vista CA 92083-8422

**TALT, ALAN R.,** lawyer; b. Stockton, Calif., June 17, 1929; s. Daniel Henry and Josephine (LeSaffre) T.; m. Marjorie Schutte, Sept. 12, 1953; children: Bradley Alan, Stephen Scott, Mark Kevin, Karen Talt Beardsley. BA, U. Calif., Berkeley, 1951, JD, 1954. Bar: Calif. 1955, U.S. Dist. Ct. (no. and so. dists.) Calif. 1955, U.S. Ct. Appeal (9th cir.) 1955. Law clk. to the chief judge U.S. Ct. Appeal (9th cir.), San Francisco, 1954-55; pvt. practice L.A. and Pasadena, Calif., 1955—; gen. counsel, sec., bd. dirs. Kirkhill Rubber Co., Brea, Calif., 1988—; gen. counsel, bd. dirs. KAPCO, Brea, 1985—; gen. counsel Caine, Farber & Gordon, Pasadena, 1986—. Asst. editor: Williston Casebook Contract Law, 1953. Pres. San Gabriel Valley Learning Soc., Pasadena, 1976-77; nat. v.p. Newman Clubs Am., 1949-50. Samuel Bell-McKee fellow, 1948; U. Calif. Berkeley Alumni scholar, 1947. Mem. Calif. State Bar, Jonathan Club, Valley Club (pres.), Ironwood Country Club. Avocations: fly fishing, philately. Estate planning, General corporate, Real property. Home: 1375 Saint Albans Rd San Marino CA 91108-1860 Office: Law Offices Alan R Talt 790 E Colorado Blvd Ste 710 Pasadena CA 91101-2190

**TAMBURINI, MICHAEL MARIO,** lawyer; b. Toledo, Sept. 4, 1955; s. Mario and Dorothea Jean Tamburini; m. Gail McEnroe, Mar. 21, 1981 (div. Dec. 1990); m. Joan Killion, June 15, 1996. BS in Bus., U. Kans., Lawrence, 1977, MBA, 1978; JD, Washington U., St. Louis, 1987. Fin. analyst Southwestern Bell, St. Louis, 1978-84; assoc. atty. Suelthaus & Kaplan, St. Louis, 1987-88; law clk. U.S. Bankruptcy Ct., Kansas City, Mo., 1988-89; ptnr. Blackwell Sanders Peper Martin LLP, Kansas City, 1989—. Trustee Multiple Sclerosis Soc., Kansas City, 1998. Mem. Kappa Sigma (bd. dirs. 1992—). Avocations: motorcycle, distance running. General civil litigation, Bankruptcy, Transportation. Office: Blackwell Sanders Peper Martin LLP 2300 Main St Ste 1100 Kansas City MO 64108-2416

**TAMEN, FRANK H.,** lawyer; b. Miami Beach, Fla.. BA in Polit. Sci., Reed Coll., 1973; JD, U. Fla., 1978. Bar: Fla. Pvt. practice Miami, 1978-80; asst. state atty. Manatee County State Atty.'s Office, Bradenton, Fla., 1981-82, Orange County State Atty.'s Office, Orlando, Fla., 1982-85, U.S. Atty.'s Office/So. Dist. of Fla., Miami, 1986—. Recipient Dir.'s award for Sustained Superior Performance, U.S. Dept. of Justice, Washington, 1991, 96. Office: US Attys Office 99 NE 4th St Miami FL 33132-2131

**TAMMELLEO, A. DAVID,** lawyer, editor, publisher; b. Providence, Aug. 9, 1935; s. Anthony and Kathleen (Gilleran) T.; m. Marylouise Kenney, Aug. 8, 1964; children: David A., Kathy. BA cum laude, Providence Coll., 1957; JD cum laude, Boston Coll., 1961. Bar: R.I. 1962, U.S. Dist. Ct. R.I., U.S. Ct. Appeals (1st cir.), U.S. Supreme Ct. Spl. investigative legal counsel State of R.I., Providence, 1961-69; chief trial counsel Monti & Monti, Providence, 1969-78; chief legal counsel Dept. Employment Security State of R.I., Providence, 1978-82; sr. ptnr. A. David Tammelleo & Assocs., Providence, 1982—; pub. Medica Press Inc., Providence, 1984—, editor-in-chief, 1984—; lectr. on hosp., med. and nursing law through U.S., 1984—; legal cons. Med. Econs. mag., 1984—. Editor: Regan Report on Hosp. Law, 1984—; Regan Report on Nursing Law, 1984—, Regan Report on Med. Law, 1984—; mem. editl. bd. RN mag., 1984-94; contbg. editor RN Jour., 1984—; columnist Legally Speaking, Advice of Counsel, 1984—; contbr. articles to legal jours. Atty., mem. biomed. ethics commn. Diocese of Providence, 1984—. Fellow R.I. Bar Found. (editl. bd. R.I. Bar jour. 1975-90, R.I. Bar Assn. (med.-legal com., joint com. with R.I. Med. Soc.); mem. ABA, Am. Judicature Assn., Am. Acad. Hosp. Attys., Nat. Health Lawyers Assn., R.I. Bar Assn., Cath. Health Assn., New Eng. Conf. Cath. Health Assn., Boston Coll. Law Sch. Deans Coun., Boston Coll. Law Sch. Alumni Assn. Avocations: sailing, tennis, jogging, astronomy, aeronautics. General practice, Health, Personal injury. Office: 10 Dorrance St Ste 500 Providence RI 02903-2018

**TAMULONIS, FRANK LOUIS, JR.,** lawyer; b. Pottsville, Pa., Sept. 26, 1946; s. Frank Louis Sr. and Cecelia Florence (Hoffman) T.; m. Jane Alice Troutman, June 26, 1976; children: Kathryn Lydia, Frank Louis III. AB, Cornell U., 1968; JD, Villanova Law Sch., 1971. Bar: Pa. 1971, U.S. Supreme Ct. 1975, U.S. Ct. Appeals (3d cir.) 1981. Law clk. to dist. judge U.S. Dist. Ct. (ea. dist.), Phila., 1971-74; assoc. Kassab, Cherry & Archbold, Media, Pa., 1974-76, Zimmerman, Lieberman & Derenzo, Pottsville, 1976—. Contbr. articles to profl. jours. Mem. Am. Trial Lawyers Assn., Def. Research Inst., Pa. Def. Inst., Inst. Pa. Trial Lawyers Assn., Pa. Bar Assn., Schuylkill County Bar Assn. Republican. Roman Catholic. Personal injury, Workers' compensation, State civil litigation. Office: Zimmerman Lieberman & Derenzo PO Box 238 111 E Market St Pottsville PA 17901-2914

**TANAKA, JEANNIE E.,** lawyer; b. L.A., Jan. 21, 1942; d. Togo William and Jean M. Tanaka. BA, Internat. Christian U., Tokyo, 1966; MSW, UCLA, 1968; JD, Washington Coll., 1984. Bar: Calif. 1984, U.S. Dist. Ct. (cen., no. dists.) Calif. 1985, U.S. Ct. Appeals (9th cir.) 1985, D.C. 1987. Instr. Aoyama Gakuin, Meiji Gakuin, Sophia U., Tokyo, 1968-75; with program devel. Encyclopedia Britannica Inst., Tokyo, 1976-78; instr. Honda, Mitsubishi, Ricoh Corps., Tokyo, 1975-80; with editorial dept. Simul Internat., Tokyo; assoc. Seki and Jarvis, L.A., 1984-86, Jones, Day, Reavis & Pogue, L.A., 1986-87, Fulbright, Jaworsky and Reavis, McGrath, L.A., 1987-89; asst. counsel Unocal, L.A., 1989-91; pvt. practice L.A., 1991—; counsel Calif. Dept. Corps., L.A., 1993—. Active Japan-Am. Soc., L.A., 1984-95, Japanese-Am. Citizens League, L.A., 1981, 92—, Japanese Am. Cultural and Cmty. Ctr., 1986-89; vol. Asian Pacific Am. Legal Ctr. So. Calif., 1985-86. Mem. Japanese-Am. Bar Assn., Mensa. Democrat. Mem. Foursquare Meth. Ch. Avocations: Japanese language, Chinese language, U.S.-Far East relations, martial arts. Administrative and regulatory, General corporate, Securities.

**TANAKA, LEILA CHIYAKO,** lawyer; b. Honolulu, Mar. 11, 1954; d. Masami and Bernice Kiyoko (Nakamura) T. B Arts and Scis. with distinction in Japanese Lang. and Am. Studies, U. Hawaii, Manoa, 1977; JD, U. Santa Clara, 1980. Bar: Hawaii 1980, U.S. Dist. Ct. Hawaii 1980. Pvt. practice Honolulu, 1980-81; law clk. to judge Hawaii State Cir. Ct. (2d cir.), Wailuku, Maui, 1981-82; spl. dep. atty. gen. Dept. of Atty. Gen., Hawaii, 1983, dep. atty. gen., 1983-88; housing unit supr., 1987-88; eviction hearings trial examiner Hawaii Housing Authority, 1986-88; mgr. departmental liability Dept. Transp., Hawaii, 1988-89; boating regulation officer Dept. of Transp., Hawaii, 1989-95; staff atty. Consumer Protection and Commerce Com. Ho. of Reps., State of Hawaii, Honolulu, 1995, staff atty. House Majority Atty.'s Office, 1996; dep. pros. atty. Office of Pros. Atty., County of Kauai, State of Hawaii, Lihue, 1997-99; dep. pros. atty., pros. atty. City of County of Honolulu State of Hawaii, Honolulu, 1999—. mem. motor vehicle industry licensing bd. Dept. Commerce and Consumer Affairs, Hawaii, 1991-99, chmn., 1997-99, Arbitrator, Court Annexed Arbitration Prog., Fifth Circuit. Mem. Am. Judicature Soc., Kauai Bar Assn., Hawaii Bar Assn., Plaza Club, Phi Kappa Phi. Buddhist. Avocations: reading, needlework, crafts, baking, music. Office: Office of Pros Atty 1060 Richards St Honolulu HI 96813

**TANCHUM, LETTY MARCUS,** lawyer; b. N.Y.C., July 20, 1949; d. Murray M. and Joyce (Marcus) Warshavsky; m. Michael Louis Tanchum, June 22, 1969; children: Meredith Jo, Robert Marcus. BA summa cum laude, Duke U., 1971, JD, 1973. Bar: N.Y. 1973. Staff atty. ABC, Inc., N.Y.C., 1973-78, asst. gen. atty., 1978-83, gen. atty., 1983-88; sr. gen. atty. Capital Cities/ABC, N.Y.C., 1986-88; v.p. legal bus. affairs Oprah Winfrey Show Harpo Prodns., Inc., Chgo., 1988-98; v.p., gen. counsel Harpo Prodns., Inc., 1999—; bd. visitors Sch. Law Duke U., Durham, N.C., 1996-99. Office: Harpo Prodns 110 N Carpenter St Chicago IL 60607-2145

**TANCS, LINDA ANN,** lawyer; b. Elizabeth, N.J., Sept. 27, 1963; d. Tibor Louis and Rose (Cecere) T. Student, U. Warwick, Coventry, Eng., 1984; BA, Rutgers Coll., 1985; JD cum laude, Seton Hall U. Sch. Law, 1993. Bar: N.J. 1993, U.S. Dist. Ct. (N.J.) 1993, N.Y. 1994. Paralegal Fox and Fox, Counsellors at Law, Newark, 1985-88, Vol. Lawyers for Arts, N.Y.C., 1988; corp. paralegal Wilentz, Goldman & Spitzer, Woodbridge, N.J., 1988-90, assoc., 1993-96; staff atty. Muze, Inc., N.Y.C., 1996-97; mem. legal dept. IMS Internat., Inc., Totowa, N.J., 1997—; v.p. Pro Agents, Inc., 1995-96; adj. prof. acctg. and legal studies dept. Middlesex County Coll., Edison, N.J., 1998—. Assoc. editor Seton Hall Law Rev. Mem. ABA, N.J. Bar Assn., N.Y. State Bar Assn. (chair young entertainment lawyers com. 1994-96), Phi Beta Kappa, Phi Sigma Iota, Delta Phi Alpha. Contracts commercial, Computer, Intellectual property. Home: 411 Roosevelt St Roselle Park NJ 07204-1509

**TANENBAUM, JAY HARVEY,** lawyer; b. N.Y.C., Nov. 17, 1933; s. Leo Aaron and Regina (Stein) T.; m. Linda Goldman, May 28, 1961; children: Susan Hillary, Steven Eric. BA, Hobart and William Smith Colls., 1954; LLB, Union U., 1957, JD, 1961. Bar: N.Y. 1957, U.S. Dist. Ct. (so. dist.) N.Y. 1961, U.S. Supreme Ct. 1967. Internat. trader Associated Metals and Minerals Corp., N.Y.C., 1960-64; pvt. practice, N.Y.C., 1964—; corp. counsel Internat. Gate Corp., Gen. Gate Corp. Mem. N.Y. State Bar Assn., N.Y. Trial Lawyers Assn., Bronx County Bar Assn. Jewish. Club: St. James (London), Le Club (N.Y.). Personal injury, FERC practice, Family and matrimonial.

**TANICK, MARSHALL HOWARD,** lawyer, law educator; b. Mpls., May 9, 1947; s. Jack and Esther (Kohn) T.; m. Cathy E. Gorlin, Feb. 20, 1982; children: Lauren, Ross. BA, U. Minn., 1969; JD, Stanford U., 1973. Bar: Calif. 1973, Minn. 1974. Law clk. to presiding justice U.S. Dist. Ct., Mpls., 1973-74; assoc. Robins, Davis & Lyons, Mpls., 1974-76; ptnr. Tanick & Heins, P.A., Mpls., 1976-89, Mansfield & Tanick, Mpls., 1989—; prof. constrn., real estate and media law U. Minn., Mpls., 1983—, Hamline U., St. Paul, 1982—; prof. constl. law William Mitchell Coll. Law, 1994. Editor: Hennepin Lawyer, Bench, Bar and Litigation mag.; contbr. articles to mags. Avocation: writing. Federal civil litigation, State civil litigation, Communications. Home: 1230 Angelo Dr Minneapolis MN 55422-4710 Office: Mansfield & Tanick 900 2nd Ave S Ste 1560 Minneapolis MN 55402-3383

**TANK, SHARON RAE,** paralegal; b. Fairfield, Iowa, July 12, 1948; d. Raymond Edward and Esther Marion (Stride) Waddell; m. Robert George Tank, June 19, 1965; children: Melissa Kay, Michelle Rene. Cert. in paralegal, Marycrest Coll., 1986. Paralegal Klockau, McCarthy, Ellison & Marquis, Rock Island, Ill., 1987-97; with Klockau, Marquis & Skorepa P.C., 1997—. Helper Girl Scouts U.S., Davenport, Iowa, 1982-83. Mem. Nat. Assn. Legal Secs. Democrat. Lutheran. Avocations: crossword puzzles, cryptoquotes, reading. Home: 1744 W 48th St Davenport IA 52806-4640 Office: Klockau Marquis & Skorepa PC 1808 3rd Ave Rock Island IL 61201-8020

**TANNE, MARTHA B.,** judge; b. Houston; d. John William and Geraldine Rebecca (Clardy) Belsey. JD, St. Mary's U., San Antonio, 1968. Judge 166th Dist. Ct., San Antonio. Episcopalian. Home: 6514 Laurel Hl San Antonio TX 78229-4237 Office: 166th Dist Ct 100 Dolorosa Rm 209 San Antonio TX 78205-3002

**TANNEN, RICKI LEWIS,** lawyer, depth psychologist/analyst, educator; b. N.Y.C., Apr. 29, 1952; d. Paul and Lillian (Singer) Lewis; m. Marc Jay Tannen, Aug. 25, 1972; children: Laine Amy, Adam Jesse. BA in Social Scis., U. Fla., 1975, MEd in Psycholinguistics, 1981, JD with honors, 1981; LLM, Harvard U., 1991; postgrad., Pacifica Grad. Inst. Bar: Fla. 1982. Tchr., guidance counselor Oak Hall Pvt. Sch., Gainesville, Fla., 1976-79; atty., jud. clk. U.S. Dist. Cts., Miami, Fla., 1981-82; rep. assoc. Ft. Lauderdale (Fla.) News, Sun-Sentinel newspaper, Ferrero, Middlebrooks, Strickland & Fischer, 1982-88; of counsel Klein & Tannen, Hollywood, Fla., 1990-91; mem., 1992—; mem. gender bias study commn. Fla. Supreme Ct., 1986, apptd. commr., reporter, 1987—; adj. prof. women and the law, media law, rhetoric, comm. law Fla. Atlantic U., 1984-88, adj. prof. dept. English, 1995—; mem. faculty Chautauqua Instn., 1995—; co-chmn. Fla. Bar Media

Law Conf., 1996; rsch. coord. Ctr. for Govtl. Responsibility, Gainesville, 1979-81; mem. Bd. Bermuda Biol. Station for Rsch., Bd. Internat. Hurricane Ctr.; panelist Human Dimensions of Climate Change; mem. Nat. Rsch. Coun. Editor: Elderly Law in Florida, 1982; author: Report of the Florida Supreme Court Gender Bias Commn.; contbr. articles to profl. jours. Bd. dirs. C.G. Jung Inst. South Fla., 1996—; dir. Inner Work Studies Program, 1995—. Mem. APA, ABA, Fla. Bar Assn. (com. on equal opportunity 1988—), Fla. Assn. women Lawyers, Assn. Psychol. Type, Assn. Transpersonal Psychology. Appellate, Constitutional, Libel. Office: 1007 S North Lake Dr Hollywood FL 33019-1314

**TANNENBAUM, JACK JOSEPH,** lawyer; b. L.A., Mar. 5, 1942; s. Milton and Etta (Steinman) T.; m. Lois Suzanne Weiner, June 9, 1963; children: Stacey Diane, Robert Charles. BA, UCLA, 1963; LLB, Loyola U., L.A., 1966. Bar: Calif. 1967, U.S. Dist. Ct. (ctrl. dist.) Calif. 1967. Atty. Liebert & Wolf, Beverly Hills, Calif., 1967-73, Legal Clinic of Jacoby & Meyers, Van Nuys, Calif., 1973-74, Law office of Martin Stolzoff, Beverly Hills, 1974, Heller & Weiner, L.A., 1974-75, Staitman & Snyder, Encino, Calif., 1975-89; ptnr. Staitman, Snyder & Tannenbaum, Encino, 1989-97, Staitman, Snyder, Tannenbaum & Dorenfeld, Encino, 1997—; judge pro tem Mcpl. Ct. L.A., 1972-85. Professional liability. Office: Snyder Dorenfeld & Tannenbaum 16633 Ventura Blvd Ste 1401 Encino CA 91436-1880

**TANNENBAUM, RICHARD NEIL,** lawyer; b. Jersey City, July 10, 1951; s. Paul H. and Sonia (Pearson) T.; children: Brette Morgan, Joshua Daniel. BA, George Washington U., 1973; JD, Ohio No. U., 1976. Bar: N.Y. 1977, U.S. Dist. Ct. (ea. dist.) N.Y. 1979, U.S. Dist. Ct. (so. dist.) N.Y. 1981, U.S. Ct. Appeals (2d cir.) 1987, U.S. Supreme Ct. 1983. Ptnr. Tannenbaum & Tannenbaum, Great Neck, N.Y., 1976-83, Tannenbaum & Reisman, Great Neck, 1983-86; staff atty. Laborers Local 1298 Legal Svcs., Hempstead, N.Y., 1984-85; of counsel Slotnick & Baker, P.C., N.Y.C., 1986-89; ptnr. Richard N. Tannenbaum, N.Y.C., 1986—; arbitrator Civil Ct. Queens County, Kew Gardens, N.Y., 1983-86, 95—; law guardian Nassau County Family Ct., Westbury, N.Y., 1978-82; vis. lectr. Law Sch., U. Iceland, Reykjavik, 1976-77. Author, composer 3 ballads, other musical compositions. Candidate for N.Y. State Senate, 7th S.D., 1980; vol. N.Y.C. Parks and Recreation, 1994. Named Outstanding Defender of Victims, Crime Victims Polit. Platform, N.Y.C., 1989. Mem. N.Y. Trial Lawyers Assn., Greak Neck Lawyers Assn. (chmn. bd. 1985, pres. 1984), N.Y. County Lawyers Assn., Songwriters Guild of Am. Avocations: piano, basketball, swimming, tennis, songwriting. Family and matrimonial, General practice, State civil litigation. Address: 213 Roundhill Rd Roslyn Heights NY 11577-1536

**TANNENWALD, PETER,** lawyer; b. Washington, Apr. 8, 1943; s. Judge Theodore and Selma (Peterfreund) T.; m. Carol B. Baum, May 25, 1969; 1 child, Jonathan Mark. AB, Brown U., 1964; LLB, Harvard U., 1967. Bar: U.S. Dist. Ct. D.C. 1968, U.S. Ct. Appeals (D.C. cir.) 1968, U.S. Supreme Ct. 1972. Assoc. Arent, Fox, Kintner, Plotkin & Kahn, Washington, 1967-74, ptnr., 1975-94; ptnr. Irwin, Campbell & Tannenwald, P.C., Washington, 1995—. Columnist The LPTV Report, 1988-92. Mem. cmty. coun. Sta. WAMU-FM, Washington, 1986-93, 94-97; dir. Brown Broadcasting Svc., Inc., Providence, 1970—; chmn. maj. law firms divsn. Nat. Capital Area affiliate United Way, 1977-79. Mem. Harvard Law Sch. Assn. D.C. (pres. 1979-80), Harvard Law Sch. Assn. (sec. 1982-84). Avocations: electronics, photography. Communications. Office: Irwin Campbell Tannenwald 1730 Rhode Island Ave NW Washington DC 20036-3102

**TANNER, DEE BOSHARD,** retired lawyer; b. Provo, Utah, Jan. 16, 1913; s. Myron Clark and Marie (Boshard) T.; m. Jane Barwick, Dec. 26, 1936 (div. Aug. 1962); children: Barry, Diane McDowell; m. Reeta Walker, Dec. 6, 1981. BA, U. Utah, 1935; LLB, Pacific Coast U., 1940; postgrad., Harvard U., 1936, Loyola U., L.A., 1937. Bar: Calif. 1943, U.S. Dist. Ct. (so. dist.) Calif. 1944, U.S. Ct. Appeals (9th cir.) 1947, ICC 1964, U.S. Dist. Ct. (ea. dist.) Calif. 1969, U.S. Supreme Ct. 1971. Assoc. Spray, Davis & Gould, L.A., 1943-44; pvt. practice L.A., 1944; assoc. Tanner and Sievers, L.A., 1944-47, Tanner and Thornton, L.A., 1947-54, Tanner, Hanson, Meyers, L.A., 1954-64; ptnr. Tanner and Van Dyke, L.A., 1964-65, Gallagher and Tanner, L.A., 1965-70; pvt. practice Pasadena, Calif., 1970-95; retired, 1995. Mem. L.A. Bar Assn., World Affairs Assn., Harvard Law Sch. Assn., Lawyers' Club L.A. Federal civil litigation. Home and Office: 1720 Lombardy Rd Pasadena CA 91106-4127

**TANNER, ERIC BENSON,** lawyer; b. St. Louis, Aug. 27, 1949; s. Robert H. and Delores (Benson) T.; m. Rosalind Grace Tanner, June 23, 1978; children: Jacob, Adam. BA, U. Mo., Columbia, 1971; JD, U. Mo., Kansas City, 1975; cert., Coll. Fin. Planning, Denver, 1988. Bar: Mo. 1975. Instr. paralegal program Avila Coll., Kansas City, 1982-84; staff atty. Legal Aid Western Mo., Kansas City, 1975-83; pvt. practice, Kansas City, 1983-86; asst. v.p. trust dept. United Mo. Bank, NA, Kansas City, 1986-90; staff atty. Shook, Hardy & Bacon, Kansas City, 1990-93; v.p. trust dept., sr. trust atty. Commerce Bank, N.A., Kansas City, 1993—; CLE lectr. on estate planning topics to various bar assns. and univs., 1975—. Contbr. articles to law jours. Mem. planned giving com. Nat. Kidney Found., Kans. and Kansas City met. area, 1995-97; vol. Habitat for Humanity, 1997, 99; bd. dirs. Prime Health, 1980-86. Mem. ABA, Mo. Bar Assn., Kansas City Met. Bar Assn., Lawyers Assn. Kansas City, Kansas City Corp. Fiduciaries Assn. (pres. 1997), Estate Planning Soc. Kansas City. Estate planning, Estate taxation, Probate. Office: Commerce Bank NA 922 Walnut St Ste 200 Kansas City MO 64106-1809

**TANNER, IRA E., JR.,** lawyer; b. Denver, Mar. 25, 1921; s. Ira E. Tanner and Irena M. Seller; m. Patricia Prey, Sept. 17, 1960; children: David, Virginia, Brooke, Sule. AB, Colo. U., 1942. Bar: Colo. Of counsel Clanahan Tanner Downing & Knowlton, Denver. Mem. ABA, Denver Bar Assn. Office: Clanahan Tanner Downing & Knowlton 1600 Broadway Ste 2400 Denver CO 80202-4924

**TANNOUS, ROBERT JOSEPH,** lawyer; b. Amman, Jordan, June 4, 1962; came to U.S., 1968; s. Jerry J. and Nadia Tannous; m. Marlo B. Tannous, Apr. 22, 1989; children: Mallory E., Alexander B. BSBA, Ohio State U., 1984, JD, 1987. Bar: Ohio 1987, U.S. Dist. Ct. (so. dist.) Ohio 1987; cert. advisor NFL Players Assn. Ptnr. Porter, Wright, Morris & Arthur LLP, Columbus, Ohio, 1987—. Trustee Children First Inc., Columbus, 1996—, Ohio Hist. Found., Columbus, 1999—; fundraiser, com. various charitable orgns., Columbus, 1987—; team walk coord. March of Dimes, 1988-90; mem. Columbus Mus. of Art, Columbus Zoo. Recipient Forty Under 40 award Bus. First, 1997; named one of Ten Outstanding Young Citizens U.S. Jr. C. of C., 1997. Mem. ABA (bus. law sect.), Ohio Sate Bar Assn., Columbus Bar Assn. (corps. law com., sports and entertainment law com., securities law com.), Capital Club, Columbus Investment Interest Group, Columbus Coun. on World Affairs, Columbus Area C. of C. (capt. club 1991-92), Alpha Lambda Delta, Phi Eta Sigma, Phi Alpha Kappa, Beta Gamma Sigma (past pres.). Republican. Episcopalian. Avocations: golf, travel, reading, Ohio State Buckeyes. Securities, Mergers and acquisitions, Finance. Office: Porter Wright Morris & Arthur LLP 41 S High St Ste 2800 Columbus OH 43215-6194

**TANSKI, JAMES MICHAEL,** lawyer; b. Bristol, Conn., Feb. 11, 1946; s. John William and Stephanie J. (Kasek) T.; m. Janet E. Burlingame, Sept. 5, 1975; children: John Matthew, Susan Burlingame. BS, U.S. Mil. Acad., 1968; JD, U. Conn., 1976. Bar: Conn. 1976, U.S. Dist. Ct. Conn. 1977, U.S. Ct. Appeals (2d cir.) 1977. Commd. 2d lt. U.S. Army, 1968, advanced through ranks to capt., 1970, resigned, 1973; assoc. Law Offices of F. Timothy McNamara, Hartford, Conn., 1976-77, Adinolfi, O'Brien & Hayes, P.C., Hartford, 1977-80; ptnr. O'Brien, Tanski, Tanzer & Young, Hartford, 1980—. Decorated Purple Heart with oak leaf cluster, Bronze Star, Air medal with 4 oak leaf clusters and 3 silver leaf clusters, Army Commendation medal with oak leaf cluster. Mem. ABA, Conn. Bar Assn. (profl. ethics com. 1982-83), Conn. Defense Lawyers Assn., Hartford County Bar Assn., Defense Research Inst. Roman Catholic. Federal civil litigation, State civil litigation, Personal injury. Office: O'Brien Tanski Tanzer et al Cityplace II 185 Asylum St Ste 2206 Hartford CT 06103-3408

**TANZER, JED SAMUEL,** lawyer, financial consultant; b. Arverne, N.Y., Nov. 16, 1947; s. David and Mildred (Bondy) T.; m. Sally Jane Ketcham, July 10, 1971. BS with honors in Social Sci., SUNY, Oneonta, 1970; JD cum laude, Syracuse U., 1978, MBA, 1978. Bar: N.Y. 1979, Fed. Dist. Ct. 1979, U.S. Tax. Ct. 1979; permanent tchg. cert. N.Y. State. Tchr., union grievance chmn. Ctrl. Sch. Dist., Windsor, N.Y., 1970-75; rsch. asst. Sch. Mgmt. Syracuse (N.Y.) U., 1977-78; sr. atty. Ayco/Am. Express Corp., Albany, N.Y., 1978-82, assoc. regional mgr., 1982-85, v.p., regional mgr., 1986-92, regional v.p., 1988-91, v.p. counseling, 1992-93, fin. cons., 1978-93; v.p. Sanford Bernstein Co., Palm Beach, Fla., 1993-99; dir. Newberger & Berman, LLC, Palm Beach, Fla., 1999—. Bd. dirs. Cobb Youth Chorus, 1988-93, treas. 1988-93; bd. dirs. Martin County Coun. for Arts, 1998—. Mem. ABA (com. state and local taxation 1981-82), N.Y. State Bar Assn., Justinian Law Soc., Beta Gamma Sigma, Kappa Delta Pi. Estate planning, Personal income taxation. Home: 10853 Egret Pointe Ln West Palm Beach FL 33412-1539

**TANZMAN, EDWARD ALAN,** lawyer; b. Chgo.; s. Jack and Mary (Grodman) T.; m. Ellen Louise Partridge. BA in Polit. Sci. with honors, U. Chgo., 1973; JD, Georgetown U., 1976. Bar: Ill. 1976, D.C. 1979. Legis. asst. U.S. Senator John A. Durkin, Washington, 1976-79; various rsch. staff positions Argonne (Ill.) Nat. Lab., 1979—, mgr. econs. and law sect., 1992—; legis. counsel Palau Nat. Congress, Koror, Palau, 1980-81; bd. dirs. Lawyers Alliance for World Security, Washington; adv. bd. DePaul U. Internat. Criminal Justice and Weapons Control, Chgo., 1998—. Co-author: Manual for National Implementation of the Chemical Weapons Convention, 1998; contbr. articles to internat. law jours. Chairperson bd. dirs. Health Rsch. Inst., Inc., Naperville, 1996—; cmty. rep. Nettelhorst Locl Sch. Coun., Chgo., 1989—; pres. Friends of Nettelhorst Sch., Chgo., 1992—. Fellowship Leadership Greater Chgo., 1993-94; recipient Award of Merit Health Rsch. Inst., Inc., 1989. Fax: 630-252-5327. Office: Argonne Nat Lab 9700 Cass Ave Argonne IL 60439-4803

**TAPHORN, JOSEPH BERNARD,** lawyer; b. Beckemeyer, Ill., Oct. 9, 1921; s. Herman Henry and Marie (Gasser) T.; m. Anna Marie Klinge, June 25, 1944 (dec. Dec. 1991); children: Robert J., Joanne M., John F.; m. Joan Campen Klemmer, July 13, 1996. BS in Agr., U. Ill., 1943; BS in Engring., George Washington U., 1949, LLB, 1950. Bar: N.Y. 1952, D.C. 1952, U.S. Dist. Ct. (so. and ea. dists.) N.Y. 1952, U.S. Dist. Ct. (no. dist.) N.Y. 1991, U.S. Dist. Ct. D.C., 1952, U.S. Ct. Appeals (D.C. cir.) 1961, U.S. Ct. Appeals (fed. cir.) 1996, U.S. Supreme Ct. 1961. Patent examiner U.S. Patent Office, Washington, 1946-49, patent classifier, 1949-50; patent agt. Pollard and Jonston, N.Y.C., 1950-52; patent atty. IBM Corp., N.Y.C., 1952-59; patent mgr., counsel IBM Corp., various locations, 1959-70; copyright counsel IBM Corp., Armonk, N.Y., 1970-78, copyright and trademark counsel, 1978-88; pvt. practice Poughkeepsie, N.Y., 1989—; chmn. bd. U.S. Dynamics, Yonkers, N.Y. 1975-77. Contbr. articles to profl. jours. Pres. Huntley Civic Assn., Eastchester, N.Y., 1958-59; trustee Copyright Soc. USA, N.Y.C., 1985—. Capt. U.S. Army, 1943-46, ETO. Mem. ABA (com. chmn. 1983—), N.Y. State Bar Assn., Dutchess County Bar Assn., Am. Intellectual Property Law Assn., N.Y. Intellectual Property Law Assn. (com. chmn. 1987-89), Ea. N.Y. Intellectual Property Law Assn., Dutchess Golf and Country Club, Americana Tennis Club. Republican. Roman Catholic. Avocations: golf, hunting, fishing, tennis, skiing. Patent, Trademark and copyright, Computer. Home and Office: 8 Scenic Dr Poughkeepsie NY 12603-5521

**TAPLEY, JAMES LEROY,** retired lawyer, railway corporation executive; b. Greenville, Miss., July 10, 1923; s. Lester Leroy and Lillian (Clark) T.; m. Priscilla Moore, Sept. 9, 1950. AB, U. N.C., 1947, JD with honors, 1950. Bar: N.C. 1951, D.C. 1962. With So. Ry. Co., Washington, 1953-83; gen. solicitor So. Ry. Co., 1967-74, asst. v.p. law, 1974-75, v.p. law, 1975-83; v.p. Washington counsel Norfolk So. Corp., Washington, 1983-87; ret., 1987. Mem. Phi Beta Kappa, Kappa Sigma. Clubs: Chevy Chase. Administrative and regulatory, Antitrust, General corporate.

**TARANTINO, LOUIS GERALD,** business consultant, lawyer; b. Bridgeport, Conn., Sept. 7, 1934; s. Louis Gerald and Mary Louise (Boyle) T. BA, U. Pa., 1955, LLB, 1958. Bar: Conn. 1958, N.Y. 1960. Assoc. Beekman & Bogue, 1959-76, ptnr., 1968-76; chmn., bd. dirs. Berkeley Mgmt. Assocs., Inc., Boston, 1984—; prin. Early Stage Advisors, LLC, Boston; pres. White Light Devel. Corp.; mem. enterprise adv. bd. Phoitonics Ctr. Boston U.; ptnr. Berkeley Investment Ptnrs., N.Y.C., Wintzen Pharms, L.P., The Netherlands, Startup Ptnrs., Boston. Mem. Bar Assn. City N.Y., N.Y. Bar Assn., Conn. Bar Assn., SAR, Huguenot Soc. Pa., St. Anthony Hall, Knickerbocker Club, India House (N.Y.C.), St. Anthony Club (Phila.). Home: One Devonshire Pl #3409 Boston MA 02109

**TARASI, LOUIS MICHAEL, JR.,** lawyer; b. Cheswick, Pa., Sept. 9, 1931; s. Louis Michael and Ruth Elizabeth (Records) T.; m. Patricia Ruth Finley, June 19, 1954; children: Susan, Louis Michael III, Elizabeth, Brian, Patricia, Matthew. BA, Miami U., Ohio, 1954; JD, U. Pa., 1959. Bar: Pa. 1960, U.S. Dist. Ct. (we. dist.) Pa. 1960, U.S. Ct. Appeals (3d cir.) 1964, U.S. Supreme Ct. 1969, U.S. Dist. Ct. (we. dist.) Tex. 1988, U.S. Ct. Appeals (5th cir.) 1989, U.S. Ct. Appeals (4th cir.) 1994, U.S. Ct. Fed. Claims 1987, U.S. Dist. Ct. Colo. 1998; cert. civil trial adv. Nat. Bd. Trial Advocacy. Assoc., owner Burgwin, Ruffin, Perry & Pohl, Pitts., 1960-68; ptnr. Conte, Courtney & Tarasi, Beaver County, Pa., 1968-78, Tarasi & Tighe, Pitts., 1978-82, Tarasi & Johnson, P.C., Pitts., 1982-95, Tarasi & Assocs. P.C., Pitts., 1995—. Mem. parish coun. St. James Ch., Sewickley, Pa.; mem. Sewickley Borough Allegheny Coun. With U.S. Army, 1954-56. Fellow Internat. Soc. Barristers; mem. Assn. Trial Lawyers Am. (gov., rep.), Pa. Trial Lawyers Assn. (pres. 1979-80), Acad. Trial Lawyers Allegheny County, Allegheny County Bar Assn., Pa. Bar Assn., West Pa. Trial Lawyers Assn. (pres. 1975), St. Thomas More Soc. (award 1991), Melvin Belli Soc. Democrat. Roman Catholic. Avocations: reading, golf, lecturing. General civil litigation, Personal injury, Toxic tort. Home: 1 Way Hollow Rd Sewickley PA 15143-1192 Office: The Tarasi Law Firm PC 510 3rd Ave Pittsburgh PA 15219-2107

**TARAVELLA, CHRISTOPHER ANTHONY,** lawyer; b. Pueblo, Colo., Sept. 19, 1951; s. Frank Louis and Ann Jean T.; m. Kathleen Kerrigan, Dec. 18, 1976; children: Nicholas M., John L. BS in Engring. Mechanics, USAF Acad., 1973; JD, U. Colo., 1976; postgrad., Harvard U., 1996. Bar: Iowa 1976, Colo. 1976, U.S. Ct. Mil. Appeals 1976, U.S. Dist. Ct. Colo. 1976, Fla. 1977, U.S. Supreme Ct. 1982, U.S. Ct. Appeals (fed. cir.) 1983, D.C. 1984, U.S. Claims Ct. 1984, Mich. 1985. Commd. 2nd lt. USAF, 1973; legal intern Staff Judge Adv. USAF, Lowry AF Base, Denver, 1973-76; advanced through grades to lt. col. USAF, Hurlburt Field, Fla., 1976-78; asst. staff judge adv. USAF, Zaragoza, Spain, 1978-81; chief cir. trial counsel USAF, Washington, 1981-83; chief Constitutional Torts Br. Civil Litigation, Washington, 1983-85; resigned USAF, 1985; asst. gen. counsel Chrysler Motors Corp., Highland Park, Mich., 1985-90; asst. gen. counsel comml. affairs, chief patent counsel Chrysler Corp., Auburn Hills, Mich., 1990-96; v.p., gen. counsel Chrysler Fin. Co. LLC, Southfield, Mich., 1997—; mem. governing com. Conf. on Consumer Fin. Law. Staff Judge Adv. USAFR, 927 Air Refueling Group, Selfridge Air NG Base, Mich., 1985-94; mem. YMCA of Met. Detroit. Mem. ABA (dir.), Am. Fin. Svcs. Assn. (gov. com. conf. on fin. law). General civil litigation, Patent, Trademark and copyright. Office: Chrysler Fin Co LLC CIMS 465-25-02 27777 Franklin Rd Southfield MI 48034-2337

**TARBET, DAVID W.,** lawyer; b. Port Arthur, Ont., Can., Sept. 27, 1941; came to U.S., 1965; s. George Barclay and Dorothy Alice Tarbet; m. Carol Houlihan Flynn, May 24, 1997; children from previous marriage: Emily Merrill, Andrew Barclay. BA, U. Toronto, 1965; PhD in English, U. Rochester, 1970; JD, SUNY, Buffalo, 1984. Bar: Mass. Prof. English SUNY, Buffalo, 1969-84; assoc. Csaplar & Bok, Boston, 1984-90, Gaston & Snow, Boston, 1990-91; mem. Hill & Barlow, Boston, 1991—; mem. Law Exch. Internat. Law Consortium, 1996—. Author articles on lit. criticim and law. Mem. Boston Bar Assn., Computer Law Assn. Contracts commercial, Communications, Intellectual property. Office: One Internat Place Boston MA 02110

**TAREN, JEFFREY LYNN,** lawyer; b. Wilkes Barre, Pa., Sept. 20, 1952; s. Arnold and Ruth Taren; m. Carolyn Therese Bieszat, May 26, 1985; children: Jordan, Mariel. BA in Polit. Sci., Rutgers Coll., 1974; JD, Boston Coll., 1977. Staff atty. Legal Assistance of Chgo., 1977-80; ptnr. Kinoy, Taren, Gerraghty & Potter, Chgo., 1980-98; hearing officer Chgo. Human Rels. Commn., 1991—; adv. bd. employment, Chgo., 1995—; bd. dirs. Nat. Lawyers Guild, Chgo., 1987-90. Author: (with others) Civil Rights Annual Review, 1995. Bd. dirs. Chgo. Lawyers Com. for Civil Rights, 1996—; chmn. Oak Park Parking Traffic Commn., 1993—. Recipient Award Hope Fair Housing Ctr., 1987, Pro Bono award Lawyers Com. for Civil Rights, 1996. Avocations: basketball, playing banjo. Office: Kinoy Taren Geraghty & Porter PC 224 S Michigan Ave Ste 300 Chicago IL 60604-2505

**TARGAN, DONALD GILMORE,** lawyer; b. Apr. 7, 1933; s. Solomon and Mollie (Simons) T.; m. Pamela Targan. BA, Juanita Coll.; JD, Am. U., 1961. Bar: N.J. 1961. Assoc. Arcus & Cooper, Atlantic City, N.J., 1961-65; atty. U.S. Atty.'s Office, Camden, N.J., 1966-69; ptnr. Targan & Kievit, Atlantic City, 1969—. Book rev. editor Am. U. Law Jour., 1960, editor-in-chief, 1961; contbr. articles to legal jours. With U.S. Army, 1954-56. Burton Smith scholar, 1961. Mem. ATLA, Assn. Trial Lawyers N.J. (bd. dirs. 1983), Am. Bd. Trial Advocates (cert. civil trial atty.), N.J. State Bar Assn. Personal injury, Family and matrimonial. Home: 1706 Shore Rd Northfield NJ 08225-2218 Office: Targan & Kievit 1 S New York Ave Atlantic City NJ 08401-8012

**TARGAN, HOLLI HART,** lawyer; b. Detroit, Jan. 3, 1960; m. Anthony Andrew Targan, Aug. 11, 1985. BA, Mich. State U., 1982; JD cum laude, Wayne State U., 1985. Bar: Md. 1985, D.C. 1988, Mich. 1990. Staff atty. Office of Comptroller of the Currency, Washington, 1985-89; assoc. Dykema Gossett, Bloomfield Hills, Mich., 1989-91; staff counsel Mich. Nat. Corp., Farmington Hills, Mich., 1991-95; prin. Law Offices of H.H. Targan, Farmington Hills, 1995-96; ptnr. Jaffe, Raitt, Heuer & Weiss, P.C., Detroit, 1996—; speaker on various electronic banking topics, 1995—. Co-author: Guide to Smart Cards and Stored Value, 1999; contbr. articles to profl. jours. Sec., vice chair B'nai B'rith Youth Orgn., Mich., 1991—. Mem. ABA (cyberspace law com.), Md. State Bar, State Bar Mich., D.C. Bar Assn., Nat. Assn. Women Bus. Owners. Administrative and regulatory, Banking, Contracts commercial. Office: Jaffe Raitt Heuer & Weiss One Woodward Ave # 2400 Detroit MI 48226

**TARKINGTON, AMY LEIGH,** lawyer, prosecutor; b. Nashville, May 31, 1963; d. Charlie Boyd and Dorothy Swann Tarkington. BA, David Lipscomb, 1985; JD, Vanderbilt U., 1988. Bar: Tenn. 1988, U.S. Ct. Appeals (6th cir.) 1989, U.S. Dist. Ct. (we. and ea. dists.) Tenn. 1990, U.S. Dist. Ct. (mid. dist.) 1991, U.S. Supreme Ct. 1993. Legis. intern Tenn. State Senate, Nashville, 1984; asst. atty. gen. Tenn. Atty. Gen., Nashville, 1988-98, sr. counsel, 1998—. Office: Tenn Atty Gens Office 425 5th Ave N Nashville TN 37243

**TARKOFF, MICHAEL HARRIS,** lawyer; b. Phila., Oct. 3, 1946. BA, U. Miami, 1968, JD, 1971. Bar: Fla. 1973, U.S. Supreme Ct. 1976, N.Y. 1983, U.S. Tax Ct. 1984. Asst. pub. defender Miami Pub. Defender's Office, Fla., 1973-77; guest lectr. U. Miami Sch. Law, 1977; ptnr. Flynn, Rubio & Tarkoff, Miami, 1977-83; ptnr. Flynn and Tarkoff, Miami, 1983-90; pvt. practice, 1990—; mem. substantial asst. in trafficking cases com. criminal law sect. Fla. Bar. Mem. Dade County Dem. Exec. Com., 1970-72, Tiger Bay; legal counsel Dade County Dem. Com., 1978. Sponsor, South Fla. coun. Boy Scouts Am.; bd. dirs. USTA umpire, Fla. sec. dist. 8, dir.; with FTA Jr. Tournament Com., del., FTA Dist. Dir. Officials. Mem. ABA, Fla. Bar Assn. (narcotics practice, legis. com. criminal law sect., crim. law sect., fed. practice com., criminal procedure rules subcom. 1989-95), Nat. Inst. Trial Advocacy (mem. faculty), Nat. Assn. Criminal Def. Lawyers (membership com., NORML legal com.), Fla. Criminal Def. Lawyers Assn. Criminal. Office: 2601 S Bayshore Dr Ste 1400 Miami FL 33133-5413

**TARONE, THEODORE T.,** lawyer; b. Palm Beach, Fla., July 15, 1968; s. Theodore T. and Alice M. Tarone. BA, Cornell U., 1990; JD cum laude, Nova Southeastern U., 1995. Clk. Dist. Atty., State of Colo., Eagle, 1993; intern Legal Aid, West Pallm Beach, Fla., 1994-95; assoc. Avis & Avis, P.A., Palm Beach, Fla., 1995—. Contbr. articles to Palm Beach Post. Mem. The Fla Bar, Palm Beach County Bar Assn., Cornell Club (bd. dirs., treas. 1998—), Palm Beach C. of C. Real property, Estate planning, General corporate. Office: Avis & Avis PA 125 Worth Ave Ste 221 Palm Beach FL 33480-4430

**TARPY, THOMAS MICHAEL,** lawyer; b. Columbus, Ohio, Jan. 4, 1945; s. Thomas Michael and Catherine G. (Sharshal) T.; m. Mary Patricia Canna, Sept. 9, 1967; children: Joshua Michael, Megan Patricia, Thomas Canna, John Patrick. A.B., John Carroll U., 1966; J.D., Ohio State U., 1969. Bar: Ohio 1969, U.S. Dist. Ct. (so. dist.) Ohio 1972, U.S. Dist. Ct. (no. dist.) Ohio 1974, U.S. Ct. Appeals (6th cir.) 1982, U.S. Supreme Ct. 1997. Assoc. Vorys, Sater, Seymour & Pease, Columbus, LLP, 1969-76, ptnr., 1977-85, 87—; v.p., chief adminstrv. officer Liebert Corp, Columbus, 1985-87. Chmn. Columbus Graphics Commn., 1980; mem. Columbus Area Leadership Program, 1975. With U.S. Army, 1969-75. Mem. ABA, Ohio Bar Assn., Columbus Bar Assn. Labor, Pension, profit-sharing, and employee benefits, General corporate. Office: Vorys Sater Seymour & Pease LLP PO Box 1008 52 E Gay St Columbus OH 43215-3161

**TARVER, MARGARET LEGGETT,** lawyer, forensic scientist; b. Birmingham, Ala., Mar. 7, 1942; d. Booker Thomas and Ernestine Wiliametta (Rutland) Leggett; divorced; children: James, Derrick. BS, Talladega (Ala.) Coll., 1962; MS, Howard U., 1966; JD, Seton Hall U., 1982. Bar: Pa., 1982, N.J., 1982, U.S. Dist. Ct. (ea. dist.) Pa., 1983, U.S. Dist. Ct. N.J., 1982. Rsch. asst.med. sch. Howard U., Washington, 1962-64; sci. cons. Bd. Edn., Washington, 1966-68; instr. Tech. Tng. Project, Newark, 1970-71; sr. learning ptnr. SUNY, Albany, 1972-74; tech. dir. N.J. State Police Lab., Hammonton, 1976—; cons., emergency med. technician U. Medicine and Dentistry N.J., 1975. Vol. atty. Phila. Lawyers Vol. Indigent Program, 1983—; bd. dirs. YWCA, Paterson, N.J., 1976-81, Women's Haven Battered Women's Program, Paterson, 1976-81. Mem. ABA, N.J. State Bar Assn. (bd. dirs. minorities in the profession sect., editor-in-chief newsletter 1990-95), Pa. Bar Assn., Burlington County Bar Assn., Phila. Bar Assn., Northeastern Assn. Forensic Scientists, Am. Acad. Forensic Scis. (jurisprudence sect. 1997), Mid-Atlantic Assn. Forensic Scientists, N.J. Assn. Forensic Scientists (bd. dirs. 1998—, mem.-at-large)), Talladega Coll. Alumni Assn. (pres. Phila. chpt. 1983-85). Avocations: pianist, organist, oil painting, tennis, bicycling. General practice, Probate, Family and matrimonial. Home: 42 Garland Ln Willingboro NJ 08046-3012 Office: NJ State Police South Regional Lab PO Box 271 Hammonton NJ 08037-0271

**TASCHNER, DANA BRADLEY,** lawyer. Sole practitioner L.A. Named Calif. Lawyer of Yr., 1998. Mem. ABA (gen. practice sect., Sole Practitioner of Yr. 1998), Fed. Bar Assn. (past co-chair trial and appellate practice com.). Office: Ste 207 2112 Century Park Ln Los Angeles CA 90067-3314

**TASHIMA, ATSUSHI WALLACE,** federal judge; b. Santa Maria, Calif., June 24, 1934; s. Yasutaro and Aya (Sasaki) T.; m. Nora Kiyo Inadomi, Jan. 27, 1957; children: Catherine Y., Christopher I., Jonathan I. AB in Polit. Sci., UCLA, 1958; LLB, Harvard U., 1961. Bar: Calif. 1962. Dep. atty. gen. State of Calif., 1962-67; atty. Spreckels Sugar divsn. Amstar Corp., 1968-72, v.p., gen. atty., 1972-77; ptnr. Morrison & Foerster, L.A., 1977-80; judge U.S. Dist. Ct. (ctrl. dist.) Calif., L.A., 1980-96, U.S. Ct. Appeals (9th cir.), Pasadena, Calif., 1996—; mem. Calif. Com. Bar Examiners, 1978-80. With USMC, 1953-55. Mem. ABA, State Bar Calif., Los Angeles County Bar Assn. Democrat. Office: US Ct Appeals PO Box 91510 125 S Grand Ave Pasadena CA 91105-1652

**TASHJIAN-BROWN, EVA S(USAN),** lawyer; b. East Orange, N.J., July 14, 1950; d. Onnik H. and Dorothy (Purcell) Tashjian; m. James Emerson Brown, Dec. 22, 1973. BA, Skidmore Coll., 1971; JD, U. Va., 1979. Bar: Va. 1979, U.S. Dist. Ct. (ea. and we. dists.) Va. 1979, U.S. Ct. Appeals (4th cir.) 1979, U.S. Supreme Ct. 1984. Mgr. personnel Wheat 1st Securities Inc., Richmond, Va., 1972-76; assoc. McGuire, Woods, Battle & Boothe, Richmond, 1979-87, ptnr., 1987—; adj. faculty law U. Richmond, 1983-84, 95. Mem. Va. Bar Assn. (exec. com. young lawyers sect.), Richmond Bar Assn., Met. Richmond Women's Bar Assn., Nat. Assn. Coll. and Univ. Attys. Avocation: hot air ballooning. Labor, Federal civil litigation, Civil rights. Home: 1170 Dover Creek Ln Manakin Sabot VA 23103-2541 Office: McGuire Woods Battle Boothe 1 James River Plz Richmond VA 23219-3229

**TASKER, MOLLY JEAN,** lawyer; b. Cumberland, Md., Feb. 13, 1945; d. Samuel Paul Tasker and Peggy Evelyn Purinton; m. Richard Mark Curtis, June 7, 1985. AA, Santa Fe Jr. Coll., 1968; BA, Fla. Atlantic U., 1970; JD, Fla. State U., 1973. Bar: Fla. 1973, U.S. Supreme Ct. 1992, U.S. Dist. Ct. (mid. dist.) Fla. 1997. Atty., advisor CIA, Washington, 1974-82, asst. gen. counsel, 1983-95, chair publs. rev. bd., 1993-95; ptnr. Tasker & Stephens, P.A., Indian Harbour Beach, Fla., 1996—; bd. dirs. Brevard County Emergency Med. Svc. Found., Melbourne, Fla., Cmty. Housing Initiative, Melbourne; guest lectr. Fla. So. Coll., Lakeland, 1997—. Exec. sec. Brevard County (Fla.) Juvenile Justice Coun., 1997—; vice-chair Brevard County Dem. Exec. Com., 1997-98; chair govtl. affairs com. C. of C., Melbourne, 1998-99. Recipient Spl. Recognition award Brevard County Legal Aid, Inc., Fla., 1997; Fulbright Travel grantee Fla. State U. Ctr. for Slavic and East European Studies, 1972. Mem. AAUW, LWV, Phi Alpha Delta, Phi Gamma Nu. Lutheran. Avocations: photography, reading, tennis, boating. Legislative, Land use and zoning (including planning), Public international. Home: 268 Lanternback Island Dr Satellite Beach FL 32937-4705 Office: 244 E Eau Gallie Blvd Indian Harbor Beach FL 32937-4874

**TASSONE, BRUNO JOSEPH,** lawyer; b. Chgo., Aug. 29, 1940; m. Cheryl A. Cerny, June 13, 1987; children: Valentina, Joseph. BSc, DePaul U., 1962; JD, Ill. Inst. Tech.-Chgo. Kent, 1969. Bar: Fla. 1980. Svc. auditor IRS, Chgo., 1963-68; tax mgr. Coopers & Lybrand, Chgo., 1968-70; lawyer Hennessy Faraci & Tassone, Chgo., 1970-83; judge Cook County, State of Ill., Chgo., 1983-89; pvt. practice Chgo., 1989—. Recipient Disting. Jurists award young lawyers sect. Chgo. Bar Assn., 1985. Mem. ABA, Am. Arbitration Assn. (arbitrator/mediator 1988), Nat. Assn. Securities Dealers (mediator 1997) Nat. Italian Am. Bar Assn. (pres. 1997-99), Justinian Soc. Lawyers (pres. 1984), Ill. State Bar Assn. (bd. govs. 1990-92, assembly mem. 1998—). Alternative dispute resolution, Personal injury, Taxation, general. Office: # 820 39 S Lasalle St Ste 820 Chicago IL 60603-1603

**TATE, EDWIN ARTHUR,** lawyer; b. El Paso, Feb. 16, 1955; s. Erwin Arthur and Geraldine Ann Tate. BA, SUNY, Binghamton, 1977; JD, Emory U., 1980. Bar: Ga. 1980. Assoc. Barwick Bentley Hayes & Karesh, Atlanta, 1980-86; ptnr. Seacrest Karesh Tate & Bicknese LLP, Atlanta, 1986—. City councilman City of Roswell, Ga., 1991—. Mem. Ga. Bar Assn., Atlanta Bar Assn., Lawyers Club Atlanta, Phi Beta Kappa. Republican. Methodist. Insurance, General civil litigation, Real property. Home: 135 Starboard Pt Roswell GA 30076-3219 Office: Seacrest Karesh Tate & Bicknese LLP 56 Perimeter Ctr E Ste 450 Atlanta GA 30346-2202

**TATE, STONEWALL SHEPHERD,** lawyer; b. Memphis, Dec. 19, 1917; m. Janet Graf; children: Adele Shepherd, Shepherd Davis, Janet Reid Walker. BA, Southwestern at Memphis (now Rhodes Coll.), 1939; JD, U. Va., 1942; LLD (hon.), Samford U., 1979, Suffolk U., 1982, Capital U., 1989, Rhodes Coll., 1993. Bar: Va. 1941, Tenn. 1942. Mem. Martin, Tate, Morrow & Marston, P.C. (and predecessor firms), Memphis, 1947—; chmn. pres.'s coun. Rhodes Coll., 1995-96, sec. bd. trustees, 1967-77, 80-84. Pres. Episcopal Churchmen of Tenn., 1961-62; sec. standing com. Episcopal Diocese of Tenn., 1969-71; pres. Chickasaw Coun. Boy Scouts Am., 1967-78. With USNR, 1942-46; comdr. USNR; ret. Decorated Order of Cloud Banner (China); recipient Silver Beaver award Boy Scouts Am., 1963, Disting. Eagle Scout award, 1980, Disting. Svc. medal Rhodes Coll., 1978, Disting. Alumni award, 1991, Lawyers' Lawyer award Memphis Bar Assn., 1990; Memphis Rotary Club Civic Recognition award, 1983; Paul Harris fellow, 1985. Fellow Am. Bar Found., Am. Coll. Trust and Estate Counsel, Internat. Acad. Estate and Trust Law, Coll. Law Practice Mgmt. (hon.), Tenn. Bar Found., Memphis and Shelby County Bar Found.; mem. ABA (chmn. standing com. on profl. discipline 1973-76, chmn. standing com. on scope and correlation of work 1977, chmn. task force on lawyer advt. 1977, pres. ABA 1978-79, chmn. standing com. on lawyer competence 1986-92, mem. coun. sr. lawyers divsn. 1997—), Am. Judicature Soc. (past bd. dirs.), Am. Law Inst., Am. Arbitration Assn. (large complex case panel 1993—), Lawyer-Pilots Bar Assn., Tenn. Bar Assn. (pres. 1963-64), Memphis and Shelby County Bar Assn. (pres. 1959-60), Nat. Conf. Bar Pres. (pres. 1972-73, Alumnus of Yr. 1996), U.S. 6th Cir. Jud. Conf. (life), U. Va. Law Sch. Alumni Assn. (mem. exec. coun. 1974-77), Rhodes Coll. Alumni Assn. (pres. 1951-53), Rotary (pres. 1982-83, bd. dirs. 1974, 80-84, 89-90), Raven Soc., Order of Coif, Phi Beta Kappa, Omicron Delta Kappa, Phi Delta Phi, Sigma Alpha Epsilon (highest effort award N.Y.C. Alumni Assn. 1979). General corporate, Estate planning, Probate. Office: Martin Tate Morrow & Marston PC Falls Bldg 22 N Front St Ste 1100 Memphis TN 38103-1182

**TATEL, DAVID STEPHEN,** federal judge; b. Washington, Mar. 16, 1942; s. Howard Edwin and Molly (Abramowitz) T.; m. Edith Sara Bassichis, Aug. 29, 1965; children: Rebecca, Stephanie, Joshua, Emily. BA, U. Mich., 1963; JD, U. Chgo., 1966. Bar: Ill 1966, U.S. Dist. Ct. (no. dist.) Ill. 1966, U.S. Dist. Ct. D.C. 1970, U.S. Ct. Appeals (7th and D.C. cirs.) 1970, U.S. Supreme Ct. 1971, U.S. Ct. Appeals (5th cir.) 1976, U.S. Ct. Appeals (11th and 4th cirs.) 1986. Instr. U. Mich., Ann Arbor, 1966-67; assoc. Sidley & Austin, Chgo. and Washington, 1967-69, 70-72; dir. Chgo. Lawyer's Com., 1969-70, Nat. Lawyers Commn. for Civil Rights Under Law, Washington, 1972-74; dir. Office for Civil Rights HEW, Washington, 1977-79; assoc., ptnr. Hogan & Hartson, Washington, 1974-77, ptnr., 1979-94; cir. judge U.S. Ct. Appeals (D.C. cir.), Washington, 1994—; lectr. Stanford U. Law Sch., 1991-92; co-chmn. Nat. Lawyers Com. for Civil Rights Under Law, Washington, 1989-91; chmn., bd. dirs. Spencer Found., Chgo., 1990-97. Mem. editl. bd. U. Chgo. Law Rev. Mem. vis. com. to law sch. U. Chgo., 1986-89, 96—; spl. master U.S. Dist. Ct. D.C., Washington, 1988-89; mem. Montgomery County Bd. Edn. Com. on Excellence in Tchg., Rockville, Md., 1985-87, Carnegie Found. for Advancement in Tchg., Stanford, Calif., 1980-82, dir., 1997—; acting gen. counsel Legal Svcs. Corp., Washington, 1975-76; bd. dirs. Refugee Policy Group, Washington, 1985-90; mem. Pew Forum on Edn. Reform, 1992-96. Mem. D.C. Bar Assn. (bd. govs. 1980-81), Chgo. Coun. Lawyers (bd. govs. 1969-70), Coun. Nat. Advisors (nat. bd. tchg. stds. 1997—, jud. conf. com. on jud. resources 1996—). Office: US Ct Appeals 333 Constitution Ave NW 3818 US Courthouse Washington DC 20001-2802

**TATEN, BRUCE MALCOLM,** lawyer, corporate; b. N.Y.C., Dec. 24, 1955; s. Bruce Malcolm and Lois Marie (Macalis) T.; m. Jacquelyn Sharbrough, May 6, 1995; children: Graye Michael, Skyler Lane. BS, Georgetown U., 1977, MS, 1978; JD, Vanderbilt U., 1983. Bar: N.Y. 1984, Ga. 1987, Tex. 1994; CPA, N.J. Acct. KPMG Peat Marwick, N.Y.C., 1978-80; assoc. Simpson, Thacher & Bartlett, N.Y.C., 1983-86, Sutherland, Asbill & Brennan, Atlanta, 1986-93; v.p., gen. counsel Keyston Internat. Inc., Houston, 1993-97; sr. v.p., chief adminstrv. officer, gen. counsel and corp. sec. Pentacon, Inc., Houston, 1997—. Mem. Am. Corp. Counsel Assn. General corporate, Mergers and acquisitions, Securities. Home: 3716 Jardin St Houston TX 77005-3649 Office: Pentacon Inc 10375 Richmond Ave Ste 700 Houston TX 77042-4170

**TATEOKA, REID,** lawyer; b. Salt Lake City, Jan. 11, 1954; s. Matt M. and Ida S. (Shimizu) T.; m. Shauna Reid, June 3, 1977; children: Jacob Reid, Elizabeth Ann, John Robinson. BA, U. Utah, 1978; JD, Brigham Young U., 1981. Bar: Utah 1981, U.S. Dist. Ct. (cen. dist.) Utah 1981, U.S. Ct. Appeals (10th cir.) 1986. Assoc. McKay, Burton, Thurman & Condie, Salt Lake City, 1981-85; ptnr., shareholder, dir. McKay, Burton & Thurman, Salt Lake City, 1985-89, pres., 1989—; lectr. on problem collections in Utah, 1988, 90. Treas. Japanese Am. Citizens League, Salt Lake City, 1983, 88-90, pres., 1991-96, bd. dirs., 1997—; active Salt Lake coun. Boy Scouts Am. Mem. Am. Inns of Cts., Phi Delta Phi (provincial pres. 1984—). Mem. LDS Ch. Avocations: skiing, golf, fishing. General civil litigation, Construction. Office: McKay Burton & Thurman Gateway Tower East Ste 600 Salt Lake City UT 84133

**TATONE, KATHY,** lawyer; b. Ft. Dodge, Iowa, Apr. 27, 1957; d. Peter and Maria Terranova; m. Marc Tatone, Aug. 29, 1978; children: Michael, Matthew. BA, U. Minn., 1981; JD cum laude, William Mitchell Coll. of Law, 1985. Bar: Minn. 1985, U.S. Ct. Appeals (8th cir.) 1985. Assoc. Karon Jepsen & Daly, St. Paul, 1985-90; ptnr. Rath Thue & Tatone, Mpls., 1990-92; pvt. practice Mpls., 1992—. Author, editor, columnist Minn. Trial Lawyers Mag., 1985—; mem. editl. bd. Barrister Mag., 1993-94; contbr. articles to profl. publs. Mem. Minn. Trial Lawyers (exec. com., bd. govs. 1990-94), Minn. Women Lawyers, Minn. State Bar Assn., Minn. Million Dollar Round Table. Personal injury. Office: 600 Highway 169 S Ste 650 Minneapolis MN 55426-1210

**TATTERSALL, HARGREAVES VICTOR, III,** lawyer; b. Bronx, Jan. 18, 1943; s. Hargreaves Victor Tattersall Jr. and Florence (Mary) Stephens; m. Bonnie Lee Opielowski (div. 1976); children: Hargreaves Victor IV, Sanderson Cole; m. Cynthia Louise Wood (div. 1995); 1 child, Jennifer Elizabeth. BSBA, U. New Haven, 1969; JD, U. Conn., 1972. Bar: Conn. 1972, Ohio 1994, U.S. Dist. Ct. Conn. 1975, U.S. Dist. Ct. (no. dist.) Ohio 1994, U.S. Supreme Ct. 1994. Assoc. gen. counsel Tilo, Inc. subs. Reynolds Metals Co., Stratford, Conn., 1973-75; ptnr. Rakosky & Smith, P.C., New London, Conn., 1975-80; sec., gen. counsel Dunham-Bush, Inc. subs. Signal Cos., Inc, West Hartford, Conn., 1980-84; v.p., sec., gen. counsel Stanadyne, Inc., Windsor, Conn., 1984-90; with Tattersall Enterprises, 1991—; ptnr. O'Rourke & Assocs., 1994-96. Chmn. Rep. Town Com., New London, 1979. Served with USN, 1960-64. Mem. ABA, Conn. Bar Assn. (exec. com. corp. counsel sect.), Ohio State Bar Assn., Cleve. Bar Assn., Am. Soc. Corp. Secs. (pres. Hartford chpt. 1987-88), Am. Corp. Counsel Assn., Am. Arbitration Assn. (nat. panel arbitrators and mediators). Roman Catholic. Contracts commercial, General corporate, Mergers and acquisitions.

**TATUM, ALLYN CARR,** lawyer, state official; b. Portia, Ark., Jan. 27, 1942; s. Algin Carr and Nina Ruth (Turney) T.; B.S. in Bus. Administrn., U. Ark., 1967, J.D., 1970; m. Lois Ann Galloway, Apr. 30, 1977; children—Lislie Rochelle, Juliet Kee. Admitted to Ark. bar, 1970; assoc. Highsmith, Harkey & Walmsley, Batesville, 1970-72; partner Highsmith, Tatum, Highsmith, Gregg & Hart, 1972-77; regional atty. Ark. Dept. Social Services, 1973-77; chmn. Ark. Workers Compensation Commn., 1977—; vis. prof. Ark. Coll., 1971-74; trust dept. advisor Citizens Bank, 1971-75; legal cons. White River Planning and Devel. Dist., 1972-77. Area Wide Comprehensive Health Planning Council, 1974-75; dir. Independence Fed. Bank, Independence Corp.; dir. Profl. Counseling Assocs. Inc., 1982-84, pres., 1985-86, also dir.; dir. Pro-Max, Inc.; mem. Atty. Gen.'s Task Force on Missing Children, 1985-87. Pres., East Side PTA, 1974-75; mem. pres. adv. council Ark. Coll., 1974-75; mem. adv. bd. Gateway Vo-Tech Sch., 1977-78; mem. Batesville (Ark.) Planning Commn., 1971-73, Community Sch. Bd., 1972-77; bd. dirs. Ark. Health Systems Found., 1974-75; bd. dirs. Delta-Hills Health Systems Agy., 1976-80, mem. exec. com., 1977; bd. dirs., exec. com. Ark. Health Coordinating Council, 1976-77; bd. dirs. North Central Ark. Mental Health Center, 1972-81, pres., 1974-80; chmn. exec. com. Region VI SW Assn. Mental Health Centers, 1977-80; bd. dirs. Batesville Community Theater, 1972; bd. dirs. Nat. Community Mental Health Inst., 1976-82, exec. com., 1977-78; bd. dirs. Nat. Council Community Mental Health Centers, 1975-82, pres., 1981-82; chmn. Ark. Gov.'s Task Force on Ark. Mental Health, 1986—; mem. adminstrv. bd., pastor parish com. First United Meth. Ch., Jacksonville, Ark. Recipient So. Senator award So. Bapt. Coll., 1974. Mem. So. Assn. Workers Compensation Adminstrs. (exec. com. 1971—, v.p. 1977, pres. 1978-79, 88-89), ABA, Ark. (chmn. com. on mental disability 1985—), Independence County (pres. 1971-72) bar assns., Ark. Trial Lawyers Assn., Nat. Health Lawyers Assn., Internat. Workers Compensation Ednl. Found. (bd. dirs. 1988—, v.p. 1988-89, 89-90), Internat. Assn. Indsl. Bds. and Commns. (nominating com. 1978-79, exec. com. 1985—, sec. 1988-89, v.p. 1989-90), Assn. Rehab., Bus. and Industry (bd. dirs. 1985—), Scot Booster Club, Ark. Mental Health Assn., Batesville C. of C., Pi Kappa Alpha, Delta Theta Phi. Clubs: Kiwanis, Batesville Country (pres. 1974-75, dir. 1975-76). Home: 2708 Northeastern Ave Jacksonville AR 72076-2502 Office: Ark Workmen's Compensation Commn Office of Chmn Justice Bldg Little Rock AR 72201

**TATUM, STEPHEN LYLE,** lawyer; b. New Orleans, Apr. 3, 1954; s. Gail Douglas and Barbara (Lyle) T.; m. Nenetta Carter, July 5, 1977; children: Carter Ann, Stephen Lyle Jr. BS in Anthropology, So. Meth. U., 1976; JD, U. Tex., 1979. Bar: Tex. 1979, U.S. Dist. Ct. (no. dist.) Tex. 1980, U.S. Dist. Ct. (ea. dist.) Tex. 1986, U.S. Dist. Ct. (we. dist.) Tex. 1991, U.S. Ct. Appeals (5th and 11th cirs.) 1981, U.S. Ct. Appeals (10th cir.) 1986, U.S. Supreme Ct. 1993; cert. in civil appellate law Tex. Bd. Legal Specialization. Law clk. Judge David O. Belew Jr. U.S. Dist. Ct., Ft. Worth, 1979-80; assoc. Cantey & Hanger, Ft. Worth, 1980-85, ptnr., 1985-90; sr. ptnr. Thompson & Knight, P.C., Ft. Worth, 1990-93; ptnr. Brown, Herman, Dean, Wiseman, Liser & Hart LLP, Ft. Worth, 1993—. Bd. dirs. Tex. Dept. Health, Austin, 1992-95, Trinity River Authority, Arlington, Tex., 1990-92; trustee Southwestern U., Georgetown, Tex., 1997—, Ft. Worth Country Day Sch., 1993—; chair bd. trustees YMCA of Tarrant County, Ft. Worth, 1987-91. Named Outstanding Young Leader of Tarrant County, Tarrant County Jaycees, Ft. Worth, 1988. Mem. Fedn. Ins. and Corp. Counsel, Internat. Assn. Def. Counsel, State Bar of Tex. (adminstrn. of justice com. 1987-91). Methodist. Avocations: soccer, golf, reading, drumming. Appellate, General civil litigation, Insurance. Office: Brown Herman Dean Wiseman Liser & Hart LLP 306 W 7th St Ste 200 Fort Worth TX 76102-4905

**TAUB, CATHY ELLEN,** lawyer; b. N.Y.C., July 22, 1958; d. Jesse and Shirley Jane Taub; m. Lowell Carl Freiberg, May 7, 1994; children: Oliver Emmett Freiberg, Julian Cole Freiberg. BA cum laude, Barnard Coll., 1980; JD with honors, George Washington U., 1983. Bar: N.Y. 1984, U.S. Dist. Ct. Md. 1984, U.S. Ct. Appeals (4th cir.) 1984. Law clk. Hon. Edward S. Northop, 1983-84; assoc. Cahill Gordon & Reindel, N.Y.C., 1984-87, 97-98; asst. v.p., corp. counsel Reliance Group Holdings, Inc., N.Y.C., 1987-92; assoc. counsel Marsh & McLennan Cos. Inc., N.Y.C., 1993-97. Mem. Assn. of the Bar of the City of N.Y. General corporate.

**TAUB, ELI IRWIN,** lawyer, arbitrator; b. N.Y.C., July 6, 1938; s. Max and Belle (Slutsky) T.; m. Nancy Denise Bell, May 15, 1983; 1 child, Jennifer. BA, Bklyn. Coll., 1960; JD, NYU, 1963. Bar: N.Y. 1964, U.S. Dist. Ct. (no. dist.) N.Y. 1979. Ptnr. Silverman, Silverman & Taub, Schenectady, N.Y., 1971-77; pres. Eli I. Taub, P.C., Schenectady, 1978—; arbitrator: Am. Arbitration Assn., N.Y. Employment Rels. Bd., 1966—; N.Y. State Pub. Employer's Rels. Bd.; hearing officer, paralegal adv. com. Schenectady County C.C.; counsel Alcoholism and Substance Abuse Coun., Schenectady County. Chmn. trustees Joseph Egan Supreme Ct. Library, Schenectady, 1980, 81, 84; pres. Schenectady County Republican Club, 1985-86; v.p. Jewish Fedn. Schenectady, 1983-86; mem. surrogate decision making com. N.Y. State Commn. on Quality of Care for the Mentally Disabled; bd. dirs. Jewish Cmty. Ctr., NE Parent and Child Soc., United Jewish Fedn. of N.E. N.Y.; adovate Nat. Coll. of Advocacy. Recipient Vol. of Yr. award Jewish Family Svcs., 1998. Mem. ATLA, Am. Arbitration Assn., Nat. Orgn. of Social Security Claimant Reps., Indsl. Rels. Rsch. Assn., N.Y. State Bar Assn., N.Y. State Trial Lawyers Assn., Schenectady County Bar Assn., Capital Dist. Trial Lawyers Assn., Injured Workers Bar Assn., B'nai B'rith (pres. 1976-77, spl. award 1982, youth svcs. award 1985). Family and matrimonial, Personal injury, Workers' compensation. Home: 105 N Ferry St Schenectady NY 12305-1610 Office: 705 Union St Schenectady NY 12305-1504

**TAUB, LINDA MARSHA,** lawyer; b. N.Y.C., Dec. 14, 1943; d. Harry Mark and Estelle Pearl (Weinberg) Lewin; m. David Stephen Taub, June 23, 1964; children: Andrew Scott, Marc Douglas, Joshua M. BA in History, L.I. U., 1975; JD, Hofstra U., 1983. Bar: N.Y. 1984, U.S. Dist. Ct. (ea. dist.) N.Y. 1984, U.S. Dist. Ct. (so. dist.) N.Y. 1986, U.S. Supreme Ct. 1991, U.S. Ct. Appeals (2d cir.) 1995. Assoc. Weinstein & Dezorett, Garden City, N.Y., 1983-84, Semon & Mondshein, Jericho, N.Y., 1985-91; ptnr. Semon & Mondshein, Woodbury, N.Y., 1991—; asst. sec. DaMart Enterprises, Inc., Syosset, N.Y., 1987—. Chmn. Hillel, Hofstra U., Hempstead, N.Y., 1997—. Mem. ABA, N.Y. State Bar Assn., Nassau County Bar Assn., Nassau County Women's Bar Assn. (chair jud. diversity com. 1996-97, bd. dirs. 1997—). General civil litigation, Real property, Family and matrimonial. Office: Semon & Mondshein 7600 Jericho Tpke Ste 200 Woodbury NY 11797-1732

**TAUB, STEPHEN RICHARD,** lawyer; b. N.Y.C., Oct. 5, 1944; s. Irving Robert and Sylvia (Cohen) T.; m. Alyson Zoe Winter, Dec. 23, 1968. BA, Queens Coll., 1965; JD, NYU, 1968. Bar: N.Y. 1969, U.S. Dist. Ct. (ea. and so. dists.) N.Y. 1970, U.S. Ct. Appeals (2nd cir.) 1971, U.S. Supreme Ct. 1972. Asst. dist. atty., bur. chief Kings County Dist. Attys. Office, Bklyn., 1970-77; pvt. practice Garden City, N.Y., 1977-96; ptnr. Ostrow and Taub, LLP, Garden City, 1996—; matrimonial case neutral evaluator Nassau County Supreme Ct., Mineola, N.Y., 1997—. Village justice Village Kensington, Great Neck, N.Y., 1986-98; acting village justice Village Old Brookville, N.Y., 1998—. Fellow Am. Acad. Matrimonial Lawyers; master N.Y. Family Law Am. Inn of Ct.; mem. ABA, N.Y. State Bar Assn., N.Y. State Magistrates Assn., Nassau County Bar Assn., Nassau County Magistrates Assn. (pres. 1993-94). Avocation: tennis. Family and matrimonial. Office: Ostrow and Taub LLP 300 Garden City Plz Ste 308 Garden City NY 11530-3359

**TAUB, THEODORE CALVIN,** lawyer; b. Springfield, Mass., Jan. 1, 1935; s. Samuel and Sara Lee (Daum) T.; m. Roberta Mae Ginsburg, Aug. 23, 1959; children: Tracy, Andrew, Adam. AB, Duke U., 1956; JD, U. Fla., 1960. Bar: Fla., 1960, U.S. Supreme Ct. Atty. Broad and Cassel, Tampa; asst. city atty. City of Tampa, 1963-67; city atty. City of Temple Terrace, Fla., 1974—; panelist in field. Contbr. articles to profl. jours. Chmn. Tampa-Hillsborough (Fla.) County Expy. Authority, 1974-84; mem. Hillsborough County Charter Commn., 1966-69, Local Govt. Mgmt. Efficiency Com., 1979, State of Fla. Environ. Efficiency Study Commn., 1986-88; founder Tampa Bay Performing Arts Ctr. Fellow: Am. Bar Found; mem. ABA (chmn. real property litigation com. 1981-86, chmn. com. on housing and urban environ. 1989-91), Am. Coll. Real Estate Lawyers (bd. govs.), Am. Land Title Assn. (lenders' counsel group), Fla. Bar Assn. (bd. cert. real estate lawyer), Fla. Jaycees (pres.), Tau Epsilon Phi. Democrat. Jewish. Land use and zoning (including planning), Real property, General civil litigation. Home: 4937 Lyford Cay Rd Tampa FL 33629-4828 Office: 100 N Tampa St Ste 3500 Tampa FL 33602-5869

**TAUBENFELD, HARRY SAMUEL,** lawyer; b. Bklyn., June 27, 1929; s. Marcus Isaac and Anna (Engelhard) T.; m. Florence Spatz, June 17, 1956; children: Anne Gail Weisbrod, Stephen Marshall. BA, Bklyn. Coll., 1951; JD, Columbia U., 1954. Bar: N.Y. 1955, U.S. Supreme Ct. 1965, U.S. Dist. Ct. (so. and ea. dists.) N.Y. 1976. Assoc. Benjamin H. Schor, Bklyn., 1955-58; ptnr. Zuckerbrod & Taubenfeld, Cedarhurst (N.Y.), N.Y.C., 1958—; bd. dirs. Cornerstone Real Estate Income Trust, 1993—, Next Generation Mktg., Inc., 1996—; village atty. Village of Cedarhurst, 1977-88, trustee, 1989—; mem. bd. Downtown Cedarhurst Bus. Improvement Dist., 1993; legis. chmn., counsel Nassau County Village Ofcls., 1979-86, v.p., 1991-93, pres., 1993-94, mem. exec. com., 1989-99, chmn. intergovtl. liaison com., 1991-93; mem. legis. com. N.Y. State Conf. Mayors, 1979-87, 92-93; mem. exec. bd. Tri-County Village Ofcls., 1991-95, pres., 1993-94; arbitrator Am. Arbitration Assn. Dist. Ct. Nassau County, 1980—, Assessment Rev. Panel, Supreme Ct., Nassau County, 1981—; mem. Constl. Bicentennial Com., 1987-89; hon. trustee Cong. Beth Shalom, Lawrence, N.Y.; nat. bd. dirs. Zionist Orgn. Am. Assoc. chmn. Am. Zionist Fedn., 1985-87; pres. Herut Zionists Am., 1977-79; v.p. Hartman YMHA, 1983-87; del. World Zionist Congress, 1977, 82, 87; mem. Zionist Gen. Coun., 1977-83; bd. govs. Jewish Agy., 1983-92; mem. exec. com. World Zionist Orgn., 1983-92; trustee United Jewish Appeal, 1986-91; bd. dirs. United Israel Appeal, 1986-91; hon. vice chmn., bd. dirs. Jewish Nat. Fund, 1987-89; nat. bd. dirs. Am. for a Safe Israel; hon. pres. World Coun. Herut Hatzoa, Jerusalem, Internat. Bd. Youthtown of Israel. Recipient Centenial award Jabotinsky Found. 1981, Betar Youth award World Betar 1982, award Internat. League for Repatriation of Russian Jews 1977, Youth Towns of Israel Leadership award 1973, Israel Bonds Leadership award 1976, Life Time Achievement award Israel Bonds 1991, Defender of Jerusalem award 1991, Israel Bonds Menachem Begin Leadership award, 1999. Mem. Internat. Assn. Jewish Lawyers and Jurists, Jewish War Vets., B'nai B'rith, Nordau Circle Club, Zionist Orgn. of Am., Cong. Beth. Shalom (Lawrence, N.Y.). Real property, Contracts commercial, Municipal (including bonds). Home: 288 Leroy Ave Cedarhurst NY 11516-1424 Office: PO Box 488 575 Chestnut St Cedarhurst NY 11516-2223

**TAURO, JOSEPH LOUIS,** federal judge; b. Winchester, Mass., Sept. 26, 1931; s. G. Joseph and Helen Maria (Petrossi) T.; m. Elizabeth Mary Quinlan, Feb. 7, 1959 (dec. 1978); children—Joseph L., Elizabeth H., Christopher M.; m. Ann Lefavour Jones, July 12, 1980. AB, Brown U., 1953; LLB, Cornell U., 1956; JD (hon.), U. Mass., 1985, Suffolk U., 1986, Northeastern U., 1990, New Eng. Sch. Law, 1992, Boston U., 1997, Brown U., 1998. Bar: Mass. 1956, D.C. 1960. Assoc. Tauro & Tauro, Lynn, Mass., 1958-59; asst. U.S. atty. Dept. Justice, Boston, 1959-60; ptnr. Jaffee & Tauro, Boston and Lynn, Mass., 1960-71; chief legal counsel Gov. of Mass., Boston, 1965-68; U.S. atty. Dept. Justice, Boston, 1972; judge U.S. Dist. Ct., Boston, 1972—; chief judge U.S. Dist. Ct., Mass., 1992-99; mem. exec. com. Cornell Law Assn., Ithaca, N.Y., 1968-71; mem. adv. coun. Cornell Law Sch., Ithaca, 1975-80; adj. prof. law Boston U. Law Sch., 1977—; mem. Jud. Conf. U.S., 1994-97, mem. com. on operation of jury sys., 1979-86, mem. adv. com. on codes of conduct, 1988-94. Trustee Brown U., 1978—, Mass. Gen. Hosp., Boston, 1968-72, Children's Hosp. Med. Ctr., Boston, 1979-94. 1st lt. U.S. Army, 1956-58. Recipient Disting. Alumnus award Cornell U. Law Sch., 1992, Brown Bear award Brown U., 1993; named one of 10 Outstanding Young Men, Greater Boston Jaycees, 1966. Fellow Am. Bar Found.; mem. Mass. Bar Assn., Boston Bar Assn. (coun. 1968-71), D.C. Bar Assn., Boston Yacht Club (Marblehead, Mass.). Republican. Roman Catholic. Avocations: sports; reading; music; films; theater. Office: 1 Courthouse Way Ste 7110 Boston MA 02210-3009

**TAVALLALI, JALAL CHAICAR,** lawyer; b. Madrid, Apr. 13, 1964; came to U.S., 1975; s. Djamchid and Nini (Chaicar) T. BA in Internat. Rels., Georgetown U., 1985, JD, 1988. Bar: N.Y. 1990, D.C. 1990, U.S. Supreme Ct. 1995. Rsch. asst. Wilkes, Artis, Hedrick & Lane, Washington, summer 1984; assoc. Goodwin & Soble, Washington, summer 1987, Wald, Harkrader & Ross, Washington, summer 1987, Milbank, Tweed, Hadley & McCloy, N.Y.C., 1988-90; mng. dir. Persico, Inc., Washington, 1986—; mng. atty. Chaikar Tavallali & Ptnrs., Washington and Baku, Azerbaijan, 1990—, Ashgabat, Turkmenistan and Tehran, Iran, 1990—; sr. assoc. New Europe Assocs., Washington and Europe, 1991-93; rschr. UN Devel. Program, N.Y.C., summer 1984. Rschr. U.S. Senator John Glenn for U.S. Pres. campaign, Washington, 1983. Mem. ABA, Am. Soc. Internat. Law, D.C. Bar Assn., Epicurean Soc. (founder 1979—), Old Stoic Soc., Phi Alpha Delta. Avocations: international affairs, travel, antiques, the arts, poetry. Private international, Contracts commercial, General corporate. Office: Chaikar Tavallali & Ptnrs 4729 Yuma St NW Washington DC 20016-2047

**TAVORMINA, JOHN WILLIAM,** lawyer; b. Elizabeth, N.J., Dec. 14, 1953; s. Joseph B. and Anne F. (Arace) T.; m. Leslie Rohrer, July 5, 1988; children: Jena Leigh, Taylor Lynn, Tori Anne. BA, Tulane U., 1975, JD, 1978. Bar: La. 1978, N.Y. 1980, Tex. 1983; cert. in personal injury, trial law, Tex. Bd. of Legal Specialization. Atty. Exxon Corp. various offices, N.Y.C., Houston, & La., 1978-87; assoc. Helm, Pletcher, Bowen & Saunders, Houston, 1987-89; ptnr. Helm, Pletcher, Bower & Saunders, Houston, 1989—. Contbr. articles to Tulane Law Rev., 1977-78; speaker at legal seminars, 1990—. Mem. Am. Bd. Trial Advocates, Tex. Bar Found., Coll. of State Bar Tex., Million Dollar Advocates Furum. General civil litigation, Personal injury. Office: Helm Pletcher Bowen & Saunders 2929 Allen Pkwy Ste 2700 Houston TX 77019-7102

**TAWEEL, A. TONY,** lawyer; b. Livonia, Mich., June 14, 1969; s. Lami A. and Hala L. Taweel; m. Suzy Tony Warra, Aug. 13, 1995. BA, U. Mich., Dearborn, 1992; JD, U. Detroit, 1995. Bar: Mich. 1996, U.S. Dist. Ct. Mich. 1996. Assoc. Charfoos & Christensen P.C., Detroit, 1996—. Mem. Syria Lodge F&AM. General civil litigation, Personal injury, Federal civil litigation. Office: Charfoos & Christensen PC 5510 Woodward Ave Detroit MI 48202-3804

**TAWSHUNSKY, ALAN NEAL,** lawyer; b. N.Y.C., Oct. 14, 1954; s. Ben and Myrtle (Fink) T. BA, Queens Coll., 1976; JD, Georgetown U., 1984. Bar: N.Y. 1985, D.C. 1986. Mathematician U.S. Energy Info. Adminstrn., Washington, 1977-84; law clk. U.S. Dist. Ct., Wilmington, Del., 1984-85; atty. Covington & Burling, Washington, 1985-90, Cadwalader, Wickersham & Taft, Washington, 1990-93, Akin, Gump, Strauss, Hauer & Feld, Washington, 1993—. Mem. ABA, D.C. Bar Assn., N.Y. State Bar Assn. Pension, profit-sharing, and employee benefits. Office: Akin Gump Strauss Hauer & Feld Ste 400 1333 New Hampshire Ave NW Washington DC 20036-1564

**TAYLOR, A. JEFFRY,** lawyer; b. L.A., Nov. 29, 1943; s. Henry Allen and Jane Clara (Bosco) T.; m. Kate Colemen Hanrahan, Apr. 10, 1965; children: Jennifer, Stefanie, Bryce, Zachary. BA, UCLA, 1965; JD, Loyola U., L.A., 1969. Bar: Calif. 1970, Vt. 1972, U.S. Supreme Ct. 1976, U.S. Tax Ct. 1985, U.S. Claims Ct. 1988, U.S. Ct. Appeals (1st cir.) 1990, U.S. Dist. Ct. (ctrl. dist.) Calif. 1970, U.S. Dist. Ct. Vt. 1972. Law clk. U.S. Dist. Judge 9th Cir. Ct. Appeals, L.A., 1969-70; trial atty. U.S. Dept. Justice Antitrust Divsn., L.A., 1970-72; corp. counsel Vt. Elec. Power Co., Rutland, 1972-79; hearing officer Vt. Dept. Edn., Montpelier, 1979-88; bar counsel Vt. Profl. Conduct Bd., Montpelier, 1979-88; adj. prof. law Vt. Law Sch., Royalton, 1978-88, 95-96; pvt. practice Rutland, 1979—. Contbr. articles Vt. Law Rev., 1997—. Vt. state counsel Clinton/Gore '92 and '96; Vt. rep. Nat. Lawyers Coun./Dem. Nat. Com.; Vt. bd. mem. UN Assn. U.S. Mem. Am. Soc. Internat. Law. Democrat. Unitarian Universalist. Avocations: opera, trout fishing. Public utilities, General corporate, Professional liability. Home: RD Box 283A Clarendon VT 05759 Office: One Justice Sq Rutland VT 05701

**TAYLOR, ALLAN BERT,** lawyer; b. Cin., June 28, 1948; s. H. Ralph and Henrietta Irene (Medalia) T.; m. Sally Ann Silverstein, June 6, 1971; children: Rachel Elizabeth, Karen Ruth. AB, Harvard U., 1970, M in Pub. Policy, 1975, JD, 1975. Bar: Conn. 1975, U.S. Ct. Appeals (D.C. cir.) 1977, U.S. Dist. Ct. Conn. 1978, U.S. Dist. Ct. (so. dist.) N.Y. 1979, U.S. Ct. Appeals (2d cir.) 1979, U.S. Supreme Ct. 1979, U.S. Ct. Appeals (1st and 10th cirs.) 1991. Law clk. to J. Skelly Wright D.C. Cir., Washington, 1975-76; law clk. to Thurgood Marshall U.S. Supreme Ct., Washington, 1976-77; assoc. Day, Berry & Howard, Hartford, Conn., 1977-83, ptnr., 1983—; overseer Bushnell Meml. Hall Corp., Hartford, 1992—. Elected mem. Hartford City Coun., 1981-87, Hartford Bd. Edn., 1989-93, v.p., 1991-93, pres., 1992-93; mem. Conn. State Bd. Edn., 1994—; bd. dirs. Conn. Assn. Bds. Edn., Hartford, 1989-93, Hartford Infant Action Project, 1990—, Hartford Stage Co., 1993—. Mem. ABA, Conn. Bar Assn., Hartford County Bar Assn., Phi Beta Kappa. Democrat. Jewish. Avocations: astronomy, reading. Federal civil litigation, Public utilities, Insurance. Home: 238 Whitney St Hartford CT 06105-2270 Office: Day Berry & Howard City Place Hartford CT 06103

**TAYLOR, AMYSUE,** lawyer; b. Columbus, Ohio, Nov. 1, 1954; m. Richard Taylor, Aug. 1, 1980; children: Richie, Kip. BSN, U. Cin., 1977; MS, Ohio State U., 1979; JD, Capital U., 1983; diploma, Nat. Inst. Trial Advocacy, 1987. Bar: Ohio 1983, U.S. Dist. Ct. (so. dist) Ohio, U.S. Ct. Appeals (6th cir.) Assoc. Zacks Luper Wolinete, Columbus, 1983-84, Jacobson Maynard Tuschman & Kalur, Columbus, 1984-88, Michael F. Colley Co. LPA, Columbus, 1989-92; pvt. practice Columbus, 1992—. Author: (chpt.) Operative Obstetrics, 1995. Mem. IRB com. Park Med. Ctr., Columbus, 1990—. Mem. Am. Trial Lawyers Assn., Ohio Trial Lawyers, Columbus Bar Assn. (chair dr./lawyer com. 1991-94), Franklin County Trial Lawyers. Office: 501 S High St Columbus OH 43215-5601

**TAYLOR, ANNA DIGGS,** judge; b. Washington, Dec. 9, 1932; d. Virginius Douglass and Hazel (Bramlette) Johnston; m. S. Martin Taylor, May 22, 1976; children: Douglass Johnston Diggs, Carla Cecile Diggs. BA, Barnard Coll., 1954; LLB, Yale U., 1957. Bar: D.C. 1957, Mich. 1961. Atty. Office Solicitor, Dept. Labor, W, 1957-60; asst. prosecutor Wayne County, Mich., 1961-62; asst. U.S. atty. Eastern Dist. of Mich., 1966; ptnr. Zwerdling, Maurer, Diggs & Papp, Detroit, 1970-75; asst. corp. counsel City of Detroit, 1975-79; U.S. dist. judge Eastern Dist. Mich. Detroit, 1979—. Hon. chair, United Way Cmty. Found., S.E. Mich., Detroit Inst. Arts, Greater Detroit Health Coun.; co-chair, vol. Leadership Coun. for S.E. Mich.; trustee Detroit Econ. Club, Detroit Inst. Arts, Henry Ford Health Sys. Mem. Fed. Bar Assn., State Bar Mich., Wolverine Bar Assn. (v.p.), Yale Law Assn. Episcopalian. Office: US Dist Ct 740 US Courthouse 231 W Lafayette Blvd Detroit MI 48226-2700

**TAYLOR, CARROLL STRIBLING,** lawyer; b. Port Chester, N.Y., Jan. 14, 1944; s. William H. Jr. and Anna P. (Stribling) T.; m. Nancy S. Tyson, Apr. 7, 1968; children: Heather, Kimberly, Tori, Tiffany, Tacy. AB, Yale U., 1965; JD, U. Calif., Berkeley, 1968. Bar: Hawaii 1969, Calif. 1969, U.S. Dist. Ct. Hawaii 1969, U.S. Dist. Ct. (cen. dist.) Calif. 1975, U.S. Ct. Appeals (9th cir.) 1975. Researcher Legis. Reference Bur., Honolulu, 1968-70; reporter Jud. Coun. Probate Code Revision Project, Honolulu, 1970-71; assoc. Chun, Kerr & Dodd, Honolulu, 1971-75; ptnr. Hamilton & Taylor, Honolulu, 1975-80; officer, dir. Char, Hamilton, Taylor & Thom, Honolulu, 1980-82, Carroll S. Taylor Atty. at Law, A Law Corp., Honolulu, 1982-86; ptnr. Taylor & Leong, Honolulu, 1986-91, Taylor, Leong & Chee, Honolulu, 1991—; adj. prof. Richardson Sch. Law U. Hawaii, Honolulu, 1981-86, 88-90, 97; mem. Disciplinary bd. of Supreme Ct. of Hawaii, 1994—, vice chair, 1997—; dir. Am. Nat. Lawyers Ins. Reciprocal, 1997—. Fellow Am. Coll. Trust and Estate Counsel; mem. ABA, Calif. Bar Assn., Hawaii Bar Assn., Hawaii Inst. Continuing Legal Edn. (pres. 1986-88), Pla. Club (Honolulu). Episcopalian. Probate, Real property, State civil litigation. Home: 46-429 Hololio St Kaneohe HI 96744-4225 Office: 737 Bishop St Ste 2060 Honolulu HI 96813-3214

**TAYLOR, CLIFFORD WOODWORTH,** state supreme court justice; b. Delaware, Ohio, Nov. 9, 1942; s. Alexander E. and Carolyn (Clifford) T.; m. Lucille Taylor; 2 children. BA, U. Mich., 1964; JD, George Washington U., 1967. Asst. prosecuting atty. Ingham County, 1971-72; ptnr. Denfield, Timmer & Taylor, 1972-92; judge Mich. Ct. of Appeals, 1992—; mem. standing com. on professionalism Mich. State Bar, 1992. Bd. dirs. Mich. Dyslexia Inst., 1991—, Friends of the Gov.'s Residence, 1991—; mem. St. Thomas Aquinas Ch. With USN, 1967-71. Fellow Mich. State Bar Found.; mem. Mich. State Bd. Law Examiners, Mich. Supreme Ct. Hist. Soc., Federalist Soc., Cath. Lawyers Guild, State Bar. Home: 736 Cowley Ave East Lansing MI 48823-3065 Office: Mich Supreme Ct PO Box 300052 Lansing MI 48909*

**TAYLOR, DAVID BROOKE,** lawyer, banker; b. Salt Lake City, Oct. 14, 1942; s. Lee Neff and June Taylor; m. Carolyn Kaufholz, May 29, 1965; children: Stewart, Allison. BA, U. Utah, 1964; JD, Columbia U., 1967. Bar: N.Y. 1967, N.C. 1995. Ptnr. Wickes, Riddell, Bloomer, Jacobi & McGuire, N.Y.C., 1967-79, Morgan, Lewis & Bockius, N.Y.C., 1979-89; banker, lawyer Chase Manhattan Bank, N.A., N.Y.C., 1989-92; pres. Geoenertec Corp., N.Y.C., 1992-93; ptnr. Fennebresque, Clark, Swindall & Hay, Charlotte, N.C., 1994-98, McGuire, Woods, Battle & Boothe, LLP, Charlotte, N.C., 1999—. Mem. ABA, N.Y. State Bar Assn., N.C. Bar Assn. Banking, General corporate, Finance. Home: 3815 Beresford Rd Charlotte NC 28211-3713 Office: McGuire Woods Battle & Boothe LLP 100 N Tryon St Ste 2900 Charlotte NC 28202-4022

**TAYLOR, DEBORAH ANN,** retired paralegal; b. Columbia, S.C.. Asst. long term care ombudsman State of Alaska Sr. Svcs., Anchorage, 1989-95, ins. counseling and asst. coord., 1993-98, info. and referral officer, 1996-98; ret., 1998; chair N.W. Alliance Info. & Referral Sys., 1997-98. Bd. dirs. Coll. Rd. Svc. Dist., Fairbanks, Alaska, 1985-87, North Star Borough Planning and Zoning Com., Fairbanks, pres. Village Green Homeowners Assn. 1983-85, Fairbanks, Grand Larry Condominium Assn., Anchorage, 1987-96. Mem. Alaska State Employees Assn. (sec. treas. 1993-95, pres. Anchorage chpt., 1991-95, sec. 1988-91), Alaska Bar Assn. (elder law, estate, probate and planning sect.).

**TAYLOR, DONALD ADAMS,** lawyer; b. St. Louis, Mar. 25, 1943; s. Robert Lewis and Mary Ellen (McCord) T.; children: Sarah, Carrie, Seth. AB, Princeton U., 1965; JD, Cornell U., 1968. Systems analyst, mktg. rep. IBM Corp., N.Y.C., 1968-71; ct. planner Court System State of N.Y., Mineola, 1971-74; dir. edn. and tng. Office Ct. Adminstrn. State of N.Y., N.Y.C., 1974-87; ptnr. Taylor and Dalton Law Offices, Manhasset, N.Y., 1987-90; sole practice Manhasset, 1990—. Pres. The Ecology Group, Sea Cliff, N.Y., 1972. Mem. Nassau County Bar Assn., Manhasset C. of C. (pres. 1991), Kiwanis (pres. 1992-93). Republican. General practice. Office: 337 Plandome Rd Manhasset NY 11030-1940

**TAYLOR, FREDERICK WILLIAM, JR. (FRITZ TAYLOR),** lawyer; b. Cleve., Oct. 21, 1933; s. Frederick William Sr. and Marguerite Elizabeth (Kistler) T.; m. Mary Phyllis Osborne, June 1, 1985. BA in History, U. Fla., 1957; MA in Near East Studies, U. Mich., 1959; JD cum laude, NYU, 1967. Bar: N.Y. 1968, Calif. 1969, U.S. Dist. Ct. (cen. dist.) Calif. 1969. Govt. rels. rep. Arabian Am. Oil Co., Dhahran, Saudi Arabia, 1959-63; oil supply coord. Arabian Am. Oil Co., N.Y.C., 1963-68; sr. counsel Arabian Am. Oil Co., Dhahran, 1969-71, gen. mgr. govt. rels. orgn., 1971-74, v.p. indsl. rels., 1974-78; assoc. O'Melveny & Myers, L.A., 1968-69; ptnr. Burt & Taylor, Marblehead, Mass., 1978-80; pres., chief exec. officer Nat. Med. Enterprises Internat. Group, L.A., 1980-82; counsel Chadbourne, Parke & Afridi, United Arab Emirates, 1982-84; ptnr. Sidley & Austin, Cairo, 1984-87, Singapore, 1987-93; spl. counsel Heller Ehrman White & McAuliffe, L.A. and Singapore, 1993-95; legal advisor, corp. counsel law divsn. Lucent Techs. Internat. Inc., Riyadh, Saudi Arabia, 1995—. Contbr. articles to profl. jours. Mem. ABA, Calif. Bar Assn., Order of Coif, Singapore Cricket Club, Tanglin Club, Changi Sailing Club, Singapore Am. Club, Dirab Golf Club. Private international, Contracts commercial, General corporate. Home: 9875 E Shadowlake Ct Claremore OK 74017-1444 Office: Lucent Techs Int Inc, PO Box 4945 Khurais Rd, Riyadh 11412, Saudi Arabia

**TAYLOR, GARY L.,** federal judge; b. 1938. AB, UCLA, 1960, JD, 1963. Assoc. Wenke, Taylor, Evans & Ikola, 1965-86; judge Orange County Superior Ct., 1986-90, U.S. Dist. Ct. (ctrl. dist.) Calif., Santa Ana, 1990—. With U.S. Army, 1964-66. Mem. Am. Coll. Trial Lawyers, State Bar Calif., Orange County Bar Assn. (bd. dirs. 1980-82, founder, chmn. bus. litigation com., Disting. Svc. award 1983). Office: US Dist Cts 751 W Santa Ana Blvd Rm 801 Santa Ana CA 92701-4509

**TAYLOR, JAY GORDON,** lawyer; b. Paducah, Ky., Nov. 18, 1940; s. William Edward Taylor and Ruah Loraze Suer; m. Barbara M. McCrea; children: Julia, Sarah, Brian. BS in Mech. Engring., U. Cin., 1964; JD, Ind. U., 1967. Bar: Ind. 1967, Ill. 1967, U.S. Dist. Ct. (no. dist.) Ill., 1970, U.S. Patent Office 1970, U.S. Ct. Appeals (7th cir.) 1975, U.S. Ct. Appeals (2d cir.) 1980, U.S. Ct. Appeals (fed. cir.) 1982, U.S. Dist. Ct. (so. and no. dists.) Ind. 1990. Ptnr. Kirkland & Ellis, Chgo., 1967-77, Haight & Hofeldt, Chgo., 1977-90, Ice Miller Donadio & Ryan, Indpls., 1990—. Capt. U.S. Army, 1967-69. Mem. ABA, Fed. Cir. Bar Assn., Am. Intellectual Property Law Assn., Intellectual Property Law Assn. Chgo., Order of Coif, Pi Tau Sigma. E-mail: taylor@imdr.com. Intellectual property. Office: Ice Miller Donadio & Ryan One American Sq Indianapolis IN 46282

**TAYLOR, JILL OLSEN,** lawyer, artist; b. Logan, Utah, June 1, 1955; d. Keith Conrad and Norma Elveda (Correll) Olsen; m. Bruce T. Taylor, July 3, 1979; children—Jenny, Benjamin, Christina. B.A. summa cum laude, Brigham Young U., 1977; J.D., Brigham Young U., 1980. Bar: Utah, 1980. Dep. county atty., Emery County, Utah, 1980-81; corp. atty. Physicians Emergency Service, Price, Utah, 1981-88; pvt. practice, Spanish Fork, Utah, 1986—. Bd. dirs., pres. Covered Bridge Canyon Homeowners Assn., 1983-89; mem. Utah County Planning Commn., 1993—, chair planning commn., 1998—. Mem. ABA, Am. Immigration Lawyers Assn. (chair Utah chpt. 1996), Utah State Bar Assn., Order of Barristers (mem. nat. bd. govs.), Phi Kappa Phi. Republican. Mormon.

**TAYLOR, JOB, III,** lawyer; b. N.Y.C., Feb. 18, 1942; s. Job II and Anne Harrison (Flinchbaugh) T.; m. Mary C. August, Oct. 24, 1964 (div. 1978); children: Whitney August, Job IV; m. Sally Lawson, May 31, 1980; 1 child, Alexandra Anne. BA, Washington & Jefferson Coll., 1964; JD, Coll. William and Mary, 1971. Bar: N.Y. 1972, U.S. Dist. Ct. (no., so. ea. and we. dists.) N.Y. 1973, U.S. Ct. Appeals (2d cir.) 1973, U.S. Ct. Claims 1974, U.S. Tax Ct. 1974, U.S. Supreme Ct. 1975, U.S. Ct. Appeals (9th cir.) 1976, U.S. Ct. Mil. Appeals 1977, U.S. Ct. Appeals (D.C. and 10th cirs.) 1977, D.C. 1981, U.S. Ct. Internat. Trade 1981, U.S. Ct. Appeals (fed. cir.) 1982, U.S. Dist. Ct. (no. dist.) Calif. 1983, U.S. Ct. Appeals (6th cir.) U.S. Dist. Ct., 1987, U.S. Ct. Appeals (3d cir.) 1990, U.S. Dist. Ct. Conn. 1996. Ptnr. Olwine, Connelly, Chase, O'Donnell & Weyher, N.Y.C., 1971-85, Latham & Watkins, N.Y.C., 1985—. Served to lt. USN, 1964-68. Mem. ABA, Assn. Bar City N.Y., La Confrerie des Chevaliers du Tastevin, Racquet and Tennis Club, Wee Burn Country Club (Darien, Conn.), New Canaan Country Club. Republican. Episcopalian. Avocations: squash, tennis, golf, reading. Antitrust, Computer, Federal civil litigation. Office: Latham & Watkins 885 3rd Ave Fl 9 New York NY 10022-4874

**TAYLOR, JOE CLINTON,** judge; b. Durant, Okla., Mar. 28, 1942; s. Luther Clinton and Virena (Parker) T.; m. Margaret Pearl Byers, June 8, 1963; children: Marna Joanne, Leah Alison, Jocelyn Camille. Student, Southeastern State Coll., 1960-62; BA, Okla. State U., 1965; JD, U. Okla., 1968. Bar: Okla. 1968. Pvt. practice Norman, Okla., 1968-69; apptd. spl. dist. judge Durant, 1969-72; assoc. dist. judge Bryan County, Okla., 1972-76; dist. judge, chief judge 19th Dist. Ct., 1976-93; presiding judge Southeastern Okla. Jud. Adminstrv. Dist., 1984-92, Choctaw Tribal Ct., 1979-83; pres. Okla. Jud. Conf., 1987-88; chmn. Assembly Presiding Judges, 1989-90; presiding judge trial div. Okla. Ct. on the Judiciary, 1991-93; Okla. Ct. of Tax Rev., 1992—; judge Okla. Ct. of Civil Appeals, Tulsa, 1993—. Chmn. bd. dirs. Durant Youth Svcs., 1976-93; bd. dirs. Bryan County Youth Svcs., Inc., 1971-93. Mem. Lions, Phi Sigma Epsilon, Delta Theta Phi. Mem. Ch. of Christ. Home: PO Box 329 Durant OK 74702-0329 Office: Ct Civil Appeals 601 State Bldg 440 S Houston Ave Tulsa OK 74127-8922

**TAYLOR, JOEL SANFORD,** lawyer; b. Hazleton, Pa., Oct. 8, 1942; s. Robert Joseph and Alice Josephine (Sanford) T.; m. Donna Rae Caron, Mar. 26, 1967; children: Jason, Adam, Jeremy. BA, Swarthmore Coll., 1965; LLB, Columbia U., 1968. Bar: N.Y. 1969, U.S. Dist. Ct. (so. and ea. dists.) N.Y. 1970, U.S. Ct. Appeals (2d cir.) 1970, Ohio 1973, U.S. Dist. Ct. (no. dist.) Ohio 1974, U.S. Supreme Ct. 1974, U.S. Dist. Ct. (so. dist.) Ohio 1975, U.S. Ct. Appeals (6th cir.) 1975, U.S. Dist. Ct. (ea. dist.) Ky. 1979. Law clk. hon. Constance B. Motley U.S. Dist. Ct., N.Y.C., 1968-69; assoc. Paul, Weiss, Rifkind, Wharton & Garrison, N.Y.C., 1969-72; exec. asst. Ohio Office of Budget & Mgmt., Columbus, Ohio, 1972-74; asst. atty. gen. Ohio Atty. Gen., Columbus, 1974-83, chief counsel, 1983-91; ptnr. Dinsmore & Shohl, Columbus, 1991—; pres. Ohio Sundry Claims Bd., Columbus, 1972-74, Ohio State Controlling Bd., Columbus, 1973-74; mem., bd. trustees Ohio State Tchrs. Retirement System, Columbus, 1986-91. Mem. ABA, Ohio State Bar Assn., Columbus Bar Assn., Environ. Law Inst., Columbia Law Alumni Assn., Alumni Coun. Swarthmore Coll., Ohio Sierra Club, Nat. Wildlife Fedn., Nature Conservancy. Environmental, General civil litigation, Administrative and regulatory. Office: Dinsmore & Shohl 175 S 3rd St Ste 1000 Columbus OH 43215-5197

**TAYLOR, JOHN CHESTNUT, III,** lawyer; b. N.Y.C., Jan. 7, 1928; s. John Chestnut and Jean Elizabeth (Willis) T.; m. Dolores Yvonne Sunstrom, Nov. 17, 1950; children: Jane Willis, John Sunstrom, Anne Holliday. B.A., Princeton U., 1947; LL.B., Yale U., 1950. Bar: N.Y. 1950, D.C. 1972. Assoc. Paul, Weiss, Rifkind, Wharton & Garrison, N.Y.C., 1950, 52-60, ptnr., 1961-85, 87-91, of counsel, 1986-87, 92—; exec. v.p., dir. AEA Investors Inc., N.Y.C., 1985-86, pres., 1986-87. Bd. dirs. AFS Intercultural Programs, Inc., N.Y.C., 1972-80, trustee, 1973-79, chmn., 1975-79; trustee Carnegie Corp. N.Y., N.Y.C., 1975-84, chmn., 1979-84; trustee, mem. exec. com. Devereux Found., 1992—, vice chmn., 1994—. Served to capt. JAGC, AUS, 1950-52. Mem. Assn. of Bar of City of N.Y., Order of Coif, Phi Beta Kappa, Phi Delta Phi. Democrat. General corporate, Entertainment. Home: 1 Hammock View Ln Savannah GA 31411-2603 Office: Paul Weiss Rifkind Wharton & Garrison Rm 200 1285 Avenue Of The Americas New York NY 10019-6065

**TAYLOR, JOHN MCKOWEN,** lawyer; b. Baton Rouge, Jan. 20, 1924; s. Benjamin Brown and May (McKowen) T.; 1 child, John McKowen. B.A., La. State U., 1948, J.D., 1950. Bar: La. 1950, U.S. Supreme Ct. 1960. Assoc. Taylor, Porter, Brooks, Fuller & Phillips, Baton Rouge, 1950-55, Huckaby, Seale, Kelton & Hayes, Baton Rouge, 1955-58; ptnr. Kelton & Taylor, Baton Rouge, 1958-61; pvt. practice law, Baton Rouge, 1961—. With AUS, 1943-46; maj. USAR, 1946—, ATO, ETO, PTO. Mem. ABA, AAAS, La. State Bar Assn., Baton Rouge Bar Assn., Mil. Order of World Wars, Am. Radio Relay League, Sigma Chi, Pi Gamma Mu, Phi Delta Phi, Baton Rouge Country Club, City of Baton Rouge Club, Baton Rouge Amateur Radio Club, SAR, Camelot Club. Republican. Presbyterian. Oil, gas, and mineral, Real property, Family and matrimonial. Home and Office: 2150 Kleinert Ave Baton Rouge LA 70806-6712

**TAYLOR, JOSEPH HENRY,** lawyer; b. Chgo., Mar. 2, 1934; s. Joseph Henry and Blanche (Murnane) T.; m. Marie Theresa Dietz, Feb. 20, 1960 (div. Dec. 21 1975); children: Lisa Marie Moose, Joseph John, Matthew Edward, Nicole; m. Joyce Louise Eriks, Jan. 1, 1977; children: Sean Philip, Ryan Joseph, Colin, Michael, Zachary. BS in Philosophy, Loyola U., Chgo., 1960, JD, 1965. Bar: Ill. 1965, U.S. Dist. Ct. (no. and so. dists.) Ill. 1965. Assoc. Pentis & Tourek, Chgo., 1965-66; pvt. practice Chgo. and Palos Heights, Ill., 1966—; prosecutor City of Palos Heights, 1976—. Alderman City of Palos Heights, 1974-76. Cpl. USMC, 1951-54. Mem. ATLA, Ill. Trial Lawyers Assn., Ill. State Bar Assn., Chgo. Bar Assn., S.W. Suburban Bar Assn. (pres. 1970), DuPage County Bar Assn., Criminal Def. Lawyer. Avocations: pilot, motorcycles, marathon runner. Criminal. Office: 7330 W College Dr Palos Heights IL 60463-1157

**TAYLOR, MARVIN EDWARD, JR.,** lawyer; b. Smithfield, N.C., Oct. 15, 1937; s. Marvin Edward and Ellen Borden Broadhurst T.; m. Karin Gunilla Guggenheim, Nov. 29, 1969; 1 child, Karin Elizabeth Guggenheim. AB, U. N.C., 1960, JD with honors, 1965. Bar: N.Y. 1966, N.C. 1968, U.S. Dist. Ct. (ea. dist.) N.C. 1973, U.S. Ct. Appeals (4th cir.) 1974, Calif. 1976. Assoc. Nixon Mudge Rose Guthrie Alexander & Mitchell, N.Y.C., 1965-67, Sanford Cannon Adams & McCullough, Raleigh, N.C., 1967-71; atty. pvt. practice, Raleigh, N.C., 1972-75, 1984—; corp. counsel Memorex Corp., Santa Clara, Calif., 1975-80; atty. pvt. practice, Hickory, N.C., 1983; dept. counsel GE Co., Hickory, N.C., 1980-82. Dir. Parents' Assn. N.C. State U., Raleigh, 1989-93, Coun. Entrepreneurial Devel, Research Triangle Park, N.C., 1985-88, chmn. pub. com., 1985-88; participant N.C. Ctr. Nonprofits Pro Bono Program, Raleigh, 1994—. With USAF, 1960-62. Mem. N.C. Bar Assn. (com. comml. banking & bus. law 1970-75, subcom. securities regulation 1972-75, bus. law sect. coun. 1982-85, 85-90, internat. law com. 1990-92, internat. law & practice sect. coun. 1992-95, pub. info. com. 1995—), Swedish-Am. C. of C. N.C. (co-founder, dir., sec./treas. 1998—), N.C. Law Rev. Staff, 1964 (rsch. editor 1965), Order of Coif. Democrat. Episcopalian. Avocations: skiing, photography, reading. Contracts commercial, General corporate, Private international. Office: 119 SW Maynard Rd Cary NC 27511-4472

**TAYLOR, MICHAEL GEORGE,** lawyer; b. Harvey, Ill., Aug. 28, 1955; s. Howard George Taylor; m. Diann Marie Taylor, Aug. 11, 1984; children: Christopher, Sarah, Nathan, Daniel. BA in Philosophy, U. Wis., 1977; MA in Philosophy, U. Mich., 1979, JD, 1984. Bar: Mich. 1984. Shareholder Leonard, Street and Deinard, Mpls., 1991—. Mem. Phi Beta Kappa. Construction, Insurance. Office: Leonard Street and Deinard 150 S 5th St Ste 2300 Minneapolis MN 55402-4238

**TAYLOR, MICHAEL LESLIE,** lawyer; b. Boonville, Mo., Nov. 2, 1954; s. Paul Howard and Nora Lee T.; m. Janet S. Finke, June 23, 1990. AA, Kansas City Communtiy Coll., 1977; BGS, U. Kans., 1979, JD, 1982. Bar: Mo. 1982, U.S. Dist. Ct. Mo. 1982, U.S. Ct. Appeals (10th cir.) 1986, U.S. Ct. Appeals (8th cir.) 1987. Assoc. atty. Watkins, Boulware, Lucas & Miner, St. Joseph, Mo., 1982-85, ptnr., 1986-87; named ptnr. Watkins, Boulware, Lucas, Miner, Murphy & Taylor, St. Joseph, Mo., 1987—; instr. Mo. Western State Coll., St. Joseph, 1985-94. Bd. mem. Midland Empire Diabetes Assn., St. Joseph, 1984; mem. United Way Allocations Com., St. Joseph, 1985-86; pres. East Hills Homes Assn., St. Joseph, 1987-89; co-chair Leadership Tomorrow, St. Joseph, 1985-88. Recipient Outstanding Vol. Svc. to the City Vol. award City St. Joseph, 1985, Lon O. Hocker Meml. Trial LAwyer award Mo. Bar Found., 1989. Fellow Am. Acad. Matrimonial Lawyers; mem. ABA, Mo. Bar Assn., St. Joseph Bar Assn. Avocations: reading, tennis, weightlifting. Family and matrimonial, General civil litigation, Personal injury. Office: Watkins Boulware Lucas Miner Murphy & Taylor 3101 Frederick Ave Saint Joseph MO 64506-2911

**TAYLOR, NANCY ELIZABETH,** lawyer; b. Salt Lake City, Apr. 6, 1956; d. Calvin Walker and Dorothy (Cope) Taylor; m. Christopher Robbins Bowen, Jan. 22, 1978; children: Elizabeth Grant Bowen, Alexandra Taylor Bowen. BS, U. Utah, 1978; JD, Cath. U., 1988. Health policy dir. Senate Com. on Labor and Human Resources, Washington, 1981-91; ptnr. Law Offices of Deborah Steelman, Washington, 1991-93; prin. shareholder Greenberg Traurig, Washington, 1993—. Testimony presentor Rep. Nat. Conf., 1992. Recipient Commr. award FDA, 1989. Mem. Nat. Health Lawyers, Women & Gov. Rels., Food and Drug Law Inst. Republican. Mem. LDS Ch. Office: Greenberg Traurig 1300 Connecticut Ave NW Washington DC 20036-1703

**TAYLOR, RICHARD CHARLES,** lawyer; b. Crookston, Minn., June 1, 1942; s. Robert E. and Frances (Freegrad) T.; m. Mary Jane Collins, Oct. 11, 1969; children: David Robert, Allison Jane, Kevin James. BS in Indsl. Engring., U. N.D., 1965, JD, 1967; postgrad., U. Calif., San Francisco, 1981; cert. of completion, Lawyers Post Grad. Clinic, 1975-76. Bar: Minn. 1967, N.D. 1967, Colo. 1971, U.S. Dist. Ct. Minn. 1979, U.S. Dist. Ct. N.D. 1982. Ptnr. Dickel, Johannson, Taylor & Rust, P.A., Crookston, 1971-98; judge U.S. Dist. Ct. 9th Jud. Dist., 1998—; mem. Minn. Lawyers' Bd. Profl. Responsibilty, St. Paul, 1983-91, Minn. Supreme Ct. Adv. Commn. on Lawyer Discipline, 1992-93. Mem. editorial bd. U. N.D. Law Rev., 1966-67. Bd. dirs., v.p. riverview Hosp. Assn., Crookston, 1979-88, Diocese of Crookston, 1984-98, Maple Lake Improvement Dist., 1989-93, Phoenix Industries, 1992-99, L&R Industries, 1988-98. Decorated Bronze Star, D.S.M. Mem. ATLA, Am. Bd. Trial Advocates, Minn. State Bar Assn. (bd. govs. 1991-98, cert. civil trial specialist 1991—), Minn Leading Attys., 14th Dist. Bar Assn. (pres. 1987-88), Minn. Trial Lawyers Assn., Minn. Def. Lawyers Assn., Minn. Diocesan atty's Assn., Am. Arbitration Assn. (panel of arbitrators), Arbitration Forum (panel of arbitrators), Am. Legion, Minakwa Country Club, Elks. Roman Catholic. Avocations: hunting, fishing, skiing. General civil litigation, Insurance, Personal injury. Home: RR 2 Box 95A Erskine MN 56535-9802

**TAYLOR, RICHARD JAMES,** lawyer; b. Merrill, Wis., Jan. 19, 1939; s. M.N. and Billie (Mead) T.; m. Nancy Hildebrand, Nov. 25, 1966. BA, U. Wis., 1962; DEF, U. Orleans, France, 1963; JD, U. Mich., 1966; postgrad., U. Paris II, 1971-72. Bar: N.Y. 1968. Assoc. Langner Parry Card & Langer, N.Y.C., 1966-68, Conboy Hewitt O'Brien & Boardman, N.Y.C., 1968-71; asst. prof. U. Paris I Law Sch., 1973-78; trademark and copyright counsel Colgate-Palmolive Co., N.Y.C., 1978—; seminar leader Am. Law and Lang., N.Y.C., 1987—; pro bono counsel Hearts and Voices, N.Y.C., 1992—; mem. com. of experts World Intellectual Property Orgn. Trademark Law Treaty, Geneva, 1993-94; lectr. intellectual property symposia. Co-author: Doing Business in France, 1973, Worldwide Trademark Transfers, 1992; contbr. chpt. to book, articles to Nat. Law Jour., Trademark Reporter, Jour. Japan Trademark Assn., Bus. Latin Am., others. Mem. ABA (chair com. on internat. trademark treaties and laws 1990-91, del. to World Trademark Symposium 1992), Internat. Trademark Assn. (chair internat. com. 1987-89, mem. internat. task force 1989-90, bd. dirs. 1992-95, mem. task force on trademark law treaty 1991-95, publ. bd. 1995—). Trademark and copyright.

**TAYLOR, RICHARD POWELL,** lawyer; b. Phila., Sept. 13, 1928; s. Earl Howard and Helen Moore (Martin) T.; m. Barbara Jo Anne Harris, Dec. 19, 1959; 1 child, Douglas Howard. BA, U. Va., 1950, JD, 1952. Bar: Va. 1952, D.C. 1956. Law clk. U.S. Ct. Appeals for 4th Circuit, 1951-52; assoc. Steptoe & Johnson LLP, Washington, 1956-61, ptnr., 1962—, chmn. transp. dept., 1978—; sec., corp. counsel Slick Corp., 1963-69, asst. sec., 1969-72, also bd. dirs., 1965-68; sec., corp. counsel Slick Indsl. Co., 1963-72; sec., bd. dirs. Slick Indsl. Co. Can. Ltd, 1966-72; bd. dirs. Intercontinental Forwarders, Inc., 1969-72. Mem. Save the Children 50th Anniversary Com., 1982; gen. counsel Am. Opera Scholarship Soc., 1974—; mem. lawyer's com. Washington Performing Arts Soc., 1982—; mem. adv. com. Rock Creek Found. Mental Health, 1982—; mem. nat. adv. bd. DAR, 1980-83, chmn., 1983—; mem. men's com. Project Hope Ball, 1980—; nat. vice chmn. for fin. Reagan for Pres., 1979-80; mem. exec. fin. com. 1981 Presdl. Inauguration; mem. President's Adv. Com. for Arts, 1982—, Rep. Nat. Com., 1983—; Md. fin. chmn. Reagan-Bush '84, Bush-Quayle '88. Served to lt (j.g.), Air Intelligence USNR, 1952-56. Mem. ABA (co-chmn. aviation com. 1964-76, chmn. 1976-77), Fed. Bar Assn., D.C. Bar Assn., Va. Bar Assn., Fed. Energy Bar Assn., Am. Judicature Soc., Assn. Transp. Practitioners, Internat. Platform Assn., Raven Soc., Order of Coif, Univ. Club, Capital Hill Club, Nat. Aviation Club, Aero Club, Congl. Country Club (Washington), Potomac (Md.) Polo Club. Episcopalian. Administrative and regulatory, General corporate, Transportation. Home: 14914 Spring Meadows Dr

Germantown MD 20874-3444 Office: 1330 Connecticut Ave NW Washington DC 20036-1704 *Everyone should devote a portion of his or her life to efforts which help ensure that our country remains free and strong and that its concept of government under law is maintained and expanded throughout the world.*

**TAYLOR, ROBERT LEE,** lawyer, former judge; b. North Wildwood, N.J., Sept. 6, 1947; s. Louis Edward and Elizabeth (Zuccato) T.; m. Julie Ann Adams, Apr. 28, 1979; children: Tracy, Jennifer, Kathryn, Robyn. BS, James Madison U., 1969; JD, Washington and Lee U., 1974. Bar: N.J. 1974, U.S. Dist. Ct. N.J. 1974, U.S. Ct. Appeals (3d cir.) 1982, U.S. Supreme Ct. 1991. Assoc. George M. James, Wildwood, 1974-78; ptnr. Way, Way, Goodkin & Taylor, Wildwood, 1978-81, Way, Way, & Taylor, Wildwood, 1981-82; pvt. practice law Stone Harbor, N.J., 1982—; judge Mid. Twp. Mcpl. Ct., N.J., 1984-89; organizer, dir. First so. State Bank, Avalon, N.J.; mem. dist. 1 ethics com. N.J. Supreme Ct., 1994-96; solicitor Lower Twp., N.J., 1994-96; diplomate N.J. Mcpl. Law. Advisor Law Explorers Boy Scouts Am., 1981, exec. bd. so. N.J. coun., 1995—; chmn. Cape May County Dem. Com., 1996-98. With U.S. Army, 1969-71. Mem. ABA, N.J. Bar Assn. (gen. coun. 1978-82), Cape May County Bar Assn. (pres. 1980-81), Cape May County Mcpl. Judges Assn. (treas. 1987-89), N.J. Jud. Conf. (del. 1978-82), Am. Legion, DAV (life), Delta Theta Phi. Democrat. Roman Catholic. Avocations: skiing, tennis. General practice, Real property, General civil litigation. Office: 9712 3rd Ave # 4 Stone Harbor NJ 08247-1931

**TAYLOR, SAMMYE LOU,** lawyer; b. Little Rock, Nov. 29, 1952; d. Orris Whitten and Mildred (Craig) T.; m. Gregory Turner Jones, Sept. 20, 1986 (div. Feb. 1998); 1 child, Alexander Taylor Jones. BA in English, U. Ark., Fayetteville, 1973; JD, U. Ark., Little Rock, 1983. Bar: U.S. Dist. Ct. (ea. and we. dists.) 1983. Assoc. Wright Lindsey & Jennings, Little Rock, 1983-88, ptnr., 1989—; mem. fed. practice com. U.S. Dist. Ct. (ea. dist.) Ark., 1998—. Mem. ABA, Ark. Bar Assn., Ark. Assn. Def. Counsel, Pulaski County Bar Assn., Am. Bd. Trial Advocates, Def. Rsch. Inst. Personal injury, Product liability, Toxic tort. Office: Wright Lindsey & Jennings 200 W Capitol Ave Ste 2200 Little Rock AR 72201-3699

**TAYLOR, TED,** lawyer; b. Fayette, Ala., June 3, 1940; B.S., U. Ala., 1962, J.D., 1966. Bar: Ala. 1966. Assoc. Hamilton, Denniston, Butler & Riddick, Mobile, Ala., 1966-67; ptnr. McDowell & Taylor, Prattville, Ala., 1967-74; ptnr. Taylor & Taylor, Prattville and Birmingham, Ala., 1974—; owner Speydthrift Farm, Lexington, 1993—, Double T Farms, Prattville, Ala., 1977—; mem. Ala. Bd. Bar Commrs., 1981. Fellow Roscoe Pound Found.; mem. 19th Jud. Cir. Bar Assn. (pres. 1973), Ala. Bar Assn., Ala. Trial Lawyers Assn. (pres. 1978), Assn. Trial Lawyers Am. (gov. 1979-80), Farrah Law Soc., U. Ala. Nat. Alumni Assn. (v.p. 1972), Autauga County Bar Assn. (pres. 1976), Am. Bd. Trial Advocacy (advocate). Personal injury. Office: 114 E Main St Prattville AL 36067-3129 also: 2130 Highland Ave S Birmingham AL 35205-4002

**TAYLOR, WILLARD B.,** lawyer; b. N.Y.C., 1940. BA, Yale U., 1962, LLB, 1965. Bar: N.Y. 1966. With firm Sullivan & Cromwell, N.Y.C.; adj. faculty NYU Law Sch. Mem. N.Y. State Bar Assn. (chair tax sect. 1983-84). Office: Sullivan & Cromwell 125 Broad St Fl 28 New York NY 10004-2489

**TAYLOR, WILLIAM AL,** state supreme court justice; b. Lusk, Wyo., Nov. 2, 1928; m. Jane Y.; 3 children. BA, U. Wyo., 1951, LLD, 1959. Bar: Wyo. 1959. Teacher Lusk, 1950-51,54-55, pvt. practice, 1959-78; city atty. Town of Lusk, 1962-74; atty. Niobrara County, Wyo., 1964-77; judge Wyo. Dist. Ct. (8th dist.), Cheyenne, 1980-93; justice Wyoming Supreme Ct., 1993—, chief justice, 1996-98; Exec. dir. Wyo. State Bar, 1977-80. Staff sgt. U.S. Army, 1951-53. Mem. Wyo. State Bar (Civil Rules com.), Wyo. Judicial Conf. (chmn. 1984-85),Tenth Cir. Bar Assn., Nat. Trial Judges, Am. Legion, Sigma Alpha Epsilon. Office: State Wyo Supreme Ct Supreme Ct Bldg Cheyenne WY 82002-0001

**TAYLOR, WILLIAM EDWARD,** lawyer; b. Detroit, Feb. 25, 1967; s. Robert Clarence and Beverly Jean T. BA, Albiono Coll., 1989; JD, U. Iowa, 1995. Assoc. Shermeta Chinko & Kilpatrick, Rochester Hills, Mich., 1996; ptnr. Gant & Talyor, PLC, Detroit, 1997—; bd. dirs. Vortex Svcs., Detroit, 1998—. Mem. Trial Lawers Am., Detroit Metro. Bar Assoc., Alpha Phi Alpha. Criminal, Bankruptcy. Office: Gant & Taylor PLC 65 Cadillac Sq Rm 2215 Detroit MI 48226-2869

**TAYLOR, WILLIAM WOODRUFF, III,** lawyer; b. Richmond, Va., July 30, 1944; s. William Woodruff Jr. and Ida (Winstead) T.; m. Susan Broadhurst, Sept. 29, 1984; children: Katherine Lowell, Matthew Gordon. AB, U. N.C., 1966; LLB, Yale U., 1969. Bar: N.C. 1969, D.C. 1970, U.S. Ct. Appeals (2nd, 4th, 5th and 11th cirs.), U.S. Supreme Ct. Law clk. to judge U.S. Dist. Ct. Del., Wilmington, 1969-70; staff atty. Pub. Defender Service, Washington, 1970-75; assoc. Ginsburg, Feldman and Bress, Washington, 1975-78; ptnr. Zuckerman, Spaeder, Goldstein, Taylor & Kolker L.L.P., Washington, 1978—; instr. dept. forensic sci. George Washington U., Washington, 1973-74; adj. prof. Columbus Sch. Law, Cath. U. Am., Washington, 1973-76; mem. D.C. Commn. on Jud. Disabilities and Tenure, 1978-83, chmn., 1979-83; vis. prof. U. N.C. Law Sch., fall 1991. Fellow Am. Coll. Trial Lawyers; mem. ABA (criminal justice sect., vice chmn. for govtl. affairs 1989-92, chair criminal justice sect. 1996-97), Nat. Inst. for Trial Advocacy (faculty 1978—, chmn. pub. defender svc. assn. 1984-89). Episcopalian. Avocations: fly fishing, tennis. Criminal, General civil litigation, Federal civil litigation. Office: Zuckerman Spaeder Goldstein Taylor & Kolker LLP 1201 Connecticut Ave NW Washington DC 20036-2638

**TEAGUE, CHARLES WOODROW,** lawyer; b. Thomasville, N.C., May 27, 1913; s. Lonnie Edwards and Dora Mae (Lassiter) T.; m. Jessie Randle Perry (div. 1976); m. Julia Brent Byrum, July 25, 1980; children: Kathy Randle Teague Jennings, Penny Randle Teague Eubanks, Charles W. Teague Jr. LLB, Wake Forest U., 1934. Bar: N.C. 1934, U.S. dist. Ct. (ea. and mid. dists.) N.C., U.S. Ct. Appeals (4th cir.), U.S. Supreme Ct. Claims atty. Liberty Mut. Ins. Co., Boston, 1934-35, High Point, N.C., 1936-38; claims atty. Lumber Mut. Casualty Ins. Co., Raleigh, N.C., 1938-42; ptnr. Teague, Campbell, Dennis & Gorham, Raleigh, 1946—; sec. N.C. R.R., Raleigh, 1960-64. Chmn. bd. elections Wake County, Raleigh, 1960-64. Lt. comdr. USN, 1942-46, PTO. Mem. N.C. Bar Assn. (chmn., bd. govs. 1960-64, councilor 1968-76, pres. 1977-78)), ABA (del.), Carolina Club, Country Club of N.C., Elk River Country Club, Kiwanis. Democrat. Presbyterian. Avocation: golf. Personal injury, Product liability, Workers' compensation. Office: Teague Campbell Dennis & Gorham 1621 Midtown Pl Raleigh NC 27609-7553

**TEARE, JOHN RICHARD, JR.,** lawyer; b. Phila., Sept. 23, 1954; divorced; 1 child, John III; m. Gale Angela Waters, June 5, 1982; children: Angela, Stephanie. BS in Criminal Justice summa cum laude, Wilmington Coll., 1987; JD cum laude, U. Richmond, 1990. Bar: W.Va. 1990, U.S. Dist. Ct. (so. dist.) W.Va. 1990, U.S. Dist. Ct. (no. dist.) W.Va. 1996, U.S. Ct. Appeals (4th cir.) 1991. Sec. guard U. Del., Newark, 1973-76; police officer City of Dover (Del.), 1976-85; summer assoc. Hirschler Fleischer Weinberg Cox & Allen, Richmond, 1989; ptnr. Bowles Rice McDavid Graff & Love, P.L.L.C., Charleston, W.Va., 1990—; counsel Charleston Police Civil Svc. Commn.; instr. Charleston Regional Police Acad., 1999. Cub scout leader Boy Scouts Am., Felton, Del., 1984-88, asst. scoutmaster, Richmond, 1988-89, Charleston, 1991—; chmn. pub. safety commn. Greater Charleston C. of C., 1991; sec. United Meth. Men, 1993; dir. Charleston Leadership Coun. on Pub. Safety, 1993-97, chmn. police dept. resource task force, 1994-97. Mem. ABA, W.Va. Bar Assn., Kanawha County Bar Assn., Def. Rsch. Inst., Def. Trial Counsel W.Va., Nat. Manufactured Housing Atty. Network, Fraternal Order of Police, Nat. Eagle Scout Assn., McNeill Law Assn., Greater Charleston C. of C., Delta Epsilon Rho. United Methodist. Avocations: camping, fishing, stamp collecting. General civil litigation, Labor, Civil rights. Home: 1565 Virginia St E Charleston WV 25311-2416 Office: Bowles Rice McDavid Graff & Love PLLC PO Box 1386 Charleston WV 25325-1386

**TEAS, RICHARD HARPER,** lawyer; b. Streator, Ill., Sept. 24, 1930; s. Bert H. and Audrey C. Teas; m. Janice K. Eikenmeyer, July 29, 1960 (dec.); children: Catherine L. Teas-Rogers, Amelia H. AB, U. Ill., 1957, LLB, 1960. Bar: Ill. 1960, U.S. Dist. Ct. (so. dist.) Ill. 1960. Probate adminstr. Continental Nat. Bank and Trust Co. of Chgo., 1960-66; ptnr. Tracy, Johnson, Bertani & Wilson Law Offices, Joliet, Ill., 1966—. Mem. Ill. State Bar Assn. (trust and estates sect. coun., standing com. on legislation), Will County Bar Assn., Am. Coll. of Trust and Estate Counsel, Estate Planning Coun. of Greater Joliet (pres. 1976). Avocations: tennis, golf. Estate planning, Probate, Estate taxation. Home: 20853 Rock Run Dr Joliet IL 60431-9323 Office: Tracy Johnson Bertani & Wilson 116 N Chicago St Ste 600 Joliet IL 60432-4234

**TEBLUM, GARY IRA,** lawyer; b. Phila., Apr. 25, 1955; s. Milton and Marlene Ann (Rosenberg) T.; m. Lisa Ida Goldsmith, May 13, 1979; children: Corey Harris, Jeremy Brett. BS, U. Del., 1976; JD cum laude, U. Pa., 1979. Assoc. Trenam, Simmons, Kemker, Scharf, Barkin, Frye & O'Neill, Tampa, Fla., 1979-84; ptnr. Trenam, Kemker, Scharf, Barkin, Frye, O'Neill & Mullis, Tampa, Fla., 1984—. Editor U. Pa. Law Rev., 1978-79. Mem. ABA, Fla. Bar Assn., Hillsborough County Bar Assn. Jewish. Securities, Contracts commercial, Corporate taxation. Home: 14039 Shady Shores Dr Tampa FL 33613-1934 Office: Trenam Kemker Scharf et al 2700 Barnett Pla Tampa FL 33601

**TECLAFF, LUDWIK ANDRZEJ,** law educator, consultant, author, lawyer; b. Czestochowa, Poland, Nov. 14, 1918; came to U.S., 1952, naturalized, 1958; s. Emil and Helena (Tarnowska) T.; m. Eileen Johnson, May 30, 1952. Mag Iuris, Oxford (Eng.) U., 1944; MS, Columbia U., 1955; LLM, NYU, 1961, JSD, 1965. Attaché Polish Fgn. Ministry, London, 1943-46; consul in Ireland, Polish Govt. in London, 1946-52; student libr. Columbia U. Sch. Libr. Sci., 1953-54; libr. Bklyn. Pub. Libr., 1954-59; rsch. librar. Fordham U. Sch. Law, 1959-62, asst. prof. law, 1962-65, assoc. prof. law, 1965-68, prof. 1968-89, prof. emeritus, 1989—, dir. law libr., 1962-86; cons. in field. With Polish Army, 1940-43, France, Eng. Recipient Clyde Eagleton award in internat. law NYU, 1965. Mem. Am. Soc. Internat. Law, Internat. Law Assn., Am. Law Librs. Assn., Internat. Coun. Environ. Law, Internat. Water Law Assn. Roman Catholic. Author: The River Basin in History and Law, 1967; Abstraction and Use of Water, 1972; Legal and Institutional Responses to Growing Water Demand, 1978; Economic Roots of Oppression, 1984, Water Law in Historical Perspective, 1985; editor: (with Albert E Utton) International Environmental Law, 1974, Water in a Developing World, 1978, International Groundwater Law, 1981, Transboundary Resources Law, 1987; contbr. articles on water law, law of the sea and environ. law to law jours. Office: Fordham U Sch Law 140 W 62nd St New York NY 10023-7407

**TEEL, ROBERT E.,** lawyer; b. Austin, Jan. 16, 1949. BBA, S.W. Tex. State U., 1971; JD, Tex. Tech. U., 1975. Bar: Tex. 1976, U.S. Dist. Ct. (no. dist.) Tex. 1976, U.S. Dist. Ct. (we. dist.) Tex. 1984, U.S. Dist. Ct. (so. dist.) Tex. 1991. Atty. Bob Huff & Assoc. Inc., Lubbock, Tex., 1976-96, sole practice, 1996—. Sr. arbitrator Better Bus. Bur., Lubbock, 1989—. With U.S. Army, 1971-73. Personal injury, Probate, General practice. Office: PO Box 1934 Lubbock TX 79408-1934

**TEETERS, BRUCE A.,** lawyer; b. Jackson Center, Ohio, Dec. 29, 1965; s. Richard Leon and Janet Elaine Teeters; m. Julie Ann Thiel, June 17, 1995; children: Madison Anna, Noah Richard. BS in Polit. Sci./Acctg., Ohio No. U., 1988; JD, U. Cin., 1991. Bar: Ohio 1991, U.S. Dist. Ct. (so. dist.) Ohio 1992. Atty. Chernesky, Heyman & Kress, Dayton, Ohio, 1991—. Bd. dirs. Bus. Adv. Com., Oakwood, Ohio, 1996—. Mem. ABA (bus. law divsn.), Ohio State Bar Assn. (bus. law divsn.), Dayton Bar Assn. General corporate, Mergers and acquisitions, Securities. Office: Chernesky Heyman & Kress Ten Courthouse Plz SW Dayton OH 45402

**TEFFT, STEVEN M.,** lawyer; b. Chgo., Aug. 6, 1957; s. James and Pearl T.; m. Laurie DiGirolamo, May 1, 1983; children: Andrew, Kathryn, Chrysan. BA, U. Ill., Chgo., 1979; JD, No. Ill. U., 1982. Asst. states atty. Peoria (Ill.) County States Attys. Office, 1982-83; atty. Pollin & Pheley, Northbrook, Ill., 1983-85. Law Office Dave Izzo, Chgo., 1985—. Roman Catholic. State civil litigation, Insurance, Personal injury. Office: Law Office Dave Izzo 2005 Wacker Ste 2400 Chicago IL 60606

**TEGENKAMP, GARY ELTON,** lawyer; b. Dayton, Ohio, Nov. 27, 1946; s. Elmer Robert and Dorothy Ann (Hummerich) T.; m. June Evelyn Barber, Aug. 2, 1969; children: Emily Stratton, Andrew Elton. BA in Polit. Sci., U. South Fla., 1969; JD, Coll. William and Mary, 1972. Bar: Va. 1972, U.S. Dist. Ct. (we. and ea. dists.) Va. 1972, U.S. Ct. Appeals (4th cir.) 1973. Law clk. to presiding judge U.S. Dist. Ct. (we. dist.) Va., U.S. Ct. Appeals (4th cir.), Abingdon, Va., 1972-73; assoc. Hunter, Fox & Trabue, Roanoke, Va., 1973-77; ptnr. Fox, Wooten and Hart P.C., Roanoke, 1977-90, Wooten & Hart, P.C., Roanoke, Va., 1991-95; asst. city atty. Office of Roanoke City Atty., 1995—. Active United Way, Roanoke Valley, 1976; legal advisor Roanoke Jaycees, 1976-77. Mem. Va. Bar Assn. (constrn. and environ. sects.), Va. Assn. Def. Attys., Roanoke Bar Assn. (chmn. com. CLE 1983-86, 6th dist. ethics com. 1988-91), Local Govt. Attys. Va. United Methodist. Avocations: coin collecting, youth sports programs. Federal civil litigation, State civil litigation, Municipal (including bonds). Home: 2524 Stanley Ave SE Roanoke VA 24014-3332 Office: Office Roanoke City Atty 464 Municipal Bldg 215 Church Ave SW Roanoke VA 24011-1517

**TEGFELDT, JENNIFER ANN,** lawyer; b. Sanford, Fla., Feb. 16, 1956; d. Carl George and Jean Helen (Wallace) T. BS in Biol. Scis., U. Calif., Davis, 1978; JD, Franklin Pierce Law Ctr., 1985. Bar: Mass. 1985, D.C. 1989, U.S. Ct. Appeals (fed. cir.) 1989, U.S. Patent Office 1984. Law clk. to Hon. Pauline Newman Ct. Appeals for the Fed. Cir., 1985-87; atty. Mason, Fenwick & Lawrence, Washington, 1987-88, Fitzpatrick, Cella, Harper & Scinto, Washington, 1989--. Contbr. articles to profl. jours. Mem. ABA, Internat. Trade Comm. Trial Lawyers Assn. (mem. exec. bd.), Am. Intellectual Property Law Assn., Fed. Cir. Bar Assn. (chair liaison com.), Am. Inn of Ct. (historian Giles S. Rich Inn 1991—). Patent, Trademark and copyright, Federal civil litigation. Office: Fitzpatrick Cella Harper Scinto 1001 Pennsylvania Ave NW Washington DC 20004-2505

**TEICH, HOWARD BERNARD,** lawyer, activist, public affairs specialist; b. Huntington, N.Y., Nov. 1, 1946; s. Samuel and Beatrice Ann (Kay) T. AB, U. Pa., 1967; JD, Boston U., 1970. Bar: N.Y., 1971, U.S. Dist. Ct. (so. dist.) N.Y. 1984. Counsel N.Y. State Senator Emanuel Gold, N.Y.C., 1971-72; law sec. N.Y. State Supreme Ct. Justin Martin Evans, N.Y.C., 1972-75; assoc. pub. Firehouse mag., N.Y.C., 1975-79; pub. Midtown South Bus., N.Y.C., 1985-87; prin. Law Offices Howard B. Teich, N.Y.C., 1980—; sr. cons. The Kamber Group, Washington, 1995—; sr. counsel McLaughlin & Stein, P.C., N.Y.C., 1997—. Founder, chair New Dem. Dimensions, N.Y.C., 1981-91, Nat. Task Force on Life Safety for Handicapped, Washington, 1979-81; bd. dirs. Boys Choir of Harlem, N.Y.C., 1983-85, Assn. on Am. Indian Affairs, 1990-97, adv. bd., 1997—; chmn. New Leadership of Israel Bonds, N.Y.C., 1977-79; pres. Am. Jewish Congress Met. Region N.Y.C., 1992—, past nat. v.p.; bd. dirs. Jewish Comty. Rels. Coun., N.Y., 1995—, past v.p., 1995-98; co-chair Jewish Heritage, N.Y.C., 1997—;dep. dir. N.Y. state citizens com. McGovern for Pres., 1972, Samuels for Gov., 1974, Carey for Gov., 1974; dep. dir. N.Y. state primary campaign Carter for Pres., 1980; co-chair N.Y. state citizens com. Glenn for Pres., 1984, Mondale/Ferraro '84, 1984; bd. dirs. Manhattan Playhouse. Recipient Robert Briscoe award Emerald Isle Immigration Soc., 1996, Israel Leadership award Israel Bonds, 1979, Martin Luther King Jr. Living-the-Dream award, Gov. George Pataki, N.Y., 1999. Mem. AJ Congress Met Region (pres. 1992—), U. Pa. Club, Assn. on Am. Indian Affairs (bd. dirs., nat. adv. bd.). Democrat. Jewish. Avocations: N.Y.C. marathon, softball, tennis, reading, theatre, dance. Home: 185 E 85th St New York NY 10028-2140 Office: 260 Madison Ave New York NY 10016-2401

**TEICHER, MARTIN,** lawyer; b. N.Y.C., Nov. 16, 1945; s. Aaron and Gertrude (Mark) T.; m. Barbara Langner, Sept. 13, 1970; children: Nina Rebecca, Ira Kenneth. BA, CUNY, Flushing, 1967; JD, NYU, 1970. Bar: N.Y. 1971, U.S. Dist. Ct. (so. and ea. dists.) N.Y. 1972, U.S. Ct. Appeals (2d cir.) 1975, U.S. Supreme Ct. 1976. Assoc. Kronish, Lieb, Shainswit, Weiner & Hellman, N.Y.C., 1970-79; atty. spl. litigation dept. Am. Cyanamid Co., Wayne, N.J., 1980-88; chief litigation counsel CIBA-GEIGY Corp., Ardsley, N.Y., 1988-97; sr. corp. counsel Pfizer, Inc., 1997—; speaker drug liability seminars; speaker on environ. ins. coverage claims, food & drug law. Mem., bd. of trustees Ahavath Torah Congregation, Englewood, N.J., 1983—, treas., 1986-88, pres., 1988-91; participant Keystone Ctr. AIDS Vaccine Liabity project, 1988-90. Mem. N.Y. State Bar Assn., Assn. of Bar of City of N.Y. (product liability com., 1981-86, tort litigation com. 1986-89, medicine and law com., 1989-91), Nat. Acad. Scis. (adv. com. on liability issues associated with AIDS vaccines 1987). Administrative and regulatory, General civil litigation, Product liability. Home: 453 Cape May St Englewood NJ 07631-4720 Office: Pfizer Inc 235 E 42nd St New York NY 10017-5755

**TEICHLER, STEPHEN LIN,** lawyer; b. Charleston, W.Va., Jan. 30, 1952; s. Alfred H. and Marjorie R. (Dunbar) T.; m. Dana Ruth Hegerle, Aug. 6, 1977; children: Adam Reed, Ryan Stephen. BA, U. Va., 1974, JD, 1977. Bar: Va. 1977, D.C. 1977. Atty. Dept. Air Force Office of Gen. Counsel, Washington, 1977-80, Baker & Botts, Washington, 1980-95; Metzger & Hollis, 1995-97; atty. Duane Morris & Heckscher, Washington, 1997—. Capt. USAF, 1977-80. Lutheran. Oil, gas, and mineral, Federal civil litigation, Public international. Home: 8315 Chapel Lake Ct Annandale VA 22003-4401 Office: Duane Morris & Heckscher 1667 K St NW Ste 700 Washington DC 20006-1608

**TEICHNER, BRUCE A.,** lawyer; b. Chgo.. BA, U. Iowa, 1981; JD, De Paul U., 1985; MBA, U. Chgo., 1997. Legal writing tchg. asst. Coll. Law De Paul U., Chgo., 1982-83; assoc. coun. Allstate Ins. Co., Northbrook, Ill. Mem. writing staff De Paul Law Rev., 1983-85; contbr. articles to profl. jours. Mem. ABA, Chgo. Bar Assn. (corp. law coms.), Am. Corp. Counsel Assn. (assoc. counsel), Phi Beta Kappa. E-mail: bteichner@allstate.com. General corporate, Securities, Private international. Office: Allstate Ins Co 3075 Sanders Rd Ste G5A Northbrook IL 60062-7127*

**TEIMAN, RICHARD B.,** lawyer; b. Bklyn., May 19, 1938. AB, Princeton U., 1959; LLB, Harvard U., 1962. Bar: N.Y. 1963. Ptnr. Winston & Strawn and predecessor Cole and Deitz, N.Y.C., 1968—. Trustee Citizens Budget Commn., 1993—. Mem. Assn. Bar City N.Y. (com. Admiralty 1975-78, 87, chair 1988-91), Maritime Law Assn. (com. Maritime Financing 1980—, chmn. subcom. Recodification U.S. Ship Mortgage Act 1986-91, chmn. subcom. U.S. Coastguard, Citizenship and Related Matters 1988-94), Phi Beta Kappa. General corporate, Admiralty, Contracts commercial. Home: 5 Pryer Ln Larchmont NY 10538-4012 Office: Winston & Strawn 200 Park Ave Rm 4100 New York NY 10166-0005

**TEITELBAUM, LEE E.,** dean, law educator; b. New Orleans, La., Nov. 4, 1941. BA magna cum laude, Harvard Coll., 1963; LLB, Harvard U., 1966; LLM, Northwestern U., 1968. Bar: Ill. Staff atty. Chgo. Lawyer Project, 1966-68; asst. prof. law U. N.D., 1968-70; assoc. prof. law SUNY, Buffalo, 1970-73; vis. assoc. prof. law U. N.Mex. Law Sch., 1972, assoc. prof. law, 1973-74, prof. law, 1974-87; prof. law, dir. Ctr. for the Study of Legal Policy Relating to Children Ind. U. Law Sch., 1980-81, vis. prof., 1987; vis. prof. U. Utah Coll. Law, 1985, prof. law, 1986—, assoc. dean acad. affairs, 1987-90, acting dean, 1988, dean, 1990-98, Alfred C. Emery prof. law, 1994—; Allan R. Tessler dean and prof. of law Cornell Law Sch., 1999—; fellow legal history program U. Wis., Madison, 1984; mem. test audit subcom., bd. trustees Law Sch. Admissions Coun.; bd. mem. Law and Soc. Assn. Author: (with A. Gough) Beyond Control: Status Offenders in the Juvenile Court, 1977 (with W.V. Stapleton) In Defense of Youth: The Role of Counsel in American Juvenile Courts, 1972; contbr. articles to profl. jours.; bd. editors Law & Soc. Rev., 1982-87, Law & Policy, Jour. Legal Edn., 1990-92. Fellow ABA (reporter ABA-IJA project on standards for juvenile justices, standards relating to the role of counsel for pvt. parties 1979); mem. Law & Soc. Assn. (bd. trustees 1977-80), Utah Minority Bar Assn. (award), Assn. Am. Law Schs. (exec. com.). Office: Univ of Utah College of Law Salt Lake City UT 84112-8909*

**TEITELBAUM, STEVEN USHER,** lawyer; b. Chgo., Nov. 29, 1945; s. Jerome H. and Marion Judith (Berlin) T.; m. Cathy Ann Rosenblatt, Mar. 11, 1984. A.B., Boston U., 1967; J.D., Union U., 1975. Bar: N.Y. 1976, U.S. Dist. Ct. (no. dist.) N.Y. 1976, U.S. Supreme Ct. 1980, U.S. Ct. Appeals (2d cir.) 1993; cert. arbitrator. Sr. atty. N.Y. State Dept. Health, Albany, 1976-79; counsel N.Y. State Office Bus. Permits, Albany, 1979-83; sole practice, Albany, 1983-95; dep. commr., gen. counsel N.Y. State Dept. Taxation and Fin., 1995—; staff judge advocate U.S. Army Res. Watervliet Arsenal, N.Y., 1978-84. Author: Streamlining the Regulatory Procedures of the Department of Agriculture, 1982. Active Found. Bd. Ctr. for Disabled, Empire State Performing Arts Ctr.; bd. trustees Albany Acad. for Girls. Served with U.S. Army, 1968-69. Mem. Am. Arbitration Assn. (arbitrator 1979—), N.Y. State Bar Assn. (com. on pub. health 1976-80, faculty on adminstrv. law 1980, com. on adminstrv. law 1980-84, 93-95, labor and employment sect., taxation sect. 1985—). Clubs: Fort Orange (Albany), Country Club Troy (N.Y.). Administrative and regulatory, State and local taxation, Taxation, general. Home: 17 Carstead Dr Slingerlands NY 12159-9266 Office: WA Harriman Office Campus Bldg 9 Rm 205 Albany NY 12227

**TEITLER, HAROLD HERMAN,** lawyer, family psychotherapist, mediator, general contractor; b. San Francisco, Feb. 14, 1936; s. Max Herman and Elsie (Kaplan) T.; m. Joan Barbara Teitler; children: Deborah, Leah, Rebekah. AB, U. Calif.-Berkeley; MA, Chapman Coll.; JD, Lincoln U., 1977. Bar: Calif., 1977. Sole practice, 1977—; mem. faculty Lincoln U. Law Sch., 1982—. Mem. Lincoln U. Law Rev. Bd. dirs. United Jewish Community Ctrs.-Brotherhoodway Ctr., 1979-82; mem. youth com. Central YMCA, San Francisco. USPHS grantee, 1962. Mem. Calif. Bar Assn., San Francisco Bar Assn., Calif. Assn. Marriage and Family Therapists, Am. Arbitration Assn. (panelist), Psi Chi, Alpha Phi Sigma. Family and matrimonial, Contracts commercial. Home: 1343 43rd Ave San Francisco CA 94122-1214

**TEKLITS, JOSEPH ANTHONY,** lawyer; b. Bellville, Ill., July 18, 1952; s. Frank Anthony and Mary (Bodish) T.; m. Deborah Ann Keevill, June 1, 1974; children: Jessica, Joseph, Michael. BA, Allentown Coll. St. Francis de Sales, 1974; JD, U. Notre Dame, 1977. Bar: Ind. 1977, Pa. 1988, U.S. Dist. Ct. (no. dist.) Ind. 1977, U.S. Dist. Ct. (so. dist.) Ind. 1977, U.S. Dist. Ct. (ea. dist.) Pa. 1988, U.S. Ct. Appeals (3d cir.) 1988, U.S. Dist. Ct. (ea. dist.) Mich. 1989, U.S. Ct. Appeals (6th cir.) 1990, U.S. Ct. Appeals (11th cir.) 1993, U.S. Supreme Ct. 1995. Legal counsel CTS Corp., Elkhart, Ind., 1977-80; mng. labor counsel Sperry Corp. (name now Unisys Corp.), Blue Bell, Pa., 1980-87, asst. gen. counsel Unisys Corp., 1987—, assoc. gen. counsel, 1995—. Mem. mgmt. com. Equal Employment Opportunity Law. Mem. ABA (labor and employment law, litigation sects., EEO com.), Delta Epsilon Sigma (pres. chpt. 1974). Republican. Roman Catholic. Labor, Federal civil litigation, Administrative and regulatory. Office: Unisys Corp Hdqrs PO Box 500 Blue Bell PA 19424-0001

**TELEPAS, GEORGE PETER,** lawyer; b. Kingston, N.Y., Nov. 20, 1935; s. Peter G. and Grace Telepas; m. Regina Tisiker, Sept. 6, 1969 (div.); m. Patricia Kilstofte, Apr. 30, 1995. BS, U. Fla., 1960; JD, U. Miami, 1965. Bar: Fla. 1965, Colo. 1986. Assoc. Preddy, Haddad, Kutner & Hardy, 1966-67, Williams & Jabara, 1967-68; pvt. practice Miami, Fla., 1968—. Mem. citizens bd. U. Miami. With USMC, 1954-56. Mem. ATLA, ABA, Fla. Bar Assn., Colo. Bar Assn., Dade County Bar Assn., Fla. Trial Lawyers Assn., Dade County Trial Lawyers Assn., Delta Theta Phi, Sigma Nu. Personal injury. Address: PH 164 1905 Sunburst Dr Vail CO 81657-5166

**TELESCA, MICHAEL ANTHONY,** federal judge; b. Rochester, N.Y., Nov. 25, 1929; s. Michael Angelo and Agatha (Locurcio) T.; m. Ethel E. Hibbard, June 5, 1953; children: Michele, Stephen. AB, U. Rochester, 1952; JD, U. Buffalo, 1955. Bar: N.Y. 1957, U.S. Dist. Ct. (we. dist.) N.Y. 1958, U.S. Ct. Appeals (2nd cir.) 1960, U.S. Supreme Ct. 1967. Ptnr. Lamb, Webster, Walz, Telesca, Rochester, N.Y., 1957-73; surrogate ct. judge Monroe County, N.Y., 1973-82; judge U.S. Dist. Ct. (we. dist.) N.Y., Rochester, 1982—, chief judge, 1989-95; apptd. to Alien Terrorist Removal Ct. by Chief Justice Rehnquist, U.S. Supreme Ct., 1996; bd. dirs. Fed. Jud. Ctr. Bd. govs. Genesee Hosp., Rochester; mem. adv. bd. Assn. for Retarded Citizens, Al Sigl Ctr., Rochester. Served to 1st lt. USMC, 1955-57. Recipient Civic medal Rochester C. of C., 1983, Hutchinson medal U.

Rochester, 1990. Mem. ABA, Am. Judicature Soc., Am. Inns. of Ct. (founder, pres. Rochester chpt.), Justinian Soc. Jurists, N.Y. State Bar Assn., Monroe County Bar Assn. Republican. Roman Catholic. Office: US Dist Ct 272 US Courthouse 100 State St Ste 212 Rochester NY 14614-1309

**TELGENHOF, ALLEN RAY,** lawyer; b. Flint, Mich., Jan. 31, 1964; s. Gerald H. and Bernice Kay Telgenhof; m. Judy Michele Campbell, Sept. 5, 1986; children: Tyler, Allyson, Will, Luke. BA, Mich. State U., 1987; JD cum laude, Thomas M. Cooley Law Sch., 1989. Bar: Mich. 1989, U.S. Dist. Ct. (ea. dist.) Mich. 1992, U.S. Ct. Appeals (6th cir.) 1992, U.S. Dist. Ct. (we. dist.) Mich. 1997. Legis. analyst Mich. Ho. of Reps., Lansing, 1989; assoc. Hicks & Schmidlin, P.C., Flint, 1990-93; pvt. practice law Clio, Mich., 1993-94; ptnr. Pointner, Joseph, Corcoran & Telgenhof, P.C., Charlevoix, Mich., 1994-98, Joseph, Corcoran & Telgenhof, P.C., Charlevoix, 1998—; advisor Clio H.S. Law Club, 1992-94; founder, pres. Clio Area Edn. Found., 1992-94; presenter in field. Trustee Clio Bd. Edn., 1992-94, Charlevoix Bd. Edn., 1995—, pres., 1997—; commr. City of Charlevoix Planning Commn., 1995-96. Mem. ABA, Charlevoix-Emmet Bar Assn. Democrat. Avocations: sports, sailing, family activities. E-mail: atelgenhof@unnet.com. Fax: 616-547-3014. General civil litigation, Criminal, Securities. Office: Joseph Corcoran & Telgenhof PC PO Box 490 203 Mason St Charlevoix MI 49720-1337

**TELLEEN, L. MICHAEL,** lawyer; b. Davenport, Iowa, Jan. 30, 1947; s. Leonard William and Margaret J. Telleen; m. Christine Louise Telleen, Sept. 2, 1973; children: Karl, Claire. BA, Carleton Coll., 1969; JD, Stanford U., 1973. Bar: Calif. 1973, U.S. Dist. Ct. (no. dist.) Calif. 1973. Assoc. Carr, McClellan, Ingersoll, Thompson & Horn, Burlingame, Calif., 1973-80, ptnr., 1980-91; shareholder, dir. Carr, McClellan, Ingersoll, Thompson & Horn, P.C., Burlingame, 1991—; bd. dirs. Pilot/Legis, Calif., 19916. Pres. United Cerebral Palsy Assn. Santa Clara/San Mateo Counties, 1977-79. Sgt. U.S. Army Res., 1970-76. Mem. Rotary Club of Belmont (pres. 1983-84). Lutheran. Avocations: golf, skiing. General corporate, Mergers and acquisitions, Securities. Office: Carr McClellan et al 216 Park Rd Burlingame CA 94010-4200

**TELLER, HOWARD BARRY,** lawyer; b. N.Y.C., May 19, 1943; m. Esther B. Teller; children: Robert, Ilene, Majorie. BS, NYU, 1966; MBA, Adelphi U., 1969; JD, U. Balt., 1973; postgrad., Temple U. Bar: Md. 1973, D.C., 1979, U.S. Dist. Ct. (fed. dist.), U.S. Tax Ct. Instr. U. Balt., 1970-72; estate and gift tax atty. IRS, Trenton, N.J., 1973-75; tax law specialist IRS, Washington, 1975-79; pvt. practice Washington, 1979-86; ptnr. Herndon, McConville, Brown, Teller & Hessler, Washington, 1986-87; of counsel Buck, Migdal & Myers, Annapolis, Md., 1991—; pvt. practice Rockville, Md., 1987—. Co-author: Tax Audits, 1980; mng. editor Forum Law Sch. newspaper, 1972; contbr. chpts. to books. Advocate for disabled/mentally challenged. Recipient Apollo Achievement Cert., NASA, 1970, Merit award U. Balt., 1972; environ. essay winner ATLA, 1971. Mem. ABA. Jewish. Avocation: golf. E-mail: hbteller@aol.com. Taxation, general, Estate planning, General corporate. Office: 11300 Rockville Pike # 112 Rockville MD 20852-3003

**TELLER, STEPHEN AIDEN,** lawyer, mediator; b. Seattle, Jan. 11, 1966; s. David and Davida Teller; m. Amy P. Summers, July 4, 1994; 1 child, Cole Teller. Student, U. Munich, Germany, 1985-87; BA in Psychology, Reed Coll., 1989; MS in Psychology, U. Wash., 1992, JD, 1993; postgrad., U. Munich, Germany, 1985-87. Bar: Wash. 1993, U.S. Dist. Ct. (we. dist.) Wash. 1994. Tchg. asst. dept. psychology U. Wash., Seattle, 1992; legal intern EEOC, Seattle, 1993; assoc. atty. Law Office of Jeffrey Needle, Seattle, 1993-98, Frank and Rosen, Seattle, 1998-99, Grant and grant, Tacoma, 1999—. Co-Author: (book chpt.) Aspects of Memory, 1992; contbr. articles to Trial Lawyers Assn. Newspaper. Mem. Wash. Employment Lawyers Assn. (treas. 1997—), Wash. Trial Lawyers Assn. (vice chair employment sect. 1998—). Democrat. Avocations: golf, skiing, family. Labor, Civil rights, Alternative dispute resolution. Office: Grant and Grant 3002 S 47th St Tacoma WA 98409-4416

**TELLERIA, ANTHONY F.,** lawyer; b. Nicaragua, June 6, 1938; s. Carlos E. and Melida (Amador) T.; m. Dolores A. Rockey, Nov. 3, 1962; children: Matthew J., Andrea F. LLB, Southwestern U., 1964. Bar: Calif 1964. Sr. ptnr. Telleria, Townley & Doran, L.A., 1971-75; pvt. practice, L.A., 1964-71, 75—. Mem. Calif. Trial Lawyers Assn., L.A. County Bar Assn., Am. Arbitration Assn. (L.A. adv. coun., accident claims com.), Consumer Attys. Assn. of L.A. Personal injury, State civil litigation, Criminal. Home: 1615 Rose Ave San Marino CA 91108-3001 Office: 150 E Colorado Blvd Ste 206 Pasadena CA 91105-3722

**TELSEY, SUZANNE LISA,** lawyer; b. N.Y.C., Mar. 18, 1958; d. Daubert and Jacqueline (Messite) T.; m. Steven C. Bennett, July 26, 1986; children: Danielle, Nicole. AB, Brown U., 1980; JD with honors, NYU, 1984. Bar: N.Y. 1985, U.S. Dist. Ct. (so. dist.) N.Y. 1985. Law clk. Hon. Pierre N. Leval U.S. Dist. Ct. (so. dist.) N.Y., N.Y.C., 1984-86; litig. assoc. Kramer, Levin, Naftalis & Frankel, N.Y.C., 1986-89; assoc. gen. counsel Bantam Doubleday Dell Pub. Group, Inc., N.Y.C., 1989-96; gen. counsel Atlas Editions, Inc., N.Y.C., 1996—. Contbr. articles to profl. jours. Mem. Assn. of the Bar of the City of N.Y. (copyright law com. 1990-94, comms. and media law sect. 1994-97), N.Y. State Bar Assn. (media law sect. 1998—), Order of the Coif. Jewish. Avocations: tennis, gardening, hiking, horseback riding, photography. Intellectual property, Trademark and copyright, Communications. Office: Atlas Editions Inc 919 3rd Ave Fl 14 New York NY 10022-3902

**TEMKO, STANLEY LEONARD,** lawyer; b. N.Y.C., Jan. 4, 1920; s. Emanuel and Betty (Alderman) T.; m. Francine Marie Salzman, Mar. 4, 1944 (dec. Dec. 1998); children: Richard J., Edward J., William D. AB, Columbia U., 1940, LLB, 1943. Bar: N.Y. 1943, D.C. 1951. Practice in N.Y.C., 1943, 46-47; law clk. Mr. Justice Wiley Rutledge, U.S. Supreme Ct., Washington, 1947-48; legal counsel Econ. Coop. Adminstrn., 1948-49; assoc. Covington & Burling, Washington, 1949-55; ptnr. Covington & Burling, 1955-90, sr. counsel, 1990—. Editor-in-chief: Columbia Law Rev, 1942-43. Trustee Beauvoir Sch., 1963-69; trustee Columbia U., 1980-91, trustee emeritus, 1991—, mem. bd. visitors Sch. Law, 1961-98, mem. emeritus, 1999—; mem. bd. govs. St. Albans Sch., 1967-73, chmn., 1971-73. 2nd lt. U.S. Army, 1943-46. Decorated Bronze Star; recipient medal for conspicuous alumni svc. Columbia U., 1979. Fellow Am. Bar Found. (chmn. rsch. com. 1970-72); mem. ABA, Am. Law Inst., D.C. Bar Assn., Columbia U. Sch. Law Alumni Assn. (pres. 1982-84), Met. Club, Nat. Press Club, Phi Beta Kappa. Administrative and regulatory, Antitrust, Health. Home: 4811 Dexter Ter NW Washington DC 20007-1020 Office: Covington & Burling 1201 Pennsylvania Ave NW PO Box 7566 Washington DC 20044-7566

**TEMMERMAN, ROBERT EUGENE, JR.,** lawyer; b. Detroit, Dec. 5, 1952; s. Robert E. and Jeanne M. (Schultz) T.; m. Lisa Diane Harvey, Sept. 14, 1985; children: Diane, Alicia, Robert III. BA, Boston Coll., 1975; JD, Santa Clara U., 1980. Bar: Calif. 1980, U.S. Dist. Ct. (no. dist.) Calif. 1980, U.S. Ct. Appeals (9th cir.) 1989, U.S. Supreme Ct. 1997. Pvt. practice Robert E. Temmerman, Jr., Atty. at Law, Campbell, Calif., 1980-98; ptnr. Temmerman & Desmarais, LLP, Campbell, Calif., 1998—, Campbell, 1998—. Co-author: Post Mortem Trust Administration, 1996. Mem. State Bar Calif. (chair exec. com. estate planning, trust and probate law sect. 1997-98). Avocations: wine making, river rafting, skiing. Estate planning, Probate, Estate taxation. Office: Temmerman & Desmarais LLP 1550 S Bascom Ave Ste 240 Campbell CA 95008-0638

**TEMPLAR, TED MAC,** lawyer; b. Arkansas City, Kans., Sept. 27, 1929; s. H. George and Helen Marie (Bishop) T.; m. Maxine Bowman, Feb. 19, 1954; children: Lance Cameron, Kenton Lane, Clayton Neil. BBA, Washburn U., 1951, JD, 1954. Bar: Kans. 1954, U.S. Dist. Ct. Kans. 1954, U.S. Ct. Appeals (10th cir.) 1961. Dep. county lawyer Cowley County, Arkansas City, Kans., 1956-58; judge city ct. Cowley County, Arkansas City, 1969-73; state rep. 79th dist. State of Kans., Topeka, 1973-77; pvt. practice Arkansas City, 1954—. 1st lt. USAR, 1951-59. Recipient Certificate Appreciation Kans. Bar Assn., 1973. Mem. Rotary Club Arkansas City, Midian Shrine, Wichita, Legion of Honor Order of DeMolay, Jaycee Internat. (senate). Republican. Avocations: hunting, fishing. Probate, Consumer commercial, General practice. Office: PO Box 1002 Arkansas City KS 67005-1002

**TEMPLE, DANA A.,** lawyer; b. Wichita, Kans., Mar. 26, 1958; d. Joseph and Donna Jean Dernovish; m. Howard Messinger, Dec. 10, 1986 (div. 1991); 1 child, Adam Hunter. BA, U. Denver, 1983, JD, 1987. Bar: Colo. 1987. Fin. sales rep. First Nat. Bank of Lakewood, Colo., 1983-85; assoc. Gelt, Fleishman & Sterling, P.C., Denver, 1989-93; ptnr. Temple & Butler, P.C., Denver, 1993; mgm., mgr. The Temple Law Offices, LLC, Denver, 1994—. Recipient Hornbeck Scholar award. Mem. ABA, Colo. Bar Assn., Denver Bar Assn., Women's Bar Assn., Colo. Trial Lawyers Assn., Phi Beta Kappa. Consumer commercial, Contracts commercial, Labor. Office: The Temple Law Office 837 E 17th Ave Apt 102 Denver CO 80218-1470

**TEMPLETON, ROBERT LINCOLN,** lawyer; b. Amarillo, Tex., Mar. 17, 1932; s. Thomas Jefferson and Mary Lillian (Jameson) T.; m. Martha Louise Williams, June 12, 1954; children: Linda Cunyus, Luanne Hopper. BA, LLB, Baylor U., 1954. Bar: Tex. 1954, U.S. Dist. Ct. (no. dist.) Tex. 1961, U.S. Ct. Appeals (5th cir.) 1964, U.S. Ct. Appeals (10th cir.) 1967, U.S. Dist. Ct. (we. dist.) Tex. 1975, U.S. Supreme Ct. 1978; cert. in civil trial and personal injury trial law Tex. Bd. Legal Specialization. Practiced in Amarillo, 1956—; ptnr. Templeton, Smithee, Hayes & Fields, Amarillo. Capt. USAF, 1954-56. Mem. ABA, ATLA, State Bar Tex. (bd. dirs. 1969-72), Tex. Trial Lawyers Assn. (bd. dirs. 1966-69). Avocations: golf, hunting, gin rummy. Home: 2319 Juniper Dr Amarillo TX 79109-3417 Office: Templeton Smithee Et Al 1313 Bank One Ctr 600 S Tyler St Amarillo TX 79101-2353

**TENENBAUM, J. SAMUEL,** lawyer; b. Frankfurt, Germany, Mar. 5, 1949; s. Josef and Chana Tenenbaum; m. Susan Kay Nabedrick, Nov. 11, 1973; 1 child, Benjamin. BA, Ohio State U., 1970; JD cum laude, Northwestern U., 1973. Bar: Ill. 1973, U.S. Dist. Ct. (no. dist.) Ill. 1974, U.S. Ct. Appeals (7th cir.) 1974, U.S. Ct. Appeals (10th cir.) 1975, U.S. Ct. Appeals (9th cir.) 1976, U.S. Supreme Ct. 1977. Law clk. to judge U.S. Dist. Ct. (no. dist.) Ill., Chgo., 1973-75; ptnr. Tenenbaum & Senerowitz and predecessor firms, Chgo., 1975-91, Schwartz, Cooper, Greenberger & Krauss, Chgo., 1991-95, Sachnoff & Weaver, Ltd., Chgo., 1995—; instr., adj. prof. clin. trial advocacy Northwestern U. Sch. Law, Chgo., 1985—. Contbr. articles to profl. jours. Pres. Beth Hillel Congregation, 1992-94; nat. chmn. Northwestern U. Law Sch. Fund, 1990-92; golf coach Jewish Cmty. Ctr. MACABBI. Avocations: golf, rafting, travel, reading. General civil litigation, Appellate. Office: Sachnoff & Weaver Ltd 30 S Wacker Dr Fl 29 Chicago IL 60606-7402

**TENGI, FRANK R.,** lawyer, insurance company executive; b. Garfield, N.J., Aug. 11, 1920; s. John and Mary (Fedush) T.; m. Shirley H. Mitchell, May 17, 1952; children: Christopher, Nancy. BS, Georgetown U., 1946; LLD, Fordham U., 1951. CPA, N.J.; lic. ins. broker, N.Y. Bar: N.Y. 1955, U.S. Supreme Ct. 1967, U.S. Ct. Claims 1967, U.S. Dist. Ct. (so. dist.) N.Y. 1967, U.S. Dist. Ct. (ea. dist.) N.Y., 1967, U.S. Tax Ct. 1968. Asst. sec. Am. Internat. Aviation Agy., Inc., N.Y.C., 1961-69; assoc. Lee Mulderig & Celentano, N.Y.C., 1965-70; asst. sec. Am. Internat. Underwriting Corp., N.Y.C., 1965—, Am. Internat. Underwriters Assn., 1965—, Starr Tech. Risks Agy., Inc., 1967-78; asst. comptroller taxation A.I.G., Inc., N.Y.C., 1971-75; asst. sec. C.V. Starr & Co., Inc., N.Y.C., 1965—; pres. Estate Maintenance Co., Inc., N.Y.C., 1969-71; mgr. reinsurance security Worldwide, Am. Internat. Group, Inc., N.Y.C., 1978-96, reins. security adv., 1996—. Mem. Mayor's Budget Adv. Com. Plainfield, 1980-81. Treas., Starr Found., 1970—. Served with U.S. Army, 1941-46; ETO. Mem. N.Y. State Bar Assn., Tax Execs. Inst. General corporate, Corporate taxation, Personal income taxation. Home: 17 Madison Ave Apt 58 Madison NJ 07940-1466 Office: 70 Pine St New York NY 10270-0002

**TENNANT, DORIS FAY,** lawyer, mediator; b. Marianna, Fla., May 26, 1950; d. Charles A. and Erbis W. Tennant; divorced; children: Corina, Hannah. BA cum laude, Emory U., 1972, MA in Tchg., 1978; cert. advanced study, Harvard U., 1980; JD, Boston U., 1989. Bar: U.S. Dist. Ct. Mass. 1989, U.S. Ct. Appeals (1st cir.) 1990. Various tchg. and adminstrv. positions Conn., Atlanta, Vt., 1972-83; prof. Marlboro (Vt.) Coll., 1983-86; assoc. Widett Slater & Goldman, Boston, 1989-93, Palmer & Dodge, Boston, 1993-95; pvt. practice Newton, Mass., 1995—; bd. dirs. Mass. Coun. on Family Mediation. Mem. Human Rights Commn., Newton, 1996—. Mem. ABA, Mass. Bar Assn., Women's Bar Assn., Boston Bar Assn. Family and matrimonial, Alternative dispute resolution. Office: 1200 Walnut St Newton MA 02461-1225

**TENNENT, TYLER D.,** lawyer; b. Detroit, Oct. 20, 1959; s. Richard James and Patricia Anne Tennent; children: Elizabeth, Nicole. BA, Mich. State U., 1981; JD, Detroit Coll. Law, 1984. Bar: Mich. 1984. Assoc. Barbier Tolleson, Mt. Clemens, Mich., 1984-89; ptnr. Clark, Klein & Beaumont, Detroit, 1989-95; mem., ptnr. Dawda, Mann, Bloomfield Hills, Mich., 1995—. Author: Michigan Environmental Law--A Practical Guide, 1997. Mem. ABA, Mich. Bar Assn. (environ. com.), Environ. Mgmt. Assn. Environmental, Real property. Office: Dawda Mann 1533 N Woodward Ave Bloomfield Hills MI 48304-2861

**TENNER, ERIN K.,** lawyer; b. Lansing, Mich., Aug. 30, 1959; d. Robert Lee and Frieda Valencia Tenner. BA, Mich. State U., 1982; JD, U. Detroit, 1985. Bar: Calif. 1986, U.S. Dist. Ct. (ce. dist.) Calif. 1986. Assoc. Pilot, Spar & Siegler, L.A., 1985—. Assoc. editor: U. Det. Law Review, 1983-85. Recipient Am. Jurisprudence award, Bancroft Whitney Co., 1983. Mem. ABA, State Bar of Calif. Contracts commercial, General corporate. Office: Ste 282 100 E Thousand Oaks Blvd Thousand Oaks CA 91360-8143

**TENNEY, DELLAPHINE WOOTEN,** retired court reporter, writer; b. Chattanooga, May 5, 1930; d. Charles Madison Wooten and Belle (Davis) Knight; m. Gene William Ailor, Aug. 2, 1948 (div. May 1959); children—Linda Hughie, Sandra Barnwell, Angela Ailor; m. Frank Leonard Stilin, Feb. 21, 1964 (div. Apr. 1971); 1 child, Andrew; m. Edward Jewett Tenney, II, Feb. 17, 1983. Student U. S.C., 1958-59, Stenotype Inst., Jacksonville Beach, Fla., 1972-74, Lippert Sch. Ct. Reporting, Plainview, Tex., 1974. Cert. court reporter, Ga., Fla., Tenn., Guam, N.H. Former personal sec. to lt. gov. of Ga., Atlanta; legal sec. Witt-Gaither-Abernathy, Chattanooga, 1971-72; pres. Accurate Reporting Service, Chattanooga, 1975-78; dean, chief exec. officer The Stenotype Ctr., Chattanooga, 1978-79; ofcl. ct. reporter Guam Superior Ct., 1979-80, N.H. Superior Ct., Concord, 1980-91; ret., 1991; pres. Life Story Inc. Author, editor, pub. Basic Stenotype Manual, 1979. Sec., Am. Cancer Soc., Aiken, S.C., 1952-53; campaign mgr. election com. for supt. edn., Aiken, 1954. Mem. NAFE, N.H. Shorthand Reporters Assn. (sec., v.p.), Nat. Court Reporters Assn. Republican. Roman Catholic. Avocations: travel, reading, book collecting, biographer, photography. Home: 26144 Constantine Rd Punta Gorda FL 33983-2607

**TENUTA, LUIGIA,** lawyer; b. Madison, Wis., June 4, 1954; d. Eugene P. and Nancy (Gardner) T. AB in Internat. Studies with honors, Miami U., Oxford, Ohio, 1976; JD, Capital U., 1981; postgrad., Pontifical Coll. Josephinum, 1987-88. Bar: Ohio 1981. With internat. mktg. dept. Dresser Industries, Columbus, Ohio, 1976-80; analyst strategic planning Dresser Industries, Columbus, 1980; mgr. internat bus. planning Dresser Industries, Stratford, Conn., 1981; pvt. practice law Columbus, 1981—. Former mem. devel. com. Miami U. Mem. Ohio Bar Assn., Columbus Bar Assn. Roman Catholic. General civil litigation, General practice. Office: 6400 Riverside Dr Dublin OH 43017-5197

**TEPLITZ, ROBERT FORMAN,** lawyer; b. Miami, Fla., Dec. 20, 1970; s. Alan Forman and Judith (Roberts) T. BA magna cum laude, Franklin & Marshall Coll., 1992; JD cum laude, Cornell U., 1995. Bar: Pa. 1995, U.S. Dist. Ct. (mid. dist.) Pa. 1997. Litigation assoc. McNees, Wallace & Nurick, Harrisburg, Pa., 1995-98; dep. chief counsel Dept. Auditor Gen., Harrisburg, 1998—. Bd. dirs. Am. Cancer Soc., Harrisburg, 1996—. Mem. Phi Beta Kappa. Office: Dept of Auditor Gen 235 Fin Bldg Harrisburg PA 17110

**TEPPER, JACQUELINE GAIL,** lawyer, sole practitioner, business consultant; b. N.Y.C., Aug. 14, 1964; d. Marvin and Elise T.; m. David Ian Robinov, May 28, 1989; children: Gregory William, Benjamin Russell. BA magna cum laude, U. Pa., 1986; JD, NYU, 1990. Bar: N.Y. 1991, Conn. 1990, U.S. Dist. Ct. (so. and ea. dists.) N.Y. 1991. Analyst 1st Boston Corp., N.Y.C., 1986-87; law clk., Judge Reena Raggi U.S. Dist. Ct. (ea. dist.) N.Y., Bklyn., 1990-91; assoc. Arnold & Porter, N.Y.C., 1991-93; v.p. bus. affairs WTA Tour, Stamford, Conn., 1993-97; sole practitioner, bus. cons. Stamford, Conn., 1998—. Editl. staff NYU Law Sch. Rev., 1988-90. Mem. N.Y.C. Bar Assn. (sports law com. 1996—), Women's Sports Found. (athletes' rights com. 1996—), Phi Beta Kappa, Pi Sigma Alpha (pres. 1985-86). Sports. Office: 96 Old Mill Ln Stamford CT 06902-1027

**TEPPER, NANCY BOXLEY,** lawyer; b. Richmond, Va., Mar. 7, 1933; d. Joseph Harry and Mathilda (Appell) Boxley; children: Amanda, Nicholas, Eliza. Student, U. Richmond, 1951; BA, Radcliffe Coll., 1953; LLB, Harvard U., 1958. Bar: N.Y. 1958, Calif., 1969. Assoc. Simpson, Thacher & Bartlett, N.Y.C., 1958-63, Robertson, Howser & Garland, Laguna Hills, Calif., 1969-70, Kindel & Anderson, Laguna Hills, 1970-77; freelance legal editor, writer Prentice-Hall, Inc., Englewood, N.J., 1963-69; pres. Nancy Boxley Tepper, Inc., Laguna Hills, 1977—; instr. U. Calif., Irvine, 1971-72. Contbr. articles to legal publs. Endowment counsel South Coast Repertory Theater and Orange County Ctr. for Performing Arts, Costa Mesa, Calif., 1985—; mem. fund raising com. Saddleback Hosp., Laguna Hills, 1989. Mem. ABA, Calif. Bar Assn., Orange County Bar Assn., Orange County Estate Planning Coun., N.Y. State Bar Assn., Harvard Club (Santa Ana, Calif., bd. dirs. 1970-72), Phi Beta Kappa. Avocations: aerobics, music, bicycling, tennis. Estate planning, Probate, Estate taxation. Office: 24031 El Toro Rd Ste 130 Laguna Hills CA 92653-3129

**TEPPER, R(OBERT) BRUCE, JR.,** lawyer; b. Long Branch, N.J., Apr. 1, 1949; s. Robert Bruce and Elaine (Ogus) T.; m. Belinda Wilkins, Nov. 26, 1971; children—Laura Katherine, Jacob Wilkins. A.B. in History, Dartmouth Coll., 1971; J.D. cum laude, St. Louis U., 1976, M.A. in Urban Affairs, 1976. Bar: Mo. 1976, Calif. 1977, Ill. 1978, U.S. Ct. Appeals (7th cir.) 1978, (8th cir.) 1976, (9th cir.) 1978, U.S. Dist. Ct. (cen., no. and so. dists.) Calif. 1978. Asst. gen. counsel St. Louis Redevel. Authority; 1976-77; assoc. Goldstein & Price, St. Louis, 1977-78, Loo, Merideth & McMillan, Los Angeles, 1978-82; sole practice, Los Angeles, 1982-84; sr. prin., CFO Kane, Ballmer and Berkman, Los Angeles, 1984—; litigation counsel to San Diego, Santa Barbara, Huntington Beach, Anaheim, Culver City, Lynwood, Norwalk, Redondo Beach, Oceanside, Ontario, Oxnard, Pasadena, Moreno Valley, Grover Beach, Glendale and Hawthorne, Calif.; spl. counsel redevel. agy. City L.A.; judge pro tempore Los Angeles County Mcpl. Ct., 1983—; grader State Bar Calif., 1980-84. Assoc. editor St. Louis U. Law Jour., 1974-76. Contbr. articles to legal jours. Grad fellow St. Louis U., 1973-76. Mem. Los Angeles County Bar Assn., Assn. Bus. Trial Lawyers, ABA. Republican. Jewish. Clubs: So. Calif. Dartmouth (bd. dirs. 1980-83), Los Angeles Athletic (Los Angeles). Land use and zoning (including planning), Environmental, State civil litigation. Home: 10966 Wrightwood Ln Studio City CA 91604-3957 Office: Kane Ballmer & Berkman 515 S Figueroa St Ste 1850 Los Angeles CA 90071-3335

**TERMINI, ROSEANN BRIDGET,** lawyer, educator; b. Phila., Feb. 2, 1953; d. Vincent James and Bridget (Marano) T. BS magna cum laude, Drexel U., 1975; MEd, Temple U., 1979, JD, 1985, grad. in food and pharmacy law, 1998. Bar: Pa. 1985, U.S. Dist. Ct. (ea. dist.) Pa. 1985, D.C. 1986. Jud. clk. Superior Ct. of Pa., Allentown, 1985-86; atty. Pa. Power & Light Co., Allentown, 1986-87; corp. counsel food and drug law Lemmon Co., Sellersville, Pa., 1987-88; sr. dep. atty. bur. consumer protection plain lang. law Office of Atty. Gen., Harrisburg, Pa., 1988-96; prof. Villanova U. Sch. Law, 1996—; Contbr. articles to profl. jours., law revs.; spkr. continuing legal edn.-plain lang. laws, environ. conf.; adj. prof. Widener U. Sch. Law, 1993—, Dickinson Sch. Law. Author: food quality pharm. publs.; contbr. articles to profl. jours, law revs.; speaker environ. conf. Active in Sr. Citizens Project Outreach, Hospice, 1986—; mem. St. Thomas More Law Bd. Recipient Plain English Prof. Food and Pharmacy Law award, Pa. Mem. ABA (various coms.), Bar Assn. D.C., Pa. Bar Assn. (ethics, exceptional children and environ. sects., Plain English award 1999), Temple U. Law Alumni Assn., Drexel U. Alumni Assn., Omicron Nu, Phi Alpha Delta. Avocations: tap dancing, hiking, cross-country skiing. Home: 1614 Brookhaven Rd Wynnewood PA 19096-2606 Office: Villanova U Law Sch Villanova PA 17120 *Notable cases include: Waste Conversion case, 1990, violation of Pa. Solid Waste Mgmt. Act.*

**TERNER, ANDOR DAVID,** lawyer; b. West Bloomfield, Mich., Feb. 17, 1970; s. Leslie Laszlo and Barbara Toby Terner; m. Joanne Rael Terner, May 26, 1996; 1 child, Jarett Benjamin. BBA, MA in acctg., U. Mich., 1993; JD, Stanford U., 1997. Bar: Calif. 1997; CPA, Mich. Acct. Arthur Andersen & Co., Detroit, 1993-94; assoc. O'Melveny & Myers LLP, Newport Beach, Calif., 1997—. Mem. Order of the Coif, Beta Gamma Sigma. General corporate, Mergers and acquisitions, Securities. Office: O'Melveny & Myers LLP 610 Newport Center Dr Newport Beach CA 92660-6419

**TERNUS, MARSHA K.,** state supreme court justice; b. Vinton, Iowa, May 30, 1951. BA, U. Iowa, 1972; JD, Drake U., 1977. Bar: Iowa. 1977, Ariz. 1984. With Bradshaw, Fowler, Proctor & Fairgrave, Des Moines, Iowa, 1977-93; justice Iowa Supreme Ct., Des Moines, 1993—. Editor-in-chief Drake Law Rev., 1976-77. Mem. Polk County Bar Assn. (pres. 1984-85), Phi Beta Kappa, Order of Coif. Office: Iowa Supreme Ct State Capital Bldg Des Moines IA 50319-0001

**TERP, THOMAS THOMSEN,** lawyer; b. Fountain Hill, Pa., Aug. 12, 1947; s. Norman T. and Josephine (Uhran) T.; m. Pamela Robinson; children: Stephanie, Brian, Adam; step-children: Taylor Mefford, Grace Mefford. BA, Albion (Mich.) Coll., 1969; JD, Coll. of William and Mary, 1973. Bar: Ohio 1973, U.S. Dist. Ct. (so. dist.) Ohio 1973, U.S. Ct. Appeals (6th cir.) 1973, U.S. Supreme Ct. 1979. Assoc. Taft, Stettinius & Hollister, Cin., 1973-80, ptnr., 1981—; bd. dirs. Starflo Corp., Orangeburg, S.C., Attorney's Liability Assurance Soc., Ltd., Hamilton, Bermuda, ALAS, Inc., Chgo. Editor-in-chief William & Mary Law Rev., 1972-73; mem. bd. editors Jour. of Environ. Hazards, 1988—, Environ. Law Jour. of Ohio, 1989—. Mem. Cin. Athletic Club, Coldstream Country Club, Epworth Assembly (Ludington, Mich.), Lincoln Hills Golf Club (Ludington), Queen City Club. Avocations: tennis, golf, travel. General civil litigation, Environmental. Office: 1800 Star Bank Ctr 425 Walnut St Cincinnati OH 45202-3923

**TERRA, SHARON ECKER,** lawyer; b. Pitts., Jan. 12, 1959; d. James and Carole Dombro Ecker; m. Edward George Terra, Feb. 8, 1987. BA, Rollins Coll., 1980; JD, Nova Law Sch., 1988. Bar: Fla. 1988, U.S. Dist. Ct. (so. dist.) Fla. 1989, Pa. 1990, U.S. Dist. Ct. (we. dist.) Pa. 1990. Staff acct. Arthur Andersen & Co., Miami, 1980-81; fin. officer Embraer Aircraft Corp., Ft. Lauderdale, Fla., 1981-82; pvt. practice Hollywood, Fla., 1988-90, Pitts., 1990—. Mem. ABA, AICPA's, Allegheny County Bar Assn., Am. Trial Lawyers Assn. Republican. General practice, Personal injury, Criminal. Home: 1057 Old Orchard Dr Gibsonia PA 15044-6081 Office: Ecker Ecker & Ecker 1116 Frick Building Pittsburgh PA 15219-6165

**TERRELL, J. ANTHONY,** lawyer; b. N.Y.C., Sept. 20, 1943; s. Claude M. and Kathleen L. (Prevost) T.; m. Karen E. Terrell, Aug. 8, 1969; 1 child, Elizabeth S. BA, NYU, 1965, LLM in Taxation, 1975; JD, Villanova U., 1968. Bar: N.Y. With Frueauff, Farrell, Sullivan & Bryan, N.Y.C., 1970-74, ptnr., 1974; assoc. Thelen Reid & Priest LLP, N.Y.C., 1974-76, ptnr., 1977—. Mem. ABA (sect. bus. law, sect. pub. utility, comm. and transp. law, vice chmn. corp. finance com.), Internat. Bar Assn. (bus. law sect.), Nat. Assn. Bond Lawyers, Belle Haven Club, Met. Club, Coral Beach and Tennis Club. General corporate, Securities, Finance. Home: Indian Harbor Greenwich CT 06830 Office: Thelen Reid & Priest LLP 40 W 57th St New York NY 10019-4001

**TERRELL, JAMES DANIEL,** lawyer; b. Kansas City, Oct. 22, 1956; s. D. Ronald and Bobbie L. (Graham) T.; m. Lori J. McAlister, May 31, 1980; children: Justin Daniel, Christopher James, Alexander Graham. BS, Ctrl. Mo. State U., 1979; JD, U. Mo., 1982. Bar: Mo. 1982, U.S. Dist. Ct. (we. dist.) 1982, U.S. Dist. Ct. (ea. dist.) Mo. 1984. Assoc. Wasinger, Parham & Morthland, Hannibal, Mo., 1982-87; ptnr. Wasinger, Parham, Morthland Terrell & Wasinger, Hannibal, 1987—. Bd. dirs. Marion County Svcs. for the Developmentally Disabled, Hannibal, 1989—. Mem. Mo. Bar Assn. (family law sect.), 10th Jud. Cir. Bar Assn., U. Mo. Alumni Assn. (life), Phi Delta Phi. Family and matrimonial, General civil litigation, Insurance. Office: Wasinger Parham Morthland Terrell & Wasinger 2801 Saint Marys Ave Hannibal MO 63401-3775

**TERRY, B. BRENT,** laywer; b. Louisville, Dec. 7, 1968; s. Bobby Swede and Eleanor (Foster) T.; m. Lee Ann, May 22, 1993. BA in History, William Jewell Coll., 1991; JD, Emory U., 1994. Bar: Ga. 1994. Sr. assoc. Attys. at Law Smith, Atlanta, 1994—. Risk mgmt. com. Briardale Bapt. Ch., Decatur, Ga., 1996-98. Mem. ABA, ATLA, Ga. Trial Lawyers Assn., Christian Legal Soc. Avocations: choral music, reading, politics, church activities, sports. Office: PO Box 450909 Atlanta GA 31145-0909

**TERRY, CRAIG ROBERT,** lawyer; b. Lake Charles, La., Oct. 18, 1955; s. Robert J. and Elodie S. (Shattuck) T.; m. Linda N. Smith, Feb. 20, 1990; children: Ian W., Lindsay N. BA, U. Tex., 1980; MA, U. Ariz., 1985, JD, 1987. Bar: Tex. 1994. Law clk. Linden, Chapa & Fields, Tucson, 1985-86, Barassi & Burris, Tucson, 1986-87; tchg. asst. dept. psychology U. Ariz., Tucson, 1984-88; contractor litigation support Tucson, 1988-90; pvt. practice Austin, Tex., 1994—; mem. adv. com. Nat. Forest Mgmt. of Ariz., Tucson, 1984. Mem. Travis County Bar Assn. (mem. alt. dispute resolution sect., family law sect., entertainment/sports law sect.), Coll. of State Bar of Tex. Alternative dispute resolution, Family and matrimonial, Entertainment. Office: 1201 Rio Grande St Ste 200 Austin TX 78701-1709

**TERRY, DAVID WILLIAM,** lawyer; b. Temple, Tex., May 21, 1958; s. Victor Lewis and Jon Gayle (Kirschner) T.; m. Katherine Ellen Noll, Dec. 5, 1987; children: Nicholas William, John Benjamin. BA, Colo. Coll., 1981; JD, South Tex. Coll. Law, 1985. Bar: Tex. 1986, U.S. Dist. Ct. (no. and ea. dists.) Tex. Briefing atty. U.S. Ct. Appeals (4th cir.), San Antonio, 1986-87; pvt. practice Dallas, 1987—. Exec. editor South Tex. Law Rev., 1985. Pres. East Dallas Cppr. Parish, 1992. Mem. Tex. Trial Lawyers Assn. (bd. dirs. 1992—), Am. Assn. Portrait Artists, Dallas Trial Lawyers Assn. (bd. dirs. 1994—), ATLA, Coll. State Bar Tex. (pro bono coll.). Democrat. Methodist. Avocations: oil painting, portraits and landscapes. Personal injury, Product liability. Office: 12221 Merit Dr Ste 1650 Dallas TX 75251-2280

**TERRY, FREDERICK ARTHUR, JR.,** lawyer; b. Buffalo, May 24, 1932; s. Frederick Arthur and Agnes Elizabeth (Tranter) T.; m. Barbara Anderson. BA, Williams Coll., 1953; LLB, Columbia U., 1956. Bar: N.Y. 1957, U.S. Dist. Ct. (so., no. and ea. dists.) N.Y., U.S. Ct. Appeals (2d cir.), U.S. Tax Ct., U.S. Supreme Ct. Law clk. U.S. Ct. Appeals (2nd cir.), 1956-57; assoc. Sullivan & Cromwell, N.Y.C., 1957-65, ptnr., 1965—. Bd. dirs. Eisenhower Exch. Fellowships, Natural Resources Def. Coun., Weinman Found.; sec., mem. bd. McIntosh Found.; trustee, chmn. com. on trust and estate gift plans Rockefeller U.; trustee Harold K. Hochschild Found.; chmn. Flagler Found. Mem. ABA, N.Y. State Bar Assn., Assn. Bar City N.Y., Century Assn., River Club, Union Club, Maidstone Club (East Hampton, N.Y.), Lyford Cay Club (Bahamas), The Bathing Corp. (Southampton, N.Y.). Estate planning. Office: Sullivan & Cromwell 125 Broad St Fl 25 New York NY 10004-2400

**TERRY, JACK CHATTERSON,** lawyer; b. Monett, Mo., Nov. 23, 1919; s. Jacob E. and Florence V. (Chatterson) T.; m. Susan W. Terry, June 7, 1941; children: Susan L. Terry Galewaler, Philip C. BA in History and Govt., U. Mo., Kansas City, 1949, JD, 1952. Bar: Mo. 1952, U.S. Supreme Ct. 1961. Sole practice Independence, Mo., 1952—; mem. Mo. Legislature, 1955-56; legis. liaison officer Jackson County (Mo.), 1967-68; atty. Inter-City Fire Protection Dist., 1955-74; city atty. City of Blue Summit (Mo.), 1971-76; atty. Jackson County (Mo.) Bd. Election Commrs., 1974-99. Pres. Independence Good Govt. League, 1961-63, Jackson County League Better Govt., 1962-66. Served as officer USAAF, 1941-46, PTO. Decorated Purple Heart, Air medal. Mem. ABA, Mo. Bar Assn., Kansas City Bar Assn., Inter-City Kiwanis (pres. 1967), Masons, Shriners. Democrat. Mem. Christian Ch. (Disciples of Christ). General practice, State civil litigation, Family and matrimonial. Home: 614 Bellevista Dr Independence MO 64055-1746 Office: 554 S Ash St PO Box 7800 Independence MO 64053

**TERRY, JOHN ALFRED,** state supreme court judge; b. Utica, N.Y., May 6, 1933; s. Robert Samuel and Julia Berenice (Collins) T. B.A. magna cum laude, Yale U., 1954; J.D., Georgetown U., 1960. Bar: D.C. 1960. Asst. U.S. atty. for D.C., 1962-67; staff atty. Nat. Commn. Reform of Fed. Criminal Laws, Washington, 1967-68; pvt. practice law Washington, 1968-69; chief appellate div. U.S. Atty.'s Office for D.C., 1969-82; judge D.C. Ct. Appeals, 1982—. Mem. D.C. Bar (bd. govs. 1977-82), ABA, Phi Beta Kappa. Office: DC Ct Appeals 500 Indiana Ave NW Washington DC 20001-2138

**TERRY, JOHN HART,** lawyer, former utility company executive, former congressman; b. Syracuse, N.Y., Nov. 14, 1924; s. Frank and Saydee (Hart) T.; m. Catherine Jean Taylor Phelan, Apr. 15, 1950; children: Catherine Jean (Mrs. Richard Thompson), Lynn Marie (Mrs. Robert Tacher), Susan Louise (Mrs. Stanley Germain), Mary Carole (Mrs. Stephen Brady). B.A., U. Notre Dame, 1945; J.D., Syracuse U., 1948. Bar: N.Y. bar 1950, D.C. bar 1972. Asst. to partner Smith & Sovik, 1948-59; asst. sec. to Gov. State of N.Y., 1959-61; sr. partner firm Smith, Sovik, Terry, Kendrick, McAuliffe & Schwarzer, 1961-73; sr. v.p., gen. counsel, sec. Niagara Mohawk Power Corp., Syracuse, 1973-87; counsel Hiscock & Barclay, Syracuse, 1987-94; atty. in pvt. practice, 1994—; mem. N.Y. State Assembly, 1962-70, 92d Congress from 34th N.Y. Dist., 1971-73; presdl. elector, 1972. State chmn. United Services Orgn., 1964-73; past pres. John Timothy Smith Found.; Founder, dir. Bishop Foery Found., Inc.; dir. St. Joseph's Hosp. Council; past pres. Lourdes Camp; bd. dirs. N.Y. State Traffic Council; past nat. bd. dirs. Am. Cancer Soc.; mem. adv. council Syracuse U. Sch. Mgmt.; past pres. Cath. Youth Orgn.; bd. dirs. Syracuse Community Baseball Club. Served to 1st lt. AUS, 1943-46. Decorated Purple Heart, Bronze Star; named Man of Year Syracuse Jr. C. of C., 1958, Man of Yr. N.Y. State Jr. C. of C., 1959, Young Man of Yr. U. Notre Dame Club Cen. N.Y., 1959; recipient U. Notre Dame Exemplar award, 1997, Rev. Theodore Hesborgh Alumni award, 1997. Mem. ABA (utility law sect.), N.Y. State Bar Assn. (chmn. com. on public utility law), Onondaga County Bar Assn. (chmn. membership and legis. coms.), D.C. Bar Assn., County Officers Assn., Citizens Found., U. Notre Dame, Syracuse U. law assns., Am. Legion, VFW, DAV, 40 and 8, Mil. Order of Purple Heart, Bellevue Country Club, Capitol Hill Club (Washington), Vero Beach Country Club. Roman Catholic. General corporate, FERC practice, General practice.

**TERRY, JOSEPH H.,** lawyer; b. Louisville, July 9, 1945; s. Wilbur H. and Reba Mae Terry; m. Donna Lynn Hogg, Apr. 21, 1967; children: Anne Griffin, Alexandra E. BA, U. Louisville, 1968; JD with distinction, U. Ky., 1971. Bar: Ky. 1971, U.S. Dist. Ct. (we. dist.) Ky. 1971, U.S. Ct. Appeals (6th cir.) 1975, U.S. Dist. Ct. (ea. dist.) Ky. 1983. Assoc., then ptnr. Middleton Reutlinger & Baird, Louisville, 1971-75; ptnr. Eldred Paxton & Terry, Princeton, Ky., 1975-79; spl. counsel Ligon Specialized Hauler Inc., Madisonville, Ky., 1979-80, pres., 1980-82; ptnr. Wyatt, Tarrant & Combs, Lexington, Ky., 1983-97, Dinsmore & Shohl, Lexington, 1997—. Contbr. articles to profl. jours. Vice chmn. Lexington Transit Auth., 1984-91, Lexington Area Sports Authority, 1998; chmn. Ky. Registry of Elections, Frankfort, 1988-95. Fellow ABA (life); mem. Ky. Bar Assn., Sports Lawyers Assn. Democrat. Presbyterian. Avocation: golf. General corporate, Mergers and acquisitions, Sports. Home: 1805 Saint Ives Cir Lexington KY 40502-7714 Office: Dinsmore & Shohl 250 W Main St Ste 2020 Lexington KY 40507-1714

**TERRY, JOSEPH RAY, JR.,** lawyer; b. Vicksburg, Miss., Aug. 10, 1938; s. Joseph Ray Sr. and Alma Blanche (Smith) T.; m. Louise Caroline Beland, July 17, 1965; children: Kathleen A., Marie L., Bernard R. JD, Loyola U., 1965. Bar: D.C. 1966, Miss. 1968, U.S. Ct. Appeals (5th cir.) 1971, Ga. 1973, U.S. Dist. Ct. (no. and so. dists.) Ga. 1973, U.S. Ct. Appeals (D.C. cir.) 1973, U.S. Supreme Ct. 1973, U.S. Ct. Appeals (8th cir.) 1974, U.S. Dist. Ct. (we. dist.) Tenn. 1983, U.S. Ct. Appeals (6th cir.) 1989. Trial atty. civil rights div. U.S. Dept. Justice, Washington, 1966-69; assoc. regional counsel U.S. Dept. HUD, Atlanta, 1969-70; ptnr. Crosland, Myer, Rindskopf & Terry, Atlanta, 1974-76; regional counsel EEOC, Atlanta, 1970-73, supr. trial atty. Litigation Cen., 1976-79; regional atty. EEOC, Memphis, 1979-96; dep. gen. counsel EEOC, Washington, 1996-99, cons., lectr., 1999—; part-time asst. atty. City of Atlanta, 1975-76; cons. NLRB, Memphis, 1981-82; adj. prof. law Emory U., 1971-75; vis. prof. law St. Louis U., 1973-74, William C. Wefel vis. prof. law, 1998—; acting program dir. EEOC, 1983, acting dist. dir., 1984-85; bd. dirs. Fed. Credit Union, 1984-91; mem. adv. com. to U.S. Dist. Ct. for western dist. Tenn., 1990-93, chmn. case mgmt. subcom., 1991-98; mem. faculty Southwestern Legal Found., Dallas, spring 1998; cons. equal employment, 1999—. Author: (jour.) Eliminating the Plaintiff's Attorney in Equal Employment Litigation: A Shakespearean Tragedy, Labor Lawyer, 1989, Memphis and Race, The Commercial Appeal, 1987. Cons. Alaska Human Rights Commn., Anchorage, 1981; bd. dirs. Nat. Kidney Found. of West Tenn., Memphis, pres., 1984-85; bd. dirs. United Meth. Neighborhood Ctr., 1985-88; bd. dirs. St. Patrick's Parish Coun., Memphis, pres., 1986-88; mem. Leadership Memphis, 1988-99; bd. dirs. Place of Grace Ministries, Carlisle, Pa., 1997—. Named Honor Law Graduate U.S. Atty. Gen., 1965. Mem. ABA (EEOC liaison com. 1987-89), Fed. Bar Assn. (bd. dirs. 1988-89, v.p. West Tenn. chpt. 1991-92, pres. 1993-94, nat. coun. 1996—, named Younger Fed. Lawyer of Yr. 1973), Supreme Ct. Hist. Soc., St. Thomas More Lawyers Guild, Salvation Army (bd. dirs. 1995-96). Roman Catholic. Avocations: tennis, golf, skiing, hiking, reading. Home: 1560 Harbert Ave Memphis TN 38104-5033

**TERRY, MICHAEL JOSEPH,** courtroom clerk; b. Mount Ayr, Iowa, Aug. 26, 1957; s. John Stanley and Kathryn Marie (Williams) T. BS in Psychology, Santa Clara U., 1979, paralegal cert., 1987. Dep. ct. clk. Santa Clara County Mcpl. Ct., San Jose, Calif., 1980-86; ct. attendent Santa Clara County Superior Ct., San Jose, 1986-87; courtroom clk. Santa Clara County Superior Ct., San Jose, Calif., 1987—. Editor: Crimson Warrior Pub., 1992—. Mem. ACLU, Courtroom Clks. Assn., World Affairs Coun., Phi Delta Phi (life). Democrat. Avocations: literature, travel, theatre. Office: Superior Ct 170 Park Center Plz San Jose CA 95113-2219

**TERRY, PANDORA ELAINE,** lawyer; b. East Point, Ga., Dec. 12, 1965; d. Perry Monroe and Doreen (Murphy) Dykes; m. Wilbur Ray Terry, Aug. 14, 1989; 1 child, Tiffany Nicole. BA in Criminal Justice, U. Ga., 1988; JD, Ga. State U., 1994. Bar: Ga. 1994, U.S. Ct. Appeals (11th cir.) 1994, U.S. Dist. Ct. (no. dist.) Ga. 1995. Rsch. asst. Capital Jury Project, 1992-93; legal extern Fed. Pub. Defender, Atlanta, 1993; rsch. asst. Ga. Justice Project, Atlanta, 1993-94; attu. pvt. practice, Jonesboro, Ga., 1994—. Mem. ABA, Assn. Trial Lawyers Am., Nat. Assn. Criminal Defense Lawyers, Am. Bus. Women's Assn., Ga. Trial Lawyers Assn., Ga. Assn. Criminal Defense Lawyers, Clayton County Bar Assn., Fayette County Bar Assn. Republican. Baptist. Criminal, Family and matrimonial, Personal injury. Home: 345 Plantation Cir Riverdale GA 30296-1106

**TERRY, ROBERT BROOKS,** lawyer; b. Kansas City, Mo., July 7, 1956; s. Frank R. and Susan S. (Smart) T.; m. Penny Susan Kanterman, July 2, 1987; children: Ryan, Kevin, Erin. Student, Vanderbilt U., 1974-75; BS in Acctg., U. Mo., 1978, JD, 1981. Bar: Mo. 1981, U.S. Dist. ct. (we. dist.) Mo. 1981, U.S. ct. Appeals (8th and 10th cirs.) 1983. Assoc. Spencer, Fane, Britt & Browne, Kansas City, Mo., 1981—; v.p., gen. counsel Farmland Industries, Inc., Kansas City, 1993—. Mem. ABA, Kansas City Mo. Bar Assn., Lawyers' Assn. Kansas City, Order of Coif. Avocation: baseball. Labor. Home: 4952 W 132 Terrace Leawood KS 66209 Office: Farmland Industries Inc PO Box 7305 3315 N Oak Trfy Kansas City MO 64116-2798

**TERRY, WARD EDGAR, JR.,** lawyer; b. Denver, Aug. 1, 1943; s. Ward E. and Peggy Helen Louise (Smith) T.; m. Juliann DiRe, Apr. 8, 1967; children: Seth S., Nicole E. BA, U. Colo., 1965, JD, 1968; LLM in Taxation, U. Denver, 1976. Bar: Colo. 1968, U.S. Dist. Ct. Colo. 1968, U.S. Tax Ct. 1980. Assoc. McMartin & Burk, Englewood, Colo., 1968-70, Modesitt & Shaw, Denver, 1970-71, Gorsuch, Kirgis, Campbell, Walker & Grover, Denver, 1971-72, Hopper and Kanouff, Denver, 1976-78; sec., dir. Ward Terry and Co., Denver, 1972-76; ptnr. Hopper, Kanouff, Smith, Peryam & Terry, Denver, 1979-91; shareholder Hopper and Kanouff, P.C., Denver, 1991-96, v.p., bd. dirs.; shareholder, v.p., sec., treas., dir. Terry, Syke & Graham, P.C., 1996-97; shareholder, dir. Clanahan, Tanner, Downing & Knowlton, P.C., Denver, 1997—; gen. ptnr. PSW Investments Ltd., Denver, 1984—. Trustee Denver Country Day Sch., Englewood, 1969-70; campaign chair Roseanne Ball Election Com., Denver, 1974. Mem. ABA (bus. law sect., real estate and probate sect., taxation sect., antitrust sect.), Colo. Bar Assn. (bus. law and taxation sect.), Denver Bar Assn., Denver Gyro Club (pres. 1994-95, v.p. 1993-94, membership chmn. 1991-92), Phi Alpha Delta. Republican. Presbyterian. Avocations: long-distance running, golf, skiing, bicycling. Securities, Mergers and acquisitions, Corporate taxation. Office: Clanahan Tanner Downing & Knowlton PC 730 17th St Ste 500 Denver CO 80202-3580

**TERSCHAN, FRANK ROBERT,** lawyer; b. Dec. 25, 1949; s. Frank Joseph and Margaret Anna (Heidt) T.; m. Barbara Elizabeth Keily, Dec. 28, 1974; 1 child, Frank Martin. BA, Syracuse U., 1972; JD, U. Wis., 1975. Bar: Wis. 1976, U.S. Dist. Ct. (ea. and we. dists.) Wis. 1976, U.S. Ct. Appeals (7th cir.) 1979, U.S. Ct. Appeals (10th cir.) 1989, U.S. Supreme Ct. 1992. From assoc. to ptnr. Frisch, Dudek & Slattery Ltd., Milw., 1975-88; ptnr. Slattery and Hausman Ltd., Milw., 1988-94, Terschan & Steinle Ltd., Milw., 1994-96, Terschan, Steinle & Ness, Milw., 1996—. Treas., sec. Ville du Park Homeowners Assn., Mequon, Wis., 1985-86; cub scout packmaster pack 3844 Boy Scouts Am., 1989-90, asst. scoutmaster Troop 865, 1991-93. Mem. ABA, Am. Bd. Trial Advocates, Wis. Bar Assn., Milw. Bar Assn., Assn. Trial Lawyers Am., Wis. Acad. of Trial Lawyers (bd. dirs. 1996—), 7th Cir. Bar Assn., Order of Coif. Republican. Lutheran. Avocations: swimming, coin collecting, reading, outdoor activities. Personal injury, General civil litigation, Federal civil litigation. Home: 10143 N Lake Shore Dr Mequon WI 53092-6109 Office: 2600 N Mayfair Rd Ste 700 Milwaukee WI 53226-1307

**TERSCHLUSE, VAL,** lawyer; b. Union, Mo., Oct. 5, 1926; s. J. Frank and Theresa C. (Hoeckelmann) T.; m. Janet M. Dickerson, July 14, 1951; children: David, Marilyn A. Hanish, Mark, Valerie M. Alderfer. JD, St. Louis Sch. Law, 1951. Bar: Mo. 1951. Pvt. practice St. Louis, 1951—. With USNR, 1944-46. Mem. Assn. Trial Lawyers Am., Fed. Bar Assn., Mo. Bar Assn., St. Louis County Bar Assn., Bar Assn. Met. St. Louis. Home: 1982 Karlin Dr Saint Louis MO 63131-1701 Office: 2300 W Port Plz Dr Ste 100 Saint Louis MO 63146-3213

**TERTERIAN, GEORGE,** lawyer; b. Beirut, Lebanon, Jan. 30, 1966; s. Ohannes Terterian and Sirvart Kelian. BA, Wayne State U., 1988, JD, 1991. Bar: Calif. 1994, U.S. Dist. Ct. (ctrl. dist.) Calif. 1994. Pvt. practice Encino, Calif., 1995—. Mem. ABA, ATLA, CAAC, Consumer Attys. Assn. of L.A., Kessab Ednl. Assn. (bd. dirs.), Phi Alpha Theta. Democrat. Avocations: travel, cooking, studying, history, athletics. General civil litigation, Personal injury. Office: Penthouse 16133 Ventura Blvd Ph A Encino CA 91436-2447

**TERZICH, MILOS,** lawyer; b. Portola, Calif., Oct. 25, 1934; s. Spaso and Saveta (Porobich) T.; children: Kimberly Ann, Sam; m. Lyane Terzich, Dec. 12, 1987. AA, Stockton Jr. Coll., 1954; BA, U. Calif., Berkeley, 1959. Bar: Calif. 1963, Nev. 1969. Atty. Office Calif. Atty. Gen., Sacramento, 1963-68; bill drafter to legis. counsel Carson City, Nev., 1968-69; assoc. Breen, Young, Whitehead et al, Reno, Nev., 1969-74, Zephyr Cove, Nev., 1974-78; pvt. practice Zephyr Cove, 1978-83, Gardnerville, Nev., 1982-91; ptnr. Terzich & Jackson, Ltd., Gardnerville, 1991—. Profl. lobbyist in Nev. Legis., 1971-83; trustee Citizens for Justice Trust Fund, Nev., 1975-87. With USMC, 1954-57. Mem. Nev. Trial Lawyers Assn. (bd. govs. 1971-88, v.p. 1983-88, gov. emeritus 1988—), Carson Valley C. of C. and Vis. Authority Inc. (bd. dirs. 1992-99, pres. 1997-98), Ducks Unltd. (area chmn. 1983-84, zone chmn. 1985-86), Masons. Republican. State civil litigation, Personal injury, Real property. Office: PO Box 1210 Gardnerville NV 89410-1210

**TESKE, STEVEN CECIL,** lawyer; b. Tucson, Ariz., Mar. 4, 1960; s. Ronald Dean and Barbara Elizabeth T.; m. Deborah Ann Appling, Mar. 12, 1983; children: DeAnna Marie, Jacquelyn Suzanne, Joshua Stephen. AA, Clayton State Coll. & U., 1981; B of Indisciplinary Studies, Ga. State U., 1983, MA in Polit. Sci., 1988, JD, 1991. Bar: Ga. 1992, U.S. Dist. Ct. (no. dist.) Ga. 1995, U.S. Ct. Appeals (11th cir.) 1997, U.S. Supreme Ct. 1997. Paralegal Ga. Dept. Labor, Atlanta, 1981-84; parole officer Ga. Bd. Pardons & Parole, Atlanta, 1984-90, deputy chief, 1990-92, cheif parole officer, 1992-94, asst. dir., 1994-95; assoc. Stephen E. Boswell, Atlanta, 1995-97; ptnr. Boswell & Teske, Jonesboro, Ga., 1997—. Mem. ABA, Am. Correctional Assn. (del assembly 1993-95), Clayton County Bar Assn. Democrat. Methodist. Avocations: stamp collecting, swimming. General civil litigation, Criminal, General corporate. Home: 1752 Brenda Dr Jonesboro GA 30236-3361 Office: Boswell & Teske PO Box 1507 Jonesboro GA 30237-1507

**TESMER, LOUISE M.,** judge, lawyer. BA, U. Wis., 1964, JD with honors, 1967. Bar: Wis. 1968. Mcpl. judge St. Francis, Wis., 1966-67; asst. dist. atty. Milwaukee County, 1967-72; judge Milwaukee County Cir. Ct., 1989-92, Milwaukee County Criminal Misdemeanor & Traffic Ct., 1992-97; judge family divsn. Milwaukee County Ct., 1997—; pvt. practice lawyer Wis., 1972—; guest lectr. U. Wis. Milw., U. Wis. Whitewater, Mt. Mary Coll. others; guest spkrs. various Milw. schs. and civic groups. Mem. Wis. Assembly, spkr. Pro Tempore, 1981, mem. various commns.; mem. bd. visitors U. Wis. Law Sch.; bd. dirs. Milw. YWCA; mem. adv. bd. Skylight Theatre, Milw. County Protective Svcs.; mem. Am. Coun. Young Polit. Leaders, del. to Soviet Union, 1974. Recipient Law Enforcement award Milw. Police Assn., 1988, Disting. Svc. to Wis. Veterans award Am. Legion, 1987, others. Mem. Wis. State Bar Assn., Mcpl. Justice Assn., Milw. Assn. Women Lawyers.

**TESON, FERNANDO ROBERTO,** law educator, consultant; b. Buenos Aires, Aug. 3, 1950; s. Roberto Julio and Marta (Grun) T.; m. Maria Teresa Martinez, Nov. 11, 1976 (div. Feb. 1992); children: Fernando, Marcelo; m. Bettina C. Rauleder, Oct. 11, 1996; 1 child, Carolina. Grad., U. Buenos Aires, 1975; lic. internat. law, U. Libre de Bruxelles, Brussels, 1982; JD, Northwestern U., 1987. Assoc. prof. law Ariz. State U., Tempe, 1984-88, prof. law, 1988—; vis. prof. San Diego Summer Program, Mex., 1987, Dublin, Ireland, 1988, Paris, 1990, 93, Hastings Law Sch., San Francisco, Spring 1990, Cardozo Law Sch., N.Y.C., Fall 1992, Ind. U., Bloomington, Spring 1993, Cornell U., Ithaca, N.Y., 1994-95; permanent vis. prof. Di Tella U., Buenos Aires, 1996—; career diplomate Argentina Govt., Buenos Aires, 1977-81; prof. George Washington/Oxford U. Internat. Human Rights Program, New College, Oxford, 1999. Author: A Philosophy of International Law, Humanitarian Intervention: An Inquiry into Law and Morality, 2d edit.; contbr. articles to profl. jours. James N. Raymond fellow Northwestern U., 1982-83. Mem. Am. Soc. Internat. Law, Am. Soc. Social and Polit. Philosophy. Avocations: music, bridge, food. Home: 1355 E McNair Dr Tempe AZ 85283-5022 Office: Ariz State U Coll of Law Tempe AZ 85287-7906

**TESSIER, DENNIS MEDWARD,** paralegal, lecturer, legal advisor, consultant; b. Royal Oak, Mich., Sept. 20, 1956; s. Medward James and Marilyn (Pitsos) T.; m. Michelle Terri Zeichick, July 28, 1990; 1 child, Brian Jae. Cert. paralegal, U. West L.A., 1987, cert. atty. practice, 1990; cert. in epidemiology, U.S. CDC, 1991. Reprodn. analyst Burroughs Corp., Detroit, 1975-76; mixologist Holiday Inn, Inc., Belair, Calif., 1977-83; spl. asst. office of the gen. counsel U.S. Jud. Intelligence Agy., Pacific Sta., L.A., 1981—; mixologist R.W. Grace Inc., Marina Del Rey, Calif., 1984-86; paralegal O'Melveny & Myers, L.A., 1986, Haight, Brown & Bonesteel, Santa Monica, Calif., 1987-93, Helsell & Fetterman, Seattle, 1993-94, Nintendo of Am. Inc., Redmond, Wash., 1994-96, Tessier Marine Custom Made Tunnel Hydroplanes, 1994—, Tousley Brain PLLC, Seattle, 1996—, Tessier Corvettes, 1996—, Tessier Am. Shelby & Mustang Restorations, 1997—; family law cons. Helping Svcs., L.A., 1990-93, L.A. Clinic, 1990; researcher Tessier & Assocs. Rsch., Topanga Canyon, Calif., 1983—, Tessier Marine, Custom Hydroplanes, 1994—, Tessier Am. Mustang and Shelby Restomods, 1995—, Tessier Corvettes, 1996—; with Starlight Found., Redmond, Wash., 1993—. Author: Beauty in Motion, 1983, Champerty and Barratry, 1998, Creek Rat Esquire, 1999; contbr. articles to profl. jours. Mem. ABA (sci. and tech. law, jud. adminstrn. sects.), ATLA, Am. Power Boat Assn., Seattle Outboard Assn., Soc. Epidemiology Rsch., Am. Power Boat Assn., Seattle Outboard Assn., Assn. Investigative Scis., U.S. Nat. Acad. Scis. Academe Industry Program (spkr. CLE). Democrat. Lutheran. Avocations: music, arts. Home: 21100 Pioneer Way Edmonds WA 98026-6947 Office: Tousley Brain PLLC 700 5th Ave Ste 5600 Seattle WA 98104-5056

**TESSLER, ROBERT LOUIS,** lawyer; b. Newark, Apr. 6, 1938; s. Max and Charlotte (Paskow) T.; m. Linda Gottlieb, 1991; 1 child, David Alan. BA, Hamilton Coll., 1959; JD, Columbia U., 1963. Bar: N.J. 1963, U.S. Dist. Ct. N.J. 1963, N.Y. 1983. Ptnr. Yankowitz & Tessler, Newark, 1963-78; assoc. Julien & Schlesinger, N.Y.C., 1978-84; ptnr. Toberoff, Tessler & Schochet, N.Y.C., 1984—; atty. Zoning Bd. of West Orange (N.J.), 1980-85. Chmn. Essex County chpt. ACLU, Newark, 1973-76; county committeeman N.J. Democratic Party, 1973-78; chmn. bd. Nat. Music Theater Network, 1989—. Mem. ATLA, N.Y. Trial Lawyers Assn., Am. Inns of Ct. Jewish. Avocation: musical theater organization devoted to developing new works in opera and musicals. Personal injury, Product liability. Office: Toberoff Tessler & Schochet 350 5th Ave Ste 5314 New York NY 10118-5314

**TESTA, RICHARD JOSEPH,** lawyer; b. Marlboro, Mass., Apr. 21, 1939; s. Joseph N. and Jeannette (Clement) T.; children: Jo-Anne, Richard J. Jr., Nancy, Susan, Karen. AB, Assumption Coll., 1959; LLB, Harvard U., 1962. Bar: Mass. 1962. Sr. ptnr. Testa, Hurwitz & Thibeault, Boston, 1973—. Mem. ABA. Roman Catholic. General corporate, General civil litigation. Office: Testa Hurwitz & Thibeault High St Tower 125 High St Fl 22 Boston MA 02110-2725

**TESTANI, ROSA ANNA,** lawyer; b. N.Y.C., Oct. 1, 1963; d. Ernesto and Antonietta (Sanita) T. BS, Fordham U., 1985; JD, Yale U., 1988. Bar: Conn. 1988, N.Y. 1989, U.S. Dist. Ct. (so. dist.) N.Y. 1990. Assoc. Skadden, Arps, Slate, Meagher & Flom, N.Y.C., 1988—. Contbr. articles to profl. jours. (Israel Peres award 1988). Fordham Presdl. Merit scholar, 1981; Phi Kappa Phi fellow, 1985. Mem. ABA, Bar Assn. of City of N.Y. Avocations: traveling, photography, cooking. General corporate, Securities. Home: 19627 Pompeii Ave Hollis NY 11423-1417

**TETI, LOUIS N.,** lawyer; b. Bryn Mawr, Pa., May 29, 1950. BA, Dickinson Coll., 1972; JD, Temple U., 1976, LLM in Tax., 1981. Bar: Pa. 1976. Ptnr. MacElree Harvey Gallagher Featherman & Sebastian Ltd., West Chester and Exton, Pa. Fellow Am. Coll. Trust and Estate Counsel; mem. ABA (ho. dels. 1985-91, 99—), Pa. Bar Assn. (chmn. young lawyers divsn. 1982-83, bd. govs. 1982-85, 91-94, 97—, pres.), Chester County Bar Assn. (sec. 1979-82, 86-88, v.p. 1989, pres.-elect 1990, pres. 1991, chair young lawyers sect. 1977, bd. divs. 1977-92), Chester County Estate Planning Coun. (pres. 1988-89). Taxation, general, Real property, Banking. Office: MacElree Harvey Law Offices 740 Springdale Dr Ste 110 Exton PA 19341-2865*

**TETTLEBAUM, HARVEY M.,** lawyer; m. Ann Safier; children: Marianne, Benjamin. AB, Dartmouth Coll., 1964; JD, Washington U. Sch. Law, 1968, AM in History, 1968. Asst. dean Washington U. Sch. Law, 1969-77; asst. atty. gne., chief counsel Consumer Protection and Anti-Trust Div., 1970-77; pvt. practice Jefferson City, Mo., 1977-90; mem., chmn. health law practice group Husch & Eppenberger, LLC, Jefferson City, Mo., 1990—. Contbr. articles to profl. jours. Treas. Mo. Rep. State Com., 1976—; v.p. Moniteau County R-1 Sch. Dist. Bd., 1991-95, pres., 1995-96; mem. Calif. R-1 Sch. Bd., 1990-96, v.p., 1993-95, pres., 1995-96. Mem. Am. Health Lawyers Assn. (bd. dirs., co-chair long-term care and the law program 1993—, chair long term care substandive law com. 1997—), Mo. Bar Assn. (health and hosp. law com., chmn. adminstrv. law com.), Am. Health Care Assn. (legal subcom. 1994—). Administrative and regulatory, Health. Home: 56295 Little Moniteau Rd California MO 65018-3069 Office: Husch & Eppenberger LLC Monroe House Ste 300 235 E High St PO Box 1251 Jefferson City MO 65102-1251

**TETZLAFF, CHARLES ROBERT,** prosecutor; b. Oct. 15, 1938; s. Donald H. and Harriet (Ranney) T.; m. Joan Seugling, July 1, 1962; children: Julie Lynn Mulrow, Carl Lawrence. BA, U. Vt., 1960; LLB, Boston U., 1963; LLM, NYU, 1964. Bar: Vt. 1964, U.S. Supreme Ct. 1970. Judge advocate USAF, 1965-68; dep. state's atty. Chittenden County, Vt., 1968-70; ptnr. Latham, Eastman, Schweyer and Tetzlaff, 1969-93; U.S. atty. dist. Vt. Office U.S. Attys., Burlington, 1993—; trustee Vt. Legal Aid, 1976-78; chair Dist. 4 Environ. Commn., 1979-83, Gov. Sentencing Study Commn., 1985-86; active Vt. Bd. Bar Examiners, 1980-84, State Police Adv. Commn., 1985-86, Gov. Bail Amendment Task Force. Capt. USAF, 1965-68. Mem. ABA, Vt. Bar Assn., Chittenden County Bar Assn. Office: US Attys Office PO Box 570 11 Elmwood Ave Burlington VT 05402

**TEVRIZIAN, DICKRAN M., JR.,** federal judge; b. Los Angeles, Aug. 4, 1940; s. Dickran and Rose Tevrizian; m. Geraldine Tevrizian, Aug. 22, 1964; children: Allyson Tracy, Leslie Sara. BS, U. So. Calif., 1962, JD, 1965. Tax acct. Arthur Andersen and Co., Los Angeles, 1965-66; atty., ptnr. Kirtland and Packard, Los Angeles, 1966-72; judge Los Angeles Mcpl. Ct., Los Angeles, 1972-78, State of Calif. Superior Ct., Los Angeles, 1978-82; ptnr. Manatt, Phelps, Rothenberg & Tunney, Los Angeles, 1982-85, Lewis, D'Amato, Brisbois & Bisgaard, Los Angeles, 1985-86; judge U.S. Dist. Ct., Los Angeles, 1986—; adv. dir. sch. pub. policy U. Calif., L.A. Adv. dir. UCLA Sch. Pub. Policy. Named Trial Judge of the Yr., Calif. Trial Lawyers Assn., 1987, L.A. County Bar Assn., 1994-95; recipient Peter the Great Gold Medal of Honor Russian Acad. Natural Scis., 1998, Ellis Island Medal of Honor award, 1999. Mem. Calif. Trial Lawyer's Assn. (trial judge of yr. 1987), L.A. County Bar Assn. (trial judge of yr. 1994-95), Malibu Bar Assn. (fed. ct. trial judge of yr. 1998). Office: US Dist Ct Royal Federal Bldg 255 E Temple St Los Angeles CA 90012-3334

**TEWES, R. SCOTT,** lawyer; b. Chgo., Mar. 23, 1956; s. Raymond Henry and Vivian Marie Tewes; m. Marcia Anne King, June 5, 1981; children: Benjamin Scott, Matthew Philip, Madeline Anne Marie, Carrie Elizabeth. BS, Bob Jones U., 1978, MS, 1980; JD, U. S.C., 1983. Bar: S.C. 1983, D.C. 1985, Ga. 1987, U.S. Supreme Ct. Assoc. Brown & Hagins, Greenville, S.C., 1983-86; law clk. to Hon. Jean Galloway Bissell U.S. Ct. Appeals Fed. Cir., Washington, 1986-87; assoc., ptnr. Kilpatrick Stockton, Atlanta, 1987—. Articles editor S.C. Law Rev., 1982-83; contbr. articles to profl. jours. Active Greenville (S.C.) County Alcohol and Drug Abuse Commn., 1985-86; trustee Killian Hill Baptist Ch., Lilburn, Ga., 1994—. Mem. S.C. Bar (practice and procedure com., bar ethics adv. com. 1985-86), Am. Intellectual Property Law Assn., Christian Legal Soc., Federalist Soc., Lic. Execs. Soc., Order of Barristers. Avocations: running, biking, skiing. Federal civil litigation, Patent, Constitutional. Office: Kilpatrick Stockton 1100 Peachtree St Ste 2800 Atlanta GA 30309

**TEZTLAFF, THEODORE R.,** lawyer. AB, Princeton U., 1966; LLB, Yale U., 1969. Bar: Ill. 1969. Formerly ptnr. Jenner & Block; gen. counsel Tenneco Inc., Greenwich, Conn. Office: Tenneco Inc 1275 King St Greenwich CT 06831-2946

**THACKER, PENNY ANN,** paralegal, office manager, tax preparer; b. Rockwood, TN, July 10, 1962; d. Tammie Andrew and Matsy Loretta (Green) Hunter; m. Jerry Lynn Thacker, July 19, 1983; children: Greg, Kendra, Elizabeth. AS in Computer Sci. and Bus. Mgmt., Roane State C.C., Harriman, Tenn., 1990; paralegal degree, Blackstone Sch. of Law, Dallas, 1997. Cert. alarm technician, NBFAA, cert. CCTV technician, TLC. State pres. C.U.R.E., Tenn., 1997. Democrat. Baptist. Home: 618 W Wheeler St Rockwood TN 37854-2033 Office: Garry Baker Elec Inc PO Box 1123 Harriman TN 37748-1123

**THACKERAY, JONATHAN E.,** lawyer; b. Athens, Ohio, July 30, 1936; s. Joseph Eugene and Betty Rutherford (Boright) T.; m. Sandra Ann McMahon; children: Jennifer, Sara, Amy, Jonathan. A.B. cum laude, Harvard U., 1958, J.D., 1961. Bar: Ohio 1961, U.S. Dist. Ct. (no. dist.) Ohio 1961, U.S. Supreme Ct. 1972, U.S. Ct. Appeals (6th cir.) 1973, U.S. Ct. Appeals (9th cir.) 1982, N.Y. 1993. Assoc. Vorys, Sater, Seymour & Pease, Columbus, Ohio, 1961; assoc. Baker & Hostetler, Cleve., 1965-72, ptnr., 1973-93; v.p., gen. counsel The Hearst Corp., N.Y.C., 1993—. Served to lt. USNR, 1961-65. Mem. ABA, Ohio Bar Assn., Cleve. Bar Assn., Am. Law Inst. Antitrust, Federal civil litigation, Communications. Office: The Hearst Corp 959 8th Ave New York NY 10019-3795 *Notable cases include: administrative proceedings leading to approval of joint newspaper operating agreements in Cincinnati, Seattle and Las Vegas; litigation of newspaper antitrust cases in Memphis, Trenton and Dallas.*

**THALACKER, ARBIE ROBERT,** lawyer; b. Marquette, Mich., Apr. 17, 1935; s. Arbie Otto and Jeanne (Emmett) T.; m. Rita Annette Skaaren, Sept. 11, 1956 (div. July 1992); children: Marc Emmett, Christopher Paul, Robert Skaaren; m. Deborah B. Garrett, Jan. 10, 1998. AB, Princeton U., 1957; JD, U. Mich., 1960. Bar: N.Y. 1961, U.S. Ct. Appeals (2d cir.) 1962. Assoc. Shearman & Sterling, N.Y.C., 1960-68, ptnr., 1968—; dir. Detrex Corp., Detroit, 1981—, chmn. bd., 1993-96. Leader Rep. Dist. Com., 1966-68; v.p., trustee Greenwich Village Soc. for Hist. Preservation; trustee The Naropa Inst.; bd. dirs. Meredith Monk House Found., Shambhala Internat. Mem. ABA, N.Y. Bar Assn., Assn. Bar City N.Y. (securities regulatory commn. 1975-78), Wine and Food Soc. (bd. dirs. 1976-78, 85-93, 94—), Chevaliers du Tastevin, Commanderie de Bordeaux, Siwanoy Country Club (bd. govs. 1976-79), Derby Club, Links Club, Verbank Hunting and Fishing Club. Securities, Private international, Mergers and acquisitions. Home: 17 Commerce St New York NY 10014-3763 Office: Shearman & Sterling 599 Lexington Ave Fl C2 New York NY 10022-6069

**THALER, CRAIG H.,** lawyer; b. Queens, N.Y., Sept. 13, 1965; s. Michael S. and Karen A. T.; m. Diane P. Heller, Nov. 17, 1991; 1 child, Justin. BA cum laude, Brandeis U., 1987; JD, Hofstra U., 1990. Bar: N.J. 1990, N.Y. 1991; U.S. Dist. Ct. N.J. Assoc. Milbank, Tweed, Hadley & McCloy, N.Y.C., 1990-95, Luskin, Stern & Eisler, LCP, N.Y.C., 1995-96; v.p., sr. counsel and asst. sec. IBJ Whitehall Bank & Trust Co., N.Y.C., 1996—. Avocations: marathon running, hiking, basketball. Finance, Banking. Office: IBJ Whitehall Bank & Trust Co One State St New York NY 10004

**THALER, PAUL SANDERS,** lawyer, mediator; b. Washington, May 4, 1961; s. Martin S. Thaler and Barbara (Friedman) Mishkin; m. Melinda Ann Frostic, Oct. 12, 1991; children: Rachel Leigh, Daniel Martin. AB, Vassar Coll., 1983; JD, Georgetown U., 1987. Bar: Md. 1987, D.C. 1988, U.S. Ct. Appeals (D.C. and 4th cirs.) 1988, U.S. Dist. Ct. Md. 1988, U.S. Ct. Appeals (fed. cir.) 1989, U.S. Dist. Ct. D.C. 1989, U.S. Ct. Internat. Trade 1990, U.S. Supreme Ct. 1992. Assoc. Cooter & Gell, Washington, 1987-93; pres. The Thaler Group, Bethesda, Md., 1993—; ptnr. The Robinson Law Firm, Washington, 1993-96, Thaler & Liebeler, 1996—; guest lectr. negotiations mediation George Washington U. Law Sch., 1996—; guest lectr. George Washington U. Sch. Law, 1996—. Treas. Montgomery Highlands Estates Homeowners Assn., Silver Spring, Md., 1990-99; mediator Superior Ct. of D.C., 1991—; mem. adv. com. Vassar Coll. Fund, 1996-99; trustee Nat. Child Rsch. Ctr., Washington, 1998—. Mem. ABA (sect. dispute resolution, vice chmn. ethics 1994-98), D.C. Bar Assn., Md. Bar Assn., Soc. Profls. in Dispute Resolution, Acad. Family Mediators. General civil litigation, Alternative dispute resolution, General practice. Home: 9429 Locust Hill Rd Bethesda MD 20814-3939 Office: Thaler & Liebeler 1919 Pennsylvania Ave NW Washington DC 20006-3404

**THALHOFER, PAUL TERRANCE,** lawyer; b. Eugene, Oreg., Oct. 27, 1954; s. Paul Albert and Elizabeth Ann (Wathen) T.; m. Cindy Ann Whitney, Aug. 7, 1977; 1 child, Brian Allen. BA, U. Colo., 1977; JD, U. Oreg., 1986. Disbursing fin. officer USMC, Okinawa, Japan, 1978-79, El Toro, Calif., 1979-80, Tustin, Calif., 1980-83; with law program dept. U. Oreg. USMC, Eugene, 1983-86; prosecuting atty. USMC, Camp Pendleton, Calif., 1986-87, def. atty., 1987, adminstrv. law atty., 1988-90, operational law atty., 1989-90; sr. legal advisor Marine Air Contingency Force USMC, Honduras, 1988; trial team leader Legal Team Delta/USMC, Camp Pendleton, Calif., 1990; legal advisor to commanding gen. USMC Forces/Operation Desert Shield, Saudi Arabia, 1990; legal advisor to comdg. gen. 3d marine aircraft ops. Desert Shield/Storm Wing, Bahrain, Saudi Arabia, 1990-91; trial team leader Legal Team Delta, Camp Pendleton, Calif., 1991-92; civil litigation atty. Bullivant, Houser, Bailey, Pendergrass & Hoffman, Portland, Oreg., 1992-93; assoc. Reif & Reif, Canby, Oreg., 1993-95; ptnr. Reif, Reif & Thalhofer, Canby, 1996—; adv. I Marine Expeditionary Force Augmentation Command Element, Camp Pendleton, Calif., 1996—. Lt. col. USMCR. Mem. Oreg. State Bar Assn., Clackamas County Bar Assn., Computer Law Assn., Vaquero Riding Club (pres. 1983), Phi Delta Phi (v.p. chpt. 1985-86). Avocations: skiing, golf, fishing. Criminal, Administrative and regulatory, General civil litigation. Home: 335 SE 7th Way Canby OR 97013-8763 Office: Reif Reif & Thalhofer 273 N Grant St Canby OR 97013-3697

**THAMES, E. GLENN, JR.,** lawyer; b. Shreveport, La., Mar. 8, 1968; s. Earl Glenn and Barbara Thames; m. Suzanne LaRa Setphens, July 15, 1989; children: Jeremy Glenn, Parker Andrew. BS, U. Ark., Little Rock, 1989; JD, Baylor U., 1992. Bar: Tex. 1992, U.S. Dist. Ct. (ea. dist.) Tex. 1994, U.S. Ct. Appeals (5th cir.) 1998. Atty. Potter, Minton, Roberts, Davis & Jones, P.C., Tyler, Tex., 1994—. Mem. ABA, Smith County Bar Assn., Smith County Young Lawyers Assn. Avocations: golf, hunting. Appellate, General civil litigation, Personal injury. Office: Potter Minton et al 500 Plaza Tower Tyler TX 75702

**THARNEY, LAURA CHRISTINE,** lawyer; b. New Brunswick, N.J., June 19, 1965; d. Thaddeus Raphael and Madeline Kay (Baumann) T. AA in Liberal Arts, Union County Coll., 1984; BA in History, Rutgers U., 1986, JD, 1991. Bar: N.J. 1991, U.S. Dist. Ct. N.J. 1991, N.Y. 1992. With Specialized Legal Svcs., N.Y. and N.J., 1991-96; dep. county counsel Office of Middlesex County Counsel, New Brunswick, 1992-94; assoc. Law Offices of Edward J. Buzak, Montville, N.J., 1994-95, Heine Assocs., P.A., Cherry Hill, N.J., 1995-96; pvt. practice Law Office of Laura C. Tharney, Milltown, N.J., 1996—. Mem. ABA, N.J. State Bar Assn. (mentor 1994—), N.Y. Bar Assn., Morris County Bar Assn. (mentor, mediator 1994—), Middlesex County Bar Assn., Phi Alpha Theta. Avocations: running, rock climbing, scuba diving. Environmental, General practice, General civil litigation. Office: 555 State Route 18 # 219 East Brunswick NJ 08816-3727

**THARP, CHRISTINE M.,** lawyer; 1 child, Casey Ann. JD, St. Mary's Sch. Law, 1980. Bar: Tex. 1980; cert. in family law Tex. Bd. Legal Specialization, 1988. Law clk. Mex. Am. Legal Def. and Edn. Fund, San Antonio, 1979; staff atty. Law Offices Charles Campion, San Antonio, 1979-86; of counsel Nicholas and Barrera, Inc., San Antonio, 1986-89; pvt. practice San Antonio, 1989—. Bd. dirs. pro bono law project mem. Bexar County Legal Aid, 1988-89, adv. bd., 1988; vol. instr. for tng. Child Advocates fo San Antonio, 1990-91; mem. Bexar County Child Support Com., 1985; co-chair Bachelor Auction, March of Dimes. Named to Outstanding Young Women of Am., 1980; recipient Cert. of Appreciation, San Antonio Foster Parents. Mem. ABA (familu law sect., enterntainment law sect.), Am. Trial Lawyers Assn. (Nat. Coll. Advocacy), Tex. Acad. Family Specialists, Bexar County Women's Bar Assn. (charter, bd. dirs. 1986-90, 92, bd. dirs. Women's Bar Found. 1989-90, 92, pub. rels. chair 1991-92), Am. Profl. Soc. on Abuse of Children, Nat. Assn. of Counsel for Children, San Antonio Family Lawyers Bar Assn. (bd. dirs. 1994—, treas. 1995-96, v.p. 1997-98, pres. 1998-99), San Antonio Bar Assn. (family law sect., fee dispute com. 1983—, chair 1987-88, 88-89), Tex. Trial Lawyers Assn. (author/lectr.), State Bar of Tex. (family law sect., lectr., mem. Coll. of the bar 1989—), Christian Legal Soc., Delta Theta Phi. Baptist. Family and matrimonial. Office: 6217 Broadway St San Antonio TX 78209-4562

**THARP, JAMES WILSON,** lawyer; b. Hoisington, Kans., Nov. 22, 1942; s. James Alfred and Jeanette B. (Wilson) Tharp Adams; children: Jennifer, Juliana, Damien. AB, U. Kans., 1965, JD, 1968. Bar: Kans. 1968, U.S. Dist. Ct. Kans. 1968, Ohio 1969, U.S. Ct. Appeals (10th cir.) 1969, U.S. Dist. Ct. (so. dist.) 1970, U.S. Ct. Appeals (6th cir.) 1974, Hawaii 1977, U.S. Dist. Ct. Hawaii 1977, U.S. Ct. Appeals (9th cir.) 1977, U.S. Supreme Ct. 1978, No. Mariana Islands 1978, U.S. Dist. Ct. No. Mariana Islands 1978, U.N. Trust Territory Pacific Islands, 1978, Rep. of Marshall Island, 1983. Asst. atty. gen State of Ohio, 1969-70; gen. counsel Ohio Dept. Edn., 1970-72; pvt. practice Columbus, Ohio, 1972-74; counsel FHA, Columbus and L.A., 1974-76; area counsel HUD, 1976-79; pvt. practice law, Honolulu, 1979—; real estate broker Hawaii, 1980—; adminstrv. hearing officer State of Hawaii, 1984—; arbitrator Hawaii Judiciary, 1987—; bd. dirs., chief academic advisor Pacific Western U. Dir., v.p. Hawaii Literacy, Inc., 1988-91; dir. Hawaii State Theatre Coun., 1988-93. Lever Brothers scholar, Scholarship Hall scholar, 1960-61. Mem. Hawaii Bar Assn. (rep. Gov.'s Coun. for Literacy 1987-91), Kansas Club Hawaii (gov. 1983-84), Masons. Avocations: reading, acting. Real property, General corporate, Consumer commercial. Office: 1210 Auahi St Ste 104 Honolulu HI 96814-4922

**THATCHER, ANNA MARIE,** lawyer, law educator; b. Shenandoah, Iowa, Apr. 24, 1948; d. Gerald Eugene and Darlene Marie Teachout; m. Graham Thatcher, Apr. 4, 1970. BA, Dakota Wesleyan U., 1970; MA, U. S.D., 1972; JD, Hamline U., 1994. Bar: Minn. Theater dir. Rapid City, S.D., 1976-87; owner Anakota Arts, Rapid City, 1982-87; arts and non-profit cons. St. Paul, 1987-94; mng. producer Periaktos Prodns., Rapid City, 1994—. Co-columnist Arts and the Law, Minn. Lawyer, 1997-98. Mem. ABA, Minn. Bar Assn. Avocations: cooking, travel. Non-profit and tax-exempt organizations. Office: Periaktos Prodns 1601 Mount Rushmore Rd # 1-368 Rapid City SD 57701-4588

**THATCHER, MATTHEW EUGENE,** lawyer; b. Tampa, Aug. 10, 1973; s. Kermit Dev and Margaret Jane (Parsons) T. BA, U. South Fla., 1995; JD, U. Fla., 1998. Law clk. Almengual & Warner, Tampa, 1996; rsch. asst. U. Fla., Gainesville, 1997; jud. clk. 13th Jud. Cir. Fla., Tampa, 1997; assoc. Almengual & Warner, 1998—. Democrat. Avocations: roller blading, writing, playing trumpet. Bankruptcy, Family and matrimonial, Insurance. Home: #1423 6306 S Macdill Ave Apt 1423 Tampa FL 33611-5056

**THAU, WILLIAM ALBERT, JR.,** lawyer; b. St. Louis, June 22, 1940; s. William Albert and Irene Elizabeth (Mundy) T.; m. Jane Hancock, Sept. 7, 1961; children: William Albert, Caroline Jane, Jennifer Elizabeth. BS in Indsl. Mgmt., Georgia Inst. Tech., 1962; JD, U. Tex., 1965. Bar: Tex. 1965. Ptnr., head of real estate sect. Jenkens & Gilchrist, Dallas, 1965—; chmn. real estate developer/builder symposium S.W. Legal Found, 1975-79; bd. dirs. Southwestern Film Archives, So. Meth. U.; lectr. Practicing Law Inst. Bd. dirs. St. Philips Sch., Tex., Dallas, 1988, So. Meth. U.; trustee Dallas Can. Acad., 1987-88. Named one of Best Lawyers in Am. Mem. ABA, Tex. State Bar Assn. (chmn real estate, probate, trust law sect.), Am. Coll. Real Estate Lawyers, Brook Hollow Golf Club. Republican. Episcopalian. Author: Negotiating the Purchase and Sale of Real Estate, 1975; editor Tex. State Bar Assn. Newsletter on Real Estate, Probate & Trust Law, 1978-81; contbr. articles to Real Estate Rev., 1983—. Contracts commercial, Real property, Construction. Office: Jenkens & Gilchrist 1445 Ross Ave Ste 3200 Dallas TX 75202-2799

**THAXTON, MARVIN DELL,** lawyer, farmer; b. Electra, Tex., June 1, 1925; s. Montgomery Dell and Ida (Scheurer) T.; m. Carolyn Moore Alexander, Aug. 30, 1949; children: Rebecca Thaxton Henderson, Gail Thaxton Fogleman, Marvin D. Jr. JD, U. Ark., 1949. Bar: Ark. 1949, U.S. Dist. Ct. (ea. dist.) Ark. 1952, U.S. Dist. Ct. (we. dist.) Ark. 1978, U.S. Dist. Ct. (we. dist.) Okla., U.S. Supreme Ct. 1987. Prin. Thaxton Furniture Co., Newport, Ark., 1949-50; ptnr. Thaxton, Hout & Howard, Attys., Newport, 1950-97; retired, 1997; spl. assoc. justice Ark. Supreme Ct., 1978, 84; examiner Ark. State Bd. Law Examiners, 1968-73, chmn. 1973. Pres. Newport C. of C., 1956, Newport Sch. Dist. Bd. Edn., 1964; past pres. Ea. Ark. Young Men's Clubs; adult leader Newport area Boy Scouts Am., 1949-54. Officer U.S. Mcht. Marine, 1945-46, PTO. Fellow Ark. Bar Found.; mem. Ark. Bar Assn. (honor cert. 1973), Newport Rotary Club (past pres., Paul Harris fellow 1990), Sigma Chi. Democrat. Methodist. Avocations: hunting, fishing, boating. General corporate, Real property, General practice. Home: 12 Lakeside Ln Newport AR 72112-3914

**THAYER, W(ALTER) STEPHEN, III,** state supreme court justice; b. N.Y.C., Jan. 13, 1946; s. Walter S. and Dorothy (Pflum) T.; m. Judith O. O'Brien, Dec. 27, 1982. B.A. in Polit. Sci., Belmont Abbey Coll., 1968; J.D., John Marshall Law Sch., Chgo., 1974. Bar: N.H. 1975, U.S. Dist. Ct. N.H. 1975, U.S. Ct. Appeals (1st cir.) 1981. Sole practice Law Offices W. Stephen Thayer, III, Manchester, N.H., 1975-81; U.S. atty. Dist. N.H., Concord, 1981-84; assoc. justice N.H. Superior Ct., 1984-86, N.H. Supreme Ct., 1986—; legal counsel N.H. State Senate, 1978-80, N.H. Rep. State Com., 1977-80; cons. GSA, Washington, 1981. Alt. del. Rep. nat. conv., 1980; presdl. elector electoral coll., 1980. Served to 1st lt. U.S. Army, 1968-71. Decorated Bronze Star. Mem. N.H. Bar Assn., N.H. Trial Lawyers Assn. Roman Catholic. Home: 1943 Elm St Manchester NH 03104-2528 Office: NH Supreme Ct One Noble Dr Concord NH 03301*

**THEIBERT, RICHARD WILDER,** lawyer, educator; b. Akron, Ohio, June 20, 1951; s. Philip Richard and Ann (Conners) T.; m. Willis Anne Burton, July 25, 1981; children: Leslie, Elizabeth, Jillian. BS, Johns Hopkins U., 1974; JD, NYU, 1978. Bar: Md. 1979, Ala. 1991. Assoc. Weinberg & Green, Balt., 1979-80, Niles, Barton & Wilmer, Balt., 1980-85, Prem and Dumler, Balt., 1985-91, Najjar Denaburg, Birmingham, Ala., 1991—; prof. U. Balt., 1987, Birmingham Sch. Law, 1991-99. Pres. Birmingham Housing Devel. Corp., 1992-98. Mem. ABA, Ala. Bar Assn., Ala. Real Estate Lawyers Assn. (v.p.), Birmingham Bar Assn. Episcopalian. Avocations: teaching, coaching. Real property, General corporate, Landlord-tenant. Home: 1000 31st St S Birmingham AL 35205-1108 Office: Najjar Denaburg 2125 Morris Ave Birmingham AL 35203-4274

**THEIS, WILLIAM HAROLD,** lawyer, educator; b. Chgo., Nov. 8, 1945; s. Clarence M. and Marion K. (McLendon) T.; m. Maria Luisa Belfiore, Dec. 5, 1973; children: Catherine, Elizabeth. AB, Loyola U., Chgo., 1967; JD, Northwestern U., 1970; LLM, Columbia U., 1977, JSD, 1982. Bar: Ill. 1970, D.C. 1971, Wis. 1998, U.S. Ct. Appeals (7th cir.) 1971, U.S. Supreme Ct. 1974, Wis. 1998. Assoc. prof. La. State U. Law Ctr., 1972-78, Loyola U. Law Sch., Chgo., 1978-81; practiced in Chgo., 1981-99; pvt. practice Winnetka, Ill., 1999—; part-time lectr. admiralty Northwestern Sch. Law, Chgo. Contbr. articles to legal jours. Served to lt. USNR, 1970-72. Mem. Am. Law Inst. Criminal, Federal civil litigation, State civil litigation. Office: Shellow Shellow & Glynn 841 Foxdale Ave Winnetka IL 60093

**THEISEN, HENRY WILLIAM,** lawyer; b. N.Y.C., Feb. 21, 1939; s. Charles and Jennie J. (Callahan) T.; m. Kathleen Anne Brennan, Jan. 23, 1966 (div. Oct. 1992); children: Gordon H., Anne, Maureen R., William R.; m. Deborah S. Lynch, June 11, 1994. BBA, Manhattan Coll., 1961; JD, Fordham U., 1966. Bar: N.Y. 1967, U.S. Dist. Ct. (no. dist.) N.Y. 1968, U.S. Ct. Appeals (2d cir.) 1971, U.S. Supreme Ct. 1974. Ptnr. Adams, Theisen & May, Ithaca, N.Y., 1967—; prosecutor City of Ithaca, 1969; estate tax atty. N.Y. State, Albany, 1976-90; county atty. Tompkins County, Ithaca, 1994—; corp. sec., bd. dirs. Paleontol. Rsch. Instn., Ithaca. Author: (fin. and estate planning) Financial and Estate Planning Records, 1996. Bd. reps. Tompkins County, Ithaca, 1976-81; panel mem. Jud. Candidate Rating Panel, Binghamton, N.Y., 1993-94; candidate Supreme Ct. Justice, N.Y., 1992. Mem. Tompkins County Bar Assn. (pres. 1990), Tompkins County C. of C. (pres. 1993), Estate Planning Coun. Tompkins County (pres. 1985), Ithaca Rotary Club. Democrat. Roman Catholic. Avocations: watercolor painting, long distance running. Probate, Real property, Municipal (including bonds). Office: Adams Theisen & May 301 The Clinton House 103 W Seneca St Ste 304 Ithaca NY 14850-4191

**THENELL, HEATHER JO,** lawyer; b. Sturgeon Bay, Wis., Jan. 18, 1969; d. Roger H. and Faye A. Isaacson; m. Matthew J. Thenell, Jan. 19, 1996. BA cum laude, Carroll Coll., Wankesha, Wis., 1990; JD, U. Wis., Madison, 1993. Atty. Quincey, Becker & Schuessler, Mayville, Wis., 1993-95, Bachman Law Firm, Appleton, Wis., 1995-98; estate protection and retirement planning atty. Aid Assn. for Lutherans, Appleton, Wis., 1998—; sec., sr. officer AAL Trust Co., FSB, Appleton, Wis., 1998—; dir., officer Midwest Mortgage Corp., Appleton, Wis., 1998—. Mentor Juvenile Diversion Program, Appleton, Wis., 1997-99; mem. Outagamie County Estate Planning Coun. Mem. Am. Bar Assn., Outagamie County Bar Assn., Wis. Bar Assn., Internat. Assn. Fin. Planners. Estate planning, Estate taxation, General corporate. Home: 2539 W Sunnyview Cir Appleton WI 54914-1147 Office: AAL 4321 N Ballard Rd Appleton WI 54919-0001

**THEOBALD, EDWARD ROBERT,** lawyer; b. Chgo., Feb. 10, 1947; s. Edward Robert Theobald Jr. and Marie (Turner) Logan; m. Bonnie J. Singer, July 18, 1970; children: Debra Marie, Kimberly Ann. BA, So. Ill. U., 1969; JD, Ill. Inst. Tech., 1974. Bar: Ill. 1974, U.S. Dist. Ct. (no. dist.) Ill. 1974. Asst. state's atty. Cook County, Chgo., 1974-79, supr. felony trial divsn., 1980-81; assoc. Conklin, Leahy & Eisenberg, Chgo., 1977; ptnr. Boharic & Theobald, Chgo., 1981-83, owner, ptnr., 1983—; legal adv. Sheriff of Cook County, Ill., 1986-89; spl. state's atty. U.S. Dist. Ct. no. dist. Ill., 1989-91; apptd. spl. corp. counsel City of Chgo., 1994. Mem. Parent adv. bd. Downers Grove (Ill.) South H.S., 1992-94. Named Number One Trial Atty. in Felony Trial Divsn. of Office of Cook County State's Atty., Felony Trial Divsn. Suprs., 1979. Mem. ABA (sect. on tort and ins. law sect. on labor and employment law, chmn. com. on sentencing alternatives young lawyers sect. 1982-83, tort and ins. practice sect., labor and employment law sect.), ATLA, Chgo. Bar Assn. (mem. bd. mgrs. 1985-87, mem. labor and employment law com. 1983—, mem. com. on coms. 1990-94, mem. membership com. 1990-95), Ill. Bar Assn., Christian Legal Soc. (bd. dirs. Ill. chpt. 1993—), Civil War Roundtable (Chgo. chpt.). Roman Catholic. Labor, Personal injury, Criminal. Home: 7104 Grand Ave Downers Grove IL 60516-3915 Office: 111 W Washington St Ste 759 Chicago IL 60602-2705

**THEOBALD, SCOTT M.,** lawyer; b. Salt Lake City, Feb. 16, 1958; s. Bruce H. and Mary E. (Farnsworth) T.; m. Carol Jane Martin, Feb. 12, 1981; children: Jason S., Lindsay J., Zoe E., Sierra N. BA in Spanish, U. Utah, 1983, BSCE, 1983; MBA, Columbia U., 1988, JD, 1988. Bar: Ariz. 1988, U.S. Dist. Ct. Ariz. 1988. Assoc. Brown & Bain, P.A., Phoenix, 1988-94, ptnr., 1994-96; ptnr. Meyer, Hendricks & Bivens, P.A., Phoenix, 1996—; vice gen. counsel Phoenix C. of C., 1995-96. Precinct committeeman Ariz. Rep. Party, Phoenix, 1988-96. Mem. Phoenix Country Club. Mormon. Avocations: hiking, travel, racquet sports, golf, films. Private international, Mergers and acquisitions, Securities. Office: Meyer Hendricks et al 3003 N Central Ave Ste 1200 Phoenix AZ 85012-2921

**THEUNE, PHILIPP CHARLES,** lawyer; b. Oceanside, N.Y., Oct. 5, 1953; s. Adalbert and Christel Theune. BS in Fin., St. John's U., Jamaica, N.Y., 1985; JD, Touro Law Ctr., Huntington, N.Y., 1992. Bar: Colo. 1992, N.Y. 1992. Mng. atty. Philipp C. Theune, L.L.C., Denver, 1992-97; v.p. Theune & Croke, P.C., Denver, 1997-98; mng. ptnr. Powell, Theune, Burke & Croke, LLP, Denver, 1998—. Served with USN, 1971-75, Viet Nam. Bankruptcy, Private international, General civil litigation. Office: Powell Theune et al 1580 Lincoln St Ste 600 Denver CO 80203-1508

**THEUS, ROMA WEAVER,** lawyer; b. Macon, Ga., Mar. 23, 1948; s. Roma and Theodosia (Mason) T.; m. Elizabeth Ann Wernicke, Sept. 29, 1991; children: Neesha Cathryn, Krishan Kumar, Naryan Joseph, Allyxandra Ann. BA, Muhlenberg Coll., 1969; JD, Harvard U., 1972. Bar: Fla., N.J., U.S. Ct. Appeals (5th and 11th cirs.), U.S. Dist. Ct. N.J., U.S. Dist. Ct. (so. and mid. dists.) Fla., U.S. Supreme Ct. Assoc. Lowenstein, Sandler, Brochin, Kohn & Fisher, Newark, 1972-74; asst. U.S. atty. U.S. Attys. Office for the Dist. of N.J., Newark, 1974-77; spl. atty. organized crime and racketeering sect. Dept. Justice, Miami, Fla., 1977-84; capital ptnr., practice area leader for litig. Holland & Knight, LLP, Ft. Lauderdale, Fla., 1984—. Contbr. articles to profl. jours. Trustee Muhlenberg Coll., Allentown, Pa., 1995—; mem. Broward County Econ. Devel. Coun., Ft. Lauderdale, Fla., 1995—. Democrat. Roman Catholic. Avocations: photography, reading, exercise, auto racing. Office: Holland & Knight LLP One E Broward Blvd Fort Lauderdale FL 33301

**THEUT, C. PETER,** lawyer; b. Center Line, Mich., July 24, 1938; s. Clarence William and Anna Marie (Martens) T.; m. Judith Fern Trombley, Aug. 4, 1962; children: Elizabeth Anne, Kristin Claire, Peter Christopher, Sarah Nicole. BA, U. Mich., 1960, LLB, 1963. Bar: Calif. 1964, Mich. 1964, U.S. Dist. Ct. (no. dist.) Ohio 1968, U.S. Dist. Ct. (ea. dist.) Mich. 1968. Assoc. Overton, Lyman & Prince, L.A., 1963-67; ptnr. Foster, Meadows and Ballard, Detroit, 1968-72; ptnr. Theut & Schellig, Mt. Clemens, Mich., 1972-80; ptnr. Hill, Lewis, Mt. Clemens, 1980-88, Butzel, Long, Detroit, 1988—, stockholder; gen. counsel Nat. Marine Bankers Assn., Mich. Boating Industries Assn.; bd. dirs. Butzel Long Global Trade Group. Mem. ABA (internat. law sect., TIPS admiralty com.), Detroit Bar Assn., Calif. State Bar Assn., Mich. State Bar Assn., Macomb County Bar Assn., Maritime Law Assn. (past chmn. recreationaal boating com.), Nat. Marine Bankers Assn. (gen. counsel), Mich. Boating Industry Assn. (gen. counsel), Lex Mundi, North Star Sail Club. Republican. Admiralty, Contracts commercial, Private international. Home: 38554 Hidden Ln Clinton Township MI 48036-1826

**THIBEAULT, GEORGE WALTER,** lawyer; b. Cambridge, Mass., Sept. 21, 1941; s. George Walter and Josephine (Maraggia) T.; m. Antoinette Miller, June 30, 1963; children—Robin M., Holly Ann. B.S., Northeastern U., 1964; M.B.A., Boston Coll., 1966, J.D., 1969. Bar: Mass. 1969. Assoc. Gaston & Snow, Boston, 1969-73; ptnr. Testa, Hurwitz & Thibeault, Boston, 1973—. Mem. ABA, Mass. Bar Assn., Am. Arbitration Assn. General corporate, Securities, Private international. Home: 181 Caterina Hts Concord MA

01742-4773 Office: Testa Hurwitz & Thibeault High St Tower 125 High St Fl 22 Boston MA 02110-2725

**THIBODEAU, THOMAS RAYMOND,** lawyer; b. St.Paul, Feb. 5, 1942; s. Raymond Anthony and Alice Marie (Parkos) T.; m. Mollie Nan Mylor, Sept. 24, 1966; 1 child, Matthew Raymond. BA in Polit. Sci. cum laude, U. St. Thomas, St. Paul, 1964; JD, U. Minn., 1967. Bar: Minn. 1967, U.S. Dist. Ct. Minn. 1967, U.S. Ct. Appeals (8th cir.) 1970, U.S. Supreme Ct. 1982, Wis. 1983, U.S. Dist. Ct. Wis. 1983; solicitor Supreme Ct. Eng. and Wales, 1996; cert. civil trial specialist Nat. Bd. Trial Advocacy. Ptnr. Johnson, Killen, Thibodeau & Seiler, Duluth, Minn., 1967—, also bd. dirs.; pres. Legal Aid Service N.E. Minn., Inc., 1969-74; mem. civil justice reform act adv. com. U.S. Dist. Ct. Minn. mem. revision Civil Jury Instruction Guide IV, 1997—. Chmn. Duluth City Charter Commn., 1976-78; vol. atty. St. Louis County Heritage and Arts Ctr., Duluth, 1980-87; pres. bd. trustees Marshall Sch., 1990-92. Recipient Disting. Alumni award U. St. Thomas, 1985. Fellow Internat. Soc. Barristers, Am. Coll. Trial Lawyers; mem. Am. Bd. Trial Advs. (adv.), Minn. Bar Assn. (chmn. specialization com. 1974-78, co-chmn. revision Civil Injury Instrn. Guide com. 1982-85), Minn. Def. Lawyers Assn. (pres. 1988-89), Acad. Cert. Trial Lawyers of Minn. (pres. elect 1993, pres. 1994-95), Internat. Assn. Def. Counsel, Assn. Def. Trial Attys. Avocations: hunting, skiing, scuba diving and other water sports, reading. Federal civil litigation, State civil litigation, Personal injury. Home: 407 Wallace Ave Duluth MN 55812-1529 Office: Johnson Killen Thibodeau & Seiler 811 Norwest Ctr Duluth MN 55802

**THIEL, ALBERT NICHOLAS, JR.,** lawyer; b. Trenton, N.J., Dec. 25, 1948; s. Albert Nicholas and Mildred Pearl (Goodrich) T.; m. Joyce Ann Hardiman, Jan. 28, 1978; children: Mary, Nicholas, Joseph, Alison. BS in Philosophy, St. Mary's Sem., 1970; JD, U. N.Mex., 1976, MBA, 1983. Bar: N.Mex., 1976, U.S. Supreme Ct., 1982. Divsn. head Legal Dept. City Albuquerque, 1977-83; pvt. practice Albuquerque, 1983-88, 90-97; ptnr. Bryan, Flynn-O'Brien & Thiel, Albuquerque, 1988-90, Robinson, Di Lando & Whitaker, Albuquerque, 1998-99, Will Ferguson and Assocs., 1999—. Labor, Personal injury, General corporate. Office: PO Box 2007 Albuquerque NM 87103-2007

**THIELE, HERBERT WILLIAM ALBERT,** lawyer; b. Gananoque, Ont., Can., Apr. 14, 1953; s. Herbert and Bertha (Shields) T.; m. Kathi M. Brown, May 29, 1982; children: Herbert R. R., Eric W. R., Brian A. J., Kelly M. M., Kevin M. H., Karl S. H. BA, U. Notre Dame, 1975; JD, U. Fla., 1978. Bar: Fla. 1978, U.S. Dist. Ct. (so. dist. trial and gen. bars) Fla. 1979, U.S. Ct. Appeals (5th and 11th cirs.) 1981, U.S. Supreme Ct. 1982, U.S. Tax Ct. 1983, U.S. Dist. Ct. (no. dist.) Fla. 1991. Assoc. Law Offices of Roger G. Saberson, Delray Beach, Fla., 1979-81; asst. city atty. City of Delray Beach, 1979-81, city atty., 1981-90; county atty. Leon County, Tallahassee, Fla., 1990—. Bd. dirs. Delray Beach Mcpl. Employees Credit Union, 1985-88. Recipient award of recognition Stetson U. Law Rev., 1989, Ralph A. Marsicano award for Local Govt. Law, Fla. Bar, 1991. Mem. ABA (vice-chmn. urban, state and local govt. com. of gen. practice sect. 1991-95, mem. labor and employment law, litigation, govt. lawyers, gen. practice and trial practice com. sects.), ATLA, FBA, Fla. Bar (exec. coun. local govt. law sect. 1986-87, sec./treas. local govt. law sect. 1987-88, chmn.-elect 1988-89, chmn., 1989-90, immediate past chmn. 1990-91, ex-officio officer 1991—, trial, real property, gen. practice and labor and employment law sects., bar com. on individual rights and responsibilities 1986-90, long-range planning com. 1991-93, continuing legal edn. com. 1998—), Tallahassee Bar Assn., Fla. Mcpl. Attys. Assn. (steering com. 1985-86, bd. dirs. 1980-89, sec./treas. 1989-90, Fla. Mcpl. Atty. of Yr. 1987), Fla. Assn. Policy Attys., Nat. Inst. Mcpl. Law Officers (pers. and labor law com., trial practices and litigation com., legal advocacy com., 11th cir. rep. 1989-90), Am. Soc. for Pub. Adminstrn., Fla. Pub. Employer Labor Rels. Assn., Fla. Assn. County Attys. (chmn. coun. county attys. 1990-91, bd. dirs. 1991-93, treas. 1993, sec. 1993-94, v.p. 1994-95, pres. 1995-97, chmn. 1996-97, officer 1997—, Recognition award 1994, Ethics in Govt. award 1998). Republican. Avocations: music, sports, philately. Home: 318 Milestone Dr Tallahassee FL 32312-3574 Office: Office of Leon County Atty Leon County Courthouse Tallahassee FL 32301

**THIELE, LESLIE KATHLEEN LARSEN,** lawyer; b. Wenatchee, Wash., Aug. 11, 1952; d. James Walter and Mary Helen (Morris) T.; m. Kenneth Edward Larsen, Sept. 13, 1986; children, James Larsen, Gabriela Dayana. BA magna cum laude, U. Redlands, 1974; postgrad., C. Albrechts U., Kiel, Fed. Republic Germany, 1977-79; JD, Duke U., 1980, LLM, 1980. Bar: Pa. 1981, U.S. Dist. Ct. (ea. dist.) Pa. 1982, U.S. Ct. Appeals (3d cir.) 1981, N.Y. 1990. Editorial asst. Inst. for Internat. Law, Kiel, Fed. Republic Germany, 1977-79; assoc. Saul, Ewing, Remick & Saul, Phila., 1981-83; assoc., then ptnr. Ehmann & Baldwin, Phila., 1983-85; pvt. practice Phila., 1985-89, Schenectady, N.Y., 1989-92; of counsel Whiteman Osterman & Hanna, Albany, N.Y., 1992—; sr. v.p. Pvt. Svcs. Corp., Phila., 1986-89; instr. Inst. for Paralegal Tng., Phila., 1986-95; legal cons. Coun. on Internat. Ednl. Exch., N.Y.C., 1988-90. Author: (with others) A Business Guide to the United States, 1987, Working Abroad, 1990; author numerous articles on internat. bus. issues. Vol. Pa. Vol. Lawyer for the Arts, 1982-88, organizer feeding program for homeless Christ Luth. Ch., Phila.; mem. exec. bd. Leadership Schenectady Alumni Assn., 1990-91, Schenectady Rotary, 1990-95; treas. Capital Region World Trade Coun., 1991-93, pres., 1993-95, mem. exec. bd., 1991-97; mem. exec. bd. N.Y. State Coun. World Trade Assns., 1994—; mem. fin. com. Mohawk Pathways coun. Girl Scouts U.S., 1992-94; chair bldg. com. Our Redeemer Luth. Ch., 1992-95; bd. dirs. GE Realty Plot Hist. Neighborhood Assn., 1998—. Fulbright scholar, 1977-79. Mem. ABA, Internat. Bar Assn., Am. Immigration Lawyers Assn., German Am. Lawyers Assn., Fulbright Assn. (bd. dirs. 1982-88, pres. 1985-86). Avocations: home repair, needlework, travel, cross-country skiing, bicycling. Private international, Immigration, naturalization, and customs, General corporate. Home: 1166 Avon Rd Schenectady NY 12308-2406

**THIEMANN, KEVIN BARRY,** lawyer; b. Jamaica, N.Y., Dec. 6, 1957; s. Norbert Joseph and Barbara Jean (Thiemann) Lynch. BS in Fgn. Service, Georgetown U., 1980; JD, Syracuse U., 1983. Bar: N.Y. 1984, U.S. Dist. Ct. (no. dist.) N.Y. 1988, U.S. Dist. Ct. (so. dist.) N.Y., 1992, Conn. 1999. Legal asst. Coffin, Inman, Christiana and Spampinato, Hudson, N.Y., 1978; summer intern dist. atty.'s office Columbia County, Hudson, 1982; law clerk Coffin, Inman and Christiana, Hudson, 1982-83 (summers); trial atty. office of gen. counsel USDA, Washington, 1983-87; assoc. DeGraff, Foy, Conway, Holt-Harris and Mealey, Albany, N.Y., 1987-88, Law Offices Robert J. Gagen, Hudson, N.Y., 1989—; counsel to Planning Bd., Town of East Greenbush, N.Y., 1989-90, Town of Hillsdale, N.Y., 1989-99; town atty. Town of Hillsdale, 1992-99; atty. Office of Regional Counsel, U.S. Dept. VA, 1997—. Mem. Internat. Fund for Animal Welfare, 1976, Defenders of Wildlife, Washington, 1984—. Mem. ABA, N.Y. State Bar Assn., U.S. Naval Inst., Internat. Fund for Animal Welfare. Avocations: sailing, hiking, horse training. Bankruptcy, General practice, Environmental. Home: 33 Maple Ln Copake Falls NY 12517-5011 Office: Law Offices Robert J Gagen 424 Warren St Hudson NY 12534-2415

**THIEROLF, RICHARD BURTON, JR.,** lawyer; b. Medford, Oreg., Oct. 27, 1948; s. Richard Burton Sr. and Helen Dorothy (Rivolta) T. BA, Columbia U., N.Y.C., 1970; JD, U. Oreg., 1976. Bar: Oreg. 1976, U.S. Dist. Ct. Oreg. 1976, U.S. Ct. Appeals (9th cir.) 1977, U.S. Dist. Ct. (no. dist.) Calif. 1980, U.S. Supreme Ct. 1993, U.S. Ct. Fed. Claims 1993. Staff atty. Orgn. of the Forgotten Am., Inc., Klamath Falls, Oreg., 1976-77, exec. dir., 1977-79; ptnr. Jacobson, Thierolf & Dickey, P.C., Medford, 1980—. Mem. City of Medford Planning Commn., 1990-92; mem. Medford Sch. Dist. 549-C Budget Com., 1991-92, chmn., 1991. Mem. ABA, Fed. Bar Assn., Oreg. State Bar (local profl. responsibility com. 1987-89, mem. fed. practice and procedure com. 1994-97, sec. 1995-97, jud. adminstrn. com. 1998—, low income legal svcs. com. 1990-93, ho. of dels. 1999—), Jackson County Bar Assn. (sec. 1988). Episcopalian. Avocation: violin. Native American, Federal civil litigation, General practice. Home: 234 Ridge Rd Ashland OR 97520-2829 Office: Jacobson Jewett Thierolf & Dickey PC Two N Oakdale Ave Medford OR 97501

**THIGPEN, RICHARD ELTON, JR.,** lawyer; b. Washington, Dec. 29, 1930; s. Richard Elton and Dorothy (Dotger) T.; m. Nancy H. Shand, Dec. 15, 1951; children: Susan B., Richard M. AB, Duke U., 1951; LLB, U. N.C., 1956. Bar: N.C., 1956, U.S. Ct. Appeals (4th cir.) 1960, U.S. Ct. Appeals (5th cir.) 1960, U.S. Ct. Appeals (10th cir.) 1974, U.S. Tax Ct. 1958, U.S. Ct. Claims 1978. Lawyer FTC, Washington, 1956-58, Thigpen & Hines, Charlotte, N.C., 1958-84, Moore & Van Allen, Charlotte, N.C., 1984-88, Poyner & Spruill, Charlotte, N.C., 1988-93; gen. counsel Richardson Sports, 1994-98. Dir. Charlotte-Mecklenburg YMCA, 1964-88, Heineman Med. Rsch. Ctr., Charlotte, 1970—, Charlotte C. of C., 1982-85. Lt. USNR, 1951-53. Fellow Am. Bar Found., Am. Coll. Tax Counsel (regent 1989-95, vice chmn. 1992, chmn. 1993-94); mem. ABA, N.C. State Bar, N.C. Bar Assn. (pres. 1988-89, chmn. tax sect. 1976-80), Sports Lawyers Assn. (bd. dirs. 1995—). Avocation: golf, travel. Sports, Taxation, general, State and local taxation. Office: 1045 Providence Rd Ste 200 Charlotte NC 28207-2568

**THISTLETHWAITE, WILLIAM H.,** lawyer; b. South Bend, Ind., Feb. 3, 1953; s. Glenn and Mildred Thistlethwaite; m. Suzanne Thistlethwaite. BS, Ind. U., 1975; JD, U. N.D., 1978. Bar: Mich. 1978, Ind. 1981. Pvt. practice law Three Rivers, Mich., 1978-83; friend of the ct., cir. ct. referee Cass County, Cassopolis, Mich., 1983-90, St. Joseph County, Centreville, Mich., 1990—. Named Outstanding Friend of the Ct., Mich. Family Support Coun., 1992. Mem. ABA, St. Joseph County Bar Assn., Referees Assn. Mich., Friend of the Ct. Assn. Office: Friend of the Court PO Box 249 Centreville MI 49032-0249

**THOMAS, ANN VAN WYNEN,** law educator; b. The Netherlands, May 27, 1919; came to U.S., 1921, naturalized, 1926; d. Cornelius and Cora Jacoba (Daansen) Van Wynen; m. A.J. Thomas Jr., Sept. 10, 1948. AB with distinction, U. Rochester, 1940; JD, U. Tex., 1943; post doctoral degree, So. Meth. U., 1952. U.S. fgn. svc. officer Johannesburg, South Africa, London, The Hague, The Netherlands, 1943-47; rsch. atty. Southwestern Legal Found., Sch. Law So. Meth. U., Dallas, 1952-67; asst. prof. polit. sci. So. Meth. U. Sch. Law, Dallas, 1968-73, assoc. prof., 1973-76, prof., 1976-85, prof. emeritus, 1985—. Author: Communism versus International Law, 1953, (with A.J. Thomas Jr.) International Treaties, 1950, Non-Intervention—The Law and its Import in the Americas, 1956, OAS: The Organization of American States, 1962, International Legal Aspects of Civil War in Spain, 1936-1939, 1967, Legal Limitations on Chemical and Biological Weapons, 1970, The Concept of Aggression, 1972, Presidential War Making Power: Constitutional and International Law Aspects, 1981, An International Rule of Law—Problems and Prospects, 1974. Chmn. time capsule com. Grayson County Commn. on Tex. Sesquicentennial, 1986-88; co-chmn. Grayson County Commn. on Bicentennial U.S. Constn., 1988-93; co-chmn. com. Grayson County Sesquicentennial, 1994-97; co-chmn. Grayson County Commn. on the Millenium, 1997—. Recipient Am. medal Nat. DAR Soc., 1992. Mem. Tex. Bar Assn., Am. Soc. Internat. Law, Grayson County Bar Assn. Home: Spaniel Hall 374 Coffee Cir Pottsboro TX 75076-3164

**THOMAS, ARCHIBALD JOHNS, III,** lawyer; b. Jacksonville, Fla., Apr. 27, 1952; s. Archibald Johns and Jean (Snodgrass) T.; m. Martha Ann Marconi, Sept. 1, 1973. BA, U. So. Fla., 1973; JD, Stetson U., 1977. Bar: Fla. 1977, U.S. Dist. Ct. (mid. dist.) Fla. 1977, U.S. Ct. Appeals (11th cir.) 1981, U.S. Supreme Ct. 1981, U.S. Claims Ct. 1990. Law clk. to U.S. magistrate U.S. Dist. Ct., Tampa, Fla., 1977-78; 1st asst. fed. pub. defender U.S. dist. Ct., Jacksonville, 1978-84; sr. ptnr. Thomas & Skinner, P.A., Jacksonville, 1984-89; pvt. practice Jacksonville, 1990—. Mem. FBA (pres. 1982-83), Nat. Assn. Criminal Def. Lawyers, Nat. Employment Lawyers Assn. (co-chmn. Fla. chpt. 1992), Jacksonville Bar Assn. Democrat. Avocation: sailing. Labor. Home: 708 Mccollum Cir Neptune Beach FL 32266-3789 Office: Riverplace Tower Ste 1640 Jacksonville FL 32207

**THOMAS, BRETT SCOTT,** lawyer; b. Knoxville, Tenn., Mar. 13, 1966; s. Claude L. and Janice Lynn Thomas; m. Jennifer Anne Hall, June 11, 1988; children: Tess Elizabeth, Trinity Hope. BA in English, Lamar U., 1988; JD, 1991. Assoc. Tucker, Hendrix & Gascoyne, P.C., Houston, 1991, Lewis & Assocs., Beaumont, Tex., 1991-93; assoc. Bush, Lewis & Roebuck, P.C., Beaumont, Tex., 1991-97, shareholder, 1997—. Mem. Calvary Bapt. Ch., Beaumont, 1982—. Mem. ATLA, Tex. Trial Lawyers Assn., Jefferson County Young Lawyers Assn. (dir. 1996-98). Democrat. Avocations: fishing, hunting, family life. Personal injury, Libel, Product liability. Home: 2110 Central Dr Beaumont TX 77706-2810 Office: Bush Lewis & Roebuck PC 1240 Orleans St Beaumont TX 77701-3612

**THOMAS, CAROL TODD,** law firm administrator; b. Rochester, Pa., May 24, 1952; d. Horace J. and Sarah Evelyn (Pack) T.; m. Robert E. Young, Aug. 16, 1975 (div. Dec. 1985); m. Geoffrey J. Suszkowski, Nov. 26, 1988. MPA, U. Denver, 1975, BA, 1974. Coord. manpower scvs. Onondaga County, Syracuse, N.Y., 1976-78; coord. community assistance Cen. N.Y. Regional Planning and Devel. Bd., Syracuse, 1978-79; from dir. adminstrn. to city mgr. Twp. of O'Hara, Pa., 1979-86; pres. OPUS, Inc., Coraopolis, Pa., 1986; city mgr. Municipality of Monroeville, Pa., 1986; exec. dir. Babst, Calland, Clements and Zomnir, P.C., Pitts., 1987-90; ptnr., cons. Mcpl. Cons. Assoc., Upper St. Clair, Pa., 1986-90; dir. adminstrn. Buckingham, Doolittle, Burroughs, A Legal Profl. Assn., Akron, Ohio, 1991-94; dir. of devel. Squire, Sanders & Dempsey, Cleve., 1994-95; dir. of adminstrn. Brouse McDowell LPA, 1995—. Participant Leadership Pitts., 1986; mem. exec. com., treas. Civic Light Opera Assocs., Pitts., 1989-90; mem. Civic Light Opera Guild, 1986-90; charter mem. Citizens League, Pitts., 1988. Mem. Assn. Legal Adminstrn., Govt. Fin. Officers Assn. (bd. dirs. 1982-86, state rep. 1984-86), Internat. City Mgmt. Assn., Women's Network (bd. dirs. 1991—, pres. 1996-98), Oakmont Country Club, Sigma Iota Epsilon, Gamma Phi Beta. Republican. Presbyterian. Home: 3559 E Prescott Cir Cuyahoga Falls OH 44223-3746

**THOMAS, CLARENCE,** United States supreme court justice; b. Savannah, Ga., June 23, 1948. BA, Holy Cross Coll., 1971; JD, Yale U., 1974. Bar: Mo. Asst. atty. gen. State of Mo., Jefferson City, 1974-77; atty. Monsanto Co., St. Louis, 1977-79; legis. asst. to Sen. John C. Danforth, Washington, 1979-81; asst. sec. for civil rights Dept. Edn., Washington, 1981-82; chmn. U.S. EEOC, Washington, 1982-90; judge U.S. Ct. Appeals, Washington, 1990-91; assoc. justice U.S. Supreme Ct., Washington, 1991—. Office: US Supreme Court Supreme Ct Bldg 1 First St NE Washington DC 20543-0001*

**THOMAS, DANIEL FRENCH,** lawyer; b. Balt., Sept. 9, 1937; s. William Daniel and Lillian Hanway (Thompson) T.; m. Sandra Jean Ailiff, Dec. 20, 1996. BA, Loyola Coll., Balt., 1959; JD, U. Md., 1962. Bar: Md. 1962, U.S. Dist. Ct. Md. 1963. Law clk. to Hon. William M. Horney Ct. of Appeals of Md., Annapolis, 1962-63; atty. Bregel & Bregel, Balt., 1963-70, Thomas & Kalichman, Balt., 1971—; lectr. Md. Inst. for Continuing Profl. Edn. of Lawyers, Balt., 1980—. Editor: Maryland Divorce and Separation Law, 1987, 92, 96; contbr. articles to profl. jours. Family and matrimonial. Home: 1101 Saint Paul St Apt 2104 Baltimore MD 21202-2673 Office: Thomas & Kalichman 7 Saint Paul St Ste 950 Baltimore MD 21202-1672

**THOMAS, DANIEL HOLCOMBE,** federal judge; b. Prattville, Ala., Aug. 25, 1906; s. Columbus Eugene and Augusta (Pratt) T.; m. Dorothy Quina, Sept. 26, 1936 (dec. 1977); children: Daniel H., Jr., Merrill Pratt; m. Catharine J. Miller, Oct. 25, 1979. LL.B., U. Ala., 1928. Bar: bar. Pvt. practice Mobile, Ala., 1929; asst. solicitor Mobile County; mem. firm Lyons, Chamberlain & Courtney, Mobile County, 1932-37, Lyons & Thomas, Mobile County, 1937-43, Lyons, Thomas & Pipes, Mobile County, 1946-51; judge U.S. Dist. Ct., Mobile, 1951-71, sr. judge, 1971—. Mem. exec. bd. Mobile Area council Boy Scouts Am., 1963—, v.p., 1967-69, pres., 1973—, mem. nat. council, 1973—, Trustee dept. archieves and history, State of Ala. Served with USNR, 1943-45. Recipient Silver Beaver award Boy Scouts Am., 1970, Silver Antelope award, 1975. Methodist. Club: Mobile Country. Home: 13 Dogwood Cir Mobile AL 36608-2308 Office: US Dist Ct 459 US Courthouse Mobile AL 36602

**THOMAS, DAVID ALBERT,** law educator; b. L.A., Feb. 4, 1944; s. Albert Rees and Betty Lou (Adams) T.; m. Paula Rasmussen, Aug. 7, 1967; children: Rebecca, David R., John H., Matthew A., Susannah, Amanda, Christina, Erin. BA, Brigham Young U., 1967; JD, Duke U., 1972; MLS, Brigham Young U., 1977. Jud. clk. U.S. Dist. Ct. Utah, Salt Lake City, 1972-73; pvt. practice Salt Lake City, 1973-74; asst. prof. Law Sch. Brigham Young U., Provo, Utah, 1974-76; assoc. prof. Law Sch. Brigham Young U., Provo, 1976-79, prof. Law Sch., 1979—, dir. law libr. Law Sch., 1974-90; accreditation site insp. ABA, Chgo., 1978—. Author: Utah Civil Procedure, 1980, (with others) A Practical Guide to Disputes Between Adjoining Landowners, 1989, Utah Civil Practice, 1992, (with others) Thomas and Backman on Utah Real Property Law, 1999; prin. author, editor-in-chief: Thompson on Real Property, Thomas Edition, 15 vols., 1994; contbr. articles to profl. jours. With U.S. Army, 1969-71, Vietnam. Mem. ABA (chair real property probate & trust sect. legis. com. 1990-98). Home: 188 E 1864 S Orem UT 84058-7864 Office: Law Sch Brigham Young U Provo UT 84602

**THOMAS, DAVID ROBERT,** lawyer; b. New Haven, Jan. 6, 1954; children: Michael Patrick, Shawn Christopher. BA, U. New Haven, 1977; JD, George Mason U., 1980. Bar: Conn. 1981, U.S. Dist. Ct. Conn. 1981. Assoc. Groob & Ressler, P.C., New Haven, 1981, Tobin & Levine, New Haven, 1981-83; pvt. practice Wallingford, Conn., 1983-85; exec. v.p., gen. counsel CMC Devel. Co., Inc., 1984-87; pres. Multitech New Eng., Inc., Wallingford, 1987-89; ptnr. Thomas & Flynn, Wallingford, 1990-92; pvt. practice Guilford, Conn., 1992-94; COO Cryotek East, Inc., New Haven, 1994-95; pvt. practive Guilford, Conn., 1996—; founder Housing Am., Inc., Home Am., Wallingford, 1990. Chmn. Community Nursery Sch., Guilford, Conn., 1989-90; coach, commr. Guilford Little League. Mem. ABA (devel. and fin. of condominium projects com. real property div. 1989), Conn. Bar Assn. (subcom. on residential practice 1988), Duck Island Yacht Club, Delta Theta Phi. Republican. Avocations: sailing, sailboat racing, running, auto racing, karate. Real property, Finance, General corporate. Home: PO Box 260 Guilford CT 06437-0260 Office: 35 State St Guilford CT 06437-2722

**THOMAS, ELIZABETH,** lawyer; b. N.Y.C., Jan. 29, 1953; d. Howard E. and Edna Patrecia (McGuire) T.; m. Ronald L. Roseman, Aug. 14, 1986; 1 Child: Catherine Blake Roseman. BA, Wellesley Coll., 1975; JD cum laude, Harvard U., 1979. Bar: Mass., 1979, Wash., 1980. Law clk. to Hon. A. David Mazzone U.S. Dist. Ct. Mass., Boston, 1979-80; atty. Evergreen Legal Svcs., Seattle, 1980-87; assoc. Preston Gates & Ellis, Seattle, 1987-89, ptnr., 1990—, chair environ. dept., 1997-98. Contbr. articles to profl. jours. Chair Energy Facility Siting Process Rev. Com.; vice-chair rate adv. com. Seattle City Light Citizens; mem. conservation programs task force N.W. Power Coun.; mem. cost allocation adv. group energy com. Seattle City Coun.; tech. advisor Demand and Resource Evaluation Project Puget Sound Power & Light. Mem. ABA (mem. pub. utilities sect., mem. natural resources & enviroment sect.), N.W. Pub. Power Assn., Phi Beta Kappa. E-mail: ethomas@prestongates.com. Public utilities, Municipal (including bonds), Natural resources. Office: Preston Gates & Ellis LLP 701 5th Ave Ste 5000 Seattle WA 98104-7078

**THOMAS, ELLA COOPER,** lawyer; b. Ft. Totten, N.Y.; d. Avery John and Ona Caroline (Gibson) C.; m. Robert Edward Lee Thomas, Nov. 22, 1938 (dec. Jan. 1985); 1 child, Robert Edward Lee Jr. Student, Vassar Coll., 1932-34, U. Hawaii, 1934-35, George Washington U., 1935-36; JD, George Washington U., 1940. Bar: U.S. Dist. Ct. D.C. 1942, U.S. Ct. Appeals (D.C. cir.) 1943, U.S. Supreme Ct. 1947, U.S. Tax Ct. 1973. Secret maps custodian U.S. Dist. Engrs., Honolulu, 1941-42; contbg. editor Labor Rels. Reporter, Washington, 1942; assoc. Smith, Ristig & Smith, Washington, 1942-45; law libr. George Washington Law Sch., Washington, 1946-53; reporter of decisions U.S. Tax Ct., Washington, 1953-75. Author: Law of Libel and Slander, 1949. Mem. Inter-Am. Bar Assn. (coun. mem. 1973—), D.C. Bar Assn. Avocations: physical fitness, crostics, mote marine lab. vol. computer.

**THOMAS, EUGENE C.,** lawyer; b. Idaho Falls, Idaho, Feb. 8, 1931; s. C.E. Thomas; m. Jody Raber; children: Michael E., Stephen R. A.B., Columbia U., 1952, J.D., 1954, LLD (hon.) Univ. Idaho, 1986, LLD (hon.), Coll. of Idaho, 1987. Bar: Idaho, 1954, U.S. Dist. Ct. Idaho 1957, US Ct. Appeals (9th cir.) 1958, U.S. Supreme Ct. 1970. Pros. atty. Ada County, Boise, Idaho, 1955-57; founding ptnr. Moffatt, Thomas, Barrett, Rock & Fields, Boise, 19578—; bd. dirs. Shore Lodge, Inc., McCall, Idaho, Nelson-Ball Paper Products, Inc., Longview, Wash., Peregrine Industries, Inc., Boise. Bd. editors ABA Jour., 1980-87. Bd. dirs. St. Luke's Regional Med. Ctr. and Mountain States Tumor Inst., Boise, 1963—, pres., chmn. bd. 1972-79; trustee Coll. of Idaho, 1980—, mem. exec. com., 1982—; trustee Associated Taxpayers of Idaho, 1983—, chmn., 1988-90. trustee Boise Futures Found., 1973—, bd. dirs., 1981—, bd. dirs. Univ./Community Health Scis. Assn., 1981—; chmn. Mayor's Select Com. on Downtown Devel., 1982-83. Named Exec. of Yr., Boise chpt. Nat. Secs. Assn., 1978, John Price lectr. 1987 ann. conf. Nat. Coll. Dist. Attys.; recipient disting. svc. award Idaho Pros. Attys., 1985, disting. svc. award Chgo. Vol. Legal Svc. Found., 1986. Fellow Internat. Acad. Trial Lawyers, Am. Bar Found. (trustee 1980-82, 86-87), Am. Law Inst.; mem. ABA (ho. of dels. 1971—, chmn. ho. of dels. 1980-82, bd. govs. 1980-82, pres. 1986-87, chmn. spl. com. on internat. affairs 1987-88), Idaho State Bar (pres. 1971-72, disting. lawyer award 1980, 86), Def. Research Inst. (state chmn. Pacific region 1978—), Idaho Assn. Def. Counsel (trustee 1966-69, pres. 1967-68), Internat. Assn. Ins. Counsel, Am. Bd. Trial Advocates, Fourth Dist. Bar Assn. (pres. 1962-63), Internat. Bar Assn. (chmn. biennial conf., governing coun. 1985-86), Conference of Pres. Union Internat. des Avocats (pres.), Nat. Conf. Bar Pres. (trustee 1974-76), Law Soc. Eng. and Wales (hon.), La Barra Mexicana (hon.), New Zealand Law Soc. (hon.), Can. Bar Assn. (hon.), Integrated Bar of the Philippines (hon.), Rocky Mountain Oil and Gas Assn. (chmn. Idaho legal com. 1978—). Clubs: Arid (dir. 1977-79), Hillcrest Country (bd. dirs. 1969-72) (Boise). General corporate, General civil litigation, Legislative. Office: Moffatt Thomas Barrett Rock & Fields PO Box 829 Boise ID 83701-5958

**THOMAS, FRANK M., JR.,** lawyer; b. Feb. 20, 1947. BA, Amherst Coll., 1969; M in City Planning, Harvard U., 1973; JD, U. Pa., 1977. Bar: Pa. 1977, U.S. Supreme Ct. 1983. Ptnr. Morgan, Lewis & Bockius, Phila. Office: Morgan Lewis & Bockius 1701 Market St Philadelphia PA 19103-2903

**THOMAS, GREGG DARROW,** lawyer; b. Jacksonville, Fla., July 31, 1951. BA magna cum laude, Vanderbilt U., 1972; JD with honors, U. Fla., 1976. Bar: Fla. 1976, D.C. 1978. Law clk. U.S. Dist. Ct. (mid. dist.) Fla., 1976-79; mem. Holland & Knight, Tampa, Fla., 1979-; ptnr., 1983-. Exec. editor U. Fla. Law Rev., 1975-76. Bd. dirs. Vol. Lawyer's Resource Ctr., 1990-95; trustee Tampa Mus. of Art, 1993—, vice chmn., 1998, chair, 1999. Mem. ABA (mem. forum com. comm. law 1983—), Am. Judicature Soc., Fla. Bar (co-chair Fla. bar media and comm. com. 1987-88, mem. grievance com. 1988, chmn. 1989-91), Fla. Bar Found. (mem. legal assistance to poor com. 1988—), Hillsborough Bar Assn., D.C. Bar, Phi Beta Kappa. Libel, Constitutional, Intellectual property. Office: Holland & Knight PO Box 1288 400 N Ashley Dr Ste 2300 Tampa FL 33602-4322

**THOMAS, HERMAN,** state judge; b. Mobile, Ala., Jan. 6, 1961; s. Daniel Thomas and Bernice Young; m. Linda Grant, June 25, 1987; children: Brooke Alexis, Andrea Michelle. BS, U. S. Ala., 1983; JD, Fla. State U., 1985. Bar: Fla., Ala., U.S. Dist. Ct. (so. dist.) Ala., U.S. Dist. Ct. Appeals (11th cir.). Adminstrv. asst. Coll. Law Fla. State U., Tallahassee, 1985-86; asst. state atty. 4th Jud. Cir. Fla., Jacksonville, 1986, 1st Jud. Cir. Fla., Pensacola, 1986-87; asst. dist. atty. 13th Jud. Cir. Ala., Mobile, 1987-90, dist. ct. judge, 1990—; adj. prof. U. S. Ala., Mobile, 1990-94, Spring Hill Coll., Mobile, 1994. Mem. sch. bd. McGill-Toolen H.S.; trustee U. S. Ala., Spring Hill Coll.; cmty. adv. Jr. League Mobile; bd. dirs. S. Ala. Med. Sci. Found., Family Exch. Ctr., Family Counseling Ctr., Parents as First Tchrs., Mobile Mental Health, Inc., Penelope Ho. Shelter, Mobile Sport Commn., Coalition Drug Free Mobile, Boys and Girls Club Greater Mobile, Inc., Am.'s Jr. Miss, Mobile Opera Bd., Ala. Civil Justice Found.; mem. A+ Coalition Better Edn.; cmty. chmn. Success by Six-United W ay; mem. adv. bd. Charter Hosp., Cath. Svc. Ctr., USA Comprehensive Sickle Cell Ctr., Autism Found. Ala.; mem. Challenge 2.0.0.0; mem. sch. bd. St. James, lector, Sunday sch. instr., youth club advisor; mem. Knights Peter Claver. 1st. lt. U.S. Army. Named Outstanding Young Man Am., 1986; recipient Disting. Citizen award. Mem. 100 Black Men Greater Mobile, Inc., U. S. Ala. Alumni (past pres., bd. dirs.), Mobile Sunrise Rotary, Mobile Inn Ct., Kappa Alpha Psi, Phi Kappa Phi. Democrat. Roman Catholic.

**THOMAS, JACQUELINE MARIE,** lawyer; b. Rochester, N.Y., June 29, 1967; d. Robert J. and Frances P. (Pata) T.; m. Jeffrey W. Raetz, May 16, 1992. BA, St. John Fisher Coll., 1988; JD cum laude, Union U., 1991. Bar: N.Y. 1992. Assoc. Bouck, Holloway, Kiernan & Casey, Albany, N.Y., 1991-

94, Lacy, Katzen, Ryen & Mittleman, Rochester, 1994—. Mem. N.Y. State Bar Assn., N.Y. State Trial Lawyers Assn., Monroe County Bar Assn. General civil litigation, Personal injury, Insurance. Office: Lacy Katzen Ryen and Mittleman 130 E Main St Ste 200 Rochester NY 14604-1620

**THOMAS, JAMES WILLIAM,** lawyer; b. N.Y.C., May 12, 1949; s. Howard and Alice (Brennan) T.; m. Cecilia Coleman Goad, July 7, 1973; children: James William, Brennan McKinney. BS, U. Dayton, 1971; JD, Ohio No. U., 1974. Bar: Ohio 1974, U.S. Dist. Ct. Ohio 1976. Ptnr. Earley & Thomas, Eaton, Ohio, 1974-89; pvt. rpactice Eaton, 1989—; village solicitor Village of Lewisburg (Ohio), 1977-81, Village of Verona (Ohio), 1979-81; asst. pros. atty. Preble County (Ohio), 1980-81. Mem. Preble County Cmty. Corrections Planing Bd. Fellow Ohio State Bar Found.; mem. ABA, Ohio State Bar Assn., Ohio State Bar Coll., Ohio Acad. Trial Lawyers, Ohio Assn. Criminal Def. Lawyers, Preble county Bar Assn. (pres. 1982-84), Comm. Improvement Corp., Eaton Country Club, Rotary (dir. 1980-87, pres. 1987-88). Republican. Roman Catholic. Avocations: boating, tennis. State civil litigation, Criminal, Real property. Home: 761 Vinland Cv Eaton OH 45320-2536 Office: 112 N Barron St Eaton OH 45320-1702

**THOMAS, JASON SELIG,** lawyer; b. Lansing, Mich., Jan. 23, 1954; s. William Ellsworth and Esta (Berg) T.; m. Edith Madeline Gettes, Oct. 28, 1995; children: Monica, Sophia. BMus, Oberlin Coll., 1976; MMus, SUNY, Stony Brook, 1978; JD, U. N.C., 1991; D of Mus. Arts, U. Wis., 1991. Bar: N.C. 1991, U.S. Dist. Ct. (ea. dist.) N.C. 1992, U.S. Dist. Ct. (mid. and we. dists.) N.C. 1995, U.S. Ct. Appeals (4th cir.) 1994. Prin. cellist Ark. Symphony Orch., Little Rock, 1978-81; asst. prof. U. Ky., Lexington, 1981-82; freelance cellist Ludwigshafen, West Germany, 1986-87; assoc. Moore & Van Allen, Raleigh, N.C., 1991-92, Hunton & Williams, Raleigh, 1992—; bd. dirs. East Carolina Legal Svcs. Corp. Contbg. author: Toxic Tort and Hazardous Substance Litigation, 1985. Bd. dirs. Cmty. Music Sch., Raleigh, 1995—. Recipient Outstanding Vol. Atty. award Wake County, N.C., 1995, 97. Mem. ABA, N.C. Bar Assn. (pro bono com. 1998), Wake County Bar Assn. Environmental, Administrative and regulatory, General civil litigation. Office: Hunton & Williams 1 Hannover Sq Ste 1400 Raleigh NC 27601-1757

**THOMAS, JEFFREY WALTON,** lawyer; b. Seattle, Nov. 12, 1960. BA, Wesleyan U., Middletown, Conn., 1984; JD, Hastings Coll. Law, San Francisco, 1989. Bar: Calif. 1989, Wash. 1992. Assoc. Pillsbury, Madison & Satro, San Francisco, 1989-91; assoc. Betts, Patterson & Moss, Seattle, 1992-95; mem. Thomas Law Offices, L.L.C., Seattle, 1995—. Mem. Madison Pk. Cmty. Coun., Seattle, 1995—. General civil litigation, Estate planning. Office: Thomas Law Offices LLC 999 3rd Ave Ste 4750 Seattle WA 98104-4042

**THOMAS, JOSEPH WESLEY,** lawyer; b. Detroit, Aug. 16, 1955; s. John Joseph and Geraldine Clare (France) T.; m. Jamie Ann MacKercher, Aug. 16, 1980. B.A., Oakland U., 1977; J.D., Thomas M. Cooley Law Sch., 1980; M.L.T., Georgetown U., 1982. Bar: D.C. 1980, Mich. 1981, U.S. Dist. Ct. D.C. 1981, U.S. Dist. Ct. (ea. dist.) Mich. 1981, U.S. Tax Ct. 1981, U.S. Ct. Appeals (D.C. cir.) 1981, U.S. Ct. Appeals (6th cir.) 1982. Assoc. Dickstein, Shapiro & Morin, Washington, 1980-81; sole practice, Troy, Mich., 1982-83; ptnr. Farhat & Thomas, P.C., Farmington Hills, Mich., 1983-86; ptnr. Driggers, Schultz, Herbst & Paterson, Troy, Mich., 1986—; panel mem. Mich. Atty. Discipline Bd. Mem. Mich. Bar Assn. (com. on unauthorized practice of law). Office: Driggers Schultz Herbst & Paterson 888 W Big Beaver Rd Suite 400 Troy MI 48084

**THOMAS, JOSEPH WINAND,** lawyer; b. New Orleans, Aug. 2, 1940; s. Gerald Henry and Edith Louise (Winand) T.; m. Claudette Condoll, Aug. 2, 1960 (div. Nov. 1985); children: Jeffery J., Anthony W.; m. Shawn B. Watkins, May 26, 1986 (div. June 1989); children: Adelle, Anne; m. Sandra J. Green, May 17, 1992; children: Winand, Elizabeth, Alice, Shepard, Julia. BS, Loyola U., Chgo., 1967; JD, Loyola U., New Orleans, 1973; MBA, Tulane U., 1984. Bar: La. 1973, U.S. Dist. Ct. (ea. dist.) La. 1973, U.S. Ct. Appeals (5th cir.) 1973, U.S. Supreme Ct. 1976, D.C. 1980. Staff atty. New Orleans Legal Assistance Corp., 1973-74; asst. atty. gen. State of La., 1974-80; pvt. practice New Orleans, 1980—; Pres., bd. dirs. New Orleans Legal Assistance Corp. Active NAACP, New Orleans, 1987-89; bd. dirs. Urban League, New Orleans. Mem. ABA, Louis Martinet Legal Soc., New Orleans Bar Assn., La. Bar Assn. Democrat. Roman Catholic. Personal injury, General civil litigation, State civil litigation. Office: 2 Canal St New Orleans LA 70130-1408

**THOMAS, LINDA S.,** lawyer; b. San Antonio, Aug. 24, 1956; d. James Samuel and Suzanne Cyrus; m. James Russell Daniel, June 12, 1976 (div. Oct. 1991); children: Brad Daniel, Allison Daniel, Amy Daniel; m. Curtis Todd Thomas, July 31, 1993. BA in Speech Pathology, Ouachita Bapt. U., Arkadelphia, Ark., 1977; JD, U. Tulsa, 1994. Bar: Okla. 1994. Speech pathologist DeQueen (Ark.) Pub. Schs., 1977-80, spl. edn. tchr., 1984-85, elem. sch. tchr., 1985-90; elem. sch. tchr. Bartlesville (Okla.) Pub. Schs., 1990-97; atty. Brewer, Worten, Robinett, Bartlesville, 1994-97, Davis Law Office, Bartlesville, 1997; sole practice Thomas Law Office, Bartlesville, 1997—. Mem. ABA, Okla. Bar Assn., Washington County Bar Assn., PEO (pres.). Family and matrimonial, General practice, Juvenile. Office: 117 W 5th St Ste 200 Bartlesville OK 74003-6615

**THOMAS, LOLA BOHN,** lawyer; b. Mpls., June 27, 1951; d. David and Dorothy (Reynolds) B.; m. Michael Thomas; children: Lili, Lynn. Grad., Yale Coll., 1972, Stanford U., 1975. Pvt. practice Miami Beach, Fla. E-mail: lolathomas@aol.com. Contracts commercial, Real property, General corporate. Office: 77 N Hibiscus Dr Miami Beach FL 33139-5117

**THOMAS, LOWELL SHUMWAY, JR.,** lawyer; b. Phila., Aug. 9, 1931; s. Lowell Shumway and Josephine (McVey) T.; m. Judith Evans, Aug. 27, 1955; children: Megan E., Heather McVey, Lowell S., Taylor G. BA, Dartmouth Coll., 1953; JD, U. Pa., 1960. Bar: Pa. 1961, U.S. Tax Ct. 1961, U.S. Dist. Ct. (ea. dist.) Pa. 1961, U.S. Ct. Appeals (3d cir.) 1961. Assoc. Duane, Morris & Heckscher, Phila., 1960-64; assoc. Saul, Ewing, Remick & Saul, Phila., 1965-68, ptnr., 1968-96, of counsel, 1997—; bd. dirs. Boardwalk Securities Corp., Peter Lumber Co., Chestnut Hill Acad., Phila., 1978-86; bd. dirs. Southeastern Pa. ARC, 1975-82, chmn., 1983-86, bd. govs., 1989-95; trustee Beaver Coll. 1987—, chmn., 1989-93. Author: Taxation of Marriage, Separation and Divorce, 1986. Lt. USN, 1953-57. Fellow Am. Coll. Tax Counsel; mem. ABA, Pa. Bar Assn., Phila. Bar Assn., Phila. Bar Found. (trustee 1980-83), Am. Law Inst. Republican. Episcopalian. Clubs: Union League (bd. dirs. 1979-82, treas. 1981-82). Corporate taxation, Personal income taxation, Pension, profit-sharing, and employee benefits. Office: Saul Ewing Remick & Saul 3800 Centre Sq W Philadelphia PA 19102

**THOMAS, MARGOT EVA,** lawyer; b. Grass Valley, Calif., Apr. 28, 1943; d. Walter Frederick and Edith Louise (Clark) T.; life ptnr. Rose Maloof; children: Matthew E. Albertson, Nicholas E. Albertson, Elizabeth R. Albertson. AB, Brown U., 1965; JD, Western New Eng. Coll., 1981. Bar: Mass. 1981. Field worker So. Christian Leadership Conf., Lisman, Ala., 1965-66; computer programmer Irving Trust Co., N.Y.C., 1966-67; social worker Phila. Dept. Welfare, 1968-70; field dir. Girl Scouts of Delaware County Pa., Upper Darby, 1971-73; project dir. Pioneer Valley Girl Scouts, Springfield, Mass., 1973-74; pvt. practice lawyer Northampton, Mass., 1981—. Pres. Northampton (Mass.) Girls Soccer Assn., 1985-91; chair Northampton (Mass.) City Dem. Com., 1989-91. Mem. Nat. Lawyers Guild, Women's Bar Assn., Mass. Bar Assn., Hampshire County Bar Assn., Mass. Assn. Women Lawyers, Mass. Lesbian and Gay Bar Assn. Real property, Probate, Alternative dispute resolution. Office: 78 Main St Northampton MA 01060-3111

**THOMAS, MARK STANTON,** lawyer; b. Leaksville, N.C., Oct. 28, 1952; s. J. Kenneth and Vivian (Butler) T.; m. Sarah Elizabeth Zeigler, June 4, 1988; 1 child, Elizabeth Christine. BA, Wake Forest U., 1975, JD, 1978. Bar: N.C. 1978, U.S. Dist. Ct. (mid. dist.) N.C. 1978, U.S. Dist. Ct. (ea. dist.) 1982, U.S. Ct. Appeals (4th cir.) 1982, U.S. Dist. Ct. (we. dist.) N.C. 1992, U.S. Supreme Ct. 1999. Assoc. Maupin Taylor & Ellis, P.A., Raleigh, N.C., 1981-85, shareholder, 1985—; v.p. N.C. Vol. Lawyers for the Arts, Raleigh, 1987-90, pres. 1990. Bd. dirs. Raleigh Little Theatre, 1985-88, atty., 1983-84; bd. dirs. Raleigh Ensemble Players, 1986-88; bd. dirs. Theatre in the Park, Raleigh, 1988-93, pres., 1991-92; mem. City of Raleigh Arts Commn., 1990-94; mem. Triangle Benefits Forum, 1990—, pres., 1994-95. Mem. ABA, N.C. Bar Assn. (chair comms. adv. com. 1989-91, co-chair com. women in legal profession 1993-94), Def. Rsch. Inst., N.C. Assn. Def. Attys. Democrat. Trademark and copyright, Pension, profit-sharing, and employee benefits, General civil litigation. Office: Maupin Taylor & Ellis PA 3200 Beech Leaf Ct Raleigh NC 27604-1085

**THOMAS, RANDALL STUART,** lawyer, educator; b. Princeton, N.J., Nov. 25, 1955; s. John Bowman and Eleanor (Graefe) T.; m. Cheri D. Ferrari; children: Cameron Stuart, Cortland Andrew, Colin Duncan, Carson F. Thomas. BA, Haverford Coll., 1977; MA, U. Mich., 1979, PhD, 1983, JD, 1985. Bar: Del. 1987, U.S. Dist. Ct. Del. 1987. Economist U. Mich., Ann Arbor, 1979-83; law clk. Fed. Dist. Ct. (ea. dist.) Mich., Ann Arbor, 1985; assoc. Potter, Anderson & Corroon, Wilmington, Del., 1986, Skadden, Arps, Slate, Meagher & Flom, Wilmington, 1987-90; assoc. prof. law U. Iowa, 1990-94, prof. law, 1994—; vis. prof. Boston U. Law Sch., 1995, U. Mich. Law Sch., 1996, Duke U. Sch. Law, 1999. Rackham fellow U. Mich., 1982-83. Democrat. Methodist. Lodge: Order of Coif. General corporate, Mergers and acquisitions, Securities. Office: U Iowa Sch Law Iowa City IA 52242

**THOMAS, RICHARD VAN,** state supreme court justice; b. Superior, Wyo., Oct. 11, 1932; s. John W. and Gertrude (McCloskey) T.; m. Lesley Arlene Ekman, June 23, 1956; children: Tara Lynn, Richard Ross, Laura Lee, Sidney Marie. B.S. in Bus. Adminstrn. with honors, U. Wyo., 1954, LL.B. with honors, 1956; LL.M., NYU, 1961. Bar: Wyo. 1956, U.S. Ct. Appeals (10th cir.) 1960, U.S. Ct. Mil. Appeals 1960, U.S. Supreme Ct. 1960. Law clk. to judge U.S. Ct. Appeals (10th Circuit), Cheyenne, 1960-63; assoc. firm Hirst & Applegate, Cheyenne, 1963-64; partner firm Hirst, Applegate & Thomas, Cheyenne, 1964-69; U.S. atty. Dist. Wyo., Cheyenne, 1969-74; justice Wyo. Supreme Ct., Cheyenne, 1974—, chief justice, 1985-86. Pres. Laramie County United Way, 1972, trustee, 1973-74, chmn. admissions and allocations com., 1968-69, chmn. exec. com., 1973, chmn. combined fed. campaign, 1974; bd. dirs. Goodwill Industries Wyo., Inc., 1974-77; exec. com. Cheyenne Crusade for Christ, 1974; v.p., exec. com. Wyo. Billy Graham Crusade, 1987; bd. dirs. Cheyenne Youth for Christ, 1978-81; chancellor Episcopal Diocese of Wyo., 1972—, lay dep. gen. conv., 1973—, chmn. search evaluation nomination com., 1976-77, lay reader, 1969—; bd. dirs. Community Action of Laramie County, 1977-82; chmn. Cheyenne dist. Boy Scouts Am., 1977-78, mem. nat. council, 1982-84, mem. Longs Peak council, 1977—, v.p. dist. ops., v.p. membership relationships, 1979-81, pres., 1981-83; mem. North Cen. Region Exec. Bd., 1986—, pres. Old West Trails Area, 1988—; chmn. Laramie County Health Planning Com., 1980-84. Served with JAGC USAF, 1957-60. Named Boss of Year, Indian Paintbrush chpt. Nat. Secs. Assn., 1974; Civil Servant of Year, Cheyenne Assn. Govt. Employees, 1973; Vol. of Yr., Cheyenne Office, Youth Alternatives, 1979; recipient St. George Episcopal award, 1982, Silver Beaver award Boy Scouts Am., 1985. Mem. Am., Laramie County bar assns., Wyo. State Bar, Phi Kappa Phi, Phi Alpha Delta, Omicron Delta Kappa, Sigma Nu. Clubs: Kiwanis (Cheyenne) (program com. 1969-70, dir. 1970-72, chmn. key club com. 1973-76, disting. pres. 1980-81), Masons (Cheyenne) (33 deg., past master); Shriners; Nat. Sojourners (Cheyenne). Office: Wyo Supreme Ct Supreme Ct Bldg 2301 Capitol Ave Cheyenne WY 82002-0001*

**THOMAS, ROBERT F.,** lawyer; b. Phila., Apr. 20, 1968; s. Robert and Delores Thomas; m. Robynne Lee Peavy, Aug. 7, 1993; 1 child, Lauryn. BA, St. Joseph's U., 1990; JD, Rutgers U., 1993. Law clk. to Hon. Francine I. Axelrod Woodbury, N.J., 1993-94; assoc. Katz Eltin Levine Kurzweil Weber & Scialabba, Cherry Hill, N.J., 1994—. Contbr. articles to profl. jours. Mem. Pi Kappa Phi. Republican. Roman Catholic. Avocations: golf, military history, space program. General civil litigation, Consumer commercial, State and local taxation. Office: Katz Eltin Levine Kurzweil Weher Scialabba 904 Kings Hwy N Cherry Hill NJ 08034-1517

**THOMAS, SIDNEY R.,** federal judge; b. Bozeman, Mont., Aug. 14, 1953; m. Martha Sheehy. BA in Speech-Comm., Mont. State U., 1975, JD cum laude, 1978. Bar: Mont. 1978, U.S. Dist. Ct. Mont. 1978, U.S. Ct. Appeals (9th cir.) 1980, U.S. Dist. Ct. (9th cir.) 1980, U.S. Ct. Fed. Claims 1986, U.S. Supreme Ct. 1994. Shareholder Moulton, Bellimgham, Longo and Mather, P.C., Billings, 1978-96; judge U.S. Ct. Appeals 9th Cir., Billings, 1996—; adj. instr. Rocky Mountain Coll., Billings, 1982-95. Contbr. articles to profl. jours. Recipient Gov.'s award for pub. svc., 1978, Outstanding Faculty award Rocky Mountain Coll., 1988. Mem. ABA, State Bar Mont., Yellowstone County Bar Assn. Office: US Ct Appeals Ninth Circuit PO Box 31478 Billings MT 59107-1478

**THOMAS, STEPHEN PAUL,** lawyer; b. Bloomington, Ill., July 30, 1938; s. Owen Wilson and Mary Katherine (Paulsen) T.; m. Marieanne Sauer, Dec. 7, 1963 (dec. June 1984); 1 child, Catherine Marie; m. Marcia Aldrich Toomey, May 28, 1988; 1 child, Ellen Antonia. BA, U. Ill., 1959; LLB, Harvard U., 1962. Bar: Ill. 1962. Vol. Peace Corps, Malawi, Africa, 1963-65; assoc. Sidley & Austin and predecessor firms, Chgo., 1965-70, ptnr., 1970—; lectr. on law Malawi Inst. Pub. Adminstrn., 1963-65. Pres. Hyde Park-Kenwood Cmty. Conf., Chgo., 1988-90; trustee Chgo. Acad. for Arts, 1991—, chmn., 1992-97; bd. dirs. Ctr. for Ethics Garrett-Evang. Theol. Sem., Evanston, Ill., 1995—, Union League Civic and Arts Found., Chgo., 1999—. Recipient Paul Cornell award Hyde Park Hist. Soc., 1981. Mem. ABA, Chgo. Bar Assn., Chgo. Fedn. of Musicians, Legal and Law Clubs Chgo., Union League Club Chgo. Democrat. Roman Catholic. Avocation: jazz piano playing. General corporate, Private international, Securities. Home: 5740 S Harper Ave Chicago IL 60637-1841 Office: Sidley & Austin 1 First Natl Plz Chicago IL 60603-2003

**THOMAS, WAYNE LEE,** lawyer; b. Sept. 22, 1945; s. Willard McSwain and June Frances (Jones) T.; m. Patricia H. Thomas, Mar. 16, 1968; children: Brigitte Elisabeth Williams, Kate Adelaide. BA, U. Fla., 1967, JD cum laude, 1971. Bar: Fla. 1971, U.S. Supreme Ct. 1975, U.S. Ct. Appeals (5th cir.) 1975, U.S. Ct. Appeals (11th cir.) 1981, U.S. Ct. Claims 1976, U.S. Dist. Ct. (mid. dist.) Fla. 1973, U.S. Dist. Ct. (so. dist. trial bar) Fla. 1975; cert. mediator and arbitrator. Law clk. U.S. Dist. Ct. (mid. dist.) Fla., 1971-73; assoc. Trenam, Simmons, Kemker, Scharf, Barkin, Frye & O'Neill, PA, Tampa, 1973-77, ptnr., 1978-81; founder, pres. McKay & Thomas, PA, Tampa, 1981-89; ptnr. Carlton, Fields, Ward, Emmanuel, Smith & Cutler, PA, 1989-95; pvt. practice Tampa, 1995—. Mem. ABA, Fla. Bar (chmn. sect. gen. practice 1981-83, mem. ethics com., vice chmn. unauthorized practice law com. 1994-98, vice chmn. fed. practice com. 1995-96, chmn. 1996-97, mem. bd. bar examiners 1986-91, chmn. 1990-91, chmn. unauthorized practice law com. 13A 1998—), Nat. Conf. Bar Examiners (multistate profl. responsibility exam. policy com. 1994—), Hillsborough County Bar Assn. (chmn. grievance com. 1985-86), Order of Coif, Fla. Blue Key, Phi Kappa Phi, Omicron Delta Kappa. Democrat. Federal civil litigation, State civil litigation, Alternative dispute resolution. Office: 707 N Franklin St Fl 10 Tampa FL 33602-4430

**THOMASCH, ROGER PAUL,** lawyer; b. N.Y.C., Nov. 7, 1942; s. Gordon J. and Margaret (Molloy) T.; children: Laura Leigh, Paul Butler. BA, Coll. William and Mary, 1964; LLB, Duke U., 1967. Bar: Conn. 1967, Colo. 1974. Assoc. atty. Cummings & Lockwood, Stamford, Conn., 1967-70; trial atty. U.S. Dept. Justice, Washington, 1970-73; ptnr. Roath & Brega, Denver, 1975-87; mng. ptnr. Denver office of Ballard, Spahr, Andrews & Ingersoll LLP, 1987—; vis. assoc. prof. of law Drake U. Sch. Law, Des Moines, 1973-74; frequent lectr. in field, U.S. and Can.; adj. faculty mem. U. Denver Coll. Law, 1976-80. Recipient Leland Forrest Outstanding Prof. award, Drake U. Sch. Law, 1973. Fellow Am. Coll. of Trial Lawyers, Colo. Bar Found.; mem. ABA, Colo. Bar Assn., Denver Country Club, Univ. Club, Denver Athletic Club. Federal civil litigation, State civil litigation, Antitrust. Office: Ballard Spahr Andrews & Ingersoll LLP 1225 17th St Ste 2300 Denver CO 80202-5535

**THOME, DENNIS WESLEY,** lawyer; b. Yakima, Wash., Feb. 1, 1939; s. Walter John and Vareta Lucille (Voris) T.; m. Penelope Lee Freeman, Aug. 27, 1961; children: Christopher, Geoffrey. BSBA, U. Denver, 1961, JD, 1967. Bar: Colo. 1967, U.S. Dist. Ct. Colo. 1967, Calif. 1971, U.S. Dist. Ct. (cen. dist.) Calif. 1971, U.S. Supreme Ct. 1971, U.S. Ct. Appeals (9th cir.) 1972. Assoc. Pehr & Newman, Westminster, Colo., 1967-69, Juggert, VaVerka & Wayman, Costa Mesa, Calif., 1975-77; house counsel Wycliffe Bible Translators, Inc., Huntington Beach, Calif., 1969-73; pvt. practice Newport Beach, Calif., 1973-75, Denver, 1977—; bd. dirs. First Fruit, Inc., Newport Beach, MOPS Internat., Inc., Denver, Reach Internat., Inc., Denver; mem. Centennial Estate Planning Coun., 1977—. Treas. Gibson for Mayor Com., Denver, 1967; bd. dirs. Christian Eye Ministry, Inc., San Diego, 1983-91, World Eye Care, Inc., 1990-91, Christian Legal Soc. Metro Denver, Inc., 1994-98; chmn. Arvada (Colo.) Covenant Ch., 1993-94; bd. dirs., sec. Wycliffe Bible Translators, Inc., Huntington Beach, Calif., 1977-83. Mem. Colo. Bar Assn. (Bill of Rights com. 1977-90, 92—), State Bar Calif., Omicron Delta Kappa. Avocations: city league volleyball. Non-profit and tax-exempt organizations, Estate planning, Probate. Office: 7515 W 17th Ave Ste C Lakewood CO 80215-3302

**THOMPSON, ALVIN W.,** judge; b. 1953. BA, Princeton U., 1975; JD, Yale U., 1978. With Robinson & Cole, Hartford, Conn., 1978-94; dist. judge U.S. Dist. Ct., Conn., 1994—. Mem. ABA, Conn. Bar Assn., Hartford County Bar Assn. Office: US Dist Ct 450 Main St Rm 240 Hartford CT 06103-3022

**THOMPSON, ANNE ELISE,** federal judge; b. Phila., July 8, 1934; d. Leroy Henry and Mary Elise (Jackson) Jenkins; m. William H. Thompson, June 19, 1965; children: William H., Sharon A. BA, Howard U., 1955, LLB, 1964; MA, Temple U., 1957. Bar: D.C. bar 1964, N.J. bar 1966. Staff atty. Office of Solicitor, Dept. Labor, Chgo., 1964-65; asst. dep. public defender Trenton, N.J., 1967-70; mcpl. prosecutor Lawrence Twp., Lawrenceville, N.J., 1970-72; mcpl. ct. judge Trenton, 1972-75; prosecutor Mercer County, Mercer County, Trenton, 1975-79; judge U.S. Dist. Ct. N.J., Trenton, 1979—, now chief judge; vice chmn. Mercer County Criminal Justice Planning Com., 1972; mem. com. criminal practice N.J. Supreme Ct., 1975-79, mem. com. mcpl. cts., 1972-75; v.p. N.J. County Prosecutors Assn., 1978-79; chmn. juvenile justice com. Nat. Dist. Attys. Assn., 1978-79. Del. Democratic Nat. Conv., 1972. Recipient Assn. Black Women Lawyers award, 1976, Disting. Service award Nat. Dist. Attys. Assn., 1979, Gene Carte Meml. award Am. Criminal Justice Assn., 1980, Outstanding Leadership award N.J. County Prosecutors Assn., 1980, John Mercer Langston Outstanding Alumnus award Howard U. Law Sch., 1981; also various service awards; certs. of appreciation. Mem. Am. Bar Assn., Fed. Bar Assn., N.J. Bar Assn., Mercer County Bar Assn. Democrat. Office: US Dist Ct US Courthouse-4000 402 E State St Trenton NJ 08608-1507

**THOMPSON, CHARLES AMOS,** lawyer; b. Rockwood, Tenn., Sept. 30, 1945; s. Amos Carson and Helen (Holloway) T.; m.Deborah Kaye Perdue, June 30, 1973 (div. Oct. 1987). BSBA, U. Montevallo, 1972; JD, Birmingham Sch. Law, 1985. Bar: Ala. 1989, U.S. Dist. Ct. (no. dist.) Ala. 1990. Pvt. practice Birmingham, Ala., 1989—. Olympic Torch bearer, 1996. Capt. USMC, 1966-69. Mem. Ala. State Bar Assn., Birmingham Bar Assn., Greater Birmingham Criminal Def. Lawyer's Assn., Birmingham Track Club (pub. rels. 1990, marathon instr. 1986—, Dr. Arthur Black award 1987). Democrat. Methodist. Avocations: running, track and field, automobile-motorcycle-house maintenance. Criminal, General practice, Probate. Home and Office: 3174 Pipe Line Rd Birmingham AL 35243-5223

**THOMPSON, DAVID RENWICK,** federal judge; b. 1930. BS in Bus., U. So. Calif., 1952, LLB, 1955. Pvt. practice law with Thompson & Thompson (and predecessor firms), 1957-85; judge U.S. Ct. Appeals (9th cir.), 1985—, sr. judge, 1998—. Served with USN, 1955-57. Mem. ABA, San Diego County Bar Assn., Am. Bd. Trial Lawyers (sec. San Diego chpt. 1983, v.p. 1984, pres. 1985). Office: US Ct Appeals 940 Front St San Diego CA 92101-8994

**THOMPSON, DONALD MIZELLE,** lawyer; b. Atlanta, Sept. 20, 1963. AA, Emory U., 1983, BA, 1985; JD, Boston U., 1988. Bar: R.I. 1988, U.S. Dist. Ct. R.I. 1988, Calif. 1991, U.S. Dist. Ct. (so., no. and ctrl. dists.) Calif. 1991, U.S. Ct. Appeals (9th cir.) 1991. Law clk. 3d dist. Ct. Ea. Middlesex, Cambridge, Mass., 1986; rsch. asst. to chief justice Paul J. Liacos Mass. Supreme Jud. Ct., Boston, 1986-87; assoc. Hinckley, Allen, Snyder & Comen, Providence, 1988-90, Bryan Cave, L.A., 1990-95, Ballard, Rosenberg & Golper, Universal City, Calif., 1995-96; asst. gen. coun., v.p. UniHealth, 1996-99; sr. counsel Tenet Health Sys., Irvine, Calif., 1999—. Emory U. faculty scholar, 1983. Mem. ABA (health law sect.), Calif. Bar Assn., R.I. Bar Assn., L.A. County Bar Assn., Nat. Health Lawyers Assn. Avocations: photography, cycling, sailing. General civil litigation, Health, Labor. Home: 305 Stonecliffe Aisle Irvine CA 92612-5728 Office: Tenet Health System 2010 Main St Ste 650 Irvine CA 92614-7272

**THOMPSON, EDWARD P.,** lawyer; b. Ann Arbor, Mich., June 8, 1946; m. N. Terrill Fentress, July 1973 (dec. Apr. 1988); children: Mark S., Carolyn T., Kimberly Anne, Bonnie H. Biggs; m. Terry Lynn Biggs, Aug. 1993. BA, Kalamazoo (Mich.) Coll., 1968; JD, U. Mich., 1970. Bar: Oreg., 1971, U.S. Fed. Ct., 1972. Clerk to ptnr. Cas, Scott, Woods & Smith, Eugene, Oreg., 1971-83; pvt. practice Eugene, 1983—. Bd. dirs. Centro Latino Americano, Eugene, 1993—; 1st v.p., bd. dirs. Western Rivers Girl Scouts, Eugene, 1970-83, United Way Lan County, 1985—; active Wesley United Meth. Ch., Eugene, 1975-84. Mem. Willamette Bus. Assn. (founder), Eugene Met. Rotary (founder, pres.). E-mail: edpthom@aol.com. Estate planning, Mergers and acquisitions, Probate. Home: 30316 Fox Hollow Rd Eugene OR 97405-9436 Office: 875 Country Club Rd Eugene OR 97401-2255

**THOMPSON, FRANK J(OSEPH),** lawyer; b. N.Y.C., Feb. 2, 1932; s. Francis P. and Margaret (Burns) T.; m. Mary-Ellen Rand, Jan. 2, 1965; children—Elizabeth, Frank P., Patricia, Susan, Ruth. B.S.E.E., Loyola U., Los Angeles, 1954, J.D., Georgetown U., 1960. Bar: D.C. 1960, Conn. 1968, U.S. Ct. Appeals (D.C. cir.) 1960, U.S. Ct. Appeals (2d cir.) 1971, U.S. Ct. Appeals (4th cir.) 1978, U.S. Ct. Appeals (fed. cir.) 1984, U.S. Dist. Ct. Conn. 1971, U.S. Dist. Ct. (so. dist.) N.Y. 1971, U.S. Patent Office, U.S. Supreme Ct. 1973. Electronic engr. Nat. Security Agy., Washington, 1956-59; electric engr. ACF Industries, Alexandria, Va., 1959-60; patent atty. gen. Electric Co., Syracuse, 1960-63; RCA, Princeton, N.J., 1963-64; Sylvania Electric, 1964-65; Perkin Electric Co., Norwalk, 1966-71; sole practice, Stamford, Conn., 1971—; lectr. Conn. Bar Assn.; hearing commr. Conn. Superior Ct., 1978—; spl. master U.S. Dist. Ct. Conn., 1994—; arbitration panelist Am. Arbitration Assn. Served with USAF, 1954-56. Recipient Certs. of Commendation, Jud. Dept. Conn., 1979, 80, 81, 82, 83, 84, 85. Mem. ABA, Conn. Bar Assn., Conn. Patent Law Assn. Trademark and copyright, Federal civil litigation, Patent. Home: 1090 Galloping Hill Rd Fairfield CT 06430-7130 Office: 111 Prospect St Stamford CT 06901-1208

**THOMPSON, GEORGE LEWIS,** lawyer; b. N.Y.C., June 12, 1944; s. Thomas Vincent and Belle (Sherman) T.; m. Daphne J. Mackey, Aug. 14, 1982. BA, Bard Coll., 1966; JD, Duke U., 1970. Bar: N.Y. 1971. Atty. advisor Gen. Counsel U.S. Dept. Transp., Washington, 1970-71; gen. atty. Rocky Mountain region FAA, Denver, 1971-74; assoc. regional counsel New Eng. region FAA, Boston, 1974-85; regional counsel N.W. Mountain region FAA, Seattle, 1985-89, asst. chief counsel, 1989—. Avocations: sailing, gardening, tennis, reading. Office: FAA NW Mountain Region 1601 Lind Ave SW Renton WA 98055-4099

**THOMPSON, GORDON, JR.,** federal judge; b. San Diego, Dec. 28, 1929; s. Gordon and Garnet (Meese) T.; m. Jean Peters, Mar. 17, 1951; children—John M., Peter Renwick, Gordon III. Grad., U. So. Calif., 1951, Southwestern U. Sch. Law, Los Angeles, 1956. Bar: Calif. 1956. With Dist. Atty.'s Office, County of San Diego, 1957-60; partner firm Thompson & Thompson, San Diego, 1960-70; U.S. dist. judge So. Dist. Calif., San Diego, 1970—, chief judge, 1984-91, sr. judge, 1994—. Mem. ABA, Am. Bd. Trial Advocates, San Diego County Bar Assn. (v.p. 1970), San Diego Yacht Club, Delta Chi. Office: US Dist Ct 940 Front St San Diego CA 92101-8994

**THOMPSON, HAROLD LEE,** lawyer; b. Dayton, Ohio, Feb. 17, 1945; s. Harold Edward Thompson and Johnita Dorothy (Cox) Metcalf; children: Aishah T., Aliya S. BS in Acctg., Cen. State U., Wilberforce, Ohio, 1967; JD, U. Conn., 1972. Bar: Ohio 1975, U.S. Dist. Ct. (so. dist.) Ohio 1975, D.C. 1976, U.S. Ct. Appeals (4th cir.) 1990. Acct. Communication Satellite

Corp., 1968-69; atty. Ohio State Legal Service, Columbus, Ohio, 1972-74; of counsel Ohio Indsl. Commn., Columbus, 1974-76; sole practice Columbus, 1976—; ptnr. Jones & Thompson, Columbus, 1984-88; prin. H. Lee Thompson Co. L.P.A., Columbus, 1988—; pres. toys and clothing H. Lee Toy Co., Columbus, 1988—; adj. prof. law Columbus State Coll., 1989; instr. Acad. Ct. Reporting, 1989; adj. prof. tax and prins. of acctg. Bliss Coll., 1990-91; mem. Am. Bd. Forensic Examiners. Reginald Heber Smith fellow U.S. Fed. Ct., 1972. Mem. ATLA (exec. mem. birth trauma litigation group), Ohio Bar Assn., Am. Coll. Legal Medicine, Ohio Acad. Trial Lawyers, Franklin County Trial Lawyers Assn., Univ. Club, Columbus Met. Club. Roman Catholic. Avocations: reading, music, jogging. Federal civil litigation, Professional liability, Personal injury. Office: 85 E Gay St Ste 810 Columbus OH 43215-3118

**THOMPSON, HOLLEY MARKER,** lawyer, strategic customer development; b. Jamestown, N.Y., Jan. 30, 1947; d. Burdette James and Mary (Novitske) Marker; children: Jennifer Kristen Simos, Kendra Elise Blair, Jennifer Lynn, Stephanie Lynn; m. Lawrence D. Thompson. AAS, Jamestown C.C., 1966; BS, Ohio U., 1969; MA, W.Va. U., 1974, JD, 1980. Bar: W.Va. 1980, U.S. Dist. Ct. (so. dist.) W.Va. 1980, Pa. 1982, U.S. Dist. Ct. (we. dist.) Pa. 1982. Tchr. math. various pub. schs., Santa Ana (Calif.), Lakewood (N.Y.) and Morgantown (W.Va.), 1970-77; atty. for students W.Va. U., Morgantown, 1980; assoc. libr., lectr. W.Va. U. Coll. Law, Morgantown, 1980-83; assoc., libr. Jackson, Kelly, Holt & O'Farrell, Charleston, W.Va., 1983-86; cons. Hildebrandt, Inc., Somerville, N.J., 1986-94; sr. dir. strategic customer devel. LEXIS Pub., Dayton, Ohio, 1994—; speaker at regional, nat. and internat. legal confs. Contbr. articles to profl. jours. Mem. ABA, Spl. Libr. Assn., Am. Assn. Law Libs., N.J. Assn. Law Libs., Legal Mktg. Assn., Phi Delta Phi. Office: LEXIS Pub 121 Chanlon Rd New Providence NJ 07974-1541

**THOMPSON, HUGH P,** state supreme court justice; b. Montezuma, Ga., July 7, 1943. Grad., Emory U., JD, 1969. Bar: Ga. 1970. Pvt. practice Milledgeville, Ga., 1970-71; judge Recorder's Ct. of Milledgeville, 1971-79, Baldwin County Ct., 1973-79; judge, chief judge Superior Ct. of Ga., 1979-94; assoc. justice Supreme Ct. of Ga., Atlanta, 1994—; instr. bus. law Ga. COll., 1971-72. Recipient Disting. Svc. award Baldwin County Jaycees, 1972; named Outstanding Young Man of Baldwin County, 1972. Mem. State Bar Ga., Jud. Coun. Ga., Ocmulgee Jud. Cir. Bar Assn. Avocations: hunting, rose gardening, golf, fishing. Office: Supreme Ct Ga State Judicial Bldg 244 Washington St SW Rm 572 Atlanta GA 30334-9007*

**THOMPSON, JAMES LEE,** lawyer; b. L.I., N.Y., Sept. 9, 1941; s. Robert Luther and Marjorie Emma (Jones) T.; m. Diana Dill Stevenson, June 29, 1963; children: James C., Thomas J. BA, Yale U., 1963; JD, U. Va., 1966. Bar: Va. 1966, Md. 1966, U.S. Ct. Mil. Appeals 1968, U.S. Dist. Ct. Md. 1972, U.S. Supreme Ct. 1978. Ptnr. Miller & Canby, Rockville, Md., 1970—, head litigation, 1975—; mem. jud. conf. U.S. Ct. Appeals (4th cir.). Mem. Thousand Acres Assn., Deep Creek Lake, Md., 1985-87. Capt. JAGC, USMC, 1966-70. Decorated D.S.M. Fellow Am. Coll. Trial Lawyers; mem. ABA, Md. State Bar Assn. (bd. govs. 1975, 78, 79, 83, 89, 94, sec. 1995, pres. 1999-00), Montgomery County Bar Assn. (pres. 1987-88, Cert. of Merit 1985), Nat. Conf. Bar Pres., Md. Bar Found., Montgomery County Bar Found. (pres. 1988-89), Loophole Club (pres. 1978-79), Phi Delta Phi. Democrat. Episcopalian. Avocations: sailing, skiing, tennis, golf, gardening. State civil litigation, General practice. Home: 419 Russell Ave Apt 110 Gaithersburg MD 20877-2836 Office: Miller & Canby 200 Monroe St Ste B Rockville MD 20850-4423*

**THOMPSON, JAMES ROBERT, JR.,** lawyer, former governor; b. Chgo., May 8, 1936; s. James Robert and Agnes Josephine (Swanson) T.; m. Jayne Carr, 1976; 1 dau., Samantha Jayne. Student, U. Ill., Chgo., 1953-55, Washington U., St. Louis, 1955-56; J.D., Northwestern U., 1959. Bar: Ill. 1959, U.S. Supreme Ct. 1964. Asst. state's atty. Cook County, Ill., 1959-64; assoc. prof. law Northwestern U. Law Sch., 1964-69; asst. atty. gen. State of Ill., 1969-70; chief criminal div., 1969, chief dept. law enforcement and pub. protection, 1969-70; 1st asst. U.S. atty. No. Dist. Ill., 1970-71, U.S. atty., 1971-75; counsel firm Winston & Strawn, Chgo., 1975-77, ptnr., chmn. exec. com., 1991—; gov. Ill., 1977-91; chmn. Pres.' Intelligence Oversight Bd., 1989-93, adv. bd. Fed. Emergency Mgmt. Agy., 1991-93; bd. govs. Chgo. Bd. Trade; bd. dirs. FMC Corp., Jefferson Smurfit Group, plc, Prime Retail Inc., Am. Nat. Can, Hollinger Internat., Inc., Union Pacific Resources, Inc., Prime Group Realty Trust, Metzler Group, Chgo. Mus. Contemporary Art, Chgo. Hist. Soc., Lyric Opera Chgo., Econ. Club Chgo., Civic Com., Comml. Club Chgo., Execs. Club Chgo. Co-author: Cases and Comments on Criminal Justice, 2 vols, 1968, 74, Criminal Law and Its Adminstration, 1970, 74. Chmn. Ill. Math. and Sci. Acad. Found.; chmn. Rep. Gov.'s Assn., 1982, Nat. Gov.'s Assn., Midwest Gov.'s Assn., Coun. Gt. Lakes Gov's., 1985. Mem. ABA, Ill. Bar Assn., Chgo. Bar Assn. Republican. Office: Winston & Strawn 35 W Wacker Dr Ste 4200 Chicago IL 60601-1695

**THOMPSON, JAMES WILLIAM,** lawyer; b. Dallas, Oct. 22, 1936; s. John Charles and Frances (Van Slyke) T.; m. Marie Hertz, June 26, 1965 (dec. 1995); children: Elizabeth, Margaret, John; m. Linda Dozier, May 2, 1998. BS, U. Mont., 1958, JD, 1962. Bar: Mont. 1962; CPA, Mont. Acct. Arthur Young & Co., N.Y.C., summer 1959; instr. bus. adminstrn. Ea. Mont. Coll., Billings, 1959-60, U. Mont., Missoula, 1960-61; assoc. Cooke, Moulton, Bellingham & Longo, Billings, 1962-64, James R. Felt, Billings, 1964-65; asst. atty. City of Billings, 1963-64, atty., 1964-66; ptnr. Felt, Speare & Thompson, Billings, 1966-72, McNamer, Thompson & Cashmore, 1973-86, McNamer & Thompson Law Firm PC, 1986-89, McNamer, Thompson, Werner & Stanley, P.C., 1990-93, McNamer Thompson Law Firm PC, 1993-98, Wright Tolliver Guthals Law Firm PC, 1999—; bd. dirs. Associated Employers of Mont., Inc., 1989-98; mem. adv. coun. Sch. Fine Arts, U. Mont., 1997—. Mem. Billings Zoning Commn., 1966-69; v.p. Billings Cmty. Action Program (now Dist. 7 Human Resources Devel. Coun.), 1968-70, pres., 1970-75, trustee, 1975—; mem. Yellowstone County Legal Svcs. Bd., 1969-70; City-County Air Pollution Control Bd., 1969-70; pres. Billings Symphony Soc., 1970-71; bd. dirs. Billings Studio Theatre, 1967-73, United Way Billings, 1973-81, Mont. Inst. Arts Found., 1986-89, Downtown Billings Assn., 1986-90, Billings Area Bus. Incubator, Inc., 1991-94, Found. of Mont. State U., Billings, 1992-98, Mont. Parks Assn., 1997—, Rimrock Opera Co., 1998—; mem. Diocesan exec. coun., 1972-75; mem. Billings Transit Commn., 1971-73; mem. City Devel. Agy., 1972-73. Mem. ABA, Am. Acad. Estate Planning Attys., Nat. Acad. Elder Law Attys., State Bar Mont., Yellowstone County Bar Assn. (bd. dirs. 1983-87, pres. 1985-86), C. of C., Elks, Kiwanis (pres. Yellowstone chpt. 1974-75), Sigma Chi (pres. Billings alumni assn. 1963-65). Episcopalian. Estate taxation, Estate planning, Probate. Home: 123 Lewis Ave Billings MT 59101-6034 Office: 10 N 27th St PO Box 1977 Billings MT 59103-1977

**THOMPSON, JEFFREY CHARLES,** lawyer; b. Mpls., June 30, 1966; s. Charles David and Sharon Alice (Hanson) T.; m. Keri Lee Plant, Aug. 10, 1991; children: Drake Jeffrey, Payton Lee, Kazlin Grace. BS in Acctg., Northwestern Coll., 1988; JD, William Mitchell Coll., 1992. Bar: Minn. 1992, Wis. 1992, U.S. Dist. Ct. Minn. 1995. Law clk. to Hon. Judge George O. Petersen Ramsey County Dist. Ct., St. Paul, Minn., 1989-92; asst. city atty. criminal divsn. City of St. Paul, 1992-93, asst. city atty. civil divsn., 1993-95; assoc. Vest & Howse, PA, Brooklyn Center, Minn., 1995—. Vice-chmn. Oak Park Cmty. Ch., Blaine, Minn., 1995-97. Republican. Mem. Christian Missionary Alliance. Avocations: golf. General civil litigation. Office: Vest & Howse PA 6300 Shingle Creek Pkwy Ste 360 Brooklyn Center MN 55430-2191

**THOMPSON, JOEL ERIK,** lawyer; b. Summit, N.J., Sept. 15, 1940; s. Maurice Eugene and Charlotte Ruth (Harrington) T.; m. Bonnie Gay Ransa, June 15, 1963 (div. Dec. 1980); m. Deborah Ann Korp, Dec. 24, 1980 (div. Jan. 1987); children: Janice Santiesteban, Amber. Student, Va. Poly. Inst., 1958, Carnegie Inst. Tech., 1960-61; BSME cum laude, Newark Coll. Engring., 1966; JD, Seton Hall, 1970. Bar: N.J. 1970, Ariz. 1975, U.S. Tax Ct. 1972, U.S. Ct. Claims 1972, U.S. Customs Ct., 1972, U.S. Ct. Mil. Appeals, 1972, U.S. Ct. Customs and Patent Appeals 1972, U.S. Dist. Ct. N.J. 1970, Ariz. 1975, U.S. Ct. Appeals (9th cir.) 1975, U.S. Supreme Ct. 1975; cert. specialist criminal law Ariz. Bd. Legal Specialization; lic. profl. engr., N.J. Sr. technician Bell Tel. Labs., Inc., Murray Hill, N.J., 1965-67; patent agent Bell Tel. Labs., Inc., Murray Hill, 1967-70, staff atty., 1970-73; sr. trial atty. N.J. Pub. Defender's Office, Elizabeth, N.J., 1973-74; assoc. Cahill, Sutton and Thomas, Phoenix, 1974-76; trial lawyer Maricopa County Pub. Defender's Office, Phoenix, 1976-80; trial lawyer, criminal law specialist Henry J. Florence, Ltd., Phoenix, 1980-86; pvt. practice Phoenix, 1987—; judge Superior Ct. Ariz., Phoenix, 1987-95; instr. Phoenix Regional Police Acad., 1976-80, Glendale C.C., 1977, Ariz. State U. Sch. of Law, 1978, Am. Inst., 1990; pres., CEO Eagle Master Corp., Phoenix, 1995—; presenter in field. Contbr. articles to profl. jours. Mem. planning com. Cammelback East Village, Phoenix, 1992-98, chmn., 1993-96; mayor's select com., Phoenix, 1997, blue ribbon com. Maricopa Assn. Govs., 1996-97. Mem. Ariz. Bar Assn., Nat. Assn. Criminal Def. Lawyers, Ariz. Attys. Criminal Justice (charter), Maricopa Bar Assn. (CLE com. 1990-94, bench and bar com. 1992-96, Cert. Appreciation), Ariz. Assn. Pvt. Investigators (hon.), Internat. Assn. Identification (hon.), Tau Beta Pi, Pi Tau Sigma. Criminal, Land use and zoning (including planning). Office: 3104 E Camelback Rd # 521 Phoenix AZ 85016-4502

**THOMPSON, JOHN MORTIMER,** lawyer; b. Milw., June 20, 1951; s. Jack M. and Dorothy M. (Kraus) T.; m. Nancy Ann Kress, Sept. 17, 1976; children: Jack, Kathleen, Michael. BA, Fla. State U., 1973; JD, Marquette U., 1976. Bar: Wis. Supreme Ct 1976, U.S. Ct. Mil. Appeals 1976, U.S. Dist. Ct. (ea., we. dists. Wis.) 1976. assoc. Trowbridge, Planert & Schaefer, Green Bay, Wis., 1981-86; assoc. Everson, Whitney, Everson & Brehm, Green Bay, 1986-87, shareholder, 1987-; Bd. dirs., legis. com. chmn. Civil Trial Counsel Wis, 1991--. Bd. dirs. Am. Cancer Soc., Green Bay, 1985-88, pres. 1988-90; co-pres. home/sch. assn. Resurrection Cath. Parish, Green Bay, 1984-85; chmn. Resurrection Cath. Parish Coun., 1990-93. Capt. USAF, 1976-81. Mem. Brown County Bar Assn. (v.p. 1990-91, pres. elect 1992--). Avocations: sports, reading. General civil litigation, Insurance, Personal injury. Home: 3319 Hyacinth Ct Green Bay WI 54301-1420 Office: Everson Whitney Everson 125 S Jefferson St Ste 106 Green Bay WI 54301-4500

**THOMPSON, JOSEPH DURANT,** lawyer; b. Ft. Knox, Ky., Jan. 10, 1967; s. Joseph Durant Jr. and Jacqueline Anderson Thompson. BS, Clemson U., 1989; JD, U. S.C., 1993. Atty. Sinkler & Boyd, P.A., Charleston, S.C., 1993—. Mem. ABA, S.C. Bar Assn., Charleston County Bar Assn., S.C. Def. Trial Lawyers Assn. Insurance, Personal injury, General civil litigation. Office: Sinkler & Boyd PA 160 E Bay St Charleston SC 29401-2120

**THOMPSON, KATHERINE GENEVIEVE,** lawyer; b. Bklyn., May 11, 1945; d. George Otway and Marie (Burke) T. BS, Good Counsel Coll., 1966; JD, Bklyn. Law Sch., 1970; LLM, NYU, 1981. Bar: N.Y. 1971, U.S. Dist. Ct. (so. and ea. dists.) N.Y. 1978, U.S. Supreme Ct. 1981. Editor Matthew Bender Pub. Co., N.Y.C., 1970-71; atty. juvenile rights div. Legal Aid Soc., N.Y.C., 1971-76, asst. atty. in charge juvenile rights div. N.Y. County office, 1976-77; sole practice N.Y.C., 1977-78; ptnr. Rothenberg, Sherman, Thompson & Halpin, N.Y.C., 1978-84, Sherman, Thompson & Halpin, N.Y.C., 1984-87, Beldock, Levine & Hoffman, N.Y.C., 1987—; mem. appellate div. 1st Dept. Screening Panel, 1981-82, appellate div. 1st Dept. Family Ct. Adv. Com., 1983-90, chmn., 1986-89. Co-author: Adoption Law and Practice, 1988; contbg. editor: Bender's Federal Practice Forms, 1971, Bender's Forms of Discovery, 1971. Bd. dirs. August Aichorn Resdl. Ctr., N.Y.C., 1979-94. Fellow Am. Bar Found., N.Y. State Bar Found.; mem. ABA (family law sect.) N.Y. State Bar Assn. (spl. com. on juvenile justice 1980-87, family law sect. 1980—), Assn. of Bar of City of N.Y. (family ct. and family law com. 1977-80, chmn. 1980-83, lectures and continuing edn. com. 1984-85, matrimonial law com. 1985-88), Womens Bar Assn., N.Y. County Lawyers Assn. (family ct. com. 1978-79). Family and matrimonial, General practice. Office: Beldock Levine & Hoffman 99 Park Ave Fl 16 New York NY 10016-1508

**THOMPSON, LARRY DEAN,** lawyer; b. Hannibal, Mo., Nov. 15, 1945; s. Ezra W. and Ruth L. (Robinson) T.; m. Brenda Anne Taggart, June 26, 1970; children: Larry Dean, Gary E. BA cum laude, Culver-Stockton Coll., Canton, Mo., 1967; MA, Mich. State U., 1969; JD, U. Mich., 1974. Bar: Mo. 1974, Ga. 1978. Indsl. rels. rep. Ford Motor Co., Birmingham, Mich., 1969-71; atty. Monsanto Co., St. Louis, 1974-77, King & Spalding, Atlanta, 1977-82; U.S. atty. U.S. Dist. Ct. (no. dist.) Ga., 1982-86; ptnr. King & Spalding, Atlanta, 1986—; mem. 11th Cir. Commn. on Lawyer Qualifications and Conduct; ind. counsel HUD investigation, 1995; mem. Ga. Bd. Bar Examiners. Editor: Jury Instructions in Criminal Antitrust Cases 1976-80, 1982. Chmn. Atlanta Urban League; mem. Ga. Bd. Edn., 1997; bd. dirs. Ga. Rep. Found. Recipient Outstanding Achievement award FBA, 1992. Mem. ABA, Nat. Bar Assn. Presbyterian. Criminal. Home: 2015 Wallace Rd SW Atlanta GA 30331-7756 Office: King & Spalding 191 Peachtree St NE Ste 40 Atlanta GA 30303-1763

**THOMPSON, LAURA KAYE,** lawyer; b. Oklahoma City, Oct. 13, 1964; m. Dan R. Thompson, Aug. 12, 1995. Student, Okla. State U., 1982-87; BA, Miss. State U., 1988; JD, U. Utah, 1992. Bar: Utah 1992, U.S. Dist. Ct. Utah 1992. Atty. Patterson, Barking, Thompson, & Larkin, Ogden, Utah, 1992—; pub. defender Davis County, Kaysville, Utah, 1997—. Mem. ABA, Weber County Bar Assn., Davis County Bar Assn., Nat. Assn. Criminal Def. Lawyers, Utah Lawyers Assn., Phi Mu Wasatch. Democrat. Southern Baptist. Avocations: dog sledding, antique refinishing, reading. Office: Patterson Barking Thompson & Larkin 427 27th St Ogden UT 84401-4201

**THOMPSON, LORAN TYSON,** lawyer; b. N.Y.C., Dec. 23, 1947; s. Kenneth Webster and Mary (Tyson) T.; m. Meera Eleanora Agarwal, Apr. 2, 1976. BA magna cum laude, Amherst Coll., 1969; MA, Harvard U., 1970, JD, 1976. Bar: N.Y. 1977, U.S. Tax Ct. 1977. Assoc. Breed, Abbott & Morgan, N.Y.C., 1976-83, ptnr., 1983-93; ptnr. Whitman Breed Abbott & Morgan LLP, N.Y.C., 1993—. Mem. ABA, N.Y. State Bar Assn. (exec. com., tax sect. 1991-98, co-chmn. com. on nonqualified employee benefits 1991-95, co-chmn. com. on qualified plans 1995-98), Assn. Bar of City of N.Y., Phi Beta Kappa. Corporate taxation, Pension, profit-sharing, and employee benefits, Taxation, general. Home: 79 W 12th St Apt 12G New York NY 10011-8510 Office: Whitman Breed Abbott & Morgan LLP 200 Park Ave New York NY 10166-0005

**THOMPSON, MOZELLE WILLMONT,** government official; b. Pitts., Dec. 11, 1954; s. Charles and Eiko (Suzaki) T. AB, Columbia U., 1976; M in Pub. Affairs, Princeton U., 1980; JD, Columbia U., 1981. Bar: N.Y. 1984, D.C. 1984, U.S. Dist. Ct. (ea. dist.) Mich. 1984, U.S. Dist. Ct. (so. and ea. dists.) N.Y. 1985, U.S. Ct. Appeals (11th cir.) 1986. Clk. to presiding judge U.S. Dist. Ct. (so. dist.) Fla., Miami, 1981-82; assoc. Skadden, Arps, Slate, Meagher & Flom, N.Y.C., 1982-90; spl. counsel to supr. Town of Babylon, N.Y., 1988-90; counsel and sec. N.Y. State Housing Fin. Agy., N.Y.C.; counsel, sec. N.Y. State Med. Care Facilities Fin. Agy., N.Y. State Affordable Housing Corp., N.Y. State Mcpl. Bond Bank Agy., N.Y. State Project Fin. Agy., N.Y.C., 1990-93; sr. v.p., gen. coun. N.Y. State Mortgage Agy., N.Y.C., 1993; dep. asst. sec. for govt. fin. policy Dept. of Treasury, Washington, 1993-96; prin. dep. asst. sec. for govt. fin. policy Dept. Treasury, Washington, 1996-97; commr. FTC, Washington, 1997—; gen. counsel North Amityville Cmty. Econ. Coun., Inc., 1989-90; pres. Greenwich Corp., 1987-93; adj. assoc. prof. Bklyn. Law Sch., 1986-91, Fordham U. Law Sch., 1992-97; mem. adv. bd. Udall Ctr., U. Ariz., Tucson, 1994—. Mem. exec. bd. Practicing Attys. for Law Students, N.Y.C., 1986-93. Mem. ABA (coms. litigation, tort and ins. practice 1984—), Nat. Coun. State Housing Agys. (co-chair legal affairs com., disclosure task force, 1991-93), Nat. Coun. Health Care Facilities Fin. Authorities (co-chair advocacy and strategic planning coms., 1991-93) N.Y. State Bar Assn., N.Y. County Lawyers Assn. (com. on fed. cts. 1984-86), D.C. Bar Assn., Assn. of Bar of City of N.Y., Assn. Princeton Grad. Alumni, Assn. Black Princeton Alumni, Columbia Law Sch. Alumni Assn., Columbia Coll. Alumni Assn., Columbia Black and Latino Alumni Assn., Columbia Coll. Class 1976 (pres. 1986—). Avocations: music, theater arts, architecture. Home: 724A 9th St SE Washington DC 20003-2804 Office: Dept of Treasury 1500 Pennsylvania Ave NW Washington DC 20220-0002

**THOMPSON, MYRON H.,** federal judge; b. 1947. BA, Yale U., 1969, JD, 1972. Asst. atty. gen. State of Ala., 1972-74; sole practice Montgomery, Ala., 1974-79; ptnr. Thompson & Faulk, Montgomery, 1979-80; judge U.S. Dist. Ct. (mid. dist.) Ala., Montgomery, 1980-91, 98—, chief judge, 1991-98. Mem. ABA, Ala. Bar Assn., Nat. Bar Assn., Ala. Lawyers Assn. Office: US Dist Ct 203 US Courthouse PO Box 235 Montgomery AL 36101-0235

**THOMPSON, NEAL LEWIS,** lawyer; b. Chattanooga, Mar. 28, 1949; s. Frank M. and Martha (Wever) T.; m. Brenda Sparks, Aug. 8, 1976; children: Frank, Matthew, Wesley. BPA, U. Miss., 1971; JD, Nashville Night Law Sch., 1976. Bar: Tenn. 1978, U.S. Ct. Appeals (6th cir.) 1992. Ct. officer Judge Campbell Carden Hamilton County Criminal Ct., Chattanooga, 1973-76; ins. adjuster Collins & Co., Chattanooga, 1976-77; pvt. practice, Chattanooga, 1978—. V.p. Chattanooga Area Hist. Assn., 1995-97, pres., 1998-99. Mem. FBA, Chattanooga Bar Assn., Citizen Taxpayers' Assn. Hamilton County (pres. 1996-97), Pachyderm Club. Republican. Presbyterian. Criminal, Workers' compensation, Personal injury. Office: 615 Lindsay St Ste 150 Chattanooga TN 37403-3438

**THOMPSON, PAUL BROWER,** lawyer; b. East Orange, N.J., Feb. 15, 1922; s. Harvey Brower and Agnes (Norman) T.; m. Audrey Hyde, Aug. 17, 1952; 1 child, Paul Brower Jr. BA, Colgate U., 1943; JD, Harvard U., 1948. Bar: N.J. 1949, U.S. Ct. Appeals (3d cir.) 1949, U.S. Dist. Ct. N.J. 1949. Assoc. Markley & Broadhurst, Jersey City, N.J., 1949-55, Lamb Langan & Blake, Jersey City, N.J., 1955-59; ptnr. Lamb Blake Thompson & Chappell, Jersey City, N.J., 1959-74; judge Esssex County Ct., Newark, 1975-79; judge Superior Ct. N.J., Newark, 1979-85, presiding judge, civil divsn., 1985-91; of counsel Tompkins McGuire Wachenfeld & Barry, Newark, 1991—. Editor (compendium) Traps for the Unwary, 1997. With USAF, 1943-46. Fellow Am. Bar Found.; mem. ABA, N.J. Bar Assn., Essex County Bar Assn., Montclair Hist. Soc. (pres. 1980), Harvard Law Sch. Assn. N.J. (pres. 1985). Republican. Congregational. Avocations: golf, gardening. Alternative dispute resolution, Federal civil litigation, General civil litigation. Home: 83 Sunset Ave Verona NJ 07044-2610 Office: Tompkins McGuire Wachenfeld & Barry 4 Gateway Ctr Newark NJ 07102-4007

**THOMPSON, RALPH GORDON,** federal judge; b. Oklahoma City, Dec. 15, 1934; s. Lee Bennett and Elaine (Bizzell) T.; m. Barbara Irene Hencke, Sept. 5, 1964; children: Lisa, Elaine, Maria. BBA, U. Okla., 1956, JD, 1961. Bar: Okla. 1961. Ptnr. Thompson, Thompson, Harbour & Selph (and predecessors), Oklahoma City, 1961-75; judge U.S. Dist. Ct. for Western Dist. Okla., Oklahoma City, 1975—; chief judge U.S. Dist. Ct. (we. dist.) Okla., 1986-93; mem. Okla. Ho. of Reps., 1966-70, asst. minority floor leader, 1969-70; spl. justice Supreme Ct. Okla., 1970-71; tchr. Harvard Law Sch. Trial Advocacy Workshop, 1981—; apptd. by chief justice of U.S. to U.S. Fgn. Intelligence Surveillance Ct., 1990-97; elected to jud. conf. of the U.S., 1997; apptd. to Edward J. Devitt Disting. Svc. Justice award selection com., 1997-99; apptd. by chief justice of U.S. to exec. com. of Jud. Conf. of the U.S., 1998—. Co-author: Mr. Integrity: Bryce Harlow, Counselor to Presidents, Bob Burke and Ralph Thompson, 1999. Rep. nominee for lt. gov., Okla., 1970; chmn. bd. ARC, Oklahoma City, 1970-72; chmn., pres. Okla. Young Lawyers Conf., 1965; mem. bd. visitors U. Okla., 1975-78. Lt. USAF, 1957-60, col. Res., ret. Decorated Legion of Merit; named Oklahoma City's Outstanding Young Man, Oklahoma City Jaycees, 1967, Outstanding Fed. Trial Judge, Okla Trial Lawyers Assn., 1980; recipient Regents Alumni award U. Okla., 1990, Disting. Svc. award, 1993; inducted Okla. Hall of Fame, 1995. Fellow Am. Bar Found.; mem. ABA, Fed. Bar Assn., Okla. Bar Assn. (chmn. sect. internat. law and gen. practice 1974-75), Oklahoma County Bar Assn. (Jud. Svc. award 1988), Jud. Conf. U.S. (com. on ct. adminstrn. 1981-89, com. on fed.-state jurisdiction 1988-91), U.S. Dist. Judges Assn. 10th Cir. (pres. 1992-94), Rotary (hon.), Order of Coif, Am. Inns of Ct. (pres. XXIII 1995-96), Phi Beta Kappa (pres. chpt. 1985-86, Phi Beta Kappa of Yr. 1991), Beta Theta Pi, Phi Alpha Delta. Episcopalian. Office: US Dist Ct 200 NW 4th St Rm 1210 Oklahoma City OK 73102-3092

**THOMPSON, RAYMOND EDWARD,** lawyer; b. Miami, Fla., July 26, 1936; s. Roy Lavern and Caroline Magdaline (Dilg) T.; 1 child, Raymond Edward Jr. BBA, U. Miami, 1959; JD, Stetson U., 1962. Bar: Fla. 1962, U.S. Dist. Ct. (so. dist.) Fla. 1962, U.S. Supreme Ct. 1971, U.S. Dist. Ct. (mid. dist.) Fla. 1996. Assoc. Hunter and Paoli, Hollywood, Fla., 1962-63, Paoli and Paoli, Hollywood, 1963-67; pvt. practice Hollywood, 1967-81, Ocala, Fla., 1981-86; with Thompson & Burton, Ocala, 1981-86; gen. counsel South Broward Park Dist., Hollywood, 1968-76, Children's Home Soc., Ft. Lauderdale, Fla., 1970-75, Assn. for Retarded Citizens-Marion, Ocala, 1985-89. Pres., gen. counsel Assn. for Retarded Citizens-Marion, Ocala, 1985-89; gen. counsel South Broward Park Dist., Hollywood, 1968-76, Children's Home Soc., Ft. Lauderdale, 1970-75; pres. Children's Home Soc., Ft. Lauderdale, 1975; bd. dirs. Marion County Fair, Inc.,1989-90. Mem. ABA, Fla. Bar Assn., Marion County Bar Assn., Broward Amateur Radio Club (pres. 1971-72), Silver Springs Radio Club (bd. dirs. 1982-84, Outstanding Profl. Contbn. award 1982), Hollywood Jaycees (treas. 1971-72, Jaycee of the Yr. 1971-72, Kiwanis (sec. 1963-81). Real property, Estate planning, Probate. Office: 628 SE 17th St Ocala FL 34471-4429

**THOMPSON, RICHARD LEON,** pharmaceutical company executive, lawyer; b. Rochester, N.Y., Dec. 5, 1944; s. Leslie L. and Marion (Cosad) T.; m. Catherine Jean Terry, July 6, 1974; children: Kristin Anne, Catherine Elizabeth. AB cum laude, SUNY, Albany, 1966; MA, Syracuse U., 1967; JD, Cath. U., 1975. Staff dir., counsel U.S. Ho. of Reps., Washington, 1973-78; dir. Abbott Labs., Washington, 1978-83; v.p. Squibb Corp., Washington, 1983-89, Bristol-Myers Squibb Corp., Washington, 1989—; chmn. legis. adv. com. Proprietary Assn., Washington, 1984; bd. dirs. Bus. Govt. Rels. Coun. Mem. com. on changing enrollments Fairfax (Va.) County Pub. Sch., 1983-84, supts. adv. com., 1984-85, mem., 1988—; mem. Fed. City Coun., 1992; chmn. legis. com. P.R.-U.S.A. Found., 1985—; co-chair edn. in 2010; bd. dirs. D.C. Hospice, Bryce Harlow Found., 1990-95. 1st lt. U.S. Army, 1968-69, Vietnam. Named one of Outstanding Young Men of Am., Jaycees, 1976. Mem. ABA, D.C. Bar Assn., Pharm. Mfrs. Assn. (chmn. Washington reps. com.1988), Congl. Country Club, Georgetown Club, City Club. Home: 1005 Woburn Ct Mc Lean VA 22102-2133 Office: Bristol-Myers Squibb Corp 655 15th St NW Ste 300 Washington DC 20005-5701

**THOMPSON, ROBERT CHARLES,** lawyer; b. Council, Idaho, Apr. 20, 1942; s. Ernest Lavelle and Evangeline Montgomery (Carlson) T.; m. Marilyn Anne Wilcox, Jan. 17, 1960 (dec. Mar. 1962); m. Patricia Joan Price, June 1, 1963 (div. 1969); m. Jan Nesbitt, June 29, 1973 (dec. May 1998); m. Shari Lewis, Feb. 7, 1999; children: Tanya, Christopher, Eric. AB, Harvard U., 1963, LLB, 1967. Bar: Mass. 1967, Calif. 1983, U.S. Dist. Ct. (ea. dist.) Mass. 1975, U.S. Ct. Appeals (1st cir.) 1976, U.S. Ct. Appeals (9th cir.) 1984, U.S. Dist. Ct. (no. dist.) Calif. 1983, U.S. Dist. Ct. (ea. dist.) Calif., 1996. Assoc. Choate, Hall & Stewart, Boston, 1967-73; asst. regional counsel EPA, Boston, 1973-75, regional counsel, 1975-82, assoc. gen. counsel, 1979-82; regional counsel EPA, San Francisco, 1982-84; ptnr. Graham & James, San Francisco, 1984-91, LeBoeuf, Lamb, Greene & MacRae, San Francisco, 1992—. Contbr. articles to profl. jours. Bd. dirs. Peninsula Indsl. and Bus. Assn., Palo Alto, Calif., 1986-98, chmn. Cambridge (Mass.) Conservation Commn., 1972-74; co-chmn. The Clift Confs. on Environ. Law, 1983-98; assoc. mem. Ban Conservation and Development Commission, 1998-. John Russell Shaw traveling fellow Harvard Coll., 1963-64; recipient Regional Administrs. Bronze medal EPA, 1976, 84. Mem. ABA (natural resources sect., com. on native Am. natural resources law, spl. com. on mktg.), Natural Resources Def. Coun., Sierra Club, Commonwealth Club, Phi Beta Kappa. Democrat. Episcopalian. Avocations: personal computers, yoga, antiques, wines, cooking. Communications, Environmental. Office: LeBoeuf Lamb Greene & MacRae One Embarcadero Ctr San Francisco CA 94111

**THOMPSON, ROBERT SAMUEL,** lawyer; b. Cleve., Nov. 2, 1930; s. Wayne Charles Thompson and Cornelia Irene (Anderson) Thompson Baker; m. Dorothy "JoAnne" Courtney; children: Robert Dale, Richard Wayne. BA, Hamilton Coll., 1953; JD, U. Mich., 1956; postgrad., Air Command and Staff Coll., Montgomery, Ala., 1967-68. Bar: Mich. 1956, Ohio 1962, U.S. Supreme Ct. 1962, Oreg. 1973. Judge advocate USAF, 1956-77; pvt. practice McMinnville, Oreg., 1977-98. Judge mcpl. ct., 1977—. Maj. USAF, 1977. Maj. USAF, 1997. Mem. Oreg. Soc. SAR (pres. 1989-90), Oreg. Mcpl. Judges Assn. (pres. 1992-93), Rotary (bd. dirs. McMinnville chpt. 1989), Am. Legion, Masons. General practice. Home and Office: 127 NW 19th St Mcminnville OR 97128-2611

**THOMPSON, RONALD EDWARD,** lawyer; b. Bremerton, Wash., May 24, 1931; s. Melville Herbert and Clara Mildred (Griggs) T.; m. Marilyn Christine Woods, Dec. 15, 1956; children: Donald Jeffery, Karen, Susan, Nancy, Sally, Claire. BA, U. Wash., 1953, JD, 1958. Bar: Wash. 1959. Asst. city atty. City of Tacoma, 1960-61; pres. firm Thompson, Krilich, LaPorte, West & Lockner, P.S., Tacoma, 1961-99; judge pro tem Mcpl. Ct., City of Tacoma, Pierce County Dist., 1972—, Pierce County Superior Ct., 1972—. Chmn. housing and social welfare com. City of Tacoma, 1965-69; mem. Tacoma Bd. Adjustment, 1967-71, chmn., 1968; mem. Tacoma Com. Future Devel., 1961-64, Tacoma Planning Commn., 1971-72; bd. dirs., pres. Mcpl. League Tacoma; bd. dirs. Pres. Tacoma Rescue Mission, Tacoma Pierce County Cancer Soc., Tacoma-Pierce County Heart Assn., Tacoma-Pierce County Coun. for Arts, Econ. Devel. Coun. Puget Sound, Tacoma Youth Symphony, Kleiner Group Home, Tacoma C.C. Found., Pierce County Econ. Devel. Corp., Wash. Transp. Policy Inst.; Coalition to Keep Wash. Moving, precinct committeeman Rep. party, 1969-73. With AUS, 1953-55; col. Res. Recipient Internat. Cmty. Svc. award Optimist Club, 1970, Patriotism award Am. Fedn. Police, 1974, citation for cmty. svc. HUD, 1974, Disting. Citizen award Mcpl. League Tacoma-Pierce County, 1985; named Lawyer of the Yr. Pierce County Legal Secs. Assn., 1992. Mem. ATLA, Am. Arbitration Assn. (panel of arbitrators), ABA, Wash. State Bar Assn., Tacoma-Pierce County Bar Assn. (sec. 1964, pres. 1979, mem. cts. and judiciary com. 1981-82), Wash. State Trial Lawyers Assn., Tacoma-Pierce County C. of C. (bd. dirs., exec. com., v.p., chmn.), Downtown Tacoma Assn. (com. chmn., bd. dirs. exec. com., chmn.), Variety Club (Seattle), Lawn Tennis Club, Tacoma Club, Optomist (Tacoma, internat. pres. 1973-74), Phi Delta Phi, Sigma Nu. Roman Catholic. General civil litigation, Real property, Personal injury. Home: 3101 E Bay Dr NW Gig Harbor WA 98335-7610 Office: Atty at Law PO Box 1189 7525 Pioneer Way Ste 101 Gig Harbor WA 98335-1165

**THOMPSON, RUFUS E.,** lawyer; b. Lubbock, Tex., Aug. 15, 1943; s. Glenn Wesley and Naomi Elvina T.; m. Sandra Jean Lemons, Aug. 8, 1965; children—Michael Glenn, Mark Gregory, Matthew Wesley. B.B.A., U. Tex., Austin, 1965, J.D., 1968. Bar: Tex. bar 1968, N.Mex. bar 1969. Assoc. firm Atwood & Malone, Roswell, N.Mex., 1968-71; ptnr. firm Atwood, Malone, Mann & Cooter, Roswell, 1971-78; U.S. Atty. Dist. N.Mex., Albuquerque, 1978-81; now ptnr. firm Modrall, Sperling, Roehl, Harris & Sisk, Albuquerque, 1981—; mem. Nat. Conf. Commrs. on Uniform State Laws, 1975-79; chmn. N.Mex. Supreme Ct. Com. on Rules of Evidence, 1972-94; U.S. Atty. for N.Mex. Com., 1978-82; mem. U.S. Atty. Gen.'s Adv. Com., 1980—, chmn., 1981. Mem. N.Mex. Democratic Party Central Com., 1972-78; mem. N.Mex. State Senate, 1973-78; mem. Gov.'s Commn. on Prevention of Organized Crime, 1985-89. Mem. Am. Bar Assn. (exec. council young lawyers sect. 1972), N.Mex. Bar Assn. (chmn. young lawyers sect. 1970). Baptist. Insurance, General civil litigation, Administrative and regulatory. Office: PO Box 2168 Albuquerque NM 87103-2168 also: Modrall, Sperling, Roehl, Harris & Sisk Nations Bank Building Ste 1000 500 4th St NW Albuquerque NM 87102-2183

**THOMPSON, SUSANNAH ELIZABETH,** lawyer; b. Fullerton, Calif., May 20, 1953; d. Harry Lowell and Susannah Elizabeth (Glover) Rupp; m. James Avery Thompson, Jr., May 16, 1987; 1 child, Sarah Mary Elizabeth Thompson. BA, Calif. State U., Fullerton, 1980; JD with hons., Am. Coll. of Law, 1989. Bar: Calif. 1989, U.S. Dist. Ct. (cen. dist.) 1989, U.S. Dist. Ct. (so. dist.) 1991. Legal asst. Minyard & Minyard, Orange, Calif., 1987-89; assoc. Simon & Simon, San Bernardino, Calif., 1989-91; pvt. practice Temecula, Calif., 1991—. Asst. editor Law Rev./Am. Coll. Law, Brea, Calif., 1989. Sec. student bar assn. Am. Coll. Law, 1987-88. Mem. ABA, Riverside County Bar Assn., Calif. Women Lawyers Assn., Inland Empire Bankruptcy Forum, Women Lawyers Assn. (chmn. mem. 1994—), Temecula C. of C. Republican. Avocations: bowling, Disneyana, reading, skating, tennis. Bankruptcy, Contracts commercial, Family and matrimonial. Office: 41593 Winchester Rd Ste 201 Temecula CA 92590-4858

**THOMPSON, TERENCE WILLIAM,** lawyer; b. Moberly, Mo., July 3, 1952; s. Donald Gene and Carolyn (Stringer) T.; m. Caryn Elizabeth Hildebrand, Aug. 30, 1975; children: Cory Elizabeth, Christopher William, Tyler Madison. *Jesse Bynum Thompson and Lelia Glorine Harris were the parents of Donald Gene Thompson. William Madison Stringer and Charity Kesiah Rogers were the parents of Minnie Carolyn Stringer (who died in 1977). The other children of Don and Carolyn are Jeanne Susanne Thompson, Daniel Scott Thompson and Bruce Rogers Thompson. Don is now married to Sandee Krell. The parents of Caryn Elizabeth Hildebrand are Robert Louis Hildebrand (who died in 1983) and Harriet "Happy" Elizabeth Jeffs, and their other children are Garrett Dennis Hildebrand and Eric Robert Hildebrand. Happy is now married to Robert Zant.* BA in Govt. with honors and high distinction, U. Ariz., 1974; JD, Harvard U., 1977. Bar: Ariz. 1977, U.S. Dist. Ct. Ariz. 1977, U.S. Tax Ct. 1979. Assoc. Brown & Bain P.A., Phoenix, 1977-83, ptnr., 1983-92; ptnr. Gallagher and Kennedy, P.A., Phoenix, 1992—; legis. aide Rep. Richard Burgess, Ariz. Ho. of Reps., 1974; mem. bus. adv. bd. Citibank Ariz. (formerly Great Western Bank & Trust, Phoenix), 1985-86. Mem. staff Harvard Law Record, 1974-75; rsch. editor Harvard Internat. Law Jour. ,1976; lead author, editor-in-chief: Arizona Corporate Practice, 1996; contbr. articles to profl. jours. Mem. Phoenix Mayor's Youth Adv. Bd. 1968-70, Phoenix Internat.; active 20-30 Club, 1978-81, sec. 1978-80, Valley Leadership, Phoenix, 1983-84, citizens task force future financing needs City of Phoenix, 1985-86; exec. coun. Boys and Girls Clubs of Met. Phoenix, 1990—; bd. dirs. Phoenix Bach Choir, 1992-94; deacon Shepherd of Hills Congl. Ch., Phoenix, 1984-85; pres. Maricopa County Young Dems., 1982-83, Ariz. Young Dems., 1983-84, sec. 1981-82, v.p. 1982-83; exec. dir. Young Dems. Am., 1985, exec. com. 1983-85; others. Fellow Ariz. Bar Found.; mem. State Bar Ariz. (vice chmn. internt. law sect. 1978, sec. securities law sect. 1990-91, vice chmn. sect. 1991-92, chmn.-elect 1992-93, chmn. 1993-94, exec. coun. 1988-96, sec. bus. law sect. 1992-93, vice chmn. 1993-94, chmn. 1994-95, exec. coun. 1996-98), Nat. Assn. Bond Lawyers, Nat. Health Lawyers, Greater Phoenix Black C. of C. (bd. dirs. 1999—), Blue Key, Phi Beta Kappa, Phi Kappa Phi, Phi Eta Sigma. Health, Securities, General corporate. Home: 202 W Lawrence Rd Phoenix AZ 85013-1226 Office: Gallagher & Kennedy PA 2600 N Central Ave Ste 1800 Phoenix AZ 85004-3099

**THOMPSON STANLEY, TRINA,** lawyer; b. Oakland, Calif., June 3, 1961; d. Woodrow Thompson and Dorothy Mae (Martin) McCullough; 1 child, Daniel Jackson Jr.; m. Calvester Ray Stanley; children: Daniel Stanley Jackson, Alexis Lynnette Stanley. AB, U. Calif., Berkeley, 1983; JD, U. Calif., 1986. Bar: Calif. 1987, U.S. Dist. Ct. (no. dist.) Calif. 1990. Tchg. asst. coun. on legal edn. opportunities U. Calif., 1984; law clk. Nat. Ctr. for Youth Law, San Francisco, 1984; clin. law clk. Alameda County Dist. Atty.'s Office, Oakland, 1985; law clk. to Hon. Henry Ramsey Alameda County Superior Ct., Oakland, 1986; sr. legal asst. Alameda County Pub. Defender's Office, 1986-87; asst. pub. defender III, Alameda County Pub. Defender's Office, Oakland, 1987-91; pvt. practice, Oakland, 1991—; co-chair Women Defenders. Editing mem. Black Law Jour., 1983-85. Bd. dirs. Oakland Ensemble Theatre, 1991-93, Family Law and Violence Ctr., Berkeley, 1990-92, First Appellate Project, 1996-97, Women Defenders, 1996—, co-chair, 1998—; PAL softball team sponsor Thompson Stanley Steelers; vol. Boys and Girls Clubs of Oakland, 1993—. Fellow Coun. on Legal Edn. Opportunities, 1983-85, grad. minority fellow, 1983-85; Yee scholar, 1985-86. Mem. ABA, Nat. Bar Assn., Calif. Pub. Defenders Assn., Alameda County Bar Assn. (bd. dirs.), Calif. Attys. for Criminal Justice (bd. dirs., President's award 1994), Alpha Kappa Alpha. Democrat. Baptist. Avocation: collecting African American historical memorabilia. Criminal, Family and matrimonial, Juvenile. Office: 440 Grand Ave Ste 210 Oakland CA 94610-5011

**THOMS, DAVID MOORE,** lawyer; b. N.Y.C., Apr. 28, 1948; s. Theodore Clark and Elizabeth Augusta (Moore) T.; m. Susan Rebecca Stuckey, Dec. 16, 1972. BA, Kalamazoo Coll., 1970; M in Urban Planning, Wayne State U., 1975, LLM in Taxation, 1988; JD, U. Detroit, 1979. Bar: Mich. 1980, N.Y. 1995. Planner City of Detroit, 1971-75; atty. Rockwell and Kotz, P.C., Detroit, 1980-87; pvt. practice David M. Thoms & Assocs., P.C., Detroit, 1987—; adj. assoc. prof. Madonna U., 1993—; presenter NYU Tax Inst. Editor Case and Comment U. of Detroit Law Rev., 1978-79. Mem. program com. Fin. and Estate Planning Coun. Detroit, 1980—; mem. adv. bd., chmn. nominating com., mem. exec. com. Met. Detroit Salvation Army, sec.-treas., vice chmn., 1994-95, chmn., 1995-96; bd. dirs. bylaws and property com., mem. nominating com., devel. com., exec. com. Mich. chpt. ARC; bd. dirs. L'Alliance Française de Grosse Pointe, French Festival of Detroit, Inc., 1986-89, 91-94, pres.; bd. dirs. Fedn. of Alliances Françaises, 1989-95, 97—, also treas., chmn. fin. com.; trustee Detroit Symphony Orch. Hall, Inc., dir., 1996-97; trustee Kalamazoo Coll., 1993—, dir., exec. com., 1995—; dir. vis. com. European art DIA, 1995-97. Recipient Burton scholarship U. Detroit, 1979; Officier dans l'Ordre des Palmes Academiques. Mem. ABA (chmn. subcom. on probate and estate planning, mem. charitable trust com.), Fed. Bar Assn., Oakland County Bar Assn., Detroit Bar Assn., State Bar Mich., N.Y. Bar Assn., Bar Assn. of City of N.Y., Fedn. Alliances Françaises-U.S.A. (bd. dirs., treas. 1991—), Am. Planning Assn. (Mich. chpt.), Detroit Athletic Club, Renaissance Club, The Grosse Pointe Club. Mem. United Church of Christ. Avocations: tennis, architectural history, music, travel, art history. Corporate taxation, Estate planning, General corporate. Office: 400 Renaissance Ctr Ste 950 Detroit MI 48243-1678

**THOMS, JEANNINE AUMOND,** lawyer; b. Chgo.; d. Emmett Patrick and Margaret (Gallet) Aumond; m. Richard W. Thoms; children: Catherine Thoms, Alison Thoms. AA, McHenry County Coll., 1979; BA, No. Ill. U., 1981; JD, Ill. Inst. Tech., 1984. Bar: Ill. 1984, U.S. Dist. Ct. (no. dist.) Ill. 1984, U.S. Ct. Appeals (7th cir.) 1985. Assoc. Foss Schuman Drake & Barnard, Chgo., 1984-86; assoc. Zukowski Rogers Flood & McArdle, Crystal Lake and Chgo., 1986-92, ptnr., 1992—; arbitrator 19th Jud. Ct. Ill., 1991—. Mem. Women's Adv. Coun. to Gov., State of Ill. Mem. ABA, LWV, Ill. State Bar Assn., Chgo. Bar Assn., McHenry County Bar Assn., Am. Trial Lawyers Assn., Acad. Family Mediators (cert.), Women's Network, Phi Alpha Delta. Mem. McHenry County Mental Health Bd., 1991-98, pres., 1995-98. Estate planning, Probate, Municipal (including bonds). Office: Zukowski Rogers Flood & McArdle 50 N Virginia St Crystal Lake IL 60014-4126 also: 100 S Wacker Dr Chicago IL 60606-4006

**THOMSON, BASIL HENRY, JR.,** lawyer, university general counsel; b. Amarillo, Tex., Jan. 17, 1945; m. Margaret Shepard, May 4, 1985; children: Christopher, Matthew, Robert. BBA, Baylor U., 1968, JD, 1973. Bar: Tex. 1974, U.S. Ct. Mil. Appeals 1974, U.S. Supreme Ct. 1977, U.S. Dist. Ct. (we. dist.) Tex. 1988, U.S. Ct. Appeals (fed. cir.) 1990. Oil title analyst Hunt Oil Co., Dallas, 1971-73; atty., advisor Regulations and Adminstrv. Law div. Office of Chief Counsel USCG, Washington, 1973-77; dir. estate planning devel. dept. Baylor U., Waco, Tex., 1977-80, gen. counsel, 1980—; adj. prof. law Baylor U.; lobbyist legis. Ind. Higher Edn., 71st Session of Tex. Legislature; mem. legis. com. Gov.'s Task Force on Drug Abuse; dir. govtl. relations Baylor U.; speaker at meetings of coll. and univ. adminstrs.; assisted in drafting legis. for Texan's War on Drugs Tex. Legislature; mem. legal adv. com. United Educators Ins. Risk Retention Group, 1994—; mem. legal svcs. rev. panel Nat. Assn. Ind. Colls. and Univs., 1997—. Active Heart O'Tex. coun. Boy Scouts Am., Heart of Tex. Coun. on Alcoholism and Drug Abuse, bd. dirs., 1987-91; mem. bd. adjustment City of Woodway. Recipient Pres.'s award Ind. Colls. and Univs. of Tex., 1994, Dist. award of merit Boy Scouts Am. Fellow Coll. State Bar Tex.; mem. ABA, FBA, Nat. Assn. Coll. and Univ. Attys. (fin., nominations and elections coms. 1994-95, bd. dirs. 1988-91), Nat. Assn. Ind. Colls. and Univs. (legal svcs. revie panel 1997—), Tex. Bar Assn., Waco Bar Assn., McLennan County Bar Assn., Owners Assn. of Sugar Creek, Inc. (dir. 1995—). Baptist. Avocations: backpacking, running, environ. concerns. Home: 100 Sugar Creek Pl Waco TX 76712-3410 Office: Baylor U PO Box 97034 Waco TX 76798-7034

**THOMSON, GEORGE RONALD,** lawyer, educator; b. Wadsworth, Ohio, Aug. 25, 1959; s. John Alan and Elizabeth (Galbraith) T. BA summa cum laude, Miami U., Oxford, Ohio, 1982, MA summa cum laude, 1983; JD with honors, Ohio State U., 1986. Bar: Ill. 1986, U.S. Dist. Ct. (no. dist.) Ill. 1986. Teaching fellow Miami U., 1982-83; dir. speech activities Ohio State U., Columbus, 1983-86; assoc. Peterson, Ross, Schloerb & Seidel, Chgo., 1986-87, Lord, Bissell & Brook, Chgo., 1987-94; asst. corp. counsel employment litig. divsn. City of Chgo., 1994—; adj. prof. dept. comm. De Paul U., Chgo., 1988-90; presenter in field. Contbr. articles to profl. jours. Fundraiser Chgo. Hist. Soc., Steppenwolf Theater Co., AIDS Legal Counsel Chgo., Smithsonian Instn., Washington, 1988—, U.S. Tennis Assn., 1990—; bd. dirs. Metro Sports Assn., 1992-94, Gerber-Hart Libr. and Archives, 1993-95, Gay and Lesbian Tennis Alliance Am., 1993-95, Team Chgo., 1994-96; mem. coord. coun. Nat. Gay and Lesbian History Month; mem. Lawyer's Com. for Ill Human Rights; dir. Chgo. Internat. Charity Tennis Classic, 1993, 94, 95, 98. Recipient Spl. Commendation Ohio Ho. of Reps., 1984, 85, Nat. Forensics Assn. award, 1982. Mem. ABA, Chgo. Bar Assn., Lesbian and Gay Bar Assn., Speech Comm. Assn. Am., Mortar Bd., Phi Beta Kappa, Phi Kappa Phi, Omicron Delta Kappa, Delta Sigma Rho-Tau Kappa Alpha, Phi Alpha Delta. Presbyterian. Avocations: tennis, flute, antiques, folk arts and crafts, reading, travel. General civil litigation, Insurance, Environmental. Home: 2835 N Pine Grove Ave Unit 2S Chicago IL 60657-6109 Office: City of Chgo Dept of Law 30 N La Salle St Ste 1020 Chicago IL 60602-2503

**THOMSON, HUGH TALBERT,** lawyer; b. San Francisco, Nov. 21, 1944; s. Douglas Hugh and Margaret Rose (Coffen) T.; children: Brian, Kimberly. B.A., U. Calif.-Berkeley, 1967; J.D., U. Calif.-Davis, 1970. Bar: Calif. 1971. Sole practice San Jose, Calif., 1971—; lectr. Continuing Edn. of Bar, Judge's Conf. Fellow Am. Acad. Matrimonial Lawyers; mem. State Bar Calif. (writer family law specialization exam. 1981, 82, 84, author Family Law News, mem. exec. com. family law sect. 1979-83), Calif. Bd. Legal Specialization for Family Law. Office: 941 W Hedding St San Jose CA 95126-1216

**THOMSON, JULIUS FAISON, JR.,** lawyer; b. Goldsboro, N.C., Apr. 26, 1923; m. Nancy Jones, Aug. 4, 1956; children: Louise Marshall Thomson East, Laurie Thomson Moore. AB, U. N.C., Chapel Hill, 1947; LLB, Wake Forest (N.C.) Coll., 1951. Bar: N.C. 1952. Mem. Goldsboro. Office: 229 E Walnut St Goldsboro NC 27530-4834

**THOREN-PEDEN, DEBORAH SUZANNE,** lawyer; b. Rockford, Ill., Mar. 28, 1958; d. Robert Roy and Marguerite Natalie (Geoghegan) Thoren; m. Steven E. Peden, Aug. 10, 1985. BA in Philosophy, Polit. Sci./Psychology, U. Mich., 1978; JD, U. So. Calif., 1982. Bar: Calif. 1982. Assoc. Bushkin, Gaines & Gaims, L.A., 1982-84, Rutan & Tucker, Costa Mesa, Calif., 1984-86; sr. counsel First Interstate Bancorp, L.A., 1986-96; of counsel Pillsbury, Madison & Sutro, L.A., 1996—; lectr. on Bank Secrecy Act and Ethics. Supervising editor U. So. Calif. Entertainment Law Jour., 1982-83, Entertainment Publishing and the Arts Handbook, 1983-84; contbr. articles to profl. publs. Mem. ABA (past vice chmn. compliance exec. com., money laundering task force, privacy task force, co chair BSA staff commentary com.), Calif. Bankers Assn. (regulatory compliance com., co-chair regulatory compliance conf., past ex-officio mem. state govt. rels. com., co-vice chair, vice-chair, Regulatory Compliance Profl. award 1997), Calif. State Bar Assn. (chair, consumer fin. com.). Avocations: riding, travel, reading, skiing. Banking, Labor. Office: Pillsbury Madison & Sutro 725 S Figueroa St Ste 1200 Los Angeles CA 90017-5443

**THORN, ANDREA PAPP,** lawyer; b. Greenwich, Conn., May 22, 1960; d. Laszlo G. and Judith (Liptak) Papp; m. Craig Thorn IV, Aug. 27, 1982; children: C. Alexander, Kelsey Amanda. BA, Dartmouth Coll., Hanover, N.H., 1982; JD, Harvard U., 1987. Bar: Mass. 1987, N.H. 1993. Assoc. Bingham Dana & Gould, Boston, 1987-89, Gaffin & Krattenmaker PC, Boston, 1989-90, Phillips, Gerstein & Holber, Haverhill, Mass., 1993-94; spl. asst. to sec. of N.Mex. Dept. of Environment, 1991-92. Mem. ABA, Mass. Bar Assn., N.H. Bar Assn. General civil litigation, Securities. Home: Phillips Academy Andover MA 01810-4161 Office: Karfunkel & Thorn PA 68 Park St Andover MA 01810-3644

**THORNBURG, LACY HERMAN,** federal judge; b. Charlotte, N.C., Dec. 20, 1929; s. Jesse Lafayette and Sarah Ann (Ziegler) T.; m. Dorothy Todd, Sept. 6, 1953; children—Sara Thornburg Evans, Lacy Eugene, Jesse Todd, Alan Ziegler. A.A., Mars Hill Coll., 1950; B.A., U. N.C., 1951, J.D., 1954. Bar: U.S. Dist. Ct. (we. dist.) N.C. Practiced law Webster, N.C., 1954-67; superior ct. judge State of N.C., 1967-83; atty. gen State of N.C., Raleigh, 1985-92; emergency judge N.C. Superior Ct., Webster, N.C., 1993-94; mem. Nat. Indian Gaming Commn., 1994-95; judge N.C. western dist. U.S. Dist. Ct., 1995—; mem. staff Congressman Taylor, Sylva, N.C., 1960, Congressman David Hall, Sylva, 1959-60; mem. N.C. Ho. of Reps., 1961-65; mem. N.C. Cts. Commn., N.C. Criminal Code Commn., Capital Planning Commn., Raleigh; chmn. Law Enforcement Coordinating Com., Raleigh, 1985—. Chmn. Jackson County Bd. of Health, Sylva, 1965-84; commr. Tryon Palace, New Bern, N.C. Served with U.S. Army, 1947-48. Mem. Lions, Masons, Shriners. Democrat. Avocations: fly fishing, skeet shooting. Office: US Dist Ct 241 US Courthouse 100 Otis St Asheville NC 28801

**THORNBURGH, RICHARD L. (DICK THORNBURGH),** lawyer, former United Nations official, former United States attorney general, former governor; b. Pitts., July 16, 1932; s. Charles Garland and Alice (Sanborn) T.; m. Virginia Walton Judson, Oct. 12, 1963; children: John, David, Peter, William. B in Engring., Yale, 1954; LLB, U. Pitts., 1957; hon. degrees, from 30 colls. and univs. Bar: Pa. 1958, U.S. Supreme Ct. 1965, D.C. 1998. Atty. Kirkpatrick & Lockhart, Pitts., 1959-69, 77-79, 87-88, 91-92, 94—; U.S. atty. for Western Pa. Pitts., 1969-75; U.S. asst. atty. gen. Dept. Justice, Washington, 1975-77; gov. State of Pa., Harrisburg, 1979-87; dir. Inst. Politics John F. Kennedy Sch. Govt., Harvard U., 1987-88; U.S. atty. gen. Washington, 1988-91; under-sec.-gen. for adminstrn. and mgmt. UN, N.Y.C., 1992-93; del. Pa. Constl. Conv., 1967-68; chmn. State Sci. and Technology Inst.; vice chair World Com. on Disability; bd. dirs. Elan Corp. plc, Nat. Mus. Indsl. History. Mem. Coun. Fgn. Rels.; trustee Urban Inst., DeWitt Wallace Fund for Colonial Williamsburg, Nat. Acad. Pub. Adminstrn. Fellow Am. Bar Found.; mem. Am. Judicature Soc. Republican. Office: Kirkpatrick & Lockhart LLP 1800 Massachusetts Ave NW Washington DC 20036-1800

**THORNBURY, WILLIAM MITCHELL,** lawyer, educator; b. Kansas City, Mo., Feb. 11, 1944; s. Paul Cobb and Marguerite Madellaine (Schulz) T.; m. Joy Frances Barrett, Feb. 2, 1973; children: Barrett Mitchell, Adele Frances. BA, UCLA, 1964; JD, U. So. Calif., 1967, postgrad. 1967-69. Bar: Calif. 1968, U.S. Dist. Ct. (cen. dist.) Calif. 1968, U.S. Dist. Ct. (no. dist.) Calif. 1973, U.S. Dist. Ct. (so. dist.) Calif. 1980, U.S. Dist. Ct. (ea. dist.) Calif. 1980, U.S. Ct. Appeals (9th cir.) 1973, U.S. Ct. Claims 1980, U.S. Ct. Internat. Trade, 1981, U.S. Ct. Customs and Patent Appeals 1980, U.S. Ct. Mil. Appeals 1980, U.S. Supreme Ct. 1973, U.S. Ct. Appeals (fed. cir.) 1984. Dep. L.A. County Pub. Defender, 1969—, dep.-in-charge traffic ct., 1982-84, supervising atty. Juvenile Svcs. div., 1984, dep. in charge, Inglewood, Calif., 1984-85; legal asst. prof. Calif. State U., L.A., 1983—; mem. adv. com. on alcohol determination State Dept. Health, 1984—; appointed to apprenticeship council by Gov. Deukmejian State of Calif., 1986—, reappointed Gov. Wilson, 1993, chmn. equal opportunity com. 1987-90, chmn. forums com., 1991-92, chair legis. com. 1993; chmn., vice chmn. Santa Monica Fair Election Practices Commn., Calif., 1981-85; advisor on drunk driving Calif. Pub. Defenders Assn., 1984—; alt. mem. L.A. County Commn. on Drunk Driving, 1983-84; mem. steering com. Santa Monica Coalition, nominations com., 1984; bd. dirs. Westside Legal Svcs., 1984-86, v.p., 1986-87, pres., 1987-88. Columnist Calif. Defender; editor Drunk Driving Manual, 1984; contbr. article to Forum. Exec. bd. dirs. Santa Monica Young Rep., 1967-72, pres. 1972-73, treas. 1973-75, bd. dirs. 1986-72; del., precinct chmn., registration chmn. L. A. County Young Rep., 1968-70; chmn. legal com. L.A. County Rep. Cen. Com., 1977-81, 83-85; chmn. jud. evaluation com., 1978-80; pres. Santa Monica Rep. Club 1986-88, bd. dirs., 1966-90; bd. dirs. West L.A. Rep. Club, 1986-91; mem. Beverly Hills Rep. Club, Rep. State Cen. com., 1983-85, 89-91, assoc. mem., 1980-83, 86-89, platform com. 1990 State Rep. Party, Non-Partisan Candidate Evaluating Coun., Inc. (bd. dirs. 1980-86, v.p. 1986-89, pres. 1989—); mem. Pasadena Rep. Club, 1984—; bd. dirs. Santa Monicans Against Crime, 1979—; chmn. 44th Assembly Dist. Rep. Cen. Com. 1974-87; chmn. Western part of L.A. County for George Murphy for U.S. Senate, 1970, John T. LaFollette for Congress, 1970; campaign chmn. Donna A. Little for City Council, 1984; adv. Pat Geffner for City Council, 1979, 81; campaign mgr. Experienced Coll. Team, 1983; mem. adv. com. Fred Beteta for Assembly, 1989-90; mem. platform com. Rep. State Party, 1990. Recipient Outstanding Chmn. award Los Angeles County Rep. Party, 1974, sec.-treas. 1968-75, chmn. legal com. 1977-82, 83-85; named Outstanding Service to Rep. Party Legal Counsel, 1978; recipient award Am. Assn. UN, 1961. Mem. ABA, L.A. County Bar Assn. (vice chmn. indigent and criminal def. com., jud. evaluation com. 1986-88, 2d vice chmn. 1989-90, 1st vice chmn., 1990-91, chair, 1991-92, criminal justice com. 1986—, criminal law and law enforcement com., 1986—), Santa Monica Bar Assn. (trustee 1976-77, 79-87, chmn. legis. and publicity com., chmn. jud. evaluation com. 1982-84, pres.-elect 1984-85, pres. 1985-86, del. to state bar conv. 1974-88, liaison to L.A. County Bar Assn. 1986-87, chmn. legis. com. 1983-84, 88), L.A. County Pub. Defenders Assn. (advisor, bd. dirs. 1980-88), Calif. Pub. Defenders Assn. (advisor), Santa Monica Hist. Soc., San Fernando Valley Criminal Bar Assn. (membership chmn. 1986-88, bd. trustees 1986—, treas. 1987-88, v.p. 1988, pres.-elect 1988, pres. 1989-90, chmn. judicial evaluations com. 1988), Assn. Trial Lawyers Am., Supreme Ct. Hist. Soc., Nat. Legal Aid and Defenders Assn., Nat. Assn. Criminal Def. Attys., Acad. Criminal Justice Scis., U. So. Calif. Law Alumni Assn., UCLA Alumni Assn., N.Y. Acad. Scis., Am. Assn. Polit. Sci., Criminal Law sect. of State Bar of Calif., Am. Soc. Criminology (life), Criminal Cts. Bar Assn., Western Region Criminal Law Educators, Santa Monica C. of C. (inebriate task force 1980), Calif. Hist. Soc., Santa Monica Coll. Patron's Assn., Nat. Assn. Criminal Def. Counsel, Navy League (life, bd. dirs. 1979—, legis. chmn. 1982, judge adv. 1983-89, 2d vice pres. 1989-90, 1st v.p. 1991-92, pres. navy league coun. 1992—), Nat. Rifle Assn. (life), Calif. Rifle and Pistol Assn. (life).

**THORNE, DAVID W.,** lawyer; b. Walla Walla, Wash., Aug. 9, 1945. BA, Wash. State U., 1967; MBA, U. Wash., 1969, JD, 1974. Bar: Wash. 1974. Mem. Davis Wright Tremaine LLP, Seattle. Mem. ABA, Am. Coll. Real Estate Lawyers, Am. Coll. Mortgage Attys., Am. Land Title Assn. Lender Counsel Group, Wash. State Bar Assn. (past mem. exec. com. real property, probate and trust sect., past chmn. 1991-92), Pacific Real Estate Inst. (past pres. 1994, founding trustee 1989-96), Phi Delta Phi. Real property. Office: Davis Wright Tremaine LLP 2600 Century Sq 1501 4th Ave Ste 2600 Seattle WA 98101-1688

**THORNE, WILLIAM ALBERT,** lawyer; b. Chgo., Feb. 20, 1924; s. William A. and Irma J. Thorne; m. Elizabeth Lee Douglas, June 19, 1948; children: Deborah, Elizabeth Ann, Margaret, Douglas. JD, Valparaiso U., 1949. Bar: Ind. 1949, U.S. Dist. Ct. (no. and so. dists.) Ind. 1949, U.S. Supreme Ct. 1960. Pvt. practice Elkhart, Ind., 1949-63; ptnr. Thorne, Grodnik, Ransel, Duncan, Byron & Hostetler, Elkhart, 1963-95, of counsel, 1995—. Bd. visitors Valparaiso U. Law Sch., 1990-96; chmn. City of Elkhart Parks and Recreation Bd., 1971-75; chmn. Elkhart Bd. Water Works, 1975-83, No. Ind. Conf. United Meth. Ch., Bd. Higher Edn. and Campus Ministry, 1994—; bd. trustees Meth. Theol. Sch. Ohio, 1993—. Cpl. U.S. Army, 1943-46. Fellow Ind. State Bar Assn. (chmn. bankruptcy sect. 1985-86, bd. govs. 1987-88). Democrat. United Methodist. Avocations: golf, reading. Bankruptcy, General corporate. Office: Thorne Grodnik Ransel Duncan Byron & Hostetler 228 W High St Elkhart IN 46516-3176

**THORNLOW, CAROLYN,** law firm administrator, consultant; b. Kew Gardens, N.Y., May 25, 1954. 1 child, Johanna Louise Ramm. B.B.A. magna cum laude, Bernard M. Baruch Coll., 1982. Gen. mgr. Richard A. Ramm Assocs., Levittown, N.Y., 1972-78; adminstr. Tunstead Schechter & Torre, N.Y.C., 1978-82, Cowan Liebowitz & Latman, P.C., N.Y.C., 1982-84, Rosenberg & Estis, P.C., N.Y.C., 1984-85; controller Finkelstein, Borah, Schwartz, Altschuler & Goldstein, P.C., N.Y.C., 1986-92; pres. Concinnity Services, Hastings, N.Y., 1984—; instr. introduction to law office mgmt. seminars Assn. Legal Adminstrs., N.Y.C., 1984. Editor: The ABA Guide to Profl. Mgrs. in the Law Office, 1996; contbr. numerous articles to profl. jours. Mem. N.Y. Assn. Legal Adminstrs. (v.p. 1982-83), Internat. Assn. Legal Adminstrs. (asst. regional v.p. 1983-84, regional v.p. 1984-85), Nat. Soc. Tax Profls. (cert. tax profl.), Am. Mgmt. Assn., Inst. Cert. Profl. Mgrs. (cert.), ABA, Inst. Cert. Mgmt. Accts., Mensa, Beta Gamma Sigma, Sigma Iota Epsilon. Home and Office: 445 Broadway Hastings On Hudson NY 10706

**THORNSBURY, MICHAEL,** judge; b. Williamson, W.Va., July 6, 1956; s. John and Maggie Z. (Thocker) T.; m. Dreama K. Keith, June 25, 1977; children: Melissa, Matthew, Elizabeth Ann. BA, Pikeville (Ky.) Coll., 1977; JD summa cum laude, U. Ky., 1980. Bar: Ky. 1980, W.Va. 1980, U.S. Dist. Ct. (so. dist.) W.Va. 1980, U.S. Dist. Ct. (ea. dist.) Ky. 1980, U.S. Appeals 1988. Chief legal aid dept. Fed. Correctional Instn., Lexington, Ky., 1978-80; pvt. practice Williamson, 1980-96; city atty. Town of Gilbert, W.Va.,

1985-90; cir. judge Mingo 30th Jud. Cir., Williamson, 1996—; asst. pros. atty. County of Mingo, Williamson, 1981-85. Mem. Mingo County Dep. Sheriff's Civil Svc. Commn., 1983-85; candidate W.Va. Ho. of Dels., 1988. Presdl. scholar Pikeville Coll., 1974. Mem. Assn. Trial Lawyer Am., Ky. Bar Assn., W.Va. Bar Assn., W.Va. Trial Lawyers Assn., W.Va. Jud. Assn., Ky. Trial Lawyers Assn., Mingo County Trial Lawyers Assn. (pres. Williamson chpt. 1986-88), Pike Coll. Alumni Assn. (bd. dirs.), Moose, Kiwanis (bd. dirs. 1997—). Democrat. Baptist. Home: 1717 W 4th Ave Williamson WV 25661-3014 Office: Mingo Cir Judge PO Box 1198 75 E 2d Ave Williamson WV 25661

**THORNTON, GUILFORD F., JR.,** lawyer; b. Brownsville, Tenn., Apr. 3, 1962; m. Anna Morrow, July 11, 1992; children: Anna Russell, Richard Taylor, Cole Farrell. BS, Vanderbilt U., 1984, JD, 1990. Bar: Tenn., U.S. Dist. Ct. (mid. dist.) Tenn. Asst. to amb. U.S. Embassy, Paris, 1986-87; prin. Stokes & Bartholomew, P.A., Nashville, 1990—. Commr. Davidson County Election Commn., Nashville, 1996—; trustee Vanderbilt U., Nashville, 1984-87. Vanderbilt Bar Assn. scholar, 1990. Mem. Nashville Bar Assn. (pres. young lawyers divsn. 1995-96, chmn. govt. rels. com. 1995-96). Republican. Presbyterian. Government contracts and claims, Public utilities, Legislative. Office: Stokes & Bartholomew PA 424 Church St Ste 2800 Nashville TN 37219-2386

**THORNTON, JOEL HAMILTON,** lawyer; b. Rome, Ga., Dec. 17, 1960; s. Billy Garner and Avis Cordle T.; m. Angelle Jacobs, July 28, 1990; 1 child, John Elias. BS, Berry Coll., 1985; JD, Ga. State U., 1993. Tchr. Floyd County Bd. Edn., Rome, Ga., 1985-89; law clk. Christian Advocates Serving Evangelism, Atlanta, 1990-93; staff atty. Am. Ctr. Law & Justice, Atlanta, 1993-95; sr. assoc. counsel ACLJ, Atlanta, 1995-98, sr. counsel, 1998—; sr. counsel European Ctr. Law & Justice, Atlanta, 1998—; spl. counsel Trinity Broadcasting Network, Santa Ana, Calif., 1995-96. Mem. Am. Trial Lawyers Assn. Presbyterian. Avocations: guitar, creative writing. Public international, Civil rights, Constitutional. Office: Am Ctr Law & Justice 1000 Regent University Dr Virginia Beach VA 23464-5037

**THORNTON, JOHN WILLIAM, SR.,** lawyer; b. Toledo, July 3, 1928; s. Cletus Bernard and Mary Victoria (Carey) T.; m. Mary Feeley, Mar. 10, 1951; children: John W. Jr., Jane Thornton Mastrucci, Deborah Thornton Hasty, Michael; m. Gabriela Marin, 1994. *Gabriela Marin was born in Targoviste, Romania, in 1960. She was educated at Politechnical University, Bucharest, graduating in 1984. During 1990-1993 she worked with a French software company on French law. She came to the U.S. in 1994. In 1997 she published 2 novels: In largul sufletului, and Obsesia de a ramane tanar. Her 3rd novel, Insula guvernatorilor, was published 1998. Two months later she became a member of Romanian Union of Writers. Presently she lives in Florida and works as freelance correspondent for Radio Romania International. She is contributing author to several newspapers, including Gracious Light, and other publications in U.S. and Romania, with editions in French and Spanish.* AB magna cum laude, U. Notre Dame, 1950, LLB summa cum laude, 1956, JD, 1969. Bar: Fla. 1956, U.S. Dist. Ct. (no., mid. and so. dists.) Fla. 1956, U.S. Ct. Appeals (5th cir.) 1956, U.S. Ct. Appeals (11th cir.) 1982. Assoc. area def. firm, Miami, Fla.; ptnr. Dixon, DeJarnette, et al, 1956-67, Stephens, Demos, Magill & Thornton, Miami, 1968-76; pvt. practice Thornton & Mastrucci, P.A. and predecessor firm, Miami, 1976—; chairperson legis. com. Fla. Med. Malpractice Claims Coun., Inc., 1984—, legis. and adminstrv. code rep. on hosp. risk mgrs. qualifications, rules and liability and nursing home rules and liability, 1986—; lectr. Fla. tort ins. law hosp. and physician series on risk mgmt. Am. Inst. Med. Law; lectr. South Fla. Hosp. Risk Mgmt. Soc.; legis. atty. Fla. Sch. Bd. Assn.; presenter legal, healthcare and ins. industry confs. *Grandparents William and Helen Thornton left Dublin, Ireland in 1881 and Grandparents John and Mary Murray left Cork, Ireland in 1878 and resided in Toledo, Ohio and Fort Wayne, Indiana, respectively. Son John, Jr. and his wife, Melinda, practice law in Dade County, Florida, as does Jane Thornton Mastrucci with son in law, engineer, Joseph Mastrucci, Frederick E. Hasty, III, son in law married to daughter Deborah, R.N., and son Michael and wife, Cathy, in Miami, as writer, educator, graphic designer, and illustrator, and wife Gabriela's DecebalThornton, all residing within a few miles of each other in the Miami area.* Contbr. articles to profl. publs. Mem. Dade County Sch. Bd., 1967—. Lt. USN, 1950-53, Korea. Mem. ABA (vice chmn. torts and ins. practice sect., active various coms.), Internat. Assn. Def. Counsel (chmn. med. malpractice com. 1975-76, chmn. profl. errors and omissions com. 1987—), Def. Rsch. Inst. (chmn. practice and procedure com. 1976-77), Fedn. Ins. and Corp. Counsel (chmn. auto and casualty ins. sect. 1987—, chmn. legis. com. 1984-88, vice chmn. ethics com. 1990-94), Fla. Def. Lawyers Assn. (bd. dirs. 1976), Internat. Assn. Ins. counsel (chmn. med. malpractice 1972-74, com. 1975-99, def. counsel com. 1976-91, reins. excess and surplus lines com. 1980-99), Dade County Def. Bar Assn., Fed. Ins. Corp. Counsel (casualty ins. law com. 1972-99, med. malpractice com. 1974-99, excess surplus and reins. com. 1976-99, publs. com. 1976-87), Maritime Law Assn. U.S., Fla. Def. Lawyers Assn. (bd. dirs., chmn. legis. com. 1974-77), Internat. Law Soc., Broward County Bar Assn., Am. Judicature Soc., Am. Health Care Assn., Coral Gables Club, Ocean Reef Club, Riviera Country Club, Sapphire Valley Country Club. Roman Catholic. Personal injury, Environmental, Insurance. Office: Thornton & Mastrucci PA 4699 Ponce De Leon Blvd Coral Gables FL 33146-2101

**THORNTON, JOSEPH PHILIP,** lawyer; b. Phila., Sept. 4, 1952; s. Joseph F. and Phyllis (Tweed) T.; m. Cynthia Moore, Oct. 21, 1977; children: Anne, Matthew, John, Mark. AB, Seton Hall U., 1974; JD, St. Louis U., 1977. Bar: N.J. 1977, Iowa 1980, Ill. 1986, U.S. Dist. Ct. (no., so. and cen. dists.) Ill. 1986, U.S. Ct. Appeals (7th cir.) 1996. Assoc. George James Law Firm, Wildwood, N.J., 1977-79; exec. asst. to chief justice Supreme Ct. of Iowa, Des Moines, 1979-82; assoc. gen. counsel Des Moines Register, 1982-85; sr. counsel pub. Tribune Co., Chgo., 1985-94; ptnr. Craven & Thornton, Springfield, Ill., 1995—. Mem. Ill. Press Assn. (gen. counsel 1995—, Legis. Svc. award 1989), Newspaper Assn. Am. (taxation com. 1995—, mem. legal affairs com. 1992-94), Ill. C. of C. (bd. dirs. 1992-94). Democrat. Roman Catholic. Communications, General civil litigation, General corporate. Office: Craven & Thornton 1005 N 7th St Springfield IL 62702-3918

**THORNTON, LUCIE ELIZABETH,** lawyer; b. Mena, Ark., Apr. 26, 1957; d. Oris Bryant and Carolyn (Cox) T.; m. Frank E. Lamothe III, Dec. 3, 1983; children: Victorine Day Lamothe, Julien Guy Lamothe. BA, Centenary Coll., Shreveport, La., 1979; JD, Tulane U., 1982. Bar: La. 1983, U.S. Dist. Ct. (ea. dist.) La. 1983. Law clk. 1st Cir. Ct. Appeals, Baton Rouge, 1982-83; assoc. Law Offices of Charles E. Hamilton III, New Orleans, 1983-85; law clk. Civil Dist. Ct. New Orleans, 1985-92; pvt. practice, New Orleans, 1992—. Mem. editorial bd. La. Appellate Ct. Handbook, 1982—. Friend of the New Orleans Zoo, 1981—; mem. New Orleans Mus. Art, 1982—; mem. La. Adv. Com. on Child Care Facilities and Child Placing Agys., 1994-98; active Jr. League of New Orleans, 1988-98, Greater Covington Jr. Svc. League, 1994-96; trustee La. Children's Mus., 1992-96; bd. dirs. Save Our Cemeteries, 1992-96, Youth Svc. Bd., 1997—; vestrywoman Christ Episcopal Ch., 1996-98, dir. Christian Formation, 1999; sustainer Jr. League New Orleans, Greater Covington Jr. Svc. League. Mem. La Bar Assn. (CLE com. 1986-87, bench-bar liaison com. 1991-94), Chi Omega. Republican. Administrative and regulatory, Personal injury. Home: 114 Random Oaks Ln Mandeville LA 70448-4565 Office: 601 Poydras St Ste 2750 New Orleans LA 70130-6014

**THORNTON, RAY,** state supreme court justice, former congressman; b. Conway, AR, July 16, 1928; s. R.H. and Wilma (Stephens) T.; m. Betty Jo Mann, Jan. 27, 1956; children: Nancy, Mary Jo, Stephanie. B.A., Yale, 1950; J.D., U. Ark., 1956. Bar: Ark. 1956, U.S. Supreme Ct 1956. Pvt. practice in Sheridan and Little Rock, 1956-70; atty. gen. Ark., 1971-73; mem. 93d-95th Congresses from 4th Ark. dist.; exec. dir. Quachita Bapt. U./Henderson State U. Joint Ednl. Consortium, Arkadelphia, Ark., 1979-80; pres. Ark. State U., Jonesboro and Beebe, 1980-84, U. Ark. System, Fayetteville, Little Rock, Pine Bluff, Monticello, 1984-89; mem. 102nd-104th Congresses from 2d Ark. dist., 1991-96; assoc. justice Ark. Supreme Ct., 1997—; chmn. Ark. Bd. Law Examiners, 1967-70; Del. 7th Ark. Constl. Conv., 1969-70. Chmn. pres.'s devel. council Harding Coll., Searcy, Ark., 1971-73. Served with USN, 1951-54, Korea. Mem. AAAS (chmn. com. on sci., engring. and public policy 1980). Office: PO Box 826 Little Rock AR 72203-0826

**THORNTON, WENDY NIX,** lawyer; b. Ruston, La., June 14, 1970; d. Gary Nix and Chris Froelich; m. Thomas Spruill Thornton, Sept. 21, 1996. BA in Comm., U. Ala., 1992; JD, Cumberland Sch. Law, 1996. Atty. Haynes & Haynes, Birmingham, Ala., 1996-97, Robert W. Lee and Assocs., Birmingham, 1997—. Mem. Ala. State Bar, Birmingham Bar Assn. Workers' compensation, Labor, Personal injury. Office: 2100 1st Ave N Ste 500 Birmingham AL 35203-4269

**THORPE, NORMAN RALPH,** lawyer, automobile company executive, retired air force officer; b. Carlinville, Ill., Oct. 17, 1934; s. Edwin Everett and Imogene Midas (Hayes) T.; m. Elaine Frances Pritzman, Nov. 1, 1968; children: Sarah Elizabeth, Carrie Rebecca. AB in Econs., U. Ill., 1956, JD, 1958; LLM in Pub. Internat. Law, George Washington U., 1967. Bar: Ill. 1958, Mich. 1988, U.S. Supreme. Ct. 1969. Commd. 2d lt. USAF, 1956, advanced through grades to brig. gen., 1983; legal advisor U.S. Embassy, Manila, 1969-72; chief internat. law hdqrs. USAF, Washington, 1972-77; staff judge adv. 21st Air Force, McGuire AFB, N.J., 1977-80, USAF Europe, Ramstein AB, Fed. Republic Germany, 1980-84; comdr. Air Force Contract Law Ctr., Wright-Patterson AFB, Ohio, 1984-88, ret., 1988; mem. legal staff, group counsel GM Def. and Power Products Gen. Motors Corp., Detroit, 1988—; legal advisor Dept. of Def. Blue Ribbon Com. on Code of Conduct, 1975; USAF del. Internat. Aero. and Astronautical Fedn., Budapest, 1983; adj. prof. U. Dayton Sch. Law, 1986-87; partnership counsel U.S. Advanced Battery Consortium, Legal Advisor U.S. Coun. Automotive Rsch., Chrysler Corp., Ford Motor Co., GM, 1990—. Contbr. articles to profl. jours. Staff mem. Commn. on Police Policies and Procedures, Dayton, 1986; trustee Dayton Philharm. Orch., 1987-88. Recipient Disting. Svc. medal Legion of Merit. Mem. ABA (chmn. com. internat. law sect. 1977-80, coun. mem. pub. contract law sect. 1986-88, chmn. com. pub. contract law sect. 1988-95, sec. pub. contract law sect. 1998-99), Air Force Assn., Dayton Coun. on World Affairs, Army/Navy Club, Detroit Econ. Club. Republican. Avocations: music, piano, gardening. Contracts commercial, Government contracts and claims, Private international. Home: 498 Abbey Rd Birmingham MI 48009-5618 Office: Gen Motors Corp Legal Staff 3031 W Grand Blvd Detroit MI 48202-3046

**THORSON, STEVEN GREG,** lawyer; b. Van Nuys, Calif., Feb. 7, 1948; s. Robert G. and Ruth C. T.; m. Patricia Lynn LaPointe, Aug. 3, 1974; 1 child, Kai Johannes. BA, St. Olaf Coll., 1977; JD, Hamline U., 1980. Bar: Minn. 1980, U.S. Dist. Ct. Minn. 1980, U.S. Tax Ct. 1980, U.S. Ct. Appeals (8th cir.) 1980. Pres. Thorson & Berg, Maple Grove, Minn., 1990-99; with Barna, Guzy & Steffen, Ltd. Attys. at Law, Mpls., 1999—; lectr. continuing legal edn., 1986—; apptd. to Minn. State Bar Assn. Commn. on Unauthorized Practice of Law, 1990-92; atty. for Columbus Twp. (Anoka County), 1981-96; mem. residential real estate com. Minn. State Bar Assn., 1992—. Mem. ch. coun. Peace Luth. Ch. Named One of Minn. Top Lawyers, Mpls/St. Paul mag., 1998. Mem. ABA, Minn. State Bar Assn., Hennepin County Bar Assn. (chmn. purchase agreement com. 1986-88), Anoka County Bar Assn. (pres. real estate sect. 1988). Avocations: alpine and nordic skiing. Real property, Land use and zoning (including planning), Municipal (including bonds). Home: 12071 Norway St NW Minneapolis MN 55448-2243 Office: 400 Northtown Fin Plz 200 Coon Rapids Blvd NW Ste 400 Minneapolis MN 55433-8024

**THOYER, JUDITH REINHARDT,** lawyer; b. Mt. Vernon, N.Y., July 29, 1940; d. Edgar Allen and Florence (Mayer) Reinhardt; m. Michael E. Thoyer, June 30, 1963; children: Erinn Thoyer Rhodes, Michael John. AB with honors, U. Mich., 1961; LLB summa cum laude, Columbia U., 1965. Bar: N.Y. 1966, D.C. 1984. Law libr. U. Ghana, Accra, Africa, 1963-64; assoc. Paul, Weiss, Rifkind, Wharton & Garrison, N.Y.C., 1966-75, ptnr., 1975—; mem. TriBar Opinion Com., 1995—. Bd. visitors Law Sch. Columbia U., N.Y.C., 1991—; bd. dirs. Women's Action Alliance, N.Y.C., 1975-89, pro bono counsel, 1975-97; mem. Women's Coun. Dem. Senatorial campaign com., 1993-97; organizing com. Alumnae Columbia Law Sch., 1996—. Mem. N.Y. County Lawyers Assn. (mem. securities and exchs. com. 1976-98), Assn. of Bar of City of N.Y. (mem. securities regulation com. 1976-79, mem. recruitment of lawyers com. 1980-82, mem. spl. com. on mergers, acquisitions and corp. control contests 1996—). Home: 1115 5th Ave Apt 3B New York NY 10128-0100 Office: Paul Weiss Rifkind Et Al 1285 Ave of Americas New York NY 10019-6028

**THRAILKILL, DANIEL B.,** lawyer; b. Fayetteville, Ark., Sept. 21, 1957. BSBA, U. Ark., 1979, J.D., 1981. Bar: Ark. 1982, Tex. 1988, U.S. Dist. Cts. (ea. and we. dists.) Ark. 1982, U.S. Ct. Appeals (8th cir.) 1983, U.S. Supreme Ct. 1985, U.S. Dist. Ct. (ea. dist.) Okla. 1995. Ptnr. Page, Thrailkill & McDaniel, P.A., Mena, Ark., 1981—; assoc. prof., lectr. Rich Mountain C.C.; assoc. justice Ark. Supreme Ct., 1996—; city atty. Cities of Mena and Hatfield. Mem. ATLA, ABA, Nat. Dist. Attys. Assn., Ark. Bar Assn., Ark. Trial Lawyers Assn., Lions, Phi Alpha Delta. Methodist. General practice, Personal injury, Real property. Home: 200 Craig St Mena AR 71953-2427 Office: Page Thrailkill & McDaniel PO Drawer 30 Courthouse Sq W Mena AR 71953

**THRALL, GORDON FISH,** lawyer; b. Jamestown, N.Y., July 28, 1923; s. Clyde Lowell and Beulah Mae (Fish) T.; m. Betty Jane Roberts, Sept. 24, 1964; 1 dau., Jenifer Jane. A.B. in History and Polit. Sci., Alfred U., 1949; J.D., Baylor U., 1953. Bar: Tex. 1953, U.S. Supreme Ct. 1957, D.C. 1958, U.S. Ct. Appeals (D.C. cir.) 1958, U.S. Ct. Mil. Appeals 1958, U.S. Dist. Ct. (ea. dist.) Tex. 1976, U.S. Ct. Appeals (5th cir.) 1986. Law clk. U.S. Dist. Ct. (ea. dist.) Tex., 1953-54; asst. prosecutor Dallas County Dist. Atty., 1954-55; assoc. firm Phinney & Hallman, Dallas, 1955-56; asst. Tex. Atty. Gen., 1957; adviser, examiner ICC, Washington, 1957-59; asst. gen. counsel Tex. State Bar, Austin, 1959-61; county atty. Reagan County, Big Lake, Tex., 1961-72; ptnr. Norman, Thrall, Angle & Guy, L.L.P., Jacksonville, Tex., 1972—. Mem. exec. com. Tex. Baptist Gen. Conv., 1965-70, adminstrv. bd., 1991-95; deacon So. Bapt. Ch.; chmn. Permian Basin dist. Concho Valley council Boy Scouts Am., Big Lake, 1965-66; chmn. Jacksonville United Fund Drive, 1987, pres., 1989; pres. Cherokee County Health Facilities Devel. Corp., 1982—; v.p., bd. dirs. Travis Towers Retirement Facility, Jacksonville, 1980—; co-trustee Summers A. Norman Found., 1988—; mem. Nan Travis Meml. Hosp. Found. Bd., 1994—. Mem. Tex. State Bar, Tex. Bar Found. (vice chmn. UPL com. 1964), Big Lake C. of C. (pres. 1963, 67), Jacksonville C. of C. (pres. 1979), Cherokee Country Club, (dir. 1981-83), Kiwanis (pres. 1978, lt. gov. div. 34 1982), Big Lake Lions (pres. 1969), Masons (32 degree). Republican. State civil litigation, Family and matrimonial, Probate. Home: 702 Ft Worth St Jacksonville TX 75766-2610 Office: Norman Thrall Angle & Guy LLP 215 E Commerce St Jacksonville TX 75766-4955

**THRASHER, JOHN EDWIN,** lawyer; b. Bloomington, Ind., May 29, 1951; s. Merlin Edwin and Edna Kathryn Thrasher; m. Nora Marie Davis, Oct. 18, 1981 (div. Mar. 1990); children: Sarah Marie, Kathryn Elizabeth. BA, Ind. U., Bloomington, 1973; JD, Ind. U., Indpls., 1978. Staff counsel Ind. State Employees Assn., Indpls., 1979; atty. Zarko Sakiris Legal Clinic, Indpls., 1979-80; sole practitioner Indpls., 1980-98; staff counsel Pub. Interest Law Group, Strafford, Vt., 1999—. Avocation: writing fiction. Appellate, Federal civil litigation, Civil rights. Home: PO Box 201 Sharon VT 05065-0201

**THREET, MARTIN EDWIN,** lawyer; b. El Paso, Tex., Sept. 1, 1933; s. Martin Albro and Frances Elizabeth (Mitchell) T.; m. Laura Elliott, Aug. 1, 1959; children—Martin, Melissa, Jennifer. B.A., N.Mex. Mil. Inst., 1955; LL.B., Vanderbilt U., 1959. Bar: N.Mex. 1959, U.S. Dist. Ct. N.Mex. 1959, U.S. Ct. Appeals (10th cir.) 1962. Ptnr., Threet, Ussery & Threet, Albuquerque, 1959-61; sr. ptnr. Threet, Threet & Glass, 1963, Threet, Threet, Glass & King, 1963-72, Threet, Threet, Glass, King & Maxwell, 1972-78, Threet, Threet, Glass, King & Hooe, 1978-80, Threet & King, 1980-97, Martin E. Threet & Assocs., 1997—; lectr. U. N.Mex., 1975-76. Served with AUS, 1958. Root Tilden scholar, 1956. Mem. N.Mex Trial Lawyers Assn., N.Mex. Bar Assn., Albuquerque Bar Assn., ABA, Comml. Law League Am. Democrat. Club: Newcomen Soc. State civil litigation, Federal civil litigation, Banking. Office: 6400 Uptown Blvd NE Suite 500 W Albuquerque NM 87110

**THRO, WILLIAM EUGENE,** lawyer; b. Elizabethtown, Ky., Nov. 8, 1963; s. Ernest Guernsey and Joan (Young) T.; m. Mary Ellen Edwards, Dec. 30, 1989; twins: Sandra Lucinda Grace Edwards-Thro and William Thomas Daniel Edwards-Thro. BA, Hanover Coll., 1986; MA, U. Melbourne, Australia, 1988; JD, U. Va., 1990. Bar: Ky. 1990, Colo. 1991, Va. 1998, U.S. Dist. Ct. (we. dist.) Ky. 1990, U.S. Dist. Ct. Colo. 1991, U.S. Ct. Appeals (6th and 10th cirs.) 1991, U.S. Ct. Appeals (3d cir.) 1993, U.S. Supreme Ct. 1993, U.S. Ct. Appeals (4th cir.) 1997, Va., 1998, U.S. Dist. Ct. (ea. dist.) Va. 1998, U.S. Dist. Ct. (we. dist.) Va. 1998, U.S. Ct. Appeals (D.C. cir.) 1999, U.S. Bankruptcy Ct. 1999. Jud. clk. Judge Ronald E. Meredith, U.S. Dist. Ct. (we. dist.) Ky., Louisville, 1990-91; asst. atty. gen. Office of Atty. Gen. State of Colo., Denver, 1991-97, Commonwealth of Va., Richmond, 1997—; mem. authors' com. West's Edn. Law Reporter, St. Paul, 1992—; sch. fin. litigation coord. Nat. Assn. Attys. Gen., 1992-97. Contbr. articles to scholarly jours. worker in various polit. campaigns. U.S. Senate Youth scholar Hearst Found., 1982; Harry S Truman scholar Truman Scholarship Found., 1984, Rotary Internat. Grad. scholar, Melbourne, 1987. Mem. ABA, Va. Bar Assn., Am. Judicature Soc., Ky. Bar Assn., Nat. Assn. Coll. and Univ. Attys., Federalist Soc., Nat. Eagle Scout Assn., Inst. for Justice, Human Action Network, Honorable Order of Ky. Cols. Republican. Home: 2924 Layne Ct Richmond VA 23233-8014 Office: Office of Atty Gen 900 E Main St Richmond VA 23219-3513

**THROESCH, DAVID,** lawyer; b. Pocahontas, Ark., Feb. 24, 1951; s. Roy and Kathleen Throesch; m. Leslie Throesch; children: Melodie, Amber. BA, Ark. State U., Jonesboro, 1973; JD, U. Ark., 1975. Bar: Ark. 1975. Pvt. practice, Pocahontas and Randolph, Ark., 1976—; pros. atty. Pocahontas and Randolph County, Ark., 1979—. Mem. Ark. Trial Lawyers Assn. (adminstrv. law chair). Democrat. Roman Catholic. Avocation: coin collection. Administrative and regulatory, Personal injury, Criminal. Home: 3722 Pyburn Ext Pocahontas AR 72455-1347 Office: PO Box 463 Pocahontas AR 72455-0463

**THRONE, DAWN RENEE,** lawyer; b. Fontana, Calif., July 15, 1970; d. Richard David Throne and Bonnie Kay Lambert; m. Harry William Wiltse, Aug. 19, 1995; 1 child, Zachary. BA in Polit. Sci., U. Hawaii, 1992; JD, U. Ariz., 1996. Bar: Nev. 1996, U.S. Dist. Ct. Nev. 1996, U.S. Ct. Appeals (9th cir.) 1997. Assoc. Jimmerson Hansen, Las Vegas, 1996—; grader Nev. State Bar Bd. Bar Examiners, Las Vegas, 1997—. Mem. Order of the Coif. Mem. LDS Ch. Family and matrimonial, General civil litigation. Office: Jimmerson Hansen 415 S 6th St Ste 100 Las Vegas NV 89101-6937

**THURMAN, ANDREW EDWARD,** lawyer; b. Raleigh, N.C., May 11, 1954; s. William Gentry and Peggy Lou (Brown) T.; m. Patricia Thurman, May 19, 1979 (dec. 1989); children: Gentry Brown, Harrison Beauchamp, Andrew Guilford; m. Tracy Fletcher, Nov. 16, 1991; 1 child, Spencer Lee. BA, Columbia U., 1976; JD, Coll. William and Mary, 1979; MPH, U. Okla., 1984. Bar: Va. 1979, Okla. 1980, U.S. Ct. Appeals (10th cir.) 1981, U.S. Supreme Ct. 1985, Pa. 1988. Staff atty. Dept. of Human Services, Oklahoma City, 1979-80; counsel State of Okla. Teaching Hosps., Oklahoma City, 1980-84; mem. Miller, Dollarhide, Dawson & Shaw, Oklahoma City, 1984-87; ptnr. Berkman, Ruslander, Pohl, Lieber & Engel, Pitts., 1988-89; of counsel Buchanan Ingersoll, Pitts., 1989; sr. v.p. and gen. counsel Forbes Health System, Pitts., 1989-96; sr. counsel Allegheny Health Edn. & Rsch. Found., Pitts., 1997-98; dep. gen. counsel Allegheny U. Hosps. West, 1998—; Pres. Council of Neighborhood Assns., Oklahoma City, 1984, Lincoln Terr. Neighborhood Assn., Oklahoma City, 1984; trustee Rader Trust, Oklahoma City, 1980—; treas. Bd. dirs. State Okla. Tchg. Hosps. Found., Oklahoma City, 1984-87, Newman Meml. Hosp., 1983-87, Willowview Hosp., Spencer, Okla., 1985-87, Allegheny U. Med. Ctrs., 1997—, AUMC/Cannonsburg Ambulance Svc., 1997—, Allegheny U. Hosps. West, 1998—, Diversified Health Group, 1998—; chair HCWP Ethics Task Force, 1993—. Fellow Am. Health Lawyers Assn.; mem. St. Anthony Hall Club of N.Y.C. (pres. 1976), Rivers Club. Democrat. Presbyterian. Avocation: reading detective novels. Health. Home: 106 Richmond Dr Pittsburgh PA 15215-1039 Office: Allegheny U Hosps W 320 E North Ave Pittsburgh PA 15212-4756

**THURMOND, GEORGE MURAT,** judge; b. Del Rio, Tex., Oct. 22, 1930; s. Roger H. and Day (Hamilton) T.; m. Elsiejean Davis, June 27, 1959; children: Carolyn Day, Georganna, Sarah Gail. BA, U. of the South, 1952; JD, U. Tex., 1955. Bar: Tex. 1955. Ptnr. Montague & Thurmond, Del Rio, 1955-69; judge Tex. Dist. Ct. (63rd dist.), Del Rio, 1970—; presiding judge 6th Adminstrv. Region, Del Rio, 1983-87; chmn. jud. sect. State Bar Tex., 1988-89. Editor: U. Tex. Law Review, 1955. Rep. Tex. Ho. of Reps., 1955-58. Mem. ABA, Tex. Bar Assn. Democrat. Episcopalian. Avocations: jogging, water sports. Office: 63d Jud Dist of Tex PO Box 1089 243 W Strickland St Del Rio TX 78840-5729

**THURSWELL, GERALD ELLIOTT,** lawyer; b. Detroit, Feb. 4, 1944; s. Harry and Lilyan (Zeitlin) T.; m. Lynn Satovsky, Sept. 17, 1967 (div. Aug. 1978); children: Jennifer, Lawrence; m. Judith Linda Bendix, Sept. 2, 1978 (div. May 1999); children: Jeremy, Lindsey. LLB with distinction, Wayne State U., 1967. Bar: Mich. 1968, N.Y. 1984, D.C. 1986, Colo. 1990, Ill. 1992, U.S. Dist. Ct. (ea. dist.) Mich. 1968, U.S. Ct. Appeals (7th cir.) 1968, U.S. Supreme Ct., 1994. Student asst. to U.S. atty. Ea. Dist. Mich., Detroit, 1966; assoc. Zwerdling, Miller, Klimist & Maurer, Detroit, 1967-68; sr. ptnr. Thurswell, Chayet & Weiner, Southfield, Mich., 1968—; arbitrator Am. Arbitration Assn., Detroit, 1969—; mediator Wayne County Cir. Ct., Mich., 1983—, Oakland County Cir. Ct. Mich., 1984—, also facilitator, 1991; twp. atty. Royal Oak Twp., Mich., 1982—; lectr. Oakland County Bar Assn. People's Law Sch., 1988. Pres. Powder Horn Estates Subdiv. Assn., West Bloomfield, Mich., 1975, United Fund, West Bloomfield, 1976. Arthur F. Lederle scholar Wayne State U. Law Sch., Detroit, 1964, grad. profl. scholar Wayne State U. Law Sch., 1965, 66. Mem. Mich. Bar Assn. (investigator/arbitrator grievance bd., atty. discipline bd., chmn. hearing panel), Mich. Trial Lawyers Assn. (legis. com. on govtl. immunit, 1984), ATLA (treas. Detroit met. chpt. 1986-87, v.p. 1989-90, pres. 1991-93), Detroit Bar Assn. (lawyer referral com., panel pub. adv. com. judicial candidates), Oakland County Bar Assn. Clubs: Wabeek Country (Bloomfield Hills), Skyline (Southfield, Mich.). Personal injury, State civil litigation. Office: Thurswell Chayet & Weiner 1000 Town Ctr Ste 500 Southfield MI 48075-1221

**TICE, DOUGLAS OSCAR, JR.,** federal judge; b. Lexington, N.C., May 2, 1933; s. Douglas Oscar Sr. and Lila Clayton (Wright) T.; m. Janet N. Capps, Feb. 28, 1959 (div. Sept. 1976); children: Douglas Oscar III, Janet E.; m. Beverley Carole Black, Aug. 8, 1982 (div. Apr. 1995); m. Martha Murdoch Edwards, June 8, 1996. BS, U. N.C., 1955, JD, 1957. Bar: N.C. 1957, U.S.

Ct. Appeals (4th cir.) 1964, Va. 1970, U.S. Dist. ct. (ea. dist.) Va. 1976, U.S. Bankruptcy Ct. (ea. dist.) Va. 1976. Exec. sec. N.C. Jud. Coun., Raleigh, 1958-59; assoc. Baucom & Adams, Raleigh, 1959-61; trial atty. Office Dist. Coun., IRS, Richmond, Va., 1961-70; corp. atty. Carlton Industries, Inc., Richmond, 1970-75; ptnr. Hubard, Tice, Marchant & Samuels, P.C., Richmond, 1975-87; judge U.S. Bankruptcy Ct. (ea. dist.), Richmond, Norfolk, Alexandria, Va., 1987-99; chief judge U.S. Bankruptcy Ct. (ea. dist.), 1999—. Co-author: Monument & Boulevard, Richmond's Grand Avenues, 1996; contbr. articles to profl. jours. Vice pres. Richmond Pub. Forum, 1976-80, com. chmn. Richmond Forum, Inc., 1986—; past pres. Richmond Civil War Roundtable, mem., 1965—; bd. dirs. Epilepsy Assn. Va., Inc., 1976-87. Capt. USAR, 1957-66. Mem. ABA, Va. Bar Assn., City of Richmond Bar Assn., Am. Bankruptcy Inst., Nat. Conf. Bankruptcy Judges, So. Hist. Assn., Va. Hist. Soc., Old Dominion Sertoma (pres. Richmond chpt. 1967). Home: 2037 W Grace St Richmond VA 23220-2003 Office: US Bankruptcy Ct 1100 E Main St Ste 341 Richmond VA 23219-3538

**TICE, LAURIE DIETRICH,** lawyer; b. Houston, Apr. 9, 1959; d. Donald Vernon and June (Reagan) Dietrich; m. Michael Dean Tice, Feb. 25, 1984 (div. May 1991); children: Rachel Michele, Rebekah Leigh. ABA approved, Southwestern Paralegal Inst., Houston, 1989; BA in History with highest honors, U. Tex., El Paso, 1994; JD, U. Tex., 1997. Bar: Tex. 1997. Legal sec. Gant & Juarez, Carlsbad, N.Mex., 1979-80; dep. clk. 5th Jud. Dist. Ct. N.Mex., Carlsbad, 1980-82; legal asst. Hinkle, Cox, Eaton, Coffield & Hensley, Roswell, N.Mex., 1982-86, Kemp, Smith, Duncan & Hammond, El Paso, Tex., 1986-92; assoc. McGinnis, Lochridge & Kilgore L.L.P., Austin, Tex., 1997—. lder, mem. resource and planning com. Univ. Presbyn. Ch., Austin, also mem. UPC Hard Knox Tennis Team. Franklin Myers Endowed Presdl. scholar, 1994-95, Judge Wilson Cohen Endowed Presdl. scholar, 1995-96, Israel Dreeben Endowed Meml. scholar, 1995-96. Mem. ABA, AAUW, Tex. Bar Assn., Travis County Bar Assn., Travis County Women Lawyers Assn. (membership com.), Austin Young Lawyers Assn., Austin Runners Club, Golden Key, Mortar Board (pres.), Beta Sigma Phi (rec. sec. 1984-85), Alpha Lambda Delta, Phi Alpha Theta (pres., sec.), Alpha Chi. Democrat. E-mail: ltice@mcginnislaw.com. General civil litigation, Labor. Home: 4404 Travis Country Cir A-2 Austin TX 78735

**TICHENOR, JAMES LEE,** lawyer, writer, filmmaker; b. Phila., Feb. 8, 1943; s. LeGrand L. and Elizabeth L. (Panetta) T.; m. Ellen Harriet Wertheim, 1968 (div. 1976); children: Dylan M., Aaron A.; m. Nancy Louise Keller, Dec. 2, 1976; children: James E., Diane E. BA, Antioch Coll., 1976; JD, Rutgers U., 1984. Bar: Pa. 1984. Pres. Cinetel Film Prodns., Phila., 1978-83; pvt. practice in law Phila., 1984-86; atty., advisor U.S. Dept. Housing and Urban Devel., Phila., 1986-91, assoc. field counsel, 1991—; vol. lawyer Phila. Vol. Lawyers for Arts, 1984-87; founding mem. Baha'i Justice Soc., 1986-88. Editor (film) Boreal Forest, 1979 (Alberta Film Festival award 1979). Chmn. Spiritual Assembly of Baha'is of Phila., 1968-94, 98—. With U.S. Army, 1964-66. Recipient Hammer award, Nat. Performance Rev. Fair Housing Processing Procedures, 1998. Mem. Wapiti Archers. Avocations: canoeing, archery, genealogy. Office: US Dept Housing and Urban Devel 100 Penn Sq E Fl 10 Philadelphia PA 19107-3322

**TIDWELL, GEORGE ERNEST,** federal judge; b. Atlanta, Aug. 1, 1931; s. George Brown and Mary (Wooddall) T.; m. Carolyn White, July 1, 1961; children: Thomas George, Linda Carol, David Loran. LL.B., Emory U., 1954. Bar: Ga. 1954. With John J. Westmoreland Sr. and Jr., Atlanta, 1954-58, Slaton, Brookins, Robertson & Tidewell, Atlanta, 1958-66; exec. asst. atty. gen. Atlanta, 1966-68; judge Civil Ct., Fulton County, Ga., 1968-71, Superior Ct., Atlanta Jud. Circuit, 1971-79, U.S. Dist. Ct. (no. dist.) Ga., Atlanta, 1979—; now chief judge. Mem. ABA, State Bar Ga., Am. Judicature Soc., Atlanta Bar Assn. Office: US Dist Ct 1967 US Courthouse 75 Spring St SW Atlanta GA 30303-3309

**TIDWELL, MOODY RUDOLPH,** federal judge; b. Kansas City, Mo., Feb. 15, 1939; s. Moody R., Jr. and Dorothy T.; m. Rena Alexandra, Jan. 28, 1966; children—Gregory, Jeremy. BA, Ohio Wesleyan U., 1961; JD, Am. U., 1964; LLM, George Washington U., 1972. Bar: U.S. Ct. Appeals (D.C. cir.) 1964, U.S. Dist Ct. D.C. 1965, U.S. Ct. Claims 1972, U.S. Ct. Appeals (10th cir.) 1979. Assoc. solicitor U.S. Dept. Interior, Washington, 1972-80; assoc. solicitor Mine Health and Safety div. Dept. Labor, Washington, 1978-80; deputy solicitor, counsellor to the sec. Dept. Interior, Washington, 1981-83; sr. judge U.S. Ct. Federal Claims, Washington, 1983—; dir., corporate sec. Keco, Inc., Cin. Recipient Disting. Service award Sec. of Interior, 1983, Meritorious Service award Sec. of Labor, 1979. Mem. ABA, FBA, D.C. Bar Assn. Office: US Ct Fed Claims 717 Madison Pl NW Washington DC 20005-1011

**TIERNEY, BETTY THORNE,** lawyer; b. East Prairie, Mo., Apr. 26, 1965; d. Troy Mc and Shirley Jeanette Latamondeer Thorne; m. Kevin James Tierney, Jan. 14, 1995; 1 child, Timothy Nicholas. BA in Polit. Sci., Ctrl. Meth. Coll., 1987; JD, Washington U., 1990. Bar: Mo. 1990, Ill. 1991, U.S. Dist. Ct. (ea. dist.) Mo. 1991, U.S. Dist. Ct. (so. dist.) Ill. 1993, U.S. Ct. Appeals (7th cir.) 1993, U.S. Ct. Appeals (5th cir.) 1995, U.S. Ct. Appeals (11th cir.) 1998. Assoc. Suelthaus & Kaplan, Clayton, Mo., 1990-92; counsel The May Dept. Stores Co., St. Louis, 1992—. Mem. Bar Assn. Met. St. Louis. Democrat. Roman Catholic. Avocations: reading, crafts, sewing, movies, exercising. Federal civil litigation, General civil litigation. Office: The May Dept Stores Co 611 Olive St Ste 1750 Saint Louis MO 63101-1721

**TIERNEY, KEVIN JOSEPH,** lawyer; b. Lowell, Mass., Dec. 13, 1951; s. Joseph Francis and Esther Rowena T. BS cum laude, Bowdoin Coll., 1973; JD, U. Maine, 1976. Bar: Maine 1976. Atty. Union Mutual Life Ins. Co., Portland, Maine, 1976-80, asst. counsel, 1980, 2d v.p., counsel, 1980-84, 2d v.p., counsel, corp. sec., 1984-86; 2d v.p., counsel, corp. sec. UNUM Corp., Portland, 1986-89, v.p., corp. counsel, sec., 1989-91, gen. counsel, sr. v.p., sec., 1991—. Bd. dirs. Pine Tree Alcoholism Treatment Ctr., Maine, 1977-84, So. Regional Alcoholism and Drug Abuse Coun., Maine, 1982-85; mem. radiation therapy tech. adv. com. So. Me. Vocat. Tech. Inst., 1985; trustee Portland Symphony Orch., 1990—. Mem. Am. Soc. Corp. Secs., Am. Corp. Counsel Assn., Maine State Bar Assn., Cumberland County (Maine) Bar Assn., Assn. of Life Ins. Counsel. General corporate, Insurance, Mergers and acquisitions. Office: UNUM Corp 2211 Congress St Portland ME 04122-0003

**TIERNEY, MICHAEL EDWARD,** lawyer; b. N.Y., July 16, 1948; s. Michael Francis and Margaret Mary (Creamer) T.; m. Alicia Mary Boldt, June 6, 1981; children: Colin, Madeleine. BA, St. Louis U., 1970, MBA, 1978, JD, 1978. Bar: Mo. Assoc., law clk. Wayne L. Millsap, P.C., St. Louis, 1977-80; staff atty. Interco. Inc., St. Louis, 1980-83; textile divsn. counsel Chromalloy Am. Corp., St. Louis, 1984-87; v.p., sec. P.N. Hirsch & Co., St. Louis, 1983-84; sr. counsel, asst. sec. Jefferson Smurfit Corp., St. Louis, 1987-92, v.p., gen. counsel, sec., 1993-98; v.p., gen. counsel, sec. Morriss Holdings L.L.C., St. Louis, 1999—. Mem. adv. bd. St. Louis Area Food Bank, 1980—. U.S. Army Security Agy., 1970-73. Mem. Racquet Club St. Louis, Old Warson Country Club. Republican. Roman Catholic. Avocations: sailing, squash. General corporate, Mergers and acquisitions, Securities. Home: 10 Twin Springs Ln Saint Louis MO 63124-1139 Office: Morriss Holdings LLC 500 Washington Ave Ste 1100 Saint Louis MO 63101-1261

**TIETIG, EDWARD CHESTER,** lawyer; b. Hollywood, Calif., Dec. 5, 1928; s. Chester and Tunis Dickerson Tietig; children: Mark, Brian, Erik, Kris. BBA, U. Cin., 1951, postgrad., 1951; JD, U. Mich., 1956. Bar: Fla., Mich., U.S. Supreme Ct., U.S. Dist. Ct. (no. and so. dists.) Fla., U.S. Ct. Appeals (5th and 11th cirs.). Pvt. practice Palm Bay, Fla., 1956—; pres., broker Farm & Grove Realty, Valkaria, Fla., 1963—; pres. Tropstock Nursery, Miami, Fla., 1978-91, Eureka Field Nursery, Miami, 1979-91, Emerald Lake Devel. and Constrn. Co., Kissimmee, Fla., 1971—; vis. lectr. U. Miami Law Sch., Coral Gables, Fla., 1972-74. Lt. s.g. USNR, 1951-63. Mem. ACLU (bd. dirs., past pres. 1991), Brevard County Bar Assn., Ad Astra Soc., Eau Gallie Yacht. Constitutional, Civil rights, Environmental. Office: 1326 Malabar Rd SE Ste 1 Palm Bay FL 32907-2502

**TIETIG, LISA KUHLMAN,** lawyer; b. St. Petersburg, Fla., Jan. 27, 1969; d. Philip John and Patricia Kay (Garriott) Kuhlman; m. Mark Edward Tietig, May 17, 1997. BS, Fla. State U., 1990, JD, 1992. Bar: Fla. 1993, U.S. Dist. Ct. (mid., no. and so. dists.) Fla. 1997. Assoc. Gardner, Shelfer, Duggar & Bist, Tallahassee, 1993, Fla. Dept. Labor and Employment Security, Tallahassee, 1994; legal writing instr. Fla. State U. Coll. Law, Tallahassee, 1994-97; ptnr. Tietig & Tietig, Merritt Island, Fla., 1997—; cons. Paula L. Walborsky, Atty. at Law, Tallahassee, 1994-96. V.p. Brevard County ACLU, Cocoa, Fla., 1997-99. Mem. Fla. Bar, Brevard County Bar Assn., Ctrl. Fla. Assn. Women Lawyers. Democrat. Civil rights, Constitutional, Labor.

**TIFFORD, ARTHUR W.,** lawyer; b. Bklyn., July 7, 1943; s. Herman and Dorothy (Kessler) T.; m. Barbara J. Sinreich, Aug. 15, 1965; children: Melissa Beth, Alexandra Lynn. BA, CUNY, 1965; JD, Bklyn. Law Sch., 1967. Bar: N.Y. 1967, Fla. 1967, U.S. Dist. Ct. (so. dist.) Fla. 1968, U.S. Ct. Mil. Appeals 1968, U.S. Ct. Appeals (5th cir.) 1971, U.S. Dist. Ct. (mid. dist.) Fla. 1979, U.S. Ct. Appeals (10th cir.) 1979, U.S. Ct. Appeals (1st cir.) 1982, U.S. Ct. Appeals (9th cir.) 1982, U.S. Ct. Appeals (11th cir.) 1981, U.S. Ct. Appeals (fed. cir.) 1985, U.S. Claims Ct. 1985, U.S. Tax Ct. 1988. Researcher, mgr. clk. Cravath, Swaine & Moore, N.Y.C., 1967; asst. U.S. atty. U.S. Dept. Justice (so. dist. Fla.), Miami, 1971-72; sole practice Miami, 1972—. Served with USMC, 1968-71, USMCR, 1971-92, ret. col. Mem. ABA, Am. Trial Lawyers Asns., Fla. Trial Lawyers Assn., Nat. Assn. Criminal Def. Lawyers, N.Y. Bar Assn., Fla. Bar Assn., Marine Corps Res. Officers Assn. (pres. Greater Miami chpt. 1978-79, 81-82, 84-85, nat. bd. dirs. 1987-89). Democrat. Avocations: writing, photography, parachuting, scuba diving, running. Home: 9980 SW 128th St Miami FL 33176-5632 Office: 1385 NW 15th St Miami FL 33125-1621

**TIGANI, BRUCE WILLIAM,** lawyer; b. Wilmington, Del., May 10, 1956; s. J. Vincent Jr. and Josephine C. (DeAngelis) T.; m. Janice Rowe, Sept. 25, 1982; children: Jessica Lynne, Bruce William Jr. Student, Georgetown U., 1974-75; BBS, U. Del., 1978; JD, Villanova U., 1981. Bar: Del. 1981, Pa. 1982, U.S. Dist. Ct. Del. 1982, U.S. Dist. Ct. (ea. dist.) Pa. 1982, U.S. Tax Ct. 1982. Assoc. Lord & Mulligan, Media, Pa., 1981-84; resident atty. Lord & Mulligan, Wilmington, 1984-87, ptnr., 1987-88; mng. ptnr. Werb, Tigani, Hood & Sullivan, Wilmington, 1988—; del. to IRS, Mid. Altantic Regional liason. Mem. lay adv. bd. The Little Sisters of Poor; active Rep. Com. of State Del. Mem. ABA, Del. State Bar Assn. (chmn. tax sect. 1991-92, real estate sect., chair trusts and estates sect., lectr. bus. and tax seminars), Wilmington Tax Group (chmn. 1994-95), Del. State C. of C. (commerce tax com.), Estate Planning Coun. Del., Inc. (bd. dirs. 1993-95), Concord Country Club, Univ. and Whist Club Wilmington, Blue and Gold Club. Avocations: golf, softball. Taxation, general, Estate planning, Real property. Office: Werb Tigani Hood & Sullivan PO Box 25046 300 Delaware Ave Wilmington DE 19899

**TIGAR, MICHAEL EDWARD,** law educator; b. Glendale, Calif., Jan. 18, 1941; s. Charles Henry and Margaret Elizabeth (Lang) T.; m. Pamet Ayer Jones, Sept. 21, 1961 (div. Mar. 1973); children: Jon Steven, Katherine Ayer; m. Amanda G. Birrell, Feb. 16, 1980 (div. Aug. 1996); 1 child, Elizabeth Torrey; m. Jane E. Blanksteen, Aug. 22, 1996. BA in Polit. Sci., U. Calif., Berkeley, 1962, JD, 1966. Bar: D.C. 1967, U.S. Ct. Appeals (2d, 4th, 5th, 6th, 7th, 8th, 9th, 10th and D.C. cirs.), U.S. Tax Ct., U.S. Supreme Ct. 1972, N.Y. 1993. Assoc. Williams & Connolly, Washington, 1966-69; editor-in-chief Selective Svc. Law Reporter, Washington, 1967-69; acting prof. law UCLA, 1969-71; pvt. practice law Grasse, France, 1972-74; assoc. William & Connolly, Washington, 1974, ptnr., 1975-77; ptnr. Tigar & Buffone, Washington, 1977-84; prof. law U. Tex., Austin, 1984-87, Joseph D. Jamail Centennial prof. law, 1987-98; of counsel Haddon, Morgan & Foreman, Denver, 1996-98; prof. law, and Edwin A. Mooers, Sr., Scholar Am. U. Washington Coll. Law, Washington, 1998—; reporter 5th Cir. Pattern Jury Instrns., Austin, 1988-90. Author: Practice Manual Selective Service Law Reporter, 1968, Law and the Rise of Capitalism, 1977, (with Jane E. Tigar) Federal Appeals: Jurisdiction and Practice, 3d edit., 1999, Examining Witnesses, 1993, Persuasion: The Litigator's Art, 1999; contbr. articles to profl. jours. Mem. ABA (vice chair 1987-88, chair elect 1988-89, chair 1989-90 sect. litigation). Avocations: sailing, cooking. Office: Washington Coll Law 4801 Massachusetts Ave NW Washington DC 20016-8196

**TIGUE, JOHN J., JR.,** lawyer; b. Pittston, Pa., Mar. 2, 1939; s. John J. Tigue and Rita Gunning; m. Grace W. Harvey, Dec. 7, 1991; children: John, James, Peter, Michael. BS, St. Peter's Coll., 1961; LLB, NYU, 1967. Bar: U.S. Dist. Ct. (so. and ea. dists.) N.Y. 1967, U.S. Supreme Ct. 1977. Acct. Peat Marwick Mitchell, N.Y.C., 1963-64; assoc. Simpson Thacher, N.Y.C., 1967-70; asst. U.S. atty. U.S. Atty.'s Office (so. dist.) N.Y., N.Y.C., 1970-73; ptnr. Kostelanetz, Ritholz, Tigue & Fink, N.Y.C., 1973-94; prin. Morvillo, Abramowitz, Grand, Iason & Silberberg, N.Y.C., 1994—. Author: (bimonthly column) Tax Litigation, 1993—; co-author: (book) Dirty Money, 1977. 1st lt. U.S. Army, 1961-63. Fellow Am. Coll. Trial Lawyers; mem. ABA, N.Y. State Bar Assn., N.Y. Coun. Def. Lawyers. Criminal, Taxation, general, General civil litigation. Office: Morvillo Abramowitz Grand Iason & Silberberg PC 9th Fl 565 5th Ave Fl 9 New York NY 10017-2426

**TIKOSH, MARK AXENTE,** lawyer; b. Arad, Banat, Romania, Aug. 17, 1955; came to U.S., 1981; s. Axente and Elena Ticosh; m. Mary Victoria Rotarescu, Sept. 10, 1979. BBA in Acctg. summa cum laude, Calif. State U., Fullerton, 1989; JD, U. of the Pacific, 1992, LLM, 1993. Bar: Calif. 1993. Acct., auditor II Orange County Probation Dept., 1984-88; pvt. practice Sacramento, Calif., 1993-94, Long Beach, Calif., 1994—; cons. U. Banat Acad. Found., Timisoara, Romania, 1997—. Editor The Transnational Lawyer, 1991. Scholarship McGeorge Legal Edn. Endowment Found., 1989-90, Dana Found., 1992-93. Mem. Calif. State Bar Assn. (estate planning trust and probate law sect.), L.A. County Bar Assn. (litigation sect.), Beta Gamma Sigma. Republican. Avocations: travel, history. Appellate, General civil litigation, Private international. Office: 800 E Ocean Blvd #100 Long Beach CA 90802

**TILEWICK, ROBERT,** lawyer; b. N.Y.C., Jan. 16, 1956; s. David and Helen (Fogel) T.; children: Naomi Seana, Benjamin Solomon. BA, Columbia U., 1977; JD, Temple U., 1985. Bar: N.Y. 1986, Ct. 1993, U.S. Dist. Ct. (so. and ea. dists.) N.Y. 1988, U.S. Ct. Appeals (2d cir.) 1989, U.S. Dist. Ct. Conn. 1991. Systems analyst, cons. Personnelmetrics, Inc., N.Y.C., 1977-80, 81-82; assoc. Cravath, Swaine & Moore, N.Y.C., 1985-87, Paul, Weiss, Rifkind, Wharton & Garrison, N.Y.C., 1987-91, 96-97, Wiggin & Dana, New Haven, Conn., 1991-96, Kalow, Springut & Bressler, N.Y.C., 1997—. Co-designer race timing system for N.Y.C. Marathon, 1977-82. NIH grantee Marine Biol. Lab., Woods Hole, Mass, 1980. Mem. ABA, N.Y.C. Bar Assn., Conn. Bar Assn., New Haven Bar Assn., Supreme Ct. Hist. Soc. Avocation: music. Federal civil litigation, General civil litigation. Office: 488 Madison Ave New York NY 10022

**TILLER, LAUREL LEE,** lawyer; b. Morton, Wash., Jan. 11, 1938; s. Edgar L. and Edna (Ball) T.; m. Priscilla Sue Prouty, Dec. 22, 1962; children: Peter B., Rachael M. BA, Willamette U., 1960; JD, U. Wash., 1963. Bar: Wash. 1963, U.S. Dist. Ct. (we. dist.) Wash. 1965, U.S. Dist. Ct. (ea. dist.) 1986, U.S. Ct. Appeals (9th cir.) 1982. Asst. atty. gen. State of Wash., Olympia, 1963-65; pvt. practice Tiller, Wheeler & Tiller, Centralia, Wash., 1965—. Mcpl. ct. judge City of Centralia, 1968-78. Mem. Wash. Bar Assn. (numerous coms. 1965—). Real property, Probate, General civil litigation. Home: PO Box 58 Centralia WA 98531-0058 Office: Tiller Wheeler & Tiller Corner Of N Rock E Pine Centralia WA 98531

**TILLER, STEVEN EDWARD,** lawyer; b. Indpls., Feb. 5, 1966; s. Ronald Eugene and Tema Lynne Tiller. BS in Chemistry, James Madison U., 1988; JD, U. Ky., 1992. Bar: Md. 1992, D.C. 1993, U.S. Dist. Ct. Md. 1994, U.S. Ct. Appeals (4th cir.) 1995, U.S. Patent Trademark Office 1995. Lab. technician ARC, Rockville, Md., 1988-89; atty. Whiteford Taylor & Preston, Balt., 1992—. Vol. Homeless Person Rep. Project, Balt., 1993—; pres., bd. dirs. JMU Alumni Assn., Balt., 1993—. Mem. Md. Bar Assn. (intellectual property subcom. 1996—), D.C. Bar Assn. (IP com. 1996—). Avocations: golf, basketball, running, music. Intellectual property, General civil litigation, Patent. Office: Whiteford Taylor & Preston LLP 7 Saint Paul St Baltimore MD 21202-1626

**TILLEY, NORWOOD CARLTON, JR.,** federal judge; b. Rock Hill, S.C., 1943; s. Norwood Carlton and Rebecca (Westbrook) T. BA, Wake Forest U., 1966, JD, 1969. Bar: N.C. 1969, U.S. Dist. Ct. (middle dist.) N.C. 1971. Law clk. to Hon. Eugene A Gordon, U.S. Dist. Judge Middle Dist. N.C., 1969-71; asst. U.S. atty. Mid. Dist. N.C., Greensboro, 1971-73, U.S. atty., 1974-77; U.S. dist. judge Mid. Dist. N.C., Durham, 1988—; ptnr. Osteen, Adams, Tilley & Walker, Greensboro, 1977-88; instr. Wake Forest U. Sch. Law, 1980. Office: US Dist Ct PO Box 3443 Greensboro NC 27402-3443

**TILLEY, RICE M(ATTHEWS), JR.,** lawyer; b. Ft. Worth, June 21, 1936; s. Rice Matthews Sr. and Lucille Geyer (Kelly) T.; children: Marisa Lynn, Angela Ainsworth, Lisa Scott, Rice Matthews III; m. Sandra Cooper, May 13, 1994. BA, Washington & Lee U., 1958; JD, So. Meth. U., 1961; LLM in Taxation, NYU, 1962. Bar: Tex. 1961. Mem. Law, Snakard & Gambill, Ft. Worth, 1964—. Bd. dirs. Van Cliburn Found., Ft. Worth Ballet Assn., Ft. Worth Symphony Orch. Assn.; bd. trustees Tex. Wesleyan Univ.; pres. Ft. Worth Opera Assn. Mem. State Bar Tex. (chmn. real estate, probate and trust law sect.), Ft. Worth C. of C. (chmn. bd.), Century II Club (pres.), Leadership Ft. Worth (chmn. bd. dirs.), Exch. Club of Ft. Worth (pres.). Republican. Estate planning, Probate, Taxation, general. Office: Law Snakard & Gambill 500 Throckmorton St Ste 3200 Fort Worth TX 76102-3859

**TILLMAN, CHAD DUSTIN,** lawyer; b. Charlotte, N.C., Feb. 28, 1970. BS in Physics, Yale U., 1991; JD, U. N.C., 1994. Bar: N.C. 1994, U.S. Dist. Ct. (we. dist.) N.C. 1994, U.S. Patent and Trademark Office 1994. Assoc. Shefte Pinckney & Sawyer, Charlotte, 1994-97, Kennedy Covington Lobdell & Hickman, Charlotte, 1997—. Avocations: writing, reading, jet skiing. Intellectual property, Patent, Trademark and copyright. Office: Kennedy Covington Lobdell & Hickman 100 N Tryon St Ste 4200 Charlotte NC 28202-4006

**TILLMAN, KAREN SUE,** lawyer; b. Garland, Tex., June 21, 1962; d. Franklin Willard and Mary Ruth Wright; m. Massie Tillman, July 2, 1993. BA, Baylor U., 1984, JD, 1986. Bar: U.S. Dist. Ct. (no. dist.) Tex. Law clk. U.S. Bankruptcy Ct., Ft. Worth, 1987-89; assoc. Hill, Heard, Gilstrap, Goetz and Moorehead, Arlington, Tex., 1989-90; litigation atty. Tandy Corp., Ft. Worth, 1990—. Dir. Ballet Concerto, Ft. Worth, 1997. Mem. Ft. Worth Club. Republican. Baptist. Avocation: piano. General civil litigation, Bankruptcy. Office: Tandy Corp 100 Throckmorton St Ste 1700 Fort Worth TX 76102-2847

**TILLMAN, MASSIE MONROE,** federal judge; b. Corpus Christi, Tex., Aug. 15, 1937; s. Clarence and Artie Lee (Stewart) T.; m. Karen Wright, July 2, 1993; children: Jeffrey Monroe, Holly. BBA, Baylor U., 1959, LLB, 1961. Bar: Tex. 1961, U.S. Dist. Ct. (no. dist.) Tex. 1961, U.S. Ct. Appeals (5th cir.) 1969, U.S. Supreme Ct. 1969; bd. cert. Personal Injury Trial Law, Tex. Ptnr. Herrick & Tillman, Ft. Worth, 1961-66; pvt. practice, Ft. Worth, 1966-70, 79-87; ptnr. Brown, Herman et al, Ft. Worth, 1970-78, Street, Swift et al, Ft. Worth, 1978-79; U.S. bankruptcy judge Ft. Worth divsn. No. Dist. Tex., 1987—. Author: Tillman's Trial Guide, 1970; Comments Editor/Case Notes Editor; mem. editl. bd. Baylor Law Rev., 1960-61. Bd. dirs. Ft. Worth Opera; mem. Ft. Worth Symphony League. Fellow Am. Bd. Trial Advocates, Tex. Bar Found.; mem. Ft. Worth/Tarrant County Bar (bd. dirs. 1969-70, v.p. 1970-71), Trial Attys.'s of Am., Nat. Conf. of Bankruptcy Judges, Am. Bankruptcy Inst. Republican. Baptist. Avocations: competition shotgun shooting, quail hunting. Office: US Bankruptcy Ct US Courthouse 501 W 10th St Fort Worth TX 76102-3637

**TILLMAN, MICHAEL GERARD,** lawyer; b. Ft. Wayne, Ind., Oct. 26, 1951; s. Robert Burl and Theresa Ellen (Till) T.; m. Joan Catharine McTigue, Dec. 19, 1981; children: Leah McTigue, Claire Tillman. BA, Harvard U., 1974; JD, U. Fla., 1984. Bar: Fla. 1985. Shareholder Scruggs & Carmichael, P.A., Gainesville, Fla., 1985-94, Coffey, Tillman, Kalishman & Owens, P.A., Gainesville, 1994-97, Wealth Strategies Collaborative, Gainesville, 1997-98, Tillman Rogers Tansey, Gainesville, 1998-99, Woodman Tillman LLC, Gainesville, 1999—; mem. legal com. Arica Inst., N.Y.C., 1992-96; fellow, faculty mem. Inst., Global Ctr. for Wealth Strategies Planning. Pres. Gainesville Estate Planning Coun., Gainesville Cmty. Found. Mem. Fla. Bar (real property and probate sect. 1990—, mem. estate and trust tax com.), Nat. Network of Estate Planning Attys. Buddhist. Avocations: teaching T'ai Chi Chuan, swimming, triathlons. Estate planning. Home: 630 NE 9th Ave Gainesville FL 32601-4440 Office: Woodman Tillman 5346 SW 91st Ter Gainesville FL 32608-7124

**TIMBAN, DEMETRIO SUNGA,** lawyer; b. Hamilton, Ohio, June 29, 1966; s. Demetrio R. and Teresita (Sunga) T. AB, U. Mich., 1988; JD, Boston U., 1992. Bar: Ma. 1993, N.Y. 1993. Staff atty. Bedford Stuyvesant Cmty. Legal Svcs. Corp., Bklyn., 1993—; exec. com. del. Legal Svcs. Staff Assoc. UAW, N.Y.C. Mem. N.Y. State Bar Assn. (resident landlord & tenant com.), Mass. Bar Assn., N.Y. County Lawyers Assn. Roman Catholic. State civil litigation, Landlord-tenant, Real property. Home: 2 Woodlake Ct Medford NJ 08055-8871

**TIMBERG, SIGMUND,** lawyer; b. Antwerp, Belgium, Mar. 5, 1911; came to U.S., 1916, naturalized, 1921; s. Arnold and Rose (Mahler) T.; m. Eleanor Ernst, Sept. 22, 1940; children—Thomas Arnold, Bernard Mahler, Rosamund and Richard Ernst (twins). A.B., Columbia U., 1930, A.M., 1930, LL.B., 1933. Bar: N.Y. 1935, U.S. Supreme Ct. 1940, D.C. 1954. Sr. atty., solicitors' office Dept. Agr., 1933-35, chief, soil conservation sect., 1935-38; staff mem. Temporary Nat. Econ. Com., 1938-39; sr. atty. SEC, 1938-42; chief, property relations and indsl. orgn. div., reoccupation br. Bd. Econ. Warfare and Fgn. Econ. Adminstrn., 1942-44; spl. asst. to atty. gen., antitrust div. Dept. Justice, 1944-45, chief judgments and judgment enforcement sect., 1946-52; sec. UN Com. on Restrictive Bus. Practices, 1952-53; cons. UN, 1953-55, 62-64; pvt. law practice, 1954-88; prof. law Georgetown U. Law School, 1952-54; faculty Parker Sch. Comparative Law, Columbia U., 1967-80; spl. counsel Senate Mil. Affairs Subcom. on Surplus Property Legislation, 1944; mem. Mission for Econ. Affairs, Am. Embassy, London, 1945; del. Anglo-Am. Telecommunications Conf., Bermuda, 1945, Geneva Copyright Conf., 1952; cons. Senate Patents Subcom., 1961, UN Patents Study, 1962-64, OAS, 1970; mem. adv. com. on fed. policy on indsl. innovation, patent and info. policy sub com., 1978-79, adv. com. on internat. investment, tech. and devel., 1979-85. Contbr. articles on antitrust, intellectual property and internat. law to legal periodicals. Mem. ABA, D.C. Bar Assn., Internat. Bar Assn., Internat. Law Assn., Am. Soc. Internat. Law, Washington Fgn. Law Soc., Am. Law Inst., Assn. Bar City N.Y., Copyright Soc. Am., Cosmos Club (Washington), Philosophy Club (Washington). Antitrust, Trademark and copyright, Private international. Home: 3519 Porter St NW Washington DC 20016-3177

**TIMBERLAKE, MARSHALL,** lawyer; b. Birmingham, Ala., July 25, 1939; s. Landon and Mary (Perry) T.; m. Rebecca Ann Griffin, Aug. 22, 1987; children: Sumner Timberlake Starling, Jane Ellison. BA, Washington and Lee U., 1961; JD, U. Ala., 1970. Bar: Ala. 1970, Ala. Supreme Ct. 1970, U.S. Dist. Ct. (no., so. and mid. dists.) Ala. 1970, U.S. Supreme Ct. 1976, U.S. Ct. Appeals (11th and 5th cirs.) 1981, U.S. Ct. Appeals (D.C. cir.) 1991. Assoc. Balch & Bingham Law Firm, Birmingham, 1970-76, ptnr., 1976—; pres. Legal Aid Soc., Birmingham, 1980-81; chmn. Ala. Supreme Ct. Commn. on Dispute Resolution, 1994-96, commr., 1996—; trustee Ala. Dispute Resolution Found., 1995—, vice chmn., 1997—. Pres. Ala. Alcohol and Drug Abuse Coun., 1994-95, dir., 1989—; v.p. Assn. Atty. Mediators, 1994—; co-chair Gov.'s Task Force on State Agy. Alternative Dispute Resolution, 1998—; bd. dirs. Partnership Assistance to the Homeless, 1998—. Capt. U.S. Army, 1962-66, Vietnam. Recipient Ann. award Dispute Resolution Inst., 1998. Fellow Ala. Law Found.; mem. ABA, Ala. State Bar (chmn. corp. banking and bus. law sect. 1981-82, chmn. bar task force on alternative dispute resolution 1992-94, Spl. Merit award 1995, co-chmn. state bar com. on ADR 1996-97, mem. spl. task force on jud. selection 1996—), Birmingham Bar Assn. (chmn. ethics com. 1975-76, chmn. unauthorized practice of law com. 1976-77, chmn. spl. projects com. 1994-95, co-chmn. com. on jud. and legal reform 1996-97, chmn. com. on jud. and legal reform 1997-98), Ala. Acad. Atty. Mediators, Redstone Club (bd. govs. 1977 -78), Rotary (Birmingham chpt., chmn. civic club found. 1984), Beaux Arts Krewe, Mountain Brook Club. Republican. Presbyterian. Avocations: tennis, thoroughbred racing, photography. General civil litigation, Public utilities, Environmental. Office: Balch & Bingham 1901 6th Ave N

Birmingham AL 35203-2618 Home: 3349 Brookwood Rd Birmingham AL 35223-2020

**TIMLIN, ROBERT J.,** judge; b. 1932. BA cum laude, Georgetown U., 1954, JD, 1959, LLM, 1964. Atty. Douglas, Obear and Campbell, 1960-61, Law Offices of A.L. Wheeler, 1961; with criminal divsn. U.S. Dept. Justice, 1961-64; atty. U.S. Atty. Office (ctrl. dist.) Calif., 1964-66, Hennigan, Ryneal and Butterwick, 1966-67; city atty. City of Corona, Calif., 1967-70; prin. Law Office of Robert J. Timlin, 1970-71, 75-76; ptnr. Hunt, Palladino and Timlin, 1971-74, Timlin and Coffin, 1974-75; judge Mcpl. Ct., Riverside, Calif., 1976-80, Calif. Superior Ct., Riverside, 1980-90; assoc. justice Calif. Ct. Appeals, 1990-94; judge U.S. Dist. Ct. (ctrl. dist.) Calif., L.A., 1994—; part-time U.S. Magistrate judge Ctrl. Dist. Calif., 1970-74. Served U.S. Army, 1955-57. Mem. ABA, Calif. Judges Assn., Phi Alpha Delta. Office: US Dist Ct PO Box 13000 4100 Main St Riverside CA 92501-3626

**TIMM, WALTER WILLIAM,** lawyer; b. St. Louis, Sept. 11, 1956; s. Walter F. and Lois B. Timm; m. Jackie Ann Timm, Nov. 30, 1979; children: Robert, Elizabeth. BSBA, U. Mo., St. Louis, 1978; MBA, Western Ill. U., 1983; JD, No. Ill. U ., 1990. Bar: Mo. 1990, Ill. 1991. Assoc. atty. Thompson & Mitchell (not Thompson Coburn), St. Louis, 1990-94; corp. counsel Angelica Corp., Chesterfield, Mo., 1994-96, asst. gen. counsel, 1997-99; now with Purina Mills Inc., Brentwood, Mo., 1999—. Chmn. bd. edn. Salem Luth. Sch., 1995-99; nat. bd. dirs. Nat. Family Partnership, Miami, Fla. Fax: 314-768-4582. E-mail: waltertimm@purina-mills.com. General corporate, Contracts commercial, Real property. Office: Purina Mills Inc 1401 S Hanley Rd Brentwood MO 63144-2987

**TIMMER, BARBARA,** lawyer; b. Holland, Mich., Dec. 13, 1946; d. John Norman and Barbara Dee (Folensbee) T. BA, Hope Coll., Holland, Mich., 1969; JD, U. Mich., 1975. Bar: Mich. 1975, U.S. Supreme Ct., 1995. Assoc. McCrosky, Libner, VanLeuven, Muskegon, Mich., 1975-78; apptd. to Mich. Women Commn. by Gov., 1976-79; staff counsel subcom. commerce, consumer & monetary affairs Ho. Govt. Ops. Com., U.S. Ho. of Reps., 1979-82, 85-86; exec. v.p. NOW, 1982-84; legis. asst. to Rep. Geraldine Ferraro, 1984; atty. Office Gen. Counsel Fed. Home Loan Bank Bd., 1986-89; gen. counsel Com. on Banking, Fin. and Urban affairs U.S. Ho. of Reps., Washington, 1989-92; asst. gen. counsel, dir. govt. affairs ITT Corp., Washington, 1992-96; ptnr. Alliance Capitol, Washington, 1994—; sr. v.p., dir. govt. rels. Home Savs. of Am., Irwindale, Calif., 1996-99; ptnr. Brand Lowell & Ryan, Washington, 1999—. Editor: Compliance With Lobbying Laws and Gift Rule Guide, 1996. Recipient Affordable Housing award Nat. Assn. Real Estate Brokers, 1990, Acad. of Women Achievers, YWCA, 1993. Mem. ABA (bus. law sect., electronic fin. svcs. subcom.), FBA (chair, exec. coun. banking law com., Exchequer Club, bd. dirs. Women in Housing and Fin., 1992-94, gen. counsel 1994—), Supreme Ct. Bar Assn., Supreme Ct. Hist. Soc., Mich. Bar Assn., Bar of Dist. Columbia. Episcopalian. Banking, Administrative and regulatory, General corporate. Office: Brand Lowell & Ryan 923 15th St NW Ste 500 Washington DC 20005-2387

**TIMMER, STEPHEN BLAINE,** lawyer; b. Holland, Mich., May 19, 1962; s. Blaine Edward and Nancy Jean (Mulder) T. BA in Econs., Eckerd Coll., 1984; JD, U. Fla., 1988; LLB (hon.), Kagawa U., Takamatsu, Japan, 1985. Atty. Burditt & Radzius, Chartered, Chgo., 1988—, Fagel & Haber; bd. dirs. The Renaissance Soc. Editor-in-chief Fla. Internat. Law Jour., 1988. Recipient fellowship St. Petersburg, Fla./Takamatsu, Japan Sister City Com., 1986. Mem. ABA, Internat. Young Lawyers Assn., Lawyers for Creative Arts, Chgo. Bar Assn., AIDS Legal Coun. Chgo. (bd. dirs. 1990—), Contemporary Mus. Art, Art Inst. Chgo., Centre du Droit de l'Art (Switzerland). Democrat. Presbyterian. Avocations: sailing, scuba diving, tennis, art collecting. Private international, General corporate, Art. Office: Fagel & Haber 140 S Dearborn St Ste 1400 Chicago IL 60603-5293

**TIMMINS, EDWARD PATRICK,** lawyer; b. Denver, June 8, 1955; s. M. Edward and Elizabeth Jean (Imhoff) T.; m. Mary Joanne Deziel, Dec. 27, 1985; children: Edward Patrick Jr., Joan Deziel. BA with honors, Harvard U., 1977; JD magna cum laude, U. Mich., 1980. Bar: Colo. 1981, U.S. Ct. Appeals (D.C. and 9th cirs.) 1982, U.S. Dist. Ct. Colo. 1984, U.S. Ct. Appeals (10th cir.) 1984. Law clk. to cir. justice U.S. Ct. Appeals (7th cir.), Chgo., 1980-81; trial atty. U.S. Dept. Justice, Washington, 1981-84; asst. U.S. atty. Denver, 1984-88; dir. Otten, Johnson, Robinson, Neff & Ragonetti P.C., Denver, 1985-96; pres. Timmins & Assocs., LLC, Denver, 1996—. Sr. editor U. Mich. Law Rev., 1979-80. Bd. dirs., vice chair Colo. Easter Seals; bd. dirs., chair Denver Pub. Schs. Found.; bd. dirs., chmn. career exploring com. Boy Scouts Am. Harvard Nat. scholar, 1976. Mem. ABA, Colo. Bar Assn. (exec. coun. jud. sect.), Denver Bar Assn., Order of Coif, Friends of Harvard Rowing. Avocations: skiing, tennis, squash. Labor, Antitrust, General civil litigation. Office: Timmins & Assocs LLC 1625 Broadway Ste 300 Denver CO 80202-4725

**TINAGLIA, MICHAEL LEE,** lawyer; b. Chgo., Dec. 21, 1952; s. Michael Leo and Josephine (Esposito) T.; m. Lucia Yolando Guzzo, Oct. 14, 1978; children: Laura, Lisa, Elena. BA, Northwestern U., 1974; JD, DePaul U., 1977. Bar: Ill. 1977, U.S. Dist. Ct. (no. dist.) Ill. 1978, U.S. Dist. Ct. (ea. dist.) Wis. 1986. Assoc. Arnold & Kadjan, Chgo., 1977-79; ptnr. Leader & Tinaglia, Chgo., 1979-86; assoc. Laser, Schostok, Kolman & Frank, Chgo., 1987-92; prin. Law Office of Michael Lee Tinaglia Ltd., Chgo., 1992-93; equity ptnr. DiMonte & Lizak, Park Ridge, Ill., 1994—; v.p., corp. counsel Tiara Med. Sys., Inc., Oak Forest, Ill. Contbr. articles to profl. jours. Alderman City Coun., Park Ridge, 1997—, mem. pub. safety com., 1997—, mem. procedures and regulations com. Mem. Ill. Bar Assn.,. Roman Catholic. Avocations: skiing, guitar. General civil litigation, Labor, Pension, profit-sharing, and employee benefits. Office: DiMonte & Lizak 1300 Higgins Rd Ste 200 Park Ridge IL 60068-5739

**TINDALL, ROBERT EMMETT,** lawyer, educator; b. N.Y.C., Jan. 2, 1934; s. Robert E. and Alice (McGonigle) T.; BS in Marine Engring., SUNY, 1955; postgrad. Georgetown U. Law Sch., 1960-61; LLB, U. Ariz., 1963; LLM, N.Y.U., 1967; PhD, City U., London, 1975; children: Robert Emmett IV, Elizabeth. Mgmt. trainee Gen. Electric Co., Schenectady, N.Y., Lynn, Mass., Glen Falls, N.Y., 1955-56, 58-60; law clk. firm Haight, Gardner, Poor and Havens, N.Y.C., 1961; admitted to Ariz. bar, 1963; prin., mem. firm Robert Emmett Tindall & Assocs., Tucson, 1963—; assoc. prof. mgmt. U. Ariz., Tucson, 1969—; vis. prof. Grad. Sch. of Law, Soochow U., Republic of China, 1972, Grad. Bus. Centre, London, 1974, NYU, 1991—; dir. MBA program U. Ariz., Tucson, 1975-81; investment cons. Kingdom of Saudi Arabia, 1981—; dir. entrepreneurship program, U. Ariz., Tucson, 1984-86; lectr. USIA in Eng., India, Middle East, 1974; lectr. bus. orgn. and regulatory laws Southwestern Legal Found., Acad. Am. and Internat. Law, 1976-80. Actor community theatres of Schenectady, 1955-56, Harrisburg, Pa., 1957-58, Tucson, 1961-71; appeared in films Rage, 1971, Showdown at OK Corral, 1971, Lost Horizon, 1972; appeared in TV programs Gunsmoke, 1972, Petrocelli, 1974. Served to lt. USN, 1956-58. Ford Found. fellow, 1965-67; Asia Found. grantee, 1972-73. Mem. Strategic Mgmt. Soc., State Bar of Ariz., Acad. Internat. Bus., Screen Actors Guild, Honourable Soc. of Middle Temple (London), Phi Delta Phi, Beta Gamma Sigma, Assoc. for Corp. Growth. Clubs: Royal Overseas League (London). Author: Multinational Enterprises, 1975; contbr. articles on domestic and internat. bus. to profl. jours. General corporate, General practice, Private international. Home: 1927 E Hawthorne St Tucson AZ 85719-4935 Office: Coll Bus and Public Adminstrn U Ariz Dept Mgmt And Policy Tucson AZ 85721-0001

**TINDER, JOHN DANIEL,** federal judge; b. Indpls., Feb. 17, 1950; s. John Glendon and Eileen M. (Foley) T.; m. Jan M. Carroll, Mar. 17, 1984. B.S., Ind. U., 1972, J.D., 1975. Bar: Ind. 1975, U.S. Dist. Ct. (so. dist.) Ind., U.S. Ct. Appeals (7th cir.), U.S. Supreme Ct. Asst. U.S. atty. Dept. of Justice, Indpls., 1975-77; pub. defender Marion County Criminal Ct., Indpls., 1977-78; chief trial dep. Marion County Pros. Office, Indpls., 1979-82; litigation counsel Harrisone Moberly, Indpls., 1982-84; U.S. atty. U.S. Dist. Ct. (so. dist.) Ind., Indpls., 1984-87; judge U.S. Dist. Ct. (so. dist.) Ind., 1987—; adj. prof. Ind. U. Sch. of Law, Indpls., 1980—; mem. Supreme Ct. Character & Fitness Com., Ind., 1982—. Co-founder Turkey Trot Invitational Race, Indpls., 1980. Recipient Cert. of Appreciation award Bur. Alcohol, Tobacco & Firearms, Indpls., 1976; Service award Marion County Prosecutor, Indpls., 1981. Mem. ABA, Ind. State Bar Assn. (dir. criminal justice sect. 1984—), Indpls. Bar Assn., 7th Circuit Ct. Bar Assn., Fed. Bar Assn. Republican. Roman Catholic. Office: US Dist Ct 304 US Courthouse 46 E Ohio St Indianapolis IN 46204-1903

**TINKER, BILL THOMAS,** lawyer; b. Torrance, Calif., Nov. 7, 1945; s. Edward E. and June A. Tinker; m. Kristi Tinker, Sept. 19, 1984; children: Mark, Michelle. BSBA, U. N.Mex., 1993; JD, U. Iowa, 1995. Bar: N.Mex. 1996. Asst. dist. atty. Dist. Atty.'s Office, Albuquerque, 1996-97; pvt. practice Albuquerque, 1997—. With U.S. Army, 1963-65. Mem. ABA, N.Mex. Bar Assn., Albuquerque Bar Assn. Democrat. Office: 1412 Lomas Blvd NW Albuquerque NM 87104-1236

**TINKER, GREGG LYNN,** lawyer; b. Seattle, Aug. 14, 1945; s. Lyle Maurice and Elberta Myrle T.; m. Cherry Lynn Leonard, Aug. 27, 1966; children: Todd Douglas, Zachary Gregg. BA in Fin., U. Wash., 1968, JD, 1974. Atty. Sullivan, Morrow & Longfelder, Seattle, 1974-79; shareholder Longfelder Tinker Kidman, Inc., Seattle, 1979—. Contbg. author: Washington Appelate Practice Handbook, 1980. Sgt. U.S. Army, 1968-71. Mem. Wash. State Bar Assn., Wash. State Trial Lawyers Assn., Wash. State Head Injury Found., King County Bar Assn. Democrat. Avocations: golf, reading, theater, symphony, travel. Personal injury, Professional liability, Product liability. Office: Longfelder Tinker Kidman Inc 101 Stewart St Ste 1010 Seattle WA 98101-1048

**TINKHAM, JAMES JEFFREY,** lawyer; b. Norfolk, Va., Oct. 25, 1961; s. James Alton Jr. and Jeanette (Munden) T. BS, U. Richmond, 1984; JD, U. Va., 1987. Bar: Va. 1987. With Faggert & Frieden, P.C., Chesapeake, Va., 1987—, ptnr., 1995—. Mng. editor Va. Tax Rev., 1986. Bd. dirs. 1st United Meth. Ch., Norfolk, 1990. Mem. ABA, Va. State Bar, Norfolk-Portsmouth Bar Assn., Phi Beta Kappa, Beta Gamma Sigma, Phi Eta Sigma, Alpha Mu Alpha, Omicron Delta Epsilon. Republican. Avocations: hunting, fishing, reading, travel. Contracts commercial, General corporate, Mergers and acquisitions. Home: 6044 Eastwood Ter Norfolk VA 23508-1111 Office: Faggert & Frieden PC 1435 Crossways Blvd Ste 200 Chesapeake VA 23320-2896

**TINNION, ANTOINE,** lawyer; b. Alston, U.K., Apr. 5, 1970; s. Robert James Coquelle and Maureen Asher Krzyzosiak. BA with honors, Oxford U., 1991; BA in Law with honors, Cambridge U., 1993; LLM, Harvard U., 1997. Bar: England and Wales, 1996, N.Y. 1998. Jr. solicitor Slaughter and May, London, 1994-96; litigation assoc. Debevoise & Plimpton, N.Y.C., 1997—. Mem. Law Soc. of England and Wales, Assn. of City Bar of N.Y. (com. on trademarks and unfair competition), Old Novocastrians Assn. Avocations: current affairs, European cinema, computers/internet. General civil litigation, Trademark and copyright, Alternative dispute resolution. Home: 182 E 95th St Apt 26E New York NY 10128-2584 Office: Debevoise & Plimpton 875 3rd Ave Fl 23 New York NY 10022-6256

**TINSLEY, NANCY GRACE,** lawyer; b. Indpls., Jan. 8, 1961; d. Frank and Virginia T.; m. Robert Kirk Stanley. BS, Purdue U., 1982; JD, Ind. U., 1990. Bar: Ind. 1990, U.S. Dist. Ct. (so. dist.) Ind. 1990, U.S. Patent and Trademark Office 1993, U.S. Ct. Appeals (7th cir.) 1997. Organic chemist Eli Lilly and Co., Indpls., 1982-89; assoc. Baker & Daniels, Indpls., 1990-98, ptnr., 1999—; Inventor and patentee (with others) inflammation inhibitor, anti-inflammatory agts. Mem. ABA, Ind. Bar Assn. (vol. atty project peace, com. on civil rights of children), Seventh Cir. Ct. Bar Assn., Indpls. Bar Assn. General civil litigation, Intellectual property, Product liability. Office: Baker & Daniels 300 N Meridian St Ste 2700 Indianapolis IN 46204-1750

**TIPPING, HARRY A.,** lawyer; b. Bainbridge, Md., Nov. 2, 1944; s. William Richard and Ann Marie (Kelly) T.; m. Kathleen Ann Palmer, July 12, 1969; 1 child, Christopher A. B.A., Gannon U., 1966; J.D., U. Akron, 1970. Bar: Ohio. Asst. law dir. City of Akron, Ohio, 1971-72, chief asst. law dir., 1972-74; ptnr. Gillen, Miller & Tipping, Akron, 1974-77, Roderick, Myers & Linton, Akron, 1977-87; prin., COO Harry A. Tipping Co. L.P.A., Akron, 1987—. Mem. Fairlawn Charter Rev. Commn., 1990—; chmn. bd. Assessment Equalization for the City of Fairlawn, 1989, 90, 97; chmn. Bd. of Tax Appeals, City of Fairlawn, Ohio, 1979-81, mem. merger com., 1980-82. With USCGR, 1966-72. Mem. ABA, Am. Bd. Trial Advocates (advocate), Akron Bar Assn., Ohio Bar Assn., Def. Rsch. Inst., Am. Arbitration Assn., Fedn. Ins. & Corp. Counsel. Republican. Roman Catholic. Clubs: Fairlawn Country (Ohio), Catawaba Island (Ohio), Firestone County (Akron, Ohio). State civil litigation, Labor, Federal civil litigation. Office: 1 Cascade Plz Ste 2200 Akron OH 44308-1135

**TIPPINS, TIMOTHY MICHAEL,** lawyer, educator; b. Troy, N.Y., Aug. 5, 1949; s. John William and Rita Dorothy (Maloney) T. BS magna cum laude, SUNY, Albany, 1971; JD, Union U., 1974. Bar: N.Y. 1975, U.S. Dist. Ct. (no. dist.) N.Y. 1975, U.S. Supreme Ct. 1982. Assoc. Arthur F. McGinn, P.C., Albany, 1975-79; pvt. practice law Troy, 1979—; asst. dist. atty. County of Rensselaer, Troy, 1978-80; dep. town atty. Town of North Greenbush, N.Y., 1976; adj. instr. Hudson Valley Community Coll., Troy, 1974-82, SUNY-Albany, 1980; adj. prof. law Union U., 1986—; speaker in field. Author: When You Face Divorce, 1982, 3d edit., 1986, New York Matrimonial Law and Practice, 2 vols., 1986; contbr. numerous articles to legal jours. Fellow Am. Acad. Matrimonial Lawyers (pres. N.Y. chpt. 1993-95, admissions com. N.Y. chpt. 1987—), Internat. Acad. Matrimonial Lawyers; mem. N.Y. State Bar Assn. (chair 1996-98, exec. com. family law sect. 1987—, sec. 1993—, co-chmn. publs. com. 1987—, spl. equitable distbn. com. 1988—, task force on family law 1994—), Albany County Bar Assn., Rensselaer County Bar Assn., Capital Dist. Trial Lawyers Assn. Republican. Avocations: reading, writing, chess. Family and matrimonial. Office: 102 3rd St Troy NY 12180-4037

**TIPTON, DREW B.,** lawyer; b. Angleton, Tex., Aug. 15, 1967; s. C.E. and Judy B. Tipton; m. Shannon M. Allen. BA in History, Tex. A&M U., 1990; JD, South Tex. Coll. of Law, 1994. Law clk. U.S. Dist. Judge John D. Rainey, Houston, 1994-95; assoc. Littler Mendelson, Houston, 1995-97, Houston, Marek & Griffin, Victoria, Tex., 1997—; speaker continuing legal edn. labor and employment law, 1995. Labor, Federal civil litigation, Civil rights. Office: Houston Marek & Griffin 120 Main Pl Ste #600 Victoria TX 77901

**TIPTON, SHEILA KAY,** lawyer; b. Martins Ferry, Ohio, Aug. 4, 1951; d. Donald Duane and Elizabeth Julia T.; m. Orrin Frink, Nov. 2, 1973 (div.); m. William Llewellyn Dawe III, Dec. 6, 1985; children: Nicholas Albert, Alexander McNeill; stepchildren: William Llewellyn IV, Christopher Michael. BS, Ohio State U., 1973; JD, Drake U., 1980. Bar: Iowa 1980, U.S. Dist. Ct. (no. and so. dists.) Iowa 1980, U.S. Ct. Appeals (8th cir.) 1980. Assoc. Bradshaw, Fowler, Proctor & Fairgrave, P.C., Des Moines, Iowa, 1980-85; ptnr., shareholder Bradshaw, Fowler, Proctor & Fairgrave, Des Moines, Iowa, 1985-99; ptnr. Dorsey & Whitey LLP, 1999—; presenter in field. Contbr. articles to profl. jours. pres. Polk County Legal Aid Soc., 1991-92; bd. dirs. Youth Home Mid-Am., 1990-97, sec., 1994-96, v.p., 1996-97; bd. dirs. des Moines Metro Opera Found., 1993-98, pres., 1997-98; bd. dirs. Des Moines Metro Opera, 1991—, v.p. devel., 1994-95, pres.-elect, 1995-96, pres., 1996-97, v.p. long range planning com., 1998—; bd. counselors Drake U. Law Sch., 1996-98. Recipient State of Iowa Govs. Vol. award, 1996. Mem. Iowa State Bar Assn. (adminstrv. law sect. coun. 1989-91, mem. bus. law sect. coun. 1993-97, co-chmn. quality life task force 1993-96, chair internat. trade com. 1992-94), Rotary (chmn. scholar com. 1994-95, bd. dirs. 1996—, sgt.-at-arms, 1997-98, sec.-treas. 1998-99, v.p. 1999—). Avocations: opera, cooking, reading, golf, travel. General corporate, Administrative and regulatory, Public utilities. Home: 13074 Lincoln Ave Des Moines IA 50325-7413 Office: Dorsey & Whitey LLP 801 Grand Ave Ste 3900 Des Moines IA 50309-8039

**TIRELLA, DAVID THEODORE,** lawyer; b. Miami, Fla., Apr. 12, 1962; s. Alfred Lewis and Julia (Papparo) T.; m. Patricia Ellen Smith, Jan. 2, 1987; children: Peter N., Carolyn S. BS in Polit Sci., Fla. State U., 1986; JD, Cumberland Sch. Law, 1989. Bar: Fla. 1989, U.S. Dist. Ct. (mid. dist.) Fla. 1990, U.S. Ct. Appeals (11th cir.) 1994. Asst. state atty. Hillsborough County State Atty.'s Office, Tampa, Fla., 1989-92; ptnr. Tirella & Tirella, Tampa, 1993-96; assoc. Eaton & Gordon, Tampa, 1996—; apptd. spl. prosecutor Hillsborough County State's Atty.'s Office, Tampa, 1991-92; spl. pub. defender Hillsborough County Pub. Defender's Office, Tampa, 1993-95; instr. Am. Inst. Paralegals, Tampa, 1995. Mem. pub. spkrs. bur. Am. Cancer Soc., Tampa, 1996—. Mem. ATLA, Fla. Bar Assn. (grievance com. Tampa 1999—), Fla. Acad. Trial Lawyers, Ferguson White Inns of Ct., Million Dollar Advocates Forum, Phi Alpha Delta. Avocations: public speaking, travel, cars. Personal injury, Criminal. Office: Cohen Jayson Skafidas Gordon & Taylor 505 E Jackson St Tampa FL 33602-4989

**TIRELLI, LINDA MARIE,** lawyer, consultant; b. Wilkes Barre, Pa., Apr. 12, 1968; d. Leonard John and Marie Jean Staisy; m. Peter Andrew Tirelli, July 7, 1990; children; Anya Nocole, Anthony Faust. BA, SUNY, Albany, 1990; JD, Quinnipiac Sch. of Law, Hamden, Conn., 1995. Bar: Conn. 1996, U.S. Dist. Ct. Conn., 1996. Assoc. Law Offices of Todd Lampert, New Canaan, Conn., 1994—; mgmt. cons., dir. Women Safe, Tiger Schulmann's Karate, Danbury, Conn., 1990—. Sec. Middle Gate Elem. Sch. Newtown, Conn., 1998—. Mem. ATLA, Conn. Trial Lawyers Assn., Conn. Bar Assn., Stamford Regional Bar Assn., New Canaan Bar Assn. Republican. Roman Catholic. Avocations: karate, boxing, scuba diving, designing, travel. Bankruptcy, Personal injury, Family and matrimonial. Home: 7 Tall Oaks Ln New City NY 10956-1506 Office: Law Office Todd Lampert 46 Main St New Canaan CT 06840-4523

**TISDALE, DOUGLAS MICHAEL,** lawyer; b. Detroit, May 3, 1949; s. Charles Walker and Violet Lucille (Battani) T.; m. Patricia Claire Brennan, Dec. 29, 1972; children: Douglas Michael Jr., Sara Elizabeth, Margaret Patricia, Victoria Claire. BA in Psychology with honors, U. Mich., 1971, JD, 1975. Bar: Colo. 1975, U.S. Dist. Ct. Colo. 1975, U.S. Ct. Appeals (10th cir.) 1976, U.S. Supreme Ct. 1979. Law clk. to chief judge U.S. Dist. Ct. Colo., Denver, 1975-76; assoc. Brownstein Hyatt Farber & Strickland, P.C., 1976-92; shareholder Popham, Haik, Schnobrich & Kaufman, Ltd., 1992-97, dir., 1995-97; ptnr. Baker & Hostetler LLP, Denver, 1997—. Federal civil litigation, Bankruptcy, Real property. Home: 4662 S Elizabeth Ct Cherry Hl Vlg CO 80110-7106 Office: Baker & Hostetler LLP 11th Fl 303 E 17th Ave Fl 11 Denver CO 80203-1235

**TISDALE, NORWOOD BOYD,** lawyer; b. N.Y.C., Aug. 1, 1945; s. Wright and Mariam Norwood (Boyd) T.; m. Laurine Gardner, Aug. 5, 1972; children: Mariam Spotswood, Mary Barden, William Norwood Boyd. BA, Duke U., 1968, M Tchg., 1970, JD, 1975. Bar: N.C. 1975. Assoc. Robert E. Lock, Jacksonville, N.C., 1975-78; ptnr. Ellis, Hooper, Warlick, Waters and Morgan, Jacksonville, 1978-88; pvt. practice Jacksonville, 1988—. Pres. Greater Jacksonville-Onslow, 1985; bd. dirs. Greater Jacksonville-Onslow C. of C., Jacksonville, 1983-85; counsel Carobell Children's Home, Jacksonville, 1979—. Mem. Rotary. Avocations: soccer, golf, sailing. Office: Norwood Boyd Tisdale 400 New Bridge St Jacksonville NC 28540-4741

**TISINGER, DAVID H.,** lawyer; b. Carrollton, Ga., May 8, 1937; s. Robert D. and Naomi E. Tisinger; m. sharon Inman, Feb. 3, 1975; children: John David, Joel Wesley. BS, Ga. Inst. Tech., 1958; LLB, U. Ga., 1963. Bar: Ga. 1962. Ptnr. Tisinger Vance & Greer, Carrollton, 1963—; instr. law U. Ga., Athens, 1964; chmn. bd. Carrollton State Bank, 1974-78. Mem. bd. regents U. Sys. of Ga., Atlanta, 1972-79. Lt. USNR, 1958-60. Fellow Am. Coll. Trial Lawyers; mem. ATLA, Def. Rsch. Inst. Avocations: farming, sailing. Personal injury, Product liability. Office: Tisinger Tisinger Vance & Greer 100 Wagon Yard Plz Carrollton GA 30117-3248

**TITLE, PETER STEPHEN,** lawyer; b. New Orleans, Nov. 24, 1950; s. Harold Benjamin and Beulah (Sterbcow) T.; m. Sheryl Gerber, June 14, 1981. B.A., Columbia U., 1972; J.D., Tulane U., 1975. Bar: La. 1975, U.S. Dist. Ct. (ea., we., mid. dists.) La., U.S. Ct. Appeals (5th cir.). Assoc. Sessions, Fishman, Rosenson, Boisfontaine, Nathan & Winn, New Orleans, 1975-81, ptnr., 1982—; instr. on property Tulane U., 1978; asst. examiner com. on Admissions to Bar, 1980-88, examiner, 1988—; lectr. on real estate. Author: Louisiana Real Estate Transactions, 1991. Mem. ABA, La. Bar Assn. (chmn. sect. on trust estates, probate and immovable property law 1983-84), New Orleans Bar Assn. (chmn. title examinations com., 1992-93), Rep. Am. Judicature Soc., Order of Coif, Phi Delta Phi. Jewish. Lodge: B'Nai Brith. Bankruptcy, General corporate, Real property. Home: 515 Hillary St New Orleans LA 70118-3833 Office: Sessions & Fishman 201 Saint Charles Ave Fl 35 New Orleans LA 70170-1000

**TITLEY, LARRY J.,** lawyer; b. Tecumseh, Mich., Dec. 9, 1943; s. Leroy H. and Julia B. (Ruesink) T.; m. Julia Margaret Neukom, May 23, 1970; children: Sarah Catherine, John Neukom. BA, U. Mich., 1965, JD, 1972. Bar: Va. 1973, Mich. 1973. Assoc. Hunton & Williams, Richmond, Va., 1972-73, Varnum, Riddering, Schmidt & Howlett, Grand Rapids, Mich., 1973—. Trustee Friends Pub. Mus., 1985-94; bd. dirs. Pub. Mus. Found., 1988-97, pres., 1992-95; bd. dirs. Camp Optimist YMCA, 1993-98, Peninsular Club, 1994—, v.p., 1996, pres. 1997. Mem. ABA, Mich. Bar Assn., Grand Rapids Bar Assn. General corporate, Pension, profit-sharing, and employee benefits. Home: 520 Roundtree Dr NE Ada MI 49301-9707 Office: Varnum Riddering Schmidt & Howlett Bridgewater Pl PO Box 352 Grand Rapids MI 49501-0352

**TITLEY, ROBERT L.,** lawyer; b. Tecumseh, Mich., Dec. 15, 1947. AB, U. Mich., 1970; JD, Duke U., 1973. Bar: Wis. 1973, Mich. 1974. Ptnr. Quarles & Brady, Milw. Mem. editorial bd. Duke Law Jour., 1972-73. Mem. ABA, State Bar Mich., State Bar Wis., Order of Coif. Trademark and copyright, Intellectual property, Federal civil litigation. Office: Quarles & Brady 411 E Wisconsin Ave Ste 2550 Milwaukee WI 53202-4497

**TITONE, VITO JOSEPH,** state supreme court justice; b. Bklyn., July 5, 1929; s. Vito and Elena (Ruisi) T.; m. Margaret Anne Viola, Dec. 30, 1956; children: Stephen, Matthew, Elena Titone Hill, Elizabeth. BA, NYU, 1951; JD, St. John's U., 1956, LL.D., 1984. Bar: N.Y. 1957, U.S. Dist. Ct. (ea. and so. dists.) N.Y., 1962, U.S. Supreme Ct. 1964, U.S. Ct. Appeals N.Y. 1985. Ptnr. Maltese & Titone, N.Y.C., 1957-65, Maltese, Titone & Anastasi, N.Y.C., 1965-68; assoc. counsel to pres. pro tem N.Y. State Senate, 1965; justice N.Y. State Supreme Ct, N.Y.C., 1969-75; assoc. justice appellate div. 2d dept., 1975-85; judge N.Y. State Ct. Appeals, Albany, 1985—; of counsel Mintz & Gold LLP, N.Y.C., 1998—; adj. prof. Coll. S.I., CUNY, 1969-72, St. John's U., Jamaica, N.Y., 1969-85. Bd. editors N.Y. Law Jour., 1999; contbr. articles to law jour. Bd. govs. Daytop Village Inc., N.Y.C.; bd. dirs. Boy Scouts Am.; bd. trustees The Am. Parkinson Disease Assn. With U.S. Army, 1951-53, to col. N.Y. State Guard. Named Citizen of Yr. Daytop Village, N.Y.C., 1969, Disting. Citizen Wagner Coll., S.I., 1983, Outstanding Contbr. Camelot Substance Abuse Network, 1983; recipient citation of merit S.I. Salvation Army Adv. Bd., 1983, Rapollo award Columbian Lawyers Assn., 1983, Disting. Judiciary award Cath. Lawyers Guild Diocese of Bklyn., 1991, Disting. Svc. award N.Y. State Lawyers Assn., Justice William Brennan award N.Y. Assn. Criminal Def. Lawyers, 1993, Life Achievement award N.Y. Conf. Italian Am. State Legislators, 1994, Ellis Island Medal of Honor, 1997, gold medal Bklyn. Bar Assn., 1997. Mem. ABA, N.Y. State Bar Assn., Richmond County Bar Assn., Supreme Ct. Justice Assn., VFW, Am. Legion (past comdr.), Charles C. Pinckney Tribute Def. Assn. of N.Y., Justinian Soc., K.C. Roman Catholic. Office: Mintz and Gold LLP 444 Park Ave S New York NY 10016-7321

**TITTSWORTH, CLAYTON (MAGNESS),** lawyer; b. Tampa, Fla., Nov. 8, 1920. Student U. Tampa, 1939-42; LLB, Stetson Law Sch., 1951. Bar: Fla. 1951; cert. cir. mediator; ptnr. Tittsworth & Tittsworth, Tampa, 1951-65, Brandon, Fla., 1964-73; pvt. practice, Brandon, 1973-83; Tittsworth and Curry P.A., Brandon, 1983-87; pvt. practice, Brandon, 1987—. Mem. ABA, Fla. Bar Assn. State civil litigation, Probate, Real property. Office: 1021 Hollyberry Ct Brandon FL 33511-7657

**TITUS, BRUCE EARL,** lawyer; b. N.Y.C., June 5, 1942. BA, Coll. William and Mary, 1964, JD, 1971. Bar: Va. 1971, D.C. 1972, Md. 1984. Asst. dir. torts br., civil divsn. U.S. Dept. Justice, 1971-82; mem. Jones, Waldo, Holbrook and McDonough, Washington; ptnr. Venable, Baetje and Howard, LLP, McLean, Va., 1986-976; prin. Rees, Broome & Diaz P.C., Vienna, Va., 1997—. Exec. editor William & Mary Law Review, 1970-71. Mem. ABA, Va. State Bar, D.C. Bar, Fairfax Bar Assn. (pres.-elect 1998—), Md. State Bar, Phi Delta Phi, Omicron Delta Kappa. General civil litigation, Alternative dispute resolution, Construction. Office: Rees Broome & Diaz PC 9th Fl 8133 Leesburg Pike Vienna VA 22182-2706

**TITUS, JON ALAN,** lawyer; b. Milw., Oct. 6, 1955; s. Mary (Irwin) Stephenson; m. Laura Jean Newman, Sept. 5, 1982; children: Katherine, Derek. BA, U. Ariz., 1977; JD, Ariz. State U., 1980. Bar: Ariz. 1980, U.S. Dist. Ct. Ariz. 1980; cert. real estate specialist. Pres. Titus, Brueckner & Berry, P.C., Scottsdale, Ariz., 1980—. Mem. Ariz. Kidney Found., 1984—, pres., 1991-92. Recipient Alumni Achievement award Ariz. State U., 1996. Mem. Ariz. Bar Assn. (chmn. securities regulation sect. 1986-87), Maricopa County Bar Assn., Scottsdale Bar Assn. (dir. 1993-95). Antitrust, Real property, Securities. Office: Titus Brueckner & Berry PC 7373 N Scottsdale Rd Ste 252B Scottsdale AZ 85253-3513

**TITUS, VICTOR ALLEN,** lawyer; b. Nevada, Mo., Sept. 2, 1956; s. Charles Allen and Viola Mae (Cliffman) T.; m. Laraine Carol Cook, Oct. 13, 1974 (div. Feb. 1982); 1 child, Matthew; m. Deborah Diane Carpenter, Apr. 10, 1984; 1 child, Jacquelynn. BS, Ctrl. Mo. State U., 1978, BA, 1978; JD, U. Mo., 1981. Bar: N.Mex. 1981, U.S. Dist. Ct. N.Mex. 1981, Mo. 1982, U.S. Ct. Appeals (10th cir. 1983), U.S. Supreme Ct. 1986, Colo. 1989, Ariz. 1995. Lawyer Jay L. Faurot, P.C., Farmington, N.Mex., 1981-83; ptnr. Faurot & Titus, P.C., Farmington, N.Mex., 1983-85; lawyer, sole proprietor Victor A. Titus, P.C., Farmington, N.Mex., 1985—; arbitrator in civil disputes Alternative Dispute Resolution-Arbitration; liquor lic. hearing officer City of Farmington, 1989-94. Contbr. articles to profl. jours. Adult Behind Youth, Boys & Girls Club, Farmington, 1987—; mem. hosp. adv. bd. San Juan Regional Med. Ctr., Farmington, 1988-93. Recipient San Juan County Disting. Svc. award N.Mex. Bar Assn., 1984; named one of Best Lawyers in Am., 1995-96, 97—. Mem. Assn. Trial Lawyers of Am., N.Mex. Trial Lawyers (bd. dirs. 1983—, pres. 1993-94), State Bar of N.Mex. (disciplinary bd. 1997—, specialization com. 1992-98, legal advt. com. 1990), San Juan County Bar Assn. (pres. 1984), Nat. Assn. Criminal Def. Lawyers (life), Colo. Trial Lawyers. Democrat. Avocation: sports. Workers' compensation, Personal injury, Criminal. Home: 5760 Pinehurst Farmington NM 87402-5078 Office: Victor A Titus PC 2021 E 20th St Farmington NM 87401-2516

**TIVENAN, CHARLES PATRICK,** lawyer; b. Newark, Feb. 20, 1954; s. Gerard Charles and Mary Jo (Vogel) T.; m. Mary Katherine Herlihy, Aug. 2, 1980; children: Moire Kathleen, Sean Patrick, Liam Francis, Michala Maureen. BA in Govt., Seton Hall U., 1975, JD, 1980. Bar: N.J. 1982, U.S. Dist. Ct. N.J. 1982, U.S. Supreme Ct. 1995. Law clk. Essex County Prosecutor's Office, Newark, summer 1978, Dwyer Connell & Lisbona, Attys., Montclair, N.J., 1978-79; legal rsch. asst. Inst. Continuing Legal Edn., Newark, 1979; jud. law clk. to Hon. John J. Dios Superior Ct., Newark, 1981-82; assoc. Timothy J. Provost, Atty., Freehold, N.J., 1982-85, Arthur Stein & Assocs., Forked River, N.J., 1985-92; sole practice Bricktown, N.J., 1992—; mediator, Early Settlement panelist Superior Ct. N.J/Ocean County, Toms River, N.J., 1987—. Mem. juvenile conf. com. South Orange (N.J.) JCC, 1974-81; condemnation commr. Ocean County, Toms River, 1986—; conflict atty. Brick Twp., Bricktown, 1994—; candidate Brick Twp. Coun., 1992; active Bricktown Dem. Club, trustee 1995-98, v.p. 1999; commr. Brick Twp. Housing Authority, Brick, 1997—; atty. advisor Brick Twp. Trial Moot Ct., 1998—. Recipient Cert. of Appreciation, Ocean County Superior Ct., 1987—, certs. of appreciation various orgns., 1985—. Mem. ABA, N.J. Bar Assn. (gen. practice, family law 1985—), Am. Trial Lawyers Assn. (N.J. affiliate, lectr. 1985—), Ocean County Bar Assn. (family law com. 1985—), KC (3d degree), Epiphany Coun. Roman Catholic. Avocations: reading, current events/politics, running, computers. Real property, General practice, Personal injury. Office: Godfrey Lake Profl Bldg 426 Herbertsville Rd Brick NJ 08724-1310

**TJOFLAT, GERALD BARD,** federal judge; b. Pitts., Dec. 6, 1929; s. Gerald Benjamin and Sarita (Romero-Hermoso) T.; m. Sarah Marie Pfohl, July 27, 1957 (dec.); children: Gerald Bard, Marie Elizabeth; m. Marcia Penman Parker, Feb. 21, 1998. Student, U. Va., 1947-50, U. Cin., 1950-52; LL.B., Duke U., 1957; D.C.L. (hon.), Jacksonville U., 1978; LLD (hon.), William Mitchell Coll. Law, 1993. Bar: Fla. 1957. Individual practice law Jacksonville, Fla., 1957-68; judge 4th Jud. Cir. Ct. Fla., 1968-70, U.S. Dist. Ct. for Middle Dist. Fla., Jacksonville, 1970-75, U.S. Ct. Appeals, 5th Cir., Jacksonville, 1975-81; judge U.S. Ct. Appeals, 11th Cir., Jacksonville, 1996—, chief judge, 1989-96; mem. Adv. Corrections Coun. U.S., 1975-87, Jud. Conf. of U.S., 1989—, Fed. Jud. Ctr. Com. on Sentencing, Probation and Pretrial Svcs., 1988-90; mem. com. adminstrn. probation system Jud. Conf. of U.S., 1972-87, chmn., 1978-87; U.S. del. 6th and 7th UN Congress for Prevention of Crime and Treatment of Offenders. Hon. life mem., bd. visitors Duke U. Law Sch.; pres. North Fla. coun. Boy Scouts Am., 1976-85, chmn., 1985-90; trustee Jacksonville Marine Inst., 1976-90, Episc. H.S., Jacksonville, 1975-90; mem. vestry St. Johns Cathedral, Jacksonville, 1969-71, 73-75, 77-79, 81-83, 85-87, 93, 95-96, sr. warden, 1975, 83, 87, 91, 92. Served with AUS, 1953-55. Recipient Merit award Duke U., 1990, Fordham-Stein prize, 1996. Mem. ABA, Fla. Bar Assn., Am. Law Inst., Am. Judicature Soc. Episcopalian. Office: US Ct Appeals US Courthouse PO Box 960 311 W Monroe St Rm 539 Jacksonville FL 32201

**TOAL, JEAN HOEFER,** state supreme court justice; b. Columbia, S.C., Aug. 11, 1943; d. Herbert W. and Lilla (Farrell) Hoefer; m. William Thomas Toal; children: Jean Hoefer, Lilla Patrick. BA in Philosophy, Agnes Scott Coll., 1965; JD, U. S.C., 1968; LHD (hon.), Coll. Charleston, 1991; LLD (hon.), Columbia Coll., 1992. Bar: S.C. Assoc. Haynsworth, Perry, Bryant, Marion & Johnstone, 1968-70; ptnr. Belser, Baker, Barwick, Ravenel, Toal & Bender, Columbia, 1970-88; assoc. justice S.C. Supreme Ct., 1988—; mem. S.C. Human Affairs Commn., 1972-74; mem. S.C. Ho. of Reps., 1975-88, chmn. house rules com., constitutional laws subcom. house judiciary com.; mem. parish coun. and lector St. Joseph's Cath. Ch.; chair S.C. Juvenile Justice Task Force, 1992-94; chair S.C. Rhodes Scholar Selection Com., 1994. Mng. editor S.C. Law Rev., 1967-68. Bd. visitors Clemson U., 1978; trustee Columbia Mus. Art; bd. trustees Agnes Scott Coll., 1996—. Named Legislator of Yr. Greenville News, Woman of Yr., U. S.C.; recipient Disting. Svc. award S.C. Mcpl. Assn., Univ. Notre Dame award, 1991, Algernon Sydney Sullivan award U. S.C., 1991. Mem. John Belton O'Neill Inn of Ct., Phi Beta Kappa, Mortar Bd., Order of the Coif. Office: Supreme Ct SC PO Box 11330 Columbia SC 29211-1330*

**TOBE, SUSAN BRING,** lawyer; b. N.Y.C., 1949; m. Richard M. Tobe. B.A., State U. Coll., Buffalo, 1971; J.D., SUNY-Buffalo, 1974. Bar: N.Y. 1975, U.S. Dist. Ct. (we. dist.) N.Y. 1976. Asst. gen. counsel Carborundum Co., Niagara Falls, N.Y., 1974-75; asst. corp. counsel City of Buffalo, 1975-78; atty.-advisor U.S. Dept. HUD, Buffalo, 1978-81; asst. atty. gen. State of N.Y., Buffalo, 1981-95; supervising atty. Pub. Interest Law Clinic, 1982; program lectr. St. Law Inst., N.Y., 1978; guest lectr. various high schs., colls., 1975-95; dir. SUNY Sch. Law Alumni Assn., Buffalo, 1979-82. Vol. Leukemia Soc., Buffalo, 1981-92, United Way Campaign, Buffalo, 1977, 88-93, Friends Community Music. Sch., Buffalo, 1984-90; mem. local organizing com., co-chair vol. com. First Night Buffalo, 1990-91, chmn. vol. com., 1991-92; com. person Dem. Party, Buffalo, 1976-78; com. mem. Instnl. Advancement State U. Coll. at Buffalo, 1987-92; mem. strategic planning com. Buffalo State Coll. Found., 1989-92, mem. devel. com., 1991-92; bd. dirs. Leadership, Buffalo, 1991-92, Buffalo State Found. chmn. award, 1992, Just Buffalo Literary Ctr., Inc., 1992-97, Buffalo Urban League, 1993—; mem. Youth Leadership, Buffalo, co-chair Criminal Justice Day. Recipient Pre-Law Disting. Alumnus award Buffalo State Coll., Spl. Recognition by Alumni, 1991, 92, Dist. Alumni award 1993. Mem. Erie County Bar Assn., N.Y. Civil Liberties Union, ABA, Women Lawyers of Western N.Y., N.Y. State Bar Assn., State Univ. Coll. Buffalo Alumni Assn. (bd. dirs. 1984-86, v.p. 1986-88, pres. 1988-92). Office: County of Erie Dept Law 69 Delaware Ave Rm 300 Buffalo NY 14202-3801

**TOBEN, BRADLEY J. B.,** dean, law educator. BA in Polit. Sci. with honors, U. Mo., St. Louis; JD with honors, Baylor U., 1977; LLM, Harvard U., 1981. Bar: Tex., Mo. Tchr. Ind. U. Sch. Law, Indpls.; of counsel Dawson & Sodd (Dallas and Corsicana); with faculty Baylor Law Sch., dean Law Sch., 1991—, Gov. Bill and Vara Faye Daniel prof. law; participant in accreditation and membership inspection of law schs. ABA, Assn. Am. Schs. Gov. apptd. Tex. commr. Nat. Conf. of Commrs. on Uniform State Laws. Mem. Am. Bar Found., Tex. Bar Found., State Bar of Tex. (active in bankruptcy specialization cert. program). Office: Baylor U PO Box 97288 Waco TX 76798-7288*

**TOBER, STEPHEN LLOYD,** lawyer; b. Boston, May 27, 1949; s. Benjamin Arthur Tober and Lee (Hymoff) Fruman; m. Susan V. Schwartz, Dec. 22, 1973; children: Cary, Jamie. Grad., Syracuse U., 1971, JD, 1974. Bar: N.H. 1974, U.S. Dist. Ct. N.H. 1974, U.S. Supreme Ct. 1978, N.Y. 1981. Assoc. Flynn, McGuirk & Blanchard, Portsmouth, N.H., 1974-79; sole practice Portsmouth, 1979-81; ptnr. Aeschliman & Tober, Portsmouth, 1981-91; prin. Tober Law Offices, P.A., Portsmouth, 1992—; lectr. Franklin Pierce Law Ctr., Concord, N.H., 1978-80. Contbr. articles to law jours. Mem. Portsmouth Charter Commn., 1976, Portsmouth Planning Bd., 1977-81; del. N.H. Constl. Conv., Concord, 1984; city councilman, Portsmouth, 1977-81. Fellow ABA (mem. ho. dels.), Am. Bar Found., N.H. Bar Assn. (pres. 1988-89, chair com. to redraft code of profl. responsibility, Disting. Svc. award, 1986, 94); mem. ATLA (gov. 1980-86), N.H. Trial Lawyers Assn. (pres. 1977), New Eng. Bar Assn. (bd. dirs. 1988-91), N.H. Bd. Bar Examiners. Democrat. Jewish. Avocations: reading, tennis. State civil litigation, Personal injury, General practice. Home: 55 T J Gamester Ave Portsmouth NH 03801-5871 Office: Tober Law Offices PA PO Box 1377 Portsmouth NH 03802-1377

**TOBEY, RAYANNE GRIFFIN,** lawyer; b. Tulsa, Okla., Mar. 29, 1970; d. Charles M. and Mary M. Griffin; m. H. Scott Tobey, Dec. 1997. BA in Polit. Sci., So. Meth. U., 1992, BA in Religious Studies, 1992; JD, U. Tulsa, 1995. Bar: Okla. 1995; Nat. Energy Law and Policy Inst. Environ. resources, energy and environ. law cert. U. Tulsa, Native Am. law cert. U. Tulsa. Assoc. Gardere & Wynne, LLP, Tulsa, Okla., 1997—. Mem. ABA, Okla. Bar Assn. Avocations: skiing, snow mobiling, reading, tennis. Oil, gas, and mineral, Natural resources, Environmental. Office: Gardere & Wynne LLP 100 W 5th St Ste 200 Tulsa OK 74103-4227

**TOBIA, RONALD LAWRENCE,** lawyer; b. Newark, Oct. 25, 1944; s. Salvatore and Marie (Melillo) T.; m. Sandra A. Boutsikaris, June 15, 1969; children: Jill, Alisandra, Joseph. BA, Lafayette Coll., 1966; JD, U. Miami, 1969. Bar: Fla. 1969, N.J. 1970. Legal asst. region 22 NLRB, Newark, 1967, 68; jud. clk. to presiding justice N.J. Superior Ct., Passaic County, 1969-70; hearing officer N.J. Pub. Employment Rels. Com., Trenton, 1970-71; sr. ptnr. Schwartz, Tobia & Stanziale, P.A., Montclair, N.J., 1972—. Contbr. articles to profl. jours. Fin. co-chmn. N.J. Rep. Com. With JAGC, U.S. Army, 1967-68. Mem. ABA, N.J. Bar Assn., Fla. Bar Assn., Essex County Bar Assn., Indsl. Rels. Rsch. Assn. Republican. Roman Catholic. Avocation: skiing. Labor, Banking. Home: 48 Old Indian Rd West Orange NJ 07052-3226 Office: Schwartz Tobia & Stanziale PA 22 Crestmont Rd Verona NJ 07044-2902

**TOBIN, BRUCE HOWARD,** lawyer; b. Detroit, July 17, 1955; s. Marshall Edward and Rhoda Maureen (Milman) T.; m. Kathleen Tobin; children: Benjamin Stewart, Jenna Rose, Lainie Nicole. BA in Social Sci., Mich. State U., 1978; JD, Detroit Coll. Law, 1982; LLM in Taxation, NYU, 1983. Bar: Mich. 1982, Fla. 1982, Nebr. 1983, U.S. Dist. Ct. (ea. dist.) Mich. 1982, U.S. Tax Ct. 1983. Assoc. Kutak, Rock & Campbell, Omaha, 1983-85; ptnr. Lebow & Tobin P.L.L.C., Farmington Hills, Mich., 1985—. Pres. West Bloomfield Sch. Bd. Mem. ABA, Fla. Bar Assn., Mich. Bar Assn. (tax com. 1985—), Nebr. Bar Assn. Jewish. Corporate taxation, Estate taxation, Real property. Office: Lebow & Tobin PLLC 7001 Orchard Lake Rd Ste 312 West Bloomfield MI 48322-3607

**TOBIN, CRAIG DANIEL,** lawyer; b. Chgo., Aug. 17, 1954; s. Thomas Arthur and Lois (O'Connor) T. BA with honors, U. Ill., 1976; JD with high honors, Ill. Inst. Tech., 1980. Bar: Ill. 1980, U.S. Dist. Ct. (no. dist.) Ill. 1980, U.S. Dist. Ct. (no. dist.) Ind. 1986, U.S. Ct. Appeals (7th cir.) 1986, U.S. Supreme Ct. 1987. Trial atty. Cook County Pub. Defender, Chgo., 1980-82; trial atty. homicide task force Pub. Defender, Chgo., 1982-84; ptnr. Craig D. Tobin and Assocs., Chgo., 1984—; lectr. Ill. Inst. for Continuing Legal Edn., Cook County Pub. Defender, Chgo., 1983, 92, Ill. Pub. Defender Assn., 1987; instr. Nat. Inst. Trial Advocacy. Named One of Outstanding Young Men in Am., 1985. Mem. ABA, Chgo. Bar Assn., Nat. Assn. Criminal Def. Lawyers. Roman Catholic. Criminal, Personal injury. Office: Craig D Tobin & Assocs 3 First National Plz Chicago IL 60602

**TOBIN, DENNIS MICHAEL,** lawyer; b. Chgo., June 3, 1948; s. Thomas Arthur and Lois (O'Connor) T.; m. Sue Wynn Henslee, June 14, 1969 (div. 1977); m. Karen Thompson, Oct. 11, 1980; children: Kyle James, Daniel Patrick. BA with honors, U. Ill., 1971; JD, Loyola U., Chgo., 1976. Bar: Ill. 1976, U.S. Dist. Ct (no. dist.) Ill. 1976, U.S. Ct. Appeals (7th cir.) 1985, U.S. Supreme Ct. 1985, Wis. 1989. Trial atty. Cook County Homicide Task Force, Chgo., 1976-84; prin. Dennis M. Tobin & Assocs., Chgo., 1984—; gen. counsel Forest Health Systems and Found., Ill., Miss., Hawaii, 1986—, Manages Behavioral Care Inc., Psychiat. Ins. Co. Am. Dir. Forest Health Systems Found.; mem. Chgo. Coun. on Fgn. Rels. Mem. ABA (forum on health law), Nat. Assn. Criminal Def. Attys., Chgo. Bar Assn. (com. on health law), Am. Soc. Law and Medicine, Ill. Assn. Criminal Def. Attys. (v.p. 1984-87), Ill. Attys. for Criminal Justice, Wis. Bar Assn., Ill. Assn. Hosp. Attys., Nat. Health Lawyers Assn., U.S. Sporting Clays Assn., Nat. Sporting Clays Assn., Gateway Gun Club. Roman Catholic. Criminal, Health. Office: 18-3 E Dundee Rd Barrington IL 60010-5292

**TOBIN, GREGORY MICHAEL,** lawyer; b. Jacksonville, Ill., Sept. 19, 1960; s. William Edward and Patricia (Pinkerton) T.; m. Carole Ann Pratt, Nov. 15, 1980; children: Benjamin, Courtney, Emily, Zachary. BS, Ill. Coll., Jacksonville, 1982; JD, St. Louis U., 1986. Bar: Ill. 1986, Va. 1986, D.C. 1986, W.Va. 1987, Mo. 1987, U.S. Dist. Ct. W.Va. 1987, U.S. Ct. Appeals (7th, 8th and 4th cirs.) 1990. Ptnr. Pratt & Tobin, East Alton, Ill., 1986—. Democrat. Roman Catholic. General civil litigation, Personal injury. Home: 12 Sycamore Dr Bethalto IL 62010-1064 Office: Pratt & Tobin PC PO Box 179 Rte 111 at Airline Dr East Alton IL 62024

**TOBIN, JAMES MICHAEL,** lawyer; b. Santa Monica, Calif., Sept. 27, 1948; s. James Joseph and Glada Marie (Meisner) T.; m. Kathleen Marie Espy, Sept. 14, 1985. BA with honors, U. Calif., Riverside, 1970; JD, Georgetown U., 1974. Bar: Calif. 1974, Mich. 1987. From atty. to gen. atty. So. Pacific Co., San Francisco, 1975-82; v.p. regulatory affairs So. Pacific Communications Co., Washington, 1982-83; v.p., gen. counsel Lexitel Corp., Washington, 1983-85; v.p., gen. counsel, sec. ALC Communications Corp., Birmingham, Mich., 1985-87, sr. v.p., gen. counsel, sec., 1987-88; of counsel Morrison & Foerster, San Francisco, 1988-90, ptnr., 1990—. Mem. ABA, Calif. Bar Assn., Mich. Bar Assn., Fed. Communications Bar Assn. Republican. Unitarian. Avocations: carpentry, travel. Administrative and regulatory, Communications, General corporate. Home: 3134 Baker St San Francisco CA 94123-1805 Office: Morrison & Foerster 425 Market St Ste 3100 San Francisco CA 94105-2482

**TOBIN, PAUL XAVIER,** lawyer, educator; b. Seattle, July 18, 1956; s. Francis Xavier and Mary-Alice Irene (Blake) T. BA in French and History, U. Mo., 1979; JD, Suffolk U., 1982; LLM in Taxation, Boston U., 1987. Bar: Mass. 1982, U.S. Ct. Appeals (1st cir.) 1983, U.S. Dist. Ct. Mass. 1983, U.S. Supreme Ct. 1986. French interpreter Travelodge, Inc., Mission, Kans., 1975-78; assoc. Holland Crowe & Drachman, P.C., Boston, 1982-85; syndication counsel U.S. Trust Co., Boston, 1985-86; ptnr. Tobin & Elfman, Boston, 1986-89; prin. Tobin, Kinsellagh & Haines, P.A., Boston, 1989-91; dir. corp. planning Sanborn Inc., Wrentham, Mass., 1991-94; gen. counsel Sanborn Internat. BV, Wrentham/Amsterdam, 1994—; adj. prof. Boston U., 1988—. Mem. Mass. Bar Assn., Phi Alpha Theta. Avocations: golf, guitar, tennis, sailing. General corporate, Contracts commercial, Securities.

**TOCK, JOSEPH,** lawyer; b. Cleve., Aug. 22, 1954; s. Julius Joseph and Marianna Yvonne (Carracio) T. BA, Kent State U., 1979; JD, Case Western Res. U., 1983. Bar: Ohio, 1983, U.S. Ct. Mil. Appeals, 1983, Colo. 1988, Guam 1995. Commd. 1st lt. USAF, 1983, advanced through grades to maj., 1994; asst. staff judge advocate, chief civil law USAF, McConnell AFB, Kans., 1983-84; asst. staff judge advocate, chief civil law USAF, Yokota Air Base, Japan, 1984-85, area def. counsel 7th cir., 1985-87; dep. staff judge advocate, chief mil. justice USAF, Kelly AFB, Tex., 1987-88; dep. county atty. El Paso County, Colo., 1989-90; pvt. practice Colorado Springs, Colo., 1990-91; staff atty. Guam Legal Svcs. Corp., 1991-92; asst. atty. gen. White Collar unit Prosecution Divsn., Agana, Guam, 1992-95; 1st asst. to chief prosecutor White Collar unit Prosecution Divsn., Agana, Guam, 1994-96; asst. atty. gen. Solicitor's Divsn., Agana, Guam, 1996-97; lead atty. for drug unit Prosecution Divsn., Agana, Guam, 1997—; dep. staff judge advocate Peterson AFB, Colo., 1990-91, Andersen AFB, Guam, 1991—; instr. family law Pikes Peak C.C., 1990-91; lectr. Continental Security Divsn., San Antonio, 1987-88, NCO prep course, Kelly AFB, Tex., 1987-88, Profl. Mil. Edn. Ctr., Yokota Air Base, 1984-87. Mem. Internat. Legal Soc. Japan, Am. Legion. Roman Catholic. Avocations: golf, handball, sailing, scuba. Office: Atty Gen Prosecution Divsn Jud Ctr Bldg 120 W O'Brien Dr Ste 2-200E Agana GU 96910-5174

**TODARO, FRANK EDWARD,** lawyer; b. Jamestown, N.Y., Dec. 5, 1957; s. Thomas A. and Marie (Ditillio) T.; m. Melinda Peters, Oct. 17, 1987. BS, Erie Community Coll., Buffalo, 1979, Brockport (N.Y.) State U., 1981; JD, Capital U., Columbus, Ohio, 1987. Bar: Ohio, U.S. Dist. Ct. (no. and so. dists.) Ohio, U.S. Ct. Appeals (6th cir.). Assoc. Frank A. Ray Co., Columbus, Ohio, 1987-93; ptnr. Ray and Todaro Co. LPA, Columbus, 1993-96; prin. Law Offices of Frank E. Todaro, Columbus, 1996—. Mem. East Dublin Civic Assn., Dublin, Ohio, 1990, treas., 1991-92, pres., 1995—. Mem. Assn. Trial Lawyers Am. (Ohio young lawyers rep. 1991-93), Ohio Bar Assn., Ohio Acad. Trial Lawyers (computer svcs. com. 1988—, home office com. 1991-92, negligence law com. 1990-91, bd. dirs. 1991-93, chair ins. law sect. 1993-95, chair advocates cir. 1997—, exec. bd. 1997—, treas. 1998, sec. 1999), Columbus Bar Assn. (trial advocacy com. 1990-91), Franklin County Trial Lawyers (membership chmn. 1989-91, newsletter editor 1990-91, trustee 1992—, treas. 1993-94, sec. 1994-95, v.p. 1995-96, pres. 1996-97, Pres.'s award 1991). E-mail: fetlaw@AC.tech.net. General civil litigation, Personal injury, Product liability. Office: 21 E State St Ste 300 Columbus OH 43215-4210

**TODARO, LAURA JEAN,** lawyer, city magistrate; b. Neligh, Nebr., June 8, 1956; d. Andrew Robert and Mary Louise (Leenerts) T. BS, U. Ill., 1978; JD, Loyola U., New Orleans, 1981. Bar: La. 1981, U.S. Dist. Ct. (ea. and mid. dists.) La. 1981, U.S. Ct. Appeals (5th cir.) 1981, U.S. Supreme Ct. 1985. Assoc. Dutel & Dutel, New Orleans, 1981-85; ptnr. Todaro & Todaro, Kenner, La., 1985—; city atty. City of Kenner, 1985-87, prosecutor, 1987-88, exec. counsel to Mayor, 1987-90, regulatory prosecutor, 1990—, city magistrate, 1992—; mem. Mayor's Adv. Coun. on Law Enforcement and Funding; bd. dirs., treas. Kenner Conv. and Visitors Bur., Inc., 1992. Bd. dirs., sec., met. bd. rep., chmn. maj. gifts campaign Kenner YMCA, 1988; bd. dirs. Met. New Orleans Battered Womens' Program, 1987-92. Mem. ABA, Fed. Bar Assn., Jefferson Parish Bar Assn., Kenner Profl. Women's Assn., Kenner Bus. Assn. (bd. dirs.), U. Ill. Alumni Assn. (local organizer), Phi Delta Phi. Republican. Roman Catholic. Avocations: sailing, water and snow skiing. State civil litigation, Family and matrimonial. Home: 75 Mckinley St Kenner LA 70065-1010 Office: City of Kenner care Clk of Ct 1801 Williams Blvd Kenner LA 70062-6296 also: 909 W Esplanade Ave Ste 202 Kenner LA 70065-2700

**TODD, ERICA WEYER,** lawyer; b. Beacon Falls, Conn., Sept. 22, 1967; d. Richard Burton and Elizabeth Jane (Weyer) T. BA in Biology, U. Bridgeport, 1989, JD, 1992; JD, Quinnipiac Coll. Sch. Law, 1994. Bar: Conn. 1992, U.S. Dist. Ct. Conn. 1993, U.S. Supreme Ct., 1998. Sr. trial asssoc. Trotta, Trotta and Trotta, New Haven, 1993—; admissions counselor Quinnipiac Coll. Sch. of Law, Hamden, 1992-93. Recipient Alumni award for Svc. to Law Sch., Quinnipiac Coll. Sch. Law, 1994. Mem. ABA, Conn. Bar Assn. (exec. com. Young Lawyers divsn. 1993—), New Haven Bar Assn. (exec. com. Young Lawyers Assn. 1994—), Def. Rsch. Inst., Assn. Trial Lawyers of Am., Ct. Trial Lawyers Assn., Conn. Def. Lawyers. Democrat. Roman Catholic. Avocation: golf. General civil litigation, Personal injury, Insurance. Home: 551 Skokorat Rd Beacon Falls CT 06403-1457 Office: Trotta Trotta & Trotta 195 Church St #815 817 PO Box 802 New Haven CT 06503-0802

**TODD, JAMES DALE,** federal judge; b. Scotts Hill, Tenn., May 20, 1943; s. James P. and Jeanette Grace (Duck) T.; m. Jeanie M. Todd, June 26, 1965; children: James Michael, Julie Diane. BS, Lambuth Coll., 1965; M Combined Scis., U. Miss., 1968; JD, Memphis State U., 1972. Bar: Tenn. 1972, U.S. Dist. Ct. (we. dist.) Tenn. 1972, U.S. Ct. Appeals (6th cir.) 1973, U.S. Supreme Ct. 1975. Tchr. sci., chmn. sci. dept. Lyman High Sch., Longwood, Fla., 1965-68, Memphis U. Sch., 1968-72; ptnr. Waldrop, Farmer, Todd & Breen, P.A., 1972-83; cir. judge div. II 26th Jud. Dist., Jackson, Tenn., 1983-85; judge U.S. Dist. Ct. (we. dist.) Tenn., Jackson, 1985—. Named Alumnus of Yr. Lambuth Coll. Alumni Assn., 1985. Fellow Tenn. Bar Found.; mem. Fed. Judges Assn., Fed. Bar Assn., Tenn. Bar Assn., Jackson Madison County Bar Assn. (pres. 1978-79). Methodist. Office: US Dist Ct 111 S Highland Ave Jackson TN 38301-6107

**TODD, RICHARD D. R.,** lawyer; b. Borger, Tex., July 17, 1962; s. William H. and Linda (Brumfield) T.; m. Lisa Ann McCown, Jan. 4, 1986; children: Richard Benjamin, Madison Claire. Student, Tex. Tech. U., Lubbock, 1984; BS in Health Care Adminstrn., Wayland Bapt. U., Plainview, Tex., 1988; JD magna cum laude, Oklahoma City U., 1991. Bar: Tex. 1992, Okla. 1992, U.S. Dist. Ct. (no. dist.) Tex. 1992, U.S. Dist. Ct. (we. dist.) Okla. 1992, U.S. Ct. Appeals (5th cir.) 1993, U.S. Supreme Ct. 1995. Paramedic/ops. mgr. Amarillo (Tex.) Med. Svcs., 1982-89; legal intern Lampkin, McCaffrey & Tawwater, Oklahoma City, 1990-92; pvt. practice Borger, Tex., 1992-95, Wichita Falls, Tex., 1995—; barrister Am. Inn of Ct., Oklahoma City, 1990-92. Editor Oklahoma City U. Law Rev., 1989-91. Percussionist First Bapt. Ch., Wichita Falls. Mem. ABA, Borger Bar Assn., State Bar Tex. (pro bono coll. 1994-95), Phi Delta Phi (vice magister 1991). Baptist. Bankruptcy, General corporate, Environmental. Office: 705 8th St Ste 920 Wichita Falls TX 76301-6539

**TODD, STEPHAN KENT,** lawyer; b. Evansville, Ind., Dec. 22, 1945; s. Rayburn W. and Juanita E. (Schmitt) T.; children from previous marriage: Whitney, Jason; m. Debra McCloskey Barnhart; 1 child, Alexandra. BS, Ohio State U., 1967; JD, Valparaiso U., 1970; LLM, U. Va., 1976. Bar: Ind. 1970, Pa. 1977, Ill. 1986, U.S. Supreme Ct. Atty., officer U.S. Army, 1970-76; atty. U.S. Steel Corp., Pitts., 1976-81, gen. atty., 1981-85; sr. gen. atty. U.S. Steel Group, USX Corp., Chgo., 1985-89; sr. gen. atty. U.S. Steel Group, USX Corp., Pitts., 1989-95, asst. gen. counsel environ. and real estate, 1995-98, gen. counsel, 1998—. Col. USAR, 1967-76, ret. Mem. ABA, Allegheny County Bar Assn., Union League Club, Am. Corp. Counsel Assn. Environmental, Personal injury, General corporate. Office: US Steel Group 600 Grant St Rm 1500 Pittsburgh PA 15219-2702

**TODD, STEPHEN MAX,** lawyer; b. Kansas City, Mo., Oct. 22, 1941; s. Louis O. and A. Maxine (Mittag); m. Carlene Harre; children: Stephanie A., Louis P. BA, Kans. State U., 1963; JD, U. Kans., 1966. Bar: Kans. 1966, U.S. Dist. Ct. Kans. 1966, U.S. Ct. Appeals (10th cir.) 1967, U.S. Supreme Ct. 1971, Mo. 1973. Assoc. Schroeder, Heeney, Groff & Spies, Topeka, 1966-72; office counsel Chgo. Title Ins. Co., Kansas City, 1973-78, regional counsel, 1978—. Author: Missouri Foreclosures of Deeds of Trust, 1983, 3d edit. 1996; contbr., editor books. Mem. ABA, Kans. Bar Assn., Mo. Bar (chmn. property law com. 1990-92), Am. Coll. Real Estate Lawyers, Kiwanis (pres. Topeka Downtown Club 1971-72, lt. gov. Mo.-Ark. dist. 1976-77, pres. Kansas City South Platte Club 1979-80), Phi Delta Phi. Real property, Insurance. Home: 5519 N Woodhaven Ln Kansas City MO 64152-4319 Office: Chgo Title Ins Co PO Box 26370 Kansas City MO 64196-6370

**TODD, STEVEN A.,** judge; b. Portland, Oreg., Dec. 27, 1955; s. Horace E. and Lois M. Todd; m. Sherry Poole, Jan. 30, 1987; 1 child, Andrew Poole. BA in Music and Polit. Sci., Northwestern U., 1978; JD, Lewis and Clark Coll., 1981. Bar: Oreg. 1981. Law clk. U.S. Dist. Ct., Portland, 1981-82, Multnomah County Cir. Ct., Portland, 1982-83; dep. dist. atty. Columbia County, St. Helen's, Oreg., 1983-87, Multnomah County, Portland, 1987-97; cir. ct. judge pro tem Multnomah County Cir. Ct., Portland, 1997—. Office: Multnomah County Cir Ct 1021 SW 4th Ave Portland OR 97204-1123

**TODD, THOMAS,** lawyer; b. Pitts., Sept. 6, 1942; s. William Thomas Jr. and Elizabeth (Alcorn) T.; m. Jamee Wadsworth, June 25, 1965; children: Heather, Spencer. BA, Williams Coll., 1964; LLB, Harvard U., 1967. Bar: Pa., U.S. Dist. Ct. (we. dist.) Pa. Assoc. Reed, Smith, Shaw & McClay, LLP, Pitts., 1967-73, ptnr., 1974—, exec. com. mem., 1979—, head bus. & fin. dept., 1991—; dir. Littleford Group, Cin., 1988—, Black Raven Enterprises, Cheyenne, Wyo., 1996—. Pres., CEO, Pitts. Symphony Soc., 1998—; chmn. Gateway Rehab. Ctr., 1996—. Mem. ABA, Nat. Assn. Bond Attys.,

Allegheny County Bar Assn., Duquesne Club, Fox Chapel Golf Club, Pitts. Golf Club, Laurel Valley Golf Club, Phi Beta Kappa. Avocations: golf, jazz, classical music, reading. Mergers and acquisitions, General corporate, Banking. Office: Reed Smith Shaw & McClay LLP 435 6th Ave Ste 2 Pittsburgh PA 15219-1886

**TOEPFER, THOMAS LYLE,** lawyer; b. Hays, Kans., Oct. 4, 1950; s. Anthony Lyle and Mary Alice (Clark) T.; m. Karen L. Culley, May 20, 1972; 1 child, Russell Thomas. AB in Econs. summa cum laude, Ft. Hays State U., 1972; JD, Washburn U., 1975. Bar: Kans. 1975, U.S. Dist. Ct. Kans. 1975, U.S. Ct. Appeals (10th cir.) 1982, U.S. Supreme Ct. 1999. Assoc. Dreiling, Bieker & Kelley, Hays, 1975-83; prosecutor City of Hays, 1977—; spl. adminstrv. law judge Workers Compensation, 1992—; sole practice Hays, 1984—. Mem. Hays Bd. Edn., 1985-93; treas. Ellis County Dems., Hays, 1980; pres. St. Nicholas Ch. Parish Coun., Hays, 1985-86; trustee Hays Med. Ctr., Hays, 1987—, Cancer Coun. Ellis County. Mem. ABA, Kans. Bar Assn., Ellis County Bar Assn. (pres. 1984-85). Democrat. Roman Catholic. General practice, General civil litigation, Probate. Home: 303 W 39th St Hays KS 67601-1518 Office: 114 W 11th St Hays KS 67601-3606

**TOFTNESS, CECIL GILLMAN,** lawyer, consultant; b. Glasgow, Mont., Sept. 13, 1920; s. Anton Bernt and Nettie (Pedersen) T.; m. Chloe Catherine Vincent, Sept. 8, 1951. AA, San Diego Jr. Coll., 1943; student, Purdue U., Northwestern U.; BS, UCLA, 1947; JD cum laude, Southwestern U., 1953. Bar: Calif. 1954, U.S. Dist. Ct. (so. dist.) Calif. 1954, U.S. Tax Ct. 1974, U.S. Supreme Ct. 1979. Pvt. rpactice palos Verdes Estates, Calif., 1954—; chmn. bd., pres., bd. dirs. Fishermen & Mchts. Bank, San Pedro, Calif., 1963-67; v.p., bd. dirs. Palos Verdes Estates Bd. Realtors, 1964-65; participant Soc. Expdn. through the Northwest Passaage. Chmn. cpaital campaign fund Richstone Charity, Hawthorne, Calif., 1983; commencement spkr. Glasgow H.S., 1981. Served to lt. (j.g.) USN, 1938-46, ETO, PTO, commdg. officer USS Ptarmigon, 1941-45. Decorated Bronze Star; mem. Physicians for Prevention of Nuclear War which received Nobel Peace prize, 1987; named Man of Yr., Glasgow, 1984. Mem. South Bay Bar Assn., Southwestern Law Sch. Alumni Assn. (class rep. 1980—), Themis Soc.-Southwestern Law Sch., Schumacher Founders Cir.-Southwestern Law Sch. (charter), Kiwanis (sec.-treas. 1955-83, v.p., pres., bd. dirs.), Masons, KT. Democrat. Lutheran. Estate planning, Estate taxation, Probate. Home: 2229 Via Acalones Palos Verdes Peninsula CA 90274-1646 Office: 2516 Via Tejon Palos Verdes Estates CA 90274-6802

**TOGMAN, LEONARD S.,** lawyer; b. Aug. 26, 1939; s. Israel and Ruth Togman; m. Barbara A. Togman, June 12, 1960; children: Melanie Sloan, Kimberly. BS in Econs., U. Pa., 1961; LLB, NYU, 1964. Bar: N.Y. 1964, Del. 1969. Trial atty. tax divsn. Dept. Justice, 1964-68; ptnr. Potter Anderson & Corroon, Wilmington, Del., 1964—. Co-author: Delaware Tax Report. Mem. Del. Bar Assn. (past chmn. tax. com.), Wilmington Tax Group (past chmn.). Avocations: golf, squash, tennis, skiing. Taxation, general, General corporate. Home: 1504 Talley Rd Wilmington DE 19803-3912 Office: Potter Anderson & Corroon PO Box 951 Wilmington DE 19899-0951

**TOHILL, JIM BARNETTE,** lawyer; b. Vicksburg, Miss., Oct. 9, 1947; s. Otho Jack and Flora (Houston) T.; m. Margaret Stone, Aug. 2, 1968; children: Houston Werlein, Shepard McAndrew. BA, Millsaps Coll., 1969; JD with distinction, U. Miss., 1974. Bar: Miss. 1974. Assoc. Watkins Ludlam Winter & Stennis, PA, Jackson, Miss., 1974-80, ptnr., 1980-90, mng. ptnr., 1988-95. Mem. Am. Coll. Real Estate Lawyers, Am. Coll. Mortgage Attys., Miss. Bar Assn. (mem. exec. com. real property sect. 1992-95, sec.-treas. 1995-96, pres. 97-98), Hinds County Bar Assn. Presbyterian. Real property, Contracts commercial. Office: 633 N State St Jackson MS 39202-3306

**TOKARS, FREDRIC WILLIAM,** lawyer, judge, educator; b. Buffalo, Apr. 23, 1953; s. Jerome and Norma Tokars; m. Sara Tokars, July 26, 1985; children: Fredric William, Michael. BBA, U. Miami, 1975; MBA in Taxation, U. Ga., 1976; JD, Woodrow Wilson Sch. Law, 1982; LLM in Taxation, Washington Sch. Law, 1988. Bar: Ga., U.S. Dist. Ct. (no. dist.) Ga., U.S. Dist. Ct. (fed. dist.), U.S. Ct. Appeals (11th cir.), U.S. Supreme Ct. Mem. tax staff Price Waterhouse, Atlanta, 1976-78; asst. dist. atty. Fulton Dist. Atty.'s Office, Atlanta, 1982-86; atty. in pvt. practice Atlanta, 1986—; judge State of Ga., Atlanta, 1989—; tchr., lectr. Fed. Law Enforcement Tng. Ctr., Glynco, Ga., 1982—, Ga. Police Acad., 1982—, AICPA, Atlanta, 1982—, Ga. Soc. CPAs, 1982—; chmn. com. on cooperation between Ga. Soc. CPAs and State Bar, 1982-87. Author: Prosecutors Role in Computer Crime, 1986; author manuals, mag. article. Active in jud. campaigns. Mem. ABA, Ga. Bar Assn., Fed. Bar Assn., Atlanta Bar Assn., Nat. Dist Attys. Assn., Assn. Trial Lawyers Am., Ga. Trial Lawyers Assn., Delta Sigma Pi, Omicron Delta Kappa. Avocations: skiing, fishing. Computer, Criminal, Taxation, general.

**TOLAN, DAVID J.,** lawyer, insurance company official; b. Detroit, Dec. 27, 1927; s. Joseph James and Helen Barbara (Blahnik) T.; m. Roseann Biwer, Feb. 15, 1958; children: Joseph, David, Julie. AB, Haverford Coll.; JD, U. Mich.; MS, Am. Coll. Bar: Wis.; CLU. Pvt. practice atty. Milw., 1952-57; agt. Northwestern Mut. Ins. Co., Milw., 1957—; prin. Tolan, Schueller & Assoc., Ltd., Milw., 1959—; lectr. AICPAs, Am. Soc. CLUs, Wis. Bar Assn., 1975—; mem. faculty CLU Inst., 1990—. Contbr. articles to profl. jours. Pres. Young Reps. Milwaukee County, 1961; bd. dirs. United Performing Arts Fund, Milw., 1966, 91, 92, Bel Canto Chorus, Milw., 1960—; scoutmaster Boy Scouts Am., 1975-77; mem. Com. for Future of Milw., 1988. With U.S. Army, 1954-57. Recipient Disting. Svc. award Assn. Milw. Assn. Life Underwriters, 1990. Mem. Am. Soc. CLUs, Assn. Advanced Life Underwriters, Estate Counselors Forum, Mid Winter Estate Planning Clini, Univ. Club (Milw.). Republican. Roman Catholic. Avocations: golf, sailing, scuba, singing. Fax: 414-240-3001. Insurance. Office: Tolan Schueller and Assocs 10144 N Port Washington Rd Mequon WI 53092-5796

**TOLAND, CLYDE WILLIAM,** lawyer; b. Iola, Kans., Aug. 18, 1947; s. Stanley E. and June E. (Thompson) T.; m. Nancy Ellen Hummel, July 27, 1974; children: David Clyde, Andrew John, Elizabeth Kay. BA, U. Kans., 1969, JD, 1975; MA, U. Wis., 1971. Bar: Kans. 1975, U.S. Dist. Ct. Kans. 1975, U.S. Supreme Ct. 1980. Ptnr. Toland and Thompson LLC, Iola, 1975—. Author: Samuel Franklin Hubbard and Permelia Caroline (Spencer) Hubbard: Pioneer Settlers in 1857 of Allen County, Kansas Territory, and their Descendants, 1985, (with others) Clark and Eliza (Wright) Toland: Their Ancestors and Descendants, 1984, David Wilson and Charlotte Elizabeth (Cooper) Wilson, 1830-1961, and Their Ancestors and Descendants, 1988. Mem. exec. com. Friends of Libr., U. Kans., 1977-92, pres., 1988-91; pres. Allen County Hist. Soc., Inc., 1990-95; founder Annual Buster Keaton Celebration, Iola, Kans., co-chmn., 1993-97; leader restoration Frederick Funston Boyhood Home, 1991-95. Co-recipient with U.S. Sen. Nancy Kassebaum First Alumni Disting. Achievement award Coll. Liberal Arts and Scis. U. Kans., 1996. Fellow Kans. Bar Found.; mem. ABA, Kans. Bar Assn. (Outstanding Svc. award 1988), Allen County Bar Assn., U. Kans. Alumni Assn. (Strickland award 1969), Phi Beta Kappa, Order of Coif, Omicron Delta Kappa (presdl. plaque 1969). Republican. Prsbyterian. Avocations: speaking on estate planning and history; historical field trips. Probate, Estate planning, Estate taxation. Home: 211 S Colborn St Iola KS 66749-3405 Office: PO Box 404 Iola KS 66749-0404

**TOLAND, JOHN ROBERT,** lawyer; b. Iola, Kans., Oct. 7, 1944; s. Stanley E. and June Elizabeth (Thompson) T.; m. Karen Alice Jeffries, Apr. 26, 1980; children: Carol Jane, Mark Charles, Scott Robert, Kent William. BA with highest distinction, U. Kans., 1966, JD, 1969. Bar: Kans. 1969, U.S. Dist. Ct. Kans. 1969, U.S. Ct. Appeals (10th cir.) 1969, U.S. Supreme Ct. 1976. Ptnr. Toland and Thompson, LLC, Iola, 1973—; city atty., Yates Center, Kans., 1976-82; spkr. sch. law seminars. Editor-in-chief Kans. Law Rev., 1968-69; mem. bd. editors Kans. Bar Assn. Jour., 1988-92. Trustee Allen County Hosp., Iola, 1979-82; bd. dirs. Iola Pub. Library, 1980-88, pres., 1983-88; bd. dirs. United Fund of Iola Inc., 1975-79, treas., 1975-77; bd. dirs. Iola Area Symphony Orch., 1994-97; ruling elder 1st Presbyn. Ch., Iola, 1983-85, 97-98; mem. Allen County Hist. Soc., Kans. State Hist. Soc., The Friends of the Eisenhower Found., U. Kans. Alumni Assn.; mem. com. on ministry John Calvin Presbytery, Presbyn Ch. (USA), 1986-88. Capt. JAGC, U.S. Army, 1969-73, Vietnam. Decorated Bronze Star, Army Commendation medal with oak leaf cluster; John Ise scholar in Econ., 1965-66, Summerfield scholar, U. Kans., 1962-66, Nat. Merit scholar, 1962-66. Fellow Kans. Bar Found.; mem. ABA, Kans. Bar Assn., Kans. Sch. Attys. Assn. (bd. dirs. 1989-93, spkr. at sch. law seminars), Allen County Bar Assn. (pres. 1980-81), Am. Legion, Rotary (pres. Iola chpt. 1980-81, Paul Harris fellow 1986), Order of Coif, VFW, Phi Beta Kappa, Phi Delta Phi, Beta Theta Pi, Sigma Pi Sigma. General practice, Probate, Education and schools. Home: PO Box 312 Iola KS 66749-0312 Office: Toland and Thompson LLC 103 E Madison St Iola KS 66749-3330

**TOLEDANO, JAMES,** lawyer; b. N.Y.C., Apr. 26, 1944; s. Ralph Robert and Nora (Romaine) T.; m. Peggy Cashman, Dec. 18, 1971; children: Gwyn Alcock, Michael Howard. AB in Polit. Sci., U. Calif., Riverside, 1968; JD, U. Calif., Berkeley, 1971. Bar: Calif. 1972. Sole practice Irvine, Calif., 1976-88; lawyer mgr. ptnr. Toledano & Wald, Irvine, Calif., 1988-98; pvt. practice Irvine, 1998—. Bd. dirs., pres. U. Calif. Riverside Alumni Assn., 1972-90; alumni regent U. Calif., 1985-87; candidate Calif. State Assembly, 1992, 94; chair Orange County Calif. Dem. Party, 1995-97. Democrat. Mem. Religious Soc. of Friends. Avocations: stamp collecting, working out, reading, writing, hiking. State civil litigation, Federal civil litigation, Appellate. Office: 18201 Von Karman Ave Ste 1170 Irvine CA 92612-1093

**TOLENTINO, CASIMIRO URBANO,** lawyer; b. Manila, May 18, 1949; came to U.S., 1959; s. Lucio Rubio and Florence (Jose) T.; m. Jennifer Masculino, June 5, 1982; 2 children: Casimiro Masculino, Cristina Cecelia Masculino. BA in Zoology, UCLA, 1972, JD, 1975. Bar: Calif. 1976. Gen. counsel civil rights div. HEW, Washington, 1975-76; regional atty. Agrl. Labor Relations Bd., Fresno, Calif., 1976-78; regional dir. Sacramento and San Diego, 1978-81; regional atty. Pub. Employment Relations Bd., Los Angeles, 1981; counsel, west div. Writers Guild Am., Los Angeles, 1982-84; dir. legal affairs Embassy TV, Los Angeles, 1984-86; sole practice Los Angeles, 1986-87; mediator Ctr. Dispute Resolution, Santa Monica, Calif., 1986-87; asst. chief counsel Dept. of Fair Employment and Housing, State of Calif., 1986-92, adminstrv. law judge dept. social svcs., 1992—. Editor: Letters in Exile, 1976; contbr. articles and revs. to Amerasia Jour. Chmn. adv. bd. UCLA Asian Am. Studies Ctr., 1983-90; chmn. bd. Asian Pacific Legal Ctr., L.A., 1983-93 (Decade award); pres. bd. civil svc. commrs. City of L.A., 1984-85, 90-93; bd. dirs. met. region United Way, 1987-95; bd. dirs. Rebuild L.A., 1992-97; mem. Asian-Pacific Am. adv. coun. L.A. Police Commn., 1995-97; mem. adv. coun. L.A. Children's Scholarship Fund, 1998—. Mem. Nat. Asian-Am. Legal Consortium (bd. dirs. 1991—), State Bar Calif. (exec. com. labor law sect. 1985-88), Los Angeles County Bar Assn., Minority Bar Assn. (sec. 1984-85), Philippine Lawyers of So. Calif. (pres. 1984-87, Award of Merit 1982). Democrat. Roman Catholic. Avocations: history, photography, travel.

**TOLES, EDWARD BERNARD,** retired judge; b. Columbus, Ga., Sept. 17, 1909; s. Alex and Virginia Frances (Luke) T.; m. Susan Evelyn Echols, Jan. 24, 1944 (dec. Oct. 1996); 1 son, Edward Bernard. A.B., U. Ill., 1932; postgrad., Law Sch., 1932-34; J.D., Loyola U., Chgo., 1936. Bar: Ill. bar 1936. Practiced in Chgo., 1936-69; asst. atty. U.S. Housing Authority, 1939-40; asst. gen. counsel, war corr. ETO; Chgo. Defender, 1943-45; U.S. bankruptcy judge No. Dist. Ill., Chgo., 1969-87. Author: Chicago Negro Judges, 1959, Negro Federal Judges, 1960, Negro Lawyer in Crisis, 1966, Black Lawyers and Judges in the U.S, 1971, also articles.; Editor: Cook County Bar News, 1961-63; Columnist: Bench and Bar, Nat. Bar Assn. Bull, 1968-75. Recipient U.S. War Dept. award for services as war corr., 1947, Ill. Jud. Coun. award, 1988; named Sr. Counsellor, Ill. State Bar Assn., 1986,. Mem. ABA, Fed. Bar Assn., Nat. Bar Assn. (Barrister of Year award 1960, C.F. Stradford award, columnist Bench and Bar Bull., historian jud. coun. 1985—), Chgo. Bar Assn. (bd. mgrs. 1969-70), Cook County Bar Assn. (Edward H. Wright award, 1962, pres. 1960-62), 7th Circuit Bar Assn. (World Peace Through Law Bar Assn.), Am. Judicature Soc., Nat. Conf. Bankruptcy Judges, Alpha Phi Alpha, Omega Psi Phi (Ode to Excellence award 1963). Democrat. Home: 4800 S Chicago Beach Dr Chicago IL 60615-7001

**TOLIN, STEFAN A.,** lawyer; b. Phila., Mar. 29, 1945. BA, Franklin & Marshall Coll., 1967; AD, U. Cairo, 1972; JD cum laude, N.C. Ctrl. U., 1976. Bar: Minn. 1977. Atty. pvt. practice, Mpls. Contbr. articles to profl. jours. With U.S. Army, 1970-71. Mem. Assn. Trial Lawyers Am., Minn. Trial Lawyers Assn. Avocation: breeding, racing and selling thoroughbreds. Personal injury, Toxic tort, Criminal. Office: 401 2d Ave Ste 540 Minneapolis MN 55401-2307

**TOLINS, ROGER ALAN,** lawyer; b. Bklyn., Jan. 25, 1936; s. Albert and Claire (Rothstein) T.; m. Doris Levine, May 15, 1960; children: Fran, Jonathan. AB with distinction, Dartmouth Coll., 1956; LLB, NYU, 1959, LLM in Taxation, 1961. Bar: N.Y. 1959. Assoc. Brennan, London & Buttenwieser, N.Y.C., 1961-67; ptnr. Goldfeld, Charak, Tolins & Lowenfels, N.Y.C., 1967-74, Tolins & Lowenfels, N.Y.C., 1975—; guest lectr. in securities law Seton Hall U. Sch. Law, 1989—. With U.S. Army, 1959-60. Mem. ABA (sect. on taxation), N.Y. State Bar Assn. General corporate, Administrative and regulatory, Corporate taxation.

**TOLL, PERRY MARK,** lawyer; b. Kansas City, Mo., Oct. 28, 1945; s. Mark Irving and Ruth (Parker) T.; m. Mary Anne Shottenkirk, Aug. 26, 1967; children: Andrea Lynne, Hillary Anne. BS in Polit. Sci. and Econs., U. Kans., 1967, JD, 1970. Bar: Mo. 1970 1970, U.S. Dist. Ct. (we. dist.) Mo. 1970, U.S. Tax Ct. 1979, U.S. Supreme Ct. 1979. With Shughart, Thomson & Kilroy P.C., Kansas City, 1970—, pres., 1995—; asst. prof. deferred compensation U. Mo., Kansas City, 1979-83; bd. dirs., pres. Heart of Am. Tax Inst., Kansas City, 1975-87. Mem., chmn. Prairie Village (Kans.) Bd. Zoning Appeals, 1977-95. Mem. ABA, Mo. Bar Assn., Nat. Health Lawyers Assn., Am. Agr. Law Assn., Mo. Merchants and Mfrs. Assn., Greater Kansas City Med. Mgrs. Assn., Lawyers Assn. Kansas City, East Kans. Estate Planning Coun. (bd. dirs., pres.), Phi Kappa Tau (bd. dirs. Beta Theta chpt.). Estate planning, Health, Pension, profit-sharing, and employee benefits. Office: Shughart Thomson & Kilroy 12 Wyandotte Plz 120 W 12th St Ste 1500 Kansas City MO 64105-1929

**TOLL, SEYMOUR IRVING,** lawyer, writer, educator; b. Phila., Feb. 19, 1925; s. Louis David and Rose (Eisenstein) T.; m. Jean Marie Barth, June 25, 1951; children: Emily Barth, Elizabeth Terry, Martha Anne, Constance Nora Frances. BAmagna cum laude, Yale U., 1948, LLB, 1951. Bar: N.Y. 1953, U.S. Dist. Ct. (ea. dist.) Pa. 1955, Pa. 1956, U.S. Ct. Appeals (3d cir.) 1956, U.S. Dist. Ct. (so. dist.) N.Y. 1958, U.S. Supreme Ct. 1958, U.S. Ct. Appeals (5th cir.) 1970. Law clk. U.S. Dist. Ct. (so. dist.), N.Y.C., 1951-52; from assoc. to ptnr. Richter, Lord, Toll & Cavanaugh, Phila., 1955-65, 69; sole practice Phila., 1965-68, 69-74; ptnr. Toll, Ebby, Langer & Marvin, Phila., 1975—; vis. lectr. U. Pa. Law Sch., 1978-86. Author: Zoned American, 1969, A Judge Uncommon, 1993 (Athenaeum Literary award 1995); jour. editor: The Retainer, 1972-73, A Court's Heritage, 1984-88; jour. assoc. editor: The Shingle, 1970-78, editor, 1979-80; contbr. numerous articles to profl. jours. Pres. Phila. Citizen's Coun. on City Planning, 1967-69; pub. dir., mem. exec. com. Phila. Housing Devel. Corp., 1967-72; bd. dirs. The Libr. Co. Phila. (pres. 1992-98). Grantee Am. Philos. Soc., 1968. Mem. ABA, Pa. Bar Assn., Phila. Bar Assn. (Fidelity Bank award 1984), Am. Coll. Trial Lawyers, 3d Cir. Jud. Conf. (permanent del.), Jr. Legal Club, Phi Beta Kappa. Democrat. Jewish. Clubs: The Franklin Inn (pres. 1981-84), Yale (Phila.). Avocations: music, sailing, travel. Federal civil litigation, Antitrust, Libel. Home: 453 Conshohocken State Rd Bala Cynwyd PA 19004-2642 Office: Toll Ebby Langer & Marvin 2 Logan Sq 18th Flr Philadelphia PA 19103-2707

**TOLLEY, EDWARD DONALD,** lawyer; b. San Antonio, Jan. 31, 1950; s. Lyle Oren and Mary Theresa Tolley; m. Beth Dekle Tolley; 1 child, Edward Spencer. BBA, U. Ga., 1971, MBA, 1974, JD, 1975. Bar: Ga. 1975, U.S. Dist. Ct. (5th cir.) 1976, U.S. Supreme Ct. 1978, U.S. Ct. Appeals (11th cir.) 1981. Ptnr. Cook, Noell, Tolley Bates and Michael and predecessor firms, Athens, Ga., 1975—; lectr. various colls., univs., civic and profl. groups. Mem. Family Counseling Assn. of Athens, Inc., mem. Gov.'s Commn. on Criminal Sanctions and Correctional Facilities, 1988-90; past bd. dirs. Am. Cancer Soc.; pres. Clarke County Bd. Edn., 1992-93. Fellow Ga. Bar Found., Am. Bd. Criminal Lawyers (bd. dirs. 1987, pres. 1996); mem. Fed. Bar Assn. (sec. 1983, treas. 1985, pres. elect Macon chpt. 1997-98), State Bar Ga. (chmn. law office and econ. com., bd. govs. 1985—, formal adv. opinion bd.), Ga. Trial Lawyers (v.p.), Ga. Assn. Criminal Def. Lawyers (pres. 1985, Indigent Def. award 1983, 88), Athens Bar Assn. (past pres.), Am. Judicature Soc., Order of Barristers. Federal civil litigation, State civil litigation. Office: Cook Noell et al 304 E Washington St Athens GA 30601-2751

**TOLMAN, STEVEN KAY,** lawyer; b. Pocatello, Idaho, Sept. 16, 1946; s. S. Ernest and June (Carver) T.; m. Geraldine Bryne, Dec. 21, 1968 (div.); children: Brett, Shawna, Kelly, Bryce, Haley; m. Donna Arnold Tolman, July 18, 1992. BA, Brigham Young U., 1968; MBA, U. Utah, 1972; JD, U. Idaho, 1975. Bar: Idaho 1975, U.S. Dist. Ct. Idaho 1975, U.S. Ct. Appeals (9th cir.) 1988. Assoc. St. Clair, Hiller, Benjamin, Wood & McGath, Ketchum, Idaho, 1975-77, Parry, Robertson, Daly & Larson, Twin Falls, Idaho, 1977-78; ptnr. Nelson, Rosholt, Robertson, Tolman & Tucker, Twin Falls, 1979-91, Hollifield Tolman & Bevan, Twin Falls, 1991-92, Hollifield & Tolman, Twin Falls, 1992-94; atty. Tolman Law Office, Twin Falls, 1994—. Sch. bd. trustee Twin Falls Sch. Dist. # 411, 1986-95. 1st lt. U.S. Army, 1968-71, Vietnam. Mem. Greater Twin Falls Area C. of C. (bd. dirs. 1985-88). Avocations: tennis, golf, skiing, hunting. Insurance, Personal injury, Contracts commercial. Office: Tolman Law Office PO Box 1276 Twin Falls ID 83303-1276

**TOLMIE, DONALD MCEACHERN,** lawyer; b. Moline, Ill., June 21, 1928; s. Ronald Charles and Margaret Blaine (Kerr) T.; m. Joann Phillis Swanson, Aug. 15, 1953; children: David M., John K., Paul N. AB, Augustana Coll., 1950, JD, U. Ill., 1953. Bar: Ill. 1953, Va. 1968. Atty. Pa. R.R., Chgo., 1953-60; asst. gen. soliciter Pa. R.R., Phila., 1961-67; gen. atty. Norfolk & Western, Roanoke, Va., 1968; gen. soliciter Norfolk & Western, Roanoke, 1968-75, gen. counsel, 1975-82; gen. counsel Norfolk (Va.) So. Corp., 1982, v.p., gen. counsel, 1983-89. Mem. Va. Bar Assn., U.S Supreme Ct. Bar Assn., Harbor Club, Cedar Point Club. Lutheran. General corporate. Home: 912 Hanover Ave Norfolk VA 23508-1227

**TOMAIN, JOSEPH PATRICK,** dean, law educator; b. Long Branch, N.J., Sept. 3, 1948; s. Joseph Pasquale and Bernice M. (Krzan) T.; m. Kathleen Corcione, Aug. 1, 1971; children: Joseph Anthony, John Fiore. AB, U. Notre Dame, 1970; JD, George Washington U., 1974. Bar: N.J., Iowa. Assoc. Giordano & Halleran, Middletown, N.J., 1974-76; from asst. to prof. law Drake U. Sch. Law, Des Moines, Iowa, 1976-83; prof. law U. Cin. Coll. Law, 1983—, acting dean, 1989-90, dean, 1990—, Nippert prof. law, 1990—; vis. prof. law U. Tex. Sch. Law, Austin, 1986-87. Author: Energy Law in a Nutshell, 1981, Nuclear Power Transformation, 1987; co-author: Energy Decision Making, 1983, Energy Law and Policy, 1989, Energy and Natural Resources Law, 1992, Regulatory Law and Policy, 1993, 2d edit., 1998. Bd. trustees Ctr. Comprehensive Alcohol Treatment, Cin., Vol. Lawyers for Poor, Cin.; mem. steering com. BLAC/CBA Round Table, Cin.; chair Thomas L. Conlan Edn. Found. Served with USAR, 1970-76. Mem. ABA, Am. Law Inst., Ohio State Bar Assn. (del.), Cin. Bar Assn. (bd. trustees). Roman Catholic. Home: 3009 Springer Ave Cincinnati OH 45208-2440 Office: U Cin Coll Law Office Dean PO Box 210040 Cincinnati OH 45221-0040*

**TOMAN, WILLIAM JOSEPH,** lawyer; b. Ripon, Wis., Apr. 4, 1956; s. Neil J. Toman and Catherine O. (Gabler) Anderson; m. Pamela A. Polenz; children: Katherine Li Kunzke-Toman, Anna Marie, Joseph Gabler. BA, Dartmouth Coll., 1978; JD, U. Wis., 1982. Bar: Wis. 1982, U.S. Dist. Ct. (we. dist.) Wis. 1982. Law clk. to presiding chief judge U.S. Dist. Ct. (we. dist.) Wis., Madison, 1982-83; assoc. Quarles & Brady, Madison, 1983-89, ptnr., 1989—. Mem. ABA, Wis. Bar Assn., Dane County Bar Assn., Fedn. of Regulatory Counsel. Insurance, Administrative and regulatory, General corporate. Office: Quarles & Brady PO Box 2113 1 S Pinckney St Madison WI 53703-2892

**TOMAR, RICHARD THOMAS,** lawyer; b. Camden, N.J., Mar. 4, 1945; s. William and Bette (Brown) T.; children: Lindsay, Leanne Meryl, Daniel Gregory. AB, Columbia Coll., 1967; JD, U. Pa., 1970. Bar: D.C. 1971, N.J. 1971, Md. 1976. Pvt. practice Washington, 1971-73; ptnr. Philipson, Mallios & Tomar, P.C., Washington, 1973-89, Margolius, Mallios, Davis, Rider & Tomar, LLP, Washington, 1989—. Mem. D.C. Trial Lawyers Assn. (bd. dirs. 1980-89). Federal civil litigation. Office: Margolius Mallios Davis Rider & Tomar LLP 1828 L St NW Ste 500 Washington DC 20036-5104

**TOMAR, WILLIAM,** lawyer; b. Camden, N.J., Oct. 10, 1916; s. Morris and Katie (Sadinsky) T.; m. Bette Brown, Nov. 28, 1942; children: Richard T., Dean Jonathon. LLB cum laude, Rutgers U., 1939. Bar: N.J. 1940, U.S. Ct. Appeals (3d cir.) 1953, U.S. Supreme Ct. 1953, Fla. 1975, D.C. 1978. Sr. ptnr. Tomar, Siminoff, Adourian & O'Brien, Haddonfield, N.J., 1958—; mem. faculty Ctr. Trial and Appellate Advocacy, Hastings Coll. Law, U. Calif., 1971-86, Nat. Coll. Advocacy, Harvard U. Law Sch., 1973-75. Mem. UN Speakers Bur., UNICEF, 1960—; mem. adv. bd. Salvation Army, 1967-84, Inst. Med. Rsch., 1967—, N.J. Capital Punishment Study Commn., 1972-73, Touro Law Sch., 1981; mem. adv. bd. N.J. Student Assistance Bd., 1987—, vice chmn., 1992-98; bd. dirs. South Jersey Assn. Performing Arts, Haddonfield Symphony Soc., 1985—; bd. dirs., pres. 1992-99; mem. exec. bd. So. N.J. Coun. Boy Scouts Am., 1985—, pres. 1992—; vice chmn., mem. bd. trustees Cooper Hosp., Univ. Med. Ctr. 1979-97, bd. mem. emeritus 1998; mem. planning com. World Peace Through Law Ctr., 1970—; trustee Cooper Med. Ctr., 1979—. Recipient Disting. Alumni award Rutgers U. Sch. Law, 1996. Fellow Am. Coll. Trial Lawyers; mem. ABA, Assn. Trial Lawyers Am. (assoc. editor jour. 1962-68, gov. 1963-64, nat. parliamentarian 1964-70, nat. exec. com. 1964-70, chmn. seminars 1965 lectr. student adv. program 1968—), World Jurist Assn. (founding mem. 1974—), N.J. Bar Assn. (fee arbitration com. 1972-74, 75-77), Trial Lawyers of N.J. (cert. by Supreme Ct. of N.J. as civil trial atty, Trial Bar award 1977), N.J. Workers Compensation Assn. (trustee 1958-83), N.Y. Trial Attys. Assn., Phila. Trial Lawyers Assn., Camden County Bar Found. (bd. trustees 1986—), Camden County Bar Assn., (com. on rels. of bench and bar 1964—, adult edn. com. 1975—). General civil litigation, Personal injury, Environmental. Office: 20 Brace Rd Cherry Hill NJ 08034-2634

**TOMASELLI, ANTHONY ALLEN,** lawyer; b. Madison, Wis., Dec. 12, 1961; s. Louis Mark and Patricia Rose (Fenske) T.; m. Lori Lynn Zoha, May 8, 1993; children: Olivia Patrice, Antonia Grace. BS, U. Wis., 1984, JD, 1988. Bar: Wis. 1988, U.S. Dist. Ct. (we. and ea. dists.) Wis. 1988, U.S. Ct. Appeals (7th and Fed. cir.), 1990. Law clk. Wis. Supreme Ct., Madison, 1988-89; assoc. Quarles & Brady, Madison, 1989-97, ptnr., 1997—. Intellectual property, Communications, General civil litigation. Office: Quarles & Brady 1 S Pinckney St Madison WI 53703-2892

**TOMBACK, JAY LOREN,** lawyer; b. Chgo., Aug. 4, 1953; s. Seymour and Marilyn Lee (Klein) T.; m. Nancy Jo Corey, July 8, 1984; 1 child, Jarrett. BS in Acctg., U. Ill., 1976; JD, John Marshall Sch. Law, 1979. Bar: Ill. 1979, Ariz. 1980, U.S. Dist. Ct. Ariz. 1980, U.S. Tax Ct. 1980. Assoc. Robert L. Lane, Ltd., Phoenix, 1980-82; prin., bd. dirs. Lane & Tomback, Ltd., Phoenix, 1982-84, Lane, Tomback & Ehrlich, Ltd., Phoenix, 1984-89, Jay L. Tomback Ltd., Phoenix, 1989—; mem. Western Pension Conf., Phoenix, 1982-92. Mem. Valley Estate Planners, Phoenix, 1980-82. Fellow Ariz. Bar Found.; mem. ABA, Internat. Assn. Fin. Planning, Am. Judicature Soc., Ill. Bar Assn., State Bar Ariz., Maricopa County Bar Assn. General corporate, Taxation, general, Estate planning. Office: Jay L Tomback Ltd 100 W Clarendon Ave Ste 1430 Phoenix AZ 85013-3509

**TOMBERS, EVELYN CHARLOTTE,** lawyer; b. Phila., Nov. 7, 1956; d. Gerold G. and Margot (Ort) Knauerhase; m. Peter C. Tombers. AS, Temple U., 1976, BA, 1977; JD, Thomas M. Cooley Law Sch., 1991. Bar: Mich. 1991. Dist. intake counselor Fla. Dept. Health Rehab. Svc., Naples, 1985-87; satellite dir. Youth Shelter S.W. Fla., Naples, 1987-88; adj. prof. Thomas M. Cooley Law Sch., Lansing, Mich., 1991-92; jud. law clk. to Justice Patricia J. Boyle Mich. Supreme Ct., Detroit, 1992-94; assoc. Harvey, Kruse, Westen and Milan, Troy, Mich., 1994-95, Bowen, Radabaugh, Milton & Brown, Troy, Mich., 1995-99, Morrison Mahoney & Miller LLP, Southfield, Mich., 1999—. Past editor (newsletter) State Bar Mich. Appellate Practice Sect. Named one of Outstanding Women Grads., Women Lawyers Am., 1991. Avocation: golf. Appellate, Insurance, Product liability. Home: 726

Englewood Ave Royal Oak MI 48073-2833 Office: Morrison Mahoney & Miller LLP 25800 Northwestern Hwy Ste 900 Southfield MI 48075-8411

**TOMICH, LILLIAN,** lawyer; b. L.A.; d. Peter S. and Yovanka P. (Ivanovic) T. AA, Pasadena City Coll., 1954; BA in Polit. Sci., UCLA, 1956, cert. secondary tchg., 1957, MA, 1958; JD, U. So. Calif., 1961. Bar: Calif. Sole practice, 1961-66; house counsel Mfrs. Bank, L.A., 1966; assoc. Hurley, Shaw & Tomich, San Marino, Calif., 1968-76, Driscoll & Tomich, San Marino, 1976—; dir. Continental Culture Specialists Inc., Glendale, Calif. Trustee St. Sava Serbian Orthodox Ch., San Gabriel, Calif. Recipient Episcopal Gramata award Serbian Orthodox Met. of Midwestern Am., 1993, Episcopal Gramata award Serbian Orthodox Bishop of Western Am., 1996; Charles Fletcher Scott fellow, 1957; U. So. Calif. Law Sch. scholar, 1958. Mem. ABA, Calif. Bar Assn., Los Angeles County Bar Assn., Women Lawyers Assn., San Marino C. of C., UCLA Alumni Assn., Town Hall and World Affairs Coun., Order Mast and Dagger, Iota Tau Tau, Alpha Gamma Sigma. General corporate, General civil litigation, Probate. Office: 2460 Huntington Dr San Marino CA 91108-2643

**TOMITA, SUSAN K.,** lawyer; b. Wailuku Maui, Hawaii, Jan. 10, 1954; d. Kazuo Tomita and Helen E.V. Ing; 1 child, Anthony. BA, Stanford U., 1976; JD, U. Santa Clara, 1979. Staff atty. Nat. Indian Youth Coun., Albuquerque, 1979-80; assoc. Luebben, Hughes & Kelly, Albuquerque, 1980-83; ptnr. Luebben, Hughes & Tomita, Albuquerque, 1983-88; shareholder Tomita & Simpson, P.C., Albuquerque, 1988—; chair elder law sect. N.Mex. State Bar, Albuquerque, 1995-96, chair Indian law sect., 1988-89, mem. com. on legal svcs. to disabled, 1993—. Author: The Handbook for Guardians and Conservators: A Practical Guide to New Mexico Law, 1997, Alternatives to Guardianships and Conservatorships, 1997. Bd. dirs. Alzheimer's Assn., Albuquerque, 1996—, Legal Aid Soc. Albuquerque, 1985-87, Indian Pueblo Legal Svcs., Santa Ana, N.Mex., 1981-83. Mem. Nat. Acad. Elder Law Attys., N.Mex. Estate Planning Coun. Democrat. Presbyterian. Avocations: bicycling, reading. Estate planning, Probate, Estate taxation. Office: Tomita & Simpson PC 4263 Montgomery Blvd NE Ste 210 Albuquerque NM 87109-6708

**TOMLIN, JAMES MILTON,** lawyer; b. Springfield, Ill., July 16, 1942; s. Bernard A. and Iona M. T.; m. Carol L. Wandell, Dec. 23, 1966 (div. Mar. 1994); children: Brian, Brad, Mitch; m. Barbara Soldwedel, Aug. 24, 1998. BS, U. Ill., 1964, JD, 1967. Bar: Ill. 1968, U.S. Dist. Ct. (no. dist.) Ill. 1973. Judge adv. gen. corps. USN, 1968-71, USNR, 1971-91; atty. Westervest, Johnson, Nicol & Keller, Peoria, Ill., 1971-73; asst. corp. counsel City of Peoria, 1973-74; pvt. practice Peoria, 1974—; Mem. law adv. bd. Ctrl. Ill. C.C., Peoria, 1990-94. Bd. dirs. Neighborhood House Assn., Peoria, 1985—, former pres., Tower Pk., Peoria Heights, 1974-84, former pres., Forest Pk. Found., Peoria, 1997—. Lt. USN, 1968-71, capt. USNR, 1971-92, ret. Avocations: skiing, golfing, bicycling. General practice, Estate planning, Probate. Office: 5823 N Forest Park Dr Peoria IL 61614-3559

**TOMLINS, NEAL EDWARD,** lawyer, accountant; b. Tulsa, Sept. 25, 1958; s. Edward E. Jr. and Bobbie (Baucum) T.; m. Megan E. Clinton, Apr. 12, 1985. BBA, So. Meth. U., 1980; JD, U. Okla., 1983. Bar: Okla. 1983, U.S. Dist. Ct. (no. dist.) Okla. 1983, U.S. Dist. Ct. (we. dist.) Okla. 1984, U.S. Ct. Appeals (10th cir.) 1988; CPA, Okla. Assoc. Holliman, Langholz et al, Tulsa, 1983-86, Baker Hoster, Tulsa, 1986-93; founder Tomlins & Goins, Tulsa, 1993—. Mem. Okla. Bar Assn., Am. Bankruptcy Inst. Bankruptcy, Contracts commercial, General corporate. Office: Tomlins & Goins Utica Plz Bldg 2100 S Utica Ave Ste 300 Tulsa OK 74114-1438

**TOMLINSON, HERBERT WESTON,** lawyer; b. Upland, Pa., Feb. 11, 1930; s. Herbert Elmer and Hilda Josephine (Schlosbon) T.; m. Mary Jean Litwhiler, Oct. 27, 1961. BS, Pa. State U., 1952, postgrad., 1956-57; JD, Dickonson Sch. Law, 1960; postgrad., Temple U. Law Sch., 1969-73; BA with highest distinction, Pa. State U., 1994. Bar: Pa. 1961, U.S. Supreme Ct. 1968; lic. pilot. Law clk., pres. Delaware County Bar Assn., 1960-61; assoc. DeFuria Larkin Defuria, Chester, Pa., 1960-62, Hodge & Balderston, Chester, Pa., 1962-65, Edward McLaughlin, Chester, Pa., 1965-67; exec. dir. Legal Svcs. Program, Deleware County, 1967-69; atty. pvt. practice, Media, Pa., 1969—; sr. staff atty. Delaware County Pub. Defender's Office, 1969—; prof. bus. law Pa. State U., 1969-75, Widener U., 1971-76, 78-80, Delaware County C.C., 1971-75; arbitrator Am. Arbitration Assn. Actor in TV commercials, 1998—. Legal counsel Disabled Vets Am.; county dir. Delaware County March of Dimes, 1966-71; rep. candidate U.S. Ho. Reps., 1976; rep. committeeman, 1966—, treas. 168th Legis. Dist., 1975-81; chmn. Media Rep. Com., 1975-76, Media Borough Auditor, 1975-79; nat. dir. Jaycees, 1965-66. Capt. USMCR, 1952-56. Named Outstanding Young Men Am. U.S. Jaycees, 1966. Mem. AAUP, ABA, Am. Assn. Trial Lawyers, Nat. Assn. Securities Dealers, Am. Arbitration Assn., Pa. Bar Assn., Pa. Trial Lawyers Assn., Delaware County Bar Assn., Delaware County Real Estate Bd., Delaware County Med. Soc. (dir. pub. health fund 1967—), Aircraft Owners and Pilots Assn., Kiwanis, Masons, Shriners, Rotary, Phi Tehta Kappa (past pres.), Phi Kappa Phi, Alpha Sigma Lambda), Screen Actors Guild. Republican. Presbyterian. Personal injury, Probate, Family and matrimonial. Home: 103 Kershaw Rd Wallingford PA 19086-6311 Office: 8 W Front St Media PA 19063-3306

**TOMLINSON, MARGARET LYNCH,** lawyer; b. Cleve., June 21, 1929; d. John Joseph and Margaret (Stevenson) Lynch; m. Alexander C. Tomlinson. AB, Smith Coll., 1950; JD, N.Y. Law Sch., 1963. Bar: N.Y. 1963, D.C. 1971, U.S Ct. Appeals (D.C. cir.) 1971. Staff officer Dept. of State, 1950-55; U.S. Del. UN Gen. Assembly, N.Y.C., 1964-68; asst. legal adviser U.S. Mission to the UN, 1963-69; asst. to Sen. Claiborne Pell, Washington, 1969-71; sr. adviser U.S. Del. to the Law of the Sea Conf., 1972-78; ptnr. Dickey, Roadman & Dickey, Washington, 1978-82; cons. office gen. counsel CIA, Washington, 1987-93; cons. Law of the Sea; bd. dirs. Coun. Ocean Law, Washington, 1984—, vice-chmn., 1994—; U.S. del. spl. session UN Gen. Assembly, 1994. Contbr. articles to profl. jours. Mem. ABA (internat. law com., chmn. law of the subcom.), Am. Soc. Internat. Law, Internat. Law Assn., D.C. Bar Assn., Nat. Press Club, 1925 F St. Club, Sulgrave Club, Cosmopolitan Club. Public international. Home: 3314 P St NW Washington DC 20007-2701

**TOMLINSON, WARREN LEON,** lawyer; b. Denver, Apr. 2, 1930; s. Leslie Aultimer and Esther (Hasler) T.; m. Lois Elaine Retallack, Aug. 8, 1953 (div. 1987); children: Stephanie Lynn, Brett Louis; m. Linda Jane Beville, May 17, 1989. BA, U. Denver, 1951; JD, NYU, 1954. Bar: Colo. 1954, U.S. Dist. Ct. Colo., U.S. Ct. Appeals (10th cir.) 1958, U.S. Supreme Ct.. 1960. Assoc. Holland & Hart, Denver, 1958-63, ptnr., 1963-85, mediator, arbitrator, 1995—. Contbr. numerous articles to profl. jours. Lt. U.S. Army, 1954-58. Fellow Coll. Labor and Employment Lawyers; mem. ABA (chmn. law practice mgmt. sect. 1988-89, charter fellow Coll. of Law Practice Mgmt. 1994). Republican. Episcopalian. Avocations: skiing, white-water rafting. Labor, General civil litigation, Construction. Home: 5017 Main Gore Dr S Apt 4 Vail CO 81657-5426 Office: Holland & Hart 555 17th St Ste 2900 Denver CO 80202-3979

**TOMLJANOVICH, ESTHER M.,** state supreme court justice; b. Galt, Iowa, Nov. 1, 1931; d. Chester William and Thelma L. (Brooks) Moellering; m. William S. Tomljanovich, Dec. 26, 1957; 1 child, William Brooks. AA, Itasca Jr. Coll., 1951; BSL, St. Paul Coll. Law, 1953, LLB, 1955. Bar: Minn. 1955, U.S. Dist. Ct. Minn. 1958. Asst. revisor of statutes State of Minn., St. Paul, 1957-66, revisor of statutes, 1974-77; dist. ct. judge State of Minn., Stillwater, 1977-90; assoc. justice Minn. Supreme Ct., St. Paul, 1990-98. Former mem. North St. Paul Bd. Edn., Maplewood Bd. Edn., Lake Elmo Planning Commn; bd. trustees William Mitchell Coll. Law, 1995—. Mem. Minn. State Bar Assn., Bus. and Profl. Women's Assn. St. Paul (former pres.). Office: Supreme Ct MN 423 Minnesota Judicial Center 25 Constitution Ave Saint Paul MN 55155-1500

**TOMME, CURTIS RABON,** lawyer; b. Brady, Tex., Feb. 18, 1956; s. William Rabon Tomme and Hannah Mae Curtis; m. Elizabeth Ann Watson, Nov. 1, 1997. BS in Indsl. Distribution, Tex. A&M U., 1978; JD, Tex. Tech U., 1988. Bar: Tex. 1989. Asst. dist. atty. Taylor County, Abilene, Tex. Bd. dirs. Salvation Army, Abilene, 1998—, Abilene A&M Club, 1997—; staff Rdy Issard for Congress Camp, Abilene, 1995-96. Mem. Abilene Bar Assn., Abilene C. of C. Office: Taylor County Criminal Dist Atty 400 Oak St Ste 110 Abilene TX 79602-1527

**TOMPERT, JAMES EMIL,** lawyer; b. Battle Creek, Mich., July 21, 1954; s. James Russell and Marjorie Mary (Storkan) T. BA, Duke U., 1976; JD, U. Mich., 1981. Bar: D.C. 1981, Md. 1985, Va. 1986. Legis. asst. to congressman U.S. Ho. of Rep., Washington, 1977-78; assoc. Baker & Hostetler, Washington, 1981-84; assoc. Cooter & Gell, Washington, 1984-86, ptnr., 1987-94; ptnr. Cooter Mangold Tompert & Wayson PLLC, Washington, 1995—. Mem. Arts Club Washington, 1989—, Univ. Club of Washington, 1997—. Mem. ABA, D.C. Bar Assn. Federal civil litigation, General civil litigation, State civil litigation. Office: Cooter Mangold Tompert & Wayson PLLC 5301 Wisconsin Ave NW Washington DC 20015-2015

**TOMPKINS, DWIGHT EDWARD,** lawyer; b. Toledo, Ohio, June 29, 1952; s. Leonard Charles and Amanda Virginia (Bunce) T.; m. Marilyn Vergara, June 15, 1974; children: Jason, Kristin. BA in Anthropology, San Diego State U., 1974; MPA, Long Beach State U., 1981; JD, Loyola U., L.A., 1990. Bar: Calif. 1990, U.S. Dist. Ct. (ctrl. dist.) Calif. 1990, U.S. Dist. Ct. (so. dist.) Calif. 1991. Analyst City of Long Beach, 1985-89; law clk. Ching, Kurtz & Blix, Santa Ana, Calif., 1989-90; assoc. Ching & Assocs., Santa Ana, 1990-91; pvt. practice Downey, Calif., 1991—; bd. dirs. Gladius, Inc., Las Vegas, Nev. Recipient Am. Jurisprudence Trial Advocacy award, 1990. Mem. Rotary (pres. 1997-98). General corporate, Estate planning. Office: 9530 Imperial Hwy Ste E Downey CA 90242-3041

**TOMPKINS, JOSEPH BUFORD, JR.,** lawyer; b. Roanoke, Va., Apr. 4, 1950; s. Joseph Buford and Rebecca Louise (Johnston) T.; m. Nancy Powell Wilson, Feb. 6, 1993; children: Edward Graves, Claiborne Forbes; 1 stepchild, Clayton Tate Wilson. BA in Politics summa cum laude, Washington and Lee U., 1971; M.P.P. in Pub. Policy, Harvard U., 1975, JD, 1975. Bar: Va. 1975, U.S. Dist. Ct. D.C. 1982, U.S. Ct. Appeals (D.C. cir.) 1976, U.S. Ct. Appeals (5th cir.) 1977, U.S. Ct. Appeals (11th cir.) 1982, U.S. Ct. Appeals (3d cir.) 1983, U.S. Ct. Appeals (6th cir.) 1985, U.S. Ct. Appeals (7th cir.) 1991, U.S. Ct. Appeals (4th cir.) 1993, U.S. Supreme Ct. 1977. Assoc. Sidley & Austin, Washington, 1975-79, ptnr., 1982—; assoc. dir. Office of Policy and Mgmt. Analysis, criminal div. U.S. Dept Justice, Washington, 1979-80, dep. chief fraud sect. criminal div., 1980-82. Contbr. articles to legal publs. Mem. Va. Bd. of Health Professions, Richmond, Va., 1984-92, vice chmn., 1984-86, chmn., 1986-88, 90-91. Recipient Spl. Commendation, U.S. Dept. Justice, 1981. Mem. ABA (criminal justice sect., mem. white collar crime com., 1980—, chmn. task force on computer crime 1982-92), Va. Bar Assn., D.C. Bar Assn., Fed. Bar Assn., Phi Beta Kappa. Democrat. Methodist. Federal civil litigation, State civil litigation, Criminal. Home: 8146 Wellington Rd Alexandria VA 22308-1214 Office: Sidley & Austin 1722 I St NW Fl 7 Washington DC 20006-3795

**TOMPKINS, MICHAEL WILLIAM,** lawyer; b. Belleville, Ill., June 29, 1965. BA in Econs., Va. Tech., 1987; JD, William and Mary, 1990. Bar: Va. 1990, U.S. Ct. Appeals (4th cir.), D.C. 1992, Md. 1996, U.S. Dist. Ct. (ea. dist.) Va. 1997. Assoc. Brincefield, Hartnett & Assocs., P.C., Alexandria, Va., 1995-98; shareholder Brincefield, Hartnett, Tompkins & Clark, P.C., Alexandria, 1999—. Mem. ABA, No. Va. Young Lawyers Assn. (pres. 1998-99), Va. State Bar (young lawyers conf. cir. rep. 1997-99), Alexandria Bar Assn., Order of Barristers. Avocation: music (four instruments). Federal civil litigation, State civil litigation, Professional liability. Office: Brincefield Hartnett Tompkins & Clark PC 526 King St Ste 423 Alexandria VA 22314-3143

**TOMPKINS, RAYMOND EDGAR,** lawyer; b. Oklahoma City, July 13, 1934; s. Charles Edgar and Eva Mae (Hodges) T.; m. Sue Anne Sharpe, June 10, 1963; children: Matthew Stephen, Christopher T., Katherine Anne. BS, Okla. State U., 1956; JD, U. Okla., 1963. Bar: Okla. 1963, U.S. Dist. Ct. (no. dist.) Okla. 1963, U.S. Dist. Ct. (we. dist.) Okla. 1964, U.S. Ct. Appeals (10th cir.) 1965, U.S. Supreme Ct. 1968, U.S. dist. Ct. (ea. dist.) Okla. 1969, U.S. Ct. Appeals (9th cir.) 1981, U.S. Ct. Appeals (4th cir.) 1986. Adminstrv. asst. U.S. Congress, 1966-68; ptnr. Linn & Helms, Oklahoma City, 1980-90, Daughery, Bradford, Haught & Tompkins, P.C., Oklahoma City, 1990-94; shareholder Conner & Winters, P.C., Oklahoma City, 1994—; mediator and arbitrator Nat. Assn. Securities Dealers. Past chmn. bd. trustees Okla. Ann. Methodist Conf., St. Luke's United Meth. Ch.; past chmn. adminstrv. bd.; mem. Okla. Bur. Investigation Commn., past chmn.; past gen. counsel Rep. State com., Interstate Oil Compact. Maj. USAR. Recipient award of Honor Oklahoma City Bi-Centennial Commn., 1976. Master Am. Inns of Ct. (emeritus); mem. ABA, Okla. County Bar Assn. (Pres.'s award 1988), Okla. Bar Assn. (chmn. bench & bar com. 1995-97, Law Day award), Am. Arbitration Assn. (mediator), Am. Judicature Soc., Assn. Atty.-Mediators (panel mem.), Blue Key, Lions (pres. Oklahome City chpt.). General civil litigation. Home: 329 NW 40th St Oklahoma City OK 73118-8419 Office: 211 N Robinson Ave Ste 1700 Oklahoma City OK 73102-7136

**TOMS, FREDERIC E.,** lawyer; b. Forest City, N.C., Apr. 19, 1941; s. J.O. and Eunice (Henson) T.; m. Pamelia, Sept. 4, 1966; children: Merritt, Cindy. AB, U. N.C., 1966, JD, 1970. Bar: N.C. 1970, U.S. Dist. Ct. (ea., so., no., we. and mid. dists.) N.C. Assoc. Brown, Fox & Deaver, Fayetteville, N.C., 1970-71; ptnr. Grimes, Dawkins, Hall & Toms, Raleigh, 1971-75; pvt. practice Raleigh, 1975-77; ptnr. Dawkins, Toms & Beebe, Cary, N.C., 1977-84, Dimmock, Reagan, Dodd & Toms, Cary, 1984-87, Toms, Reagan & Montgomery, Cary, 1987—. Mem. Rotary. Personal injury, Consumer commercial.

**TONA, THOMAS,** lawyer; b. Flushing, N.Y., July 30, 1968; s. Thomas Peter and Lorraine T. BA, Hofstra U., 1990, JD, 1993. Bar: N.Y. 1994, U.S. Dist. Ct. (so. and ea. dists.) 1994. Assoc. Generosa & Carusona, P.C., Mineola, N.Y., 1993-94, Deutsch & Schneider, Queens, N.Y., 1994-95, Cartier, Hogan, Sullivan, Bernstein & Auerbach, Patchogue, N.Y., 1996—. Advisor Hofstra U. Sch. of Law Moot Ct., Hempstead, N.Y., 1993; judge Pace Law Sch. Moot Ct., Westchester, N.Y., 1996. Mem. ABA, N.Y. State Bar Assn., Suffolk County Bar Assn., Nat. Inst. for Trial Advocacy (cert.), Sons of Italy. Roman Catholic. Personal injury, Insurance, State civil litigation. Office: Cartier Hogan Sullivan Bernstein & Auerbah 77 Medford Ave Patchogue NY 11772

**TONE, PHILIP WILLIS,** retired lawyer, former federal judge; b. Chgo., Apr. 9, 1923; s. Elmer James and Frances (Willis) T.; m. Gretchen Altfillisch, Mar. 10, 1945; children: Michael P., Jeffrey R., Susan A. BA, U. Iowa, 1943, JD, 1948. Bar: Iowa 1948, Ill. 1950, D.C. 1950. Law clk. Justice Wiley B. Rutledge, Supreme Ct. U.S., Washington, 1948-49; assoc. firm Covington & Burling, Washington, 1949-50; assoc., ptnr. firm Jenner & Block, Chgo., 1950-72, 80-97; judge U.S. Dist. Ct., Chgo., 1972-74, U.S. Ct. Appeals (7th cir.), Chgo., 1974-80; spl. counsel Nat. Commn. on Causes and Prevention of Violence, 1968-69, U.S. Senate subcom. to investigate individuals representing interests of fgn. govts., 1980; Chmn. Ill. Supreme Ct. Rules Com., 1968-71, sec., 1963-68; mem. Com. on Jud. Br. of Jud. Conf. of U.S., 1987-91; gen. counsel U.S. Golf Assn., 1988-92; mem. Fed. Jud. Fellows Commn., 1986-92; chmn. Fed. Jud. Ctr. Found. Contbr. articles to legal periodicals. With AUS, 1943-46. Grad. fellow Law Sch. Yale U., 1948. Fellow Am. Coll. Trial Lawyers (regent 1984-87, pres. 1988-89); mem. ABA, Am. Bar Found., Am. Law Inst., Ill. Bar Assn. (bd. govs. 1960-64), Chgo. Bar Assn. (bd. mgrs. 1966-69), Am. Judicature Soc., Law Club Chgo. (pres. 1979-80), Legal Club Chgo. Federal civil litigation, General civil litigation, Antitrust.

**TONEY, WILLIAM DAVID, II,** lawyer; b. Houston, June 14, 1971; s. William David and Jeanie Thomason (Smith) T.; m. Ginger Lee Grief, Oct. 12, 1996. BA in Polit. Sci., U. North Tex., 1993; JD, Baylor U., 1996. Bar: Tex. 1996, U.S. Dist. Ct. (so. and ea. dists.) Tex. 1996. Law clk. Mills, Shirley, Eckel & Bassett, Houston, 1995, assoc., 1996—. Mem. ABA (litigation sect.), FBA, State Bar Tex., Tex. Assn. Def. Counsel, Houston Bar Assn. (litigation sect., spl. olympics, tennis and golf. coms.), Houston Young Lawyers Assn., Harris County Bar Assn., Phi Delta Phi. Personal injury, Professional liability, Insurance. Office: Mills Shirley Eckel & Bassett LLP 600 Travis St Ste 3950 Houston TX 77002-3088

**TONG, PETER P.,** patent lawyer. PhD, Calif. Inst. Tech., 1985; MBA, Santa Clara U., 1992, JD, 1994. Bar: Calif. 1994. Engr. Hewlett Packard, Palo Alto, Calif., 1985-90, legal assoc., 1991-94, patent lawyer, 1994-95; patent lawyer McCutchen, Doyle, Palo Alto, 1995-97, Fliesler, Dubb, Meyer & Lovejoy, San Francisco, 1997—; CEO IP Learn, Mountain View, Calif., 1998—. Patentee in field. Mem. Caltech Alumni Assn. (pres. 1992-94), MBA Alumni Assn. Santa Clara Univ. (pres. 1996-97). Intellectual property. Office: Fliesler Dubb Meyer & Lovejoy 4 Embarcadero Ctr Lbby 4 San Francisco CA 94111-4112

**TONOGBANUA, A. ROBERT,** lawyer; b. Manila, The Philippines, Apr. 18, 1969; came to U.S,. 1969; s. Gabino Conwi and Teresita (Chua) T. BS, St. Joseph's U., 1991; JD, Temple U., 1996. Bar: N.J., U.S. Dist. Ct. N.J. Claims atty. Zurich Ins., Marlton, N.J., 1996-97; assoc. Margolis Edelstein, Westmont, N.J., 1997—. Mem. Camden County Bar Assn., N.J. State Bar Assn., Inst. on Disabilities, Sigma Xi. Democrat. Roman Catholic. Avocations: vocalist, tennis. Personal injury, Environmental, Toxic tort. Home: 3004 Sherry Ct Voorhees NJ 08043-3001 Office: Margolis Edelstein 216 Haddon Ave Ste 750 Westmont NJ 08108-2809

**TONRY, RICHARD ALVIN,** lawyer, pecan farmer; b. New Orleans, June 25, 1935; s. Richard Gordon and Dolores Theresa (Kroger) T.; m. Joy Ann Willmouth, Feb. 3, 1950; children: Richard A., Tara Ann, Cullen Adair. BA magna cum laude, Spring Hill Coll., Mobile, Ala., 1961, M Philosophy summa cum laude, 1962; JD, Loyola U. of South, New Orleans, 1967. Bar: La. 1967, U.S. Dist. Ct. (ea. dist.) La. 1967, U.S. Ct. Appeals (5th cir.) 1972, U.S. Supreme Ct. 1972. Ptnr. McBride & Tonry, Arabi, La., 1967-73, Tonry & Mumphrey, Chalmette, La., 1973-80; mem. La. Ho. of Reps., 1976, U.S. Ho. Reps., Washington, 1977; ptnr. Tonry & Ginart, Chalmette, 1990—; pecan farmer, Lumberton, Miss., 1991—. Chmn. Heart Fund of St. Bernard, Chalmettee, 1971-73. Named Outstanding Young Man of St. Bernard, St. Bernard Jaycees, 1973. Mem. ABA, ATLA, La. Bar Assn. (ho. of dels. 1973-74), La. Trial Lawyers Assn. (bd. dirs. 1972-75). Democrat. Roman Catholic. Avocations: hunting, gardening. Personal injury, Criminal, General civil litigation. Home: 1177 W Main Ave Lumberton MS 39455-8335

**TOOBIN, JEFFREY ROSS,** writer, legal analyst; b. N.Y.C., May 21, 1960; s. Jerome and Marlene Sanders T.; m. Amy Bennett McIntosh, May 31, 1986; children: Ellen Frances, Adam Jerome. AB, Harvard U., 1982, JD, 1986. Bar: N.Y. 1987. Law clerk Hon. J. Edward Lumbard, N.Y.C., 1986-87; assoc. counsel Indep. Counsel Lawrence Walsh, Washington, 1987-89; asst. U.S. Atty. Ea. Dist. N.Y., Bklyn., 1990-93; legal analyst ABC News, N.Y.C., 1996—; staff writer The New Yorker, N.Y.C., 1993—. Author: Opening Arguments: A Young Lawyer's First Case-United States v. Oliver North, 1991, The Run of His Life: The People v. O.J. Simpson, 1996, A Vast Conspiracy: The Real Story of the Sex Scandal that Nearly Brought Down a President, 2000; contbr. articles to The New Yorker. Office: The New Yorker 20 W 43rd St New York NY 10036-7400

**TOOHEY, BRIAN FREDERICK,** lawyer; b. Niagara Falls, N.Y., Dec. 14, 1944; s. Matthew Frederick and Marilyn Gertrude (Hoag) T.; m. Mary Elizabeth Monihan; children: Maureen Elizabeth, Matthew Sheridan, Margaret Monihan, Mary Catherine, Elizabeth Warner. BS, Niagara U., 1966; JD, Cornell U., 1969. Bar: N.Y. 1969, N.Mex. 1978, Ohio 1980. Ptnr. Cohen, Swados, Wright, Hanifin & Bradford, Buffalo, 1973-77; pvt. practice Santa Fe, 1977-79; of counsel Jones, Day, Reavis & Pogue, Cleve., 1979-80, ptnr., 1981—. Mem. Citizens League Greater Cleve., 1982—. Ltd. JAG Corps, USNR, 1970-73. Mem. ABA, N.Y. State Bar Assn., State Bar N.Mex., Ohio State Bar Assn., Greater Cleve. Bar Assn. Roman Catholic. E-mail: bftoohey@jonesday.com. Federal civil litigation, Insurance. Home: 25 Pepper Creek Dr Cleveland OH 44124-5279 Office: Jones Day Reavis & Pogue N Point 901 Lakeside Ave E Cleveland OH 44114-1116

**TOOLE, BRUCE RYAN,** lawyer; b. Missoula, Mont., June 21, 1924; s. John Howard and Marjorie Lee (Ross) T.; m. Loris Knoll, Sept. 29, 1951; children: Marjorie, Ryan, Allan. JD, U. Mont., 1949. Bar: Mont., U.S. Ct. Appeals (9th & Fed. cirs.), U.S. Supreme Ct., U.S. Claims Ct. Sole practice Missoula, 1950; dep. county atty. Missoula County, 1951; ptnr. Crowley Law Firm, Billings, Mont., 1951-92; of counsel Crowley Law Firm, Billings, 1992—. Editor Mont. Lawyer, 1979-83. Mem. Mont. Com. for Humanities, Missoula; v.p. Billings Preservation Soc.; precinctman Yellowstone County Reps. With U.S. Army, 1944-45, ETO. Fellowship grantee NEH, Harvard U., 1980. Fellow Am. Coll. Trial Lawyers, Am. Bar Found.; mem. Am. Bd. Trial Advs., State Bar Mont. (pres. 1977-78), Yellowstone County Bar (pres. 1973, chmn. com. on mediation 1992), Internat. Assn. Def. Counsel. Avocations: politics, history, photography, metal work. General civil litigation, Alternative dispute resolution. Home: 3019 Glacier Dr Billings MT 59102-0711 Office: Crowley Law Firm 490 N 31st St Ste 500 Billings MT 59101-1288

**TOOLE, JOHN HARPER,** lawyer; b. Johnson City, N.Y., Apr. 4, 1941; s. Edward Joseph and Anne (Junius) T.; m. Lamar Sparkman, May 30, 1969; children: John Carter, Lucy Bland. BS, U. Va., 1963; JD, Washington Coll. of Law, 1971. Bar: Va. 1971, D.C. 1972. From assoc. to ptnr. Lewis, Mitchell & Moore, Tysons Corner, Va., 1971-77; ptnr. Watt, Tieder, Killian, Toole & Hoffar, Tysons Corner, 1978-82; ptnr., of counsel McGuire, Woods, Battle & Boothe, Tysons Corner, 1983—. 1st. Lt. U.S. Army, 1963-66. Mem. ABA, Va. State Bar, Va. Bar Assn., D.C. Bar Assn. Real property, Contracts commercial, Banking. Office: McGuire Woods Battle & Boothe PO Box 9346 8280 Greensboro Dr Ste 900 Mc Lean VA 22102-3892

**TOOLE, WILLIAM WALTER,** lawyer; b. Phila., Feb. 17, 1959; s. James Francis and Patricia (Wooldridge) T.; m. Claudina Ghianni, May 20, 1989; 1 child, Lauren Marie. BA, Haverford Coll., 1982; MBA, Wake Forest U., 1989, JD, 1989. Bar: N.C. 1989, Md. 1990, U.S. Dist. Ct. Md. 1990, U.S. Ct. Appeals (4th cir.) 1991, Va. 1992. Journalist Rural Hall (N.C.) Ind., 1983-84; comml. fisherman Destin, Fla., 1984-85; law clk. to Hon. Louis B. Meyer N.C. Supreme Ct., Raleigh, 1989-90; atty. Piper & Marbury, Balt., 1990-93; ptnr. Robinson, Bradshaw & Hinson PA, Balt., 1993—; adj. prof. UNC, Charlotte. Editor-in-chief monthly newsletter Md. Environ. Law Newsletter; contbr. chpt. to Md. Environ. Law Handbook. Bd. dirs. Gaston Day Sch.; action team leader Water Quality Protection Bd. Mem. Haverford Alumni Assn. (regional rep. 1990-98), Carolina Raptor Ctr., Torch Club. Environmental.

**TOOMEY, THOMAS MURRAY,** lawyer; b. Washington, Dec. 9, 1923; s. Vincent L. and Catherine V. (McCann) T.; m. Grace Donohoe, June 22, 1948; children: Isabelle Marie Toomey Hessick, Helen Marie, Mary Louise, Thomas Murray. Student, Duke U., 1943-44, Catholic U. Am., 1942-43, 47-49; J.D., Catholic U. Am., 1949. Bar: D.C. 1949, Md. 1952. Sole practice Washington and Md., 1949—; bd. dirs. Allied Capital Corp, Washington, Chgo., Detroit, San Francisco, Atlanta, Frankfurt, Germany, Fed. Ctr. Plz. Corp., Donohoe Cos., Inc., Washington, Nat. Capital Bank, Washington. Chmn. aviation and transp. coms. Met. Washington Bd. Trade, 1954-76, bd. dirs., 1962-77; chmn. dedication Dulles Internat. Airport, 1962; trustee Cath. U. Am., 1981—; founding trustee Heights Sch. Served to 1st lt. USMC, 1942-46, 50-52. Recipient Ann. Alumni Achievement award Cath. U., 1977, Most Disting. Alumnus award St. John's Coll. High Sch. D.C., 1994. Mem. ABA, D.C. Bar Assn., Md. Bar Assn., Bar Assn. D.C., Am. Judicature Soc., Comml. Law League Am., Friendly Sons St. Patrick (pres. 1983), Sovereign Mil. Order of Malta (Fed. Assn. U.S.A.), Congl. Golf and Country Club, Kenwood Golf and Country Club, Univ. Club, Army and Navy Club (Washington), Tower Club, Lago Mar Beach Club (Ft. Lauderdale, Fla.). Home: 6204 Garnett Dr Bethesda MD 20815-6618 Office: 4701 Sangamore Rd Bethesda MD 20816-2508

**TOONE, THOMAS LEE,** lawyer; b. Kermit, Tex., Oct. 28, 1947; s. Herbert Hoover and Kathlyn (Collins) T.; m. Jane Elizabeth McCaslin, July 23, 1993; children: Thomas Lee Jr., John Kevin. BA in Zoology and Pre-Med, U. Tex., 1970, JD, 1973. Bar: Tex. 1973, Ariz. 1976, U.S. Dist. Ct. Ariz. 1976, U.S. Ct. Appeals (9th cir.) 1981, U.S. Supreme Ct. 1982; cert. specialist personal injury and wrongful death, PADI Open Water; lic. pilot, airplane single engine land. State senate legal counsel Tex. State Senate, Austin, Tex., 1970-73; elections atty. Tex. Sec. State, Austin, 1973-75; judge adv. USNG Res., 1973-76; trial atty. Beer & Toone, P.C., Phoenix, Ariz., 1975—; mem.

faculty Nat. Inst. Trial Adv., Crash Survival Investigation Advanced Course; judge pro tempore Maricopa County Superior Ct. 1st lt. USNG, 1970-76. Fellow Ariz. Bar Found.; mem. ABA, Maricopa County Bar Assn. (sec., bd. dirs./treas., pres. elect 1995—), Am. Bd. Trial Advs. (assoc. mem., sec. 1998—), Nat. Transp. Safety Bd. Bar Assn. (founding mem.), Ariz. Assn. Def. Counsel, Lawyer-Pilots Bar Assn., Def. Rsch. Inst., Internat. Assn. Def. Counsel. Avocations: rodeo events, snowskiing, tennis, jogging, hiking. Aviation, Personal injury, Insurance. Office: Beer & Toone PC 76 E Mitchell Dr Phoenix AZ 85012-2330

**TOOTHMAN, JOHN WILLIAM,** lawyer; b. Bryn Mawr, Pa., Dec. 6, 1954; s. Nolan Ernest Toothman and Caroline Nell Reed Pawl; m. Elizabeth McGee; 1 child, William. BS ChemE with honors, U. Va., 1977, MS ChemE, 1979; JD cum laude, Harvard U., 1981. Bar: D.C. 1981, Va. 1987, U.S. Dist. Ct. (ea. dist.) Va. 1987, U.S. Ct. Fed. Claims 1987, U.S. Ct. Appeals (4th and fed. cir.) 1987, U.S. Supreme Ct. 1987, Md. 1990, U.S. Dist. Ct. Md. 1990, U.S. Bankruptcy Ct. (ea. dist.) Va. 1994, U.S. Dist. Ct. Colo. 1998. Assoc. Howrey & Simon, Washington, 1981-83, Akin, Gump, Strauss et al, Washington, 1983-84; trial atty. civil div. U.S. Dept. Justice, Washington, 1984-86; assoc. John Grad & Assocs., Alexandria, Va., 1986-88; ptnr. Grad, Toothman, Logan & Chabot, P.C., Alexandria, 1988-89, Shulman, Rogers, Gandal, Pordy & Ecker, P.A., Alexandria, 1989-93; founder The Devil's Advocate & Toothman & White, P.C., 1993—; guest lectr. George Washington U. Law Sch., 1988; lectr. in field. Author: (with Douglas Danner) Danner & Toothman Trial Practice Checklists, 1989; contbr. articles to profl. jours. NSF fellow, 1977. Mem. ABA (Ross Essay award 1995), Am. Corp. Counsel Assn., Sigma Xi, Tau Beta Pi. Federal civil litigation, General civil litigation, Contracts commercial. Address: 400 N Columbus St Ste 250 Alexandria VA 22314-2264

**TOPEL, DAVID LOUIS,** lawyer; b. Wilmington, Del., June 16, 1953; s. Henry and Phyllis Lee (Parkes) T. BA, U. Del., 1975; JD, Widener U., 1978. Bar: Pa. 1979, U.S. Dist. Ct. (ea. dist.) Pa. 1980, U.S. Ct. Appeals (3d cir.) 1980. Trial atty. major trials divsn. City Solicitor's Office of Phila., 1979-82; assoc. Obermayer Rebmann Maxwell & Hippel, Phila., 1982-84; ptnr. Sprecher Felix Visco Hutchison & Young, Phila., 1984-89; sole practice Phila., 1989—; guest lectr. Thomas Jefferson Univ. Hosp., Phila., 1983-87. Editor, pub. (mag.) Progress Notes, 1983-89. Recipient Outstanding Alumnus award Widener U. Sch. Law, 1984; nationally ranked swimmer U.S. Masters Swimming Assn. Mem. Pa. Bar Assn., Am. Soc. Law & Medicine, Pi Sigma Alpha. Avocations: screenwriting. State civil litigation, Health, Personal injury. Office: 212 Monroe St Philadelphia PA 19147-3309

**TOPHAM, LEE EVANS,** defender. MBA, Plymouth State Coll., 1988; JD, Franklin Pierce Law Ctr., Concord, N.H., 1991. Bar: N.H. 1991, U.S. Dist. Ct. N.H. 1991. Staff atty. N.H. Pub. Defender, Keene, 1991-93; staff atty. N.H. Pub. Defender, Concord, 1993-95, mng. atty., 1995—. Town moderator Town of Wilmot, N.H., 1998—. Mem. N.H. Bar Assn., N.H. Assn. Criminal Def. Lawyers, Frank Rowe Kenison Am. Inn of Ct. (barrister). Office: NH Pub Defender 117 N State St Concord NH 03301-4493

**TOPLITZ, GEORGE NATHAN,** lawyer; b. Winsted, Conn., June 13, 1936; s. Morris and Rose (Dolinsky) T.; m. Janet S. Strauss, July 30, 1961 (div.); children: Jill, Wendy, Anna; m. Kimilene A. Snead, Nov. 25, 1979. BA, U. Conn., 1958; LLB, Boston U., 1961. Bar: N.Y. 1964, U.S. Dist. Ct. (so. dist.) N.Y. 1968, U.S. Dist. Ct. (ea. dist.) N.Y. 1968, U.S. Ct. Appeals (2d cir.) 1986, U.S. Supreme Ct. 1987. Claims atty. Royal-Globe Ins. Co., surety dept., N.Y.C., 1963-65; surety atty. Transam. Inst. Co., N.Y.C., 1965-67; assoc. Max E. Greenberg, Cantor, Reiss, N.Y.C., 1967—, ptnr., 1974-88; ptnr. Max E. Greenberg, Cantor, Trager, Toplitz, 1988—; lectr. Am. Mgmt. Assn., 1974-76, Am. Assn. Cost Engrs., 1974-75, Sch. Continuing Edn. NYU, 1975; NW Ctr. Profl. Edn., 1988. With U.S. Army, 1961-63. Recipient Letter of Commendation for acting vol. spl. master Supreme Ct. N.Y., 1982, 84, 85, 86, 87, 88, 89, 90, Fed. mediator, U.S. Dist. Ct. (ea. dist.), N.Y., 1992. Mem. ABA, N.Y. State Bar Assn., N.Y. County Lawyers Assn., Assn. Trial Lawyers Am., Internat. Platform Assn. Federal civil litigation, State civil litigation, Government contracts and claims. Office: 100 Church St New York NY 10007-2601

**TOPOL, ROBIN APRIL LEVITT,** lawyer; b. N.Y.C., Apr. 2; d. Anatole Roy and Phyllis Patricia (Redman) Levitt; m. Clifford Miles Topol, Oct. 23, 1982. Student, Stanford U., Eng., 1974; BA, Barnard Coll., 1976; JD, NYU, 1979; postgrad. exec. mgmt. program, Yale U., 1987. Bar: N.Y. 1980, Fla. 1981. Ptnr. real estate dept., comml. real estate and leasing Kurzman & Eisenberg, White Plains, N.Y., 1996—. Trustee alumni bd. dirs. Yale U. Sch. Mgmt., 1987-88. Mem. ABA (vice chmn. real property com. 1986-90), N.Y. County Bar Assn. (real estate com. 1986-96), Women's Bar Assn. (chmn. real estate com. 1980-96). Avocations: tennis, golf, running. Real property. Office: Kurzman & Eisenberg 1 N Broadway White Plains NY 10601-2310

**TOPP, SUSAN HLYWA,** lawyer; b. Detroit, Oct. 9, 1956; d. Michael Leo and Lucy Stella (Rusak) Hlywa; m. Robert Elwin Topp, July 25, 1985; children: Matthew, Sarah, Michael and Jamie (triplets). BS in Edn. cum laude, Ctrl. Mich. U., 1978; JD cum laude, Wayne State U., Detroit, 1991. Bar: Mich. 1992, U.S. Dist. Ct. (ea. dist.) Mich. 1992. Conservation officer Mich. Dept. Natural Resources, Pontiac, 1980-88; environ. conservation officer Mich. Dept. Natural Resources, Livonia, 1988-93; pvt. practice Gaylord, Mich., 1993; ptnr. Rolinski & Topp, PLC, Gaylord, 1993; assoc. Plunkett & Cooney, PC, Gaylord, 1993—; adj. faculty Audubon Internat. Active Rocky Mountain Mineral Law Found., Urban Land Inst. Recipient Am. Jurisprudence award Wayne State U., 1987, Trial Advocacy award, 1988. Mem. ABA (nat. resources and environ. law com.), AAUW, Mich. State Bar Assn. (environ. law sect.), Mich. C. of C. Roman Catholic. Avocations: backpacking, skiing, scuba diving, back-country camping, canoeing. Environmental, Oil, gas, and mineral, Real property. Office: Plunkett & Cooney PC Hidden Valley Exec Ctr PO Box 280 Gaylord MI 49734-0280

**TORGERSON, LARRY KEITH,** lawyer; b. Albert Lea, Minn., Aug. 25, 1935; s. Fritz G. and Lu (Hillman) T. BA, Drake U., 1958, MA, 1960, LLB, 1963, JD, 1968; MA, Iowa U., 1962; cert., The Hague (The Netherlands) Acad. Internat. Law, 1965, 69; LLM, U. Minn., 1969, Columbia U., 1971, U. Mo., 1976; PMD, Harvard U., 1973, EdM, 1974. Bar: Minn. 1964, Wis. 1970, Iowa 1970, U.S. Tax Ct. 1971, U.S. Supreme Ct. 1972, U.S. Dist. Ct. Minn. 1964, U.S. Dist. Ct. (no. dist.) Iowa 1971, U.S. Dist. Ct. (ea. dist.) Wis. 1981, U.S. Ct. Appeals (8th cir.) 1981. Asst. corp. counsel 1st Bank Stock Corp. (88 Banks) Mpls., 1963-67; asst. corp. counsel 1st. Svc. Corp., (27 ins. agys., computer subs.) Mpls., 1965-67; v.p., trust officer Nat. City Bank, Mpls., 1967-69; sr. mem. Torgerson Law Firm, Northwood, Iowa, 1969-87; trustee, gen. counsel Torgerson Farms, Northwood, 1977—, Redbirch Farms, Kensett, Iowa, 1987—, Sunburst Farms, Grafton, Iowa, 1987—, Gold Dust Farms, Bolan, Iowa, 1988—, Torgerson Grain Storage, Bolan, 1988—, Indian Summer Farms, Bolan, 1991—, Sunset Farms, Bolan, 1992—, Sunrise Farms, Grafton, 1994—; CEO, gen. counsel Internat. Investments, Mpls., 1983-96, Transoceanic, Mpls., 1987-96, Torgerson Capital, Northwood, 1996—, Torgerson Investments, Northwood, 1984—, Torgerson Properties, Northwood, 1987—, Torgerson Ranches, Sundance, Wyo., 1998—, Hawaiian Investments UnLtd., Maui, Hawaii, 1998—, Internat. Investments UnLtd., San Pedro, Belize, 1999—. Recipient All-Am. Journalism award, Thomas Arkle Clark Outstanding Achievement award, Dennis E. Brumfield Outstanding Achievement award, Johnny B. Guy Outstanding Leadership award, Silver Bullet Outstanding Achievement award Drake ATO; named one of Outstanding Young Men of Am. U.S. Jaycees, Hon. Rotarian; Hagen scholar, Honor Scholarship. Mem. ABA, Am. Judicature Soc., Iowa Bar Assn., Minn. Bar Assn., Wis Bar Assn., Hennepin County Bar Assn., Mensa, Drake Student-Faculty Coun., Drake Student Alumni Coun. (chmn.), Jaycees, Harvard Bus. Sch. Study (pres., exec. com., univ. editor in chief), Psi Chi, Circle K (pres. local chpt.), Phi Alpha Delta, Omicron Delta Kappa (pres. local chpt.), Pi Kappa Delta (pres. local chpt.), Alpha Tau Omega (pres.local chpt., Silver Bullet Outstanding Leadership award), Pi Delta Epsilon (founder, chpt. pres.), Alpha Kappa Delta, Alpha Scholastic Hon. (U. editor-in-chief), Harvard Bus. Sch. Exec. Com. (U. editor-in-chief). Lutheran. General corporate, Real property, Taxation, general.

**TORKILDSON, RAYMOND MAYNARD,** lawyer; b. Lake City, S.D., Nov. 19, 1917; s. Gustav Adolph and Agnes (Opitz) T.; m. Sharman Elizabeth Vaughn, Sept. 8, 1956; children—Stephen, Thomas. S.B., U. S.D., 1946; J.D., Harvard U., 1948. Bar: Calif. 1949, Hawaii 1950. Assoc. James P. Blaisdell, Honolulu, 1949-52; ptnr. Moore, Torkildson & Rice and successors, Honolulu, 1955-64; exec. v.p. Hawaii Employers Council, Honolulu, 1964-67; ptnr. Torkildson, Katz, Fonseca, Jaffe, Moore & Hetherington and predecessors, Honolulu, 1967-72, sr. ptnr., 1972-92, of counsel, 1993—. Mem. mgmt. com. Armed Forces YMCA, Honolulu, 1971; treas. Hawaii Republican Com. 1977-83. Served with U.S. Army, 1941-46; lt. col. Res. ret. Mem. ABA, Hawaii Bar Assn. Roman Catholic. Clubs: Oahu Country, Pacific (Honolulu). Labor.

**TORKILDSON, THOMAS MILES,** lawyer; b. Honolulu, Sept. 9, 1963; s. Raymond Maynard and Sharman Elizabeth (Vaughn) T.; m. Sylvia Rebecca De La Paz. BA, Brown U., 1988; JD, Baylor U. Sch. Law, 1992. Bar: Tex 1993. Asoc. Carinhas Chosey & Sullivan, Brownsville, Tex., 1993, The De Anda Law Firm, Laredo, Tex., 1993-95; mng. atty. The Torkildson Law Firm, El Paso, Tex., 1995—; auto safety cons., El Paso, 1995-97. Author: Personal Injuries: Understanding the Legal Aspects, 1997. Mem. ATLA. Avocations: bicycling, skiing, autocross racing. E-mail: triallaw@trial-law.org. General civil litigation, Personal injury, Family and matrimonial. Office: The Torkildson Law Firm 220 Thunderbird Dr Ste 11 El Paso TX 79912-3911

**TORMEY, JOHN JOSEPH, III,** lawyer; b. Nurnberg, Germany, Aug. 18, 1962; came to U.S., 1962; BA, Harvard U., 1984; JD, UCLA, 1987. Bar: N.Y. 1988, Calif. 1988, D.C. 1988, U.S. Dist. Ct. (so. and ea. dists.) N.Y. 1988, Calif. 1989. Assoc. Pryor Cashman Sherman & Flynn, N.Y.C., 1987-90; counsel The Walt Disney Co., N.Y.C., 1990-94; sr. litigation counsel Miramax Films, N.Y.C., 1994-96; atty. pvt. practice, N.Y.C., 1997—. Entertainment, General practice, Intellectual property. Office: 217 E 86th St PMB 221 New York NY 10028-3617

**TORNSTROM, ROBERT ERNEST,** lawyer, oil company executive; b. St. Paul, Jan. 17, 1946; s. Clifford H. and Janet (Hale) T.; m. Betty Jane Hermann, Aug. 5, 1978; children: Carter, Gunnar, Katherine. BA, U. Colo., 1968, JD, 1974; diploma grad. sch. mgmt. exec. program, UCLA, 1990. Bar: Colo. 1974, U.S. Dist. Ct. Colo. 1974, Calif. 1975, U.S. Dist. Ct. (cen. dist.) Calif. 1975. Atty. Union Oil Co. of Calif., Los Angeles, 1974-76, counsel internat. div., 1977-78; regional counsel Union Oil Co. of Calif., Singapore, 1976-77; sr. atty. Occidental Internat. Exploration and Prodn. Co., Bakersfield, Calif., 1978-81, mng. counsel, 1981-85, v.p., assoc. gen. counsel, 1985-88, v.p., regional ops. mgr., 1988-91; pres. Occidental Argentina, Buenos Aires, 1991-93, Occidental of Russia, Moscow, 1993-94; dir. comml. negotiations Occidental Internat., 1994-96; chmn. of bd. Sullivan Petroleum Co., 1997—; bd. dirs., chmn. bd. Parmaneft Joint Venture, Vanyogannef JV, Moscow; bd. dirs. Calif. Land and Cattle Co., King City, 602 Operating Corp.; exec. bd. Cmty. House, Bakersfield; legal cons. Island Creek Coal Co., Lexington, Ky. Served to capt. U.S. Army, 1968-71, Vietnam. Decorated Bronze Star. Recipient Am. Jurisprudence award Bancroft-Whitney Co., 1974; named Eagle Scout, Boy Scouts Am. Mem. Am. Soc. Internat. Law, Am. Corp. Counsel Assn., Soc. Mayflower Descendants, Moscow Country Club, Stockdale Country Club. Republican. Episcopalian. Avocations: skiing, tennis, golf, riding, collecting classic automobiles. Private international, Oil, gas, and mineral, General corporate. Home: 310 Mount Lowe Dr Bakersfield CA 93309-2468 Office: 14800 Sunnybank Ave Bakersfield CA 93312-8702

**TORO, AMALIA MARIA,** lawyer; b. Hartford, Conn., Nov. 6, 1920; d. Frederick and Maria (Casale) T. BA, U. Conn., 1942; JD, Yale U., 1944. Bar: Conn. 1944. Assoc. Wiggin & Dana, New Haven, 1944-46; atty., dir., chief elections div. Office Sec. of State, Conn., 1946-75; judge Ct. Common Pleas State of Conn., 1975; pvt. practice Hartford, Conn., 1975—; alt. pub. mem. Conn. Bd. Mediation and Arbitration, 1996—. Former mem. Ford Found Com. on Voting and Election Systems; mem. State Employees' Retirement Commn., 1956-75, past vice-chmn. Recipient AMITA award in law, 1970, Humanitarian award Columbus Day Celebration Com., 1986. Mem. Greater Hartford Bus. and Profl. Women (pres. 1989-91, Woman of the Yr. award 1969), Conn. Bar Assn. (Merit award 1973), Conn. Assn. Mcpl. Attys. (past pres.), Greater Hartford U. Conn. Alumni Assn. (past pres.). Estate planning, Personal injury, Probate. Office: 234 Pearl St Hartford CT 06103-2113

**TORPEY, SCOTT RAYMOND,** lawyer; b. Detroit, July 4, 1955; s. Raymond George and Carmela Rose (Aquaro) T. BA in English, Wayne State U., 1978; JD, U. Detroit, 1982. Bar: Mich. 1984, D.C. 1985, N.Y. 1990, Ill. 1990, Calif. 1991, U.S. Dist. Ct. (ea. and we. dist.) Mich., U.S. Dist. Ct. (so., we., no. and ea. dists.) N.Y. 1990, U.S. Dist. Ct. (no., cen. and so. dists.) Ill. 1990, U.S. Dist. Ct. (D.C. dist.) 1989, U.S. Dist. Ct. (cen., so., no. and ea. dists.) Calif., 1991, U.S. Tax Ct., U.S. Ct. Appeals (D.C., fed., 2d, 6th, 7th and 9th cirs.), U.S. Supreme Ct. 1988. Assoc. Long & Levit, San Francisco, 1982-83, Keating, Canham & Wells, Detroit, 1983-85; litigation ptnr. Kohl, Secrest, Wardle, Lynch, Clark & Hampton, Farmington Hills, Mich., 1985—. Editor Tax Law Jour., 1981, Corp., Fin. and Bus. Law Jour., 1982. Mem. ABA, Fed. Bar Assn., Lawyer-Pilots Bar Assn., Bar Assn. San Francisco, Mich. State Bar Assn. (chmn. aviation torts com. of aviation law sect. 1992—). Republican. Avocations: sports, music, sports cars. Aviation, Product liability, General civil litigation. Office: Kohl Secrest Wardle Lynch Clark & Hampton 30903 Northwestern Hwy Farmington MI 48334-2556

**TORREGROSSA, JOSEPH ANTHONY,** lawyer; b. Bklyn., Sept. 23, 1944; s. Joseph and Marie (Faraone) T.; m. Ann S. Gormally, July 11, 1970; children—Brennan, Maresa. A.B., Villanova U., 1966, J.D., 1969. Bar: N.Y. 1970, Pa. 1971, U.S. Dist. Ct. (ea. dist.) Pa. 1971, U.S. Ct. Appeals (3d cir.) 1973, U.S. Supreme Ct. 1975. Law Clk. to judge U.S. Dist. Ct. (ea. dist.) Pa., 1969-71; assoc. Morgan, Lewis & Bockius, Phila., 1971-77; ptnr. Morgan, Lewis & Bockius, Phila., 1977-97; appelate mediation dir. U.S. Ct. Appeals, Phila., 1998—; lectr. in field. Mem. Phila. Bar Assn., Pa. Bar Assn., ABA. Federal civil litigation, State civil litigation.

**TORRENS, DANIEL,** lawyer; b. Phila., Oct. 30, 1969. BA, Ariz. State U., 1992; JD, U. Nebr., 1996. Bar: Ariz. 1996, Colo. 1997, U.S. Dist. Ct. Ariz. 1996, U.S. Ct. Appeals (9th cir.) 1997. Assoc. Struckmeyer & Wilson, Phx., 1996-98, Turley, Swan & Childers, Phx., 1998—. Mem. ABA, Ariz. Bar Assn., Colo. Bar Assn., Def. Rsch. Inst., Delta Theta Phi. General civil litigation, Insurance, Personal injury. Office: Turley Swan & Childers 3101 N Central Ave Ste 1300 Phoenix AZ 85012-2656

**TORRES, ERNEST C.,** federal judge; b. 1941. AB, Dartmouth Coll., 1963; JD, Duke U., 1968. Assoc. Hinckley, Allen, Salisbury & Parsons, 1968-74; ptnr. Saunders & Torres, 1974-80; assoc. justice R.I. Superior Ct., 1980-85; asst. v.p. Aetna Life and Casualty, 1985-86; ptnr. Tillinghast, Collins & Graham, 1986-87; judge U.S. Dist. Ct. R.I., Providence, 1988—; pres. East Greenwich (R.I.) Town Coun., 1972-74; state rep. R.I. Ho. of Reps., 1975-80, dep. minority leader, 1977-80. Recipient Disting. Svc. award Jaycees, 1974; named Man of Yr., Prince Henry Soc. R.I., 1988, Prince Henry Soc. Mass., 1995; Alfred P. Sloan scholar Dartmouth Coll. Mem. ABA, ATLA, FBA, R.I. Bar Assn., Jaycees (Dist. Svc. award 1974), Prince Henry Soc. of R.I., Prince Henry Soc. of Mass. Office: US Dist Ct 1 Exch Ter 216 Fed Bldg & Courthouse Providence RI 02903

**TORREY, CLAUDIA OLIVIA,** lawyer; b. Nashville, June 10, 1958; d. Claude Adolphus and Rubye Mayette (Prigmore) T. BA in Econ., Syracuse U., 1980; JD, N.Y. Law Sch., 1985. Bar: N.Y. State 1988. Legal intern Costello, Cooney & Fearon, Syracuse, N.Y., 1979; legal clk. First Am. Corp., Nashville, 1981; legal asst. James I. Meyerson, N.Y.C., 1982-85; jud. law clk. N.Y. State Supreme Ct., N.Y.C., 1985; interim project supr., legal asst. CUNY Ctrl. Office, 1985-86; legal analyst Rosenman & Colin Law Firm, N.Y.C., 1986-87; asst. counsel N.Y. State Legis., Albany, 1988-90; atty., cons. pvt. practice, Nashville, Cookeville, Tenn., 1991—; bd. mem. Children's Corner Day Care Ctr., Albany, N.Y., 1989-90. Ch. rep. FOCUS exec. coun. Westminster Presbyn. Ch., Albany, 1990; v.p. dormitory coun., flr. rep. Syracuse U., 1977-79. Mem. ABA (young lawyers divsn. liaison to ABA forum on health law 1994-96), Internat. Platform Assn., N.Y. State Bar Assn., Alpha Kappa Alpha (treas. Syracuse U. chpt. 1977-78, pres. 1979). Avocations: singing, reading, harp, travel, art. Health, Education and schools, General practice. Home and Office: PO Box 150234 Nashville TN 37215-0234

**TORRUELLA, JUAN R.,** federal judge; b. 1933. BS in Bus. and Fin., U. Pa., 1954; LLB, Boston U., 1957; LLM, U. Va., 1984; MPA, U. P.R., 1984; LLD, St. John's U., 1995. Judge U.S. Dist. Ct. P.R., San Juan, 1974-82, chief judge, 1982-84; judge U.S. Ct. Appeals (1st cir.), San Juan, 1984-94, chief judge, 1994—; former mem. jud. conf. com. on the Adminstrn. of the Fed. Magistrate Sys; mem. jud. conf. exec. com. on Internat. Jud. Reform. Mem. ABA, Fed. Bar Assn., Assn. Labor Rels. Practitioners P.R. and V.I., D.C. Bar Assn., P.R. Bar Assn. Address: EDIF Federal 150 Ave Carlos Chardon San Juan PR 00918-1703*

**TORSHEN, JEROME HAROLD,** lawyer; b. Chgo., Nov. 27, 1929; s. Jack and Lillian (Futterman) T.; m. Kay Pomerance, June 19, 1966; children: Jonathan, Jacqueline. BS, Northwestern U., 1951; JD, Harvard U., 1955. Bar: Ill. 1955, U.S. Dist. Ct. (no. dist.) Ill. 1955, U.S. Ct. Appeals (7th cir.) 1958, (8th cir.) 1961, (9th and D.C. cirs.) 1972, U.S. Supreme Ct. 1972. Assoc. Clausen, Hirsh & Miller, Chgo., 1955-62; pres. Jerome H. Torshen, Ltd., Chgo., 1963-87, Torshen, Schoenfield & Spreyer, Ltd., Chgo., 1987-94, Torshen, Spreyer, Ltd., Chgo., 1994, Torshen, Spreyer & Garmisa, Ltd., Chgo., 1994-97, Torshen, Spreyer, Garmisa & Slobig, Ltd., Chgo., 1997—; spl. asst. atty. gen. Ill., 1965-70; assoc. counsel Spl. Commn. Ill. Supreme Ct., 1969; counsel Ill. Legis. Redistricting Commn., 1971-72; spl. state's atty. Cook County, Ill., 1979-81, 83-86; spl. counsel Met. San. Dist. Greater Chgo., 1977-81, 84-88. Contbr. articles to profl. jours. Counsel Cook County Dem. Cen. Com., Chgo., 1982-87; bd. dirs. Jewish Family and Community Svc., Parents' Coun. Washington U., St. Louis, 1988-92; mem. collectors' group Mus. Contemporary Art; sustaining fellow Art Int. Chgo. Served with U.S. Army, 1951-52. Recipient Torch of Learning award Am. Friends of Hebrew U., 1985, Outstanding Civic Duty award, Union League Club of Chgo., 1967. Fellow Am. Coll. Trial Lawyers; mem. ABA, Chgo. Bar Assn. (commn. on jud. evaluation 1986-90), Bar Assn. 7th Cir. Appellate Lawyers Assn. (founder, pres. 1976-77), Decalogue Soc., Standard Club, Sixty Club of Chgo. Federal civil litigation, State civil litigation, Insurance. Office: 105 W Adams St Ste 3200 Chicago IL 60603-4109

**TOSCANO, OSCAR ERNESTO,** lawyer; b. Ecuador, Jan. 24, 1951; s. Hugo and Maruja (Lopez) T.; children: Marina, Tracy, Oscar Emerson. BA, UCLA, 1975; JD, Loyola U., L.A., 1978. Bar: Calif. 1978, U.S. Dist. Ct. (9th dist.) Calif. 1978. Pvt. practice Glendale, 1978—. Mem. Assn. Trial Lawyers Am., L.A. Trial Lawyers Assn. (bd. govs.), Calif. Trial Lawyers Assn., Los Angeles County Bar, Mex.-Am. Bar Assn., State Bar Calif., Hispanic Alumni Scholarship Found. Avocations: tennis, chess, trial work. Criminal, Family and matrimonial, Insurance. Office: 625 W Broadway Glendale CA 91204-1041

**TOSH, KAREN,** lawyer; b. Marion, Ky., Mar. 24, 1950; d. Enoch and Anna T.; m. Tracey Maclin, July 26, 1996. BA, St. Mary's U., 1992; MS, Murray State U., 1976; JD, U. Louisville, 1980. Bar: Ky. 1981, Ala. 1991, Mass. 1996. Ptnr. Scent & Scent, Paducah, Ky., 1984-92, Sanderson-Tosh, Paducah, 1992-97; counsel family law Hill & Barlow PC, Boston, 1998—. Fellow Am. Acad. Matrimonial Lawyers. Office: Hill & Barlow PC 1 International Pl Boston MA 02110-2602

**TOSTEVIN, BRECK C.,** lawyer; b. Feb. 7, 1961; m. Jana E. Sudkamp, Feb. 12, 1992; 1 child, Keegan. AB, Occidental Coll., 1983; JD, Hastings Coll. Law, 1988. Bar: Calif. 1988, Alaska 1989, U.S. Dist. Ct. Alaska 1989. Legis. aide Congressman Leon Panetta, Washington, 1983-85; intern Calif. Atty. Gen.'s Office, San Francisco, 1988; law clk. Alaska Supreme Ct., Anchorage, 1988-89; asst. atty. gen. Alaska Dept. Law, Anchorage, 1989—. Mem. ABA, Alaska Bar Assn., Anchorage Inn of Ct. Office: Alaska Dept Law 1031 W 4th Ave Ste 200 Anchorage AK 99501-5903

**TOSTI, JEANNE MARIE,** lawyer; b. Chgo., Sept. 6, 1948. BSN cum laude, St. John Coll. Cleve., 1970; MSN, Kent State U., 1985; JD, Cleve. Marshall Coll. Law, 1992. Bar: Ohio 1992, U.S. Dist. Ct. (no. dist.) Ohio 1998. Assoc. atty. Becker & Mishkind L.P.A., Cleve., 1992—. Mem. Assn. Trial Lawyers Am., Ohio Assn. Trial Lawyers, Ohio State Bar Assn., Cleve. Bar Assn. Personal injury. Office: Becker & Mishkind Co LPA 1660 W 2d St Ste 660 Cleveland OH 44113

**TOTH, JOHN MICHAEL,** lawyer; b. Detroit, Feb. 20, 1956; s. John and Joyce Loraine (Axford) T.; m. Lorie Ann Gill, Sept. 25, 1981; children: Jennifer, Jon, Aaron. AB, U. Mich., 1977; JD, Villanova U., 1981. Bar: Mich. 1982, U.S. Dist. Ct. (ea. dist.) Mich. 1982, Ohio 1991. Assoc. Moll, Desenberg & Bayer, Detroit, 1981-86, ptnr., 1987-91; ptnr. Small, Toth, Baldridge and Van Belkum, Bingham Farms, Mich., 1991—. Mem. Mich. State Bar Assn. (character and fitness dist. I 1991-94, standing com. 1994—), Detroit Athletic Club. Personal injury, Insurance, Professional liability. Office: Small Toth Baldridge & Van Belkum 30100 Telegraph Rd Ste 250 Bingham Farms MI 48025-4562

**TOTTEN, R. BART,** lawyer; b. Newport, R.I., June 19, 1963; s. Randolph B. and Nancy S. Totten. BS in Indsl. Engring. with honors, U. Fla., 1986; JD, U. Va., 1989. Atty. Holland & Knight, Miami, Fla., 1989-93, Adler Pollock & Sheehan P.C., Providence, 1993—. Mem. adv. bd. dirs. Big Bros. of R.I., Providence, 1993—. General civil litigation, Computer. Office: Adler Pollock & Sheehan 2300 Bank of Boston Plz Providence RI 02903

**TOUBY, KATHLEEN ANITA,** lawyer; b. Miami Beach, Fla., Feb. 20, 1943; s. Harry and Kathleen Rebecca (Hamper) T.; m. Joseph Thomas Woodward; children: Mark Andrew, Judson David Touby. BS in Nursing, U. Fla., 1965, MRC in Rehab. Counseling, 1967; JD with honors, Nova U., 1977. Bar: Fla. 1978, D.C. 1978. Counselor, Jewish Vocat. Svc., Chgo., 1967-68; rehab. counselor Fla. Dept. Vocat. Rehab., Miami, 1968-70; spl. asst., asst. U.S. atty. U.S. Dept. Justice, Miami, 1978-80; assoc. firm Pyszka & Kessler, P.A., Miami, 1980-83; ptnr. firm Touby & Smith, P.A., Miami, Fla., 1983-89, Touby, Smith, DeMahy and Drake P.A., 1989-94, Touby & Woodward, P.A., 1994—; chmn. adv. exec. bd. Paralegal Edn. program Barry U., 1986-87; lectr. Food and Drug Law Inst., 1987-89, 91; lectr. environ. law Exec. Enterprises, 1987-88; lectr. trial techniques, Hispanic Nat. Bar Assn., St. Thomas Law Sch.; adj. prof. product liability Can. Govt., U.S. Trade and Mktg. Dept., 1989-95. Co-author (with Smith and O'Reilly) The Environmental Litigation Deskbook, 1989; contbr. chpts. to Trial Strategies in American Inns of Ct. publ. Fla. Rules of Civil Procedure, 1997; contbr. articles to profl. jours.; Mem. ABA, Am. Inns of Ct., pres., 1998— (pres.-elect St. Thomas Law Sch. chpt. 1997-98, pres. 1998—), Dade County Bar Assn., Fed. Bar Assn. (bd. dirs. 1989—, v.p. 1991-92, pres.-elect So. Fla. chpt. 1992-93, pres. 1993-94), Dade County Bar Assn. (legal aid, pub. svcs. com. 1988), Phi Delta Phi (province pres. 1982-85, bd. dirs. 1985-87). Roman Catholic. General civil litigation, Personal injury, Insurance. Home: 450 Sabal Palm Rd Miami FL 33137-3352 Office: Touby & Woodward PA 250 Bird Rd Ste 308 Miami FL 33146-1424

**TOUBY, RICHARD,** lawyer; b. Sioux City, Iowa, Nov. 17, 1924; s. Louis and Rebecca (Keck) T.; m. Marion Lascher, Aug. 6, 1949; children: Jill Diane, Kim Paula. LLB, U. Miami, 1948; LLM, Duke U., 1950. Bar: Fla. 1948. Faculty U. Miami, Coral Gables, Fla., 1948-63; mem. 8th Air Force Meml. Assn., 305 Bomb Group (H) Assn., 1994—. 1st Lt. USAF, 1943-45. General corporate, General practice, Contracts commercial. Office: 19 W Flagler St Ste 907 Miami FL 33130-4407

**TOUCHY, DEBORAH K. P.,** lawyer, accountant; b. Pasadena, Tex., Dec. 9, 1957; d. Donald Carl and Bobbie Jo (Jackson) Putzka; m. Harry Roy Touchy, Jr., Feb. 23, 1980. BBA, Baylor U., 1979; JD, U. Houston, 1988. Bar: Tex. 1989; CPA, Tex.; cert. in estate planning and probate law Tex. Bd. Legal Specialization. Sr. mgr. tax KMPG Peat Marwick, Houston, 1980-86; assoc. Fizer Beck Webster & Bentley, Houston, 1989-90; pvt. practice law Houston, 1990—; chmn. spl. events Jr. League Houston, 1997-98. Editor Houston Law Rev., 1988-89. Chmn. ticket sales incentives Chi Omega, Houston, 1985; active ticket sales Mus. Fine Arts, Houston, 1984; facilities chmn. Woodland Trails West Civic Orgn., Houston, 1982-83; pres. Women

Attys. in Tax & Probate, 1994-95. Recipient Outstanding Alumi award Beta Alpha Psi, 1997. Mem. ABA (estate-probate sect. 1989—, vice chmn. commn. property com. 1994—), AICPA (taxation sect., estate and gift tax com. 1992-95, 1998—), Tex. Soc. CPAs (bd. dirs. 1995—, chmn. tax inst. com. 1996-97, estate planning com. 1990-94, 96—), Houston Chpt. CPAs (chmn. taxpayer edn. 1985-86, chmn. membership com. 1992-93, v.p. 1993-94, 96-97, chmn. tax forums 1994-95, long range planning com. 1995-96, treas.-elect 1997-98, chmn. leadership devel. 1997-98, treas. 1998-99, chmn. annual charity event 1999—, bd. dirs. 1999—), Houston Bar Assn. (estate-probate sect. 1989—), State Bar Tex. (estate-probate sect. 1989—, mem. elder law com. 1991-97), Houston Estate and Fin. Forum, Baylor U. Women's Assn. (treas. 1993-94, chmn. fin. com. 1994-95, parliamentarian 1995-96, sec. 1996-97, pres. 1997-98), Chief Justice-Advocates, Tex. Bd. Legal Specializations (cert. estate planning, probate law 1994), Order of Coif, Omicron Delta Kappa, Phi Delta Phi, Beta Alpha Psi (Outstanding Alumni 1997). Estate planning, Probate, Taxation, general. Office: 2932 Plumb St Houston TX 77005-3058

**TOUHY, JOHN M.,** lawyer; b. Chgo., Apr. 30, 1955; s. John Andrew and Enid L. T.; m. Judy O'Malley; children: Andrew, Matthew, Evan, Meredith. BA, U. Chgo., 1977; JD, NYU Sch. Law, 1980. Bar: Ill. 1980, U.S. Dist. Ct. (no. dist.) Ill. 1983, U.S. Ct. Appeals (7th cir.) 1981. Assoc. Mayer, Brown & Platt, Chgo., 1980-87; ptnr., 1987—. Bd. dirs. Lawyer's Assistance Program. Mem. ABA, Chgo. Bar Assn., Chgo. Legal Club, Chgo. Lincoln Inns Ct., Chgo. Delta Upsilon Alumni Assn. General practice, Libel, Contracts commercial. Office: Mayer Brown & Platt 190 S Lasalle St Ste 3100 Chicago IL 60603-3441

**TOUMEY, DONALD JOSEPH,** lawyer; b. Bronxville, N.Y., Apr. 22, 1956; s. Hubert John and Dorothy Agnes Toumey. BA, Williams Coll., 1978; JD, Yale U., 1981. Bar: N.Y. 1982, D.C. 1985, U.S. Supreme Ct. 1986. Law clk. to judge U.S. Ct Appeals (2d cir.), N.Y.C., 1981-82; spl. asst. to gen. counsel U.S. Dept. Treasury, Washington, 1982-85; assoc. Sullivan & Cromwell, N.Y.C., 1985-90; ptnr., 1990—. Republican. Banking, Securities, Mergers and acquisitions. Home: 250 E 54th St New York NY 10022-4810 Office: Sullivan & Cromwell 125 Broad St New York NY 10004-2489

**TOUPS, MITCHELL A.,** lawyer; b. Beaumont, Tex., June 7, 1957; s. George A. and Peggy (Meents) T.; m. Julie Perkins, July 23, 1983. BBA in fin., Lamar U., 1980; JD, Tex. Tech U., 1982. Bar: Tex. 1983, U.S. Dist. Ct. (ea. dist.) Tex., (so. dist.) Tex., U.S. Ct. Appeals (5th cir.), U.S. Supreme Ct. Ptnr. Weller, Green, McGown & Toups, Beaumont, Tex., 1983—. George Mahan scholar, Tex. Tech U., 1982. Mem. ABA, ATLA, Tex. Bar Assn., Jefferson County Bar Assn., Tex. Trial Lawyers Assn., Order of the Coif, Pi Kappa Alpha, (Powers award 1978), Phi Kappa Phi. Episcopalian. Office: Weller Treen McGown & Toups PO Box 350 Beaumont TX 77704-0350

**TOUS, RAUL F.,** lawyer; b. Havana, Cuba, 1935; came to U.S., 1960; m. Adriana Zaldivar, Feb. 4, 1961; 1 child, Ana Maria Tous Abi Steiman. LLD, U. Santo Tomas, Villanueva, Cuba, 1959, M Econs., 1960; postgrad., Rutgers U., 1970, N.Y. Law Sch., 1971. Bar: N.J. Internat. export credit mgr. Reynolds Metals, Richmond, Va., 1960-62; spl. agt. Prudential Ins. Co., Springfield, N.J., 1962-65; export credit mgr. Quaker Oats Co., N.Y.C., 1965-68; legal and compliance atty. E.I. DuPont, N.Y.C., 1968-71; ptnr. D'Agostino, Breiktopf & Tous, Newark, 1971-72; pvt. practice, Newark, 1972-96; ptnr. Tous & Perez, P.A., Newark, 1996—. Immigration, naturalization, and customs, Family and matrimonial, Real property. Office: Tous & Perez PA 838 Broad St Newark NJ 07102-2710

**TOUSEY, ROBERT RYAN,** lawyer; b. L.I., N.Y., May 31, 1958; s. Fred Lester and Alice Marie (Ryan) T.; m. Betty Grivakis, Nov. 20, 1988 (div. June 1994); children: Christopher, Stephanie. BS, U. Md., 1984; JD, U. Balt., 1989. Bar: Md. 1989, U.S. Dist. Ct. Md. 1990, U.S. Ct. Appeals (4th cir.) 1991, U.S. Tax Ct. 1991, U.S. Supreme Ct. 1992. Sr. tax cons. Ernst & Young, Balt., 1989-91; trial atty. Owens, Robertson & Parler, Balt., 1991-94, Law Office of Stephen L. Miles, Balt., 1994—; law sch. rep. ABA Law Student Divsn., Balt., 1987-88. Sr. editor U. Balt. Law Forum, 1986 (Exceptional Svc. award 1988). Past mem. Howard County Drug Abuse Adv. Bd., Ellicott City, Md., 1993-95; Congl.candidate, 3d Dist. Md., 1994; active, religious edn. tchr., team capt. Heritage for Hope campaign St. Augustine's Roman Cath. Ch.; pres. Mid-Atlantic regional coun. Parents Without Ptnrs.; Md. state pub. policy chair Am. Cancer Soc. Sgt. USAF, 1978-82. Recipient Outstanding Svc. award County Exec. Ecker, Ellicott City, 1995, Spl. Congl. Recognition cert., 1997. Mem. Md. State Bar Assn., Am. Cancer Soc. (divsn. dir., pub. policy chair, past pres. Howard County unit 1990-92), Parents Without Ptnrs. (Mid Atlantic Regional coun. pres.). Republican. Avocations: public service, baseball, movies, travel. Personal injury, Criminal, Workers' compensation. Home: 3133 Normandy Woods Dr Apt H Ellicott City MD 21043-4585 Office: 1130 N Charles St Baltimore MD 21201-5506

**TOUSLEY, RUSSELL FREDERICK,** lawyer; b. New Haven, Nov. 19, 1938; s. Russell F. and Della (Ermer) T.; m. Sarah Morford, July 23, 1963; children: Ellen Elizabeth, Kenneth Morford. BA cum laude, Yale Coll., 1960; JD, U. Wash., 1967. Bar: Wash. 1967. Assoc. Davis Wright, Seattle, 1967-69; v.p. Safecare Co., Inc., Seattle, 1969-78, Winmar Co., Inc., Seattle, 1977-78; ptnr. Tousley Brain, PLLC, Seattle, 1978—. Trustee Seattle Opera Assn., 1980—, pres., chmn. bd., 1985-87; trustee Seattle Chamber Music Festival, 1990-93; moderator Plymouth Congl. Ch., Seattle, 1975-77, 83-85, trustee, 1969-93, adminstrn., property and fin. bd., 1999—. Lt. (j.g.) USN, 1960-64. Mem. ABA, Wash. State Bar Assn., Seattle-King County Bar Assn., Internat. Coun. Shopping Ctrs. (assoc.), Rainier Club, Seattle Tennis Club, Rotary. Avocations: opera, reading, collecting mint U.S. regular issue stamps. E-mail: rftousley@tousley.com. Real property, Finance, Private international. Office: Tousley Brain PLLC Key Tower 56th Flr 700 5th Ave Ste 5600 Seattle WA 98104-5056

**TOW, L. MICHELLE,** lawyer; b. San Diego, May 31, 1960; m. Marvin Tow, Sept. 4, 1988. BA, Loretto Heights Coll., Denver, 1982; JD, Nat. U. Sch. Law, San Diego, 1992. Bar: Calif. 1993, U.S. Dist. Ct. (so. dist.) Calif. 1993, U.S. Ct. Appeals (9th cir.). Judicial extern Calif. Ct. Appeals (4th dist.), San Diego, 1992; law clk. Law Office of Kendall Squires, San Diego, 1992-93; pvt. practice San Diego, 1993—; instr. Kelsey-Jenny Coll., San Diego, 1997. Editor exec. lead articles Nat. U. Law Rev., 1993. Vol. San Diego Sister City Soc., 1992; pro bono atty., 1993—. Recipient Am. Jurisprudence award Lawyers Co-op Publishing, 1990-92; disting. grad. Nat. U. Sch. Law, 1992. Mem. Calif. Bar Assn., San Diego Bar Assn., San Diego Employer's Assn., Delta Theta Phi. Avocations: reading, politics, swimming. Consumer commercial, Contracts commercial, Landlord-tenant. Office: 5030 Camino De La Siesta San Diego CA 92108-3119

**TOWERY, CURTIS KENT,** judge; b. Hugoton, Kans., Jan. 29, 1954; s. Clyde D. and Jo June (Curtis) T. BA, Trinity U., 1976; JD, U. Okla., 1979; LLM in Taxation, Boston U., 1989. Mem. Curtis & Blanton, Pauls Valley, Okla., 1980-81; lawyer land and legal dept. Trigg Drilling Co., Oklahoma City, 1981-82; adminstrv. law judge Okla. Corp. Commn., Oklahoma City, 1982-85; counsel Curtis & Blanton, Pauls Valley, Okla., 1985-88; adminstrv. law judge Okla. Dept. Mines, Oklahoma City, 1985-88, assoc. gen. counsel, 1989-92; contracts and purchasing adminstr., atty. Okla. Turnpike Authority, Oklahoma City, 1992-93; asst. gen. counsel Okla. Corp. Commn., 1993-97; spl. judge City of Oklahoma City, 1997—; adminstrv. law judge Okla. Dept. of Labor, 1998; v.p., trust officer Bank One Trust, Oklahoma City, 1998—; bd. dirs. First Nat. Bank Pauls Valley, 1983-88. Assoc. bd. Okla. Mus. Art, 1985-88, Okla. Symphony Orch., 1987-92; assoc. bd. Ballet Okla., 1987-92, sec., 1990-91, v.p., 1988-89; mem. Oklahoma City Estate Planning Coun., Ruth Bader Ginsburg Am. Inn of Ct., 1999—. Mem. ABA, Tex. Bar Assn., Okla. Bar Assn., Tex. Bar Assn., Am. Assn. Petroleum Landmen, Internat. Assn. Energy Economists, Men's Dinner Club, Faculty House, Rotary, Elks, Phi Alpha Delta, Sigma Nu. Democrat. Presbyterian. Avocations: flying, golf, traveling, investment analysis. Home: PO Box 14891 Oklahoma City OK 73113-0891 Office: 1200 NW 63d St Ste 200 Oklahoma City OK 73116

**TOWERY, JAMES E.,** lawyer; b. Los Alamos, N.Mex., July 12, 1948; s. Lawson E. and Irma (Van Apeldorn) T.; m. Kathryn K. Meier, July 20, 1991; 1 child, Mark J. BA, Princeton U., 1973; JD, Emory U., 1976. Assoc. Morgan Beauzay Hammer, San Jose, Calif., 1977-79; ptnr. Morgan & Towery, San Jose, Calif., 1979-89; assoc. Hoge Fenton Jones & Appel, San Jose, Calif., 1989-90, ptnr., 1990—. Chmn. bd. trustees Alexian Bros. Hosp., San Jose, Calif., 1995-98. Mem. ABA (ho. of dels. 1989-98, standing com. client protection 1996—, chair 1998-00), State Bar Calif. (v.p. and chair discipline com. 1994-95, bd. govs. 1992-96, pres. 1995-96, presiding arbitrator, fee arbitration program 1990-92), Santa Clara County Bar Assn. (counsel 1984-85, treas. 1987, pres. 1989). Professional liability, Health, Personal injury. Office: Hoge Fenton Jones 60 S Market St San Jose CA 95113-2351

**TOWEY, EDWARD ANDREW,** lawyer; b. Rochester, Minn., Oct. 14, 1945; s. Andrew Edward T. and Julia F. Nelson; m. Anne K. Weber, May 24, 1975; children: Brigit Kathleen, Edward Andrew Jr., Patricia Anne. BS in Bus., U. Minn., 1968; JD, Valparaiso U., 1973. Bar: Minn. 1973, U.S. Dist. Ct. 1974, U.S. Ct. Appeals 1975. Assoc. Ulvin, Sullivan & Towey, St. Paul, 1973-80, Towey and Assocs., St. Paul, 1980-85; gen. counsel, sec. Hammel, Green and Abrahamson, Inc., Mpls., 1985—; pres. Greenspan, Inc., Mpls., 1990—; lectr. AIA, Minn., 1990—. Contbr. article to profl. jour. Pres. bd. dirs. Youth Svc. Bur., St. Paul, 1980-82, Midway YMCA, St. Paul, 1982-84. Sgt. U.S. Army, 1968-70, Vietnam. Mem. ABA, Minn. State Bar Asssn., Hennepin County Bar Assn. Construction, Professional liability, General corporate. Office: Hammel Green and Abrahamson 1201 Harmon Pl Minneapolis MN 55403-1920

**TOWNS, WILLIAM ROY,** lawyer; b. Houston, Nov. 19, 1952; s. Wilbur and Doris Rollins Towns; m. Jamie L. Lewis, Aug. 19, 1979; children; Graham C., Sienna L. BA in Govt., U. Tex., Austin, 1976; JD cum laude, U. Houston, 1980. Bar: Tex. 1980, U.S. Dist. Ct. (so. dist.) Tex. 1980, U.S. Ct. Appeals (7th cir.) 1982. Law clk. U.S. Dist. Ct. (so. dist.), Galveston, Tex., 1980-82; assoc. Royston, Rayzor, Vickery & Williams, Houston, 1982-87, ptnr., 1987—; adj. prof. U. Houston Law Ctr., 1998—. Contbr. articles to profl. jours. Mem. Houston Bar Assn., Maritime Law assn., Southeast Admiralty Law Assn., Garland Walker Am. Inn of Ct. Avocations: music, reading, golf, baseball. Toxic tort, General civil litigation, Health. Office: Royston Rayzor Vickery & Williams 600 Travis St Ste 2200 Houston TX 77002-2986

**TOWNSEND, BRIAN DOUGLAS,** paralegal; b. Tokyo, Sept. 22, 1961; s. Thomas and Juanita Evora (Sanford) T.; m. Gloria Ann Wigfall, Aug. 23, 1986; children: Brian D. Jr., Brianna A. BA in Criminology, U. Md., 1983. Legal aide Kirkland & Ellis, Washington, 1984-85; legal asst. to mng. clk. Cadwalader, Wickersham & Taft, Washington, 1985-87; paralegal specialist, Office of Chief Counsel U.S. Dept. Transp. Maritime Adminstrn., Washington, 1987-90, U.S. Dept. Treasury, IRS, Washington, 1990-92; litigation support specialist U.S. Dept. Justice, Tax Divsn., Washington, 1992-93; paralegal specialist Resolution Trust Corp., Washington, 1993-95, FDIC, Washington, 1996-98, U.S. Dept. Treasury, OIG, Washington, 1998-99; program specialist FOIA/PA U.S. Dept. Treasury, OFAC, Washington, 1999—. Avocations: bowling, fishing, swimming, chess, football. Office: OFAC US Dept Treasury 1500 Pennsylvania Ave NW Washington DC 20220-0001

**TOWNSEND, BYRON EDWIN,** lawyer; b. Louisville, Feb. 27, 1956; s. Julius Charles III and Jeryl Townsend; m. Vicki L. Stolberg, Apr. 4, 1987. BA, U. Fla., 1977, JD, 1980. Bar: Fla. 1981, U.S. Dist. Ct. (mid. dist.) Fla. 1985; bd. cert. Fla. Bar Worker's Compensation. Assoc. Blake & Assocs., Tampa, Fla., 1982-84; staff counsel Aetna Casualty & Surety Co., Tampa, 1984-87; pvt. practice Tampa, 1987-90; ptnr. Barrs, Willamson, Stolberg Townsend Gonzalez, P.A., 1990—. Mem. ABA, Fla. Bar Assn., Hillsborough County Bar Assn. (bar workers compensation sect., trial lawyers sect.), Assn. Trial Lawyers Am., Assn. Fla. Trial Lawyers. Avocations: volleyball, tennis, stamp collecting. Workers' compensation, Personal injury, Insurance. Home: 248 Blanca Ave Tampa FL 33606-3328 Office: 2503 W Swann Ave Tampa FL 33609-4017

**TOWNSEND, JOHN FREDERICK, JR.,** lawyer; b. Indpls., June 19, 1942; s. John Frederick and Mary (Later) T.; m. Sue C. Townsend, Sept. 4, 1970; children: John Frederick III, Carol Ann. BA, U. Mich., 1964; JD, Harvard U., 1967. Bar: Ind. 1967, U.S. Dist. Ct. (so. dist.) Ind. 1967, U.S. Ct. Appeals (7th cir.) 1969. Ptnr. Townsend & Montross (and predecessor firm), Indpls., 1967—. Fellow Am. Coll. Trial Lawyers, Ind. Coll. Trial Lawyers (pres. 1982-83); mem. Assn. Trial Layers Am. (bd. govs. 1988-91), Phi Beta Kappa, Phi Kappa Phi. Avocations: golf, music, water sports. Personal injury, Product liability, Insurance. Office: 230 E Ohio St Indianapolis IN 46204-2160

**TOWNSEND, JOHN MICHAEL,** lawyer; b. West Point, N.Y., Mar. 21, 1947; s. John D. and Vera (Nachman) T.; m. Frances M. Fragos, Oct. 8, 1994; 1 child, James E. BA, Yale U., 1968, JD, 1971. Bar: N.Y. 1972, U.S. Dist. Ct. (so. and ea. dists.) N.Y. 1975, U.S. Ct. Appeals (2nd cir.) 1975, U.S. Supreme Ct. 1975, U.S. Ct. Appeals (8th cir.) 1982, U.S. Ct. Appeals (7th and 10th cirs.) 1986, D.C. 1990, U.S. Dist. Ct. D.C. 1990, U.S. Ct. Appeals (D.C. cir.) 1990, U.S. Ct. Appeals (4th cir.) 1991. Assoc. Hughes Hubbard & Reed, LLP, N.Y.C., 1971-73, 75-80, ptnr., 1980—; assoc. Hughes Hubbard & Reed, Paris, 1973-74; arbitrator U.S. Dist. Ct. (ea. dist.) N.Y., Am. Arbitration Assn., bd. dirs., exec. com.; trustee U.S. Coun. Internat. Bus. Editl. bd. ADR Currents. 1st lt. USAR, 1971-75. Mem. ABA, Am. Law Inst., Internat. Bar Assn., Assn. Bar City N.Y., Union Internat. des Avocats, Univ. Club, Yale Club (N.Y.C.), Yale Law Sch. Assn. (exec. com.). Democrat. Episcopalian. Fax: (202) 721-4646. Antitrust, Alternative dispute resolution, Private international. Office: Hughes Hubbard & Reed LLP 1775 I St NW Washington DC 20006-2402

**TOWNSEND, WILLIAM JACKSON,** lawyer; b. Grayson, Ky., June 4, 1932; s. Robert Glenn and Lois Juanita (Jackson) T. BS, Wake Forest U., 1954; Student U. Ky., 1957, U. Louisville, 1958, U. N.C., 1960. Bar: N.C. 1965. Claims adjuster State Farm Ins. Co., 1963; sole practice, Fayetteville, N.C., 1965—; pub. adminstr. Robeson County, N.C., 1966; dir., treas. Colonial Foods, Inc., St. Paul, N.C., 1959—; tax atty. City of Lumberton, 1966-67 . Served as 1st lt. U.S. Army, 1954-56. Mem. N.C. Bar Assn., N.C. State Bar, Cumberland County Bar Assn., N.C. Bar Assn., Scabbard and Blade (pres.), Delta Theta Phi. Presbyterian. Club: Kiwanis (treas. Fayetteville 1973-82). Personal injury, Family and matrimonial, General corporate. Office: PO Box 584 2109 Elvira St Apt 806 Fayetteville NC 28303-4867

**TOWNSLEY, TODD ALAN,** lawyer; b. Bloomington, Ind., Mar. 25, 1966; s. Kenneth Raymond and Wilma Irene Townsley; m. Elizabeth Anne Arrington, Feb. 13, 1993; children: Justin Morales, Lex Alan. BA, Ind. U., 1988; JD, Harvard U., 1991. Bar: U.S. Dist. Ct. (mid. dist.) La. 1992. Assoc. Cox, Cox, Townsley & Fowler, Lakes Charles, La., 1991-94; ptnr. The Townsley Law Firm, Lakes Charles, La., 1995—. Editor Harvard Jour. Law and Pub. Policy, 1990-91. Coach Little League Baseball, Lake Charles, La., 1994—. Mem. ATLA, La. Trial Lawyers Assn., S.W. La. Bar Assn. Methodist. Personal injury. Office: The Townsley Law Firm 3102 Enterprise Blvd Lake Charles LA 70601-8722

**TRABARIS, DOUGLAS WILLIAM,** lawyer; b. Oak Park, Ill., Apr. 8, 1959; s. George Peter and Mimi (Karras) T.; m. Valerie Ellen Keys, Feb. 14, 1988. BA, U. Ill., 1981; JD, ITT/Chgo. Kent, 1984. Bar: Ill. 1985, Ohio 1991. Special asst. atty. gen. Ill. Commerce Commn., Chgo., 1985-88, adminstrv. law judge, 1988-89; atty. MCI Telecommunications Corp., Chgo., 1989-90; sr. atty., 1990-94; regional atty. TCG, 1995-98; sr. atty. AT&T Corp., 1998—; pres. Nivek Corp. Chgo., 1987—. Treas. Hellenic Profl. Soc., Chgo., 1986-87, v.p., 1987-88. Mem. Am. Hellenic Inst., Ill. Bar, Ohio Bar. Greek Orthodox. Avocation: skiing. Home: 321 Woodlawn Ave Glencoe IL 60022-2137 Office: AT&T Corp 222 W Adams St Ste 1500 Chicago IL 60606-5307

**TRACHSEL, WILLIAM HENRY,** corporate lawyer; b. El Paso, Tex., Apr. 20, 1943. BS in Aerospace Engring., U. Fla., 1965; JD, U. Conn., 1971. Bar: Conn. 1971. With United Tech. Corp., Hartford, Conn., 1965-93, v.p., sec. and dep. gen. counsel, 1993-98, sr. v.p., gen. counsel, sec., 1998—. Mem. ABA, Am. Corp. Counsel Assn. Office: United Tech Corp United Tech Bldg Hartford CT 06101

**TRACHTENBERG, JUDITH,** lawyer, educator; b. Newark, May 21, 1949; d. Bertram and Estelle (Meyers) T. Diplôme, McGill U., Montreal, Que., Can., 1970; BA in Math. and French, Rutgers U., 1971; MAT in French, Ind. U., 1973, JD, 1978. Bar: Ind. 1978, N.J. 1985, Pa., 1985. Various tchg. positions, 1973-76; assoc. Montgomery, Elsner, & Pardieck, Seymour, Ind., 1978-80; pvt. practice Columbus, Ind., 1980-82; mng. atty. Women's Legal Clinic, South Bend, Ind., 1982-84; v.p. Ctr. for Non-Profit Corps., Princeton, N.J., 1985-91; instr. Fairleigh Dickinson U. and Seton Hall U., Madison and South Orange, N.J., 1990—; pvt. practice Roosevelt, N.J., 1991—; cons. Ctr. for Non-Profit Corps., North Brunswick, 1992—. Editor: (book chpt.) Bender's Federal Tax Service, 1992; mem. editl. bd. Non-Profit Sector Resource Institute, 1994—. Mem. charter class Leadership N.J., New Brunswick, 1986-87; sec., trustee Roosevelt Arts Project, 1988—; chair, trustee Mercer St. Friends Ctr., Trenton, N.J., 1991-97; trustee Storytelling Arts, 1998—; sec., treas. Friends Ctr. Fund, 1998—; mem. numerous charitable orgns. Recipient Equal Justice medal Legal Svcs. of N.J., 1995. Fax: (609) 448-4676. Office: PO Box 132 27 N Rochdale Ave Roosevelt NJ 08555

**TRACHTMAN, JERRY H.,** lawyer; b. Phila., Aug. 10, 1945. BSEE, Pa. State U., 1967; JD, U. Fla., 1976. Bar: Fla. 1976, U.S. Dist. Ct. (mid. dist.) Fla. 1978, U.S. Supreme Ct. 1980, U.S. Ct. Appeals (11th cir.) 1989; cert. aviation law. Elec. engr. N.Am. Aviation, Columbus, Ohio, 1967-68; Apollo spacecraft systems engr. N.Am. Aviation, Kennedy Space Ctr., Fla., 1968-71; Skylab project engr. Martin Marietta, Kennedy Space Ctr., 1971-74; pvt. practice Satellite Beach, Fla., 1976-80; atty., mng. ptnr. Trachtman and Henderson, P.A., Melbourne, Fla., 1980—; adj. prof. aviation law Fla. Inst. Tech., Melbourne, 1983-90; mem. adv. bd. Kaiser Coll., Melbourne, 1994—. Recipient Apollo achievement award NASA. Mem. ATLA, Fla. Bar Assn. (chmn. aviation law com. 1995, vice chmn. 1993-95), Lawyer-Pilots Bar Assn., NTSB Bar Assn. (founder 1984—), Acad. Fla. Trial Lawyers. Aviation, Personal injury, State civil litigation. Office: 1990 W New Haven Ave Ste 201 Melbourne FL 32904-3923

**TRACI, DONALD PHILIP,** retired lawyer; b. Cleve., Mar. 13, 1927; m. Lillian Traci Calafiore; 11 children. BS cum laude, Coll. of the Holy Cross, Worcester, Mass., 1950; JD magna cum laude, Cleve. State U., 1955; LLD (hon.), U. Urbino, Italy, 1989. Bar: Ohio 1955, U.S. Dist. Ct. (no. and so. dists.) Ohio 1955, U.S. Ct. Appeals (3d, 6th and 7th cirs.), U.S. Dist. Ct. (we. and ea. dists.) Pa., U.S. Supreme Ct. 1965. Ptnr. Spangenberg, Shibley, Traci, Lancione & Liber, Cleve., 1955-94; ret., 1994—; lectr. York U., Toronto, Ont., Can., Case Western Res. U., Cleve. Marshall Law Sch., U. Mich., Akron U., U. Cin., Ohio No. U., Harvard U. Trustee Cath. Charities Diocese of Cleve., past pres. Bd. Cath. Edn.; former chmn. bd. regents St. Ignatius H.S., Cleve.; mem. pres.'s coun. Coll. of Holy Cross; Eucharist min. St. Rose of Lima Ch. With USN, 1945-46. Fellow Am. Coll. Trial Lawyers, Internat. Acad. Trial Lawyers (past pres.), Am. Bd. Trial Advocacy; mem. ABA, ATLA (trustee Lambert Chair Found., lectr. trial practice), Ohio State Bar Assn. (lectr. trial practice), Ohio Acad. Trial Lawyers (past chmn. rules seminar, lectr. trial practice), Cuyahoga County Bar Assn. (lectr. trial practice), Cleve. Acad. Trial Lawyers (lectr. trial practice), Trial Lawyers for Pub. Justice (sustaining founder), Cleve. Bar Assn. (chmn. Advocacy Inst., trustee, CLE com., jud. selection com., spl. justice ctr. com., fed. ct., common pleas ct. and ct. appeals com., pres. 1986), Jud. Conf. U.S. 6th Cir. Ct. (life), Jud. Conf. 8th Jud. Dist. Ohio life), Knights of Malta, Knights of Holu Sepulchre of Jerusalem, Delta Theta Phi. Personal injury, Federal civil litigation, General civil litigation. Home: 12700 Lake Ave Apt 505 Lakewood OH 44107-1547 Winter Address: 5760 Midnight Pass Rd Apt 210D Sarasota FL 34242-3025

**TRACT, MARC MITCHELL,** lawyer; b. N.Y.C., Sept. 20, 1959; s. Harold Michael and Natalie Ann (Meyerowitz) T.; m. Sharon Beth Widrow; children: Melissa Hope, Harrison Michael, Sarah Michelle. BA in Biology, Ithaca Coll., 1981; JD, Pepperdine U., 1984. Bar: N.Y. 1985, N.J. 1985, D.C. 1986. Assoc. Kroll & Tract, N.Y.C., 1985-90, ptnr., 1990-94; ptnr. Rosenman & Colin LLP, N.Y.C., 1994—; bd. dirs. Sorema N.Am. Reinsurance Co., N.Y.C., Navigators Group Inc., N.Y.C., Chatham Reinsurance Corp., San Francisco, C.A., AXA Nordstern Art Ins. Corp. Am., N.Y.C., Fortress Ins. Co., Rosemont, Ill., N.Y.C., Oriska Corp., Oriskany, N.Y. Mem. ABA, Assn. of Bar of City of N.Y., N.Y. State Bar Assn., N.J. State Bar Assn., N.Y. County Lawyers Assn., Am. Coun. Germany, Old Westbury Golf and Country Club, Met. Club, Econ. Club N.Y. Republican. Insurance, General corporate, Mergers and acquisitions. Office: Rosenman & Colin LLP 575 Madison Ave Fl 11 New York NY 10022-2511

**TRACTENBERG, CRAIG R.,** lawyer; b. Phila., Dec. 5, 1956; s. Jerome and Diane (Epstein) T.; m. Anna P. McDonald, June 9, 1981; children: David, Jeremy. BA, La Salle Coll., Phila., 1979; JD, Temple U., 1981. Bar: Pa. 1981, N.J. 1983, U.S. Dist. Ct. (ea. dist.) Pa. 1981, U.S. Dist. Ct. N.J. 1983, U.S. Ct. Appeals (2d cir.) 1983, U.S. Ct. Appeals (3rd cir.) 1990, U.S. Supreme Ct. 1987. Assoc. Abraham, Pressman & Bauer, P.C., Phila., 1981-87, ptnr., 1987-97; shareholder Buchanan Ingersoll, Profl. Corp., Phila., 1998—; bd. dirs. Rita's Water Ice Franchising, Inc. Contbg. editor Franchise Law Quar., Franchise Law Digest, U. Mich. Jour. Law Rev., Franchise Update, Sum., 1991; contbr. articles to law jours. and profl. publs. Bd. dirs. Har Zion Temple, Penn Valley, Pa., 1988—, Friends of ALS, 1989. Mem. ABA (faculty forum com. on franchising 1989), Pa. Bar Assn. (chmn. com. on franchising), Phila. Bar Assn., N.J. Bar Assn. (com. on fundraising), Internat. Franchise Assn., Rotary (pres. Bryn Mawr, Pa. chpt. 1989),. Republican. Avocations: running, golf, electronics. Franchising, Contracts commercial, Bankruptcy. Home: 249 Ithan Creek Rd Villanova PA 19085-1339 Office: Buchanan Ingersoll Profl Corp 1835 Market St Fl 14 Philadelphia PA 19103-2968

**TRACY, BARBARA MARIE,** lawyer; b. Mpls., Oct. 13, 1945; d. Thomas A. and Ruth C. (Roby) T. BA, U. Minn., 1971; JD, U. Okla., 1980. Bar: Okla. 1980, U.S. Dist. Ct. (we. dist.) Okla. 1980, U.S. Dist. Ct. (no. dist.) Tex. 1991, U.S. Supreme Ct. 1988, U.S. Dist. Ct. (ea. dist.) Tex. 1995. Assoc. Pierce, Couch, Hendrickson, Johnston & Baysinger, Oklahoma City, 1980-82; ptnr. Rizley & Tracy, Sayre, Okla., 1982-84; pvt. practice Oklahoma City, 1984-90; gen. atty. U.S. Army Corps Engrs., Ft. Worth, 1991—. Mem. citizens adv. bd. O'Donoghue Rehab. Inst., Oklahoma City. Mem. ABA, Okla. Bar Assn., Fed. Bar Assn., Internat. Tng. in Commn. (pres. Ace Club chpt.). Democrat. Roman Catholic. Avocations: photography, flying, water sports. Office: 819 Taylor St Fort Worth TX 76102-6114

**TRACY, J. DAVID,** lawyer, educator; b. Ft. Worth, Jan. 1, 1946; s. Dennis Ford and Virginia Eloise (Hall) T.; m. Jeral Ann Wilson, June 3, 1967; children: Bradley Wilson, Jennifer Diann. BA with honors, U. Tex., 1968, JD, 1970; LLM, So. Meth. U., 1971. Bar: Tex. 1971, U.S. Tax Ct. 1971, U.S. Ct. Appeals (5th cir.) 1976, U.S. Supreme Ct. 1978; cert. in estate planning, probate and tax law Tex. Bd. Legal Specialization. Ptnr. Tracy & Holland, LLP, Ft. Worth; bd. dirs. Ft. Worth Conv. and Vis. Bur., sec., 1987-89; adj. prof. advanced corp. taxation So. Meth. U., 1975-77; lectr. continuing legal edn.; council mem. real estate, probate and trust law sect. State Bar Tex., 1983-87; newsletter editor 1987-89, chmn., 1991-92; mem. Coll. State Bar Tex., tax law adv. commn. Tex. Bd. Legal Specialization, 1987—. Contbr. articles to law jours. Mem. adv. bd. dirs. Tarrant County Conv. Ctr., 1983-89, chmn., 1986-87. Named Outstanding Young Lawyer of Tarrant County, Tarrant County Young Lawyers Assn., 1982. Fellow Am. Coll. Trust and Estate Counsel, Tex. Bar Found., Tarrant County Bar Found.; mem. ABA, Ft. Worth Club, Colonial Country Club, Phi Delta Phi. Presbyterian. Estate planning, Taxation, general, Pension, profit-sharing, and employee benefits. Office: 306 W 7th St Ste 500 Fort Worth TX 76102-4905

**TRACY, WILLIAM FRANCIS, II,** lawyer; b. Decatur, Ill., Mar. 7, 1947; s. William Francis and Agnes Madonna (Ryan) T.; m. Elaine Baxter, Jan. 23, 1970; children: Katherine, Colleen, Ryan. AB, St. Louis U., 1969; JD, Northwestern U., 1972. Bar: Mo. 1972, Ill. 1977. Law clk. U.S. Dept. of Justice, Washington, summer 1971; jr. ptnr. Bryan, Cave, McPheeters & McRoberts, St. Louis, Mo., 1972-77; assoc. Doss, Simpson & Tracy, Monticello, Ill., 1977-78; ptnr., Miller, Tracy, Braun, Funk & Paisley LTD,

Monticello, 1978—; spl. asst. atty. gen. State of Ill., Monticello, 1980-83, pub. adminstr., conservator, guardian, Piatt County, Ill., 1978-90. Pres. Community Council, Bement, Ill., 1979. Mem. ABA, Mo. Bar Assn., Ill. Bar Assn., Piatt County Bar Assn. Club: Monticello Golf (treas., bd. dirs. 1982-84). Lodges: Rotary (treas. 1983-84), Lions (pres. 1981), K.C. (adv. 1981-82). Probate, Estate planning, Estate taxation. Home: 807 N State St Monticello IL 61856-1145

**TRAGER, DAVID G.,** federal judge; b. Mt. Vernon, N.Y., Dec. 23, 1937; s. Sol and Clara (Friedman) T.; m. Roberta E. Weisbrod, May 2, 1972; children: Mara Emet, Josiah Samuel, Naomi Gabrielle. B.A., Columbia Coll., 1959; LL.B., Harvard U., 1962. Bar: N.Y. Assoc. Berman & Frost, 1963-65, Butler, Jablow & Geller, 1965-67; asst. corp. counsel Appeals Div. City of N.Y., 1967; law clk. Judge Kenneth B. Keating, N.Y. State Ct. Appeals, 1968-69; asst. U.S. atty. chief, appeals div., 1970-72; U.S. atty. Ea. Dist. N.Y., Bklyn., 1974-78; prof. Bklyn. Law Sch., 1972-94, dean, 1983-94; judge U.S. Dist. Ct. (ea. dist.) N.Y., Bklyn., 1994—; chmn. Mayor's Com. on Judiciary, 1982-89, N.Y. State Temp. Commn. on Investigation, 1983-90. Mem. N.Y.C. Charter Rev. Commn., 1986-89. With USAR, 1962-65, USNR, 1965-69. Mem. ABA, N.Y. State Bar Assn., Assn. Bar City N.Y., Fed. Bar Council (pres. 1986-88), Am. Law Inst., Am. Judicature Soc. Office: US Courthouse 225 Cadman Plz E Brooklyn NY 11201-1818

**TRAGER, MICHAEL DAVID,** lawyer; b. N.Y.C., Feb. 15, 1959; s. Philip and Ina (Shulkin) T.; m. Mariella Gonzalez, Sept. 12, 1987; children: Nicholas, Alexander. BA, Wesleyan U., Middletown, Conn., 1981; JD, Boston U., 1985. Bar: Mass. 1985, Conn. 1986, Fla. 1988, D.C. 1989. Staff atty. enforcement divsn. Securities & Exchange Com., Washington, 1985-87; assoc. Morgan, Lewis & Bockius, Miami, Fla., 1987-88; participating assoc. Fulbright & Jaworski, Washington, 1989-92; ptnr. Trager & Trager, Washington, 1992-93; of counsel Fulbright & Jaworski, Washington, 1993-94, ptnr., 1995—. Bd. dirs. Jewish Nat. Fund-Mid-Atlantic Region, 1993-97; officer Horace Mann PTA. Mem. ABA (bus. law sect. fed. regulation securities com. and civil litigation and SEC enforcement matters subcom., litigation sect. securities litigation com. and SEC enforcement subcom., class action and derivative litigation com. and securities litigation subcom.), D.C. Bar (corp., fin. and securities law sect. corp. counsel and planning group for broker-dealer programs 1992-94, broker-dealer regulation com.), Mass. Bar, Fla. Bar., Conn. Bar. Federal civil litigation, Securities, Administrative and regulatory. Office: Fulbright & Jaworski 801 Pennsylvania Ave NW Fl 3-5 Washington DC 20004-2623

**TRAGOS, GEORGE EURIPEDES,** lawyer; b. Chgo., July 15, 1949; s. Euripedes G. and Eugene G. (Gatziolis) T.; m. Donna Marie Thalassites, Nov. 18, 1978; children: Louise, Gina, Peter. BA, Fla. State U., 1971, JD, 1974. Bar: Fla., U.S. Dist. Ct. (mid., so. dists.) Fla., U.S. Dist. Ct. (we. dist.) Tenn., U.S. Ct. Appeals (5th, 11th cirs.). Legis. aide Fla. Ho. of Reps., 1972-73; tax analyst tax and fin. com., 1973-74; chief, felony asst. states atty. State of Fla., Clearwater, 1974-78; partner firm Case, Kimpton, Tragos & Burke, P.A., Clearwater Beach, 1978-83; chief criminal div. U.S. Atty.'s Office for Middle Dist. Fla., Tampa, 1983-85; lead trial asst. Pres. Organized Crime Drug Enforcement Task Force, Tampa, 1985; sole practice Clearwater, 1985—. Contbr. articles to profl. jours. and frequent lectr. Mem. Clearwater Bar (pres. 1994), Fla. Bar Assn. (chmn. fed. practice com. 1986, chmn. criminal law sect., chmn. bar evidence com. 1990), Fla. Assn. Criminal Def. Lawyers (pres. 1991), Fla. Acad. Trial Lawyers, Am. Trial Lawyers Assn., Fla. State U. Alumni Assn. Law Sch. (bd. dirs.), Tampa Bay Fed. Bar Assn. (v.p. 1989), Clearwater Beach Jaycees (pres. 1979), Fla. U. Gold Key Club (pres. 1972), Ahepa. Democrat. Mem. Greek Orthodox Ch. Avocations: boating, tennis. E-mail: greeklaw@gte.net. Office: 600 Cleveland St Ste 700 Clearwater FL 33755-4158

**TRAMONTE, JAMES ALBERT,** lawyer; b. New Orleans, Mar. 6, 1951; s. August Joseph and Genevieve Tramonte; m. Stephanie Thomas, Aug. 12, 1972; children: James Albert Jr., Karen Elizabeth, David August, Patrick Thomas, Mark Joseph. Student, U. Miss., 1968-70; BS in Acctg., La. State U., New Orleans, 1973; JD, Tulane U., 1976; LLM in Taxation, NYU, 1977. Bar: La. 1976, U.S. Tax Ct. 1977, U.S. Ct. Claims 1978, U.S. Ct. Appeals (5th cir.) 1981, U.S. Ct. Appeals (11th cir.) 1981, Ga. 1989; cert. tax atty., La.; CPA, La. Ptnr. Hurt, Richardson, Garner, Todd & Cadenhead, Atlanta, 1988-92; gen. counsel Ctrl. Health Svcs., Inc., 1993-96, Simione Ctrl. Holdings, Inc., Atlanta, 1993-97; exec. v.p. LDC Direct, Ltd. Co., Atlanta, 1998-99; chief legal officer R.S. Andrews Enterprises, Inc., Atlanta, 1999—. Author: Estate Planning for Divorced and Remarried Persons, 1986; co-author Loyola Law Rev. 5th Cir. Symposium, 1986. Mem. ABA (sect. on taxation), La. State Bar Assn. (sect. on taxation, chmn. formulary com. 1981-82, chmn. liaison com. with dist. dir. IRS 1982-83), AICPA, Ga. State Soc. CPAs (taxation com. 1989). Roman Catholic. Mergers and acquisitions, General corporate, Intellectual property. Home: 5509 Mt Vernon Way Dunwoody GA 30338-2815

**TRAMONTI, JOHN, JR.,** lawyer; b. Providence, Dec. 24, 1930; s. John and Patricia Tramonti. BA, Providence Coll.; JD, Boston Coll., 1952. Bar: R.I. 1952. Sole practitioner Providence. Mem. Am. Bd. Trial Advocates, Nat. Assn. Criminal Def. Attys., R.I. Assn. Trial Attys., R.I. Assn. Criminal Def. Attys. Criminal. Office: 15 Westminster St Ste 808 Providence RI 02903-2415

**TRAN, JULIE HOAN,** lawyer; b. Dalat, Vietnam, May 25, 1970; came to U.S., 1975; d. My Ich and Ngu Thi Tran. BA in English, Baylor U., 1992; JD, Cornell Law Sch., 1995, postgrad. Bar: Tex. 1996, N.Y. 1996. Assoc. Akin, Gump, Strauss, Hauer & Feld, L.L.P., Houston, 1995-99, N.Y.C., 1999—; co-chmn., lectr. Conference on Creating and Structuring Internat. Joint Ventures, 1999; mem. Firm Hiring Com., 1988-99. Gen. editor Jour. of Pub. Law and Policy, 1994-95. Mem. ABA, Houston Bar Assn., N.Y. Bar Assn., Phi Delta Phi. General corporate, Private international, Mergers and acquisitions. Office: Akin Gump Strauss Hauer & Feld LLP 590 Madison Ave New York NY 10022-2524

**TRAN, MINH QUANG,** lawyer; b. Saigon, Vietnam, Sept. 17, 1960; came to U.S., 1975; s. Van Quang and Mai Thi (Duong) T. BSChemE, Rice U., 1984; JD, South Tex. Coll. Law, 1994; postgrad., U. Houston. Bar: Tex. 1994, U.S. Dist. Ct. (so., no. and ea. dists.) Tex. 1995, U.S. Ct. Appeals (fed. cir.) 1999. Process engr. Allied-Signal, Baton Rouge, 1984-87; sr. process engr. Occidental Chem. Corp., Houston, 1987-92; legal intern Pravel, Hewitt, Kimball & Krieger, Houston, 1992; intellectual property intern to Hon. Norman Black U.S. Dist. Ct. (so. dist.) Tex., Houston, 1992-93; assoc. Hardin, Beer, Hagstette & Davidson, Houston, 1993; gen. counsel Agar Corp. Inc., Houston, 1994—. Author: Patent Law Primer for Federal Court, 1993. Mem. adv. bd. Houston Police Dept., 1996. Fellow AIChE; mem. ABA, Tex. Bar Assn., Houston Intellectual Law Assn. (active coms.). Buddhist. Avocations: camping, gardening, travel, biking. Intellectual property, General corporate, Federal civil litigation. Home: 11343 Bayou Place Ln Houston TX 77099-4243 Office: AGAR Corp Inc 1600 Townhurst Dr Houston TX 77043-3284

**TRANCHINA, FRANK PETER, JR.,** lawyer; b. New Orleans, July 18, 1953; s. Frank P. and Effie (Volpe) T.; m. Susan Kendrick, Sept. 28, 1995. BA, Loyola U., New Orleans, 1976, JD, 1979. Bar: La. 1979, U.S. Ct. Appeals (5th cir.) 1981, Calif. 1994. Assoc. Law Offices Guy W. Olano, Jr., Kenner, La., 1979-86, Satterlee, Mestayer & Freeman, New Orleans, 1986-88; ptnr. Tranchina & Martinez, A.P.L.C., New Orleans, 1988-98, Tranchina & Assocs., New Orleans, 1998—; lectr. in field, 1989—; asst. grader for civil code I, La. Bar Exam., 1989-97. Contbr. articles to legal jours. Fellow Am. Acad. Matrimonial Lawyers (bd. cert. family law specialist La.); mem. ABA (trial techniques com. family law sect., law practice mgmt. com.), La. State Bar (chmn. CLE family law sect. 1989-90, treas. 1990, vice chmn. 1991-92, chmn. 1992-94), New Orleans Bar Assn., Toastmasters (pres. Metairie, La. 1981-84), Jefferson Parish Bar Assn. (chmn. CLE 1989-90, 91-92 domestic rels. sect.). Family and matrimonial. Home: 51 Cardinal Ln Mandeville LA 70471-6758

**TRANTER, TERENCE MICHAEL,** lawyer; b. Cin., Nov. 26, 1944; s. John Lawrence and Florence Ellen (McGann) T.; m. Doris Ann Tepe, June 22, 1968; children—Amy, Terry, Michael, Christopher. A.B., Georgetown U., 1966; J.D., U. Cin., 1969. Bar: Ohio 1969, U.S. Dist. Ct. (so. dist.) Ohio 1969, U.S. Ct. Appeals (6th cir.) 1969. Asst. atty. gen. State of Ohio, Cin., 1970-71; sole practice law, Cin., 1969—; mem. Ohio Ho. of Reps., Columbus, 1976-92; referee Domestic Relations Ct., Hamilton County, Ohio, 1975. Vice chmn. Hamilton County Democratic Exec. Com., Cin., 1984—; mem. Ohio Dem. Cen. Com., Columbus, 1984-92; mem. city council Golf Manor, Ohio, 1971-76. Mem. ABA, Ohio Bar Assn., Cin. Bar Assn., Ohio Bd. Realtors, Cin. Bd. Realtors. Democrat. Roman Catholic. Lodges: K.C., Eagles. Avocation: fishing. General practice. Home: 7303 Fair Oaks Dr Cincinnati OH 45237-2923 Office: 606 American Bldg Cincinnati OH 45202

**TRAPP, DAVID JAMES,** lawyer, educator; b. L.A., Mar. 2, 1959; s. Robert Frank and Nancy Hoyt T. BS in Criminology, Calif. State U., 1982; JD, Santa Clara U., 1985. Bar: Calif. 1985, U.S. Dist. Ct. (no. dist.) Calif. 1985. Assoc. McKeehan, Bernard & Wood, Fremont, Calif., 1986-91; attorney Finch & Chavez, Campbell, Calif., 1991-93; pvt. practice San Jose, Calif., 1993—; instr. U. Phoenix, San Jose, 1993—. Author: The Raconteur, 1999. Mem. Christian Legal Soc. of Santa Clara County (dir. 1998—). Roman Catholic. Avocations: fishing, chess, literature. Bankruptcy, General practice. Office: 540 Bird Ave Ste 200 San Jose CA 95125-1528

**TRAPP, RANDA MCDANIEL,** lawyer; b. San Diego, Nov. 26, 1954; d. Bennie McDaniel and Dorothy Nell Lemons; m. Larry Trapp, May 24, 1980; children: Lawrence, Langston. BA, San Jose State U., 1981; JD, Georgetown U., 1985. Atty. State Calif. Dept. Justice, San Diego, 1985-90, Hillyer & Irwin, San Diego, 1990-95, Sempra Energy, San Diego, 1995—; pres. Earl B. Gilliam Bar Assn., San Diego, 1989-90; dir. Lawyers Club, San Diego, 1991-94. Pres. San Diego Br. NAACP, 1996-98; trustee San Diego County Retirement Bd., 1996—. With USN, 1974-79. Recipient Thurgood Marshall award NAACP, San Diego, 1994, Thurgood Marshall award Earl B. Gilliam Bar Assn., San Diego, 1998, Tribute to Women in Industry award YWCA, San Diego, 1998, Phenomenal Woman award Earl B. Gilliam Bar Assn., San Diego, 1998. Democrat. Avocations: skiing, walking, tennis. Fax: 619-699-5181. Office: Sempra Energy 101 Ash St San Diego CA 92101-3017

**TRAUB, RICHARD KENNETH,** lawyer; b. Lakewood, N.J., Aug. 4, 1950; s. Harold W. and Muriel N. (Zurlin) T.; m. Barbara Lynn Wright, July 9, 1972; children: Russell S., Melissa L. BBA, U. Miami, Coral Gables, Fla., 1972, JD cum laude, 1975. Bar: Fla. 1975, N.Y. 1976, N.J. 1976, U.S. Dist. Ct. N.J. 1976, U.S. Supreme Ct. 1979, U.S. Dist. Ct. (ea. & so. dists.) N.Y. 1981. Ptnr. Wilson, Elser, Moskowitz, Edelman & Dicker, N.Y.C., 1975-95, Traub Eglin Lieberman Straus, Hawthorne, N.Y., 1996—; ptnr. Time for Patty Stables, N.J., 1992—; officer, dir. X-Ray Duplications, Inc., N.J.; ptnr., founder Fractured Greetings, N.J.; mem., lectr. Fedn. Ins. and Corp. Counsel, 1993—, mem. admissions com., industry cooperation ins. coverage and alt. dispute resolution coms.; lectr. Inst. for Internat. Rsch., Washington, 1988, Engring. News Record Constrn. Claims Conf., 1991. Author: Legal and Professional Aspects of Construction Management, 1990, The Year 2000 and Potential Liabilities and Otherwise, 1999; contbr. articles to profl. jours. Bd. dirs. Pop Warner Football Assn., Holmdel, N.J., 1989—. Mem. ABA (forum com. on constrn. industry 1989, tort and ins. practice sect. 1985—, computer litigation sect.), N.Y. State Bar Assn., N.J. Bar Assn., Fla. Bar Assn., Fedn. Ins. and Corp. Counsel (spkr. The Millenium Bug ins. coverage sect., vice chair ins. coverage and Y2K sects., vice chair tech. com., mem. admissions com.), Def. Rsch. Inst. Insurance, Construction, Environmental. Office: Traub Eglin Lieberman Straus Mid-Westchester Exec Park Three Skyline Dr Hawthorne NY 10532 also: 505 Main St Hackensack NJ 07601-5900

**TRAUTH, JOSEPH LOUIS, JR.,** lawyer; b. Cin., Apr. 22, 1945; s. Joseph L. and Margaret (Walter) T.; m. Barbara Widmeyer, July 4, 1970; children: Jennifer, Joseph III, Jonathan, Braden, Maria. BS in Econs., Xavier U., 1967; JD, U. Cin., 1973. Bar: Ohio 1973, U.S. Dist. Ct. (so. dist.) Ohio 1973, U.S. Ct. Appeals (6th cir.) 1973, U.S. Supreme Ct. 1988. Ptnr. Keating, Muething & Klekamp, PLL, Cin., 1973-80, Keating, Muething & Klekamp, Cin., 1980—; speaker real estate law, 1974—. Contbr. articles to real estate publs. Mem. Rep. Leadership Coun., Cin., 1987—, Parish Coun., Cin., 1990. Mem. Cin. Bar Assn. (grievance com., real estate com., negligence com.). Roman Catholic. Avocations: running, tennis, reading. General civil litigation, Real property, Land use and zoning (including planning). Office: Keating Muething & Klekamp 1800 Provident Tower 1 E 4th St Ste 1400 Cincinnati OH 45202-3717

**TRAUTMAN, HERMAN LOUIS,** lawyer, educator; b. Columbus, Ind., Sept. 26, 1911; s. Theodore H. and Emma (Guckenberger) T.; m. Marian Lucille Green, Sept. 1, 1940; children: Stephen M., Pamela C.; LLB with distinction Ind. U., 1937, BA, 1946, JD with distinction, 1946; postgrad., NYU, 1953, Ford Found. faculty fellow, Harvard U., 1954-55. Bar: Ind. 1937, U.S. Tax Ct., U.S. Ct. Appeals (6th cir.) Tenn. Sole practice, Evansville, Ind., 1937-43; pres. Crescent Coal Co., Evansville, 1941-43; prof. law U. Ala. Tuscaloosa, 1946-49; prof. law Vanderbilt U., 1949—, prof. law emeritus, 1977; NYU vis. prof., 1955, U. Mich., Ann Arbor, 1963-64; ptnr. Trautman & Trautman, Nashville, 1976-85; sole practice, Nashville, 1986—. Served to lt. comdr. USN, 1943-46. Mem. ABA, Am. Law Inst., Tenn. Bar Assn., Nashville Bar Assn., Nat. Conf. Jud. Adminstrs., Estate Planning Coun., Order of Coif, Phi Gamma Delta, Belle Meade Club, Univ. Club, Kiwanis. Methodist. Probate, Estate taxation, Taxation, general. Address: PO Box 150862 Nashville TN 37215-0862

**TRAVERS, SHERRI HAUSSNER,** lawyer, mediator; b. East St. Louis, July 25, 1947; d. Richard E. and Pauline M. Haussner; m. Mack J. Travers; children: Allian Hamilton, J.R. Shell, Annilee. BS in Math. summa cum laude, Lamar U., 1968, MS in Math., 1969, BS in Computer Sci. magna cum laude, 1987; JD, South Tex. U., 1990. Bar: Tex. 1990. Ptnr. Travers & Travers LLP, Katy, Tex. Office: Travers & Travers LLP 20501 Katy Fwy Ste 124 Katy TX 77450-1940

**TRAVIS, TODD ANDREW,** lawyer; b. Hackensack, N.J., May 25, 1962; s. John Robert and Gayle J. Travis; m. Susan D. Travis, Aug. 15, 1987; children: Jordan, Brandon. BA in Speech Comm. and Polit. Sci., U. Denver, 1984, JD, 1994. Ptnr. Bahr, Kreidle & Travis P.C., Littleton, Colo., 1994-98; pvt. practice Denver, 1994—. Hornbeck scholar U. Denver, 1981. Mem. ATLA, Colo. Trial Lawyers Assn., Arapahoe County Bar Assn. Republican. Personal injury, Insurance. Office: 50 S Steele St Ste 222 Denver CO 80209-2807

**TRAXLER, WILLIAM BYRD, JR.,** federal judge; b. Greenville, S.C., May 1, 1948; s. William Byrd and Bettie (Wooten) T.; m. Patricia Alford, Aug. 21, 1972; children: William Byrd III, James McCall. BA, Davidson Coll., 1970; JD, U. S.C., 1973. Assoc. William Byrd Traxler, Greenville, 1973-75; asst. solicitor 13th Jud. Ct., Greenville, 1975-78, dep. solicitor, 1978-81, solicitor, 1981-85, resident cir. judge, 1985-92; U.S. Dist. judge Dist. of S.C., Greenville, 1992-98; judge U.S. Ct. of Appeals (4th cir.), Greenville, 1998—. Recipient Outstanding Svc. award Solicitors Assn., S.C., 1987, Leadership award Probation, Parole & Pardon Svcs., S.C., 1990. Office: PO Box 10127 Greenville SC 29603-0127

**TRAYLOR, CHET D.,** state supreme court justice; b. Columbia, La., Oct. 12, 1945; s. John Hardy and Bernice (Bogan) T.; children: Mary Therese, Leigh Ann, Anna Marie. BA in Govt., N.E. La. State U., 1969; JD, Loyola U., 1974. Bar: La. Judge 5th Jud. Dist. Ct., Franklin, Richland and West Carroll Parishes, La., 1985-97; assoc. justice La. Supreme Ct., 1997—; past legal advisor La. State Police; past investigator La. Dept. Justice; asst. dist. atty., Franklin Parish, 1975-76. Founding bd. mem. Winnsboro Econ. Devel. Found.; mem. Rocky Mountain Conservation Fund. With U.S. Army. Mem. ABA, La. Bar Assn., La. Dist. Judges Assn., NRA (life), Franklin Parish Mental Health Assn. (past bd. dirs.), Winnsboro Lions Club (past bd. dirs.), Greenwings (founder John Adams chpt.). Methodist. Office: Supreme Ct 301 Loyola Ave New Orleans LA 70112-1814*

**TRAYLOR, ROBERT ARTHUR,** lawyer; b. Syracuse, N.Y., Jan. 15, 1949; s. Robert Arthur and Julia Elizabeth (McNulty) T.; m. Bonita Lynn Schmidt, Nov. 26, 1977. BS, LeMoyne Coll., 1970; JD cum laude, Syracuse U., 1975. Bar: N.Y., U.S. Dist. Ct. (no. dist.) N.Y., U.S. Tax Ct. Assoc. Love, Balducci & Scaccia, Syracuse, N.Y., 1976-77; estate tax atty. IRS, Syracuse, 1977-81; assoc. Scaccia Law Firm, Syracuse, 1981—. Contbr. articles to profl. jours. Of counsel St. Ann Sch., Syracuse, 1981—, mem. coordinating com. Vision 2000 1994—, mem. bd., 1998—. With U.S. Army, 1970-72. Mem. ABA, Onondaga County Bar Assn. (vol. lawyer program 1993—, Vol. Lawyer of Month 1994), World Wildlife Fedn. Republican. Roman Catholic. Avocations: motorsports, military history, Catholic education. General civil litigation, Probate, Real property. Home: 112 Knowland Dr Liverpool NY 13090-3130 Office: Scaccia Law Firm State Tower Bldg Ste 402 Syracuse NY 13202-1798

**TRAYNHAM, JERRY GLENN,** lawyer; b. Greenville, S.C., May 25, 1945; s. Jerry Broadus and Doris Irene Traynham; m. Kathleen Perryman, Oct. 30, 1968 (div. Apr. 1983); children: Penelope Anne, Elizabeth Blaise; m. Elizabeth Susan Southard, Mar. 16, 1985. BS in Journalism, U. Fla., 1972; JD, Tex. A&M U., Houston, 1975. Bar: Tex. 1975, Fla. 1976, U.S. Dist. Ct. (no. and mid. dists.) Fla., U.S. Ct. Appeals (5th cir.) 1980, U.S. Ct. Appeals (11th cir.) 1981, U.S. Supreme Ct. 1981. Assoc. Michaels & Patterson, Tallahassee, 1975-76, Patterson & Black, Tallahassee, 1976-77; ptnr. Patterson & Traynham, Tallahassee, 1977—. Participating atty. ACLU, Fla., 1978—. With U.S. Army, 1967-71, Vietnam. Mem. Tallahassee Bar Assn. (editor newsletter 1980-82), Tallahassee Tennis Assn. (treas., v.p. 1986-91, bd. dirs. 1991—, Disting. Svc. and President's award 1990). Democrat. Avocations: tennis, horsemanship, sailing, astronomy, running. Appellate, Civil rights, Labor. Office: Patterson & Traynham 315 Beard St Tallahassee FL 32303-6227

**TRAYNOR, JOHN MICHAEL,** lawyer; b. Oakland, Calif., Oct. 25, 1934; s. Roger J. and Madeleine (Lackmann) T.; m. Shirley Williams, Feb. 11, 1956; children: Kathleen Traynor Millard, Elizabeth Traynor Fowler, Thomas. BA, U. Calif., Berkeley, 1955; JD, Harvard U., 1960. Bar: Calif. 1961, U.S. Supreme Ct. 1966. Dep. atty. gen. State of Calif., San Francisco, 1961-63; spl. counsel Calif. Senate Com. on Local Govt., Sacramento, 1963; assoc. firm Cooley Godward, LLP, San Francisco, 1963-69, ptnr., 1969—; adviser 3d Restatement of Unfair Competition, 1988-95, 3d Restatement of Torts; Products Liability, 1992-97, Apportionment, 1994—, 1988 Revs. 2d Restatement of Conflict of Laws, 3rd Restatement of Restitution, 1997—; lectr. U. Calif. Boalt Hall Sch. Law, Berkeley, 1982-89, 1996—; chmn. EarthJustice Legal Def. Fund (formerly Sierra Club Legal Defense Fund), 1989-91, pres. 1991-92, trustee, 1974-96. Mem. bd. overseers Inst. for Civil Justice The RAND Corp., 1991-97; bd. dirs. Environ. Law Inst., 1991-97, Sierra Legal Defence Fund (Can.), 1990-96. Served to 1st lt. USMC, 1955-57. Fellow AAAS, Am. Bar Found. (life); mem. Am. Law Inst. (coun. 1985—, 2d v.p. 1993-98, 1st v.p. 1998—), Bar Assn. San Francisco (pres. 1973). Federal civil litigation, State civil litigation, Intellectual property. Home: 3131 Eton Ave Berkeley CA 94705-2713 Office: Cooley Godward LLP 1 Maritime Plz Ste 2000 San Francisco CA 94111-3510

**TRCA, RANDY ERNEST,** lawyer; b. Mason City, Iowa, Mar. 29, 1957; s. Ernest Edward and Emily (Hrubes) T. BS, N.W. Mo. State U., 1978; JD, U. Iowa, 1981, MBA, 1982. Bar: Iowa 1981, U.S. Dist. Ct. (no. and so. dists.) Iowa 1982. Pvt. practice law Iowa City, 1982—. Mem. edn. com. Iowa City C. of C., 1982-88. Mem. Iowa State Bar Assn. Democrat. Roman Catholic. Avocations: golfing, skiing, jogging, travel, culture. Bankruptcy, Personal injury, Family and matrimonial. Home: 1915 Muscatine Ave Iowa City IA 52240-6409 Office: 1232 E Burlington St Iowa City IA 52240-3212

**TREACY, GERALD BERNARD, JR.,** lawyer; b. Newark, July 29, 1951; s. Gerald B. Sr. and Mabel L. (Nesbitt) T.; m. Joyce M. Biazzo, Apr. 6, 1974. BA summa cum laude, Rider Coll., 1973; JD, UCLA, 1981. Bar: Calif. 1981, Wash. 1982, D.C. 1995. Tchr. English Arthur L. Johnson Regional High Sch., Clark, N.J., 1973-77; assoc. Gibson, Dunn & Crutcher, L.A., 1981-82; ptnr. Perkins Coie, Bellevue, Wash., 1982-94, McGuire Woods Battle & Boothe, McLean, Va. and Bellevue, Va., 1994-96, Egger, Betts, Austin, Treacy, Bellevue, Wash., 1996-98; mem. Treacy Law Group, Bellevue, 1998—; chmn. bd. dirs. estate planning adv. bd. U. Wash., Seattle, 1990-92; presenter TV Seminar, Where There's a Will, PBS affiliate. Author: Washington Guardianship Law, Administration and Litigation, 1988, supplemented, 1991, 2d edit., 1992, supplemented, 1993, Supporting Organizations, 1996. Mem. endowment fund com. United Way, Seattle, 1987-89, exec. com. Washington Planned Giving Coun., 1993-94, 96-98; bd. dirs., mem. adv. bd. ARC, Seattle, 1985-89, Arthritis Gift, 1987-89, Seattle Symphony, 1992, Seattle U., 1996. Mem. Eastside King County Estate Planning Coun., Order of Coif. Avocations: photography, hiking, ethnic and classical music, poetry, host/writer Gilbert & Sullivan radio show. Estate planning, Probate, Estate taxation. Office: 777 108th Ave NE Ste 2200 Bellevue WA 98004-5147

**TREACY, VINCENT EDWARD,** lawyer; b. Mass., Jan. 30, 1942. AB, Boston Coll., 1964; JD with honors, George Washington U., 1971. Bar: Va. 1972, D.C. 1973, Md. 1999; U.S. Supreme Ct. 1976. Atty. Fed. Labor Rels. Coun., Washington, 1971-73; legis. atty. Am. law divsn. Congrl. Rsch. Svc., Libr. Congress, Washington, 1973-98; sole practitioner Washington, 1998—; legis. cons. Romanian Legal Analysis and Legis. Drafting Conf., Senate and Chamber Duputies Romania, Bucharest, 1996. Mem. law rev. staff George Washington Law Rev., 1970. Mem. ABA, FBA, George Washington Law Alumni Assn. (pres. Capitol Hill chpt. 1986-87), Order of Coif. Labor, Pension, profit-sharing, and employee benefits.

**TREADWAY, JAMES CURRAN,** lawyer, investment company executive, former government official; b. Anderson, S.C., May 21, 1943; s. James C. and Maxine (Hall) T.; m. Susan Pepper Davis, Sept. 6, 1969; children: Elizabeth Pepper Hall, Caroline Worrell Harper. AB summa cum laude, Rollins Coll., 1964; JD summa cum laude, Washington and Lee U., 1967. Bar: Ga. 1967, Mass. 1968, D.C. 1970. Assoc. Candler, Cox, McClain & Andrews, Atlanta, 1967-68, Gadsby & Hannah, Boston and Washington, 1968-72; ptnr. Dickstein, Shapiro & Morin, Washington, 1972-82; commr. SEC, Washington, 1982-85; ptnr. Baker & Botts, Washington, 1985-87; exec. v.p., chmn. dept. merchant banking, exec. com. Paine Webber Group Inc., N.Y.C., 1987—; chmn. Nat. Commn. on Fraudulent Fin. Reporting, 1985-87; chmn. bd. dirs. Washington & Lee U. Sch. Law, 1992-94; spl. expert adviser, witness various U.S. congl. coms.; lectr. in field. Editor-in-chief Wash. & Lee U. Law review, 1966-67. Recipient Wildman Medal Am. Acctg. Assn., 1989. Mem. Mass. Bar Assn., Ga. Bar Assn., D.C. Bar Assn., Chevy Chase (Md.) Club, Bedford (N.Y.) Golf and Tennis Club, City Tavern Club, Met. Club, Univ. Club (Washington), Verbank Hunting and Fishing Club (Uniondale N.Y.; dir. 1995—), Order of Coif, Phi Beta Kappa, Omicron Delta Kappa. Republican. Roman Catholic. Home: Laurel Ledge RD 4 Croton Lake Rd Bedford Corners NY 10549 Office: PaineWebber Group Inc 1285 Ave of Americas New York NY 10019-6028

**TREANOR, WILLIAM MICHAEL,** law educator; b. Morristown, N.J., Nov. 16, 1957; s. William Joseph and Margaret Loretto (Lenaghan) T.; m. Allison Derivaux Ames, Oct. 15, 1994; children: William Paul Ames, Katherine Derivaux. BA, Yale U., 1979, JD, 1985; AM in History, Harvard U., 1982. Spl. asst. to dep. commr. U.S. Office Edn., Washington, 1979-80; speechwriter to sec. U.S. Dept. Edn., Washington, 1980; law clk. to Hon. James L. Oakes U.S. Ct. Appeals, 2d Cir., Brattleboro, Vt., 1985-86; spl. asst. to chmn. Com. on Govt. Integrity, N.Y.C., 1987; spl. asst. U.S. atty. U.S. Atty.'s Office, Washington, 1990; assoc. counsel Office of Ind. Counsel, Washington, 1987-90; assoc. prof. law Fordham U., N.Y.C., 1991—. Contbr. articles to profl. jours. Democrat. Office: US Dept Justice 950 Pennsylvania Ave NW Washington DC 20530-0001

**TRECEK, TIMOTHY SCOTT,** lawyer; b. Racine, Wis., Sept. 26, 1968; s. Robert Thomas and Mona Marie Trecek; m. Karyn Marie Kwiatkowski, Aug. 27, 1994; children: Gabrielle Grace, Danielle Terese. BS in Polit. Sci., Marquette U., 1990, JD, 1993. Bar: Wis. 1993, U.S. Dist. Ct. (ea. dist.) Wis. 1993. Atty. Kasdorf, Lewis & Swietlik, Milw., 1993-95, Habush, Habush, Davis & Rottier, Milw., 1995—. Mem. ABA, Wis. Acad. of Trial Lawyers (com. mem. bd. attys. profl. responsibility), Wis. State Bar Assn., Assn. of Trial Lawyers of Am. Roman Catholic. Avocations: golfing, family. Personal injury, General civil litigation. Office: Habush Habush Davis & Rottier 777 E Wisconsin Ave 2300 Milwaukee WI 53202-5381

**TREDENNICK, STEVEN BURROUGHS,** lawyer; b. Newport News, Va., June 26, 1943; s. John C. and Jacqueline (Burroughs) T.; m. D. Diane French, June 11, 1966; children: Steven Randolph, Christopher Scott. BA,

U. Tex., El Paso, 1965; JD, U. Va., 1968; cert., Coll. for Fin. Planning, 1984. Bar: Va. 1968, Tex. 1970, N.Mex. 1984. Assoc. Goodman, Hallmark & Akard, El Paso, Tex., 1972-74; pvt. practice Steven Tredennick, P.C., El Paso, 1974-79; sr. shareholder Mayfield and Perrenot, P.C., El Paso, 1979-05; atty. Steven Tredennick Atty. at Law, Round Rock, Tex., 1996—; mem. U.S.-Mex. task force Atlantic coun. of U.S., Washington, 1985. Editor newsletter Franchising in the Americas. Chmn. Sun Bowl luncheon Rotary Club of El Paso, 1993-94; chmn. Tex. Lyceum Assn., 1989; chmn. various coms. U. Tex., El Paso, 1980—; sponsor, spkr., writer The Franchise Ctr., 1993-95. Capt. U.S. Army, 1968-72. Recipient Rising Star of Tex. award Tex. Bus. Mag., 1983; named to Best Lawyers in Am., Woodward/White, Inc., 1995—. Fellow Tex. Bar Found. (life); mem. ABA, El Paso Bar Assn. (past program chair 1972—), State Bar of Va. (assoc.). Episcopalian. Avocations: music, reading, golf, volunteer work. Home and Office: 4028 Sable Oaks Dr Round Rock TX 78664-6251

**TREECE, RANDY LIONEL,** lawyer; b. Paducah, Ky., Apr. 16, 1956; s. Franklin William and Leona Marie (Kelley) T.; m. Devonda Kaye Corzine, May 30, 1976; children: Natalie, Elliot, Tifanie, Savanah. AA, Paducah C.C., 1976; BSBA in Profl. Acctg., So. Ill. U., 1977; JD, Vanderbilt U., 1984. Staff acct. Ernst & Young, St. Louis, 1977-79; sr. acct. Ernst & Young, Denver, 1979-81; assoc. Stoll, Keenon & Park, Lexington, Ky., 1984-86; ptnr. Whitlow, Robert, Houston & Straub, Paducah, Ky., 1986—. Co-author: (book) Kentucky Tax Law, 1990, 2d edit., 1994; contbr. articles to profl. jours. Mem. ABA (small bus. com. 1992-95), Ky. Bar Assn., AICPA, Ky. Soc. CPAs (small bus. com. 1991-95). Estate planning, General corporate, Probate. Office: Whitlow Roberts Houston & Straub 300 Broadway St Paducah KY 42001-0733

**TREMAINE, H. STEWART,** lawyer; b. St. Paul, Mar. 17, 1919; s. Hugh Milner and Sally (Fox) T.; m. Harriet Lupton, July 10, 1948; children: Sally, Victoria, Katherine. BA, U. Wash., 1940; LLB, Yale U., 1946. Bar: Oreg. 1947, Wash. 1947. Ptnr. Davis Wright Tremaine, Portland, Oreg., 1947—. Capt. USMC, 1942-45. Decorated Purple Heart (2). Mem. Arlington Club, Waverley Club, Multnomah Athletic Club (pres.). Republican. Presbyterian. Avocations: golf, hiking, climbing, fishing, bridge. Corporate taxation, Estate planning. Office: Davis Wright Tremaine 1300 SW 5th Ave Ste 2200 Portland OR 97201-5682

**TRENT, CLYDE NATHANIEL,** legal assistant; b. Pitts., Nov. 25, 1945; s. Isaiah and Grace Sarah (Massie) T.; m. Mary Julia Kelly, Nov. 22, 1974; children: Robert, Nathaniel. BA, U. Pitts., 1979; paralegal cert., Pa. State U., 1984; AS, C.C. Allegheny, Monroeville, Pa., 1986; paralegal cert., U. Pitts., 1987. Letter carrier U.S. Postal Svc., Pitts., 1968-80; legal asst. Strassburger & McKenna, Pitts., 1980-85, Feldstein Law Office, Pitts., 1985-90, Elderly Citizens Ctr., Mt. Lebanon, Pa., 1990-91; claims examiner Office Econ. Security, Pitts., 1991—; adv. bd. mem. Legal Intellect, Inc., Monroeville, 1988—. Mem. Western Pa. Hist. Soc., Pitts., 1993—. With U.S. Army, 1965-67. Mem. Am. Criminal Justice, Pitts. Paralegal Assn. (com. 1990), Pa. State Alumni (vol. 1986-94), Lambda Alpha Epsilon (pres. 1979-80), Phi Theta Kappa. Avocations: horseback riding, student pilot, cooking, historical research.

**TRENT, JOHN THOMAS, JR.,** lawyer; b. Hammond, Ind., Mar. 11, 1954; s. John Thomas and Sally (Ritter) T.; m. Laura Marie Nelson, Aug. 5, 1978; children: Lauren, Valerie, Alex. AB, Wabash Coll., 1976; JD, Vanderbilt U., 1979. Bar: Tenn. 1979, U.S. Dist. Ct. (mid. dist.) Tenn. Mng. dir. Boult, Cummings, Conners & Berry P.L.C., Nashville, 1979—; frequent panelist and speaker to real estate and other groups. Chmn. adminstr. bd. and other coms. and offices, West End United Meth. Ch., Nashville, 1983—99; mem. bd. dirs. Cumberland Sci. Mus., 1997—, Jr. Achievement Tenn. Fellow Nashville Bar; mem. ABA, Nat. Assn. Industrial and Office Parks (past bd. dirs. Nashville chpt.), Tenn. Bar Assn., Nashville Bar Assn., Nat. Assn. Bond Lawyers, Assn. Attys. and Execs. in Corp. Real Estate. Real property, Appellate, Municipal (including bonds). Office: Boult Cummings Conners & Berry PLC 414 Union St Ste 1600 Nashville TN 37219-1744

**TRETSCHOK, DALE DEEGE,** lawyer; b. Pitts., Aug. 31, 1941; s. Carl Edward and Hildegard Marie (Deege) T.; m. Carole Diane Tully, Aug. 3, 1963; children: Cody, Tully. BS, U. Ariz., 1963, JD, 1966. Bar: Ariz. 1966, U.S. Ct. Mil. Appeals 1966, U.S. Dist. Ct. Ariz. 1970, U.S. Ct. Appeals (9th cir.) 1980. Ptnr. Davis, Eppstein & Tretschok, Tucson, 1970-78; shareholder Tretschok McNamara & Clymer, P.C., Tucson, 1979-96, Tretschok, McNamara, Patten and Lohmann, Tucson, 1996-99, Tretschok, McNamara & Patten, P.C., Tucson, 1999—; speaker at seminars on workers compensation to various groups. Capt. U.S. Army, 1966-70. Mem. ABA, Ariz. Trial Lawyers Assn., Assn. Trial Lawyers Am., Ariz. State Bar (workers' compensation sect.), Nat. Orgn. Social Security Claimants' Reps. (sustaining). Workers' compensation, Pension, profit-sharing, and employee benefits. Office: Tretschok McNamara & Patten PC PO Box 42887 Tucson AZ 85733-2887

**TREVENA, JOHN HARRY,** lawyer; b. Dunedin, Fla., Dec. 28, 1961; s. Ernest Lewis and Lenora Geraldine (Adelson) T.; m. Susan Lee Corris, Nov. 23, 1988; 1 child, Samuel Alan. BA in criminal justice, Univ. S. Fla., 1982; Fla. Police standards, Pinellas Police Acad., 1982; JD, Stetson Univ., 1985. Bar: Fla., U.S. Dist. Ct. (mid. dist.) Fla. 1986. Pvt. practice Largo, Fla.; editorial bd. Fla. Bar Jour., Fla. Bar News, 1990-93. *John H. Trevena, Board Certified Criminal Trial Lawyer, former Assistant State Attorney and former Police Officer, consults statewide with other attorneys in all criminal matters, particularly capital murder and complex white collar cases. Mr. Trevena has appeared in national and international media, including CBS 48 Hours, Fox News Channel, The Los Angeles Times, the BBC and the ABA Journal. Mr. Trevena is often called upon for legal commentary on high profile criminal cases.* Mem. Clearwater and Am. Bar Assn., Fla. Bar Assn., Fla. Assn. Criminal Def. Lawyers, Pinellas County Trial Lawyers Assn., Pinellas County Criminal Def. Lawyers Assn., Nat. Assn. Criminal Def. Lawyers, Am. Judicature Soc., Fla. Bar Bd. Legal Specialization and Edn. (bd. cert. criminal trial lawyer). Roman Catholic. Democrat. Criminal. Home: 423 Buttonwood Ln Largo FL 33770-4060 Office: 801 W Bay Dr Ste 509 Largo FL 33770-3220

**TREVETT, KENNETH PARKHURST,** lawyer; b. Boston, Sept. 22, 1947; s. Laurence Davies and Naomi (Smith) T.; m. Barbara Kent, June 10, 1978; stepchildren: Kimberly, Dennison, Tanya. BA in English (hon.), Colgate U., 1969; JD cum laude, Suffolk U., 1979. Bar: Mass. 1980, U.S. Dist. Ct. Mass. 1980, Maine 1983. With office of pub. affairs Sec. of State, Commonwealth of Mass., Boston, 1978; asst. dean for adminstrn. Tufts U. Sch. Vet. Medicine, Boston, 1979-82; asst. to dir., house counsel Jackson Lab., Bar Harbor, Maine, 1982-89; gen. counsel Dana-Farber Cancer Inst., Boston, 1989-96; pvt. practice, Boston, 1996; COO, gen. counsel Schepens Eye Rsch. Inst., 1996—. Co-author: An Evaluation of the De-institutionalization of the Massachusetts Department of Youth Services, 1972; co-developer: (edn. CD-ROM on licensing) Technology Transfer Series; contbr. several invited papers on legal and ethical aspects of biotech. and medicine. Mem. Gov.'s Tech. Strategy Task Force, Augusta, Maine, 1983-84, Maine Sci. and Tech. Commn., 1988-89; trustee 2d v.p., Mt. Desert Island Hosp., 1984-89; 1st v.p. Assn. Ind. Rsch. Insts., 1990-92, pres., 1993-95. Democrat. Unitarian. Avocations: golf, writing. General corporate, Health. Office: Schepens Eye Rsch Inst 20 Staniford St Boston MA 02114-2508

**TREVETT, THOMAS NEIL,** lawyer; b. Rochester, N.Y., Mar. 14, 1942; S. Frank E. and Andrea (Kuhn) T.; m. Margaret H. Hepburn, July 29, 1967; children; Monica, Millicent, Thomas. BS, St. John Fisher Coll., 1964; JD, Albany Law Sch., 1967. Bar: N.Y. 1967, U.S. Dist. Ct. (we. dist.) N.Y. 1968. Assoc. Thomas J. Meagher, Rochester, 1967-68, Trevett, Lenweaver, Salzer, and predecessor Gough, Skipworth, Summers, Eves & Trevett, Rochester, 1968—; pres. Trevett, Lenweaver, Salzer, and predecessor Gough, Skipworth, 1985-89. State Dem. committeeman; bd. dirs. Genesee region March Dimes, Rochester Area Multiple Sclerosis Soc., chmn. bd., 1992-94; chmn. bd. trustees McQuaid Jesuit N.S., 1997. Mem. ABA, N.Y. State Bar Assn., (ho. of dels. 1981, chmn. Ins. Negligence and Compensation Law sect. 1989-90, John E. Leach award, 1996), Monroe County Bar Assn. (trustee 1996—, pres. 1999—), Def. Rsch. Inst., Fedn. Ins. Corp. Counsel, Wayne County Bar. Assn. (pres. 1978-79). Roman Catholic. Estate planning, Personal injury, Real property. Office: 700 Reynolds Arc Rochester NY 14614-1803 also: 2003 Main St Ontario NY 14519

**TREVISANI, ROBERT ARMAND,** lawyer, educator; b. Boston, Sept. 9, 1933; s. John and Olga (Zanni) T.; m. H. Patricia Meister, Feb. 6, 1960; children: Pamela, Margaret, Robert M., Peter. BA, Boston Coll., 1955, LLB, 1958; LLM in Taxation, NYU, 1959. Bar: Mass. 1959, N.Y. 1961, D.C. 1965. Trial atty. U.S. Treasury Dept., N.Y.C., 1960-64; assoc. Cedar & Cedar, Worcester, Mass., 1964-66, Gadsby & Hannah, Boston and Washington, 1966-68; ptnr. Gadsby & Hannah LLP, Boston and Washington, 1968—; adj. prof. law Boston U. Grad. Sch. Law, 1972-95, Boston Coll. Law Sch., Newton, Mass., 1997—; chmn. sect. legal practice Internat. Bar Assn., London, 1994-96. Pres. Commonwealth Charitable Found., 1972—; trustee Ida Coll., Newton, 1990—; dir. HomePort Bancorp., Inc. Fellow Am. Bar Found.; mem. London Ct. Internat. Arbitration. Private international, Mergers and acquisitions, Corporate taxation. Office: Gadsby & Hannah LLP 225 Franklin St Boston MA 02110-2804

**TREVOR, LEIGH BARRY,** lawyer; b. Galesburg, Ill., Aug. 29, 1934; s. Dean Spaulding and Jean Elizabeth (Barry) T.; m. Mary Witherell, Aug. 8, 1978; children: John W. Hoffman, Ann Kete, Stephen S., Julia B. Kramer, Elizabeth P. Grad., Phillips Acad., 1952; AB magna cum laude, Harvard U., 1956, LLB, 1962. Bar: Ohio 1963, U.S. Dist. Ct. D.C. 1970. Assoc. Jones, Day, Reavis & Pogue, Cleve., 1962-68, ptnr., 1969—, ptnr.-in-charge, 1990-93; sec. Dix & Eaton, Inc., Cleve.; lectr. on hostile corp. takeovers, other corp. law topics. Contbr. articles to profl. jours. Trustee State Troopers of Ohio, 1985—; pres. Stakeholders in Am., Mpls., 1987-88; trustee Cleveland State U. Found., 1990-94, Gt. Lakes Theater Festival, 1991-94. Lt. (j.g.) USN, 1956-59. Fellow Ohio State Bar Found.; mem. Ohio State Bar Assn. (mem. tender offer subcom. 1982—, chmn. corp. law com. 1989-91, coun. of dels. 1991—), Cleve. Bar Assn., D.C. Bar Assn., Phi Beta Kappa. Republican. Episcopalian. General corporate, Mergers and acquisitions. Home: 3 Hidden Vly Rocky River OH 44116-1143 Office: Jones Day Reavis & Pogue 901 Lakeside Ave Cleveland OH 44114-1116

**TREXLER, WYNN RIDENHOUR,** paralegal; b. Salisbury, N.C., Sept. 15, 1941; d. Lee R. and Olena (Ludwig) Ridenhour; m. Frederick C.D. Trexler, June 14, 1959; children: Dale, Wendy, Chris, Matt. Grad. high sch., Salisbury. Legal sec. Woodson & Woodson and successor firm Woodson, Hudson & Busby, Salisbury, 1959-60, 64-67; teller Home Savs. & Loan Assn., Salisbury, 1961-63; legal sec. Burke, Donaldson & Holshouser, Salisbury, 1968-77, Carlton, Rhodes & Wallace, Salisbury, 1977-81; paralega Mona Lisa Wallace, Salisbury, 1981-86; freelance paralegal Piedmont Paralegal Svc., Salisbury, 1986—. Mem. Nat. Assn. Legal Assts. (cert.), Nat Assn. Legal Secs. (cert.), N.C. Paralegal Assn. (charter, bd. dirs. 1980-86, liaison), N.C. Acad. Trial Lawyers (assco., legal assts. sect., edn. com. 1984—), Profl. Legal Assts. Democrat. Lutheran. Avocations: photography, collecting and restoring antiques, driving and showing British cars, raising ostrich. Home: PO Box 275 Faith NC 28041-0275 Office: Piedmont Paralegal Svc 2450 Artz Rd Salisbury NC 28146-1164

**TRICARICO, JOSEPH ARCHANGELO,** lawyer; b. N.Y.C., May 6, 1940; s. Nicholas and Frances Tricarico; m. Mildred Grandi, Feb. 12, 1972; 1 child, Nicholas. BS, St. Johns U., 1963, JD, 1967. V.p. trust counsel U.S. Trust Co. N.Y., N.Y.C., 1973—. Author: Generation-Skipping Transfers: A Primer, 1984. Pro bono arbitrator small claims ct. Civil Ct. of City of N.Y., S.I., 1981—; trustee Eger Health Care Ctr., S.I., 1990—. Mem. ABA (com. bus. law 1990—, vice chair com. generation-skipping transfers 1993—, com. taxation 1984—), Am. Corp. Counsel Assn. (com. securities litigation 1991—, com. environ. law 1992—), N.Y. Bankers Assn. (spl. counsel trust legis. and regulatory com. 1991—), N.Y. Bar Assn., New York County Lawyers Assn. (com. on legis. 1989—), Am. Judges Assn. (hon. judge 1985—). Bankruptcy, Probate, Securities. Office: US Trust Co NY 114 W 47th St New York NY 10036-1510

**TRIEWEILER, TERRY NICHOLAS,** state supreme court justice; b. Dubuque, Iowa, Mar. 21, 1948; s. George Nicholas and Anne Marie (Oastern) T.; m. Carol M. Jacobson, Aug. 11, 1972; children: Kathryn Anne, Christina Marie, Anna Theresa. BA, Drake U., 1970, JD, 1972. Bar: Iowa 1973, Wash. 1973, U.S. Dist. Ct. (so. dist.) Iowa 1973, U.S. Dist. Ct. (we. dist.) Wash. 1973, Mont. 1975, U.S. Dist. Ct. Mont. 1977. Staff atty. Polk County Legal Services, Des Moines, 1973; assoc. Hullin, Roberts, Mines, Fite & Riveland, Seattle, 1973-75, Morrison & Hedman, Whitefish, Mont., 1975-77; sole practice, Whitefish; justice Mont. Supreme Ct., Helena, 1991—; lectr. U. Mont. Law Sch., 1981—; mem. com. to amend civil proc. rules Mont. Supreme Ct., Helena, 1984, commn. to draft pattern jury instrns., 1985; mem. Gov.'s Adv. Com. on Amendment to Work Compensation Act, adv. com. Mont. Work Compensation Ct. Mem. ABA, Mont. Bar Assn. (pres. 1986-87), Wash. Bar Assn., Iowa Bar Assn., Assn. Trial Lawyers Am., Mont. Trial Lawyers Assn. (dir., pres.). Democrat. Roman Catholic. Home: 1615 Virginia Dale St Helena MT 59601-5823 Office: Mont Supreme Ct Justice Bldg Rm 410 215 N Sanders St Helena MT 59601-4522*

**TRIFFIN, NICHOLAS,** law librarian, law educator; b. Boston, May 30, 1942; s. Robert and Lois (Brandt) T.; m. Mary M. Bertolet, June 1, 1965 (div. June 1975); children: Amyk (dec.), A. Robert; m. Madeleine J. Wilken, May 30, 1981. BA cum laude, Yale U., 1965, JD, 1968; MLS, Rutgers U., 1978. Bar: N.Y. 1969, Conn. 1973, U.S. Dist. Ct. Conn. 1973, U.S. Ct. Appeals (2nd cir.) 1973, U.S. Tax Ct. 1974. Assoc. Willkie Farr & Gallagher, N.Y.C., 1968-70; dean students Johnson (Vt.) State Coll., 1970-72; assoc. Di Sesa & Evans, New Haven, 1972-76; head pub. services, instr. law U. Conn., W. Hartford, 1977-81; law library dir., assoc. prof. Hamline U., St. Paul, 1982-84; dir. law library Pace U., White Plains, N.Y., 1984-98; prof. Pace U., 1984—; bd. dirs. Hale Found.; bd. advisors Oceana Pub., Inc., 1987-95; chief info. svcs. Inst. Internat. Comml. Law, 1993-94, dir., 1994—; adj. prof. Hartford Coll., 1978-80; lectr. Peking U., summer 1997; vis. scholar Yale U. Law Sch., fall 1998. Author: Law Books Published, 1984-95, Law Books in Print, 5th edit., 1987, 6th edit., 1991, 7th edit., 1995, Law Books in Review, 1984-92, Drafting History of the Federal Rules of Criminal Procedure, 1991; columnist Law Libr. Jour., 1983-84. Justice of peace, Conn., 1976-78. Mem. Am. Assn. Law Librs. (chmn. reader svcs. spl. interest sect. 1982-83, chmn. legal history and rare books spl. interest sect. 1991-92, chmn. constn. and bylaws com. 1994-95), Westchester Acad. Libr. Dirs. Orgn., Inc. (v.p. 1990-91, pres. 1991-92, exec. bd. dirs. 1992-94), Law Libr. New Eng. (pres. 1981-82), Minn. Assn. Law Librs. (v.p. 1983-84), Westchester Libr. Assn. (exec. bd. 1990-91), Myositis Assn. Am., Mory's Club, Beta Phi Mu. Mem. Soc. of Friends. Avocations: kayaking, rare books, opera. Office: Pace U Law Sch 78 N Broadway White Plains NY 10603-3710 *Society delights in putting barriers between people. Our greatest task is to remove these barriers - to use every encounter with others as an opportunity to empathize and to expand the horizons of our understanding - and to see that fundamentally we are all one.*

**TRIMBLE, JAMES T., JR.,** federal judge; b. Bunkie, La., Sept. 13, 1932; s. James T. Sr. and Mabel (McNabb) T.; m. Murel Elise Biles, Aug. 18, 1956; children: Elise Ramsey, Mary Olive Beacham, Martha McNabb Elliott, Sarah Palmer Trimble. Attended, U. Southwestern La. (formerly Southwestern La. Inst.), 1950-52; BA in Law, La. State U., 1955, JD, 1956. Bar: La. 1956. With Gist, Murchison & Gist (now Gist, Methvin, Hughes & Munsterman), 1959-78, Trimble, Percy, Smith, Wilson, Foote, Walker & Honeycutt, 1979-86; U.S. magistrate U.S. Dist. Ct. (we. dist.) La., 1986-91, judge, 1991—. Lt. USAF, 1956-59. Mem. Fed. Judges Assn., Southwest La. Bar Assn., La. Bar Assn., La. Bar Found. Avocations: jogging, gardening, tennis. Office: 611 Broad St Ste 237 Lake Charles LA 70601-4380

**TRIMBLE, PAUL JOSEPH,** retired lawyer; b. Springfield, Mass., Oct. 9, 1930; s. Peter Paul and Bernnese (Myrick) T.; m. Suzanne Hrudka; children: Troy, Derrick, Andrew. B.A., Am. Internat. U., Springfield, Mass., 1952; LL.B., U. Tex., Austin, 1955. Bar: Calif., Tex., Ill., Alaska. Counsel Mobil Oil Corp., Joliet, Ill., 1964-72; assoc. counsel Fluor Corp., Irvine, Calif., 1972-73, corp. counsel, 1973-74, sr. corp. counsel, 1974, asst. gen. counsel, 1974-80, gen. counsel, 1980-82, sr. v.p., gen. counsel, 1982-96, sr. v.p. law, gen. counsel, 1984-96, corp. sec., 1992-96, cons., 1996—. Mem. ABA, Calif. Bar Assn., Tex. Bar Assn., Ill. Bar Assn., Alaska Bar Assn. Republican.

**TRIMBLE, SANDRA ELLINGSON,** lawyer; b. Buffalo, Wyo., May 10, 1952; d. Andrew C. and Edna E. Ellingson; children: Samuel James, Stephen Joseph. BA with highest distinction, Colo. State U., 1974; MEd, Sul Ross State U., 1977; JD cum laude, Georgetown U., 1989. Bar: Md. 1989, D.C. 1990. Contract specialist USAF, Pope AFB, N.C., 1979-81; purchasing rep. Damson Oil Corp., Houston, 1982-86; summer assoc. Fried Frank Harris Shriver & Jacobson, Washington, 1988; law clk. Sullivan & Cromwell, Washington, 1988-89; assoc. Cleary Gottlieb Steen & Hamilton, Washington, 1989-97; of counsel Orrick Herrington & Sutcliffe LLP, Washington, 1997—. Assoc. notes editor Georgetown Law Jour., 1988-89. Recipient Disting. Achievement in Advocacy award Internat. Acad. Trial Lawyers, 1989; Nat. Merit scholar, 1970; law fellow Georgetown U. Law Ctr., 1987-88. Mem. ABA, Phi Beta Kappa. Finance, General corporate, Securities. Office: Orrick Herrington & Sutcliffe LLP 3050 K St NW Ste 200 Washington DC 20007-5135

**TRIMMIER, CHARLES STEPHEN, JR.,** lawyer; b. Chgo., June 25, 1943; s. Charles Stephen and Lucille E. (Anderson) T.; m. Rae Wade Trimmier, Aug. 19, 1966; children: Charles Stephen, Hallie Wade. B.A., U. Ala., Tuscaloosa, 1965, J.D., 1968. Bar: Ala. 1968. From assoc. to ptnr. Rives, Peterson, Pettus and Conway, Birmingham, Ala., 1968-77; pres. TrimmierLaw Firm, L.L.C., Birmingham, Mobile, Montgomery, Muscle Shoals, Dothan and Decatur, Ala., Orlando, Palm Beach and Panama City, Fla. 1977—; gen. counsel Nat. Assn. State Chartered Credit Union Suprs., Ala. Credit Union League, Fla. Credit Union League, La. Credit Union League. Mem. ABA (bus. and banking law sect., credit union com.), Ala. Bar Assn., Birmingham Bar Assn., Comml. Law League, Ala. Law Inst., La. Credit Union League, Shades Valley Jaycees (sec. 1973). Episcopalian. Editor-in-chief: Ala. Law Rev. 1968. Contracts commercial, General corporate, Private international. Home: 3819 River View Cir Birmingham AL 35243-4801 Office: Trimmier Law Firm LLC PO Box 1885 Birmingham AL 35201-1885

**TRIMMIER, ROSCOE, JR.,** lawyer; b. Charlotte, N.C., July 22, 1944; s. Roscoe and Susie Elizabeth (Stitt) T.; divorced; 1 child, Leigh Snowden. AB, Harvard U., 1971, JD, 1974. Bar: Mass. 1974, U.S. Dist. Ct. Mass. 1975, U.S. Ct. Appeals (1st cir.) 1975, U.S. Supreme Ct. 1979, U.S. Claims Ct. 1983. Assoc. Ropes & Gray, Boston, 1974-83, ptnr., 1983—; mem. hearing com. Bd. Bar Overseers, 1983-89; bd. dirs., v.p. Family Counseling & Guidance Ctr., Inc., Boston, 1980-93; gov. Mus. of Sci., 1981-93; mem. exec. com. Jud. Nominating Commn., 1991-96; corp. mem. Mass. Gen. Hosp., 1992—; overseer N.E Med. Ctr. Hosps., 1992—. Served to 1st lt. U.S. Army, 1965-68. Fellow Am. Bar Found. (life), Mass. Bar Found. (life), Am. Coll. Trial Lawyers; mem. ABA (standing com. on fed. judiciary), Mass. Bar Assn., Boston Bar Assn., Am. Law Inst., Mass. Black Lawyers Assn. (life). Federal civil litigation, State civil litigation, Environmental. Home: 1265 Beacon St Brookline MA 02446-5200 Office: Ropes & Gray 1 International Pl Fl 4 Boston MA 02110-2624

**TRINDER, RACHEL BANDELE,** lawyer; b. Ibadan, Nigeria, Feb. 21, 1955; came to U.S., 1977; d. Victor William John and Margaret (Almond) T. BA with honors, Oxford U., 1977, MA, 1994; LLM, U. Va., 1978. Bar: D.C. 1979, U.S. Dist. Ct. 1979, U.S. Ct. Appeals (D.C. cir.) 1980, U.S. Supreme Ct. 1986. Assoc. Zuckert, Scoutt & Rasenberger, LLP, Washington, 1978-85, ptnr., 1985—; v.p. aviation spl. interest cpht. Transp. Rsch. Forum, 1988-90, exec. v.p., 1990-91, gen. counsel, 1989-91; mem. bd. advisors 3d Ann. Symposium on Law and Outer Space, 1991, program dir., mem. bd. advisors, 4th Ann., 1991-92. Contbr. articles to legal jours. Bd. govs. Internat. Student House, 1986-93, mem. exec. com., asst. treas., 1987-88, mem. bd. advisors, 1993-97. Fellow English Speaking Union, 1977. Mem. FBA (chair space law com. 1990-94, chair internat. law sect. 1994-96), Internat. Bar Assn., Inter-Pacific Bar Assn., Internat. Inst. Space Law (life), Internat. Aviation Women's Assn. (dir.-at-large 1996-98), Internat. Inst. Air and Space Law (bd. govs., exec. com. 1992—), Internat. Aviation Club (bd. govs. 1984-86, pres. 1986), Aero Club (bd. govs. 1993—, chair legal com. 1993-95, sec. 1996-97, 2d v.p. 1997-98, 1st v.p. 1998-99). Aviation, Private international, General corporate. Home: 1266 Dartmouth Ct Alexandria VA 22314-4784 Office: Zuckert Scoutt & Rasenberger LLP 888 17th St NW Washington DC 20006-3939

**TRIO, EDWARD ALAN,** lawyer, accountant; b. Newark, N.J., Dec. 29, 1952; s. Edward B. and Dorothy J. (Salvia) T.; m. Patricia Ann Sherwood, June 19, 1982; children: Edward Joseph, Michael John. B.B.A., U. Notre Dame, 1974; J.D., Hamline U., St. Paul, 1977; LL.M. in Taxation with honors, Chgo.-Kent Coll. Law, 1984. Bar: Ill. 1977, U.S. Dist. Ct. (no. dist.) Ill. 1977, U.S. Tax Ct. 1979, U.S. Supreme Ct. 1984. C.P.A. Staff auditor Donald E. Bark, C.P.A., Arlington Heights, Ill., 1972-77; assoc. Graf & Gulbrandsen, Morton Grove, Ill., 1977-80; ptnr. Schneider, Graf & Trio, Morton Grove, 1980-82; tax specialist Deloitte Haskins & Sells, Chgo., 1982-85; assoc. Gould & Ratner, Chgo., 1985-90, ptnr., 1991—. Mem. ABA, AICPA, Ill. State Bar Assn., Chgo. Bar Assn., KC. Roman Catholic. Estate planning, Personal income taxation, Probate. Home: 909 N Derbyshire Ave Arlington Heights IL 60004-5776 Office: Gould & Ratner 222 N La Salle St Ste 800 Chicago IL 60601-1086

**TRIPLETT, AUSTIN HENRY,** lawyer, mediator; b. Chgo., Aug. 17, 1955; s. Henry Luther and Nora Mae Triplett; m. Nedra H. Joyner, June 19, 1982; children: Ariel Clare, Blair Katelin. BS, So. Ill. U., 1979; cert. in data processing, Harold Washington Coll., Chgo., 1982; postgrad., U. Ill., Springfield, 1983-84; JD, No. Ill. U., 1995; postgrad., Ill. Inst. Tech., 1996—. Bar: Ill. 1995; cert. mediator, divorce mediator. Mgmt. trainee, duty mgr. Westin Hotels/UAL, Inc., Chgo., 1979-83; adv. mktg. rep. IBM, Springfield and Chgo., 1983-92; spl. asst. to dir. admissions No. Ill. U. Sch. Law, DeKalb, 1993-95; asst. atty. gen. Office Ill. Atty. Gen., Chgo., 1995—, bur. chief, 1998; presiding ptnr. Hart Evans & Assocs., Chgo., 1981-87; gen. counsel, fin. matters mem. Triplett, Henley, Savage and Assocs. LLC, Memphis and Chgo., 1994—; cons. sr. leader IBM Global Svcs. Chgo. Metro, 1999—. Am. Field Svc. scholar, Germany, 1970. Mem. ABA, Ill. Bar Assn. (sect. coun. 1995—, reporter task force on minorities in justice sys. 1996-97), Chgo. Bar Assn., Ill. Trial Lawyers Assn., Kappa Alpha Psi (life). Republican. Roman Catholic. Avocations: judo, reading, travel. Office: Office Ill Atty Gen 100 W Randolph St Chicago IL 60601-3218

**TRIPLETT, TIMOTHY WAYNE,** lawyer; b. Washington, Mo., Sept. 19, 1954; s. Lewis and Ruth (Kappelmann) T.; children: Grant, Andrew, Anne. BS summa cum laude, SW Bapt. Coll., 1975; JD cum laude, U. Mo., 1977. Bar: Kans. 1978, Mo. 1984. Assoc. Blackwell Sanders Matheny Weary & Lombardi, Kansas City, Mo., 1978-82; ptnr. Blackwell Sanders Matheny Weary & Lombardi, Overland Park, Kans., 1982—. Participant Annual Johnston County Community Coll. Benefit, Overland Park. Mem. Kans. Bar Assn., Kansas City Met. Bar Assn., Johnson County Bar Assn., Mo. Bar Assn., Kans. Assn. Ins. Def. Counsel, SW Bapt. U. Alumni Assn. (pres. Greater Kansas City chpt. 1991-92), Overland Park C. of C. Construction, Public utilities, Product liability. Office: Blackwell Sanders Matheny Weary & Lombardi 2300 Main St Ste 1000 Kansas City MO 64108-2416

**TRIPP, KAREN BRYANT,** lawyer; b. Rocky Mount, N.C., Sept. 2, 1955; d. Bryant and Katherine Rebecca (Watkins) Tripp; m. Robert Mark Burleson, June 25, 1977 (div. 1997); 1 child, Hamilton Chase Barnett. BA, U. N.C., 1976; JD, U. Ala., 1981. Bar: Tex. 1981, U.S. Dist. Ct. (so. dist.) Tex. 1982, U.S. Dist. Ct. (ea. dist.) Tex. 1991, U.S. Dist. Ct. (no. dist.) Tex. 1998, U.S. Ct. Appeals (fed. cir.) 1983, U.S. Supreme Ct. 1994. Law clk. Tucker, Gray & Espy, Tuscaloosa, Ala., 1978-81; law clk. to presiding justice Ala. Supreme Ct., Montgomery, summer 1980; atty. Exxon Prodn. Rsch. Co., Houston, 1981-86, coord. tech. transfer, 1986-87; assoc. Arnold, white and Durkee, Houston, 1988-93, shareholder, 1994-98; shareholder Winstead, Sechrest & Minick, Attys. at Law, Houston, 1998; pres. Blake Barnett & Co., 1996—; pvt. practice, 1999—; Creator, program planner, master of ceremonies 1st and 2d intellectual prperty law confs. for women corp. counsels. Editor Intellectual Property Law Rev., 1995-99; contbr. articles to profl. jours. Mem. ABA (intellectual property law sect., ethics com. 1992-96), Houston Bar Assn. (interprofl. rels. com. 1988-90), Houston Intellectual Property Lawyers Assn. (mem. outstanding inventor com. 1982-84, chmn. 1994-95, sec. 1987-88, treas. 1991-92, bd. dirs. 1992-94, 98—, nominations com. 1993, 96), Tex. Bar Assn. (antitrust law com. 1984-85, chmn. internat.

law com. intellectual property law sect. 1987-88, inernat. transfer tech. com. 1983-84), Women's Fin. Exch., Am. Intellectual Property Lawyers Assn. (patent law com. 1995), Women in Tech. (founder), Phi Alpha Delta. Democrat. Episcopalian. Patent, Trademark and copyright, Intellectual property. Office: 1100 Louisiana St Ste 2690 Houston TX 77002-5216

**TRIPP, NORMAN DENSMORE,** lawyer; b. Binghamton, N.Y., Apr. 11, 1938; s. Merritt Frederick and Eleonore Graves (Satterley) T.; m. Jane Grace Mighton, June 15, 1962; children: Jennifer, Norman, Christine, Michael. BA, U. Miami, 1962; JD magna cum laude, Cleve. State U., 1967. Bar: Ohio, Fla. Chmn. Tripp Scott P.A., Fort Lauderdale, Fla.; gen. counsel Cert. Tours (Delta Dream Vacations). Past mem. bd. adjustment City of Fort Lauderdale; mem. Ft. Lauderdale Downtown Devel. Authority; mem. South Fla. Annenberg Challenge, Broward County; mem. City of Ft. Lauderdale Downtown Devel. Bd.; bd. trustees State of Fla. C.C. System, U. Miami, Coral Gables, Fla. Mem. Am. Soc. Travel Agts., ABA, Broward County Bar Assn., Fla. Bar Assn., Ocean Reef Club (Key Largo), Fort Lauderdale Yacht Club, Fort Lauderdale Country Club,. Contracts commercial, Real property, Insurance. Office: Tripp Scott PA PO Box 14245 Fort Lauderdale FL 33302-4245

**TRIPP, PAUL WAYNE,** lawyer; b. Adel, Ga., Oct. 16, 1969; s. Mack Carliss and Nancy Jane Tripp; m. Tracey Lynn Hay, Mar. 21, 1998. BS, U. Ctrl. Fla., 1989; MBA, JD, U. Fla., 1997. Bar: Fla. 1998, U.S. Dist. Ct. (mid., so. and no. dists.) Fla. 1998. Asst. to contr. Am. Machinery, Orlando, Fla., 1988-90; summer assoc. Tew Zinober Barnes Zimmet Unice, Clearwater, Fla., 1997; assoc. Rudnick & Wolfe, Tampa, Fla., 1998—. Instr. Hillsborough Lit. Counsel, 1998. Sgt. U.S. Army, 1990-94. Republican. Southern Baptist. Bankruptcy, General civil litigation, Land use and zoning (including planning). Office: Rudnick & Wolfe 101 E Kennedy Blvd Ste 2000 Tampa FL 33602-5149

**TRIPP, THOMAS NEAL,** lawyer, political consultant; b. June 19, 1942; s. Gerald Frederick and Kathryn Ann (Siebold) T.; m. Ellen Marie Larrimer, Apr. 16, 1966; children: David Larrimer, Bradford Doublas, Corinne Catherine. BA cum laude, Mich. State U., 1964; JD, George Washington U., 1967. Bar: Ohio 1967, U.S. Ct. Mil. Appeals 1968, U.S. Supreme Ct. 1968, Wyo. 1991. Pvt. practice Columbus, Ohio, 1969—, Wilson, Wyo., 1991—; real estate developer, Columbus, 1969—; chmn. bd. Black Sheep Enterprises, Columbus, 1969—; polit. cons. David A. Keene & Assocs., Washington, 1986-96; vice chmn. bd. Sun Valley-Elkhorn Assn., Idaho, 1983-85, chmn, 1986-91; vice chmn. Sawtooth Sports, Ketchum, Idaho, 1983-85; legal counsel Wallace F. Ackley Co., Columbus, 1973—; vice chmn. Triathlon LLC, 1996—; presiding judge Ohio Mock Triathlon Competition, 1986-94; chmn. bd. dirs. White House, 1996; bd. dirs. U.S. Prison Industries; mem. small bus. adv. coun. FCC; dep. spl. adviser to pres. N.Am. Free Trade Agreement. Trustee Americans for Responsible Govt., Washington, GOPAC; mem. Peace Corps Adv. Coun., 1981-85; mem. U.S. Commn. on Trade Policy and Negotiations, 1985-88; campaign mgr., fin. chmn. Charles Rockwell Saxbe, Ohio Ho. of Reps., 1974, 76, 78, 80; campaign mgr. George Bush for Pres., 1980, nat. dep. field dir., nat. dep. polit. dir., 1980; mem. alumni admissions coun. Mich. State U., 1984—, George Washington U., 1988—; regional co-chmn. Reagan-Bush, 1984, mem. nat. fin. com., 1984; mem. Victory '84 fin. com.; mem. Victory '88 fin. com. Bush-Quayle; co-chmn. Ohio Lawyers for Bush/Quayle, 1988; Rep. candidate 2d U.S. Congl. Dist., Idaho, 1988; candidate U.S. Senate, Wyo., 1996; transition dir. Ohio Sec. of State, 1990-91; mem. bd. trustees Columbus Acad. Pvt. Co-ed Secondary Sch., 1991-94; chair bd. dirs. T.R.E.E. Coalition, 1991—p; bd. trustees Prescott (Ariz.) Coll., 1998—. 1st lt. U.S. Army, 1967-69. Fellow Pi Sigma Alpha, Vietnam Vet. Am., Phi Delta Phi. Republican. Workers' compensation, Personal injury, Real property. Home: 5420 Clark State Rd Columbus OH 43230-1956

**TRITTER, DANIEL F.,** lawyer, writer; b. N.Y.C., Jan. 20, 1934; s. Maurice J. and Hermina (Ronay) T.; m. Rita Frances Shane, June 22, 1958; 1 child, Michael Shane. BA, Williams Coll., 1954; MA, Columbia U., 1957; cert., Inst. on East Cen. Europe, 1957; JD, Benjamin N. Cardozo Sch. Law, 1982. Bar: N.Y. 1984, U.S. Dist. Ct. (so. dist., ea. dist.) 1984, U.S. Supreme Ct. 1987. Writer, exec. Diener & Dorskind, Inc., N.Y.C., 1960-71, M.L. Grant, Inc., N.Y.C., 1971-79; pvt. practice, N.Y.C., 1984—; adj. prof. Williams Coll., 1984, Touro Law Sch., 1989, Benjamin N. Cardozo Sch. Law, 1999. Contbr. essays to profl. jours. Bd. govs. N.Y. chpt. Arthritis Found., 1985-90. Spl. agt. CIC, U.S. Army, 1957-60. Mem. Assn. Trial Lawyers Am., Law and Humanities Inst. (pres. 1986-91, v.p. 1991—), Williams Club. Democrat. Avocations: classical music, writing, sports. Entertainment, General civil litigation. Office: 330 W 42nd St Fl 32 New York NY 10036-6902

**TROCANO, RUSSELL PETER,** lawyer; b. Hackensack, N.J., Sept. 7, 1963; s. Rosario Mario and Barbara Ann (Costa) T. BA, Seton Hall U., 1984; JD, Fordham U., 1987, LLM, 1992. Bar: N.J. 1987, N.Y. 1988. Law clk. to presiding justice County of Middlesex, New Brunswick, N.J., 1987-88; assoc. Sellar Richardson Law Firm, Newark and Roseland, N.J., 1988; Morgan Melhuish Monaghan Law Firm, Livingston, N.J., 1988-89; prin., owner Russell P. Trocano, Ridgewood, N.J., 1989—. Mem. San Guisseppe Societa de Santa Croce de Camerina, Paterson, N.J., 1989—. Fordham U. scholar, 1987. Mem. ABA, N.J. Bar Assn., N.Y. State Bar Assn., Bergen County Bar Assn., Passaic County Bar Assn., Brehon Law Soc., Arthur T. Vanderbilt Inn of Cts., Phi Alpha Theta. Roman Catholic. Avocations: mineral collecting, travel, reading. Consumer commercial, Bankruptcy, General practice. Home: 60 S Maple Ave Ridgewood NJ 07450-4542 Office: 7 E Ridgewood Ave Ridgewood NJ 07450-3807

**TROFFKIN, HOWARD JULIAN,** lawyer, diversified company executive; b. Port Chester, N.Y., Jan. 30, 1937; s. Irving and Frieda Troffkin; m. Rhea Dorothy, May 12, 1963; children—Stephen, Barbara. BS in Chemistry, St. Lawrence U., 1959; postgrad. Columbia U. Sch. Engring., 1959-60; J.D., Georgetown U., 1970. Bar: Va. 1971, D.C. 1972. Research chemist Am. Cyanamid Co., 1961-66, legal trainee, 1966-67, pat. agt., 1967-71; assoc. Pennie, Edmonds, Morton, Taylor & Adams, Washington, 1971-77; patent atty. W.R. Grace & Co., Columbia, Md., 1977-86, sr. patent counsel 1987-98; pvt. practice, 1998—. Patentee in chemistry field. Mem. Willerburn Civic Assn., 1971-75. Served with AUS, 1960-61. Mem. ABA, Va. Bar Assn., D.C. Bar Assn., Washington Pat. Lawyers Assn., Md. Patent Law Assn. (pres. 1981-83), Am. Intellectual Property Law Assn., Am. Chem. Soc. Jewish. Avocations: woodcrafting, travel. Patent, Intellectual property, Trademark and copyright. Home and Office: 7808 Ivymount Ter Potomac MD 20854-3218

**TROGE, ANN MARIE,** lawyer, magistrate; b. Charles City, Iowa, Feb. 9, 1963; d. Jack L. and Jean M. Troge. BA in Tchg., U. No. Iowa, 1985; JD, Drake U., 1992. Bar: Iowa 1992, U.S. Dist. Ct. (no. dist.) Iowa 1992. Assoc. Sutton Law Office, Charles City, 1992-93; ptnr. Sutton & Troge Law Office, Charles City, 1994-98; magistrate Floyd County, Charles City, 1994—; pvt. practice, Charles City, 1999—; adj. instr. North Iowa Area C.C., Mason City, Iowa, 1997—. Past v.p. City Improvement Assn., Charles City; bd. dirs. Stony Pont Players, Charles City. Mem. Iowa State Bar, Iowa Trial Lawyers Assn., Iowa State Bar Rev. Sch., Inc. (Farmington juvenile law com. 1997—), Rotary (former bd. dirs.). Roman Catholic. Avocations: music, acting. Family and matrimonial, Juvenile, General practice. Home and Office: 1208 Clark St Charles City IA 50616-2815

**TROILO, ARTHUR, III,** lawyer; b. Frankfurt, Germany; came to U.S., 1953; s. Arthur Charles Jr. and Nancy Ann (Sullivan) T.; 1 child, Douglas Arthur. BFA, U. Tex., 1977; JD, U. Houston, 1984. Bar: Tex. 1985, D.C. 1991, U.S. Dist. Ct. (D.C. dist.) 1985, U.S. Dist. Ct. Tex. 1985, U.S. Ct. Appeals (D.C., fed. and 5th cirs.) 1988, U.S. Ct. Fed. Claims, U.S. Supreme Ct. 1988. Assoc. Davidson & Troilo, San Antonio, 1984-90; dep. gen. counsel U.S. GSA, Washington, 1990-92; gen. counsel U.S. Office of Personnel Mgmt., Washington, 1992-93; ptnr. Maloney & Burch, Washington, 1993-94; regional dir. Sen. Kay Bailey Hutchison, San Antonio, 1994-96; chief charitable trust sect. Tex. Atty. Gen.'s Office, Austin, 1997—; former govt. mem. Adminstrv. Conf. of the U.S., 1992-93. Author: Ethical Restrictions on Federal Officials You Should Know About, 1993, St. Mary's Law Journal Symposium, 1993. Bd. dirs. Alamo Area Big Bros. and Sisters, 1989-90. Named one of Outstanding Young Men Am., 1988. Mem. D.C. Bar, San Antonio Bar Assn., The Coll. of State Bar of Tex. Avocations: amateur baseball. Home: 14130 Sage Trl San Antonio TX 78231-1975 Office: PO Box 12548 Austin TX 78711-2548

**TROJACK, JOHN EDWARD,** lawyer; b. St. Paul, Mar. 30, 1946; s. Albert G. and Eleanor (Mader) T.; m. Mary Jo LaNasa, Oct. 12, 1979; 4 children. BA, U. Minn., 1968; JD, William Mitchell Coll. Law, St. Paul, 1976. Bar: Minn. 1976, U.S. Dist. Ct. Minn. 1976, U.S. Ct. Appeals (8th cir.) 1980, U.S. Supreme Ct. 1980. Assoc. John E. Daubney, St. Paul, 1976-78; ptnr. Wagner, Rutchick & Trojack, P.A., St. Paul, 1978-83; sole practice St. Paul, 1983—; arbitrator Hennepin County Dist. Ct., 1986—; vol. atty. So. Minn. Legal Svcs. Corp., St. Paul, 1982—; Conciliation Ct. referee Ramsey County Dist. Ct., St. Paul, 1979—. Served with USN, 1968-72, capt. USNR. Mem. Minn. Bar Assn. (chair gen. practice sect. 1983-85), Ramsey County Bar Assn. (real property com., family law com., dist. ethics com.), Naval Res. Assn., Res. Officers Assn., The Harvesters Club, Phi Alpha Delta. General practice, State civil litigation, Probate. Address: 1549 Livingston Ave Ste 108 Saint Paul MN 55118-3415

**TROMBLEY, MICHAEL JEROME,** lawyer; b. Bay City, Mich., Dec. 10, 1933; s. Clare F. and Sarah I. (Ingersol) T.; m. Anna K. Simons (div. 1963); children: Peter, Tad; m. Sandra V. Bybee (dec. 1980); children: Christine, Jacques; m. Sherry V. Cribbs, June 10, 1981. A.A., Menlo Coll., 1953; B.A., Stanford U., 1955; LL.B., U. Mo., 1960. Bar: Mo. 1960, Fla. 1974. Sole practice, Columbia, Mo., 1960-68; ptnr. Alexander, Wayland, Trombley, Butcher, Columbia, Mo., 1964-68; sole practice, 1969-79; ptnr. Trombley, Matheny & Schommer, Sebring, Fla., 1980-84, Trombley, Lobozzo, Schommer, Disler & Acoorsi, Sebring, 1984—. Charter pres. Estate Planning Council of Highlands County, Fla., 1979-80. Served to 1st lt. USMCR, 1955-57. Mem. Am. Judicature Soc., Acad. Fla. Trial Lawyers, Nat. Acad. Elder Law Attys. Republican. Episcopalian. Clubs: Masons, Shriners, Elks. State civil litigation, Federal civil litigation, Estate planning. Office: 329 S Commerce Ave Sebring FL 33870-3607

**TRONFELD, JAY,** lawyer; b. Phila.; s. Sidney I. and Cecilia (Zalkin) T.; m. Caren Herzberg, Aug. 30, 1970; children: Andrew Clinton, Caye Margaret. BA, U. Richmond, 1966; JD, U. Tenn., 1971. Bar: Va. Law clk. Doumar, Pincus, Knight & Harlan, Norfolk, Va., 1971; lawyer Donmar, Pinens, Knight & Harlan, Norfolk, Va., 1971-72; pres. Jay Tronfeld & Assoc., Richmond, Va., 1972—; pres. Richmond Trial Lawyers Assn., 1991-92; lectr. in field. Served with USAF Res., 1967. Mem. ABA, Am. Trial Lawyers Assn., Va. Trial Lawyers Assn., Richmond Bar Assn. Avocations: fishing, gardening, traveling. Personal injury. Office: Jay Tronfeld and Assoc 4020 W Broad St Richmond VA 23230-3916

**TROOP, (WALTER) MICHAEL,** prosecutor; m. Lillian Troop; 2 children. BPA, U. Miss.; JD, U. Ky. Asst. prof. bus. law U. Miss., 1974-77; with Ky. Gen. Assembly, 1974; trial commr. Hopkins County Dist. Ct., Ky., 1977-80; pvt. practice Madisonville, Ky., 1977-88; commr. Ky. State Police, 1988-91; also sec. justice cabinet; U.S. atty. we. dist. Ky. Office U.S. Atty., Louisville, 1993—; mem. Atty. Gen.'s Adv. Com. Office: US Attys Office Bank of Louisville Bldg 510 W Broadway Fl 10 Louisville KY 40202-2237*

**TROOST, FRANK WILLIAM,** judge; b. Joliet, Ill., June 8, 1916; s. Elizabeth Troost; m. Anne Emerson Bowden, Oct. 5, 1940; children: Frank William, John Bowden, Martha Maria Frantz. BBA, U. So. Calif., 1937, LLB, 1939. Judge Culver Jud. Dist. Mcpl. Ct., 1965-85. Mem. Calif. Judges Assn. (seminar leader, v.p., bd. dirs.), S.W. L.A. Bar Assn. (founder, pres.), Marina Del Rey Bar Assn., Culver City Bar Assn., U. So. Calif. Law Alumni (pres.). Home: 3650 Fairland Blvd Los Angeles CA 90043-1109

**TROST, EILEEN BANNON,** lawyer; b. Teaneck, N.J., Jan. 9, 1951; d. William Eugene and Marie Thelma (Finlayson) Bannon; m. Lawrence Peter Trost Jr., Aug. 27, 1977; children: Lawrence Peter III, William Patrick, Timothy Alexander. BA with great distinction, Shimer Coll., 1972; JD cum laude, U. Minn., 1976. Bar: Ill. 1976, U.S. Dist. Ct. (no. dist.) Ill. 1976, Minn. 1978, U.S. Tax Ct. 1978, U.S. Supreme Ct. 1981. Assoc. McDermott, Will & Emery, Chgo., 1976-82, ptnr., 1982-93; v.p. No. Trust Bank Ariz. N.A., Phoenix, 1993-95; ptnr. Sonnenschein Nath & Rosenthal, Chgo., 1995—. Mem. Am. Coll. Trust and Estate Coun., Minn. Bar Assn., Internat. Acad. Estate and Trust Law. Roman Catholic. Estate planning, Probate, Estate taxation. Office: Sonnenschein Nath & Rosenthal 8000 Sears Tower Chicago IL 60606

**TROTT, DENNIS C(HARLES),** lawyer; b. Ft. Wayne, Ind., Oct. 31, 1946; s. Charles and Eileen (Collins) T.; m. Nancy J. Servis, Aug. 4, 1973; children: Eileen Susanne, Duncan Eric. AB, Ind. U., 1968; JD, U. Mich., 1973. Bar: N.Y. 1974, U.S. Dist. Ct. (so. dist.) N.Y. 1974, U.S. Ct. Appeals (2d cir.) 1974, U.S. Dist. Ct. (ea. dist.) N.Y. 1978, U.S. Ct. Mil. Appeals 1985, U.S. Ct. Internat. Trade 1986, U.S. Tax Ct. 1986, U.S. Supreme Ct. 1986, U.S. Ct. Claims 1988, U.S. Ct. Appeals (fed. cir.) 1990, U.S. Ct. Appeals (3rd and 6th cirs.) 1991. Assoc. Haight, Gardner, N.Y.C., 1973-75, Breed, Abbott, N.Y.C., 1975-77; pres., chief exec. officer Luke Enterprises, Inc., N.Y.C., 1988—; ptnr. Trott & Appel, N.Y.C., 1989-91; pvt. practice N.Y.C., 1991—. Bd. dirs. Neighborhood Housing Services of N.Y.C., 1985-89. Served with U.S. Army, 1968-70. Mem. Assn. Bar City N.Y., N.Y. County Lawyers Assn., Maritime Law Assn., Nat. Trust for Hist. Preservation. General corporate, Banking, Admiralty. Home: 304 Sherman St Brooklyn NY 11218-1507 Office: 305 Broadway Rm 700 New York NY 10007-1109

**TROTT, STEPHEN SPANGLER,** federal judge, musician; b. Glen Ridge, N.J., Dec. 12, 1939; s. David Herman and Virginia (Spangler) T.; divorced; children: Christina, Shelley. BA, Wesleyan U., 1962; LLB, Harvard U., 1965; LLD (hon.), Santa Clara U., 1992. Bar: Calif. 1966, U.S. Dist. Ct. (cen. dist.) Calif. 1966, U.S. Ct. Appeals (9th cir.) 1983, U.S. Supreme Ct. 1984. Guitarist, mem. The Highwaymen, 1958—; dep. dist. atty. Los Angeles County Dist. Atty.'s Office, Los Angeles, 1966-75; chief dep. dist. atty. Los Angeles County Dist. Atty.'s Office, 1975-79; U.S. dist. atty. Central Dist. Calif., Los Angeles, 1981-83; asst. atty. gen. criminal div. Dept. Justice, Washington, 1983-86; mem. faculty Nat. Coll. Dist. Attys., Houston, 1973—; chmn. central dist. Calif. Law Enforcement Coordinating Com., Houston, 1981-83; coordinator Los Angeles-Nev. Drug Enforcement Task Force, 1982-83; assoc. atty. gen. Justice Dept., Washington, 1986-88; chmn. U.S. Interpol, 1986-88; judge U.S. Ct. of Appeals 9th Cir., Boise, Idaho, 1988—. Trustee Wesleyan U., 1984-87; bd. dirs., pres. Children's Home Soc., Idaho, 1990—; pres., bd. dirs. Boise Philharm. Assn., 1995—, v.p., 1997-99, pres., 1999—. Recipient Gold record as singer-guitarist for Michael Row the Boat Ashore, 1961, Disting. Faculty award Nat. Coll. Dist. Attys., 1977. Mem. Am. Coll. Trial Lawyers, Wilderness Fly Fishers Club (pres. 1975-77), Brentwood Racing Pigeon Club (pres. 1977-82), Idaho Racing Pigeon Assn., Magic Castle, Internat. Brotherhood Magicians, Idaho Classic Guitar Soc. (founder, pres. 1989—). Republican. Office: US Ct Appeals 9th Cir 667 US Courthouse 550 W Fort St Boise ID 83724-0101

**TROTTA, FRANK P., JR.,** lawyer; b. New Rochelle, N.Y., Jan. 19, 1955. BA, SUNY, Albany, 1975; JD, Union U., Albany, 1978; LLM, NYU, 1986; MBA, Columbia U., 1992. Bar: N.Y. U.S. Dist. Ct. (no. and ea. dists.) N.Y. 1979, U.S. Ct. Mil. Appeals 1978, U.S. Dist. Ct. (so. and ea. dists.) N.Y. 1980, U.S. Ct. Internat. Trade 1980, U.S. Tax Ct. 1982, U.S. Supreme Ct. 1982, U.S. Ct. Appeals (D.C. cir.) 1983, U.S. Ct. Customs and Patent Appeals 1984, D.C. 1985, Conn. 1988, Pa. 1991. Assoc. Weil, Gotshal & Manges, N.Y.C., 1978-81; pvt. practice Washington, N.Y.C., 1981-86, New Rochelle, 1981-92, Greenwich, Conn., 1986—; mem. bd. govs. Fund for Justice and Edn., 1987-90, ABA, 1987-90; mem. faculty Practicing Law Inst., 1979; governing mem. Nat. Jud. Coll., 1987-90, Am. Bar Endowment, 1987-90, ABRA Pension Fund, 1987-90; chmn. bd. advisors Columbia U. Grad. Sch. Bus., Inst. for Non-for-Profit Mgmt., 1992-95. Mem. nat. com. Cath. Campaign Am.; chmn. New Rochelle Rep. Party, 1982-85; mem., bd. dirs. Boys Town of Italy, 1997—. Legislative. Address: 1 Fawcett Pl Ste 132 Greenwich CT 06830-6553

**TROTTER, RICHARD CLAYTON,** lawyer; b. Houston, June 2, 1950; s. John Clayton and Frances (Barrington) T.; m. Susan Hendrick, Dec. 28, 1972; children: Fredrick, Frances, Susie, Byron, Ricky, Alma. BBA, U. Tex., 1973, JD, 1976. Bar: Tex. 1976, U.S. Dist. Ct. (we. and no. dists.) Tex. 1978, Fla. 1982, U.S. Ct. Appeals (5th cir.) 1978, U.S. Ct. Appeals (7th cir.) 1987, U.S. Supreme Ct. 1988. Law clk. to Hon. John H. Wood, Jr. U.S. Dist. Ct., San Antonio, 1976-78; postdoctoral Oxford U., Eng., 1978-80; corp. counsel GM, Orlando, Fla., 1980-83; pvt. practice San Antonio, 1989—; asst. prof. Tex. Tech. U., Lubbock, 1983-86, 87-89, Trinity U., San Antonio, 1989—; assoc. prof. Regent U., Virginia Beach, Va., 1986-87. Author: Lone Star Law, 1991; editor proceedings So. Bus. Law, 1990; contbr. articles to profl. jours. Mem. Tex. Trial Lawyers Assn., So. Bus. Law Assn. (sec.-treas. 1988-89, v.p., editor 1987-90, pres. 1991-92), Coll. State Bar Tex., Honor Soc. Internat. Scholars. Republican. Avocations: running, flying, basketball. Libel, Contracts commercial, Personal injury. Office: Branton & Hall PC 737 Travis Park Plz San Antonio TX 78205-1786

**TROUT, LINDA COPPLE,** state supreme court justice; b. Tokyo, Sept. 1, 1951. BA, U. Idaho, 1973, JD, 1977; LLD (hon.), Albertson Coll. Idaho, 1999. Bar: Idaho 1977. Judge magistrate divsn. Idaho Dist. Ct. (2d jud. divsn.), 1983-90; dist. judge Idaho Dist. Ct. (2d jud. divsn.), Lewiston, 1991-92; acting trial ct. adminstr. Idaho Dist. Ct. (2d jud. divsn.), 1987-91; justice Idaho Supreme Ct., 1992—, chief justice, 1997—; instr. coll. law U. Idaho, 1983, 88. Mem. Idaho State Bar Assn., Clearwater Bar Assn. (pres. 1980-81).

**TROUTMAN, E. MAC,** federal judge; b. Greenwood Township, Pa., Jan. 7, 1915; s. Emmett Theodore and Kathryn (Holman) T.; m. Margaret Petrick, Nov. 23, 1944; children—Jane A., Jean K. A.B., Dickinson Coll., 1934, LL.B., 1936. Bar: Pa. 1937. With Phila. and Reading Coal and Iron Co., 1937-58, gen. counsel, 1954-58; gen. atty. Phila. and Reading Corp., 1958-67; gen. counsel Reading Anthracite Co., 1958-61, Reserve Carbon Corp., 1961-66, So. Carbon Corp., 1966-67; solicitor Blue Mountain Sch. Dist., 1963-67, Blue Mountain Area Sch. Authority, 1963-67, Orwigsburg Municipal Authority, 1966-67, Am. Bank and Trust Co., Reading and Pottsville, Pa., 1957-67; exec. sec., gen. counsel Pa. Self-Insurers Assn., 1962-67; U.S. judge Eastern Dist. Pa., from 1967, sr. judge, 1982-98; retired, 1998. Bd. dirs. Greater Pottsville Indsl. Devel. Corp., 1963-67, Pa. C. of C., 1955-65, Greater Pottsville Area C. of C., 1961-64, Orwigsburg Community Meml. Assn., 1950-66, Schuylkill County Soc. Crippled Children, 1945-67; v.p., dir. Pottsville Hosp. and Warne Clinic, 1960-67. Served with AUS, World War II. Mem. ABA, Pa. Bar Assn., Schuylkill County Bar Assn. (vice chancellor 1955-57, chmn. jud. vacancies and unauthorized practice coms. 1960, chmn. medico-legal com. 1963-65). Lutheran (pres. coun. 1961—). Home: Kimmel's Rd Orwigsburg PA 17961

**TROUTMAN, J. GREGORY,** lawyer; b. Louisville, Dec. 7, 1966. BA in Polit. Sci. cum laude, U. Louisville, 1989, JD, 1992; LLM in Taxation, Boston U., 1993. Bar: Ky. 1992, U.S. Fed. Claims Ct. 1994, U.S. Dist. Ct. (we. dist.) Ky. 1995, U.S. Dist. Ct. (ea. dist.) Ky. 1998, U.S. Ct. Appeals (6th cir.) 1998, U.S. Ct. Appeals (7th cir.) 1999. Pvt. practice Louisville, 1992-94; assoc. Morris, Garlove, Waterman & Johnson, Louisville, 1994—. Vol. Camapign Northup for Congress, 1996, 98; bd. dirs. Spring Mill Bible Camp, Mitchell, Ind., 1994—. Mem. Ky. Bar Assn., Louisville Bar Assn. Fax: 502-589-3219. E-mail: JGT@mgwj.com. Office: Morris Garlove Waterman & Johnson 1000 One Riverfront Plaza Louisville KY 40202

**TROUTWINE, GAYLE LEONE,** lawyer; b. Kansas City, Mo., Feb. 26, 1952. BS, N.W. Mo. State U., 1973; JD with honors, U. Mo., 1978. Bar: Mo. 1978, Oreg. 1983, U.S. Dist. Ct. (we. dist.) Mo., Wash. 1984, U.S. Ct. Appeals (9th cir.) 1984, U.S. Dist. Ct. (we. dist.) Wash., U.S. Supreme Ct., Hawaii 1995. Ptnr. Williams & Troutwine, P.C., Portland, Oreg., 1986—; speaker in field. Contbr. articles to profl. jours. Steering com. mem. Breast Implant Litigation, 1992—, Tobacco Litigation; bd. mem. Portland Area Women's Polit. Caucus, 1992-95, Oreg. Women's Polit. Caucus, 1996—; mem. Jud. Steering com., 1994. Named Queen of Torts Wall St. Jour., 1996. Mem. ATLA (bd. govs.), Hawaii State Bar, Mo. Bar, Oreg. State Bar (exec. bd. litigation sect. 1984-88, chmn. 1987-88, procedure and practice com. 1985-88, bd. govs. 1990-93), Wash. State Bar, Oreg. Trial Lawyers Assn. (bd. govs. 1987-91), Calif. Trial Lawyers Assn., Hawaii Trial Lawyers Assn., Wash. Trial Lawyers Assn., Women Lawyers Assn., Greater Kansas City (sec. 1981-82), Western Trial Lawyers Assn. (bd. govs. 1992—). Democrat. Personal injury, Federal civil litigation, State civil litigation. Office: Williams and Troutwine PC 1001 SW 5th Ave Ste 1900 Portland OR 97204-1135

**TROVER, ELLEN LLOYD,** lawyer; b. Richmond, Va., Nov. 23, 1947; d. Robert Van Buren and Hazel (Urban) Lloyd; m. Denis William Trover, June 12, 1971; 1 dau., Florence Emma. AB, Vassar Coll., 1969; JD, Coll. William and Mary, 1972. Assoc. editor Bancroft-Whitney, San Francisco, 1973-74; owner Ellen Lloyd Trover Atty.-at-Law, Thousand Oaks, Calif., 1974-82; ptnr. Trover & Fisher, Thousand Oaks, 1982-89; pvt. practice law, Thousand Oaks, 1989-98; mng. ptnr. The Lloyd-Trover Partnership, 1998—. Editor: Handbooks of State Chronologies, 1972. Trustee, Conejo Future Found., Thousand Oaks, 1978-91, trustee emeritus, 1992—, vice chmn., 1982-84, chmn., 1984-88; pres. Zonta Club Conejo Valley Area, 1978-79; trustee Hydro Help for the Handicapped, 1980-85, Atlantis Found., 1994—. Mem. State Bar Calif., Va. State Bar, Phi Alpha Delta. Democrat. Presbyterian. Probate, Estate taxation. Home: 11355 Presilla Rd Camarillo CA 93012-9230 Office: 1107E E Thousand Oaks Blvd Thousand Oaks CA 91362-2816

**TROWBRIDGE, JEFFERY DAVID,** lawyer; b. Santa Monica, Calif., Mar. 6, 1956; s. John Munro and Betty Jane (Taylor) T.; m. Linda Patrice Olbert, Aug. 5, 1978; children: Brian, Daniel, Patrick. BA, U. Colo., 1978; JD, U. Calif., San Francisco, 1981. Bar: Calif. 1981, U.S. Dist. Ct. (no. dist.) Calif. 1981. Assoc. Law Offices Dennis M. Sullivan, Oakland, Calif., 1981-87; pvt. practice, Oakland, 1987—. Counsel pro bono, bd. dirs. Ctr. for AIDS Svcs., Oakland, 1990; mem. fin. adminstrn. adv. com. Am. Lung Assn., Alameda County, 1988—, bd. dirs., 1989—, sec. bd. dirs., 1990, pres.-elect 1991—, pres. 1992-93; mem. corp. bd. College Ave. Presbyn. Ch., 1989—. Boettcher Found. scholar, Denver, 1974-78. Mem. Calif. State Bar Assn., Alameda County Bar Assn., Order of Coif, Thurston Soc., Rotary (sec. svcs. Piedmont-Montclair club 1988—). Avocations: jogging, guitar. State civil litigation, General practice, General corporate. Office: 180 Grand Ave Ste 1550 Oakland CA 94612-3703

**TROWER, WILLIAM KEVIN,** lawyer; b. Pitts., Aug. 15, 1958; s. William Harvey and Clara Belle Trower; 1 child, Richard. BA, Point Park Coll., Pitts., 1981; JD cum laude, Duquesne U., 1992. Bar: Pa. 1992. With affiliate rels. Sheridan Broadcasting, Pitts., 1979-91; with media rels. United Way, Pitts., 1991-93; in pub. affairs WTAE-TV, Pitts., 1993-95; atty. Law Offices of Byrd R. Brown, Pitts., 1993—. Mem. Law Rev., Duquesne U., 1991. Mem. Kappa Alpha Psi. General practice, General civil litigation. Office: 515 Court Pl Pittsburgh PA 15219-2002

**TROWERS, TERESA CARDENAS,** lawyer; b. Manzanillo, Oriente, Cuba, Oct. 3, 1951; came to the U.S., 1967; d. Andres A. and Rosa M. Ricardo Cardenas; m. Eugene A. Trowers, June 7, 1986; children: Teresa, Olivia, Jennifer. BA, U. Ill., Chgo., 1977; BS, Emory U., 1978; MS, Govs. State U., 1983; LLD, Tex. Tech. U., 1996. Bar: U.S. Dist. Ct. (no. dist.) Tex. 1998. Med. records dir. Mt. Sinai Hosp., Chgo., 1979-82; quality assurance coord. Lakeshore Hosp., Chgo., 1982-83; med. records dir. Luth. Gen. Hosp., San Antonio, 1983-91; social security handler West Tex. Legal Svcs., Lubbock, 1996-97; pvt. practice law Lubbock, 1998—; owner Trowers Medicolegal Cons., Lubbock, 1998—. Columnist Lubbock County Dem. Party Newsletter. Adv. bd. mem. Child Advocacy, Lubbock, 1998—; mem. Symphony Guill, Lubbock, 1998—; mem. com. Windmill Playrights Festival. Recipient Steve Condos award, 1999. Mem. Am. Health Info. Mgmt., Mexican ABA, Tex. Bar Assn. (professionalism com.), Tex. State Bar Coll., Tex. Criminal Def. Lawyers, Tex. Trial Lawyers Assn., South Plains Family Law Assn. (v.p., pres.-elect). Democrat. Roman Catholic. Avocations: travel, reading, cooking, gardening, entertaining. Personal injury, Criminal, Family and matrimonial. Office: 916 Main St Ste 609 Lubbock TX 79401-3403

**TROY, RICHARD HERSHEY,** lawyer; b. Boston, Sept. 24, 1937; married. AB, Georgetown U., 1959; postgrad., U. Munich, Fed. Republic Germany, 1959-60; LLB, Harvard U., 1963. Bar: Mass. 1963, N.Y. 1965, U.S. Dist. Ct. (so. and ea. dists.) N.Y. 1965, U.S. Ct. Appeals (2d cir.) 1968, U.S. Supreme Ct. 1969, Conn. 1985. Law clk. to presiding justice U.S. Dist. Ct. N.H., Concord, 1963-64; assoc. Shearman & Sterling, N.Y.C., 1964-73; asst. gen. counsel, asst. sec. Combustion Engring., Inc., Stamford, Conn.,

1974-81, v.p., assoc. gen. counsel, 1982-85, v.p., dep. gen. counsel, 1985-90; v.p., dep. gen. counsel Asea Brown Boveri, Inc., Stamford, 1990; v.p., assoc. gen. counsel UST, Inc., Greenwich, Conn., 1990-92; v.p. fin., law and adminstrn. Cell Pathways, Inc., Denver and Tucson, 1992-97; sr. v.p. corp. devel., gen. counsel and sec. Cell Pathways, Inc., Horsham, Pa., 1997—; speaker in field. Contbr. articles to profl. publs. Mem. Am. Soc. Corp. Secs. (bd. dirs. 1988-91, chmn. securities law com. 1984-89, chmn. proxy system com. 1990-93), Conn. Bar Assn. (mem. exec. com. corp. sect. 1986—), Westchester Fairfield Corp. Counsel Assn. (bd. dirs. 1978-83, pres. 1982). General corporate, Securities, General civil litigation. Office: Cell Pathways Inc 702 Electronic Dr Horsham PA 19044-2229

**TROY, ROBERT SWEENEY, SR.,** lawyer; b. Quincy, Mass., Aug. 13, 1949; s. Robert F. and Winifred (Sweeney) T.; m. Sabina Greene, Oct. 12, 1985; children: Robert Sweeney Jr., Michael Francis, Matthew Thomas. AB, Georgetown U., 1971; JD, Boston Coll., 1974. Bar: Mass. 1974, Fla. 1976, U.S. Dist. Ct. Mass. 1976, U.S. Ct. Appeals 1977, U.S. Ct. Mil. Appeals 1982, U.S. Supreme Ct. 1990. Asst. dist. atty. Cape and Islands, Mass., 1974-76; counsel Town of Bourne, Mass., 1978—; counsel Town of Duxbury, Mass., 1986—, Barnstable County, 1992—. Mem. Mass. Bar Assn. (bd. dels. 1977-80), Barnstable County Bar Assn., Plymouth County Bar Assn., Town Counsel Assn. Home: PO Box 125 West Barnstable MA 02668-0125 Office: 90 Route 6A Sandwich MA 02563-5301

**TROYER, TRACY LYNN,** lawyer; b. Hamilton, Ohio, Nov. 17, 1969; s. Gary Allen and Mary Beth Pursifull; m. Phillip James Troyer, Jan. 2, 1993. BS in Bus. Mktg., Ind. U., 1991, JD, 1994. Bar: Va. 1994, Ind. 1995, U.S. Dist. Ct. (so. dist.) Ind. 1995. Assoc. Hinkle, Keck & Hinkle, Danville, Ind., 1995-96, Boeglin Law Office, Ft. Wayne, Ind., 1996-97; ptnr. Boeglin & Troyer, Ft. Wayne, Ind., 1998—; mem. Ft. Wayne Estate Planning Coun., 1997—. Co-author: Basic Probate Procedure, 1998. Mem., vice chair Altrusa Profl. Group, Ft. Wayne, 1997—. Mem. Tri Kappa. Family and matrimonial, Estate planning, Probate. Office: Boeglin & Troyer 4214 Hobson Ct Fort Wayne IN 46815-8648

**TRUE, ROY JOE,** lawyer; b. Shreveport, La., Feb. 20, 1938; s. Collins B. and Lula Mae (Cady) T.; m. Patsy Jean Hudsmith, Aug. 29, 1959; children: Andrea Alane, Alyssa Anne, Ashley Alisbeth. Student, Centenary Coll., 1957; BS, Tex. Christian U., 1961; LLB, So. Meth. U., 1963, postgrad., 1968-69. Bar: Tex. 1963. Pvt. practice, Dallas, 1963—; pres. Invesco Internat. Corp., 1969-70, True & Sewell and predecessors, 1975—; bus. adviser, counselor Mickey Mantle, 1969-95; dir. The Mickey Mantle Found., 1995-98. Mem. editl. bd. Southwestern Law Jour, 1962-63. Served with AUS, 1956. Mem. ABA, Dallas Bar Assn., Tex. Assn. Bank Counsel, Phi Alpha Delta. Banking, Contracts commercial, General corporate. Home: 5601 Ursula Ln Dallas TX 75229-6429 Office: 8080 N Central Expy Fl 9 Dallas TX 75206-1838

**TRUETT, HAROLD JOSEPH, III (TIM TRUETT),** lawyer; b. Alameda, Calif., Feb. 13, 1946; s. Harold Joseph and Lois Lucille (Mellin) T.; 1 child, Harold Joseph IV; m. Anna V. Billante, Oct. 1, 1983; 1 child, James S. Carstensen. BA, U. San Francisco, 1968, JD, 1975. Bar: Calif. 1975, Hawaii 1987, U.S. Dist. Ct. (ea., so., no., and cen. dists.) Calif. 1976, Hawaii 1987, U.S. Ct. Appeals (9th cir.) 1980, U.S. Supreme Ct. 1988, U.S. Ct. Fed. Claims, 1995. Assoc. Hoberg, Finger et al, San Francisco, 1975-78, Bledsoe, Smith et al, San Francisco, 1979-80, Abramson & Bianco, San Francisco, 1980-83; mem. Ingram & Truett, San Rafael, 1983-90; prin. Law Office of H.J. Tim Truett, San Francisco, 1991-93, Winchell & Truett, San Francisco, 1994—; lectr. trial practice Am. Coll. Legal Medicine, 1989, 90, Calif. Continuing Edn. of the Bar. Bd. dirs. Shining Star Found. 1991—, Marin County, Calif.; mem. Marin Dem. Coun., San Rafael, 1983-90. Lt., aviator USN, 1967-74. Mem. ABA, Hawaii Bar Assn., Assn. Trial Lawyers Am., Calif. Bar Assn. (com. for adminstrn. of justice, conf. of dels.), San Francisco Bar Assn., Calif. Trial Lawyers Assn., Lawyers Pilots Assn. Roman Catholic. State civil litigation, Aviation, Personal injury. Home: 2622 Leavenworth St San Francisco CA 94133-1614

**TRUEX, SHELLEY ANNE,** lawyer; b. Johnson City, N.Y., Sept. 22, 1968; d. Gordon Elbert and Diane Marie Truex; m. Mark Ambrose Quarantillo, Aug. 1, 1998. BA, SUNY, Binghamton, 1989; JD, Union U., 1992. Bar: N.Y. 1993. Staff atty. Niagara County Legal Aid, Inc., Niagara Falls, N.Y., 1993-94; assoc. Gregory A. Pope & Assocs., Lockport, N.Y., 1994-97; owner, ptnr. Quarantillo & Truex, Niagara Falls, 1997—. Mem. N.Y. State Bar Assn., Erie County Bar Assn., Niagara Falls Bar Assn., Lockport Bar Assn. Family and matrimonial, Estate planning, Juvenile. Office: Quarantillo & Truex 625 6th St Niagara Falls NY 14301-1752

**TRUHLAR, DORIS BROADDUS,** lawyer; b. Oklahoma City, Sept. 18, 1946; d. Elbridge Sidney and Doris Mary (Prock) Broaddus; divs.; children: Samara Taryle, Brett Taryle (dec.); m. Robert John Truhlar, June 24, 1978; children: Ivy, Holly. B in journalism, U. Mo., 1967; MA, U. Denver, 1976, JD with honors, 1980. Bar: Colo. 1981, U.S. Dist. Ct. Colo. 1981, U.S. Ct. Appeals (10th cir.) 1981, U.S. Supreme Ct., 1996. Law clk. to Hon. Robert H. McWilliams, Jr. U.S. Ct. Appeals (10th cir.), Denver, 1980-81; corp. sec., gen. counsel Hart Exploration and Prodn. Co., Englewood, Colo.; ptnr. Truhlar and Truhlar, LLP, Littleton, Colo., 1985—; adj. prof. U. Denver Coll. Law, 1986-88, 90-91, mem. adv. com. advocacy skills program, 1990; spkr. CLE Programs; expert witness regarding attys. fees; mem. Thursday Night Bar Adv. Bd., 1995—, chair, 1996-98. Trainer attys. and vols. who work with abused and neglected children; active various vol. programs; vestry bd. Good Shepherd Episcopal Ch., 1992-95; mem. adv. com. Metro Parenting and Divorce Ctr., 1995-98, transition team Gov. Bill Owens Judiciary com., Colo., 1998. Recipient Woman of Achievement, Entreprneur of Yr. award Met. YWCA of Denver, 1993, Denver Gridiron award, 1st pl. Editl. Writing award Nat. Edn. Writers Assn., Chalres B. Dillion awrd for outstanding pub. svc., 1997, also several Mo. Press Assn. awards and newspaper writing awards; honoree for outstanding svc. in providing legal svcs. to the poor Barristers' Ball, 1998. Mem: ABA, Am. Trial Lawyers Assn., Denver Bar Assn. (Vol. Atty. of Yr. award), Colo. Bar Assn. (organizer, tchr. pro se div. clinics, ethics com. 1984-91, calling com.), Colo. Women's Bar Assn. (co-chair jud. com. 1995-98, bd. dirs., historian 1998—), Arapahoe County Bar Assn. (Cmty. Svc. award, Pro Bono Atty. 1992, coord. Channel 4 Ask-a-Lawyer, cmty. svc. chair, cmty. svc. chair 1998—). Family and matrimonial, General practice. Office: 1901 W Littleton Blvd Littleton CO 80120-2022

**TRUITT, ROBERT RALPH, JR.,** lawyer; b. Lincoln-Chaves Counties, N.Mex., Jan. 21, 1948; s. Robert Ralph and Dorothy (Butler) T.; m. Susan Donovan, Nov. 28, 1981; children: Patrick Lynn, Maureen Elizabeth. BA, BBA, Southwestern U., 1970; JD, U. Tex., 1973. Bar: Tex. 1973, U.S. Ct. Appeals (5th cir.) 1976, U.S. Dist. Ct. (we. dist.) Tex. 1977, U.S. Dist. Ct. (no. dist.) Tex. 1981. Assoc. Turpin, Smith & Dyer, Midland, Tex., 1973-77; sole practice Midland, 1977—. Chmn. planning and zoning com., City of Midland, 1979-80; chmn., dir. and treas. Midland Downtown Lions Fire Prevention and Hist. Found., 1980—; dir. and sec.-treas. Midland Downtown Lions Youth Found., 1992-98, Midland Masonic Hist. Mus. and Libr. Found., 1996—; dir. Presdl. Mus., 1998—. Mem. Tex. Bar Assn., Midland County Bar Assn. Banking, Bankruptcy, State civil litigation. Office: 901 W Texas Ave Midland TX 79701-6167

**TRUJILLO, LORENZO A.,** lawyer, educator; b. Denver, Aug. 10, 1951; s. Filbert G. and Marie O. Trujillo; m. Ellen Alires; children: Javier Antonio, Lorenzo Feliciano, Kristina Alires. BA, U. Colo., 1972, MA, 1974, postgrad.; EdD, U. San Francisco, 1979; JD, U. Colo., 1993. Bar: Colo. 1994, U.S. Dist. Ct. Colo. 1994, U.S. Ct. Appeals (10th cir.) 1994, U.S. Supreme Ct. 1999; cert. edn. tchr., prin., supt., Colo., Calif. Exec. assoc. Inter-Am. Rsch. Assocs., Rosslyn, Va., 1980-82; exec. dir. humanities Jefferson County Pub. Schs., Golden, Colo., 1982-89; pvt. practice edn. cons. Lakewood, Colo., 1989-93; gen. corp. counsel Am. Achievement Schs., Inc., Lakewood, Colo., 1994-96; atty. Frie, Arndt & Trujillo Law Firm, Arvada, Colo., 1994-96, ptnr., 1995-97; dist. hearing officer, dir. of instrn. Adams County Sch. Dist. 14, 1997—, dir. human resources, 1998-99, dist. attendance officer, prin. H.S., 1999—; co-chair Mellon fellowships The Coll. Bd., N.Y.C., 1987-93; cons. U.S.I.A. Fulbright Tchr. Exch. Program, Washington, 1987-93; editl. advisor Harcourt, Brace, Jovanovich Pub., Orlando, Fla., 1988-93; mem. Colo. Supreme Ct. Multicultural Commn., 1996-98, Colo. Supreme Ct. Multicultural Com., 1999—. Contbr. numerous articles to profl. jours. Mem. panel of arbitrators Am. Arbitration Assn., 1994. Recipient Legal Aid Clinic Acad. award Colo. Bar Assn., 1993, Pro Bono award, 1993, Loyola U. Acad. award, 1993, Gov.'s award for excellence in the arts State of Colo., 1996. Mem. Colo. chpt. Am. Assn. Tchrs. of Spanish and Portuguese (pres. 1985-88), Am. Immigration Lawyers Assn., Nat. Sch. Bds. Coun. Sch. Attys., Nat. Assn. Judiciary Interpreters and Translators, Colo. Bar Assn. (probate and trust sect., grievance policy com. 1995-97, ethics com. 1995-96), U. San Francisco Alumni Assn. (founder, pres. 1987-90), Phi Delta Kappa (chair internat. edn. com. 1988-89), Phi Alpha Delta. Avocation: violinist. Education and schools, General practice, Estate planning. Office: Adams County Sch Dist 14 Divsn Human Resources 4720 E 69th Ave Commerce City CO 80022-2380

**TRUNZO, THOMAS HAROLD, JR.,** lawyer; b. McKeesport, Pa., Oct. 23, 1948; s. Thomas H. Trunzo; m. Deborah A. Arnesen, Feb. 6, 1982; children: Melissa, Kirsten. BA, Tufts U., 1976; JD, Vt. Law Sch., 1980. Bar: N.H. 1980, Mass. 1981, Vt. 1988. Ptnr. Mullaly & Trunzo Law Offices, West Lebanon, N.H., 1980-87; pvt. practice Lebanon, N.H., 1987—. Active sch. bd. Orford (N.H.) Sch. Dist., 1988-95; mem. Orford Planning Bd., 1991-93; moderator Riverdell Sch. Dist., Oxford, 1998—. Mem. Assn. Trial Lawyers Am., Nat. Lawyers Guild, N.H. Bar Assn. (Pro bono award 1987), Vt. Bar Assn., Grafton County Bar Assn. Democrat. General practice, Family and matrimonial, Real property. Home: RR 1 Box 42 Orford NH 03777-9707 Office: Citizens Bank Bldg PO Box 825 20 W Park St Ste 415 Lebanon NH 03766-1322

**TRUSKOWSKI, JOHN BUDD,** lawyer; b. Chgo., Dec. 3, 1945; s. Casimer T. and Jewell S. (Kirk) T.; m. Karen Lee Sloss, Mar. 21, 1970; children: Philip K., Jennifer B. BS, U. Ill., 1967; JD, U. Chgo., 1970. Bar: Ill. 1970, U.S. Dist. Ct. (no. dist.) Ill. 1970, U.S. Tax Ct. 1977. Assoc. Keck, Mahin & Cate, Chgo., 1970-71, 74-78, ptnr., 1978-97; ptnr. Lord, Bissell & Brook, Chgo., 1997—. Author, editor Callaghan's Federal Tax Guide, 1987. Lt., USNR, 1971-74. Mem. ABA, Ill. State Bar Assn., Chgo. Bar Assn. Republican. Presbyterian. Avocations: model railroading, stamp collecting. Corporate taxation, Taxation, general, Personal income taxation. Home: 251 Kimberly Ln Lake Forest IL 60045-3862 Office: Lord Bissell & Brook Harris Bank Bldg 115 S Lasalle St Ste 3200 Chicago IL 60603-3972

**TRUST, BRIAN,** lawyer; b. Bklyn., Mar. 7, 1956; s. Ronald and Phyllis T.; married; children: Matthew J., Steven N. BA, Bklyn. Coll., 1977; MA, NYU, 1979, JD, 1986. Bar: N.Y. 1987, U.S. Dist. Ct. (so. dist.) N.Y. Assoc. Simpson, Thacher & Bartlett, N.Y.C., 1986-96, counsel, 1996—. Editor Norton Bankruptcy Law and Practice, 2d edit., 1993—. Mem. ABA, Assn. Bar City N.Y. Avocations: guitar, computers. Bankruptcy. Office: Simpson Thacher & Bartlett 425 Lexington Ave Fl 15 New York NY 10017-3954

**TRYBAN, ESTHER ELIZABETH,** lawyer; b. Chgo., Aug. 14, 1958; d. Chester Joseph and Lottie Elizabeth (Napora) T. AAS with honors, Elgin (Ill.) C.C., 1977, AS with honors, 1982; BS with honors, Roosevelt U., Chgo., 1986; JD, U. Chgo., 1989. Bar: Ill. 1989, U.S. Dist. Ct. (no. dist.) Ill. 1989, U.S. Ct. Appeals (7th cir.) 1990, U.S. Supreme Ct., 1996. Supr. adminstrv. svcs. law dept. Motorola, Inc., Schaumburg, Ill., 1977-86; staff law clk. U.S. Bankruptcy Ct., No. Dist. Ill., Chgo., 1989-90; asst. corp. counsel City of Chgo., 1990—. Mem. ABA, Nat. Lawyers Guild, Assn. Former Bankruptcy Law Clks, Ill. State Bar Assn., Chgo. Bar Assn. (chair govt. svc. com. 1996-97). Roman Catholic. Avocations: reading, football, traveling. Office: City Chgo Dept Law 30 N Lasalle St Ste 900 Chicago IL 60602-2503

**TSAMIS, DONNA ROBIN,** lawyer; b. Yonkers, N.Y., Sept. 26, 1957; d. Donald Charles and Lenore Angela (Boccia) Lanza; m. Vasili Tsamis, June 18, 1983; children: Niki Alexandra, Victoria Angela. BA summa cum laude, Fordham U., 1979, JD, 1982. Bar: N.Y. 1983, U.S. Dist. Ct. (so. and ea. dist.) N.Y., U.S. Supreme Ct. 1993. Assoc. Jackson, Lewis, Schnitzler & Krupman, N.Y.C., 1982-86, White Plains, N.Y., 1986—; ptnr. Jackson, Lewis, Schnitzler & Krupman, 1990—. Vice chmn. ann. luncheon com. Girl Scouts U.S.A., Westchester, 1989-92. Mem. Westchester Women's Bar Assn. (chmn. Forum on Alternative Work Schedules for Atty. 1989, bd. dirs. 1990, 92, chmn. lawyering parenting com. 1989-91), Westchester Assn. Women Bus. Owners, Columbian Lawyers Assn. (bd. dirs. 1990-94). Avocations: travel, swimming, tennis. Labor. Office: Jackson Lewis Schnitzler & Krupman 1 N Broadway Ste 1502 White Plains NY 10601-2320

**TSE, CHARLES YUNG CHANG,** drug company executive; b. Shanghai, China, Mar. 22, 1926; s. Kung Chao and Say Ying (Chen) T.; m. Vivian Chang, Apr. 25, 1955; 1 dau., Roberta. BA in Econs, St. John's U., Shanghai, 1949; MS in Acctg, U. Ill., 1950; JD, N.Y. Law Sch., 1990. Asst. to controller Am. Internat. Group, N.Y.C., 1950-54; asst. mgr. Am. Internat. Group, Singapore-Malaysia, 1955-57; with Warner-Lambert Co., Morris Plains, N.J., 1957-86; area mgr. S.E. Asia Warner-Lambert Co., 1966-68, regional dir. S.E. Asia, 1968-69, v.p. Australasia, 1970-71, pres. Western Hemisphere Group, 1971-72, pres. Pan Am. Mgmt. Center, 1972-76, pres. European Mgmt. Center, 1976-78, pres. Internat. Group, 1979-86, sr. v.p. corp., 1980-83, exec. v.p. corp., 1984-85, vice chmn., 1985-86; dir. Foster Wheeler Corp., Livingston, N.J., 1984-98, Superior Telecom., Inc., 1996—, Com. of 100; mem. faculty bus. adminstrn. dept. Fairleigh Dickinson U., 1961-64; pres. Cancer Rsch. Inst., Inc., N.Y.C., 1991-92. Bd. visitors CCNY, 1974-78; trustee Morristown Meml. Hosp. (N.J.), 1982-86; bd. dirs. Bus. Council for Internat. Understanding, 1984-87. Mem. NAM (dir. 1984-86), Assn. of the Bar of the City of N.Y. (mem. Asian affairs com. 1991—). General corporate, Private international, Mergers and acquisitions. Office: 300 Park Ave Fl 17 New York NY 10022-7402

**TSISMENAKIS, VASILIA HELEN A.,** lawyer; b. Bklyn., May 21, 1968; d. Artemios and Stella (Kapassakis) T. BA, Fordham U., 1988, JD, 1991. Bar: N.J. 1991, N.Y. 1992, U.S. Supreme Ct. 1996. Assoc. Mudge rose Guthrie Alexander & Ferdon, N.Y.C., 1991-94, Battle Fowler LLP, N.Y.C., 1994—; legal advisor Pan Cretan Assn. of Am., N.Y.C., 1995—. Mem. N.Y. State Hellenic Am. Rep. Assn., N.Y.C., 1997—. Mem. ABA. Greek Orthodox. Avocations: classical dance, bicycling. Real property, Estate taxation. Office: Battle Fowler LLP 75 E 55th St New York NY 10022-3205

**TSO, TOM,** law educator; b. Teecnospos, Ariz., Mar. 7, 1945; s. Horace Hosteen and Lena (Saltwater) T.; m. Louise Anne Chee, Jan. 8, 1970; children: Travis, Dempsey, Delsey Renee, Dorothy Mae, Wanda L. BS in Polit. Sci., City U. L.A., 1988; JD (hon.), CUNY. Plant operator Air Reduction Co., Teecnospos, 1968-69; tribal park ranger Navajo Nation, Window Rock, Ariz., 1969; interpreter, investigator, ct. advocate Legal Aid & Defender Svc., Window Rock, 1970-73; ct. advocate, equal opportunity asst. Navajo Housing Authority, Window Rock, 1973-74; interpreter, investigator, ct. advocate Legal Aid & Defender Svc., Window Rock, 1974; tribal ct. advocate Law Firm of Louis Denetsosie, Window Rock, 1976-77; dir. tribal law devel. and litigation unit DNA-People's Legal Svcs., Window Rock, 1977-81; dist. ct. judge Window Rock Dist. Ct., Window Rock, 1981-85; chief justice Navajo Nation Supreme Ct., Window Rock, 1985-91; with Bur. Indian Affairs Agy., 1991; cmty. rels. advisor Mobil Exploration and Producing U.S. Inc., Cortez, Colo., 1994-96; tchr. law advocacy Crownpoint (N.Mex.) Inst. Tech., 1996—; cons. ENRON Corp., Houston, 1998—; chmn. adv. tng. com. Legal Svcs. Corp., Washington, 1977-78; mem. advocate tng. com. Ariz. Statewide Legal Svcs., 1978-79; chmn. Navajo Nation Bar Admissions Com., Window Rock, 1979-81; bd. dirs. Nat. Indian Justice Ctr., San Francisco, 1985-92; mem. Ariz. State Gov.'s Adv. Coun. Juvenile Justice, 1988-93; mem. labor mgmt. com. Gallup-McKinley County Pub. Schs., 1994—; mem., vp. Navajo Engring. and Constrn. Authority, Shiprock, N.Mex., 1995—; mem. adv. bd. Tribal Law and Policy Inst., San Francisco, 1997—. assisting cons. Navajo Legal Glossary, Fed. Dist. Ct., 1983; contbr. articles to profl. jours. Bd. dirs. Gallup Friendship House, Gallup, N.Mex., 1979-80; pres. Day Care Ctr., Ft. Defiance, Ariz., 1978-79; mem. Window Rock Christian Reformed Ch., 1978-85; mem. adv. bd. to the Gov.'s Office on Women/Children in Poverty, Phoenix, 1986-87. Sgt. USMC, 1965-67, Vietnam. Decorated Purple Heart; recipient Petra Found. award, 1991, award of appreciation Indian Bar Assn., 1991, State Bar Ariz., 1992, Disting. Jud. Svc. award State Bar N.Mex., 1992. Mem. Navajo Nation Bar Assn. (v.p. 1979-81, chmn. bar admission com. 1979-81, cert. appreciation 1985), Fleet Marine Assn., Disabled Ams. Assn. Mem. Christian Reformed Ch.

**TU, PETER,** lawyer; b. Singapore, Singapore, Feb. 20, 1964; s. Chen-Nan Tu and Yit-Yoong Yong; m. Peggy Ng, Mar. 12, 1990; children: Thomas, Taylor. SBChemE, SB in Biology, MIT, 1986; MBA in Fin., Seton Hall U., South Orange, N.J., 1987; JD, Seton Hall U., Newark, 1994. Bar: N.J. 1994, U.S. Dist. Ct. N.J. 1994, U.S. Ct. Appeals (3d cir.) 1995, U.S. Dist. Ct. (so. dist.) N.Y. 1996. Law clk. to Hon. Stewart G. Pollock, Morristown, N.J., 1994-95; law clk. to Hon. Leonard I. Garth Newark, 1995-96; assoc. Weil, Gotshal & Manges LLP, N.Y.C., 1996—. Editor symposium Seton Hall Law Rev., 1993-94; contbg. editor Jour. Proprietary Rights, 1996—. Ednl. counselor MIT, 1998—; gen. counsel CAMIT, N.Y.C., 1998—. Whipple Meml. scholar Seton Hall Law Sch., 1991-94. Mem. N.J. Bar Assn. (2d vice chmn. minorities in profession sect. 1996—, mem. exec. com. gen. coun. 1996—, mem. task force on diversity 1998—), MIT Alumni Club (no. N.J.). Avocations: chess, bridge, tennis. Office: Weil Gotshal & Manges LLP 767 5th Ave Fl Concl New York NY 10153-0119

**TUBMAN, WILLIAM CHARLES,** lawyer; b. N.Y.C., Mar. 16, 1932; s. William Thomas and Ellen Veronica (Griffin) T.; m. Dorothy Rita Krug, Aug. 15, 1964; children: William Charles Jr., Thomas Davison, Matthew Griffin. BS, Fordham U., 1953, JD, 1960; postdoctoral, NYU Sch. Law, 1960-61. Bar: N.Y. 1960, U.S. Ct. Appeals (2d cir.) 1966, U.S. Supreme Ct. 1967, U.S. Ct. Customs and Patent Appeals 1971. Auditor Peat, Marwick Mitchell & Co., N.Y.C., 1956-60; sr. counsel Kennecott Corp., N.Y.C., 1960-82; sr. counsel Phelps Dodge Corp., N.Y.C., 1982-85, sec., 1985-95, v.p., 1987-95; pres. Phelps Dodge Found., Phoenix, 1988-95. Author: Legal Status of Minerals Beyond the Continental Shelf, 1966. Mem. scholarship adv. coun. U. Ariz., 1990-92; active Big Bros., Inc., N.Y.C., 1963-73; trustee Phoenix Art Mus., 1989-94; bd. dirs. St. Joseph Hosp. Found., 1994—, chmn., 1994-95; bd. dirs. The Phoenix Symphony, 1994-95. Recipient Disting. Svc. cert. Big Brothers Inc., 1968. Mem. ABA, N.Y. State Bar Assn., Maricopa County Bar Assn. Democrat. Roman Catholic. Securities, General corporate, Antitrust.

**TUCCIARONE, ENRICO GREGORY,** lawyer; b. Pitts., July 25, 1969; s. Pietro Tucciarone and Donna Marie Bisegna; m. Tricia A. Keith, Apr. 1, 1995. BA in History, U. Pitts., 1991; JD cum laude, Thomas M. Cooley Law Sch., 1994. Bar: Mich. 1995, U.S. Dist. Ct. (ea. dis.) Mich. 1995. Assoc. atty. Neal Neal & Stewart P.C., Flint, Mich., 1995-98, Willmarth Tanoury Ramar et al, Detroit, 1998—. Vol. various house and jud. candidates, Lansing and Flint, Mich., 1994—; mem. Genesee County Republicans, Flint, 1995—; vol. legal cons. Genesee County (Mich.) Republican Party, 1998. Mem. ABA, Genesse County Bar Assn., Greater Flint Toastmasters. Avocations: golf, archery, mountain biking, camping. Insurance, Personal injury, State civil litigation. Office: Willmarth Tanoury Ramar et al 535 Griswold St Ste 1730 Detroit MI 48226-3698

**TUCHMAN, STEVEN LESLIE,** lawyer, theatre critic; b. Indpls., Sept. 3, 1946; s. Frederick and Lillian (Alper) T. BA, Ind. U., 1968, JD, 1971; cert. internat. law, City Coll. London, 1970. Bar: Ind. 1971. Advisor Den Danske Bank, Copenhagen, Denmark, 1971-73; assoc. Melvin Simon and Assoc., Inc., Indpls., 1973-81; pvt. practice Indpls., 1981-90; critic Sta. WFYI-FM, Indpls., 1981-90; ptnr. Lewis & Kappes, Indpls., 1990—; critic Sta. WTHR-TV, Indpls., 1987-95; columnist The New Times, Indpls., 1989; adj. prof. real estate law Ind. U. Sch. Bus., 1983-84; mediator Marion County Mcpl. and Superior Ct. mediation program, 1987—. Contbr. articles to profl. jours. V.p. Dance Kaleidoscope, Indpls., 1980-81; pres. Festival Dance Theatre, Indpls. and N.Y.C., 1983-84; chmn. task force subcom. Indpls. Pub. Schs. Referendum, 1985; subcom. chmn. exec. com. Internat. Violin Competition Indpls., 1986-89; chmn. real estate com. community adv. coun. Jr. League Indpls., 1987—, Indpls. Com. Fgn. Rels., 1990—; bd. dirs. Planned Parenthood Cen. Ind., 1987—, v.p. 1989-91, pres. 1991—; steering com., affiliate pres.' coun. nat. com. Planned Parenthood Fedn. Am.; mem. Jewish Community Rels., 1988-90. Mem. Ind. State Bar Assn. (ho. dels. 1986—), Indpls. Bar Assn. (com. long range plans 1987-88, Disting. award), ABA, Am. Immigration Lawyers Assn. (chmn. Ind. chpt., 1994-96, mem. bd. govs., 1994-96), Ind. Supreme Ct. Disciplinary Commn. (grievance com.), Indpls. Bar Found., Am. Theatre Critics Assn., Kiwanis, Phi Delta Phi. General corporate, Immigration, naturalization, and customs, Real property. Office: 1210 One American Sq PO Box 82053 Indianapolis IN 46282

**TUCK, THOMAS CHRISTOPHER,** lawyer; b. Winston-Salem, N.C., Jan. 6, 1972; s. Ira Thomas and Kathryn (Crudup) T.; m. Kendra Sieber. BA, U. N.C., 1993; JD, Marquette U., 1996. Bar: Wis. 1996, U.S. Dist. Ct. (ea. dist.) Wis. 1996. Atty. Habush, Habush, Davis and Rottier, S.C., Milw., 1996-98, Ness, Motley, Loadholt, Richardson & Poole, P.A., Charleston, S.C., 1998—. Mem. Marquette Law Rev., 1995-96, Marquette Sports Law Jour., 1994-96. Mem. ABA, ATLA, Wis. Acad. Trial Lawyers, State Bar Wis., Milw. Bar Assn. Episcopalian. Avocations: tennis, golf. Product liability. Office: Ness Motley Loadholt Richardson & Poole PA PO Box 1137 Charleston SC 29402-1137

**TUCKER, BERRY KENNETH,** lawyer; b. Chgo., Sept. 23, 1946; s. Sheldon K. and Regina E. (Winter) T.; m. Sherry L. Soref, Nov. 20, 1970; children: Jami Leigh, David William. BS in Mgmt., No. Ill. U., 1969; JD, Loyola U., Chgo., 1972. Bar: Ill. 1972, U.S. Dist. Ct. (no. dist.) Ill. 1972, U.S. Ct. Appeals (fed. cir.) 1983. Asst. counsel Ill. Dept. Mental Health, Chgo., 1972-74; asst. chief counsel Ill. Dept. Transp., Chgo., 1974-78; div. chmn. Nat. R.R. Adjustment Bd., Chgo., 1978-80; sr. ptnr. Berry K. Tucker & Assoc. Ltd., Chgo., 1980—; chief counsel Aunt Marthas Youth Svc. Ctr., Wake Forest, Ill., 1974—. Mem. water com. Village of Flossmoor (Ill.), 1987-88. Mem. Ill. Bar Assn. (mem. sect. counsel adminstrv. law com. 1973-76), Chgo. Bar Assn. (mem. environ. law com. 1975-78). Avocations: auto restoration, raquetball, golf. General corporate, Juvenile, Personal injury. Office: Berry K Tucker & Assocs Ltd 5210 W 95th St Ste 100 Oak Lawn IL 60453-2460

**TUCKER, BOWEN HAYWARD,** lawyer; b. Providence, Apr. 13, 1938; s. Stuart Hayward and Ardelle Chase (Drabble) T.; m. Jan Louise Brown, Aug. 26, 1961; children: Stefan Kendric Slade, Catherine Kendra Gordon. AB in Math., Brown U., 1959; JD, U. Mich., 1962. Bar: R.I. 1963, Ill. 1967, U.S. Supreme Ct. 1970. Assoc. Hinckley & Allen, Providence, 1962-66; sr. atty. Caterpillar, Inc., Peoria, Ill., 1966-72; counsel FMC Corp., Chgo., 1972-82, sr. litigation counsel, 1982-95, assoc. gen. counsel, 1995—. Chmn. legal process task force Chgo. Residential Sch. Study Com., 1973-74, mem. Commn. on Children, 1983-85, Ill. Com. on Rights of Minors, 1974-77, Com. on Youth and the Law, 1977-79; mem. White House Conf. on Children, ednl. svcs. subcom., 1979-80; chairperson Youth Employment Task Force, 1982-83; mem. citizens com. on Juvenile Ct. (Cook County), 1978-94, chmn. detention subcom., 1982-94; mem. econ. effects adv. com. Rand Inst. Civil Justice, 1990-92; bd. dirs. Voices Ill. Children, 1998—. 1st lt. U.S. Army, 1962-69. Mem. ABA, Am. Law Inst., Ill. State Bar Assn., R.I. Bar Assn., Chgo. (chmn. com. on juvenile law, 1976-77), Engine Mfrs. Assn. (chmn. legal com. 1972), Chgo. Lincoln Inn of Ct. (sec., treas. 1996-98), Constrn. Industry Mfrs. Assn. (exec. com. of Lawyers' Coun. 1972, 1975-79, vice chmn. 1977, chmn. 1978-79), Mfrs. Alliance (products liability coun. 1974-95, vice chmn. 1981-83, chmn. 1983-85), Product Liability Adv. Coun. (bd. dirs. 1986—, exec. com. 1990-97, vice chmn. 1991-93, chmn. 1993-95), ACLU (bd. dirs. Ill. div. 1970-79, exec. com. 1973-79, sec. 1975-77), Am. Arbitration Assn. (mem panel of arbitrators 1985-96), Phi Alph Delta. Club: Brown Univ. of Chgo. (nat. alumni schs. program 1973-85, v.p. 1980-81, pres. 1981-86), Law Club of City of Chicago. General civil litigation, Product liability, Juvenile. Home: 107 W Noyes St Arlington Heights IL 60005-3747 Office: 200 E Randolph St Ste 6700 Chicago IL 60601-6436

**TUCKER, EDWIN WALLACE,** law educator; b. N.Y.C., Feb. 25, 1927; s. Benjamin and May Tucker; m. Gladys Lipschutz, Sept. 14, 1952; children: Sherwin M., Pamela A. BA, NYU, 1948; LLB, Harvard U., 1951; LLM, N.Y. Law Sch., 1963, JSD, 1964; MA, Trinity Coll., Hartford, Conn., 1967. Bar: N.Y. 1955, U.S. Dist. Ct. (ea. and so. dists.) N.Y. 1958, U.S. Ct. Appeals (2d cir.) 1958, U.S. Supreme Ct. 1960. Pvt. practice, N.Y.C., 1955-63; Disting. Alumni prof. and prof. bus. law U. Conn., Storrs, 1963—, mem. bd. editors occasional paper and monograph series, 1966-70. Author: Adjudication of Social Issues, 1971, 2d edit., 1977, Legal Regulation of the

Environment, 1972, Administrative Agencies, Regulation of Enterprise, and Individual Liberties, 1975, CPA Law Review, 1985; co-author: The Legal and Ethical Environment of Business, 1992; book rev. editor Am. Bus. Law Jour., 1964-65, adv. editor, 1974—; co-editor Am. Bus. Jour., 1965-73; mem. editl. bd. Am. Jour. Small Bus., 1979-86; editor Jour. Legal Studies Edn., 1983-85, editor-in-chief, 1985-87, adv. editor, 1987—; mem. bd. editors North Atlantic Regional Bus. Law Rev., 1984—. With USAF, 1951-55. Recipient medal of excellence Am. Bus. Law Assn., 1979. Mem. Acad. Legal Studies in Bus., North Atlantic Regional Bus. Law Assn. Home: 11 Eastwood Rd Storrs Mansfield CT 06268-2401

**TUCKER, KATHRYN LOUISE,** lawyer, educator; b. N.Y.C., July 29, 1959; d. Robert J. and Kathryn Louise (Norton) Sisk; m. Scott L. Tucker, July 1, 1989; children: Torin Norton, Montana Taiga. BA, Hampshire Coll., Amherst, Mass., 1981; JD, Georgetown U., 1985. Bar: Wash. 1985, U.S. Dist. Ct. (we. dist.) Wash., U.S. Dist. Ct. (ea. dist.) Wash., U.S. Ct. Appeals (9th cir.), U.S. Ct. Appeals (2d cir.) 1995, U.S. Supreme Ct. Assoc. Perkins Coie, Seattle, 1988-96; of counsel Perkins Cole, Seattle, 1996—; dir. legal affairs Compassion in Dying, Seattle, 1997—; affiliate prof. law U. Wash. Law Sch., Seattle, 1996—. Author articles on patient rights at the end of life and end-of-life decision making; subject of articles; appeared on network news programs. Mem. ABA. Democrat. Avocations: whitewater kayaking, cross-country skiing. Constitutional, Health, Professional liability. Office: Perkins Coie 1201 3d Ave Seattle WA 98101

**TUCKER, MARCUS OTHELLO,** judge; b. Santa Monica, Calif., Nov. 12, 1934; s. Marcus Othello Sr. and Essie Louvonia (McLendon) T.; m. Indira Hale, May 29, 1965; 1 child, Angelique. BA, U. So. Calif., 1956; JD, Howard U., 1960. Bar: Calif. 1962, U.S. Dist. Ct. (cen. dist.) Calif. 1962, U.S. Ct. Appeals (9th cir.) 1965, U.S. Ct. Internat. Trade 1970, U.S. Supreme Ct. 1971. Pvt. practice, Santa Monica, 1962-63, 67-74; dep. atty. City of Santa Monica, 1963-65; asst. atty. U.S. Dist. Ct. (Cen. Dist.) Calif., 1965-67; commr. L.A. Superior Ct., 1974-76; judge mcpl. ct. Long Beach (Calif.) Jud. Dist., 1976-85; judge superior ct. L.A. Jud. Dist., 1985—; supervising judge L.A. County Dependency Ct. L.A. Superior Ct., 1991-92, presiding judge Juvenile divsn., 1993-94; asst. prof. law Pacific U., Long Beach, 1984, 86; justice pro tem U.S. Ct. Appeals (2nd cir.), 1981; mem. exec. com. Superior Ct. of L.A. County, 1995-96. Mem. editl. staff Howard U. Law Sch. Jour., 1959-60. Pres. Community Rehab. Industries Found., Long Beach, 1983-86, Legal Aid Found., L.A., 1976-77; bd. dirs. Long Beach coun. Boy Scouts Am., 1978-92. With U.S. Army, 1960-66. Named Judge of Yr. Juvenile Cts. Bar Assn., 1986, Disting. Jurist Long Beach Trial Trauma Coun., 1987, Honoree in Law Handy Community Ctr., L.A., 1987, Bernard S. Jefferson Jurist of Yr. John M. Langston Bar Assn. Black Lawyers, 1990, Judge of Yr. Long Beach Bar Assn., 1993; recipient award for Law-Related Edn. Constl. Rights Found./L.A. County Bar Assn., 1992, commendation L.A. County Bd. Suprs., 1994. Fellow Internat. Acad. Trial Judges; mem. ABA, Calif. Judges Assn. (chmn. juvenile law com. 1986-87), Langston Bar Assn. (pres. bd. dirs. 1972, 73), Calif. Assn. Black Lawyers, Santa Monica Bay Dist. Bar Assn. (treas. 1969-71), Am. Inns of Ct., Selden Soc. Avocations: comparative law, traveling. Office: 415 W Ocean Blvd Dept 245 Long Beach CA 90802-4512

**TUCKER, MICHAEL LANE,** lawyer; b. Feb. 13, 1955; s. Robert Lane and Bonnie Jean (Childers) T.; m. Paula Jane Arrowood, Nov. 22, 1975; children: Melissa, Amy, Laura. BA in Polit. Sci., Wright State U., 1977; JD, U. Dayton, 1980. Bar: Ohio 1980, U.S. Dist. Ct. (so. dist.) 1980, U.S. Ct. Appeals (6th cir.) 1988. Assoc. Brannon & Cox Law Offices, Dayton, Ohio, 1980-84, Brannon & Hall Law Offices, Dayton, 1984-87; ptnr. Brannon, Hall & Tucker, Dayton, 1987-90, Hall, Tucker & Fullenkamp, Dayton, 1990-93, Hall, Tucker, Fullenkamp & Singer, Dayton, 1993—. Family and matrimonial, Personal injury, General civil litigation. Office: Hall Tucker Fullenkamp & Singer 131 N Ludlow St Ste 1000 Dayton OH 45402-1160

**TUCKER, RICHARD BLACKBURN, III,** lawyer; b. Pitts., Oct. 28, 1943; s. Richard B. Jr. and Alice (Reed) T.; m. Dorothy Dohoney, Aug. 24, 1974; 1 child, R. Wade. BA, U. Va., 1965; JD, Columbia U., 1968. Bar: Pa. 1970, R.I. 1971, U.S. Supreme Ct. 1984. Vista vol. Greater Kansas City (Mo.) Legal Aid & Defender Soc., 1968-69; atty. R.I. Legal Svcs., Providence, 1970-76, Tucker Arensberg, P.C., Pitts., 1976—. Active western Pa. chpt. Nat. Hemophilia Found., Pitts., 1976-82. Mem. Pa. Bar Assn., Allegheny County Bar Assn. (vice-chmn. appellate practice com. 1994-95, chmn., 1996-97). Democrat. Episcopalian. Avocations: tennis, skiing. General civil litigation, Appellate. Home: 217 Edgeworth Ln Sewickley PA 15143-1052 Office: Tucker Arensberg PC One Ppg Pl Ste 1500 Pittsburgh PA 15222-5413

**TUCKER, SHERRY E.,** lawyer; b. High Point, N.C., July 25, 1947; d. Raymond Jacob and Irma (Davis) T. BA, U. N.C., Asheville, 1973; MA, Appalachian State U., 1974; JD, N.C. Ctrl. U., 1977. Bar: N.C., U.S. Dist. Ct. (ea. dist.) N.C., U.S. Ct. Appeals (4th cir.); cert. mediator N.C. Superior Ct., Raleigh, 1995—. Pvt. practice law Chapel Hill, N.C., 1978-89; atty. Title Ins. Co., Chapel Hill, 1989-92; pvt. practice law Raleigh, N.C., 1992-95; assoc. Sanford Holshouser Law Firm, Raleigh, 1995—. Contbr. articles to profl. jours. Bd. mem. The Childhood Trust, Chapel Hill, 1991—. Mem. ABA, N.C. State Bar (com. mem. PALS com. 1993—), N.C. Bar Assn., Pi Gamma Mu. Avocations: horseback riding, piano, golf, tennis. Alternative dispute resolution, Real property, General corporate. Office: Sanford Holshouser Law Firm Ste 600 219 Fayetteville Street Mall # 1000 Raleigh NC 27601-1366

**TUCKER, WATSON BILLOPP,** lawyer; b. Dobbs Ferry, N.Y., Nov. 16, 1940; s. Watson Billopp and Mary (Prema) T.; children: Robin, Craig, Christopher, Alexander, John. BS, Northwestern U., Evanston, Ill., 1962; JD magna cum laude, Northwestern U., 1965. Bar: Ill. 1965, U.S. Dist. Ct. (no. dist.) Ill. 1966, U.S. Supreme Ct. 1971, U.S. Dist. Ct. (no. dist.) N.Y. 1976, U.S. Ct. Appeals (2d, 3d, 5th, 6th, 7th, and 9th cirs.). Ptnr. Mayer, Brown & Platt, Chgo., 1972-99, Tucker & Brown LLC, DeKalb, Ill., 1999—; trial lawyer Aon Corp., Chgo. Fellow Am. Coll. Trial Lawyers. General civil litigation, Antitrust, Securities. Office: Tucker & Brown LLC 115 N 1st St Dekalb IL 60115-3201

**TUCKER, WILLIAM P.,** lawyer, writer; b. Kingston, N.Y., Jan. 26, 1932; s. Philip and Mary (McGowan) T.; m. Dolores F. Beaudoin, June 10, 1961; children: Andrew M., Thomas B., Mary A. BA with honors, Hunter Coll., 1958; JD with honors, St. John's U., 1962. Bar: N.Y. 1962, U.S. Dist. Ct. (ea. dist.) N.Y. 1963, Fla. 1980. Assoc. Mendes & Mount, N.Y.C., 1962-63; ptnr. Cullen and Dykman, Bklyn. and Garden City, N.Y., 1963-98, Golden, Wexler & Sarnese, Garden City/Purchase/S.I., 1998—; former gen. counsel Broadway Nat. Bank, Wartburg Luth. Svcs., Luth. Ctr. for the Aging, Martin Luther Ter. Apts., Inc., Interfaith Med. Ctr.; former gen. counsel Roosevelt Savs. Bank, Olympian Bank, GreenPoint Bank, Ridgewood Savs. Bank, Atlantic Liberty Savs., F.A., Bethpage Fed. Credit Union, Mcpl. Credit Union, Lincoln Savs. Bank, Bklyn. Savs. Bank, Met. Savs. Bank, Crossland Savs. Bank, Bushwick Savs. Bank, Anchor Savs. Bank; former spl. counsel OCI Mortgage Corp., Bklyn C. of C., Downtown Bklyn. Bus. Assn., Bank of N.Y., Chase Manhattan Bank, Fleet Bank, Kraft Credit Union, Apple Bank for Savs., Barclays Bank of N.Y.; chmn. bd. dirs. Broadway Nat. Bank. Author: DP-or Billy and Jerry in the Promised Land. Past mem. Selective Svc. Bd.; past pres. St. Vincent Ferrer Home Sch. Assn.; del. Diocesan Union Holy Name Socs.; mem. coun. St. Johns's U.; mem. coun. of regents St. Francis Coll., Bklyn.; bd. dirs. Faith Home Found., St. Josephs Coll. Mem. Am. Coll. Real Estate Lawyers, N.Y. State Bar Assn., Fla. Bar Assn., Savs. Banks Lawyers Assn. Bklyn., N.Y. Land Title Assn., Suffolk County Bar Assn., Savs. Bank Assn. N.Y. State (law com.), Bklyn. Mcpl. Club, Knight of Malta. Avocations: co-owner Salem Keizer Volcanoes N.W. League baseball team. Banking, Real property, General practice. Home: 23 Bunker Hill Dr Huntington NY 11743-5705 Office: Golden Wexler & Sarnese 377 Oak St Ste 202 Garden City NY 11530-6547

**TUCK-RICHMOND, DOLETTA SUE,** prosecutor; b. Hugo, Okla., June 18, 1966; d. Benny Doyle and Tommie Marie (Cousins) T.; m. Lyle Richmond, Sept. 30, 1995. AS, Murray State Coll., Tishomingo, Okla., 1986; BS magna cum laude, S.E. Okla. State U., 1988; JD with highest honors, U. Okla., 1991. Bar: Okla. 1991, U.S. Dist. Ct. (we., ea., and no. dists.), U.S. Ct. Appeals (10th cir.). Summer assoc. Andrews Davis, Oklahoma City, 1989-90; instr. in legal rsch, writing and oral advocacy U. Okla., Norman, 1989-91; assoc. Crowe & Dunlevy, Oklahoma City, 1991-93, Tulsa, Okla., 1993-94; pvt. practice Antlers, Okla., 1994; exempt orgn. specialist IRS, Oklahoma City, Okla., 1994-95; asst. atty. gen. State of Okla., Oklahoma City, 1995—; asst. U.S. atty. U.S. Atty's. Office (we. dist.) Okla., Oklahoma City, 1999—. Author: Joint Defense Agreements Can It Help Your Client, 1998, King For a Day: An Overview of Federal and State Qui Jam Provisions, 1999; contbg. author, editor: Oklahoma Environmental Law Practitioner's Handbook, 1992. Firm com. mem., participant Harvest Food Dr., Oklahoma City, 1991; chairperson Okla. Young Lawyers Rape Victims Assistance Com., 1992-94; bd. dirs. Okla. County Young Lawyers Divsn., 1993; participant, vol. Legal Aide of Western Okla., 1991. Named Miss Murray State Coll., Student Senate Pres., Tishomingo, Okla., 1986-86, Order of Coif U. Okla., Norman, Okla., 1991, Okla. Law Review U. Okla., Norman, 1991. Mem. FBA, Okla. Bar Assn. (bd. dirs., young lawyers divsn. 1993-95, mock trial com. 1994-95, liaison mental health com. 1994-95), Am. Agrl. Law Assn., Phi Delta Phi, Phi Kappa Phi (Spl. Act award for U.S. Atty. 1996, 97). Democrat. Baptist. Avocations: tennis, reading, writing, knitting, sports events. Home: 1624 SW 128th Pl Oklahoma City OK 73170-5018 Office: US Atty's Office Western Dist of Okla 210 Park Ave Ste 400 Oklahoma City OK 73102-5628

**TUDOR, BYNUM ELLSWORTH, III,** lawyer; b. Winston-Salem, N.C., Mar. 19, 1960. BSBA, U. N.C., 1981; MBA, JD, Wake Forest U., 1986. Bar: Tenn. 1986. Assoc. Dearborn & Ewing, Nashville, 1986-92, Baker, Worthington, Crossley & Stansberry, Nashville, 1993-94; shareholder Tudor & Lindsey, P.C., Nashville, 1994—. Mem. ABA, Tenn. Bar Assn., Nashville Bar Assn., Middle Tenn. Employee Benefits Coun., Tenn. Valley Employee Benefits Coun., Phi Delta Phi. Democrat. Pension, profit-sharing, and employee benefits, Insurance, Labor. Home: 716 Clematis Dr Nashville TN 37205-1030 Office: Tudor & Lindsey PC 303 Church St Ste 200 Nashville TN 37201-1797

**TUDOR, JOHN MARTIN,** lawyer, educator; b. Kenton, Ohio; s. Arthur Davis and Marjorie Maxie (Martin) T.; m. Anda Maija Vilums, Aug. 26, 1961; children: Mara Y. Tudor Ward, Andrew Roland. BA, Ohio State U., 1959; JD, Duke U., 1962. Bar: Ohio 1962, U.S. Dist. Ct. (no. dist.) Ohio 1963, U.S. Supreme Ct. 1973, U.S. Ct. Appeals (6th cir.) 1987, U.S. Dist. Ct. (ctrl. dist.) Ill. 1995. Assoc. Squire, Sanders & Dempsey, Cleve., 1962-65; ptnr. Mahon, Tudor & Van Dyne, Kenton, 1965-88, Tudor, Blue & Cloud, Columbus, Ohio, 1969-88, Tudor, Cloud & Cesner, Kenton, 1988-90; pvt. practice Tudor Law, LLC, Kenton, 1990—; gen. counsel Am. BanCorp., Columbus, 1974-80; pres., dir. Village BancShares, Inc., Kenton, 1980-90, mng. mem. Latvian-Am. Trading Co., Ltd., 1997—. Author: We The People, 1987; contbr. articles to profl. jours. Founder Hardin County Hist. Soc., Kenton, 1966. Mem. ATLA, Am. Inns of Ct., Hardin County Bar Assn. (pres.), Eagle Scouts Assn. Republican. Presbyterian. Avocations: snow skiing, sail boating. General corporate, Probate, General civil litigation. Home: 411 Cecelia St Kenton OH 43326-1451 Office: 22 N Main St Kenton OH 43326-1552

**TUFARO, RICHARD CHASE,** lawyer; b. N.Y.C., July 9, 1944; s. Frank P. and Stephania A. (Maida) T.; m. Helen M. Tufaro, June 25, 1977; children: Mary C., Edward F., Paul R., Cynthia M. AB magna cum laude, Dartmouth Coll., 1965; LLB cum laude, Harvard U., 1968. Bar: N.Y. 1969, D.C. 1992, Md. 1994; U.S. Dist. Ct. (so. dist.) N.Y. 1973, U.S. Dist. Ct. (ea. dist.) N.Y. 1978, U.S. Dist Ct. (D.C. dist.), 1994; U.S. Dist. Ct. (Md. dist.), 1996, U.S. Ct. Apls. (2d cir.) 1973, (5th cir.) 1976, (9th cir.) 1979, (6th cir.) 1980, (4th cir.), 1995; U.S. Ct. Claims, 1985, U.S. Ct. Appeals (3d cir.) 1990, U.S. Ct. Appeals (D.C. cir.) 1992; U.S. Sup. Ct., 1975. Law clk. Appellate-Div. N.Y. State, N.Y.C., 1970-71, assoc. Milbank, Tweed, Hadley & McCloy, N.Y.C., 1971-72, adminstrv. asst. White House Domestic Coun., Washington, 1972-73, assoc. Milbank, Tweed, Hadley & McCloy, N.Y.C., 1973-77, ptnr. 1978—. Served to capt. U.S. Army, 1968-70. Decorated Bronze Star with oak leaf cluster. Mem. ABA, Am. Mgmt. Assn., Phi Beta Kappa. Federal civil litigation, State civil litigation, Contracts commercial. Home: 7109 Heathwood Ct Bethesda MD 20817-2915 Office: 1825 I St NW Ste 1100 Washington DC 20006-5417

**TUFFLEY, FRANCIS DOUGLAS,** lawyer; b. Lewistown, Mont., Feb. 10, 1946; s. Francis Darby and Norma Hermione (Arildson) T.; m. Mary Carolyn Dyar, June 27, 1970; children: Jessica Carolyn, Bradley Dyar. Student U. Wash., 1964-66; BA in Polit. Sci., U. Puget Sound, 1968; JD magna cum laude, Gonzaga U., 1976. Bar: Wash. 1976, U.S. Dist. Ct. (ea. dist.) Wash. 1976, U.S. Dist. Ct. (we. dist.) Wash. 1979, U.S. Ct. Appeals (9th cir.) 1979. Assoc. Paine, Lowe, Coffin, Herman & O'Kelley, Spokane, Wash., 1976-79; sole practice, Spokane, 1979-83; assoc. Burns & Ricketts, P.S., Seattle, 1983-84; ptnr. Tuffley & Assocs., P.S., Seattle, 1984-90; assoc. Beresford Booth Baronsky & Trompeter, Inc., P.S., 1990—; counsel Vis. Nurses Assn., Spokane, 1979-81, Wash. State Psychol. Assn., 1985-87. Mem. procurement com. Wampum, Spokane, 1979-81; mem. steering com. McDermott for Gov., Spokane, 1980, steering com. Donahue for Judge, 1982; co-chmn. Wasson for Judge Com., Spokane, 1981; active YMCA Indian Guides, 1984—; commr. Westhill (Wash.) Water Dist., 1988—; mem. Wash. State Jud. Coun., 1988—. Served to capt. USAF, 1968-73. Mem. Wash. State Bar Assn. (state tel-law task force 1978, lawyer referral com. 1978-83, legis. com. 1986-90), Spokane County Bar Assn. (chmn. tel-law project 1977-80, trustee 1979-83, Ann. award of Merit 1981), Spokane Young Lawyer's Assn. (pres. 1979-81, trustee 1978-81), King County Bar Assn. (judiciary and courts com. 1985-89, bench-bar delay reduction task force 1987-89), Wash. State Trial Lawyers Assn. (legis. steering com. 1985-90, vice chmn. conv. com. 1986-87, chmn. membership com. 1987-89, chmn. ct. congestion com. 1987-89, bd. dirs. 1987-90), Bainbridge Island Sportsman's Club. Democrat. Methodist. State civil litigation, Personal injury, Insurance. Home: 6550 NE Dapple Ct Bainbridge Island WA 98110 Office: Beresford Booth Baronsky & Trompeter Inc PS 1201 3rd Ave Ste 1400 Seattle WA 98101-3029

**TUFTE, BRIAN N.,** lawyer; b. Mpls., Dec. 9, 1961; s. Obert N. and Doris H. T.; m. Julie S. Bart, June 4, 1993; children: Jessica, Brianna. BA in Physics/Math., St. Olaf Coll., 1984; JD magna cum laude, William Mitchell Coll. Law, 1994. Bar: Minn. 1994, U.S. Dist. Ct. Minn. 1994, U.S. Ct. Appeals (8th and fed. cirs.) 1994, U.S. Patent and Trademark Office. Sr. integrated cir. design engr. Honeywell Inc., Solid State Elecs. Ctr., Plymouth, Minn., 1985-93; assoc. atty. Nawrocki, Rooney & Siverston, P.A., Mpls., 1993-98; founding ptnr. Crompton, Seager & Tufte, LLC, Mpls., 1998—. Mem. Am. Intellectual Property Law Assn., Minn. Intellectual Property Law Assn., Minn. Bar Assn., Hennepin County Bar Assn. Intellectual property, Patent, Trademark and copyright. Office: Crompton Seager & Tufte LLC 331 2nd Ave S Ste 895 Minneapolis MN 55401-2246

**TUHOLSKE, JACK R.,** lawyer; b. Feb. 14, 1954; m. Lillian Westrapp, Sept. 8, 1979; children: Oliver, Benjamin, Cascade. Student, U. Rochester, 1972-75; BA in Polit. Sci., U. Wash., 1977; JD with honors, U. Mont., 1985. Pvt. practice Missoula, Mont., 1985—; adj. prof. environ. law U. Mont., Missoula, 1997—, supr. Environ. Law Clinic, 1995—, lectr., 1985—. Author: Forest Plans and Fisheries, 1985; contbr. articles to profl. jours. Patroller, dir. Nat. Ski Patrol, Lolo Pass, Mont., 1981-87; v.p., bd. dirs. Sussex Sch., Missoula, 1993-96. Recipient Legal Achievement award Mont. Wildlife Fedn., 1988, Conservation award Alliance for Wild Rockies, 1995. Administrative and regulatory, Environmental, Natural resources. Home: PO Box 7458 Missoula MT 59807-7458 Office: 401 Washington St Missoula MT 59802-4526

**TUKE, ROBERT DUDLEY,** lawyer, educator; b. Rochester, N.Y., Dec. 5, 1947; s. Theodore Robert and Doris Jean (Smith) T.; m. Susan Devereux Cummins, June 21, 1969; children: Andrew, Sarah. BA with distinction, U. Va., 1969; JD, Vanderbilt U., 1976. Bar: Tenn. 1976, U.S. Dist. Ct. (mid. dist.) Tenn. 1976, U.S. Ct. Appeals (6th cir.) 1976, U.S. Ct. Appeals (4th cir.) 1978, U.S. Ct. Appeals (fed. cir.) 1993, U.S. Supreme Ct. 1986, U.S. Ct. Internat. Trade 1993. Assoc. Farris, Warfield & Kanaday, Nashville, 1976-79, ptnr., 1980-94; ptnr. Tuke Yopp & Sweeney, Nashville, 1994—; adj. prof. law Vanderbilt U. Law Sch., Nashville; faculty PLI, 1995—; mem. AMA Drs.' Adv. Network. Author: (with others) Tennessee Practice, 1992—; editor Vanderbilt Law Rev.; contbr. articles to profl. jours. Mem. Tenn. Adoption Law Study Commn., 1993-96, Metro CATV Com. Capt. USMC, 1969-73. Decorated Cross of Gallantry; Patrick Wilson Merit scholar. Mem. ABA, Nat. Health Law Assn., Nat. Assn. Bond Lawyers, Am. Acad. Adoption Attys. (bd. dirs.), Tenn. Bar Assn., Nashville Bar Assn., Nashville C. of C. (bd. gov.), Order of Coif. Democrat. Episcopalian. Avocations: rowing, running, cycling, hiking, travel. General corporate, Securities, Health. Office: NationsBank Plz 414 Union St Ste 1100 Nashville TN 37219-1718

**TULLY, BERNARD MICHAEL,** lawyer; b. Pitts., Aug. 28, 1952; s. Joseph J. and Mary Lorraine T.; m. Feb. 15, 1991; children: Elizabeth, Kevin, Michael, Jessica, Katie. BA, Duquesne, Pitts., 1974; JD, Ohio No. U., 1979. Asst. dist. atty. Pitts., 1979-85; assoc. Stokes, Lurie & Cole, Pitts., 1985-87; pvt. practice Pitts., 1987—; solicitor Allegheny County Treas., Pitts., 1994-98. Personal injury, Criminal. Office: Grant Bldg 310 Grant St Ste 729 Pittsburgh PA 15219-2200

**TULLY, ROBERT GERARD,** lawyer; b. Dubuque, Iowa, Sept. 7, 1955; s. Thomas Alois and Marjorie May (Fosselman) T. BA, U. Notre Dame, 1977; postgrad., U. Notre Dame, London, summer 1979; JD, Drake U., 1981. Bar: Iowa 1981, U.S. Dist. Ct (no. and so. dists.) Iowa 1981, U.S. Ct. Appeals (8th cir.) 1981, U.S. Supreme Ct. 1986. Assoc. Verne Lawyer & Assocs., Des Moines, 1981-93; bd. dirs. Dubuque Lumber Co., sec., treas., 1984-87; lectr. Nat. Collegiate Mock Trial Drake U., Des Moines, 1984-93, atty., coach, 1985-93; bd. counselors Drake U. Law Sch., 1986-92, chmn. alumni rels. com. Contbr. articles to profl. jours. Com. mem. Dubuque County Dem. party, 1976-78, Polk County Dem. party, 1982-83, 87-89, 92—, del. state convs., 1988; bd. dirs. nat. Coun. Alcoholism and Other Drug Dependencies for Des Moines Area (pres. 1985-92); mem. nat. commn. on future of Drake U. Fellow Iowa Acad. Trial Lawyers (compiler various profl. publs.); mem. ABA, ATLA (state del. 1991—, bd. govs. 1993—, mem. key peron com.), Nat. Assn. Student Bar Assns. (v.p. 1980-81), Iowa Bar Assn. (Uniform Jury Instructions rules com., young lawyers sect., com. legal svcs. for elderly chmn. fed. practice com., law related edn. com.), Assn. Trial Lawyers Iowa (pres. 1992-93, pres.-elect 1991-92, v.p. legis. 1988-91, bd. govs. 1985—, Outstanding Key Person 1983-84, 91-92, chmn. key person com. 1985-88), Polk County Bar Assn. (bd. dirs. 1993—, grievance com.), Iowa Citizens Action Network (bd. dirs. 1989—), Blackstone Inn of Ct., Notre Dame Club of Des Moines (pres. 1981-83), Drake Student Bar Assn. (pres. 1980-81), Phi Alpha Delta. Roman Catholic. Personal injury, State civil litigation, Federal civil litigation. Home: 838 Stone Ridge Pl Dubuque IA 52001-1362 Office: Michael J Galligan Law Firm 300 Walnut St Des Moines IA 50309-2249

**TUMOLA, THOMAS JOSEPH,** lawyer; b. Newtown Square, Pa., Jan. 18, 1941; s. Joseph Thomas and Vera P. Tumola; m. Sarabelle Hare, Aug. 19, 1972; children—Thomas Joseph, Jr., Cristabell Hill. B.S. in Econs., Villanova U., 1962, J.D., 1966; postgrad Temple U., 1970-72. Bar: Pa. 1967, U.S. Ct. Apls. (3d cir.) 1967, U.S. Dist. Ct. (ea. dist.) Pa. 1968, U.S. Tax Ct. 1971. Law clk. U.S. Ct. Apls. 3d cir., Phila., 1966-68; assoc. Clark, Ladner, Fortenbaugh & Young, Phila., 1968-73, ptnr., 1974-97; ptnr. Duane, Morris & Heckscher, 1996—; mem. adv. task force on revision of Pa. Navigation Commn. Law, 1978. Mem. ABA, Pa. Bar Assn., Phila. Bar Assn., Gamma Phi. Clubs: Union League, Villanova (Phila.). Contbr. articles to legal jours. Consumer commercial, General corporate, State and local taxation. Home: 807 Bowman Ave Wynnewood PA 19096-1602 Office: One Liberty Pl 42nd Fl Philadelphia PA 19103-7396

**TUMOLO, MICHAEL L.,** corporate lawyer. V.p., counsel Toys 'R' Us, Paramus, N.J., 1981—. Office: Toys R Us 461 From Rd Paramus NJ 07652-3524

**TUNE, JAMES FULCHER,** lawyer; b. Danville, Va., May 13, 1942; s. William Orrin and Susan Agnes (Fulcher) T.; m. Katherine Del Mickey, Aug. 2, 1969; children: Katherine Winslow, Jeffrey Bricker. BA, U. Va., 1964; MA, Stanford U., 1970, JD, 1974. Bar: Wash. 1974, U.S. Dist. Ct. (we. dist.) Wash. 1974. Assoc. Bogle & Gates, Seattle, 1974-79, ptnr., 1980-99, head comml./banking dept., 1985-93, mng. ptnr., 1986-93, chmn., 1994-99; ptnr. Dorsey & Whitney LLP, Seattle, 1999—, chmn. Seattle exec. com., 1999—; bd. dirs. BIEC Internat. Inc., Kalama, Wash., BHP Steel Bldg. Products USA Inc., Sacramento, BHP Coated Steel Corp., Rancho Cucumonga, Calif., BHP Steel Ams. Inc., Long Beach, Calif., Nichirei Foods, Inc., Seattle, Passport Cuising Internat., Inc., Seattle; chmn. Seattle-King City Econ. Devel. Coun., 1992. Chmn. Seattle Repertory Theatre, 1995. Lt. USN, 1964-69, Vietnam. Woodrow Wilson fellow, 1964, Danforth Found. fellow, 1964. Mem. ABA, Wash. State Bar Assn. (lectr. CLE 1976, 78, 84), Seattle-King County Bar Assn., Seattle C. of C. (vice chmn. City Budget Task Force 1980-82), Phi Beta Kappa, Ranier Club, Seattle Tennis Club, Rotary. Presbyterian. Banking, Contracts commercial, General corporate. Office: Dorsey & Whitney LLP US Bank Bldg Ctr 1420 5th Ave Ste 4200 Seattle WA 98101-2375

**TUNGATE, DAVID E.,** lawyer, educator; b. Columbus, Ohio, Apr. 22, 1945; s. Ernest O. and Diantha (Woltz) T.; m. Mary Ann V. Montaleone, Jan. 27, 1968; children: David, Melissa. BA, U. Ill., Champaign, 1967, JD, 1970. Bar: U.S. Dist. Ct. (we. dist.) Pa. 1970, Superior Ct. Pa., 1971, Supreme Ct. Pa., 1971, U.S. Ct. Appeals (3d cir.) 1973, U.S. Ct. Claims 1987, U.S. Dist. Ct (ea. dist.) Wis. 1989, U.S. Ct. Appeals (fed. cir.) 1990. Assoc. Eckert, Seamans, Cherin & Mellott, Pitts., 1976-75, ptnr., 1976—; adj. prof. Carnegie Mellon U., Pitts., 1991—, U. Pitts. Sch. of Law, 1996—. Contbr. articles to profl. jours.; author bus. book revs. Pitts. Post-Gazette, 1986—. Chmn. Zoning Hearing Bd. Upper St. Clair, 1991—. Mem. ABA, Penn. Bar Assn., Allegheny County Bar Assn. General civil litigation, Contracts commercial, Computer. Office: Eckert Seamans Cherin & Mellott 42d Fl USX Tower 600 Grant St Pittsburgh PA 15219-2702

**TUNGATE, JAMES LESTER,** lawyer; b. Columbus, Ohio, Sept. 27, 1947; s. Ernest O. Jr. and Diantha (Woltz) T.; m. Susan Sumner, Aug. 25, 1973; children: Edward Ernest, James Aaron. B.S., Ill. Wesleyan U., 1969; M.A., Northwestern U.-Ill., 1970, Ph.D., 1972; J.D., U. Ill.-Urbana, 1979; hon. D.H.L., London Sch. (Eng.), 1972. Bar: Ill. 1979, U.S. Supreme Ct. 1985. Spl. instr. Northwestern U., Evanston, Ill., 1971; prof., chmn. Loyola U., New Orleans, 1971-76; state dir. News Election Service, New Orleans, 1972-74; dir. Inst. Religious Communications, New Orleans, 1974-76; asst. to state's atty. Iroquois County, Watseka, Ill., 1978; ptnr. Tungate & Tungate, Watseka, 1979—; media cons. Inst. Politics, New Orleans, 1973-76; legal cons., lectr. Iroquois Mental Health Ctr., Watseka, 1980—; lectr. law Kankakee Community Coll., Ill., 1982. Author: Romantic Images in Popular Songs, 1972; Readings in Broadcast Law, 1975. Dir. Iroquois Mental Health Ctr., 1980—; chmn. Iroquois County chpt. ARC, 1982-84, 85—; dir. Iroquois Republican Council, 1983—. Recipient Internat. Radio and TV Found. award; Harnow scholar U. Ill., 1976. Mem. Ill. Bar Assn., Iroquois County Bar Assn. (Law Day chmn., pres. 1998—), Chgo. Bar Assn., Pi Alpha Delta. Republican. Methodist. Lodges: Masons (master 1982-83), Scottish Rite (most wise master 1997-98, 33-degree 1999), Mohammed Shrine. Banking, General practice, Probate. Home: 146 W Hislop Dr Cissna Park IL 60924-8718 Office: Tungate Law Offices 744 E Walnut St PO Box 337 Watseka IL 60970-0337

**TUOZZOLO, JOHN JOSEPH,** lawyer; b. Norwalk, Conn., July 20, 1948; s. Anthony and Helen (Marsico) T.; m. Karen A. McCoy, Dec. 26, 1970; children: Barbara-Ann, Christopher, Karen. BA, U. Dayton, 1970; JD, Coll. William and Mary, 1973; MBA, U. Conn., Storrs, 1981; MS in Taxation, U. Hartford, 1985. Bar: Conn. 1973, U.S. Dist. Ct. Conn. 1976. Assoc. Ventura, Ventura and West, Danbury, Conn., 1974-77; ptnr. Jaber and Tuozzolo, Danbury, 1977-78, Cutsumpas, Collins, Hannafin, Garamella, Jaber & Tuozzolo, Danbury, 1978—; adj. prof. Western Conn. State U., Danbury, 1977—; presenter at seminars. Contbg. author: Connecticut Real Property Law, 1984. Chmn. Behtel (Conn.) Rep. Town Com., 1978-82, bd. dirs. Western Conn. chpt. ARC, Danbury, 1986-93, Brookfield/Danbury YMCA, 1991—; adminstrv. com. United Way, Danbury, 1991—. Lt. col. JAGC, USAR, 1973—. Mem. Conn. Bar Assn. (exec. com. probate and extates, tax sect.), Danbury Bar Assn., YMCA, Nat. Acad. Elder Law Attys. Republican. Roman Catholic. Estate planning, Personal income taxation, Real property. Home: 73 Woodside Cir Torrington CT 06790-2238 Office: Cutsumpas Collins Hannafin Garamella Jaber & Tuozzolo 148 Deer Hill Ave Danbury CT 06810-7770

**TUPPER, KENT PHILLIP,** lawyer; b. Huron, S.D., July 24, 1931; s. Ezra Lynn and Mildred Virginia (Nason) T.; m. Joan Maria McGinley, Dec. 18, 1954; children: Kent Michael, Kay Maria Tupper-Bunker. BA, U. Minn., 1956; JD, William Mitchell Coll. Law, 1963. Bar: Minn. 1963, U.S. Dist. Ct. Minn. 1964, U.S. Supreme Ct. 1971, U.S. Ct. Appeals (8th cir.) 1972. Indsl. psychologist Chrysler Corp., Detroit, 1956-57; claim examiner Hardware Mut. Ins., Mpls., 1957-63; ptnr. Tupper & Rosenbower, Mpls., 1964-67; dir., atty. Leech Lake Reservation Legal Svcs., Cass Lake, Minn., 1967-69; ptnr. Tupper, Smith, Seck, Mattson et. al., Walker, Minn., 1969-84, Tupper Law Offices, Mpls., 1984-93; chief judge Skakopee Mdewakaton Tribal Ct., Prior Lake, Minn., 1985-93; ret., 1993; legal counsel Minn. Chippewa Tribe, Cass Lake, 1974-91; bd. dirs. Leech Lake Legal Svcs., Cass Lake, 1969-77. Del. State Dem. Conv., 1972. Sgt. USMC, 1951-54. Episcopalian. Native American, Personal injury, General corporate.

**TURBIN, RICHARD,** lawyer; b. N.Y.C., Dec. 25, 1944; s. William and Ruth (Fiedler) T.; m. Rai Saint Chu-Turbin, June 12, 1976; children: Laurel Mei, Derek Andrew. BA magna cum laude, Cornell U., 1966; JD, Harvard U., 1969. Bar: Hawaii 1971, U.S. Dist. Ct. Hawaii 1971. Asst. atty. gen. Western Samoa, Apia, 1969-70; dep. pub. defender Pub. Defender's Office, Honolulu, 1970-74; dir. Legal Aid Soc. Hawaii, Kaneohe, 1974-75; sr. atty., pres. Law Offices Richard Turbin, Honolulu, 1975—; legal counsel Hawaii Crime Commn., 1980-81. Co-author: Pacific; author: Medical Malpractice, Handling Emergency Medical Cases, 1991; editor Harvard Civil Rights-Civil Liberties Law Rev., 1969. Legal counsel Dem. Party, Honolulu County, 1981-82; elected Neighborhood Bd., 1985, elected chair, 1990-97; bd. dirs. Hawaii chpt. ACLU, 1974-78, East-West Ctr. grantee, 1971, 72. Mem. ATLA, ABA (chair internat. torts and ins. law and practice com., mem. governing coun., chair tort and ins. practice sect. 1999—, chair-elect 1998-99), Hawaii Bar Assn., Hawaii Trial Lawyers Assn. (bd. govs.), Hawaii Jaycees (legal counsel 1981-82), Chinese Jaycees Honolulu (legal counsel 1980-81), Honolulu Tennis League (undefeated player 1983), Hawaii Harlequin Rugby Club (sec., legal counsel 1978-82), Pacific Club, Outrigger Canoe Club. Jewish. Personal injury, State civil litigation, Workers' compensation. Home: 4557 Kolohala St Honolulu HI 96816-4953 Office: 737 Bishop St Ste 1850 Honolulu HI 96813-3201

**TURCKE, PAUL ANDREW,** lawyer; b. Anchorage, Oct. 4, 1965. BA, Whitman Coll., 1987; JD, U. Idaho, 1993. Bar: Idaho 1993, S.D. 1994, U.S. Dist. Ct. Idaho 1993, U.S. Ct. Appeals (9th cir.) 1997. Law clk. to hon. Gerald Schroeder 4th Dist. Ct., Boise, Idaho, 1993-94; assoc. Moore & Kandaras, Rapid City, S.D., 1994-95; dep. pub. defender Kootenai County Pub. Defender's Office, Coeur d'Alene, Idaho, 1995-96; dep. prosecuting atty. Bonner County, Sandpoint, Idaho, 1996; shareholder Moore Smith Busten & Turcke, Boise, 1996—. Fax: 208-331-1202. E-mail: pturcke@micron.net. Environmental, Municipal (including bonds), Natural resources. Office: Moore Smith Buxten & Turcke 999 Main St Ste 910 Boise ID 83702-9011

**TUREK, DOUGLAS D.,** lawyer; b. Woodville, Tex., June 6, 1970; s. David E. and Linda M. Turek. BA in History, U. Tex., 1991; JD, U. Houston, 1994. Bar: Tex., 1995, U.S. Dist. Ct. (so. dist.) Tex., 1996, U.S. Ct. Appeals (5th cir.), 1996. Assoc. atty. Glickman, Herlong & Hughes LLP, Houston, 1995—. Dir. Neartown Youth Baseball League, Houston, 1996-97, coach, 1997-98. Mem. ABA, State Bar Tex., Houston Bar Assn. (dir. law practice mgmt. 1998—), Houston Young Lawyer's Assn., Phi Delta Phi. Avocations: golf, hunting, fishing, backpacking, camping. General civil litigation, Labor, Contracts commercial. Office: Glickman Herlong & Hughes LLP 1001 Fannin St Ste 1460 Houston TX 77002-6799

**TUREN, BARBARA ELLEN,** lawyer; b. Newark, Nov. 4, 1951; d. Samuel and Elaine (Goldfarb) T.; m. Leonard Paul Caplan, May 22, 1982 (div. June 1987); 1 child, Andrew. BA with distinction, George Washington U., Washington, 1973; MA with honors, London U., 1974; JD magna cum laude, Seton Hall U., 1990. Bar: N.J. 1990, U.S. Dist. Ct. N.J. 1990, U.S. Ct. Appeals (3d cir.) 1991, U.S. Supreme Ct. 1995. Fundraiser Am. Pl. Theatre, N.Y.C., 1978-79; lit. scout Warner Theatre Prodns., N.Y.C., 1979-80; lit. cons. Theatre Now, Inc., N.Y.C., 1980-82; lit. and talent agt. Don Buchwald & Assocs., N.Y.C., 1982-85; assoc. Hannoch Weisman, Roseland, N.J., 1990-92, Vogel, Chait, Schwartz and Collins, Morristown, N.J., 1992-93; dep. atty. gen. Divsn. Law and Pub. Safety, State of N.J., Newark, 1994—; adj. prof. law Seton Hall U. Sch. Law, Newark, 1994—. Pre-sch. vol. Head Start, Washington, 1970-73; lit. vol. N.Y.C. Sch. System, 1978-85. Recipient Cert. of Membership Seton Hall Constl. Law Jour., Newark, 1989-90. Mem. ABA, N.J. Bar Assn. Jewish. Avocations: travel, theatre, reading, collecting rare books. General civil litigation, Administrative and regulatory, Government contracts and claims.

**TURETSKY, AARON,** lawyer; b. Bklyn., Mar. 23, 1951; s. Victor and Edith (Levine) T.; m. Edna M. Real, July 21, 1990; children: Persephone Fatima, Aaron Jr. BA summa cum laude, Hunter Coll., N.Y.C., 1979; JD magna cum laude, N.Y. Law Sch., 1986. Bar: N.J. 1986, U.S. Dist. Ct. N.J. 1986, N.Y. 1987, U.S. Dist. Ct. (so. and ea. dist.) N.Y. 1987, U.S. Dist. Ct. (no. dist.) N.Y. 1988. Appellate law rsch. asst. appellate div. 2d dept. Supreme Ct. State of N.Y., 1986-87; atty. North Country Legal Svcs., Inc., Plattsburgh, N.Y., 1987-89; assoc. Holcombe & Bruno, Plattsburgh, 1989-90; pvt. practice, Keeseville, N.Y., 1990—; law guardian Essex County Family Ct., 1990—; impartial hearing officer for children with disabilites, 1996—. Chmn. Essex County, N.Y. Conservative Com., 1990—; N.Y. St. Conservative Party N.E. regional vice. chmn., 1992—; eucharistic min. Cath. Community, Keeseville, N.Y. Mem. N.Y. State Bar Assn., Clinton County Bar Assn., Essex County Bar Assn., Elks, KC, Phi Beta Kappa. Roman Catholic. General practice, Family and matrimonial, Education and schools. Office: PO Box 367 Keeseville NY 12944-0367

**TURK, ANDREW BORDERS,** lawyer; b. San Diego, June 26, 1966; s. Rudy Henry and Wanda Lee (Borders) T.; m. BarbaraJay Kiftmeyer, Oct. 3, 1993. BA summa cum laude, Ariz. State U., 1988; JD, U. Wash., 1992. Bar: Ariz. 1993, Wash. 1993, U.S. Dist. Ct. Ariz. 1993, U.S. Ct. Appeals (9th cir.) 1993. Assoc. Muchmore & Wallwork, P.C., Phoenix, 1993-95, Jennings, Strouss & Salmon, P.L.C., Phoenix, 1996—. Co-author: Arizona Environmental Law Manual, 1994, rev. edit., 1998; contbr. articles to profl. jours. Mem. bicycle adv. com. City of Tempe, Ariz., 1993—, vice chair, 1996, mayoral appointee, chair subcom. on edn., 1996—. Mem. Maricopa County Young Lawyers Assn. (bd. dirs. 1997—, sec. 1998), Ariz. State Bar Assn. (civil practice and procedures com. 1998—, pres.-elect 1999), Phi Beta Kappa, Phi Alpha Delta. Avocations: cycling, golf, history, comic book, music. General civil litigation, Toxic tort, Contracts commercial. Office: Jennings Strouss & Salmon 2 N Central Ave Phoenix AZ 85004-2322

**TURK, JAMES CLINTON,** federal judge; b. Roanoke, Va., May 3, 1923; s. James Alexander and Geneva (Richardson) T.; m. Barbara Duncan, Aug. 21, 1954; children—Ramona Leah, James Clinton, Robert Malcolm Duncan, Mary Elizabeth, David Michael. A.B., Roanoke Coll., 1949; L.L.B., Washington and Lee U., 1952. Bar: Va. bar 1952. Assoc. Dalton & Poff, Radford, Va., 1952-53; ptnr. Dalton, Poff & Turk, Radford, 1953-72; U.S. senator from Va., 1959-72; judge U.S. Dist. Ct. (we. dist.) Va., Roanoke, 1972-73, chief judge, 1973—; dir. 1st & Mchts. Nat. Bank of Radford. Mem. Va. Senate, from 1959, minority leader.; Trustee Radford Community Hosp., 1959—. Served with AUS, 1943-46. Mem. Order of Coif, Phi Beta Kappa, Omicron Delta Kappa. Baptist (deacon). Home: 1002 Walker Dr Radford VA 24141-3018 Office: US Dist Ct 246 Franklin Rd SW # 220 Roanoke VA 24011-2214

**TURK, JAMES CLINTON, JR.,** lawyer; b. Radford, Va., Oct. 27, 1956; s. James Clinton and Barbara (Duncan) T.; m. Allison Blanding, Oct. 16, 1993; children: Lindsey Leigh, Katherine Alexandra, Alma Rae. BA in Econs., Roanoke Coll., 1979; JD, Samford U., 1984. Bar: Va. 1984, U.S. Dist. Ct. (ea. and we. dists.) Va. 1984, U.S. Bankruptcy Ct. 1985, U.S. Ct. Appeals (4th cir.) 1985, U.S. Supreme Ct. 1988; cert. specialist in civil and criminal trial advocacy Nat. Bd. Trial Advocacy. Ptnr. Stone, Harrison, Turk & Showalter, P.C., Radford, 1985—; adj. prof. criminal justice dept. Radford U. Sec. Radford Rep. Com., 1984—; fundraising chmn. Am. Heart Assn., Radford, 1986—; bd. dirs. New River Valley Workshop, Inc., v.p., 1990-92, pres., 1992-93; bd. dirs. new River C.C. Ednl. Found.; apptd. chmn. and dir. Va. Student Assistance Authorities by Gov. George Allen, 1994—; escheator City of Radford and Pulaski County; rep. western dist. CJA Panel Attys., Va.; mem. 4th Cir. Jud. Conf. Mem. ATLA (sustaining, fellow Coll. of Advocacy), ABA, Am. Bd. Trial Advs., Va. Bar Assn. (civil litigation sect. coun. 1991—, criminal litigation sect. coun. 1994—), Nat. Assn. Criminal Def. Lawyers (life; death penalty com. and indigent def. com.), Va. Trial Lawyers Assn., Jaycees, Rotary. Republican. Roman Catholic. Avocations: weightlifting, skiing, travel. Criminal, State civil litigation, Personal injury. Home: 460 Quailwood Dr Blacksburg VA 24060-6724 Office: Stone Harrison Turk & Showalter PC PO Box 2968 Radford VA 24143-2968

**TURKHEIMER, PAUL ADAM,** lawyer; b. New Rochelle, N.Y., Dec. 20, 1962; s. Allan fRank and Sherrie Linda (Goldman) T.; m. Harriet Michele Sternberg, Dec. 21, 1986; children: Ally Rachel, Bari Sarah, Zachary Steven. BS, Ind. U., 1984; JD, U. Balt., 1990. Bar: Md. 1990, D.C. 1992. Assoc. Farrington, Smallwood & Wells, Landover, Md., 1990-93, Smallwood & Wells, Landover, 1993-95, Meyers, Billlingsley, Rodbell & Rosenbaum, Riverdale, Md., 1995—; ptnr. Meyers, Billingsley, Rodbell & Rosenbaum, Rivewrdale, Md., 1999—. Professional liability, Personal injury, General civil litigation. Office: Meyers Billingsley Rodbell & Rosenbaum 6801 Kenilworth Ave Ste 400 Riverdale MD 20737-1331

**TURKHUD, ROHIT SUMANT,** lawyer; b. Bombay, India, June 17, 1959; came to U.S. 1982; s. Sumant Bhasker and Roda (Shroff) T.; m. Nandita R. Kodikal, July 22, 1989. B.Commerce, U. Bombay, 1979, LLB, 1982; LLM, U. Pa., 1983. Bar: N.Y. 1984, U.S. Dist. Ct. (so. and ea. dist.) N.Y., 1987. Assoc. Law Offices of Milan Ganik, N.Y.C., 1984-85, Law Offices of Sheldon Zelig, N.Y.C., 1985-89, Law Offices of Lance Kuba, N.Y.C., 1989; ptnr. Nelson & Turkhud, N.Y.C., 1990-94; of counsel Nallaseth & Naganada, N.Y.C., 1994; pvt. practice N.Y.C., 1994—. Mem. Am. Immigration Lawyers Assn., N.Y. County Lawyers Assn. (immigration and nationality law com. 1990—). Avocations: travel, table-tennis, tennis, dancing. Immigration, naturalization, and customs.

**TURLEY, LINDA,** lawyer; b. Altus, Okla., July 16, 1958; d. Windle and Shirley (Lacey) Turley; m. Thomas J. Stutz, Mar. 30, 1985; 1 child, Lacey. BS, Georgetown U., 1980; JD with honors, U. Tex., 1983. Bar: Tex. 1983; bd. cert. in personal injury trial law. Atty., head product liability dept. Law Offices of Windle Turley, P.C., Dallas, 1986-95; ptnr. Turley & Stutz, P.C., Dallas, 1997—; mem. task force on Tex. rules of civil procedure Tex. Supreme Ct., 1992-93. Mem. ATLA (bd. govs. 1993-96, chair women trial lawyers' caucus 1989-90, chair product liability sect. 1996-97), Tex. Trial Lawyers Assn. (bd. dirs. 1989—). Personal injury, Product liability, General civil litigation. Office: 6440 N Central Expy Ste 610 Dallas TX 75206-4135

**TURLEY, ROBERT JOE,** lawyer; b. Sterling, Ky., Dec. 6, 1926; s. R. Joe and Mavis Clare (Sternberg) T.; m. Mary Lynn Sanders, Dec. 17, 1948 (dv.); children: Leighton Turley Isaacs, Lynn Turley McComas, R. Joe, Mavis Lee Turley Scully. Student, Berea Coll., 1944-45, St. Mary's Coll., Calif., 1945-46; LLB, U. Ky., 1949. Bar: Ky. 1949, U.S. Dist. Ct. (ea. dist.) Ky. 1950, U.S. Supreme Ct. 1959. Ptnr. Mooney & Turley and successor firms, Lexington, Ky., 1949-84; ptnr. Turley & Moore, Lexington, 1984-89, of counsel, 1989-93; chmn. Fed. Jud. Selection Commn. Ky., 1985-89; gen counsel Shriners Hosps. for Children, 1976-77, trustee, 1981-90, emeritus trustee, 1990—. Author: The Choices Are Yours; contbr. articles to legal jours. With USNR, 1944-46. Diplomate Nat. Bd. Trial Advocacy, 1980. Fellow Am. Coll. Trial Lawyers, Ky. Bar Found. (life); mem. Ky. Bar Assn., Lafayette Club, St. Ives Jour. Club, Champions Trace Golf Club, Masons, Shriners. Federal civil litigation, General civil litigation, State civil litigation. Home: 111 Woodland Ave Lexington KY 40502-6415

**TURMEL, STACEY LYNN,** lawyer; b. Pt. Colborne, Ont., Can., Dec. 19, 1967; Came to U.S., 1982; d. Maurice Joseph and Donna Jean (Grau) T. BSBA in Fin., U. Ctrl. Fla., 1991; JD cum laude, Stetson U., 1994. Bar: Fla. 1994, U.S. Dist. Ct. (mid. dist.) Fla. 1994, U.S. Ct. Appeals (11th cir.) 1996. Jr. assoc., law clk. Levine, Hirsch, Segall & Northcutt, P.A., Tampa, Fla., 1994-95; litig. assoc. Maney, Damsker & Jones, P.C., Tampa, Fla., 1995-99, Turmel & Quinn, P.A., Tampa, Fla., 1999—. With USAR, 1989-92. Mem. ATLA, Hillsborough County Bar Assn., Family Inns of Ct., Phi Delta Phi. Democrat. Roman Catholic. Avocations: cycling, sailing, sea kayaking, rollerblading. Family and matrimonial, General civil litigation, Probate. Office: Turmel & Quinn PA 412 E Madison St Ste 803 Tampa FL 33602

**TURNAGE, JEAN A.,** state supreme court justice; b. St. Ignatius, Mont., Mar. 10, 1926. JD, Mont. State U., 1951; D Laws and Letters (non.), U. Mont., 1995. Bar: Mont. 1951, U.S. Supreme Ct. 1963. Formerly ptnr. Turnage, McNeil & Mercer, Polson, Mont.; formerly Mont. State senator from 13th Dist.; pres. Mont. State Senate, 1981-83; chief justice Supreme Ct. Mont., 1985—. Mem. Mont. State Bar Assn., Nat. Conf. Chief Justices (past pres.), Nat. Ctr. State Courts (past chair). Office: Mont Supreme Ct 215 N Sanders St Helena MT 59601-4522

**TURNBULL, E. R. (NED TURNBULL),** state judge; b. Lexington, Ky., Feb. 13, 1961; s. E.R. Turnbull and Nancy (McBryde) Unger; m. Leslee Allison King, July 22, 1988; children: Rand, King, Sid. BA, So. Meth. U., 1984; JD, U. Tulsa, 1990. Bar: Okla. 1990. Asst. dist. atty. major crimes divsn. Tulsa County Dist. Atty.'s Office, Tulsa, 1990-94; state dist. judge Dist. Ct. of State of Okla., Tulsa, 1995—, chief judge criminal divsn., 1998—; revised Okla. criminal felony murder statute and Tulsa County criinal ct. rules; mem. rules com. Okla. Ct. Criminal Appeals, 1996, mem. emergency appellate divsn., 1996. Bd. dirs. Youth Svcs. Tulsa, 1992—, Tri-County Coun. for Aging, Tulsa, 1994-97. Named Outstanding Young Oklahoman, Okla. Jr. C. of C., 1996, gov.'s commendation and exec. dept. proclamation State of Okla., 1996. Mem. Okla. Bar Assn., Okla. Trial Judges Assn., Tulsa County Bar Assn., Rotary. Presbyterian. Avocations: exercise, reading, child rearing. Office: Tulsa County Ct House 500 S Denver Ave Tulsa OK 74103-3838

**TURNBULL, H. RUTHERFORD, III,** law educator, lawyer; b. N.Y.C., Sept. 22, 1937; s. Henry R. and Ruth (White) T.; m. Mary M. Slingluff, Apr. 4, 1964 (div. 1972); m. Ann Patterson, Mar. 23, 1974; children: Jay, Amy, Katherine. BA, Johns Hopkins U., 1959; LLB with hon., U. Md., 1964; LLM, Harvard U., 1969. Bar: Md., N.C. Law clerk to Hon. Emory H. Niles Supreme Bench Balt. City, 1959-60; law clerk to Hon. Roszel C. Thomsen U.S. Dist. Ct. Md., 1962-63; assoc. Piper & Marbury, Balt., 1964-67; prof. Inst. Govt. U. N.C., Chapel Hill, 1969-80, U. Kans., Lawrence, 1980—; prof. spl. edn., courtesy prof. law U. Kans. Editor-in-chief Md. Law Review. Cons., author, lectr., co-dir. Beach Ctr. on Families and Disability, U. Kans.; pres. Full Citizenship Inc., Lawrence, 1987-93; spl. staff-fellow U.S. Senate subcom. on disability policy, Washington, 1987-88; bd. dirs. Camphill Assn. N.Am., Inc., 1985-87; trustee Judge David L. Bazelon Ctr. Mental Health Law, 1993-99. With U.S. Army, 1960-65. Recipient Nat. Leadership award Nat. Assn. Pvt. Residential Resources, 1988, Nat. Leadership award Internat. Coun. for Exceptional Children, 1996, Nat. Leadership award Am. Assn. on Mental Retardation, 1997; Public Policy fellow Joseph P. Kennedy, Jr. Found., 1987-88. Fellow Am. Assn. on Mental Retardation (pres. 1985-86, bd. dirs. 1980-86, Nat. Leadership award 1997); mem. ABA (chmn. disability law commn. 1991-95), U.S.A. Assn. for Retarded Citizens (sec. and dir. 1981-83), Assn. for Persons with Severe Handicaps (treas. 1988, bd. dirs. 1987-90), Nat. Assn. Rehab. Rsch. and Tng. Ctrs. (chair govt. affairs com. 1990-93), Internat. Assn. Scientific Study of Mental Deficiency, Internat. League of Assns. for Persons with Mental Handicaps, Johns Hopkins U. Alumni Assn. Democrat. Episcopalian. Home: 1636 Alvamar Dr Lawrence KS 66047-1714 Office: U Kans 3111 Haworth Hall Lawrence KS 66044-7516

**TURNBULL, REGINALD HARRISON,** lawyer; b. Springfield, Mo., Nov. 3, 1946; s. John Howard and Margaret Maurine Turnbull; m. Anita K. Propst, Dec. 18, 1972; children: Bryce C., Kyle D., Ryan H. BA, N.W. Mo. State U., 1972; JD, U. Mo., Kansas City, 1976. Bar: Mo. 1976, U.S. Dist. Ct. (we dist.) Mo. 1976. Law clk. Jackson County Cir. Ct., Kansas City, Mo., 1976-77; asst. atty. gen. Mo. Atty. Gen., Jefferson City, Mo., 1977-81; dep. dir. for human resources Mo. Dept. of Mental Health, Jefferson City, 1981-91; assoc. atty. Waltz & Jordan, Jefferson City, Mo., 1991-96; shareholder, atty. Riner Turnbull and Walker P.C., Jefferson City, 1996—. Pres. Jefferson City Parks and Recreation Commn., 1984-90, Jefferson City Parents and Tchrs. Orgn., 1994-96; scout master Troup 1, Jefferson City, 1991-94. Mem. Jefferson City Breakfast Rotary Club, Nat. Acad. of Elder Law Attys., Mo. Bar Assn. (probate trust com.), Nat. Orgn. of Social Security Claimant's Reps. Fax: 573-635-6584. E-mail: ribull@aol.com. Estate planning, Family and matrimonial, Bankruptcy. Home: 135 Forest Hill Ave Jefferson City MO 65109-0963 Office: Riner Turnbull & Walker PC 305 E Mccarty St Jefferson City MO 65101-3155

**TURNER, BRUCE EDWARD,** lawyer; b. Wichita Falls, Tex., Oct. 31, 1947; s. Charles William and Marie Jeanne (Masson) T.; m. Barbara Lu Oakes, Oct. 8, 1982; children: Gradie, Anna Marie, Kelly. BA, Tex. Tech U., 1970, JD, 1973; LLM, NYU, 1974. Bar: Tex. 1974, U.S. Dist. Ct. (so. dist.) Tex. 1975, U.S. Tax Ct. 1975, U.S. Ct. Appeals (8th cir.) 1979, U.S. Dist. Ct. (no. dist.) Tex. 1988; bd. cert. comml. real estate. Assoc. Dillingham, Schleider & Marquelette, Houston, 1974-76, Johnston & Feather, Dallas, 1976-80; tax counsel Atlantic Richfield Co., Dallas, 1980-81; corp. counsel Lehndorff, Dallas, 1981—; owner Turner & Assocs., Dallas, 1983—; spkr., contbg. writer Advanced Real Estate Seminar, 1994. Mem. Tex. Bar Assn., Dallas Bar Assn., ICC Practitioners. Republican. Methodist. Club: Downtown Mens (Dallas). Estate taxation, Real property. Home: 3708 Southwestern Blvd Dallas TX 75225-7220 Office: 16901 Dallas Pkwy Ste 204 Addison TX 75001-5225

**TURNER, DAVID ELDRIDGE,** lawyer; b. Washington, Jan. 16, 1947; s. Olan Eldridge and Bernice Adele (Bothwell) T.; children: Matthew David, Elizabeth Kristine, Jacob Michael. BS, Pa. State U., 1969; JD cum laude, Temple U., 1974. Bar: Pa. 1974, U.S. Dist. Ct. (ea. and mid. dists.) Pa. 1974, U.S. Ct. Appeals (3d cir.) 1983, U.S. Supreme Ct. 1985. With Liberty Mut. Ins. Co., Allentown, Pa., 1969-71; ptnr. Rhoda, Stoudt & Bradley, Reading, Pa., 1974-80, Kozloff, Diener, Turner & Payne P.C., Wyomissing, Pa., 1980-84; pres. Bingaman, Hess, Coblentz & Bell, P.C., Reading, 1985—; instr. Pa. State U., Berks County, 1974-80; jud. appointee Berks County Ct. of Common Pleas, Reading, 1982-83. Supr. Robeson Twp. Bd. Suprs., Berks County, Pa., 1980-82. Mem. ABA, Pa. Bar Assn., Berks County Bar Assn., Pa. Trial Lawyers Assn., Pa. Def. Inst., Endlich Law Club, Mensa. Avocations: sculpture, rock climbing. State civil litigation, Federal civil litigation, Insurance. Office: Bingaman Hess Coblentz & Bell 601 Penn Square Ctr PO Box 61 Reading PA 19603-0061

**TURNER, DUNCAN CALVERT,** lawyer; b. Gulfport, Miss., Jan. 28, 1953; s. Francis McRae and Elizabeth Calvert T.; m. Rebecca Reuter, Dec. 29, 1977; children: Aaron, Laura, Samuel. BS, U.S. Mil. Acad., 1974; MBA, U. Miss., 1990, JD, 1990. Bar: Miss. 1990, U.S. Dist. Ct. 1990, Wash. 1991, U.S. Ct. Fed. Claims 1995. Commd. 2d. lt. U.S. Army, 1974, advanced through grades to maj., 1986; atty. Bogle & Gates, Seattle, 1990-96, Badgley Mullins Law Group, Seattle, 1996—. Avocations: music, golf, hiking. General civil litigation, Professional liability, Labor. Office: Badgley Mullins Law Group 5100 Wash Mutual Tower 1201 3rd Ave Seattle WA 98101-3029

**TURNER, ELIZABETH RUTH,** lawyer; b. Bethesda, Md., July 22, 1964; d. Robert Davison and Nancy (Reed) T. BA in History, Wesleyan U., Middletown, Conn., 1986; JD, Harvard U., 1990. Bar: Tex. 1990, U.S. Ct. Claims 1996. Ptnr. Hughes & Luce, L.L.P., Dallas, 1990—. Contbr. articles to profl. jours. Vol. Dallas Area Habitat for Humanity, 1992—. Mem. ABA, State Bar Tex., Dallas Bar Assn. Avocations: acting, singing. Estate planning. Office: Hughes & Luce LLP 1717 Main St Ste 2800 Dallas TX 75201-4685

**TURNER, HUGH JOSEPH, JR.,** lawyer; b. Paterson, N.J., Oct. 5, 1945; s. Hugh Joseph and Louise (Sullivan) T.; m. Charlene Chiappetta, Feb. 11, 1983. BS, Boston U., 1967; JD, U. Miami, Coral Gables, Fla., 1975. Bar: Fla. 1975, U.S. Dist. Ct. (so., no. and mid. dists.) Fla. 1975, U.S. Ct. Appeals (11th cir.) 1981, U.S. Supreme Ct. 1984. Tchr. Browne & Nichols, Cambridge, Mass., 1968-72; ptnr. Smathers & Thompson, Miami, Fla., 1981-87, Kelley Drye & Warren, Miami, 1987-93, English, McCaughan & O'Bryan, Ft. Lauderdale, 1993—; chmn. Fla. Bar internat. law sect., 1988-89. Contbg. author book on internat. dispute resolution Fla. Bar, 1989; contbr. articles to profl. jours. Bd. dirs. Japan Soc. South Fla., Miami, 1989—; mem. Sea Ranch Lakes Village Coun. Mem. ABA, Def. Rsch. Inst. Avocation: running. General civil litigation, Product liability, Private international. Office: English McCaughan O'Bryan 100 NE 3rd Ave Ste 1100 Fort Lauderdale FL 33301-1144

**TURNER, JAMES THOMAS,** judge; b. Clifton Forge, Va., Mar. 12, 1938; s. James Thomas and Ruth (Greene) T.; m. Patricia Sue Renfrow, July 8, 1962; 1 child, James Thomas. BA, Wake Forest Coll., 1960; JD, U. Va., 1965. Bar: Va. 1965, U.S. Ct. Appeals (4th and fed. cirs.), U.S. Supreme Ct. Assoc. firm Williams, Worrell, Kelly & Greer, Norfolk, Va., 1965, ptnr., 1971-79; U.S. magistrate U.S. Dist. Ct., Eastern Dist. Va., Norfolk, 1979-87; judge, U.S. Ct. Fed. Claims, 1987—. Mem. ABA, FBA, Va. Bar Assn., Norfolk and Portsmouth Bar Assn. (sec. 1975-79). Office: US Ct Fed Claims 717 Madison Pl NW Washington DC 20005-1011

**TURNER, JEROME,** federal judge; b. Memphis, Feb. 18, 1942; s. Cooper and Eugenia (Morrison) T.; m. Shirley Broadhead, Oct. 18, 1969 (div. July 1986); children: Alexandra Cox, Christian Annette; m. Kay Farese, Aug. 22, 1987. BA, Washington and Lee U., 1964, LLB cum laude, 1966; LLM in Jud. Process, U. Va., 1998. Bar: Tenn. 1966. Law clk. to judge Robert M. McRae U.S. Dist. Ct., Memphis, 1966-67; assoc. Canada, Russell & Turner, Memphis, 1967-73, ptnr., 1974-78; ptnr. Wildman, Harrold, Allen, Dixon & McDonnell, Memphis, 1978-87; judge U.S. Dist. Ct. (we. Dist.) Tenn., Memphis, 1988—. Author: Law Rev. Comment, Washington and Lee Law Rev., 1964, 65; editor: Law Rev., 1966. Treas. Elect Don Sundquist to Congress Com., 1981-82, Reelect Don Sundquist to Congress Com., 1983-86. Fellow Tenn. Bar Found., Memphis and Shelby County Bar Found. (bd. dirs. 1982-83, 87, 96-98); mem. Memphis and Shelby County Bar Assn. (pres. 1988, treas. 1984, bd. dirs. 1978-79), Fed. Bar Assn., Tenn. Bar Assn., Leo Bearman Sr. Am. Inn of Ct. (pres. 1995-96, 97), Order of Coif, Omicron Delta Kappa. Roman Catholic. Avocations: hunting, tennis, reading, gardening. Office: US Dist Ct Clifford Davis Fed Bldg 167 N Main St Ste 951 Memphis TN 38103-1875

**TURNER, KAY FARESE,** lawyer, law educator; b. Jackson, Miss., Aug. 14, 1945; d. John B. and Orene Ellis Farese; m. Robert B. Dodge, May 26, 1963 (div. Oct. 1971); 1 child, Johnathan Park; m. William Oliver Luckett, Jr., Dec. 30, 1972 (div. Aug. 1983); children: William Oliver III, Whitney Haimes; m. Jerome Turner, Aug. 22, 1987. BA, Rhodes Coll., 1966; JD, U. Miss., 1973; cert., Harvard Law Sch., 1986. Bar: Miss. 1973, U.S. Dist. Ct. (no. dist.) Miss. 1973, U.S. Ct. Appeals (5th cir.) 1981, Tenn. 1983, U.S. Dist. Ct. (we. dist.) Tenn. 1983. Assoc. Luckett & Barnwell, Clarksdale, Miss., 1974-76; ptnr. Luckett, Luckett & Thompson, Clarksdale, Miss., 1976-82, Luckett, Luckett & Luckett, Clarksdale, Memphis, 1983-84; prin. Kay Farese Luckett, Memphis, 1984-87, Kay Farese Turner, Memphis, 1987—; adj. prof. U. Memphis Sch. Law, 1996—. Named in Best Lawyers Am., Memphis, 1995—. Fellow Am. Acad. Matrimonial Lawyers; mem. ABA, Miss. Bar. Assn., Memphis (sec., treas. 1997—), Am. Inns Ct., III, Memphis-Shelby County Bar Assn. Republican. Roman Catholic. Avocations: tennis, travel, art, writing, fishing. Federal civil litigation, State civil litigation, Family and matrimonial. Office: Morgan Keegan Twr 50 N Front St Ste 770 Memphis TN 38103-1104

**TURNER, LARRY LEO,** lawyer; b. Elizabeth City, N.C., Sept. 17, 1959; s. Willie Larry and Emma Louise (Billups) T.; children: Hillary Elizabeth, Nicholas Larry. BA, U. N.C., 1981; JD, Georgetown U., 1984. Bar: Pa. 1986. Assoc. Montgomery, McCracken, Walker & Rhoads, LLP, Phila., 1986-94, hiring ptnr., ptnr. litigation dept., 1994—, co-chmn. comml. ins. def. group, 1995—, vice chmn. litigation dept., 1998—. Former mem. bd. dirs. Phila. Vol. Lawyers for Arts, White & Williams Scholars, Phila., 1997—; mem. Leadership, Inc., Phila., 1998. Mem. Internat. Trademark Assn., Pa. Bar Assn., Phila. Bar Assn. (past mem. bd. govs. and young lawyers exec. com.), Def. Rsch. Inst., Barristers Assn. Address: 123 S Broad St Philadelphia PA 19109-1029

**TURNER, LESTER NATHAN,** lawyer, international trade consultant; b. Colmar, Ky., July 11, 1933; s. Clifford G. and Minnie G. (Ensor) T.; m. Sandra B. Ward, July 3, 1976; children: Kimberly L., Michele M., Renee S., Mark L., Jeffrey S., Derek Kyle. BS, Lincoln Meml. U., 1955; JD, U. Mich., 1959. Bar: Mich. 1960, U.S. Dist. Ct. (ea. and we. dist.) Mich., U.S. Ct. Appeals (6th cir.), U.S. Supreme Ct. 1982. Law clk. to presiding justice, research atty. Mich. Supreme Ct., Lansing, 1960-62; ptnr. Sinas, Dramis, Brake & Turner, Lansing, 1960-78; sole law practice, internat. bus. cons. internat. cons. bus. and law primarily in Mid. East Countries with emphasis on Palestinian Nat. Authority, Lansing, Harbor Springs, Mich., 1978—; prin., CEO Palestinian Tourism Co. Ltd., Palestinian Co. Transp. Ltd., North Bay Ltd.; Mem. std. jury instrn. com. Mich. Supreme Ct., Lansing, 1963-73; cons. higher commn. investment and fin. Palestinian Pres., 1997—. Mem. Mich. State Bar Assn., Mich. Trial Lawyers Assn. (bd. dirs. 1963-74, vice pres. 1974). Methodist. E-mail: tcb@freeway.net. Fax: 616-526-0922. Education and schools, Federal civil litigation, General practice. Home and Office: 1005 Timber Pass Harbor Springs MI 49740-9221

**TURNER, OTIS HAWES,** lawyer; b. Arkadelphia, Ark., Oct. 18, 1927; s. Cleve C. and Laura Eva (Flanagin) T.; m. Molly Sue Stauber, June 17, 1956; children: Neal, Tab. BA, Ouachita Bapt. Coll., 1951; LLB, U. Ark., 1955. Bar: U.S. Supreme Ct. 1964, U.S. Dist. Ct. (ea. and we. dists.) Ark. 1955. Ptnr. McMillan, Turner & McCorkle, Arkadelphia, Ark., 1955-73, 75-89; judge 8th Jud. dist. Ark., Arkadelphia, 1973-74; assoc. justice Ark. Supreme Ct., Little Rock, 1990; ptnr. McMillan, Turner & McCorkle, 1991—. With U.S. Army, 1946-48. Fellow Am. Coll. Trial Lawyers, Am. Bd. Trial Advocates. Democrat. Baptist. Avocations: golf, woodworking. General civil litigation, Personal injury, Product liability. Office: McMillan Turner McCorkle & Curry 929 Main St Arkadelphia AR 71923-5931

**TURNER, ROBERT F.,** lawyer; b. Roswell, N. Mex., Dec. 17, 1963; s. Bob F. and Mary H. T.; m. Dawn M. Franke; children: Robert F. II, Elizabeth. BA in Psychology, N. Mex. State U., 1987; JD, U. Tex., 1992. Bar: N.M. 1994. Juvenile pub. defender Travis County, Austin, Tex., 1992-93; pvt. practice Deming, N. Mex., 1994—. Named Personal Injury Atty. of Yr., Consumer Bus. Rev., 1998. Mem. Benevolent Order Elks. Personal injury, General practice, General civil litigation. Home and Office: 112 E Maple St Deming NM 88030-4141

**TURNER, ROBERT JOSEPH,** lawyer; b. Newnan, Ga., Jan. 18, 1964; s. W. Ross and Christine (Dukes) T. BS in Molecular Biology, Vanderbilt U., 1986; JD, Memphis Sch. Law, 1991. Bar: Tenn. 1991, U.S. Supreme Ct. 1996. Ptnr. Hildebrand, Nolan, Porter et al, Nashville, 1991-94; mng. atty. Turner Law Offices, P.C., Nashville, 1994—; pres. Profl. Flight Svc., Inc., Nashville, 1996—, The Profl. Corp., Nashville, 1996—, Profl. Devel. Corp., Nashville, 1996—. Recipient cert. of appreciation Met. Police Explorers, Nashville, 1994. Avocation: flying. General corporate, State civil litigation, Estate planning. Office: 208 3rd Ave N Ste 300 Nashville TN 37201-1642

**TURNER, SHAWN DENNIS,** lawyer; b. Salt Lake City, Apr. 19, 1959; s. Gerald Lewis and Cynthia Sue Turner; m. Pamela M. Morgan, May 31, 1985; children: Erin K., Jessica L. BS, U. Utah, 1984; MBA, Cornell U., 1986; JD, Brigham Young U., 1990. Bar: Utah 1990, U.S. Dist. Ct. Utah 1992, U.S. Ct. Appeals (10th cir.) 1992, U.S. Tax Ct. 1992, U.S. Ct. Claims 1993. Law clk. Utah Atty. Gen.'s Office, Salt Lake City, 1988-89; assoc. McKay Burton & Thurman, Salt Lake City, 1990-91; shareholder Brown, Larson, Jenkins & Halliday, Salt Lake City, 1991-96; ptnr. Larson, Kirkham & Turner, Salt Lake City, 1996—; tax cons. Deloitte Haskins & Sells, Salt Lake City, 1986-87; agt. Attys. Title, Salt Lake City, 1996—; mem. Advantage Title Co., Salt Lake City, 1997—. Mem. Utah State Bar Assn. (tax sect., litig. sect., estate planning sect.), U.S. Chess Found. Taxation, general, General civil litigation, Appellate. Office: Larson Kirkham & Turner 4516 S 700 E Ste 100 Salt Lake City UT 84107-8319

**TURNER, STEPHEN MILLER,** lawyer, oil company executive; b. Omaha, Mar. 13, 1939; s. Clinton Heron and Margaret Elizabeth (Miller) T.; m. Claudine Mengin, Aug. 10, 1968; children: Marshall C., Scott M. BA, William Jewell Coll., 1961; JD, U. Iowa, 1964; LLM, U. Chgo., 1966. Bar: Ohio 1969, D.C. 1975, N.Y. 1982. Asst. U.S. atty. U.S. Dept. Justice, Sioux City, Iowa, 1966-67; U.S. atty. No. Dist. of Iowa, Sioux City, 1967-68; assoc. Squire, Sanders & Dempsey, Cleve., 1968-74; mng. ptnr. Squire, Sanders & Dempsey, Brussels, 1975-82; ptnr. Squire, Sanders & Dempsey, N.Y.C., 1982-89; sr. staff assoc. Pres.'s Counsel on Exec. Reorgn., Washington, 1969-70; sr. v.p., gen. counsel Texaco Inc., White Plains, N.Y., 1989—. Ohio Bar Assn., N.Y. State Bar Assn., D.C. Bar Assn., Burning Tree Country Club (Greenwich). Republican. Presbyterian. Home: 67 Londonderry Dr Greenwich CT 06830-3509 Office: Texaco Inc 2000 Westchester Ave White Plains CT 06830*

**TURNER, TOM,** editor; b. Oakland, Calif., 1942; m. Mary Jorgensen; children: Bret and Kathryn (twins). BA in Polit. Sci., U. Calif., 1965. Vol. Peace Corps, Turkey, 1965-67; grant analyst Head Start, 1968; editor, adminstrv. asst. Sierra Club, 1968-69; various positions including exec. dir. Friends of the Earth, 1969-86, also editor Not Man Apart; staff writer, dir. publs. Earthjustice Legal Def. Fund, 1986—. Author: Wild By Law: the Sierra Club Legal Defense Fund and the Places It Has Saved, 1990, Sierra Club: 100 Years of Protecting Nature, 1991; contbr. to The Ency. of the Environment, 1994, also chpts. to books; contbr. articles to Sierra, Defenders, Wilderness, San Francisco Chronicle, San Francisco Examiner, L.A. Times, Oakland Tribune,Washington Post, Mother Earth News, Outside, others. Office: Earthjustice Legal Def Fund 180 Montgomery St Ste 1400 San Francisco CA 94104-4236

**TURNHEIM, JOY KAREN,** lawyer; b. Jersey City, N.J., Apr. 21, 1965; d. Palmer and Gloria Grace (Freer) T. AB, Dartmouth Coll., 1985; JD, Northwestern U., 1988; MBA with distinction, DePaul U., 1993; MPhil, NYU, 1997. Bar: Ill. 1988, U.S. Dist. Ct. (no. dist.) Ill. 1988. Law clk. to Hon. Sophia H. Hall Ill. Circuit Ct., Chgo., 1988-89; assoc. Nathanson & Wray, Chgo., 1989-90, Horvath & Wigoda, Chgo., 1990; pvt. practice Law Offices Joy K. Turnheim, 1991—; exec. dir. Chenny Troupe, Chgo., 1993; adj. prof. Columbia Coll., 1992-94; chpt. atty. Assn. Women in Metals Industry, 1989-91. Treas. Presbyn. Women in 4th Ch., Chgo., 1989-94; chmn. Silver Apple Ball, Chgo., 1990; moderator Kairos Fellowship, Chgo., 1990-92; deacon 4th Presbyn. Ch., 1992-95; mem. Jr. League Chgo., 1992—; chair Project CON!CERN, 1995—; founding mem., women's bd. Community Support Svcs., 1992-95; mem. Friends of Red Cross, 1990-94. Mem. ABA, Ill. State Bar Assn., Chgo. Bar Assn., Chgo. Soc. Clubs, Am. Inns of Ct. (Wigmore chpt.). Avocations: tennis, skiing, golf.

**TURO, RON,** lawyer; b. Fort Wayne, Ind., Apr. 2, 1955; s. John B. and Joan L. (Gluntz) T.; m. Claire Teresa Fetterman T., May 24, 1980; children: Andrew Jacob, Patricia Erin, Dominic Earl. BA in History with honors, Pa. State U., 1978; JD, Dickinson Sch. Law, 1981. Bar: Pa. 1981, U.S. Dist. (mid. dist.) Pa. 1982, U.S. Supreme Ct. 1987, U.S. Ct. Appeals (3d cir.) 1989. Ast. pub. defender Cumberland County, Carlisle, Pa., 1981-84; ptnr. Griffie & Turo, Carlisle, 1984-89; pvt. practice Carlisle, 1989—. Founder West Shore Police Recognition Dinner, Camp Hill, Pa., 1985—; mem. Pa. Assn. Retarded Citizens, 1996—; mem. Nat. Cath. Com. on Scouting, 1988—, vice chmn. for fin., dist. com., 1996—; chmn. Region III, Pa., N.J., 1993-95, parliamentarian and legal coun., 1991—, advisor religious act, 1998—; mem. Big Bros./Big Sisters Carlisle select com., 1993-98; bd. dirs. AHEDD, Inc., 1993-94, vice chmn. 1994-95, chmn., 1995—; trustee David E. Baker Scholarship Trust, 1997—. Recipient St. George Emblem Boy Scouts Am., 1983, Eagle Scout 1969, Golden AAD Emblem, 1989. Mem. Nat. Lawyer's Assn., Nat. Assn. Criminal Def. Lawyers, Pa. Bar Assn., Pa. Assn. Criminal Def. Lawyers, Cumberland County Bar Assn. (social chmn. 1985-98, pub. rels. com. 1998—), St. Thomas More Soc. (v.p. 1996-98, treas. 1998—), Trinity H.S. Alumni Orgn. pres. 1988-90), Mensa (local sec. 1990-92, editor 1992-95), KC (pres. Capital area chpt. 1989, Knight of Yr. 1981, grand knight 1985-87, 93-95, fin. sec. 1996—, dist. dep. 1998—). Republican. Roman Catholic. Avocations: scouting, scuba diving, travel. General civil litigation, Criminal. Home: 539 Baltimore Pike Mount Holly Springs PA 17065-1028 Office: 32 S Bedford St Carlisle PA 17013-3302

**TURPIN, JOHN RUSSELL, JR.,** lawyer; b. Houston, July 10, 1948; s. John R. and Nell (Pliler) T.; m. Susan G. Loney, Jan. 3, 1975; children: Sarah T., Susan Gail. BA, U. Tex., 1970, JD, 1973. Bar: Tex. 1973. Lawyer sole practice Austin, Tex., 1973-81, Corpus Christi, Tex., 1981—. Democrat. Avocations: raising my daughters, gardening, reading. Real property, Probate, Family and matrimonial. Home: 6530 Brockhampton St Corpus Christi TX 78414-3506 Office: 5959 S Staple PO Box 81401 Corpus Christi TX 78468-1401

**TURRENTINE, HOWARD BOYD,** federal judge; b. Escondido, Calif., Jan. 22, 1914; s. Howard and Veda Lillian (Maxfield) T.; m. Virginia Jacobsen, May 13, 1965 (dec.); children: Howard Robert, Terry Beverly; m. Marlene Lipsey, Nov. 1, 1991. AB, San Diego State Coll., 1936; LLB, U. So. Calif., 1939. Bar: Calif. 1939. Practiced in San Diego, 1939-68; judge Superior Ct. County of San Diego, 1968-70, U.S. Dist. Ct. (so. dist.) Calif., Calif.; sr. judge U.S. Dist. Ct. (so. dist.) Calif., San Diego, 1970—. Served with USNR, 1941-45. Mem. ABA, Fed. Bar Assn., Am. Judicature Soc. Office: US Dist Ct 940 Front St San Diego CA 92101-8994

**TUSCHMAN, JAMES MARSHALL,** lawyer; b. Nov. 28, 1941; s. Chester and Harriet (Harris) T.; m. Ina S. Cheloff, Sept. 2, 1967; children: Chad Michael, Jon Stephen, Sari Anne. BS in Bus., Miami U., Oxford, Ohio, 1963; JD, Ohio State U., 1966. Bar: Ohio 1966, U.S. Ct. Appeals (6th and 7th cirs.), U.S. Supreme Ct. Assoc. Shumaker, Loop & Kendrick, Toledo, 1966-84, ptnr., 1970-84; co-founder, chmn. ops. com. Jacobson Maynard Tuschman & Kalur, Toledo, 1985-97; mem. exec. com., COO Ohio Ferrous Group Omnisource Corp., Toledo, 1998—; chmn. bd., sec. Tuschman Steel Co., Toledo, 1969-76; vice-chmn. bd. Kripke Tuschman Industries, Inc., 1977-85, dir. 1977-86; chmn. bd., sec. Toledo Steel Supply Co., 1969-86; ptnr. Starr Ave. Co., Toledo, 1969-86. Mem. bd. trustees U. Toledo; past trustee, chmn. fin. com., past treas. Maumee Valley Country Day Sch.; past trustee, v.p., treas. Temple B'nai Istrel, 1984-88. Fellow Internat. Soc. Barristers; mem. Am. Bd. Trial Advocates, Ohio Bar Assn., Toledo Bar Assn., Ohio Civil Trial Lawyers Assn., Toledo Club (bd. dirs.), Inverness Country Club, Zeta Beta Tau, Phi Delta Phi. Personal injury, Insurance. Home: 2579 Olde Brookside Rd Toledo OH 43615-2233 Office: Omnisource Corp 5130 N Detroit Ave Toledo OH 43612-3515

**TUSKEY, JOHN P.,** law educator; b. South Bend, Ind., Nov. 19, 1957; s. Clarence Francis and Martha Ann T.; m. Laura Jeanne Ishmael, June 26, 1998. BBA in Acctg., U. Notre Dame, 1980, JD, 1983. Bar: Ind. 1983, U.S. Dist. Ct. (no. and so. dists.) Ind. 1983, U.S. Ct. Appeals (7th cir.) 1992, Ill. 1994, U.S. Supreme Ct. 1997. Ptnr. Tuskey & Tuskey, Mishawaka, Ind., 1983-86; law clk. U.S. Ct. Appeals (7th cir.), South Bend, Ind., 1986-93; assoc. Bullaro, Carton & Stone, Chgo., 1993-94; sr. rsch. counsel Am. Ctr. Law and Justice, Virginia Beach, Va., 1994—; asst. prof. Regent U. Law Sch., Virginia Beach, 1998—; vis. asst. prof. Regent U. Law Sch., 1994-96. Contbr. articles to profl. jours. Mem. Federalist Soc., Fellowship Cath. Scholars. Roman Catholic. Avocations: reading, bicycling, motorsports, football, basketball. Office: Am Ctr Law and Justice 100 Regent University Dr Virginia Beach VA 23464-5037

**TUTT, LOUISE THOMPSON,** lawyer; b. Centerville, Iowa, Nov. 10, 1937; d. Lawrence Eugene and Alice Helen (Thompson) T. B.A., U. Ariz., 1963, J.D., 1969. Bar: Calif. 1972, U.S. Dist. Ct. (so. dist.) Calif. 1972, Mo. 1976. Practice law, San Diego and LaJolla, Calif., 1972-75; appeals referee Div. Employment Security, Jefferson City, Mo., 1977-79; counsel Labor and Indsl. Rels. Commn., Jefferson City, Mo., 1979-80; legal adviser Div. Workers Compensation, Jefferson City, 1980-94, St. Louis, 1994—. Bd. dirs. LaJolla Sinfonia, 1975. Democrat. Home: 6445 Nottingham Ave Saint Louis MO 63109-2614

**TUTTLE, ROGER LEWIS,** lawyer, educator; b. Wyandotte County, Kans., Nov. 9, 1930; s. Emmett Joseph and Freda Alberta (Lewis) T.; m. Beverly Jean Campbell, Aug. 3, 1957; children—Pamela Anne, Deborah Jean Tuttle Edwards. B.A., U. Kans., 1952; J.D., U. Miss., 1958. Bar: Miss. 1958, U.S. Dist. Ct. (so. dist.) Miss. 1958, U.S. Dist. Ct. (no. dist.) Miss. 1959, U.S. Dist. Ct. (ea. dist.) La. 1963, U.S. Ct. Appeals (4th cir.) 1964, Va. 1965, U.S. Dist. Ct. (ea. dist.) Va. 1971, U.S. Supreme Ct. 1971, U.S. Dist. Ct. (we. dist.) Va. 1976, Okla. 1982, U.S. Dist. Ct. (no. dist.) Okla. 1983, U.S. Ct. Appeals (10th cir.) 1983. Assoc. Neill, Clark & Townsend, Indianola, Miss., 1958-61, Heidelberg, Woodliff & Franks, Jackson, Miss., 1961-62; area atty. Exxon, New Orleans and Charlotte, N.C., 1962-65; asst. counsel Lawyers Title Ins. Corp., Richmond, Va., 1965-71; gen. atty. A.H. Robins Co., Richmond, 1971-76; asst. gen. counsel Dan River Inc., 1976-82; prof. law Oral Roberts U., Tulsa, 1982-85, dean, 1985-87, clin. prof. med. jurisprudence, 1987-88; chief legal officer, corp. sec. Oral Roberts Ministries, 1986-88; of counsel Freed & Haskins, Richmond, 1988-89, Conner & Edwards, Richmond, 1989, Davis & Tuttle, 1989-90, pvt. practice, 1990—. Mem. Spl. Adv. Counsel to Mayor, Richmond, 1971-76; mem. Richmond Air Pollution Control Bd., 1972-73; bd. dirs. Richmond Met. Authority, 1973-76. Served to lt. col. M.I., USAR, 1952-73. Decorated Mil. Cross (Belgium), Bronze Star, Army Commendation Medal with oak leaf cluster; named Prof. of Yr., Oral Roberts U., 1984-85. Mem. Va. Bar Assn., Miss. Bar Assn., Okla. Bar Assn. (civil procedure com., mem. continuing legal edn. com.), Assn. Trial Lawyers Am., Am. Coll. Legal Medicine, Assn. Former Intelligence Officers, Army CIC Vets. Assn., Phi Alpha Delta, Pi Kappa Alpha. Republican. Presbyn. Clubs: Masons, Scottish Rite, Shriners. Contbr. articles to legal publs. Health, General civil litigation, Personal injury. Office: 13624 Northwich Dr Midlothian VA 23112-4932

**TUTTLE, WILLIAM ROGER,** lawyer, financial advisor; m. Meredith Anne Weatherbee, July 21, 1959; children: William Stetson, Samuel Alexander, Andrew Roger. Banking cert., Brown U., 1971; BS in Acctg., Bentley Coll., 1973, MS in Fin., 1980; cert. exec. devel. program, U. Mass., 1974; JD, Suffolk U., 1977; cert. in fin. studies, Fairfield U., 1981; LLM, Boston U., 1987. Bar: Mass. 1977, U.S. Dist. Ct. Mass. 1978, U.S. Supreme Ct. 1982; lic. real estate broker. With South Shore Nat. Bank, Mass., 1957-59, Home Savs. Bank, Boston, 1959-85; lawyer, pres. Abington (Mass.) Legal Ctr., 1985—. Publ. (weekly bank report) New England Bank and Thrift Stock Report, 1985-93. Mem. judicial nominating coun. S.E. dist. Commonwealth of Mass., 1991—; mem. Mass. Rep. State Com., former dep. chmn., asst. treas.; mem. Abington Rep. Town Com.; coach Abington Sr. Little League Baseball, Abington Youth Soccer League; trustee Massasoit C.C., Brockton, Mass., 1997—. Mem. Boston Econ. Club. E-mail: tuttleesq@aol.com. Home: 101 Highfields Rd Abington MA 02351-2449 Office: Abington Legal Ctr 79 Bedford St PO Box 2091 Abington MA 02351-0591

**TWANMOH, VALERIE HURLEY,** lawyer, mediator, arbitrator; b. Englewood, N.J., May 27, 1957; d. Orval Franklin Jr. and Judith Ann (Kaplan) Hurley; m. Joseph Richard Twanmoh, June 21, 1981; children: Kai Hurley, Darren Hurley, Ross Hurley. BA, Hamilton Coll., 1979; JD, U. Conn., 1982. Bar: N.J. 1982, U.S. Dist. Ct. N.J. 1982, Mich. 1984, U.S. Dist. Ct. (we. dist.) Mich. 1984, U.S. Dist. Ct. (ea. dist.) Mich. 1986, Md. 1995; cert. civil and divorce mediator, N.J., 1996—. Intern Congressman James J. Howard, Washington, 1977; assoc. Cholette, Perkins & Buchanan, Grand Rapids, Mich., 1983-86, Conlin, Conlin, McKenney & Philbrick, Ann Arbor, Mich., 1986-87; ptnr. Rogers & Twanmoh, P.C., Ann Arbor, 1988-93, Valerie Hurley Twanmoh, P.C., Ann Arbor, 1993-94; mediator, arbitrator Fallston, Md., 1994—; intern Civil Mediation Inst., Seton Hall Law Sch., 1995; comml. arbitrator Am. Arbitration Assn., Southfield, Mich., 1994—. Bd. dirs. Ctr. for Occupational and Personalized Edn.-O'Brien Ctr., 1992-94, Nat. Assn. Mothers' Ctrs., 1995—, FACETS, 1995—; mem. com. Planned Parenthood Mid-MIch., Ann Arbor, 1987-90; vice-chair for orgn. Dukakis for Pres. campaign, Ann Arbor, 1988; campaign dir. Rebecca McGowan for U. Mich. Regent, 1992. Mem. ABA, Mich. State Bar Assn., Washtenaw County Bar Assn., Women Lawyers' Assn. (Washtenaw region v.p. program 1989, v.p.-pres. elect 1990-92, pres. 1992-93), Women Lawyers' Assn. Mich. (dir. at large 1993—), Lions (treas. 1989). Democrat. Avocations: tennis, piano, reading. Labor, Civil rights.

**TWARDY, STANLEY ALBERT, JR.,** lawyer; b. Trenton, N.J., Sept. 13, 1951; s. Stanley Albert Twardy and Dorothy M. Stonaker. BS with honors, Trinity Coll., 1973; JD, U. Va., 1976; LLM, Georgetown U., 1980. Bar: Conn. 1976, D.C. 1978, U.S. Supreme Ct. 1979, U.S. Ct. Appeals (2d cir.) 1984. Assoc. Whitman & Ransom, Greenwich, Conn., 1976-77; counsel com. on small bus. U.S. Senate, 1977-79, counsel to Senator Lowell Weicker Jr., 1979-80; ptnr. Silver, Golub & Sandak, Stamford, Conn., 1980-85; U.S. atty. Dist. of Conn., New Haven, 1985-91; chief of staff Office of Gov. Lowell Weicker, Conn., 1991-93; ptnr. Day, Berry & Howard, Stamford, Conn., 1993—. Mem. vestry St. John's Episcopal Ch., Stamford, 1983-86; bd. dirs. Drugs Don't Work!, 1989-93, 94—, chmn. program com., 1989-91; mem. nat. alumni exec. com. Trinity Coll., 1985-90, mem. athletic adv. com., 1992—, bd. trustees, 1996—; bd. dirs. Spl. Olympics World Summer Games Organizing Com., Inc., 1993-95, Easter Seals Rehab. Ctr. S.W. Conn., Inc., 1993—; chmn. City of Stamford Police Chief Selection Panel, 1993-94; mem. area adv. com. U. Conn. at Stamford, 1993-96; mem. strategic planning mgmt. com. U. Conn., 1993-95; bd. dirs. Stamford Hosp. Health Found., 1995—; trustee Trinity Coll., 1996—. Mem. ABA, Conn. Bar Assn., Assn. Trial Lawyers Am., Conn. Trial Lawyers Assn., Phi Beta Kappa. Federal civil litigation, Constitutional, Criminal.

**TWEEL, DONNA SHANK,** lawyer; b. Huntington, W.Va., Jan. 3, 1960. BA, Marshall U., 1982; JD cum laude, U. Dayton, 1990. Bar: Ohio 1990. Jud. staff atty. State of Ohio Ct. Appeals, 2d dist., Dayton, 1990-94; assoc. Turner & McNamee Co., LPA, Dayton, 1994-96, Chernesky, Heyman & Kress, PLL, Dayton, 1996—. Mem. U. Dayton Law Rev. Coun. mem. Village of Waynesville, Ohio, 1993-96. Mem. ABA, Ohio State Bar Assn., Dayton Bar Assn., Dayton Women's Bar Assn. (bd. dirs. 1998—). General corporate, Mergers and acquisitions. Office: Chernesky Heyman & Kress PLL 1100 Courthouse Plz SW Dayton OH 45402

**TWERSKY, JONATHAN,** lawyer; b. Kiev, Ukraine, July 31, 1961; came to U.S., 1976; s. David and Polina Twersky; m. Ninah Beliavsky, Mar. 27, 1988; children: Michaella S., Delilah L. AA in Hebrew Lit., Yeshiva U., 1982, BA in Polit. Sci., 1982; JD, Benjamin Cardozo Sch. Law, 1985. Bar: N.Y., U.S. Dist. Ct. (ea. and so. dist.) N.Y. Staff atty., svcs. staff atty. Bklyn. br. Legal Svcs. for N.Y.C., 1985-92, dir. housing law unit, 1992—. Bd. dirs. Shorefront Jewish Cmty. Counsel, Bklyn., 1997—. Mem. Phi Delta Phi. Office: Legal Svcs for NYC Bklyn Br 186 Joralemon St Ste 703 Brooklyn NY 11201-4326

**TWIETMEYER, DON HENRY,** lawyer; b. Rochester, N.Y., June 4, 1954; s. Frederick Herman and Norma Frances (Porter) T.; m. Victoria Lynne Engleman, July 1, 1989; children: Laura Elizabeth, Jill Ann Cafarelli, Anthony R. Cafarelli. BA in Polit. Sci., Econs. with honors, SUNY, Buffalo, 1976; JD, Union U., 1979; LLM in Taxation, U. Miami, 1980; MBA in Acctg., Rochester Inst. Tech., 1983. Bar: N.Y. 1980, Fla. 1980, U.S. Dist. Ct. (we. dist.) N.Y. 1980, U.S. Dist. Ct. (so. dist.) Fla. 1980, U.S. Tax Ct. 1980, U.S. Ct. Appeals (5th and 11th cirs.) 1981, U.S. Supreme Ct. 1994, U.S. Bankruptcy Ct. 1994; CPA, N.Y. Tax acct. Davie, Kaplan & Braverman, Rochester, 1980-82; assoc. DeHond-Stowe Law Office, Rochester, 1982-84, Lacy, Katzen, Ryen & Mittleman, Rochester, 1984-87; mng. atty. DeHond Law Office, Rochester, 1987-91, prin., 1991-92; assoc. Fix, Spindelman, Brovitz, Turk, Himelein & Shukoff, Rochester, 1992-98; of counsel Saperston & Day, P.C., Rochester, 1998—; lectr. estate and gift taxes Found. Acctg. Edn., 1987-96. Author: Review and Update for Experienced Practitioners: Fiduciary, Estate and Gift Taxation, 1987-96. V.p. coun. Hope Luth. Ch., 1989-91, active meml. fund com., 1990-91, chmn. bldg. use com., 1990-91; chmn. missions and social concerns com. Bethlehem Luth. Ch., 1992—, mem. ch. coun., 1993-95, pres. ch. coun., 1994-95, deacon, 1994-95; mem. orgn. com. Luth. Charities Rochester Region, 1993-95, pres., dir., 1995—; dir. Prevention Ptnrs., Inc., 1997—, fin. com., 1997—; mem. planned and deferred giving com. The Genesee Hosp. Found., 1998—. Mem. ABA (tax sect., entertainment and sports industries forum) Fla. Bar Assn. (tax sect., out of state practitioners divsn., real property, probate and trust sect.), N.Y. State Bar Assn. (tax sect., entertainment and sports law sect, trusts and estates sect.), Monroe County Bar Assn. (tax sect. and trusts and estates sect., exec. coun. 1996—, elder law com., intellectual property law com.), N.Y. State Soc. CPAs, Am. Assn. Atty.-CPAs, Estate Planning Coun. Rochester, Rotary (internat. svc. com. 1994—, Rotary Internat. Found. com. 1994—, chairperson com. 1996—, Rochester Rotary Golf Tournament com. 1995—, planned giving com. 1997—), Phi Beta Kappa, Phi Alpha Delta, Omicron Delta Epsilon, Phi Eta Sima. Republican. Lutheran. Avocations: golf, tennis, skiing, philately. E-mail: dtwietmeyer@saperstonday.com. Fax#: (716) 325-5458. Entertainment, Estate planning, Taxation, general. Office: 800 First Federal Plz Rochester NY 14614-1916

**TWIFORD, ALICE KATE,** lawyer; b. York, Pa., Mar. 16, 1956; d. James R., Sr. and Helen M. (McTague) Markle; m. Lester D. Twiford, Nov. 14, 1981. BS, York Coll. of Pa., 1976; JD, Coll. of William and Mary, 1991, LLM, 1992. Bar: Va. Commd. 2d lt.r U.S. Army, 1976, advanced through grades to capt., 1980, resigned, 1988; pvt. practice Williamsburg, Va., 1992—. Chmn. Social Svcs. Adv. Bd., James City County, Va., 1992- 96. Mem. ABA, Va. State Bar (bd. of govs. gen. practice sect., 1993—), Williamsburg Area Trial Lawyers Assn. (pres. 1993-94). General practice, Taxation, general, Juvenile. Office: 161 John Jefferson Rd # C Williamsburg VA 23185-5640

**TWIFORD, H. HUNTER, III,** lawyer; b. Memphis, Sept. 19, 1949; s. Horace Hunter and Elizabeth (Andrews) T.; m. Frances Dill, June 27, 1970; children—Elizabeth Smith, Horace Hunter IV. B.A., U. Miss., 1971, J.D., 1972. Bar: Miss. 1972, U.S. Dist. Ct. Miss. 1972, U.S. Ct. Appeals (5th cir.) 1972, U.S. Ct. Appeals (11th cir.) 1977, U.S. Supreme Ct. 1977. Assoc., Holcomb, Dunbar, Connell, Merkel & Tollison, Clarksdale, Miss., 1972-75; ptnr. Garmon, Wood & Twiford, Clarksdale, 1977-78, Wood & Twiford, P.A., Clarksdale, 1978-85, Twiford & Webster, P.A., Clarksdale, 1985-90, Tollison, Austin & Twiford (Clarksdale, Oxford, Hernando, Southaven), 1990-94; Twiford Webster & Gresham, 1994—; adj. prof. Coahoma C.C., Clarksdale, 1976—; city atty. Town of Friars Point, Miss., 1981-89, Town of Jonestown, Miss., 1973-76; mcpl. judge City of Clarksdale, 1974-76; city atty. City of Clarksdale, Miss., 1985—. Author: Mississippi Annexation Law, 1992. Mem. vestry St. George's Episc. Ch., Clarksdale, 1974-76, 82-83, 87-90, sr. warden, 1984-86; mem. Coahoma County C. of C., Clarksdale, 1975—, bd. dirs. indsl. found., 1989—; mem. Gov.'s Commn. on Drug Abuse, Jackson, Miss., 1976-80; sec. Clarksdale-Coahoma County Joint Airport Bd., Clarksdale, 1981-86; dir. Indsl. Devel. Authority Coahoma County, Miss., 1988—. Mem. Assn. Trial Lawyers Am., Miss. Trial Lawyers Assn., Nat. Assn. Criminal Def. Lawyers, Nat. Inst. Mcpl. Legal Officers (chmn. pers. sect. 1989, state chmn. Miss. 1991-96),Internat. Municipal Lawyers Assn., (formerly NIMLO), Miss. Bar Assn. (bar commr. 1998—), Miss. Mcpl. Assn. (pres. attys. sect. 1995-96), Coahoma County Bar Assn. Lodge: Rotary (pres. 1984-85, Paul Harris fellow). General practice, Labor. Office: Twiford Webster & Gresham 144 Sunflower Ave Clarksdale MS 38614-4219

**TWIG, JACK** See BRANCH, JOHN WELLS

**TWILLEY, JOSHUA MARION,** lawyer; b. Dover, Del., Mar. 23, 1928; s. Joshua Marion and Alice Hunn (Dunn) T.; m. Rebecca Jane Buchanan, Dec. 27, 1952; children—Stephanie, Jeffrey, Linda, Edgar, Joshua; m. 2d, Rosemary Miller, Dec. 1, 1972. B.A. cum laude, Harvard U., 1950, J.D., 1953. Bar: Del. 1953, U.S. dist. ct. Del. 1960, U.S. Sup. Ct. 1976. Sole practice, Dover, 1955-72; sr. ptnr. Twilley, Jones & Feliceangeli, Dover, 1972-88; Twilley, Street & Brayerman, 1988-95, Twilley & Street, 1995—; pres. Del. Indsl. Enterprises, Inc.; chmn. Incorporating Svcs. Ltd., Del. Incorporating Svcs. Ltd.; bd. dirs. First Nat. Bank Wyo.; sec. Sunshine Builders, Inc. mem. Del. Pub. Service Commn., 1975—, vice chmn. 1995—; pres. Kent County levy ct., 1970-75. Mem. exec. com. Del. Democratic Com., 1970-93; pres. Elizabeth Murphey Sch., 1957—. Served with U.S. Army, 1953-55. Mem. ABA, Del. Bar Assn., Kent County Bar Assn. Democrat. Lutheran. Avocations: gardening, landscape architecture. Real property, Probate, Banking. Home: 124 Meadow Glen Dr Dover DE 19901-5544 Office: 426 S State St Dover DE 19901-6724

**TWISS, ROBERT MANNING,** prosecutor; b. Worcester, Mass., Aug. 2, 1948; s. Robert Sullivan Jr. and Marion (Manning) T.; m. Joan Marie Callahan, Aug. 4, 1979. BA, U. Mass., 1970; JD, U. San Francisco, 1975; MA in Criminal Justice, Wichita State U., 1979; LLM, Georgetown U., 1981. Bar: Mass. 1976, Calif., 1988, U.S. Ct. Mil. Appeals 1976, U.S. Dist. Ct. Mass. 1976, U.S. Ct. Appeals (1st cir.) 1976, U.S. Ct. Appeals (5th cir.) 1986, U.S. Ct. Appeals (9th cir.) 1988, U.S. Dist. Ct. (ea. and cen. dist.) Calif. 1989. Atty. office chief counsel IRS, Washington, 1980-86; trial atty. criminal div. U.S. Dept. Justice, Washington, 1986-87; asst. U.S. atty. U.S.

Dept. Justice, Sacramento, 1987-93, 94—, chief organized crime and narcotics, 1991-92, 1st asst. U.S. atty., 1992-93, U.S. atty., 1993, exec. assst. U.S. atty., 1994. Contbr. articles to profl. jours. Capt. JAGC, U.S. Army, 1976-80. Named to McAuliffe Honor Soc. U. San Francisco, 1975; recipient Markham award Office Chief Counsel IRS, Washington, 1985. Avocation: athletics. Office: Office US Atty 501 I St Fl 10 Sacramento CA 95814-7306

**TWITCHELL, E(RVIN) EUGENE,** lawyer; b. Salt Lake City, Mar. 4, 1932; s. Irvin A. and E. Alberta (Davis) T.; m. Joyce A. Newey, Aug. 9, 1957 (div. May 1989); children: Robert R., Lauren E., David J., Michael S.; m. Linda Sue Wilson, 1991; children: Bonnie Wilson, Jimmy Wilson, Benjamin Wilson, Stefanie Wilson. Student, Brigham Young U., 1954-55; BA, Calif. State U., Long Beach, 1959; JD, UCLA, 1966. Bar: Mich. 1977, U.S. Dist. Ct. (ea. dist.) Mich., U.S. Supreme Ct. 1987. Contract adminstr. Rockwell No. Am. Aviation, Seal Beach, Calif., 1966-68; sr. contracts adminstr. McDonnell Douglas Corp., Long Beach, Calif., 1968-73; in-house counsel Albert C. Martin & Assocs., L.A., 1973-77; instr. bus. law Golden West Coll., Huntington Beach, 1973-74; corp. counsel, corp. sec. Barton Malow Co., Southfield, Mich., 1977-97, ret., 1997; mem. Detroit EEO Forum, 1983-87; arbitrating and cons., 1997—. Pres. Corona (Calif.) Musical Theater, 1975-76; dist. chmn. Boy Scouts of Am.-North Trails, Oakland County, Mich., 1978-80; treas. Barton Malow PAC, Southfield, 1983-97. Sgt. USAF, 1950-52. Mem. ABA, Mich. Bar Assn., Am. Arbitration Assn. (arbitrator Detroit, Ala., Ga., and Fla. areas 1985-97, arbitrator Ala.-Ga. area 1997—), Am. Corp. Counsel Assn. (v.p., dir. 1983-97). Republican. Mem. LDS Ch. Avocations: cartooning, painting, karate, music, theatre, writing. Construction, Alternative dispute resolution, Labor. Home and Office: 142 Gammage Rd Eufaula AL 36027-5874

**TWOMEY, THOMAS A., JR.,** lawyer; b. N.Y.C., Dec. 8, 1945; s. Thomas A. and Mary (Maloney) T.; m. Judith Hope Twomey, Dec. 15, 1979; stepchildren: Erling Hope, Nisse Hope. *Great-great-grandfather, Michael Twomey, was born in Macroom, County Cork, Ireland, and immigrated to Boston in 1841 during the Great Famine. The family, thereafter, settled in Sheepshead Bay, Brooklyn, where father, Thomas Twomey, was born in 1915. Grandmother Grace Ketchcham's ancestry is traced to Englishman, Edward Ketcham, and his son, John, who helped found Southold and Huntington Towns on Long Island in mid-17th Century. Other ancestors helped found Southampton, Islip, Hempstead, Jamaica, and New Utrecht, serving as legislators, Town officials, and an occasional pirate.* BA, Manhattan Coll., 1967; postgrad., U.Va., 1967-68; JD, Columbia U., 1970. Bar: N.Y. 1972, U.S. Tax Ct. 1974. Asst. town atty. Town of Southampton N.Y., 1973-74; spl. asst. dist. atty. Suffolk County, N.Y., 1973-74; pvt. practice law Riverhead, N.Y., 1974-75; ptnr. Hubbard & Twomey, Riverhead, 1976-79, Twomey, Latham, Shea & Kelley, Riverhead, 1980—; chair N.Y. State East End Econ. and Environ. Task Force, 1993; mem. deans coun. Stonybrook Sch. Medicine, 1991—; adj. prof. environ. law Southampton Coll., 1977-78. *Over the last 25 years, Mr. Twomey helped build his law firm into one of the largest in Suffolk County, with 45 attorneys and staff. Martindale-Hubbell has given its highest rating to the firm for legal competence and reliability. All of its attorneys are involved in community organizations, including Mr. Twomey who recently raised $3.6 million to expand and restore the East Hampton Library, of which he is now the President. As Chair of the Lecture Series of The East Hampton 350th Anniversary, he recently edited Awakening the Past, a history of the Town, and now serves as Town historian.* Bd. dirs. East End Arts Coun., Riverhead, 1983, Guild Hall East Hampton, 1993—, East Hampton Libr., 1994—; trustee L.I. Power Authority, 1989-94; town historian, Town of East Hampton, editor town history. Recipient Environ. award, U.S. EPA, 1980. Mem. ABA, Suffolk County Bar Assn., State Energy Coun., N.Y. State Fresh Water Wetlands Appeals Bd. Democrat. Real property, State civil litigation, Estate planning. Home: 9 Two Holes of Water Rd East Hampton NY 11937-0902 Office: Twomey Latham Shea & Kelley 33 W 2nd St Riverhead NY 11901-2701

**TYACK, THOMAS MICHAEL,** lawyer; b. Columbus, Ohio, June 20, 1940; s. George E. and E. Naomi (Ballard) T.; m. Patricia J. Clark, Sept. 7, 1969; children: Jonathan, Jeffrey, James, Justin. BA cum laude, Ohio State U., Columbus, 1962, Jd, 1965. Bar: Ohio 1965, U.S. Ct. Appeals (6th cir.) 1970, U.S. Supreme Ct. 1970, U.S. Dist. Ct. (so. dist.) Ohio 1972. Ptnr. Tyack, Scott & Colley, Columbus, 1965-79, Tyack Scott & Wiseman, Columbus, 1979-81; prin. Thomas M. Tyack Assocs. Co., L.P.A., Columbus, 1981-90; ptnr. Tyack & Blackmore Co., L.P.A., Columbus, 1991-94; pres. Tyack, Blackmore Co., L.P.A., Columbus, 1994—; bar examiner Ohio supreme Ct., 1975-80; lectr., legal asst. program Capital U., Ohio, 1977-90. Fellow Am. Coll. Trial Lawyers; mem. ABA, Ohio Bar Assn., Columbus Bar Assn., Franklin Ct. and Trial Lawyers, Assn. Trial Lawyers Am., Ohio Acad. Trial Lawyers, Ohio Acad. Trial Lawyers, Ohio Acad. Criminal Def. Lawyers, NDCDL. Republican. Methodist. Criminal, Personal injury, Family and matrimonial. Office: 536 S High St Columbus OH 43215-5605

**TYLER, BRIAN JOSEPH,** lawyer; b. Hanover, Pa., Mar. 22, 1966; s. Joseph Glenn and Rose Marie (Neiderer) T. BA, Gettysburg U., 1991; JD, Widener U., 1996. Dep. clk. U.S. Bankruptcy Ct., Harrisburg, Pa., 1991-92; program adminstr. Chpt. 13 Trustee Office, Harrisburg, 1992-96; assoc. Purcell, Krug & Haller, Harrisburg, 1996—; lectr., faculty Pa. Bar Inst., Mechanicsburg, 1997-98; mediator U.S. Bankruptcy Ct., Harrisburg, 1998. Bd. dirs. Harrisburg Cmty. Theatre, 1997-99. With USAF, 1984-88. Mem. Pa. Bankruptcy Bar Assn. (v.p. mid. dist. 1998-99), Leadership Harrisburg Area. Bankruptcy, Consumer commercial, Private international. Office: Purcell Krug & Haller 1719 N Front St Harrisburg PA 17102-2392

**TYLER, DAVID MALCOLM,** lawyer; b. Detroit, Sept. 12, 1930; s. Alfred D. and Esther May (Williams) T.; m. Karol Anne DeWulf, May 1, 1981; children: Deborah Tyler Haddad, Claudia, David M. Jr., Heidi Waggoner, Holly Waggoner. BA, Wayne State U., 1952; JD, U. Mich., 1959. Bar: Mich. 1959, U.S. Dist. Ct. (ea. dist.) Mich. 1959, U.S. Ct. Appeals (6th cir.) 1973. Rsch. clk. U.S. Dist. Ct. We. Dist., Grand Rapids, Mich., 1959; atty. Cholett, Perkins & Buchanan, Grand Rapids, Mich., 1960-61, Sommer, Sorlwartz, Silver, Schartz & Tyler, Detroit, 1962-77, Tyler, Reynolds & Kenny, Detroit, 1977-86, Sullivan, Ward, Bone, Tyler & Asher, Southfield, Mich., 1986—; lectr. Def. Rsch. Inst., Inst. for Continuing Legal Edn., U. Mich. Contbg. author Mich. Law of Damages. Lt. USN, 1953-56. Mem. State Bar Mich. Assn. (chmn. negligence sect. 1981, chmn. automobile reparations com. 1976, co-chmn. products liability task force 1977), Mich. Def. Trial Counsel (pres. 1986), Country Club Detroit, Lost Tree Club. State civil litigation, Personal injury, Product liability. Office: Sullivan Ward Bone Tyler & Asher 258100 Northwestern Hwy Southfield MI 48037

**TYLER, JOHN E., III,** lawyer; b. Kansas City, Mo.. BA, U. Notre Dame, 1986, JD, 1989. From assoc. to ptnr. Lathrop & Gage L.C., Kansas City, 1989-99; gen. counsel, sec. Ewing Marion Kauffman Found., Kansas City, 1999—. Pres. Genesis Sch., Kansas City, 1995-96, 96-97; pres. Archbishop O'Hara H.S., Kansas City, 1994-95, 95-96, 96-97; chair tax increment fin. commn. city of Raytown, Mo., 1997—; bd. dirs. Ctr. for Mgmt. Assistance, Kansas City, pres., 1999—. Named Man of Yr. Leukemia Soc., Kansas City, 1998, Bernie Hoffman award for cmty. svc. Cmty. Svc. Awards Found., 1997. Mem. ABA, Mo. Bar Assn. (Thomas D. Cochran award for cmty. svc. 1995), Kans. Bar Assn., Kansas City Metro. Bar Assn. (young lawyer of yr. 1998). General civil litigation, Condemnation, Non-profit and tax-exempt organizations. Home: 11112 E 83d Terr Raytown MO 64138 Office: Ewing Marion Kauffman Found 4801 Rockhill Rd Kansas City MO 64110-2046

**TYLER, PAUL RICHARD,** lawyer; b. Lenox, Iowa, Dec. 22, 1942; s. Victor Hugh and Wilma Elene (Choate) T.; m. Eileen M. Walter, Aug. 30, 1964; children: Robert D., Stephen W., Anne C. BA with honors, U. Iowa, 1964, JD with distinction, 1967. Bar: Iowa 1967, Wis. 1967. Atty. Northwestern Mut. Life Ins. Co., Milw., 1967-69; assoc. Dickinson, Throckmorton, Parker et al, Des Moines, 1969-71, ptnr., 1971-87; shareholder Dickinson, Mackaman, Tyler & Hagen PC, Des Moines, 1987—. Bd. dirs. Pub. Health Nursing Assn., Des Moines, 1977-81, Hospice Cen. Iowa, 1988-94. Mem. ABA, Iowa Bar Assn. (chmn. legal forms com. 1982-88, co-chmn. ann. meeting 1987, bd. govs. 1995-99), Wis. Bar Assn., Polk County Bar Assn. (treas. chmn. grievance com. 1984-87, bd. dirs. 1989-93, 95—), Lincoln Inne, Des Moines Club, Phi Beta Kappa. Democrat. Presbyterian. Office: 1600 Hub Tower 699 Walnut St # 699 Des Moines IA 50309-3929

**TYNCH, DAVID RAY,** lawyer; b. Portsmouth, Va., June 8, 1947; s. John and Inez (Conner) T.; m. April Diane Smith, May 15, 1971; children: Ashley Dawn, Alisa Christine, David Arthur. BS, Old Dominion U., 1971; JD, St. Mary's U., San Antonio, 1981; LLM, So. Meth. U., 1983. Bar: Tex. 1982, Va. 1983. Tchr. City of Portsmouth, 1971-72; salesman/mktg. Smithfield (Va.) Foods, 1972-73; assoc. Leighton & Hood, San Antonio, 1980-82, Hofheimer, Nusbaum, McPhaul & Brenner, Norfolk, Va., 1983-86; mng. ptnr., lawyer Cooper, Spong & Davis, P.C., Portsmouth, 1986—; dir. Nat. 1099, Virginia Beach, Va., 1989—, Nat. Lawyers Locate Svc., Virginia Beach, 1995, Cenit Bank FSB, Norfolk, 1994—, Homestead Savs. Bank, Portsmouth, 1985-94. Dir. Ports Events, Inc., Portsmouth, 1990—, Maryview Found., Portsmouth, 1991—, Portsmouth Schs. Found., 1991—, Urban Partnership State of Va., 1994; dir., sec. Portsmouth Partnership, 1990—; commr. City of Portsmouth Mcpl. Fin. Commn., 1986-95; commr., chmn. City of Portsmouth Parking Authority, 1989-95. Maj. USAF, 1973-79. Mem. ABA, Va. State Bar Assn., Norfolk-Portsmouth Bar Assn., Portsmouth C. of C. (dir., chmn. 1993), Portsmouth Sports Club (dir., pres. 1991). Methodist. Avocations: golf, boating. Non-profit and tax-exempt organizations, Corporate taxation, Taxation, general. Home: 3502 Cardinal Ln Portsmouth VA 23703-3632 Office: Cooper Spong & Davis PC 500 Ctrl Fidelity Bank Bldg PO Box 1475 Portsmouth VA 23705-1475

**TYNER, DEBORAH G.,** judge; b. Mich., June 28, 1956; d. Herb and Suzanne Tyner; m. Scott Raderman, July 26, 1979 (dec. Apr. 1982); m. Richard A. Herman, Dec. 10, 1983; 2 children. BA, U. Mich., 1977; JD, Wayne State U., 1981; grad., Nat. Jud. Coll., 1991. Bar: Mich. 1981, U.S. Dist. Ct. (ea. dist.) Mich. 1982. Asst. prosecutor County of Wayne, Detroit, 1980-85; atty. Milton Zussman, P.C., Southfield, Mich., 1985-86; ptnr., atty. Sommers, Schwartz, Silver & Schwartz, Southfield, 1986-90; judge Oakland County Cir. Ct., Pontiac, Mich., 1991—; co-chmn. criminal atty. appointment sys. Joint Bench Bar Com. Trustee Multiple Sclerosis Soc. Recipient Brotherhood award Jewish War Vets., 1991, Barristers award B'nai B'rith award, 1991, honoree State of Israel Bonds, 1999; Adams Pratt Found. fellow. Mem. State Bar Mich. (past mem. rep. assembly), Oakland County Bar Assn., Mich. Judges Assn. (exec. and legis. coms.). Office: Oakland County Cir Ct 1200 N Telegraph Rd Pontiac MI 48341-1032

**TYNER, JOHN JOSEPH, III,** lawyer; s. John Joseph Jr. and Martha Irene (Gherson) T.; m. Donna King; children: Michael, Thomas. Student, U. Zagreb (Yugoslavia), 1976; BS in Pol. Sci. & History, Willamette U., 1977; JD, Gonzaga U., 1982. Bar: Oreg. 1982. Title examiner Pioneer Natl. Title Co., Beaverton, Oreg., 1977-79; pvt. practice Tyner & Assoc., Hillsboro, Oreg., 1982—. Budget com. Tualatin Hills Park & Recreation Dist., 1983; bd. dir. Washington County Pub. Affairs Forum, 1985; chmn. Washington Dem. Party, 1986-87, 1990-92. Legislative Action award Oreg. Trial Lawyers Assn., 1987. Mem. Oreg. State Bar (bd. govs. 1998—, house del. 1996-98), Oreg. Criminal Def. Lawyers Assn. (bd. dirs. 1994-98, v.p. 1997-98, Pres.'s award 1998), Washington County Bar Assn. (treas. 1987), Multnomah County Bar Assn. (bd. dirs. Young Lawyers Divsn. 1986), Kiwanis Club Cedar Hills (1st v.p. 1988). Criminal, General civil litigation, Personal injury. Office: Tyner & Assocs 347 SW Oak St Hillsboro OR 97123-3934

**TYTANIC, CHRISTOPHER ALAN,** lawyer; b. Oklahoma City, July 12, 1961; s. Stanley Martin and Stella Rose (Fillips) T. AA, Oscar Rose Jr. Coll., 1981; BA, U. Okla., 1983, JD, 1986. Bar: Okla. 1986. Legal intern Zuhdi & Denum, Oklahoma City, 1986; atty. Kerr-McGee Corp., Oklahoma City, 1986—; spkr. in field. Recipient Letzeiser award U. Okla.; named Scholastic All-Am., 1982. Mem. ABA, Okla. Bar Assn., Nat. Polled Hereford Assn., Okla. Polled Hereford Assn., Mineral Soc. Lawyers of Okla. City, Assn. Internat. Petroleum Negotiators, Phi Beta Kappa, Phi Theta Kappa, Pi Sigma Alpha, Omicron Delta Kappa, Phi Delta Phi. Avocations: golf, hunting, fishing. Natural resources, Private international, Mergers and acquisitions. Home: 3245 S Westminster Rd Oklahoma City OK 73150-1312 Office: Kerr-McGee Corp 123 Robert S Kerr Ave Oklahoma City OK 73102-6444

**UBALDI, MICHAEL V.,** lawyer; b. Stockton, Calif., May 2, 1948; s. Ben Raymond and Audrey Grace (Smalley) U.; m. Terryanne Ubaldi (div. Apr. 1990); children: Jennifer N., Justin M.; m. Linda A. Ubaldi, Feb. 14, 1991. BA, Calif. State U., Sacramento, 1971; JD, U. Calif., San Francisco, 1974. Bar: Calif. 1974. Assoc. Bullen, McKone & McKinley, Sacramento, 1974-81; ptnr. Duncan, Ball, Evans & Ubaldi, Sacramento, 1981—. Bd. dirs. Sutter Hosps. Found., Sacramento, 1985-92, Make-A-Wish Found., Sacramento, 1990-98, Mercy Hosps. Found., Sacramento, 1993—. Mem. No. Calif. Assn. Def. Counsel (bd. dirs. 1998—). Avocations: golf, art, travel. Personal injury. Office: Duncan Ball Evans & Ubaldi 641 Fulton Ave Fl 2D Sacramento CA 95825-4800

**UBINGER, JOHN W., JR.,** lawyer; b. Pitts., Jan. 31, 1949. BBA cum laude, Ohio U., 1970; JD, U. Notre Dame, 1973. Bar: Pa. 1973. Ptnr. Jones, Day, Reavis & Pogue, Pitts.; instr. environ. dispute resolution Duquesne U. Bd. dirs. Pa. Environ. Coun., chmn. task force on reuse of indsl. sites, 1994-95; bd. dirs., treas. Allegheny Land Trust; adv. com. Allegheny County Dept. Air Pollution Control, 1992-95, Allegheny County Contaminated Sites Redevel. Study, 1994-95. Mem. ABA (natural resources, energy and environ. law sect.) Pa. Bar Assn. (chmn. environ., mineral and natural resources law sect. 1990-91), Allegheny County Bar Assn. (chmn. environ. law sect. 1991), Air and Waste Mgmt. Assn. (chmn. We. Pa. Sect. 1989-90), Environ. Law Inst. (assoc.). Environmental, Alternative dispute resolution. Office: Jones Day Reavis & Pogue 1 Mellon Bank Ct 500 Grant St Pittsburgh PA 15219-2502

**UDALL, THOMAS,** congressman; b. Tucson, May 18, 1948; s. Stewart and Lee Udall; m. Jill Z. Cooper; 1 child, Amanda Cooper. BA, Prescott Coll., 1970; LLB, Cambridge U., Eng., 1975; JD, U. N.Mex., 1977. Law clk. to Hon. Oliver Seth U.S. Ct. Appeals (10th cir.), Santa Fe, 1977-78; asst. U.S. atty. U.S. Atty.'s Office, 1978-81; pvt. practice Santa Fe, 1981-83; chief counsel N.Mex. Health & Environ. Dept., 1983-84; ptnr. Miller, Stratvert, Togerson & Schlenker, P.A., Albuquerque, 1985-90; atty. gen. State of N.Mex., 1991-98; mem. 106th Congress from NM 3rd dist., 1999—, small bus. com.; mem. resources com. Dem. candidate U.S. Ho. Reps., 1988; past pres. Rio Chama Preservation Trust; mem. N.Mex. Environ. Improvement Bd., 1986-87; bd. dirs. La Compania de Teatro de Albuquerque, Santa Fe Chamber Music Festival, Law Fund. Mem. Nat. Assn. Attys. Gen. (pres. 1996), Kiwanis. Democrat. Office: US Ho of Reps 502 Cannon Hob Washington DC 20515-0001

**UDASHEN, ROBERT NATHAN,** lawyer; b. Amarillo, Tex., June 10, 1953; s. Leo Joe and Esther K. (Klugsberg) U.; m. Dale Lynn Sandgarten, Aug. 15, 1976. BA with high honors, U. Tex., 1974, JD, 1977. Bar: Tex. 1977, U.S. Ct. Appeals (5th cir.) 1978, U.S. Dist. Ct. (no. and so. dists.) Tex. 1978, U.S. Ct. Appeals (11th cir.) 1981, U.S. Supreme Ct. 1981, U.S. Dist. Ct. (ea. dist.) Tex. 1989, U.S. Dist. Ct. (we. dist.) Tex. 1991. Staff atty. Staff Counsel for Inmates, Huntsville, Tex., 1977-79; assoc., ptnr. Crowder, Mattox & Udashen, Dallas, 1979-85; ptnr. Udashen & Goldstucker, Dallas, 1985-87; pvt. practice, 1987-94; ptnr. Milner, Lobel, Goranson, Sorrels, Udashen & Wells, Dallas, 1995—; bd. dirs. Open, Inc., Dallas; instr. trial advocacy Sch. Law So. Meth. U., 1993-95; adj. prof. criminal procedure Sch. Law So. Meth. U., 1998-99. Contbr. articles to profl. jours. Adv. bd. Coalition for Safer Dallas, 1994. Mem. State Bar Tex. (penal code com. 1992-93), Nat. Assn. Criminal Def. Lawyers, Tex. Criminal Def. Lawyers Assn., Dallas Criminal Def. Lawyers Assn. Criminal. Office: Milner Lobel Goranson Sorrels Udashen & Wells 2515 Mckinney Ave Ste 1500 Dallas TX 75201-7604

**UDELL, LEI (LISA) KAREN,** lawyer; b. LaCrosse, Wis., June 10, 1961; d. Carl James and Carolyn Alberta Narveson; m. David Sterling Udell, Jan. 3, 1987; children: Taylor Caroline, Lauren Morissa. BA magna cum laude, U. Puget Sound, 1983; JD magna cum laude, Cornell U., 1992. Bar: Calif. 1993, U.S. Dist. Ct. (so. dist.) Calif. 1993, U.S. Dist. Ct. Ariz. 1994, U.S. Dist. Ct. (ctrl. dist.) Calif. 1998. Sr. fin. analyst Houlihan, Lokey, Howard & Zukin, L.A., 1985-88; law clk. 9th cir. U.S. Ct. Appeals, Pasadena, Calif., 1992-93; atty. Sheppard, Mullin, Richter & Hampton, San Diego, 1993—. Contbr. articles to profl. publs. Troop leader Girl Scouts Am., Coronado, Calif., 1996—. Mem. Fed. Bar Assn. (membership chair 1998, newsletter editor 1997-98), Assn. Bus. Trial Lawyers, Calif. Bar Assn., San Diego County Bar Assn., Lawyers Club San Diego. General civil litigation, Federal civil litigation, State civil litigation. Office: Sheppard Mullin Richter & Hampton 501 W Broadway Fl 19 San Diego CA 92101-3536

**UENO, TAKEMI,** lawyer; b. Bklyn., June 8, 1966; d. Hiromi and Ryuko (Kobayashi) U. AB magna cum laude, Harvard & Radcliffe Colls., 1987; MA with distinction, London Sch. of Econs., 1988; MPhil, Columbia U., 1990; JD cum laude, Harvard U., 1993. Bar: N.Y. 1994, D.C. 1996. Assoc. Winthrop, Stimson, Putnam & Roberts, N.Y.C., 1993—. Mem. Assn. of Bar of City of N.Y. (mem. com. on internat. human rights, 1995-98, com. on fgn. and comparative law 1994-95). Democrat. Avocations: classical music, ballet, reading, travel. General civil litigation. Office: Winthrop Stimson Putnam & Roberts One Battery Pk Plz New York NY 10004

**UFBERG, MURRAY,** lawyer; b. Danville, Pa., July 30, 1943; s. Alfred Eugene and Leah (Abrams) U.; m. Margery Ann Fishman, June 29, 1969; children: Aaron, Joshua, Rachel. BA, Bucknell U., 1964; JD, Duquesne U., 1968. Bar: Pa. 1969, U.s. Dist. Ct. (mid. dist.) Pa. Assoc. Rosenn, Jenkins & Greenwald, Wilkes-Barre, Pa., 1969-74; ptnr. Rosenn, Jenkins & Greenwald, L.L.P., Wilkes-Barre, 1974—; vice chair Greater Wilkes-Barre Partnership, Inc.; mem. legal com. Pa. Savs. Leagues, Inc. Chmn. United Way Wyo. Valley Gen. Campaign, Wilkes-Barre, 1990, bd. dirs. 1992-99; past pres. Ohav Zedek Synagogue, Wilkes-Barre, 1986-88, Jewish Cmty. Ctr. Wyoming Valley, 1982-83, Seligman J. Strauss Lodge/B'nai B'rith, Wilkes-Barre, 1970-74; bd. dirs., chmn. cmty. rels. coun. Jewish Cmty. Bd., 1993-97; chmn. Jewish Cmty. Bd. of Wyoming Valley, 1997—, pres. Jewish Fedn. Greater Wilkes-Barre; vice chmn. bd. trustees Coll. Misericordia; mem. Luzerne County adv. com. Pa. Economy League; mem. pres.'s adv. coun. Keystone Coll.; mem. Pres. Adv. Coun. Keystone Coll. Recipient Disting. Svc. award Wilkes-Barre Jaycees, 1979. Mem. ABA, Pa. Bar Assn., Luzerne County Bar Assn. (chmn. cmty. rels. com. 1997—), Wilkes-Barre Law and Libr. Assn., Duquesne U. Law Alumni Assn. (bd. govs.). Jewish. Avocations: sports, recreational reading. Contracts commercial, Real property, General corporate. Home: 644 Charles Ave Kingston PA 18704-4806 Office: Rosenn Jenkins & Greenwald 15 S Franklin St Wilkes Barre PA 18711-0076

**UFFORD, CHARLES WILBUR, JR.,** lawyer; b. Princeton, N.J., July 8, 1931; m. Isabel Letitia Wheeler, May 20, 1961; children: Eleanor Morris Ufford Léger, Catherine Latourette Ufford-Chase, Alison Wistar Ufford Salem. BA cum laude (Francis H. Burr scholar), Harvard U., 1953, LLB, 1959; postgrad. (Lionel de Jersey Harvard studentship), Cambridge U., Eng., 1953-54. Bar: N.Y. 1961, U.S. Tax Ct. 1963. Assoc. Riggs, Ferris & Geer, N.Y.C., 1959-61; from assoc. to ptnr. Jackson, Nash, Brophy, Barringer & Brooks, 1961-78; ptnr. Skadden, Arps, Slate, Meagher & Flom, N.Y.C., 1978-92, of counsel, 1993-96. Contbr. articles to legal jours. Trustee Nat. Squash Racquets Ednl. Found., N.Y.C., 1972-81; mem. Princeton monthly Meeting, Soc. of Friends, clk., 1986-88, 99; mem. exec. com. Friends Com. on Nat. Legislation, 1997-98; dir. Pennswood Village, 1998—. Nat. Intercollegiate Squash Racquets champion, 1952-53; mem. NCAA All-Am. Soccer 1st team, 1952. Fellow Am. Coll. Trust and Estate Counsel (transfer tax study com. 1990-93); mem. ABA, N.Y. Bar Assn. (chmn. trusts and estates law sect. 1984), Assn. Bar City N.Y., N.Y. State Office of Ct. Adminstrn. (Surrogates Ct. Adv. Com., 1994-96), U.S. Squash Racquets Assn. (hon. life; trustee endowment fund 1984-96), Internat. Lawn Tennis Club U.S.A. (dir. 1982—). Probate, Estate taxation, Estate planning. Office: 150 Mercer St Princeton NJ 08540-6827 *Integrity, perseverance, compassion and humor are all very well--but the key is to be blessed by a Divine Improvidence.*

**UGHETTA, WILLIAM CASPER,** lawyer, manufacturing company executive; b. N.Y.C., Feb. 8, 1933; s. Casper and Frieda (Bohland) U.; m. Mary L. Lusk, Aug. 10, 1957; children: William C., Robert L., Edward F., Mark R. AB, Princeton U, 1954; LLB, Harvard U., 1959. Bar: N.Y. 1959. Assoc. Shearman & Sterling, N.Y.C., 1959-67; asst. sec. Corning Glass Works, N.Y., 1968-70, sec., counsel, 1971-72, v.p., gen. counsel, 1972-82, sr. v.p., gen. counsel, 1983-98; bd. dirs. Chemung Canal Trust Co., Covance Inc. Bd. dirs. Steuben Area coun. Boy Scouts Am.; officer Corning Mus. Glass, Corning Glass Works Found.; trustee Corning C.C. Lt. (j.g.) USN, 1954-56. Mem. Assn. of Bar of City of N.Y., ABA, N.Y. State Bar Assn., Am. Corp. Counsel Assn. (trustee 1982-85), Princeton Club (N.Y.C.), Univ. Club (N.Y.C.), Corning Country Club. General corporate. Home: 13 North Rd Corning NY 14830-3235

**UHL, CHRISTOPHER MARTIN,** lawyer, educator; b. Balt., Feb. 21, 1958; s. Robert Henry and Marie Antoinette (Carosella) U.; m. Gael Anna Evandelista, Feb. 16, 1991; children: Christopher Martin Uhl, Grace Molinari Uhl. BS in Acctg., Northeastern U., 1989, MBA, 1991; JD, New Eng. Sch. Law, 1992. Bar: Mass. 1993, N.Y. 1993, U.S. Dist. Ct. Mass. 1993, D.C. 1994, Maine 1994, U.S. Dist. Ct. D.C. 1994, U.S. Dist. Maine 1994, Conn. 1995. Fingerprint technician FBI, Washington, 1976-79; project mgr. various constrn. cos., Balt., 1979-87, Admiral Constrn. Co., Boston, 1987-91; asst. dist. atty. Worcester (Mass.) Dist. Atty.'s Office, 1992-96; prin. Christopher Uhl, Attorney at Law, Worcester, 1997—; prof. Becker Coll., Worcester, 1993-97. Bd. dirs. Am. Cancer Soc., Boston, 1990-96; ward coord. Reelect Dist. Atty. Campaign, Worcester, 1994; elected mem. Southborough Rep. Town Com., Southborough Housing Authority, Northborough/Southborough Regional Sch. Com. Named Hon. Mem. Rep. State Com. Republican. Roman Catholic. Roman Catholic. Fax: (508) 797-4210. Criminal, Construction, General civil litigation. Office: 5 State St Worcester MA 01609-2893

**UHLE, WILLIAM K.,** lawyer; b. Huntington, W.V., June 19, 1952; s. Alvin Otton and Virginia Lucille Uhle; m. Linda Patterson, Nov. 19, 1983; children: Megal Elizabeth, Matthew Otto. BA in Econs., Stanford U., 1974, BA in Polit. Sci., 1974; JD, U. Oreg., 1977. Atty. in solo practice, Oregon City, Oreg., 1978-84, Portland, Oreg., 1984-87; ptnr. Thuemmel & Uhle, Portland, 1987—. Mem. Nat. Assn. Criminal Def. Lawyers, Oreg. Criminal Def. Lawyers (life). Home: 13630 SW Tarleton Ct Portland OR 97224-1679 Office: Thuemmel & Uhle 210 SW Morriston St Ste 600 Portland OR 97204

**ULLMAN, JAMES A.,** lawyer; b. Buffalo, Dec. 14, 1946; s. Robert A. and Sonya A. Ullman; m. Vivian E. Klein, Sept. 5, 1970; children: Alysa, Andrew, Lindsay. BA, U. Mich., 1968; JD, SUNY, Buffalo, 1971. Bar: N.Y. 1972, Ariz. 1972, U.S. Dist. Ct. Ariz., U.S. Dist. Ct. (we. dist.) N.Y., U.S. Supreme Ct. 1984. Ptnr. Dagett & Ullman, Phoenix, 1973-76; sole practice Phoenix, 1976-87, 93-98; ptnr. Eaton Dodge & Lazarus, Phoenix, 1987-89, Heron Burchette et al., Phoenix, Washington, 1988-90, Jennings Strouss & Salmon, Phoenix, 1990-93; sr. mem. O'Connor, Cavanagh, Anderson, Killingsworth & Beshears, Phoenix, 1998—; instr. Maricopa C.C., Phoenix, 1996; adj. prof. law Western Internat. U., Phoenix, 1996-97. Contbr. articles to profl. jours. Chmn., mem. State C.C. Bd., 1990-97; pres., mem. State Bd. Edn., Ariz., 1991-97. Mem. Edn. Law Assn. (past pres.). Avocations: gourmet cooking, travel. Franchising, Education and schools, Trademark and copyright. Office: O'Connor Cavanagh Anderson Killingsworth & Beshears 1 E Camelback Rd Ste 1100 Phoenix AZ 85012-1691

**ULLMAN, ROGER ROLAND,** lawyer, realtor; b. Darby, Pa., Nov. 16, 1948; s. David Ulrich and Carolyn Elizabeth (Wensink) U.; m. Minnie Lean Zanzinger, May 26, 1968; children: Roger II, Craig, David. BA, W.Va. Wesleyan Coll., 1970; MBA, Pepperdine U., 1976; JD, Del. Law Sch., Wilmington, 1980. Officer USMC, 1970-77; realtor Pa., 1977—; solo practice law, Swarthmore, Pa., 1981—. Vol. Boy Scouts Am., 1977—. With USAR, 1989—. Mem. Rotary. Fax: (610) 543-8789. Real property, Probate, Personal injury. Home: 199 Harvard Ave Swarthmore PA 19081-1625

**ULREY, PRESCOTT DAVID,** lawyer; b. Atlanta, Apr. 1, 1966; s. David Michael Ulrey and Barbara Ann (Johnson) Middendorf. AB, U. Calif., Berkeley, 1988; MALD, Fletcher Sch. Law & Diplomacy, 1991; JD, Columbia U., 1994. Bar: N.Y. 1995. Atty. Brown & Wood, N.Y.C., 1994-97, N.Y.C. Office Mgmt & Budget, N.Y.C., 1997—. Mem. ABA, Bar Assn. City N.Y. Office: NYC Office Mgmt & Budget 75 Park Pl New York NY 10007-2146

**ULRICH, CLIFFORD ALBERT,** lawyer; b. Manhasset, N.Y., July 7, 1967; s. Werner Richard Ulrich and Marie Jane Sciacca; m. Mary Michelle Lamanna, July 23, 1994; children: Jessica Marie, Alan Matthew. BSME, Case Western Res. U., 1989; JD, N.Y. Law Sch., 1996. Bar: N.Y. 1997, U.S. Patent and Trademark Office 1998. Project engr. Gesipa Fasteners U.S.A., Trenton, N.J., 1990-92; assoc. Kane, Dalsimer, Sullivan, Kurucz, Levy, Eisele & Richard, N.Y.C., 1996—. Mem. ABA, N.Y. State Bar Assn., N.Y. Intellectual Property Law Assn. Patent, Intellectual property. Office: Kane Dalsimer Sullivan Kurucz Levy Eisele & Richard 711 3rd Ave New York NY 10017-4014

**ULRICH, PAUL GRAHAM,** lawyer, author, publisher, editor; b. Spokane, Wash., Nov. 29, 1938; s. Donald Gunn and Kathryn (Vandercook) U.; m. Kathleen Nelson Smith, July 30, 1982; children—Kathleen Elizabeth, Marilee Rae, Michael Graham. BA with high honors, U. Mont., 1961; JD, Stanford U., 1964. Bar: Calif. 1965, Ariz. 1966, U.S. Supreme Ct. 1969, U.S. Ct. Appeals (9th cir.) 1965, U.S. Ct. Appeals (5th cir.) 1981. Law clk. judge U.S. Ct. Appeals, 9th Circuit, San Francisco, 1964-65; assoc. Lewis and Roca, Phoenix, 1965-70, ptnr., 1970-85; pres. Paul G. Ulrich P.C., Phoenix, 1985-92, Ulrich, Thompson & Kessler, P.C., Phoenix, 1992-94, Ulrich & Kessler, P.C., Phoenix, 1994-95, Ulrich, Kessler & Anger, P.C., Phoenix, 1995—; owner Pathway Enterprises, 1985-91; judge pro tem divsn. 1, Ariz. Ct. Appeals, Phoenix, 1986; instr. Thunderbird Grad. Sch. Internat. Mgmt., 1968-69, Ariz. State U. Coll. Law, 1970-73, 78, Scottsdale C.C., 1975-77, also continuing legal edn. seminars. Author and pub.: Applying Management and Motivation Concepts to Law Offices, 1985; editor, contbr.: Arizona Appellate Handbook, 1978—, Working With Legal Assistants, 1980, 81, Future Directions for Law Office Management, 1982, People in the Law Office, 1985-86; co-author, pub.: Arizona Healthcare Professional Liability Handbook, 1992, supplement, 1994, Arizona Healthcare Professional Liability Defense Manual, 1995, Arizona Healthcare Professional Liability Update Newsletter, 1992—; co-author: Federal Appellate Practice Guide: Ninth Circuit, 1994, 2d edit., 1999; contbg. editor Law Office Econs. and Mgmt., 1984-97, Life, Law and the Pursuit of Balance, 1996, 2d edit., 1997. Mem. Ariz. Supreme Ct. Task Force on Ct. Orgn. and Adminstrn., 1988-89; mem. com. on appellate cts. Ariz. Supreme Ct., 1990-91; bd. visitors Stanford U. Law Sch., 1974-77; adv. com. legal assisting program Phoenix Coll., 1985-95; atty. rep. 9th Cir. Jud. Conf., 1997—. With U.S. Army, 1956. Recipient continuing legal edn. award State Bar Ariz., 1978, 86, 90, Harrison Tweed spl. merit award Am. Law Inst./ABA, 1987. Fellow Ariz. Bar Found. (founding 1985—); mem. ABA (chmn. selection and utilization of staff pers. com., econs. of law sect. 1979-81, mem. standing com. legal assts. 1982-86, co-chmn. joint project on appellate handbooks 1983-85, co-chmn. fed. appellate handbook project 1985-88, chmn. com. on liaison with non-lawyers orgns. Econs. of Law Practice sect. 1985-86), Am. Acad. Appellate Lawyers, Am. Law Inst., Am. Judicature Soc. (Spl. Merit citation 1987), Ariz. Bar Assn. (chmn. econs. of law practice com. 1980-81, co-chmn. lower ct. improvement com. 1982-85, co-chmn. Ariz. appellate handbook project 1976—), Coll. Law Practice Mgmt., Maricopa County Bar Assn. (bd. dirs. 1994-96), Calif. Bar Assn., Phi Kappa Phi, Phi Alpha Delta, Sigma Phi Epsilon. Democrat. State civil litigation, Federal civil litigation, Appellate. Home: 2529 E Lupine Ave Phoenix AZ 85028-1823 Office: Ste 250 3707 N Seventh St Phoenix AZ 85014-5057

**ULRICH, ROBERT GARDNER,** retail food chain executive, lawyer; b. Evanston, Ill., May 6, 1935; s. Charles Clemens and Nell Clare (Stanley) U.; m. Diane Mary Granzin, June 6, 1964; children—Robert Jeffrey, Laura Elizabeth, Meredith Christine. LL.B. (Law Rev. key), Marquette U., Milw., 1960. Bar: Wis. 1960, Ill. 1960, N.Y. 1981. Law clk. to fed. dist. judge Milw., 1961-62; atty. S.C. Johnson & Son, Inc., Racine, Wis., 1962-65, Motorola, Inc., Franklin Park, Ill., 1965-68; atty., then asst. gen. counsel Jewel Cos., Inc., Melrose Park, Ill., 1968-75; v.p., gen. counsel Gt. Atlantic & Pacific Tea Co., Inc., Montvale, N.J., 1975-81; sr. v.p., gen. counsel, sec. Gt. Atlantic & Pacific Tea Co., Inc., 1981—. Mem. Am. Bar Assn., N.Y. State Bar Assn. General corporate. Home: 500 Weymouth Dr Wyckoff NJ 07481-1217 Office: Gt Atlantic & Pacific Tea Co Box 418 2 Paragon Dr Montvale NJ 07645-1718*

**ULRICH, THEODORE ALBERT,** lawyer; b. Spokane, Wash., Jan. 1, 1943; s. Herbert Roy and Martha (Hoffman) Ulrich; m. Nancy Allison, May 30, 1966; children: Donald Wayne, Frederick Albert. BS cum laude, U.S. Mcht. Marine Acad., 1965; JD cum laude, Fordham U., 1970; LLM, NYU, 1974. Bar: N.Y. 1971, U.S. Ct. Appeals (2nd cir.) 1971, U.S. Supreme Ct. 1974, U.S. Ct. Claims 1977, U.S. Customs Ct. 1978, U.S. Ct. Internat. Trade 1981, U.S. Ct. Appeals (5th cir.) 1988, U.S. Ct. Appeals (D.C. cir.) 1992, Colo. 1993, U.S. Ct. Appeals (10 cir.) 1994. Mng. clk. U.S. Dept. Justice, N.Y.C., 1968-69, law clk. to federal dist. judge, 1969-70; assoc. Cadwalader, Wickersham & Taft, N.Y.C., 1970-80, ptnr., 1980-94; ptnr. Popham, Haik, Schnobrich & Kaufman, Ltd., Denver, 1994-96; sole practice law Denver, 1996—. Co-author: Encyclopedia of International Commercial Litigation, 1991, Arbitration of Construction Contracts, V, 1991; contbg. author: Marine Engineering Economics and Cost Analysis, 1995; author, editor Fordham Law Rev., 1969. Leader Boy Scouts Am., Nassau County, N.Y., 1984-94, Denver, 1994—. Lt. comdr. USCGR, 1965-86. Mem. ABA, Colo. Bar, Denver Bar, Maritime Law Assn., Am. Soc. Internat. Law, Soc. Naval Architects and Marine Engrs., U.S. Naval Inst., Am. Arbitration Assn. Contracts commercial, Federal civil litigation, Private international. Home and Office: 4300 E 6th Ave Denver CO 80220-4940

**ULTIMO, PAUL JOSEPH,** lawyer; b. Bklyn., Mar. 19, 1964; s. Frank Daniel and Kathryn Linda (Spingola) U.; 1 child, Anthony Joseph. BBA, Nat. U., 1992; JD, Western State U., 1995. Bar: U.S. Dist. Ct. (ctrl. dist.) Calif. 1996. Of counsel Curd, Galindo & Smith LLP, Long Beach, Calif. Donor Dem. Party, South Orange County, Calif., 1998. Recipient Am. Jurisprudence award in constnl. law Bancroft Whitney, 1995, Am. Jurisprudence award in comml. code Bancroft Whitney, 1995. Mem. ABA, Orange County Bar Assn. Roman Catholic. Avocations: water skiing, golfing, boating, sailing. Criminal, Federal civil litigation, State civil litigation. Home: 25422 Remesa Dr Mission Viejo CA 92691-5463 Office: The Ultimo Bldg 1411 E Borchard Ave Santa Ana CA 92705-4414 also: Curd Galindo & Smith LLP Shoreline Sq Tower 301 E Ocean Blvd Ste 460 Long Beach CA 90802-4832

**ULVEN, MARK EDWARD,** lawyer; b. Sioux City, Iowa, Mar. 23, 1954; s. Marvin Edward and Bonnie Mae Ulven; m. Kathleen Lynn Lanini, Jan. 9, 1982 (div. June 1993); m. Debra Anne Cappellino, Sept. 3, 1993; children: Alexandra, Allison. BS, U. S.D., 1976; MA, U. Mo., 1982; JD, Georgetown U., 1994. BAr:Pa. Instr. U. Mo., Columbia, 1981-82; asst. editor Texarkana (Tex.) Gazette, 1982-83; legis. asst. U.S. Ho. of Reps., Washington, 1983-86, U.S. Senate, Washington, 1986-92; legis. analyst Dorsey & Whitney, Washington, 1992-94; assoc. Jones Day Reavis & Pogue, Washington, 1994-98, Klett, Lieber, Rooney & Schorling, Pitts., 1998—. Contbr. articles to profl. jours. Recipient Am. Jurisprudence award, 1994, award for editl. cartooning/illustration Va. Press Assn., 1989. Mem. Allegheny County Bar Assn. Republican. Episcopalian. Avocations: drawing and painting. Federal civil litigation, State civil litigation. Home: 2006 White Oak Ct Moon Township PA 15108-9050 Office: Klett Lieber Rooney & Schorling One Oxford Centre Pittsburgh PA 15219

**UMEBAYASHI, CLYDE SATORU,** lawyer; b. Honolulu, Sept. 2, 1947; s. Robert S. and Dorothy C. Umebayashi; m. Cheryl J. Much, June 27, 1975. BBA in Travel Industry Mgmt., U. Hawaii, 1969, JD, 1980. Spl. dept. atty. gen. Labor and Indsl. Rels. Appeals Bd., Honolulu, 1980-81; atty., dir., shareholder Kessner, Duca, Umebayashi, Bain & Matsunaga, Honolulu, 1981—; commr. Hawaii Criminal Justice Commn. Bd. dirs. Wesley Found., Honolulu, 1993-97. Mem. Hawaii State Bar Assn. Workers' compensation, Personal injury, Real property. Office: Kessner Duca Umebayashi Bain & Matsunaga 220 S King St Fl 19 Honolulu HI 96813-4526

**UMMER, JAMES WALTER,** lawyer; b. Pitts., July 16, 1945; s. Walter B. and Rose P. (Gerhardt) U.; m. Janet Sue Young, Dec. 21, 1968; children: James Bradley, Benjamin F. BA, Thiel Coll., 1967; JD, Duke U., 1972. Bar: Pa. 1972. Trust officer Pitts. Nat. Bank, 1972-75; tax atty., shareholder Buchanan Ingersoll P.C., Pitts., 1975-92; prin. Hirtle, Callaghan & Co., Pitts., 1992-93; shareholder Babst, Calland, Clements and Zomnir, Pitts., 1993—; dir. SPEC Group, Inc., Pitts., Pa., 1994—; chmn. Morgan Franklin & Co., Pitts., Golf Course Cos., Orlando, Fla. Trustee Thiel Coll., Greenville, Pa., 1984—, The Rehab. Inst. Pitts., 1984—, Snee-Reinhardt Charitable Found., Pitts., 1987—; mem. bd. visitors Duke U. Divinity Sch., 1999—. Fellow Am. Coll. Probate Counsel; mem. Estate Planning Coun. Western Pa. (pres. 1986-87), Tax Club (Pitts.), Duquesne Club, Rolling Rock Club, Oakmont Country Club. Republican. Presbyterian. Estate planning, Taxation, general, Probate. Home: 200 Woodland Farms Rd Pittsburgh PA 15238-2024 Office: Babst Calland Clements & Zomnir 2 Gateway Ctr Fl 8 Pittsburgh PA 15222-1425

**UNDERBERG, MARK ALAN,** lawyer; b. Niagara Falls, N.Y., July 9, 1955; s. Alan Jack and Joyce Love (Wisbaum) U.; m. Diane Englander, Mar. 22, 1986; children: Andrew Englander, James Englander. BA, Cornell U., 1977, JD, 1981. Bar: N.Y. 1981. Law clk. to chief judge U.S. Ct. Appeals (3d cir.), Wilmington, Del., 1981-82; assoc. Debevoise & Plimpton, N.Y.C., 1982-87; mng. dir., dep. gen. counsel Henley Group, Inc., N.Y.C., 1987-90, mng. dir., gen. counsel, 1990-92; v.p., gen. counsel Abex Inc., Hampton, N.H., 1992-95; v.p., gen. counsel Fisher Sci. Internat. Inc., Hampton, N.H., 1991-97, cons. 1997-98; counsel Paul, Weiss, Rifkind, Wharton & Garrison, N.Y.C., 1998—. Editor-in-chief Cornell Law Rev., 1980-81. Mem. ABA, Assn. of Bar of City of N.Y., Genesee Valley Club, University Club. General corporate, Securities. Office: Paul Weiss Rifkind Wharton & Garrison Rm 200 1285 Avenue Of The Americas New York NY 10019-6065

**UNDERHILL, JOANNE PARSONS,** lawyer; b. Chgo., Oct. 6, 1950; d. Charles Erwin Jr. and Justine Parsons; m. James C. Underhill, Jr., June 20, 1981; children: Maureen, James Charles. BA cum laude, Yale U., 1973; JD, Am. U., Washington, 1979. Bar: D.C. 1979, Colo. 1987, U.S. Dist. Ct. Washington 1980, U.S. Ct. Appeals (D.C. cir.) 1980, U.S. Ct. Appeals (10th cir.) 1985. Assoc. Howrey & Simon, Washington, 1979-83; trial atty. Fed. Home Loan Bank Bd., Washington, 1983-85; asst. gen. counsel Fed. Home Loan Bank Bd. and FSLIC, Washington, 1985-86; spl. counsel Gorsuch & Kirgis, Denver, 1986-87; shareholder Popham, Haik, Snobrich & Kaufman, Ltd., Denver, 1988-94, Underhill & Underhill, P.C., Greenwood Village, Colo., 1994—; mem. Pks., Trails and Recreation Commn., Greenwood Village, 1991—, chair, 1992-95; pub. mem. Colo. Bd. Accountancy, Denver, 1994—; del. Statehouse Conf. on Small Bus., Denver, 1997. Bd. dirs. Colo. Women's C. of C., Denver, 1993-96; chair Colo. Women's Leadership Coalition, Denver, 1996-97, Women's Leadershi Cir., Girl Scouts Mile Hi Coun., 1997—. Recipient Woman of Distinction award Girl Scouts Mile Hi Coun., Denver, 1997, The Power of One award Colo. Woman '98, 1998. Mem. ABA, Colo. Women's Bar Assn. (bd. dirs. 1994-95), Colo. Bar Assn. (Amicus curiae com. 1993-95), Arapahoe County Bar Assn. Democrat. Methodist. General civil litigation, General practice, Professional liability. Office: Underhill & Underhill PC 5290 Dtc Pkwy Ste 150 Greenwood Village CO 80111-2721

**UNDERWOOD, ANTHONY PAUL,** lawyer; b. Atlanta, June 25, 1955; s. Paul L and Charlene B. (Snider) U.; m. Joan Carol Butler, May 27, 1978; children: Andrew Ryan, Elizabeth Kaitlin, Caroline MacKenzie. BA, U. North Ala., 1977; MA, Samford U., 1980, JD, 1980; MS, Johns Hopkins U., 1983; LLM, Judge Adv. Gen.'s Sch., 1994. Bar: Ala. 1980, U.S. Claims Ct. 1982, U.S. Ct. Mil. Appeals 1982. Trial atty. U.S. Army, various locations, 1980-87; sr. assoc. Doke & Riley, Dallas, 1987-89; legal counsel, dir. contracts Hughes Aircraft Co., Torrence, Calif., 1989-93; mgr., contracts Hughes Missile Systems Co., Tucson, Ariz., 1993-95; dir., contracts & licensing Lockheed Martin Internat. Launch Svcs., San Diego, 1995—. Author: A Progressive History of the Young Men's Business Club of Birmingham, Ala.: 1946-70, 1980. Lt. col. USAR, 1980—. Mem. ABA (vice chair various coms., pub. contract law sect). Republican. Avocations: travel, running, reading, attending sports events. Private international, Intellectual property, Government contracts and claims. Office: Lockhead Martin Internat Launch Svcs Inc 101 W Broadway Ste 2000 San Diego CA 92101-8221

**UNDERWOOD, R. MICHAEL,** lawyer; b. Oak Ridge, Tenn., May 2, 1950; s. William Robert and Althea (Grant) U.; m. Zilpha Philip Rawson, June 24, 1987. BA, SUNY, Buffalo, 1976; JD, U. Tenn., 1978. Bar: Fla. 1980, U.S. Dist. Ct. (no. and mid. dists.) Fla. 1980, U.S. Ct. Appeals (11th cir.) 1984, U.S. Supreme Ct. 1988. Sr. atty. Fla. Dept. Banking and Fin., Tallahassee, 1983-90, Katz Kutter Haigler, Tallahassee, 1990-92; shareholder Rutledge Ecenia Underwood Purnell & Hoffman, P.A., Tallahassee, 1992-99, Akerman, Senterfitt & Eidson, P.A., Tallahassee, 1999—; chmn. Fla. Adv. Bd. on Unclaimed Property, 1997—; prin. drafter of many statutes and regulations in the areas of securities regulation, unclaimed property (escheat), banking and fin. svcs.; expert witness on securities regulation and unclaimed property. Contbr. articles to profl. jours. Mem. ABA (com. on state regulaiton of securities 1990—). Democrat. Episcopalian. Avocations: backpacking, canoeing, Bible study. Securities, Administrative and regulatory, General civil litigation. Office: Akerman Senterfitt & Eidson PA 301 S Bronough St Ste 200 Tallahassee FL 32301-1722 also: PO Box 10555 Tallahassee FL 32302-2555

**UNGAR, ROBERT ARTHUR,** lawyer, lobbyist; b. N.Y.C., Oct. 31, 1955; s. Albert Joseph and Elayne Lee (Fruhling) U.; m. Eileen P. Doherty, June 11, 1988. BS summa cum laude, Mercy Coll., 1983; JD, St. John's U., 1987. Bar: Conn. 1987, N.Y. 1988. Pres. Alton Cons., Inc., Great Neck, N.Y., 1975-81; mgr. met. zone N.Y. Motorola Inc., Queens, N.Y., 1981-85; br. mgr. Wang Info. Svcs. Corp., N.Y.C., 1985-86; asst. to dean sch. law St. John's U., Queens, 1986-87; counsel to insp. gen. Fire Dept. N.Y.C. Dept. Investigation, Bklyn., 1987-88; atty. Sullivan & Liapakis, P.C., N.Y.C., 1988-90; first asst. commr. N.Y.C. Fire Dept., Bklyn., 1990; sr. ptnr. Ungar, Gerstman & Pomerance, Garden City, N.Y., 1990-92; pvt. practice Robert A. Ungar, P.C., 1993—; pres. Robert A. Ungar Assocs., Inc., 1995—; adj. prof. law Mercy Coll., 1990-92. Chmn. drug task force Cmty. Planning Bd. #7, Queens, 1988-89; legis. counsel N.Y.C. Fire Marshals Devevolent Assn., N.Y.C., Fire Alarm Dispatchers Benevolent Assn., Met. Buglar and Fire Alarm Assn., N.Y.C. EMS and Paramedics Union; gen. counsel N.Y.C. Fire Dept. Ner Tamid Soc. Recipient outstanding community svc. award Community Planning Bd. Queens #1, 1981; named Hon. Battalion Chief N.Y.C. Fire Dept., 1989. Mem. ABA, N.Y. State Bar Assn., Queens County Bar Assn., Assn. of Bar of City of N.Y., Assn. Trial Lawyers Am., N.Y. State Trial Lawyers Assn. (bd. dirs.), Nassau County Bar Assn., Capitol Hill Club (Washington), Fire Bell Club, N.Y. Press Club. Avocations: electronics, radio communications. Personal injury, Legislative, Family and matrimonial. Home: 150-16 17 Ave Whitestone NY 11357-3121 Office: 595 Stewart Ave Ste 410 Garden City NY 11530-4736

**UNGARETTI, RICHARD ANTHONY,** lawyer; b. Chgo., May 25, 1942; s. Dino Carl and Antoinette (Calvetti) U.; children: Joy A., Paul R. BS, DePaul U., 1964, JD, 1970. Bar: Ill. 1970, U.S. Dist. Ct. (no. dist.) Ill. 1970, U.S. Supreme Ct. 1980. Assoc. Kirkland & Ellis, Chgo., 1970-74; ptnr. Ungaretti & Harris, Chgo., 1974—. Mem. adv. coun. DePaul Coll. Law, Chgo., 1988. Mem. ABA, Chgo. Bar Assn., Ill. State Bar Assn., Internat. Coun. Shopping Ctrs., Am. Coll. Real Estate Lawyers, Justinian Soc., Urban Land Inst. (assoc.), Lamda Alpha. Avocations: golf, fishing, hunting. Real property, Land use and zoning (including planning), Landlord-tenant. Office: Ungaretti & Harris 3500 Three First Nat Plz Chicago IL 60602

**UNGARO-BENAGES, URSULA MANCUSI,** federal judge; b. Miami Beach, Fla., Jan. 29, 1951; d. Ludivico Mancusi-Ungaro and Ursula Berliner; m. Michael A. Benages, Mar., 1988. Student, Smith Coll., 1968-70; BA in English Lit., U. Miami, 1973; JD, U. Fla., 1975. Bar: Fla. 1975. Assoc. Frates, Floyd, Pearson et al, Miami, 1976-78, Blackwell, Walker, Gray et al, Miami, 1978-80, Finley, Kumble, Heine et al, Miami, 1980-85, Sparber, Shevin, Shapo et al, Miami, 1985-87; cir. judge State of Fla., Miami, 1987-92; U.S. dist. judge Miami, 1992—; mem. Fla. Supreme Ct. Race & Ethnic & Racial Bias Study Commn., Fla., 1989-92, St. Thomas U. Inns of Ct., Miami, 1991-92. Bd. dirs. United Family & Children's Svcs., Miami, 1981-82; mem. City of Miami Task Force, 1991-92. Mem. ABA, Fed. Judges Assn., Fla. Assn. Women Lawyers, Dade County Bar Assn., Eugene Spellman Inns of Ct. U. Miami. Office: US Dist Ct 301 N Miami Ave Fl 11 Miami FL 33128-7702

**UNGER, CHARLES JOSEPH,** lawyer; b. Alexandria, Va., Oct. 30, 1955; s. Gerald Bertram and Bette (Bernstein) U. BA, Northwestern U., 1973-77; JD, U. Ill., 1977-80. Bar: Calif. 1981, U.S. Dist. Ct. (ctrl. dist.) Calif. 1991. Law clerk Flanagan, Booth, Santa Ana, Calif., 1980-81; assoc. atty. Flanagan, Booth, Santa Ana, 1981-86; ptnr. Flanagan, Booth & Unger, Santa Ana, 1986—; instr., DUI Defense U. So. Calif., L.A., 1985-97; therapist Foothill Ctr. for Personal and Family Growth, 1997—. Columnist Glendale (Calif.) News Press. Psychology doctorate Am. Behavioral Studies Inst., Tustin, Calif., 1985-97. Mem. Glendale Bar Assn. (pres. 1996-97). Democrat. Jewish. Criminal. Office: Flanagan Booth & Unger 1156 N Brand Blvd Glendale CA 91202-2504

**UNGER, GERE NATHAN,** physician, lawyer; b. Monticello, N.Y., May 15, 1949; s. Jessie Aaron and Shirley (Rosenstein) U.; m. Alicen J. McGowan, July 21, 1990; children: Elijah, Breena, Ari, Sasha, Arlen. JD, Bernadean U., 1979; MD, Inst. Polytecnico, Mexico City, 1986; D Phys. Medicine, Met. U., Mexico City, 1987; postgrad., Boston U., 1993, Harvard Law Sch., 1994-96; LLM in Health Law, U. Glasgow, 1999. Dipomate Am. Bd. Forensic Examiners, Am. Bd. Med. Legal Analysis in Medicine and Surgery, Am. Bd. Forensic Medicine, Am. Bd. Risk Mgmt. Med. dir. Vietnam Vets. Post-Traumatic Stress Disorder Program, 1988-90; emergency rm. physician, cons. in medicaid fraud Bronx (N.Y.)-Lebanon Hosp., 1990—; clin. legal medicine Paladin Profl. Group, P.A., Palm Beach, Fla., 1992-98; pres. Albany Law Jour. Co., Inc., 1998—; jurisconsult Office of Gere Unger, M.D., J.D., 1999—; mediator, arbitrator, negotiator World Intellectual Property Orgn., 1994; mem. peer rev. com. Nat. Inst. on Disability and Rehab. Rsch., Office Spl. Edn., U.S. Dept. Edn., 1993; mem. clin. ethics com. Inst. Medecine Legale et de Medecine Sociale, Strasbourg, France, 1994; mem. surg. critical care com. Am. Soc. Critical Care Medicine, 1992; N.Y. state capt. Am. Trial Lawyers Exch., 1992. Editl. rev. bd. Am. Bd. Forensic Examiners, 1993, Jour. Neurol. and Orthopaedic Medicine and Surgery, 1993. Commandant Broward County Marine Corps League, 1995—. With USMC, 1968-72. Fellow Internat. Coll. Surgeons (mem. ethics com. 1994, mem. emergency response program Ea. region 1994), Am. Acad. Neurol. and Orthopaedic Surgeons, Am. Coll. Legal Medicine, Am. Coll. Forensic Examiners, Exec. Practice Mgmt.; mem. ABA, ATLA, FBA (mem. health com., rep. ABA 1994, chmn. med. malpractice/tort com. and FBA liaison to AMA), Nat. Coll. Advocacy, Internat. Bar Assn., Am. Coll. Physician Execs. (chair forum on law and med. mgmt. 1995), Kennedy Inst. Ethics, Nat. Health Lawyers Assn., Am. Soc. of Laser Medicine and Surgery, Nat. Assn. of Forensic Econs., Nat. Lawyers Assn. (chmn. Native Am. law sect.), Internat. Soc. Police Surgeons (advisor 1998—). Avocations: flying, boating. Office: 8 Elk St Ste 3 Albany NY 12207-1010

**UNGER, PETER VAN BUREN,** lawyer; b. Cin., Nov. 15, 1957; s. Sherman Edward and Polly Van Buren (Taylor) U.; m. Laura Meth Simone, June 29, 1991; children: Simone Taylor, Natalie Van Buren. BA in History, Polit. Sci., Miami U., Oxford, Ohio, 1980; JD, U. Cin., 1983; LLM in Securities, Georgetown U., 1987. Bar: Ohio 1984, D.C. 1985, U.S. Supreme Ct. 1991. Law clk. chief judge U.S. Dist. Ct. (so. dist.) Fla., Ft. Lauderdale, 1983-85; staff atty. enforcement divsn. SEC, N.Y.C., 1986-88; assoc. Fulbright & Jaworski, Washington, 1988-89, participating assoc., 1990-94, ptnr., 1995—. Mem. ABA (bus. law sect., com. fed. regulation of securities, sub-com. on civil litigation and SEC enforcement matters 1989—, litigation sect. com. on securities litigation sub-com. on SEC enforcement practice 1990—), Securities Industry Assn. (compliance and legal divsn.), D.C. Bar Assn. (corp., fin. and securities law sect. steering com.). Securities. Home: 3308 N St NW Washington DC 20007-2807 Office: Fulbright & Jaworski LLP 801 Pennsylvania Ave NW Washington DC 20004-2615

**UNGER, RICHARD MAHLON,** lawyer; b. Walterboro, S.C., June 14, 1945; s. Henry Wayne and Keith (Jeffries) U.; m. Katherine L. Smith, Mar. 29, 1967; children: Richard M. Jr., Dorothy Katherine. BA, Wofford Coll., 1967; JD, U. S.C., 1970. Bar: S.C. 1967, U.S. Dist. Ct. S.C. 1967, U.S. Ct. Appeals (4th cir.) 1974. Legal advisor S.C. Dept. of Edn., Columbia, 1972; assoc. Edens, Woodward & Butler, 1972-74; ptnr. Woodward, Butler & Unger, 1974-80, Woodward & Unger, 1980-85, Woodward, Leventis, Unger, Ormand & Herndon, Columbia, 1985-90, Woodward, Leventis, Unger, Herndon & Cothran, Columbia, 1990-91, Woodward, Leventis, Unger, Daves, Herndon & Cothan, Columbia, 1991-95, Leventis & Unger, P.C., Columbia, 1996, Rogers Townsend & Thomas PC, Columbia, 1996—; gen. counsel Drak Devel. Corp., 1980—. Chmn. City of Columbia Zoning Bd. Adjustments, 1988-93; mem. fin. com. Jim Leventis for Congress, 1988; bd. dirs. Palmetto Land Title Assn., 1994-99. Capt. U.S. Army, 1971, Vietnam. Mem. ABA (com. on regulations and land sales 1988—, com. on real property, probate and trust law 1988—, com. on tax 1995—), S.C. Bar Assn. (ho. of dels./probate, estate planning and trust sect., tax sect. 1993—, real estate sect.), Nat. Acad. of Elder Law Attys., Greater Columbia C. of C. (bd. dirs. 1995—, mem. bd. dirs. 1996—), Windermere Club, Masons. Avocations: fishing, boating, hunting. E-mail: unger@rit-law.com. Real property, Probate, General corporate. Office: Rogers Townsend & Thomas PO Box 100200 1441 Main St 10th Fl Columbia SC 29202-3200

**UNGERECHT, TODD EDWARD,** lawyer; b. Pasco, Wash., Jan. 29, 1965; s. Roger L. and Julie A. (Boblet) U. BA in History, BA in Polit. Sci., Gonzaga U., 1987, JD, 1990. Bar: Wash. 1990, U.S. Dist. Ct. (ea. dist.) Wash. 1991. Assoc. Leavy, Schultz & Sweeney, P.S., Pasco, 1990-91, Houger, Miller & Stein, P.S., Richland, Wash., 1991-93; dep. pros. atty., civil atty. Franklin County Pros. Atty.'s Office, Pasco, 1993-94; legis. asst., dist. rep. for Congressman Doc Hastings, U.S. Ho. of Reps., Washington, 1994-97; assoc. Roach Law Offices, P.S., Pasco, 1997—. Committeeman Wash. State Rep. Com., Pasco, 1993-94; campaign mgr. Friends of Doc Hastings, Kennewick, Wash., 1996; bd. dirs. Tri-Cities YMCA, 1998—. Mem. Benton-Franklin Bar Assn. (sec.-treas. 1993-94), Toastmasters, Rotary (bd. dirs. Pasco-Kennewick 1998—), Phi Delta Phi, Alpha Sigma Nu. Roman Catholic. Avocations: history, music, travel, golf. Legislative, Government contracts and claims, Estate planning. Office: Roach Law Offices 428 W Shoshone St Pasco WA 99301-5347

**UNGERLEIDER, ROBERT NORMAN,** lawyer; b. Englewood, N.J.; s. Emil and Lillian Stone U.; m. Linda L. Salsman, Sept. 23, 1967; children: Michelle E. Ungerleider Friedman, Deborah E. Ungerleider Tight. BA, Rutgers U., 1962, LLB, 1965. Bar: N.J. 1965, Ill. 1975, U.S. Dist. Ct. (no. dist.) N.J. 1965, U.S. Dist. Ct. (no. dist.) Ill. 1975. Staff atty. Middlesex County Legal Svc. Corps., Perth Amboy, N.J., 1968-70; exec. dir. Perth Amboy Model Cities Adminstrn., 1970-72; sr. assoc. SPA/Redco, Inc., Chgo., 1972-74; assoc. Sheldon L. Baskin, Esq., Chgo., 1974-86; ptnr. Katz, Randall, Weinberg, Chgo., 1986—; mem. blue ribbon adv. bd. Cook County Recorder of Deeds, Chgo., Mcpl. Ct. adv. com., Chgo. Co-editor Tenant-Landlord Handbook Illinois, 1976; exec. editor ABA Jour. on Affordable Housing and Comty. Devel. Law., 1993—; contbr. articles to ABA Jour. Mem. Mental Health Nd, Middlesex County, N.J., 1969, New Brunswick, comty. adv. bd. N.J. Pub. Broadcasting, Trenton, 1969; bd. dirs., pres. Chiavalle Montesorri Sch., Evanston, Ill., 1974-76. Recipient cert. of recognition Coun. for Jewish Elderly, 1978; named Advocate of Yr., Ray Graham Assn. for Physically Handicapped, 1978. Mem. ABA (governing com. Forum on Affordable Housing 1995—), Ill. State Bar Assn., Chgo. Bar Assn. Avocations: travel, sports, books, music. Real property, Landlord-tenant, Non-profit and tax-exempt organizations. Home: 100 Williamsburg Rd Evanston IL 60203-1813 Office: Katz Randall & Weinberg 333 W Wacker Dr Chicago IL 60606-1220

**UNIS, RICHARD L.,** judge; b. Portland, Oreg., June 11, 1928. BS, U. Oreg., JD. Bar: Oreg. 1954, U.S. Dist. Ct. Oreg. 1957, U.S. Ct. Appeals (9th cir.) 1960, U.S. Supreme Ct. 1965. Judge Portland Mcpl. Ct., 1968-71; judge Multnomah County Dist. Ct., 1972-76, presiding judge, 1972-74; former judge Oreg. Cir. Ct. 4th Judicial Dist., 1977-90; former sr. dep. city atty. City of Portland; assoc. justice Oreg. Supreme Ct., Portland, 1990-96; spl. master U.S. Dist. Ct. House, Portland; adj. prof. of local govt. law and evidence Lewis & Clark Coll. Northwestern Sch. Law, 1969-76, 77-96; spl. master supr. La.-Pacific Inner-Seal Siding nationwide class action litig.; faculty mem. The Nat. Judicial Coll., 1971-96; former faculty mem. Am. Acad. Judicial Edn. Author: Procedure and Instructions in Traffic Court Cases, 1970, 101 Questions and Answers on Preliminary Hearings, 1974. Bd. dirs. Oreg. Free from Drug Abuse; mem. Oreg. Adv. Com. on Evidence Law Revision, chmn. subcom., 1974-79. Maj. USAFR, JAGC, ret. Recipient Meritorius Svc. award U. Oregon sch. Law, 1988; named Legal Citizen of Yr. Oreg. Law Related Edn., 1987; inducted into The Nat. Judicial Coll.

Hall of Honor, 1988. Mem. Am. Judicature Soc. (bd. dirs. 1975), Am. Judges Assn., Multnomah Bar Found., Oregon Judicial Conf. (chmn. Oreg. Judicial Coll. 1973-80, legis. com. 1976—, exec. com. of judicial edn. com., judicial conduct com.), N.Am. Judges Assn. (tenure, selection and compensation judges com.), Dist. Ct. Judges of Oreg. (v.p., chmn. edn. com.), Nat. Conf. Spl. Ct. Judges (exec. com.), Oreg. State Bar (judicial adminstrn. com., sec. local govt. com., com. on continuing certification, uniform jury instrn. com., exec. com. criminal law sect., trial practice sect. standards and certification com., past chmn., among others), Oreg. Trial Lawyers Assn. (named Judge of Yr. 1984). Office: US Dist Ct House 1000 SW 3rd Ave Portland OR 97204-2930

**UNKELBACH, L. CARY,** lawyer; b. New York, July 25, 1950; d. Kurt and Evelyn (Haskell) U.; m. David W. Olmstead, Sept. 11, 1993. BA, William Smith Coll., Geneva, N.Y., 1972; JD, U. Denver, 1979. Bar: Colo. 1979, U.S. Dist. Ct. Colo. 1979, U.S. Ct. Appeals (10th cir.) 1987. Dep. dist. atty. Jefferson County Dist. Attys. Office, Golden, Colo., 1979-84; asst. atty. gen. Atty. Gen.'s Office, Denver, 1984-86; assoc. John Faught PC, Englewood, Colo., 1986-90; asst. county atty. Arapahoe County, Littleton, Colo., 1990—. V.p., bd. mem. 2nd Appletree West Condo Assn., Denver, 1985-92. Mem. Colo. County Attys. Assn. (bd. dirs. 1997—). Avocations: hiking, snowshoeing, travel, photography, animals. Home: PO Box 532 Franktown CO 80116-0532 Office: Acapahoe County Atty Office 5334 S Prince St Littleton CO 80120-1136

**UNPINGCO, JOHN WALTER SABLAN,** federal judge; b. 1950. BA, St. Louis U., 1972; MBA, JD, NYU, 1976; LLM, Georgetown U., 1983. Bar: Guam 1977, D.C. 1983, Calif. 1992. Atty. Ferenz, Bramhall, Williams & Gruskin, Guam, 1976-77; atty. Office Staff Judge Advocate USAF, 1977-85, 85-87, civilian atty., Office Staff Judge Advocate, 1985-87; counsel U.S. Naval Air Warfare Ctr., China Lake, Calif., 1987-92; fed. judge U.S. Dist. Ct. (Guam dist.), 1992—; part-time instr. U. Md. Far East divsn., Yokota Air Base, Tokyo, 1983-87, European divsn., RAF Mildenhall, Suffolk, U.K., 1979-82, U. Guam, 1994—. Mem. ABA, State Bar Calif., Guam Bar Assn., Internat. Legal Soc. Japan, D.C. Bar Assn., NWC Community Fed. Credit Union (bd. dirs. 1991-92). Office: Pacific News Bldg 238 Archbishop FC Flores St 6th Fl Agana GU 96910

**UNRUH, ROBERT JAMES,** lawyer, educator; b. Tulsa, Nov. 16, 1929; s. Robert James and Mary Marguerittte Unruh; m. Paula Combest, Mar. 21, 1951; children: Jilda, James, Allison. BA, U. Tulsa, 1951, JD with honors, MA, 1954. Bar: Okla. 1954, U.S. Ct. Appeals (8th and 10th cirs.), U.S. Supreme Ct. 1972. Ptnr. Ungerman, Grable, Ungerman, Leiter & Unruh, Tulsa, 1957-62, Blackstock & Unruh, Tulsa, 1963-67, Unruh & Leiter, Tulsa, 1973-89; pvt. practice, Tulsa, 1968-72, 90—. Past chmn. Okla. and Tulsa County Rep. Conv., Tulsa; past bd. dirs. Tulsa Philharm. With U.S. Army, 1955-56. Named to Athletic Hall of Fame, U. Tulsa. Mem. Okla. Bar Assn., Tulsa Bar Assn., Tulsa Title and Probate Lawyers Assn., Tulsa Country Club (pres. 1972), Exchange Club (pres. Tulsa 1970), Sword and Key, Phi Gamma Kappa, Delta Theta Phi, Phi Alpha Theta, Pi Gamma Mu. Avocation: Golf. Estate planning, General practice, Real property. Home: 2927 S Quaker Ave Tulsa OK 74114-5309 Office: 9 E 4th St Ste 300 Tulsa OK 74103-5109

**UNTHANK, G. WIX,** federal judge; b. Tway, Ky., June 14, 1923; s. Green Ward and Estell (Howard) U.; m. Marilyn Elizabeth Ward, Feb. 28, 1953. J.D., U. Miami, Fla., 1950. Bar: Ky. 1950. Judge Harlan County, 1950-57; asst. U.S. atty., Lexington, Ky., 1966-69; commonwealth atty. Harlan, 1970-80; judge U.S. Dist. Ct. (ea. dist.) Ky., Pikeville, 1980-88; sr. judge U.S. Dist. Ct. (ea. dist.) Ky., London, 1988—. Served with AUS, 1940-45, ETO. Decorated Purple Heart, Bronze Star, Combat Inf. badge. Mem. ABA, Am. Judicature Soc., Ky. Bar Assn., Fla. Bar Assn. Democrat. Presbyterian. Office: Sr Judge's Chambers PO Box 5112 London KY 40745-5112

**UNTIED, WESLEY KYLE,** lawyer; b. Newark, Ohio, May 1, 1959; s. Wesley Monroe and Judy Ann (King) U.; m. Cathy Renee McIntosh, June 6, 1987; children: Vincent Michael, Elizabeth Adrienne, Alexandra Anne. BS, Ohio State U., 1982; JD, Capital U., 1985. Bar: Ohio 1985, U.S. Dist. Ct. (so. dist.) Ohio 1987, U.S. Supreme Ct. 1995. Assoc. Schaller, Campbell & Untied, Newark, 1985-91, ptnr., 1992—. Mem. Licking County Rep. Exec. Com., Newark, 1988—, Licking County Bd. Elections, 1992—; various offices Centenary United Meth. Ch., 1985—. Named Outstanding Young Profl., Ohio State U. Coll. Agr., 1994. Mem. Ohio State U. Alumni Assn. (adv. coun. 1995—), Newark Area C. of C. (bd. dirs. 1998—), Ducks Unltd., Masons. Probate, Real property, General practice. Office: Schaller Campbell & Untied 32 N Park Pl Newark OH 43055-5517

**UPTON, ARTHUR EDWARD,** lawyer; b. N.Y.C., Aug. 30, 1934; s. Arthur Joseph and Helene Clara (Heblich) U.; m. Patricia Ann Fleming, Aug. 17, 1957; children: Kevin, Brian, Kerry, Maureen. BS in Acctg., Fordham U., 1956; JD, St. John's U., N.Y.C., 1965. Bar: N.Y. 1967, U.S. Dist. Ct. (ea. and so. dist.) 1967, U.S. Tax Ct. 1967. Pvt. practice Syosset, N.Y., 1974-82, 87-91; ptnr. Golden, Upton & Wexler, Lynbrook, N.Y., 1982-87; sr. ptnr. Upton, Cohen & Slamowitz, Syosset, 1991—. Bd. dirs. St. Mary's Children and Family Ctr., Syosset, 1993—; bd. overseers Lynn U., Boca Raton, Fla., 1994—. Mem. ABA, N.Y. State Bar Assn., Nassau County Bar Assn., K.C. (past grand knight). Republican. Roman Catholic. Avocations: theatre, reading, travel, sports. Consumer commercial, Real property, Probate. Home: 4 Hunt Dr Jericho NY 11753-1142 Office: Upton Cohen & Slamowitz 485 Underhill Blvd Ste 103 Syosset NY 11791-3433

**URAM, GERALD ROBERT,** lawyer; b. Newark, July 11, 1941; s. Arthur George and Mildred (Stein) U.; m. Melissa Gordon, May 27, 1995; children: Michael, Alison, Carolyn Gordon Lewis. BA, Dartmouth Coll., 1963; LLB, Yale U., 1967. Bar: N.Y. 1967. Assoc. Paul, Weiss, Rifkind, Wharton & Garrison, N.Y.C., 1967-74; v.p., corp. counsel Prudential Bldg. Maintenance Corp., N.Y.C., 1974; ptnr. Davis & Gilbert, N.Y.C., 1974—; lectr. N.Y. Law Sch. Bd. dirs. St. Francis Friends of Poor, Inc. Mem. ABA, N.Y. State Bar Assn., Assn. Bar City of N.Y. Contbr. to profl. publs. Landlord-tenant, Real property. Office: 1740 Broadway Fl 3 New York NY 10019-4315

**URANGA, JOSE NAVARETTE,** lawyer, corporate; b. El Paso, Tex., Sept. 30, 1946; s. Jose and Lucia (Navarette) U.; m. Joan Torgersen, Aug. 7, 1971; children: Todd J., David E., Lauren A. BA, N.Mex. State U., 1969; MA, U. Tex., 1976; JD, Georgetown U., 1972. Bar: Tex. 1974, D.C. 1974, U.S. Supreme Ct. 1978, U.S. Ct. Appeals (D.C. cir.) 1979, U.S. Dist. Ct. D.C. 1979, Calif. 1991. Asst. staff judge advocate U.S. Army Judge Advocate Gen.'s Corps, San Antonio, 1974-77; asst. atty. gen. Office Tex. Atty. Gen., San Antonio, 1978-79; trial atty. U.S. Dept. Justice, Land & Natural Resources Div., Washington, 1979-80; spl. asst. to U.S. atty. gen. U.S. Dept. Justice, Washington, 1980-81; sr. counsel Cummins Engine Co., Inc., Columbus, Ind., 1981-84; dir. environ., health & safety Diamond Shamrock Chems. Corp., Dallas, 1984-87; asst. gen. counsel Rockwell Internat., Dallas, 1987-89; v.p. environ. & regulatory affairs Pioneer Chlor Alkali Co., Houston, 1989-90; sr. counsel Aerojet Gen. Corp., Sacramento, Calif., 1990—. Asst. scoutmaster Troop 1377 Boy Scouts Am., Kingwood, Tex., 1989—; pro tem judge Sacramento County Small Claims Ct., 1995—. Recipient Army Commendation Medal, 1977. Mem. ABA, Tex. State Bar Assn., Calif. State Bar Assn., Washington Bar Assn. Avocations: coin collecting, Am. polit. items, photography. Environmental, General corporate. Office: Aerojet General Corp PO Box 13222 Sacramento CA 95813-6000

**URBAN, CHARLES J.,** lawyer; b. Urbana, Ill., Aug. 8, 1963; s. Raymond J. and Nancy K. Urban; children: Charles J. II, Joshua A. BS, U. Ill., 1985; JD, So. Ill. U., 1988. Bar: Ill. 1989, U.S. Dist. Ct. (ctrl. and no. dists.) Ill. Assoc. Goldsworthy Fifield & Hasselberg, Peoria, Ill., 1988-96; pntr. Hasselberg, Williams, Grebe & Snodgrass, Peoria, 1997—. Bd. dirs. ctrl. Ill. divsn. March of Dimes, Peoria, 1991-96. Mem. Ill. Bar Assn., Peoria County Bar Assn., Am. Inns of Ct. Family and matrimonial, General civil litigation, Bankruptcy. Office: Hasselberg Williams Grebe & Snodgrass 124 SW Adams St Ste 360 Peoria IL 61602-1320

**URBAN, DONALD WAYNE,** lawyer; b. Belleville, Ill., Oct. 9, 1953; s. Andrew Anthony and Eileen Marie (Tibbitt) U.; m. Mary Beth Evans, June 9, 1979 (div. Oct. 1994); m. Georgianna Dowling, Feb. 2, 1995; 1 child, Andrew Jared. BA, So. Ill. U., 1976; JD, Washington U., 1979. Assoc. Sprague & Sprague, Belleville, 1979-96; ptnr. Sprague & Urban, Belleville, 1996—; author, lectr. Ill. Inst. for CLE, Springfield. Author: Blasting & Subsidence Illinois Institute for Continuing Legal Education Handbook, 1983, vol. 2, 1986, vol. 3, 1989. Pres. Looking Glass Playhouse, Lebanon, Ill., 1988-90, 95-97; spokesman St. Clair County Bicentennial, Belleville, 1989. Mem. Gamma Theta Upsilon. Democrat. Avocation: community theatre. Personal injury, Bankruptcy, Estate planning. Home: 815 Belleville St Lebanon IL 62254-1312 Office: Sprague & Urban 26 E Washington St Belleville IL 62220-2101

**URBAN, LISA BREIER,** lawyer; b. Queens, N.Y., Apr. 28, 1964. BA, SUNY, Stonybrook, 1985; JD, Fordham U., 1990. Bar: N.Y. 1991. Mng. ptnr. Breier, Deutschmeister & Urban, P.C., N.Y.C., 1991—. E-mail: lawbdu@aol.com. Real property, Landlord-tenant, Contracts commercial. Office: Breier Deutschmeister & Urban PC 299 Broadway Ste 702 New York NY 10007-1901

**URBANSKI, STEPHEN KARL,** lawyer; b. Kingston, Pa., Jan. 29, 1964; s. Edward Kamil Urbanski and Bernadine Helen Mros; m. Lori Ann Duda, June 17, 1995 (div. Oct. 1996); m. Lisa Ann Hearst, July 19, 1998; children: Patricia, Kathleen. BA, Wilkes U., 1985; JD, Temple U., 1988. Bar: Pa. 1988, N.J. 1990. Asst. pub. defender Office of Luzerne County Public Defender, Wilkes-Barre, Pa., 1989; assoc. Anapol Schwartz Weiss & Schwartz, Phila., 1990, Leonard Zack and Assoc., Phila., 1991; pvt. practice Wilkes-Barre, 1992-95; sr. ptnr. Haggerty & Urbanski, Kingston, Pa., 1995—; lectr. Coll. Misericordia, Dallas, Pa., 1992, Marywood U., Scranton, Pa., 1992, 93. Editor (periodical) Classless Action, 1987-88; author: One Vote Can't Make a Difference, 1998. Bd. dirs. Cultural Heritage Coun., Kingston, 1993—; mem. Kingston Republican Com., 1998—; councilman Municipality of Kingston, 1998—. With U.S. Army, 1983-85. Roman Catholic. Criminal, Family and matrimonial. Home: 82 3d Ave Kingston PA 18704-5724 Office: Haggerty & Urbanski 840 W Market St Kingston PA 18704-3337

**URBINA, RICARDO M.,** judge; b. 1946. BA, Georgetown U., 1967, JD, 1970. Trial atty. Pub. Defender Svc. for D.C., 1970-72; prin. Urbina & Libby, Washington, 1972-73, Law Office of Ricardo M. Urbina, Washington, 1973-74; prof. law, dir. criminal justice program Howard U., Washington, 1974-81; assoc. judge D.C. Superior Ct., 1981-94; judge U.S. Dist. Ct. D.C., 1994—; adj. prof. Antioch Sch. Law, 1976, Georgetown U. Law Ctr., Washington, 1982, George Washington U. Nat. Law Ctr., Washington, 1993—; instr. Nat. Inst. Trial Advocacy, 1976, 78; vis. instr. trial advocacy Howard Law Sch., 1996—. Mem. ABA, D.C. Hispanic Bar Assn., Nat. Bar Assn., Hispanic Nat. Bar Assn., Washington Bar Assn., D.C. Bar Assn., Women's Bar Assn., Fahy Inns of Ct. (emeritus), Counsellors of Washington D.C., Coun. for Ct. Excellence, Phi Delta Phi. Office: US Dist Ct DC US Courthouse Rm 4311 333 Constitution Ave NW Washington DC 20001-2802

**URBOM, WARREN KEITH,** federal judge; b. Atlanta, Nebr., Dec. 17, 1925; s. Clarence Andrew and Anna Myrl (Irelan) U.; m. Joyce Marie Crawford, Aug. 19, 1951; children: Kim Marie, Randall Crawford, Allison Lee, Joy Renee. AB with highest distinction, Nebr. Wesleyan U., 1950, LLD (hon.), 1984; JD with distinction, U. Mich., 1953. Bar: Nebr. 1953. Mem. firm Baylor, Evnen, Baylor, Urbom, & Curtiss, Lincoln, Nebr., 1953-70; judge U.S. Dist. Ct. Nebr., 1970—; chief judge U.S. Dist. Ct. Dist. Nebr., 1972-86, sr. judge, 1991—; mem. com. on practice and procedure Nebr. Supreme Ct., 1965-95; mem. subcom. on fed. jurisdiction Jud. Conf. U.S., 1975-83; adj. instr. trial advocacy U. Nebr. Coll. Law, 1979-90; bd. dirs. Fed. Jud. Ctr., 1982-86; chmn. com. on orientation newly apptd. dist. judges Fed. Jud. Ctr., 1986-89; mem. 8th Cir. Com. on Model Criminal and Civil Jury Instrns., 1983—; mem. adv. com. on alternative sentences U.S. Sentencing Com., 1989-91. Contbr. articles to profl. jours. Trustee St. Paul Sch. Theology, Kansas City, Mo., 1986-89; active United Methodist Ch. (bd. mgrs., bd. global ministries 1972-76, gen. com. on status and role of women, 1988-96, gen. conf. 1972, 76, 80, 88, 92, 96); pres. Lincoln YMCA, 1965-67; bd. govs. Nebr. Wesleyan U., chmn. 1975-80. With AUS, 1944-46. Recipient Medal of Honor, Nebr. Wesleyan U. Alumni Assn., 1983. Fellow Am. Coll. Trial Lawyers; mem. ABA, Nebr. Bar Assn. (ho. of dels. 1966-70, Outstanding Legal Educator award 1990), Lincoln Bar Assn. (Liberty Bell award 1993, pres. 1968-69), Kiwanis (Disting. Svc. award 1993), Masons (33 deg.), Am. Inns of Ct. (Lewis F. Powell Jr. award for Professionalism and Ethics 1995). Methodist. Home: 4421 Ridgeview Dr Lincoln NE 68516-1516 Office: US Dist Ct 586 Fed Bldg 100 Centennial Mall N Lincoln NE 68508-3859

**URCIS, JOSE,** lawyer; b. Havana, Cuba, Aug. 20, 1951; s. Rafael Urcis and Amalia Apel; m. Marsha R. Baucom, Dec. 31, 1978 (div. June 1984); children: Rafael, Julia. BA, CCNY, 1973; JD, U. Pa., 1976. Bar: Calif. 1976, U.S. Dist. Ct. (cen. dist.) Calif. 1977. Atty. Law Office of Bohm & Urcis, Santa Ana, Calif., 1977-82; pvt. practice Santa Ana, 1982—. Personal injury. Office: 920 W 17th St Ste A Santa Ana CA 92706-3576

**URELIUS, SHAWN RENEA,** lawyer; b. Ft. Dodge, Iowa, Feb. 13, 1963; d. Norman Dean and Ruby Lee Urelius. BA summa cum laude, N.E. Mo. State U., Kirksville, 1985, BS summa cum laude, 1985; JD, U. Va., 1988. Bar: Tex. 1988, D.C. 1990, Va. 1991. Assoc. Haynes and Boone, Dallas, 1988-91, McSweeney, Burtch & Crump, Richmond, Va., 1991-97; asst. gen. counsel Hamilton Beach/Proctor Silex, Inc., Richmond, 1997—. Mem. ABA, Tex. State Bar Assn., D.C. Bar Assn., Va. Bar Assn. General civil litigation, General corporate, Environmental. Office: Hamilton Beach Proctor-Silex Inc 4421 Waterfront Dr Glen Allen VA 23060-3375

**URIS, ALAN M.,** lawyer; b. N.Y.C., Apr. 4, 1934; m. Sheila Jones, June 24, 1970; 1 child, Genevieve Uris. BA, Dartmouth Coll., 1955; LLB, NYU, 1958. Bar: Vt. 1970, N.Y. 1959. Atty. Uris & Lisa, N.Y.C., 1965-70, Uris & Hutton, Westfield, Vt., 1970-84; asst. dist. atty. Dist. Atty.'s Office Queens County, 1984-87; sole practice N.Y.C., 1987-94; of counsel DeVagno, Borchert, Levine & LaSpina, Whitestone, N.Y., 1994—; town atty. Warren, Vt. Mem. Queens County Bar Assn., Queens County Asst. Dist. Attys. Assn. Democrat. Jewish. Personal injury. Home: 13-29 Michael Pl Bayside NY 11361 Office: DeVagno Borchert Levine & LaSpina 19-02 Whitestone Expy White Stone NY 11357-3099

**URIS, HARVEY R.,** lawyer; b. Paterson, N.J., 1954. BA cum laude, Boston U., 1976, JD cum laude, 1979. Bar: N.Y. 1980. Ptnr. Skadden, Arps, Slate, Meagher & Flom LLP, N.Y.C. Office: Skadden Arps Slate Meagher & Flom LLP 919 3rd Ave New York NY 10022-3902

**UROWSKY, RICHARD J.,** lawyer; b. N.Y.C., June 28, 1946; s. Jacob and Anne (Granick) U. BA, Yale U., 1967, JD, 1972; BPhil, Oxford U., Eng., 1970. Bar: N.Y. 1973, U.S. Dist. Ct. (so. dist.) N.Y. 1973, U.S. Ct. Appeals (2d cir.) 1973, U.S. Supreme Ct. 1977. Law clk. to Justice Reed U.S. Supreme Ct., Washington, 1972-73; assoc. Sullivan & Cromwell, N.Y.C., 1973-80, ptnr., 1980—. Mem. ABA, Assn. of the Bar of the City of N.Y., Fed. Bar Coun., N.Y. County Lawyers Assn., Yale Club, Links, Lyford Cay Club. Federal civil litigation, Antitrust, Securities. Office: Sullivan & Cromwell 125 Broad St Fl 28 New York NY 10004-2489

**URQUHART, STEPHEN E.,** lawyer; b. Quincy, Mass., Mar. 2, 1949; s. Raymond Miles and M. Eileen (MacDonald) U.; m. Katherine Driscoll, Mar. 15, 1970; 1 child, Stephen M. AB, Boston Coll., 1976, JD, 1979. Bar: Mass. 1979, U.S. Dist. Ct. Mass. 1980. Legis. aide Mass. Ho. of Reps., Boston, 1976; counsel B.C. Legal Assistance Bur., Waltham, Mass., 1976-79; assoc. Law Offices of Robert J. Ladd (formerly Law Offices of Roland I. Wood), North Andover, Mass., 1980-88, Law Offices Nicholas Macaronis, Lowell, Mass., 1988-91, Law Offices Ernest W. Piper, Jr., Boston, 1991—. Precinct capt. Edward M. Kennedy for Senator, Mass. 1979-80; campaign worker various Dem. candidates. Recipient cert. of merit United World Federalists, 1974. Mem. ABA, Mass. Bar Assn., Mass. Acad. Trial Attys., Am. Arbitration Assn., Internat. Platform Assn., Assn. Trial Lawyers Am., Phi Beta Kappa, Phi Delta Phi. Methodist. Club: Clan Urquhart (Va.). Avocations: model shipbuilding, Scottish history and music, reading, travel. State civil litigation, Insurance, Personal injury. Home: PO Box 610 Danville NH 03819-0610 Office: 256 Friend St Boston MA 02114-1801

**URQUIA, RAFAEL, II,** lawyer; b. San Salvador, El Salvador, May 11, 1944; came to U.S., 1950; s. M. Rafael and Luz (Bolaños) U.; m. Thelma Louise Faught; 1 child, Alexandra. BS, Georgetown U., 1966, JD, 1969; LD, U. Madrid, 1972. Bar: N.Y. 1975, U.S. Ct. Appeals (2d cir.) 1975. Sr. assoc. Curtis, Mallet-Prevost, Colt & Mosle, N.Y.C., 1972-78; internat. counsel Internat. Multifoods Corp., Mpls., 1979-82; pvt. practice N.Y.C., 1983-87; ptnr. Thomas Re & Ptnrs., N.Y.C., 1987-90, Fox & Horan, N.Y.C., 1990—. Author book rev. Speaker Rep. Presdl. Campaign, 1988. Fellow OAS, 1967, Inst. Spanish Culture, 1970. Mem. ABA, Assn. of Bar of City of N.Y. (mem. inter.-Am. affairs com. 1984-87). Roman Catholic. Avocations: rare books, art. Private international, General corporate, Contracts commercial. Home: 200 E 66th St D-1802 New York NY 10021-6728 Office: Fox & Horan 1 Broadway Fl 7 New York NY 10004-1048

**URSU, JOHN JOSEPH,** lawyer; b. 1939. BA, U. Mich., 1962, JD, 1965. Bar: Mich. 1966, Ky. 1970, Minn. 1972. Trial atty. FTC, 1965-67; staff mem. Pres.'s Commn. on Civil Disorders, 1967; advisor to commr. FTC, 1968-69; legal counsel GE, 1969-72; divsn. atty. 3M, 1972-74, sr. atty., 1974-76, assoc. counsel, 1976-81, asst. gen. counsel, 1981-86, assoc. gen. counsel, 1986-90, dep. gen. counsel, 1990-92, gen. counsel, 1992-93; v.p. legal affairs & gen. counsel 3M, St. Paul, 1993-96, sr. v.p. legal affairs and gen. counsel, 1997—; adj. faculty William Mitchell Coll. Law, 1978-82. General corporate, Product liability, Antitrust. Office: 3M Gen Offices 3 M Ctr # 220-14w7 Saint Paul MN 55144-0001

**USATINE, WARREN ALAN,** lawyer; b. Bklyn., June 26, 1970; s. Stewart L. and Sandra Usatine. BA, U. Va., 1992; JD, U. Pa., 1995. Bar: N.J. 1995, U.S. Dist. Ct. N.J., 1995, U.S. Supreme Ct. 1995. Atty. Cole, Schotz, Meisel, Forman & Leonard, P.A., Hackensack, N.J., 1995—. Contbr. articles to profl. jours. Avocations: golf, baseball, classical and jazz music. Federal civil litigation, State civil litigation, Bankruptcy. Office: Cole Schotz Meisel Forman & Leonard PA 25 Main St Hackensack NJ 07601-7015

**USSERY, ALBERT TRAVIS,** lawyer, investment company executive; b. Gulfport, Miss., Mar. 12, 1928; s. Walter Travis and Rosamond (Sears) U.; m. Margaret Grosvenor Paine, Nov. 22, 1950; children: Margaret Rosamond, John Travis, Marilyn Ann, Meredith Lee. AB, Washington U., St. Louis, 1950; LLB, U. N.Mex., 1951, JD, 1968; LLM, Georgetown U., 1955. Bar: N.Mex. 1951. Ptnr. Gallagher and Ussery, Albuquerque, 1951-53, Threet, Ussery & Threet, Albuquerque, 1957-60; assoc. with Alfred H. McRae, Albuquerque, 1961-63; ptnr. McRae, Ussery, Mims, Ortega & Kitts, Albuquerque, 1964-65; chmn. Am. Bank Commerce, 1966-70, pres., 1967-70; ptnr. Ussery, Burciaga & Parrish, Albuquerque, 1969-79; pres. Ussery & Parrish, P.A., Albuquerque, 1980—; spl. counsel to Albuquerque on water law, 1956-66; chmn. Rio Grande Valley Bank, Albuquerque, 1972-83, Bank of S.W., 1980-83; lectr. mil. law U. N.Mex., 1956, instr. corp. fin., 1956-57, lectr. bus. law, 1960-61; bd. dirs. 1st City Investment Brokers, Inc., 1983-85, Lovelace Med. Systems and Techs., Inc., 1983-84. Chmn. water adv. com. Albuquerque Indsl. Devel. Svc., 1960-66; vice chmn. N.Mex. Coun. on Econ. Edn., 1969-74; mem. N.Mex. Regional Export Expansion Council, 1969-74, mem. Albuquerque Armed Forces Adv. Assn., 1977—. Trustee Village Los Ranchos de Albuquerque, 1970-72; chmn. adv. bd. Lovelace-Bataan Med. Ctr., 1976-78; trustee Lovelace Med. Found., 1978-96, vice chmn., 1988-96; trustee Lovelace Respiratory Rsch. Inst., 1996—, chmn., 1966—; bd. dirs. Goodwill Industries N.Mex., 1957-65, Albuquerque Travelers Assistance, 1956-66, Family Consultation Svc., 1961-64, Albuquerque Symphony Assn., 1964-68, Hispanic Culture Found., 1983-92, Lovelace Health Plan Inc., 1985-89; bd. dirs. N.Mex. Arthritis Found., 1969-74, pres., 1971. Mem. Am., Fed., Albuquerque (treas. 1957-60) bar assns., State Bar N.Mex., Estate Planning Coun. Albuquerque (pres. 1962), N.Mex. Zool. Soc. (dir., pres. 1977-78), Am. Legion (comdr. 1962-63), Lawyers Club. (pres. 1983-84). Lodge: Kiwanis (dir. 1957-60). General corporate, Banking, Real property. Home: 37 Chaco Loop Sandia Park NM 87047-8505 Office: Ussery & Parrish PA 200 Rio Grande Valley Bldg 501 Tijeras Ave NW Albuquerque NM 87102-3174

**USSERY, HARRY MACRAE,** investor, lawyer; b. Rockingham, N.C., Jan. 27, 1920; s. Robert Roy and Maggie Estelle (MacRae) U.; m. Olive Dual Simmons, Mar. 19, 1949. AA, Wake Forest U., 1947; JD, George Washington U., 1950. Bar: D.C. 1950. Assoc. firm Geiger & Harmel, Washington, 1950-52; ptnr. firm McNeill & Ussery, Washington, 1952-53; gen. counsel, dir. Harry R. Byers, Inc., Engring. and Constrn. Power Plants, Washington and Denver, 1953-59; procurement counsel Martin Marieta Corp., Denver, 1959-62; authorized agt. RCA, Camden N.J., 1962-69; staff counsel, mgr. internat. subcontract ops. Burns & Roe Constrn. Corp., Paramus, N.J., 1969-74; staff counsel Burns & Roe Indsl. Svcs. Corp., 1975-78; asst. to pres., Burns & Roe Svcs. Corp., Oradell, N.J., 1978-81; investor, Santa Fe, 1981—; broker Collector Cars, 1990—; founder, chmn. Assn. Mortgage Investors, Inc., 1983-86; chmn. Santa Fe Mortgage Investments, Inc., 1984-86; spl. city atty for annexations-contracts, Santa Fe, 1985-87; editor Investors Voice, 1983-86; chief moderator, dir., Dist. Roundtable, Sta. WWDC, Washington, 1950-53; cons., estate planning counsel Tom Lovell Trust, 1986—. Served with USAAF, 1941-45. Recipient Cmty. Chest campaign awards, 1951, 52. Mem. ABA, Am. Judicature Soc., Nat. Contract Mgmt. Assn., D.C. Bar Assn. (exec. coun. Jr. bar sect. 1954-56), George Washington U. Law Assn., Wake Forest U. Alumni Assn., Geneal. Soc. Santa Fe (state commr.), Council Scottish Clans Assns., St. Andrew's Soc., Clan MacRae Soc., Scottish Am. Mil. Soc., Sons Am. Revolution (pres. Santa Fe chpt. 1995-98, pres. N.Mex. Soc. 1997-98), Clan Donald and Assoc. Scots N.Mex., Delta Theta Phi. Republican. Presbyterian. Club: Santa Fe Vintage Car (pres., editor newsletter 1985-94). Author: The Origin of the Surname of Ussery, 1983 (founder-pres. The House of Usser, Internat., a Norman-Celtic family soc. 1993—); contbr. articles to various publs. and hist. socs. Address: 149 Tano Rd Santa Fe NM 87501-7557

**UTRATA, CARL IGNATIUS,** corporate counsel, corporate executive; b. Trnava, Slovak Republic, Sept. 23, 1940; came to U.S., 1949, naturalized, 1955; s. Joseph and Irma Mary Utrata; m. Mary Ann M. Nypaver, June 17, 1972; children: Edward Joseph, Stephanie Ann. BS in Fgn. Service, Georgetown U., 1963; JD, Case Western Res. U., 1971. Bar: Ohio 1972, U.S. Dist. Ct. (no. dist.) Ohio 1983, U.S. Ct. Appeals (6th cir.) 1987. Indsl. rels. staff asst. Republic Steel Corp., Buffalo, 1967-68; safety-labor supr. Republic Steel Corp., Cleve., 1969-84, coord., mgr. equal employment opportunity, 1972-79, corp. dir. equal employment opportunity, 1979-84; pvt. practice, 1985-91; corp. counsel ISK Bioscis. Corp., Mentor, Ohio, 1991-98; lectr. seminars; tng. media producer. Pres. Lakewood Neighbors Assn., Ohio, 1974, libr. levy chmn., 1975, mem. zoning initiative com., 1976-78; trustee Coun. on Human Rels., Cleve., 1982-88, pres., 1985-88; assoc. v.p. United Way Svcs., Cleve., 1984-85; trustee legal Aid Soc. Cleve., 1986-88; cofounder, pres. bus., industry and edn. con. Urban League Cleve., 1978-79. With U.S. Army, 1963-65, ETO. Mem. ABA (pesticide subcom. 1995-98), Am. Crop Protection Assn. (law com. 1995-98), Cleve. Employers Equal Opportunity Assn. (co-founder, chmn. 1982, pres.' cup 1983). General corporate, Labor, Administrative and regulatory. Home and Office: 1506 Arthur Ave Cleveland OH 44107-3804

**UTRECHT, JAMES DAVID,** lawyer; b. Camp Polk, La., May 23, 1952; s. James C. and Susan (McDevitt) U.; married; children: Ann Elizabeth, Claire Susan. BBA, U. Cin., 1974, JD, 1977. Bar: Ohio 1977. Ptnr. Utrecht Law Offices, Troy, Ohio, 1977—; asst. law dir. City of Troy, 1984—. Mem. ABA, Ohio Bar Assn., Ohio State Bar Assn., Miami County Bar Assn., Troy Area C. of C. (bd. dirs. 1986—), Elks. Republican. Roman Catholic. Banking, General practice, Personal injury. Home: 570 Brookwood Dr Troy OH 45373-4373 Office: Utrecht Law Offices 12 Plum St Troy OH 45373-3250

**UTRECHT, PAUL F.,** lawyer; b. The Hague, The Netherlands, Aug. 31, 1960; s. Robert Packard and Arnolda (Cohen) U. BA, Claremont McKenna Coll., 1980; student, Sorbonne, Paris, 1980; JD, U. Calif., Berkeley, 1983. Bar: Calif. 1985, U.S. Ct. Appeals (9th cir.) 1986, U.S. Supreme Ct. 1990. Law clk. to Judge M. Joseph Blumenfeld U.S. Dist. Ct., Hartford, Conn.,

1983-84; assoc. Pillsbury Madison & Sutro, San Francisco, 1984-87, Law Offices of S.G. Archibald, Paris, 1987; pvt. practice San Francisco, 1987—. Contbr.: Rule 11 and Other Sanctions, 1986. General civil litigation, Probate, Appellate. Office: 235 Montgomery St Ste 810 San Francisco CA 94104-2906

**UTTER, ROBERT FRENCH,** retired state supreme court justice; b. Seattle, June 19, 1930; s. John and Besse (French) U.; m. Elizabeth J. Stevenson, Dec. 28, 1953; children: Kimberly, Kirk, John. BS, U. Wash., 1952; LLB, 1954. Bar: Wash. 1954. Pros. atty. King County, Wash., 1955-57; individual practice law Seattle, 1957-59; ct. commr. King County Superior Ct., 1959-64, judge, 1964-69; judge Wash. State Ct. Appeals, 1969-71; judge Wash. State Supreme Ct., 1971-95, chief justice, 1979-81; ret., 1995; lectr. in field, leader comparative law tour People's Republic of China, 1986, 87, 88, 91, USSR, 1989, Republic of South Africa, 1997, Ukraine, Hungarian and Czech Republic, 1998; adj. prof. constl. law U. Puget Sound, 1987, 88, 89, 90, 91, 92, 93, 94; cons. CEELI, 1991, 93—, USIA, 1992; visitor to Kazakhstan, Kyrgystan Judiciary, 1993, 94, 95, 96, Outer Mangolia, 1997; lectr. to Albanian Judiciary, 1994, 95. Editor books on real property and appellate practice. Pres., founder Big Brother Assn., Seattle, 1955-67; pres., founder Job Therapy Inc., 1963-71; mem. exec. com. Conf. of Chief Justices, 1979-80, 81-86; pres. Thurston County Big Bros./Big Sisters, 1984; lectr. Soviet Acad. Moscow, 1991; USIA visitor to comment on jud. system, Latvia, 1992, Kazakstan, 1993-94; trustee Linfield Coll. Named Alumnus of Yr., Linfield Coll., 1973, Disting. Jud. Scholar, U. Ind., 1987, Judge of Yr., Wash. State Trial Lawyers, 1989, Outstanding Judge, Wash. State Bar Assn., 1990, Outstanding Judge, Seattle-King County Bar Assn., 1992, Conder-Faulkner lectr. U. Wash. Sch. Law, 1995, Disting. Alumnus Sch. Law U. Wash., 1995. Fellow Chartered Inst. Arbitrators; mem. ABA (commentator on proposed constns. of Albania, Bulgaria, Romania, Russia, Lithuania, Azerbaijan, Uzbekistan, Byelarus, Kazakhstan & Ukraine), Am. Judicature Soc. (Herbert Harley award 1983, Justice award 1998, sec. 1987—, chmn. bd. dirs., mem. exec. com.), Order of Coif. Baptist.

**VACCA, ANTHONY,** lawyer; b. Graniteville, R.I., Sept. 28, 1925; s. Charles and Jennie V.; m. Rose Catherine, Ovt. 6, 1951; children: Frances Jane, Carolyn Mary. PhB, Providence Coll., 1948; JD, Northeastern U., 1951. Bar: R.I. 1951, U.S. Dist. Ct. R.I., 1952, U.S. Supreme Ct. 1979. Instr. U. R.I. Coll. Law, 1961-62; judge Probate Ct., Smithfield, R.I., 1969-77; atty. pvt. practice, 1977—. Del. R.I. Constitutional Conv., 1964-69; mem. Spl. Legis. Commn. Probate Judges, 1975; ration com. Town of Smithfield, 1961, charter commn., 1974, price stabilization bd., 1976. With USN, 1943-45. Fellow Am. Coll. Probate Coun.; mem. R.I. Bar Assn. (exec. com. 1967-68, chmn. com. continuing legal edn. 1970, mem. ho. of dels. 1974, treas. 1975-76, sec. 1976-77, com. superior ct. bench=bar 1983). Independent. Roman Catholic. Probate, Personal injury. Home: 43 Maplecrest Dr Greenville RI 02828-2912 Office: 596 Newport Ave Pawtucket RI 02861-3237

**VACCARO, CHARLES G.,** federal judge; b. Sept. 15, 1940; married. BS, Calif. State U., 1962; MS, Fla. State U., 1963; JD, U. Colo., 1973. Bar: Ark. 1974, U.S. Dist. Ct. (ea. and we. dists.) Ark. 1978, U.S. Supreme Ct. 1978, Fla. 1989. Engr. Bethlehem (Pa.) Steel Corp.; tchr. in U.S. and France, CEO of wood products mfg. co.; tech. projects coord. U.S. Govt., Washington; polit/econs. officer U.S. Govt., Nigeria; sr. dist. advisor U.S. Fgn. Svc., Vietnam; dep. dist. atty.; U.S. Magistrate judge U.S. We. Dist. Ct., Hot Springs Nat. Park, Ark. Home: 16323 Willowpark Dr Tomball TX 77375-9013

**VACCO, DENNIS C.,** lawyer; b. Buffalo, Aug. 16, 1952; s. Carmen A. and Mildred V.; m. Kelly McIlroy; children: Alex, Connor. BA, Colgate U., 1974; JD, SUNY, Buffalo, 1978. Bar: N.Y. 1978, Fed. Ct. 1978, 82. Asst. dist. atty. Office of Erie County Dist. Atty., Buffalo, 1978-82, chief G.J. bureau, 1982-88; U.S. Atty. We. Dist. N.Y. Buffalo, 1988-93; atty. gen. State of New York, Albany, 1993-98; v.p. for govtl. affairs Waste Mgmt. Inc., 1998—; chmn. Atty. Gen.'s Environ. Subcom., Atty. Gen.'s Subcom. on Organized Crime and Violent Crime; mem. Nat. Environ. Enforcement Coun. Co-chair Erie County Community Commn. on Alcohol and Substance Abuse; bd. dirs. United Way of Erie County. Recipient Environ. Enforcement Leadership award Atty. Gen. Dept. of Justice, Washington, 1991. Mem. N.Y. State Bar Assn., Erie County Bar Assn., Nat. Dist. Attys. Assn., N.Y. State Dist. Attys. Assn., NCCJ, Hamburg Devel. Corp., 100 Club of Buffalo, U. Buffalo Law Alumni Assn. (bd. dirs.). Republican. Roman Catholic. Avocations: travel, sports.

**VACHIER, CAROLINE,** lawyer. BA, Montclair State Coll., 1987; JD, Rutgers U. Sch. Law, 1990. Law clk. State of N.J. Office Adminstrv. Law, Newark, 1990-91; dep. atty. gen. State of N.J. Divsn. Law, Newark, 1991—; chair cmty. adv. bd. Montclair State U., Upper Montclair, N.J., 1993—. Office: State of New Jersey Divsn Law 124 Halsey St Fl 5 Newark NJ 07102-3017

**VACHSS, ANDREW HENRY,** lawyer, author, juvenile justice and child abuse consultant; b. N.Y.C., Oct. 19, 1942; s. Bernard and Geraldine (Mattus) V. BA, Case Western Res. U., 1965; JD magna cum laude, New Engl. Sch. Law, 1975. Bar: N.Y. 1976, U.S. Dist. Ct. (so. and ea. dists.) N.Y. 1976. Program rep. USPHS, Ohio, 1965-66; unit supr N.Y.C. Dept. Social Svcs., 1966-69; urban coord. Community Devel. Found., Norwalk, Conn., 1969-70; dir. Uptown Community Orgn., Chgo., 1970-71; dep. dir. Medfield (Mass.)-Norfolk Prison Project, 1971-72; dir. intensive treatment unit ANDROS II, Roslindale, Mass., 1972-73; project dir. Mass. Dept. Youth Svcs., Boston, 1972-73; dir. Juvenile Justice Planning Project, N.Y.C., 1975-85; pvt. practice N.Y.C., 1976—; organizer, coord. Calumet (Ind.) Community Congress, 1970; bd. dirs. Libra Inc., Cambridge, Mass., Advocacy Assocs., N.Y. and N.J.; adj. prof. Coll. New Resources, N.Y.C., 1980-81; lectr. trainer, speaker to numerous orgns.; cons. on juvenile justice and child abuse to numerous orgns., 1971—. Author: The Life-Style Violent Juvenile: The Secure Treatment Approach, 1979, (novels) Flood, 1985, Strega, 1987, Blue Belle, 1988, Hard Candy, 1989, Blossom, 1990, Sacrifice, 1991, Shella, 1993, Another Chance To Get It Right, 1995, Down in the Zero, 1994, Footsteps of the Hawk, 1995, Batman: The Ultimate Evil, 1995, False Allegations, 1996, Safe House, 1998, Choice of Evil, 1999 (graphic novels) Predator: Race War, 1995, Hard Looks, 1996, (collected short stories) Born Bad, 1994, Everybody Pays, 1999; editor-in-chief New Eng. Law Rev., 1974-75; contbg. editor Parade; contbr. articles to legal publs. Bd. of counselors, Civitas Childtrauma Programs, Baylor Coll. of Medicine; mem. expert adv. panel on catastrophic child abuse N.Y. State Office of Mental Health. Recipient Grand Prix de Lit. Policiére, 1988, Falcon award Maltese Falcon Soc. Japan, 1988, Deutschen Krimi Preis, Die Jury des Bochumer Krimi Archivs, 1989; Indsl. Area Found. Tng. Inst. fellow, 1970-71, John Hay Whitney Found. fellow, 1976-77. Mem. Nat. Assn. Counsel for Children, Am. Profl. Soc. on Abuse of Children, PEN, Writers Guild of Am. E-mail: www.vachss.com. Juvenile. Office: Ste 2805 420 Lexington Ave New York NY 10170-2899

**VADEN, FRANK SAMUEL, III,** lawyer, engineer; b. San Antonio, Nov. 13, 1934; s. Frank Samuel Jr. and Helen Alyne (Roberts) V.; m. Caroline Chittenden Gerdes, Feb. 20, 1960; children: Christina Louise (Mrs. Eugene Linton), Olivia Anne (Mrs. Warren Augenstein), Cecilia Claire (Mrs. Scott Johnson). BSEE and BS in Indsl. Engring., Tex. A&M U., 1957; JD, So. Meth. U., 1963. Bar: Tex. 1963, U.S. Dist. Ct. (we. and so. dists.) Tex. 1963, U.S. Ct. Appeals (5th, 9th, 11th and Fed. cirs.) 1963, U.S. Supreme Ct. 1986; registered U.S. Patent and Trademark Office 1964. Assoc. Arnold & Roylance, Houston, 1963-66; ptnr. Arnold, White & Durkee, Houston, 1966-73, mng. ptnr., 1973-78; prin. Frank S. Vaden III, P.C., Houston, 1978-80; sr. ptnr. Vaden, Eickenroht & Thompson, L.L.P., Houston, 1980-98; ptnr. Felsman, Bradley, Vaden, Gunter & Dillon, L.L.P., Houston, 1999—; bd. dirs. Phoenix Annydrous, Inc., Houston; lectr. in field. Author: Invention Protection for Practicing Engineers, 1971; contbr. numerous articles to profl. jours. Capt. S.C., U.S. Army, 1957-67. Fellow Tex. Bar Found. (sustaining), Houston Bar Found. (sustaining); mem. ABA (mem. standing com. on specialization 1993-96), Tex. Bar Assn. (chair intellectual property law sec. 1984-85), Houston Bar Assn., Am. Intellectual Property Law Assn., Houston Intellectual Property Law Assn. (pres. 1985-86), U.S. Trademark Assn., Licensing Exec. Soc. (chmn. Houston chpt. 1987-88). Republican. Episcopalian. Patent, Trademark and copyright, Intellectual property. Office: Felsman Bradley Vaden Gunter & Dillon LLP 1 Riverway Ste 1100 Houston TX 77056-1920

**VAIDEN, KRISTI L.,** lawyer. BA, St. Olaf Coll., 1971; JD, Washington U., 1978. Bar: U.S. Ct. Appeals (D.C. cir.) 1979, Mo. 1980, N.J. 1991. Rsch. asst. Nat. Assessment of Ednl. Progress, Denver, 1972-74; adminstrv. asst. Coun. for Ednl. Devel. and Rsch., Washington, 1975-76; law clk. U.S. Dist. Ct. Ea. Dist. Mo., St. Louis, 1979-82; atty. Peabody Coal Co., St. Louis, 1983-85, Southwestern Bell Tel. Co., St. Louis, 1985-90; sr. counsel Bell Comm. Rsch., Morristown, N.J., 1990-97; asst. gen. counsel The Prudential Ins. Co., Newark, 1997—; adj. prof. Washington U. Sch. Law, St. Louis, 1981-84; mem. civil justice reform act adv. com. U.S. Dist. Ct. N.J., 1999. Contbr. articles to profl. jours. Trustee Packanack Cmty. Ch., Wayne, N.J., 1996; cable TV com. mem. Township of Wayne, 1998—. Mem. ABA, Am. Corp. Counsel Assn. (chair intellectual property com. 1994-96, chair coun. nat. coms. 1998, leadership devel. com. 1999, Robert I. Townsend Jr. award 1996), N.J. Corp. Counsel Assn. (bd. dirs. 1998—). Computer, Communications, Contracts commercial. Office: The Prudential Ins Co Am 80 Livingston Ave Roseland NJ 07068-1798

**VAIL, BRUCE RONALD,** lawyer; b. Plainfield, N.J., Dec. 30, 1959; s. William Charles and Jane Edith (Roblin) V.; m. Debra Ann Matuszczak, Oct. 5, 1954. BA, U. N.C., Greensboro, 1981; JD, U. Miss., 1984. Bar: Miss. 1984, Ga. 1989. Reference specialist U. Miss. Sch. Law Libr., Oxford, 1983-84; law clk. U.S. Magistrate Jerry A. Davis-U.S. Dist. Ct., Aberdeen, Miss., 1984-86, Chief Judge L.T. Senter Jr.-U.S. Dist. Ct., Aberdeen, Miss., 1986-88; staff atty. 11th cir. U.S. Ct. Appeals, Atlanta, 1989-94; assoc. Glaze & Glaze P.C., Jonesboro, Ga., 1994—. Book rev. editor Jour. Space Law, 1983-84; on-air personality Sta. WUAG-FM, 1979-81. Pres. Kimmeridge Homeowners Assn., Inc., Peachtree City, Ga., 1996—, Elder Abuse Coun. Clayton Co., Jonesboro, 1995—; mem. adv. bd. Leadership Clayton, Jonesboro, 1995—. Mem. ABA, Atlanta Bar Assn., Clayton Co. Bar Assn., Phi Alpha Delta. Presbyn. Avocations: travel, geneology. Federal civil litigation, Municipal (including bonds), General corporate. Office: Glaze & Glaze 120 N Mcdonough St Jonesboro GA 30236-3692

**VAJTAY, STEPHEN MICHAEL, JR.,** lawyer; b. New Brunswick, N.J., Mar. 18, 1958; s. Stephen Michael and Veronica Gizella (Fehèr) V.; m. Gabriella Katherine Soltèsz, Aug. 5, 1989; children: Stephen, Andrew, Gregory, Daniel. BA, Rutgers U., 1980; JD, Georgetown U., 1983; LLM, NYU, 1989. Bar: N.J. 1984, U.S. Tax Ct. 1985. Assoc. McCarter and English, Newark, N.J., 1983-91, ptnr., 1991—; trustee Hungarian Scout Assn. in Exteris, Garfield, N.J., 1985—; trustee Partnership for a Drug-Free N.J., Inc., Montclair, 1993—; adj. prof. law Seton Hall U. Sch. Law, Newark, 1995—; spkr. at lectrs. and seminars, 1992—. Contbr. articles to profl. jours. Mem. Bd. of Adjustment, New Brunswick, N.J., 1993-98. Mem. ABA, N.J. Bar Assn. (1st vice chmn. tax sect.), Essex County Bar Assn., Phi Beta Kappa. Roman Catholic. Corporate taxation, Mergers and acquisitions, Taxation, general. Office: McCarter and English Four Gateway Ctr 100 Mulberry St Newark NJ 07102

**VAKERICS, THOMAS VINCENT,** lawyer; b. Lorain, Ohio, Mar. 26, 1944; s. Paul Peter and Margaret Theresa (Dobos) V.; m. Kathryn Ida Rogers, Aug. 7,1965; children: Meredith Vakerics Ehler, Mitchell Thomas. BA, Bowling Green State U., 1965; JD with honors, George Washington U., 1968. Bar: U.S. Dist. Ct. D.C. 1968, U.S. Ct. Appeals (D.C. cir.) 1969, U.S. Supreme Ct. 1974, U.S. Ct. Internat. Trade 1982, U.S. Ct. Appeals (Fed. cir.) 1982. Antitrust trial atty. FTC, Washington, 1969-73; assoc. Gore, Cladouhos & Brashares, Washington, 1973-75; ptnr. O'Connor & Hannan, Washington, 1975-84, Bayh, Tabbert & Capehart, Washington, 1984-86, Morgan, Lewis & Bockius, Washington, 1986-88, Winthrop, Stimson, Putnam & Roberts, Washington, 1988-94, Perkins Coie, 1994—; vis. prof. Nihon U., Tokyo, 1981-88. Author: Antitrust Basics, 1985, Antidumping, Countervailing Duty and Other Trade Actions, 1987; contbr. articles to profl. jours. Mem. ABA (vice chmn. internat. antitrust law com. sect. internat. law and practice 1992-95), Internat. Bar Assn., D.C. Bar Assn., Solar Energy Rsch. Inst. (editl. adv. bd. Solar Energy Law Reporter 1979-82), Order of Coif, Phi Delta Phi, Pi Sigma Alpha, Phi Alpha Delta, Sigma Chi. Democrat. Roman Catholic. Antitrust, Private international. Home: 12820 Tewksbury Dr Herndon VA 20171-2427 Office: Perkins Coie 607 14th St NW Ste 800 Washington DC 20005-2000

**VAKIL, VIRGIE MAY,** lawyer; b. Hershey, Pa., Oct. 4, 1943; d. John Henry and Mary Dorothy (Phillips) Tshudy; m. Hassan C. Vakil, Mar. 9, 1967; children—Jeffrey Jahan, Mark Mehdi. Diploma in nursing Harrisburg Hosp. (Pa.), 1964, Ga. State U., Atlanta, 1970; B.A. summa cum laude, West Chester State U., 1976; J.D., Temple U., 1981. R.N., Pa., Ga. Nurse, Allegheny Gen. Hosp., Pitts., 1964-66; nurse Piedmont Hosp., Atlanta, 1966-67, instr. nursing, 1968; utilization rev. analyst Blue Cross/Blue Shield Del., Wilmington, 1971; sole practice, Media, Pa., 1981-87; assoc. Gibbons, Buckley, Smith, Palmer & Proud, P.C., Media, 1987-91, shareholder Kelly, Grimes, Pietrangelo & Vakil, 1991—. Contbg. author: Practices, 1983, Nurses Legal Handbook, 1985, 1992. Bd. dirs. women in bus. com. Delaware County C. of C., 1981-85; Republican committeewoman Upper Providence Twp. (Pa.), 1982-86; bd. dirs. Community Care Programs, 1986-88, Del. County Home Care Assn., 1988—, Upper Providence Citizens Assn., 1987-90. Mem. ABA, Pa. Bar Assn., Assn. Trial Lawyers Am., Delaware County Bar Assn. (chmn. med./dental law com. 1985, 89, 93, 94, bd. dirs. 1990-92, Guy Dufuria Am. Inn of Ct. 1990—), LWV, Psi Chi, Pi Gamma Mu, Phi Alpha Delta. Republican. Home: 690 Meadowbrook Ln Media PA 19063-4213 Office: 36 E Second St Media PA 19063-4213

**VAKILI, ALIDAD,** lawyer; b. Tehran, Iran, Mar. 9, 1968; came to the U.S., 1978; s. Houshang and Glenna Wekill; m. Ommid Vakili, July 12, 1964. BA in Philosophy, U. Calif., San Diego, 1991; JD, Calif. Western Sch. Law, 1994. Bar: Calif. 1995. Assoc. Vakili & Leus, L.A., 1995-96; ptnr. Vakili & Hordon, San Diego, 1996-98; prin. atty. Vakili & Assocs., San Diego, 1998—; v.p. Iranian Am. Lawyers Assn., L.A., 1996. Mem. ABA, San Diego County Bar Assn. (co-chair bus. sect. 1998-99). Avocations: reading, writing. General civil litigation, Contracts commercial, General corporate. Office: Vakili & Assocs 101 W Broadway 9th Flr San Diego CA 92101-8201

**VAKRINOS, THEODORE CHRISTOS,** lawyer; b. Athens, Greece, Nov. 3, 1955; came to U.S., 1981; LLB, Aristoteles U., Thessaloniki, Greece, 1978; postgrad., Albert-Ludwigs-U., Freiburg, Germany, 1979-81. Ptnr. Vakrinos Kontogiannis & Assoc., Athens, 1981—; legal cons. Tex., 1992—, Washington, 1993—, Calif., 1996—, Ill., 1999—. Mem. ABA, Am. Hellenic Ednl. Progressive Assn., Southwestern Legal Found. (adv. bd. mem. Internat. and Comparative Law Ctr.), Athens Bar Assn., Dallas Bar Assn. Real property, Private international. Home: 1808 E Timberview Ln Arlington TX 76014-1561 Office: Vakrinos Kontogiannis & Assocs, 58 Omirou St, 10672 Athens Greece Office: 7822 Ridgecrest Dr Alexandria VA 22308-1053

**VALADEZ, ROBERT ALLEN,** lawyer; b. McAllen, Tex., May 27, 1960; s. Ventura S. and Maria G. (De los Santos) V.; m. Kelly Curll Valadez; 1 child, Ashley Marie. BBA, U. Tex., 1982; JD, 1985. Bar: Tex. 1985, U.S. Dist. Ct. (so., we., ea. & no. dists.) Tex. Briefing atty. Tex. Supreme Ct., Austin, 1985-86; assoc. Fulbright & Jaworski, San Antonio, 1986-89, participating assoc., 1989-92; assoc. Wright & Greenhill, San Antonio, 1992-93; shareholder Shelton & Valadez, San Antonio, 1993—. State civil litigation, Personal injury, Product liability. Home: 1739 Fawn Gate San Antonio TX 78248-1326 Office: Shelton & Valadez 800 Airport Ctr 112 E Pecan St Ste 2600 San Antonio TX 78205-1528

**VALCARCE, JIM J.,** lawyer; b. Reno, Apr. 20, 1969; s. Paul and Karrol Valcarce; m. Tauni Rodgers, Sept. 14, 1995; 1 child, Joseph Fortune. BS, Utah State U., 1990; JD, Drake U., 1994. Gen. counsel Kakerak Inc., Nome, Alaska, 1994-95; dist. atty. Bethel, Alaska, 1995-96; atty. Hedland, Brennan, Heidemann & Cooke, Bethel, 1996—; Gen. counsel Village of Kwinhagak, Alaska, 1997, AVCP, Bethel, 1998. Mem. Scottish Rite (32 degree), Harmony Lodge (freemason). Avocations: archaeology, collecting native art, collecting wine. Personal injury, Criminal, Admiralty. Home and Office: Hedland Brennan Heideman & Cooke PO Box 555 Bethel AK 99559-0555

**VALDEZ, FRANCES VALDEZ,** lawyer; b. San Antonio, Tex., Sept. 7, 1954; d. Juan Ortiz and Basilisa Flores Valdez; m. Joe Albert Gonzales, Sept. 26, 1981; children: Ana Lisa, Martin Esteban. BA, Yale U., 1977; JD, U. Tex., 1980. Bar: Tex. 1980, U.S. Dist. Ct. (no. dist.) Tex. 1981, U.S. Ct. Appeals (5th cir.) 1981, U.S. Ct. Appeals (10th cir.) 1981. Trial atty. office of the solicitor U.S. Dept. Labor, Dallas, 1980-84; briefing atty. no. dist. Tex. U.S. Bankruptcy Ct., Dallas, 1984-85; dir., shareholder, atty. Geary Glast & Middleton P.C., Dallas, 1985-92; regulatory/environ. atty. J.C. Penney Co. Inc., Plano, Tex., 1992-98; pres. Valdez Valdez & Assocs. P.C., Dallas, 1998—; mem. adv. panel The Bus. Forum, 1993-96; bd. dirs. MiEscuelita. Law vol. Cath. Charities, Dallas, 1992-95; mentor, spkr. Nike Club, Dallas, 1994-96. Mem. Dallas Bar Assn. (spkr. com. mem. environ. sect. 1992—, internat. sec. 1991—), Mex.-Am. Bar Assn., Bankruptcy Bar Assn. (co-chair ct. liaison com., chair), Yale Club of Dallas, Hispanic C. of C. (planning com. chair, spkr. com. chair 1985—). Democrat. Roman Catholic. Avocations: cycling, basketball one on one, flower & wreath arranging, writing. Environmental, Federal civil litigation, Labor. Home: 9109 Livenshire Dr Dallas TX 75238-2820 Office: Valdez Valdez & Assocs 1201 Main St Ste 850 Dallas TX 75202-3920

**VALE, VICTOR JOHN EUGENE, II,** lawyer; b. Heampstead, N.Y., Oct. 6, 1958; s. Victor E. and Caroline Katherine Frances V. BBA, Midd. Tenn. State U., 1990; JD, Marquet Univ., 1993. Bar: Fla., 1994, Wis., 1993; U.S. Dist. Ct. (ea. dist.) Wis., 1993. Pvt. practice Ft. Pierce, 1994—; vice-chmn. econ. devel. com., Port St. Lucie, Fla., 1994—; chmn. met. planning orgn. citizen's adv. com., St. Lucie County, Fla., 1994—. Contbg. author: Wisemen on Criminal Procedures, 1993; editor: Grenig on Civil Procedure, 1993. V.p. Port St. Lucie Rep. Club, 1994—; Rep. state committeeman, 1996—. Staff sgt. U.S. Army, 1976-86. Recipient Law Student award Bur. Nat. Affairs, Washington, 1993; cert. appreciation Comm. on Bicentennial of U.S. Constn., Washington, 1992, 93. Mem. Disabled Am. Vets., Federalist Soc. (pres. 1992-93), Omicron Delta Epsilon, Sigma Xi. Roman Catholic. Avocations: golf, tennis, sailing, skiing, chess. Family and matrimonial, General civil litigation, General corporate.

**VALENCIANO, RANDAL GRANT BOLOSAN,** lawyer; b. Waimea, Hawaii, Nov. 17, 1958; s. Placido Dias and Maria (Bolosan) V.; m. Debbie F.I.; children: Marisa Claire Ihara, Dreana Rae Ihara, Randon Grant Ihara. BS, U. Oreg., 1980; JD, U. Wash., 1983. Bar: Hawaii 1983. Dep. pub. def. State of Hawaii, 1983-84; dep. prosecutor County of Kauai, 1984-87; ptnr. Valenciano & Zenger, Lihue, 1989-91; arbitrator 5th Jud. Cir. State of Hawaii, 1988-91; mem. Defender Coun. State of Hawaii, 1989-91. Lawyer, coach Waimea High Sch. Mock Trial Team, 1986-88; bd. dirs. Hawaii United Meth. Union, Honolulu, 1987-91. Mem. Hawaii State Bar Assn., Kauai Bar Assn. (v.p. 1988-89), Kauai County Coun. (vice chair 1990-92). Democrat. Avocation: sports card collecting, bonsai plants. Criminal, Family and matrimonial, General civil litigation. Home: Pua Nani St Lihue HI 96766 Office: 3016 Umi St Ste 211A Lihue HI 96766-1346

**VALENTE, DOUGLAS,** lawyer; b. Bronx, N.Y., Sept. 18, 1966; s. John S. and Marguerite M. Valente; m. Stacey J. Klein, 1994. BA, SUNY, Stony Brook, 1988; JD, Touro Coll., 1991; MA, NYU, 1998. Bar: N.Y. 1992, U.S. Dist. Ct. (ea. dist.) N.Y. 1992, U.S. Dist. Ct. (so. dist.) N.Y. 1995. Assoc. Law Office of Richard H. Cunningham, Smithtown, N.Y., 1992-93; pvt. practice Northport, N.Y., 1993-95, 96—; ptnr. Valente & Delmont, Northport, 1995-96. Mem. Am. Philos. Assn., N.Y. State Bar Assn., Suffolk County Bar Assn. Bankruptcy, Criminal, General practice. Office: 490 Main St Northport NY 11768-1953

**VALENTE, PETER CHARLES,** lawyer; b. N.Y.C., July 3, 1940; s. Francis Louis and Aurelia Emily (Cella) V.; m. Judith Kay Nemeroff, Feb. 19, 1966; children: Susan Lynn, David Marc. BA, Bowdoin Coll., 1962; LLB, Columbia U., 1966; LLM, N.Y.U., 1971. Bar: N.Y. 1967. Assoc. Tenzer Greenblatt LLP, N.Y.C., 1967-73, ptnr., 1973—, ptnr. in charge trusts and estates dept. Co-author column on wills, estates and surrogate's practice N.Y. Law Jour. Fellow Am. Coll. Trust and Estate Counsel; mem. ABA, N.Y. State Bar Assn. (lectr. on wills, trusts and estates), Assn. of Bar of City of N.Y., N.Y. County Lawyers' Assn. (former bd. dirs. and chmn. com. on surrogates' ct., lectr. on wills, trusts and estates), Phi Beta Kappa. Probate, Estate planning, Estate taxation. Office: Tenzer Greenblatt LLP 405 Lexington Ave New York NY 10174-0002

**VALENTI, DENNIS R.,** lawyer; b. Royal Oak, Mich., Apr. 1, 1958; s. Philip S. and Iris M. V.; m. Diane P. Scherer, Apr. 5, 1986; 1 child, Patrick J. BBA, Western Mich. U., 1980; MBA, Mich. State U., 1985; JD, U. Detroit, 1991. Bar: Mich. 1991, U.S. Dist. Ct. (ea. dist.) Mich. 1991. Fed. bank examiner FDIC, Washington, 1980-84; fin. officer NBD-Bancorp, Detroit, 1985-88; prof. Ea. Mich. U., Ypsilanti, 1988-95; atty. pvt. practice, Ann Arbor, Mich., 1991-96, Ferguson & Widmayer, Ann Arbor, Mich., 1996—; adj. prof. Wayne State U., Detroit, 1989-96. Mem. State Bar Mich. (bus. law sect., probate and estate planning sect.), Washtenaw County Bar Assn. (estates and trusts sect., co-chair tax sect. 1997—), Optimist Club (pres. 1996). Mergers and acquisitions, Contracts commercial, Estate planning. Office: Ferguson & Widmayer 538 N Division St Ann Arbor MI 48104-1136

**VALENTI, MICHAEL A.,** lawyer; b. Cleve., Jan. 26, 1960; s. Richard A. and Josephine A. Valenti; m. Kelly Jeane Vance, Jan. 26, 1990; children: Alexander P., Nicholas R., Dylan V. BA in French, Coll. of Holy Cross, 1982; JD, Am. U., 1986. Bar: Ky. 1987, U.S. Dist. Ct. (we. and ea. dists.) Ky. 1987, U.S. Ct. Appeals (fed. cir.) 1988, U.S. Ct. Appeals (6th cir.) 1989, U.S. Dist. Ct. (so. dist.) Ind. 1996, Colo. 1998. Assoc. Greenbaum, Doll & McDonald, Louisville, 1986-87, Hirn, Reed & Harper, Louisville, 1987-95; ptnr. Hirn, Reed, Doheny & Harper, Louisville, 1997, Zoppoth, Valenti & Hanley, Louisville, 1997—; chmn. bd. dirs. RMD Corp. Pro bono svc. work Legal Aid Soc., Louisville. Mem. Ky. Bar Assn. (continuing legal edn. awarad 1996). General civil litigation, General corporate, Intellectual property. Office: Zoppoth Valenti & Hanley 2121 Citizens Pla Louisville KY 40202-2823

**VALENTINE, H. JEFFREY,** legal association executive; b. Phila., Sept. 28, 1945; s. Joshua Morton and Olga W. (Wilson) V.; 1 child, Karyn. BS, St. Louis U., 1964, postgrad., 1966-68. Programmer, systems analyst Honeywell Electronic Data Processing, Wellesley Hills, Mass., 1964-66; account exec. Semiconductor div. Tex. Instruments, New Eng., 1966-68; New Eng. sales exec., Mid-Atlantic regional mgr. Electronic Instrumentation Co., 1968-70; pres. Nat. Free Lance Photographers Assn., Doylestown, Pa., 1970-89; pres., dir. Towne Print & Copy Ctrs. Inc.; v.p., exec. dir. Nat. Paralegal Assn., 1982—; pres. Paralegal Assocs., Inc., 1982—; chief operating officer Doylestown Parking Corp., 1977-88; bd. dirs. Law Enforcement Supply Co., Solebury, Valtronics Supply Co., Towne Print & Copy Centers Inc., Solebury, Doylestown Stationery and Office Supply, Energy Mktg. Assocs., Inc., Solebury, Paralegal Placement Network; pres. Paralegal Pub. Corp., 1983-90; pub. Paralegal Jour.; pres. Valco Enterprises Inc., 1986—, Paralegal Employment Sys., Inc., 1988, Solebury Press, Inc., 1989—; ptnr. J&S Gen. Contractors, 1993—, J&S Landscaping Tree Svc., 1993—; owner Specialized Computer Consulting, 1992—. Author: Photographers Bookkeeping System, 1973, rev. edit., 1978, Photographers Pricing Guides, 1971, 72, 74, 75, Available Markets Director's - 4 Vols., 1973-77, National Model Sources Directory, Nat. Paralegal Salary and Employment Survey, 1985-86, 88, 90-92, 93-94; also articles, bulls. and pamphlets. Exec. sec. Doylestown Bus. Assn., 1972-78, pres., 1979, 83, v.p., 1981. Recipient Internat. Men of Achievement award, 1988; named Personalities of the Am., 1988. Mem. London Coll. Applied Scis., Nat. Fedn. Paralegal Assns., Photog. Industry Coun., Nat. Assn. Legal Assts., Am. Soc. Assn. Execs., Soc. Assn. Mgrs., Nat. Fedn. Ind. Business (mem. action coun. com.), Nat. Parking Assn., Nat. Office Products Assn., Graphic Arts Assn. Delaware Valley, Nat. Assn. Federally Licensed Firearms Dealers, Nat. Compostition Assn., Internat. Platform Assn. Office: PO Box 406 Solebury PA 18963-0406

**VALENTINE, MICHAEL JOHN,** lawyer; b. Hackensack, N.J., Oct. 1, 1957; s. William Glen and Joan Lorenzetti V.; m. Jennifer A. Barnes, Sept. 3, 1983; children: Michael Beowulf, Zachary John. BS, U. Houston, 1981, JD, 1986. Bar: Tex. 1986, U.S. Dist. Ct. (so. dist.) Tex. 1989, U.S. Dist. Ct. (no., ea. and we. dists.) Tex. 1995, U.S. Ct. Appeals (5th cir.) 1995, U.S. Tax Ct. 1989, U.S. Supreme Ct. 1995. Sr. tax cons. Touche Ross & Co., Houston,

1986-88; assoc. atty. Urquhart & Hassel, Houston, 1989-94; gen. counsel Warren Elec. Co., Houston, 1994—. Charter mem. Hedonistic Halloween Soc., Houston, 1984; treas. Knights of Bula, Houston, 1993. Disting. Svc. award Faculty U. Houston Law Ctr., 1986. Mem. ABA, Tex. Bar Assn., Houston Bar Assn., Italian-Am. Lawyers Assn., Tau Kappa Epsilon (bd. dirs., chmn. 1994—). Roman Catholic. General corporate, Taxation, general, Estate planning. Office: Warren Electric Co PO Box 67 2929 Mckinney St Houston TX 77003-3823

**VALENZUELA, MANUEL ANTHONY, JR.,** lawyer; b. L.A., Dec. 4, 1955; s. Manuel and Artimesa B. (Ruiz) V.; m. Guadalupe Roa, Nov. 8, 1980; children: Manuel Anthony III, Nancy Christine. BA in Polit. Sci., UCLA, 1978; MPA, U. So. Calif., 1982; JD, Southwestern U., L.A., 1987. Bar: Calif. 1987, U.S. Dist. Ct. (cen. dist.) Calif. 1987, U.S. Ct. Appeals (9th cir.) 1988, U.S. Supreme Ct. 1991. Legis. analyst L.A. City Coun., 1981-88; legal extern ACLU, L.A., 1985; assoc. county counsel County of Los Angeles, 1988-89, sr. assoc county counsel, 1989-90, dep. county counsel, 1990-94, sr. dep. county counsel, 1994-98, prin. dep. county counsel, 1998—. Mem. L.A. County Bar Assn. (exec. com. govtl. law sect. 1990-91, 95-96, 96—, sec. govtl. law sect. 1991-92, 2d vice chair govtl. law sect. 1992-93, 1st vice chair govtl. law sect. 1993-94, chair govtl. law sect. 1994-95, bd. trustees 1995-96), Mexican Am. Bar Assn. (bd. dirs. 1990, 91), L.A. County Counsel Assn. (bd. dirs. 1989-99), UCLA Latino Alumni Assn. (founder, bd. dirs. 1989-90, scholarship com. 1995—). Democrat. Roman Catholic. Avocations: tennis, backpacking, reading. Home: 9647 Val St Temple City CA 91780-1438 Office: Office of County Counsel 648 Hall of Adminstrn 500 W Temple St Los Angeles CA 90012-2713

**VALERIE JACOBSON, BRODSKY,** lawyer; b. Charlottesville, Va., Jan. 21, 1964; d. Sidney Leon Jacobson and Linda Keller Longman; m. Neal Paul Brodsky, May 29, 1988; children: Sara Rose, Rachel Amanda. BBA, Coll. William and Mary, 1986, JD, 1989. Bar: Va. Ptnr. Vandeventer Black LLP, Norfolk, Va., 1989—; pro bono prosecutor Norfolk Commonwealth's Atty. Office, Va., 1996. Contbr. articles to profl. jours., newspapers, chpt. to book. Bd. dirs. Women's Am. ORT, Norfolk, Va., 1995—, The Planning Coun., Norfolk, 1995, Jewish Family Svcs., Norfolk, 1998—. Mem. ABA, Am. Immigration Lawyers Assn. (invited spkr. annual conf. 1998), Va. State Bar Assn., Va. Bar Assn., Norfolk-Portsmouth Bar Assn., Hampton Roads C. of C. (adv. bd. 1997—). Immigration, naturalization, and customs. Office: Vandeventer Black LLP 500 World Trade Ctr Norfolk VA 23510-1679

**VALERIO, PAT J,** lawyer; b. Aberdeen, Wash., Aug. 19, 1962; d. Joseph Richard and Mary Allen (Finch) V. BA in Polit. Sci., Seattle U., 1984; JD, U. Wash., 1987. Bar: Wash. 1988, U.S. Dist. Ct. (we. dist.) Wash. 1990. Legal advisor Cath. Cmty. Svcs., Seattle, 1985-86; rsch. designer Evergreen Legal Svcs., Seattle, 1986; trial atty. Assoc. Counsel for the Accused, Seattle, 1989—; mem. Pro Bono Com., 1989. Vol. Legal Svcs., Seattle, 1995. Mem. Ind. Bar Assn. Avocations: writing, animal rights, doll collecting, tango. Criminal. Office: Associated Counsel for the Accused 110 Prefontaine Pl S Ste 200 Seattle WA 98104-2674

**VALETUTTO, DAVID MICHAEL,** lawyer; b. Vineland, N.J., May 1, 1966; s. Laurence Vincent and Beverli June Valetutto. BBA, Baylor U., 1989; JD, South Tex. Coll. Law, 1993. Bar: Tex. 1993, Tex. Supreme Ct. 1993, U.S. Dist. Ct. (so. dist.) Tex. 1993, U.S. Ct. Appeals (5th cir.) 1994, U.S. Dist. Ct. (no. and ea. dists.) Tex. 1998, U.S. Dist. Ct. Colo. 1998. Assoc. Watts & Glover, LLP, Houston, 1993-94; ptnr. Valetutto, Shellist, Lore & Lazarz, P.C., Houston, 1994-97; assoc. Law Offices of Windle Turley, P.C., Dallas, 1997-98; of counsel Robert Kwok & Assocs., P.C., Houston, 1998—. Mem. ATLA, Tex. Trial Lawyers Assn., Houston Bar Assn., Houston Young Lawyers Assn., Delta Theta Phi. Fax: 713-773-3960. Personal injury, Labor, Product liability. Office: Robert Kwok & Assocs PC 6100 Corporate Dr Ste 530 Houston TX 77036-3492

**VALLE, LAURENCE FRANCIS,** lawyer; b. N.Y.C., Feb. 16, 1943; s. Mario John and Marian Josephine (Longinotti) V.; m. Joan Strachan, June 11, 1966 (dec.); children: Christopher John, Stacia Lyn. BS, U. Miami, 1966, JD, 1969. Bar: Fla. 1969, U.S. Ct. Mil. Appeals 1970, U.S. Dist. Ct. (so. and mid. dists.) Fla. 1975, U.S. Ct. Appeals (D.C. cir.) 1975, U.S. Ct. Appeals (5th and 11th cirs.) 1981, U.S. Dist. Ct. (we. dist.) Tex. 1989. Assoc. Underwood, Gillis & Karcher PA, Miami, Fla., 1973-77; ptnr. Underwood, Gillis, Karcher & Valle PA, Miami, 1977-87, Dixon, Dixon, Nicklaus & Valle, Miami, 1987-90, Nicklaus, Valle, Craig & Wicks, Miami, 1990-95, Valle & Craig, P.A., Miami, 1995—; of counsel Greater Miami Marine Assn., 1983—. Contbr. articles to profl. jours. Served to capt. U.S. Army, 1970-74. Mem. ABA, Fla. Bar Assn. (chmn. grievance com., 1982-85), Assn. Trial Lawyers Am., SE Admiralty Law Inst., Maritime Law Assn. of U.S., Bankers Club Miami. Republican. Roman Catholic. Avocations: tennis, running, water skiing, snow skiing. Admiralty, Personal injury, Workers' compensation. Office: Valle & Craig PA PO Box 19670 Miami FL 33101-9670

**VALLIANT, JAMES STEVENS,** lawyer; b. Glendale, Calif., Sept. 29, 1963; s. William Warren and Carol Dee (Heath) V.; m. Holly Lynne White. BA, NYU, 1984; JD, U. San Diego, 1989. Bar: Calif. 1989. Law instr. U. San Diego, 1988-89; dep. dist. atty. Dist. Atty.'s Office, San Diego, 1989—; host talk show WJM Prodns., Hollywood, Calif., 1996. Contbr. articles in objectivism and early Christianity. Recipient Citation of Appreciation MADD, 1993. Office: Dist Attys Office 330 W Broadway San Diego CA 92101-3825

**VALLONE, RALPH, JR.,** lawyer; b. Phila., Apr. 15, 1947; s. Ralph and Carmen Maria (Perez) V. BA, Yale U., 1966, M. Philosophy (Carnegie fellow), 1966; LLD Harvard U., 1972. Bar: P.R., 1972, U.S. dist. ct. P.R., 1972, U.S. Sup. Ct., 1972. Ptnr. Ralph Vallone Law Firm, San Juan, P.R., 1972—; prof. comml. law Interam. U. Law Sch., P.R., 1972—; chief hearing examiner for Environ. Quality Bd. of P.R. Author: Tiene Usted un Caso de Malapractica Medica, 1985, Second Vision, 1994. Past Trustee Bronx Mus. Arts. Mem. P.R. Inst. Registry Law, Jud. Conf. of P.R. Federal civil litigation, Banking, General corporate. Office: 1411 Ashford Fl 2D Santurce San Juan PR 00907-1435

**VALOIS, ROBERT ARTHUR,** lawyer; b. N.Y.C., May 13, 1938; s. Frank Jacob and Harriet Frances (LaCroix) V.; m. Ruth Emilie Skacil, Dec. 23, 1961; children: Marguerite Jeannette, Robert Arthur Jr. BBA, U. Miami, 1962; JD, Wake Forest U., 1972. Bar: N.C. 1972, Fla. 1972, U.S. Ct. Appeals (4th cir.) 1973, U.S. Dist. Ct. (ea. and mid. dists.) 1974, U.S. Supreme Ct. 1975, U.S. Ct. Appeals (6th cir.) 1986. Field examiner NLRB, Winston-Salem, N.C., 1962-70; from assoc. to ptnr. Maupin, Taylor, Ellis & Adams, P.A., Raleigh, N.C., 1972—; chmn. labor and employment sect. Maupin, Taylor & Ellis, P.A., Raleigh, N.C., 1972-97; chmn. bd. dirs., pres. Maupin, Taylor & Ellis, P.A., Raleigh, 1997—; vice chmn. Legal Svcs. Corp., Washington, 1984-90, bd. dirs. Served with USN, 1956-59. Mem. Greater Raleigh C. of C. (chmn. fed. govt. com. 1991—), Capitol City Club. Democrat. Presbyterian. Labor.

**VAMOS, FLORENCE M.,** lawyer; b. N.Y.C., Apr. 9; d. Joseph Calabro and Louise Marie (Riccio) Horvath; m. Joseph S. Vamos. BA magna cum laude, U.Minn., 1974; JD, William Mitchell Coll. Law, St. Paul, 1978. Bar: Ind. 1978, Mich. 1982, U.S. Dist. Ct. (so. dist.) Ind. 1978, U.S. Dist. Ct. (no. dist.) Ind. 1979, U.S. Dist. Ct. (so. dist.) Mich. 1981, U.S. Dist. Ct (ea. dist.) Mich. 1982. Pvt. practice law South Bend, Ind., 1978-90, Mishawaka, Ind., 1990—. Mem. Ind. State Bar Assn., Mich. State Bar Assn., Cass County (Mich.) Bar Assn., St. Joseph County (Ind.) Bar Assn., Nat. Inst. Trial Advocacy. General practice, Trademark and copyright, Family and matrimonial.

**VAN, PETER,** lawyer; b. Boston, Sept. 7, 1936; s. Frank Lewis and Ruth (Spevack) V.; m. Faye Anne Zinck, 1991; children: Jami Lynne, Robert Charles. BA, Dartmouth, 1958; LLD, Boston Coll., 1961. Bar: Mass. 1962. Assoc. Brown, Rudnick, Freed and Gesmer, Boston, 1961-63; assoc. Fine and Ambrogne, Boston, 1963-65, ptnr., 1966-73, sr. ptnr., 1973—, mng. ptnr., chmn. exec. com., 1988-90; ptnr., mem. exec. com. Mintz, Levin, Cohn, Ferris, Glovsky and Popeo, P.C., Boston, 1990-97; ptnr. Bingham, Dana LLP, Boston, 1997—. Mem. fin. com., overseer Beth Israel Hosp. Boston. Mem. Masons. Real property, Banking, Contracts commercial. Office: 150 Federal St Boston MA 02110-1713

**VAN ALFEN, SCOTT B.,** lawyer, associate; b. Salt Lake City, Feb. 11, 1967; s. Curtis Nicolas and Jeanette Bieler Van A.; m. Dana Leigh Bruner, Apr. 29, 1989; children: Jessica Ashley, Braden Scott. BS in Bus. Mgmt., Brigham Young U., 1991; JD, U. Nebr., 1994. Bar: Nev. 1994, U.S. Dist. Ct. Nev. 1994, U.S. Ct. Appeals (9th cir.) 1997. Litigation atty. Christensen Law Offices, Las Vegas, 1994—. Varsity scout advisor Boy Scouts Am., Las Vegas, 1995. Mem. Assn. Trial Lawyers Am., Nev. Trial Lawyers Assn. Republican. Mem. LDS Ch. Avocations: kayaking, camping, water skiing, cycling, remote control airplanes. Personal injury, Family and matrimonial, Probate. Office: Christensen Law Offices 1000 S Valley View Blvd Las Vegas NV 89107-4413

**VAN ANTWERPEN, FRANKLIN STUART,** federal judge; b. Passaic, N.J., Oct. 23, 1941; s. Franklin John and Dorothy (Hoedemaker) Van A.; m. Kathleen Veronica O'Brien, Sept. 12, 1970; children: Joy, Franklin W., Virginia. BS in Engring. Physics, U. Maine, 1964; JD, Temple U., 1967; postgrad., Nat. Jud. Coll., 1980. Bar: Pa. 1969, U.S. Dist. Ct. (ea. dist.) Pa. 1971, U.S. Ct. Appeals (3d cir.) 1971, U.S. Supreme Ct. 1972. Corp. counsel Hazeltine, Corp., N.Y.C., 1967-70; chief counsel Northampton County Legal Aid Soc., Easton, Pa., 1970-71; assoc. Hemstreet & Smith, Easton, 1971-73; ptnr. Hemstreet & VanAntwerpen, Easton, 1973-79; judge Ct. Common Pleas of Northampton County (Pa.), 1979-87, U.S. Dist. Ct. (ea. dist.) Pa., Phila., 1987—; appointed to U.S. Sentencing Commn. Jud. Working Group, 1992-93, U.S. Jud. Conf. Com. on Defender Svcs., 1997; trial judge U.S. vs. Scarfo, 1988-89; adj. prof. Northampton County Area C.C., 1976-81; solicitor Palmer Twp., 1971-79; gen. counsel Fairview Savs. and Loan Assn., Easton, 1973-79. Recipient Booster award Bus. Indsl. and Profl. Assn., 1979, George Palmer award Palmer Twp., 1980, Man of Yr. award, 1981, Law Enforcement Commendation medal Nat. Soc. SAR, 1990; named an Alumnus Who Has Made a Difference in the World, U. Maine, 1991. Mem. ABA (com. on jud. edn.), Fed. Bar Assn. (hon.), Pa. Bar Assn., Northampton County Bar Assn., Am. Judicature Soc., Fed. Judges Assn., Pomfret Club, Nat. Lawyers Club Washington, Union League Club, Pa. Soc. Club, Sigma Pi Sigma. Office: US Dist Ct Holmes Bldg 2nd and Ferry St Easton PA 18042

**VAN ARTSDALEN, DONALD WEST,** federal judge; b. Doylestown, Pa., Oct. 21, 1919; s. Isaac Jeans and May Mable (Danenhower) Van A.; m. Marie Catherine Auerbach, June 20, 1953. Student, Williams Coll., 1937-40; LL.B., U. Pa., 1948. Bar: Pa. 1948, U.S. Supreme Ct. 1956. Practiced in Doylestown, 1948-70; dist. atty. Bucks County (Pa.), 1954-58; judge U.S. Dist. Ct. Pa. (ea. dist.), Phila., from 1970, now sr. judge, 1987. Served with Canadian Army, 1940-42; Served with AUS, 1942-45. Mem. Order of the Coif. Office: US District Court 3124 US Courthse Ind Mall W 601 Market St Philadelphia PA 19106-1796

**VANASKIE, THOMAS IGNATIUS,** judge; b. Shamokin, Pa., Nov. 11, 1953; s. John Anthony and Delores (Wesoloski) V.; m. Dorothy Grace Williams, Aug. 12, 1978; children: Diane, Laura, Thomas. BA magna cum laude, Lycoming Coll., 1975; JD cum laude, Dickinson U., Carlisle, Pa., 1978. Bar: Pa. 1978, U.S. Dist. Ct. (mid. dist.) Pa. 1980, U.S. Ct. Appeals (3rd cir.) 1982, U.S. Supreme Ct. 1983. Law clk. to chief judge U.S. Dist. Ct. (mid. dist.) Pa., Scranton, 1978-80; assoc. Dilworth, Paxson, Kalish & Kauffman, Scranton, 1980-85, ptnr., 1986-92; prin. mem. Elliott, Vanaskie & Riley, 1992-94; judge U.S. Dist. Ct. (mid. dist.) Pa., Scranton; counsel Gov. Robert P. Casey Com., Harrisburg, Pa., 1987-92; mem. automation and tech. com. U.S. Cir. Ct. 3d cir., 1998, co-chair 3d cir. task force on info. resources, 1998—. Contbr. articles to profl. jours. Mem. Scranton Waste Mgmt. Com., 1989; trustee Scranton Prep. Sch., 1997—. Recipient James A. Finnegan award Finnegan Found. Mem. Judicature, Pa. Bar Assn., Fed. Judges Assn. (bd. dirs. 1998). Democrat. Avocations: golf, reading. Office: US Dist Ct Fed Courthouse 4th Fl Washington Ave & Linden St Scranton PA 18501

**VANBEBBER, GEORGE THOMAS,** federal judge; b. Troy, Kans., Oct. 21, 1931; s. Roy Vest and Anne (Wenner) V.; m. Alleen Sara Castellani. AB, U. Kans., 1953, LLB, 1955. Bar: Kans. 1955, U.S. Dist. Ct. Kans. 1955, U.S. Ct. Appeals (10th cir.) 1961. Pvt. practice, Troy, 1955-58, 1961-82; asst. U.S. atty. Topeka, Kansas City, Kans., 1958-61; county atty. Doniphan County, Troy, 1963-69; mem. Kans. House of Reps., 1973-75; chmn. Kans. Corp. Commn., Topeka, 1975-79; U.S. magistrate Topeka, 1982-89; judge U.S. Dist. Ct., Kansas City, Kan., 1989-95, chief judge, 1995—. Mem. ABA, Kas. Bar Assn. Episcopalian. Office: US Dist Ct 529 US Courthouse 500 State Ave Kansas City KS 66101-2403

**VAN BLUNK, HENRY EDWARD,** lawyer; b. Phila., Oct. 20, 1968; s. James Joseph Jr. and Beatrice Marie (Kilpatrick) Van B. BS in Acctg., Pa. State U., 1990; JD, Widener U., Wilmington, Del., 1993; MBA, Widener U., Chester, Pa., 1993. Bar: Pa. 1993, N.J. 1993, U.S. Dist. Ct. N.J. 1994, U.S. Dist. Ct. (ea. dist.) Pa. 1996, U.S. Ct. Appeals (3rd cir.) 1998. Law clk. to Hon. Tullio Gean Leompolla U.S. Magistrate Judge/U.S. Dist. Ct. (ea. dist.) Pa., Phila., 1994; shareholder Liederbach, Hahn, Foy & Petro, P.C., Richboro, Pa., 1994—. Mem. ABA, Pa. Bar Assn., Bucks County Bar Assn., Republican Club. Roman Catholic. General practice, Real property, Contracts commercial. Home: 310 Daleview Ct Yardley PA 19067-3442 Office: Liederbach Hahn Foy & Petri 892 2d Street Pike Richboro PA 18954

**VAN BROEKHOVEN, ROLLIN ADRIAN,** federal judge; b. Dallas, June 3, 1940; s. Harold and Loraine (Chafer) Van B.; m. Diana Gullett, Oct. 6, 1962; children: Gretchen, Heidi. BS, Wheaton Coll., 1962; JD cum laude, Baylor U., 1968; LLM, George Washington U., 1975; DPhil, Oxford U., 1991. Bar: Tex. 1968, U.S. Ct. Mil. Appeals 1970, U.S. Ct. Claims 1970, U.S. Supreme Ct. 1975. Commd. 2d lt. U.S. Army, 1962, advanced through grades to maj., 1969; trial atty., Ft. Hood, Tex., 1968-70, Heidelberg, W.Ger., 1970-71; gen. counsel U.S. Army Procurement Agy., Frankfurt, W.Ger., 1971-74; asst. gen. counsel Dept. Army, Washington, 1975-77; resigned, 1977; dep. counsel NAVSUP, Dept. Navy, Washington, 1977-80; judge Armed Svcs. Bd. Contract Appeals, Washington, 1980—. Editor-in-chief Baylor Law Rev., 1968. Contbr. articles to legal jours. Contbg. author textbooks. Pres., PTA, Frankfurt, 1972-74; mem. Frankfurt Community Adv. Coun., 1972-74; mem. Child Abuse Council, Killeen, Tex., 1968-69; elder, chmn. Evangelical Free Ch., Manassas, Va., 1980-84; bd. dirs. Trinity Sem., Deerfield, Ill., 1982-88; trustee Outreach, Inc., Grand Rapids, Mich., 1977—; mem. gen. bd. Evang. Free Ch. of Am., 1982—, mem. standards com. Evans Coun. for Fin. Accountability, 1982—; bd. regents, bd. incorp mems Dallas Theol. Seminary, 1988—; chmn. standards com., bd. dirs. Evang. Coun. Fin. Accountability, 1982—. Recipient Spl. Recognition award Mariano Galvez U., Guatemala, 1984; decorated in service. Mem. ABA, Tex. Bar Assn., Fed. Bar Assn., Nat. Conf. Bd. Contract Appeals Mems. Republican. Home: 8026 Whitting Dr Manassas VA 20112-4705

**VAN CAMP, BRIAN RALPH,** judge; b. Halstead, Kans., Aug. 23, 1940; s. Ralph A. and Mary Margaret (Bragg) Van C.; m. Diane D. Miller, 1992; children: Megan M., Laurie E. AB, U. Calif., Berkeley, 1962, LLB, 1965. Bar: Calif. 1966. Dep. atty. gen. State Calif., 1965-67; agy. atty. Redevel. Agy., City of Sacramento, 1967-70; asst./acting sec. Bus. and Trans. Agy., State of Calif., 1970-71; commr. of corps. State of Calif., Sacramento, 1971-74; partner firm Diepenbrock, Wulff, Plant & Hannegan, Sacramento, 1975-77, Van Camp & Johnson, Sacramento, 1978-90; sr. ptnr. Downey, Brand, Seymour & Rohwer, 1990-97; judge Superior Ct., Sacramento County, 1997—; lectr. Continuing Edn. Bar, Practicing Law Inst., Calif. CPA Soc. Contbr. articles to profl. jours. Mem. Rep. State Ctrl. Com. Calif., 1974-78; pres. Sacramento Area Commerce and Trade Orgn., 1986-87; mem. electoral coll. Presdl. Elector for State of Calif., 1976; mem. Calif. Health Facilities Fin. Authority, 1985-89; mem. Capital Area Devel. Authority, 1989-97, chmn., 1990-97; mem. Calif. Jud. Coun. Task Force on Quality of Justice, 1998-99; bd. dirs. Sacramento Symphony Assn., 1973-85, 92-94, Sacramento Symphony Found., 1993—, Sacramento Valley Venture Capital Forum, 1986-90, League to Save Lake Tahoe, 1988-95, Valley Vision, Inc., 1993-97; elder Fremont Presbyn. Ch., 1967—. Recipient Sumner-Mering Meml. award Sacramento U. of Calif. Alumni Assn., 1962, Thos. Jefferson award Am. Inst. Pub. Svc., 1994, Excellence in Achievement award Calif. Alumni Assn., 1997; named Outstanding Young Man of Yr., Sacramento Jaycees, 1970, Internat. Young Man of Yr., Active 20-30 Club Internat., 1973. Mem. Calif. State Bar (mem.com. on corps. 1977-80, partnerships and unincorporated bus. assns. 1983-87), Sacramento County Bar Assn., Calif. C. of C. (chmn. statewide energy task force 1979-85, bd. dirs. 1982-97, chmn. edn. com. 1988-90), Sacramento Met. C. of C. (co-chmn. econ. devel. com. 1979, bd. dirs. 1986-88), Boalt Hall Alumni Assn. (bd. dirs. 1991-94), Lincoln Club Sacramento Valley (bd. dirs., pres. 1984-86), U. Calif. Men's Club (pres. 1968), Sutter Club, Kanadhar Ski Club, Rotary Club Sacramento (pres. 1993-94, Paul Harris Fellow award 1995), Comstock Club (pres. 1976-77). Republican. Presbyterian. E-mail: bvcj@courts.co.sacramento.ca.us. Office: 720 9th St Sacramento CA 95814-1311

**VANCE, BEVERLY DIANE,** lawyer; b. Hattiesburg, Miss., Sept. 13, 1942; d. John Joseph Schilling and Edna Ross (Lott) Faciane; m. Ronald J. Christie, Nov. 11, 1961 (div. 1973); children: Pamela D., Heather B., Carol A.; m. John Vance, Jan. 19, 1975. BA in History summa cum laude, SUNY, Buffalo, 1980, JD, 1984. Bar: N.Y. 1986, U.S. Dist. Ct. N.Y. 1987. Atty. Allen, Lippes & Shone, Buffalo, 1984-85, Gross & Shuman, Buffalo, 1985-86; atty. Diebold & Farmelo, Buffalo, 1986-93, ptnr., 1993—. Mem. ABA, ATLA, Erie County Bar Assn. (matrimonial and family law com.), N.Y. Bar Assn., N.Y. State Coun. Divorce Mediation. Roman Catholic. Avocations: sailing, cross country skiing. Family and matrimonial. Office: Diebold & Farmelo 1500 Statler Towers Buffalo NY 14202-7502

**VANCE, MICHAEL CHARLES,** lawyer; b. Marshalltown, Iowa, May 31, 1951; s. Randall Scott and Irma Vance; m. Bonnie K. Becker, Jan. 1, 1995; children: Thomas Randall, Patrick Michael. BA in Polit. Sci. and Econs., U. Iowa, 1973, JD with distinction, 1976. Bar: Iowa 1976, U.S Dist. Ct. (so. dist.) Iowa 1976, U.S. Tax Ct. 1991. Sole practice Mt. Pleasant, Iowa, 1976—; atty. City of Wayland, Iowa, 1976—; instr. bus. law Iowa Wesleyan Coll., Mt. Pleasant, 1977-78; asst. county atty. Henry County, Mt. Pleasant, 1979-97, jud. magistrate, 1997—. Mem., bd. dirs. Community Mental Health of Henry, Louisa and Jefferson Counties, Mt. Pleasant, 1977-82; chairperson Henry County Dems., Mt. Pleasant, 1978-83; pres. Mt. Pleasant Sesquicentennial Assn., 1984-86, St. Alphonsus Ch. Parish Council (pres. 1983-85), Mt. Pleasant, 1985— (trustee). Mem. ABA, Iowa Bar Assn. (bd. govs. 1996—), Henry County Bar Assn. (sec.-treas. 1977-78, v.p. 1978-79, pres. 1979-80, 88-91), Iowa Trial Lawyers Assn., Iowa Conf. Bar Assn. Presidents (bd. dirs. 1979-81), Iowa Assn. Jud. Magistrates (bd. dirs. 1998—), Mt. Pleasant C. of C. (bd. dirs. 1991-93, named Citizen of Yr. 1985), Mt. Pleasant Jaycees (bd. dirs. 1978-83), Rotary, KC, Omicron Delta Kappa, Omicron Delta Epsilon. Roman Catholic. General practice, General civil litigation, Probate. Home: 2005 Bittersweet Cir Mount Pleasant IA 52641-8301 Office: PO Box 469 101 N Jefferson St Mount Pleasant IA 52641-2039

**VANCHO, JANINE,** lawyer; b. San Francisco, May 11, 1961; d. Jon C. and Inez Beatrice Culwell; m. John Anthony Vancho, Nov. 30, 1981; 1 child, Justin. JD, Thomas Jefferson Sch. Law, San Diego, 1997. Bar: Calif. 1998. Assoc. Brownwood & Rice, San Diego, 1996—. Insurance, State civil litigation, Personal injury. Office: Brownwood & Rice 525 B St San Diego CA 92101

**VAN CLEVE, WILLIAM MOORE,** lawyer; b. Mar. 17, 1929; s. William T Van Cleve and Catherine (Baldwin) Moore Van Cleve; m. Georgia Hess Dunbar, June 27, 1953; children: Peter Dunbar, Robert Baldwin, Sarah Van Cleve Van Doren, Emory Basford. Grad., Phillips Acad., 1946; AB in Econs., Princeton U., 1950; JD, Washington U., St. Louis, 1953. Bar: Mo. 1953. Assoc. Dunbar and Gaddy, St. Louis, 1955-58; ptnr. Bryan Cave LLP (and predecessor firm), St. Louis, 1958—, chmn., 1973-94; bd. dirs. Emerson Electric Co. Trustee Washington U., 1983—, vice chmn. bd. trustees, 1988-93, 95—, chmn., 1993-95, mem. exec. com., 1985—; pres. Eliot Soc., 1982-86; chmn. Law Sch. Nat. Coun., 1986-93; commr. St. Louis Sci. Ctr., 1993—; bd. dirs., pres. Parents As Tchrs. Nat. Ctr., 1991—. Mem. ABA, Bar Assn. Met. St. Louis, Mound City Bar Assn., St. Louis County Bar Assn., Order of Coif (hon.). Democrat. Episcopalian. Clubs: Princeton (pres. 1974-75), Noonday (pres. 1985), St. Louis Country, Bogey (pres. 1990-91), Round Table (St. Louis). General corporate, Estate planning, Non-profit and tax-exempt organizations. Home: 8 Dromara Rd Saint Louis MO 63124-1816 Office: Bryan Cave LLP 211 N Broadway Fl 36 Saint Louis MO 63102-2733

**VAN CONAS, KENDALL ASHLEIGH,** lawyer; b. Panorama City, Calif., Mar. 6, 1966; d. Philip and Grace Ella (Reid) Cohen; m. Andrew George Van Conas, Apr. 11, 1992; children: Julia Grace, Natalie Ashleigh. BA, UCLA, 1988; JD, Southwestern U., L.A., 1992. Bar: Calif. 1992, U.S. Dist. Ct. (ctrl. dist.) Calif. 1992. Assoc. Cohen & Cohen, Camarillo, Calif., 1992—. Bd. dirs. Dream Found., Santa Barbara, Calif., 1996—. Mem. Calif. Bar Assn., Ventura County Bar Assn. (vice chmn. probate sect. 1997—), Rotary (bd. dirs. Camarillo 1994-97). Estate planning, Probate, Family and matrimonial. Office: Cohen & Cohen 445 Rosewood Ave Camarillo CA 93010-5929

**VAN DAM, MARGOT NICOLE,** lawyer; b. Calif., June 5, 1962. BA in Econs., U. Pa., 1984; MBA, Cornell U., 1986; JD, U. So. Calif., 1989. Bar: Calif. 1989. Internship Calif. State Atty. Gen's. Office, 1988; jud. externship with Hon. J. Spencer Letts U.S. Dist. Ct. (ctrl. dist.) Calif., 1988; sr. counsel Mattel, Inc., L.A., 1996—. Media. Office: Mattel Inc 333 Continental Blvd El Segundo CA 90245-5012

**VANDEGRIFT, LEE BARTLETT,** commisioner; b. Wichita, Kans., May 16, 1953; s. Alfred Eugene Peter and Clara Ann Vandegrift; m. Mauricia Gay Hornback, May 25, 1985; 1 child: Blair Elaine. BA, Evergreen State Coll., 1975; JD, U. Wash., 1978. Bar: U.S. Dist. Ct. (ea., we. dists.) Wash. Assoc. Law Office Peter Young, Wenatchee, Wash., 1978-81; shareholder Young, Monnette & Vandergrift, P.S., Wenatchee, 1981-95; superior ct. commr. Chelan County and Douglas County Superior Ct., Wenatchee, 1995—. Bd. dirs. Mission Vista, Inc., Wenatchee, 1984-94, Translink, Wenatchee, 1989—, Habitat for Humanity, Wenatchee, 1998—. Mem. Supriorr Ct. Judges Assn. Office: Chelan County Superior Ct PO Box 880 Wenatchee WA 98807-0880

**VAN DE KAMP, JOHN KALAR,** lawyer; b. Pasadena, Calif., Feb. 7, 1936; s. Harry and Georgie (Kalar) Van de K.; m. Andrea Fisher, Mar. 11, 1978; 1 child, Diana. BA, Dartmouth Coll., 1956; JD, Stanford U., 1959. Bar: Calif. 1960. Asst. U.S. atty. L.A., 1960-66, U.S. atty., 1966-67; dep. dir. Exec. Office for U.S. Attys., Washington, 1967-68, dir., 1968-69; spl. asst. Pres.'s Commn. on Campus Unrest, 1970; fed. pub. defender L.A., 1971-75; dist. atty. Los Angeles County, 1975-83; atty. gen. State of Calif., 1983-91; ptnr. Dewey Ballantine, L.A., 1991-96, of counsel, 1996—; pres. Thoroughbred Owners, Calif., 1996—; bd. dirs. United Airlines. Mem. Calif. Dist. Attys. Assn. (pres. 1975-83), Nat. Dist. Attys. Assn. (v.p. 1975-83), Peace Officers Assn. L.A. County (past pres.), Nat. Assn. Attys. Gen. (exec. com. 1983-91), Conf. Western Attys. Gen. (pres. 1986). General practice, General civil litigation, Administrative and regulatory. Office: Dewey Ballantine 333 S Hope St Ste 3000 Los Angeles CA 90071-3039

**VAN DEMARK, RICHARD EDWARD,** lawyer; b. Sioux Falls, S.D., June 6, 1955; s. Robert Eugene and Bertie Marie (Thompson) Van D.; m. Michelle Margaret Volin, June 5, 1982; children: Andrew Porter, Hannah Elizabeth. AB, Vassar Coll., 1977; postgrad., Princeton (N.J.), 1977-79; MBA, U. Chgo., 1981; JD, Northwestern U., 1984. Bar: Ill. 1984. Assoc. Bell, Boyd & Lloyd, Chgo., 1984-91, ptnr., 1992-93; investment exec. Dain Rauscher, Inc., Sioux Falls, S.D., 1996—. Trustee Vassar Coll., 1982—. Mem. ABA, S.D. Bar Assn., Ill. Bar Assn., Chgo. Bar Assn., Phi Beta Kappa, Omicron Delta Epsilon. Real property, General corporate. Home: 321 E 27th St Sioux Falls SD 57105-3032 Office: Dain Rauscher Inc 101 N Main Ave Ste 301 Sioux Falls SD 57104-6450

**VAN DEMARK, RUTH ELAINE,** lawyer; b. Santa Fe, N.Mex., May 16, 1944; d. Robert Eugene and Bertha Marie (Thompson) Van D.; m. Leland Wilkinson, June 23, 1967; children: Anne Marie, Caroline Cook. AB, Vassar Coll., 1966; MTS, Harvard U., 1969; JD with honors, U. Conn., 1976. Bar: Conn. 1976, Ill. 1977, U.S. Dist. Ct. Conn. 1976, U.S. Dist. Ct. (no. dist.) Ill., U.S. Ct. Appeals (7th cir.) 1984, U.S. Supreme Ct. 1983. Instr. legal rsch. and writing Loyola U. Sch. Law, Chgo., 1976-79; assoc. Wildman,

Harrold, Allen & Dixon, Chgo., 1977-84, ptnr., 1985-94; prin. Law Offices of Ruth E. Van Demark, Chgo., 1995—; mem. rules com. Ill. Supreme Ct., 1999—, chair appellate rules subcom., 1996—; mem. dist. ct. fund adv. com. U.S. Dist. Ct. (no. dist.) Ill., 1997—. Assoc. editor Conn. Law Rev., 1975-76. Mem. adv. bd. Horizon Hospice, Chgo., 1978—, YWCA Battered Women's Shelter, Evanston, Ill., 1982-86; del.-at-large White House Conf. on Families, L.A., 1980; mem. alumni coun. Harvard Divinity Sch., 1988-91; vol. atty. Pro Bono Advocates Chgo., 1982-92, bd. dirs., 1993-99, chair devel. com., 1993; bd. dirs. Friends of Pro Bono Advocates Orgn., 1987-89, New Voice Prodns., 1984-86, Byrne Piven Theater Workshop, 1987-90, Luth. Social Svcs. Ill., 1998—; founder, bd. dirs. Friends of Battered Women and Their Children, 1986-87; chair 175th Reunion Fund Harvard U. Div. Sch., 1992. Mem. ABA, Ill. Bar Assn., Conn. Bar Assn., Chgo. Bar Assn., Appellate Lawyers Assn. Ill. (bd. dirs. 1985-87, treas. 1989-90, sec. 1990-91, v.p. 1991-92, pres. 1992-93), Women's Bar Assn. Ill., Jr. League Evanston (chair State Pub. Affairs Com. 1987-88, Vol. of Yr. 1983-84), Chgo. Vassar Club (pres. 1979-81), Cosmopolitan Club (N.Y.C.). Federal civil litigation, State civil litigation, Appellate. Home: 1127 Asbury Ave Evanston IL 60202-1136 Office: 225 W Washington St Ste 2200 Chicago IL 60606-3408

**VANDENBERG, RAYMOND LEONARD, JR.,** lawyer; b. Little Rock, Feb. 21, 1948; s. Raymond Leonard and Beatrice Lois (Hilbert) V.; m. Margaret Ann Keegan, Mar. 14, 1987; children: christopher Hilbert, Theodore William. AB, Cornell U., 1970; JD, U. Mich., 1975. Assoc. Thacher, Proffitt & Wood, N.Y.C., 1975-78; assoc. Finley Kimble Wagner, N.Y.C., 1978-84, ptnr., 1984-87; pres. Vande Vision Entertainment, N.Y.C., 1987-91; atty. pvt. practice, N.Y.C., 1991-96; pres. Vandenberg & Assocs., N.Y.C., 1997-98; ptnr. Vandenberg & Felin, LLP, N.Y.C., 1998—. Vestry mem. St. Bartholomew's Ch., N.Y.C., 1989-98, warden, 1991-95. Mem. N.Y. Athletic Club, Knickerbocker Club. Avocation: running. Federal civil litigation, General civil litigation, State civil litigation. Home: 429 Stellar Ave Pelham NY 10803-2124 Office: Vandenberg & Felin LLP 110 E 42nd St New York NY 10017-5611

**VANDENBURGH, BEVERLY ANN,** lawyer; b. Chgo., Oct. 25, 1930; d. John W. and Florence A. (Wallen) Hibbott; m. Edward C. Vandenburgh, Apr. 11, 1959 (div. 1985); children: Lynn, J. Derek; m. Kenneth Vaughan Dake, Apr. 19, 1986. BS, Northwestern U., 1952; JD, DePaul U., 1958. Bar: Ill. 1959. Patent atty. Swift & Co., Chgo., 1959-61; pvt. practice Barrington, Ill., 1962-90; ret., 1990—. Vice pres. Countryside Ctr. for Handicapped, Long Grove, Ill., 1965. Mem. ABA (editor patent, trademark and copyright sect. Chgo. chpt. 1963-79, past sect. chmn. tax sect.), Ill. Bar Assn., Phi Beta Kappa, Barrington Women's (incorporator, chmn.). Republican. Baptist. Avocations: travel, fishing, snorkeling, handiwork, reading. Estate planning, Taxation, general, Patent. Home: 73 Sawmill Creek Dr Nellysford VA 22958-9538

**VANDEN EYKEL, IKE,** lawyer; b. Slayton, Minn., Mar. 25, 1949; s. Martin D. and Wilma J. V.; m. Cathy A., Aug. 5, 1978; childre; Eric, Lindsey, Steven. BS, Drake U., 1971; JD, Baylor U., 1973. Bar: Tex. 1973, U.S. Dist. Ct. (no. dist.) Tex. 1973, U.S. Supreme Ct. 1976. Assoc. Stroud & Smith, Dallas, 1973-78; ptnr. Secugson, Doiuglass, Falooner & Vanden Eykel, Dallas, 1978-90; ptnr. Koons, Fuller & Vanden Eykel, Dallas, 1990-95, mng. ptnr., 1995—. Author: Successful Lone Star Divorce, 1998. Fellow Am. Acad. Matromonial Lawyers, Internat. Acad. Matromonial Lawyers; mem. Am. Coll. Family Trial Lawyers (diplomate). Republican. Methodist. Avocations: golf, tennis. E-mail: ike@kfur-law.com. Family and matrimonial. Office: Koons Fuller Vanden Eykel & Robertson 2311 Cedar Springs Rd Ste 300 Dallas TX 75201-7811

**VANDERBILT, ARTHUR T., II,** lawyer; b. Summit, N.J., Feb. 20, 1950; s. William Runyon and Jean (White) V. BA, Wesleyan U., Middletown, Conn., 1972; JD, U. Va., 1975. Bar: N.J. 1975, U.S. Dist. Ct. N.J. 1975, U.S. Supreme Ct. 1978. Jud. clk. to presiding justice N.J. Superior Ct., 1975-76, dep. atty. gen., 1976-78, asst. counsel to gov., 1978-79; ptnr. Carella, Byrne, Bain & Gilfillan, Roseland, N.J., 1979—; chmn. Supreme Ct. Ethics Com.; mem. Supreme Ct. Adv. Com. Profl. Ethics. Author: Changing Law 1976, Jersey Justice, 1978, Law School, 1981, Treasure Wreck, 1986, Fortune's Children, 1989 (Book of the Month Club, Readers Digest and fgn. edits.), New Jersey's Judicial Revolution, 1997, Golden Days, 1998, Jersey Jurists, 1998, The Making of a Bestseller, 1999. Mem. ABA (Scribes award 1976), N.J. Bar Assn., Am. Judicature Soc., Nat. Assn. Bond Lawyers, The Authors Guild, Inc., Nat. Writers Union. Republican. Presbyterian. Avocation: writing. Municipal (including bonds), Administrative and regulatory, Public utilities. Office: Carella Byrne Bain & Gilfillan 6 Becker Farm Rd Roseland NJ 07068-1735

**VANDERGINST, DENNIS ALLEN,** lawyer; b. Moline, Ill., July 16, 1962; s. Kenneth James and Barbara Ann (Garard) V.; m. Jean Elizabeth Pauwels, July 10, 1992. BA, No. Ill. U., 1985; JD, DePaul U., 1989. Bar: Ill. 1989, U.S. Dist. Ct. (no. dist.) Ill. 1989, U.S. Ct. Appeals (7th cir.) 1990, U.S. Dist. Ct. (ctrl. dist.) Ill. 1992, Iowa 1994, Wis. 1996. Law clk., atty. Law Offices Elliott Samuels, Chgo., 1987-90; atty. pvt. practice, Chgo., 1990-91, Wylie, Mulherin, Rehfeldt & Varchetto, Wheaton, Ill., 1991-92; ptnr. Braud/Westensee, Rock Island, Wheaton, Ill., 1992-99, Braud, Westensee & Van Der Ginst, Rock Island, Wheaton, 1999—; adj. prof. Black Hawk Coll., Moline, Ill., 1993—. Mem. ABA (medicine and law com., products, gen. liability and consumer law com., automobile law com., litigation sect., tort law and ins. sect.), ATLA (interstate trucking litigation group, motor vehicle collision hwy. and premises liability sect., ins. sect. 1994—), Ill. State Bar Assn., Ill. Trial Lawyers Assn. (procedural rules com. 1994—, membership com., legis. com. 1994—, med. negligence com., ins. law com., product liability com. 1994—), Iowa State Bar Assn. (law panels com. 1994—, svcs. to the elderly com.), Iowa Trial Lawyers Assn., Rock Island County Bar Assn., Jaycees, KC, Winnebago County Bar Assn. (profl. responsibility com., legal/med. com., editl. bd., profl. responsibility com.), Chgo. Bar Assn. (class litigation com. 1998—, ins. law com., tort litigation com. 1998—). Personal injury, Product liability, Insurance. Office: Braud Westensee & Van der Ginst 1705 2nd Ave 6th Flr Rock Island IL 61201-8718

**VANDER LAAN, ALLAN C.,** lawyer; b. Grand Rapids, Mich.; s. Allan Carroll and Barbara Vander L. BA, Calvin Coll., 1978; JD, Thomas M. Cooley Law Sch., Lansing, Mich., 1981. Bar: U.S. Dist. Ct. (we. dist.) Mich., U.S. Ct. Appeals (6th cir.). Asst. prosecutor Barry County, Hastings, Mich., 1982-86; lawyer Denenberg, Tuffley & Jamieson, Grand Rapids, Mich., 1986-93, Morrison, Mahoney & Miller, Grand Rapids, 1994-95, Roberts, Betz & Bloss P.C., Grand Rapids, 1995-99, Rekiel & Assocs., Grand Rapids, 1999—. Mem. Grand Rapids Bar Assn. Insurance, Personal injury, Product liability. Office: Rekiel & Assocs 4102 Embassy Dr SE Grand Rapids MI 49546-2417

**VANDER LAAN, MARK ALAN,** lawyer; b. Akron, Ohio, Sept. 14, 1948; s. Robert H. and Isabel R. (Bishop) Vander L.; m. Barbara Ann Ryzenga, Aug. 25, 1970; children: Aaron, Matthew. AB, Hope Coll., 1970; JD, U. Mich., 1972. Bar: Ohio 1973, U.S. Dist. Ct. (so. dist.) Ohio 1973, U.S. Ct. Appeals (6th cir.) 1978, U.S. Supreme Ct. 1981. Assoc. Dinsmore, Shohl, Coates & Deupree, Cin., 1972-79; ptnr. Dinsmore & Shohl, Cin., 1979—; spl. counsel Ohio Atty. Gen.'s Office, 1983—; spl. prosecutor State of Ohio, 1985-94; city solicitor City of Blue Ash, Ohio, 1987—, City of Silvirton, Ohio, 1999—; trustee Cin. So. Railway, 1994—. Mem. Cin. Human Rels. Commn., 1980-86; mem. Leadership Cin. Class XIII, 1989-90; trustee Legal Aid Soc. of Cin., 1981-94, pres., 1988-90. Mem. ABA, Ohio Bar Assn., Cin. Bar Assn. (ethics com. 1983—), Sixth Cir. Jud. Conf. (life), Potter Stewart Inn of Ct. (master), Queen City Club. General civil litigation, General corporate. Office: Dinsmore & Shohl 1900 Chemed Ct 255 E 5th St Cincinnati OH 45202-4700

**VAN DERMYDEN, SUE ANN,** lawyer; b. Wahpeton, N.D., Mar. 6, 1965; d. Roger and Helen Slotten; m. Richard Van Dermyden, July 6, 1991; children: Courtney, Tori. BA in Polit. Sci., Calif. State U., Chico, 1990; JD, U. of the Pacific, 1993. Bar: Calif. 1993, U.S. Dist. Ct. (ea. dist.) Calif. 1993. Assoc. Nossaman, Guthner, Knox & Elliott, Sacramento, 1996-97, Schachter, Kristoff, Orenstein & Berkowitz, LLP, Sacramento, 1997—. Mem. Bldg. Industry Assn. (membership com. 1994—), McGeorge Sch. Law Alumni Assn. (bd. dirs. 1995—). Labor, General civil litigation. Office: Schachter Kristoff Orenstein & Berkowitz 980 9th St Ste 1500 Sacramento CA 95814-2735

**VANDERPOEL, JAMES ROBERT,** lawyer; b. Harvey, Ill., Sept. 27, 1955; s. Waid Richard and Ruth (Silberman) V.; m. Deanne Czabaranek, May 1987; children: Jacqueline, Robert, Jennifer. BS in Fin., Ind. U., 1978; JD, Santa Clara U., 1982. Bar: Calif. 1982, U.S. Dist. Ct. (no. dist.) Calif. 1982. Group contracts mgr. Motorola Computer Group, Tempe, Ariz., 1984—. Avocations: basketball, hiking, golf, snorkeling, gardening. Contracts commercial, Computer, Intellectual property. Office: Motorola Computer Group 2900 S Diablo Way Tempe AZ 85282-3214

**VANDERVOORT, TERRE LYNNE,** prosecutor; b. Battle Creek, Mich., Oct. 15, 1965; d. Peter Millard and Nancy Dare Vandervoort; m. David Michael Rader, Sept. 21, 1996. BS in Bus. cum laude, Miami U., Oxford, Ohio, 1987; JD, Ohio State U., 1990. Bar: Ohio 1990. Assoc. Sitterley & Vandervoort, Lancaster, Ohio, 1990-92; asst. prosecutor City of Lancaster, 1992-96, law dir., city prosecutor, 1996—; lectr. on effective prosecution Ohio Atty. Gen., Columbus, 1997; law enforcement trainer. Bd. mem. Lighthouse, Inc., Lancaster, 1992—, Cmty. Corrections Bd., Lancaster, 1996—. Recipient Victims of Crime Pub. Policy Leadership award, 1995; Violence Against Women Act grantee Fed. Govt., Lancaster, 1998. Republican. Methodist. Office: City Law Dirs Office 104 E Main St Lancaster OH 43130-3726

**VAN DER WAL, JEANNE HUBER,** lawyer, stockbroker, consultant; b. Flushing, N.Y., Feb. 7, 1954; d. William Joseph and Georgene (Lukes) Huber; m. Peter van der Wal, May 8, 1982. AB magna cum laude, Colgate U., 1975; JD, Suffolk U., 1978. Bar: D.C. 1979, U.S. Dist. Ct. D.C. 1979, U.S. Ct. Appeals (D.C. cir.) 1979, U.S. Supreme Ct. 1983. Regulatory atty. Kimberly-Clark Corp., Washington, 1978-83; corp. counsel Kimberly-Clark Corp., Roswell, Ga., 1983-86; pvt. practice cons. Northridge, Calif., 1986-87; account exec. Drexel Burnham Lambert, Beverly Hills, Calif., 1987—; corp. rep. U.S. Mex. C. of C., Washington and Mex., 1979-83; corp. rep. ASTM, Phila., 1981-83; cons. Industry Sector Adv. Com. on Paper and Paper Products for Trade Policy Matters, Dept. of Commerce, Washington, 1982-85. Participant Women's Equality Day, The White House, 1984; mem. exec. women's briefing on commerce Rep. Nat. Com., Washington, 1985; Rep. Presdl. Task Force, Washington, 1985-87. N.Y. Regents scholar, 1971-75. Mem. ABA, Bar Assn. D.C., D.C. Bar Assn., Century City C. of C. (vice chair internat. bus. com.), Brit.-Am. C. of C. (vice chair activities com.), U.S.-Mexico C. of C., Australian-Am. C. of C., Internat. Bankers Assn., Internat. Platform Assn., Phi Beta Kappa. Republican. Roman Catholic. Clubs: Willow Springs Country (Roswell, Ga.) (bd. dirs., v.p. 1984-85, bd. dirs., sec. 1985-86). Avocations: real estate, sailing, golf, skiing. Administrative and regulatory, Contracts commercial, General corporate. Home: 18930 Harnett St Northridge CA 91326-3007

**VAN DER WALDE, PAUL D.,** lawyer, entrepreneur; b. Boston, Aug. 22, 1966; s. Peter H. and Roberta L. Van Der Walde. BS in Bus., Ariz. State U., 1989; JD, Santa Clara U., 1993. Bar: Calif., Ariz., U.S. Dist. Ct. (no. dist.) Calif. Atty. Mitchell, Stock & Burrow, San Jose, Calif., 1991-93, Law Offices of Daniel Cornell, San Jose, 1993-94; ptnr. Cornell & Van Der Walde, Palo Alto, Calif., 1994-97, Van Der Walde & Assocs., Cupertino, Calif., 1997—; pres. Legal Connection, Cupertino, 1998—; mem. exec. com. Santa Clara Legal Referral Svcs., San Jose, 1998-99; bd. govs. Legal Connection, 1998—. Mem. ATLA, Santa Clara County Bar Assn., Consumer Attys. Calif. Avocations: skiing, hiking, whitewater rafting, cooking, the finer things in life. General civil litigation. Office: Van Der Walde & Assocs 20370 Town Center Ln Ste 100 Cupertino CA 95014-3226

**VANDER WEIDE, VERNON JAY,** lawyer; b. East Grand Rapids, Mich., Apr. 3, 1940; s. Henry Thomas and Della (Van Zoeren) V.W.; m. Gretchen Laurie Clemmons, Sept. 11, 1965; children: Jennifer, Stephanie, Vanessa. AA, Grand Rapids Jr. Coll., 1960; BA, U. Mich., 1962, LLB, 1965; LLM, George Washington U., 1971. Bar: D.C. 1970, Mich. 1970, Minn. 1977, U.S. Dist. Ct. Minn. 1977. Staff asst. House Rep. Conf., Washington, 1965-66; staff atty. ICC, Washington, 1969-70; br. chief atty. SEC, Arlington, Va., 1970-76; shareholder Wiese & Cox, Mpls., 1970-76; shareholder, bd. dirs. Head, Seifert & Vander Weide, Mpls., 1982—; lectr. Continuing Legal Edn. Corp. Orgn., 1981, 87. Writer, analyst, columnist for neighborhood newspaper, Mpls., 1982-94. Mem. task force Supt.'s Blue Ribbon Commn., Mpls., 1982; bd. deacons Westminster Presbyn. Ch., Mpls., 1993-95. Capt. U.S. Army, 1966-69. Mem. Minn. Bar Assn., Hennepin County Bar Assn. Avocations: sailing, investments, reading, teaching, family. General civil litigation, Securities, General corporate. Office: Head Seifert & Vander Weide 120 S 6th St Minneapolis MN 55402-1803

**VAN DEVANDER, CHARLES WAYNE,** lawyer; b. Artesia, N.Mex., Oct. 3, 1962; s. Dorsey Clark and Mary Jo (Jacobs) Van D.; m. Sherri Lynn McClanahan, Aug. 27, 1987 (div. Dec. 1990); m. Beverly Ann Blank, Nov. 19, 1994. BS in Acctg., Ariz. State U., 1992; JD, U. Denver, 1995, LLM in Taxation, 1997. Bar: Colo. 1995, CHLU, CPA. Restaurant mgr. Restaurant Enterprises Group, Phoenix, 1987-90; law clk. Security Life of Denver, 1994-96, atty., 1996—; cons. Desert Traditions LLC, Denver, 1997—. Co-author, co-editor: (tech. manuals) Split Dollar A to Z, 1998, Estate Planning A to Z (2 vols.), 1998. Vol. Read Aloud Program Denver Pub. Libr., 1997, student tutoring MLK Elem., 1992-95. Mem. Colo. Bar Assn., Denver Bar Assn. Avocations: fly fishing, golf, sports card collecting. Estate planning, Insurance. Office: Security Life of Denver Ins Co 1290 Broadway Ste 666 Denver CO 80203-5699

**VANDEVER, WILLIAM DIRK,** lawyer; b. Chgo., Aug. 1, 1949; s. Lester J. and Elizabeth J. V.; m. Kathi J. Zellmer, Aug. 26, 1983; children: Barton Dirk, Brooke Shelby. BS, U. Mo., Kansas City, 1971, JD with distinction, 1974. Bar: Mo. 1975, U.S. Dist. Ct. (we. dist.) Mo. 1975. Dir. Popham Law Firm, Kansas City, Mo., 1975—; lectr. in field, Kansas City Mo., 1979—. Issue editor U. Mo.-Kansas City Law Rev., 1974. Fellow Am. Bd. Trial Advs. (Best Lawyers in Am.-tort law); mem. ABA, ATLA, Mo. Assn. Trial Attys., Kansas City Met. Bar Assn. (treas., sec., pres., elected to 16th Jud. Commn. 1988-94), Kansas City Bar Found. (treas. 1992, sec. 1994, pres. 1996-98), Interest on Lawyer Trust Accts. of Mo. (bd. govs.), Kansas City Mem. Svcs. (pres. 1988—, commr. 16th jud. cir. selection com.), U. Mo. Kansas City Found. (fin. com. 1998), Phi Delta Phi, Beta Theta Pi. Avocations: tennis, skiing, running, reading. Personal injury, Construction. Home: 11380 W 121st Ter Shawnee Mission KS 66213-1978 Office: Popham Law Firm 1300 Commerce Trust Bldg Kansas City MO 64106

**VANDEWALLE, GERALD WAYNE,** state supreme court chief justice; b. Noonan, N.D., Aug. 15, 1933; s. Jules C. and Blanche Marie (Gits) VandeW. BSc, U. N.D., 1955, JD, 1958. Bar: N.D., U.S. Dist. Ct. N.D. 1959. Spl. asst. atty. gen. State of N.D., Bismarck, 1958-75, 1st asst. atty. gen., 1975-78; justice N.D. Supreme Ct., 1978-92, chief justice, 1993—; mem. faculty Bismarck Jr. Coll., 1972-76; chair Nat. Ctr. for State Cts. Rsch. adv. coun.; mem. fed.-state jurisdiction com. Jud. Conf. of the U.S. Editor-in-chief N.D. Law Rev, 1957-58. Active Bismarck Meals on Wheels. Recipient Sioux award U. N.D., 1992, Ednl. Law award N.D. Coun. Sch. Attys., 1987, Love Without Fear award Abused Adult Resource Ctr., 1995, N. Dakota State Bar Assoc. Dist. Service Award, 1998. Mem. ABA (co-chair bar admissions com., mem. coun. sect. legal edn. and admissions), State Bar Assn. N.D., Burleigh County Bar Assn., Conf. of Chief Justices (1st v.p., bd. dirs., chair fed.-state tribal rels. com.), Am. Contract Bridge League, Order of Coif, N.D. Jud. Conf. (exec. com.), Phi Eta Sigma, Beta Alpha Psi (Outstanding Alumnus award Zeta chpt. 1995), Beta Gamma Sigma, Phi Alpha Delta. Roman Catholic. Clubs: Elks, K.C. Office: ND Supreme Ct State Capitol 600 E Boulevard Ave Bismarck ND 58505-0660

**VANDIVIER, BLAIR ROBERT,** lawyer; b. Rapid City, S.D., Dec. 24, 1955; s. Robert Eugene and Barbara Jean (Kidd) V.; m. Elizabeth Louise Watson, July 26, 1980; children: Jessica Elizabeth, Jennifer Louise. BS magna cum laude, Butler U., 1978; JD cum laude, Ind. U., 1981. Bar: Ind. 1981, U.S. Dist. Ct. (so. dist.) Ind. 1981, U.S. Tax Ct. 1985. Assoc. Henderson, Daily, Withrow, Johnson & Gross, Indpls., 1981-83; assoc., ptnr. Johnson, Gross, Densborn & Wright, Indpls., 1983-85, of counsel, 1985-87; v.p., sec. Benchmark Products, Inc. (formerly Benchmark Chem. Corp.), Indpls., 1985-91, pres., 1991—, also bd. dirs.; ptnr. Gross & Vandivier, Indpls., 1987-89; of counsel Riley, Bennett & Egloff, Indpls., 1990—; mgmt. rep. Pro Com, L.L.C., 1991—; v.p. Seleco Inc., Indpls., 1988-93, pres., 1993—. Mem. com. Conner Prairie Settlement Fund Dr., Indpls., 1983-85, Riley Run, 1987—; mem. regulatory study com. City of Indpls., 1993-98. Mem. ABA, Ind. Bar Assn., Indpls. Bar Assn (bd. dirs. young lawyers divsn. 1982-85), Am. Electroplaters and Surface Finisher's Soc. (chmn. nat. law com. 1986-97, pres. Indpls. br. 1989, bd. mgrs. 1997—, tech. conf. bd. 1991-97, chmn. surface finishers ann. tech. conf. and exhbn. 1994, chmn. surface finishers focus group 1994—, Tech. Conf. Bd. Recognition award 1996), Nat. Assn. Metal Finishers (bd. dirs. 1998—, exec. com. 1998—), Metal Finishing Suppliers Assn. (spl. projects svcs. com., 1988-93, chmn. 1993—, chmn. hazardous materials br. 1991-93, trustee 1992-95, v.p. 1995-97, pres. 1997-99, past pres. 1999—), Highland Golf Club, Highland Country Club (chmn. ins. com. 1989-94, golf. com. 1992-94, bd. dirs. 1995-97, chmn. fin. com. 1996-97) Surface Finishing Industry Coun. (bd. dirs., sec. 1997-98, pres. 1999), Econ. Club Indpls., Metal Finishing Found. (pres. 1999), Delta Tau Delta (chmn. 1987-97, bd. dirs. Beta Zeta Found. 1986, Outstanding Alumnus Beta Zeta chpt. 1986). Republican. Episcopalian. Avocations: golf, reading. Contracts commercial, Real property, General corporate. Home: 8927 Woodacre Ln Indianapolis IN 46234-2848 Office: Benchmark Products Inc PO Box 68809 Indianapolis IN 46268-0809

**VANDOVER, SAMUEL TAYLOR,** lawyer; b. St. Louis, Jan. 28, 1942; s. Lewis Samuel and Mary Lou (Dimond) V.; m. Gail L. Chartrand, Sept. 9, 1966; children: Victoria G. Billimack, Virginia G., Lewis S. BS, St. Louis U., 1964, JD, 1967. Bar: Mo. 1967, U.S. Dist. Ct. (ea. dist.) Mo. 1968, U.S. Ct. Appeals (8th cir.) 1974, U.S. Supreme Ct. 1977. Assoc. Law Offices of Edward L. Dowd, St. Louis, 1967-69; asst. pub. defender St. Louis County, 1969-71; assoc. Heneghan, Roberts & Godfrey, St. Louis, 1971-73; ptnr. Godfrey & Vandover, St. Louis, 1973-77; prin. Godfrey, Vandover & Burns, Inc., St. Louis, 1977—; prosecuting atty. City of Kirkwood, Mo., 1977-80; mem. com. on rules Mo. Supreme Ct., Jefferson City, 1980-82. Recipient Lon O. Hocker Meml. Trial Lawyer award Mo. Bar Found., 1973. Mem. Am. Bd. Trial Advs., Internat. Assn. Def. Counsel, St. Louis Metro Bar Assn. (award of merit 1977), Media Club. Roman Catholic. Avocations: hunting, fishing. General civil litigation, Insurance, Personal injury. Home: 530 Gray Barn Ln Warson Woods MO 63122-1602 Office: Godfrey Vandover & Burns Inc 720 Olive St Fl 21 Saint Louis MO 63101-2338

**VAN DYKE, HENRY JOSEPH,** lawyer; b. Bklyn., Apr. 1, 1955; s. Henry and Marie C. (Loechner) Van D.; m. Mary Eileen Murphy, July 4, 1981; children: Kristen E., Michael H., Erik J., Katherine A., Kelly E., Mark J. BA in Govt. & Internat. Studies, U. Notre Dame, 1976; JD, Boston Coll., 1979. Bar: N.Y. 1982. Atty. Rosch & Rosch, Bellston Spa, N.Y., 1979-82; atty. advisor Office Hearings/Appeals, Social Security Adminstrn., Albany, 1982-89; chief counsel U.S. Dept. Energy, Schenectady (N.Y.) Naval Reactors Office, 1989—. Pres. St. Ambrose Home Sch. Assn., Latham, N.Y., 1993-98, v.p., 1991-93; legal advisor Coalition Concerned Caths., Albany, 1988-98, chmn., 1995-97. Republican. Home: 7 Margaret Dr Loudonville NY 12211-1110 Office: Schenectady Naval Reactors Office PO Box 1069 Schenectady NY 12301-1069

**VAN DYKE, PETER TYSON,** lawyer; b. Glens Falls, N.Y., Mar. 3, 1942; s. Robert Tyson and Jonise Katherine (Rezzemini) Van D.; m. Prudence H., Dec. 10, 1942; children: Elizabeth, Katherine, Carolyn. BS, U. R.I., 1964; JD with hons., SUNY, Albany, 1968; LLM, George Washington U., 1973. Bar: N.Y. 1969, Okla. 1972, U.S. Supreme Ct., U.S. Ct. Appeals (10th cir.), Okla., N.Y., U.S. Dist. Ct. (ea. dist.) N.Y., U.S. Dist. Ct. (we., ea. and no. dists.) Okla., U.S. Dist. Ct. (no. dist.) Tex. Atty. Lytle Sale & Curlee, Oklahoma City, 1972-97, McAfee & Taft, Oklahoma City, 1997—; counsel Okla. chpt. Nat. Elec. Contractor's Assn., 1980—. Elder Trinity Bapt. Ch., Norman, 1988—. Capt. U.S. Army, 1969-73. Republican. Baptist. Labor. Office: McAfee & Taft 2 Leadership Sq 10th Fl Oklahoma City OK 73102

**VAN EYSDEN, INGA,** lawyer; b. Poughkeepsie, N.Y., Jan. 9, 1959; d. Wilbur Raymond and Doris Marion (Schefferaas) Van E. BFA, Phila. Coll. Art, 1982; JD cum laude, Am. U., 1989. Bar: N.Y. 1990, U.S. Dist. Ct. (so. and ea. dist.) N.Y. 1990. Asst. corp. counsel N.Y.C. Law Dept., 1989-96, dep. asst. chief, 1996-98, asst. chief, 1998—. Office: City of New York Law Dept 100 Church St Rm 6c9 New York NY 10007-2601

**VAN FLEET, GEORGE ALLAN,** lawyer; b. Monterey, Calif., Jan. 20, 1953; s. George Lawson and Wilma Ruth (Williams) Van F.; m. Laurie Elise Koch, July 20, 1975; children: Katia Elaine, Alexander Lawson. BA summa cum laude, Rice U., 1976; JD, Columbia U., 1977. Bar: Tex. 1978, U.S. Dist. Ct. (so. dist.) Tex. 1978, U.S. Dist. Ct. (we. dist.) Tex. 1987, U.S. Dist. Ct. (no. dist.) Tex, 1988, U.S. Dist. Ct. (ea. dist.) Tex. 1991, U.S. Tax Ct., 1984, U.S. Ct. Appeals (5th cir.) 1978, U.S. Ct. Appeals (11th cir.) 1981, U.S. Ct. Appeals (D.C. cir.) 1982, U.S. Ct. Appeals (fed. cir.) 1993, U.S. Supreme Ct. 1981. Law clk. U.S. Ct. Appeals (2d cir.), N.Y.C., 1977; assoc. Vinson & Elkins, Houston, 1977-84, ptnr., 1984—; mem. NAFTA Tri-Nat. Task Force on Competition Policy; co-chair Antitrust Practice Group. Editor: Compliance Manuals for the New Antitrust Era, 1989; co-author: Federal Civil Procedure Before Trial—Fifth Circuit, 1997, The Competition Laws of NAFTA, Canada, Mexico, and the United States, 1997, Business and Commercial Litigation in federal Courts, 1998; contbr. articles to profl. jour. Mem. bd. visitors Columbia U., 1992—; mem. City of Houston Ethics Com., 1992-98, chmn. 1995-98; dir. Tex. Appleseed Found., 1998—. Recipient Ordroneaux prize Columbia U., 1977; James Kent scholar Columbia U., 1974-77. Fellow Tex. Bar Found.; mem. ABA (com. chmn. 1987-95, mem. coun. 1996—), Houston Bar Assn. (sect. chair 1991-93), Tex.-Mex. Bar Assn. (chmn. 1998—), Phi Beta Kappa. Democrat. Jewish. Antitrust, General civil litigation, Professional liability. Home: 3430 S Parkwood Dr Houston TX 77021-1238 Office: Vinson & Elkins LLP 1001 Fannin St Ste 2300 Houston TX 77002-6760

**VANGELISTI, RICHARD J.,** lawyer; b. Delta, Colo., Feb. 28, 1967. BA magna cum laude, Ariz. State U., 1991; JD, So. Meth. U., 1995. Bar: U.S. Dist. Ct. (ea. dist.) Tex. 1996, U.S. Dist. Ct. (no. and so. dists.) Tex. 1997, U.S. Dist. Ct. (we. dist.) Tex. 1998. Jud. intern U.S. Dist. Judge Joe Kendall No. Dist. Tex., Dallas, 1993; summer assoc. Fulbright & Jaworski LLP, Dallas, 1994, Gardere & Wynne LLP, Dallas, 1994; jud. clk. U.S. Dist. Judge Richard A. Schell Ea. Dist. Tex., Beaumont, 1995-97; assoc.. Fulbright & Jaworski LLP, Dallas, 1997—. Contbr. articles to profl. jours. Mem. Dallas Bar Assn., Dallas Assn. Young Lawyers, Order of the Coif. General civil litigation. Office: Fulbright & Jaworski LLP 2200 Ross Ave Ste 2800 Dallas TX 75201-2784

**VAN GILDER, DEREK ROBERT,** lawyer, engineer; b. San Antonio, Feb. 26, 1950; s. Robert Ellis and Genevieve Delphine (Hutter) Van G. Student, U.S. Mil. Acad., 1969-71; BS in Civil Engring., U. Tex., 1974, JD, 1981; MBA, U. Houston, 1976. Bar: Tex. 1981, U.S. Ct. Appeals (5th and 9th cirs.) 1982, Calif. 1982, U.S. Dist. Ct. (cen. dist.) Calif. 1982, U.S. Dist. Ct. (ea. and so. dists.) Tex. 1982, U.S. Dist. Ct. (we. dist.) Tex. 1983, U.S. Dist. Ct. (no. dist.) Tex. 1988, U.S. Supreme Ct. 1988, D.C. 1990, U.S. Patent/Trademark 1990. Engr. various engring cos., Houston, Longview and Austin, Tex., 1974-81; assoc. Thelen, Marrin, Johnson & Bridges, Los Angeles, 1981-82, Bean & Manning, Houston, 1982-85; pvt. practice Van Gilder & Assocs., Houston, 1985-94, Law Office of Derek R. Van Gilder, Bastrop, Tex., 1995—; instr. Houston C.C., 1981-82; life mem., committeeman Houston Livestock Show & Rodeo, 1991—. Bd. dirs. Children's Advocacy Ctr. of Bastrop County, treas. 1996-90. Mem. ABA, ASCE, NSPE, Bastrop C. of C., Houston Bar Assn., Coll. State Bar Tex., Am. Arbitration Assn. (panel of arbitrators), Tex. Soc. Profl. Engrs., Rotary Club Bastrop County (v.p. 1996-97, pres.-elect 1997-98, pres. 1998-99). Republican. Roman Catholic. Avocations: racquetball, golf, Scuba diving, photography. Construction, Patent, General civil litigation. Office: 916 Main St Bastrop TX 78602-3810

**VAN GRAAFEILAND, ELLSWORTH ALFRED,** federal judge; b. Rochester, N.Y., May 11, 1915; s. Ivan and Elsie (Gohr) VanG.; m. Rosemary Vaeth, May 26, 1945; children—Gary, Suzanne, Joan, John, Anne. AB, U. Rochester, 1937; LLB, Cornell U., 1940. Bar: N.Y. 1940. Practiced in Rochester; now sr. judge U.S. Ct. Appeals for 2d Cir. Fellow Am. Bar Found., N.Y. Bar Found.; mem. ABA (ho. dels. 1973-75), N.Y. State Bar Assn. (v.p. 1972-73, pres. 1973-74, chmn. negligence compensation and ins. sect. 1968-69), Monroe County Bar Assn. (past pres.), Am. Coll. Trial Lawyers., Masons, Kent Club, Oak Hill Country Club. Home: 1 Tiffany Ct Pittsfield NY 14534-1067 Office: US Ct Appeals Fed Bldg 100 State St Ste 423 Rochester NY 14614-1309

**VAN GRAAFEILAND, GARY P.,** lawyer. BA, Union Coll., 1968; JD, Cornell U., 1972. Bar: N.Y. 1973. Asst. gen. counsel Eastman Kodak, Rochester, N.Y., 1989-92, sr. v.p., gen. counsel, sec., 1992—. Office: Eastman Kodak Co 343 State St Rochester NY 14650-0001

**VAN GRACK, STEVEN,** lawyer; b. Memphis, Oct. 6, 1948; s. Irving and Edna (Schwartz) Van G.; m. Gail Beverly Lang, Nov. 18, 1972 (div.); children: Adam, Ryan, Brandon; m. Susan M. Freeland, May 21, 1993. BA, U. Md., 1970, JD, 1974. Bar: Md. 1974, D.C. 1976, U.S. Dist. Ct. Md. 1976, U.S. Dist. Ct. D.C. 1976, U.S. Ct. Appeals (4th cir.) 1977, U.S. Supreme Ct. 1978. Law clk. to presiding justice Montgomery County Cir. Ct., Rockville, Md., 1974-75; assoc. Joseph Roesser Law Offices, Silver Springs, Md., 1975-78; ptnr. Ebert & Bowytz, Washington, 1978-80; mng. ptnr. Van Grack, Axelson & Williamowsky, Rockville, 1980—; instr., lectr. Montgomery Coll., Germantown, Md., 1983-85. Cubmaster packs 1343 and 1449 Boy Scouts Am.; coach Rockville Baseball Assn.; campaign mgr. Com. to Elect the Sitting Judges, Rockville, 1982; mayor City of Rockville, 1985-87; gen. counsel Montgomery County Dem. Cen. Com., Kensington, Md., 1978-82; trustee Shady Grove Adventist Hosp. Found; bd. dirs. Washington Met. Council Govts.; co-chmn. Montgomery County March of Dimes WalkAm. Com., 1998, 99; Dem. cand. 8th Congressional Dist. Md., 1994. With USAR, 1970-71. Recipient Fifth Annual Pro Bono Svc. award Montgomery County Bar Found.1998, Extraordinary Commitment to the Delivery of Legal Svcs. award Montgomery County Bar Found., 1999; named one of Outstanding Young Men of Am., Jaycess, 1978, 81. Mem. ABA, ATLA, Md. Bar Assn., Montgomery County Bar Assn., Md. Trial Lawyers Assn., Rockville C. of C. (bd. dirs.). Jewish. Avocations: running, swimming, exercising, coin collecting, polit. button collecting. Personal injury, State civil litigation, Criminal. Home: 808 Fordham St Rockville MD 20850-1018 Office: Van Grack Axelson & Williamowsky 110 N Washington St Fl 5 Rockville MD 20850-2223

**VAN GRUNSVEN, PAUL ROBERT,** lawyer; b. Green Bay, Wis., Mar. 11, 1961; s. David Edward and Carol Ann (Janssen) Van G. BS, Marquette U., 1983, JD, 1986; LLM in Health Law, De Paul U., 1995. Bar: Wis. 1986, U.S. Dist. Ct. (ea. dist.) Wis. 1986. Mem. Techmeier & Van Grunsven, S.C., Milw., 1986=89, shareholder, 1989—; adj. prof. Marquette U. Law Sch., Milw., 1995—. Recipient Am. Jurisprudence award Lawyer's Coop. Pub. Co., 1986. Mem. ATLA, Wis. Trial Lawyers for Public Justice, Wis. Acad. Trial Lawyers (bd. dirs., co-editor The Verdict), Wis. Bar Assn., Milw. Bar Assn. (co-chair health law sect.). Roman Catholic. Avocations: golf, football, baseball, basketball. Personal injury, Health, General civil litigation. Office: Techmeier & Van Grunsven SC 411 E Wisconsin Ave Ste 1100 Milwaukee WI 53202-4464

**VAN GUNDY, GREGORY FRANK,** lawyer; b. Columbus, Ohio, Oct. 24, 1945; s. Paul Arden and Edna Marie (Sanders) Van G.; m. Lisa Tamara Langer. B.A., Ohio State U., Columbus, 1966, J.D., 1969. Bar: N.Y. bar 1971. Asso. atty. firm Willkie Farr & Gallagher, N.Y.C., 1970-74; v.p. legal, sec. Marsh & McLennan Cos., Inc., N.Y.C., 1974-79; v.p., sec., gen. counsel Marsh & McLennan Cos., Inc., 1979—. Mem. ABA, Phi Beta Kappa. Roman Catholic. Club: University (N.Y.C.). General corporate. Home: 232 Fox Meadow Rd Scarsdale NY 10583-1640 Office: Marsh & McLennan Cos Inc 1166 Avenue Of The Americas New York NY 10036-2708

**VAN HOOMISSEN, GEORGE ALBERT,** state supreme court justice; b. Portland, Oreg., Mar. 7, 1930; s. Fred J. and Helen F. (Flanagan) Van H.; m. Ruth Madeleine Niedermeyer, June 4, 1960; children: Geroge T., Ruth Anne, Madeleine, Matthew. BBA, U. Portland, 1951; JD, Georgetown U., 1955, LLM in Labor Law, 1957; LLM in Jud. Adminstrn., U. Va., 1986. Bar: D.C. 1955, Oreg. 1956, Tex. 1971, U.S. Dist. Ct. Oreg. 1956, U.S. Ct. Mil. Appeals 1955, U.S. Ct. Customs and Patent Appeals 1955, U.S. Ct. Claims 1955, U.S. Ct. Appeals (9th cir.) 1956, U.S. Ct. Appeals (D.C. cir.) 1955, U.S. Supreme Ct. 1960. Law clk. for Chief Justice Harold J. Warner Oreg. Supreme Ct., 1955-56; Keigwin teaching fellow Georgetown Law Sch., 1956-57; dep. dist. atty. Multnomah County, Portland, 1957-59; pvt. practice Portland, 1959-62; dist. atty. Multnomah County, 1962-71; dean nat. coll. dist. attys., prof. law U. Houston, 1971-73; judge Cir. Ct., Portland, 1973-81, Oreg. Ct. Appeals, Salem, 1981-88; assoc. justice Oreg. Supreme Ct., Salem, 1988—; adj. prof. Northwestern Sch. Law, Portland, Willamette U. Sch. Law, Portland State U.; mem. faculty Am. Acad. Judicial Edn., Nat. Judicial Coll.; Keigwin Teaching fellow Georgetown U. Law Sch. Mem. Oreg. Ho. of Reps., Salem, 1959-62, chmn. house jud. com. With USMC, 1951-53; col. USMCR (ret.). Recipient Disting. Alumnus award U. Portland, 1972. Master Owen M. Panner Am. Inn of Ct.; mem. ABA, Oreg. State Bar, Tex. Bar Assn., Oreg. Law Inst. (bd. dirs.), Arlington Club, Multnomah Athletic Club, Univ. Club. Roman Catholic. Office: Oreg Supreme Ct 1163 State St Salem OR 97310-1331

**VANHOVE, LORRI KAY,** lawyer, financial services executive; b. Madison, S.D., Dec. 10, 1956; d. Robert Harold Vanhove and Doris Darlene (Beck) Vanhove Strub. BS, S.D. State U., 1979; JD, U. Neb., 1982. Bar: S.D. 1982, U.S. Dist. Ct. S.D. 1982, Minn. 1985. Cons. fin. planning Fed. Land Bank of Omaha, 1982-85; mgr. advanced fin. planning IDS Fin. Services Inc., Mpls., 1985—. Speaker various civ. groups. William Holt scholar U. Neb., 1980, Yale C. Holland scholar U. Neb., 1981. Mem. ABA, S.D. Bar Assn. (contr. articles to jour.), Minn. Bar Assn., Hennipen County Bar Assn., Phi Delta Phi. Probate, Personal income taxation, Pension, profit-sharing, and employee benefits. Home: 10400 Buckingham Dr Eden Prairie MN 55347-2939 Office: IDS Fin Services Inc Ids Tower # 10 Minneapolis MN 55402-2100

**VAN KAMPEN, AL,** lawyer; b. Detroit; s. Al J. and Laureen Ann Van Kampen; m. Lisa Alice Gonnason, Sept. 1, 1990; children: Kyle, grant. BA in Econs., U. Mich., 1979, JD, 1983. Bar: Wash. 1983. Ptnr. Bogle & Gates, Seattle, 1983-99; v.p. A.V. Kurt Constrn. Co., Ferndale, Mich., 1980-92. Editor, co-author: Contribution and Claims Reduction in Antitrust Litigation, 1986, Sample Jury Instructions in Civil Antitrust Cases, 1999. Mem. Mayor's Citizen Forecast Com., Seattle, 1987. Mem. ABA, Wash. State Bar Assn. (chair antitrust sect.). Avocations: sailing, skiing. Antitrust, Intellectual property, Health. Office: Van Kampen & Assocs 600 Stewart St Ste 305 Seattle WA 98101-1257

**VAN KERREBROOK, MARY ALICE,** lawyer; b. Houston, Aug. 21, 1961; d. Richard Rene and Phyllis Law (Banks) Van K. BA in Econs., Northwestern U., 1983; JD, So. Meth. U., 1986. Bar: Tex. 1986, U.S. Dist. Ct. (so. dist.) Tex. 1987, U.S. Ct. Appeals (5th cir.) 1988, U.S. Dist. Ct. (ea. dist.) Tex. 1989. Assoc. Wilson, Cribbs, Goren & Flaum, P.C., Houston, 1986-94, shareholder, 1994—. Trustee Tex. Com. on Natural Resources, Dallas, 1988—; mem. exec. com. Galveston Bay Found., Webster, Tex., 1991-93; pres. Katy Prairie Conservancy, Houston, 1995—. General civil litigation, Appellate, State and local taxation. Office: Wilson Cribbs Goren & Flaum PC 2200 Lyric Ctr 440 Houston TX 77002-1624

**VAN KEUREN, PETER SCOTT,** lawyer; b. Manchester, Conn., July 26, 1961; s. William Charles and Dorothy Helen Van Keuren; m. Kimberly Ann Pollock, Mar. 20, 1993; children: Lindsay, Steven. B of Bldg. Constrn., U. Fla., 1983, JD, 1989. Bar: Fla.; cert. gen. contractor, Fla. Project mgr. Merrill, Stewart and Wilson, Inc., West Palm Beach, Fla., 1983-86; atty. David L. Gorman, P.A., North Palm Beach, Fla., 1989-96; v.p. Van Keuren Constrn., Inc., Jupiter, Fla., 1996-98; pres. Primary Bldg. Inspections, Inc., Jupiter, 1998—; sole practitioner Jupiter, 1996—. Assoc. Gen. Contractors scholar, 1987-89. Republican. Roman Catholic. Avocation: golf. Home: 5 Hitching Post Cir Tequesta FL 33469-1506 Office: 1001 Alternate Ala Jupiter FL 33477

**VAN KIRK, THOMAS L.,** lawyer; b. Pa., June 25, 1945; s. Theodore and Mary Jane (Young) Van K.; children: Thomas Jr., Christopher. BA, Bucknell U., 1967; JD cum laude, Dickinson U., 1970. Bar: Pa., U.S. Dist. Ct. (we. and ea. dists.) Pa. 1971, U.S. Ct. Appeals (3d cir.) 1972, U.S. Supreme Ct. 1976. Clk. Pa. Superior Ct., 1970-71; assoc. Buchanan Ingersoll, Pitts., 1971-77, ptnr., 1978—, chief oper. officer, 1985—; bd. dirs. Buchanan Ingersoll P.C.; v.p. State Pa. Economy League; bd. dirs. Western Pa. Economy League, chair, 1998. Chmn. Allegheny County Heart Assn. Walk, 1992; chair Pitts. Downtown Partnership, 1995-97; bd. dirs., vice chair Rivers Club Pitts.; bd. dirs. Capital divsn. Pa. Economy League, sec./treas., 1995; bd. dirs. Pitts. Cultural Trust, 1998. Fellow Am. Bar Found.; mem. ABA, Allegheny County Bar Assn., Duquesne Club, Rivers Club, Racquet Club Phila., The Club at Nevillewood. Democrat. Lutheran. Antitrust, Public international, Federal civil litigation. Home: 1010 Osage Rd Pittsburgh PA 15243-1014 Office: Buchanan Ingersoll PC 301 Grant St Fl 20 Pittsburgh PA 15219-1410

**VAN LEUVEN, ROBERT JOSEPH,** lawyer; b. Detroit, Apr. 17, 1931; s. Joseph Francis and Olive (Stowell) Van L.;m. Merri Lee Van Leuven; children: Joseph Michael, Douglas Robert, Julie Margaret. student Albion Coll., 1949-51; BA with distinction Wayne State U., 1953; JD, U. Mich., 1957. Bar: Mich. 1957. Since practiced in Muskegon, Mich.; ptnr. Hathaway, Latimer, Clink & Robb, 1957-68, ptnr. McCroskey, Libner & Van Leuven, 1968-81, ptnr. Libner-Van Leuven, 1982—; past mem. council negligence law sect. State Bar Mich. Bd. dirs. Muskegon Children's Home, 1965-75. Served with AUS 1953-55. Fellow Mich. Bar Found., Mich. Trial Lawyers Assn., Am. Coll. Trial Lawyers; mem. Assn. Trial Lawyers Am., Delta Sigma Phi. Club: Muskegon Country. General civil litigation, Civil rights, Personal injury. Home: 1309 Randolph Ave Muskegon MI 49441-3249 Office: Libner-Van Leuven Muskegon Mall 400 Comerica Muskegon MI 49443

**VANNATTA, SHANE ANTHONY,** lawyer; b. Williston, N.D., May 5, 1968; s. Marlyn Laverne and Karen (Rossland) V. BA in Polit. Sci. with high honors, U. Mont., 1990, JD with honors, 1993. Bar: Mont. 1993, U.S. Dist. Ct. Mont. 1993. Clk./intern Worden Thane & Haines, P.C., Missoula, Mont., 1991-93, assoc., 1993-96, sr. assoc., 1996—. Contbr. articles to profl. jours. In-house campaign exec. United Way of Missoula, 1994—. Mem. Western Mont. Bar Assn. (treas. 1997-98, sec. 1998—), Mont. State Bar (new lawyers sect., pres. 1996-97), Missoula New Lawyers Assn. (pres. 1993-94), Missoula C. of C. (chair Leadership Missoula 1998—). Roman Catholic. Avocations: Tae Kwon-Do (cert. 2d dan), bicycling. Contracts commercial, Trademark and copyright, General civil litigation. Office: Worden Thane & Haines PC 111 N Higgins Ave Ste 600 Missoula MT 59802-4494

**VANNI, ROBERT JOHN,** lawyer; b. Richmond, Va.; s. Anthony John and Jeanette (Genovese) V. BSBA, Babson Coll., 1966; JD, NYU, 1969; cert., U. Catholique L'Ouest, Angers, France, 1971; MBA, Columbia U., 1977. Bar: N.Y. 1969. Asst. econ. affairs officer UN Secretariat, N.Y.C., 1969-72; assoc. Shearman & Sterling, N.Y.C., 1972-79; gen. counsel N.Y.C. Dept. Cultural Affairs, N.Y.C., 1979-86; gen. counsel, asst. sec. N.Y. Pub. Libr., Astor Lenox and Tilden Founds., N.Y.C., 1986—; chair, of counsel N.Y.C. cultural instns., 1987—; bd. advisors Nat. Ctr. Philanthropy and the Law, 1997—. Bd. dirs. Afghanistan Relief Com., N.Y.C., 1980-86, Am.-Italy Soc., N.Y.C., 1983-95, Jazz Found. Am., N.Y.C., 1990-95; trustee Louis Armstrong Edn. Found., 1997—. Named one of Outstanding Young Men in Am. Mem. Nat. Assn. Coll. and Univ. Attys. (co-chair com. on museums and librs. 1996—), N.Y.C. Bar Assn. (chair com. on internat. trade 1983-87, mem. long range planning com., nonprofit orgn. com.). Office: N Y Pub Libr 5th Ave and 42d St New York NY 10018

**VAN OEVEREN, EDWARD LANIER,** lawyer, biologist, physician; b. Washington, Apr. 12, 1954. BA with high distinction, U. Va., 1976; M.D., Med. Coll. Va., 1995; JD, U. Va., 1981; BS with distinction, George Mason U., 1983; MPH, Johns Hopkins U., 1998. Bar: Va. 1981, U.S. Dist. Ct. (ea. dist.) Va. 1988, U.S. Temporary Emergency Ct. Appeals 1989; lic. physician, Va. Pvt. practice legal cons. Falls Church, Va., 1984-85; pvt. practice law Falls Church, 1986-89, pvt. practice law and biology, 1989—; intern Med. Coll. Va., 1996-97; resident in preventive medicine Johns Hopkins U., Balt., 1997-99. Editor: Federal Special Court Litigation, 1982. Election officer Fairfax County (Va.) Electoral Bd., 1989-90, 94-99. Capt. Va. Army NG, 1996-97; 1st lt. USAR, 1995-96, capt., 1997—. Mem. AMA, APHA, Assn. Preventive Medicine Residents, Va. State Bar Assn., George Mason U. Alumni Assn. (scholarship, awards, rules and policies coms. 1989-91), Alpha Chi. Avocation: photography. Personal injury, Aviation, Federal civil litigation. Home: 3304 Patrick Henry Dr Falls Church VA 22044-1514

**VAN PELT, FRED RICHARD,** lawyer; b. Joplin, Mo., June 26, 1958; s. Fred L. and Dorthy (Carlton) Van P.; m. Kay A. Willenbrink; children: Fred Ryan, Natalie Marie. BA, Pitts. State U., 1980; JD, U. Mo., 1983. Sole practice law Springfield, Mo., 1983-84; pres., shareholder Van Pelt and Van Pelt, Springfield, 1984—; pres. V.P./H. Motels Inc., Joplin, 1994—. v.p., bd. dirs. CASA of SW Mo., Springfield, 1988—; mem. Child Protection Team of DFS, Springfield, 1989-92. Fellow Am. Acad. Matrimonial Lawyers; mem. ATLA, Mo. Bar Assn., Mo. Assn. Trial Lawyers, Springfield Metro. Bar Assn. Family and matrimonial, Personal injury. Office: U-100 1200 E Woodhurst Dr Springfield MO 65804

**VAN PRAAG, ALAN,** lawyer; b. Bklyn., Mar. 6, 1947; s. Leopold Marcus and Rose (Wexell) Van P.; divorced; 1 child, Melissa Rose; m. Lynne Diamond, Nov. 24, 1991. BA, Hunter Coll., 1968; JD, Bklyn. Law Sch., 1971. Bar: U.S. Dist. Ct. (ea. dist.) N.Y. 1972, U.S. Dist. Ct. (so. dist.) N.Y. 1974, U.S. Ct. Appeals (2d cir.) 1976, U.S. Ct. Appeals (3rd cir.) 1978, U.S. Ct. Appeals (4th cir.) 1980, U.S. Ct. Appeals (11th cir.) 1994. Atty. Dept. of Navy, Bklyn., 1971-74; assoc. Poles Tublin Patestides, N.Y.C., 1974-80, ptnr., 1980-88, Snow Becker Krauss P.C., 1988-93, ptnr., 1993—; dir., gen. counsel Egyptian Am. C. of C., N.Y.C., 1986-90. Contbr. articles to Bklyn. Law Rev., 1970-71, ABA Litigation Jour., 1986. Chmn. Vol. Com. Rusk Inst. Rehab., N.Y., 1976-88. Mem. Maritime Law Assn. (chmn. subcom. bankruptcy 1988—, vice chmn. com. practice and procedures 1984—, stevedoring com. 1994, chmn. subcom. to advise Dept. State with regard to a conv. for reciprocal enforcement of money judgments 1996—), ABA (mem. sect. internat. law 1974—), N.Y. Trial Lawyers Assn. (admiralty, pvt. internat. bankruptcy). Admiralty, Private international, Bankruptcy. Home: 355 S End Ave Apt 34L New York NY 10280-1060 Office: Snow Becker Krauss PC 605 3rd Ave Fl 25 New York NY 10158-0125

**VAN RYZIN, GARY JAMES,** lawyer, accountant; b. Appleton, Wis., Apr. 26, 1953; s. Howard John and Roseanne Jean (Verbeten) Van R.; m. Pamela Jean Casey, Aug. 23, 1975; children: Kimberly, Andrew, Benjamin. MA, U. Ga., 1976; MBA in Acctg., Rosary Coll., 1979; MS in Bus., U. Wis., 1989, JD, 1994. CPA, Wis.; Bar: Wis., 1996, U.S. Dist. Ct. (we. dist.) Wis.; cert. assn. exec., cert. mgmt. acct. Projects mgr. Nat. Roofing Contractors Assn., Chgo., 1977-80; v.p. fin. Credit Union Nat. Assn., Madison, Wis., 1980-88; CFO Bus. Graphics Group, Madison, 1989-94, Full Compass Sys., Ltd., Middleton, Wis., 1994—. Recipient Winners Circle award Am. Soc. Assn. Execs., 1987. Fellow Wis. Inst. CPAs, AICPA; mem. Inst. Cert. Mgmt. Accts., Inst. Mgmt. Accts., ABA (taxation divsn.), Wis. Bar Assn., Constrn. Industry Fin. Mgrs. Assn., Beta Gamma Sigma, Kappa Tau Alpha. E-mail: gary@fullcompass.com. Home: 50 Fuller Dr Madison WI 53704-5925 Office: Full Compass Sys Ltd 8001 Terrace Ave Middleton WI 53562-3194

**VAN SCHOONENBERG, ROBERT G.,** corporate lawyer; b. Madison, Wis., Aug. 18, 1946; s. John W. and Ione (Henning) Schoonenberg. BA, Marquette U., 1968; MBA, U. Wis., 1972; JD, U. Mich., 1974. Bar: Calif. 1975, Fla. 1976. Atty. Gulf Oil Corp., Pitts., 1974-81; sr. v.p., gen. counsel, sec. Avery Dennison Corp., Pasadena, Calif., 1981—; judge pro tem Pasadena Mcpl. Ct., 1987-89. Dir., v.p. fin. adminstrn. Am. Cancer Soc., San Gabriel Vally Unit, 1987—; v.p., treas., dir., v.p. investments Pasadena Symphony Assn.; bd. dirs. Pasadena Recreation and Parks Found., 1983-84; mem. Pasadena Citizens Task Force on Crime Control, 1983-84; dir. Boy Scouts, San Gabriel Valley Coun., dir. public coun.; bd. dirs. Verugo Hills Hosp. Found. Mem. ABA, Am. Corp. Counsel Assn. (bd. dirs.), Am. Soc. Corp. Secs. (bd. dirs., pres. Southern Calif. chpt.), L.A. County Bar Assn. (past chair, corp. law dept. sect.), Corp. Counsel Inst. (bd. govs.), Jonathon Club, Flint Canyon Tennis Club, Pasadena Athletic Club, Wis. Union. Clubs: Athletic (Pasadena); Wis. Union. General corporate, Securities, Intellectual property. Office: Avery Dennison Corp 150 N Orange Grove Blvd Pasadena CA 91103-3534

**VAN SICKLE, BRUCE MARION,** federal judge; b. Minot, N.D., Feb. 13, 1917; s. Guy Robin and Hilda Alice (Rosenquist) Van S.; m. Dorothy Alfreda Hermann, May 26, 1943; children: Susan Van Sickle Cooper, John Allan, Craig Bruce, David Max. BSL, U. Minn., 1941, JD, 1941. Bar: Minn. 1941, N.D. 1946. Pvt. practice law, Minot, 1947-71; judge U.S. Dist. Ct. N.D., 1971-85, sr. judge, 1985—; mem. N.D. Ho. of Reps., 1957, 59. Served with USMCR, 1941-46. Mem. ABA, N.D. Bar Assn., N.W. Bar Assn., Ward County Bar Assn., Am. Trial Lawyers Assn., Am. Coll. Probate Counsel, Am. Judicature Soc., Bruce M. Van Sickle Inns of Ct., Masons, Shriners, Elks, Delta Theta Phi. Office: US Dist Ct US Courthouse Rm 428 PO Box 670 Bismarck ND 58502-0670

**VAN TINE, MATTHEW ERIC,** lawyer; b. Tomahawk, Wis., June 21, 1958; s. Kenneth G. and Louise (Olson) Van T.; m. Rena Marie David, Apr. 30, 1988; 1 child, Kristen. AB cum laude, Harvard Coll., 1980; JD magna cum laude, Boston U., 1983. Bar: Ill., 1983, Mass., 1983; U.S. Dist. Ct. Mass., 1984, U.S. Dist. Ct. (no. dist.) Ill., 1986. Law clk. to Hon. Raymond J. Pettine U.S. Dist. Ct. R.I., Providence, 1983-84; assoc. Palmer & Dodge, Boston, 1984-85, Schiff, Hardin & Waite, Chgo., 1985-88; asst. corp. counsel City of Chgo., 1988-92; assoc. to ptnr. Saunders & Monroe, Chgo., 1993—. Exec. editor: Boston University Law Rev., 1982-83. Mem. ABA, Chgo. Bar Assn., Inns of Ct. General civil litigation, Labor, Government contracts and claims. Office: Saunders & Monroe 1600 NBC Tower 455 N Cityfront Plaza Dr Chicago IL 60611-5503

**VAN WAGNER, ALBERT EDWIN, JR.,** lawyer; b. Bronxville, N.Y., Jan. 28, 1946; s. Albert Edwin and Margaret (Libby) Van W.; m. Marie Teresa; 1 child, Eric. BS, Ariz. State U., 1976, MBA, 1977, JD, 1978. Bar: Ariz. 1979, U.S. Dist. Ct. Ariz. 1979, U.S. Ct. Appeals (9th cir.) 1979. Assoc. Eldridge & Brown, Phoenix, 1979-80; ptnr. Eldridge & Van Wagner, Phoenix, 1981-84; sole practice Phoenix, 1984-90; ptnr. Van Wagner & Erhart, Phoenix, 1991—. council mem. City of Hitchfield Park (Ariz.), 1992—, vice mayor, 1996-98. With USMC, 1966-68. Mem. Assn. Trial Lawyers Am., Marisopa County Bar Assn. Democrat. Avocations: bridge, golf. Personal injury, Product liability. Office: 649 N 3rd Ave Phoenix AZ 85003-1522

**VANWINKLE, JOHN RAGAN,** lawyer; b. Ft. Knox, Ky., Dec. 18, 1951; s. John Lloyd and Kate (Morris) VanW.; m. Cathy M. VanWinkle, Dec. 9, 1983; stepchildren: William Gabriel Gammons, Virginia Leigh Gammons. BS, State Coll. Ark., Conway, 1974; JD, U. Ark., 1980. Bar: Ark. 1980, U.S. Ct. Appeals, U.S. Supreme Ct. Caseworker Mental Retardation Devel. Disabilities Svc., Ft. Smith, Ark., 1974-77; dep. pros. atty. Pros. Atty.-12th Dist., Ft. Smith, 1980-81; ptnr. Person & VanWinkle, Ft. Smith, 1982-86, Sexton, Kirkpatrick, Nolan, VanWinkle & Caddell, Ft. Smith, 1986-89, Hewett, Shock & VanWinkle, Ft. Smith, 1989-91; chancery judge 12th Jud. Cir., Ft. Smith, 1991-92; ptnr. Rose & VanWinkle, Fayetteville, Ark., 1993—, Rose, VanWinkle & Woods, Fayetteville, 1998—. Bd. dirs. Family Support Svcs., 1995—, N.W. Ark. Regional Indsl. Devel. Corp., 1996—; v.p. Habitat for Humanity, 1996—; Dem. nominee for Congress 3d Congl. Dist.-Ark., Ft. Smith, 1992; chmn. Sebastian County Dem. Ctr. Com., Ft. Smith, 1989-91; del. Dem. Nat. Conv., 1988. Mem. ATLA, Ark. Trial Lawyers Assn. Methodist. Avocations: golf, reading. Personal injury, Criminal, Libel. Office: Rose VanWinkle & Woods 112 W Center St Ste 400 Fayetteville AR 72701-6089

**VAN WINKLE, WESLEY ANDREW,** lawyer, educator; b. Kansas City, Mo., Sept. 22, 1952; s. Willard and Cleone Verlee (O'Dell) Van W.; m. Ruth Kay Shelby, Apr. 10, 1984. B degree, U. Nebr., 1972; JD, San Francisco Law Sch., 1987. Bar: Calif. 1987, U.S. Dist. Ct. (no. dist.) Calif. 1987, U.S. Supreme Ct. 1994. Atty. Bagetelos & Fadem, San Francisco, 1987-91; pvt. practice Berkeley, Calif., 1991—; prof. law San Francisco Law Sch., 1990—; apptd. mem. Calif. Appellate Indigent Def. Oversight Adv. com., 1997—. Editor (legal newspaper/rev.) Res Ipsa Loquitur, 1986. Mem. Calif. Attys. for Criminal Justice, Calif. Appellate Def. Counsel (pres. 1998-99), San Francisco Law Sch. Alumni Assn. (bd. dirs.), Delta Theta Phi. Democrat. Criminal. Office: PO Box 5216 Berkeley CA 94705-0216

**VAN ZANDT, DAVID E.,** dean; b. Princeton, N.J., Feb. 17, 1953; m. Lisa A. Huestis; children: Caroline, Nicholas. AB summa cum laude, Princeton U., 1975; JD, Yale U., 1981; PhD in Sociology, U. London, 1985. Bar: Ill. Clk. to Hon. Pierre N. Leval U.S. Dist. Ct. (so. dist.) N.Y., 1981-82; clk. to Hon. Harry A. Blackmun U.S. Supreme Ct., Washington, 1982-83; atty. Davis, Polk & Wardwell, 1984-85; mem. faculty Northwestern U. Law Sch., Chgo., 1985—; dean Northwester U. Law Sch., Chgo., 1995—; mem. planning com. Northwestern U. Corporate Counsel Inst., Northwestern U. Corp. Counsel Ctr. Author: Living in the Children of God, 1991; mng. editor Yale Law Jour., 1980-81; contbr. articles to profl. jours. Office: Northwestern U Sch Law Office of Dean 357 E Chicago Ave Chicago IL 60611*

**VAN ZILE, PHILIP TAYLOR, III,** lawyer, educator; b. Detroit, Feb. 17, 1945; s. Philip Taylor II and Ruth (Butzel) Van Z.; m. Susan Jones, Sept. 12, 1981; children: Caroline Sage, Philip Taylor IV. BA, Oberlin Coll., 1968; MDiv, Union Theol. Sem., 1971; JD, Mich. State U., 1975. Bar: Mich. 1976, D.C. 1976, U.S. Dist. Ct. (ea. dist.) Mich. 1976, U.S. Ct. Appeals (6th cir.) 1976, U.S. Supreme Ct. 1977, Pa. 1981. Law clk. Mich. Ct. Appeals, Detroit, 1976-78, Mich. Supreme Ct., Detroit and Lansing, Mich., 1978-80; asst. corp. counsel Office of Corp. Counsel, Washington, 1980-87; assoc. Killian & Gephart, Harrisburg, Pa., 1987-89; prin. Law Office of Philip T. Van Zile, Harrisburg, 1989-91; assoc. coun. Office Chief Coun. Pa. Dept. Conservation and Natural Resources, Harrisburg, 1991—; assoc. realtor M.C. Walker Realty, Mechanicsburg, Pa., 1997—; teaching fellow Detroit Coll. Law, 1976-80; teaching asst. Detroit Gen. Hosp., 1978-80; teaching assoc. Acad. Med. Arts and Bus., Harrisburg, 1990-91. Contbr. articles to profl. jours. Ordained elder Mechanicsburg Presbyn. Ch., 1995—, chmn. vol. ministries, 1995, chmn. peacemaking, 1996, chmn. staff, 1997—. Mem. ABA, Kenwood Club (Chevy Chase, Md.). Administrative and regulatory, Environmental, Government contracts and claims. Office: Pa Dept Conservation/Natural Resources Office Chief Counsel 400 Market St Harrisburg PA 17101-2301

**VAN ZOMEREN, BARBARA RUTH,** lawyer; b. Mankato, Minn., June 4, 1969; d. Bernard Henry and Elizabeth Ruth Van Z.; m. John Michael Chaussee, Apr. 4, 1998. BA, U. Minn., 1992; JD, Hamline U. Sch. Law, 1995. Bar: Minn. 1995. Law clk. St. Louis City, Duluth, Minn., 1995-96; lawyer Farm Credit Svcs., Mankato, 1996-97, Doherty, Rumble & Butler, St. Paul, 1997—. Vol. Minn. 4-H, Minn. FFA. Mem. ABA, Minn. State Bar Assn. Meth. Avocations: golfing, hunting, fishing. General corporate, Environmental, Contracts commercial. Office: Doherty Rumble & Butler 30 7th St E Ste 2800 Saint Paul MN 55101-4999

**VARANESE, MICHELE L.,** lawyer; b. Highland Park, Mich., Sept. 6, 1964; d. Daniel Wayne and Shirlyan (Starks) H. Student, L.A. Valley Coll., 1982-83; BA, Calif. State U., Northridge, 1988; JD, Southwestern U., 1991; LLM in Taxation, U. S.D., 1996. Bar: Calif., 1991. Mem. support staff HealthPace div. of Coroon & Black Ins., Studio City, Calif., 1985; asst. adminstr. For Kids' Sake, Tarzana, Calif., 1985-86; law clk., extern tax div. U.S. Atty.'s Office, L.A., 1990; pvt. practice San Fernando Valley, Calif., 1992—. Mem. choir North Rim Christian Fellowship, Northridge, 1989—; vol. food preparer Salvation Army, Van Nuys Calif., 1992—. Mem. L.A. Bar Assn. (real estate, tax and estate planning sect.), Women Lawyers Assn. L.A., Calif. Young Lawyers Assn., San Fernando Valley Estate Planning Coun., So. Calif. Coun. of Elder Law Attys. Avocations: cooking, dancing, movies.

**VARAT, JONATHAN D.,** dean, law educator; b. 1945. BA, U. Pa., Phila., 1967, JD, 1972. Law clk. to judge Walter Mansfield U.S. Ct. Appeals (2d cir.), N.Y.C., 1972-73; law clk. to justice Byron White U.S. Supreme Ct., Washington, 1973-74; assoc. O'Melveny & Myers, Los Angeles, 1974-76; acting prof. UCLA, 1976-81, prof., 1981—, assoc. dean, 1982-83, 91-92; dean UCLA Sch. Law, 1998—. Office: UCLA Sch Law 405 Hilgard Ave Los Angeles CA 90095-9000

**VARDAMAN, JOHN WESLEY,** lawyer; b. Montgomery, Ala., Apr. 22, 1940; s. John Wesley and Elizabeth (Merrill) V.; m. Marianne Fay, June 14,

1969; children: Thomas, Shannon, John Wesley III, Davis. BA, Washington & Lee U., 1962; JD, Harvard U., 1965. Bar: D.C. 1966, U.S. Dist. Ct. (D.C.) 1967, U.S. Supreme Ct. 1970. Law clk. to justice Hugo Black U.S. Supreme Ct., 1965-66; assoc. Wilmer, Cutler & Pickering, Washington, 1966-70; ptnr. Williams & Connolly, Washington, 1970—; gen. counsel U.S. Golf Assn., 1999—. Contbr. articles to profl. jours. Mem. ABA, Am. Coll. Trial Lawyers, William B. Bryant Am. Inn of Ct., Met. Club, Congl. Country Club (Bethesda, Md.). Baptist. Avocation: golf. Federal civil litigation, Criminal, Environmental. Office: Williams & Connolly 725 12th St NW Washington DC 20005-5901

**VARELA, LAURA JOAN,** lawyer; b. Culpepper, Va., Sept. 29, 1969; d. Manuel Jr. and Joan Elizabeth V. BA, U. Fla., Gainesville, 1991, JD, 1994. Assoc. atty. Law Office of Stanley Shorman, Hollywood, Fla., 1994-95; staff atty. Keller, Houck & Shinkle PA, Miami, 1995; assoc. atty. Brent G. Siegel PA, Gainesville, Fla., 1995—; treas. Young Lawyers Divsn. 8th cir., Gainesville, Fla., 1997—. Mem. 8th Jud. Cir. Bar Assn., Acad. Fla. Trial Lawyers, Phi Beta Kappa. Avocations: cooking, golf, wine tasting. General civil litigation, Personal injury. Office: Brent G Siegel PA 4046 W Newberry Rd Gainesville FL 32607-2343

**VARELLAS, SANDRA MOTTE,** judge; b. Anderson, S.C., Oct. 17, 1946; d. James E. and Helen Lucille (Gilliam) Motte; m. James John Varellas, July 3, 1971; children: James John III, David Todd. BA, Winthrop U., 1968; MA, U. Ky., 1970, JD, 1975. Bar: Ky. 1975, Fla. 1976, U.S. Dist. Ct. (ea. dist.) Ky. 1975, U.S. Ct. Appeals (6th cir.) 1976, U.S. Supreme Ct. 1978. Instr. Midway Coll., Ky., 1970-72; adj. prof. U. Ky. Coll. Law, Lexington, 1976-78; instr. dept. bus. adminstrn. U. Ky., Lexington, 1976-78; atty. Varellas, Pratt & Cooley, Lexington, 1975-93, Varellas & Pratt, Lexington, 1993-97, Varellas & Varellas, Lexington, 1998—; Fayette County judge exec., Ky., 1980—; hearing officer Ky. Natural Resources and Environ. Protection Cabinet, Frankfort, 1984-88. Committeewoman Ky. Young Dems., Frankfort, 1977-80; pres. Fayette County Young Dems., Lexington, 1977; bd. dirs. Ky. Dem. Women's Club, Frankfort, 1980-84, bd. dirs., Bluegrass Estate Planning Coun., 1995-98; grad. Leadership Lexington, 1981; chairwoman Profl. Women's Forum, Lexington, Ky., 1985-86, bd. dirs., 1984-87, Aequum award com., 1989-92; mem. devel. coun. Midway Coll., 1990-92; co-chair Gift Club Com., 1992. Named Outstanding Young Dem. Woman, Ky. Young Dems., Frankfort, 1977, Outstanding Former Young Dem., Ky. Young Dems., 1983. Mem. Ky. Bar Assn. (treas. young lawyers divsn. 1978-79, long range planning com. 1988-89), Fla. Bar, Fayette County Bar Assn. (treas. 1977-78, bd. govs. 1978-80), LWV (nominating com. 1984-85), Greater Lexington C. of C. (legis. affairs com. 1994-95, bd.d irs. coun. smaller enterprises 1992-95). Club: The Lexington Forum (bd. dirs. 1996-99), Lexington Philharm. Guild (bd. dirs. 1979-81, 86—), Nat. Assn. Women Bus. Owners (chmn. cmty. liaison/govtl. affairs com. 1992-93), Lexington Network (bd. dirs. and sec. 1994-98). Office: Varellas & Varellas 167 W Main St Ste 1310 Lexington KY 40507-1711

**VARGA, S. GARY,** lawyer; b. Washington, Aug. 2, 1946; s. Julius Lester and Lillian Mae Varga; 1 child, Von Christopher. BS in Econs., Ohio State U., 1968; JD, Duke U., 1971; cert. trial advocacy, U. Calif., San Francisco. Bar: Iowa 1971, S.C. 1971, U.S. Ct. Appeals (4th cir.) 1971, Calif. 1976, U.S. Ct. Appeals (9th cir.) 1976, U.S. Supreme Ct. 1976. Clk. to Judge Donald Russell U.S. Ct. Appeals for 4th Circuit, 1971-73; pvt. practice, Carmel, Calif., 1976—; bd. dirs., pres. Maiden Am., Inc., Carmel, 1992—, Fuzzybops, Inc., Carmel, 1994—. Mem. Monterey County Planning Commn., Salinas, Calif. Capt. JAGC, U.S. Army, 1971-76. Recipient cert. of appreciation Am. Heart Assn., Calif., 1994. Mem. Kiwanis. General civil litigation, Contracts commercial, Real property. Office: 26613 Carmel Center Pl Ste 201 Carmel CA 93923-8653

**VARGAS, DIANA MONICA,** lawyer; b. Queens, N.Y., Nov. 18, 1970; d. Jay A. Vargas and Diana Martinez; m. Dave A. Singh, July 3, 1998. BA, NYU, 1992; JD, St. John's U., 1995. Bar: N.Y. 1996, U.S. Dist. Ct. (so. and ea. dists.) N.Y. 1996. Assoc. Scheurer, Wiggin & Hardy, N.Y.C., 1996-97; pvt. practice, Mineola, N.Y., 1997—; law guardian Nassau County Legal Panel, 1997—. Mem. Nassau County Bar Assn. Roman Catholic. Family and matrimonial, General practice, Private international. Office: 221 Mineola Blvd Mineola NY 11501-2545

**VARN, WILFRED CLAUDE,** lawyer; b. DeLand, Fla., Mar. 14, 1919; s. Claude Grady and Marjorie Amelia (Boor) V.; m. Betty Jean Davenport, Nov. 12, 1949; children: Mary Patricia Varn Moore, Wilfred Claude Jr., George Seward. BSBA, U. Fla, 1947, LLB, (reconferred JD 1967), 1948. Bar: Fla. 1948, U.S. Dist. Ct. (no. dist.) Fla. 1948, U.S. Dist. Ct. (mid. dist. and trial bar so. dist.) Fla. 1956, U.S. Ct. Appeals (5th cir.) 1958, U.S. Supreme Ct. 1959, U.S. Ct. Appeals (5th and 11th cirs.), 1981. Ptnr. Spear and Varn, Panama City, Fla., 1948-54; asst. U.S. Atty. Dept. Justice No. Dist. Fla., 1954-58, U.S. Atty., 1958-61; ptnr. Ervin, Varn, Jacobs & Ervin, Tallahassee, Fla., 1961—. Vice chancellor Episcopal Diocese of Fla., Jacksonville, 1994—; Rep. state com. mem. 1961-66. 2d lt. U.S. Army, 1942-46. PTO. Decorated Legion of Merit, U.S. Army, 1972. Fellow Am. Coll. of Trial Lawyers, Am. Bar Found.; mem. Fla. Bar Assn. (50 yr. Membership award 1998), Kiwanis Club (bd. dirs.). Avocations: painting, exercise, travel, hiking, swimming. General civil litigation, General practice, Condemnation. Home: 705 Kenilworth Rd Tallahassee FL 32312-3045 Office: Ervin Varn Jacobs & Ervin 305 S Gadsden St Tallahassee FL 32301-1811

**VARNER, CARLTON A.,** lawyer; b. Creston, Iowa, July 14, 1947. BA, U. Iowa, 1969; JD magna cum laude, U. Minn., 1972. Bar: Calif. 1972. Mng. ptnr. Sheppard Mullin Richter & Hampton, L.A., 1991-98. Author: The Microsoft Case, Exclusionary Innovation, 1998, California Antitrust Law, 1999; co-author: Antitrust Law Developments, 4th edit., 1998. Mem. ABA, L.A. County Bar Assn. (chmn. antitrust sect. 1993-94). Fax: 213-620-1398. E-mail: cvarner@smrh.com. Antitrust. Office: Sheppard Mullin Richter & Hampton LLP 333 S Hope St Fl 48 Los Angeles CA 90071-1406

**VARNER, ROBERT EDWARD,** federal judge; b. Montgomery, Ala., June 11, 1921; s. William and Georgia (Thomas) V.; children: Robert Edward, Carolyn Stuart.; m. Jane Dennis Hannah, Feb. 27, 1982. BS, Auburn U., 1946; JD, U. Ala., 1949. Bar: Ala. 1949. Atty. City of Tuskegee, 1951; asst. U.S. atty. U.S. Dist. Ct. (mid. dist.) Ala., 1954-58; U.S. dist. judge U.S. Dist. Ct. (mid. dist.) Ala., Montgomery, 1971-86, sr. judge, 1986—; pvt. practice Montgomery, 1958-71; ptnr. Jones, Murray, Stewart & Varner, 1958-71; guest lectr. bus. law Huntingdon Coll. Pres. Montgomery Rotary Charity Found.; v.p., fin. chmn. Tukabatchee Area coun. Boy Scouts Am.; mem. Macon County Bd. Edn., 1950-54. With USNR, 1942-46. Recipient Silver Beaver award Boy Scouts Am. Mem. ABA, FBA, ATLA, Montgomery Bar Assn. (pres. 1971), Macon County Bar Assn., Jud. Conf. U.S. (mem. com. on operation of jury sys.), Rotary (pres. club 1961), Phi Alpha Delta (Outstanding Alumnus award 1996), Phi Delta Theta. Republican. Methodist. Office: US Dist Ct 300 US Courthouse PO Box 2046 Montgomery AL 36102-2046

**VARNEY, ROBERT T.,** lawyer; b. Hopedale, Ill., Apr. 23, 1961; s. George H. and Mary M. Varney; m. Victoria K. Spear, June 23, 1990; children: Christopher, Alex. BS, U. Ill., 1983, JD, 1986. Bar: Ill., Mass., U.S. Dist. Ct. (no., ctrl. and so. dists.) Ill., U.S. Ct. Appeals (7th cir.). Assoc. Williams & Montgomery, Chgo., 1986-89; assoc. Sanchez & Daniels, Chgo., 1989-94, ptnr., 1994—; arbitrator McLean County, Bloomington, Ill., 1998—, Cook County, Chgo., 1990—. Mem. ABA, Internat. Assn. Def. Counsel, Ill. Bar Assn., Ill. Def. Coun., Chgo. Bar Assn., McLean County Bar Assn., Def. Rsch. Inst. Avocations: golf, racquetball. General civil litigation, Insurance, Labor. Office: Sanchez & Daniels 237 E Front St Bloomington IL 61701-5211

**VARONA, DANIEL ROBERT,** lawyer, insurance company executive; b. Bklyn., Oct. 26, 1944; s. Theodore A. and Elsie Varona; m. Camille Mastronardi Feb. 14, 1986; children: David, Christopher, Julia. BS in Psychology, CCNY, 1971; JD, N.Y. Law Sch., 1977. Atty.office of gen. counsel N.Y. State Ins. Dept., N.Y.C., 1977-79; gen. coun., sec. Ideal Mut. Ins. Co. & Optimum Holding Corp., N.Y.C., 1979-85; sec. and counsel North Atlantic Life Ins. Co., Jerico, N.Y., 1985-87; gen. counsel, sec., chief adminstrv. officer Companion Life/Mut. Omaha Cos., Rye, N.Y., 1987—. With USN, 1964-68. N.Y. State Regents scholar, 1962-64, Vietnam War Svc. scholar N.Y. State, 1968-71. Mem. N.Y. State Bar Assn. (chair life, health and accident com., torts ins. and compensation sect.), Westchester Bar Assn., Putnam Bar Assn. Avocations: gardening, martial arts. Insurance, General corporate, Administrative and regulatory. Office: Companion Life/ Mut Omaha 401 Theodore Fremd Ave Rye NY 10580-1422

**VASQUEZ, JESSICA FRANCES,** lawyer; b. N.Y.C., June 5, 1974; d. Francisco and Madeline V. AB, Bryn Mawr Coll., Pa., 1996; JD, N.Y. Law Sch., 1999. Tchr. Higher Achievement Program, Washington, 1994; clerical asst. Athena Inst. for Women's Wellness, Haverford, Pa., 1995-96; legal intern Ctr. for Battered Women's Legal Svcs., N.Y.C., 1997, 98-99, ACLU, N.Y.C., 1997-98, Siskind, Susser, Haas & Ryan, N.Y.C., 1997-98; co-chair The Law Sch. Domestic Violence Consortium, N.Y.C., 1997-99, N.Y. Law Sch. Domestic Violence Project, 1997-99; student chair Courtroom Advs. Project. Mem. Assn. Bar City N.Y., Latino Law Students Assn. (sec. 1997-98), Legal Assn. for Women (exec. bd. 1997-98). Democrat. Family and matrimonial, Immigration, naturalization, and customs. Office: CBWLS 67 Wall St Ste 2411 New York NY 10005-3101

**VASQUEZ, JUAN FLORES,** judge; b. San Antonio, June 24, 1948; s. Jose and Amelia (Flores) V.; m. Mary Theresa Schultz, Aug. 22, 1970; children: Juan Jr., Jaime. BA, U. Tex., 1972; JD, U. Houston, 1977; LLM in Taxation, NYU, 1978. Bar: Tex. 1977, U.S. Dist. Ct. (so. dist.) Tex. 1982, U.S. Dist. Ct. (we. dist.) Tex. 1985, U.S. Ct. Appeals (5th cir.) 1982, U.S. Supreme Ct. 1996, U.S. Tax Ct. 1978. Acct. Coopers & Lybrand, L.A., 1972-74; tax atty. Office of Chief Coun. IRS, Houston, 1978-82, Leighton, Hood & Vasquez, San Antonio, 1987; pvt. practice San Antonio, 1987-95; judge U.S. Tax Ct., Washington, 1995—. Mem. ABA, Mex.-Am. Bar Assn. Tex. and San Antonio, Nat. Hispanic Bar Assn., Nat. Judicial Coll., Hispanic Bar Assn. D.C., Coll. State Coll. Tex., Tex. State Bar Assn., San Antonio Bar Assn. Office: US Tax Ct 400 2nd St NW Washington DC 20217-0002

**VASSALLO, JOHN A.,** lawyer; b. N.Y.C., Aug. 19, 1937; s. John and Gilda (Di Desidero) V.; divorced; children: John C., Elena, Edward F. AB, Columbia U., 1959, LLB, 1962. Bar: N.Y. 1963, U.S. Dist. Ct. (so. and ea. dists.) N.Y. 1964, U.S. Ct. Appeals (2nd cir.) 1965. Assoc. Saxe, Bacon & O'Shea, N.Y.C., 1962-68; ptnr. Barovick & Konecky, N.Y.C., 1968-70, Kurtz & Vassallo, N.Y.C., 1970-78, Franklin, Weinrib, Rudell & Vassallo, N.Y.C., 1978—. Fellow Am. Acad. Matrimonial Attys. (bd. govs.); mem. N.Y. State Bar Assn., Am. Coll. Family Trial Laywers (diplomate), Friars Club. Family and matrimonial, General civil litigation. Home: 285 Central Park W New York NY 10024-3006 Office: Franklin Weinrib Rudell & Vassallo 488 Madison Ave New York NY 10022-5702

**VASSILAKIS, THEODORE,** judge, lawyer; b. Alexandria, Egypt, Sept. 18, 1942; came to U.S., 1970; s. Nicholaos and Maria (Panagiotakis) V.; m. Ellen Kourtides, Apr. 1, 1976. BA in Polit. Sci., Panteios U., Athens, Greece, 1964; LLD in Law, U. Thessaloniki, Greece, 1967; LLM in Corp. Law, NYU, 1979. Bar: Athens, Greece 1994, N.Y. 1985, U.S. Dist. Ct. (so. and ea. dists. 1988), U.S. Supreme Ct. 1996. Adminstrv. officer Greek Ministry of Commerce, Athens, 1967-70; protocol officer Greek Embassy, Osaka, Japan, 1970; comml. attache Consulate Gen. Greece, N.Y.C., 1970-76; legal cons. Seward Rafael & Kourides, N.Y.C., 1977-81; field underwriter N.Y. Life Ins. Co., N.Y.C., 1981-84; real estate agt. Cooper Hill, N.Y.C., 1984-85; atty.-at-law Bonaguidi & Assocs., N.Y.C., 1985-90; adminstrv. law judge N.Y. State Office Temporary & Disability Assistance, N.Y.C., 1990—; founding ptnr. Corcoran & Vassilakis, Attys. at Law, N.Y.C., 1998—. Sub-lt. Greek Mil., 1964-66. Mem. Pan-Macedonian Orgn. (hon. mem.), N.Y. State Adminstrv. Law Judges Assn. (co-pres. 1993—), Alexander the Great Found. (founding mem., gen. counsel 1991—), Hellenic-Am. C. of C. Home: 405 E 56th St New York NY 10022-2412

**VASTI, THOMAS FRANCIS, III,** lawyer; b. Poughkeepsie, N.Y., Sept. 22, 1966; s. Thomas F. Jr. and Faith Vasti; m. Suzanne Hammond, Aug. 17, 1991; children: Annelise Nicole, Matthew Thomas. BA, U. Notre Dame, 1988; JD, St. John's, 1991. Bar: N.Y. 1992, Conn. 1992, U.S. Dist. Ct. (ea. dist.) N.Y. 1995, U.S. Dist. Ct. (so. dist.) N.Y. 1995. Law clk. Vasti & Rutberg, Pleasant Valley, N.Y., 1988-91; assoc. Vasti & Sears, Pleasant Valley, 1991-96; v.p., sr. atty. Vasti & Sears, P.C., Pleasant Valley, 1996—; spkr. Landlord/Tenant Litigation Nat. Bus. Inst., 1995. Treas., head coach No. Dutchess Raiders Pop Warner, Millbrook, N.Y., 1991—. Mem. ABA, ATLA, N.Y. State Bar Assn., N.Y. State Trial Lawyers Assn., Dutchess County Bar Assn., Pleasant Valley C. of C. (v.p., trustee 1992—), KC, Notre Dame Alumni Club (sec. mid. Hudson Valley 1997, 98, v.p. 1999—). Republican. Roman Catholic. Avocations: youth sports coaching, golf, hunting, fishing, trombone playing. Personal injury, General civil litigation, Family and matrimonial. Office: Vasti & Sears PC Rte 44 PO Box 656 Pleasant Valley NY 12569-0656

**VASVARI, THOMAS M.,** lawyer; b. Youngstown, Ohio, Nov. 25, 1964; s. Thomas D. and Rosemarie V.; m. Christine L. Gentile, June 3, 1989. BA, Youngstown State U., 1987; JD, Case Western Res. U., 1990. Atty. pvt. practice, Youngstown, Ohio, 1990-94; law clk. Ohio 7th Dist. Ct. Appeals, Youngstown, 1991-94; assoc. McLaughlin, McNally & Carlin, Youngstown, 1994-98; ptnr. Carlin & Vasvari, Poland, Ohio, 1998—. Mem. Nat. Bd. Trial Advocacy. General civil litigation, Personal injury, Product liability. Office: Carlin & Vasvari 625 Main St PO Box 5369 Poland OH 44514-0369

**VATER, CHARLES J.,** lawyer; b. Pitts., Feb. 8, 1950; s. Joseph A. and Helen M. (Genellie) V.; m. Diane E. Vater, June 10, 1972; children: Allison D., Elizabeth A. BA, U. Notre Dame, 1971; JD, U. Pitts., 1975. Bar: Pa. 1975, U.S. Dist. Ct. (we. dist.) Pa. 1975, U.S. Ct. Appeals (3d cir.) 1979. Assoc. Tucker Arensberg, P.C., Pitts., 1975-80, ptnr., shareholder, 1980—, mng. shareholder. Contbr. articles to profl. jours. Mem. Allegheny County Bar Assn. (probate coun. 1988-98, 99—), Estate Planning Coun. Pitts. (bd. dirs. 1988-90, 95-97, sec. 1999), Order of Coif, Phi Beta Kappa. Estate planning, Probate, Contracts commercial. Home: 1615 Trolist Dr Pittsburgh PA 15241-2650 Office: Tucker Arensberg 1 Ppg Pl Ste 1500 Pittsburgh PA 15222-5413

**VAUGHAN, AUDREY JUDD,** paralegal, musician; b. Washington, May 8, 1936; d. Deane Brewster and Elizabeth (Melamed) Judd; m. Arthur Harris Vaughan Jr., Feb. 7, 1959 (div. June 1976); 1 child, Erik Brewster. BA, Cornell U., 1958; postgrad., Eastman Sch. Music, 1959-62; cert. in paralegal studies, UCLA, 1977. Tchr. music Rochester (N.Y.) Sch. Sys., 1961-64, Gooden Sch., Sierra Madre, Calif., 1975-78; paralegal Nossaman, Kruger & Marsh, L.A., 1978-80, Latham Watkins, L.A., 1980-84, Ammirato Palumbo, Pasadena, Calif., 1984-99; sr. paralegal Santochi, Gable, Dwyer & Takahashi, Glendale, Calif., 1999—; dir. Los Grillos, medieval and renaissance music performing group, Pasadena, 1965—. Organizer studies and presentations, bd. dirs., spkr. LWV, Pasadena, 1965-73; mem. Baroquen Consort and Baroque Instrumental Ensemble, Silverlake Baroque Ensemble, 1997-99. Mem. L.A. Paralegal Assn. (com. for paralegal edn., spkr. 1985-99). Avocations: singing, playing renaissance instruments, playing harpsichord, hiking. Home: 2034 Glenview Ter Altadena CA 91001-2808

**VAUGHAN, HERBERT WILEY,** lawyer; b. Brookline, Mass., June 1, 1920; s. David D. and Elzie G. (Wiley) V.; m. Ann Graustein, June 28, 1941. Student, U. Chgo., 1937-38; SB cum laude, Harvard U., 1941, LLB, 1948. Bar: Mass. 1948. Assoc. Hale and Dorr, Boston, 1948-54, jr. ptnr., 1954-56, sr. ptnr., 1956-82, co-mng. ptnr., 1976-80; pres. Herbert W. Vaughan, P.C., sr. ptnr. Hale and Dorr, 1982-89, of counsel, 1990-95, ret. ptnr., 1996; bd. dirs., mem. fin. com. Boston and Maine R.R., 1961-64. Asst. sec. and mem. adv. coun., The Trustees of Reservations; mem. Com. of Fund for Preservation of Wildlife and Natural Areas; mem. bd. trustees, Am. Friends of New Coll. (Oxford Univ.). Fellow Am. Bar Found. (life); mem. ABA, Chesterton Soc. (internat. com.), Mass. Bar Assn., Boston Bar Assn., Am. Law Inst., Am. Coll. Real Estate Lawyers, Am. Coun. Trustees and Alumni (mem. alumni leadership coun.), Bay Club, Badminton and Tennis Club, Union Club (Boston), Boston Econ. Club, Longwood Cricket Club (Brookline, Mass.). Real property. Office: Hale and Dorr LLP 60 State St Ste 25 Boston MA 02109-1816

**VAUGHN, KATHRYN SUE,** lawyer; b. Beaumont, Tex., June 5, 1967; d. Oris and Jeannette Wright Vaughn. BA in English cum laude, Lamar U., 1988; JD magna cum laude, U. Houston, 1992. Bar: Tex. 1992, U.S. Dist. Ct. (so. dist.) Tex. 1993, U.S. Dist. Ct. (ea. dist.) Tex. 1993, U.S. Ct. appeals (5th cir.) 1994. Assoc. Baker & Botts, Houston, 1992—. Mem. Tex. Bar Assn. (labor and employment sect.), Houston Bar Assn., Houston Young Lawyers Assn. Labor. Office: Baker & Botts One Shell Plaza 910 Louisiana St Ste 3600 Houston TX 77002-4916

**VAUGHN-CARRINGTON, DEBRA MILLER,** lawyer; b. Detroit, July 9, 1951; d. Roy Orlando and Juanita Zenobia (Miller) Vaughn; m. Gregory Lewis Carrington, Oct. 19, 1985. BA, Memphis State U., 1978; JD, Howard U., 1984. Bar: D.C. 1987, U.S. Ct. Appeals. Newscaster/reporter Sta. WGOW-WSKZ-AM-FM, Chattanooga, 1979-80; air personality Sta. WDOD-AM-FM, Chattanooga, 1979-80; legal researcher Washington, 1985-87, pvt. practice,, 1987-88; assoc. communications law Law Offices Lauren A. Colby, Frederick, Md., 1988-89; assoc. Law Offices J. Lincoln Woodard, Washington, 1989; head communications law div., spl. asst. to sr. ptnr. Cade & Reid, Washington, 1989—. Mem. ABA, Bar Assn. D.C., Women's Bar Assn. D.C., U.S. Ct. Appeals Bar Assn., Fed. Communications Bar Assn., Phi Alpha Delta, Sigma Gamma Rho. Democrat. Roman Catholic. Avocations: piano, organ, swimming, needlepoint, reading. Communications, General corporate, Entertainment. Office: Cade & Reid 600 New Hampshire Ave NW Washington DC 20037-2403

**VAZQUEZ, CARLOS MANUEL,** law educator; b. Havana, Cuba, Jan. 22, 1958; came to U.S., 1962; s. Carlos Jesus and Lourdes Raida (Molina) V.; m. Mary Katherine Qualiana, Aug. 3, 1993; children: Elena Maria, Elias Mateo. BA, Yale U., 1979; JD, Columbia U., 1983. Bar: D.C. 1985, U.S. Ct. Appeals (D.C., 6th and 9th cirs.) 1985, U.S. Supreme Ct. 1989. Law clk. Legal Advisor's Office U.S. Dept. of State, Washington, 1983; law clk. to Judge Stephen Reinhardt U.S. Ct. Appeals (9th cir.) Calif., L.A., 1983-84; assoc. Covington & Burling, Washington, 1985-90; vis. assoc. prof. law Georgetown U. Law Ctr., Washington, 1990-91, assoc. prof. law, 1991-96, prof. of law, 1996—. Contbr. articles to law jours. Recipient Pro Bono Svc. award Internat. Human Rights Law Group, Washington, 1986. Mem. ABA, Am. Soc. Internat. Law, Hispanic Nat. Bar Assn., D.C. Bar (co-chair pub. internat. law com. 1995—). Roman Catholic. Avocations: traveling, music, literature. Office: Georgetown Univ Law Ctr 600 New Jersey Ave NW Washington DC 20001-2022

**VAZQUEZ, MARTHA ALICIA,** judge; b. Santa Barbara, Calif., Feb. 21, 1953; d. Remigio and Consuelo (Mendez) V.; m. Frank Mathew, Aug. 7, 1976; children: Cristina Vazquez Matthew, Nicholas Vazquez Matthew, Nathan Vazquez Matthew. BA in Govt., U. Notre Dame, 1975, JD, 1978. Bar: N.Mex. 1979, U.S. Dist. Ct. (we. dist.) N.Mex. 1979. Atty. Pub. Defender's Office, Santa Fe, 1979-81; ptnr. Jones, Snead, Wertheim, Rodriguez & Wentworth, Santa Fe, 1981-93; judge U.S. District Ct., 10th Circuit, Santa Fe, 1993—. Chmn. City Santa Fe Grievance Bd. Mem. N.Mex. Bar Assn. (fee arbitration com., chmn. trial practice sect. 1984-85, mem. task force on minority involvement in bar activities), Santa Fe Bar Assn. (jud. liasion com.), Nat. Assn. Criminal Def. Lawyers, Assn. Trial Lawyers Am., N.Mex. Trial Lawyers Assn. Democrat. Roman Catholic. Office: US Courthouse PO Box 2710 Santa Fe NM 87504-2710

**VAZZANA, JAMES ANTHONY,** lawyer; b. Rochester, N.Y., Dec. 15, 1964; s. Joseph Anthony and Joan (Terrana) V.; m. Dina Gugino, June 29, 1991. BA, U. Rochester, 1987; JD, U. Dayton, 1990. Bar: N.Y. 1991, U.S. Dist. Ct. (we. dist.) N.Y. 1993. Assoc. Pauley and Barney, P.C., Rochester, N.Y., 1990-95, Law Office Brian J. Barney, Rochester, N.Y., 1995, Woods, Oviatt, Gilman, Sturman & Clarke LLP, Rochester, N.Y., 1995—. Fin. chmn. Com. to Return Supreme Ct. Justice Kenneth Fisher, Rochester, 1995, Com. to Re-elect Family Ct. Judge Anthony J. Sciolino, Rochester, 1996. Mem. N.Y. State Bar Assn. (family law sect. 1991—), Monroe County Bar Assn. (fee arbitration com. 1994-97, juvenile law com. 1995—, sec. family law sect. 1997, v.p. 1998, exec. coun. 1997), Italian Am. Businessmans Assn. (v.p. 199597, pres. 1998—), Aquinas Inst. Sports Booster, Theta Delta Chi. Avocations: family, travel, golf, cooking, gardening. Family and matrimonial. Office: Woods Oviatt Gilman Sturman & Clarke LLP 700 Crossroads Bldg 2 State St Rochester NY 14614-2004

**VEACH, ROBERT RAYMOND, JR.,** lawyer; b. Charleston, S.C., Nov. 28, 1950; s. Robert Raymond and Evelyn Ardell (Vegter) V.; m. Lori Sue Erickson, May 27, 1989. Student, St. Olaf Coll., 1968-70; BS in Acctg., Ariz. State U., 1972; JD, So. Meth. U., 1975. Bar: Tex. 1975, Nebr. 1975, U.S. Dist. Ct. Nebr. 1975, U.S. Dist. Ct. (no. dist.) Tex. 1975, Temporary Emergency Ct. Appeals 1975. Acctg. instr. Sch. Bus. So. Meth. U., Dallas, 1973-74; law clk. to Hon. Joe E. Estes U.S. Dist. Ct. No. Dist. Tex.-Temp. Emergency Ct. Appeals, Dallas, 1975-76; assoc. Locke Purnell Boren Laney & Neely, Dallas, 1976-80; v.p. The Lomas & Nettleton Co., Dallas, 1980-83, Rauscher Pierce Refsnes, Inc., Dallas, 1983-87; pres. RPR Mortgage Fin. Corp., Dallas, 1985-87; sr. shareholder Locke Purnell Rain Harrell, Dallas, 1987-97; exec. v.p. PC Holdings, Inc., Dallas, 1998—; pvt. practice Dallas, 1998—; allied mem. N.Y. Stock Exch., 1985-87; lectr. securities and banking confs.; bd. dirs. pvt. corps.; trustee Correctional Properties Trust, chmn. audit and finance com., 1998—. Author legal articles. Dir. North Tex. affiliate Am. Diabetes Assn., Dallas, 1978-81; mem. Gov.'s Task Force Wash. State Housing Commn., 1982-83. Mem. ABA, State Bar of Tex., Nebr. State Bar Assn., Fed. Bar Assn., Dallas Bar Assn. Republican. Methodist. Avocations: golf, antique Am. firearms. General corporate, Finance, Securities. Home: 4223 Brookview Dr Dallas TX 75220-3801 Office: 2911 Turtle Creek Blvd Dallas TX 75219-6247

**VEAL, REX R.,** lawyer; b. Lafayette, Ga., May 2, 1956; s. Boyd Herman and Barbara Ann (Sharp) V.; m. Vicky Elizabeth Wilkins, Dec. 13, 1980; children: Matthew Aaron and Richard Andrew (twins). BA, U. Tenn., 1978, JD, 1980. Bar: Tenn. 1981, U.S. Dist. Ct. (ea. dist.) Tenn. 1981, U.S. Ct. Appeals (10th cir.) 1981, U.S. Ct. Appeals (6th cir.) 1984, U.S. Ct. Appeals (4th cir.) 1987, Ga. 1991, U.S. Dist. Ct. (no. dist.) Ga. 1991, U.S. Ct. Appeals (11th cir.) 1991, D.C. 1993, U.S. Dist. Ct. D.C. 1993, U.S. Ct. Appeals (D.C. and fed. cir.) 1993. Assoc. Finkelstein, Kern, Steinberg & Cunningham, Knoxville, Tenn., 1980-83; atty. FDIC, Knoxville, 1983-84, sr. atty., 1984-88; counsel liquidation FDIC, Washington, 1988-89, assoc. gen. counsel, 1989-90; spl. counsel Resolution Trust Corp., Washington, 1989-90; ptnr. Powell, Goldstein, Frazer & Murphy, Atlanta and Washington, 1990—; lectr. in field. Contbr. articles to profl. jours. Mem. ABA, Tenn. Bar Assn., Ga. Bar Assn., Atlanta Bar Assn. Avocations: jogging, collecting books. Contracts commercial, Finance, Real property. Home: 6201 Blackberry Hl Norcross GA 30092-1375 Office: Powell Goldstein Frazer & Murphy 191 Peachtree St NE Fl 16 Atlanta GA 30303-1740 also: 1001 Pennsylvania Ave NW Ste 6 Washington DC 20004-2505

**VEASEY, EUGENE NORMAN,** state supreme court chief justice; b. Wilmington, Del., Jan. 9, 1933; s. Eugene E. and Elizabeth B. (Norman) V.; m. Suzanne Johnson, Aug. 4, 1956; children: Andrew Scott, Dluglas Ross, E. Norman Jr., Marian Elizabeth. AB, Dartmouth Coll., 1954; LLB, U. Pa., 1957. Bar: Del. 158, U.S. Supreme Ct. 1963. Dep. atty. gen. State of Del., 1961-62; chief dep., 1962-63; ptnr. Richards, Layton & Finger, Wilmington, Del., 1963-92; chief justice Del. Supreme Ct., 1992—. Contbr. articles to profl. jours. Bd. advisors U. Pa. Inst. for Law and Econs. Capt. Del. Air N.G., 1957-63. Fellow Am. Bar Found., Am. Coll. Trial Lawyers, Am. Intellectual Property Law Assn.; mem. Del. Bd. Bar Examiners (chmn. 1973-80), Del. Bar Assn. (pres. 1982-83, chmn. corp. law com. 1969-74, chmn. rules com. Del. Supreme Ct. 1974-80), ABA (chair bus. law sect. 1994-95, chair spl. com. on ethics 2000 1997—), Am. Law Inst. (bd. dirs. conf. chief jusice 1994-96, chair professionalism com. 1994-98, 1st v.p. 1998, pres.-elect 1998—), Nat. Ctr. State Cts. (pres. 1999—, chair bd. dirs. 1999—). Republican. Episcopalian. Office: Del Supreme Ct PO Box 1997 Wilmington DE 19899-1997

**VEAZEY, GARY EUGENE,** lawyer; b. Birmingham, Ala., Dec. 17, 1957; s. Arthur Eugene and Phyllis Lee V.; m. Kathy S. Veazey, Dec. 31, 1986; children: Martin M., Katherine Lee. BBA, Mid. Tenn. State U., 1980; JD, U. Memphis, 1983. Bar: Tenn. 1983; U.S. Dist. (we. dist.) Tenn. 1986. Assoc. Peice, Rice, Bratcher, Nichols & Stone, Memphis, 1983-86; ptnr. Rice, Rice, Bursi & Veazey, Memphis, 1986-89, Rice, Rice, Smith, Bursi &

Veazey, Memphis, 1989-94, Rice, Smith, Bursi, Veazey, Amundsen & Jewell, Memphis, 1994—. Bd. dirs. World Pro Fun Tour, Inc., Memphis, 1985-87. Mem. Tenn. Bar Assn., Memphis Bar Assn., Tenn. Trial Lawyers Assn. Personal injury, General civil litigation, Criminal. Office: Rice Smith Bursi Veazey Amundsen & Jewell 44 N 2nd St Fl 10 Memphis TN 38103-2251

**VEEDER, PETER GREIG,** lawyer; b. Pitts., Aug. 13, 1941. AB, Princeton U., 1963; JD, U. Pitts., 1966. Bar: Pa. 1966, D.C. 1976. Lawyer Thorp Reed & Armstrong, Pitts., 1970-99; of counsel Thorp, Reed & Armstrong, Pitts., 1999—. Environmental. Office: Thorp Reed & Armstrong One Riverfront Ctr 20 Stanwix St Ste 900 Pittsburgh PA 15222-4895

**VEGA, BENJAMIN URBIZO,** retired judge, television producer; b. La Ceiba, Honduras, Jan. 18, 1916; m. Janie Lou Smith, Oct. 12, 1989; AB, U. So. Calif., 1938, postgrad., 1939-40; LLB, Pacific Coast U. Law, 1941. Bar: Calif. 1947, U.S. Dist. Ct. (so. dist.) Calif. 1947, U.S. Supreme Ct. 1958. Assoc. Anderson, McPharlin & Connors, L.A., 1947-48, Newman & Newman, L.A., 1948-51; dep. dist. atty. County of L.A., 1951-66; judge L.A., County Mcpl. Ct., East L.A. Jud. Dist., 1966-86, retired, 1986; leader faculty seminar Calif. Jud. Coll. at Earl Warren Legal Inst., U. Calif-Berkeley, 1978. Mem. Calif. Gov.'s Adv. Com. on Children and Youth, 1968; del. Commn. of the Califs., 1978; bd. dirs. Los Angeles-Mexico City Sister City Com.; pres. Argentine Cultural Found., 1983. Recipient award for outstanding services from Mayor of L.A., 1973, City of Commerce, City of Montebello, Calif. Assembly, Southwestern Sch. Law, Disting. Pub. Service award Dist. Atty. L.A. Mem. Conf. Calif. Judges, Mcpl. Ct. Judges' Assn. (award for Outstanding Services), Beverly Hills Bar Assn., Navy League, L.A. County, Am. Judicature Soc., World Affairs Council, Rotary (hon.), Pi Sigma Alpha. Home: 101 California Ave Apt 1207 Santa Monica CA 90403-3525

**VEGA, GREGORY A.,** prosecutor; b. East Chicago, Ind.. BS in Acctg., Ind. U., 1975; JD, Valparaiso U., 1980. Honors program trial atty. Office of Chief Counsel IRS, Chgo.; with U.S. Atty.'s Office for No. Dist. of Ind., 1983-87; asst. U.S. atty. in maj. frauds and econ. crimes unit U.S. Atty.'s Office, San Diego, 1987; U.S. atty. so. dist. Calif. U.S. Dept. Justice, 1999—; instr. Atty. Gen.'s Advocacy Inst., Nat. Inst. Trial Advocacy. Mem. Hispanic Nat. Bar Assn. (past pres. 1997-98), State Bar Calif. (chmn. criminal law adv. commn. 1992-93, bd. legal specialization 1993-96), San Diego County Bar Assn. (jud. evaluation com. 1993), San Diego La Raza Lawyers Assn. (past bd. dirs.). Office: Rm 6293 880 Front St San Diego CA 92101-8893*

**VEGA, MATTHEW ANTHONY,** lawyer; b. Memphis, July 10, 1968; s. Romeo and Barbara Lynn Vega; m. Jennifer Vega (Webster), Dec. 16, 1989; children: Shelby, Anna, Matthew. BA, Freed-Hardeman U., 1990; JD, Yale U., 1993. Bar: Ala. 1994. Assoc. Sirote & Permutt PC, Birmingham, Ala., 1993-97; corp. counsel Bruno's Inc., Birmingham, 1997-99; sr. corp. counsel Advantica Restaurant Group, Inc., Spartanburg, S.C., 1999—; mem. adv. bd. Freed Hardeman U., Henderson, Tenn., 1998; mem. edit. bd. The Ala. Lawyer, Montgomery, 1998. Co-editor Alabama Employer's Desk Manual, 1993-97. Mem. ABA, Ala. State Bar Assn., Birmingham Bar Assn., Rainbow Omega (bd. dirs.). Mem. Ch. of Christ. Civil rights, Labor, General civil litigation. Home: 317 Trantham Ct Inman SC 29349-7056 Office: Advantica Restaurant Group Inc 203 E Main St Spartanburg SC 29319-0002

**VEITCH, THOMAS HAROLD,** lawyer; b. Lake Odessa, Mich., June 9, 1938; s. Harold L. and Alice Lowe (Danes) V.; m. Ruta Purvins, 1963 (div. 1977); children: Kimura Lee, Gregory T.; m. Anne C. Veitch, Feb. 4, 1978; children: Stephanie Suzanne, Catherine. BS, Ctrl. Mich. U., Mt. Pleasant, 1960; JD, St. Mary's U., San Antonio, 1973. Bar: Tex. 1973. Mng. ptnr. Veitch & Britt PC, San Antonio, 1974-81; pres. Veitch & Assocs., San Antonio, 1981-95; ptnr. Soules & Wallace, San Antonio, 1995—; dir. Tex. Legal Protection Plan, Austin, 1996—. Author: What You Need to Know to Settle With Insurance Companies, 1991, The Consultant's Guide to Litigation Services, How to be an Expert Witness, 1992. Bd. mem. Selective Svc., Local Bd. 113, 1982—; trustee San Antonio Rotary Youth Edn. Found., 1995—. Mem. Am. Assn. Ins. Mgmt. Cons. (dir. 1994—), CPCU Soc. (nat. com. mem. cons. and litigation sect. 1994—, pres. Alamo chpt. 1974), Assn. Atty.-Mediators (pres. 1996), San Antonio Bar Found. (trustee 1995—), St. Mary's Law Alumni Assn. (trustee 1996-98), Rotary of San Antonio, Oak Hills Lions (pres. 1977), Sabor Toastmasters (pres. 1989). Avocations: golf, reading, travel, learning Spanish. Insurance, Probate, Estate planning. Office: Soules & Wallace 100 W Houston St Ste 1500 San Antonio TX 78205-1433

**VELA, FILEMON B.,** federal judge; b. Harlingen, Tex., May 1, 1935; s. Roberto and Maria Luisa Cardenas V.; m. Blanca Sanchez, Jan. 28, 1962; children: Filemon, Rafael Eduardo, Sylvia Adriana. Student, Tex. Southmost Coll., 1954-56, U. Tex., 1956-57; JD, St. Mary's U., San Antonio, 1962. Bar: Tex. 1962. Mem. Vela & Vela, 1962-63; atty. Mexican-Am. Legal Def. Fund, 1962-75; pvt. practice law Brownsville, 1963-75; judge dist. 107, Tex. Dist. Ct., 1975-80; judge U.S. Dist. Ct. (so. dist.) Tex., Brownsville, 1980—; instr. Law Enforcement Coll. City commr., Brownsville, 1971-73. Served with U.S. Army, 1957-59. Mem. State Bar Tex. Democrat. Office: US Dist Ct 206 Federal Bldg 500 E 10th St Brownsville TX 78520-5121

**VELTROP, JAMES D.,** lawyer; b. Jefferson City, Mo., Nov. 5, 1958; s. James Henry and Joanne Daray V.; m. Carroll Ourslen, Nov. 19, 1989; children: Sophia, Nicholas, Drew. AB, Mo. U., 1981, MA, 1983; JD, Harvard U., 1986. Bar: Conn., Md., D.C., U.S. Supreme Ct. Law clk. to Hon. Judith Rogers U.S. Ct. Appeals, Washington, 1986-87; assoc. Skadden, Arps, Slate, Meagler & Flom, Washington, 1987-96, Brussels, 1987-96; ptnr. Pepe & Hazard, Hartford, Conn., 1996-97, Axinn, Veltrop & Harkrider LLP, Hartford, 1997—. Co-author: Procedure and Enforcement in E.C. and U.S. Competition Law, 1993, Due Process and Anticompetitive Practices, 1994, Mergers and Acquisitions in the Health Care Industry, 1994, Le Controle Juridictionnel en Matiere de Droit de la Concurrence et des Concentrations, 1994. Mem. ABA, Conn. Bar Assn., Harvard-Radcliffe Club. Intellectual property, Antitrust, Federal civil litigation. Office: Axinn Veltrop & Harkrider One City Pl Hartford CT 06103

**VENABLE, GIOVAN HARBOUR,** lawyer; b. Winston-Salem, N.C., Dec. 10, 1956; d. Joel William and Jo Ann (Harbour) V. AB in Music magna cum laude, Dartmouth Coll., 1979; MDiv, Harvard U., 1983; JD, Stanford U., 1988. Bar: Calif. 1989, D.C. 1990, U.S. Supreme Ct. 1994; ordained minister Congregational Ch. 1984. Assoc. Wyman Bautzer Kuchel & Sibert, L.A., 1988-90; assoc. Gipson Hoffman & Pancione, L.A., 1990-92; pvt. practice L.A., 1992—. Contbr. articles to profl. jours.; editor Cal West Congregationalist, 1990—. Active 1st Congl. Ch., L.A., 1983—; mem. Intermission, L.a., 1989—. Mem. Ebell Club (v.p. membership 1988—), Phi Beta Kappa. Avocations: piano, running, travel, tennis. Entertainment, Real property. Office: 419 N Larchmont Blvd Los Angeles CA 90004-3013

**VENERUSO, JAMES JOHN,** lawyer; b. Bklyn., Feb. 4, 1951; s. Jack and Ann (Maugeri) V.; m. Lillian B. Curto, Aug. 16, 1975; children: Jacquelyn, James, Stephen. BA, Iona Coll., 1972; JD, Widener U., 1975. Bar: N.Y. 1976, U.S. Ct. Claims 1977, U.S. Supreme Ct. 1979, U.S. Dist. Ct. (so. dist.) N.Y. 1979, Fla. 1980. Assoc. Griffin, Kane, Letsen & Coogan, Yonkers, N.Y., 1975-81; mng. ptnr. Griffin, Letsen, Coogan & Veneruso, Bronxville, N.Y., 1981-94, Griffin Coogan & Veneruso, P.C., Bronxville, 1994—. Bd. dirs. Big Bros.-Big Sisters, Yonkers, 1978-79, 83-84. Assoc. editor Jour. Corp. Law, Widener Law Sch., 1973-74; bd. editors Pace Law Rev., 1979-80; gen. counsel Throggs Neck Extended Care Facility Family Coun. Mem. N.Y. State Bar Assn., Westchester County Bar Assn. (features editor 1983, chmn. banking com., 1993—), Yonkers Lawyers Assn. (sec. 1982-83, fin. sec. 1983-84), N.Y. State Bankers Assn. (legal com. 1988—), Heartsong Found. (dir., gen. counsel pro bono 1992—), Greyston Found. (bd. dirs. 1999—), Bronxville C. of C. (bd. dirs. 1990-93, legal counsel 1993-95), Family Svcs. Soc. (bd. dirs. gen. counsel pro bono 1991-95), N.Y. State Banking Assn. (legal adv. com. 1992—), Greyston Found. (bd. dirs. gen. coun.), N.Y. State Bar Assn. (condominium and coops. com. 1990—), Westchester 2000 (bd. mem. 1998—), John Marshall Honor Soc., Delta Lambda Sigma (pres. 1973-74). Democrat. Roman Catholic. Contracts commercial, Real property, Banking. Home: 100 Dellwood Rd Bronxville NY 10708-2006 Office: Griffin Coogan & Veneruso PC 51 Pondfield Rd Bronxville NY 10708-3805

**VENKER, THOMAS EDWARD,** lawyer; b. St. Louis, Nov. 27, 1954; s. Thomas Edward and Dolores Marie Venker; m. Sharon Teresa McNerney, Jan. 2, 1981; children: Thomas E. III, David A., Daniel J. BS, U. Va., 1977; JD, St. Louis U., 1980. Bar: Mo. 1980. Assoc. The Stolar Partnership, St. Louis, 1980-84, ptnr., 1984—. Treas. AFS-United Mo. Area Team, St. Louis, 1997—. Mem. ABA. Taxation, general, Estate planning, Corporate taxation. Home: 12 Bopp Ln Saint Louis MO 63131-3115 Office: The Stolar Partnership 911 Washington Ave Fl 7 Saint Louis MO 63101-1243

**VENNING, ROBERT STANLEY,** lawyer; b. Boise, Idaho, July 24, 1943; s. William Lucas and Corey Elizabeth (Brown) V.; m. Sandra Macdonald, May 9, 1966 (div. 1976); 1 child, Rachel Elizabeth; m. Laura Siegel, Mar. 24, 1979; 1 child, Daniel Rockhill Siegel. AB, Harvard U., 1965; MA, U. Chgo., 1966; LLB, Yale U., 1970. Bar: Calif., U.S. Dist. Ct. (no. dist.) Calif., 1971, U.S. Dist. Ct. (cen. dist.) Calif. 1973, U.S. Ct. Appeals (9th cir.) 1977, U.S. Supreme Ct. 1977, U.S. Ct. Appeals (fed. cir.) 1986, U.S. Ct. Appeals (D.C. cir.) 1987. Assoc. Heller Ehrman White & McAuliffe, San Francisco, 1970-73, 73-76, ptnr., 1977—, mem. exec. com., 1991-94; vis. lectr. U. Wash., Seattle, 1973, Boalt Hall Sch. Law, U. Calif., Berkeley, 1982-85, 89, Sch. Bus., Stanford U., 1986-87. Editor Yale Law Jour., 1969-70. Early neutral evaluator U.S. Dist. Ct. (no. dist.) Calif., 1987—; mem. Natural Resources Def. Coun. Fellow Am. Bar Found. (life); mem. ABA, San Francisco Bar Assn. (past chair judiciary com.), CPR Inst. for Dispute Resolution, Olympic Club. Federal civil litigation, General civil litigation, State civil litigation. Office: Heller White & McAuliffe 333 Bush St San Francisco CA 94104-2806

**VENTKER, DAVID NEIL,** lawyer; b. Laredo, Tex., Feb. 6, 1957; s. David R. and Nancy M. (Sorenson ) V.; m. Katherine Louise Wheeler, Oct. 1, 1983; children: Sarah, Emily. BA in Econs., Ohio State U., 1979, JD, 1982. Bar: Ohio 1982, Va. 1989, N.C. 1999, U.S. Ct. Mil. Appeals 1985. Commd. U.S. Navy, 1982, advanced through grades to lt. comdr., 1989; counsel defense U.S. Navy, Charleston, S.C., 1983-85; counsel trial U.S. Navy, Sigonella, Italy, 1985-87; staff judge advocate Atlantic Fleet/NATO, 1987-89; ptnr. Huff, Poole & Mahoney, PC, 1989—. Contbr. articles to profl. jours. Mem. Maritime Law Assn. of U.S. (procter in admiralty), Va. State Bar Assn., N.C. State Bar Assn., Ohio Bar Assn. Presbyterian. Office: Huff Poole & Mahoney PC 4705 Columbus St Virginia Beach VA 23462-6749

**VENTO, M. THÉRÈSE,** lawyer; b. N.Y.C., June 30, 1951; d. Anthony Joseph and Margaret (Stechert) V.; m. Peter Michael MacNamara, Dec. 23, 1977; children: David Miles, Elyse Anne. BS, U. Fla., 1974, JD, 1976. Bar: Fla. 1977, U.S. Dist. Ct. (so. and mid. dists.) Fla. 1982, U.S. Ct. Appeals (5th and 11th cirs.) 1981, U.S. Supreme Ct. 1985. Clk. to presiding justice U.S. Dist. Ct. (so. dist.) Fla., Miami, 1976-78; assoc. Mahoney, Hadlow & Adams, Miami, 1978-79; assoc. Shutts & Bowen, Miami, 1979-84, ptnr., 1985-95; founding ptnr. Gallwey Gillman Curtis Vento & Horn, P.A., Miami, 1995—. Trustee Miami Art Mus., 1988—, The Beacon Coun., 1995-97, Law Sch. Alumni Coun., U. of Fla., 1994—. Fellow Am. Bar Found.; mem. Dade County Bar Assn. (dir. young lawyers sect. 1978-83, editor newsletter 1981-83), Fla. Assn. for Women Lawyers, Fla. Bar Assn. (bd. govs., young lawyers div. 1983-85, civil procedure rules com. 1983-90, exec. coun. trial lawyers sect. 1996—), The Miami Forum (v.p. 1987-88, bd. dirs. 1989-91). General civil litigation, Libel. Home: 3908 Main Hwy Miami FL 33133-6513 Office: Gallwey Gillman Curtis Vento & Horn PA 200 SE 1st St Ste 1100 Miami FL 33131-1909

**VENTRES, DANIEL BRAINERD, JR.,** lawyer; b. Washington, Dec. 2, 1930; s. Daniel Brainerd and Sarah Helen (Dunlap) V.; m. Sarah Stevenson, May 22, 1954 (div. 1978); children: Katherine Ventres Canipelli, William Brainerd; m. Judith Martin, Dec. 27, 1984. BA in Bus. Adminstrn. and Econs., Ohio Wesleyan U., 1952; JD, George Washington U., 1957. Bar: Minn. 1960, U.S. Dist. Ct. Minn. 1965, U.S. Supreme Ct. 1969, U.S. Ct. Mil. Appeals 1972, U.S. Ct. Appeals (8th cir.) 1989. Appraiser, legal asst. Redevel. Land Agy., Washington, 1955-56; procurement and legal staff The Martin Co., Denver, 1957-59, Mpls. Honeywell Co., 1959-60; ptnr. Carlsen, Greiner & Law, Mpls., 1960-84, MacIntosh & Commers, Mpls., 1984-86; of counsel Gray, Plant, Mooty, Mooty & Bennett, PA, Mpls., 1986-94, Gislason, Dosland, Hunter & Malecki, PA, Minnetonka, Minn., 1994-95; pvt. practice Mpls., 1995—; assoc. counsel Amateur Athletic Union, Indpls., 1974-80, U.S. Swimming Team, Colorado Springs, Colo., 1978-80; chmn. ad hoc com. on dispute resolution alternatives in family law Minn. Supreme Ct., Mpls., 1993-96; adj. prof. family law Hamline U. Law Sch., St. Paul, 1993; referee settlement conf. program Hennepin County Dist. Ct., Mpls., 1994—; lectr. Nat. Bus. Inst. Seminars, 1994. Mem. Ind. Sch. Dist. 274 Bd. Edn., Hopkins, Minn., 1965-72; chmn., legis. coord. Suburban Sch. Dist. Joint Bd., Hopkins, 1972; v.p. adminstrn. U.S. Swimming Com.; U.S. swimming ofcl. Olympic Games, PanAm. Games, Aquatic World Games; chmn., dir. Minn. AAU swimming, Minn. AAU, 1968-80. Officer USMC, 1952-54; col. USMCR, 1972-78. Mem. ABA, FBA (bd. dirs., v.p. Minn. chpt. 1961—, Minn. rep. alternat dispute resolution com. 1995-96, chmn. subcom. on alternate dispute reolution practices, procedures and processes Minn. chpt. 1996—), Am. Acad. Matrimonial Lawyers, Am. Arbitration Assn. (arbitrator, mediator, evaluator Mpls. 1995-98), Minn. Bar Assn. (cert. arbitrator, mediator and evaluator, lectr. CLE 1988-95), Hennepin County Bar Assn., Masons. Family and matrimonial, Real property, Consumer commercial. Office: 625 2d Ave S Ste 419 Minneapolis MN 55402

**VENTRES, JUDITH MARTIN,** lawyer; b. Ann Arbor, Mich., Feb. 10, 1943; d. D. Lawrence and Donna E. (Webb) Moran; children: Laura C. Martin, Paul M. Martin, A. Lindsay McGill; m. Daniel B. Ventres Jr., Dec. 27, 1984. BA, U. Mich., 1963; postgrad., U. Jean Moulin, Inst. du Droit, Lyon, France, 1981; JD, U. Minn., 1982. Bar: Minn. 1982, Fla. 1991, Colo. 1994, U.S. Tax Ct. 1989, U.S. Dist. Ct. Minn. 1989, U.S. Ct. Appeals (8th cir.) 1989. Tax supr., dir. fin. planning, asst. nat. dir. Coopers & Lybrand, Mpls., 1981-84; dir. fin. planning Investors Diversified Services subs. Am. Express, Mpls. and N.Y.C., 1984-85; sr. tax mgr., dir. fin. planning KPMG Peat Marwick Main & Co., Mpls., 1985-89; prin. Martin & Assocs., PA, Mpls., Minn., 1989—; faculty Minn. CLE, 1994; adv. bd. Nicollet/Ebenezer, 1996. owner Alternatax, Inc. Mem. Mpls. C. of C. Campaign, Downtown Coun. Coms., Mpls., 1982-84, Metro Tax Planning Group, 1984-86, Mpls. Estate Planning Coun., 1985—, Planned Giving Coun.; class chmn. fundraising campaign U. Minn. Law Sch., Mpls., 1985, 98; bd. dirs. Ensemble Capriccio, chmn. fundraising com., 1998—; usher Christ Presbyn. Ch., Edina, Minn., 1983—; mem. adv. coun. on planned giving ARC. Mem. ABA (task force on legal fin. planning), Minn. Bar Assn., Hennepin County Bar Assn., Fla. Bar Assn., Colo. Bar Assn., Minn. Soc. CPAs (instr. continuing legal edn. 1983-84, continuing profl. edn. 1982-86, individual, trust and estate provisions Tax Reform Act 1986, continuing legal edn. -estate planning 1994), Minn. Planned Giving Coun., Am. Assn. Ind. Investors (speaker), Am. Soc. CLUs, Minn. Soc. CLUs, Minn. Women Lawyers, Fla. Women Lawyers, Lex Alumnae, U. Mich. Alumni Assn. (coun. govs. 1989—, pres.-elect, scholarship chmn.), U. Minn. Alumni Club (bd. dirs. 1996, coun. govs. 1988-96, pres., treas. mem. com.), Minn. World Trade Assn., Internat. Assn. Fin. Planners, Edina C. of C., Interlachen Club, Athletic Club, Lafayette Club, U. Minn. Alumni Assn. (mem. univ. issues com., nat. bd. dirs. 1996—). Probate, Personal income taxation, Estate planning. Home: 1355 Vine Pl Mound MN 55364-9635 Office: Martin & Assocs PA 1650 W 82nd St Ste 1460 Minneapolis MN 55431-1466

**VENTRY, CATHERINE VALERIE,** lawyer; b. Bronxville, N.Y., Feb. 19, 1949; d. Victor and Catherine Regina (Dillon) V. AB in Logic and Philosophy, Vassar Coll., 1971; postgrad., Boston U., 1972; JD, N.Y. Law Sch., 1978. Bar: N.Y. 1979, U.S. Dist. Ct. (so. and ea. dists.) N.Y. 1979. Adj. asst. prof. John Jay Coll. of Criminal Justice, N.Y.C., 1978-80; adj. asst. prof. bus. law Coll. Mount St. Vincent Lehman Coll., N.Y.C., 1978-82; staff atty. City of N.Y. Dept. Housing Preservation and Devel. Litigation Bureau, N.Y.C., 1981-84; pvt. practice N.Y., 1984—; Tax editor Prentice-Hall Pub. Co., Englewood Cliffs, N.J., 1980-81. Mem. N.Y. State Bar, Rockland County Women's Bar, Rockland County Bar Assn., MENSA. Avocations: rock music, song writing. General civil litigation, Criminal, Workers' compensation. Office: 873 Union Ave New Windsor NY 12553-5034

**VENTURA, BRUCE ANTHONY,** lawyer; b. Petersburg, Va., July 20, 1959; s. Luis S. and Margaret L. (Dennison) V. Honors in econs., U. Coll. Cardiff, Wales, U.K., 1980; BA with honors, U. Ill., 1981; JD, U. Calif., Berkeley, 1984. Bar: Calif. 1984, D.C. 1986. Assoc. Paul, Hastings, Janofsky & Walker, Washington, 1984-89; sr. internat. atty. RJR Internat., Winston-Salem, N.C., 1989-92; v.p., gen. counsel RJR Nabisco, Hong Kong, 1992-95, Nabisco Internat., N.Y.C., 1996-98, RJR Nabisco Internat., Geneva, Switzerland, 1998—; exec. editor Internat. Tax and Bus. Lawyer, Berkeley, Calif., 1982-84; dir. Internat. Law Soc.; treas. UN Assn., Urbana, Ill., 1980-81; v.p. Illini Forensic Assn., Urbana, 1979-81. Named Edmund S. James scholar U. Ill., 1977-81. Mem. ABA, Royal Order of the Buffalo Bar (chmn. 1984—). Private international, General corporate, Contracts commercial. Office: C/O RJR Geneva HQ PO Box 408 Winston Salem NC 27102-0408

**VERA, RONALD THOMAS,** lawyer; b. Pomona, Calif., Oct. 16, 1946; s. Marcelino and Mary (Regaldo) V.; m. Christina Vega, June 10, 1972; children: Noah, Luis, Adam, Paul. BS, Mich. State U., 1970; JD, UCLA, 1973. Bar: Calif., 1974. Atty. Calif. Rural Legal Assistance, El Centro, Calif., 1973-77; dep. dir. Calif. Rural Legal Assistance, San Francisco, 1977-79; staff atty. Mex.-Am. Legal Defense & Ednl. Fund, San Francisco, 1979-85; assoc. scholar Tomas Rivera Ctr. for Policy Studies, Claremont, Calif., 1985-86; ptnr. Barbosa & Vera, L.A., 1986-90; of counsel Best, Best & Krieger, Riverside, Calif., 1990-92; pvt. practice Claremont, 1994—; vis. prof. law Loyola U. Law Sch., L.A., 1992-93, adj. prof. law, 1993-99. Contbr. articles to Ednl. Jours. Bd. dirs. Contra Costa Pers. Commn., Contra Costa County, Calif., 1984-86, Nat. Ctr. for Fair and Open Testing, Cambridge, Mass., 1986-94, Damien Prep. High Sch., La Verne, Calif., 1990-94, Pub. Counsel, 1989-92, Pomona Valley Med. Ctr., 1992—, Calif. Consortium of Edn. Found., 1995—. Recipient fellowship NEH, Harvard U. Law Sch., Cambridge, Mass., 1980, Tomas Rivera Ctr. for Policy Studies, Clarement, Calif., 1985-86. Mem.. ABA, Calif. State Bar Assn. (chair client security fund commn. 1993-97), L.A. County Bar Assn. Education and schools, Environmental, Municipal (including bonds). Office: 223 W Foothill Blvd Fl 2 Claremont CA 91711-2708

**VERCAMMEN, KENNETH ALBERT,** lawyer; b. Edison, N.J., Aug. 7, 1959; s. Albert Peter and Carol Ann (Rasche) V.; m. Cynthia Ann Bachenski, July 9, 1989. BS, U. Scranton, 1981; JD, U. Del., 1985. Bar: N.J., Pa. 1985, N.Y. 1986, D.C. 1987. Mng. atty. Metuchen, N.J., 1990—; adj. prof. Middlesex County Coll., Edison, 1990-91. Contbr. articles to profl. jours. Mem. Am. Cancer Soc., Edison, 1989—; counselor Cen. Jersey Road Runners, 1987. Named a Top Young Profl. by Am. Cancer Soc., New Brunswick, 1988, 89. Mem. KC. Roman Catholic. Avocations: cross-country running, soccer. Personal injury, Criminal, Contracts commercial. Office: 407 Main St Metuchen NJ 08840-1850

**VERDIRAME, PETER J.,** lawyer; b. N.Y.C., Apr. 8, 1954; s. Peter A. V. and Cosima M. Matichecchia; m. Michelle S. Russo. Bar: N.Y. 1982, U.S. Dist. Ct. (so. dist.) N.Y. 1987, U.S. Dist. Ct. (ea. dist.) N.Y. 1985, U.S. Dist. Ct. (no. dist.) N.Y. 1988), U.S. Ct. Appeals (2d cir.) 1996. Ptnr. Chesney Murphy & Moran, Baldwin, N.Y., 1987—. arbitrator small claims ct. civil ct. City of N.Y., 1992-97. Judge Civil Trial Inst. St. John's Law Sch., 1995, 96. Mem. Nassau County Bar Assn., N.Y. State Trial Lawyers Assn. Professional liability, Personal injury, Insurance. Office: Chesney & Murphy & Moran 2305 Grand Ave Baldwin NY 11510-3152

**VERDON, JANE KATHRYN,** lawyer; b. Manchester, N.C., 1943. BA, Newton Coll. (Boston Coll.), 1964; JD, U. San Diego, 1991. Bar: N.C. 1992. Legal intern San Diego City Atty. - Criminal Divsn., 1991; law clk. criminal def. Cheshire, Parker, Hughes and Manning, Raleigh, N.C., 1991-92; pvt. practice Raleigh, 1992—; creative dir., corp. v.p., ptnr. Internat. Creative Sys.; account exec., publicity dir., TV spokesperson H. Richard Silver, Inc.; fashion, beauty editor, spokesperson for major consumer mags., newspapers, TV; advt. and promotion in all areas of health, beauty and fashion. Assoc. fashion editor, assoc. mng. editor Seventeen Mag.; fashion dir. Woman's World Mag.; contbg. editor, writer for newspapers and consumer mags., radio and TV features, brochures, scripts, promotional programs, mediation, negotiations; TV and comml. appearances. Mem. AFTRA, ABA, N.C. Bar Assn., N.C. Trial Lawyers Assn., N.J. Foster Parents' Assn., Lawyers' Club. State civil litigation, Alternative dispute resolution, Criminal. Office: 514 Daniels St Raleigh NC 27605-1317

**VER DUGHT, ELGENE CLARK,** lawyer/mediator; b. Des Moines, Oct. 8, 1951; s. Elvyn Eugene and Betty Louise (Clark) Ver D.; m. Julliann Esther Dieckmann, June 15, 1974; children: Janna, Jared. BA, U. Mo., 1973; JD cum laude, Hamline U., 1976. Bar: Mo. 1976, U.S. Dist. Ct. (we. dist.) Mo. 1976, U.S. Supreme Ct. 1979, U.S. Ct. Appeals (8th cir.) 1981. Ptnr. Ver Dught Law Offices, Higginsville, Mo., 1976—; city atty. Corder, Mo., 1977-85, Wellington, Mo., 1978-85, Napoleon, Mo., 1979-85; prosecuting atty. County of Lafayette, Lexington, Mo., 1979-80; city atty. Blackburn, Mo., 1982-87; city prosecutor Higginsville, Mo., 1986-88; counsel C-1 Sch. Dist., Higginsville, 1987-88, 90—; exec. dir., founder Mediation Svcs. Mo.; cons. Ver Dught Farms, Lexington and Higginsville, Mo., 1978—; founder Mediation Svcs. of Mo. V.p. Lafayette County Dems., Mo., 1977; bd. dirs., adv. coun. Foster Grandparent Assn. Mem. Nat. Acad. Family Mediators (sr.), Assn. Family and Conciliation Cts. Democrat. Reorganized Ch. Jesus Christ Latter Day Saints. Lodge: Rotary (pres. Higginsville club 1983-84, Paul Harris fellow, 1984). Alternative dispute resolution, State civil litigation, Family and matrimonial. Home: RR 2 Box 173 Higginsville MO 64037-9528 Office: 1814 N Main St # 174 Higginsville MO 64037-1525 also: 13910 Noland Ct Ste B-1 Independence MO 64055-3353

**VERHOFF, CATHERINE LOUISE,** lawyer; b. Osaka, Japan, July 27, 1953; d. Robert Brannon and Midori (Kojima) Phillips; m. Randolph Warren Pregibon; 1 child, Nicole Midori Verhoff. BA, U. Akron, 1975; JD, NYU Law Sch., 1993. Bar: N.Y., N.J. Exec. dir. Salem (Ohio) Cmty. Theatre, 1977-82; musical theatre dir. The Youngstown (Ohio) Playhouse, 1982-84; dir. personnel Lehren/McGovern Constrn. Mgmt., Inc., N.Y.C., 1984-85; bus. mgr. Old Stratford Renovation and Restoration, N.Y.C., 1985-86, Steve Gold, Inc., N.Y.C., 1986-87; dir. ops. Nat. Resources Def. Coun., N.Y.C., 1987-93; assoc. Kramer, Levin, Naftalis & Fankel, N.Y.C., 1993—. Democrat. Avocations: Formula One racing, wine tasting and collecting, modern dance, travel. Home: 40 Gordonhurst Ave Montclair NJ 07043-2416 Office: Kramer Levin Naftalis & Frankel 919 3d Ave New York NY 10022

**VERKAMP, JOHN PAUL,** lawyer; b. Ft. Smith, Ark., June 10, 1965; s. Herman Frank and Dolores Sophie V.; m. Darla Shawn, July 6, 1985; children: Luke, Logan, Landon. BSA in Agrl. Mechanization & Agrl. Bus., U. Ark., 1988, JD, 1991. Bar: Ark. 1991, U.S. Dist.Ct. (ea. and we. dists.) Ark. 1991, U.S. Ct. Appeals (8th cir.) 1994. Assoc. atty. Walters Law Firm, Greenwood, Ark., 1991-92; ptnr. Walters, Hamby & Verkamp, P.A., Greenwood, 1992—; city atty. City of Charleston, Ark., 1991-98, City of Ozark, Ark., 1994-98, City of Branch, Ark., 1995-98, City of Ratcliff, Ark., 1995-98. Chmn. annexation com. City of Ozark, 1998; election commr. Franklin County, 1998; mem. adv. bd. Batter Women's Task Force, Ft. Smith, Ark., 1998; bd. dirs. St. Edward Hospice, Ft. Smith, 1997-98, Ark. Child Abuse and Negligence Prevention Bd., 1998. Named Pro Bono Atty., Ark. Vol. Lawyers for Elderly, 1998. Mem. Ark. Bar Assn., South Sebastian County Bar Assn. (pres. 1997-98). Republican. Roman Catholic. Avocations: writing short stories, writing poetry, hunting, fishing, landscaping. Home: 501 E Main St Charleston AR 72933-9020 Office: Walters Hamby & Verkamp PA 1405 W Center St Ste 3 Greenwood AR 72936-3402

**VERMES, L. ROBERT,** lawyer; b. Sussex, N.J., Jan. 7, 1945; s. Leslie R. and Alice E. (Gerry) V.; m. June Ellen Shero, July 4, 1974; children: Carly Dara, Brittain Nel, Courtney Lyn. BS, Northwestern U., 1967; JD, U. of La Verne, 1979. Bar: Calif. 1980, U.S. Dist. Ct. Calif. Sr. claims examiner Fremont Indemnity Corp., L.A., 1977-79, assoc., 1979-82; assoc. Towner, Kristiansen, Bellanca & Hill, Tustin, Calif., 1982-84; ptnr. Kriner, Hebner & Vermes, Santa Ana, Calif., 1984-87; sr. ptnr. Charton, Vermes & Rovenger, Santa Ana, 1987—; pvt. practice Irvine, Calif., 1998—; instr. Stress/Psychiatric Case Mgmt. workshops and seminars, Inst. Safety and Sys. Mgmt. USC, 1989—, cert. program worker's compensation adminstrn., U. Calif., Irvine; instr. I.E.A. Bd. dirs. High Hopes Head Trauma. Mem. ABA, State

Bar Calif., Orange County Bar Assn., Cornell Caduceus Soc., Northwestern U. Alumni Assn. (v.p. admission coun.), Trinity Sch. Alumni Assn., Coll. of Legal-Medicine Associade in Law, Sigma Alpha Epsilon. Workers' compensation, State civil litigation. Home: 5412 Amalfi Dr Irvine CA 92612-3400

**VERNAVA, ANTHONY MICHAEL,** lawyer; b. N.Y.C., May 13, 1937; s. Michel Antonio Vernava and Ana Avellina Guerriero. BS, Georgetown U., 1959; JD, Harvard U., 1962; LLM, NYU, 1965; MA in L.Am. Studies/ Internat. Fin., George Washington U., 1999. Bar: N.Y. 1962, U.S. Dist. Ct. (so. and ea. dists.) N.Y. 1963, U.S. Ct. Appeals (2nd cir.) 1963, Mich. 1965, U.S. Dist. Ct. (ea. dist.) Mich. 1966, U.S. Tax Ct. 1966, U.S. Supreme Ct. 1966, Ill. 1973. Atty. Reid & Priest, N.Y.C., 1962-63, IBM Corp., Armonk, N.Y., 1963-65; assoc. prof. Wayne State U., Detroit, 1965-68, prof., 1968-72; pvt. practice law Detroit and Chgo., 1972-75; prof. law So. Meth. U., Dallas, 1975-76; prof. law, consulting atty. U. Detroit Sch. Law, 1976-95; pvt. practice internat. cons. Fairfax, Va., 1995—; arbitrator Mich. Employment Rels. Commn., Detroit, 1988-95. Contbr. articles to profl. jours. Mem. ABA, N.Y. State Bar. Avocations: international travel, pre-Colombian civilizations, boating, hiking. Private international, Securities, Corporate taxation. Office: PO Box 99 Oakton VA 22124-0099

**VERNER, JIMMY LYNN, JR.,** lawyer, expert witness; b. Ft. Bragg, N.C., N.C., Dec. 13, 1953; s. Jimmy Lynn and Betty (Smith) V. BA in Polit. Sci. cum laude, Utah, 1975, cert. in internat. rels., 1974; MA in Polit. Sci., Emory U., 1976; JD, U. San Diego, 1979. Bar: Miss. 1980, U.S. Dist. Ct. (no. and so. dists.) Miss., U.S. Ct. Appeals (5th cir.) 1980, Tenn. 1982, U.S. Dist. Ct. (we. dist.) Tenn., U.S. Supreme Ct. 1983, Tex. 1986, U.S. Dist. Cts. (no., ea. and we. dists.) Tex. 1986, U.S. Ct. Appeals (D.C. cir.) 1988; cert. in family and civil trial law Tex. Bd. Legal Specialization. Faculty rsch. asst. U. San Diego, 1977-78; law clk. to Hon. William C. Keady U.S. Dist. Ct. for No. Dist. Miss., Greenville, 1979-81; ptnr. Akers & Verner, Greenville, 1981-82, Seeligson, Douglass, Falconer & Vanden Eykel, Dallas, 1985-90, Koons, Fuller & Vanden Eykel, Dallas, 1990-93; assoc. Martin, Tate, Morrow & Marston, Memphis, 1982-85; ptnr. Verner & Brumley, P.C., Dallas, 1993—; adj. prof. law Memphis State U., 1985; instr. Dallas-Am. Inst. Banking, 1986-89; lectr. in field, 1987—. Exec. editor San Diego Law Rev., 1978-79; editor Legal Update Newsletter, 1997—; contbr. articles to law jours. Bd. dirs. Habitat for Humanity, Dallas, 1985, Plano (Tex.) Bd. Adjustment, 1986-88. Fellow Dallas Bar Found.; mem. ABA, State Bar Tex., Tex. Acad. Fmily Law Specialists, Dallas Bar Assn. (bd. dirs. 1992-94). Avocations: skiing, horses, travel, Internet, reading. E-mail: jvevuer@verner-brumley.com. Family and matrimonial. Office: 3131 Turtle Creek Blvd Ste 1020 Dallas TX 75219-5439

**VERNIERO, PETER,** judge; married; 2 children. BA summa cum laude, Drew U., 1981; JD, Duke U., 1984. Law clk. to Justice Robert L. Clifford, 1984; with Pitney, Hardin, Kipp & Szuch, Morristown, N.J., 1985-87; dir. Herold & Haines P.A., Warren, N.J.; chief counsel, chief of staff Gov. Christine Whitman, Trenton, N.J.; atty. gen. State of N.J., Trenton, 1996-99; justice N.J. Supreme Ct., Trenton, 1999—; adj. prof. bus. law County Coll. Morris, 1986. Exec. dir. Rep. State Com., 1989-90. Office: Supreme Ct Box 970 Trenton NJ 08625

**VERNON, CRAIG K.,** lawyer; b. Alexandria, Va., Oct. 17, 1968; s. E. Kent and Maurine Vernon; m. Liliana Vernon, June 29, 1991; children: J. Dax, Aitana M. BS in Econs., Brigham Young U., 1993; JD, U. Idaho, 1996. Ptnr. Goicoechea Law Offices, Spokane, Wash., 1996-97; atty. Howard & Owens P.A., Coeur D Alene, Idaho, 1997—. Mem. ATLA, Wash. State Trial Lawyers Assn., Idaho Trial Lawyers Assn. Democrat. Insurance, Personal injury. Office: Howard & Owens PA 1250 W Ironwood Dr Ste 320 Coeur D Alene ID 83814-2682

**VERNON, DARRYL MITCHELL,** lawyer; b. N.Y.C., May 4, 1956; s. Leonard and Joyce (Davidson) V.; m. Lauren Lynn Bernstein, Aug. 21, 1982. BA in Math., Tufts U., 1978; JD, Yeshiva U., 1981. Bar: N.Y. 1982, U.S. Dist. Ct. (so. and ea. dists.) N.Y. 1982, U.S. Ct. Appeals (2d cir.) 1987. Assoc. Hochberg & Greenberg, N.Y.C., 1981-82; ptnr. Greenberg & Vernon, N.Y.C., 1982-83, Law Offices of Darryl M. Vernon, N.Y.C., 1983—; pres., ptnr. Vernon & Ginsburg, LLP, N.Y.C., 1989—. Contbr. articles to profl. jours. Samuel Belkin scholar Yeshiva U., 1979. Mem. ABA, ATLA, Assn. Bar City N.Y. (com. legal issues pertaining to animals). Real property, Landlord-tenant, Animal welfare. Office: 261 Madison Ave New York NY 10016-2303

**VERON, J. MICHAEL,** lawyer; b. Lake Charles, La., Aug. 24, 1950; s. Earl Ernest and Alverdy (Heyd) V.; m. Melinda Anne Guidry, Jan. 2, 1993; children: John Heyd, Katharine Leigh, Dylan Michael Earl. BA, Tulane U., 1972, JD, 1974; LLM, Harvard U., 1976. Bar: La. 1974, U.S. Dist. Ct. (we. dist.) La. 1977, U.S. Dist. Ct. (ea. dist.) La. 1979, U.S. Dist. Ct. (mid. dist.) La., 1983, U.S. Dist. Ct. (ea. dist.) Tex. 1992), U.S. Ct. Appeals (5th cir.) 1981, U.S. Ct. Appeals (fed. cir.) 1996, U.S. Tax Ct. 1988. Law clk. to presiding justice La. Supreme Ct., New Orleans, 1974-75; sole practice Lake Charles, 1976-78; ptnr. Scofield, Gerard, Veron, Singletary & Pohorelsky (formerly Scofield, Gerard, Veron, Hoskins & Soileau), Lake Charles, 1978—; instr. legal method and rsch. Boston U., 1975-76; lectr. environ. law McNeese State U., 1976-79; faculty Tulane Trial Adv. Inst., 1980; adj. proj. La. State U. Sch. Law, 1993—. Mem. bd. editors Tulane Law Rev., 1972-73, assoc. editor, 1973-74. Mem. athletic adv. com. Tulane U., 1983-86; pres. Krewe of Barataria, 1980-86; bd. dirs. Friends of Gov.'s Program for Gifted Children, Inc., 1985. Named to La. State U. Law Ctr. Hall of Fame, 1993. Mem. U.S. Golf Assn. (sectional affairs com.), La. Golf Assn. (bd. dirs., pres. 1990), Order of Coif, Maritime Law Assn., Lake Charles Country Club (pres. 1986), Tulane Green Wave (pres. Lake Charles chpt. 1984), English Turn Golf & Country Club. Roman Catholic. Avocations: golf, gin rummy, athletics. Federal civil litigation, General civil litigation, State civil litigation. Home: 230 Laurel St Lake Charles LA 70605-5524 Office: Scofield Gerard Veron Singletary & Pohorelsky 1114 Ryan St Lake Charles LA 70601-5252

**VERRELLI, ANTHONY LOUIS,** lawyer; b. Bronx, Feb. 19, 1967; s. Sebastiano and Josephine V.; m. Sungho Pak, Feb. 16, 1997. BA cum laude, Iona Coll., 1989; MA summa cum laude, St. John's U., 1991; JD, Seton Hall U., 1994. Bar: N.J. 1994, N.Y. 1995, U.S. Dist. Ct. (so. and ea. dists.) N.Y. 1995. Atty. pvt. practice, Bronx, 1994—. St. John's U. Grad. Sch. scholar, Jamaica, N.Y., 1991. Mem. N.Y. State Trial Lawyers Assn., Bronx County Bar Assn. Avocations: soccer, hiking, golf. Personal injury, Real property, Pension, profit-sharing, and employee benefits. Office: 2701 Williamsbridge Rd Bronx NY 10469-4109

**VERRILL, CHARLES OWEN, JR.,** lawyer; b. Biddeford, Maine, Sept. 30, 1937; s. Charles Owen and Elizabeth (Handy) V.; m. Mary Ann Blanchard, Aug. 13, 1960 (dec.); children: Martha Anne, Edward Blanchard, Ethan Christopher, Elizabeth Handy, Matthew Lawton, Peter Goldthwait; m. Diana Baber, Dec. 11, 1993. AB, Tufts U., 1959; LLB, Duke U., 1962. Bar: D.C. 1962. Assoc. Weaver & Glassie, 1962-64; assoc. Barco, Cook, Patton & Blow, 1964-66, ptnr., 1967; ptnr. Patton, Boggs & Blow, 1967-84, Wiley, Rein & Fielding, Washington, 1984—; adj. prof. internat. trade law Georgetown U. Law Ctr., Washington, 1978—, Charles Fahy Disting. adj. prof., 1993, Internat. Trade Law, Duke U. Law Sch., 1998—; conf. chmn. The Future of Internat. Steel Industry, Bellagio, Italy, 1984, U.S. Agenda for Uruguay Round, Airlie House, Warrenton, Va., 1986, Polish Joint Venture Law, Cracow, Poland, 1987, Internat. Steel Industry II, Bellagio, 1987, Bulgaria and the GATT, Washington, 1977; chair, spkr. Protection of Intellectual Property from Theft and Piracy Abroad Southwestern Legal Found. Fgn. Investment Symposium, 1995, chair, panel on NAFTA 2 1/2 Years Later, 1996. Local dir. Tufts U. Ann. Fund, 1965-69; mem. Duke Law Alumni Coun., 1972-75; trustee Internat. Law Inst., 1981—, chmn. bd. trustees, 1983-87; trustee Bulgarian Am. Friendship Soc., 1992—, Christ Ch., Dark Harbor, Maine; apptd. to roster of dispute settlement panelists World Trade Orgn., 1995, 97; chmn. adv. bd. Inst. for Attitudinal Studies, 1997—. Mem. ABA, Internat. Bar Assn., D.C. Bar Assn., Order of Coif, Theta Delta Chi, Phi Delta Phi, Met. Club (Washington), Chevy Chase Club (Md.), Tarratine Club (Dark Harbor, Maine). Private international. Home: 3000 Q St NW Washington DC 20007-3080 Office: 1776 K St NW Washington DC 20006-2304

**VERRONE, PATRIC MILLER,** lawyer, writer; b. Glendale, N.Y.C., Sept. 29, 1959; s. Pat and Edna (Miller) V.; m. Margaret Maiya Williams, 1989; children: Patric Carroll Williams, Marianne Emma Williams. BA, Harvard U., 1981; JD, Boston Coll., 1984. Bar: Fla. 1984, Calif. 1988, U.S. Dist. Ct. (mid. dist.) Fla. 1984, U.S. Dist. Ct. (ctrl. dist.) Calif. 1995, U.S. Ct. Appeals (9th cir.) 1995. Assoc. Allen, Knudsen, Swartz, DeBoest, Rhoads & Edwards, Ft. Myers, Fla., 1984-86; writer The Tonight Show, Burbank, Calif., 1987-90; adj. prof. Loyola Law Sch., L.A., 1998-99. Dir., producer, writer The Civil War--The Lost Episode, 1991; writer The Larry Sanders Show, 1992-94, The Critic, 1993-95; producer, writer The Simpsons, 1994-95, Muppets Tonight!, 1995-97 (Emmy award Best Children's Program 1998), Pinky and the Brain, 1998, Futurama, 1998—; editor Harvard Lampoon, 1978-84, Boston Coll. Law Rev., 1983-84, Fla. Bar Jour., 1987-88, L.A. Lawyer, 1994—; issue editor: Ann. Entertainment Law Issue, 1995-99; contbr. articles to profl. jours. including Elysian Fields Quar., Baseball and the American Legal Mind, White's Guide to Collecting Figures. Bd. dirs. Calif. Confedn. of Arts, 1994-98, Mus. Contemporary Art, 1994-95. Mem. ABA (vice chair arts, entertainment and sports law com. 1995-96), Calif. Bar, Calif. Lawyers for Arts, L.A. County Bar Assn. (sec. barristers exec. com., chair artists and the law com., steering com. homeless shelter project, intellectual property and entertainment law sect., state appelate jud. evaluation com., legis. activity com.), Fla. Bar Assn., Writers Guild Am. West (exec. com. animation writers caucus), Harvard Club Lee County (v.p. 1985-86), Harvard Club So. Calif. Republican. Roman Catholic. Avocation: baseball. Entertainment. Home and Office: PO Box 1428 Pacific Palisades CA 90272-1428

**VERSKA, KIMBERLY ANNE,** lawyer; b. Pitts., Nov. 21, 1968; d. Barry Saul and Monica Louise Yahr; m. Stephen Michael Verska, Sept. 1, 1996. BS in Langs. summa cum laude, Georgetown U., 1991; JD cum laude, Harvard U., 1995. Bar: Ga. 1995. Dir. Soviet-Am. Bur. on Human Rights, Moscow, 1991-92; atty. Sutherland, Asbill & Brennan, Atlanta, 1995-97, Alston & Bird, LLP, Atlanta, 1997—. Co-author: Structuring Strategic Business Alliances, 1998; exec. editor Harvard Jour. Law and Pub. Policy, 1994-95. Gen. counsel Ga. Fedn. Young Rep. Clubs, Atlanta, 1997—; counsel Atlanta Jaycees, 1998—. Mem. Ga. Bar Assn. (corp. and banking sect. 1995—, internat. sect. 1997—, bd. dirs. internat. sect. 1998—), Phi Beta Kappa. Avocations: languages, travel, political opinion and activism. Mergers and acquisitions, Private international, General corporate. Office: Alston & Bird LLP 1201 W Peachtree St NW Ste 4200 Atlanta GA 30309-3424

**VERTUN, ALAN STUART,** lawyer; b. N.Y.C., Feb. 11, 1951; s. Simon and Dorothy (Weber) V.; m. Marion Vertun, May 20, 1983; children: Laura, Jeffrey, Amy. AB, UCLA, 1973; JD, Southwestern U., 1976. Bar: Calif. 1976. Atty. Potscrubber, Inc., L.A., 1978-81, NIS Corp., L.A., 1981-84; pvt. practice L.A., 1984—. Vol. Am. Cancer Soc., L.A., 1985-95, LIFE, L.A., 1984-87. Mem. Los Angeles County Bar Assn. Personal injury, General corporate, General civil litigation. Office: 4250 Wilshire Blvd # 203 Los Angeles CA 90010-3508

**VESELY, TORI ANN,** lawyer; b. Portage, Wis., Aug. 24, 1965; d. Paul R. and Claudia K. Vesely. BA in Polit Sci., Carthage Coll., 1987; JD, Marquette U., 1990. Bar: Wis., 1990, U.S. Dist. Ct. (ea. and we. dists.) Wis. 1990. Asst. corp. counsel Sauk County, Baraboo, Wis., 1993—. Vol. Spl. Olympics, Merrill, Wis., 1991. Mem. State Bar Wis., Wis. Child Support Enforcement Assn., Sauk County Bar Assn. Family and matrimonial, Workers' compensation, General civil litigation. Office: Sauk Co Child Support Agy 515 Oak St Baraboo WI 53913-2416

**VESSEL, ROBERT LESLIE,** lawyer; b. Chgo., Mar. 21, 1942; s. Louis Frank and Margaret Ruth (Barber) V.; m. Diane White, Oct. 12, 1966; m. Lise Vessel, Dec. 19, 1992. BA, U. Ill., 1964; JD, Seton Hall U., 1973; LLM in Taxation, U. Miami, Coral Gables, Fla., 1980. Bar: N.J. 1973, Fla. 1981, U.S. Dist. Ct. (so. and mid. dists.) Fla. 1981, U.S. Ct. Appeals (11th cir.) 1981; bd. cert. civil trial, Fla. Assoc. Bennett & Bennett P.A., East Orange, N.J., 1973-76; ptnr. Kantor & Vessel, P.A., Wayne, N.J., 1976-81; assoc. Haddad Josephs & Jack, P.A., Coral Gables, Fla., 1981-85; ptnr. Mitchell Alley Rywant & Vessel, Tampa, 1985-89, Moffitt & Vessel, P.A., Tampa, 1989-94, Vessel & Morales, P.A., Tampa, 1994—. With USNR, 1964-66. Mem. Assn. Trial Lawyers Am., Nat. Inst. Trial Advocacy, Acad. Fla. Trial Lawyers, Hillsboro County Bar Assn. Avocation: sailing. Personal injury, Federal civil litigation. Office: Vessel & Morales PA 1411 N Westshore Blvd Ste 203 Tampa FL 33607-4529

**VESTNER, ELIOT N., JR.,** lawyer, bank executive; b. Bronxville, N.Y., Aug. 4, 1935; s. Eliot N. and Priscilla Alden (Fuller) V.; m. Elizabeth Gwin, Jan. 1, 1966 (div. 1992); children: Alice-Lee, Charles Fuller; m. Louise R. Cutler, Aug. 11, 1995. B.A., Amherst Coll., 1957; M.A., U. Mich., 1958; LL.B., Columbia U., 1962. Bar: N.Y. 1963. Assoc. Debevoise, Plimpton, Lyons & Gates, N.Y.C., 1962-68; spl. counsel N.Y. State Bank Dept., 1968-70; spl. asst. to Gov. Nelson A. Rockefeller, 1970-72; 1st dep. supt. N.Y. State, 1972-75, supt. banking, 1974-75; sr. v.p., gen. counsel Irving Trust Co., 1975-82, exec. v.p., 1982-87; exec. counsel Bank of Boston, 1987-96, exec. dir. pensions, 1996—; dir. Boston-AIG Co., 1994—; bd. dirs. Previnter, Mexico. Republican. Home: East India Row 4A/B Boston MA 02110 Office: Bank of Boston PO Box 2016 Boston MA 02106-2016

**VETA, D. JEAN,** lawyer; b. Cheyenne, Wyo., Oct. 19, 1954; d. John and Margaret Veta. Student, Williams Coll., 1973-74; BA summa cum laude, Tulane U., 1977, JD magna cum laude, 1981. Bar: D.C. Ct. Appeals, 1981, U.S. Dist. Ct., Washington, 1982, U.S. Ct. Appeals, Washington, 1982, U.S. Ct. Appeals (4th cir.), 1994. Law clk., Hon. Harold H. Greene U.S. Dist. Ct. D.C., 1981-82; assoc. Covington & Burling, Washington, 1982-89, ptnr., 1989-98; dep. gen. counsel U.S. Dept. Edn., Washington, 1998—. Mem. editl. bd., contbr. chpt.: The Woman Advocate, 1995; mem. bd. adv. editors Tulane Law Rev., New Orleans, 1992—. Bd. dirs. Beth El House, Inc., Alexandria, Va., 1992-99; bd. dirs. Tulane Alumni Assn., 1993-95. Thomas J. Watson Found. fellow, Eng., Sweden, Denmark, 1977. Mem. ABA (coun. mem. litigation sect. 1995-98, divsn. dir. 1994-95, chair various coms. 1986-94, sec. litigation sect. 1998—), Women's Bar Assn.

**VETTER, JOANNE REINIGER,** paralegal; b. Rochester, N.Y., Aug. 19, 1947; d. Carl Gotlieb and Stella (Dmytriw) Reiniger; m. Ernest J. Vetter, Oct. 7, 1967 (dec. Jan. 1993); 1 child, John; stepchildren: Stephen, Anne Robb. BS in Bus. Administrn., U. Akron, 1981; Paralegal Cert., Hammel Coll., Akron, Ohio, 1988. Paralegal Richard P. Martin LPA, Stow, Ohio, 1990-91; Pvt. Atty. Involvement coord. for Summit, Portage and Medina counties Western Res. Legal Svcs., Akron, 1991—; asst. state dir. Am. Inst. for Paralegal Studies, Walsh Coll., Canton, Ohio, 1993-94; mem. adv. bd. legal assisting program U. Akron, 1993—; mem. adv. bd. Hammel Coll., 1990-92. Mem. ABA, Ohio State Bar Assn., Akron Bar Assn. (Liberty Bell award 1992), Northeastern Ohio Paralegal Assn. (bd. dirs., past pres.), Dirs. of Vols. in Am., Women in the Wind Motorcycle Club, Omicron Delta Kappa. Roman Catholic. Avocations: woodworking, gardening, motorcycle.

**VETTORI, PAUL MARION,** lawyer; b. Washington, Sept. 6, 1944; s. Mariano L. and Bessie (Southerd) V.; m. Judith Ann Gersack, June 19, 1965; children: Joseph, Damon, Jason, Justin. AB, U. Md., Coll. Park, 1967; JD, U. Md., Balt., 1970. Bar: Md. 1970, U.S. Dist. Ct. Md. 1970, U.S. Ct. Appeals (4th cir.) 1970. Assoc. Frank, Bernstein, Conaway & Goldman, Balt., 1971-74; asst. atty. gen. Md. Atty. Gen.'s Office, Balt., 1974-75; ptnr. Shapiro, Vettori & Olander, Balt., 1975-81, Frank, Bernstein, Conaway & Goldman, Balt., 1981-91, Kenny, Vettori & Robinson, P.A., Balt., 1992-97, White, Miller, Kenny & Vettori, LLP, Towson, Md., 1997—. Mem. ABA, Md. State Bar Assn., Balt. County Bar Assn., Howard County Bar Assn., Rotary (pres.). Avocation: sports. General civil litigation. Office: White Miller Kenny & Vettori LLP 300 Lafayette Bldg 40 W Chesapeake Ave Towson MD 21204-4803

**VIA, PATRICIA PRESTIGIACOMO,** lawyer; b. Jackson Heights, N.Y., Oct. 15, 1960; d. Giochinno Anthony and Caroline Prestigiacomo; m. Dennis Keith, Apr. 30, 1994; 1 child, Stephen Anthony. BA in Polit. Sci., U. Md., 1982, JD, 1985. Bar: Md. 1985, U.S. Dist. Ct. Md. 1988, U.S. Ct. Appeals (4th cir.), 1990. Atty. Braude Margulies & Rephan, Balt., 1985-88; assoc. county atty. Montgomery County Attys. Office, Rockville, 1988—. Mem. Montgomery County Bar Assn. Democrat. Roman Catholic. Avocations: softball, golfing, cooking. Office: Montgomery County Attys Office 101 Monroe St Fl 3 Rockville MD 20850-2540

**VICE, LAVONNA LEE,** lawyer; b. Lexington, Ky., May 27, 1952; d. Keith Romould and Helen (Singer) V. BA summa cum laude, U. Balt., 1980, JD, 1983. Bar: Md. 1983, U.S. Ct. Appeals (4th cir.) 1987, U.S. Dist. Ct. Md. 1988, D.C. 1989, U.S. Supreme Ct. 1989. Trial atty. Ellin & Baker, Balt., 1983—; lectr., writer, rschr. med., surg. and hosp. standards of care. Mem. ABA, ATLA, Md. State Bar Assn., D.C. Bar Assn., Balt. City. Bar Assn. Professional liability, Personal injury, General civil litigation. Office: Ellin & Baker 1101 Saint Paul St Ste 201 Baltimore MD 21202-2691

**VICKERY, BYRON LAMAR,** lawyer; b. Columbus, Ohio, Apr. 26, 1937; s. Chester Byron and Ruth Kirstein (Ausst) V.; m. Joyce Geiser, July 22, 1960 (div. 1987); children: Gregory, Kirsten, Andrea, Colleen, Chad, Alexandra, Taylor; m. Deanna Kay Feller, Feb. 22, 1989. BA in Polit. Sci., Ohio State U., LLB. Bar: Ohio 1965, Mich. 1966, Ky. 1988. Personal injury. Office: 500 S Front St Columbus OH 43215-7619

**VICKERY, EDWARD DOWNTAIN,** lawyer; b. Fort Worth, Tex., May 1, 1922; s. Charles Richard and Margaret May V.; m. Dorothy Butler, Jan. 30, 1943; children: Anne Vickery Stevenson, E.D. Vickery, Jr. AS, North Tex. Agrl. Coll., 1941; BA, U. Tex., 1947, JD, 1948. Bar: Tex. 1948, U.S. Dist. Ct. (so. dist.) Tex. 1948, U.S. Ct. Appeals (5th cir.) 1950, Bd. Immagration Appeals 1952, U.S. Supreme Ct. 1953. From assoc. to sr. partner Royston, Rayzor, Vickery & Williams, Houston, 1948-55, sr. partner, 1955—; bd. dirs. First Nat. Bank Bellaire, Tex. Coastal Bank, Mayde Creek Bank; adv. dir. Tradition Bank, Houston. Deacon First Presbyn. Ch., Houston, 1958-64, elder 1965-94; mem. Brazos Presbyn. Ch., 1972-77, chmn. 1976-77; bd. trustees Austin (Tex.) Presbyn. Theol. Sem., 1976-85, 86-95, v. chmn. 1978-83, chmn. 1983-85, 89-95; bd. trustees Tex. Presbyn. Found. 1978-85. Fellow ATLA, Internat. Acad. Trial Lawyers (Am. chpt.); mem. Internat. Assn. Insurance Counsel, Am. Judicature Soc., Maritime Law Assn. U.S. (exec. com. 1977-80), Hist. Soc. Supreme Ct. U.S., Tex. Assn. Defense Counsel (bd. dirs. 1965-67), Tex. Bar Found. (Houston chpt.), Tulane Admiralty Law Inst. (program, planning com., adv. bd., 1965-92), Propellor Club U.S. (nat. pres. 1965-66, 66-67, nat. first v.p. 1964-65, nat. exec. com. 1961-85, port of Houston pres. 1961-62), U. Tex. Littlefield Soc., Chancellor's Coun., T Assn., Longhorn Found., Law Sch. Found., Mariners Club, Houston Club, Lakeside Country Club. Admiralty, Insurance, Personal injury. Home: 610 Wellesley Dr Houston TX 77024-5507 Office: Royston Rayzor Vickery & Williams LLP 600 Travis St Ste 2200 Houston TX 77002-2986

**VICKERY, EUGENE BENTON, JR.,** lawyer; b. New Orleans, Nov. 23, 1936; s. Eugene Benton and Esther (Cleveland) V.; m. Anne Saunders Porteous, Aug. 25, 1961; children—Eugene Benton III, Saunders P., Ninette C., William A. A.B., Williams Coll., 1962; J.D., Loyola U., New Orleans, 1967. Bar: La. 1967, U.S. Dist. Ct. (ea. and we. dist.) La. 1967, U.S. Ct. Appeals (5th cir.) 1967. Supr. computer systems, sr. tech. programmer Shell Oil Co., New Orleans Data Center, 1962-67; jr. ptnr. Porteous, Toledano, Hainkel & Johnson, New Orleans, 1968-73; ptnr. Sutterfield & Vickery, New Orleans, 1974-82; sole practice, New Orleans, 1982—; procurator-adv. Met. Tribunal for Archdiocese of New Orleans. Trustee, St. George's Epis. Sch., 1975-83, chmn., 1978-79; mem. La. Landmarks Soc., Met. Crime Commn., Uptown Neighborhood Improvement Assn. New Orleans and River Region C. of C. Served with U.S. Army, 1956-59. Mem. ABA, La. Bar Assn., New Orleans Bar Assn., La. Assn. Def. Counsel, New Orleans Assn. Def. Counsel, Def. Research Inst., Am. Judicature Soc., Am. Arbitration Assn. (panel of arbitrators 1968—), Notaries Assn. New Orleans, Delta Phi. Republican. Roman Catholic. Clubs: Boston, La., Williams (N.Y.C.). General corporate, Insurance, Probate. Home and Office: 5526 Chestnut St New Orleans LA 70115-3109

**VICKERY, RONALD STEPHEN,** lawyer; b. Houston, June 28, 1965; s. Patrick Nelson and Martha Sue (Gilpen) V.; m. Leigh Oliver Smith, Nov. 15, 1968; children: William, Samuel. BBA, Baylor U., 1987, JD, 1990. Bar: U.S. Dist. Ct. (ea. dist.) Tex. 1992; bd. cert. personal injury trial law. Assoc. Ramey & Flock, P.C., Tyler, Tex., 1992-96, shareholder, 1997—. Bd. dirs. Tyler Teen Ct., 1995—, Historic Tyler, 1997—. Mem. Smith County Young Lawyers Assn. (pres. 1995-96), Smith County Bar Assn. (treas. 1997-98). Republican. Baptist. Avocations: golf, hunting. General civil litigation, Personal injury, Insurance. Home: 1520 Holly Creek Dr Tyler TX 75703-0905 Office: Ramey & Flock PC PO Box 629 Tyler TX 75710-0629

**VICTOR, MICHAEL GARY,** lawyer, physician; b. Detroit, Sept. 20, 1945; s. Simon H. and Helen (Litsky) V.; m. Karen Sue Hutson, July 20, 1975; children: Elise Nicole, Sara Lisabeth. Bar: Ill. 1980, U.S. Dist. Ct. (no. dist.) Ill. 1980, U.S. Ct. Appeals (7th cir.) 1981; diplomate Am. Bd. Legal Medicine. Pres. Advocate Adv. Assocs., Chgo., 1982-95; asst. prof. medicine Northwestern U. Med. Sch., Chgo., 1982—; pvt. practice law Barrington, Ill., 1982—; dir. emergency medicine Loretto Hosp., Chgo., 1980-85, chief. sect. of emergency medicine St. Josephs Hosp., Chgo., 1985-87; v.p. Med. Emergency Svcs. Assocs., Buffalo Grove, Ill., 1989; v.p. MESA Mgmt. Corp.; of counsel Bollinger, Ruberry & Garvey, Chgo. Author: Informed Consent, 1980; Brain Death, 1980; (with others) Due Process for Physicians, 1984, A Physicians Guide to the Illinios Living Will Act, The Choice is Ours!, 1989. Recipient Service awards Am. Coll. Emergency Medicine, 1973-83. Fellow Am. Coll. Legal Medicine (bd. govs. 1996-97, alt. del. to AMA House of Dels. 1996-97), Chgo. Acad. Legal Medicine; mem. Am. Coll. Emergency Physicians (pres. Ill. chpt. 1980, med.-legal-ins. council 1980-81, 83-84), ABA, Ill. State Bar Assn., Am. Soc. Law and Medicine, Chgo. Bar Assn. (med.-legal council 1981-83), AMA, Ill. State Med. Soc. (med.-legal council 1980-86, 88), Chgo. Med. Soc. Jewish. State civil litigation, Health. Home and Office: 153 Aberdoor Ln Inverness IL 60067

**VICTOR, RICHARD STEVEN,** lawyer; b. Detroit, Mich., Aug. 3, 1949; s. Simon H. and Helen (Litsky) V.; m. Denise L. Berman, Nov. 26, 1978; children: Daniel, Ronald, Sandra. Bar: Mich. 1975, U.S. Dist. Ct. (ea. dist.) Mich. 1975. Assoc. Law Offices of Albert Best, Detroit, 1975; ptnr. Best & Victor, Oak Park, Mich., 1976-80; sole practice Oak Park, 1981-85; ptnr. Law Offices of Victor, Robbins and Bassett and predecessor firms, Birmingham, Mich., 1986-93; ptnr. Victor and Robbins and predecessor firms, Birmingham, 1993-98, Bloomfield Hills, Mich., 1998—; instr. in family law Oakland U., Rochester, Mich., 1976—; bd. dirs. Agy. for Jewish Edn., 1990; legal advisor family law Sta. Ask the Lawyer WXYT radio. Author: (column) Legally Speaking, Stepfamily Bull., 1984—; author, genera editor: Michigan Practitioners Series: Family Law and Practice, 1997; tech. advisor Whose Mother Am I? Aaron Spelling Prodns./ABC Movies. Mem. community adv. bd. Woodland Hills Med. Ctr., 1981—; v.p. Bloomfield (Mich.) Sq. Homeowners Assn., 1985—, pres. 1988; chmn. legis. com. Birmingham Schs. PTA, 1987—. Recipient Award of Meritorious Svc. to the Children of Am., Nat. Coun. of Juvenile and Family Ct. Judges, 1993, Child Advocate of Yr. award Chld Abuse and Neglect Coun., 1994, Disting. Svc. award Oakland County Bar Assn., 1994, Lifetime Achievement award State Bar Mich., 1999. Fellow Mich. State Bar Found., Am. Acad. Matrimonial Lawyers (bd. mgrs. Mich. chpt. 1999—, com. chair); mem. ABA (guest lectr. sem. 1988, exec. com. on custody 1989—), Mich. Bar Assn. (treas. family law sect. 1987-88, sec. 1988-89, chmn. continuing legal edn. com. family law sect., 1986-90, corr. sec. 1988-89, chmn. elect 1989-90, chmn. family law sect. 1990-91, Appreciation award from family law sect. 1987-89, Lifetime Achievement award family law sect. 1999, co-founder SMILE), Oakland County Bar Assn. (chmn. lawyer's admission com. 1981, unauthorized practice of law 1982, oldtimer's night 1984-85, speakers bur. 1985), Family Law Coun. (chmn. legis. com.), Grandparent Rights Orgn. (founder, exec. dir. 1984—, newsletter editor), B'nai B'rith Barristers. Jewish. Avocation: playing piano. Family and matrimonial, Personal injury. Office: Law Office of Victor and Robbins 100 W Long Lake Rd Ste 250 Bloomfield Hills MI 48304-2774

**VICTORINO, LOUIS D.,** lawyer; b. Lemoore, Calif., May 27, 1945; s. Louis and Mayme (Garcia) V.; m. Kathleen Gilman Berl, June 7, 1975. BA, Stanford U., 1967; JD, UCLA, 1970. Assoc./ptnr. Pettit & Martin, San Francisco, L.A., 1970-84; ptnr. Seyfarth, Shaw, Fairweather & Geraldson, L.A., 1984-88, Pillsbury & Madison, L.A., 1988-93, Fried, Frank, Harris,

Shriver & Jacobson, L.A., 1993—; adv. bd. Govt. Contractor, Washington, 1990—; legal advisor Commn. Govt. Procurement, 1971. Co-author: Proving & Pricing Construction Claims, 1990, Government Contractor Briefing Papers Collection, 1987-95. Mem. ABA (pub. contract law sect., reg. pres. 1975, editl. bd. Pub. Contract Law Jour. 1992-95), Fed. Bar Assn. (reg. v.p.), Ct. Fed. Claims Bar Assn., Bd. Contract Appeals Bar Assn. Government contracts and claims. Office: Fried Frank Harris Shrive & Jacobson 725 S Figueroa St Ste 1200 Los Angeles CA 90017-5443

**VICTORSON, MICHAEL BRUCE,** lawyer; b. Fairmont, W.Va., July 13, 1954; s. Morton Jerome and Deborah (Jacobson) V.; m. Janet Harris, Mar. 8, 1981; children: David Solomon, Sara Lorraine. BA, W.Va. U., 1976, JD, 1979. Bar: W.Va. 1979, U.S. Dist. Ct. (so. and no. dists.) W.Va. 1979, U.S. Dist. Ct. (ea. dist.) Ky. 1986, U.S. Ct. Appeals (4th cir.) 1980, U.S. Supreme Ct., 1992. Assoc. Love, Wise, Robinson and Woodroe, Charleston, W.Va., 1979-83; assoc. Robinson & McElwee LLP, Charleston, 1983-84, ptnr., 1985—; speaker at profl. seminars. Contbr. articles to profl. publs. Chmn. appeal bd. U.S. Selective Svc. System, So. Dist. W.Va., Charleston, 1983—; lawyers' chmn. United Way Kanawha Valley, Charleston, 1988-90, 91-92, chmn. profl. div., 1992-93, mem. admissions com., 1990-92; bd. dirs. Med. Eye Bank W.Va., Charleston, 1989—; trustee B'nai Jacob Synagogue, 1992-94, v.p. 1997—, Federated Jewish Charities of Charleston, Inc., 1998—; mem. visiting com. W. Va. U. Coll. of Law, 1996—. Mem. ABA, Internat. Assn. Jewish Lawyers and Jurists, Am. Law Firm Assn. (products liability steering com., bd. dirs. 1998—), W.Va. Bar Assn., W.Va. State Bar Assn., Kanawha County Bar Assn., Def. Rsch. Inst., Def. Trial Counsel W.Va. (charter, bd. govs. 1992-98), Nat. Assn. R.R. Trial Counsel, Order of Coif, Phi Beta Kappa, Phi Delta Phi, Phi Kappa Phi, Pi Sigma Alpha. General civil litigation, Environmental. Office: Robinson and McElwee LLP PO Box 1791 Charleston WV 25326-1791

**VICTORY, JEFFREY PAUL,** state supreme court justice; b. Shreveport, La., Jan. 29, 1946; s. Thomas Edward and Esther (Horton) V.; m. Nancy Clark Victory, Jan. 20, 1973; children: Paul Bradford, William Peter, Christopher Thomas, Mary Katherine. BA in History and Govt., Centenary Coll., 1967; JD, Tulane U., 1971. Bar: La. 1971. Ptnr. Tucker, Jeter, Jackson & Victory, Shreveport, 1971-82; dist. ct. judge 1st Jud. Dist. Ct., Shreveport, 1982-90; appellate judge 2d Circuit Ct. of Appeal, Shreveport, 1991-95; assoc. justice Supreme Ct. La., 1995—. Bd. dirs. CODAC Drug Abuse, Shreveport; mem. La. Sentencing Commn. La. NG, 1969-75. Mem. ABA, Shreveport Bar Assn., La. Bar Assn. Republican. Baptist. Avocations: tennis, motorcycles, classic cars. Office: Supreme Ct 301 Loyola Ave New Orleans LA 70112-1814*

**VIDERMAN, LINDA JEAN,** paralegal, corporate executive; b. Follansbee, W.Va., Dec. 4, 1957; d. Charles Richard and Louise Edith (LeBoeuf) Roberts; m. David Gerald Viderman Jr., Mar. 15, 1974; children: Jessica Renae, April Mae, Melinda Dawn. AS, W.Va. No. Community Coll., 1983; Cert. income tax prep., H&R Block, Steubenville, Ohio, 1986. Cert. surg. tech.; cert. fin. counselor; lic. ins. agt. Food prep. pers. Bonanza Steak House, Weirton, W.Va., 1981-83; ward clk., food svcs. Weirton Med. Ctr., 1982-84; sec., treas. Mountaineer Security Systems, Inc., Wheeling, W.Va., 1983-96; owner, operator The Button Booth, Colliers, W.Va., 1985—; paralegal, adminstr. Atty. Dominic J. Potts, Steubenville, Ohio, 1987-92; gen. ptnr., executrix Panhandle Homes, Wellsburg, W.Va., 1988-96; sec./treas., executrix Panhandle Homes, Inc., 1996—; ins. agt. Milico, Mass. Indemnity, 1991-92, L&L Ins. Svcs., 1992-94; paralegal Atty. Fred Risovich II, Weirton, 1991-93; sec. The Hon. Fred Risovich II, Wheeling, 1993; paralegal atty. Christopher J. Paull, Wellsburg, W.Va., 1993—; owner Wellsburg Office Supply, 1993-94; owner, dir. Viderman & Assocs., Wellsburg, 1998—; notary pub., 1991—. Contbr. articles numerous jours.; author numerous poems. Chmn. safety com. Colliers (W.Va.) Primary PTA, 1985-87; mem., sec. LaLeche League, Steubenville, Ohio, 1978-80; vol. counselor W.Va. U. Fin. Counseling Svc., 1990—; IRS vol. Vol. Income Tax Assistance Program, 1991—. Mem. W.Va. Writers Assn., Legal Assts. of W.Va., Inc., Am. Affiliate of Nat. Assn. Legal Assts., W.Va. Trial Lawyers Assn., Wellsburg Art Assn., Brooke County Genealogical Soc., Phi Theta Kappa. Jehovah's Witness. Avocations: Christian ministry, home computing, camping, genealogy, home schooling. Home: RR2 Box 28 Wellsburg WV 26070-9500 Office: Panhandle Homes Inc RR 2 Box 27A Wellsburg WV 26070-9500

**VIE, GEORGE WILLIAM, III,** lawyer; b. Tampa, Fla., Mar. 21, 1961; s. George William Jr. and Cheri Ann (Bass) V. BS magna cum laude, U. Houston, Clear Lake, Tex., 1985; JD, U. Tex., 1988. Bar: Tex. 1989, U.S. Dist. Ct. (so. dist.) Tex. 1990, U.S. Ct. Appeals (5th cir.) 1990, U.S. Mil. Ct. Appeals 1995, U.S. Supreme Ct. 1995; bd. cert. civil appellate law Tex. Bd. Legal Specialization. Legal asst. Bankston, Wright & Greenhill, Austin, Tex., 1985-89; atty. Bankston, Wright & Greenhill, Austin, 1989-90; ptnr. Mills, Shirley, Eckel & Bassett, Galveston, Tex., 1990—; spkr. in field. Contbr. articles to legal publs. Fellow Tex. Bar Found.; mem. FBA, State Bar Tex., Phi Kappa Phi, Sigma Phi Epsilon. Appellate, Constitutional, Civil rights. Office: Mills Shirley Eckel & Bassett 2228 Mechanic St Ste 400 Galveston TX 77550-1591

**VIENER, JOHN D.,** lawyer; b. Richmond, Va., Oct. 18, 1939; s. Reuben and Thelma (Kurtz) V.; m. Karin Erika Bauer, Apr. 7, 1969; children: John D. Jr., Katherine Bauer. BA, Yale U., 1961; JD, Harvard U., 1964. Bar: N.Y. State 1965, U.S. Supreme Ct. 1970, U.S. Dist. Ct. (so. dist.) N.Y. 1974, U.S. Tax Ct. 1975. Assoc. Satterlee, Warfield & Stephens, N.Y.C., 1964-69; sole practice N.Y.C., 1969-76; founder, bd. dirs., gen. counsel Foxfire Fund Inc., 1968-88; sr. ptnr. Christy & Viener, N.Y.C., 1976-98, Salans, Hertzfeld, Heilbronn, Christy & Viener, N.Y.C., 1999—; gen. counsel, bd. dirs. Landmark Communities, Inc., 1970—, Am. Continental Properties Group, 1978, NF&M Internat., Inc., 1976—, Singer Fund, Inc., 1979—, Immunotherapy, Inc., 1997—, Tupper Broadcasting Group Cos., 1996—, Viener Found., 1991—; gen. counsel Nat. Cancer Found. Cancer Care, 1982-85, Troster, Singer & Co., 1970-77; bd. dirs. Gen. Financiere Immob. et Commer. S.A., 1985-89; spl. counsel fin. instns., investment banking and securities concerns; real estate and tax advisor. Bd. dirs. York Theatre Co., 1999—. Mem. Meeker Brook Sporting Assn., Fairfield County Hounds, Manursing Island Club, Washington Club, Palm Beach Polo. Real property, Securities, Corporate taxation. Office: Salans Hertzfeld Heilbronn Christy & Viener 620 5th Ave New York NY 10020-2402

**VIERTEL, GEORGE JOSEPH,** lawyer, arbitrator, mediator, consulting engineer; b. N.Y.C., June 10, 1912; s. William and Marie Dorothy (Reichert) V.; 1 child, Elise V. DeShazo. BSCE, NYU, 1934; LLB, LaSalle U., Chgo., 1952; cert., Old Dominion U., 1963; student, Alliance Francaise, Paris, 1971; JD (hon.), Bernadean U., 1973; PhD (hon.), Am. U., 1977. Bar: Va. 1954, D.C., 1972, Md., 1981, U.S. Dist. Ct. (ea. dist. Va.) 1954, U.S. Ct. Appeals (4th cir.) 1954, U.S. Tax Ct. 1954, U.S. Supreme Ct. 1957, U.S. Claims Ct. 1961, U.S. Dist. Ct. Hawaii 1962, U.S. Ct. Appeals (9th cir.) 1963, U.S. Dist. Ct. (D.C. dist.) 1972, U.S. Ct. Appeals (7th cir.) 1972, U.S. Ct. Appeals (D.C. cir.) 1973, Ct. Appeals Md. 1981, U.S. Ct. Mil. Appeals 1973, U.S. Dist. Ct. Md. 1981; registered profl. engr. Md., Va., D.C., N.Y., Wis.; cert. expedited dispute settler; cert. arbitrator Superior Ct. D.C.; lic. real estate broker, Md. Freelance constrn. estimator, 1952-57; asst. engr. N.Y.C. Housing Authority, 1934, Bd. Transp. N.Y.C, 1933-34; supr. constrn. M. Shapiro & Son, N.Y.C.; engr. N.Y.C. Bd. Water Supply; asst. resident engr. Langley Field Sta., Va.; civil engr. Nat. Adv. Com. for Aeronautics (now known as NASA), Langley Field, 1940-48; assoc. Williams, Coile, Blanchard, Architects and Engrs., Newport News, Va., 1948-50; ptnr., chief engr. Assoc. Architects and Engrs., Newport News, 1950-61; asst. to dir. Office of Constrn. and Facility Mgmt. U.S. Dept. Energy, Washington, 1977-79; sole practice law Va., 1954—, Washington, 1972—, Md., 1981—; arbitrator, mediator Montgomery County Cir. Ct., Balt. City Cir. Ct., among others. Contbr. articles to profl. jours. Lt. U.S. Army Corps Engrs., 1934-39. Fellow ASCE (life, pres. local chpt. 1965-67); mem. Bar Assn. Montgomery County, Soc. Profls. in Dispute Resolution. Alternative dispute resolution, General practice, General civil litigation. Home: 4407 Pinetree Rd Rockville MD 20853-1320 Office: 9525 Georgia Ave Ste 105 Silver Spring MD 20910-1439

**VIETOR, HAROLD DUANE,** federal judge; b. Parkersburg, Iowa, Dec. 29, 1931; s. Harold Howard and Alma Johanna (Kreimeyer) V.; m. Dalia Artemisa Zamarripa Cadena, Mar. 24, 1973; children: Christine Elizabeth, John Richard, Greta Maria. BA, U. Iowa, 1955, JD, 1958. Bar: Iowa 1958. Law clk. U.S. Ct. Appeals 8th Circuit, 1958-59; ptnr. Bleakley Law Offices, Cedar Rapids, Iowa, 1959-65; judge Iowa Dist. Ct., Cedar Rapids, 1965-79, chief judge, 1970-79; U.S. dist. judge U.S. Dist. Ct. for So. Dist. Iowa, Des Moines, 1979-96, chief judge, 1985-92, sr. U.S. dist. judge, 1997—; lectr. at law schs., legal seminars U.S. and Japan. Contbr. articles to profl. jours. in U.S. and Japan. Served with USN, 1952-54. Mem. ABA, Iowa Bar Assn. (pres. jr. sect. 1966-67), Iowa Judges Assn. (pres. 1975-76), 8th Cir. Dist. Judges Assn. (pres. 1986-88). Office: US Dist Ct 221 US Courthouse 123 E Walnut St Des Moines IA 50309-2035

**VIG, VERNON EDWARD,** lawyer; b. St. Cloud, Minn., June 19, 1937; s. Edward Enoch and Salley Johanna (Johnson) V.; m. Susan Jane Rosenow, June 10, 1961; 1 child, Elizabeth Karen. BA, Carleton Coll., 1959; LLB, NYU, 1962, LLM, 1963; postdoctoral Université de Paris, Faculté de Droit, 1964. Bar: N.Y. 1962; Avocat, Paris 1992. Assoc. Cleary, Gottlieb, Steen & Hamilton, Paris, 1964-65; assoc. Donovan, Leisure, Newton & Irvine, N.Y.C. and Paris, 1965-72, ptnr., 1972-86; ptnr. LeBoeuf, Lamb, Greene & MacRae, N.Y.C., 1986—. Sr. warden Grace Ch., Bklyn., 1986—. George F. Baker scholar, Fullbright scholar, 1963-64, Ford Found. scholar, 1963-64. Mem. ABA (internat. trade com.), N.Y. State Bar Assn. (chmn. antitrust 1987-88), Assn. of Bar of City of N.Y., Internat. Bar Assn., Union Internationale des Avocats. Episcopalian. Clubs: Heights Casino (Bklyn.); Merriewold (Forestburgh, N.Y., bd. dirs. 1985-91). Private international, General corporate, Antitrust. Office: LeBoeuf Lamb Greene & MacRae 125 W 55th St New York NY 10019-5369

**VIGIL, CAROL JEAN,** lawyer, judge, child support hearing officer; b. Santa Fe, Oct. 24, 1947; d. Martin Jr. and Evelyn (Abeita) V.; m. Philip D. Palmer, Dec. 16, 1977; 1 child, Sparo Arika Vigil-Palmer. BS, U. N.Mex., 1974, JD, 1978. Bar: N.Mex. 1979. Atty. Indian Pueblo Legal Svcs., Santa Ana Pueblo, N.Mex., 1978-80; appellate div. atty. gen. State of N.Mex., Santa Fe, 1980-84; sole practice Santa Fe, 1984-87, spl. commr. domestic violence and mental competency, 1994-98; judge Divsn. III First Jud. Dist. Ct., Santa Fe, 1998—; tribal atty. Tesuque Pueblo, N.Mex., 1985-88; tribal prosecutor Eight No. Indian Pueblo Council Child Abuse Prosecution Project, San Juan Pueblo, N.Mex., 1986-88; apptd. by Gov. Caruthers Commn. on Rape Prevention & Prosecution, 1988—; mem. com. to study racial bias N.Mex. Supreme Ct., 1998—; mem. com. abuse/neglect mediation. Sec. No. N.Mex. Legal Services, Santa Fe, 1981-82, chmn., 1982-83, vice chmn. 1984-85; bd. dirs. Santa Fe Mountain Ctr., 1985-86; bd. dirs., sec., treas., Pueblo Ins. Agy., 1985-86. Reginald Heber Smith fellow, 1978-80; recipient Outstanding Women award Gov. N.Mex., 1993, one of 10 people who made a difference award The New Mexican, 1995. Mem. ABA, N.Mex. Bar Assn. (pro bono com. 1986-88, chair Indian law sect. 1987-88, N.Mex. task force on minority involvement in state bar 1988—, Supreme Ct. rules of evidence com. 1993—), Pueblo North Mktg. Ctr. (bd. dirs. 1988, chair 1989), Indian Bar Assn., Oliver Seth Inn of Ct., Delta Theta Phi (barrier free futures, bd. dirs., chair 1997—). Democrat. Roman Catholic. Avocation: art: print and original drawings. Civil rights, Family and matrimonial. Home: PO Box 481 Tesuque NM 87574-0481 Office: 1st Jud Dist Ct Divsn III PO Box 2268 Santa Fe NM 87504-2268

**VIGIL, DANIEL AGUSTIN,** academic administrator; b. Denver, Feb. 13, 1947; s. Agustin and Rachel (Naranjo) V.; m. Claudia Cartier. BA in History, U. Colo., Denver, 1978, JD, 1982. Bar: Colo. 1982, U.S. Dist. Ct. Colo. 1983. Project mgr. Mathematics Policy Rsch., Denver, 1978; law clk. Denver Dist. Ct., 1982-83; ptnr. Vigil and Bley, Denver, 1983-85; asst. dean sch. law U. Colo., Boulder, 1983-89; assoc. dean sch. law U. Colo., 1989—; apptd. by chief justice of Colo. Supreme Ct. to serve on Colo. Supreme Ct. Ad Hoc Com. on miniority participation in legal profession, 1988-94; adj. prof. U. Colo. Sch. Law; mem. Gov. Colo. Lottery Commn., 1990-97. Editor (newsletter) Class Action, 1987-88; co-editor (ethics com. column) Colo. Lawyer, 1995-97. Bd. dirs. Legal Aid Soc. Met. Denver, 1986—, chmn. bd. dirs., 1998—; past v.p. Colo. Minority Scholarhip Consortium, pres. 1990-91; mem. Task Force on Community Race Rels., Boulder, 1989-94; past mem. jud. nomination rev. com. U.S. Senator Tim Wirth. Mem. Colo. Bar Assn. (mem. legal edn. and admissions com. 1989-94, chmn. 1989-91, bd. govs. 1991, 97—), Hispanic Nat. Bar Assn. (chmn. scholarship com. 1990-95), Colo Hispanic Bar Assn. (bd. dirs. 1985-89, pres. 1990), Denver Bar Assn. (joint com. on minorities in the legal profession), Boulder County Bar Assn. (ex-officio mem., trustee), Phi Delta Phi (faculty sponsor). Roman Catholic. Avocations: skiing, cosmology. Home: 828 3d Ave PO Box 518 Lyons CO 80540-0518 Office: U Colo Sch Law PO Box 401 Boulder CO 80303

**VIGNERI, JOSEPH WILLIAM,** lawyer; b. Decatur, Ill., July 28, 1956; s. Joseph Paul and Thelma Lucille (Pettus) V.; m. Martha Suzanne Smith, May 19, 1984; children: Craig Ashley, Emily Carmela. BA in Polit. Sci., Millikin U., 1980; JD cum laude, St. Louis U., 1983. Bar: Ill. 1983, U.S. Dist. Ct. (ctrl. dist.) Ill. 1983, U.S. Supreme Ct. 1990. Assoc. Rosenberg, Rosenberg, Bickes, Johnson & Richardson, Decatur, 1983-86; ptnr. Brilley & Vigneri, Decatur, 1986-88; pvt. practice, Decatur, 1988-92; ptnr. Vigneri & Robinson, Decatur, Ill., 1993-95; pvt. practice Decatur, 1995—; past mem. job. svc. employer com. Ill. Dept. Employment Security. Past mem. profl. adv. com. Vis. Nurses Assn.; past bd. dirs., treas. Macon County Mental Health Assn. Mem. ABA (sect. real property, probate and trust law, com. spl. needs and tech. com., vice chmn. gen. practice com. 1991-92, family law subcom., editor newsletter), Ill. Bar Assn. (sec. individual rights sect. 1986, mem. bus. advice and fin. planning sect. coun. 1995-97), Decatur Bar Assn. (continuing legal edn. com. 1994-95, tech. com. 1996-97). Republican. Roman Catholic. Avocations: reading, travel, computers. Criminal, Bankruptcy, Family and matrimonial. Home: 65 Ridge Lane Dr Decatur IL 62521-5456 Office: PO Box 857 136 W Washington St Decatur IL 62525-0857 also: 212 W Vine St Taylorville IL 62568-1957

**VILCHEZ, VICTORIA ANNE,** lawyer; b. Tampa, Fla., Aug. 10, 1955; d. Angel and Mary Ida (Guarisco) V.; children: Matthew Stephen Williams, Michael Paul Williams, Heather Margaret Williams. B.A., Fla. State U., 1977; J.D., Mercer U., 1980. Bar: Fla. 1980. Trial atty. Office Pub. Defender, Miami, Fla., 1980-83; pvt. practice, Miami, 1983-84, Lake Worth, Fla., 1984-85; ptnr. Williams & Williams, Lake Worth, 1985-91; pvt. practice, West Palm Beach, Fla., 1991—; traffic magistrate Palm Beach County Ct.; rep. Nat. Conf. on Women and Law, Atlanta, 1978. Vol. Cath. Home for Children, Miami, 1983-84; mem. Council of Cath. Women, Miami, 1983-84; class 1994 Leadership Palm Beach County. Recipient cert. of achievement 8th Nat. Conf. Juvenile Justice, 1981; Mercer U. grantee, 1977. Mem. Fla. Bar, Fla. Assn. Women Lawyers (sec., newsletter editor Palm Beach County chpt. 1985-86), Palm Beach County Bar Assn., Acad. Fla. Trial Lawyers, Fla. State U. Alumni Assn., Palm Beach County Hispanic Bar Assn. (pres.-elect 1990-91, pres. 1991-92, bd. dirs. 1990—, treas. 1993-94, 94-97), Legal Aid Soc. Palm Beach (bd. dirs. 1992—), Rotary (Royal Palm Beach club), Royal Palm Beach Jaycees, Kiwanis, Delta Theta Phi. Democrat. Roman Catholic. Family and matrimonial, Criminal, Juvenile. Office: 1803 S Australian Ave Ste A West Palm Beach FL 33409-6454

**VILETTO, HAROLD ERNST,** lawyer; b. Peekskill, N.Y., Sept. 21, 1956; s. Harold Nicholas and Gisela (Koenig) V.; m. Valentina Viletto, May 16, 1987; children: Joseph, Victoria. BS, Georgetown U., 1978; JD, Cath. U., 1984. Bar: Md., D.C., Pa. Assoc. Law Office of Alan Muldauer, Rockville, Md., 1985-87, Law Office of Charles Rand, Rockville, Md., 1987-89, Sweeney, Sheehan & Spencer, Phila., 1989-97; sr. staff atty. Hartford Staff Law Office, Phila., 1997, mng. atty., 1997—. Soccer coach Cheltenham (Pa.) Jayvees, 1994—; Little League coach Cheltenham Athletic Assn., 1994—. Roman Catholic. Insurance, General civil litigation. Home: 920 Melrose Ave Melrose Park PA 19027-2926 Office: 1515 Market St Philadelphia PA 19102-1921

**VILLA, JAMES GERARD,** lawyer; b. Amsterdam, N.Y., Mar. 7, 1944; s. Joseph and Catherine (Collistra) V.; children: Catherine Flynn, James Daniel; m. Debra Monaghan Nazar, Sept. 2, 1995. AB, Fordham Coll., Bronx, N.Y., 1966; JD, Albany Law Sch., 1970. Bar: Vt. 1970, N.Y. 1999, D.C. 1999, U.S. Supreme Ct. 1991, U.S. Dist. Ct. (so. and ea. dists.) N.Y. 1994. Law clk. to chief Judge Bernard J. Leddy, U.S. Dist. Ct., Burlington, Vt., 1970-72; assoc. Dinse, Erdman, Knapp & McAndrew, Burlington, Vt., 1972-75, Langrock, Sperry & Parker, Middlebury, Vt., 1975-78; acting judge, pvt. practice, Burlington, Vt., 1976-82; gen. counsel, v.p. licensing Hazelett Strip-Casting Corp., Colchester, Vt., 1982-90; mem. Villa & Monaghan Nazar, Brooklyn Heights, N.Y., 1991—; counsel, mem. adv. bd. Orgn. Chinese Am., N.Y.C., 1994—; bd. govs. Med. Ctr. Hosp., Vt. Health Fund., Burlington, Vt., 1982-89. Co-Inventor, Matrix Coatings Improved Continuous Casting Process on Apparatus, 1988, 93. Bd. mem. Brownstone Bklyn. Rep. Club, N.Y., 1998—, Multiple Sclerosis Soc. of Vt., Burlington, 1984-89. Recipient Outstanding Cmty. Svc. award Orgn. of Chinese Am. N.Y.C., 1996. Mem. N.Y. County Lawyers, Bklyn. Bar Assn., Am. Corp. Coun. Assn., Vt. Bar Assn. Roman Catholic. Avocation: sailing. Intellectual property, Private international, General corporate. Office: Villa & Monaghan Nazar 82 Schermerhorn St Apt 4B Brooklyn NY 11201-5026

**VILLA, JOHN KAZAR,** lawyer; b. Ypsilanti, Mich., June 9, 1948; s. John Joseph and Susie (Hoogasian) V.; m. Ellen A. Edwards, June 3, 1990. AB, Duke U., 1970; JD, U. Mich., 1973. Bar: D.C. 1973. Trial atty. U.S. Dept. Justice, Washington, 1973-77; assoc. Williams & Connolly, Washington, 1977-81; ptnr. Williams & Connolly, 1981—. Author: legal treatises. Federal civil litigation, Professional liability. Office: Williams & Connolly 725 12th St NW Washington DC 20005-5901

**VILLALOBOS, RAUL,** lawyer; b. El Paso, Tex., Feb. 23, 1931; s. Pablo and Pilar O. Villalobos; m. Glenda Charlene Villalobos. BBA, U. Tex., El Paso, 1972; JD, U. Houston, 1973. Bar: Tex., U.S. Supreme Ct., U.S. Dist. (so. and we. dist.) Tex., U.S. Tax Ct. With U.S. Army, 1951-53. General practice, Personal injury. Home: PO Box 640543 El Paso TX 79904-0543

**VILLARREAL, FERNANDO MARIN,** lawyer; b. Mathis, Tex., Oct. 2, 1956; s. Pablo and Dora Villarreal; m. Yvonne Dominguez, Sept. 30, 1995. AA, McLennan C.C., Waco, Tex., 1977; BBA, Baylor U., 1979; JD, U. Houston, 1983. Bar: Tex. Pvt. practice, Waco, Tex.; justice of peace, McLennan County, Waco, 1992—. V.p. McLennan County Dem. Com., Waco; past pres. League United L.Am. Citizens, Waco. Mem. McLennon County Bar Assn. (bd. dirs.). Democrat. Roman Catholic. Avocations: reading, walking, gardening. General practice, Family and matrimonial. Office: 1001 S 18th St # B Waco TX 76706-1948

**VILLASANA, GEORGE ANTHONY,** lawyer; b. Queens, N.Y., Oct. 14, 1967. BS in Acctg., Pa. State U., 1989; M of Acctg., Fla. Internat. U., Miami, 1990; JD, Am. U., 1995; LLM in Tax, Georgetown U., 1998. Bar: Fla. 1995. Staff atty. SEC, Washington, 1995-97; assoc. Shutts & Bowen LLP, Miami, Fla., 1997-99, Holland & Knight LLP, Miami, 1999—. Mem. ABA, Fla. Bar, Dade County Bar Assn. Mergers and acquisitions, Securities, General corporate. Office: Holland and Knight LLP 701 Brickell Ave Ste 3000 Miami FL 33131-2898

**VILLAUME, FRANK EUGENE, III,** lawyer; b. St. Paul, Nov. 29, 1945; s. Frank Eugene and Marie DeRoma Villaume; m. Mary Jo Conway, Oct. 18, 1975; 1 child, Frank E. IV. BA, U. St. Thomas, 1967; JD, William Mitchell Coll. Law, 1972. Bar: Minn. 1972, U.S. Dist. Ct. Minn. 1976, U.S. Ct. Appeals (8th cir.) 1978. Asst. city atty. City of St. Paul, 1973-80, dep. city atty., 1980-82, asst. city atty., supr. litigation, 1985—; assoc. Kueppers, Kueppers, von Feldt & Salmen, St. Paul, 1982-85; mem. local rules adv. com. U.S. Dist. Ct. Minn. Vol. meal server Cath. Charities: Lowry Shelter, St. Paul, 1996—; vol. laborer Habitat for Humanity, St. Paul, 1997—. Named Leading Lawyer in Minn., Am. Rsch. Corp., 1994. Mem. Minn. Def. Lawyers Assn. (chmn. local govtl. liability sect.), Ramsey County Bar Assn. (2nd dist. ethics com.). Office: City of St Paul 15 Kellogg Blvd W Rm 550 Saint Paul MN 55102-1621

**VILLAVASO, STEPHEN DONALD,** lawyer, urban planner; b. New Orleans, July 12, 1949; s. Donald Philip and Jacklyn (Tully) V.; m. Regina Smith, Apr. 17, 1971; children: Christine Regina, Stephen Warner. BS in Econs., U. New Orleans, 1971, M in Urban and Regional Planning, 1976; JD, Loyola U., New Orleans, 1981. Bar: La. 1982; recognized ct. expert in land use, planning and zoning. Urban and regional planner Barnard & Thomas, New Orleans, 1976-78; dir. analysis and planning Office of Mayor, City of New Orleans, 1978-81; counsel for planning and devel. Office of City Atty., City of New Orleans, 1983-84; dir. planning and environ. affairs Tecon Realty, New Orleans, 1981-83; v.p. for planning and project mgmt. Morphy, Makofsky, Mumphrey & Masson, New Orleans, 1984-89; bus. devel. mgr. Waste Mgmt., Inc., New Orleans, 1989-96; pres. Villavaso & Assocs., LLC, New Orleans, 1996—; bd. dirs. Regional Loan Corp.; guest lectr., adj. prof. Coll. of Urban and Pub. Affairs, U. New Orleans, 1976—; spl. instr. grad. studies in urban planning So. U. New Orleans, 1987—. Bd. dirs. New Orleans Traffic and Transp. Bur., 1981-86, Riverfront Awareness, New Orleans, 1984-86; bd. dirs. Vols. Am. Greater New Orleans, 1987-96, vice chmn., 1990, chmn. bd., 1992-95. With USN, 1971-74. Named one of Outstanding Young Men of Am., 1980, 82. Mem. ABA, Am. Inst. of Cert. Planners, Am. Planning Assn. (pres. La. div. 1980-84, disting. svc. award 1985), Urban Land Inst., La. Bar Assn., U. New Orleans Alumni Assn. (bd. dirs. 1990—), Phi Kappa Phi, Delta Sigma Pi (pres. 1971), Omicron Delta Kappa. Democrat. Roman Catholic. Avocations: philately, camping, travel. Land use and zoning (including planning), Environmental. Home: 6304 Beauregard Ave New Orleans LA 70124-4502

**VILLAVICENCIO, DENNIS (RICHARD),** lawyer; b. North Hollywood, Calif., June 20, 1967; s. Richard Adolph and Sandra Marie V. BA, San Diego State U., 1990; JD, U. San Diego, 1993. Bar: Supreme Ct. Calif. 1993, U. S. Dist. Ct. (so. dist.) Calif. 1993. Intern San Diego City Atty's. Office, 1990; law clerk Law Office John Allen, Carlsbad, Calif., 1991-93; intern U. San Diego Environ. Law Office, 1993; assoc. Law Office John Allen, Carlsbad, Calif., 1993-98; ptnr. Allen & Villavicencio, L.L.P., Carlsbad, Calif., 1998—. Mem. Kappa Sigma (alumnus advisor 1995—). Securities, Alternative dispute resolution, General civil litigation. Office: Allen & Villavicencio LLP 1925 Palomar Oaks Way Carlsbad CA 92008-6526

**VIMONT, RICHARD ELGIN,** lawyer; b. Lexington, Ky., Aug. 3, 1936; s. Richard Thompson and Christine Frazee (Anderson) V.; m. Louise Marie Salyer, Sept. 10, 1960; children: Richard Thompson II, Margaret Anderson; m. 2d, Martha Jane Murray, Nov. 13, 1982 (div.); m. Mary Ann Farley, May 31, 1997. BS, U. Ky., 1958, JD, 1960. Bar: Ky. 1960, U.S. Dist. Ct. (ea. dist.) Ky. 1960, U.S. Dist. Ct. (we. dist.) Ky. 1964, U.S. Ct. Appeals (6th cir.) 1964, U.S. Supreme Ct. 1966. Assoc. Brown, Sledd and McCann, 1960-64; ptnr. Core, Vimont and Combs, 1964-68, Breckinridge, Vimont and Amato, 1968-70, Anggelis, Vimont and Bunch, 1970-78, Vimont and Wills PLLC, Lexington, Ky., 1978—; mng. mem., 1998—; city commr., Lexington, 1971-72; chmn. Lexington Mounted Police Bd., chair 1997—, asst. commonwealth atty., 1973-75; vis. prof. Transylvania U., 1978-80, Midway Coll., 1992; bd. dirs. Ky. World Trade Ctr., 1990-97, Equitania Ins. Co.; mng. dir. Equitania Ins. Co., 1990-93, pres., CEO, 1993—; gen. counsel Pavenstedt Pauli (U.S.A.), Inc., 1990-92; adj. prof. U. Kent. Coll. of Law, 1998. Bd. dirs. Lexington Ballet Co., 1989-90. Fellow U. Ky., U. Kent; mem. ABA, Am. Acad. Trial Attys., Ky. Bar Assn., Ky. Acad. Trial Attys., Fayette County Bar Assn., Lexington C. of C., Thoroughbred Club of Am., Lexington Polo Club, Lexington, Lafayette Club, Spindletop Hall Club (bd. dirs. 1978-81, 86-90), Rotary (sec. Lexington endowment 1994-97, Paul Harris fellow). Democrat. Mem. Disciple of Christ Ch. Insurance, Construction, Equine. Office: 155 E Main St Fl 3 Lexington KY 40507-1300

**VINAL, GREGORY MICHAEL,** lawyer; b. N.Y.C., Mar. 26, 1963; s. Eugene Robert and Mary Elizabeth V.; m. Jeanne Marie Vezina, Oct. 17, 1992; children: Elizabeth Mary, Gregory Michael Jr. BS in Bus. Adminstrn. cum laude, SUNY, Buffalo, 1985, MBA in Fin., 1989, JD, 1989; LLM in Taxation, NYU, 1993. Bar: N.Y. 1990, Conn. 1989, U.S. Dist. Ct. (we. dist.) N.Y. 1995, U.S. Tax Ct. 1990, U.S. Bankruptcy Ct. 1996. Tax cons. Deloitte & Touche, Stamford, Conn., 1989-92, Buffalo, 1992-94; ptnr. Vinal & Vinal, Buffalo, 1994—. State civil litigation, Personal injury, General practice. Home: 335 Lebrun Rd Buffalo NY 14226-4168 Office: Vinal & Vinal 335 Le Brun Rd Buffalo NY 14226-4168

**VINAL, JEANNE MARIE,** lawyer; b. Buffalo, Apr. 8, 1964; d. Frederic Joseph and Rita Teresa Vezina; m. Gregory M. Vinal, Oct. 17, 1992; children: Elizabeth, Gregory. AB, Colgate U., 1986; JD, SUNY, Buffalo, 1989. Bar: Conn. 1989, N.Y. 1990, U.S. Dist. Ct. (we. dist.) N.Y. 1990, U.S.

Bankruptcy Ct. 1990, U.S. Dist. Ct. (no. dist.) N.Y. 1999. Assoc. Phillips, Lytle et al, Buffalo, 1989-90, Grosse, Rossetti et al, Buffalo, 1990-93; ptnr. Vinal & Vinal, Buffalo, 1994—. Dir. Literacy Vols. Buffalo, 1990-92. George Cobb fellow Colgate U., 1984. Mem. Women's Bar Assn. State N.Y. (dir. 1990-93, dir., treas. We. N.Y. chpt. 1990-93), N.Y. State Bar Assn., Interclub Coun. We. N.Y. (past pres.), Erie County Bar Assn. Democrat. Roman Catholic. State civil litigation, Personal injury, General practice. Home: 335 Lebrun Rd Buffalo NY 14226-4168 Office: Vinal & Vinal 35 Le Brun Rd Amherst NY 14226-4168

**VINAR, BENJAMIN,** lawyer; b. Rock Island, Ill., Apr. 10, 1935; s. Isidore and Bessie (Shaman) V.; m. Rochelle Weinfeld, June 17, 1962; children: Jacqueline, Dov, Elana, Daniella. BA, U. Ill., 1957; LLB, NYU, 1960. Bar: N.Y. 1961, U.S. Dist. Ct. (so. dist.) N.Y. 1962, U.S. Ct. Appeals (2nd cir.) 1964, U.S. Supreme Ct. 1966, U.S. Dist. Ct. (ea. dist.) N.Y. 1971. Assoc. Donovan, Leisure, Newton & Irvine, N.Y.C., 1961-71; pvt. practice N.Y.C., 1971-76, Garden City, N.Y. and N.Y.C., 1986—; ptnr. Siff & Newman, P.C., N.Y.C., 1976-86. Contbr. articles to profl. jours. Mem. nat. law com. Anti-Defamation League, N.Y.C., 1975—; pres. Queens Jewish Community Coun., N.Y.C., 1979-81, Young Israel of Queens Valley, N.Y.C., 1984-86; v.p. Nat. Coun. Young Israel, 1986-90, YM-YMHA of Northern Queens, N.Y.C., 1989-91; bd. dirs. Met. Coun. on Jewish Poverty, N.Y.C., 1984-89. Mem. Assn. of Bar of City of N.Y., Nassau Bar Assn., NYU Law Rev. Alumni Assn. (pres. 1981-83), B'nai Brith (v.p. lawyers unit 1985—), Order of Coif, Phi Beta Kappa, Phi Kappa Phi. Democrat. Appellate, Insurance, State civil litigation.

**VINCENTI, MICHAEL BAXTER,** lawyer; b. Balt., Dec. 28, 1950; s. Rudolph and Betty (Jones) V.; m. Patricia Lynn Bishopp, Apr. 14, 1984; children: Sarah, Elizabeth. BA, Johns Hopkins U., 1972; JD, NYU Sch. Law, 1975. Bar: Ill. 1975, Ky. 1979. Assoc. Sonnenschein, Nath & Rosenthal, Chgo., 1975-79; from assoc. to ptnr. Wyatt, Tarrant & Combs, Louisville, 1979—; guest instr. Jefferson Cmty. Coll., Louisville, 1988-98. Sec., gen. counsel Louisville Sci. Ctr., 1993—; dir., counsel bd. trustees Chance Sch., Louisville, 1995-98. Mem. ABA, ALTA (lender's counsel group), Internat. Coun. Shopping Ctrs., Ill. Bar Assn., Am. Land Title Assn., Am. Coll. Real Estate Lawyers, Ky. Bar Assn., Louisville Bar Assn., Ill. Bar Assn., Rotary, Louisville Boat Club, Lex Mundi. Episcopalian. Avocations: racquetball, tennis, traveling, reading. Fax: 502-589-0309; E-mail: mvincenti@wyattfirm.com. Real property, Contracts commercial, Landlord-tenant. Office: Wyatt Tarrant & Combs 500 W Jefferson St Ste 2700 Louisville KY 40202-2898

**VINCENTI, SHELDON ARNOLD,** law educator, lawyer; b. Ogden, Utah, Sept. 4, 1938; s. Arnold Joseph and Mae (Burch) V.; children: Matthew Lewis, Amanda Jo. AB, Harvard U., 1960, JD, 1963. Bar: Utah 1963. Sole practice law, Ogden, 1966-67; ptnr. Lowe and Vincenti, Ogden, 1968-70; legis. asst. to U.S. Rep. Gunn McKay, Washington, 1971-72, adminstrv. asst., 1973; prof., assoc. dean U. of Idaho Coll. of Law, Moscow, Idaho, 1973-83, dean, prof. law, 1983-95, prof. law, 1995—. Home: 2480 W Twin Rd Moscow ID 83843-9114 Office: U Idaho Coll Law 6th & Rayburn St Moscow ID 83843

**VINES, WILLIAM DORSEY,** lawyer; b. Kingsport, Tenn., May 28, 1942; s. William D. and Ozella Mae (Eastridge) V.; m. Norma Rene Cobb, Nov. 24, 1964 (div. Jan. 1980); children: David, Gregory, Derek; m. Dawn Marie Cioppa, Mar. 31, 1984; 1 child, Rachel. JD, U. Tenn., 1965. Bar: Tenn. 1966, U.S. Dist. Ct. (ea. dist.) Tenn. 1966, U.S. Ct. Appeals (6th cir.) 1967, U.S. Supreme Ct. 1972; cert. civil trial specialist commn. on Continuing Legal Edn. and Specialization of Tenn./Nat. Bd. Trial Advocates; cert. Rule 31 Mediator/Tenn. Supreme Ct. Atty. Knoxville, 1966-72; ptnr. Butler, Vines & Babb, Knoxville, 1972—. Fellow Tenn. Bar Found.; mem. Knoxville Bar Assn. (past. pres.), Am. Inns of Ct. (master of bench emeritus). Avocations: flying, skiing, trout fishing. E-mail: Wvines@bvblaw.com. General civil litigation, Alternative dispute resolution, Personal injury. Office: Butler Vines & Babb PO Box 2649 Knoxville TN 37901-2649

**VINICOMBE, CHARLES JAMES,** lawyer; b. Bklyn., July 12, 1962; s. James Charles and Virginia Rose V.; m. Michele Lee Buchman, Dec. 4, 1993. BA, Seton Hall U., 1984; JD, Wake Forest U., 1987. Bar: N.J., N.C.; U.S. Dist. Ct. N.J., U.S. Dist. Ct. (mid. dist. N.C.), U.S. Ct. Appeals (3rd and 4th cirs.). Assoc. Carruthers & Roth, Greensboro, N.C., 1987-89; assoc. Drinker, Biddle & Reath, Princeton, N.J., 1989-96, ptnr., 1996—; adj. faculty Seton Hall Law Sch., Newark, 1996-97. Articles editor Wake Forest Lw Rev., 1986-87; contbr. articles to profl. jours. Law Faculty scholar Wake Forest Law Sch., Winston-Salem, N.C., 1986-87. Mem. N.J. Bar Assn., ABA, Def. Rsch. Inst., Jaycees (v.p., sec., pub. rels. dir. North Plainfield, N.J. 1980-84). Avocations: reading, hiking, fishing. Home: 73 Crickhollow Ct Belle Mead NJ 08502-1429 Office: Drinker Biddle & Reath LLP 105 College Rd E Princeton NJ 08540-6622

**VINING, ROBERT LUKE, JR.,** federal judge; b. Chatsworth, Ga., Mar. 30, 1931; m. Martha Sue Cates; 1 child, Laura Orr. BA, JD, U. Ga., 1959. With Mitchell & Mitchell, 1958-60; ptnr. McCamy, Miner & Vining, Dalton, 1960-69; solicitor gen. Conasauga Judicial Cir., 1963-68; judge Whitfield County Superior Ct., Dalton, 1969-79; judge U.S. Dist. Ct. (no. dist.) Ga., 1979-95, chief judge, 1995—; now sr. judge. Served to staff sgt. USAF, 1951-59. Office: US Dist Ct PO Box 6226 Rome GA 30162-6226

**VINKEMULDER, H. YVONNE,** retired lawyer; b. Grand Rapids, Mich., Aug. 21, 1930; d. Arthur and Frances (DeWitt) V. Student, Calvin Coll., 1948-50, Blodgett Hosp. Sch. Nursing, 1950-52; BA, Trinity Coll., 1956; JD, U. Miami, Coral Gables, Fla., 1983. Bar: Wis. 1983. Staff nurse Little Traverse Hosp., Petoskey, Mich., 1952-53, Swedish Covenant Hosp., Chgo., 1953-55; campus nurse Trinity Coll., Chgo., 1955-57; head nurse Colo. Coll., Colorado Springs, 1957-61; sec. Inter-Varsity Christian Fellowship, Chgo., 1961-65; asst. to dir. devel. Inter-Varsity Christian Fellowship, Chgo. and Madison, Wis., 1965-74; dir. devel. Inter-Varsity Christian Fellowship, Madison, 1974-80, dir. planned giving, 1979-81, 90-96, gen. counsel, 1983-96; ret., 1996; cons. in devel. various orgns., 1976-80; lectr. internat. law Fgn. Language Inst., Tianjin, China, 1989. Columnist The Branch, 1976-79; contbg. author: A Guide to Wisconsin Non Profit Corporations, 1990; contbr. articles to mags. Bd. dirs. Internat. Fellowship of Evang. Students, Inc., Boston, 1975-85, Schloss Mittersill Christian Conf. Inc., Madison, 1985-93, 94—; clk. Faith Bapt. Ch., Madison, 1985-95; mem. stds. com. Evang. Coun. Fin. Accountability, 1989-96; mem. steering com. Evang. Legal Forum, 1988-90, gen. bd. Buckeye Evang. Free Ch. Mem. Wis. State Bar Assn., Christian Legal Soc. Mem. Evang. Free Ch. Home: 801 Acewood Blvd Madison WI 53714-3209

**VINROOT, RICHARD ALLEN,** lawyer, mayor; b. Charlotte, N.C., Apr. 14, 1941; s. Gustav Edgar and Vera Frances (Pickett) V.; m. Judith Lee Allen, Dec. 29, 1964; children: Richard A., Laura Tabor, Kathryn Pickett. BS in Bus. Adminstrn., U. N.C., 1963, JD, 1966. Bar: N.C. 1966, U.S. Dist. Ct. (ea., mid. and we. dists.) N.C. 1969, U.S. Ct. Appeals (4th cir.) 1969. Ptnr. Robinson, Bradshaw & Hinson, P.A., Charlotte, 1969—; mayor City of Charlotte, 1991-95; bd. dirs. Martin-Marietta Materials Inc. Tchr. sr. h.s. sunday sch. Myers Park Presbyn. Ch., 1970—, ruling elder, 1970-76, 78-84, 96—, chmn. of session, 1984; mem. Charlotte City Coun., 1983-91. With U.S. Army, 1967-68, Vietnam. Recipient Bronze Star, 1968; named Mcpl. Leader of the Yr. Am. City & County Mag., 1995. Mem. ABA, VFW, N.C. Bar Assn., Mecklenburg County Bar Assn. (sec. 1976, bd. dir. 1970-76), Mecklenburg County Vietnam Vets. Assn., Mecklenburg County Eagle Scouts Assn., Am. Legion, Phalanx Lodge Mason.. Republican. Presbyterian. General practice, General civil litigation, Construction. Office: Robinson Bradshaw & Hinson PA 1900 Independence Ctr 101 N Tryon St Ste 1900 Charlotte NC 28246-0103

**VINSON, C. ROGER,** federal judge; b. Cadiz, Ky., Feb. 19, 1940. BS, U.S. Naval Acad., 1962; JD, Vanderbilt U., 1971. Bar: Fla. 1971. Commd. ensign USN, 1962, advanced through grades to lt., 1963, naval aviator, until 1968, resigned, 1968; assoc. to ptnr. Beggs & Lane, Pensacola, Fla., 1971-83; judge U.S. Dist. Ct. (no. dist.) Fla., Pensacola, 1983-97, chief judge, 1997—; mem. Jud. Conf. Adv. Com. on Civil Rules, 1993—; mem. 11th Cir. Pattern Instrn. Com. Office: US Courthouse 5th fl 1 N Palafox St Pensacola FL 32501-5625

**VINSON, WILLIAM THEODORE,** lawyer, diversified corporation executive. BS, USAF Acad., 1965; JD, UCLA, 1969. Bar: Calif. 1970. Judge advocate USAF, 1970-74; trial counsel Phillips Petroleum, San Mateo, Calif., 1974-75; atty. Lockheed Corp., Westlake Village, Calif., 1975-90; v.p. & sec. Lockheed Corp., Westlake Village, 1990-92, v.p., gen. couns., 92-95; v.p., chief counsel Lockheed Martin Corp., Westlake Village, 1995-98; cons. Lockheed Corp., Westlake Village, 1998. General corporate, Government contracts and claims, Private international. Office: Lockheed Martin Corp 310 N Westlake Blvd Ste 200 Westlake Vlg CA 91362-3791

**VIOLANTE, JOSEPH ANTHONY,** lawyer; b. Jersey City, June 15, 1950; s. Carmine Joseph and Rosa (Cardillo) V.; m. Linda Lee Munn, July 5, 1972; children: Joseph Anthony II, Christy Anne, Gina Lee. Student, St. Peter's Coll., Jersey City, 1972-74; BA, U. N.Mex., 1975; JD, U. La Verne (Calif.), 1980. Bar: Calif. 1981, U.S. Dist. Ct. (cen. dist.) Calif. 1982, (6th dist.) Ohio 1992, U.S. Ct. Appeals (fed. cir.) 1990, U.S. Ct. Appeals (D.C. cir.) 1991, U.S. Ct. Vets. Appeals 1990. Sole practice Thousand Oaks, Calif., 1981-85; atty., cons. Bd. Vet. Appeals, Washington, 1985-90; staff counsel DAV, Washington, 1990-92, legis. counsel, 1992-96, dep. nat. legis. dir., 1996-97, nat. legis. dir., 1997—; mem. adv. bd. Bowie Cable T.V., 1989-91, bd. dirs., 1992-94. Co-host cable TV show Vets. Forum, 1991-94. Asst. coach Am. Youth Soccer Orgn., Thousand Oaks, 1981-84, Little League, Thousand Oaks, 1981-84; del. John Glenn Calif. Dem. Presdl. Primary, Thousand Oaks, 1984; active campaign Combined Fed., Washington, 1985; mem. presdl. del. Prisoners of War/Missing in Action, Southeast Asia, 1996. With USMC, 1969-72. Mem. ABA (vice chmn. vets. benefit com. 1991-98), DAV (life, comdr. 1990-91), VFW (life, comdr. 1984-85), KC, Calif. Bar Assn., Fed. Cir. Bar Assn. (chmn. vets appeal com. 1992-96, co-chmn. legis. com. 1996—), FBA (at-large bd. mem., vets. com. 1991-92), D.C. Bar Assn., Italian-Am. Bar Assn., Nat. Italian-Am. Found., Coun. of 1,000, Nat. Italian Am. Found. (nat. mentors program), Am. Legion, Italian Am. War Vets., Marine Corps League, 3d Marine Divsn. Assn. (life), 2d Bn. 4th Marine Assn. Democrat. Roman Catholic. Avocations: collecting coins, soccer, softball, reading. Legislative, Administrative and regulatory, Government contracts and claims. Home: 2515 Ann Arbor Ln Bowie MD 20716-1562 Office: DAV Nat Svc & Legis Hdqrs 807 Maine Ave SW Washington DC 20024-2410

**VIRELLI, LOUIS JAMES, JR.,** lawyer; b. Phila., Nov. 4, 1948; s. Louis James and Elsie Antoinette (Colombo) V.; m. Barbara Ann Rotella, Aug. 22, 1970; children: Louis J. III, Christopher F. BE in Mech. Engring., Villanova U., 1970; JD, U. Tenn., 1972. Bar: Pa. 1973, U.S. Patent and Trademark Office, 1973, U.S. Ct. Customs and Patent Appeals 1974, U.S. Dist. Ct. (we. dist.) Pa. 1976, U.S. Dist. Ct. (ea. dist.) Pa. 1977, U.S. Ct. Appeals (9th cir.) 1980, U.S. Ct. Appeals (D.C. cir.) 1982, U.S. Supreme Ct. 1982. Patent atty. Sperry New Holland Co., New Holland, Pa., 1973-74; assoc. counsel Westinghouse Co., Pitts., 1974-76; assoc. Paul & Paul, Phila., 1976-80, ptnr., 1980-84; patent counsel Nat. Starch and Chem. Corp., Bridgewater, N.J., 1984-88; asst. gen. counsel, intellectual property Nat. Starch & Chem. Co., Bridgewater, N.J., 1988-92, gen. counsel, intellectual property, 1992-95; asst. gen. counsel Patents Unilever U.S., Inc., Edgewater, N.J., 1988-95; v.p. gen. patent counsel Unilever N.V., P.L.C., Edgewater, N.J., 1995-96, sr. v.p., gen. patent counsel, 1997—; arbitrator U.S. Dist. Ct. (ea. dist.) Pa., Phila., 1982-84. Mem. ABA, N.J. Patent Law Assn., Phila. Patent Law Assn., Assn. Corp. Patent Counsels. Patent, Trademark and copyright, General corporate. Office: Unilever US Inc 45 River Rd Edgewater NJ 07020-1017 also: Unilever PLC, Unilever House Blackfriars, London England

**VIRK, RACHEL LEWIS,** lawyer; b. Lowell, Mass., Nov. 22, 1961; d. Gary Lee and Diane Lewis; m. Vijay Vir Singh Virk, Sept. 22, 1996. Bar: Va. 1989. Atty. Robert A. Ades & Assocs. P.C., Springfield, Va., 1990—. Family and matrimonial. Office: Robert A Ades & Assocs PC 5419 Backlick Rd Ste B Springfield VA 22151-3937

**VISCOUNTY, PERRY JOSEPH,** lawyer; b. Orange, Calif., Sept. 29, 1962; s. Thomas Alexander and Terry Lea (Davey) V.; m. Mary Katherine Powell, July 24, 1993; children: John H., Matthew W. BS, U. Southern Calif., 1984, JD, 1987. Bar: Calif. 1987, U.S. Dist. Ct. (no., ea., ctrl. and so. dist.) Calif. 1987, U.S. Ct. Appeals (9th cir.) 1987, U.S. Supreme Ct. 1996. Ptrn. Sheppard, Mullin, Richter & Hampton, Costa Mesa, Calif., 1987-98; ptnr. Latham & Watkins, Costa Mesa, Calif., 1998—. Author: Trade Secrets Practice in California, 1996; contbr. articles to profl. jours and newspaper. Mem. Internat. Trademark Assn. (meetings com.), Calif. State Bar (founder, edn. com. 1993), OCPLA (chmn. trade secret com.), OC Bar Found. (Willey W. Manuel Pro Bono award, 1993, Svcs. award, 1994), Young Exec. Am. (nat. bd. dir. 1997, bd. dir. 1996-97), Orange County Patent Law Assn. Avocations: golf, tennis, volleyball and reading. Office: Latham & Watkins & Hampton 650 Town Center Dr Ste 2000 Costa Mesa CA 92626-7135

**VISION, BLANCHE STEIN,** retired judge; b. Chgo., Apr. 4, 1922; d. Abe and Ida (Mash) Stein; m. Philip H. Vision, Sept. 30, 1967 (dec. Mar. 1997). BA, U. Chgo., 1943; JD, Columbia U., 1948. Bar: Oreg. 1949, D.C. 1950, U.S. Ct. Appeals (7th cir.) 1967. House counsel Goldblatt Bros. Dept. Stores, Chgo., 1950-51; dir. sta. rels. Keystone Broadcasting System, Chgo., 1952-60; sr. atty. FTC, Chgo., 1961-80; adminstrv. law judge Office Hearings and Appeals. Social Security Adminstrn., Chgo., 1980-83; arbitrator Better Bus. Bur. Greater Chgo., 1970-80; judge Judicate Nat. Pvt. Ct. Sys., 1987-92. Bd. dirs. Property Owners and Residents Assn., Sun City West, Ariz., 1985, Sun Cities Art Mus., 1985, Sun Cities Transit System, Inc., 1985-89, Sun Cities Symphony Guild, 1987-88, Sun Cities Symphony Assn., 1987-89, Sun Health Found. Aux., 1988. Recipient FTC Meritorious Svc. award. Mem. ABA, AAUW (v.p. Sun City West chpt. 1984), D.C. Bar Assn., Am. Arbitration Assn. (panel of arbitrators), Phi Beta Kappa. Home: 13225 W Castlebar Dr Sun City West AZ 85375-2502

**VITAL, PATRICIA BEST,** lawyer; b. Pitts., Mar. 26; d. Clarence D. and Billie Lorraine (Wilson) B.; m. Leo Vital, Mar. 30. BA magna cum laude, U. Tenn., Chattanooga, 1989; JD with honors, U. Tenn., 1992. Bar: Ga. 1994, Tenn. 1993, U.S. Dist. Ct. (ea. dist.) Tenn. 1993, U.S. Dist. Ct. (no. dist.) Ga. 1995, U.S. Ct. Appeals (6th cir.) 1993, U.S. Ct. Appeals (11th cir.) 1995, U.S. Supreme Ct. 1996. Legal asst. Gleason & Assoc. Law Firm, Rossville, Ga., 1981-82; med. staff coord. Hutcheson Med. Ctr., Ft. Oglethorpe, Ga., 1982-86; rsch. asst. U. Tenn. Law Coll., Knoxville, 1991-92; from law clk. to assoc. atty. Lusk, Carter & McGhehey, Chattanooga, 1990-93; pvt. practice Chattanooga, 1993—; mediator Vital Dispute Resolution Svcs., Chattanooga, 1996—; law clk. Hamilton County Attys. Office, Chattanooga, summer 1990; devel. coun. co-chair class 1992 U. Tenn. Coll. Law, alumni network mentoring program, 1995—, deans cir., 1992—; pres. adult scholars program U. Tenn., Chattanooga, 1988-89, adult scholars program adv. coun., scholarship com., 1994—; presenter in field; adj. prof. pre-trial litigation, legal asst. studies program U. Tenn., fall, 1997; instr. Law Sch. Admission Test preparation course KAPLAN, Inc., 1999—; commn. continuing legal edn. and specialization Tenn. Supreme Ct., 1996—; panel mediator (Ea. and Mid. dists.) Tenn. Fed. Mediation Programs, U.S. Dept. Justice, Am. with Disabilities, Chattanooga Better Bus. Bur., Hamilton County Tenn. Divorce Mediation, Am. Health Lawyers ADR Svc. Co-author: Tennessee Alternative Dispute Resolution Handbook, 1997; contbr. articles to profl. jours. Mentor Hamilton County Bd. Edn., 1995-96; cmty. resource person Ooltewah Middle and Chattanooga Phoenix Middle Schs., 1994-96; capt. attys. team presch. phon-a-thon Siskin Found., 1994-95; mem. Chattanooga Chamber Found. Leadership Chattanooga Class, 1997-98; nat. adv. bd. Ctr. for Enterprise Edn., Peabody Coll. Edn., Vanderbilt U., 1998—. Mem. ABA (ethics 2000 adv. coun. 1998, dispute resolution sect. Boston Conf. Planning Com. 1998—, co-chair dispute resolution sect. State and Local Bar Com. 1998—), AAUW, Fed. Bar Assn., Nat. Inst. Dispute Resolution, Nat. Assn. Mediators in Edn., Am. Health Lawyers Assn., Nat. Assn. Women Bus. Owners (local chpt. bd. dirs. 1994), Am. Soc. Law, Medicine and Ethics, Tenn. Bar Assn. (com. chair, sec. ho. of dels. 1995—, com. chair law related edn. 1996-97, bd. dirs. law office tech. and mgmt. 1994-96, sec-treas., chair-elect, chair dispute resolution 1995-98, Merit award 1995, mem. editl. bd. TBALink), Mediation Assn. Tenn. (chair continuing mediation edn., curriculum com. 1996—), Tenn. Trial Lawyers Assn., Tenn. Assn. Med. Staff Svcs., Tenn. Assn. Ptnrs. in Edn., Ga. State Bar Assn., Chattanooga Bar Assn. (bd. govs. 1996-97, chair bd. govs. task force on the future Tenn. judicial sys. 1995—, centennial planning com. 1996-97, chair continuing legal edn. com. 1994-95, chair ethics rules rev. com. 1998—, chair dispute resolution com. 1998—, First Beyond the Call of Duty award 1995), Chattanooga Trial Lawyers Assn. (dir., gov. bd. 1995—), Southeast Tenn. Lawyers Assn. Women (dir. at-large 1996-97), Better Bus. Bur., S.E. Tenn. Coun. on Children & Youth, Chattanooga Area C. of C., Phi Delta Phi. Avocations: whitewater rafting, mountain hiking, aerobics, reading. Fax: (423) 267-2376. E-mail: Best-LAW@webtv.net and vitalmediate@webtv.net. Health, General practice, General civil litigation. Office: Vital Law Offc & Dispute Resolution Svcs 604 James Bldg 735 Broad St Chattanooga TN 37402-1804

**VITALE, JAMES DREW,** lawyer; b. Livingston, N.J., Mar. 14, 1967; s. Joseph Anthony and Elizabeth Kathryn Vitale. BA, Rutgers U., Newark, 1990; JD, Rutgers U., Camden, N.J., 1994. Bar: N.J. 1994, U.S. Dist. Ct. N.J. 1994, N.Y. 1995. Atty. Am. Internat. Group, N.Y.C., 1994-97; assoc. Rosenman & Colin, LLP, N.Y.C., 1997-98; regulatory compliance counsel Zurich U.S. Ins. Group, Schaumburg, Ill., 1998—; mem. home warranty task force Calif. Bur. Electronic and Appliance Repair, Sacramento, 1998—. Mem. New York County Lawyers Assn. (com. on ins. 1998—, com. on constrn. law 1998—), Assn. Bar City N.Y., U.S. Soo Bahk Do, Moo Dukh Kwan Fedn. Democrat. Roman Catholic. Avocations: golf, martial arts. Insurance, General corporate, Administrative and regulatory. Home: 11 Oakview Ave Maplewood NJ 07040-2213 Office: Zurich US Ins Group 1400 American Ln Schaumburg IL 60196-5452

**VITITOE, JAMES WILSON,** lawyer; b. Oklahoma City, Mar. 14, 1947; s. Theodore Curtis Vititoe and Eula Mae (Cope) Seboth; m. Karen Dutcher, May 29, 1984; children: Justin Ryan, Travis James. BA in Psychology, Coll. William & Mary, 1971; JD, Southwestern U., 1976. Bar: Iowa 1977, Calif. 1977. Atty. Law Office of Edward Masry, L.A., 1977-84; ptnr. Masry & Vititoe, Studio City, Calif., 1985—. Named Outstanding Lawyer Yr. Congressman Mervin Dymally, 1992, 93. Mem. ATLA, Consumers Atty. Assn. L.A. (bd. govs. 1998), Consumer Attys. Assn. Calif. (Consumer Advocate of Yr. award 1997), Calif. Applicants Assn., Toastmasters (L.A.), Jonathan Club. Avocations: jogging, travel, theater, movies. Personal injury, Professional liability, Toxic tort. Office: Masry & Vititoe 5707 Corsa Ave Fl 2 Westlake Village CA 91362-6499

**VITKOWSKY, VINCENT JOSEPH,** lawyer; b. Newark, Oct. 3, 1955; s. Boniface and Rosemary (Ofack) V.; m. Mary Gunzburg, May 16, 1981 (div. 1997); children: Vincent Jr., Victoria. BA, Northwestern U., 1977; JD, Cornell U., 1980. Bar: N.Y. 1981. Assoc. Hart and Hume, N.Y.C., 1980-84, Kroll & Tract, N.Y.C., 1984-87; of counsel Nixon, Hargrave, Devans & Doyle, N.Y.C., 1988-89; ptnr. Buchalter, Nemer, Fields & Younger, N.Y.C., 1990-95, Edwards & Angell, N.Y.C., 1996—; lectr. in field. Contbr. articles to profl. jours. Mem. ABA (com. chmn.), Am. Arbitration Assn. (inernat. panel arbitrators), Internat. Bar Assn. (com. officer), Internat. Law Assn., Assn. Bar City of N.Y., Cornell Club, Human Rights Watch, IBA Human Rights Inst., Lawyers Com. for Human Rights. General civil litigation, Private international. Home: 1 Irving Pl New York NY 10003 Office: Edwards & Angell 750 Lexington Ave Fl 12 New York NY 10022-1253

**VLACHOS-KEASTEAD, KONSTANTINA,** lawyer; b. Jersey City, N.J., Oct. 29, 1960; d. George K. and Panagioula (Golematis) Vlachos; m. Scott Brion Keastead, Nov. 28, 1993. BA in Psychology and Criminial Justice, Moravian Coll., 1982; JD, Nova U., 1985. Bar: N.J. 1985. Pvt. practice atty. Kearny, N.J., 1985—. Active mem. St. George Greek Orthodox Ch., Clifton, N.J., First Presbyn. Ch. of Arlington, Kearny. Mem. ABA, N.J. State Bar Assn. Office: 824 Kearny Ave Kearny NJ 07032-3236

**VLADECK, JUDITH POMARLEN,** lawyer; b. Norfolk, Va., Aug. 1, 1923. BA, Hunter Coll., 1945; JD, Columbia U., 1947. Bar: N.Y. 1947, U.S. Supreme Ct. 1962. Assoc. Conrad & Smith, N.Y.C., 1947-51; sole practice N.Y.C., 1951-57; mem. Vladeck, Elias, Vladeck & Engelhard P.C., N.Y.C., 1957—; sr. ptnr. Vladeck, Waldman, Elias & Englehard, P.C., N.Y.C.; bd. dirs. Group Health Ins., Inc., Am. Arbitration Assn.; adj. prof. Fordham Law Sch.; mem. Civil Justice Reform Act Adv. Group of So. Dist. of N.Y.; adv. coun. CPR Jud. Project. Mem. adv. bd. Inst. for Edn. and Rsch. on Women and Work, Cornell U.; bd. dirs. N.Y. Civil Liberties Union, 1963-68; bd. dirs., counsel Tamiment Inst., Inc.; bd. dirs. lawyers' coordinating com. AFL-CIO; bd. mem. Non-Traditional Employment for Women. Recipient Edith Spivack award, 1998, ORT Jurisprudence award, 1996; elected to Hunter Coll. Hall of Fame, 1988. Fellow Am. Bar Found., Coll. of Labor and Employment Lawyers; mem. ABA (co-chmn. labor law and equal employment coms.), N.Y. State Bar Assn. (labor law com.), Assn. of Bar of City of N.Y., N.Y. County Lawyers Assn., Fed. Bar Assn., Women's Bar Assn., Am. Arbitration Assn. (panel of arbitrators), Columbia Law Sch. Alumni Assn. (bd. dirs.), Harlem Inst. Fashion (counsel, bd. dirs.). Labor, General civil litigation. Home: 115 Central Park W New York NY 10023-4153 Office: Vladeck Waldman Elias & Engelhard 1501 Broadway Ste 800 New York NY 10036-5560

**VLAHAKIS, PATRICIA,** lawyer; b. Stamford, Conn., May 22, 1956. BA summa cum laude, Bryn Mawr Coll., 1978; JD, Columbia U., 1981. Bar: N.Y. 1982. Ptnr. Wachtell, Lipton, Rosen & Katz, N.Y.C., 1981—; lectr. on mergers and acquisitions, securities law. Contbr. articles to profl. jours. Bd. dirs. Phoenix House Found., Inc. Named one of 50 Top Women Lawyers Nat. Law Jour., 1998. Mem. ABA. E-mail: PAVlahakis@wlrk.com. Securities, Mergers and acquisitions. Office: Wachtell Lipton Rosen & Katz 51 W 52nd St Fl 29 New York NY 10019-6150*

**VOCHT, MICHELLE ELISE,** lawyer; b. Detroit, Sept. 27, 1956. BA with honors, U. Mich., 1978; JD, Wayne State U., 1981. Bar: Mich., U.S. Dist. Ct. (ea. and we. dist.) Mich., U.S. Ct. Appeals (6th cir.), 1981. V.p., treas. Roy, Shecter & Vocht PC, Detroit, Bloomfield Hills, Mich., 1981—; pro bono teaching faculty Detroit chpt. Fed. Bar Assn.; mediator Mediation Tribunal Wayne County Cir. Ct., 1989—; pre-sentencing probation officer 48th Dist. Ct., 1989-90. Mem. com. for re-election Mich. Supreme Ct. Justice, 1986; mem. Rep. Assembly, Oak County, 1992—; exec. bd. Birmingham Women's Community Ctr., 1987-88; bd. dirs. Community Adv. Bd.-Arbor Clin. Group, Inc., 1989-91; mem. drug and alcohol abuse spl. task force County of Oakland, 1989—. Mem. Assn. Trial Lawyers Am., Am. Inns of Ct. (barrister 1984-87), Mich. Trial Lawyers Assn., Women Lawyers Assn., Oakland Trial Lawyers Assn. (exec. bd. dirs. 1982-84, 88—, sec. 1990—, v.p. 1991-92, pres. 1992-95), Oakland County Bar Assn., State Bar Assn. Mich. (chmn. gen. practice sect. 1984-86, sec. 1982-83, vice chmn. 1983-84, mem. civil procedure com. 1982-84, assoc. mem. lawyers and judges assistance com. 1988-89, hearing and panelist atty. discipline bd. 1982—, labor and employment sect., health care sect., computer law sect., chair drafting com. 1995-97, com. on state trial ct. adminstrn. 1995-98, com. on profession 1997), Mich. Employment Law Assn., Interna. Platform Assn., Indsl. Rels. Rsch. Assn. Roman Catholic. Avocations: hiking, history, humanities, and sciences. Labor, Federal civil litigation, State civil litigation. Home: 901 N Adams Rd Birmingham MI 48009-5646 Office: Roy Shecter & Vocht PC 36700 Woodward Ave Ste 205 Bloomfield Hills MI 48304-0930

**VOELKER, LOUIS WILLIAM, III,** lawyer; b. Gary, Ind., Apr. 17, 1969; s. Louis W. and Carol Jean V.; m. Elizabeth Applegarth, Mar. 13, 1993; children: Elijah, Madeline. BA, Purdue U., 1991; JD, Ind. U., 1995. Bar: Ind. 1995, U.S. Dist. Ct. (no. and so. dists.) Ind. 1995. Assoc. Eichhorn & Eichhorn, Hammond, Ind., 1995—. Adminstrv. bd. dirs. Door Village United Meth. Ch., LaPorte, Ind., 1996—. Mwm. Ind. Bar Assn., Lake County Bar Assn., Order of Barristers. Republican. Avocations: music, songwriting. State civil litigation, Professional liability. Office: Eichhorn & Eichhorn 200 Russell St # 6 Hammond IN 46320-1818

**VOGEL, BERNARD HENRY,** lawyer; b. N.Y.C., May 23, 1941; s. Harold and Bertha (Steinberg) V.; m. Alyce Vogel, June 13, 1965; children: Jennifer Lyn, Jonathan Harlan. BA, Queens Coll., 1963; LLB, Bklyn. Law Sch., 1966, JD, 1967. Bar: N.Y. 1967, U.S. Dist. Ct. (so. and ea. dists.) N.Y. 1974. Assoc. Seavey Gallet & Fingerit, N.Y.C., 1968-72; ptnr. Seavey Fingerit & Vogel, N.Y.C., 1972-80; mng. ptnr. Seavey Fingerit Vogel & Oziel, N.Y.C., 1980—; lectr. coop. orgns., N.Y.C., 1980—; lectr., author articles Fedn. N.Y. Housing Coops., N.Y.C., 1984—; arbitrator Am. Arbitration Assn., N.Y.C., 1980—; adv. bd., bd. dirs. various corps., N.Y.C., 1968—. Mem. Queens County Bar. Real property, General civil litigation, General corporate. Home: 27 Hummingbird Dr Roslyn NY 11576-2534

Office: Seavey Fingerit Vogel & Oziel 60 E 86th St New York NY 10028-1009

**VOGEL, CEDRIC WAKELEE,** lawyer; b. Cin., June 4, 1946; s. Cedric and Patricia (Woodruff) V. BA, Yale U., 1968; JD, Harvard U., 1971. Bar: Ohio 1972, Fla. 1973, U.S. Tax Ct. 1972, U.S. Supreme Ct. 1975. Ptnr. Vogel, Heis, Wenstrup & Cameron, Cin., 1972-96; sole practice, 1997—; bd. dirs. Pro Srs., 1994—. Chmn. mem.'s com. Cin. Art Mus., 1987-88; chmn. auction Cin. Hist. Soc., 1985; local pres. English Speaking Union, 1979-81, nat. bd. dirs., 1981; chmn. Keep Cin. Beautiful, Inc., 1994-96; active Bravo! Cin. Ballet, 1989; chmn. Act II Nutcracker Ball, 1987-88; bd. dirs. Merc Libr., 1991-98; bd. dirs. Cin. Preservation Assn., 1990-93, Cin. Opera Guild, 1997-99; vice chmn. Children's Heart Assn. Reds Rally, 1989; bd. dirs. Cin. Country Day Sch., 1983, pres. Alumni Coun. and Ann. Fund, 1983. Mem. Cin. Bar Assn., Fla. Bar Assn., Harvard Law Sch. Assn. Cin. (pres. 1997-99, Heimlich Inst. (trustee 1987—), Yale Alumni Assn. (del. 1984-87), Cin. Yale Club (pres. 1980-81, 96-97), Cincinnatus, The Lawyers Club Cin. (pres. 1995), Harvard Club of Cin. (bd. dirs. 1996-98, pres. 1999). Republican. Probate, Consumer commercial, General practice. Home: 2270 Madison Rd Cincinnati OH 45208-2659 Office: 817 Main St Ste 800 Cincinnati OH 45202-2183

**VOGEL, CHARLES NICHOLAS,** lawyer; b. Fargo, N.D., Mar. 13, 1943; s. Mart R. and Lois Hess (Fluetsch) V.; m. Ene Kolvastik; 1 child, David Teodor. AB, Lawrence U., 1965; JD, U. Chgo., 1968. Bar: N.D. 1968, U.S. Dist. Ct. N.D. 1969, U.S. Ct. Appeals (8th cir.) 1988. Tchg. asst. Stanford U., Palo Alto, Calif., 1968-69; pvt. practice Fargo, N.D., 1969—; Pres. Red River Estate Planning, Fargo, N.D., 1985-86. Pres. Fargo Symphony Orch., 1982. Fellow Am. Coll. Trust and Estate Counsel (state rep. 1991-95); mem. ABA, N.D. State Bar Assn., Cass County Bar Assn. (pres. 1988-89, Kiwanis (pres. 1987-88). Avocations: bridge, sports, sailing. Pension, profit-sharing, and employee benefits, Probate, Estate planning. Office: Vogel Law Firm 502 1st Ave N Fargo ND 58102-4804

**VOGEL, HOWARD STANLEY,** lawyer; b. N.Y.C., Jan. 21, 1934; s. Moe and Sylvia (Miller) V.; m. Judith Anne Gelb, June 30, 1962; 1 son, Michael S. B.A., Bklyn. Coll., 1954; J.D., Columbia U., 1957; LL.M. in Corp. Law, NYU, 1969. Bar: N.Y. 1957, U.S. Supreme Ct. 1964. Assoc. Whitman & Ransom, N.Y.C., 1961-66; with Texaco Inc., 1966—, gen. atty., 1970-73, assoc. gen. counsel, 1973-81, gen. counsel Texaco Philanthropic Found. Inc., 1979-82, gen. counsel Jefferson Chem. Co., Texaco Chems. Can. Inc., 1973-82, assoc. gen. tax counsel, gen. mgr. adminstrn., White Plains, N.Y., 1981—; gen. tax counsel Texaco Found. Inc., 1995—. Pres., dir. 169 E. 69th Corp., 1981—. Served to 1st lt. JAGC, U.S. Army, 1958-60. Mem. ABA, Assn. Bar City N.Y., Fed. Bar Council, Assn. Ex-Mems. of Squadron A (N.Y.C.). Club: Princeton (N.Y.C.). Corporate taxation, General corporate, Securities. Home: 169 E 69th St Apt 9D New York NY 10021-5163 Office: 2000 Westchester Ave White Plains NY 10650-0001

**VOGEL, JENNIFER LYN,** lawyer; b. Queens, N.Y., June 20, 1969; d. Bernard Henry and Alyce Susan Vogel. BA, Washington U., St. Louis, 1991; JD, Bklyn. Law Sch., 1994. Assoc. Seavey Vogel & Oziel, Mineola, N.Y., 1994—. Landlord-tenant. Office: Seavey Vogel & Oziel LLP 33 Willis Ave Ste 200 Mineola NY 11501-4411

**VOGEL, JOHN WALTER,** lawyer; b. Dansville, N.Y., Sept. 19, 1948; s. Walter Earl and Betty (Elston) V.; m. Pamela Hill; children: Michael John, Jennifer Alexandra. BA, SUNY, Albany, 1970; JD, Syracuse U., 1976. Bar: N.Y. 1976, U.S. Dist. Ct. (we. dist.) N.Y. 1979, U.S. Tax Ct. 1980, U.S. Supreme Ct., 1980, U.S. Dist. Ct. (no. dist.) N.Y. 1985, U.S. Ct. Appeals (2d cir.) 1985. Assoc. Edward J. Degnan Law Offices, Caniesteo, N.Y., 1976-77; atty. N.Y. State Dept. Agrl. & Markets, Albany, 1977-78; sole practice law Dansville, 1978—; v.p., legal counsel Dansville Econ. Devel. Corp., 1983—; closing atty. Farmers Home Adminstrn., Dansville, 1982—. Dir. Livingston County (N.Y.) Drug Abuse Prevention Council, 1981-82. Served with U.S. Army, 1970-73. Mem. N.Y. State Bar Assn., Livingston County Bar Assn. (sec., treas. 1980-82, v.p. 1984-85, pres. 1985-86), Assn. Trial Lawyers Am., N.Y. State Trial Lawyers Assn., Dansville C. of C. (bd. dirs. 1985—). Republican. Presbyterian. General practice, Personal injury, State civil litigation. Home: 261 Main St Dansville NY 14437-1111 Office: 125 Main St Dansville NY 14437-1611

**VOGEL, MICHAEL SCOTT,** lawyer; b. N.Y.C., Apr. 19, 1966; s. Howard S. and Judith A. (Gelb) V.; m. Catherine T. Kenney, Aug. 10, 1991; children: Edward A. K. Vogel, Charles T. V. Kenney. BA, Yale U., 1988; JD, Columbia U., 1991. Bar: Conn., 1991, N.Y., 1992, U.S. Dist. Ct. (so. dist.) N.Y., 1992, U.S. Dist. Ct. (ea. dist.) N.Y., 1993, U.s. Ct. Appeals (2d, 3d cirs.), 1996, N.J., 1998, U.S. Dist. Ct. N.J., 1998. Assoc. Duker & Barrett, N.Y.C., 1991-97; ptnr. Allegaert Berger & Vogel LLP, N.Y.C., Princeton, N.J., 1997—. General civil litigation, Appellate, Toxic tort. Office: Allegaert Berger & Vogel LLP 111 Broadway New York NY 10006-1901

**VOGELMAN, LAWRENCE ALLEN,** law educator, lawyer; b. Bklyn., Feb. 24, 1949; s. Herman and Gertrude (Wohl) V.; m. Deborah Malka, Jan. 24, 1971 (div. Aug. 1980); m. Marcia Sikowitz, Mar. 3, 1985. BA, Bklyn. Coll., 1970; JD, Bklyn. Law Sch., 1973. Bar: N.Y. 1974, U.S. Dist. Cts. (so. and ea. dists.) N.Y. 1975, U.S. Ct. Appeals (2d cir.) 1975, U.S. Ct. Appeals (3d cir.) 1983, U.S. Supreme Ct. 1983, N.H. 1994, DNH 1994. Trial atty. Legal Aid Soc., N.Y.C., 1973-77; assoc. appellate counsel Criminal Appeals Bur., N.Y.C., 1977-78; clin. prof. law Benjamin N. Cardozo Sch. Law, Yeshiva U., N.Y.C., 1979-93; dep. dir. N.H. Pub. Defender, Concord, N.H., 1993-97; coun. Shuchman, Krause-Elmslie, P.L.L.C., 1997—. adj. prof. law Franklin Pierce Law Ctr., 1994—; faculty Inst. for Criminal Def. Advocacy, 1995—; program dir. Max Freund Litigation Ctr., 1984—; team leader Emory U. Trial Techniques Program, Atlanta, 1981-89, N.J. region, Nat. Inst. Trial Advocacy, 1997—; mem. faculty N.E. region, Nat. Inst. Trial Advocacy, 1980—, Tom C. Clark Ctr. for Advocacy, Hofstra U. Sch. Law, 1980—, Legal Aid Socs. Trial Advocacy Program, 1986—, Widener U. Law Sch. Intensive Trial Program, 1987—, U. San Francisco Intensive Trial Advocacy Program, 1991—; mem. indigent's assigned counsel panel, appellate div. First Dept., N.Y.C., 1979-94; criminal justice act panel U.S. Dist. Ct. (so. and ea. dists.) N.Y., 1985-94, dist. N.H., 1997—; adminstrv. law judge N.Y.C. Environ. Control Bd., 1980-81; pres. bd. of trustees Woodward Park Sch., 1990-94; legal adv. bd. N.H. Civil Liberties Union. Author, editor: Cases and Materials on Clinical Legal Education, 1979; editor revisions to Eyewitness Identification. Fellow Am. Bd. Criminal Lawyers; mem. Assn. of Bar of City of N.Y., Assn. of Legal Aid Attys. (exec. v.p. 1977-78, exec. com. 1984-86, bargaining com. chairperson 1974-79), Soc. Am. Law Tchrs., Assn. Trial Lawyers Am. (exec. com. civil rights sect.), Nat. Assn. Criminal Def. Lawyers (bd. dirs.), N.H. Assn. Criminal Def. Lawyers, N.Y. State Defenders Assn., Order of Barristers, Am. Inns of Ct. (master Daniel Webster Inn of Ct.), Fortune Soc. (exec. com., bd. dirs.). Democrat. Jewish. Home: 1311 White Cedar Blvd Portsmouth NH 03801-6540 Office: Shuchman & Krause-Elmslie PLLC PO Box 220 Exeter NH 03833-0220 *Notable cases include: People vs. Joel Steinberg, represented co-defendant, Hedda Nussbaum in homicide death Lisa Steinberg; U.S. vs. Falvey, in which Irish Rep. Army supporters were acquitted of gun running because of knowledge and approval of CIA; Bell vs. Coughlin, which involved highly-publicized homicide of 2 N.Y. police officers; People vs. Roche, which established agy. def. to drug sale in State of N.Y.'s highest ct.; U.S. vs. Joseph, which appealed convictions in Brinks case.*

**VOGELSANG, BETH TYLER,** lawyer; b. Miami, July 5, 1962; d. George C. Vogelsang and Martha Iacobucci; m. Richard C. Tyler, May 29, 1982; children: Ryan Carter, Stephanie Nicole, Travis Scott. BA cum laude, Pepperdine U., 1982; JD magna cum laude, U. Miami, 1985. Bar: Fla. 1985, U.S. Dist. Ct. (so. dist.) Fla. 1985; bd. cert. marital & family Fla. Bar Assn., 1992. Assoc. Law Offices George C. Vogelsang, Miami, 1985-90; ptnr. The Vogelsang Law Firm, Miami, 1990-96; of counsel A.J. Barranco & Assoc., Miami, 1996-98; ptnr. Barranco, Kircher & Vogelsang, Miami, 1998—. Mem. First Family Law Am. Inn of Ct. Democrat. Family and matrimonial, Personal injury. Office: Barranco Kircher & Vogelsang PA 150 W Flagler St Ste 1400 Miami FL 33130-1537

**VOGET, JANE J.,** city official, lawyer; b. Montréal, Que., Can., Jan. 2, 1949; d. Frederick Wilhelm and Mary Kay (Mee) V. BA in German and Anthropology, So. Ill. U., 1971, MS in Planning and Cmty. Devel., 1977; JD, Lewis and Clark Coll., 1990. Bar: Wash. 1991. Program mgr. Ill. Dept. Local Govt. Affairs, Springfield, 1975-78, U.S. Dept. Housing and Urban Devel., Washington, 1978; mem. staff The White House, Office Asst. to Pres. for Intergovtl. Affairs, Washington, 1979-80; housing project mgr. Multnomah County, Portland, Oreg., 1985-88; sr. project mgr. City of Seattle, 1989—; pvt. practice, Seattle, 1991—. Author, co-author govtl. publs. Vol. lawyer West Seattle Legal Clinic, 1994—, Na Hanu 'O ku'ulei Aloha, 1996—. Mem. ABA (mem. affordable housing fin. com. 1991-96), Wash. State Bar Assn. (real property probate and trust sect.), King County Bar Assn. (Housing Justice Project atty.), Orca Alliance (bd. dirs.). Avocations: swimming, Hawaiian music and dance, animal rights advocate. Office: 500 Union St Ste 450 Seattle WA 98101-2332 also: City of Seattle 618 2nd Ave Seattle WA 98104-2289

**VOGL, FRANK E.,** lawyer; b. Dubuque, Iowa, Jan. 5, 1943; s. August L. and Mary (Hanson) V.; m. Julie Ann Leary, Nov. 28, 1981; children: James, Christina. BA, Loras Coll., Dubuque, 1965; JD, Georgetown U., 1968. Appellate atty. NLRB, Washington, 1968-72; ptnr. Best & Flanagan, Mpls., 1974—. Labor, Immigration, naturalization, and customs. Office: Best & Flanagan 601 2d Ave S Minneapolis MN 55404

**VOGT, MARTHA DIANE,** lawyer; b. Albertville, Ala., Sept. 22, 1952; m. Robert A. Vogt, May 26, 1973. BA, Oakland U., 1974; JD, Wayne Law Sch., 1980. Bar: Mich. 1980, U.S. Ct. Appeals (4th cir.) 1985, Fla. 1988, U.S. Ct. Appeals (6th cir.) 1990, U.S. Ct. Appeals (11th cir.) 1996. Ptnr. Clark, Klein & Beaumont, Detroit, 1980-92, Bavol & Vogt, Tampa, Fla., 1992-95; pvt. practice Law Office of M. Diane Vogt, Tampa, Fla., 1995—; adj. prof. Wayne Law Sch., Detroit, 1987-92; instr. U. South Fla., 1995. Author: The Silicone Solution, 1999; co-author: Lawyer Retention: Improving Job Satisfaction for Lawyers. Mem. ABA, DRI, State Bar of Mich. Assn., The Fla. Bar Assn. General civil litigation, Product liability. Office: 100 N Tampa St Ste 2100 Tampa FL 33602-5809

**VOIGHT, ELIZABETH ANNE,** lawyer; b. Sapulpa, Okla., Aug. 6, 1944; d. Robert Guy and Garneeta Ruth (Bell) Voight; m. Bodo Barske, Feb. 22, 1985; children: Anne Katherine, Ruth Caroline. BA, U. Ark.-Fayetteville, 1967, MA, 1969; postgrad., U. Hamburg (W.Ger.), 1966-67; J.D., Georgetown U., 1978. Bar: N.Y. 1979. Lectr. German Oral Roberts U., Tulsa, 1968-69; tchr. German D.C. pub. schs., 1971-73; instr. German Georgetown U., Washington, 1973-74; adminstrv. asst. to dean Sch. Fgn. Svc. Georgetown U., 1974-77; law clk. Cole Corette & Abrutyn, Washington, 1977-78; atty. Walter, Conston, Alexander & Green, P.C., N.Y.C., 1978-88, Munich, 1990—; atty. Hasche Sigle Eschenlohr Peltzer, Munich, 1990—. Author: (with Dr. Otto Schmidt) German Commercial Code, German-English Text, 4th edit., 1999; translator articles for profl. jours. Chmn. regional screening Am. Field Svc., N.Y.C., 1981-86; founding mem. Am. Berlin Opera Found. German Acad. Exchange Program fellow, 1966-67; adv. coun. Georgetown U. Ctr. German and European Studies. Mem. Assn. Bar City N.Y., N.Y. State Bar Assn., Munich Bar Assn., Internat. Fiscal Assn., Internat. Bar Assn., Am. C. of C. in Germany (Munich regional com.), Phi Beta Kappa, Kappa Kappa Gamma. Contracts commercial, General corporate, Mergers and acquisitions.

**VOIGT, STEVEN RUSSELL,** lawyer; b. Geneva, Nebr., Dec. 29, 1952; s. James Leroy and Martha Anne (Erikson) V.; m. Barbara Jeane Molcyk, Apr. 23, 1983; children: Kelsey Marie, Katelyn Anne. BS, U. Nebr., 1975, JD, 1978. Bar: Nebr. 1978, U.S. Dist. Ct. Nebr. 1978, U.S. Tax Ct. 1980. Assoc. Nye, Hervert, Jorgensen & Watson, Kearney, Nebr., 1978-80; ptnr. Giese, Butler & Voigt, Kearney, 1980-82, Butler & Voigt, Kearney, 1982-85, Butler, Voigt & Brewster, Kearney, 1985-97, Butler, Voigt & Stewart P.C., Kearney, 1997—; bd. dirs. Western Nebr. Legal Svcs., Scottsbluff, pres. bd. 1997—; pub. defender County of Kearney, Minden, Nebr., 1982—; pres. Nebr. Lawyers Trust Account Found., Lincoln, 1986-90. Mem. ABA (exec. coun. young lawyers div. 1985-86), Assn. Trial Lawyers Am., Nebr. State Bar Assn. (vice chair judiciary com.), Nebr. Criminal Defense Atty's. Assn., Sertoma (pres. Kearney chpt. 1983-84), Kearney Country Club (pres. of bd. dirs. 1995), Masons, Shriners. Avocations: golf, bicycling. Consumer commercial, Criminal, Family and matrimonial. Home: 5207 Avenue G Pl Kearney NE 68847-8598 Office: Butler Voigt & Stewart PC 2202 Central Ave Ste 200 Kearney NE 68847-5359

**VOIGTS, L.R.,** lawyer; b. Greene, Iowa, Oct. 2, 1927; s. Dick Voigts and Marie Koester; m. Darlene R. Voigts, Aug. 6, 1950; children: Douglas, Jane, Nancy. BA, Wartburg Coll., 1948; JD, Drake U., 1955. Bar: Iowa, U.S. Dist. Ct. (8th cir.) Iowa. Jud. law clk. U.S. Dist. Ct. (no. dist.) Iowa, 1955; ptnr. Nyemaster Goode Voigts West Haisell & O'Brien, Des Moines, 1955—. Fellow Am. Coll. Trial Lawyers; mem. ABA (ho. of dels. 1989-96), C. Edwin Moore Inn of Ct. (master), Iowa Acad. Trial Lawyers. Republican. Lutheran. General civil litigation. Home: 614 40th St Des Moines IA 50312-3320 Office: Nyemaster Goode Voigts West Haisell & O'Brien 700 Walnut St Ste 1600 Des Moines IA 50309-3800

**VOJCANIN, SAVA ALEXANDER,** lawyer; b. Oak Lawn, Ill., Oct. 15, 1964; s. Jovan and Lili (Yovanovich) V. Diplomate, Culver Mil. Acad., 1981; BA with distinction, DePauw U., 1985; JD, Washington U., 1988. Bar: Ill. 1988, U.S. Dist. Ct. (no. dist.) Ill. 1989, U.S. Dist. Ct. (no. dist.) Tex. 1996. Assoc. Schaffenegger, Watson & Peterson Ltd., Chgo., 1988-91; assoc. Clausen Miller P.C., Chgo., 1991-98, ptnr., 1999—. Editor: Law, Culture and Values, 1989. Mem. Mayor's Adv. Coun. on Immigrant and Refugee Affairs, Chgo., 1992-97; active St. Basil Orthodox Ch. of Lake Forest, 1997—. Mem. Serbian Bar Assn. Am. (bd. dirs.), Chgo. Bar Assn. Insurance, Construction, Public international. Office: Clausen Miller PC 10 S LaSalle St Chicago IL 60603-1098

**VOLK, KENNETH HOHNE,** lawyer; b. Hackensack, N.J., Nov. 8, 1922; s. Henry L. and Constance (Brady) V.; m. Joyce Geary, May 11, 1954; children: Christopher H., Cynthia. BS, U.S. Naval Acad., 1946; LLB, Yale U., 1953. Ptnr. Burlingham, Underwood, N.Y.C., 1955-92; of counsel McLane, Graf, Raulerson & Middleton, Portsmouth, N.H., 1992—; speaker various symposia and confs. on maritime law. Assoc. editor Am. Maritime Cases; contbr. articles to profl. jours. Pres. Maritime Assocs., N.Y.C., 1967-68; chmn. bd. dirs. Seamen's House YMCA, N.Y.C., 1971-76; sec., bd. dirs. Seamen's Ch. Inst., N.Y.C., 1977-92; bd. dirs. Strawbery Banke Mus., Portsmouth, N.H.; mem. adv. bd. Tulane Admiralty Law Inst.. Fellow Am. Bar Found., Am. Coll. Trial Lawyers; mem. ABA, Assn. Bar of City of N.Y., Maritime Law Assn. U.S. (exec. com. 1977-80, pres. 1990-92), Comite Maritime Internat. (titulary mem.), Quaker Hill Country Club (pres. 1976-78). Republican. Espicopalian. Avocations: reading, hiking, fishing. Admiralty, Federal civil litigation, Private international. Office: McLane Graf Raulerson 30 Penhallow St Portsmouth NH 03801-3816

**VOLK, PAUL S.,** lawyer; b. Concord, Mass., Aug. 6, 1957; s. Paul and Amaryllis Ann V.; m. Deborah Ann Pensack, Feb. 13, 1982. BA cum laude, U. Vt., 1980; JD summa cum laude, New England Sch. Law, 1986. Bar: Vt. 1987, U.S. Dist. Ct. Vt. 1987, U.S. Ct. Appeals (2d cir.) 1991, U.S. Dist. Ct. (no. dist.) N.Y. 1995. Assoc., contract pub. defender Blodgett & Watts, Burlington, Vt., 1986-89; ptnr. Blodgett, Watts & Volk, P.C., Burlington, 1989—; supervising atty. student legal svc. U. Vt., Burlington, 1988—. Mem. ACLU (dir. 1994—), Vt. Bar Assn. (mem. criminal law com.), Vt. Assn. Criminal Def. Lawyers (dir. 1991—, pres. 1998). Democrat. Avocations: downhill skiing, tennis, golfing, mountain sports, music. Criminal, Family and matrimonial, Constitutional. Office: Blodgett Watts & Volk PC PO Box 8 Burlington VT 05402-0008

**VOLLACK, ANTHONY F.,** former state supreme court justice; b. Cheyenne, Wyo., Aug. 7, 1929; s. Luke and Opal Vollack; m. D. Imojean; children: Leah, Kirk. Bar: Colo. 1956. Pvt. practice law Colo., from 1956; former state senator; judge Colo. Dist. Ct. (1st jud. dist.), 1977-85; justice Colo. Supreme Ct., 1986-98, chief justice, 1995-98, ret., 1998. Office: Colo Supreme Ct Colorado State Judicial Bldg 2 E 14th Ave Denver CO 80203-2115

**VOLLMER, RICHARD WADE,** federal judge; b. St. Louis, Mar. 7, 1926; s. Richard W. and Beatrice (Burke) V.; m. Marilyn S. Stikes, Sept. 17, 1949. Student, Springhill Coll., 1946-49; LLB, U. Ala., 1953. Bar: Ala. 1953, U.S. Dist. Ct. (so. dist.) Ala. 1956, U.S. Ct. Appeals (5th cir.) 1963, U.S. Ct. Appeals (11th cir.) 1983. Judge U.S. Dist. Ct. (so. dist.) Ala., 1990—. Mem. Mobile Bar Assn. (pres. 1990), Rotary (Paul Harris fellow 1988). Roman Catholic.

**VOLMERT, DEBORAH JEAN,** lawyer; b. Belleville, Ill., June 9, 1968; d. David A. and Mary Faye Mehrmann; m. Douglas Ambrose Volmert, May 20, 1995; 1 child, Brett Douglas. BS, Truman State U., 1990; JD, Washington U., 1993. Bar: Ill. 1993, U.S. Dist. Ct. (so. dist.) Ill. 1993, Mo. 1994, U.S. Ct. Appeals (7th cir.) 1995, U.S. Dist. Ct. (ea. dist.) Mo. 1997. Atty. Thompson & Mitchell, Belleville, Ill., 1993-97, The Stolar Partnership, Belleville, 1997—; sec. Belleville Main St., Inc., 1998—, also bd. dirs. Bd. dirs. Hoyleton (Ill.) Youth and Family Svcs., 1995—. Mem. ABA, Nat. Assn. Bond Lawyers, Ill. State Bar Assn., Monroe County Bar Assn. (pres. 1997-98), St. Clair County Bar Assn. Consumer commercial, Bankruptcy. Office: The Stolar Partnership PO Box 484 Belleville IL 62222-0484

**VON BERNUTH, CARL W.,** diversified corporation executive, lawyer. BA, Yale U., 1966, LLB, 1969. Bar: N.Y. 1970, Pa. 1990. Corp. atty. White & Case, 1969-80; assoc. gen. counsel Union Pacific Corp., N.Y.C., 1980-83, dep. gen. counsel fin. and adminstrn., 1984-88; v.p., gen. counsel Union Pacific Corp., Bethlehem, Pa., 1988-91, sr. v.p., gen. counsel, 1991-97; sr. v.p., gen. counsel and sec. Union Pacific Corp., Omaha, 1997—. General corporate, Securities. Office: Union Pacific Corp 1416 Dodge St Rm 1230 Omaha NE 68179-0001

**VON DER HEYDT, JAMES ARNOLD,** federal judge; b. Miles City, Mont., July 15, 1919; s. Harry Karl and Alice S. (Arnold) von der H.; m. Verna E. Johnson, May 21, 1952. A.B., Albion (Mich.) Coll., 1942; J.D., Northwestern, 1951. Bar: Alaska 1951. Pvt. law practice Nome, 1953-59; judge superior ct. Juneau, Alaska, 1959-66; U.S. dist. judge, now sr. judge U.S. Dist. Ct. Alaska, Alaska, 1966—; U.S. commr. Nome, Alaska, 1951—; U.S. atty. div. 2 Dist. Alaska, 1951-53; mem. Alaska Ho. of Reps., 1957-59. Author: Mother Sawtooth's Nome, 1990. Pres. Anchorage Fine Arts Mus. Assn. Recipient Disting. Alumni award Albion Coll., 1995. Mem. Alaska Bar Assn. (mem. bd. govs. 1955-59, pres. 1959-60), Am. Judicature Soc., Masons (32d degree), Phi Delta Phi, Sigma Nu. Club: Mason (32 deg.), Shriner. Avocation: researching Arctic bird life, creative writing. Office: US Dist Ct 222 W 7th Ave Unit 4 Anchorage AK 99513-7564

**VONINSKI, JOHN R.,** lawyer; b. Syracuse, N.Y., Dec. 22, 1948; s. Andrew and Anne V.; m. Sharon Barnard Voninski, Aug. 5, 1972. BA, SUNY, 1971, postgrad., 1971-72; JD, Seattle U., 1974. Bar: N.Y. Atty. Michaels & Michaels, Syracuse, 1974-76; sr. dep. county atty. Onondaga County Atty's. Office, Syracuse, 1976-85; asst. atty. gen.-in-charge N.Y. State Atty. Gen's. Office, Syracuse, 1985-95; counsel N.Y. State Supreme Ct., Syracuse, 1995—. Avocation: aircraft piloting. Home: 3740 Oran Delphi Rd Manlius NY 13104-8615 Office: NY State Supreme Court 401 Montgomery St Syracuse NY 13202-2151

**VON KALINOWSKI, JULIAN ONESIME,** lawyer; b. St. Louis, May 19, 1916; s. Walter E. and Maybelle (Michaud) von K.; m. Penelope Jayne Dyer, June 29, 1980; children by previous marriage: Julian Onesime, Wendy Jean von Kalinowski. BA, Miss. Coll., 1937; JD with honors, U. Va., 1940. Bar: Va. 1940, Calif. 1946. Assoc. Gibson, Dunn and Crutcher, L.A., 1946-52, ptnr., 1953-85, mem. exec. com., 1962-82, adv. ptnr., 1985—; CEO, chmn. Litigation Scis., Inc., Culver City, Calif., 1991-94; chmn. emeritus Litigation Scis., Inc., Torrance, Calif., 1994-96, Dispute Dyamics, Inc., Torrance, Calif., 1996—; instr. Columbia Law Sch., Parker Sch. Fgn. and Cooperative Law, summer 1981; instr. antitrust law and litigation So. Meth. Sch. of Law, summer 1982-84, bd. visitors, 1982-85; v.p., bd. dirs., mem. exec. com. W.M. Keck Found.; mem. faculty Practising Law Inst., 1971, 76, 78, 79, 80; instr. in spl. course on antitrust litigation Columbia U. Law Sch., N.Y.C., 1981; mem. lawyers dels. com. to 9th Cir. Jud. Conf., 1953-67; UN expert Mission to People's Republic China, 1982. Contbr. articles to legal jours.; author: Antitrust Laws and Trade Regulation, 1969, desk edit., 1981; gen. editor: World Law of Competition, 1978, Antitrust Counseling and Litigation Techniques, 1984; gen. editor emeritus Antitrust Report. With USN, 1941-46, capt. Res. ret. Fellow Am. Bar Found., Am. Coll. Trial Lawyers (chmn. complex litigation com. 1984-87); mem. ABA (ho. of dels. 1970, chmn. antitrust law sect. 1972-73), State Bar Calif., L.A. Bar Assn., U. Va. Law Sch. Alumni Assn., Calif. Club, L.A. Country Club, La Jolla Beach and Tennis Club, Phi Kappa Psi, Phi Alpha Delta. Republican. Episcopalian. Antitrust, Federal civil litigation, General civil litigation. Home: 12320 Ridge Cir Los Angeles CA 90049-1151

**VON MANDEL, MICHAEL JACQUES,** lawyer; b. Yokohama, Japan, Oct. 20, 1941; came to the U.S., 1946; s. Michael Maximillan and Suzanne (Jacques) V.M.; m. Mary Denise Bienvenue, Dec. 22, 1984; 1 child, Michelle Denise. AB in Econs., Georgetown U., 1964; JD, Cath. U., 1968; LLM in Taxation, NYU, 1970. Bar: Washington 1969, Conn. 1969, Ill. 1976, U.S. Dist. Ct. (no. dist.) Ill. 1976, Fla. 1977, U.S. Ct. Appeals (7th cir.) 1976. Trial atty. FTC, Washington, 1968-69; trial atty. tax divsn. U.S. Dept. Justice, Washington, 1970-76; pvt. practice Chgo., 1976-93; ptnr. Von Mandel & Von Mandel, Chgo., 1994—; adj. prof. grad. tax program DePaul U., Chgo., 1980-83. Contbr. chpts. to books. Mem. ABA (tax and litigation sects. 1976—), Chgo. Bar Assn. (fed. tax com. 1976—), Fed. Bar Assn. (bd. dirs. 1981-93), Bar Assn. 7th Fed. Cir., Union League Club. Roman Catholic. Taxation, general, Corporate taxation, Federal civil litigation. Office: von Mandel & von Mandel 135 S La Salle St Ste 2216 Chicago IL 60603-4108

**VON MEHREN, ARTHUR TAYLOR,** lawyer, educator; b. Albert Lea, Minn., Aug. 10, 1922; s. Sigurd Anders and Eulalia Marion (Anderson) von M.; m. Joan Elizabeth Moore, Oct. 11, 1947; children—George Moore, Peter Anders, Philip Taylor. S.B., Harvard U., 1942, LL.B., 1945, Ph.D., 1946; Faculty of Law, U. Zurich, 1946-47; Faculte de Droit, U. Paris, 1948-49; Doctor iuris (h.c.), Katholeke U., Leuven, 1985. Bar: Mass. 1950, U.S. Dist. Ct. Mass. 1980. Law clk. U.S. Ct. Appeals (1st cir.), 1945-46; asst. prof. law Harvard U., 1946-53, prof., 1953-76, Story prof., 1976-93, prof. emeritus, 1993—, dir. East Asian legal studies program, 1981-83; acting chief legislation br., legal div. Occupation Mil. Govt. U.S.,Germany, 1947-48, cons. legal div., 1949; tchr. Salzburg Seminar in Am. Studies, summers 1953, 54; Fulbright research prof. U. Tokyo, Japan, 1956-57, Rome, Italy, 1968-69; cons. legal studies Ford Found., New Delhi, 1962-63; vis. prof. U. Frankfurt, summer 1967, City Univ. Hong Kong, 1995; Ford vis. prof. Inst. Advanced Legal Studies, U. London, 1976; assoc. prof. U. Paris, 1977; Goodhart prof. legal sci. U. Cambridge, 1983-84, fellow Downing Coll., 1983-84, hon. fellow, 1984—; fellow Wissenschaftskolleg zu Berlin, 1990-91. Author: The Civil Law System: An Introduction to the Comparative Study of Law, 1957, 2d edit. (with J. Gordley), 1977, Law in the United States: A General and Comparative View, 1988; co-author: The Law of Multistate Problems:Cases and Materials in the conflict of Laws, 1965, Conflict of Laws: American, Comparative, International, 1998, International Commercial Arbitration, 1999; mem. editl. bd. Am. Jour. Comparative Law, 1952-86; contbr. articles to profl. jours.; editor: Law in Japan-The Legal Order in a Changing Soc., 1963; mem. editorial com. Internat. Ency. Comparative Law, 1969—; mem. adv. bd. Internat. Ctr. for Settlement of Investment Disputes Rev.-Fgn. Investment Law Jour., 1985—. Mem. U.S. Del. Hague Conf. pvt. internat. law, 1966, 68, 76, 80, 85, 93, 96. Named to Order of the Rising Sun, golden rays Japanese Govt., 1989; Guggenheim fellow, 1968-69; inst. fellow Sackler Inst. Advanced Studies, 1986-87. Mem. ABA (Leonard J. Theberge Award for Pvt. Internat. Law 1997, Sect. of Internat. Law and Practice), Am. Acad. Arts and Scis., Internat. Acad. Comparative Law, Institut de Droit Internat., Japanese Am. Soc. Legal Studies, Am. Soc. Comparative Law (bd. dirs., pres.), Am. Soc. Polit. and Legal Philosophy, Institut Grand-Duchal (corr.), Phi Beta Kappa. Office: Harvard Law Sch/ AR-231 1545 Massachusetts Ave Cambridge MA 02138-2903

**VON PASSENHEIM, JOHN B.,** lawyer; b. Calif., Nov. 25, 1964; s. Burr Charles and Kathryn E. (Kirkland) Passenheim. BA in English with honors, U. Calif.-Santa Barbara, 1986; JD, U. Calif., Hastings, 1989. Bar: Calif. 1989, U.S. Dist. Ct. (so. dist.) Calif. 1991. Pvt. practice San Diego, 1990—; organizer Rock The Vote, San Diego, 1992; primary atty. Calif. Lawyers for the Arts, San Diego; panelist Ind. Music Seminar, 1992, 93, 94; mem. Surfrider Found. Nat. Adv. Bd., 1995—; gen. counsel Greyboy Records, Posh

Boy Records, Alchemical, Inc. Contbg. staff DICTA mag., 1990-94; editor (legal column) It's the Law, 1990-93. Exec. counsel San Diego chpt. Surfrider Found., 1991-95; vol. atty. San Diego Vol. Lawyer Program, 1990-93. Entertainment, General practice, General civil litigation. Office: 4425 Bayard St Ste 240 San Diego CA 92109-4089

**VON SAUERS, JOSEPH F.,** lawyer; b. N.Y.C.; s. Joseph F. and Margaret von Sauers; m. June A. von Sauers. BEE, Manhattan Coll., 1980; MBA, Pepperdine U., 1987; JD, Southwestern U., 1991; LLM, Columbia U., 1995. Bar: Calif. 1992, D.C. 1993, Minn. 1993, Tex. 1993, Colo. 1994, U.S. Patent and Trademark Office. Contracts negotiator Hughes Aircraft Co., El Segundo, Calif., 1985-92; atty. Jones, Day, Reavis & Pogue, Dallas, 1992-94, Loeb & Loeb, LLP, L.A., 1995-97, Gray, Cary, Ware & Freidenrich, Palo Alto, Calif., 1997-98; dep. gen. coun. Roland Corp. U.S., L.A., 1998—; active Calif. Lawyers for Arts, L.A., 1996; guest spkr. Loyola U., L.A., 1996. Contbr. articles to profl. jours. Mem. Am. Legion. Comdr. USNR. Recipient Kuwait Liberation medal Saudi Arabian/Kuwaiti Govts., 1992, 96; Wildman scholar Southwestern U., 1987-91. Mem. Naval Res. Assn., L.A. County Bar Assn. Avocations: sailing, golf, tennis. Intellectual property, Entertainment, Contracts commercial.

**VON WALDOW, ARND N.,** lawyer; b. Moenchen-Gladbach, Germany, Mar. 15, 1957; came to U.S., 1966; s. Hans Eberhard and Brigitte H. (Schulze-Kadelbach) von W.; m. Esther R. Haguel, May 25, 1987; children: Rachel J., Danielle M. BA, Syracuse U., 1980; JD, U. Pitts., 1983. Bar: La. 1983, Pa. 1989. Assoc. Sessions & Fishman, New Orleans, 1983-90, Eckert, Seamans, Cherin & Mellott, Pitts., 1990-91; ptnr. Meyer, Darragh, Buckler, Bebenek & Eck, Pitts., 1991—; mem. Product Liability Adv. Coun., Chgo., 1991—. Mem. ABA, Def. Rsch. Inst., Phi Beta Kappa. Product liability, Contracts commercial, Insurance. Home: 1738 Hempstead Ln Pittsburgh PA 15241-1376 Office: Reed Smith Shaw & McClay 435 6th Ave Ste 2 Pittsburgh PA 15219-1886

**VOORHEES, RICHARD LESLEY,** federal judge; b. Syracuse, N.Y., June 5, 1941; s. Henry Austin and Catherine Adeline (Fait) V.; m. Barbara Holway Humphries, 1968; children: Martha Northrop, Steven Coerte. BA, Davidson Coll., 1963; JD, U. N.C., Chapel Hill, 1968. Bar: N.C. 1968, U.S. Dist. Ct. (we. dist.) N.C. 1969, U.S. Tax Ct. 1969, U.S. Ct. Appeals (4th cir.) 1978, U.S. Dist. Ct. (mid. dist.) N.C. 1981. Mem., ptnr. Garland, Alala, Bradley & Gray, Gastonia, N.C., 1968-80; pvt. practice Gastonia, N.C., 1980-88; judge U.S. Dist. Ct., Charlotte, N.C., 1988—, chief judge, 1991-98. Mem. N.C. State Rep. Exec. Com., Gaston County Rep. Com., chmn., 1979-83, U.S. Jud. Conf. Com., 1993—, case mgmt. and ct. adminstrn. com., 4th Cir. Ct. Appeals Jud. Coun., 1992-93; chmn. Gaston County Bd. Elections, Gastonia, 1985-86; alt. del. Rep. Nat. Conv., Kansas City, Kans., 1976. 1st lt. U.S. Army, 1963-65, U.S. Army Res., 1963-69. Mem. N.C. Bar Assn., Fed. Judges Assn., Dist. Judges Assn. Avocation: boating. Office: US Dist Ct WDNC 195 Fed Bldg 401 W Trade St Charlotte NC 28202-1619

**VORAN, JOEL BRUCE,** lawyer; b. Kingman, Kans., Mar. 24, 1952; s. Bruce H. and Venora M. (Layman) V.; m. Marsha A. Kooser, May 26, 1979; children: Erica, Ben, Ashley. BA, U. Kans., 1974; JD, U. Tex., 1977. Bar: Mo. 1977, U.S. Dist. Ct. (we. dist.) Mo. 1977, U.S. Tax Ct. 1986. From assoc. to ptnr. Lathrop & Gage L.C., Kansas City, Mo., 1977—; adv. dir. Mark Twain Bank, Kansas City, 1985-89. Bd. dirs. Kansas City YMCA, 1979—; city chmn. Prairie Village (Kans.) Rep. Party, 1985-88; participant Kansas City Tomorrow Project, 1989-90. Mem. ABA, Mo. Bar Assn., Kansas City Met. Bar Assn., Kansas City Lawyers Assn., Delta Tau Delta (bd. dirs., pres. 1977-87; alumni pres. Kansas City chpt. 1989-90), Friends of Art Club. Republican. Roman Catholic. Avocations: tennis, golf, jogging. General corporate, Taxation, general, Probate. Home: 2949 W 118th Ter Leawood KS 66211-3047 Office: Lathrop & Gage LC 2345 Grand Blvd Ste 2400 Kansas City MO 64108-2642

**VORREITER, PATRICIA JOAN,** lawyer; b. Savanna, Ill., July 5, 1940; d. Harry and Florence K. (Fitzpatrick) Wolfe; m. John Vorreiter, Dec. 28, 1962; children: Janelle, Riane, Loren. BA, Colo. State U., 1962; JD, Santa Clara (Calif.) U., 1980. Bar: Calif. 1980, U.S. Dist. Ct. (no. dist.) Calif. 1980. Assoc. Mackey & Friedland, San Jose, Calif., 1980-81; sole practice Sunnyvale, Calif., 1981—. Elder Sunnyvale Presbyn. Ch., 1988-90, deacon, 1984-86; v.p., bd. dirs. Life's Garden Inc., Sunnyvale, 1986-88; bd. dirs. Condo Assn., Sunnyvale; trustee San Jose Presbytery, 1991—; mem. Sunnyvale City Coun., 1995—. Mem. ABA, Calif. Bar Assn., Santa Clara Bar Assn. (family law com. 1987), Sunnyvale-Cupertino Bar Assn. (lawyer referral com. 1986-88, bd. dirs. 1988—), Nat. League Cities (housing, cmty. & econ. devel. policy com.), Women in Mcpl. Govt. (bd. dirs.), League Calif. Cities (housing, cmty. & econ. devel. com. 1995—), Calif. Space & Tech. Alliance (bd. dirs.). Democrat. Avocations: running, aerobics, bicycling. Probate, Family and matrimonial. Home: 937 Aster Ct Sunnyvale CA 94086-6701 Office: 333 W Maude Ave Ste 201 Sunnyvale CA 94086-4373

**VORT, ROBERT A.,** lawyer; b. Newark, N.J., Sept. 24, 1943; s. Saul S. and Ruth J. (Jacobson) V.; m. Elizabeth Hornstein, June 25, 1968 (div. Nov. 1979); m. Marcelle Greenstein, Nov. 18, 1979 (div. Jan. 1991); children: Joel, Abigail, Rebeccah; m. Tina Kruh, Feb. 4, 1996; 1 child, Hannah. BS in Econs., U. Pa., 1965; JD, Columbia U., 1968. Bar: N.J. 1968, N.Y. 1970, U.S. Ct. Appeals (2d and 3d cirs. 1975), U.S. Ct. Appeals (9th cir.) 1980, U.S. Ct. Appeals (5th cir.) 1981, U.S. Ct. Appeals (fed. cir.) 1984, U.S. Dist. Ct. N.J. 1968, U.S. Dist. Ct. (so. and ea. dists.) N.Y. 1984, U.S. Supreme Ct. 1977. Law clk. to Hon. Theodore I. Botter Superior Ct. of N.J., 1968-69; assoc. Davis & Cox, 1969-71, Israel B. Greene, 1971-73; sole practitioner, 1973-82; ptnr. Balk, Goldberger, Seligsohn, O'Connor & Rhatican, 1982-84, Kirsten, Friedman & Cherin, 1986; sole practitioner, 1984-85, 87-88; ptnr. Goldberg, Mufson & Spar, West Orange, N.J., 1988-91; counsel Donald Friedman, West Orange, 1991-92; sole practitioner Tenafly, N.J., 1969—. Mem. ABA (litigation sect., family law sect., legal econs. sect.), N.J. State Bar Assn. (appellate practice subcom.), Bergen County Bar Assn. Appellate, General civil litigation, Family and matrimonial. Office: PO Box 142 45 Central Ave Tenafly NJ 07670-1741

**VORYS, ARTHUR ISAIAH,** lawyer; b. Columbus, Ohio, June 16, 1923; s. Webb Isaiah and Adeline (Werner) V.; m. Lucia Rogers, July 16, 1949 (div. 1980); children: Caroline S., Adeline Vorys Cranson, Lucy Vorys Noll, Webb I.; m. Ann Harris, Dec. 13, 1980. BA, Williams Coll., 1945; LLB, JD, Ohio State U., 1949. Bar: Ohio 1949. From assoc. to ptnr. Vorys, Sater, Seymour & Pease LLP, Columbus, 1949-82, sr. ptnr., 1982-93, of counsel, 1993—; supt. ins. State of Ohio, 1957-59; bd. dirs Vorys Bros., Inc., others. Trustee, past pres. Children's Hosp., Greenlawn Cemetery Found.; trustee, former chmn. Ohio State U. Hosps.; regent Capital U.; del. Rep. Nat. Conv., 1968, 72. Lt. USMCR, World War II. Decorated Purple Heart. Fellow Ohio State Bar, Columbus Bar Assn.; mem. ABA, Am. Judicature Soc., Rocky Fork Headley Hunt Club, Rocky Fork Hunt and Country Club, Capital Club, Phi Delta Phi, Chi Psi. General corporate, Insurance, Mergers and acquisitions. Home: 5826 Havens Corners Rd Columbus OH 43230-3142 Office: Vorys Sater Seymour & Pease LLP PO Box 1008 52 E Gay St Columbus OH 43215-3161

**VOSBURG, BRUCE DAVID,** lawyer; b. Omaha, June 17, 1943; s. Noble Perrin and Dena V. (Ferrari) V.; m. Susan Simpson, May 27, 1972; children: Margaret Amy, Wendy Christine, Bruce David. BA, U. Notre Dame, 1965; BSME, 1966; JD, Harvard U., 1969. Bar: Nebr. 1969, Ill. 1970, U.S. Supreme Ct. 1974. Law clk. U.S. Dist. Ct. Nebr., 1969-70; assoc. Kirkland & Ellis, Chgo., 1970-72; ptnr. Fitzgerald & Schorr, Omaha, 1972—. Author: Financing Small Businesses, 1981, Securities Law Practice, 1987, Securities Law-Going Public, 1989, Trade Secret Protection, 1994, Protecting Intellectual Property, 1998, Intellectual Property Law, 1998. Pres. Children's Crisis Ctr., 1984-85, bd. dirs., 1973-84; pres. Nebr. Tennis Assn., 1976-77; mem. Leadership Omaha, 1979; chmn. bd. dirs. City of Omaha Parks and Recreation, 1985-92; founding dir. Friends of the Parks, 1988; bd. dirs. Omaha Pub. Libr. Found., 1997—, pres., 1999—; bd. dirs. Western Heritage Mus., 1998—. Fellow Nebr. Bar Found.; mem. ABA, Nat. Assn. Bond Attys., Nebr. Bar Assn. (chmn. securities com.), Omaha Bar Assn. (exec. coun. 1983-86), Rotary (dir. 1993—), Mo. Valley Tennis Assn. (chmn. grievance com. 1978—), Tau Beta Pi. Republican. Roman Catholic. Intellectual property, General corporate, Securities. Office: 1100 Woodmen Towers Omaha NE 68102

**VOSIK, WAYNE GILBERT,** lawyer; b. Phila., July 22, 1945; s. Alexander Frank and Dorothy Marie (Yarnell) V.; m. Helga Maria Kuepper, Oct. 31, 1970 (div. Nov. 1995); m. Mary Helen Welch, Mar. 21, 1997; children: Melissa Marie Vosik Osborne, Douglas Wayne. BA, Temple U., 1967, JD, 1970. Bar: Pa. Asst. dist. atty. Phila. Dist. Atty.'s Office, 1970-72; sec., gen. counsel Ins. Fedn. Pa., Phila., 1972-74; gen. counsel, asst. sec. Acad. Ins. Group, Valley Forge, Pa., 1974-78; pvt. practice Feasterville, Pa., 1979-92; v.p. legal and govt. affairs, asst. sec., dir. human rels. Am. Travellers Corp., Bensalem, Pa., 1992-97; pvt. practice Newtown, Pa., 1997—; cons. ins. dept. U.S. V.I., St. Thomas, 1993; bd. dirs. Greater Delaware Valley Health Underwriters Assn., Phila.; instr. Am. Coll., Brwyn Mawr, Pa., 1998—. Fin. com. U.S. Senator Rick Santorum, 1994. Mem. ABA, Pa. Bar Assn., Pa. Health Underwriters Assn. (mem. legis. com. 1997—), Life Office Mgmt. Assn. (co-editor, chmn. accident & health edn. com. 1996—), Phi Alpha Delta. Republican. Methodist. Avocation: coaching youth soccer. Insurance, Administrative and regulatory, Legislative. Home: 63 Bobbie Dr Warminster PA 18974-1638 Office: 444 S State St Ste C-1 Newtown PA 18940-1945

**VOSS, BARRY VAUGHAN,** lawyer; b. St. Paul, July 25, 1952; s. James Lee and Stella Marie (Stewart) V.; m. Marilyn Williams, Jan. 25, 1980; children: Rori, Tiffini, Aaron. BA, U. Minn., 1975; JD, Hamline U., 1978. Bar: Minn. 1978, U.S. Dist. Ct. Minn. 1980, U.S. Ct. Appeals (8th cir.) 1982. Pres. Voss and Hickman, P.A., Mpls., 1978—; spkr. in field. Author: A Case of Cold Steel, 1999. Bd. dirs. Ramsey County Corrections Adv. Bd., St. Paul, 1977-79, Eden House Program, 1998—. Recipient Most Well-Prepared award Minn. Lawyers Judges' Choice, 1991. Mem. Am. Trial Lawyers Assn. (fire loss com.), Minn. Assn. Criminal Def. Attys. (bd. dirs. 1992-96), Minn. Trial Lawyers Assn., Minn. State Bar Assn. (civil litigation and criminal law sects.), Hennepin County Bar Assn. Democrat. Lutheran. Avocations: public speaking, sports, reading. Criminal, General civil litigation, Entertainment. Office: Voss and Hickman PA 527 Marquette Ave Ste 2355 Minneapolis MN 55402-1323

**VOSS, KENNETH ERWIN,** lawyer; b. Milw., Apr. 10, 1930; s. Andrew Hubert and Helen Lillian Voss; m. Charlotte Denise Gutierrez, Dec. 31, 1957; children: Christopher, Peter, Lisa, Michael, Timothy, Mark. BA, St. Francis Sem., Milw., 1952; JD, Marquette U., 1960. Bar: Wis. 1960, U.S. Dist. Ct. (ea. dist.) Wis. 1960, U.S. Supreme Ct. 1960. Gen. counsel Johnson Controls, Inc., Milw., 1960-84; pvt. practice Wickwire, Gavin & Gibbs, Vienna, Va and Madison, Wis., 1984-86, Milw., 1984-86, 90-91, Fiorenza & Hayes, Milw., 1988-90, Suran & Suran, Milw., 1991—. Author: (chpt.) Businessman's Guide to Construction, 1979, (chpt.) A Guide for the Foreign Investor, 1984, (chpts.) Wisconsin Construction Law, 1985. Sgt. U.S. Army, 1960-65. Mem. Am. Arbitration Assn. (arbitrator 1968—), State Bar Wis. (mem. rels. com. 1995—, bd. dirs. pub. contract and constrn. law sect.). Roman Catholic. Alternative dispute resolution, Construction, Estate planning. Office: Suran and Suran 9001 N 76th St Ste 303 Milwaukee WI 53223-1911

**VRANICAR, GREGORY LEONARD,** lawyer; b. Milw., June 28, 1950; s. Leonard B. and Margery Jean (Anderson) V.; m. Marilyn J. Vrbenec, May 1, 1982; children: Mark A., David G. BA, Grinnell Coll., 1972; JD, U. Iowa, 1975. Bar: Iowa 1975, Mo. 1978, U.S. Dist. Ct. (we. dist.) Mo. 1978, U.S. Ct. Appeals (8th cir.) 1980, U.S. Ct. Appeals (10th cir.) 1983. Assoc. Rich, Granoff, Levy & Gee, Kansas City, Mo., 1978-83, ptnr., 1983-90; ptnr. Seigfreid, Bingham, Levy, Selzer & Gee, Kansas City, 1990-94; fund devel. dir. Midwest Christian Counseling Ctr., Kansas City, 1994-95, acting exec. dir., 1996-97, exec. dir., 1997—. Dir. Coterie Theatre, Inc., Kansas City, 1988-94, pres., 1991-92; pres. Sr. Companion Program, Kansas City, 1987-88, adv. coun., 1985—; mem. peace and social justice com. Cure of Ars Ch., Leawood, Kans., 1990—; alumni bd. Grinnell Coll., 1993—. Capt. USAF, 1975-78. Democrat. Roman Catholic. Avocations: jogging, swimming. General civil litigation, Labor, Non-profit and tax-exempt organizations. Home: 9726 Aberdeen St Shawnee Mission KS 66206-2149 Office: Midwest Christian Couseling Ctr 4520 Madison Ave Ste 301 Kansas City MO 64111-3541

**VRANICAR, MICHAEL GREGORY,** lawyer; b. Hammond, Ind., Mar. 11, 1961; s. Melvin G. and Maryann R. (Szarek) V.; m. Marianna C. Livas, May 28, 1994. BSEE, U. Ill., 1983; JD, U. San Diego, 1987. Bar: Calif. 1987, Ill. 1988. Engr. Gen. Dynamics, San Diego, 1983-88; judge advocate USMC, Okinawa, Japan, 1988-91; assoc. Stellato & Schwartz, Chgo., 1992-94; ptnr. Plesha & Vranicar, Chgo., 1995—; arbitrator Cook County Arbitration Bd., Chgo., 1994—; judge regional competition Nat. Moot Ct., Chgo., 1992. Maj. USMC Res., 1996—. Mem. Chgo. Bar Assn., Okinawa Bench and Bar Assn., Am. Legion. Republican. Roman Catholic. General civil litigation, General corporate, General practice. Office: 10540 S Western Ave Ste 103 Chicago IL 60643-2529

**VRATIL, JOHN LOGAN,** lawyer; b. Great Bend, Kans., Oct. 28, 1945; s. Frank and Althea (Shuss) V.; m. Kathy Hoefer, June 21, 1971 (div. Dec. 1985); m. Anne Whitfill, Mar. 7, 1986 (div. Dec. 1992); children: Alison, Andy, Ashley. BS in Edn., U. Kans., 1967; postgrad., U. Southampton, Eng., 1967-68; JD, U. Kans., 1971; postgrad., U. Exeter, Eng., 1972. Bar: Kans. 1971, U.S. Dist. Ct. Kans. 1971, U.S. Ct. Appeals (10th and 8th cirs.) 1975. From assoc. to ptnr. Bennett, Lytle, Wetzler & Winn, Prairie Village, Kans., 1972-83; with Lathrop & Gage, Overland Park, Kans., 1983—; mem. Kans. State Senate, 1998—. Contbr. articles to profl. jours. Mem. recreation commn. Prairie Village, 1982-83, mem. planning commn., 1983-84; v.p. Usher Mansion Hist. Found., Lawrence, Kans., 1990—. Mem. ABA, Kans. Bar Assn. (pres. 1995-96, gov. 1988-97), Kans. Bar Found. (bd. trustees 1996—), Johnson County Bar Assn. (pres. 1979), Kans. Sch. Attys. Assn. (pres. 1985), Overland Park C. of C. (bd. dirs. 1985-94, pres. 1988). Republican. Avocations: sports, hunting, reading. General civil litigation, Education and schools, Contracts commercial. Home: 9534 Lee Blvd Leawood KS 66206-2261 Office: Lathrop & Gage 9401 Indian Creek Pky Overland Park KS 66210-2005

**VRATIL, KATHRYN HOEFER,** federal judge; b. Manhattan, Kans., Apr. 21, 1949; d. John J. and Kathryn Ruth (Fryer) Hoefer; children: Alison K., John A., Ashley A. BA, U. Kans., 1971, JD, 1975; postgrad., Exeter U., 1971-72. Bar: Kans. 1975, Mo. 1978, U.S. Dist. Ct. Kans. 1975, U.S. Dist. Ct. (we. dist.) Mo. 1978, U.S. Dist. Ct. (ea. dist.) Mo. 1985, U.S. Ct. Appeals (8th cir.) 1978, U.S. Ct. Appeals (10th cir.) 1980, U.S. Ct. Appeals (11th dist.) 1983, U.S. Supreme Ct., 1995. Law clk. U.S. Dist. Ct., Kansas City, Kans., 1975-78; assoc. Lathrop Koontz & Norquist, Kansas City, Mo., 1978-83; ptnr. Lathrop & Norquist, Kansas City, 1984-92; judge City of Prairie Village, Kans., 1990-92; bd. dirs. Kans. Legal Bd. Svcs., 1991-92. Bd. editors Kans. Law Rev., 1974-75, Jour. Kans. Bar Assn., 1992—. Mem. Kansas City Tomorrow (XIV); bd. trustees, shepherd-deacon Village Presbyn. Ch.; nat. adv. bd. U. Kans. Ctr. for Environ. Edn. and Tng., 1993-95; bd. dirs. Kans. Legal Svcs., 1991-92. Fellow Kans. Bar Foun., Am. Bar Found.; mem. ABA (edtl. bd. Judges Jour. 1996—), Am. Judicature Soc., Nat. Assn. Judges, Fed. Judges Assn., Kans. Bar Assn., Mo. Bar Assn., Kansas City Met. Area Bar Assn., Wyandotte County Bar Assn., Johnson County Bar Assn., Assn. Women Judges, Lawyers Assn. Kansas City, Supreme Ct. Hist. Soc., Kans. State Hist. Soc., U. Kans. Law Soc. (bd. govs. 1978-81), Kans. U. Alumni Assn. (mem. Kansas City chpt. alumni bd. 1990-92, nat. bd. dirs. 1991—, bd. govs. Adams Alumni Ctr. 1992—, mem. chancellor's club 1993—, mem. Williams ednl. fund 1993—, mem. Jayhawks for higher edn. 1993-95), Homestead Country Club Prairie Village (pres. 1985-86), Sons and Daus of Kans. (life), Rotary, Jr. League Wyandotte and Johnson Counties, Order of Coif, Kans. Inn of Ct. (master 1993—), Overland Park Rotary, Univ. Club, Phi Kappa Phi. Republican. Presbyterian. Avocations: cycling, sailing. Office: 511 US Courthouse 500 State Ave Kansas City KS 66101-2403

**VREELAND, NEAL C.,** lawyer; b. Wellsville, N.Y., Nov. 25, 1947; s. Howard C. and Marilyn E. Vreeland; m. Gail Sewalt, Aug. 10, 1968; 1 child, Justin K. BS, U. Vt., 1969; JD, SUNY Buffalo, Amherst, 1976. Bar: N.Y. 1977, U.S. Dist. Ct. (we. dist.) N.Y. 1977, Vt. 1978, U.S. Dist. Ct. Vt. 1978. Assoc. Kavinoky Cook, Buffalo, N.Y., 1976-77; prin. Williams Williams & Vreeland, Poultney, Vt., 1978-84, Carroll George & Pratt, Rutland, Vt., 1984-97, Pratt Vreeland Kennelly & Zonay, Rutland, 1997—; adj. prof. Green Mountain Coll., Poultney, 1981-85. Town agt. Town of Poultney, 1988—, planning commr., 1988-91; planning commr. Rutland Regional Planning Commn., 1991. Capt. U.S. Army, 1969-73. Mem. ABA, Vt. Bar Assn., Vt. Trial Lawyer's Assn., Rutland County Bar Assn. General civil litigation, Construction, Contracts commercial. Office: Pratt Vreeland Kennelly & Zonay PO Box 280 64 N Main St Rutland VT 05702

**VRIESMAN, TODD L.,** lawyer; b. Milw., May 14, 1956; s. Dar. W. and Elaine V. (Yungner) V.; m. Michele Renee Irish, Aug. 21, 1982; children: Kyle L., Andrew T., Laura M. BA, Carthage Coll., Kenosha, Wis., 1978; JD, U. Denver, 1981. Bar: Colo. 1981, U.S. Dist. Ct. Colo. 1981, U.S. Ct. Appeals (9th and 10th cir.) 1981, U.S. Supreme Ct. 1992. Jud. law clk. to Hon. Alfred A. Arraj U.S. Dist. Ct., Denver, 1981-82; assoc. Kirkland & Ellis, Denver, 1982-89, ptnr., 1989-95; ptnr. Petrie, Bauer & Vriesman LLP, Denver, 1996—. Contbr. article to profl. jours. Mem. Colo. Bar Assn., Denver Bar Assn. Lutheran. General civil litigation. Office: Petrie Bauer Vriesman LLP 1775 Sherman St Ste 2500 Denver CO 80203-4319

**VUKELICH, JOHN EDWARD,** lawyer; b. Virginia, Minn., June 5, 1948; s. John Edward and Marguerite Smith V.; m. Lisa Carlson, Mar. 25, 1994; 1 child, Nicholas John. AB, Brown U., 1970; JD cum laude, William Mitchell Coll., 1970. Bar: Minn. 1975, U.S. Dist. Ct. Minn. 1975, U.S. Ct. Appeals (8th cir.) 1975. Assoc., ptnr. Dudley & Smith, St. Paul, 1975-85; atty. pvt. practice, Eden Prairie, Minn., 1986-94; assoc. Schwebel, Goetz & Sieben, Mpls., 1994—. With U.S. Army, 1970-76. Mem. Am. Trial Lawyers Assn., Minn. Trial Lawyers Assn. Avocations: woodworking, hunting, hockey. Insurance, Personal injury. Home: 4928 Ridge Rd Edina MN 55436-1012

**VUKELICH, MILO MICHAEL,** lawyer; b. Cody, Wyo., May 22, 1962; s. Michael Milo and Lila Kathleen (Sidwell) V.; m. Cheryl Ann Bragonier, May 27, 1989; 1 child, Alyssa Kathleen MacRae. BSc, U. Wyo., 1984, JD, 1987; M in Internat. Mgmt., Am. Grad Sch. Internat. Mgmt., 1995. Bar: Wyo. 1987, Mont. 1996, U.S. Dist. Ct. Wyo. 1987, U.S. Ct. Appeals (10th cir.) 1988, U.S. Supreme Ct. 1989. Assoc. Simpson and Kepler, Cody, Wyo., 1987-88; asst. attorney gen. State of Wyo., Cheyenne, 1988-90, sr. asst. attorney gen., 1990-94; tax counsel, special asst. attorney gen. Mont. Dept. Revenue, Helena, 1996-99, Unisys Corp., Blue Bell, Pa., 1999—. Avocations: music, reading, information technology, computer technology. Home: 133 Briarwood Ln Helena MT 59601-0135 Office: Unisys Corp Info Svcs Group Blue Bell PA 19422

**VULEVICH, EDWARD, JR.,** prosecutor; b. Nov. 5, 1933; s. Edward J. and Minnie R. V.; m. Diane Misko; children: Erin, Jan, John. AB, U. Ala., 1955, JD, 1957. Bar: Ala., U.S. Supreme Ct., U.S. Ct. Appeals (11th cir.) Ala., U.S. Ct. Appeals (5th cir.) Ala. Atty. U.S. Dept. Justice, Mobile, Ala., 1969—, chief civil divsn. Office: US Attys Office 169 Dauphin St Ste 200 Mobile AL 36602-3271

**VULLO, MARIA THERESE,** lawyer; b. Bklyn., Oct. 4, 1963; d. Peter R. and Mary L. (Simone) V. BA in Polit. Sci., Coll. Mt. St. Vincent, 1984; JD, N.Y.U., 1987. Bar: N.Y. 1988, U.S. Ct. Appeals (2nd cir.) 1990, U.S. Dist. Ct. (so. and ea. dists.) N.Y. 1990, U.S. Ct. Appeals (10th cir.) 1994, Tax Ct., 1995, U.S. Ct. Appeals (9th cir.) 1999. Law clk. to Hon. John A MacKenzie U.S. Dist. Ct. Va., Norfolk, 1987-88; assoc. Paul, Weiss, Rifkind, Wharton & Garrison, N.Y.C., 1988-96, ptnr., 1996—; spl. counsel Ho. Subcom. on Employment and Housing, Washington, 1989-90. Mem. ABA, N.Y. Bar Assn., Bar of City of N.Y., Order of the Barristers. Democrat. Avocations: travel, politics, public interest. General civil litigation. Office: Paul Weiss Rifkind Wharton & Garrison Rm 202 1285 Avenue Of The Americas New York NY 10019-6028

**VYSKOCIL, MARY KAY,** lawyer; b. N.Y.C., May 22, 1958; d. Gerard John and Kay Theresa (Murphy) V. BA summa cum laude, Dominican Coll., Blauvelt, N.Y., 1980; JD, St. John's U., Jamaica, N.Y., 1983. Bar: N.Y. 1984, U.S. Dist. Ct. (so., ea. and no. dists.) N.Y. 1984, U.S. Dist. Ct. Conn. 1988, U.S. Dist. Ct. (no. dist.) Calif. 1988, U.S. Ct. Appeals (2d cir.) 1984, U.S. Ct. Appeals (3d cir. 1985), U.S. Ct. Appeals (4th and 6th cirs.) 1993, U.S. Ct. Appeals (9th cir.) 1992, U.S. Ct. Appeals (11th cir.) 1996, U.S. Supreme Ct. 1989; cert. in secondary edn., N.Y. Assoc. Simpson Thacher & Bartlett, N.Y.C., 1983-90, ptnr., 1991—; co-chair consumer subcom., gender working group 2d cir. Task Force on Racial, Ethnic and Gender Fairness, N.Y.C., 1995-97. Co-author: Modern Reinsurance Law and Practice, 1996. Trustee St. Joseph's Sem., Yonkers, N.Y., 1986—, Dominican Coll., 1987—; mem. alumni bd. dirs. St. John's U. Sch. Law, 1996—, dean search comm., 1998—. Recipient 40 Under Forty award Nat. Law Jour., 1995. Mem. Assn. Bar City N.Y. (fed. cts. com. 1996—, chair ins. com. 1993-96), ABA (co-chair subcom. ins. coverage com. of litigation sect. 1997—). Roman Catholic. Avocations: swimming, reading, travel, horseback riding. General civil litigation, Insurance, Federal civil litigation. Office: Simpson Thacher & Bartlett 425 Lexington Ave Fl 15 New York NY 10017-3954

**WAAGE, MERVIN BERNARD,** lawyer; b. Spirit Lake, Iowa, May 12, 1944; s. Bernard and Pearl Peterson W.; children: Love Lee, Mark Warren. BA, Northwestern Coll., Roseville, Minn., 1966; MDiv, Southwestern Sem., 1969; JD, So. Methodist U., 1974. Bar: Tex. 1974, U.S. Dist Ct. (no. dist.) Tex. 1974, U.S. Dist. Ct. (ea. dist.) Tex. 1976, U.S. Supreme Ct. 1977, U.S. Tax Ct. 1978, U.S. Ct. Claims, 1978, U.S. Dist. Ct. (we. dist.) Tex. 1988, U.S. Ct. Appeals (5th cir.) 1989. Asst. dist. atty. Denton County (Tex.) Atty.'s Office, 1974-76; pvt. practice law Denton, Tex., 1977—; bankruptcy trustee, 1980-87. Mem. Tex. Bar Assn., Tex. State Bar (bankruptcy com.), Tex. Bd. Legal Specialization (cert. in consumer bankruptcy 1986, cert. in bus. bankruptcy 1988). Republican. Baptist. Avocations: singing, jogging, camping. Bankruptcy. Home: 107 Lexington Ln Denton TX 76205-5473 Office: Waage & Waage LLP 8350 S Stemmons St Denton TX 76205-2424

**WACHS, ALAN SCOTT,** lawyer; b. N.Y.C., Feb. 26, 1969; s. Murray B. Wachs and Marilyn K. Kronish; m. Fawn L. Payne, May 8, 1993; children: Rachel, Benjamin, Samuel. BA, U. North Fla., 1990; JD, Fla. State U., 1993. Bar: U.S. Dist. Ct. (mid. dist.) Fla. 1994, Fla. 1996, U.S. Dist. Ct. (no. dist.) Fla. 1997, U.S. Ct. Appeals (11th cir.) 1997, U.S. Dist. Ct. (so. dist.) Fla. Atty. Kirschner & Nain, Jacksonville, Fla., 1993-98, Holland & Knight, Jacksonville, 1998—. Mem. Jacksonville Bar Assn., Def. Rsch. Inst. General civil litigation, Landlord-tenant. Office: 50 N Laura St Ste 3900 Jacksonville FL 32202-3622

**WACHSMAN, HARVEY FREDERICK,** lawyer, neurosurgeon; b. Bklyn., June 13, 1936; s. Ben and Mollie (Kugel) W.; m. Kathryn M. D'Agostino, Jan. 31, 1976; children: Dara Nicole, David Winston, Jacqueline Victoria, Lauren Elizabeth, Derek Charles, Ashley Max, Marea Lane, Melissa Roseanne. B.A., Tulane U., 1958; M.D., Chgo. Med. Sch., 1962; J.D., Bklyn. Law Sch., 1976. Bar: Conn. 1976, N.Y. 1977, Fla. 1977, D.C. 1978, U.S. Supreme Ct. 1980, Pa. 1984, Md. 1986, Tex. 1987. Diplomate Nat. Bd. Med. Examiners; cert. Am. Bd. Legal Medicine, Am. Bd. Profl. Liability Attys. (pres.); cert. civil trial advocate Nat. Bd. Trial Advocacy (trustee). Intern surgery Kings County Hosp. Ctr., Bklyn., 1962-63; resident in surgery Kingsbrook Med. Ctr., Bklyn., 1964-65; resident in neurol. surgery Emory U. Hosp., Atlanta, 1965-69; practice medicine specializing in neurosurgery Bridgeport, Conn., 1972-74; ptnr. Pegalis & Wachsman, Great Neck, N.Y., 1977—; adj. prof. neurosurgery SUNY, Stony Brook; adj. prof. law St. John's U. Sch. Law; bd. trustees SUNY, chmn. health sci. and hosp. com.; pres., CEO Found. Excellence & Ethics in Medicine. Author: American Law of Medical Malpractice, Vol. I, 1980, 2d edit., 1992, American Law of Medical Malpractice, Vol. II, 1981, 2d edit., 1993, American Law of Medical Malpractice, Vol. III, 1982, 2d edit., 1994, Cumulative Supplement to American Law of Medical Malpractice, 1981, 82, 83, 84, 85, American Law of Medical Malpractice, 2d edit., Vols. I, II and II, Lethal Medicine, 1993; mem. editl. bd. Legal Aspects of Med. Practice, 1978-82. Trustee SUNY, chmn. health sci. and hosp. com. Fellow Am. Coll. Legal Medicine (mem. bd. govs. 1986, chmn. edn. com. 1983—, chmn. 1985 nat. meeting, New Orleans, chmn. 1988 nat. meeting, Va., bd. dirs. ACLM Found.), Am. Acad. Forensic Scis., Royal Soc. Medicine, Royal Soc. Arts (London), Royal Soc. Medicine (London), Roscoe Pound Found. of Assn. Trial Lawyers Am.; mem. ABA, Am. Soc. Law and Medicine, Congress Neurol. Surgeons, Assn. Trial Lawyers Am., Soc. Med. Jurisprudence (trustee), N.Y. Bar Assn., Conn. Bar Assn., Fla. Bar Assn., D.C. Bar Assn., N.Y. Acad. Scis., Assn. Trial Lawyers Am. (bd. govs.), N.Y. Trial Lawyers Assn., Conn. Trial

Lawyers Assn., Fla. Acad. Trial Lawyers, Md. Trial Lawyers Assn., Tex. Trial Lawyers Assn., Pa. Trial Lawyers Assn., Nat. Bar Assn. (mem. com. on South Africa), Nassau County Bar Assn., Fairfield County Med. Soc., Nassau-Suffolk Trial Lawyers Assn. Club: Cosmos (Washington). Office: 175 E Shore Rd Great Neck NY 11023-2430 *In my pursuit of knowledge and excellence in the fields of neurosurgery and the law, I have found that arming oneself with the power of knowledge is truly the key to helping others. Let one's goal in life be to help others, and he shall always find fulfillment, challenge and hope.*

**WACHSMUTH, ROBERT WILLIAM,** lawyer; b. Crowell, Tex., Jan. 20, 1942; s. Frederick W. and Dorothy (McKown) W.; children: Wendi Leigh, Ashley Beth, Matthew McKown. BA, U. Tex., 1965, JD, 1966, grad. bus. sch., 1976. Bar: Tex. 1966, U.S. Dist. Ct. (we. dist.) Tex. 1970, U.S. Ct. Appeals (5th cir., 11 cir.) 1975, U.S. Supreme Ct. 1979, U.S. Dist. Ct. (so. dist.) Tex. 1987. Assoc. Foster, Lewis, Langley, Gardner and Banack, San Antonio, 1969-73; of counsel H.B. Zachry Co., San Antonio, 1973-79; ptnr. Johnson, Johnston, Bowlin, Wachsmuth and Vives, San Antonio, 1973-79, Kelfer, Coatney & Wachsmuth, San Antonio, 1979-81, Kelfer, Coatney, Wachsmuth & Saunders, San Antonio, 1981-83, Brock & Kelfer, P.C., San Antonio, 1983-88, Coatney & Wachsmuth, P.C., San Antonio, 1989-92, Gendry, Sprague & Wachsmuth, P.C., San Antonio, 1992-94, The Kleberg Law Firm, P.C., San Antonio, 1994—; panel arbitrators Fed. Ct. Annexed Program, San Antonio, 1987—, Bexar County Arbitration Program, San Antonio, 1988; instr. San Antonio Jr. Coll., 1972-74; bd. cert./civil trial law Tex. Bd. Legal Specialization, 1981—; mem. faculty constrn. mgmt. and contrn. exec. program Tex. A&M U. Contbr. articles to profl. jours. Bd. dirs. Halfway House San Antonio. Capt., mil. judge USMCR, 1966-69, Vietnam. Mem. ABA, Tex. State Bar Assn. (bd. dirs., treas., sec., vice chmn. constrn. law sect. 1989-92, chmn. 1992-93), Am. Arbitration Assn. (panel of arbitrators, panel of mediators), San Antonio Bar Assn. (chmn. alternative dispute resolution com.), Fed. Bar Assn., Am. Subcontractors Assn. (gen. counsel San Antonio chpt. 1984-92), Assn. Gen. Contractors (gen. counsel San Antonio chpt. 1995—), Plaza Club (social com.), Masons, Scottish Rite, Shriners, Optimists (pres. 1977-78). Republican. Episcopalian. Avocations: hunting, skiing, spectator sports. Antitrust, General civil litigation, Construction. Office: The Kleberg Law Firm PC 112 E Pecan St Ste 2200 San Antonio TX 78205-1521

**WACTOR, JON KARL,** lawyer; b. Agana, Guam, Apr. 16, 1957; s. Edwin LeRoy and Mary Louise (Barrett) W.; m. Joan Bradley June 17, 1989; children: Jon Nicholas, Alexandra. BA, U. Ariz., 1979, JD, 1982. Bar: Ariz., Calif.; Ariz. Supreme Ct. 1982, U.S. Dist. Ct., U.S. Ct. Appeals (9th cir.), U.S. Supreme Ct. 1994. Asst. Ariz. Atty. Gen., Phoenix, 1982-85; senior enforcement counsel EPA, San Francisco, 1985-89; assoc. Gray, Cary, Ames & Frye, San Diego, 1989-91; ptnr. Adams, Duque & Hazeltine, San Diego, 1991-94; mgn. ptnr., San Francisco office Luce, Forward, Hamilton & Scripps, 1994, 97; ptnr. Luce, Forward, Hamilton & Scripps LLP, San Francisco, 1994—. Editor Law Rev. U. Ariz., 1980-81; contbr. to profl. jours. Recipient Bronze medal EPA, San Francisco, 1987. Mem. Calif. Bar Assn., San Francisco Bar Assn. (environ. sect.), Maricopa County Bar Assn. (editor jour. 1984-85, Mem. of Yr. award 1985). Office: Luce Forward Hamilton & Scripps LLP 121 Spear St Ste 200 San Francisco CA 94105-1582

**WADDELL, JOHN EMORY,** lawyer; b. Dothan, Ala., Sept. 1, 1948; s. J.L. and Lillie Mae Waddell; m. Melanie Elizabeth Edwards, May 5, 1974; children: Kelli Elizabeth, Haley Drue, Spencer Pace. Student, George C. Wallace Community Coll.; BS in Mktg. and Bus. Adminstrn., Troy State U., 1970; JD, Samford U., 1973. Bar: Fla. 1973, U.S. Dist. Ct. (so. dist.) Fla. 1973, U.S. Tax Ct. 1973, Ala. 1974, Ga. 1974, U.S. Dist. Ct. (no. dist.) Fla. 1975, U.S. Dist. Ct. (mid. dist.) Ala. 1975. Sole practice Dothan, 1975—; pub. defender City of Dothan, 1975-80, mcpl. judge, 1980-86. Named one of Outstanding Young Men Am., 1985. Mem. Ala. Bar Assn., Fla. Bar Assn., Ga. Bar Assn., Assn. Trial Lawyers Am., Ala. Trial Lawyers Assn. (bd. govs. 1983-86). Methodist. Avocations: golf, boating. Personal injury, Probate, Family and matrimonial. Home: 111 N Englewood Dr Dothan AL 36303-3007 Office: 214 W Troy St # 7024 Dothan AL 36303-4455

**WADDELL, PHILLIP DEAN,** lawyer; b. Covington, Ky., Nov. 14, 1948; s. Ewell Edward and Sarah Isobel (Dean) W.; m. Jill Annette Tolson, Aug. 23, 1975; children: Nathan Ewell, James Seth. BA, Centre Coll. Ky., 1971; JD, No. Ky. U., 1982. Bar: Ky. 1982, Ohio 1983, Tenn. 1986. V.p., mgr. escrow Eagle Savings Assn., Cin., 1973-83; v.p. Union Planters Nat. Bank, Memphis, 1983-84; sr. v.p., liason First Nat. Bank & Trust Co., Oklahoma City, 1984-86; sr. v.p., sec., gen. counsel First Mortgage Strategies Group, Inc., Memphis, 1986-92; atty. pvt. practice, Memphis, 1992—. Mem. ABA, Am. Judicature Soc., Ky. Bar Assn., Tenn. Bar Assn. Republican. Presbyterian. Lodge: Kiwanis. General corporate, Real property, Contracts commercial. Home: 2095 Allenby Rd Memphis TN 38139-4343 Office: 1789 Kirby Pkwy Ste 2 Memphis TN 38138-3657

**WADE, EDWIN LEE,** writer, lawyer; b. Yonkers, N.Y., Jan. 26, 1932; s. James and Helen Pierce (Kinne) W.; m. Nancy Lou Sells, Mar. 23, 1957; children: James Lee, Jeffrey K. BS, Columbia U., 1954; MA, U. Chgo., 1956; JD, Georgetown U., 1965. Bar: Ill. 1965. Fgn. svc. officer U.S. Dept. State, 1956-57; mktg. analyst Chrysler Internat., S.A., Switzerland, 1957-61; intelligence officer CIA, 1961-63; industry analyst U.S. Internat. Trade Commn., 1963-65; gen. atty. Universal Oil Products Co., Des Plaines, Ill., 1965-72; atty. Amsted Industries, Inc., Chgo., 1972-73; chief counsel dept. gen. svcs. State of Ill., Springfield, 1973-75; sr. atty. U.S. Gypsum Co., Chgo., 1975-84; gen. atty. USG Corp., 1985, corp. counsel, 1986, asst. gen. counsel, 1987, corp. sec., 1987-90, corp. sec., asst. gen. counsel, 1990-93; prin. Edwin L. Wade, 1993-95; instr. Roosevelt U., Chgo., 1995-96. Fellow Chgo. Bar Assn. (life); mem. ABA, Ill. Bar Assn., Union League Club Chgo., Am. Philatelic Soc., Royal Philatelic Soc. Can., Toastmasters Internat. General corporate, Public international, Constitutional. Home: 434 Mary Ln Crystal Lake IL 60014-7257 Office: Let's Talk Sense Publishing Co PO Box 6716 Chicago IL 60680-6716

**WADE, JEFFREY LEE,** lawyer; b. Louisville, Oct. 5, 1946; s. Louis Harold and Lelia May (Powell) W.; m. Linda Lee Ochs, May 17, 1969; children: Jody Martin, Betsy Ellen, Anna Lee. BA in Arts and Scis., U. Ky., 1968; MSW, Fla. State U., 1973; JD, U. Louisville, 1982. Bar: Ky. 1982, U.S. Dist. Ct. (we. dist.) Ky. 1985, U.S. Dist. Ct. (ea. dist.) Ky. 1991, U.S. Tax Ct. 1985, U.S. Ct. Appeals (6th cir.) 1985, U.S. Supreme Ct. 1992. Social worker Ky. Dept. Child Welfare, Lexington, 1969-71; cons. Fla. Drug Abuse Program, Tallahassee, 1973; mgmt. cons. Resource Planning Corp., Washington, 1973-75; social worker Ky. Cabinet for Human Resources, Louisville, 1975-79; asst. commonwealth atty. Commonwealth Atty., 46th Jud. Dist., Brandenburg, Ky., 1982-86; asst. county atty. Meade County Atty., Brandenburg, Ky., 1985-88; atty., assoc. Stone & Darnall, Attys.-at-Law, Brandenburg, Ky., 1982-83, Wade & Darnall, Attys.-at-Law, Brandenburg, Ky., 1983-92; pvt. practice Jeffrey L. Wade, Atty.-at-Law, Brandenburg, Ky., 1992—; master commr. Meade Cir. Ct., 1993-97; bd. dirs. Communicare, Inc., Elizabethtown, Ky., chmn., 1996-97. Mem. staff Jour. Family Law, 1980-82; Brandeis brief editor (newspaper) The Louisville Law Examiner, 1980-82. Trustee, tchr. Brandenburg United Meth. Ch., 1985-95; coach Meade County Soccer, Brandenburg, 1987-89, Meade County Little League, Brandenburg, 1982-86; pres. Brandenburg PTO, 1984-86. Recipient fellowship NIMH, 1971, scholarship U. Ky. Med. Sch., 1968, Epidemiol. Rsch. Tng. fellowship U. Ky. Med. Sch., 1968, Trustee scholarship U. Ky., 1964. Mem. Assn. Trial Lawyers Am., Meade County Bar Assn. (pres. 1982-90), Louisville Bar Assn., Ky. Acad. Trial Attys., Nat. Orgn. Social Security Clairmonts Reps. Democrat. Avocations: running, tennis, guitar, writing poetry. Personal injury, Family and matrimonial, Criminal. Home: 1108 Ambridge Dr Louisville KY 40207-2471 Office: 623 W Main St Ste 100 Louisville KY 40202-2978

**WADLEY, W. THOMAS,** lawyer; b. Tampa, Fla., Aug. 3, 1957; s. William Morrill Wadley and Allison Ray; m. Catherine Norton, Jan. 2, 1993 (div. May 1997). BA, Auburn U., 1979; JD, Stetson U., 1981. Bar: Fla. 1982, U.S. Dist. Ct. (mid. dist.) Fla. 1982, U.S. Ct. Appeals (11th cir.) 1988; bd. cert. criminal trial lawyer Fla. Bar, 1994—; bd. cert. criminal trial adv. Nat. Bd. Trial Advocacy, 1998—. Lawyer Myron J. Mensh P.A., St. Petersburg, Fla., 1982-84, Yanchuck, Thompson, Young & Berman, St. Petersburg, 1984-90, Rahdert & Anderson, St. Petersburg, 1990-91; pvt. practice law St. Petersburg, 1991-95, Yanchuck, Berman & Kavoukus, St. Petersburg, 1995—; pres. Pinellas County Criminal Def. Lawyers Assn., 1996. Mem. ATLA, Nat. Assn. Criminal Def. Lawyers, Fla. Assn. Criminal Def. Lawyers. Avocation: private pilot. Criminal, Personal injury. Home: Apt 511 13795 Feather Sound Cir E Clearwater FL 33762-2244 Office: Yanchuck Berman & Kavoukus 800 2nd Ave S Ste 380 Saint Petersburg FL 33701-4026

**WAECHTER, ARTHUR JOSEPH, JR.,** lawyer; b. New Orleans, Nov. 20, 1913; s. Arthur Joseph and Elinor (Reckner) W.; m. Peggy Weaver, Feb. 20, 1939; children: Susan Porter Waechter McClellan, Sally Ann Waechter McGehee, Robert. AB, Tulane U., 1934, LLB, 1936. Bar: La. 1936. Since practiced in New Orleans; ptnr. Jones, Walker, Waechter, Poitevent, Carrere & Denegre, 1942—; prof. law Sch. Law Tulane U., 1947-68, prof. emeritus, 1968—; bd. dirs. Canal Barge Co., Inc. Bd. visitors Tulane U., 1959-64; bd. advisers to editors Tulane Law Rev. Assn., 1960—; bd. adminstrs. Tulane Ednl. Fund, 1968-83, emeritus bd. adminstrs., 1983—. Served to lt. (j.g.) USNR, 1943-46. Mem. ABA, La. Bar Assn. (gov. 1968-70), New Orleans Bar Assn. (pres. 1961-62), Internat. Assn. Def. Counsel, Tulane U. Alumni Assn. (pres. 1962-63), Maritime Law Assn. U.S., Am. Law Inst., Am. Judicature Soc., Am. Coll. Real Estate Lawyers (gov. 1983-86), Order of Coif, Pickwick Club, Boston Club, Stratford Club, La. Club, So. Yacht Club, The Plimsol (New Orleans), Phi Kappa Sigma, Phi Delta Phi. General corporate, Contracts commercial, Real property. Home: 100 Christwood Blvd Covington LA 70433-4606 Office: Jones Walker Waechter Poitevent Carrere & Denegre 201 Saint Charles Ave Ste 5200 New Orleans LA 70170-5100

**WAEGER, ROBERT WRIGHT,** insurance executive, lawyer; b. N.Y.C., Aug. 30, 1946; s. Robert Werner and ELizabeth (Nostrand) W.; m. Cicily Altenburg, Aug. 23, 1969 (div.); children: Cindy, Patrice, Holly, Bobby, Danny; m. Marie Clark, June 19, 1990. BS in Acctg., St. Francis Coll., 1968; JD, Duquesne U., 1976. House counsel, regional claims atty. Nationwide Ins. Co., Columbus, Ohio, 1971-81; ptnr. Skarlatos, Zonarich and Waeger, Pa., 1981-85; v.p. claims Pa. Hosp. Ins. Co., Mechanicsburg, 1985—; adj. prof. Millersville (Pa.) U., 1988—. Bd. dirs. Allendale Civic Assn., Camp Hill, Pa., 1984-85, St. Francis Alumni Bd., Loretto, Pa., 1975—; chmn. United Way, Mechanicsburg, 1988—. Mem. Hosp. Ins. Forum (chmn. claims com. 1989—), Pa. Trial Lawyers Assn., Pa. Def. Inst., Dauphin County Bar Assn., Pa. Bar Assn., Aircraft Owners and Pilots Assn. (Eagle Pilot award 1984). Avocation: flying. Home: PO Box 234 Harrisburg PA 17108-0234 Office: PHICO Ins Co PO Box 85 Mechanicsburg PA 17055-0085

**WAGGONER, JAMES CLYDE,** lawyer; b. Nashville, May 7, 1946; s. Charles Franklin and Alpha (Noah) W.; m. Diane Dusenbery, Aug. 17, 1968; children: Benjamin, Elizabeth. BA, Reed Coll., 1968; JD, U. Oreg., 1974. Bar: Oreg. 1974, U.S. Dist. Ct. Oreg. 1975, U.S. Ct. Appeals (9th cir.) 1980, U.S. Tax Ct. 1979, U.S. Supreme Ct. 1979. Clerk to presiding justice Oreg. Supreme Ct., Salem, 1974-75; assoc. Martin, Bischoff & Templeton, Portland, Oreg., 1975-78, ptnr., 1978-82; ptnr. Waggoner, Farleigh, Wada, Georgeff & Witt, Portland, 1982-89, Davis Wright Tremaine, Portland, 1990—. Contbr. articles to profl. jours. Fulbright scholar U. London, 1968-69. Mem. ABA, Oreg. Bar Assn., Multnomah Bar Assn., Reed Coll. Alumni Assn. (v.p. 1988, pres. 1989, bd. mgmt.) Alzheimers Assn. of Columbia-Willamette (v.p. 1992, pres. 1993), Order Coif, Phi Beta Kappa. Democrat. Avocations: wood turning, calligraphy. Real property, Bankruptcy, Consumer commercial. Office: Davis Wright Tremaine 1300 SW 5th Ave Ste 2300 Portland OR 97201-5630

**WAGNER, ANNICE MCBRYDE,** federal judge. BA, Wayne State U., law degree. With Houston and Gardner; gen. counsel Nat. Capital Housing Authority; people's counsel D.C.; assoc. judge Superior Court D.C., 1977-90; assoc. judge D.C. Ct. Appeals, 1990—, now chief judge; mem. teaching team, trial advocacy workshop Harvard U. Office: Dist of Columbia Court of Appeals 500 Indiana Ave NW Ste 6000 Washington DC 20001-2131*

**WAGNER, ARTHUR WARD, JR.,** lawyer; b. Birmingham, Ala., Aug. 13, 1930; s. Arthur Ward and Lucille (Lockheart) W.; m. Ruth Shingler, May 11, 1957; children: Celia Wagner Minter, Julia Wagner Dolce, Helen Wagner McAfee. BSBA, U. Fla., 1954, JD, 1957. Bar: Fla. 1957, U.S. Dist. Ct. (so. dist.) Fla. 1957, U.S. Dist. Ct. (mid. dist.) Fla. 1975. Ptnr. Wagner, Johnson, & McAfee, P.A., West Palm Beach, Fla., 1959—; lectr. in field. Author: Art of Advocacy: Jury Selection, 1981; co-author: Anatomy of Personal Injury Lawsuit I & II, 1968 and 1981. Mem. 15th Jud. Nominating Com., Palm Beach City, 1979-82, 4th Dist. Nominating Commn., Palm Beach City, 1982-86; mem. pres.'s coun. U. Fla.; vestry, chancellor Holy Trinity Parish; bd. dirs. U. Fla. Found., 1996-2000. Fellow Internat. Acad. Trial Lawyers, Am. Coll. Trial Lawyers, Internat. Soc. Barristers, Am. Bd. Trial Advs.; mem. Assn. Trial Lawyers Am. (pres. 1975-76, hon. life trustee Roscoe Pound Found.), So. Trial Lawyers Assn. (pres. 1991), U. Fla. Law Coll. Alumni (mem. bd. govs.). Democrat. Episcopalian. Personal injury, General civil litigation, Administrative and regulatory. Office: Wagner Johnson & McAfee PA 1818 S Australian Ave West Palm Beach FL 33409-6452

**WAGNER, BARBARA,** lawyer; b. Amherst, Mass., Aug. 10, 1951; d. Robert Wanner and Sally (Marsh) W.; m. William C. Partin, Sept. 10, 1977; children: Sally Marsh Wagner Partin, William Robert Wagner Partin. BA, Yale U., 1973; MSBA, Boston U., 1977; JD, Columbia U., 1981. Bar: N.Y. 1982, Ohio 1988. Tchg. asst. ESL Albert-Einstein-Oberschule and Walter Gropius Gesamtschule, Berlin, Germany, 1974-76; translator German-English Brigade Map Supply Ctr. U.S. Army, Berlin, 1976-77; lectr. English phonology Tchr.'s Coll., Berlin, 1976-77; lectr. bus. fin. U. Md., Rota, Spain, 1978; assoc. Shearman & Sterling, N.Y.C., 1981-83, Haythe & Curley, N.Y.C., 1983-85, Skadden, Arps, Slate, Meagher & Flom, N.Y.C., 1985-87, Smith & Schracke, Dayton, Ohio, 1987-88, Frost & Jacobs, Cin., 1988-91; sr. counsel Chiquita Brands Internat., Inc., Cin., 1991-92, asst. gen. counsel, 1992-98, assoc. gen. counsel, 1998—; adj. prof. Coll. Law U. Cin.; spkr. in field. Mem. ABA, Ohio Bar Assn., Cin. Bar Assn., Cin. Yale Club (dir. alumni schs. com. 1990—, pres. 1998-99). Avocations: gardening, photography. General corporate, Securities, Finance. Office: Chiquita Brands International Inc 250 E 5th St Cincinnati OH 45202-5190

**WAGNER, BRENDA CAROL,** lawyer; b. Fayetteville, N.C., Apr. 18, 1951; d. David H. and Mollie C. W. BS, N.C. Ctrl. U., 1973, JD, 1976. Bar: N.C. 1977, D.C. 1979, Md. 1987, U.S. Dist. Ct. (mid. dist.) N.C. 1977, U.S. Dist. Ct. D.C. 1987, U.S. Dist. Ct. Md. 1991, U.S. Ct. Appeals (4th cir.) 1983. Hearing officer N.C. ABC Bd., Raleigh, 1978-79; rsch. dir. N.C. Dept. Adminstrn., Raleigh, 1979-80; asst. pub. defender N.C. Pub. Defender, 27A Jud. Dist., Gastonia, 1980-81; asst. corp. counsel D.C. Govt., Washington, 1986-87; hearing officer D.C. Dept. Pub. Housing, Washington, 1991-97. Commr. N.C. Property Tax Study Commn., Raleigh, 1981-82; mem. League Women Voters, Washington, 1996—; life mem. Urban League, Washington, 1996—; bd. dirs. Legal Svcs. Bd., Raleigh, 1978-80, United Way, Gastonia, 1980-81, Planning Bd., Rocky Mount, N.C., 1983-86. Mem. ABA, ATLA, Nat. Bar Assn., Women's Bar Assn. D.C. Office: Wagner & Assocs 733 15th St NW Ste 908 Washington DC 20005-2112

**WAGNER, BRIAN J.,** lawyer; b. Detroit, Apr. 17, 1967; s. John R. and Carolyn F. Wagner. BA, U. Mich., 1990; JD, Detroit Coll. of Law, 1994. Law clk. Wayne County Cir. Ct., Detroit, 1994-97; pvt. practice Grosse Pointe, Mich., 1997-98; atty. Petersmarck Callahan Bauer & Barbour P.C., Detroit, 1998—. Mem. Detroit Bar Assn., Mich. Bar Assn. General civil litigation, Product liability, Criminal. Office: Petersmarck Callahan Bauer & Barbour PC One Kennedy Square Ste 1300 Detroit MI 48226

**WAGNER, CURTIS LEE, JR.,** judge; b. Kingsport, Tenn., Nov. 8, 1928; m. Jeanne E. Allen (dec.); children: Curtis L. III, Rex A. Student Tenn. Poly. Inst., 1947-49; LLB, U. Tenn., 1951. Bar: Tenn. 1952. Assoc. Kramer, Dye, McNabb and Greenwood, Knoxville, Tenn., 1951-54; atty.-adv. gen. crimes and fraud sect. Criminal Div., Dept. Justice, Washington, 1954-56, trial atty. Dept. Justice, 1954-60, assigned to Ct. of Claims sect. Civil Div., 1956-60; spl. asst. to JAG for communications, transp. and utilities, Office JAG, Dept. Army, Washington, 1960-64, chief Regulatory Law Div., 1964-74, mem. civilian lawyer career com., 1960-74, chmn. JAG incentive awards com. 1960-74, mem. Army Staff Awards Bd., 1964-74, mem. Army Environ. Policy Council, 1972-74. Adminstrv. law judge FERC, Washington, 1974-79, chief adminstrv. law judge, 1979—. Dist. commr. Nat. Capital Area council Boy Scouts Am., 1967-69; mem. Bd. Govts. Watergate of Alexandria Condo, 1996—; commr. Alexandria Redevel. and Pub. Housing Commn., 1996—. Decorated Meritorious Civilian Service award, Exceptional Civilian Service award; recipient citation for outstanding performance Dept. Army, 1961-74; Scouter's Tng. award Boy Scouts Am., 1965, Scoutmaster's Key, 1966, Commr.'s Key, 1968, Commr.'s Arrowhead Honor, 1966, Silver Beaver award, 1969. Mem. Order of Arrow, Soc. Profls. in Dispute Resolution. Methodist. Clubs: Annapolis Yacht (parliamentarian). Office: Fed Energy Regulatory Commn 888 1st St NE Washington DC 20426-0002

**WAGNER, DAVID JAMES,** lawyer; b. Cleve., Feb. 7, 1946; m. Martha Wilson, June 22, 1979; 1 child, Diana Jane. BS, USAF Acad., 1969; JD, Georgetown U., 1973. Bar: Colo. 1973, U.S. Supreme Ct. 1975, U.S. Dist. Ct. of Colo. 1973, U.S. Tax Ct. 1974. Asst. assoc. gen. counsel Presdl. Clemency Bd., Washington, 1974-75; sec., gen. counsel Cablecomm-Gen. Inc., Denver, 1975-77; adj. prof. law Metro. State Coll., Denver, 1975-80; atty., mng. prin. Wagner & Waller, P.C., Denver, 1977-84; chmn. bd. GILA Comm., Inc., Denver, 1987; pvt. practice David Wagner & Assocs., P.C., Englewood, Colo., 1984—. Editor Am. Criminal Law Rev., Georgetown U. Law Sch., 1972-73. Trustee Kent Denver Sch., Cherry Hills Village, Colo., 1990-96, treas., 1992, pres., 1992-96; treas., dir. Denver Chamber Orch., 1979-81; dir. Leadership Denver Assn., 1978-80; trustee Colo. Sch. Mines, 1999. Capt. USAF, 1973-75. Republican. Episcopalian. Securities. Office: David Wagner & Assocs PC Penthouse 8400 E Prentice Ave Ph Englewood CO 80111-2927

**WAGNER, ERIC ROLAND,** lawyer; b. Napa, Calif., July 10, 1964; s. Jim Roland and Louise W.; m. Lori Lynn Welsh, July 29, 1990; children: Ryan, Katherine. BA, U. Calif., Berkeley, 1986; JD, Pepperdine U., 1989. Bar: Calif. 1989, D.C. 1998, U.S. Ct. Appeals (9th and 6th cirs.) 1998, U.S. Supreme Ct. 1998. Atty. Brayton, Harley & Curtis, Novato, Calif., 1993-96; atty. Scranton Law Firm, Concord, Calif., 1996—; law clk. Calif. Ct. Appeals (2d dist.), L.A., 1988. Bd. dirs. Boys & Girls Club, Napa, Calif., 1990-93. Mem. Washington Trial Lawyers Assn., Calif. Bar Assn., Washington Bar Assn., Consumer Attys. Calif. State civil litigation, General civil litigation, Personal injury. Office: PO Box 121 Rodeo CA 94572-0121

**WAGNER, GARY TED,** lawyer; b. N.Y.C., Apr. 2, 1960; s. Adolph and Ruth (Heiferman) W. BA, Queens Coll., N.Y., 1982; JD, Temple U., Phila., 1985. Bar: Pa. 1985, N.J. 1985, N.Y. 1988. Assoc. Blank Rome Comisky & McCauley, Phila., 1985-87, Parker Chapin Flattau & Klimpl, N.Y.C., 1987-88; assoc. gen. counsel Robert Martin Co., Elmsford, N.Y., 1989—. Mem. Midnight Run, Dobbs Ferry, N.Y., 1994—, UJA Fedn., Westchester County, 1990—, Bronx H.S. Sci. Alumni Assn., 1985—. Mem. Westchester-Fairfield County Corp. Counsel Assn., The Corporate Bar. Avocations: tennis, hiking. Real property. Office: Robert Martin Co 100 Clearbrook Rd Ste 1 Elmsford NY 10523-1108

**WAGNER, JAMES PEYTON,** lawyer; b. McKinney, Tex., July 22, 1939; s. Otto James and Jane Peyton (Adams) W.; m. Patricia Anne Squires, June 16, 1962; children: Jarrod Shannon, Anne Paige, Leslie Lauren, James Russell. BA, Tex. Tech. U., Lubbock, 1961; LLB, So. Meth. U., 1964. Bar: Tex. 1964, U.S. Dist. Ct. (no. dist.) Tex. 1965, U.S. Ct. Appeals (3rd and 5th cirs.) 1996, U.S. Supreme Ct. 1996. Atty. United American Ins. Co., Dallas, 1969-70, Employer's Ins. of Wausau, Dallas, 1970-73, Crumley Murphy and Shrull, Ft. Worth, 1973-77, Fillmore & Camp, Ft. Worth, 1977-78, Penner, Jones, Keith & Wagner, Ft. Worth, 1978-80, The Wagner Law Firm, Ft. Worth, Dallas, 1964-69, 80-85;, 1997—; prin. Keith and Wagner, P.C., Ft. Worth, 1985-89; assoc. Brockermeyer & Assocs., Ft. Worth, 1989-90; ptnr. Fielding, Barrett & Taylor, Ft. Worth, 1990-97. Author, contbr. course book: State Bar of Texas Personal Injury and Workers Compensation Practice Skills, 1987, 89. Mem. ATLA, State Bar Tex., Tarrant County Bar Assn., Coll. of State Bar Tex., Brain Injury Assn. Baha'i World Faith. Avocations: oenology, music. Insurance, Personal injury, Product liability. Home: 4240 Sudith Ln Midlothian TX 76065-6332 Office: The Wagner Law Firm 2702 One Bank Tower 500 Throckmorton St Fort Worth TX 76102-3708

**WAGNER, JOHN LEO,** lawyer, former magistrate judge; b. Ithaca, N.Y., Mar. 12, 1954; s. Paul Francis and Doris Elizabeth (Hoffschneider) W.; m. Marilyn Modin, June 18, 1987. Student, U. Nebr., 1973-74; BA, U. Okla., 1976, JD, 1979. Bar: Okla. 1980, U.S. Dist. Ct. (we. dist.) Okla. 1980, U.S. Dist. Ct. (no. and ea. dists.) Okla. 1981, U.S. Ct. Appeals (10th cir.) 1982. Assoc. Franklin, Harmon & Satterfield Inc., Oklahoma City, 1980-82; ptnr. Franklin, Harmon & Satterfield, Inc., Oklahoma City, 1982; assoc. Kornfeld, Franklin & Phillips, Oklahoma City, 1982-85, ptnr., 1985; magistrate judge U.S. Dist. Ct. No. Dist. Okla., Tulsa, 1985-97; dir. Irell & Manella LLP Alt. Dispute Resolution Ctr., Newport Beach, Calif., 1997—. Pres. U. Okla. Coll. Law Assn., 1991-92. Mem. ABA, Internat. Acad. Mediators, Fed. Magistrate Judge's Assn. (dir. 10th cir. 1987-89), 10th Cir. Edn. Com., Okla. Bar Assn., Council Oak Am. Inn of Cts. (pres. 1992-93), Jud. Conf. U.S. (com. ct. adminstrn. and case mgmt. 1992-97), CPR-Georgetown Commn. Ethics and Standards in ADR. Republican. Alternative dispute resolution, Federal civil litigation, Environmental. Office: Irell & Manella LLP Alt Dispute Resolution Ctr 840 Newport Center Dr Ste 450 Newport Beach CA 92660-6321

**WAGNER, JOSEPH HAGEL,** lawyer; b. Balt., June 4, 1947; s. Herman B. and Mary Louise (Hagel) W.; m. Hilary Reuss Becton, June 10, 1972; children: James Becton, Christopher Lowther. BA, Villanova U., 1969; JD, Syracuse U., 1972. Editor Bucks County Law Reporter, 1983-85, asst. editor, 85-86. Chmn. ch. com. ARC Bloodmobile, 1984-87; v.p. Bucks County Estate Planning Council, 1984-87, pres., 1987-88; former pres., v.p. New Britain Borough Civic Assn. Served to capt. USAR, 1972-81. Mem. Bucks County Bar Assn. (treas. 1983-85, bd. dirs. 1981-83). Republican. Roman Catholic. Probate, Estate planning, Real property. Home: 25 Linda Ln Warrington PA 18976-1044 Office: 332 N Main St Doylestown PA 18901-3715

**WAGNER, LYNN EDWARD,** lawyer; b. Mt. Holly, N.J., Feb. 10, 1941; s. Edward John and Alma Elizabeth (Mason) W.; m. Maureen Elizabeth Bach, May 25, 1973; children: Daniel Preston, Matthew Evan. BS, Drexel U., 1965; JD, Duke U., 1968. Bar: Mass. 1968, U.S. Dist. Ct. Mass. 1968, Fla. 1972, U.S. Dist. Ct. (mid. dist.) Fla. 1972, U.S. Ct. Appeals (5th cir.) 1972, U.S. Supreme Ct. 1972, Pa. 1975, U.S. Dist. Ct. (we. dist.) Pa. 1975, U.S. Ct. Appeals (4th cir.) 1977, U.S. Ct Appeals (11th cir.) 1978, U.S. Ct. Appeals (D.C. cir.) 1980, U.S. Ct. Appeals (3d cir.) 1985, U.S. Dist. Ct. (so. dist.) Fla. 1991, U.S. Dist. Ct. (no. dist.) Fla. 1992; cert. cir. ct. mediator, Fla. Assoc. Foley, Hoag & Elliot, Boston, 1968-70; asst. prof. law U. Fla., Gainesville, 1971-73; sr. trial atty. U.S. EEOC, Washington, 1973-74; assoc. Pitts, Eubanks, Ross & Rumberger, Orlando, Fla., 1974-75; ptnr. Berkman, Ruslander, Pohl, Lieber & Engel, Pitts., 1975-84, Kirkpatrick & Lockhart, Pitts., 1985-86, Rumberger, Kirk, Caldwell, Cabaniss, Burke & Wechsler, Orlando, 1986-91, Cabaniss, Burke & Wagner, Orlando, 1991-94, Baker & Hostetler, Orlando, 1995-97, Rumrell, Wagner & Costabel, Orlando, 1997—; gen. counsel North Star Media, Inc., 1997—; gen. counsel Impact Comms., Inc., 1989-95; bd. dirs. Fla. Legal Svcs., Inc. With USAR, 1960-61. Scholarship recipient Sch. Law, Duke U., Durham, N.C., 1965-68. Mem. ABA (litigation sect., employment law sect., forum on constrn. industry, dispute resolution section), Mass. Bar Assn., Pa. Bar Assn. (labor sect., dispute resolution sect.), Fla. Bar Assn. (labor sect., fed. ct. practice sect., dispute resolution sect.), Am. Arbitration Assn. (mem. arbitration & mediation panels for employment, securities and comml.), Nat. Assn. Securities Dealers (arbitration and mediation panels for securities and employment), Fla. Acad. Profl. Mediators, Fla. Acad. Trial Lawyers, Am. Judicator Soc. Avocations: fishing, boating, nature study. General civil litigation, Construction, Labor. Home: 526 Alokee Ct Lake Mary FL 32746-2218 Office: Rumrell Wagner & Costabel 2400 Maitland Ctr Pkwy #225 PO Box 540537 Orlando FL 32854-0537

**WAGNER, MARK ALAN,** lawyer; b. Papua New Guinea, Feb. 9, 1966; s. Merlyn Dean and Janet Bertha W.; m. Cheryl Rae Varoz, June 29, 1989; 1 child, Samantha. BS, U. Utah, 1988, JD, 1992. Bar: Utah. Jud. clk. U.S.

Dist. Ct. Utah, Salt Lake City, 1993; from assoc. to shareholder Parr, Waddops, Brown, Gee, & Loveless, Salt Lake City, 1994—; staff atty. Freedom of Info. Hotline Soc. Profl. Journalists, Salt Lake City, 1994—. Mng. editor Utah Law Rev., Salt Lake City, 1991-92. Com. Salt Lake City Mayor's Task Force, 1997—; vol. Am. Cancer Soc., 1987, 95—. Mem. ABA, ATLA, Utah Trial Lawyers Assn., AIA, Order of Coif. General civil litigation, Computer, Pension, profit-sharing, and employee benefits. Office: Parr Waddups et al 185 S State St Ste 1300 Salt Lake City UT 84111-1537

**WAGNER, MICHAEL DUANE,** lawyer; b. Shiner, Tex., July 4, 1948; s. Martin Matthew and Mary Margaret (Prasek) W.; m. Patricia Ann Miller, July 1, 1972; children: Matthew Miller, Michael Patrick. BA, Tex. Christian U., 1970; JD, St. Mary's Sch. Law, San Antonio, 1973. Bar: Tex. 1973, U.S. Supreme Ct. 1977. Assoc. counsel United Svcs. Automobile Assn., San Antonio, 1973-78, asst. v.p., counsel, 1978-80; v.p., counsel United Svcs. Automobile Assn., San Antonio, 1980-98, sr. v.p., gen. counsel, 1999—; counsel investment mgmt. co. United Services Automobile Assn., San Antonio, 1980—, pres., chmn. bd. dirs. fed. credit union, 1981-84. Counsel United San Antonio Found., 1982; rep. Target 90/Goals for San Antonio, 1985; chmn. bd. advisors Daus. Charity Svcs. San Antonio; trustee Boysville, 1988; bd. dirs. De Paul Family Ctr., San Antonio, 1985, Cancer Therapy and Rsch. Ctr., Friends of McNay, ARC, San Francisco, Archdiocese of San Antonio. Named one of Outstanding Young Men in Am., U.S. Jr. C. of C., 1984. Mem. ABA, Fed. Bar Assn., State Bar of Tex. (ethics and grievance com.) San Antonio Bar Assn., Phi Delta Theta, Phi Alpha Delta. Roman Catholic. Avocations: running, home renovation. General corporate, Securities, Labor.

**WAGNER, MICHAEL G.,** lawyer; b. Bklyn., July 12, 1949; s. Irving and Vivian (Lederman) W.; m. Martha Rosario Estevez, Nov. 21, 1979; children: Roxanne, Eric, Jeannien, Nicole, Shawn. BSBA, Ithaca Coll., 1971; JD, Bklyn. Law Sch., 1974. Bar: N.Y. 1975, U.S. Dist. Ct. (ea. dist.) N.Y., U.S. Dist. Ct. (so. dist.) N.Y., U.S. Ct. Appeals (2d. cir.). Counselor Mental Health Info. Svc., N.Y.C., 1974-76; ptnr. Klein, Wagner & Morris, N.Y.C., 1976—; lawyer; b. Bklyn., July 12, 1949; s. Irving and Vivian (Lederman) W.; m. Martha Rosario Estevez, Nov. 21, 1979; children—Roxanne, Eric, Jeannien, Nicole, Shawn B.S.B.A., Ithaca Coll., 1971; J.D., Bklyn. Law Sch., 1974. Bar: N.Y. 1975, U.S. Dist. Ct. (ea. dist.) N.Y., U.S. Dist. Ct. (so. dist.) N.Y., U.S. Ct. Appeals (2d cir.). Counselor Mental Health Info. Service, N.Y.C., 1974-76; ptnr. Klein, Wagner & Morris, N.Y.C., 1976—; lectr. on social security rights VA, 1984. Mem. N.Y. Social Security Bar Assn. (bd. dirs., treas., pres.), Bklyn. Bar Assn., Rockland Bar Assn., Queens Bar Assn., Delta Mu Delta (v.p. 1970-71). Democrat. Jewish. Mem. ABA, N.Y. Social Security Bar Assn. (bd. dirs., treas, pres.), Nat. Orgn. Social Security Claimant's Reps., Queens Bar Assn., Delta Mu Delta (v.p. 1970-71). Democrat. Jewish. Pension, profit-sharing, and employee benefits, Workers' compensation, Federal civil litigation. Home: 16 Harvey Ln U Saddle Riv NJ 07458-2110 Office: Klein Wagner & Morris LLP 277 Broadway Fl 9 New York NY 10007-2001

**WAGNER, RAYMOND THOMAS, JR.,** lawyer, corporation executive; b. St. Louis, June 8, 1959; s. Raymond T. and Loretto (Muenster) W.; m. Ann L. Trousdale, Feb. 20, 1987. BA, St. Louis U., 1981, MBA, 1984; JD, U. Mo., Kansas City, 1985; LLM in Taxation, Washington U., St. Louis, 1993. Bar: Mo. 1985, Ill. 1986, U.S. Supreme Ct. 1989, U.S. Tax Ct. 1989. Legal rsch. and writing instr. U. Mo., Kansas City, 1983-84; law clk. to chief justice Mo. Supreme Ct., Jefferson City, 1985-86; assoc. Gilmore & Bell, St. Louis, 1986-87, Suelthaus & Kaplan P.C., St. Louis, 1987-89; gen. counsel Mo. Dept Revenue, 1989-90; counsel to gov. State of Mo., Jefferson City, 1990-91; dir. revenue Mo. Dept. Revenue, 1991-93; of counsel Armstrong Teasdale Schlafly & Davis, St. Louis, 1993; dir. revenue Ill. Dept Revenue, Springfield, 1993-95; legal and legis. v.p. Enterprise Rent-A-Car, St. Louis, 1995—; adj. prof. law LLM taxation program sch. law Washington U., St. Louis, 1993—; chmn. Gov.'s Ethics Com., 1991-92, Mo. Hwy. Reciprocity Commn., 1991-93; commr. Multistate Tax. Commn., 1991-93, Mo. Mil. Adv. Commn., 1991-93. Twp. coord. Jefferson Twp., Webster Groves, Mo., 1988; precinct capt. Gravois Twp., Webster Groves, 1988; bd. dirs. Shelter the Children, St. Louis, 1988-95; bd. dirs. Foster Care Coalition St. Louis, 1995—, pres. 1998—; chmn. platform com. Mo. Rep. Conv., 1992; exec. bd. dirs. St. Louis U. Sch. Bus.; mem. chancellor's coun. U. Mo., St. Louis, 1998—. Mem. ABA, Ill. Bar Assn., Mo. Bar Assn., Bar Assn. Met. St. Louis (chmn. law student svcs. com. 1986-87, chmn. social com. 1987-88, mem. exec. com. young lawyers assn. 1988-89, co-chmn. administrv. law com., govt. liaison com. young lawyers sect. 1989-90, chmn. legis. com. 1991—), Regional Commerce and Growth Assn. (vice chair pub. policy coun. 1996, chair pub. policy coun. 1998—), Associated Industries Mo. (bd. dirs. 1996—), Mo. C.of C. (bd. dirs. 1998—). Republican. Roman Catholic. General corporate, Securities, Taxation, general. Home: 313 Saint Andrews Ct Ballwin MO 63011-2504 Office: Enterprise Rent-A-Car 600 Corporate Park Dr Saint Louis MO 63105-4204

**WAGNER, THOMAS JOSEPH,** lawyer, insurance company executive; b. Jackson, Mich., June 29, 1939; s. O. Walter and Dorothy Ann (Hollinger) W.; m. Judith Louise Bogardus, Jan. 15, 1961; children—Ann Louise, Mark Robert, Rachel Miriam. B.A., Earlham Coll., 1957; J.D., U. Chgo., 1965. Bar: Ill. 1968, U.S. Supreme Ct. 1975. Asst. to gov. State of Ill., Springfield, 1966-67, legal counsel, adminstrv. asst. to treas., 1967-70; adminstrv. asst. to U.S. senator Adlai E. Stevenson, Washington, 1970-77; sr. v.p. govt. affairs div. Am. Ins. Assn., Washington, 1977-80; staff v.p. Ina Corp., 1980-82; v.p., chief counsel Property Casualty Group, CIGNA Corp., Phila., 1982-86, v.p., assoc. gen. counsel, 1986-88, sr. v.p., corp. sec., 1988-91, exec. v.p., gen. counsel, 1992—; trustee Eisenhower Exchange Fellowships, Inc.; bd. dirs. Inst. Law and Econs., U. Penn. Past chmn. Phila. Crime Commn. Africa-Asia Pub. Svc. fellow Syracuse U., 1965-66. Mem. ABA (bus. law com.), Am. Corp. Counsel Assn., U.S.-Pacific Econ. Cooperation Coun. Insurance, Legislative. Office: Cigna Corp PO Box 7716 1 Liberty Place 55th Fl Philadelphia PA 19192-1550

**WAGNER, WENCESLAS JOSEPH,** law educator; b. Warsaw, Poland, Dec. 12, 1917; came to U.S., 1948; s. Joseph W. Wegner and Margaret M. de Ferrein; m. Dianne A. Moc, July 23, 1950 (div. Aug. 1970); children: Joseph V., Alexandra D., Margaret E.; m. Magdalena M. Niezychowska, Sept. 21, 1979 (dec. 1989); m. Janina Daniela Morgiewicz, Feb. 14, 1994. LLM, U. Warsaw, 1939; D in Law, U. Paris, 1947; LLM, Northwestern U., 1950, JD, 1953, D of Jud. Sci., 1957; D h.c., Nicolas Copernicus U., Torun, Poland, 1992. Bar: Ind. 1965. Asst. to full prof. law Notre Dame (Ind.) U., 1953-62; prof. law Ind. U., Bloomington, 1962-71, U. Detroit, 1971-89; disting. vis. prof. law U. Seton Hall, Newark, 1969-70; vis. prof. law various univs., various cities, Poland, 1970-71, 90-93; chmn. coun. European Faculty of Law, Warsaw, 1997—; vis. prof. law U. Paris, U. Rennes, 1969-70; internat. invited spkr. and lectr., numerous univs. and other instns. Author over 250 publs. in English, French, Polish, German and Portuguese; bd. editors Am. Jour. Comparative Law, 1963-89. Pres. Am. Coun. Polish Culture, 1958-60; v.p. Polish Home Army Vets., Chgo., 1990—. 2d lt., Polish Secret Army during German Occupation, 1941-45, Warsaw. Fulbright grantee, Commn. Internat. Exchs. Scholars, 4 times; Knight Comdr. Order of St. John of Jerusalem (Malta), 1990—. Mem. Am. Fgn. Law Assn. (v.p. 1964-66), Internat. Movement of Cath. Lawyers (v.p. 1972-89), Assn. Am. Law Schs. (chmn. internat. meetings com. 1966-89), numerous other orgns. Roman Catholic. Avocations: philately, tennis, skiing, musi. Home: 3365 Sandleheath The Meadows Sarasota FL 34235

**WAGONER, DAVID EVERETT,** lawyer; b. Pottstown, Pa., May 16, 1928; s. Claude Brower and Mary Kathryn (Groff) W.; children: Paul R., Colin H., Elon D., Peter B., Dana F.; m. Jean Morton Saunders; children: Constance A., Jennifer L., Melissa J. BA, Yale U., 1950; LLB, U. Pa., 1953. Bar: D.C. 1953, Pa. 1953, Wash. 1953. Law clk. U.S. Ct. Appeals (3d cir.), Pa., 1955-56; law clk. U.S. Supreme Ct., Washington, 1956-57; ptnr. Perkins & Coie, Seattle, 1957-96; panel mem. of arbitration forum worldwide including People's Republic of China, B.C. Internat. Comml. Arbitration Ctr., Hong Kong Internat. Arbitration Centre, Asian/Pacific Ctr. for Resolution of Internat. Bus. Disputes and the Ctr. for Internat. Dispute Resolution for Asian/Pacific Region. Mem. sch. com. Mcpl. League Seattle and King County, 1958—, chmn., 1962-65; mem. Seattle schs. citizens coms. on equal ednl. opportunity and adult vocat. edn., 1963-64; mem. Nat. Com. Support Pub. Schs.; mem. adv. com. on community colls., to 1965, legislature interim com. on edn., 1964-65; mem. community coll. adv. com. to state supt. pub. instrn., 1965; chmn. edn. com. Forward Thrust, 1968; mem. Univ. Congl. Ch. Council Seattle, 1968-70; bd. dirs. Met. YMCA Seattle, 1968; bd. dirs. Seattle Pub. Schs., 1965-73, v.p., 1966-67, 72-73, pres., 1968, 73; trustee Evergreen State Coll. Found., chmn. 1986-87, capitol campaign planning chmn.; trustee Pacific NW Ballet, v.p. 1986. Served to 1st lt. M.C., AUS, 1953-55. Fellow Am. Coll. Trial Lawyers (mem. ethics com., legal ethics com.), Chartered Inst. Arbitrators, Singapore Inst. Arbitrators; mem. ABA (chmn. standing com. fed. jud. imprisonment, chmn. appellate advocacy com., mem. commn. on separation of powers and jud. independence), Wash. State Bar Assn., Seattle-King County Bar Assn., Acad. Experts, Swiss Arbitration Assn., Comml. Bar Assn. London, Nat. Sch. Bds. Assn. (bd. dirs., chmn. coun. Big City bds. edn. 1971-72), English-Speaking Union (v.p. Seattle chpt. 1961-62), Chi Phi. Alternative dispute resolution. Home: 4215 E Blaine St Seattle WA 98112-3229 Office: Internat Arbitration Chambers US BankCtr 1420 5th Ave Fl 22 Seattle WA 98101-4087

**WAGSHAL, JEROME STANLEY,** lawyer, philatelic consultant; b. Washington, June 20, 1928; s. Philip and May (Wolf) W. BA with distinction, George Washington U., 1950; LLB, Yale U., 1953. Bar: U.S. Dist. Ct. D.C. 1953, U.S. Ct. Appeals (D.C. cir.) 1953, U.S. Supreme Ct. 1958, N.Y. 1970. Instr. U.S. Naval Sch. of Naval Justice, 1953-57; trial atty. Dept. of Justice Antitrust Div., 1957-68; v.p., gen. counsel Ecol. Sci. Corp., 1968-69; ptnr. Dickstein, Shapiro & Galigan and successor firms, 1970-73; founding ptnr. Pearce & Wagshal, Washington, 1973-75; sole practice, Washington, 1975. Contbr. articles to legal and philatelic jours. Past 1st v.p. Georgetown Citizens Assn. Served to lt., USNR, 1953-57. Recipient Ashbrook Cup, 1970, Chase Cup, 1987, Neinken award, 1987, U.S. Philatelic Classics Soc., Schreiber Cup, Am. Philatelic Soc., 1970. Mem. ABA, D.C. Bar, Order of Coif, Phi Beta Kappa, Omicron Delta Kappa, Pi Gamma Mu, Phi Eta Sigma, Delta Sigma Rho. Clubs: Yale (N.Y.C.); Boca Del Mar Country (Boca Raton, Fla.), City Tavern (Washington). Antitrust, Federal civil litigation, State civil litigation. Home: 6942 Villas Dr W Boca Raton FL 33433-5030 Office: 5920 Empire Way Rockville MD 20852-2861

**WAGSTAFF, ROBERT HALL,** lawyer; b. Kansas city, Mo., Nov. 5, 1941; s. Robert Wilson and Katherine Motter (Hall) W. AB, Dartmouth Coll., 1963; JD, U. Kans., 1966. Bar: Kans., Alaska, Wyo., U.S. Ct. Appeals (9th cir.), U.S. Supreme Ct.; cert. flight and instrument instr.; reg. airline transport pilot. Asst. atty. gen. State of Kans., 1966-67; asst. dist. atty. Office of Fairbanks (Alaska) Dist. Atty., 1967-69; ptnr. Boyko & Walton, Anchorage, 1969-70; sr. ptnr. Wagstaff et al., Ancorage, 1970—; adj. prof. law Embry-Riddle U., 1985. Chmn., bd. dirs. Alaska Youth Advocates, 1974-75; pres. U.S. Aerobatic Found., Oshkosh, Wis., 1986-94. Recipient Air Sports medal Fedn. Aeronautique Internat., Paris, 1991. Mem. ACLU (nat. bd. dirs. N.Y. 1972-78), ABA, Alaska Acad. Trial Lawyers, Alaska Bar Assn. (bd. govs. 1985-88, pres. 1987-88), Alaska Jud. Coun., Lawyer-Pilots Bar Assn. (regional v.p.), Nat. Lawyers Guild, Assn. Trial Lawyers Am., Nat. Assn. Criminal Defense Lawyers, Nat. Transp. Safety Bd. Assn., Am. Bd. Trial Advocates. Personal injury, Product liability, Aviation. Office: 425 G St Ste 610 Anchorage AK 99501-2137

**WAHL, ROBERT JAMES,** lawyer; b. Ft. Wayne, Jan. 11, 1958. BA, Miami U., Oxford, Ohio, 1980; JD, Stetson U., 1983. Law clk. U.S. Bankruptcy Ct. (mid. dist.) Fla., Tampa, 1983-84; atty. Blasingame, Forizs & Smiljanic, PA, St. Petersburg, Fla., 1984-97, James, Hoyer, Newcomer, Forizs & Smiljanich, PA, St. Petersburg, 1998—. Bankruptcy, General civil litigation. Office: James Hoyer Newcomer Forizs & Smiljanich PA 300 1st Ave S Ste 500 Saint Petersburg FL 33701-4200

**WAHLEN, EDWIN ALFRED,** lawyer; b. Gary, Ind., Mar. 12, 1919; s. Alfred and Ethel (Pearson) W.; m. Alice Elizabeth Condit, Apr. 24, 1943 (div. 1983); children: Edwin Alfred, Virginia Elizabeth, Martha Anne; m. Elizabeth L. Corey, Nov. 23, 1984. Student, U. Ala., 1936-38; A.B., U. Chgo., 1942, J.D., 1948. Bar: Ill. 1948. Practiced in Chgo., 1948—; mem. firm Haight, Goldstein & Haight, 1948-55; ptnr. Goldstein & Wahlen, 1956-59, Arvey, Hodes, Costello & Burman (and predecessor), 1959-91, Wildman, Harrold, Allen & Dixon, 1992—. Author: Soldiers and Sailors Wills: A Proposal For Federal Legislation, 1948. Served to 2d lt. AUS, 1942-46. Decorated Silver Star medal, Bronze Star medal. Mem. ABA, Ill. Bar Assn., Chgo. Bar Assn., Order of Coif, Phi Beta Kappa, Phi Alpha Delta. General corporate, Real property, Contracts commercial. Home: 1250 Breckenridge Ct Lake Forest IL 60045-3875 Office: 225 W Wacker Dr Chicago IL 60606-1224

**WAINESS, MARCIA WATSON,** legal management consultant; b. Bklyn., Dec. 17, 1949; d. Stanley and Seena (Klein) Watson; m. Steven Richard Wainess, Aug. 7, 1975. Student, UCLA, 1967-71, 80-81, UCLA Grad. Sch., 1987-88. Office mgr., paralegal Lewis, Marenstein & Kadar, L.A., 1977-81; office mgr. Rosenfeld, Meyer & Susman, Beverly Hills, Calif., 1981-83; adminstr. Rudin, Richman & Appel, Beverly Hills, 1983; dir. adminstrn. Kadison, Pfaelzer, L.A., 1983-87; exec. dir. Richards, Watson and Gershon, L.A., 1987-93; legal mgmt. cons. Wainess & Co., L.A., 1993-99; dir. law firm svcs. Dutch Franklin Bus. Svcs., Inc., 1999—; faculty UCLA Legal Mgmt. & Adminstrn. Program, 1983, U. So. Calif. Paralegal Program, L.A., 1985; adv. bd. atty. asst. tng. program UCLA, 1984-88; adj. faculty U. West L.A. Sch. Paralegal Studies, 1997-98. Mem. ABA (chair Displaywrite Users Group 1986, legal tech. adv. coun. litig. support working group 1986-87), Inst. Mgmt. Consultants, L.A. County Bar Assn. (exec. com. law office mgmt. sect.), San Fernando Valley Bar Assn., Assn. Legal Adminstrs. (mem. editl. adv. bd. 1998—, bd. dirs. 1990-92, asst. regional v.p. Calif. 1987-88, regional v.p. 1988-89, pres. Beverly Hills chpt. 1985-86, membership chair 1984-85, chair new adminstrn. sect. 1982-84, mktg. mgmt. sect. com. 1989-90, internat. conf. com.), Beverly Hills Bar Assn. (chair law practice mgmt. sect. 1998—). Avocations: historic preservation, antiques, interior design. Office: 11601 Wilshire Blvd Fl 23D Los Angeles CA 90025-1770

**WAINWRIGHT, GEORGE,** judge; b. Wilson County, N.C., Dec. 10, 1943; s. George Sr. and Susan Wainwright; m. Carol McChesney; children: Kennon, Ashton. Undergrad. degree, U. N.C., 1966; JD, Wake Forest U., 1984. Agribus. and real estate positions Wilson, 1966-81; with Wheatly, Wheatly, Nobles & Weeks, Beaufort, N.C., 1986-90; apptd. judge Dist. Ct., 1991; resident Superior Ct. judge for N.C. Jud. Dist. 3B, 1994; justice Supreme Ct. N.C., 1999—. With USCGR, 1966-72. Morehead scholar, 1966. Mem. N.C. Bar Assn., Lookout Rotary Club. Presbyterian. Office: Supreme Ct NC Justice Bldg PO Box 1841 Raleigh NC 27602*

**WAISANEN, CHRISTINE M.,** lawyer, writer; b. Hancock, Mich., May 27, 1949; d. Frederick B. and Helen M. (Hill) W.; m. Robert John Katzenstein, Apr. 21, 1979; children: Jeffrey Hunt, Erick Hill. BA with honors, U. Mich., 1971; JD, U. Denver, 1975. Bar: Colo. 1975, D.C. 1978. Labor rels. atty. U.S. C. of C., Washington, 1976-79; govt. rels. specialist ICI Americas, Inc., Wilmington, Del., 1979-87; dir. cultural affairs City of Wilmington, 1987; founder, chief writer Hill, Katzenstein & Waisanen, 1988—. Chmn. Delaware State Coastal Zone Indsl. Control Bd., 1993—. Mem. Fed. Bar Assn., Jr. League of Wilmington (v.p. 1985-86), Women's Rep. Club of Wilmington (bd. dirs. 1988-93). Republican. Presbyterian. Administrative and regulatory, Environmental, Land use and zoning (including planning). Home: 1609 Mt Salem Ln Wilmington DE 19806-1134

**WAITE, DAVID ERNEST,** lawyer; b. Chester, Pa., Mar. 17, 1951; s. Clayland M. and Mary E. (Hopkins) W.; m. Anna Hawkins, Nov. 14, 1977; children: Frank, Billie Gail, Jack. BS in Econs. with distinction and honors, U. Ky., 1981, JD, 1984. Bar: Ky. 1984, Tenn. 1990, U.S. Dist. Ct. (ea. dist.) Ky. 1984, U.S. Dist. Ct. (ea. dist.) Tenn. 1990, U.S. Ct. Appeals (6th cir.) 1990, U.S. Ct. Claims 1991, U.S. Supreme Ct. 1991. Asst. county atty. Bourbon County, Paris, Ky., 1984-85; sole practice Paris, Ky., 1985-90; atty. City of North Middletown, Ky., 1987-90; assoc. Milligan Law Firm, Knoxville, Tenn., 1990-94; ptnr. Brown & Waite, Knoxville, Tenn., 1994-96; sole practice, 1996—. Mem. Ky. Bar Assn., Assn. Trial Lawyers Am., Tenn. Bar Assn., Knoxville Bar Assn., Anderson County Bar Assn., Tenn. Trial Lawyer's Assn. Democrat. Episcopalian. Personal injury, Product liability, Professional liability. Office: Law Office of Donna Keene Holt 108 Durwood Rd Knoxville TN 37922

**WAITE, FREDERICK PAUL,** lawyer; b. Troy, N.Y., Nov. 17, 1945; s. John Graves and Helena Ferber Waite; m. Sherrian Patricia Knight, Dec. 27, 1969; children: Angharad H.K., Penelope V.K. AB cum laude, Princeton (N.J.) U., 1967; JD cum laude, Harvard U., 1971. Bar: N.Y. 1972, D.C. 1975, U.S. Dist. Ct. (no. dist.) N.Y. 1972, U.S. Supreme Ct. 1974, U.S. Mil. Ct. 1974, U.S. Ct. Internat. Trade 1984, U.S. Ct. Appeals (fed. cir.) 1984. Assoc. Crowell & Moring, Washington, 1976-77; assoc., ptrn. Cadwalader, Wickersham & Taft, Washington, 1978-89; ptnr. Davis, Graham & Stubbs, Washington, 1989-92; mng. dir. Ackerson & Bishop PC, Washington, 1992-94; shareholder, ptnr. Popham, Haik, Schnobrich & Kaufman PC, Washington, 1994-97; prtn. Hollan & Knight LLP, Washington, 1997—. Co-author: International Court of Justice Opinion Briefs, 1978. Capt. USAF, 1972-76. Mem. ABA, D.C. Bar Assn., Washington Internat. Trade Assn., Wire Assn. Internat. Avocations: travel, history, ice hockey, reading. Administrative and regulatory, Private international, Appellate. Office: Holland & Knight LLP 2100 Pennsylvania Ave NW Washington DC 20037-3295

**WAITE, JEFFREY C.,** lawyer, educator; b. Carlisle, Pa., Jan. 10, 1955; s. Leonard Francis and Helen Mary Waite; m. Elizabeth J. Winters, Sept. 1, 1984; children: Jeffrey Scott, Gregory Douglas, Kevin Andrew. BA summa cum laude, Long Island U., Bklyn., 1976; MA, Kent State U., 1978; JD, Ohio State U., 1981. Bar: Ohio 1981, U.S. Dist. Ct. (so. dist.) Ohio 1982, U.S. Ct. Appeals (6th cir.) 1984, U.S. Supreme Ct. 1984. Jud. law clk. to Hon. Chas. A. Anderson U.S. Bankruptcy Ct., Dayton, Ohio, 1981-83; mng. ptnr. E.S. Gallon & Assocs., Cin., 1990-93; ptnr. Monnie Waite & O'Connor, Cin., 1994-97; mng. ptnr. Jeffrey Waite & Assocs., Cin., 1997—; adj. asst. prof. U. Cin., 1997—; vice chmn. joint com. Cin. Bar Assn. and The Acad. of Medicine, 1998—. Co-author: Ohio Workers' Compensation Law Practice Guide, 1996. Trustee Wyoming (Ohio) Presbyn. Ch. Mem. ATLA, Ohio State Bar Assn. (cert. workers compensation specialist), Ohio Acad. Trial Lawyers, Cin. Bar Assn., Hamilton County Trial Lawyers Assn. (treas.), Lions Club (past pres.). Workers' compensation, Personal injury. Office: Jeffrey Waite & Assocs 830 Main St Ste 500 Cincinnati OH 45202-2123

**WAITE, RICHARD WHITEHEAD,** lawyer, retired military officer; b. Meadville, Pa., Dec. 8, 1940; s. Richard Marvin and Dorothy Elaine Waite; m. Audrey Lee Collins, May 20, 1961; 1 child: Shawn Paul. MS, Ctrl. Mo. State U., 1976; MPA, Ariz. State U., 1989, JD, 1989. Bar: Ariz. 1989, U.S. Tax Ct. 1989, Colo. 1990, D.C. 1990. Commd. 2d lt. USAF, 1960, advanced through grades to col., 1981; ret., 1986; law clk. Ariz. Ct. Appeals, Phoenix, 1990-91; dep. county atty. Coconino County, Flagstaff, Ariz., 1991-95, 96—, dir. pretrial svcs., 1995-96. Mem. Air Force Assn. (pres. Sedona chpt. 1991-93), Sedona Airport Assn. (bd. dirs. 1992-95), Arroyo Roble Owners Assn. (bd. dirs., sec. 1994-96), Ariz. State U. Alumni Assn. (bd. dirs., treas. Sedona chpt. 1990-94), USAFR Officers Assn., Am. Legion (post #3), Pi Alpha Alpha. Republican. Avocation: antique restoration. Home: 160 Sugar Loaf Dr Sedona AZ 86336-6241 Office: Coconino County Atty 100 E Birch Ave Flagstaff AZ 86001-4625

**WAKE, ROBERT ALAN,** lawyer; b. Ft. Belvoir, Va., Oct. 7, 1952; s. Robert Warner and Esther Jeannette (Schreiber) W.; m. Marcia Greenbaum, July 17, 1977; children: Benjamin Ehren, Koren Alison. BS, MIT, 1974; PhD, Brown U., 1979; JD, Harvard U., 1988. Bar: Maine 1988. Lectr. U. Wis., Milw., 1979-81; asst. prof. U. Maine, Orono, 1981-82, U. Calif., Santa Cruz, 1982-85; law clk. to chief justice Vincent L. McKusick Portland, Maine, 1988-89; asst. atty. gen. State of Maine, Augusta, 1989-93; fin. surveillance counsel Maine Bur. Ins., Augusta, 1993—. Author poems. Mem. Common Cause, 1980—; chpt. pres. Maine State Employees Assn.; vice-chair Maine Dem. Party Rules Com.; pres. Gorham-Sebago Lake Regional Land Trust. Mem. ABA, Maine Bar Assn., Am. Math. Soc., ACLU, Am. Contract Bridge League, Ins. Regulatory Examiners Soc. Democrat. Jewish. Avocations: basketball, hiking, tennis, writing. Home: 1 Covered Bridge Rd Windham ME 04062-4609 Office: Maine Bureau of Insurance 34 State House Sta Augusta ME 04333-0001

**WAKEFIELD, ROBERT,** lawyer, retired marine corps officer; b. Oakland, Calif., Nov. 24, 1936; s. Hal Wesley and Elizabeth Luella Wakefield; m. Lysbeth Brooks, June 6, 1960 (div. Sept. 1978); m. Dorothy Irene Liston, Sept. 23, 1978; children: Victoria A. Conway, Gregory Scott. BA, U. Calif., Berkeley, 1959; grad., USMC Command-Gen. Staff Coll., 1974; grad. with highest distinction, U.S. Naval War Coll., 1982; MA with honors, Ctrl. Mich. U., 1983; JD cum laude, U. Idaho, 1992. Bar: Idaho 1992, U.S. Dist. Ct. Idaho 1992, Colo. 1993, also Nez Perce and Coeur d'Alene tribal cts. Commd. 2d lt. USMC, 1959, advanced through grades to col.; ret., 1989; law clk. 2d Dist. Ct., Moscow, Idaho, 1992-93, N.Mex. Ct. Appeals, Las Cruces, 1996-97; ptnr. Liston, Wakefield & Dwelle, Moscow, 1993-96, 97—; prof. clin. studies Indian program law U. Idaho Coll. Law, Nex Perce and Coeur d'Alene Reservations, 1992-96. Contbr. articles to mil. publs. Decorated Legion of Merit, Purple Heart, 13 Air medals. Mem. 2d Dist. Bar Assn., Marine Corps Assn., Am. Inns. Ct. Republican. Episcopalian. Avocations: scuba diving, hunting, fishing. Family and matrimonial, Estate planning, Native American. Office: Liston Wakefield & Dwelle 609 S Washington St Ste 206 Moscow ID 83843-3064

**WAKS, STEPHEN HARVEY,** lawyer; b. Decatur, Ill., Apr. 9, 1947; s. Paul and Regina (Geisler) W. BA, U. Wis., 1969; JD, U. Calif., San Francisco, 1974. Bar: Calif. 1974, U.S. Ct. Appeals (9th cir.) 1977, U.S. Tax Ct. 1977. Assoc. Wohl, Cinnamon, Hagedorn, Dunbar & Johnson, Sacramento, 1978-79; mem. Waks Law Corp., Sacramento, 1979—; instr. U. Calif.-Davis, 1982—, Golden Gate U., 1983—. Co-author: Real Estate Taxation, 1983. bd. dirs. Am. River Bank, Sacramento. Mem. ABA, Calif. Bar Assn., Sacramento County Bar Assn., Phi Delta Phi. Real property, Personal income taxation. Office: 555 Capitol Mall Ste 450 Sacramento CA 95814-4582

**WALBAUM, ROBERT C.,** lawyer; b. Springfield, Ill., Nov. 13, 1933; s. George Crum and Mary Emma (Taylor) W.; m. Anita P. Walbaum, Aug. 6, 1960; children—John Taylor, Charles Robert. Student Bradley U., Peoria, Ill., 1951-53; B.S. in Commerce, U. Ill.-Urbana, 1955; J.D., Washington U., St. Louis, 1960. Bar: Ill. 1961, U.S. Dist. Ct. (so. dist.) Ill. 1964, U.S. Ct. Apls. (7th cir.) 1973, U.S. Supreme Ct. 1989. With Chgo. Title & Trust Co., 1960-61; asst. states atty. County of Sangamon, Ill., Springfield, 1961-63; sole practice, Springfield, 1963—; atty. City Springfield, 1964-69, Village Pleasant Plains, Ill., 1970-93; tech. advisor Ill. Dept. Law Enforcement, 1969-73; counsel Springfield Park Dist., 1984—; dir. Pleasant Plains State Bank, 1982-95. Mem. Sangamon County Bd. Suprs., 1962-75, chmn., 1974; bd. dirs. Washington St. Mission, Springfield, 1966-90, pres., 1983-86. Served with U.S. Army, 1955-57. Mem. ABA, Ill. State Bar Assn., Sangamon County Bar Assn., Phi Alpha Delta. Republican. Episcopalian. Clubs: Illini Country, Sangamo, Am. Bus. (Springfield). Probate, General corporate, Banking. Address: 1049 W Woodland Ave Springfield IL 62704-2863

**WALCHER, ALAN ERNEST,** lawyer; b. Chgo., Oct. 2, 1949; s. Chester R. and Dorothy E. (Kullgren) W.; m. Penny Marie Walcher; children: Dustin Alan, Michael Alan, Christopher Ray; 1 stepchild, Ronald Edwin Culver. BS, U. Utah, 1971, cert. in internat. rels., 1971, JD, 1974. Bar: Utah 1974, U.S. Dist. Ct. Utah 1974, U.S. Ct. Appeals (10th cir.) 1977, Calif. 1979, U.S. Dist. Ct. (cen. dist.) Calif. 1979, U.S. Ct. Appeals (9th cir.) 1983, U.S. Dist. Ct. (ea., no., and so. dists.) Calif. 1994. Sole practice, Salt Lake City, 1974-79; ptnr. Costello & Walcher, L.A., 1979-85, Walcher & Scheuer, 1985-88, Ford & Harrison, 1988-91, Epstein Becker & Green, 1991—; judge pro tem Los Angeles Mcpl. Ct., 1986-91; dir. Citronia, Inc., Los Angeles, 1979-81. Trial counsel Utah chpt. Common Cause, Salt Lake City, 1978-79. Robert Mukai scholar U. Utah, 1971. Mem. Soc. Bar and Gavel (v.p. 1975-77), ABA, Fed. Bar Assn., Los Angeles County Bar Assn., Century City Bar Assn., Assn. Bus. Trial Lawyers, Phi Delta Phi, Owl and Key. Club: Woodland Hills Country (Los Angeles). State civil litigation, Federal civil litigation, Government contracts and claims. Home: 17933 Sunburst St Northridge CA 91325-2848 Office: Epstein Becker & Green 1875 Century Park E Ste 500 Los Angeles CA 90067-2506

**WALD, BERNARD JOSEPH,** lawyer; b. Bklyn., Sept. 14, 1932; s. Max and Ruth (Mencher) W.; m. Francine Joy Weintraub, Feb. 2, 1964; children—David Evan, Kevin Mitchell. B.B.A. magna cum laude, CCNY; J.D. cum laude, NYU, 1955. Bar: N.Y. 1955, U.S. Dist. Ct. (so. dist.) N.Y. 1960,

U.S. Dist. Ct. (ea. dist.) N.Y. 1960, U.S. Ct. Appeals (2d cir.) 1960, U.S. Supreme Ct. 1971. Mem. Herzfeld & Rubin, P.C. and predecessor firms, N.Y.C., 1955—. Mem. ABA, N.Y. State Bar Assn., Assn. Bar City N.Y., N.Y. County Lawyers Assn. Contracts commercial, General corporate, Private international. Office: Herzfeld & Rubin PC 40 Wall St Ste 5400 New York NY 10005-2301

**WALD, JULIA POOL,** lawyer; b. Bombay, Aug. 11, 1941; came to U.S., 1942; d. John Lawrence and Patricia Pool; m. Albert Weiler Wald, Jan. 14, 1967 (div. Dec. 1984); children: Laura Helen, Michael Harold. BA, Wellesley Coll., 1963; MA, U. Calif., Berkeley, 1967; JD, U. Idaho, 1977. Bar: Calif. 1977. Assoc. Bryson & Rochester, 1980-84, Heller, Erhman, White & McAuliffe, 1984-87, Lukens, Cooper, Perry & Drummond, 1987-89; ptnr. Bird & Wald, San Francisco, 1989-94; pvt. practice San Francisco, 1994-98, Wald & Kramer, LLP, San Francisco, 1998—. Contbr. articles to profl. jours. Mem. State Bar Calif. (cert. legal specialist bd. legal specialization), San Francisco Bar Assn., San Francisco Estate Planning Coun., San Francisco Bay Area Tax Lawyers. Democrat. Unitarian. Avocations: bird watching, opposing homelessness. Office: 260 California St Fl 7 San Francisco CA 94111-4396

**WALD, PATRICIA MCGOWAN,** federal judge; b. Torrington, Conn., Sept. 16, 1928; d. Joseph F. and Margaret (O'Keefe) McGowan; m. Robert L. Wald, June 22, 1952; children—Sarah, Douglas, Johanna, Frederica, Thomas. BA, Conn. Coll., 1948; LLB, Yale U., 1951; HHD (hon.), Mt. Vernon Jr. Coll., 1980; LLD (hon.), George Washington Law Sch., 1983, CUNY, 1984, Notre Dame U., John Jay Sch. Criminal Justice, Mt. Holyoke Coll., 1985, Georgetown U., 1987, Villanova U. Law Sch., Amherst Coll., N.Y. Law Sch., 1988, Colgate U., 1989, Hofstra Law Sch., 1991, New Eng. Coll., 1991, Hoffstra U., 1991, Vermont Law Sch., 1995. Bar: D.C. 1952. Clk. to judge Jerome Frank U.S. Ct. Appeals, 1951-52; asso. firm Arnold, Fortas & Porter, Washington, 1952-53; mem. D.C. Crime Commn., 1964-65; atty. Office of Criminal Justice, 1967-68, Neighborhood Legal Svc., Washington, 1968-70; co-dir. Ford Found. Project on Drug Abuse, 1970, Ctr. for Law and Social Policy, 1971-72, Mental Health Law Project, 1972-77; asst. atty. gen. for legis. affairs U.S. Dept. Justice, Washington, 1977-79; judge U.S. Ct. Appeals (D.C. cir.), 1979—, chief judge, 1986-91. Author: Law and Poverty, 1965; co-author: Bail in the United States, 1964, Dealing with Drug Abuse, 1973; contbr. articles on legal topics. Trustee Ford Found., 1972-77, Phillips Exeter Acad., 1975-77, Agnes Meyer Found., 1976-77, Conn. Coll., 1976-77; mem. Carnegie Council on Children, 1972-77. Mem. ABA-Ctrl. and Ea. European Law Inst. (exec. bd. 1994-99, bd. editors ABA Jour. 1978-86), Am. Law Inst. (coun. 1979—, exec. com. 1985-99, 2d v.p. 1988-93, 1st v.p. 1993-98), Am. Acad. Arts and Scis., Phi Beta Kappa. Office: US Ct Appeals 333 Constitution Ave NW Washington DC 20001-2802

**WALD, ROBERT LEWIS,** lawyer; b. Worcester, Mass., Sept. 9, 1926; s. Lewis and Freda Ann (Rosenfield) W.; m. Patricia Ann McGowan, June 22, 1952; children: Sarah Elizabeth, Douglas Robert, Johanna Margaret, Frederica Nora, Thomas Robert. AB, Harvard U., 1947; LLB, Yale U., 1951. Bar: Mass. 1951, D.C. 1959, U.S. Ct. Appeals (4th cir.) 1957, U.S. Supreme Ct. 1957, U.S. Ct. Appeals (D.C. cir.) 1959, U.S. Ct. Appeals (6th cir.) 1975. Clerk to Judge Irving R. Kaufman U.S. Dist. Ct. (so. dist.) N.Y., 1951-52; asst. to gen. counsel FTC, Washington, 1954-56; ptnr. Wald, Harkrader, Ross and predecessor firms, Washington, 1961-87, Nussbaum & Wald, Washington, 1989-96; sr. counsel Baach Robinson & Lewis, Washington, 1996—; dir. Romanian-Am. Enterprise Fund, 1994-97, chmn., 1994-96; dir. Internat. Human Rights Law Group, 1991—. Served to lt. USNR, 1944-46, 52-53. Mem. ABA, D.C. Bar Assn. Administrative and regulatory, Antitrust, General practice. Home: 2101 Connecticut Ave NW Washington DC 20008-1728 Office: Baach Robinson & Lewis One Thomas Circle NW Washington DC 20005

**WALD, SHERRI SUNDEM,** lawyer; b. Sioux Falls, S.D., Jan. 17, 1957; d. Richard and Carol Marie Sundem; m. James Michael Wald, Sept. 17, 1988; 1 child, Sigrid Sundem Wald. BA, U. S.D., 1979, JD, 1983. Bar: S.D. 1983, U.S. Dist. Ct. S.D. 1983, U.S. Ct. Appeals (8th cir.) 1983. Law clerk S.D. Cir. Ct. (6th cir.), Pierre, S.D., 1983-84; asst. atty. gen. Office of Atty. Gen., Pierre, 1984—; mem. S.D. State Criminal Law Com. Co-chair L.W.V., Pierre, 1989-90; edn. com. Luth. Meml. Ch., Pierre, 1997. Mem. State Bar S.D. (criminal law com. 1984-99), AAUW, Nat. Assn. State Medicaid Fraud Control Units (exec. com. 1988-90), Nat. Assn. State Bd. Accountancy (chair legal com. 1997). Home: 512 N Grand Ave Pierre SD 57501-2116 Office: Office Atty Gen 500 E Capitol Ave Pierre SD 57501-5070

**WALDBAUM, ALAN G.,** lawyer; b. Seattle, Dec. 31, 1968; s. Kenneth W. and Susan G. Waldbaum. BBA, U. Wash., 1991; JD, U. Mich., 1994. Bar: Wash. 1994. Assoc. Davis Wright Tremaine, Seattle, 1994-98; assoc. counsel Teledesic, 1999—. Bd. dirs. Jewish Family Svc., Seattle, 1996—, King County Literacy Coalition, Seattle, 1996-98. Mem. ABA, Wash. State Bar Assn., King County Bar Assn. Avocations: screenwriting, basketball, skiing, swimming, drums. Communications, General corporate. Office: 1445 120th Ave NE Bellevue WA 98005-2127

**WALDECK, JOHN WALTER, JR.,** lawyer; b. Cleve., May 3, 1949; s. John Walter Sr. and Marjorie Ruth (Palenschat) W.; m. Cheryl Gene Cutter, Sept. 10, 1977; children: John III, Matthew, Rebecca. BS, John Carroll U., 1973; JD, Cleve. State U., 1977. Bar: Ohio 1977. Product applications chemist Synthetic Products Co., Cleve., 1969-76; assoc. Arter & Hadden, Cleve., 1977-85, ptnr., 1986-88; ptnr. Porter, Wright, Morris and Arthur, Cleve., 1988-90, ptnr. in charge, 1990-96; ptnr. Walter & Haverfield, Cleve., 1996—. Chmn. Bainbridge Twp. Bd. Zoning Appeals, Chagrin Falls, Ohio, 1984-94; trustee Greater Cleve. chpt. Lupus Found. Am., 1978-91, sec., 1979-86; trustee LeBlond Housing Corp., Cleve., 1990-96, sec., 1996, Univ. Circle, Inc., 1993-97, Fairmount Ctr. for Performing and Fine Arts, Novelty, Ohio, 1993-96, sect., 1994-95; bd. dirs. Geauga County Mental Health Alcohol and Drug Addiction Svc. Bd., Chardon, Ohio, 1988-97, treas., 1991-93, vice-chmn., 1993-95, chmn., 1995-97; mem. bd. advisors Palliative Care Svcs., Cleve. Clinic Cancer Ctr., 1989-91. Mem. Ohio State Bar Assn. (real property sect. bd. govs. 1992), Greater Cleve. Bar Assn. (real property, corp. banking sect. co-chair real estate law inst. 1990, 95, 96). Roman Catholic. Avocations: beekeeping, gardening, jogging. Real property, General corporate, Finance. Home: 18814 Rivers Edge Dr W Chagrin Falls OH 44023-4968 Office: Walter & Haverfield 50 Public Square 1300 Terminal Tower Cleveland OH 44113

**WALDER, NOELEEN GWYNAETH,** lawyer; b. Easton, Conn., June 8, 1970; d. Eugene and Loretta W. BA with distinction, Stanford U., 1992; JD cum laude, Harvard U., 1995. Bar: N.Y. Policy advisor N.Y. State Assembly, Rochester, 1995; assoc. Winthrop, Stimson, Putnam & Roberts, N.Y.C., 1996-98, Skadden, Arps, Slate, Meagher & Flom, LLP, N.Y.C., 1998—. Mem. ABA, Assn. Bar City N.Y., Phi Beta Kappa. Avocations: photography, Italian, modern dance, ethnography. General civil litigation, Trademark and copyright. Home: 175 W 12th St 5M New York NY 10011 Office: Skadden Arps Slate Meagher Flom LLP 919 3d Ave New York NY 10022-3902

**WALDMAN, DANIEL,** lawyer. BA, Harvard U., 1977; JD, Columbia U., 1980. Bar: D.C. 1980. Clk. to Judge William A. Norris U.S. Ct. Appeals (9th cir.), 1980-82; with firm Arnold & Porter, Washington, 1982-96; gen. counsel Commodity Futures Trading Commn., Washington, 1996—. Office: US Commodity Futures Trading Commn 1155 21st St NW Washington DC 20036-3308*

**WALDMAN, JAY CARL,** judge; b. Pitts., Nov. 16, 1944; s. Milton and Dorothy (Florence) W.; m. Roberta Tex Landy, Aug. 28, 1969. B.S., U. Wis., 1966; J.D., U. Pa., 1969. Bar: Pa. 1970, D.C. 1976, U.S. Supreme Ct. 1976. Assoc., Rose, Schmidt, Dixon & Hasley, Pitts., 1970-71; asst. U.S. atty. western dist. Pa., Pitts., 1971-75; dep. asst. U.S. Atty. Gen., Washington, 1975-77; counsel Gov. of Pa., Harrisburg, 1978-86; sr. ptnr., Dilworth, Paxson, Kalish & Kauffman, Phila., 1986-88; judge U.S. Dist. Ct. (ea. dist.) Pa., 1988—. Dir. Thornburgh for Gov. campaign., Pa., 1977-78; commr. Pa. Convention Ctr. Authority, 1986-88. Fellow Am. Bar Found.; mem. ABA, Fed. Bar Assn., Union League Phila. Republican. Office: US Dist Ct Pa 9613 US Courthouse 601 Market St Philadelphia PA 19106-1713

**WALDMAN, SEYMOUR MORTON,** lawyer; b. N.Y.C., Aug. 6, 1926; s. Louis and Bella B. Waldman; m. Lois Citrin, Aug. 5, 1951; children: David, Daniel, Michael, Ellen. BA, Columbia U., 1948, LLB, 1950. Bar: N.Y. 1950, U.S. Ct. Appeals (1st, 2d, 3d, 4th, 5th, 6th and D.C. cirs.), U.S. Dist. Ct. (so. dist.) N.Y., U.S. Dist. Ct. (ea. dist.) N.Y., U.S. Supreme Ct. 1956. From assoc. to ptnr. Waldman & Waldman, N.Y.C., 1950-82; ptnr., of counsel Vladeck, Waldman, Elias & Engelhard, P.C., N.Y.C., 1982—; atty. Village of Croton-Hudson, N.Y., 1972—; chair zoning bd. appeals Village of Croton-Hudson, 1963-72, trustee hosp. for Joint Diseases Orthopaedic Inst., 1968-93. With USN, 1944-46. Mem. ABA, N.Y. State Bar Assn., Assn. of the Bar of the City of N.Y., Phi Beta Kappa. Avocation: tennis. Office: Vladeck Waldman Elias & Engelhard PC 1501 Broadway Ste 800 New York NY 10036-5560

**WALDO, JAMES CHANDLER,** lawyer; b. Seattle, Oct. 23, 1948; s. Burton Chandler and Margaret (Hoar) W.; m. Sharon B. Barber; children: Sara K., William K., John J. Grad., Whitman Coll., 1970; JD, Willamette U., 1974. Bar: Wash. 1974, U.S. Ct. Appeals (9th cir.) 1976. Exec. asst. Dept. of Labor, Washington, 1974-76; asst. U.S. atty. Justice Dept., Seattle, 1976-79; of counsel ESTEP & LI, Seattle, 1979-80; prin. Gordon, Thomas, Honeywell, Malanca, Peterson & Daheim, P.L.L.C., Seattle, 1981—; chmn. N.W. Renewable Resources Ctr., Seattle, 1984-97, Wash. State Energy Strategy Com., 1991-93; mem. Wash. Dept. Natural Resources Aquatic Lands Adv. Com., 1994. Trustee Western Wash. U., Bellingham, 1981-93. Recipient Outstanding Alumnus of Yr. Whitman Coll., 1994, Dir.'s award Wash. Dept. Fisheries, 1986, Pres.'s award Assn. Wash. Bus., 1988, Outstanding Citizen award Western Assn. Fish & Wildlife Agys., 1987. Republican. FERC practice, Environmental, Government contracts and claims. Office: Gordon Thomas Honeywell Malanca Peterson & Daheim PLLC 1201 Pacific Ave Ste 2200 Tacoma WA 98402-4314 Address: PO Box 1157 Tacoma WA 98401-1157

**WALDO, JOSEPH THOMAS,** lawyer; b. Roanoke, Va., Mar. 11, 1950; s. Harry Creekmur and Janet (Odom) W.; children: Joseph Patrick, Ashley Lauren. AB, U. N.C., Chapel Hill, 1972; JD, Coll. of William & Mary, 1978. Bar: Va. 1978, U.S. Dist. Ct. (ea. dist.) Va. 1978, U.S. Bankruptcy Ct. 1978, U.S. Ct. Appeals (4th cir.) 1979, U.S. Tax Ct. 1981. Ptnr., founder Waldo & Tilhou, Virginia Beach, Va., 1978-84; prin. ptnr. Pender & Coward, Virginia Beach, 1984-98; pvt. practice Norfolk, Va., 1998—. Pres. Virginia Beach SPCA, 1989-91, bd. dirs., 1986-91; bd. dirs. Greater Ocean View Found., 1988-92, Norfolk Sch. Bd., 1992—. Mem. ABA, Va. Bar Assn., Virginia Beach Bar Assn., Norfolk Portsmouth Bar Assn., William & Mary Law Sch. Alumni Assn. (bd. dirs., sec., treas. 1984-87). Episcopalian. Contracts commercial, Real property, Construction. Home: 321 Duke St Apt 125 Norfolk VA 23510-1270 Office: Eminent Domain Prop Rights 253 W Freemason St Ste 201 Norfolk VA 23510-1220

**WALDORF, GERALDINE POLACK,** lawyer; b. N.Y.C., Jan. 10, 1942; d. Marcel and Pauline (Kornbluh) Polack; m. Donald S. Waldorf, June 22, 1963; children: Heidi A., Lawrence W., Mahlon R. AB magna cum laude, Vassar Coll., 1963; MA, Sarah Lawrence Coll., 1969; JD, Columbia U., 1979; LLM in Taxation, NYU, 1986. Bar: N.Y. 1979. Assoc. Kelley, Drye & Warren, N.Y.C., 1979-84; pvt. practice, Nanuet, N.Y., 1984-88, 92—; of counsel Davidson, Dawson & Clark, N.Y.C., 1988-92. Co-author: New York Practice Guide: Probate and Estate Administration, 1985. Bd. dirs. Am. Cancer Soc., Rockland County, N.Y., 1971-77, 85-91; adv. com. Georgetown U. Child Devel. Ctr., Washington, 1991—. Harlan Fiske Stone scholar Columbia U. Sch. Law, N.Y.C., 1976-78. Mem. ABA, Women's Bar Assn. of State of N.Y., N.Y. State Bar Assn., Assn. of Bar of City of N.Y., Rockland County Bar Assn., Rockland County Tax and Estate Planning Coun. (bd. dirs. 1986-91). Estate planning, Probate, Estate taxation. Office: 57 N Middletown Rd Nanuet NY 10954-2312

**WALDREP, CHARLIE DAVID,** lawyer; b. Gainesville, Ga., Nov. 13, 1948; s. Robert Ernest and Bonnie Lou (Black) W.; m. Suzanne Elizabeth, Aug. 12, 1972 (div. 1997); children: Stacy, Megan, Brittany. BA, Jacksonville State U., 1971; JD cum laude, Samford U., 1976. Bar: Ala. 1976, U.S. Dist. Ct. (no. and mid. dist.) 1976, U.S. Ct. Appeals (5th and 11th cir.) 1984. Atty. Forstman & Waldrep, Birmingham, Ala., 1976-78, Gorham & Waldrep, P.C., Birmingham, 1978—. Mem. State Dem. Exec. Com., 1986-90; chmn. Gov. Folsom's Task Force on Edn. Reform, 1993; acting chief of staff Gov. Jim Folsom, 1993-94; chief of transition Gov. Jim Folsom, 1993; bd. dirs. John Croyle's Big Oak Ranch Inc., 1982-91, Positive Maturity, 1988-93; trustee Leukemia Soc. Am., 1989-94; pres. Birmingham Downtown Dem. Club, 1983-84, founding mem. City of Birmingham Park and Recreation, 1985-93, Parkway Christian Acad. Parents and Tchrs. Fellowship, 1987-89; mem. Ala. Mfg. Housing Commn., So. Regional Edn. Bd., Edn. Commn. States. With Ala. Air N.G., 1971-77. Mem. ABA, ATLA, Fed. Energy Bar Assn., Ala. State Bar Assn., Ala. Trial Lawyers Assn., Christian Legal Soc., Jacksonville State U. Nat. Alumni Assn. (pres. 1983-85), Kiwanis (pres. 1986-87). Baptist. General civil litigation, Civil rights. Office: Gorham & Waldrep PC 2101 6th Ave N Ste 700 Birmingham AL 35203-2761

**WALDRON, JONATHAN KENT,** lawyer; b. Washington, Feb. 11, 1949; s. Russell Lee and Ruth Magdalena Waldron; m. Janet Amy Roltsch, Dec. 8, 1973; children: Nathan Jay, Nicole Lee. BS in English, USCG Acad., 1971; JD, U. Miami, 1981. Bar: Fla. 1981, D.C. 1990. Officer USCG, 1971-91; sr. counsel Marine Spill Response Corp., Washington, 1991-95; ptnr. Dyer Ellis & Joseph, Washington, 1996—, 1997—. Recipient Schneider award Dept. Transp., 1990. Mem. Maritime Law Assn. Avocation: tennis. Administrative and regulatory, Environmental, Private international. Home: 3302 Lauren Oaks Ct Oak Hill VA 20171-1742 Office: Dyer Ellis & Joseph 600 New Hampshire Ave NW Washington DC 20037-2403

**WALDRON, KENNETH LYNN,** lawyer; b. Cape Girardeau, Mo., Oct. 18, 1941; s. Leonard Vernal and Edna Marion (Baskerville) W.; children: Leonard, Matthew, Charles. Student, Westminster Coll., 1959-61; BS, U. Mo., 1963, JD, 1966. Bar: Mo. 1966, U.S. Dist. Ct. (ea. dist.) Mo. 1968, U.S. Ct. Appeals (8th cir.) 1971, U.S. Supreme Ct. 1975. Salesman Nat. Biscuit Co., various locations, 1963-66; assoc. Buerkle & Lowes, Jackson, Mo., 1966-71; ptnr. Waldron & Assocs., Jackson, 1971-91; pres., CEO Eagle Environ. Products, Inc.; pres. Quail Springs Farm and Kennels, Inc., Stonewall Enterprises, Inc., Jackson Kids Stuff, Ltd. Served to capt. U.S. Army, 1966-68. Decorated 2 Legions of Merit; named one of Outstanding Young Men in Am., 1972, 74, 76. Mem. Mo. Bar Assn., Assn. Trial Lawyers Am., Mo. Assn. Trial Attys., Am. Soc. Law and Medicine, Nat. Inst. Mcpl. Law Officers, Jackson Jaycees (Mo. legal counsel 1972-74, disting. service award 1968, 74), Am. Legion, Rotary. Republican. Baptist. Avocations: tennis, golf, hunting, bird dog field trials, music (vocal & guitar). Personal injury, General civil litigation. Home: PO Box 270 Jackson MO 63755-0270 Office: Waldron & Assocs PO Box 270 Jackson MO 63755-0270

**WALDROP, NORMAN ERSKINE, JR.,** lawyer; b. Gadsden, Ala., Feb. 27, 1946; s. Norman E. Sr. and Margaret Alice Waldrop; m. Margaret Ann Waldrop, Sept. 13, 1969; children: Margaret Carson, Norman Erskine III. BS, Auburn U., 1968; JD, U. Ala., 1971. Bar: Ala. 1971. Trial atty., ptnr. Armbrecht, jackson, DeMouy, Crowe, Holmes & Reeves, Mobile, Ala., 1971—; mem. code commn., Ala. Judicial Inquiry Commn., Montgomery, 1994-99; chmn. so. dist. Ala. adv. bd., Mobile, 1992-96. Capt. USAR Transp. Svc., 1971-77, Mobile. Mem. Nat. Assn. Railroad Trial Counsel, Am. Bd. Trial Advocates, Maritime Law Assn., Fedn. Ins. & Corp. Counsel, Order of Coif, Omicron Delta Kappa. Avocations: tennis, golf. Personal injury, Professional liability. Office: Armbrecht Jackson DeMouy PO Box 290 Mobile AL 36601-0290

**WALES, GWYNNE HUNTINGTON,** lawyer; b. Evanston, Ill., Apr. 18, 1933; s. Robert Willett and Solace (Huntington) W.; m. Janet McCobb, Feb. 8, 1957; children—Thomas Gwynne, Catherine Anne, Louise Carrie. A.B., Princeton U., 1954; J.D., Harvard U., 1961. Bar: N.Y. 1962. Assoc. White & Case, N.Y.C., 1961-69; ptnr. White & Case, 1969—; resident ptnr. White & Case, Brussels, 1969-75, Ankara, Turkey, 1998—. Served with USN, 1954-58. Mem. ABA, N.Y. State Bar Assn., Am. Law Inst., Union Internat. des Avocats. Club: Round Hill (Greenwich, Conn.). Private international, Corporate taxation, Personal income taxation. Home: Hafta Sokak 16, 06700 Gaziosmanpasa Ankara, Turkey Office: White & Case Piyade Sokak, 18 Portakal Cicegi Kat 2, 06550 Camkaya Ankara, Turkey

**WALES, ROSS ELLIOT,** lawyer; b. Youngstown, Ohio, Oct. 17, 1947; s. Craig C. and Beverly (Bromley) W.; m. Juliana Fraser, Sept. 16, 1972; children: Dod Elliot, James Craig. AB, Princeton U., 1969; JD, U. Va., 1974. Bar: Ohio 1974, U.S. Dist. Ct. (so. dist.) Ohio 1974, U.S. Ct. Appeals (5th cir.) 1979. Assoc. Taft, Stettinius & Hollister, Cin., 1974-81, ptnr., 1981—; pres. U.S. Swimming, Inc., Colorado Springs, 1979-84, U.S. Aquatic Sports, Inc., Colorado Springs, 1984-88, 94-98. Pres. Cin. Active to Support Edn., 1987-88; chmn. sch. tax levy campaign, Cin., 1987; trustee The Childrens Home Cin., 1987—, v.p., 1995-98, pres., 1998—; bd. sec. Cin. State Tech. and C.C., 1995-98, vice-chmn., 1998—; sec. Greater Cin. Arts and Edn. Ctr., 1996—. Mem. ABA, Ohio Bar Assn., Cin. Bar Assn., Internat. Swimming Fedn. of Lausanne, Switzerland (sec. 1988-92, v.p. 1992—). Presbyterian. General corporate, Private international, Health. Office: 1800 Star Bank Ctr 425 Walnut St Cincinnati OH 45202-3923

**WALKER, A. HARRIS,** lawyer, manufacturing executive, retired; b. Lincoln, Ill., Feb. 7, 1935; s. Arthur M. and Margaret (Harris) W.; m. Ann Pontious, Aug. 27, 1960; children: Christine, Stuart, Melinda. BA, Northwestern U., 1956; JD, U. Mich., 1963; MBA, U. Chgo., 1969. Bar: Ill. 1963, U.S. Dist. Ct. (no. dist.) Ill. 1964, U.S. Ct. Appeals (7th cir.) 1963. Assoc. Peterson, Lowry, Rall, Barber & Ross, Chgo., 1963-66; atty. Am. Hosp. Supply Co., Evanston, Ill., 1966-71; sr. atty. A.B. Dick Co., Chgo., 1971-74, asst. gen. counsel, 1974-86, v.p., gen. counsel, sec., 1986-97, also bd. dirs., officer of various subs.; retired, 1997. Presbyterian. General corporate.

**WALKER, BETTY STEVENS,** lawyer; b. N.Y.C., Feb. 3, 1943; d. Randolph Blakney and Anne (Stevens) Wood; m. Paul Thomas Walker, Aug. 27, 1942; children: Camarf, Tarik, Kumi. BA in Polit. Sci. and History, Spelman Coll., 1964; JD, Harvard U., 1967. Bar: U.S. Dist. Ct. (DC) 1981, U.S. Ct. Appeals (DC cir.) 1977, U.S. Supreme Ct. 1996. Coord. southern schs. Legal Def. and Ednl. Fund, N.Y.C., 1964; asst. prof. polit. sci. Shaw U., Raleigh, N.C., 1968-69; faculty fellow Shaw U., Raleigh, 1969-70; corp. atty. Southern Railway Co., Washington, 1974-77; exec. asst. to adminstr. Farmers Home Adminstrn. USDA, Washington, 1977-81; assoc. Walker & Walker Assoc., P.C., Washington, 1981—. Democrat. Mem. African Meth. Ch. Personal injury. Office: Walker & Walker Assoc PC 2807 18th St NW Washington DC 20009

**WALKER, CLARENCE WESLEY,** lawyer; b. Durham, N.C., July 19, 1931; s. Ernie Franklin and Mollie Elizabeth (Cole) W.; m. Ann-Heath Harris, June 5, 1954; children: Clare Ann, Wesley Gregg. A.B., Duke U., 1953, LL.B., 1955. Bar: N.C. 1955. Assoc. Mudge Stern Baldwin & Todd, 1955-59; ptnr. Kennedy, Covington, Loddell & Hickman, Charlotte, N.C., 1959—; bd. dirs. Lawyers Mut. Liability Ins. Co., Legal Services Corp. N.C., Oakwood Homes Corp. Glendale Group, Ltd.; lectr. N.C. Bar Found. Continuing Legal Edn. Insts., N.C. Jud. Planning Com., 1978-79; pres. Pvt. Adjudication Found. Chmn. bd. mgrs. Charlotte Meml. Hosp. and Med. Ctr., 1981-87; trustee N.C. Ctrl. U., 1979-83; vice-chmn. Charlotte-Mecklenburg Hosp. Authority, 1998-99; adv. bd. Ctrl. Piedmont Paralegal Sch.; chmn. Charlotte-Mecklenburg Hosp. Found.; trustee Charlotte Country Day Sch., 1977-81; state chmn. Nat. Found. March of Dimes, 1968-70; chmn. Charlotte Park and Recreation Commn., 1970-73; bd. dirs. Charlotte Symphony, 1965-71, Bethlehem Ctr., 1975-77, N.C. Recreators Found., 1973-75; adv. bd. Charlotte Children's Theatre, 1972; bd. dirs. Charlotte C. of C., 1970-72; bd. visitors Duke U. Law Sch.; dir., gen. campaign chmn. United Way Ctrl. Carolinas, 1985. Fellow Am. Bar Found.; mem. N.C. Bar Assn. (pres. 1978-79, gov. 1971-75), ABA (state del. 1980-89, assembly del., bd. govs. 1997-2000) 26th Jud. Dist. Bar Assn., Mecklenburg Bar Found. (trustee), Am. Law Inst., Order of Coif, Phi Eta Sigma, Phi Beta Kappa. Democrat. Methodist. General corporate, Securities, Public utilities. Home: 1047 Ardsley Rd Charlotte NC 28207-1815 Office: Kennedy Covington Lobdell & Hickman Bank of Am Corp Ctr 100 N Tryon St Ste 4200 Charlotte NC 28202-4006

**WALKER, CRAIG MICHAEL,** lawyer; b. Vt., 1947; m. Patricia A. Magruder; two children. BA, Williams Coll., 1969; JD, Cornell U., 1972. Bar: N.Y. 1973, U.S. Dist. Ct. (so. dist.) N.Y. 1975, U.S. Ct. Appeals (2d cir) 1975, U.S. Supreme Ct 1976. Assoc. Alexander & Green, N.Y.C., 1972-80, ptnr., 1980-86, chmn. litigation dept., 1985-86; ptnr. Walter, Conston, Alexander & Green P.C., N.Y.C., 1987-89, Rogers & Wells LLP, N.Y.C., 1990—. Contbr. author: New York Forms of Jury Instruction, 1992; contbr. articles to profl. jours. Fellow Am. Bar Found.; mem. ABA, N.Y. State Bar Assn., Def. Rsch. Inst., Fed. Bar Coun. Democrat. Antitrust, Technology, Securities.

**WALKER, DANIEL JOSHUA, JR.,** lawyer; b. Gibson, N.C., Nov. 27, 1915; s. Daniel Joshua and Annie (Hurdle) W.; m. Sarah Elizabeth Nicholson, June 14, 1941. AB, U. N.C., 1936, JD, 1948. Bar: N.C. 1948, U.S. Dist. Ct. (mid. dist.) N.C. 1956, U.S. Ct. Appeals (4th cir.) 1956. Clk. Superior Ct. Alamance County, Graham, N.C., 1948-53; ptnr. Long, Ridge, Harris & Walker, Graham, 1953-67; county atty. Alamance County, 1964-77, county mgr., 1971-76; sr. mem. Walker Harris & Pierce, Graham, 1967-71; ptnr. Allen & Walker and predecessor, Burlington, N.C., 1977-91; pvt. practice Graham, 1991—; of counsel Floyd, Allen & Jacobs, Greensboro, Burlington, 1991—. Mem. Human Rels. Coun. of Alamance County, 1963-71, chmn., 1970; mem. N.C. Environ. Mgmt. Commn., 1972-77; pres. Alamance County Young Dem. Club, 1950; chmn. Alamance County Dem. Exec. Com., 1956-58; mem. N.C. Dem. Exec. Com., 1958-66; trustee Tech. Inst. of Alamance, 1964-71, Presbyn. Found., Presbyn. Ch. of U.S., 1969-73; moderator Orange Presbytery, 1980, mem. coun., 1972-74; bd. dirs. Alamance County United Fund, Cherokee coun. Boy Scouts Am., Burlington Cmty. YMCA; mem. adv. bd. Salvation Army, 1980—, chmn., 1990-91. Capt. AUS, 1942-46, ETO. Decorated Bronze Star. Mem. ABA, N.C. Bar Assn., Alamance County Bar Assn. (pres. 1977-78), N.C. Assn. County Attys. (pres. 1972, County Atty. of Yr. 1971), 15th Jud. Dist. Bar Assn. (pres. 1967-68), Alamance County C. of C. (pres. 1981), Phi Alpha Delta, Burlington Kiwanis (pres. 1957, Alamance County Citizen of Yr. 1969). Probate, Condemnation. Office: PO Box 772 Graham NC 27253-0772

**WALKER, E. ALLEN,** lawyer; b. Provo, Utah, July 4, 1963; s. G. Perrin and Charlotte Joy (Johnson) W.; m. Stephanie Joell Reed, July 20, 1990; children: Kyrsten, Brittany, Jordan. BA, Brigham Young U., 1986, JD, 1989. Bar: Wash. 1990, U.S. Dist. Ct. (we. dist.) Wash. 1990. Assoc. Law Offices of Clayton R. Dickinson, Tacoma, Wash., 1990-92; ptnr. Walker Bradshaw, P.C., Tacoma, 1993—. Mem. Wash. State Bar Assn., Tacoma-Pierce County Bar Assn. Republican. Mem. Ch. of Latter Day Saints. Avocation: religious instruction. Family and matrimonial, Criminal, Personal injury. Office: Walker Bradshaw PC 2607 Bridgeport Way W Ste 2C Tacoma WA 98466-4725

**WALKER, EDWARD GARRETT,** lawyer; b. Roanoke Rapids, N.C., Oct. 19, 1950; s. Aubrey O'Neal and Christine Ferguson Walker; m. Jane Tuckwiller, Sept. 10, 1982; children: Charles Aubrey, Elizabeth Garrett. BA in English, U. N.C., 1972, JD with high honors, 1975. Bar: N.C. 1975. Law clk. to chief justice Susie Sharp N.C. Supreme Ct., Raleigh, 1975-76; lawyer Smith Helms Mulliss & Moore LLP, Greensboro, N.C., 1976—; adj. prof. law Wake Forest U. Law Sch., Winston-Salem, N.C., 1993-95. Assoc. editor N.C. Law Rev., 1974-75. Mem. ABA (real property sect.), Am. Coll. Real Estate Lawyers, N.C. Bar Assn. (chmn. real property sect. 1985-86), Phi Beta Kappa, Order of Coif. Contracts commercial, Land use and zoning (including planning), Real property. Home: 2 Loch Ridge Dr Greensboro NC 27408-3868 Office: Smith Helms Mulliss & Moore LLP 300 N Greene St Ste 1400 Greensboro NC 27401-2171

**WALKER, FRANCIS JOSEPH,** lawyer; b. Tacoma, Aug. 5, 1922; s. John McSweeney and Sarah Veronica (Meechan) W.; m. Julia Corinne O'Brien, Jan. 27, 1951; children: Vincent Paul, Monica Irene Hylton, Jill Marie Nudell, John Michael, Michael Joseph, Thomas More. BA, St. Martin's Coll., 1947; JD, U. Wash., 1950. Bar: Wash. Asst. atty. gen. State of Wash., 1950-51; pvt. practice law, Olympia, Wash., 1951—; gen. counsel Wash. Cath. Conf., 1967-76. Lt. (j.g.) USNR, 1943-46; PTO. Probate, Estate taxation, Consumer commercial. Home and Office: 2723 Hillside Dr SE Olympia WA 98501-3460

**WALKER, GEORGE KONTZ,** law educator; b. Tuscaloosa, Ala., July 8, 1938; s. Joseph Henry and Catherine Louise (Indorf) W.; m. Phyllis Ann Sherman, July 30, 1966; children: Charles Edward, Mary Neel. BA, U. Ala., 1959; LLB, Vanderbilt U., 1966; AM, Duke U., 1968; LLM, U. Va., 1972; postgrad. (Sterling fellow), Law Sch. Yale U., 1975-76. Bar: Va. 1967, N.C. 1976. Law clk. U.S. Dist. Ct., Richmond, Va., 1966-67; assoc. Hunton, Williams, Gay, Powell & Gibson, Richmond, 1967-70; pvt. practice Charlottesville, Va., 1970-71; asst. prof. Law Sch. Wake Forest U., Winston-Salem, N.C., 1972-73, assoc. prof. Law Sch., 1974-77, prof. Law Sch., 1977—; mem. bd. advisors Divinity Sch. Wake Forest U., 1991-94; Charles H. Stockton prof. internat. law U.S. Naval War Coll., 1992-93; vis. prof. Marshall-Wythe Sch. Law, Coll. William and Mary, Williamsburg, Va., 1979-80, U. Ala. Law Sch., 1985; cons. Naval War Coll., 1976—, Nat. Def. Exec. Res., 1991—, Naval War Coll., Operational Law Adv. Bd., 1993—. Co-author: Moore's Federal Practice, 3rd edit., 1997; contbr. articles to profl. jours. With USN, 1959-62, capt. USNR, ret. Woodrow Wilson fellow, 1962-63; recipient Joseph Branch Alumni Svc. award, Wake Forest, 1988; named Hon. Atty. Gen. N.C., 1986. Mem. ABA, Va. Bar Assn., N.C. Bar Assn. (v.p. 1997-98), Am. Soc. Internat. Law (exec. coun. 1988-91), Internat. Law Assn., Am. Judicature Soc., Am. Law Inst., Maritime Law Assn., Order of Barristers, Order of the Coif (hon.), Piedmont Club, Phi Beta Kappa, Sigma Alpha Epsilon, Phi Delta Phi. Democrat. Episcopalian. Home: 3321 Pennington Ln Winston Salem NC 27106-5439 Office: Wake Forest U Sch Law PO Box 7206 Winston Salem NC 27109-7206

**WALKER, IRVING EDWARD,** lawyer; b. Balt., Jan. 31, 1952; s. Bertram and Mildred (Shapiro) W.; m. Laura Sachs, May 21, 1978; children: Brandon Harris, Aaron Seth, Emily Celeste. BA, Duke U., 1973; JD, U. Md., 1978. Bar: Md. 1978, U.S. Dist. Ct. Md. 1978, U.S. Ct. Appeals (4th cir.) 1980, U.S. Supreme Ct. 1995. Assoc. Frank, Bernstein, Conaway & Goldman, Balt., 1978-85, ptnr., 1986-91; prin. Miles & Stockbridge, Balt., 1991—; chair Bankruptcy & Creditors Rights Group, 1991—. Contbg. author: Bankruptcy Deskbook, 1986. Bd. dirs. Jewish Community Ctr. Greater Balt., 1986-88, Temple Emanuel of Balt., Inc., 1996—. Mem. ABA (mem. chpt. 11 subcom. 1993), Md. Bar Assn., Bar Assn. Balt. City (chmn. bankruptcy and bus. law com. 1989-90), Am. Bankruptcy Inst., Bankruptcy Assn. Dist. Md. (pres. 1992-93, chmn. Balt. chpt. 1989-91), Order of Coif. Avocations: soccer, weightlifting. Bankruptcy, Federal civil litigation. Office: Miles & Stockbridge 10 Light St Ste 1100 Baltimore MD 21202-1487

**WALKER, JEREMY THOMAS,** lawyer; b. Manchester, N.H., Oct. 2, 1967; s. Jerome Kenneth and Patricia Carol Walker; m. Argyro Georgoulas, Aug. 25, 1991; children: Rebecca Sophia, Krysten Elizabeth. BA in Liberal Arts, St. Anselm Coll., 1989; BS in Civil Engring., U. Notre Dame, 1990; JD, William and Mary, 1996. Bar: N.H. 1996, U.S. Dist. Ct. N.H. 1996. Civil engr. Radian Corp., Herndon, Va., 1990-93; atty. McLane Law Firm, Manchester, 1996—. Advisor United Way, Manchester, 1996-97. Mem. N.H. Trial Lawyers. Federal civil litigation, Intellectual property. Office: McLane Graf, Raderson & Middleton 900 Elm St PO Box 326 Manchester NH 03105-0326

**WALKER, JOHN MERCER, JR.,** federal judge; b. N.Y.C., Dec. 26, 1940; s. John Mercer and Louise (Mead) W.; m. Cristy West, June 20, 1980 (div. Apr. 1983); m. Katharine Kirkland, Feb. 14, 1987. BA, Yale U., 1962; JD, U. Mich., 1966. Bar: N.Y. 1969, U.S. Dist. Ct. (so. dist.) N.Y. 1971, U.S. Ct. Appeals (2d cir.) 1972, U.S. Supreme Ct. 1977, U.S. Ct. Appeals (D.C. cir.) 1982. Maxwell Sch. Pub. Adminstrn. fellow, state counsel Republic of Botswana, Africa, 1966-68; assoc. Davis, Polk and Warwell, N.Y.C., 1969-70; asst. U.S. atty. U.S. Dist. Ct. (so. dist.) N.Y., 1971-75; assoc. to ptnr. Carter, Ledyard and Milburn, N.Y.C., 1975-81; asst. sec. enforcement ops. Dept. Treasury, Washington, 1981-85; judge U.S. Dist. Ct. (so. dist.) N.Y., 1985-89, U.S. Ct. Appeals (2nd cir.), 1989—; adj. prof. NYU Law Sch., 1995—; gen. counsel Nat. Coun. on Crime and Deliquency, N.Y.C., 1977-81; chmn. Fed. Law Enforcement Tng. Ctr., Washington, 1981-85; spl. counsel Adminstrv. Conf. U.S., Washington, 1986-92; mem. budget com. jud. conf. Inst. Jud. Adminstrn., 1992—, dir., 1992—. Del. Rep. Nat. Conv., Detroit, 1980. With USMCR, 1963-67. Recipient Alexander Hamilton award Sec. of Treas., Washington, 1985, Secret Service Honor award, 1985. Mem. ABA, D.C. Bar Assn., Assn. Bar City of N.Y., Fed. Judges Assn. (pres. 1993-95). Republican. Episcopalian. Office: US Cir Ct 157 Church St New Haven CT 06510-2100

**WALKER, JOHN SUMPTER, JR.,** lawyer; b. Richmond, Ark., Oct. 13, 1921; s. John Sumpter, Martha (Wilson) W.; m. Eljana M. duVall, Dec. 31, 1947; children: John Stephen, Barbara Monika Ann, Peter Mark Gregory. *Daughter Barbara is executive director of the Independent Bankers of Colorado organization. The former state banking commissioner was appointed by Colorado governor Roy Romer to be the first woman to serve in that position in the state. She also serves as special counsel with McKenna & Cuneo, a Denver law firm. She was staff attorney for the U.S. Securities and Exchange Commission for four years. She holds a journalism degree from the University of Colorado and a law degree from the University of Denver. She is married to Philip Feigin, executive director, North American Securities Administrators Association, Inc., Washington D.C.* BA, Tulane U., 1942; MS, U. Denver, 1952, JD, 1960; diploma Nat. Def. U., 1981. Bar: Colo. 1960, U.S. Dist. Ct. Colo. 1960, U.S. Supreme Ct., 1968, U.S. Ct. Appeals (10th cir.) 1960, U.S. Tax Ct., 1981. With Denver & Rio Grande Western R.R. Co., 1951-61, gen. solicitor, 1961-89; pres. Denver Union Terminal Ry. Co. Apptd. gen. counsel Moffat Tunnel Commn., 1991; life mem. Children's Diabetes Fund. With U.S. Army, 1942-46. Decorated Bronze Star. Mem. Colo. Bar Assn., Arapahoe County Bar Assn., Alliance Francaise (life), Order of St. Ives, U. Denver Chancellors' Soc., Cath. Lawyers Guild, Denver Athletic Club. Republican. Roman Catholic. General corporate.

**WALKER, JONATHAN LEE,** lawyer; b. Kalamazoo, Mar. 8, 1948; s. Harvey E. and Olivia M. (Estrada) W. BA, U. Mich., 1969; JD, Wayne State U., 1977. Bar: Mich. 1977, Colo. 1996, U.S. Dist. Ct. (ea. dist.) Mich. 1983. Assoc. Moore, Barr & Kerwin, Detroit, 1977-79; ptnr. firm Barr & Walker, Detroit, 1979-82; assoc. firm Richard M. Goodman, P.C., Detroit, 1983-87; hearing officer Mich. Civil Rights Commn., Detroit, 1983-86; pvt. practice Detroit, 1988-89, Birmingham, Mich., 1990-98; dep. pub. defender Office of State Pub. Defender, Colorado Springs, Colo., 1998—; participant Detroit Bar Assn. Vol. Lawyer Program. Bd. dirs. Cmty. treatment Ctr.-Project Rehab., Detroit, 1983-89; mem. scholarship com. Latino en Marcha Scholarship Fund, Detroit, 1984; treas. youth assistance program Citizens Adv. Coun., 1987. Mem. ATLA, State Bar Mich. Found., Wayne County Mediation Tribunal (mediator), Am. Arbitration Assn. (arbitrator), Nat. Lawyers Guild (exec. bd. Detroit chpt. 1988-92, pres. Detroit chpt. 1988-90), Mich. Trial Lawyers Assn. (co-chair coalition com. 1988-90, exec. bd. 1988-96, co-chair pro bono com. 1991-96), State Bar Mich. (com. on underrepresented groups in law 1980-92, chmn. 1983-85, mem. com. jud. qualifications 1985-86, Latin Am. affairs coun. 1978-96), Legal Aid and Def. Assn. (bd. dirs. 1990-95), Hispanic Bar Assn., Trial Lawyers for Pub. Justice (founder 1981, mem. amicus com. 1985-86, state capt. 1991-95), Ctr. for Auto Safety, Washtenaw County Bar Assn. Product liability, Criminal. Office: 25 N Cascade 400 Colorado Springs CO 80903

**WALKER, L. MARK,** lawyer; b. Ada, Okla., July 10, 1957; s. Richard G. and Beverly C. (Jones) W.; m. Frances L. Fisher, Feb. 24, 1989; 1 child, Michael Alan. BBA in Econs. with spl. distinction, U. Okla., 1980, JD, 1983. Bar: Okla. 1983. Shareholder, dir. Crowe & Dunlevy, P.C., Oklahoma City, 1983—. Contbr. articles to profl. jours. Mem. ABA, Okla. Mineral Lawyers Soc., Okla. Bar Assn., Order of Coif. Environmental, Oil, gas, and mineral. Home: 4705 Shadow Creek Dr Edmond OK 73034-5900 Office: Crowe & Dunlevy PC 20 N Broadway Ave Ste 1800 Oklahoma City OK 73102-8273

**WALKER, LEE ANNE,** lawyer; b. Edmonton, Alta., Can., Aug. 12, 1949; d. Jock and Leila Anne (Mithaug) Walker; m. Thomas Peters, Defc. 30, 1995. JD, U. Utah, 1979. Bar: Utah 1979. CEO Handivan Inc., Salt Lake City, 1987—. Address: 4790 Cherry St Salt Lake City UT 84123-3609

**WALKER, RANDALL WAYNE,** lawyer; b. Pampa, Tex., Mar. 13, 1956; s. Jimmy Wayne and Dorothy Evelyn (Mercer) W.; m. Patricia Gale Vernon Walker, Dec. 12, 1992; children: Alissa Gail Walker Warner, Angie Marie Walker Grimsey, Cory Wayne, Nicholas Russell Rattan. AA, Clarendon (Tex.) Coll., 1980; BS, West Tex. State U., Canyon, 1984; JD, Tex. Tech. U., Lubbock, 1986. Bar: Tex., 1987. Pvt. practice Clarendon, Tex., 1987-91; asst. atty. gen. Tex. Atty. Gen. Office, Wichita Falls, Tex., 1991—; mng. atty. Tex. Atty. Gen. Office, Wichita Falls, 1992—. Cubmaster Boy Scouts Am., Clarendon, 1988-89. Mem. State Bar Tex., Wichita County Bar Assn., Lions (v.p. Clarendon 1989). Avocations: fishing, camping, woodworking. Office: Attorney General Office 813 8th St Wichita Falls TX 76301-3305

**WALKER, RICHARD HENRY,** lawyer; b. Wilmington, Del., Dec. 29, 1950; s. Henry H. and Mary L. (Meister) W. BA, Trinity Coll., 1972; JD, Temple U., 1975. Bar: Pa. 1976, U.S. Supreme Ct. 1977, N.Y. 1978, D.C. 1981. Law clk. to Hon. Collins J. Seitz U.S. Ct. Appeals (3rd cir.), Wilmington, Del., 1975-76; assoc., ptnr. Cadwalader, Wickersham & Taft, N.Y.C., 1976-91; regional dir. N.E. office U.S. SEC, N.Y.C., 1991-95; gen. counsel U.S. SEC, Washington, 1996-98, dir. enforcement, 1998—. Fellow Am. Bar Found. Office: SEC 450 5th St NW Rm 8213 Washington DC 20549-0001

**WALKER, ROBERT KIRK,** lawyer; m. Joy Holt; children: R. Kirk Jr., Marilyn Joy Walker Fisher, James Holt. Student, U. South, Sewanee; LLB, U. Va., 1948, JD, 1970. Bar: Va. 1948, Tenn. 1948. Assoc. Strang, Fletcher & Carriger, Chattanooga, 1949-55; ptnr. Strang, Fletcher, Carriger, Walker, Hodge & Smith, Chattanooga, 1955-71; mayor City of Chattanooga, 1971-75; mng. ptnr. Strang, Fletcher, Carriger, Walker, Hodge & Smith, Chattanooga, 1975-97, of counsel, 1998; life mem. U.S. Jud. Conf. 6th cir., 1966—; hearing officer Bd. Profl. Responsibility of Supreme Ct. of Tenn., 1976-84. Chmn. Chattanooga-Hamilton County Com. on Bicentennial of U.S. Constn., 1987-90, chmn. Miller Park Bd., 1974—; chmn. bd. Ctr. City Corp. (Miller Park Plz.), 1986-89; founding chmn. Leadership Chattanooga, 1983-85; chmn. Soldiers & Sailors Meml. Auditorium Redevel. com., 1988-92; chmn. Tivoli Theatre Renovation and Restoration study com., 1979-82, mem. Chattanooga Venture Tivoli Bldg. com. 1986-89, mem. Ovation! Campaign exec. com., 1986-89; gen. campaign chmn. United Way Chattanooga, 1991, bd. dirs., 1990-96, vice chmn., 1991, exec. com., 1990-92; trustee U. Chattanooga Found., 1989—, exec. com., 1994—; mem. U. Tenn. Chattanooga Chancellors Roundtable, 1981-84; mem. Tonya Pub. Affairs adv. com., U. South, 1980—; mem. Chattanooga Sch. Consolidation Referendum coms., 1994, 96, Chattanooga Sales Tax Referendum com., 1996; mem. nat. coun. Boy Scouts of Am., 1966-76, exec. bd. Cherokee Area Coun. 1958—, v.p., 1967-69; vice chmn. adv. bd. U. Tenn. Govt.-Industry-Law Ctr., 1965-66; exec. bd. Chattanooga Area Heart Assn., 1966-75; exec. bd. Hamilton County Law Enforcement Commn., 1962-67; mem. Chattanooga-Hamilton County Health Dept. adv. com., 1966-71; mem. Tenn. Law Revision Commn., 1970-71; v.p. Tenn. Mcpl. League, 19791-75; chmn. Tenn. Local Govt. study commn., 1973-74; bd. dirs. Nat. Human Svcs. Inst. Families and Children, treas., 1974-76; mem. Nat. Conf. Social Welfare & U.S. Dept. HEW Task Force on Orgn. & Delivery of Human Svcs. in U.S., 1976-77; numerous other civic offices and activities. Lt., USN, World War II and Korea. Honored by Tenn. Gen. Assembly for Svc. Contbns. to Perpetuate Pub. Good, 1998; recipient Dorothy Patten Love of Chattanooga award, 1991; receipitn award for disting. contbns. on 30th anniversary Chattanooga State Tech. C.C., 1996; recipient numerous medals and awards Freedoms Found., including George Washington honor medals for pub. address, 1981, 88, 93, 97; recipient Ctrl. H.S. Disting. Alumni award, 1993; Dr. John. E. Huckaba City Beautiful award 1996 presented to Robert Kirk and Joy Walker, Scenic Cities Beautiful com.; hon. mem. Am. Women in Radio & TV; numerous other awards. Fellow Am. Bar Found., Tennessee Bar Found. (charter), Chattanooga Bar Found. (charter; chmn. 1991-97); Tenn. Bar Assn. (pres. 1965-66), Chattanooga Bar Assn. (pres. 1962-63, Ralph H. Kelley Humanitarian award 1994); mem. Chattanooga Audubon Soc. (exec. bd. 1981-84), Rotary Club of Chattanooga (bd. dirs. 1987-88, 89-90, 96-97, 1st v.p. 1989-90, pres.-elect 1994-95, pres. 1995-96, Paul Harris fellow 1990—), Kiwanis (hon., Disting. Svc. award 1992), Greater Chattanooga Area C. of C. (edn. com. 1962-71, chmn. spl. 4-yr. state coll. com. 1966-71, chmn. ednl. task force 1967-71, dir. 1969-75, 81-82, v.p. 1982), Optimist Club of Chattanooga (pres. 1958-59), Optimist Internat. (past lt. gov., Man of Yr. 1956), Mountain City Club of Chattanooga, Chattanooga Golf & Country Club, Alpha Hon. Scholastic Soc. Non-profit and tax-exempt organizations, Legislative, Probate. Office: Strang Fletcher Carriger Walker Hodge & Smith 1 Union Sq Chattanooga TN 37402-2505

**WALKER, TIMOTHY BLAKE,** lawyer, educator; b. Utica, N.Y., May 21, 1940; s. Harold Blake and Mary Alice (Corder) W.; m. Sandra Blake; children: Kimberlee Corder, Tyler Blake, Kelley Loren. AB magna cum laude, Princeton U., 1962; JD magna cum laude, U. Denver, 1967, MA in Sociology, 1969. Bar: Colo. 1968, Calif. 1969, Ind. 1971. Asst. prof. law U. Pacific, 1968-69; vis. assoc. prof. U. Toledo, 1969-70; assoc. prof. Indpls. Law Sch., Ind. U., 1970-71; assoc. prof. U. Denver, 1971-75, prof., 1975-99; prof. emeritus, 1999—; dir. adminstrn. of justice program U. Denver, 1971-78; sole practice law Denver, 1972-79; of counsel Robert T. Hinds, Jr. & Assocs. (P.C.), Littleton, Colo., 1980-85; ptnr., of counsel Cox, Mustain-Wood, Walker & Schumacher, Littleton, 1985—; cons. in field; rsch. on lay representation in adminstrv. agys., Colo., 1975-76. Contbr. articles to profl. publs.; lectr., symposium editor: Denver Law Jour., 1966-67; editor-in-chief: Family Law Quar., 1983-92. Mem. Ind. Child Support Commn., 1970-71; pres. Shawnee (Colo.) Water Consumers Assn., 1975-84, 93-95; del. Colo. Rep. Conv., 1978. Colo. Bar Assn. grantee, 1975-76. Fellow Am. Sociol. Assn., Am. Acad. Matrimonial Lawyers, Internat. Acad. Matrimonial Lawyers; mem. ABA (vice chmn. child custody subcom., sec. sect. family law 1992-93, vice-chairperson, sec. family 1993-94, chairperson-elect sect. family law 1994-95, chairperson sect. family law 1995-96, mem. child custody task force, chmn. alimony maintenance and support com.), Calif. Bar Assn., Colo. Bar Assn., Ind. Bar Assn., Colo. Trial Lawyers Assn. (cons.). Presbyterian. Home: 7329 Rochester Ct Castle Rock CO 80104-9281 Office: 1900 Olive St Denver CO 80220-1857 also: 6601 S University Blvd Littleton CO 80121-2913 *Law and justice require the combination of intellectual self-discipline and an awareness of human dignity. The path of the law is often twisted and circuitous, and my goal has been to leave the trail better than I found it.*

**WALKER, TIMOTHY LEE,** lawyer; b. Whittier, Calif., Sept. 25, 1947; s. Maurice Samuel and Esther (Scoleri) W.; m. Claire M. Duarte, Aug. 16, 1969; children: Kristen, Matthew, Megan, Kendra. BS, U. Calif., Santa Barbara, 1969; JD, Loyola U., 1972. Bar: Calif. 1972, U.S. Dist. Ct. (cen. dist.) Calif. 1973; diplomate Am. Bd. of Trial Advocates. Assoc. Shield & Smith, L.A., 1972-76, ptnr., 1976-91; ptnr. Walker Haggerty & Behar, 1991—; bd. dirs. Assn. Southern Calif. Defense Counsel, L.A., pres. 1986. Fellow Am. Coll. Trial Lawyers, Internat. Soc. Barristers; mem. Internat. Assn. Defense Counsel, Def. Rsch. Inst. (bd. dirs. 1992-98), Arbitration L.A. Superior Ct. Avocation: sports. Construction, Personal injury, Federal civil litigation. Office: Ford Walker Haggerty & Behar 1 World Trade Ctr Fl 27 Long Beach CA 90831-0002

**WALKER, VAUGHN R.,** federal judge; b. Watseka, Ill., Feb. 27, 1944; s. Vaughn Rosenworth and Catharine (Miles) W. AB, U. Mich., 1966; JD, Stanford U., 1970. Intern economist SEC, Washington, 1966, 68; law clk. to the Hon. Robert J. Kelleher U.S. Dist. Ct. Calif., L.A., 1971-72; assoc. atty. Pillsbury Madison & Sutro, San Francisco, 1972-77, ptnr., 1978-90; judge U.S. Dist. Ct. (no. dist.) Calif., San Francisco, 1990—; mem. Calif. Law Revision Commn., Palo Alto, 1986-89. Dir. Jr. Achievement of Bay Area, San Francisco, 1979-83, St. Francis Found., San Francisco, 1991-97, 99—. Woodrow Wilson Found. fellow U. Calif., Berkeley, 1966-67. Fellow Am. Bar Found.; mem. ABA (jud. rep., antitrust sect. 1991-95), Lawyers' Club of San Francisco (pres. 1985-86), Assn. Bus. Trial Lawyers (dir. 1996-98), Am. Law Inst., Am. Saddlebred Horse Assn., San Francisco Mus. Modern Art, Bohemian Club, Olympic Club, Pacific-Union Club. Office: US Dist Ct 450 Golden Gate Ave Ste 36052 San Francisco CA 94102-3482

**WALKER, WALTER HERBERT, III,** lawyer, writer; b. Quincy, Mass., Sept. 12, 1949; s. Walter H. Jr. and Irene M. (Horn) W.; m. Anne M. DiScuillo, June 17, 1982; children: Brett Daniel, Jeffrey St. John. BA, U. Pa., 1971; JD, U. Calif., San Francisco, 1974. Bar: Calif. 1974, Mass. 1981. Appellate atty. ICC, Washington, 1975-77; trial atty. Handler, Baker, Greene & Taylor, San Francisco, 1977 80; ptnr. Sterns and Walker and predecessor firm Sterns, Smith, Walker & Grell, San Francisco, 1981-88; ptnr. firm Walker & Durham, San Francisco, 1988—. Author: A Dime to Dance By, 1983 (Best 1st Novel by Calif. Author), The Two Dude Defense, 1985, Rules of The Knife Fight, 1986, The Immediate Prospect of Being Hanged, 1989, The Appearance of Impropriety, 1992. Mem. ATLA, Consumer Attys. of Calif., San Francisco Trial Lawyers Assn., Mystery Writers Am. Democrat. Club: Hastings Rugby. Personal injury, Insurance, Product liability. Home: 604 Seminary Dr Mill Valley CA 94941-3169 Office: 50 Francisco St Ste 160 San Francisco CA 94133-2108

**WALKER, WOODROW WILSON,** lawyer, cattle and timber farmer; b. Greenville, Mich., Feb. 19, 1919; s. Craig Walker and Mildred Chase; m. Janet K. Keiter, Oct. 7, 1950; children: Jonathan Woodrow, William Craig, Elaine Virginia. BA, U. Mich., 1943; LLB, Cath. U., 1950. Bar: D.C. 1950, U.S. Supreme Ct. 1958, Va. 1959. Atty. Am. law div. legis. reference Libr. Congress, Washington, 1951-60; pvt. practice, Arlington, Va., 1960—; counsel Calvary Found., Arlington, 1970-85, first pres., 1972; judge moot ct. George Mason Law Sch., 1986; owner-operator Walker Farm Front Royal, Va., 1972—. Co-author rsch. publs. for U.S. Govt.; featured in Washington Post. V.p. Jefferson Civic Assn., Arlington, 1955-61; pres. Nellie Custis PTA, Arlington, 1960-61; sec. Arlington County Bd. Equalization Real Estate Assessment, 1962, chmn. 1963; com. chmn. Arlington Troop 108 Boy Scouts Am., 1964-69; mem. Arlington County Pub. Utilities Commn., 1964-66, vice chmn., 1965-66; pres. Betschler Class Adult Sunday Sch., Calvary United Meth. Ch., Arlington, 1965. Served with U.S. Army, 1943-45, PTO. Cited for notable deed in conduct of his legal duties Washington Post, 1996. Mem. ABA, Arlington County Bar Assn., Va. Farm Bur., Va. Cattleman's Assn. Methodist. Democrat. Consumer commercial, Contracts commercial, General practice. Home: 2822 Ft Scott Dr Arlington VA 22202-2307 Office: 2055 N 15th St Ste 203 Arlington VA 22201-2613

**WALKUP, CHARLOTTE LLOYD,** lawyer; b. N.Y.C., Apr. 28, 1910; d. Charles Henry and Helene Louise (Wheeler) Tuttle; m. David D. Lloyd, Oct. 19, 1940 (dec. Dec. 1962); children: Andrew M. Lloyd, Louisa Lloyd Hurley; m. Homer Allen Walkup, Feb. 4, 1967. AB, Bassar Coll., 1931; LLB, Columbia U., 1934. Bar: N.Y. 1935, U.S. Supreme Ct. 1939, U.S. Dist. Ct. D.C. 1953, Va. 1954. Asst. solicitor Dept. Interior, Washington, 1934-45; asst. gen. counsel UNRRA, Washington and London, 1945-48; assoc. and cons. firms Washington, 1953, 55, 60; atty., spl. asst. Office Treasury, Washington, 1961-65, asst. gen. counsel, 1965-73; cons. Rogers & Wells, Washington, 1975-86. Editor Columbia Law Rev., 1933-34. Pres. Alexandria Cmty. Welfare Coun., 1950-52; bd. dirs. Alexandria Coun. Human Rels., 1958-60, New Hope Found., 1977. Recipient Meritorious Svc. award Dept. Treasury, 1970, Exceptional Svc. award, 1973, Career Svc. award Nat. Civil Svc. League, 1973; named Hon. fellow Harry S. Truman Libr. Inst. Mem. Columbia U. Alumni Assn., Phi Beta Kappa. Democrat. Episcopalian. Administrative and regulatory, Public international. Home: Apt 1251 4800 Fillmore Ave Alexandria VA 22311-5077

**WALKUP, HOMER ALLEN,** lawyer, writer; b. Dunloup, W.Va., Jan. 28, 1917; s. Homer Allen and Lillie Belle (Harris) W.; m. Edna Mae Tucker, Nov. 19, 1941 (dec. 1966); m. Charlotte M. Tuttle Lloyd, Feb. 4, 1967; children: Homer Allen, Randolph Michael, Pamela Susan. AB, W.Va. U., 1935, LLB, 1938; LLM, Georgetown U., 1947. Bar: W.Va. 1938, U.S. Supreme Ct. 1946, U.S. Ct. Fed. Claims 1978, U.S. Ct. Appeals (fed. cir.) 1982, U.S. Ct. Claims 1982, U.S. Ct. Appeals Armed Forces 1984. Sole practice, W.Va., 1938-42; complaint atty. W.Va. Office OPA, Charleston, 1942; commd. ensign USNR, 1942, advanced through grades to capt., 1963; appellate judge Navy Ct. Mil. Rev., 1966-68; dep. asst., JAG of Navy, 1968-73; ret., 1973; sole practice, Summersville, W.Va., 1974—. Mem. governing bd. Alexandria (Va.) Cmty. Mental Health Ctr., 1988—; bd. dirs. United Way Nat. Capital Area, 1990—. Mem. ABA, ATLA, Fed. Bar Assn., W.Va. State Bar, W.Va. Bar Assn., Bar Assn. D.C., Fed. Cir. Bar Assn., Judge Advs. Assn. (bd. dirs.), Navy-MarCorps Retired Judge Advs. Assn., Am. Judicature Soc., Mil. Order World Wars, Res. Officers Assn., Ret. Officers Assn., Order of Coif. Democrat. Presbyterian. Club: Mil. Dist. Washington Officers. Contbr. in field. Military, Administrative and regulatory. Office: Ste 1251 4800 Fillmore Ave Alexandria VA 22311-5077

**WALKUP, JOHN KNOX,** state attorney general; m. Betsy Walkup; children: Alice, Margaret. BA magna cum laude, Centre Coll. Ky.; JD, Harvard U. Law clk. to Chief Justice Tenn. Supreme Ct., 1972-73; formerly in pvt. practice Burson & Walkup, Memphis; chief counsel, staff dir. subcom. govtl. affairs U.S. Senate; chief dep. atty. gen. State of Tenn., 1985-89, solicitor gen., 1989-93, atty. gen., 1997-99; former ptnr. Gullett, Sanford, Robinson & Martin, Nashville; with Wyatt, Tarrant & Combs, Nashville, 1999—; former part-time asst. county atty. Shelby County, Tenn.; lectr. Law Sch. Vanderbilt U., 1993-95. Mem. ABA, Tenn. Bar Assn., Nashville Bar Assn. Office: Wyatt Tarrant & Combs 511 Union St Ste 1500 Nashville TN 37219-1750

**WALL, DONALD ARTHUR,** lawyer; b. Lafayette, Ind., Mar. 17, 1946; s. Dwight Arthur and Myra Virginia (Peavey) W.; m. Cheryn Lynn Heinen, Aug. 29, 1970; children: Sarah Lynn, Michael Donald. BA, Butler U., 1968; JD, Northwestern U., 1971. Bar: Ohio 1971, U.S. Dist. Ct. (no. dist.) Ohio 1973, U.S. Supreme Ct. 1980, Ariz. 1982, U.S. Dist. Ct. (no. dist.) W.Va. 1982, U.S. Ct. Appeals (6th cir.) 1982, U.S. Dist. Ct. Ariz. 1983, U.S. Ct. Appeals (9th and 10th cirs.) 1984, U.S. Ct. Appeals (5th cir.) 1988. Assoc. Squire, Sanders & Dempsey, Cleve., 1971-80, ptnr., 1980-82; ptnr. Squire, Sanders & Dempsey, Phoenix, 1983—; spkr. at profl. meetings; program moderator. Contbr. articles to profl. jours. Trustee Ch. of the Saviour Day Ctr., Cleveland Heights, 1979-82; mem. adminstrv. bd. Ch. of Saviour, Cleveland Heights, 1980-83; fin. com. Paradise Valley (Ariz.) United Meth. Ch., 1986-87; bd. dirs., divsn. commr. North Scottsdale (Ariz.) Little League, 1983-92; bd. dirs. Epilepsy Found. N.E. Ohio, 1976-82, pres., 1981-82; bd. dirs. N.E. Cmty. Basketball Assn., 1993—; bd. visitors U. Ariz. Law Sch., 1996—; bd. mgrs. Scottsdale-Paradise Valley YMCA, 1999—. Mem. ABA (torts and ins. practice and litigation sect., past chmn. r.r. law com., litigation sect.), Def. Rsch. Inst., Ariz. Bar Assn. (labor and trial practice sects.), Maricopa County Bar Assn., Am. Judicature Soc., Ariz. Assn. Def. Counsel. Methodist. Federal civil litigation, State civil litigation, Labor. Office: Squire Sanders & Dempsey LLP 40 N Central Ave Ste 2700 Phoenix AZ 85004-4498

**WALL, JOHN DAVID,** lawyer; b. Houston, Apr. 6, 1967; s. Jerry Don and Jacquelyn (Finney) W.; m. Kimberly Robyn Weber, Sept. 16, 1995. BSBA in Acctg./Data Procesing, U. Ark., 1989, JD, 1992. Bar: Ark. 1992, Okla. 1993, U.S. Dist. Ct. (ea. and we. dists.) Ark. 1993. Ptnr. Bassett Law Firm, Fayetteville, Ark., 1992—. Pres. Sigma Nu Alumni Housing Bd., Fayetteville, 1994—. Mem. ABA, Ark. Bar Assn., Okla. Bar Asn. Methodist. Avocations: golf, handball, computers, bar-be-que. Workers' compensation, Computer, General civil litigation. Office: Bassett Law Firm 221 N College Ave Fayetteville AR 72701-4238

**WALL, JOSEPH R.,** federal lawyer; b. Milw., Jan. 2, 1957; s. Paul B. and Nina A. Wall; 1 child, Justin M. BS in Acctg., Marquette U., 1979, JD magna cum laude, 1984. Bar: Wis., U.S. Dist. Ct. (ea. dist.) Wis., U.S. Ct. Appeals (7th cir.); CPA, Wis. Pub. acct. Touche Ross & Co., Milw., 1979-81; asst. dist. atty. Milw. County Dist. Atty.'s Office, 1984-86; asst. U.S. atty. U.S. Dept. Justice (ea. dist.) Wis., Milw., 1986—; advisor St. Benedict The Moor Legal Clinic, Milw., 1983-90; mem. 7th Cir. Criminal Jury Instrn. Revision Com., Chgo., 1997-98. Contbr. articles to profl. jours. Site organizer Safe and Sound, Milw., 1998; reading tutor Milw. Pub. Schs., 1998. Avocation: long distance running. Office: 517 E Wisconsin Ave Rm 530 Milwaukee WI 53202-4504

**WALL, KENNETH E., JR.,** lawyer; b. Beaumont, Tex., Apr. 6, 1944; s. Kenneth E. and W. Geraldine (Peoples) W.; m. Marjorie Lee Hughes, Dec. 21, 1968; children—Barbara, Elizabeth, Kenneth. Grad. Lamar U., 1966, U. Tex.-Austin, 1969. Bar: Tex. 1969, U.S. Supreme Ct. 1979. Asst. city atty., Beaumont, 1969-73, city atty., 1973-84; with firm Olson & Olson, Houston, 1984—; dir. Tex. Mcpl. League Ins. Trust, 1979-84, vice chmn., 1983-84; counsel S.E. Tex. Regional Planning Commn., 1974, 76. Active Boy Scouts Am., Girl Scouts U.S.A. Mem. Nat. Inst. Mcpl. Law Officers (chmn. com. on local govt. pers. 1979-81, 82-84), State Bar Tex., Tex. City Attys. Assn. (pres. 1982-83), Jefferson County Bar Assn. (dir. 1975-77), Houston Bar Assn., Phi Delta Phi. Methodist. Land use and zoning (including planning), State and local taxation, Municipal (including bonds). Office: 333 Clay St Houston TX 77002-4000

**WALL, ROBERT ANTHONY, JR.,** lawyer; b. Hartford, Conn., Mar. 3, 1945; s. Robert Anthony and Eileen (Fitzgerald) W.; children: Andrea, Melanie, Victoria, Robert, Natalie; m. Diana M. Wall. BA, Georgetown U., Washington, 1968; JD, Am. U., Washington, 1973. Bar: Conn. 1974, U.S. Ct. Appeals (D.C. cir.) 1974, U.S. Dist. Ct. Conn. 1974, U.S. Supreme Ct. 1977. Ptnr. Wall, Wall & Frauenhofer, Torrington, Conn., 1974-87; pvt. practice Torrington, 1987—. Mem. State of Conn. Rep. Ctrl. Com., 1976-79. Mem. Conn. Trial Lawyers Assn. (bd. govs. 1984-86), Ct. Washington #67 Foresters of Am. (trustee 1988—). Roman Catholic. Personal injury. Home: 55 Quail Run Torrington CT 06790-2550 Office: 8 Church St Torrington CT 06790-5247

**WALL, THOMAS EDWARD,** lawyer; b. Ft. Worth, Mar. 24, 1949; s. David Edward and Mary (Friedel) W.; m. Denna Chu, Aug. 3, 1980. BA, Tex. U., 1972; cert. in Criminal Justice, UCLA, 1979; JD, U. LaVerne, 1975; postgrad., USC, L.A., 1979-81. Bar: Calif. 1977, U.S. dist. Ct. (so. dist. ) Calif. 1977, (no. dist.) 1980, U.S. Ct. Appeals (9th cir.) 1988, U.S. Supreme Ct. 1989. Pvt. practice Rancho Palos Verdes, Calif., 1977—; juvenile traffic referee L.A. County Superior Ct., 1993—; ethics officer L.A. County Met. Transp. Authority, 1996—; cons. L.A. County Bar AIDS Project, L.A. County Bar Sexual Abuse Project; instr., UCLA Experimental Coll., 1977; speaker, Montebello Sch. Dist., Calif., 1989—. Editor: Beverly Hills Bar Jour., 1978-79; contbr. articles to profl. jours. Judge Pro Temp L.A. Superior Ct., 1988—, L.A. Mcpl. Ct., 1988—, Santa Monica Judicial Dist., 1988—; arbitrator, Calif. State Bar Fee Dispute Program, L.A., 1989—; cmty. rater City of L.A. Police Dept., 1997—; dir. Homeowners Assn., 1997—. Appointed to Com. on Profl. Responsiblity, Calif. State Bar Ann., 1989—, L.A. County Bar Assn., 1988—; recipient Certificate of Appreciation Calif. State Bar, 1993. Mem. Calif. State Bar Assn. (Wiley W. Manuel award for pro bono legal svcs. 1993), L.A. County Bar Assn. (com. appellate jud. evaluations), Culver City Bar Assn., Optimist Club (1st v.p. 1990—, pres. 1992-93). Avocations: reading, watching sports, movies, travel, eating. Personal injury, Insurance, General civil litigation. Office: Thomas Wall Law Offices 28729 S Western Ave Ste 206 Rancho Palos Verdes CA 90275

**WALLACE, DON, JR.,** law educator; b. Vienna, Austria, Apr. 23, 1932; s. Don and Julie (Baer) W. (parents Am. citizens); m. Daphne Mary Wickham, 1963; children: Alexandra Jane, Sarah Anne, Benjamin James. B.A. with high honors, Yale U., 1953; LL.B. cum laude, Harvard U., 1957. Bar: N.Y. 1957, D.C. 1978. Assoc. Fleischmann, Jaeckle, Stokes and Hitchcock, N.Y.C., 1959-60, Paul, Weiss, Rifkind, Wharton and Garrison, N.Y.C., 1957-58, 60-62; rsch. asst. to faculty mem. Harvard Law Sch., Cambridge, Mass., 1958-59; regional legal adv. Middle East AID, Dept. State, 1963-65, dep. asst. gen. counsel, 1965-66; assoc. prof. law Georgetown U. Law Ctr., Washington, 1966-71, prof., 1971—; chmn. Internat. Law Inst., Washington, 1969—; cons. AID, 1966-70, UN Centre on Transnat. Corps., 1977-78; counsel Wald, Harkrader & Ross, Washington, 1978-86, Arnold & Porter, 1986-89, Shearman & Sterling, 1989-98, Morgan, Lewis & Bockius, 1998—; legal advisor State of Qatar, 1979-82; chmn. adv. com. on tech. and world trade Office of Tech. Assessment, U.S. Congress, 1976-79; mem. Sec. of State's Adv. Com. on Pvt. Internat. Law, 1979—; mem. U.S. del. UN Conf. on State Succession in Respect of Treaties, Vienna, 1978; mem. U.S. del. new internat. econ. order working group UN Commn. Internat. Trade Law, Vienna, 1981—; vis. com. Harvar dLaw Sch., 1996—. Co-author: Internat. Business and Economics: Law and Policy; author: International Regulation of Multinational Corporations, 1976, Dear Mr. President: The Needed Turnaround in America's International Economic Affairs, 1984; editor: A Lawyer's Guide to International Business Transactions, 1977-87; contbr. numerous articles on internat. trade and law to profl. jours., books revs. on law and bus. to profl. jours. Coord. Anne Arundel County (Md.) Dem. Nat. Com., 1972-79; sec. Chesapeake Found., 1972-73; nat. chmn. Law Profs. for Bush and Quayle, 1988, 92, for Dole and Kemp, 1996; v.p., bd. govs. UNIDROIT Found., Rome, 1997—.$Dat. co-chmn. Law Profs. for. Fulbright fellow, 1967, Eisenhower Exch. fellow, 1976. Mem. ABA (chmn. sect. internat. law 1978-79), Ho. of Dels. 1982-84), Am. Law Inst., Internat. Law Assn., Shaybani Soc. of Internat. Law (v.p.), Ctrl. and Ea. European Law Initiative (mem. adv. bd.), World Trade Orgn. (mem. panel of judges), Cosmos Club, Met. Club. Home: 2800 35th St NW Washington DC 20007-1411 Office: Georgetown U Law Ctr 600 New Jersey Ave NW Washington DC 20001-2022

**WALLACE, EDNA MARIE,** paralegal; b. Indpls., July 22, 1945; d. William T. and Agnes L. (Pierce) Branson; m. James Michael Wallace; children: Penny Sue Wallace-Steele, Brandi Michael Wallace-Coffin. Paralegal Cert., Am. Inst. Paralegal Studies, Oak Brook Terrace, Ill., 1988. Paralegal, office adminstr. Baldwin & Baldwin, Danville, Ind., 1985-90; paralegal Tucker, Surface, Fehribach, Indpls., 1990-92; paralegal, office adminstr. Hebenstreit & Moberly, Indpls., 1992-96; paralegal Kroger, Gardis & Regas, Indpls., 1996—; Author CLE seminar. Mem. paralegal adv. bd. St. Mary of the Woods Coll., 1999—. Mem. Nat. Fedn. Paralegal Assns. (registered paralegal), Indpls. Bar Assn. (chair paralegal exec. com. 1998—), Ind. Paralegal Assn., Bus./Profl. Women, Order Eastern Star, Job's Daus. (adult leader 1986—, bd. dirs. ednl. found. 1997—), Epsilon Sigma Alpha (pres. chpt. 1988-90). Republican. Baptist. Office: Kroger Gardis & Regas 111 Monument Cir Ste 900 Indianapolis IN 46204-5125

**WALLACE, ELAINE WENDY,** lawyer; b. Worcester, Mass., Feb. 16, 1949; d. Louis S. and Ida (Zeiper) W. BA, Yeshiva U., 1971; JD, John F. Kennedy Sch. Law, 1976. Sole practice Oakland, Calif. Civil rights, Government contracts and claims, Labor. Home: 2430 Palmetto St # 1 Oakland CA 94602-2923 Office: 2430 Palmetto St # 2 Oakland CA 94602-2923

**WALLACE, FRANKLIN SHERWOOD,** lawyer; b. Bklyn., Nov. 24, 1927; s. Abraham Charles and Jennie (Etkin) Wolowitz; student U. Wis., 1943-45; BS cum laude, U.S. Mcht. Marine Acad., 1950; LLB, JD, U. Mich., 1953; m. Eleanor Ruth Pope, Aug. 23, 1953; children: Julia Diane, Charles Andrew. *Franklin Wallace's wife Eleanor is the Former Iowa 10K record holder (1955-59), the former Illinois senior Olympic record holder (5,000 M, 1,500 M, 800 M, 1955-59), winner of the Bronze medal 1987 National Senior Olympics (1,500 M) and an All-American (5K and 10K 1950-54, 55-59, 60-65). She was the secretary at the Cornbelt Running Club and is the commissioner of Rock Island Park and Recreation Board. His daughter Julia is married to Donivier Campbell. They have two daughters, Emmaline 7 and Eden 4. She is the managing editor of the Arizona Republic, Phoenix and a former Pulitzer Prize judge. His son Charles graduated from U. Mo. in 1991 and John Marshall Law School in 1994. He is an attorney with the firm of O'Conner, Schiff and Myers, Chicago.* Bar: 1954. Practiced in Rock Island; ptnr. firm Winstein, Kavensky & Wallace; asst. state's atty. Rock Island County, 1967-68; local counsel UAW at John Deere-J.I. Case Plants. Former bd. dirs. Tri City Jewish Ctr.; former trustee United Jewish Charities of Quad Cities; former bd. dirs. Blackhawk Coll. Found. Mem. ABA, Ill. Bar Assn. (chmn. jud. adv. polls com. 1979-84), Rock Island County Bar Assn., Am. Trial Lawyers Assn., Ill. Trial Lawyers Assn., Nat. Assn. Criminal Def. Lawyers, Ill. Appellate Lawyers Assn., Am. Judicature Soc., Blackhawk Coll. Found. Democrat. Jewish. Labor, Family and matrimonial, General civil litigation. Home: 3405 20th Street Ct Rock Island IL 61201-6201 Office: Rock Island Bank Bldg Rock Island IL 61201

**WALLACE, HERBERT NORMAN,** lawyer; b. Syracuse, N.Y., Oct. 19, 1937; s. Louis H. and Betty (Wagner) W.; m. Frances Adele Groobman, June 1, 1963 (div. Sept. 1976); children: Craig, Julie; m. Frances Mae Souza, Nov. 12, 1977; 1 child, John. BA, Davis & Elkins Coll., 1959; JD, Syracuse U., 1962. Bar: N.Y. 1962, U.S. Dist. Ct. (no. dist.) N.Y. 1962. Asst. atty. gen. State of N.Y., Albany, 1963-66; asst. atty. gen in charge of Poughkeepsie (N.Y.) office State of N.Y., Poughkeepsie, 1966-79; counsel to banking com. N.Y. State Senate, Albany, 1979-84, counsel to Senator Rolison, asst. majority leader, 1984-88; sole practice Poughkeepsie, N.Y., 1979-86, 94—; ptnr. Wallace & Moore, Poughkeepsie, 1986-94. Mem. Poughkeepsie Rep. Com., 1977-91. Recipient Ellis Island medal of hon. NECO, 1997. Mem. N.Y. State Bar Assn., Dutchess County Bar Assn. Jewish. Condemnation, General practice, Real property. Home: 65 Cardinal Dr Poughkeepsie NY 12601-5703 Office: 299 Main Mall Poughkeepsie NY 12601-3144

**WALLACE, J. CLIFFORD,** federal judge; b. San Diego, Dec. 11, 1928; s. John Franklin and Lillie Isabel (Overing) W.; m. Elaine J. Barnes, Apr. 8, 1996; 9 children. B.A., San Diego State U., 1952; LL.B., U. Calif., Berkeley, 1955. Bar: Calif. 1955. With firm Gray, Cary, Ames & Frye, San Diego, 1955-70; judge U.S. Dist. Ct. for So. Dist. Calif., 1970-72; judge U.S. Ct. Appeals for 9th Circuit, San Diego, 1972-96, sr. circuit judge, 1996—. Contrbr. articles to profl. jours. Served with USN, 1946-49. Mem. Am. Bd. Trial Advocates, Inst. Jud. Adminstrn. Mem. LDS Ch. (stake pres. San Diego East 1962-67, regional rep. 1967-74, 77-79). Office: US Ct Appeals 9th Cir 940 Front St Ste 4192 San Diego CA 92101-8918 *My principles, ideals and goals and my standard of conduct are embodied in the Gospel of Jesus Christ. They come to fruition in family life, service, industry and integrity and in an attempt, in some small way, to make my community a better place within which to live.*

**WALLACE, JOHN PAUL,** lawyer; b. New Hartford, N.Y., May 5, 1962; s. John Luther and Kathryn Marie Wallace. BS in Gen. Studies, Regents Coll., Albany, N.Y., 1991; JD, U. Dayton, 1994. Bar: N.Y., U.S. Dist. Ct. (no. dist.) N.Y. Lawyer Meltzer Law Office, Syracuse, N.Y., 1995—. Republican. Christian. General practice, Criminal, Family and matrimonial. Home: 6344 E Taft Rd North Syracuse NY 13212

**WALLACE, KEITH M.,** lawyer; b. Evansville, Ind., Apr. 2, 1956; s. B. Joe and M. Joyce (Nicolaides) W.; 1 child, Elizabeth Anne. BA in Psychology, Ind. U., 1978; JD, Valparaiso U., 1983. Bar: Ky. 1984, Ind. 1983, U.S. Dist. Ct. (so. dist.) Ind. 1983, U.S. Ct. Appeals (7th cir.) 1985, U.S. Supreme Ct., 1997. Comml. credit analyst Old Nat. Bank, Evansville, 1978-79; assoc. Cubbage & Thomason, Henderson, Ky., 1983-84, Perdue & Stigger, Evansville, 1984-86; ptnr. Jones & Wallace, Evansville, 1987-90; fgn. expert Peking U. Law Dept., People's Republic China, 1990-91; ptnr. Wright, Evans & Daly, Evansville, 1991-95, Jones & Wallace, Evansville, 1996—; asst. city atty., Evansville, 1984-90; hearing officer City of Evansville Dept. Code Enforcement, 1992—. Steward Christian Fellowship Ch., Evansville, 1988-90; vol. Evansville Rescue Mission, 1987-92, Habitat for Humanity, 1992—; bd. dirs. Impact Ministries, 1992—; exec. dir. Families Thru Internat. Adoptions, Inc., 1995—. Mem. Ind. Bar Assn., Ky. Bar Assn., Evansville Bar Assn., Christian Legal Soc., Evansville Runners Club. General corporate, Environmental, Real property. Office: PO Box 1065 123 NW 4th St Rm 520 Evansville IN 47708-1715

**WALLACE, MATTHEW MARK,** lawyer; b. Detroit, Nov. 19, 1958; s. Robert James and Judith Anita Wallace; m. Emily Mosher, Nov. 1, 1980; children: Luke David, Elizabeth Ann. BBA with distinction, U. Mich., 1980; JD, Wayne State U., 1986. Bar: Mich. 1986, U.S. Dist. Ct. (ea. dist.) Mich. 1986, U.S. Supreme Ct. 1992. Audit asst., tax asst., tax sr. Arthur Andersen & Co., Detroit, 1980-84; contr. RPM Pizza of Mich., Livonia, 1984-85; with Davidson, Staiger, Adair & Hill, Port Huron, Mich., 1986-94, CFO, 1992-94; pvt. practice Port Huron, 1994—; adj. prof. taxation Walsh Coll. of Accountancy and Bus. Adminstrn., 1988-98. Bd. dirs. Port Huron Area Estate Planning Coun., 1990-92; mem. Blue Water Rental Housing Assn., 1988—, bd. dirs., 1988-93, 94—, pres., 1988-90, 95-96; mem. adv. bd. Port Huron Neighborhood Improvement Project, 1987-88; mem. Olde Town Revitalization Coun., 1988-94; mem. fund raising com. Mercy Hosp. Devel. Coun., 1989-90; vol. Boy Scouts Am. Blue Water Coun., 1996—, cubmaster Pack 110, 1996—; vol. Keewahdin Elem. Sch., 1998—, chess club coord., 1998; active Grace Episcopal Ch., Port Huron, 1986—, mem. bd. govs., 1996-98, fin. com., 1996—, chmn. fin. com., 1997-98, treas., 1997—, tchr. Sunday sch., 1991—; bd. dirs. Try Sail Inc. Cmty. Program, 1991-96; bd. dirs. Lakeshore Legal Svcs. Inc., legal aid, 1989-95, audit com., 1989-95, pension trustee, 1993-95; mem. audit com. St. Clair County chpt. ARC, 1998. Mem. ABA, AICPAs, Mich. Assn. CPAs, Mich. Bar Assn., St. Clair County Bar Assn., Am. Assn. Atty.-CPAs, Am. Immigratin Lawyers Assn., Fed. Bar Assn., Greater Port Huron C. of C. (bd. dirs. 1992-94), Rotary (bd. dirs. 1994-98, pres. 1996-97), Port Huron Yacht Club (various offices). Avocations: sailing, skiing, camping. Contracts commercial, Estate planning, Real property. Office: 707 Huron Ave Port Huron MI 48060-3703

**WALLACE, PAUL ROBERT,** lawyer; b. Phila., Oct. 23, 1964; s. Joseph Francis and Virgina Marie (Snock) W.; m. Lisa Anne Almeida, May 28, 1988; children: Benjamin Lees. Elyssa Carolina. BA, U. Md., 1986; JD, Cath. U. Am., 1989. Bar: Pa. 1990, Del. 1990, U. S. Dist. Ct. Del. 1991, U.S. Ct Appeal (3d cir.) 1991, U.S. Supreme Ct. 1993. Mgmt. analyst U.S. Dept. Agr., Washington, 1984-89; dep. atty gen. Dept. Justice State of Del., Wilmington, 1989—; mem. legisl. rev. com. Del. Dept. Justice, Wilmington, 1995—. Author numerous Del. criminal statutes including DUI law, Child Abuse murder law and Zero Tolerance law, 1995—. Lectr. Doctor-Lawyer Drug Edn. Program, Wilmington, 1990—, pres. Corpus Christi Home & Sch. Assn. With USMCR, 1982-86. Recipient Kathryn F. Gruber Meml. award Blinded Vets. Assn., Washington, 1985, 86; Cert. Merit USDA, Washington, 1988. Mem. Del. State Bar Assn. (former vice chair criminal law sect., judicial nominating com.), Nat. Dist. Attys. Assn., Assn. of Govt. Attys. in Capital Litigation, Assn. Deputy Attys (exec. com.), Alpha Phi Sigma. Republican. Roman Catholic. Office: Dept Justice State of Del 820 N French St Fl 7 Wilmington DE 19801-3509

**WALLACE, SEAN DANIEL,** lawyer; b. Walnut Creek, Calif., June 17, 1960; s. Daniel M. and Patricia Marie (Coyne) W.; m. Eileen Marie Lynch, May 29, 1999. BA, Hampden-Sydney Coll., 1982; JD, U. Md., 1985. Bar: Md. 1985, U.S. Dist. Ct. Md. 1986 (co-chmn. so. divsn. joint adv. com.), D.C. 1986, U.S. Dist. Ct. D.C. 1986, U.S. Ct. Appeals (4th, D.C. and Fed. cirs.) 1986. Spl. asst. to U.S. rep. Steny H. Hoyer, Washington, 1982; assoc. Knight, Manzi, Brennan & Ostrom, Upper Marlboro, Md., 1985-88; assoc. county atty. Prince George's County, Md., 1988-95, dep. county atty., chief litig., 1995-98; county atty. Prince George's County, 1999—; bd. dirs. moot ct. U. Md. Law Sch., Balt., 1983-85. Mem. youth adv. com. City of Bowie, Md., 1976-78, security ops. staff Dem. Nat. Convention, N.Y.C., 1980, inquiry com. Md. Atty. Grievance Commn., 1986—; chmn. convention Young Dems. of Md., 1982; bd. dirs. Associated Cath. Charities Archdiocese Washington, 1994—, chmn. fin. com., 1996-98, bd. vice chair, 1999. Named one of Outstanding Young Men in Am. U.S. Jaycees, 1982, 84. Mem. ABA, Md. Assn. of Counties (co-chmn. govt. liability workgroup 1995-96), Prince George's County Bar Assn., Md. Bar Assn. (bd. dirs. 1997-99, treas. 1999—), J. Dudley Digges Inn of Ct., Nat. Eagle Scout Assn. Democrat. Roman Catholic. Federal civil litigation, State civil litigation. Home: 2701 Lyn Pl Bowie MD 20715-2362 Office: Prince George's County Office of Law County Adminstrn Bldg Ste 5121 Upper Marlboro MD 20772

**WALLACE, STEVEN CHARLES,** judge; b. Lubbock, Tex., Jan. 19, 1953; s. Charles Andrew Wallace and Alice Hillene (McMillin) Stone; m. Kathleen Louise Merrill, Apr. 3, 1976; children: Christine Merrill, Zachary Charles, Steven Kyle. BA, Tex. Tech U., 1975, JD, 1979. Bar: Tex. 1979, U.S. Dist. Ct. (no. dist.) Tex. 1980, U.S. Ct. Appeals (5th cir.) 1981. Asst. county atty. Parker County, Weatherford, Tex., 1979-80; asst. dist. atty. Tarrant County, Ft. Worth, 1980-83; pvt. practice Ft. Worth, 1983-90; judge Tarrant County Ct. at Law # 2, Ft. Worth, 1991—; chmn. prosecution and adjudication subcom. Tarrant 2000 Task Force, 1987—. Recipient Am. Jurisprudence award Bancroft Whitney Co., 1979. Fellow Coll. State Bar of Tex.; mem. Am. Judges Assn. (bd. govs.), State Bar Tex., Tarrant County Bar Assn., Ridotto Club, Ridgelea Country Club, Phi Alpha Delta, Phi Alpha Theta. Avocations: golf, fishing, music, traveling, astronomy. Office: County Ct at Law # 2 100 W Weatherford St Fort Worth TX 76102-2115

**WALLACH, DAVID MICHAEL,** lawyer; b. Fort Worth, Nov. 13, 1954; s. David Edward and Zelma Jane (Gilbreath) W.; m. Susan Danell Hailey, Aug. 16, 1975; children: Landon James, Tyler Field, Carter Hailey. BA, Tex. Christian U., 1975; JD, U. Houston, 1979. Bar: Tex. 1979, U.S. Dist. Ct. (no. dist.) Tex. 1979, U.S. Ct. Appeals (5th and 11th cirs.) 1979, U.S. Dist. Ct. (so. dist.) Tex. 1986, U.S. Dist. Ct. (we. dist.) Tex. 1992. Assoc. Shannon, Gracey, Ratliff & Miller, Fort Worth, 1979-83, ptnr., 1983-91; shareholder Wallach & Moore PC, Fort Worth, 1991—. Contbr. articles to profl. jours. Named Boss of Yr. Fort Worth Legal Secs. Assn., 1991. Fellow Tex. Bar Found.; mem. Tex. Assn. Def. Counsel (v.p. programs 1993-96, bd. dirs. 1989-96, 97—, v.p. North Tex. region 1997—, pres.'s award 1992), Def. Rsch. Inst., Tarrant County Civil Trial Lawyers Assn. (pres. 1988-89, exec. v.p. 1987-88), State Bar Tex., Tarrant County Bar Assn., North Tex. Soc. for Health Care Risk Mgmt., Health Industry Coun. Dallas-Fort Worth Region, Shriners, Scottish Rite, Masons. Republican. Methodist. Avocations: golf, snow skiing, racquetball. E-mail: mwallach@wallachmoore.com. Personal injury, Product liability, Professional liability. Office: Wallach & Moore PC 1300 Summit Ave Ste 300 Fort Worth TX 76102-4417

**WALLACH, ERIC JEAN,** lawyer; b. N.Y.C., June 11, 1947; s. Milton Harold and Jacqueline (Goldschmidt) W.; m. Miriam Grunberger, Mar. 21, 1976; children: Katherine, Emily, Peter. BA, Harvard U., 1968, JD, 1972. Bar: N.Y. 1973, U.S. Dist. Ct. (so. and ea. dists.) N.Y. 1973, U.S. Dist. Ct. (no. dist.) N.Y. 1989, U.S. Ct. Appeals (2nd cir.) 1973, (3d cir.) 1996, U.S. Tax Ct. 1976. Assoc. Webster & Sheffield, N.Y.C., 1972-77; assoc. Rosenman & Colin, N.Y.C., 1977-80, ptnr., 1981-96, mem. mgmt. com., 1993-96, chmn. employment practice group, 1985-96; ptnr., chmn. employment practice group Kasowitz, Benson, Torres & Friedman LLP, N.Y.C., 1996—; presenter CLE programs, Practising Law Inst., Cambridge Inst., others. Mem. editl. bd. You and the Law, 1992-96; contbr. articles to profl. jours. Sec.-treas. Art Dealers Assn. Am., Inc., N.Y.C., 1985-96; trustee C.G. Jung Found. for Analytical Psychology; trustee Am. Jewish World Svc., Inc., N.Y.C., 1989-97, chmn., 1995-97; dir. N.Y. Jr. Tennis League. Mem. Harvard Club N.Y.C. (admissions com. 1992-94), Sunningdale Country Club, Poughkeepsie Tennis Club. Democrat. Avocations: sports, travel, reading. Labor, General civil litigation. Home: 20 W 64th St New York NY 10023-7180 also: 16 Buttonwood Ln Rhinebeck NY 12572-2402 Office: Kasowitz Benson Torres & Friedman LLP 1301 Ave of Ams New York NY 10019

**WALLACH, STEVEN ERNST,** lawyer, pilot; b. N.Y.C., Mar. 21, 1944; s. Eduard Herbert Wallach and Karin (Wassermann) Grunebaum; m. Stefany Gay Rosehill (div. Oct. 1990); children: Shelby Karin, Shawna Beth; m. Geri Joan Grieco, Nov. 21, 1992. BS, USAF Acad., 1965; MS summa cum laude, U. So. Calif., 1971; JD magna cum laude, Nova U., 1986. Bar: Fla. 1986, D.C. 1988, U.S. Dist. Ct. (so. dist.) Fla. 1987, U.S. Dist. Ct. (mid. dist.) Fla. 1989, U.S. Dist. Ct. Ariz. 1989. Systems analyst Hughes Aircraft Co., L.A., 1971-72; airline pilot Ea. Air Lines, Miami, 1972-91; atty. Barwick, Dillian & Lambert pa, Miami Shores, Fla., 1987-96; atty., ptnr. Thornton Davis & Murray, P.A., Miami, 1996-98; aviation mgmt. cons. PRC Speas, Lake Success, N.Y., 1977-83, TRAMCO, Cambridge, Mass., 1977-77. Trustee Karin Grunebaum Cancer Found., Cambridge, 1979—. Capt. USAF, 1965-70. Decorated DFC. Avocation: flying. Aviation, Product liability.

**WALLEN, KATE RABASSA,** lawyer; b. N.Y.C., Apr. 13, 1960. BA, Dartmouth Coll., 1982; JD cum laude, Cardozo Sch. Law, N.Y.C., 1985. Bar: N.J. 1985, U.S. Dist. Ct. N.J. 1985. Atty. N.Y. Life Ins. Co., N.Y.C., 1985-86; assoc. Horn Goldberg Gorny & Daniels, Atlantic City, 1986-93; of counsel Wallen & Beakley, Atlantic City, 1993-96; ptnr. Wallen & Wallen, Atlantic City, 1996—; no-fault claims arbitrator Am. Arbitration Assn., Somerset, N.J., 1993—; mem. Dist. I Ethics Com., Atlantic, 1991-95; personal injury arbitrator N.J. Superior Ct. Atlantic and Cape May Counties, Atlantic City, 1993—. Notes and comments editor Cardozo Law Rev., 1984-85. Personal injury, Insurance. Office: Wallen & Wallen 1125 Atlantic Ave Ste 421 Atlantic City NJ 08401-4806

**WALLENDER, MICHAEL TODD,** lawyer; b. Schenectady, N.Y., Apr. 8, 1950; s. Kenneth Clark and Martha Lee (Getty) W.; m. Joyce Ann Mushaw, June 3, 1978; children: Kristina Lee, Michael David. BA, Colgate U., 1972; JD, Harvard U., 1975. Law asst. N.Y. State Supreme Ct. Appellate Div., Albany, 1975-76; assoc. DeGraff, Foy, Conway, Holt-Harris & Mealey, Albany, 1976-80, ptnr., 1981-90; counsel N.Y. State Assn. Realtors, Albany, 1981—, Albany County Bd. Realtors, 1985-92, Capital Regional Multiple Listing Svc., Albany, 1986—, Greater Capitol Assn. Realtors, 1992—. Author: Realtors and the Law of Agency, 1988. Mem. ATLA, ABA, Lawyers for Justice in Ireland, N.Y. State Bar Assn., Albany County Bar Assn., Ft. Orange Club, Mohawk Golf Club, Colgate Club (capital dist. chpt., Albany), Saratoga Reading Rm. Avocation: thoroughbred horse racing. Federal civil litigation, Environmental, General corporate. Home: 28 Cheshire Pl Niskayuna NY 12309-4939 Office: 90 State St Ste 1501 Albany NY 12207-1714

**WALLER, JOHN HENRY, JR.,** state supreme court justice; b. Mullins, S.C., Oct. 31, 1937; s. John Henry and Elnita (Rabon) W.; m. Jane McLaurin Cooper, Nov. 16, 1963 (div.); children: John Henry III, Melissa McLaurin; m. Debra Ann Meares, May 9, 1981; children: Ryan Meares, Rand Ellis. AB in Psychology, Wofford Coll., 1959; LLB, JD, U. S.C., 1963. Mem. S.C. Ho. of Reps., 1967-77, S.C. Senate, 1977-80; judge S.C. Cir. Ct., 1980-94; assoc. justice S.C. Supreme Ct., 1994—; mem. S.C. Cir. Ct. Adv. Com., 1981-94, chmn., 1991-94; mem. S.C. Jud. Std. Com., 1991-94, chmn., 1992-94. Capt. U.S. Army, 1959-60. Mem. Millins Rotary Club (1st pres.), Masons, Shriners. Avocations: woodworking, golf, water sports, snow skiing. Office: SC Supreme Ct 103 Main St PO Box 1059 Marion SC 29571-1059 Office: SC Supreme Ct Supreme Court PO Box 11330 Columbia SC 29211-1330*

**WALLER, PAUL PRESSLEY, JR.,** lawyer; b. East St. Louis, Ill., May 16, 1924; s. Paul Pressley and Rosamond Agnes (Mulqueeny) W.; m. Dolores A. Hartman; children: Mary Eleanor Waller Frascella, Paul P. III, Joseph H., J. Michael Waller, Kathleen A. Feist, Anne M. Meirink, Margaret M. Szendrey, Maureen R. Waller. JD, St. Louis U., 1948. Bar: Mo. 1949, Ill. 1950, U.S. Ct. Appeals (8th cir.) 1957, U.S. Supreme Ct. 1958. Assoc. Oemke & Dunham, East St. Louis, 1950-52; pvt. practice law East St. Louis, 1953-68, Belleville, Ill., 1969; ptnr. O'Connell & Waller, Belleville, 1969-82; spl. asst. atty. gen. State of Ill., 1962-69, 83-86. Pres. St. Clair County Health and Welfare, St. Clair County Law Libr.; v.p. Legal Aid Soc. St. Clair County; bd. dirs. United Fund; chmn. St. Clair County chpt. ARC. With USN, 1943-46. Mem. St. Clair County Bar Assn., Ill. Bar Assn., Mo. Bar Assn., Bar Assn. Met. St. Louis, Serra (dist. gov.), K.C. (dist. dep.), Elks, Nat. Coun. Cath. Men (nat. chmn. com. on legislation). Democrat. Probate, General practice. Home: 121 Woods Edge Dr Belleville IL 62221-0453 Office: 211 S Jackson St Belleville IL 62220-2254

**WALLER, WILLIAM LOWE, JR.,** state supreme court justice; b. Miss., Feb. 9, 1952; s. Bill Sr. and Carroll (Overton) W.; m. Charlotte Brawner, Aug. 4, 1979; children: William, Jeannie, Clayton. Student, Delta State U.; BA in Bus., Miss. State U., 1974; JD, U. Miss., 1977; grad., U.S. Army War Coll. Bar: Miss. 1977. Ptnr. Waller and Waller, 1977-97; judge City of Jackson, Miss., 1995-96; justice Miss. Supreme Ct., Jackson, 1997—; chmn. lawyer referral svc. Miss. State Bar, 1987-89; panelist Miss. Pro Bon Svc. Tchr. Sunday sch. First Bapt. Ch., Jackson, Miss.; past gen. counsel Ctrl. Miss. chpt. Lupus Found. Am.; bd. dirs., chmn. Jackson Coun. Neighborhoods. Col. Miss. Nat. Guard, asst. chief of staff. Mem. ABA, Miss. Bar Assn., Christian Legal Soc., Am. Legion, Miss. Nat. Guard Assn. (sec., chmn. legis. com., bd. dirs.). Office: PO Box 117 Jackson MS 39205-0117

**WALLIN, JAMES PETER,** lawyer; b. Huntington, N.Y., May 9, 1958; s. Jerome Peter and Margaret Mary (Gilvarry) W.; m. Julia Katherine Springen, Aug. 11, 1984; children: James Peter Jr., Thomas George, Katherine Grace, Sarah Elizabeth. BA in Econs., SUNY, Stony Brook, 1980; JD, N.Y. Law Sch., 1983. Bar: N.Y. 1984. Counsel Alliance Capital Mgmt., N.Y.C., 1982-86; assoc. Cole & Dietz (now Winston & Strawn), N.Y.C., 1986-87; counsel The Dreyfus Corp., N.Y.C., 1987-88; gen. counsel Yamaichi Capital Mgmt. Inc., N.Y.C., 1988-92, Yamaichi Internat. (Am.) Inc., N.Y.C., 1992-94, Evergreen Asset Mgmt. Corp., 1994-97; dir. risk mgmt. Morgan Stanley Dean Witter Advisors, N.Y.C., 1997—; mem. faculty Practicing Law Inst., N.Y.C., 1992—. Author: (seminar materials) Broker Dealer Regulation, 1992. Avocations: aviation, skiing. Securities, General corporate, Private international. Home: PO Box 151 Cold Spring Harbor NY 11724 Office: Two World Trade Ctr New York NY 10048

**WALLINGER, M(ELVIN) BRUCE,** lawyer; b. Richmond, Va., Dec. 27, 1945; s. Melvin W. and Ellen Scott (Barnard) W.; m. Rosemary Moore Hynes, Aug. 8, 1970; children: Mary Moore, Ann Harrison, Carrie. BA, U. Va., 1968, JD, 1972. Bar: Va. 1972, U.S. Dist. Ct. (we. dist.) Va. 1972, U.S. Ct. Appeals (4th cir.) 1976, U.S. Supreme Ct. 1978, U.S. Dist. Ct. (ea. dist.) Va. 1986; cert. comml. mediator Am. Arbitration Assn. Assoc. Wharton, Aldhizer & Weaver, Harrisonburg, Va., 1972-76, ptnr., 1976-98; mng. ptnr. Wharton, Aldhizer & Weaver, Harrisonburg, 1998—. Bd. dirs. Shrine Mont, Inc., Orkney Springs, Va.; trustee Stuart Hall Sch., Staunton, Va., Shenandoah County Libr. Foun., Edinburg, Va. Fellow ABA, Am. Coll. Trial Lawyers, Va. Law Found.; mem. Va. Bar Assn. (exec. com. 1996-99), Harrisonburg Bar Assn. (pres. 1984), Va. State Bar (pres. young lawyers conf. 1981-82, chmn. 6th dist. disciplinary com. 1988-89), Va. Assn. Def. Attys. (pres. 1989-90). Republican. Episcopalian. Avocations: biking, scuba diving. Alternative dispute resolution, General civil litigation, Labor. Office: Wharton Aldhizer & Weaver 100 S Mason St Harrisonburg VA 22801-4022

**WALLIS, BEN ALTON, JR.,** lawyer; b. Llano County, Tex., Apr. 27, 1936; s. Ben A. and Jessie Ella (Longbotham) W.; children from previous marriage: Ben a. III, M. Jessica; m. Joan Mery, 1987. BBA, U. Tex., 1961, JD, 1971; postgrad., Law Sch. So. Meth. U. Bar: Tex. 1966, U.S. Dist. Ct. (no. dist.) Tex. 1971, U.S. Ct. Appeals D.C. 1974, U.S. Dist. Ct. D.C. 1975, U.S. Dist. Ct. (we. dist.) Tex. 1975, U.S. Dist. Ct. (no. dist.) Calif. 1983, U.S. Ct. Appeals (5th cir.) 1975, U.S. Ct. Appeals (8th cir.) 1980, U.S. Ct. Appeals (11th cir.) 1981, U.S. Dist. Ct. (ea. dist.) Wis. 1983, U.S. Supreme Ct. 1974. Pvt. practice Llano, 1966-67, Dallas, 1971-73; investigator, prosecutor State Securities Bd. Tex., 1967-71; v.p. of devel. Club Corp. Am., Dallas, 1973; assoc. counsel impeachment task force U.S. Ho. of Reps. Com. on Judiciary, Washington, 1974; prin. Law Offices of Ben Wallis, P.C., San Antonio, 1974—. Chmn. Nat. Land Use Conf., 1979-81; mem. Gov.'s Areawide Planning Adv. Com., 1975-78; pres. Inst. Human Rights Rsch., 1979-82. Mem. ATLA, FBA, State Bar Tex. (former chmn. agr. tax com.), D.C. Bar Assn., San Antonio Bar Assn., Delta Theta Phi, Delta Sigma Pi. Republican. Baptist. Condemnation, General practice, General civil litigation. Office: GPM South Tower 800 NW Loop 410 Ste 350 San Antonio TX 78216-5619

**WALLIS, OLNEY GRAY,** lawyer, educator; b. Llano, Tex., July 27, 1940; s. Ben Alton and Jessie Ella (Longbotham) W.; m. Linda Lee Johnson, June 29, 1963; children—Anne, Brett. B.A., U. Tex., 1962, J.D., 1965. Bar: Tex. 1965, U.S. Dist. Ct. (so. dist.) Tex. 1966, U.S. Ct. Mil. Appeals 1968, U.S. Supreme Ct. 1970, U.S. Dist. Ct. (we. dist.) Tex. 1976, U.S. Ct. Appeals (5th cir.) 1977, U.S. Tax Ct. 1980, U.S. Ct. Appeals (10th cir.) 1981, U.S. Ct. Appeals (11th cir.) 1983, U.S. Dist. Ct. (no. dist.) Tex. 1985, U.S. Dist. Ct. (ea. and we. dists.) Ark. 1985, U.S. Ct. Appeals (8th cir.) 1985. Assoc., Brown & Cecil, Houston, 1965-66; asst. U.S. atty. Dept. Justice, Houston, 1971-74; mem. Jefferson, Wallis & Sherman, Houston, 1975-81; mem. Wallis & Pruitt, Houston, 1981-87, Wallis and Short, 1987—; instr. U. Md., Keflauik, Iceland, 1968-69; mem. faculty continuing legal edn. U. Houston, 1981-84. Served to capt. USAF, 1966-70. Decorated Air Force Commendation medal, 1970; recipient Disting. Service award U.S. Dept. Justice, 1973. Mem. Assn. Trial Lawyers Am., Am Judicature Soc., Tex. Trial Lawyers Assn., Houston Trial Lawyers Assn., Houston Bar Assn., Houston Bar Found., Phi Delta Phi, Phi Kappa Tau. Democrat. Episcopalian. Criminal, Federal civil litigation, State civil litigation. Office: Wallis & Short 4300 Scotland St Houston TX 77007-7328

**WALLISCH, MICHAEL A.,** lawyer; b. Pitts., Nov. 26, 1952; s. Fred M. and Patricia Loretta Wallisch; m. Patricia Ann Sullivan, Nov. 9, 1985; children: Thomas Michael, Amy Michelle. Pvt. practice Pitts. Office: 310 Grant St Ste 1030 Pittsburgh PA 15219-2200

**WALLISON, FRIEDA K.,** lawyer; b. N.Y.C., Jan. 15, 1943; d. Ruvin H. and Edith (Landes) Koslow; m. Peter J. Wallison, Nov. 24, 1966; children: Ethan S., Jeremy L., Rebecca K. AB, Smith Coll., 1963; LLB, Harvard U., 1966. Bar: N.Y. 1967, D.C. 1982. Assoc. Carter, Ledyard & Milburn, N.Y.C., 1966-75; spl. counsel divsn. market regulation SEC, Washington, 1975; exec. dir., gen. counsel Mcpl. Securities Rulemaking Bd., Washington, 1975-78; ptnr. Rogers & Wells, N.Y.C. and Washington, 1978-83, Jones, Day, Reavis & Pogue, N.Y.C. and Washington, 1983-98; mem. Govtl. Acctg. Standards Coun., Washington, 1984-90, Nat. Coun. on Pub. Works Improvement, Washington, 1985-88; vice chair environ. fin. adv. bd. EPA, 1988-92. Contbr. articles to profl. jours. Fellow Am. Bar Found.; mem. Nat. Assn. Bond Lawyers, N.Y.C. Bar Assn. Securities, Finance.

**WALLS, GEORGE RODNEY,** lawyer; b. New Orleans, Sept. 30, 1945; s. Preston Rodney and Bobbe Cleo (Sharp) W.; m. Nancy Ellen Smith, June 29, 1974; children: Scott Christian, Brian Cannon. BA, U. Md., 1967, JD, 1970. Bar: Md. 1971, D.C. 1971, U.S. Dist. Ct. D.C. 1971, U.S. Supreme Ct. 1977. Assoc. counsel GAC Fin. Inc., Allentown, Pa., 1970-73; sr. atty. Quality Inns Internat., Inc., Silver Spring, Md., 1973-76; gen. counsel, sec. Suburban Bancorp., Bethesda, Md., 1976-86; sr. assoc. gen. counsel, corp. sec. Sovran Fin. Corp., Norfolk, Va., 1986-90; sr. assoc. gen. counsel C&S/Sovran, Norfolk, Va., 1990-91; asst. gen. counsel NationsBank Corp./Bank of Am., Charlotte, N.C., 1991—. Mem. Md. Bar Assn., D.C. Bar Assn., N.C. Bar Assn., Am. Assn. Corp. Secs. Presbyterian. Banking, General corporate. Home: 12425 Pine Valley Club Dr Charlotte NC 28277-4023 Office: Bank of Am Plaza Nci 002 29 01 Charlotte NC 28255-0001

**WALMER, JAMES L.,** lawyer; b. Wabash, Ind., Oct. 18, 1948; s. Warren D. and Josephine (Clupper) W.; m. Carolyn Gwen Lackey, Apr. 23, 1977; children: Ryan, Christian, Jonathan, Geoffrey. BS, Ball State U., 1971; JD, U. Tulsa, 1973. Bar: Okla. 1974, Ind. 1974, U.S. Dist. Ct. (no. and ea. dists.) Okla. 1974, U.S. Dist. Ct. (so. dist.) Ind. 1974, U.S. Dist. Ct. (no. dist.) Ind. 1975. Sole practice Warsaw, Ind., 1974—; dep. prosecutor Kosciusko County, Warsaw, 1976-96; town atty. Winona Lake, Ind., 1976—, Pierceton, Ind., 1980—. Chmn. bd. dirs. Cardinal Ctr. Inc., Warsaw, 1978-84; mem. philanthropy com. Ball State U., Muncie, Ind., 1986—; pres. Lincoln PTO, 1989-90; co-pres. Harrison PTO, 1993-94; coach Warsaw Cmty. Baseball League, 1990, asst. coach, 1991-93; trustee First United Meth. Ch., 1992-94; dir. Ind. Prosecutors Child Support Alliance, 1994-96; bd. dirs. Warsaw Little League, 1994-98, coach, 1994-96, 98. Mem. ABA, Ind. Bar Assn. (chmn. surrogacy com. family law sect. 1987-88), Kosciusko County Bar Assn. (treas. 1979—), Okla. Bar Assn., Ind. Mcpl. Lawyers Assn. Republican. Methodist. Lodges: Optimists (v.p. 1979-80), Shriners, Masons. General practice, Family and matrimonial. Home: 1705 E Springhill Rd Warsaw IN 46580-1805 Office: PO Box 1056 Warsaw IN 46581-1056

**WALNER, ROBERT JOEL,** lawyer; b. Chgo., Dec. 22, 1946; s. Wallace and Elsie W.; m. Charlene Walner; children: Marci, Lisa. BA, U. Ill., 1968; JD, De Paul U., 1972; M in Mgmt. with distinction, Northwestern U., 1991. Bar: Ill. 1972, U.S. Dist. Ct. (no. dist.) Ill. 1972, U.S. Ct. Appeals (7th cir.) 1972, Fla. 1973. Atty. SEC, Chgo., 1972-73; pvt. practice Chgo., 1973—; adminstrv. law judge Ill. Commerce Commn., Chgo., 1973-76; atty. Allied Van Lines, Inc., Broadview, Ill., 1976-79; sr. v.p., gen. counsel, sec. The Balcor Co., Skokie, Ill., 1979-92; prin. fin. ops. Balcor Securities divsn. The Balcor Co., Skokie, 1984-92, pres., 1989-92; of counsel Lawrence, Walner & Assocs., Ltd., Chgo., 1992-93; sr. v.p., gen. counsel, sec. Grubb & Ellis Co., Northbrook, Ill., 1994—; mem. securities adv. com. to Ill. Sec. of State, 1984-94; mem. editl. bd. Real Estate Securities Jour., Real Estate Securities and Capital Markets; program chmn. Regulators and You seminar. Contbr. chpts. to books, articles on real estate and securities law to profl. jours.; assoc. editor De Paul U. Law Rev. Mem. Kellogg Career Devel. Com., 1992-94, Kellogg Bus. Adv. Com., 1992—; mem. enterprise forum MIT, 1992—, mem. exec. com., 1993-94. With USAR, 1968-73. Mem. ABA, Ill. Bar Assn., Chgo. Bar Assn., Am. Real Estate Com. (pres. com. 1985-90), Real Estate Syndication Com. (chmn. 1982-85), Ill. Inst. Continuing Legal Edn., N.Am. Securities Adminstrs. Assn. Inc. (industry adv. com. to real estate com., 1987-89), Real Estate Securities and Syndication Inst. of Nat. Assn. Realtors (chmn. regulatory and legis. com., 1984, 87, specialist, real estate investment, group v.p., 1987, exec. com. 1987-90), Nat. Real Estate Investment Forum (chmn. 1985, 88), Real Estate Investment Assn. (founder, exec. com. 1990-92), Kellogg Alumni Club (bd. dirs., event chmn. 1996-98, v.p., exec. com. 1998—), Beta Gamma Sigma. Securities, General corporate, General civil litigation.

**WALPER, ROBERT ANDREW,** lawyer; b. Balt., Jan. 12, 1968; s. William Edward and Doris Ann W.; m. Holly Ann Wolford, May 27, 1995. BBS, Temple U., 1991, JD, 1994; LLM in Taxation, Villanova U., 1999. Bar: Pa. 1994, U.S. Dist. Ct. (ea. dist.) Pa. 1994. Atty. Fox, Rothschild, O'Brien & Frankel, LLP, Phila., 1996—. Recipient Terrence Klasky award Temple U., Phila., 1994, Rhea Liebman award, 1994. Mem. Montgomery Bar Assn., Greater Willow Grove C. of C. Contracts commercial, General corporate, Real property. Office: Fox Rothschild O'Brien & Frankel LLP 1250 S Broad St Ste 1000 Lansdale PA 19446-5343

**WALPIN, GERALD,** lawyer; b. N.Y.C., Sept. 1, 1931; s. Michael and Mary (Gordon) W.; m. Sheila Kainer, Apr. 13, 1957; children: Amanda Eve, Edward Andrew, Jennifer Hope. BA, CCNY, 1952; LLB cum laude, Yale Law Sch., 1955. Bar: N.Y. 1955, U.S. Supreme Ct. 1965, U.S. Ct. Appeals (2d cir.) 1960, (6th cir.) 1969, (3d cir.) 1976, (8th cir.) 1982, (9th cir.) 1983, (llth cir.) 1983, (7th cir.) 1984, U.S. Ct. Claims 1984. Law clk. to Hon. E.J. Dimock U.S. Dist. Ct. (so. dist.) N.Y., N.Y.C.; law clk. to Hon. F.P. Bryan U.S. Dist. Judge (so. dist.) N.Y., N.Y.C., 1955-57; asst. U.S. atty., chief spl. prosecutions U.S. Atty. Office, N.Y.C., 1960-65; sr. ptnr. Rosenman & Colin and predecessor firm, N.Y.C., 1965—, chmn. litigation dept., 1985-96; adv. com. Fed. Ct. So. Dist. N.Y., 1991—; co-chmn. lawyers divsn. Anti-Defamation League, N.Y., 1994-97; bd. dirs. Ctr. for Individual Rights, 1997—. Editor Yale Law Jour., 1953-54, mng. editor, 1954-55; contbr. articles to profl. jours. Pres., trustee Parker Jewish Inst. for Health Care and Rehab., New Hyde Park, N.Y., 1979-87, chmn., trustee, 1987-90; bd. dirs. Fund for Modern Cts., N.Y.C., 1985-91; mem. law com. Am. Jewish Com., 1980—; mem. Com. for Free World, N.Y.C., 1983-91; trustee, mem. exec. com. United Jewish Appeal-Fedn. Jewish Philanthropies, N.Y.C., 1984-96; mem. Nassau County Crime Commn., 1970; pres. Kensington Civic Orgn., Gt. Neck, N.Y., 1972-73. Recipient Quality of Life award United Jewish Appeal Fedn., 1978, Human Rels. award Am. Jewish Com., 1982, Gift of Life award Jewish Inst. Geriatric Care, 1987, Learned Hand award Am. Jewish Com., 1990, Human Rels. award Anti-Defamation League, 1998. Mem. ABA, Assn. Bar City N.Y., Fed. Bar Coun. (chmn. modern cts. com. 1989, v.p. 1991-95, chmn. bench and bar liaison com. 1994-95, vice chmn. 1995-97, chmn. bd. dirs. 1997-99), Federalist Soc. (chmn. litigation sect. 1996—), Univ. Club, Yale Club. Republican. Jewish. General civil litigation, Criminal, Securities. Home: 875 Park Ave New York NY 10021-0341 Office: Rosenman & Colin 575 Madison Ave Fl 20 New York NY 10022-2511 *My life should be an appropriate response to God and this country for providing me with the opportunities I have had: Contribution to our society and strengthening of our country's steadfast opposition to discrimination for or against anyone based on race, religion or sex.*

**WALPOLE, JAMES R.,** lawyer; b. Oswego, N.Y., Aug. 31, 1944; s. Richard and Margaret Mary Walpole; children: Sarah, Mark, Ethan. BA, John Carroll U., 1966; JD, Case Western Res. U., 1969. Bar: Ohio 1969, D.C. 1971, Ill. 1994, U.S. Ct. Appeals (D.C., 3d, 4th, 7th, 8th and 11th cirs.), U.S. Supreme Ct. 1973. Trial atty. U.S. Dept. Justice, Washington, 1971-74; sr. counsel Am. Mining Congress, Washington, 1975-79; ptnr. Holland & Hast, Washington, 1979-85, Chadbourne & Parke, Washington, 1985-92; v.p. environment FMC Corp., Chgo., 1992-95; sr. environ. counsel Sears Roebuck & Co., Chgo., 1995—; mem. adv. com. U.S. C. of C., Washington, 1987-92; adj. prof. environ. law Cath. U., Washington, 1975-79. Author publs. in field. Bd. dirs. Griffin Theater Co., 19946. Roman Catholic. Avocations: Civil War, fishing. Environmental, Mergers and acquisitions, Administrative and regulatory. Office: Sears Roebuck Hdqrs 3333 Beverly Rd # B6-326B Hoffman Estates IL 60192

**WALSH, CHARLES MICHAEL,** law educator; b. East Liverpool, Ohio, Feb. 23, 1966; s. Charles Michael Walsh and Linda Sue Marinro; m. Deborah Rae Hall, Aug. 17, 1991; 1 child, Michael. BS in Acctg., U. Akron, 1988, JD, 1991. Bar: Ohio 1991, U.S. Dist. Ct. (no. dist.) Ohio 1992, U.S. Ct. Appeals (6th cir.) 1995. Jud. law clk. Ohio 9th Dist. Ct. Appeals, Akron, 1991-93; dir. trial litigation clinic U. Akron Sch. Law, 1993—; vis. asst. prof. law Case Western Res. U. Sch. Law, Cleve., 1998—. Trustee Stow (Ohio)-Munroe Falls Pub. Libr., 1998—. Mem. ABA, Ohio State Bar Assn., Akron Bar Assn. Republican. Lutheran. Office: Case Western Res Univ Sch of Law 11075 East Blvd Cleveland OH 44106-5409

**WALSH, DAVID GRAVES,** lawyer; b. Madison, Wis., Jan. 7, 1943; s. John J. and Audrey B. Walsh; married; children: Michael, Katherine, Molly, John. BBA, U. Wis., 1965; JD, Harvard U., 1970. Bar: Wis. Law clk. Wis. Supreme Ct., Madison, 1970-71; ptnr. Walsh, Walsh, Sweeney & Whitney, Madison, 1971-86; ptnr.-in-charge Foley & Lardner, Madison, 1986—; bd. dirs. Nat. Guardian Life, Madison, 1981—; lectr. U. Wis., Madison, 1974-75, 77-78. Chmn. State of Wis. Elections Bd., Madison, 1978. Lt. USN, 1965-67, Vietnam. Recipient Disting. Bus. Alumnus award U. Wis. Sch. Bus., 1997. Maple Bluff Country Club (Madison) (pres. 1987). Roman Catholic. Avocations: tennis, golf, fishing. Communications, Bankruptcy, Contracts commercial. Home: 41 Fuller Dr Madison WI 53704-5962 Office: Foley & Lardner PO Box 1497 Madison WI 53701-1497

**WALSH, DAVID JAMES,** lawyer; b. Dubuque, Iowa, Aug. 10, 1949; s. James and Helen Walsh; m. Alice Chebba; children: Elizabeth, James. BA, Loras Coll., 1971; JD, U. Wis., 1974; MBA, Alaska Pacific U., 1990; postgrad. in Internat. Bus., City U. London, 1991. Bar: Wis. 1974, Alaska 1975. Asst. dist. atty. State of Alaska, Anchorage, 1975-78; pvt. practice Anchorage, 1974-75, 78-90; co-founder, chmn. exec. com. Internat. Assn. Ins. Suprs., 1992-95; dir. ins. State of Alaska, 1990-95; gen. counsel Domestic Brokerage Group Am. Internat. Group, N.Y.C., 1995-98; pres. Nat. Assn. Ins. Commrs., 1994—; mem. Gov.'s Transition Team, 1982-83; mem. U.S./Alaska R.R. Transfer Team, 1982-84; vice chmn. State Rolyalty Oil and Gas Adv. Bd., 1985-87. Chmn. Anchorage Mcpl. Assembly, 1976-86; bd. dirs. Alaska Mcpl. League, 1976-86, pres., 1980; mem. exec. bd. Greater N.Y. coun. Boy Scouts Am., 1997—. Mem. Assn. Internationale de Droit des Assurances (presdl. coun. 1995—). Insurance, Private international, Administrative and regulatory. Office: Swiss Am Holding Corp 175 King St Armonk NY 10504-1606

**WALSH, GERRY O'MALLEY,** lawyer; b. Houston, Dec. 22, 1936; d. Frederick Harold and Blanche (O'Malley) W. B.S., U. Houston, 1959; J.D., S. Tex. Coll. Law, 1966. Bar: Tex. 1966, U.S. Dist. Ct. (so. dist.) Tex. 1967, (we. dist.) Tex. 1976; cert. elem. tchr. Tex. Elem. tchr. Houston, 1959-65; instr. bus. law U. Houston, 1966-67; pvt. practice, Houston, 1966—; lectr. legal, jud. and civic orgns. Adviser, den mother Sam Houston coun. Boy Scouts Am.; mem. Mus. Fine Arts. Recipient den mother award Sam Houston coun. Boy Scouts Am. Mem. ABA, Houston Zool. Assn., Houston Archeol. Soc., Bus. and Profl. Women's Assn. (Woman of Yr. 1973), Am. Judicature Soc., Tex. Criminal Lawyers Assn., Harris County Criminal Lawyers Assn., Tex. Trial Lawyers Assn., State Bar Tex., Houston Bar Assn., U. Houston Alumni Assn., So. Tex. Coll. Law Alumni Assn., Nat. Criminal Def. Lawyers Assn., Zeta Tau Alpha (best mem. and rec. sec. 1958), Sigma Chi (award 1958). Criminal, Family and matrimonial, General practice.

**WALSH, JAMES HAMILTON,** lawyer; b. Astoria, N.Y., May 20, 1947; s. Edward James and Helen Smith (Hamilton) W.; m. Janice Ausherman, Aug. 3, 1968; children: Tracy, Courtney, Eric. B.A. in Psychology, Bridgewater Coll., 1968; J.D., U. Va., 1975. Bar: Va. 1975, U.S. Dist. Ct. (ea. and we. dists.) Va. 1975, U.S. Ct. Appeals (4th cir.) 1976, U.S. Supreme Ct. 1982. Assoc. McGuire, Woods, Battle & Boothe (and predecessor firms), Richmond, Va., 1975-82, ptnr., 1982—; instr. Nat. Inst. Trial Adv.; adj. prof. U. Richmond, 1992, 93; spl. prosecutor U.S. Dist. Ct. (ea. dist.) Va., 1979, 84. Mem. bd. trustees Bridgewater (Va.) Coll., mem. exec. com.; mem. staff Va. Law Rev. With U.S. Army, 1969-72. Mem. ABA (mem. antitrust sect. health care com., litigation sect.), Va. State Bar (bd. govs. antitrust sect. 1984-90, chmn. 1986), Va. Bar Assn. (chmn. criminal law sect., 1997, 98), Richmond Bar Assn., Order Coif, Phi Delta Phi. Episcopalian. Clubs: Willow Oaks. Contbr. articles to profl. jours. Antitrust, General civil litigation, Product liability. Home: 113 Adingham Ct Richmond VA 23229-7761 Office: McGuire Woods Battle & Boothe 1 James Ctr 910 E Cary St Richmond VA 23219-4004

**WALSH, JAMES JOSEPH,** lawyer; b. New Orleans, June 21, 1948; s. Francis Michael and Violet (Young) W.; m. Priscilla Robson Ferris, Oct. 12, 1972; children: Caitlin Marian, Alison Robson. BA, La. State U., 1970, JD, 1975. Bar: La. 1975, Mich. 1977, U.S. Ct. Appeals (6th cir.) 1981, U.S. Supreme Ct. 1991. Law clk. Mich. Ct. Appeals, Detroit, 1975-77; assoc. Bodman, Longley & Dahling, Detroit, 1977-84, ptnr., 1984—, head litigation practice group; counsel Outdoor Advt. Assn. Mich. Editor: La. Law Rev., 1975. Named to Hall of Fame, La. State U. Law Sch., 1988. Mem. ABA, State Bar Mich., Detroit Bar Assn., Fed. Bar Assn., Detroit Athletic Club. Avocations: fishing, gardening, carpentry. Federal civil litigation, General civil litigation, Appellate. Home: 8025 Mast Rd Dexter MI 48130-9301 Office: Bodman Longley & Dahling 100 Renaissance Ctr Fl 34 Detroit MI 48243-1001

**WALSH, J(OHN) B(RONSON),** lawyer; b. Buffalo, Feb. 20, 1927; s. John A. and Alice (Condon) W.; m. Barbara Ashford, May 20, 1966; 1 child, Martha. AB, Canisius Coll., 1950; JD, Georgetown U., 1952. Bar: N.Y. 1953, U.S. Supreme Ct. 1958, U.S. Ct. Internat. Trade 1969, U.S. Ct. Customs and Patent Appeals 1973. Trial atty. Garvey & Conway, N.Y.C., 1953-54; vol. atty. Nativity Mission, N.Y.C., 1953-54; ptnr. Jaeckle, Fleischmann, Kelly, Swart & Augspurger, Buffalo, 1955-60; pvt. practice Buffalo, 1961-75; ptnr. Jaeckle, Fleischmann & Mugel, Buffalo, 1976-80; with Walsh & Cleary, P.C., Buffalo, 1980-84; pvt. practice, 1984—; spl. counsel Ecology and Environment, Inc., Lancaster, N.Y., 1989—; trial counsel antitrust div. Dept. Justice, Washington, 1960-61; spl. counsel on disciplinary procedures N.Y. Supreme Ct., 1960-76; appointee legal disciplinary coordinating com. State of N.Y., 1971; legis. counsel, spl. counsel to mayor Buffalo, 1995—; counsel to sheriff Erie County, 1969-72; legis counsel Niagara Frontier Transp. Authority; cons. Norfolk So. R.R., Ecology and Environment on Govtl. Affairs; guest lectr. univs. and profl. groups. Author: (TV series) The Law and You (Freedom Found. award, ABA award, Internat. Police Assn. award). Past pres. Ashford Hollow Found. Visual and Performing Arts; past trustee Dollar Bills, Inc.; past co-producer Grand Island Playhouse and Players. With U.S. Army, 1945-46. Recipient Gold Key Buffalo Jr. C. of C., 1962, award Freedom Found., 1966. Fellow Am. Bar Found.; mem. ABA (del. internat. conf. Brussels 1963, Mexico City 1964, Lausanne, Switzerland 1964, Award of Merit com. 1961-70, sec., vice chair, chmn. sect. bar activities 1965-69, mem. ho. of dels. 1969-70, mem. crime prevention and control com. 1968-70, vice chair sr. lawyers divsn., com. legislation and adminstrn. regulations 1992—, vice chair sr. lawyers divsn. membership com. 1993-94), N.Y. Trial Lawyers Assn., Am. Immigration Lawyers Assn., Am. Judicature Soc., N.Y. State Bar Assn. (past exec. sec.), Erie County Bar Assn., Buffalo Bar Assn., Nat. Pub. Employer Labor Relations Assn., Capital Hill Club of Buffalo, Am. Assn. Airport Execs., N.Y. State Bus. Coun. (environ. law subcom., chmn. subcom.), Buffalo Irish Club (bd. dirs.), Buffalo Athletic Club (past bd. dirs., past v.p.), Buffalo Canoe Club, Buffalo Club, Ft. Orange of Albany Club, KC, Knights of Equity, Leoknights, Phi Delta Phi, Delta Gamma. Roman Catholic. Legislative, Environmental, Immigration, naturalization, and customs. Home: 95 North Dr Eggertsville NY 14226-4158 Office: 368 Pleasant View Dr Lancaster NY 14086-1316 also: 210 Ellicott Sq Bldg Buffalo NY 14203-2402

**WALSH, JOSEPH LEO, III,** lawyer; b. St. Louis, Dec. 7, 1954; s. Joseph Leo and Joan Marie (Bocklage) W.; m. Eileen Rose Boland, June 11, 1982; children: Katie Rose, Joseph L. IV, Brian James, John Patrick, Mary Elizabeth. BS cum laude, Loras Coll., 1977; JD, St. Mary's U., 1984. Bar: Tex. 1984, U.S. Dist. Ct. (so. dist.) Tex. 1985, Mo. 1986, U.S. Dist. Ct. (ea. dist.) Mo. 1989, U.S. Ct. Appeals (8th cir.) 1989, U.S. Supreme Ct. 1991. Assoc. Chamberlain, Hrdlicka, White, Johnson & Williams, Houston, 1984-86; atty. Haley, Fredrickson & Walsh, St. Louis, 1986-88; assoc. Gray & Ritter, St. Louis, 1988-95; pvt. practice St. Louis, 1995—; pro bono legal clinic St. Patrick Ctr., 1991—, Holy Guardian Angel Settlement, 1995—; jud. clk. U.S. Dist. Ct. (we. dist.) Tex., 1984. Co-author: Missouri Bar CLE Treatise on Torts, 2d edit., 1990; sr. assoc. editor St. Mary's U. Sch. Law Jour., 1983-84. Active Holly Hills Neighborhood Assn., 1991-93; v.p. Our Lady of Pillar Men's Club, 1998, pres., 1999—. Recipient Torts and Evidence award Lawyers' Co-op Pub. Co., 1982; named to Nat. Order Barristers, 1984. Mem. Assn. Trial Lawyers Am., Mo. Assn. Trial Attys., Bar Assn. Met. St. Louis, Lawyers Assn. St. Louis, Phi Delta Phi (pres. 1984). Roman Catholic. General civil litigation, Personal injury, Product liability. Home and Office: 10469 White Bridge Ln Saint Louis MO 63141-8415 Office: 720 Olive St Ste 750 Saint Louis MO 63101-2330

**WALSH, JOSEPH THOMAS,** state supreme court justice; b. Wilmington, Del., May 18, 1930; s. Joseph Patrick and Mary Agnes (Bolton) W.; m. Madeline Maria Lamb, Oct. 6, 1955; children: Kevin, Lois, Patrick, Daniel, Thomas, Nancy. BA, LaSalle Coll., 1952; LLB, Georgetown U., 1955. Bar: D.C. 1955, Del. 1955. Atty. Ho. of Reps., Dover, Del., 1961-62; chief counsel Pub. Svc. Commn., Dover, 1964-72; judge Del. Superior Ct., Wilmington, 1972-84; vice chancellor Ct. of Chancery, Wilmington, 1984-85; justice Del. Supreme Ct., Wilmington, 1985—. Capt. U.S. Army, 1955-58. Democrat. Roman Catholic. Office: Del Supreme Ct Carvel State Bldg Wilmington DE 19801-3509*

**WALSH, KEVIN PETER,** lawyer; b. Waterbury, Conn., Apr. 6, 1961. BA, Providence Coll., 1983, Providence Coll., 1983; JD, Suffolk U., 1986. Bar: Conn. 1986, Mass. 1987, Maine 1987, U.S. Dist. Ct. Conn. 1988, U.S. Supreme Ct. 1994. Assoc. Lovejoy Hoffernan Rimer & Cuneo, Norwalk, Conn., 1986-87, Cella McKeon, North Haven, Conn., 1987-89; ptnr. Cella McKeon & Williams, North Haven, 1989—. Mem. ATLA, Ins. Def. Rsch. Inst., Conn. Def. Rsch. Inst., Conn. Trial Lawyers Assn. Federal civil litigation, General civil litigation, Product liability. Office: Cella McKeon & Williams 21 Washington Ave North Haven CT 06473-2310

**WALSH, LEATRICE D.,** lawyer; b. Providence, R.I., May 20, 1946; d. Henry and Ethel (Bailey) Harper; divorced; 1 child, Raymond L. III. BSN, U. R.I., 1968; JD, New Eng. Sch. of Law, 1993. Bar: R.I. 1993, U.S. Dist. Ct. R.I. 1994, U.S. Supreme Ct. 1998. Pvt. practice Cranston, R.I., 1993—; legal cons. Kent County Vis. Nurses Assn., Warwick, R.I., 1994—. Mem. ABA, R.I. Bar Assn. Consumer commercial, Family and matrimonial, General civil litigation. Office: 1441 Park Ave Cranston RI 02920-6632

**WALSH, MILTON O'NEAL,** lawyer; b. Memphis, Tenn., June 17, 1941; s. J. Milton and Rebie (Willis) W.; m. Janet Parker; children: Susan, Neal. BS, La. State U., 1964, JD, 1971. Bar: La. 1971. Salesman Met. Ins. Co., Baton Rouge, 1963-65; claims adjustor Safeco Ins. Co., Baton Rouge, 1965-68; law clk. Franklin, Moore, Beychok & Cooper, Baton Rouge, 1968-71, assoc., 1971-73; ptnr. Franklin, Moore, Cooper & Walsh, Baton Rouge, 1973-74, Franklin, Moore & Walsh, Baton Rouge, 1974-90; prin. O'Neal Walsh and Assocs., Baton Rouge, 1990—; chmn. rules com. Baton Rouge City Ct., 1975-76, liaison com. 19th Jud. Dist. Ct., 1977; instr. in bus. law La. State U., 1974. Mem. ABA (mem. products liability com. 1978-79), Baton Rouge Bar Assn., La. Bar Assn., La. Assn. Def. Counsel (bd. dirs. 1982-84, 96-97), Internat. Assn. Def. Counsel (mem. casualty ins. com. 1980-81, mem. faculty 14th ann. counsel trial acad. 1986), Def. Rsch. Inst. (state chmn. 1980-82, regional v.p. 1983-86, bd. dirs. 1986-89, 96-98, mem. arbitration com., Scroll of Merit award 1981, 82), Am. Bd. Trial Advocates, Assn. Def. Trial Attys. (state chmn. 1984—, S.W. mem. chmn. 1985-95, v.p./pres.-elect 1995-96, pres. 1996-97, mem. exec. coun. 1990-93), Sherwood Forest Country Club (bd. dirs. 1977-79, pres. 1979), Phi Delta Phi. General civil litigation, Insurance. Office: O'Neal Walsh & Assocs 501 Louisiana Ave Baton Rouge LA 70802-5921

**WALSH, RICHARD MICHAEL,** lawyer; b. Portland, Oreg., Nov. 8, 1958; s. Robert Thomas and Elizabeth Ann (Stott) W.; m. Teresa Ann Emfinger; children: Samantha Ann, Michael Richard, Kevin Collier. BS in Polit. Sci., Portland State U., 1983; JD, U. Oreg., 1986. Bar: Oreg. 1986. Assoc. Schouboe Marvin & Furniss, Portland, 1986-88; ptnr. Olson Rowell & Walsh, Salem, Oreg., 1988-93; pvt. practice Salem, 1993-99; prin. Richard Walsh and Assocs., 1999—. Atty. Oreg. Workers Compensation. Oreg. Law Sch. Alumni scholar, 1983-84, Oreg. Law Found. scholar, 1985. Mem. ABA, Oreg. State Bar, Oreg. Trial Lawyers Assn., Oreg. Fed. Dist. Bar., Am. Trial Lawyers Assn., Lions Club, Phi Delta Phi. Democrat. Roman Catholic. Avocations: bicycling, backpacking, racquetball. General civil litigation, Personal injury, Workers' compensation. Office: 876 Welcome Way SE Ste 200 Salem OR 97302-3936

**WALSH, ROBERT ANTHONY,** lawyer; b. Boston, Aug. 26, 1938; s. Frank and Emily Angelica (Bissitt) W.; m. Angela Rosalie Barile, Aug. 3, 1966; children: Maria, Robert II, Amy. SB, MIT, 1960; MS, Fla. Inst. Tech., 1967; JD, Suffolk U., 1971. Bar: Mass. 1971, U.S. Dist. Ct. Mass. 1972, U.S. Patent Office 1972, Can. Patent Office 1973, Ill. 1976, U.S. Supreme Ct. 1976, U.S. Ct. Appeals (Fed. cir.) 1982, U.S. Ct. Mil. Appeals 1983, Vt. 1996; registered profl. engr., Mass. Engr. Saturn Boeing, Michaud, La., 1964-65; program analyst RCA, Cape Canaveral, Fla., 1965-68; patent trainee, engr. Avco Research Lab., Everett, Mass., 1968-72; patent atty. GTE Labs., Waltham, Mass., 1972-73; group patent counsel Bell & Howell Co., Chgo., 1973-78; patent counsel ITT E. Coast Patents, Nutley, N.J., 1978-80, patent counsel internat., 1980-82, sr. patent counsel internat., 1982-86; dir. internat. patents ITT Corp., N.Y.C., 1986-87; gen. patent counsel ITT Def. Tech. Corp., Nutley, 1987-89; chief patent counsel Allied-Signal Aerospace Co., Phoenix, 1989-94; atty. IBM Corp., Essex Junction, Vt., 1994—; ednl. counselor admissions MIT, No. N.J., 1978-89, Ariz., 1989-94; with Office of Judge Adv. Gen., Washington. Col. USAF, 1960-92. (ret.). Mem. ABA (co-chmn. subcom. PTC sect. 105), Tri-State USAFR Lawyers Assn. (Meritorious Achievement award 1980), KC (fin. sec. Scottsdale, Ariz. 1993-95), Internat. Patent Club (pres. 1988-89), Am. Intellectual Property Law Assn., Aerospace Industry Assn. (chmn. Intellectual Property com.), Chgo. Patent Law Assn., N.J. Patent Law Assn., Ariz. Patent Law Assn. (bd. dirs.), Sigma Xi. Roman Catholic. Patent, Trademark and copyright. Home: 171 Yacht Haven Dr Shelburne VT 05482-7776 Office: Intellectual Property Law Dept 915 1000 River St Essex Junction VT 05452-4201

**WALSH, ROBERT K.,** dean. AB, Providence Coll., 1964; JD, Harvard U., 1967. Bar: Calif. 1967, Ark. 1979. Assoc. McCatchen, Black, Verleger & Shea, L.A., 1967-70; asst. prof. Villanova (Pa.) U., 1970-71, assoc. prof., 1971-73, prof., 1973-76; ptnr. Friday, Eldredge & Clark, Little Rock, 1981-89; dean, prof. Wake Forest Sch. Law, Winston-Salem, N.C., 1989—. Mem. ABA (chair accreditation com. 1984-86, chair standards rev. com. sect. legal edn. 1991—), N.C. Bar Assn. (chair bar bench and law schs. com. 1990-92, v.p., bd. govs. 1994-95). Office: Wake Forest Sch Law Worrell Profl Ctr PO Box 7206 Winston Salem NC 27109-7206*

**WALSH, ROBERT PATRICK, JR.,** lawyer; b. Oak Park, Ill., Apr. 12, 1959; s. Robert Patrick and Marie Terese (Murnane) W.; m. Laura Helen Barry, July 6, 1985; children: Robert Patrick III, Barry Joseph, Daniel Casey, Casey Murnane. BA, St. John's U., Collegeville, Minn., 1981; JD, Loyola U., Chgo., 1986. Bar: Ill. 1986, U.S. Dist. Ct. (no. dist.) Ill. 1986. Assoc. Robert A. Clifford and Assocs., Chgo., 1986-94, Corboy, Demetrio & Clifford, 1994-95, Clifford Law Offices, 1995—. Mem. ABA, Ill. Bar Assn., Chgo. Bar Assn., Assn. Trial Lawyers Am., Ill. Trial Lawyers Assn., Fenwick Bar Assn., PIXX. Roman Catholic. Personal injury, Insurance, State civil litigation. Office: Clifford Law Offices PC 120 N La Salle St Fl 31 Chicago IL 60602-2412

**WALSH, SEAN M.,** lawyer, audio-video computer forensics consultant; b. N.Y.C., Dec. 26, 1947; s. John W. and Catherine M. Walsh; m. Christine Ann Kull, June 10, 1978; children: Kathleen, Sean, Stephen. BS, Fordham U., 1970, JD, 1973. Bar: N.Y. 1974. Chief, asst. dist. atty. Dist. Atty.'s Office, N.Y.C., 1973-96; pres. Walsh Assocs. Forensic Cons., Douglaston, N.Y., 1997—; officer/dir. Law Enforcement Video Assocs., Ft. Worth, 1989-95. Author: Video and the Law, 1979; inventor non-linear video wire tapping rec. sys. Vice-chmn. N.Y.C. Cmty. Planning Bd., 1986—; pres. Queens (N.Y.) Civic Congress, 1996—, past pres./dir. Douglaston Civic Assn. Recipient Outstanding Cmty. Bd. Work, N.Y.C., 1973, Outstanding Svc. to N.Y. State Police, 1992, Van Zandt Cmty. Svc. award, 1999; named Marshall to Little Neck Douglaston Meml. Day Parade, 1990. Mem. Assn. Bar City N.Y. (Comm. com. 1983-85, Computer com. 1997—), N.Y. County Lawyer's Assn. (various coms. 1976-91), Queens County Bar Assn. (Criminal Law com. 1997—), High Tech. Crime Investigation Assn. (pres. local chpt. 1994-96, internat. v.p. 1999). Avocations: sailing, skiing, scuba diving. Home: PO Box 238 Little Neck NY 11363-0238

**WALSH, TARA JANE,** lawyer; b. Palo Alto, Calif., Sept. 2, 1969; d. William Desmond and Mary Jane Walsh. BA, U. So. Calif., 1991; JD, Fordham U., 1994. Bar: Calif. 1994, U.S. Dist. Ct. (no. and ea. dists.) Calif., U.S. Ct. Appeal (9th cir.). Assoc. Ropers, Majestic Kohn-Bentley, Redwood City, Calif., 1994-97, Miller Starr & Regalia, Menlo Park, Calif., 1997—. Vol. Rep. Party, 1994—; bd. dirs. Am. Ireland Fund, San Francisco, 1996—. Mem. ABA, San Francisco Bar Assn., San Mateo Bar Assn., Santa Clara Bar Assn. Roman Catholic. Avocations: snowboarding, mountain hiking, volleyball. Real property, General corporate. Office: Miller Starr & Regalia 545 Middlefield Rd Ste 200 Menlo Park CA 94025-3400

**WALSH, THOMAS F.,** lawyer; b. Pittsfield, Mass., July 18, 1955; s. Thomas Francis and Joan Patricia (Shaughnessy) W.; m. Marianne York, Aug. 4, 1979; children: Charity L., Victoria A., Hannah J., Thomas F. B in Environ. Sci., SUNY at Syracuse, 1977, B in Landscape Architecture, 1978; JD, U. Mich., 1985. Landscape architect A.E. Bye & Assocs., Greenwich, Conn., 1978-82; assoc./counsel Nixon, Hargrave, Devans & Doyle, Rochester, N.Y., 1985-95; environ. ptnr. Jaeckle Fleischmann & Mugel, Rochester, 1996—; mem. N.Y. State Super Fund Mgmt. Bd., Albany, 1996—, N.Y. State Bus. Coun., Inc., Albany, 1987—; chair Local Emergency Planning Com., Monroe County, N.Y., 1990—, chair, 1999. Contbr. articles to profl. jours. Chair Parks and Recreation Adv. Bd., Brighton, N.Y., 1991—. Mem. N.Y. State Bar Assn., Monroe County Bar Assn. (chair environ. com. 1991-93), Rochester Yacht Club. Republican. Roman Catholic. Avocations: skiing, sailing, painting. Environmental, Land use and zoning (including planning), General civil litigation. Office: Jaeckle Fleischmann & Mugel LLP 39 State St Rochester NY 14614-1311

**WALSH, THOMAS JAMES, JR.,** lawyer; b. Memphis, Oct. 22, 1947; s. Thomas James and Lois Rhine (Gibson) w.; m. Jean Clay McKee, May 31, 1969; children: Courtney Michelle, Meredith McKee. BA, Yale Coll., 1969; JD, U. Va., 1975. Bar: Tenn. 1975, U.S. Dist. Ct. (we. dist.) Tenn. 1976, U.S. Ct. Appeals (5th cir.) 1982, U.S. Ct. Appeals (6th cir.) 1985, U.S. Ct. Appeals (11th cir.) 1986, U.S. Supreme Ct. 1986, U.S. Ct. Appeals (10th cir.) 1991, U.S. Ct. Appeals (8th cir.) 1992, U.S. Ct. Appeals (3d cir.) 1998. Assoc. Canada, Russell & Turner, Memphis, 1975-78; assoc. Wildman, Harrold, Allen, Dixon & McDonnell, Memphis, 1978-80, ptnr., 1981-89; ptnr. McDonnell, Boyd, Smith & Solmson, Memphis, 1989-90, McDonnell Boyd, Memphis, 1990-94; atty. Wolff Ardis, P.C., Memphis, 1995-97; sr. counsel McKnight, Hudson, Lewis, Ford & Harrison, Memphis, 1997—; hearing officer Bd. of Profl. Responsibility Supreme Ct. Tenn., 1988-95. Chmn. bd. dirs. Multiple Sclerosis Soc. mid-south chpt., Memphis, 1978, World Affairs Coun. Memphis, 1985—; vol. atty. pro bono panel for sr. citizens, Memphis, 1982—; v.p. Bapt. Peace Fellowship of N.Am., Memphis, 1984-89; coun. chmn. Prescott Meml. Bapt. Ch., Memphis, 1993-95. Mem. Class award Leadership Memphis, 1985, Community Class award Unitarian Universalist Fellowship, Memphis, 1989. Mem. ABA, Tenn. Bar Assn., Memphis Bar Assn. Democrat. Avocations: photography, baseball. General civil litigation, Product liability, Banking. Office: PO Box 171375 Memphis TN 38187-1375

**WALSH, THOMAS JOHN, SR.,** lawyer; b. Omaha, Aug. 6, 1927; s. John R. and Mary P. (Wokersien) W.; m. Virginia Frederick, June 10, 1950; children: Ellen, Thomas John, Jean, Dan, Jim, Pat, William. LLB, Creighton U., 1951. Bar: Nebr. 1951, U.S. Dist. Ct. Nebr. 1951, U.S. Ct. Appeals (8th cir.) 1954. Law clk. to judge U.S. Ct. Appeals (8th cir.), Omaha, 1951-54; dep. pub. defender Douglas County, Nebr., 1954-56; ptnr. Haney & Walsh, 1956-68; sr. ptnr. Walsh, Walentine, Miles, Fullenkamp & O'Toole, 1968-84, Walsh, Fullenkamp & Doyle, Omaha, 1984—. Pres. Nebr. Lawyers Trust Account Found., 1985. Fellow Am. Coll. Trial Lawyers; mem. Am. Bd. Trial Advs., Nebr. Bar Assn. (exec. com. 1977-83), Omaha Bar Assn. General civil litigation, Personal injury, Insurance. Office: Walsh Fullenkamp & Doyle 11440 W Center Rd Omaha NE 68144-4410

**WALSH, THOMAS JOSEPH,** lawyer; b. Kansas City, Mo., Oct. 3, 1932; s. Thomas E. and Clare E. (O'Leary) W.; m. Ellen B. Butler; children: Carolyn, David, Kathy. AB, U. Mo., 1953; JD, Georgetown U., 1958. Bar: D.C. 1958, Mo. 1958. Sole practice Lee's Summit, Mo., 1958—. Mem. 4th Congl. Dist. Youth Council, 1985—; vice chmn. Mo. Council on Criminal Justice, 1977-80; sec. Jackson County Bd. Election Commrs., 1993-96, chmn. 1997—. Served to 1st lt. U.S. Army, 1953-55. Mem. Mo. Bar Assn., Assn. Trial Lawyers Am., Met. Kansas City Bar Assn., Knights of Columbus. Democrat. Roman Catholic. Lodge: Optimists (lt. gov. 1963-64, pres. 1960-61). General practice, State civil litigation, Family and matrimonial. Home: 210 NW Hillcrest Ln Lees Summit MO 64063-2103 Office: 528 W 3rd St Lees Summit MO 64063-2248

**WALTER, DONALD ELLSWORTH,** federal judge; b. Jennings, La., Mar. 15, 1936; s. Robert R. and Ada (Lafleur) D'Aquin; m. Charlotte Sevier Donald, Jan. 5, 1942; children: Laura Ney, Robert Ellsworth, Susannah Brooks. BA, La. State U., 1961, JD, 1964. Bar: La. 1964, U.S. Supreme Ct. 1969. Assoc. Cavanaugh, Brame, Holt & Woodley, 1964-66, Holt & Woodley, Lake Charles, La., 1966-69; U.S. atty. U.S. Dept. Justice, Shreveport, La., 1969-77; lawyer Hargrove, Guyton, Ramey & Barlow, Shreveport, La., 1977-85; judge U.S. Dist. Ct. (west. dist.) La., Monroe, 1985-92, Shreveport, La., 1993—. Served with AUS, 1957-58. Office: US Dist Ct 300 Fannin St Ste 4200 Shreveport LA 71101-3122

**WALTER, GLENN RICHARD,** lawyer; b. Lancaster, Pa., May 16, 1962; s. Richard Kupp and Gayle Marie Walter; m. Nancy Donita Messer, Jan. 11, 1992; children: Jessica Morgan, Kyle Reed, Sydney Paige. BSBA, U. Pa., Bloomsburg, 1984; JD, U. Tenn., 1987. Bar: Tenn., U.S. Dist. Ct. (ea. dist.) Tenn., U.S. Ct. Appeals (6th cir.). Atty. Kramer Rayson Leake Rodgers & Morgan, Knoxville, 1987-96, Lewis King Krieg Waldrop & Catron, Knoxville, 1996—. Mem. ABA (spl. projects coord. young lawyers divsn. 1997-98), Tenn. Bar Assn. (bd. govs. 1997—, pres. young lawyers divsn. 1998—). Insurance, General civil litigation, Labor. Office: Lewis King Krieg Waldrop & Catron 620 Market St Knoxville TN 37902-2231

**WALTER, MICHAEL CHARLES,** lawyer; b. Oklahoma City, Nov. 25, 1956; s. Donald Wayne and Viola Helen (Heffelfinger) W. BA in Polit. Sci., BJ, U. Wash., 1980; JD, Univ. Puget Sound, 1983. Bar: Wash. 1985, U.S. Dist. Ct. (9th cir. 1985). Ptnr. Keating, Bucklin & McCormack, Seattle, 1985—; instr. Bellevue (Wash.) C.C., 1983—. FAX: 206-223-9423. Mem. ABA, Wash. State Bar Assn., Reporters Com. for Freedom of Press, Seattle-King County Bar Assn., Wash. Assn. Def. Counsel, Seattle Claims Adjustors Assn., Wash. Assn. Mcpl. Attys., Def. Rsch. Inst., Am. Planning Assn., Def. Rsch. Inst. Avocations: running, swimming, hiking, coin collecting, photography. Fax: (206) 223-9423. Insurance, Municipal (including bonds), State civil litigation. Home: 11920 27th Pl SW Burien WA 98146-2438 Office: Keating Bucklin & McCormack 4141 SeaFirst 5th Ave Pla Seattle WA 98104

**WALTER, TERI A.,** lawyer, real estate broker; b. Des Moines, Nov. 3, 1958; d. James P. and Betty J. (Bish) Leporte. AA, Des Moines Area C.C., Ankeny, Iowa, 1979; BA in Econs. magna cum laude, U. Houston, 1985, JD, 1988. Bar: Tex. 1988, U.S. Dist. Ct. (so. dist.) Tex. 1989. Assoc. Smith, Wright & Weed, Houston, 1986-89, Baker Brown, Sharman & Parker, Houston, 1989-90, Whittington, Pfeiffer & Vacek, Houston, 1991-96; ptnr. Walter, Burdzinski & Co., LLP, Houston, 1997—. V.p. fundraising Alley Theatre Guild, Houston, 1995-96, v.p. membership, 1996-98; grad. Ledership 20/20, 1998. Mem. ABA, Tex. Bar Assn., Assn. Women Attys. (mem. jud. evaluation com. 1996-98), Greater S.W. Houston C. of C., Houston Assn. Realtors. Libertarian. Avocation: flying. Personal injury, Real property. Office: Walter Burdzinski & Co LLP 3730 Kirby Dr Ste 520 Houston TX 77098-3979

**WALTERS, BILL,** state senator, lawyer; b. Paris, Ark., Apr. 17, 1943; s. Peter Louis and Elizabeth Cecelia (Wilhelm) W.; m. Joyce Leslie Garrett Moore, Jan. 9, 1964 (div. 1970); children: Jamie, Sherry Ann; m. Shirley Ann Dixon, Aug. 20, 1971; 1 child, Sandra. BS, U. Ark., 1966, JD, 1971. Bar: Ark. 1971, U.S. Dist. Ct. Ark. 1971. Asst. prosecuting atty. 12th Jud. Dist. Ark., Ft. Smith, 1971-74; pvt. practice Greenwood, Ark., 1975—; mem. Ark. Senate, Little Rock, 1982—; bd. dirs., sec.-treas. Mineral Owners Collective Assn. Inc., Greenwood; v.p., bd. dirs. Sebastian County Abstract & Title Ins. Co., Greenwood and Ft. Smith, Ark.; mem. Ark. Real Estate Commn., Ark. Abstract and Title Commn. Committeeman Rep. Ctrl. Com. Ark., Ft. Smith, 1980; search pilot CAP, Ft. Smith. Decorated Silver Medal of Valor; recipient Cert. of Honor Justice for Crime's Victims, 1983. Mem. Ark. Bar Assn., South Sebastian County Bar Assn. (pres. 1991-94), Profl. Landmen's Assn. Roman Catholic. Home: PO Box 280 Greenwood AR 72936-0280 Office: 44 Town Square St Greenwood AR 72936-4019

**WALTERS, DAVID MCLEAN,** lawyer; b. Cleve., Apr. 4, 1917; s. William L. and Marguerite (McLean) W.; m. Betty J. Latimer, Mar. 25, 1939 (dec. 1983); 1 child, Susan Patricia (Mrs. James Edward Smith); m. Rebecca Brewer, Feb. 14, 1991. BA, Baldwin-Wallace Coll., 1938, LHD (hon.); LLB, Cleve. Sch. Law, 1943; JD, U. Miami, 1950; LHD (hon.), St. Thomas of Villanova U. Bar: D.C. 1950, Fla. 1950, Fed. 1950. Judge adminstrv. practices U.S. Dept. Justice, Washington, 1940-50; sr. law ptnr. firm Walters & Costanzo, Miami, Fla., 1950-80; of counsel firm Walters, Costanzo, Russell, Zyne, 1980-85; amb. to Vatican, 1976-78; fellow internat. medicine, bd. advisors Med. Sch., Boston U., 1985. Chmn. Fla. Harbor Pilot Commn., 1952-54, City of Miami Seaport Commn., 1953-54, Nat. Leukemia Soc., 1965-66, Archbishops Charities Dr., 1975-76; spl. bond counsel Dade County, 1957-58; gen. counsel Dade County Port Authority, 1957-58; vice-chmn. Nat. Dem. Fin. Coun., 1960-77; mem. Gov.'s Adv. Bd. on Health and Rehabilitative Svc., 1976-77; sec.-treas. Inter-Am. Ctr. Authority, 1960-74; bd. advisor St. Thomas Law Sch., 1985-88; personal rep. Pres. Reagan F.D.R. Meml. Commn., 1985; bd. dirs. Barry U.; chmn. bd. trustees Variety Children's Hosp.; pres. Miami Children's Hosp. Found., 1980—; trustee Gregorian Inst. Found., Rome. Served with Counter Intelligence Corps., U.S. Army, 1943-46. Decorated Bronze Star medal., Knight of the Grand-cross, Order St. Gregory the Great; recipient Silver medallion NCCJ, Resolution of Commendation award for civic contbn. Fla. Legislature, 1988. Mem. Am., Fla., Fed., D.C., Interam. bar assns., Am. Assn. Knights of Malta (v.p.), Serra Club, Sovereign Mil. Order Malta (master knight 1975—, exec. com. papal visit to U.S. 1987), Omicron Delta Kappa, Lambda Chi Alpha. Democrat. Roman Catholic. Home: 9202 SW 78th Pl Miami FL 33156-7590 Home (summer): 5 St Helens, Marine Parade Sandycove, Dublin Ireland Office: 3000 SW 62nd Ave Miami FL 33155-3065

**WALTERS, DENNIS H.,** lawyer; b. Rochelle, Ill., Mar. 2, 1950; s. Harold R. and Helen M. (Eshbaugh) W.; m. Marilyn E. Hoban, Jan. 1, 1984. BA, Ill. Wesleyan U., 1972; MS in Bus. Adminstrn., Boston U., 1975; JD, Harvard U., 1979. Bar: Wash. 1979, Alaska, 1985, U.S. Ct. Appeals (9th cir.) 1991, U.S. Supreme Ct. 1991; lic. comml. pilot, flight instr. Assoc. Karr Tuttle Campbell, Seattle, 1979, shareholder, 1987—, head of appellate practice, 1991—. Trustee, pres. Vision Svcs., Seattle, 1980-86; trustee Literacy Coun. of Kitsap, 1993-96. With U.S. Army, 1972-76. Named Citizen of Day, Sta. KIXI, Seattle, 1985. Mem. ABA, Seattle-King County Bar Assn. (chmn. aviation sect. 1984-85), Lawyer-Pilots Bar Assn., Wing Point Golf and Country Club. Avocations: flying, golf, boating. Aviation, General civil litigation, Environmental. Home: 25853 Canyon Rd NW Poulsbo WA 98370-9752 Office: Karr Tuttle Campbell 1201 3rd Ave Ste 2900 Seattle WA 98101-3028

**WALTERS, GOMER WINSTON,** lawyer; b. Johnstown, Pa., Sept. 24, 1937; s. Philip Thomas and Margaret Elizabeth (Peat) W.; m. Jean Mary Jester, June 13, 1964 (divorced 1988); children: Bruce Joseph, Matthew Howel, Melinda Jean. BE, Yale U., 1960; JD, George Washington U., 1965. Bar: Ill. 1965, Pa. 1972, U.S. Dist. Ct. (no. dist.) Ill. 1965, U.S. Dist. Ct. (we. dist.) Pa. 1972, U.S. Dist. Ct. (no. dist.) Ohio 1973, U.S. Ct. Appeals (3 and 7th cirs.) 1981, U.S. Supreme Ct. 1982, U.S. Ct. Appeals (fed. cir.) 1982. Assoc. Kirkland & Ellis, Chgo., 1965-70, ptnr., 1970-72; patent atty. Westinghouse Electric Corp., Pitts., 1972-73; assoc. Walsh, Case & Coale, Chgo., 1973-74, Lee & Smith, Chgo., 1975; ptnr. Haight & Hofeldt, Chgo., 1975-90, Wood, Phillips, Van Santen, Clark & Mortimer, Chgo., 1990-95; pvt. practice, Chgo., Ligonier, Pa., 1995—; chmn.'s council Crow Canyon Archaeol. Ctr., 1987—, trustee, 1996—; dir., treas. Primitive Arts Soc. of Chgo., 1991-96. Mem. ABA, Chgo. Bar Assn., Am. Intellectual Property Law Assn., Intellectual Property Law Assn., Univ. Club Chgo., Tower Club. Federal civil litigation, Patent, Trademark and copyright. Office: Cliffwood 1300 Route 271 S Ligonier PA 15658-9248

**WALTERS, JESSE RAYMOND, JR.,** justice; b. Rexburg, Idaho, Dec. 26, 1938; s. Jesse Raymond and Thelma Rachael (Hodgson) W.; m. Harriet Payne, May 11, 1959; children: Craig T., Robyn J. Scott. Student, Ricks Coll., 1957-58; BA in Polit. Sci., U. Idaho, 1961, JD, 1963; postgrad., U. Washington, 1962; LLM, U. Va., 1990. Bar: Idaho 1963; U.S. Dist. Ct. Idaho 1964, U.S. Ct. Appeals (9th cir.) 1970. Law clk. to chief justice Idaho Supreme Ct., 1963-64; solo practice Boise, Idaho, 1964-77; atty. Idaho senate, Boise, 1965; dist. judge 4th Jud. Dist., Idaho, 1977-82, adminstrv. dist. judge, 1981-82; chief judge Idaho Ct. Appeals, Boise, 1982-97; chmn. magistrate's commn. 4th jud. dist.; chmn. Supreme Ct. mem. services; chmn. Criminal Pattern Jury Instrn. Com.; mem. Civil Pattern Jury Instrn. Com. Republican committeeman Boise, 1975-77; mem. Ada County Rep. Ctrl. Com., 1975-77. Mem. Idaho Bar Assn. (bankruptcy com.), Idaho Adminstrv. Judges Assn., ABA, Am. Judicature Soc., Assn. Trial Lawyers Am., Idaho Trial Layers Assn., Coun. Chief Judges Ct. Appeals (pres. 1994-95), Boise Estate Planning Coun., Jaycees (nat. dir. 1969-70, pres. Boise chpt. 1966-67), Lions, Elks, Eagles. Mormon. Office: Supreme Ct of Idaho PO Box 83720 Boise ID 83720-3720

**WALTERS, JOEL W.,** lawyer; b. Kansas City, Mo., Sept. 12, 1960; s. Harry and Margaret Ruth (Armstrong) W.; m. Gail Susan Einstein, Mar. 2, 1992; children: Evan Daniel, Stephanie Lianne. BSBA, U. Mo., Columbia, 1981; JD with distinction, U. Mo., Kansas City, 1984. Bar: Mo. 1984, Fla. 1986, U.S. Dist. Ct. (we. dist.) Mo. 1986, U.S. Dist. Ct. (mid. dist.) Fla. 1986, U.S. Dist. Ct. (so. dist.) Fla. 1988, U.S. Ct. Appeals (8th and 11th cirs.) 1986. Law clk. to Hon. Robert T. Donnelly Supreme Ct. of Mo., Jefferson City, 1984-86; assoc. Abel, Band, Brown, Russell & Collier, Chartered, Sarasota, Fla., 1986-91; founding shareholder, ptnr. Brown Clark & Walters, Sarasota, 1991—; cert. mediator Supreme Ct. of Fla., 1992—; arbitrator nat. panel Am. Arbitration Assn., Miami, Fla., 1994—; spkr. in field. Bd. dirs., pres. Police Athletic League, Sarasota, 1990—; bd. dirs. Longboat Key (Fla.) Recreation Ctr., 1994—; mem. adv. bd. dirs. Sunnyland coun. Boy Scouts Am., 1991-92. Mem. Sarasota County Bar Assn., Acad. Fla. Trial Lawyers, Charlotte County Bar Assn. Avocations: boating, tennis, fishing, diving, skiing. Construction, Contracts commercial, Banking. Home: 584 Cutter Ln Longboat Key FL 34228-3706 Office: Brown Clark & Walters PA 1819 Main St Ste 1100 Sarasota FL 34236-5999

**WALTERS, JOHNNIE MCKEIVER,** lawyer; b. Hartsville, S.C., Dec. 20, 1919; s. Tommie Ellis and Lizzie Lee (Grantham) W.; m. Donna Lucile Hall, Sept. 1, 1947; children: Donna Dianne Walters Gent, Lizbeth Kathern Walters Kukorowski, Hilton Horace, John Roy. AB, Furman U., 1942, LLD, 1973; LLB, U. Mich., 1948. Bar: Mich. 1948, N.Y. 1955, S.C. 1961, D.C. 1973. Atty. office chief counsel IRS, Washington, 1949-53; asst. mgr. tax div. law dept. Texaco, Inc., N.Y.C., 1953-61; ptnr. firm Geer, Walters, & Demo, Greenville, S.C., 1961-69; asst. atty. gen. tax div. Dept. Justice, Washington, 1969-71; commr. IRS, 1971-73; ptnr. firm Hunton & Williams, Washington, 1973-79, Leatherwood Walker Todd & Mann, P.C., Greenville, 1979-95; exec. v.p., gen. counsel Colonial Trust Co., 1996—; bd. dirs. Textile Hall Corp., Greenville, Santee Cooper, Moncks Corner, S.C. Mem. S.C. Coun. on Competitiveness, 1987-91; bd. dirs. Greenville Hosp. System Found., S.C. State Mus. Found. With USAAF, 1942-45. Fellow Am. Coll. Tax Counsel (founding regent), Am. Coll. Trust and Estate Counsel, Am. Bar Found., S.C. Bar Found. (bd. dirs. 1988-92); mem. ABA (taxation sect.), S.C. Bar (chmn. taxation sect. 1983-84), Rotary (pres. local club 1968-69). Republican. Baptist. Taxation, general, Estate planning, Probate. Office: Colonial Trust Co PO Box 2817 Greenville SC 29602-2817 Home: 1804 N Main St Greenville SC 29609-4729

**WALTERS, SUMNER J.,** former judge, lawyer; b. Van Wert, Ohio, Oct. 4, 1916; s. Sumner Eliot and Kittie Mae (Allen) W.; m. Marjorie Louise Acheson, May 22, 1948; 1 child, Sumner Eliot. JD, Ohio No. U., 1940. Pvt. practice Van Wert, 1940-41, 1968-71; ptnr. Walters & Koch Attys., Van Wert, 1941-46, Stroup & Walters Attys., Van Wert, 1946-68, Walters, Young & Walters Attys., Van Wert, 1971-80; judge Van Wert Mcpl. Ct., 1980-87; vis. judge State of Ohio, 1987-96; ret., 1997; pros. atty. Van Wert County, 1948-60; acting judge Van Wert Mcpl. Ct., 1960-80; village solicitor Middlepoint, Ohio, 1960-80; pres. Van Wert Indsl. Devel. Corp., 1966-76; trustee Van Wert County Found., 1960—, Marsh Found., 1970—. pres. Van Wert County Humane Soc., 1963 —. With Corps Mil. Police, 1942-45, ETO. Named Outstanding Citizen Van Wert Jr. C. of C., 1965. Mem. Ohio Bar Assn. (exec. com. 1968-71), Ohio Mcpl. Judges Assn., Am. Legion, VFW, Masons, Shriners, KT (Knight York Cross of Honor), Sigma Phi Epsilon. Avocations: fishing, golf, woodworking. Home and Office: 1018 Rosemont Dr Van Wert OH 45891-2640

**WALTHER, ZERITA,** paralegal; b. N.Y.C., Nov. 22, 1927; d. James Alexander and Sarah Rebecca (Esperance) Potter; m. George P. Walther II; children: Joseph, Leona. BS in Edn., Met. Inst., London, 1973; cert. in labor studies, Cornell U., 1979; paralegal cert., Manhattanville Coll., 1984. Tchr. OEO, L.I. City, N.Y., 1966-69, Washington Bus. Inst., N.Y.C., 1969-70; editorial asst., feature writer N.Y. Times, N.Y.C., 1973-85; legal asst. Marcus, Rippa & Gould, White Plains, N.Y., 1985-88; corp. legal asst. Kim Taylor Profls., White Plains, 1988-92; casting cons., 1962-63; bd. dirs., cons. Rockingchair Press News Svc., Elmsford, N.Y., 1978-93. Soprano Westfair Chamber Singers, Westchester, Fairfield Counties, 1991-94, White Plains Coalition Singers, 1993—, Our Lady of Mt. Carmel Adult Choir, Elmsford, 1989-94, St. Christopher's Adult Choir, Buchanan, 1994—. Sec. Women of Westchester, 1978-80; mem. Westchester Black Women's Polit. Caucus, 1989-91; coord. Elmsford chpt. Women in Self Help, 1982-84; mediator, vol. BBB, White Plains, 1983-85, Westchester Mediation Ctr., Yonkers, N.Y., 1988-91; legis. asst. to 12th dist. Westchester County legislator, White Plains, 1984-92; cert. ombudsmon N.Y. State Office for the Aging, 1994—, VITA/TCE, AARP tax aide, Peekskill, 1995—; chaplain Chaplain program Hudson Valley Hosp. Ctr., Peekskill, Cortlandt, N.Y., 1998—. Lily Endowment Found. and Smithsonian Inst. scholar Sarah Lawrence Coll., summer 1979. Democrat. Roman Catholic. Avocations: singing (opera, classical, show tunes, gospel), numerology and astrology. Office: PO Box 431 Crugers NY 10521-0431

**WALTON, DAN GIBSON,** lawyer; b. Houston, Mar. 26, 1950; s. Dan Edward and Lucy Frances (Gibson) W.; m. Martha Sandlin, June 24, 1972; children: Cole Gibson, Emily Wyatt. BA with honors, U. Va., 1972; JD with honors, U. Tex., 1975. Bar: Tex. 1975, U.S. Dist. Ct. (so. dist.) Tex. 1977, U.S. Ct. Appeals (D.C. cir.) 1975, U.S. Ct. Appeals (5th cir.) 1981; bd. cert. in civil trial law and personal injury. Law clk. to hon. Malcolm R. Wilkey D.C. Ct. Appeals (D.C. cir.), 1975-76; assoc. Vinson & Elkins, Houston, 1976-82, ptnr., 1982—; bd. dirs. The Meth. Health Care Sys., Houston. Bd. dirs. South Tex. Coll. Law, Houston, 1994, Covenant House Tex., Houston, 1993, Briarwood Sch./Brookwood Cmty., Houston, 1991; trustee St. John's Sch., Houston, 1997, Good Samaritan Found., 1998; co-chancellor Tex. Ann. Conf., United Meth. Ch., Houston, 1996. Fellow Am. Bar Found., Tex. Bar Found., Houston Bar Found. (chair 1994), Houston Bar Assn. (pres. 1998-99), Garland Walker Am. Inn of Ct. (master), Am. Bd. Trial Advocates (assoc.), Internat. Assn. Def. Counsel, Tex. Assn. Def. Counsel. Avocation: golf. General civil litigation, Construction, Professional liability. Home: 3203 Ella Lee Ln Houston TX 77019-5923 Office: Vinson & Elkins LLP 2300 First City Tower 1001 Fannin St Ste 3201 Houston TX 77002-6706

**WALTON, EDMUND LEWIS, JR.,** lawyer; b. Salisbury, Md., Sept. 4, 1936; s. Edmund Lewis and Iris Tull (White) W.; m. Barbara Post, Sept. 18, 1965; children: Southy E., Kristen P. BA, Coll. William and Mary, 1961, JD (Godwin scholar), 1963. Bar: Va. 1963, U.S. Dist. Ct. (ea. dist.) Va. 1964, U.S. Supreme Ct. 1971, U.S. Dist. Ct. (we. dist.) Va. 1972, U.S. Ct. Appeals (4th cir.) 1980. Grad. asst. Coll. William and Mary, 1961-62; assoc. Simmonds, Coleburn, Towner & Carman, Arlington, Fairfax, Va., 1963-68; ptnr. Simmonds, Coleburn, Towner & Carman, Arlington, Fairfax, 1968-74, Putbrese and Walton, McLean, Va., 1976; pvt. practice McLean, Va., 1976-82; sr. ptnr. Walton and Adams P.C., McLean, 1983—; judge pro tem Fairfax County Cir. Ct., 1977—; commr. in chancery, 1990-97, legis. com. Va. State Bar, 1974-76; bus. law sect. exec. com. 1983-88, sec. 1984-85, vice chmn. 1985-86, chmn. 1986-87. Editor William and Mary Law Sch. Rev. 1961-63. Bd. dirs. Home Run Acres Civic Assn. 1968-70, v.p. 1969-70; bd. dirs. McLean Citizens Assn., 1976-79, 1st v.p. 1977-78; bd. dirs., pres. Rocky Run Citizens Assn., 1973-74; bd. dirs. Langley Sch. Inc., 1975-77, treas. 1976-77; mem. Fairfax County Rep. Com., 1966-82, chmn. 1970-72; del. Rep. Nat. Conv. 1972; mem Va. Rep. Ctrl. Com. 1974-77, exec. com. 1976-77; chmn. Providence Dist. Rep. Com., 1968-70; mem. 10th Congl. Dist. Rep. Com. 1970-77, vice chmn. 1974-76, chmn. 1976-77, mem. 8th Congl. Dist. Rep. Com. 1967-70; v.p. Arlington County Young Reps., 1965-66, counsel Arlington County Rep. Com. 1965-66; bd. dirs. McLean Planning Com. 1975-79, chmn. 1976-77; bd. dirs. McLean Office Sq. Condominium Assn., 1979-83, pres. 1979-82; chmn. Tysons Corner Citizens Task

Force 1977-78; mem. Fairfax County Coun. on Arts; bd. dirs. Fairfax YMCA 1974-75; bd. dirs. Friends of Turkey Run Farm, 1981—, counsel 1981—, mem. exec. com. 1981-83. With U.S. Army 1956-59. Named McLean (Va.) Bus. Citizen of Yr. 1996. Fellow ABA Found. (life), Va. Law Found. (dir. 1991-97, mem. com. on continuing legal edn. 1990-91, chmn. 1992-93); mem. ABA, Am. Law Inst., Va. Bar Assn. (spl. com. to study rules of ethics 1981-84, membership com. 1981-84, exec. com. 1982-88, chmn. 1984-85, pres.-elect 1985-86, pres. 1986-87), Va. Continuing Legal Edn. Bd. (chmn. 1995-98), Arlington County Bar Assn., Fairfax County Bar Assn. (cts. com. 1975-77, dir. 1976-77), McLean Bar Assn. (dir. 1978-79, 80-83, sec. 1978-79, pres. 1980-82), Va. Trial Lawyers Assn., Am. Judicature Soc., William and Mary Law Sch. Assn. (dir. 1970-76), Fairfax County C. of C. (dir. ex officio 1981-83), McLean C. of C. (bd. dirs. 1995-96, McLean Bus. and Profl. Assn. (dir. 1976-85, 89-90, pres. 1981-83), Washington Golf and Country Club, Daufuskie Island Club, Lowes Island Club, Phi Alpha Delta. Episcopalian. State civil litigation, General corporate, Banking. Home: 2032 Mayfair Mclean Ct Falls Church VA 22043-1760 Office: PO Drawer EE 6862 Elm St Ste 400 Mc Lean VA 22101-3833

**WALTON, JON DAVID,** lawyer; b. Clairton, Pa., Sept. 18, 1942; s. Thomas Edward and Matilda Lucy (Sunday) W.; m. Carol Jeanne Rowland, Sept. 15, 1964; children: David Edward, Diane Elizabeth. BS, Purdue U., 1964; JD, Valparaiso U., 1969. Bar: Pa. 1969. Atty. U.S. Steel Corp. (now USX Corp.), Pitts., 1969-73; asst. gen. counsel Harbison-Walker Refractories, Pitts., 1973-75; gen. counsel Harbison-Walker Refractories, 1975-81, v.p., gen. counsel, 1981-83; regional gen. counsel Dresser Industries, Inc. (now Indresco Corp.), Pitts., 1983-86; gen. counsel, sec. Allegheny Ludlum Corp., Pitts., 1986-90, v.p., gen. counsel, sec., 1990-96; v.p., gen. counsel, sec. Allegheny Teledyne Inc., Pitts., 1996—, sr. v.p., gen. counsel, sec., 1997—; trustee Westminster Coll., 1997—. Pres., bd. dirs. Music for Mt. Lebanon, 1996—; chmn. bd. dirs. Pitts. Youth Golf Found., 1991-98; clk. of session Southminster Presbyn. Ch., 1998—. Mem. ABA, Pa. Bar Assn., Allegheny County Bar Assn., Am. Soc. Corp. Secs. (former pres. regional group), Pa. Chamber Bus. and Industry (bd. dirs., exec. com.), Am. Corp. Counsel Assn., Am. Arbitration Assn. (panel arbitrators), Duquesne Club, Valley Brook Country Club, Rolling Rock Club. General corporate. Home: 137 Hoodridge Dr Pittsburgh PA 15228-1803 Office: Allegheny Teledyne Inc 1000 Six PPG Pl Pittsburgh PA 15222-5479

**WALTON, LEWIS R.,** lawyer, writer; b. Santa Monica, Calif., Dec. 28, 1941; s. Lee Redford and Mabel B. (Nielsen) W.; m. Jo Ellen Walton, Dec. 19, 1971; 1 child, Richard. BA, La Sierra Coll., 1963; JD magna cum laude, U. San Diego, 1967, cert. tax law, 1989, LLM in Taxation, 1990. Bar: Calif. 1968, U.S. Supreme Ct. 1971, U.S. Tax Ct. 1973. Assoc. Clayton, Stark, Corona, Calif., 1970-71; pvt. practice Bakersfield, Calif., 1972—. Author: Omega, 1981, Omega II, 1995, Six Extra Years, 1981, Lucifer Diary, 1997. Bd. sec. SJCH Cmty. Hosp., Kern County, Calif., 1973-86; mem. presdl. task force Rep. Party, 1984-88; legal officer CAP, Calif., 1991-93; spl. advisor Congl. Adv. Bd., Washington, 1982-89. Lt. USCG, 1967-70, Vietnam. Recipient Burkan award ASCAP, 1966. Avocation: aviation. Personal income taxation. Office: 8825 Hwy 155 Glennville CA 93221

**WALTON, ROBERT PRENTISS,** lawyer; b. Cleve., Jan. 11, 1938; s. Robert Clark and Elizabeth (Bowman) W.; m. Rosalie S., May 29, 1965; children—Jenifer S., Robert D. B.A., Yale U., 1959; LL.B., U. Va., 1962. Bar: N.Y. 1963, Conn. 1962, Va. 1962, U.S. Supreme Ct. 1967. Assoc. gen. counsel NYU, 1977-83, sr. assoc. counsel, 1983—; asst. U.S. atty. So. Dist. N.Y., 1970-75; mem. McGarrahan & Heard, N.Y.C., 1975-77. Recipient Am. Jurisprudence prize Bancroft Whitney Co., 1962. Mem. N.Y. State Bar Assn. General civil litigation, Contracts commercial, Construction. Home: 69 Midland St Cold Spring Harbor NY 11724-1805 Office: 70 Washington Sq S New York NY 10012-1019

**WALTON, STANLEY ANTHONY, III,** lawyer; b. Chgo., Dec. 10, 1939; s. Stanley Anthony and Emily Ann (Pouzar) W.; m. Karen Kayser, Aug. 10, 1963; children: Katherine, Anne, Alex. BA, Washington and Lee U., 1962, LLB, 1965. Bar: Ill. 1965, U.S. Dist. Ct. (no. dist.) Ill. 1966, U.S. Ct. Appeals (7th cir.) 1966. Ptnr. Winston & Strawn, Chgo., 1965-89, Sayfarth Shaw Fairweather, Chgo., 1989-96. Trustee Village of Hinsdale (Ill.), 1985-89; bd. dirs. Washington and Lee Law Sch., Lexington, Va., 1975-78, bd. dirs. univ. alumni, 1983-87, pres. 1986-87; bd. dirs. UNICEF, Chgo., 1983; pres. Hinsdale Hist. Soc., 1979-81, St. Isaac Jogues PTA, 1980 . Mem. ABA, Phi Alpha Delta. Republican. Roman Catholic. Club: Hinsdale Golf. Federal civil litigation, State civil litigation. Home and Office: 6679 Snug Harbor Dr Willowbrook IL 60514-1826

**WALTON-EVERETT, LAURA,** lawyer; b. Cleve., Aug. 27, 1970; d. Thomas Smith Walton and Irma Celeste Terrell; m. Juan Mario Everett, Aug. 20, 1994; 1 child, Rashaan Malik Everett. BS, U. Calif., Berkeley, 1992, JD, 1995. Bar: Calif. 1995. Dep. dist. atty. L.A. Dist. Atty., 1996—. Mem. Nat. Black Prosecutors Assn. Avocations: traveling, mentoring. Office: LA Dist Atty 210 W Temple St Los Angeles CA 90012-3210

**WALTZER, JOEL REUBEN,** lawyer; b. New Orleans, May 9, 1963; m. Toni Ann Waltzer; 1 child, Noah Evan. BSBA, Boston U., 1985; JD, Harvard U., 1988. Bar: La. 1989. Jud. clk. La. Supreme Ct., New Orleans, 1988-89; environ. law fellow Tulane Environ. Law clinic, New Orleans, 1989-90; assoc. Kanner & Assocs., New Orleans, 1990-92; ptnr. Waltzer & Assocs., New Orleans, 1992—; com. mem. La. Law Inst., Baton Rouge, 1993-94; bd. dirs. Coalition to Restore Coastal La., Baton Rouge, 1995-97; treas. Friends of the Lake, Baton Rouge, 1995—. Pres. Vista Park Civic Assn., New Orleans, 1995—. Recipient Brown Pelican legal award Gov. of La., 1990. Mem. ABA, Am. Trial Lawyers Assn., La. Trial Lawyers, La. Bar Assn. Avocations: fishing, basketball, softball. General civil litigation, Environmental, Personal injury. Office: Waltzer & Assocs 144 Elk Pl Ste 1710 New Orleans LA 70112-2698

**WALZ, GREGORY STEPHEN,** lawyer; b. St. Cloud, Minn., Mar. 8, 1957; s. Wendelin George and Ilse Marie Walz; m. Sandra Jean Theis, Nov. 17, 1987; children: Nicole, Joseph, Jacob, Jessica. BA, St. Johns U., Collegeville, Minn., 1981; JD, William Mitchell Coll. Law, St. Paul, 1987. Bar: Minn. 1987, U.S. Dist. Ct. Minn. 1987. Atty. Walz Law Office, St. Cloud, 1990—. Personal injury, Family and matrimonial, Criminal. Office: Walz Law Office PO Box 1794 Saint Cloud MN 56302-1794

**WALZER, JAMES HARVEY,** lawyer, author; b. Neptune, N.J., Jan. 24, 1949; s. Elwood John and Mary Elizabeth (Harvey) W.; m. Gloria Jean Demkowski, May 29, 1971; children: Sara, Emily, Amanda, Adam. BA, Bowdoin Coll., 1972; JD, Cleve. State U., 1975. Bar: N.J. 1975, U.S. Dist. Ct. N.J. 1975. Pvt. practice, Newark, 1975-78, Livingston, N.J., 1978-81, Boonton, N.J., 1981—; legal forms editor All-State Legal, a div. of All-State Internat., Inc., Cranford, N.J., 1978—96. Author: Employment, Agency, Service Agreements, 1986, Motor Vehicle Law and Practice--Forms, 1988, Civil Practice Forms, 5 vols., 1990, 8 vols., 5th edit., 1998; editor, author: Legal Forms, 7 vols., 1995-96. Mem. Manville (N.J.) Bd. Adjustment, 1976. Mem. ABA, N.J. Bar Assn., Morris County Bar Assn., Elks. Democrat. General practice, Real property, Family and matrimonial. Home: 18 Magda Ln Somerville NJ 08876-4217 Office: 103 William St PO Box 675 Boonton NJ 07005-0675

**WAMPLER, ROBERT JOSEPH,** lawyer; b. Greensboro, Ind., Mar. 3, 1936; s. Cruden V. and Mary L. (James) W.; m. Karen A. Wiggins, Feb. 19, 1977; children: Eric J., Kelly L., Michael J. AB, Yale U., 1959; JD, Ind. U., 1963. Bar: Ind. 1963, U.S. Dist. Ct. (so. dist.) Ind. 1963, U.S. Supreme Ct. 1966, U.S. Ct. Appeals (7th cir.) 1972. Assoc. Kightlinger & Gray, Indpls., 1963—, ptnr., 1968—, sr. ptnr., 1971—. Author handbook on product liability; co-author: Trial Advocacy in Indiana, 1989. Sec., bd. dirs. Ivy Ridge Civic Assn., Indpls., 1975—. Fellow Indpls. Bar Found.; mem. Indpls. Bar Assn. (chmn. litigation sect. 1987), Ind. Bar Assn., Internat. Assn. Def. Counsel, Def. Trial Counsel Ind., Masons, Order of Coif, Phi Delta Phi. Republican. Episcopalian. General civil litigation, Professional liability, Alternative dispute resolution. Home: 5939 Cape Cod Ct Indianapolis IN 46250-1845 Office: Kightlinger & Gray 151 N Delaware St Ste 660 Indianapolis IN 46204-2574

**WANDER, HERBERT STANTON,** lawyer; b. Cin., Mar. 17, 1935; s. Louis Marvin and Pauline (Schuster) W.; m. Ruth Cele Fell, Aug. 7, 1960; children: Daniel Jerome, Susan Gail, Lois Marlene. AB, U. Mich., 1957; LLB, Yale U., 1960. Bar: Ohio 1960, Ill. 1960. Law clk. to judge U.S. Dist. Ct. (no. dist.) Ill., 1960-61; ptnr. Pope Ballard Shepard & Fowle, Chgo., 1961-78, Katten Muchin & Zavis, Chgo., 1978—; trustee Michael Reese Found., 1991—; bd. dirs. Tel. & Data Systems, Chgo., Advance Ross Corp., 1991-96; mem. legal adv. com. to the bd. govs. N.Y. Stock Exch., 1989-92; mem. legal adv. bd. Nat. Assn. Securities Dealers, Inc., 1996-99. Editor: (jour.) Bus. Law Today, 1992-93; editor-in-chief: (jour.) The Bus. Lawyer, 1993-94; contbr. numerous articles to profl. jours. Bd. dirs. Jewish Fedn. Met. Chgo., 1972—, pres., 1981-83; bd. dirs. Jewish United Fund, 1972—, pres., 1981-83, chmn. pub. affairs com., 1984-87, gen. campaign chmn., 1993; former regional chmn. nat. young leadership cabinet United Jewish Appeal; vice-chmn. large city budgeting conf. Coun. Jewish Fedns., 1979-82, bd. dirs., 1980—, exec. com., 1983-84. Mem. ABA (sec. bus. law sect. 1992-93, vice-chair 1993-94, chair-elect 1994-95, chair 1995-96, apptd. to commn. on multidisciplinary practice 1998), Ill. State Bar Assn., Chgo. Bar Assn., Yale Law Sch. Assn. (exec. com. 1982-86), Std. Club, Econ. Club, Northmoor Country Club, Phi Beta Kappa. Mergers and acquisitions, Securities, General corporate. Home: 70 Prospect Ave Highland Park IL 60035-3329 Office: Katten Muchin & Zavis 525 W Monroe St Ste 1600 Chicago IL 60661-3693

**WANDERMAN, SUSAN MAE,** lawyer; b. N.Y.C., Mar. 12, 1947; d. Leo and Muriel D. Wanderman. AB, Wheaton Coll., Norton, Mass., 1967; JD, St. John's U., 1970; LLM, NYU, 1976. Bar: N.Y. 1971, U.S. Dist. Ct. (ea. and so. dists.) N.Y. 1972, U.S. Ct. Appeals (2d cir.) 1973, U.S. Supreme Ct. 1974. Asst. legal officer, legal dept. Chem. Bank, N.Y.C., 1972-75; 2d v.p. legal dept. Chase Manhattan Bank N.A., N.Y.C., 1975-82; asst. gen. counsel Citicorp Services, Inc., N.Y.C., 1982-84, v.p. Citibank, N.A., N.Y.C., 1984—; instr. bus. law and law for the layman LaGuardia Community Coll., 1976-77; law day speaker Queens County Supreme Ct., 1979-83; mem. Community Bd. 6, Queens County, N.Y.C., 1987—. Contbr. articles to legal publs. Past vol. N.Y. State Bar Assn. Lawyers in the Classroom. Mem. ABA, N.Y. State Bar Assn., Queens County Bar Assn. Computer, Pension, profit-sharing, and employee benefits, Banking. Office: Citibank NA One Court Sq Long Island City NY 11120

**WANEK, JERROLD,** lawyer; b. Council Bluffs, Iowa, July 10, 1958; s. Gene Joseph and Twila K. (Altman) W.; m. Carolyn Diane Moore, Dec. 31, 1986; children: Joseph J.A., Christopher R.A, Sophia M.B. BA, U. Iowa, 1980; JD, Drake U., 1983. Bar: Iowa 1983, U.S. Dist. Ct. (no. and so. dists.) Iowa 1983, U.S. Ct. Appeals (8th cir.) 1984, Nebr. 1991, U.S. Dist. Ct. Nebr. 1992; cert. bus. bankruptcy specialist Acad. of the Comml. Law League of Am., 1993-98. Assoc. Garten, Garten & Landess, Des Moines, 1983-85; ptnr. Garten & Landess, Des Moines, 1985-87, Garten & Wanek, Des Moines, 1987—. Mem. ABA, Iowa State Bar Assn., Polk County Bar Assn., Nebr. Bar Assn., Fed. Bar Assn. Comml. Law League Am. (bankruptcy sect. 1985—), Acad. Comml. and Bankruptcy Law Specialists. Democrat. Lutheran. General civil litigation, Consumer commercial, Bankruptcy. Office: Garten & Wanek 835 Ins Exchange Bldg Des Moines IA 50309

**WANG, ALBERT HUAI-EN,** lawyer; b. Tainan, Taiwan, Feb. 21, 1967; s. Tien-Yu and Shiu-Yin (Chen) W. BA, UCLA, 1990, MA, 1990; JD, Cornell U., 1994. Bar: N.Y. 1995. Tax specialist KPMG Peat Marwick, L.A., 1990-91; assoc. Willkie Farr & Gallagher, N.Y.C., 1994-99; corp. assoc. Schulte Roth & Zabel LLP, N.Y.C., 1999—. Regent scholar U. Calif., 1986. Mem. ABA, N.Y. State Bar Assn., Chinese Fin. Soc., Phi Beta Kappa. E-mail: albert.wang@srz.com. General corporate, Securities, Private international. Office: Schulte Roth & Zabel LLP 900 3rd Ave Fl 19 New York NY 10022-4774

**WANG, CHARLESTON CHENG-KUNG,** lawyer, engineer; b. Tainan, Republic of China, Oct. 17, 1956; came to U.S., 1972; s. Shan-Cheng and I-Tsen (Cheng) W.; m. Shirley Liao, Mar. 14, 1981; children: Vivian, Arthur Rex. BS in Econs. and Chem. Engring., U. Del., 1977; MBA in Internat. Bus., Xavier U., 1979; JD, No. Ky. U., 1982; postgrad., U. Cin., 1989, No. Territory U. Darwin, Australia, 1999. Bar: Ohio 1982, U.S. Dist. Ct. (so. dist.) Ohio 1983, U.S. Dist. Ct. (ea. dist.) Ky. 1983, U.S. Ct. Appeals (6th cir.) 1983; diplomate Am. Bd. Indsl. Hygiene; cert. indsl. hygienist. Chem. engr. Procter & Gamble, Cin., 1979-81, NIOSH, Cin., 1981-84; mng. ptnr. Groeber & Wang, Cin., 1982-85; compliance officer U.S. Dept. Labor, Cin., 1985-88; v.p., gen. counsel Environ. Enterprises, Inc., Cin., 1988—; adj. prof. No. Ky. U., 1983—, U. Cin., 1985—. Author: How to Manage Workplace Derived Hazards and Avoid Liability, 1987, OSHA Compliance & Management Handbook, 1991; assoc. editor No. Ky. Law Rev., 1980-82; contbr. articles to profl. jours. Mem. Am. Acad. Indsl. Hygiene, Am. Inst. Chem. Engrs., Am. Conf. Govt. Indsl. Hygienists, Chinese Am. Assn. Cin. (pres. 1987-88). Avocation: swimming. Home: 11321 Terwilligers Valley Ln Cincinnati OH 45249-2744 Office: Wanglaw Bldg 6924 Plainfield Rd Cincinnati OH 45236-3734

**WANGER, OLIVER WINSTON,** federal judge; b. L.A., Nov. 27, 1940; m. Lorrie A. Reinhart; children: Guy A., Christopher L., Andrew G., W. Derek, Oliver Winston II. Student, Colo. Sch. Mines, 1958-60; BS, U. So. Calif., 1963; LLB, U. Calif., Berkeley, 1966. Bar: Calif. 1967, U.S. Dist. Ct. (ea. dist.) Calif. 1969, U.S. Tax Ct. 1969, U.S. Dist. Ct. (cen. dist.) Calif. 1975, U.S. Dist. Ct. (so. dist.) Calif. 1977, U.S. Dist. Ct. (no. dist.) Calif. 1989, U.S. Ct. Appeals (9th cir.) 1989. Dep. dist. atty. Fresno (Calif.) County Dist. Atty., 1967-69; ptnr. Gallagher, Baker & Manock, Fresno, 1969-74; sr. ptnr. McCormick, Barstow, Sheppard, Wayte & Carruth, Fresno, 1974-91; judge U.S. Dist. Ct. (ea. dist.) Calif., Fresno, 1991—; adj. prof. law Humphreys Coll. Law, Fresno, 1968-70. Fellow Am. Coll. Trial Lawyers, Internat. Acad. Trial Lawyers; mem. Am. Bd. Trial Advs. (pres. San Joaquin Valley chpt. 1987-89, nat. bd. dirs. 1989-91), Am. Bd. Profl. Liability Attys. (founder, diplomate), Calif. State Bar (mem. exec. com. litigation sect. 1989-92, mem. com. on fed. cts. 1989-90), San Joaquin Valley Am. Inn of Ct. (pres. 1992-93), Beta Gamma Sigma. Office: US Dist Ct 5104 US Courthouse 1130 O St Fresno CA 93721-2201

**WANKE, RONALD LEE,** lawyer; b. Chgo., June 22, 1941; s. William F. and Lucille (Kleinwachter) W.; m. Rose Klonowski, Oct. 23, 1987. BSEE, Northwestern U., 1964; JD, DePaul U., 1968. Bar: Ill. 1968. Assoc. Wood, Dalton, Phillips, Mason & Rowe, Chgo., 1968-71, ptnr., 1971-84; ptnr. Jenner & Block, Chgo., 1984—; lectr. John Marshall Law Sch., Chgo., 1985-94. Co-author: (book chpt.) International Intellectual Property Law, 1997; contbr. articles to Software Law Jour., 1987, Internat. Legal Strategy, 1995. Mem. ABA, Computer Law Assn., Intellectual Property Law Assn. Chgo. (chmn. inventor svcs. com. 1976, chmn. fed. rules com. 1981). Computer, Patent, Trademark and copyright. Home: 1806 N Sedgwick St Chicago IL 60614-5306 Office: Jenner & Block 1 E Ibm Plz Fl 4000 Chicago IL 60611-7603

**WARD, DENITTA DAWN,** lawyer; b. Gardner, Kans., Apr. 29, 1963; d. Gerald Dee Ascue and Patricia Diane (Henderson) Ray; m. Kent Alan Ward, July 6, 1991; children: Alexander Patrick, Olivia Caitlyn. BA, U. Kans., 1985; JD magna cum laude, Georgetown U., 1989. Bar: Md. 1989, U.S. Ct. Appeals (fed. cir.) 1990, D.C. 1991, U.S. Ct. Internat. Trade 1991. Rsch. asst. Georgetown U., Washington, 1988-89; jud. clk. U.S. Ct. Appeals for Fed. Cir., Washington, 1989-90; assoc. Donovan Leisure Rogovin Huge & Schiller, Washington, 1990-94; atty. Fed. Election Commn., Washington, 1994-96, Marriott Internat., Inc., 1996-98. Mng. editor Law and Policy in Internat. Bus., 1988-89. Mem. ABA, Ct. of Appeals for Fed. Cir. Bar Assn., Ct. of Appeals of Fed. Cir. Former Jud. Clks. Assn., Order of Coif, Omicron Delta Kappa, Pi Sigma Alpha. Avocations: travel, gardening. Federal civil litigation, Contracts commercial, Labor. Home: 6999 Firerock Ct Boulder CO 80301-3814

**WARD, HIRAM HAMILTON,** federal judge; b. Thomasville, N.C., Apr. 29, 1923; s. O.L. and Margaret A. W.; m. Evelyn M. McDaniel, June 1, 1947; children: William McDaniel, James Randolph. Student, Wake Forest Coll., 1945-47; J.D., Wake Forest U., 1950, LLD (hon.), 1996. Bar: N.C. bar 1950. Practiced law Denton, N.C., 1950-51; staff atty. Nat. Prodn. Authority, Washington, 1951-52; partner firm DeLapp, Ward & Hedrick, Lexington, N.C., 1952-72; U.S. dist. judge Mid. Dist. N.C., 1972—, chief judge, 1982-88, sr. judge, 1988—; mem. com. on Codes of Conduct of Jud. Conf., U.S., 1990-95; mem. Fourth Cir. Jud. Coun., 1984-87. Contbr. legal opinions to Fed. Supplement, F.2d & F.R.D., 1972—. Bd. visitors Wake Forest U. Sch. Law, 1973—; Mem. N.C. Bd. Elections, 1964-72; trustee Wingate Coll., 1969-72. Served with USAAF, 1940-45. Decorated Air medal, Purple Heart; recipient Liberty Bell award N.C. Bar Assn., 1994. Mem. ABA, N.C. Bar Assn., Am. Judicature Soc., N.C. State Bar, Masons, Lions, Phi Alpha Delta (hon. life). Republican. Baptist. Home: 188 Forest Park Dr Denton NC 27239-8013 Office: Hiram H Ward US Courthouse 246 Fed Bldg 251 N Main St Winston Salem NC 27101-3914

**WARD, HORACE TALIAFERRO,** federal judge; b. LaGrange, Ga., July 29, 1927; m. Ruth LeFlore (dec.); 1 son (dec.). AB, Morehouse Coll., 1949; MA, Atlanta U., 1950; JD, Northwestern U., 1959. Bar: Ga. 1960. Instr. polit. sci. Ark. A.M. and N. Coll., 1950-51, Ala. State Coll., 1951-53, 55-56; claims authorizer U.S. Social Security Adminstrn., 1959-60; assoc. firm Hollowell Ward Moore & Alexander (and successors), Atlanta, 1960-69; individual practice law Atlanta, 1971-74; judge Civil Ct. of Fulton County, 1974-77, Fulton Superior Ct., 1977-79; U.S. Dist. Ct. judge No. Dist. Ga., Atlanta, 1979-93; sr. judge U.S. Dist. Ct. No. Dist. Ga., Atlanta, 1993—; lectr. bus. and sch. law Atlanta U., 1965-70; dep. city atty., Atlanta, 1969-70, asst. county atty., Fulton County, 1971-74. Former Trustee Friendship Baptist Ch., Atlanta; mem. Ga. adv. com. U.S. Civil Rights Commn., 1963-65; assisting lawyer NAACP Legal Def. and Edn. Fund, Inc., 1960-70; mem. Jud. Selection Commn., Atlanta, 1972-74, Charter Commn., 1971-72; mem. Ga. Senate, 1964-74, jud. com., rules com., county and urban affairs com.; mem. State Democratic Exec. com., 1966-74; former bd. dirs. Atlanta Legal Aid Soc.; bd. dirs. Atlanta Urban League, Fed. Defender Program, No. Dist. Ga.; trustee Met. Atlanta Commn. on Crime and Delinquency, Atlanta U., Fledgling Found. Mem. Am. Bar Assn., Nat. Bar Assn. (chmn. jud. council 1978-79), State Bar Ga., Atlanta Bar Assn., Gate City Bar Assn. (pres. 1972-74), Atlanta Lawyers Club, Phi Beta Kappa, Alpha Phi Alpha, Phi Alpha Delta, Sigma Pi Phi. Office: US Dist Court 2388 US Courthouse 75 Spring St SW Atlanta GA 30303-3309

**WARD, JAMES A.,** lawyer; b. Waukesha, Wis.. BA in Polit. Sci., Carroll Coll., Waukesha, 1971; JD, So. Meth. U., 1974. Bar: Wis. 1974, U.S. Dist. Ct. (ea. and we. dists.) Wis. 1974, U.S. Supreme Ct. 1979. Atty. Krause & Ward, Waukesha, 1974-78; sole practitioner Waukesha, 1978-80; atty. Congdon, Ward & Walden, S.C., Waukesha, 1981—. Mem. Rotary (newsletter editor). Probate, Estate planning, General civil litigation. Office: Cogndon Ward & Walden SC 707 W Moreland Blvd Waukesha WI 53188-2400

**WARD, JOE HENRY, JR.,** retired lawyer; b. Childress, Tex., Apr. 18, 1930; s. Joe Henry and Helen Ida (Chastain) W.; m. Carlotta Agnes Abreu, Feb. 7, 1959; children: James, Robert, William, John. BS in Acctg., Tex. Christian U., 1952; JD, So. Meth. U., 1964. Bar: Tex. 1964, Va. 1972, D.C. 1974; CPA, Tex. Mgr. Alexander Grant & Co. CPA's, Dallas, 1956-64; atty. U.S. Treasury, 1965-68; tax counsel U.S. Senate Fin. Com., 1968-72; pvt. practice Washington, 1972-83; asst. gen. counsel, tax mgr. Epic Holdings, Ltd. and Crysopt Corp., 1983-87; pvt. practice Washington and Va., 1987-95; ret., 1995. Lt. USNR, 1952-56. Mem. ABA, AICPA, Am. Assn. Atty.-CPA's, Univ. Club. General corporate, Corporate taxation, Estate planning. Home: 2639 Mann Ct Falls Church VA 22046-2721

**WARD, KENNETH WAYNE,** lawyer; b. Knoxville, July 16, 1965; s. Tommy Jr. and Edna Irene W.; m. Lora E. Baker, Apr. 15, 1989; children: Michael Birt, Meghan Baker. B of Indsl. Engring., Ga. Inst. Tech., 1988; JD, U. Tenn., 1992. Bar: Tenn. 1992, U.S. Dist. Ct. (ea. dist.) Tenn. 1992. Assoc. Kennerly, Montgomery & Finley, Knoxville, 1992—. Deacon Ctrl. Bapt. Ch. of Bearden, Knoxville, 1997—. Mem. ABA, Tenn. Bar Assn., Tenn. Defense Lawyers Assn., Knoxville Bar Assn., Defense Rsch. Inst. Avocations: golf, fishing, hiking. Insurance, Product liability, General civil litigation. Office: Kennerly Montgomery & Finley 550 W Main St Fl 4 Knoxville TN 37902-2515

**WARD, MICHAEL W.,** lawyer; b. Chgo., Aug. 16, 1950; s. John Francis and Mary Frances (Brophy) W.; m. Amy Louise Alsopiedy, June 29, 1974; children: Daniel Joseph, James Patrick. BA, U. Notre Dame, 1972; JD, Ill. Inst. Tech., 1976. Bar: Ill. 1976, U.S. Dist. Ct. (no. dist.) Ill. 1976, U.S. Ct. Appeals (7th cir.) 1976, U.S. Supreme Ct. 1980, U.S. Dist. Ct. (no. dist.) Ill. 1982, U.S. Ct. Appeals (6th cir.) 1985. Asst. state's atty. Cook County, Chgo., 1976-80; assoc. O'Keefe, Ashenden, Lyons & Ward, Chgo., 1980-85, ptnr., 1986—. v.p. Northshore Fellowship League, Evanston, Ill., 1982-84; mem. St. Nicholas Sch. Bd., Evanston, 1984-86; bd. dirs. New Horizons Youth Group, Evanston, 1979-85; mem. adv. bd. Cath. Charities, 1989—; mem. fin. coun. St. Nicholas Ch., Evanston, 1988—. Mem. Ill. State Bar Assn. (pub. utilities section council 1988-90, Chgo. Bar Assn., Fed. Comm. Bar Assn. (charter mem. midwest coordinating com.). Roman Catholic. Communications, Taxation, general, General civil litigation. Home: 1012 Mulford St Evanston IL 60202-3317 Office: O'Keefe Ashenden Lyons & Ward 30 N La Salle St Ste 4100 Chicago IL 60602-2507

**WARD, NICHOLAS DONNELL,** lawyer; b. N.Y.C., July 30, 1941; s. Francis Xavier and Sarah Delamater (Donnell) W.; m. Elizabeth Reed Lowman, Sept. 6, 1968 (dec.); m. Virginia Ann McArthur, June 7, 1985 (div. 1993). BA, Columbia Coll., 1963; LLB, Georgetown U., 1966. Bar: D.C. 1967, U.S. Supreme Ct. 1977. Assoc. Hamilton & Hamilton, Washington, 1967-72, ptnr., 1973-85; ptnr. Muir & Ward, Chartered, 1986-87, Noterman and Ward, Washington, 1987-90; pvt. practice Washington, 1990—; instr. paralegal progams U. Md., College Park, 1975-77, Georgetown U., Washington, 1977, 89; mem. adv. com. on Superior Ct. rules of probate and fiduciary procedure, Superior Ct. of D.C., 1975—, cons. Register of Wills, 1987-88, rules cons., 1988-89; mem. Jud. Conf., D.C., 1981—, D.C. Cir., 1981, 84, 85; mem. faculty Mus. Mgmt. Inst., Berkeley, Calif., 1979-86; adj. prof. Sch. Law Cath. U., 1986-88. Editor legal form book: Will and Testamentary Trust Forms, 1974, 2d edit. 1982, 3d edit. 1993 (ABA Spl. Recognition award 1982); state editor Wilkins' Drafting Wills and Trust Agreements, D.C. Supplement; author-reviser Digest of D.C. Probate Law for The Probate Counsel, 1990—; contbr. articles to profl. jours.; performer and author phonograph record: The Roast Beef of Old England, Come Dance With Me In Ireland. Trustee Benjamin Franklin U., Washington, 1976-79; ann. corp. mem. Children's Hosp. of D.C., Washington, 1971-81; trustee Conf. Meml. Assn., Inc., Washington, 1975-77; knight Mil. and Hospitaller Order of Saint Lazarus of Jerusalem, 1977—; Receiver Commandery of the Atlantic, 1987—; officer The Am. Soc. Most Venerable Order of Hosp. of St. John of Jerusalem, 1992—; pres. gen. Gen. Soc. of War of 1812, 1984-87; gen. sec. Gen. Soc. SR, 1976-85; gov. gen. Hereditary Order of Descendants of Col. Govs., 1983-85; gov. Soc. of Col. Wars in D.C., 1982-84; mem. steering com. Friends of Music at Smithsonian, 1986—. Staff sgt. USAR, 1966-72. Recipient Samuel Green award N.H. Soc. of Cin., 1991. Fellow Am. Coll. Trust and Estate Counsel (state chmn. 1987-92), Nat. Assn. Coll. and Univ. Attys. (sec.-treas. 1979-86, chmn. sect. on univ. mus. and collections 1981-86); mem. Bar Assn. of D.C. (bd. dirs. 1979-81, treas. 1982-85, trustee rsch. found. 1986-88, 1990—, pres. 1992-93, Marvin E. Preis award 1980), D.C. Estate Planning Coun. (bd. dir. 1985-87, membership com. 1983-86), ABA (real property, probate and trust law sect., chmn. com. on charitable giving 1990-92, state reporter on current probate and drafting: charitable giving 1990-92, state reporter on current probate and trust law decisions 1983-92, mem. com. on exempt orgns. sect. taxation 1991—, mem. at large com. on nonprofit corps. sect. bus. 1989—), Am. Law Inst. (planning com. and faculty continuing legal edn. program, legal problems of mus. adminstn. 1975—), Selden Soc., Am. Soc. for Legal History, Associated Musicians of Greater N.Y., Am. Fedn. Musicians, D.C. Jaycees (bd. dir. Downtown chpt. 1971-72, legal counsel, 1972-74), D.C. Bar (trustee client's security fund 1981-1990, chmn. 1983-90, chmn. sect. 8, estates, trust and probate sect. 1984-86, cert. appreciation for contbns. to continuing legal edn. 1989), Am. Counsel Assn. (sec.-treas. 1987-89), Am. Arbitration Assn. (panel of arbitrators), Cosmos Club (bd. mgmt. 1984-86, 87-90, sec. 1986-87), Met. Club, City Tavern Club (reciprocity com. 1989—, bd. govs. 1992—), Union Club, St. Nicholas Soc. of City N.Y. (bd. mgrs. 1985-89), The Barristers (v.p. 1989-90), The Counsellors, Soc. Cin., N.H. Soc., Alpha Delta Phi, Phi Delta Phi (pres. Barrister Inn 1977-78, Samuel Green award 1991). Episcopalian. Avocation: golf, flutist. Estate planning, Probate, Education and schools. Home: 1684 32nd St NW Washington DC

20007-2969 Office: 1000 Potomac St NW Ste 300 Washington DC 20007-3547

**WARD, ROBERT JOSEPH,** federal judge; b. N.Y.C., Jan. 31, 1926; s. Joseph G. and Honor V. (Hess) W.; m. Florence C. Maisel, Apr. 15, 1951 (dec. Mar. 1994); children: Laura Alice, Carolyn; m. Renée J. Sokolow, May 28, 1995. SB, Harvard Coll., 1945, LLB, 1949. Bar: N.Y. 1949. Practiced in N.Y.C., 1949-51, 61-72; asst. dist. atty. N.Y. County, 1951-55; asst. U.S. atty. So. Dist. N.Y., 1956-61; judge U.S. Dist. Ct. (so. dist.) N.Y., 1972-91, sr. judge, 1991—. With USNR, 1944-46. Mem. N.Y. State Bar Assn., Assn. of Bar of City of N.Y., Fed. Bar Coun. Office: US Dist Ct US Courthouse Foley Sq New York NY 10007-1501

**WARD, ROBERT RICHARD,** lawyer; b. Spencer, Iowa, Nov. 7, 1948. BA, U. Calif., Berkeley, 1971; MBA, Calif. State U., Hayward, 1974; JD, Pepperdine U., 1978. Bar: Calif. 1978; U.S. Dist. Ct. (cen. dist.) 1979; U.S. Supreme Ct. 1978. Sr. ptnr. Mainstreet Law Offices, Inc., Yorba Linda, Calif., 1981—; real estate broker Award Properties, Yorba Linda, Calif., 1990—; bd. dirs. Colorbrite, Inc., Huntington Beach, Calif., 1990-96, Nat. Recreational Corp., San Jose, 1983-96, Ednl. Found., Yorba Linda, 1992-94, Sino Am., Dalian, China, 1992-96. Co-author: Alaska Pipeline Legislation, 1977. Pres. Placentia (Calif.) C. of C.; chmn. Planning Commn., Placentia; bd. dirs. Yorba Linda C. of C. Mem. Orange County Bar Assn., ATLA, Rotary Club, Exchange Club. Avocations: hunting, fly fishing, scuba diving. General corporate, Personal injury, Estate planning. Office: Main St Law Offices Inc 4895 Main St Yorba Linda CA 92886-3413

**WARD, THOMAS MONROE,** lawyer, law educator; b. Raleigh, N.C., Mar. 6, 1952; s. Melvin Francis and Margaret Alice (Fulcher) W.; m. Ann Frances Sharky, July 28, 1980. B.S.B.A., U. N.C., 1974, J.D., 1978. Bar: N.C. 1978, U.S. Dist. Ct. (ea. dist.) N.C. 1978. Ptnr. Ward, Ward, Willey & Ward, New Bern, N.C., 1978-96; Harris, Shields, Creech & Ward, PA, 1997—; instr. bus. law Craven Community Coll., New Bern, 1982-85. Bd. dirs. Footlight Theatre/Lollipop Playhouse Inc., New Bern, 1980-89, Craven Chpt. N.C. Cmty. Found., 1994—; vol. Craven County Recreation Dept., New Bern, 1982-86; chmn. Richard Dobbs Spaight Constl. Commemorative Com., 1985-89; dir. Craven county affiliate N.C. Commns. Found. Mem. Craven County Bar Assn., N.D. Bar Assn., N.C. Acad. Trial Lawyers, Assn. Trial Lawyers Am., Phi Beta Kappa, Beta Gamma Sigma. Democrat. Methodist. Lodge: Rotary. Bankruptcy, General civil litigation, Real property. Office: Harris Shields Creech & Ward PA PO Box 1168 New Bern NC 28563-1168

**WARD, WILLIAM FRANCIS,** lawyer; b. N.Y.C., Nov. 20, 1951; s. Edward Francis and Ruth Alice (Young) W.; m. Joan Louise Yanzek, Oct. 8, 1983. BA cum laude, Holy Cross Coll., Worcester, Mass., 1973; JD, Temple U., Phila., 1977. Bar: Pa. 1977, U.S. Dist. Ct. (ea. dist.) Pa. 1977, D.C. 1979, U.S. Dist. Ct. (we. dist.) Pa. 1979, U.S. Ct. Appeals (3d cir.) 1983, U.S. Supreme Ct., 1982. Law clk. to presiding judge U.S. Dist. Ct. (ea. dist.) Pa., Phila., 1977-78; asst. U.S. atty. U.S. Atty's. Office, Pitts., 1979-85, chief econ. crime sect., 1983-85; ptnr. Meyer, Unkovic and Scott, Pitts., 1986-96; first dep. atty. gen. Office of Atty. Gen., Harrisburg, Pa., 1996—; lectr. USNR, 1980, U.S. Postal Service, Pitts., 1981. Contbr. articles to profl. jours. Mem. Allegheny County Republican Exec. Com. Recipient Spl. Achievement award, U.S. Atty. Gen., 1980, Spl. Commendation award, 1984, FBI award White Collar Crime Squad, 1985, U.S. Postal Inspection Service award, 1985. Mem. ABA, Pa. Bar Assn., Fed. Bar Assn., Pa. Assn. Criminal Def. Lawyers, Assn.Trial Lawyers in Criminal Ct., Allegheny County Bar Assn., Am. Judicature Soc., St. Thomas More Soc. Roman Catholic. Criminal, Federal civil litigation, State civil litigation. Home: 266 Jefferson Dr Pittsburgh PA 15228-2111 Office: Office of Atty Gen 16th Fl Strawberry Sq Harrisburg PA 17120

**WARDEN, JOHN L.,** lawyer; b. Evansville, Ind., Sept. 22, 1941; s. Walter Wilson and Juanita (Veatch) W.; m. Phillis Ann Rodgers, Oct. 27, 1960; children: Anne W. Clark, John L., W. Carson. AB, Harvard U., 1962; LLB, U. Va., 1965. Bar: N.Y. 1966, U.S. Ct. Appeals (2d cir.) 1966, U.S. Dist. Ct. (so. and ea. dists.) N.Y. 1967, U.S. Ct. Appeals (10th cir.) 1971, U.S. Supreme Ct. 1972, U.S. Ct. Appeals (D.C. cir.) 1980. Assoc. Sullivan & Cromwell, N.Y.C., 1965-73, ptnr., 1973—. Pres. U. Va. Law Sch. Found.; trustee Am. Ballet Theatre. Fellow Am. Coll. Trial Lawyers; mem. ABA, Am. Law Inst., N.Y. State Bar Assn., Assn. Bar City N.Y., N.Y. County Lawyers Assn., Knickerbocker Club, Down Town Assn. Club, Doubles Club, Bedford Golf and Tennis Club, Lyford Cay Club. Republican. Episcopalian. Editor-in-chief Va. Law Rev., 1964-65. Antitrust, Mergers and acquisitions, General civil litigation. Office: Sullivan & Cromwell 125 Broad St Fl 28 New York NY 10004-2489

**WARDEN, WILLIAM C.,** lawyer. Exec. v.p., gen. counsel, sec., chief adminstrv. officer Lowe's Cos., Inc., North Wilkesboro, N.C. Office: Lowe's Cos Inc PO Box 1111 North Wilkesboro NC 28659-1111*

**WARDLAW, KIM A.M.,** federal judge; b. San Francisco, July 2, 1954; m. William M. Wardlaw Sr., Sept. 8, 1984. Student, Santa Clara U., 1972-73, Foothill C.C., Los Altos Hills, Calif., 1973-74; AB in Comm. summa cum laude, UCLA, 1976, JD with honors, 1979. Bar: Calif., U.S. Dist. Ct. (cen. dist.) Calif. 1979, U.S. Dist. Ct. (so. dist.) Calif. 1982, U.S. Dist. Ct. Nev. 1985, U.S. Dist. Ct. (no. dist.) Calif. 1992, U.S. Dist. Ct Mont. 1993, U.S. Dist. Ct. Minn. 1994, U.S. Dist. Ct. (no. dist.) Ala. 1994, U.S. Dist. Ct. (so. dist.) Miss. 1995, U.S. Supreme Ct. Law clk. U.S. Dist. Ct. Cen. Dist. Calif., 1979-80; assoc. O'Melveny and Myers, 1980-87, ptnr., 1987-95; circ. judge U.S. Dist. Ct. Calif., L.A., 1995—; presdl. transition team Dept. Justice, Washington, 1993; mayoral transition Team City of L.A., 1995—; bd. govs., vice-chair UCLA Ctr. for Comm. Policy, 1994—; cons. in field. Co-author: The Encyclopedia of the American Constitution, 1986; contbr. articles to profl. jours. Pres. Women Lawyers Pub. Action Grant Found., 1986-87; del. Dem. Nat. Conv., 1992; founding mem. L.A. Chamber Orchestra, 1992—; active Legal Def. and Edn. Fund, Calif. Leadership Coun., 1993—, Blue Ribbon of L.A. Music Ctr., 1993—. Named one of Most Prominent Bus. Attys. in L.A. County, L.A. Bus. Jour., 1995; recipient Buddy award NOW, 1995. Mem. ABA, NOW, Mex.-Am. Bar Assn. L.A. County, Calif. Women Lawyers, Women Lawyers Assn. L.A., L.A. County Bar Assn. (trustee 1993-94), Assn. Bus. Trial Lawyers (gov. 1988—), Orgn. Women Execs., Downtown Women Ptnrs, Chancery Club, Breakfast Club, Hollywood Womens Polit. Com., City Club Bunker Hill, Phi Beta Kappa. Office: US Dist Ct 9th Cir 125 S Grand Ave Pasadena CA 91105-1621

**WARE, G. LANE,** lawyer; b. Green Bay, Wis., Mar. 24, 1939; s. Gordon L. and Irene P. Ware; m. Linda Lee Kramer, Sept. 9, 1967; children: Hilary, Justin. BS, Northwestern U., 1961; JD, U. Wis., 1965. Bar: Wis. 1965, U.S. Dist. (we. dist.) Wis. Pres. Ruder, Ware & Michler, Wausau, Wis., 1972—; bd. dirs. Wis. Lawyers Mutual Ins. Co., Madison. Bd. dirs. Murco Found., Wausau, 1979—, Wausau Health Found., 1986—, Leigh Yawkey Woodson Art Mus., Wausau, 1994—. Fellow Am. Bar Found.; mem. Am. Law Inst., Am. Judicature Soc., State Bar Wis. (pres. 1989-90), Wis. Law Found. (pres. 1998—), U. Wis. Law Alumni Assn. (pres. 1998—). General corporate, Securities. Office: Ruder Ware & Michler PO Box 8050 Wausau WI 54402-8050

**WARE, HENRY NEILL, JR.,** lawyer; b. Richmond, Va., Nov. 26, 1954; s. Henry Neill and Elizabeth Ware; m. Marilynn Susan Hamrick, Nov. 11, 1985; children: Henry N. III, Alexander Shepard, Robert Lowry. BA, U. Va., 1977; JD, U. Richmond, 1983. Bar: Va. 1983, U.S. Dist. Ct. (ea. dist.) Va. 1983, U.S. Ct. Appeals (4th cir.) 1983, U.S. Ct. Appeals (6th cir.) 1992. Assoc. May & Miller, Richmond, 1983-85, McGuire, Woods, Battle & Boothe, Richmond, 1985-93; prin. Cook Ware Lonnes & Heyward, Richmond, 1993—. Mem. Commonwealth Club, Deep Run Hunt Club. Republican. Episcopalian. Avocations: hunting, falconry. General civil litigation, Contracts commercial, Product liability. Office: Cook Ware Lonnes & Heyward PC 4461 Cox Rd Ste 100 Glen Allen VA 23060-3331

**WARE, JAMES W.,** federal judge; b. 1946. BA, Calif. Luth. U., 1969; JD, Stanford U., 1972. Assoc. Blase, Valentine & Klein, Palo Alto, Calif., 1972-77, ptnr., 1977; judge Santa Clara County Superior Ct., U.S. Dist. Ct. (no. dist.) Calif., 1990—; pro bono East Palo Alto Law Project. Active Am. Leadership Forum; mem. bd. visitors Stanford Law Sch.; active Martin Luther King Papers Project. 2nd lt. USAR, 1969-86. Office: US Dist Cts 280 S 1st St Rm 4150 San Jose CA 95113-3002

**WARING, BRADISH J.,** lawyer; b. New Orleans, Mar. 6, 1952; s. Simons Vanderhorst and Mary Barnwell (Rhett) W.; m. Amelia B., May 27, 1978; children: Amelia S., Mary B.R., Louisa V. BA, U. S.C., 1975, JD, 1977. Bar: U.S. Dist. Ct. S.C. 1978, U.S. Ct. Appeals (4th cir.) 1978, U.S. Supreme Ct. 1987, S.C. 1978. From assoc. to ptnr. Young, Clement, Rivers & Tisdale, Charleston, S.C., 1977—; corp. counsel Town of Sullivan's Island, S.C., 1979-81; chair emeritus Am. Law Firm Assn. Sch. Law., L.A., 1998—. Bd. dirs., treas. Charleston Day Sch., 1996—; vestry mem., sec. St. James Episcopal Ch., Goose Creek, S.C., 1991—; apptd. chair Commrs. Plottage Charleston Br., 1993-94. Fellow S.C. Bar Found.; mem. S.C. Bar Assn. (bd. govs. 1997—, ho. dels. 1985—), Fedn. Ins. & Corp. Counsel. Avocations: sailing, golf, hunting, travel. Insurance, General civil litigation, Product liability. Office: Young Clement Rivers & Tisdale 28 Broad St Charleston SC 29401-3070

**WARIS, MICHAEL, JR.,** lawyer; b. Phila., July 3, 1921; s. Michael and Esther (March) W.; m. Mary Luschyk, June 2, 1956. B.S. in Econs., U. Pa., 1942, J.D. cum laude, 1944. Bar: Pa., D.C. Law clk. to judge U.S. Tax Ct., Washington, 1946-48; trial counsel IRS, Washington, 1948-52; legis. atty. Legislation and Regulations div. IRS Washington, 1952-55; assoc. tax legis. counsel U.S. Treasury Dept., Washington, 1955-62; ptnr. Baker & McKenzie, Washington, 1962-88, of counsel, 1988—; adj. prof. Georgetown U. Law Sch., Washington, 1963-73. Bd. dirs. United Service Orgn. Nat. Capital Area, 1978-79; mem. adv. group to U.S. Commr. of IRS, Washington, 1979-80. Named Master of the Bench, J. Edgar Murdock Am. Inn of Ct., 1988. Fellow ABA; mem. Fed. Bar Assn., Bar Assn. D.C., Ukrainian-Am. Bar Assn. (past chmn. bd. govs.), Cosmos Club, Met. Club, Beta Gamma Sigma. Ukrainian Catholic. Corporate taxation, Taxation, general, Legislative. Home: 6707 Tusculum Rd Bethesda MD 20817-1521 Office: Baker & McKenzie 815 Connecticut Ave NW Washington DC 20006-4004

**WARNER, CHARLES COLLINS,** lawyer; b. Cambridge, Mass., June 19, 1942; s. Hoyt Landon and Charlotte (Collins) W.; m. Elizabeth Denny, Aug. 24, 1964; children: Peter, Andrew, Elizabeth. BA, Yale U., 1964; JD cum laude, Ohio State U., 1970. Bar: Ohio 1970. Assoc. Porter, Wright, Morris & Arthur and predecessor, Columbus, 1970-76, ptnr., 1976—, also mgr. labor and employment law dept., 1988-92. Pres. Peace Corps Svc. Coun., Columbus, 1974-76, Old Worthington (Ohio) Assn., 1976-78, Alliance for Quality Edn., Worthington, 1987-89, Worthington Ednl. Found., 1994-96, Opera Columbus, 1999—; chmn. lawyers sect. United Way, Columbus, 1983-84; mem. alumni adv. coun. Ohio State U. Fellow Am. Bar Found., Ohio Bar Found., Columbus Bar Found., Coll. Labor and Employment Lawyers; mem. ABA (subcom. chmn. EEO com. 1986-89, co-chair-elect 1998—, exec. com. Met. Bar Caucus 1992-94, chmn. state & local bar ADR com. 1995-98), Ohio State Bar Assn. (coun. of dels. 1993—, chmn. fed. cts. com. 1992-94), Ohio Met. Bar Assn. (pres. 1991-92), Columbus Bar Assn. (pres. 1991-92, bd. govs. 1982-87, 88-93), FBA, Ohio Assn. Civil Trial Attys. (exec. bd. 1988-97), Nat. Coun. Ohio State U. Law Alumni Assn. (pres. 1996-97), Capital Club, Yale Club (pres. 1979-81). Avocations: clarinet, singing, tennis. Federal civil litigation, General civil litigation, Labor. Home: 145 E South St Columbus OH 43085-4129 Office: Porter Wright Morris & Arthur 41 S High St Ste 2800 Columbus OH 43215-6194

**WARNER, CHARLES FORD,** lawyer; b. Anderson, Ind., Aug. 18, 1918; s. Ford and Rebecca Ellen (Leathers) W.; m. Elizabeth Ann Wilson, June 16, 1945; children: John, Virginia. BA, U. Wash., 1941, JD, 1947. Bar: Wash. 1947. Instr., tchg. asst. in bus. law U. Wash., Seattle, 1946-47; assoc. Walthew, Oseran, Seattle, 1947-52; ptnr. Walthew, Warner & Keefe, Seattle, 1952-87; sr. ptnr. Wallthew, Warner, Costello, Thompson & Eagan, Seattle, 1987-93, semi-ret., 1993—. Govs. com. workers compensation. Wash. State Ho. of Reps., Olympia, 1966-67, mem. Ind. appeals com. 1966-67); mem. civil rights adv. com. Firlands Hosp., Seattle, 1963-65. 1st lt. inf. U.S. Army, 1941-45, ETO, NATUSA. Decorated Bronze Star. Mem. Wash. State Bar Assn. (adv. com. prepaid legal svcs. 1975-76), Wash. State Trial Lawyers Assn. (founding incorporator, regional v.p. 1966), King County Bar Assn., Overlake Golf and Country Club (Medina, Wash.) (trustee 1972-75). Avocations: golf, fly fishing, tennis. Workers' compensation, Education and schools, Personal injury. Home: 3600 Hunts Point Rd Bellevue WA 98004-1114 Office: Walthew Warner Et Al 123 3d Ave S Seattle WA 98104

**WARNER, JEANNETTE SLOAN,** lawyer; b. Mpls., Jan. 5, 1960. BA, Vanderbilt U., 1982, JD, 1989; LLM in Tax., NYU, 1998. Bar: U.S. Dist. Ct. (so. dist.) N.Y. 1990. Assoc. Milbank Tweed Hadley & McCloy, N.Y.C., 1989-91; pvt. practice N.Y.C., 1991—. Mem. N.Y. Jr. League, 1991—; mem. women's com. Kip's Bay Boys & Girls Club, N.Y.C., 1997—. Mem. Assn. of the Bar of the City of N.Y. Episcopalian. Estate planning, Estate taxation, Real property. Office: 110 E 59th St Ste 600 New York NY 10022-1304

**WARNER, PAUL M.,** prosecutor. BA, Brigham Young U., 1973, JD, 1976, MPA, 1984. With Utah Atty. Gen.'s Office, 1991-98; U.S. atty. Utah dist. U.S. Dept. Justice, 1998—. Office: 185 South St Ste 400 Salt Lake City UT 84111*

**WARNOCK, WILLIAM REID,** lawyer; b. Detroit, Mich., July 25, 1939; s. William G. and Margery E. (Ford) W.; m. Sandra L. Klarich, Dec. 27, 1961; children: Cheryl Lynn, Laura Ellen. BBA, U. Mich., 1961, JD with distinction, 1964. Bar: Ill. 1964, U.S. Dist. Ct. (no. dist.) Ill. 1965, U.S. Supreme Ct. 1972, Mich. 1995. With Ross & Hardies, Chgo., 1964-70; regional counsel U.S. Dept. HUD, Chgo., 1970-73; ptnr. Roan & Grossman, Chgo., 1973-82; sole practice Chgo., 1982-85; ptnr. Siegel & Warnock, Chgo., 1985-91; of counsel Donovan & Olsen, Chgo., 1991; pres. William R. Warnock P.C., LaGrange, Ill., 1992—; cons. Ill. Dept. Bus. and Econ. Devel., Chgo., 1977-78, Ill. Housing Devel. Authority, Chgo., 1973-78, Council State Housing Financing Agys., Washington, 1975-78; past pres., chmn. Atty.'s Title Guaranty Fund, Inc., Chgo., 1986-88, also bd. dirs., 1976—. Author: (legal references) Land Use and Zoning, 1974-88, Ward on Title Examination, 1975, Illinois Real Property Service: Real Estate Exchanges, 1988, Environmental Law and the Real Estate Lawyer, 1989-90. Mem. Ill. State Bar Assn., Am. Coll. Real Estate Lawyers, DuPage Club. Republican. Methodist. Avocations: boating, woodworking. Fax: 708-482-0977. Real property, Land use and zoning (including planning). Home: 165 Briarwood N Oak Brook IL 60523-8720

**WARR, JOHN ARTHUR,** lawyer; b. Vicenza, Italy, June 18, 1969; s. Thomas James and Paula Jean (Peiser) W.; m. Shannon Elaine Allison, Sept. 23, 1995; 1 child, Lawton Alistair. BA, Tulane U., 1991; JD, Ga. State U., 1995. Bar: Ga. 1995. Asst. dist. atty. south Ga. jud. cir. Dist. Atty.'s Office, Bainbridge, Ga., 1996—. Mem. Decatur County Bar Assn. (sec.-treas. 1997, v.p. 1998). Presbyterian. Avocations: golf, reading. Office: Dist Atty's Office PO Box 1843 Bainbridge GA 31718-1843

**WARREN, ANNE SCHAEFER,** lawyer; b. New Orleans, Jan. 23, 1965; d. Everett Gordon Schaefer Jr. and Frances Darrah McCall; m. G. Martin Warren Jr., May 22, 1993; 1 child, Meredith. BA, La. State U., 1987; JD, Loyola U., 1993. Bar: Miss. 1993, La. 1994. Assoc. Bryant & Clark, Gulfport, Miss., 1994-95, Laird & Goff, Gulfport, 1995—. Mem. exec. bd. Jr. Aux. of Gulfport, 1994-2000, Ctr. for Prevention of Child Abuse, Gulfport, 1998—. Mem. Miss. Bar Young Lawyers Divsn. (sec. 1999-2000), Harrison County Young Lawyers (sec. 1995-96, v.p. 1996-97, pres. 1997-98). Methodist. Real property, General civil litigation. Home: 45 Greenbriar Dr Gulfport MS 39507-4247 Office: Laird and Goff PO Box 160 Gulfport MS 39502-0160

**WARREN, BRADFORD LLOYD,** lawyer; b. Indpls., Oct. 2, 1948; s. Claude Marion and Nina Jean (Davidson) W. AB, Ind. U., Bloomington, 1970; JD, Ind. U., Indpls., 1973. Bar: Ind. 1973, U.S. Dist. Ct. (so. dist.) Ind. 1973, U.S. Supreme Ct. 1983. Tax staffman Arthur Andersen & Co., Indpls., 1972-74; ptnr. Warren, Snider & Warren, Indpls., 1974-77; sole practice Indpls., 1977—; Active Libertarian Party Ind. 1976—, candidate U.S. Ho. Reps., 1984, candidate U.S. Senate, 1986. Mem. Ind. U. Alumni Assn., Delta Tau Delta (bd. dirs., sec., treas. Beta Alpha Shelter 1976-94). Lodge: Order of Demolay, Chevalier citation. Probate, Personal income taxation, Estate planning. Home: 5204 N Winthrop Ave Indianapolis IN 46220-3259 Office: 926 E 52nd St Indianapolis IN 46205-1124

**WARREN, ELIZABETH,** law educator. BS, U. Houston, 1970; JD, Rutgers U., 1976. Robert Braucher vis. prof. law Harvard U., Cambridge, Mass., 1992-93, Leo Gottlieb prof. law, 1995—. Contbr. articles to profl. jours. Named one of 50 Top Women Lawyers Nat. Law Jour., 1998. Office: Harvard U Law Sch Hauser 200 Cambridge MA 02138*

**WARREN, JESSICA MENDES,** laweyr; b. Laredo, Tex., Dec. 16, 1970; d. Hector G. and Mary (Kallil) M.; m. John Warren, Apr. 18, 1998. BA, U. Tex., 1992; JD, Baylor U., 1995. Bar: Tex. 1995, U.S. Dist. Ct. (we. dist.) Tex. 1997. Assoc. atty. Bean & Manning, L.L.P., Houston, 1995-98, Harris & Harris, Inc., Austin, Tex., 1998—. Vol. Women's Advocacy Project, Austin, Tex., 1998, Toys for Tots, Houston, 1996, 97. Mem. Tex. Young Lawyers Assn. Roman Catholic. Avocations: horseback riding, music. Administrative and regulatory, General civil litigation. Office: Harris & Harris The Atrium 8701 Mopac Ste 400 Austin TX 78759-8364

**WARREN, JOHN HERTZ, III,** lawyer; b. Charleston, S.C., June 6, 1946; s. John Hertz Jr. and Louise (Hammett) W.; m. Helen Smith, Oct. 7, 1968; children: Louise Capers, Caroline Gregorie, John Alexander. BS in English, Coll. Charleston, 1967; JD, U. S.C., 1972. Bar: S.C. 1972, U.S. Dist. Ct. S.C. 1973, U.S. Ct. Appeals (4th cir.) 1973. Assoc. Brockinton & Brockinton, Charleston, 1972-73; assoc., then ptnr. Sinkler, Gibbs & Simons, Charleston, 1973-85; ptnr. Hutcheson & Warren, Charleston, 1986-92, Warren & Sinkler, Charleston, 1993—. Pres. Charleston Symphony Orch., 1984-85; trustee Hist. Charleston Found., 1987—, pres., 1994—; trustee Coll. of Charleston Found., 1987—, pres., 1995—; bd. dirs. Med. Soc. Health Sys., Inc., 1993—. Mem. ABA, S.C. Bar Assn., Charleston County Bar Assn., Ocean Cruising Club (London), Carolina Yacht Club. Episcopalian. Banking, General corporate, Real property. Home: 6350 Oak Grove Plantation Rd Wadmalaw Island SC 29487 Office: 171 Church St Ste 340 Charleston SC 29401-3140

**WARREN, J(OHN) MICHAEL,** lawyer; b. Port of Spain, Trinidad and Tobago, Dec. 16, 1939; came to U.S., 1946; s. John Milton and Isma Thelma (Farmer) W.; m. JoAnn Darlene Westermeier, June 24, 1961; children: John Douglas, Denise Marie, Stephanie Ann Larsen, Lynne Catherine Thatcher. BA, Tchr.'s Cert., Ea. Mich. U., 1961; JD, U. Mich., 1964. Bar: Mich. 1965. Assoc. Foster, Campbell, Lindermer & McGurrin, Lansing, 1965-70; exec. com. ptnr. Foster, Lindermer, Swift & Collins, Lansing, 1970-80, pres., 1974-80; pres. Warren, Cameron, Faust & Asciutto, Okemos, Mich., 1981—; bd. dirs. Maxco, Inc., Lansing, Camp, Inc., Jackson, Mich. Pres. Chief Okemos coun. Boy Scouts Am., Lansing, 1989-91; pres. Lansing Region Comty. Found., 1994. Named Man of Yr., Gaelic League of Lansing, 1979; recipient Silver Beaver award Boy Scouts Am., 1990, Whitney Young award, 1996. Mem. Lansing Regional C. of C. (pres. 1980, Tireless award 1980). Avocations: genealogy, golf, reading. Home: 2150 Heritage Ave Okemos MI 48864-3614 Office: Warren Cameron Faust & Asciutto PO Box 26067 Lansing MI 48909-6067

**WARREN, JOHNNY WILMER,** lawyer, judge; b. Milledgeville, Ga., Sept. 2, 1946; s. Johnnie Linton and Allene (Harden) W.; m. Hannah Hall, Aug. 27, 1967; children: Hannah Michelle, Heather Elizabeth. AA, Mid. Ga. Coll., 1967; BBA, Ga. Coll., 1977, JD, 1979, M in Mgmt. Info. Sys., 1993. Bar: Ga. 1979, U.S. Dist. Ct. (so. and mid. dists.) Ga. 1979, U.S. Tax Ct. 1979, U.S. Ct. Appeals (11th cir.) 1981, U.S. Supreme Ct. 1984. Radio announcer, engr. Dublin (Ga.) Broadcasting Co., 1967-72; pres., gen. mgr. Dublico, Inc., Dublin, 1972-79; pvt. practice law Dublin, 1979—; judge Laurens County Small Claims Ct., Dublin, 1979-83; chief magistrate Magistrate Ct. Laurens County, Dublin, 1983-96, chmn. tng. coun., 1985—; instr. Inst. of Continuing Legal Edn. in Ga., 1983—, bus. law Ga. Coll., 1989—. Author: Magistrate Court Handbook, 1984, supplements, 1985-90, How to Collect Your Small Claim in Georgia, 1987, Georgia Magistrate Court Guide with Forms, 1993, 98; editor Ga. Magistrate Ct. Newsletter, 1989-96. Mem. Dublin Planning and Zoning Appeals Bd., 1981-85, Dublin Planning and Zoning Commn., 1985-97, vice-chmn., 1989-97; pres. Dublin Fine Arts Assn., 1986-88. Mem. ABA, State Bar Ga. (bd. govs. 1985-93, chmn. publs. com. 1988-90), Dublin Cir. Bar Assn. (sec.-treas. 1982-83, v.p. 1983-84, pres. 1984-85), Ga. Coun. Magistrate Judges (pres. 1989-90, exec. com. 1990-96), D.C. Bar Assn. Methodist. Avocations: computers, photography. General practice, Real property, Consumer commercial. Home and Office: PO Box 775 Dublin GA 31040-0775

**WARREN, KEITH ASHLEY,** lawyer; b. Cambridge, Md., Dec. 26, 1943; s. William Lester and Exa Martha (Ashley) W.; m. Ingrid T. Peterson, July 20, 1968; children: Lisa, Mark, Blake. BA, U. Ky., 1965, JD, 1968. Bar: Ky. 1968, U.S. Ct. Mil. Appeals 1969, U.S. Supreme Ct. 1972, Tenn. 1977. Trial atty. Nat. Labor Rels. Bd., Memphis, 1973-76; assoc. McKnight, Hudson, Lewis, Memphis, 1976-80, ptnr., 1980—; spl. labor rels. coun. Govt. of Shelby County, Memphis, 1979-81; bd. advisors Hospitality Human Resources, Lincoln, Nebr., 1992—. Pres. Fisherville (Tenn.) Civic Club, 1992—. Capt. USAF, 1968-73. Mem. Ky. Bar Assn. (labor law sect. 1968—), Tenn. Bar Assn. (labor law sect. 1977—), Memphis Bar Assn. (employment law sect. 1977—), Nat. Law Network (labor litigation sect. 1994—). Republican. Methodist. Avocation: snow skiing. Labor, Federal civil litigation, Civil rights. Home: 11590 Macon Rd Eads TN 38028-9734 Office: McKnight Hudson Lewis 6750 Poplar Ave Ste 301 Memphis TN 38138-7415

**WARREN, RUSSELL ALLEN,** lawyer; b. St. Louis, Oct. 28, 1965; s. Frank Allen and Edna Anna W.; m. Janice Davidse, Oct. 10, 1992. BA, St. Louis U., 1988, JD, 1991. Bar: Mo. 1992, U.S. Dist. Ct. (ea. dist.) Mo. 1992, Ill. 1993. Assoc. Elbein & Goldberg, St. Louis, 1990-93; pvt. practice St. Louis, 1993—. Pres. Canvas Cove Homeowners Assn., O'Fallon, Mo., 1998—, Canvas Cove archtl. control com., 1998—. Mem. ABA, Ill. Bar Assn., Mo. Bar Assn. Republican. Presbyterian. Avocations: fishing, canoeing, camping, philately, tennis. Criminal, Probate, Transportation. Office: 1221 Locust St Ste 1000 Saint Louis MO 63103-2382

**WARREN, STEWART DAVID,** lawyer; b. Newark, Aug. 4, 1946; s. Robert W.; m. Laura Anne Wichman, May 18, 1990; children: Beth, Michael. BS in Acctg., Rider Coll., 1968; JD, Rutgers U., 1971. Dep. atty. gen. N.J. Divsn. Criminal Justice, Trenton, 1971-94, N.J. Divsn. Law, Trenton, 1994—. Commdr. flotilla USCG, Trenton, 1995—. Alumni scholar Rutgers U., 1964-71. Mem. Raoul Wallenberg Com. N.J. (v.p. 1984-91), Pi Gamma Mu. Office: Office of Atty Gen PO Box 93 Trenton NJ 08625-0093

**WARREN, WILLIAM BRADFORD,** lawyer; b. Boston, July 25, 1934; s. Minton Machado and Sarah Ripley (Robbins) W.; children: John Coolidge, Sarah W. Jaffe; m. Arete B. Swartz, Sept. 20, 1985. AB magna cum laude, Harvard U., 1956, LLB cum laude, 1959. Bar: N.Y. 1960. Assoc. Dewey Ballantine, N.Y.C., 1959-68; ptnr. Dewey Ballantine, LLP, 1968—; lectr. Inst. Fed. Taxation, N.Y. U., So. Fed. Tax Inst., Practicing Law Inst. Pres. Cintas Found., N.Y.C.; bd. dirs. John Carter Brown Libr., Providence, R.I.; adv. bd. dirs. Met. Opera Assn., N.Y.C. Mem. Am. Law Inst., Am. Coll. Trust and Estate Counsel (former regent), Acad. Am. Poets (bd. dirs.), Internat. Acad. Estate and Trust Law (former exec. com.), N.Y. State Bar Assn. (chmn. com. taxation of trust and estates sect. 1980-83), Assn. Bar City N.Y., Soc. Mayflower Descs., Harvard Club, Knickerbocker Club, Century Club, Grolier Club (past pres.). Home: 520 E 86th St New York NY 10028-7534 Office: Dewey Ballantine LLP 1301 Avenue Of The Americas New York NY 10019-6022

**WARSHAW, ALLEN CHARLES,** lawyer; b. Harrisburg, Pa., Aug. 27, 1948; s. Julius and Miriam (Nepove) W.; m. Shirley Anne Nes, Aug. 23, 1970; children: Christopher James, Andrew Charles, William Robert. BA, U. Pa., 1970; JD, Villanova U., 1973. Bar: Pa. 1973, U.S. Dist. Ct. (ea. and mid. dists.) Pa. 1974, U.S. Ct. Appeals (3d cir.) 1975, U.S. Supreme Ct. 1977, Calif. 1978. Staff atty. Office Atty. Gen., State of Pa., Harrisburg, 1973-79, chief civil litigation, 1979-85, dir. civil law, 1985-86; ptnr. Duane, Morris & Heckscher, Harrisburg, 1986—. Coach, past pres. Mechanicsburg

Soccer Assn.; Dem. committeeperson, area leader Cumberland County; mem. exec. com. Cumberland County Dem. Party. Fellow Am. Bar Found.; mem. ABA, Fed. Bar Assn., Am. Bankruptcy Inst., Pa. Bar Assn., Dauphin County Bar Assn., Turnabout Mgmt. Assn. Bankruptcy, General civil litigation, Civil rights. Home: 1035 Mccormick Rd Mechanicsburg PA 17055-5970 Office: Duane Morris & Heckscher 305 N Front St Ste 500 Harrisburg PA 17101-1239

**WARSHAW, MICHAEL THOMAS,** lawyer; b. Jersey City, June 29, 1950; s. Thomas T. and June C. (Lancaster) W.; m. Mary Jane Egidio, July 12, 1986. BA in Sociology, Coll. of the Holy Cross, 1972; JD, Bklyn. Law Sch., 1975. Bar: N.J. 1976, U.S. Dist. Ct. N.J. 1976, U.S. Ct. Appeals (3d cir.) 1982, N.Y. Ct. of Appeals 1987, U.S. Supreme Ct. 1982. Law sec. to judge N.J. Superior Ct., 1975-76; assoc. Drazin & Warshaw PC, Red Bank, N.J., 1976-88, Magee & Graham, Wall, N.J., 1988-90; pres. Michael T. Warshaw, PC, Red Bank, 1990-95; shareholder Warshaw & Barnes, PC, Red Bank, 1995—; adj. prof. bus. law Brookdale C.C., Lincroft; speaker Mock Trial Sem., Young Lawyers div. N.J. Bar Assn., 1984, Discovery Sem., 1986; mem. com. on mcpl. cts. N.J. Supreme Ct., 1984-88. Chmn. Red Bank Cath. H.S. Devel. Adv. Coun., 1994—, elder law seminar Trenton Diocese, 1996; trustee Brookdale C.C. Found., 1995—. Mem. ABA, N.J. Bar Assn. (young lawyers divsn., exec. com. 1983-86), N.J. Bar Found. (spkrs. bur.), Monmouth County Bar Assn. (civil practice com. 1985—, chair alternative dispute resolution com.), Christian Bros. Acad. Alumni Assn. (pres. 1993-95), Phi Delta Phi. Republican. Roman Catholic. Avocations: golf, youth athletics. General civil litigation, Personal injury, Estate planning. Home: 18 Quaker Rd Middletown NJ 07748-3193 Office: 10 W Bergen Pl Ste 202 Red Bank NJ 07701-1500

**WARTHEN, HARRY JUSTICE, III,** lawyer; b. Richmond, Va., July 8, 1939; s. Harry Justice Jr. and Martha Winston (Alsop) W.; m. Sally Berkeley Trapnell, Sept. 7, 1968; children: Martha Alsop, William Trapnell. BA, U. Va., 1961, LLB, 1967. Bar: Va. 1967, U.S. Ct. Appeals (4th cir.) 1967, U.S. Dist. Ct. (ea. dist.) Va. 1969. Law clk. to judge U.S. Ct. Appeals (4th cir.), Richmond, Va., 1967-68; assoc. Hunton & Williams, Richmond, 1968—; lectr. U. Va. Law Sch., Charlottesville, 1975-77, in field. Trustee exec. com. Hist. Richmond Found., 1986-95, 96—; trustee Woodrow Wilson Birthplace and Mus., 1997—; dir. exec. com. Preservation Alliance of Va., 1991-97, pres., 1994-96; elder, trustee endowment fund Grace Covenant Presbyn. Ch.; moderator Hanover Presbytery, Presbyn. Ch. (USA), 1988. Lt. U.S. Army, 1962-64. Fellow Am. Coll. Trust and Estate Counsel, Va. Law Found.; mem. ABA, Richmond Bar Assn., Va. Bar Assn. (chmn. sect. on wills, trusts and estates 1981-89), Antiquarian Soc. Richmond (pres. 1977-78, 98-99), Country Club Va., Deep Run Hunt Club. Republican. Probate, Estate taxation. Home: 1319 Shallow Well Rd Manakin-Sabot VA 23103-2305 Office: Hunton & Williams Riverfront Plaza East Tower PO Box 1535 Richmond VA 23218-1535

**WASHBURN, JOHN JAMES,** lawyer, financial services company executive; b. Chelsea, Mass., Sept. 15, 1956; s. Kathryn Lorraine (Webster) W. BSBA cum laude, Suffolk U., Boston, 1978; MBA, Suffolk U., 1983; JD, New Eng. Sch. Law, 1987; LLM in Taxation, Boston U., 1989. Bar: Mass. 1987, Ill. 1996, U.S. Dist. Ct. Mass. 1988, U.S. Ct. Appeals (1st, 3d and 4th cirs.) 1988, U.S. Tax Ct. 1989, U.S. Ct. Claims 1991, U.S. Ct. Appeals (D.C. cir.) 1992, U.S. Ct. Appeals (7th cir.) 1996, U.S. Supreme Ct. 1996, U.S. Dist. Ct. (no. and ctrl. dists.) Ill. 1996. Intern Boston Mcpl. Ct., Suffolk County Dist. Atty.'s Office; assoc. Boxer & Assocs., Boston, 1987-88; pvt. practice North Reading, Mass., 1988—, Westchester, Ill., 1996—; v.p. legal Nat. Translink Corp., Westchester, Ill., 1995—; cons. FGL Commodity Svcs. New England, 1988-92. Editor Confinement jour., 1986-87, B.U. Taxation jour., 1988-89; contbr. articles to profl. jours. Mem. North Reading Rep. Town Com., 1989-95, vice chmn., 1992-95; del. Mass. Rep. State Conv., 1990, 94; selectman North Reading, 1991-94, chmn., 1993-94, fin. com., 1994-95, clk., 1995; bd. dirs. Essex-Middlesex Sanitary Dist., 1991-95; Mass. Justice of Peace. Mem. ATLA, Ill. State Bar Assn., DuPage County Bar Assn., Chgo. Bar Assn., Am. Soc. Notaries, Phi Alpha Delta, Delta Sigma Pi. Republican. Avocations: golf, numismatics. Personal injury, General civil litigation, Consumer commercial. Office: Nat Translink Corp 1301 W 22nd St Ste 410 Oak Brook IL 60523-2088 also: PO Box 264 PO Box 498 North Reading MA 01864-0498

**WASHINGTON, ERIC,** judge. Assoc. Fulbright and Jaworski, Houston; legis. dir., counsel Rep. Michael Andrews; spl. counsel corp. counsel, prin. dep. corp. counsel; ptnr. Hogan & Hartson, Washington, 1990-95; apptd. Superior Ct.; judge D.C. Ct. Appeals, 1999—. Office: DC Ct Appeals 6th Fl 500 Indiana Ave NW Washington DC 20001*

**WASHINGTON, KAREN ROBERTS,** lawyer; b. Dallas, Mar. 29, 1960; d. Thomas Edwin and Mary Lee (Jones) Roberts; m. Bruce Edward Washington, Aug. 16, 1986. BA in Spanish, Tex. Tech U., 1981; JD, U. Tex., 1984. Bar: Tex. 1984, U.D. Dist. Ct. (no. dist.) Tex. 1985, U.S. Dist. Ct. (so. and we. dists.) Tex. 1988, U.S. Supreme Ct. 1989, U.S. Ct. Appeals (5th cir.) 1989, U.S. Dist. Ct. (ea. dist.) Tex. 1996. Briefing atty. 5th Ct. Appeals Tex., Dallas, 1984-85; asst. city atty. City of Dallas, 1985-86; assoc. Godwin, Carlton & Maxwell, Dallas, 1986-89, mem. firm, 1990-93; mem. firm Thorpe Hatcher & Washington, L.L.P., Dallas, 1994—. V.p. gen. counsel Theatre 3. Mem. Nat. Employment Lawyers Assn., Assn. Women Execs., Dallas Bar Assn., Assn. Atty. Mediators, Greater Dallas and North Tex. Presuit Mediation Program, Patrick E. Higginbothan Am. Inn of Ct., State Bar Coll., Altrusa Club Downtown Dallas, Alpha Phi. Episcopalian. General civil litigation, Civil rights, Labor. Office: Thorpe Hatcher & Washington LLP 2929 Carlisle St Ste 250 Dallas TX 75204-4069

**WASHINGTON, VALDEMAR LUTHER,** judge; b. Balt., June 21, 1952; s. G. Luther and Vivian Irene (Edwards) W.; m. Ada Catherine Miller, Aug. 11, 1984; children: Valdemar Luther II, Christopher James. BA in Communications, Mich. State U., 1974; JD, U. Mich., 1976. Bar: Mich. 1977, U.S. Dist. Ct. (ea. div.) Mich. 1977. Assoc. Baker, Baker and Selby, Bay City, Mich., 1977; dir. Acctg. Aid Soc. of Greater Flint (Mich.), 1978; sole practice Flint, 1978-81, 81-86; ptnr. Robinson, Washington, Smith and Stanfield, P.C., Flint, 1981; judge Genesee County Cir. Ct., Flint, 1986—, chief judge, 1990-91. Pres. adv. bd. McCree Theatre, Flint, 1983; bd. dirs. Big Sisters Orgn., Flint, 1983; mem. legal redress com. NAACP, Flint, 1984-86. Mem. Mich. Bar Assn., Genesee County Bar Assn., Assn. Trial Lawyers Am., Mich. Trial Lawyers Assn., Genesee County Trial Lawyers Assn., Mensa. Episcopalian. Avocations: swimming, reading. Office: 328 S Saginaw St Ste 9001 Flint MI 48502-1943

**WASKA, RONALD JEROME,** lawyer; b. Helena, Mont., Aug. 18, 1942; s. Charles Daniel and Mildred (Jablonski) W.; m. Elizabeth Ann Helten, Dec. 3, 1973; children: Amber Ann, Autumn Ann. BA, U. Tex., 1964; JD in Law, U. Houston, 1969. Bar: Tex. 1969, U.S. Supreme Ct. 1975, U.S. Dist. Ct. (no., so., we., and ea. dists.) Tex., U.S. Tax Ct., U.S. Ct. Appeals (5th, 8th and 11th cirs.). Asst. U.S. atty. Civil and Criminal Div., chief Criminal Div. So. Dist. of Tex., Houston, 1970-75; pvt. practice law Houston, 1976—. Recipient Outstanding Performance Rating Dept. of Justice, Washington, 1970-75, AV Rating Martindale-Hubbell, 1974. Fellow Tex. Bar Found., Houston Fed. Bar; mem. ABA, Houston Bar Assn., Tex. Trial Lawyers Assn., Assn. Trial Lawyers Am., Fed. Bar Assn. (Outstanding svc. 1974, Younger Fed. Lawyer award 1974), Assn. of Criminal Attys., Bar Assn. of 5th Fed. Cir., Tex. Assn. of Criminal Attys., Harris County Assn. Criminal Attys., Phi Alpha Delta, Pi Kappa Alpha. Republican. Roman Catholic. Avocations: writing, music, sports. Criminal, Federal civil litigation, State civil litigation. Office: 952 Echo Ln Ste 180 Houston TX 77024-2753

**WASKO, LAWRENCE DENNIS,** lawyer; b. Yonkers, N.Y., Oct. 27, 1932; s. Joseph Ambrose and Florence Audrey (Brown) W.; m. Ann Elaine Dowd, Feb. 23, 1963; children: Mark Ambrose, Maura Ann. AB, Harpur Coll., Endicott, N.Y., 1958; JD, Georgetown U., 1963. Air transp. examiner Civil Aeronautics Bd., Washington, 1958-62; dir. research Air Transport Assn., Washington, 1963; assoc. to sr. ptnr. Seamon, Wasko & Ozment, Washington, 1964-90; adj. prof. internat. bus. diplomacy Georgetown U., Washington, 1974-85; bd. dirs. Va. Nat. Bank-Fairfax, Springfield, 1974-77, First Comml. Bank, Arlington, 1977-80. Bd. trustees Nat. Hosp. for Orthopedics and Rehab., Alexandria, 1983-84; mem. program com. Landegger Program in Internat. Bus. Devel., Georgetown U., Sch. of Fgn. Svc., 1989—. Mem. Bar Assn. D.C., Washington Golf and Country Club, Delta Theta Phi. Home: 7002 Holyrood Dr Mc Lean VA 22101-1552 Office: Connecticut Bldg 9th Fl 1150 Connecticut Ave NW Washington DC 20036-4104

**WASKO, STEVEN E.,** lawyer; b. Chgo., May 10, 1954; s. Theodore J. and Beverly W.; m. Elaine L. Enger, Oct. 3, 1981 (div. Aug. 1996); 1 child, Christine. B in Spl. Studies cum laude, Cornell Coll., 1976; JD cum laude, Kent U., 1979. Bar: Ill. 1979, U.S. Dist. Ct. (no. dist.) Ill. 1979. Assoc. atty. Blanshan & Summerfield, Park Ridge, Ill., 1979-81; ptnr. Summerfield & Wasko, Park Ridge, 1981-86; sole practitioner Steven Wasko and Assocs., Park Ridge, 1986-90, mng. ptnr., 1992-95; ptnr. Wasko & Michaels, Park Ridge, 1990-91, Steponate & Wasko Ltd., Park Ridge and Chgo., 1995—; dir. Kolan Corp., Park Ridge, 1988—. Great Books leader Field Sch. Dist., Park Ridge, 1997—. Avocations: jogging, watercolors and fine art. Family and matrimonial. Office: 1580 N Northwest Hwy Park Ridge IL 60068-1444

**WASMAN, JANE G.,** lawyer; b. Miami Beach, Fla., May 9, 1956. BA magna cum laude, Princeton U., 1978; JD, Harvard U., 1981. Bar: Calif. 1981, D.C. 1983, N.Y. 1990. Assoc. Jones, Day Revis & Pogue, L.A., 1981-85; assoc. counsel U.S. Senate Com. on Vets. Affairs, Washington, 1987-89; assoc. Fried, Frank, Harris, Shriver & Jacobson, N.Y.C., 1989-95; dir. litigation Schering-Plough Corp., Kenilworth, N.J., 1995-98; staff v.p. European ops.-legal, chief counsel Europe Schering-Plough Corp., Kenilworth, 1998—. Mem. Am. Corp. Counsel Assn., Phi Beta Kappa. Private international, General civil litigation, Administrative and regulatory. Office: Schering-Plough Corp 2000 Galloping Hill Rd Kenilworth NJ 07033-1328

**WASSERMAN, MICHAEL FRANCIS,** lawyer; b. Poughkeepsie, N.Y., Mar. 24, 1965; s. Richard Stanley and Marilyn Rose (Gallmeier) W. BA, Wesleyan U., 1990; JD magna cum laude, U. Minn., 1993. Bar: Va. 1993, D.C. 1994, Md. 1994, U.S. Dist. Ct. D.C. 1994, U.S. Dist. Ct. (ea. dist.) Va. 1996, U.S. Dist. Ct. Md. 1996, U.S. Supreme Ct. 1997. Asst. corp. counsel D.C. Govt., 1994; law clk. to Hon. Vanessa Ruiz D.C. Ct. Appeals, Washington, 1994-96; assoc. Pepper Hamilton LLP, Washington, 1996-97, Sidley & Austin, Washington, 1997—. Author: (with others) Europe Without Frontiers: A Lawyer's Guide, 1989; editor Minn. Law Rev., 1992-93. Mem. Am. Soc. Legal History, Selden Soc., Order of the Coif. Dem. Avocations: legal history, hiking, canoeing. Appellate, Federal civil litigation, Product liability. Home: 1600 28th St NW Washington DC 20007-2952 Office: Sidley & Austin 1722 Eye St NW Washington DC 20006-3795

**WASSERMAN, RICHARD LEO,** lawyer; b. Balt., Aug. 6, 1948; s. Jack B. and Claire (Gutman) W.; m. Manuele Delbourgo, May 13, 1973; children: Alexander E., Lauren E. AB, Princeton U., 1970, JD, Columbia U., 1973. Bar: N.Y. 1975, Md. 1978, U.S. Dist. Ct. (so. and ea. dists.) N.Y. 1975, U.S. Dist. Ct. Md. 1978, U.S. Ct. Appeals (2d cir.) 1975, U.S. Ct. Appeals (4th cir.) 1979, U.S. Supreme Ct. 1982. Law clk. to hon. Roszel C. Thomsen U.S. Dist. Ct. Md., Balt., 1973-74; assoc. Proskauer Rose Goetz & Mendelsohn, N.Y.C., 1974-78; assoc. Venable, Baetjer & Howard, Balt., 1978-81, ptnr., 1982—. Fellow Am. Coll. Bankruptcy, Md. Bar Found.; mem. ABA (bus. bankruptcy com.), Md. Bar Assn. (sec. coun. bus. law sect. 1989-92), Bar Assn. Balt. City (chmn. banking, bankruptcy and bus. law com. 1987-88), Bankruptcy Bar Assn. Dist. Md. (bd. dirs. 1988—, pres. 1990-91), Assn. Bar City N.Y., Am. Bankruptcy Inst., Princeton U. Alumni Assn. Md. (bd. dirs. 1980-98, pres. 1985-87), Suburban Club Baltimore County (bd. govs. 1982-89, 94-98, 2d v.p. 1986-87, sec. 1987-88, pres.-elect 1994-95, pres. 1995-97). Democrat. Jewish. Avocations: tennis, bridge. Bankruptcy, Contracts commercial, Banking. Office: Venable Baetjer & Howard LLP 1800 Mercantile Bank Bldg Baltimore MD 21201

**WASSERMAN, STEPHEN ALAN,** lawyer; b. Cleve., Apr. 7, 1948; s. Myron Earl and Eve Ruth (Milstein) W.; m. Sandra Shulamith Moltz, Oct. 20, 1978. BA, U. Wis., 1970; JD, Northeastern U., Boston, 1978. Bar: Mass. 1978, U.S. Dist. Ct. Mass. 1978. Housing atty. Neighborhood Legal Svcs., Lynn, Mass., 1978-83; ptnr. Barmack, Boggs and Wasserman, Lynn, 1983-91; pvt. practice Salem, Mass., 1991-97, 98—, Boston, 1997-98. Bd. dirs. North Shore Cmty. Action Program, Peabody, Mass., 1995—. Avocations: reading, baseball, jogging. Personal injury, Landlord-tenant, Toxic tort. Office: 60 Washington St Salem MA 01970-3515

**WASSERMAN, SYLVIA KATZ,** lawyer; b. Milw., Mar. 30, 1916; d. Abraham and Anna Esther Katz; m. Eugene Wasserman (dec. Mar. 1970); children: Barbara Wasserman Vinson, Louis. BA, U. Ill., 1937; B of Law, Northwestern U., 1939, JD, 1970. Lawyer Office of Daniel D. Carmell, Chgo., Legal Br. N.Y. Ordinance Dist., N.Y.C.; lawyer, brief editor Bala Cynwyd, Pa.; lawyer Sheboygan, Wis., 1951—. Commr. Sheboygan Police and Fire Commn., 1980-93; bd. dirs. Friendship House, Sheboygan, 1974-96. Recipient Commendation award Friendship House, 1986. Mem. ABa, Ill. Bar Assn., Sheboygan Bar Assn. Democrat. Jewish. Probate, Family and matrimonial, General practice. Home: 215 Superior Ave Sheboygan WI 53081-2957 Office: 2808 Kohler Memorial Dr Sheboygan WI 53081-3166

**WASSERMAN, WILLIAM PHILLIP,** lawyer; b. Los Angeles, Sept. 13, 1945; s. Al and Ceil (Diamond) W.; married; children: Sam, George. BA, U. Calif., Berkeley, 1967; JD, U. Calif., 1970. Bar: Calif. 1971, U.S. Tax Ct. 1971. Ptnr. Ernst & Young LLP, Los Angeles, 1970—; lectr. in field.; participant in numerous programs, confs., and workshops in field in field. Mem. Editorial adv. bd.: Real Estate Taxation: A Practitioner's Guide, 1984—, Federal Tax Annual: Real Estate, 1982; contbr. numerous articles to profl. jours. Mem. ABA (nat. chmn Tax Sect. com. on real estate problems 1985-87), State Bar Calif., Los Angeles County Bar Assn., Calif. Bd. Legal Specialization (cert. taxation law specialist). Taxation, general. Office: Ernst & Young LLP 725 S Figueroa St Los Angeles CA 90017-5524

**WASSON, KAREN REED,** lawyer; b. Augsburg, West Germany, Aug. 18, 1966; d. Frank III and Carol Ensign Reed; m. Dean Patrick Wasson, Apr. 5, 1997; children: Jason Llewellyn, Trista L., Tiffany D., Shea A. BS, Fla. State U., 1988; JD, U. Ga., 1991. Bar: Ga., Fla. Asst. dist. atty. Gwinnett County Dist. Atty.'s Office, Lawrenceville, Ga., 1991-97; with Law Offices of Nolan Carter. Contbr. articles to profl. jours. Mem. Supporters of the Shield, Lawrenceville, 1994-97. Mem. Assn. Trial Lawyers Am., Fla. Trial Lawyers Assn., Orange County Bar Assn. Republican. Methodist. Avocations: golf, gardening, reading. State civil litigation, Professional liability, Personal injury. Home: 2406 Wekiva Walk Way Apopka FL 32703-4840 Office: Law Offices of Nolan Carter 1218 E Robinson St Orlando FL 32801-2116

**WASSON, ROY D.,** lawyer; b. Kingsville, Tex., Dec. 4. 1950; s. Virgil Dale and Magdalina Isabella (Flowers) W.; m. Carol Ann Fenello, May 23, 1987. BA, Ea. Ky. U., Richmond, 1975; JD with distinction, U. Ky., 1981. Bar: Fla. 1981, U.S Supreme Ct. 1987, U.S. Ct. Appeals (11th cir.) 1982, U.S. Dist. Ct. (so. dist.) Fla., 1981, U.S. Dist. Ct. (mid. dist.) 1983. Assoc. Kimbrell & Hamann, Miami, Fla., 1981-87; pvt. practice Miami, 1987—. Mem. ABA, Assn. Trial Lawyers Am., Acad. Fla. Trial Lawyers (bd. dirs., past chair amicus curiae com., past chair appellate practice sect.), Fla. Bar (chair appellate practice sect., appellate rules com. 1988-97), Dade County Trial Lawyers Assn., Dade County Bar Assn. (appellate cts. com.), Order of Coif. Democrat. Avocations: sailing, scuba diving. Labor. Office: 1320 S Dixie Hwy Miami FL 33146-2926

**WATANABE, ROY NOBORU,** lawyer; b. Honolulu, July 23, 1947; s. Tadao I. and Clara Y. W.; m. Myrna E. Watanabe, June 8, 1970 (div. Oct. 1983); m. Mona Mangan, Oct. 24, 1987. AB, Columbia Coll., 1969; JD, Columbia U., 1973. Bar: N.Y. 1974, U.S. Dist. Ct. (so. and ea. dists.) N.Y. 1976, U.S. Ct. Appeals (2d cir.) 1976. Honors program atty. Office of Labor Rels., Office of Mayor, N.Y.C., 1973-76; assoc. Frankle & Greenwald, N.Y.C., 1976, Cohn, Glickstein, Lurie, Ostrin, Lubell & Lubell, N.Y.C., 1976-79; ptnr. Cohn, Glickstein & Lurie (formerly Cohn, Glickstein, Lurie, Ostrin, Lubell & Lubell, N.Y.C., 1979-88, Spivak, Lipton, Watanabe, Spivak & Moss, 1989—; guest lectr. labor law Boston Coll., 1982, Union U., 1983, 85, Mercer U., 1997, NYU Law Sch., 1998; faculty Practicing Law Inst., N.Y.C., 1987; panelist, lectr. regional conf. N.Y. State Bar Assn. labor and employment law sect. and Nat. Labor Rels. Bd., N.Y.C., 1986; author, commentator 50th ann. labor conf. NYU, 1997. Contbg. author: NLRA Law and Practice, 1991. Cooperating atty. Asian Am. Legal Def. & Edn. Fund., N.Y.C., 1982—. Nat. Def. Fgn. Language fellow, Columbia U., 1967. Mem. Assn. of Bar of City of N.Y. (labor and employment law com. 1980-83, 86-89, legal and edn. and admission to bar com. 1984-85), N.Y. State Bar Assn. (exec. com., co-chair practice before N.Y. State Labor Rels. Bd. and Nat. Labor Rels. Bd. com. 1989-93, labor arbitration com. 1983—, entertainment, arts and sports law sect. 1989—). Labor, Pension, profit-sharing, and employee benefits, Entertainment. Office: Spivak Lipton Et Al 1700 Broadway New York NY 10019-5905

**WATERHOUSE, RACHEL L.,** lawyer; b. Orlando, Fla., Oct. 17, 1962; d. Linton S. and Louise J. Waterhouse; m. James M. Sokolowski, May 26, 1984 (div. Nov. 1998); 1 child, Sarah Louise. BA, U. S.C., 1984; JD cum laude, Stetson U., 1988. Bar: Fla. 1988, Tenn. 1989, U.S. Dist. Ct. (mid. dist.) Tenn. 1989, U.S. Dist. Ct. (we. dist.) Tenn. 1994, U.S. Ct. Appeals (6th cir.) 1994, U.S. Supreme Ct. 1994, U.S. Dist. Ct. (ea. dist.) Tenn. 1995. Jud. law clk. hon. Thomas A. Higgins U.S. Dist. Ct., Nashville, 1989-91; atty. King & Ballow, Nashville, 1991-94; asst. atty. gen. Tenn. Atty. Gens. Office, Nashville, 1994-95; asst. U.S. atty. U.S. Dept. Justice, Nashville, 1995—. Co-author: Americans With Disabilities Act, 1994; notes editor Stetson Law Rev., 1987. Stephen ministry Episcopal Ch., Nashville, 1989-91; bd. dirs. Focus, Nashville, 1991-94. Named to Outstanding Young Women of Am., 1988. Mem. ABA, Fla. Bar Assn., Nashville Bar Assn. (various coms.), Lawyers Assn. for Women (various coms.). Avocations: running, reading, hiking. Office: US Attys Office Dept Justice 110 9th Ave S Ste A961 Nashville TN 37203-3870

**WATERMAN, DAVID MOORE,** lawyer; b. San Francisco, July 23, 1947; s. Joseph and Muriel Yvette (Moore) W.; children: Kymberley Anne, Kevin David. BA, U. Ariz., 1970, JD, 1973; postgrad., U. Wash., 1978-80. Bar: Ariz. 1973, U.S. Dist. Ct. Ariz. 1973, U.S. Ct. Appeals (9th cir.) 1973. Assoc. Law Offices of William Berlat, Tucson, 1973-74, Law Offices of David K. Wolfe, Tucson, 1976-78, Rabinovitz, Dix & Rehling, Tucson, 1981-84; ptnr. Dix, Rehling & Waterman, Tucson, 1984-86, Dix & Waterman, Tucson, 1986-91; propr. Law Offices of David M. Waterman, 1991-95; ptnr. Taylor & Assocs., Tucson, 1996-98; pvt. practice Tucson, 1998—; adj. prof. bus. law U. Puget Sound, Tacoma, Wash., 1978-80; instr. Highline C.C., Midway, Wash., 1978-79, U. Phoenix, 1992-93; staff assoc. Office of Atty. Gen., Seattle, 1978. Mem. ABA, ATLA, Ariz. Assn. Lawyers for Injured Workers, So. Ariz. Workers' Compensation Applicant's Assn. (pres. 1986-88), State Bar Ariz. Worker's Compensation (co-chair sect. 1985), Am. Soc. Law and Medicine. Workers' compensation, Personal injury. Office: 900 E River Rd Ste 204 Tucson AZ 85718-5675

**WATERMAN, WILLIAM, JR.,** lawyer; b. Chgo., July 17, 1937. AB, Harvard U., 1959, LLB, 1962. Bar: Ill. 1962, N.Y. 1966, U.S. Ct. Dist. Ct. (so. and ea. dists.) 1968, U.S. Ct. Appeals (2nd cir.) 1975, U.S. Supreme Ct. 1976. Legal advisor Ministry Fin. No. Nigeria, Kaduna, 1963; asst. lectr. U. Lagos, Nigeria, 1963-64; assoc. Spear and Hill, N.Y.C., 1965-68; pvt. practice N.Y.C., 1969—. Co-author: Immigration Law and Defense, 1977, 4th rev. edit. 1986; contbr. articles to profl. jours. Mem. Am. Immigration Lawyers Assn., Nat. Lawyers Guild, N.Y. State Bar Assn., Assn. of Bar of City of N.Y. Immigration, naturalization, and customs, Family and matrimonial, General corporate. Address: 305 Broadway Fl 7 New York NY 10007-1109

**WATERS, H. FRANKLIN,** federal judge; b. Hackett, Ark., July 20, 1932; s. William A. and Wilma W.; m. Janie C. Waters, May 31, 1958; children—Carolyn Denise, Melanie Jane, Melissa Ann. B.S., U. Ark., 1955; LL.B., St. Louis U., 1964. Engr., atty. Ralston-Purina Co., St. Louis, 1958-66; ptnr. Crouch, Blair, Cypert & Waters, 1967-81; judge U.S. Dist. Ct. (we. dist.) Ark., from 1981, chief judge, sr. judge, 1997—. Former bd. dirs. Springdale Schs.; former bd. govs. Washington Regional Med. Ctr. Mem. ABA, Ark. Bar Assn., Springdale C. of C. (past bd. dirs.). Office: US Dist Ct PO Box 1908 Fayetteville AR 72702-1908

**WATERS, LAUGHLIN EDWARD,** federal judge; b. L.A., Aug. 16, 1914; s. Frank J. and Ida (Bauman) W.; m. Voula Davanis, Aug. 22, 1953; children: Laughlin Edward, Maura Kathleen, Deirdre Mary, Megan Ann, Eileen Brigid. A.B., UCLA, 1939; J.D., U. So. Calif., 1946. Bar: Calif. 1946. Dep. atty. gen. Calif., Los Angeles, 1946-47; individual practice law Los Angeles, 1947-53; sr. ptnr. Nossaman, Waters, Krueger & Marsh, 1961-76; U.S. atty. So. Dist. Calif., 1953-61; judge U.S. Dist. Ct. (cen. dist.) Calif., 1976—, now sr. judge; cons. U.S. Dept. State in London, 1970; mem. U.S. Del. to Conf. Environ. Problems in Prague, 1971, White House Conf. on Aging, 1970-71; sr. dist. judge rep. Jud. Coun.; judge Atty Gen.'s Adv. Inst. Mem. Calif. Legislature, 1946-53; vice chmn. Rep. State Ctrl. Com., 1950-51, chmn., 1952-53; bd. dirs. Legal Aid Found., 1954-60; past pres. Cath. Big Brothers. Served as capt. U.S. Army, 1942-46. Decorated Bronze Star with oak leaf cluster, Purple Heart with oak leaf cluster, Combat Inf. badge. Fellow Am. Bar Found., Am. Coll. Trial Lawyers; mem. ABA (chmn. com. on housing and urban devel. 1977-79), Fed. Bar Assn. (founder, past pres.), L.A. County Bar Assn., Am. Judicature Soc., Assn. Bus. Trial Lawyers, U. So. Calif., UCLA Law Assn., Am. Legion , U. So. Calif. Legion Lex, Order Blue Shield, Town Hall, Polish Order Merit Cross with Swords, Hon. Citizen of Chambois, Trun, France, 10th Polish Dragoons (hon.), Soc. Friendly Sons St. Patrick (past pres., Medallion of Merit award), Knights of Malta, Anchor Club, Calif. Club, L.A. Club (past pres.). Roman Catholic. Office: US Dist Ct 255 E Temple St Los Angeles CA 90012-3334

**WATERS, MICHAEL D.,** lawyer, educator; b. Cullman, Ala., Apr. 7, 1950; s. Verlou E. and Mary Anna Waters; m. Julia Bumeds, July 27, 1973 (div. Nov. 1980); m. Melinda Mitchell, May 29, 1982; children: David, Mitchell, Laura. BA, Duke U., 1972; MA, Oxford (Eng.) U., 1975, Oxford (Eng.) U., 1975; JD, U. Ala., 1977. Assoc. Bradley, Arauf, Rose & Wite, Birmingham, Ala., 1977-78; legal advisor Gov. of Ala., Montgomery, 1979-80; assoc. Miller Hamilton Snider & Odom, Mobile, Ala., 1980-82, ptnr., 1982-87; ptnr. Miller Hamilton Snider & Odom, Montgomery, Ala., 1987-97, Balch & bingham, Montgomery, 1997—; chmn. Ala. Bd. Bar Exam., Montgomery, 1991-94. Author: Proxy Regulation, 1992, supplement, 1993. Trustee Farrah Law Sch., U. Ala., Tuscaloosa, 1992—. Banking, Securities, General corporate. Home: 3261 Lancaster Ln Montgomery AL 36106-2634 Office: Balch & Bingham LLP 2 Dexter Ave Montgomery AL 36104-3574

**WATHEN, DANIEL EVERETT,** state supreme court chief justice; b. Easton, Maine, Nov. 4, 1939; s. Joseph Jackson and Wilda Persis (Dow) W.; m. Judith Carol Foren, July 14, 1960; children: Julanne Carol, Daniel Arthur. AB, Ricker Coll., 1962; JD, U. Maine, 1965; LLM (hon.), U. Va. Law Sch., 1988. Bar: Maine 1965. Atty. Wathen & Wathen, Augusta, Maine, 1965-77; trial judge Superior Ct. Maine, Augusta, 1977-81; appellate judge Supreme Jud. Ct. Maine, Augusta, 1981-92; state chief justice Supreme Jud. Ct. Maine, 1992—.

**WATKINS, CHARLES MORGAN,** lawyer; b. Newport News, Va., Sept. 12, 1954; s. Walter Edmond and Joanne Kathryn (Halla) W.; m. Margie Elizabeth Valentine, July 16, 1983; children: Kathryn Grace, Mark Emerson, James Morgan. AB, Franklin & Marshall Coll., 1976; JD, Dickinson Sch. of Law, 1981. Bar: D.C. 1981, U.S. Ct. Claims 1983, U.S.Ct. Appeals (Fed. cir.) 1987, U.S. Tax Ct. 1987. Atty. office of chief counsel IRS, Washington, 1981-85; mem. Webster, Chamberlain & Bean, Washington, 1986—; instr. in tax law, Ch. Law and Tax Report; ruling elder McLean Presbyn. Ch. Author: Nondiscrimination Rules for Employee Benefit Plans, 1988, (with others) Issues for Exempt Organizations: A Guide for State Associations, 1987; contbr. articles to profl. jours. Mem. ABA, Christian Legal Soc., Christian Mgmt. Assn. Republican. Presbyterian. Avocations: camping, canoeing, hiking, tennis. Non-profit and tax-exempt organizations, Pension, profit-sharing, and employee benefits, Taxation, general. Office: Webster Chamberlain & Bean Ste 1000 1747 Pennsylvania Ave NW Washington DC 20006-4693 *Churches and other religious organizations must carry out their worship and other charitable work in a manner that is morally and ethically correct, wise in its accumulation and distribution of resources, and sensitive to the true needs of their beneficiaries.*

**WATKINS, SUSAN GAIL,** lawyer; b. Independence, Mo., May 17, 1962; d. Floyd L. and Judy G. (Bell) W.; m. Richard L. Davis, Jr., Jan. 10, 1992; children: Eva, Andrea, Grant, Kyle. BA, Graceland Coll., 1983; JD, U. Mo., 1986. Bar: Mo. 1986, U.S. Dist. Ct. (we. dist.) Mo. 1986, U.S. Ct.

Appeals 1990. Assoc. Les D. Wight, P.C., Independence, 1986-87; ptnr. Snoke & Watkins, Independence, 1987-90, Watkins Law Offices, 1990—; asst. prosecuting atty. Jackson County, Mo., 1991-94; instr. Draughon Bus. Coll., Independence, 1987-90; exec. dir. Independence Youth Ct., 1988—; judge Independence Mcpl. Ct., 1995—. Bd. dirs. Music Arts Inst., Stone Ch. Presch.; mem. Independence Jr. Svc. League. Mem. ABA, ATLA, Mo. Assn. Trial Attys., Assn. Women Lawyers, Mo. Assn. Criminal Def. Lawyers, East Jackson County Bar Assn. (bd. dirs.), Kansas City Bar Assn. (young lawyers sect.), Mo. Mcpl. Judges Assn., Ednl. Adv. Coun., L.E.A.D. Independence C. of C., Phi Alpha Delta. Mem. Reorganized Ch. of Jesus Christ of Latter-day Saints. Avocations: swimming, sailing, skiing, scuba diving, music. Family and matrimonial, Landlord-tenant, General practice. Office: Watkins Law Offices 221 W Lexington Ave Ste 250 Independence MO 64050-3736

**WATSON, CRAIG STERLING,** lawyer; b. Detroit, Mar. 19, 1958; s. George Ray and Joan Fay (Steele) W. BA, U. New Orleans, 1981; JD, La. State U., 1984. Bar: La. 1984, Tex. 1985, U.S. Dist. Ct. (mid. dist.) La. 1984, U.S. Dist. Ct. (ea. dist.) La. 1985, U.S. Dist. Ct. (so. dist.) Tex. 1986, U.S. Dist. Ct. (we. dist.) La. 1990, U.S. Ct. Appeals (5th cir.) 1987, U.S. Ct. Appeals (4th cir.) 1988. Assoc. Cave and McKay, Baton Rouge, 1984-93, McKay & Watson, Baton Rouge, 1993-96; pvt. practice Baton Rouge, 1997—. Campaign vol. Edwin Edwards for Gov. La., 1983, Bryan Bush for Dist. Atty. Baton Rouge, 1985, John Breaux for U.S. Senate, 1986; dep. campaign coord. Tauzin for Gov. With USCG 1975-79, Res. ret. Mem. ABA, La. Bar Assn., Baton Rouge Bar Assn. (mem. fed. bar liaison com 1984—), Tex. Bar Assn., Assn. Trial Lawyers Am., La. Trial Lawyers Assn. Democrat. Lutheran. Avocations: marathon running, sports, coin collecting. Admiralty, Federal civil litigation, Personal injury. Office: Cave & McKay 3909 Plaza Tower Dr Baton Rouge LA 70816-4356

**WATSON, DONALD NATHANIEL,** lawyer; b. Elberton, Ga., May 1, 1953; s. Thomas Clark and Alice Roberta (Blackwell) W.; m. Paula Jean Lockett, June 16, 1984; children: Alyson, Nathaniel, Cimone. BA, Yale U., 1975; JD, U. Miami, 1980. Bar: Fla., U.S. Dist. Ct. (so. dist.) Fla., U.S. Ct. Appeals (11th cir.). Asst. state atty. Legal Svcs. Greater Miami, Inc., Fla., 1979-80, Legal Aid Svc. Broward County, Fla., 1980-84, Broward County State Atty.'s Office, Fla., 1984-88; ptnr. Gary, Williams, Parenti, Finney, Lewis, McManus, Watson & Sperando, Stuart, 1988—. Bd. dirs. Share Ctrl. Fla., 1996-97; trustee St. Mark Missionary Bapt. Ch., Ft. Pierce, Fla., 1996-97. Mem. Nat. Bar Assn., ABA, ATLA, T.J. Reddick Bar Assn., Martin County Bar Assn., Acad. Fla. Trial Lawyers, Fla. Bar Assn. (grievance com. 1994-95), Omi Psi Phi. Democrat. Avocations: bowling, skating, swimming. Home: 1556 SE Faculty Ct Port Saint Lucie FL 34952-7603 Office: Gary Williams Parenti Finney Lewis McManus Watson & Sperando 221 SE Osceola St Ste 300 Stuart FL 34994-2289

**WATSON, FORREST ALBERT, JR.,** lawyer, bank executive; b. Atlanta, May 7, 1951; s. Forrest Albert and Virginia Doris (Ritch) W.; m. Marlys Wise, Oct. 16, 1982; children: Annaliese Marie Elizabeth, Forrest Albert Watson III. AB, Emory U., 1973; JD, U. Ga., 1975; postgrad., Mercer U., 1979-80. Bar: Ga. 1975, U.S. Dist. Ct. (mid. dist.) Ga. 1976, U.S. Tax Ct. 1976, U.S. Ct. Appeals (5th cir.) 1977, U.S. Supreme Ct. 1980; cert. data processor; CFP. Assoc. Banks, Smith & Lambdin, Barnesville, Ga., 1976-78; ptnr. Watson & Lindsey, Barnesville, 1978-82; v.p., gen. counsel United Bank Corp., Barnesville, 1981-91, chief ops. officer, 1990—, exec. v.p., gen. counsel, 1991—, mem., bd. dirs., exec. v.p., 1991; pres. United Bank Mortgage; exec. v.p., sr. trust officer United Bank, Griffin, Ga., 1995—; pres. United Bank Mortgage, 1993-95; gen. counsel Lamar State Bank, Barnesville, 1976-84; judge Small Claims Ct., Lamar County, Ga., 1976, City Ct. of Milner, Ga., 1977; lectr. IBM, 1984-85; atty. City of Meansville, Ga., 1976, City of Milner, 1977; bd. dirs. United Bank Corp. Assoc. editor Ga. Jour. Internat. Law, 1975. Gen. counsel Lamar County Devel. Authority, Barnesville, 1977; bd. dirs. Legaline Inc., Atlanta, 1983-85. Mem. ABA, Ga. Bar Assn., Cir. Ct. Bar Assn., Griffin Cir. Bar Assn., Ga. Rural Health Assn. (trustee 1981-82), S.E. Bank Card Assn. (operating com. 1986-91), Assn. Cert. Fin. Planners, Assn. Inst. Cert. Computer Profls., Internat. Assn. Fin. Planners. Methodist. Avocations: art, antiques, travel. Banking. Home: PO Box 347 Zebulon GA 30295-0347 Office: United Bank Corp PO Box 1337 110 Griffin St Zebulon GA 30295

**WATSON, GLENN ROBERT,** lawyer; b. Okla., May 2, 1917; s. Albert Thomas and Ethel (Riddle) W.; m. Dorothy Ann Mosiman, Feb. 25, 1945; 1 dau., Carol Ann. Student, East Cen. State U., Okla., 1933-36; LL.B., Okla. U., 1939. Bar: Okla. 1939, Calif. 1946. Pvt. practice law Okla., 1939-41; ptnr., pres. Richards, Watson & Gershon, Los Angeles, 1946—; city atty. Industry, Calif., 1958-65, 78-83, Commerce, Calif., 1960-61, Cerritos, Calif., 1956-64, Victorville, Calif., 1962-63, Carson, Calif., 1968—, Rosemead, Calif., 1960-76, Seal Beach, Calif., 1972-78, South El Monte, Calif., 1976-78, Avalon, Calif., 1976-80, Artesia, Calif., 1976-97. Served with USNR, 1942-46. Mem. ABA, Los Angeles County Bar Assn., Am. Judicature Soc., Lawyers Club of Los Angeles (past pres.), Los Angeles World Affairs Council, La Canada C. of C. (past pres.), Order of Coif, Phi Delta Phi, Delta Chi. Oil, gas, and mineral, Real property, Municipal (including bonds). Home: 800 W 1st St Los Angeles CA 90012-2412 Office: Richards Watson & Gershon 333 S Hope St Los Angeles CA 90071-1406

**WATSON, JACK CROZIER,** retired state supreme court justice; b. Jonesville, La., Sept. 17, 1928; s. Jesse Crozier and Gladys Lucille (Talbot) W.; m. Henrietta Sue Carter, Dec. 26, 1958; children: Carter Crozier (dec.), Wells Talbot. BA, U. Southwestern La., 1949; JD, La. State U., 1956; completed with honor, Appellate Judges Seminar, N.Y. U., 1974, Sr. Appellate Judges Seminar, 1980. Bar: La. 1956. Atty. King, Anderson & Swift, Lake Charles, La., 1956-58; prosecutor City of Lake Charles, 1960; asst. dist. atty. Calcasieu Parish, La., 1961-64; ptnr. Watson & Watson, Lake Charles, 1961-64; judge 14th Jud. Dist., La., 1964-72; judge ad hoc Ct. Appeals, 1st Circuit, Baton Rouge, 1972-73; judge Ct. Appeals, 3rd Circuit, Lake Charles, 1973-79; assoc. justice La. Supreme Ct., New Orleans, 1979-96, ret., 1996; faculty advisor Nat. Coll. State Judiciary, Reno, 1970, 73; adj. prof. law summer sch. program in Greece, Tulane U., 1988-97; adj. prof. law So. U., Baton Rouge, 1998-99; del. NEH Seminar, 1976; La. del to Internat. Conf. Appellate Magistrates, The Philippines, 1977; mem. La. Jud. Coun., 1986-92. 1st lt. USAF, 1950-54. Mem. ABA, La. Bar Assn., S.W. La. Bar Assn. (pres. 1973), Law Inst. State of La., La. Coun. Juvenile Ct. Judges (pres. 1969-70), Am. Judicature Soc., S.W. La. Camellia Soc. (pres. 1973-74), Am. Legion (post comdr. 1963), Lake Charles Yacht Club (commodore 1974), Blue Key, Sigma Alpha Epsilon, Phi Delta Phi, Pi Kappa Delta. Democrat. Baptist. Home: 868 Del Mar Downs Rd Solana Beach CA 92075-2312

**WATSON, JAMES LOPEZ,** federal judge; b. N.Y.C., May 21, 1922; s. James S. and Violet (Lopez) W.; m. D'Jaris Hinton Watson, July 14, 1956 (dec. Nov. 1989); children: Norman, Karen, Kris. B.A. in Govt, N.Y. U., 1947; LL.B., Bklyn. Law Sch., 1951. Bar: N.Y. bar 1951. Mem. N.Y. Senate from 21st Senatorial Dist., 1954-63; judge Civil Ct. N.Y., 1964-66; acting judge N.Y. State Supreme Ct., 1965; judge U.S. Customs Ct., 1966-80; judge U.S. Ct. Internat. Trade, N.Y., 1980—, now sr. judge. Bd. dirs. N.Y.C. Police Athletic League. Served with inf. AUS, World War II, ETO. Decorated Purple Heart, Combat Inf. badge. Mem. ABA, N.Y. State Bar Assn., Fed. Bar Council, World Peace Through Law. Home: 676 Riverside Dr New York NY 10031-5529 Office: US Ct Internat Trade 1 Federal Plz New York NY 10278-0001

**WATSON, JOHN MICHAEL,** lawyer; b. Kansas City, Tex., May 9, 1956; s. Jarvis Schedey and Edwina Louise Watson; m. Margaret Marie Blackshear; children: Maggie, John. BA, Washington and Lee U., 1979; JD, U. Houston, 1981. Bar: Tex. 1982, U.S. Dist. Ct. (so., no., ea. and we. dists.) Tex. 1994. Counsel Union Bank Houston, 1982-85; asst. gen. counsel, v.p. Allied Bank Tex., Houston, 1985-88; asst. gen. counsel, sr. v.p. First Interstate Bank Tex., N.A., Houston, 1988-96; sr. counsel, v.p. Wells Fargo Bank, Houston, 1996—; dir. The Agnes Carter Helms Sch., Camden, Tex., 1986-89, Supreme Ct. Bd. Disciplinary Appeals, Houston, 1996—. Mem. Tex. Assn. Bank Counsel (dir. 1989-92). Republican. Methodist. Banking, Contracts commercial, State civil litigation.

**WATSON, JOHN W.,** lawyer; b. Roanoke, Va., Jan. 27, 1945; s. Manly Arthur and Linda Faye (Givens) W.; m. Susan Rebecca Meredith, May 29, 1965; children: Nicholas M., Emily W. BA, Vanderbilt U., 1967; JD, U. Conn., 1979. Bar: Conn. 1979, U.S. Dist. Ct. Conn. 1979, Mass. 1983. Pub. defender Office of Pub. Defender, Hartford, Conn., 1980-81, New Haven, Conn., 1981-94, Hartford, Conn., 1994—. Pres. local bd. ACLU, New Haven, Conn., 1978-85; bd. dirs. Unitarian Soc. New Haven, Hamden, Conn., 1987— (past pres.). With U.S. Army, 1970-71. Mem. Conn. Bar Assn., Nat. Legal Aid & Defenders Orgn., Conn. Trial Lawyers Assn. Unitarian Universalist. Avocations: acting, travel, bicycling. Office: Office Pub Defender 101 Lafayette St Hartford CT 06106-1509

**WATSON, KIPP ELLIOTT,** lawyer; b. L.A., Oct. 30, 1950; s. Benjamin And Irene Cohen; m. Emily Strauss; 1 child, Lisa Jo. BA, NYU, 1977; JD, Benjamin N. Cardozo Sch. Law, 1980. Bar: N.Y. Pvt. practice N.Y.C., 1984-98; of counsel Mark B. Stumer & Assocs., N.Y.C., 1998—. Roothbert fellow, N.Y.C., 1979. Mem. N.Y.State Bar Assn. (civil rights com.), Nat. Employment Lawyers Assn. N.Y. (bd. dirs., newsletter editor), Dem. Club (pres. 1993). Avocations: computer programming, chess, wheelchair basketball-forward for N.Y. Rollin' Knicks. Civil rights, Labor, Personal injury. Office: Mark B Stumer & Assocs 101 5th Ave Rm 10E New York NY 10003-1008

**WATSON, LAUREL ANNE,** lawyer; b. San Diego, Dec. 18, 1956; d. John and Nila (Landell) W. BA, U. Calif. Santa Barbara, 1978; JD, S.W. Univ. L.A., 1981; LLM in Tax., U. Pacific, 1996; LLM in Internat. Law, Golden Gate U., 1999. Mgr. contracts Raytheon Electronics, Santa Barbara, 1981-86, Tracor Inc., Santa Barbara, 1986-88, GM Hughes Electronics, Santa Barbara, 1988-91; legal asst. State of Calif., Sacramento, 1992-93; CEO Watson Tech. Group, Woodside, Calif., 1994—. Mem. Churchill Club. Republican. Presbyterian. Avocations: triathlon, skiing, kayaking, sailing, golf.

**WATSON, MARK HENRY,** lawyer, business writer; b. Camden, N.J., Apr. 12, 1938; s. Donald Robert and Elizabeth Rozanne (Rowan) W.; m. Patricia A. Olsen, Aug. 27, 1960 (dec.); 1 son, Mark; m. 2d, Suzanne M. Young, Dec. 31, 1966; children—Matthew, Betsy, Daniel, William, Michael. B.A. with honors, Rutgers U., 1959, J.D., 1964; postgrad. U.Del., 1959-61. Bar: N.J. 1965. Assoc., Brown, Connery, Kulp & Wille, Camden, N.J., 1966-67; sole practice, Camden, 1967-69, Haddonfield, N.J., 1980—; owner Internat. Commerce Svcs., Audubon, N.J., 1993—; house counsel S. Jersey Realty Abstract Co., Camden, 1969-70, N.Y.-N.J. div. Kaufman & Broad Homes, 1970-71; pres. C.F. Seabrook (N.J.) Co., 1971-76, Koster Nursery, Inc., 1976-80; bus. advisor, writer; arbitrator Am. Arbitration Assn., 1972—; adj. prof. bus. law Camden County Coll., Blackwood, N.J., 1979-80. Del. White House Conf. on Small Bus., 1980; organizer N.J. Small Bus. Unity Council; chmn. N.J. Small Bus. Devel. Council. Adv. Bd., 1988. Named Small Bus. Media Adv. of Yr., U.S. Small Bus. Adminstrn., 1981, 82. Mem. ABA, N.J. Bar Assn., Camden County Bar Assn. Author: Succeeding in Your Own Business: Do It Right the First Time, 1982; contbr. articles on small bus. to newspapers. Contracts commercial, General corporate. Home: 310 Copley Rd Haddonfield NJ 08033-3651 Office: 523 S White Horse Pike Audubon NJ 08106-1312

**WATSON, NORMA H.,** editor. Rsch. asst. Nat. Opinion Rsch. Ctr., Chgo., 1953-58, asst. study dir., 1958-59; cons. Health Ins. Plan Greater N.Y., 1960-61; pub. info. writer Environ. Def. Fund, N.Y.C., 1974-77, editor, 1977-96, sr. editor, 1996—. Office: Environ Def Fund Letter 257 Park Ave S New York NY 10010-7304

**WATSON, PHIL,** lawyer; b. Des Moines, June 19, 1941; s. Vinton C. and Margaret L. Watson; m. Judith Ann Watson, Aug. 22, 1965; children: Laura A., Phil. BS in Econs., Simpson Coll., Indianola, Iowa, 1964; JD, Drake U., 1967. Bar: Iowa 1967. Atty. Bertroche-Watson, Des Moines, 1967-75; sole practitioner Des Moines, 1975—; pres. Iowa Credit Assn., Des Moines, 1989, Indianola Devel. Co., 1993. Bd. dirs. Nat. Balloon Classic, Indianola, 1986-90. Mem. Iowa State Bar Assn., Polk County Bar Assn. Republican. Avocation: bicycling. Consumer commercial, Probate, Real property. Home: 203 S Kenwood Blvd Indianola IA 50125-2111 Office: 535 E Army Post Rd Des Moines IA 50315-5930

**WATSON, REBECCA WUNDER,** lawyer; b. Chgo., Feb. 17, 1952; d. David Hart and Shirley May (Dahlin) Wunder; m. Keith C. Thomson, Oct. 6, 1979 (div. Dec. 1989); m. Gregory B. Watson, Jan. 20, 1996. BA, U. Denver, 1974, MA in LS, 1975, JD, 1978. Bar: Wyo. 1978, Colo. 1989, D.C. 1995, Mont. 1995. Law clk. U.S. Dist. Ct. for Dist. Wyo., Cheyenne, 1978-80; assoc., then ptnr. Burgess & Davis, Sheridan, Wyo., 1980-88; pvt. practice, Denver, 1988-90; asst. gen. counsel for energy policy Dept. Energy, Washington, 1990-93; of counsel Crowell & Moring, Washington, 1993-95; ptnr. Gough Shanahan Johnson & Waterman, Helena, Mont., 1995—. Contbr. author: ABA Natural Resource Law Handbook, 1993; contbr. articles to law jours. Mem. ABA (chmn. natural resource com. sect. adminstrv. law 1994-97, chmn. pub. lands com. sect. natural resources, energy and environ. law 1997—), Wyo. Bar Assn., Mont. Bar Assn., Phi Beta Kappa. Republican. Avocations: cooking, reading, travel, hunting. Natural resources, Environmental, Legislative. Home: Little Blackfoot River Rch 560 Dana Ln Garrison MT 59731-9741 Office: Gough Shanahan Et Al 33 S Last Chance Gulch St Helena MT 59601-4132

**WATSON, RICHARD PRATHER,** lawyer, small business consultant; b. Westfield, Ill., Apr. 18, 1938; s. Jesse L and Ardie E. (Prather) W.; m. Rena Jo Stegner, Feb. 14, 1960; children: Richard Gregg, Steven T., Rachel Marie. BS in Acctg., Eastern Ill. U., Charleston, 1950; MS, Butler U., 1953; JD, Ind. U., 1957; cert. acctg., Fin. Sch. U.S.A.; grad., Gen. Motors Inst. Jr. Exec. Tng. Program. Bar: Ind. 1957, U.S. Dist. Ct. (so. dist.) Ind. 1957, U.S. Ct. Appeals (7th cir.) 1957, U.S. Ct. of Claims 1963. Evaluator dept. safety responsiblity State of Ill., Springfield, 1950; instr. acctg. U.S. Army Fin. Ctr., Ft. Harrison, Ind., 1953; dept. foreman Delco-Remy div. Gen. Motors Co., Anderson, Ind., 1953-57; adminstrv. asst. Ind. Toll Rd. Commn., Indpls., 1954-57; chief hearing judge Pub. Service Commn. Ind., Indpls., 1958-62; corp. counsel Ind. Sec. of State, Indpls., 1962-64; ptnr. Carvey, Watson & McNevin, Indpls.; judge pro tem Marion County Superior Ct., 1971-73, Marion Criminal Ct., 1975, Marion Mcpl. Ct., 1976-78; sr. assoc. Watson & Rochford, Indpls.; pvt. practice cons. to small bus. Indpls., 1981-87; pvt. practice Watson & Leatherbury, Indpls., 1987—; small business and corp. owner, chief exec. officer Watson Mgmt. Corp., Watson Shopping Ctr., The Village Inn, Grandma's Italian Kitchen, Italian/Italian, Inc.; former owner State House Deli, State House Inn, Earline's Cocktail Lounge; cons. to numerous cos.; lectr. in fin. and small bus. Chmn. civilian bd. Indpls. Police Motorcycle Drill Team; mem. Indpls. Mus. Art; bd. dirs. Indpls. Vets. Day Council, Northeastwood Football Assn., Avocat Nat. La Societte des 40 Hommes et 8 Chevaux; chmn., bd. dirs. Avalon Hills Civic Assn. Mem. ABA, Ind. State Bar Assn., Indpls. Bar Assn., Am. Judicature Soc., Assn. Trial Lawyers Am., Ind. Trial Lawyers Assn., Am. Assn. Hosp. Attys., Ind. Assn. Hosp. Attys., Am. Legion, Ind. U. Alumni Assn., Nat. C. of C., Fraternal Order of Police, Nat. Boxcar Assn. Republican. Methodist. Clubs: Morse-Indpls. Yacht (past commodore); Indpls. Athletic, Athenaeum Turners, Ind. U. Men's; Ind. Soc. (Chgo.). Avocations: public speaking, fishing, hunting, drawing and painting, swimming and boating. Consumer commercial, General corporate, General practice. Office: Watson & Leatherbury PO Box 501914 8888 Keystone Xing Indianapolis IN 46250

**WATSON, ROBERT FRANCIS,** lawyer; b. Houston, Jan. 9, 1936; s. Louis Leon and Lora Elizabeth (Hodges) W.; m. Marietta Kiser, Nov. 24, 1961; children: Julia, Melissa, Rebecca. BA, Vanderbilt U., 1957; JD, U. Denver, 1959. Bar: Colo. 1959, U.S. Dist. Ct. (no. dist.) Tex. 1967, U.S. Supreme Ct. 1968, Tex. 1973, U.S. Ct. Appeals (5th cir.) 1973, U.S. Dist. Ct. (so. dist.) Tex. 1980, U.S. Ct. Appeals (11th cir.) 1981. Law clk. U.S. Dist. Ct. Colo., 1960-61; trial atty. SEC, Denver, 1961-67; asst. regional adminstr. SEC, Ft. Worth, 1967-72, regional adminstr., 1972-75; ptnr. Law, Snakard & Gambill, P.C., Ft. Worth, 1975-98, of counsel, 1998—; counsel City of Ft. Worth Police Investigation Commn., 1975; spl. counsel Office Atty. Gen. State Ariz., 1977-78. Contbr. articles to profl. jours. Mem. Ft. Worth Crime Commn., 1987-93; pres. bd. trustees Trinity Valley Sch., Ft. Worth; adv. dir., pres. Lena Pope Home for Dependent and Neglected Children, Ft. Worth. Honoree 27th Ann. Rocky Mountain State-Fed.-Provincial Securities Conf. Mem. ABA, FBA, State Bar Tex., Colo. Bar Assn. (life fellow), Tex. Bar Found., Tex. Bus. Law Found. (bd. dirs. 1988-93), Tarrant County Bar Assn., Tarrant County Bar Found., U. Denver Law Sch. Alumni Coun., Coll. of State Bar Tex., Ft. Worth Club, Shady Oaks Country Club (Ft. Worth), Phi Delta Phi. Republican. Presbyterian. Securities, Federal civil litigation, General corporate. Office: USPA&IRA 4100 S Hulen St Fort Worth TX 76109-4953 also: Law Snakard & Gambill PC 500 Throckmorton St Ste 3200 Fort Worth TX 76102-3819

**WATSON, ROBERT JAMES,** lawyer; b. Oceanside, N.Y., Mar. 30, 1955; s. Ralph Joseph and Mildred Adeline (Knapp) W.; m. Ann M. Goade, May 27, 1988; children: Emily Allyn, Caroline Elisabeth. BA, Biscayne Coll., 1976; JD, U. Fla., 1979. Bar: Fla. 1979, U.S. Dist. Ct. (so. dist.) Fla. 1980, U.S. Dist. Ct. (no. dist.) Fla. 1981, U.S. Dist. Ct. (mid. dist.) Fla. 1982, U.S. Ct. Appeals (11th cir.) 1982. Asst. pub. defender Law Offices of Elton Schwarz, Ft. Pierce, Fla., 1979-81; ptnr. Wilkinson & Watson P.A., Stuart, Fla., 1981-86; pvt. practice Stuart, 1986-90; ptnr. Frierson & Watson, Stuart, 1990—. Mem. Fla. Bar Assn., Nat. Assn. Criminal Def. Lawyers, Acad. Fla. Trial Lawyers, Martin Assn. Criminal Def. Lawyers, Fla. Assn. Criminal Def. Lawyers. Democrat. Roman Catholic. Avocation: golf, running, skiing. Criminal, Personal injury, Civil rights. Home: 9 Emarita Way Stuart FL 34996-6704 Office: Frierson & Watson 3601 SE Ocean Blvd Ste 004 Stuart FL 34996-6737

**WATSON, ROBERTA CASPER,** lawyer; b. Boise, Idaho, July 11, 1949; d. John Blaine and Joyce Lucile (Mercer) C.; m. Robert George Watson, July 22, 1972; 1 child, Rebecca Joyce. BA cum laude, U. Idaho, 1971; JD, Harvard U., 1974. Bar: Mass. 1974, U.S. Dist. Ct. Mass. 1975, U.S. Supreme Ct. 1979, U.S. Ct. Appeals (1st cir.) 1979, U.S. Tax Ct. 1979, Fla. 1985, U.S. Dist. Ct. (mid. dist.) Fla. 1985, U.S. Dist. Ct. (so. dist.) Fla. 1987. Assoc. Peabody & Brown, Boston, 1974-78, Mintz, Levin, Cohn, Ferris, Glovsky & Popeo, Boston, 1978-84; sr. dir. Wolper Ross & Co., Miami, 1983-85; assoc. Trenam, Kemker, Scharf, Barkin, Frye, O'Neill & Mullis, P.A., Tampa, Fla., 1985-87, ptnr., 1988—. Co-author: A Physician's Guide to Professional Corporations; co-editor-in-chief COBRA Adv. Newsletter; contbr. articles to profl. jours. Pres. Performing Arts Ctr. Greater Framingham, Mass., 1983; bd. dirs., Northside Mental Health Ctr., 1987—, pres. 1999—; trustee Unitarian Universalist Found., Clearwater, Fla., 1986—; bd. dirs. dist. 6 Cmty. Health Purchasing Alliance, pers. com. chair, 1998—. Named bd. mem. of yr. Fla. Cmty. Mental Health, 1994. Mem. ABA (chair employee benefit com. sect. taxation 1995-96, chair employee benefits interest group health law sect. 1998—), Fla. West Coast Employee Benefits Coun. (bd. dirs., treas. 1997-98, v.p. 1998—), Harvard Club (bd. dirs. West Coast Fla. chpt.), Tampa Club, Order Ea. Star. Democrat. Avocations: music, metaphysics, Lincoln historian. Pension, profit-sharing, and employee benefits, Health. Home: 124 Adalia Ave Tampa FL 33606-3304 Office: Trenam Kemker et al 2700 Barnett Pla Tampa FL 33602

**WATSON, S.A.,** lawyer, retired judge; b. Hot Springs, Ark., July 11, 1942; s. Sterl A. and Naomi Pauline (Thrasher) W.; m. Wanda Batt, May 2, 1968; children: Angel Watson Brothers, Clinton Jeremy. JD, U. Ala., 1966. Bar: Ala. 1967, U.S. Dist. Ct. Ala. 1968, U.S. Supreme Ct. 1970. Assoc. Humphrey, Lutz & Smith, Huntsville, Ala., 1967-68; asst. dist. atty. 23d Jud. Cir., Huntsville, Ala., 1968-69, chief asst. dist. atty., 1969-72, dist. judge, 1972-74, cir. judge, 1974-87; ptnr. Hornsby, Watson & Meginniss, Huntsville, Ala., 1988—; chair Madison County jud. commn. 23d Jud. Cir., 1978-83; faculty advisor Nat. Jud. Coll., Reno, 1982; spl. judge Ala. Ct. Criminal Appeals, Montgomery, 1983; spl. justice Ala. Supreme Ct., Montgomery, 1996-97; mem. faculty trial advocacy tng. program La. State U. Sch. Law, 1996, 97, 99. Personal injury, General civil litigation. Home: 1929 Cherry Tree Rd Gurley AL 35748-9318 Office: Hornsby Watson and Meginniss 1110 Gleneagles Dr SW Huntsville AL 35801-6404

**WATSON, STEPHEN ALLISON, III,** lawyer; b. Spokane, Wash., Aug. 17, 1957; s. Stephen Allison Jr. and Joan (Sauter) W.; m. Jeanie Faust; children: Angelie, Alyssa, Stephen. BA in Polit. Sci., Northwestern U., 1979; JD, Case We. U., 1982. Bar: Ohio 1983, U.S. Dist. Ct. (no. dist.) Ohio 1983. Counsel, environ. claims mgr. Argonaut Ins. Co., Chgo., 1982-86; mgr. hazardous waste unit Zurich Ins. Co., Schaumburg, Ill., 1989-91; mgr. environ. line bus. Zurich Ins. Co., Schaumburg, 1991-94; program exec., dir. regulatory svcs. Foster Wheeler Environ. Co., Livingston, N.J., 1995—; mng. dir., also bd. dirs. Foster Wheeler Environ. Co. Nigeria Ltd., 1997—; cons. Office Spl. Dep., Chgo., 1995-96; lectr. in field. Contbr. articles to profl. jours. Mem. ABA (natural resource, energy and environ. law sect.), Def. Rsch. Inst. (environ. law com.). Republican. Avocations: golf, photography, sailing. Environmental, Private international, Public international. Office: Foster Wheeler Environ Corp 8 Peach Tree Hill Rd Livingston NJ 07039-5701

**WATSON, THOMAS C.,** lawyer; b. Poplar Bluff, Mo., Feb. 26, 1945; s. William C. and Dorothy E. (Whitson) W.; children: Thomas II, Nathan, Edward, Clay, Luke; m. Sharlene Wonders, Mar. 19, 1994. BS, U. Memphis, 1967, MEd, 1968; JD, Washington U., St. Louis, 1972. Bar: Mo. 1972, D.C. 1973. Assoc. Morgan, Lewis & Bockius, Washington, 1973-78, ptnr., 1978-79; ptnr. Crowell & Moring, Washington, 1979-95, Watson & Renner, 1996—. Avocations: hiking, biking, computers, hunting wild fowl. General corporate, General civil litigation, Toxic tort. Office: Watson & Renner 2000 M St NW Suite 330 Washington DC 20036-3307

**WATSON, THOMAS ROGER,** lawyer; b. Concord, N.H., May 14, 1951; s. Roger Edward and Mary (Hannigan) W. BA in Polit. Sci. cum laude, U. N.H., 1973; JD, Franklin Pierce Law Ctr., 1978. Bar: N.H. 1978, U.S. Dist. Ct. N.H. 1978, U.S. Ct. Appeals (1st cir.) 1978, Maine 1982, U.S. Dist. Ct. Maine 1982, U.S. Supreme Ct. 1986. Ptnr. Tybursky & Watson, Portsmouth, N.H., 1979-86, Tybursky, Watson & Harman, Portsmouth, 1987-88, Taylor, Keane, Blanchard, Lyons & Watson, P.A., Portsmouth, 1988-94, Watson, Lyons, & Bosen, P.A., Portsmouth, 1994—; del. N.H. Constl. Conv., Concord, 1974. Mem. Maritime Heritage Commn., 1986-95, City of Portsmouth Hist. Dist. Commn., 1992, City of Portsmouth Planning Bd., 1992-94; bd. dirs. N.H. Small Bus. Devel. Ctr., 1993-95, N.H. Main St. Ctr., 1998—; mem. adv. bd. Ballet New England, 1997—; bd. advisors N.H. Small Bus. Devel. Ctr., 1992-95. Mem. ABA, Assn. Trial Lawyers Am. (state del. 1996—, chair-elect 1997-98, chair 1998-99, exec. com. 1998—, Outstanding State Del. 1997), N.H. Bar Assn. (bd. govs. 1985-90), N.H. Trial Lawyers Assn. (bd. govs. 1989—, sec. 1982-92, treas. 1993-94, pres. elect 1994-95, pres. 1995-96, recipient Pres.'s award 1993, 97), Rockingham County Bar Assn., Franklin Pierce Law Ctr. Alumni Assn. (pres. 1985-86), N.H. Bar Found. (bd. govs. 1987-90), Greater Portmouth C. of C. (bd. dirs. 1988-92, chmn. 1990-92), Portsmouth Hist. Soc. (trustee 1994—, pres. 1995-97), Portsmouth Atheneum (proprietor 1991—). General civil litigation, Family and matrimonial, Personal injury. Office: Watson Lyons & Bosen PA PO Box 469 Portsmouth NH 03802-0469

**WATSON, WELLS,** lawyer; b. Lake Charles, La., Apr. 11, 1963; s. Jack Crozier and Sue (Carter) W. BA, U. Miss., 1987; JD cum laude, Tulane U., 1990. Bar: La. 1990. Law clk. for Chief Judge Fred Heebe U.S. Dist. Ct., New Orleans, 1990-91; lawyer Baggett, McCall, Burgess & Watson, Lake Charles, La., 1991—. Mem. La. Trial Lawyers Assn. (chmn. new lawyers, bd. govs. 1994), Am. Trial Lawyers (La. gov. of new lawyers). Personal injury, Admiralty, Toxic tort. Home: 6916 Shadow Ln Lake Charles LA 70605-9009 Office: Baggett McCall Burgess & Watson 3006 Country Club Rd Lake Charles LA 70605-5920

**WATSON-WESLEY, DENISE J.,** lawyer; b. Chgo., June 24, 1946; d. Moses Ferguson and Ozella Gant; m. Stephen J. Wesley, June 4, 1979 (div. Jan. 1993); m. Logan Watson III; children: Logan IV, DeeNa Watson Walker. BS in Bus. Edn., DePaul U., 1976; JD, St. Louis U., 1984. Legal sec. various law firms, Chgo., 1965-76; tchr. Robert Morris Coll., Chgo., 1965-79, Ritter N.J. St. Louis C.C., 1979-84; pub. defender Pub. Defandant Office, 1985-87; projector Cir. Atty. Office, 1988-89; law clk. 22nd Jud. Cir., 1989-95; city atty. Office of Comptr., 1989-95; pvt. practice law White & Watson, L.C., 1995—. Mem. Mound City Bar. Avocations: aerobics, Evangelization. E-mail: djwatson@cswbell.net. General corporate, Entertainment, Finance. Office: White & Watson LC 500 Washington Ave Ste 1150 Saint Louis MO 63101-1236

**WATT, JOSEPH MICHAEL,** state supreme court justice; b. Austin, Tex., Mar. 8, 1947. BA in History, Tex. Tech U., 1969; JD, U. Tex., 1972. Bar:

Tex. 1972, Okla. 1974. Pvt. practice, Altus, Okla., 1972-85; judge Dist. Trial Ct., 1985-91; gen. counsel to gov. State of Okla., Oklahoma City, 1991-92; justice Okla Supreme Ct., Okahoma City, 1992—. Fax: 405-521-6982. Office: Okla State Supreme Ct State Capitol Rm 240 Oklahoma City OK 73105

**WATTERS, RICHARD DONALD,** lawyer; b. Midland, Mich., May 3, 1951; s. Donald Wayne and Madalyn Bird (Tinetti) W.; m. Ann Elizabeth Hutchison, May 24, 1975; children: Kelly E., Nathan Paul. BS in Indsl. Engring., Bradley U., 1973; JD cum laude, St. Louis U., 1976. BAr: Mo. 1976, U.S. Dist. Ct. (we. and ea. dists.) Mo. 1976, Ill. 1977, U.S. Ct. Appeals (8th cir.) 1981. Assoc. Lashly & Baer, P.C., St. Louis, 1976-81, ptnr., 1981—, dept. chmn., 1989—; instr. St. Louis U. Sch. Law, 1977-79. Chmn., pres. United Cerebral Palsy Assn. St. Louis, 1985-88; bd. dirs. Canterbury Enterprises, sheltered workshop, St. Louis, 1988-94, participant Leadershp St. Louis, 1988-89; ethics com. DePaul Health Ctr., 1990—. Mem. Am. Health Lawyers Assn., Mo. Soc. Hosp. Attys. (bd. dirs. 1988-94, pres. 1990-91), Mo. Bar Assn. (vice chmn. health and hosp. com. 1988-90), Bar Assn. Metro. St. Louis (co-chmn. med.-legal com.). Republican. Avocation: sailing. Health, Administrative and regulatory, General corporate. Office: Lashly & Baer PC 714 Locust St Saint Louis MO 63101-1699

**WATTS, C. ALLEN,** lawyer; b. Winter Haven, Fla., Oct. 7, 1946; s. Charles Meredith and Lois Jeanette (Thornhill) W.; m. Joyce Elaine McDeavitt DeLoach, Dec. 29, 1967 (div. Oct. 1980); m. Margaret Jean Morris, Sept. 28, 1982; children: Ashley, Kristin, Kelly, Mark, Evan, Caitlin. BA in Religion, Stetson U., 1967, JD magna cum laude, 1971. Bar: Fla. 1971, N.C. 1977, U.S. Ct. Apeals (5th and 11th cirs.) 1981, U.S. Ct. Appeals (4th cir.) 1982, U.S. Supreme Ct. 1979. Ptnr. Fogle & Watts, Deland, Fla., 1972-76; assoc. prof. law Campbell U., Buies Creek, N.C., 1976-78; ptnr. Watts & Biernacki, Deland, Fla., 1978-81; assoc. Watts & Karl, Deland, Fla., 1981-83; ptnr. Fishback Davis et al, Daytona Beach, Fla., 1983-86, Cobb Cole & Bell, Daytona Beach, Fla., 1986—. Bd. advisors Stetson U. Coll. of Arts & Scis., Deland, 1992—; bd. dirs. 1000 Friends of Fla., Tallahassee, 1993—; vice chair Volusia County Bus. Devel. Corp., Daytona Beach, 1993-95, 98—; bd. counsel Volusia County Sch. Bd., Deland, 1990-97. Author: (with others) Florida Environmental & Land Use, 1996; editor-in-chief Stetson Law Rev., 1970-71; contbr. articles to profl. jours. Mem. Fla. Bar (appellate rules com. 1983-85, 94—), Deland Jaycees (pres. 1974-75, Outstanding Young Man award 1978), Fla. Jaycees (dist. pres. 1975-76), Rotary (Daytona Beach, Fla.), Lake Beresford Yacht Club. Democrat. Episcopalian. Avocations: gardening, travel. Administrative and regulatory, Environmental, Constitutional. Office: Cobb Cole & Bell 150 Magnolia Ave Daytona Beach FL 32114-4346

**WATTS, JAMES DARIEL,** lawyer, educator; b. Independence, Mo., Dec. 15, 1957; s. Lester Dariel and Donna Mae (Dawson) W.; m. Karen Elizabeth Harms, Aug 14, 1982; children: Whitney Catherine, Abigail Charlotte, William Charles, Andrew Christopher, Michael Conrad. BA in Govt., U. Mo., Columbia, 1980; JD, U. Mo., Kansas City, 1984, LLM in Urban Affairs, 1986. Bar: mo. 1985, U.S. Dist. Ct. (we. dist.) Mo., U.S. Ct. Appeals (8th cir.). Assoc. Levy & Craig, Kansas City, 1996-97; jud. law clk. Jackson County Cir. Cts., 16th Jud. Dist., Div. II, Kansas City, Mo., 1988; assoc. Wirken & King, Kansas City, 1988-92; sr. mgr., midwest dir. bus. incentive Ernst & Young LLP, Kansas City, Mo.; lectr. U. Cin., 1987. Mem. Kansas City (Mo.) Hist. Found., 1987—, Kansas City Consensus, 1988—; active Friends of the Zoo, 1985—. Mem. ABA, Mo. Bar Assn., Kansas City Bar Assn., Nat. Trust for Historic Preservation, Kansas City Tomorrow Class XIII, I.P.T., U.L.I. Roman Catholic. Avocations: golf, winetasting, hist. rehab. bldgs. Land use and zoning (including planning), Real property. Home: 13237 Barkley St Shawnee Mission KS 66209-3915 Office: One Kansas City Pl 1200 Main St Kansas City MO 64105-2122

**WATTS, STEPHEN HURT, II,** lawyer; b. Lynchburg, Va., Feb. 21, 1947; s. James Owen Jr. and Sarah Webb (Key) W.; m. Beverley Allan Brockenbrough, July 16, 1969 (div. 1986): children: Day Lowry, Stephen Hurt Jr.; m. Sally Yates Wood, May 24, 1986 (div. 1995); m. Mollie Crawford Talbott;, March 24, 1999. BA, Washington & Lee U., 1968; JD, U. Va., 1972. Bar: Va. 1972, W.Va. 1973. Law clk. Taylor, Michie & Callahan, Charlottesville, Va., 1970-72; assoc. Spilman, Thomas, Battle & Klostermeyer, Charleston, W.Va., 1972-75; ptnr. Watts & Watts, Lynchburg, Va., 1975-77; v.p., counsel Commonwealth Gas Pipeline Corp., Richmond, 1977-81; gen. counsel Commonwealth Natural Resources, Inc., Richmond, 1980-81; assoc. McGuire, Woods & Battle, Richmond, 1981-83; ptnr. McGuire, Woods, Battle & Boothe, L.L.P., Richmond, 1983—. Bd. dirs. Lower Fan Civic Assn., Richmond, 1987-91, TheatreVirginia, Richmond, 1992-93, Va. Oil and Gas Assn., 1993; pres., bd. dirs. Studio Theatre Richmond, 1991-93; chmn. outreach com. Grace and Holy Trinity Episcopal Ch., Richmond, 1993. Mem. ABA, Va. State Bar (dir. adminstrv. law sect., chmn. 1995-96), Fed. Energy Bar Assn. Administrative and regulatory, FERC practice, Public utilities. Home: 2022 Grove Ave Richmond VA 23220-4534 Office: McGuire Woods Battle & Boothe One James Center 901 E Cary St Richmond VA 23219-4057

**WATTS, STEVEN RICHARD,** lawyer; b. Toledo, Oct. 5, 1955; s. James Hupp and Lona Jane Katherine (Miller) W.; m. Marcia Ann Jackson, Mar. 6, 1982. BA in History, Ohio State U., 1978; JD summa cum laude, U. Dayton, 1981. Bar: Ohio 1981, U.S. Dist. Ct. (so. dist.) Ohio 1981. Assoc. Smith & Schnacke, Dayton, Ohio, 1981-84; assoc. Porter, Wright, Morris & Arthur, Dayton, 1984-89, ptnr., 1990; ptnr. Chernesky, Heyman & Kress P.L.L., Dayton, 1990—. Mem. ABA, Ohio State Bar Assn., Dayton Bar Assn. Presbyterian. Avocation: golf. General corporate, Securities. Home: 1101 Viewpoint Dr Dayton OH 45459-1442 Office: Chernesky Heyman & Kress PLL 1100 Courthouse Pla SW Dayton OH 45402

**WAX, HAROLD WILFRED,** lawyer; b. L.A., Apr. 13, 1925; s. Saul M. and Bertha W.; m. Beverly J. Wax, Apr. 6, 1952 (dec. Feb. 1988); children: Jon M., Alan J., Pamela Y., Maureen B. Adlen. BA, U. So. Calif., 1949, JD, 1951. Bar: Calif. 1952, U.S. Ct. Appeals 1952, U.S. Supreme Ct. 1975. Atty. Loeb & Loeb, L.A., 1952-53, Rose, Klein & Marias, L.A., 1953-59, Wax & Sayble, L.A., 1959-67, Wax & Appell, L.A., 1967-87, Wax & Wax, L.A., 1987—. With U.S. Army, 1943-46. Recipient Eugene Marias Lifetime Achievement award, Calif. Applicant Attys. Assn., San Diego, 1997. Mem. Calif. Applicant Attys. Assn. (pres. 1969), Lawyers Club L.A. County (pres. 1976), Woodland Hills Shrine Club (pres. 1965), Ionic Masonic Lodge (Master 1977). Democrat. Jewish. Avocation: tennis. Workers' compensation, Pension, profit-sharing, and employee benefits. Office: Wax & Wax 411 N Central Ave Ste 520 Glendale CA 91203-2081

**WAXMAN, RANDI J.,** lawyer, educator; b. Phila., Jan. 4, 1964. B.Accountancy, George Washington U., 1985; JD, Georgetown U., 1988. CPA, Md.; bar: PA, MD, D.C. Assoc. Melrod Redman, Gartlan, P.C., Washington, 1988-92; prin. Law Offices of Randi J. Waxman, P.C., Washington, 1992—; assoc. prof. dept. bus. Columbia Union Coll., Takoma Park, Md., 1992—. Bd. dirs. Resolve, Washington, 1994-98, Grosvenor Home Owner's Assn., Bethesda, Md., 1989—. Mem. AICPA, Md. Bar Assn., D.C. Bar Assn. Office: Columbia Union College 7600 Flower Ave Takoma Park MD 20912-7794

**WAXMAN, SETH PAUL,** lawyer; b. Hartford, Conn., Nov. 28, 1951; s. Felix H. and Frieda (Goodman) W.; m. Debra F. Goldberg, Mar. 20, 1977; children: Noah, Sarah, Ethan. AB summa cum laude, Harvard U., 1973; JD, Yale U., 1977. Bar: D.C. 1978, U.S. Dist. Ct. D.C., U.S. Ct. Appeals (D.C., 1st-11th cirs.) 1979, U.S. Supreme Ct. 1981. Law clk to Judge Gerhard A. Gesell Washington, 1977-78; ptnr. Miller Cassidy Larroca & Lewin, Washington, 1978-94; assoc. dep. atty. gen. U.S. Dept. Justice, Washington, 1994-96, dep. solitor gen., 1996-97, acting dep. atty. gen., 1997, solicitor gen. of the U.S., 1997—; instr. Nat. Inst. for Trial Advocacy. Contbr. numerous articles on litigation to legal jours. Michael C. Rockefeller fellow Harvard U., 1973-74; recipient Cardozo award for civil rights Anti-Defamation League, 1987. Mem. ABA (mem. standing com. on professionalism, Pro Bono Publico award 1988), Jud. Conf. U.S. Federal civil litigation, Constitutional, Criminal. Office: US Dept Justice Rm 5712 Washington DC 20530-0001

**WAXMAN, SHELDON ROBERT,** lawyer; b. Chgo., Apr. 22, 1941; s. Henri and Ann (Sokolsky) W.; m. Katherine Slamski, Aug. 23, 1979; children: Josiah, Zoe. BA, U. Ill., 1963; JD, DePaul U., 1965. Bar: Ill. 1965, U.S. Supreme Ct. 1976, Mich. 1985. Staff atty. Argonne (Ill.) Nat. Lab., 1968-71; asst. U.S. Atty., Chgo., 1971-74; owner firm Shelly Waxman & Assocs., Chgo. and South Haven, Mich., 1976—. Author: In the Teeth of the Wind, 1995; editor-in-chief New Z Letter; contbr. articles to profl. jours. Founder Freedom Lawyers of Am., People for Simplified Tax Law, Nukes to the Sun. Civil rights, General civil litigation, Criminal. Office: PO Box 309 South Haven MI 49090-0309

**WAXSE, DAVID JOHN,** lawyer; b. Oswego, Kans., June 29, 1945; s. I. Joseph and Mary (Poole) W.; m. Linda Schilling (div.); children: Rachel, Ryan, Rebecca; m. Judy Pfannenstiel, May 29, 1982; 1 child, Elayna. BA, U. Kans., 1967; teaching cert., Columbia U., 1968, JD, 1971. Bar: Kans. 1971, U.S. Ct. Appeals (10th cir.) 1971, U.S. Supreme Ct. 1975, U.S. Ct. Appeals (8th Cir.) 1998. Dean of students Intermediate Sch. 88, N.Y.C., 1968-70; spl. edn. tchr. Peter Cooper Sch., N.Y.C., 1970-71; assoc. Payne & Jones, Olathe, Kans., 1971-74, ptnr., 1974-84; of counsel Shook, Hardy & Bacon, Overland Park, Kans., 1984-86, ptnr., 1986-95; shareholder Shook, Hardy & Bacon P.C., Overland Park, 1993-95; ptnr. Shook, Hardy & Bacon L.L.P., Overland Park, Kans., 1995—; shareholder Shook, Hardy & Bacon P.C., Overland Park, 1993-95, v.p., asst. gen. counsel, 1995—; mcpl. judge City of Shawnee, Kans., 1974-80; atty. City of DeSoto, Kans., 1972-79; adj. prof. U. Kans. Sch. Law, Lawrence, 1981-82; mem. juv. code adv. com. Kans. Jud. Coun., 1979-83, guardianship adv. com., 1982-83, atty. fees adv. com., 1986-87; mem. Civil Justice Reform Act Adv. Com., U.S. Dist. Ct. for Dist. Kans., 1991-95; mem. Kans. Commn. on Jud. Qualifications, 1992—, vice-chmn. 1994-97, chair, 1997-99; v.p. Kans. Legal Svcs., Inc., 1980-82, pres., 1985-87; bd. advisors Kans. Coll. Advocacy, 1979-80; bd. trustees, lawyers' com. Civil Rights Under Law, 1997—. Author: (with others) Kansas Employment Law, 1985, Litigating Employment Law Cases, 1987, Kansas Employment Law Handbook, 1991, supplements, 1992, 95, Kansas Annual Survey, 1990—. Mem. Kan. Gov.'s Adv. Com. on Criminal Justice, 1974-77; mem. Kans. Justice Commn., 1997-99; gen. counsel Western Mo. Dist. ACLU, 1976-78, 86-97, v.p., 1983-86, nat. bd. dirs., 1979-86, 91—, chmn. children's rights com., 1980-86; mem. AIDS Pol. Network, 1987—, med. treatment issues com., 1991-96, constn. com., 1991—; mem. med./tech. com. AIDS Coun. Greater Kans. City, 1986-98, ethics com. consortium Midwest Bioethics Ctr., 1990—; bd. dirs. Parents Anonymous Kans., 1978-83, pres., 1979; bd. dirs., mem. fin. com. Kans. Com. for Prevention Child Abuse, 1980-83. Fellow Am. Bar Found., Kans. Bar Found.; mem. ABA (chmn. children's rights com. and family law sects. 1985-86), Am. Judicature Soc. (bd. dirs. 1997—, adv. com. for ctr. for judicial conduct 1997—), Am. Employment Law Coun., Kans. Bar Assn. (chmn. legal aid com. 1978-83, bd. govs. 1988—, v.p. 1996-97, pres.-elect 1997-98, pres. 1998-99, Pres.' Outstanding Svc. award 1982), Kans. City Met. Bar Assn., Johnson County Bar Assn. (chmn. legal aid com. 1975-82, 92-96), Common Cause, Sierra Club. Federal civil litigation, Civil rights, Labor. Home: 9976 Hemlock Dr Shawnee Mission KS 66212-3447 Office: Shook Hardy and Bacon LLP 10801 Mastin Ste 1000 84 Corporate Woods Overland Park KS 66210-1669

**WAY, BRIAN H.,** lawyer; b. Naha, Japan, Feb. 11, 1969; s. John H. and Imelda A. Way. BS, U. Mich., 1991; JD, Columbia U., 1995. Bar: N.Y. 1996, U. S. Dist. Ct. (so. dist.) N.Y. 1996. Law clk. to judge U.S. Dist. Ct. (so. dist.) N.Y., N.Y.C., 1995-97; assoc. Hughes Hubbard & Reed, N.Y.C., 1997—. Editor Columbia Human Rights Law Rev., 1993-95. Mem. Assn. of Bar of City of N.Y. (sec. patents com. 1998—). Democrat. Avocations: tennis, travel. General civil litigation, Intellectual property, Patent. Office: Hughes Hubbard & Reed One Battery Park Plaza New York NY 10004

**WAYLAND, R. EDDIE,** lawyer; b. Knoxville, Mar. 11, 1953; s. Herman H. and Myrtle G. (Jeri) W.; m. Melinda Malone; children: Houston, Malone, Marian. BS, U. Tenn., 1975, JD, 1978. Bar: Tenn., U.S. Ct. Appeals (6th cir.) 1979, U.S. Ct. Appeals (3d cir.) 1980, U.S. Ct. Appeals (2d and 7th cirs.) 1991, U.S. Ct. Appeals (4th and 9th cirs.) 1994. Assoc., then ptnr. King & Ballow, Nashville, 1978—. Gen. counsel Nashville C. of C., 1994; bd. dirs. Nashville Better Bus. Bur., 1990-95. Mem. ABA, ATLA, Tenn. Bar Assn. (chmn. labor law sect. 1984-86), Nat. Inst. for Trial Advocacy. E-mail: REW@king-ballow.com. Labor, General civil litigation, Communications. Office: King & Ballow 315 Union St Ste 1100 Nashville TN 37201-1401

**WAYLAND, SHARON MORRIS,** law librarian; b. Ft. Worth, July 5, 1951; d. Wesley B. Morris and Lelia L. Curl; children: Brian, Curtis. BA magna cum laude, U. Tex., Arlington, 1973; MLS summa cum laude, U. North Tex., 1982. Asst. dir. Tarrant County Law Libr., Ft. Worth, 1982-89, dir., 1990—; law book reviewer Legal Info. Alert, Chgo., 1989—. Mem. Am. Assn. Law Librs., Southwestern Assn. Law Librs., Tarrant County Assn. Law Librs. (past pres.), Dallas Assn. Law Librs. Avocations: gardening, oil painting, sewing. Office: Tarrant County Law Libr 100 W Weatherford St Rm 420 Fort Worth TX 76102-2115

**WAYNE, ROBERT JONATHAN,** lawyer, educator; b. Fresno, Calif., Apr. 4, 1951; s. William W. and Blanche Wayne; m. Dorothy A. Madden, Oct. 23, 1981; children: Daniel, Julia. BS, U. Oreg., 1971; JD, UCLA, 1974. Bar: Calif. 1974, Wash. 1975, U.S. Dist. Ct. (we. dist.) Wash. 1975, U.S. Ct. Appeals (9th and D.C. cirs.) 1975, U.S. Supreme Ct. 1979. Law clk. U.S. Ct. Appeals (D.C. cir.), 1974-75; assoc. Perkins, Coie, Stone, Olsen & Williams, Seattle, 1975-76; dep. prosecutor King County Prosecutor's Office, Seattle, 1976-78; pvt. practice, Seattle, 1978—; instr. trial advocacy U. Wash., Seattle, 1977—; instr. trial advocacy Nat. Inst. Trial Advocacy, Seattle, 1979—, asst. team leader, 1990, team leader, 1991-99, team leader nat. session, 1993, program dir. N.W. region, 1998—. Mem. ATLA, NACDL (life, chmn. lawyers assistance strike force 1993-94), Wash. State Trial Lawyers Assn. (chmn. tort sect. 1983-85), Wash. State Bar Assn. (chmn. criminal law sect. 1982-83, 86-87, exec. com. 1980-88), Seattle-King County Bar Assn. (jud. screening com. 1988-91), Wash. Assn. Criminal Def. Lawyers (founder, bd. govs. 1986-89, 99—, chmn. lawyers assistance strike force 1986-90, 91-93, chmn. ann. meeting 1989-90), Order of Coif, Order of Barristers. Avocations: skiing, flying. Criminal, General civil litigation, Personal injury. Office: 1301 5th Ave Seattle WA 98101-2603

**WEARN, JAMES MCCARTNEY,** lawyer; b. N.Y.C., July 15, 1942; s. F. Stafford and Mildred Field (King) W.; m. Patricia Watts, Nov. 27, 1981; children. BA, Washington and Lee U., 1964; JD, George Washington U., 1967. Bar: Fla. 1967. Pvt. practice, West Palm Beach, Fla.; dist. atty. South Lake Worth Inlet Dist., 1973-96; town atty. Town of Manalapan, Fla., 1974—, also former mcpl. judge. Councilman Town of Palm Beach, Fla., 1982-84, mem. retirement bd. trustes, 1990—, vice chmn., 1992—, mem. charter commn., vice chmn. 1997—; bd. dirs. Fla. Gov.'s Hurricane Conf., 1995—; chmn. planning com. Fla. State Svc. Coun., 1992-94, chmn. orgn., 1995—; mem. S.E. Regional Mgmt. Com., 1994-95; bd. dirs. Palm Beach County chpt. ARC, 1978-98, mem. exec. com., 1978=98, vol. legal counsel and chmn. com. on legal affairs and chpt. policy, 1978-90, 95-96, assoc. legal counsel, 1990=95, 96—, founder Fairgrounds Operation (during Hurricane Andrew), 1992. Capt. U.S. Army, 1968-70, Vietnam. Recipient Sue Whitmore award Palm Beach County chpt. ARC, 1988. Mem. ABA, ATLA, Fla. Bar (grievance com. 1981-84, chmn. 1982-84), Acad. Fla. Trial Lawyers, Fla. Mcpl. Attys. Assn., Palm Beach County Trial Lawyers Assn., Palm Beach County Bar Assn. (chmn. investiture com. 1976-77, vice chmn. civil practice com. 1977-78, mem. cir. ct. adv. com. 1978-79), SAR, S.R., West Palm Beach Fishing Club, Everglades Club, Beach Club (tennis com. 1977—), Sailfish Club (invitational gold cup team tournament com. 1994-98, co-chmn. 1996-97, vice chmn. 1997-98), Rotary (charter West Palm Beach, bd. dirs. 1986-98, treas. 1986-94, sec. 1994-95, v.p. 1995-96, pres. 1996-97), Phi Kappa Psi. Avocations: deep sea fishing, snow skiing, tennis. General practice, State civil litigation, Municipal (including bonds). Home: 260 Jamaica Ln Palm Beach FL 33480-3322 Office: 2023 N Flagler Dr West Palm Beach FL 33407-6109

**WEATHERHEAD, LESLIE R.,** lawyer; b. Tacoma, Sept. 28, 1956; s. A. Kingsley and Ingrid A. (Lien) W.; m. Anali C. Torrado, June 24, 1985; children: Spencer, Madeleine, Audrey. BA, U. Oreg., 1977; JD, U. Wash., 1980. Bar: Wash. 1980, Oreg. 1996, U.S. Ct. Appeals (9th cir.) 1981, U.S. Dist. Ct. (ea. dist.) Wash. 1984, U.S. Ct. Internat. Trade 1984, Hawaii 1987, U.S. Dist. Ct. (we. dist.) Wash. 1989, Idaho 1989, U.S. Dist. Ct. Idaho 1989, U.S. Supreme Ct. 1994, Colville Tribal Ct. 1993, U.S. Ct. Apeals (10th cir.) 1995, U.S. Ct. Fed. Claims 1995, U.S. Ct. Appeals (fed. cir.) 1999. Asst. terr. prosecutor Territory of Guam, Agana, 1980-83; spl. asst. U.S. Atty. Dist. of Guam and No. Marianas, Agana, 1982-83; atty. Witherspoon, Kelley, Davenport & Toole, Spokane, 1984—; lawyer-rep. 9th cir. jud. conf., 1989-95, lawyer-rep. chmn., 1995; adj. faculty Gonzaga U. Sch. of Law, 1994-95. Contbr. articles on Indian law, administrv. investigations and fed. jurisprudence to profl. jours. Bd. dirs. Spokane Opera Co., 1989-96, pres., 1992-94. Mem. ABA, Fed. Bar Assn. (pres. ea. dist. 1996-97), Hawaii Bar Assn., Idaho Bar Assn., Wash. State Bar Assn., Oreg. State Bar Assn. Avocations: sailing, scuba, skiing. Federal civil litigation, Criminal, Administrative and regulatory. Office: Witherspoon Kelley Davenport & Toole 428 W Riverside Ave Spokane WA 99201-0301

**WEATHERSBY, JAMES ROY,** lawyer; b. Pine Bluff, Ark., Aug. 28, 1935; s. Willard Alton and Francis (McCormick) W.; children: Jim, Brad; m. Lydia Huber, Jan. 20, 1990. BScE, U. Tenn., 1958; JD, Vanderbilt U., 1964. Bar: Ala. 1965, Tenn. 1965, Ga. 1971, U.S. Dist. Ct. (no. dist.) Ala. 1966, U.S. Dist. Ct. (no. dist.) Ga. 1971, U.S. Dist. Ct. (middle dist.) Ga. 1985, U.S. Dist. Ct. (so. dist.) Ga. 1990, U.S. Dist. Ct. (ea. dist.) Tenn. 1997, U.S. Ct. Appeals (D.C., 4th, 5th, 7th, 8th and 11th cirs.), U.S. Supreme Ct. 1969. Labor counsel Rust Engring. Co., Pitts., Pa., Birmingham, Ala., 1964-70; ptnr. Wilson & Wilson, Atlanta, 1971-76; ptnr., head labor sect. Powell Goldstein Fraser & Murphy, Atlanta, 1976-90; mng. ptnr. Ogletree Deakins Nash Smoak & Stewart, Atlanta, 1991-95, Littler Mendelson, Atlanta, 1996—; dep. atty. gen. State of Ga., Atlanta, 1974—; gen. counsel Assoc. Builders & Contractors of Ga., Atlanta, 1976—; bd. dirs. Kamtech Inc., Glen Falls, N.Y. Mem. ABA, Lawyers Club Atlanta, Ga. Bar Assn., Atlanta Bar Assn. Labor. Home: 5056 Green Pine Dr NE Atlanta GA 30342-2402 Office: Littler Mendelson 3348 Peachtree Rd NE Atlanta GA 30326-1008

**WEATHERUP, ROY GARFIELD,** lawyer; b. Annapolis, Md., Apr. 20, 1947; s. Robert Alexander and Kathryn Crites (Hesser) W.; m. Wendy Gaines, Sept. 10, 1977; children: Jennifer, Christine. AB in Polit. Sci., Stanford U., 1968, JD, 1973. Bar: Calif. 1972, U.S. Dist. Ct. 1973, U.S. Ct. Appeals (9th cir.) 1975, U.S. Supreme Ct. 1980. Assoc. Haight, Brown & Bonesteel, Santa Monica, Santa Ana, L.A., 1972-78, ptnr., 1979—; judge Moot Ct. UCLA, Loyola U., Pepperdine U.; arbitrator Am. Arbitration Assn.; mem. com. Book Approved Jury Instrns. L.A. Superior Ct. Mem. ABA, Calif. Acad. Appellate Lawyers, Los Angeles County Bar Assn., Town Hall Calif. Republican. Methodist. Appellate, State civil litigation, Insurance. Home: 17260 Rayen St Northridge CA 91325-2919 Office: Haight Brown & Bonesteel PO Box 680 1620 26th St Ste 4000 Santa Monica CA 90404-4060

**WEAVER, DONNA BECK,** lawyer; b. June 20, 1952. BA, U. Calif., Berkeley, 1974; JD, Golden Gate U., 1977. Cert. family law specialist Calif. Bd. Legal Specialization. Lawyer Trope & Trope, L.A. Fellow Am. Acad. Matrimonial Lawyers; mem. L.A. County Bar Assn. (mem. exec. com. family law sect.), San Luis Obispo County Bar Assn. (past pres.). Family and matrimonial. Office: Trope & Trope 12121 Wilshire Blvd Los Angeles CA 90025-1123

**WEAVER, ELIZABETH A.,** state supreme court chief justice; b. New Orleans; d. Louis and Mary Weaver. BA, Newcomb Coll.; JD, Tulane U. Elem. tchr. Glen Lake Cmty. Sch., Maple City, Mich.; French tchr. Leelanau Sch., Glen Arbor, Mich.; pvt. practice Glen Arbor, Mich.; law clk. Civil Dist. Ct., New Orleans; atty. Coleman, Dutrey & Thomson, New Orleans; atty., title specialist Chevron Oil Co., New Orleans; probate and juvenile judge Leelanau County, Mich., 1975-86; judge Mich. Ct. of Appeals, Mich., 1987-94; justice Mich. Supreme Ct., Lansing, 1995—; mem. Mich. Com. on Juvenile Justice, Nat. Conv. State Adv. Groups on Juvenile Justice for U.S.; chair Gov.'s Task Force on Children's Justice, Trial Ct. Assessment Commn., Office Juvenile Justice and Deliquency Prevention; treas. Children's Charter of Cts. of Mich. Chairperson Western Mich. U. Continuing Legal Adv. Bd.; mem. steering com. Grand Traverse/Leelanau Commn. on Youth; mem. Glen Arbor Twp. Zoning Bd.; mem. chamber arts north Leelanau County; mem. citizen's adv. coun. Arnell Engstrom Children's Ctr.; mem. cmty. adv. com. Pathfinder Sch. Treaty Law Demonstration Project; active Grand Traverse/Leelanau Mental Health Found. Named one of five Outstanding Young Women in Mich., Mich. Jaycees. Fellow Mich. State Bar Found.; mem. ABA, Mich. Bar Assn. (chair continuing legal edn. adv. bd., chair crime prevention ctr., chair juvenile law com.), Nat. Coun. Juvenile and Family Judges, La. Bar Assn., Grand Traverse County Bar Assn., Leelanau County Bar Assn., Antrim County Bar Assn., Delta Kappa Gamma (hon.). Office: Mich Supreme Ct 3300 Grandview Plz 10850 E Traverse Hwy Traverse City MI 49684-1364

**WEAVER, MICHAEL JAMES,** lawyer; b. Bakersfield, Calif., Feb. 11, 1946; s. Kenneth James and Elsa Hope (Rogers) W.; m. Valerie Scott, Sept. 2, 1966; children: Christopher James, Brett Michael, Karen Ashley. AB, Calif. State U., Long Beach, 1968; JD magna cum laude, U. San Diego, 1973. Bar: Calif., 1973, U.S. Dist. Ct. (so. dist.) Calif. 1973, U.S. Ct. Appeals (9th cir.) 1975, U.S. Supreme Ct. 1977. Law clk. to chief judge U.S. Dist. Ct. (so. dist.) Calif., San Diego, 1973-75; assoc. Luce, Forward, Hamilton & Scripps, San Diego, 1975-80, ptnr., 1980-86; ptnr. Sheppard, Mullin, Richter & Hampton, San Diego, 1986-99, Latham & Watkins, San Diego, 1999—; judge pro tem San Diego Superior Ct.; master of the Bench of the Inn, Am. Inns of Ct., Louis M. Welch chpt.; lectr. Inn of Ct., San Diego, 1981—, Continuing Edn. of Bar, Calif., 1983—, Workshop for Judges U.S. Ct. Appeals (9th cir.), 1990; mem. task force on establishment of bus. cts. sys. Jud. Coun. Calif., 1996-97. Editor-in-chief: San Diego Law Rev., 1973; contbr. articles to profl. jours. Bd. dirs., pres. San Diego Kidney Found., 1985-90; bd. dirs. San Diego Aerospace Mus., 1985-97; trustee La Jolla (Calif.) Playhouse, 1990-91. Served to lt. USNR, 1968-74. Fellow Am. Coll. Trial Lawyers; mem. San Diego Assn. Bus. Trial Lawyers (founding mem., bd. govs.), San Diego Def. Lawyers Assn. (dir.), Am. Arbitration Assn., 9th Cir. Jud. Conf. (del. 1987-90), Calif. Supreme Ct. Hist. Assn. (bd. dirs. 1998—), Safari Club Internat. (San Diego chpt.), San Diego Sportsmen's Club. Republican. Presbyterian. Avocations: reading, family activities, flying, skiing. Federal civil litigation, General civil litigation, State civil litigation. Office: Latham & Watkins 701 B St Ste 2100 San Diego CA 92101-8197

**WEAVER, PAUL DAVID,** lawyer; b. Chgo., Feb. 15, 1943; s. Paul Stanley and Margaret Elizabeth (Wurster) W.; m. Carol Lynne Homan, July 1, 1978; children: Paul Tyson, Samuel Lincoln. AB, Yale U., 1965; JD, U. Mich., 1971. Bar: Mass. 1971, Ohio 1972. Mgr. west coast Big 3 Industries, Houston, 1965-68; assoc. Goodwin, Procter & Hoar, Boston, 1971-78; sec., gen. counsel Houghton Mifflin Co., Boston, 1979-88, sr. v.p., gen. counsel, 1989—. Mem. Beverly (Mass.) Hosp. Corp., 1978—; town counsel Town of Wenham, Mass., 1976—, moderator, 1987—. Mem. ABA, Mass. Bar Assn., Boston Bar Assn., Assn. Am. Publs. (chmn. lawyers com. 1985-86), Am. Soc. Corp. Secs., Mass. City Solicitors/Town Counsels Assn., Mass. Moderators Assn., Myopia Hunt Club (Hamilton, Mass.), Yale Club (N.Y.C.), Phi Delta Phi. Avocations: antiques, skiing. General corporate, Trademark and copyright, General practice. Home: 88 Walnut Rd Wenham MA 01984-1611 Office: Houghton Mifflin Co 222 Berkeley St Fl 5 Boston MA 02116-3748

**WEAVER, SANDJAI,** prosecutor; b. Phila., Feb. 7, 1955; d. Floyd Grant and Eddie Mae Weaver; 1 child, Theresa Rhae. BS in Adminstrv. Justice, Tex. So. U., 1982; JD, Ohio No. U., 1987. Bar: Pa. Legal intern Heardin County Prosecutors, Kenton, Ohio, 1985-87, Cmty. Legal Svcs., Lima, Ohio, 1987-88; asst. dist. atty. Phila. Dist. Attys. Office, 1990—; dist. atty. rep. North Ctrl. Neighborhood Adv. Coun., Phila., 1991-98; participant, educator LEAPP Temple U., Phila., 1993, Intensive Trial Adv. Program-Widener U. Law, Del., 1998. Active Christian Stronghold Ch., 1994—. Avocations: painting, drawing, playing saxophone, reading. Home: 2323 N Gratz St Philadelphia PA 19132-4338 Office: Phila DAs Office 1421 Arch St Fl 10 Philadelphia PA 19102-1507

**WEAVER, TIMOTHY ALLAN,** lawyer; b. Elkhart, Ind., Nov. 30, 1948; s. Arthur and Joan Lucile (Yoder) W.; m. Catherine Anne Power, Nov. 23, 1974; children: Daniel Timothy, Christopher Matthew, David Colwell. AB, Brown U., 1971; JD, U. Ill., 1974. Bar: Ill. 1974, U.S. Dist. Ct. (no. dist.) Ill. 1975, U.S. Ct. Appeals (7th cir.) 1975, U.S. Dist. Ct. (no. dist. trial bar)

Ill. 1982, U.S. Dist. Ct. (ea. dist.) Wis. 1999. Asst. pub. defender Cook County Pub. Defender, Chgo., 1974-75; trial atty. Chgo. Transit Authority, 1975-78; assoc. Philip E. Howard Ltd., Chgo., 1978; assoc. Pretzel & Stouffer, Chartered, Chgo., 1978-82, ptnr., 1982—. Editor: Medical Malpractice, 1989, 92, 96; contbr. chpts. to books. Mem. ABA, Ill. Bar Assn., Ill. Assn. Def. Trial Counsel, Am. Soc. Law and Medicine, The Law Club of Chgo. General civil litigation, Personal injury, Product liability. Office: Pretzel & Stouffer One S Wacker Dr #2500 Chicago IL 60606

**WEBB, CURTIS RANDALL,** lawyer; b. Twin Falls, Idaho, Apr. 23, 1958; s. Lloyd J. and Barbara W.; m. Kristy Diane Buckland, Dec. 19, 1986; children: Katharine, Clark, Alexander, Nicole, Anne. BA, Utah State U., 1981; JD, Brigham Young U., 1984. Bar: Idaho 1984, U.S. Dist. Ct. Idaho 1984, U.S. Supreme Ct. 1988, U.S. Ct. Fed. Claims, 1988, U.S. Ct. Appeals (fed. cir.) 1991, U.S. Ct. Appeals (1st cir.) 1995. Assoc. Webb, Burton, Carlson, Pederson & Paine, Twin Falls, Idaho, 1984-86; ptnr. Webb, Burton, Carlson & Pederson, Twin Falls, 1986-91, Webbm Oederseb & Webb, Twin Falls, 1991-93, Lloyd J. & Curtis R. Webb, Twin Falls, 1993—; mem. Adv. Commn. on Childhood Vaccines, Washington 1993-95, chmn. 1995. Bd. dirs. Idaho Conservation League, 1991-93, Idaho Rivers United, 1991—. Mem. ATLA, Idaho Trial Lawyers Assn. Democrat. Mem. LDS Ch. Product liability, Personal injury. Home: 2158 Addison Ave E Twin Falls ID 83301-5365 Office: Lloyd J & Curtis R Webb 155 2d Ave N Twin Falls ID 83301

**WEBB, JANE MARIE,** lawyer; b. Wellington, Shropshire, Eng., Jan. 14, 1945; came to the U.S., 1969; BA, U. London, Eng., 1966; BA in English summa cum laude, Waynesburg Coll., 1981; JD, U. Pitts., 1984. Bar: Pa. 1984. Law clk. presiding judge Glenn R. Toothman Jr. Greene County, Waynesburg, Pa., 1982-84; assoc. McCall, Stets & Hardisty, Waynesburg, 1984-86; asst. dist. atty. Greene County Dist. Atty.'s Office, Waynesburg, 1986-87; assoc. Nernberg & Laffey, Pitts., 1988-89, Toothman & Toothman, Waynesburg, 1989-91; ptnr., founding mem., shareholder, dir., officer Chambers Webb, P.C., Waynesburg, 1991-96; pvt. practice Waynesburg, 1996—; instr. Waynesburg (Pa.) Coll., 1986—. Editor (legal jour.) The Greene Reports, 1992—; editor, author (newsletter) The Greene Sheet, 1992—. Lt., treas., mem. Morris Twp. Vol. Fire Co., Nineveh, Pa., 1972-81; asst. dir. Greene County Emergency Mgmt. Agy., 1977-79; bd. dirs. Nat. Football League Players Assn.-Greene County Celebrity Golf Classic, Waynesburg, 1995. Mem. NAFE, Pa. Bar Assn. (del. ho. of dels. 1994—, exec. com. conf. of county bar leaders 1994—, gov.-at-large bd. govs. 1995-97, sec. 1998—), Greene County Bar Assn., Allegheny County Bar Assn., Xi Psi Epsilon. Avocations: skiing, long distance running. General practice, Real property, Family and matrimonial. Home: RR 1 Box 192A Graysville PA 15337-9314 Office: 32 S Church St Ste 208 Waynesburg PA 15370-1832

**WEBB, JOHN,** retired state supreme court justice; b. Rocky Mount, N.C., Sept. 18, 1926; s. William Devin and Ella (Johnson) W.; m. Martha Carolyn Harris, Sept. 13, 1958; children: Caroline Webb Smart, William Devin. Student, U. N.C., 1946-49; LLB, Columbia U., 1952. Judge Superior Ct., Wilson, N.C., 1971-77, N.C. Ct. Appeals, Raleigh, 1977-86; justice Supreme Ct. N.C., Raleigh, 1986-99; ptnr. Webb & Webb, Raleigh, N.C., 1998—. Served with USN, 1944-46. Mem. N.C. Bar Assn. Democrat. Baptist. Home: 808 Trinity Dr W Wilson NC 27893-2131 Office: Webb & Webb 19 W Hargett St Raleigh NC 27601-1391

**WEBB, JOHN GIBBON, III,** lawyer; b. Flint, Mich., June 1, 1944; s. John Gibbon Jr. and Martha W.; m. Fain Murphey, July 6, 1968; children: Jennifer Horn, Philip, Andrew, John Matthew. AB, Davidson Coll., 1966; JD, Vanderbilt U., 1970. Bar: N.Y. 1971, N.J. 1981. Assoc. Curtis, Mallet-Prevost, Colt & Mosle, N.Y.C., 1970-80; gen. counsel, v.p. & sec. J.M. Huber Corp., Edison, N.J., 1980-95; pvt. practice Mt. Olive, N.J., 1996—. Episcopalian. Private international, General corporate, Contracts commercial. Office: 500 International Dr Ste 300 Budd Lake NJ 07828-1381

**WEBB, KATHLEEN ROCHFORD,** lawyer; b. Santa Ana, Calif., Apr. 30, 1956; d. Thomas Francis and Eileen (Travers) Rochford; m. William Alan Webb, May 27, 1978; children: Alan Travers, Shannon Kristin. BBA, Memphis State U., 1981, JD, 1987. Bar: Tenn. 1988. Assoc. Murphy, DeZonia & Webb, Memphis, 1987—; real estate broker Rochford & Assocs., Cordova, Tenn., 1976-88; instr. U. Memphis, 1985—. Leader Girl Scouts USA, Memphis, 1993—. Mem. Memphis Bar Assn. (chair real estate sect.), ABA, Tenn. Bar Assn., Real Estate Industry Trade Assn. (pres. 1996), Women's Coun. Realtors (local pres. 1983-84, State Woman of Yr. 1984, pres. 1988), Memphis Area Assn. Realtors (dir. 1986-87, trustee 1988-90, Affiliate of Yr. 1991). Republican. Roman Catholic. Avocations: exercise, outdoor activities, girl scouts. Real property. Office: Murphy DeZonia & Webb 6389 N Quail Hollow Rd Ste 102 Memphis TN 38120-1422

**WEBB, MORRISON DESOTO,** lawyer, communications company executive; b. Danbury, Conn., Dec. 25, 1947; s. Jean Francis III and Nancy (Bukeley) W.; m. Stacie Luise Jacob, May 27, 1979; children: Nicholas Beale, Nathaniel Rodman. BA in English magna cum laude, Amherst Coll., 1969; JD cum laude, Harvard U., 1976. Bar: N.Y. 1977, U.S. Dist. Ct. (ea. and so. dists.) N.Y. 1977, Mass. 1980. Assoc. Rogers & Wells, N.Y.C., 1976-80; atty. New England Telephone, Boston, 1980-83, gen. atty., 1983-84; v.p., gen. counsel NYNEX Bus. Info. Systems Co., White Plains, N.Y., 1984-86; corp. dir. NYNEX Corp. Strategic Mktg.-Networks, White Plains, N.Y., 1986-87; pres. NYNEX Govt. Affairs Co., Washington, 1987-91; v.p., gen. counsel, sec. New Eng. Telephone Co., Boston, 1991-95; exec. v.p., gen. counsel, sec. NYNEX Corp., 1995-97; exec. v.p., external affairs & corp. comms. Bell Atlantic, 1997—; bd. dirs. Bell Atlantic. Co-chmn. Carnegie Hall Corp. Fund; corp. adv. com. Mus. Fine Arts, Boston; trustee Folger Shakespeare Libr. Served to lt. (j.g.) USNR, 1969-73. Mem. ABA, Nat. Policy Assn. (trustee), New England Legal Found. (trustee). Republican. Administrative and regulatory, Communications, General corporate. Home: 120 Rye Ridge Rd Harrison NY 10528-1011 Office: Bell Atlantic Corp 1195 Ave of the Americas New York NY 10036*

**WEBB, RICHARD CRAIG,** lawyer; b. Columbia, S.C., Mar. 18, 1965; s. James Roger and Margaret Ann Webb; m. Clair Manning Turner, May 4, 1991; children: R. Hampton T., H. Gillian G. BA, Furman U., 1987; JD, U. S.C., 1990. Bar: S.C. 1990, U.S. Dist. Ct. S.C. 1991, U.S. Ct. Appeals (4th cir.) 1991, D.C. 1993. Assoc. Holmes & Thompson, Charleston, S.C., 1990-94; mng. dir. Webb Sports Internat., Charleston, 1994-98; pvt. practice Charleston, 1994-98; assoc. Davis, Craver, Hagood & Kerr, P.A., Charleston, 1998—. Author: (with others) S.C. Jurisprudence — Sports Law, 1994; contbr. articles to profl. jours. Usher St. Philip's Episopal Ch., Charleston, 1991—. Mem. Carolina Yacht Club, Order of Coif, Order of Wig and Robe. Avocations: family, rock climbing. Contracts commercial, General corporate, Sports. Office: Davis Craver Hagood & Kerr PA 171 Church St Ste 120 Charleston SC 29401-3136

**WEBB, RODNEY SCOTT,** judge; b. Cavalier, N.D., June 21, 1935; s. Chester and Aylza (Martin) W.; m. Betty M. Lykken, Aug. 31, 1957; children: Sharon, Crystal, Todd, Wade, Susan. BS, U. N.D., 1957, JD, 1959. Bar: N.D. 1959, U.S. Dist. Ct. N.D. 1965, U.S. Ct. Appeals (8th cir.) 1981. Assoc. Ringsak, Webb, Rice & Metelman, Grafton, N.D., 1959-81; state's atty. Walsh County, Grafton, 1966-74; mcpl. judge City of Grafton, 1975-81; spl. asst. atty. gen. State of N.D., 1970-81; U.S. atty. Dist. of N.D., Fargo, 1981-87, judge U.S. Dist. Ct. N.D., 1987—, Fargo, chief judge, 1996—. Col. JAG, N.D. Army N.G., ret. Mem. N.D. State Attys. Assn. (past pres.). Lutheran. Office: US Dist Ct 655 1st Ave N Ste 410 Fargo ND 58102-4952

**WEBB, THOMAS IRWIN, JR.,** lawyer; b. Toledo, Sept. 16, 1948; s. Thomas Irwin and Marcia Davis (Winters) W.; m. Polly S. DeWitt, Oct. 11, 1986; 1 child, Elisabeth Hurst. BA, Williams Coll., 1970; postgrad., Boston U., 1970-71; JD, Case Western Res. U., 1973. Bar: Ohio. Assoc. Shumaker, Loop & Kendrick, Toledo, 1973-79, ptnr., 1979—, chmn. corp. law dept., 1992-94, mgmt. com., 1994-99; dir. Calphalon Corp., 1990-98, Yark Oldsmobile, Inc. Coun. mem. Village of Ottawa Hills, Ohio, Divsn. Securities, 1979-85, adv. com., commr. of taxation, 1999—; trustee Kiwanis Youth Found. of Toledo, 1982—; dir. Toledo Area Regional Trans it Authority, 1989-91; trustee Arts Commn. Greater Toledo, 1993—, exec. com., 1994—, v.p., 1994-96, pres., 1996-97; trustee Jr. Achievement of Northwestern Ohio, Inc., 1992—, Lourdes Coll. Found., 1995—. Mem. ABA, Ohio Bar Assn. (corp. law com. 1989—), Toledo Bar Assn., Northwestern Ohio Alumni Assn. of Williams Coll. (pres. 1974-83), Toledo-Rowing Found. (trustee 1985—), Toledo Area C. of C. (trustee 1991-98, exec. com. 1993-98), Order of Coif, Crystal Downs Country Club, Toledo Country Club, The Toledo Club (trustee 1984-90, pres. 1987-90), Williams Club N.Y. Republican. Episcopalian. General corporate, Mergers and acquisitions, Securities. Office: Shumaker Loop & Kendrick 1000 Jackson St Toledo OH 43624-1573

**WEBB ANDERSON, JOANN MARIE,** lawyer, community advocate; b. St. Louis, Nov. 19, 1942; d. Jeff and Nancy Mae (Harris) Webb; m. Clifton Earl Anderson, Dec. 30, 1966; children: Ronald James Anderson, Nancy Delia Anderson. Student, U. Mo., Columbia and St. Louis, 1960-62; BA in History, St. Louis U., 1967, JD, 1978; grad., Ind. U., 1974-75. Bar: Mo. 1979, U.S. Dist. Ct. U.S. V.I. 1981, U.S. Dist. Ct. (ea. dist.) Mo. 1979, U.S. Ct. Appeals (8th cir.) 1979, U.S. Ct. Appeals (3d cir.) 1982. Staff atty. Legal Svcs. Ea. Mo., St. Louis, 1979-80; staff atty., mng. atty. Legal Svcs. V.I., Christiansted, Frederiksted, 1980-81; asst. atty. gen. Govt. of V.I., St. Croix, 1981-83; supervising atty. civil divsn. Dept. of Justice, Office of Atty. Gen., St. Croix, 1984-85, acting chief and supervising atty., 1985-87; exec.dir. Navy Relief Soc./Japan Aux., Yokusuka, 1988-89; of counsel Law Office of Arthur C. Kellung, St. Louis, 1997; sole practitioner St. Louis, 1997—. Bd. dirs. Archway Cmtys., Inc., St. Louis, 1998—; mem. polit. action com. Coalition of 100 Black Women, St. Louis, 1990; mem. planning and focus group Hyde Park Neighbors/Trinity Sq., St. Louis, 1990—. Mem. Bar Assn. Met. St. Louis (edn. com.), Jr. League of St. Louis, Zeta Phi Beta. Roman Catholic. Avocations: neighborhood development, historical preservation, reading, grandparenting, international travel. Labor, Personal injury. Home: 1420 Bremen Ave Saint Louis MO 63107-2918 Office: 1428 Salisbury St Saint Louis MO 63107-2939

**WEBBER, JAMES CARL,** lawyer; b. Santa Ana, Calif., Sept. 23, 1957; children: Claire Elizabeth, Amanda Constance. BA in Comms., Calif. State U., Fullerton, 1981; JD, U. So. Calif., L.A., 1985. Bar: Calif. 1985, U.S. Dist. Ct. (cen. dist.) Calif. 1985, U.S. Ct. Appeals (9th cir.) 1985, Wash. 1987, U.S. Dist. Ct. (we. dist.) Wash. 1986, U.S. Dist. Ct. (ea. dist.) Wash. 1988, U.S. Dist. Ct. (so. dist.) Calif. 1990. Atty. Drummy Garret King & Harrison, Costa Mesa, Calif., 1985-87, Davis Wright Tremaine, Bellevue, Wash., 1987-91, Weissburg & Aronson, San Diego, 1991, O'Shea Barnard Martin, Bellevue, 1991-92; sr. asst. city atty. Seattle Law Dept., 1993-98; spl. counsel Littler Mendelson, Seattle, 1998—. Bd. dirs., v.p. Seattle Mens' Chorus, 1997—; sec., bd. dirs. Bellevue Repertory Theater, 1988-91. Avocations: music, theater, writing. Labor, State civil litigation, Federal civil litigation. Office: Littler Mendelson 999 3d Ave Ste 3800 Seattle WA 98104

**WEBER, ALBAN,** association executive, lawyer; b. Chgo., Jan. 29, 1915; s. Joseph A. and Anna (von Plachecki) W.; m. Margaret Kenny, Dec. 29, 1951; children: Alban III, Peggy Ann, Gloria, Brian. AB, Harvard U., 1935, JD, 1937; MA, Northwestern U., 1962; LLM, John Marshall Law sch., 1967. Bar: Ill. 1938, Mich. 1985, Fla. 1997, U.S. Supreme Ct. 1946. Ptnr. Weber & Weber, 1937-41; gen. counsel Fgn. Liquidation Commn., State Dept., 1946; trust officer Lake Shore Nat. Bank, Chgo., 1952-55; univ. counsel Northwestrn U., Evanston, Ill., 1955-70; pres. Fedn. Ind. Ill. Colls. and Univs., Evanston, 1971-85; of counsel Schuyler, Roche & Zwirner, Evanston, 1984-94; pres. Benjamin Frankoin Fund, Inc., 1965-75, Northwestern U. Press, Inc., 1961-80; chmn. State Assn. Execs. Coun., 1981. Pres. N.E. Ill. coun. Boy Scouts Am., 1970-71, dist. chmn. Gulfstream coun., 1994-95; alderman City of Chgo., 1947-51. Comdr. USNR, 1941-45, rear adm., 1969-75. Recipient Silver Beaver award Boy Scouts Am., Meritorious Svc. award Loyola U., 1978, Edn. for Freedom award Roosevelt U., 1984. Mem. Nat. Assn. Coll. and Univ. Attys. (pres. 1962), Harvard Law Soc. Ill. (pres. 1984), Navy League (pres. Evanston coun. 1967-70), Univ. Risk Mgmt. Assn. (pres. 1965), Naval Order U.S. (nat. comdr. 1970-72), Law Club, Econs. Club, Harvard Club, Execs. Club, Chgo. Yacht Club, White Lake Yacht Club, Kiwanis (lt. gov., pres. Port St. Lucie club), St. Lucie River Power Squadron (comdr.), Anchor Line Yacht Club (commodore). Home: 1555 SE Sunshine Ave Port Saint Lucie FL 34952-6011

**WEBER, ARNOLD I.,** lawyer; b. Little Cedar, Iowa, Oct. 4, 1926; divorced; children: Katherine Weber Hickle, Thomas, Margaret Weber Robertson. PhB magna cum laude, Marquette U., 1949; MA, Harvard U., 1950; JD, George Washington U., 1954, LLM, 1956. Bar: D.C. 1954, Md. 1961, Calif. 1962, U.S. Dist Ct. D.C. 1954, (no. dist.) Calif. 1962, (cen. dist.) Calif. 1992, U.S. Ct. Claims 1960, U.S. Tax Ct. 1965, U.S. Ct. Appeals (D.C. cir.) 1954, (9th cir.) 1962, (fed. cir.) 1991, U.S. Supreme Ct. 1959. Lawyer Housing and Home Fin., Washington, 1954; pvt. practice Washington, 1954-55; lawyer Tariff Commn., Washington, 1954-55, FCC, Washington, 1955-56, IRS, Washington, 1956-61; assoc. Brobeck, Phleger & Harrison, San Francisco, 1961-64; sr. gen. atty. So. Pacific Transp., San Francisco, 1964-84; western tax counsel Santa Fe Pacific Corp., San Francisco, 1985-88; pvt. practice San Francisco, 1988—. With USNR, 1944-54, PTO. Mem. ABA, Olympic Club, Bar Assn. San Francisco, State Bar of Calif. Alternative dispute resolution, General civil litigation, Probate. Office: 57 Post St Ste 502 San Francisco CA 94104-5020

**WEBER, FRED J.,** retired state supreme court justice; b. Deer Lodge, Mont., Oct. 6, 1919; s. Victor N. and Dorothy A. (Roberts) W.; m. Phyllis M. Schell, June 2, 1951; children: Anna Marie, Donald J., Mark W., Paul V. B.A., U. Mont., 1943, J.D., 1947. Bar: Mont. 1947. Atty. Kuhr & Weber, Havre, Mont., 1947-55, Weber, Bosch & Kuhr, and successors, 1956-80; justice Supreme Ct. Mont., Helena, 1981-95. Served to capt. inf. U.S. Army, 1943-46. Fellow Am. Bar Found., Am. Coll. Probate Counsel; mem. ABA, Am. Judicature Soc.

**WEBER, FREDRIC ALAN,** lawyer; b. Paterson, N.J., July 31, 1948; s. Frederick Edward and Alida (Hessels) W.; m. Mary Elizabeth Cook, June 18, 1983. BA in History, Rice U., 1970; JD, Yale U., 1976. Bar: Tex. 1976, U.S. Dist. Ct. (so. dist.) Tex. Assoc. Fulbright & Jaworski, Houston, 1976-80, participating assoc., 1980-83, ptnr., 1983—. Dir. Houston Symphony Soc., 1993—. Recipient Benjamin Scharps prize Yale Law Sch., 1976, Ambrose Gherini prize Yale Law Sch., 1976. Mem. ABA, Am. Coll. Bond Counsel, Nat. Assn. Bond Lawyers (bd. dirs. 1988-89, treas. 1989-90, pres.-elect 1991, pres. 1991-92), Houston Bar Assn. Finance, Municipal (including bonds), Securities. Office: Fulbright & Jaworski LLP 1301 Mckinney St Ste 5100 Houston TX 77010-3031

**WEBER, GAIL MARY,** lawyer; b. Austin, Minn., Dec. 7, 1954; d. Clemence Peter and Aryls Marion (Mulick) W.; m. Thomas Jeffrey Miller, Sept. 24, 1983; 1 child, Paula Suzanne. AA, Austin C.C., 1975; BA in Psychology and English with high scholastic honors, St. Cloud State U., 1978; JD, Hamline U., 1983. Bar: Minn. 1983, U.S. Supreme Ct. Minn. 1983, U.S. Dist. Ct. Minn. 1984. Child care specialist Gerard Schs., Austin, 1978-80; legal intern St. Paul Dept. Edn., 1981-82; law clk. Alton, Severson, Sovis & Groves, Apple Valley, Minn., 1982; law clk. Heuer Madden & Gruesner, Mpls., 1983, assoc., 1983-85; assoc. Heuer, Weber & Assocs., Mpls., 1986-88, Robbins & Rashke, Mpls., 1986-93; ptnr. Robbins Rashke & Weber, Edina, 1993—; pvt. practice Edina, Minn., 1985-92; coach high sch. mock trial program, Mpls., 1986—, vol. Chrysalis, Mpls., 1986-98; co-chmn. Legis. Action Com., Minn. Women Lawyers, 1987-89. Mem. ACLU, 1990, Minn. Civil Liberties Union, 1990, Big Sisters, St. Paul, 1980-82, Greenpeace; Sunday sch. tchr., 1995-98; co-leader Daisy Scouts, 1996-97. Recipient Appreciation award Chrysalis Ctr. for Women, 1989-97. Mem. Minn. Trial Lawyers Assn., Nat. Employment Lawyers Assn. (Minn. chpt.), Fed. Bar Assn., Minn. Soc. Criminal Justice (sec. 1988, v.p. 1989, bd. dirs.), Minn. Women Lawyers (bd. dirs. 1989-91), Minn. Trial Lawyers Assn., LWV (asst. editor newsletter 1987-89, bd. dirs., chair edn. study 1994-95), Delta Theta Phi. Democrat. Roman Catholic. Avocations: reading, theater, karate, opera, golf. Personal injury, Criminal, Labor. Office: 7600 Parklawn Ave Ste 410 Edina MN 55435-5130

**WEBER, GERALD RICHARD,** legal association administrator, educator; b. Middletown, Conn., June 2, 1964; s. Gerald Richard Sr. and Norma Jean W.; m. Stephanie Stuckey, May 27, 1996 (div. Dec. 1997). BS in Fin. and Law summa cum laude, Ill. State U., 1986; JD summa cum laude, U. Ga., 1989. Bar: Ga., 1990, U.S. Ct. Appeals (5th and 11th cirs.) U.S. Supreme Ct., 1990, U.S. Dist. Ct. (no. and mid. dists.) Ga., 1990. Jud. clk. to Hon. Thelma Wyatt Cummings Fulton Superior Ct., Atlanta, 1987; jud. clk. to Hon. Carolyn Dineen King U.S. Ct. Appeals (5th cir.), Houston, 1989-90; assoc. Dow, Lohnes & Albertson, Atlanta, 1990-91; legal dir. Am. Civil Liberties Union, Atlanta, 1991—; adj. prof. Emory U. Sch. Law, Atlanta, 1997—, Ga. State U. Coll. Law, Atlanta, 1998—; chair legal com. Task Force for Homeless, 1992—; barrister Joseph Henry Lumpkin Inns of Ct., 1994-96; bd. dirs. Ga. First Amendment Found., 1994—, Ga. Ctr. Law in Pub. Interest, 1998—; mem. Atlanta steering com. Lawyers Com. Civil Rights Under Law, 1996—; panelist in field; lectr. in field. Symposium editor Ga. Law Rev.; contbr. articles to mags. and profl. jours.; appearances in numerous local and nat. TV and radio shows. Bd. trustees U. Ga. Libr., 1996-97; pres. Leadership Atlanta, 1997-98; pres. Cabbagetown Neighborhood Improvement Assn., 1998—, rep. neighborhood planning unit-N, 1998—; mem. adv. com. AID Atlanta, 1998—; mem. adv. bd. Jeanette Rankin Found., 1997—; election monitor S. African Elections, 1994; bd. dirs. Table of Elements. Recipient Cert. Appreciation, U.S. Dept. Justice, 1998; named one of 21 Young Lawyers Leading Us Into 21st Century, ABA, 1995, Forty Top Georgians Under 40, Ga. Trend Mag., 1997. Mem. FBA, State Bar Ga. (co-chair individual rights sect. 1998—, mem. various coms.), Lawyers Club Atlanta, Order of Coif. Democrat. Lutheran. Avocations: Theremin musician, tennis, biking, fossil collecting. Office: Am Civil Liberties Union Ga 142 Mitchell St SW Ste 301 Atlanta GA 30303-3428

**WEBER, HERMAN JACOB,** federal judge; b. Lima, Ohio, May 20, 1927; s. Herman Jacob and Ada Minola (Esterly) W.; m. Barbara L. Rice, May 22, 1948; children: Clayton, Deborah. BA, Otterbein Coll., 1949; JD summa cum laude, Ohio State U., 1951. Bar: Ohio 1952, U.S. Dist. Ct. (so. dist.) Ohio 1954. Ptnr. Weber & Hogue, Fairborn, Ohio, 1952-61; judge Fairborn Mayor's Ct., 1956-58; acting judge Fairborn Mcpl. Ct., 1958-60; judge Greene County Common Pleas Ct., Xenia, Ohio, 1961-82, Ohio Ct. Appeals (2d dist.), Dayton, 1982-85, U.S. Dist. Ct. (so. dist.) Ohio, Cin., 1985—; chmn. Ohio Jud. Conf., Columbus, 1980-82; pres. Ohio Common Pleas Judges Assn., Columbus, 1975. Vice mayor City of Fairborn, 1955-57, council mem., 1955-59. Served with USNR, 1945-46. Office: US Dist Ct 801 100 E 5th St Cincinnati OH 45202-3905

**WEBER, JOHN WALTER,** insurance company executive; b. Rochester, N.Y., Jan. 10, 1959; s. Donald J. and Patricia M. (Mangon) W.; m. Tracy Ann Sitler, Nov. 4, 1989. BS, U. Conn., 1984. Claims supr. Hartford Ins. Group, Southington, Conn., 1986-90; regional claims mgr. Housing Authority Risk Retention Group, Cheshire, Conn., 1990—. Mem. U. Conn. Alumni Assn. Avocations: jogging, reading, softball, cooking.

**WEBER, LAURA ANN,** lawyer; b. Green Bay, Wis., Feb. 16, 1969; d. Jonathan N. Weber and Ruth Ann Riebe. BA, Marquette U., 1991, JD cum laude, 1994. Bar: Wis. 1994. Assoc. Clair Law Offices, S.C., Delavan, Wis., 1995—. E-mail: clairlaw@elknet.net. Estate planning, Probate, Real property. Office: Clair Law Offices SC PO Box 445 Delavan WI 53115-0445

**WEBER, RICHARD J.,** lawyer; b. Marshfield, Wis., Mar. 4, 1934; s. Herbert C. and Esther J. Weber; m. Diane M. Weber, June 21, 1961; children: Daniel, David, Suzanne. Bar: Wis. 1961, U.S. Dist. Ct. (we. and ea. dists.) Wis. 1961. Asst. editor law rev. Marquette U., Milw., 1960-61; law clk. Wis. Supreme Ct., Madison, 1961-62; assoc. Terwilliger Wakeen Piehler & Conway, Wausau, Wis., 1962-66; mng. ptnr. Kelley Weber Pietz & Slater S.C., Wausau, 1968—; lectr. U. Wis., Madison, 1975-76, 87, Wis. Cont. Legal Edn., Madison, 1975, 80. Dir. Wausau Crimestoppers, Wausau, 1995—. Mem. ABA, Am. Trial Lawyers Assn., Wis. Acad. Trial Lawyers, Wis. League Municipalities, Marathon County Bar Assn. (pres. 1990), Wausau Elks Lodge. Roman Catholic. Avocations: golf, running, boating, fishing. General civil litigation, Condemnation, Municipal (including bonds). Office: Kelley Weber Pietz & Slater SC 530 Jackson St Wausau WI 54403-5531

**WEBER, SCOTT LOUIS,** lawyer; b. Livingston, N.J., Oct. 21, 1968; s. David Bernard and Janice Risa Weber; m. Irene Barbara Lubawy, May 24, 1992. BA, Rutgers Coll., 1990; JD, Boston Coll., 1993. Bar: N.J. 1993, U.S. Dist. Ct. N.J. 1993, N.Y. 1994, Pa. 1994, U.S. Dist. Ct. (so. and ea. dists.) N.Y. 1998. Atty., assoc. Pitney, Hardin, Kipp & Szuch, Morristown, N.J., 1993-97, Latham & Watkins, Newark, 1997—; mediator Superior Cts., Morris County, N.J., 1996-97; vol. atty., tng. coord. Jersey Battered Women's Legal Advocacy Program, Morris County, 1993-97. Mem. ABA, Cap and Skull Honors Soc., Pi Sigma Alpha. Avocations: fitness, bonsai, opera and blues music, golf. General civil litigation, Antitrust, Product liability. Office: Latham & Watkins One Newark Ctr Newark NJ 07101

**WEBERPAL, MICHAEL ANDREW,** lawyer; b. Sycamore, Ill., Sept. 16, 1951; s. Michael Andrew Sr. and Mary Elizabeth (Egan) W.; m. Michelle Vinet, Aug. 20, 1971. BA in Econs., U. Wis., Milw., 1975; JD, U. Wis., Madison, 1978; LLM, So. Meth. U., 1992. Bar: Wis. 1978, Tex. 1980, U.S. Dist. Ct. (we. dist.) Wis. Assoc. LaRowe & Gerlach, Reedsburg, Wis., 1978-79; tax specialist Laventhol & Horwath, Dallas, 1980-81; sr. atty. Otis Engrng. Corp. (subsidiary of Halliburton Co.), Dallas and London, 1983-88; sr. tax counsel Halliburton Co., Dallas, 1988-92, sr. atty., asst. sec., 1992-93; v.p., gen. counsel, sec. Highlands Ins. Co., Houston, 1993-97; gen. counsel, sec. Landmark Graphics Corp. subs. Halliburton Co., Houston, 1997—. Mem. ABA, State Bar Tex., State Bar Wis., Houston Bar Assn. Republican. Roman Catholic. Avocations: skiing, jogging, golf. General corporate, Corporate taxation, Private international. Home: 6230 Inwood Dr Houston TX 77057-3508 Office: Landmark Graphics Corp 15150 Memorial Dr Houston TX 77079-4304

**WEBOSTAD, WESLEY ERIC,** lawyer; b. Seattle, Jan. 24, 1963; s. Wesley Julius and Celeste Webostad; m. Holly Yvette Hewes, Mar. 19, 1994; 1 child, Colin Bernard. BSEE, U. Calif., Irvine, 1986; JD, Santa Clara U., 1991. Bar: Calif. 1992, U.S. Dist. Ct. (no. dist.) Calif. 1992, U.S. Patent and Trademark Office, 1992. Quality engr. Ford Aerospace Corp., Newport Beach, Calif., 1986-88; assoc. Davis & Schroeder, Monterey, Calif., 1992-93, LaRiviere, Grubman & Payne, Monterey, 1993-95; patent counsel Micron Tech., Inc., Boise, Idaho, 1995—; legal-extern Judge Claudia Wilken, U.S. Dist. Ct. (no. dist.) Calif., San Francisco, 1991. Assoc. editor Santa Clara Law Rev., 1991-92. Mem. Am. Intellectual Property Law Assn. Fax: 208-368-5606. E-mail: ewebostad@micron.com. Office: Micron Tech Inc 8000 Federal Way Boise ID 83716-9632

**WEBSTER, C. EDWARD, II,** lawyer, judge; b. Cody, Wyo., Mar. 27, 1944; s. Constant E. and Lucille (Moncur) W. B.A. in Bus. Administrn., U. Wyo., 1967, J.D., 1969. Bar: Wyo. 1969. Legis. asst. U.S. Senator Clifford P. Hansen, 1969-72; ptnr. Housel and Webster, Cody, Wyo., 1973-79; pvt. practice, Cody, 1979-99; prin. Webster & Thompson, LLC, 1999—; judge mcpl. ct.; justice of peace. Pres. Cody Stampede, 1980-84. Mem. ABA, Cody C. of C. (pres. 1974-75), Eagles Club (Cody). Republican. Mem. LDS Ch. State civil litigation, Oil, gas, and mineral, Real property. Office: 1226 11th St Cody WY 82414-3523

**WEBSTER, PETER BRIDGMAN,** lawyer; b. Boston, Jan. 11, 1941; s. John Archibald and Mildred (Bridgman) W.; m. Elaine Gerber, Dec. 20, 1964; children: Amy Elizabeth, Peter Bridgman, Timothy James. AB, Bowdoin Coll., 1962; LLB, Cornell U., 1965. Bar: Maine 1965, U.S. Dist. Ct. Maine 1965. Assoc., then sr. ptnr. Verrill & Dana, Portland, Maine, 1965—; mem. grievance commn. Maine Bd. Bar Overseers, Augusta, 1979-88, chmn., 1984-88, mem. 1986-94, chmn. 1990-92; adj. prof. law U. Maine, Portland, 1981; mem. Maine Commn. on Ethics and Govtl. Practices, 1991—, chair 1997—, chair Lawyers' Fund for Client Protection. Recipient Alumni Svc. award Bowdoin Coll., 1999. General corporate, Banking, Education and schools. Home: 185 W Main St Yarmouth ME 04096-8400

**WEBSTER, PETER DAVID,** judge; b. Framingham, Mass., Feb. 12, 1949; s. Waldo John and Helen Anne (Borovek) W.; m. Michele Page Hernandez, Jan. 13, 1989; 1 stepchild, Alana Perryman. BS, Georgetown U., 1971; JD, Duke U., 1974; LLM, U. Va., 1995. Bar: Fla. 1974, U.S. Dist. Ct. (mid. dist.) Fla. 1975, U.S. Ct. Appeals (5th cir.) 1975, U.S. Dist. Ct. (so. dist.) Fla. 1977, U.S. Dist. Ct. (no. dist.) Fla. 1978, U.S. Supreme Ct. 1978, U.S. Ct. Appeals (11th cir.) 1981. Law clk. U.S. Dist. Judge, Jacksonville, Fla., 1974-75; assoc. Bedell, Bedell, Dittmar, Smith & Zehmer, Jacksonville, 1975-

78; ptnr. Bedell, Bedell, Dittmar & Zehmer, Jacksonville, 1978-85; cir. judge State Fla., Jacksonville, 1986-91; judge Dist. Ct. of Appeal, First Dist., State of Fla., Tallahassee, 1991—; master of bench Chester Bedell Am. Inn of Ct., 1988-91, Tallahassee Am. Inn of Ct., 1992—; chmn. com. on standard jury instrns. in civil cases, chmn. court reporter cert. planning com.; mem. com. on trial ct. info. sys.; com. on confidentiality of records of jud. br. Fla. Supreme Ct. Contbg. author: Sanctions: Rule 11 and Other Powers, 1986, Florida Criminal Rules and Practice Manual, 1990. Bd. dirs. Jacksonville Area Legal Aid, Inc., 1978-82, River Region Human Svcs., Inc., Jacksonville, 1986-88; mem. adv. bd. P.A.C.E. Ctr. for Girls, Inc., Jacksonville, 1986-91; com. mem. Shawnee dist. North Fla. coun. Boy Scouts Am., 1974-78; mem. delinquency task force Mayor's Commn. on Children and Youth, City of Jacksonville, 1988-91; officer, mem. exec. bd. Suwanee River Area coun. Boy Scouts, 1991-96. Mem. Fla. Conf. Appellate Judges, Jacksonville Bar Assn., Tallahassee Bar Assn., Phi Beta Kappa, Phi Alpha Theta, Phi Eta Sigma. Office: 1st Dist Ct Appeal 301 Martin Luther King Blvd Tallahassee FL 32399-1850

**WEBSTER, WILLIAM HODGES,** lawyer; b. N.Y.C., Oct. 26, 1946; s. Eugene Burnett and Verna May Webster; m. Joan Leslie Strawder, Dec. 30, 1967; 1 child, Sydney Kristen. BA cum laude, NYU, 1972; JD, U. Calif., Berkeley, 1975. Bar: Calif. 1976, U.S. Dist. Ct. (no. dist.) Calif. 1976, U.S. Tax Ct. 1984. Rsch. assoc. Nat. Econ. Devel. & Law Ctr., Berkeley, 1974-76, staff atty., 1976-81, mng. atty., 1981-83; ptnr. Hunter & Anderson, Oakland, Calif., 1983-86, mng. ptnr., 1986-93; mng. ptnr. Webster & Anderson, Oakland, Calif., 1993—. Contbr. articles to profl. jours. Mem. Mayor's Com. on Responsible Investments, City of Berkeley, 1990, Mayor's Housing Task Force, City of Berkeley, 1986. Recipient Cert. of Merit, Nat. Congress for Cmty. Econ. Devel., 1983. Mem. Nat. Assn. Bond Lawyers, Calif. Bar Assn. (bus. law sect.), Charles Houston Bar Assn., Kappa Alpha Psi. Democrat. Avocations: yoga, bicycling, swimming, chess, reading. Municipal (including bonds), Non-profit and tax-exempt organizations, General corporate. Office: Webster and Anderson 469 9th St Ste 240 Oakland CA 94607-4068

**WEBSTER COBB, DEIRDRÉ LOUISE,** lawyer; b. Washington, Sept. 12, 1962; d. Joseph William Webster Jr. and Jacqueline Lillian (Dennis) Patterson; m. Robert Glenn Cobb, Oct. 18, 1997. BA in Polit. Sci., Chatham Coll., 1984; JD, U. Pitts., 1987. Bar: Pa. 1987, D.C. 1988, N.J. 1992; cert. supervisory mgmt., N.J., 1988. Gov.'s fellow State N.J., Trenton, 1987-88; asst. counsel Office People's Counsel, Washington, 1988-89; atty. City Coun. Com. Judiciary, Washington, 1989; exec. asst. N.J. Dept. Personnel, Trenton, 1989-93; counsel, asst. to dir. AFSCME Counsel, Trenton, 1993-94; regulatory officer N.J. Dept. Labor, Trenton, 1994-98; barrister Sidney Reitman Employment Law Am. Inn Ct., N.J., 1995-97; commr. N.J. Adv. Com. Status of Women, 1996-98; mem. com. complementary dispute resolution N.J. Supreme Ct., 1996-98. V.p. TLC Assocs., Willingboro, N.J., 1995—; mem. exec. com. Rainbow Gala, Am. Diabetes Assn. N.J., 1997—. Recipient Louis Kaplhan Human Rels. award Am. Jewish Com., Pitts., 1980, Clinton-Myetta Daddler Law award Negro Ednl. Emergency Drive, Pitts., 1986-87, Student Leadership award, 1987; Humphrey-Jamison scholar Chatham Coll., Pitts., 1980. Mem. Assn. Black Women Lawyers N.J. (v.p. 1993-95, pres. 1995-97), N.J. Bar Assn. Avocations: reading, tennis. Office: NJ Dept Cmty Affairs Divsn on Women PO Box 801 Trenton NJ 08625-0801

**WECHSLER, MARY HEYRMAN,** lawyer; b. Green Bay, Wis., Jan. 8, 1948; d. Donald Hubert and Helen (Polcyn) Heyrman; m. Roger Wechsler, Aug. 1971 (div. 1977); 1 child, Risa Heyrman; m. David Jay Sellinger, Aug. 15, 1981; 1 stepchild, Kirk Benjamin; 1 child, Michael Paul. Student, U. Chgo., 1966-67, 68-69; BA, U. Wash., 1971; JD cum laude, U. Puget Sound, 1979. Bar: Wash. 1979. Assoc. Law Offices Ann Johnson, Seattle, 1979-81; ptnr. Johnson, Wechsler, Thompson, Seattle, 1981-83; pvt. practice Seattle, 1984-87; ptnr. Mussehl, Rosenberg et al, Seattle, 1987-88, Wechsler, Becker, Erickson, Ross, Roubik & Hunter, Seattle, 1988—; mem. Bd. of Ct. Edn., 1998, 99; bd. dirs. U. Wash. Law Sch. Child Advocacy Clinic, 1996—; mem. Walsh Commn. on Jud. Selection, 1995-96; mem. Wash. State Supreme Ct. commn. on domestic rels., 1996-97; mem. law-related edn. com., 1997; chair edn. com. Access to Justice Bd., 1996-99, bd. ct. edn., 1998-99; presenter in field. Author: Family Law in Washington, 1987, rev. edit., 1988, Marriage and Separation, Divorce and Your Rights, 1994; contbr. articles to legal publs. Mem. Wash. State Ethics Adv. Com., 1992-95; bd. dirs. Seattle LWV, 1991-92. Fellow Am. Acad. Matrimonial Lawyers (sec.-treas. Wash. state chpt. 1996, profl. com. nat. 1996-97, v.p. 1997, 98, pres. 1999); mem. ABA (chmn. Wash. state 1987-88), Wash. State Bar Assn. (exec. com. family law sect. 1985-91, chair 1988-89, ct. improvement com. 1998—, legis. com. 1991-96, Outstanding Atty. of Yr. family law sect. 1988, comms. com. 1997-98), Wash. Women Lawyers, King County Bar Assn. (legis. com. 1985—, vice-chair 1990-91, chair family law sect. 1986-87, chair domestic violence com. 1986-87, trustee 1988-90, policy planning com. 1991-92, 2d v.p. 1992-93, 1st v.p. 1993-94, pres. 1994-95, long-range planning com. 1998—, awards com. 1997—, Outstanding Atty. award 1999), Nat. Conf. of Bar Pres. (commn. com. 1994-95, long range planning com. 1998-99), King County Bar Found. (trustee 1997—). Family and matrimonial, State civil litigation. Office: Wechsler Becker Erickson Ross Roubik & Hunter 701 5th Ave Seattle WA 98104-7016

**WEDDINGTON, SARAH RAGLE,** lawyer, educator, speaker, writer; b. Abilene, Tex., Feb. 5, 1945; d. Herbert Doyle and Lena Catherine Ragle. BS magna cum laude, McMurry Coll., 1965, hon. doctorate, 1979; JD, U. Tex., 1967; hon. doctorate, Hamilton Coll., 1979, Southwestern U., 1989, Austin Coll., 1993, Nova Southeastern U., 1999. Bar: Tex. 1967, D.C. 1979, U.S. Dist. Ct. (we., no. and ea. dists.) Tex., U.S. Ct. Appeals (5th cir.) U.S. Supreme Ct. Pvt. practice law Austin, 1967-77; gen. counsel Dept. Agr., Washington, 1977-78; spl. asst. to Pres., Washington, 1978-79, asst. to Pres., 1979-81; chmn. Interdepartmental Task Force on Women, 1978-81; mem. Pres.'s Commn. on Exec. Exchange, 1981; Carl Hatch prof. law and pub. adminstrn. U. N.Mex., Albuquerque, 1982-83; pvt. practice law Austin, Tex., 1985—; dir. Tex. Office State-Fed. Rels., Austin, Washington, 1983-85; vis. prof. govt. Wheaton Coll., Norton, Mass., 1981-83; sr. lectr. Tex. Woman's U., Denton, 1981-90, 93, U. Tex., Austin, 1986—. Author: A Question of Choice, 1992; contbg. editor Glamour mag., 1981-83. Mem. Tex. Ho. of Reps., 1973-77. Recipient Woman of Yr. award Tex. Women's Polit. Caucus, 1973, Time Mag. Outstanding Young Am. Leaders, 1979, Leadership awards Ladies Home Jour., 1980, spl. recognition Esquire mag., 1984, Elizabeth (Betty) Boyer award Equity Action League, 1992, Woman Who Dares award Nat. Coun. Jewish Women, 1993, Woman of Distinction award Nat. Conf. for Coll. Women Student Leaders, 1993, Colby award for Pub. Svc. Sigma Kappa, 1996, Hummingbird award Leadership Am., 1998; named Lectr. of Yr. Nat. Assn. for Coll. Activities, 1990. Mem. Tex. Bar Assn. Family and matrimonial, Constitutional, General practice. Office: S Weddington Law Offices 709 W 14th St Austin TX 78701-1707

**WEDDLE, JUSTIN SETH,** lawyer; b. N.Y.C., Feb. 2, 1970; s. Stephen Shields and Meredith Baldwin Weddle; m. Ferrell Motlow, May 26, 1996. BA in Philosophy, Haverford Coll., 1992; JD, Columbia U., 1995. Bar: N.Y. 1996, Mass. 1996, U.S. Dist. Ct. (so. dist.) N.Y. 1996. Law clk. hon. Peter K. Leisure U.S. Dist. Ct. (so. dist.) N.Y., N.Y.C., 1995-96; assoc. Debevoise & Plimpton, N.Y.C., 1996-99; asst. U.S. atty. so. dist. U.S. Atty.'s Office, N.Y.C., 1999—. Mng. editor Columbia Law Rev., 1994-95. Kent scholar Columbia Law Sch., 1994-95. Mem. Assn. of the Bar of the City of N.y. (sec. corrections com. 1998—), Columbia Law Sch. Assn. (dir. 1998—). General civil litigation, Criminal. Office: US Attorney's Office One St Andrew's Plz New York NY 10007

**WEDDLE, RANDALL JAY,** lawyer; b. South Bend, Ind., Mar. 20, 1944; s. James O. and Lois Weddle; m. Carol S. Hoffer, Aug. 15, 1965; children: Justin, Aaron. BA, Ind. U., 1966, JD, 1971. Bar: Alaska 1972. Assoc. Faulkner Banfield Duogan & Holmes, Juneau, Alaska, 1971-74; shareholder Faulkner Banfield Doogan & Holmes, Juneau, Alaska, 1974-78, Anchorage, 1978-98; shareholder, pres. Holmes Weddle & Barcott (formerly Faulkner Banfield Doogan & Holmes), Anchorage, 1998—. 1st lt. U.S. Army, 1966-68. General civil litigation, Workers' compensation, Insurance. Office: Holmes Weddle & Barcott 701 W 8th Ave Ste 700 Anchorage AK 99501-3453

**WEDEKIND, DAVID N.,** lawyer; b. Knoxville, Tenn., June 1, 1955; s. Roy Adam and Jean Willard Wedekind; m. Gail Elizabeth McCamy, July 29, 1979; children: Angeline Elizabeth, Sarah Jean, David Blaine. BS in Mktg., U. Tenn., 1977; JD, U. Memphis, 1981. Bar: Tenn. 1981, U.S. Dist. Ct. (ea. dist.) Tenn. 1982, U.S. Ct. Appeals (6th cir.) 1989. Assoc. Hodges, Poughty & Carson, Knoxville, 1981-85; ptnr. Hodges, Doughty & Carson, Knoxville, 1985—; bd. dirs. TVA&I Fair, Knoxville; spkr. in field. Mem. ABA, Tenn. Bar Assn., Knoxville Bar Assn., Def. Rsch. Inst. Republican. Roman Catholic. Avocations: golfing, hiking. Workers' compensation, General civil litigation, Insurance. Office: Hodges Doughty & Carson 617 W Main St Knoxville TN 37902-2602

**WEDGLE, RICHARD JAY,** lawyer; b. Denver, Dec. 2, 1951; s. Joseph M. and Lillian E. (Brown) W.; m. Susan R. Mason, Oct. 17, 1987. BA, U. Calif., Berkeley, 1974; JD, U. Denver, 1978. Bar: Colo. 1978, U.S. Dist. Ct. Colo. 1978, U.S. Ct. Appeals (10th cir.) 1980. Ptnr. Cox, Wedgle & Padmore, P.C., Denver, 1978-85, Barnes, Wedgle & Shpall, P.C., Denver, 1986-87, Wedgle and Shpall, P.C., Denver, 1987-98, Wedgle and Friedman, P.C., Denver, 1998—. Vol. coord. Dick Lamm for Gov., 1974, citizen adv. office, 1975; bd. dirs. Cherry Creek Improvement Assn., 1985-88. Mem. ABA, Colo. Bar Assn., Denver Bar Assn., Jewish Cmty. Ctr. Avocations: running, biking, gardening. Federal civil litigation, State civil litigation, Family and matrimonial. Home: 365 Marion St Denver CO 80218-3927 Office: Wedgle & Friedman PC 730 17th St Ste 230 Denver CO 80202-3546

**WEDGWOOD, RUTH,** law educator, international affairs expert; b. N.Y.C.; d. Morris P. and Anne (Williams) Glushien; m. Josiah Francis Wedgwood; May 29, 1982; 1 child, Josiah Ruskin Wedgwood. BA magna cum laude, Harvard U., 1972; fellow, London Sch. Econs., 1972-73; JD, Yale U., 1976. Bar: D.C., N.Y., U.S. Supreme Ct. Law clk. to Hon. judge Henry Friendly U.S. Ct. Appeals (2d cir.), N.Y.C., 1976-77; law clk. to justice Harry Blackmun U.S. Supreme Ct., Washington, 1977-78; spl. asst. to asst. atty. gen. U.S. Dept. Justice, Washington, 1978-80; asst. U.S. atty. U.S. Dist. Ct. (so. dist.) N.Y., N.Y.C., 1980-86; prof. law Yale U., New Haven, 1986—, faculty fellow Inst. for Social and Policy Studies, 1989—; faculty fellow Berkeley Coll., Yale U., 1989—; faculty internat. security program Yale U., 1992—, faculty UN studies program, 1992—; dir. Yale UN Legal Studies, 1996—; mem. Sec. of State's Adv. Com. Internat. Law, 1993—; dir., sr. fellow project internat. orgns. and law Coun. Fgn. Rels., 1994—; Charles Stockton prof. internat. law U.S. Naval War Coll., Newport, R.I., 1998-99; mem. Hart-Rudman Commn. on Nat. Security in 2025, Dept. Def. Adv. Commn., 1999—; mem. acad. adv. com. to spl. rep. of UN Sec.-Gen. for Children and Armed Conflict, 1999—. Exec. editor Yale Law Jour., 1975-76; author: The Revolutionary Martyrdom of Jonathan Robbins, 1990, The Use of Force in International Affairs, 1992, American National Interest and the United Nations, 1996, Toward an International Criminal Court?, 1999; mem. bd. editors Yale Jour. Law and Humanities, 1988-98; mem. bd. editors Am. Jour. Internat. Law, 1998—; contbr. articles to profl jours. and popular publs. including N.Y. Times, Washington Post, Christian Sci. Monitor, Internat. Herald Tribune, Washington Times, Fgn. Affairs; commentator for CNN, Fox. Nat. Pub. Radio, Pub Broadcasting Systems. Prin. rapporteur U.S. Atty. Gen.'s Guidelines on FBI Undercover Ops., Informant Use and Racketeering and Gen. Crime Investigations, 1980; bd. dirs. Lawyers Com. for Human Rights, N.Y.C., 1988-94; mem. policy adv. com. UN Assn. of U.S.A., 1998—. Recipient Israel Peres prize, 1976; Ford Found. Rsch. grant; Rockefeller Found. fellow. Mem. ABA, Am. Law Inst., Am. Soc. Internat. Law (exec. com. 1995-98), Internat. Law Assn. (v.p. 1994—, program chmn. Am. br. 1992), Assn. Am. Law Sch. (chmn. sect. internat. law 1995-96), Assn. of the Bar of the City of N.Y. (arms control and internat. security affairs com., chmn. 1989-92, chmn. internat. affairs coun. 1992-95, exec. com. 1995-99), Union Internationale des Avocats, U.S.A. (chpt. bd. govs. 1993-98), Coun. on Fgn. Rels., Elizabethan Club, Mory's Assn., Yale Club (N.Y.C.), Lawn Club. Office: Yale U Sch Law PO Box 208215 New Haven CT 06520-8215 also: Coun on Fgn Rels 58 E 68th St New York NY 10021-5939 *Notable cases include: U.S. vs. Kostadinov, involving a Bulgarian spy traded for 25 East Bloc detainees; U.S. vs. Gold, Orosz, Egerhazi and Kompar, involving a million dollar racketeering/landlord arson ring in N.Y.C. that defrauded Lloyd's of London Sasse Syndicate; U.S. vs. Kazemzadeh and DeVelasco, involving pub. corruption in N.Y.C. Health and Hospitals Corporation and in the fed. WIC program.*

**WEDIG, REGINA SCOTTO,** lawyer; b. Pensacola, Fla., July 30, 1955; d. Anthony P. and Janet (Treadway) Scotto; m. Eric M. Wedig. BA magna cum laude, Loyola U., 1977; MA, Tulane U., 1979; JD, La. State U., 1984. Bar: Tenn. 1984, U.S. Dist. Ct. (ea., mid. and we. dists.) Tenn. 1984, La. 1985, U.S. Dist. Ct. (ea., mid. and we. dists.) La. 1985, U.S. Ct. Appeals (5th cir.) 1985, U.S. Ct. Appeals (11th cir.) 1998. Assoc. Harkavy, Shainberg, Kosten, et al, Memphis, 1984-88; assoc. Bordelon, Hamlin & Theriot, New Orleans, 1988-94, ptnr., 1994—; chmn. moot ct. bd. Paul M. Herbert Law Sch., La. State U., Baton Rouge, 1983-84. Editor: (newsletter) LSU-Coastal Law Newsletter, 1983-84; author: (law jour.) La. Bar Jour., 1996. Mem. La. Bar Assn., Tenn. Bar Assn., New Orleans Bar Assn. Contracts commercial, Real property, Probate. Office: Bordelon Hamlin & Theriot 701 S Peters St New Orleans LA 70130-1588

**WEED, RAY ARNOLD,** lawyer; b. Lubbock, Tex., May 30, 1934; s. Thomas Arnold and Rosalie (Syfrett) W.; m. Barbara Ware, Dec. 22, 1955 (div. 1961); children: Stanley Arnold, Stephen Kelsey; m. Kathleen Burks, Dec. 19, 1987. BBA, Tex. Tech. U., 1957; JD, U. Tex., 1964. Bar: Tex. 1964, U.S. Dist. Ct. (we. and so. dists.) Tex., U.S. Ct. Appeals (5th cir.), U.S. Supreme Ct. Assoc. Groce, Hebdon, Fahey and Smith, San Antonio, 1964-69; ptnr., shareholder Groce, Locke & Hebdon, San Antonio, 1969-91; shareholder, pres. Ball & Weed, PC, San Antonio, 1991. Capt. U.S. Army, 1957-64. Fellow Am. Coll. Trial Lawyers, Tex. Bar Found., San Antonio Bar Found.; mem. Tex. Assn. Def. Counsel, Fed. Inst. and Corp. Counsel, Am. Bd. Trial Advs. (pres. San Antonio chpt. 1990), Def. Counsel San Antonio (founder 1992, pres. 1993). Republican. Avocation: ranching. Product liability, Personal injury. Office: Ball & Weed 745 E Mulberry Ave Ste 500 San Antonio TX 78212-3191

**WEEKS, ARTHUR ANDREW,** lawyer, law educator; b. Hanceville, Ala., Dec. 2, 1914; s. A.A. and Anna S. (Seibert) W.; m. Carol P. Weeks; children: John David, Carol Christine, Nancy Anna. A.B., Samford U., 1936; LL.B., U. Ala., 1939, J.D., 1939; LL.M., Duke U., 1950; LL.D. (hon.), Widener U., 1980. Bar: Ala. 1939, Tenn. 1948. Sole practice Birmingham, Ala., 1939-41, 1946-47, 1954-61; dean, prof. law Cumberland U. Sch. Law, 1947-54; dean, prof. Samford U., 1961-72, prof. law, 1972-74; prof. law Cumberland Sch. Law, Samford U., 1984—; prof. law Del. Sch. Law of Widener U., Wilmington, 1974-82, dean, 1974-80, interim dean, 1982-83, dean emeritus, prof., 1983—. Served to capt. AUS, 1941-46. Mem. ABA, Tenn. Bar Assn., Ala. Bar Assn., Birmingham Bar Assn., Del. Bar Assn. (assoc.), Phi Alpha Delta, Phi Kappa Phi, Delta Theta Phi. Home: 1105 Water Edge Ct Birmingham AL 35244-1437

**WEEKS, JANET HEALY,** supreme court justice; b. Quincy, Mass., Oct. 19, 1932; d. John Francis and Sheila Josephine (Jackson) Healy; m. George Weeks, Aug. 29, 1959; children: Susan, George. AB in chemistry, Emmanuel Coll., Boston, 1954; JD, Boston Coll., 1958; LLD (hon.), U. Guam, 1984. Bar: Mass. 1958, Guam 1972. Trial atty. U.S. Dept. Justice, Washington, 1958-60, Trapp & Gayle, Agana, Guam, 1971-73; ptnr. Trapp, Gayle, Teker, Weeks & Friedman, Agana, 1973-75; judge Superior Ct. Guam, Agana, 1975-96; justice 1st Supreme Ctr. Guam, 1996-99; chmn. task force cts., prosecution and def. Terr. Crime Commn., 1973-76; mem. Terr. Crime Commn. Bd., 1975-76, Guam Law Revision Commn., 1981—; rep. Nat. Conf. State Trial Judges, 1982. Mem. Cath. Sch. Bd. Guam, 1973. Mem. ABA, Nat. Assn. Women Judges (charter), Am. Judges Assn., Fed. Bar Assn. (chpt. sec. 1974), Guam Bar Assn., Internat. Club (Guam). Office: 120 W Obrien Dr Hagatna GU 96910-5174

**WEEKS, RHODA LETHEA,** lawyer; b. Harper City, Liberia, Apr. 3, 1967; d. Rocheforte L. Weeks and Fannie Elizabeth (Thomson) Goll. BA in Econs. summa cum laude, Howard U., 1988; JD, Harvard U., 1991. Bar: N.Y. 1992, Mass. 1992, D.C. 1992. Assoc. Skadden, Arps, Slate, Meagher & Flom, L.L.P., Washington, 1991-97; counsel IMF, Washington, 1997—. Contbr. articles to profl. jours. Mem. ABA, Women in Housing and Fin. Baptist. Avocation: tennis. Office: IMF 700 19th St NW Washington DC 20431-0001

**WEEKS, TRESI LEA,** lawyer; b. Brownwood, Tex., Dec. 3, 1961; d. Dean Moore and Patsy Ruth (Evans) Adams; m. Kevin Weeks, Oct. 26, 1998. BA in Fgn. Svc., BA in French, Baylor U., 1984, JD, 1987. Bar: Tex. 1987, U.S. Dist. Ct. (no. dist.) Tex. 1988, U.S. Ct. Appeals (5th cir.) 1989. Atty. Richard Jackson & Assocs., Dallas, 1987-91, Amis, Bell & Moore, Arlington, Tex., 1992-98. Vol. Legal Svcs. of North Tex., Dallas, 1988-97, Dallas Com. for Fgn. Visitors, 1989-92; bd. dirs. Plano Internat. Presch., 1995-96. Recipient Pro Bono Svc. award Legal Svcs. of North Tex., 1989, 90, 91. Mem. AAUW (pub. policy dir. Plano, Tex. br. 1992, 93-94, v.p. 1994-95), State Bar Tex. (mem. mentor program for lawyers com. 1994-98, mem. local bar svcs. com. 1994-96), Dallas Bar Assn., Dallas Women Lawyers Assn. (bd. dirs. 1989-90, v.p. 1992, pres. 1993). Avocations: scuba diving, reading, bicycling, hiking, growing herbs. Personal injury, Insurance, State civil litigation.

**WEEMS, KYLE RICHARD,** lawyer; b. Greeneville, Tenn., May 30, 1937; m. Catherine L. Weems, Dec. 22, 1962; children: Richard, Catherine Elizabeth. LLB, U. Tenn., 1961. Bar: Tenn. 1961, U.S. Supreme Ct. 1965, U.S. Ct. Appeals (6th and 11th cirs.), U.S. Tax Ct. Ptnr. Weems & House, Chattanooga; lectr., spkr. in field; mem. U.S. panel of trustees U.S. Dist. Ct. (ea. dist.) Tenn. Contbr. articles to profl. publs. Capt. JAGC U.S. Army, 1962-66, maj., USAR, 1967-73. Fellow Tenn. Bar Found., Am. Coll. Bankruptcy; mem. ABA, Am. Bankruptcy Inst., Southeastern Bankruptcy Law Inst. (bd. dirs. 1976—), Tenn. Bar Assn., Chattanooga Bar Assn., Chattanooga Trial Lawyers Assn., Tenn. Trial Lawyers Assn. Bankruptcy, General corporate, Probate. Office: Weems & House 1810 Mccallie Ave Chattanooga TN 37404-3025

**WEG, HOWARD JAY,** lawyer; b. Los Angeles, Nov. 15, 1954; m. Karlene Bernards, June 4, 1981; children: Adam, Jennifer. BA, UCLA, 1976; JD, Southwestern U., 1979; LLM, Yale U., 1980. Bar: Calif. 1979, U.S. Dist. Ct. (cen., so., ea. and no. dists.) Calif. 1980, U.S. Tax Ct. 1980, U.S. Ct. Appeals (9th cir.) 1980. Assoc. Fine, Perzik & Friedman, Los Angeles, 1980-82, Dennis, Juarez, Reeser, Shafer & Young, Los Angeles, 1982-84; assoc. Gendel, Raskoff, Shapiro & Quittner, Los Angeles, 1984-88, ptnr., 1989-90; ptnr. Morrison & Foerster, 1990-94, Orrick, Herrington & Sutcliffe, 1994-99, Peitzman, Glassman & Weg, L.A., 1999—. Author: (with others) Financial Institutions in the 1980's, 1982, (jour.) The Secured Creditor's Rights to Rents from Real Property, 1988,Introduction to Federal Regulation of Plant Closings and Mass Layoffs, 1989. Mem. ABA (corp., banking and bus. law sect., Chapter 11 and Avoiding Powers subcoms. Bus. Bankruptcy com.), Fin. Lawyers Conf., L.A. County Bar Assn., Bankruptcy Study Group, Calif. State Bar Assn. (exec. com. bus. law sect.). Bankruptcy, Banking, Contracts commercial. Office: Peitzman Glassman & Weg 2049 Century Park E Ste 1100 Los Angeles CA 90067-3113

**WEGNER, JUDITH WELCH,** law educator, dean; b. Hartford, Conn., Feb. 14, 1950; d. John Raymond and Ruth (Thulen) Welch; m. Warren W. Wegner, Oct. 13, 1972. BA with honors, U. Wis., 1972; JD, UCLA, 1976. Bar: Calif. 1976, D.C. 1977, N.C. 1988, U.S. Supreme Ct. 1980, U.S. Ct. Appeals. Law clk. to Judge Warren Ferguson, U.S. Dist. Ct. for So. Dist. Calif., L.A., 1976-77; atty. Office Legal Counsel and Land & Natural Resources Divsn. U.S. Dept. Justice, Washington, 1977-79; spl. asst. to sec. U.S. Dept. Edn., Washington, 1979-80; vis. assoc. prof. U. Iowa Coll. Law, Iowa City, 1981; asst. prof. U. N.C. Sch. Law, Chapel Hill, 1981-84, assoc. prof., 1984-88, prof., 1988—, assoc. dean, 1986-88, dean, 1989-99; sr. scholar Carnegie Found. for Advancement of Tchg., 1999—; spkr. in field. Chief comment editor UCLA Law Rev., 1975-76; contbr. articles to legal publs. Mem. ABA (chmn. planning com. African Law Sch. Initiative 1994, co-chmn. planning com. 1994 mid-yr. deans meeting sect. on legal edn. and admission to bar), N.C. Assn. Women Attys. (Gweneth Davis award 1989), N.C. State Bar Assn., Assn. Am. Law Schs. (mem. exec. com. sect. on law & edn. 1985-88, mem. exec. com. sect. on local govt. law 1989-92, mem. accreditation com. 1986-88, chmn. 1989-91, program chmn. 1992 ann. meeting, program chmn. 1994 ann. meeting, mem. exec. com. 1992-96, pres. 1995), Soc. Am. Law Tchrs., Nat. League Cities (coun.-mentor program 1989-91), Women's Internat. Forum, Order of Coif (nat. exec. com. 1989-91), Phi Beta Kappa. Democrat. E-mail: judithúwegner@unc.edu. Office: Carnegie Found Adv of Tchg 555 Middlefield Rd Menlo Park CA 94025-3443 also: U NC Sch Law Van Hecke-Wettach Hall Campus Box 3380 Chapel Hill NC 27599-3380

**WEHDE, ALBERT EDWARD,** lawyer; b. Milw., Feb. 14, 1935; s. Albert Christian and Mary Hubbel (Dewey) W.; m. Joan M. Forney, Nov. 4, 1978; children: John C., Edward T. BS, Marquette U., 1956, JD, 1960. Bar: Wis. 1960, Calif. 1968. Atty. AEC, Albuquerque, 1963-66; counsel Lockheed Aircraft Co., Sunnyvale and Redlands, Calif., 1966-73; assoc. Schultz & Manfield, Palo Alto, Calif., 1973-74; sr. counsel FMC Corp., Santa Clara, Calif., 1974-95; atty. AEW Internat. Cons., Santa Clara, 1995—; bd. dirs. Tech. Fed. Credit Union, San Jose, Calif., chmn., 1994-96. Pres. Mountain View (Calif.) Babe Ruth League, 1976; trustee Mid-Peninsula Family Services Assn., Palo Alto, 1973-74. Served to capt. U.S. Army, 1960-63. Mem. ABA (chmn. region VII pub. contracts sect. 1977-81), Santa Clara County Bar Assn. (co-chmn. corp. counsel sect. 1983-84, mem. exec. com.), Am. Corp. Counsel Assn. (chpt. sec., pres. 1988, bd. dirs. 1983—). Democrat. Roman Catholic. Avocations: gourmet cooking, music, sports. Private international, Government contracts and claims. Home: 1106 Lorne Way Sunnyvale CA 94087-5157 Office: AEW Internat Cons 1400 Coleman Ave Ste F27 Santa Clara CA 95050-4359

**WEICKER, RAYMOND, III,** lawyer, army officer; b. Ft. Benning, Ga., May 20, 1970; s. Raymond Thomas II and Dianne (Cenimo) W. AB in Environ. Studies, Franklin and Marshall Coll., 1992; JD, Bklyn. Law Sch., 1995. Bar: N.J. 1995, N.Y. 1996, U.S. Dist. Ct. N.J. 1995. Commd. 2d lt. U.S. Army, 1992, advanced through grades to capt., 1995; with Judge Adv. Gen.'s Corps, 101st Airborne Divsn., Ft. Benning, Ga., 1995—. Mem. Phi Kappa Psi. Republican. Roman Catholic. Office: OSJA HHC 101st Airborne Div Attn: AF2B-JA Fort Campbell KY 42223

**WEIDEMEYER, CARLETON LLOYD,** lawyer; b. Hebbville, Md., June 12, 1933. BA in Polit. Sci., U. Md., 1958; JD, Stetson U., 1961. Bar: Fla. 1961, D.C. 1971, U.S. Dist. Ct. (mid. dist.) Fla. 1963, U.S. Ct. Appeals (5th cir.) 1967, U.S. Ct. Appeals (D.C. cir.) 1976, U.S. Supreme Ct. 1966, U.S. Ct. Appeals (11th cir.) 1982. Rsch. asst. Fla. 2d Dist. Ct. Appeals, 1961-65; ptnr. Kalle and Weidemeyer, St. Petersburg, Fla., 1965-68; asst. pub. defender 6th Jud. Cir., Fla., 1966-69, 81-83; ptnr. Wightman, Weidemeyer, Jones, Turnbull and Cobb, Clearwater, Fla., 1968-82; pres. Carleton L. Weidemeyer, P.A. Law Office, 1982—; guest lectr. Stetson U., 1978-80; lectr. estate planning seminars; bd. dirs. 1st Nat. Bank and Trust Co., 1974-78, Fla. Bank of Commerce, 1973-77. Author: (handbook) Arbitration of Entertainment Claims, Baltimore County's Second District, The Emerging Thirties, 1990, Area History, Baltimore County, 1990, History of Musicians' Association of Clearwater, Local 729, AFM, 1999; editor Ad Lib mag., 1978-81; contbr. numerous articles to profl. jours. and geneal. pubs.; performer This Is Your Navy Radio Show, Memphis, 1951-52; leader Polka Dots, The Jazz Notes, 1976—; mem. St. Paul Ch. Orch., Fla. Hist. Soc., 1973—, Md. Hist. Soc., 1990—, Pinellas County Estate Planning Assn., 1997—; performer Clearwater Jazz Holiday, 1980, 81, co-chmn., 1981. Bd. advisors Musician Ins. Trust; trustee Francis G. Prasse Meml. Scholarship Trust, 1984—; mem. planned giving com. Upper Pinellas Assn. Retarded Citizens, 1996—, Tampa Bay Rsch. Inst., 1999—; adv. com. Fla. Sheriff Youth Ranches, 1997—; bd. dirs. Pinellas Ctr. for Visually Impaired, 1999—. Served with USN, 1951-54. Mem. SAR, Musicians Assn. Clearwater (pres. 1976-81), Fla.-Ga. Conf. Musicians (sec., treas. 1974-76), NRA, ABA (sr. bar sect.), Fed. Bar Assn., Fla. State Hist. Soc., Md. Hist. Soc., Greater St. Petersburg Musicians Assn., Clearwater Bar Assn. (probate divsn.), Am. Fedn. Musicians (internat. law com. pres. so. conf. musicians 1979-80), Nat. Geneal. Soc., Clearwater Genealogy Soc., Md. Geneal. Soc., Augustan Soc., Lancaster (Pa.) Geneal. Soc., Pinellas (Fla.) Geneal. Soc. (lectr. 1995—), Balt. County Geneal. Soc., Lancaster Mennonite Hist. Soc., Navy Hurricane Hunters, Sons Union Vets. Civil War, Md. Hist. Soc., Catonsville (Md.) Hist. Soc., Am. Legion, German Am. Geneal. Assn., DAV Fleet Res., Masons, Egypt Temple Shrine, Moose, Sertoma (bd. dirs.

Clearwater chpt. 1984-96, v.p. 1989-92), Phi Delta Phi, Sigma Pi, Kappa Kappa Psi. General practice, Estate planning, Entertainment. Home: 2261 Belleair Rd Clearwater FL 33764-2761 Office: 501 S Fort Harrison Ave Clearwater FL 33756-5317

**WEIDLICH, PAUL SCOTT,** lawyer; b. Glen Ridge, N.J., Apr. 12, 1967; s. Jay Clark and Susan Kee W.; m. Ashley Cassandra Paul, Aug. 27, 1994. BCE, Lafayette Coll., Easton, Pa., 1989; JD, George Washington U., 1992. Bar: N.J. 1992, N.Y. 1993, Tenn. 1998, U.S. Supreme Ct. 1997, U.S. Patent and Trademark Office 1998. Assoc. Schenck, Price, Smith & King, Morristown, N.J., 1992-98; assoc. Spears, Moore, Rebman & Williams, Chattanooga, 1998—. Mcpl. prosecutor Harding Twp., N.J., 1996-98. Mem. Tenn. Bar Assn., Chattanooga Bar Assn., Tenn. Intellectual Property Law Assn. General civil litigation, Intellectual property, Patent. Office: Spears Moore Rebman & Williams PO Box 1749 Chattanooga TN 37401-1749

**WEIDNER, LAUREN FINDER,** lawyer; b. N.Y.C., Jan. 21, 1965. B in Commerce, McGill U., 1986; JD, U. Calif., San Francisco, 1991. Bar: Calif. 1991, U.S. Dist. Ct. (no. and ctrl. dists.) Calif. 1991, U.S. Dist. Ct. (so. dist.) Calif. 1996. Assoc. Sedgwick, Deteut, Moran & Arnold, San Francisco, 1991-95, Higgs Fletcher & Mack, San Diego, 1996-97, Gilbert, Kelly, Crowley & Jennett, San Diego, 1997—. Co-chair El Rancho del Ray Playground Renovation Com., Chula Vista, Calif., 1997-98; commr. City of Chula Vista Parks and Recreation, 1998—. Mem. San Diego Bar Assn. General civil litigation, Personal injury, Professional liability. Office: Gilbert Kelly Crowley & Jennett 401 B St Ste 1150 San Diego CA 92101-4283

**WEIGHT, MICHAEL ANTHONY,** lawyer, former judge; b. Hilo, Hawaii, Jan. 5, 1940; s. Leslie A. and Grace B. (Brown) W.; m. Victoria Noel; children: Rachael R., Elizabeth G., Thomas P. BA in History, U. Rochester, 1961; LLB, Vanderbilt U., 1967. Bar: Hawaii 1967, U.S. Ct. Appeals (9th cir.) 1968, U.S. Supreme Ct. 1972. Pvt. practice, Honolulu, 1974-97; former judge Dist. Ct. (1st cir.) Hawaii; asst. fed. pub. defender Dists. of Hawaii and Guam, 1997—. Bd. dirs. Bishop Mus. Assn. 1st lt. USMC, 1961-63. Mem. ABA, Hawaii Bar Assn. Criminal. Office: Fed Pub Defenders Office 300 Ala Moana Blvd Honolulu HI 96850-0001

**WEIL, ANDREW L.,** lawyer; b. Highland Park, Ill., Dec. 19, 1960; s. Edward A. and Julie R. Weil. BA in Econs. with honors, Northwestern U., 1983, JD, 1986. Bar: Ill. Ptnr. Sonnenschein Nath & Rosenthal, Chgo., 1986—; corp. sec. Donnelly Enterprise Solutions Inc., Chgo., 1997—. Note and comment editor: Northwestern U. Jour. Internat. Law and Bus., 1984-86. Mem. Phi Beta Kappa. General corporate, Securities, Contracts commercial. Office: Sonnenschein Nath & Rosenthal 8000 Sears Tower Chicago IL 60606

**WEIL, CASS SARGENT,** lawyer; b. N.Y.C., Nov. 6, 1946; s. Theodore and Ruth Frances (Sargent) W.; m. Susan Mary Heinrich, Oct. 29, 1983 (div. 1987). BA, SUNY, Stonybrook, 1968; JD cum laude, William Mitchell Coll. of Law, 1980. Bar: Minn. 1980, U.S. Dist. Ct. Minn. 1980, U.S. Ct. Appeals (8th cir.) 1980, Wis. 1984, U.S. Ct. Appeals (7th cir.) 1984; cert. bankruptcy law specialist, consumer and bus. Am. Bd. Certification. Assoc. J.R. Kotts & Assoc., Mpls., 1980-81, Wagner, Rutchick & Trojack, St. Paul, 1981-83; ptnr. Zohlmann & Weil, Wilmar, Minn., 1983, Peterson, Franke & Riach, P.A., St. Paul, 1983-91, O'Connor & Hannan, Mpls., 1991-94, Moss & Barnett, P.A., Mpls., 1994—. Editor: Minn. Legal Forms, Bankruptcy, 1983, 87, 91, 92, 93. Recipient Leading Am. Atty. award Am. Rsch. Corp., 1994, 96, 98, Minn. Top Lawyers Mpls. St. Paul Mag., 1998. Mem. Minn. Bar Assn. (vice chmn. bankruptcy sect. 1984-88, chairperson 1988-89), Wis. Bar Assn., Am. Bankruptcy Inst., Comml. Law League Am., Order of Barristers. Democrat. Jewish. Bankruptcy, Consumer commercial, Contracts commercial. Office: Moss & Barnett PA 4800 Norwest Ctr Minneapolis MN 55402

**WEIL, PETER HENRY,** lawyer; b. N.Y.C., Nov. 20, 1933; s. Frank L. and Henrietta Amelia (Simons) W.; m. Helen Fay Kolodkin, Dec. 18, 1960; children: Karen W. Markus, Frank L. BA cum laude, Princeton U., 1954; LLB cum laude, Harvard U., 1957. Bar: N.Y. 1957, U.S. Dist. Cts. (so. and ea. dists.) N.Y. 1972. Assoc. Weil, Gotshal & Manges, N.Y.C., 1958-62; from assoc. to ptnr. Kaye Scholer, N.Y.C., 1962-95, ret., 1995; lectr. SMU Inst. on Comml. Financing, 1985-94, Banking Law Inst., 1987-89. Author: Asset Based Lending: An Introductory Guide to Secured Financing, P.L.I., 1989, 3d edit., 1996. Fellow Am. Coll. of Commercial Fin. Lawyers; former chmn. N.Y. bd. overseers, former bd. govs. Hebrew Union Coll., Jewish Inst. Religion, Cin., N.Y.C., Los Angeles, Jerusalem. With U.S. Army 1957-58. Mem. Ringwood Golden Master Volleyball Team, U.S. Nat. Champions, 1983. Mem. ABA, Assn. of Bar of City of N.Y. (banking law com. 1975-78). Banking, Contracts commercial, Bankruptcy.

**WEIL, ROBERT IRVING,** lawyer, arbitrator, mediator, retired judge; b. N.Y.C., Apr. 6, 1922; s. Irving Julius and Esther (Aisenstein) W.; m. Carol Ethel Tannenbaum, Nov. 6, 1946 (div. 1953); children: David Irving, Timothy Robert; m. Dorothy Granet Kornhandler, Sept. 12, 1958. AB, UCLA, 1943; MS in Journalism, Columbia U., 1944; JD, U. So. Calif., L.A., 1951. Bar: Calif. 1951, U.S. Dist. Ct. (cen. dist.) Calif. 1951, U.S. Supreme Ct. 1961. Assoc. Pacht, Tannenbaum & Ross, L.A., 1951-54; ptnr. Tannenbaum, Steinberg & Shearer, Beverly Hills, Calif., 1954-58, Aaronson, Weil & Friedman, L.A., 1958-75; judge Calif. County Superior Ct., L.A., 1975-90; pvt. practice L.A., 1990—; v.p. L.A. Police Commn., 1973-75; chmn. Calif. Ctr. for Jud. Edn. and Rsch., Emoryville, 1989-90; lectr., seminar leader Calif. Jud. Coll., Berkeley, 1981—, The Rutter Group, L.A., 1981—. Co-author: California Practice Guide: Civil Procedure Before Trial, 1983; contbr. articles to profl. jours. Mem. ABA, Am. Judges Assn., Calif. Judges Assn. (pres. 1985-86, v.p. 1993-94), Pres.'s award 1987, v.p. 1993, Edn. award 1997), L.A. County Bar Assn., L.A. Copyright Soc., Beverly Hills Bar Assn. Avocations: writing, reading, travel, theatre. E-mail: robertweil@worldnet.att.net. Alternative dispute resolution. Home and Office: 2686 Claray Dr Los Angeles CA 90077-2017

**WEILBACHER, DAVID PAUL,** lawyer, consultant; b. Denver, Feb. 15, 1948; s. Paul Herman and Grace (Lewis) W.; m. Patricia Ann Hayne, Nov. 10, 1969; children: James David, Katrina Ann. AA, West Hills Coll., 1968; JD, Santa Barbara Coll. Law, 1984. Bar: Calif., 1987, U.S. Tax Ct. 1996. Pvt. practice Arroyo Grande, Calif., 1987—. Capt. USMC, 1969-74. Home: PO Box 51 Arroyo Grande CA 93421-0051 Office: 1248 Grand Ave Ste A Arroyo Grande CA 93420-2429

**WEILER, MARY PAULINE,** lawyer, nurse; b. Portland, Oreg., Nov. 11, 1957; d. Alfred John Weiler and Pauline Marguerite Roberts. BSN, BA in Psychology, U. Wash., 1980; JD cum laude, Lewis & Clark Coll., 1989. Bar: Ariz. 1989, Wash. 1990, Oreg. 1990, U.S. Dist. Ct. Ariz. 1989. Adminstr./dir. Kimberly Svcs., Inc., Portland, Oreg., 1984-86; med. cons. Spears, Lubersky et al, Portland, Oreg., 1986-88; atty. Gallagher & Kennedy, Phoenix, 1989-90; sr. health plan counsel, dir. contract adminstrn. Kaiser Found. Health Plan of the Northwest, Portland, 1990—. Advisor Animal Aid, Portland, 1988—. Mem. Oreg. State Bar Assn. (mem.-at-large exec. com. health law sect. 1995-97, mem. corp. counsel sect. 1995—), Wash. State Bar Assn. (health law sect. 1990—, corp. counsel sect. 1995—). Democrat. Avocations: sailing, reading. Health, General corporate, Legislative. Office: Kaiser Found Health Plan NW 500 NE Multnomah St Ste 100 Portland OR 97232-2031

**WEILER, TODD DAVID,** lawyer; b. Augusta, Ga., May 4, 1967; s. Wayne D. and Yvonne Elizabeth (Black) W.; m. Elizbeth A. Gordon, Aug. 2, 1991; children: Tyman T., London G. BS, Brigham Young U., 1990, JD, 1996. Bar: Utah 1996, U.S. Dist. Ct. Utah 1996, U.S. Ct. Appeals (10th cir.) 1996. Assoc. Parry, Anderson & Mansfield, Salt Lake City, 1995—. Republican. Mormon. General civil litigation, Labor, General practice. Office: Parry Anderson & Mansfield 1248 W 1900 S Woods Cross UT 84087-2338

**WEILL, (LIGE) HARRY, SR.,** lawyer; b. Chattanooga, Sept. 12, 1916; s. David Robert Weill Sr. and Elsie Rose (Wertheimer) W.; m. Marcelle Baum, Dec. 10, 1947; children: Lige Harry Jr., Elsie Florence, Marcelle Audrey. BA, U. Va., 1936; JD, Harvard U., Cambridge, Mass., 1940; LLD, Harvard U., New Haven, Conn., 1940. Bar: Tenn. 1948, U.S. Ct. Appeals (6th cir.) 1954, U.S. Tax Ct. 1976, U.S. Supreme Ct. 1983. Assoc. Frazier & Roberts, 1940, 1944-59; ptnr. Roberts & Weill, 1959-62; sr. ptnr. Weill & Weill, Chattanooga; instr. contract law, McKenzie Coll.; founder Rossville (Ga.) Bank, 1963. Past pres. Mizpah congregation Julius and Bertha Ochs Meml. Temple; bd. dirs. Girls Club Chattanooga; mem. Estate Planning Coun. Chattanooga; past pres. Jaycees Jr. C of C Chattanooga; mem. bd. dirs. Kiwanis Club; Lt. U.S. Army, 1941-44, PTO. Named mem. of Thomas Jefferson Soc. of Alumni Univ. Va., 1986; scholar Univ. Va., 1932. Mem. ABA, Assn. Trial Lawyers Am., Am. Judicature Soc., Tenn. Bar Assn. (bd. dirs.), Tenn. Trial Lawyers Assn., Chattanooga Bar Assn., Chattanooga Trial Lawyers Assn., B'Nai Brith Internat. Assn., Walden Club, Am. Legion, Zeta Beta Tau. Avocations: gardening, skiing, walking. Personal injury, Probate, Estate taxation.

**WEIMAN, ENRIQUE WATSON,** lawyer; b. Rio de Janeiro, Jan. 1, 1946; came to U.S., 1947; BA, U. Tampa, 1968, JD, 1976; LLM, Atlanta Law Sch., 1976. Bar: Ga.1984. Staff atty. Eason Kennedy and Assocs., Atlanta, 1984-85; mng. ptnr. Hyatt Legal Svcs., Sandy Springs, Ga., 1985-90; pres. Weiman & Perry, P.C., Stone Mountain, Ga., 1990—. Contbr. to local newspaper. Capt. USMC, 1969-71, Res., 1972-80. Avocations: tennis, swimming, sailing. General practice. Home: 5575 S Pines Ct Stone Mountain GA 30087 Office: Weiman & Perry 739 Main St Ste 9 Stone Mountain GA 30083-3089

**WEIMER, GREGORY ALOYISUS,** lawyer; b. Ridgewood, N.J., June 15, 1961; m. Allison Ruth Hastings, Sept. 12, 1992. BA, U. Vt., 1984; JD cum laude, Vt. Law Sch., South Royalton, 1988. Bar: Vt. 1989, Maine 1990, N.H. 1993. Law clk. Vt. Trial Cts., Bennington, 1988-89; assoc. Wilson Powell Lang & Faris, Burlington, Vt., 1989-90, Friedman & Babcock, Portland, Maine, 1990-92; ptnr. Hastings Law Office, Fryeburg, Maine, 1992—; rsch. editor Vermont Law Review, 1987-88. Mem. Fryeburg Planning Bd., 1994—; soccer coach Fryeburg Acad., 1992—. Avocations: bird hunting, soccer. General civil litigation, Insurance, Land use and zoning (including planning). Office: Hastings Law Office 71 Main St Fryeburg ME 04037-1105

**WEIMER, PETER DWIGHT,** mediator, lawyer, corporate executive; b. Grand Rapids, Mich., Oct. 14, 1938; s. Glen E. and Clarabel (Kauffman) W.; children: Melanie, Kim; m. Judith Anne Minor. BA, Bridgewater Coll., 1962; JD, Howard U., 1969. Cert. mediator Supreme Ct. Va. Assoc. counsel Loporto & Weimer Ltd., Manassas, Va., 1970-75; chief counsel Weimer & Cheatle Ltd., Manassas, 1975-79, Peter D. Weimer, P.C., Manassas, 1979-83; pres., mediator Mediation Ltd., Manassas, 1981—; pres. Citation Properties, Inc., Manassas, 1971-93; pres. Preferred Rsch. of No. Va., Inc., 1985-89, Pro Rsch. Inc., 1989-93, Pro Mgmt., Inc., 1990—; cons. Continental Title & Escrow, Inc., 1992-96. Mem. Va. Mediation Network. Address: PO Box 1616 Manassas VA 20108-1616

**WEINACHT, JOHN WILLIAM,** lawyer; b. Orange, Tex., Nov. 13, 1963; s. Charles and Mary Ann W.; m. Luz Marina Lara, Aug. 21, 1985; children: Lara, Jake, Claire. BA, U. Tex., 1987; JD, Baylor U., 1989. Bar: Tex. 1989, N. Mex. 1994, U.S. Dist. Ct. (all dists.) Tex. 1993, U.S. Dist. Ct. N. Mex. 1994, U.S. Ct. Appeals (5th cir.) 1993, U.S. Ct. Appeals (10th cir.) 1995, U.S. Ct. Internat. Trade 1995; U.S. Supreme Ct. 1995. Atty. pvt. practice, Pecos, Tex., 1989—; county atty. Reeves County, Pecos, Tex., 1993-96; spl. counsel Reeves County Detention Ctr., Pecos, Tex., 1997—. Mem. ABA, Tex. Trial Lawyers Assn., Reeves County Bar Assn., Trans-Pecos Bar Assn. Democrat. General civil litigation, General practice, Personal injury. Office: 420 S Cypress St Pecos TX 79772-4012

**WEINBERG, SHELLEY ANN,** lawyer; b. Newark, Mar. 17, 1955; d. Martin R. and Ruby Weinberg; m. Gary Kessel, Oct. 17, 1998. BFA, Syracuse U., 1977; JD, Touro Law Sch., Jacob D. Fuchsberg Law Ctr., 1987. Bar: N.J. 1988, U.S. Dist. Ct. N.J. 1988. Assoc. Larry A. Chamish, Esq., Newark, 1988-90, Wysoker, Glassner & Weingartner, New Brunswick, N.J., 1990, Nelinson, Roche & Carter, East Orange, N.J., 1991-92, Miller & Pincus, Esqs., Livingston, N.J., 1992-93; pvt. practice law, 1993—. Pub. Interest Law fellow Touro Law Sch., 1986. Mem. ATLA, N.J. State Bar Assn., Essex and Morris County Bar Assns. (workers compensation sect.), Nat. Orgn. Social Security Claimants Reps. Democrat. Avocations: fine art, travel, Spanish language. Pension, profit-sharing, and employee benefits, Workers' compensation, Civil rights. Office: 17 Academy St Ste 609 Newark NJ 07102-2905 also: Headqtrs Plaza North Tower 14th Flr Morristown NJ 07963 also: 535 N 7th St Newark NJ 07107

**WEINBERG, STEVEN LEWIS,** lawyer; b. N.Y.C., Aug. 22, 1961; s. Harry and Florence Weinberg. BA in Polit. Sci., SUNY, Binghamton, 1982; JD, Union U., Binghamton, 1985. Bar: N.Y. 1987, U.S. Ct. Appeals (2d cir.) 1987, U.S. Dist. Ct. (no., so., and ea. dists.) N.Y. 1987. Asst. dist. atty. Queens Dist. Atty., Kew Gardens, N.Y., 1985-87; atty. Gotesman Wolgel Secuda Malomy & Flynn P.C., N.Y.C., 1987—. Ct. justice Village of Thomaston, Gt. Neck, N.Y., 1997—. General civil litigation, Appellate. Office: Gottesman Wolgel Secuda Malomy & Flynn PC 29 John St New York NY 10038-4005

**WEINBERGER, ALAN DAVID,** lawyer, corporate executive; b. Washington, July 31, 1945; s. Theodore George and Shirley Sunshine (Gross) W.; m. Lauren Myra Kaminski, Dec. 2, 1979; children: Mark Henry, Benjamin Charles. BA, NYU, 1967, JD, 1970; LLM, Harvard U., 1973. Bar: N.Y. 1971, D.C. 1978, U.S. Supreme Ct. 1980. Assoc. White & Case, N.Y.C., 1970-72; founding law prof. Vt. Law Sch., South Royalton, 1973-75; atty. SEC and Fed. Home Loan Bank Bd., Washington, 1977-81; founder, chmn. bd. dirs., CEO The ASCII Group Inc., Washington, 1984—; founder, chmn. bd. dirs. Tech. Net, Inc., Bethesda, Md., 1995; mem. adv. bd. Ashton Tate Inc., Torrance, Calif., 1986-87; sponsor, agt. All Union Fgn. Trade Acad., Acad. Nat. Economy of USSR in U.S.A., 1988-90; chmn. U.S. adv. bd. Moscow State U. of Commerce, 1992—; chmn. govt. affairs com. Computer Tech. Industry Assn., 1993-95. Author: White Paper to Reform Business Education in Russia, 1996; law rev. editor NYU Sch. Law, 1970. Named one of Top 25 Most Influential Execs. in Computer Industry, Computer Reseller News, 1988. Mem. Nat. Orgn. on Disability (CEO coun.), D.C. Bar Assn., Order of Coif, Kenwood Country Club. Avocation: tennis. Computer, General corporate. Office: ASCII Group Inc 7101 Wisconsin Ave Bethesda MD 20814-4871

**WEINBERGER, HAROLD PAUL,** lawyer; b. N.Y.C., Mar. 12, 1947; s. Fred and Elaine (Schonfeld) W.; m. Toby Ann Strassman, Dec. 15, 1968; children—James David, Karen Ellen. BA, CCNY, 1967; JD, Columbia U., 1970. Bar: N.Y. 1971, U.S. Dist. Cts. (so., ea. and no. dists.) N.Y. 1972, U.S. Ct. Appeals (2d cir.) 1972. Law clk. to presiding justice U.S. Ct. Appeals (2d cir.) N.Y.C., 1970-71; assoc. Kramer, Levin, Naftalis, Nessen, Kamin & Frankel, LLP, N.Y.C., 1971-77, ptnr., 1978—. Recipient John Ordronaux prize Columbia U. Law Sch., 1970. Mem. Assn. Bar City N.Y. (com. fed. legislation 1975-78, com. on products liability 1983-86, mem. com. on trademarks and unfair competition 1995-97). Democrat. Jewish. Federal civil litigation, State civil litigation, Intellectual property. Home: 336 Central Park W New York NY 10025-7111 Office: Kramer Levin Naftalis & Frankel LLP 919 3rd Ave New York NY 10022-3902

**WEINBERGER, PETER HENRY,** lawyer; b. Cleve., Nov. 15, 1950; s. Eric and Eva (Grant) W.; m. Laurie Ann Novak, Aug. 26, 1972; children: Kelly, Adam. AB in Psychology, Syracuse U., 1972; JD, Case Western Res. U., 1975. Bar: Ohio 1975, U.S. Ct. Appeals (6th cir.) 1975, U.S. Ct. Appeals (4th cir.) 1986, Pa. 1995, U.S. Supreme Ct. 1995. Ptnr. Kube & Weinberger, Cleve., 1975-88, Spangenberg, Shibley & Liber, Cleve., 1988—; lectr. to bar assns., Case Western Res. U. Sch. Law. Contb. articles to legal jours. Chmn. Solon (Ohio) Cable TV Adv. Com., 1984-85; mem. Solon Civil Svc. Commn., 1985-87, vice chmn., 1986-87; bd. dirs. 1st Unitarian Ch. Cleve., pres., 1992-93. Mem. ABA, Ohio Bar Assn., Cleve. Bar Assn. (chmn. young lawyers sect. 1980-81, charter mem. coun. litigation sect. 1987—), Cuyahoga Bar Assn. (pres. 1991-92, chmn. grievance com. 1984-86, trustee 1987—, cert. of appreciation 1985, 89, outstanding svc. award 1986), Assn. Trial Lawyers Am., Ohio Acad. Trial Lawyers (trustee 1999—), Cleve. Acad. Trial Attys. (pres. 1984-85, spl. merit award 1985), 8th Dist. Jud. Conf. (charter mem. commn. on pre-trials), Cuyahoga Bar Found. (pres. 1998—), Am. Bd. of Trial Advs. (adv.). Democrat. Unitarian. Personal injury. Home: 34910 Forest Ln Cleveland OH 44139-1441 Office: Spangenberg Shibley & Liber 2400 National City Ctr Cleveland OH 44114

**WEINBLATT, SEYMOUR SOLOMON,** lawyer; b. Bklyn., May 6, 1922; s. David and Lillian (Kantor) W.; m. Dorothy Robinovitz, Mar. 16, 1946 (div. May 1973); children: Jeffrey Howard, Jan Robin; m. Elizabeth Jean King Shelton, June 3, 1973; children: Eric H. Waser, Mark S. Waser (dec.). BA in Zoology, Ind. U., 1947; JD with honors, Rutgers U., 1950, postgrad., 1950-53. Bar: N.J. 1951, U.S. Dist. Ct. N.J. 1951, U.S. Supreme Ct. 1957, U.S. Ct. Appeals (3d cir.) 1975. Atty. City of Manville, N.J., 1962-64, atty. bd. edn., 1962-66; of counsel Strauss & Tauriello, Flemington, N.J., 1984—. Mem. bd. edn. Twp. of Bethlehem, 1977-80, pres. bd. edn., 1979; mem. planning and zoning bd. Town of Juno Beach, Fla., 1998—. Mem. ABA, Hunterdon County (N.J.) Bar Assn., Am. Legion, Jewish War Vets. Jewish. Avocations: real estate, sports, journalism. Fax: (561) 622-6767. E-mail: junoweinblatt@att.net. Criminal, Family and matrimonial, Personal injury. Home: 911 Ocean Dr Apt 803 Juno Beach FL 33408-1700 Office: Strauss & Tauriello 63 Main St Ste 204 Flemington NJ 08822-1452

**WEINER, CHARLES R.,** federal judge; b. Phila., June 27, 1922; s. Max and Bessie (Chairney) W.; m. Edna Gerber, Aug. 24, 1947; children: William, Carole, Harvey. Grad., U. Pa., 1947, M.A., 1967, Ph.D., 1972; LL.B., Temple U., 1950. Bar: Pa. bar 1951. Asst. dist. atty. Philadelphia County, 1952-53; mem. Pa. Senate from Phila. County, 1952-67, minority floor leader, 1959-60, 63-64, majority floor leader, 1961-62; U.S. dist. judge Eastern Dist. Pa., 1967—; now sr. judge; Mem. Phila. County Bd. Law Examiners, 1959—. Mem. Pres.'s Adv. Commn. Inter-Govtl. Rels., Phila., Pub. Policy Com., Phila. Crime Prevention Assn., Big Bros. Assn.; mem. Pa. Bd. Arts and Scis.; trustee, exec. com. Fedn. Jewish Philanthropies of Phila., Allied Jewish Appeal of Phila.; bd. dirs. Mental Health Assn. of Pa., Phila. Psychiat. Ctr., Phila. Tribune Charities, Phila. Wharton Ctr. Parkside YMCA, Jewish Publ. Soc. Am., The Athenaeum, and others. Recipient Phila. Fellowship award; Founder's Day award Temple U.; Alumni award U. Pa.; Founder's award Berean Inst.; others. Mem. ABA, Pa. Bar Assn., Phila. Bar Assn., Am. Law Inst. Office: US District Ct 6613 US Courthouse Ind Mall W 601 Market St Philadelphia PA 19106-1713

**WEINER, DAIN PASCAL,** lawyer, artist; b. Sacramento, Calif., June 14, 1967; s. David and Melode Weiner. BA in Psychology and History, U. Calif., Davis, 1989, JD, 1992. Bar: Calif. 1992, U.S. Dist. Ct. (ea. dist.) Calif. 1993. Tax appeal officer El Dorado County Bd. Equalization, Placerville, Calif., 1997—. Mem. Salcantay Alpine Club (pres. 1993). Avocations: mountaineering, camping, skiing, travel, swimming. Criminal, Personal injury. Office: 3294 Royal Dr Ste 201 Cameron Park CA 95682-8503

**WEINER, DAVID P.,** lawyer; b. Portland, Oreg., Feb. 9, 1948. BA, Claremont McKenna Coll., 1969; JD magna cum laude, Willamette U., 1972. Law clk. U.S. Dist. Ct. Oreg., Portland, 1972-73; from assoc. to ptnr. Samuels, Yoelin, Weiner, Kanton & Seymour, Portland, 1973-96; of counsel Greene & Markley, P.C., Portland, 1996—; mem. discipline rules and procedures com. Oreg. Supreme Ct., 1986—. Mem. ABA (real property sect. B-4 opinion letter com. 1994—), Oreg. State Bar (chair real property com. on opinion letters 1988—, Multnomah County Bar, Oreg. Golf Assn. (pres. 1998—). Real property, Contracts commercial. Office: Greene and Markley PC 1515 SW 5th Ave Ste 600 Portland OR 97201-5449

**WEINER, EARL DAVID,** lawyer; b. Balt., Aug. 21, 1939; s. Jacob Joseph and Sophia Gertrude (Rachanow) W.; m. Gina Helen Priestley Ingoglia, Mar. 30, 1962; children: Melissa Danis Balmain, John Barlow. A.B., Dickinson Coll., 1960; LL.B., Yale U., 1968. Bar: N.Y. 1969. Assoc. Sullivan & Cromwell, N.Y.C., 1968-76, ptnr., 1976—; adj. prof. Rutgers U. Sch. Law, 1987-88; bd. dirs. Solvay Techs. Inc., Hedwin Corp., The Acting Co., vice chair, 1992—, v.p., 1991-92. Gov. Bklyn. Heights Assn., 1980-87, pres., 1985-87, adv. com., 1987—; gov. The Heights Casino, 1979-84, pres., 1981-84; trustee Bklyn. Bot. Garden, 1985—, chmn. 1999—; trustee Green-Wood Cemetery, 1986—, Bklyn. Hosp. Ctr., 1998—; bd. advisors Dickinson Coll., Carlisle, Pa., 1986-90, chmn., 1988-90, trustee, 1988—, vice chmn. 1998—; mem. adv. com. East Rock Inst., 1988—. Lt. USN, 1961-65. Mem. ABA, N.Y. State Bar Assn., Assn. of Bar of City of N.Y. General corporate, Private international. Office: Sullivan & Cromwell 125 Broad St Fl 28 New York NY 10004-2489

**WEINER, ELEANOR FAITH SRAGO,** lawyer; d. Benjamin and Jessie Althea (Lovovitch) Srago; m. Robert S. Weiner, Aug. 24, 1958; children: Michael James, Karin Elizabeth. BA, Skidmore Coll., 1957; JD, Northwestern U., 1962. Law clk. Hon. Vito Concilio Superior Ct., Newark, N.J., 1964-67; ptnr. Eleanor S. Weiner, Esq., Green Village, N.J., 1967—. Rep. of battered women; com. mem. Govs. Conf. on Children and Youth, Indpls., 1981. Chgo. Title and Trust scholarship, 1961. Mem. Morris County Bar Assn., Kappa Beta Pi. Avocations: art and art history, music, tennis, swimming, sailing. Home: 1 Hemlock Ln Morristown NJ 07960-6774 Office: 667 Shunpike Rd Ste 3 Green Village NJ 07935-3021

**WEINER, JODY CARL,** lawyer, author; b. Chgo., Oct. 19, 1948; s. Leo and Sarah J. Weiner; m. Nancy S. Calef, Mar. 4, 1993. BA, U. Wis., 1970; JD, DePaul U., 1974. Bar: Ill. 1974, U.S. Dist. Ct. (no. dist.) Ill. 1974, U.S. Ct. Appeals (6th and 7th cirs.) 1975, Calif. 1989, U.S. Dist. Ct. (no. dist.) Calif. 1989. Assoc. Law Offices Frazin & Frazin, Chgo., 1974-77; ptnr. Muslin & Weiner, Chgo., 1977-80; pvt. practice, Chgo., 1980-85; sr. assoc. Law Offices James Duryea Jr., San Francisco, 1989-91; pvt. practice, San Francisco, 1991—; corp. counsel Skyy Vodka, San Francisco, 1995—. Author: (novels) Raise Your Other Right Hand, 1991, Prisoners of Truth, 1997. Cons., advisor Artist Guild San Francisco, 1996—, Gorilla Found., Woodside, Calif., 1998-99, Eureka Theatre, San Francisco, 1998—. Mem. ABA, San Francisco Bar Assn. General civil litigation, General corporate, Entertainment. Office: 846 Filbert St San Francisco CA 94133-2627

**WEINER, KENNETH BRIAN,** lawyer; b. N.Y.C., Oct. 13, 1954; s. Irwin I. and Elayne B. (Biffer) W. BSCE, Case Western Res. U., 1976; JD summa cum laude, N.Y. Law Sch., 1986. Bar: N.Y. 1986, Washington 1997; registered profl. engr., N.J. Quality control engr. Cosmic Constrn. Co., Newport News, Va., 1976-77; project engr., geotech. engr. Mueser Rutledge Cons. Engrs., N.Y.C., 1977-86; assoc. Olwine, Connelly, Chase, O'Donnel & Weyner, N.Y.C., 1986-91, Ballard Spahr Andrews & Ingersoll LLP, Washington, 1992; assoc. Reid & Priest LLP, Washington, 1992-95, ptnr., 1996-98; ptnr. Thelen Reid & Priest LLP, Washington, 1998—. Contbr. articles to profl. jours. Mem. Aircraft Owners and Pilots Assn., Mooney Aircraft Pilots Assn. Avocations: flying, skiing. Contracts commercial, Construction, Finance. Office: Thelen Reid & Priest LLP 701 Pennsylvania Ave NW Washington DC 20004-2608

**WEINER, LAWRENCE,** lawyer; b. Phila., Aug. 20, 1942; s. Robert A. and Goldie Weiner; m. Jane M. Coulthard, Feb. 28, 1976; 1 child, Kimberly. BS in Econs., U. Pa., 1964, JD, 1967. Bar: Pa. 1967, U.S. Dist. Ct. (ea. dist.) Pa. 1967, Fla. 1970, U.S. Dist. Ct. (so. dist.) Fla. 1976, U.S. Ct. Appeals (5th cir.) 1976, U.S. Tax Ct. 1984. Assoc., ptnr. Blank, Rome, Klaus & Comisky, Phila., 1967-71, 1975-77; ptnr. Weiner & Weisenfeld, P.A., Miami Beach, Fla., 1971-73, Pettigrew & Bailey, Miami, Fla., 1973-75; pres. Lawrence Weiner, P.A., Miami, 1977-83; ptnr. Spieler, Weiner & Spieler, P.A., Miami, 1983-89, Weiner & Cummings, P.A., Miami, 1989-94, Weiner, Cummings & Vittoria, Miami, 1994—; lectr. Wharton Sch. U. Pa., Phila., 1968-70; instr. bus. law and acctg. Community Coll. Phila., 1967-70; lectr. estate planning various non-lawyer groups, Miami, 1972—. Mem. Fla. Bar (liaison non-lawyers groups 1980-87), Pa. Bar Assn., Phila. Bar Assn., Dade County Bar Assn. (chmn. ins. com. 1977-78, probate law com. 1992—). Democrat. Jewish. Probate, General corporate, Estate planning. Office: Weiner Cummings & Vittoria 1428 Brickell Ave Ste 400 Miami FL 33131-3436

**WEINER, RONALD ALLEN,** lawyer; b. Detroit, Mar. 30, 1962; s. Samuel Paul and Phyllis Diane W.; m. Amy Marilyn Hoffman Weiner, July 7, 1990; children: Hannah, Abigail. BA in Polit. Sci., U. Mich., Ann Arbor, 1983; JD, Syracuse (N.Y.) U. Coll. Law, 1987. Bar: Mich. 1987; U.S. Dist. Ct. (ea. dist.). Asst. prosecuting atty. Macomb County Prosecutor, Mt. Clemens, Mich., 1987-90; atty. Zamplas, Johnson, Walker & Cavanagh PC, Bloomfield

Hills, Mich., 1990-92, Lakin, Worsham & Victor PC, Southfield, Mich., 1992-95, Zamler, Mellen & Shiffman PC, Southfield, Mich., 1995—. Contbr. articles to profl. jours. Mem. Mich. Trial Lawyers Assn., Assn. Trial Lawyers Am. Democrat. Jewish. Personal injury. Office: Zamler Mellen & Shiffman PC 23077 Greenfield Rd Ste 557 Southfield MI 48075-3727

**WEINER, SAMUEL,** lawyer; b. Phila., Feb. 2, 1955; s. Paul David Weiner and Evelyn Ruth Monash; m. Sondra A. Petteruti, Aug. 20, 1983; children: Evonne, Alexis, Nikki. BS, U. Vt., 1977; JD, Vt. Law Sch., 1980; M in Tax Law, Boston U., 1981. Bar: Mass. 1981, N.J. 1983, U.S. Dist. Ct. N.J. 1981. Tax cons. Price Waterhouse, Boston, 1981-83; atty. Klein Chapman, Clifton, N.J., 1983-84, Cole, Schotz, Meisel, Forman & Leonard, P.C., Hackensack, N.J., 1984—. Author: Starting a Limited Liability Company, 1995; contbr. articles to profl. jours. Bd. trustees Tomorrow's Children, Hackensack, 1993—. Mem. N.J. State Bar Assn. Avocations: triathons, running, skiing, traveling, reading. Taxation, general, Probate, Estate planning. Office: Cole Schotz Meisel Forman & Leonard PC 2 Main St Hackensack NJ 07601-7006

**WEINER, STANLEY P.,** lawyer; b. Kansas City, Mo., July 22, 1941; m. Susan M. Levine, Sept. 1, 1962; children: Caren M., Tracy B., Scott R. BBA in Acctg., U. Mich., 1963, JD, 1967. Bar: Mo. 1967. Law clk. U.S. Tax Ct., Washington, 1967-69; assoc. Hornle, Morris & Huckseller, Phila., 1969-73; ptnr. Smith, Gill, Fisher & Butts, Kansas City, Mo., 1973-78, Grier, Shaltzman & Weiner, Kansas City, 1978-84, Shook, Hardy & Bacon LLP, Kansas City, 1984—. Pres. Lawyers Trust Fund Found., Jefferson City, Mo., 1985-88, Jewish Cmty. Ctr., Kansas City, 1990-93; chmn. Heart of Am. Tax Inst., Kansas City, 1978. Recipient Pres.'s award The Mo. Bar, Charles Evans Whittaker award Lawyers Assn., Kansas City. Fellow Am. Coll. Tax Counsel. Office: Shook Hardy & Bacon LLP 1200 Main St Ste 3000 Kansas City MO 64105-2139

**WEINER, STEPHEN L.,** lawyer; b. N.Y.C., 1946; m. Nan E. Weiner. AB, Columbia Coll., 1967; JD cum laude, Columbia U., 1970. Bar: N.Y. 1971, U.S. Dist. Ct. (so. and ea. dists.) N.Y. 1971, U.S. Ct. Appeals (2d cir.) 1971. Assoc. Hughes Hubbard & Reed, N.Y.C., 1970-72; asst. dist. atty. N.Y. County Dist. Atty., N.Y.C., 1972-75; law sec. to Hon. Leon B. Polsky N.Y. Supreme Ct., N.Y.C., 1975-78; spl. counsel N.Y. State Commn. Investigation, N.Y.C., 1978-79; ptnr. Hoffinger Friedland, N.Y.C., 1979-96; pvt. practice N.Y.C., 1996—; chmn. and commr. N.Y. State Commn. Investigation, 1996—; mem. nat. evaluation team, assigned counsel plan, 1st jud. dept., sch. pub. affairs, Am. U., Washington, 1991. Mem. ind. jud. screening panel Supreme Ct. Dem. County Com., 1986, ind. jud. screening panel surrogates ct. and civil ct., 1990; mem. N.Y. Gov.'s transition team, 1994-95; bd. dirs. Legal Aid Soc., 1995—, Ctr. Cmty. Alternatives, 1995—; mem. N.Y. Unified Ct. Sys. Office Ct. Adminstrn. Adv. Com. Criminal Law and Procedure, 1994—; mem. appellate divsn. N.Y. Supreme Ct. First Jud. Dept. Disciplinary com., policy com., 1989-92, hearings panel, 1986-97, spl. counsel to policy com., 1998—. Mem. ABA (criminal justice, family law, litigation sects.), Nat. Assn. Criminal Def. Lawyers (mem. ethics adv. com. 1989-96), Fed. Bar Coun., N.Y. State Bar Assn. (del. ho. of dels. 1991-97, mem. second century com., 1993-96, mem. various coms. and sects.), N.Y. Criminal Bar Assn. (co-chair com. legislation 1981-84), N.Y. State Assn. Criminal Def. Lawyers (charter), Assn. Bar City of N.Y. (chair com. criminal justice ops. and budget 1987-90, coun. criminal justice 1990-93, mem. delegation to N.Y. State Bar Assn. ho. of dels. 1991-97, mem. various coms. and couns.), Soc. of Columbia Grads., Phi Delta Phi. Avocations: fishing, sailing, boating, photography. Federal civil litigation, State civil litigation, Criminal. Office: care White & Case 1155 Avenue Of The Americas New York NY 10036-2711

**WEINGARDEN, MITCHELL IAN,** lawyer; b. N.Y.C., Apr. 30, 1959; s. Harold Danny and Diane Joyce Weingarden; m. Janet Esther Handelman, Sept. 3, 1984; children: Pamela, Ilyssa, Thea. BS, SUNY, Binghamton, 1980; JD, Emory U., 1983. Bar: N.Y. 1984, U.S. Dist. Ct. (so. and ea. dist.) N.Y. Asst. dist. atty. Kings County Dist. Atty.'s Office, Bklyn., 1983-88; v.p. R.H. Macy & Co. Inc., N.Y.C., 1989-93; instr. NYU, 1997—; ptnr. Law Offices of Mitchell I. Weingarden, White Plains, N.Y., 1993—; adminstrv. law judge N.Y.C. Dept. of Fin., 1995—. Chmn. Town of Bedford Dem. Com., 1997-99; mem. Westchester County Dem. Com., 1997—. General civil litigation, Contracts commercial, Labor. Office: 30 Glenn St Fl 2 White Plains NY 10603-3254

**WEINGARTEN, SAUL MYER,** lawyer; b. Los Angeles, Dec. 19, 1921; s. Louis and Lillian Dorothy (Alter) W.; m. Miriam Ellen Moore, Jan. 21, 1949; children: David, Steven, Lawrence, Bruce. AA, Antelope Valley Coll., 1940; AB, UCLA, 1942; cert., Cornell U., 1943; JD, U. Southern Calif., 1949. Prin. Saul M. Weingarten Assocs., Seaside, Calif., 1954—; atty. City of Gonzales, Calif., 1954-74, City of Seaside, 1955-70; gen. counsel Redevel. Agy., Seaside, 1955-76, Security Nat. Bank, Monterey, Calif., 1968-74; bd. dirs., exec. com. Frontier Bank, Cheyenne, Wyo., 1984—, Mariposa Hall Inc., 1989—. Author: Practice Compendium, 1950; contbr. articles to profl. jours. Del. Internat. Union of Local Authorities, Brussels, Belgium, 1963, 73; candidate state legislature Dem. Com., Monterey County, 1958; counsel Monterey Peninsula Mus. of Art, Inc., 1972-80; gen. counsel Monterey County Symphony Assn., Carmel, Calif., 1974-98, Mountain Plains Edn. Project, Glasgow, Mont., 1975-81; chmn. fund raising ARC, Monterey, 1964; chmn., bd. dirs. fund raising United Way, Monterey, 1962-63; pres., bd. dirs. Alliance on Aging, Monterey, 1968-82; bd. dirs. Family Svc. Agy., Monterey, 1958-66, Monterey County Cultural Coun., 1986—, Clark Found., 1982—; dir., mem. exec. com. Monterey Bay Performing Arts Ctr., 1990. Served to commdr. USN, 1942-46, 50-54, Korea. Grad. fellow Coro Found., 1949-50. Mem. Calif. Bar Assn., Monterey County Bar Assn., Monterey County Trial Lawyers Assn., Rotary (pres. 1970-71, 82-83), Commonwealth Club, Meadowbrook Club. Jewish. Avocations: tennis, travel. General practice, State civil litigation, Family and matrimonial. Home: 4135 Crest Rd Pebble Beach CA 93953-3008 Office: 1123 Fremont Blvd Seaside CA 93955-5759

**WEINGER, STEVEN MURRAY,** lawyer; b. Chgo., Feb. 7, 1954; s. Paul and Joan (Taxay) W.; children: Blake, Paige, Haley. BA, Hampshire Coll., 1975; JD, U. Chgo., 1978. Bar: Fla. 1979, Ill. 1979, U.S. Dist. Ct. (so. dist.) Fla. 1979, U.S. Ct. Appeals (5th cir.) 1980, U.S. Ct. Appeals (11th cir.) 1981, U.S. Supreme Ct. 1982, U.S. Dist. Ct. (mid. dist.) Fla. 1989. Mem. faculty U. Miami Sch. Law, Coral Gables, Fla., 1978-79; ptnr. Kurzban, Kurzban & Weinger, P.A., Miami, Fla., 1979—. Bd. dirs. Sunrise Cmty. for Mentally Retarded, Miami, United Cerebral Palsy Tallahassee, Inc., Palmer-Trinity Sch., Miami. Recipient Chmn.'s award Sunrise Cmty. for Mentally Retarded, 1987; honoree United Cerebral Palsy in South Fla., 1995, Fla. Assn. Rehab. Facilities, 1996, United Cerebral Palsy Assn., 1997. Mem. ABA, Assn. Trial Lawyers Am., Fla. Assn. Trial Lawyers. Federal civil litigation, Health, General civil litigation. Office: Kurzban Kurzban & Weinger 2650 SW 27th Ave Fl 2D Miami FL 33133-3003

**WEINIG, RICHARD ARTHUR,** lawyer; b. Durango, Colo., Mar. 23, 1940; s. Arthur John and Edna (Novella) W.; m. Barbara A. Westerlund, June 16, 1964. BA in Polit. Sci., Stanford U., 1962, postgrad. in Soviet Studies, 1962-65; JD, U. Calif., San Francisco, 1971. Bar: Alaska 1971, U.S. Dist. Ct. Alaska 1971, U.S. Ct. Appeals (9th cir.) 1978, U.S. Supreme Ct. 1979. Assoc. Burr, Pease & Kurtz, Anchorage, 1971-73, Greater Anchorage Area Borough, 1973-75, Municipality of Anchorage, 1975-82; ptnr. Pletcher & Slaybaugh, Anchorage, 1982-88, Pletcher, Weinig & Merriner, Anchorage, 1988—. Mem. editl. bd. Hastings Law Jour. Active Stanford U. Young Republicans, 1961-65, Sierra Club, Mountaineering Club, Knik Canoyers and Kayakers of Alaska, Alaska Ctr. for Environ. Mem. ABA, Alaska Bar Assn., Anchorage Bar Assn., NRA. Republican. Presbyterian. Condemnation, Personal injury, Insurance. Office: Pletcher Weinig Fisher Dennis & Porchello 800 E Dimond Blvd Ste 3-620 Anchorage AK 99515-2045

**WEINMAN, GLENN ALAN,** lawyer; b. N.Y.C., Dec. 9, 1955; s. Seymour and Iris Rhoda (Bergman) W. BA in Polit. Sci., UCLA, 1978; JD, U. So. Calif., 1981. Bar: Calif. 1981. Assoc. counsel Mitsui Mfrs. Bank, L.A., 1981-83; assoc. McKenna, Conner & Cuneo, L.A., 1983-85, Stroock, Stroock & Lavan, L.A., 1985-87; sr. counsel Buchalter, Nemer, Fields & Younger, L.A., 1987-91; ptnr. Keck, Mahin & Cate, L.A., 1991-93; sr. v.p., gen. counsel Western Internat. Media Corp., L.A., 1993-96; v.p. law and human resources, sec. Guess?, Inc., L.A., 1996—, sec. law and human resources, 1998—; also bd. dirs.; bd. dirs. Guess? Retail Inc., Guess? Licensing, Inc., Guess.com., Inc. Mem. ABA (corp. banking and bus. law sect., com. on savs. instns., com. on banking law corp. counsel sect.), Calif. Bar Assn. (bus. law sect., com. fin. instns. 1989-91, com. consumer svcs. 1991-94), L.A. County Bar Assn. (corp. legal depts. sect., bus. and corps. law sect., subcom. on fin. instns.), Calif. Fashion Assn., Am. Apparel Mfrs. Assn. (govt. rels. com. 1997—), Legion Lex, U. So. Calif. Law Alumni Assn., Phi Alpha Delta. Avocation: tennis. Banking, General corporate, Contracts commercial. Office: Guess? Inc 1444 S Alameda St Los Angeles CA 90021-2433

**WEINMANN, RICHARD ADRIAN,** lawyer; b. N.Y.C., Oct. 15, 1917; s. Randolph and Mae (Korber) W.; m. Bert Millicent Landes, Dec. 26, 1946; children: Harriet Joan, Elaine, Anita; m. Ginger Grace Rich, 1999. LLB, Bklyn. Law Sch., 1948; LLM, NYU, 1953. Bar: N.Y. 1958, U.S. Dist. Ct. (so. dist.) N.Y. 1960; U.S. Dist. Ct. (ea. dist.) N.Y. 1960, U.S. Ct. Appeals (2d cir.) 1965, U.S. Supreme Ct. 1964. Ptnr. Sipser, Weinstock & Weinmann, N.Y.C., 1953-71; sole practice N.Y.C., 1972—; guest lectr. seminars; mem. staff Cornell U. Sch. Indsl. and Labor Relations; panel arbitrator Fed. Mediation and Conciliation Svc. Am. Arbitration Assn. Suffolk and Nassau Counties Pub. Employment Relations Bds. N.Y. State; N.J. State Bd. Mediation, N.Y. State Employment Rels. Bd. Committeeman Nassau County (N.Y.), 1965—; former mem. legal adv. bd. Union Lawyers Ednl. Conf. Served with AUS, 1943-46. Mem. ABA, ACLU, N.Y. State Bar Assn., Indsl. Rels. Rsch. Assn., B'nai B'rith. Labor, General practice.

**WEINSCHEL, ALAN JAY,** lawyer; b. Bklyn., Feb. 9, 1946; m. Barbara Ellen Schure, Aug. 20, 1967; children: Lawrence, Adam, Naomi. BA, Bklyn. Coll., 1967; JD, NYU, 1969. Bar: N.Y. 1970, U.S. Dist. Ct. (so. and ea. dists.) N.Y. 1973, U.S. Ct. Appeals (2d cir.) 1979, U.S. Ct. Appeals (9th cir.) 1986, U.S. Ct. Appeals (3d cir.) 1993, U.S. Ct. Appeals (7th cir.) 1996. Assoc. Breed, Abbott & Morgan, N.Y.C., 1969-74; assoc. Weil, Gotshal & Manges, N.Y.C., 1974-78, ptnr., 1978—; lectr. Practising Law Inst., Ohio Legal Ctr., Am. Mgmt. Assn., Law Jour. Seminars, Law and Bus. Seminars, Glasser Legalworks. Trustee N.Y. Inst. Tech., Old Westbury, N.Y., 1969-76, Temple Sinai, Roslyn, N.Y., 1981-87, 89-95. Capt. U.S. Army res., 1969-74. Mem. ABA (editl. bd. Antitrust Devels. 1981-87), N.Y. State Bar Assn. (chmn. antitrust sect. 1993-95), Assn. Bar of City of N.Y. Antitrust, General civil litigation, Intellectual property. Office: Weil Gotshal & Manges 767 5th Ave Fl Concl New York NY 10153-0119

**WEINSHIENK, ZITA LEESON,** federal judge; b. St. Paul, Apr. 3, 1933; d. Louis and Ada (Dubov) Leeson; m. Hubert Troy Weinshienk, July 8, 1956 (dec. 1983); children: Edith Blair, Kay Anne, Darcy Jill; m. James N. Schaffner, Nov. 15, 1986. Student, U. Colo., 1952-53; BA magna cum laude, U. Ariz., 1955; JD cum laude, Harvard U., 1958; Fulbright grantee, U. Copenhagen, Denmark, 1959; LHD (hon.), Loretto Heights Coll., 1985; LLD (hon.), U. Denver, 1990. Bar: Colo. 1959. Probation counselor, legal adviser, referee Denver Juvenile Ct., 1959-64; judge Denver Mcpl. Ct., 1964-65, Denver County Ct., 1965-71, Denver Dist. Ct., 1972-79; judge, then sr. judge U.S. Dist. Ct. Colo., Denver, 1979—. Precinct committeewoman Denver Democratic Com., 1963-64; bd. dirs. Crime Stoppers. Named one of 100 Women in Touch with Our Time Harper's Bazaar Mag., 1971, Woman of Yr., Denver Bus. and Profl. Women, 1969; recipient Women Helping Women award Soroptimist Internat. of Denver, 1983, Hanna G. Solomon award Nat. Coun. Jewish Women, Denver, 1986. Fellow Colo. Bar Found., Am. Bar Found.; mem. ABA, Denver Bar Assn., Colo. Bar Assn., Nat. Conf. Fed. Trial Judges (exec. com., past chair), Dist. Judges' Assn. of 10th Cir. (past pres.), Colo. Women's Bar Assn., Fed. Judges Assn., Denver Crime Stoppers Inc. (bd.dirs.), Devner LWV, Women's Forum Colo., Harvard Law Sch. Assn., Phi Beta Kappa, Phi Kappa Phi, Order of Coif (hon. Colo. chpt.). Office: US Dist Ct US Courthouse Rm C-418 1929 Stout St Denver CO 80294-1929

**WEINSTEIN, ALAN EDWARD,** lawyer; b. Bklyn., Apr. 20, 1945; s. John and Matilda W.; m. Patti Kantor, Dec. 18, 1965; children: Steven R., David A. AA, U. Fla., 1964; BBA, U. Miami (Fla.), 1965, JD cum laude, 1968. Bar: Fla. 1968, U.S. Dist. Ct. (so. dist.) Fla. 1968, U.S. Ct. Appeals (5th cir.) 1969, U.S. Supreme Ct. 1973, U.S. Ct. Appeals (4th & 11th cirs.) 1981. Assoc. Cohen & Hogan, Miami Beach, Fla., 1968-71; pvt. practice Miami Beach, 1972-81; sr. ptnr. Weinstein & Preira, Miami Beach, 1981-92; prin. Law Offices of Alan E. Weinstein, Miami, 1992—; lectr. continuing legal edn. programs. Mem. ABA (criminal and family law sect. 1968—, white collar crime commn. 1986—), Nat. Assn. Criminal Def. Lawyers, 1st Family Law Am. Inn of Court, Fla. Bar Assn. (criminal and family law sect. 1968—, ethics com. 1987-88, bench/bar com. 1988-89, grievance com. 1999—), Fla. Criminal Def. Attys. Assn. (pres. 1978-79), Fla. Assn. Criminal Def. Lawyers (treas. 1989-90), Miami Beach Bar Assn., Soc. Wig and Robe, Phi Kappa Phi. Avocations: marlin fishing, reading, travel. Criminal, Family and matrimonial. Office: 1801 West Ave Miami FL 33139-1431

**WEINSTEIN, ANDREW H.,** lawyer; b. Pitts., Oct. 5, 1943; s. Adolph J. and Meta I. (Schwartz) W.; m. Susan Balber, Aug. 11, 1968; children: Jodi L., Toby M., Jamie M. BSBA, Duquesne U., 1965; JD, U. Pitts., 1968; LLM in Tax Law, NYU, 1969. Bar: Pa. 1969, U.S. Tax Ct. 1969, Fla. 1970, U.S. Dist. Ct. (so. dist.) Fla., U.S. Ct. Fed. Claims. Trial atty. IRS, L.A., 1969-70, Miami, Fla., 1970-73; ptnr. Glass, Schultz, Weinstein & Moss, Coral Gables, Fla., 1973-80, Holland & Knight, Miami, 1980—. Contbr. articles to profl. jours. Bd. dirs. New World Symphony, Miami, Performing Arts Found., Zool. Soc. Fla. Fellow Am. Coll. Tax Counsel; mem. ABA (tax sect. com., chmn. subcom. 1981-87, chmn. CLE subcom., adminstrv. practice com.), The Fla. Bar Assn. Republican. Avocations: golf, swimming, travel. Corporate taxation, Estate taxation, Personal income taxation. Office: Holland & Knight 701 Brickell Ave Ste 3000 Miami FL 33131-2898

**WEINSTEIN, DAVID AKERS,** lawyer; b. Denver, Apr. 9, 1942; s. Sam and Rowena May (Akers) W.; m. Gayle Ann Sunshine. BA, U. Colo., 1963; JD, U. Denver, 1967. Bar: Colo. 1967, N.Y. 1970, Ohio 1972, Wis. 1993, U.S. Dist. Ct. Colo., U.S. Ct. Appeals (10th and fed. cirs.). Atty. U.S. Patent and Trademark Office, Washington, 1967-70, Gen. Foods Corp., White Plains, N.Y., 1970-71, Borden Inc., Columbus, Ohio, 1971-77; pvt. practice Denver, 1977-91, 98—; atty.-spl. counsel Reinhart, Boerner Van Deuren Norris & Rieselbach, Denver, 1991-94, Holme, Roberts & Owen, Denver, 1994-96; ptnr. Dorsey & Whitney, Denver, 1996-97; legal cons. Republic of Bulgaria Patent Office, Sofia, 1996, Govt. of Egypt Trademark Office, Cairo, 1997-99, Govt. of Jordan Ministry of Industry & Trade, 1999. Author: How to Protect Your Creative Work, 1987, How to Protect Your Business, Professional & Brand Names, 1990. Past pres., bd. dirs. Colo. Lawyers for the Arts, Denver. Mem. Am. Intellectual Property Law Assn., Copyright Soc. U.S.A., Internat. Trademark Assn., Licensing Execs. Soc. Trademark and copyright. Office: 1700 Broadway Ste 1800 Denver CO 80290-1801

**WEINSTEIN, DIANE GILBERT,** federal judge; b. Rochester, N.Y., June 14, 1947; d. Myron Birne and Doris Isabelle (Robie) Gilbert; m. Dwight Douglas Sypolt; children: Andrew, David. BA, Smith Coll., Northampton, Mass., 1969; postgrad., Stanford U., 1977-78, Georgetown U., 1978; JD, Boston U., 1979. Bar: D.C. 1979, Mass. 1979. Law clk. to judge D.C. Ct. Appeals, Washington, 1979-80; assoc. Peabody, Lambert & Meyers, Washington, 1980-83; asst. gen. counsel Office of Mgmt. and Budget, Washington, 1983-86; dep. gen. counsel U.S. Dept. Edn., Washington, 1986-88, acting gen. counsel, 1988-89; legal counselor to V.P. of U.S., White House; counsel Pres.'s Competitiveness Coun., Washington, 1989-90; judge U.S. Ct. Fed. Claims, Washington, 1990—. Recipient Young Lawyer's award Boston U. Law Sch., 1989. Mem. Fed. Am. Inn of Ct. (Master), Federalist Soc. Republican. Office: US Ct Fed Claims 717 Madison Pl NW Washington DC 20005-1011

**WEINSTEIN, HARRIS,** lawyer; b. Providence, May 10, 1935; s. Joseph and Gertrude (Rusitzky) W.; m. Rosa Grunberg, June 3, 1956; children: Teme Feldman, Joshua, Jacob. BS in Math., MIT, 1956, MS in Math., 1958; LLB, Columbia U., 1961. Bar: D.C. 1962. Law clk. to judge William H. Hastie U.S. Ct. Appeals (3d cir.), Phila., 1961-62; with Covington & Burling, Washington, 1962-67, 69-90, 1993—; chief counsel Office of Thrift Supervision U.S. Dept. of Treasury, Washington, 1990-92; asst. to solicitor gen. U.S. Dept. Justice, 1967-69; pub. mem. Adminstrv. Conf. of U.S., 1982-90; lectr. U. Va. Law Sch., 1995; mgmt. com. Undiscovered Mgrs., LLC, 1998—. V.p. Jewish Social Svc. Agy., 1995-98; mem. MIT Corp., 1989-95. Mem. Nat. Press Club. General civil litigation, Banking. Home: 7717 Georgetown Pike Mc Lean VA 22102-1411 Office: Covington & Burling PO Box 7566 1201 Pennsylvania Ave NW Washington DC 20004-2401

**WEINSTEIN, JACK BERTRAND,** federal judge; b. Wichita, Kans., Aug. 10, 1921; s. Harry Louis and Bessie Helen (Brodach) W.; m. Evelyn Horowitz, Oct. 10, 1946; children: Seth George, Michael David, Howard Lewis. BA, Bklyn. Coll., 1943; LLB, Columbia, 1948; LLD (hon.), Bklyn. Law Sch., Yeshiva U., Albany Law Sch., Hofstra Law Sch., L.I. U.; Yale U. Bar: N.Y. 1949. Assoc. Columbia Law Sch., 1948-49; law clk. N.Y. Ct. Appeals Judge Stanly H. Fuld, 1949-50; ptnr. William Rosenfeld, N.Y.C., 1950-52; mem. faculty Columbia Law Sch., 1952-67, prof. law, 1956-67, adj. prof., 1967-97; U.S. judge (Eastern Dist. N.Y.), 1967-93, chief judge, 1980-88; sr. judge Ea. Dist. N.Y., 1993—; vis. prof. U. Tex., 1957, U. Colo., 1961, Harvard U., 1982, Georgetown U., 1991, Bklyn. Law Sch., 1988-97, others; counsel N.Y. Joint Legis. Com. Motor Vehicle Problems, 1952-54, State Sen. Seymour Halpern, 1952-54; reporter adv. com. practice and procedure N.Y. State Temp. Commn. Cts., 1955-58; adv. com. practice N.Y. Judicial Conf., 1963-66; adv. com. rules of evidence U.S. Jud. Conf., 1965-75, mem. com. jurisdiction, 1969-75, mem., 1983-86; mem. 2d Cir. Jud. Coun., 1982-88, U.S. Jud. Conf., 1983-86, others in past. Author: (with Morgan and Maquire) Cases and Materials on Evidence, 4th edit, 1965, (with Maguire, Chadbourne and Mansfield, 5th edit.), 1971, 6th edit., 1975, (with Mansfield, Abrams and Berger), 9th edit., 1997, (with Rosenberg) Cases and Materials on Civil Procedure, 1961, rev. edit, (with Smit), 1971, (with Smit, Rosenberg and Korn), 1976, (with Korn and Miller) New York Civil Procedure, 9 vols., rev. edit, 1966, Manual of New York Civil Procedure, 1967, Basic Problems of State and Federal Evidence, 1976, (with Berger) Weinstein's Evidence, 7 vols., 1967, rev. edit., 1993, Revising Rule Making Procedures, 1977, A New York Constitution Meeting Today's Needs and Tomorrow's Challenges, 1967, Disaster, A Legal Allegory, 1988, (with Greenawalt) Readings for Seminar on Equality and Law, 1979, (with Murphy) Readings for Seminar in Individual Rights in a Mass Society, 1990-91, (with Berger) Readings for Seminar in Science and Law, (with Feinberg) Mass Torts, 1992, 94, Individual Justice in Mass Litigation, 1995. Chmn. N.Y. Dem. adv. com. on Constl. Conv., 1955; bd. dirs. N.Y. Civil Liberties Union, 1956-62, Cardozo Sch. Law, Conf. on Jewish Social Studies, 1980-88; nat. adv. bd. Am. Jewish Congress, 1960-67, CARE, 1985-90, Fedn. Jewish Philanthropies, 1985-94; chmn. lay bd. Riverside Hosp. Adolescent Drug Users, 1954-55. Lt. USNR, 1943-46. Mem. ABA, N.Y. State Bar Assn., Assn. of Bar of City of N.Y., Nassau County Bar Assn., Am. Law Inst., Soc. Pub. Tchrs. Law (Eng.), Am. Acad. Arts and Scis. Jewish. Office: US Dist Ct US Courthouse 225 Cadman Plz E Brooklyn NY 11201-1818

**WEINSTEIN, JORDAN HARVEY,** lawyer; b. Cheyenne, Wyo., July 16, 1953; s. Seymour and Janet A. Weinstein; m. Deborah Lynne Fruchtman; children: Jennifer, David, Allison, Melissa. BA, U. Mich., 1974; LLB, Osgoode Hall Law Sch., Toronto, Can., 1978. Bar: Mass. 1979, U.S. Dist. Ct. Mass. 1979. Assoc. Weinstein Bernstein & Burwick, Worcester, Mass., 1979-90, ptnr., 1990-92, mng. ptnr., 1992—. nat. v.p., chmn. U.S. Maccabrah steering com., head U.S. del. Maccabi USA/Sports for Israel, Phila., 1997—. Fellow Mass. Bar Found.; mem. ABA, Mass. Bar Assn., Worcester County Bar Assn., Mass. Trial Lawyers Assn., Mass. Acad. Trial Lawyers. Avocations: recruiting and organizing national teams to represent U.S. at World Maccabi Games. General civil litigation, Personal injury, Contracts commercial. Home: 23 Holly Cir Holden MA 01520-1160 Office: Weinstein Bernstein & Burwick 10 Mechanic St Worcester MA 01608-2420

**WEINSTEIN, MARK MICHAEL,** lawyer; b. N.Y.C., Apr. 20, 1942; s. Nathan and Caroline (Levine) W.; m. Adrienne Peni Kuba, Aug. 15, 1965; children: Samantha Beth, Caleb Jonathan. AB, Columbia Coll., 1964; LLB, U. Pa., 1968. Assoc. Paul Weiss, Rifkind, Wharton and Garrison, N.Y.C., 1968-76; asst. v.p., dep. gen. counsel Warner Communications Inc., N.Y.C., 1976-78, v.p., 1978-85; v.p., gen. counsel Viacom Internat. Inc., N.Y.C., 1985-87, sr. v.p., gen. counsel and sec., 1987-93, sr. v.p. govt. affairs, 1993-97; mng. mem. Weinstein Legal Search and Cons., N.Y.C., 1997—, Bridgestone Legal Staffing, LLC, N.Y.C., 1999—. Office: Weinstein Legal Search and Consulting Ste 2900 885 3d Ave New York NY 10022

**WEINSTEIN, MARTIN JAMES,** lawyer; b. Washington, D.C., Jan. 31, 1959; m. Amy Cooper, Apr. 14, 1991. BA, Dartmouth Coll., 1981; JD, Univ. Va., 1984. Bar: D.C. 1985, Md. 1985, Ga. 1990. Assoc. Howrey & Simon, Washington, 1984-88; trial atty. U.S. Dept. Justice, Washington, 1988-89; asst. U.S. atty. U.S. Dept. Justice, U.S. Atty's Office, Atlanta, 1989-96; ptnr. Foley & Lardner, Washington, 1996—; chmn. compliance, counseling White Collar Practice Group; adv. U.S. Dept. State., Washington, 1996; participant Commonwealth Films, Boston, 1996; founder, gen. coun. Silverstar Inns, L.L.C., Telluride, Colo., 1995—; founder Capital Opportunities, Ltd., Chevy Chase, Md., 1985-96. Contbr. articles to profl. jours. Recipient Federal Law Enforcement Officers Prosecutorial award Fed. Law Enforcement, 1995, The John Marshall award U.S. Dept. Justice, 1995. Private international, Criminal, Government contracts and claims. Office: Foley & Lardner 3000 K St NW Ste 500 Washington DC 20007-5143

**WEINSTEIN, WILLIAM JOSEPH,** lawyer; b. Detroit, Dec. 9, 1917; s. Joseph and Bessie (Abromovitch) W.; m. Evelyn Ross, Apr. 5, 1942 (dec.); children: Patricia, Michael; m. Rose Sokolsky, Oct. 25, 1972. LLB, Wayne State U., 1940. Bar: Mich. 1940, U.S. Dist. Ct. (ea. and so. dists.) Mich. 1940, U.S. Ct. Appeals (6th cir.) 1951, U.S. Ct. Appeals (9th cir.) 1972. Ptnr. Charfoos, Gussin & Weinstein, Southfield, Mich., 1951-54, Charfoos, Gussin, Weinstein & Kroll, Detroit, 1955-59, Gussin, Weinstein & Kroll, P.C., Detroit, 1965-73, Weinstein, Kroll & Gordon, P.C., Detroit, 1973-85; pvt. practice Southfield, 1985-87, Bloomfield Hills, Mich., 1987—; mem. std. jury instrn. com. Mich. Supreme Ct. 1965-72. Contbr. articles to legal jours. Maj. gen. USMCR, 1941-75. Decorated Bronze Star with Combat V, Legion of Merit (2), Purple Heart (2). Recipient Disting. Alumnus award Wayne State U. Law Sch., 1968. Mem. Mich. Bar Assn. (chmn. negligence sect. 1962-63), Am. Coll. Trial Lawyers, Internat. Acad. Trial Lawyers, USN League (nat. v.p. 1971-72), Tam-o-Shanter Club (Orchard Lake, Mich.), St. Andrews Country Club (Boca Raton, Fla.). Federal civil litigation, State civil litigation, Personal injury. Home and Office: 3922 Wabeek Lake Dr E Bloomfield Hills MI 48302-1261

**WEINSTOCK, GREGG D.,** lawyer; b. Bklyn., July 22, 1964; s. Leonard and Rita Weinstock; m. Wendy G. Weinstock; children: Zachary, Jacob, Amy. BA, Johns Hopkins U., 1985; JD, George Washington U., 1988. Bar: N.Y., N.J., Conn., D.C., U.S. Supreme Ct., U.S. Dist. Ct. N.J., U.S. Dist. Ct. (ea. and so. dists.) N.Y., U.S. Ct. Appeals (2d cir.), U.S. Dist. Ct. Conn. Assoc. Cullen and Dykman, Bklyn., 1988-91; ptnr. Garbaroni & Scher P.C., N.Y.C., 1991—. Assoc. editor George Washington Jour. Internat. Law and Econs., 1987-88. Coach Valley Stream (N.Y.) Soccer Club, 1998—; asst. coach Valley Stream Knicks Basketball League, 1998. Mem. ABA, N.Y. State Bar Assn. Avocations: running, reading. State civil litigation, Personal injury, General civil litigation. Office: Garbarini & Scher PC 1114 Ave of Americas New York NY 10036

**WEINTRAUB, BRUCE SCOTT,** lawyer; b. Manhasset, N.Y., May 28, 1957; s. Jerome L. and Annabelle (Steinfeld) W. BS, SUNY at Stony Brook, 1978; MS, L.I. Univ., 1981; JD, Yeshiva U., 1988. Assoc. Scully Scott Murphy & Presser, Garden City, N.Y., 1988-91, Rosenman & Colin, N.Y.C., 1991-93; patent atty. Becton Dickinson and Co., Franklin Lakes, N.J., 1994-98, sr. intellectual property counsel, 1999—. Mem. ABA, N.Y. State Bar Assn., Am. Intellectual Property Law Assn., Licensing Execs. Soc. Intellectual property, Patent. Office: Becton Dickinson and Co 1 Becton Dr Franklin Lakes NJ 07417-1880

**WEIR, ROBERT H.,** lawyer; b. Boston, Dec. 7, 1922; s. Abraham and Beatrice (Stern) W.; A.B., Harvard U., 1944, LL.B., 1948; m. Ruth Hirsch, July 2, 1954 (dec. Nov. 1965); children—Anthony, David, Michael H.; m. 2d, Sylvia T. Frias; children—Nicole F., Daniella F. Admitted to Mass. bar, 1948, Wash. bar, 1952, Calif. bar, 1957; spl. asst. to atty. gen. U.S. Dept. Justice, Seattle, 1948-53, Washington, 1953-56; practiced in San Jose, also Palo Alto, Calif., 1957—. Instr. taxation of real estate U. Calif. at San Jose and San Francisco, 1957—; lectr. U. So. Calif. Tax Inst. Mem. prison com. Am. Friends Service Com. Bd. dirs. San Jose Light Opera Assn., Inc. Served with U.S. Army, 1942-45. Mem. Am., Santa Clara County bar assns., State Bar Calif., Am. Judicature Soc. Author: Advantages in Taxes, 1960. Tax columnist Rural Realtor, Chgo., 1959—. Speaker taxation annual meetings Nat. Assn. Real Estate Bds., 1958-60. Author: Taxes Working for You, 1966; How to Make the Most of Depreciation Write Off. Contbr. articles to profl. jours. Antitrust, Estate planning, Taxation, general. Address: 27743 Via Ventana Los Altos CA 94022-3241

**WEIS, JOSEPH FRANCIS, JR.,** federal judge; b. Pitts., Mar. 12, 1923; s. Joseph Francis and Mary (Flaherty) W.; m. Margaret Horne, Dec. 27, 1958; children: Maureen, Joseph Francis, Christine. BA, Duquesne U., 1941-47; J.D., U. Pitts., 1950; LLD (hon.), Dickinson Coll., 1989. Bar: Pa. 1950. Individual practice law Pitts., 1950-68; judge Ct. Common Pleas, Allegheny County, Pa., 1968-70, U.S. Dist. Ct. (we. dist.) Pa., 1970-73; judge U.S. Ct. Appeals (3d cir.), Pitts., 1973-99, sr. judge, 1999—; lectr. trial procedures, 1965—; adj. prof. law U. Pitts., 1986—; chmn. Fed. Cts. Study Com., Jud. Conf. Com. on Experiment to Videotape Trial Proceedings within the 3rd Cir., Internat. Jud. Conf. the Joint Am.-Can. Appellate Judges Conf., Toronto, 1986, London, 1985, futurist subcom. bicentennial com. Ct. Common Pleas, Allegheny County, Pa., 1988; participant programs legal medicine, Rome, London; mem. Am.-Can. Legal Exchange, 1987. Contbr. articles to legal jours. Mem. Mental Health and Mental Retardation Bd., Allegheny County, 1970-73; mem. Leukemia Soc., 1970-73, Knights of Malta, Am. Legion, 4th Armored Div. Assn., Disabled Am. Vets., Cath. War Vets., Mil. Order of the World Wars; mem. bd. adminstrn. Cath. Diocese Pitts., 1971-83; trustee Forbes Hosp. System, Pitts., 1969-74. Capt. AUS, 1943-48. Decorated Bronze Star, Purple Heart with oak leaf cluster; recipient St. Thomas More award, 1971, Phillip Amram award, 1991, Edward J. Devitt Disting. Svc. to Justice award, 1993, History Makers award, 1997. Fellow Internat. Acad. Trial Lawyers (hon.), Am. Bar Found.; mem. ABA (chmn. appellate judges' conf. 1981-83), Pa. Bar Assn., Allegheny Bar Assn. (past v.p.), Acad. Trial Lawyers Allegheny County (past pres), Am. Judicature Soc., Jud. Conf. U.S. (chmn. civil rules com. 1986-87, com. on adminstrn. bankruptcy system 1983-87, subcom. on jud. improvements 1983-87, chmn. standing com. rules of practice and procedure 1988), Inst. Jud. Adminstrn., KC. Home: 225 Hillcrest Rd Pittsburgh PA 15238-2307 Office: US Ct Appeals US PO & Courthouse 7th & Grant St Rm 513 Pittsburgh PA 15219*

**WEIS, LAURA VISSER,** lawyer; b. Mich., June 6, 1961; d. Roger Leonard and Genevieve (Gore) V.; m. Barton Dale Weis, Jan. 12, 1991. BA cum laude, U. Va., 1983, JD, 1986. Bar: Calif. 1987, D.C. 1988, Va. 1991. Assoc. Shaw, Pittman, Potts & Trowbridge, Washington, 1986-90, Christian, Barton, Epps, Brent & Chappell, Richmond, Va., 1990—. Co-author: (with others) National Institute on Construction Law & Practice, 1987, Law and Business, 1988. Del. Nat. Rep. Inst. for Internat. Affairs, Czechoslovakia, 1990. Mem. ABA, Va. State Bar, Calif. Bar Assn., D.C. Bar Assn., Richmond Bar Assn. (exec. com., sec. real estate sect.), Philanthropy By Design (bd. dirs. 1992-95), Comml. Real Estate Women of Richmond, Va., French-Am. C. of C. (bd. dirs., asst. sec. 1988-90). Real property, General corporate. Office: Christian Barton Epps Brent & Chappell 909 E Main St Fl 12 Richmond VA 23219-3002

**WEISBERG, ADAM JON,** lawyer; b. Cocoa Beach, Fla., June 5, 1963; s. Melvin H. Weisberg and Joan Julie (Carney) Vargo; m. Cheryl Lynn Scupp, June 25, 1994. BS in Bus. Econs., Rider Coll., 1985; JD, N.Y. Law Sch., 1988. Bar: N.Y. 1989, N.J. 1989, U.S. Dist. Ct. 1989, Fla. 1991. Law clk., asst. prosecutor Middlesex County Prosecutors Office, New Brunswick, N.J., 1988-90; workers' compensation atty. Levinson Axelrod Wheaton, Edison, N.J., 1990-91; trial atty. workers compensation Richard J. Simon, Esq., New Brunswick, 1991-92; pvt. practice lawyer New Brunswick, 1992—; pres. Asbury Music Co., Belmar, N.J. Mem. ABA, N.J. Bar Assn., Middlesex County Bar Assn., Monmouth County Bar Assn., Assn. Criminal Def. Lawyers. Avocations: fishing, surfing. Criminal, Workers' compensation, Personal injury. Office: Monmouth Exec Plz II 1300 Highway 35 Ste 201 Ocean NJ 07712-3531 also: 46 Bayard St New Brunswick NJ 08901-2152

**WEISBERG, DAVID CHARLES,** lawyer; b. N.Y.C., June 25, 1938; s. Leonard Joseph and Rae M. (Kimberg) W.; m. Linda Gail Kerman, Aug. 27, 1975; children: Leonard Jay, Risa Beth. AB, U. Mich., 1958; LLB, Harvard U., 1961. Bar: N.Y. 1962, U.S. Dist. Ct. (so. and ea. dists.) N.Y. 1965, U.S. Supreme Ct. 1970. Assoc. firm Dreyer & Traub, Bklyn., 1962, Lee Franklin, Mineola, N.Y., 1962-65; pvt. practice Patchogue, N.Y., 1965-67, 77-80; ptnr. Bass & Weisberg, Patchogue, 1967-77, Davidow, Davidow, Russo & Weisberg, Patchogue, 1981-82, Davidow, Davidow, Weisberg & Wismann, Patchogue, 1982-87, Davidow, Davidow & Wismann, Patchogue, 1988-92, Weisberg & Wismann, Patchogue, 1992—; assoc. justice and justice Village of Patchogue, 1968-70, village atty., 1970-85; spl. asst. dist. atty. Suffolk County, Patchogue, 1970-85; assoc. estate tax atty., appraiser N.Y. State Dept. Taxation and Fin., Hauppauge, N.Y., 1975-85; lectr. estate tax Suffolk County Acad. Law, 1976-84, negligence law, 1994. Law chmn. Suffolk County Dem. Com., N.Y., 1975-85; bd. dirs. Temple Beth El of Patchogue. With USAR, 1961-62. Mem. ATLA, N.Y. State Bar Assn., Suffolk County Bar Assn., Nassau-Suffolk Trial Lawyers Sect., Lions (pres. Medford 1978-79, 2d v.p. 1984-85). Avocations: bicycling, skiing, backpacking. General civil litigation, Personal injury, Estate planning. Office: Weisberg & Wismann 110 N Ocean Ave Patchogue NY 11772-2004

**WEISBERGER, JOSEPH ROBERT,** state supreme court chief justice; b. Providence, Aug. 3, 1920; s. Samuel Joseph and Ann Elizabeth (Meighan) W.; m. Sylvia Blanche Pigeon, June 9, 1951; children: Joseph Robert, Paula Ann, Judith Marie. AB, Brown U., 1942; JD, Harvard U., 1949; LLD (hon.), R.I. Coll., Suffolk U., Mt. St. Joseph Coll.; DCL (hon.), Providence Coll.; DHL (hon.), Bryant Coll.; LLD (hon.), Roger Williams Coll., 1992, Brown U., 1992, Constantine U., 1997; LLD, So. New England Sch. Law, 1998. Bar: Mass. 1949, R.I. 1950. With Quinn & Quinn, Providence, 1951-56; solicitor Glocester, R.I., 1953-56; judge Superior Ct. R.I., Providence, 1956-72; presiding justice R.I. Superior Ct., Providence, 1972-78; justice R.I. Supreme Ct., Providence, 1978—, 1978—; chief justice R.I. Supreme Ct., Providence, 1993—; adj. prof. U. Nev., 1986—; mem. faculty Nat. Jud. Coll.; vis. lectr. Providence Coll., Suffolk Law Sch., Roger Williams Coll.; Chmn. New Eng. Regional Conf. Trial Judges, 1962, 63, 65; chmn. New Eng. Regional Commn. Disordered Offender, 1968-71, R.I. Com. Adoption on Rules Criminal Procedure, 1968-72, chmn. of R.I. Adv. Com. Corrections, 1973, Nat. Conf. State Trial Judges ABA, 1977-78; exec. com. Appelate Judges Conf. ABA, 1979—, vice chmn., 1983-85, chmn., 1985-86; bd. dirs. Nat. Ctr. for State Cts., 1975-81. Chmn. editorial bd. Judges Jour., 1973-75. Pres. R.I. Health Facilities Planning Coun., 1967-70; chmn. Gov. R.I. Coun. Mental Health, 1968-73; moderator Town of East Providence, 1954-56; mem. R.I. Senate, 1953-56, minority leader, 1955-56; vice chmn. bd. trustee R.I. Hosp., 1968-92, St. Joseph's Hosp., trustee, 1962—. Lt. comdr. USNR, 1941-46. Recipient Erwin Griswold award Nat. Jud. Coll., 1989; named to R.I. Hall of Fame; Paul Harris fellow Rotary Internat. Fellow Am. Bar Found.; mem. ABA (ho. of dels., task force on criminal justice stds. 1977-79, exec. com. appellate judges' conf. 1979-95), KC, R.I. Bar Assn., Am. Judges Assn. (gov.), Inst. Jud. Adminstrn., Am. Judicature Soc. (Herbert Harley award 1990), Am. Law Inst., Order of St. Gregory (knight comdr. with star 1989, Goodrich award for Svc. 1995), Phi Beta Kappa (past pres. Alpha chpt. Brown U.). Home: 60 Winthrop St Riverside RI 02915-2624 Office: RI Supreme Ct 250 Benefit St Providence RI 02903-2719 *My professional life for the last 43 years has been occupied with judicial duties. I have been blessed with the opportunity to meet ever changing challenges and to attempt to solve a myriad of problems. These opportunities have been rewarding and absorbing. I consider judicial work to be a great privilege.*

**WEISBURD, EVERARD J.,** lawyer; b. Holly Grove, Ark., July 11, 1913; s. Harry Weisburd and Amee Johnson; m. Helen R. Waller, Sept. 12, 1943; children: Arthur M., Mary Jane. LLB, U. Ark., 1938. Bar: Ark., U.S. Dist. Ct. (ea. dist.) Ark. Democrat. Jewish. Family and matrimonial, State civil litigation, Probate. Office: 120 Ross Ave West Memphis AR 72301-3040

**WEISBURD, STEVEN I.,** lawyer; b. Bklyn., Sept. 18, 1949; s. Walter Bennett Weisburd and Sandra (Goldstein) Schmidt; m. Irene Soohoo-Weisburd; children: Bryan Joshua, Amy Rebecca, Daniel Timothy. BSEE, U. Hartford, 1971; JD, Temple U., 1974. Bar: Pa. 1974, N.Y. 1977. Assoc. Seidel, Gonda & Goldhammer, Phila., 1974-76; assoc. Ostrolenk, Faber, Gerb & Soffen, N.Y.C., 1976-79, ptnr., 1980—. Mem. ABA, N.J. Patent Law Assn., N.Y. Patent, Trademark, and Copyright Law Assn., Inc. Patent, Trademark and copyright, Computer. Home: 315 W 70th St New York NY 10023-3504

**WEISCHADLE, DOUGLAS ERIC,** lawyer, literary agent; b. Trenton, N.J., May 13, 1971; s. David E. and Mary Ann (Piscopo) W. BS, Trenton State Coll., 1992; JD, New England Sch. Law, 1995. Bar: Mass. 1995, N.J. 1995, D.C. 1996, U.S. Dist. Ct. Mass. 1996, U.S. Dist. Ct. N.J. 1996. Legis. aide N.J. Gen. Assembly, Trenton, 1991; law clk. N.J. Atty. Gen., Trenton, 1993, Mass. Atty. Gen., Boston, 1993; project asst., U.S. Senate Sen. Frank Lautenberg, Washington, 1994; ptnr. Weischadle & Weischadle, Quincy, Mass., 1995—; lit. agt., pres. The Gatsby Group, Inc., Boston, 1996—. Recipient Cum Laude award Am. Classic League, N.Y.C., 1985. Mem. ABA, Mass. Bar Assn., Mass. Acad. Trial Attys., Boston Bar Assn., D.C. Bar Assn., N.J. Bar Assn. Avocations: reading, writing, travel, science. Office: PO Box 692017 1212 Hancock St Quincy MA 02269

**WEISENBURGER, THEODORE MAURICE,** retired judge, poet, educator, writer; b. Tuttle, N.D., May 12, 1930; s. John and Emily (Rosenay) W.; children: Sam, Jennifer, Emily, Todd, Daniel, Dwight, Holly, Michael, Paul, Peter; m. Maylyne Chu, Sept. 19, 1985; 1 child, Irene. BA, U. N.D., 1952, LLB, 1956, JD, 1969; BFT, Am. Grad Sch. Internat. Mgmt., Phoenix, 1957. Bar: N.D. 1963, U.S. Dist. Ct. N.D. 1963. County judge, tchr. Bensen County, Minnewaukan, N.D., 1968-75, Walsh County, Grafton, N.D., 1975-87; trial judge Devils Lake Sioux, Ft. Totten, N.D., 1968-84, Turtle Mountain Chippewa, Belcourt, N.D., 1974-87; U.S. magistrate U.S. Dist. Ct., Minnewaukan, 1972-75; Justice of the Peace pro tem Maricopa County, Ariz., 1988-92; instr. Rio Salado C.C., 1992—; tchr. in Ethiopia, 1958-59. Author: Poetry and Other Poems, 1991. 1st lt. U.S. Army, 1952-54. Recipient Humanitarian award U.S. Cath. Conf., 1978, 82, Right to Know award Sigma Delta Chi, 1980, Spirit of Am. award U.S. Conf. Bishops, 1982. Home: 4353 E Libby St Phoenix AZ 85032-1732

**WEISER, FRANK ALAN,** lawyer; b. L.A., Dec. 12, 1953; s. Carl and Rose (Klein) W.; m. Susan Koenig, Aug. 12, 1983. BA, UCLA, 1976; JD, Southwestern U., L.A., 1979; LLM in Taxation, U. San Diego, 1986. Bar: Calif. 1979, U.S. Dist. Ct. (cen. dist.) Calif. 1981, U.S. Tax Ct. 1982, U.S. Ct. Appeals (9th cir.) 1982, U.S. Supreme Ct. 1987, U.S. Ct. Claims 1987, U.S. Ct. Mil. Appeals 1988, U.S. Ct. Appeals (fed. cir.) 1989, U.S. Ct. Internat. Trade 1989, U.S. Ct. Appeals Temporary Emergency Ct., 1989, U.S. Ct. Vets. Appeals 1990, U.S. Dist. Ct. (no. and so. dists.) Calif. 1993. Tax cons., advanced underwriter Transam. Occidental Life Ins. Co., L.A., 1979-80; assoc. Law Offices Herman English, 1980-81; atty., owner Frank A. Weiser-A Law Corp., L.A., 1981—; judge pro tem L.A. County Mcpl. Ct., 1987—. Editor So. Calif. mag., 1987—; contbr. articles to profl. jours. Bd. suprs. Michael Antonovich Election Com., 1988; mem. World Affairs Coun., L.A.; mem. U.S. Ct. of Vets. Appeals, 1990; assoc. mem. Calif. Rep. Cen. Com. Recipient official resolutions from Calif. State Legislature, 1989, joint rules com. resolution for state assembly and sate senate, 1990, Calif. State Assembly and Senate, 1989, L.A. County Bd. of Suprs., 1989, City Coun. of L.A., 1987, Congressional Cert. of Appreciation; tribute to him placed into official Congl. record, 1989; Nat. Merit scholar, 1971. Mem. ABA (internat. labor com., arts control and disarmament com., internat. employment practices com., editorial advisor internat. law and practice sect. publs. com., internat. property, estate and trust com., fgn. investment in U.S. com.), Fed. Bar Assn. (internat. law com.), Inter-Am. Bar Assn., Am. Judicature Soc., Assn. Trial Lawyers Am., Calif. Trial Lawyers Assn., L.A. Trial Lawyers Assn., Internat. Bar Assn., World Affairs Coun. L.A., World Inst. Achievement, L.A. Athletic Club. Estate planning, Land use and zoning (including planning), Private international. Office: 3460 Wilshire Blvd Ste 903 Los Angeles CA 90010-2230

**WEISER, MARTIN JAY,** lawyer; b. N.Y.C., Mar. 20, 1943; s. Jack J. and Esther (Attias) w.; m. Pamela D. Morgan, Sept. 4, 1966; children: Nicole, Jennifer. BA, Temple U., 1964; JD, Bklyn. Law Sch., 1967; LLM, NYU, 1975. Cert. tchr., N.Y.; bar: N.Y. 1967; U.S. Dist. Ct. (ea. dist.) N.Y. 1975, U.S. Dist. Ct. (so. dist.) N.Y., 1990. Assoc. Newman & O'Malley, N.Y.C., 1967-69; ptnr., pres. Raiskin, Weiser & Donofrio, P.C., N.Y.C., 1970—; counsel Metro N.Y. Oldsmobile Dealers Assn., 1988. Bd. dirs. East Hills, N.Y. Assn., 1986-87; v.p. Rio Assn., 1988, bd. dirs., pres., 1988—. Mem. N.Y. County Lawyers Assn., Nassau Bar Assn., N.Y. State Trial Lawyers Assn., Assn. Trial Lawyers of Am., Car and Truck Leasing Assn. Am., Inst. for Safety Analysis, Nob Hill Club (v.p. 1985-86). Personal injury, General civil litigation, Insurance. Office: Weiser & Assocs PC 215 Lexington Ave New York NY 10016-6023

**WEISFELD, SHELDON,** lawyer; b. McAllen, Tex., Feb. 20, 1946; s. Morris and Pauline (Horwitz) W.; m. Eve F. Weisfeld, Jan. 23, 1994; 1 child, Raquel Paolina. BBA, U. Tex., 1967; postgrad., Nat. U. Mex., Mexico City, 1969; JD, U. Houston, 1970. Bar: Tex. 1971, U.S. Dist. Ct. (so. dist.) Tex. 1978, U.S. Dist. Ct. (we. dist.) Tex. 1995, U.S. Ct. Appeals (5th cir.) 1978, U.S. Ct. Appeals (11th cir.) 1981, U.S. Supreme Ct. 1982. Pvt. practice Austin, Tex., 1973-77; pvt. practice law Brownsville, Tex., 1980—; asst. fed. pub. defender U.S. Dist. Ct. (so. dist.) Tex., Brownsville, 1977-80; dir., sec.-treas. Flying Nurses Inc. Mem. Nat. Assn. Criminal Def. Lawyers, Tex. Criminal Def. Lawyers (dir.), ABA, ACLU Tex. (bd. dirs.), Fed. Bar Assn., State Bar Tex., Cameron County (Tex.) Bar Assn., Hidalgo County (Tex.) Bar Assn., Rotary Club, B'nai B'rith. Democrat. Office fax: (956) 544-7446. Criminal, Federal civil litigation. Office: 1324 E 7th St Brownsville TX 78520-7241

**WEISGALL, JONATHAN MICHAEL,** lawyer; b. Balt., Mar. 17, 1949; s. Hugo David and Nathalie (Shulman) W.; m. Ruth Macdonald, June 3, 1979; children: Alison, Andrew, Benjamin. BA, Columbia Coll., 1970; JD, Stanford U., 1973. Bar: D.C. 1974, N.Y. 1974, U.S. Supreme Ct. 1982, Marshall Islands 1983. Law clk. to judge U.S. Ct. Appeals (9th cir.), San Francisco, 1973-74; assoc. Covington & Burling, Washington, 1974-79; from assoc. to ptnr. Ginsburg, Feldman, Weil & Bress, Washington, 1980-83; sole practice Washington, 1983-99; v.p. Legis. and Regulatory Affairs MidAmerican Energy Holdings Co., 1995—; adj. prof. law Georgetown U. Law Ctr. Author: Operation Crossroads: The Atomic Tests at Bikini Atoll, 1994; exec. prodr. documentary film Radio Bikini. Chmn. bd. dirs. Ctr. for Energy Efficiency and Renewable Techs.; trustee Arena Stage, Washington; bd. dirs. Meet the Composer. Mem. Geothermal Energy Assn. (v.p., bd. dirs.), Phi Beta Kappa. Jewish. E-mail: jweisgall@aol.com. Federal civil litigation, Public international, Legislative. Home: 5309 Edgemoor Ln Bethesda MD 20814-1323 Office: 2101 L St NW Washington DC 20037-1524

**WEISMAN, DAVID,** lawyer; b. North Miami Beach, Fla., Oct. 26, 1955; s. William and Arline Weisman; m. Betsy Greenberg, June 10, 1979; children: Robin, Alex, Brooke. BBA, U. Miami, 1976; JD, U. Fla., 1978. Bar: Fla. 1987, U.S. Dist. Ct. (so. dist.) Fla. 1980; bd. cert. real estate lawyer. Tax acct. Touche Ross & Co., Miami, Fla., 1979; assoc. atty. Pallot Poppell Goodman & Slotnick, Miami, 1979-82; ptnr., atty. Abrams Anton PA, Hollywood, Fla., 1982—; lectr. in field. Contbr. articles to profl. jours. Pres. Hamlet of Davie Homeowners Assn., 1997-98. Mem. ABA (real property, probate and trust law sect.), The Fla. Bar (exec. coun. real property sect.), South Broward Bar Assn. (officer and bd. dirs. 1988-91, pres. 1990-91), Hollywood C. of C. (bd. dirs. 1990-97, legal counsel 1992-95. Real property, Landlord-tenant, General corporate. Office: Abrams Anton PA 2021 Tyler St Hollywood FL 33020-4518

**WEISMAN, MITCHELL ARTHUR,** lawyer; b. Cleve., Sept. 20, 1958; s. Fred and Lois Jane (Kutler) W.; m. Mary Elizabeth Beathard, June 16, 1984; children: Matthew, Megan, Molly. BBA, Emory U., 1980; JD, Ohio State U., 1983. Bar: Ohio. Ptnr. Weisman, Goldberg & Weisman, Cleve., 1983—; speaker in field. Mem. ATLA, Ohio Bar Assn., Cleve. Bar Assn., Cuyahoga County Bar Assn. (bd. trustees 1990-93), Bar Assn. Greater Cleve. (young lawyers exec. com. 1987-90, chmn. civil litigation sect. 1987-88), Cleve. Acad. Trial Lawyers, Ohio State Bar Assn., Ohio Acad. Trial Lawyers, Cleve. Baseball Fedn. (bd. dirs. 1996—), Phi Sigma Tau, Masons, Cleve. Racquet Club. Avocations: softball, waterskiing, snow skiing, racquetball, squash. Home: 5917 Briardale Ln Solon OH 44139-2301 Office: Weisman Goldberg & Weisman 101 W Prospect Ave Cleveland OH 44115-1093

**WEISMAN, PAUL HOWARD,** lawyer; b. Los Angeles, Oct. 14, 1957; s. Albert L. and Rose J. (Zimman) W.; m. Allison L. Minas, Oct. 19, 1985. BA cum laude, U. Calif., Davis, 1979; JD, Loyola U., Los Angeles, 1982. Bar: Calif. 1982. Tax atty. legis. and regulations div. office of chief counsel Dept. of Treasury IRS, Washington, 1982-83; tax atty. dist. counsel/office of chief counsel Dept. of Treasury IRS, L.A., 1983-87; tax atty. Law Offices of Paul H. Weisman, L.A., 1987—; registered players contract rep. Nat. Football League Players Assn. Co-author BNA Tax Mgmt. Portfolio 404 2d Federal Tax Collection Procedure, publs. in field. Participant vol. Income Tax Assistance, L.A., 1981-83. Mem. San Fernando Valley Bar Assn., Beverly Hills Bar Assn. (co-chmn. tax ct. prose program). Republican. Avocations: sports, running, art, music, politics. Estate planning, Sports, Personal income taxation.

**WEISS, ADAM WILLIAM,** lawyer; b. Bklyn., Aug. 3, 1970; s. Ronald S. and Zelda W. BA, Yeshiva U., 1992; JD magna cum laude, NYU, 1995. Assoc. Russo, Darnell & Ludato LLP, East Meadow, N.Y., 1996—. Dean Allison Reppy scholar N.Y. Law Sch., 1992-95. Mem. ABA, N.Y. State Bar Assn., N.Y.C. Bar Assn. Jewish. Personal injury, Insurance, State civil litigation. Office: Russo Darnell & Ludato LLP 915 E 12th St East Meadow NY 11554

**WEISS, ALLAN,** lawyer; b. Louisville, Aug. 7, 1940; s. Morris M. and Evalyn (Brown) W.; m. Anne Pierce, Feb. 6, 1971; 1 child, John Allan. B.S. in Law, U. Louisville, 1962, J.D., 1964. Bar: Ky. 1964, U.S. Dist. Ct. (we. dist.) Ky. 1965, U.S. Dist. Ct. (ea. dist.) Ky. 1973, U.S. Ct. Appeals (6th cir.) 1972; cert. arbitrator NASD Regulations Inc., 1998. Law clk., Ky. Supreme Ct., 1964-65; with Ferreri, Fogle, Pohl & Picklesimer, 1998—. Contbr. articles to profl. jours. Mem. adv. com. Learn More-Earn More Project Louisville Bd. Edn., 1965-68, chmn. citizens adv. com. 1967-68; bd. dirs. Louisville Sch. Autistic Children, 1973-83, pres., 1976-77; bd. dirs. Arts Forum, Inc., 1980-84, assoc. editor Beaux Arts mag., 1980-81; bd. dirs. Bingham Child Guidance Clinic, 1979-90, treas., 1983, v.p., 1984; mem. Sunday Sch. com. The Temple, 1976-78; com. mem. Bur. of Jewish Edn.-High Sch. of Jewish Studies, 1980-82; pres. Ky. Legal Services Inc., 1984, bd. dirs. 1981-85; bd. dirs. Cmty. Health Charities, 1990-99. Bingham fellow, 1997.Mem. Ky. State Bar Assn., Louisville Bar Assn. (chmn. pre-paid legal ins. com. 1982), Internat. Assn. Def. Counsel, Ky. Def. Counsel, Lawyers Alliance for World Security (bd. dirs.). Democrat. E-mail: aweiss@aye.net. Workers' compensation, Insurance, Alternative dispute resolution. Home: 3014 Shallcross Way Louisville KY 40222-6102 Office: Ferreri Fogle Pohl & Picklesimer 203 Speed Bldg 333 Guthrie Grn Louisville KY 40202-1829

**WEISS, ANDRÉ,** lawyer; b. N.Y.C., Dec. 3, 1952; s. William and Elisabeth (Lowenger) W.; m. Deborah A. Weiss, Dec. 14, 1980; children: Talia Rachel, Keren Ashley, Abby Rebecca. BA, NYU, 1974; JD, Syracuse U., 1977. Atty. Securities & Exch. Commn., Washington, 1977-79; assoc. Shearman & Sterling, N.Y.C., 1979-86; ptnr. Schulte Roth & Zabel, N.Y.C., 1986—. Mem. N.Y. City Bar Assn. (securities regulation com. sec. 1989—), Calif. Bar Assn. Avocations: swimming, chess. Office: Schulte Roth & Zabel 900 3rd Ave Fl 19 New York NY 10022-4774*

**WEISS, ANDREW RICHARD,** lawyer, mediator, educator, optician; b. Hartford, Conn., Jan. 11, 1945; s. Irving and Clara E. (Miller) W.; m. Sara N. Brookwood, Apr. 3, 1981 (dec. June 1982); m. Avril M. Bell, Oct. 14, 1989. BA, Dartmouth Coll., 1967; MA, U. Wis., 1968; postgrad., Boston U., 1970; JD, Boston Coll., 1977. Bar: Mass. 1977, U.S. Dist. Ct. Mass. 1978, U.S. Supreme Ct. 1992. Tchr. English, Saddle River (N.J.) Country Day Sch., 1968-69; rsch. and writing asst. Soun-View Throg's Neck Cmty. Mental Health Ctr., Bronx, 1969-70; legal adv. Mass. Advocacy Ctr., Boston, 1975-77; pvt. practice, Boston, 1978-89; atty. Resolution, Wellesley, Mass., 1989—; instr. New Eng. Sch. Whole Health Edn., 1995—, dean faculty, 1997—; instr. meditation Cambridge Ctr. Adult Edn., 1994—. Trustee Thacher Montessori Sch., Milton, Mass., 1981—, Newbury Insight Meditation Ctr., 1995—; pres. Zaltho Found., Inc., Concord, Mass., 1994—. Mem. Mass. Bar Assn., Soc. Profls. Dispute Resolution, Internat. Alliance Holistic Lawyers, Order Interbeing Internat. (exec. coun. 1992—). Avocations: music, motorcycles, hiking, pets. Alternative dispute resolution, Estate planning, Non-profit and tax-exempt organizations. Home and Office: 20 Elm St Maynard MA 01754-2630

**WEISS, ARNOLD HANS,** lawyer, consultant; b. Nurnberg, Germany, July 25, 1924; m. Artemis Lychos, May 5, 1956; children: Daniel L., Andrew A. B.A., U. Wis., 1951, J.D., 1952. Bar: Wis. 1953, D.C. 1958. Atty. advisor Office Gen. Counsel U.S. Treasury, 1953-60; atty. Inter Am. Devel. Bank, 1960-61, dep. gen. counsel, 1961-70, gen. counsel, 1970-77; ptnr. Arent, Fox, Kintner, Plotkin & Kahn, Washington, 1977-90; cons. Chevy Chase, Md., 1991; sec., gen. counsel Emerging Markets Corp., Washington, 1995—. With U.S. Army, 1942-47; served to lt. col. JAGC USAR, 1948-62. Decorated Bronze Star. Mem. ABA, Am. Soc. Internat. Law, Inter-Am. Bar Assn., Internat. Bar Assn., D.C. Bar Assn., Univ. Club of D.C., Univ. Club of Mexico City, Army and Navy Club (Washington). Private international, Public international, Contracts commercial. Office: Emerging Markets Corp 2001 Pennsylvania Ave NW Washington DC 20006-1850

**WEISS, CHRISTOPHER JOHN,** lawyer; b. Oswego, N.Y., Sept. 1, 1952; s. Robert Leo and Flora Elizabeth Weiss; m. Corinne Fratt, Mar. 28, 1973; children: Allison Ardis, Natalie Elizabeth, Christine Corinne, Kathryn Creigh. BS, Fla. State U., 1970, JD, 1977. Bar: Fla. 1977, U.S. Dist. Ct. (mid. and so. dists.) Fla. 1977, U.S. Supreme Ct. 1977. Ptnr. Holland and Knight, Maguire, Voorhis & Wells, P.A., Orlando, Fla., 1977—; lectr., author various constrn. litigation issues, 1977—. Mem. Orlando Rep. Com., 1975—. Mem. Fla. Bar, Orange County Bar Assn. (constrn. com. 1987—), Am. Arbitration Assn. (nat. panelist 1982—), Assoc. Gen. Contractors, Assoc. Builders and Contractors, Constrn. Fin. Mgrs. Assn. Avocations: camping, fishing, reading. Contracts commercial, State civil litigation. Office: Holland & Knight-Maguire Voorhis & Wells PA PO Box 1526 Orlando FL 32802-1526

**WEISS, EDITH BROWN,** law educator; b. Salem, Oreg., Feb. 19, 1942; d. Leon Michael and Edith E. Brown; m. Charles Weiss, Jr., July 24, 1969; children: Jed, Tamara. AB, Stanford U., 1963; JD, Harvard U., 1966; PhD, U. Calif., Berkeley, 1973; DDL (hon.), Chgo.-Kent Coll. Law, 1993. Bar: D.C. 1967, U.S. Ct. Claims 1967, U.S. Ct. Customs and Patent Appeals 1967, U.S. Ct. Mil. Appeals. Atty. advisor ACDA, Washington, 1966-68; rsch. assoc. Columbia U., N.Y.C., 1970-72, Brookings Instn., Washington, 1972-74; asst. prof. civil engring. and politics Princeton U., 1974-78; prof. law Georgetown U., Washington, 1978—, Francis Cabell Brown prof. international. law, 1996—; cons. UN Environ. Program, 1974-78, 94-97, UN U., 1983—; assoc. gen. counsel internat. law EPA, 1990-92; chmn. com. on rsch. on global environ. change Social Sci. Rsch. Coun., 1989-94; spl. legal advisor N.Am. Commn. Environ. Coop., 1996—. Author: (with Jacobson) Engaging Countries: Strengthening Compliance with International Environment Accords, 1998, In Fairness to Future Generations: International Law, Common Patrimony and Intergenerational Equity, 1989, Environmental Change and International Law, 1992; mem. bd. editors Am. Jour. Internat. Law, Global Governance, Environment, Transnat. Press, UN U Press; contbr. articles to profl. jours. Recipient Dinkelspiel award Stanford U., 1963, Leland T. Chapin award, 1962, Mellinkoff award, 1963; Harold and Margaret Sprout award, 1979, Elizabeth Haub prize, 1994, Prominent Woman in Internat. Law award Am. Soc. Internat. Law, 1996; Woodrow Wilson fellow, 1968. Mem. ABA (standing com. world order), Am. Soc. Internat. Law (chmn. ann meeting 1979, exec. coun. 1981-85, v.p. 1983-85, pres. 1994-96, Cert. Merit 1990), NAS (environ. studies bd. 1981-84, vice chair U.S. nat. com. for SCOPE 1984-85, water sci. and tech. bd., commn. on geoscis., environment and resources 1992-95), Internat. Inst. Applied Sys. Analysis (vice chair U.S. nat. com. 1993-98), Coun. Fgn. Rels., Am. Law Inst., Internat. Coun. Environ. Law, Cousteau Soc. (coun. advs.), Japanese Inst. Global Environ Strategies (bd. dirs. 1996—), Bannockburn Civic Assn., Phi Beta Kappa, Sigma Xi. Office: Georgetown U Law Ctr 600 New Jersey Ave NW Washington DC 20001-2075

**WEISS, EDWARD ABRAHAM,** lawyer; b. Chgo., Jan. 26, 1931; s. Morris Isaac and Gizella (Zeiger) W.; m. Phyllis Seibel, Oct. 1, 1983; children: Jennifer, Nathan, Chris, Darin, Corey. BSBA, U. Calif.-Berkeley, 1953; JD (Frank M. Angellotti scholar, John Norton Pomeroy scholar), Hastings Coll. Law, U. Calif.-San Francisco, 1959. Bar: Calif. 1960, U.S. Supreme Ct. 1971;

CPA, Calif. Acct., Aitel & Aitel, CPAs, San Francisco, 1953, 55-57, 57-79; assoc. Dreher & Frankel, Oakland, Calif., 1959-61; sole practice, Oakland, 1961-71, Walnut Creek, Calif., 1973—; sr. ptnr. Weiss & Paul, Oakland, 1967-69, Weiss & Wald, Oakland, 1969-71, Weiss & Pincus, 1988-89; exec. v.p., gen. counsel Am. Plan Investment Corp., San Francisco, 1971-72; lectr., instr. J.F. Kennedy Law Sch., 1973-75. Mem. aviation adv. com. Bd. Suprs.; bd. dirs. Jewish Welfare Fedn. Alameda and Contra Costa Counties, 1963-69; founder, bd. dirs. Beth Olam Meml. Chapel, 1971-72; bd. dirs. Jewish Community Relations Council Alameda and Contra Costa Counties, 1963-65, 67-68; pres. Congregation B'nai Sholom, 1969-71. Mem. Comml. Law League, ABA, State Bar Calif., Alameda County Bar Assn., Contra Costa County Bar Assn., Lawyer-Pilots Bar Assn., Thurston Honor Soc., Order of Coif. State civil litigation, Real property, Consumer commercial. Home: 865 Corrie Pl Pleasant Hill CA 94523-2176

**WEISS, ERIC MARTIN,** lawyer; b. N.Y.C., Mar. 31, 1955; s. Abraham and Violet Weiss; m. Stacey Blumenson, Jan. 7, 1963; children: Benjamin, Alexander. BS, NYU, 1976; MBA, U. Chgo., 1978; JD, Duke U., 1984. CPA, N.Y.; bar: N.Y. 1985, U.S. Dist. Ct. (so. dist.) N.Y. 1985. Staff acct., tax specialist Coopers & Lybrand, N.Y.C., 1978-81; assoc. Davis Polk & Wardwell, N.Y.C., 1984-87, Skadden Arps Slate Meagher & Flom, N.Y.C., 1987-90, Solomon & Fornari P.C., N.Y.C., 1991; exec. v.p., gen. counsel Active Internat., Pearl River, N.Y., 1992—. Mem. ABA, N.Y. State Bar Assn., Assn. Bar City N.Y., Am. Corp. Counsel Assn. Office: Active Internat 1 Blue Hill Plz Pearl River NY 10965-3104

**WEISS, HARLAN LEE,** lawyer; b. Washington, Dec. 6, 1941; s. Richard Stanley and Ethel (Schulman) W.; m. Elaine Sharon Schooler, Feb. 14, 1971; children: Rachel Shayna, Brian Adam. BA, U. Md.-College Park, 1963; JD with honors, U. Md.-Balt., 1966. Bar: Md. 1967, D.C. 1967, U.S. Dist. Ct. Md. 1967, U.S. Dist. Ct. D.C. 1967, U.S. Ct. Appeals (D.C. cir.) 1968, U.S. Ct. Appeals (4th cir.) 1977, U.S. Supreme Ct. 1970. Law clk. Ct. Appeals of Md., 1966-67; assoc. Surrey & Morse and predecessors, Washington, 1967-72; assoc. Sachs, Greenebaum, Taylor, Washington, 1972-76, ptnr., 1976-90; mem. Kivitz & Liptz, LLC, Chevy Chase, Md., 1990; mem. Jud. Conf. D.C., 1978-79; arbitrator Am. Arbitration Assn. State civil litigation, Insurance, Federal civil litigation. Home: 12017 Cheyenne Rd Gaithersburg MD 20878-2011 Office: 650 Barlow Bldg 5454 Wisconsin Ave Chevy Chase MD 20815-6901

**WEISS, JONATHAN ARTHUR,** lawyer; b. May 1, 1939. BA, Yale U., 1960, LLB, 1963. Bar: D.C. 1994, N.Y. 1967. Mng. atty. Neighborhood Legal Svcs., Washington, 1964-66, Mobilization for Youth Legal Svcs., N.Y.C., 1969-71; with Ctr. on Welfare Law, Columbia U. Law Sch., N.Y.C., 1967-69; dir. Legal Svcs. for Elderly, N.Y.C., 1971—; lectr. Hebrew U., Jerusalem, 1966; vis. prof. Tex. So. U. Law Sch., Houston, 1971; adj. prof. Yeshiva U. Cardozo Law Sch., N.Y.C., falls 1983-85. Co-author, editor: The Law and the Elderly, 1976; contbr. numerous articles and revs. to law and philos. jours. and newspapers. Bd. dirs. N.Y. Civil Liberties Union, Asian Am. Legal Def. Fund, Disability Legal Def. Fund, Gay and Lesbian Legal Def. Fund. Recipient Disting. Scholar medal Hofstra U., 1972; Fulbright scholar, 1966. Mem. ABA (mem. Adv. Coun. ethics 2000 com.), Native Am. Bar Assn. Democrat. Federal civil litigation, Health, Labor. Office: Legal Svcs for Elderly 130 W 42d St New York NY 10036

**WEISS, LEON ALAN,** lawyer; b. Cleve., Mar. 6, 1942; s. Benjamin J. and Anne N. (Rose) W.; m. Marilou Rippner, Feb. 6, 1965 (div. 1972); m. Ellen A. Wolf, May 7, 1997. BS, Bucknell U., 1963; JD, Case Western Res. U., 1966. Bar: Ohio 1966, U.S. Dist. Ct. (no. dist.) Ohio 1966, U.S. Ct. Appeals (6th cir.) 1966. Assoc. Rippner Schwartz & Carlin, Cleve., 1966-70; pvt. practice, Cleve., 1970-79; ptnr. Reminger & Reminger, Cleve., 1979—. Fellow Am. Coll. Trust and Estate Counsel; mem. Ohio Bar Assn., Cleve. Bar Assn. Probate, Estate planning, State civil litigation. Office: Reminger & Reminger 113 Saint Clair Ave Ste 700 Cleveland OH 44114-1273

**WEISS, LEON JEFFREY,** lawyer; b. Detroit, June 22, 1951; s. Rubin and Elizabeth W.; m. Michelle Dombrowski, Dec. 30, 1988; children: Hayley, Adam, Emily, Molly. BA in Polit. Sci., U. Mich., 1974; JD, Nova Southeastern U., 1977. Bar: Fla. 1977, U.S. Dist. Ct. (so. dist.) Fla. 1980, Mich. 1983, U.S. Dist. Ct. (ea. dist.) Mich. 1984. Asst. pub. defender Dade County Pub. Defender, Miami, Fla., 1977-80; ptnr. Resnick, Rosenthal & Weiss, Miami, 1980-83; pvt. practice Law Offices Leon J. Weiss, Detroit, 1983—, Boca Raton, Fla., 1983—; mem. negligence law sect. and criminal law sect. State Bar Mich., 1985—. Vol. Rose Cancer Ctr., Beaumont Hosp., Royal Oak, Mich., 1984—; sponsor Save The Children, Westport, Conn., 1995—. Named to Pro Bono Honor Roll, Mich. Bar, 1994—. Mem. Mich. Trial Lawyers Assn. Zen Humanist. Avocations: writing, golfing, reading, traveling. General civil litigation, Criminal, Personal injury. Office: 31731 Northwestern Hwy Ste 152 Farmington Hills MI 48334

**WEISS, LEONARD ARYE,** lawyer; b. Rochester, Pa., Aug. 4, 1923; s. Joseph Weiss and Margaret Czeisler; m. Shirley Sanders, Dec. 21, 1947; children: Jeffrey A., Cathee M. LLB, Albany Law Sch., 1948; LLD (hon.), Coll. St. Rose, 1997. Bar: U.S. Dist. Ct. (no. dist.) N.Y. 1948. Justice City Ct. Albany, N.Y., 1976-77, Supreme Ct., N.Y.C., 1979-94; assoc. justice appellate divsn. third dept. N.Y.C., 1981-94, presiding justice appellate divsn. third dept., 1991-93; president Assn. Justices Supreme Ct., N.Y.C., 1984-85; presiding mem. Coun. Jud. Assns., N.Y. State Bar Assn., N.Y.C., 1988. Chair Albany County Dem. Com., 1994—; exec. com. N.Y. State Dem. Com., 1994—; commr. Pub. Svc. Commn. N.Y. State, 1999. Pvt. U.S. Army, 1942-44. Administrative and regulatory, Alternative dispute resolution, Appellate. Office: McNamee Lochner Titus & Williams 75 State St Ste 12 Albany NY 12207-2503

**WEISS, MARK ANSCHEL,** lawyer; b. N.Y.C., June 20, 1937; s. George and Ida (Galin) W.; m. Joan Roth, June 8, 1958; children—Rebecca, Sarabeth, Jonathan, Deborah. A.B., Columbia U., 1958; LLB magna cum laude, Harvard U., 1961; Bar: N.Y. 1961, D.C. 1962, U.S. Supreme Ct. 1965. Assoc. Covington & Burling, Washington, 1961-66, 69-70, ptnr., 1970—; spl. asst. to Under Sec. Treasury Dept., Washington, 1966-68, spl. asst. to sec., 1968-69. Mem. editl. adv. bd. Electronic Banking Law and Commerce Report. Mem. D.C. Bar, ABA, Fed. Bar Assn. (vice chmn. banking law com.), City Club (Washington). Banking, Antitrust, Private international. Office: Covington & Burling PO Box 7566 1201 Pennsylvania Ave NW Washington DC 20044

**WEISS, RHETT LOUIS,** lawyer; b. Kyushu, Japan, May 22, 1961; came to U.S., 1961; s. Armand Berl and Judith (Bernstein) W.; m. Kristen Sue Krieger, Oct. 11, 1987; children: Aaron Bradford, Alexander Donald, Andrew Franklin. BS in Mgmt. cum laude, Tulane U., 1983; JD, Coll. William and Mary, 1986; exec. internat. bus. cert., Georgetown U., 1996. Bar: Va. 1986, D.C. 1993, N.Y. 1995, U.S. Ct. Appeals (4th cir.) 1986, U.S. Tax Ct. 1987, U.S. Dist. Ct. (we. dist.) Va. 1989, U.S. Bankruptcy Ct. (we. dist.) Va. 1989, U.S. Dist. Ct. (ea. dist.) Va. 1989, U.S. Bankruptcy Ct. (ea. dist.) Va. 1996. Vice pres., chief ops. officer First Fed. Savs. Bank Shenandoah Valley, Front Royal, Va., 1990-92; sr. atty. Weil, Gotshal & Manges LLP, Washington, 1992-97; dir. strategic relocation/expansion svcs., mem. mgmt. com. Bus. Incentives Group, KPMG Peat Marwick LLP, McLean, Va., 1997-99; pres., CEO DEALTEK, L.C., McLean, Va., 1999—; former prin., dir. Adamson, Crump, Sharp & Weiss, P.C., Front Royal; bd. dirs. Pentathlon Corp., Winchester, Va., Assns. Internat. Inc., McLean, Va., Weiss Pub. Co., Inc., Richmond, Va.; asst. town atty., counsel to Front Royal Planning Commn., 1987-90. Author: Portfolio Transactions: The Anatomy of a Deal, 1994, The Basics of Successful Negotiating, 1994, The Negotiating Process: Optimizing Give and Take, 1995, 96, 97, Doing Global Business in a United States Foreign-Trade Zone, 1996, 97, Sales and Use Tax-Exempt Construction: An Innovative Economic Development Tool to Help Land the Deal, 1997, Facility Development, Expansion and Operations: The Major Tax and Related Cost Aspects, 1998, Doing a Deal in the U.S.: Incentives and the Project Negotiation Process, 1998. Bd. dirs. Blue Ridge Arts Coun., Inc., 1987-92, v.p., 1989-90, pres., 1990-91; bd. dirs. Front Royal Little Theatre, Inc., 1988-89, Front Royal Warren County Unit Am. Heart Assn., 1991-92, Lord Fairfax C.C. Ednl. Found., 1991-94, Build-A-Future Found., 1994—, v.p., 1997—; Shenrapawa dist. chmn. Shenandoah area coun. Boy Scouts Am., 1988-89, coun. treas., 1991-92, coun. bd. dirs., 1987-94; adv. com. Small Bus. Assistance Ctr., Lord Fairfax C.C.; mem. Seaton Elem. Sch. devel. team D.C. Pub. Schs. Ptnrs. In Edn. Program, 1994-96; coach Southwestern Youth Assn., 1998—. Recipient Nat. Quality Dist. award Boy Scouts Am., 1988, 89, Statuette award, 1992. Fellow John Marshall Soc. of Va. Bar Assn.; mem. ABA, Nat. Coun. Urban Econ. Devel., Am. Econ. Devel. Coun., D.C. Bar (vice chmn. comml. trans. com. 1994-96, vice chmn. real property trans. com. 1996-97, chmn. 1997-98, real estate, housing and land use sect.), Va. State Bar, N.Y. Bar, Va. Econ. Developers Assn., So. Econ. Devel. Coun., Valley Estate Planning Coun. (bd. govs. 1989-92, pres. 1992), Nat. Coun. Urban Econ. Devel., Am. Econ. Devel. Coun., Front Royal-Warren County C. of C. (bd. dirs. 1989-92, pres. 1990-91), Country Club Fairfax (Va.), Delta Tau Delta (sec. 1980-81), Beta Gamma Sigma, Beta Alpha Psi. Avocations: cars, outdoors, skiing, golf, travel, music. Finance, General corporate, Real property. Home: 7419 Kincheloe Rd Clifton VA 20124-1831 Office: DEALTEK LC 6878 Fleetwood Rd Ste D Mc Lean VA 22101-3618

**WEISS, RONALD PHILLIP,** lawyer; b. Springfield, Mass., Apr. 28, 1947; s. Kermit Paul and Fay Roslyn (Robinovitz) W.; m. Janet Faye Landon, June 15, 1969; children: Emily, Katherine. BA, Dartmouth Coll., 1968; JD, U. Pa., 1972. Bar: Mass. 1972, U.S. Dist. Ct. Mass. 1975, U.S. Tax Ct. 1979. Assoc. Bulkley, Richardson and Gelinas, Springfield, Mass., 1972-78; ptnr. Bulkley, Richardson & Gelinas, LLP, Springfield, 1978—; pres. Estate Planning Coun. Hampden County, 1979-81; trustee Mass. Continuing Legal Edn. Inc., 1978-81. Author: (with others) Drafting Wills and Trusts in Massachusetts, 1990, 92, 94; editor: (with others) Massachusetts Corporate Tax Manual, 1986. Trustee Springfield Symphony Orch., 1986—, v.p. 1988-89, pres. 1989-91, chmn. 1991-94; mem. bd. advisors U. Mass. Family Bus. Ctr., 1992—; trustee Jewish Fedn. Greater Springfield, 1986-90; mem. appropriations com. Town of Longmeadow, Mass., 1990-96, chmn. 1991-92, 95-96. Mem. ABA, Mass. Bar Assn. (chmn. taxation sect. 1978-81, bd. dels. 1979-81), Mass. Bar Found., Hampden County Bar Assn., Rotary. General corporate, Mergers and acquisitions, Estate planning. Office: Bulkley Richardson & Gelinas LLP 1500 Main St Ste 2700 Springfield MA 01115-0001

**WEISS, SHERMAN DAVID,** lawyer; b. Detroit, Dec. 26, 1929; s. Abraham and Eva (Lieberman) W.; m. Lorraine Gloria Moss, Apr. 5, 1952; children—Roger Kevin, Diane Leslie, Linda Beth. Student U. Ill., 1947-48; B.S.C., Roosevelt U., 1951; J.D., Chgo.-Kent Coll. Law, 1957. Bar: Ill. 1958, U.S. Dist. Ct. (no. dist.) Ill. 1958, U.S. Ct. Appeals (7th cir.) 1965. Mem. Deutsch & Kurlan, Chgo., 1959-60, Brody and Gore, Chgo., 1960-62, Arnstein, Gluck, Weitzenfeld and Minow, Chgo., 1963-65; asst. sec., asst. v.p. Walter E. Heller Internat. Corp., Chgo., 1965-75, Imperial Leather & Sportswear, Ltd., Los Angeles, 1975-76; exec. v.p. Roth Carpet Mills, Santa Monica, Calif., 1977-78; sr. research rep. Greenwich Assocs., 1985-87; cons. fin. and bus. mgmt., L.A., 1979—; adj. prof. law John Marshall Sch. Law, Chgo., 1966-67. Bd. dirs. Met. YMCA Chgo., 1961-64; gen. counsel Leukemia League Ill., 1960-70. Served with U.S. Army, 1952-54. Mem. Ill. Bar Assn., ABA. Jewish. Case editor Chgo.-Kent Law Rev., 1956-57. Private international, General corporate, Contracts commercial. Home: 3955 Declaration Ave Calabasas CA 91302-5740

**WEISS, STEPHEN L.,** lawyer; b. Chgo., Nov. 24, 1941. BS in Econ., U. Pa., 1962; LLB, Yale U., 1965. Bar: Ariz. 1965. Assoc. Langerman Begam & Lewis, Phoenix, 1965-68, Dushoff Sacks & Corcoran, Phoenix, 1969-70; assoc. Gorey & Ely, Phoenix, 1971-75, ptnr., 1976; ptnr. Ely & Bettini, Phoenix, 1977; pvt. practice Phoenix, 1978—. Mem. ATLA, Ariz. Trial Lawyers Assn. (dir. 1980—). Workers' compensation. Office: PO Box 36940 Phoenix AZ 85067-6940

**WEISS, TERRI LYNN,** lawyer; b. Oct. 9, 1957. AB, Georgetown U., 1978, JD, 1981. Bar: N.Y. 1982, U.S. Dist. Ct. (so. and ea. dists.) N.Y. 1982, U.S. Ct. Appeals (2nd cir.), 1982. Assoc. Morgan, Lewis & Bockius, N.Y.C., 1981-86, Rosenman & Colin, N.Y.C., 1986-90; ptnr. Marino & Weiss P.C., White Plains, N.Y., 1990—. Mem. editl. bd. Jour. Am. Acad. Matrimonial Lawyers; Matrimonial Strategist; contbr. articles to profl. jours.; lectr. profl. orgns. Neutral evaluator Matrimonial Alt. Dispute Resolution Program, N.Y. County, N.Y.C., 1997—; arbitrator Domestic Rels. Fee Dispute Resolution Program, White Plains, N.Y., 1996—, Nat. Assn. Securities Dealers, N.Y.C., 1989—; bd. of profl. med. conduct N.Y. State Office Profl. Med. Conduct, N.Y. State Bd. Health, N.Y.C., 1988-98. Fellow Am. Acad. Matrimonial Lawyers (amicus com. N.Y. chpt. 1994—), Internat. Acad. Matrimonial Lawyers; mem. N.Y. State Bar Assn. (exec. com. family law sect. 1996—), Westchester Women's Bar Assn. Family and matrimonial, State civil litigation. Office: Marino & Weiss PC 162 Grand St White Plains NY 10601-4803

**WEISSBARD, SAMUEL HELD,** lawyer; b. N.Y.C., Mar. 3, 1947; children: Andrew Joshua, David S. BA, Case Western Res. U., 1967; JD with highest honors, George Washington U., 1970. Bar: D.C. 1970, U.S. Supreme Ct. 1974, Calif. 1998. Assoc. Fried, Frank, Harris, Shriver & Kampelman, 1970-73, Arent, Fox, Kintner, Plotkin & Kahn, 1973-78; prin. Weissbard & Fields, P.C., 1978-83; shareholder, v.p. Wilkes, Artis, Hedrick & Lane, Washington, 1983-86; ptnr. Foley & Lardner, Washington, 1986-97, L.A., 1997-98; co-chair creditors' rights workout and bankruptcy group Foley & Lardner, Washington, 1992-95; sr. counsel Cox, Castle & Nicholson, L.L.P., Newport Beach, Calif., 1998—. Editor in chief George Washington U. Law Rev., 1969-70. Bd. dirs. Luther Rice Soc., George Washington U., 1985-87, Atlanta Coll. Art, 1993, Nat. Learning Ctr., 1993-96, Georgetown Arts Commn. and gen. counsel 1995-96; Chmn. steering com. of Lawyer's Alliance for Nat. Learning Ctr. and Capital Children's Mus., 1989-90; mem. steering com. DC/NLC Don't Drop Out Campaign, 1992,93, bd. dirs., 1994-96; devel. com. Shelter for the Homeless, 1998—. Recipient John Bell Larner medal, 1970. Mem. ABA, D.C. Bar, Georgetown Bus. and Profl. Assn. (bd. dirs. 1993-96, sec., gen. counsel 1993-97), Orange County Bus. Assn. (legis. com. 1998—), Order of Coif. Real property, General corporate. Office: Cox Castle Nicholson LLP 19800 Macarthur Blvd Ste 600 Irvine CA 92612-2435

**WEISSENBERGER, HARRY GEORGE,** lawyer; b. Berlin, Fed. Republic of Germany, Aug. 20, 1928; s. Georg Wilhelm and Gabriele Anna (Hochberg) W.; m. Margaret Looper, Dec. 23, 1950; children: Carol Weissenberger Schlicht, Harry George Jr., Bruce Lee. Student, Swiss Inst. Tech., 1946-47; BEE, Ga. Tech. Inst., 1950; JD, Emory U., 1952; LLM, George Washington U., 1956. Bar: Ga. 1952, U.S. Dist. Ct. (no. dist.) Ga. 1952, U.S. Ct. Appeals (4th cir.) 1952, U.S. Supreme Ct. 1956, U.S. Ct. Customs and Patent Appeals 1956, Mo. 1957, U.S. Dist. Ct. (ea. dist.) Mo. 1957, U.S. Ct. Appeals (8th cir.) 1957, Mich. 1961, U.S. Dist. Ct. (we. dist.) Mich. 1961, U.S. Ct. Appeals (7th cir.) 1961, Calif. 1964, U.S. Dist. Ct. (no. and cen. dists.) Calif. 1964, U.S. Ct. Appeals (9th cir.) 1964, U.S. Dist. Ct. (ea. dist.) Calif. 1974, U.S. Dist. Ct. (we. dist.) Tex. 1976, U.S. Dist. ct. (so. dist.) Calif. 1982, U.S. Ct. Appeals (Fed. cir.) 1982. Examiner U.S. Patent Office, Washington, 1955-56; assoc. Bruninga & Sutherland, St. Louis, 1956-58, Sutherland, Polster & Taylor, St. Louis, 1958-59; assoc. Price & Heneveld, Grand Rapids, Mich., 1959-61, ptnr., 1961-63; ptnr. Mellin, Hanscom & Hursh, San Francisco, 1963-67, Mellin, Hursh, Moore & Weissenberger, 1967-74, Phillips, Moore, Weissenberger, Lempio & Strabala, San Francisco, 1974-76; ptnr. Phillips, Moore, Weissenberger, Lempio & Majestic, San Francisco, 1976-78, Newport Beach, Calif., 1978-81; ptnr. Weissenberger & Peterson, Newport Beach, 1982-86, Laguna Hills, Calif., 1986-90; ptnr. Weissenberger, Peterson, Uxa & Myers, Laguna Hills, 1990-93; pvt. practice atty. Laguna Hills, 1993-99; of counsel Stout, Uxa, Buyan & Mullins, Irvine, Calif., 1999—. Mem. Indsl. League Orange County, 1982-93. Served to 1st lt. USAF, 1953-55. Recipient Honored Citizen award Orange County Bd. Suprs., 1992. Mem. Calif. Bar Assn., Am. Intellectual Property Law Assn., Orange County Patent Law Assn. (pres. 1985), Am. Arbitration Assn., Rotary (chpt. bd. dirs. 1988-94, 98, pres. 1991-92, Rotarian of the Yr. award 1989). Republican. Presbyterian. Patent, Trademark and copyright. Office: Ste 300 4 Venture Irvine CA 92618-7384

**WEISSENBORN, ANNE ADKINS,** lawyer; b. Circleville, Ohio, Feb. 15, 1939; d. Joseph W. Jr. and Eleanor Y. (Yeagley) Adkins; m. Ernest W. Weissenborn, Apr. 11, 1970; 1 child, Elizabeth Anne. BA, Western Coll. Women, Oxford, Ohio, 1961; MA, Johns Hopkins Sch. Internat. Studies, Washington, 1964; MEd, Harvard U., 1968; JD, Cath. U., Washington, 1977. Bar: Md. 1977, D.C. 1980. Program specialist U.S. Office Edn., Washington, 1963-65; tchr. African Am. Inst., Dar es Salaam, Tanzania, 1965-66; program asst. African-Am. Inst., Washington, 1968, 69; instr. The Western Coll., Oxford, 1969-71; cons. Trans-Century Corp., Washington, 1972-75; atty. Fed. Election Commn., Washington, 1977-87, sr. atty., 1987—. Bd. dirs. Allied Silver Spring (Md.) Interfaith Svcs. for Srs.; founding pres., bd. dirs. Shaw Cmty. Ministry, Washington, 1991—. Mem. Bar Assn. D.C., Western Coll. Alumnae Assn. (trustee 1996—). Mem. Christ Cong. Ch. Home: 10021 Raynor Rd Silver Spring MD 20901-2124 Office: Fed Election Commn 999 E St NW Washington DC 20239-0004

**WEISSENBORN, SHERIDAN KENDALL,** lawyer; b. Trenton, N.J., Oct. 3, 1948; d. Howard Weinstein and Shirleye Rose (Stanley) W.; m. Lee Edward, Mar. 19, 1977; stepchildren: Jim, Carol, Stephen. BA, U. Miami, 1970, JD, 1973. Bar: Fla. 1973, U.S. Dist. Ct. (so. dist.) Fla. 1974, U.S. Supreme Ct. 1980, U.S. Ct. Appeals (11th cir.) 1982, U.S. Dist. Ct. (mid. dist.) Fla. 1984. Ptnr. Papy & Weissenborn, P.A., Coral Gables, Fla., 1974—. Mem. Fla. Bar Assn. Federal civil litigation, State civil litigation, Antitrust. Home: 14620 SW 82nd Ave Miami FL 33158-1902 Office: Papy & Weissenborn PA 3001 Ponce De Leon Blvd # 502 Coral Gables FL 33134-6824

**WEISSMAN, WILLIAM R.,** lawyer; b. N.Y.C., Aug. 16, 1940; s. Emanuel and Gertrude (Halpern) W.; m. Barbra Phylis Gershman; 1 child, Adam; stepchildren: Eric, Jace, Julie Greenman. BA, Columbia U., 1962, JD cum laude, 1965. Bar: N.Y. 1965, D.C. 1969, U.S. Dist Ct. (no. dist.) Tex. 1965, U.S. Dist. Ct. (so. and ea. dists.) N.Y. 1977, U.S. Ct. Appeals (5th cir.) 1966, U.S. Ct. Appeals (D.C. dir.) 1969, U.S. Ct. Appeals (9th cir.) 1973, U.S. Ct. Apeals (2d and 3d cirs.) 1974, U.S. Ct. Appeals (10th cir.) 1979, U.S. Ct. Appeals (11th cir.) 1981, U.S. Supreme Ct. 1968. News dir., progrm dir. WKCR-FM, N.Y.C., 1960-62; law clk. U.S. dist. judge, Dallas, 1965-66; trial atty. antitrust divsn. Dept. Justice, Washington, 1966-69; spl. asst. U.S. atty. Washington, 1967; assoc. Wald, Harkrader & Ross, Washington, 1969-72, ptnr., 1973-85; ptnr. Piper & Marbury LLP, Washington, 1986—; instr. D.C. Bar continuing legal edn. program Georgetown U. Law Sch., Washington, 1980-89; environ. regulation course Exec. Enterprises, Inc., 1985-95. Mem. editl. bd. Jour. Environ. Regulation, 1991-95, Environ. Regulation & Permitting, 1995—. Parliamentarian Arlington County Dem. Com., 1971-75; mem. Arlington (Va.) County Tenant-Landlord Commn., 1973-77, chmn. 1975-77. Mem. ABA, ASTM (E-50 com. environ. assessment 1998—), Fed. Bar Assn., D.C. Bar Assn., Columbia U. Washington Club (bd. dirs. 1987-93). Jewish. Administrative and regulatory, Environmental, Federal civil litigation. Home: 3802 Lakeview Ter Falls Church VA 22041-1313 Office: Piper & Marbury LLP 1200 19th St NW Fl 7 Washington DC 20036-2430

**WEIST, WILLIAM BERNARD,** lawyer; b. Lafayette, Ind., Dec. 23, 1938; s. Bernard Francis and Frances Loretta (Doyle) W.; m. Rosemary Elaine Anderson, Apr. 30, 1963; children: Sean M., Cynthia A. BBA, U. Notre Dame, 1961; JD, U. Louisville, 1970. Bar: Ky. 1971, Ind. 1971, U.S. Dist. Ct. (no. and so. dists.) Ind. 1971. Bank examiner Fed. Res. Bank, St. Louis, 1966-67; Trust officer Citizens Fidelity Bank, Louisville, 1967-71; pvt. practice Fowler, Ind., 1971—; bd. dirs. Benton Fin. Corp., Fowler, Fowler State Bank; prosecuting atty. 76th Jud. Cir., Benton County, Ind., 1975—. Capt. USAF, 1961-65. Fellow Ind. Bar Found. (charter mem.),; mem. Ind. State Bar Assn., Ind. Prosecuting Attys. Assn. (pres. 1979), Ind. Prosecuting Attys. Coun. (chmn. 1989), Nat. Dist. Attys. Assn. (bd. dirs.), Columbia Club (Indpls.), Elks, KC. Avocations: golf, reading. Probate, Estate planning, General practice. Home: 1000 E 5th St Fowler IN 47944-1520 Office: Weist Bldg Grant Ave Fowler IN 47944-1379

**WEITENDORF, KURT ROBERT,** lawyer; b. Lakewood, Ohio, June 15, 1955; s. Robert Daniel and Joy Louise (Miller) W.; m. Joan E. Booth, Oct. 31, 1997. Student, U. Ky., 1973-74; BA, Ohio State U., 1977; JD, U. Akron, 1980. Assoc. Roderick, Myers & Linton, Akron, 1980-85, ptnr., 1986-95; mng. atty. Akron office Davis and Young Co. L.P.A., 1995-96; ptnr. Roderick, Myers & Linton, Akron, 1996—. Mem. ABA, Ohio State Bar Assn., Akron Bar Assn. (trustees), Def. Rsch. Inst. Avocations: golf, scuba, skiing. Personal injury, Product liability, State civil litigation. Office: Roderick Myers & Linton 1500 One Cascade Plz Akron OH 44308-1108

**WEITZ, HARVEY,** lawyer; b. Bklyn. Aug. 16, 1934; AB, Bklyn. Coll.; JD, Bklyn. Law Sch. Bar: N.Y. 1954, U.S. Dist. Ct. (ea. and so. dists.) N.Y. 1956. Diplomate Am. Bd. Profl. Liability Attys. Ptnr. Schneider, Kleinick, Weitz, Damashek & Shoot, N.Y.C., 1966—; dean N.Y. State Trial Lawyers Institute; adj. prof. Bklyn Law Sch.; spl. master Supreme Ct. 1980-84. Author: A Compendium of the Art of Summation; Weitz on Automobile Litigation: The No-Fault Handbook; editor in chief Trial Lawyers Quar., 1972-80. Served with U.S. Army. Fellow Internat. Acad. Trial Lawyers, Internat. Soc. Barristers, Roscoe Pound Found.; mem. N.Y. State Trial Lawyers Assn. (bd. dirs.), Trial Lawyers for Pub. Justice (bd. dirs.), Am. Bd. Trial Advocates (nat. bd. mem.), ATLA (bd. govs. 1981-93, nat. secy. 1986-87), N.Y. State Trial Lawyers Assn. (pres. 1980-82), Bklyn. Law Sch. Alumni Assn. (bd. dirs.), Inner Circle of Advocates, Nat. Forensic Ctr. (mem. adv. panel), N.Y. State Bar (lectr.), Nat. Practice Inst. (lectr.), Assn. of the Bar, N.Y. County Lawyers Assn. (lectr.), N.Y.C. Trial Lawyers Assn. Personal injury. Office: Schneider Kleinick Weitz Damashek & Shoot 233 Broadway Fl 5 New York NY 10279-0050

**WEITZEL, J. DENNIS,** lawyer; b. Austin, Tex., Oct. 11, 1956; s. Kenneth Douglas and Norma S. Weitzel; m. Lori Mason, June 12, 1982; 5 children. Student, U. Tulsa, 1974-77, U. Tex., 1977-78; JD, U. Tex., 1981. Bar: Tex., U.S. Ct. Appeals (5th cir.), U.S. Dist. Ct. (no., so., ea. and we. dists.) Tex. Assoc. Cantey and Hanger, Fort Worth, 1981-84; ptnr. Stradley, Schmidt, Stephens and Wright, Dallas, 1985-87, Burleson, Pate and Gibson, Dallas, 1987-95, Fox Weitzel and Howell LLP, Dallas and Houston, 1995-96, Weitzel and Howell LLP, Dallas, 1996—. Dir. Parkland Found., Dallas, 1992—. Fellow Tex. Bar Found.; mem. Tex. Trial Lawyers Assn. (bd. dirs. 1995—). Avocations: tennis, photography. Insurance, Professional liability, Personal injury. Office: 2414 N Akard St Ste 700 Dallas TX 75201-1750

**WEITZMAN, LINDA SUE,** lawyer; b. Phila., July 27, 1959; d. Gerald and Elaine Weitzman. BA, Emory U., 1981; JD, U. Miami, 1984. Bar: Fla. 1984, Ga. 1989, U.S. Dist. Ct. (so. dist.) Fla. 1990. Assoc. Weiner, Shapiro & Rose, Miami; clk. Judge Mary Ann MacKenzie, Miami; in house counsel KRC Enterprises Inc., Ft. Lauderdale, Fla.; pvt. practice Coral Gables, Fla., 1989—. Mem. Am. Cancer Soc. Mem. ABA, Dade County Bar Assn., Viscayans. E-mail: lswatty@gateway.net. General civil litigation, Real property, Contracts commercial. Home and Office: 1514 Highland Ln Delray Beach FL 33444-4161

**WEITZMAN, MARC HERSCHEL,** lawyer; b. Milw., Feb. 1, 1950; s. J. Leonard and Esther (Charne) W.; m. Natalyn Ann Gipstein, Oct. 5, 1980; children: Benjamin, Marissa, Laura, Emily. BA, U. Calif., Santa Barbara, 1972; JD, Western State U., 1976. Bar: Calif. 1978, U.S. Dist. Ct. (cen. dist.) Calif. 1979, U.S. Ct. Appeals (9th cir.) 1981, U.S. Supreme Ct. 1987. Atty. State Compensation Ins. Fund, Long Beach, Calif., 1979-82, State Farm Ins. Co., Costa Mesa, Calif., 1982-85; assoc. Grancell, Grancell & Marshall, Santa Ana, Calif., 1985-88; ptnr. Hertz & Weitzman, Huntington Beach, Calif., 1988-89; pvt. practice Seal Beach, Calif., 1989—. Judge pro tem State of Calif. Divsn. Indsl. Rels.-Divsn. Indsl. Accidents, Norwalk, 1986—, Long Beach, 1984—, Santa Ana, 1995—; cert. workers' compensation specialist Calif. Bd. Legal Specialization-State Bar Calif., 1988—; arbitrator State of Calif. Divsns. Indsl. Rels. and Indsl. Accident, 1991. Mem. L.A. County Bar Assn., Orange County Bar Assn., Orange County Workers' Compensation Def. Assn., So. Calif. Rehab. Exch., Long Beach Bar Assn. Workers' compensation. Office: 3010 Old Ranch Pkwy Ste 200 Seal Beach CA 90740-2750

**WELBORN, GORDON LEE,** lawyer; b. Roseburg, Oreg., Dec. 28, 1960; s. Kenneth Lee and Ginger Mary Welborn; m. Dina Mary Gambee, June 12, 1982; children: Chase, Whitney, Laurel. BS, Portland State U., 1983; JD, Lewis and Clark U., 1986. Bar: Oreg. 1987, Wash. 1994. Atty. Safeco Ins., Lake Oswego, Oreg., 1987-92, Moscato, Byerly, Skopil, Portland, Oreg., 1992-93; from assoc. to ptnr. Hoffman, hart & Wagner, Portland, Oreg., 1993—, resident ptnr., 1998—. Avocations: golf, outdoors. Personal injury, Professional liability, General civil litigation. Office: Hoffman Hart and Wagner 755 SW 7th St Redmond OR 97756-2708

**WELBORN, REICH LEE,** lawyer; b. Winston-Salem, N.C., Nov. 1, 1945; s. Bishop M. and Hazel (Weatherman) W.; m. Martha Huffstetler, Aug. 27, 1966; children: Judson Allen, Spencer Brooks. AB, U. N.C., 1968, JD with honors, 1971. Bar: N.C. 1971. Assoc. Moore & Van Allen, PLLC and predecessor Powe Porter & Alphin, P.A., Durham, N.C., 1971-76; ptnr. Moore & Van Allen and predecessor Powe Porter & Alphin, P.A., Durham, N.C., 1976—; v.p. Family Counseling Svc., Durham, 1978-79. Recipient Order of Long Leaf Pine award Gov. of N.C., 1981, Spl. Citation, 1983. Mem. ABA, N.C. Bar Assn., Durham County Bar Assn. (v.p. 1987-89, pres. 1989-90), N.C. State Bar, Croasdaile Club (pres. 1989-90), Sertoma (pres. Durham chpt. 1987-88), N.C. Jaycees (pres. 1981-82), Durham C. of C. (bd. dirs. 1992-93, 98). General corporate, Real property, Securities. Home: 7 Lanecrest Pl Durham NC 27705-1854 Office: Moore & Van Allen PLLC 2200 W Main St Ste 800 Durham NC 27705-4658

**WELBORNE, JOHN HOWARD,** lawyer, railway company executive; b. Los Angeles, July 24, 1947; s. William Elmo and Pauline Cornwell (Schoder) W.; m. Mary Martha Lampkin, Oct. 8, 1994. AB, U. Calif.-Berkeley, 1969; MPA, UCLA, 1974; JD, U. Calif.-Davis, 1977. Bar: Calif. 1977, D.C. 1980. Congl. intern Congressman John V. Tunney, Washington, 1969; assoc. firm Adams, Duque & Hazeltine, L.A., 1979-84, of counsel, 1984-96; gen. counsel Magnum Software Corp., Chatsworth, Calif., 1989-98; mgmt. cons., 1971—; dir. Pueblo Viejo Devel. Corp., 1979-88, Union Hardware & Metal Co.; pres. Angels Flight Railway Co., L.A., 1995—; COO Calif. Sesquicentennial Found., 1996-97. Contbr. articles to profl. jours. Mem. cen. bus. dist. project adv. com., downtown strategic plan adv. com., chmn. open space task force, mem. South Park task force City of L.A. Cmty. Redevel. Agy.; mem. L.A. Philharm. Men's Com., 1978-89; pres. L.A. County Host Com. for Olympic Games, 1984; mem. exec. com. Citizens' Task Force for Cen. Libr. Devel., L.A., 1981-83; bd. dirs. Angels Flight Railway Found., L.A. chpt. ARC, 1986-89, Children's Bur. L.A., 1982-88, El Pueblo Park Assn., 1983-89, Friends of the USC Librs., Inner City Law Ctr., 1992-95, Los Amigos del Pueblo, L.A. Libr. Assn., 1983-89, 92—, Windsor Sq. Assn., 1980-87, L.A. Beautiful, 1982-85, Pershing Sq. Restoration Campaign, 1986-87, Children's Bur. Found., 1997—; bd. dirs. In the Wings div. Music Ctr. Los Angeles County, 1982-86, pres., 1984-85; bd. dirs., officer L.A. 200 Com., 1978-91; bd. councilors U. So. Calif. Sch. Pub. Adminstrn., 1983-89; mem. adv. bd. The L.A. Conservancy; trustee Windsor Sq.-Hancock Park Hist. Soc., 1983-86, Nat. Trust Hist. Preservation; fellow Amundsen Inst. U.S.-Mex. Studies, 1987. Capt. Adj. Gen.'s Corps, U.S. Army, 1970-71, USAR, 1972-79. Decorated Army Commendation medal with oak leaf cluster; Cross of Merit 1st class (Fed. Republic Germany). Mem. ABA, D.C. Bar Assn., State Bar Calif., Ordre des Coteaux de Champagne, Confrerie Saint-Etienne d'Alsace, Calif. Vintage Wine Soc. Episcopalian. Office: Angels Flight Railway PO Box 712345 Los Angeles CA 90071-7345

**WELCH, DAVID WILLIAM,** lawyer; b. St. Louis, Feb. 26, 1941; s. Claude LeRoy Welch and Mary Eleanor (Peggs) Penney; m. Candace Lee Capages, June 5, 1971; children: Joseph Peggs, Heather Elizabeth, Katherine Laura. BSBA, Washington U., St. Louis, 1963; JD, U. Tulsa, 1971. Bar: Okla. 1972, Mo. 1973, U.S. Dist. Ct. (we. dist.) Mo. 1973, U.S. Dist. Ct. (ea. dist.) Mo. 1974, U.S. Ct. Appeals (8th cir.) 1977, U.S. Ct. Appeals (7th cir.) 1991. Contract adminstr. McDonnell Aircraft Corp., St. Louis, 1965-66; bus. analyst Dun & Bradstreet Inc., Los Angeles, 1967-68; atty. U.S. Dept. Labor, Washington, 1972-73; ptnr. Moller Talent, Kuelthau & Welch, St. Louis, 1973-88, Lashly & Baer, St. Louis, 1988-96, Armstrong Teasdale LLP, St. Louis, 1996—. Author: (handbook) Missouri Employment Law, 1988; contbr. book chpts. Missouri Bar Employer-Employee Law, 1985, 87, 89, 92, 94, Missouri Discrimination Law, 1999; co-editor: Occupational Safety and Health Law, 1996. Mem. City of Creve Coeur Ethics Commn., 1987-88, Planning and Zoning Commn., 1988-96; bd. dirs. Camp Wyman, Eureka, Mo., 1982—, sec., 1987-88, 2nd v.p. 1988-89, 1st v.p. 1990-92, pres., 1992-94. Mem. ABA, Fed. Bar Assn., Mo. Bar Assn., Okla. Bar Assn., St. Louis Bar Assn., Kiwanis (bd. dirs. St. Louis 1979—, sec. 1982-83, 93-94, v.p. 1983-84, 88-90, 92-93, Man of Yr. award 1985). Democrat. Mem. Christian Ch. (Disciples of Christ). Avocations: travel, landscaping, music. Labor. Home: 536 N Mosley Rd Saint Louis MO 63141-7633 Office: Armstrong Teasdale 1 Metropolitan Sq Ste 2600 Saint Louis MO 63102-2740

**WELCH, EDWARD P.,** lawyer; b. Columbus, Ohio, Mar. 12, 1950; s. Charles E. and Charma L. (Overbeck) W.; m. Noreen R. Welch, Sept. 8, 1973. BS in Bus. Adminstrn., Georgetown U., 1972; JD, Villanova U., 1976. Bar: Del. 1976, U.S. Dist. Ct. Del. 1977, U.S. Ct. Appeals (3d cir.) 1981, U.S. Supreme Ct. 1981, N.Y. 1982, U.S. Ct. Appeals (fed. cir.) 1985, (5th cir.) 1992. Law clk. Del Ct. Chancery, Wilmington, 1976-77; assoc. Prickett, Ward, Burt & Sanders, Wilmington, 1977-79; assoc. Skadden, Arps, Slate, Meagher & Flom, Wilmington, 1979-84, ptnr., 1984—; mem. com. charged with drafting evidence code Del., com. charged with drafting dir. liability legis., Wilmington 1977-78, Ct. Chancery Rules Com., Wilmington, 1990—. Author: Folk, Ward & Welch: Folk on the Delaware General Corporation Law, 1988, 2d edit., 1992; bimonthly Nat. Law Jour.; co-editor: Folk On The Delaware General Corporation Law Fundamentals, 1993. Bd. dirs. United Cerebral Palsy of Del., Wilmington, 1977-87, The Mary Campbell Ctr., 1987—; co-chmn. United Cerebral Palsy's Camp Manito, Wilmington, 1982-83; trustee The Tatnall Sch., Wilmington, 1992-95. Recipient Community Svc. award United Cerebral Palsy of Del., Wilmington, 1981. Mem. Del. Bar Assn. (mem. coun. corp. law, Young Lawyers award 1986), The Rodney Square Club, Corp. Law Coun. General corporate. Office: Skadden Arps Slate Meagher & Flom PO Box 636 One Rodney Sq Wilmington DE 19801

**WELCH, JOSEPH DANIEL,** lawyer; b. University City, Mo., Feb. 1, 1952; s. Robert Joseph and Mary Virginia (Church) W.; m. Sharon Susan Filipek, Mar. 16, 1973; children: Eric Ryan, Christopher Joseph, Colin Andrew, Maria Nicole, Theresa Katherine. BA cum laude, St. Louis U., 1974, JD, 1977. Bar: Mo. 1977, U.S. Dist. Ct. (ea. and we. dists.) Mo. 1977, U.S. Ct. Appeals (8th cir.) 1984, U.S. Supreme Ct. 1994. Assoc. Ely & Cary, Hannibal, Mo., 1977-79; ptnr. Ely, Cary & Welch, Hannibal, Mo., 1979-82, Ely, Cary, Welch & Hickman, Hannibal, Mo., 1982—; mem. Mississippi River Pky. Commn., St. Paul, 1988-95, head Mo. del., 1988; mem. Nat. Heritage Corridor Commn., Washington, 1990-96; speaker various orgns. Editor: Year in Review-Bankruptcy, 1991-94, co-author, 1988-90; speaker various profl. orgns.; contbr. articles to profl. jours. Bd. dirs. Mark Twain Area Physician's Recruitment Assn., Hannibal, 1984-85, Hannibal Free Pub. Libr., 1980-82, Hannibal C. of C., 1978-80; pres. Hannibal Ctrl. Bus. Devel., Inc., 1982-85; mem. Mo. Right-to-Life, 1977—; community adv. bd. St. Elizabeth Hosp., 1985-86; Birthright of Hannibal, Inc., 1980—, Holy Family Sch. Bd., 1990-95. Recipient acad. scholarship St. Louis U., 1970-74, recognition for Significant Contribution to Bush Adminstrn., Dept. Interior, 1993. Mem. ATLA, Mo. Assn. Trial Lawyers., Mark Twain Astron. Soc. (co-founder). Roman Catholic. Avocations: parenting, basketball, tennis, boating, creative writing. Banking, Bankruptcy, General practice. Home: 601 Country Club Dr Hannibal MO 63401-3033 Office: Cary Welch and Hickman LLP 1000 Center St Hannibal MO 63401-3449

**WELCH, LAWRENCE ANDREW, JR.,** lawyer; b. Memphis, Apr. 5, 1961; s. Lawrence A. and Dorothy (Foust) W.; m. Lisa Carol Garland Sept. 19, 1987; children: Jennifer Leigh, Lawrence Andrew III. BS in Bus. Adminstrn., Christian Bros. Coll., 1983; JD, Memphis State U., 1990. Bar: Tenn. 1990, U.S. Dist. Ct. (ea. dist.) Tenn. 1991, U.S. Ct. Appeals (6th cir.) 1992. Mem. Milligan & Coleman, Greeneville, Tenn., 1990-94; sole practitioner Greeneville, 1994—. Mem. ABA (litigation sect., legal malpractice com.), Tenn. Defense Lawyer Assn., Tenn. Bar Assn., Greene County Bar Assn. Republican. Presbyterian. General civil litigation, Personal injury, Workers' compensation. Home: 58 Woodcrest Cir Greeneville TN 37745-0521 Office: 313 E Bernard Ave Greeneville TN 37745-5013

**WELCH, LOUISE BRIDGMAN,** lawyer; b. Louisville, June 28, 1949; d. Charles Whitefield Jr. and Margie Louise (Beam) W.; m. Robert Edward Mackley, June 12, 1976 (div. Mar. 1984). BA, Wellesley Coll., 1971; MA, U. Louisville, 1976, JD, 1990. Bar: Ky. 1991, Ind. 1991. Owner Main Travel Agy., Inc., Louisville, 1978-88; atty. Adminstrv. Office of the Cts., Louisville, 1991-93; pvt. practice law Louisville, 1994—. Bd. dirs. Seven Counties Svc. Inc., Louisville, 1997. Family and matrimonial, Juvenile. Office: PO Box 4284 Louisville KY 40204-0284

**WELCH, WILLIAM,** lawyer; b. Logansport, Ind., June 17, 1918; s. George W. and Alyce W.; m. Jean Louise Knauss, Mar. 5, 1949; children: Brian W., Sarah L. McNaught. BA, DePauw U., 1940; JD, U. Mich., 1948. Bar: Ind. 1948, U.S. Dist. Ct. (so. dist.) Ind. 1948, U.S. Ct. Claims 1948, U.S. Ct. Appeals (7th cir.) 1952, U.S. Tax Ct. 1955, U.S. Supreme Ct. 1974. From assoc. to ptnr. McHale, Cook & Welch P.C., Indpls., 1948—, also past chmn. bd.; trustee Citizens Gas and Coke, Indpls. Trustee DePauw U., Greencastle, Ind. Lt. comdr. USNR, 1941-46, PTO. Fellow Am. Bar Found., Ind. Bar Found., Indpls. Bar Found.; mem. 7th Cir. Bar Assn. (bd. govs., pres. 1991-92). Banking, Public utilities, Securities. Office: McHale Cook & Welch PC 1100 Chamber of Comm Bldg 310 N Meridian St Indianapolis IN 46204-1709

**WELCH-MCKAY, DAWN RENEE,** legal assistant; b. Lincoln, Nebr., Jan. 21, 1965; d. David Eugene and Helen Bessie (Hypes) W. BA in Pre-Law, Hawaii Pacific U., 1988; postgrad., U. Alaska, Anchorage, 1995—. Cert. Emergency Med. Tech. II, Alaska, 1994. Supr. Sizzler Family Steakhouse, Anchorage, 1981; dept. mgr. sales Jay Jacobs, Anchorage, 1982-83; resident asst. Hawaii Pacific U., Kaneohe, 1987-88; legal asst., intern Atkinson, Conway & Gagnon, Anchorage, 1988; contract paralegal Anchorage, 1989—; legal asst. Bogle & Gates, Anchorage, 1989, Bradbury, Bliss & Riordan, Anchorage, 1990-91; owner Welch's Ind. Paralegal Svc., Anchorage, 1991-94; ind. contractor, Anchorage, 1991-94. Vol. Rep. Party of Alaska, 1987, State of Alaska Cmty. Clean-Up, 1981-82, Concerned Citizens of Anchorage, 1981-82; med. asst., EMT II British Petroleum, 1993-96. Hawaii Pacific U. grantee, 1987-88; named to Outstanding Young Women Am., 1987. Mem. NAFE, Nat. Fedn. Paralegal Assns., Alaska Assn. Legal Assts., Nat. Assn. Legal Assts. Avocations: hiking, body surfing, biking, softball. Home: PO Box 303 Boissevain VA 24606-0303

**WELCOME, PATRICIA,** lawyer; b. St. Christopher, W.I., July 4, 1958. BA, U. V.I., 1987; JD cum laude, Tex. So. U., 1990. Bar: V.I. 1991, U.S. Ct. Appeals (3d cir.) 1993. Law clk. to Hon. Eileen Petersen Territorial Ct. V.I., 1990-92; asst. legal counsel Legis. of V.I., St. Croix, 1992; assoc. Douglas L. Capdeville, St. Croix. Recipient Am. Jurisprudence award for Bus. Assn., 1989, award for Consumer Protection, 1989. Mem. ABA, V.I. Bar Assn. (scholarship 1988-90, pres. elect. 1997-98, pres. 1998-99, chair young lawyers com. 1992-93, bar ethics coms. 1994—). Insurance, General civil litigation, Toxic tort. Office: Law Offices of Douglas L Capdeville PO Box 4191 2107 Company St St Croix VI 00822-4191*

**WELGE, JACK HERMAN, JR.,** lawyer; b. Austin, Tex., Sept. 12, 1951; s. Jack Herman and Regina Victoria (Hunger) W.; m. Frances Ava Roddy Avent, Dec. 23, 1977; children: Kirsten Frances Page Welge, Kathleen Ava Regina Welge. BA, U. Tex., 1974; JD, St. Mary's U., 1977. Bar: Tex. 1977, U.S. Dist. Ct. (ea. dist.) Tex. 1979, U.S. Dist. Ct. (no. dist.) Tex. 1982, U.S. Ct. Appeals (5th cir.) 1983, U.S. Supreme Ct., 1984; cert. family law Tex. Bd. Legal Specialization 1984. Asst. dist. atty. Gregg County Criminal Dist. Atty., Longview, Tex., 1978-79; assoc. Law Office of G. Brockett Irwin, Longview, 1979-81; judge Mcpl. Ct. of Record, Longview, 1979-81; ptnr. Adams & Sheppard, Longview, 1981-83; pvt. practice, 1983—; of counsel East Tex. Assn. for Abused Families, Longview, 1985-90. Bd. dirs. Longview Mus. and Arts Ctr., 1991-94, East Tex. Coun. on Alcoholism and Drug Abuse, Longview, 1981-83, Longview Cmty. Theater, 1979-82, East Tex. Assn. for Abused Families, Longview, 1983-85; bd. dirs. Salvation Army, 1994—, chmn. 1997; vestry Trinity Episcopal Ch., Longview, 1993-96; co-chair legal profl. divsn. Gregg Co. United Way, 1996-97. Mem. State Bar of Tex. (pro bono coll., contested custody case panel, protective case panel, Gregg County lawyers pro bono project, Outstanding Contbn. award 1990, Disting. Svc. award 1993, 95, Outstanding Pro Bono Atty. 1994, 97), N.E. Tex. Bar Assn., Rotary (pres. Longview club 1987-88, Paul Harris fellow 1982, 20 Yrs. Perfect Attendance 1999), Gregg County Bar Assn. (pres. 1983), Gregg County Family Law Coun., Tex. Acad. Family Law Specialists, East Tex. Knife and Fork Club (pres. 1983-84), Mason, Delta Theta Phi (dean 1977, Bickett Senate), Delta Upsilon (Tex. chpt. found. bd. 1974-78). Family and matrimonial, General civil litigation, Probate. Office: PO Box 3624 413 S Green St Longview TX 75601-7534

**WELIKSON, JEFFREY ALAN,** lawyer; b. Bklyn., Jan. 8, 1957; s. Bennet Joseph and Cynthia Ann Welikson; m. Laura Sanders, Aug. 19, 1979; children: Gregory Andrew, Joshua Stuart. BS, U. Pa., 1976, MBA, 1977; JD, Harvard U., 1980. Bar: N.Y. 1981; CPA, N.Y. Assoc. Shearman & Sterling, N.Y.C., 1980-83; staff counsel Reliance Group Holdings Inc., N.Y.C., 1983-84, dir. legal dept., 1984-85, asst. v.p., corp. counsel, 1985-88, v.p., asst. gen. counsel, asst. sec., 1988-94; exec. v.p., gen. counsel, sec. Reliance Nat. Ins. Co., N.Y.C., 1994—. Contbg. editor Harvard U. Internat. Law Jour., 1979-80. Mem. ABA, Assn. Bar of City of N.Y., Am. Corp. Counsel Assn. General corporate, Securities, Mergers and acquisitions. Office: Reliance Nat Ins Co 77 Water St New York NY 10005-4401

**WELLER, CHARLES DAVID,** lawyer; b. Hartford, Conn., Oct. 19, 1944; s. Harry Deets and Betty Jane (Allenbaugh) W. BA, Yale U., 1966; JD, Case Western Res. U., 1973. Bar: Ohio 1973, U.S. Dist. Ct. (so. dist.) Ohio 1974, U.S. Dist. Ct. (no. dist.) Ohio 1976, U.S. Ct. Appeals (6th cir.) 1987, U.S. Ct. Appeals (4th cir.) 1994, U.S. Supreme Ct. 1978. Math tchr. U.S. Peace Corps, Johore Bahru, Malaysia, 1966-68; spl. asst. U.S. Peace Corps, Washington, 1969; dep. dir. so. region U.S. Peace Corps, Atlanta, 1969-70; asst. atty. gen. antitrust sect. Ohio Atty.'s Gen. Office, Columbus and Cleve., Ohio, 1973-82; of counsel Jones, Day, Reavis & Pogue, Cleve., 1982-94; ptnr. Baker & Hostetler LLP, Cleve., 1994—; trustee Health Action Coun., Cleve., 1982-95, Health Sys. Agy. of North, 1983-92, Cleve. Health Edn. Mus., 1991-97. Mem. ABA (antitrust sect. and forum com. on health law), Yale Alumni Assn. Cleve. (trustee). Antitrust, Health, General civil litigation. Home: 12521 Lake Shore Blvd Cleveland OH 44108-1134 Office: Baker and Hostetler LLP 3200 National City Ctr Cleveland OH 44114-3485

**WELLFORD, HARRY WALKER,** federal judge; b. Memphis, Aug. 6, 1924; s. Harry Alexander and Roberta Thompson (Prothro) W.; m. Katherine E. Potts, Dec. 8, 1951; children: Harry Walker, James B. Buckner P., Katherine T., Allison R. Student, U. N.C., 1943-44; BA, Washington and Lee U., 1947; postgrad. in law, U. Mich., 1947-48; LLD, Vanderbilt U., 1950. Bar: Tenn. 1950. Atty. McCloy, Myar & Wellford, Memphis, 1950-60, McCloy, Wellford & Clark, Memphis, 1960-70; judge U.S. Dist. Ct., Memphis, 1970-82; judge U.S. Ct. Appeals (6th cir.), Cin. and Memphis, 1982-92, sr. judge, 1992—; mem. pres.' adv. coun. Rhodes Coll. Chair Senator Howard Baker campaigns, 1964-66; chair Tenn. Hist. Commn., Tenn. Constnl. Bicentennial Commn., 1987-88; mem. charter drafting com. City of Memphis, 1967, Tenn. Am. Revolution Bicentennial Commn., 1976, com. on Adminstrn. Fed. Magistrates Sys., Jud. Conf. Subcom. Adminstrn. of Criminal Law Probation; clk. session, commr. Gen. Assembly; elder Presbyn. Ch.; moderator Memphis Presbytery, 1994. Recipient Sam A. Myar award for svc. to profession and community Memphis State Law U., 1963. Mem. Phi Beta Kappa, Omega Delta Kappa. Office: US Ct Appeals Clifford Davis Federal Bldg 167 N Main St Ste 1176 Memphis TN 38103-1824

**WELLINGTON, CAROL STRONG,** law librarian; b. Altadena, Calif., Jan. 30, 1948; d. Edward Walters and Elizabeth (Leonards) Strong; m. David Heath Wellington, May 27, 1978; 1 child, Edward Heath. BA, Lake Forest (Ill.) Coll., 1969; MLS, Simmons Coll., 1973. Libr. Hill & Barlow, Boston, 1973-88, Peabody & Arnold LLP, Boston, 1988—. Mem. Am. Assn. Law Librs., Assn. Boston Law Librs. (v.p. 1979-80, pres. 1980-81), Spl. Librs. Assn., Law Librs. New England. Office: Peabody & Arnold LLP 50 Rowes Wharf Fl 7 Boston MA 02110-3342

**WELLINGTON, HARRY HILLEL,** lawyer, educator; b. New Haven, Aug. 13, 1926; s. Alex M. and Jean (Ripps) W.; m. Sheila Wacks, June 22, 1952; children: John, Thomas. AB, U. Pa., 1947; LLB, Harvard U., 1952; MA (hon.), Yale U., 1960. Bar: D.C. 1952. Law clk. to U.S. Judge Magruder, 1953-54, Supreme Ct. Justice Frankfurter, 1955-56; asst. prof. law Stanford U., 1954-56; mem. faculty Yale U., 1956—, prof. law, 1960—, Edward J. Phelps prof. law, 1967-83, dean Law Sch., 1975-85, Sterling prof. law, 1983-92, Sterling prof. emeritus law, 1992—, Harry H. Wellington prof. lectr., 1995—; pres., dean, prof. law N.Y. Law Sch., N.Y.C., 1992—; Ford fellow London Sch. Econs., 1965; Guggenheim fellow; sr. fellow Brookings Instn., 1968-71; Rockefeller Found. fellow Bellagio Study and Conf. Ctr., 1984; faculty mem. Salzburg Seminar in Am. Studies, 1985; John M. Harlan disting. vis. prof. N.Y. Law Sch., 1985-86; review person ITT-SEC; moderator Asbestos-Wellington Group; cons. domestic and fgn. govtl. agys.; trustee N.Y. Law Sch.; bd. govs. Yale U. Press; mem. jud. panel, exec. com. Ctr. Public Resources Legal Program; Harry H. Wellington lectr., 1995—. Author: with Harold Shepherd) Contracts and Contract Remedies, 1957, Labor and the Legal Process, 1968, (with Clyde Summers) Labor Law, 1968, 2d edit., 1983, (with Ralph Winter) The Unions and the Cities, 1971, Interpreting the Constitution, 1990; contbr. articles to profl. jours. Mem. ABA, Bar Assn. Conn., Am. Law Inst., Am. Arbitration Assn., Am. Acad. Arts and Scis., Common Cause (nat governing bd.). Office: NY Law Sch 57 Worth St New York NY 10013-2959 also: Yale U Sch Law New Haven CT 06520

**WELLINGTON, RALPH GLENN,** lawyer; b. Three Rivers, Mich., June 18, 1946; s. Cleon G. and Gladys M. (Cole) W.; m. Margaret Brennan; children: Ralph Glenn II, Jeffrey Scott, Tyler Cahill. BA, Kalamazoo Coll., 1968; JD, U. Mich., 1970. Bar: Pa. 1971, U.S. Dist. Ct. (ea. dist.) Pa. 1971, U.S. Dist. Ct. (mid. dist.) Pa. 1976, U.S. Ct. Appeals (3d cir.) 1978, U.S. Ct. Appeals (6th cir.) 1985, U.S. Supreme Ct. 1987. Atty. Schnader Harrison Segal & Lewis, Phila., chmn., 1998—; frequent lectr. on litigation and ethics in U.S.A. and abroad. Contbr. articles to profl. jours. Trustee Kalamazoo Coll., 1992-98. Fellow Am. Coll. Trial Lawyers; mem. ABA, Nat. Assn. R.R. Trial Counsel, Aviation Ins. Assn., Lawyer-Pilots Bar Assn., Phila. Bar Assn. (chair profl. responsibility com. 1988), Phila. Cricket Club, Pyramid Club. Lutheran. Avocations: squash, golf, jazz piano. General civil litigation, Securities, Transportation. Home: 604 W Hartwell Ln Philadelphia PA 19118-4114 Office: Schnader Harrison Segal & Lewis 1600 Market St Ste 3600 Philadelphia PA 19103-7240

**WELLMAN, DAVID JOSEPH,** lawyer; b. Port Huron, Mich., Feb. 13, 1947; s. Joseph Elliot and Annabel Jones Wellman; m. Elizabeth A. Wellman, Oct. 27, 1990; 1 child, Todd David. BA, Ctrl. Mich. U., 1969; JD, Detroit Coll. Law, 1973. Of counsel Colombo & Colombo, Bloomfield, Mich., 1990—. General corporate, Mergers and acquisitions, Corporate taxation. Office: Colombo & Colombo 1701 N Woodward Ave Ste 50 Bloomfield Hills MI 48304-2239

**WELLMAN, THOMAS PETER,** lawyer; b. Farrell, Pa., Feb. 25, 1932; s. Peter Michael and Bessie Thomas (George) W.; m. Jeanne Ann Harding, July 9, 1971; children: Elizabeth Thomas, Katherine Thomas. BA, Miami U., Oxford, Ohio, 1956; JD, Ohio State U., 1959. Bar: Ohio 1959, U.S. Dist. Ct. (no. dist.) Ohio 1961. Asst. atty. gen. State of Ohio, Columbus, 1959-60; sr. atty. Wellman & Jeren Co., L.P.A., Youngstown, Ohio, 1960—; mng. ptnr. Tablack, Wellman, Jeren, Hackett & Skoufatos Co., L.P.A., Youngstown, 1973—. Mem. Canfield (Ohio) Income Tax Rev. Bd., 1981—. With U.S. Army, 1952-54. Mem. Ohio State Bar Assn. (workers compensation sect. 1991—), Mahoning County Bar Assn. (chmn. unauthorized practice of law com. 1984-85, mem. inquiry com. 1990—). Presbyterian. Avocation: sailing. Workers' compensation, Pension, profit-sharing, and employee benefits. Office: 67 Westchester Dr Youngstown OH 44515-3902

**WELLNITZ, CRAIG OTTO,** lawyer, English language educator; b. Elwood, Ind., Dec. 5, 1946; s. Frank Otto and Jeanne (Albright) W.; m. Karen Sue Thomas, Apr. 13, 1974 (div. Sept. 1987); children: Jennifer Suzanne, Anne Katherine; m. Carol L. Hinesley, Jan. 23, 1988. BA, Purdue U., 1969; MA, Ind. U., 1972; JD, Ind. U.-Indpls., 1978. Bar: Ind. 1978, U.S. Dist. Ct. (so. dist.) Ind. 1978, U.S. Supreme Ct. 1983, U.S. Ct. Appeals (7th and Fed. cirs.) 1984, U.S. Dist. Ct. (no. dist.) 1990; registered mediator, Ind. Instr. Danville Jr. Coll., Ill., 1972-74, S.W. Mo. State U., Springfield, Mo., 1974-75; ptnr. Coates, Hatfield, Calkins & Wellnitz, Indpls., 1978—; pub. defender criminal divsn. Marion Superior Ct., Marion County, 1979-88, master commr. criminal divsn., 1988-96, registered mediator, 1998—; instr. U. Indpls., 1981-82; mem. adj. faculty dept. English Butler U., Indpls., 1982—; instr. English Ind. U.-Purdue U., Indpls., 1987-90; pres. Ind. Account Mgmt., Inspls., 1985-94; v.p. Carol Craig Assocs., Indpls., 1987—; lectr. in field. Columnist A Jury of Your Peers, 1984-86. Vice committeeman Indpls. Rep. precinct, 1978; chmn. fin. com. St. Luke's United Meth. Ch., 1985-87; sponsor Christian Children's Fund, 1990—; active Am. Mus. Natural History, Indpls. Zoo, Children's Mus. Indpls., The Royal Oak Found. Postgrad. study grantee S.W. Mo. State U., Springfield, 1975. Mem. ABA, AAUP, MLA, ATLA, Def. Rsch. Inst., Nat. Assn. Retail Collection Attys., Am. Collectors Assn., Ind. Bar Assn., Ind. Trial Lawyers Assn., Indpls. Bar Assn., Nat. Coun. Tchrs. English, Smithsonian Assocs., Libr. Congress Assocs., Internat. Platform Assn., Nat. Spkrs. Assn., Spkrs. U.S.A., Internat. Spkrs. Network, Broad Ripple Village Assn., Columbia Club, Rivera Club Indpls., Elks. E-mail: Indplslaw@aol.com., http://www.thebook.com/collection. Personal injury, Consumer commercial, State civil litigation. Office: 1 Indiana Sq Ste 2335 Indianapolis IN 46204-2012

**WELLON, ROBERT G.,** lawyer; b. Port Jervis, N.Y., Apr. 18, 1948; s. Frank Lewis and Alice (Stevens) W.; m. Jan Montgomery, Aug. 12, 1972; children: Robert F., Alice Wynn. AB, Emory U., 1970; JD, Stetson Coll. Law, 1974. Assoc. Turner, Turner & Turner, Atlanta, 1974-78; ptnr. Ridley, Wellon, Schwieger & Brazier, Atlanta, 1978-86; of counsel Wilson, Strickland & Benson, Atlanta, 1987—; adj. prof. Atlanta Law Sch., 1981-94; adj. prof. law Emory U. Sch. of Law, 1995—. Gov.'s task force chmn. Atlanta 2000, 1978; exec. com., treas., 2nd v.p. Atlanta Easter Seals Soc., 1983-88; rep. Neighborhood Planning Unit, 1981-83; adminstrv. bd. Northside United Meth. Ch. Served with USAR, 1970-76. Recipient Judge Joe Morris award Stetson Coll. Law, St. Petersburg, 1974, Charles E. Watkins svc. award 1995). Mem. Fla. Bar, State Bar. Ga. (professionalism com. 1994—), Atlanta Bar Assn. (bd. dirs. 1978-88, pres. 1986-87, bd. trustees CLE), Lawyers Club Atlanta, Old War Horse Lawyers Club, Atlanta Found. for Psychoanalysis (exec. com. 1997—), Charles Longstreet Weltner Family Law Inn of Ct. (pres. 1997—), Atlanta Found. for Psychoanalysis, Inc. (bd. dirs. 1994, exec. com. 1997—). Methodist. Family and matrimonial, Personal injury, State civil litigation. Office: 1100 One Midtown Pla 1360 Peachtree St NE Atlanta GA 30309-3283

**WELLS, BENJAMIN GLADNEY,** lawyer; b. St. Louis, Nov. 13, 1943; s. Benjamin Harris and Katherine Emma (Gladney) W.; m. Nancy Kathryn Harpster, June 7, 1967; children: Barbara Gladney, Benjamin Harpster. BA magna cum laude, Amherst (Mass.) Coll., 1965; JD cum laude, Harvard U., 1968. Bar: Ill. 1968, Tex. 1973, U.S. Tax Ct. 1973, U.S. Ct. Claims 1975, U.S. Ct. Appeals (5th cir.) 1981, U.S. Dist. Ct. (so. dist.) Tex. 1985, U.S. Dist. Ct. (we. dist.) Tex. 1993. Assoc. Kirkland & Ellis, Chgo., 1968-69; assoc. to ptnr. Baker & Botts, L.L.P., Houston, 1973—. Contbr. articles to profl. jours. Mem. planned giving com. St. John's Sch., Houston (chmn. 1987-98); Harvard Legal Aid Bureau, 1966-68. Capt. U.S. Army, 1969-72. Fellow Am. Coll. Tax Counsel; mem. ABA (vice chair corp. tax com. sect. on taxation 1999—), Houston Tax Roundtable (pres. 1994-95), The Forest Club, The Houston Club, Phi Beta Kappa. Presbyterian. Corporate taxation, Taxation, general. Office: Baker & Botts LLP One Shell Plaza 910 Louisiana St Ste 3330 Houston TX 77002-4916

**WELLS, CHARLES TALLEY,** state supreme court justice. Bar: Fla. 1965, U.S. Dist Ct. (middle dist. of Fla.), U.S. Ct. Appeals,(5th cir.) now (11th cir.) 1966, U.S. Supreme Ct., 1969, U.S. Dist. Ct., U.S. Dist. Ct. (So. dist), Fla., 1976, U.S. Ct. of Claims, 1990. Trial atty. U.S. dept justice Washington, 1969; pvt. practice maguire, Voohris and Wells, PA, Orlando, Fla., 1965-68, 1970-75, Wells, Gattis, Hollowes & Carpenter, PA, Orlando, Fla., 1976-94; justice Fla. Supreme Ct., Tallahassee. Methodist. Office: Fla Supreme Ct Supreme Ct Bldg 500 S Duval St Tallahassee FL 32399-6556

**WELLS, GARY B.,** lawyer, accountant; b. Salt Lake City, May 27, 1963; s. BBA, Idaho State U., 1985; JD, Brigham Young U., 1991. Bar: Calif. 1991; CPA, Calif. Acct. Arthur Andersen & Co., Denver, 1985-86, Brown, Fink, Boyce & Co., Sacramento, 1986-88; assoc. Baker, Manock & Jensen, Fresno, Calif., 1991-97; pvt. practice law and acctg., Fresno, 1997—; lectr. Computing Inst. Seminars, Pocatello, Idaho, 1987-92. Co-author: Quattro: From Beginning through Macros with Applications in Finance and Accounting, 1989, Financial Applications Using Quattro Pro 3.0, 1991, Financial Analysis Using Quattro Pro 6.0, 1996. J. Reuben Clark scholar Brigham Young U. Mem. State Bar Calif., Fresno County Bar Assn., Internat. Assn. for Fin. Planning (pres. Fresno chpt. 1999), Calif. Soc. CPAs,

Beta Alpha Psi, Phi Kappa Phi, Beta Gamma Sigma. Estate planning, Taxation, general, Appellate. Office: 2251 E Beechwood Ave Ste 101 Fresno CA 93720-0329

**WELLS, JOSHUA JOSEPH,** lawyer; b. Syracuse, N.Y., Mar. 7, 1971; s. Richard Alan and Portia Lynn Wells. BS, Cornell U., 1993; JD, Boston U., 1996. Bar: N.Y. 1997, U.S. Dist. Ct. (no., so., ea. and we. dists.) N.Y. 1997. Assoc. Harris Beach & Wilcox, Syracuse, 1996-97, Landman Corsi Ballaine & Ford P.C., N.Y.C., 1997—. Mem. ABA, New York County Lawyers Assn. Federal civil litigation, Environmental, Transportation. Home: 33 Greenwich Ave New York NY 10014-2701 Office: Landman Corsi Ballaine & Ford 120 Broadway Fl 27 New York NY 10271-2799

**WELLS, LESLEY B.,** judge; b. Muskegon, Mich., Oct. 6, 1937; d. James Franklin and Inez Simpson Wells; m. Arthur V. N. Brooks, June 20, 1959 (div.); children: Lauren Elizabeth, Caryn Alison, Anne Kristin, Thomas Eliot; m. Charles F. Clarke, Nov. 13, 1998. BA, Chatham Coll., 1959; JD cum laude, Cleve. State U., 1974; cert., Nat. Jud. Coll., 1983, 85, 87, Nat. Jud. Coll., 89. Bar: Ohio 1975, U.S. Dist. Ct. (no. dist.) Ohio 1975, U.S. Supreme Ct. 1989. Pvt. practice Cleve., 1975; ptnr. Brooks & Moffet, Cleve., 1975-79; dir., atty. ABAR Litigation Ctr., Cleve., 1979-80; assoc. Schneider, Smeltz, Huston & Ranney, Cleve., 1980-83; judge Ct. of Common Pleas, Cleve., 1983-94, U.S. Dist. Ct. (no. dist.) Ohio 6th Cir., Cleve., 1994—; adj. prof. law and urban policy Cleve. State U., 1979-82. Editor, author: Litigation Manual, 1980. Past pres. Cleve. Legal Aid Soc.; legal chmn. Nat. Women's Polit. Caucus, 1981-82; chmn. Gov.'s Task Force on Family Violence, Ohio, 1983-87; mem. biomed. ethics com. Case Western Res. U. Med. Sch., 1985-94; master N.W. Ordinance U.S. Constn. Commn., Ohio, 1986-88, Burton Inn of Ct., 1989—, counselor, 1993, pres., 1998-99; trustee Rosemary Ctr., 1986-92, Miami U., 1988-92, Urban League Cleve., 1989-90, Chatham Coll., 1989-94. Recipient Superior Jud. award Supreme Ct. Ohio, 1983, J. Irwin award Womenspace, Ohio, 1984, award Womens City Club, 1985, Disting. Alumna award Chatham Coll., 1988, Alumni Civic Achievement award Cleve. State U., 1992, Golden Gavel award Ohio Judges Assn., 1994, Outstanding Alumni award Cleve. Marshall Law Alumni Assn., 1994, Greater Cleve. Achievement award YWCA, 1995. Mem. ABA (coun. litigation sect. 1996-99), Am. Law Inst., Ohio Bar Assn., Ohio Womens Bar Assn., Cleve. Bar Assn. (Merit Svc. award 1983), Cuyahoga County Bar Assn., Nat. Assn. Women Judges, Philos. Club Cleve. Office: 338 US Courthouse 201 Superior Ave E Cleveland OH 44114-1201

**WELLS, PETER NATHANIEL,** judge, lawyer; b. Ogdensburg, N.Y., May 13, 1938; s. John Harris and Mary Theresa (Houlihan) W.; m. Diana Barry Wells, Apr. 8, 1967; children: Mary, Sarah, Matthew. BS in Polit. Sci., Manhattan Coll., 1960; LLB, Boston Coll., 1963. Bar: N.Y. 1963, U.S. Dist. Ct. (no. dist.) N.Y. 1967, U.S. Dist. Ct. (we. dist.) N.Y. 1971, U.S. Ct. Appeals (2d cir.) 1974, U.S. Ct. Appeals (3d cir.) 1978, U.S. Supreme Ct. 1974. Asst. atty. gen. State of N.Y., 1964-68; assoc. Costello, Cooney & Fearon, Syracuse, N.Y., 1968-70, ptnr., 1970-76; ptnr. Williams, Micale & Wells, Syracuse, 1976-88; Mackenzie Smith Lewis, Michell & Hughes, Syracuse, 1988; surrogate ct. judge Onodaga County, 1989—; mem. EPTL-SCPA Legis. adv. com. of N.Y. State. Editl. bd. Warren's Heaton on Surrogate Ct. Chmn. Dewitt Republican Com., 1976-87; town justice Dewitt, N.Y., 1987-88; pres. N.Y. State Surrogate's Assn., 1999—. Served with USAR, 1963-69. Mem. ABA, N.Y. State Bar Assn., Onondaga County Bar Assn., Def. Rsch. Inst., Upstate Trial Lawyers Assn., N.Y. State Surrogate's Assn. (pres. 1999—). Roman Catholic. Clubs: Cavalry, Manlius (N.Y.). Home: 100 Downing Rd Syracuse NY 13214-1503 Office: Surrogate Ct Chambers Onondaga County Courth Syracuse NY 13202

**WELLS, ROBERT ALFRED,** lawyer; b. Louisiana, Mo., Dec. 1, 1942; s. Harry Armstrong and Irene Jacobson W.; m. Binney Kitchel, Dec. 21, 1968; children: Hylah, Theodore. BA with honors, DePauw U., 1964; JD cum laude, Univ. Mich., 1967. Bar: U.S. Tax Ct. 1973, U.S. Supreme Ct. 1976, U.S. Mil. Ct. Appeals 1978. Assoc. Dewey, Ballantine, Bushby, Palmer & Wood, N.Y.C., 1967-68, McLane, Graf, Raulerson & Middleton, Manchester, N.H., 1971—. Bd. dirs. Am. Lung Assn. of N.H., pres., 1980-81, sec., 1990—; bd. dirs. Am. Lung Assn., 1988-94, mem. exec. com., 1987—; active St. Andrew's Episc. Ch., Hopkinton, N.H., 1971—, vestry mem., 1974-77, warden, 1979-85; trustee Protestant Episc. Ch. of N.H., 1985—; mem. Town of Hopkinton Planning Bd., 1977-79; co-chmn. Hopkinton Master Plan Revision Com., 1986-88; chmn. State Adv. Com. to the U.S. Civil Rights Commn., 1985-89; bd. dirs. Pat's Peak Ednl. Found., Inc., 1982-87, bd. dirs. Youth Soccer Assn.; trustee Heritage Heights/ Homewood, 1994—, Soc. for Protection of N.H. Forests, 1988-94, 95-96, sec., 1995-96. Lt. USN, 1968-70. Mem. Am Coll. Trust & Estate Counsel, N.H. Bar Assn. (chmn. elderly legal devel. Program 1978-81, continuing legal education program 1981-85, fee dispute resolution com. 1986-88), Internat. Assn. of Fin. Planners (edn. com. 1985—), Phi Beta Kappa. Episcopalian. Probate, Estate planning, Administrative and regulatory. Office: PO Box 326 Manchester NH 03105-0326

**WELLS, SAMUEL JAY,** lawyer; b. Sand Springs, Okla., Feb. 3, 1924; s. Robert Lester and Ada Blanche W.; m. Mary Elizabeth Rice; children: Samuel Jay Wells Jr., Robert V., Duncan W. BA in Psychology, U. Mo., 1956, JD, 1956. Atty. County Atty. Office, Kansas City, 1956-60, Kans. Dept. Revenue, Kansas City, 1974-86; atty. Spl. Asst. Atty. Gen., Topeka, 1959; v.p. Wells Corp., Shawnee Mission, Kans., 1970—; dir., v.p. Mission Groves Inc., Ft. Pierce, Fla., 1970-85; pres. Westborough Devel. Corp., Kansas City, Kans., 1972—. With USAF, 1943. Mem. Kans. Trial Lawyers Assn. (bd. govs. 1972—), Masons, Shriner, Tau Kappa Epsilon, Delta Theta Phi. Democrat. Personal injury, Workers' compensation. Home: 3601 Shawnee Mission Pkwy Shawnee Mission KS 66205-2711

**WELLS, STEVEN W.,** lawyer; b. Ft. Walton Beach, Fla., Sept. 8, 1960; s. H. Wayne and Shirley A. W.; m. Lisa Stieler, May 20, 1983; Robert, James, Jessica. BA in Comm., Mich. State U., 1982; JD with distinction, Detroit Coll. of Law, 1985. Bar: Mich. Asst. prosecutor Oakland County, Pontiac, Mich., 1985-88; mng. ptnr. Schnelz, Bondy & Wells, P.C., Troy, Mich., 1988-93; shareholder, mng. ptnr. Cross Wrock, P.C., Detroit, 1993—. Contbr. articles to State Bar Jour., presentations to legal forums. Fellow Mich. Bar Assn.; ABA, ATLA, Detroit Bar Assn., Mich. Trial Lawyers Assn., Nat. Dist. Attys. Assn. Avocations: golf, tennis, coaching youth baseball, soccer. Communications, General civil litigation. Office: Cross Wrock PC 201 W Big Beaver Rd Ste 220 Troy MI 48084-4157

**WELLS, WAYNE ALTON,** lawyer; b. Abilene, Tex., Sept. 29, 1946; s. Thomas Edsel and Velma Pauline (Moseley) W.; married; children: Susannah, Emily. BA, U. Okla., 1969, JD, 1972. Bar: Supreme Ct. Okla. 1972, U.S. Dist Ct. (western dist.) Okla. 1973, U.S. Dist. Ct. (ea. dist.) Okla. 1985, U.S. Dist. Ct. (no. dist.) Okla. 1982, U.S. Ct. Appeals (10th cir.) 1976. Assoc. Lampkin, Wolfe, Burger, Abel, McCaffery & Norman, Oklahoma City, 1972-76; sole practice Edmond, Okla., 1976—. Athletic advisory bd. dirs. U.S. Olympic Com., Colorado Springs, 1973-76. Recipient Gold medal free style wrestling Internat. Olympics, Munich, 1972; named champion wrestler Nat. Colligate Athletic Assn., 1968, U.S. Wrestling Hall of Fame, 1982. Mem. Okla. Bar Assn., Okla. Trial Lawyers Assn. (adv. bd. 1980), Okla. County Bar Assn., Citizens Savs. Athletic Found. Republican. Avocations: skiing, hunting, flying. Personal injury, Insurance, Workers' compensation.

**WELMAKER, FORREST NOLAN,** lawyer; b. McKinney, Tex., Aug. 13, 1925; s. Felix E. and Forrest Love (Baker) W.; div.; children: Forrest Nolan Jr., Mary Elizabeth Welmaker Young, Byron Skillin. BBA, U. Tex., 1950, LLD, 1953. Bar: Tex. 1953, U.S. Dist. Ct. (so. and we. dists.) Tex. 1956, U.S. Ct. Appeals (5th cir.) 1956, U.S. Tax Ct. 1959, U.S. Supreme Ct. 1956. Pvt. practice San Antonio, 1953—. Past bd. dirs., officer United Fund San Antonio, San Antonio chpt. ARC, Children Welfare Bur. San Antonio, San Antonio YMCA. Capt. USNR, 1943-46, PTO, 1950-52, Korea. Fellow Tex. Bar Found., San Antonio Bar Found.; mem. San Antonio Bar Assn. (past bd. dirs., v.p., pres.), Tex. Assn. Def. Counsel, San Antonio Res. Officer Assn., Tex. Bar Assn. (past bd. dirs.), San Antonio Pla. Club, San Antonio German Club. Episcopalian. Avocations: handball, boating. General civil litigation, General practice, Personal injury. Home: 114 W Brandon Dr San Antonio TX 78209-6404

**WELSH, ALFRED JOHN,** lawyer, consultant; b. Louisville, May 10, 1947; s. Elvin Alfred and Carol (Kleymeyer) W.; m. Lee Mitchell, Aug. 1, 1970; children: Charles Kleymeyer, Kathryn Thomas. BA, Centre Coll., 1969; JD, U. Ky., 1972; LLM in Internat. Law cum laude, U. Brussels, 1973. Bar: Ky. 1972, U.S. Dist. Ct. (we. and ea. dists.) Ky. 1972, U.S. Ct. Appeals (6th cir.) 1972. Atty. Ky. Atty. Gen. Office, Frankfort, 1973-74; legis. counsel to congressman Ho. of Reps., Washington, 1974-77; mng. ptnr. Nicolas Welsh Brooks & Hayward, Louisville, 1977—, Boone Welsh Brooks and Hayward Internat. Law; hon. counsel of Belgium, 1983—; econ. devel. advisor Kimgdom of Belgium; mem. Ky. Econ. Adv. Coun.; pres. Transcontinental Trading Cons., Ltd.; participant in North African Mideast Econ. Summit Conf., Morocco, 1994; bd. dirs. Intervention Resources, Inc. Bd. dirs. Greater Louisville Swim Found., 1983-94, exec. com., 1994—; bd. dirs. Louisville com. Coun. Fgn. Rels., 1993—, also pres.; bd. dirs. Jefferson County Alcohol and Drug Abuse Found., Louisville, 1986—, Intervention Resource, Inc., Louisville, 1998—, Internet. Resolve; mem. econ. task force of Ky. Legis. Agts. Decorated knight Order of the Crown (Belgium). Mem. ABA (internat. law sect., commn. on impairment), Ky. Bar Assn. (bd. dirs. 1981-82, pres. young lawyers divsn. 1981-82), Am. Judicature Soc., Louisville C. of C. Democrat. Presbyterian. Avocations: swimming, water polo, soccer. General corporate, Personal injury, Private international. Office: Barristers Hall 1009 S 4th St Louisville KY 40203-3207

**WELSH, JOHN BERESFORD, JR.,** lawyer; b. Seattle, Feb. 16, 1940; s. John B. and Rowena Morgan (Custer) W. Student U. Hawaii, 1960, Georgetown U., 1960; BA, U. Wash., 1962, LLB, 1965. Bar: Wash. 1965. Staff counsel Joint Com. on Govtl. Cooperation, 1965-66; asst. atty. gen. Dept. Labor and Industries, 1966-67; atty. Legis. Coun., acting as counsel to Pub. Health Com., Labor Com., Pub. Employees Collective Bargaining Com., Com. on State Instns. and Youth Devel., State of Wash., 1967-73; sr. counsel Wash. Ho. of Reps., counsel to Ho. Com. on Social and Health Svcs., Olympia, 1973-86; atty. Ho. spkr., 1973; counsel Ho. Com. Human Svcs., 1987-91, 93-95, Ho. Com. on Health Care, 1987—, Ho. Com. on Trade and Econ. Devel., 1995-98, Joint Select Com. on Nurse Delegation, 1995-98; Joint Select Com. on Oral Health, 1996; legal cons. Gov's. Planning Commn. Vocat. Rehab., 1968, Gov.'s Commn. on Youth Involvement, 1969; envoy from Gov. Wash. to investiture of Prince of Wales, London, 1969; faculty Conf. Liceasure, Enforcement and Regulation, Nat. Conf. State Legislatures, Denver, 1977, New Orleans, 1977, San Francisco, 1984, Orlando, Fla., 1985, Denver 1986, Kansas City, Mo., 1987, Washington, 1988, Indpls., 1989, Seattle, 1990, Ft. Lauderdale, Fla., 1991, Albuquerque, 1992, Boston, 1994, San Antonio, 1995, Norfolk 1997; mem. steering com., 1986-90, legis. issues com., 1986—, Coun. on Licensure, Enforcement and Regulation, 1984, 86-90, 87-88, Coun. of State Govts. com. on suggested state legis., 1988—, sub. com. scope and agenda, 1988-95; vol. Hampton Rds. U.S. Naval Mus., mem. gov's. state medal merit com., 1986—. Hon. prof. health adminstrn. Eastern Wash. U., 1982. Mem. Wash. Bar Assn., Govtl. Lawyers Assn., Nat. Health Lawyers Assn., Soc. des Amis du Musee de l'Armee, Paris, English Speaking Union, La Societe Napoleonienne (pres.), Medals Soc. Am., Sons of Union Veterans of the Civil War, Custer Battlefield Hist. & Mus. Assn., 8th Army Air Force Hist. Assn., Northwest Hist. Assn. (bd. dirs.), The Colonial Williamsburg Found., Nat. Trust Historic Preservation, Napoleonic Alliance (bd. dirs.), Friends of Willie & Joe, Phi Delta Phi. Office: Wash Ho Reps PO Box 40600 Olympia WA 98504-0600

**WELSH, KELLY RAYMOND,** lawyer, telecommunications company executive; b. Chgo., July 6, 1952; s. Raymond J. and Mary Jane (Kelly) W.; m. Ellen S. Alberding, June 28, 1985; children: Katherine A., Julia S. AB cum laude, Harvard U., 1974, JD magna cum laude, 1978; MA, Sussex U., Eng., 1975. Assoc. Mayer, Brown & Platt, Chgo., 1979-85, ptnr., 1985-89; corp. counsel City of Chgo., 1989-93; v.p., assoc. gen. counsel Ameritech Corp., Chgo., 1993-96, exec. v.p., gen. counsel, 1996—. Chmn. Met. Pier and Exposition Authority, Chgo., 1994—. Mem. ABA, Chgo. Bar Assn., Chgo. Coun. Lawyers, Chgo. Coun. Fgn. Rels. (mem. Chgo. com.), Legal Club Chgo. Office: Ameritech Corp 30 S Wacker Dr Fl 39 Chicago IL 60606-7413*

**WELT, PHILIP STANLEY,** lawyer, consultant; b. Freeport, N.Y., July 5, 1959; s. Morris and Rose (Offenberg) W.; m. Karen Teresa Gault, May 22, 1994. BBA summa cum laude, Hofstra U., 1983; MBA, Columbia U., 1988; JD cum laude, NYU, 1995. Bar: N.J. 1995, N.Y. 1995; U.S. Dist. Ct. N.J. 1995, U.S. Dist. Ct. (so. and ea. dists.) N.Y. 1996, U.S. Ct. Appeals (2d cir.), 1997; CPA, N.Y. Sr. mgr. Deloitte & Touche, N.Y.C., 1983-92; assoc. Reboul MacMurray Hewitt Maynard & Kristol, N.Y.C., 1993, Davis Polk & Wardwell, N.Y.C., 1994, 96—; jud. clk. U.S. Dist. Ct. N.J., Newark, 1995-96; bd. dirs., treas. Pub. Interest Law Found., N.Y.C., 1993-94; guest spkr. Boy Scouts Am., Nassau County, 1984-91, Nat. Assn. Accts., N.Y./N.J., 1988-92, others. Sr. editor Columbia Jour. World Bus., 1986-88; sr. exec. editor Ann. Survey Am. Law, 1993-95; contbr. articles to profl. jours. Vol. income tax asst. Dept. Treasury, IRS, N.Y.C., 1981-87; vol. Variety-The Children's Charity, N.Y.C., 1985-87; advisor Friends of Jon Kaiman, Nassau County, 1995. Provost's scholar Hofstra U., 1981-83, Deloitt & Touche fellow Columbia U., 1986-88; recipient Appreciation cert. Dept. Treasury, IRS, 1981-87, Variety, 1985-87, Bovenaan Outstanding Cmty. Svc. award Hofstra U., 1983, Orison S. Marden Moot Ct. Advocacy award NYU Sch. Law, 1993, Seymore A. Levy meml. award, 1995. Mem. ABA, ATLA, AICPAs, N.Y. State Soc. CPAs, Beta Alpha Psi, Beta Gamma Sigma. Avocations: golf, rock climbing, photography, philately, amateur radio. Communications, Finance, Public international. Home: 157 Mountain Wood Rd Stamford CT 06903-2107 Office: Davis Polk and Wardwell 450 Lexington Ave New York NY 10017-3911

**WELTCHEK, ROBERT JAY,** lawyer; b. Elizabeth, N.J., July 28, 1955; s. Leslie Mayer and Patricia Marjorie (Schoenhaut) W.; m. Holly Prager; children: Nolan Joseph, Emily Rachel. BA, Rutgers U., 1977; JD with honors, U. Md., 1980. Bar: Md. 1980, U.S. Dist. Ct. Md. 1980, U.S. Ct. Appeals (4th cir.) 1981. Assoc. Bertram M. Goldstein P.A., Balt., 1980-82; ptnr. Goldstein, Weltchek & Assocs., Balt., 1983-89, Gebhardt & Smith, Balt., 1989-93, Snyder, Weltchek & Vogelstein, P.A., Balt., 1993-97, Snyder, Weiner, Weltchek, Vogelstein & Brown, Balt., 1997—. Mem. ABA, Md. State Bar Assn., Fed. Bar Assn., Balt. City Bar Assn., Assn. Trial Lawyers Am., Md. Trial Lawyers Assn. Democrat. Jewish. Avocations: tennis, racquetball. Personal injury, Federal civil litigation, State civil litigation. Home: 10606 Candlewick Rd Stevenson MD 21153-9999 Office: Snyder Weiner Weltchek Vogelstein & Brown 1829 Reisterstown Rd Baltimore MD 21208-6320 *Notable cases include: Maynard vs. George Washington U. Med. Ctr., Superior Ct. D.C., 1990, which involved $5 million jury verdict for the plaintiff in med. malpractice action.*

**WELTY, CHARLES DOUGLAS,** lawyer; b. Houston, Mar. 16, 1952; s. Charles I. and Jane Douglas (Mullane) W.; m. Anita Katherine Blair, Feb. 24, 1986. BA, Rice U., 1974; JD, U. Va., 1982. Bar: N.Y. 1983, D.C. 1984, Va., 1988, U.S. Supreme Ct. 1996. Assoc. Lord, Day & Lord, N.Y.C., 1982-84; pvt. practice Washington, 1984-86; assoc. Eckert, Seamans et. al., Washington, 1986-88; pvt. practice Arlington, Va., 1988-91; ptnr. Welty & Blair, P.C., Arlington, Va., 1991—. Sr. editor Va. Jour. Internat. Law, 1980-82. Lt. USN, 1974-79, Indian Ocean. Mem. Federalist Soc., Fed. Am. Inn of Court, The Army & Navy Club (Washington), Va. Bar Assn. General corporate, Estate planning, Probate. Office: Welty & Blair PC 2111 Wilson Blvd Ste 550 Arlington VA 22201-3051

**WELTZ, PAUL MARTIN,** lawyer; b. N.Y.C., Jan. 23, 1937; s. David Donald and Selma (Lahnstein) W.; m. Wendy Frisch; children: Jeffrey, Michael. BA, NYU, 1958; JD, Fordham U., 1961. Bar: N.Y. 1975, U.S. Dist. Ct. (so. dist.) N.Y. 1975, U.S. Ct. Appeals 1975. Spl. legal asst. to justices N.Y. State Supreme Ct., 1963-64, law sec. to justice, 1964-66; law sec. to justice Appellate divsn. N.Y. State Superior Ct., 1966-74, dir. office of projects devel., 1975-77, adminstr. indigent defendants program, family and criminal, 1975-77, chief law ast. to justices, 1977-81; sole practitioner N.Y.C., 1981—. Mem. Hollywood Golf Club (v.p. 1998—), Elberon Bathing Club (prs. 1975-85). State civil litigation, Estate planning, Family and matrimonial. Home: 1003 Elberon Ave Long Branch NJ 07740-4708 Office: 350 5th Ave Ste 7610 New York NY 10118-7699

**WEMPLE, PETER HOLLAND,** lawyer, educator; b. N.Y.C., Aug. 8, 1958; s. George Barr and Suzanne (Fonay) W.; m. Susan Thornton; children: David Michael, Sarah Kathryn. BA, Harvard U., 1981; JD, John Marshall Law Sch., 1985. Bar: Ind. 1985, Ill. 1986. Assoc. Ice Miller Donadio & Ryan, Indpls., 1985-86, McKenna, Storer, Rowe, White & Farrug, Chgo., 1986—; adj. prof. law John Marshall Law Sch., Chgo., 1988—. Mem. John Marshall Law Rev., 1983-85. Mem. ABA, Ill. Bar Assn., Chgo. Bar Assn., Ill. Assn. Def. Trial Counsel. Federal civil litigation, State civil litigation, Personal injury. Office: McKenna Storer Rowe White & Farrug 200 N La Salle St Ste 3000 Chicago IL 60601-1083

**WENDEL, CHARLES ALLEN,** lawyer; b. Lockport, N.Y., Aug. 13, 1942; s. Harold Henry and Doris Lillian (Gardner) W.; m. Helen W. Roberts, June 23, 1973; children: William Charles, Jonathan David. BChem Engring., Rensselaer Poly Inst., 1964; JD, Am. U., 1968. Bar: N.Y. 1969, Va. 1971, D.C. 1980, U.S. Ct. Appeals (fed. and 4th cirs.), U.S. Dsit. Ct. (ea. and we. dists.) Va., U.S. Supreme Ct. Patent examiner U.S. Patent and Trademark Office, Washington, 1964-66; patent trainee Union Carbide Corp., Washington, 1966-68; patent atty. Union Carbide Corp., N.Y.C., 1968-70; assoc., then ptnr. Stevens, Davis, Miller & Mosher, Arlington, Va., 1970-83; ptnr. firm Wegner & Bretschneider, Washington, 1983-85; assoc. solicitor U.S. Patent and Trademark Office, 1985-88; assoc. Lyon & Lyon, Washington, 1988-90; founding ptnr. Parkhurst, Wendel & Rossi, Alexandria, Va., 1990-95. Contbr. articles to profl. jours. Mem. Va. State Bar (patent trademark copyright sect., chmn. 1977-78), Am. Intellectual Patent Law Assn., Patent Lawyers Club Washington (prs. 1982-83), Delta Theta Phi. Republican. Patent, Intellectual property. Office: Parkhurst & Wendel LLP 1421 Prince St Ste 210 Alexandria VA 22314-2805

**WENDELL HSU, LINDA SHARON,** lawyer; b. Lima, Peru, June 7, 1967; came to U.S., 1967; d. Robert Earl Wendell and Karen Yvonne Davidsen; m. Peter R. Hsu, Aug. 29, 1998. BA in Econs., San Diego State U., 1989; JD, U. San Diego, 1992. Bar: Calif. 1992, U.S. Dist. Ct. (no., cen. and so. dists.) Calif. 1993. Law clk. Thorsnes, Bartolotta, McGuire & Padilla, San Diego, 1990-91; law clk., atty. Friedberg & Bunge, San Diego, 1991-93; atty. Law Offices Edward Robinson, Redondo Beach, Calif., 1993-94, Tharpe & Howell, Santa Barbara, Calif., 1994-96, Selman Breitman, San Francisco, 1996—. Democrat. Avocations: literature, politics, aerobics, running, hiking. Insurance, Appellate, General civil litigation. Office: Selman Breitman 1 Sansome St Ste 1900 San Francisco CA 94104-4448

**WENDT, JOHN ARTHUR FREDERIC, JR.,** lawyer; b. Cleve.; s. John Arthur Frederic and Martha Ann (Hunter) W.; m. Marjorie Rickard Richardson, Oct. 2, 1962; children: Wendy Wendt Wood, Eric A., John A. F. III, Hilary H.; m. Dorothy Fay Nuttall, Dec. 29, 1976. AB with honors, U. Mich., 1942; JD, U. Colo., 1951. Bar: Colo. 1951, U.S. Dist. Ct. Colo. 1951, U.S. Ct. Appeals (10th cir.) 1957, U.S. Supreme Ct. 1971. Assoc. Tippit, Haskell & Welborn, Denver, 1953-58; ptnr. Wendt & Kistler, Denver, 1958-62; ptnr. Wendt Law Offices, Aspen, Colo., 1971-81, Delta, Colo., 1985—; dist. atty. 9th Jud. Dist. Colo., 1965-69; judge Pitkin County, Colo., 1971-78; dist. atty. 7th Jud. Dist. Colo., 1981-85; farmer; judge Cedaredge County, 1986—; contract mediator, Colo. Judiciary, 1995—. Chmn. Delta County Planning Commn., 1991-94. Maj. U.S. Army, 1942-46, 51-53. Decorated Purple Heart, Silver Star, Bronze Star (2). Mem. Am. Arbitration Assn. (mem. panel), Acad. Family Mediators, Colo. Bar Assn. (gov. 1965-71, 82,85, 87-96), Pitkin County Bar Assn. (pres. 1971-72), Delta County Bar Assn. (pres. 1986-89), Am. Judicature Soc., 7th Jud. Dist. Bench-Bar Com., Colo. Coun. Mediation, U.S. Equestrian Team (chmn. Colo. chpt. 1976-86), Masters of Fox Hounds Assn., M.F.H. Roaring Fork Hounds (dist. commr. 1992-99), Black Canyon Pony Club, U.S. Pony Clubs, Inc. (gov. 1996—), Phi Kappa Psi, Phi Delta Phi, Phi Beta Kappa. Republican. Epsicopalian. General corporate, State civil litigation, Family and matrimonial. Home: Lenado Farm 2130 Spruce Ln Cedaredge CO 81413-9565 Office: PO Box 94 540 Main St Delta CO 81416-1834

**WENNER, CHARLES RODERICK,** lawyer; b. New Haven, Jan. 10, 1947; s. Charles Bellew and Joan Rhoda (Morrison) W.; m. Jovira C. Vergara, June 11, 1999. BS, Coll. Charleston, 1969; JD, U. Conn., 1973. Bar: Conn. 1974, D.C. 1977. Law clk. Conn. Superior Ct., Hartford, 1973-74; staff atty. SEC, Washington, 1974-76, spl. counsel to chmn., 1976-77; assoc. Fulbright & Jaworski, Washington, 1977-81, ptnr., 1981—; lectr. law Sch. Law U. Conn., 1973-74. Trustee Calvary United Meth. Ch., Arlington, Va., 1993-95, 97-98; counselor Gospel Mission of Washington, 1991—; bd. dirs. Operation Friendship Internat., Inc., Washington, 1993—. Recipient Am. Hist. award DAR, Charleston, 1969. Mem. ABA, D.C. Bar Assn. Methodist. Avocations: running. Securities. Home: Apt 105 1101 S Arlington Ridge Rd Arlington VA 22202-1922 Office: Fulbright & Jaworski 801 Pennsylvania Ave NW Fl 3-5 Washington DC 20004-2623

**WENNERMARK, JOHN DAVID,** lawyer; b. Hot Springs, Ark., Jan. 30, 1940; s. John Harold and Roberta (Brown) W.; m. Beverly Ann Shumate, Apr. 15, 1967; children: John D. Jr., Catherine, Valorie, Leslie, Jared, Jennifer, Christopher. AA, San Antonio Coll., 1960; BA, ST. Mary's U., 1964, JD, 1964. Bar: Tex. 1964, U.S. Dist. Ct. (we. dist.) Tex. 1966, U.S. Ct. Appeals (5th cir.) 1989. Pvt. practice, San Antonio, 1964—. Author study guide Corporations, 1964. Mem. Mensa, Phi Theta Kappa, Phi Delta Phi, Delta Epsilon Sigma. Mormons. Avocations: scuba diving, golf, camping, running, tennis. State civil litigation, Personal injury, Workers' compensation. Home: 120 W Hosack St Boerne TX 78006-2626 Office: 112 Villita St San Antonio TX 78205-2729

**WENTWORTH, THEODORE SUMNER,** lawyer; b. Bklyn., July 18, 1938; s. Theodore Sumner and Alice Ruth (Wortmann) W.; m. Sharon Linelle Arkush, 1965 (dec. 1987); children: Christina Linn, Kathrun Allison; m. Diana Webb von Welanetz, 1989; 1 stepchild, Lexi von Welanetz. AA, Am. River Coll., 1958; JD, U. Calif., Hastings, 1962. Bar: Calif. 1963, U.S. Dist. Ct. (no. and ctrl. dists.) Calif., U.S. Ct. Appeals (9th cir.), U.S. Supreme Ct.; cert. trial specialist; diplomate Nat. Bd. Trial Advocacy; assoc. Am. Bd. Trial Advocates. Assoc. Adams, Hunt & Martin, Santa Ana, Calif., 1963-66; ptnr. Hunt, Liljestrom & Wentworth, Santa Ana, Calif., 1967-77; pres. Solabs Corp.; chmn. bd., exec. v.p. Plant Warehouse, Inc., Hawaii, 1974-82; prin. Law Offices of Wentworth & Paoli, Newport Beach & Temecula, Calif.; judge pro tem Superior Ct. Attys. Panel Harbor Mcpl. Ct.; owner Eagles Ridge Ranch, Temecula, 1977—. Pres., bd. dirs. Santa Ana-Tustin Cmty. Chest, 1972; v.p., trustee South Orange County United Way, 1973-75; pres. Orange County Fedn. Funds, 1972-73; bd. dirs. Orange County Mental Health Assn. Mem. ABA, Am. Bd. Trial Advocates (assoc.), State Bar Calif., Orange County Bar Assn. (dir. 1972-76), Am. Trial Lawyers Assn., Calif. Trial Lawyers Assn. (bd. govs. 1968-70), Orange County Trial Lawyers Assn. (pres. 1967-68), Lawyer-Pilots Bar Assn., Aircraft Owners and Pilots Assn., Bahia Corinthian Yacht Club, Pacific Club, Newport. Research in vedic prins., natural law, quantum physics and mechanics. Personal injury, Product liability. Office: 4631 Teller Ave Ste 100 Newport Beach CA 92660-8105 also: 41530 Enterprise Cir S Temecula CA 92590-4816

**WENZEL, FRANCIS GEORGE, JR.,** lawyer; b. Phila., Oct. 6, 1953; s. Francis George and Marie Louise (Devine) W.; 1 child, Ruth Marie. BS in math., Pa. State U., 1974; JD, Dickinson Sch. Law, 1977. Bar: Pa. 1977, U.S. Dist. Ct. (ea. dist. Pa.) 1978, U.S. Ct. Appeals (3d cir.) 1982. Law clerk Office of Staff Judge Advocate Marine Corps Base Camp LeJune, Jacksonville, N.C., 1976, Dauphin County Pub. Def. Office, Harrisburg, Pa., 1976-77; judge advocate Jt. Law Ctr. Marine Corp. Air Station, Jacksonville, 1978-80; atty. LaBraum & Doak, Phila., 1980-84, Griffin, Aponick & Musto, Wilkes-Barre, Pa., 1984-89, Rosenn, Jenkins & Greenwald, Wilkes-Barre, Pa., 1989-96, Marshall, DEnnehey, Warner, Coleman & Goggin, Scranton, Pa., 1996—; mem. Tech. Task Force Bloomsburg, 1990-93. Contbr. articles to profl. jours. Bd. dirs., pres., contract negotiator Bloomsburg Area Sch. Dist., 1989—; mem. spl. projects Parish Coun. St. Columbia Roman Catholic. Ch., Bloomsburg, 1987—. Capt. U.S. Marine Corps, 1974-80. Mem. Pa. Bar Assn., Penn. Def. Inst. Republican. Personal injury, Insurance, General civil litigation. Home: 248 East St Bloomsburg PA 17815-1845 Office: Marshall Dennehey Warner Coleman & Goggin 507 Linden St Ste 800 Scranton PA 18503-1636

**WEPRIN, BARRY ALAN,** lawyer; b. Bklyn., Sept. 29, 1952; s. Saul and Sylvia (Matz) W.; m. Patricia J. Langer, Sept. 16, 1979, children: Alexander, Matthew. AB, Harvard U., 1974; M Pub. Adminstrn., Princeton U., 1978;

JD, NYU, 1978. Bar: N.Y. 1979, U.S. Dist. Ct. (so. and ea. dists.) N.Y. 1980, U.S. Supreme Ct. 1983. Law clk. to judge U.S. Dist. Ct., Bklyn., 1978-80; assoc. Wachtell, Lipton, Rosen & Katz, N.Y.C., 1980-85; counsel N.Y. State Housing Finance Agy., N.Y.C., 1985—, N.Y. State Med. Care Facilities Finance Agy., N.Y.C., 1985—. Editor NYU Law Rev., 1977-78. Nat. Merit scholar, 1974. Mem. N.Y. State Bar Assn., Assn. of Bar of City of N.Y. Democrat. Home: 415 Claflin Ave Mamaroneck NY 10543-3907 Office: NY State Housing Fin Agy 3 Park Ave New York NY 10016-5902

**WERDEGAR, KATHRYN MICKLE,** state supreme court justice; b. San Francisco; d. Benjamin Christie and Kathryn Marie (Clark) Mickle; m. David Werdegar; children: Maurice Clark, Matthew Mickle. Student, Wellesley Coll., 1954-55; AB with honors, U. Calif., Berkeley, 1957; JD with highest distinction, George Washington U., 1962; JD, U. Calif., Berkeley, 1990. Bar: Calif. 1964, U.S. Dist. Ct. (no. dist.) Calif. 1964, U.S. Ct. Appeals (9th cir.) 1964, Calif. Supreme Ct. 1964. Legal asst. civil rights divsn. U.S. Dept. Justice, Washington, 1962-63; cons. Calif. Study Commn. on Mental Retardation, 1963-64; assoc. U. Calif. Ctr. for Study of Law and Soc., Berkeley, 1965-67; spl. cons. State Dept. Mental Hygiene, 1967-68; cons. Calif. Coll. Trial Judges, 1968-71; atty., head criminal divsn. Calif. Continuing Edn. of Bar, 1971-78; assoc. dean acad. and student affairs, assoc. prof. Sch. Law, U. San Francisco, 1978-81; sr. staff atty. Calif. 1st Dist. Ct. Appeal, 1981-85, Calif. Supreme Ct., 1985-91; assoc. justice Calif. 1st Dist. Ct. Appeal, 1991-94, Calif. Supreme Ct., San Francisco, 1994—. Author: Benchbook: Misdemeanor Procedure, 1971, Misdemeanor Procedure Benchbook, 1975, 83; contbr. California Continuing Education of the Bar books; editor: California Criminal Law Practice series, 1972, California Uninsured Motorist Practice, 1973, I California Civil Procedure Before Trial, 1977. Recipient Charles Glover award George Washington U., J. William Fulbright award for disting. pub. svc. George Washington U. Law Sch. Alumni Assn., award of excellence Calif. Alumni Assn., Roger J. Traynor Appellate Justice of Yr. award, Justice of Yr. award Consumer Attys. of Calif., also 5 Am. Jurisprudence awards, others. Mem. Nat. Assn. Women Judges, Calif. Judges Assn., Nev./Calif. Women Judges Assn., Order of the Coif. Office: Calif Supreme Court 350 Mcallister St San Francisco CA 94102-4712

**WERDER, HORST HEINRICH,** lawyer; b. Stettin, Germany, Aug. 13, 1924; m. Petina Allen. BS, Columbia U., 1949, JD, 1951. Bar: N.Y. 1952, Ill. 1962. Ptnr. Haseltine & Lake, N.Y.C., 1952-61, Baker & McKenzie, Chgo., 1961-89. Mem. Columbia U. Club of S.W. Fla., Mich. Shores Club (Wilmette, Ill.). Intellectual property, Private international, Trademark and copyright. Office: 3115 Gulf Shore Blvd N Naples FL 34103-3943

**WERLE, MARK FRED,** lawyer; b. N.Y.C., Jan. 22, 1964; s. Fred Carl and Trude Marie W.; m. Michelle Lynne Geiringer, Aug. 20, 1989; children: Melissa, Jocelyn. BA, Hofstra U., 1987, JD, 1989. Bar: N.Y. 1990, Conn. 1990, Vt. 1997. Atty. Jacobowitz, Spessard, Garfinkel & Lesman, N.Y.C., 1992-95; gen. counsel North Atlantic Utilities, Inc., Sea Cliff, N.Y., 1995-97; atty. Ryan Smith & Carbine, Rutland, Vt., 1997—. Mem. ABA, N.Y. State Bar Assn., Vt. Bar Assn., Vt. Hotel & Restaurant Assn., Rutland C. of C., Killington C. of C. Avocations: music, sports, computers, travel. FERC practice, Insurance, Product liability. Home: 285 Thundering Brook Rd Killington VT 05751-9512 Office: Ryan Smith & Carbine PO Box 310 Rutland VT 05702-0310

**WERLEIN, EWING, JR.,** federal judge; b. Houston, Sept. 14, 1936; s. Ewing and Ruth (Storey) W.; m. Kay McGibbon Werlein, June 29, 1963; children: Ewing Kenneth, Emily Kay. BA, So. Meth. U., 1958; LLB, U. Tex., 1961. Bar: Tex. 1961, U.S. Dist. Ct. (so. dist.) Tex. 1965, U.S. Dist. Ct. (ea. dist.) Tex. 1990, U.S. Ct. Appeals (5th cir.) 1970, U.S. Ct. Appeals (10th cir.) 1980, U.S. Claims Ct. 1985, U.S. Tax Ct. 1985, U.S. Supreme Ct. 1983. Ptnr. Vinson & Elkins, Houston, 1964-92; dist. judge U.S. Dist. Ct. (so. dist.) Tex., 1992—. Trustee So. Meth. U., Dallas, 1976-92, Asbury Theol. Sem., Wilmore, Ky., 1989—; mem. gen. bd. pub. United Meth. Ch., Nashville, 1974-84, chmn., 1980-84, chancellor Tex. ann. conf., 1977—; mem. exec. com. World Meth. Counh., 1981-96, treas, 1991-93. Capt. USAF, 1961-64. Fellow Am. Coll. Trial Lawyers, 1984, Internat. Soc. Barristers, 1987; recipient Disting. Alumni award SMU Alumni Assn., 1994. Fellow Am. Bar Found., Tex. Bar Found., Houston Bar Found.; mem. State Bar Tex. (dir. 1990-93), Nat. Conf. Bar Pres., Houston Bar Assn. (pres. 1988-89), Houston C. of C. (life), SAR, Order of Coif, Petroleum Club, Houston Club, Phi Beta Kappa. Office: US Dist Ct Tex US Courthouse 515 Rusk St Ste 9136 Houston TX 77002-2605

**WERLIN-GORENSTEIN, BARBARA CAROL,** lawyer, counselor; b. Troy, N.Y., Oct. 31, 1955; d. Samuel Jacob and Pearl Lucille Werlin; m. Stuart Ray Gorenstein, Nov. 18, 1984; children: Benjamin, Samuel. BA in Psychology, Russell Sage Coll., 1976; MS in Psychology, Rensselaer Polytechnic Inst., 1977; JD, Union U., 1981. Bar: N.Y., U.S. Dist. Ct. (no. dist.) N.Y. 1984, U.S. Supreme Ct. 1987. Various positions N.Y. State Atty. Gen.'s Office, Albany, 1979-86; counselor Albany, 1994—, pvt. practice, 1986—. Campaigner Westmere and Guilderland Sch. Bd. Candidates, 1991-96; Christmas wrap vol. Am. Cancer Soc., Albany, 1996; vol. Westmere and Guilderland Sch. PTA, 1993—; founder, facilitator Mother's Support Group, Albany, 1988-90. Mem. ABA, Albany Women's Bar Assn. (program chair 1980s), Albany County Bar Assn., Am. Counseling Assn., Am. Assn. for Adult Devel. and Aging, Guiderland C. of C., Phi Kappa Phi, Phi Alpha Delta. Avocations: drawing, sewing, cooking, creative writing, writing music. General practice. Home and Office: 3 Bonnie Dr Guilderland NY 12084-9761

**WERNER, CHERYL E.,** prosecutor; b. Ft. Wayne, Ind., June 13, 1971; d. William L. and Charlene W. AB, U. Mich., 1992; JD, U. Toledo, 1996. Bar: Ohio, Mich. Law clk. Dixon & Dixon, Toledo, 1995-96; atty. Dixon & Hayes, Toledo, 1996-97, Lennard, Graham & Goldsmith, Monroe, Mich., 1997-98; asst. prosecuting atty. Office of the Prosecuting Atty., Monroe, 1998—. Mem. Monroe County Bar Assn. (sec. 1998—), Women Lawyers Assn. of Mich. (v.p. Monroe County chpt. 1998—). Independent. Roman Catholic. Avocations: piccolo, flute in concert band. Office: Office of the Prosecuting Atty 125 E 2d St Monroe MI 48161

**WERNER, THOMAS M.,** lawyer; b. Des Moines, June 1, 1954; s. Charles T. and Olivia M. W.; m. Debra L. Miller, May 5, 1990. BA in journalism, Drake U., 1976, JD, 1979. Bar: Iowa 1980, U.S. Dist. Ct. (so. dist.) Iowa 1980, U.S. Ct. Appeals (8th cir.) 1980, U.S. Dist. Ct. (no. dist.) Iowa 1981. Asst. county atty. Polk County, Des Moines, 1980-82; with Anderson & Werner, Des Moines, 1982—. Mem. Iowa Trial Lawyers Assn., Des Moines Golf and Country Club. Avocations: travel, golf. Labor, Workers' compensation, Personal injury. Office: Anderson & Werner 520 35th St Des Moines IA 50312-3403

**WERNICK, CLAUDIA NICOLE,** lawyer, consultant; b. N.Y.C., Nov. 15, 1963; d. Saul Wernick and Kay McCauley. BA, George Washington U., 1985; JD, Rutgers U., 1992. Bar: N.Y. 1993, N.J. 1992. Lawyer Schlesinger & Sussman, N.Y.C., 1992-94; v.p. Bozell Worldwide, N.Y.C., 1994-97; prin. Wernick & Assocs., L.L.C., N.Y.C., 1998—. Vol. East Harlem Tutorial Program, N.Y.C., 1992—. Recipient Acad. Women Achievers award YWCA of City of N.Y., 1996. Fax: 212-545-7112. Office: Wernick & Associates 55 Park Ave New York NY 10016-3018

**WERSHALS, PAUL L.,** lawyer; b. Bklyn., July 10, 1942. AA in Bus. Adminstrn., Midwest Inst. Bus. Adminstrn., 1963; BS in Bus. Adminstrn., Babson Coll., 1965; JD, Suffolk U., 1969; LLM, NYU, 1975. Bar: N.Y. 1974, U.S. Supreme Ct. 1974. Mem. Nassau County Assigned Counsel Defender Plan; mem. legal com., citizens adv. com. for cablevision Town of North Heampstead, N.Y., 1976-97. Mem. Sen. Michael J. Tully's legis. adv. com., 1982-97; dir. Great Neck (N.Y.) Sr. Citizens Ctr., Inc., Town of North Hempstead, 1985-89. Mem. Am. Judges Assn., N.Y. State Trial Lawyers Assn., Nassau County Bar Assn. (arbitrator 1981—, mem. arbitration tribunal panel 1984—), Great Neck (N.Y.) Lawyers Assn. (bd. dirs. 1973—, sec. 1981-84,pres. 1985, chmn. bd. dirs. 1986-87), Phi Alpha Delta (mem. moot ct.). General practice, Probate, Real property. Office: 10 Cuttermill Rd Great Neck NY 11021-3201

**WERT, ROBERT CLIFTON,** lawyer; b. Pleasantville, N.J., Jan. 8, 1944; s. Clifton Robert and Anna Louise (McLarren) W.; m. Grace Elizabeth Dunbar, Dec. 16, 1967; children: Andrew, Amy, Bethany, Laura. BS in Acctg., Temple U., 1965, JD, 1868; grad., JAG Sch., 1982, Command & Gen. Staff Coll., 1984, U.S. Army JFK Spl. Warfare Ctr, 1987. Bar: Pa. 1968, U.S. Dist. Ct. (ea. dist.) Pa. 1968, U.S. Ct. Mil. Appeals 1969, US. Supreme Ct. 1981. Commd. 2d lt. mil. police USAR, 1965, advanced through ranks to lt. col., 1984, ret., 1990; mil. judge U.S. Army, Okinawa, Japan, 1970-73, chief trial counsel, 1973; staff judge adv. Valley Forge Army Hosp. U.S. Army, 1973-74; chief trial counsel U.S. Army, Fort Dix, N.J., 1974-76; chief legal asst. and claims U.S. Army, 1976-77, ret., 1990; chief staff counsel Southeastern Penn Transp. Authority, Phila., 1977-78, acting chief counsel, 1978-80, gen. counsel, 1980-84, dept. gen. mgr., 1984-86; exec. dir. Blank Rome Comisky & McCauley, Phila., 1986—; owner Insulco, King of Prussia, Pa., 1972-79; co-owner Master Page Inc., Malvern, Pa., 1985—; vice chair Charlestown Twp. Bd. Suprs. Bd. dirs. Evang. Assn. for Promotion of Edn., St. David's, Pa., Ea. Coll., 1988—, Crime Prevention Assn. Charitable Giving, Phila., 1991—; bd. dirs. Crime Prevention Assn., Phila., 1988—, chair exec. com., 1992-94, 98—, treas., 1994-96, v.p., 1997-98; pres. Charlestown Townwatch, 1980—; coord. Twp. Emergency, 1984-99; vice-chair bd. supr. Charlestown Twp., 1998—; deacon, Sunday Sch. supt., mem. bldg. com., chmn. property com. Ch. of the Savior, Wayne, Pa.; bd. dirs., asst. treas. Adv. Meth. Ch., Phila. Decorated Meritorious Svc. medal, Army Achievement medal, Overseas Svc. medal, Nat. Def. Svc. medal, various Res. decorations; recipient Pa. Gov.'s award, 1989. Mem. Assn. of Legal Adminstrs., Phila. Bar Assn., Temple U. Law Alumni Assn. (exec. com. 1995-96), Masons. Avocation: woodworking. General corporate, Transportation, Military. Office: Blank Rome Comisky & McCauley One Logan Sq Philadelphia PA 19103-6998

**WERTHEIM, JOHN V.,** lawyer; b. Santa Fe, Feb. 12, 1968; s. Jerry and Mary Carole Wertheim; m. Bianc Ortiz, Dec. 30, 1994. BA in History, Yale U., 1990; JD, U. N.Mex., 1995. Fin. analyst, corp. fin. Alex. Brown & Sons, Inc., Balt., 1990-91; N.Mex. dir. Clinton for Pres., Albuquerque, 1992; bus. cons. in pvt. practice, Albuquerque, 1993-96; campaign mgr. Bruce King for Gov., Albuquerque, 1994; assoc. atty. The Jones Law Firm, Santa Fe, 1997—; mng. dir. Wertheim Doyle & Co., Albuquerque, 1998—. Reading tutor Dolores Gonzales Elem., Albuquerque, 1996; Dem. Party nominee U.S. Ho. of Reps., 1996. Named Outstanding Young Man of N.Mex., N.Mex. Assn. Ret. Tchrs., 1996. Mem. N.Mex. Bar Assn., N.Mex. Trial Lawyers Assn., Kiwanis. Jewish. Avocations: hiking, running, rafting, skiing. Antitrust, General civil litigation, Personal injury. Home: 401 Dartmouth Dr SE Albuquerque NM 87106-2223 Office: PO Box 4298 Albuquerque NM 87196-4298

**WERTKIN, ROBIN STUART,** lawyer; b. Pitts., Oct. 4, 1955; s. Edward and Hilda Lynn W.; m. Jennifer R.T. Olbum, July 24, 1996; children: Elija Allswede, Eric H. BS, U. Pitts., 1977, JD, 1981. Bar: Pa. 1981, U.S. Dist. Ct. (we. dist.) Pa. 1981, U.S. Ct. Appeals (3d cir.) 1985. Law clk. Ct. of Common Pleas of Fayette County, Pa., Uniontown, 1981-82; atty. Evans, Ivory, P.C., Pitts., 1982—. Mem. Acad. Rail Labor Attys., Acad. Trial Lawyers Allegheny County. Avocations: skiing, golf. Personal injury, Admiralty, Product liability. Office: Evans Ivory C 1311 Frick Bldg Pittsburgh PA 15219

**WESCOTT, LAURENCE STEWART,** lawyer; b. Balt., Mar. 13, 1930; s. William Lawrence and Marie (Driscoll) W.; m. Elaine Cecilia Cullen, May 3, 1958; children: William Laurence, Susannah Stewart McNelis, Patrick Collen. BA, Washington Coll., Chestertown, Md., 1951; LLB, U. Md., 1954. Bar: Md. 1954, U.S. Ct. Appeals (4th cir.) 1955, U.S. Ct. Appeals (D.C. cir.) 1982, U.S. Ct. Appeals (3d cir.) 1970, U.S. Ct. Appeals (6th cir.) 1995. Field atty. NLRB, Balt., 1958-61, 63-65; personnel adminstr. Bendix Corp., Towson, Md., 1961-63; atty. Shawe & Rosenthal, Balt., 1965-68, Cook & Cluster, Balt., 1968-70; ptnr. Venable Baetser & Howard, Balt., 1971-94, Serotte Rockman & Wescott, Balt., 1994—. Mem. bd. vis. and govs. Washington Coll., Chestertown, Md., 1976-82, 86—. With U.S. Army, 1954-56. Mem. ABA, Md. State Bar Assn., Balt. County Bar Assn., Towson Bus. Assn. (pres. 1997-98), Elks Club. Republican. Roman Catholic. Avocations: golf, reading, travel. Labor, Alternative dispute resolution. Home: 502 Limerick Cir Unit 201 Timonium MD 21093-7755 Office: Serotte Rockman & Wescott 409 Washington Ave Ste 610 Baltimore MD 21204-4903

**WESELY, NATHAN,** lawyer; b. Osceola, Nebr., Aug. 5, 1958; s. Elden and Connie Wesely; m. Lisa Wesely, Apr. 4, 1987; children: Sarah, Kate, John, Adam. BS in Indsl. Engring., U. Nebr., 1980; MBA, U. Tex., 1985, JD, 1986. Bar: Tex. 1986, La. 1997, U.S. Dist. Ct. (so. dist.) Tex. 1988, U.S. Ct. Appeals (5th cir.) 1990, U.S. Dist. Ct. (ea. dist.) 1991, U.S. Supreme Ct., 1992, U.S. Dist. Ct. (we. dist.) Tex. 1993,. Cost engr. IBM, Austin, Tex., 1980-83; assoc. atty. Clark, Thomas, Winters & Newton, Austin, 1986-88, Bracewell & Patterson, Houston, 1988-95; employment atty. Trans Tex. Gas Corp., Houston, 1995-98; ptnr. labor and employment law Royston, Rayzor, Vickery & Williams, Houston, 1999—. Bd. mem. Bd. Adjustments, Bellaire, Tex., 1996. E-mail: nathan.wesely@roystonlaw.com. Labor, General civil litigation. Home: 4406 Acacia St Bellaire TX 77401-4302 Office: Royston Rayzor Vickery & Williams LLP 600 Travis 2200 Chase Tower Houston TX 77002

**WESLEY, RICHARD C.,** state supreme court justice; b. Canandaigua, N.Y., Aug. 1, 1949; s. Charles and Beatrice W.; m. Kathryn Rice; 2 children. BA summa cum laude, SUNY, Albany, 1971; JD, Cornell U., 1974. Assoc. Harris, Beach & Wilcox, 1974-76; with Welch, Streb & Porter, 1976-77; ptnr. Streb, Porter, Meyer & Wesley, 1977-86; justice Supreme Ct. 7th Jud. Dist., 1986—; supervising judge Criminal Cts. 7th Jud. Dist., 1991; judge appellate div. Supreme Ct. 4th Dept., 1994—, U.S. Ct. Appeals, 1996—; now assoc. judge N.Y. Ct. Appeals, Albany; creator Felony Screening Program, 1993; lectr. in field; bd. trustees Ctr. Dispute Resolution, Pre-Trial Svcs. Corp. Editor: Cornell Law Rev. Asst. counsel to Assembly Rep. leader James L. Emery, 1979-1982; assemblyman N.Y. State 136th Assembly Dist., 1982-84, 84-86; chair Livingston County Alcohol and Drug Abuse Prevention Coun.; bd. trustees United Ch. Livonia, Chances and Changes, Charles Settlement House; bd. dirs. Myers' Found.; driver Livonia Vol. Ambulance. Named Legislator of Yr., Livingston-Wyoming Assn. Retarded Citizens, 1988; recipient Disting. SUNY Alumni award SUNY Alumni Assn., 1997. Fellow N.Y. State Bar Found.; mem. Livingston County Bar Assn. (sec.), Supreme Ct. Justices Assn. (pres. 7th jud. dist.). Fax: 716-243-7915. Office: NY Ct Appeals Ct Appeals Hall 20 Eagle St Albany NY 12207-1009*

**WESLEY, WILLIAM MATTHEW,** lawyer; b. Green Bay, Wis., Dec. 19, 1943. BEE, Marquette U., 1966; JD cum laude, Loyola U., Chgo., 1971. Bar: Ill. 1971, U.S. Dist. Ct. (no. dist.) Ill., U.S. Ct. Appeals (7th cir. and fed. cir.), U.S. Supreme Ct. 1992. Engr. Tex. Instruments, Motorola; ptnr. McAndrews, Held & Malloy, Ltd., Chgo. Hearing officer Ill. Pollution Control Bd., 1972-85. Named one of Leading Experts in Patent Law, Euromoney Mag., 1997, 98, 99. Mem. ABA, Chgo. Bar Assn., Am. Intellectual Property Law Assn., Fed. Cir. Bar Assn., Intellectual Property Law Assn. Chgo., Internat. Trade Commn. Trial Lawyers Assn. (exec. com. 1991—), Tau Beta Pi, Eta Kappa Nu, Alpha Sigma Nu. Fax: 312-707-9155. Intellectual property, Public international, Patent. Office: McAndrews Held & Malloy Ltd 500 W Madison St Fl 34 Chicago IL 60661-2511

**WESSEL, PETER,** lawyer; b. N.Y.C., N.Y., Feb. 2, 1952; s. Harry Nathan Jr. and Charlene (Freimuth) W.; married Vicki Brodsky Scheck; children: Daniel, Elizabeth, Justin Scheck, Matthew Scheck. BS, Syracuse U., 1974, MPA, JD, 1980. Bar: N.Y. 1981, U.S. Dist. Ct. (no., so., ea. and we. dists.) N.Y. 1981, Fla. 1984, U.S. Ct. Mil. Appeals, 1988, U.S. Ct. Appeals (2d cir.) 1988, U.S. Supreme Ct. 1988. Confidential law clk. to Hon. David F. Lee Jr. N.Y. Supreme Ct., 1980-82; sr. atty. criminal def. div. The Legal Aid Soc., N.Y.C., 1982-87; pvt. practice N.Y.C., 1987—. Notes and comments editor Syracuse Law Rev., 1979-80; contbr. articles to profl. jours. Robert M. Anderson award for Writing and Legal Scholarship, 1980, Neal Brewster scholar, 1977-78, Syracuse U. Coll. Law scholar 1978-79, Louis Waters Meml. scholar, 1979-80, Hiscock, Cowie, Bruce & Lee scholar, 1979-80; Martindale-Hubbell a-v rated. Mem. ABA, N.Y. State Bar Assn., Assn. of Bar of City of N.Y., Fla. Bar Assn., Nat. Assn. Criminal Def. Lawyers, N.Y. State Assn. Criminal Def. Lawyers, N.Y. State Defender Assn., N.Y. State Trial Lawyers Assn., N.Y. County Lawyers Assn., N.Y. Criminal Bar Assn. Criminal, General civil litigation, Personal injury.

**WEST, CAROL CATHERINE,** law educator; b. Phila., May 23, 1944; d. Scott G. and Helen (Young) West. BA, Miss. U. for Women, 1966; MLS, U. So. Miss., 1984; JD, U. Miss., 1970. Pub. svcs. law libr. U. Va., Charlottesville, 1966-67; catalog law libr. U. Miss., Oxford, 1967-70; legis. reference libr. Miss. Legislature, Jackson, 1970-75; law libr. Miss. Coll., Jackson, 1975-94, prof. law, 1975—; del. White House conf. Libr. and Info. Svcs., 1991; cons. to Parliament of Armenia, 1995, Parliament of Tanzania, 1997; mem. Miss. Task Force on Gender Fairness in the Cts.; mem. bd. commr. Miss. Libr. Comm., 1993-98. Mem. ABA, Miss. Bar, Hinds County Bar (bd. dirs. 1994-96), Miss. Women Lawyers Assn. (bd. dirs. 1991-93), Miss. Libr. Assn. Methodist. Office: Miss Coll Law Sch 151 E Griffith St Jackson MS 39201-1302

**WEST, DAVID BLAIR,** lawyer; b. Del Rio, Tex., Dec. 4, 1950; s. William Gaston and Margarite (Miller) W.; m. Carol Davis, Dec. 25, 1953. BA, Austin Coll., Sherman, Tex., 1973; MA in Pub. Affairs, U. Tex., 1975, JD, 1981. Bar: Tex. 1981; cert. in civil trial law. Exec. sec. jud. planning com. Supreme Ct. Tex., Austin, 1977-79; law clk. U.S. Dist. Ct. (we. dist.) Tex., Austin, 1982-83, U.S. Ct. Appeals (5th cir.), Austin, 1983-84; assoc. Cox & Smith Inc., San Antonio, 1984-89, atty./shareholder, 1990—; bd. dirs. Bexar County Detention Ministries, San Antonio, 1996-98; mem. Citizens Com. on Tex. Jud. Sys., Supreme Ct. of Tex., 1993. Author articles. Elder, 1st Presbyn. Ch., San Antonio, 1986-96; mem. Tex. Pub. Policy Found., San Antonio, 1997-98. Mem. San Antonio Bar Assn. (program com. 1997-98), Order of the Alamo, Conopus (prs. 1997). Republican. Avocation: writing musicals. General civil litigation, Contracts commercial. Office: Cox & Smith Inc 112 E Pecan St Ste 1800 San Antonio TX 78205-1521

**WEST, JOSEPH KING,** judge; b. Yonkers, N.Y., Sept. 11, 1929; s. Ralph and Nellie (Brown) W.; m. Shirley Arvene Gray, July 3, 1954; children: Rebecca, Joseph K. BS, Howard U., Washington, 1952; JD, Bklyn. Law Sch., 1961. Bar: U.S. Supreme Ct. 1962, N.Y. 1962, U.S. Dist. Ct. (so. dist.) N.Y. 1962. Asst. corp. counsel City of Yonkers, N.Y., 1964-65; asst. dist. atty. Pros. Office, White Plains, N.Y., 1965-82; city ct. judge Yonkers (N.Y.) City Ct., 1983-84; county ct. judge Westchester Judicial Ct., White Plains, 1985-99; supervising judge Criminal Cts. 9th Jud. Dist. Dutchess, Orange, Putnam, Rockland and Westchester Counties, 1991-98; state supreme ct. justice State of New York, 1999—. Bd. dirs. St. Joseph's Med. Ctr.; adv. bd. Yonkers Big. Bros./Big Sisters. 1st lt. U.S. Army, 1952-56. Mem. Westchester County Bar Assn., Yonkers Lawyers Assn., Alpha Phi Alpha. Avocations: sports, walking, tennis, piano. Office: Westchester County Ct 111 Dr Martin Luther King Jr B White Plains NY 10601-2509

**WEST, KENNETH EDWARD,** lawyer; b. Phila., June 30, 1963; s. Edward Brown and Delores Ann (Brooks) W.; m. Cheryl Y. Tolerico; children: Jessie Marie, Brooks T., Jennifer Zevra. BS, Pa. State U., 1985; JD, Villanova U., 1988. Bar: Pa. 1988, U.S. Dist. Ct. (ea. dist.) Pa. 1990, U.S. Dist. Ct. N.J. 1988; lic. real estate agent, Pa. Assoc. Pachtman, Douglass & Assocs., Folsom, Pa., 1988-90; ptnr. Douglass, West & Riley, Drexel Hill, Pa., 1990-93, Douglass, West & Assocs., Drexel Hill, Pa., 1993—; Mem. bancruptcy conf. U.S. Dist. Ct. (ea. dist.) Pa. Mem. Pa. Trial Lawyers Assn., Del. County Bar Assn. Avocations: squash, raquetball. Bankruptcy, Personal injury, Real property. Home: 1015 Antler Dr Glen Mills PA 19342-9601 Office: Douglass West & Assocs 830 N Landsdowne Ave Drexel Hill PA 19026-1526

**WEST, LEE ROY,** federal judge; b. Clayton, Okla., Nov. 26, 1929; s. Calvin and Nicie (Hill) W.; m. MaryAnn Ellis, Aug. 29, 1952; children: Kimberly Ellis, Jennifer Lee. B.A., U. Okla., 1952, J.D., 1956; LL.M. (Ford Found. fellow), Harvard U., 1963. Bar: Okla. 1956. Individual practice law Ada, Okla., 1956-61, 63-65; faculty U. Okla. Coll. Law, 1961-62; Ford Found. fellow in law teaching Harvard U., Cambridge, Mass., 1962-63; judge 22d Jud. Dist. Okla., Ada, 1965-73; mem. CAB, Washington, 1973-78; acting chmn. CAB, 1977; practice law Tulsa, 1978-79; spl. justice Okla. Supreme Ct., 1965; judge U.S. Dist Ct. (we. dist.) Okla., 1979-94; sr. judge U.S. Dist. Ct. (we. dist.), Okla., 1994—. Editor: Okla. Law Rev. Served to capt. USMC, 1952-54. Mem. U. Okla. Alumni Assn. (dir.), Phi Delta Phi (pres. 1956), Phi Eta Sigma, Order of Coif. Home: 6500 E Danforth Rd Edmond OK 73034-7601 Office: US Dist Ct 3001 US Courthouse 200 NW 4th St Rm 1210 Oklahoma City OK 73102-3092

**WEST, ROBERT GRADY,** lawyer; b. Dallas, Aug. 13, 1947; s. Robert Sorrells and Thelma Grady W.; m. Marsha Lee Riegert, June 5, 1971; children: Kathryn Lee, Laura Elaine. BA, Midwestern State U., 1969; JD, U. Tex., 1972. Bar: Tex. 1972, U.S. Dist. Ct. (no. dist.) Tex. 1975, U.S. Dist. Ct. (ea. dist.) Tex. 1992, U.S. Ct. Appeals (5th cir.) 1976. Assoc. McGown, Godfrey, Decker, McMackin, Shipman & McClane, Ft. Worth, 1972-77, ptnr., 1977-88; ptnr. Decker, McMackin & McClane, Ft. Worth, 1988-90, Decker, Jones, McMackin, McClane, Hall & Bates, Ft. Worth, 1990-93; assoc. Michener, Larimore, Swindle, Whitaker, et al, Ft. Worth, 1993-98; ptnr. Michener, Larimore, Swindle, Witaker, et al, Ft. Worth, 1999—. Bd. regents Midwestern State U., Wichita Falls, Tex., 1992-98; dir. Grace Found., Dallas, 1990-92; mem. Tex. Ctr. Legal Ethics & Professionalism, 1994—, Leadership Ft. Worth, 1984. Mem. Am. Assn. Profl. Landmen, State Bar Tex., Tarrant County Bar Assn. Presbyterian. Avocations: travel, musical theatre, walking, volunteering. Real property, Probate, Non-profit and tax-exempt organizations. Office: Michener Larimore Swindle Whitaker et al 3500 City Ctr Tower II 301 Commerce St Fort Worth TX 76102-4140

**WEST, S. SCOTT,** lawyer, mechanical engineer; b. Houston, Apr. 2, 1963; s. Walter Maxwell West, Jr. and Barbara Sue Williams; m. Kimbala Kay Turner, Mar. 14, 1992; children: Tiffany Turner, Maddison West, Garret West, Gunner West. BSME, U. Tex., 1985; JD, S. Tex. Coll. Law, 1989. Bar: Tex. 1990, U.S. Ct. Appeals (5th cir.) 1992, U.S. Dist. Ct. (so. dist.) Tex 1990, U.S. Dist. Ct. (ea. dist.) Tex. 1997; cert. personal injury trial law. Design engr. Channel--Track and Tube-Way, Houston, 1985-90; assoc. lawyer Stephens & Clark, Houston, 1990-93; ptnr. Stephens & Stephens, Houston, 1994-96; named ptnr. Stephens, Stephens & West, Houston, 1997; prin. The West Law Firm, Sugar Land, Tex., 1997—; spkr. in field. Recipient Am. Jurisprudence award Civil Trial Practice, 1989. Mem. ABA, Assn. Trial Lawyers Am. (sustaining mem., exec. com. dir. product liability sect. 1997—, Tex. gov. new lawyers div. 1995—, liaison product liability sect. 1995-96), Tex. Trial Lawyers Assn. (assoc. dir. 1994—), Houston Bar Assn., Fort Bend Bar Assn., Houston Trial Lawyers Assn. (dir. 1994—), Tex. Supreme Ct. (unauthorized practice law com. 1997-99), Million Dollar Advs. Forum (life), State Bar Coll., Phi Delta Phi, Tau Beta Pi. Democrat. Avocations: snow skiing, scuba diving, karate, sky diving, hunting. Personal injury, Product liability, General civil litigation. Office: The West Law Firm 1600 Highway 6 Ste 450 Sugar Land TX 77478-4920

**WESTBERG, JOHN AUGUSTIN,** lawyer; b. Springfield, Mass., Oct. 12, 1931; s. Carl Joseph and Elizabeth Rebecca (Glassmire) W.; BA, Coll. William and Mary, 1955; JD, U. Va., 1959; m. Mina Lari, Aug. 21, 1976; children: Christine, Steven, Jennifer, Saman. Bar: N.Y. 1960, D.C. 1969, U.S. Supreme Ct. 1968. Assoc. Lord, Day and Lord, N.Y.C., 1959-64; legal adv. AID, Washington, 1964-65, regional legal adv. for Mid. East, Am. Embassy, Teheran, Iran, also AID affairs officer, 1965-68; founder John A. Westberg & Assocs., Inc., Teheran, 1968, pres., 1968-79; ptnr. Wald, Harkrader & Ross, London and Washington, 1981-87; pvt. practice, Washington, 1987-89; ptnr. Westberg & Johnson, Washington, 1989-96; of counsel Pepper, Hamilton LLP, Washington, 1996-98. Bd. dirs. Damavand Coll.; mem. N.Y. County Dem. Com., 1963. 1st lt. U.S. Army, 1955-57, Korea. Mem. Am. Soc. Internat. Law, D.C. Bar, Fed. Bar Assn., Iran Am. C. of C. (bd. govs. 1973-77), Shaybani Soc. (v.p.), Cosmos Club. Author: International Transactions and Claims Involving Government Parties--Case Law of the Iran-United States Claims Tribunal, 1991; contbr. articles to bus. and law jours. Avocations: tennis, skiing. Mem. ABA, Internat. Bar Assn., Am. Soc. Internat. Law, Assn. Bar City N.Y., Iran Am. C. of C. (bd. govs. 1973-77), Shaybani Soc., Cosmos Club. Private international, Alternative dispute resolution, Government contracts and claims. Home: Tadjrish Maghsoudbak, 6 Sepah Salar/Dehghom, Tehran Iran Office: Parsliam/Pol-e-Rumi Kharzar St, No 35 Khosro Ln, Teheran 19149, Iran

**WESTBROOK, JAMES EDWIN,** lawyer, educator; b. Camden, Ark., Sept. 7, 1934; s. Loy Edwin and Helen Lucille (Bethea) W.; m. Elizabeth Kay Farris, Dec. 23, 1956; children: William Michael, Robert Bruce, Matthew David. BA with high honors, Hendrix Coll., 1956; JD with distinction, Duke U., 1959; LLM, Georgetown U., 1965. Bar: Ark. 1959, Okla. 1977, Mo. 1982. Assoc. Mehaffy, Smith & Williams, Little Rock, 1959-62; asst. counsel, subcom. of U.S. Senate Jud. Com., Washington, 1963; legis. asst. U.S. Senate, Washington, 1963-65; asst. prof. law U. Mo., Columbia, 1965-68, asst. dean, 1966-68, assoc. prof., 1968-70, prof., 1970-76, 80—, James S. Rollins prof. law, 1974-76, 80—, Earl F. Nelson prof. law, 1982-99, emeritus prof., 1999—, interim dean, 1981-82; dean U. Okla. Coll. Law, Norman, 1976-80; George Allen vis. prof. law, U. Richmond, 1987; vis. prof. law Duke U., 1988, Washington U., St. Louis, 1996; reporter Mid-Am. Assembly on Role of State in Urban Crisis, 1970; dir. Summer Internship Program in Local Govt., 1968; cons. various Mo. cities on drafting home-rule charters; mem. Gov.'s Adv. Coun. on Local Govt. Law, 1967-68, Fed. Practice Com. U.S. Dist. Ct. (we. dist.) Mo., 1986-90; chmn. Columbia Charter Revision Commn., 1973-74; mem. spl. com. labor relations Mo. Dept. Labor and Indsl. Rels., 1975; mem. Task Force on Gender and Justice, Mo. Jud. Conf., 1990-93; mem. com. to rev. govtl. structure of Boone County, Mo., 1991. Author: (with L. Riskin) Dispute Resolution and Lawyers, 1987, supplement, 1993, 2d edit., 1997, abridged edit. of 2d edit., 1998; contbr. articles to profl. jours. Chair search com. for chancellor U. Mo., Columbia, 1992, chair search com. for provost, 1998. Mem. ABA, Nat. Acad. Arbitrators, Assn. Am. Law Schs. (chmn. local govt. law round table com. 1972), Ctrl. States Law Sch. Assn. (pres. 1982-83), Mo. Bar Assn. (vice chmn. labor law com. 1986-87, chmn. 1987-88, Spurgeon Smithton award 1995), Order of Coif, Blue Key, Alpha Chi. Roman Catholic. Home: 3609 S Woods Edge Rd Columbia MO 65203-6606 Office: U Mo Sch Law Columbia MO 65211-0001

**WESTBROOK, WILLIAM V.,** lawyer; b. San Angelo, Tex., Oct. 2; s. William V. Jr. and Barbara (Thompson) W.; m. Patricia L. Westbook. BBA, U. Miss., 1973, JD, 1975. Bar: Miss. Spl. asst. atty. gen. Miss. Dept. Justice, Jackson, 1977-83; ptnr. White & Morse, Gulfport, Miss., 1984-92, Eaton & Cottrell, Gulfport, 1992-94, Bryant, Clark, Dukes, Blakeslee, Ramsay & Hammond, Gulfport, 1994—. Trustee Presbytery of Miss., 1995—. Mem. Gulfport Yacht Club (sec. 1994—). Presbyterian. General civil litigation, Contracts commercial, General corporate. Office: Bryant Clark Dukes Et Al 2223 14th St Gulfport MS 39501-2006

**WESTENHOVER, GARY FLOYD,** lawyer; b. Denton, Tex., May 6, 1955; s. Glenn J. and Florene B. (Hutchins) W.; m. Mary J. Maulsby, May 10, 1980; children: Jennifer A. Shepherd, J. Ryan, Ashley N. AA, Weatherford Coll., 1975; BA, U. Tex., 1976, JD, 1980. Bar: Tex. 1981; bd. cert. in estate planning and probate law, Tex. Com. counsel Tex. State Senate, Austin, 1977-80; assoc. Bishop, Lamsens & Brown, Ft. Worth, 1981, Simon, Anisman, Doby, Wilson & Liles, Ft. Worth, 1981-83; pvt. practice Weatherford, Tex., 1983—; city atty. City of Reno, Tex., 1986—. Active Ft. Worth Bus. and Estate Planning Coun., 1994-97; pres. Am. Heart Assn., Weatherford, 1986. Mem. State Bar Tex., Parker County Bar Assn. (pres. 1986, treas. 1983-97), Tarrant County Probate Bar Assn. Avocation: golf. Estate planning, Probate, Estate taxation. Office: 101 S Main St Weatherford TX 76086-4319

**WESTERHAUS, DOUGLAS BERNARD,** lawyer; b. Marion, Kans., Jan. 11, 1951; s. Edwin Gerard and Bernadine (Ullman) W.; m. Susan Elizabeth Scott, Aug. 20, 1973 (div. Jan. 1979); m. Karen Sue Giersch, Sept. 20, 1980 (div. Aug. 1997); children: John Joseph, Jamie Lynn, Jeffrey Michael; m. Victoria Lee Ruhga, March, 1998. BSBA, Kans. U., 1973, JD, 1976. Bar: Kans. 1976, U.S. Dist. Kans. 1976, U.S. Supreme Ct. 1980. Assoc. Harper & Hornbaker, Junction City, Kans., 1976-78; ptnr. Harper & Hornbaker, Junction City, 1978-80; prin. Westerhaus Law Office, Marion, Kans., 1980-86; pres. Hydrogen Energy Corp., 1986-91, also bd. dirs.; staff atty. THORN Ams., Inc., dba Rent-A-Ctr., Wichita, Kans., 1991-95, chief counsel human resources, 1995-96, assoc. gen. counsel, 1996-97; dir. Field Human Resources, 1997-98; exec. v.p. Mr. Goodcents Franchise Sys., Inc., 1999—; atty. City of Grandview Plaza, Kans. 1977-80, City of Lehigh, Kans. 1980-86, Marion County, 1981-85; gen. counsel The Hydrogen Energy Corp., Kansas City, Mo. 1984-86, Marion Die & Fixture, 1980-86. Bd. dirs. St. Luke's Hosp., Marion, 1985-86. Mem. ABA, Kans. Bar Assn. (chmn. Lawyer Referral Commn. 1979-84, Outstanding Service award 1984), Marion County Bar Assn. (pres. 1985), Sedgwick County Bar Assn. Republican. Roman Catholic. General corporate, Labor. Home: 12813 King St Overland Park KS 66213-4416

**WESTERN, MARION WAYNE,** lawyer; b. Deseret, Utah, May 4, 1936; s. Francis Marion and Myrtle Brunson Western; m. Kathleen Ricks, May 16, 1959 (dec. Aug. 1978); children: Ellen Western Camp, Marc F., Amy Western Meador, James R.; m. Delores Biggs, Jan. 19, 1985. BS in Chemistry, Utah State U., 1961; JD with honors, George Washington U., 1964. Bar: Calif. 1966, U.S. Ct. Appeals (9th cir.) 1966, Utah 1975, U.S. Ct. Appeals (fed. cir.) 1983, U.S. Patent and Trademark Office 1965. Examiner U.S. Patent Office, Washington, 1961-64; patent atty. Shell Oil Co., San Francisco, 1964-73, Criddle & Thorpe, Salt Lake City, 1973-75; ptnr. Criddle, Thorpe & Western, Salt Lake City, 1976-79, Criddle & Western, Salt Lake City, 1979-80, Thorpe, North & Western, Sandy, Utah, 1980—. Avocations: outdoors, fishing, photography, poetry, classical music. Alternative dispute resolution, Contracts commercial, Construction. Office: Thorpe North & Western 8180 S 700 E Sandy UT 84070-0562

**WESTERVELT, CHARLES EPHRAIM, JR.,** lawyer; b. Columbus, Ohio, Mar. 10, 1922; s. Charles Ephraim and Winifred Reed (Wells) W.; m. Melba Louise Kuhlman, Mar. 3, 1946; children: John Charles, Kirk Thomas, Todd William, Reed Matthew. BA, Ohio State U., 1943, LLB and JD, 1948. Ptnr. Graves & Westervelt, Columbus, 1948-53; chief right of way atty. Ohio Turnpike Commn., Columbus, 1953-55, asst. to exec. dir., 1956; pvt. practice C.E. Westervelt Jr., Westerville, Ohio, 1956—. Trustee Westerville Pub. Libr., 1958-75; twp. clk. Genoa Twp., Ohio, 1960-72, mem. vol. fire dept., 1970-95; various offices Westerville Hist. Soc., 1948—. With USAAF, ETO, 1943-46. Decorated Air medal with 4 oak leaf clusters. Mem. Phi Beta Kappa. Republican. United Methodist. Avocations: reading, gardening, camping, fishing, genealogy. Estate planning, Probate, Estate taxation. Home: 7974 Africa Rd Westerville OH 43082-8818 Office: 18 W College Ave Westerville OH 43081-2104

**WESTFALL, GREGORY BURKE,** lawyer; b. Stamford, Tex., June 30, 1963; s. William Jake Westfall and Martha Ann Burke; m. Mollee Elizabeth Bennett, Oct. 1, 1994. BBA with highest honors, U. Tex., Arlington, 1990; JD summa cum laude, Tex. Tech. U., 1993. Bar: Tex. 1993, U.S. Dist. Ct. Tex. (no. dist.) 1993. Assoc. Law Office of Tom Hall, Ft. Worth, 1990-94; assoc. Jeff Kearney & Assocs., Ft. Worth, 1994—. Contbr. articles to profl. jours. Sgt. U.S. Army, 1984-87. Recipient Order of the Coif Tex. Tech. U., 1993. Mem. ATLA, Nat. Assn. Criminal Def. Lawyers, Tex. Trial Lawyers Assn., Tex. Criminal Def. Lawyers Assn., Coll. of State Bar of Tex., Tarrant County Trial Lawyers Assn. (bd. dirs. 1995—), Tarrant County Criminal Def. Lawyers Assn. Criminal, Personal injury. Office: Jeff Kearney & Assocs 120 W 3rd St Ste 300 Fort Worth TX 76102-7415

**WESTIN, DAVID LAWRENCE,** lawyer; b. Flint, Mich., July 29, 1952; s. Lawrence Rae and Mary Louise (Holman) W.; m. Victoria Peters; children: Victoria, Elizabeth, Matthew. BA, U. Mich., 1974, JD, 1977. Bar: D.C. 1979. Law clk. U.S. Ct. Appeals (2d cir.), N.Y.C., 1977-78, U.S. Supreme Ct., Washington, 1979; assoc. Wilmer, Cutler & Pickering, Washington, 1979-84, ptnr., 1985-91; sr. v.p., gen. counsel Capital Cities/ABC, Inc., N.Y.C., 1991-93; pres. of prodn. ABC TV Network, N.Y.C., 1993-94, pres., 1994-97, pres. of news, 1997—; lectr. Harvard U. Law Sch., Cambridge, Mass., 1986; adj. prof. Georgetown U. Law Ctr., Washington, 1989-91. Bd. dirs. Lincoln Ctr. Film. Soc., 1994—, Am. Arbitration Assn., 1991—. Democrat. Presbyterian. Club: Chevy Chase (Md.). Private international, General civil litigation, Contracts commercial. Home: 1717 Desales St NW Washington DC 20036-4401 Office: ABC TV Network 47 W 66th St Fl 5 New York NY 10023-6201

**WESTMAN, CARL EDWARD,** lawyer; b. Youngstown, Ohio, Dec. 12, 1943; s. Carl H. and Mary Lillis (Powell) W.; m. Carolyn J., July 17, 1965; children: C. Forrest, Stephanie A. BBA, Sam Houston State U., 1966; JD, U. Miami, 1969, LLM in Taxation, 1972. Bar: Fla. 1969; lic. USCG capt. Ptnr. Frost & Jacobs, 1983-93, Roetzel & Andress, 1993-98, Steel, Hector & Davis, Naples, Fla., 1999—. Mem. S.W. Fla. coun. Boy Scouts Am. Eagle Bd. of Rev., 1987—; trustee David Lawrence Found. for Mental Health, Inc., 1976-86, chmn. 1985-86; trustee Pikeville Coll., 1993—, Naples Cmty. Hosp., 1992—, Cmty. Health Care, Inc., 1995—, chmn. profl. capabilities com. physician credentialing, NCH Healthcare Sys., 1998—; past pres. bd. trustees, elder Moorings Presbyn. Ch.; chmn. S.W. Fla. Adv. Bd., Rosenstiel Sch. of Marine and Atmospheric Sci., U. Miami. Mem. ABA, Fla. Bar, Collier County Bar Assn., Estate Planning Coun., Coral Reef Yacht Club, Useppa Island Club. Estate planning, Probate, General practice. Home: 1952 Crayton Rd Naples FL 34102-5070 Office: 5551 Ridgewood Dr Ste 101 Naples FL 34108-2718

**WESTON, MICHAEL C.,** lawyer; b. Asheville, N.C., Aug. 13, 1938; m. Mary Ann Damme; two children. AB in English, Brown U., 1960; JD, U. Mich., 1963. Bar: Mich. 1964, Ill. 1973. Assoc. Clark Hill, Detroit, 1963-68; from sec. to pres. corp. and indsl. consortium Econ. Devel. Corp. of Greater Detroit, 1969-73; chief staff atty. Northwestern U., Evanston, Ill., 1973-81, v.p. legal affairs, 1981-89; v.p. and gen. counsel, 1990—; lectr. minority bus. devel. Inst. Continuing Legal Edn., conflicts of interest Nat. Coun. Univ. Rsch. Adminstrs. Contbr. articles to profl. jours. Chmn. Univ. Gallery Com., 1982-85; bd. dirs. Northwestern U. Press. Mem. ABA (sec. taxation, com. on exempt orgns., ho. of dels., lectr. Inst. on Minority Bus. Devel.), Chgo. Coun. Lawyers, Nat. Assn. Coll. and Univ. Attys. (lectr. fed. tax matters, outside activities faculty mems. univ.-cmty. rels., med. risk mgmt., bd. dirs. 1985-88, 92-97, pres. 1995-96). Education and schools, Health, Taxation, general. Office: Northwestern U 633 Clark St Evanston IL 60208-0001

**WESTPHAL, JAMES PHILLIP,** lawyer; b. Mpls., Nov. 12, 1961; s. William Paul and Kathryn Joy (Homme) W. BS, U. Minn., 1983, JD, 1986. Bar: Minn. 1987, U.S. Dist. Ct. Minn. 1987. Assoc. Victor Seiler & Assocs., Mpls., 1987-92; pvt. practice Mpls., 1993—. Mem. ABA, Hennepin County Bar Assn. Democrat. Lutheran. Personal injury, Bankruptcy, Criminal. Office: 301 4th Ave S 270 Grain Exch Bldg Minneapolis MN 55415

**WETSCH, LAURA JOHNSON,** lawyer; b. Fargo, N.D., Nov. 18, 1959; d. Ronald Lee Johnson and Jacqualene Lee (Goudie) Johnson Trefz; m. John Robert Wetsch, Aug. 29, 1981; children: Julie Elizabeth, Katherine Anne, John Michael. AA, Bismarck (N.D.) State Coll., 1980; BA, U. N.D., 1982, JD, 1985. Bar: N.D. 1985, N.C. 1992. Law clk. to Hon. Patrick A. Conmy, U.S. Dist. Ct. for N.D., Bismarck, 1985-88; pvt. practice, Langdon, N.D., 1988-91; assoc. Jordan Price Wall Gray Jones & Carlton, PLLC, Raleigh, N.C., 1992-99; dir., v.p. legal affairs Hytec Cons., Inc., Cary, N.C., 1999—; of counsel Joyce L. Davis & Assocs., Raleigh, 1999—; instr. bus. and criminal law U. N.D.-Lake Region, Cavalier, 1990-91; instr. paralegal studies Ctrl. Carolina C.C., Sanford, N.C., 1991-92; instr. bus. law Wake Tech. C.C., Raleigh, 1992-93. Author, editor (pamphlet) Crime Survivors Handbook, 1996; editor N.D. Women Lawyers Assn. Newsletter, 1990-91; contbr. articles to profl. jours. Vol. mediator and arbitrator Burleigh County Housing Authority, Bismarck, 1986-88; concessions co-chmn. Sanderson H.S. Band Boosters, 1996-98; curbside cons. in employment law, N.C. Ctr. for Nonprofits, 1998. Mem. Nat. Employment Lawyers Assn., N.C. Bar Assn. (citizen edn. com. young lawyers divsn. 1994-96, chmn. membership svcs. com. young lawyers divsn. 1996-97), N.C. Acad. Trial Lawyers, Wake County Bar Assn. Democrat. Roman Catholic. Labor, Civil rights, General civil litigation. Office: Jordan Price Wall Gray Jones & Carlton 225 Hillsborough St Ste 200 Raleigh NC 27603-1765

**WETTERMARK, JAMES HART,** lawyer; b. Mobile, Ala., Nov. 28, 1953; s. Alfred Boyce and Helen M. (McCown) W.; m. Joan L. Coppinger, June 28, 1984. BS, Auburn U., 1975; JD, U. Ala., 1978. Bar: Ala. 1978, Tenn. 1990, Ga. 1991, U.S. Dist. Ct. (no., mid., so. dist.) Ala., (no. dist.) Ga., U.S. Ct. Appeals (5th, 11th, 6th cirs.). Ptnr. Burge & Wettermark, Birmingham, Ala. Mem. Assn. Trial Lawyers Am., Ala. Bar Assn., Ga. Bar Assn., Tenn. Bar Assn. Avocations: golf, tennis, flying. Personal injury, General civil litigation, Product liability. Home: 4229 Abingdon Trl Birmingham AL 35243-1737 Office: Burg & Wettermark PC 2300 Southtrust Tower Birmingham AL 35203-3204

**WETZEL, JAMES K.,** lawyer; b. Biloxi, Miss., Apr. 2, 1954; s. Percy James and Norma Lee (Porter) W.; m. Garnette A. Quarles, Aug. 24, 1975; 1 child, Garner. AS, Miss. Gulf Coast Jr. Coll., Perkington, Miss., 1974; BS in Polit. Sci., U. So. Miss., Hattiesburg, 1976; JD, Miss. Coll., Jackson, 1979. Bar: Miss. 1979, U.S. Dist. Ct. (so. dist.) Miss. 1980, U.S. Ct. Appeals (5th cir.) 1981. Law clk. to Justice Harry Walter, Miss. Supreme Ct., Jackson, 1979-80; assoc. atty. Hopkins, Dodson et al, Gulfport, Miss., 1980-82; city atty. City of Gulfport, 1985-89; sr. ptnr., owner James K. Wetzel, P.A., Gulfport, 1982—. Mem. ABA, ATLA, Miss. Trial Lawyers Assn., Am. Inns of Ct. Roman Catholic. Personal injury, Labor, Contracts commercial. Office: James K Wetzel & Assocs 1701 24th Ave Gulfport MS 39501-2972

**WETZLER, RICHARD S.,** lawyer; b. Marysville, Kans., Nov. 30, 1946; s. Charles S. and Esther E. Wetzler; m. Cheryl S. Bailey, July 23, 1977; children: Erika, Kristin, Andrew. BA, U. Kans., 1968, JD, 1971. Bar: Kans. 1971. Trial atty. USDA, Washington, 1971-72; asst. dist. atty. Johnson County Dist. Atty., Olathe, Kans., 1973-78; ptnr. Bennett, Lytle, Wetzler, Prairie Village, Kans., 1978-97, Holman, Hansen & Colville, Prairie Village, 1998—; city atty. City of Leawood, Kans., 1985—; bd. dirs. Lakewood Village, Lenexa, Kans., 1993—. Mem. Prairie Village Kiwanis (pres. 1985-95), Leawood Rotary Club (pres. elect). Municipal (including bonds), General civil litigation, Family and matrimonial. Office: Holman Hansen & Colville 9400 Mission Rd Shawnee Mission KS 66206-2042

**WEWERS, MARK ERIC,** lawyer; b. Kansas City, Kans., Mar. 9, 1969; s. James L. and Vicki L. Wewers; m. Kimberly K. Zoller, May 14, 1994. BA, U. Kans., Lawrence, 1991; JD, Oklahoma City U., 1994. Bar: Tex. 1994, U.S. Dist. Ct. (no. dist.) Tex. 1995, U.S. Dist. Ct. (ea. dist.) Tex. 1997, U.S. Dist. Ct. (so. dist.) Tex. 1998, U.S. Ct. Appeals (5th cir.) 1998, U.S. Ct. Appeals (8th cir.) 1999. Atty. Roberts, Cunningham & Stripling, Dallas, 1994—; mem. Oklahoma City U. Law Rev., 1992-94. Mem. Dallas Bar Assn. General civil litigation, Transportation, Labor. Office: Roberts Cunningham & Stripling LLP 800 Preston Commons W 8117 Preston Rd Dallas TX 75225-6332

**WEXELBAUM, MICHAEL,** lawyer; b. Bklyn., Aug. 12, 1946; s. Joseph and Beatrice (Skurnick) W.; m. Cynthia Debra Schorr, Apr. 15, 1973 (dec. 1984); children: Joshua David, Stephanie Faye; m. Joan Brenda Math, Aug. 21, 1994; stepchildren: Jonathan David Kaye, Matthew Lawrence Kaye, Julie Dana Kaye. BA in Econs., Bucknell U., 1968; JD, NYU, 1971. Bar: N.Y. 1972, U.S. Dist. Ct. (so. and ea. dists.) N.Y. 1973. Assoc. Sherman, Citron & Karasik, P.C., N.Y.C., 1972-80; ptnr., head litigation dept. Sherman, Citron & Karasik, P.C., 1980—. Arbitrator Am. Arbitration Assn. and Gen. Arbitration Coun. of Textile and Apparel Industries, N.Y.C., 1982—. Mem. Bankruptcy Lawyers Bar Assn., Lawyers Assn. Textile and Apparel Industries (bd. govs.), Am. Arbitration Assn. (arbitrator). Democratic. Jewish. Avocations: tennis, skiing, biking, theatre. General civil litigation, Contracts commercial, General practice. Home: 85 Norrans Ridge Dr Ridgefield CT 06877-4237 Office: Sherman Citron & Karasik PC Carnegie Hall Tower 152 W 57th St New York NY 10019-3310

**WEXLER, DANNIEL JUSTIN,** lawyer; b. S.I., N.Y., Feb. 25, 1963; s. Harry K. Wexler and Jacqueline Desjardins Corn; m. Susan Jean Lacey, Oct. 9, 1994; children: Ashli Lacey Scarpinato, Emma Rose. BA, SUNY, Stony Brook, 1986; JD, U. So. Calif., 1989. Bar: Calif. 1989. Assoc. White & Case, L.A., 1989-91, Horton Barbaro & Reilly, Santa Ana, Calif., 1991-96, Zabner & Assocs., Westlake Village, Calif., 1996-97; sr. assoc. quinlivan & Kaniewski, Newport Beach, Calif., 1997—. Mem. Nat. Network of Estate Planning Attys., Legion Lex Inn of Cts. (bd. dirs. 1989-93), Planned Giving Round Table. Democrat. Jewish. Avocation: tennis. Estate planning, Estate taxation, Probate. Office: Quinlivan & Kaniewski 1401 Dove St Ste 580 Newport Beach CA 92660-2492

**WEXLER, JANICE KAY,** lawyer, educator; b. Madison, Wis., Apr. 2, 1954; d. Jay Milo and Lorelei K. (Kabaker) W.; m. Joel E. Davidson, Oct. 18, 1980 (div. Dec. 1992); children: Joshua A. Davidson, Ari W. Davidson; m. Scott N. Grover, Mar. 15, 1993. BA, U. Wis., 1976, JD, 1979. Bar: Wis. 1979. Lawyer Bell Law Offices, SS, Madison, 1979-87; dir. continuing legal edn. seminars State Bar Wis., Madison, 1987-95; exec. dir. Madison Area Builders Assn., 1995-96, United Refugees of Wis., Madison, 1996; lectr. U. Wis. Law Sch., Madison, 1996—; econ. support supr. State of Wis., Madison, 1996-97; lawyer Krekeler & Scheffer, S.C., Madison, 1997—; mem. adv. bd. Wis. Womens Bus. Initiative Corp., Madison, 1995—. Author (handbook) Legal Guide for the Elderly, 1996. Adv. PTO Falk Sch., Madison, 1994-97. Mem. ABA (adv. task force 1995), State Bar Wis., Dane County Bar Assn. Democrat. Jewish. Home: 1137 Sunridge Dr Madison WI 53711-3366 Office: Krekeler and Scheffer SC 15 N Pinckney St Madison WI 53703-2833

**WEXLER, JOAN G.,** dean, law educator; b. N.Y.C., Nov. 25, 1946; m. Marvin Wexler, June 16, 1968 (div.); children: Matthew Eric, Laura Page. BS with honors and distinction, Cornell U., 1968; MA in Teaching, Harvard U., 1970; JD, Yale, 1974. Judicial law clerk for Judge Jack B. Weinstein U.S. Dist. Ct. (ea. dist.), N.Y., 1974-75; assoc. Debevoise & Plimpton, N.Y.C., 1975-77; asst. prof. law NYU Sch. Law, 1978-81, assoc. prof. law, 1981-85; prof. law Bklyn. Law Sch., 1985—, assoc. dean acad. affairs, prof. law, 1987-94, acting dean, prof. law, 1994, dean, pres. and prof. law, 1994—; spkr. in field; evaluator trust adminstrn. and estate adminstrn. courses N.Y. State Banking Assn., 1993; mem. planning com. Bench and Bar Conf. Fed. Bar Found., 1995; mem. planning com. Workshop on Family and Juvenile Law Am. Assn. Law Schs., Washington, 1993. Contbr. articles to profl. jours. Bd. dirs. Downtown Bklyn. Devel. Assn., 1992-96, Fed. Bar Coun. Found., 1993-98, Fund for Modern Cts., 1994—, Assn. of the Bar of the City of N.Y. Fund, 1994-96. Fellow Am. Bar Found., Practising Law Inst.; mem. ABA (vice chairperson sect. legal edn. and admissions new deans' seminar planning com. 1995-96, ind. law sch. com. 1996-97, continuing legal edn. com. 1997-98), Am. Law Inst., Fed. Bar Coun. Found. (pres. 1999—, chair nominating com. 1998), N.Y. State Bar Assn. (com. on children and the law 1993-97, com. on legal edn. and admission to the bar 1994—), N.Y. Women's Bar Assn. (bd. dirs. 1988-91, v.p. 1987-88, 92-93, spl. recognition award 1996), Assn. of the Bar of the City of N.Y. (ad hoc com. on AIDS 1987-88, ad hoc com. on surrogate parenting 1986-88, com. on family ct. and family law 1989-92, nominating com. 1992-93, 99—, long range planning com. 1992-95, com. on matrimonial law 1985-89, 92-95, com. on honors 1994-97, v.p. 1996-97, chair com. on honors 1997-99), Pres.'s Coun. of Cornell Women. Home: 1045 Nine Acres Ln Mararoneck NY 10543-4706 Office: Bklyn Law Sch 250 Joralemon St Brooklyn NY 11201-3700

**WEXLER, LEONARD D.,** federal judge; b. Bklyn., Nov. 11, 1924; s. Jacob and Bessie (Herman) W.; m. Barbara Blum, Mar. 1953; children: Allison Wexler Smeitanka, Robert, William. BS, Ind. U., 1947, JD, NYU, 1950. Bar: N.Y. 1983, U.S. Dist. Ct. (ea. dist.) N.Y. 1983. Assoc. Siben & Siben Esqs., Bay Shore, N.Y., 1950-56; ptnr. Meyer & Wexler Esqs., Smithtown, N.Y., 1956-83; judge U.S. Dist. Ct. (eastern dist.) N.Y., 1983—; now sr. judge; atty. Suffolk County Police Conf., 1956-83; 1st atty. Suffolk County Patrolmen's Benevolent Assn., 1960-75; 1st atty. Suffolk County Detectives Assn., 1964-70; temporary state chmn., legal counsel Com. for Rev. Juvenile Justice System, N.Y. State Bar Assn.; speaker, lectr.; 1st adminstr. Assigned Counsel Plan N.Y. State, 1966-83. Served with U.S. Army, 1943-45. Mem. Suffolk County Criminal Bar Assn. (founder 1965, dir. 1956-60). Republican. Jewish. Avocations: travelling; sailing. Home: 94 W Bayberry Rd Islip NY 11751-4905 Office: US Dist Ct US Courthouse 300 Rabro Dr Hauppauge NY 11788-4256

**WHALEN, COLLEEN HISER,** lawyer, nurse; b. Troy, N.Y., June 11, 1952; d. Theodore Edwin and Madelyn Hiser. AD, Maria Coll., Albany, N.Y., 1979; BS, Russell Sage Coll., Troy, 1986; JD, Albany Law Sch., 1989. RN, N.Y. Staff nurse St. Mary's Hosp., Troy, 1979—; assoc. atty. Maynard, O'Connor & Smith, Albany, 1989-92, Carter, Conboy, Case, Blackmore & Napierski, Albany, 1992-98; atty., of counsel Castillo & Siegel, Albany, 1998—; legal cons. John Ahearn Rescue Squad, Mechanicsville, N.Y., 1986—; adj. prof. SUNY, Utica/Rome, 1994. Vol. firefighter Mechanicville Fire Dept., 1978—; vol. rescue squad John Ahearn Rescue Squad, 1979—. Mem. N.Y. State Bar Assn., Albany County Bar Assn., Capital Dist. Women's Bar ASsn., Justinian Honor Soc., Phi Kappa Phi. Personal injury, General civil litigation. Office: Castillo & Siegel 817 Madison Ave Albany NY 12208-3798

**WHALEN, JAMES LAWRENCE,** protective services official, lawyer, educator; b. Cin., Jan. 8, 1962; s. Lawrence Edward and Donna Lee (Faulkner) W.; m. Mary Colleen Anneken, Apr. 28, 1984; children: Kelly, Amy, Nicholas, Julie. BS in Criminal Justice, U. Cin., 1988; JD, No. Ky. U., 1992. Bar: Ohio, D.C. Police officer Metro-Dade Police Dept., Miami, Fla., 1982-85; police officer Cin. (Ohio) Police Divsn., 1986-92, police lt., 1992—; pvt. practice lawyer Cin., 1992—; cert. instr. Ohio Police Officers Tng. Assn., State of Ohio, 1990—; prof. No. Ky. U., Highland Heights, 1994—; instr. in field. Recipient Career Enhancement award Rotary Club, Cin., 1991. Mem. ABA, Ohio Bar Assn., Cin. Bar Assn., Fraternal Order of Police. Roman Catholic. Avocations: family activities, home remodeling, athletics. General civil litigation, Estate planning, Family and matrimonial. Office: Cin Police Divsn 310 Ezzard Charles Dr Cincinnati OH 45214-2805

**WHALEN, JEANMARIE,** lawyer; b. Mt. Kisco, N.Y., Dec. 20, 1961; d. Robert Joseph and Ann Rita Whalen. BA in Politics, Cath. U., 1984; JD, Whittier Coll., 1990. Bar: N.Y. 1991, Conn. 1991, Fla. 1993. Atty. Lichtblau & Goldenberg, PA, North Palm Beach, Fla., 1993-94, Slawson, Cunningham, Whalen & Stewart, Palm Beach Gardens, Fla., 1994—; lectr. in field. Recipient Voluntary Bar Pres.' award Fla. Coun. Bar Assn., 1997, 98. Mem. Acad. Fla. Trial Lawyers (bd. dirs. 1996-97, chair women's caucus 1996-97), Fla. Assn. for Women Lawyers (exec. bd. 1996—, treas. 1996-97, pres.-elect Palm Beach chpt. 1996-97, 97-98, pub. rels. dir. 1997-98, seminar chair 1997—, pres.-elect 1998-99). Republican. Roman Catholic. Avocations: running, tennis, skiing, swimming. Personal injury, Insurance, General civil litigation. Office: 2401 Pga Blvd Ste 140 Palm Beach Gardens FL 33410

**WHALEN, LAURENCE J.,** federal judge; b. 1944. BA, Georgetown Coll., 1967; JD, Georgetown U., 1970, LLM in Taxation, 1971. Judge U.S. Tax Ct., Washington, 1987—; atty. Crowe & Dunlevy, Oklahoma City, Hamel & Park, Washington; spl. asst. to Asst. Atty. Gen.; trial atty., tax div. U.S. Dept. Justice. With USAR, 1971. Mem. ABA ( taxation, litigation and bus. law sects.), Fed. Bar Assn. Office: US Tax Ct 400 2nd St NW Washington DC 20217-0002

**WHALEN, PAUL LEWELLIN,** lawyer, educator, mediator; b. Lexington, Ky.; s. Elza Boz and Barbara Jean (Lewellin) W.; m. Teena Gail Tanner, Jan. 26, 1985; children: Ashley, Lars, Lucy. BA, U. Ky.; JD, Northern Ky. U.; cert., Bonn U., Fed. Republic Germany, 1981; student, U.S. Army J.A.G. Sch., 1988; diploma, USAF Squadron Officers Sch., 1998. Bar: W.Va. 1984, U.S. Ct. Appeals (6th cir.) 1984, Ky. 1985, U.S. Ct. Appeals (4th cir.) 1985, Ohio 1993. Assoc. Geary Walker, Parkersburg, W.Va., 1984-85; prin. Paul L. Whalen, Ft. Thomas, Ky., 1985—; advisor Families with Children from China, 1998—; prof. pub. contract law Air Force Inst. Tech., 1999—; hearing officer Ky. Dept. IDEA; atty. Dept. of Air Force, Office of Chief Trial Atty. Contract Law Ctr., Wright Patterson AFB, 1988-99; hearing officer, prosecutor Ky. Dept. Edn. Profl. Stds. Bd., 1995-97. State sec. Ky. Young Dems., 1981-82; mem. Campbell County Foster Care Rev. Bd., Newport, Ky., 1986, Leadership No. Ky.; bd. dirs. Ky. Coun. Child Abuse, Inc. Com. for Kids; mem. Ft. Thomas Bd. Edn., 1987-99,, chmn., 1990-94; dir. Ky. Sch. Bd. Assn., 1993-98; mem. Ky. Commn. on Human Svcs. Recipient Commendation No. Ky. Legal Aid, 1986-99. Mem. No. Ky. Bar Assn., Optimist Club, Kiwanis Club, Phi Alpha Delta. Democrat. Methodist. Avocations: freelance writing, stamp collecting, politics, amateur radio, bicycling. Consumer commercial, Family and matrimonial, Government contracts and claims. Home: 113 Ridgeway Ave Fort Thomas KY 41075-1333 Office: PO Box 22 Fort Thomas KY 41075 *Notable cases include: Givan vs. Ask Realty, Ky. App., 788 S.W. 2d 503, 1990, establishing that a real estate broker has a fiduciary relationship* *with seller even though he may be sub-agent; Ocento Electric, Inc., ASBCA No. 36789, 88-3 BCA, 21,188, regarding timeliness of appeals to bds. of contract appeals.*

**WHALEY, JAMES THADDEUS,** lawyer, accountant. BS, U. Ill., 1990, JD, 1995. Bar: Ill. 1995, Calif. 1996; CPA, Ill. Acct. Price Waterhouse, Chgo., 1990-92; assoc. Jenner & Block, Chgo., 1995-96, Brobeck Phleger & Harrison, San Diego, 1996-97, Wilson, Sonsini, Goodrich & Rosati, Palo Alto, Calif., 1997—. General corporate, Mergers and acquisitions, Securities. Office: Wilson Sonsini et al 650 Page Mill Rd Palo Alto CA 94304-1001

**WHALEY, NANCY JEAN,** lawyer; b. Ft. Thomas, Ky., Apr. 4, 1965; d. Omer L. and Frances A. (Sowder) Humphress; m. John Thomas Whaley, Oct. 5, 1996. BA, Eureka Coll., 1987; JD, Emory U., 1991. Bar: Ga. 1991. Atty. Clark & Smith P.C., Atlanta, 1991-92, Chpt. 13 Trustee, Atlanta, 1992—. Co-founder Ga. Women on the Run for Office, Atlanta, 1995—. Capt. USAFR, 1986—. Mem. Ga. Assn. Women Lawyers (pres. 1998—), Air Force Assn., Delta Zeta (convention com. 1998). Republican. Southern Baptist. Avocations: golf, scuba diving, running. Home: 965 Greyfield Pl NW Atlanta GA 30328-4812 Office: Chpt 13 Trustee 100 Peachtree St NW Ste 300 Atlanta GA 30303-1911

**WHARTON, HUGH DAVIS, III,** lawyer, judge; b. Buffalo, June 1, 1940; s. Hugh Davis and Helen Bricka (McAuliffe) W.; m. Patricia Granville Ditton, June 20, 1964 (div. Apr. 1982); children: Jennifer Wharton, Gregory Paul, Michael David. BA, Princeton U., 1961; JD, Yale U., 1964. Bar: Alaska 1965, Colo. 1965, Calif. 1969. Asst. atty. gen. State of Alaska, Juneau, 1964-65; chief law clk. to Judge Doyle, U.S. Dist. Ct., Denver, 1965-66; field rep. U.S. OEO, Office of Pres., Kansas City, Mo., 1966-67; field rep. U.S. OEO, Office of Pres., San Francisco, 1967-69, dep. regional atty. Western region, 1969-71, regional atty., 1971-73; city atty. City of Livermore, Calif., 1973-74; regional atty. Western region U.S. Dept. Energy, San Francisco, 1974-80; pvt. practice, San Francisco, 1980—; adminstrv. law judge City and County of San Francisco, 1984—; judge pro tem Superior Ct., 1990—. Pres. Golden Gate Bus. Assn., San Francisco, 1989-92; mem. bd. dirs. United Way of the Bay Area, 1989—; candidate for supr. City and County of San Francisco, 1982, 84, candidate for muni judge, 1988; mem. vol. bd. dirs. San Francisco Gen. Hosp., 1983-88; pres. Diamond Hts. Cmty. Assn., San Francisco, 1987-90. Recipient John W. Gardner Disting. Leadership award United Way, 1992. Mem. State Bar of Calif., Bay Area Lawyers for Individual Freedom. Democrat. Episcopalian. Avocations; politics, travel, fitness, classic cars. Probate, Non-profit and tax-exempt organizations, General practice.

**WHARTON, JAMES CARL,** lawyer, educator; b. Bellingham, Wash., Aug. 4, 1936; s. James J. Wharton; m. Sarah L. Wharton, Sept. 2, 1973; 1 child, Denise E. BA in Chemistry, U. Wash., 1959; MS in Chemistry, U. Idaho, 1968; JD, U. San Francisco, 1974. Bar: Calif. 1975; cert. jr. coll. tchr., Calif.; cert. ski instr. Nuc. engr. Phillips Petroleum Corp. Idaho, Idaho Falls, 1959-69; staff rschr. Lawrence Livermore Nat. Lab., Livermore, Calif., 1969-76; sole practice bankruptcy and estate planning Livermore, 1977-91; environ. and contract specialist U. Calif., 1991—; instr. law Armstrong Coll., Berkeley, 1979-81. Contbr. articles to profl. publs. Chmn. energy and environ. com. City of Livermore, 1992—; ski instr. Heavenly Ski Area, 1995—. Mem. Calif. State Bar Assn., Alameda County Bar Assn., Livermore-Amador Valley Bar Assn., Dublin C. of C., Exchange Club. Democrat. Bankruptcy, Personal injury, Real property.

**WHARTON, JAMES T.,** lawyer; b. Cresson, Pa., July 7, 1930; s. Denver and Edna (Myers) W.; m. Sara Ann Breen, June 18, 1955 (dec.); children: Michael T., Sharon A., Patrick J., Maureen A., Christopher R., Mark E., Timothy J., James T.; m. Beverly K. Wharton, Oct. 19, 1982. BA, Pa. State U., 1952; LLB, Georgetown U., 1956. Bar: Md., D.C. Ptnr. McCarthy and Wharton, Rockville, Md., 1961-84; mng. ptnr. Wharton Levin Ehemantraut, Klein and Nash, Annapolis, Md., 1984—; bd. dirs. Criswell Chevrolet, Inc., Gaithersburg, Md., 1990—; mem. jud. nominating com. State of Md., 1979-86. Fellow Am. Coll. Trial Lawyers; mem. Md. State Bar Assn. (bd. govs. 1972-73), Montgomery County Bar Assn. (sec. 1965, pres. 1974-75). Republican. Product liability, Personal injury, General civil litigation. Home: 109 Terrapin Ln Stevensville MD 21666-3721 Office: Wharton Levin 104 West St Annapolis MD 21401-2802

**WHATLEY, JACQUELINE BELTRAM,** lawyer; b. West Orange, N.J., Sept. 26, 1944; d. Quirino and Eliane (Gruet) Beltram; m. John W. Whatley, June 25, 1966. BA, U. Tampa, 1966; JD, Stetson U., 1969. Bar: Fla. 1969, Alaska 1971. Cert. real estate law specialist. Assoc. Gibbons, Tucker, McEwen Smith & Cofer, Tampa, Fla., 1969-71; pvt. practice, Anchorage, 1971-73; ptnr. Gibbons, Tucker, Miller, Whatley & Stein, P.A., Tampa, 1973—, pres., 1981—. Bd. dirs. Travelers Aid Soc., 1982-94; trustee Humana Women's Hosp., Tampa 1987-93, Keystone United Meth. Ch., 1986-89, 99—. Mem. ABA, Fla. Bar Assn. (real estate cert. com. 1993-95), Alaska Bar Assn., Tenn. Walking Horse Breeders and Exhibitors Assn. (v.p. 1984-87, dir. for Fla. 1981-87, 1990-93, 97-99, adv. com. Tenn. Walking Horse Nat. Celebration 1994-97), Fla. Walking and Racking Horse Assn. (bd. dirs. 1988-89, pres. 1980-82), Athena Club (Tampa). Republican. Methodist. Real property, Contracts commercial. Home: PO Box 17595 Tampa FL 33682-7595 Office: 101 E Kennedy Blvd Ste 1000 Tampa FL 33602-5146

**WHATLEY, WILLIAM WAYNE, JR.,** lawyer; b. Dothan, Ala., Dec. 12, 1958; s. William Wayne Whatley Sr. and Emily Carol (Hudgens) Vandemark; m. Joy Thompson Campbell, Oct. 4, 1997. BA, U. Ala., 1981, JD, 1984. Bar: Ala. 1984, U.S. Dist. Ct. (mid. and no. dists.) Ala. 1985, U.S. Ct. Appeals (11th cir.) 1985, U.S. Dist. Ct. (so. dist.) Ala. 1986, U.S. Supreme Ct. 1997. Staff atty. Ala. Ct. Criminal Appeals, Montgomery, 1984-85; asst. atty. gen. State of Ala., Montgomery, 1985-87, asst. atty. gen. criminal litigation divsn., 1987-88; asst. atty. gen., dir. Ala. Medicaid Fraud Control Unit, Montgomery, 1988-92, dep. atty. gen., 1992-96; pvt. practice Montgomery, 1996—. Office: 529 S Perry St Ste 12-A Montgomery AL 36104-4651

**WHEAT, JOHN NIXON,** lawyer; b. Liberty, Tex., Dec. 15, 1952; s. Thomas Allen and Dora (Arrendell) W. BA, Tulane U., 1975; JD, St. Mary's U., San Antonio, 1977. Bar: Tex. 1978, U.S. Dist. Ct. (ea. dist.) Tex. 1978, U.S. Ct. Appeals (5th cir.) 1979. Law clk. U.S. Dist. Ct. Ea. Dist. Tex., Beaumont, 1978-79; pvt. practice The Wheat Firm, Liberty, Tex., 1979—. Vice chmn. Chambers-Liberty County Navigation Dist., 1994-99, chmn., 1999—; pres. chpt. 10 Sons of Republic of Tex. Mem. ABA, Tex. Bar Assn., Liberty-Chambers County Bar Assn., Houston Bar Assn., Tower Club of Beaumont, Magnolia Ridge County Club, Knights of Neches, Delta Theta Phi. Republican. Episcopalian. Avocations: ranching, hunting, riding, philosophy. Real property, Probate, Banking. Office: 714 Main St PO Box 10050 Liberty TX 77575-7550

**WHEATLEY, CHARLES HENRY, III,** lawyer, biomedical technology company executive; b. Balt., Aug. 11, 1932; s. Charles Henry Jr. and Rebecca W. (Cloud) W.; m. Charlotte Beryl Davis, June 11, 1955; children: Charles H. IV, Craig A., Cheryl L. W. Jackson. *Descendant of Robert Burns, Scottish poet; grandchildren: Tyler C., Travis A., Caitlin K., Emma E. Wheatley, Regan L. Jackson. Sisters and brothers in law: Elaine W., Raymond L. Jacobs, Lois W., Andrew J. Schultz, Katherine W., Herman S. Roemer, Dorothy W., Calvin E. Plitt. Daughters in law: Kimberly R., Elaine L. Wheatley. Nieces: Elaine J. Bousman, Carole R. Hickey, Jean K., Mollie W. Roemer, Cathy S. Santee. Nephews: Andrew J. Jr., Frank C. Schultz, Calvin E. Plitt, Jr. Grandparents: Mary B., Charles H. Wheatley Sr., Carlena, Walter Cloud. Father and Mother in law: Esther B., Delbert M. Davis.* BA in Polit. Sci. with hons., Western Md. Coll., 1954; JD with hons., U. Md., 1959. Bar: Md. 1960, D.C. 1981, U.S. Supreme Ct. 1964. Tchr. Carroll County Pub. Schs., Westminster, Md., 1955-56; officer, judge advocate U.S. Army, 1957-62; law clk. assoc. judge William R. Horney Md. Ct. Appeals, Annapolis, 1959-60; pvt. practice Md. and Washington, 1960—; mem. Md. legislature Ho. of Dels., Annapolis, 1962-66; pres., COO Cell Works, Inc., Balt., 1997—; real estate, ins. exec. AID Realty & Ins. Co., Balt., 1960—; adj. coll. instr. Western Md. coll., Westminster, 1963-65, Villa Julie Coll., 1980-86, Balt. Cmty. Col., 1966-72; mem. adv. bd. Fleet Bus. Sch., Annapolis, Md., 1986—, Balt. Cmty. Col., 1986—; chmn. bd., ceo Regional Mfg. Inst., Balt., 1993-96; nat. del. White House Conf. on Small Bus., Washington, 1985. *Originated "Planned Unit Development" and "Adequate Facilities" Zoning Ordinances, Baltimore City Council, Maryland to ensure well planned community development. Originated first statewide Maryland prepaid legal services. Incorporated one of the first commercial space launch companies in the world. Consultant in law office automation Maryland and American Bar Associations. Sponsored first mandatory seatbelt and teenage driver education legislation in Maryland legislature. Chaired Baltimore City Council Capital Budget Committee for inner harbor development. Sponsored resolution establishing "language signs for the deaf" as foreign language alternative in Maryland schools. Designed first statewide educational support staff personnel organization in Maryland State Teachers Association.* Contbr., editor: (weekly newspaper) Maryland Teacher, 1974-77; guest News Makers program WJZ-TV, 1985; contbr. articles to profl. jours. Md. del. Md. State Constitutional Convention, Annapolis, 1967-68; councilman Balt. City Coun., 1971-74. 1st lt. JAG U.S. Army, 1957-62. Received Cell Works Co. Computerworld-Smithsonian Science Innovation laureate award, 1999. Mem. Md. Commn. Mfg. Competitiveness, Md. State Bar Assn., Dist. Columbia Bar. Assn., Md. State Tchrs. Assn. (exec. sec. 1974-77), Order of the Coif, Pi Gamma Mu. Democrat. Methodist. Avocations: education, music, writing, basketball, skiing. General corporate, Health, Legislative. Office: Cell Works Inc 5202 Westland Blvd Baltimore MD 21227-2349

**WHEATON, ROBIN LEE,** lawyer; b. Flint, Mich., July 29, 1948; s. Richard George and Roberta Jean (Schmiedeknecht) W.; m. Barbara Jean Bright, Oct. 18, 1968; children: Shane Matthew, Ashley Sarah, Joshua David. Student, C.S. Mott C.C., Flint, 1971-72; BA, U. Mich., Flint, 1974; JD, U. Detroit, 1977. Bar: Mich. 1978. Pvt. practice Flint, 1980—. Bd. dirs. Am. Heart Assn., Flint, 1988-92. With U.S. Army, 1968-70, Vietnam. Decorated Bronze medal with V device, Purple Heart with oak leaf cluster. Personal injury, Criminal, State civil litigation. Office: 1003 Church St Flint MI 48502-1011

**WHEELAN, R(ICHELIEU) E(DWARD),** lawyer; b. N.Y.C., July 10, 1945; s. Richard Fairfax and Margaret (Murray) W. BS, Springfield (Mass.) Coll., 1967; MS, Iona Coll., 1977; JD, Pace U., 1981. Bar: N.Y. 1982, Minn. 1983, Colo. 1989, Tex. 1990, U.S. Dist. Ct. (no dist.) Calif. 1982, (so. dist.) Tex. 1991, U.S. Internat. Trade 1982, U.S. Ct. Appeals (2d cir.) 1982, (9th cir.) 1983, (5th cir.) 1993, U.S. Supreme Ct. 1994, U.S. Tax Ct. 1998; bd. cert. criminal law, trial advocacy. Lt. of detectives White Plains (N.Y.) Police Dept., 1969-81; area counsel IBM, Armonk, N.Y., 1981-89; gen. counsel Kroll Assocs. (Asia), Hong Kong, 1989-91; pvt. practice, Houston, 1991—. Mem. ABA (mem. sentencing guidelines com.), Nat. Assn. Criminal Def. Lawyers (life mem., mem. death penalty com., champion adv. bd.), Coll. of State Bar Tex., Pro Bono Coll. StateBar Tex., Tex. Assn. Criminal Def. Lawyers. Criminal, Personal income taxation. Office: 440 Louisiana St Houston TX 77002-1639

**WHEELER, EDD DUDLEY,** lawyer; b. Macon, Ga., July 19, 1940; m. Frances Schnelker Rouhslange, Feb. 12, 1974; children: Diana Kaye, Catherine Anne, Emily Clare. BS, USAF Acad., 1962; MPA, U. Okla., 1968; PhD, Emory U., 1971; JD, Am. U., 1979. Bar: Ga. 1979, U.S. Dist. Ct. (no. dist.) Ga., U.S. Supreme Ct. 1991. Pvt. practice Macon, 1979-83; assoc. dir. Law & Econs. Ctr. Emory U., Atlanta, 1983-84; pvt. practice Tucker, Ga., 1984-91; commd. 2d lt. USAF, 1962, advanced through grades to lt. col., 1976, ret., 1978; spl. asst. atty. gen. Ga. Atty. Gen. Office, Atlanta, 1987-88; pres. Cronus, Inc., Atlanta, 1989-91; fed. adminstrv. law judge, 1991—. Author: From Games of God to Bubba's Field: A Century of the Modern Olympic Games, 1995, The Knot which Is Great within Us: Poems on Life, Law, and Other Imperfections, 1997. County commr. Bibb County Bd. of Commrs., Macon, 1980-82. Fellow Ga. Bar Found.; mem. Ga. Bar Assn., Com. on Lawyer Professionalism (reporter 1986-87). Episcopalian. Constitutional, General practice, Alternative dispute resolution. Office: 3598 Midvale Cv Tucker GA 30084-3208

**WHEELER, HAROLD AUSTIN, SR.,** lawyer, former educational administrator; b. Montverde, Fla., Oct. 5, 1925; s. Bureon Kylus and Susan Ella (Bible) W.; m. Myrtle Edna Suggs, Sept. 30, 1949; children—Brenda Lynn, Harold Austin, Stephen Wayne, Donna Kay. B.S.B.A., U. Fla., 1950; M.Ed., Fla. Atlantic U., 1970; J.D., U. Miami (Fla.), 1973, LL.M., 1977. C.P.A., Fla.; bar: Fla. 1973. Auditor to supr. auditor Fla. State Auditing Dept., 1950-62; asst. supt. fin. and acctg. Palm Beach County, Fla. Pub. Schs., 1962-65; dir. fin., treas. Fla. Pub. Schs., Dade County, 1966-81. Mem. AICPA, Fla. Inst. CPA, Fla. Bar Assn., Assn. Sch. Bus. Ofcls. of U.S. and Can., Kiwanis (life mem.). Democrat. Baptist. Administrative and regulatory, Taxation, general, Real property. Home: 6695 SW 112th St Miami FL 33156-4856

**WHEELER, JAMES JULIAN,** lawyer; b. Independence, Mo., Mar. 20, 1921; s. Luther I. and Edith (Hesler) W.; m. Janet L. Esau, Apr. 28, 1951; children: Linnell Gretzinger, Robert W. LLB, U. Mo., 1948. Bar: Mo. 1948, U.S. Dist. Ct. (ea. dist.) Mo. 1956. Prosecuting atty. County of Chariton, Mo., 1950-54, probate judge, 1974-75; circuit judge 9th Judicial Circuit Court, Mo., 1976-82; sole practice Keytesville, Mo., 1948-74, 82—. Served as cpl. USMC, 1941-46, PTO. Mem. ABA, Mo. Bar Assn., Am. Judicature Soc., Assn. Trial Lawyers Am. Democrat. General practice, Criminal, State civil litigation. Home: 112 Kennedy Ave Keytesville MO 65261 Office: 304 Walnut St Keytesville MO 65261-1064

**WHEELER, JOHN WATSON,** lawyer; b. Murfreesboro, Tenn., Sept. 11, 1938; s. James William and Grace (Fann) W.; m. Dorothy Anita Pressgrove, Aug. 5, 1959; children: Jeffrey William, John Harold. BS in Journalism, U. Tenn., 1960, JD, 1968. Bar: Tenn. 1968, U.S. Dist. Ct. (ea. dist.) Tenn. 1968, U.S. Supreme Ct. 1974, U.S. Ct. Appeals (6th cir.) 1975. Editor The Covington (Tenn.) Leader, 1963-65; adminstrv. asst. to lab. dir. UT-AEC Rsch. Lab., Oak Ridge, Tenn., 1965-68; assoc. Hodges, Doughty & Carson, Knoxville, Tenn., 1968-72; ptnr. Hodges, Doughty & Carson, Knoxville, 1972—; mem. commn. to study Applellate Cts. in Tenn.; chair U.S. Magistrate Merit Selection Panel, Ea. Dist., Tenn., 1991; mem. Bankruptcy Judge Merit Selection Panel, Ea. Dist. Tenn., 1992-94; chmn. Hist. Soc., U.S. Dist. Ct. (ea. dist.) Tenn. Mem. organizing com. Tenn. Supreme Ct. Hist. Soc. Lt. U.S. Army, 1961-63, capt. Res. Fellow Am. Bar Found. (life), Tenn. Bar Found.; mem. ABA (ho. of dels. 1986—), Tenn. Bar Assn. (pres. 1989-90, bd. govs. 1981-91), Nat. Conf. Bar Pres., Am. Inns. of Ct. (master of bench), Internat. Assn. Def. Counsel, So. Conf. Bar Pres., Fox Den Country Club. Republican. Lutheran. Avocations: golf, travel. General civil litigation, Insurance, Workers' compensation. Home: 12009 N Fox Den Dr Knoxville TN 37922-2540 Office: Hodges Doughty & Carson PO Box 869 Knoxville TN 37901-0869

**WHEELER, KAREN HANNAH,** lawyer; b. Denver, June 14, 1962; d. Stanley L. and Betty. M. Hannah; m. Eric W. Wheeler, Aug. 4, 1989; children: Eric John, Andrew Jordan, William Joseph. BA, Colo. State U., 1984; JD, U. Neb., 1987. Bar: Colo. 1987, U.S. Dist. Ct. Colo. 1987, U.S. Ct. Appeals (10th cir.) 1987. Assoc. Hall & Evans, Denver, 1987-90; shareholder Levy & Lambdin, P.C., Englewood, Colo., 1990—. Mem. ABA, Colo. Bar Assn. Avocations: running, golf, writing. General civil litigation, Environmental, Personal injury. Office: Levy and Lambdin PC 6400 Fiddlers Green Pkwy Ste 900 Englewood CO 80111-2739

**WHEELER, MALCOLM EDWARD,** lawyer, law educator; b. Berkeley, Calif., Nov. 29, 1944; s. Malcolm Ross and Frances Dolores (Kane) W.; m. Donna Marie Stambaugh, July 21, 1981; children: Jessica Ross, M. Connor. SB, MIT, 1966; JD, Stanford U., 1969. Bar: Calif. 1970, Colo. 1992, U.S. Dist. Ct (cen. dist.) Calif. 1970, U.S. Ct. Appeals (9th cir.) 1970, U.S. Ct. Appeals (10th cir.) 1973, U.S. Dist. Ct. (no., so., ea. and cen. dists.) Calif. 1975, U.S. Ct. Appeals (11th cir.) 1987, U.S. Ct. Appeals (D.C. cir.) 1987, U.S. Supreme Ct. 1976, U.S. Ct. Appeals (3d cir.) 1989, (4th cir.) 1992, (8th cir.) 1993, (5th cir.) 1995, (Fed. cir.) 1998. Assoc. Howard, Prim, Smith, Rice & Downs, San Francisco, 1969-71; assoc. prof. law U. Kans., Lawrence, 1971-74; assoc. Hughes Hubbard & Reed, Los Angeles, 1974-77, ptnr., 1977-81, 83-85, cons., 1981-83; ptnr. Skadden, Arps, Slate, Meagher & Flom, Los Angeles, 1985-91; dir. Parcel, Mauro, Hultin & Spaanstra P.C., Denver, 1991-98, Wheeler Trigg & Kennedy, P.C., Denver, 1998—; vis. prof. U. Iowa, 1978, prof., 1979; prof. U. Kans., Lawrence, 1981-83; chief counsel U.S. Senate Select Com. to Study Law Enforcement Undercover Activities, Washington, 1982-83. Mem. editorial bd. Jour. Products Liability, 1984—; bd. editors Fed. Litigation Guide Reporter, 1986—; contbr. articles to profl. jours. Mem. ABA, Calif. Bar Assn., Colo. Bar Assn., Am. Law Inst. Federal civil litigation, General civil litigation, Product liability. Home: 100 Humboldt St Denver CO 80218-3932

**WHEELER, MARK ANDREW, SR.,** lawyer; b. Pitts., Feb. 14, 1963; s. Andrew Mate Wheeler and Anna Ruth (Whitfield) W.; m. Darla Jo Fusselman, May 10, 1993; children: Mark Andrew Jr., Lauren Anna, Layne Allison, Livia Arden. BA in Philosophy, Hampden-Sydney Coll., 1985; JD, W.Va. U., 1991. Bar: Pa. 1992, U.S. Dist. Ct. (we. dist.) Pa. 1993; ordained to ministry Lighthouse Ch., 1997. Staff litigator W.Va. U. Coll. Law Legal Clinic, Morgantown, 1991-92; jud. clk. Mahoning County, Youngstown, Ohio, 1991-92; pvt. practice Reynoldsville, Pa., 1993—, Clarion, Pa., 1994—; legal cons. S.T. & E., Inc., Punxsutawney, Pa., 1993—, Jefferson County Gun Owners Assn., Brookville, Pa., 1994—, Crimestoppers of Jefferson County, Brookville, 1993-94, Five Star Homes, Inc., 1995-97, Bembeng Cons., Inc., 1994—. Bd. dirs. Reynoldsville Area Indsl. Bd., 1993-96; mem. exec. dist. com. Boy Scouts Am., Dubois, Pa., 1993—; bd. dirs. Reynoldsville Pub. Libr. Assn., 1993-96; mem. Dubois Christian and Missionary Alliance Ch., mem. choir, 1995—. Mem. ABA, ATLA, Internat. Platform Assn., Pa. Bar Assn. (young lawyers divsn., chair zone 7), Am. Ctr. for Law and Justice, Pa. Trial Lawyers Assn., Pa. Assn. Notaries, Jefferson County Bar Assn., Western Pa. Trial Lawyers Assn., Clarion County Bar Assn., Nat. Eagle Scout Assn. Republican. Avocations: songwriting, public speaking, home renovation, car restoration. General civil litigation, Criminal, Family and matrimonial. Office: PO Box 176 512 Main St Reynoldsville PA 15851-1335 also: PO Box 770 Clarion PA 16214-0770

**WHEELER, V.M., III,** lawyer; b. New Orleans, Apr. 26, 1958; s. Virgil M. Jr. and Gloria Ann (DeGruy) W. BBA, Loyola U., New Orleans, 1978; MBA, So. Meth. U., 1979; JD, Tulane U., 1984. Bar: La. 1984, U.S. Dist. Ct. (ea. dist.) La. 1984, U.S. Ct. Appeals (5th cir.) 1984, U.S. Supreme Ct. 1993. Assoc., corp. fin. dept. Howard Weil Labouisse Friedrichs, Inc., New Orleans, 1982-83, asst. v.p., 1983-84; assoc. Jones, Walker, Waechter, Poitevent, Carrere & Denegre, New Orleans, 1984-86; v.p. corp. fin. dept. Shearson Lehman Hutton Inc., N.Y.C. and Dallas, 1986-90; v.p. Kidder, Peabody & Co., Inc., N.Y.C., Houston, 1990-91; mng. dir. corp. fin. group Price Waterhouse, Houston, 1991-92; dir. corp. fin. group Nationsbanc Capital Markets, Inc., Houston, 1992-94; with investment banking group Cain Bros. & Co., Houston, 1994-97; ptnr. Kendrick & Wheeler, L.L.P., New Orleans, 1995—; bd. dirs. Cucos Inc. Contbr. articles to profl. jours. Mem. LaPlace (La.) Drainage Dist., 1995—; mem. citizens task force Jefferson Parish Hosp. Svc. Dist., 1997-98; mem. Gov.'s Econ. Devel. Commn., State of La., 1986; mem. adv. bd. Assoc. Cath. Charities Adult Group Homes, 1982-83; bd. dirs. Bright Sch., 1983-86, 95—; mem. pub. advocacy com. New Orleans com. Nat. Alzheimer's Assn., 1995. Mem. ABA, La. Bar Assn., New Orleans Bar Assn., Blue Key, Beta Gamma Sigma. Beta Alpha Psi. Democrat. Roman Catholic. Avocations: golf, skiing, flying, tennis. Finance, Real property, State civil litigation. Home: 210 Hector Ave Metairie LA 70005-4118 Office: Kendrick & Wheeler LLP 203 Carondelet St Ste 200 New Orleans LA 70130-3011

**WHELPLEY, DAVID B., JR.,** lawyer; b. Akron, Ohio, Apr. 21, 1964; s. David B. and JoAnn D. W.; m. Teresa E. Dugger, Oct. 21, 1989; m. David III, Austin, Hannah. BS cum laude, Clemson U., 1986; JD, Emory U., 1989. Bar: N.C. 1989, Ga. 1989. Ptnr. Kilpatrick Stockton LLP, Charlotte, N.C., 1989—; adv. Legal Svcs. N.C., Raleigh, 1997-98. Mem. exec. bd. Theatre Charlotte, 1995-99; bd. dirs. Mecklenburg County Register Deeds Adv. Bd., 1995-98, Mecklenburg County Transp. Plan Adv. Bd., 1998-99. Mem. ABA (mem. com.), N.C. Bar Assn. (mem. com.). Avocations: traveling, skiing, hiking. Contracts commercial, Finance, Mergers and acquisitions. Office: Kilpatrick Stockton LLP 3500 One First Union Ctr 301 S College St Charlotte NC 28202-6000

**WHICHARD, WILLIS PADGETT,** law educator, former state supreme court justice; b. Durham, N.C., May 24, 1940; s. Willis Guilford and Beulah (Padgett) W.; m. Leona Irene Paschal, June 4, 1961; children: Jennifer Diane, Ida Gilbert. AB, U. N.C., 1962, JD, 1965; LLM, U. Va., 1984, SJD, 1994. Bar: N.C. 1965. Law clk. N.C. Supreme Ct., Raleigh, 1965-66; ptnr. Powe, Porter, Alphin & Whichard, Durham, 1966-80; assoc. judge N.C. Ct. Appeals, Raleigh, 1980-86; assoc. justice N.C. Supreme Ct., Raleigh, 1986-98; dean and prof. law Campbell U.; instr. grad. sch. bus. adminstrn. Duke U., 1978; vis. lectr. U. N.C. Sch. Law, 1986-98. Contbr. articles to profl. jours. Rep. N.C. Ho. of Reps., Raleigh, 1970-74; senator N.C. Senate, 1974-80, chair numerous coms. and commns.; N.C. legis. rsch. commn., 1971-73, 75-77, land policy coun., 1975-79; bd. dirs. Sr. Citizens Coordinating Coun., 1972-74; chair local crusade Am. Cancer Soc., 1977, state crusade chair, 1980, chair pub. issues com., 1980-84; pres., bd. chmn. Downtown Durham Devel. Corp., 1980-84; bd. dirs. Durham County chpt. ARC, 1971-79; Durham county campaign dir. March of Dimes, 1968, 69, chmn., 1969-74, bd. dirs. Triangle chpt., 1974-79; bd. advisors Duke Hosp., 1982-85, U. N.C. Sch. Pub. Health, 1985-96, U. N.C. Sch. Social Work, 1989—; bd. visitors N.C. Ctrl. U. Sch. Law, 1987—; mem. law sch. dean search com. U. N.C., 1978-79, 88-89, self-study com., 1985-86; pres. N.C. Inst. Justice, 1984-94; bd. dirs. N.C. Ctr. Crime and Punishment, 1984-94. Staff sgt. N.C. Army NG, 1966-72. Recipient Disting. Service award Durham Jaycees, 1971, Outstanding Legis. award N.C. Acad. Trial Lawyers, 1975, Outstanding Youth Service award N.C. Juvenile Correctional Assn., 1975, Citizen of Yr., Eno Valley Civitan Club, Durham, 1982, Faith Active in Pub. Life award N.C. Council of Churches, 1983, Outstanding Appellate Judge award N.C. Acad. Trial Lawyers, 1983, inducted Durham High Sch. Hall of Fame, 1987. Mem. ABA, N.C. Bar Assn. (v.p. 1983-84), Durham County Bar Assn., U. N.C. Law Alumni Assn. (pres. 1978-79, bd. dirs. 1979-82), Nat. Guard Assn. (judge advocate 1972-73, legis. com. 1974-76), Order of Golden Fleece, Order of Grail, Order of Old Well, Amphoterothen Soc., Order of Coif, Phi Alpha Theta, Phi Kappa Alpha. Democrat. Baptist. Clubs: Durham-Chapel Hill Torch (pres. 1984-85), Watauga (Raleigh, pres. 1994-95). Home: 5608 Woodberry Rd Durham NC 27707-5335 Office: Wiggins Sch Law Campbell Univ PO Box 158 Buies Creek NC 27506-0158

**WHINSTON, STEPHEN ALAN,** lawyer; b. Stamford, Conn., Mar. 27, 1948; s. Alfred Leonard and Rose (Eisgrau) W.; m. Joan Lenett, June 4, 1978; children: Stephanie Portnoy, Brian Arasim, Joshua. BA, Colgate U., 1970; JD, Case Western Res. U., 1973. Bar: Pa. 1973, U.S. Dist. Ct. (ea. dist.) Pa. 1973, U.S. Ct. Appeals (3d cir.) 1973, U.S. Ct. Appeals (8th cir.) 1995. Trial atty. U.S. Dept. Justice, Washington, 1974-79, sr. trial atty., 1979-83; atty. Berger & Montague, P.C., Phila., 1983-85, shareholder, 1986—. Bd. dirs. Disabilities Law Project, Phila., 1989—, Jewish Fedn. Housing, Inc., Cherry Hill, N.J., 1994-96. Mem. Pa. Prison Soc. (bd. dirs.). Avocation: music. Securities, Civil rights, General civil litigation. Office: Berger & Montague PC 1622 Locust St Philadelphia PA 19103-6305

**WHIPKEY, LISA J.,** lawyer; b. Greensburg, Pa., Feb. 9, 1970; d. Larry R. and Mardi K. Whipkey. BA in History, SUNY, Geneseo, 1992; JD, Pa. State U., Carlisle, 1995. Bar: Pa. 1996, N.J. 1996, U.S. Dist. Ct. N.J. 1996. Assoc. Kummer, Knox, Naughton & Hansbury, Parsippany, N.J., 1996—. Vol. Big Bros./Big Sisters Morris County, N.J., 1998—. Mem. ABA, N.J. State Bar Assn., Pa. Bar Assn., Morris County Bar Assn., Worrall F. Mountain Inn of Ct., Phi Alpha Theta, Delta Theta Phi. General civil litigation, Environmental, Land use and zoning (including planning). Office: Kummer Knox Naughton & Hansbury 299 Cherry Hill Rd Parsippany NJ 07054-1111

**WHIPPLE, DEAN,** federal judge; b. 1938. BS, Drury Coll., 1961; postgrad., U. Tulsa, 1961-62; JD, U. Mo., Kansas City, 1965, postgrad., 1965. Pvt. practice Lebanon, Mo., 1965-75; cir. judge div. II 26th Jud. Cir. Mo., 1975-87; dist. judge U.S. Dist. Ct., Kansas City, Mo., 1987—; prosecuting atty. Laclede County, Mo., 1967-71. Mem. Cen. United Meth. Ch., Kansas City. With Mo. N.G., 1956-61; USAR, 1961-66. Mem. Mo. Bar Assn. (mem. pub. info. com. 1971-72, mem. judiciary com. 1971-72, mem. bd. govs. 1975-87, mem. exec. com. 1983-84, 86-87, mem. planning com. for ann. meeting 1985, 87, chmn. 1986, mem. selection com. for Lon Hocker award 1986), Mo. Trial Judges Assn., 26th Jud. Bar Assn., Laclede County Bar Assn. (pres. 1968-69, 72-73), Kansas City Met. Bar Assn., Kansas City Inn of Ct. (instr. 1988-93), Mo. Hist. Soc., Phi Delta Phi. Office: US Courthouse 400 E 9th St Kansas City MO 64106-2607

**WHIPPS, EDWARD FRANKLIN,** lawyer; b. Columbus, Ohio, Dec. 17, 1936; s. Rusk Henry and Agnes Lucille (Green) W.; children: Edward Scott, Rusk Huot, Sylvia Louise, Rudyard Christian. B.A., Ohio Wesleyan U., 1958; J.D., Ohio State U., 1961. Bar: Ohio 1961, U.S. Dist. Ct. (so. dist.) Ohio 1962, U.S. Dist. Ct. (no. dist.) Ohio 1964, U.S. Ct. Claims 1963, U.S. Supreme Ct. 1963, Miss. 1965, U.S. Ct. Appeals (6th cir.) 1980. Assoc. George, Greek, King & McMahon, Columbus, 1961-66; ptnr. George, Greek, King, McMahon & McConnaughey, Columbus, 1966-79, McConnaughey, Stradley, Mone & Moul, Columbus, 1979-81, Thompson, Hine & Flory, Columbus, 1981-93; prin. Edward F. Whipps & Assocs., Columbus, 1993-94; ptnr. Whipps & Wistner, Columbus, 1995—; founder, trustee Creative Living, Inc., 1969—; trustee, v.p. Unverferth House, Inc., 1989; trustee Eagle Scholarship Trust. Host: TV programs Upper Arlington Plain Talk, 1979-82; TV program Bridging Disability, 1981-82, Lawyers on Call, 1982—, U.A. Today, 1982-86, The Ohio Wesleyan Experience, 1984—. Mem. Ohio Bd. Psychology, 1992—; mem. Upper Arlington (Ohio) Bd. Edn., 1971-80, pres., 1978-79; mem. bd. alumni dirs. Ohio Wesleyan U., 1975-79; trustee Walden Ravines Assn., 1992-96, pres. 1993-96. Mem. ABA, Columbus Bar Assn., Ohio State Bar Assn., Assn. Trial Lawyers Am., Ohio Acad. Trial Lawyers, Franklin County Trial Lawyers Assn., Am. Judicature Soc., Columbus Bar Found., Ohio Bd. Pscyhology, Columbus C. of C., Upper Arlington Area C. of C. (trustee 1978—), Lawyers Club, Barrister Club, Columbus Athletic Club, Nat. Football Found. & Hall of Fame, Columbus Touchdown Club, Downtown Quarterback Club, Ohio State U. Faculty (Columbus) Club, Ohio State U. Golf Club, Highlands Country Club, Delta Tau Delta (nat. v.p. 1976-78). Republican. Federal civil litigation, State civil litigation, Family and matrimonial. Home: 472 Green Hollow Rd SW Pataskala OH 43062-9706 Office: Whipps & Wistner 500 S Front St Columbus OH 43215-7619 *Personal philosophy: Commitment to personal growth, the development of interpersonal relationships, the rule of law and a firm belief in the unique value of every individual in a holographic universe are the primary factors seen in my approach to life.*

**WHITAKER, GARRY BRUCE,** lawyer; b. Murfreesboro, N.C., Apr. 20, 1959. BA in Politics, Wake Forest U., 1980, JD, 1983. Bar: N.C., U.S. Dist. Ct. (middle dist.) N.C. Assoc. Martin & Van Hoy, Mocksville, N.C., 1983-85; ptnr. Powell & Whitaker, Winston Salem, N.C., 1985-91, Crawford & Whitaker, Winston Salem, 1991-95; prin. Garry Whitaker, P.C, Winston Salem, 1995—; legal counsel N.C. Eye Bank, Winston-Salem, 1998. Past pres. Winston-Salem Jr. C. of C.; mem. class of '97, Leadership Winston=Salem, 1996-97. Mem. ATLA, N.C. Acad. Trial Lawyers, N.C. Bar Assn. Office: 1 N Marshall St Ste 350 Winston Salem NC 27101-2847

**WHITAKER, GLENN VIRGIL,** lawyer; b. Cin., July 23, 1947; s. Glenn M. and Doris (Handlon) W.; m. Jennifer Lynn Angus, Oct. 22, 1990. BA, Denison U., 1969; JD, George Washington U., 1972. Bar: Md. 1972, D.C. 1973, Ohio 1980. Law clk. to judge U.S. Dist. Ct., Balt., 1972-73; assoc. O'Donoghue and O'Donoghue, Washington, 1973-76; trial atty. civil div. U.S. Dept. Justice, Washington, 1976-78, spl. litigation counsel, 1978-80; ptnr. Graydon, Head & Ritchey, Cin., 1980-92, Voyrs, Sater, Seymour & Pease, Cin., 1992—; emeritus master of bench Potter Stewart Inn of Ct., Cin., 1985—; adj. prof. law Coll. Law U. Cin.; mem. Am. Bd. Trial Advocates. Fellow Am. Coll. Trial Lawyers; mem. ABA, ATLA, Ohio Bar Assn., D.C. Bar Assn., Md. Bar Assn., Cin. Bar Assn. Avocations: hiking, exploring. General civil litigation, Criminal, Personal injury. Office: Vorys Sater Seymour & Pease 221 E 4th St Ste 2100 Cincinnati OH 45202-5133

**WHITAKER, MARY FERNAN,** lawyer; b. Kansas City, Mo., May 29, 1958; d. James Paul and Mildred Louise (Connor) Fernan; m. Mark Dwight Whitaker, May 28, 1983; children: Paul Connor, James Sullivan, Helen Foster. BSN, George Mason U., 1982, JD, 1987. Bar: Va. 1987, Pa. 1995; cert. swim coach, Md. cert. swim judge. Nurse George Washington Med. Ctr., Washington, 1980-82, Mt. Vernon Hosp., Alexandria, Va., 1982-84; atty. Legal Svcs. No. Va., Arlington, 1987, Office Rev. and Appeals, EEOC, Falls Church, Va., 1987-88; pvt. practice Annadale, Va., 1988-93, Pottsville, Pa., 1993-95, Coopersburg, Pa., 1995-96, Solomons, Md., 1996—; adj. faculty paralegal program No. Va. C.C., 1992; counselor, mem. legal com. My Sister's Pl., Washington, 1987-93; mem. pro bono panel Legal Svcs. No. Va., Falls Church, 1997—. Vol. ARC, Alexandria, 1987; vol. atty. Women's Legal Def. Fund, Washington, 1989-91, Legal Svcs. No. Va., 1997—; mem. Shelter Outreach Program, 1990-93; v.p. Ravensworth Bristow Civic assn., 1990-93; head makeup design for cmty. theatre troupe Camelot Players, 1990-91; tchr. 3d grade religious edn. St. Michael's Ch. Choir, 1991-92, tchr. 8th grade religious edn., 1992-93, choir, 1992-93; tchr. 7th grade religious edn. St. Joseph Ch., 1995-96; swimmer U.S. Masters, 1997, 98; cert. stroke and turn judge Md. Swimming, 1998—. U.S. Master Swimmer, 1997-98. Mem. Va. State Bar Assn., Fairfax Bar Assn., Phi Delta Phi. Roman Catholic. Avocations: bicycling, swimming. Office: PO Box 881 Solomons MD 20688-0881

**WHITAKER, RONALD STEPHEN,** lawyer; b. Cleve., Oct. 26, 1957; s. Wilbert S. and Dolores J. Whitaker; m. Carolyn M. Conyers, Sept. 29, 1984; children: Christopher, Chelsea. BA, UCLA, 1980, JD, 1983. Bar: Calif. 1983, U.S. Dist. Ct. (cen. dist.) Calif., 1983, U.S. Dist. Ct. (so. dist.) Calif., 1984, U.S. Dist. Ct. (ea. dist.) Calif., 1993, U.S. Ct. Appeals (9th cir.) 1983. Assoc. Ritter, Winne & Rodriguez, L.A., 1983-86; assoc. Spray, Gould & Bowers, L.A., 1986-88, prin., 1988-91; shareholder, founding mem. Robinson, Dilando & Whitaker, L.A., 1991—. Mem. ABA, Am. Bd. Trial Advocates, Def. Rsch. Inst., L.A. County Bar Assn., Nat. Bar Assn., John M. Langston Bar Assn. Republican. Avocations: basketball, softball. Insurance, Labor, General civil litigation. Office: Robinson Dilando & Whitaker 800 Wilshire Blvd Ste 1100 Los Angeles CA 90017-2615

**WHITBECK, JILL KARLA,** lawyer; b. Bangkok, Jan. 17, 1968; d. Joseph Kern Walter and Ruth Ann Tucker; m. Christopher Lee Whitbeck, July 20, 1991; children: Jasmine Claire, Donald Joseph. BA, Calif. Luth. U., 1990; JD, Pepperdine U. Sch. Law, 1993. Bar: Nev. 1993, U.S. Dist. Ct. Nev. 1994. Atty. Laxalt & Nomura, Reno, 1993-94, Edward M. Bernstein & Assocs., Reno, 1994-97, Law Offices of White & Meany, Reno, 1997—. Deaconess, sch. bd. New Beginnings Child Devel. Ctr., Washoe Valley, Nev., 1998. Mem. ABA, ATLA, Nev. Trial Lawyers Assn., No. Nev. Women Lawyers Assn., Nev. State Bar Assn., Washoe County Bar Assn. Republican. Mem. Christian Ch. Product liability, Toxic tort, Personal injury. Office: Law Offices of White & Meany 3185 Lakeside Dr Reno NV 89509-4503

**WHITE, BENJAMIN BALLARD, JR.,** lawyer; b. Princeton, W.Va., Mar. 19, 1927; s. Benjamin Ballard and Zylpha Katherine (Karnes) W.; m. Gloria Lee Jones, Nov. 7, 1947 (dec. 1958); 1 child, Benjamin Ballard III; m. Wanda Ann Bowling, Sept. 2, 1959; children: Leigh Anne, Leonard Elbert. JD, Washington & Lee U., 1951. Bar: W.Va. 1951, U.S. Ct. Appeals (4th cir.) W.Va. 1956. Pvt. practice Princeton, 1951, 53-55; jr. ptnr. Ross & White, Bluefield, W.Va., 1952, Sanders & White, Princeton, 1956-60; pvt. practice Whites' Law Offices, Princeton, 1961-80; sr. ptnr. White & Ambrose, Princeton, 1981-83, Whites' Law Offices, Princeton, 1983—; v.p. New River Investments, Princeton, 1977—. Pres. Princeton Police Civil Svc. Commr., 1967-81. With U.S. Army, 1945-46. Mem. W.Va. State Bar, W.Va. Bar Assn., Mercer County Bar Assn. (pres. 1971), Def. Rsch. Inst., Internat. Assn. Def. Counsel, Elks, Moose. Republican. Presbyterian. Insurance, General civil litigation, Personal injury. Office: Whites' Law Offices 1426 E Main St Princeton WV 24740-3064

**WHITE, BYRON R.,** former United States supreme court justice; b. Ft. Collins, Colo., June 8, 1917; m. Marion Stearns; children: Charles, Nancy. Grad., U. Colo., 1938; Rhodes scholar, Oxford (Eng.) U.; grad., Yale Law Sch. Clk. to chief justice U.S., 1946-47; atty. firm Lewis, Grant & Davis, Denver, 1947-60; dep. atty. gen. U.S., 1961-62; assoc. justice Supreme Ct., U.S., 1962-93; ret., 1993. Served with USNR, World War II, Pacific. Mem. Phi Beta Kappa, Phi Gamma Delta, Order of Coif. Address: US Supreme Ct Supreme Ct Bldg 1 First St NE Washington DC 20543-0001

**WHITE, C. THOMAS,** state supreme court justice; b. Humphrey, Nebr., Oct. 5, 1928; s. John Ambrose and Margaret Elizabeth (Costello) W.; m. Joan White, Oct. 9, 1971; children: Michaela, Thomas, Patrick. JD, Creighton U., 1952. Bar: Nebr. County atty. Platte County (Nebr.), Columbus, 1955-65; judge 21st Dist. Ct. Nebr., Columbus, 1965-77; justice Nebr. Supreme Ct., Lincoln, 1977—, chief justice, 1995—. Served with U.S. Army, 1946-47. Roman Catholic. Clubs: Elks, KC. Office: Nebr Supreme Ct 2215 State Capitol Lincoln NE 68509

**WHITE, DANIEL BOWMAN,** lawyer; b. Charlotte, N.C., Apr. 12, 1948; s. William Garner and Elizabeth (Bowman) W.; m. Sarah de Saussure Peterson, May 29, 1976; children: Bentley Parker, Sarah de Saussure. AB, Davidson Coll., 1970; JD, U. S.C., 1976. Bar: S.C. 1976, U.S. Dist. Ct. S.C. 1976, U.S. Ct. Appeals (4th cir.) 1978, U.S. Ct. Appeals (fed. cir.) 1990. Ptnr. Gibbes, Gallivan, White & Boyd P.A., Greenville, S.C., 1976—. Comments editor U. S.C. Law Rev., 1975-76. Commr. Greenville Zoning Commn., 1980-85; mem. Supreme Ct. Bd. Commrs. on Grievances and Discipline, 1988-91. 1st lt. U.S. Army, 1971-73. Decorated Bronze Star; Dana scholar Davidson Coll., N.C., 1966-70. Mem. S.C. Bar (ho. dels. 1986—, bd. govs. 1992-95), Def. Rsch. Inst., Nat. Assn. R.R. Trial Counsel, Greenville Young Lawyers Club (pres. 1981), Fed. Cir. Jud. Conf., Internat. Assn. Def. Counsel. Episcopalian. Federal civil litigation, State civil litigation, Environmental. Home: 24 Sirrine Dr Greenville SC 29605-1137 Office: Gibbes Gallivan White & Boyd PA 330 E Coffee St Greenville SC 29601-2804

**WHITE, DEBORAH SUE YOUNGBLOOD,** lawyer; b. Fairview, Okla., July 29, 1954; d. G. Dean and Beatrice J. (Hiebert) White. BS with honors, Okla. State U., 1976, MA with honors, 1979; JD cum laude, Boston Coll. Law Sch., 1991; MPH in Health Care Mgmt., Harvard U., 1992. Bar: Colo., N.Mex., U.S. Ct. Appeals (10th cir.). Judicial law clk. Colo. Supreme Ct., 1992-94; assoc. atty. Patton Boggs, L.L.P., Denver, 1994-97, Vaglica & Meinhold, Colorado Springs, 1997—. Mem. ABA, Colo. Bar Assn., N.Mex. Bar Assn., Minoru Yasui Am. Inns of Ct. (exec. coun. 1995-97), Phi Kappa Phi. Avocation: travel. Administrative and regulatory, General civil litigation. Office: Vaglica & Meinhold 105 E Moreno Ave Ste 1oo Colorado Springs CO 80903-3933

**WHITE, EDITH JEAN,** lawyer; b. Orange, Tex., Oct. 19, 1945. BA, U. Minn., 1967; JD, U. San Diego, 1979. Bar: Calif. 1979, U.S. Dist. Ct. (so. dist.) Calif. 1979. Pvt. practice San Diego, 1979—. Bd. dirs. Assn. for Cmty. Housing Solutions, San Diego, 1993— (pres. 1997), San Diego Alliance for the Mentally Ill, 1992—; mem. adv. bd. Psychiat. Emergency Response Team, San Diego, 1993-97. Avocations: travel, writing, photography, scuba diving. Estate planning, Labor. Office: 3232 4th Ave San Diego CA 92103-5702

**WHITE, EDWARD ALFRED,** lawyer; b. Elizabeth, N.J., Nov. 23, 1934. BS in Indsl. Engring., U. Mich., 1957, JD, 1963. Bar: Fla. 1963, U.S. Ct. Appeals (5th cir.) 1971, U.S. Supreme Ct. 1976, U.S. Ct. Appeals (11th cir.) 1981. Assoc. Jennings, Watts, Clarke & Hamilton, Jacksonville, Fla., 1963-66, ptnr., 1966-69; ptnr. Wayman & White, Jacksonville, 1969-72; pvt. practice, Jacksonville, 1972—; mem. aviation law com. Fla. Bar, 1972-94, chmn., 1979-81, bd. govs., 1984-88, admiralty com., 1984—, chmn., 1990-91, chmn. pub. relations com., 1986-88, exec. coun. trial lawyers sect., 1986-91, chmn. admiralty cert. com., 1995-97. Fellow Am. Bar Found.; mem. ABA (vice chmn. admiralty law com. 1995—), Fla. Bar Assn. (bd. cert. civil trial lawyer, bd. cert. admiralty lawyer), Jacksonville Bar Assn. (chmn. legal ethics com. 1975-76, bd. govs. 1976-78, pres. 1979-80), Assn. Trial Lawyers Am. (sustaining mem. 1984—), Acad. Fla. Trial Lawyers (diplomate), Fla. Coun. Bar Assn. Pres.'s, Lawyer-Pilots Bar Assn., Am. Judicature Soc., Maritime Law Assn. (proctor in admiralty), Southeastern Admiralty Law Inst. (bd. dirs. 1982-84, chmn./pres. 1994). Fax: 904-356-6508. Personal injury, Admiralty, General civil litigation. Home: 1959 Largo Rd Jacksonville FL 32207-3926 Office: 601 Blackstone Bldg 233 E Bay St Jacksonville FL 32202-3452

**WHITE, EDWARD GIBSON, II,** lawyer; b. Lexington, Ky., Nov. 7, 1954; s. Russell Edwin White and Betty Lee White-Estabrook; m. Cynthia Ann Reisz, Mar. 10, 1979; children: Edward Gibson III, William Elliot, John Alexander, Albert Grahm. BA, U. Tenn., Chattanooga, 1980; JD, U. Tenn., Knoxville, 1983. Bar: Tenn. 1983, U.S. Dist. Ct. (ea. dist.) Tenn. 1984, U.S. Ct. Appeals (6th cir.) 1985. Assoc. Hodges, Doughty & Carson, Knoxville, 1983-87, ptnr., 1988—. Pledge vol. Knoxville Mus. Art, 1986—. Mem. ABA (litigation sect. 1985—), Tenn. Bar Assn. (interprofl. code com. 1989—, med./legal com. 1991—), Knoxville Bar Assn. (treas. 1995-96, continuing legal edn. com. 1985-86, 88-91, chmn. 1992-94, mem. naturalization com. 1985-87, bd. govs. 1993-94, pres. elect 1996, pres. 1997, Pres.'s award 1992), Tenn. Def. Lawyers Assn., Def. Rsch. Inst. (med./legal com. 1985—), Am. Bd. Trial Advocates, Knoxville Bar Found., U. Tenn. Pres.'s Club, Univ. Club, Cherokee Country Club. Republican. Avocations: tennis, golf, boating, water sports, bird hunting. General civil litigation, Insurance, Personal injury. Office: Hodges Doughty & Carson 617 Main St # 869 Knoxville TN 37902-2602

**WHITE, F(LOYD) AL,** lawyer; b. Gallipolis, Ohio, Nov. 7, 1944; s. Floyd A. Jr. and Josphine A. (Keefer) W. AA, Kans. Jr. Coll., 1964; BA, U. Mo., 1966; JD, U. Mo., Kansas City, 1972. Bar: Mo. 1972, Kans. 1982, U.S. Dist. Ct. (we. dist.) Mo. 1972, U.S. Dist. Ct. Kans. Pvt. practice Kansas City, Mo., 1998—; 1st asst. pub. defender Clay County, Mo., 1974-76. Editor U. Mo. Law Rev., 1971-72. 1st lt. U.S. Army, 1961-68. Mem. ABA, Nat. Assn. Criminal Def. Lawyers, Mo. Bar Assn., Kans. Bar Assn., Mo. Assn. Criminal Def. Lawyers, Kans. Assn. Criminal Def. Lawyers, Clay County Bar Assn. Baptist. Criminal, Military, General practice. Home: 8 NE 62nd Pl Kansas City MO 64118-4140 Office: 5440 N Oak Kansas City MO 64118-4605

**WHITE, GEORGE W.,** federal judge; b. 1931. Student, Baldwin-Wallace Coll., 1948-51; J.D., Cleveland-Marshall Coll. Law, 1955. Sole practice law Cleve., 1956-68; judge Ct. Common Pleas, Ohio, 1968-80; judge U.S. Dist. Ct. (no. dist.) Ohio, 1980-95, chief judge, 1995—; referee Ct. Common Pleas, Cuyahoga County, 1957-62. Councilman, Cleve., 1963-68. Mem. ABA, Fed. Bar Assn., 6th Circuit Jud. Coun. (exec. com. 1995—). Office: US Dist Ct 300 US Courthouse 201 Superior Ave NE Cleveland OH 44114-1201

**WHITE, GEORGE WENDELL, JR.,** lawyer; b. Washington, Nov. 9, 1915; s. George Wendell and Blanche E. (Berry) W.; m. Elnor L. Musson, Apr. 5, 1940; children: Randall C., Wendy Lou Gibson, Cynthia Lee Miller. AB, U. Md., College Park, 1937; LLB, U. Md., Balt., 1939. Bar: Md. 1939. Assoc. Weinberg & Green, Balt., 1940-50; sr. ptnr. White, Miller, Kenny & Vettori, LLP, Towson, Md. Nat. campaign mgr. Nixon-Agnew, 1972, 76. Sgt. U.S. Army, 1942-45. Mem. ABA, Am. Coll. Trial Lawyers, Am. Bd. Trial Advocates, Md. Trial Lawyers Assn. (pres. 1988—), Elks, Optimists, Gamma Eta Gamma (nat. pres. 1939-42). Democrat. Methodist. Federal civil litigation, General civil litigation, Personal injury. Home: 36 S Charles St Baltimore MD 21201-3020 Office: 40 W Chesapeake Ave Ste 300 Baltimore MD 21204-4843

**WHITE, HARRY EDWARD, JR.,** lawyer; b. Menominee, Mich., Apr. 26, 1939; s. Harry Edward and Verena Charlotte (Leisen) W.; m. Mary P.A. Sheaffer, June 7, 1980. BS in Fgn. Svc., Georgetown U., Washington, 1961; LLB, Columbia U., 1964. Bar: N.Y. 1965, U.S. Supreme Ct. 1970, U.S. Dist. Ct. (so. dist.) N.Y. 1979, U.S. Tax Ct. 1980. Assoc. Milbank, Tweed, Hadley & McCloy, N.Y.C., 1964-65, 67-73, ptnr., 1974—. Contbr. chpts. to books, articles to legal jours. Served with M.I., U.S. Army, 1965-66, Vietnam. Decorated Bronze Star. Mem. ABA, Internat. Bar Assn., N.Y. State Bar Assn. (chmn. taxation com. internat. law practice sect. 1987-90, co-chmn. exempt orgns. com. tax sect. 1987-88), Internat. Law Assn., Am. Soc. Internat. Law, Assn. Bar of City of N.Y., Internat. Fiscal Assn. Republican. Roman Catholic. Corporate taxation, Taxation, general, Personal income taxation. Home: 333 E 55th St New York NY 10022-8316 Office: Milbank Tweed Hadley & McCloy 1 Chase Manhattan Plz Fl 47 New York NY 10005-1413

**WHITE, HELENE NITA,** federal judge; b. Jackson Heights, N.Y., Dec. 2, 1954; d. Frank William and Ruth (Gruber) W. AB, Columbia U., 1978; JD, U. Pa., 1978. Bar: Pa. 1979, Mich. 1979. Law clk. to justice Mich. Supreme Ct., Southfield, 1978-80; judge Common Pleas Ct., Detroit, 1981, 36th Dist Ct., Detroit, 1981-83, Wayne Cir. Ct., Detroit, 1983-92, Mich. Ct. Appeals, Detroit, 1992—. Bd. dirs., chmn. bylaws com. Met. Detroit YWCA, 1986-87, Coalition Temporary Shelter, 1986—, chmn. nominating com., 1988—; mem. bd. advisors Sojourner Found., 1988.; adv. bd. Detroit Women's Forum, 1988—; program com. Bus. and Profl. Div. of Jewish Welfare Fedn., 1987—. Mem. ABA, Pa. Bar Assn., Detroit Bar Assn., Nat. Assn. Women Judges (chmn. publicity 1984, membership com. 1985—), Women Lawyers Assn. Mich. Jewish.

**WHITE, JAMES BOYD,** law educator; b. Boston, July 28, 1938; s. Benjamin Vroom and Charlotte Green (Conover) W.; m. Mary Louise Fitch, Jan. 1, 1978; children: Emma Lillian, Henry Alfred; children by previous marriage: Catherine Conover, John Southworth. A.B., Amherst Coll., 1960; A.M., Harvard U., 1961, LL.B., 1964. Assoc. Foley, Hoag & Eliot, Boston, 1964-67; asst. prof. law U. Colo., 1967-69, assoc. prof., 1969-73, prof., 1973-75; prof. law U. Chgo., 1975-83; Hart Wright prof. law and English U. Mich., Ann Arbor, 1983—; vis. assoc. prof. Stanford U., 1972. Author: The Legal Imagination, 1973, (with Scarboro) Constitutional Criminal Procedure, 1976, When Words Lose Their Meaning, 1981, Heracles' Bow, 1985, Justice as Translation, 1990, "This Book of Starres", 1994, Acts of Hope, 1994. Sinclair Kennedy Traveling fellow, 1964-65; Nat. Endowment for Humanities fellow, 1979-80, 92; Guggenheim fellow, 1993; vis. scholar Phi Beta Kappa, 1997-98. Mem. AAAS, Am. Law Inst. Office: U Mich Law Sch 625 S State St Ann Arbor MI 48109-1215

**WHITE, JAMES RICHARD,** lawyer; b. McKinney, Tex., Jan. 22, 1948; s. James Ray and Maxine (Brown) W.; children: Nicole Olivia, Mandi Leigh, James Derek. BBA, So. Meth. U., 1969, MBA, 1970, JD, 1973, LLM, 1977. Bar: Tex. 1973, U.S. Tax Ct. 1975, U.S. Supreme Ct. 1989, U.S. Ct. Appeals (5th cir.) 1989); cert. Comml. Real Estate Law Tex. Bd. Legal Specialization. Assoc. Elliot, Meer, Vetter, Denton & Bates, Dallas, 1973-74, Atwell, Cain & Davenport, Dallas, 1974-75; atty. Sabine Corp., Dallas, 1975-77; assoc. Brice & Barron, Dallas, 1977-79; ptnr. Millard & Olson, Dallas, 1979-82, Johnson & Swanson, Dallas, 1982-83, Winstead, Sechrest & Minick P.C., Dallas, 1983—; mem. staff Southwestern Law Jour., Dallas, 1971-73; mem. So. Meth. U. Moot Ct. Bd., Order Barristers, Dallas, 1972-73; prof. North Lake Coll., Dallas, 1985; bd. dirs. Tex. Assn. Young Lawyers, Austin, 1980-82; sec. bd. dirs. Dallas Assn. Young Lawyers, 1976-80. Contbr. articles to profl. jours. Chmn. bd. dirs. Tex. Lawyers Credit Union, Austin, 1980-82; pres. North Tex. Premier Soccer Assn., Dallas, 1979-81; v.p. Lake Highlands Soccer Assn., 1995-96, pres., 1996—; mem. regional mobility task force Real Estate Coun., City of Dallas, 1991-92, mem. downtown revitalization com., 1995-97; mem. Dallas Indsl. Devel. Bd., 1992-93, Dallas Higher Edn. Authority Bd., 1994-96; spkr.'s bur. and accreditation divsn. World Cup USA '94. Mem. ABA (mem. title ins. and survey, mortgage loan origination and structure com., mortgage financing and opinion, non-traditional comml. real estate fin. coms.), Tex. Bar Assn. (cert. 1973, mem. mortgage loan opinion com.), Tex. Coll. Real Estate Attys., Coll. State Bar Tex. Methodist. Avocations: soccer, golf, skiing, racquetball. E-mail: jrwhite@winstead.com. Real property, Finance, Banking. Home: 8003 Hundley Ct Dallas TX 75231-4728 Office: Winstead Sechrest & Minick 5400 Renaissance Tower 1201 Elm St Ste 5400 Dallas TX 75270-2199

**WHITE, JEFFERY HOWELL,** lawyer; b. Tyler, Tex., Aug. 4, 1959; s. Bluford D. and Tempie R. (Tunnell) W.; m. Michael Anne Mackley, May 21, 1989; children: Kristin, Alex. BS in History, So. Ark. U., 1983; JD, Oklahoma City U., 1986. Bar: Tex. 1987. Assoc. Dean White, Canton, Tex., 1986-90; asst. dist. atty. Van Zandt Co., Canton, 1991-94; ptnr. Elliott Elliott & White, Canton, 1994-97; pvt. practice Canton, Tex., 1997—. Mem. Van Zandt County Bar Assn., Tex. Criminal Def. Lawyers Assn., Tex. State Bar (dist. 1-A grievance com. 1996—). Democrat. United Methodist. Avocations: golf, tennis, spectator sports. Criminal, Family and matrimonial, Juvenile. Home: PO Box 102 Canton TX 75103-0102 Office: 157 N Buffalo St Canton TX 75103-1353

**WHITE, JERUSHA LYNN,** lawyer; b. Kansas City, Mo., Nov. 30, 1950; d. Riley Vaughn and Edith Blynn (Ringen) W.; m. Larry D. Hancock, Jan. 5, 1969 (div. 1973); m. Stephen Perry Wasson, Nov. 30, 1978 (div. 1985); m. Charles Beam Westley, Feb. 14, 1994. AS, State Fair Community Coll., 1974; BS, Cen. Mo. State U., 1978; JD, U. Mo., Kansas City, 1981. Bar: Mo. 1981. With Montgomery Ward & Co., Sedalia, Mo., 1968-69, Parkhurst Mfg. Co., Sedalia, 1969-71, United Farm Agy., Sedalia, 1972-73, Montgomery Ward & Co., 1973-74, Howard Truck & Equipment Co., Sedalia, 1974-75, McGraw-Edison Co., Sedalia, 1975-76, Rival Mfg. Co., Sedalia, 1977-78; buyer Hotel Equipment Co., Century City, Calif., 1978; law clk. Legal Aid of Western Mo., Kansas City, 1979-80, Horowitz & Shurin, P.C., Kansas City, 1980-81; assoc. Steve Borel/Steve Streen, Kansas City, 1982-83; pvt. practice, Sedalia, 1983-85; ptnr. Cope, Schuber & White, 1985-86; staff atty. Hyatt Legal Svcs., 1986-88; asst. dist. counsel U.S. Army Corps of Engrs., 1988—. Mem. ABA, Mo. Bar Assn. Democrat. Presbyterian. Government contracts and claims. Home: 6717 NW Chinquapin Ct Kansas City MO 64151-2326 Office: Corps Engrs 700 Federal Bldg 601 E 12th St Kansas City MO 64106-2826

**WHITE, JILL CAROLYN,** lawyer; b. Santa Barbara, Calif., Mar. 20, 1934; d. Douglas Cameron and Gladys Louise (Ashley) W.; m. Walter Otto Weyrauch, Mar. 17, 1973. BA, Occidental Coll., L.A., 1955; JD, U. Calif., Berkeley, 1972. Bar: Fla. 1974, Calif. 1975, D.C. 1981, U.S. Dist. Ct. (no. and mid. dists.) Fla., U.S. Ct. Appeals (5th and 11th cirs.), U.S. Supreme Ct. Staff mem. U.S. Dept. State, Am. Embassy, Rio de Janeiro, 1956-58; with psychol. rsch. units Inst. Human Devel., Inst. Personality Assessment and Rsch., U. Calif., Berkeley, 1961-68; adj. prof. criminal justice program U. Fla., Gainesville, Fla., 1976-78; pvt. practice immigration and nationality law, Gainesville, 1976—. Contbr. articles to profl. jours. Mem. ABA, Am. Immigration Lawyers Assn. (bd. dirs. Ctrl. Fla. chpt. 1985-94, 95-96, 97-99, chmn. Ctrl. Fla. chpt. 1988-89, co-chmn. so. regional liaison com. 1990-92, nat. bd. dirs. 1988-89), Bar Assn. 8th Jud. Cir. Fla., Fla. Bar (immigration and nationality law cert. com. 1994-99, chmn. cert. com. 1997-98), Gainesville Area C. of C., Gainesville Area Innovation Network, Altrusa. Democrat. Immigration, naturalization, and customs. Office: 2830 NW 41st St Ste C Gainesville FL 32606-6667

**WHITE, JOE E., JR.,** lawyer; b. Roswell, N.Mex., Oct. 27, 1962. BA in Polit. Sci., Ctrl. State U., 1985; JD, U. Okla., 1988. Bar: Okla. Assoc. Hughes, White, Adams & Grant, Oklahoma City, Okla., 1985-93, ptnr., 1993-94; ptnr. White & Adams, Oklahoma City, Okla., 1995—; barrister Am. Inns of Ct., Oklahoma City, 1994—. Trustee Okla. Student Loan Authority, Oklahoma City, 1992-96; vice chmn. bd. dirs. U. Ctrl. Okla. Found., Edmond, 1992—. Democrat. Baptist. Criminal, General practice, General civil litigation. Office: White & Adams 25th Fl 204 N Robinson Ave Bldg 25 Oklahoma City OK 73102-6803

**WHITE, JOHN JOSEPH, III,** lawyer; b. Darby, Pa., Nov. 23, 1948; s. John J. Jr. and Catherine (Lafferty) W.; m. Catherine M Staley, Dec. 9, 1983. BS, U. Scranton, 1970; MPA, Marywood Coll., 1977; JD, Loyola U., New Orleans, 1983. Bar: Pa. 1983, U.S. Dist. Ct. (ea. dist.) Pa. 1983, N.J. 1984, U.S. Dist. Ct. N.J. 1984, U.S. Tax Ct. 1984, U.S. Ct. Appeals (3d cir.) 1983, U.S. Dist. Ct. (mid. dist.) Pa. 1984, D.C. 1985, U.S. Supreme Ct. 1987. Exec. dir. Scranton (Pa.) Theatre Libre, Inc., 1973-77; pub. Libre Press Inc., Scranton, 1977-83; pvt. practice Phila., 1983—; pres. Washington Franklin Investment Corp., 1992—; owner Mercury Transp. Co., Inc., Lansdowne, Pa., 1987—; N.Am. agt. Palacky U. Med. Sch., Olomouc, Czech Republic, 1995—. Founder, pub. Metro Mag., 1977-83. Founder, Scranton Pub. Theatre, 1976; dir. Scranton Theatre Libre, Inc., 1973. Capt. USAF, 1970-73; lt. col. Res., 1973—. Mem. ABA, Pa. Trial Lawyers Assn., Phila. Bar Assn., Phila. Trial Lawyers Assn., Air Force Assn. (chpt. pres. 1975—), Phi Delta Phi Internat. Legal Frat. Democrat. Roman Catholic. Avocations: jogging, art collecting. E-mail: lawfirmusa@aol.com. Personal injury, Private international, General civil litigation.

**WHITE, KATHERINE PATRICIA,** lawyer; b. N.Y.C., Feb. 1, 1948; d. Edward Christopher and Catherine Elizabeth (Walsh) W. BA in English, Molloy Coll., 1969; JD, St. John's U., 1971. Bar: N.Y. 1972, U.S. Dist. Ct. (ea. and so. dists.) N.Y., 1973, U.S. Supreme Ct. 1976. Atty. Western Electric Co., Inc., N.Y.C., 1971-79; sr. atty. AT&T Corp., N.Y.C., 1979-96, chief regulatory counsel-New Eng., 1996-97, law and govt. affairs v.p., gen.

atty., 1997—; adj. prof. law N.Y. Law Sch., N.Y.C., 1987-88, Fordham U. Sch. Law, 1988-91; bd. dirs. First Security Benefit Life Ins. Co. N.Y. Vol. Sloan Kettering Inst., 1973, North Shore U. Hosp., 1975, various fed., state and local polit. campaigns; judge N.Y. State Bicentennial Writing Competition, N.Y.C., 1977-78; chmn. Com. to Elect Supreme Ct. Judge, N.Y.C., 1982. Mem. Am. Corp. Counsel Assn., N.Y. State Bar Assn. (bus. and banking law com. real estate law sect., corp. counsel sect.), Assn. Bar City N.Y. (adminstrv. law com. 1982-85, young lawyers com. 1976-79, judge nat. moot ct. competition 1979-91), Cath. Lawyers Guild for Diocese of Rockville Centre (pres. 1980-81), St. John's U. Sch. Law Alumni Assn. (pres. L.I. chpt. 1986-88), Women's Nat. Rep. Club (bd. govs. 1988-91), Met. Club. Avocations: racing sailboats, figure skating, golf, tennis. Administrative and regulatory, Contracts commercial, Public utilities. Home: 1035 5th Ave Apt 14D New York NY 10028-0135 Office: AT&T 32 Avenue Of The Americas New York NY 10013-2473

**WHITE, KATHERINE RUSSELL,** lawyer; b. Washington, Oct. 1, 1949; d. Peregrine and Junita (Russell) W. BA, Goucher Coll., 1971; JD, U. Md., 1976. Bar: Md. 1976, N.C. 1986. Clk. Hon. Marshall Levin, Balt., 1974-76, Hon. Richard A. Gilbert, Annapolis, Md., 1976-77; reporter The Sun, Balt., 1977-80, The Charlotte (N.C.) Observer, 1981-86; asst. atty. gen. Dept. Justice, Raleigh, N.C., 1986-89; assoc. Everett, Gaskins, Hancock, Raleigh, N.C., 1989-95; atty. pvt. practice, Raleigh, N.C., 1995-98; exec. dir., gen. counsel N.C. Bd. Ethics, Raleigh, 1998—; vis. lectr., comms. law N.C. State U., 1992—. Contbg. author: North Carolina Focus, 1989, 96, State Government, 1996. Mem. Nat. Freedom of Info. Coalition, Dallas, 1990— (Achievement award 1995); chmn. Haven House, Inc., Raleigh, 1996-97, bd. dirs., 1986-97. Mem. ABA, Newspapers Assn. Am. (mem. new media fedn. bd.), N.C. Bar Assn. (ethics com. 1990-91), Wake County Bar Assn. Home: 309 N Bloodworth St Raleigh NC 27601-1107 Office: NC Bd Ethics 116 W Jones St Raleigh NC 27603-1300

**WHITE, KENDRED ALAN,** lawyer; b. Madisonville, Tenn., Oct. 2, 1938; s. Leonard A. and Nora (Clyde) W.; m. Peggy Ann Cowling, Aug. 24, 1963; children: Jonathan C., Erik K., Lauren A. BS, U. Tenn., 1961, JD, 1964. Bar: Tenn. 1964, U.S. Dist. Ct. (ea. dist.) Tenn. 1966, U.S. Supreme Ct. 1971. Pvt. practice law Madisonville, 1964—; mem. hearing com. Bd. of Profl. Responsibility, Tenn. Supreme Ct., 1982-85; bd. dirs. Vol. Fed. S&L, Madisonville. With USAF, 1958-64. Fellow Tenn. Bar Found.; mem. ABA, Tenn. Bar Assn., Phi Delta Phi (province pres. 1996—). Republican. Baptist. Avocation: travel. Real property.

**WHITE, LETITIA H.,** lawyer; b. Lafayette, Ind., Apr. 12, 1951; d. Thomas Purcell White and Jean Holliday Phipps. AB, Ind. U., 1974; JD, South Tex. Coll., 1985. Bar: Tex. Assoc. Burlington Resources, Houston, 1986-98; sr. atty. Coastal Corp., Houston, 1998—; corp., sec.-treas. Norrant Enterprise, Houston, 1996-98, d-Zeiner, Inc., Houston, 1997-98. Republican. Avocation: running. Real property, Construction, Oil, gas, and mineral. Office: Coastal Corp Nine Greenway Plz Houston TX 77046

**WHITE, LINDA DIANE,** lawyer; b. N.Y.C., Apr. 1, 1952; d. Bernard and Elaine (Simons) Schwartz; m. Thomas M. White, Aug. 16, 1975; 1 child, Alexandra Nicole. AB, U. Pa., 1973; JD, Northwestern U., 1976. Bar: Ill. 1976. Assoc. Walsh, Case, Coale & Brown, Chgo., 1976-77, Greenberger & Kaufmann (merged into Katten, Muchin), Chgo., 1977-82; ptnr. Greenberger & Kaufmann (merged into Katten, Muchin), 1982-85, Sonnenschein Nath & Rosenthal, Chgo., 1985—. Mem. ABA (real property fin. com., comml. leasing com., real property, probate and trust law sect. 1987—), Ill. Bar Assn., Chgo. Bar Assn., Practicing Law Inst. (chmn. program on negotiating comml. leases 1995-99, real estate law adv. com.). Real property, Contracts commercial, Landlord-tenant. Office: Sonnenschein Nath & Rosenthal 8000 Sears Tower 233 S Wacker Dr Ste 8000 Chicago IL 60606-6342

**WHITE, MARTIN FRED,** lawyer; b. Warren, Ohio, Nov. 12, 1952; s. Benjamin and Bella Dorothy (Bernstein) W. BA, Ohio State U., 1973; JD, 1977. Bar: U.S. Dist. Ct. (no. dist.) Ohio, 1981, Pa., 1993. Atty. pvt. practice, Warren, Ohio, 1977—; spl. counsel Ohio Atty. Gen., Columbus, Ohio, 1991—. Mem. Am. Trial Lawyers Assn., Ohio Acad. Trial Lawyers, Mahoning-Trumbull Trial Lawyers Assn., Ohio Acad. Criminal Def. Attys., Ohio Bar Assn., Trumbull County Bar Assn. Personal injury, State civil litigation, Criminal. Office: PO Box 1150 Warren OH 44482-1150

**WHITE, MARY JO,** prosecutor. U.S. atty. So. Dist. N.Y., Manhattan, 1993—. Office: US Attys Office 1 Saint Andrews Plz New York NY 10007-1781*

**WHITE, MICHAEL LEE,** lawyer; b. Dilley, Tex., Mar. 27, 1953; s. Deryl and Ruby Alice (Gillis) W. BA, Tex. A&M U., 1975; JD, U. Houston, 1978. Bar: Tex. 1979. Briefing atty. 14th Ct. Appeals, Houston, 1979; contracts analyst Texaco Inc., Houston, 1979-80, legis. coord., 1980-82; mgr. state govt. rels. Pennzoil Co., Houston, 1982-85, mgr. employee comms., pub. affairs liaison, 1985-87, mgr. media comms., 1987-88; dir. govt. affairs Met. Transit Authority Harris County, Houston, 1988-90; v.p. C. of C. divsn. Greater Houston Partnership, 1990-94; legis. cons., mediator Austin, Tex., 1994—. Fellow Houston Bar Found.; mem. ABA, State Bar Tex., Houston Bar Assn., Tex. Lyceum Assn. (bd. dirs., exec. com. 1984-89), Travis County Bar Assn. Avocations: golf, tennis, skiing, reading. Legislative, Alternative dispute resolution. Office: PO Box 1667 Austin TX 78767-1667

**WHITE, NANCY LEE,** lawyer; b. St. Joseph, Mo., Aug. 24, 1953; d. Robert Lee and Mary Margaret (Stamp) W.; m. Thomas Gerard Hanley, Sept. 24, 1977 (div. Aug. 12, 1995); 1 child, Mary Margaret. BA, DePauw U., 1975; JD, Loyola U., 1981. Bar: Ill. 1981, Ariz. 1987, Calif. 1998, U.S. Dist. Ct. (no. dist.) Ill. 1981, U.S. Dist. Ct. Ariz. 1987, U.S. Dist. Ct. (so. dist.) Calif. 1998. Assoc. Sidley & Austin, Chgo., 1981-87; from assoc. to ptnr. Streich Lang, Phoenix, 1987—; mem. appts. com. State Bar Ariz., 1997—. Cmty. adv. bd. Cmty. AIDS Coun., Phoenix, 1993-97; gen. counsel Phoenix C. of C., 1996-97; bd. dirs. Ariz. Leadership 2000 & Beyond, Phoenix, 1996—, Xicanindio Artes, Phoenix, 1996—, The Christmas House Found., 1997—. Recipient Athena award Phoenix C. of C., 1994. Mem. Ariz. Women Lawyers Assn. (bus. devel. com. 1996—), Phoenix C. of C. (chmn. NAFTA task force 1992-95). Democrat. Roman Catholic. Avocations: gourmet cooking, inernational travel, weight lifting. Contracts commercial, Finance, Private international. Office: Streich Lang Renaissance One 2 N Central Phoenix AZ 85004

**WHITE, NORMAN,** lawyer, educator; b. Lake Wales, Fla., Oct. 17, 1948; s. Marvin Peyton White and Martha Louise Whitehurst; m. Elaine Honeycutt, June 17, 1969; children: Matthew, Forrest. BS in Journalism, U. Fla., 1969, JD, 1972. Bar: Fla. 1973, U.S. Dist. Ct. (mid. dist.) Fla. 1973. Asst. state atty. State of Fla., Office of State Atty., Barton, 1973-74; ptnr. Bradley-Johnson, Lake Wales, 1975—. Pres. Lake Wales Family YMCA, 1992; trustee Winterhaven (Fla.) Hosp., 1985—, Lake Wales Hosp., 1989—. Mem. Fla. Bar Assn. (chmn. 10th jud. cir. grievanc com.), Rotary (pres. 1990). Methodist. Avocations: classic novels, tennis, golf. State civil litigation, Personal injury. Office: PO Box 1260 Lake Wales FL 33859-1260

**WHITE, PATRICIA DENISE,** dean, law educator; b. Syracuse, N.Y., July 8, 1949; d. Theodore C. and Kathleen (Cowles) Denise; m. Nicholas P. White, Feb. 20, 1971; children: Olivia Lawrence, Alexander Cowles. BA, U. Mich., 1971, MA, JD, 1974. Bar: D.C. 1975, Mich. 1988, Utah 1995. Assoc. Steptoe & Johnson, Washington, 1975-76; vis. asst. prof. Coll. of Law U. Toledo, 1976-77; assoc. Caplin & Drysdale, Washington, 1977-79; asst. prof. Law Ctr. Georgetown U., 1979-84, assoc. prof. Law Ctr., 1985-88; vis. prof. Law Sch. U. Mich., Ann Arbor, 1988-94; prof. U. Utah, Salt Lake City, 1994-98; counsel Parson, Behle and Latimer, Salt Lake City, 1995-98; dean, prof. Ariz. State U. Coll. Law, 1999—; counsel Bodman, Longley and Dahling, Detroit, Ann Arbor, 1990-95. Contbr. articles to profl. jours. Office: Ariz State U Coll Law McAllister & Orange Sts Box 877906 Tempe AZ 85287*

**WHITE, RICHARD CLARENCE,** lawyer; b. Sioux City, Iowa, Oct. 31, 1933; m. Beverly Frances Fitzpatrick, Feb. 22, 1955; children—Anne, Richard, William, Christopher. B.A.; LL.B., Stanford U., 1962. Bar: Calif. 1963, U.S. Supreme Ct. 1970, N.Y. 1983. Assoc. O'Melveny & Myers, L.A., 1962-70, ptnr., 1970-94; lectr. in field. Bd. dirs. Equal Employment Adv. Coun., Washington, 1976-80, 83, Performing Arts Ctr. of Orange County 1983-86. Capt. USMC, 1954-59. Fellow Coll. Labor and Employment Lawyers (founding, bd. govs.); mem. ABA (co-chmn. com. on practice and procedure labor and employment law sect. 1977-80, mem. equal opportunity law com. 1980-85, co-chmn. com. on insts. and meetings 1985-87, coun. 1987-97). Labor, Administrative and regulatory.

**WHITE, RODNEY CURTIS,** paralegal, legal assistant; b. Pueblo, Colo., Aug. 20, 1958; s. Richard Robert and Mary Alice (Valdez) W. Student, Pueblo C.C., 1987-89; Diploma Paralegal/Legal Asst., So. Career Inst., Boca Raton, Fla., 1990, student, 1996—. Freelance paralegal Pueblo, 1991-95; UA technician/security Crossroads Managed Care Sys., Pueblo, 1995—, billing clerk/client intake, 1998—; investigator/legal rschr. various law firms, 1989-90; notary public, 1989—. Campaign coord. Elect George Bush for Pres. campaign, So. Colo., 1988-89, Rau for County Clerk and Recorder; pres. Viva Bush com. Rep. Nat. Hispanic Assembly, Washington, 1985-89; mem. Rep. Nat. Com., Washington, 1988-89; Colo. state hosp. employee rep. Am. Fed. State County Mcpl. Employees, Pueblo, 1985-88; fund raiser Crime Stopper, Pueblo. Mem. Colo. Trial Lawyers Assn. Republican. Home: 2581 Lynwood Ln Pueblo CO 81005-2719

**WHITE, RONNIE L.,** state supreme court justice. AA, St. Louis C.C., 1977; BA, St. Louis U., 1979; JD, U. Mo., Kansas City, 1983. Bar: Mo. Law intern Jackson County Prosecutors Office; legal asst. U.S. Def. Mapping Agy.; trial atty. Office of Pub. Defender; mem. Mo. Ho. of Reps., 1989-93; judge Mo. Ct. Appeals, 1994; spl. judge Mo. Supreme Ct., 1994-95, justice, 1994-95, assoc. justice, 1995—; adj. faculty Washington U. Sch. Law, 1997—. Office: PO Box 150 Jefferson City MO 65102-0150*

**WHITE, SUSAN PAGE,** lawyer; b. Riverside, Calif., Nov. 24, 1961; d. David Edward and Joanne (Churchill) Page; m. Mark William Simon White, Dec. 1, 1990. BA, Wheaton (Ill.) Coll., 1983; JD, Loyola U., L.A., 1988. Bar: Calif. 1988, U.S. Dist. Ct. (cen. dist.) Calif. 1989. Mgr. Interface Community Battered Women's Shelter, Newbury Park, Calif., 1983-85; assoc. Lillick & McHose, L.A., 1988-90, Troop Steuber Pasich Reddick & Tobey LLP, L.A., 1990—. Republican. Baptist. Insurance, Entertainment, State civil litigation. Home: 925 Dickson St Marina Dl Rey CA 90292-5512 Office: 2029 Century Park E Ste 2400 Los Angeles CA 90067-3010

**WHITE, THOMAS S.,** lawyer; b. Sharon, Pa., Aug. 27, 1949; s. Herbert F. and Ruth J. W.; m. Linda K. Clark, May 12, 1973; children: Kimberly, Nicholas. BA, Case Western Reserve U., 1973; JD, Gonzaga U., 1976. Bar: Wash. 1980, U.S. Dist. Ct. (we. dist.) Wash. 1983, U.S. Dist. Ct. (we. dist.) Pa. 1983, U.S. Ct. Appeals (3rd cir.) 1983. Legal advisor Spokane Legal Svcs., Wash., 1977; revenue officer State of Wash., Everett, 1979-80; dep. pros. atty. Snohomish County, Everett, 1980; postal insp. U.S. Postal Svc., Pa., W.V., 1981-84; regional insp. atty. U.S. Postal Svc., Phila., 1984-85; insp. atty., nat. money laundering advisor U.S. Postal Svc., Washington, 1985-93; insp. atty. Seattle divsn. U.S. Postal Svc., Seattle, 1993—. Active Spotsylvania County Boy Scouts, Fredericksburg, Va., 1988-89; trustee Peace United Meth. Ch., Fredricksburg, 1988-89. Recipient Meritorious Svc. honor award U.S. Postal Svc., 1988, 90-91, Spl. Achievement award, 1988, 93, 97. Mem. ABA (criminal justice sect.), Wash. State Bar Assn. Methodist. Avocations: gardening, fishing, camping. Office: 3d & Union PO Box 400 Seattle WA 98111-4000

**WHITE, WALTER HIAWATHA, JR.,** lawyer; b. Milw., Aug. 21, 1954; s. Walter H. and Winifred (Parker) W.; m. Sonja Athene Rein, Dec. 30, 1977. Student, Leningrad Pedagogical Inst., USSR, 1976; BA, Amherst Coll., 1977; JD, U. Calif., Berkeley, 1980. Bar: Wis. 1980, U.S. Dist. Ct. (ea. dist.) Wis. 1980, U.S. Ct. Appeals (7th cir.) 1980, U.S. Supreme Ct. 1983. Assoc. Michael, Best & Friedrich, Milw., 1980-88; commr. securities State of Wis., 1988-91; ptnr. Quarles & Brady, Milw., 1991-94; mng. dir. Steptoe & Johnson Internat., Moscow, 1994-99; ptnr. Bryan Cave, London, 1999—; trustee Milw. Found., 1992—; vice chmn. dist. com. Bd. Attys. Profl. Responsibility, Milw., 1984-87; bd. dirs. Wis. Trust Found., Madison, Church Mut. Ins. Co., Merrill, Wis., Ctrl. Asian Am. Enterprise Fund. Editor Black Law Jour., 1978-80; mem. editorial bd. Barrister Mag.; contbr. articles to profl. jours. Mem. Cardinal Stritch Coll. Bus. Adv. Bd., Milw., 1982-85, health law com. Wis. Civil Liberties Union, Milw., 1985—, Gov.'s Adv. Bd. to Legal Services Corp., Madison, 1982-87; sec. Milw. Forum Inc., 1982—; pres. Milw. Urban League, 1985; bd. dirs. WUWM Pub. Radio Sta., Milw., 1983-86, Family Service Milw., Inc., 1987-89, Neighborhood House of Milw., Inc., 1987—. John Woodruff Simpson fellow, 1977; Named one of the 86 most interesting people in Milw., Milw. Mag., 1986. Mem. ABA (chair young lawyers div. 1989-90, commn. on opportunities for minorities in the profession, del. assn. Soviet lawyers, co-chair commonwealth of ind. states law com. of internat. law and practice sect. 1990-91), Nat. Bar Assn., Assn. Internat. des Jeunes Avocats, Milw. Bar Assn., Wis. Black Lawyers Assn. (bd. dirs. 1982-83), Milw. Young Lawyers Assn. (pres. 1984-85, pres.'s award 1985), Bd. Bar Examiners, Milw. Found. Avocations: Russian lit., rowing, squash. Health, General corporate, Private international. Office: Bryan Cave, 29 Queen Annes Gate, London England SW14 9BU Office: 700 13th St NW Washington DC 20005-3960

**WHITE, WILLIAM NELSON,** lawyer; b. Balt., Sept. 8, 1938; s. Nelson Cardwell and Ellen Atwell (Zoller) W.; m. Mary Kathleen Bitzel, Sept. 2, 1960 (div. 1971); children: Craig William, Jeffrey Alan, Colin Christopher; m. Christine Lewin Hanna, July 8, 1978. LLB, U. Md., 1968, JD, 1969. Bar: Md. 1972, U.S. Ct. Appeals (4th cir.) 1975, U.S. Dist. Ct. Md. 1976, U.S. Spreme Ct. 1976. Asst. state's atty. Balt., 1972; assoc. Brooks & Turnbull, Balt., 1973-76; pvt. practice Balt., 1977—; counsel St. Andrews Soc. Balt., 1989—; former counsel, bd. dirs. St. George's Soc. Former elder, pres. deacons, trustee Roland Park Presbyn. Ch.; mem. worship, music and sacrament coun., elder Second Presbyn. Ch. Mem. ABA, Md. Bar Assn., Baltimore County Bar Assn., U. Md. Alumni Assn. for Greater Balt. (pres. 1977), Supreme Ct. Hist. Soc. Avocations: history, philosophy, classical music, tennis, sailing. State civil litigation, Insurance, Personal injury. Office: 305 W Chesapeake Ave # Ll-3 Baltimore MD 21204-4421

**WHITEHEAD, DAVID BARRY,** lawyer; b. San Francisco, Oct. 14, 1946; s. Barry and Fritzi-Beth (Bowman) W.; m. René Dayan, May 26, 1990. AB in History, Stanford U., 1968, JD, 1971. Bar: Calif. 1972, U.S. Dist. Ct. (no. dist.) Calif. 1972, U.S. Ct. Appeals (9th cir.) 1972, U.S. Dist. Ct. (cen. dist.) Calif. 1974. Assoc. Cullinan Hancock Rothert & Burns, San Francisco, 1972-74; assoc. Cullinan Burns & Helmer, San Francisco, 1975-77, ptnr., 1977-78; ptnr. Burns & Whitehead, San Francisco, 1979-85, Whitehead & Porter, San Francisco, 1986-97, Whitehead, Porter & Gordon LLP, San Francisco, 1998—; bd. dirs. Rainbow Music, Inc., San Francisco, ITP, Inc., Sunnyvale, Calif.; founding dir. A. Lincoln High Sch. San Francisco, 1989—. Mem. San Francisco Rep. Steering Com., 1984-89; bd. dirs. Enterprise for High Sch. Students, San Francisco, 1982-86, San Francisco chpt. Easter Seal Soc., 1986—, Opera West Found., San Francisco, 1986—, Traveler's Aid Soc., San Francisco, 1989—, Hosp. de la Familia, 1995—. 1st lt. USAR, 1968-71. Mem. ABA, Calif. Bar Assn., San Francisco Bar Assn., Calif. Scholarship Fedn. (life) Family Club San Francisco (bd. dirs. 1986-89, 93-95), World Trade Club, Abraham Lincoln High Sch. San Francisco Alumni Assn. (founding dir.). Roman Catholic. Avocations: tenor, writer, director, actor. General corporate, Securities, Probate. Home: 1896 Pacific Ave Apt 502 San Francisco CA 94109-2302 Office: Whitehead Porter & Gordon LLP 220 Montgomery St Fl 18 San Francisco CA 94104-3402

**WHITEHEAD, JAMES FRED, III,** lawyer; b. Atlanta, July 3, 1946; s. James Fred Jr. and Jessie Mae (Turner) W.; m. Joanne Christina Mayo, June 21, 1969 (div. Feb. 1992); children: Matthew Nicholas, Rebecca Catherine; m. Nancy Karean Hatley, May 28, 1992; stepchildren: Brandon, Madison. AB with distinction, Stanford U., 1968; JD, U. Mich., 1975. Bar: Wash. 1975, U.S. Dist. Ct. (we. dist.) Wash. 1975, U.S. Ct. Appeals (9th cir.) 1975, U.S. Supreme Ct. 1976, U.S. Dist. Ct. (ea. dist.) Wash. 1994, Alaska 1995, U.S. Dist. Ct. Alaska 1995. Assoc. LeGros, Buchanan, Paul & Madden, Seattle, 1975-79; dir., officer LeGros, Buchanan, Paul & Whitehead, Seattle, 1979-92; ptnr. McGee, Reno & Whitehead, Seattle, 1993; of counsel Holmes Weddle & Barcott, Seattle, 1993-97, shareholder, 1997—; organizer, lectr. Pacific Northwest Admiralty Law Inst., Seattle, 1981—; chmn. Internat. Maritime Law Conf., Seattle, 1996. Assoc. editor Am. Maritime Cases, 1991—; contbr. articles to profl. jours. Mem. ABA, Maritime Law Assn. of U.S. Avocations: tennis, golf, birding. Admiralty, Personal injury, Insurance. Office: Holmes Weddle & Barcott Ste 2600 First Interstate Center Seattle WA 98104

**WHITEHEAD, JAMES MADISON,** law librarian; b. Mobile, Ala., July 16, 1929; s. James Manikee and Fanny (Salmon) W.; m. Elena Hulings, June 11, 1955; children: James M.M., John Douglass, Kenneth Clark, Julia Harker. BA, U. Chgo., 1951; JD, Tulane U., 1959; MS, La. State U., 1963; PhD, U. Pitts., 1981. Bar: La. 1959. Acting head pub. svscs. La. State U., New Orleans, 1965; head sci. library U. Colo., Boulder, 1965-66; asst. prof. head dept. circulation Va. Poly. Inst., Blacksburg, 1967-70; adminstrv. asst. Va. Poly. Ins. and State U., Blacksburg, 1970-71; asst. prof., assoc. prof., law librarian Coll. William and Mary, Williamsburg, Va., 1971-76; asst. prof. SUNY, Geneseo, 1978-80, Atlanta U., 1980-84; pvt. practice Stone Mountain, Ga., 1984-85; libr. IV U. Ga. Law Library, Athens, 1985-95; ret., 1995; cons. ultra microfiche adv. group Ency. Britannica, Blacksburg, 1969. Author: Logos of Library and Information Science: Apperceptions on the Institutes of Bibematics with Commentaries on the General Humanistic Method and the Common Philosophy, 1981. Asst. cubmaster Webelos, leader Boy Scouts Am., Blacksburg, 1969-70, patrol dad, adviser, 1970-71. Cpl. USMC, 1952-54. Mem. La. Bar Assn., Masons, Beta Phi Mu. Republican. Christian Scientist. Avocations: fishing, dog and cat care, poetry and play writing, reading. Home: 104 Hurst St Williamsburg VA 23185-3305

**WHITEHEAD, JOHN WAYNE,** law educator, organization administrator, author; b. Pulaski, Tenn., July 14, 1946; s. John M. and Alatha (Wiser) W.; m. Virginia Carolyn Nichols, Aug. 26, 1967; children: Jayson Reau, Jonathan Mathew, Elisabeth Anne, Joel Christofer, Joshua Benjamen. BA, U. Ark., 1969, JD, 1974. Bar: Ark. 1974, U.S. Dist. Ct. (ea. and we. dists.) Ark. 1974, U.S. Supreme Ct. 1977, U.S. Ct. Appeals (9th cir.) 1980, Va. 1981, U.S. Ct. Appeals (7th cir.) 1981, U.S. Ct Appeals (4th and 5th cirs.). Spl. counsel Christian Legal Soc., Oak Park, Ill., 1977-78; assoc. Gibbs & Craze, Cleve., 1978-79; sole practice law Manassas, Va., 1979-82; pres. The Rutherford Inst., Charlottesville, Va., 1982—, also bd. dirs.; frequent lectr. colls., law schs.; past adj. prof. O.W. Coburn Sch. Law. Author: The Separation Illusion, 1977, Schools on Fire, 1980, The New Tyranny, 1982, The Second American Revolution, 1982, The Stealing of America, 1983, The Freedom of Religious Expression in Public High Schools, 1983, The End of Man, 1986, An American Dream, 1987, The Rights of Religious Persons in Public Education, 1991, Home Education: Rights and Reasons, 1993, Religious Apartheid, 1994, several others; writer, dir.: (TV video series) Grasping for the Wind (Silver World medal N.Y. Film Festival), 1998; contbr. numerous articles to profl. jours.; contbr. numerous chpts. to books. Served to 1st lt. U.S. Army, 1969-71. Named Christian Leader of Yr. Christian World Affairs Conf., Washington, 1986; recipient Bus. and Profl. award Religious Heritage Am., 1990, Hungarian Freedom medal, Budapest, 1991. Mem. ABA, Ark. Bar Assn., Va. Bar Assn. Office: The Rutherford Inst PO Box 7482 Charlottesville VA 22906-7482

**WHITEHILL, CLIFFORD LANE,** lawyer; b. Houston, Apr. 14, 1931; s. Clifford R. and Catalina (Yarza) W.; m. Daisy Mae Woodruff, Apr. 18, 1959; children: Clifford Scott, Alicia Anne, Stephen Lane. BA, Rice U., 1954; LLB, U. Tex., 1957; LLM, Harvard U., 1958. Bar: Tex. 1957, Minn. 1962. Assoc. Childress, Port and Crady, Houston, 1957-59; auditor Haskins and Sells, 1959; asst. gen. counsel Tex. Butadiene and Chem. Co., N.Y.C., 1959-62; with Gen. Mills, Inc., Mpls., 1962-94, gen. counsel, 1975-94, sr. v.p., gen. counsel, 1981—, sec., 1981-94; sr. v.p. gen. counsel, sec. Darden Restaurants, 1995-99. Mem. Minn. Minority Corp. Counsel; mem. corp. adv. bd., mem. adv. com. Nat. Chamber Litigation Ctr.; trustee William Mitchell Coll. Law; assoc. bd. dirs. Minn. Opera; bd. dirs. Minn. Uruguay Ptnrs. Am., Nat. Hispanic Scholarship Fund, Fund Legal Aid Soc., Minn. Spl. Olympics, Greater Minn. Coun. Chs. Minn.; chmn. Better Bus. Bur.; chmn. coun. Better Bus. Burs.; mem. exec. com. Ctr. Pub. Resources. Mem. ABA, Minn. Bar Assn., Tex. Bar Assn., Am. Arbitration Assn. (bd. dirs.), Nat. Assn. Mfrs. (bd. dirs., state dir.), UN Assn. U.S., Assn. of Gen. Counsel, Harvard Club, Lafayette Club, Bay Hill Club. Republican. Roman Catholic. Avocations: boating, flying, skiing, tennis. General corporate, Public international, Corporate taxation. Office: Darden Restaurants Inc PO Box 593330 5900 Lake Ellenor Dr Orlando FL 32809-4634

**WHITEHOUSE, SHELDON,** attorney general, lawyer; b. N.Y.C., Oct. 20, 1955; s. Charles Sheldon and Mary (Rand) W.; m. Sandra Christine Thornton, Sept. 20, 1986; 2 children. BA, Yale U., 1978; JD, U. Va., 1982. Bar: W.Va. 1982, R.I. 1983, U.S. Dist. Ct. R.I. 1984, U.S. Supreme Ct. 1986, U.S. Ct. Appeals (1st cir.) 1984. Atty. Providence, 1983-84, spl. asst. atty. gen., 1985-89, chief regulatory unit, 1988-90, asst. atty. gen., 1989-90; exec. counsel Office of Gov., 1991, dir. gov. policy office, 1991-92; dir. Dept. Bus. Regulation, 1992-94; U.S. atty for dist. of R.I., 1994-98; atty. gen. State of R.I., 1999—.

**WHITE-HURST, JOHN MARSHALL,** lawyer; b. Washington, May 30, 1942; s. Bernard Marshall and Viola (Hailman) W.-H.; m. Elizabeth Kibler, Oct. 17, 1964 (dec. 1981); 1 child, Elizabeth Marshall; m. Barbara Ann Paliwoda, July 7, 1984. BA, U. Richmond, 1964, JD, 1972. Bar: Va. 1972. Pvt. practice Chase City, Va., 1973-94; asst. commonwealth's atty. Mecklenburg County, Boydton, Va., 1975-89, commonwealth's atty., 1989—; bd. dirs. Va. Legal Aid Soc., Inc., Lynchburg, 1985-92. Bd. dirs. Southside Regional Juvenile Group Home, South Boston, Va., 1980-85, Cmty. Diversion Program, Farmville, Va., 1988-95. Capt. U.S. Army, 1964-68. Mem. Nat. Dist. Atty. Assn., Va. Bar Assn., Va. Trial Lawyers Assn., Mecklenburg County Bar Assn. (pres. 1980-81, 91-92), Local Govt. Attys. Va. (bd. dirs. 1974-77), Chase City Lions (pres. 1976), Am. Legion, Mason, Moose. Baptist. Avocations: fishing, computers. Office: Commonwealth Atty Office MecKlenburg County PO Box 7 Boydton VA 23917-0007

**WHITEMAN, JOSEPH DAVID,** retired lawyer, manufacturing company executive; b. Sioux Falls, S.D., Sept. 12, 1933; s. Samuel D. and Margaret (Wallace) W.; m. Mary Kelly, Dec. 29, 1962; children: Anne Margaret, Mary Ellen, Joseph David, Sarah Kelly, Jane. B.A., U. Mich., 1955, J.D., 1960. Bar: D.C. 1960, Ohio 1976. Assoc. Cox, Langford, Stoddard & Cutler, Washington, 1959-64; sec., gen. counsel Studebaker group Studebaker Worthington, Inc., N.Y.C., 1964-71; asst. gen. counsel. United Telecommunications, Inc., Kansas City, Mo., 1971-74; v.p., gen. counsel, sec. Weatherhead Co., Cleve., 1974-77, Parker Hannifin Corp., Cleve., 1977-98; ret., 1998. Immediate past chmn. bd. dirs. St. Lukes Med. Ctr. Served as lt. USNR, 1955-57. Mem. ABA, Beta Theta Pi, Phi Delta Phi. Republican. Roman Catholic. Home: PO Box 424 2508 Robinson Springs Rd Stowe VT 05672 Office: Parker Hannifin Corp 6035 Parkland Blvd Cleveland OH 44124-4141

**WHITENER, HUGH DAVE,** lawyer, educator; b. Charlotte, N.C., May 22, 1944; s. Hugh Dave and Marie (Jenkins) W.; m. Sandra Rinehart, Oct. 3, 1964; children: Tripp, Laura. BA, Erskine Coll., Due West, S.C., 1966; JD, U. S.C., 1969. Bar: S.C. 1969. Atty. Calvo & Lee, Columbia, S.C., 1969-71; ptnr. Calvo & Whitener, Columbia, 1971-80, Whitener, Knight & Medlin, Columbia, 1980-85, Whitener & Wharton, Columbia, 1985—; adj. prof. U. S.C. Law Sch., Columbia, 1987—; bd. dirs., atty. Better Bus. Bur., Columbia 1988—; spkr. in field. Author: (fiction) Class Menagerie, 1998. Methodist. Avocation: fiction writing. Home: 225 Spring Valley Rd Columbia SC 29223-5939 Office: Whitener & Wharton PA 2001 Park St Columbia SC 29201-2006

**WHITESELL, DARRYL DUANE,** lawyer; b. Lynchburg, Va., Nov. 15, 1968; s. Lester Caryle and Patricia Milnor (Clauss) W.; m. Kristina Marie Hall Whitesell, June 26, 1993; 1 child, William Tyler. BA in Acctg., Lynchburg (Va.) Coll., 1991; JD, Coll. William & Mary, Williamsburg, Va., 1997. Bar: Va.; CPA. Acct. Cherry, Bekaert & Holland, Lynchburg, Va., 1991-94; atty. Edmunds & Williams, Lynchburg, Va., 1997—; dir. VASCPA, Lynchburg (Va.) Chpt., 1993-94, Meals on Wheels, Lynchburg, Va., 1997—. Contbr. articles to profl. jours. Mem. ABA, Va. Bar Assn., Va. Soc. CPAs, Am. Instr. CPAs. General corporate, Estate planning, Taxation, general. Office: Edmunds & Williams PC 800 Main St Ste 400 Lynchburg VA 24504-1533

**WHITESELL, ERIC DWIGHT,** lawyer; b. Staunton, Va., Apr. 17, 1952; s. Thomas Marshall and Anastasia Itsa (Hadjateleanou) W.; m. Nancy Gayle Webb Fodela, Nov. 10, 1973 (div. Feb. 1989); 1 child, Thomas Ryan; m. charlotte Earlene Wright, Apr. 6, 1989. BS, Va. Commonwealth U., 1974, MBA, 1975; JD, U. Richmond, 1977; LLM, Coll. of William and Mary, 1979. Bar: Va. 1979, U.S. Dist. Ct. (we. dist.) Va. 1980, U.S. Tax Ct. 1979, U.S. Ct. Appeals (4th cir.) 1992. Ptnr. Gillespie Hart Altizer & Whitesell, P.C., Tazewell, Va., 1979—. Sec.-treas. Thompson Valley Cmty. Assn., Tazewell, 1992—. Mem. Va. Bar Assn., Va. Assn. Def. Attys. Presbyterian. Avocation: farming. General practice. Office: Gillespie Hart Altizer & Whitesell Main and Elk St Tazewell VA 24651

**WHITESIDE, MARY ANN,** lawyer. JD, U. Colo. Bar: Colo., U.S. Dist. Ct. Colo., U.S. Ct. Appeals (10th cir.), U.S. Supreme Ct. Dep. securities commr. Colo. Divsn. Securities; first asst. atty. gen. in charge of labor and civil rights Colo. Atty. Gen.'s Office; dir., chief adminstrv. law judge State Pers. Bd.; lawyer Divsn. Workers' Compensation, Denver; mem. ad hoc com. on appellate rules Colo. Supreme Ct.; fellow sr. execs. program Harvard U. John F. Kennedy Sch. Govt., 1994. Contbr. chpt. to books. Office: Dept Labor Divsn Workers Co Tower II Ste 400 1515 Arapaltor St Denver CO 80202-3150

**WHITESIDE, WILLIAM ANTHONY, JR.,** lawyer; b. Phila., Feb. 23, 1929; s. William Anthony and Ellen T. (Hensler) W.; m. Eileen Ann Ferrick, Feb. 27, 1954; children: William Anthony III, Michael P., Eileen A., Richard F., Christopher J., Mary P. BS, Notre Dame U., 1951; LLB, U. Pa., 1954. Bar: Pa. 1955. Assoc. Speiser, Satinsky, Gilliland & Packel, Phila., 1956-58, ptnr., 1958-61; ptnr. Fox, Rothschild, O'Brien & Frankel, Phila., 1961—. Trustee Am. Coll. Mgmt. and Tech., Dubrovnik, Croatia; chmn. emeritus bd. trustees and exec. com., emeritus trustee, Rochester Inst. of Tech.; mem. pres. adv. coun. U. Notre Dame; bd. dirs. PAL, mem. exec. com.; emeritus trustee Germantown Acad., past pres. 1st lt. USAF, 1954-56. Named Man of Yr. Notre Dame club Phila., 1967. Mem. ABA, Pa. Bar Assn., Phila. Bar Assn., N.Y. Union League Club, Pyramid Club, Wissahickon Skating Club, Pa Soc. Republican. Roman Catholic. Private international, Pension, profit-sharing, and employee benefits, Labor. Home: 7808 Cobden Rd Laverock PA 19038-7256 also: 901 Gardens Plz Ocean City NJ 08226-4719 Office: Fox Rothschild O'Brien & Frankel 2000 Market St Ste 10 Philadelphia PA 19103-3231

**WHITFORD, JOSEPH P.,** lawyer; b. N.Y.C., Apr. 30, 1950. BA, Union Coll., 1972; JD, Syracuse U., 1975; LLM in Taxation, George Washington U., 1978. Bar: N.Y. 1976, D.C. 1977, Wash. 1979. Staff atty. divsn. corp. fin. SEC, Washington, 1975-78; assoc. Foster Pepper & Shefelman, Seattle, 1978-83, mem., 1983—; chmn. bd. dirs. MIT Forum on the Northwest, 1992-93. Securities, Finance, General corporate. Office: Foster Pepper & Shefelman PLLC 1111 3rd Ave Ste 3400 Seattle WA 98101-3299

**WHITING, HENRY H.,** state supreme court justice. LLB, Univ. Va., 1949. Former judge 26th Jud. Cir. of Va.; sr. justice Va. Supreme Ct., Richmond, 1987—. Office: Va Supreme Ct 101 N 9th St Fl 4 Richmond VA 23219-2307

**WHITING, REID A.,** lawyer; b. Batavia, N.Y., Oct. 8, 1955; s. J. Reid and Mary Ann W.; m. Jacalyn Ann Fay Whiting, Aug. 17, 1979; children: Reid A II., Jake M., John F., Cal McC. BA, U. Rochester, N.Y., 1977; JD, Albany Law Sch., N.Y., 1980. Bar: N.Y. State 1981; U.S. Dist. Ct. (we. dist.) 1981. Asst. county atty. Genesee Co. Atty., Batavia, N.Y., 1981-95; ptnr. Rizzo and Whiting, LeRoy, N.Y., 1983-90; pvt. practice LeRoy, N.Y., 1990-96; ptnr. Boylan, Morton & Whiting LLP, LeRoy, N.Y., 1996—. Coach LeRoy Little League, 1995-99; dir., coach Youth Basketball, LeRoy, N.Y., 1996-99. Mem. N.Y. State Bar Assn., Genesee County Bar Assn., Stafford Country Club, Inc., Northwoods Sportsmen's Assn. Roman Catholic. Avocations: golf, tennis. hunting, fishing, coaching youth sports. Banking, General practice, Real property. Home: 89 E Main St Le Roy NY 14482-1235 Office: Boylan Morton & Whiting LLP 45 W Main St Le Roy NY 14482-1305

**WHITING, RICHARD ALBERT,** lawyer; b. Cambridge, Mass., Dec. 2, 1922; s. Albert S. and Jessie (Coleman) W.; m. Marvelene Nash, Feb. 22, 1948 (div. 1984); children—Richard A. Jr., Stephen C., Jeffrey D., Gary S., Kimberly G.; m. Joanne Sherry, Oct. 14, 1984. AB, Dartmouth Coll., 1944; JD, Yale U., 1949. Bar: D.C. 1949. Assoc. Steptoe & Johnson, Washington, 1949-55, ptnr., 1956-86, of counsel, 1987—; adj. prof. Vt. Law Sch., South Royalton, 1985-90; mem. exec. com. Yale Law Sch. Assn., New Haven, 1985-88; mem. adv. bd. The Antitrust Bull., N.Y.C., 1975—. Contbr. articles to profl. jours. Trustee Colby-Sawyer Coll., 1987-97. 1st lt. U.S. Army, 1945-46. Mem. ABA (council mem. Antitrust Law sect. 1977-85, del. to Ho. Dels. 1982-83, chmn. 1984-85). Presbyterian. Antitrust. Home: PO Box 749 Grantham NH 03753-0749 Office: 1330 Connecticut Ave NW Washington DC 20036-1704

**WHITING, STEPHEN CLYDE,** lawyer; b. Arlington, Va., Mar. 20, 1952; s. Richard A. Whiting; m. Patrice Quinn, May 24, 1980; children: Kelsey, Daniel, Seth, Samuel. BA magna cum laude, Dartmouth Coll., 1974; JD, U. Va., 1978. Bar: Maine 1978, U.S. Dist. Ct. Maine 1978. Ptnr. Douglas, Whiting, Denham & Rogers, Portland, Maine, 1978-98; founder The Whiting Law Firm, P.A., Portland, 1998—; Maine state dir. Am. Ctr. Law and Justice, 1998—. Co-author: Trying the Automobile Injury Case in Maine, 1993, Premises Liability: Preparation and Trial of a Difficult Case in Maine, 1994, Trying Soft Tissue Injury Cases in Maine, 1995. Mem. ATLA, Maine Bar Assn., Maine Trial Lawyers Assn., Phi Beta Kappa. General civil litigation, Insurance, Personal injury. Office: The Whiting Law Firm PA 75 Pearl St Ste 213 Portland ME 04101-4101

**WHITLEY, JOE DALLY,** lawyer; b. Atlanta, Nov. 12, 1950; s. Thomas Youngie and Mary Jo (Dally) W.; m. Kathleen Pinion, Sept. 27, 1975; children: Lauren Jacqueline, Thomas McMillan. BA, U. Ga., 1972, JD, 1975. Bar: Ga. 1975, U.S. Supreme Ct. 1989. Assoc. Kelly, Denney, Pease & Allison, Columbus, Ga., 1975-78; asst. dist. atty. Chattahoochee Jud. Cir., Columbus, 1978-79; assoc. Hirsch, Beil & Partin, P.C., Columbus, 1979-81; U.S. atty. Dept. Justice, Macon, Ga., 1981-87; dep. asst. atty. gen., Criminal Div. Dept. Justice, Washington, 1987-88, dep. assoc. atty. gen., 1988-89, acting assoc. atty. gen., 1989; ptnr. Smith, Gambrell & Russell, Atlanta, 1989-90; U.S. atty. Dept. of Justice, Atlanta, 1990-93; ptnr. Kilpatrick Stockton, Atlanta, 1993-97, Alston & Bird, Atlanta, 1997—; mem. atty. gen.'s adv. com. Dept. Justice, Washington, 1982-85; chmn. organized crime and violent crime subcom. Atty. Gen.'s Adv. Com., 1990-93, mem. investigative subcom., chmn. white collar crime subcom., 1993—. Treas. Muscogee County Young Reps., Columbus, 1979-80. Mem. Ga. Bar Assn., Macon Bar Assn., Young Lawyers Club (pres. Columbus chpt. 1980-81), Lawyers Club of Atlanta. Republican. Presbyterian. Criminal. Office: Alston & Bird 1201 W Peachtree St NW Atlanta GA 30309-3424

**WHITLOCK, JULIE MARIE,** lawyer; b. Omaha, May 28, 1968; d. Larry F. and Barbara E. Schucht; m. Kevin M. Whitlock, June 25, 1994. BA in Fgn. Affairs, U. Va., 1990; JD, U. Richmond, 1994. Bar: Va. 1994, U.S. Dist. Ct. (ea. dist.) Va. 1994, U.S. Ct. Appeals (4th cir.) 1995. Ptnr. Thorsen Marchant & Scher LLP, Richmond, Va., 1996-98; assoc. Thompson & McMullan, PC, Richmond, 1998—. Mem. Chesterfield Jr. Woman's Club. General civil litigation, Labor, Intellectual property. Office: Thompson & McMullan PC 100 Shockoe Slip Ste C Richmond VA 23219-4140

**WHITLOCK, WILLIE WALKER,** lawyer; b. Mineral, Va., Nov. 16, 1925; s. Edward Jackson and Lottie Alma (Talley) W.; m. Eula Madeline Dymacek, July 15, 1950; children: John D., Jane Whitlock Sisk. BS in Bus., Coll. William and Mary, 1950; LBL, Va. Coll. Law, 1953. Bar: Va. 1955, U.S. Dist. Ct. Va. 1957. Atty. Town of Mineral, 1965-97, County of Louisa, 1976-79; mem. adv. bd. Jefferson Nat. Bank, Mineral, 1972-98. Chmn. Louisa County Dem. Com., Louisa, Va., 1978-82, 32d Legis. Dist. Va., 1978-82. Sgt. U.S. Army, 1945-46. Mem. Va. State Bar, Piedmont Bar Assn. (pres. 1976), Louisa County Bar Assn. (pres. 1968-99), Am. Legion, Lions, Masons. Baptist. Home and Office: PO Box 130 Mineral VA 23117-0130

**WHITLOW, JAMES ADAMS,** lawyer; b. Mayfield, Ky., Jan. 29, 1968; s. Charles William and June (Hawkens) W. BA, Transylvania U., 1990; JD, Harvard U., 1993. Bar: N.C. 1994. Assoc. Parker Poe Adams & Bernstein, L.L.P., Charlotte, N.C., 1993-95, Akin, Gump, Strauss, Hauer & Feld, L.L.P., Dallas, 1995-97, Rubin, Baum, Levin, Constant, Friedman & Bilzin, Miami, 1997—. General corporate, Mergers and acquisitions, Entertainment. Office: Rubin Baum Levin Constant Friedman & Bilzin 2500 First Union Fin Ctr Miami FL 33131

**WHITMAN, CHARLES S., III,** lawyer; b. N.Y.C., Apr. 19, 1942; s. Charles S. Jr. and Janet (Russell) W; m. Christina L. Madden, Oct. 20, 1979; 1 child, Elizabeth R. AB, Harvard U., 1964, LLB, 1967; LLM, Cambridge U., 1989. BAr: N.Y. 1967, U.S. Supreme Ct. 1972. Asst. to chmn. U.S. SEC, Washington, 1971-74; gen. counsel Mitchell Hutchins Inc., N.Y.C., 1974; assoc. Davis Polk & Wardwell, N.Y.C., 1968-71, 74-76, ptnr., 1977—. Bd. dirs. Manhattan Eye, Ear and Throat Hosp., N.Y.C., 1990—. Mem. Am. Law Inst. Republican. Presbyterian. Securities, General corporate. Office: Davis Polk & Wardwell 450 Lexington Ave New York NY 10017-3911

**WHITMER, FREDERICK LEE,** lawyer; b. Terre Haute, Ind., Nov. 5, 1947; s. Lee Arthur and Ella (Diekhoff) W.; m. Valeri Cade; children: Caitlin Margaret, Meghan Connors, Christian Frederick. BA, Wabash Coll., 1969; JD, Columbia U., 1973. Bar: N.Y. 1975, U.S. Dist. Ct. (so. dist.) N.Y. 1975, N.J. 1976, U.S. Dist. Ct. N.J. 1976, U.S. Ct. Appeals (3d cir.) 1977, U.S. Ct. Appeals (fed. cir.) 1983, U.S. Ct. Appeals (2d cir.) 1987, U.S. Supreme Ct. 1988, U.S. Ct. Appeals (7th cir.) 1994. Assoc. Kaye, Scholer, Fierman, Hays & Handler, N.Y.C., 1973-76, Pitney, Hardin & Kipp, Morristown, 1976-78; ptnr. Pitney, Hardin, Kipp & Szuch, Morristown, 1979—. Mem. ABA, N.J. Bar Assn., Phi Beta Kappa. Republican. Lutheran. Antitrust, Trademark and copyright, Federal civil litigation. Home: 190 Hurlbutt St Wilton CT 06897-2706 Office: Pitney Hardin Kipp & Szuch PO Box 1945 Morristown NJ 07962-1945

**WHITMER, J. A.,** lawyer; b. South Bend, Ind., Mar. 24, 1952; d. Charles Inman and Kathleen Louise W.; m. John S. Frizzo, July 13, 1991; stepchildren: Jacinda Leigh Frizzo, Steven Richard Frizzo, Nathaniel Joseph Frizzo. BA magna cum laude, Hanover Coll., 1974; JD summa cum laude, U. Notre Dame Law Sch., 1982. Bar: Calif. 1982, U.S. Dist. Ct. (ctrl. dist.) Calif. 1982, Ind. 1983, U.S. Dist. Ct. (no. and so. dists.) Ind. 1983. Assoc. atty. Surr & Hellyer, San Bernardino, Calif., 1982-84, Barnes & Thornburg, South Bend, Ind., 1984-85, Thorne, Grodnik, Ransel, Duncan, Byron & Hostetler, Elkhart, Ind., 1985-91; pvt. practice Elkhart, Ind., 1992—. Mem. Am. Bar Assn., Ind. State Bar Assn., Elkhart City Bar Assn., Kiwanis Club of Elkhart (bd. dirs. 1995-98). Avocations: antiques, gardening, reading. General practice, General corporate, Bankruptcy. Office: 421 S 2nd St Ste 405 Elkhart IN 46516-3227

**WHITMER, LESLIE GAY,** federal official; b. Lexington, Ky., July 31, 1941; s. Leslie Allen and Gaynelle Kimbrell (McPherson) W.; m. Patricia Ann Welch, July 5, 1969; 1 child, Mary Gay. BS, U. Ky., 1963, JD, 1965. Bar: Ky. 1966, U.S. Dist. Ct. Ky. 1972, U.S. Supreme Ct. 1972. Atty. advisor gen. Office of Gen. Counsel, U.S. Dept. Agr., Chgo., 1966-69; dir. bar counsel Ky. Bar Assn.; editor Ky. Bar Jour., 1974-83; registrar Supreme Ct. Ky., 1975-83; clk. U.S. Dist. Ct. (ea. dist.) Ky., 1983—, mem. civil justice reform act adv. group, 1992—; adj. prof. law U. Ky. Coll. Law, 1980, 82; mem. Gov.'s Task Force on Office Pub. Advocacy, 1982; exec. dir. Ky. Bar Ctr., 1979-83; sec.-treas. Ky. Bar Title Ins. Agy. Inc., 1973-83; asst. sec.-treas. Ky. Bar Found., 1979-83; exec. dir. Ky. Fed. Jud. Selection Commn., 1978-83; bd. dirs., sec.-treas. Ky. Legal Services Plan, Inc., 1978-83. Contbr. articles to legal jours. Recipient Recognition of Merit award U. Ky. Coll. Law Alumni Assn., 1983. Mem. Ky. Bar Assn. (bd. dirs., bar counsel, treas. 1973-83, discipline com. 1987-98), Fed. Bar Assn. (bd. dirs. 1998—), Psi Chi, Phi Alpha Delta, Spindletop Hall Club, U.K. Faculty Club. Office: Federal Courthouse Lexington KY 40507

**WHITMORE, BRUCE G.,** lawyer. BA, Tufts U., 1966; JD, Harvard U., 1969. Bar: N.Y. 1970, Calif. 1973, Pa. 1979. Gen. atty. ARCO Transp. Co., 1985-86; assoc. gen. counsel corp. fin. ARCO, 1986-90; v.p., gen. counsel ARCO Chem. Co., 1990-94; sr. v.p., gen. counsel, corp. sec. Atlantic Richfield Co., L.A., 1995—. Mem. ABA. Office: ARCO 333 S Hope St Fl 20 Los Angeles CA 90071-1406

**WHITNEY, CHARLES LEROY,** lawyer; b. Aurora, Nebr., Oct. 1, 1918; s. Charles Leroy and Alta Leona (Entriken) W.; m. Emily Louise Rothman, Nov. 17, 1942; children: Charles Leroy III, Anne Rothman, Mary Elizabeth, William Shafer. AB, York Coll.; LLB, U. Nebr. Bar: Nebr. 1946. Pvt. practice Aurora, 1946-59; ptnr. Whitney and Newman, Aurora, 1959-73; sr. ptnr. Whitney, Newman, Mersch & Otto, Aurora, 1974-87, of counsel, 1987—. Bd. dirs. Prairie Plains Inst., Aurora. Served to lt. USNR, 1942-46, PTO. Mem. Nebr. State Bar Assn., Aurora C. of C., Am. Legion (past comdr. local post). Democrat. United Methodist. Avocations: fishing, woodworking, photography. General practice, Probate, Real property. Home: 40 Rosewood Cir Aurora NE 68818-1420 Office: Whitney Newman Mersch & Otto PO Box 228 Aurora NE 68818-0228

**WHITNEY, DAVID,** prosecutor; b. Alamosa, Colo., Apr. 25, 1942; s. Robert F. and Clarissa I. (Wilson) W.; m. Martha Green, Sept. 26, 1980; children from previous marriage: LeAnn Gonzalez, Christopher. AB in Philosophy, UCLA, 1968, JD, 1971, postgrad., 1971-72. Bar: Calif. 1972, U.S. Dist. Ct. (cen. dist.) Calif. 1973, U.S. Ct. Appeals (9th cir.) 1981, U.S. Supreme Ct. 1985. Dep. pub. defender L.A., 1972-74, pvt. practice, 1974-78; pvt. practice San Bernardino, Calif., 1978-86; dep. dist. atty. Dist. Atty.'s Office, San Bernardino, 1986—, death penalty coord., psychiat. issues coord., 1988—, lead atty. major crimes unit, 1996—; expert witness, lectr. in field. Chmn. Fire Commn., Forest Falls, Calif., 1988—. Mem. Calif. Dist. Attys. Assn. (mem. state death penalty com. 1995—), Forensic Mental Health Assn. Calif. (pub. policy com. 1996—), Criminal Cts. Bar Assn. (bd. dirs. 1982-84), County Bar Assn. (jud. evaluation com. 1987-89, co-chmn. 1988, bench/bar com. 1989, chmn. office mgmt. adv. com. 1995, domestic violence prosecutions com. 1995). Democrat. Office: Office of Dist Atty 316 Mountain Vw San Bernardino CA 92415-0001

**WHITNEY, ENOCH JONATHAN,** lawyer; b. Jacksonville, Fla., Oct. 7, 1945; s. Enoch Johnson and Iris Ida (Sperber) W.; m. Diane Marie Dupuy, Aug. 29, 1968; children: Elizabeth, William, Edward. BA, Fla. State U., 1967, JD, 1970; grad., FBI Nat. Law Inst., 1989. Bar: Fla. 1970, U.S. Dist. Ct. (no. dist.) Fla. 1970 U.S. Dist. Ct. (mid. dist.) Fla. 1982, U.S. Dist. Ct. (so. dist.) Fla. 1989, U.S. Ct. Appeals (5th cir.) 1971, U.S. Ct. Appeals (11th cir.) 1981, U.S. Supreme Ct. 1974. Rsch. asst. Fla. 1st Dist. Ct. Appeals, Tallahassee, 1971; asst. atty. gen. Fla. Dept. Legal Affairs, Tallahassee, 1971-74; asst. gen. counsel Fla. Dept. Hwy. Safety & Motor Vehicles, Tallahassee, 1974-79, gen. counsel, 1979-82, 86—; gen. counsel Fla. Parole and Probation Commn., Tallahassee, 1982-85; instr. Fla. Hwy. Patrol Tng. Acad., Tallahassee, 1977-82, 86—. Named Able Toastmaster, Toastmasters Internat., 1977. Mem. ABA, Tallahassee Bar Assn. (ex officio dir. 1989-97), Fla. Govt. Bar Assn. (pres. 1977-78), Fla. Bar (bd. govs. 1989-97, charter mem. govt. law sect. 1991, appellate law sect. 1994, bd. cert. appellate lawyer 1994, budget com. 1992-95, 96-99), Fla. Coun. Bar Assn. Pres. (life), Fla. State U. Alumni Assn. (life), Fla. Supreme Ct. Hist. Soc., Supreme Ct. U.S. Hist. Soc., Atty. Gen.'s Hist. Soc. Fla., Fla. Sheriff's Assn., Govs. Club, Capital Tiger Bay Club, Fla. Assn. Police Attys., Kiwanis (pres. Tallahassee 1984-85, lt. gov. fla. dist. 1986-87). Democrat. Roman Catholic. Avocations: antique collecting, reading. Home: 5001 Vernon Rd Tallahassee FL 32311-4534 Office: Fla Dept Hwy Safety & Motor Vehicles 2900 Apalachee Pky Tallahassee FL 32399-6552

**WHITNEY, JOHN FRANKLIN,** lawyer; b. Green Bay, Wis., Aug. 10, 1953; s. John Clarence and Helen (Mayer) W. BA, Tulane U., 1975; JD, Georgetown U., 1978. Bar: La. 1978. Assoc. Phelps, Dunbar, New Orleans, 1978-82; assoc. Barham & Churchill, New Orleans, 1983-85, ptnr., 1985-88; pvt. practice law New Orleans, 1988-89; counsel Lea & Gibbens, New Orleans, 1989-90; ptnr. Breazeale, Sachse & Wilson, New Orleans, 1990—. Fellow La. Bar Found. (life); mem. ABA, Fed. Bar Assn., Fed. Energy Bar Assn. Republican. Roman Catholic. Avocations: golf, racquetball. Federal civil litigation, State civil litigation, Securities. Home: 4007 St Charles Ave Apt 305 New Orleans LA 70115-4774 Office: Breazeale Sachse & Wilson 909 Poydras St Ste 2400 New Orleans LA 70112-4004

**WHITNEY, KATHLEEN MARIE,** lawyer, educator; b. Maywood, Calif., Dec. 3, 1946; m. William Joseph Rohr, July 1, 1986; children: Aran Hunter, Kristie Jennifer. BA, Calif. State U., 1979; JD, Western State U., 1984; LLM, U. San Diego, 1996. Bar: Calif. 1985, U.S. Ct. Appeals (9th cir.). Assoc. various litigation firms, 1985-92; immigration and naturalization lawyer for Haitian refugees, 1992-95; prof. law Western State U., Fullerton, Calif., 1992—. Bd. dirs., legal counsel Internat. Childcare, Columbus, Ohio, 1990-97; vol. Episcopal Svc. Alliance, Santa Ana, Calif., 1988-90. Recipient civic award Orange County Met. Area, 1996. Mem. Calif. State Bar Assn. (com. legal profls. with disabilities). Office: Western State U 1111 N State College Blvd Fullerton CA 92831-3000

**WHITNEY, LARRY GENE,** lawyer; b. Muncie, Ind., July 25, 1946; s. John Wesley and Fannie Mae (Wallace) W.; m. Gail B; children: Tamara D., Tiffany D. BS cum laude, Ball State U., 1969; JD, Ind. U., 1972. Bar: Ind. 1972, U.S. Ct. Appeals (4th cir.) 1974, D.C. 1975, U.S. Ct. Appeals (6th and 9th cirs.) 1975, U.S. Dist Ct. D.C. 1976, U.S. Dist. Ct. (so. dist.) Ind. 1981, U.S. Ct. Appeals (7th cir.) 1988. Trial atty. criminal div. U.S. Dept. Justice, Washington, 1972-75; asst. U.S. atty. U.S. Atty.'s Office, Washington, 1975-79; chief counsel Marion County Prosecutor's Office, Indpls., 1979-82; adj. prof. law Ind. U. Law Sch., Indpls., 1982-83; pvt. practice Whitney, Klopchin, Ross & Draper, Indpls., 1982-85; lawyer Coons & Saint, Indpls., 1985-92; cons. Indpls. Bus. Devel. Found., 1982-87. Mem. infrastructure com. C. of C., Indpls., 1991, Pub. Defender Commn., Indpls., 1991, Ctr. for Leadership Devel., Indpls., 1992, fin. com. Am. Heart Assn., Indpls., 1983-84. Mem. NAACP (life), Nat. Bar Assn., Am. Trial Lawyers, Marion County Bar Assn. (bd. dirs., pres. 1990-91, Rufus C. Kuykendall award 1992), Indpls. Bar Assn., Indpls. Urban League. Avocations: tennis, sailing, travel, reading. General civil litigation, Personal injury, General corporate. Office: Saint Simonseu Thomas and Whitney 127 E Michigan St Fl 5 Indianapolis IN 46204-1518

**WHITNEY, WILLIAM BERNARD,** lawyer; b. Ft. Worth, Dec. 19, 1941; s. William Bernard and Mary Elizabeth (Garrett) W.; m. Renate Baltmanis, Aug. 27, 1966; children: Marilyn Whitney Byrum, William Baltmanis. BA, U. Kans., 1963, JD, 1965. Bar: Tex. 1965, U.S. Dist. Ct. (no. dist.) Tex. 1971, U.S. Ct. Appeals (5th cir.) 1976; cert. in estate planning and probate, Tex. Assoc. Garrett and Stahala, Ft. Worth, 1966-70, Crumley Murphy & Shrull, Ft. Worth, 1970-79, Handy Morgan and Meeks, Hurst, Tex., 1979-80; pvt. practice, Ft. Worth, 1980—. Deacon, tchr., trustee Rosen Heights Bapt. Ch., Ft. Worth, 1980—; vice chmn. Southwestern coun. Southwestern Bapt. Theol. Sem., 1994-98. Mem. Tarrant County Bar Assn. (editor Bar News 1970), Tarrant County Probate Bar Assn. (bd. dirs. 1992-94), Otimists (bd. dirs. Ft. Worth 1982-83, pres. 1989-90). Estate planning, Probate. Home: 4101 Ranier Ct Fort Worth TX 76109-5026 Office: 6500 W Vickery Blvd Fort Worth TX 76116-9109

**WHITSON, LISH,** lawyer; b. Washington, Oct. 13, 1942; s. I. Lish and Clytie B. (Collier) W.; m. Barbara Lee Sullivan, Sept. 16, 1965; children: L. Richard, Kimberly S. BA in Philosophy, Pa. State U., 1965; JD, U. Wash., 1972. Bar: Wash. 1973, U.S. Dist. Ct. (we. dist.) 1973, U.S. Dist. Ct. (ea. dist.) 1977, U.S. Supreme Ct. 1977. Assoc. Seattle-King County Pub. Defender Assn., 1972-76; assoc. Helsell, Fetterman, Martin, Todd & Hokanson, Seattle, 1976-81, ptnr., 1981-98; of counsel Badgley Mullins, Seattle, 1998—. Bd. dirs., past chmn. Downtown Emergency Svc. Ctr., Seattle, 1981-97; bd. dirs. Allied Arts, 1988-96, pres., 1994-96; trustee Seattle Youth Symphony Orch., bd. dirs., 1986-95; mem. alumni bd. U. Wash. Law Sch., 1993—, treas., 1997—. Fellow Am. Bar Found., Am. Coll. Trial Lawyers; mem. ABA (young lawyers divsn. rep. to exec. coun. 1979, mem. standing com. on lawyer referral svc. 1990-96, chmn. 1992-96, commn. on women in the profn. 1998—), ATLA, Am. Bd. Trial Advocates (assoc.), Wash. State Bar Assn. (gov. 1995-98), King County Bar Found. (mem. pres. coun.), Seattle-King County Bar Assn. (pro bono com. chmn. 1981-84, bd. dirs. 1988-91, young lawyers sect. 1977-79, chmn. 1979, Pro Bono Svc. award 1993), Fed. Bar Assn., Am. Judicature Soc. (bd. dirs. 1981-86), Seattle Pub. Def. Assn. (bd. dirs. 1982-86), Wash. Athletic Club. General civil litigation, Product liability, Personal injury. Office: Badgley-Mullins Law Group 2101 3rd Ave Ste 5100 Seattle WA 98121-2321

**WHITTEN, BEATRICE EHRENBERG,** lawyer; b. Charleston, S.C., Oct. 19, 1959; d. David Owen and Susan Rush (Hills) W.; m. C. Patrick Leopold, Dec. 30, 1989; children: Jesse Lawrence, Susan Cameron. AS in Criminal Justice, Trident Tech. Coll., Charleston, 1980; BS in Criminal Justice, Charleston So. U., 1987; JD, U. S.C., 1990. Bar: S.C. 1990; cert. civil mediator. Assoc. Thomas W. Greene, Charleston, S.C., 1990-91; assoc./ptnr. Lucey & Whitten, PA, Charleston, 1991-93; pvt. practice Mt. Pleasant, S.C., 1993—; adj. faculty Trident Tech. Coll., Charleston, 1994—; instr. legal writing U. S.C., Columbia, 1988-90. Mem. S.C. Bar Assn. (bar pro bono program 1990—). Avocations: canoeing, camping. Administrative and regulatory, Probate, Family and matrimonial. Office: 745 Johnnie Dodds Blvd # B Mount Pleasant SC 29464-3021

**WHITTEN, C. G.,** lawyer; b. Abilene, Tex., Apr. 1, 1925; s. C.G. and Eugenia (St. Clair) W.; m. Alene Henley, Nov. 25, 1945; children: Julie, Jennifer, Blake; m. Carol Owen, Apr. 22, 1977. JD, U. Tex.-Austin, 1949. Bar: Tex. 1949, U.S. Dist. Ct. (no. dist.) Tex. 1950, U.S. Supreme Ct. 1955. Assoc. Grisham & King, Abilene, Tex., 1949-52; ptnr. Jameson & Whitten, 1952-54, Jameson, Whitten, Harrell & Wilcox, 1954-58, Whitten, Harrell, Erwin & Jameson, 1958-68, Whitten, Sprain, Wagner, Price & Edwards, 1968-79, Whitten, Haag, Cobb & Hacker, 1979-82; sr. ptnr. Whitten, Haag, Hacker, Hagin & Cutbirth, 1983-87; pres. Whitten, Hacker, Hagin, Anderson & Rucker, P.C., 1987-92; of counsel Whitten & Young, 1992—; gen. counsel Pittencrieff Comms., Inc., 1992-97, sr. v.p., dir., 1994-97; pres. Abilene Improvement Corp., 1994—; mem. tax. increment funding dist., 1995—, mem. adv. coun. U. of Tex. Press, 1995—, chmn. 1998—. Mem. Abilene Ind. Sch. Dist. Bd. Edn., 1956-76, pres. 1972-76. General corporate. Office: PO Box 208 Abilene TX 79604-0208

**WHITTERS, JAMES PAYTON, III,** lawyer, university administrator; b. Boston, Oct. 23, 1939; s. James P. Jr. and Norene (Jones) W.; m. Elizabeth Robertson, July 19, 1969; children: James P. IV, Catharine A. BA in History, Trinity Coll., Hartford, Conn., 1962; JD, Boston Coll., 1969; postgrad, U. Mass., Boston. Bar: Mass. 1969, U.S. Dist. Ct. Mass. 1970, U.S. Ct. Appeals (1st cir.) 1972. Assoc. Ely, Bartlett, Brown & Proctor, Boston, 1969-74; assoc. Gaston Snow & Ely Bartlett, Boston, 1974-79, ptnr., 1979-88; ptnr. Gaston & Snow, Boston, 1988-91; of counsel Peabody & Brown, Boston, 1991-95; dir. Office Career Svcs. Suffolk U. Law Sch., Boston, 1995—; adj. prof. Am. legal history Suffolk U. Law Sch., 1997—; bd. dirs., sec. Robertson Factories, Inc., Taunton, Mass., 1979—; v.p. Alkalol Co., Taunton, 1976-97, sr. v.p., 1997—; vis. tchr. Groton (Mass.) Sch., 1993-94; mem. Mass. Conflict Intervention Mediation Team, 1995—. Bd. dirs. New Eng. com. NAACP Legal Def. Fund, 1982—, Beacon Hill Nursery Sch., 1976-78, Mass. Appleseed Ctr. Law and Justice, 1997—; chmn. Mass. Outdoor Advt. Bd., Boston, 1975-81; vice chmn. Mass. Jud. Nominating Coun., Boston, 1983-87; trustee Trinity Coll., 1983-95; trustee, sec. Hurricane Island Outward Bound Sch., 1977-87; bd. dirs. Mass. affiliate Am. Heart Assn., 1979-98, chmn., 1989-91; bd. dirs. Greater Boston Legal Svcs., 1982-84, 93-99, Mass. Assn. Mediation Programs and Practitioners, 1993-98. Lt. (j.g.) USN, 1962-65. Recipient Alumni Excellence award Trinity Coll., 1987. Mem. Boston Bar Assn., Mass. Bar Assn., ABA, The Country Club (Brookline, Mass.). Democrat. Unitarian. Avocations: reading history, mountain climbing & jogging. Home: 44 Mount Vernon St Boston MA 02108-1302

**WHITTIER, MONTE RAY,** lawyer; b. Pocatello, Idaho, June 28, 1955; s. Raymond Max and Marjorie Lucille (Pea) W.; m. Denise Womack, May 29, 1982; children: Jason Dennis, Sarah Michelle, Sadie Mckenzie. BS in Acctg., U. Utah, 1976; JD, U. Idaho, 1978. Bar: Idaho 1978, U.S. Dist. Ct. Idaho, 1979, U.S. Supreme Ct. 1985, U.S. Tax Ct. 1989, U.S. Ct. Appeals (9th cir.) 1991, Idaho, 1979. Ptnr., shareholder Whittier & Souza, Pocatello, 1979-89; shareholder, mng. atty. Whittier, Souza & Naftz, Pocatello, 1989-97; asst. gen. counsel Melaleuca, Inc., Idaho Falls, 1997—. Vol. Internat. Spl. Olympics, South Bend, Ind., 1987, Mpls., 1991; mem. Magistrate Commn. 6th Jud. Dist., Pocatello, 1989-91; bd. dirs. Bannock Baseball, Inc., 1996-97.

Mem. ATLA, Idaho Trial Lawyers Assn. (bd. dirs. 6th Jud. Dist. Pro Bono award 1994), Civitan (pres. Bannock chpt. 1983-84, bd. dirs. 1981-87, 92-93, lt. gov. Intermountain chpt. 1986-87, Outstanding Pres. award 1984, Outstanding Svc. award 1982-83, 86-88, 91). Avocations: bicycling, skiing, golfing, Spl. Olympics vol. activities. General corporate, General civil litigation, Personal injury. Office: Melaleuca Inc 3910 S Yellowstone Hwy Idaho Falls ID 83402-6003

**WHITTLESEY, JOHN WILLIAMS,** lawyer, consultant, arbitrator; b. Newton Upper Falls, Mass., Aug. 18, 1917; s. John Eddy and Dorothy (Williams) W.; m. Barbara Baur, June 13, 1942; children—J. Baur, Diana, Paul Woodman. B.A., Harvard U., 1937, LL.B., 1940; LL.M., Columbia U., 1947. Bar: Mass. 1940, N.Y. 1953, U.S. Dist. Ct. (so. and ea. dist.) N.Y., 1972, U.S. Ct. Appeals (2d cir.) 1972, U.S. Supreme Ct. Labor atty. U.S. C. of C., Washington, 1946-51; asst. industry mem. Wage Stblzn. Bd., Washington, 1951-52; counsel Fisher & Rudge, N.Y.C., 1952-53; chief labor counsel Union Carbide Corp., Danbury, Conn., 1953-82; sole practice law, Chappaqua, N.Y., 1982—; of counsel Wisehart & Koch, 1984—, Keane & Beane, White Plains, N.Y., 1985-89; adminstrv. law judge Office Hearings and Appeals Social Security Adminstrn., 1990-93; cons. in field; chmn. occupational safety and health com. N.Y. Bus. Coun., Albany, 1975-87; chmn. N.Y.C. Labor and Human Resources Com., 1987-89. Committeeman Westchester Republican County Com., White Plains, N.Y., 1957—; committeeman New Castle Rep. Town Com., Chappaqua, N.Y., 1957—, chmn., 1969-73. Served to capt. U.S. Army, 1940-45, ETO. New Directions grantee OSHA, 1984-85. Mem. ABA, N.Y. State Bar Assn., Westchester County Bar Assn., N.Y.C. Bar Assn., Am. Arbitration Assn. Republican. Congregationalist. Avocations: sailing, philately. Labor, Workers' compensation, Pension, profit-sharing, and employee benefits. Home and Office: 310 Douglas Rd Chappaqua NY 10514-3100 Office: Wisehart & Koch 9 W 44th St New York NY 10036-6601

**WHITWORTH, J. BRYAN, JR.,** oil company executive, lawyer; b. Baton Rouge, Aug. 14, 1938; s. Jennings Bryan Sr. and Virginia Ann (Calvert) W.; m. Sue Alice Walters, July 15, 1961 (Jan. 1982); children: Catherine Ann, Elizabeth, Suzanne Virginia; m. Donna Axum, Mar. 1, 1984. BS Pre-Law, U. Ala., 1961, LLM, 1964. Assoc. Cabaniss, Johnston, Gardner & Clark, Birmingham, Ala., 1964-66; gen. AT&T, Washington and N.Y.C., 1966-71; atty. Phillips Petroleum Co., Bartlesville, Okla., 1971-77, sr. counsel, 1977-79, assoc. gen. counsel, 1979-81, v.p. govt. relations, 1981-95, sr. v.p., gen. counsel and govt. relations, 1995—; bd. dirs. Salk Inst. Biotechnology/ Industry Assn. Inc., San Diego; mem. policy devel com. Am. Petroleum Inst., Washington, 1982—, Gov.'s Task Force on Higher Edn. in Okla. and the Council for Reorgn. of State Govt., Oklahoma City, 1985-87; bd. dirs. First Nat. Bank & First Bancshares Inc., Bartlesville. Former editor-in-chief Ala. Law Rev., U. Ala. Mem. Okla. Bar Assn., N.Y. Bar Assn., D.C. Bar Assn., Bartlesville Area C. of C. (v.p., bd. dirs. 1985-87, pres. 1987-88). Lodge: Rotary. Office: Phillips Petroleum Co 18 Phillips Bldg 4th and Keeler Ave Bartlesville OK 74004*

**WHORISKEY, ROBERT DONALD,** lawyer; b. Cambridge, Mass., May 9, 1929; s. John Joseph and Katherine Euphemia (MacDonald) W.; m. Martha Beebe Poutas, Apr. 16, 1966; children: Alexandra, Jonathan, Eliza. AB, Harvard U., 1952; JD, Boston Coll., 1958; LLM, NYU, 1960. Bar: Mass. 1958, N.Y. 1963, U.S. Tax Ct. 1961, U.S. Claims Ct. 1969, U.S. Dist. Ct. (so. dist.) N.Y. 1969, U.S. Ct. Customs 1971, U.S. Ct. Appeals (2d cir.) 1972, U.S. Ct. Appeals (3d cir.) 1983, U.S. Ct. Appeals (D.C. cir.) 1991, U.S. Supreme Ct. 1974. Sr. trial atty. Office Chief Counsel, IRS, N.Y.C., 1960-67; assoc. Curtis, Mallet-Prevost, Colt & Mosle, N.Y.C., 1967-70, ptnr., 1970—, exec. com., 1978-82, chmn. tax dept., 1982-87; bd. dirs. Internat. Tax Inst., v.p., lectr., 1980-84, chmn. bd., pres., lectr., 1985-87; lectr. Practicing Law Inst., World Trade Inst., Tax Execs. Inst., Am. Mgmt. Assn., Coun. for Internat. Tax Edn.; bd. dirs. Life Ins. Co. of Boston and N.Y., Inc. Author: Foreign Trusts, 1977, Annual Institute on International Taxation, 1966, 80, 81, (with Sidney Pine, Ralph Seligman) Tax and Business Benefits of the Bahamas, 1986; contbg. author: International Boycotts, CCH Federal Tax Service, 1988, CCH Smart Tax CD-ROM: Third Party Information, John Wiley and Sons, Inc.'s Transfer Pricing, 1993, Transfer Pricing Under IRC & 482: Overview and Planning, Part I, 1996, Accuracy Related Penalty Regulations for Transfer Pricing, Part II, 1997, Third Party Information, Part III, 1997, U.S. Taxation of International Operations, Rarren, Gorham Lamont, 1998—. Trustee, treas. Montessori Sch. Westchester, 1974-77; mem. bd. ethics Village of Larchmont, N.Y., 1988—. With U.S. Army, 1952-54. Mem. ABA (com. on alternative tax sys. tax sect. 1994—, com. on ct. procedure tax sec. 1997—), N.Y. State Bar Assn. (com. on practice and procedure tax sect. 1990—), Assn. of the Bar of the City of N.Y., Harvard Club, Larchmont Yacht Club. Democrat. Roman Catholic. Taxation, general, Corporate taxation, Estate taxation. Office: Curtis Mallet-Prevost Colt & Mosle 101 Park Ave Fl 34 New York NY 10178-0061

**WHORLEY, JAMES MARSHALL,** lawyer; b. Murfreesboro, Tenn., Aug. 4, 1963; s. John Frank Whorley and Elizabeth Frances Bradley; m. Chris Holley, Dec. 19, 1987; children: Marshall, Holley. BS with high honors, U. Tenn., 1985; MBA, U. Tex., 1987, JD with honors, 1990. Bar: Tex. 1991, U.S. Dist. Ct. (so. dist.) Tex. 1992, U.S. Dist. Ct. (we. dist.) Tex. 1994; bd. cert. family law Tex. Bd. Legal Specialization. Assoc. Looper, Reed, Mark and McGraw, Houston, 1991-94; pvt. practice, Temple, Tex., 1994—. Mem. Tex. Acad. Family Law Specialists. Home: 515 W Royal Ave Temple TX 76501-1631 Office: 1912 W Avenue H Temple TX 76504-5232

**WHYTE, KEVIN J.,** lawyer; b. Morgantown, W.Va., Feb. 7, 1960; s. Thomas J. and Margaret Ann W.; m. Ellen C. Pantelich White, Apr. 27, 1996; 1 child, Ryan Patrick. BA, U. Va., Charlottesville, 1982; JD, U. Richmond, Va., 1985. Bar: Pa. 1987—, W.Va. 1986—. Law clk. Fed. Dist. Ct., Charleston, W.Va., 1985-87; assoc. Berkman Ruslander, Pitts., 1987-88; assoc., ptnr. Doepken, Keevican & Weiss, Pitts., 1988—; mem. Eastern Mineral Law Found., 1993—. Fin.Devel. Com. Am. Red Cross, Pitts., 1996-98. Mem. Rivers Club, St. Clair Country Club. Roman Catholic. General corporate, Mergers and acquisitions. Office: Doepkin Keevican & Weiss 58th Fl USX Tower Pittsburgh PA 15219

**WHYTE, RONALD M.,** federal judge; b. 1942. BA in Math., Wesleyan U., 1964; JD, U. So. Calif., 1967. Bar: Calif. 1967, U.S. Dist. Ct. (no. dist.) Calif. 1967, U.S. Dist. Ct. (cen. dist.) Calif. 1968, U.S. Ct. Appeals (9th cir.) 1986. Assoc. Hoge, Fenton Jones & Appel, Inc., San Jose, Calif., 1971-77, mem., 1977-89; judge Superior Ct. State of Calif., 1989-92, U.S. Dist. Ct. (no. dist.) Calif., San Jose, 1992—; judge pro-tempore Superior Ct. Calif., 1977-89; lectr. Calif. Continuing Edn. of Bar, Rutter Group, Santa Clara Bar Assn., State Bar Calif.; legal counsel Santa CLara County Bar Assn., 1986-89; mem. county select com. Criminal Conflicts Program, 1988. Bd. trustees Santa Clara County Bar Assn., 1978-79, 84-85. Lt. Judge Advocate Gen.'s Corps, USNR, 1968-71. Recipient Judge of Yr. award Santa Clara County Trial Lawyers Assn., 1992, Am. Jurisprudence award. Mem. Calif. Judges Assn., Assn. Bus. Trial Lawyers (bd. govs. 1991-93), Santa Clara Inn of Ct. (exec. com. 1993—), San Francisco Bay area Intellectual Property Inn of Ct. (exec. com. 1994—). Office: US Courthouse 280 S 1st St Rm 2112 San Jose CA 95113-3002

**WIACEK, BRUCE EDWARD,** lawyer; b. N.Y.C., Aug. 3, 1943; s. A. Edward and Ann Catherine (Miller) W.; m. Dianne Gail Masumian, Aug. 26, 1984; 1 child, Lauren Alysse. BA, Fordham U., 1965, MA, 1971, JD, 1978; MS in Edn., Iona Grad. Sch., 1974; LLM, NYU, 1981. Bar: N.Y. 1979, U.S. Dist. Ct. (so. and ea. dists.) N.Y. 1979. Tchr. Cardinal Spellman High Sch., N.Y.C., 1967-73, Tarrytown (N.Y.) Pub. Sch., 1973-79; supervisor labor relations Sperry Corp., Great Neck, N.Y., 1979-84; ptnr. Wiacek & Corcoran, White Plains, N.Y., 1984-87; pvt. practice White Plains, N.Y., 1987-89; proprietor Tefft Legal Forms, White Plains, N.Y., 1989-90; arbitrator small claims City Ct. of White Plains, 1985—; assoc. prof. Iona Coll., Yonkers, N.Y., 1988-90. Legal columnist The Advocate, 1978—. Dir. legal asst. program Seton Coll., Yonkers. N.Y., 1985-89. Roman Catholic. Avocations: antique automobiles, post-war toy trains. Labor, General practice. Home: 1180 Midland Ave Bronxville NY 10708-6466

**WICH, DONALD ANTHONY, JR.,** lawyer; b. Apr. 13, 1947; s. Donald Anthony and Margaret Louise (Blatz) W. BA with honors, Notre Dame U., Ind., 1969; JD, Notre Dame U., 1972. Bar: Fla. 1972, U.S. Dist. Ct. (so. dist.) Fla. 1972, U.S. Ct. Appeals (5th and 11th cirs.) 1982, U.S. Supreme Ct. 1976; cert. civil trial lawyer, 1983. Assoc. VISTA, Miami, Fla., 1972-74; atty. Legal Svcs., Miami, 1973-75; adj. prof. law U. Miami, 1974-75; ptnr. Wich, Wich & wich, P.A., Ft. Lauderdale, Fla., 1992—; pres., dir. Legal Aid of Broward, Ft. Lauderdale, 1976-82; mem. 17th Cir. Jud. Nominating Commn., 1998—. Treas. St. Thomas More Sch. of So. Fla., 1989-99. Mem. ABA, ATLA, Am. Arbitration Assn., North Broward Bar Assn. (pres. 1983-84), Acad. Fla. Trial Lawyers Assn. (sustaining mem.), Broward County Trial Lawyers Assn. (pres. 1988-89, sustaining mem.), Broward Bar Assn. (chmn. legis. com. 1984-85, exec. com. 1986-92, 94—, chmn. bench-bar com. 1993-94, chmn. clk.-bar com. 1993—, pres. 1997-98, 17th cir. jud. nominating commn.), Tex. Trial Lawyers Assn., N.Y. Trial Lawyers Assn., Pompano Beach C. of C. (pres. 1989-90, dir. 1984-87, 92—, govtl. affairs chmn. 1983-84, art show chmn. 1984-85, seafood festival chmn. 1986-90), Notre Dame Frederick Sorin Soc., Rotary (bd. dirs. 1987-91), Woodhouse (bd. dirs. 1990-91). Personal injury, General civil litigation, Real property. Office: Wich Wich & Wich PA 2400 E Commercial Blvd Fort Lauderdale FL 33308-4030

**WICHINSKY, GLENN ELLIS,** lawyer; b. Monticello, N.Y., Dec. 22, 1952; s. Michael A. Wichinsky and Ann (Pesekow) Kaplan; m. Lillian Carol Rindom, June 6, 1976; children: Laura, David. BA in Polit. Sci., U. Miami, 1974; JD, U. Pacific, 1982. Bar: Fla. 1982, Nev. 1983, U.S. Dist. Ct. Nev. 1984. Legis. asst. Calif. Assembly, Sacramento, 1978-80; legal advisor Community Legal Svcs., Sacramento, 1980-81; jud. clk. Sacramento County Superior Ct., Sacramento, 1981-82; assoc. Rogers, Monsey, Woodbury, Las Vegas, Nev., 1983; pvt. practice Las Vegas and Boca Raton, Fla., 1983—. Chmn. transp. com. Palm Beach County (Fla.) Coop., 1987-89, Palm Beach County Task Force for Responsible Representation, 1989-91; mem. Palm Beach County Comprehensive Planning Adv. Com., 1988, Zoning Bd. Adjustment, 1991—, West Boca Action Com., Boca Raton, 1986-90. Music scholar U. Miami, 1970. Mem. ABA (com. on air and space law), Internat. Assn. Gaming Attorneys, Fla. Bar Assn. (aviation law com.), Palm Beach County Bar Assn., South Palm Beach County Bar Assn., Tau Epsilon Phi (pres. 1973-74). Democrat. Jewish. Avocations: skiing, travel, aviation, meterology. General corporate, Administrative and regulatory, Probate. Office: 1200 N Fed Hwy Ste 200 Boca Raton FL 33432

**WICK, LAWRENCE SCOTT,** lawyer; b. San Diego, Oct. 1, 1945; s. Kenneth Lawrence and Lorrayne (Scott) W.; m. Beverly Ann DeRoss, Aug. 26, 1972 (div.); children: Ryan Scott, Andrew Taylor, Hayley Lauren. BA, Northwestern U., Evanston, Ill., 1967; JD, Columbia U., 1970. Atty. Leydig Voit & Mayer Ltd., Chgo., 1978-84, shareholder, 1984-98; ptnr. Wildman, Harrold, Allen & Dixon, Chgo., 1998—; v.p., sec., gen. counsel Lionheart Prodns., Ltd., Chgo., 1995—. Contbr. articles to profl. jours. and encys. Bd. govs. Brand Names Edn. Found., 1994-95; exec. dir. Lefkowitz Internat. Trademark Moot Ct., 1994-95; bd. dirs. Tangley Oaks Homeowners Assn., 1997—, treas., 1998-99, pres., 1999—. Mem. ABA. Internat. Trademark Assn., Copyright Soc. U.S., Pharm. Trade Marks Group (London), Am. Film Inst., Chgo. Bar Assn. Republican. Presbyterian. Avocations: international travel, film, swimming. Trademark and copyright, Federal civil litigation, Intellectual property. Home: 317 Rothbury Ct Lake Bluff IL 60044-1927 Office: Wildman Harrold Allen and Dixon 225 W Wacker Dr Ste 3000 Chicago IL 60606-1224

**WICKER, THOMAS CAREY, JR.,** judge; b. New Orleans, Aug. 1, 1923; s. Thomas Carey and Mary (Taylor) W.; children: Thomas Carey III, Catherine Anne; m. Jane Anne Trepanier, Dec. 29, 1995. BBA, Tulane U., 1944, LLB, 1949, JD, 1969. Bar: La. 1949. Law clk. La. Supreme Ct., New Orleans, 1949-50; asst. U.S. Atty., 1950-53; practiced in New Orleans, 1953-72; mem. firm Simon, Wicker & Wiedemann, 1953-67; partner firm Wicker, Wiedemann & Fransen, 1967-72; dist. judge Jefferson Parish (La.), 1972-85, judge, Court of Appeals 5th cir., 1985-98, mem. faculty Nat. Jud. Coll., 1979-93, Tulane U. Sch. Law, 1978-83. Past bd. visitors Tulane U.; bd. dirs. La. Jud. Coll.; past pres. Sugar Bowl. Author: (with others) Judicial Ethics, 1982, (with others) Modern Judicial Ethics, 1992; editor Tulane Law Review, 1949. Lt. (j.g.), USNR, 1944-46. Mem. ABA (jud. div. council), La. (chmn. jr. bar sect. 1958-59, gov. 1958, mem. ho. of dels. 1960-72), Jefferson Parish, bar assns., Tulane U. Alumni Assn. (past pres.), Am. Judicature Soc., La. Dist. Judges Assn. (past pres.), Order of Coif, Beta Gamma Sigma, Pi Kappa Alpha. Episcopalian. Clubs: Rotary (pres. 1971-72), Metairie (La.) Country. Avocations: golf, photography, military history. Home: 500 Rue Saint Ann Apt 127 Metairie LA 70005-4639 Office: La Ct Appeal 5th Cir Gretna Courthouse Fl 4 Gretna LA 70053

**WICKERHAM, RICHARD DENNIS,** lawyer; b. Plainfield, N.J., Oct. 9, 1950; s. Richard Frame and Margaret Theresa (Waldron) W.; m. Margaret Ann Music, June 29, 1989. BS in Fgn. Svc., Georgetown U., 1972; JD, Fordham U., 1975. Bar: N.Y. 1976, U.S. Dist. Ct. (no. dist.) N.Y. 1977. Pvt. practice atty., counsellor at law Schenectady, N.Y., 1976—; law guardian Schenectady, 1976-85; atty., Office of Aging County of Schenectady, N.Y., 1981—; mem., Com. on Profl. Stds. N.Y. Supreme Ct., Appellate Divsn. (3rd. jud. dept.), Albany, N.Y., 1996—. Mem. St. Clare's Hosp. Found. Leadership, Schenectady, 1990—. Recipient Cert. of Appreciation and Merit, The Lawyers' Fund for Client Protection of the State of N.Y., Albany, 1994. Mem. Rotary Internat., Schenectady County C. of C. Roman Catholic. Avocations: rowing, salt water fishing. Probate, Estate planning, General civil litigation. Home: 484 Hutchinson Rd Scotia NY 12302-6515 Office: PO Box 1167 28 Jay St Schenectady NY 12305-1900

**WICKLUND, DAVID WAYNE,** lawyer; b. St. Paul, Aug. 7, 1949; s. Wayne Glenwood and Elna Katherine (Buresh) W.; m. Susan Marie Bubenko, Nov. 17, 1973; children: David Jr., Kurt, Edward. BA cum laude, Williams Coll., 1971; JD cum laude, U. Toledo, 1974. Bar: Ohio 1974. Assoc. Shumaker, Loop & Kendrick, Toledo, 1974-80, ptnr., 1981—; adj. instr. law, U. Toledo, 1988. Editor-in-chief U. Toledo Law Rev. 1973-74. Mem. ABA, Ohio State Bar Assn. (mem. bd. govs. antitrust sect.), Toledo Bar Assn., Inverness Club. Antitrust, General civil litigation, Bankruptcy. Office: Shumaker Loop & Kendrick N Courthouse Sq 1000 Jackson St Toledo OH 43624-1573

**WICKS, CHARLES CARTER,** lawyer; b. Goshen, Ind., May 28, 1945; s. Charles Sterling and Christine (Carter) W.; m. Penny Rae Krull, Oct. 31, 1970; children: Jay, Kristin, Scott. BA, Tulane U., 1967; JD, Ind. U., 1970. Bar: Ind. 1970, U.S. Ct. Mil. Appeals 1971. Ptnr. Matthews Petsche-Wicks, South Bend, Ind., 1974-78, Virgil, Cawley, Platt & Wicks, Elkhart, Ind., 1978; pvt. practice Elkhart, 1978-88, 89—, dep. pros. atty., 1978—; ptnr. Wicks & Rieff, Elkhart, 1988-89; lectr. forensic medicine Goshen Coll. Sch. Nursing. Mem. Rep. Cen. Com., Goshen, 1978—. Mem. vestry St. James Episcopal ch., 1977-79, 81-84, 86-88, sr. warden, 1989, diocesan coun. Episcopal Diocese No. Ind., 1988-89. Capt. USAF, 1970-74. Mem. ABA, ATLA, Ind. Bar Assn., Assn. Trial Lawyers Am., Ind. Trial Lawyers Assn., Elkhart County Estate Planning Coun. (pres. 1982-83), Elkhart County Past Masters' Assn. (pres. 1984, 89), Elkhart C. of C., Goshen C. of C., Goshen County Past Masters Assn., Am. Legion, Masons (master 1980, trustee 1983-85, comdr. in chief, chmn. degree com. Scottish Rite), Shriners (pres. Goshen club 1983, dir. 21st degree 1985-94), Moose, Elkhart Kiwanis (bd. dirs. 1986-87), Christiana Creek Country Club, Benk Oak Golf Club, Greater Elkhart Pachyderm Club (pres. 1989—), Nat. Pachyderm Club (bd. dirs. 1998—). Personal injury, Family and matrimonial, State civil litigation. Home: 26207 Hilly Ln Elkhart IN 46517-2243 Office: 514 S Main St PO Box 1884 Elkhart IN 46515-1884

**WICKS, JEFFREY DONALD,** lawyer; b. Springfield, Mo., Jan. 8, 1971; s. Jack and Janet Wicks. BA, U. Mo., Columbia, 1993; JD, Washburn U., 1996. Bar: Kans. Assoc. Turner & Boisseau, Chartered, Great Bend, Kans., 1996—. Mem. Kans. Bar Assn., Order of the Barristers. Home: 3021 SW Randolph Ave Apt 104 Topeka KS 66611-1748 Office: Turner & Boisseau Chartered 3900 Broadway Ave Great Bend KS 67530-3525

**WIDDEL, JOHN EARL, JR.,** lawyer; b. Minot, N.D., Nov. 17, 1936; s. John Earl Sr. and Angela Victoria W.; m. Yvonne J. Haugen, Dec. 21, 1973; children: John P., James M., Susan N., Andrea K. B in Philosophy, BSBA, U. N.D., 1966, BSBA, 1971. Bar: N.D. 1971, U.S. Dist. Ct. N.D., 1971, U.S. Ct. Appeals (8th cir.) 1989. Ptnr. Thorsen & Widdel, Grand Forks, N.D., 1971-97; shareholder Law Offices ND, PC; mcpl. judge City of Grand Forks, 1972—; ct. magistrate Grand Forks County, 1975. Mem. N.D. Foster Parent Program, 1974-87, Nat. Conf. of Bar Pres.; mem. bd. dirs. YMCA, Grand Forks, 1982; dist. chmn. Boy Scouts Am., 1987-88; corp. mem. United Hosp. With U.S. Army, 1960-62. Mem. Am. Acad. Estate Planning Attys., State Bar Assn. N.D. (bd. govs. 1983-88, pres. 1986-87), Greater Grand Forks County Bar Assn. (pres. 1982), N.E. Cen. Jud. Dist. (pres. 1983), Grand Forks Cemetery Assn. (bd. dirs. 1984—, pres. 1989-94), Grand Forks Hist. Soc. (pres. 1983), Grand Forks Jaycees, Antique Automobile Club Am. (nat. bd. dirs. 1984—, v.p. 1985—), sec.-treas. 1989, pres. N.D. region 1977-78, 83-84), Sertoma (bd. dirs. 1994—, pres. 1997-98), Elks (exalted ruler 1985-86), Masonic Bodies (Kem Temple Potentate 1995), Nat. Assn. Estate Planning Coun. (accredited estate planner, 1994), N.D. Mcpl. Judges Assn. (dir. 1993—). Roman Catholic. General practice, Probate, Real property. Home: Box 5624 Grand Forks ND 58206-5624 Office: Thorsen & Widdel PO Box 5624 Grand Forks ND 58206-5624

**WIDENER, HIRAM EMORY, JR.,** federal judge; b. Abingdon, Va., Apr. 30, 1923; s. Hiram Emory and Nita Douglas (Peck) W.; children: Molly Berendt, Hiram Emory III. Student, Va. Poly. Inst., 1940-41; B.S., U.S. Naval Acad., 1944; LL.B., Washington and Lee U., 1953, LL.D., 1977. Bar: Va. 1951. Pvt. practice law Bristol, Va., 1953-69; judge U.S. Dist. Ct. Western Dist. Va., Abingdon, 1969-71; chief judge U.S. Dist. Ct. Western Dist. Va., 1971-72; judge U.S. Ct. Appeals 4th Circuit, Abingdon, 1972—; U.S. commr. Western Dist. Va., 1963-66; mem. Va. Election Laws Study Commn., 1968-69. Chmn. Rep. party 9th Dist. Va., 1966-69; mem. Va. Rep. State Ctrl. Com., 1966-69, state exec. com., 1966-69. Served to lt. (j.g.) USN, 1944-49; to lt. USNR, 1951-52. Decorated Bronze Star with combat V. Mem. Am. Law Inst., Va. Bar Assn., Va. State Bar, Phi Alpha Delta. Republican. Presbyterian. Home and Office: 180 E Main St Rm 123 Abingdon VA 24210-2839

**WIDMANN, EDWARD HEALY,** lawyer; b. Pasadena, Calif., July 28, 1940; s. Frederick Carpenter and Nancy (Healy) W.; m. Nancy Louise DuClos, Aug. 25, 1962; children: Brian E., Beth Louise, Devin Bok-Sun. BA, Claremont Men's Coll., 1962; JD, U. Denver, 1965. Bar: Colo. 1965, U.S. Dist. Ct. Colo. 1965, U.S. Ct. Appeals (10th cir.) 1965, U.S. Supreme Ct. 1981. Ptnr. Hall & Evans, Denver, 1965—. Mem. ABA, Colo. Bar Assn. (pres. litig. sect. 1980), Colo. Def. Bar Assn. Democrat. Federal civil litigation, State civil litigation, Personal injury. Home: 703 Ash St Denver CO 80220-4928 Office: Hall and Evans 1200 17th St Ste 1700 Denver CO 80202-5817

**WIECHMANN, ERIC WATT,** lawyer; b. Schenectady, N.Y., June 12, 1948; s. Richard Jerdone and Ann (Watt) W.; m. Merrill Metzger, May 22, 1971. BA, Hamilton Coll., 1970; JD, Cornell U., 1974. Bar: Conn. 1975, U.S. Dist. Ct. (so. and ea. dists.) N.Y. 1975, U.S. Dist. Ct. Conn. 1975, U.S. Dist. Ct. D.C. 1981, U.S. Ct. Appeals (2nd cir.) 1975, U.S. Ct. Appeals (9th cir.) 1980, U.S. Ct. Appeals D.C. 1982, U.S. Ct. Appeals (5th cir.) 1986, U.S. Ct. Appeals (10th cir.) 1989, U.S. Supreme Ct. 1978. Assoc. Cummings & Lockwood, Stamford, Conn., 1974-82; ptnr. Cummings & Lockwood, Stamford, 1982—; mng. ptnr. Hartford office, 1996—; spl. pretrial master U.S. Dist. Ct. Conn. 1984—; state atty. trial referee, 1986—, mem. law revision commn., evidence code oversight com.; mem. civil task force, civil jury instrn. com. Conn. Superior Ct. Contbr. articles to profl. jours. Mem. Zoning Bd. Appeals, New Canaan, Conn., 1984-85. Mem. ABA (vice chmn. toxics and hazardous law com.), Def. Rsch. Inst., Internat. Assn. Def. Counsel (mem. faculty Def. Trial Acad. 1996, chair toxic and hazardous substance com.), Internat. Soc. Barristers, Conn. Bar Assn. (exec. com. antitrust sect. 1982—, ct. rules adv. com, chmn. 1991-93), Fed. Bar Coun., Hartford Club, Golf Club Avon. Republican. Episcopalian. General civil litigation, Product liability, Antitrust. Home: 21 Foxcroft Run Avon CT 06001-2509

**WIEDER, BRUCE TERRILL,** lawyer, electrical engineer; b. Cleve., Dec. 9, 1955; s. Ira J. and Judith M. (Marx) W. BSEE, Cornell U., 1978; MBA, U. Tex., 1980, JD with honors, 1988. Bar: Tex. 1988, U.S. Dist. Ct. (we. dist.) Tex. 1989, U.S. Patent and Trademark Office 1989, U.S. Ct. Appeals (fed. cir.) 1990, D.C. 1991, U.S. Supreme Ct. 1992, U.S. Dist. Ct. (no. dist.) Tex. 1995, Va. 1997, U.S. Dist. Ct. (ea. dist.) Va. 1997. Engr. Motorola, Inc., Austin, Tex., 1979-85; assoc. Arnold, White & Durkee, Austin, 1988-90; law clk. U.S. Ct. Appeals (Fed. cir.), Washington, 1990-91; assoc. Burns, Doane, Swecker & Mathis, Alexandria, Va., 1991-97, ptnr., 1998—; adj. prof. Georgetown U. Law Ctr., 1998—. Mem. IEEE, ABA, Am. Intellectual Property Law Assn., Alpha Phi Omega (life), Beta Gamma Sigma (life). Patent, Trademark and copyright, Computer. Office: Burns Doane Swecker & Mathis 1737 King St Ste 500 Alexandria VA 22314-2727

**WIEGAND, ROBERT, II,** lawyer; b. New Orleans, Feb. 11, 1947; s. Robert Nelson and Olivia Eustis (Eaves) W.; m. Pamela Danos, Apr. 23, 1976; children: Stephen B., Kelly M., Julianna. BA in History, Tulane U., 1970, JD, 1972; LLM in Taxation, U. Denver, 1977. Bar: La. 1972, U.S. Dist. Ct. (ea. dist.) La. 1972, U.S. Ct. Appeals (5th cir.) 1975, Colo. 1976, U.S. Dist. Ct. Colo. 1976. Assoc. Deutsch & Kerrigan, New Orleans, 1972-76, Banta & Hoyt, Englewood, Colo., 1977-78; ptnr. Allspach & Wiegand, Denver, 1978-80; prin. Wiegand and Assocs. P.C., Denver, 1980-83; prin. O'Connor & Hannan, Denver, 1983-86, of counsel, 1986-89; of counsel Pendleton & Sabian, P.C., Denver, 1989-90; pres., CEO, SPM Group Inc., Denver, 1986-88; prin. Wiegand Attys. & Counselors, Englewood, 1992—; corp. counsel SPM Group, Inc., Denver, 1980-90, Info. Solutions, Inc., Denver, 1984-91, Rhodea Co., 1987-91, Big Sur Waterbeds Inc., 1980-86. Councilman City of Greenwood Village, Colo., 1985-89, precinct committeeman, 1986—. Mem. Colo. Bar Assn. (bus. law sect. on Colo. corp. code and uniform ltd. partnership act), La. Bar Assn. Republican. Episcopalian. Club: University ( Denver). General corporate, Securities, Corporate taxation. Office: Wiegand Attys and Counselors 5261 S Quebec St Englewood CO 80111-1805

**WIEGERS, EDWARD G.,** lawyer; b. St. Louis, Mar. 20, 1928; s. Edward G. and Elsie C. W.; m. Shirley M. Grein, Sept. 4, 1954; children: Edward III, Mary Ann. BS in Bus. Adminstrn., U. Mo., 1950; LLB, JD, St. Louis U., 1957. Dir. legal svcs. Met. St. Louis Sewer Dist., 1957-90; judge City of Florissant, Mo.; gen. counsel Black Jack (Mo.) Fire Protection Dist.; pvt. practice St. Louis County. Sgt. USAF, 1951-53. Mem. Mo. Bar Assn., Bar Assn. St. Louis. Home: 618 Broadmoor Dr Apt A Chesterfield MO 63017-3123

**WIEGLEY, ROGER DOUGLAS,** lawyer; b. Buffalo, Dec. 8, 1948; s. Richard John and Georgianna (Eggleston) W. BA, SUNY, Buffalo, 1970; JD magna cum laude, U. Wis., 1977. Bar: Wis. 1977, Hawaii 1978, N.Y. 1982, D.C. 1982, Calif. 1986. Spl. asst. U.S. atty. U.S. Justice Dept., Honolulu, 1978-81; spl. asst. to gen. counsel Dept. of the Navy, Washington, 1981-82; assoc. Sullivan & Cromwell, Washington, 1982-88; ptnr. Sidley & Austin, Washington, 1988-94, Winthrop, Stimson, Putnam & Roberts, Washington, 1994-98; dir. Credit Suisse First Boston, N.Y.C., 1999—; gen. counsel Benson, Inc. and Sentry, San Jose, Calif., 1985-86; arbitrator nat. panel Am. Arbitration Assn., 1988—. Author: Trade and Export Finance, 1997; contbr. numerous articles to profl. jours. Mem. pvt. sector study on cost control, Washington, 1982-83. Served with USN, 1973-82. Finance, Mergers and acquisitions, General corporate. Office: Credit Suisse First Boston Eleven Madison Ave New York NY 10010-3629

**WIEHL, JAMES GEORGE,** lawyer; b. Chgo., Sept. 11, 1954; s. George Donald and Mildred Rita (Sweet) W.; m. Julie Marie Gill, Aug. 3, 1979. BA in Govt., U. Notre Dame, Ind., 1976; JD, U. Notre Dame, 1979. Bar: Mo. 1979, U.S. Dist. Ct. (ea. dist.) Mo. 1979, U.S. Ct. Appeals (8th cir.) 1979. Head nat. healthcare practice group Sonnenschein, Nath & Rosenthal, St. Louis, 1991—; bd. dirs. Midwest Migrant Health Info., Inc.; presenter in field. Author: The Managed Care Manual, The Direct Contracting Manual; contbr. articles to profl. jours. Pres. devel. bd. Cardinal Glennon Children's Hosp., St. Louis, 1993. Mem. ABA (forum com. on health law), Mo. Bar Assn. (health law com.), Nat. Health Lawyers Assn., St. Louis Met. Bar Assn., Am. Acad. Hosp. Attys., Cath. Health Assn. of U.S., Mo. Soc. Hosp. Attys. (bd. dirs.). Health, Antitrust, Corporate taxation. Office: Sonnenschein Nath & Rosenthal One Metropolitan Sq Ste 3000 Saint Louis MO 63102

**WIEHL, LIS W.,** law educator; b. Seattle, Aug. 9, 1961; d. Richard Lloyd and Inga (Wolfsberg) W.; m. Robb London; children: Jacob, Danielle. JD,

Harvard U., 1987; MA, U. Queensland, Brisbane, Australia, 1985; BA, Columbia U, 1983, U. Helsinki, Helsinki, Finland, 1978-79. Bar: Washington.; U.S. Dist. Ct.; U.S. Ct. Appeals (9th Cir.). Assoc Perkins Coie Law Firm, Seattle, WA, 1987-90; fed. prosecutor U.S. Attys. Office, Seattle, 1990-95; asst. prof. Law Sch., dir of trial advocacy program U. Wash., Seattle, 1995—; counsel Perkins Coie Law Firm, Seattle; exec. asst. U.S. atty., Seattle, summer 1998; prin. dep. chief investigative counsel to U.S. Ho. of Reps. Com. on Judiciary, 1998-99. Author: law review U. Wash., 1987, U. Mich., 1998; contbr. articles to New York Times, ABA Jour. Treas. Lawyers Students Engaged in Resolution, Seattle, 1995—. Recepient Distinction in Teaching award Harvard U., 1987. Mem. Fed. Bar Assn., Order of the Coif.

**WIENER, JACQUES LOEB, JR.,** federal judge; b. Shreveport, La., Oct. 2, 1934; s. Jacques L. and Betty (Eichenbaum) W.; m. Sandra Mills Feingerts; children: Patricia Wiener Shifke, Jacques L. III, Betty Ellen Wiener Spomer, Donald B. BA, Tulane U., 1956, JD, 1961. Bar: La. 1961, U.S. Dist. Ct. (we. dist.) La. 1961. Ptnr. Wiener, Weiss & Madison, Shreveport, 1961-90; judge U.S. Ct. Appeals (5th cir.), New Orleans, 1990—; mem. coun. La. State Law Inst., 1963; master of the bench Am. Inn of Ct., 1990-98. Pres. United Way N.W. La., 1975, Shreveport Jewish Fedn., 1969-70. Fellow Am. Coll. Trust & Estates Counsel, Am. Bar Found., La. Bar Found.; academician Internat. Acad. Trust & Estate Law; mem. ABA, La. State Bar Assn., Shreveport Bar Assn. (pres. 1982), Am. Law Inst. Avocations: fly fishing, upland game bird hunting, photography, travel. Office: Court of Appeals Building 600 Camp St Rm 244 New Orleans LA 70130-3425

**WIENER, SCOTT DAVID,** lawyer; b. Phila., May 11, 1970; s. Richard and Elaine (Chaplin) W. AB, Duke U., 1992; JD, Harvard U., 1996. Law clk. justice Alan Handler Supreme Ct. N.J., Trenton, 1996-97. Contbr. articles to profl. jours. Pres. Alpha Epsilon Pi, Duke U., 1990-91; chair Lambda, Harvard Law Sch. Gay and Lesbian Orgn., Cambridge, Mass., 1993-96. Fulbright scholar, Chile, 1992-93. Avocations: fitness, reading, animals. Address: PO Box 1032 Turnersville NJ 08012-0852

**WIER, RICHARD ROYAL, JR.,** lawyer, inventor; b. Wilmington, Del., May 19, 1941; s. Richard Royal and Anne (Kurtz) W.; m. Anne E. Edwards, Nov. 25, 1978; children—Melissa Royal, Emma Kurtz; children from previous marriage: Richard Royal, III, Mimi Poole. BA in English, Hamilton Coll., 1963; LLB, U. Pa., 1966; postgrad., Temple U., 1981-82. Bar: D.C. 1967, Del. 1967, Pa. 1980, U.S. Dist. Ct. Del., U.S. Ct. Appeals (3d cir.), U.S. Supreme Ct. Assoc. Connolly, Bove & Lodge, Wilmington, 1966-68; dep. atty. gen. State of Del., Wilmington, 1968-70; state prosecutor Del. Dept. Justice, Wilmington, 1970-74; atty. gen. State of Del., Wilmington, 1975-79; ptnr. Prickett, Jones, Elliott, Kristol & Schnee, Wilmington, 1979-92; pvt. practice Wilmington, 1993—; lectr. criminal and labor law various instns. Named one of Top Four Labor/Employment Attys. in Del., Del. Today, 1996. Active United Way campaign, 1976, 77; mem. supervisory bd. Gov.'s Commn. on Criminal Justice; bd. dirs. Del. Coun. Crime and Justice, 1982-89; mem. adv. coun. Diabetes Control, 1990-92; dir. Project Assist, 1992-95, Commn. on Outreach, 1994—. Recipient Law Enforcement award Newark Police Dept., 1974; Law Enforcement Commendation medal Nat. Soc. SAR, 1976; Ideal Citizen award Am. Found. for Sci. Creative Intelligence, 1976; Commendation Del. Gen. Assembly Senate, 1976, 77, 80; named one of Top Four Labor/Employment Attys. in Del., Del. Today, 1996. Mem. ABA, Nat. Dist. Attys. Assn. (state dir.), Del. Bar Assn. (chmn. criminal law sect. 1987-91, co-chmn. on drug crisis 1993—, vice chmn. labor law sect. 1987-88, chmn. 1989-90), Pa. Bar Assn., D.C. Bar Assn., Nat. Assn. Attys. Gen. (hon. life, exec. com.), Soc. Attys. Gen. Execs. (emeritus), Am. Judicature Soc., Am. Del. Trial Lawyers Assn., Nat. Assn. Extradition Ofcls. (hon. life, regional v.p., exec. dir.), Italian Radio/TV Assn. (hon., Outstanding Achievement award), Internat. Platform Assn., Pi Delta Epsilon. E-mail: rwier@wierlaw.com. Criminal, Labor, Personal injury. Office: 1220 N Market St Ste 600 Wilmington DE 19801-2598

**WIESE, KURT ROWLAND,** lawyer; b. Fulton, Mo., Nov. 3, 1955; s. Donald Edgar Wiese and Bonnie Oliver Shaddock; m. Anne Carroll Gordon, July 8, 1978; children: Evelyn, Hollis. BS, Tulane U., 1978; JD, U. Ariz., 1984. Sr. atty. South Coast Air Quality Mgmt. Dist., Diamond Bar, Calif., 1989—; adj. prof. Western State U. Coll. Law, Fullerton, 1993—; instr. environ. compliance Calif. State U., Fullerton, 1998—. Mem. L.A. County Bar Assn. (environ. law sect., chair air quality com. 1996), Phi Beta Kappa, Order of Coif, Newport Harbor Yacht Club. Home: 666 Catalina Laguna Beach CA 92651-2545

**WIETHOLTER, THOMAS ANDREW,** lawyer; b. Covington, Ky., Mar. 28, 1951; s. Henry Joseph and Esther Andrews W.; m. Susan Humbert Wietholter, May 14, 1988 (div. Aug. 27, 1996); 1 child, Jessica. AAS in Fine Sci., N. Ky. U., Highland Heights, 1980, BS in Pub. Adminstrn., 1981; JD, Salmon P. Chase, Highland Heights, 1986. Asst. fire chief Newport (Ky.) Fire Dept., 1973-99; cons. pvt. practice, Edgewood, Ky., 1978—; atty. Klette & Klette, Ft. Mitchell, Ky., 1994—. Mem. Local Govt. Statute Revision Commn., Frankfort, Ky., 1978-80, No. Ky. elec. Auth., Covington, Ky., 1992-97; treas. Mcpl. Atty. Assoc. of Ky., 1998-99. Mem. ABA, Ky. Bar Assn., Ohio Bar Assn., N. Ky. Bar Assn. Roman Catholic. Avocations: coin collecting, target shooting. Family and matrimonial, Personal injury, Municipal (including bonds). Home: 3066 Magnolia Ct Edgewood KY 41017-3351 Office: Klette & Klette 250 Grandview Dr Fort Mitchell KY 41017-5667

**WIGELL, RAYMOND GEORGE,** lawyer; b. Chgo., Apr. 18, 1949; s. Raymond Carl and Amanda D. (Santiago) W.; m. Barbara E. Buettner, June 28, 1980; children: Katherine, Elizabeth, Charles. BA, U. Ill., Chgo., 1971; JD, John Marshall Law Sch., 1975; LLM in Taxation, DePaul U., 1991. Bar: Ill. 1975, U.S. Dist. Ct. (no. dist.) Ill. 1975, U.S. Ct. Appeals (7th cir.) 1978, U.S. Supreme Ct. 1979, U.S. Tax Ct. 1987. Pvt. practice law Raymond G. Wigell, Chgo., 1975-77; trial atty. Cook County Pub. Defender, Chgo., 1977-78; pres., owner, atty. Wigell & Assocs., Chicago Heights, Ill., 1978—; instr. MacCormac Jr. Coll., Chgo., 1976-77; lectr. in bus. law Oakton C.C., Des Plaines, Ill., 1976-84; adj. prof. Govs. State U., University Park, Ill., 1984-92. Commn. chair inquiry bd. Atty. Registration Disciplinary Commn. Supreme Ct. Ill., Chgo., 1985-90, commn. chair hearing bd., 1990-95. With USN, 1971-77. Mem. U. Ill. Alumni Assn. (life mem.). Roman Catholic. General corporate, Criminal, General civil litigation. Office: Wigell & Assocs Atty at Law 418 Dixie Hwy Chicago Heights IL 60411-1739

**WIGGER, JARREL L.,** lawyer; b. Wiesbaden, Germany, May 12, 1963; s. Philip Lee and Ervinetta (Maxey) W.; m. Rose Marie Riley, Aug. 1, 1987; children: Amy Elizabeth, Jordan Lee. BA in English, The Citadel, 1985; JD, Wake Forest U., 1988. Bar: S.C. 1988, U.S. Dist. Ct. S.C. 1993, U.S. Ct. Mil. Appeals 1991, U.S. Supreme Ct. 1998. Student prosecutor Forsyth County Dist. Atty. Office, Winston-Salem, N.C., 1988; assoc. Drose, Davidson & Bennett, Charleston, S.C., 1992-94, jr. ptnr., 1995-98; ptnr. Davidson, Bennett & Wigger, Charleston, 1999—; real estate cons. Co-editor, author: U.S. Navy Mass Casualty Handbook, 1991. Lt. USN, 1986-92. Mem. ABA, ATLA, S.C. Trial Lawyers Assn., S.C. Bar Assn., Charleston County Bar Assn., Claimant Assn. for Workers Compensation, Assn. Citadel Men (life), Citadel Brigadier Found., Charleston Area Citadel Club, Citadel Old Timers Wrestling Club (pres. 1996—), Sigma Tau Delta. Avocations: runing, guitar, wrestling, coaching. General civil litigation, Personal injury, Workers' compensation. Office: 8086 Rivers Ave N Charleston SC 29406-9235

**WIGGIN, THOMAS BYRON,** lawyer; b. Hoboken, N.J., May 11, 1967; s. Thomas Eugene Wiggin and Anne Mary Moore. Bachelor's degree, George Washington U., 1989; JD, N.Y. Law Sch., 1992. Bar: N.Y. 1993, N.J. 1993. Assoc. Edmonds Torres Martinez & Mazza, N.Y.C., 1992-94; ptnr. Scheurer & Wiggin, N.Y.C., 1994-96, Scheurer Wiggin & Hardy, N.Y.C., 1996—. Mem. Assn. Bar City of N.Y. (election law com.), N.Y. Law Sch. Alumni (CLE com.). Criminal, Civil rights, General civil litigation. Office: Scheurer Wiggin & Hardy 250 W 57th St Ste 515 New York NY 10107-0522

**WIGGINS, CHARLES EDWARD,** judge; b. El Monte, Calif., Dec. 3, 1927; s. Louis J. and Margaret E. (Fanning) W.; m. Yvonne L. Boots, Dec. 30, 1946 (dec. Sept. 1971); children: Steven L., Scott D.; m. Betty J. Koontz, July 12, 1972. B.S., U. So. Calif., 1953, LL.B., 1956; LL.B. (hon.) Ohio Wesleyan, 1975, Han Yang. U., Seoul, Korea, 1976. Bar: Calif. 1957, D.C. 1978. Lawyer, Wood & Wiggins, El Monte, Calif., 1956-66, Musick, Peeler & Garrett, Los Angeles, 1979-81, Pierson, Ball & Dowd, Washington, 1982-84, Pillsbury, Madison & Sutro, San Francisco, 1984; mem. 90-95th congresses from 25th and 39th Calif. Dists.; judge U.S. Ct. Appeals (9th cir.), 1984-96, sr. judge, 1996—. Mayor City of El Monte, Calif., 1964-66; mem. Planning Commn. City of El Monte, 1956-60; mem. Commn. on Bicentennial of U.S. Constitution, 1985—, mem. standing com. on rules of practice and procedure, 1987—. Served to 1st lt. U.S. Army, 1945-48, 50-52, Korea. Mem. ABA, State Bar Calif., D.C. Bar Assn. Republican. Lodge: Lions.

**WIGGINS, JAMES L.,** lawyer. U.S. atty. for mid. dist. Ga. U.S. Dept. Justice, Macon, Ga., 1994-96; ptnr. Almand & Wiggins, Macon. Office: Almand & Wiggins 504 Anson Ave Eastman GA 31023-1530

**WIGGINS, ROBERT L.,** lawyer; b. Greenville, S.C., Mar. 20, 1949; s. Robert L. and Donna O'dell W.; m. Vicki Castee, Feb. 24, 1967 (div. Nov. 1990); children: Michelle, Jenny, Emily, Alex; m. Ann Allison Korns, Sept. 26, 1994. BA, Clemson U., 1971; JD, U. Ala., 1974. Bar: Ala. 1979, U.S. Ct. Appeals (5th and 11th cirs.) 1979, U.S. Supreme Ct. 1979, U.s. Dist. Ct. (all dists.) Ala. 1979. Ptnr. Wiggins & Guinn, Birmingham, Ala., 1975-85, Grodon Silberman Wiggins & Childs, Birmingham, Ala., 1985—; lectr. Miles Coll. Sch. Law, Bimingham, 1976-79. Mem. Ala. Bar Assn., Birmingham Bar Assn. Democrat. Presbyterian. Avocations: gardening, reading. Civil rights, Labor, Federal civil litigation. Office: Gordon Silberman Wiggins & Childs 1400 Southtrust Tower Birmingham AL 35203-3221

**WIGHTMAN, ANN,** lawyer; b. Dayton, Ohio, July 29, 1958; d. William L. and Mary Ann (Lamb) W. AB, Ohio U., 1980; JD, Case Western Res. U., 1984. Bar: Ohio 1984, U.S. Dist. Ct. (so. dist.) Ohio 1984, U.S. Ct. Appeals (6th cir.) 1991, U.S. Ct. Appeals (7th cir.) 1992, U.S. Supreme Ct. 1993. Assoc. Smith & Schnacke, Dayton, 1984-89; sr. assoc. Faruki Gilliam & Ireland, Dayton, 1989-91, ptnr., 1991—; adj. prof. U. Dayton Sch. Law, 1988-93; chmn. Artemis House, Inc., Dayton, 1988-90, bd. dirs., 1985-95; arbitrator Am. Arbitration Assn.; mem., bd. dirs. Legal Aid Soc. Dayton, Inc., 1996—; bd. dirs. Impact Weekly. Mem. Vol. Lawyer's Project, Dayton, 1988-96; mem. Challenge 95 Task Force, Dayton, 1989-90, Up and Comer, Dayton, 1990; vol. arbitrator Montgomery County Common Pleas Ct., 1989—; bd. dirs. ACLU of Ohio Found., 1991-94; mem. Leadership, Dayton, 1992. Mem. ABA (trial and environ. sects.), Ohio Bar Assn., Phi Beta Kappa. Federal civil litigation, State civil litigation, Environmental. Home: 240 W Dixon Ave Dayton OH 45419-2902 Office: Faruki Gilliam & Ireland 10 N Ludlow St Ste 600 Dayton OH 45402-1875

**WIGLER, ANDREW JEFFREY,** lawyer; b. Bklyn., Aug. 11, 1965; s. Jerome L. and Florence (Hoffstein) W.; m. Nancy D. Wigler, Feb. 22, 1992. BA, Albany State U., 1987; JD, Yeshiva U., N.Y.C., 1990. Bar: N.J. 1990, U.S. Dist. Ct. N.J. 1990, N.Y. 1991, U.S. Dist. Ct. (so. and ea. dists.) N.Y. 1991, U.S. Ct. Appeals (2nd cir.) 1991, D.C. 1993. Legis. intern Hon. Thomas J. Bartosiewicz, Albany, N.Y., 1986; legis. aide Hon. Anthony J. Genovesi, Albany, 1987; assoc. Reisman, Peirez, Reisman & Calica, Garden City, N.Y., 1993-94; assoc. Berger & Ackman, P.C., N.Y.C., 1990-93, ptnr., 1994-95; ptnr. Law Offices of Andrew J. Wigler, Esq., Great Neck, N.Y., 1995—; atty. in pvt. practice Advanced Mortgage Sys., L.L.C., Great Neck, N.Y., 1995—; bd. dirs. Advanced Mortgage Sys., LLC, N.Y.C. Committeeman Queens County Dem. Com., 1993, Kings County Dem. Com., 1990. Recipient First Place Brief award Phillip C. Jessup Moot Ct. Competition, N.Y., 1989, Best Brief award Cardozo Advocacy Competition, N.Y.C., 1988. Mem. ABA, N.Y. State Women's Bar Assn., Nassau County Bar Assn., N.Y. State Bar Assn., N.Y. County Lawyers Assn., Washington Bar Assn. Democrat. Family and matrimonial, General civil litigation, General practice.

**WILBURN, MARY NELSON,** retired lawyer, writer; b. Balt., Feb. 18, 1932; d. David Alfred and Phoebe Blanche (Novotny) Nelson; m. Adolph Yarbrough Wilburn, Mar. 5, 1957; children: Adolph II, Jason David. AB cum laude, Howard U., 1952; MA, U. Wis., 1955, JD, 1975; cert. in trans., Georgetown U., 1997. Bar: Wis. 1975, U.S. Supreme Ct. 1981. Commr. Nat. Coun. of Negro Women Commn. on Edn., 1986—; bd. dirs. Bd. of Office of Employee Appeals, D.C.; judge NAACP ACT-SO Competition, 1994—, Leadership Am., 1991—; vol. One Ch. One Addict, 1995—, bd. dirs., 1997—; mem. bd. edn. Cath. Archdiocese of Washington, 1995—; bd. dirs. Office Employee Appeals, D.C., 1997—, One Ch.-One Inmate, 1997—; vol. Black Revolutionary War Patriots' Found., 1998—. Mem. Internat. Fedn. Women Lawyers (exec. coun. 1996—), Am. Translators Assn., Howard U. Alumni Assn., Links, Inc., Leadership Greater Washington (bd. dirs. 1992-94, v.p. 1995-96), Coun. Black Catholics, Alpha Kappa Alpha.

**WILCHINS, HOWARD MARTIN,** lawyer; b. Paterson, N.J., Mar. 6, 1945; s. Philip Aaron and Esther (Blake) W.; m. Margaret Mandon, Sept. 6, 1970; children—Julie, Daniel. AB, Mich. State U., 1966; JD, U. Chgo., 1969. BAR: D.C. 1969, U.S. Supreme Ct. 1975. Trial atty. FPC, Washington, 1969-70; spl. asst. to N.Y. Public Service Commn., Albany, 1970-72; dep. sect. chief AEC, Washington, 1972-75; dep. gen. counsel-litigation U.S. Ry. Assn., Washington, 1975-81, gen. counsel, 1981-84; dep. chief enforcement div. FCC Common Carrier Bur., Washington, 1984-90; v.p. Arnold S. Tesh Advisors, Washington, 1990-92; sr. litigation atty. Office Nuclear Safety Enforcement, U.S. Dept. Energy, Washington, 1992—; mem. faculty Trial Practice Inst., U.S. CSC, 1977-79. Bd. dirs. United Jewish Appeal Greater Washington, 1984-90, 92-96; bd. dirs. Charles E. Smith Jewish Day Sch., 1983—, v.p., 1986-88, pres., 1988-90; mem. Hillel of Greater Washington, 1990—, v.p., 1992-94, pres., 1994-96; bd. dirs., mem. Capital Camps, 1990-96; bd. dir. Jewish Edn. Svc. N.Am., 1996—. Mem. ABA, D.C. Bar Assn., Fed. Comm. Bar Assn. (co-chmn. com. on arbitration and mediation 1991-94), Am. Arbitration Assn. Home: 5 Feather Rock Pl Rockville MD 20850-3114 Office: US Dept Energy Office Nuclear Safety Enforc Washington DC 20585-0001

**WILCOX, DEBRA KAY,** lawyer; b. Colorado Springs, Colo., Sept. 7, 1955; children: Justin, Lauren. BA in English, U. No. Colo., 1977; JD, U. Denver, 1986. Bar: Colo. 1987, U.S. Dist. Ct. Colo. 1988. Rsch. analyst Colo. Legis. Coun., Denver, 1978-80, 81-83; govt. affairs staff Alliance of Am. Insurers, Chgo., 1980-81; law clk. and assoc. Rotole, Jaunarajs, Walker & Lumbye, Denver, 1986-88; of counsel Jay M. Finesilver, P.C., Denver, 1988-90, Cogswell & Eggleston, Denver, 1990, Kobayashi & Assocs., P.C., Denver, 1990-94, Pencom, Inc., Denver, 1994-95, Land Am. Fin. Group Inc., Phoenix, 1995—; mem. jud. tchg. faculty Colo. Dept. Jud. Adminstrn., P.C., Denver, 1988, mem. state collection agy. bd., 1992. Co-author: A History of Colorado's Legislative Leaders, 1979. Mem. acctg. com. Newton Mid. Sch., 1996-99, chmn., 1998-99. Recipient Arnold M. Chuktow award, U. Denver, 1986; named Outstanding Young Women in Am., 1976, 1986. Mem. ABA (mem. host com. young lawyers divsn. 1988), Colo. Bar Assn. (mem. availability of legal svcs. com.), Denver Bar Assn., Sigma Sigma Sigma (v.p. 1988-90, mem. nat. ednl. found. bd. 1990-92). Consumer commercial, General civil litigation, Government contracts and claims. Office: LandAmerica Fin Group Inc 3636 N Central Ave Ste 350 Phoenix AZ 85012-1929

**WILCOX, DONALD ALAN,** lawyer; b. Grantsburg, Wis., July 18, 1951; s. John Charles and Lois Margaret (Finch) W.; m. Rachel Ann Johnson, Dec. 28, 1973; children: Benjamin Ray, Joseph Charles (dec.), Sara Johanna. BS, USAF Acad., 1973; JD, Georgetown U., 1979. Bar: Minn. 1979. Commd. 2d lt. USAF, 1973, advanced through grades to capt., resigned, 1979; assoc Holmquist & Holmquist, Benson, Minn., 1979-81; ptnr. Holmquist & Wilcox, 1981-90; shareholder Wilcox, Erhardt & Spates, P.A., Benson, 1990-91; pvt. practice Benson, 1991—; gen. counsel Swift County-Benson Hosp., 1981—, Farmers Mut. Coop., Bellingham, Minn., 1986—, Agralite Coop., Benson, 1986—, Kandiyohi Electric Coop., 1995—; atty. City of Benson, 1985—; examiner of titles, Swift County, Benson, 1986—, Federated Tel. Coop., Chokio, Minn., 1988—. Mem. Benson Planning Commn., 1979—; pres. Our Redeemer's Luth. Ch., Benson, 1985-86, 93-94; pres., bd. dirs. Swift County Homes, Inc., Benson, 1984-92. Recipient Lawyers Coop. Pub. award Lawyers Coop. Pub. Co., 1979. Mem. Minn. Bar Assn., Twelfth Dist. Bar Assn. (pres. 1995-96), Benson C. of C. (bd. dirs. 1981-84), Kiwanis (treas. Benson 1982-84, 97—). Avocations: reading, golf, skiing. Contracts commercial, Probate, Real property. Home: 604 13th St S Benson MN 56215-2017 Office: 1150 Wisconsin Ave Benson MN 56215-1841

**WILCOX, GREGORY B.,** lawyer; b. Des Moines, Sept. 22, 1954; s. Lawrence R. and Mary T. Wilcox; m. Melinda S. Wilcox, Sept. 4, 1976; children: Andrew, Austin, Morgan. BBA, U. Iowa, 1976; JD, Drake U., 1982. Bar: Iowa. V.p. Wilcox Enterprises, Inc., West Des Moines, Iowa, 1976-79; atty. Nyemaster Law Firm, Des Moines, 1982—, shareholder, dir., 1987—. Assoc. articles editor Drake Law Sch., 1981-82; contbr. articles to profl. jours. Dir. Iowa State Chpt. March Dimes, Des Moines, 1993—; dir., sec. Iowa Sports Found., Des Moines, 1996—. Mem. ABA, Iowa State Bar Assn. (chair forms com. 1988-91, chair profl. corp. com. 1993-95), Polk County Bar Assn., Order of the Coif. Office: Nyemaster Law Firm 700 Walnut St Ste 1600 Des Moines IA 50309-3899

**WILCOX, JON P.,** state supreme court justice; b. Berlin, Wis., Sept. 5, 1936; m. Jane Ann; children: Jeffrey, Jennifer. AB in Polit. Sci., Ripon Coll., 1958; JD, U. Wis., 1965. Pvt. practice Steele, Smyth, Klos and Flynn, LaCrosse, Wis., 1965-66, Hacker and Wilcox, Wautoma, Wis., 1966-69, Wilcox, Rudolph, Kubasta & Rathjen, Wautoma, 1969-79; elected judge Waushara County Cir. Ct., 1979-92; apptd. justice Wis. Supreme Ct., 1992-97, elected justice 10-yr. term, 1997; commr. Family Ct., Waushara County, 1977-79; vice chmn., chmn. Wis. Sentencing Commn., 1984-92; chief judge 6th Jud. Dist., 1985-92; mem. State-Fed. Jud. Coun., 1992—, Jud. Coun. Wis., 1993-98; mem. Prison Overcrowding Task Force, 1988-90; mem. numerous coms. Wis. Judiciary; mem. faculty Wis. Jud. Coll., 1986-97; chmn. Wis. Chief Judges Com., 1990-92; co-chair comm. on judiciary as co-equal br. of govt. Wis. State Bar, 1995-97; lectr. in field. Contbr. (with others): Wisconsin News Reporters Legal Handbook: Wisconsin Courts and Court Procedures, 1987. Bd. visitors U. Wis. Law Sch, 1970-76. Lt. U.S. Army, 1959-61. Named Outstanding Jaycee Wautoma, 1974; recipient Disting. Alumni award Ripon Coll., 1993. Fellow Am. Bar Found.; mem. ABA (com. on continuing appellate edn.), Wis. Bar Assn. (bench bar com.), Wis. Law Found. (bd. dirs.), Tri-County Bar Assn., Dane County Bar Assn., Trout Unltd., Ruffed Grouse Soc., Ducks Unltd., Rotary, Phi Alpha Delta. Office: Supreme Court State Capitol PO Box 1688 Madison WI 53701-1688

**WILCOX, MARK DEAN,** lawyer; b. Chgo., May 25, 1952; s. Fabian Joseph and Zeryle Lucille (Tase) W.; m. Catherine J. Wertjes, Mar. 12, 1983; children: Glenna Lynn, Joanna Tessie, Andrew Fabian Joseph. BBA, U. Notre Dame, 1973; JD, Northwestern U., 1976; CLU, Am. Coll., 1979, ChFC, 1992. Bar: Ill. 1976, U.S. Dist. Ct. (no. dist.) Ill. 1976, Trial Bar 1982, U.S. Ct. Appeals (7th cir.) 1987, U.S. Supreme Ct. 1989. Staff asst. Nat. Dist. Attys. Assn., Chgo., 1974-75; trial asst. Cook County States Atty., Chgo., 1975; intern U.S. Atty. No. Dist. Ill., Chgo., 1975-76; assoc. Lord, Bissell & Brook, Chgo., 1976-85, ptnr., 1986—. Bd. mgrs. YMCA Metropolitan Chgo., exec. com. Internat. Spl. Olympics. Mem. ABA (tort and ins. practice sect.), Am. Soc. CLU and ChFC, Chgo. Bar Assn. (ins. law com.), Def. Rsch. Inst., Trial Lawyers Club Chgo., Notre Dame Nat. Monogram Club, Union League Club (Chgo.), Beta Gamma Sigma. Insurance, Professional liability, General civil litigation. Office: Lord Bissell & Brook 115 S La Salle St Ste 3200 Chicago IL 60603-3972

**WILCOX, MARTHA ANNE,** lawyer; b. Miami, Fla., Jan. 13, 1948; m. Ralph Ogden, Jan. 31, 1981; children: Helen, Chris. BA in Philosophy, Speech summa cum laude, Ind.-Purdue U., 1976; JD, Ind. U., 1976. Bar: Ind. 1976, Colo. 1984, U.S. Dist. Ct. (so. dist.) Ind. 1976, U.S. Dist. Ct. (no. dist.) Ind. 1980, U.S. Dist. Ct. Colo. 1984, U.S. Ct. Appeals (7th cir.) 1976, U.S. Ct. Appeals (10th cir.) 1983, U.S. Supreme Ct. 1984. Pub. defender Marion County Criminal Ct., 1977-74; adj. prof. appellate advocacy, practice Ind. U., 1976-77; pvt. practice Indpls., 1977-78; spl. judge civil and criminal divs. Marion County Superior Ct., 1975-80, appellate pub. defender, 1982-83; ptnr. Wilcox, Ogden & DuMond, Indpls., 1979-83, Wilcox & Ogden, Denver, 1983—. Editor-in-Chief Genesis Lit. and Philos. Jour. Mem. of com. on character and fitness Ind. Supreme Ct., 1982-84; pres., vice pres. Student Govt.; mem., capt., coach varsity debate team; student rep. to Faculty Senate and Univ. Budget Com.; state chmn. Older Hoosiers Law Day, 1979; founding mem., mem. bd. dirs. Network of Women in Bus., Inc., 1976-81; speakers bur. Ind. U., 1976-84, search, screen com. for dean of the Sch. of Liberal Arts, 1982; bd. dirs. YWCA of Met., Indpls.; team mem. on brief, oral argument Nat. Moot Ct., bd. dirs, coach. Recipient of acad. scholars, Nat. and Regional Collegiate Debate Competition award, Disting. Alumi award Ind.-Purdue U., 1981, Outstanding Debater award 1972, 1973; named Outstanding Young Women of Am. 1982; winner of Collegiate Persuasive Speaking Competition. Fellow Ind. Bar Found. (charter mem. 1980); mem. ABA (faculty mem. ann. conf. on atty. discipline 1982), Assn. Trial Lawyers Am., Ind. State Bar Assn. (litigation sect., co-chmn. of Nat. Moot Ct. Com. 1978, judge 1980), Am. Arbitration Assn. (panel mem. 1981—), Colo. Bar Assn., Denver Bar Assn., Indpls. Bar Assn. (legal ethics com. 1979-84), Alpha Tau Alpha, Sigma Tau Delta. Personal injury, Federal civil litigation, Professional liability. Office: Wilcox & Ogden PC 1750 Gilpin St Denver CO 80218-1206

**WILCOX, MICHAEL WING,** lawyer; b. Buffalo, July 21, 1941; s. Paul Wing and Barbara Ann (Bauter) W.; m. Diane Rose Dell, June 18, 1966; children: Timothy, Katherine, Matthew. AB, UCLA, 1963; JD, Marquette U., 1966. Bar: Wis. 1966, U.S. Ct. Appeals (7th cir.) 1967. Law clk. to judge U.S. Ct. Appeals (7th cir.), Chgo., 1966-67; with Boardman, Suhr, Curry & Field, Madison, Wis., 1967-83; ptnr. Quarles & Brady, Madison, 1983-90, Stolper, Koritzinsky, Brewster & Neider, Madison, 1990-94, Stolper & Wilcox, Madison, 1995—; lectr. in field. Author: (with others) Marital Property Law in Wisconsin, 1986. Fin. com. Meriter Found. Mem. ABA (chmn. marital property com. of real property probate and trust law sect. 1986-89), Wis. State Bar Assn. (chmn. taxation sect. 1983-84), Am. Coll. Trust and Estate Counsel, Rotary (pres. Madison West chpt. 1998-99), Blackhawk Country Club. Estate planning, Probate, Estate taxation. Home: 6318 Keelson Dr Madison WI 53705-4367 Office: Stolper & Wilcox 6510 Grand Teton Plz Madison WI 53719-1029

**WILD, NELSON HOPKINS,** lawyer; b. Milw., July 16, 1933; s. Henry Goetseels and Virginia Douglas (Weller) W.; m. Joan Ruth Miles, Apr. 12, 1969; children: Mark, Eric. A.B., Princeton U., 1955; LL.B., U. Wis., 1961. Bar: Wis. 1962, Calif. 1967; cert. specialist in probate, estate planning and trust law State Bar of Calif. Research assoc. Wis. Legis. Council, Madison, 1955-56; assoc. Whyte, Hirschboeck, Minahan, Harding & Harland, Milw., 1961-67, Thelen, Marin, Johnson & Bridges, San Francisco, 1967-70; sole practice law San Francisco, 1970—; mem. State Bar Calif. Client Trust Fund Commn., 1983, mem. exec. com. conf. dels., 1985-88. Contbr. articles to legal jours. Bd. dirs. Neighborhood Legal Assistance Found., San Francisco, 1974-85, chmn. bd., 1978-81. Served with USAF, 1956-58. Mem. ABA, Calif. Bar Assn., San Francisco Bar Assn., Am. Bar Found., Lawyers of San Francisco Club (gov. 1975, treas. 1981, v.p. 1982, pres.-elect 1983, pres. 1984), Calif. Tennis Club (bd. dirs. 1995-97, pres. 1997). Probate, General corporate, Estate planning. Office: 220 Montgomery St Ste 1006 San Francisco CA 94104-3419

**WILD, ROBERT WARREN,** lawyer; b. Syracuse, N.Y., Mar. 25, 1942; s. Robert Sumner and Evelyn I. (Yorman) W.; m. Elizabeth Trowbridge, Sept. 5, 1965; children: Robert Mason, Alexander Lewis, Elizabeth Anne. BS, MIT, 1964; JD, Cornell U., 1970. Bar: N.Y. 1971, D.C. 1973. Engr. Smithsonian Astrophysical Obs., Cambridge, Mass., 1965-67; atty., advisor U.S. Dept. Justice, Washington, 1970-72; law clk. to Hon. Justice William H. Rehnquist U.S. Supreme Ct., Washington, 1972-73; ptnr. Nixon, Hargrave, Devans & Doyle, Rochester, N.Y., 1973—. Mem. Monroe County Bar Assn. (trustee 1990-91, 92-94, treas. 1992-94, counsel 1994—). Pension, profit-sharing, and employee benefits, Labor, Taxation, general. Office: Nixon Hargrave Devans & Doyle LLP Clinton Sq PO Box 1051 Rochester NY 14603-1051

**WILD, VICTOR ALLYN,** lawyer, educator; b. Logansport, Ind., May 7, 1946; s. Clifford Otto and Mary E. (Helvey) W.; m. Wesley Hobbs, July 25, 1975; 1 child, Rachel. BS in Pub. Adminstrn., U.Ariz., 1968, JD, 1974. Bar: Ariz. 1975, U.S. Dist. Ct. Ariz. 1975, Mass. 1984, U.S. Dist. Ct. Mass. 1984, U.S. Ct. Appeals (1st cir.) 1985, U.S. Ct. Appeals (9th cir.). Chief escrow officer Lawyers Title Co., Denver, 1971-72; escrow officer Lawyers Title Co., Tucson, 1970-71; law clk. Pima County Atty., Tucson, 1973-75, dep. county atty., 1975-81, chief criminal dep., 1981-84; asst. U.S. Atty. Dist. of Mass., Boston, 1984—; chief gen. crimes unit U.S. Atty.'s Office, Boston, 1986-89; seminar instr. Mass. Continuing Legal Edn., Internat. Assn. Law Enforcement Investment Analysts, Dept. of Justice Office Internat. Affairs, Dept. of Labor, FBI, U.S. Postal Svc., Secret Svc., State Bar Ariz., Tucson and Phoenix, 1981-84; instr. U. Ariz., Tucson, 1981-84, Pima Community Coll., Tucson, 1981-84. Mem. vestry St. Michael's Episc. Ch., Marblehead, Mass., 1986—, lay Eucharistic min., 1988—, parish warden, 1992—; mem. Boston Ctr. for Internat. Visitors, 1989—; bd. dirs. Crime Resistors, Inc., Tucson, 1983, CODAC, Tucson, 1983, 88-Crime, Inc., Tucson, 1983, Marblehead Seaport Trust, 1987—; chmn. Marblehead Capital Planning Commn., 1989—; bd. dirs. Marblehead Citizen Scholarship Found., 1997—; mem. PhD rev. com. Law Policy and Soc. Northeastern U., 1991-92. Mem. editl. bd. Episcopal Times, Diocese of Mass., 1988—; bd. dirs. Davenport House Child Enrichment Ctr., Marblehead, 1986-89. With USAF, 1968-70. Recipient Commendation awards Dept. Labor, Dept. State, USCG, USIA, U.S. Postal Svc., Dept. Treasury, EOUSA Rev., Software Pub. Assn., Mass. Ins. Fraud Bur.; named Prosecutor of Yr., Office Insp. Gen., U.S. Dept. Labor, 1986, DOJ Spec. Achievement Award, 1993, 95, 96. Master Boston Inn of Ct.; mem. Ariz. Bar Assn., Mass. Bar Assn., Tau Kappa Epsilon, Delta Sigma Pi, Phi Kappa Delta. Office: US Attys Office Ste 9200 US Courthouse One Courthouse Way Boston MA 02210

**WILDE, JINHEE KIM,** lawyer; b. Seoul, Korea, Aug. 16, 1958; d. Grace Myung-sook and John Jeong-Kuk Gehrim; m. David B. Wilde, June 19, 1982; children: Winston, Brendon. BA, U. Chgo., 1981; JD, Loyola U. Sch. Law, 1985. Legal advisor Spkr. Ill. Ho. Reps., Springfield, 1986; prosecutor Chgo. Law Dept., 1986-88; litigation atty. Block, Levy & Assocs., Chgo., 1988; dep. recorder Cook County Recorder of Deeds, Chgo., 1989; atty. adv. office of gen. counsel to Inspector Gen. Nominee U.S. Dept. Agriculture, Washington, 1989-95; of counsel Arent Fox Kintner Plotkin & Kahn, Washington, 1996—. Commr. Chesapeake Bary Critical Bay Critical Area Commn., Annapolis, Md., 1996—; mem. Dem. Ctrl. Com., Md., 1998; bd. dirs. Coalition of Asian Pacific Am. Dems., Md., 1998; exec. v.p. Asian Pacific Am. Heritage Coun., Washington, 1992. Mem. Women's Bar Assn. (com. chair 1996-99). Democrat. Roman Catholic. Private international, Oil, gas, and mineral, Administrative and regulatory. Office: Arent Fox Kintner Plotkin & Kahn 1050 Connecticut Ave NW Washington DC 20036-5314

**WILDE, WILLIAM RICHARD,** lawyer; b. Markesan, Wis., Mar. 1, 1953; s. Leslie Maurice and Elaine Margaret (Schweder) W.; m. Carolyn Margaret Zieman, July 17, 1981 (div. 1987); 1 child, Leah Marie; m. Barbara Joan Rohlf, Jan. 6, 1990. BA, U. Wis., Milw., 1975; JD, Marquette U., 1980. Bar: Wis. 1980, U.S. Dist. Ct. (ea. and we. dists.) Wis. 1980. Dist. atty. Green Lake County, Green Lake, Wis., 1980-83, corp.counsel, 1981; ptnr. Curtis, Wilde and Neal, Oshkosh, Wis., 1983-97, Wilde Law Offices, Oshkosh, 1997—. Mem. Assn. Trial Lawyers Am., Wis. Bar Assn., Wis. Acad. Trial Lawyers (Amicus Curiae Brief com. 1987-92, bd. dirs., assoc. editor The Verdict, treas. 1993, sec. 1994, v.p. 1995, pres.-elect 1996, pres. 1997), Wis. Assn. Criminal Def. Lawyers (bd. dirs. 1987-91), Winnebbago County Bar Assn., Green Lake County Bar Assn. Personal injury, Insurance, General civil litigation. Office: Wilde Law Offices 1901 S Washburn PO Box 3422 Oshkosh WI 54903-3422 also: PO Box 282 Markesan WI 53946-0282

**WILDER, CHARLES WILLOUGHBY,** lawyer, consultant; b. Newton, Mass., Jan. 27, 1929; s. Philip Sawyer and Elisabeth (Clark) W.; m. Elinor Gardner Dean, Nov. 2, 1957; children: Michael, Stephen, Elisabeth. BA, Bowdoin Coll., 1950; LLB, Columbia U., 1957. Bar: N.Y. 1958. Assoc. White & Case, N.Y.C., 1957-58; law clk. to judge U.S. Ct. Appeals (2d cir.), N.Y.C., 1958-59; atty. Gen. Electric Co., 1959-67; from counsel to v.p., dep. gen. counsel, sec. Tex. Gulf Sulphur Co. (name changed to Texasgulf Inc. 1973), N.Y.C. and Stamford, Conn., 1967-90; v.p., dep. gen. counsel, sec. Elf Aquitaine, Inc., Stamford, 1983-90; now legal cons. Served to lt. (j.g.) USNR, 1951-54. Mem. ABA, N.Y. State Bar Assn., Assn. Bar City N.Y. Democrat. General corporate. Office: Elf Aquitaine Inc 444 Madison Ave Fl 20 New York NY 10022-6903

**WILDER, JAMES SAMPSON, III,** lawyer, judge; b. Knoxville, Tenn., Mar. 15, 1949; s. James Sampson and Florence Louise (Summers) W. BS, Lambuth Coll., Jackson, Tenn., 1971; JD, Memphis State U., 1974. Bar: Tenn. 1974, U.S. Dist. Ct. (we. dist.) Tenn. 1975, U.S. Supreme Ct. 1981, U.S. Ct. Appeals (6th cir.) 1982. Assoc. Lt. Gov. John S. Wilder, Somerville, Tenn., 1974-75, ptnr., 1975-76; ptnr. Wilder, Wilder & Johnson, Somerville, 1976-83; pvt. practice James S. Wilder III, Somerville, 1983-95; gen. sessions judge Fayette County, Somerville, Tenn., 1985-90; assoc. Petkoff and Lancaster, Memphis, 1995—. Scoutmaster troop 95 Boy Scouts Am., Somerville, 1975-77, com. person, 1977—. Paul Harris fellow Rotary, Somerville, 1977. Mem. ABA, Assn. Trial Lawyers Am., Tenn. Bar Assn., Tenn. Trial Lawyers Assn. (dir. 1983-86), Fayette County C. of C. (dir. 1979—), Somerville Rotary (dir. 1976—, charter pres. 1976-78). Methodist. Avocations: hunting, fishing. State civil litigation, Federal civil litigation, Personal injury. Home: PO Box 187 Somerville TN 38068-0187 Office: Washington Courtyard 305 Washington Ave Memphis TN 38103-1911

**WILDER, MICHAEL STEPHEN,** insurance company executive; b. New Haven, Conn., Sept. 8, 1941. BA, Yale U., 1963; JD, Harvard U., 1966. Bar: Conn. 1966. Atty. Hartford (Conn.) Fire Ins. Co., 1967-69, asst. gen. counsel, 1969-71, assoc. gen. counsel, 1971-75, gen. coun., sec., 1975-87, sr. v.p., gen. counsel, sec., 1987-95; sr. v.p., gen. counsel The Hartford Fin. Svcs. Group, Inc., 1995—. Mem. ABA, Conn. Bar Assn. Office: Hartford Fin Svcs Group Inc Hartford Plz Hartford CT 06115

**WILDER, ROLAND PERCIVAL, JR.,** lawyer; b. Malden, Mass., June 21, 1940; s. Roland Percival and Clarissa (Hunting) W.; m. Susan McAra Randell, Sept. 3, 1965; children: Roland Percival III, William Randell. BA, Washington and Jefferson Coll., 1963; JD, Vanderbilt U., 1966. Bar: D.C. 1967, U.S. Dist. Ct. D.C. 1967, U.S. Ct. Appeals (D.C. cir.) 1967, U.S. Supreme Ct. 1972, U.S. Ct. Appeals (4th, 5th and 6th cirs.) 1976, U.S. Ct. Appeals (8th and 9th cirs.) 1977, U.S. Ct. Appeals (2d cir.) 1978, U.S. Ct. Appeals (11th cir.) 1981, U.S. Dist. Ct. Md. 1994, U.S. Ct. Appeals (3d cir.) 1997, U.S. Dist. Ct. Colo. 1997, U.S. Dist. Ct. (ea. dist.) Mich. 1999. Atty. Office of Solicitor U.S. Dept. Labor, Washington, 1967-69; asst. counsel civil rights office of solicitor U.S. Dept. Labor, Washington, 1969-70, counsel civil rights office of solicitor, 1970-71; supr. atty. office gen. counsel NLRB, Washington, 1972-74; assoc. gen. counsel Internat. Brotherhood Teamsters, Washington, 1974-85; sr. mem. Baptiste & Wilder P.C., Washington, 1985—; lectr. numerous continuing legal edn. programs various states, 1970—. Mng. editor Vanderbilt U. Law Rev., 1965-66; contbr. articles to profl. jours. V.p. Arlington (Va.) Cubs Youth Club, Inc., 1975-81; coach Fairfax (Va.) Hockey Club, 1979-83. Mem. ABA, D.C. Bar Assn., Assn. Trial Lawyers Am., Phi Delta Phi, Pi Sigma Alpha, Phi Alpha Theta, Roosevelt Soc., Joint Council Flight Attendant Unions (hon. flight attendant 1985). Democrat. Avocations: history, tennis, skiing. Labor, Federal civil litigation, Pension, profit-sharing, and employee benefits. Home: 6244 Williamsburg Blvd Arlington VA 22207-1151 Office: Baptiste & Wilder PC 1150 Connecticut Ave NW Ste 500 Washington DC 20036-4194

**WILDER, SHARON BETH,** lawyer; b. Silver Springs, Md., June 26, 1968; d. Alan H. and Marilyn I. Wilder. BA, Boston U., 1990; JD, George Washington U., 1993. Bar: Md. 1993; cert. child passenger safety technician Nat. Hwy. Traffic Safety Adminstrn. Investigator Montgomery County Divsn. Consumer Affairs, Rockville, Md., 1994—. Office: Montgomery County Divsn Consumer Affairs 100 Maryland Ave Rockville MD 20850-2322

**WILDER, WILLIAM F.,** lawyer; b. Prescott, Ariz., Aug. 29, 1938; s. Carleton Stafford and Judith (Carlock) W.; m. Liisa Wilder, Oct. 18, 1975; children: Rebecca Files, Andrew. BS in Bus. Adminstrn., U. Ariz., 1962, LLB, 1964. Bar: Ariz. 1964. Atty., shareholder Ryley, Carlock & Applewhite, Phoenix, 1964—. Bd. dirs., chmn. Ariz. Heart Assn., 1977-83; trustee Desert Bot. Garden, Phoenix, 1996—; bd. dirs. Arizonans for Cultural Devel., 1994—, Phoenix Cmty. Alliance, 1993—. Served with USN, 1956-58. Mem. Nat. Assn. Bond Attys. Avocations: fishing, hiking, camping, tennis, skiing, travel.

**WILDER, WILLIAM RANDELL,** lawyer; b. Alexandria, Va., May 18, 1968; s. Roland Percival Jr. and Susan McAra W.; m. Jennifer Slack, June 14, 1997. BA, Va. Tech., 1990; JD, William & Mary Coll., 1993. Bar: D.C. 1996, Tex. 1997, Va. 1993, U.S. Ct. Appeals (4th cir.) 1998, U.S. Ct. Appeals (5th cir.) 1998, U.S. Dist. Ct. (ea. dist.) Va., U.S. Dist. Ct. D.C. 1998, U.S. Dist. Ct. (we. dist.) Va., U.S. Dist. Ct. (so. dist.) Tex. 1997. Atty. Law Office Earl Shaffer, Arlington, Va., 1994-97; assoc. Baptiste & Wilder, P.C., Washington, 1997—. Mem. ABA (Regional Champion nat. appellate adv. competition), Assn. Trial Lawyers Am., Va. Trial Lawyers Assn., Order of Barristers. Labor, Aviation, Federal civil litigation. Office: Baptiste & Wilder PC 1150 Connecticut Ave NW Ste 500 Washington DC 20036-4194

**WILDEROTTER, JAMES ARTHUR,** lawyer; b. Newark, July 25, 1944; s. Arthur Walter and Dorothy Theresa (King) W.; m. Cheryl Lynn Clifford; children: James, Kristin, Kathryn. BA, Georgetown U., 1966; JD, U. Ill., 1969. Bar: D.C. 1969, U.S. Supreme Ct. 1974. Assoc. Covington & Burling, Washington, 1969-71; spl. asst. to Under Sec. Commerce, Washington, 1971-73; exec. asst. to Sec. HUD, Washington, 1973-74; assoc. dept. atty. gen. U.S. Washington, 1974-75, assoc. counsel to Pres. U.S., 1975-76; gen. counsel U.S. Energy Research and Devel. Adminstrn., Washington, 1976-77; of counsel Morgan, Lewis & Bockius, Washington, 1977-78; ptnr. Jones, Day, Reavis & Pogue, Washington, 1978-91, 95—; v.p., gen. counsel Internat. Paper Co., Purchase, N.Y., 1991-94. Editor in chief: U. Ill. Law Rev., 1968-69. Gen. counsel rules com. Rep. Nat. Conv., 1980; sec. James S. Brady Presdl. Found., 1982-88; gen. counsel Nat. Sudden Infant Death Syndrome Found., 1986-90, sec. Sudden Infant Death Syndrome Alliance, 1990-93. With USN, 1962-68. Mem. ABA. Republican. Roman Catholic. General corporate, Administrative and regulatory. Home: 518 Duke St Alexandria VA 22314-3738 Office: Jones Day Reavis and Pogue 51 Louisiana Ave NW Washington DC 20001-2113

**WILDSMITH, QUENTIN,** lawyer; b. Christianstead, V.I., Dec. 15, 1968; s. Graham Wildsmith and Peggy Vitale; m. Marina Wildsmith, June 3, 1990; children: Bryton, Grayson. BA in English, Coll. William and Mary, 1990; JD, St. Louis U., 1993. Bar: Mo. 1993, Wash. 1995, U.S. Dist. Ct. (we. dist.) Wash. 1997. Asst. pub. defender III Mo. Pub. Defender, St. Louis, 1993-97; atty. MacDermid Liebert & Morgan P.S., Silverdale, Wash., 1997—; trustee, treas. Hospice Kitsap County, Silverdale, 1997—. Mem. Wash. State Bar Assn. (exec. com. law practice mgmt. and tech. sect. 1998). Estate planning, General corporate. Office: MacDermid Liebert & Morgan PS 9226 Bayshore Dr NW Ste 103 Silverdale WA 98383-9196

**WILE, PHILIP HODGES,** law educator; b. Cleve., Dec. 2, 1930; s. Ralph H. and Elizabeth (Mower) W.; m. Nancy D. Wile, Oct. 26, 1952 (dec. Jan. 1992); children: James, Elizabeth Wile Meyerowitz, Janet Wile Melikian; m. JoAnne S. Steninger, May 29, 1993. AB, Stanford U., 1952, JD, 1957. Bar: Calif. 1957. Assoc. Kimble, Thomas, Snell, Jamison & Russell, Fresno, Calif., 1957-61; asst. prof. law Stanford (Calif.) Sch. Law, 1961-62; ptnr., shareholder Thomas, Snell, Jamison, Russell & Asperger, Fresno, 1962-87; prof. law, dir. tax programs U. Pacific McGeorge Sch. Law, Sacramento, 1987—. Author: Federal Income Tax—A Case Book on the Basics, 1995; contbr. articles to law jours. Pres. Sacramento Traditional Jazz Soc. Found., 1996-99. Mem. ABA, Order of Coif. Office: U Pacific McGeorge Sch Law 3200 5th Ave Sacramento CA 95817-2705

**WILEMAN, GEORGE ROBERT,** lawyer; b. Ironton, Ohio, June 1, 1938; s. George Merchant and Marguerite (McCormack) W.; children: John Chandler, Julie Jo. AB, Duke U., 1960; JD, Georgetown U., 1963. Bar: Ohio 1968, Tex. 1977, U.S. Supreme Ct. 1993. Pvt. practice Dallas, 1977—. Mem. Coll. State Bar of Tex. Republican. Avocations: boating, running. Personal injury, Professional liability. Home: 5200 Keller Springs Rd Apt 1136 Dallas TX 75248-2750 Address: The Roles Building 2651 N Harwood St Ste 550 Dallas TX 75201-1565

**WILEY, EDWIN PACKARD,** retired lawyer; b. Chgo., Dec. 10, 1929; s. Edwin Garnet and Marjorie Chastina (Packard) W.; m. Barbara Jean Miller, May 21, 1949; children: Edwin Miller, Clayton Alexander, Stephen Packard. BA, U. Chgo., 1949, JD, 1952. Bar: Wis. 1952, Ill. 1952, U.S. Dist. Ct. (ea. dist.) Wis. 1953, U.S. Supreme Ct. 1978. Assoc. Foley & Lardner, Milw., 1952-60, ptnr., 1960-98; ret.; bd. dirs. Genetic Testing Inst., Inc., other corps. and founds. Co-author: Bank Holding Companies: A Practical Guide to Bank Acquisitions and Mergers, 1988, Wisconsin Uniform Commercial Code Handbook, 1971; author: Promotional Arrangements: Discrimination in Advertising and Promotional Allowances, 1976; editor in chief U. Chgo. Law Rev., 1952; contbr. articles to legal jours. Bd. dirs. Blood Ctr. of Southeastern Wis., pres., 1978-82; pres. Blood Ctr. Rsch. Found., Inc., 1983-87; v.p. Friends of Schlitz Audubon Ctr., Inc., 1975-87; active United Performing Arts Fund of Milw.; pres. Wis. Conservatory of Music, 1968-74; pres. First Unitarian Soc. Milw., 1961-63; v.p. Mid-Am. Ballet Co., 1971-73, Milw. Ballet Co., 1973-74; pres. Florentine Opera Co., 1983-86; bd. dirs. Milw. Symphony Orch., pres., 1993-95; bd. dirs. Milw. Pub. Mus., Inc., sec. 1992—; bd. dirs. Wis. History Found. Mem. ABA, State Bar of Wis., Milw. Bar Assn., Am. Law Inst., Order of Coif, Univ. Club, Phi Beta Kappa (pres. Greater Milw. assn. 1962-63). Unitarian-Universalist. Antitrust, Banking, Private international. Home: 929 N Astor St Unit 2101 Milwaukee WI 53202-3488

**WILEY, RICHARD EMERSON,** lawyer; b. Peoria, Ill., July 20, 1934; s. Joseph Henry and Jean W. (Farrell) W.; m. Elizabeth J. Edwards, Aug. 6, 1960; children: Douglas S., Pamela L. B.S. with distinction, Northwestern U., 1955, J.D., 1958; LLM, Georgetown U., 1962; LLD (hon.), Cath. U. of Am., 1998. Bar: Ill. 1958, D.C. 1972. Pvt. practice Chgo., 1962-70; gen. counsel FCC, Washington, 1970-72, mem., 1972-74, chmn., 1974-77, chmn. FCC's adv. com. on advanced TV svc., 1987-96; mng. ptnr. Wiley, Rein & Fielding, Washington, 1983—; prof. law John Marshall Law Sch., U. Chgo., 1963-70. Chmn. adv. bd. Inst. for Tele-Info., Columbia U., 1989—. Capt. AUS, 1959-62. Recipient Emmy award Nat. Acad. Arts, 1997, Medal of Honor, Electronic Industries Am., 1996. Fellow Am. Bar Found.; mem. ABA (mem. ho. of dels. 1969-71, 77-84, chmn. young lawyers sect., 1977-84, chmn. Forum com. on communications 1969, chmn. bd. editors ABA Jour. 1984-89, chmn. com. on scope and correlation of work 1989, chmn. adminstrv. law and regulatory practice 1993-94), Fed. Bar Assn. (pres. 1977), Fed. Communications Bar Assn. (pres. 1987), Ill. Bar Assn., Chgo. Bar Assn., Adminstrv. Conf. U.S. (coun., sr. fellow), Phi Delta Phi, Phi Delta Kappa. Methodist. Communications. Home: 3818 N Woodrow St Arlington VA 22207-4345 Office: Wiley Rein & Fielding 1776 K St NW Ste 1100 Washington DC 20006-2304

**WILF, MERVIN M.,** lawyer; b. Phila., Mar. 10, 1926; s. Benjamin and Bessie (Kovalsky) W.; m. Virginia F. Coleman, Feb. 18, 1990; children: Michael J., Susan R., Kathy E. A.B., Pa. State U., 1946; J.D. magna cum laude, U. Pa., 1955. Bar: Pa. 1956, Mass. 1991. Assoc., then partner firm White and Williams, Phila., 1955-71; partner firm Townsend, Elliot & Munson, Phila., 1971, Hudson, Wilf & Kronfeld, Phila., 1972-80, Mervin M. Wilf Ltd., 1981-89, 92—; of counsel Hale and Dorr, Boston, 1990-92; adj. prof. law U. Pa. Law Sch.; lectr. law Rutgers U. Law Sch., Villanova U. Law Sch.; vis. prof. law Temple U. Law Sch. Articles editor: U. Pa. Law Rev, 1954-55; contbr. articles to legal jours. Pres. Nat. Mus. Am. Jewish History, Phila., 1975-78; bd. overseers Gratz Coll., Phila., 1965—. Served with USMC, 1944-45. Fellow Am. Coll. Tax Counsel, Am. Coll. Trust and Estate Counsel; mem. ABA (standing com. on profl. edn. 1978-83, mem. council sect. taxation 1977-80, chair employee benefits com. 1970-72), Phila. Bar Assn. (chmn. council sect. taxation 1984-86), Am. Law Inst., Am. Law Inst.-ABA (com. on continuing profl. edn. 1986—). Jewish. Club: Union League (Phila.). Estate planning, Taxation, general, Pension, profit-sharing, and employee benefits. Office: 3901 Mellon Bank Ctr 1735 Market St Philadelphia PA 19103-7595 also: 2 Berkeley Pl Cambridge MA 02138

**WILHELM, ROBERT OSCAR,** lawyer, civil engineer, developer; b. Balt., July 7, 1918; s. Clarence Oscar and Agnes Virginia (Grimm) W.; m. Grace Sanborn Luckie, Apr. 4, 1959. BSCE, Ga. Tech. Inst., 1947, MSIM, 1948; JD, Stanford U., 1951. Bar: Calif. 1952, U.S. Supreme Ct. Mem. Wilhelm, Thompson, Wentholt and Gibbs, Redwood City, Calif., 1952—; gen. counsel Bay Counties Gen. Contractors; pvt. practice civil engring., Redwood City, 1952—; pres. Bay Counties Builders Escrow, Inc., 1972-88. With C.E., AUS, 1942-46. Mem. Bay Counties Civil Engrs. (pres. 1957), Peninsula Builders Exchange (pres. 1958-71, dir.), Calif. State Builders Exchange (treas. 1971), Del Mesa Carmel Cmty. Assn. (bd. dirs. 1997-99), Mason, Odd Fellows, Eagle, Elks. Author: The Manual of Procedures for the Construction Industry, 1971, Manual of Procedures and Form Book for Construction Industry, 9th edit., 1995; columnist Law and You in Daily Pacific Builder, 1955—; author: Construction Law for Contractors, Architects and Engineers. Construction, Government contracts and claims. Home: 134 Del Mesa Carmel Carmel CA 93923-7950 Office: 702 Marshall St Ste 510 Redwood City CA 94063-1826

**WILHOIT, HENRY RUPERT, JR.,** federal judge; b. Grayson, Ky., Feb. 11, 1935; s. H. Rupert and Kathryn (Reynolds) W.; m. Jane Horton, Apr. 7, 1956; children: Mary Jane, H. Rupert, William. LLB, U. Ky., 1960. Ptnr. Wilhoit & Wilhoit, 1960-81; city atty. City of Grayson, Ky., 1962-66; county atty. Carter County, Ky., 1966-70; judge U.S. Dist. Ct. (ea. dist.) Ky., 1981-96, chief judge, 1998—. Recipient Disting. Service award U. Ky. Alumni Assn., 1980. Mem. ABA, Ky. Bar Assn. Office: US Dist Ct 320 Fed Bldg 1405 Greenup Ave Ashland KY 41101-7542

**WILK, ADAM ROSS,** lawyer; b. N.Y.C., July 27, 1963; s. Alwyn Norman and Gussie Ray W.; m. Janice Lynn Moore, Oct. 22, 1988; children: Brian, Taylor. BA in Psychology, SUNY, Albany, 1985; JD, George Washington U., 1988. Assoc. Doctor & Doctor, P.C., Washington, 1988-89; assoc. Protas & Spivok Chtd., Rockville, Md., 1989-90; prin. Carr, Morris & Graeff, P.C., Washington, 1990—. Democrat. Jewish. Avocations: golf, sports, children. General civil litigation, Consumer commercial, General practice. Office: Carr Morris & Graeff PC 1120 G St NW Ste 930 Washington DC 20005-3842

**WILKE, BARBARA R.,** lawyer; b. Omaha, Nov. 23, 1946; d. Thomas M.B. Hicks and Eleanor (Greusel) Murray; m. Alvin Wilke, May 24, 1980; 1 child, Lisa Ann. BA, Roosevelt U., 1971; JD, John Marshall U., 1987. Bar: Ill. 1987, U.S. Dist. Ct. Ill. 1987. Sole practice Schaumburg, Ill., 1987—. Mem. ABA, Ill. State Bar Assn. Family and matrimonial, Bankruptcy, Criminal. Office: 1000 E Woodfield Rd Schaumburg IL 60173-4728

**WILKEN, CLAUDIA,** judge; b. Mpls., Aug. 17, 1949. BA with honors, Stanford U., 1971; JD, U. Calif., Berkeley, 1975. Bar: Calif. 1975, U.S. Dist. Ct. (no. dist.) Calif. 1975, U.S. Ct. Appeals (9th cir.) 1976, U.S. Supreme Ct. 1981. Asst. fed. pub. defender U.S. Dist. Ct. (no. dist.) Calif., San Francisco, 1975-78, U.S. magistrate judge, 1983-93, dist. judge, 1993—; ptnr. Wilken & Leverett, Berkeley, Calif., 1978-84; adj. prof. U. Calif., Berkeley, 1978-84; prof. New Coll. Sch. Law, 1980-85; mem. jud. br. com. Jud. Conf. U.S.; past mem. edn. com. Fed. Jud. Ctr.; chair 9th cir. Magistrates Conf., 1987-88. Mem. ABA (mem. jud. adminstrn. divsn.), Alameda County Bar Assn. (judge's membership), Nat. Assn. Women Judges, Order of Coif, Phi Beta Kappa. Office: US Dist Ct No Dist 1301 Clay St # 2 Oakland CA 94612-5217

**WILKERSON, CAROLYN S.,** labor relations consultant; b. Oakdale, Tenn.. BA in Mgmt., Antioch Coll., 1989; JD, Capital Law Sch., 1994. Legal sec. Shipman, Utrecht & Dipon, Troy, Ohio, 1976-78; adminstrv. asst. Ohio Edn. Assn., Columbus, 1978-95, labor cons., 1995—. Mem. ABA, Ohio Bar Assn., Mahoning Bar Assn. Mem. LDS Ch. Home: PO Box 9892 Boardman OH 44513-0892 Office: Ohio Edn Assn 830 E Midlothian Blvd Youngstown OH 44502-2583

**WILKERSON, JAMES NEILL,** lawyer; b. Tyler, Tex., Dec. 17, 1939; s. Hubert Cecil and Vida (Alexander) W.; m. Cal Cantrell; children: Cody, Ike. AA, Tyler Jr. Coll., 1960; BBA, U. Tex., 1966, JD, 1968. Bar: Tex. 1968, U.S. Supreme Ct. 1973, U.S. Dist. Ct. (we. dist.) Tex. 1974. Pvt. practice Georgetown, Tex., 1977—; instr. Cen. Tex. Coll., Copperaas Cove, Tex., 1973-74; asst prof. law U.S. Mil. Acad., West Point, N.Y., 1971-73; pres. C&N Bus. Developers, 1992—. Pres. Beautify Georgetown Assn., 1977-80, 81-82; pres. U. Tex. Young Reps., 1964-65; co-chmn. Bush for Pres., 1988, Reagan-Bush campaign, 1980; mem. Williamson County Rep. Com., 1977-81; chmn. Hist. Preservation Com., 1979-85; trustee 1st United Meth. Ch., 1994—, chmn. bd. trustees, 1996—. Col. USAR, 1968—, trial judge JAGC, 1975-91, appellate judge Army Ct. Mil. Rev., 1991-93. Decorated Legion of Merit, Bronze Star, Air medal. Mem. Tex. State Bar Coll., Williamson County Bar Assn., Sertoma (v.p. 1981-83, 87, sec. 1988-89, pres. 1992-93), Lions (pres. 1982-83), Vietnam War Vets. Estate planning, Probate. Office: PO Box 1090 Georgetown TX 78627-1090 also: PO Box 876 Mason TX 76856-0876

**WILKINS, HERBERT PUTNAM,** retired state supreme court chief justice; b. Cambridge, Mass., Jan. 10, 1930; s. Raymond Sanger and Mary Louisa (Aldrich) W.; m. Angela Joy Middleton, June 21, 1952; children: Douglas H., Stephen M., Christopher P., Kate W. McManus. A.B., Harvard U., 1951, LL.B. magna cum laude, 1954; LL.D., Suffolk U., 1976; J.D., New Eng. Sch. Law, 1979; LL.D., So. New Eng. Law Sch., 1998. Bar: Mass. 1954. Assoc. firm Palmer & Dodge, Boston, 1954-59; ptnr. Palmer & Dodge, 1960-72; assoc. justice Mass. Supreme Jud. Ct., 1972-96, chief justice, 1996-99; vis. prof. Boston Coll. Law Sch., Newton, Mass., 1999—. Editor: Harvard U. Law Rev, 1953-54. Bd. overseers Harvard U., 1977-83, pres. bd., 1981-83; trustee Milton Acad., 1971-76, Phillips Exeter Acad., 1972-78; mem. Concord (Mass.) Planning Bd., 1957-60; selectman Town of Concord, 1960-66, town counsel, 1969-72; town counsel Town of Acton, Mass., 1966-72. Mem. Am. Law Inst. (council), Am. Coll. Trial Lawyers (jud. fellow). Republican. Unitarian-Universalist. Office: Boston Coll Law Sch 885 Centre St Newton MA 02459-1154

**WILKINS, MICHAEL JON,** judge; b. Murray, Utah, May 13, 1948; s. Jack L. and Mary June (Phillips) W.; m. Diane W. Wilkins, Nov. 9, 1967; children: Jennifer, Stephanie, Bradley J. BS, U. Utah, 1975, JD, 1976. Bar: Utah 1977, U.S. Dist. Ct. Utah 1977, U.S. Ct. Appeals (10th cir.) 1987, U.S. Supreme Ct. 1986. Mng. ptnr. Wilkins, Oritt & Headman, Salt Lake City, 1989-94; judge Utah Ct. Appeals, 1994—; mem. Gov.'s Adv. Com. on Corp., Salt Lake City, 1989-94; mem. Utah Supreme Ct. Complex Steering Com., 1993-94; mem. Judiciary Standing Com. on Info., Automation and Records, 1995—, chmn., 1995—; mem. Legis. Compensation Commn., 1994-95. Trustee Utah Law Related Edn. Project, Inc., Salt Lake City, 1991-95, chmn., 1992-94. 1st lt. U.S. Army, 1968-72. Mem. LDS Ch. Office: PO Box 40230 Salt Lake City UT 84114-0230

**WILKINS, WILLIAM WALTER, JR.,** federal judge; b. Anderson, S.C., Mar. 29, 1942; s. William Walter and Evelyn Louise (Horton) W.; m. Carolyn Louise Adams, Aug. 15, 1964; children: Lauren, Lyn, Walt. BA, Davidson Coll., 1964; JD, U. S.C., 1967. Bar: S.C., 1967, U.S. Dist. Ct. S.C. 1967, U.S. Ct. Appeals (4th cir.) 1969, U.S. Supreme Ct. 1970. Law clk. to judge U.S. Ct. Appeals 4th Cir., 1969; legal asst. to U.S. Senator Strom Thurmond, 1970; ptnr. Wilkins & Wilkins, Greenville, S.C., 1971-75; solicitor 13th Jud. Cir., 1974-81; judge U.S. Dist. Ct., Greenville, 1981-86, U.S. Ct. Appeals (4th cir.), 1986—; lectr. Greenville Tech. Coll., 1973-97; chmn. U.S. Sentencing Commn., 1985-94. Editor-in-chief S.C. Law Rev., 1967; contbr. articles to legal jours. Served with U.S. Army, 1967-69. Named Outstanding Grad. of Yr. U. S.C. Sch. Law, 1967. Mem. S.C. Bar Assn., Wig and Robe. Republican. Baptist. Office: US Cir Ct 4th Ct Federal Bldg PO Box 10857 300 E Washington St Rm 222 Greenville SC 29603-0857*

**WILKINSON, JAMES ALLAN,** lawyer, healthcare executive; b. Cumberland, Md., Feb. 10, 1945; s. John Robinson and Dorothy Jane (Kelley) W.; m. Elizabeth Susanne Quinlan, Apr. 14, 1973; 1 child, Kathryn Barrett. BS in Fgn. Svc., Georgetown U., 1967; JD, Duquesne U., 1978. Bar: Pa., U.S. Dist. Ct. (we. dist.) Pa. Legis. analyst Office of Mgmt. and Budget, Washington, 1972-73; dep. exec. sec. Cost of Living Coun., Washington, 1973-74; sr. fin. analyst U.S. Steel Corp., Pitts., 1974-82; ptnr. Buchanan Ingersoll, Pitts., 1982-88; exec. v.p., gen. counsel Meritcare, Pitts., Pa., 1988—; sr. v.p. Culwell Health Inc., 1991—; adj. prof. U. Pitts. Sch. Law, 1988-91. Author: Financing and Refinancing Under Prospective Payment, 1985, Family Caregivers' Guide Planning and Decision Making for the Elderly, 1998; contbr. articles to profl. jours. Chmn. Oversight Com. on Organ Transplantation, Pitts., 1986—; sec.-treas. bd. dirs. Pitts. Symphony Soc., 1986-98, exec. com. bd. dirs., 1999—; bd. dirs. Western Pa. Com. of Prevention of Child Abuse, 1987-90, Comprehensive Safety Compliance, 1988-91,

Buchanan Ingersoll Profl. corp., 1988-90, Parental Stress Ctr., 1990-94; sec. Ross Mountain Club, 1995-98; bd. dirs. Carnegie Inst., 1997—, Carnegie Mus. Natural History, 1997—, Andy Warhol Mus., 1998—. Mem. Am. Soc. Law and Medicine, Am. Health Lawyers Assn., Audobon Soc. Southwestern Pa. (treas. 1996—), Duquesne Club. Republican. Episcopalian. Health, General corporate, Mergers and acquisitions. Home: 1005 Elmhurst Rd Pittsburgh PA 15215-1819 Office: Meritcare Inc 625 Stanwix St Ste 1220 Pittsburgh PA 15222-1417

**WILKINSON, JAMES HARVIE, III,** federal judge; b. N.Y.C., Sept. 29, 1944; s. James Harvie and Letitia (Nelson) W.; m. Lossie Grist Noell, June 30, 1973; children: James Nelson, Porter Noell. BA, Yale U., 1963-67; JD, U. Va., 1972; JD (hon.), U. Richmond, 1997, U. S.C., 1998. Bar: Va. 1972. Law clk. to U.S. Supreme Ct. Justice Lewis F. Powell, Jr., Washington, 1972-73; asst. prof. law U. Va., 1973-75, assoc. prof., 1975-78; editor Norfolk (Va.) Virginian-Pilot, 1978-81; prof. law U. Va., 1981-82, 83-84; dep. asst. atty. gen. Civil Rights div. Dept. Justice, 1982-83; judge U.S. Ct. Appeals (4th cir.), 1984—, chief judge, 1996—. Author: Harry Byrd and the Changing Face of Virginia Politics, 1968, Serving Justice: A Supreme Court Clerk's View, 1974, From Brown to Bakke: The Supreme Court and School Integration, 1979, One Nation Indivisible: How Ethnic Separatism Threatens America, 1997. Bd. Visitors U. Va., 1970-73; Republican candidate for Congress from 3d Dist. V a., 1970; bd. dirs. Fed. Jud. Ctr., 1992-96. Served with U.S. Army, 1968-69. Mem. Va. State Bar, Va. Bar Assn., Am. Law Inst. Episcopalian. Home: 1713 Yorktown Dr Charlottesville VA 22901-3035 Office: US Ct Appeals 255 W Main St Ste 230 Charlottesville VA 22902-5058

**WILKINSON, RANDELL L.,** judge; b. San Bernardino, Calif., Nov. 3, 1950; s. Alvis L. and Emma J. Wilkinson; m. Cheryl T. Hjorten; children: Laura, Marilyn, John, Lisa, Christa, Amber. Student, Occidental Coll., 1968-69; BA in History, Brigham Young U., 1974, JD, 1976. Bar: Calif. 1977, U.S. Dist. Ct. (cen. dist.) Calif. 1985. Dep. dist. atty. Orange County Dist. Atty.'s Office, Santa Ana, Calif., 1977-86; judge Orange County Ctrl. Mcpl. Ct., Santa Ana, 1986-90, Orange County Superior Ct., Santa Ana, 1990—; lectr., mem. internat. representing U.S. legal sys. Bar Assn. Campina Grande, Brazil, State Bar of Paraiba, Brazil, 1998. Mem. Calif. Judges Assn. Republican. Mem. LDS Ch. Avocations: travel, hiking. Office: Orange County Superior Ct 700 Civic Center Dr W Santa Ana CA 92701-4045

**WILKINSON, RICHARD K.,** lawyer; b. Burlington, Vt., June 4, 1957; s. Earl J. and Marcia E. (Learned) W.; m. Debbie Kay Draper, Oct. 27, 1979; children: Emily Kim, David Mack, Ethan Allen. BA, James Madison U., Harrisonburg, Va., 1979; JD, Coll. William and Mary, 1983. Bar: Va. 1983, U.S. Dist. Ct. (we. dist.) Va. 1983, Bankruptcy Ct. (we. dist.) Va. 1984. Assoc. Wolfe & Farmer, Norton, Va., 1983-86, Shackelford & Honenberger, Orange, Va., 1987-89; pvt. practice Gordonsville, Va., 1989-94; assoc. Atwell, Somerville & Assocs., Ltd., Orange, Va., 1994—; town atty., Gordonsville, 1995—; sec. Orange Recreation Assn., 1995-97. Dir. Community Diversion Incentive Prog., Culpeper, Va., 1987-95, Gordonsville Housing Alliance, Va., 1988-90. Mem. Va. State Bar Assn., Piedmont Bar Assn., Gordonsville Lions Club (pres. 1992-93). General practice, Criminal. Home: 305 Cadmus Cir Gordonsville VA 22942-9103 Office: Nations Bank Bldg 113 W Main St Fl 3 Orange VA 22960-1524

**WILKS, LARRY DEAN,** lawyer; b. Columbia, S.C., Jan. 8, 1955; s. Ray Dean and Jean (Garrett) W.; m. Jan Elizabeth McIllwain, May 2,1981; children: John Ray, Adam Garrett. BS, U. Tenn., 1977, JD, 1980. Bar: Tenn. 1981, U.S. Dist. Ct. (mid. dist.) Tenn. 1981, U.S. Supreme Ct. 1986, U.S. Ct. Appeals (6th cir.) 1993, U.S. Dist. Ct. (we. dist.) Tenn. 1996. Assoc. Mayo & Norris, Nashville, 1981-82; sole practice Springfield, Tenn., 1982-84; ptnr. Walton, Jones & Wilks, 1984, Jones & Wilks, 1984-89. Chmn. Dem. Orgn. Robertson County Tenn., 1986-93. Fellow Tenn. Bar Found.; mem. ABA, ATLA, Tenn. Bar Assn. (assoc. gen. counsel 1991-94, gen. counsel 1994-99, bd. profl. responsibility 1993-98, bd. govs. 1991—, young lawyers divsn. lifetime fellow, asst. treas. 1999-00), Tenn. Assn. Criminal Def. Lawyers, Tenn. Trial Lawyers Assn., Robertson County Bar Assn. (pres. 1993-96), Nat. Assn. Criminal Def. Laywers, Tenn. Young Lawyers Conf. (bd. dirs. 1987, editor quar. newsletter 1987-88, Mid. Tenn. v.p. 1988-89, v.p. 1989-90, pres.-elect 1990-91, pres. 1991-92). Methodist. Criminal, Personal injury, Product liability. Office: 509 W Court Sq Springfield TN 37172-2413

**WILL, ROBERT JOHN,** lawyer; b. St. Louis, May 17, 1963; m. Stephanie Rutkoski, Aug. 8, 1987; children: Thomas, Rachel. BA, St. Louis U., 1984; JD, George Washington U., 1987. Bar: Mo. 1987, U.S. Dist. Ct. (ea. and we. dists.) Mo., Ill., 1988, U.S. Dist. Ct. (so. dist.) Ill. 1990, U.S. Ct. Appeals (7th and 8th cirs.) 1988. Mem. Lewis, Rice & Fingersh, St. Louis, 1987—. Mem. Vol. Lawyers Assn., St. Louis, 1987—. Nat. Merit scholar, 1981. Mem. ABA, Mo. Bar Assn., Ill. Bar Assn., Phi Beta Kappa, Order of Coif. Roman Catholic. General civil litigation. Home: 433 Hazelgreen Dr Saint Louis MO 63119-1319 Office: Lewis Rice & Fingersh LC 500 N Broadway Ste 2000 Saint Louis MO 63102-2147

**WILLARD, DAVID CHARLES,** lawyer; b. Tacoma, Wash., July 10, 1955; s. Robert Jackson and Emma (Raad) W. BA, U. South Fla., 1977; JD, South Tex. Coll. Law, 1981. Bar: La. 1990, U.S. Dist. Ct. (ea. dist.) La. 1992, U.S. Dist. Ct. (we. dist.) La. 1993, U.S. Dist. Ct. (mid. dist.) La., U.S. Ct. Appeals (5th cir.), U.S. Supreme Ct. Ptnr. Willard & Long, Lafayette, La., 1992—. Preferred mem. Nat. Rep. Senatorial Com., Washington, 1990; life mem. Rep. Presdl. Task Force, Washington, 1992. Bem. ABA, La. State Bar Assn., Lafayette Parish Bar Assn., Assn. Trial Lawyers Am., La. Trial Lawyers Assn., NFL Players Assn. (advisor 1992), Omicron Delta Kappa. Espicopalian. Avocations: soccer, chess. Criminal, Personal injury, Constitutional. Office: Willard & Long First National Bank Tower 600 Jefferson St Ste 920 Lafayette LA 70501-8917

**WILLARD, GLENN MARK,** lawyer; b. Port Huron, Mich., Aug. 19, 1959; s. Stephen Randall Willard (dec.) and Louise Marie Bowers (dec.); m. Joanna Lynn Reeder, Oct. 16, 1982; children: Micah, Lindsay, Jordan, Jared, Adrienne, Titus, Samuel, Maria. BS, Mich. State U., 1982; MA, Regent U., 1995, JD, 1995. Bar: Mich. 1995, U.S. Dist. Ct. (we. dist.) Mich. 1995, U.S. Ct. Appeals (6th cir.) 1995, U.S. Ct. Appeals (7th cir.) 1997, Colo. 1998, U.S. Dist. Ct. Ariz. 1998, U.S. Ct. Appeals (4th cir.) 1998. Legis. aide State Senator Harmon Cropsey, Lansing, Mich., 1983-89; mem. Workers' Compensation Appeal Bd., Lansing, 1989-91, chmn., 1991; law clk. judge Joseph Baker Va. Ct. Appeals, Norfolk, 1994-95; law clk. judge Robert Holmes Bell U.S. Dist. Ct. (we. dist.) Mich., Grand Rapids, 1995-96; law clk. judge John Coffey U.S. Ct. Appeals (7th cir.), Milw., 1996-97; assoc. Bopp, Coleson & Bostrom, Terre Haute, Ind., 1997—. Civil rights, Constitutional, Federal civil litigation. Office: Bopp Coleson & Bostrom 1 S 6th St Terre Haute IN 47807-3510

**WILLARD, GREGORY DALE,** lawyer; b. Pittsfield, Ill., Feb. 8, 1954; s. Wesley Dale and Rosmary (Stark) W.; m. Ann Julia Grier, June 3, 1978; children: Michael, David, John. BA summa cum laude, Westminster Coll., Fulton, Mo., 1976; JD cum laude, U. Ill., 1979. Bar: Mo., U.S. Dist. Ct. (ea. dist.) Mo., U.S. Ct. Appeals (8th Cir.). Staff asst. to Pres. Exec. Office of the Pres. The White House, Washington, 1976-77; ptnr. Bryan Cave, St. Louis, 1979—; co-chmn. bankruptcy com. Met. Bar Assn., St. Louis, 1983-84. Bd. Dirs. St. Louis Children's Hosp., 1985-89, Found. for Spl. Edn., 1990—, Congress Neurol. Surgeons, 1998—. Mem. Congress of Neurol. Surgeons, Noonday Club. Bankruptcy, Banking, Consumer commercial. Office: Bryan Cave 211 N Broadway Saint Louis MO 63102-2733

**WILLARD, ROBERT EDGAR,** lawyer; b. Bronxville, N.Y., Dec. 13, 1929; s. William Edgar and Ethel Marie (Van Ness) W.; m. Shirley Fay Cooper, May 29, 1954; children: Laura Marie, Linda Ann, John Judson. B.A. in Econs., Wash. State U., 1954; J.D., Harvard U., 1958. Bar: Calif. 1959. Law clk. to U.S. dist. judge, 1958-59; pvt. practice L.A., 1959-82; assoc. firm Flint & Mackay, 1959-61; pvt. practice, 1962-64; mem. firm Willard & Baltaxe, 1964-65, Baird, Holley, Baird & Galen, 1966-69, Baird, Holley, Galen & Willard, 1970-74, Holley, Galen & Willard, 1975-82, Galvin & Willard, Newport Beach, Calif., 1982-86; pvt. practice Newport Beach, 1987-89; mem. firm Davis, Punelli Keathley & Willard, Newport Beach, 1990—; Dir. various corps. Served with AUS, 1946-48, 50-51. Mem. ABA, Los Angeles County Bar Assn., State Bar Calif., Assn. Trial Lawyers Am., Am. Judicature Soc., Acacia Frat. Congregationalist. Club: Calcutta Saddle and Cycle. Federal civil litigation, State civil litigation, Real property. Home: 1840 Oriole Dr Costa Mesa CA 92626-4758 Office: 610 Newport Center Dr Ste 1000 Newport Beach CA 92660-6449

**WILLARD-JONES, DONNA C.,** lawyer; b. Calgary, Alberta, Can., Jan. 19, 1944; m. Douglas E. Jones. BA with honors, U. B.C., 1965, student, 1965-66; JD, U. Oreg., 1970. Bar: Ala. 1970, U.S. Dist. Ct. Ala. 1970, U.S. Ct. Appeals (9th cir.) 1971, U.S. Customs Ct. 1972, U.S. Tax Ct. 1975, U.S. Supreme Ct. 1981. Assoc. Boyko & Walton, 1970-71, Walton & Willard, 1971-73; ptnr. Gruenberg & Willard, 1974, Gruenberg, Willard & Smith, 1974-75, Richmond, Willoughby & Willard, 1976-81, Willoughby & Willard, 1981-89; pvt. practice Anchorage, 1990—; chmn. fed. adv. group Implementation of Civil Justice Reform Act of 1990, 1991-92; lawyer rep. 9th Cir. Jud. Conf., 1979-80; mem. spl. com. on contempt Ala. Supreme Ct., 1991-92; chmn. Bankruptcy Judge Merit Screening com., 1979; mem. Am. Judicature Soc., 1973-92, Am. Trial Lawyers Assn., 1981-92; bd. dirs. Ala. Legal Svcs. Corp., 1979-80; spkr. in field. Mem. U. B.C. Law Rev.; assoc. editor Oreg. Law Rev.; copy editor Ala. Bar Rag, 1979-84, contbg. editor, 1979-92; annual reviser Probate Counsel, 1972-88. Mem. Anchorage Port Commn., 1987-93, chmn., 1990-93; chmn. Ala. State Officers Compensation Commn., 1986-92; mem. Anchorage Transp. Commn., 1983-87, chmn., 1986-87; vice-chmn. Ala. Code Revision Commn., 1976-78; bd. trustees Ala. Indian Arts, Inc., 1970-92; mem. Chilkat Dancer Ala., 1965—. Fellow Am. Bar Found. (life); mem. ABA (ho. dels. 1980-84, 86—, bd. govs. 1992—, sec. 1996—), Nat. Conf. Bar Pres. (exec. coun. 1985-88), Nat. Conf. Bar Founds. (bd. trustees 1983-90), Am. Arbitration Assn., We. States Bar Conf. (pres. 1983-84), Ala. Bar Assn. (Bd. Govs. Disting. Svc. award 1991, bd. govs. 1977-80, numerous coms.),. Presbyterian. Fax: 907-278-0449. Bankruptcy, General corporate, Construction. Office: 124 E 7th Ave Anchorage AK 99501-3608 also: Am Bar Assn 750 N Lake Shore Dr Chicago IL 60611-4403

**WILLCOX, BRECKINRIDGE LONG,** lawyer; b. San Diego, Aug. 2, 1944; s. Arnold Augur and Christine Graham (Long) W.; m. Laura Henderson, Nov. 21, 1973; children: Blair Breckinridge, Christopher Henderson. BA, Yale U., 1966; JD, Duke U., 1969. Bar: Ma. 1969, U.S. Dist. Ct. (D.C. dist.) 1969, Hawaii 1972. Criminal div. staff U.S. Dept. Justice, Washington, 1975-81, sr. litigation counsel, 1981-84; U.S. Atty. U.S. Dept. Justice, Balt., 1986—; ptnr. McKenna, Conner & Cuneo, Washington, 1984-86. Served to capt. USMC, 1970-73. Mem. ABA, Md. Bar Assn., D.C. Bar Assn., Hawaii Bar Assn. Office: Arent Fox Kintner & Kahn 1050 Connecticut Ave NW Washington DC 20036-5314

**WILLCOX, RODERICK HARRISON,** lawyer; b. Columbus, Ohio, Jan. 10, 1934; s. Richard V. and Marcella A. (Rehl) W.; m. Rita Kay Click, July 2, 1955; children: Sharon Marie Willcox Hazlewood, Kathy Lynn, Patricia Ann Willcox Hanna, Roderick Harrison Jr. BA, Williams Coll., 1955; LLB, U. Mich., 1958. Ptnr. Chester, Willcox & Saxbe, Columbus, Ohio, 1971—. General corporate, Estate planning, Estate taxation. Office: Chester Willcox & Saxbe LLP 17 S High St Ste 900 Columbus OH 43215-3442

**WILLE, KARIN L.,** lawyer; b. Northfield, Minn., Dec. 14, 1949; d. James Virginia Wille. BA summa cum laude, Macalester Coll., 1971; JD cum laude, U. Minn., 1974. Bar: Minn. 1974, U.S. Dist. Ct. Minn. 1974. Atty. Dresselhuis & Assoc., Mpls., 1974-75; assoc. Dorsey & Whitney, Mpls., 1975-76; atty. Dayton-Hudson Corp., Mpls., 1976-84; gen. counsel B. Dalton Booksellers, Edina, Minn., 1985-87; assoc. Briggs & Morgan, Mpls., 1987-88; shareholder Briggs and Briggs, 1988—; co-chair Upper Midwest Employment Law Inst., 1983—. Mem. ABA, Minn. State Bar Assn. (labor and employment sect., corp. counsel sect., dir. 1989-91), Hennepin County Bar Assn. (labor and employment sect.), Minn. Women Lawyers, Phi Beta Kappa. Education and schools, Labor, Non-profit and tax-exempt organizations. Office: Briggs & Morgan 80 S 8th St Ste 2400 Minneapolis MN 55402-2157

**WILLEMS, DANIEL WAYNE,** lawyer; b. Harvey, Ill., Apr. 4, 1957; s. Abraham and Phyllis Mae W.; m. Denise Smith, June 14, 1980; children: Mary Elizabeth, Dinah Ruth. BA, Ctrl. Coll., Iowa, 1982; JD, U. Iowa, 1985. Bar: Iowa 1985, U.S. Dist. Ct. (no. and so. dists.) Iowa. Atty. M. Gene Blackburn Law Office, Fort Dodge, Iowa, 1985-88; pvt. practice Cedar Rapids, Iowa, 1988—. Real property, Personal injury, Family and matrimonial. Home and Office: 641 40th St SE Cedar Rapids IA 52403-4343

**WILLENS, MATTHEW LYLE,** lawyer; b. Chgo., Oct. 24, 1969; s. Nathan and Shirley Willens; m. Lena Rosa Maria DiFilippo, Nov. 28, 1998. BS, No. Ill. U., 1991; JD, Loyola U., 1995. Bar: Ill. 1995, U.S. Dist. Ct. (no. dist.) Ill. 1995, U.S. Dist. Ct. (cen. dist.) Ill. 1998. Sr. assoc. Rapoport Law Offices, P.C., Chgo., 1995—. Mem. ATLA, Ill. Trial Lawyer's Assn., Chgo. Bar Assn., N.W. Suburban Bar Assn. Personal injury, Product liability, Transportation. Office: Rapoport Law Offices PC 10275 W Higgins Rd Ste 370 Rosemont IL 60018-3885

**WILLER, REBECCA SHARON,** lawyer; b. Bklyn., Mar. 15, 1966; d. Maurice and Grace Ann (Sacks) W. AB, Barnard Coll., 1987; JD, NYU, 1990. Bar: N.Y. 1991. Legal intern Hon. George A. Murphy, N.Y. State Supreme Ct., Mineola, 1988; rsch. asst. Sch. of Law, NYU, N.Y.C., 1988-90; assoc. Phillips, Nizer, Benjamin, Krim & Ballon, N.Y.C., 1990-91; atty. bur. proprietary sch. supervision N.Y. State Dept. Edn., N.Y.C., 1992—. Jerusalem fellow Aish Hatorah, 1985. Mem. ABA, N.Y. State Bar Assn., Assn. Trial Lawyers Am., NOW, B'nai B'rith. Avocations: drawing, music. Office: NY State Edn Dept 1 Park Ave New York NY 10016-5802

**WILLETT, JONATHAN S.,** lawyer; b. N.Y.C., Jan. 2, 1960; s. Edward and Roslyn Willett; m. Julianne Willett, Mar. 20, 1995; 1 child, Isabelle. BA in Philosophy, U. Colo., 1982; JD, U. Denver, 1986. Dep. state pub. defender Colo. State Pub. Defender, Denver, 1986-89, Golden, 1989-92; atty. Chalat & Co., Denver, 1992-93; pvt. practice Denver, 1993—; lectr. Colo. Criminal Def. Bar, Denver, 1989, Nat. Bus. Inst., Denver, 1998. Counsel to bd. dirs. Ctr. on Deafness, Denver, 1995-97. Mem. Colo. Criminal Def. Bar. Criminal, General civil litigation, Appellate. Office: 1515 Arapahoe St Ste 1555 Denver CO 80202-2118

**WILLETT, THOMAS EDWARD,** lawyer; b. N.Y.C., Nov. 8, 1947; s. Oscar Edward and Alice (Fleming) W.; m. Marilyn Kenney, Dec. 28, 1969; children: Thomas Justin, Christopher Joseph. BS, USAF Acad., Colo., 1969; JD with distinction, Cornell U., 1972. Bar: N.Y. 1973, U.S. Ct. Claims 1973, U.S. Supreme Ct. 1977. Judge advocate USAF, Syracuse, N.Y., 1973-75, Kincheloe AFB, Mich., 1975-77; judge advocate USAF Hdqs., Washington, 1977-79; assoc. Harris, Beach & Wilcox, Rochester, N.Y., 1979-84, ptnr., 1985—. Pres. Monroe County Legal Assistance Corp., Rochester, 1983-89. Capt. USAF, 1969-79. Mem. ABA, N.Y. State Bar Assn., Monroe County Bar Assn., Order of Coif. General corporate, Banking, Securities. Office: Harris Beach & Wilcox Granite Bldg 130 Main St E Rochester NY 14604-1687

**WILLEY, CHARLES WAYNE,** lawyer; b. Dillon, Mont., Oct. 7, 1932; s. Asa Charles and Elizabeth Ellen Willey; m. Helene D., July 21, 1962 (div.); children: Stephen Charles, Heather Helene, Brent David, Scott D.; m. Alexis W. Grant, Jan. 26, 1986. BS with honors, Mont. State U., 1954; JD with high honors, U. Mont., 1959. Bar: Mont. 1959, Calif. 1960, U.S. Ct. Claims 1975, U.S. Tax Ct. 1975, U.S. Ct. Appeals (9th cir.) 1959, U.S. Ct. Appeals (Fed. cir.) 1983, U.S. Supreme Ct. 1972. Law clk. to presiding judge U.S. Ct. Appeals (9th cir.), 1959-60; ptnr. Price, Postel & Parma, Santa Barbara, Calif., 1960-77; pvt. practice Santa Barbara, 1977—; prof. law corp.; instr. Santa Barbara City Coll., 1961-63, U. Calif., Santa Barbara, 1963-64; lectr. Mont. Tax Inst., 1990, 92, Am. Agr. Law Assn., 1993, 96. Chief editor Mont. Law Rev., 1958-59. Pres. Legal Aid Found. Santa Barbara, 1970; mem. Laguna Blanca Sch. Bd., pres. 1980-81; v.p. Phoenix of Santa Barbara. Served to capt. USAF, 1954-56. Mem. Santa Barbara County Bar Assn. (pres. 1972-73), Phi Kappa Phi, Phi Eta Sigma, Phi Delta Phi. Republican. Episcopalian. Lodge: Kiwanis. Avocations: reading, writing, traveling. Estate planning, Real property, State civil litigation. Office: 1114 State St Ste 315 Santa Barbara CA 93101-2735

**WILLEY, STEPHEN DOUGLAS,** lawyer, certified public accountant; b. Mt. Pleasant, Iowa, Apr. 30, 1950; s. Charles David Willey and Sally Ann (Hall) Stringer; m. Martha Frances Wood, June 3, 1978; children: Stephen David, John Brandon, Mark Charles, Andrew Joseph (twins). Student, U.S. Mil. Acad., 1969-70; BBA, U. Tex., Arlington, 1973; JD, U. Tex., 1978. Bar: Tex. 1978, U.S. Dist. Ct. (no. dist.) Tex. 1983, U.S. Tax Ct. 1985, U.S. Ct. Claims, 1988; cert. estate planning and probate law Tex. Bd. Legal Specialization. Acct. Ernst & Ernst CPAs, Ft. Worth, 1972-74; atty. Hilgers, Watkins, Ledbetter & Hays, Austin, Tex., 1976-78; acct. Rolater, Ducote & Belew, CPAs, Dallas, 1978-79; assoc. Hill, Heard & Oneal, Attys., Arlington, Tex., 1979-81; pvt. practice Arlington, 1981—; adj. prof. Blaw, Tex. Wesleyan U.; lectr. in field. Pres. bd. Boys Clubs Arlington; mem. Northwest Arlington Homeowners Assn., YMCA Indian Guides, Meth. Men's club, Ch. choir; chmn. dist. com. Boy Scouts of Am., 1990-93. Mem. AICPA, Tex. Soc. CPAs, Am. Assn. Atty. CPAs, Arlington Bar Assn., (dir. 1997—), Dallas Bar Assn. (tax sect. real property, probate and trust sect.), Tex. State Bar (tax sect. real estate probate and trust law sect.), Coll. State Bar of Tex., Tex. Acad. Probate Counsel, Tarrant County Bar Assn., Tarrant County Debtor's Bar, Tex. Acad. Probate and Trust Lawyers, Internat. Assn. Fin. Planning, Nat. Assn. Estate Planning Couns. (accredited estate planner), Mid-Cities Assn. CPAs (dir. 1997—), Arlington C. of C., U. Tex. Alumni Assn. (dir. 1997—), Rotary. Estate planning, Pension, profit-sharing, and employee benefits, Estate taxation. Office: 920 W Mitchell St Arlington TX 76013-2537

**WILLI, JAMES NORMAN,** lawyer; b. Houston, Apr. 3, 1963; s. Herman Jr. and Lydia Mae Willi; m. Tracy Jill Moore, Aug. 20, 1994; children: Alexander James, Andrew Thomas. BSEE, U. Tex., 1985; MBA, U. Houston, 1989; JD cum laude, South Tex. U., 1995. Bar: Tex. 1996, Colo. 1997, U.S. Dist. Ct. (so. dist.) Tex. 1996, U.S. Dist. Ct. (no., ea. and we. dists.) Tex. 1998; registered profl. engr., Tex. Elec. engr. Houston Lighting & Power Co., 1986-96; pres. James N. Willi, PC, Houston, 1996-99, Willi & Padgett, PLLC, Houston, 1999—. Mem. South Tex. Law Rev., 1993-94. Named Hon. Admiral of the Tex. Navy, State of Tex., 1988. Mem. ABA, NACDL, NRA (life), Tex. State Rifle Assn. (life), Ex-Students Assn. U. Tex. (life), Houston Bar Assn., Harris County Criminal Lawyers Assn., Phi Delta Phi. Republican. Lutheran. Avocations: skeet shooting, downhill skiing, scuba diving. Criminal. Office: Willi & Padgett PLLC 4822 Omeara Dr Houston TX 77035-3410

**WILLI, TRACY JILL,** lawyer; b. Mpls., Apr. 26, 1967; d. Glendon E. and Marlene M. Moore; m. James Norman Willi, Aug. 20, 1994; children: Alexander, Andrew. BA in Biology, U. Tex., 1989; JD, South Tex. U., 1992. Bar: Tex., Colo., U.S. Dist. Ct. (so. dist.) Tex. Import/export clk. Internat. Customs Svc., Houston, 1984-85; legal asst. Woodard, Hall & Primm, Houston, 1989; law clk. Marathon Oil Co., Houston, summer 1991; assoc. Womble & Spain, Houston, 1992—. Bd. dirs. South Tex. U. Coll. Law, Houston, 1991-92. Travel fellow Rotary, 1994; recipient European Econ. Cmty. Writing scholarship Nat. Custom Brokers and Freight Forwarders Assn., 1989. Mem. Houston Bar Assn. (bd. editors, cite rschr. Houston Lawyer Mag. 1990-91, jud. reception com., appellate practice sect. 1998, appellate inst. com., appellate practice sect. 1998). Office: Womble & Spain 909 Fannin St Houston TX 77010-1001

**WILLIAMS, ALEXANDER, JR.,** judge; b. 1948. BA, Howard U., 1970, JD cum laude, 1973. Pvt. practice Hyattsville and Beltsville, Md., 1974-86; gen. counsel Town of Farimount Heights, Md., 1975-86, Town of Glenarden, Md., 1980-86; asst. pub. defender Prince George's County, Md., 1977-78, state atty., 1987-94; judge U.S. Dist. Ct., Md., 1994—; adj. prof. Howard U., Washington, 1978—. Bd. deacons, assoc. pastor Walker Meml. Bapt. Ch.; bd. dirs. Greater Laurel-Beltsville Hosp.; active Am. Heart Assn., Nat. Forum State Leaders, No. Forum Concerned Citizens of Prince George's County. Mem. ABA, Nat. Bar Assn., D.C. Bar Assn., J. Franklyn Bourne Bar Assn., Md. State Bar Assn., Prince George's County Bar Assn., Md. State Attys. Assn. (bd. dirs.), Alliance Black Elected Ofcls., Masons. Office: US Dist Ct Md 6500 Cherrywood Ln Rm 445A Greenbelt MD 20770-1249

**WILLIAMS, ANN CLAIRE,** federal judge; b. 1949; m. David J. Stewart. BS, Wayne State U., 1970; MA, U. Mich., 1972; JD, U. Notre Dame, 1975. Law clk. to Hon. Robert A. Sprecher, 1975-76; asst. U.S. atty. U.S. Dist. Ct. (no. dist.) Ill., Chgo., 1976-85; faculty Nat. Inst. for Trial Advocacy, 1979—, also bd. dirs.; judge U.S. Dist. Ct. (no. dist.) Ill., 1985—; chief Organized Crime Drug Enforcement Task Force for North Ctrl. Region, 1983-85; mem. ct. adminstrn. and case mgmt. com. Jud. Conf. U.S., 1990-97, chair, 1993-97. Trustee U. Chgo. Lab Sch.; sec. bd. trustees U. Notre Dame; founder Minority Legal Resources, Inc. Mem. FBA (pres.-elect), Fed. Judges Assn., Nat. Assn. Women Judges, Ill. State Bar Assn., Ill. Jud. Coun., Cook County Bar Asn., Women's Bar Assn. Ill., Black Women's Lawyers Assn. Greater Chgo. Office: US Dist Ct 219 S Dearborn St Ste 1988 Chicago IL 60604-1801

**WILLIAMS, ANTHONY JEROME,** lawyer; b. Lubbock, Tex., Jan. 11, 1963; s. Vera Lee Williams. BA magna cum laude, Tex. Tech U., 1985, JD, 1990. Bar: Tex. 1991. Atty. I, Office City Atty., Lubbock, 1991-94; assoc. Fadduol and Glasheen, Lubbock, 1994; pvt. practice Law Office Anthony Williams, Lubbock, 1994—; instr. South Plains Coll., Lubbock, 1993-94. Bd. dirs. Dunbar Neighborhood Assn., Lubbock, 1995. Fellow Sloan Found., 1985; Martin Luther King scholar Tex. Tech U. Sch. Law, 1990. Avocations: gourmet cooking, gardening. Personal injury, Criminal, Civil rights. Home: 1804 E 25th St Lubbock TX 79404-1308 Office: 1114 10th St Lubbock TX 79401-2700

**WILLIAMS, BARBARA JUNE,** lawyer; b. Lansing, Mich., Jan. 6, 1948; d. Ben Allan and Virginia Jane (Searing) W.; m. John Paul Halvorsen, Oct. 21, 1971. AA, Stephens Coll., 1968; BA, U. Ill.-Champaign, 1970; JD, Rutgers U., 1974. Bar: N.J. 1974, N.Y. 1981. Assoc., Bookbinder, Coulagori & Bookbinder, Burlington, N.J., 1974-76, Law Offices of Cyrus Bloom, Newark, 1976-78, Warren, Goldberg, Berman & Lubitz, Princeton, N.J., 1978-84; staff atty. Rutgers U. Sch. of Law, Newark, 1984-85; assoc. Strauss & Hall, Princeton, 1985-87; of counsel Weg & Myers, P.C., New York, 1987—. Assoc. editor Rutgers Camden Law Jour., 1973-74; contbr. articles to profl. jours. Mem. Nat. Sch. Bds. Assn. (bd. dir. nat. coun. sch. attys. 1981-86), ABA, N.J. Bar Assn. (dir. govt. law sect. 1981-84), Mercer County Bar Assn., Princeton Bar Assn., Assn. Trial Lawyers Am., NOW, Lawrence Arts Assn., Lawrence Twp. Federal civil litigation, Education and schools, Insurance. Home: 90 Denow Rd Trenton NJ 08648-2047

**WILLIAMS, BETTY OUTHIER,** lawyer; b. Woodward, Okla., Sept. 11, 1947; d. Robert E. and Ethel M. (Castiller) Outhier; children: Amanda J., Emily Rebecca. BA, Oklahoma City U., 1969; JD, Vanderbilt U., 1972. Bar: Okla. 1972, U.S. Dist. Ct. (no. dist.) Okla. 1972, U.S. Dist. Ct. (ea. dist.) Okla. 1973, (U.S. Ct. Appeals (10th cir.) 1973, U.S. Supreme Ct. 1980, U.S. Dist. Ct. (we. dist.) Okla. 1988. Atty. Regional Heber Smith Cmty. Lawyer Fellowship, Tulsa, 1972-73; asst. U.S. atty. Muskogee, Okla., 1973-81, U.S. atty., 1981-82; ptnr. Robinson, Locke, Gage, Fite & Williams, Muskogee, 1982-96, Robinson, Gage & Williams, Muskogee, 1996-97, Gage & Williams, Muskogee, 1997—; Chair local rules com. U.S. Bankruptcy Ct. Ea. Dist., Okla., 1994, U.S. Dist. Ct. Ea. Dist. Okla., 1995; adj. settlement judge U.S. Dist. Ct. Ea. Dis. Okla., 1998—. Mem. editl. bd. Okla. Law Enforcement Ops. Bull., 1993-94. Pres. Bus. and Profl. Women, Muskogee, 1975-77, 83; pres., bd. dirs. YWCA, Muskogee, 1975-82; bd. dirs. Green County Mental Health, Muskogee, 1986-88, WISH, 1990—; trustee Frontier Heritage Found., 1990-98; chmn. bd. commrs. Muskogee Housing Authority; adminstrv. bd. chmn., St. Paul United Meth. Ch., Muskogee, 1999. Named One of Outstanding Young Career Women, Bus. and Profl. Women, 1974. Fellow Okla. Bar Found. (trustee 1989—, v.p. 1994, pres. elect. 1995, pres. 1996); mem. ABA, Okla. Bar Assn. (mem. editl. bd. 1996—), Muskogee County Bar Assn. (pres. 1984-85), Soroptomists (pres. 1986-88), Gamma Phi Beta (alumnae pres. 1993—). Republican. Methodist. Federal civil litigation, Bankruptcy, State civil litigation. Home: 4326 Oklahoma St Muskogee OK 74401-2351 Office: Gage & Williams PO Box 87 Muskogee OK 74402-0087

**WILLIAMS, CHARLES AUGUST,** lawyer; b. Miami, Fla., Feb. 21, 1957; s. Harry and Mary Ann Williams; m. Sheri-lyn Prescott, May 30, 1992; children: Nicholas, Matthew, Michael, Heather, Andrew. BA, Mercer U.,

1977, JD, 1980. Assoc. Walton, Lantaff, Miami/Ft. Lauderdale, Fla., 1980-84; ptnr. Williams & Williams, Lake Worth, Fla., 1985-91, Williams & Wender, Lake Worth, 1991—. Roman Catholic. Avocations: golf, fishing. Workers' compensation. Office: Williams & Wender PA 917 N Dixie Hwy Lake Worth FL 33460-2530

**WILLIAMS, CHARLES JUDSON,** lawyer; b. San Mateo, Calif., Nov. 23, 1930; s. John Augustus and Edith (Babcock) W.; children: Patrick, Victoria, Apphia. AB, U. Calif., Berkeley, 1952, LLB, 1955. Bar: Calif. 1955, U.S. Supreme Ct., 1970. Assoc. Kirkbride, Wilson, Harzfeld and Wallace, San Mateo County, Calif., 1956-59; sole practice Solano County, Calif., 1959-64, Martinez, Calif., 1964—, Benicia, Calif., 1981-88; city atty. Pleasant Hill, Calif., 1962-80, Yountville, Calif., 1965-68, Benicia, 1968-76, 80-82, Lafayette, Calif., 1968—, Moraga, Calif., 1974-92, Danville, Calif., 1982-88, Pittsburg, Calif., 1984-93, Orinda, Calif., 1985-97; lectr. Calif. Continuing Edn. Bar 1964-65, U. Calif. Extension 1974-76, John F. Kennedy U. Sch. Law 1966-69; spl. counsel to various Calif. cities; legal advisor Alaska Legis. Council 1959-61; advisor Alaska sup. ct. 1960-61; advisor on revision Alaska statues 1960-62; atty. Pleasant Hill Redevel. Agy. 1978-82; sec., bd. dirs. Vintage Savs. & Loan Assn., Napa County, Calif., 1974-82; bd. dirs. 23d Agrl. Dist. Assn., Contra Costa County, 1968-70. Author: California Code Comments to West's Annotated California Codes, 3 vols., 1965, West' California Code Forms, Commercial, 2 vols., 1965, West's California Government Code Forms, 3 vols., 1971, Supplement to California Zoning Practice, 1978, 80, 82, 84, 85, 87, 89, 91, 94, 95, 96, 97, 98, 99; contbr. articles to legal jours. Mem. ABA, Calif. Bar Assn., Contra Costa County Bar Assn. Administrative and regulatory, State civil litigation. Office: 1330 Arnold Dr Ste 149 Martinez CA 94553-6538

**WILLIAMS, CLAY RULE,** lawyer; b. Milw., Sept. 25, 1935; s. George Laverne and Marguerite Mae (Rule) W.; m. Jeanne Lee Huber, Jan. 18, 1986; children: Gwynne, Amy, Daniel, Sarah. BA, Lawrence U., 1957; LLB, U. Mich., 1960. Bar: Wis. 1960, U.S. Dist. Ct. (ea. and we. dists.) Wis. 1964, U.S. Ct. Appeals (7th cir.) 1965, U.S. Ct. Mil. Appeals 1963, U.S. Supreme Ct. 1963. Assoc. Gibbs, Roper & Fifield, Milw., 1963-67; ptnr. Von Briesen, Purtell & Roper, Milw., 1967—; mem. Gov.'s Task Force Creation Bus. Ct., 1994—; instr. profl. seminars. Author: Berry, Davis, Deguire and Williams, Wisconsin Business Corporation Law, 1992; contbr. articles to profl. publs. Mem. Shorewood (Wis.) Sch. Bd., 1976-79. Capt. USAF, Judge Adv. Corps., 1960-63. Mem. ABA (sect. antitrust law, corp. counseling com., task force on Uniform Securities Act, com. on securities litigation), Wis. Bar Assn. (co-chmn. com. to revise corp. laws 1986-90, chmn. standing com. on bus. corp. law 1990-97, Pres.'s Award of Excellence 1990, 97), Milw. Bar Assn. (probate and real property sect., joint bench-bar com. Ct. Appeals, 1986-88, long-range planning com. 1987), 7th Cir. Bar Assn., Fedn. Ins. and Corp. Counsel, Def. Rsch. Inst., Am. Law Inst., Assn. Bar City N.Y., Wis. Bar Found., Milw. Club, Univ. Club. Republican. Episcopalian. Avocations: hunting, fishing, squash, skiing, reading. Securities, General civil litigation, General corporate. Office: von Baiesen Purtell & Roper 411 E Wisconsin Ave Milwaukee WI 53202-4461 also: 126 S Albany St Spring Green WI 53588-8809

**WILLIAMS, CYNTHIA ANNE,** lawyer; b. Gary, Ind., Aug. 29, 1961; d. Joseph A. and Ruth Ann Williams; m. Steven J. Hamstra. BA, Ind. U., Ft. Wayne, 1984; JD, Ind. U., Bloomington, 1987, MLS, 1998. Bar: Ind. 1987, U.S. Dist. Ct. (no. and so. dists.) Ind. 1987. Jud. law clk. Ind. Ct. Appeals, Indpls., 1987-89; assoc. Ferguson & Ferguson, Bloomington, Ind., 1989—. Mem. ABA, Ind. State Bar Assn., Monroe County Bar Assn., Ind. Mcpl. Law Assn. Real property, Public utilities, Contracts commercial. Office: Ferguson & Ferguson 403 E 6th St Bloomington IN 47408-4017

**WILLIAMS, DAVID WELFORD,** federal judge; b. Atlanta, Mar. 20, 1910; s. William W. and Maude (Lee) W.; m. Ouida Maie White, June 11, 1939; children: David Welford, Vaughn Charles. A.A., Los Angeles Jr. Coll., 1932; A.B., UCLA, 1934; LL.B., U. So. Calif., 1937. Bar: Calif. 1937. Practiced in Los Angeles, 1937-55; judge Mcpl. Ct., Los Angeles, 1956-62, Superior Ct., Los Angeles, 1962-69, U.S. Dist. Ct. (cen. dist.) Calif., Los Angeles, 1969—; now sr. judge U.S. Dist. Ct. (cen. dist.) Calif.; judge Los Angeles County Grand Jury, 1965. Recipient Russwurm award Nat. Assn. Newspapers, 1958; Profl. Achievement award UCLA Alumni Assn., 1966. Office: US Dist Ct US Courthouse 312 N Spring St Ste 1621 Los Angeles CA 90012-4718

**WILLIAMS, DENNIS VAUGHN,** lawyer, educator; b. Wilkinsburg, Pa., June 3, 1946; s. Thomas Ulysses and Margaret Louise (Pfefferman) W.; m. Shirley Ann Kramer, July 26, 1979; children: Kristin Elizabeth, Katrina Alexandra, Leah Nicole, Shaun Leighton. BBA, Ohio U., 1968; JD, Duquesne U., 1973. Par: Pa. 1973, U.S. Dist. Ct. (we. dist.) Pa. 1973, U.S. Ct. Appeals (3d cir.) 1982, U.S. Supreme Ct. 1987. Gen. counsel Domestic Abuse Office-Women's Shelter, Erie, Pa., 1977-81, Hospitality House-Women's Shelter, Erie, 1981—; instr. Mercyhurst Coll., Erie, 1984—; pvt. practice Erie, 1973—; bd. dirs. Lakeview Devel., Inc., Erie, 1975—; instr. Pa. Dep. Sheriff Tng. Act. Bd. dirs. Am. Cancer Soc., 1986—. With U.S. Army, 1968-70, res. 1970-74. Mem. ABA, Pa. Bar Assn., Pa. Trial Lawyers Assn., Am. Legion. Democrat. Greek Orthodox. Lodge: Elks. Criminal, Family and matrimonial, Personal injury. Home: 3845 Beech Ave Erie PA 16508-3112 Office: Williams & Adair 332 E 6th St Erie PA 16507-1610

**WILLIAMS, DONALD NEAL,** lawyer; b. Sanford, Fla., Feb. 13, 1959; s. Volie Adkins and Constance (Lott) W. BA in Polit. Sci., Western Carolina U., 1981; JD, Fla. State U., 1984. Bar: Fla. 1984, U.S. Dist. Ct. (mid. dist.) Fla. 1984. Assoc. Rumberger, Kirk, Orlando, Fla., 1984-87, Markel, McDonough & O'Neal, Orlando, 1987-89, McDonough, O'Neal & O'Dell, Orlando, 1989-91; ptnr. McDonough, O'Neal & D'Dell, Orlando, 1991-93, McDonough, O'Dell, Wieland & Williams, Orlando, 1993-97; pvt. practice Orlando, 1997—. Charter mem. Future Leaders Council Central Fla., Orlando, 1987—. Mem. ABA, Orange County Bar Assn., Fla. Def. Lawyers Assn. Democrat. Presbyterian. Avocations: golf, basketball, softball, skiing, water skiing. Insurance, Personal injury, Construction. Home: 2805 Marsala Ct Orlando FL 32806-5555 Office: 609 E Central Blvd Orlando FL 32801-2916

**WILLIAMS, EDWARD J.,** lawyer; b. LaCrosse, Wis., June 18, 1947; s. Joseph Christopher and Amanda Theodora Williams; m. Carolyn Goehrs, June 30, 1947; children: Gregory, Andrew, Keri Lynn, Katie. BS, U. Wis., La Crosse, 1969; JD, U. Louisville, 1973. Bar: Fla. 1974, Wis. 1979, U.S. Dist. Ct. (so. dist.) Fla. 1974, U.S. Dist. Ct. (ea. dist.) Wis. 1979, U.S. Dist. Ct. (we. dist.) Wis. 1994. Asst. county atty. Broward County, Ft. Lauderdale, Fla., 1973-76; asst. city atty. City of Oakland Park, Fla., 1976-79; atty. Mulcahy & Wherry, S.C., Milw., Green Bay, Oshkosh, Wis., also Ft. Lauderdale, 1979-91, Godfrey & Kahn, S.C., Oshkosh, 1991—. Author and contbr. to book, articles to mags. Chair Leadership Oshkosh, 1988—. Served with U.S. Army, 1970-76. Mem. Oshkosh C. of C. (bd. dirs. 1988-89). Labor, Land use and zoning (including planning), Education and schools. Office: Godfrey & Kahn SC 219 Washington Ave Fl 2D Oshkosh WI 54901-5029

**WILLIAMS, FRANK J.,** judge, historian, writer; b. Providence, Aug. 24, 1940; s. Frank and Natalie L. (Corelli) W.; m. Virginia E. Miller, Aug. 24, 1966. BA, Boston U., 1962, JD, 1970, MS in Taxation, Bryant Coll., 1986, LHD Lincoln Coll., 1987. Bar: R.I. 1970, U.S. Dist. Ct. R.I. 1970, U.S. Supreme Ct. 1976. Assoc. Tillinghast, Collins & Graham, Providence, 1970-75, Leonard Decof Ltd., Providence, 1976-78; law clk. Graham, Reid, Ewing & Stapleton, Providence, 1969; law clk., adminstrv. asst. R.I. atty. gen., Providence, 1967-68; pres. Frank J. Williams Ltd., attys.-at-law, Providence, 1978-95; assoc. justice R.I. Superior Ct., 1995—; judge of probate Town of Hopkinton (R.I.), 1978-82, 84-90, solicitor, 1978-82, 84-87; judge of probate Town of West Greenwich, R.I., 1984-86, 92-95, solicitor, 1984-92, asst. solicitor, 1992—; dep. judge of probate, 1987-92; solicitor Town of Coventry, R.I., 1972-74, 76-78, Town of Barrington, R.I., 1993-95, Town of Bristol, R.I., 1995, Town of South Kingstown, R.I., 1995; past spl. counsel Towns of Westerly, Bristol, Hopkinton, South Kingstown, City of Providence; atty. Town of Smithfield Sewer Authority, 1974-90; legis. counsel R.I. Retail Fedn., 1975-93, Credit Info. Bur., R.I. Mortgage Bankers Assn., 1992-95; adj. prof. Roger Williams Sch. of Law, 1997—; lectr. bus. and legal practices R.I. Sch. Design, Providence, 1976-80; mem. panel of arbitrators Am. Arbitration Assn., panel of mediators R.I. Superior Ct., 1993-95; mem. R.I. Bd. of Bar Examiners, 1987-95, chair, 1995; chair R.I. Housing and Mortgage Fin. Corp., 1995, The Lincoln Forum, 1996—. Pres. Lincoln Group of Boston, 1976-88; pres. Abraham Lincoln Assn. Springfield, Ill. 1986-95, Ulysses S. Grant Assn., 1990—; elected del. R.I. Constitutional Conv., 1986; elected town moderator Richmond, R.I., 1989, 1992-95; dist. moderator Chaniho Regional Sch. Dist., 1994; bd. dirs. John E. Fogarty Found. for Mentally Retarded, South County Hosp., 1995, Narragansett council Boy Scouts Am., 1969-80, 98—; chmn. Lincoln adv. com. Brown U.; mem. Lincoln prize adv. com. Gettysburg Coll. Served to capt. U.S. Army, 1962-67; Vietnam. Decorated Bronze Star, Republic of Vietnam Gallantry Cross with silver star, combat infantryman's badge, Air medal with 2 oak cleaf clusters, Army Commendation Medal. Mem. ABA, R.I. Bar Assn. (ho. of dels. 1986-93, chmn. new lawyers adv. com. 1976-87, chmn. mcpl. law com. 1993), Nat. Coll. Probate Judges, Am. Antiquarian Soc., Pi Sigma Alpha. Roman Catholic. Office: 1111 Main St Hope Valley RI 02832-1610

**WILLIAMS, GARY RANDALL,** lawyer; b. Gainesville, Ga., Oct. 16, 1946; s. Ernest Eugene and Ruby Louise (Conner) W.; m. Linda (Meg) Eberhart, May 12, 1990. AA, SUNY, Albany, 1973; LLB, LaSalle U., 1969; JD, Woodrow Wilson Coll. Law, 1976. Bar: Ga. 1978, U.S. Tax Ct. 1978, U.S. Dist. Ct. (no. dist.) Ga. 1979, U.S. Ct. Claims 1980, U.S. Ct. Appeals (11th cir.) 1981; Cert. Tax Profl., 1988, U.S. Supreme Ct. 1997; cert. practitioner of taxation. Atty. IRS, Washington, 1977-80; pvt. practice Marietta, Ga., 1980-81, 82-86, Hiram, Ga., 1992-94, Dallas, Ga., 1994—; lawyer ADP Pension Svcs., Inc., El Toro, Calif., 1981-82; tax specialist Ga. Dept. Revenue, Atlanta, 1986-92; judge protem Paulding County Probate Ct., 1997—. Affiliate atty. Am. Ctr. for Law and Justice. With U.S. Army, 1966-73. Mem. NRA, State Bar Ga., Paulding County Bar Assn. (sec., treas. 1994, pres. 1998-99), Nat. Assn. Estate Planners and Couns., Nat. Assn. Tax Practitioners. Avocations: computers, automobiles. Probate, Taxation, general, Pension, profit-sharing, and employee benefits. Office: 302 W I Pkwy Dallas GA 30132-5061

**WILLIAMS, GLEN MORGAN,** federal judge; b. Jonesville, Va., Feb. 17, 1920; s. Hughy May and Hattie Mae W.; m. Jane Slemp, Nov. 17, 1962; children: Susan, Judy, Rebecca, Melinda. A.B. magna cum laude, Milligan Coll., 1940; J.D., U. Va., 1948. Bar: Va. 1947. Pvt. practice law Jonesville, 1948-76; judge U.S. Dist. Ct. (we. dist.) Va., 1976-88, sr. judge, 1988—; commonwealth's atty. Lee County, Va., 1948-51; mem. Va. Senate, 1953-55. Mem. editorial bd.: Va. Law Rev, 1946-47. Mem. Lee County Sch. Bd., 1972-76; trustee, elder First Christian Ch., Pennington Gap, Va. Lt. USN, 1942-46, MTO. Recipient Citation of Merit Va. Def. Lawyers Assn., Oustanding Alumnus award Milligan Coll., 1980, Svc. to Region award Emory & Henry Coll., 1996. Mem. ABA, Va. State Bar (citation of merit), Va. Bar Assn. (citation of merit), Fed. Bar Assn., Va. Trial Lawyers Assn. (Meritorious Svc. award 1986, Disting. Svc. award), Am. Legion, 40 and 8. Clubs: Lions, Masons, Shriners. Office: US Dist Ct Fed Bldg PO Box 339 Abingdon VA 24212-0339

**WILLIAMS, GREGORY HOWARD,** dean, law educator; b. Muncie, Ind., Nov. 12, 1943; s. James Anthony Williams; m. Sara Catherine Whitney, Aug. 29, 1969; children: Natalia Dora, Zachary Benjamin, Anthony Bladimir, Carlos Gregory. BA, Ball State U., 1966; MA, U. Md., 1969; PhD, George Washington U., 1982, MPH, 1977, JD, 1971; LLD, Calif. Western Sch. Law, 1997, DHD, 1999. Bar: Va. 1971, D.C. 1972. Dep. sheriff Delaware County, Muncie, Ind., 1963-66; tchr. Falls Ch. Public Sch., Va., 1966-70; legis. asst. U.S. Senate, Washington, 1971-73; dir. exptl. programs George Washington U., 1973-77; prof. law U. Iowa Coll. Law, Iowa City, 1977-93; assoc. v.p. Acad. Affairs U. Iowa, 1991-93; dean, prof. law Ohio State U., Columbus, 1993—. Author: Law and Politics of Police Discretion, 1984, Iowa Guide to Search and Seizure, 1986, Life on the Color Line: The True Story of a White Boy Who Discovered He Was Black, 1995. Mem. Iowa Adv. Commn. to U.S. Commn. on Civil Rights, Washington, 1978-86; chmn., mem. Iowa Law Enforcement Acad., Camp Dodge, 1979-85. Recipient Cert. of Appreciation Black Law Students Assn., 1984, GW Edn. Opportunity Program, 1977, Disting. Alumnus award George Washington U., Nat. Law Ctr., 1994, L.A. Times Book prize Current Interest Category, 1995, Disting. Alumnus award Ball State U., 1996. Mem. Assn. Am. Law Schs. (pres. exec. com. 1999). Office: Ohio State U Coll of Law 55 W 12th Ave Columbus OH 43210-1338

**WILLIAMS, HENRY NEWTON,** lawyer; b. Dickson, Tenn., May 14, 1917; s. H. Newton and Cora Ethel (Wynns) W.; m. LaVerna Pearl Wharton, July 12, 1944 (dec.); children: John Wharton, George Wynns. BS, Middle Tenn. State U., 1937; MA, U. Tenn., 1938; PhD, U. Chgo., 1951; JD, Vanderbilt U., 1952; LL.M., Columbia U., 1954. Bar: Tenn. 1953, D.C. 1960, U.S. Supreme Ct. 1956, U.S. Ct. Appeals (3d cir.) 1954, (9th and 10th cirs.) 1955, (D.C. cir.) 1957. Asst. prof. polit. sci. Vanderbilt U., 1946-53; assoc. prof. law Mercer U., Macon, Ga., 1954-56; atty. U.S. Dept. Justice, 1956-68, FTC, Washington, 1968-70; dep. gen. counsel Selective Svc. System, Washington, 1970-76, gen. counsel, 1976—. Col. U.S. Army, 1942-46. J. P. Chamberlain fellow Columbia U. Law Sch., 1953-54; Edward Hilman fellow U. Chgo., 1939-40; Univ. fellow, 1938-39. Mem. Am. Law Inst., ABA, Fed. Bar Assn., Tenn. Bar Assn., D.C. Bar Assn. Episcopalian. Contbr. articles to law and polit. sci. jours. Home: 11811 Judson Rd Silver Spring MD 20902-2054 Office: Selective Svc System Office of the Dir 1515 Wilson Blvd Fl 4th Arlington VA 22209-2425

**WILLIAMS, HENRY WARD, JR.,** lawyer; b. Rochester, N.Y., Jan. 12, 1930; s. Henry Ward and Margaret Elizabeth (Simpson) W.; m. Christina M.; children: Edith Williams Linares, Margaret Williams Warren, Sarah Williams Farrand, Ann Williams Treacy, Elizabeth DeLancey, Victoria Maureen. AB, Dartmouth Coll., 1952; LLB, U.Va., 1958. Bar: N.Y. 1959, U.S. Dist. Ct. (we. dist.) N.Y. 1959, U.S. Dist. Ct. (so. dist.) Mich. 1982, U.S. Ct. Appeals (2d cir.) 1963, U.S. Tax Ct. 1960, U.S. Supreme Ct. 1968, D.C. 1978. Ptnr. Harris, Beach & Wilcox, Rochester, 1958-78, Robinson, Williams, Angeloff & Frank, Rochester, 1978-80, Weidman, Williams, Jordon, Angeloff & Frank, Rochester, 1980-82, The Williams Law Firm, Rochester, 1982—. Editor Va. Law Rev., 1957-58. Chmn. Geva, Genesee Finger/Lakes Regional Planning Coun., 1973-89; majority leader Monroe County Legislature, 1967-73; mem. alumni coun. Dartmouth Coll., 1995—; mem. Nat. Ski Patrol Sys. Lt. (j.g.) USN, 1952-55. Mem. ABA, N.Y. State Bar Assn., Monroe County Bar Assn. (trustee 1982-85), Rochester Yacht Club, Royal Can. Yacht Club, Lake Yacht Racing Assn. (pres. 1985-87, hon. pres. 1988-90), Royal Ocean Racing Club, Raven Soc., Order of Coif, Omicron Delta Kappa. General practice. Office: The Williams Law Firm 12 Rochester St Scottsville NY 14546

**WILLIAMS, HOWARD RUSSELL,** lawyer, educator; b. Evansville, Ind., Sept. 26, 1915; s. Clyde Alfred and Grace (Preston) W.; m. Virginia Merle Thompson, Nov. 3, 1942; 1 son, Frederick S.T. AB, Washington U., St. Louis, 1937; LLB, Columbia U., 1940. Bar: N.Y. 1941. With firm Root, Clark, Buckner & Ballantine, N.Y.C., 1940-41; prof. law, asst. dean U. Tex. Law Sch., Austin, 1946-51; prof. law Columbia U. Law Sch., N.Y.C., 1951-63; Dwight prof. Columbia Law Sch., 1959-63; prof. law Stanford U., 1963-85, Stella W. and Ira S. Lillick prof., 1968-82, prof. emeritus, 1982, Robert E. Paradise prof. natural resources, 1983-85, prof. emeritus, 1985—; Oil and gas cons. President's Materials Policy Commn., 1951; mem. Calif. Law Revision Commn., 1971-79, vice chmn., 1976-77, chmn., 1978-79. Author or co-author: Cases on Property, 1954, Cases on Oil and Gas, 1956, 5th edit., 1987, Decedents' Estates and Trusts, 1968, Future Interests, 1970, Oil and Gas Law, 8 vols., 1959-64 (with ann. supplements/rev. 1964-95), abridged edit., 1973, Manual of Oil and Gas Terms, 1957, 10th edit., 1997. Bd. regents Berkeley Bapt. Divinity Sch., 1966-67; trustee Rocky Mountain Mineral Law Found., 1964-66, 68-85. With U.S. Army, 1941-46. Recipient Clyde O. Martz Tchg. award Rocky Mountain Mineral Law Found., 1994. Mem. Phi Beta Kappa. Democrat. Home: 360 Everett Ave Apt 4B Palo Alto CA 94301-1422 Office: Stanford U Sch Law Nathan Abbott Way Stanford CA 94305

**WILLIAMS, J. BRYAN,** lawyer; b. Detroit, July 23, 1947; s. Walter J. and Maureen June (Kay) W.; m. Jane Elizabeth Eisele, Aug. 24, 1974; children: Kyle Joseph, Ryan Patrick. AB, U. Notre Dame, 1969; JD, U. Mich., 1972. Bar: Mich. 1972, U.S. Dist. Ct. (ea. dist.) Mich. 1972. CEO Dickinson, Wright, PLLC (and predecessor firm), Detroit, 1972—. Mem. ABA, Mich. Bar Assn., Detroit Bar Assn., Notre Dame Club of Detroit (pres. 1984), Oakland Hills Country Club, Nat. Club Assn. (bd. dirs., sec. 1995-97, treas. 1997-98, v.p. 1998—), Detroit Regional C. of C. (bd. dirs.), Chamber Music Soc. of Detroit (bd. dirs.), Econ. Club Detroit (bd. dirs.), Detroit Legal News Co. (bd. dirs.). Roman Catholic. Banking, General corporate. Home: 993 Suffield Ave Birmingham MI 48009-1242 Office: 500 Woodward Ave Ste 4000 Detroit MI 48226-3416

**WILLIAMS, J. MAXWELL,** lawyer, arbitrator and mediator; b. Spartanburg, S.C., Aug. 11, 1943. BA, Vanderbilt U., 1965; JD, U. Fla., 1971. Bar: Fla. 1971, Tenn. 1980, U.S. Dist. Ct. (mid. dist.) Fla. 1973, U.S. Dist. Ct. (so. dist.) Fla. 1972, U.S. Dist. Ct. (we. dist.) Tenn. 1984, U.S. Ct. Appeals (5th cir.) 1974, U.S. Supreme Ct. 1974; cert. mediator, Fla., Tenn. Atty. Kimbrell & Hamaan, Miami, Fla., 1971-73, State of Fla., Tampa, 1974-75; county atty. Hillsborough County, Tampa, 1976-79; chief group counsel, asst. sec. W.R. Grace & Co., Memphis, 1980-98; v.p., gen. counsel Memphis Light, Gas and Water, 1998—. Steering com. Shelby County Rep. Party, Memphis, 1991-95. With USMCR. Named Vol. of Yr., Memphis Legal Svcs., 1992, one of Outstanding Young Men in Am., 1980. Mem. Nat. Assn. Security Dealers (mediator, arbitrator 1996—), Memphis Bar Assn. (chair alt. dispute resolution com. 1996-98), Am. Arbitration Assn. (West Tenn. adv. coun. 1995—, mediator, arbitrator 1994—), Rotary. Baptist. Avocations: swimming, tennis, travel. Alternative dispute resolution, Environmental, Public utilities. Home: 7242 Neshoba Cir Germantown TN 38138-3749 Office: Memphis Light Gas and Water 220 S Main St Memphis TN 38103-3917

**WILLIAMS, J. VERNON,** lawyer; b. Honolulu, Apr. 26, 1921; s. Urban and W. Amelia (Olson) W.; m. Malvina H. Hitchcock, Oct. 4, 1947 (dec. May 1970); children—Carl H., Karin, Frances E., Scott S.; m. Mary McLellan, Sept. 6, 1980. Student, Phillips Andover Acad., 1937-39; B.A. cum laude, Amherst Coll., 1943; LL.B., Yale, 1948. Bar: Wash. 1948. Assoc. Riddell, Riddell & Hemphill, 1948-50; ptnr. Riddell, Williams, Bullitt & Walkinshaw (and predecessor firms), 1950-95; prin. Graham & James L.L.P./Riddell Williams, P.S., Seattle, 1996—; sec., dir. Airborne Freight Corp., 1968-79, gen. counsel, 1968-96. Chmn. March of Dimes, Seattle, 1954-55; Mem. Mayor's City Charter Rev. Com., 1968-69; chmn. Seattle Bd. Park Commrs., 1966-68; co-chmn. parks and open space com. Forward Thrust, 1966-69; dir. bd. and commrs. br. Nat. Recreation and Parks Assn., 1968-69; chmn. Gov.'s adv. com. Social and Health Services, 1972-75; Bd. dirs. Seattle Met. YMCA, 1965—, pres., 1976-79; trustee Lakeside Sch., 1971-79; mem. alumni council Phillips Andover Acad., 1970-73, Yale Law Sch., 1969-77; chancellor St. Mark's Cathedral, Seattle, 1964—. Served with USAAF, 1943-45. Mem. Univ. Club, Seattle Tennis Club, Birnam Wood Golf Club. General corporate, Real property, Aviation. Home: 1100 38th Ave E Seattle WA 98112-4434 Office: 4500 1001 4th Ave Plz Seattle WA 98154-1065

**WILLIAMS, JACKIE N.,** prosecutor; b. Roosevelt, Okla., Oct. 4, 1943; s. David Coleman and Grace Pearl (Southard) W.; children: Douglas Kennedy, Eric Neil. BBA, Wichita State U., 1967; JD, Washburn U. Law Sch., 1971. Bar: Kans. 1971. Asst. atty. gen. Kans. Atty. Gen.'s Office, Topeka, 1971-73; asst. dist. atty. Wichita, Kans., 1973-77; adminstrv. asst. U.S. Congressman Dan Glickman, Washington, D.C., 1977; asst. U.S. atty. Wichita, 1977-96; U.S. atty. Kans., 1996—. Office: Epic Center 301 N Main St Ste 1200 Wichita KS 67202-4812*

**WILLIAMS, JOEL CASH,** lawyer; b. Dacula, Ga., Dec. 19, 1942; s. Joel Cash and Cora Belle W.; m. M'Liss Gurneym Dec. 11, 1976; children: Laurel M'Liss, Morgan Delannoy. BA, Shorter Coll., 1964; LLB, Mercer U., 1967. Bar: Ga., 1966, Ga. (no. dist.), 1967, Ga. (mid. dist.), 1967. Intern Atty. Gen. Ga., Atlanta, 1966, deputy asst. atty. gen., 1967-68, asst. atty. gen., 1968-69; legal counsel U.S. Senator Richard Russell, Washington, 1970-71, U.S. Senator David Gambrell, Washington, 1971; asst. to pres. Savannah (Ga.) Foods & Industry, 1971-78, v.p. corp. affairs, 1978-97; ptnr. Powell, Goldstein, Frazer & Murphy, Atlanta, 1998—; chmn. adv. bd. 1st Liberty Bank, Savannah, 1993-97. Editor-in-chief Mercer LAw Rev., 1966-67. Chmn. bd. dirs. Savannah C. of C., United Way, Savannah, 1987-88. Mem. State Bar Ga. (corp. coun.), Ga. C. of C. (bd. dirs. 1994—). General corporate, Environmental, Public international. Office: Powell Goldstein Frazer & Murphy 191 Peachtree St NE Ste 1600 Atlanta GA 30303-1736

**WILLIAMS, JOHN ANDREW,** lawyer; b. Toccoa, Ga., Oct. 18, 1962; s. Sanford Herbert and Linda (Way) W.; m. Dawn Marie Alsop, Aug. 10, 1996; 1 child, Jeannie. BA in Polit. Sci., U. Ga., 1984, MA in Polit. Sci., 1986; JD, NYU, 1993. Bar: S.C. 1993, N.C. 1997, U.S. Dist. Ct. S.C. 1993, U.S. Dist. Ct. (mid. dist.) N.C. 1997, U.S. Dist. Ct. (we. dist.) N.C. 1998, U.S. Ct. Appeals (4th cir.) 1996. Assoc. Nelson, Mullins, Riley & Scarborough, Greenville, S.C., 1993-95; sole practitioner Greenville, 1995-96; assoc. Edwards, Ballard, Clark, Barrett and Carlson, Winston-Salem, N.C., 1996-99, Moye, O'Brien, O'Rourke, Hogan & Pickert, Atlanta, 1999—; mem. NYU Ctr. for Labor and Employment Law, N.Y.C., 1996—. Contbr. articles to profl. jours. Chmn. Upstate Young Reps., Greenville, 1995-96, Bob Dole for Pres., Greenville County, S.C., 1996. 1st lt. USAF, 1986-90. Mem. ABA, N.C. Bar Assn., S.C. Bar Assn. Republican. Methodist. Avocations: reading, jogging, politics. Labor. Home: 605 Gwinnett Square Cir Duluth GA 30096 Office: Moye O'Brien O'Rourke Hogan & Pickert 999 Peachtree St Atlanta GA 30309

**WILLIAMS, JULIE LLOYD,** lawyer; b. Washington, May 24, 1950; d. Walter Herbert and Jean (Grabill) W.; m. Don Scroggin, May 9, 1981; 1 child, Patrick Conner. BA, Goddard Coll., 1971; JD, Antioch Sch. Law, 1975. Bar: Va. 1975, D.C. 1976. Assoc. Fried, Frank, Harris, Shriver, Washington, 1975-83; assoc. gen. counsel Fed. Home Loan Bank Bd., Washington, 1983-86, dep. gen. counsel, 1986-89; dep. chief counsel Office of Thrift Supervision, Washington, 1989-91, sr. dep. chief counsel, 1991-93; dep. chief counsel Comptr. of the Currency, Washington, 1993-94, chief counsel, 1994-98, acting comptr., 1998—. Co-author: (handbook) How to Incorporate: A Handbook for Entrepreneurs & Professionals, 1987; author: Savings Institutions: Mergers, Acquisitions & Conversions, 1988. Mem. ABA (banking law com.), Women in Housing and Fin. Home: 3064 Q St NW Washington DC 20007-3080 Office: Office Comptroller Currency 250 E St SW Washington DC 20024-3208

**WILLIAMS, KAREN HASTIE,** lawyer, think tank executive; b. Washington, Sept. 30, 1944; d. William Henry and Beryl (Lockhart) Hastie; m. Wesley S. Williams, Jr.; children: Amanda Pedersen, Wesley Hastie, Bailey Lockhart. Cert., U. Neuchatel, Switzerland, 1965; BA, Bates Coll., 1966; MA, Tufts U., 1967; JD, Cath. U. Am., 1973. Bar: D.C. 1973. Staff asst. internat. gov. relations dept. Mobil Oil Corp., N.Y.C., 1967-69; staff asst. com. Dist. Columbia U.S. Senate, 1970, chief counsel com. on the budget, 1977-80; law clk. to judge Spottswood Robinson III U.S. Ct. Appeals (D.C. Cir.), Washington, 1973-74; law clk. to assoc. justice Thurgood Marshall U.S. Supreme Ct., Washington, 1974-75; assoc. Fried, Frank, Harris, Shriver & Kampelman, Washington, 1975-77, 1975-77; adminstr. Office Mgmt. and Budget, Washington, 1980-81; of counsel Crowell & Moring, Washington, 1982, ptnr., 1982—; Bd. dirs. Crestar Fin. Services Corp., Fannie Mae, Washington Gas Light Co., Continental Airlines. Trustee Greater Washington Research Ctr., chair. Mem. ABA (pub. contract law sect., past chair), Nat. Bar Assn., Washington Bar Assn., Nat. Contract Mgmt. Assn., NAACP (bd. dirs. legal defense fund). Office: Crowell & Moring Ste 1200W 1001 Pennsylvania Ave NW Washington DC 20004-2505

**WILLIAMS, KAREN JOHNSON,** federal judge; b. Orangeburg, S.C., Aug. 4, 1951; d. James G. Johnson and Marcia (Reynolds) Johnson Dantzler; m. Charles H. Williams, Dec. 27, 1968; children: Marian, Ashley, Charlie, David. BA, Columbia Coll., 1972; postgrad., U. S.C., 1973, JD cum laude, 1980. Bar: S.C. 1980, U.S. Dist. Ct. S.C. 1980, U.S. Ct. Appeals (4th cir.) 1981. Tchr. Irmo (S.C.) Mid. Sch., 1972-74, O-W High Sch., Orangeburg, 1974-76; assoc. Charles H. Williams P.A., Orangeburg, 1980-92; circuit judge U.S. Ct. Appeals (4th cir.), 1992—; mem. exec. bd. grievance commn. S.C. Supreme Ct., Columbia, 1983-92. Mem. child devel. bd. First Bapt. Ch., Orangeburg; bd. dirs. Orangeburg County Mental Retardation Bd., 1986-94, Orangeburg-Calhoun Hosp. Found.; bd. visitors Columbia Coll., 1988-92; dir. Reg. Med. Ctr. Hosp. Found., 1988-92; mem. adv. bd. Orangeburg-Calhoun Tech. Coll., 1987-92. Mem. ABA, Am. Judicature Soc., Fed.

Judges Assn., S.C. Bar Assn., Orangeburg County Bar Assn. (co-chair Law Day 1981), S.C. Trial Lawyers Assn., Bus. and profl. Women Assn., Rotary, Order of Wig and Robe, Order of Coif. Home: 2503 Five Chop Rd Orangeburg SC 29115-8185 Office: 1021 Middleton St Orangeburg SC 29115-4783*

**WILLIAMS, LEE DWAIN,** lawyer; b. Enid, Okla., Sept. 2, 1950; s. Lawrence and Wilma Jean (Richards) W. BA Polit. Sci., U. Calif., Santa Barbara, 1974; postgrad., U. Calif., 1974; JD, UCLA, 1977. Bar: Calif. 1977, U.S. Dist. Ct. (cen. dist.) Calif. 1977. Assoc. Irell & Manella, L.A., 1977-79, Riordan & McKinzie (formerly Riordan, Caps, Carbone & McKinzie), L.A., 1979-84; prin. Law Offices of Lee D. Williams, L.A., 1984-88; ptnr. Williams & Kilkowski, L.A., 1988—; bd. dirs. Peoplemover, INc., Manhattan Beach, Calif. Vol. atty. Pub. Counsel, La., 1978-80; trustee Children's Inst. Internat., L.A., 1981—, v.p., 1982-83, 98—, treas., 1995-97. Mem. Calif. State Bar. Democrat. Avocations: Basketball, skiing, reading, theatre. General corporate, Federal civil litigation, State civil litigation. Office: 25th Fl 1900 Avenue of the Stars Los Angeles CA 90067

**WILLIAMS, MARCUS DOYLE,** judge; b. Nashville, Oct. 24, 1952; s. John Freelander and Pansy (Doyle) W.; m. Carmen Myrie, May 21, 1983; children: Aaron Doyle, Adam Myrie. BA with honors, Fisk U., 1973; JD, Cath. U. of Am., 1977. Bar: Va. 1977, D.C. 1978. Asst. commonwealth's atty. County of Fairfax, Fairfax, Va., 1978-80; asst. county atty. County of Fairfax, Faifax, Va., 1980-87; dist. ct. judge 19th Jud. Dist., Va., 1987-90; judge 19th Jud. Cir., Va., 1990—; lectr. bus. legal studies George Mason U., Fairfax, 1980-95; instr. pvt. investigators North Va. Community Coll., Fairfax, 1979; mem. Fairfax Criminal Justice Adv. Bd., 1980-86; faculty advisor Nat. Jud. Coll., 1991, faculty, 1992—; Am. participant lectr. for USIA, 1990; lectr. George Mason U. Law Sch., 1987. Book reviewer for ABA Jour., 1981-84; contbr. articles to legal jours. Bd. visitors Cath. U. Law Sch., 1998—. Recipient cert. of appreciation for outstanding svc. Burke-Fairfax Jack & Jill, Cert. of Appreciation, Nat. Forum for Black Pub. Adminstrs. and Black Women United for Action, 1995; Thomas J. Watson Found. fellow, 1977, Otis Smith award BLSA of Cath. U. Law Sch. Mem. ABA (chair subcom. Victims of Crimes), Fairfax Bar Assn. (CLE com., vice chmn. 1986-87), Am. Bus. Law Assn., Am. Judges Assn., Phi Alpha Delta, Beta Kappa Chi, Omega Psi Phi. Methodist. Office: Cir Ct 4110 Chain Bridge Rd Fairfax VA 22030-4009

**WILLIAMS, MARK COLBURN,** lawyer; b. N.Y.C., May 20, 1963; s. Robert Colburn and Beatrice Ruth (Walfish) W. Student, Haverford (Pa.) Coll., 1981-83; BA, Columbia U., 1987; JD, N.Y. Law Sch., 1990. Bar: N.Y. 1992, U.S. Ct. Appeals (fed. cir.) 1992, U.S. Dist. Ct. (D.C. dist.) 1992. Assoc. Jones Hirsch Connors & Bull, N.Y.C., 1990-92; atty., adviser Fed. Energy Regulatory Commn., Washington, 1992—. Contbr. articles to profl. jours. Active N.Y. and Bronx County Dem. Com., 1976-92. Mem. ABA (chmn. legis. subcom. to study the introduction med. practice parameters, 1990-91, ins. regulation com., adminstrv. & regulatory sect.), N.Y. State Bar Assn. (pub. utility law com.), N.Y. County Lawyers' Assn. (chmn. adminstrv. law com. 1993—). Office: Wright Talisman 1200 G St NW Ste 600 Washington DC 20005-3838

**WILLIAMS, MARK SHELTON F.,** lawyer; b. Missoula, Mont., Oct. 12, 1964; s. Shelton C. and Donna L. (Finstad) W.; m. Susan E. Schild, Sept. 5, 1993. BA, Middlebury Coll., 1987; JD with honors, U. Mont., 1992. Bar: Mont. 1992, U.S. Dist. Ct. Mont. 1992, U.S. Ct. Appeals (9th and 10th cirs.) 1992. Acct. officer Chem. Bank, N.Y.C., 1987-89; law clk. U.S. Ct. Appeals 10th cir., Denver, 1992-93; atty. Williams & Ranney P.C., Missoula, 1993—. Editor-in-chief Mont. Law Rev., 1991. Mem. Leadership Missoula, 1994-95. Mem. ABA, Mont. Young Lawyers (pres. 1995-96), Montana Law Found. (bd. dirs.), Phi Delta Phi. Avocations: ski racing, sail boarding, mountain biking. General civil litigation, Insurance, Environmental. Office: Williams & Ranney PC 235 E Pine St Missoula MT 59802-4512

**WILLIAMS, MARY BETH,** lawyer; b. Marshfield, Wis., Aug. 8, 1948; d. Delos A. and Leona E. (Kademan) Kobs; m. Ernest F. Wittwer, July 15, 1967 (div. Jan. 1989); children: Jake, Freddie; m. Paul L. Williams, July 22, 1989. BBA, U. Wis., 1983, JD, 1986. Bar: Wis. 1986, U.S. Dist. Ct. (we. dist.) Wis. 1986, U.S. Dist. Ct. (ea. dist.) Wis. 1988. Assoc. Wickhem & Gage, S.C., Janesville, Wis., 1986-88, Brennan, Steil, Basting & MacDougall, S.C., Janesville, 1988-91; pvt. practice law Janesville, 1991—; mem. legal secs. program adv. com. Blackhawk Tech. Coll., Janesville, 1992—; mem. alcohol license adv. com. City of Janesville, 1994—. Mem. ABA, State Bar Wis., Rock County Bar Assn. Avocations: reading, puzzle solving, piano playing, genealogy, historical restoration. Real property, Estate planning, Probate. Office: 20 S Main St Ste 5 Janesville WI 53545-3959

**WILLIAMS, MAUREEN,** lawyer, former accountant. BSBA, Creighton U., 1985; JD, Hamline U., 1991. Bar: Minn. 1991, U.S. Dist. Ct. 1994, U.S. Ct. Appeals 1994; CPA 1988. CPA Ginoli & Co., Peoria, Ill., 1986, Woodward & Co., Kansas City, Mo., 1986-88; law clk. State Minn., Mankato, 1992-93; pvt. practice Mpls., 1993—. Republican. Roman Catholic. Avocations: reading, biking. Appellate, Criminal. Office: PO Box 581304 Minneapolis MN 55458-1304

**WILLIAMS, MICHAEL EDWARD,** lawyer; b. Ft. Worth, Aug. 10, 1955; s. Jerrol Evans and Helen Louise (Hoffner) W.; m. Jackie Ann Gordinier, Dec. 30, 1978; children: Margaret Eileen, James Andrew. BA, U. Calif., Riverside, 1977; JD, U. San Diego, 1980. Bar: Calif. 1980, U.S. Dist. Ct. (so. dist.) Calif. 1980, U.S. Tax Ct. 1981, U.S. Dist. Ct. (ea. and cen. dists.) Calif. 1982, U.S. Dist. Ct. (no. dist.) Calif. 1985. Assoc. Jamison & McFadden, Solana Beach, Calif., 1980-86, Dorazio, Barnhorst & Bonar, San Diego, 1986; sole practice Encinitas, Calif., 1987—. Atty. pro bono Community Resource Ctr., Encinitas, Calif., 1984—; vice moderator San Diego Presbytery, Presbyn. Ch. U.S.A., 1998, moderator, 1999. Mem. Calif. State Bar Assn. (fee arbitrator 1992—), San Diego County Bar Assn. (client rels. com. 1990—, fee arbitration com. 1991—, ct. arbitrator). Democrat. Presbyterian. State civil litigation, Bankruptcy, Contracts commercial. Office: 4405 Manchester Ave Ste 206 Encinitas CA 92024-7902

**WILLIAMS, MILTON LAWRENCE,** judge, educator; b. Aug. 14, 1932; s. Richard and Helen (Riley) W.; m. Rose King, Oct. 22, 1960; children: Milton Lawrence, Darrie T. BS, NYU, 1960; LLB, N.Y. Law Sch., 1963. Bar: N.Y. 1965, U.S. Dist. Ct. (so. and ea. dists.) N.Y. 1967, U.S. Supreme Ct. 1968, U.S. Customs Ct. 1971. Regional counsel SBA, N.Y.C., 1966-68; assoc. gen. counsel Knapp Commn., N.Y.C., 1970-71; exec. dir. Mckay Commn., N.Y.C., 1972; judge N.Y.C. Criminal Ct., 1977-84; acting justice N.Y. State Supreme Ct., 1978-84; adminstrv. judge criminal term N.Y. State Supreme Ct. 1st Jud. Dist., 1983-85, justice, 1985—; dep. chief adminstrv. judge N.Y.C. Cts., 1985-93; assoc. justice appellate divsn. 1st Dept., 1994—. Mem. N.Y. State Commn. on Sentencing Guidelines, N.Y.C., 1983-86; bd. trustees St. Patrick's Cathedral, Inner City Scholarship Fund, St. John's U. With USN, 1951-55. Mem. Assn. of Bar of City of N.Y., Sigma Pi Phi, Zeta Boule, Knight of Malta. Roman Catholic. Office: Assoc Justice Appellate Divsn First Dept 27 Madison Ave New York NY 10010-2201

**WILLIAMS, NEIL, JR.,** lawyer; b. Charlotte, N.C., Mar. 22, 1936; s. Lyman Neil and Thelma (Peterson) W.; m. Sue Sigmon, Aug. 23, 1958; children: Fred R., Susan S. AB, Duke U., 1958, JD, 1961. Bar: Ga. 1962, U.S. Dist. Ct. (no. dist.) Ga. 1977, U.S. Ct. Appeals (11th cir.) 1977. Assoc. Alston & Bird (and predecessor firm), Atlanta, 1961-65, ptnr., 1966—, mng. ptnr., 1984-96; bd. dirs. Nat. Data Corp., Atlanta, Printpack, Inc., Atlanta, Atty's Liability Assurance Soc., Inc., Chgo. Chmn. bd. trustees Duke U., 1983-88, trustee, 1980-93; chmn. bd. trustees Vasser Woolley Found., Atlanta, 1975—, Leadership Atlanta, 1976-80; trustee Brevard Music Ctr., 1977-86, 91—, Presbyn. Ch. USA Found., Jeffersonville, Ind., 1983-90, Research Triangle Inst., 1983-88, The Duke Endowment, Charlotte, N.C., 1997—; bd. dirs. Atlanta Symphony Orch., 1970-76, 84-93, 95-98, pres. 1988-90; Woodruff Arts Ctr., 1987-98; bd. counsellors The Carter Ctr., Atlanta, 1987-96; Cen. Atlanta Progress, 1984-96; bd. dirs. Am. Symphony Orch. League, Washington, 1990—, chmn., 1995—. Recipient Disting. Alumni award Duke U., 1991, Rhyne award, 1996. Mem. ABA, Am. Bar Found., State Bar Ga., Am. Law Inst., Atlanta C. of C. (bd. dirs., 1992-97, vice chmn. 1994-97), Phi Beta Kappa, Omicron Delta Kappa. Clubs: Piedmont Driving, Commerce (Atlanta); University (N.Y.C.). Contracts commercial, General corporate, Securities. Home: 3 Nacoochee Pl NW Atlanta GA 30305-4164 Office: Alston & Bird 1 Atlantic Ctr 1201 W Peachtree St NW Atlanta GA 30309-3424

**WILLIAMS, NELSON GARRETT,** lawyer, mediator, arbitrator; b. Detroit, Feb. 16, 1926; s. Nelson Wallace and Sylvia Marie (Bowen) W.; m. Marian Pearl Stemme, May 29, 1948 (dec. 1972); children: Elizabeth, Margaret, Roberta. BA, Bowling Green State U., 1947; MA, U. Mich., 1950; MEd, U. South Fla., 1980; JD with honors, Fla. State U., 1987. Bar: Fla. 1987. Editor Huron County Tribune, Bad Axe, Mich., 1947-48; asst. prof. Keuka Coll., Keuka Park, N.Y., 1954-57, Ball State Tchrs. Coll., Muncie, Ind., 1957-63; lectr. Ind. U., Bloomington, 1963-65; assoc. prof. Dana Coll., Blair, Nebr., 1965-69, Sch. of Ozarks, Point Lookout, Mo., 1969-72; exec. dir Am. Cancer Soc., Gainesville, Fla., 1972-74; tchr. Sumter Correctional Inst., Bushnell, Fla. 1974-84; staff atty. Withlacoochee Area Legal Svcs., Floral City, Fla., 1987-89; ret. Withlacoochee Area Legal Svcs., Floral County, Fla., 1989. Author: Labor Journalism, 1963; contbr. articles to popular jours. Grad. fellow U. Fla., 1951-54, Fla. Bar Found. pub. svc. fellow, 1984-87; econs. fellow Case Inst. Tech., 1954, U. Wis., 1958. Mem. Fla. Bar Assn., AAUP (chpt. pres. 1968-69), AFSCME (local v.p., del. 1978-84), Assn. for Union Democracy, Soc. Profl. Journalists, Train Collectors Assn., Am. Flyer Collectors Club, Toy Train Operating Soc., Sigma Delta Chi, Phi Alpha Theta, Pi Sigma Alpha, Pi Gamma Mu, Phi Kappa Phi. Democrat. Avocation: collecting and writing about antique electric toy trains. Home: 7589 S Grovewood Loop Floral City FL 34436-2915

**WILLIAMS, PARHAM HENRY, JR.,** law educator; b. Lexington, Miss., June 8, 1931; s. Parham Henry and Mary Gladys (Hoover) W.; m. Polly Fay Franklin, Sept. 5, 1954; children: Mary Martha, Parham Henry III, John Franklin, Daniel Dickson. BA, U. Miss., 1953, JD, 1954; LLM (Sterling fellow), Yale U., 1965. Bar: Miss. 1954, U.S. Supreme Ct., 1966. Dist. atty. 4th Jud. Dist. Miss., 1957-63; assoc. prof. law U. Miss., University, 1963-65, prof., 1966-71, dean, 1971-85, Whitten chairholder, 1996; v.p., dean Cumberland Sch. Law, Samford U., 1985-96, v.p., dean Chapman U., Anaheim, Calif.; commr. to Nat. Conf. Commrs. on Uniform State Laws, 1972-85; chmn. Ala. Humanities Found., 1990-91. Law adminstrn. fellow NYU, 1968, Sterling fellow Yale U., 1965. Fellow Am. Bar Found.; mem. ABA, Miss. Bar Assn. Office: Chapman Univ Sch of Law 1240 S State College Pkwy Anaheim CA 92806-5240

**WILLIAMS, PERCY DON,** lawyer; b. Dallas, Sept. 19, 1922; s. Percy Don and Frances (Worrill) W.; m. Helen Lucille Brunsdale, Aug. 4, 1954; children—Anne Lucy, Margaret Frances, Elizabeth Helen. B.A. with honors, So. Methodist U., 1942, M.A., 1943; LL.B. magna cum laude, Harvard U., 1946. Bar: Tex. 1951. Instr. So. Meth. U. Law Sch., 1946-47; asst. prof., then assoc. prof. U. Tex. Law Sch., Austin, 1947-49; lectr. U. Va. Law Sch., 1951; law clk. to Justice Tom C. Clark U.S. Supreme Ct., 1949-51; pvt. practice Houston, 1952—; master dist. ct. Harris County, Tex., 1980-95. Contbr. articles to legal jours. Decorated Order of Sacred Treasure Gold Rays, Rosette, Japan. Fellow Tex. Bar Found.; mem. ABA, State Bar Tex. (col.), Fed. Bar Assn., Houston Bar Assn., Am. Law Inst., Am. Judicature Soc., Order of Coif, Phi Beta Kappa, Phi Eta Sigma, Pi Sigma Alpha, Tau Kappa Alpha, Kappa Sigma. Clubs: Houston, Houstonian. General corporate, Contracts commercial, General practice. Home: 31 Briar Hollow Ln Houston TX 77027-9301 Office: 5685 1st Interst Bank Plz Houston TX 77002

**WILLIAMS, QUINN PATRICK,** lawyer; b. Evergreen Park, Ill., May 6, 1949; s. William Albert and Jeanne Marie (Quinlan) W.; children: Michael Ryan, Mark Reed, Kelly Elizabeth. BBA, U. Wis., 1972; JD, U. Ariz., 1974. Bar: Ariz. 1975, N.Y. 1984, U.S. Dist. Ct. Ariz. 1976. V.p., sec., gen. counsel Combined Comm. Corp., Phoenix, 1975-80; sr. v.p. legal and adminstrn. Swensen's Inc., Phoenix, 1980-86; of counsel Winston & Strawn, Phoenix, 1985-87, prtr., 1987-89; ptnr. Snell & Wilmer, Phoenix, 1989—. Chmn. Ariz. Tech. Incubator, 1993-94, Ariz. Venture Capital Conf., 1993, 94; co-chmn. Gov.'s Small Bus. Advocate Exec. Coun., 1993—; bd. dirs. Greater Phoenix Econ. Coun., 1996—, Scottsdale Partnership; vice chair Gov. Regulatory Coun., 1995-97; sec. GSPED High Tech. Cluster, 1993—. Served with USAR, 1967-73. Mem. ABA, State Bar Ariz., Maricopa County Bar Assn., N.Y. Bar Assn., Internat. Franchise Assn., Scottsdale C. of C. (bd. dirs.), Paradise Valley Country Club, Scottsdale Charros. Republican. Roman Catholic. General corporate, Franchising, Securities. Home: 8131 N 75th St Scottsdale AZ 85258-2781 Office: Snell & Wilmer One Arizona Ctr Phoenix AZ 85004

**WILLIAMS, RAIFAEL WORLEY,** lawyer; b. Nashville, July 27, 1970; s. John and Constance Williams; m. Sabrina Smith, Apr. 4, 1996. BA, Morehouse Coll., 1992; JD, Northeastern U., 1995. Bar: Ga. 1996, Ga. Supreme Ct. 1996, U.S. Dist. Ct. Ga. 1996. Law clk. hon. John Nixon U.S. Dist. Ct. (mid. dist.) Tenn., Nashville, 1993; law clk. Gromfine & Taylor, Alexandria, Va., 1993-94, ACLU, Chgo., 1994, Internat. Brotherhood Teamsters, Washington, 1994-95; trial atty. Nat. Labor Rels. Bd., Indpls., 1995—. Coord. Martin Luther King Ctr. for Nonviolent Social Change, Atlanta, 1990-91. Mem. ABA (labor and employment law sect.), ATLA, Nat. Bar Assn., Atlanta Bar Assn., Workers' Dislocation Subcom. (pub. cochair 1998—), Phi Beta Kappa, Golden Key Nat. Honor Soc. Avocations: baseball, volleyball, reading. Office: Nat Labor Rels Bd Region 25 575 N Pennsylvania St Indianapolis IN 46204-1526

**WILLIAMS, REBECCA LYNN,** lawyer, nurse; b. LaGrange, Ill., Jan. 24, 1959; d. Richard Fowler and Anita (Albro) W. BSN magna cum laude, Duke U., 1981; JD, Loyola U., 1986. Bar: Ill. 1986, U.S. Dist. Ct. (no. dist.) Ill. 1986. Nurse Children's Meml. Hosp., Chgo., 1981-84, St. Jude's Hosp., Vieux Fort, St. Lucia, 1983; assoc. McDermott, Will & Emery, Chgo., 1986-88, Winston & Strawn, Chgo., 1988-93; ptnr. Sonnenschein Nath & Rosenthal, Chgo., 1993-98; of counsel Davis Wright Tremaine LLP, Seattle, 1998—. Contbr. articles to profl. jours. Patron various civic, environ., charitable and polit. groups. Mem. ABA, ANA, Am. Health Lawyers Assn. Avocations: scuba diving, reading, hiking, photography. Health. Office: Davis Wright Tremaine LLP 2600 Century Sq 1501 4th Ave Seattle WA 98101-1688

**WILLIAMS, RICHARD LEROY,** federal judge; b. Morrisville, Va., Apr. 6, 1923; s. Wilcie Edward and Minnie Mae (Brinkley) W.; m. Eugenia Kellogg, Sept. 11, 1948; children: Nancy Williams Davies, R. Gregory, Walter L., Gwendolyn Mason. LLB, U. Va., 1951. Bar: Va. 1951. Ptnr. McGuire, Woods & Battle and predecessor firms, 1951-72; judge Cir. Ct. City of Richmond, 1972-76; ptnr. McGuire, Woods & Battle, 1976-80; dist. judge U.S. Dist. Ct., Richmond, Va., 1980—, sr. judge, 1992—. 2d lt. Air Corps., U.S. Army, 1940-45. Fellow Am. Coll. Trial Lawyers; mem. Va. State Bar, Va. Bar Assn., Richmond Bar Assn. Office: US Dist Ct/Lewis F Powell 1000 E Main St Ste 228 Richmond VA 23219-3525

**WILLIAMS, RITA TUCKER,** lawyer; b. Atlanta, Jan. 26, 1950; d. Claude Edward and Lillian Bernice (Barber) Tucker; m. Raymond Williams, Jr., Jan. 1, 1973; children: Monet Danielle, Brandon Raynard, Blake Hassan. BA, Spelman Coll., 1972; MA, U. Mich., 1976; JD, Emory U., 1987. Bar: Ga. 1987. Tchr. pub. schs., Suisun, Calif., 1977-82; assoc. Alston & Bird, Atlanta, 1987-89, Bernard & Assocs., Decatur, Ga., 1989-90; prin. Williams & Assocs., Decatur, 1990—; instr. seminar Nat. Inst. Trial Advocacy, Emory U., Atlanta, spring 1992-95, tutor 1st yr. law students, 1996. Named Outstanding Alumna, Emory U. Law Sch., 1996. Mem. ABA, State Bar Ga. Assn., Ga. Trial Lawyers Assn., Omicron Delta Kappa. Democrat. Office: 220 Church St Decatur GA 30030-3328

**WILLIAMS, ROBERT DANA,** lawyer; b. Hyannis, Mass., Feb. 21, 1939; s. Harold Warren and Winifred Josephine (Shores) W.; m. Gaye Carol Gorringe, May 30, 1964 (div. 1974); children: Sarah Ann, Amy Alden; m. Barbara Ellen Bruce, Aug. 7, 1976; children: Dana Ariana Brix, Nathaniel Shepard. AB magna cum laude, Harvard U., 1961, LLB, 1964. Bar: Mass. 1965. Rsch. asst. Am. Law Inst., Cambridge, Mass., 1964-65; assoc. Warner & Stackpole, Boston, 1965-71; ptnr. Warner & Stackpole, 1971-85; of counsel Hinckley, Allen, Tobin & Silverstein, Boston, 1985-87; ptnr. Hinckley, Allen, Snyder & Comen, Boston, 1987-90, Wayne, Lazares & Chappell, Boston, 1990-95, Masterman, Culbert & Tully, LLP, Boston, 1995—; firm rep. New Eng. Entrepreneurship Coun., Inc. Boston, 1986-89. Bd. govs., exec. com. Concord (Mass.) Mus., 1980-86, capital campaign steering com., 1990-92; bd. dirs. Found. of Mass. Eye and Ear Infirmary, Boston, 1980-91; trustee, sec. Guidance Camps, Inc., 1968-86; trustee Mass. Eye and Ear Infirmary, 1971-99, bd. mgrs., 1980-91, chmn. nominating com., 1984-91; dir., sec. Napoleonic Soc. of Am., Clearwater, Fla., 1985-95; bd. dirs. Psychomotor Inst., Inc., Cambridge, Mass., 1979-95. Mem. Orgn. Am. Historians, Am. Soc. Legal History (com. on documentary preservation 1980-88), Phi Beta Kappa. Congregationalist. Avocations: history, antiquarian books. General corporate, Mergers and acquisitions, Securities. Home: 41 Monument St Concord MA 01742-1841 Office: Masterman Culbert & Tully LLP One Lewis Wharf Boston MA 02110-3985

**WILLIAMS, ROGER COURTLAND,** lawyer; b. Atlanta, June 11, 1944; s. Ralph Roger and Beatrice (Hill) W.; m. Jo Ann Davenport, June 9, 1968; children: Melissa, Kimberly, Courtland. BS, U. Ala., 1966, JD, 1969. Bar: Ala. 1969, U.S. Dist. Ct. (no. and mid. dists.) Ala. 1969, U.S. Supreme Ct. 1972. V.p. Williams, Williams & Williams, P.C., Tuscaloosa, Ala., 1969-90; pres. Williams, Williams & Williams, P.C., Tuscaloosa, 1990—. Mem. bd. trustees Tuscaloosa Acad., 1987—, pres., 1990-94; bd. dirs. Children's Hands On Mus., Tuscaloosa, 1986-97. 1st lt. U.S. Army, 1969-71. Mem. ABA, Ala. State Bar Assn. (vice chmn. ADR com. 1997-98), Assn. Trial Lawyers Am., Nat. Acad. Arbitrators, Am. Arbitration Assn., Jaycees (nat. assoc. legal counsel 1979-80, state pres. 1978-79, pres. Ala. Found. 1980-81, Internat. Senator), Toastmasters (pres. 1975), Kiwanis (bd. dirs. 1974, 90, v.p. 1995-98, pres. 1998-99), Indian Hills Country Club (bd. dirs. 1996—). Methodist. General practice, General civil litigation, Alternative dispute resolution. Office: Williams Williams & Williams PC PO Box 2690 Tuscaloosa AL 35403-2690

**WILLIAMS, RONALD DOHERTY,** lawyer; b. New Haven, Conn., Apr. 6, 1927; s. Richard Hugha nd Ethel W. (Nelson) w.; m. Laura Costarelli, Aug. 25, 1951; children: Craig F., Ronald D., Ellen A., Jane E. BA, U. Va., 1951; LLB, 1954. Bar: Conn. 1954. Assoc. Pullman, Comley, Bradley & Reeves, Bridgeport, Conn., 1954-60; ptnr., 1960-88, Williams, Cooney & Sheehy, 1989—; mem. Fed. Jud. Com., 1988-91, com. unauthorized practice law, 1988-94, com. to study rules civil practice & procedure, 1984-86; atty. state trial referee, 1984-90. Selectman Town fo Easton (Conn.), 1975-85, justice of the peace, 1977—, town atty., 1985—; mem. Bridgeport Area Found., 1971-90, adv. com. U. Bridgeport Law Sch., 1982-92; mem. statewide grievance com., 1985-91, chmn., 1989-91; mem. exec. bd. Sch. Law Quinnipiac Coll., 1994—. Served with U.S. Army, 1945-46. Fellow Am. Coll. Trial Lawyers; mem. ABA, Am. Bd. Trial Advs., Conn. Bar Assn. (bd. govs. 1975-78), Bridgeport Bar Assn. (pres. 1975), Conn. Def. Lawyers Assn. (pres. 1984-85), Trial Attys. Am. Republican. Roman Catholic. Personal injury, Insurance, State civil litigation. Home: 14 Newman Dr Easton CT 06612-1915 Office: 1 Lafayette Cir Bridgeport CT 06604-6021

**WILLIAMS, SHARON A.,** lawyer; b. Portland, Oreg., Nov. 8, 1960. BS in Polit. Sci. with honors, Portland State U., 1982; JD, Willamette U., 1985. Bar: Oreg. 1985, U.S. Dist. Ct. Oreg. Assoc. Birkland & Houze, Portland, 1985-87, Thompson, Adams, DeBast & Ray, Beaverton, Oreg., 1987-89, Sorensen-Jolink, Trubo, Koch & McIlhenny, Portland, 1989-93; ptnr. Sorensen-Jolink, Trubo, Williams, McIlhenny & Williams LLP, Portland, 1993—. Bd. dirs. Tualatin Valley Mental Health Ctr., Beaverton, Oreg., 1988-92. Mem. Oreg. State Bar Assn. (com. on balancing career and family 1992-94), Multnomah Bar Assn., Oreg. Acad. Family Law Practitioners, Wash. County Bar Assn. (mem. jud. selection com. 1998—). Avocations: travel, family, cooking. Family and matrimonial, Juvenile. Office: Sorensen-Jolink Trubo Williams McIlhenny & Williams LLP 1020 SW Taylor St Ste 880 Portland OR 97205-2513

**WILLIAMS, SPENCER MORTIMER,** federal judge; b. Reading, Mass., Feb. 24, 1922; s. Theodore Ryder and Anabel (Hutchison) W.; m. Kathryn Bramlage, Aug. 20, 1943; children: Carol Marcia (Mrs. James B. Garvey), Peter, Spencer, Clark, Janice, Diane (Mrs. Sean Quinn). AB, UCLA, 1943; postgrad., Hastings Coll. Law, 1946; JD, U. Calif., Berkeley, 1948. Bar: Calif. 1949, U.S. Supreme Ct. 1952. Assoc. Beresford & Adams, San Jose, Calif., 1949, Rankin, O'Neal, Center, Luckhardt, Bonney, Marlais & Lund, San Jose, Evans, Jackson & Kennedy, Sacramento; county counsel Santa Clara County, 1955-67; adminstr. Calif. Health and Welfare Agy., Sacramento, 1967-69; judge U.S. Dist. Ct. (no. dist.) Calif., San Francisco, from 1971, now sr. judge; County exec. pro tem, Santa Clara County; adminstr. Calif. Youth and Adult Corrections Agy., Sacramento; sec. Calif. Human Relations Agy., Sacramento, 1967-70. Chmn. San Jose Christmas Seals Drive, 1953, San Jose Muscular Dystrophy Drive, 1953, 54; team capt. fund raising drive San Jose YMCA, 1960; co-chmn. indsl. sect. fund raising drive Alexian Bros. Hosp., San Jose, 1964; team capt. fund raising drive San Jose Hosp.; mem. com. on youth and govt. YMCA, 1967-68; Candidate for Calif. Assembly, 1954, Calif. Atty. Gen., 1966, 70; Bd. dirs. San Jose Better Bus. Bur., 1955-66, Boys City Boys' Club, San Jose, 1965-67; pres. trustees Santa Clara County Law Library, 1955-66. Served with USNR, 1943-46; to lt. comdr. JAG Corps USNR, 1950-52, PTO. Named San Jose Man of Year, 1954. Mem. ABA, Calif. Bar Assn. (vice chmn. com. on publicly employed attys. 1962-63), Santa Clara County Bar Assn., Sacramento Bar Assn., Internat. Assn. Trial Judges (pres. 1995-96), Calif. Dist. Attys. Assn. (pres. 1963-64), Nat. Assn. County Civil Attys. (pres. 1963-64), 9th Cir. Dist. Judges Assn. (pres. 1981-83), Fed. Judges Assn. (pres. 1982-87), Kiwanis, Theta Delta Chi. Office: US Dist Ct 280 S 1st St Rm 5150 San Jose CA 95113-3002

**WILLIAMS, STEPHEN FAIN,** federal judge; b. N.Y.C., N.Y., Sept. 23, 1936; s. Charles Dickerman and Virginia (Fain) W.; m. Faith Morrow, June 11, 1966; children: Susan, Geoffrey Fain, Sarah Margot Nu, Timothy Dwight, Nicholas Morrow. B.A., Yale U., 1958; J.D., Harvard U., 1961. Bar: N.Y. 1962, Colo. 1977. Assoc. Debevoise, Plimpton, Lyons & Gates, N.Y.C., 1962-66; asst. U.S. atty. So. Dist. N.Y., 1966-69; asst. prof. law U. Colo., Boulder, 1969-77; prof. U. Colo., 1977-86; judge U.S. Ct. Appeals (D.C. cir.), Washington, 1986—; vis. prof. UCLA, 1975-76; vis. prof., fellow in law and econs. U. Chgo., 1979-80; vis. William L. Hutchison prof. energy law So. Meth. U., 1983-84; cons. Adminstrv. Conf. U.S., 1974-76, FTC, 1983-85; mem. Boulder Area Growth Study Commn., 1972-73. Contbr. articles to law revs., mags. Served with U.S. Army, 1961-62. Mem. Am. Law Inst. Office: US Courthouse 3rd Constitution Ave NW Washington DC 20001

**WILLIAMS, STEVEN MARK,** lawyer; b. Guthrie, Okla., Mar. 25, 1954; s. Bob G. and Martha Jane Williams; m. Caron F. Henderson, Dec. 29, 1989 (div.); children: Casey, Blake, Steven Jr. BBA in Acctg., U. Tex., 1975; JD, Tex. Tech. U., 1979. Bar: Tex. Atty. El Paso Natural Gas Co., 1979-81, Transco Energy Co., Houston, 1981-83, Diamond Shamrock Corp., Dallas, 1983-85; assoc. Troy Douthitt, Wichita Falls, Tex., 1986-87; pvt. practice Wichita Falls, 1988—. Football coach, Boys Clubs Am., Wichita Falls, 1998. Named Texhoma's Best Atty., Wichita Falls Times Record News. Mem. ATLA, Tex. State Bar Assn., Tex. Trial Lawyers Assn., Wichita County Bar Assn. Personal injury, Criminal, Bankruptcy. Office: 901 Lamar St Wichita Falls TX 76301-3414

**WILLIAMS, TERESA ANN GOODE,** lawyer; b. Edmond, Okla., Oct. 29, 1959; d. Fred Noble and Lucy Edwinna (Rials) Goode; m. Kirk Owen Williams, May 26, 1984; children: Chance O., Clint L., Cristen M., Caitlyn E. AA, Rose State Coll., 1986; BBA, U. Ctrl. Okla., 1987; JD, U. Okla., 1991. Bar: Okla. 1991, U.S. Dist. Ct. (we. and no. dists.) Okla. 1991, U.S. Ct. Appeals (10th cir.) 1991. Legal sec. C.H. Spearman, Jr., Edmond, 1978-82; legal asst., sec. Coleman, Walke & Briggs, Oklahoma City, 1982-87, Geary L. Walke, P.C., Oklahoma City, 1987-89; legal rsch. clk. Prof. Joyce Palomar, Norman, Okla., 1990; summer legal clk. Edwards, Sonders & Propester, Oklahoma City, 1990; summer legal clk. Crowe & Dunlevy, Oklahoma City, 1990, assoc., 1991—. Contbr. articles to profl. jours. Mem. pks. commn. City of Moore, Okla., 1988-91, mem. planning commn., 1988-91. Recipient Civitan award, 1977; named Outstanding Young Women of Am., 1983. Mem. ABA (young lawyers divsn. health care law com., health law forum com., sect. of patent, trademark and copyright law), Okla. Bar Assn. (sec. health law sect., intellectual property sect.), Oklahoma County Bar Assn., Cleveland County Bar Assn., Nat. Health Lawyers Assn.-Am. Acad. Hosp. Attys., Okla. Health Lawyers Assn., Am. Health Info. Mgmt. Assn. (ambulatory care sect., quality assurance sect.), Ruth Bader Ginsburg

Inns of Ct. (barrister). Avocations: church activities, children, snow skiing, water sports. Health, General corporate, Intellectual property. Office: Crowe & Dunlevy 1800 Mid-America Tower 20 N Broadway Ave Ste 1800 Oklahoma City OK 73102-8273

**WILLIAMS, THEODORE JOSEPH, JR.,** lawyer; b. Pitts., July 23, 1947; s. Theodore Joseph and Isabel (McAnulty) W.; m. Sherri Lynne Foust, July 4, 1970; children: Kelley Shields, Jonathan Stewart, Jordan Fuller. BA, Purdue U., 1969; JD, U. Tulsa, 1974. Bar: Ill. 1975, Colo. 1996, U.S. Ct. Appeals (7th cir.) 1975, U.S. Dist. Ct. (no., so. and cen. dists.) Ill. 1975, Mo. 1978, U.S. Ct. Appeals (8th cir.) 1978, U.S. Dist. Ct. (ea. and we. dists.) Mo. 1978, U.S. Supreme Ct. 1978, D.C. 1981, U.S. Ct. Appeals (D.C. cir.) 1988, U.S. Dist. Ct. D.C 1988, U.S. Ct. Mil. Appeals 1991, U.S. Ct. Appeals (10 cir.) 1996. Asst. city prosecutor City of Tulsa, 1974; trial atty., law dept. Chgo. and North Western R.R., Chgo., 1975-78; assoc. Thompson and Mitchell, St. Louis, 1978-81; assoc. Shepherd, Sandberg & Phoenix, P.C., St. Louis, 1981-84, ptnr., 1984-88; ptnr., chmn. transp. law dept. Armstrong, Teasdale, Schlafly & Davis, St. Louis, 1988—. Assoc. editor Law. Jour., U. Tulsa, 1974. Treas. sch. bd. Mary Queen of Peace Sch., Webster Groves, Mo., 1986, v.p., 1987. Lt. col. USAR, 1991—. Mem. ABA (vice chmn. rail and motor carrier law com., torts and ins. practice law sect. 1989-90, chair-elect 1990-91, chair 1991-92), Ill. Bar Assn., Mo. Bar Assn., Def. Rsch. Inst. (chair, railroad law commn. 1996), Nat. Assn. R.R. Trial Coun., We. Conf. Ry. Coun., Assn. ICC Practitioners, Maritime Law Assn., Internat. Assn. Def. Coun., Transp. Lawyers Assn., Assn. Transp. Practitioners, D.C. Bar Assn., Colo. Bar Assn. Republican. Roman Catholic. Personal injury, Product liability, Transportation. Office: Armstrong Teasdale Schlafly & Davis One Metropolitan Sq Saint Louis MO 63102

**WILLIAMS, THOMAS ARTHUR,** lawyer; b. Wilmington, N.C., Sept. 26, 1943; s. Louis C. and Mary Alice (Elmore) W.; m. Karen Barbara Hoster, Feb. 2, 1978; children—Morgan, Duncan; stepchildren: Quentin, Marady. B.S. In Journalism, Okla. State U., 1966; J.D.S., U. Okla., 1972. Bar: Okla. 1972, U.S. Dist. Ct. (we. dist.) Okla. 1972, U.S. Dist. Ct. (ea. and no. dists.) Okla. 1973, U.S. Ct. Appeals (10th cir.) 1973. Assoc. Jones, Atkinson, Williams, Bane & Klingenberg, Oklahoma City, 1972-73, Jones, Williams, Bane, Ray & Klingenberg, Oklahoma City, 1973-74; owner Bane & Williams, Oklahoma City, 1974-76; ptnr. Kratz, Thomas, Williams & Patton, Oklahoma City, 1978-79; ptnr. Drummond, Patton, Williams & Tullius, Oklahoma City, 1979-81; ptnr. Williams, Patton, Patton & Hyde, Oklahoma City, 1981-83; prof. corrections law Rose State Coll., 1976-78; judge Temporary Ct. Appeals 124, Okla., 1982. Mem. Okla. Bar Assn. (exec. bd. family law sect. 1987-89, membership chmn. 1987-89), Oklahoma County Bar Assn., Okla. Criminal Def. Lawyers Assn., ABA, Phi Delta Phi. Bankruptcy, Probate, Estate planning.

**WILLIAMS, THOMAS RAYMOND,** lawyer; b. Meridian, Miss., Aug. 26, 1940. BS, U. Ala., 1962, LLB, 1964. Bar: Ala. 1964, Tex. 1979, U.S. Supreme Ct. 1980, D.C. 1983. Ptnr. McDermott, Will & Emery, Washington. Mem. D.C. Bar Assn., Ala. State Bar Assn., State Bar Tex. Administrative and regulatory, Federal civil litigation, Franchising. Office: McDermott Will & Emery 600 13th St NW Fl 12-8 Washington DC 20005-3005

**WILLIAMS, WILLIAM JAMES,** lawyer; b. Augusta, Ga., May 24, 1945; s. W.E. and Lorine B. Williams; m. Brenda Susan Rabun, July 31, 1974; children: Jennifer S., Amanda B. BA, U. Ga., Athens, 1967, JD, 1971. Bar: Ga. 1983, U.S. Dist. Ct. (so. dist.) Ga. 1972, U.S. Ct. of Appeals (11th cir.) 1983. Assoc. Sanders Hester & Holley, Augusta, 1971-73, ptnr., 1973-78; ptnr. Dye & Williams, Augusta, 1978-79, Johnston Wilkin & Williams, Augusta, 1979—; spl. hearing examiner Ga. Dept. Human Resources, Atlanta, 1987-89. With Ga. Army Nat. Guard, 1967-73. Mem. Ga. Trial Lawyers Assn., Augusta Bar Assn. Methodist. Avocations: golf, fishing, hunting. General civil litigation, Probate, Family and matrimonial. Office: Johnston Wilkin & Williams 235 Davis Rd Augusta GA 30907-2407

**WILLIAMS, WILLIAM JOHN, JR.,** lawyer; b. New Rochelle, N.Y., Feb. 6, 1937; s. William John and Jane (Gormley) W.; m. Barbara Reuter. BA, Holy Cross Coll., Worcester, Mass., 1958; LLB, NYU, 1961. Bar: N.Y. 1961. Practiced in N.Y.C., 1962—; ptnr. firm Sullivan & Cromwell, 1969—. Trustee NYU Law Sch. Found., 1977—, Holy Cross Coll., 1988-96. Fellow Am. Bar Found.; mem. ABA, Am. Law Inst., N.Y. State Bar Assn., Assn. of Bar of City of N.Y., U.S. Golf Assn. (mem. exec. com. 1978-87, sec. 1980-81, v.p. 1982-85, pres. 1986-87). Democrat. Roman Catholic. General corporate, Private international, Securities.

**WILLIAMSON, DEBORAH DAYWOOD,** lawyer; b. Greenville, S.C., Mar. 8, 1954; d. Narcief M. Daywood and Margaret Elizabeth (Guy) Robbins; m. George F. Williamson, Nov. 9, 1974; children: Christal Elizabeth, Victoria Whitney. BA, San Antonio Coll., 1973, S.W. Tex. U., 1974, U. Tex., El Paso, 1977; JD, U. Houston, 1981. Bar: Tex. 1982, U.S. Dist. Ct. (we. dist.) Tex. 1983, U.S. Dist. Ct. (so. dist.) Tex. 1986, U.S. Dist. Ct. (no. dist.) Tex. 1989, U.S. Dist. Ct. Ariz. 1991, U.S. Ct. Appeals (5th cir.) 1983. Atty. Cox & Smith Inc., San Antonio, 1982—. Author: (with others) Single Asset Real Estate Bankruptcies, 1996; columnist Am. Bankruptcy Inst. Jour., 1985—. Fellow Tex. Bar Found., Am. Coll. Bankruptcy, San Antonio Bar Found.; master Am. Inns of Ct., William Session; mem. Am. Bankruptcy Inst. (pres. 1998-99), San Antonio Bankruptcy Bar Assn. Bankruptcy. Office: Cox & Smith Inc 112 E Pecan St Ste 1800 San Antonio TX 78205-1521

**WILLIAMSON, EDWIN DARGAN,** lawyer, former federal official; b. Florence, S.C., Sept. 23, 1939; s. Benjamin F. and Sara (Dargan) W.; m. Kathe Gates, July 12, 1969; children: Samuel Gates, Edwin Dargan Jr., Sara Elizabeth. BA cum laude, U. of the South, 1961, DCL (hon.), 1992; JD, NYU, 1964. Bar: N.Y. 1965, D.C. 1988. Assoc. Sullivan & Cromwell, N.Y.C., 1964-70, ptnr., 1971-76; ptnr. Sullivan & Cromwell, London, 1976-79, N.Y.C., 1979-88, Washington, 1988-90, 93—; legal adviser U.S. Dept. State, Washington, 1990-93, Permanent Ct. of Arbitration, 1991—. Regent U. of the South, Sewanee, Tenn., 1981-87, chmn., 1985-87, coun. fgn. rels., 1995—; bd. dirs. Nat. Dance Inst., N.Y.C., 1984-88, Episcopal Ch. Found., N.Y.C., 1986-94; vestryman St. James Episcopal Ch., N.Y.C., 1984-88. Mem. U.S. Coun. Internat. Bus., Bus. and Industry Adv. Com. to OECD (vice chmn. com. on multinat. enterprise and investments 1993—, vice-chmn. BIAC expert group on Multinat. mgmt. investment 1996-99, vice-chmn. BIAC 1998—), Internat. Rep. Inst. (rule of law adv. bd. 1993—), Racquet and Tennis Club (N.Y.C.), Met. Club. Republican. Private international, Public international, Securities.

**WILLIAMSON, JAMES ROBERT, JR.,** lawyer; b. Morgantown, W.Va., Nov. 9, 1961; s. James Robert Williamson and Katheryn Williamson Kay; m. Elizabeth Anne Warlick, June 16, 1984; children: Lindsey, Molly, Anne. BS in Bus. Adminstrn., Vanderbilt U., 1983; JD, W.Va. U., 1986. Bar: Ga. 1986, W.Va. 1986, Fla. 1990. Assoc. King & Spalding, Atlanta, 1986-90, Stichter, Riedel, Blain & Prosser, Tampa, Fla., 1990-91, Bisbee, Rickertsen & Herzog, Atlanta, 1991-93; ptnr. Scroggins & Williamson, Atlanta, 1993—. Steptoe & Johnson scholar W. Va. U. Law Sch., 1984-86. Mem. Atlanta Bar Assn. (mem. bankruptcy sect.), Ga. State Bar Assn. (mem. bankruptcy sect., bd. dirs. 1998), Ansley Golf Club. Methodist. Bankruptcy, General civil litigation. Office: 1500 Candler Bldg 127 Peachtree St NE Atlanta GA 30303-1810

**WILLIAMSON, RICHARD THOMAS,** lawyer, real estate broker; b. New Orleans, La., Sept. 24, 1958; s. Thomas Mose and Catherine Anne (Arnold) W. AA, Long Beach (Calif.) C.C., 1982; BS, U. So. Calif., 1986; postgrad., Calif. State U., Long Beach, 1988; JD, Southwestern U., L.A., 1992. Bar: Calif.; cert. real estate appraiser. Pres., CEO Campus Systems, L.A., 1982-86; bus. cons. Intelligent Solutions, Long Beach, Calif., 1986-87; real estate broker Coldwell Banker, Long Beach, 1987—; assoc. Landis & Assocs., Long Beach, Calif., 1992—; cons. TVO Med. Group, Long Beach, 1986, Leather 'N More, Fountain Valley, Calif., 1988-90; mem. adv. bd. Coldwell Banker, Long Beach, Calif., 1988-90. Bd. dirs. Homeless Relief Program, Long Beach, 1987-91. With USAF, 1976-78. Grantee, scholar Haynes Found., L.A., 1982-86. Mem. ABA, ATLA, Calif. Assn. Realtors. Office: Landis & Assocs 5580 E 2nd St Ste 209 Long Beach CA 90803-3959

**WILLIAMSON, RONALD THOMAS,** lawyer; b. Paterson, N.J., Nov. 12, 1948; s. Thomas Sim and Jessie Carnegie (Sandilands) W.; m. Nancy Anne Hough, June 13, 1982; children: Kate Elizabeth, Brad Francis Thomas. BA, Rutgers U., 1970; JD cum laude, Widener U., 1975. Bar: Pa. 1976, U.S. Dist. Ct. (ea. dist.) Pa. 1976, U.S. Supreme Ct. 1979, U.S. Ct. Appeals (3d cir.) 1980. Assoc. Modell, Pincus, Hahn and Reich, Phila., 1976-77; asst. dist. atty., chief of appeals County of Montgomery, Norristown, Pa., 1977-85; sr. dep. atty. gen. appeals and legal svcs. sect. Pa. Atty. Gen., Harrisburg, 1997—, 1997—; instr. search and seizure Southeastern Tng. Ctr., Pa. State Police, Worcester, 1979-85; legal instr. Montgomery County C.C., Whitpain, Pa., 1984. Contbr. to profl. publs. Bd. dirs. Denbigh Group Foster Home, Bridgeport, Pa., 1979-83, pres., 1984; mem. Cen. Montgomery Optimist Club, Norristown, 1980-81. Mem. Pa. Bar Assn., Montgomery County Bar Assn. (chmn. appellate ct. practice com.). Republican. Presbyterian. Avocations: tennis, squash, sailing, triathlon, reading. Office: Pa Office Atty Gen 2490 Blbd ff Generals Norristown PA 19403-5234

**WILLIAMS UMLAUF, NATALIE R.,** lawyer; b. Frankfurt, Germany, July 7, 1965; came to U.S., 1965; d. Nathaniel and Jacqueline P. (Williams); m. Erik G. Umlauf, Oct. 3, 1997. BS, Cornell U., 1986; JD, Yale U., 1990. Bar: N.Y. 1990. Assoc. Debevoise & Plimpton, N.Y.C., 1990-93, 94-95; law clk. to Hon. sonia Sotomayor So. Dist. N.Y., N.Y.C., 1993-94; assoc. counsel to the Pres. White House, Washington, 1995-96; assoc. Debevoise & Plimpton, N.Y.C., 1996—; adj. prof. Columbia Law Sch., N.Y.C., 1998—. Bd. dirs. Classic Stage Co., N.Y.C., 1996—. Mem. N.Y.C. Bar Assn. (fed. cts. com.). Democrat. General civil litigation, Product liability. Home: 18 Hamilton Ter New York NY 10031-6403 Office: Debevoise & Plimpton 875 3d Ave New York NY 10022

**WILLINGER, LOWELL D.,** lawyer; b. Mar. 8, 1942. BA, Cornell U., 1964; LLB, Harvard U., 1967. Bar: N.Y. 1968. Assoc. Hofferman, Gartlir, Gottlieb & Gross, N.Y.C., 1968-69, Goldstein, Durfeen, Shames & Hyde, N.Y.C., 1969-78, Carlo, Luria, Glassner, Cook & Kufeld, N.Y.C., 1978-82; assoc., sr. counsel Proskauer, Rose, N.Y.C., 1982—. Mem. N.Y.C. Bar Assn. (real property law com. 1998—), Phi Beta Kappa. Real property, Landlord-tenant. Office: Proskauer Rose 1585 Broadway New York NY 10036-8200

**WILLINGHAM, CLARK SUTTLES,** lawyer; b. Houston, Nov. 29, 1944; s. Paul Suttles and Elsie Dell (Clark) W.; m. Jane Joyce Hitch, Aug. 16, 1969; children: Meredith Moores, James Barrett. BBA, Tex. Tech U., 1967; JD, So. Meth. U., 1971, LLM, 1984. Bar: Tex. 1971. Ptnr. Kasmir, Willingham & Krage, Dallas, 1972-86, Finley, Kumble et al, Dallas, 1986-87, Brice & Mankoff, Dallas, 1988-98, Moseley & Standerfer, PC, Dallas, 1999—; mem. Tex. Bd. Vet. Med. Examiners, 1991-95, pres., 1994; bd. dirs. Tex. Beef Coun., pres., 1989. Contbr. articles to profl. jours. Exec. com. Dallas Summer Musicals, 1979-93, pres., 1994-95. Mem. ABA (chmn. agrl. com. tax sect. 1984-86), State Bar Tex. (chmn. agrl. tax com. 1985-87), Dallas Bar Assn., Am. Law Inst., Nat. Cattlemen's Beef Assn. (bd. dirs., pres 1998 ), U.S. Meat Export Fedn. (exec. com. 1991-93), Beef Industry Coun. (exec. com. 1990-91, promotion chmn. 1992-94), Tex. Cattle Feeders Assn. (bd. dirs., pres. 1988), Dallas Country Club. Republican. Episcopalian. Personal income taxation, Corporate taxation, Estate taxation. Home: 3824 Shenandoah St Dallas TX 75205-1702 Office: Moseley & Standerfer 3878 Oak Lawn Ave Ste 400 Dallas TX 75219-4469

**WILLIS, BETH ANNE,** paralegal; b. Tonawanda, N.Y., Dec. 10, 1970; d. James David and Barbara Anne Willis. Student, Gloucester County Coll., 1996-98, Rutgers U., 1998—. Legal asst. Brown & Connery, Westmont, N.J., 1993-97; paralegal Archer & Greiner, Haddonfield, N.J., 1997—. Mem. Gloucester County Paralegal Assn., South Jersey Paralegal Assn., Soccer Internat., Phi Theta Kappa. Avocations: soccer, golf, tennis, reading. Home: 604 Yorkshire Ct Sewell NJ 08080-2516 Office: Archer & Greiner One Centennial Sq Haddonfield NJ 08033

**WILLIS, BRUCE DONALD,** judge; b. Mpls., Jan. 29, 1941; s. Donald Robert and Marie Evelyn (Edwards) W.; m. Elizabeth Ann Runsvold, July 17, 1971; children: Andrew John, Ellen Elizabeth. BA in English, Yale U., 1962; LLB, Harvard U., 1965. Bar: Minn., 1965, U.S. Dist. Ct. Minn. 1965, U.S. Ct. Fed. Claims 1989, U.S. Ct. Appeals (8th cir.) 1991, U.S. Supreme Ct. 1992. Assoc. Popham, Haik, Schnobrich & Kaufman, Ltd., Mpls., 1965-71, ptnr., 1971-95; judge Minn. Ct. Appeals, 1995—; mem. adv. bd. Minn. Inst. Legal Edn., 1985—, mem. jud. adv. bd. for the Law and Organizational Econs. Ctr. of the Univ. of Kansas, 1997—. Contbr. articles to profl. jours. Del. Rep. Nat. convs., 1976, 88; vice chmn. Ind.-Rep. Party Minn., 1979-81; mem. State Ethical Practices Bd., 1990-95, sec. 1990-91, vice chmn. 1991-92, chmn., 1992-93; mem. Minn. Commn. on Jud. Selection, 1991-94; mem. Minn. Bd. Jud. Stds., 1997—; mem. adv. com. on rules of civil appellate procedure Minn. Supreme Ct., 1997—. Named one of 1990's Lawyers of Yr., Minn. Jour. Law and Politics, 1991, one of Minn.'s Best Trial Lawyers, Minn. Lawyer, 1991. Mem. ABA, Minn. Bar Assn., Rolling Green Country Club. Mem. United Ch. of Christ. Home: 2940 Walnut Grove Ln N Plymouth MN 55447-1567 Office: Minn Jud Ctr 25 Constitution Ave Saint Paul MN 55155-1500

**WILLIS, DAWN LOUISE,** paralegal, small business owner; b. Johnstown, Pa., Sept. 11, 1959; d. Kenneth William and Dawn Louise (Joseph) Hagins; m. Marc Anthony Ross, Nov. 30, 1984 (div.); m. Jerry Wayne Willis, Dec. 16, 1989 (div.). Grad. high sch., Sacramento, Calif. Legal sec. Wilcoxen & Callahan, Sacramento, 1979-87, paralegal asst., 1987-88; legal adminstr. Law Office Jack Vetter, Sacramento, 1989-99; owner, mgr. Your Girl Friday Secretarial and Legal Support Svcs., Sacramento, 1991—; legal sec. Foley & Lardner, Sacramento, 1999—. Vol. ARC, 1985, Spl. Olympics, 1997—. Mem. Consumer Attys. of Calif., Sacramento Legal Secs. Assn. Democrat. Lutheran. Avocations: water sports, camping, reading, cooking. Office: Foley & Lardner 300 Capitol Mall Ste 1125 Sacramento CA 95814

**WILLIS, JEFFREY LYNN,** lawyer; b. Stillwater, Okla., Jan. 26, 1951; s. William R. and Jean Louise (Evans) w.; children: Jeffrey, James, Julia, Meredith. BA, No. Ariz. U., 1972; JD, Washington and Lee U., 1975. Bar: Va. 1975, D.C. 1976, Ariz. 1977, U.S. Supreme Ct., 1984, Nev., 1992, Hawaii 1997, Calif. 1998. Assoc. Von Baur, Coburn, Simmons & Turtle, Washington, 1975-77, Streich, Lang, Weeks & Cardon, Phoenix, 1977-82; ptnr. Streich Lang, Tucson, 1982—, mng. ptnr., 1992-96. Author: Arizona Legal Forms, 1988. Mem. Senator McCain's Fed. Jud. Selection Com., Tucson, 1990. Fellow Ariz. Bar Found.; mem. ABA, Tucson Country Club. Federal civil litigation, General civil litigation, State civil litigation. Office: Streich Lang Ste 1700 One S Church Ave Tucson AZ 85701-1413

**WILLIS, JOHN ALEXANDER,** lawyer; b. Queens, N.Y., Feb. 3, 1966; s. John Joseph Willis and Dorothy Elizabeth (Savides) White. BA, SUNY, Stony Brook, 1989; JD, Nova Southeastern Law Ctr., 1994. Bar: Fla. 1994, U.S. Ct. Appeals (11th cir.) 1994, N.Y. 1995, U.S. Dist. Ct. (so. dist.) Fla. 1995, U.S. Supreme Ct., 1999. Acct. coord. Met. Life Ins. Co., Hauppauge, N.Y., 1989-91; cert. legal intern Palm Beach County State's Atty Office, West Palm Beach, Fla., 1994; assoc. David & French, P.A., Boca Raton, Fla., 1994—. Mem. ATLA, Acad. Fla. Trial Lawyers, South Palm Beach County Bar Assn. Avocations: golf, computers, softball. General civil litigation, Insurance, Personal injury. Office: David & French PA 2600 N Military Trl Ste 125 Boca Raton FL 33431-6330

**WILLIS, SHARI RENEE LYNE,** lawyer; b. Salina, Kans., Dec. 15, 1970; d. James Lucky Rose II and Vera Fern Lyne; m. Jeffrey Todd Willis, Aug. 7, 1993; children: Jordan Nicole, Katlyn Michelle, Laken Andrew. BS in Psychology, Kans. State U.; JD with honors, Washburn U. Bar: Kans., 1996, U.S. Dist. Ct. Kans., 1996, U.S. Ct. Appeals (10th cir.), 1996, U.S. Supreme Ct., 1996. Assoc. McDonald Tinker Skaer Quinn & Herrington, Wichita, Kans., 1996—. Pres., co-founder Katlyn's Hope Inc., Wellington, Kans., 1995. Recipient Cali award of excellence C.A.L.I., 1995. Mem. Kans. Bar Assn., Wichita Bar Assn., Sumner County Bar Assn. Republican. Methodist. Labor, General civil litigation, Insurance. Home: 303 S Elm St Wellington KS 67152-2747 Office: McDonald Tinker Skaer 300 W Douglas Ave Wichita KS 67202-2916

**WILLY, THOMAS RALPH,** lawyer; b. Phila., Sept. 30, 1943; s. Albert Ralph and Dorothy Rose (Driver) W.; m. Kay Harris, Jan. 12, 1968; children—Elyn Alexandria, Jon Charles. B.A. in History, U. Mo.-Kansas City, 1966, J.D. with distinction, 1974. Bar: Mo. 1974, U.S. Tax Ct. 1982. Assoc. Deacy & Deacy, Kansas City, Mo., 1974-75, Logan, Hentzen, Haitbrink & Moore, Kansas City, 1975; ptnr. Hentzen, Haitbrink & Moore, Kansas City, 1976-78, Hentzen, Moore & Willy, Kansas City, 1978-80, Moore and Willy Profl. Corp., Kansas City, 1980-87, pres., dir. 1987-94; shareholder, dir. Van Osdol, Magruder, Erickson & Redmond, P.C., Kansas City, 1994—; cons. Ctr. for Mgmt. Assistance, Kansas City; presenter living will project, Midwest Bioethics Ctr. Pres. Kansas City Swiss Soc., 1989-91, bd. dirs. 1993-96; bd. dirs. Greater Kansas City People to People, 1995-98; active Greater Kansas City Coun. Philanthropy, Mid-Am. Planned Giving Coun., Nat. Com. on Planned Giving, Midwest Bioethics Ctr., Friends of Art, Kansas City, Kansas City Consensus, Hist. Kansas City Found. Served to capt. USAF, 1966-70. Mem. ABA, (sect. internat. law, sect. bus. law), Mo. Bar Assn., Lions (bd. dirs. Leawood 1986-88, 90-92, sec. 1988-90, v.p. 1996-97). General corporate, Non-profit and tax-exempt organizations, Estate planning. Home: 10314 Lee Blvd Shawnee Mission KS 66206-2629 Office: 2700 Commerce Tower 911 Main St Kansas City MO 64105-2007

**WILMARTH, ARTHUR EDWARD, JR.,** law educator; b. Olean, N.Y., Feb. 16, 1951; s. Arthur Edward and Helen Mae (Sinon) W.; m. Ellen Kay Whetham, Oct. 15, 1983. BA, Yale U., 1972; JD, Harvard U., 1975. Bar: D.C. 1976, U.S. Supreme Ct. 1984, Pa. 1992. Assoc. Arent, Fox, Kintner, Plotkin & Kahn, Washington, 1975-79, Jones, Day, Reavis & Pogue, Washington, 1979-84; ptnr. Jones, Day, Reavis & Pogue, 1985-86, Barley, Snyder, Senft & Cohen, Lancaster, Pa., 1992-94; assoc. prof. law George Washington U., Washington, 1986—; exch. lawyer Kenneth, Brown, Baker & Baker, London, 1977-78; legal cons. Conf. State Bank Suprs., Washington, 1979—; adv. bd. state and local legal ctr. Acad. State and Local Govt., 1992—. Office: George Washington U Law Sch 720 20th St NW Washington DC 20052-0001

**WILMER, CHARLES MARK,** lawyer; b. Phoenix, Dec. 31, 1938; s. Mark Bernard and Genevieve (Tibshraeny) W.; m. Sandra Jean Provo; children: Charles M. Jr., Thomas C., Jeffrey A., Brian N. LLB, U. Ariz., 1964. Bar: Ariz. 1964, U.S. Dist. Ct. Ariz. 1964. Pvt. practice, Phoenix, 1964—; judge pro tem Ariz. Ct. Appeals, 1985, 93. Contbr. numerous articles to law jours. Recipient Disting. Svcs. award Ariz. Ct. Appeals, 1985. Fellow Ariz. Bar Found. (founding); mem. Ariz. State Bar (bd. legal specialization 1979), Maricopa County Bar Assn. Avocation: all outdoor activities. Workers' compensation. Office: 722 E Osborn Rd Ste 120 Phoenix AZ 85014-5275

**WILMOTH, WILLIAM DAVID,** lawyer; b. Elkins, W.Va., July 11, 1950; s. Stark Amasa and Goldie (Johnson) W.; m. Rebecca Weaver, Aug. 21, 1971; children: Charles, Anne, Samuel, Peter. BS in Fin. cum laude, W.Va. U., 1972, JD, 1975. Bar: W.Va. 1975, U.S. Dist. Ct. (so. dist.) W.Va. 1975, U.S. Dist. Ct. (no. dist.) W.Va. 1976, U.S. Ct. Appeals (4th cir.) 1977, U.S. Supreme Ct. 1981, Pa. 1986. Law clk. to presiding judge U.S. Dist. Ct. (no. dist.) W.Va., Elkins, 1975-76; assoc. Bachmann, Hess, Bachmann & Garden, Wheeling, W.Va., 1976-77; asst. U.S. atty. U.S. Dept. Justice, Wheeling, 1977-80; ptnr. Schrader, Byrd, Byrum & Companion, Wheeling, 1980-93; U.S. atty. U.S. Dist. Ct. (no. dist.) W.Va., Wheeling, W.Va., 1993-99; ptnr. Steptoe & Johnson, Wheeling, 1999—. Past pres., bd. dirs. nat. trail coun. Boy Scouts Am., Wheeling; bd. dirs. Wheeling Nat. Heritage Area Corp., Wheeling YMCA, State Coll. Sys. W.Va., past chmn. Mem. ABA, Def. Research Inst., Def. Trial Lawyers W.Va., Rotary Club Wheeling (past pres.). Democrat. Health, Insurance, Criminal. Home: RR 4 Box 106 Wheeling WV 26003-9314 Office: Steptoe & Johnson PO Box 150 Wheeling WV 26003-0020

**WILNER, ALAN M.,** judge; b. Balt., Jan. 26, 1937. AB, Johns Hopkins U., 1958, MLA, 1966; JD, U. Md., 1962. Assoc. Sherbow, Shea & Doyle, Balt., 1962-65; asst. atty. gen. State of Md., 1965-68; assoc. Venable, Baetjer & Howard, Balt., 1968-71; asst., then chief legis. officer, govs. staff, 1971-77; assoc. judge Ct. of Spl. Appeals, 1977-90, chief judge, 1990-96; judge Ct. of Appeals, Md., 1996—; adj. faculty U. Md. Sch. of Law, U. Balt. Sch. of Law. Mem. ABA, Md. Bar. Found., Md. State Bar Assn., Balt. County Bar Assn. Office: Md Ct of Appeals County Cts Bldg 401 Bosley Ave Towson MD 21204-4420*

**WILNER, MORTON HARRISON,** retired lawyer; b. Balt., May 28, 1908; s. Joseph A. and Ida (Berkow) W.; m. Zelda Dunkelman, Nov. 3, 1940; children: James D., Thomas B., Lawrence J., Theodora. B.S. in Econs, U. Pa., 1930; J.D., Georgetown U., 1934. Bar: D.C. 1933. Gen. counsel emeritus Armed Forces Benefit Assn.; vice chmn. AFBA Indsl. Bank; bd. dirs. Armed Forces Benefit Svcs., Inc.; mem. emeritus Giant Food, Inc. Past pres. Jewish Community Center of Greater Washington.; Emeritus life trustee U. Pa.; past pres. Nat. Child Research Center; bd. govs. St. Albans Sch., 1968-72. Served to maj. USAAF; dep. dir. aircraft div. WPB 1942-45. Decorated Legion of Merit; recipient Ourisman Meml. award for civic achievement, 1970; Ben Franklin award U. Pa., 1973; alumni award of merit, 1975; Friar of Yr. award U. Pa., 1976; Wharton Sch. Club Joseph Wharton award, 1980; named to U. Pa. Baseball Hall of Fame, 1997. Mem. Fed. Bar Assn., ABA (ho. dels. 1971-73), D.C. Bar Assn., Internat. Bar Assn., Fed. Communications Bar Assn. (pres. 1969-70). Clubs: Army and Navy, Woodmont Country. Home: 2701 Chesapeake St NW Washington DC 20008-1042 Office: AFBA 909 N Washington St Ste 100 Alexandria VA 22314-1556

**WILSEY, STEVEN M.,** lawyer; b. St. Petersburg, Fla., Apr. 7, 1967; s. George F. and Elizabeth H. Wilsey; m. Vivian G. Wilsey, July 19, 1997. BS in Fin., Fla. State U., 1989; BS in Acctg., U. Fla., 1991, JD, 1992. Bar: Fla., 1992, U.S. Tax Ct., 1992. Ptnr. Fisher and Wilsey, P.A., St. Petersburg, Fla., 1992—. Mem. Suncoasters, St. Petersburg, 1998—; dir. Family Resources, Inc., St. Petersburg, 1995—. Mem. ABA, Fla. Bar Assn., Fla. Inst. CPAs, St. Petersburg Bar Assn. (past chair tax sect. 1992—), Exch. Club, Phi Delta Phi. Republican. Episcopalian. Probate, Estate taxation, Real property. Office: Fisher and Wilsey PA 275 4th St N Saint Petersburg FL 33701-3290

**WILSMAN, JAMES MICHAEL,** lawyer; b. Port Huron, Mich., Oct. 7, 1939; s. Leo George and Fay P. Wilsman; m. Sandra Keith, June 28, 1962 (div. Sept. 1988); children: Sarah, David. BA, Hiram (Ohio) Coll., 1961; JD, U. Mich., 1964. Bar: Ohio 1964, U.S. Dist. Ct. Ohio 1965, U.S. Ct. Appeals (6th cir.) 1965. Assoc. Squire, Sanders & Dempsey, Cleve., 1964-66; ptnr. Parks, Eisele, Bates & Wilsman, Cleve., 1966-86, Hahn Loeser & Parks, Cleve., 1986-90, Kelley, McCann & Livingstone, Cleve., 1990-93, Wilsman & Schoonover, Cleve., 1993—. Pres. Citizens League of Greater Cleve., 1974-76. Mem. ABA, Ohio Bar Assn. (family law sect. Cleve. chpt. 1986—), Cleve. Bar Assn. (chmn. family law sect. 1986—), Shaker Heights Country Club. Avocation: golf. Family and matrimonial, General civil litigation. Home: 19801 Van Aken Blvd Apt 210F Cleveland OH 44122-3651 Office: Wilsman & Schoonover 1920 Bond Ct Bldg 1300 E 9th St Cleveland OH 44114-1503

**WILSON, ABRAHAM,** lawyer; b. Zhitomir, Ukraine, Nov. 19, 1922; came to U.S., 1923; s. Isaac and Katie (Garshoig) W.; m. Gloria Bachman, July 26, 1949 (div. Dec. 1965); 1 child, Chana; m. Christine Haftkowycz, July 23, 1966; children: Marko A., Raissa. BS, Rutgers U., 1947, MS in Chemistry, 1950, PhD in Chemistry, 1951; JD cum laude, Seton Hall U., 1974. Bar: N.J. 1974, U.S. Dist. Ct. N.J. 1974, U.S. Patent Office 1974, U.S. Dist. Ct. (so. and ea. dists.) N.Y. 1984, U.S. Supreme Ct. 1984. Sr. scientist Colgate Palmolive Co., Jersey City, 1951-55; sr. chemist Am. Cyanamid Co., Bound Brook, N.J., 1955-62, group leader phys. chemistry rsch., 1962-72, sr. scientist, 1972-74; counsel, asst. to pres. Triangle-Price Co., Inc., South Brunswick, N.J., 1974-76; pvt. practice Piscataway, N.J., 1976-86; ptnr. Sherman, Kuhn, Justin, Wilson & Spadoro, P.A., Edison, 1986-89, Rubin, Rubin, Malgran & Kuhn, Piscataway, 1989-90, Smith & Schechter, Piscataway, 1990-94; pvt. practice Piscataway, 1993—; instr. phys. chemistry Rutgers U., 1951-56; gen. counsel Enzon, Inc., South Plainfield, N.J., 1981-87, outside counsel, 1987-90. Built Frank Lloyd Wright House, Millstone, N.J., 1955-56; patentee in field. Councilman Borough of Millstone, N.J., 1959-61, mayor, 1962-64; bd. dirs. Piscataway Community TV Authority, 1986-98, chmn. bd. dirs., 1986-88; bd. dirs. Middlesex County ARC, 1986—; mem.

environ. commn. Twp. of Piscataway, 1988—. 2nd lt. USAF, 1943-46, PTO. Vis. fellow Imperial Coll. Sci. Tech., London, 1961-62. Mem. Am. Chem. Soc., N.J. Bar Assn., N.J. Patent Bar Assn., Middlesex County Bar Assn., Am. Intellectual Property Assn. Democrat. Jewish. Fax no.: (732) 885-3409; email: awilson@owestinternet.net. General practice, Patent, Real property. Office: 508 Ellis Pky Piscataway NJ 08854-4515

**WILSON, ALMA,** state supreme court justice; b. Pauls Valley, Okla.; d. William R. and Anna L. (Schuppert) Bell; m. William A. Wilson, May 30, 1948 (dec. Mar. 1994); 1 child, Lee Anne. AB, U. Okla., 1939, JD, 1941, LLD (hon.), 1992. Bar: Okla. 1941. Law clk. fed. ct. Muskogee, Okla., 1941-43; pvt. practice Oklahoma City, 1943-47, Pauls Valley, 1948-69; judge Pauls Valley Mcpl. Ct., 1967-68; spl. judge Garvin & McLain Counties, Norman, Okla., 1969-75; dist. judge Cleveland County, Norman, Okla., 1975-79; justice Okla. Supreme Ct., Oklahoma City, 1982—, now chief justice, 1995-96. Mem. alumni bd. dirs. U. Okla.; mem. Assistance League; trustee Univ.Okla. Meml. Union. Recipient Guy Brown award, 1974, Woman of Yr. award Norman Bus. and Profl. Women, 1975, Okla. Women's Hall of Fame award, 1983, Okla Hall of Fame, 1996, Pauls Valley Hall of Fame, 1997, Pioneer Woman award, 1985, Disting. Svc. Citation U. Okla., 1985. Mem. AAUW, Am. Judicature Soc., Garvin County Bar Assn. (past pres.), Okla. Bar Assn. (co-chmn. law and citizenship edn. com.), Okla. Trial Lawyers Assn. (Appellate Judge of Yr. 1986, 89), Luther Bohanon Am. Inns Ct. XXIII, Altrusa, Am. Legion Aux. Office: Okla Supreme Ct State Capitol Oklahoma City OK 73105*

**WILSON, BRUCE BRIGHTON,** retired transportation executive, lawyer; b. Boston, Feb. 6, 1936; s. Robert Lee and Jane (Schlotterer) W.; m. Elizabeth Ann MacFarland, Dec. 31, 1958; children: Mabeth, Mary, Bruce Robert, Caroline Daly. AB, Princeton U., 1958; LLB, U. Pa., 1961. Bar: Pa. 1962. Assoc. Montgomery, McCracken, Walker & Rhoads, Phila., 1962-69; atty. U.S. Dept. Justice, Washington, 1969-79; dep. asst. atty. gen. antitrust div. U.S. Dept. Justice, 1971-76; spl. counsel Consol. Rail Corp., Phila., 1979-81, gen. counsel litigation and antitrust, 1981-82, v.p., gen. counsel, 1982-84, v.p. law, 1984-87, sr. v.p. law, 1987-97, sr. v.p. merger, 1997; bd. dirs. Phila. Indsl. Devel. Corp.; mem. mgmt. com. Concord Resources Group, 1989-91. Mem. corp. adv. bd. Phila. Mus. Art; chmn. Radnor Twp. Cable Comms. Coun., 1993—. Fellow Salzburg Seminar in Am. Studies (Austria), 1965; fellow Felz Inst. State and Local Govt., 1967. Mem. ABA, Phila. Bar Assn., Corinthian Yacht Club, Beach Club Cape May. General corporate, Antitrust. Home: 224 Chamounix Rd Wayne PA 19087-3606

**WILSON, BRUCE SANDNESS,** lawyer; b. Mar. 24, 1959; s. James C. and Jeanne T. Wilson; m. Lisa Westfall, Oct. 22, 1988; children: Jennifer, Andrew, Julia. BA, U. Va., 1981, JD, 1986. Bar: D.C. 1989, Va. 1988, Eng. and Wales 1996. Legis. asst. to Hon. Steve L. Neal U.S. Ho. of Reps., Washington, 1981-83; jud. clk. to Hon. Pasco M. Bowman U.S. Ct. Appeals (8th cir.), Kansas City, Mo., 1986-87; assoc. Covington & Burling, Washington and London, 1987-94, ptnr., 1994—. Mem. ABA (bus. sect.). General corporate, Finance, Securities. Office: Covington & Burling 1201 Pennsylvania Ave NW Washington DC 20004-2401

**WILSON, CHARLES FRANK,** lawyer, law educator; b. Scranton, Pa., July 11, 1943; s. Victor Peter and Rose (Sposito) W.; m. Diane P. Cardoni, June 30, 1973 (dec. 1979); m. Kathleen Geary, Sept. 16, 1983; children: Nicole, Lisa. BS in Edn., Villanova U., 1965; JD, Dickinson U., 1969. Bar: U.S. Dist. Ct. (mid. dist.) Pa. 1969, U.S. Ct. Appeals (3d cir.) 1975. Assoc. Laster, Strohl, Kane, Mattes & McDonald, Scranton, Pa., 1969-71, Epstein, O'Neill & Utan, Scranton, 1971-83; asst. dist. atty. Dist. Attys. Office, Scranton, 1974-80; ptnr. Epstein, Utan, Wilson & Marsili, Scranton, 1983—; instr. bus. law Pa. State U., 1971. Contbr. articles to profl. jours. Mem. ABA, Lackawanna County Bar Assn., Pa. Bar Assn., Pa. Trial Lawyers Assn., Scranton Lions Club. Republican. Roman Catholic. Avocations: fishing, boating, snorkeling. Personal injury, Workers' compensation, General practice. Office: Epstein Utan Wilson & Marsili 800 Penn Security Bank Bldg 142 N Washington Ave Scranton PA 18503-2200

**WILSON, CHARLES HAVEN,** lawyer; b. Waltham, Mass., July 27, 1936; s. Charles Haven Sr. and Kathryn (Sullivan) W.; children: Kathryn Wilson Self, Charles H. Jr. AB in Govt. magna cum laude, Tufts U., 1958; MS in Journalism, Columbia U., 1959; JD, U. Calif., Berkeley, 1967. Bar: D.C. 1968, U.S. Supreme Ct. 1972. Sr. law clk. to Chief Justice Earl Warren, 1967-68; from assoc. to counsel Williams & Connolly, Washington, 1968-90; sr. counsel ACLU of Nat. Capital Area, Washington, 1992-98; sr. staff atty. Bazelon Ctr. for Mental Health Law, Washington, 1998—; adj. prof. constitutional law Georgetown U. Law Ctr., 1971, 72. With U.S. Army, 1959-62. Mem. ABA (litigation sect. coun. 1976-79, dir publs. 1975-90, founding editor jour. Litigation 1974, bd. editors ABA Jour. 1985-91), Order of Coif. Democrat. Roman Catholic. Avocation: reading. General civil litigation, Civil rights, Constitutional. Office: Bazelon Ctr for Mental Health Law S 1212 1101 15th St NW Washington DC 20005-5002

**WILSON, CHARLES R.,** lawyer. BS, U. Notre Dame, JD. Bar: Fla. Law clk. to Hon. Joseph W. Hatchett U.S. Ct. Appeal for 11th Cir.; county judge 13th Jud. Cir. of Fla., 1987-90; sole practitioner Fla., 1981-86; U.S. magistrate judge U.S. Dist. Ct. (mid. dist.) Fla., 1990-94; U.S. atty. Middle Dist. Fla., 1994—. Mem. Fla. Bar Assn. (bd. govs. young lawyers sect.), Hillsborough County Bar Assn. (pres. young lawyers sect., Most Productive Young Lawyer award 1990). Office: US Atty 400 N Tampa St Ste 3200 Tampa FL 33602-4774

**WILSON, CHRISTIAN BURHENN,** lawyer; b. Balt., Feb. 24, 1946; s. Christian Columbus and Ruth Louise Frieda (Burhenn) W.; m. Kay Spencer Lewis, June 20, 1974. BA, Towson State U., 1968; JD, U. Balt., 1975. Bar: Md. 1976, U.S. Dist. Ct. Md. 1976, U.S. Supreme Ct. 1980. Staff atty. Monumental Properties, Inc., Balt., 1977-79; counsel Mall Mgmt. and Assocs., Balt., 1979-85; sole practice Bel Air, Md., 1986—; sr. lectr. Towson (Md.) State U., 1982-91. Served to 2d lt., Md. N.G., 1969-70. Mem. ABA, Md. State Bar Assn., Harford County Bar Assn., Sigma Delta Kappa. Republican. Lutheran. Real property, Landlord-tenant, Consumer commercial. Home: 257 Victory Ln Bel Air MD 21014-5431 Office: 139 N Main St # 306 Bel Air MD 21014-8808

**WILSON, CLAUDE RAYMOND, JR.,** lawyer; b. Dallas, Feb. 22, 1933; s. Claude Raymond and Lottie (Watts) W.; m. Emilynn Wilson; children: Deidra Wilson Graves, Melissa Woodard Utley, Michele Woodard Dunn. BBA, So. Meth. U., 1954, JD, 1956. Bar: Tex. 1956; CPA, Calif., Tex. Asso. firm Cervin & Melton, Dallas, 1956-58; atty. Tex. & Pacific R.R. Co., Dallas, 1958-60; atty. office regional counsel IRS, San Francisco, 1960-63; sr. trial atty. office chief counsel IRS, Washington, 1963-65; ptnr. Wilson & White L.L.P., Dallas, 1965-98, Vial, Hamilton, Koch & Knox LLP, Dallas, 1998—; chmn., Dallas dist. dir. IRS Adv. Commn., 1990-91. Mem. ABA, AICPA (coun. 1989-93), State Bar Tex., Dallas Bar Assn. (pres. sect. taxation 1969-70), Tex. Soc. CPAs (pres. 1989-90, pres. Dallas chpt. 1983-84), Greater Dallas C. of C. (chmn. appropriations and tax com. 1990-91), Crescent Club, Montaigne Club, Dallas Petroleum Club, Masons, Shriners, Delta Sigma Phi, Delta Theta Phi. Republican. Episcopalian. Taxation, general, State and local taxation, Personal income taxation. Office: Vial Hamilton Koch & Knox 4400 Bank One Ctr 1717 Main St Dallas TX 75201-7388

**WILSON, CYNTHIA DIANE,** lawyer; b. Detroit, Nov. 9, 1954; d. Henry and Naomi (Ross) W. Student, Mich. State U., 1971-73; BA in Psychology, Wayne State U., 1975; JD, Antioch Sch. of Law, Washington, 1979; Cleo Fellow, U. Cin. Sch. of Law, summer 1976. Bar: Mich. 1986, U.S. Dist. Ct. (ea. dist.) Mich. 1986. Dir. pub. edn. legal svcs. project Washington Lawyers' Com. for Civil Rights Under Law, Washington, 1978-82; exec. dir. Washington Parent Group, 1981-82; v.p. Galaxy of Stars Artist Mgmt., Washington, 1982-83; spl. projects asst. City of Detroit Council (Mich.), 1983-84; spl. cons., entertainment Jacksons' Victory Tour, Los Angeles and New York, 1984; spl. cons. USA for Africa, Los Angeles, 1985; exec. dir. Greater Mich. Minority C. of C., Detroit, 1986-87; pvt. practice Southfield and Detroit, Mich., 1987—; co-chmn. Los Angeles Human Relations Commn., Los Angeles, 1985; exec. dir. and gen. counsel Tower Exec. Sts. Assn., Detroit 1989—; dir. For Our Children's Sake, N.Y.C., 1986—; cons. Ballet Cultural Azteca, Saginaw, Mich., 1987—, Mich. Council for the Arts, Detroit, 1987—, Nat. Endowment for the Arts, Washington, 1983—. Co-author: A Primer for Parent and Community Involvement, 1981 (recipient Resolution award 1982). Legal counsel Oakland County Bus. Consortium and Investment Group, Southfield, 1988—. Named Outstanding Community Lawyer, Nat. Conf. of Black Lawyers, Washington, 1981, Outstanding Young Woman of Am., Ala. 1983, Legal Svcs. Corp. Fellow, Washington 1981; recipient certificate of merit D.C. Citizens for Better Pub. Edn., Washington 1979-80, cert. of appreciation Nat. Conf. of Black Lawyers, Washington, 1981, Resolution and award, D.C. Council, Washington, 1982. Mem. ABA, Oakland County Bar Assn., Wolverine Bar Assn. Avocations: writing, art, herbal gardening remedies, croptal and vibration healing. Entertainment, Insurance, General corporate. Office: 100 W Hickory Grove Rd Apt B4 Bloomfield Hills MI 48304-2163

**WILSON, DANA MICHELLE SIRKIS,** lawyer; b. Silver Spring, Md., Apr. 24, 1967. B in Gen. Studies, U. Md., 1989; JD, U. Md., Balt., 1992. Bar: Md., D.C., U.S. Dist. Ct. Md., U.S. Dist. Ct. D.C., U.S. Ct. Appeals (4th cir.). Jud. clk. Judge John C. Eldridge Md. Ct. Appeals, Annapolis, 1992-93; lawyer Shapiro and Olander, PA, Balt., 1993—. Consumer commercial, Labor. Office: Shapiro and Olander PA 36 S Charles St Fl 20 Baltimore MD 21201-3020

**WILSON, DARRYL CEDRIC,** lawyer, law educator, consultant, arbitrator; b. Chgo., Nov. 5, 1961. BFA, BBA, So. Meth. U., 1982; JD, U. Fla., 1984; LLM, John Marshall Law Sch., 1989. Bar: Ill. 1986, U.S. Ct. Appeal (7th cir.) 1986, Fla. 1995, U.S. Supreme Ct. 1995; cert. mediator/arbitrator, Ill., Fla. Law clk. Ctr. for Govtl. Responsibility, Gainesville, Fla., 1984-85; Reginald Heber Smith law fellow Cook County Legal Assistance, Harvey, Ill., 1985-86, staff atty. property specialist, 1986-87; pro bono coord. Cook County Legal Assistance, Oak Park, Ill., 1987; corp. atty. intellectual property divsn. Soft Sheen Products Corp., Chgo., 1987; real estate atty. UAW, Ford Legal Svcs., Lansing, Ill., 1988-89; of counsel Steck & Spataro, Chgo., 1989-93; pvt. practice Wilson and Assocs., Chgo., 1989—; prof. law Detroit Coll. Law, 1992-94; mng. ptnr., gen. counsel Freico Diversified Svcs., 1988—; prof. law Stetson U. Sch. Law, 1994—; cons. Pvt. Minority Small Bus. Assocs., Chgo., 1992, Detroit, 1992; mem. U.S. Copyright Arbitration Royalty Panel. Contbr. articles to profl. and acad. jours. Mem. ABA, Am. Intellectual Property Lawyers Assn., Black Entertainment and Sports Lawyers Assn., Internat. Intellectual Property Lawyers Assn., Ill. Bar Assn., Fla. Bar Assn., Sports Lawyers Assn., Lawyers for Creative Arts., Am. Arbitration Assn. (comml. arbitration panel mem.), World Intellectual Property Orgnl., Ct. of Arbitration for Sport. Avocations: music, sports, history. Real property, Intellectual property, General practice. Office: Stetson U Coll Law Saint Petersburg FL 33711 also: Wilson & Assoc PO Box 530052 Saint Petersburg FL 33747-0052

**WILSON, DEANNE MARIE,** lawyer; b. L.A., Apr. 5, 1944; d. William Wayne and Marie Antoinette (Arnerich) W.; m. Phillip Bradford Plank, Nov. 21, 1970 (div. Jan. 1990); 1 child, Bartlett Alfred Plank; m. Laurence Bernard Orloff, Apr. 26, 1992. AB in Sociology, Stanford U., 1966; JD, Seton Hall U., 1980. Bar: N.J. 1980, U.S. Dist. Ct. N.J. 1980, U.S. Ct. Appeals (3d cir.) 1984, N.Y. 1988, U.S. Tax Ct. 1988, U.S Supreme Ct. 1990. Law clk. Schenck Price Smith Knig, Morristown, N.J., 1979-80, N.J. Supreme Ct., Morristown, 1980-81; assoc. Lowenstein, Sandler, Brochin, Kohl, Fisher, Boylan, Roseland, N.J., 1981-83, Orloff Lowenbach Stifelman & Siegel, Roseland, N.J., 1983-87, Ellenport & Holsinger, Roseland, N.J., 1988; ptnr. Greenberg Margolis, Roseland, N.J., 1989-93; mng. atty. Mound Cotton & Wollan, East Hanover, N.J., 1993—; Bd. dirs. N.J. Inst. Continuing Edn., East Brunswick; mem. Supreme Ct. Civil Practice Commn., Trenton, N.J., 1985-93, Superior Ct. Commn. Women in Cts., Trenton, 1991-94. Fundraiser People for Whitman, Clark, N.J., 1992-94, Stanford (Calif.) U., 1988-91; master Arthur T. Vanderbilt Inns of Ct., Montclair, N.J., 1994—. Mem. ABA, N.J. State Bar Assn. (trustee 1993—), Essex County Bar Assn. (chair equity jurisprudence 1990—), Morris COunty Bar Assn. Republican. Roman Catholic. Avocations: scuba diving, travel, cooking, dog training. Environmental, Insurance, General civil litigation. Office: Mound Cotton & Wollan Box 78 72 Eagle Rock Ave Bldg 2 East Hanover NJ 07936-3151

**WILSON, DONALD KENNETH, JR.,** lawyer, publisher; b. Lancaster, Pa., Mar. 5, 1954; s. Donald Kenneth and Gloria (Payne) W.; m. Lauren Elaine O'Connor, Sept. 3, 1977; children: Donald, Tameka, Veronica, Matthew. BA, U. So. Calif., 1976; JD, N.Y. Law Sch., 1979. Bar: Calif. 1979, U.S. Ct. Appeals (9th cir.) 1979, U.S. Ct. Appeals (ea. dist.) Mich., 1996, U.S. Ct. Appeals, Colo. 1997. Ptnr. Law Office, L.A., 1987-92; pres., chief operating officer Quincy Jones Productions, L.A., 1983-86; assoc. Garey, Mason & Sloane, L.A., 1979-82; pres., CEO 4 Kids Music, L.A., 1989—, Dotevema Music, L.A., 1989—; of counsel Law Offices Johnnie L. Cochran Jr., L.A., 1992—. Producer: (video documentary) Frank Sinatra, 1984 (Vira award 1985, Grammy nomination 1985); contb. articles to newspapers. Trustee First African Meth. Episc. Ch., 1989-97; mem. NAACP, L.A., 1990. Recipient Citizenship award, Am. Legion, 1972; named Outstanding Young Men of Am., 1982, 83, Outstanding Contbr. to Community, Entertainment Civic Orgn., 1986. Avocations: tennis, reading, walking, fishing. Office: Law Offices Johnnie L Cochran Jr 4929 Wilshire Blvd Ste 1010 Los Angeles CA 90010-3825

**WILSON, DOUGLAS DOWNES,** lawyer; b. Astoria, N.Y., Jan. 20, 1947; s. Douglas and Mildred P. (Payne) W.; children: Douglas S., Debra J. AB, Grove City Coll., 1968; JD, Am. U., 1970; LLM, George Washington U., 1974. Bar: Md. 1971, D.C. 1971, U.S. Ct. Appeals (D.C. cir.) 1972, U.S. Ct. Mil. Appeals 1972, U.S. Supreme Ct. 1975, Va. 1978, U.S. Ct. Claims, U.S. Ct. Appeals (4th cir.), U.S. Dist. Ct. (we. dist.) Va. 1978, U.S. Dist. Ct. (ea. dist.) Va. 1979, U.S. Dist. Ct. (ea. dist.) Ky. 1981. Staff judge advocate Air Force Office Sci. Rsch., Arlington, Va., 1971-74; trial atty. Office Chief Trial Atty., Dept. Air Force, Wright Patterson AFB, Ohio, 1974-77; assoc. Martin, Hopkins & Lemon, P.C., Roanoke, Va., 1977-78; ptnr. Gardner, Moss & Brown, Washington and Roanoke, 1978-83; ptnr. Parvin Wilson & Barnett, P.C., 1984-96; mem. Wilson & Assocs., PC, 1996—; guest lectr. Old Dominion U., Norfolk, U. Wis., Madison, Alaska Pacific U., Anchorage, Va. Tech., Blacksburg. Deacon, First Presbyn. Ch., Roanoke, 1979-82, elder, 1989-92; mem. Roanoke Valley Estate Planning Coun., 1979-82; dir. Legal Aid Soc., Roanoke Valley, 1982-84; chmn. long range planning commn. Roanoke City Sch. Bd., 1986-93. Capt. USAF, 1971-77. Decorated Air Force Commendation medal with oak leaf cluster. Mem. ABA (pub. contract law sect.), Md. Bar Assn., D.C. Bar Assn., Fed. Bar Assn., Va. Bar Assn. (bd. govs., constrn. law sect. 1989-92), Nat. Assn. Bond Lawyers, Am. Road and Trans. Builders Assn., Va. Road and Trans. Builders Assn. (dir. 1993-96), Tenn. Road Builders Assn., Elks (exalted ruler 1973-74), Forest Ridge Civic Assn. (dir. 1974-77). Government contracts and claims, Labor, Construction. Home: 1410 West Dr SW Roanoke VA 24015-3736 Office: 1410 West Dr SW Roanoke VA 24015-3736

**WILSON, EDWARD N.,** lawyer; b. Bklyn., July 31, 1936; s. Elmer N. and Dorothy R. Wilson; m. Anne E. Wilburn; children: Maria-Teresa, Alicia Marie. AB, Holy Cross Coll., 1958; JD, Columbia U., 1963. Bar: N.Y. 1964, U.S. Ct. Appeals (2d cir.) 1966. Assoc. Willkie Farr & Gallagher, N.Y.C., 1963-72; v.p., sec., gen. counsel Loral Corp., N.Y.C., 1972-82; of counsel Eisenberg, Honig & Fogler, N.Y.C., 1982-93, Law Office of Michael Simon, N.Y.C., 1993—. Lt. (j.g.) USNR, 1958-60. Mem. ABA (corp. bus. sect., intellectual property sect.), N.Y. State Bar Assn. (corp. bus. sect., intellectual property sect.), Assn. of the Bar of the City of N.Y. Democrat. Roman Catholic. General corporate, Finance, Securities. Home: 38 Garden Pl Brooklyn NY 11201-4502 Office: Law Office of Michael Simon 317 Madison Ave New York NY 10017-5201

**WILSON, ELIZABETH DAVIS,** lawyer; b. Russellville, Ky., Feb. 24, 1958; d. Robert Americus Wilson and Martha Louise Oakley Wilson Dodson; m. James C. Dodson, Nov. 5, 1988 (div. Mar. 1997); children: Victor, Julia. BA, Vanderbilt U., 1980; postgrad., Georgetown U.; JD, U. Louisville, 1983. Bar: Ky., Pa., Md., U.S. Dist. Ct. Legal and legis. aide to Senator W. Ford, U.S. Senate, Washington, 1983-88; chief legis. lobbyist Humane Soc. U.S., Washington, 1988-89; pvt. practice, Russellville, Ky., 1989T; pub. defender Commonwealth of Ky., 199-95; asst. county atty. Logan County, Russellville, 1995—. Mem. Ky. Bar Assn. (ho. of dels. 1996—), 7th Jud. Bar Assn. (pres. 1995—). Family and matrimonial, Consumer commercial, Personal injury. Office: PO Box 366 350 W 4th St Russellville KY 42276-1323

**WILSON, GARY DEAN,** lawyer; b. Wichita, Kans., June 7, 1943; s. Glenn E. and Roe Zella (Mills) W.; m. Diane Kay Williams, Dec. 29, 1965; children: Mark R., Matthew C., Christopher G. BA, Stanford U., 1965, LLB, 1968. Bar: D.C. 1970, U.S. Dist. Ct. D.C. 1970, U.S. Ct. Appeals (D.C. cir.) 1972, U.S. Ct. Appeals (7th cir.) 1979, U.S. Ct. Appeals (2d cir.) 1983. Law clk. U.S. Ct. Appeals, 2d cir., N.Y.C., 1968-69, U.S. Supreme Ct., Washington, 1969-70; assoc. Wilmer, Cutler & Pickering, Washington, 1970-75, ptnr., 1976—; acting prof. law Stanford (Calif.) Law Sch., 1981-82. Bd. visitors Stanford Law Sch., 1990-92. Democrat. Federal civil litigation, Antitrust, Intellectual property. Home: 4636 30th St NW Washington DC 20008-2127 Office: Wilmer Cutler & Pickering 2445 M St NW Ste 900 Washington DC 20037-1435

**WILSON, GEORGE J.,** lawyer; b. Amityville, N.Y., May 7, 1957; s. George and Jeanine W.; m. Elizabeth Wilson; children: Nina Anne, Sarah Elizabeth. BA magna cum laude, Hofstra U., 1979; JD, St. John's U., 1984. Bar: N.Y. 1985, U.S. Dist. Ct. (so. and ea. dists.) N.Y. 1989. Assoc. Kelly Rode Kelly Burke, Mineola, N.Y., 1984-93; ptnr. Kelly Rode Kelly, Mineola, 1993—; cons. various ins. carriers. Mem. N.Y. State Bar Assn., Nassau/Suffolk Trial Lawyers Assn., Nassau County Bar Assn. Roman Catholic. Avocations: special education, jogging, sports. State civil litigation, Federal civil litigation, Appellate. Home: 12 Hawthorne St West Hempstead NY 11552-3145 Office: Kelly Rode & Kelly 330 Old Country Rd Ste 305 Mineola NY 11501-4170

**WILSON, HUGH STEVEN,** lawyer; b. Paducah, Ky., Nov. 27, 1947; s. Hugh Gipson and Rebekah (Dunn) W.; m. Clare Maloney, Apr. 28, 1973; children: Morgan Elizabeth, Zachary Hunter, Samuel Gipson. BS, Ind. U., 1968; JD, U. Chgo., 1971; LLM, Harvard U., 1972. Bar: Calif. 1972, U.S. Dist. Ct. (cen. dist.) Calif. 1972, U.S. Dist. Ct. (so. dist.) Calif. 1973, U.S. Ct. Appeals (9th cir.) 1975, U.S. Dist. Ct. (no. dist.) Calif. 1977, U.S. Supreme Ct. 1978, U.S. Dist. Ct. (ea. dist.) 1980. Assoc. Latham & Watkins, Los Angeles, 1972-78, ptnr., 1978—. Recipient Jerome N. Frank prize U. Chgo. Law Sch., 1971. Mem. ABA, Los Angeles County Bar Assn., Order of Coif, Calif. Club., Coronado Yacht Club. Republican. Avocations: lit., zoology. Federal civil litigation, General corporate, Mergers and acquisitions.

**WILSON, JAMES CHARLES, JR.,** lawyer; b. Birmingham, Ala., Sept. 13, 1947; s. James C. and Angelina (Serio) W.; m. Ann Bullock, Mar. 1, 1975; children: Brent Trammell, Lucy Bullock. BA, Tulane U., 1969, JD, 1972; MBA, Samford U., 1995. Ptnr. Bradley, Arant, Rose & White, Birmingham, 1972-90, Lange, Simpson, Robinson & Somerville, Birmingham, 1990-93, Sirote & Permutt, P.C., Birmingham, 1993-96; v.p. and gen. counsel Shop-A-Snak Food Mart, Inc., Birmingham, 1996; pres. Lucent Holdings, Inc., Golden, Miss., 1997-98; ptnr. Baker, Johnston & Wilson LLP, Birmingham, Ala., 1999—; adj. prof. internat. bus. transactions and internat. law U. Ala., Tuscaloosa, 1983-85, 89-96, internat. bus. transactions Cumberland Sch. Law, 1990-95. Author: Alabama Business Corporation Law, 1980; co-author: Corporate Law for the Healthcare Provider: Organization, Operation, Merger and Bankruptcy, 1993, Alabama Business Corporation Law Guide, 1995. Mem. adv. bd. Jr. League of Birmingham, 1984; bd. dirs. Ala. chpt. Am. Liver Found., 1993-97, sec., 1994-95; trustee The Altamont Sch., 1995—, v.p., 1996-98, pres., 1998—. With U.S. Army, 1972-76. Mem. ABA (sect. internat. law, tax and corp., banking and bus. law), Internat. Bar Assn., Nat. Health Lawyers Assn., Am. Hosp. Atty's. Assn., Ala. Bar Assn., Birmingham Bar Assn. (chmn. pub. rels. com. 1990), Birmingham Golf Assn. (pres., v.p., treas. 1982-84). Lodge: Rotary (pres. Birmingham-Sunrise club 1986-87). General corporate, Securities, Private international. Office: 1 Independence Plz Ste 322 Birmingham AL 35209-2634

**WILSON, JAMES EDWARD, JR.,** lawyer; b. Ft. Benning, Ga., Nov. 7, 1954; s. James E. Wilson and Joanne J. (Fister) Dimmitt; m. Joanna C. Favaro, Aug. 22, 1981; children: Katy, Sarah, Annie, Jessica, Henry. BS, U. Nev., 1977; JD, U. of The Pacific, 1981. Bar: Nev. 1981, Calif. 1983, U.S. Dist. Ct. Nev. 1981, U.S. Ct. Appeals (9th cir.) 1981. Dep. dist. atty. Elko (Nev.) County Dist. Atty. Office, 1981-82, dist. atty., 1983-85; pvt. practice Carson City, Nev., 1986—. Pres. PTO, Carson City, 1990; coach Am. Youth Soccer Orgn., Carson City, 1989-90. Mem. ABA, Assn. Trial Lawyers Am., Nev. Trial Lawyers Assn. Republican. Mem. LDS Ch. Personal injury, General civil litigation, Criminal. Office: 496 W Ann St Carson City NV 89703-3904

**WILSON, JAMES GWYNN,** defender; b. Burley, Idaho, Mar. 22, 1962; s. John Fredrick W. and Gwendolyn Gwynn; m. Sharon Barwick, Aug. 15, 1985; children: Christopher James, Scott Ian. BA in Anthropology, Brigham Young U., 1988; JD, U. Idaho, 1991. Bar: N. Mex. 1992, U.S. Dist. Ct. N. Mex. 1992. Intern Canyon County Prosecutor, Caldwell, Idaho, 1990, C. Alan Grider, Clarkson and Washington, Idaho, 1991; clk. Branch Law Firm, Albuquerque, 1991-92, assoc., 1992; atty. 1 N. Mex. Pub. Defender, Clovis, 1993-94, pub. defender 3, 1994-97, pub. defender 4, 1997—; judge Curry County Teen Ct., Clovis, 1997—. Bd. dirs. Youth Opportunities Unltd., Clovis, N. Mex., 1994, 97, 98, v.p. bd., 1994, 95, pres. bd. dirs., 1995-96; mem. regional adv. com. for mental health Region IV, N.Mex. Dept. Health, Behavioral Health Scis. Divsn., 1999—. Mem. Clovis Noonday Kiwanis (bd. dirs. 1998-99, 1st v.p. 1999—). Office: N Mex Pub Defender Dept 621 N Main St Clovis NM 88101-6656

**WILSON, JAMES WILLIAM,** retired lawyer; b. Spartanburg, S.C., June 19, 1928; s. James William and Ruth (Greenwaldt) W.; m. Elizabeth Clair Pickett, May 23, 1952; children: Susan Alexandra Wilson Albright, James William. Student, Tulane U., 1945-46; BA, U. Tex., Austin, 1950, LLB, 1951. Bar: Tex. 1951. Practiced in Austin, 1951-79; ptnr. McGinnis, Lochridge & Kilgore (and predecessors), 1960-76; of counsel Stubbeman, McRae, Sealy, Laughlin & Browder, 1976-79; sr. v.p. and gen. counsel Brown & Root, Inc., Houston, 1980-93, also dir.; of counsel Sewell & Riggs, Houston, 1993-95; asst. atty. gen., 1957-58; counsel to senate majority posting com. and legis. asst. to senate majority leader Lyndon B. Johnson, 1959-60; adj. prof. U. Tex. Law Sch., 1962-63, 95-97. Lt. (j.g.) USNR, 1952-55. Fellow Tex. Bar Found.; mem. ABA, Tex. Bar Assn., Am. Law Inst., Order of Coif, Phi Beta Kappa. General civil litigation, Construction, Environmental. Home: 3412 Timberwood Cir Austin TX 78703-1013

**WILSON, JEFFREY DALE,** lawyer; b. Pocatello, Idaho, May 20, 1955; s. Robert D. and Frances C. (Priest) W.; m. Margo A. Hoyt, Dec. 21, 1978; children: Robert J., Carrie A., Brooke M., Brian M. BA, Brigham Young U., 1979; JD, U. Kans., 1982. Bar: Okla. 1982, Tex. 1985. Assoc. Hall, Estill, Hardwick, Gable, Collingsworth & Nelson, Tulsa, 1982-84; corp. atty. Diamond Shamrock Corp., Dallas, 1985; assoc. Brice & Mankoff, Dallas, 1986-88, Winstead, McGuire, Sechrest & Minick, Dallas, 1988-90; internat. legal advisor GGS Co., Ltd., Tokyo, 1990-91, Jeffrey D. Wilson, Esq., Portland, Oreg., 1992—. Assoc. editor Kans. Law Review, 1980-82; contbg. author: Texas Foreclosure Law, 1990. Mem. ABA, Okla. Bar Assn., State Bar of Tex., Inter-Pacific Bar Assn. LDS. Avocations: sports, writing, music. Private international, Securities, Mergers and acquisitions. Office: 2002 Wembley Park Rd Lake Oswego OR 97034-2616

**WILSON, JOSEPH LOPEZ,** lawyer; b. El Aguaje, Sinaloa, Mex., Feb. 25, 1960; naturalized citizen, 1991; s. Adrian Lopez and Maria Juana (Lopez) Castro: m. Francine Cobb, Aug. 9, 1980 (div. 1985); 1 child, Eric Joseph; m. Lorraine Ann Evans, De. 21, 1987; children: Tabatha, Eric, Tiffany, Carlos. BS, U. Nebr., 1983; JD, Creighton U., 1986. Bar: Nebr. 1986, U.S. Dist. Ct. Nebr. 1986. Paralegal then atty. Chicano Awareness Ctr., Omaha, 1983-84, 87-88; atty. Cath. Hispanic Ministries, Omaha, 1986; pvt. practice law Omaha, 1987-88; with Legal Aid Soc., 1988-90; assoc. Krieger & Krieger, Omaha, 1990-91, Law Offices of Ivory Griggs, 1991-92, JLW-4-LAW, Omaha, 1992—; mem. Hispanic adv. com. Legal Aid Soc. Omaha, 1988-90. Mem. Hispanic adv. com. Met. Tech. C.C., Omaha, 1987—; mem. scholarship com. Creighton Law Sch., 1984-86; bd. dirs. Chicano Awareness Ctr. Mem. ABA, Nebr. Bar Assn., Hispanic Bar Assn., Assn. Trial Lawyers Am., Am. Immigration Lawyers Assn., Nebr. Notary Assn. Avocations: tennis, chess, fishing. Immigration, naturalization, and customs. Office: JLW-4-Law 11128 John Galt Blvd Ste 440 Omaha NE 68137-2397

**WILSON, JOSEPH MORRIS, III,** lawyer; b. Milw., July 26, 1945; s. Joseph Morris Jr. and Phyllis Elizabeth (Cresson) W.; children: Elizabeth J., Eric M.; m. Dixie Lee Brock, Mar. 23, 1984. BA, Calif. State U., Chico, 1967; MA, U. Washington, 1968; JD summa cum laude, Ohio State U., 1976. Bar: Alaska 1976, U.S. Dist. Ct. Alaska 1976, U.S. Ct. Appeals (9th cir.) 1986. Recruiter and vol. U.S. Peace Corps, People's Republic of Benin, 1969-73; legal intern U.S. Ho. of Reps., Washington, 1975; ptnr. Guess & Rudd P.C., Anchorage, 1976-88, chmn. comml. dept., 1981-82, ptnr. compensation com., 1982-84; mgr. Alaska taxes, sr. tax atty. BP Exploration Inc., Alaska, 1990-99; bus. law instr. U. Alaska, Anchorage, 1977-78. Mem. ABA, Alaska Bar Assn. Democrat. Club: World Affairs Coun. Avocations: music, sports, travel. State and local taxation, General corporate, Corporate taxation. Home and Office: 2556 Palmera Cir Las Vegas NV 89121-4016

**WILSON, JULIA ANN YOTHER,** lawyer; b. Dallas, Sept. 6, 1958; d. Julian White and Mary Ann (Estes) Yother; m. Eugene Richard Wilson, 1983. BA, East Ctrl. U., Ada, Okla., 1980; JD, U. Okla., 1983. Bar: Okla. 1990, Calif. 1993, D.C. 1995; U.S. Ct. Appeals (9th cir.) Calif. 1993, U.S. Supreme Ct. 1993, U.S. Dist. Ct. (ctrl. dist.) Calif. 1993, U.S. Dist. Ct. (we. dist.) Okla., 1997. Assoc. Law Office of George Rodda Jr., Newport Beach, Calif., 1984-96; sole practice law Oklahoma City, 1996-97; assoc. Coldiron, Wilson & Assocs., Oklahoma City, 1997—. Served to 1st lt. USAR, 1980-86. Mem. ABA, D.C. Bar Assn., Calif. Bar Assn., Oklahoma County Bar Assn., Okla. Bar Assn. (litigation sect.), Orange County Bar Assn. Banking, General corporate, General civil litigation. Office: Coldiron Wilson & Assocs 1800 E Memorial Rd Ste 106 Oklahoma City OK 73131-1827

**WILSON, KAREN LEROHL,** lawyer; b. Albuquerque, Sept. 15, 1950; d. John Kenneth Sr. and Ann Castleman (Lawrence) LeRohl; children: Teddy, Tommy. BA, William & Mary U., 1972; JD, Am. U., 1978; LLM, George Washington U., 1982. Bar: Va. 1979, Calif. 1984, U.S. Claims Ct. 1980, U.S. Ct. Appeals (4th cir.) 1981, U.S. Supreme Ct. 1982. Supr. law dept. Prudential Ins. Co., Washington, 1972-74; law clk. Arnold & Porter, Washington, 1975-78; atty., advisor Def. Logistics Agy., Alexandria, Va., 1978-80, Office Sec. Def., Washington, 1980-84; counsel TRW Corp., Redondo Beach, Calif., 1984-87; asst. group counsel Hughes Aircraft Co., El Segundo, Calif., 1987-92; group contr., dir. govt. rels. and compliance Allied Signal Inc., Torrance, Calif., 1992-94, v.p. bus. ethics and govt. compliance, 1994-97, v.p. govt. fin. and process excellence, 1998—. Mem. adv. bd.: Fed. Contracts Report; contbr. articles to profl. jours. Recipient Presdl. Sports award Pres. Carter, Washington, 1980; Disting. Youth award U.S. Army, 1976. Mem. ABA (dep. chmn. 1980), Fed. Bar Assn., Va. Bar Assn., Calif. Bar Assn., Nat. Contract Mgmt. Assn. (nat. advisor, trustee), Fin. Execs. Inst. (chmn. govt. bus. com.), Ethics Officers Assn., Inst. Mgmt. Accts., Inst. Internal Auditors, William and Mary Coll. Alumni Assn. (v.p. greater L.A. 1987-88), Am. Corp. Counsel Assocs., Aerospace Industries Assn. (vice chmn. procurement and fin. exec. com.), Inst. Noetic Scis., Cameron Sta. Tennis Club (pres. 1980), Michelob Light Tennis Club (capt. 1983). Republican. General corporate, Government contracts and claims. Office: Allied Signal Aerospace M/S Torr-38-1-01422 2525 W 190th St Torrance CA 90504-6002

**WILSON, KAREN WILKERSON,** paralegal; b. Reidsville, N.C., June 28, 1957; d. William Henry and Jean Gloria (Tiller) W.; married. Student, N.C. State U., 1975-77, Western Carolina U., Cullowhee, N.C., 1978-80; diploma, Profl. Ctr. Paralegal Studies, Columbia, S.C., 1988. Paralegal Ken H. Lester, Esquire, Columbia, 1989—; spkr. Alumni Profl. Ctr. Paralegal Studies, Columbia, 1988-95. Mem. ATLA, S.C. Trial Lawyers Assn. (paralegal rep. 1993-96). Democrat. Methodist. Office: Lester & Jones 1716 Main St Columbia SC 29201-2820

**WILSON, KEVIN LANG,** lawyer; b. Odessa, Tex., Dec. 3, 1962; s. Walter and Barbara W.; m. Janice L. Jones, July 17, 1993. BBA, Baylor U., 1984, JD, 1987. Bar: Tex. 1987, U.S. Dist. Ct. Tex. 1990. Asst. dist. atty. Ector County, Odessa, 1990-94; ptnr. Ashley & Wilson. Mem. Tex. Bd. Pub. Accountancy, Tri-Svc. Lions Club (pres. 1990-91). Avocation: residential rental properties. Personal injury, Criminal. Office: Ashley & Wilson 513 N Grant Ave Odessa TX 79761-5120

**WILSON, LESTER ARNAULD, III,** lawyer; b. Durham, N.C., Nov. 9, 1948; s. Lester Arnauld Jr. and Lillian May (McFetridge) W.; m. Cordelia Ruffin Plunkett, July 6, 1985; children: Thomas Middleton, Elizabeth Michie. BA, U. Va., 1970; JD, Emory U., 1973. Bar: Va. 1973, U.S. Dist. Ct. (ea. dist.) Va. 1973. Asst. city atty. City of Norfolk, Va., 1973-75; pvt. practice Charlottesville, Va., 1975-78, 92—; asst. commonwealth atty. Conty of Albemarle, Charlottesville, 1978-82, dep. commonwealth atty., 1982-90, commonwealth atty., 1990-92; dir. student legals svcs. U. Va., 1998—; bd. dirs. Community Diversion Incentive Program, Charlottesville, 1990-92, Jefferson Area Crime Stoppers, Charlottesville, 1988-92. Mem. Va. State Bar, Va. Bar Assn., Charlottesville-Albemarle Bar Assn. Episcopalian. Avocation: canoeing. General practice. Office: 204 University Way Charlottesville VA 22903-1822

**WILSON, LEVON EDWARD,** law educator, lawyer; b. Charlotte, N.C., Apr. 2, 1954; s. James A. and Thomasina Wilson. BSBA, Western Carolina U., 1976; JD, N.C. Ctrl. U., 1979. Bar: N.C. 1981, U.S. Dist. Ct. (mid. dist.) N.C. 1981, U.S. Tax Ct. 1981, U.S. Ct. Appeals (4th cir.) 1982, U.S. Supreme Ct. 1984; lic. real estate broker, N.C.; cert. mediator N.C. Alternative Dispute Resolution Commn. Pvt. practice Greensboro, N.C., 1981-85; asst. county atty. Guilford County, Greensboro, 1985-88; asst. prof. N.C. Agrl. & Tech. State U., Greensboro, 1988-91; asst. prof. Western Carolina U., Cullowhee, N.C., 1991-96, assoc. prof., head dept. bus. adminstrn., law and mktg., 1996—; pres. Trade Brokers Cons.; legal counsel, bd. dirs. Rhodes Assocs., Inc., Greensboro, 1982—; legal counsel Guilford County Sheriff's Dept., Greensboro, 1985-88; bd. dirs. Webster Enterprises, Inc. Contbr. articles to profl. jours. Bd. dirs. Post Advocacy Detention Program; active mem. Prison Litigation Study Task Force, Adminstrn. Justice Study Com. Recipient Svc. award Blacks in Mgmt., 1980, Excellence in Tchg. award Jay I. Kneedler Found. of Western Carolina U., 1994-95; Student in Free Enterprise fellow. Mem. ABA, N.C. Bar Assn., Acad. Legal Studies in Bus., Southeastern Acad. Legal Studies in Bus. (former editor-in-chief Jour. of Legal Studies in Bus., mng. editor), N.C. Assn. Police Attys., N.C. Real Estate Eudcators Assn., So. Acad. Legal Studies in Bus., Phi Delta Phi, Beta Gamma Sigma. Democrat. Methodist. Home: PO Box 620 Cullowhee NC 28723-0620 Office: Western Carolina U Coll of Bus Cullowhee NC 28723

**WILSON, MABLE JEAN,** paralegal; b. Pine Bluff, Ark.; d. James Arthur and Ruthia Mae (Dansby) Watson; children: Dana Eileen, Dana Kent Fuller. BS, cert. in paralegal studies, U. So. Calif., 1982-86. Dep. sheriff L.A. County, 1971-80; ind. paralegal Wilson's Divorce Clinic, L.A., 1980—. Participant Dist. Atty. Victim Witness Program, L.A., 1991; active Brotherhood Crusade, L.A., 1992. Recipient Merit award L.A. County Bar Assn., 1993. Mem. Assn. Family and Conciliation Cts., Folk Power Inc. (bd. dirs. 1993—), Alpha Svc. Co. (v.p. 1993—, profl. women's adv. bd., Women's Inner Circle of Achievement). Avocations: interior decorating, making stained glass windows, ceramics, painting, writing poetry. Office: 3860 Crenshaw Blvd Ste 201 Los Angeles CA 90008-1816

**WILSON, MICHAEL B(RUCE),** lawyer; b. Boise, Idaho, Aug. 5, 1943; s. George E. and Helen E. (Hughes) W.; m. Sarah J. Copeland, June 18, 1966; children: David B., Janet L. BS in Math., Oreg. State U., 1965, MS in Gen. Sci., 1966; JD, Lewis and Clark Coll., 1978. Bar: Oreg. 1978, U.S. Ct. Mil. Appeals 1978. Commd. 2d lt. USAF, 1966, advanced through grades to maj., 1978, served in Vietnam, 1968; chief of logistics 3d Weather Wing, Offut AFB, Nebr., 1969-71; chief maintenance 2d Weather Wing, Wiesbaden AFB, Fed. Republic Germany, 1971-75; chief civil law HQ Chanute TTC, Chanute AFB, Ill., 1978-80; chief civil and mil. affairs HQ 17th Air Force, Sembach AFB, Fed. Republic Germany, 1980-83; dir. telecommunications and contract law Air Force Communications Command, Scott AFB, Ill., 1983-87; counsel U.S. West Communications, Englewood, Colo., 1988—; chmn. Joint Svcs. Telecommunications Working Group, 1983-87, Air Force Comml. Communications Working Group, Scott AFB, 1985-87, AFCC Comml. Communications Working Group, Scott AFB, 1985-87, DOD Comml. Telecommunications Com. Liason Officer Boy Scouts Am., Sembach AFB, 1981-83; mem. U.S. West Coun. of Leaders. Recipient Mgmt./Adminstrv. Excellence award Interagy. Com. on Info. Resources Mgmt., 1987. Mem. ABA, Fed. Communications Bar Assn., Armed Forces Communications Electronics Assn., Nat. Contract Mgmt. Assn. Government contracts and claims, Communications, Computer.

**WILSON, MICHAEL MOUREAU,** lawyer, physician; b. Cheverly, Md., Dec. 30, 1952; s. Kenneth Moureau and Helen (Rice) Smith. BS, MIT, 1974; JD, Georgetown U., 1977, MD, 1986. Bar: D.C. 1977, N.Y. 1980, U.S. Dist. Ct. D.C. 1980, U.S. Dist. Ct. Md. 1992, U.S. Ct. Appeals (D.C. cir.) 1980, U.S. Supreme Ct. 1981. Law clk. Hon. John B. Hannum U.S. Dist. Ct., Phila., 1977-78; assoc. Cravath Swaine & Moore, N.Y.C., 1978-79; asst. to gen. counsel NSF, Washington, 1979-82; resident in psychiatry St. Elizabeth Hosp., Washington, 1986-89; pvt. practice med. malpractice litigation Washington, 1989—. Notes editor Am. Criminal Law Rev., 1976-77. Mem. ABA, Assn. Trial Lawyers Am., D.C. Trial Lawyers Assn., Phi Beta Kappa. Personal injury. Office: 1700 K St NW Ste 1007 Washington DC 20006-3815

**WILSON, PETER SINCLAIR,** financial services executive; b. Gloversville, N.Y., Sept. 16, 1958; s. Peter Sinclair and Lise (Steiner) W.; m. Patricia Marie Neugebauer, Aug. 20, 1983; children: Tyler Gideon, Bonnie Corinne, Kaitlyn Aileen. BS in Acctg., LeMoyne Coll., 1980; JD, Union U., 1983. Bar: N.Y. 1984, U.S. Dist. Ct. (no. dist.) N.Y. 1985, U.S. Tax Ct. 1986, Mass. 1993. Staff acct. Coopers & Lybrand, Syracuse, N.Y., 1983-84; assoc. Krolick & DeGraff, Albany, 1984-89; prin. DeGraff Wilson Ralston & Dwyer, P.C., Albany, 1989-94; pres. Clermont Ptnrs. Inc., Albany, 1994—; dir. fin. Firestix Industries L.P., 1995—. Office: Firestix Industries LP PO Box 6 Burnt Hills NY 12027-0006

**WILSON, REBECCA LYNN,** lawyer; b. Glen Ellyn, Ill., July 22, 1965; d. Wayne Robert Wilson and Rosemary Phylis (Stoecklin) Maglio. BA, U. Wis., 1987; JD, William Mitchell Coll., 1990; cert. mediation, Lakewood (Minn.) C.C., 1994. Bar: Minn. 1990, U.S. Dist. Ct. Minn. 1992. Law clk., assoc. Jack S. Jaycox Law Offices, Bloomington, Minn., 1988-93; assoc. Steffens, Wilkerson & Lang, Edina, Minn., 1993, Wilkerson, Lang & Hegna, Bloomington, 1993-95, Wilkerson, Hegna & Walsten, Bloomington, 1996—. Mem. ABA, Minn. State Bar Assn., Hennepin County Bar Assn. Family and matrimonial, General civil litigation. Office: Wilkerson Hegna & Walsten Ste 1100 3800 W 80th St Bloomington MN 55431-4426

**WILSON, RHYS THADDEUS,** lawyer; b. Albany, Ga., May 9, 1955; s. Joseph Farr Jr. and Betty Ann (Wilkins) W.; m. Carolyn Reid Saffold, June 2, 1984. AB, Duke U., 1976; JD, U. Ga., 1979; LLM, Emory U., 1985. Bar: Ga. 1979. Pvt. practice law Atlanta, 1979-89; sr. v.p., gen. counsel Monarch Capital Group, Inc., Atlanta, 1989-92, Jackson & Coker, Inc., Atlanta, 1992-93; pres. Jackson & Coker Locum Tenens, Inc., Atlanta, 1993-95; ptnr. Robins, Kaplan, Miller & Ciresi, Atlanta, 1995—; spkr. continuing legal edn. seminars. Contbr. articles to profl. jours. Mem. ABA, Ga. Bar Assn. (chmn. internat. law sect. 1987-88, exec. com. corp. and banking law sect. 1987-89, editorial bd. Ga. State Bar Jour. 1986-89), Atlanta Bar Assn. (editor newsletter 1984-86, Outstanding Svc. award 1986), Assn. for Corp. Growth, Atlanta Network Alliance, The Exec. Com. TEC, Atlanta Venture Forum, Capital City Club. Episcopalian. Mergers and acquisitions, Securities, General corporate.

**WILSON, RICHARD RANDOLPH,** lawyer; b. Pasadena, Calif., Apr. 14, 1950; s. Robert James and Phyllis Jean (Blackman) W.; m. Catherine Goodhugh Stevens, Oct. 11, 1980; children: Thomas Randolph, Charles Stevens. BA cum laude, Yale U., 1971; JD, U. Wash., 1976. Bar: Wash. 1976, U.S. Dist. Ct. (we. dist.) Wash. 1976, U.S. Ct. Appeals (9th cir.) 1977. Assoc. Hillis, Phillips, Cairncross, Clark & Martin, Seattle, 1976-81, ptnr., 1981-84; ptnr. Hillis, Cairncross, Clark & Martin, Seattle, 1984-87; ptnr. Hillis Clark Martin & Peterson, Seattle, 1987—, chmn. land use and environ. group; bd. dirs. Quality Child Care Svcs., Inc., Seattle; pres. Plymouth Housing Group, Seattle, 1998—, trustee, 1994—; lectr. various bar assns., 1980—. Contbr. articles to profl. jours. Chmn. class agts. Yale U. Alumni Fund, New Haven, 1985-87, class agt., 1971—, mem. class coun., 1991-96, mem. Western Wash. exec. com. Yale capital campaign, 1992-97, vice chmn. leadership gifts com. Yale 25th reunion, 1995-96; mem., vice chmn. Medina (Wash.) Planning Commn., 1990-92; chmn. capital campaign Plymouth Congrl. Ch., Seattle, 1995, moderator, pres. ch. coun., 1998—. Mem. ABA, Wash. State Bar Assn. (dir. environ. and land use law sect. 1985-88), Seattle-King County Bar Assn., Kingsley Trust Assn. (pres. 1996-98), Yale Assn. of Western Wash. Congregationalist. Avocations: acting, singing, rare book collecting. Real property, Land use and zoning (including planning), Environmental. Home: 2305 86th Ave NE Bellevue WA 98004-2416 Office: Hillis Clark Martin & Peterson 1221 2nd Ave Ste 500 Seattle WA 98101-2925 *Notable cases include: Barrie vs. Kitsap County, 1980; Sore vs. Snohomish County, 1983; Conv. Ctr. Coalition vs. City of Seattle, 1986; Orion Corp. vs. State, 1987, Cougar Mountain Assocs. vs. King County, 1988; King County vs. Central Puget Sound Growth Management Hearings Board, 1998, 1999.*

**WILSON, ROBERT BRYAN,** judge; b. San Mateo, Calif., Aug. 14, 1958; s. Robert Darrel and Helen Ann (Zidek) W.; m. Jacqueline A. Hallinan, Aug. 19, 1989. BS, No. Mich. U., 1980; JD, W.Va. Coll. Law, 1986. Bar: U.S. Dist. Ct. (no. and so. dists.) W.Va. 1986, U.S. Ct. Appeals (4th cir.) 1996, U.S. Supreme Ct. 1998. Atty. W.Va. Dept. Tax and Revenue, Charleston, 1986-92; pvt. practice Charleston, 1992-93, 95; assoc. Forman & Crane, L.C., Charleston, 1993-95; pvt. Erisa practice Charleston, 1992—; counsel ednl. com. W.Va. Senate, Charleston, 1991-92; adminstrv. law judge W.Va. Human Rights Commn., Charleston, 1995—. Avocations: cross country skiing, white water canoeing, traveling. Home: 1120 Swan Rd Charleston WV 25314-1426

**WILSON, ROBERT FOSTER,** lawyer; b. Windsor, Colo., Apr. 6, 1926; s. Foster W. and Anne Lucille (Svedman) W.; m. Mary Elizabeth Clark, Mar. 4, 1951 (div. Feb. 1972); children: Robert F., Katharine A.; m. Sally Anne Nemec, June 8, 1982. BA in Econs., U. Iowa, 1950, JD, 1951. Bar: Iowa 1951, U.S. Dist. Ct. (no. and so. dists.) Iowa 1956, U.S. Ct. Appeals (8th cir.) 1967. Atty., FTC, Chgo., 1951-55; pvt. practice, Cedar Rapids, Iowa, 1955—; pres. Lawyer Forms, Inc.; dir. Lawyers Forms, Inc. Democratic state rep. Iowa Legislature, Linn County, 1959-60; mem. Iowa Reapportionment Com., 1968; pres. Linn County Day Care, Cedar Rapids, 1968-70; del. to U.S. and Japan Bilateral Session on Legal and Econ. Rels. Conf., Tokyo, 1988, Moscow Conf. on Law and Bilateral Rels., Moscow, 1990; U.S. del. to Moscow conf. on legal and econ. rels., 1990. Sgt. U.S. Army, 1944-46. Mem. ATLA, Am. Arbitration Assn. (mem. panel arbitrators), Am. Legion (judge advocate 1970-75, 1987-93), Iowa Trial Lawyers Assn., Iowa Bar Assn., Linn County Bar Assn., Delta Theta Phi. Club: Cedar View Country. Lodges: Elks, Eagles. Personal injury, Probate, Workers' compensation. Home: 100 1st Ave NE Cedar Rapids IA 52401-1128 Office: 810 Dows Bldg Cedar Rapids IA 52403-7010

**WILSON, ROBERT LEE, JR.,** lawyer; b. Ahoskie, N.C., Oct. 2, 1954; s. Robert Lee and Mozelle (Rogers) W.; m. Alice Martin, May 22, 1976; children: Robert Lee III, Katherine Sterling. BA, U. N.C., 1976; JD, Wake Forest U., 1981. Bar: N.C. 1981, U.S. Dist. Ct. (ea. dist.) N.C. 1983, U.S. Ct. Appeals (4th cir.) 1984. Assoc. Hollowell & Silverstein, P.A., Raleigh, N.C., 1982-89, Maupin, Taylor & Ellis, P.A., Raleigh, 1989-98; ptnr. Smith Helms Mulliss & Moore, L.L.P., Raleigh, 1998—. Co-author: (chpt.) Legal Medicine, 1989; contbr. (monthly) Health Law Notes, 1985-89. Bd. dirs. Nolan D. Bunn Found., Raleigh, 1989-95, N.C. State U. Alumni of Delta Upsilon Found., 1982-92. Mem. ABA (health law sect.), Am. Health Lawyers Assn., N.C. Bar Assn. (exec. coun., sec., treas., vice chmn. health law sect. 1986-88, 96—, vice chmn. 199—), N.C. Soc. Health Care Attys. (officer 1985-89, 92-94, bd. dirs. 1991-94). Presbyterian. E-mail: bobúwilson@shmm.com. Health, Administrative and regulatory, General corporate. Home: 3420 Doyle Rd Raleigh NC 27607-3302 Office: Smith Helms Mulliss & Moore LLP 2800 Two Hannover Sq Raleigh NC 27601

**WILSON, ROGER CALVIN,** lawyer; b. Atlanta, Mar. 20, 1963; s. Calvin Jr. and Jewel M. Wilson; m. Virginia Grace Mokarry, Dec. 30, 1995. BA in Internat. Affairs, George Washington U., 1985; JD, U. Ga., 1989; LLM in Internat. Law, NYU, 1995. Bar: Ga. 1990, D.C. 1992, U.S. Dist. Ct. (no. dist.) Ga., U.S. Ct. Appeals (fed. and 11th cirs.), U.S. Ct. Internat. Trade. Law clk. Judge R. Kenton Musgrave, N.Y.C., 1989-91; atty. Morgan, Lewis & Rockius, Washington, 1991-95, Evert & Weathersby, Atlanta, 1995—. Editor-in-chief Ga. Jour. Internat. and Comparative Law, 1988-89. Vassar Wooley scholar U. Ga. Sch. Law, Athens, 1985-89. Mem. John Randolph Club, Phi Beta Kappa. General civil litigation, Product liability, Private international. Office: Evert & Weathersby 3405 Piedmont Rd NE Ste 225 Atlanta GA 30305-1764

**WILSON, ROGER GOODWIN,** lawyer; b. Evanston, Ill., Sept. 3, 1950; s. G. Turner Jr. and Lois (Shay) W.; m. Giovinella Gonthier, Mar. 7, 1975. AB, Dartmouth Coll., 1972; JD, Harvard U., 1975. Bar: Ill. 1975, U.S. Dist. Ct. (no. dist.) Ill. 1976, U.S. Ct. Appeals (7th cir.) 1977, U.S. Dist. Ct. (no. dist.) Ind. 1985. Assoc. Kirkland & Ellis, Chgo., 1975-81, ptnr., 1981-86; sr. v.p., gen. counsel, corp. sec. Blue Cross/Blue Shield, 1986—; speaker Nat. Healthcare Inst., U. Mich., 1987-93, Am. Law Inst.-ABA Conf. on Mng. and Resolving Domestic and Internat. Bus. Disputes, N.Y.C., 1988, Washington, 1990; cert. health cons. program Purdue U., 1993-94, Inst. for Bus. Strategy Devel., Northwestern U., 1993-94, The Health Care Antitrust Forum, Chgo., 1995, Nat. Health Lawyers Assn. Managed Care Law Inst., 1995, Nat. Health Lawyers Assn. Conf. on Tax Issues in Healthcare Orgns., 1996. Contbg. editor Health Care Fraud and Abuse Newsletter, 1998—. Advisor Constl. Rights Found., Chgo., 1982-87; mem. So. Poverty Law Ctr., Montgomery, Ala., 1981—. Mem. ABA, Nat. Health Lawyers Assn. (spkr. 1984), Legal Assistance Found. of Chgo. (bd. dirs. 1998—), Chgo. Coun. Lawyers (bd. govs. 1988-92), Coun. Chief Legal Officers (conf. bd. 1995—), Coun. Corp. Governance (donf. bd. 1998—), Dartmouth Lawyers Assn., Legal Assistance Found. Chgo. (bd. dirs. 1998—), Sinfonietta (bd. dirs. 1987—), Univ. Club, Mid-Am. Club, Phi Beta Kappa. Avocations: French lang. and culture. Health, General corporate, Insurance. Home: 151 N Michigan Ave Apt 2819 Chicago IL 60601-7522 Office: Blue Cross/Blue Shield 225 N Michigan Ave Ste 200 Chicago IL 60601-7601

**WILSON, STEPHEN VICTOR,** federal judge; b. N.Y.C., Mar. 26, 1942; s. Harry and Rae (Ross) W. B.A. in Econs., Lehigh U., 1963; J.D., Bklyn. Law Sch., 1967; LL.M., George Washington U., 1973. Bars: N.Y. 1967, D.C. 1971, Calif. 1972, U.S. Ct. Appeals (9th cir.) U.S. Dist. Ct. (so., cen. and no. dists.) Calif. Trial atty. Tax div. U.S. Dept. Justice, 1968-71; asst. U.S. atty., L.A., 1971-77, chief spl. prosecutions, 1973-77; ptnr. Hochman, Salkin & Deroy, Beverly Hills, Calif., from 1977; judge U.S. Dist. Ct. (cen. dist.) Calif., L.A., 1985—; adj. prof. law Loyola U. Law Sch., 1976-79; U.S. Dept. State rep. to govt. W.Ger. on 20th anniversary of Marshall Plan, 1967; del. jud. conf. U.S. Ct. Appeals (9th cir.), 1982-86. Co-editor Tax Crimes--Corporate Liability, BNA Tax Management Series, 1983; contbr. articles to profl. jours. Recipient Spl. Commendation award U.S. Dept. Justice, 1977. Mem. ABA, L.A. County Bar Assn., Beverly Hills Bar Assn. (chmn. criminal law com.), Fed. Bar Assn. Jewish. Contbr. articles to profl. jours. Home: 9100 Wilshire Blvd Beverly Hills CA 90212-3415 Office: US Courthouse 312 N Spring St Ste 217J Los Angeles CA 90012-4704

**WILSON, SUSAN ELIZABETH,** lawyer; b. Charlottesville, Va., Aug. 17, 1957; d. Colon Hayes Jr. and Patricia Ann (Webb) W. AA, Emory U., 1977, BA, 1979; MA in Journalism, U. Ga., 1984, JD, 1991. Bar: Ga. 1991, N.C. 1992, U.S. Dist. Ct. (we. dist.) N.C. 1994. Judicial intern Supreme Ct. Ga., Atlanta, 1989; summer clk., summer assoc. B.J. Rounds & Assocs., Athens, Ga., 1990, 91; vol., ind. contractor Pisaah Legal Svcs., Asheville, N.C., 1991-92; ptnr. Wilson & Rudolph, Black Mountain, N.C., 1992; atty. Buncombe County Dept. Social Svcs., Asheville, 1992—; mem. adv. bd. Buncombe County Teen Ct., 1994—, chair adv. bd., 1996—; mem. adv. bd. Buncombe Alternatives, Inc., 1995—, vice-chair, 1998—; mem. adv. bd. Earn and Learn, 1997—. Mem. Phi Sigma Tau. Episcopalian. Avocations: reading, hiking, music. Home: 6 Squirrel Ridge Dr Weaverville NC 28787-8316 Office: Buncombe County IV-D 40 Coxe Ave Asheville NC 28801-3307

**WILSON, T. MICHAEL,** lawyer; b. Wichita, Kans., July 22, 1947. BBA, Wichita State U., 1969; JD, Washburn U., 1972. Bar: Kans., U.S. Supreme Ct., U.S. Ct. Appeals (10th cir.), U.S. Dist. Ct. Kans. Ptnr. Stinson Lasswell & Wilson, L.C., Wichita, 1972—. Fellow Am. Acad. Matrimonial Lawyers; mem. ABA, ATLA (bd. govs., bd. editors family law), Kans. Bar Assn., Kans. Trial Lawyers Assn., Wichita Bar Assn. Avocations: golf, skiing. Fax: 316-264-3791. E-mail: stinson@southwind.net. Family and matrimonial. Office: Stinson Lasswell & Wilson LC 300 W Douglas Ave Ste 430 Wichita KS 67202-2916

**WILSON, THOMAS BUCK,** lawyer; b. Hartford, Conn., Nov. 25, 1939; s. Thomas S. and Mildred M. (Buck) W.; m. Gayle L. Davis, Aug. 26, 1967; children: Peter B., Jennifer D., Matthew T. BA, Trinity Coll., 1961; JD, U. Conn., 1967. Bar: Conn. 1967, U.S. Dist. Ct. Conn. 1967, u.S. Ct. Appeals (2nd cir.) 1975, U.S. Supreme Ct. 1973. Atty. Suisman, Shapiro, Wool, Brennan & Gray, P.C., New London, Conn., 1967—; town atty., Ledyard, Conn., 1971-79, 83-91, 95—, Plainfield, Conn., 1982-90; apptd. state atty. trial ref. State of Conn., 1988—; judge Mohegan Tribal Gaming Disputes Ct., 1996—. Author with other Conn. Lawyer's Basic Practice Manual Conn. Civil Procedure, 1972, rev. 1986. First lt. USAF, 1961-64. Mem. ABA, Conn. Bar Assn., New London County Bar Assn., U. Conn. Law Sch. AlumniAssn. (pres. 1983-84), Lions (pres. 1988-89, 97—), KC. Democrat. Roman Catholic. Avocations: hiking, fishing. General practice, Personal injury. Office: Suisman Shapiro Wool Brennan & Gray Union Plaza New London CT 06320-6410

**WILSON, THOMAS MATTHEW, III,** lawyer; b. Ware, Mass., Feb. 22, 1936; s. Thomas Matthew Jr. and Ann Veronica (Shea) W.; m. Deborah Ord Lockhart, Feb. 10, 1962; children: Deborah Veronica, Leslie Lockhart, Thomas Matthew IV. BA, Brown U., 1958; JD, U. Md., 1971. Bar: Md. 1972, U.S. Ct. Appeals (4th cir.) 1976, U.S. Supreme Ct. 1977. Sales mgr. Mid-Ea. Box Mfg. Co., Balt., 1966-74; asst. atty. gen., chief antitrust divsn. State of Md., Balt., 1974-79; ptnr. Tydings & Rosenberg, LLP, Balt., 1979—. Author: Defending an Antitrust Action Brought by a State, 1987, The Spectre of Double Recovery in Antitrust Federalism, 1989; co-author: Reciprocity and the Private Plaintiff, 1972; mem. editl. adv. bd. Bur. of Nat. Affairs Antitrust and Trade Regulation Report, 1979—. Mem. ABA (sect. on antitrust law 1974—, chmn. state antitrust enforcement com. 1986-89, antitrust sect. coun. 1990-93, coord. com. on legal edn. 1993—), Md. Bar Assn. (antitrust subcom. 1975-78), Internat. Bar Assn. (sect. on bus. law, antitrust law and monopolies com. 1983—), Churchwarden's Chess Club. Republican. Antitrust, Franchising, Appellate. Home: Baobab Farm Hampstead MD 21074 Office: Tydings & Rosenberg LLP 100 E Pratt St Baltimore MD 21202-1009

**WILSON, THOMAS RUSSELL,** lawyer; b. Des Moines, Jan. 10, 1965; s. Russell Harry and Beverly Ann (Burchfield) W. BS, U. Iowa, 1986; JD, Harvard U., 1990. Bar: Calif. 1990. Fgn. lawyer Nauta Dutilh, Rotterdam, The Netherlands, 1990; fellow European Commn., Brussels, 1991; assoc. Morgan, Lewis & Bockius, L.A., 1992-94; br. gen. counsel Valeo, S.A., Paris, 1994-97; assoc. Brobeck Phleger & Harrison, LLP, Palo Alto, Calif., 1997—. Mem. State Bar of Calif. (intellectual property sect.), Bar Assn. San Francisco (com. sports and entertainment law). E-mail: twilson@bi-obeck.com. Computer, Intellectual property, Private international. Home: 1478 Page St Apt 4 San Francisco CA 94117-2081 Office: Brobeck Phleger & Harrison 2 Embarcadero Pl 2200 Geng Rd Palo Alto CA 94303-3322

**WILSON, VIRGIL JAMES, III,** lawyer; b. San Jose, Calif., July 25, 1953; s. Virgil James Wilson Jr. and Phyllis Emily (Mothorn) Brasser; m. Sara Fahey; children: Gabriel James Hekili, Alexander Robert Kaimoku, Hayley Noelani, Maia E. Kailani. BA with honors, U. Calif., Santa Cruz, 1975; JD cum laude, U. Santa Clara, 1981. Bar: Calif. 1981, U.S. Dist. Ct. (no. dist.) Calif. 1981, Hawaii 1982, U.S. Dist. Ct. Hawaii 1982, U.S. Ct. Appeals (9th cir.) 1987, U.S. Supreme Ct. 1987, Oreg. 1990, U.S. Dist. Ct. Oreg. 1998; lic. pvt. investigator, Hawaii. Atty. James Krueger P.C., Wailuku, Maui, 1981-83; resident counsel Sterns & Ingram, Honolulu, 1983-89; pvt. practice Kailua, Hawaii, 1989—; of counsel Law Offices of Ian L. Mattoch, 1993-96; assoc. Thorp, Purdy, Jewett, Urness & Wilkinson, P.C., Springfield, Oreg., 1998—; owner Wilson Investigations, Santa Cruz, 1978-81, Honolulu, 1981—. Mem. ATLA, Hawaii Bar Assn., Calif. State Bar Assn., Oreg. Bar Assn., Oreg. Trial Lawyers Assn. Avocation: profl. magician. Personal injury, Product liability, General civil litigation. Office: Thorp Purdy Jewett Urness & Wilkinson PC Pacific Continntl Bank Bldg 1011 Harlow Rd Ste 300 Springfield OR 97477-1142 also: PO Box 70167 Eugene OR 97401-0139

**WILSON, WESLEY M.,** retired lawyer, writer; b. Mangum, Okla., June 21, 1927; s. Frank Henry and Fern (McCool) W.; m. Marjorie Helen Montague, Sept. 7, 1957; children: Larry Arthur, Bruce Alan. BS, Ill. Inst. Tech., Chgo., 1952; MBA, U. Chgo., 1954; JD, U. Wash., 1960. Bar: Wash., 1960. With AT&T Long Lines, Chgo., 1948-50; equipment engr. Western Elec. Co., Chgo., 1952-54; pers. asst., pers. dir. West Coast Telephone Co., Everett, Wash., 1954-57; atty. NLRB, Seattle, 1960-69; labor rels. atty. Wilson & Lofland, Yakima, Wash., 1970-85; part-time mgmt. cons. Donworth & Assocs., Seattle, 1957-58; instr. pers. rels. U. Wash., Seattle, 1958; instr. labor rels. City U., Yakima, 1980-84. Author: Labor Law Handbook and 10 supplements, 1963, 68-85, The Labor Relations Primer, 1973, Know Your Job Rights, 1976, Countries and Cultures of the World, Then and Now, (3 vols.), 1997, Five Languages Made Simpler, French, Italian, English, Spanish, German, 1997, Curious Customs and Bizarre Beliefs Around the World, 1999. With U.S. Merchant Marines, 1945-46, U.S. Army, 1946-48. Mem. Wash. State Bar Assn., Yakima County Bar Assn. (pres. 1984-85). Avocations: travel, history, economics, languages, backpacking. Home: 3300 Carpenter Rd SE Apt 113 Olympia WA 98503-4012

**WILSON, WILLIAM BERRY,** lawyer; b. Cape Girardeau, Mo., June 17, 1947; s. Charles F. and Anita (Bartlum) W.; m. Suzanne T. Wilson; children: Matthew James, Sarah Talbot. BA summa cum laude, Westminster Coll., 1969; JD, U. Mich., 1972. Bar: Fla. 1972, U.S. Dist. Ct. (mid. dist.) Fla. 1972, U.S. Ct. Appeals (11th cir.) 1972, U.S. Supreme Ct. 1976; bd. cert. Civil Trial Lawyer, 1983—. Ptnr. Maguire, Voorhis & Wells P.A., Orlando, Fla., 1977-98; mng. dir. Maguire, Voorhis & Wells P.A., Orlando, 1982-84, pres., 1984-97, chmn., 1997-98; ptnr. Holland & Knight LLP, Orlando, 1998—; mem. exec. com. and trust com., bd. dirs. SunTrust Bank Ctrl. Fla., N.A. Bd. dirs. Econ. Devel. Authority, Orlando, 1992-97, chmn. 1994-95, subcom. chmn. Project 2000, Orlando, 1985-87; bd. dirs. Fla. Symphony, Orlando, 1985-93, Fla. TaxWatch, Inc., 1992-98, Rotary, Univ. Club, Country Club of Orlando, Citrus Club, 1994—, chmn., 1998—; bd. dirs. U. Ctrl. Fla. Found., 1996—, Jr. Achievement, 1998—; trustee Orlando Mus. Art, 1993—, pres., 1997—; bd. overseers Crummer Sch. Bus. Rollins Coll., 1994—; chmn. Fla. Residential Property & Casualty Joint Underwriting Assn., 1995—. Mem. ABA, Fla. Bar Assn. (mem. exec. coun. trial lawyers sect. 1987—, chmn. 1996-97, code and rules of evidence com. 1986-88, chmn. 1996-97), Orange County Bar Assn. (chmn. fed. and state practice sect. 1982-84, jud. rels. com. chmn., 1987—, chmn. professionalism com. 1997-99), Am. Bd. Trial Advocacy, Def. Rsch. Inst., Fla. Def. Lawyers Assn, Greater Orlando C. of C. (bd. dirs., exec. com. 1997—). Republican. Presbyterian. Avocations: tennis, scuba diving. E-mail: bwilson@hklaw.com. Federal civil litigation, State civil litigation, Construction. Office: Holland & Knight LLP PO Box 1526 200 S Orange Ave Orlando FL 32801-3410

**WILSON, WILLIAM R., JR.,** judge; b. 1939. Student, U. Ark., 1957-58; BA, Hendrix Coll., 1962; JD, Vanderbilt U., 1965. Atty. Autrey & Goodson, Texarkana, Ark., 1965-66, Wright, Lindsey & Jennings, Little Rock, 1969-72, Wilson & Hodge, Little Rock, 1972-74; prin. William R. Wilson Jr., P.A., Little Rock, 1974-80, Wilson & Engstrom, Little Rock, 1980-83, Wilson, Engstrom & Vowell, Little Rock, 1984, Wilson, Engstrom, Corum & Dudley, Little Rock, 1984-93; judge U.S. Dist. Ct. (ea. dist.) Ark., Little Rock, 1993—; chair Ark. Supreme Ct. Com. on Model Criminal Jury Instrns., 1978—; active Ark. Supreme Ct. Com. on Civil Practice, 1982—. Lt. USN, 1966-69. Named Disting. Alumnus, Hendrix Coll., 1993, Outstanding Lawyer, Pulaski County Bar Assn., 1993. Mem. ABA, ATLA, Am. Bd. Trial Advocates (Nat. Civil Justice award 1992), Am. Coll. Trial Lawyers, Internat. Acad. Trial Lawyers, Internat. Soc. Barristers, Ark. Bar Assn. (Outstanding Lawyer 1991), S.W. Ark. Bar Assn., Ark. Trial Lawyers Assn. (pres. 1982, Outstanding Trial Lawyer 1988-89). Office: US Dist Ct Ea Dist 600 W Capitol Ave Rm 153 Little Rock AR 72201-3329

**WILSON-COKER, PATRICIA ANNE,** lawyer, social service administrator, educator; b. Willimantic, Conn., Aug. 26, 1950; d. Bertram W. and Mary Evelyn (Spurlock) Wilson; m. Edward H. Coker (div. 1973). BA, U. Conn., 1977, MSW, JD, 1981. Bar: Conn. 1981. Asst. prof. social work, dir. Ctr. for Child Welfare Studies St. Joseph Coll., West Hartford, Conn., 1981-86; assoc. prof. social work, chair social work & child welfare St. Joseph Coll., West Hartford, 1986-88; exec. asst. to commr., statewide dir. divsn. children protective svcs. Conn. Dept. Children and Youth Svcs., Hartford, 1988-91, mediation panelist, Juan F. consent decree, 1990-91; monitoring panelist dept. children and youth svcs. Fed. Dist. Ct., New Haven, 1991-92; dir. social svc. planning & interdisciplinary program devel. Dept. Social Svcs., Hartford, Conn., 1992-93; dir. adminstrv. hearings and appeals Dept. Social Svcs., Middletown, Conn., 1993-95; regional administr. north ctrl. region Dept. Social Svcs., Conn., 1995-99; commr. Dept. Social Scis., Hartford, Conn., 1999—; instr. U. Conn., Storrs, summer 1977, social rsch. asst. philosophy dept., summer 1978; legal social work intern juvenile unit Hartford (Conn.) Legal Aid Soc., 1978-79, legal rschr. juvenile unit, summer 1979, legal rschr., fall 1979; instr. Ea. Conn. State U., Willimantic, spring 1980; cons. New Eng. Clin. Assocs., West Hartford, 1985-86, Office of Policy & Mgmt., State Conn., Hartford, 1988, Perisky and Daniels, Hartford, 1988; apptd. Juvenile Justice Adv. Com. to the Office of Policy and Mgmt., State Conn., 1983-89, Conn. Task Force on Family Violence, 1985-86, Criminal Sanctions Task Force, 1987, Child Support Task Force, 1987-88, Conn. Children's Commn., 1988-91; assoc. prof. St. Joseph Coll., West Hartford, 1981-88, So. Conn. State Coll., New Haven, 1990—; trustee ednl. policies St. Joseph Coll., 1980-97, chair, 1997; lectr. and presenter in field. Contbr. articles to profl. jours. Recipient Judge Thomas Gill award Conn. Children in Placement Program, 1991, Annual award Conn. Coun. on Adoption, 1991; named Educator of Yr., Conn. Girl Scout Coun., 1987. Office: Dept Social Svcs 25 Sigourney St Hartford CT 06106-5001

**WILT, VALERIE RAE,** lawyer; b. Springfield, Ohio, June 8, 1963; m. Gregory L. Wilt, July 11, 1987; children: Arianne Rae, Samantha Moore. BA, Miami U., Oxford, Ohio, 1985; JD cum laude, U. Dayton, 1988. Bar: Ohio 1988, U.S. Dist. Ct. (so. and we. dists.) Ohio 1988, U.S. Ct. Appeals (6th cir.) 1994. Assoc. Bieser, Greer & Landis, Dayton, Ohio, 1988-90; ptnr. Juergens Wilt & Strilecky's, Springfield, 1991—; spkr. on risk mgmt. for vol. workshops; spkr. to Springfield Legal Secs. Assn. on Case Mgmt. Mem. Rep. Nat. Com., 1994-98; vol. spkr. career day United Way. Named Lawyer of Yr. Greater Dayton Area Lawyers Vol. Projects, 1989. Mem. Ohio State Bar Assn., Clark County Bar Assn., Springfield Law Libr. Assn., Springfield-Clark County C. of C. Republican. Roman Catholic. Avocations: reading, athletics, speaking. General practice. Office: Juergens Wilt & Strileckys 200 N Fountain Ave Springfield OH 45504-2596

**WIMBROW, PETER AYERS, III,** lawyer; b. Salisbury, Md., Apr. 11, 1947; s. Peter Ayers Jr. and Margaret (Johnson) W. BS, East Tenn. State U., 1970; JD, Washington and Lee U., 1973. Bar: Md. 1973, U.S. Dist. Ct. Md. 1974, U.S. Ct. Appeals (4th cir.) 1979, U.S. Supreme Ct. 1979, U.S. Tax Ct. 1981, U.S. Ct. Appeals (D.C. cir.) 1981, U.S. Ct. Appeals (3d cir.) 1985. Sole practice Ocean City, Md., 1974—. Photographer, cast mem.: (film) Clear and Present Danger; contbg. editor Coconut Times. Mem. City Solicitor Feasibility Study Com., Ocean City; mem. WWII com. Berlin Heritage Found. Mem. ABA, ATLA, Md. State Bar Assn. (bd. govs., program com., membership com., centennial com., mem. coun. solo & small firm practice sect.), Worcester County Bar Assn. (sec., treas., v.p., pres., chmn. com. on athletic endeavors), Md. Trial Lawyers Assn., Md. Criminal Def. Attys. Assn., Appellate Jud. Nominating Commn., Nat. Criminal Def. Attys. Assn. Democrat. Civil rights, General civil litigation, Criminal. Home: Seatime Condominium 136 St 502-n Ocean City MD 21842 Office: PO Box 56 4100 Coastal Hwy Ocean City MD 21843

**WIMMER, NANCY T.,** lawyer; b. Newark, Jan. 13, 1951; d. Harold and Gilda (Schwartz) Tainow; m. Howard A. Wimmer, Sept. 1, 1974; 2 children. BS magna cum laude, Temple U., 1973, JD, 1994. Bar: Pa. 1995. Staff atty. Cmty. Health Law Project, Camden, N.J., 1993-96; legal cons. elder law project Temple U., Phila., 1994; mng. atty., dir. Cancer Patient Legal Advocacy Network, Pa., 1994-99; assoc. counsel, dir. legal advocacy for patients Temple Legal Aid Office, 1999—. Recipient Courage award Am. Cancer Soc., 1998. Mem. Pa. Bar Assn., Phila. Bar Assn., Northeast Reg. Ca. Inst. (adv. bd.), Linda Creed Br. Ca. Found. (adv. bd.), Nat. Br. Ca. Coalition. Health, Elder, Insurance.

**WIMPFHEIMER, MICHAEL CLARK,** lawyer; b. N.Y.C., July 9, 1944; s. Henry and Ruth (Rapp) W.; m. Susanne Rabner, June 11, 1968; children: Jan Steven, Barry Scott, Luba Rachel. BA, Columbia U., 1964; JD, Harvard U., 1967. Bar: N.Y. 1967, U.S. Dist. Ct. (ea. and so. dists.) N.Y. 1974, U.S. Ct. Appeals (2d cir.) 1974, U.S. Ct. Mil. Appeals 1979, U.S. Claims Ct., 1992. Ptnr. Wimpfheimer & Wimpfheimer, N.Y.C., 1970—. V.p. Union of Orthodox Jewish Congregations of Am., N.Y.C., 1978—. Comdr. JAGC USNR ret., 1968-92. Mem. ABA, N.Y. State Bar Assn., Bronx County Bar Assn. Jewish. Estate planning, General practice, Real property. Home: 2756 Arlington Ave Riverdale Bronx NY 10463-4807 Office: Wimpfheimer & Wimpfheimer 330 W 58th St Ste 600 New York NY 10019-1818

**WIMPFHEIMER, STEVEN,** lawyer; b. N.Y.C., Dec. 5, 1941; s. Kurt and Ruth (Prochnik) W.; m. Ruth L. Feigenbaum, June 26, 1966; children: Robert, Debra, Amy. BS, Syracuse U., 1963; LLB, Bklyn. Law Sch., 1966. Bar: N.Y. 1966, U.S. Supreme Ct. 1974, U.S. Dist. Ct. (so. and ea. dists.) N.Y. 1976. Assoc. Borden, Skidell, Fleck, Hunter Esquires, Jamaica, N.Y., 1968-69; law asst. Supreme Ct., Queens County, Jamaica, 1969-71, confidential law clk. to justice, 1971-75; assoc. Lippe, Ruskin, Schlissel, Esquires, Mineola, N.Y., 1975-79; ptnr. Wimpfheimer & Sherman, Esquires, Garden City, N.Y., 1979-93; pvt. practice Garden City, N.Y., 1993—; adj. assoc. prof. Adelphi U., Garden City, 1979-86; bd. advisors Adelphi U. Lawyers' Asst. Program, Garden City, 1986-93; arbitrator Am. Arbitration Assn., Garden City, 1984—. Contbr. articles to profl. jours. Pres. Lake Success (N.Y.) Jewish Ctr., 1987-88, Royal Ranch Club, Floral Park, N.Y., 1978-79, Jamaica lodge B'nai B'rith, 1973-75. Capt. U.S. Army, 1967-68, Vietnam. Recipient Torch of Liberty, B'nai B'rith Anti-Defamation League, Queens, N.Y., 1979. Mem. N.Y. State Bar Assn., Queens County Bar Assn. (bd. mgrs. 1989—, treas. 1995-97, v.p. 1997-99, pres. 1999—), Nassau County Bar Assn., Real Estate Tax Rev. Bar Assn. Avocations: tennis, cycling, photography. Condemnation, Real property, General civil litigation. Office: 666 Old Country Rd Garden City NY 11530-2004

**WIMS, TRAVIS MARTIN,** lawyer; b. Kansas City, Mo., June 23, 1969; s. Larry Jack and Betty Sue Wims; m. Kee Stewart, Sept. 7, 1996. BS in Bus., U. Mo., 1991; JD, Washburn U., 1994. Chief adverse actions USAF, Shaw AFB, S.C., 1994-95, chief preventive law, 1995-96; spl. asst. U.S. Atty. USAF, Columbia, S.C., 1994-96; chief preventive law USAF, Tinker AFB, Okla., 1996-98, area def. counsel, 1998—.

**WINCHELL, WILLIAM OLIN,** mechanical engineer, educator, lawyer; b. Rochester, N.Y., Dec. 31, 1933; s. Leslie Olin and Hazel Agnes (Apker) W.; m. Doris Jane Martenson, Jan. 19, 1957; children: Jason, Darrell, Kirk. BME, GMI Engring. and Mgmt. Inst., 1956; MSc, Ohio State U., 1970; MBA, U. Detroit, 1976; JD, Detroit Coll. Law, 1980. Bar: Mich. 1981, U.S. Dist. Ct. (ea. dist.) Mich. 1981, U.S. Ct. Appeals (6th cir.) 1982, U.S. Supreme Ct. 1985, N.Y. 1988; registered profl. engr., Mich., N.Y. Cons. Gen. Motors Corp., Detroit and Warren, Mich. and Lockport, N.Y., 1951-87; pvt. practice Royal Oak, Mich., 1981—; assoc. prof., chmn. dept. indsl. engring. and mech. Alfred (N.Y.) U., 1987-90; assoc. prof. mfg. engring. Ferris State U., Big Rapids, Mich., 1990-91, 93-96; vis. assoc. prof., program coord. Purdue U., Warren, Mich., 1991-92, 96—; lectr. Lawrence Technol. U., Southfield, Mich., 1996-98. Mem. Royal Oak Long Range Planning Commn., 1980. Served to lt. commdr. USNR, 1956-76. Burton fellow Detroit Coll. Law, 1978. Fellow Am. Soc. Quality Control (v.p. 1985-89); mem. ABA, Mich. Bar Assn., Soc. Mfg. Engrs., Inst. Indsl. Engrs., Am. Soc. Engring. Educators, Tau Beta Pi, Beta Gamma Sigma. Roman Catholic. Club: North Star Sail. Avocations: sailing, woodworking.

**WINDER, DAVID KENT,** federal judge; b. Salt Lake City, June 8, 1932; s. Edwin Kent and Alma Eliza (Cannon) W.; m. Pamela Martin, June 24, 1955; children: Ann, Kay, James. BA, U. Utah, 1955; LLB, Stanford U., 1958. Bar: Utah 1958, Calif. 1958. Assoc. firm Clyde, Mecham & Pratt Salt Lake City, Utah, 1958-66; law clk. to chief justice Utah Supreme Ct., 1958-59; dep. county atty. Salt Lake County, 1959-63, chief dep. dist. atty., 1965-66; asst. U.S. atty. Salt Lake City, 1963-65; partner firm Strong & Hanni, Salt Lake City, 1966-77; judge U.S. Dist. Ct., Salt Lake City, Utah, 1977-79; judge U.S. Dist. Ct., Utah, 1979-93, chief judge, 1993-97, sr. judge, 1997—; examiner Utah Bar Examiners, 1975-79, chmn., 1977-79; mem. jud. resources com. Served with USAF, 1951-52. Mem. Am. Bd. Trial Advocates, Utah State Bar (Judge of Yr. award 1978), Salt Lake County Bar Assn., Calif. State Bar. Democrat. Office: US Dist Ct 110 US Courthouse 350 S Main St Salt Lake City UT 84101-2106

**WINDER, RICHARD EARNEST,** legal foundation administrator, writer, consultant; b. Vernal, Utah, Sept. 23, 1950; s. William Wallace and Winnifred (Jenkins) W.; m. Janice Fay Walker, Apr. 19, 1975; children: Scott Christian, Eric John, Brian Geoffrey, Laura Jeanne, Amy Elizabeth. BA magna cum laude, Brigham Young U., 1974, JD cum laude, 1978; MBA with honors, U. Michigan, Flint, 1988. Bar: Utah 1978, U.S. Dist. Ct. Utah 1978, Mich. 1979, U.S. Dist. Ct. (ea. and we. dists.) Mich. 1979. Tchg. asst., grad. instr. Brigham Young U., Provo, Utah, 1976-78; law clk. Willingham & Coté, E. Lansing, Mich., 1978-79, atty., 1979-87; exec. v.p. Mgmt. Leasing, Inc., Battle Creek, Mich., 1987-88, Mgmt. Options, Inc., Lansing, Mich., 1988-91; fin. mgr. Mich. State Bar Found., Lansing, Mich., 1991-94, dep. dir., fin. mgr., 1994—; panelist 9th Nat. Legis. Conf. Small Bus., San Antonio, 1987; adj. prof. Davenport Coll. Bus., Lansing, 1990-92, mgmt. adv. com., 1993-96; mem. founding steering com. Capital Quality Initiative, Lansing, 1992-96; liaison State Bar Mich. Long Range Planning Process, 1996-97; co-founder, rsch. prin. Quality Dynamics Rsch. Inst., Haslett, Mich., 1994-97; rsch. prin. Leadership Dynamics Rsch. Inst., Haslett, 1998—. Author: (with others) Value Sharing: Value Building, 1990, Corporate Orienteering, 1995; contbr., bd. editors: Summary of Utah Real Property Law, 1978. Vol. leader Boy Scouts Am., Chief Okemos Coun., Lansing, 1978—. Fellow Mich. State Bar Found.; mem. ABA, Am. Soc. Quality Control (chmn. Lansing-Jackson sect. 1994-95, spkr. and writer 1992—), Mich. Bar Assn., Utah Bar Assn., Lansing Regional C. of C. (small bus. coun., MBA task force Bus. and Edn. com. 1988-92, recipient Chmn.'s award 1992), Beta Gamma Sigma. Republican. Mem. LDS Ch. Avocations: writing, speaking, computer technology, research, teaching. Office: Mich State Bar Found 306 Townsend St Lansing MI 48933-2012

**WINDHAM, JOHN FRANKLIN,** lawyer; b. Fayette, Ala., Jan. 21, 1948; s. Grover B. Windham Jr. and Nancy Katherine (McAdams) Haynie; 1 child, John Franklin Jr.; m. Denise Roche McNair, Apr. 6, 1999; 1 stepchild, Brittany Danielle McNair. BA, U. West Fla., 1970; JD, U. N.C., 1975. Bar: Fla. 1975, U.S. Dist. Ct. (no. dist.) Fla. 1976, U.S. Ct. Appeals (11th cir.) 1983, U.S. Supreme Ct. 1984. Acctg. supr. Monsanto Co., Research Triangle Park, N.C., 1970-72; law clk. to U.S. Atty Pensacola, Fla., 1974; assoc. Beggs & Lane, Pensacola, 1975-79, ptnr., 1979—; adj. asst. prof. bus. law Troy State U., Pensacola, 1983-90. Mem. exec. com. Fla. divsn. Am. Cancer Soc., 1982-93, 95—, chmn. bd. 1998-99, chmn. elect bd. 1997-98; chmn. legis. and planned giving, 1986-88, chmn. inc. devel., 1989-91, chmn. ad hoc adv. com., 1991—, legal advisor, 1992—, bd. dirs., 1993—, mem. scholarship com., 1995—, mem. Winn Dixie adv. com., 1996—, chmn. dist. VII steering com., 1995-96. v.p, 1996-97, chmn. field ops. com., 1996-98; chmn. bd. Escambia Christian Sch., Pensacola, 1976-86; deacon Ch. of Christ, 1985-95; mem. adv. bd. Interim Healthcare, 1993-96, Panhandle Rehab. Injury Mgmt. and Evaluation, 1993-96; mem. founding bd. East Hill Christian Ch., 1995-97; bd. govs. Pensacola chpt. Order Granaderos e Dames de Galvez, 1990-98, pres. 1995-98; mem. U. West Fla. Found., 1983-85. Mem. Fla. Bar (workers compensation rules com., 1995—), Fla. Def. Lawyers Assn., Fla. Workers Compensation Inst., Southeastern Admiralty Law Inst. (bd. dirs. 1986-89), U. West Fla. Nat. Alumni Assn. (bd. dirs.), Kiwanis (pres. Pensacola 1978-79, 88-89). Republican. Avocations: church activities. Federal civil litigation, State civil litigation, Workers' compensation. Office: Beggs & Lane PO Box 12950 Pensacola FL 32576-2950

**WINDHAM, TIMOTHY RAY,** lawyer; b. Jackson, Miss., Oct. 11, 1963; s. Albert S. and Olivia J. (Ray) W.; m. Susan Charlene Carroll, Feb. 16, 1985. BBA, Millsaps Coll., Jackson, Miss., 1983; JD, Loyola Law Sch., L.A., 1998. Area sales mgr. McRae's Dept. Stores, Vicksburg, Miss., 1987-90; store mgr. S and K Menswear, Jackson, 1990-91; gen. mgr. Abbey Healthcare, L.A., 1991-93; regional exec. Supercare Healthcare, Industry, Calif., 1993-94; account mgr. Nat. Med. Care, L.A., 1994-97; account exec. Apria Healthcare, L.A., 1997-98; atty. Lewis, D'Amato, Brisbois and Bisgaard, L.A., 1998—. Dist. commr. Boy Scouts Am., 1971—; founding mem. Miss. Indian Cultural Soc., Jackson, 1981—. Recipient Am. Jurisprudence award Bancroft Whitney, 1996-97, Am. Bd. Trial Advocates award, 1998. Mem. ABA, ATLA, Calif. Assn. Health Svcs. at Home (adv. com. 1991—), Healthcare Sales Profls., Phi Delta Phi (magister 1997-98). Libertarian. Avocation: golf. Personal injury, Health, General civil litigation. Home: 426 Heather Heights Ct Monrovia CA 91016-1547 Office: Lewis D'Amato Brisbois and Bisgaard LLP 221 N Figueroa St Ste 1200 Los Angeles CA 90012-2646

**WINE, DONALD ARTHUR,** lawyer; b. Oelwein, Iowa, Oct. 8, 1922; s. George A. and Gladys E. (Lisle) W.; m. Mary L. Schneider, Dec. 27, 1947; children: Mark, Marcia, James. B.A., Drake U., 1946; JD, State U. Iowa, 1949. Bar: Iowa 1949, D.C. 1968. Pvt. practice in Newport and Wine, 1949-61; U.S. atty. So. Dist. Iowa, 1961-65; of counsel Davis, Brown, Koehn, Shors & Roberts, Des Moines. Bd. dirs. Des Moines YMCA, 1963-75; bd. dirs. Salvation Army, 1969—, chmn., 1971; bd. dirs. Davenport YMCA, 1961; bd. dirs. Internat. Assn. Y's Men, 1957-59, area v.p., 1961; bd. dirs. Polk County Assn. Retarded Persons, 1991-95; mem. internat. com. YMCA's U.S. and Can., 1961-75; v.p. Iowa Council Chs.; pres. Des Moines Area Religious Coun. Found., 1992-97; chmn. bd. trustees First Bapt. Ch., 1975; trustee U. Osteo. Medicine and Health Scis., 1980-95; Organizer Young Dems., Iowa, 1946; co-chmn. Scott County Citizens for Kennedy, 1960. Served to capt., navigator USAAF, 1943-45. Decorated D.F.C. Mem. ABA (chmn. com. jud. adminstrn. jr. bar sect. 1958), Iowa Bar Assn. (pres. jr. bar sect. 1957), Polk County Bar Assn. (sec. 1973-74), Des Moines C. of C. (chmn. city-state tax com. 1978-79, chmn. legis. com. 1979-84, bd. dirs. 1981), Des Moines Club, Masons, Kiwanis (pres. Downtown club 1969), Order of Coif, Sigma Alpha Epsilon. Office: Davis Brown Koehn Shors & Roberts 2500 Financial Ctr 666 Walnut St Des Moines IA 50309-3904

**WINE, L. MARK,** lawyer; b. Norfolk, Va., Apr. 16, 1945; s. Melvin Leon and Mildred Sylvia (Weiss) W.; m. Blanche Weintraub, June 8, 1969; children—Kim, Lara, Dana. B.A. with high honors, U. Va., 1967; J.D., U. Chgo., 1970. Bar: D.C. 1970, U.S. Supreme Ct. 1977. Assoc., Kirkland & Ellis, Washington, 1970-72; trial atty. land and natural resources div. Dept. of Justice, Washington, 1972-78; ptnr. Kirkland & Ellis, Washington, 1978—. Mem. ABA. Environmental, Administrative and regulatory, Federal civil litigation. Office: Kirkland & Ellis 655 15th St NW Ste 1200 Washington DC 20005-5793

**WINE-BANKS, JILL SUSAN,** lawyer; b. Chgo., May 5, 1943; d. Bert S. and Sylvia Dawn (Simon) Wine; m. Ian David Volner, Aug. 21, 1965; m. Michael A. Banks, Jan. 12, 1980. BS, U. Ill.-Champaign-Urbana, 1964; JD, Columbia U., 1968; LLD (hon.), Hood Coll., 1975. Bar: N.Y. 1969, U.S. Ct. Appeals (4th cir.) 1969, U.S. Ct. Appeals (6th and 9th cirs.) 1973, U.S. Supreme Ct. 1974, D.C. 1976, Ill. 1980. Asst. press. and pub. rels. dir. Assembly of Captive European Nations, N.Y.C., 1965-66; trial atty. criminal div. organized crime and racketeering sect. and labor racketeering sect. U.S. Dept. Justice, 1969-73; asst. spl. prosecutor Watergate Spl. Prosecutor's Office, 1973-75; lectr. law seminar on trial practice Columbia U. Sch. Law, N.Y.C., 1975-77; assoc. Fried, Frank, Harris, Shriver & Kampelman, Washington, 1975-77; gen. counsel Dept. Army, Pentagon, Washington, 1977-79; ptnr. Jenner & Block, Chgo., 1980-84; solicitor gen. State of Ill. Office of Atty. Gen., 1984-86, dep. atty. gen., 1986-87; exec. v.p., chief oper. officer ABA, Chgo., 1987-90; pvt. practice law, 1990-92; bd. dirs. Cenvill Devel. Corp., 1991-92; v.p. Motorola Internat. Network Ventures Inc. and dir. transaction and govt. rels. group, Network Ventures Divsn., Motorola, 1992-97, chmn. bd., St Peters Telecom and Omni Capital Inc.; dir. Strategic Alliances, Vendor Mgmt. Motorola Cellular Infrastructure Group, 1997-99; v.p. Alliances, Maytag Corp., 1999—; mem. EEC disting. vis. program European Parliament, 1987; bd. dirs. Cenvill Devel. Corp., 1991-92; chmn. bd. dirs. St. Petersburg Telecom, Russia, 1994-97, Omni Capital Ptnrs., Inc., 1994-97; mem. bd. assocs. program for the study of cultural values & ethics U. Ill. Recipient Spl. Achievement award U.S. Dept. Justice, 1972, Meritorious award, 1973, Cert. Outstanding Svc., 1975; decoration for Disting. Civilian Svc., Dept. Army, 1979; named Disting. Visitor to European Econ. Community. Mem. Internat. Women's Forum, The Chgo. Network, Econ. Club. Address: 8700 W Bryn Mawr Ave Chicago IL 60631-3512

**WINER, STEPHEN I.,** lawyer; b. Mpls., Jan. 30, 1965; s. Edward Lewis and Sandra Paulette W.; m. Julie Ellen Falk, June 8, 1997. BA summa cum laude, U. Minn., 1987; JD cum laude, Northwestern U., 1990. Bar: Minn. 1987, Tex. 1994. Assoc. Dorsey & Whitney LLP, Mpls., 1990-93; asst. gen. counsel AIM Mgmt. Group Inc., Houston, 1993—. Mem. ABA, Order of Coif. Avocation: investments. Securities, Computer, General corporate. Office: AIM Mgmt Group Inc 11 E Greenway Plz Ste 100 Houston TX 77046-1100

**WINES, LAWRENCE EUGENE,** lawyer, corporate executive, financial consultant; b. St. Louis, Jan. 17, 1957; s. Frank Peter and Audrey Margret (Murphy) W. BA, U. Mo., 1984; JD, St. Louis U., 1987; MBA, Columbia State U., 1996, PhD, 1998. Bar: Mo., U.S. Dist. Ct. (we. dist.) Mo.; registered fin. planner. Mem. staff Gephardt for President, Washington, 1987-88; sole practice Ferguson, Mo., 1989-90; ptnr. Progressive Consulting, Ferguson, 1988-93, Wines & Stein attys., P.C., Ferguson, 1990-95, Wines Law Office, L.C., 1995—; pres. Wines Properties, Inc., Wines Enterprises, Inc.; prin. Wines Law Offices, L.C., 1995—. Cons. fundraising Missourias for Mike Wolff, St. Louis, 1988-92, John Shear Election Com., St. Louis, 1988-95, Congresswoman Joan Kelly Horn, St. Louis, 1990-92, Quinn for Sec. State, St. Louis, 1991-92; Ferguson Com. man St. Louis County Dem. Com., 1987-92; vol. Congressman Richard Gephardt, St. Louis and Washington, 1984—. Recipient: Presdl. Svc. award U. Mo. St. Louis Alumni Assn., 1989-90, Disting. Svc. award Disabled Student Union, 1991, Disting. Vol. award U. Mo. St. Louis, 1987; named Outstanding Male Young Dem. Mo. Young Dems., 1986. Mem. ABA, ATLA, Mo. Bar Assn., Mo. Assn. Trial Attys., Bar Assn. Met. St. Louis, St. Louis County Bar Assn., Lincoln County Bar Assn., St. Louis Rams Quarterback Club. Roman Catholic. Avocations: weighlifting, shooting, archery. Personal injury, Criminal, Product liability. Office: 905 S Florissant Rd Saint Louis MO 63135-3254

**WINFREE, GREGORY DAINARD,** lawyer; b. New Hyde Park, N.Y., Feb. 24, 1965; s. Walter Lehman, Jr. and Ruth W.; m. Frances Harris, Sept. 30, 1995. BS, St. John's U., 1986; JD, Georgetown U., 1989. Litigation assoc. Venable, Baetjer, Howard & Civiletti, Washington, 1989-91; trial atty. U.S. Dept. Justice, Washington, 1991-93; litigation counsel Union Carbide Corp., Danbury, Conn., 1993—. Patent for load distributing golf shirt, 1998. Bd. dirs. Hord Found., Danbury, Conn., 1998—, Union Carbide Found., Danbury, 1998—; v.p. Mason's Army Jr. Golf Program, Washington. Mem. ABA (minority in-house counsel group, treas. 1996—). Avocations: music, golf, tennis, fly fishing. E-mail: winfregd@ucarb.com. Toxic tort, Legislative, Alternative dispute resolution. Office: 39 Old Ridgebury Rd Danbury CT 06817-0001

**WINFREY, DIANA LEE,** lawyer; b. Kansas City, Mo., July 17, 1955; d. James William and Louise Augusta (Harrison) W. BA in Spanish, U. Mo., 1978, JD, 1984. Bar: Mo. 1984, Calif. 1985. Tchr. Pan-Am. Workshop, Mexico City, 1979; law clk. Mo. Ct. of Appeals, Kansas City, 1984-85; assoc. Early, Maslach, Leavy & Nutt, L.A., 1985-87, Wilson, Elser, et al, L.A., 1987-88, Wood, Lucksinger & Epstein, L.A., 1988-90, Coony & Bihr, Beverly Hills, Calif., 1990-95; sole practitioner Woodland Hills, Calif., 1995—. Asst. editor The Urban Lawyer Jour., 1983-84. Member Heal the Bay, Santa Monica, Calif., 1991—. Recipient Outstanding Achievement and Svc. award U. Mo., 1978. Mem. ABA, Calif. Bar Assn., Mo. Bar Assn., L.A. County Bar Assn., Beverly Hills Bar Assn., Am. Bd. Trial Attys., Inns of Ct. Democrat. General practice, General civil litigation, General corporate. Office: Hale Braden & Hinchcliffe LLP 9th Fl 3415 S Sepulveda Blvd Fl 9 Los Angeles CA 90034-6060

**WING, ADRIEN KATHERINE,** law educator; b. Aug. 7, 1956; d. John Ellison and Katherine (Pruitt) Wing; children: Che-Cabral, Nolan Felipe. AB magna cum laude, Princeton U., 1978; MA, UCLA, 1979; JD, Stanford, 1982. Bar: N.Y. 1983, U.S. Dist. Ct. (so. and ea. dists.) N.Y. 1983, U.S. Ct. Appeals (5th and 9th cirs.). Assoc. Curtis, Mallet-Prevost, Colt &

Mosle, N.Y.C., 1982-86, Rabinowitz, Boudin, Standard, Krinsky & Lieberman, 1986-87; assoc. prof. law U. Iowa, Iowa City, 1987-93; prof. U. Iowa, 1993—; mem. alumni council Princeton U., 1983-85, trustee Class of '78 Alumni Found., 1984-87, 93—, v.p. Princeton Class of 1978 Alumni, 1993-98; mem. bd. visitors Stanford Law Sch., 1993-96. Mem. bd. editors Am. J. Comp. Law, 1993—. Mem. ABA (exec. com. young lawyers sect. 1985-87), Nat. Conf. Black Lawyers (UN rep., chmn. internat. affairs sect. 1982-95), Internat. Assn. Dem. Lawyers (UN rep. 1984-87), Am. Soc. Internat. Law (exec. coun. 1986-89, 96-99, exec. com. 1988-99, group chair S. Africa 1993-95, nom. com. 1991, 93, membership com. 1994-95), Am. Friends Svc. Com. (bd. dirs. Middle East 1998—), Black Alumni of Princeton U. (bd. dirs. 1982-87), Transafrica Scholars Forum Coun. (bd. dirs. 1993-95), Iowa City Foreign Rels. Coun. (bd. dirs. 1989-94), Iowa Peace Inst. (bd. dirs. 1993-95), Coun. on Fgn. Rels., Internat. Third World Legal Studies Assn. (bd. dirs. 1996—, nom. trustee Princeton com. 1997—). Democrat. Avocations: photography, jogging, writing, poetry. Office: U Iowa Sch Law Boyd Law Bldg Iowa City IA 52242

**WINGATE, HENRY TRAVILLION,** federal judge; b. Jackson, Miss., Jan. 6, 1947; s. J.T. and Eloise (Anderson) W.; m. Turner Arnita Ward, Aug. 10, 1974. BA, Grinnell Coll., 1969; JD, Yale U., 1973; LLD (hon.), Grinnell Coll., 1986. Bar: Miss. 1973, U.S. Dist. Ct. (so. dist.) Miss. 1973, U.S. Ct. Appeals (5th cir.) 1973, U.S. Mil. Ct. 1973. Law clk. New Haven (Conn.) Legal Assistance, 1971-72, Community Legal Aid, Jackson, 1972-73; spl. asst. atty. gen. State of Miss., Jackson, 1976-80; asst. dist. atty. (7th cir.), Jackson, 1980-84; asst. U.S. atty. U.S. Dist. Ct. (so. dist.), Jackson, 1984-85; judge U.S. Dist. Ct. (so. dist.) Miss., Jackson, 1985—; lectr. Miss. Prosecutors Coll., 1980-84, Law Enforcement Tng. Acad., Pearl, Miss., 1980-84, Miss. Jud. Coll., 1980-84, Nat. Coll. Dist. Attys., 1984-85; adj. prof. law Golden Gate U., Norfolk, Va, 1975-76, Tidewater Community Coll., 1976, Miss. Coll. Sch. Law, 1978-84. Former mem. adv. bd. Jackson Parks and Recreation Dept.; former mem. bd. dirs. SCAN Am. of Miss., Inc., Jackson Arts Alliance, Drug Rsch. and Edn. Assn. in Miss., Inc., United Way Jackson; mem. exec. com. Yale U. Law sch., 1989—; chmn. bd. dirs. YMCA, 1978-80. Racquetball State Singles Champion Jr. Vets. Div., 1981, State Singles Champion Srs. Div., 1982, Outstanding Legal Service award NAACP (Jackson br. and Miss. br.), 1982, Civil Liberties award Elks, 1983, Community Service award Women for Progress Orgn., 1984. Mem. ABA (co-chmn. sect. litigation liaison with judiciary 1989-91), Miss. Bar Assn., Hinds County Bar Assn., Fed. Bar Assn., Yale Club Miss. Avocations: reading, theater, racquetball, jogging, bowling. Home: 6018 Huntview Dr Jackson MS 39206-2130 Office: James O Eastland Courthouse 245 E Capitol St Ste 109 Jackson MS 39201-2414

**WINGER, BRIAN NEIL,** lawyer; b. Ulysses, Kans., July 31, 1967; s. Donald Eugene and Judith Ann Winger; m. Beth Louise Winger, Dec. 20, 1993. BS, Okla. Christian U., 1990; JD, Oklahoma City U., 1994. Bar: Okla. 1996, U.S. Dist. Ct. (we. dist.) Okla. 1996. Investment property advisor Kabili & Co. Investments, Boulder, Colo., 1994-96; dir. estate planning Okla. Christian U., Oklahoma City, 1996-97, gen. counsel, 1997—. Republican. Mem. Ch. of Christ. Office: Okla Christian U PO Box 11000 Oklahoma City OK 73136-1100

**WINGERTER, JOHN RAYMOND,** lawyer; b. Erie, Pa., June 30, 1942; s. Raymond J. and Magdalene (Pfeil) W.; m. Susan Tracy Smith, Aug. 5, 1967; children: Julie, Kara, Lori, Darcie, Daryle. BA, Norwich U., 1964; JD, U. Notre Dame, 1968. Bar: Pa. 1967, U.S. Dist. Ct. (we. dist.) Pa. 1967, U.S. Ct. Appeals (3d cir.) 1971, U.S. Supreme Ct. 1973. Assoc. Carney, Palmisano & Walsh, Erie, Pa., 1967-69; ptnr. Carney & Good, Erie, 1969—. Trustee Gannon U. Mem. ABA, Pa. Bar Assn. (ho. dels. 1983—), Erie Bar Assn. (exec. com.), Assn. Trial Lawyers Am., Pa. Trial Lawyers Assn. Republican. Roman Catholic. Clubs: Erie Yacht, Lake View Country Club. Federal civil litigation, State civil litigation, Personal injury. Home: 1540 S Shore Dr Erie PA 16505-2438 Office: Carney & Good 254 W 6th St Erie PA 16507-1398

**WINGET, WALTER WINFIELD,** lawyer; b. Peoria, Ill., Sept. 12, 1936; s. Walter W. Winget and Arabella (Robinson) Richardson; m. Alice B. Winget, Sept. 23, 1993; children: Marie, Marshall. AB cum laude, Princeton U., 1958; JD, U. Mich., 1961. Bar: R.I. 1962, Ill. 1962, U.S. Supreme Ct. 1971; cert. civil trial advocate. Assoc. Edwards & Angell, Providence, 1961-64; sole practice Peoria, 1964-77; ptnr. Winget & Kane, Peoria, 1977—; asst. pub. defender Peoria, 1969-70; bd. dirs. various corps. Atty., bd. dirs. Better Bus. Bur. Cen. Ill., Inc. 1973-92, chmn., 1979-81. Served to sgt. U.S. Army, 1961-62. Mem. Ill. Bar Assn., Ill. Trial Lawyers Assn., Peoria County Bar Assn. (pres. 1991-92), Rice Pond Preserve. Republican. Episcopalian. Club: Peoria Country. Avocations: competitive target shooting, big game and duck hunting. Federal civil litigation, State civil litigation, General corporate. Home: 6712 N Post Oak Rd Peoria IL 61615-2347 Office: Winget & Kane 416 Main St Ste 807 Peoria IL 61602-1177

**WINKELMAN, JOHNNY MARTIN,** lawyer, real estate development consultant; b. Bell, Calif., Nov. 17, 1946; s. Roy Hugh and Phyllis Lorrane (Jansen) W.; m. Brenda Jean Scott, July 4, 1979; children: Brian, Jennifer, Kristina, Diana. AA, Southwestern Coll., 1974; LLB, Western State U., 1976, JD, 1979. Bar: Calif. 1979, U.S. Dist. Ct. (so. dist.) Calif. 1979. Carpenter Local 1492, Los Angeles, 1969-70; constrn. mgr. Winkelman Constrn., Whittier, Calif., 1970-71; bldg. insp. City of Chula Vista, Calif., 1971-76; sr. bldg. insp. City of Nat. City, Calif., 1976-79; law practice San Diego, 1979—; cons., instr. Southwestern Coll., 1979-85; corp. counsel Palm Homes, Inc., Chula Vista, 1979-88; tribal councilor Viejas Band Mission Indians, Alpine, Calif., 1985-91; advisor Bd. Appeals City of Chula Vista, 1981-88; CEO Viejas Casino & Turf, Club, 1991-99. Served with U.S. Army, 1966-68. Mem. Calif. State Bar, San Diego County Bar Assn., Kiwanis. Baptist. Lodge: Rotary. Avocations: skiing, travel, all-terrain cycle excursions. Office: 5000 Willows Rd Alpine CA 91901-1656

**WINKLER, ALLEN WARREN,** lawyer; b. Chgo., Dec. 11, 1954; s. Maurice A. and Florence (Klein) W.; m. Bett C. Gibson, Nov. 1, 1986. BS, No. Ill. U., 1977; JD, Tulane U., 1981. Bar: La. 1982, Ill. 1982, U.S. Dist. Ct. (ea. dist.) La. 1982, U.S. Dist. Ct. (mid. dist.) La. 1987. Atty. La. Legal Clinic, New Orleans, 1982-84; pvt. practice law New Orleans, 1984-85; staff atty. Oak Tree Savs. Bank, S.S.B., New Orleans, 1985-87, sr. atty., asst. v.p., 1987-90; atty. FDIC/Resolution Trust Corp., Baton Rouge, 1991-92; sr. atty. FDIC/Resolution Trust Corp., Atlanta, 1992-95; sr. corp. counsel Fleet Fin., Inc., Atlanta, 1996-97; pres. Legal Ease Inc., Atlanta, 1996—; corp. counsel Prudential Bank, Atlanta, 1997; gen. counsel, v.p. NCS Mortgage Svcs., Norcross, Ga., 1998—; mem. faculty Franklin Coll. Ct. Reporting, Metairie, La., 1981-88; cons., guest lectr. paralegal studies Tulane U., New Orleans, 1982-90; guest lectr. U. New Orleans, 1988-90. Vol. Hawkins for Judge campaign, New Orleans. Mem. La. Bar Assn., Ill. Bar Assn. Consumer commercial, Real property, Contracts commercial. Home: 1322 Colony Dr Marietta GA 30068-2886 Office: NCS Mortgagge Svcs 5335 Triangle Pkwy Norcross GA 30092-2599

**WINKLER, CHARLES HOWARD,** lawyer, investment management company executive; b. N.Y.C., Aug. 4, 1954; s. Joseph Conrad and Geraldine Miriam (Borok) W.; m. Joni S. Taylor, Aug. 28, 1993. BBA with highest distinction, Emory U., 1976; JD, Northwestern U., 1979. Bar: Ill. 1979, U.S. Dist. Ct (no. dist.) Ill. 1979. Assoc. Levenfeld & Kanter, Chgo., 1979-80; assoc. Kanter & Eisenberg, Chgo., 1980-84, ptnr., 1985-86; ptnr. Neal Gerber & Eisenberg, Chgo., 1986-96; sr. mng. dir., COO Citadel Investment Group, LLC, Chgo., 1996—; sr. mng. dir. Citadel Trading Group, Chgo., 1996—, Titan Securities LLC, Chgo., 1996—, Aragon Investments Ltd., Chgo., 1996—; bd. dirs. Kensington Global Strategies Fund, Ltd., Antaeus Internat. Investments, Ltd., Jackson Investment Fund Ltd., Citadel Investment Group (Europe) Ltd. Author: (with others) Basic Tax Shelters, 1982, Limited Liability Companies: The Entity of Choice, 1995; mng. editor Northwestern Jour. Internat. Law and Bus., 1979. Mem. ABA (mem. sect. on taxation), Beta Gamma Sigma. Taxation, general, General corporate, Securities. Home: 50 E Bellevue Pl Chicago IL 60611-1129 Office: Citadel Investment Group LLC 225 W Washington St Fl 9 Chicago IL 60606-2418

**WINKLER, DANA JOHN,** lawyer; b. Wichita, Kans., Jan. 2, 1944; s. Donald Emil and Hazel Claire (Schmitter) W.; m. Mary Ann Seiwert, Oct. 14, 1967; 1 child, Jonathan. BA, Wichita State U., 1967; JD, Washburn Law Sch., 1971. Staff writer Wichita (Kans.) Eagle & Beacon, 1961-67; ptnr. Davis, Bruce, Davis & Winkler, Wichita, 1972-77; asst. city atty. City of Wichita, 1977-99; dir. Wichita Mcpl. Fed. Credit Union, 1980—, pres., 1982, 99—, sec.-treas., 1994-98, v.p., 1998-99; dir. Deaf and Hard of Hearing Counseling Svc., 1979-80. Vol. Sedgwick County United Way, Wichita, 1973-74; vice-chmn. Wichita Pub. Schs. Spl. Edn. Adv. Coun., 1987-89. 1st lt. U.S. Army, 1967-69. Mem. Kans. Bar Assn., Wichita Bar Assn., Masons. Republican. Roman Catholic. Home and Office: 1621 Harlan St Wichita KS 67212-1842

**WINNING, JOHN PATRICK,** lawyer; b. Murphysboro, Ill., Oct. 29, 1952; s. William T. Jr. and Lillian (Albers) W.; m. Jessica Anne Yoder, June 17, 1978 (div. July 1999); children: Erika Anne, Brian Patrick, Derek Matthew. AB with distinction, Mo. Bapt. Coll., 1974; JD, St. Louis U., 1979. Bar: Mo. 1979, U.S. Dist. Ct. (ea. dist.) Mo. 1979, U.S. Ct. Appeals (8th cir.) 1979, U.S. Dist. Ct. (so. dist.) Tex. 1985, U.S. Ct. Appeals (5th cir.) 1987, U.S. Dist. Ct. (we. dist.) Tex. 1988, Tex. 1989. Assoc. Chused, Strauss, Chorlins, Goldfarb, Bini & Kohn, St. Louis, 1979-81; assoc. counsel Mfrs. Hanover Fin. Services, Phila., 1981-83; corp. counsel Cessna Fin. Corp., Wichita, Kans., 1983-85; atty. Southwestern Bell Publs., Inc., St. Louis, 1985-90; pvt. practice St. Louis, 1990—; pres. Butler Hill Investments, Inc., St. Louis, 1990-91; prin. Success Mgmt. Group, 1991-96, DPPC Mgmt. Group, St. Louis, 1996-97; sec., bd. dirs. Winning Equipment Co.; asst. prof. bus. adminstn. Mo. Bapt. Coll., 1986-91. Treas. Concerned Citizens of Chesterfield, 1989-91; deacon, mem. fin. com. 1st Bapt. Ch., Ellisville, Mo., 1992-93, vice chmn. fin. com., 1993-94, chmn. fin. com., 1994-95, vice chmn. deacons, 1993-95, chmn. deacons, 1997-98, dir. Sunday sch., 1993-94; bd. trustees, chmn. athletic com., 1992-97, 98—, chmn. by-laws com. Mo. Bapt. Coll., 1992-96, sec. presdl. search com., 1994, mem., exec. com. bd. trustees, 1994-97, 98—; mgr. St. Louis Flames Youth Baseball, 1992-95; mgr. St. Louis Thunder Youth Baseball, 1995-97; coach St. Clare Bulls Basketball Team, 1994-97, St. Louis Wolfpack Youth Baseball, 1997-98; asst. scoutmaster troop 313, merit badge counselor Boy Scouts Am., 1997—; Camporee staff New Horizons dist. Boy Scouts Am., 1998—, adult leader tng. staff, 1998—, camping com., 1998—, dist. roundtable staff, 1999—. Named one of Outstanding Young Men of Am., 1987, Outstanding Alumnus, Mo. Bapt. Coll., 1987-88; named to Athletic Hall of Fame, Mo. Bapt. Coll., 1989; recipient Wood Badge Adult Leadership Tng. award Boy Scouts Am., 1998. Mem. Nat. Lawyers Assn., Eagle Scouts Assn., Met. St. Louis Bar Assn., Christian Legal Soc., Acad. Family Mediators, Assn. Family and Conciliation Cts., Mo. Bapt. Coll. Alumni Assn. (pres. 1980-81, 88-90), St. Louis Assn., Christian Attys., West County C. of C., Chesterfield C. of C. Republican. Southern Baptist. Avocations: coaching baseball and basketball, reading, camping. General corporate, Family and matrimonial, Real property. Home: 321A Barrington Sq Saint Louis MO 63122 Office: 13100 Manchester Rd Ste 214 Saint Louis MO 63131-1730

**WINOGRADE, AUDREY,** lawyer; b. N.Y.C., Jan. 14, 1937; d. Joseph and Mildred (Weisbart) Weiner; m. Richard Earl Winograde, Dec. 7, 1960 (div. Jan. 1971); children: Leslie Jo, Jana; m. Paul Lewis Levinson, Sept. 19, 1989. BBA, CUNY, 1957; teaching credential, UCLA/Calif. State U., Northridge, 1960; JD cum laude, Southwestern U., L.A., 1986. Bar:Calif. 1986, U.S. Dist. Ct. (cen. dist.) Calif. 1986, U.S. Ct. Appeals (9th cir.) 1986. Tchr. L.A. City Schs., 1958-62, 71-78; advt. salesperson The Hollywood Reporter, L.A., 1966-70; regional sales mgr. Carol Little, L.A., 1978-80; nat. sales mgr. Bijou, L.A., 1980-81; owner, adminstr. James Reva Having Fun, L.A., 1981-83; law clk. Chaleff & English, Santa Monica, Calif., 1984-86, assoc., 1986-92, ptnr., 1993—; adj. prof. juvenile law Southwestern U. Sch. Law, L.A., 1993; spkr. in field. Fundraiser Kathleen Brown for Gov.; criminal law advisor Com. to Elect Gray Davis, L.A., 1994; judge pro-tem L.A. Mcpl. Ct., 1993—; bd. dirs. Camp Pacific Heartland; vol. lawyer Sybil Brand Inst., 1990—. Recipient Bradley Scholarships Southwestern U. Sch. Law, L.A., 1984-86. Mem. ABA (sentencing and corrections com. 1990—), Women Lawyers L.A. (bd. dirs. 1988-96, sec.-treas. 1991-92), Calif. State Bar Assn. (del. from Los Angeles County 1988-94), Southwestern U. Sch. Law Alumni Assn. (pres. 1993-95, bd. trustees 1993—), Am.-Jewish Congress (rel. rights com. 1996—). Avocations: reading, exercising, movies, theatre. Criminal, Juvenile, Administrative and regulatory. Office: Chaleff & English 1337 Ocean Ave Santa Monica CA 90401-1029

**WINOGRADSKY, STEVEN,** lawyer; b. N.Y.C., Sept. 22, 1949; s. Harry J. and Hazel (Sadoff) W.; m. Rosemary K. West, Dec. 8, 1985. BA in Polit. Sci., Calif. State U., Northridge, 1971; JD, U. San Fernando, 1977. Bar: Calif., 1977. V.p. bus. affairs Clearing House, Ltd., Hollywood, Calif., 1980-86; mng. dir. music, bus. and legal affairs MCA Home Entertainment and Universal Pictures and TV, Universal City, Calif., 1986-89; dir. music, bus. affairs Hanna-Barbera Prodns., Inc., L.A., 1989-91; pres. Winogradsky Co., Granada Hills, Calif., 1992—. Mem. Calif. State Bar, Calif. Copyright Conf. (bd. dirs. 1986-94, v.p. 1994-95, pres. 1995-97), Assn. Ind. Music Pubs. (bd. dirs. 1989-90, pres. 1991-94). Office: Winogradsky Co 11240 Magnolia Blvd Ste 104 North Hollywood CA 91601-3790

**WINSHIP, BLAINE H.,** lawyer; b. Ithaca, N.Y., Apr. 3, 1951; s. Hershell F. and June M. (Nickless) W.; m. Karin M. Byrne, Dec. 21, 1979. AB magna cum laude, Dartmouth Coll., 1973; JD, Cornell U., 1976. Bar: Ill. 1976, Fla. 1982. Assoc. Sonnenschein, Nath & Rosenthal, Chgo., 1976-82; ptnr. Winship & Byrne, Miami, Fla., 1983—. Contbg. author: ABA Criminal Antitrust Manual, 1982. Mem. bd. trustees StageWorks, Tampa, Fla., 1984-86, pres., 1986. Rufus Choate scholar Dartmouth Coll., 1972-73. Mem. Miami City Club, Fla. Bar Assn. (vice chmn., antitrust and trade regulation com., exec. com. bus. law sect.), Phi Beta Kappa. Antitrust, Federal civil litigation. Home: 1014 Hardee Rd Coral Gables FL 33146-3330 Office: Winship & Byrne Ste 1870 200 S Biscayne Blvd Miami FL 33131-2310

**WINSHIP, PETER,** law educator; b. Pensacola, Fla., Jan. 5, 1944; s. Stephen and Frances Norinne (Hayford) W.; m. Marion Christina Nelson, June 18, 1966; children: Verity Elizabeth, Adam Edward. AB, Harvard U., 1964, LLB, 1968; LLM, London Sch. of Econs., 1973; postdoctoral, Yale U., 1973-74. Bar: Tex. 1975, U.S. Dist. Ct. (no. dist.) Tex. 1981, (so. dist.) 1999, U.S. Ct. Appeals (5th and 11th cirs.) 1981. Legal advisor Ethiopian Ministry of Commerce, Addis Ababa, 1968-70; lectr. Haile Selassie I U., Addis Ababa, 1970-72; prof. law So. Meth. U., Dallas, 1974-90, James Cleo Thompson Sr. Trustee prof., 1990—; vis. prof. U. Calif., Berkeley, 1979-80, UCLA Sch. Law, 1986, Coll. William & Mary, 1990, U. Pa., 1992, U. Miami, 1997, U. Conn., 1999—. Co-author: Texas Litigation Guide, Vols. 7-10, 1979, Commercial Transactions, 1985; editor: Background Documents of the Ethiopian Commercial Code, 1974. Mem. Am. Law Inst., Internat. Inst. for Unification Pvt. Law (corr. 1983—), UN Commn. on Internat. Trade Law (nat. corr. 1990). Home: 3448 Amherst Ave Dallas TX 75225-7624 Office: So Meth U Sch Law Dallas TX 75275-0001

**WINSLOW, JOHN FRANKLIN,** lawyer; b. Houston, Nov. 15, 1933; s. Franklin Jarnigan and Jane (Shipley) W. BA, U. Tex., 1957, LLB, 1960. Bar: Tex. 1959, D.C. 1961. Atty., Hispanic law div. Library Congress, Washington, 1965-68; counsel, com. on the judiciary Ho. of Reps., Washington, 1968-71; atty., editor Matthew Bender & Co., Washington, 1973-79; atty. FERC, Washington, 1979-84; sole practice Washington, 1984—; researcher Hispanic Law Research, Washington, 1979—. Author: Conglomerates Unlimited: The Failure of Regulation, 1974; editor: Fed. Power Service, 1974-79; contbr. articles to Washington Monthly, Nation, 1975—. Mem. Tex. Bar Assn., D.C. Bar Assn. Administrative and regulatory, Public international.

**WINSTEAD, GEORGE ALVIS,** law librarian, biochemist, educator, consultant; b. Owensboro, Ky., Jan. 14, 1916; s. Robert Lee and Mary Oma (Dempsey) W.; m. Elisabeth Donelson Weaver, July 18, 1943. BS, We. Ky. U., 1938; MA, George Peabody Coll., 1940, MLS, 1957, MEd, 1958. Head chemistry and biology dept. Belmont Coll., Nashville, 1952-56; head chemistry dept. George Peabody Coll., Vanderbilt U., Nashville, 1956-58; assoc. law librarian Vanderbilt U., Nashville, 1958-76; dir. Tenn. State Supreme Ct. Law Libraries, Nashville, 1976—; law cons. Tenn. Youth Legis., Nashville, 1976—; cons. civic clubs, local colls., 1976—, Tenn. State Govt. Depts. Archives, Nashville, 1976—. Author: Tenn. State Law Library Progress Reports, 1975, Supreme Court Library Personnel Guide, 1981, Designing Future Law Libraries' Growth and Expansion, 1982, Problem Identification and Solutions in Law Libraries, Tenn. Supreme Courts, 1985. Mem. Col. Tenn. Gov.'s staff, Nashville, 1978. With USAAF, 1943-46. Named to Gov.'s Staff of Ky. Cols., Lexington, 1988. Fellow Am. Inst. Chemists, SAR. Baptist. Avocations: camping, hiking, traveling, crafts, antique cars. Home: 3819 Gallatin Rd Nashville TN 37216-2609 Office: Tenn Supreme Ct Libr Nashville TN 37219

**WINSTON, HAROLD RONALD,** lawyer; b. Atlantic, Iowa, Feb. 7, 1932; s. Louis D. and Leta B. (Carter) W.; m. Carol J. Sundeen, June 11, 1955; children: Leslie Winston Yannetti, Lisa Winston Shaw, Laura Winston Moritz. BA, U. Iowa, 1954, JD, 1958. Bar: Iowa 1958, U.S. District Ct. (no. and so. dists.) Iowa 1962, U.S. Tax Ct. 1962, U.S. Ct. Appeals (8th cir.) 1970, U.S. Supreme Ct. 1969. Trust Officer United Home Bank & Trust Co., Mason City, Iowa, 1958-59; mem. Breese & Cornwell, 1960-62, Breese, Cornwell, Winston & Reuber, 1963-73, Winston, Schroeder & Reuber, 1974-79, Winston, Reuber, Swanson & Byrne, P.C., Mason City, 1980-92, Winston, Reuber & Byrne, 1992-96, Winston & Byrne P.C., 1996—. Police judge, Mason City, 1961-73. Contbr. articles to profl. jours. Past pres. Family YMCA, Mason City, Cerro Gordo County Estate Planning Coun.; active local charitable orgns. Capt. USAF, 1955-57. Fellow Am. Coll. Trust and Estate Counsel, Am. Bar Found. (life), Iowa Bar Found. (life); mem. ABA, Iowa Bar Assn. (gov., lectr. ann. meeting 1977-79), 2d Jud. Dist. Bar Assn. (lectr. meeting 1981-82), Cerro Gordo County Bar Assn. (past pres.), Am. Judicature Soc., Assn. Trial Lawyers Am., Mason City Country Club, Kiwanis, Masons. Republican. Presbyterian (elder). Probate, General corporate, General practice. Office: Winston & Byrne 119 2d St NW Mason City IA 50401-3105

**WINSTON, JUDITH ANN,** lawyer; b. Atlantic City, Nov. 23, 1943; d. Edward Carlton and Margaret Ann (Goodman) Marianno; m. Michael Russell Winston, Aug. 10, 1963; children: Lisa Marie, Cynthia Eileen. BA magna cum laude, Howard U., Washington, 1966; JD, Georgetown U., 1977. Bar: D.C. 1877, U.S. Supreme Ct. Dir. EEO project Coun. Great City Schs., Washington, 1971-74; legal asst. Lawyers Com. for Civil Rights Under Law, Washington, 1975-77; spl. asst. to dir. Office for Civil Rights, HEW, Washington, 1977-79; exec. asst., legal cousnel to chair U.S. EEO Commn., Washington, 1979-80; asst. gen. counsel U.S. Dept. Edn., 1980-86; dep. dir. Lawyers Com. for Civil Rights Under Law, 1986-88; dep. dir. pub. policy Women's Legal Def. Fund, Washington, 1988-90, chair employment discrimination com., 1979-88, ednl. cons., 1974-77; asst. prof. law Washington Coll. Law of Am. U., 1990-93, assoc. prof. law, 1993-95; gen. cousnel U.S. Dept. Edn., Washington, 1993—; exec. dir. Pres.'s Initiative on Race, 1997-98. Author: Desegregating Schools in the Great Cities: Philadelphia, 1970, Chronicle of a Decade 1961-70, 1970, Desegregating Urban Schools: Educational Equality/Quality, 1970; contbr. articles to profl. jours. Pres. bd. dirs. Higher Achievement Program. Recipient Margaret Brent award Woman Lawyer of Achievement, Am. Bar Assn. Commn. on Women in the Profession, 1998; named Woman Lawyer of Yr., Women's Bar Assn., 1997. Fellow ABA Found.; mem. ACLU (pres. Nat. Capital Area, bd. dirs.), Fed. Bar Assn. (chair gen. counsels sect. 1993—), D.C. Bar Assn. Thurgood Marshall award 1999), Washington Coun. Lawyers, Washington Bar Assn., Nat. Bar Assn., Lawyers Com. for Civil Rights Under Law (treas., bd. dirs.), Links Inc., Alpha Kappa Alpha, Phi Beta Kappa, Delta Theta Phi. Democrat. Episcopalian. Home: 1371 Kalmia Rd NW Washington DC 20012-1444 Office: Dept Edn 600 Independence Ave SW Washington DC 20202-0002

**WINSTON, ROBERT W., JR.,** lawyer, mediator; b. St. Louis, Sept. 18, 1939; s. Robert W. and Lucille McNeely W.; m. Joan M. Makuta, July 27, 1963; children: Christopher, Jennifer, Tamara. BA in Fin., U. Wash., 1961, JD, 1966. Bar: Wash. 1966, U.S. Dist. Ct. (ea. dist.) Wash. 1966, U.S. Ct. Appeals (9th cir.) 1972, U.S. Supreme Ct. 1982. Law clk. to Hon. Charles Powell U.S. Dist. Ct. (ea. dist.), Spokane, 1966-67; ptnr. Winston & Cashatt, PS, Spokane, Wash., 1972-82; assoc. Winston, Cashatt, Repsold, McNichols, Connelly & Driscoll, Spokane, 1967-71; founder, pres. Winston, Stevens & Clay, PS, Spokane, 1983—. Trustee We. Wash. U., Bellingham, 1971-77; trustee, chmn. bd. Children's Home Soc. Wash., Spokane, 1975-76; Wash. del. White House Conf. on Children, 1970, White House Conf. on Youth, 1971. With U.S. Army, 1961-63. Recipient Award of Merit, We. Wash. U., 1977. Mem. Spokane Bar Assn., State Wash. Bar Assn., Wash. Coun. Sch. Attys. (trustee 1976-79), Manito Golf & Country Club (pres. 1994). Avocations: golf, travel. Education and schools, Labor, Alternative dispute resolution. Office: Winston Stevens & Clay PS 421 W Riverside Ave Ste 412 Spokane WA 99201-0402

**WINTER, LESLIE ANTONE,** lawyer; b. Balt., Aug. 21, 1946; s. Henry Leslie and Maxine Sealy Winter; m. Sue Ellen Marder (div. Sept. 1997); children: Rebecca, Jennifer, Samuel. BA, U. Md., 1969, JD, 1972; LLM, George Washington U., 1978. Bar: Md. 1972, U.S. Dist. Ct. Md. 1972. Assoc. Smith Somerville & Case, Balt., 1973-76, Evans, Kohler & George, Balt., 1976-79; ptnr. Ruppersburger, Winter, Clark & Mister, Tinomium, Md., 1979-87; counsel Polovoy, McCoy & Vincent, Balt., 1987-90; owner Advance Title Svcs., Inc., Towson, Md., 1990—. Author: Tax Planner and Preparation for Horseowners, 1990-95, Bookkeeper for Horse Owners, 1990-95. Mem. Md. State Bar Assn., Balt. County Bar Assn. Real property, Estate planning, General corporate. Office: 600 Baltimore Ave Ste 202 Towson MD 21204-4084

**WINTER, RALPH KARL, JR.,** federal judge; b. Waterbury, Conn., July 30, 1935; married. B.A., Yale U., 1957, J.D., 1960. Bar: Conn. 1973. Research assoc., lectr. Yale U., 1962-64, asst. prof. to assoc. prof. law, 1964-78, William K. Townsend prof. law, 1978-82; spl. cons. subcom. on separation of powers U.S. Senate Com. on Judiciary, 1968-72; sr. fellow Brookings Inst., 1968-70; adj. scholar Am. Enterprise Inst., 1972-82; judge U.S. Ct. Appeals (2d cir.), New Haven, 1982-97, chief judge, 1997—; vis. prof. law U. Chgo., 1966; mem. adv. com. civil rules Jud. Conf. U.S., 1987-92, chair adv. com. rules evidence, 1993-96. Contbr. articles to profl. jours. Office: Second Circuit US Courthouse 141 Church St New Haven CT 06510-2030*

**WINTERSHEIMER, DONALD CARL,** state supreme court justice; b. Covington, Ky., Apr. 21, 1932; s. Carl E. and Marie A. (Kohl) W.; m. Alice T. Rabe, June 24, 1961; children: Mark D., Lisa Ann, Craig P., Amy T., Blaise Q. BA, Thomas More Coll., 1953; MA, Xavier U., 1956; JD, U. Cin., 1959; LHD (hon.), No. Ky. U., 1999. Bar: Ky. 1960, Ohio 1960. Pvt. practice Covington, Ky., 1960-76; city solicitor City of Covington, 1962-76; judge Ky. Ct. Appeals, Frankfort, 1976-83; justice Ky. Supreme Ct., Frankfort, 1983—, chmn. criminal rules com., 1988-94, chmn. continuing jud. edn. com., 1983—, chmn. rules com., 1994—; del. Foster Parent Rev. Bd., 1985—; mem. adv. bd. Sta. WNKU-FM, 1984-94, Am. Soc. Writers on Legal Subjects. Trustee Sta. WNKU-FM. Recipient Cmty. Svc. award Thomas More Coll., 1968; recipient Disting. Alumnus award Thomas More Coll., 1982, Disting. Alumni award Coll. Law/U.Cin., 1998; named Disting. Jurist Chase Coll. Law, 1983, Outstanding Jurist Phi Alpha Delta Law Frat., 1990. Mem. ABA, Am. Judicature Soc., Ky. Bar Assn., Ohio Bar Assn., Cin. Bar Assn., Inst. Jud. Adminstrn. Democrat. Roman Catholic. Home: 224 Adams Ave Covington KY 41014-1712 Office: Ky Supreme Ct Capitol Building Room 235 700 Capitol Ave Frankfort KY 40601-3410

**WINTHROP, GRIFFITH JOEL,** lawyer; b. N.Y.C., June 1, 1936; s. Griffith Joel and Frances (Brown) W.; m. Lorna Scott Laughland, June 27, 1976; children: Griffith III, Nathanael Green, Elizabeth, Benjamin. BA, Harvard U., 1958; JD, New Eng. Sch. Law, 1980. Bar: Mass. 1980, N.Y. 1987. Commd. ensign USN, 1959, advanced through grades to lt. comdr., 1968, ret., 1979; atty. Dept. Social Svcs., Essex County, Mass., 1980-86; pvt. practice Canandaigua, N.Y., 1987—. Chmn. clock com. Merrill Vol. Firemen, Canandaigua, 1986—. Recipient Harold S. Ulen award Harvard U., 1958. Mem. Canandaigua Rotary (bd. dirs. 1991). Avocations: sailing, reading. Criminal, Family and matrimonial, Probate. Office: 47 Ontario St Canandaigua NY 14424-1852

**WINTHROP, LAWRENCE FREDRICK,** lawyer; b. L.A., Apr. 18, 1952; s. Murray and Vauneta (Cardwell) W.; BA with honors, Whittier Coll., 1974; JD magna cum laude, Calif. Western Sch., 1977. Bar: Ariz. 1977, Calif. 1977, U.S. Dist. Ct. Ariz. 1977, U.S. Dist. Ct. (so. dist.) Calif. 1981, U.S. Ct. Appeals (9th cir.) 1981, U.S. Dist. Ct. (cen. dist.) Calif. 1983, U.S. Supreme Ct. 1983. Assoc. Snell and Wilmer, Phoenix, 1977-83, ptnr., 1984-93, Doyle, Winthrop, P.C., Phoenix, 1993—. judge pro tem Maricopa County Superior

Ct., 1987-97, Ariz. Ct. Appeals, 1992—; lectr. Ariz. personal injury law and practice and state and local tax law Tax Exec. Inst., Nat. Bus. Inst., Profl. Edn. Systems, Inc., Ariz. Trial Lawyers Assn., Maricopa County Bar Assn.; bd. dirs. Valley of the Sun Sch., 1989-97, chmn., 1994-96; mem. Vol. Lawyers Program, Phoenix, 1980—. Fellow Ariz. Bar Found., Maricopa Bar Found.; mem. ABA, Calif. Bar Assn., Ariz. Bar Assn. (mem. com. on exam, 1995—), Ariz. Tax Rsch. Assn. (bd. dirs. 1989-93), Maricopa County Bar Assn., Ariz. Assn. Def. Counsel (bd. dirs., pres. 1988-89, chmn. med.-mal-practice com. 1993-95), Aspen Valley Club, LaMancha Racquet Club. Republican. Methodist. Avocations: music, golf, tennis. Editor-in-chief Calif. Western Law Rev., 1976-77. General civil litigation, Personal injury. Home: 6031 N 2nd St Phoenix AZ 85012-1210 Office: Doyle and Winthrop PC PO Box 10417 2800 N Central Ave Ste 1550 Phoenix AZ 85004-1057

**WINTHROP, SHERMAN,** lawyer; b. Duluth, Minn., Feb. 3, 1931; s. George E. and Mary (Tesler) W.; m. Barbara Cowan, Dec. 16, 1956; children: Susan Winthrop Crist, Bradley T., Douglas A. BBA, U. Minn., 1952; JD, Harvard U., 1955. Bar: Minn. 1955, U.S. Dist. Ct. Minn. 1955, U.S. Tax Ct. Law clk. to chief justice Minn. Supreme Ct., St. Paul, 1955-56; ptnr. Oppenheimer, Wolff & Donnelly, St. Paul, 1956-79; chmn. Winthrop & Weinstine P.A., St. Paul, 1979—; bd. dirs. Bremer Fin. Corp., St. Paul, Minn. Mem. ABA, Minn. Bar Assn. (chair exec. coun., bus. law sect. 1992-93), Ramsey County Bar Assn. Avocations: tennis, travel, family. Banking, General corporate, Real property. Home: 1672 Pinehurst Ave Saint Paul MN 55116-2158 Office: Winthrop & Weinstine PA 3200 Minn World Trade Ctr 30 7th St E Saint Paul MN 55101-4914

**WINZENREID, JAMES ERNEST,** lawyer, entrepreneur; b. Wheeling, W.Va., June 9, 1951; s. Ernest Christian and Dorothy Emma (Wolf) W.; m. Rebecca Lee Rice, Aug. 11, 1979; children: Diana Lee, Lauren Rice. AB, W. Liberty State Coll., 1973; MBA, W.Va. U., 1979; JD, Duquesne U., 1987; LLM, Wayne State U., 1989. Bar: Pa. 1987, U.S. Dist. Ct. (we. dist.) Pa. 1987. Staff asst. Wheeling Pitts. Steel Corp., Wheeling, 1974-78, supr. indl. relations, 1978; mgr. profl. planning and devel. Copperweld Corp., Pitts., 1978-79; mgr. human resources Copperweld Corp., Glassport, Pa., 1979-81; plant mgr. Copperweld Corp., Glassport, 1981-83; group mgr. human resources Copperweld Corp., Pitts., 1984-85, market program mgr., 1986-87; with lab. and employment dept. Eckert, Seamans, Cherin & Mellott, Pitts., 1986-87; corp. staff rep. Tecumseh (Mich.) Products Co., 1987-89; v.p. human resources devel. Lafarge (Va.) Corp., 1989-94; v.p. human resources western region Lafarge Constrn. Materials, Calgary, Alta., Can., 1994-96, Lafarge Can. Inc., Calgary, 1996-99; v.p. human resources Alstrom Transport, Inc., N.Y.C., 1999—. Mng. editor Juris mag., 1986. Bd. dirs. Wheeling Symphony Soc., 1977-86, Wheeling Jaycees, 1976-78; mem. adv. bd. Jr. Achievement Southwestern Pa., 1981-83. Named Outstanding Young Men Am. U.S. Jaycees, 1979. Mem. ASTD, ABA, Pa. Bar Assn., Allegheny Bar Assn., Am. Soc. Human Resources Mgmt., Human Resource Planning Soc., Human Resources Assn. Calgary, Human Resources Inst. Alberta, Phi Alpha Delta. Republican. Lutheran. Avocations: golf, reading. Labor. Home: 47 Overbrook Dr Bridgeport OH 43912-1412 Office: Alstom Transport Inc 420 Lexington Ave Ste 810 New York NY 10170

**WINZER, P.J.,** lawyer; b. Shreveport, La., June 7, 1947; d. C.W. Winzer and Pearlene Hall Winzer Tobin. BA in Polit. Sci., So. U., Baton Rouge, 1968; JD, UCLA, 1971. Bar: Bar: Calif. 1972, U.S. Supreme Ct. 1986. Staff atty. Office of Gen. Counsel, U.S. HEW, Washington, 1971-80; asst. spl. counsel U.S. Office of Spl. Counsel Merit Systems Protection Bd., Dallas, 1980-82; regional dir. U.S. Merit Systems Protection Bd., Falls Church, Va., 1982—. Mem. Calif. Bar Assn., Fed. Cir. Bar Assn., Delta Sigma Theta. Office: US Merit System Protection 5203 Leesburg Pike Ste 1109 Falls Church VA 22041-3471

**WIRKEN, JAMES CHARLES,** lawyer; b. Lansing, Mich., July 3, 1944; s. Frank and Mary (Brosnahan) W.; m. Mary Morse, June 12, 1971; children: Christopher, Erika, Kurt, Gretchen, Jeffrey, Matthew. BA in English, Rockhurst Coll., 1967; JD, St. Louis U., 1970. Bar: Mo. 1970, U.S. Dist. Ct. (we. dist.) Mo. 1970. Asst. prosecuter Jackson County, Kansas City, Mo., 1970-72; assoc. Morris, Larson, King, Stamper & Bold, Kansas City, Mo., 1972-75; dir. Spradley, Wirken, Reismeyer & King, Kansas City, Mo., 1976-88, Wirken & King, Kansas City, Mo., 1988-93; pres. The Wirken Group, Kansas City, Mo., 1993—; adj. prof. law U. Mo., Kansas City, 1984-89; founder, chmn. Lender Liability Group. Author: Managing a Practice and Avoiding Malpractice, 1983; co-author Missouri Civil Procedure Form Book, 1984; mem. editorial bd. Mo. Law Weekly, 1989—, Lender Liability News, 1990—, Emerging Trends and Theories of Lender Liability, 1991. Mem. ABA (exec. coun.), Nat. Conf. Bar Pres. (coun. 1992-96), Nat. Caucus of Met. Bar Leaders (exec. coun., pres. 1988-94), Am. Trial Lawyers Assn., L.P. Gas Group (founder, chair 1986-90), Mo. Bar Assn. (bd. govs. 1977-78, chmn. econs. and methods practice com. 1982-84, quality and methods of practice com. 1989-91, vice chmn. young lawyers sect. 1976-78), Mo. Assn. Trial Attys. (bd. govs. 1983-85), Kansas City Met. Bar Assn. (pres. young lawyers sect. 1975, chair legal assistance com. 1977-78, chair tort law com. 1982, pres. 1990). Federal civil litigation, State civil litigation, Personal injury. Home: 47 W 53rd Kansas City MO 64112 Office: The Wirken Group PC 2600 Grand Blvd Ste 440 Kansas City MO 64108-4600

**WIRTH, PETER,** lawyer; b. Halgehausen, Germany, July 17, 1950; came to U.S., 1956; BA, U. Wis., 1972; JD, Harvard U., 1975. Bar: Mass. 1975. Assoc. Palmer & Dodge, Boston, 1975-81, ptnr., 1982-96, of counsel, 1996—; exec. v.p., chief legal officer Genzyme Corp., 1996—; lectr. grad. tax program Boston U., 1982-85. Mem. ABA, Mass. Bar Assn., Phi Beta Kappa. General corporate, Securities, Finance. Office: Genzyme Corporation One Kendall Square Cambridge MA 02139

**WIRTZ, RICHARD STANLEY,** law educator, former dean; b. Chgo., June 15, 1940; s. William Willard and Jane (Quisenberry) W.; m. Margaret Hickman, Oct. 12, 1966; children: Elizabeth, Margaret. BA magna cum laude, Amherst Coll., 1961; MPA, Princeton U., 1963; JD, Stanford U., 1970. Bar: Wash., 1971. Law clerk to Hon. Robert A. Ainsworth U.S. Ct. Appeals ( 5th cir.), 1970-71; assoc. Davis, Wright, Todd, Riese & Jones, Seattle, 1971-74; asst. prof. U. Tenn. Law Coll., Knoxville, 1974-77, assoc. prof., 1977-87, prof., 1987—. Acad. Affairs assoc. dean, 1988-91, acting dean, 1991-92, dean, 1992-98; vis. assoc. prof. Cornell U. Law Sch., 1977-78; chairperson sect. on tchg. methods Assn. Am. Law Schs., 1991-92. Contbr. articles to profl. jours. With U.S. Army, 1963-64. Recipient SBA Outstanding Tchr. award, 1987, Harry W. Laughlin Faculty Svc. award, 1987, Harold C. Warner Outstanding Tchr. award, 1984, Univ. Tenn. Law Coll. Fellow Am. Bar Found., Tenn. Bar Found.; mem. ABA (vice chmn. curriculum com. sect. legal edn. and addmissions to the bar 1995—), So. Assn. Colls. & Schs. (hon. officer 1995—), Tenn. Bar Assn., Tenn. Lawyers Assn. for Women. Democrat. Avocations: soccer refereeing, racquetball. Office: Univ Tenn Coll Law 1505 Cumberland Ave Knoxville TN 37916-3199*

**WISE, AARON NOAH,** lawyer; b. Hartford, Conn., Feb. 14, 1940; s. Joseph J. and Ethel (Sklar) W.; m. Genevieve Ehrlich, Dec. 17. 1966; children: Haywood Martin, Paul Russell, Renee Alicia. AB, Boston U., 1962; JD, Boston Coll., 1965; LLM in Comparative/Internat. Law, NYU, 1971; certificat de Doctorate, d' Université en Droit, U. Paris Law Sch., 1970. Bar: N.Y., U.S. Dist. Ct. (so. dist.) N.Y. Internat. atty. Schering-Plough, Kenilworth, N.J., 1969-74; ptnr. Conboy Hewitt O'Brien & Boardman, N.Y.C., 1974-80, Wise Lerman & Katz P.C. (formerly Rosenbaum Wise Lerman & Katz), N.Y.C., 1981-95, Klepner & Cayea, N.Y.C., 1995-98, Brand, Layea & Brand, LLC, 1998—; lectr. bus. and legal groups U.S., Europe, Latin Am. Author: International Sports Law and Business (Kluwer Law Internat., 1997, 3 vols.), Foreign Businessman's Guide to U.S. Law-Practice-Taxation; contbr. articles to pubs. in U.S. and Europe. Mem. ABA, N.Y. State Bar Assn. Avocations: multi-lingual including French, Spanish, Portuguese, Italian, Russian, Japanese and German. Private international, General corporate, Contracts commercial. Home: 38 Cummings Cir West Orange NJ 07052-2264 Office: Brand Cayea & Brand LLC 720 5th Ave Fl 14 New York NY 10019-4107

**WISE, DONALD EDWARD,** lawyer; b. Bristol, Tenn.; s. Donald Edward Sr. and Nancy June Wise; m. Pamela Kay, Aug. 10, 1991; children: Jackson Tyler, Zachary Andrew. BS, East Tenn. State U., Johnson City, 1989; JD, Samford U., Birmingham, Ala., 1993. Bar: Va. 1993, Tenn. 1994, U.S. Dist. Ct. (we. dist.) Va. 1993, U.S. Dist. Ct. (ea. dist.) Tenn. 1994, U.S. Ct. Appeals (6th cir.) 1993, U.S. Ct. Appeals (4th cir.) 1994. Atty. Arrington, Schelin & Herrell, P.C., Birstol, Va., 1991—. Mem. ABA, ATLA, Workplace Injury Litigation Group, Nat. Orgn. Social Security Claimants Reps. Republican. Presbyterian. Labor, Workers' compensation. Home: 3631 Island Rd Blountville TN 37617-3707 Office: Arrington Schelin & Hervell 1315 Euclid Ave Bristol VA 24201-3830

**WISE, HELENA SUNNY,** lawyer; b. Ridgecrest, Calif., Dec. 3, 1954; d. Strother Eldon and Mary Helen (Harinek) W.; children: Marie Evelyn, Shawnie Helene. BA with honors, UCLA, 1976; JD with highest honors, Loyola Marymount U., 1979. Bar: Calif. 1979, U.S. Dist. Ct. (ctrl. dist.) Calif. 1980, U.S. Ct. Appeals (9th cir.) 1980, Nev. 1992, Ariz. 1992. Ptnr. Geffner & Satzman, Los Angeles, 1980-87; pvt. practice Burbank, Calif., 1987—. Columnist Los Angeles Lawyer mag., 1985-86. Chmn., founder Barristers Child Abuse Com., L.A., 1982-86; mem. exec. bd. Vols. in Parole, L.A., 1983-90; mem. Dem. Chair's Circle, L.A., 1985; mem. adv. bd. Over Easy Found., 1987—; vol. Love is Feeding Everyone. Fellow ABA (exec. coun. labor and employment law 1986-89, liaison young lawyers sect., bd. dirs. young lawyers divsn. 1986-88, mem. MSN team Nat. Com. on Child Abuse, del., teller Ho. of Dels. 1978-79), L.A. County Bar Assn. (v.p. sr. bar 1984-86, pres. young lawyers sect.), State Bar Calif. (bd. dirs. Calif. Young Lawyers Assn., labor law ad hoc com. on wrongful discharge, mem. juv. law com., UCLA alumni rep., USAC 1992-94, student rels. com. 1992-94), Am. Legion Women's Auz. Avocations: photography, skiing, playing organ. Office: 3111 W Burbank Blvd Ste 101 Burbank CA 91505-2350

**WISE, ROBERT POWELL,** lawyer; b. Jackson, Miss., Nov. 13, 1951; s. Sherwood Willing and Elizabeth (Powell) W. AB, Colgate U., 1973; MA, U. Va., 1975; JD, Washington & Lee U., 1979. Bar: Miss. 1979, U.S. Dist. Ct. Miss. 1979, U.S. Ct. Appeals (5th cir.) 1988. Ptnr. Wise, Carter, Child & Caraway, Jackson, 1979—. Lic. lay reader, chalice bearer St. Andrews Episc. Cathedral, Jackson, 1984—; pres. Caledonian Soc. Miss., Jackson, 1987, bd. dirs., 1985-90; bd. dirs. Belhaven Improvement Assn., 1991—, pres., 1994-97, English Speaking Union of Miss., Jackson, 1985-92, Nat. Kidney Found. Miss., 1987—, v.p., 1988-92, pres. 1993-94; pres. Belhaven Security Assn., 1992-93. Mem. ABA, Fed. Comm. Bar Assn., Miss. Bar Assn. Construction, Administrative and regulatory, Consumer commercial. Home: 1602 Linden Pl Jackson MS 39202-1215 Office: Wise Carter Child & Caraway 600 Heritage Bldg Jackson MS 39201-2688

**WISE, ROGER LAMBERT,** lawyer; b. Pitts., Dec. 19, 1945; s. Lambert A. and Elizabeth S. (Schultz) W.; m. Karen M. Wise, May 16, 1970; children: Matthew, Tara. BS, U. Pitts., 1967, JD, 1973. Bar: Pa. 1973, W.Va. 1992, U.S. Dist. Ct. (we., mid., ea. dists.) Pa., (so. dist.) W.Va. 1992, U.S. Ct. Appeals (3d cir.) 1974. Law clk. Hon. Ruggerio J. Aldisert 3d Cir., Pitts., 1973-75; atty. USX Corp., Pitts., 1975-85; assoc. Grigsby, Gaca & Davies, Pitts., 1985-89, ptnr., 1990-93; ptnr. Heintzman, Warren & Wise, Pitts., 1993—. 1st lt. USAF, 1969-72. Mem. ABA, ASTM, Am. Welding Soc., Pa. Bar Assn., Allegheny County Bar Assn. Product liability, Personal injury, Construction. Office: Heintzman Warren Wise & Fornella PC 35th Fl Gulf Tower 707 Grant St Pittsburgh PA 15219-1908

**WISE, SHERWOOD WILLING,** lawyer; b. Hazlehurst, Miss., Aug. 13, 1910; s. Joseph Sherwood and Myra (Willing) W.; m. Elizabeth Carter Powell, July 28, 1937; children: Elizabeth Wise Copeland, Sherwood Willing, Joseph Powell, Robert Powell and Louise Wise Hardy (twins). B.A., Washington and Lee U., 1932, J.D., 1934, LLD (hon.), 1997. Bar: Miss. 1934. Practiced law Jackson; counsel Wise Carter Child & Caraway, 1941-87; commr. Miss. Bar, 1958-60; gen. counsel Miss. Power & Light Co., 1961-80. Author: Wise Carter Child & Caraway, One Missisipi Law Firm, 1883-1986, 1988, The Cathedral of St. Andrew, 1839-1989, 1989, St. Andrew's Episcopal Day School: A Case for Continuity and Stability in Christian Values, 1983, The Way I See It, Then and Now, 1996. Co-founder Jackson Symphony Orch., 1944; pres. Jackson Cmty. Chest, 1950; Miss. chmn. Ducks Unlimited, Inc., 1961-71; mem. exec. com. Episcopal Diocese Miss., 1941, past mem. dept. missions and standing com., also trustee, 1958-88; del. Episc. Gen. Conv., 1952, 64, 67, 69, 70, 79; mem. joint commn., ecumenical rels. Episc., Ch., 1967-73; co-founder, chmn. St. Mark's Ednl. Day care Ctr., 1967; a founder, organizer St. Andrew's Episc. Day Sch., Jackson, 1947, trustee, 1947-72, 78-82; trustee Nat. Cathedral Assn., 1975-77; del. Democratic Nat. Conv., 1940; trustee State Dept. Archives and History, 1947, King, Jackson Jr. League Carnival Ball, 1971. Served to lt. comdr. USNR, 1942-46. Recipient Disting. Alumnus award Washington and Lee U., 1983. Fellow Am. Coll. Trial Lawyers, Am. Inns of Ct. (Charles Clark chpt.), Magna Charta Barons, Gen. Soc. of War of 1812 (pres. Miss. 1992-94), The Sovereign Colonial Soc., Am. of Royal Descent, Order First Families of Miss. 1699-1817, SCV; mem. ABA (com. on civil rights and racial unrest 1962, standing com. fed. judiciary 1969-75, Miss. state del. to ho. of dels. 1981-87), Nat. Conf. Lawyers and Environ. Design Profls. (chmn. 1979-85), Nat. Soc. SAR, Sons of the Revolution, Miss. Bar Assn. (pres. 1961-62), Hinds County Bar Assn. (pres. 1958-59), Edison Electric Inst. (legal com. 1962-80), Nat. Assn. R.R. Trial Counsel, Am. Judicature Soc., Scribes, Jackson C. of C. (past v.p., dir.), Newcomen Soc., Cum Laude Soc., Kappa Sigma, Omicron Delta Kappa, Phi Delta Phi. Clubs: Rotary (past dir., Paul Harris fellow), Jackson Country (past bd. govs.), Capital Club, Jackson Yacht (past gov.). Federal civil litigation, General corporate, Public utilities. Home: 3839 Eastover Dr Jackson MS 39211-6731 Office: PO Box 651 Jackson MS 39205-0651

**WISE, WARREN ROBERTS,** retired lawyer; b. Beaver City, Nebr., Oct. 8, 1929; s. Harold Edward and Doris Lorene (Roberts) W.; m. Marcia Hench, Oct. 14, 1961; children: Debra, David, Susan. BS, U. Nebr., 1950, LLB, 1953; LLM, Georgetown U., 1960. Atty. U.S. Dept. Justice Lands Div., Washington, 1955-61, U.S. Dept. Justice Tax Div., Washington, 1961-63; assoc. counsel Mass. Mut. Life Ins. Co., Springfield, 1963-67, asst. gen. counsel, 1967-72, 2d v.p., assoc. gen. counsel, 1972-74, v.p., assoc. gen. counsel, 1974-85, sr. v.p., assoc. gen. counsel, 1985-88, exec. v.p., gen. counsel, 1988-93; ret., 1993. Author: Business Insurance Agreements, 1970, 80, 91; editor; Massachusetts Life Insurance Law, 1980. Chmn. bd. East Coast Conf., Evang. Covenant Ch., 1987-89, chmn. pension bd., 1984-86, exec. bd., 1995—; bd. dirs. Mass. Family Inst., 1994-98, vol. policy analyst, 1994-98. Mem. ABA (chmn. life ins. law com. torts and ins. sect. 1992-93), Assn. Life Inst. Counsel (bd. dirs. 1987-92, pres. 1992-93), Longmeadow Country Club, Laurel Oak Country Club. Republican. Avocation: golf. Home: 7831 Allen Robertson Pl Sarasota FL 34240-8634

**WISEHART, ARTHUR MCKEE,** lawyer; b. Evanston, Ill., July 3, 1928; s. Arthur J. and Dorothy H. (Rice) W.; m. Mary Elizabeth Dodson, 1953; children: William, Ellen, Arthur, Charles. B.A., Miami U., Oxford, Ohio, 1950; M.P.A., Wayne State U., 1953; J.D., U. Mich., 1954. Bar: N.Y. 1955. With firm Chadbourne, Parke, Whiteside & Wolff, N.Y.C., 1954-59; with Am. Airlines, Inc., 1959-69, corp. sec., asst. gen. counsel, 1968-69; sr. v.p., gen. counsel, sec. REA Express, 1969-74; dir., sec. REA Holding Corp., 1969-74; sr. partner Law Offices of Arthur M. Wisehart, 1974-75, Wisehart & Koch, 1975—, 1981—; dir. Hoover Co., 1975-76. Author articles. Mem. ABA, Assn. of Bar of City of N.Y., Order of Coif, Delta Chi. Presbyterian. Clubs: Princeton. General civil litigation, Civil rights, Labor. Office: Wisehart & Koch 19 W 44th St Ste 412 New York NY 10036-5993

**WISEHEART, MALCOLM BOYD, JR.,** lawyer; b. Miami, Fla., Sept. 18, 1942; s. Malcolm B. and Dorothy E. (Allen) W.; m. Michele I. Romanens, Dec. 11, 1976. BA, Yale U., 1965; MA in English Jurisprudence, Cambridge U., 1973; JD with honors, U. Fla., 1970. Bar: Fla. 1970, Eng. and Wales 1970, Jamaica 1970, Trinidad and Tobago 1971, D.C. 1980. Assoc. Helliwell, Melrose & DeWolf, Miami, 1970-72; sr. ptnr. Malcolm B. Wiseheart, Jr., P.A., Miami, 1973-86; sr. ptnr., Wiseheart & Joyce, P.A., Miami, 1986-88; sec., gen. counsel Wiseheart Found.; spl. master Dade County Property Appraisal Adjustment Bd., 1977-90; pres. Fla. Law Inst., 1980-99; trustee, mem. exec. com. Players State Theater, 1982-84; bd. dirs. Sta. WLRN Pub. Radio, 1982, Coun. Internat. Visitors; trustee Ransom Everglades Sch., 1995-97. Named Most Outstanding, U. Fla. Law Rev. Alumnus, 1981. Mem. Fla Bar (chmn. grievance com. 1978-81), Dade County Bar Assn. (dir. 1971-74, 86-89, treas. 1974-75, sec. 1975-77), Order of Coif, Yale Club (Miami pres. 1976-77), United Oxford and Cambridge Univs. Club (London). Real property, State civil litigation, Landlord-tenant. Office: Wiseheart Bldg 2840 SW 3rd Ave Miami FL 33129-2317

**WISEMAN, MICHAEL MARTIN,** lawyer; b. N.Y.C., Oct. 25, 1953; s. Robert Lawrence and Katherine Loise (Martin) W.; m. Helen Ann Garten, May 18, 1984. BA, Harvard U., 1975, JD, 1978. Bar: N.Y. 1979, Mass. 1978, U.S. Dist. Ct. (so. and ea. dists.) N.Y. 1979, U.S. Supreme Ct. 1988. Assoc. Sullivan & Cromwell, N.Y.C., 1978-85, ptnr., 1985—; mem. N.Y. State Banking Law Com. Contbr. articles to profl. jours. Fellow Am. Bar Found.; mem. ABA (vice chair banking, currency and treasury com. of adminstrv. law sect. 1991-94), Assn. Bar City N.Y. (chair com. on banking law 1985-91, chair 1988-91), Am. Law Inst. Banking, Finance, Securities. Office: Sullivan & Cromwell 125 Broad St Fl 28 New York NY 10004-2489

**WISEMAN, THOMAS ANDERTON, JR.,** federal judge; b. Tullahoma, Tenn., Nov. 3, 1930; s. Thomas Anderton and Vera Seleta (Poe) W.; m. Emily Barbara Matlack, Mar. 30, 1957; children: Thomas Anderton III, Mary Alice, Sarah Emily. B.A., Vanderbilt U., 1952, LL.B., 1954; LLM, U. Va., 1990. Bar: Tenn. Pvt. practice Tullahoma, 1956-63; ptnr. Haynes, Wiseman & Hull, Tullahoma and Winchester, Tenn., 1963-71; treas. State of Tenn., 1971-74; ptnr. Chambers & Wiseman, 1974-78; judge U.S. Dist. Ct. (mid. dist.) Tenn., Nashville, 1978—, chief judge, 1984-91, sr. judge, 1995—; rep. 6th cir. Jud. Conf. of the U.S., 1997—, chair dist. judges conf., 1998-99; mem. Tenn. Ho. of Reps., 1964-68; adj. prof. law Vanderbilt U. Sch. Law. Asso. editor: Vanderbilt Law Rev, 1953-54. Democratic candidate for gov., Tenn., 1974; Chmn. Tenn. Heart Fund, 1973, Middle Tenn. Heart Fund, 1972. Served with U.S. Army, 1954-56. Fellow Tenn. Bar Found.; mem. Fed. Judges Assn. (bd. dirs. 1982-87, v.p. 1982-91, 87-91, 6th cir. rep. to jud. conf. U.S.), Masons (33 deg.), Shriners, Amateur Chefs Soc. Presbyterian. Office: US Dist Ct 777 US Courthouse 801 Broadway Nashville TN 37203-3816

**WISHEK, MICHAEL BRADLEY,** lawyer; b. Pasadena, Calif., June 25, 1959; s. Homer Cedric and Donna Jean (Arnold) W.; m. Shari Patrice Rubin, June 7, 1981 (div. Feb. 1986); m. Dorothea Jean Palo, Feb. 12, 1988; children: Kirstin Alyce, Lauren Ashley. BS in Polit. Sci and Philosophy, Claremont Men's Coll., 1981; JD, U. Calif., Davis, 1985. Bar: Calif. 1986, U.S. Dist. Ct. (ea. dist.) Calif. 1986. Assoc. Michael S. Sands, Inc., Sacramento, 1986-91; ptnr. Rothschild & Wishek, Sacramento, 1991-96, Rothschild, Wishek & Sands, Sacramento, 1996—; mem. Milton L. Schwartz Am. Inn of Ct., 1992-97; adj. instr. trial practice U. Calif., Sch. Law, Davis. Mem. ABA, Calif. Bar Assn., Sacramento County Bar Assn. (co-chmn. criminal law sect. 1988-90), Calif. Attys. for Criminal Justice, Criminal Def. Lawyers of Sacramento (bd. dirs. 1993—, v.p. 1996). Democrat. Avocations: snow skiing, backpacking, sailing. Criminal. Office: 901 F St Ste 200 Sacramento CA 95814-0733

**WISHENGRAD, MARCIA H.,** lawyer; b. Hudson, N.Y., Feb. 10, 1936; d. Joseph and Jessie (Diamond) W.; m. Robert J. Metzger, Sept. 3, 1961; 1 child, Jocelyn M. BA, Cornell U., 1957, JD, 1960. Bar: N.Y. 1960, U.S. Dist. Ct. (so. and ea. dists.) N.Y. 1962, U.S. Supreme Ct. 1964. Atty. Monroe County Family Court, Rochester, N.Y., 1963-65, Monroe County Legal Aid Soc., Rochester, 1965-67; sr. urban renewal atty. City of Rochester, 1971-74; dep. county atty. Monroe County, Rochester, 1974-93; pvt. practice Rochester, 1963—. Bd. visitors State Sch. Industry, Rochester; pres. Arc of Monroe County, 1991-93; v.p. Arc Found. of Monroe, 1990—. Mem. N.Y. State Bar Assn., Monroe County Bar Assn., Greater Rochester Assn. of Women Attys. (judicial com.). Republican. Jewish. Avocations: boating, tennis, reading. Family and matrimonial. Office: 36 W Main St Ste 312 Rochester NY 14614-1701

**WISLER, JAMES LYNN,** lawyer; b. Emporia, Kans., May 6, 1943; s. Clyde C. and Iris A. Wisler; children: Simone, Mac, Hilary, Charity, Tess, Mike. BA, U. Kans., 1965, JD, 1975. Bar: Kans. 1975. Mem. Schroer Rice PA, Topeka, Kans., 1992—. Mem. ATLA, Kans. Trial Lawyers Assn., Topeka Bar Assn., Kans. Bar Assn., Douglas County Bar Assn. Democrat. Roman Catholic. Personal injury, Workers' compensation, Civil rights. Home: 1016 Parkview Rd Lawrence KS 66049-3323 Office: Schroer Rice PA 115 SE 7th St Topeka KS 66603-3901

**WISNER, CYNTHIA FICKE,** lawyer, law educator; b. Cin., Aug. 17, 1957; d. Howard William and Verna Lee (Schriever) Ficke; m. Neal R. Wisner, Jan. 5, 1980; children: April Leigh, Shelbi Lynn. BS, Kent State U., 1978; JD, U. Mich., 1981. Bar: Mich. 1981, U.S. Dist. Ct. (ea. dist.) Mich. 1981, U.S. Tax Ct. 1982. Assoc. Jaffe, Snider, Raitt and Heuer, Detroit, 1981-83; assoc. Honigman Miller Schwartz and Cohn, Detroit, 1983-86, ptnr., 1987-93; ptnr. Howard & Howard Attys., P.C., Bloomfield Hills, Mich., 1993-94; gen. counsel The Detroit Med. Ctr., 1994—; adj. prof. U. Detroit Mercy, 1987—;presenter at profl. confs. Co-editor Health Law Focus newsletter, 1991-93. Tchr. Sunday jr. ch., Wed. midweek ch. Trinity Evangel. Presbyn. Ch., Plymouth, Mich., 1990—. Mem. ABA (health law forum), Mich. Soc. Hosp. Attys., Nat. Health Lawyers Assn., Acctg. Aid Soc., Kent State U. Alumni Assn., U. Mich. Alumni Assn. Avocations: fishing, reading, teaching. Health, Taxation, general, General corporate. Office: The Detroit Med Ctr 3990 John R St Detroit MI 48201-2018

**WISSER, ELLEN,** lawyer, educator; b. N.Y.C., May 7, 1930; d. Samuel and Essie (Chentko) Borenstein; m. Allen Wisser, Apr. 1, 1951; children—Ronni Ilise, Jamie Robert, Kerry Marc. Student Am. Acad. Dramatic Arts, N.Y.C., 1948-49; B.A. cum laude, Bklyn. Coll., 1953, M.A., 1955; J.D., U. Bridgeport (Conn.), 1982. Bar: Conn. 1983, U.S. Dist. Ct. Conn. 1984, U.S. Supreme Ct., 1986. Tchr. N.Y.C. Bd. Edn., 1953-62, Bridgeport Bd. Edn., 1963-84; sole practice, Westport/Bridgeport, Conn., 1983—; legal cons., dir. Bridgeport Youth Law Edn. Program, 1983-85; dir. Conn. Consortium for Law-Related Edn., Inc., 1982—; speaker in field; dir. Westport Speech and Hearing Ctr., 1964-66. Mem. Mayor's Conf. on Status of Edn. 1984. Recipient Am. Jurisprudence awards, 1978-79. Mem. ABA, Conn. Bar Assn. (family law sect., juvenile justice com. women's law com. 1984), Bridgeport Bar Assn., Assn. Trial Lawyers Am., Conn. Trial Lawyers Assn., NEA (state del.-rep. assembly 1972-77, evaluator 1973), Conn. Edn. Assn. (dir. 1974-77, legis. comm. 1972-78, Bridgeport Edn. Assn. (v.p. 1973-74, 83-84, labor negotiator 1983, chmn. joint com. tchr. evaluation 1979-84), Phi Alpha Delta (Douglass chpt. treas. 1978-79, del. nat. conv. 1979). Family and matrimonial, General practice, Workers' compensation. Home: 7 Black Birch Rd Westport CT 06880-2603

**WISWALL, FRANK LAWRENCE, JR.,** lawyer, educator; b. Albany, N.Y., Sept. 21, 1939; s. Frank Lawrence and Clara Elizabeth (Chapman) W.; m. Elizabeth Curtiss Nelson, Aug. 9, 1975; children by previous marriage: Anne W. Kowalski, Frank Lawrence III. BA, Colby Coll., 1962; JD, Cornell U., 1965; PhD in Law, Cambridge U., 1967. Bar: Maine 1965, N.Y. 1968, U.S. Supreme Ct. 1968, D.C. 1975; lic. master near coastal steam and motor vessels, 1960—. Assoc. Burlingham, Underwood, Barron, Wright & White, N.Y.C., 1967-73; maritime legal adviser Rep. of Liberia, 1968-88; v.p. com. Maritime Internat., 1997—; intern Maritime Law Inst., 1999; mem. legal com. Internat. Maritime Orgn., London, 1972-74, vice chmn. 1974-79, chmn., 1980-84; tutorial supr. internat. law Clare Coll., Cambridge, Eng., 1966-67; vis. lectr. Cornell Law Sch., 1969-76, 82; lectr. U. Va. Law Sch. and Ctr. for Oceans Law and Policy, 1978-82; prof. law Cornell U., 1984; Johnsen prof. maritime law Tulane U., 1985; vis. prof. law World Maritime U., Malmo, Sweden, 1986—; prof. Internat. Maritime Law Inst., Malta, 1991—, mem. governing bd., 1992—; prof. admiralty law Maine Maritime Acad., 1993-94; del. Internat. Conf. Marine Pollution, London, 1973; del., chmn. drafting com. Internat. Conf. Carriage of Passengers and Luggage by Sea, Athens, 1974; del. Internat. Conf. on Safety of Life at Sea, London, 1974, 3d UN Conf. on Law of Sea, Caracas, Venezuela, 1974, 3d UN Conf. on Law of Sea (all subsequent sessions); del., chmn. com. final clauses Internat. Conf. on Limitation of Liability for Maritime Claims, London, 1976; del. UN Conf. Carriage of Goods by Sea, Hamburg, 1978, XIII Diplomatic Conf. on Maritime Law, Brussels, 1979; chmn. com. of the whole Internat. Conf. Carriage of Hazardous Substances by Sea, 1984; del. internat. conf. on Maritime Terrorism, Rome, 1988; counsel various marine casualty bds. of investigation, 1970—, harbormaster, Port of Castine, 1960-62. Author: The Development of Admiralty Jurisdiction and Practice Since 1800, 1970; editor-in-chief Benedict on Admiralty, Vols. 6, 6A-6F (Internat. Maritime Law), 1992—; contbr. articles to profl. jours. Ofcl. prin. Diocese of

Mid-Atlantic States, Anglican Cath. Ch., 1988—, chancellor Missionary Diocese of N.E., 1993—; spkr. assembly laity Anglican Cath. Ch., 1995—. Recipient Yorke prize U. Cambridge, 1968-69. Fellow Royal Hist. Soc.; mem. Nat. Lawyers Assn., Comité Maritime Internat. (exec. councillor 1989-96, v.p. 1997—), Maritime Law Assn. U.S. (chmn. com. on intergovtl. orgns. 1983-87, chmn. com. on CMI 1987-95), Ecclesiastical Law Soc., Selden Soc., Am. Soc. Legal History, U.K. Assn. Average Adjusters, U.S. Assn. Average Adjusters, Maine Bar Assn., Assn. Bar City N.Y., U.S. Navy League (pres. Penobscot coun. 1997), United Oxford and Cambridge U. Club (London), Century Assn., Alpha Delta Phi, Phi Delta Phi. Admiralty, Private international, Public international. Office: PO Box 201 Castine ME 04421-0201

**WITHERS, W. WAYNE,** lawyer; b. Enid, Okla., Nov. 4, 1940; s. Walter O. and Ruby (Mackey) W.; m. Patricia Ann Peppers, Dec. 12, 1974; children: Jennifer Lynn, Whitney Lee. BA, U. Okla., 1962; JD, Northwestern U., 1965. Bar: Okla. 1965, Mo. 1970, U.S. Ct. Appeals (8th cir.), 1972, U.S. Supreme Ct. 1972, U.S. Ct. Appeals (fed. cir.) 1984, U.S. Ct. Appeals (D.C. cir.) 1985, U.S. Ct. Claims, 1988. Staff atty. FTC, Washington, 1965-68; co. atty. Monsanto Co., St. Louis, 1966-78, asst. gen. counsel, 1978-85; gen. counsel Monsanto Agrl. Co., St. Louis, 1985-87, v.p., gen. counsel, 1987-89; sr. v.p., sec., gen. counsel Emerson Electric Co., St. Louis, 1989—; v.p. Internat. Food Biotech. Coun., Washington, 1989-90; bd. dirs. Internat. Life Scis. Inst., Washington, 1989-90. Contbr. articles to profl. jours. Mem. ABA (sec. corp. law dept.), Am. Law Inst., Assn. Gen. Counsel, Bar Assn. Met. St. Louis, Indsl. Biotech. Assn. (chmn. law com.), Environ. Law Inst. (assoc.), Nat. Agrl. Chem. Assn. (chmn. law com. 1983-85), The Conf. Bd. Coun. for Gen. Counsel (vice chmn. 1992-99), MAPI Law Coun. Administrative and regulatory, General corporate, Environmental. Home: 608 Claymont Estate Dr Chesterfield MO 63017-7060 Office: Emerson Electric Co 8100 W Florissant Ave Saint Louis MO 63136-1494

**WITHERWAX, CHARLES HALSEY,** lawyer, arbitrator, mediator; b. Schroon Lake, N.Y., July 24, 1934; s. Halsey Jerome and Elizabeth Daisy (Bingham) W.; m. Marianne Jehander, June 24, 1980. BS in Marine Transp., N.Y. State Maritime Coll., 1956; LLB, Union U., 1959. Bar: N.Y. 1962, U.S. Dist. Ct. (so. dist.) N.Y. 1962, U.S. Supreme Ct. 1968, Hawaii 1971, U.S. Dist. Ct. Hawaii 1971, U.S. Ct. Appeals (9th cir.) 1984, U.S. Tax Ct. 1984, Nev. 1991, D.C. 1993, U.S. Ct. Appeals (2d cir.) 1995. Assoc. prof. N.Y. State Maritime Coll., Fort Schuyler, N.Y., 1963-64; asst. v.p., bond claims atty. Chubb Ins. Group, N.Y.C., 1961-70; v.p., gen. counsel Hawaiian Ins. Group, Honolulu, 1970-74; ptnr. Davis, Witherwax, Playdon & Gerson, Honolulu, 1974-78; prin. atty. Witherwax, Pottenger & Nishioka, Honolulu, 1978-91; of counsel D'Amato & Lynch, N.Y.C., 1992—. Author: (manual) Hawaii Construction Law, Mechanics Liens and Bond Claims, 1985, co-author, 1987. Bronx county chmn. N.Y. State Conservative Party, 1962-67; state sec. N.Y. State Conservative Party, 1967-70. Lt. comdr. USNR, 1959-79. Mem. ABA (vice chair fidelity and surety com. 1978-83), Internat. Assn. Def. Counsel. Roman Catholic. Avocations: sailing, travel, golf. Insurance, Construction, General civil litigation. Office: D'Amato & Lynch 37th Flr 70 Pine St Fl 37 New York NY 10270-0002

**WITKIN, ERIC DOUGLAS,** lawyer; b. Trenton, N.J., May 14, 1948; s. Nathan and Norma Shirley (Stein) W.; m. Regina Ann Bilotta, June 8, 1980; children: Daniel Robert, Sarah Ann. AB magna cum laude, Columbia U., 1969; JD, Harvard U., 1972. Bar: N.Y. 1973, D.C. 1989, U.S. Dist. Ct. (so. and ea. dists.) N.Y. 1974, U.S. Ct. Appeals (2d and D.C. cirs.) 1974, U.S. Supreme Ct. 1977, U.S. Dist. Ct. D.C. 1989. Assoc. Poletti, Freidin, Prashker & Gartner, N.Y.C., 1972-80, ptnr., 1980-85; sr. atty. labor Kaye, Scholer, Fierman, Hays & Handler, N.Y.C., 1985-88; of counsel Akin, Gump, Strauss, Hauer & Feld, Washington, 1988-90; counsel Benetar, Bernstein, Schair & Stein, N.Y.C., 1990-99; ptnr. Roberts & Finger, LLP, N.Y.C., 1999—. treas., founder Property Owners Against Unfair Taxation, N.Y.C., 1983-90; trustee Congregation Emanu-El of Westchester, 1996—. Lawrence Chamberlain scholar Columbia U., N.Y.C., 1968; recipient Alumni medal Alumni Fedn. Columbia U., 1982. Mem. ABA (labor and employment law sect.), N.Y. State Bar Assn. (labor and employment law sect., com. on equal employment opportunity law), Assn. of Bar of City of N.Y. (spl. com. on sex and law 1975-82, com. on labor and employment law 1982-85, 92-94), Westchester County Bar Assn., Columbia Coll. Alumni Assn. (pres. 1988-90, bd. dirs. 1974—, Robert Lincoln Carey prize, Alumni prize 1969, Lions award 1990), Alumni Fedn. Columbia U. (alumni trustee nominating com. 1990-97, pres. 1997-99), Am. Soc. Pers. Adminstrn. (contbr. monthly newsletter 1986-88), Soc. Human Resource Mgmt., Soc. Columbia Grads. (bd. dirs. 1994-97), Human Resources Assn. N.Y., Phi Beta Kappa. Club: Harvard (N.Y.C.). Avocations: piano, sailing. Labor, Federal civil litigation, State civil litigation. Home: 103 Wendover Rd Rye NY 10580-1939 Office: Roberts & Finger LLP 767 3rd Ave New York NY 10017-2023

**WITMAN, LEONARD JOEL,** lawyer; b. N.Y.C., Nov. 7, 1950; s. Seymour and Ruth W.; m. Mona Soled, Aug. 25, 1950; children: Rachel, Leah. BA, Rutgers Coll., 1972; JD, N.Y. Law Sch., 1975. Bar: N.J. 1975, U.S. Dist. Ct. N.J. 1975, U.S. Ct. Appeals (2d cir.) 1975, U.S. Dist. Ct. (so. and ea. dists.) N.Y., 1976, U.S. Tax Ct. 1976. Tax law specialist IRS, Newark, 1975-78; assoc. Lampf, Lipkind, West Orange, N.J, 1978-81; ptnr. Brach, Eichler, Rosenberg, Silver, Bernstein, Hammer & Gladstone, Roseland, N.J., 1981-89, Witman, Stadmauer & Michaels, P.A., Florham Park, N.J., 1990—; Adj. law prof. Seton Hall U., N.J. Author: Top Heavy Pension Plans, 1985; contbr. articles to profl. jours. Mem. ABA, N.J. Bar Assn., (chmn. employee benefit com. 1984-86, chmn. taxation sect. 1987-88), Essex County Bar Assn., Morris County Bar Assn. Jewish. Pension, profit-sharing, and employee benefits, Taxation, general. Home: 31 Conkling Rd Flanders NJ 07836-9106 Office: Witman Stadtmauer & Michaels 26 Columbia Tpke Florham Park NJ 07932-2213

**WITMEYER, JOHN JACOB, III,** lawyer; b. New Orleans, Dec. 18, 1946; s. John J. and Thais Audrey (Dolese) W. BS, Tulane U., 1968; JD with distinction, Duke U., 1971. Bar: N.Y. Assoc. Mudge Rose Guthrie & Alexander, N.Y.C., 1971-76; ptnr. Ford Marrin Esposito & Wittmeyer (now Ford, Marrin, Esposito, Witmeyer & Gleser LLP), N.Y.C., 1976—. Bd. trustees Gregorian U. Found., 1999—; adv. coun. Paul Tulane Coll., Tulane U., 1998—. General civil litigation, General corporate. Office: Ford Marrin Esposito Witmeyer & Gleser LLP Wall St Plz New York NY 10005-1875

**WITORT, JANET LEE,** lawyer; b. Cedar Rapids, Iowa, Mar. 10, 1950; d. Charles Francis Svoboda and Phyllis Harriet (Wilber) Miller; m. Stephen Francis Witort, Oct. 27, 1979. Student, U. Colo., 1968-69, U. Iowa, 1971; BA, U. No. Colo., 1972; JD, Loyola U., 1979. Bar: Ill. 1979, U.S. Dist. Ct. (no. dist.) Ill. 1979, U.S. Dist. Ct. (no. dist.) Ill. 1979, U.S. Supreme Ct. 1987. Paralegal Fed. Nat. Mortgage Assn., Chgo., 1973-75, Sidley & Austin, Chgo., 1975-76; assoc. Frankel, McKay & Orlikoff, Chgo., 1979-81; atty. Mut. Trust Life Ins. Co., Oak Brook, Ill., 1981-86; assoc. counsel, asst. sec. N.Am. Co. for Life and Health Ins., Chgo., 1986-88; sr. atty. AMA, Chgo., 1988-89; gen. coun., sec. AMA Ins., Chgo., 1989-91, v.p. gen. counsel, sec., 1991-93; asst. gen. counsel Prudential Ins. and Fin. Svcs., Chgo., 1984-98; sr. counsel Allianz Life Ins. Co. of N.Am., 1998—. Author: (with others) The Legal Assistant-A Self Statement, 1974, (with others) Requirements and Limitations Imposed by Corporate Law, 1989, updated, 1992. Vol. Rep. Campaign, Chgo., 1974-76, 90-93, Children's Hosp. Guild, North Oaks, Minn., 1993—, v.p. 1994-95, pres. 1996; vol. Sci. Mus. Minn., St. Paul, 1994—; trustee Hindsdale Ill. Pub. Libr., 1987-93, v.p., 1991-93; bd. dirs. Suburban Libr. Sys., Burr Ridge, Ill., 1988-91, sec. 1990-91; bd. dirs. Children's Hosp. Assn., St. Paul, 1995-96; active Jr. League, St. Paul, 1997—. Mem. ABA, Am. Soc. Med. Assn. Coun., Ill. Bar Assn., Chgo. Assn. Paralegal Assts. (sec. 1973-74), Chgo. Bar Assn. (chair life & health ins. subcom. 1992-93), Womans Bar Assn. of Ill. (mem. ins. com. 1987-93), Ill. Paralegal Assn. (v.p. 1975-76), Nat. Fed. Paralegal Assns. (midwest reg. dir. 1975-76), Am. Corp. Counsel Assn. (membership com. 1988-90), Phi Alpha Delta, Student Bar Assn. (class rep. 1976-77). Republican. Avocations: golf, travel, skiing. Insurance, Real property, General corporate. Office: 1750 Hennepin Ave Minneapolis MN 55403-2115

**WITT, ALAN MICHAEL,** lawyer, accountant; b. Chgo., Apr. 13, 1952; s. Robert and Lois W.; m. Pamela Beth Ander, Dec. 29, 1976; children: Caryn, Kenneth, Amy. BS in Acctg., U. Ill., 1974, JD. Bar: Ill. 1977. Tax and audit cons. Weisbard, Strauss & Snider, Chgo., 1977-81; sole practice Wheeling, Ill., 1977—; tax mgr. Laventhol & Horwath, Chgo., 1981-83; tax ptnr. Ostrow, Reisin, Berk & Abrams, Ltd., 1983—; mng. dir., 1992-95; lectr. law Lewis Coll. Law, Glen Ellyn, Ill., 1980, Kent Coll. Law, Chgo., 1981—. Co-author: Year End Tax Planning, 1982, 3rd rev. edit., 1986; editor: The Tax Advisor Tax Clinic, 1990-96; co-editor: Callaghan's Legal Checklists, 1985-96; contbg. editor: Hanbook for Tax Advisors, 1990—. Mem. ABA, AICPAs (accredited personal fin. splst.), Ill. State Bar Assn., Chgo. Bar Assn., Ill. CPAs Soc., Beta Gamma Sigma, Tau Kappa Epsilon. Estate taxation, Corporate taxation, Estate planning. Home: 1155 Wayne Ave Deerfield IL 60015-2824 Office: Ste 2600 455 N Cityfront Plaza Dr Chicago IL 60611-5506

**WITT, JOHN WILLIAM,** lawyer; b. Los Angeles, Aug. 30, 1932; s. John Udo and Alice (Westervelt) W.; m. Lenora Jane Ticknor, Sept. 1, 1961; children: John David, Stephanie Anne Witt Mills, William Westervelt. AB, U. So. Calif., 1954, JD, 1960. Bar: State Bar Calif. 1961, U.S. Dist. Ct. (ctrl. dist.) Calif. 1961, U.S. Dist. (so. dist.) Calif. 1967, U.S. Supreme Ct. 1969. Dep. city atty. City of San Diego, 1961-64, chief criminal dep. city atty., 1964-67, chief dep. city atty., 1967-69, city atty., 1969-96; spl. counsel Lounsbery Ferguson Altona & Peak, LLP, San Diego, 1996—. Contbr. articles to profl. jours. Pres. Boys' Clubs San Diego, 1985-87; bd. dirs. St. Paul's Episcopal Home, Inc., San Diego, 1982-88, 97—; exec. bd. San Diego County Council Boy Scouts Am, 1970-81, chmn. leadership tng. com., 1970-73, Bicentennial chmn., 1974-76, chmn. Jamboree com., 1977. Served with USMC, 1954-57, col. res. ret. Named Pub. Lawyer of Yr. San Diego County Bar Assn., 1986, Disting. Eagle Scout Boy Scouts Am., 1975. Mem. ABA (state and local govt. law sec., coun. mem. 1980-84, 85-89, 96-98, chair 1992-93, mem. ho. dels. 1993-96, Nelson award 1996), Internat. Mcpl. Law Officers Assn. (pres. 1985-86, bd. trustees 1976-87, Outstanding Nat. Pub. Svc. award 1986), League Calif. Cities (bd. dirs. 1985-96), League Calif. Cities City Atty.'s Dept. (pres. 1976-77), Calif. Dist. Attys. Assn. (bd. dirs. 1980-82), Southwestern Legal Found. (adv. bd. mem. mcpl. legal studies ctr. 1981—), State Bar Calif. (exec. com. pub. law sect. 1980-83), San Diego County Bar Assn. (chair pub. lawyers com. 1997-98), San Diego Lions Club (bd. trustees welfare found. 1983-87, 90-97, chair 1992-93, pres. 1990-91, Diocesan standing com. 1974-78, 82-86, Diocesan bd. dirs. 1998—, dep. to gen. convention 1985-97), Phi Alpha Delta. Republican. Episcopalian. Avocations: writing, travel, sports. Municipal (including bonds), Land use and zoning (including planning), Alternative dispute resolution. Office: Lounsbery Ferguson Altona & Peak LLP 19th Fl 550 West C St 19th Fl San Diego CA 92101-3540

**WITTE, JOHN, JR.,** law educator; b. St. Catharines, Ont., Can., Aug. 14, 1959; s. John and Gertie (van Harten) W.; m. Eliza Ellison, Nov. 18, 1995; children: Hope, Alison. BA, Calvin Coll., 1982; JD, Harvard U., 1985. Bar: Ga. 1986. Dir. Law and Religion Program Emory U., Atlanta, 1987—, Jonas Robitscher Prof. Law, 1993—; participant Lilly Project on Religion, Culture, and the Family, U. Chgo. Divinity Sch., 1992—; pub. lectr. Trinity Coll., Dublin, Ireland, Oxford (Eng.) U., U. Toronto, U. Tex., Tel Aviv U., U. Heidelberg (Germany), U. Tübingen (Germany), Columbia U., McGill U. (Montreal), Harvard U. (Cambridge, Mass.), Free U. Amsterdam, U. Chgo., U. Calif. Berkeley, Ind. U. (Bloomington), numerous other instns. in N.Am., Western Europe, Israel, and South Africa; dir. Pew Charitable Trusts projects and coord. Law and Religion Program, including Christianity and Democracy project, 1989-92, Religious Human Rights project, 1992-95, and Problem of Proselytizing project, 1995—. Author: From Sacrament to Contract: Marriage, Religion, and Law in the Western Tradition, 1997, Christianity and Democracy in Global Context, 1993, Human Rights in Judaism, 1997, The Weightier Matters of the Law: Essays on Law and Religion, 1989, A Christian Theory of Social Institutions, 1986, Proselytism and Orthodoxy in Russia, 1999, Religion and the American Constitutional Experiment, 1999; contbr. over 80 chpts. to books and articles to profl. jours. in fields of law and religion, European and Am. legal history, ch.-state rels., and legal philosophy; gen. editor Emory U. Studies in Law and Religion, 1989—. Alexander von Humboldt-Stiftung sr. fellow, Germany, 1995; recipient Most Outstanding Educator award United Meth. Found. Christian Higher Edn., Nashville, 1994; grantee Pew Charitable Trusts, Inc., 1989, 92, 95, Lilly Endowment, 1999. Office: Emory Univ Law School 1301 Clifton Rd NE Atlanta GA 30322-1013

**WITTEBORT, ROBERT JOHN, JR.,** lawyer; b. Chgo., Dec. 29, 1947; s. Robert John and Marguerite (Shaughnessy) W.; m. Nancy Joan Hertel, July 2, 1988. BA, Yale U., 1969; JD, Notre Dame U., 1974. Bar: Ill. 1974, U.S. Dist. Ct. (no. dist.) Ill. 1974, U.S. Ct. Appeals (7th cir.) 1975, U.S. Tax Ct. 1977, U.S. Ct. Mil. Appeals 1982. Assoc. Hopkins & Sutter, Chgo., 1974-77; gen. counsel, asst. dir. Ill. Housing Devel. Authority, Chgo., 1977-82; ptnr. Chapman and Cutler, Chgo., 1982-90; sr. ptnr. Law Offices Robert J. Wittebort, Jr., 1990—; co-founder, exec. v.p., gen. counsel Chgo. Bldg. Svcs., Inc., 1990-97; sr. v.p. DHR Internat. Inc., 1997—. Contbg. editor: Business Law, 4th edit., 1977; contbg. author: Notre Dame Lawyer, 1974; author: The Chicago Club 1960-1994, 1995, The Saddle & Cycle Club 1895-1995, 1998. Bd. dirs. Music of the Baroque, Met. Housing Devel. Corp., Chgo.; trustee Chgo. Acad. Scis. Comdr. USNR, 1969—. Mem. Nat. Assn. Bond Lawyers, Naval Order U.S. (vice comdr.-gen.), Ill. Commandery Naval Order U.S. (comdr. 1987-88), Chgo. Club, Saddle & Cycle Club, The Casino, Lambda Alpha. Republican. Municipal (including bonds), Securities, Real property.

**WITTELS, BARNABY CAESAR,** lawyer; b. Phila., Mar. 28, 1948; s. David G. and Beatrice Tanya (Graitcr) W.; m. Heidi Jo Linsk, Sept. 8, 1974 (div. Aug. 1997); children: Kate Sophie, William David; m. Mary M. Labaree, Sept. 20, 1998. BA cum laude, Temple U., 1970; MA in Pol. Sci., Boston U., 1972, JD, 1975. Bar: Pa. 1975, U.S. Dist. Ct. (ea. dist.) Pa. 1985, U.S. Ct. Appeals (2d, 3d and 4th cir.) 1986. Asst. defender Defender Assn. of Phila., 1975-80; law clk. to Hon. Stanley Kubacki, 1980-84; ptnr. Wittels, Newman & Bomstein, 1980-82; assoc. LaCheen & Alva, 1982-86; ptnr. LaCheen & Assoc., 1986—. Contbr. column to newspapers. Chair Northwest Victim Svcs., Phila., 1981-84, mem. bd. dirs., 1983-90, chair, 1997— (outstanding svc. & leadership 1990), founding mem.; com. man 21st Divsn. Dem. Party, Phila., 1985-90, various polit. and jud. campaigns, 1980—. Mem. NACDL, Phila. Bar Assn. (fee dispute com. 1996—, chmn. 1998—, mem. com. to elect good judges 1987-88, Pa. Bar Asn., Pa. Assn. Criminal Def. Lawyers, Phila. Bar Found. (Apothaker award 1983). Democratic. Jewish. Avocations: writing, baseball, football, reading, woodworking. Criminal, Appellate, Consumer commercial. Office: LaCheen & Assoc 3100 Lewis Tower Bldg Philadelphia PA 19102

**WITTENBRINK, JEFFREY SCOTT,** lawyer; b. Cairo, Ill., May 24, 1960; s. Howard Samuel and Cherie Ellen (Martin) W.; m. Tamara Inez Parker, Aug. 5, 1989; children: Charlotte Jane, Jeffrey Scott Jr. BA, La. State U., 1984, JD, 1987. Bar: La. 1988, U.S. Dist. Ct. (ea. and mid. dists.) La. 1988, U.S. Dist. Ct. (we. dist.) La. 1989, U.S. Ct. Appeals (5th cir.) 1989, U.S. Supreme Ct. 1996. Law clk. to Judge William H. Brown, 19th Jud. Dist. Ct., Baton Rouge, 1987-88; assoc. Roy, Kiesel, Aaron & Tucker, Baton Rouge, 1988-91, Winston G. DeCuir & Assocs., Baton Rouge, 1991-93; pvt. practice Baton Rouge, 1993—; arbitrator Baton Rouge City Ct., 1993—; instr. CPCU's, Baton Rouge, 1991, Office Emergency Planning State of La., 1993. Contbr. articles to Around the Bar legal newsletter, 1987—. Coach debate team Cath. H.S., Baton Rouge, 1987-91, mock trial team Baton Rouge H.S., 1989-93; treas. Ingleside United Meth. Ch., Baton Rouge, 1991-92, trustee, bd. dirs., 1991—, chair pastor-parish com., 1992—; mem., lectr. La. Vol. Lawyers for Arts, Baton Rouge, 1988—; bd. dirs. La. Crafts Coun., Baton Rouge, 1990—. Mem. ABA, ATLA, La. Bar Assn., Baton Rouge Bar Assn. (mem. newsletter com. 1987—, vol. indigent panel 1992—, chair CLE 1992—, chmn. membership com. 1993, chair Law Expo com. 1998, Pres.'s award 1993), Dean Henry George McMahon Am. Inn of Ct. (barrister, reporter 1993-95), Cortana Kiwanis (bd. dirs. 1994-97, pres.-elect 1997-98, pres. 1998-99). Avocations: photography, fencing, writing. Family and matrimonial, General civil litigation, Personal injury. Office: 533 Europe St Baton Rouge LA 70802-6408

**WITTHAUER, ROBERT TAYLOR,** lawyer; b. Pascagoula, Miss., June 22, 1970; s. Robert Alfred and Helen Ruth Witthauer; m. Jamie Yunsil Hong, Nov. 1, 1997. BBA, Miss. State U., 1992; JD, U. Miss., 1995. Bar: Tenn. 1995, Miss. 1996. Assoc. Shumacker & Thompson, Chattanooga, 1995-96; ptnr. Cliett, Witthauer & McRae, West Point, Miss., 1996-99; assoc. Petkoff & Lancaster, Memphis, 1999—. Mem. Miss. Bar Assn. (bus. law sect. 1997—), Tenn. Bar Assn., Memphis Bar Assn., Columbus C. of C., Rotary. Republican. Avocations: fishing, shooting. General civil litigation, Insurance, Consumer commercial. Home: 130 S Front St #408 Memphis TN 38103 Office: Petkoff & Lancaster 305 Washington Ave Memphis TN 38103

**WITTIG, RAYMOND SHAFFER,** lawyer, technology transfer advisor; b. Allentown, Pa., Dec. 13, 1944; s. Raymond Battie and Alice (Shaffer) W.; m. Beth Glover, June 21, 1975; children: Meaghan G., Allison G. BA, Pa. State U., 1966, MEd, 1968; JD, Dickinson Sch. Law, 1974. Bar: Pa. 1974, U.S. Ct. Appeals (D.C. cir.) 1978. Rsch. psychologist Intext Corp., Scranton, Pa., 1968; minority counsel Small Bus. Com., U.S. Ho. Reps., Washington, 1975-84; pvt. practice Washington, 1984-92; tech. transfer group leader Geo-Ctrs., Inc., Newton Ctr., Mass., 1992—. Capt. U.S. Army, 1969-71. Mem. AAAS, ABA, Nat. Order Barristers, Tech. Transfer Soc., Licensing Execs. Soc. Legislative, Administrative and regulatory, Government contracts and claims.

**WITWER, SAMUEL WEILER, JR.,** lawyer; b. Chgo., Aug. 5, 1941; s. Samuel Weiler and Ethyl Loraine (Wilkins) W.; m. Susan P. Stewart, Sept. 18, 1971; children: Samuel Stewart, Michael Douglas. AB with honors, Dickinson Coll., 1963; JD, U. Mich., 1966. Bar: Ill. 1967, U.S. Dist. Ct. (no. dist.) Ill. 1967, U.S. Ct. Appeals (7th cir.) 1972, U.S. Supreme Ct. 1973, U.S. Ct. Appeals (6th cir.) 1985, U.S. Dist. Ct. (ea. dist.) Mich., 1987. Assoc. Witwer, Moran, Burlage & Atkinson, Chgo., 1967-74; ptnr. Witwer, Poltrock & Giampietro, 1974— ; mem. Fed. Trial Bar Admissions Com. No. Dist. Ill., 1982—. Governing mem. Chgo. Zool. Soc., 1986-90; trustee United Meth. Homes and Services, Chgo., 1974—, Dickinson Coll., Carlisle, Pa., 1976-97; mem. Cook County Home Rule Commn., Chgo., 1974-75; chmn. Agy. Appeals Com. Chgo., 1975-78; atty. Glenview Park Dist., 1982—; spl. asst. atty. gen. Auditor Gen. Ill., 1984-92. Mem. ABA, Meth. Bar Assn. (pres. 1972-73), Chgo. Bar Assn., Ill. Bar Assn., Law Club of Chgo., Sigma Chi, Phi Delta Phi. Republican. Methodist. Club: Union League. Federal civil litigation, State civil litigation. Home: 1330 Overlook Dr Glenview IL 60025-5166 Office: Witwer Poltrock & Giampietro 125 S Wacker Dr Chicago IL 60606-4402

**WIZNIA, CAROLANN KAMENS,** lawyer; b. Boston, Apr. 30, 1950. BA, Brandeis U., 1972; JD, Boston Coll., 1975. Bar: Conn. 1976. Pvt. practice New Haven, 1976—. Mem. ABA, Conn. Bar Assn. Consumer commercial, Probate, General practice. Office: 850 Howard Ave New Haven CT 06519-1106

**WLADIS, MARK NEIL,** lawyer; b. Elizabeth, N.J., May 18, 1964; s. George L. and Roberta W. (Wolgin) W.; m. Diane F. Wladis, Nov. 18, 1990; children: Jacqueline P., Harrison S. BA, Muhlenberg Coll., 1986; JD, Syracuse U., 1989, LLM in Taxation, 1993. Bar: N.Y. 1990, Fla. 1995, U.S. Dist. Ct. (no. dist.) N.Y. 1991, U.S. Tax Ct. 1992. Tax assoc. Coopers & Lybrand, Syracuse, N.Y., 1989-90; assoc. Nottingham, Engel, Gordon & Kerr, Syracuse, N.Y., 1991-92; ptnr. Melvin & Melvin, LLP, Syracuse, N.Y., 1993—. Bd. dirs. Ctrl. N.Y. Lupus Soc., Syracuse, 1992-94, Jewish Fedn., Syracuse, 1996—. Mem. Lafayette Golf and Country Club (bd. dirs. 1994-95). General corporate, Taxation, general, Probate. Office: Melvin & Melvin LLP 217 S Salina St Ste 700 Syracuse NY 13202-1390

**WOESSNER, WARREN DEXTER,** lawyer; b. May 31, 1944; s. Warren Wendling and Flora Coffin (Dexter) W.; m. Iris Freeman, Jan. 6, 1990. BA, Cornell U., 1966; PhD in Chemistry, U. Wis., Madison, 1971, JD cum laude, 1981. Bar: Wis. 1981, N.Y. 1982, Minn. 1984, U.S. Patent Office 1981, U.S. Supreme Ct. 1999. Sr. rsch. scientist Miles Labs., Madison, Wis., 1972-78; assoc. Kenyon & Kenyon, N.Y.C., 1981-84; assoc. Merchant, Gould, Smith, Edell, Welter & Schmidt., Mpls., 1984-88, ptnr., 1989-93; ptnr. Schwegman, Lundberg, Woessner & Kluth, Mpls., 1993—. Sr. editor Abraxas Press, Inc., 1981—, bd. dirs., 1981-84; contbr. to books, articles to profl. jours. Bd. dirs. Sta. WORT-FM, Madison, 1975-78; council Small Mag. Editors and Pubs., San Francisco, 1975-77, Coffee House Press, Mpls., 1988-99. Nat. Endowment for Arts Individual fellow creative writing, 1974; Wis. Arts. Bd. Individual fellow, 1975, 76; Loft-McKnight fellow, 1985. Mem. ABA, Am. Intellectual Property Law Assn. (chair, chem. practice com. 1993-95), PTO Biotech. Customer Ptnrship., Am. Chem. Soc. Patent. Office: Schwegman Lundberg et al 120 S 8th St Ste 1600 Minneapolis MN 55402-2811

**WOFFORD, CINDY LYNN,** lawyer; b. Athens, Tex., Feb. 3, 1952; d. William Avant and Nell (England) W.; m. Dan Henry Lee III, Dec. 1, 1993. BA, Stephen F. Austin U., 1974; JD, U. Tex., 1978; LLM in Tax., So. Meth. U., 1986. Bar: Tex. 1978, U.S. Dist. Ct. (ea. dist.) Tex. 1980, Md. 1989, D.C. 1989, U.S. Tax Ct. 1989. Assoc. Cox, Roady, Dawson/Sheinfeld, Maley & Kay, Houston, 1978-81, Superior Oil Co., Houston, 1981-83, Ray, Hemphill, Trotti, Finfrock, Dallas, 1983-84, Frank C. Hider, P.C., Dallas, 1984-86; chief counsel IRS, Washington, 1987-88; assoc. Linda J. Ravdin, PC, Washington, 1989-93; prin. Ravdin & Wofford PC, Washington, 1993—. Author: Divorce and Separation, Tax Management Portfolio; contbr. articles to profl. jours. Mem. ABA (domestic rels. com. tax sect.), State Bar Tex., State Bar Md., D.C. Bar Assn. Presbyterian. Family and matrimonial, Estate planning, Personal income taxation. Office: Ravdin & Wofford PC 1700 K St NW Ste 650 Washington DC 20006-3812

**WOHL, KENNETH ALLAN,** lawyer; b. Denver, May 26, 1950; s. Milton and Leah (Liss) W. BA with honors, U. Calif., Berkeley, 1972; JD, U. Denver, 1975. Bar: Calif. 1975, U.S. Dist. Ct. (cen. dist.) Calif. 1975, Colo. 1976, U.S. Dist. Ct. Colo. 1976, U.S. Dist. Ct. (we. dist.) Tex. 1988. Trial atty. U.S. Equal Employment Opportunity Commn., Denver, 1976-79; regional counsel Mexican-Am. Legal Def. and Ednl. Fund, Denver, 1979-81; employment litigation cons. Denver, 1981-82; adminstrv. law judge State of Ariz., Tucson, 1982-83; sr. trial atty. U.S. Equal Employment Opportunity Commn., 1983-90; employment law counsel Continental Airlines, 1990-95; mgr. employment dispute resolution US West, 1995-97; asst. dir. EEO, U. Ariz., Tucson, 1997-98; pvt. practice Wheat Ridge, Colo., 1998-99; corp. counsel Colo. West Mental Health, 1999—; cons. Rocky Mountain Assn. Indsl. Psychologists, Denver, 1977-79. Del. Colo. Dem. Conv., Denver, 1976. Mem. Calif. Bar Assn., Colo. Bar Assn., Jefferson County 1st Dist. Bar Assn., Ariz. Fair Employment Practices Com. Avocations: hiking, short story writing. Civil rights, Federal civil litigation, Labor. Home and Office: 1151 County Road 106 Carbondale CO 81623-2391

**WOHL, RONALD GENE,** lawyer; b. N.Y.C., Dec. 10, 1934; s. Arthur and Bernice (Deutch) W.; m. Linda Susan Meltsner, May 2, 1965; children: Allison Brooke Wohl George, Arthur Evan, Amanda Kate. AB, Syracuse U., 1956, LLB, 1961; LLM, Bklyn. Law Sch., 1967. Bar: N.Y. 1962, U.S. Dist. Ct. (so. and ea. dists.) N.Y. 1963, U.S. Ct. Appeals (2d cir.) 1964, U.S. Supreme Ct. 1965, U.S. Dist. Ct. (no. dist.) N.Y. 1977, U. S. Dist. Ct. Conn. 1980, U.S. Tax Ct. 1986. Law clk. to judge Jacob Mishler U.S. Dist. Ct. (ea. dist.) N.Y., 1963-64; assoc. Edward Gettinger & Peter Gettinger, N.Y.C., 1962-63, 68-70; asst. U.S. atty. U.S. Dept. of Justice, N.Y.C., 1964-68; ptnr. Squadron, Gartenberg, Ellenoff & Pleasant, N.Y.C., 1970-71; pvt. practice N.Y.C., 1971-74; ptnr. Ferster, Bruckman, Wohl, Most & Rothman, LLP, N.Y.C., 1974-96, sr. counsel, 1997-98; sr. counsel Goetz, Fitzpatrick, Most & Bruckman LLP, 1999—. Trustee Roslyn (N.Y.) Union Free Sch. Dist., 1981-93. Mem. N.Y. Bar Assn., N.Y. Dist. Attys. Assn., Assn. of Bar of City of N.Y., Nassau County Bar, Soc. of Med. Jurisprudence. Avocation: photography. General civil litigation, Federal civil litigation, Personal injury. Home: 70 The Intervale Roslyn NY 11576-1905 Office: Goetz Fitzpatrick Most & Bruckman LLP One Penn Plz New York NY 10119

**WOHLFORTH, ERIC EVANS,** lawyer; b. N.Y.C., Apr. 17, 1932; s. Robert Martin and Mildred Campbell (Evans) W.; m. Caroline Penniman, Aug. 3, 1957; children: Eric Evans, Charles Penniman. AB, Princeton U., 1954; LLB, U. Va., 1957. Bar: N.Y. 1958, Alaska 1967. Assoc. Hawkins, Delafield & Wood, N.Y.C., 1957-66; ptnr. McGrath & Wohlforth, Anchorage, 1966-70; commr. revenue State of Alaska, Anchorage, 1970-72; ptnr. McGrath, Wohlforth & Flint, Anchorage, 1972-74, Wohlforth & Flint, Anchorage, 1974-87, Wohlforth, Flint & Gruening, 1987-88, Wohlforth, Argetsinger, Johnson & Brecht, 1988-98, Wohlforth, Vassar, Johnson & Brecht, 1999—; mem. Alaska Investment Adv. Com., 1973-80. Chancellor Episcopal Diocese of Alaska, 1972—; mem., trustee, vice-chair Alaska Permanent Fund Corp., 1995—, chmn. 1997—. Mem. Alaska Bar Assn., Assn. of Bar of City of N.Y. Municipal (including bonds), Finance. Home: 7831 Ingram St

Anchorage AK 99502-3965 Office: 900 W 5th Ave Ste 600 Anchorage AK 99501-2029

**WOHLREICH, JACK JAY,** lawyer; b. Newark, Feb. 8, 1946; s. Charles Carl and Erna D. (Epstein) W.; m. Jane Friedlander, June 21, 1969; children: Erin Michelle, Caleb Joshua. BA in Polit. Sci., Am. U., 1968, JD, 1971; postdoctoral, George Washington U., 1972. Bar: Md. 1972, D.C. 1972, U.S. Dist. Ct. Md. 1972, U.S. Dist. Ct. D.C. 1972, U.S. Ct. Appeals (4th cir.) 1973, U.S. Supreme Ct. 1975, Ill. 1976, U.S. Dist. Ct. (no. dist.) Ill. 1976. Participant N.J. Dept. Community Affairs internship program Woodrow Wilson Sch./Princeton U., 1968; asst. chief counsel FDA divsn. HHS, Washington, 1971-75; assoc. gen. counsel, chief of litigation, FDA counsel Baxter Internat., Deerfield, Ill., 1975-91; head FDA and health care practice group Dressler, Goldsmith, Shore & Milnamow, Ltd., Chgo., 1991—; mem. Congl. Leadership for Future Com., staff asst., 1971; faculty Practicing Law Inst., 1989—, Nat. Insts. Trial Adv., So. Meth. U., 1989, Soc. for Profl. Advancement, Princeton, N.J., 1989; mem. adv. bd. Pragmaton; guest lectr. Regulatory Affairs Profl. Soc., 1992, Internat. Business Com., 1993, various insts. Contbg. editor Am. U. Law Rev., 1969-71. Asst. to candidate/advanceman Dem. Nat. Com., 1968, Kennedy for Pres. Com., Washington, 1968; chief of advance R. Sargent Shriver, 1970-71; founding mem. Gaithersburg (Md.) Hebrew Congregation, 1974; rep. Ill. Sch. Dist. 107 Caucus, 1985-88. Mem. ABA, Chgo. Bar Assn. (mem. minority coun. demonstration program steering com.), Ill. Bar Assn., D.C. Bar Assn., Md. Bar Assn., Food and Drug Law Inst. (chairperson ann. meeting program biologics sect., program dir. device update, biologic's update, instr. Biologies Workshop 1994), Pharm. Mfrs. Assn., Health Industries Mfrs. Assn., Am. Blood Resources Assn. (chmn. legal com., chmn. assoc. law sect. 1985-88), Regulatory Affairs Profl. Soc., Tau Epsilon Phi. Avocations: collecting and restoring antique cars, collecting wines. Personal injury, Health, Federal civil litigation. Home: 954 Deerfield Rd Highland Park IL 60035-3521 Office: Dressler Goldsmith Shore & Milamow Ltd 2 Prudential Pla Ste 4700 Chicago IL 60601

**WOJCIECHOWSKI, MARC JAMES,** lawyer; b. Wiesbaden, Germany, June 1, 1965; came to U.S., 1969; s. William Alios and Theresa Lorraine W.; m. Mary Hood, Aug. 11, 1990. BS in Criminal Justice summa cum laude, Southwest Tex. State U., 1987; JD, U. Houston, 1990. Bar: Tex. 1990, U.S. Dist. Ct. (so. dist.) Tex. 1992, U.S. Ct. Appeals (5th cir.) 1998. Assoc. Weller, Wheelus & Green, Beaumont, Tex., 1990-91, Wetzel & Herron, LLP, The Woodlands, Tex., 1991-95; ptnr. Herron, Williamson & Wojciechowski, LLP, Houston, 1995-97; prin. Wojciechowski & Assocs., PC, Houston, 1998—. Mem. The Woodlands Cmty. Assn., 1991—. Recipient scholarship award Tex. Assn. Police Chiefs, 1985-86. Mem. Tex. Assn. Def. Counsel. Roman Catholic. Avocations: racquetball, weight lifting, jogging, travelling. Insurance, General civil litigation, Contracts commercial. Office: Wojciechowski & Assocs PC 2 Northpoint Dr Ste 450 Houston TX 77060-3227

**WOJNAROWSKI, RICHARD ROBERT,** lawyer; b. Chgo., Dec. 25, 1953. BA, St. Xavier Coll., 1975; JD, DePaul U., 1978. Bar: Ill. 1978. Sole practice, Worth, Ill., 1978—; instr. real estate law St. Xavier Coll., Chgo., 1980—. Mem. ABA, Ill. State Bar Assn., St. Xavier Coll. Alumni Bd. Roman Catholic. Office: 11212 S Harlem Ave Worth IL 60482-1804

**WOLCZYK, JOSEPH MICHAEL,** lawyer; b. Auburn, N.Y., June 16, 1955; s. Constantine J. and Mary E. (Burke) W.; 1 child, Sarah Marie. AA, Auburn (N.Y.) C.C., 1975; BA, SUNY, Buffalo, 1977; MA, U. Notre Dame, 1978; JD, Valparaiso U., 1982; AAS, Cayuga (N.Y.) C.C., 1987. Bar: N.Y. 1984, U.S. Dist. Ct. (no. dist.) N.Y. 1985, D.C. 1986, U.S. Ct. Appeals (fed. cir.) 1989, Maine 1990. Pvt. practice Auburn, 1984—; atty., engr. Integrated Concepts, Inc., Rochester, N.Y., 1989-90; v.p. legal ops. White Earth Environ., Auburn, 1988-90; owner Commonwealth Funding of Auburn, 1986-87. Author: Small Town Solo, 5 The Compleat Lawyer 4. Mem. exec. bd. Boy Scouts Am. #366, Auburn, 1991-95; incorporator, bd. dirs. Tomatofest of Ctrl. N.Y., Auburn, 1988; vice chmn. Auburn Zoning Bd. Appeals, 1986-88; bd. dirs. Legal Svcs. of Ctrl. N.Y., 1995-98. Named one of Outstanding Young Men of Am., 1988. Mem. ABA (sec. law student divsn. 1981, Silver Key 19810, D.C. Bar, Maine Bar Assn., Irish Lawyers Assn. N.Y., Cayuga Mus. of History (treas. 1991-94, pres. 1994-96), Rotary Club Auburn (pres. 1988-90, Group Study Exch. team to Japan 1985, 96, Group Study Exch. dist. chmn. 1993-97, chmn. dist. 7150 found. com. 1996-99, chmn.), Auburn/Cayuga C.C. Alumni Assn. (bd. dirs. 1997—). Avocations: sailing, bicycling, hiking, skiing. Real property, General corporate, Private international. Office: 164 State St Auburn NY 13021-1845

**WOLERY, DON EDWARD,** lawyer; b. Portsmouth, Ohio, Nov. 14, 1951; s. John Joseph and Betty Kathleen (Robinson) Stevens; 1 child, Stacy Kathleen; m. Beth Ann Armbrecht, Oct. 22, 1987. BS in Edn., Ohio State U., 1974; JD, Capital U., 1979. Bar: Ohio 1979, U.S. Dist. Ct. (so. dist.) Ohio 1983. Atty. pvt. practice, Columbus, 1979—; inst. Main St. Elem. Sch., Columbus, 1993-97. With U.S. Army, 1969-71. Recipient Lazarus award Columbus C. of C., 1995. Mem. Ohio Assn. Criminal Defense Lawyers, Ohio Acad. Trial Lawyers, Ctrl. Ohio Assn. Criminal Defense Lawyers, Masons. Avocations: martial arts, golf. Criminal, Family and matrimonial, Personal injury. Office: 789 S Front St Columbus OH 43206-1905

**WOLF, ALAN STEVEN,** lawyer; b. Jersey City, Jan. 5, 1955; s. Lester Joel and Beatrice (Spiegel) W.; m. Donna Snow Wolf, Aug. 31, 1980; children: Lauren, Bradley. BA, Dartmouth Coll., 1977; JD, Southwestern U., L.A., 1980. Bar: Calif. 1980, U.S. Dist. Ct. (no., so., ea. and cen. dists.) Calif. 1980. With Alvarado, Rus & McClellen, Orange, Calif., 1981-84; ptnr. Cameron Dreyfuss & Wolf, Orange, 1984-89; pres. Gordon & Wolf, Newport Beach, Calif., 1989-91, Wolf & Pfeifer, Newport Beach, Calif., 1991-97, Wolf & Richards, Newport Beach, 1997—. Pres., founding dir. Laguna Beach (Calif.) Pop Warner Football, 1995-96, sec., 1996; chief Indian Princess Tribe, Laguna Beach, 1993. Mem. U.S. Foreclosure Network (bd. dirs. 1990-95, Com. Mem. of Yr. 1994), Calif. Mortgage Bankers Assn. (chmn. legal issues com. 1994-95), Dartmouth Club (pres. Orange County club 1991); fellow Am. Coll. Mortgage Attys. Avocations: computers, Internet. Finance, Bankruptcy, Real property. Office: Wolf & Richards 18 Corporate Plaza Dr Newport Beach CA 92660-7901

**WOLF, AUSTIN KEITH,** laywer; b. Peoria, Ill., Feb. 7, 1923; s. Gustave Albert and Daisy Lazard W.; m. Beverly Silver, June 19, 1949 (wid. May 1981); children: Nancy, Judy; m. Ellen Wolf, Nov. 28, 1982. BA, Yale U., 1948; LLB, Harvard U., 1951. Ptnr. Cohen & Wolf PC, Bridgeport, Conn., 91-98; atty. trial referee Superior Ct., 1983—; lectr. Conn. Bar Assn., 1981—. Bd. editors: Conn. Bar Jour., 1979-84. Mem. exec. com. Planning and Zoning, 1968—. Sgt. USMC, 1941-46, PTO. Mem. ABA, Bridgeport Bar Assns., Conn. Bar Assn. (ho. of dels. 1979-83), Am. Coll. Real Estate Lawyers. Land use and zoning (including planning), Real property. Office: Cohen & Wolf PC PO Box 1821 1115 Broad St Bridgeport CT 06601-1021

**WOLF, BRUCE,** lawyer; b. Phila., Dec. 16, 1955; s. Charles and Mary (Saionz) W. BA, Temple U., 1977; JD, Drake U., 1981. Bar: Pa. 1981, U.S. Dist. Ct. (ea dist.) Pa. 1981, U.S. Ct. Appeals (3d cir.) 1981. Assoc. LaCheen & Alva, Phila., 1981-88; pvt. practice Phila., 1989—; mem. Fed. Criminal Justice Act Panel, Phila., 1998—. Committeeman Phila. Dem. Party 63rd ward, 1994—. Mem. Phila. Bar Assn., Pa. Assn. Criminal Def. Lawyers. Democrat. Jewish. Fax: (215) 922-2194. Criminal, General practice, Family and matrimonial. Office: 612 S 6th St 1st Fl Philadelphia PA 19147-2108

**WOLF, CARL,** lawyer; b. Phila., Dec. 3, 1950; s. Harry and Yetta (Boorstein) W. BA, Pa. State U., 1972; JD, U. San Diego, 1976. Bar: Calif. 1976, U.S. Dist. Ct. (no. dist.) Calif. 1976. VISTA and staff atty. San Francisco Neighborhood Leagl Assistance Found., 1977-80; assoc. Allan Lerch & Assocs., San Francisco, 1981-83; ptnr. Hammill & Wolf, San Francisco, 1983-93; pvt. practice, San Francisco, 1993-95; ptnr. Callaway & Wolf, San Francisco, 1995—. Bd. dirs. Bay Area Lawyers for Individual Freedom, San Francisco, 1981-87, AIDS Legal Referral Panel, San Francisco, 1988-92, San Francisco Legal Assistance Found., 1992-95. Mem. State Bar Calif. (ethnic minority rels. com. 1984-87, Wiley Manuel award for pro bono svcs. 1991). Avocation: travel. Personal injury, General civil litigation. Office: Callaway & Wolf 785 Market St Ste 1150 San Francisco CA 94103-2003

**WOLF, CYD BETH,** lawyer, entrepreneur; b. N.Y.C., Oct. 6, 1957; d. Aaron Joseph and Sally (Marcus) W.; m. Germano Fabio Fabiani, Nov. 18, 1990; children: Alessandra Julia Fabiani, Francesca Isabella Fabiani. BA in Urban Studies with honors, U. Pa., 1977; JD, U. Balt., 1983. Bar: Md. 1983, U.S. Dist. Ct. Md. 1983, U.S. Ct. Appeals (6th and 11th cir.) 1986, U.S. Ct. Appeals (4th and 5th cir.) 1989. Assoc. Weinberger, Weinstock, Sagner, Stevan & Harris, Balt., 1983-86, Semmes, Bowen & Semmes, Balt., 1986-90, Piper & Marbury, Balt., 1990-95; private practice Balt., 1995-98, Owings Mills, Md., 1998—. Contbr. articles to profl. jours. Leadership com. Univ. Balt. Ednl. Found. 1983—, fundraiser 1983—, mentor 1983—. Mem. ABA, Am. Bankruptcy Inst., Md. State Bar Assn. (banking sect., bus. sect.), Bankruptcy Bar Assn. Md., Comml. Law League Am. (bankruptcy and insolvency sect.), Bar Assn. Balt. City (banking sect., bankruptcy sect., bus. sect.). Avocations: tennis, swimming, painting, drawing, fiction and nonfiction reading and writing. Consumer commercial, Bankruptcy. Home: 5 Hillchase Ct Baltimore MD 21208-6306 Office: Cyd Beth Wolf Atty at Law 6 Park Center Ct Ste 202 Owings Mills MD 21117-5604

**WOLF, G. VAN VELSOR, JR.,** lawyer; b. Balt., Feb. 19, 1944; s. G. Van Velsor and Alice Roberts (Kimberly) W.; m. Ann Holmes Kavanagh, May 19, 1984; children: George Van Velsor III, Timothy Kavanagh (dec.), Christopher Kavanagh, Elisabeth Huxley. BA, Yale U., 1966; JD, Vanderbilt U., 1973. Bar: N.Y. 1974, U.S. Dist. Ct. (so. dist.) N.Y. 1974, U.S. Ct. Appeals (2d cir.) 1974, Ariz. 1982, U.S. Dist. Ct. Ariz. 1982, U.S. Ct. Appeals (9th cir.) 1982. Agrl. advisor U.S. Peace Corps., Tanzania and Kenya, 1966-70; assoc. Milbank, Tweed, Hadley & McCloy, N.Y.C., 1973-75; vis. lectr. law Airlangga U., Surabaya, Indonesia, 1975-76; editor-in-chief Environ. Law Reporter, Washington, 1976-81; cons. Nat. Trust Hist. Preservation, Washington, 1981; assoc. Lewis & Roca, Phoenix, 1981-84, ptnr., 1984-91; ptnr. Snell & Wilmer, Phoenix, 1991—; vis. lectr. law U. Ariz., 1990, Vanderbilt U., 1991, U. Md., 1994, Ariz. State U., 1995; cons. Nat. Trust Hist. Preservation, Washington, 1981. Editor: Toxic Substances Control, 1980; editor in chief Environ. Law Reporter 1976-81; contbr. articles to profl. jours. Bd. dirs. Ariz. divsn. Am. Cancer Soc., 1985-96, sec., 1990-92, vice-chmn., 1992-94, chmn. 1994-96, bd. dirs. S.W. divsn., 1996—, chmn., 1996-98; bd. dirs. Herberger Theatre Ctr., 1998—, Phoenix Little Theater, 1983-90, chmn. 1986-88. Mem. ABA (vice-chmn. SONREEL commn. state and regional environ. coop. 1995-98, co-chmn. 1998—, vice-chmn. environ. audits task force 1998-99, vice-chmn. SONREEL ann. meeting planning com. 1998-99), Assn. of Bar of City of N.Y., Ariz. State Bar Assn. (coun. environ. & nat. res. law sect. 1988-93, chmn. 1991-92, CLE com. 1992-98, chmn. 1997-98), Maricopa County Bar Assn., Ariz. Acad., Union Club N.Y.C., Univ. Club Phoenix, Phoenix Country Club. Environmental, Legislative. Office: Snell & Wilmer 1 Arizona Ctr Phoenix AZ 85004-0001

**WOLF, GARY WICKERT,** lawyer; b. Slinger, Wis., Apr. 19, 1938; s. Leonard A. and Cleo C. (Wickert) W.; m. Jacqueline Weltzin, Dec. 17, 1960; children: Gary, Jonathan. BAA, U. Minn., 1960, JD cum laude, 1963. Bar: N.Y. 1964, U.S. Ct. Appeals (2d cir.) 1969, U.S. Dist. Ct. (so. dist.) N.Y. 1969, U.S. Supreme Ct. 1971. Assoc. Cahill, Gordon & Reindel, N.Y.C., 1963-70, ptnr., 1970—; bd. dirs. N.J. Resources Corp., N.J. Natural Gas Co. Mem. N.Y. State Bar Assn. (com. on securities regulation), N.Y.C. Bar Assn. (com. on pub. utility regulation), Anglers Club (N.Y.C.), Downtown Assn. (N.Y.C.), Mashomack Fish and Game Club. Securities, General corporate, Public utilities. Home: Pleasantville Rd New Vernon NJ 07976 Office: Cahill Gordon & Reindel 80 Pine St Fl 17 New York NY 10005-1790

**WOLF, KEVIN EARL,** lawyer; b. Siren, Wis., May 27, 1959; s. Earl Francis and Jacquelyn Joy Wolf; m. Louise Anne Nelles, Aug. 16, 1986; children: Joshua Earl, Jacob Gerard. BBA, U. Wis., 1981, JD, 1984. Bar: Wis. Assoc. atty. Ruder, Ware & Michler, Wausau, Wis., 1984-92, shareholder, 1992—. Bd. dirs. Wausau Area Performing Arts Found., 1994—, pres., 1998; bd. dirs. Wausau Cmty. Theatre, 1984-95, pres., 1988-89. Mem. ABA, ATLA, State Bar Wis., Moratown County Bar, Civil Trial Counsel Wis., Eis. Acad. Trial Lawyers, KC. Roman Catholic. Avocations: books, performing arts, music. General civil litigation, Contracts commercial, Labor. Home: 1715 Woodland Ridge Rd Wausau WI 54403-2388 Office: Ruder Ware & Michler PO Box 8050 Wausau WI 54402-8050

**WOLF, LAWRENCE,** lawyer; b. L.A.. BA, Calif. U., Northridge, 1972; JD, U. Calif., Santa Clara, 1975. Bar: Calif. 1975. Atty. City of Santa Monica, Calif., 1975-77, L.A. County Pub. Defender, 1977-79; pvt. practice law L.A., 1979—; coord. law confs. Calif. Juvenile Cts., Inglewood, 1983. Mem. L.A. County Bar Assn., Juvenile Cts. Bar Assn. Criminal, Juvenile, Administrative and regulatory. Office: 10390 Santa Monica Blvd Ste 300 Los Angeles CA 90025

**WOLF, LILLIAN F.,** lawyer; b. Blythe, Calif., Dec. 13, 1962; d. James Clifford and Carmen Miranda Wolf. BA in History, San Francisco State U., 1986; JD, U. San Francisco, 1991. Bar: Calif., U.S. Dist. Ct. (no. dist.) Calif. Assoc. Berman, Berkley & Lasky LLP, San Francisco, 1992—. Mem. Calif. Bar Assn. (employment law sect.), Queen's Bench (employment law com., bus. devel. com.). Democrat. Roman Catholic. Avocations: travel, opera, football, baseball. General civil litigation, Civil rights, Labor. Office: Berman Berkley & Lasky LLP 601 Montgomery St Fl 3D San Francisco CA 94111-2603

**WOLF, MARCUS ALAN,** lawyer; b. Mansfield, Ohio, July 6, 1946; s. Carl Merle and Eunice Virginia (Beekman) W.; children: Stephanie Ariah, Marcus André. BA, Northeast La. U., 1969; JD, Ohio No. U., 1980. Bar: Ohio 1980, U.S. Dist. Ct. (no. dist.) Ohio 1980. Tchr. Clearfork Valley Schs., Butler, Ohio, 1969-70, Shelby City Schools, Shelby, Ohio, 1972-77; prin. Marcus A. Wolf Co. L.P.A. (formerly Thompson & Wolf Co. L.P.A.), Mansfield, 1980—. Mem. exec. com. Richland County Dem. Com., 1986-93, precinct committeeman, 1988, 90-93; chmn. adminstrv. bd. Main St. United Meth. Ch.; mem. dist. 7 Mansfield Power Squadron, 1985—. Mem. ABA, Ohio Bar Assn., Richland County Bar Assn., Masons. Methodist. Avocations: boating, fishing, skiing, hunting. Family and matrimonial, Criminal. Home: 457 Davis Rd Mansfield OH 44907-1121 Office: Marcus A. Wolf Co LPA 13 Park Ave W Mansfield OH 44902-1714

**WOLF, MARK LAWRENCE,** federal judge; b. Boston, Nov. 23, 1946; s. Jason Harold and Beatrice (Meltzer) W.; m. Lynne Lichterman, Apr. 4, 1971; children: Jonathan, Matthew. BA cum laude, Yale U., 1968; JD cum laude, Harvard U., 1971; hon. degree, Boston Latin Sch., 1990. Bar: Mass. 1971, D.C. 1972, U.S. Supreme Ct. 1976. Assoc. Surrey, Karasik & Morse, Washington, 1971-74; spl. asst. to dep. atty. gen. U.S. Dept. Justice, Washington, 1974-75, spl. asst. to atty. gen., 1975-76; dep. U.S. atty. U.S. Dept. Justice, Boston, 1981-85; from assoc. to ptnr. Sullivan & Worcester, Boston, 1977-81; judge U.S. Dist. Ct. Mass., Boston, 1985—; lectr. Harvard U. Law Sch., Cambridge, Mass., 1990—; adj. prof. Boston Coll. Law Sch., 1992. Bd. dirs. Albert Schweitzer Fellowship, Boston, 1974—, pres., 1989-97, chmn., 1997—; chmn. John William Ward Fellowship, Boston, 1986—. Recipient cert. appreciation U.S. Pres., 1975, Disting. Service award U.S. Atty. Gen., 1985. Mem. Boston Bar Assn. (council 1982-85), Am. Law Inst. Office: US Dist Ct 1 Courthouse Way Boston MA 02210-3002

**WOLF, MARSHALL JAY,** lawyer; b. Cleve., Nov. 20, 1941; s. Sol J. and Ruth (Shapiro) W.; m. Judith Shermer, Ja. 29, 1967; children: Randi Caryn, Robert Howard. BA, Miami U., 1964; JD, Case Western Reserve U., 1967. Bar: Ohio 1967, U.S. Dist. Ct. (no. dist.) Ohio 1969. Law clk. to Common Pleas Ct. Cuyahoga County, Ohio, 1967-69; assoc. Metzenbaum, Gaines, Finley & Stern, Cleve., 1969-75; ptnr., dir. Metzenbaum, Gaines & Stern, Cleve., 1975-81, Schwarzwald, Robiner, Wolf & Rock, Cleve., 1981-88, Wolf & Akers, Cleve., 1988—; chief U.S. del., 1st World Congress Family Law and Children's Rights, Sydney, Australia, 1993. Editor: (with others) Managing Clients & Cases, 1986; contbr. articles to profl. jours. Trustee, Temple on the Heights, Pepper Pike, Ohio, 1971-81; mem. Cuyahoga County Dem. Exec. Com., Cleve., 1972-76; pres. Univ. Hts. Dem. Com., 1974-76. Fellow Am. Acad. Matrimonial Lawyers (pres. Ohio chpt.), Internat. Acad. Matrimonial Lawyers; mem. ABA (family law sect. coun. 1984-94, chair 1992-93), Ohio Acad. Trial Lawyers (chmn. family law com. 1976-77, Disting. Svc. award 1977), Cuyahoga County Bar Assn. (chmn. family law sect. 1981-84). Family and matrimonial. Home: 3958 W Meadow Ln Cleveland OH 44122-4775 Office: Wolf & Akers 1515 East Blvd Bldg 1717 Cleveland OH 44106-1720

**WOLF, MARTIN EUGENE,** lawyer; b. Balt., Sept. 9, 1958; s. Eugene Bernard and Mary Anna (O'Neil) W.; m. Nancy Ann Reinsfelder, May 9, 1980; children: Matthew Adam, Allison Maria, Emily Elizabeth. BA, Johns Hopkins U., 1980; JD, U. Md., 1991. Bar: Md. 1991, U.S. Dist. Ct. Md. 1992, U.S. Ct. Appeals (4th cir.) 1992, U.S. Ct. Appeals (2d cir.) 1993, U.S. Ct. Appeals (3d cir.) 1998. Mgmt. trainee Giant Foods, Inc., Landover, Md., 1980-82, dept. mgr., 1982-83, ops. analyst, 1983-86, fin. coord., 1986-89; law clk. Piper & Marbury, L.L.P., Balt., 1989-91, assoc., 1991-96; prin. Law Office of Martin E. Wolf, Abingdon, Md., 1996—; dir. Giant Food Fed. Credit Union, Landover, 1984-89; pres. Stalagmite Properties, Ltd., Abingdon, Md., 1995-96; tchg. asst. U. Md. Sch. Law, Balt., 1992-94, adj. prof., 1996—. Mem. ABA, Md. State Bar Assn., Harford County Bar Assn., Harford County Bar Found. (Vol. Svc. award 1992, 94). Republican. Roman Catholic. Avocations: Lacrosse, hockey. Appellate, General civil litigation, Land use and zoning (including planning). Home: 11 Mitchell Dr Abingdon MD 21009-1628

**WOLF, MAURICE,** lawyer; b. London, Eng., Oct. 15, 1931; came to U.S., 1947; s. D.I. and Esther (de Miranda) W.; m. Yolanda Pazmino, May 4, 1963; children: J. David, Monica Maria. Cert., Universidad Nacional Autonoma de Mexico, Mexico City, 1957; BA with honors, UCLA, 1959; LLB, Columbia U., 1962. Bar: N.Y. 1962, D.C. 1964, U.S. Supreme Ct. 1980. Atty., advisor Office Satellite Communications, FCC, Washington, 1962-66, counsel, 1966-72; sr. counsel Inter-Am. Devel. Bank, Washington, 1972-77; sr. ptnr. Wolf, Arnold & Cardoso P.C., Washington, 1977—; vis. prof. internat. law Am. U. Sch. Law, 1996-97, co-dir. summer internat. law program, Santago, Chile, 1997; vis. lectr. U. Ga., 1998. Co-author: Doing Business With The International Development Agencies in Washington, 1983; mem. editl. adv. bd. Internat. Legal Materials, 1997—; contbr. articles to profl. jours. Mem. parents fund coun. Williams Coll., 1984—; mem. parents adv. coun. Kenyon Coll., 1986—, chmn. acad. affairs, 1988—; pres. Riverside Civic Assn., Fairfax, Conn., 1969-70, 77-80, v.p., 1976-77; co-chmn. Mt. Vernon Coun., Fairfax, 1969-70; bd. dir. Inter-Am. Bar Found., 1995—. Harlan Fiske Stone scholar, Columbia U., 1962. Mem. Am. Arbitration Assn. (mem. internat. panel), N.Y. Bar Assn., D.C. Bar Assn. (chmn. internat. investment fin. subcom. 1978, vice-chair internat. law steering com. 1999—), Am. Soc. Internat. Law, Inter-Am. Bar Assn., Fed. Bar Assn., Columbia Soc. Internat. Law (pres. 1961-62), Internat. Bar Assn. (mem. adv. editl. com.), Inter-Am. Bar Found. (bd. dirs.), Williams Club. Avocations: photography, cooking. Private international, Public international, General corporate. Office: Wolf Arnold & Cardoso PC 1150 18th St NW Washington DC 20036-3816

**WOLF, NEAL LLOYD,** lawyer; b. Chgo., Feb. 8, 1949; s. Ira and Bettye (Brainin) W.; m. Caren Ellen Mirsky, June 11, 1972 (div. Apr., 1995); children: Michael Elliot, Brian Martin. AB magna cum laude, Princeton U., 1970; JD, U. Chgo., 1974. Bar: Ariz. 1974, U.S. Dist. Ct. Ariz. 1974, U.S. Ct. Appeals (9th cir.) 1975, Ill. 1983, U.S. Dist. Ct. (no. dist.) Ill. 1983, U.S. Ct. Appeals (7th cir.) 1983, U.S. Ct. Appeals (8th cir.) 1985, U.S. Supreme Ct., 1985, U.S. Dist. Ct. (no. dist.) Tex., 1990. Ptnr. Lewis and Roca, Phoenix, 1974-83, Winston & Strawn, Chgo., 1983-86, 89—, Ross & Hardies, Chgo., 1986-89. Mem. ABA. Avocations: golf, reading, movies, tennis. Bankruptcy, Contracts commercial, Federal civil litigation. Office: Winston & Strawn 35 W Wacker Dr Ste 4200 Chicago IL 60601-1695

**WOLF, ROBERT THOMAS,** lawyer; b. N.Y.C., Apr. 14, 1936; s. Simon and Rose (Salzhauer) W.; divorced; 1 child, Lisa Eve. BS in Econs., U. Pa., 1955; LLB, Bklyn. Law Sch., 1963. Bar: N.Y. 1964. Asst. corp. counsel City of N.Y., 1970-80; ptnr. Weinberger & Wolf, Bronx, N.Y., 1980-83, Weinberger, Wolf, Rodrigues & Malach, Bronx, 1983-87, Weinberger, Wolf & Malach, Bronx, 1987-88, Wolf & Malach, Bronx, 1988-90; sole practice Bronx, 1990—. With U.S. Army, 1957-59. Mem. N.Y. State Bar Assn., Bronx County Bar Assn., Assn. Trial Lawyers Am., N.Y. State Trial Lawyers Assn. Avocations: sports, reading, swimming, Spanish literature and conversation. Personal injury, Product liability, Civil rights. Office: 327 E 149th St Bronx NY 10451-5685

**WOLF, WILLIAM JOHN,** lawyer; b. Grosse Pointe, Mich., Jan. 18, 1963; s. John William and Marilyn Ann (Wazny) W.; m. Debra Rae Gibson. BA, Alma Coll., Alma, Mich., 1984; JD, Wake Forest U., Winston-Salem, N.C., 1987. Bar: N.C., Fed. Ct. Atty. Womble Carlyle Sandridge & Rice, Winston-Salem, 1987-90, Nye, Phears & Davis, Durham, 1990-92; ptnr., atty. Nye & Wolf, Durham, 1992-93; atty. Bugg & Wolf PA, Durham, 1993—. Pres. Durham Young Lawyers, 1995. Mem. N.C. Bar Assn., N.C. Assn. Constrn. (law sect. 1989—), Durham Cty. Bar Assn. Construction. Office: Bugg & Wolf 411 Andrews Rd Ste 160 Durham NC 27705-6507

**WOLFE, DEBORAH ANN,** lawyer; b. Detroit, May 4, 1955; d. Adam and Mary A. (Smyth) Wolfe; m. Lester D. McDonald, May 23, 1987; children: Molly, Thomas. Student, Ariz. State U., Tempe, 1973-76; BA in Polit. Sci., Bus., Tex. Christian U., Ft. Worth, 1977; postgrad., So. Meth. U., 1977-78; JD, U. San Diego, 1980; grad., Gerry Spence's Trail Lawyer, 1999. Bar: Calif. 1981, Ariz. 1982. Sole practice San Diego, 1981-83; ptnr. Kremer & Wolfe, San Diego, 1983-86; assoc. D. Dwight Worden, Solana Beach, Calif., 1986-89; pvt. practice San Diego, 1989-91; owner Wolfe & McDonald, 1991-96; shareholder Nugent & Newnham, San Diego, 1996—; judge F. Lee Bailey Moot Ct. Competition, San Diego, 1984; instr. San Diego Inn of Ct. Evidence, 1988-95. Floutist San Diego City Guard Band, 1981-93, Grossmont Sinfonia, La Mesa, 1982-83, Classical/Chamber Music Quartet, San Diego, 1983-87, Foothills United Meth. Ch. band, 1997—; leader Girl Scouts. Named Legal Eagles Calif. Lawyer mag., 1996. Mem. Assn. Trial Lawyers Am., Consumer Attys. Calif., Consumer Attys. San Diego (pres. 1996, Outstanding Trial Lawyer award 1987, Outstanding Trial Lawyer award 1996, Trial Lawyer of Yr. award 1996), Lawyers Club (San Diego), San Diego Trial Lawyers Assn. (Outstanding Trial Lawyers award 1987), Am. Inns of Ct. (master). Professional liability, Personal injury, Insurance. Office: Nugent & Newnham 1010 2nd Ave Ste 2200 San Diego CA 92101-4913

**WOLFE, HARRIET MUNRETT,** lawyer; b. Mt. Vernon, N.Y., Aug. 18, 1953; d. Lester John Francis Jr. and Olga Harriet (Miller) Munrett; m. Charles Briant Wolfe, Sept. 10, 1983. BA, U. Conn., 1975; postgrad., Oxford U. (Eng.), 1976; JD, Pepperdine U., 1978. Bar: Conn. 1979. Assoc. legal counsel, asst. sec. Citytrust, Bridgeport, Conn., 1979-90; v.p., sr. counsel, asst. sec. legal dept. Shawmut Bank Conn., N.A., Hartford, 1990-96; sole practice law, 1996-97; sr. v.p., counsel, sec. Webster Fin. Corp., Waterbury, Conn., 1997—; mem. govt. rels. com. Electronic Funds Transfer Assn., Washington, 1983—. Mem. Conn. Bar Assn. (mem. legis. com. banking law sect.), ABA, Conn. Bankers Assn. (trust legis. com.), Guilford Flotilla Coast Guard Aux., U.S. Sailing Assn., Phi Alpha Delta Internat. (Frank E. Gray award 1978, Shepherd chpt. Outstanding Student award 1977-78). Banking, General corporate, Securities. Home: 621 Northwood Dr Guilford CT 06437-1124 Office: Webster Fin Corp Webster Plaza Waterbury CT 06702

**WOLFE, J. MATTHEW,** lawyer; b. Pitts., Mar. 29, 1956; s. James Michael and Mary Evangeline (Andrews) W.; m. Deborah Ann Smith, Oct. 2, 1982; children: James M. Jr., Ross M. BA, U. Pa., 1978; JD, Villanova U., 1981. Bar: Pa. 1981, U.S. Dist. Ct. (ea. dist.) Pa. 1985, U.S. Ct. Appeals (3rd cir.) 1985, U.S. Supreme Ct., 1992, U.S. Dist. Ct. (we. dist.) Pa. 1997. Atty. Cmty. Legal Svcs., Phila., 1981-82; pvt. practice Phila., 1981-82, 89-95, 97—; asst. counsel Pa. Dept. of Transp., Phila, 1983-86; spl. prosecutor Pa., 1984-86; spl. asst. dist. atty. Berks County, Reading, Pa., 1984-86; dep. atty. gen. Commonwealth of Pa., Phila., 1986-89; spl. asst. dist. atty. Phila., 1991-92; chief counsel Pa. Dept. Law and Industry, 1995-97; atty. Law Offices of Alice Ballard, 1999—; gen. counsel Univ. Bus. Machines, Inc., Upper Darby, Pa., 1989-95; instr. Pa. Bar Inst., Harrisburg, 1984; Pa. workers compensation rules com. Pa. Dept. Laor & Industry, 1995-97, Pa. Worker's Compensation Fraud task force, 1996-97. Assoc. editor The Docket newspaper, 1980-81; contbr. articles to The Univ. City Trumpet newspaper, 1981-95. Ward leader 27th Ward Rep. Com., Phila., 1979—; bd. dirs. University City Town Watch, 1983-85; mem. Spruce Hill Cmty. Assn., Phila., 1980—, bd. dirs., 1982-96, 99—; chmn. Univ. City Rep. Com., 1990-96; mem. Sch. Bd.

Task Force on Scholastics and Sports, Phila., 1986, Cedar Park Neighbors, 1986—; mem. neighborhood adv. coun. 19th Police Dist., Phila., 1987-93; vice chmn. Woodland Dist. Phila. coun. Boy Scouts Am., 1989-91. Mem. ABA, Pa. Bar Assn. (mem. com. legal ethics and profl. responsibility 1986-95), Phila. Bar Assn. (instr. 1995), West Phila. C. of C. (bd. dirs. 1989-95, gen. counsel 1993-95, 98—), Pi Sigma Alpha, Phi Delta Theta (editor Phi Oracle newsletter). Roman Catholic. Home and Office: 4256 Regent Sq Philadelphia PA 19104-4439

**WOLFE, JAMES RONALD,** lawyer; b. Pitts., Dec. 10, 1932; s. James Thaddeus and Helen Matilda (Corey) W.; m. Anne Lisbeth Dahle Eriksen, May 28, 1960 (dec. 1996); children: Ronald, Christopher, Geoffrey. B.A. summa cum laude, Duquesne U., 1954, DHL (hon.), 1997; LL.B. cum laude, NYU, 1959. Bar: N.Y. 1959. Assoc. Simpson Thacher & Bartlett, N.Y.C., 1959-69, ptnr., 1969-95, counsel, 1996-99. Co-editor: West's McKinney's Forms, Uniform Commercial Code, 1965. Served to 1st lt. U.S. Army, 1955-57. Mem. ABA, N.Y. State Bar Assn., Assn. Bar City N.Y., Am. Judicature Soc. Republican. Roman Catholic. Banking, General corporate, Finance. Home: 641 King St Chappaqua NY 10514-3807 Office: Simpson Thacher & Bartlett 425 Lexington Ave New York NY 10017-3954

**WOLFE, PHILIP BRANNON,** lawyer; b. Russell, Kans., Mar. 13, 1951; s. Donald E. and Ruth (Ochs) Wolfe. BBA, Washburn U., 1973, JD, 1976. Bar: Kans. 1976, U.S. Dist. Ct. Kans. 1976. Assoc. Dean and Nichols, Topeka, 1976-77; ptnr. Nichols and Wolfe, Topeka, 1977—. Vice-pres. Topeka Pub. Schs. Found., 1988, pres. 1989. Mem. ABA,f Kans. Bar Assn. (chmn. membership com. 1988), Topeka Bar Assn., Nat. Assn. Bond Lawyers, Rotary (bd. mem. local chpt. 1988), Greater Tofpeka C. of C. (chmn. bd. dirs. 1986). Republican. Congregationalist. Municipal (including bonds), Real property, State and local taxation. Office: Nichols & Wolfe 1120 Bank Towers Topeka KS 66603

**WOLFE, ROGER ALLEN,** lawyer; b. Charleston, W.Va., Aug. 25, 1948; s. Jackson Clark and Imogene Ashley Wolfe; m. Bonnie Wolfe, Dec. 11, 1970 (div. Mar. 1982); children: Matthew, Theresa; m. Cheryl Harris, Apr. 2, 1983; children: Katherine, Rebecca. BA in Psychology, W.Va. U., 1970, JD, 1973. Bar: W.Va. 1970, U.S. Ct. Appeals (4th cir.) 1975, U.S. Supreme Ct. 1979. Law clk. U.S. Dist. Ct., Charleston, 1973-74; ptnr. Jackson & Kelly, Charleston, 1974—. Mem. W.Va. State Bar (chair employment law com. 1993—), Order of the Coif. Avocations: music, gardening, reading, family activities, outdoor activities. Labor. Office: Jackson & Kelly PO Box 553 Charleston WV 25322-0553

**WOLFE, SUSAN J.,** lawyer; b. San Bernardino, Calif., Mar. 30, 1950; d. James A. and Anna Lee (Prothro) Leonard; m. Ralph G. Devoe, Nov. 16, 1975; children: Catherine, Laura. Ba in Lit., U. Chgo.; JD, Stanford U., 1981. Bar: Calif. 1981, U.S. Dist. Ct. (no. dist.) Calif. 1981. Assoc. Wilson, Sonsini, Goodrich & Rosati, Palo Alto, Calif., 1981-85, Nolan & Armstrong, Palo Alto, 1990-93; corp. counsel Seagate Software, Scotts Valley, Calif., 1993—. Author: The Last Billable Hour, 1989 (Edgar award 1990). Democrat. Office: Seagate Software PO Box 66360 Scotts Valley CA 95067-0360

**WOLFF, DEBORAH H(OROWITZ),** lawyer; b. Phila., Apr. 6, 1940; d. Samuel and Anne (Manstein) Horowitz; m. Morris H. Wolff, May 15, 1966 (div.); children: Michelle Lynn, Lesley Anne; m. Walter Allan Levy, June 7, 1987. BS, U. Pa., 1962, MS, 1966; postgrad., Sophia U., Tokyo, 1968; JD, Villanova U., 1979; LLM, 1988. Tchr. Overbrook High Sch., Phila., 1962-68; homebound tchr. Lower Merior Twp., Montgomery County, 1968-71; asst. dean U. Pa., Phila., 1975-76; law clk. Stassen, Kostos and Mason, Phila., 1977-78; assoc. Spencer, Sherr, Moses and Zuckerman, Norristown, Pa., 1980-81; ptnr. Wolff Assocs., 1981—; lectr. law and estate planning, Phila., 1980—; Recipient 3d Ann. Community Svc. award Phila. Mayor's Com. for Women, 1984; named Pa. Heroine of Month, Ladies Home Jour., July 1984. Founder Take a Brother Program; bd. dirs. Germantown Jewish Ctr.; high sch. sponsor World Affairs Club, Phila., 1962-68; mem. exec. com., sec. bd. Crime Prevention Assn., Phila., 1965—; v.p. bd. dirs. U. Pa. Alumnae Bd., Phila., 1965—, pres. bd. dirs., 1993—, v.p. organized classes, bd. crime prevention; chmn. urban conf. Boys Club Am., 1987; active Hahnaman Brain Tumor Rsch. Bd.; v.p., bd. dirs. Crime Prevention. Mem. Lions (pres. Germantown Club 1997—). General corporate, Probate, Taxation, general. Home and Office: 422 W Mermaid Ln Philadelphia PA 19118-4204

**WOLFF, ELROY HARRIS,** lawyer; b. N.Y.C., May 20, 1935; s. Samuel and Rose Marian (Katz) W.; children: Ethan, Anna Louise. A.B., Columbia U., 1957, LL.B., 1963. Bar: N.Y. 1963, D.C. 1969. Assoc. Kaye, Scholer, Fierman, Hays & Handler, N.Y.C., 1963-65; atty.-adviser to commr. FTC, Washington, 1965-67; sr. trial atty. Dept. Transp., 1967-69; assoc. Leibman, Williams, Bennett, Baird & Minow, Washington, 1969-70, ptnr., 1970-72; ptnr. Sidley & Austin, Washington, 1972—; mem. adv. com. on practice and procedure FTC, 1969-71; chmn. adv. com. on procedural reform CAB, 1975. Served to 1st lt. USAF, 1957-60. Mem. ABA (chmn. spring meeting program 1992-94, coun. 1995-98), Union Internationale des advocats (chmn. competition law com. 1994-98), Army and Navy Club. Antitrust, Administrative and regulatory, Federal civil litigation. Office: Sidley & Austin 1722 I St NW Washington DC 20006-3795

**WOLFF, FRANK MARTIN,** lawyer; b. Ft. Bragg, N.C., July 25, 1956; s. William H. and Ina B. Wolff; m. Joy Hartzler, Aug. 20, 1977; children: Christopher, Victoria. BA, Bob Jones U., Greenville, S.C., 1977; JD, U. Fla., 1980. Bar: Fla. 1980. Assoc. Maguire Voorhis & Wells, Orlando, Fla., 1980-83, Dean Mead, Orlando, 1983-86; ptnr. Rooks Wolff Nardella, Orlando, 1986-87, Wolff Hill McFarlin & Herron, Orlando, 1987—. Mem. Orange County Bar Assn. (chair bankruptcy subcom. 1990-91), Ctrl. Fla. Bankruptcy Assn. (bd. dirs. 1993-96), Univ. Club. Bankruptcy. Office: Wolff Hill McFarlin & Herron 1851 W Colonial Dr Orlando FL 32804-7013

**WOLFF, FRANK PIERCE, JR.,** lawyer; b. St. Louis, Feb. 27, 1946; s. Frank P. and Beatrice (Stein) W.; m. Susan Scallet, May 11, 1984; children: Elizabeth McLane, Victoria Hancox. BA, Middlebury Coll., 1968; JD, U. Va., 1971. Bar: Mo. 1971, U.S. Ct. Appeals (5th cir.) 1974, U.S. Ct. Appeals (8th cir.) 1975, U.S. Supreme Ct. 1975. Ptnr. Lewis, Rice & Fingersh, St. Louis, 1971-90; ptnr., sect. leader, bus. and transactional counseling sect., mem. oper. group Bryan Cave LLP, St. Louis, 1990—; bd. dirs. Wood Ceilings, Inc. Bd. dirs. Leadership St. Louis, 1985-88, Washington U. Child Guidance Clinic, St. Louis, 1976-79, Jewish Family and Children's Svc., St. Louis, 1981-83, John Burroughs Sch., 1995—, BJC Health Sys., Inc., 1998—; gen. counsel Mo. Bot. Garden, St. Louis, 1981—, Mo. Hist. Soc., St. Louis, 1997—; spl. counsel Saint Louis Symphony Soc., 1989—; trustee St. Louis Children's Hosp., 1995—, chairperson mission vision and values com., 1996-97, mem. exec. com., 1997—; co-chmn. Parks Task Force, 2004 Inc. . Capt. USAR, 1968-76. Mem. ABA, Mo. Bar Assn., Bar Assn. Met. St. Louis (chmn. corp. sect. 1984-85), Noonday Club, Westwood County Club (chmn. fin. com. 1989-91, treas. 1989-91, v.p. 1991-93, pres. 1993-95, exec. com. 1989-95). General corporate, Antitrust, Non-profit and tax-exempt organizations. Home: 17 Clerbrook Ln Saint Louis MO 63124-1202 Office: Bryan Cave 211 N Broadway Ste 3600 Saint Louis MO 63102-2733

**WOLFF, KURT JAKOB,** lawyer; b. Mannheim, Germany, Mar. 7, 1936; s. Ernest and Florence (Marx) W.; m. Sanda Lynn Dobrick, Dec. 28, 1958; children; Tracy Ellin, Brett Harris. AB, NYU, 1955; JD, U. Mich., 1958. Bar: N.Y. 1958, U.S. Supreme Ct. 1974, Hawaii 1985, Calif. 1988. Atty. pvt. practice, N.Y.C., 1958—; assoc. Hays, Sklar & HErzberg, N.Y.C., 1958-60; sr. assoc. Nathan, Mannheimer, Asche, Winer & Friedman, N.Y.C., 1960-65; sr. assoc. Otterbourg, Steindler, Houston & Rosen, N.Y.C., 1965-68, sr. ptnr., 1968-70, dir., treas., 1970—, CEO, 1982-99, gen. counsel, 1999—; spl. master N.Y. Supreme Ct., 1977-85; vol. master U.S. Dist. Ct. (so. dist.) N.Y., 1978-82. Lectr., U. Mich. Law Sch.; mem. com. of visitors U. Mich. Law Sch., 1993—; spl. mediator Dept. Disciplinary Com. Appellate Divsn. First Judical Dept., 1991—. Contbr. articles to profl. jours. Mem. ABA (chmn. ins. com. econs. sect. 1980-82, editor arbitratino newsletter, arbitration com. sect. litigation), N.Y. State Bar Assn. (lectr.), Am. Arbitration Assn. (arbitrator), N.Y.C. Bar Assn. (arbitration com. 197-83, state cts. of superior jurisdiction com. 1983-86, mem. com. legal edn. & admission to the bar 1991-94), Hawaii State Bar Assn., Calif. State Bar Assn., Gen. Arbitration Coun. Textile Industry N.Y.C., Fed. Bar Coun. Federal civil litigation, State civil litigation, Contracts commercial. Home: 4 Juniper Ct Armonk NY 10504-1356 also: 48-641 Torrito Ct Palm Desert CA 92260 also: John Hancock Bldg 175 E Delaware Pl Apt 6504 Chicago IL 60611-7731 Office: 230 Park Ave New York NY 10169-0005

**WOLFF, MICHAEL A.,** state supreme court judge. Grad., Dartmouth Coll., 1967; JD, U. Minn., 1970. Lawyer Legal Svcs.; mem. faculty St. Louis U. Sch. Law, 1975-98; judge Mo. Supreme Ct., 1998—; chief counsel to gov., 1993-94, spl. counsel, 1994-98. Co-author: Federal Jury Practice and Instructions. chief counsel to Gov. St. Louis, 1993-94, spl. counsel, 1994-98. Office: Supreme Ct MO PO Box 150 Jefferson City MO 65102*

**WOLFF, PAUL MARTIN,** lawyer; b. Kansas City, Mo., July 22, 1941; s. Joseph L. and Eleanor B. Wolff; m. Rhea S. Schwartz, Oct. 9, 1976. BA, U. Wis., 1963; LLB, Harvard U., 1966. Bar: D.C. 1968, U.S. Ct. Appeals (D.C. and 2d cir.) 1968, U.S. Supreme Ct. 1975, U.S. Ct. Appeals (10th and fed. cirs.) 1981, U.S. Ct. Appeals (8th cir.) 1982, U.S. Tax Ct. 1982, U.S. Ct. Claims 1984. Law clk. to Judge James R. Durfee U.S. Ct. Claims, Washington, 1966-67; assoc. Williams & Connolly, Washington, 1967-75, ptnr., 1976—; adj. prof. Catholic U. Law Sch., 1970-73. Co-author: Forensic Sciences; contbr. articles to legal jours. Bd. dirs. Washington Coun. for Civil Rights Under Law, 1980-90, Renwick Alliance, Washington, 1987-93, Am. Jewish Com., Washington, 1988-92, Washington Legal Clinic for Homeless, 1988-99, Opportunities for Older Ams. Found., 1988-92, Washington Performing Arts Soc., 1990—, Emeritus Found., 1992—; dir. D.C. Sports Commn., Com. Pub. Edn.; trustee Fed. City Coun., Am. U., Corcoran Mus. of Art. Mem. Georgetown Club, Econ. Club Washington (dir.), Phi Beta Kappa. Democrat. Avocations: photography, gardening, fly fishing, sculpting. Fax: 202-434-5580. General civil litigation, Federal civil litigation, Banking. Home: 4770 Reservoir Rd NW Washington DC 20007-1905 also: Oak Ridge Warrenton VA 20186 Office: Williams & Connolly 725 12th St NW Washington DC 20005-5901

**WOLFGANG, JAYSON RICHARD,** lawyer; b. Allentown, Pa., May 14, 1966; s. Calvin A. and M. Louise Wolfgang; m. Louise M. Hathaway, Sept. 21, 1991; children: Rachel L., Ryan J. BA in Criminology, Ind. U. of Pa., 1988; JD, The Dickinson Sch. Law, 1991. Assoc. Mette, Evans & Woodside, Harrisburg, Pa., 1991-96, Buchanan Ingersoll PC, Harrisburg, Pa., 1997—. Bd. dirs. Modern Transp. Partnership, Harrisburg, 1998, The Art Ctr. Sch. and Galleries, 1999—; grad. Leadership Harrisburg Pa., 1997-98; vice chair Middlesex Twp. (Pa.) Recycling Study Com., 1995-97. Avocations: travel, golf, hunting, fishing. General civil litigation. Office: Buchanan Ingersoll PC 213 Market St Fl 3 Harrisburg PA 17101-2132

**WOLFRAM, CHARLES WILLIAM,** law educator; b. Cleve., Feb. 28, 1937; s. Carl P. and Dona M. (Minitch) W.; m. Nancy Russell Bass, Dec. 18, 1965; children: Catherine Dana, Peter Russell. AB, Notre Dame U., 1959; LLB, U. Tex., 1962. Bar: D.C. 1962, Minn. 1974. Assoc. Covington & Burling, Washington, 1962-64; mem. FAA Contract Appeals Panel, Washington, 1964-65; asst. prof. law U. Minn., 1965-67, assoc. prof., 1967-70, prof., 1970-81; prof. law Cornell U., Ithaca, N.Y., 1982-84; Charles Frank Reavis Sr. prof. law Cornell U., Ithaca, 1984—; assoc. dean acad. affairs Cornell U., Ithaca, 1986-90, interim dean, 1998-99; vis. prof. U. So. Calif. Law Center, 1976-77. Author: (with J. Morris Clark) Professional Responsibilty: Issues for Minnesota Attorneys, 1976, Modern Legal Ethics, 1986; contbr. chpts. to books, articles to profl. jours. Mem. Am. Law Inst. (chief reporter Restatement of Law Governing Lawyers 1986—), Order of Coif. Democrat. Office: Cornell Law Sch 106 Myron Taylor Hall Ithaca NY 14853-4901

**WOLFSON, NICHOLAS,** law educator; b. N.Y.C., Feb. 29, 1932; m. Judith Wolfson, Sept. 8, 1955; children: Amy, Adam. AB with highest honors, Columbia U., 1953; JD cum laude, Harvard U., 1956. Bar: N.Y. 1956, Mass. 1966. Atty. SEC, Washington, 1958-60; pvt. practice N.Y.C. and Boston, 1960-66; br. chief, spl. counsel, asst. dir. SEC, 1967-72; prof. U. Conn., 1972—, Ellen Ash Peters prof., 1990-92, George & Helen England prof., 1995—; vis. scholar Hoover Instn. on War, Revolution and Peace, Stanford (Calif.) U., fall 1985; lectr. in field. Author: The Modern Corporation: Free Markets vs. Regulation, 1984, Corporate First Amendments Rights and the SEC, 1990, Twentieth Century Fund Report: Conflicts of Interest: Investment Banking, 1976, Hate Speech, Sex Speech, Free Speech, 1997; co-author: Regulation of Brokers, Dealers and Securities Markets, 1977; contbr. articles to profl. jours. Past mem. exec. com. Nat. Jewish Cmty. Rels. Adv. Coun. Mem. ABA (chair legal edn. com. sect. bus. law 1984-88), Assn. Am. Law Schs. (chair bus. assns. sect. 1978). Office: U Conn Sch of Law 65 Elizabeth St Hartford CT 06105-2290

**WOLIN, ALFRED M.,** federal judge; b. Orange, N.J., Sept. 17, 1932; s. George and Juliet (Rosenstock) W.; m. Jane Zapiekov, Mar. 27, 1960; children: Roger, Marc. BA, U. Mich., 1954; LLB, JD, Rutgers U., 1959. Pvt. practice Elizabeth, N.J., 1960-80; judge Union County Dist. Ct., Elizabeth, N.J., 1980-85, Union County Superior Ct., Elizabeth, N.J., 1985-87, U.S. Dist. Ct., Newark, N.J., 1987—; atty. Roselle Bd. Adjustment, 1965-74; legis. aide to Senator Matthew J. Rinaldo, N.J. Senate, 1970-72; spl. asst. prosecutor Union County, 1970; congl. field rep. 12th congl. dist., 1972-79; mcpl. prosecutor Town of Westfield, N.J., 1973-74. Chief staff atty. Union County Legal Aid Soc., 1964-74; mem. Union County Ethics Com., sec., 1970-78, exec. com. Statewide Speedy Trial Com., Conf. Presiding Criminal Judges, Criminal Practice Com.; active Temple Emanuel, Jewish Fedn. Cen. N.J. SPC 2 U.S. Army, 1954-56, Germany. Mem. ABA, Am. Judicature Soc., N.J. Bar Assn. (judicial selection, discipline of the bar, lawyer referral coms.), Union County Bar Assn. (sec. 1970-74, pres. elect 1975, pres. 1976, judicial appointments com.), Fed. Judges Assn. Jewish. Office: US Dist Ct US Courthouse PO Box 999 Newark NJ 07101-0999 *Notable cases include: (as judge) presided over trademark rights suit involving Procter & Gamble vs. Revlon, 1990, which alleged that Revlon's creation of Ivory Coast shampoo infringed on name of Procter & Gamble's Ivory soap. The suit was settled for an undisclosed amount.*

**WOLIS, KENNETH ARNOLD,** lawyer; b. N.Y.C., July 3, 1931; s. Sol and Esther (Wolis) W.; m. Nizha Arbib, Feb. 9, 1963; 1 child, Robert. BA, NYU, 1953; JD, U. Miami, 1958. Bar: Fla. 1958, U.S. Dist. Ct. (so. dist.) Fla. 1959, U.S. Ct. Appeals (11th cir.) 1959, U.S. Supreme Ct. 1971. Atty. Von Zamft & Kravitz, Miami, Fla., 1958-59, Meltzer & Nesbitt, Miami, 1960; sole practitioner North Miami, Fla., 1960-64, Miami, 1964-70, Hollywood, Fla., 1971—; atty. Apt. and Hotel Assn. Hollywood, 1973-97, Ravenswood Mgmt. Assn., Ft. Lauderdale, Fla., 1990-97, Three Horizons East Condominium, North Miami, 1988-97. Mem. Zoning Bd., Town of Surfside, Fla., 1961-63; trustee. Emerald Hills Homeowners Assn., 1999. With U.S. Army, 1954-56. Mem. Masons, Shriners, Scottish Rite (pres. 1992), Hollywood Lions Club. Avocations: reading, walking. Fax: (954) 963-8156. Probate, Personal injury, General practice. Office: 4600 Sheridan St Hollywood FL 33021-3409

**WOLK, BRUCE ALAN,** law educator; b. Bklyn., Mar. 2, 1946; s. Morton and Gertrude W.; m. Lois Gloria Krepliak, June 22, 1968; children: Adam, Daniel. BS, Antioch Coll., 1968; MS, Stanford U., 1972; JD, Harvard U., 1975. Bar: D.C. 1975. Assoc. Hogan & Hartson, Washington, 1975-78; prof. U. Calif. Sch. Law, Davis, 1978—, acting dean, 1990-91, dean, 1993-98. Danforth Found. fellow, 1970-74, NSF fellow, 1970-72, Fulbright sr. research fellow, 1985-86. Mem. ABA, Am. Law Inst. Office: Univ Cal-Davis Sch Law King Hall 400 Mrak Hall Dr Davis CA 95616-5201

**WOLK, STUART RODNEY,** lawyer, educator, author; b. N.Y.C., May 15, 1938; s. Charles and Cressie (Bresky) W.; m. Priscilla Wahl, Feb. 3, 1968; 1 dau., Melissa Cressie. BA, Queens Coll., 1958; MA, Grad. Faculty of New Sch. Social Rsch., 1960; JD, Bklyn. Law Sch., 1961; PhD, St. Andrews Coll. (Eng.), 1964, D.H.L. London Inst., 1973. Bar: N.Y. 1961, D.C. 1961, U.S. Supreme Ct. 1964, N.J. 1975, U.S. dist. ct. (ea. and so. dists.) N.Y., U.S. dist. ct. N.J., U.S. dist. ct. D.C., U.S. Dist. Ct. Conn., U.S. Tax Ct., U.S. Ct. Mil. Appeals, U.S. Claims Ct., U.S. Ct. Appeals (D.C. cir.), U.S. Ct. Appeals (2d and 5th cirs.), Conn. 1984. Asst. staff judge adv. for procurement law USAF, 1961-62, asst. staff judge adv. for procurement and labor law, 1963-65; asst. gen. counsel Def. Electronic Supply Ctr., 1962-63; asst. div. counsel Litton Systems, Inc. div. Litton Industries, Inc., New Rochelle, N.Y., 1965-66; contract counsel Kollsman Instrument Corp., Syosset, N.Y., 1966-67; assoc. gen. counsel, dir. govt. contracts Bulova Watch Co., N.Y.C., 1967-69; sr. ptnr. Wolk Neuman & Bakshi, and predecessors, Washington, N.Y.C., Hartford, Conn., Trenton and Montville, N.J., 1969—, Wolk, Neuman & Maziarz; adj. prof. mgmt. and law Roth Grad. Sch., Bus., LIU Prof. Mgmt., former acad. dir. exec. masters degree program, curricula chair, gen. mgmt.; prof. Hartford Grad. Ctr. Sch. Mgmt. Served to col. JAGC, USAFR, 1958-85; sr. res. designee to dir. Sec. USAF Pers. Coun., 1985-88. Alvin-Johnson Prize scholar, 1958-61; Bancroft-Whitney scholar, 1961. Mem. N.J. Bar Assn., N.Y. State Bar Assn., D.C. Bar Assn., Conn. Bar Assn., Houston Bar Assn., Res. Officers Assn., Nat. Council Fin. Edn. (bd. govs.). Contbg. author: Your Book of Financial Planning; author: Legal Aspects of Computer Use; contbr. numerous articles to legal jours. Administrative and regulatory, General corporate, Labor. Office: 1 Craig Ct Montville NJ 07045-9605 also: 3201 New Mexico Ave NW Ste 247 Washington DC 20016-2756 also: 30 E 40th St New York NY 10016-1201 also: 275 Windsor St Hartford CT 06120-2910 also: 311 White Horse Ave Trenton NJ 08610-1411

**WOLKEN, GEORGE, JR.,** patent lawyer; b. Jersey City, Nov. 11, 1944; s. George and Lilac (Straub) W.; children: Jill, Daniel, Michael. BS summa cum laude, Tufts U., 1966; PhD, Harvard U., 1971; JD, Capital U., 1981. Asst. prof. chemistry Ill. Inst. Tech., Chgo., 1974-76; researcher Battelle, Columbus, Ohio, 1976-78, rsch. mgr., 1978-82; pvt. practice patent law Columbus, 1982-95; of counsel Porter, Wright, Morris, Arthur, Columbus, 1995-98, Skjerven, Morrill, MacPherson, Franklin & Friel, San Jose, Calif., 1999—. Contbr. numerous articles to sci. and profl. jours. Fax: (408) 453-7979.

**WOLLE, CHARLES ROBERT,** federal judge; b. Sioux City, Iowa, Oct. 16, 1935; s. William Carl and Vivian (Down) W.; m. Kerstin Birgitta Wennerstrom, June 26, 1961; children: Karl Johan Knut, Erik Vernon, Thomas Dag, Aaron Charles. AB, Harvard U., 1959; JD, Iowa Law Sch., 1961. Bar: Iowa 1961. Assoc. Shull, Marshall & Marks, Sioux City, 1961-67, ptnr., 1968-80; judge Dist. Ct. Iowa, Sioux City, 1981-83; justice Iowa Supreme Ct., Sioux City and Des Moines, 1983-87; judge U.S. Dist. Ct. (so. dist.) Iowa, Des Moines, 1987-92, chief judge, 1992-99; faculty Nat. Jud. Coll., Reno, 1983—. Editor Iowa Law Rev., 1960-61. Vice pres. bd. dirs. Sioux City Symphony, 1972-77; sec., bd. dirs. Morningside Coll., Sioux City, 1977-81. Fellow Am. Coll. Trial Lawyers; mem. ABA, Iowa Bar Assn., Sioux City C. of C. (bd. dirs. 1977-78). Avocations: sports, art, music, literature. Home: 1601 Pleasant View Dr Des Moines IA 50315-2129 Office: US Dist Judge 103 US Courthouse 123 E Walnut St Des Moines IA 50309-2035

**WOLLER, JAMES ALAN,** lawyer; b. Adrian, Mich., Dec. 27, 1946; s. Robert Arthur and Florence Emma (Jacob) W.; m. Jill Ann Samis, Aug. 18, 1968 (div. Aug. 1978); 1 child, Emily Erin; m. Elizabeth Julia Frey, May 22, 1982 (div. Apr. 1999). BA, U. Mich., 1969; JD, Columbia U., 1974. Bar: N.J. 1974, U.S. Dist. Ct. N.J. 1974, U.S. Tax Ct. 1976, U.S. Supreme Ct. 1995. Assoc. McCarter & English, Newark, 1974-79; v.p. Pfaltz & Woller, P.A., Summit, N.J., 1979-86, pres., 1987—. Editor Columbia U. Human Rights Law Rev., 1973-74. Mem. ABA, N.J. Bar Assn., Union County Bar Assn., Summit Bar Assn. (pres. 1987-88), Downtown Club (trustee 1997-99, treas. 1999—), Raritan Yacht Club (fin. sec. Perth Amboy, N.J. 1988-89, treas. 1989-92, vice commodore 1993-94, commodore 1994-95), Columbia Law Sch. Assn. N.J. (trustee 1992-97, v.p. 1997—). Republican. Methodist. Avocation: sailing. General corporate, Banking, Real property. Home: 434 Lawrence St Apt 20 Perth Amboy NJ 08861-2148 Office: Pfaltz & Woller PA 382 Springfield Ave Ste 217 Summit NJ 07901-2780

**WOLLINS, DAVID HART,** lawyer; b. N.Y.C., Nov. 1, 1952; s. Donald John Wollins and Constance Joy Graham; m. Leslie Bjerg Lilly, Apr. 1, 1989; children: Alexandra Bjerg Lilly W., David Hart Jr. BS in Fin. and Mktg., U. Pa., 1974; JD, New Eng. Sch. Law, 1978. Bar: N.Y. 1979, U.S. Dist. Ct. (ea. and so. dists.) N.Y. 1979, U.S. Dist. Ct. Colo. 1986, U.S. Ct. Appeals (10th cir.) 1986, U.S. Ct. Appeals (fed., D.C. and 2d cirs.) 1990, U.S. Ct. Appeals (9th cir.), 1992, U.S. Ct. Claims 1983, U.S. Supreme Ct. 1994. Pres. Nature's Way Recycling Co., Boston, 1974-75; summer assoc. Phillips, Nizer, Benjamin, Krim & Ballon, N.Y.C., 1976-78, assoc., 1978-86; of counsel Cortez and Friedman, P.C., Englewood, Colo., 1986-87; mem. firm, co-head litigation dept. Brenman, Raskin, Friedlob & Tenenbaum, P.C., Denver, 1987-91; shareholder, head litigation dept. McGeady Sisneros & Wollins, P.C., Denver, 1991-95; spl. counsel Jonathan J. Hellman & Assoc., P.C., Englewood, Colo., 1995-96; mng. ptnr. Wollins, Hellman & Green, Denver, 1996—; pro bono atty., City N.Y., 1978-86. Author short stories and numerous poems. Mem. N.Y. Bar Assn., Colo. Bar Assn., Colo. Trial Lawyers Assn., Denver Bar Assn. Fax: 303-758-8111. Federal civil litigation, General civil litigation, Securities. Home: 311 Bannock St # A/C Denver CO 80223-1103 Office: Wollins Hellman & Green 720 S Colorado Blvd Ste 620S Denver CO 80246-1943

**WOLLMAN, ROGER LELAND,** judge; b. Frankfort, S.D., May 29, 1934; s. Edwin and Katherine Wollman; m. Diane Marie Schroeder, June 21, 1959; children: Steven James, John Mark, Thomas Roger. BA, Tabor Coll., Hillsboro, Kans., 1957; JD magna cum laude, U. S.D., 1962; LLM, Harvard U., 1964. Bar: S.D. 1964. Sole practice, Aberdeen, 1964-71; justice S.D. Supreme Ct., 1971-85, chief justice, 1978-82; judge U.S. Ct. Appeals (8th cir.), 1985—, chief judge, 1999—; states atty. Brown County, Aberdeen, 1967-71. Served with AUS, 1957-59. Office: US Ct Appeals US Courthouse & Fed Bldg 400 S Phillips Ave Rm 315 Sioux Falls SD 57104-6851*

**WOLNITZEK, STEPHEN DALE,** lawyer; b. Covington, Ky., Mar. 13, 1949; s. Frederick William Jr. and Mary Ruth (Meiners) W.; m. Katherine Anita Bishop, Dec. 15, 1972; children: Marcus Stephen, Justin Bishop. BA cum laude, U. Notre Dame, 1970; JD, U. Cin., 1974. Bar: Ky. 1975, U.S. Dist. Ct. (ea. dist.) Ky. 1976, U.S. Supreme Ct. 1978, U.S. Dist. Ct. (we. dist.) Ky. 1981, U.S. Ct. Appeals (6th cir.) 1991. Dep. sheriff Kenton County, Covington, 1971-75; assoc. Taliaferro & Smith, Covington, 1975-80; ptnr. Taliaferro, Smith, Mann, Wolnitzek & Schachter, Covington, 1980-86; officer Smith, Wolnitzek, Schachter & Rowekamp P.S.C., Covington, 1986-96; pres. Wolnitzek, Rowekamp, Bender & Bonar, P.S.C., Covington, 1996-98, Wolnitzek, Rowekamp & Bonar, P.S.C., Covington, 1998—; Bd. dirs. Ky. Legal Svcs. Plan Inc., 1984-96; adj. prof. Samuel Chase Coll. Law, No. Ky. U., 1995-98; mem. Ky. Jud. Retirement and Removal Commn. (now Ky. Jud. Conduct Commn.), 1995—, chair, 1996—;. Mem. exec. com. Kenton County Boys-Girls Club, 1981—, sec., 1995, v.p., 1996, pres., 1997; mem. exec. com. Ky. Law Enforcement Coun., Frankfort, 1984-93, vice chmn., 1991-93, chair cert. com., 1986-93; mem. City Coun., Ft. Wright, Ky., 1984-85, mem. Bd. Adjustment, 1986-97, vice chair, 1995-97; pres. No. Ky. Comty. Ctr., Covington, 1985-86; mem. bd. visitors Chase Coll. Law, no. Ky. U., 1995-97; bd. dirs. Kenton Housing Inc., 1986—, sec., 1991-93, v.p., 1993-95, pres., 1995-97; trustee No. Ky. Youth Leadership Found., 1992—, exec. com. bd. dirs., 1992—, pres., 1996—. Recipient Roy Taylor award No. Ky. Legal Aid Soc., 1985, Disting. Lawyer award No. Ky. Bar Assn., 1998; named Vol. of Yr., Community Chest United Appeal, Cin., 1986. Fellow Am. Bar Found., Ky. Bar Found. (charter life; bd. dirs. 1989-94, 95—), No. Ky. Bar Found. (charter life); mem. Ky. Bar Assn. (bd. govs. 1984-96, chmn. ho. of dels. 1986, v.p. 1992-93, pres. 1994-95), Assn. Def. Attys., Coun. Sch. Bd. Attys. (bd. dirs. 1981-87), Samuel P. Chase Am. Inns of Ct. (master 1994-99), Ky. Def. Counsel, DRI, Notre Dame Club Cin., U. Cin. Alumni Assn. (bd. trustees, bd. dirs.), Fraternal Order Police. Democrat. Roman Catholic. Avocations: sports, reading. Insurance, Education and schools, State civil litigation. Home: 1836 Beacon Hl Covington KY 41011-3684 Office: Wolnitzek Rowekamp & Bonar PSC 502 Greenup St # 352 Covington KY 41011-2522

**WOLOWITZ, DAVID,** lawyer; b. Washington, Apr. 3, 1946; s. William H. and Frances H. Wolowitz; m. Roxanne S. Tooker, Aug. 29, 1970. AB, Washington U., 1968; MA, Harvard U., 1971; JD, U. Mich., 1975. Bar: N.H. 1975, U.S. Dist. Ct. N.H. 1975, U.S. Dist. Ct. (1st cir.) 1981, Mass. 1985. Staff atty. N.H. Legal Assistance, Concord, 1975-76; mng. atty. N.H. Legal Assistance, Portsmouth, 1977-79, N.H. Pub. Defender, Exeter, 1979-83; atty., ptnr. Sanders & McDermott, Hampton, N.H., 1983-91; atty., dir. McLane Law Firm, Portsmouth, 1991—; guest faculty trial advocacy program Harvard Law Sch., 1983—. Jewish. General civil litigation, Personal injury, Labor. Office: McLane Law Firm 30 Penhallow St Portsmouth NH 03801-3816

**WOLPER, BEATRICE EMENS,** lawyer; b. New Haven, Nov. 28, 1945. BA, U. Cin., 1974; JD cum laude, No. Ky. U., 1978. Bar: Ohio 1979. Assoc., then ptnr. Emens, Kegler, Brown, Hill & Ritter, Columbus, Ohio, 1979-97; ptnr. Chester, Willcox & Saxbe, LLP, Columbus, 1997—; pres., founder Women's Bus. Bd., Columbus, 1984—; bd. mem., exec. com. Ctr. Sci. and Industry, Columbus, 1994—; bd. dirs. Attys. for Family Hold Enterprises, N.Y.C. Author: Family Business Basics, 1998. Participant NAFTA, Washington, 1993; del. White House Conf. on Small Bus., Washington, 1995. Named Entrepreneur of the Yr., YWCA, Columbus, 1993, Women of Achievement, Ernst & Young/Inc. Mag., Columbus, 1993. Mem. Internat. Women's Forum (pres. Ohio chpt. 1994—), Columbus Bar Assn. (chair securities commn. 1987-89), Capital Club (chair 1994-96), Columbus C. of C. (bd. mem. 1994—). Avocations: fly fishing, geology, hiking, reading. General corporate, Estate planning. Home: 9592 Lake Of The Woods Dr Galena OH 43021-9622 Office: Chester Willcox & Saxbe LLP 17 S High St Ste 900 Columbus OH 43215-3442

**WOLSON, CRAIG ALAN,** lawyer; b. Toledo, Feb. 20, 1949; s. Max A. and Elaine B. (Cohn) W.; m. Janis Nan Braun, July 30, 1972 (div. Mar. 1986); m. Ellen Carol Schulgasser, Oct. 26, 1986; children: Lindsey, Michael and Geoffrey (triplets). BA, U. Mich., 1971, JD, 1974. Bar: N.Y. 1975, U.S. Dist. Ct. (so. and ea. dists.) N.Y. 1975, U.S. Ct. Appeals (2d cir.) 1975, U.S. Supreme Ct. 1978. Assoc. Shearman & Sterling, N.Y.C., 1974-81; v.p., asst. gen. counsel Thomson McKinnon Securities Inc., N.Y.C., 1981-85; v.p., sec., gen. counsel J.D. Mattus Co., Inc., Greenwich, Conn., 1985-88; also bd. dirs. J.D. Mattus Co., Inc. and affiliated cos., Greenwich; v.p., asst. gen. counsel Chem. Bank, N.Y.C., 1988-95; of counsel Williams & Harris, N.Y.C., 1995-96; ptnr. Williams & Harris LLP, N.Y.C., 1996-97; counsel Brown & Wood L.L.P., N.Y.C., 1997-98, Mayer, Brown & Platt, N.Y.C., 1999—; dep. clk. Lucas County Courthouse, Toledo, 1968-69, 71-72. Articles and adminstrv. editor U. Mich. Law Rev., 1973-74. Mem. ABA, N.Y. State Bar Assn., Assn. of Bar of City of N.Y. (securities regulation com. 1994-97, corp. law com. 1997—), Corp. Bar. Assn. of Westchester and Fairfield, Phi Beta Kappa, Phi Eta Sigma, Pi Sigma Alpha. Avocations: reading, playing piano, fine dining, theater. Securities, General corporate. Home: 41 Bonnie Brook Rd Westport CT 06880-1507 Office: Mayer Brown & Platt 21st Flr 1675 Broadway Fl 21 New York NY 10019-5820

**WOMACK, CHARLES RAYMOND,** lawyer; b. McMinnville, Tenn., July 4, 1905; s. John Watson and Frances Isabel (Denton) W.; m. Sally Lee Carver, June 19, 1949; children: Mary Carolyn Womack Corson, John Winston. LLB, Memphis State U., 1944. Bookkeeper So. Supply Co., Jackson, Tenn., 1932-37, sec., 1937-55, treas., 1955-68, pres., 1955-68, chmn. bd., 1968-70; pvt. practice law Jackson, Tenn., 1971—; trustee Freed-Hardeman U., Henderson, Tenn., 1970-90. Republican. Mem. Ch. of Christ. Avocations: golf, fishing, hunting, travel, reading. Probate, Pension, profit-sharing, and employee benefits, General practice. Home: 409 Wisdom St Jackson TN 38301-4329 Office: CR Womack Atty 420 E Main St Jackson TN 38301-6328

**WOMACK, GUY LEE,** lawyer, marine officer; b. Atlanta, Jan. 23, 1953; s. Ivey Lee and Mary Jane (Jenkins) W.; m. Kathy Sue Jones, Sept. 19, 1970; children: Paige Ann, Geoffrey Lee, Amy Elizabeth. BA in Polit. Sci., U. Ga., 1977; JD, Woodrow Wilson Coll. Law, 1980. Bar: Ga. 1980, U.S. Ct. Mil. Appeals 1981, U.S. Supreme Ct. 1989, U.S. Ct. Appeals (5th cir.) 1993, (11th cir.) 1997, U.S. Dist. Ct. (so. dist.) Tex. 1990, (so. dist.) Ala. 1997, U.S. Ct. Appeals (4th cir.) 1997. Commd. 2d lt. USMC, 1980, advanced through grades to lt. col., 1995; exec. officer Co. I 2d Bn. USMC, Camp LeJeune, N.C., 1981-82, def. counsel 2d div., 1982-83, prosecutor, dep. staff judge advocate 2d Marine div., 1983-84; prosecutor USMC, Guantanamo Bay, Cuba, 1984-86; student amphibious warfare sch. USMC, Quantico, Va., 1986-87; house counsel/prosecutor Naval Investigative Service Legal Services Support Sect. USMC, Camp LeJeune, 1987—; asst. U.S. atty. U.S. Dist. Ct. (so. dist.) Tex., 1990-96; pvt. practice, 1997—. Chmn. Law Day Observance Naval Legal Service Office, Guantanano Bay, 1986. Mem. ABA (Pub. Service award 1986), Assn. Trial Lawyers Am., State Bar Tex., State Bar Ga., Tex. Criminal Def. Lawyers Assn., Ga. Assn. Criminal Def. Lawyers, Marine Corps Assn. (life), Nat. Assn. Chiefs Police, Nat. Rifle Assn. (life), Profl. Assn. Diving Instrs. (pres. scuba instr. council Guantanamo 1984-86). Republican. Baptist. Avocations: scuba diving, running, tae kwon do, shooting sports, reading. Fax: (713) 224-2815. E-mail: gwomack@ix.netcom.com. Home: 3730 Brookvale Ct Kingwood TX 77345-1229 Office: 440 Louisiana St Ste 800 Houston TX 77002-1635

**WOMACK, MARY PAULINE,** lawyer; b. Chattanooga, Tenn., Dec. 3, 1942; d. Abner and Lucille (Thomas) W. BS, U. Chattanooga, 1964; JD, Woodrow Wilson Coll. Law, 1984. Bar: Ga. 1988, U.S. Dist. Ct. (no. dist.) Ga. 1988. Pvt. practice Atlanta, 1988—. DeKalb County Dems., 66th dist., regional com. State of Ga. Mem. Ga. Bar Assn., Sigma Delta Kappa (past regional v.p.). Criminal, Personal injury, Landlord-tenant. Home: 3445 Ashwood Ln Atlanta GA 30341-4534 Office: Ste 1950 100 Peachtree St NW Atlanta GA 30303-1906

**WOMACK, TOM D.,** lawyer; b. Forrest City, Ark., Oct. 28, 1946; s. Thomas Isaac and Ida Mae (Bannon) W.; m. Linda C. Cornish, Aug. 18, 1973; children: Thomas Andrew, John Derek. BS, Ark. State U., 1968; JD, U. Memphis, 1972. Bar: Ark. 1972, U.S. Dist. Ct. (ea. dist.) Ark. 1972, U.S. Ct. Appeals (8th cir.), U.S. Supreme Ct. 1977, U.S. Tax Ct. 1980. Assoc. Barrett, Wheatley, Smith & Deacon, Jonesboro, Ark., 1972-74, ptnr., 1975-93; ptnr. Womack, Landis, Phelps, McNeil & McDaniel, Jonesboro, Ark., 1993—. Contbr. articles to law jours. Chpt. chmn. Craighead County Red Cross, Jonesboro, Ark., 1985; chmn., bd. dirs. Greater Jonesboro C. of C., 1987-88; bd. dirs. Ark. Cmty. Found., 1999—. Recipient Gavel award Ark. Bar Assn., 1984. Fellow Am. Coll. Trust and Estate Counsel; mem. Ark. Bd. Legal Specialization (tax law splst. 1986—). Baptist. Avocation: fishing. General corporate, Corporate taxation, Probate. Office: Womack Landis Phelps McNeil & McDaniel 301 W Washington Ave Jonesboro AR 72401-2778

**WONG, ELIZABETH ANNE,** lawyer; b. Houston, Oct. 3, 1967; d. Edward P. and Jennie L. Wong. BA in Psychology, U. So. Calif., L.A., 1989; JD, Southwestern U., 1994. Bar: Calif. 1994, U.S. Dist. Ct. (ctrl. dist.) Calif. 1994, Tex. 1995. Lawyer, editor West Group, Rochester, N.Y., 1996-97; legal editor Daily Jour. Corp., L.A., 1997; assoc. Waters McCluskey & Boehle, Santa Monica, Calif., 1997—. Editor Tex. Jurisprudence 3rd edit., 1996-97, State Trial Handbooks, 1996-97; articles editor Ohio Jurisprudence, 1996-97, N.J. Pleading & Practice, 1996-97; contbr. articles to profl. jours. Mem. So. Calif. Def. Counsel, Def. Rsch. Inst. General civil litigation, Insurance, Product liability. Office: Waters McCluskey & Boehle 3250 Ocean Park Blvd Ste 300 Santa Monica CA 90405-3219

**WONG, FRANCISCO RAIMUNDO,** law educator, lawyer; b. Havana, Cuba, Oct. 29, 1944; came to U.S., 1961; s. Juan Wong and Teresa Diaz de Villegas; divorced; 1 child, Richard Alan; m. Elena Shifrin, June 8, 1997. BA, No. Mich. U., 1965; MA, U. Mich., 1970, PhD, 1974; JD, U. Calif., Berkeley, 1976. Bar: Calif. 1980, Fla. 1986, U.S. Dist. (no. dist.) Calif. 1990. Prof. law City Coll. San Francisco, 1971—, chmn. dept., 1979-85; dir., assoc. dean Miami (Fla.) Dade Coll., 1985-86; pvt. practice, Kentfield and Greenbrae, Calif., 1980—; book reviewer West Pub. Corp., St. Paul, 1990-98; diplomat-scholar U.S. Dept. State, Washington, 1976; guest spkr. Sta. KQED-TV and KCSM-TV, San Francisco, 1994; polit. analyst Univision/KDTV, San Francisco, 1984—; visiting scholar Sch. Bus., U. Calif., Berkeley, 1982. Editor: Foreign Affairs Anthology, 1998-99. Bd. dirs. La Familia Marin, San Rafael, Calif., 1981-85, Small Bus. Inst., Kentfiedl, 1981-83; panelist Mexican-Am. Legal Def. Fund Citizen Outreach, San Francisco, 1984; mem. Cuban-Am. Nat. Coun., 1985—. Horace C. Rackham fellow U. Mich., 1970-71; summer fellow U. Calif., 1995. Mem. Calif. State Bar (editl. adv. bd. Calif. Lawyer 1991-93), Latino Ednl. Assn. (treas. 1979-85, bd. dirs.), World Affairs Coun. No. Calif. Roman Catholic. Avocations: travel, reading, films. Office: City Coll San Francisco 50 Phelan Ave San Francisco CA 94112-1821

**WONG, JAMES THOMAS,** lawyer; b. N.Y.C., Sept. 15, 1955; s. Swee Chee and Dorothy Chuan-Ying (Yang) W.; m. Patricia Uyehara, Aug. 15, 1981; children: Thomas, Jordan, Cory, Sara. BA cum laude, U. Pa., 1976; JD, Case Western Res. U., 1979. Bar: Pa. 1979, U.S. Dist. Ct. (ea. dist.) Pa. 1979, Hi. 1982, U.S. Ct. Appeals (9th cir.) 1982. Dep. atty. gen., asst. gen. counsel Commonwealth of Pa., 1980-82; assoc. Law Offices Richard K. Quinn, Honolulu, 1982-85; ptnr. Libkuman, Ventura, Ayabe & Hughes, Honolulu, 1985-91; sr. trial atty., staff counsel AIG Ins. Cos., Honolulu, 1991-94; mng. atty. Law Offices of James T. Wong, Honolulu, 1995—. Bd. dir. Asian Am. Council Greater Phila., 1980-82. Mem. ABA, Pa. Bar Assn., Hi. Bar Assn., Am. Arbitration Assn. Lutheran. Federal civil litigation, State civil litigation, Personal injury. Home: 173 Kokololio Pl Honolulu HI 96821-2563 Office: 500 Ala Moana Blvd Honolulu HI 96813-4920

**WONG, LINDA,** lawyer; b. Hackensack, N.J., Nov. 15, 1953; d. Quing and Alice Wong; m. Richard Peres, June 14, 1980; children: Lindsay Peres, Jessica Peres. BA, Rutgers U., 1976, JD, 1982. Atty. Office Legis. Svcs., Divsn. Legal Svcs., Trenton, N.J., 1982-84, N.J. Dept. of the Pub. Adv., Divsn. Devel. Disabled, Trenton, 1984-90; asst. dir. divsn. civil rights N.J. Dept. Law and Pub. Safety, Trenton, 1990-94; ptnr. Wong, Tsai & Fleming, Edison, N.J., 1994—; adj. instr. Rutgers U., New Brunswick, N.J., 1994-95; mem. Supreme Ct. Com., N.J., 1994-96; presenter in field. Contbr. articles to profl. jours. Mem. ABA, N.J. State Bar Assn. (chairperson), N.J. Assn. Pacific Am. Lawyer Assn., Nat. Asian Pacific ABA, N.J. NOW. Labor, Education and schools, General civil litigation. Office: Wong Tsai & Fleming 2035 Lincoln Hwy Ste 1050 Edison NJ 08817-3352

**WONG, REUBEN SUN FAI,** lawyer; b. Honolulu, Mar. 12, 1936; s. Lin and Ella Mew Quon (Ching) W.; m. Vera Hui, Dec. 4, 1966; children: Delwyn, Irwyn. BSCE, U. Hawaii, 1958; JD, U. Ill., 1964. Bar: Hawaii 1964, U.S. Dist. Ct. Hawaii 1964, U.S. Ct. Appeals (9th cir.) 1967, U.S. Supreme Ct. 1974. Law clk. Supreme Ct. of Hawaii, Honolulu, 1964-65; dep. corp. counsel City and County of Honolulu, 1965-67; adminstrv. asst. Hawaii Ho. of Reps., Honolulu, 1967; ptnr. Chuck & Fujiyama, Honolulu, 1967-76; sole practice Honolulu, 1976—; lectr. U. Hawaii, 1967-70. Vice chairperson Legislature's Adv. Study Commn. on Water Resources, Honolulu, 1982-85. Served to capt. USAF, 1959-62. Mem. ABA, Am. Judicature Soc., Assn. Trial Lawyers Am., Am. Arbitration Assn. (mem. panel of arbitrators), Hawaii C. of C. (bd. dirs. 1976-80, v.p. 1977-78), Chinese C. of C., Phi Alpha Delta. Lodge: Aloha Temple. Real property, General civil litigation, Banking. Home: 15 Homelani Pl Honolulu HI 96817-1113 Office: 220 S King St Ste 2288 Honolulu HI 96813-4538

**WONG, RICHARD C.,** lawyer; b. N.Y.C., May 31, 1964. AB, Cornell U., 1985; JD, U. Buffalo, 1988. Bar: N.Y. Atty. Weil, Gotshal & Manges LLP, N.Y.C. E-mail: richard.wong@weil.com. Office: Weil Gotshal & Manges LLP 767 5th Ave New York NY 10022-1695

**WONG, RICHARD LEE,** lawyer; b. Austin, Tex., May 5, 1964; s. Richard and Narcissus Faye (Lee) W. BA, Calif. State U., Hayward, 1987; JD, Georgetown U., 1990. Mem. Office of Presdl. Pers. The White House, Washington, 1989-90; with Sedgwick Detert Moran & Arnold, San Francisco, 1990-91; dist. office staff U.S. Senator John Seymour, San Francisco, 1991-92; atty.-advisor U.S. Dept. Transp., Washington, 1992—. Mem. Chinese Christian Ch. of Greater Washington. Recipient Nat. Performance Review Reinventing Govt. award, 1997. Mem. Asian Pacific Bar Assn., U.S. Naval Inst., Conf. on Asian Pacific Am. leadership. Transportation, Administrative and regulatory, Legislative. Address: 1211 S Eads St Apt 601 Arlington VA 22202-2890

**WONNELL, HAROLD EDWARD,** lawyer; b. Columbus, Ohio, July 2, 1923; s. Clarence Edward and Daisy (Van Fossen) W.; m. Nancy Kathleen Thomas, Aug. 20, 1940; children: Vikki Priest, Andre Jo Correale, Deirdre Jo Davis, Gabrielle A. Morton. BSBA, Ohio State U., 1949, LLB, 1951, JD, 1967. Spl. agt., field agt. in L.A. and Portland, on staff of J. Edgar Hoover, FBI, Washington, 1951-55; mem. pub. rels. and investigation Thoroughbred Racing Assn., Chgo., 1955-57; pvt. practice in law Columbus, Ohio; lawyer Wonnell & Wonnell Co., L.P.A., Columbus, 1957—; spkr. Ohio No. U. Coll. of Law, 1961-69. Author: Ohio Traffic Law Handbook, 1969, 85. Judge Franklin County Common Pleas, Columbus, 1985-86; mem. past pres., dr. chmn. Charity Newsies, Columbus, 1962-97; past pres., bd. dirs. Big Bros./Big Sisters, Columbus, 1955-94; past chmn., bd. mgmt. Ctrl. YMCA, Columbus, 1961-73. With U.S. Marines, 1942-46. Recipient Svc. award Divsn. of Police, Lions Club. Fellow Ohio Sate Bar Found., Acad. of Law and Sci., Roscoe-Pound-Am. Trial Lawyers Found.; mem. ATLA, Ohio State Bar Assn. (chmn. various coms.), Columbus Bar Assn. (chmn. various coms.), Fed. Bar Assn., Soc. of Former Spl. Agts. of FBI (past pres. Columbus chpt.), Ohio Acad. Criminal Trial Lawyers. Democrat. Avocations: golf, reading, travel. General practice, Criminal, Personal injury. Home: 324 Jackson St Columbus OH 43206-1246 Office: Wonnell & Wonnell Co LPA 330 S High St Columbus OH 43215-4510

**WONNELL, THOMAS BURKE,** lawyer; b. Jan. 29, 1970. BA, U. Calif., San Diego, 1993; JD, Washington and Lee U., 1996. Bar: Alaska 1996, U.S. Dist. Ct. Alaska 1996, U.S. Ct. Appeals (9th cir.) 1998. Asst. mcpl. prosecutor Municipality of Anchorage, 1996-98; pvt. practice, Anchorage, 1998—. Criminal, Family and matrimonial, General civil litigation. Office: 2600 Denali St Ste 460 Anchorage AK 99503-2754

**WOO, CHRISTOPHER,** lawyer; b. Honolulu, Nov. 5, 1972; s. Vernon Y.T. and Arlene G. Woo. BA in Econs. and Philosophy, Claremont McKenna Coll., 1995; JD, U. Hawaii, 1998. Bar: Hawaii 1998, U.S. Dist. Ct. Hawaii 1998. Law clk. Law Offices of Michael McCarthy, Honolulu, 1995-96; law clk. Hurd & Luria, Honolulu, 1996-98, assoc., 1998—. Mem. Hawaii State Bar Assn., Fed. Bar Assn. Dist. of Hawaii, Outrigger Canoe Club. General civil litigation. Office: Hurd & Luria 201 Merchant St Ste 1500 Honolulu HI 96813-2928

**WOO, VERNON YING-TSAI,** lawyer, real estate developer, judge; b. Honolulu, Aug. 7, 1942; s. William Shu-Bin and Hilda Woo; m. Arlene Gay Ischar, Feb. 14, 1971; children: Christopher Shu-Bin, Lia Gay. BA, U. Hawaii, 1964, MA, 1966; JD, Harvard U., 1969. Pres. Woo Kessner Duca & Maki, Honolulu, 1972-87; pvt. practice law Honolulu, 1987—; judge per diem Honolulu Dist. Family Ct., 1978-84, 95—. Bd. dirs. Boys and Girls Club of Honolulu,. 1985—, pres., 1990-92. Mem. ABA, Hawaii Bar Assn., Honolulu Bd. Realtors, Pacific Club. Real property. Home: 2070 Kalawahine Pl Honolulu HI 96822-2518 Office: 1019 Waimanu St Ste 205 Honolulu HI 96814-3409

**WOOD, ALLISON LORRAINE,** lawyer; b. N.Y.C., May 30, 1962; d. Walter C. and Joan T. Wood. BA, Pace U., 1984; JD, DePaul U., 1987; postgrad., Northwestern U. Bar: Ill. 1987, U.S. Dist. Ct. (no. dist.) Ill. 1989, Fed. Trial Bar 1990. Judicial extern U.S. Bankruptcy Ct., Chgo., 1987; pub. defender, Office of Pub. Defender Cook County, Ill., 1987-89; counsel The Peoples Gas Light and Coke Co., Chgo., 1989-93; assoc Albert, Bates, Whitehead & McGaugh, Chgo., 1993—; adj. prof. DePaul U. Coll. Law, 1992—; hearing bd. panelist Atty. Registration Disciplinary Commn. Tutor, lectr. Minority Legal Edn. Resources, Inc., Chgo.; bd. dirs., sec. Ctrs. for New Horizons; mem. Target Hope-Mentor; spkr. We Care Role Model. Mem. ABA, Ill. State Bar Assn., Chgo. Bar Assn., Cook County Bar Assn. (bd. dirs., treas.), DePaul U. Coll. of Law Alumni Bd. Consumer commercial, General civil litigation, Bankruptcy. Office: Albert Bates Whitehead & McGaugh 1 S Wacker Dr Ste 1990 Chicago IL 60606-4616

**WOOD, DIANE PAMELA,** judge; b. Plainfield, N.J., July 4, 1950; d. Kenneth Reed and Lucille (Padmore) Wood; m. Dennis James Hutchinson, Sept. 2, 1978 (div. May 1998); children: Kathryn, David, Jane. BA, U. Tex., 1971, JD, 1975. Bar: Tex. 1975, D.C. 1978, Ill. 1993. Law clk. U.S. Ct. Appeals (5th cir.), 1975-76, U.S. Supreme Ct., 1976-77; atty.-advisor U.S. Dept. State, Washington, 1977-78; assoc. law firm Covington & Burling, Washington, 1978-80; asst. prof. law Georgetown U. Law Ctr., Washington, 1980-81; asst. prof. law U. Chgo., 1981-88, prof. law, 1988-95, assoc. dean, 1989-92, Harold J. and Marion F. Green prof. internat. legal studies, 1990-95, sr. lectr. in law, 1995—; spl. cons. antitrust divsn. internat. guide U.S. Dept. Justice, 1986-87, dep. asst. atty. gen. antitrust divsn., 1993-95; cir. judge U.S. Ct. Appeals (7th cir.), 1995—. Contbr. articles to profl. jours. Bd. dirs. Hyde Park-Kenwood Cmty. Health Ctr., 1983-85. Mem. Am. Soc. Internat. Law, Am. law Inst., Internat. Acad. Comparative Law, Phi Alpha Delta. Democrat.

**WOOD, HARLINGTON, JR.,** federal judge; b. Springfield, Ill., Apr. 17, 1920; s. Harlington and Marie (Green) W. A.B., U. Ill., 1942, J.D., 1948. Bar: Ill. 1948. Practiced in Springfield, 1948-69; U.S. atty. So. Dist. Ill., 1958-61; mem. firm Wood & Wood, 1961-69; assoc. dep. atty. gen. for U.S. attys. U.S. dept. Justice, 1969-70; assoc. dep. atty. gen. Justice Dept., Washington, 1970-72; asst. atty. gen. civil div. Justice Dept., 1972-73; U.S. dist. judge So. Dist. Ill., Springfield, 1973-76; judge U.S. Ct. Appeals (7th cir.), 1976—; adj. prof. Sch. Law, U. Ill., Champaign, 1993; disting. vis. prof. St. Louis U. Law Sch., 1996—. Chmn. Adminstrv. Office Oversight Com., 1988-90; mem. Long Range Planning Com., 1991-96. Office: US Ct Appeals PO Box 299 600 E Monroe St Springfield IL 62701-1626

**WOOD, JAMES JERRY,** lawyer; b. Rockford, Ala., Aug. 13, 1940; s. James Ronald and Ada Love Wood; m. Earline Luckie, Aug. 9, 1959; children: James Jerry, William Gregory, Diana Lynn. AB, Samford U., 1964, JD, 1969. Bar: Ala. 1969, U.S. Supreme Ct. 1976. Dir. legal affairs Med. Assn. State of Ala., 1969-70; asst. atty. gen. State of Ala., 1970-72; asst. U.S. atty. Middle Dist. Ala., 1972-76; pvt. practice, 1977-78; pres. Wood & Parnell, P.A., Montgomery, Ala., 1979-89; pvt. practice Montgomery, 1990—; gen. counsel Ala. Builders Self-Insurance Fund, Home Builders of Ala.; chmn. character and fitness com. Ala. State Bar, 1981-84, 86-89, chair task force on quality of life, 1990-92, chair task force on mem. svcs., 1994-96. Capt. USAR, 1974-79. Mem. ABA (ho. of dels. 1990-98), FBA (pres. Montgomery chpt. 1974-75), Am. Nat. Inns of Ct., Ala. Assn. Workers Compensation Group Self-Insured Funds (chmn.), Ala. Bar Assn., Montgomery Bar Assn., Ala. Def. Lawyers Assn., Ala. Law Inst., Def. Rsch. Inst., Montgomery Capital Rotary (pres. 1986-87, 96-97). Republican. Baptist. E-mail: jjwood@mindspring.com. General corporate, Construction, Workers' compensation. Office: PO Box 4189 Montgomery AL 36103-4189

**WOOD, JENNIFER LYNN,** lawyer; b. Redwood Falls, Minn., Mar. 14, 1964; d. David George and Jacqueline (Palmer) W. BA cum laude, Gustavus Adolphus Coll., 1986; JD cum laude, U. Minn., 1995. Bar: Minn. 1995. Law clk. Dist. Ct. Minn., Mpls., 1995-97; assoc. Zalk & Eayrs, Mpls., 1997-98; shareholder Zalk & Wood, Mpls., 1999—. Humphrey fellow Humphrey Inst. Policy Forum, Mpls., 1995-96. Mem. Minn. State Bar Assn., Minn. Justice found., Hennepin County Bar Assn. Family and matrimonial. Office: Zalk & Wood PA 5861 Cedar Lake Rd S Minneapolis MN 55416-1481

**WOOD, JOSHUA WARREN, III,** lawyer, foundation executive; b. Portsmouth, Va., Aug. 31, 1941; s. Joshua Warren and Mary Evelyn (Carter) W.; m. Marcia Neal Ramsey, Feb. 29, 1964; children: Lauren Elaine, Joshua Warren IV. AB, Princeton U., 1963; JD, U. Va., 1971. Bar: Va. 1971, N.J. 1976, U.S. Supreme Ct. 1977, N.Y. 1982. Comml. banking asst. Bankers Trust Co., N.Y.C., 1967-68; assoc. McGuire, Woods & Battle, Richmond, Va., 1971-75; v.p., gen. counsel, sec. The Robert Wood Johnson Found., Princeton, N.J., 1975—; mem. Commn. on Health Care Dispute Resolution, AMA; mem. AAA/ABA/AMA Commn. on Alternative Dispute Resolution in Health Care. Mem. editl. bd. Va. Law Rev., 1969-71. Capt. arty. U.S. Army, 1963-67. Decorated Army Commendation medal. Mem. ABA, Princeton Bar Assn., N.Y. Bar Assn., Va. Bar Assn., N.J. Bar Assn., Nat. Health Lawyers Assn., Am. Arbitration Assn. (bd. dirs., mem. panel of arbitrators, task force Mass torts & alternative dispute resolution), Order of Coif, Princeton Club. Corporate taxation, Finance, Alternative dispute resolution. Office: College Rd PO Box 2316 Princeton NJ 08543-2316

**WOOD, KIMBA M.,** judge; b. Port Townsend, Wash., Jan. 2, 1944. BA cum laude, Conn. Coll., 1965; MSc, London Sch. Econs., 1966; JD, Harvard U., 1969. Bar: U.S. Dist. Ct. D.C. 1969, U.S. Ct. Appeals D.C. 1969, N.Y. 1972, U.S. Dist. Ct. (ea. and so. dists.) N.Y. 1974, U.S. Ct. Appeals (2d cir.) 1975, U.S. Supreme Ct. 1980, U.S. Dist. Ct. (we. dist.) N.Y. 1981. Assoc. Steptoe & Johnson, Washington, 1969-70; with Office Spl. Counsel, OEO Legal Svcs., Washington, 1970-71; assoc., then ptnr. LeBoeuf, Lamb, Leiby & MacRae, N.Y.C., 1971-88; judge, U.S. Dist. Ct. (so. dist.) N.Y., N.Y.C., 1988—. Mem. ABA (chmn. civil practice, procedure com. 1982-85, mem. coun. 1985-88, jud. rep. 1989-91), N.Y. State Bar Assn. (chmn. antitrust sect. 1983-84), Fed. Bar Coun. (trustee from 1978, v.p., 1984-85), Am. Law Inst. Office: US Dist Ct US Courthouse 500 Pearl St New York NY 10007-1316

**WOOD, ROBERT ALEXANDER,** lawyer; b. Cleve., Sept. 4, 1939; m. Dorita M. Wood, June 18, 1966; children: Melissa, Robert Gregory; m. Zoe Breen, Apr. 25, 1992; children: Liana, Ashley, Cara. BA, U. Mich., 1961; JD, Cleve. Marshall Sch. Law, 1969. Bar: Conn. 1972, Ohio 1969, U.S. Ct. Mil. Appeals 1973. Pvt. practice Avon, Conn., 1972-89; claims counsel Lawyers Title Ins. Co., Richmond, Va., 1989-91; dist. counsel Stewart Title, Norfolk, Va., 1991-93; asst. gen. counsel Midland Title Security, Inc., Cleve., 1993—; lectr. in field. Jr. warden Trinity Cathedral, Cleve., 1996—. Comdr. JAGC USNR, 1961-83. Mem. Ohio Bar Assn., Cleve. Bar Assn. (real estate sect.), Naval Res. Lawyers Assn., Ohio Land Title Assn. Insurance. Office: Midland Title Security Inc 1360 E 9th St Ste 500 Cleveland OH 44114-1705

**WOOD, ROBERT CHARLES,** financial consultant; b. Chgo., Apr. 8, 1956; s. Roy Edward and Mildred Lucille (Jones) W.; m. Jennifer Jo Briggs, Oct. 1984; children: Jacqueline Jones, Reagan Keith. BA in History, BBA in Real Estate, So. Meth. U., 1979, JD, 1982. Bar: Tex. 1983. Appraiser McClellan-Massey, Dallas, 1977-79; researcher, acquisitions officer Amstar Fin. Corp., Dallas, 1979-80; prin. Robert Wood Cons., Dallas, 1981-98; prin. Welch & Wood Attys. and Y2K Consulting, 1998—; cons. Plan Mktg. Cos., 1983-84; pvt. practice law, Dallas, 1983-84; gen. counsel Diversified Benefits, Inc., Dallas, 1984-86; nat. accts. mgr. L. omas & Nettleton Real Estate Group, Dallas, 1987-88; sr. pension cons., prin. Eppler, Guerin &Turner, 1988-93; chmn. adv. coun. on devel. Medisend, 1991; nat. consulting coord. fin. advisors coun., v.p. Callan Assocs., San Francisco, 1994-95; atty. at law, 1995—. Author: Electionomics: How the Money Managers View the Election, 1992, After the Congress Vote: How the Managers See Things Now, 1993, Y2K--The Year 2000 Issue: How Y2K Affects the Markets, 1998; mem. So. Meth. U. Law Rev., 1981-82; contbr. articles to profl. publs. Bd. dirs. Am. Cancer Soc., Dallas unit, 1982-87, mem. spl. events com., 1986-87, crusade com., 1987-88, corp. devel. bd. chmn. 1989—. Mem. Tex. Bar Assn., Phila. Bar Assn., Phi Gamma Delta. Avocations: skiing, tennis, bicycling. E-mail: rccwood@aol.com.

**WOOD, ROBERT WARREN,** lawyer; b. Des Moines, July 5, 1955; s. Merle Warren and Cecily Ann (Sherk) W.; m. Beatrice Wood, Aug. 4, 1979; 1 child, Bryce Mercedes. Student, U. Sheffield, Eng., 1975-76; AB, Humboldt State U., 1976; JD, U. Chgo., 1979. Bar: Ariz. 1979, Calif. 1980, U.S. Tax Ct. 1980, N.Y. 1989, D.C. 1993, Mont. 1998; Roll of Solicitors of Eng. and Wales, 1998. Assoc. Jennings, Strouss, Phoenix, 1979-80, McCutchen, Doyle, San Francisco, 1980-82, Broad, Khourie, San Francisco, 1982-85; assoc. Steefel, Levitt & Weiss, San Francisco, 1985-87, ptnr., 1987-91; ptnr. Bancroft & McAlister, San Francisco, 1991-93; prin. Robert W. Wood, P.C., San Francisco, 1993—; instr. in law U. Calif. San Francisco, 1981-82. *With over twenty years of domestic and international experience, Robert W. Wood is well known as a tax attorney and specialist in taxation and mergers and acquisitions. He represents entrepreneurs, U.S. and foreign investors, privately held companies and publicly traded entities. He regularly renders advice to companies and shareholders on the structuring and closing of taxable and tax-free acquisitions, and is routinely engaged by companies, law and accounting firms to provide specialized advice in this field. He also advises litigants and attorneys on the tax treatment of damage awards and settlement payments, an area in which he is a recognized U.S. authority.* Author: Taxation of Corporate Liquidations: A Complete Planning Guide, 1987, 2nd edit., 1994, The Executive's Complete Guide to Business Taxes, 1989, Corporate Taxation: Complete Planning and Practice Guide, 1989, S Corporations, 1990, The Ultimate Tax Planning Guide for Growing Companies, 1991, Taxation of Damage Awards and Settlement Payments, 1st edit., 1991, 2nd edit., 1998, Tax Strategies in Hiring, Retaining and Terminating Employees, 1991, The Home Office Tax Guide, 1991; co-author: (with others) California Closely Held Corporations: Tax Planning and Practice Guide, 1987, Legal Guide to Independent Contractor Status, 2nd edit., 1996; editor: California Small Busines Guide, 4 vols., 1998, Home Office Money & Tax Guide, 1992, Tax Aspects of Settlements and Judgements, 1993, 2d edit., 1998; editor-in-chief The M & A Tax Report; editor: Limited

Liability Companies: Formation, Operation and Conversion, 1994, Limited Liability Partnerships: Formation, Operation and Taxation, 1996; mem. editl. bd. Real Estate Tax Digest, The Practical Accountant, Jour. Real Estate Taxation. Fellow Am. Coll. Tax Counsel; mem. Calif. Bd. Legal Specialization (cert. specialist taxation), Candian Bar Assn., Bohemian Club, Law Coun. Australia. Republican. Mergers and acquisitions, Corporate taxation, Personal income taxation. Office: 477 Pacific Ave # 300 San Francisco CA 94133-4614

**WOOD, STEVEN NOEL HOUSLEY,** lawyer; b. Tucson, Dec. 12, 1967; s. John C. Wood and Pauli R. LeCoque; m. Sally Jo Housley, Aug. 5, 1989; children: Adam E., Benjamin I., Joseph R. BA, Calif. Luth. U., 1989; JD, U. Calif., Berkeley, 1992. Bar: Calif. 1992, U.S. Dist. Ct. (no. dist.) Calif. 1992, U.S. Ct. Appeals (9th cir.) 1992. Assoc. Stoddard Falco & Pfeiffer, Walnut Creek, Calif., 1992-96; ptnr. Stoddard Pfeiffer Bergquist & Wood LLP, Walnut Creek, 1996—. Mem. Christian Legal Soc., Contra Costa Bar Assn. Avocations: family, church, sports. General civil litigation, General corporate, Real property. Office: Stoddard Pfeiffer Bergquist & Wood LLP 1470 Maria Ln Ste 300 Walnut Creek CA 94596-5399

**WOOD, TRACEY A.,** lawyer; b. Milw., June 21, 1967; d. Kenneth J. and Susan J. (Hayden) Wood; m. Steven W. Roller, Dec. 12, 1990 (div. Oct. 1997); 1 child, Alexander Case Roller. BA, Marquette U., 1988; JD, U. Wis., 1993. Bar: Wis. 1993, U.S. Dist. Ct. (we. and ea. dists.) Wis. 1993, U.S. Ct. Appeals (7th cir.) 1993. Atty. Kalal & Assocs., Madison, 1993-96, Thomas, Kelly, Habermehl & Wood, S.C., Madison, 1996-98; ptnr. Van Wagner & Wood, S.C., Madison, 1998—. Mem. Nat. Assn. Criminal Def. Lawyers, Wis. Assn. Criminal Def. Lawyers, Dane County Criminal Def. Lawyers Assn. (pres. 1998). Avocations: bicycling, hiking, cross-country skiing. Criminal, Juvenile. Office: Van Wagner & Wood SC 3 S Pinckney St Madison WI 53703-2866

**WOOD, TROY JAMES,** lawyer; b. Eugene, Oreg., Nov. 25, 1969; s. Byron Arthur and Barbara Ann (Boylan) W.; m. Julie Lynn Tracy, June 15, 1996. BA, U. of the Pacific, Stockton, Calif., 1992; JD, U. of the Pacific, Sacramento, 1995. Bar: Oreg. 1995, Idaho 1995. Corp. cousnel May Tracking Co., Salem, Oreg., 1995-96; atty. Albertson's, Boise, Idaho, 1996—; mem. supervisory com. to bd. dirs. Albertson's Employ Fed. Credit Union, Boise, 1998—. Mem. property com. Immanuel Luth. Ch., Boise, 1998—. Cpl. USMCR, 1988-93. Mem. ABA, Oreg. Bar Assn., Idaho Bar Assn. Avocations: fly fishing, hunting, rugby, camping and other outdoor recreation. Contracts commercial, General corporate, Real property. Office: Albertson's Legal Dept PO Box 20 Boise ID 83726-0020

**WOOD, WILLIAM EDWARD,** lawyer; b. N.Y.C., Sept. 30, 1948; s. Ernest Harvey and Ruth Ratcliff W.; m. Susan Kamont Wehrlen, June 10, 1972; children: Sarah Harvey, William McKinnie. AB, Colgate U., 1970; JD, Washington and Lee U., 1973. Bar: N.C. 1973, U.S. Dist. Ct. (ea. dist.) N.C. 1976, U.S. Ct. Appeals (4th cir.) 1982. From asst. dist. attorney to chief dist. ct. judge 13th Judicial District of N.C., Whiteville, 1973-80, chief dist. ct. judge, 1980-84; pvt. practice Whiteville, 1984—; mediator Whiteville, N.C., 1992—. Mem. N.C. Acad. Trial Lawyers, 13th Dist. Bar Assn., Columbus County Bar Assn. Democrat. Episcopalian. Avocations: classic car restoration, custom motorcycles. Office: William E Wood Attorney 100 Courthouse Sq Whiteville NC 28472-3338

**WOOD, WILLIAM MCBRAYER,** lawyer; b. Greenville, S.C., Jan. 27, 1942; s. Oliver Gillan and Grace (McBrayer) W.; m. Nancy Cooper, 1973 (dec. 1993); children: Walter, Lewis; m. Jeanette Dobson Haney, June 25, 1994. BS in Acctg., U. S.C., 1964, JD cum laude, 1972; LLMin Estate Planning (scholar), U. Miami, 1980. Bar: S.C. 1972, Fla. 1979, D.C. 1973, U.S. Tax Ct. 1972, U.S. Ct. Claims 1972, U.S. Supreme Ct. 1977. Intern ct. of claims sect., tax divsn. U.S. Dept. Justice, 1971; law clk. to chief judge U.S. Ct. Claims, Washington, 1972-74; ptnr. firm Edwards Wood, Duggan & Reese, Greer and Greenville, 1974-78; asst. prof. law Cumberland Law Sch., Samford U., Birmingham, Ala., 1978-79; faculty Nat. Inst. Trial Advocacy: N.E. Regional Inst., 1979, 83-90, 95-97, Fla. Regional Inst., 1989; teaching team 5th intensive trial techniques course Hofstra U., 1983; assoc. then capital ptnr. firm Shutts & Bowen, Miami, 1980-85; sole practice Miami, 1985—; also Rock Hill, S.C., 1994—. Contbg. editor: The Lawyers PC; Fla. editor: Drafting Wills and Trust Agreements; substantive com. editor ABA: The Tax Lawyer, 1983—. Pres. Piedmont Heritage Found., Inc. 1975-78; del. State Rep. Conv., 1985, 87, 90; exec. committeeman Miami-Dade County Republicans, 1988-94, co-gen. counsel, 1990-91; apptd. Miami-Dade County Indsl. Devel. Authority, 1990-94; mem. vestry Episc. Ch., 1993-94. With USAF, 1965-69, Vietnam. Decorated Air Force Commendation medal; recipient Am. Jurisprudence award in real property and tax I, 1971; winner Grand prize So. Living Mag. travel photo contest, 1969. Mem. ABA (taxation sect., teaching law com., 1994—), Greer C. of C. (pres. 1977, Outstanding leadership award 1976), Greater Greenville C. of C. (dir. 1977), Order Wig and Robe, Estate Planning Council South Fla., Omicron Delta Kappa. Club: Bankers (bd. govs. 1989-94). Lodge: Masons, Rotary. Estate planning, Estate taxation, Probate. Office: 5345 Wilgrove Mint Hill Rd Charlotte NC 28227-3467

**WOODARD, HEATHER ANNE,** lawyer; b. Washington, Oct. 2, 1970; d. Philip Allen and Valerie Ann W. BA, Boston Coll., 1992; JD, U. Pacific, 1996. Bar: U.S. Dist. Ct. (no. dist.) Calif. 1996, U.S. Ct. Appeals (9th cir.) 1996, U.S. Dist. Ct. (ctrl. dist.) Calif. 1997. Law clk. Marin County Dist. Atty., San Rafael, Calif., 1995, 96; assoc. Lieff Cabraser Heimann & Bern, San Francisco, 1996—. Mem. ABA, ATLA, Bar Assn. San Francisco. Democrat. Roman Catholic. Avocations: travel, skiing, scuba diving, golf, wine tasting. Product liability, General civil litigation, Alternative dispute resolution. Office: Lieff Cabraser 275 Battery St Fl 30 San Francisco CA 94111-3305

**WOODARD, MARK DAVIS,** lawyer, association executive, lobbyist; b. Washington, Jan. 14, 1949; s. Vascoe Cramer and Wilma (Davis) W. BA, U. Md., 1973; JD, U. Balt., 1980. Bar: Md. 1980, U.S. Dist. Ct. Md. 1981, D.C. 1987, U.S. Bankruptcy Ct. 1981. Assoc. Grief, Cohen and Alpert, Balt., 1981-82, Potler, Belsky & Weiner, Balt., 1983-84; mng. atty. Hyatt Legal Services, Silver Spring, Md., 1984-85; pvt. practice Silver Spring, 1986; dir. legal and legis. services Md. Assn. Bds. Edn., Annapolis, 1987-88; v.p. govtl. rels. Health Facilities Assn. Md., Annapolis Junction, Md., 1997—; asst. exec. dir. Md. Assn. Counties, Annapolis, 1988-94; intergovtl. rels. officer Prince George's County Sch. Sys., 1994-98; v.p. govt. rels. Health Facilities Assn. Md., 1998—. Supreme Ct. editor Balt. Law Forum; contbr. articles to profl. jours. Mgr. vols. Mondale-Ferraro presdl. campaign, Balt., 1984; mem. issues com. Stewart Bainum for Congress campaign, Silver Spring, 1986; treas. Com. to Elect Dana Dembrow Del., Silver Spring, 1986. Mem. ABA, Md. Bar Assn., D.C. Bar Assn., Md. Com. Full Funding Edn., Coun. Sch. Bd. Attys., Green St. Coalition, Md. Assn. Counties (edn. com). Democrat. Mem. United Ch. of Christ. Avocations: reading, bridge, sports, cooking, walking. Home: 13218 Trebleclef Ln Silver Spring MD 20904-6866 Office: Health Facilities Assn Md Junction Bus Pk 10010 Junction Dr Ste 116 Annapolis Junction MD 20701-1172

**WOODBURN, RALPH ROBERT, JR.,** lawyer; b. Haverhill, Mass., Nov. 3, 1946; s. Ralph Robert and Josephine Marie (McClure) W.; m. Janet M. Smith, Sept. 15, 1985. BA, Mich. State U., 1967; JD, Harvard U., 1972; LLM, Boston U., 1981. Bar: Mass. 1972, U.S. Tax Ct. 1987. Assoc. Bowers, Fortier & Lakin, Boston, 1972-76; from assoc. to ptnr. Haussermann, Davison & Shattuck, Boston, 1976-83; ptnr. Palmer & Dodge, Boston, 1983—; tchr. Harvard Ctr. for Lifelong Learning, Cambridge, Mass., 1986-89; chmn. Wellesley Cable Access Bd., 1993-95. Contbr. articles to Boston Bar Jour. and Estate Planning. Treas. Exeter Assn. of New Eng., Boston, 1985-89, v.p., 1989-91, pres., 1991-93. Fellow Am. Coll. Trust and Estate Counsel; mem. ABA, Boston Bar Assn. (chmn. probate legislation 1983-93), Brae Burn Country Club (Newton, Mass.), Harvard Club of Boston, Boston Probate and Estate Planning Forum (program chair 1996-97, moderator 1997-98), Harvard Travellers Club. Estate planning, Probate, Estate taxation. Home: 25 Cypress Rd Wellesley MA 02481-2918 Office: Palmer & Dodge 1 Beacon St Boston MA 02108-3190

**WOODBURY, ROBERT CHARLES,** lawyer; b. Sheridan, N.Y., July 7, 1929; s. Wendell F. and Lillian S. (Towne) W.; m. Martha Bayard Page, Jan. 25, 1958. *Wife, Martha, descended from the widow Bayard, sister of Peter Stuyvesant past governor of New Amsterdam. Daughter of Beatrice Bayard and Stanley Hart Page. Page is a graduate of St. Anne's School, Charlottesville, and Middlebury College, Vermont. Served as Economic Development Planner, Department of Commerce, Washington (1956-58); Assistant Editor, Fortune Magazine, New York (1965-67), Research Assistant, MacKenzie & Co., New York, 1968-70; Founder, Vice President and Director, Woodbury Vineyards Winery, 1979-91 and President and Director, Woodbury Farms, 1969-98. Founder, President and Director of the Chautauqua County Arts Council, 1975-77; Stock Broker and Manager, Fredonia, NY Office, Bodell OvercashAnderson, Co., Jamestown, NY, 1993-.* BEE, Rensselaer Poly. Inst., 1950; JD, Cornell U., 1953. Bar: N.Y. 1954, U.S. Dist. Ct. (so. dist.) N.Y. 1965, U.S. Dist. Ct. (we. dist.) N.Y. 1979, U.S. Ct. Appeals (4th cir.) 1964, U.S. Ct. Claims 1961, U.S. Ct. Mil. Appeals 1956, U.S. Patent Office 1961; lic. profl. engr., N.Y. Project engr. Army reactors program U.S. Atomic Energy Commn., 1957-60; assoc. Reid & Priest, N.Y.C., 1962-70; pvt. practice Dunkirk, N.Y., 1971—; ptnr. Aular & Woodbury, Dunkirk, N.Y., 1973-81, Morten & Woodbury, Dunkirk, N.Y., 1982-88; gen. counsel N.Y. State Temp. Commn. Environ. Impact Major Pub. Utility Facilities, 1970-71; del. N.Y. 8th Jud. Dist. Rep. Jud. Nominating Conv., 1985—; chmn. bd. dirs. Woodbury Farms, Ltd., 1965-98, Woodbury Vineyards, 1968-91. Assoc. trustee Buffalo Gen. Hosp. Found., 1994-96; trustees coun. Buffalo Gen. Healthcare Sys., 1996-98, steering com. 1996-98; mem. trustees coun. Kaleida Health Sys., Buffalo, 1998—; founding pres. Chautauqua County Arts Coun., 1971; town atty. Town of Sheridan, 1972-75; dist. counsel city sch. dist. City of Dunkirk, 1973-82; co-founder No. Chautauqua Indsl. Roundtable, 1979; co-chmn. Chmn.'s Club, Chautauqua County Rep. Com. 1988-98; v.p., dir., counsel Historic Harbor Devel., Inc., 1996—. Lt. USN, 1954-57. Fellow N.Y. Bar Found.; mem. N.Y. State Bar Assn. (chmn. com. atomic energy law 1967-69, chmn. com. pub. utility law 1969-71, mem. action unit 5 regulatory reform N.Y. 1980-83), Bar Assn. No. Chautauqua (pres. 1979), Cornell Law Assn., Rensselaer Alumni Assn., Dunkirk C. of C. (pres. 1979), Mid-Day Club Buffalo, Chautauqua Yacht Club. Republican. Presbyterian. Avocations: skiing, wine, sailing. General corporate, Contracts commercial, Nuclear power. Home: 3300 S Roberts Rd Fredonia NY 14063-9418 Office: PO Box 800 87 E 4th St Dunkirk NY 14048-2225

**WOODCOCK, JOHN ALDEN,** lawyer; b. Bangor, Maine, July 6, 1950; s. John Alden Woodcock and Joan (Carlin) Nestler; m. Beverly Ann Newcombe, July 14, 1973; children: John A., Patrick C., Christopher C. AB, Bowdoin Coll., 1972; MA, U. London, 1973; JD, U. Maine, 1976. Bar: Maine 1976, U.S. Dist. Ct. Maine 1976. Assoc. Stearns, Finnegan & Needham, Bangor, 1976-80; asst. dist. atty. Penobscot County, Bangor, 1977-78; ptnr. Mitchell & Stearns, Bangor, 1980-91, Weatherbee, Woodcock, Burlock & Woodcock, Bangor, 1991—. Mem. alumni coun. Bowdoin Coll., Brunswick, Maine, 1992—, pres., 1995-96, trustee, 1996—; bd. dirs. Ea. Maine Med. Ctr., Bangor, 1980—, chmn, 1996—, Ea. Maine Healthcare, Bangor, 1989—. Master Ballou Inn of Ct.; fellow Maine Bar Found.; mem. ABA, Maine State Bar Assn., Penobscot County Bar Assn. General civil litigation, Insurance, Personal injury. Home: 110 Main Rd N Hampden ME 04444-1404 Office: Weatherbee Woodcock Burlock & Woodcock 136 Broadway Bangor ME 04401-5206

**WOODHOUSE, GAY VANDERPOEL,** state attorney general; b. Torrington, Wyo., Jan. 8, 1950; d. Wayne Gaylord and Sally (Rouse) Vanderpoel; m. Randy Woodhouse, Nov. 26, 1983; children: Dustin, Houston. BA with honors, U. Wyo., 1972, JD, 1977. Bar: Wyo. 1978, U.S. Dist. Ct. Wyo., U.S. Supreme Ct. Dir. student Legal Svcs., Laramie, Wyo., 1976-77; assoc. Donald Jones Law Offices, Torrington, 1977-78; asst. atty. gen. State of Wyo., Cheyenne, 1978-84, sr. asst. atty. gen., 1984-89, spl. U.S. atty., 1987-89, chief dept. atty. gen., 1995-98, atty. gen., 1998—. Chmn. bd. Pathfinder, 1987; bd. dirs. S.E. Wyo. Mental Health; chmn. Wyo. Tel. Consumer Panel, Casper, 1982-86; spl. projects cons. N.Am. Securities Adminstrs. Assn., 1987-89; advisor Cheyenne Halfway House, 1984-93. Mem. Laramie County Bar Assn. Republican. Avocations: inline speed skating, stained glass. Office: 123 Capitol Bldg Cheyenne WY 82002-0001

**WOODHOUSE, THOMAS EDWIN,** lawyer; b. Cedar Rapids, Iowa, Apr. 30, 1940; s. Keith Wallace and Elinor Julia (Cherny) W.; m. Kiyoko Fujiie, May 29, 1965; children: Miya, Keith, Leighton. AB cum laude, Amherst Coll., 1962; JD, Harvard U., 1965. Bar: N.Y. 1966, U.S. Supreme Ct. 1969, Calif. 1975. Assoc. Chadbourne, Parke, Whiteside & Wolff, N.Y.C., 1965-68; atty./adviser AID, Washington, 1968-69; counsel Pvt. Investment Co. for Asia S.A., Tokyo, 1969-72; ptnr. Woodhouse Lee & Davis, Singapore, 1972-74; assoc. Graham & James, San Francisco, 1974-75; asst. gen. counsel Natomas Co., San Francisco, 1975-81; mem. Lasky, Haas, Cohler & Munter, San Francisco, 1982-90; trust adminstr. Ronald Family Trust A, 1989—, Gordon P. Getty Family Trust, 1994—; sole practice, Berkeley, 1990—; of counsel Wilson, Sonsini, Goodrich & Rosati, Palo Alto, Calif., 1992-95; instr. law faculty U. Singapore, 1972-74; CEO, Vallejo Investments, 1997—. chmn. Police Rev. Com. of Berkeley (Calif.), 1980-84; mem. Berkeley Police Res., 1986—; bd. dirs. Friends Assn. of Svcs. for Elderly, 1979-84; clk. fin. com. Am. Friends Svc. Com. of No. Calif., 1979-83; pres. Zyzzyva Inc., lit. quar., 1985-87. Trustee Freedom from Hunger, 1989—, Dominican Sch. of Philosophy and Theology, 1998—. With U.S. Army, 1958. Fellow Am. Bar Found. (life); mem. Calif. Bar Assn., Assn. Internat. de Bibliophilie, Harvard Club, Univ. Club, Tanglin Club, Cricket Club, Book Club Calif., Roxburghe Club, Travellers Club, Grolier Club. Republican. Roman Catholic. General corporate, Private international, Patent. Home and Office: 1800 San Antonio Ave Berkeley CA 94707-1618

**WOODINGTON, KENNETH P.,** lawyer; b. Camden, N.J., June 14, 1947; s. George Royden and Opal Ruth (Bradfield) W.; m. Elizabeth Farnsworth Young, July 8, 1972; children: Paul, John. BA, U. Ga., 1969; JD, Duke U., 1972. Bar: S.C. 1973, U.S. Dist. Ct. S.C. 1975, U.S. Ct. Appeals (4th cir.) 1975, U.S. Supreme Ct. 1988. Law clk. Supreme Ct. S.C., Columbia, 1972-74; sr. asst. atty. gen. S.C. Atty. Gen.'s Office, Columbia, 1974—. Co-author: South Carolina Appellate Practice, 1985. Elder, Shandon Presbyn. Ch., Columbia, 1983—, lay pastoral min., 1992—. Mem. Phi Beta Kappa. Avocations: cycling, golf, genealogy, personal computers. Office: SC Atty Gen's Office 1000 Assembly St Columbia SC 29201-3117

**WOOD KAHARI, BRENDA MARIE,** lawyer; b. Washington, Jan. 29, 1951; d. Sylvester and Laverne Morris; m. Muzanenhamo Eric Kahari, June 13, 1981; children: Brent, Morris. BA, U. Dayton, 1972; JD, Howard U., 1975; LLM, Georgetown U., 1982. Bar: Ohio 1975, D.C. 1977. Legal intern Dept. State/U.S. AID, Washington, 1974-75; assoc. atty. Squire, Sanders & Dempsey, Cleve., 1975-78; assoc. counsel Pepco, Washington, 1978-81; legal advisor Ministry of Justice, Harare, Zimbabwe, 1981-86; pvt. practice B.W. Kahari Law Office, Harare/Washington, 1986; office affil. Soble Internat. Law, 1996; bd. dirs. Olmur Investments, Harare; trustee Zimbabwe Health Care Trust, 1996—; bd. dirs. Nat. Anglican Theol. Colls., Zimbabwe, 1996. Author, reporter and spkr. in field of trademarks. Fellow Chartered Inst. Internat. Arbitrators; mem. Ohio Bar Assn., D.C. Bar Assn., Law Soc. Zimbabwe. Intellectual property, Private international, Contracts commercial. Home: 96 Montgomery Rd Highlands, Harare Zimbabwe Office: BW Kahari, 38 Samora Machel Ave, Harare Zimbabwe

**WOODKE, ROBERT ALLEN,** lawyer; b. Schaller, Iowa, Dec. 23, 1950; s. Everett Albert and Helen Marie (Breihan) W.; m. Jan Melanie Lawrence, Aug. 15, 1987 (div. 1997). BS, Iowa State U., 1973; JD, Creighton U., 1977. Bar: Iowa 1977, Minn. 1978, U.S. Dist. Ct. (no. dist.) Iowa 1977, U.S. Dist. Ct.Minn. 1980. Law clk. Minn. 5th Dist. Ct., Marshall, 1977-78; assoc. Powell Law Office, Bemidji, Minn., 1978-82; pvt. practice Bemidji, 1982—; cons. Mgmt. Tng. Inst., Bemidji, 1987-88. Contbg. author: Flying Solo: A Survival Guide for Solo Lawyers, 1984, 2d edit., 1994, Going to Trial, 1989, Personal Injury Handbook, 1991. Recipient Ann. Legal Svc. award N.W. Minn. Legal Svcs., Moorehead, 1987. Mem. ABA (coun. mem. sect. gen. practice 1994-98; co-editor-in-chief Legal Tech. and Practice Guide 1996-98, mem. editl. bd. to 1998), Minn. Trial Lawyers Assn., Minn. Bar Assn. (chair sect. of gen. practice 1990-92), Beltrami County Bar Assn. (pres. 1988-89), 15th Dist. Bar Assn. (treas. 1986-87, pres. 1997-98), Downtown Bus. and Profl. Assn., Bemidji C. of C., Jaycees (v.p. 1986-87), Lions Club (2d v.p. Bemidji chpt. 1987-88, 1st v.p. 1988—, pres. 1989—). Republican. Lutheran. Personal injury, General civil litigation, General practice. Office: Brouse Woodke & Meyer 1106 Paul Bunyan Dr NE Bemidji MN 56601-3255

**WOODLAND, IRWIN FRANCIS,** lawyer; b. New York, Sept. 2, 1922; s. John James and Mary (Hynes) W.; m. Sally Duffy, Sept. 23, 1954; children: Connie, J. Patrick, Stephen, Joseph, William, David, Duffy. BA, Columbia U., 1948; JD, Ohio State U., 1959. Bar: Calif. 1960, Wash., 1991, U.S. Dist. Ct. (cen. dist.) Calif. 1960, U.S. Dist. Ct. (no. dist.) Calif. 1962, U.S. Dist. Ct. (so. dist.) Calif. From assoc. to ptnr. Gibson, Dunn & Crutcher, L.A., 1959-88; Bd. dirs. Sunlaw Energy Corp., Vernon, Calif. With USAF, 1942-45, ETO. Mem. ABA, Calif. Bar Assn., L.A. Bar Assn., Wash. State Bar Assn., Fed. Energy Bar Assn., Am. Mgmt. Assn., Phi Delta Phi, Jonathan Club, Bel Air Bay Club. Roman Catholic. Antitrust, General civil litigation, FERC practice. Office: Gibson Dunn & Crutcher 333 S Grand Ave Ste 4400 Los Angeles CA 90071-3197

**WOODLAND, STEVEN DEE,** lawyer; b. Logan, Utah, Aug. 27, 1951; s. Daniel Platt and Althea (Rawlins) W.; m. Darlene Anderson, Apr. 19, 1974; children: Jonathan, Natalie, Camille, Ryan, Jeffrey. BS, Brigham Young U., 1974, JD magna cum laude, 1977. Bar: Ariz. 1978, Utah 1979, U.S. Dist. Ct. Utah, U.S. Ct. Appeals (10th cir.) 1986, U.S. Tax Ct. 1981, U.S. Supreme Ct. 1989. Jud. law clk. to Hon. Richard H. Chambers, U.S. Ct. Appeals (9th cir.), San Francisco, 1977-78; assoc. Van Cott, Bagley, Cornwall & McCarthy, Salt Lake City, 1978-83, ptnr., 1983-98; judge pro tem Third Dist. Ct., Salt Lake City, 1996—; ptnr. Stoel Rives, Salt Lake City, 1998—; lectr. Utah Fed. Tax Inst. Salt Lake City, 1981; bd. adv. CPA Forum, 1992-93; lectr. Utah Info. Tech. Assn. Seminar, 1992. Mem. dist. com. Boy Scouts Am., 1989-97. J. Reuben Clark scholar Brigham Young U., Provo, 1977. Mem. ABA (tax sect.), Utah Bar Assn. (tax sect., lectr. ann meeting 1982, lectr. probate sect. 1984), Ariz. Bar, We. Pension & Benefit Conf. (program com. 1987, lectr. 1996), Salt Lake Area C. of C. (govt. affairs com. 1989-96). Mem. LDS Church. Avocations: hiking, backpacking, foreign affairs. Pension, profit-sharing, and employee benefits, Corporate taxation, Taxation, general. Office: Stoel Rives 201 S Main St Ste 1100 Salt Lake City UT 84111-4904

**WOODLEY, ANN E.,** lawyer, educator; b. Greenville, S.C., July 23, 1956; d. Donald Robert Woodley and Elizabeth Van Dyke. BA in Polit. Sci. and Journalism summa cum laude, U. Ariz., 1978; JD cum laude, Ariz. State U., 1981. Bar: Ariz. 1981, U.S. Dist. Ct. Ariz. 1981, D.C. 1983, U.S. Dist. Ct. D.C. 1984, U.S. Ct. Appeals (D.C. and 9th cirs.) 1984, U.S. Ct. Appeals (7th cir.) 1986, U.S. Supreme Ct. 1987, Ohio 1991, Calif. 1992. Law clk. to chief judge U.S. Dist. Ct. Ariz., Phoenix, 1981-83; assoc. Winston & Strawn, Washington, 1983-88; asst. prof. law U. Akron (Ohio) Sch. Law, 1988-95, assoc. prof. law, 1995—. Mem. ABA, Am. Trial Lawyers Assn., Ariz. Bar Assn., D.C. Womens Bar Assn., Soc. Profls. in Dispute Resolution (assoc.), Nat. Inst. Dispute Resolution. Democrat. Presbyterian. E-mail: woodley@uakron.edu. Federal civil litigation, State civil litigation, Alternative dispute resolution. Office: U Akron Sch Law Akron OH 44325-0001

**WOODLOCK, DOUGLAS PRESTON,** judge; b. Hartford, Conn., Feb. 27, 1947; s. Preston and Kathryn (Ropp) W.; m. Patricia Mathilde Powers, Aug. 30, 1969; children: Pamela, Benjamin. BA, Yale U., 1969; JD, Georgetown U., 1975. Bar: Mass. 1975. Reporter Chgo. Sun-Times, 1969-73; staff mem. SEC, Washington, 1973-75; law clk. to Judge F.J. Murray U.S. Dist. Ct. Mass., Boston, 1975-76; assoc. Goodwin, Procter & Hoar, Boston, 1976-79, 83-84, ptnr., 1984-86; asst. U.S. atty. Boston, 1979-83; judge U.S. Dist. Ct., Boston, 1986—; instr. Harvard U. Law Sch., 1980, 81; mem. U.S. Jud. Conf. Com. on Security Space and Facilities, 1987-95; chmn. New Boston Fed. Courthouse Bldg. Com., 1987-98. Articles editor Georgetown Law Jour., 1973-75; contbr. articles to profl. jours. Chmn. Commonwealth of Mass. Com. for Pub. Counsel Svcs., 1984-86, Town of Hamilton Bd. Appeals, 1978-79. Recipient Dir.'s award U.S. Dept. Justice, 1983, Thomas Jefferson award for Pub. Architecture, AIA, 1996. Mem. ABA, Mass. Bar Assn., Boston Bar Assn., Am. Law Inst., Am. Judicature Soc., Am. Bar Found., Fed. Judges Assn. (bd. dirs. 1996—), Mass. Hist. Soc. Office: US Courthouse 1 Courthouse Way Ste 4110 Boston MA 02210-3006

**WOODROW, RANDALL MARK,** lawyer; b. Anniston, Ala., June 17, 1956; s. Herbert Milisam and Rose (Marshall) W.; m. Carolyn Ann Jackson, Jan. 7, 1977; children: Amanda Lauren, Emily Claire, Taylor Jackson, Douglas Cockrell. BA in Polit. Sci., Jacksonville (Ala.) State U., 1978; JD, Samford U., 1981. Bar: Ala. 1981. Law clk. to judge U.S. Dist. Ct. (no. dist.) Ala., 1981-82; ptnr. Doster & Woodrow, Anniston, Ala., 1990—; asst. dist. atty. 7th Jud. Cir., Anniston, 1983; adj. prof. Jacksonville State U., 1985-86. Chmn. crusade Calhoun County Cancer Soc., Anniston, 1983; mem. adminstrv. bd. dirs. 1st United Meth. Ch., Anniston, 1984—; pres. Boys Clubs of Anniston, Inc., 1985; mem. Calhoun County Econ. Devel. Coun., 1995—; mem. Jacksonville (Ala.) Planning Commn., 1995—; mem. City of Jacksonville Bd. Edn., 1996—. Mem. ABA, Ala. Bar Assn., Calhoun County Bar Assn., Calhoun County C. of C. Federal civil litigation, State civil litigation, General corporate. Home: 509 6th St NE Jacksonville AL 36265-1617 Office: Doster & Woodrow 1000 Quintard Ave Anniston AL 36201-5788

**WOODRUFF, RANDALL LEE,** lawyer; b. Anderson, Ind., July 31, 1954; s. Billy Max and Phyllis Joan (Helmick) W.; m. Lucetta Farnham, Aug. 15, 1976. BA, Ind. U., 1976, JD, 1985. Bar: Ind. 1985, U.S. Dist. Ct. (no. and so. dists.) Ind. 1985, U.S. Supreme Ct. 1989. Exec. dir Cmty. Justice Ctr., Anderson, 1979-85; assoc. Shearer, Schrock & Woodruff, Anderson, 1985-87; pvt. practice Anderson, 1987-97, Woodruff Law Offices, P.C., Anderson, 1997—; bd. dirs. East Cen. Legal Svcs. Program, Anderson, 1986-89; trustee Chpt. 7 Bankruptcy Panel, So. Dist. Ind., 1991—. Bd. dirs. Offender Aid & Restoration of the U.S., 1988-93. Mem. Ind. Assn. Criminal Def. Lawyers, Ct. Appointed Spl. Advocates (bd. dirs. 1988), Madison County Bar Assn. (sec./treas. 1990, v.p. 1991, pres. 1992). Methodist. Criminal, Personal injury, General practice. Office: 109 E 9th St Anderson IN 46016-1509

**WOODS, CHRISTOPHER JOHN,** lawyer, solicitor; b. Eng., Feb. 17, 1957; s. William Ernest and Jean W.; m. Sarah Karen Preston, Sept. 1, 1990; children: Henry, James. BA in Law, Nottingham Trent, Eng., 1979. Bar: Eng. 1984, Hong Kong 1988, N.Y. 1999. Trainee solicitor Norton Rose, London, 1982-84; solicitor Clifford Chance, London and Hong Kong, 1984-90; solicitor, ptnr. Simmons & Simmons, Hong Kong and N.Y.C., 1990—. Co-author: Technology Transfer in the PRC, 1988. Mem. Internat. Trademark Assn. (com. 1990). Avocations: classic cars, mountain biking. Intellectual property, Trademark and copyright, Computer. Office: Simmons & Simmons 570 Lexington Ave New York NY 10022-6837

**WOODS, CURTIS E(UGENE),** lawyer; b. Ft. Leavenworth, Kans., May 29, 1950; s. Cecil Eugene and Velma Marie (Storms) W.; m. Kathleen L. Kopach, June 8, 1985; children: Colin Eric, Cameron Robert, Alexandra Marie. BA, U. Mo., Kansas City, 1972; JD, Northwestern U., Chgo., 1975. Bar: Ill. 1975, Mo. 1976, U.S. Dist. Ct. (no. dist.) Ill., U.S. Dist. Ct. (we. dist.) Mo., U.S. Dist. Ct. Kans., U.S. Ct. Appeals (7th, 8th and 10th cirs.). Law clk. U.S. Ct. Appeals (7th cir.), Chgo., 1975-76; assoc. Spencer Fane Britt & Browne, Kansas City, 1976-81; ptnr. Spencer Fane Britt & Browne, Kansas City, Mo., 1982-94, Sonnenschein Nath & Rosenthal, Kansas City, 1994—. Contbr. articles to profl. jours. Recipient William Jennings Bryan award Northwestern U., 1974. Mem. ABA, Mo. Bar Assn., Kansas City Bar Assn., Order of Coif. Antitrust, Federal civil litigation, Trademark and copyright. Office: Sonnenschein Nath Rosenthal 4520 Main St Ste 1100 Kansas City MO 64111-7700

**WOODS, DENNIS LYNN,** lawyer; b. Frankfort, Ind., Aug. 19, 1951; s. Willis McClure and Evelyn Colleen (Street) W. BS, Ind. U., 1973, JD, 1976. Bar: Ind. 1976, U.S. Dist. Ct. (so. dist.) Ind. 1976, U.S. Dist. Ct. (no. dist.) Ind. 1977. Dep. pros. atty. Tippecanoe County, Lafayette, Ind., 1977-78; chief dep. pros. atty. Tippecanoe County, Lafayetee, Ind., 1978, felony dep. pros. atty., 1979; pvt. practice Fowler, Ind., 1979—; pres. Cmty. and Family Resource Ctr., Inc., Lafayette, 1991-92; adj. prof. trial advocacy Purdue U. Mem. Nat. Assn. Counsel for Children, Ind. State Bar Assn., Ind. Assn. Welfare Attys., Benton County Bar Assn., C. of C. Democrat. Avocations: tennis, computer, jogging. General practice, State civil litigation, Criminal. Home: 2618 Trace 26 West Lafayette IN 47906-1888 Office: PO Box 232 Fowler IN 47944-0232

**WOODS, GEORGE EDWARD,** judge; b. 1923; m. Janice Smith. Student, Ohio No. U., 1941-43, 46, Tex. A&M Coll., 1943, Ill. Inst. Tech., 1943; JD, Detroit Coll. Law, 1949. Sole practice, Pontiac, Mich., 1949-51; asst. pros. atty. Oakland City, Mich., 1951-52; chief asst. U.S. atty., Ea. Dist. Mich., 1953-60, U.S. atty., 1960-61; assoc., Honigman, Miller, Schwartz and Cohn, Detroit, 1961-62; sole practice, Detroit, 1962-81; judge, U.S. Bankruptcy Ct., 1981-83, U.S. Dist. Ct. (ea. dist.) Mich., Detroit, 1983-93, sr. judge, 1993—. Served with AUS, 1943-46. Fellow Internat. Acad. Trial Lawyers, Am. Coll. Trial Lawyers; mem. Fed. Bar Assn., State Bar Mich. Office: US Dist Ct 277 US Courthouse 231 W Lafayette Blvd Detroit MI 48226-2700

**WOODS, GERALD MARION IRWIN,** lawyer; b. New Orleans, Dec. 18, 1947; s. Marion and Cecilia Fredericka (Durr) W. BBA, Loyola U., 1971, JD, 1976; postgrad. acctg., tax, U. New Orleans, 1986—. Bar: La. 1976, U.S. Dist. Ct. (ea. dist.) La. 1977, U.S. Ct. Appeals (5th cir.) 1978, D.C. 1982, U.S. Supreme Ct. 1982, U.S. Tax Ct. 1982, U.S. Mil. Ct. 1983, U.S Ct. Appeals (11th cir.) 1983. Comptroller ARC, New Orleans, 1971-79; assoc., acct. McGovern and Assocs., New Orleans, 1975-78; asst. dist. atty. New Orleans Dist. Atty.'s Office, 1979-80; in-house counsel Dormal Corp., New Orleans, 1982-83, A. Copeland Enterprises, Inc., New Orleans, 1983-85; assoc. McGovern, New Orleans, 1985-87, Richard Reynolds & Assocs., La., 1987—; atty. Record Data, Inc. subs. TRW, Inc., La., 1987—; estate and gift tax atty., No. La. IRS, 1987—; assoc. McGovern & Reynolds Assocs., New Orleans, 1987; v.p. Alliance Good Gov., Jefferson, La., 1982—; in-house counsel My Favorite Year, Inc., New Orleans, 1983-85. Recipient Silver Key award (2) ABA, 1974-76; named one of Outstanding Young Men of Am. Mem. New Orleans Bar Assn., Fed. Bar Assn., Jefferson Bar Assn., Loyola U. Alumni Assn., Delta Theta Phi (dist. chancellor 1976—), Blue Key (v.p. 1976). Democrat. Roman Catholic. Avocations: hunting, fishing, camping, car ralleys. Real property. Home: 2108 Roosevelt Blvd Kenner LA 70062-5909 Office: F Edward Hebert Fed Bldg 600 S Maestri Pl STOP # 33 New Orleans LA 70130

**WOODS, GRANT,** lawyer, former state attorney general; b. Elk City, Okla., May 19, 1954; m. Marlene Galán; children: Austin, Lauren, Cole, Dylan. BA, Occidental Coll., 1976; JD, Ariz. State U., 1979. Atty. gen. Ariz., 1990-99; ptnr. Goldstein, McGroder & Woods Ltd., 1999—. Founder Mesa Boys and Girls Club. Mem. State Bar Ariz., Ariz. Trial Lawyers Assn. Criminal. Office: Goldstein McGroder & Woods Ltd 2200 E Camelback Rd Ste 221 Phoenix AZ 85016-3497*

**WOODS, HARRY ARTHUR, JR.,** lawyer; b. Hartford, Ark., Feb. 15, 1941; s. Harry Arthur and Viada (Young) W.; m. Carol Ann Meschter, Jan. 21, 1967; children: Harry Arthur III, Elizabeth Ann. BA in Econs., Okla. State U., 1963; JD, NYU, 1966. Bar: N.Y. 1966, Okla. 1970. Assoc. White & Case, N.Y.C., 1966-67; assoc. Crowe & Dunlevy, Oklahoma City, 1971-75, ptnr., 1975—. Councilman City of Edmond, 1975-79, mayor pro tem, 1977-79. Capt. JAGC U.S. Army, 1967-71. Mem. ABA, Am. Law Inst., Okla. Bar Assn., Oklahoma County Bar Assn. (Outstanding Svc. award 1982, Golden Gavel award 1983, 98, Neil Bogan Professionalism award 1998), Ruth Bader Ginsburg Inn of Ct. (pres. 1998-99), Okla. City Bar Assn. Democrat. Methodist. Avocations: flying, jogging, bicycling, photography, astronomy. Federal civil litigation, State civil litigation, Product liability. Office: Crowe & Dunlevy 1800 Mid-America Tower 20 N Broadway Ave Ste 1800 Oklahoma City OK 73102-8273

**WOODS, HENRY,** federal judge; b. Abbeville, Miss., Mar. 17, 1918; s. Joseph Neal and Mary Jett (Wooldridge) W.; m. Kathleen Mary McCaffrey, Jan. 1, 1943; children—Mary Sue, Thomas Henry, Eileen Anne, James Michael. B.A., U. Ark., 1938, J.D. cum laude, 1940. Bar: Ark. bar 1940. Spl. agt. FBI, 1941-46; mem. firm Alston & Woods, Texarkana, Ark., 1946-48; exec. sec. to Gov. Ark., 1949-53; mem. firm McMath, Leatherman & Woods, Little Rock, 1953-80; judge U.S. Dist. Ct. (ea. dist.) Ark., 1980-95, sr. judge, 1995—; referee in bankruptcy U.S. Dist. Ct., Texarkana, 1947-48; spl. assoc. justice Ark. Supreme Ct., 1967-74, chmn. com. model jury instrns., 1973-80; chmn. bd. Ctr. Trial and Appellate Advocacy, Hastings Coll. Law, San Francisco, 1975-76; mem. joint conf. com. ABA-AMA, 1973-78, Ark. Constl. Revision Study Commn., 1967-68. Author treatise comparative fault.; Contbr. articles to legal jours. Pres. Young Democrats Ark., 1946-48; mem. Gubernatorial Com. Study Death Penalty, 1971-73. Mem. ABA, Ark. Bar Assn. (pres. 1972-73, Outstanding Lawyer award 1975), Pulaski County Bar Assn., Assn. Trial Lawyers Am. (gov. 1965-67), Ark. Trial Lawyers Assn. (pres. 1965-67), Internat. Acad. Trial Lawyers, Internat. Soc. Barristers, Am. Coll. Trial Lawyers, Am. Bd. Trial Advocates, Phi Alpha Delta. Methodist. Home: 42 Wingate Dr Little Rock AR 72205-2556 Office: US Dist Ct 600 W Capitol Ave Ste 360 Little Rock AR 72201-3323

**WOODS, JOSEPH REID,** lawyer, arbitrator; b. Milroy, Ind., Oct. 11, 1929; s. John Melvin and Mary Lorenda (Johnston) W.; m. Avis Lorene Woods, June 14, 1958; children—John P., Edward W., Ann L. B.S., Ind. U., 1952, J.D., 1963. Bar: Ind. 1963. Practice law, Indpls., 1963—; ins. claims adjuster State Farm Ins. Co., 1958-62; spl. agt. Office Naval Intelligence, resident agt. in charge, Des Moines, 1954-57. Mem. Bd. Edn. Franklin Twp. Community Sch. Corp., 1970-82, pres., 1972-74, 76, 78, 81; Served as cpl. AUS, 1952-54. Recipient Service award Am. Arbitration Assn., Bd. Edn., 1982. Mem. Ind. Trial Lawyers Assn. Presbyterian (elder). Family and matrimonial, General practice, Personal injury. Home: 6305 Fairlane Dr Indianapolis IN 46259-1718 Office: Woods & Woods PC 135 N Pennsylvania St Ste 2330 Indianapolis IN 46204-4403

**WOODS, KERIN MARGARET,** lawyer; b. Norwich, Conn., Mar. 3, 1959; d. Donald Grimes and Sheila (O'Connor) W.; m. Karl-Eirk Sternlof, May 4, 1995; children: Emma Woods Sternlof, Nora George Connor Sternlof. BA, Coll. Holy Cross, 1980; JD, U. Conn., 1983. Bar: Conn. 1983, U.S. Dist. Ct. Conn. 1983, R.I. 1987, U.S. Dist. Ct. R.I. 1989, U.S. Ct. Appeals (2d cir.) 1997, Mashantucket Pequot Tribal Ct. 1996. Lawyer Suisman, Shapiro, Wool, Brennan, Gray & Greenburg, P.C., New London, Conn., 1983-87, Faulkner & Boyce, P.C., New London, 1987-93, Anderson & Ferdon, P.C., Norwich, 1993—; spl. master civil divsn. State of Conn. Superior Ct., Hartford, 1997—. Mem. ATLA, Conn. Trial Lawyers Assn. (lectr. seminars 1992, 94, bd. govs. 1996—, asst. editor jour. 1985-90), R.I. Trial Lawyers Assn., Conn. Bar Assn., New London Ct. Bar Assn. Avocations: photography, reading, cooking. Personal injury, Pension, profit-sharing, and employee benefits, General civil litigation. Office: Anderson & Ferdon PC PO Drawer 749 101 Water St New London CT 06320-6310

**WOODS, ROBERT EDWARD,** lawyer; b. Albert Lea, Minn., Mar. 27, 1952; s. William Fabian and Maxine Elizabeth (Schmit) W.; m. Cynthia Anne Pratt, Dec. 26, 1975; children: Laura Marie Woods, Amy Elizabeth Woods. BA, U. Minn., 1974, JD, 1977; MBA, U. Pa., 1983. Bar: Minn. 1977, U.S. Dist. Ct. Minn. 1980, U.S. Ct. Appeals (8th cir.) 1980. Assoc. Moriarty & Janzen, Mpls., 1977-81, Berger & Montague, Phila., 1982-83; assoc. Briggs and Morgan, St. Paul and Mpls., 1983-84, ptnr., 1984—; sr. v.p. corp. devel. Ins Web Corp., Redwood City, Calif., 1999—; adj. prof. William Mitchell Coll. Law, St. Paul, 1985; exec. com., bd. dirs. LEX MUNDI, Ltd., Houston, 1989-93, chmn. bd. 1991-92; bd. dirs. Midwest Asia Ctr., 1993-95, chmn. bd., 1994-95. Author (with others) Business Torts, 1989; sr. contbg. editor: Evidence in America: The Federal Rules in the States, 1987. Mem. ABA, Minn. State Bar Assn., Hennepin County Bar Assn., Ramsey County Bar Assn. (chmn. corp., banking and bus. law sect. 1985-87), Assn. Trial Lawyers Am., Wharton Club of Minn., Phi Beta Kappa. Federal civil litigation, Securities, General civil litigation. Home: 28 N Deep Lake Rd North Oaks MN 55127-6506 Office: Briggs & Morgan 2400 IDS Ctr 80 S 8th St Ste 2400 Minneapolis MN 55402-2157

**WOODS, TERRENCE PATRICK,** lawyer; b. Portsmouth, Va., June 11, 1944; s. Donald Peter and Helen Tucker Woods; m. Linda Nekervis Kleinz, Apr. 23, 1971; children: Katherine, Timothy, Kevin, Michael. BA, U. Ariz., 1966; JD, Ariz. State U., 1973. Bar: Ariz. 1973, U.S. Dist. Ct. Ariz. 1973, U.S. Ct. Appeals (9th cir.) 1976. Assoc. Johnson, Tucker, Jessen & Dake, Phoenix, Ariz., 1973-74, Jones, Teilborg, Sanders, Haga & Parks, Phoenix, 1974-78; shareholder Broening, Oberg, Woods, Wilson & Cass, P.C., Phoenix, 1978—, also bd. dirs.; judge advocate gen. dept. USAF, Ariz. Air N.G., 1977-89. Asst. adjutant gen. Ariz. N.G., Phoenix, 1989-93; judge Ariz. Ct. Mil. Appeals, Phoenix, 1997—. Brigadier gen. USAFR, 1966-93. Mem. Air Force Assn. (life), N.G. Assn. of U.S., Ariz. Assn. Def. Counsel, State Bar Ariz., Maricopa County Bar Assn. Republican. Roman Catholic. Avocation: baseball coach. Personal injury, Insurance, Toxic tort. Office: Broening Oberg Woods Wilson & Cass PC 1122 E Jefferson St Phoenix AZ 85034-2224

**WOODS, THOMAS FABIAN,** lawyer; b. St. Paul, June 27, 1956; s. William Fabian and Maxine Elizabeth (Schmit) W.; m. Rona Pilar Quiñanola, Oct. 26, 1985 (div. Dec. 1991); 1 child, Sara Anne; m. Lora Denise Hammers, Aug. 14, 1992. BS in Geophysics, U. Minn., 1979; MS in Geophysics, U. Wyo., 1987; JD, U. Wis., 1992, profl. devel. degree in engring., 1998. Bar: Wis. 1992, U.S. Dist. Ct. (we. dist.) Wis. 1992, U.S. Patent Office 1992; registered geophysicist Calif. Jr. wireline engr. Schlumberger Internat., Argentina, 1979-80; gen. velocity engr. Seismograph Svc. Corp., Houston, 1980-81; seismologist, mgr. Seiscom-Delta United Internat., Ltd., Singapore, 1981-83; exploration geophysicist Amoco Corp., Denver, 1986-88; engring. geophysicist Harding-Lawson Assocs., Novato, Calif., 1988; patent law clk. Honeywell, Inc., Mpls., 1990-91; patent law clk. Rayovac Corp., Madison, Wis., 1991-92, patent atty., 1992-96, patent counsel, 1996; patent atty. Medtronic, Inc., Mpls., 1996-99; European patent counsel Medtronic, Inc., Maastricht, The Netherlands, 1999—; cons. Bison Instruments, Inc., Mpls., 1985, Kans. Oil Co., Manhattan, 1985. Contbr. articles to Oil and Gas Jour. and SEG; patentee in field. Grantee U. Wyo., 1985-86, U. Wis., 1989-90. Mem. ABA, AAAS, Am. Intellectual Property Law Assn., Wis. Intellectual Property Law Soc. (pres. U. Wis. Law Sch. 1990-92), Wis. Intellectual Property Law Assn., Minn. Intellectual Property Law Assn. Achievements include rsch. in field of seismology; coordination and supervision of 800-level vertical seismic profile experiment in Sunland Park, New Mex. Patent, Trademark and copyright. Home: Klimmenderstraat 2, 6343 AC Klimmen The Netherlands Office: Medtronic BRC, Endepolsdomein 5, 6229 GW Manstruchts The Netherlands

**WOODS, WILLIAM HUNT,** lawyer; b. Toledo, Ohio, May 30, 1946; s. William Stanley and Marie Hunt W.; m. Mary Catherine Clucus, Aug. 5, 1972; children: Rebecca Lucile, William Clucus. BS in Edn., Ohio State U., 1968, JD cum laude, 1973. Bar: Ohio 1973, U.S. Dist. Ct. (no. and so. dists.) Ohio 1974, U.S. Ct. Appeals (6th cir.) 1980. Tchr. Perrysburg (Ohio) Pub. Schs., 1968-70; atty. McNamara & McNamara, Columbus, Ohio, 19736. Contbr. articles to profl. jours. Pres. North Columbus Jaycees, 1979-80. Fellow Columbus Bar Found.; mem. ABA (vice chair fidelity & surety law com. 1996-91, 93—), Ohio State Bar Assn., Columbus Bar Assn. Democrat. Presbyterian. Avocations: genealogy, Civic War history, auto racing, golf. Insurance, Fidelity and surety, General civil litigation. Office: McNamara & McNamara 88 E Broad St Ste 1250 Columbus OH 43215-3558

**WOODS, WINTON D.,** law educator; b. Balt., Jan. 11, 1938; s. W.D. and Nancy N. W.; m. Barbara Lewis; children: Tad, Adam, Brooke, Lindsy, Jessica. AB Econ./Gov., Ind. U., 1961, JD with distinction, 1965. Bar: Ind., Ariz.; U.S. Supreme Ct. Law clk. U.S. Dist. Ct. (no. dist.) Calif., Sacramento, 1965-67; prof. law U. Ariz., Tucson, 1967—; reporter U.S. Dist. Ariz. Civil Justice Reform Act Com., 1992—; pres. Law Office Computing, Inc., 1990—; dir. Courtroom of the Future Project, U. Ariz., 1993—. Contbr. articles to profl. jours; author: The Lawyers Computer Book, 1990. Mem. bio-ethics com. UMC, Tucson, 1984-96. Recipient Fulbright award, 1979, Educator of Yr. award Internat. Comm. Industry Assn., 1996-97; fellow NEH, 1972, Nat. Inst. for Dispute Resolution, 1982. Fellow Coll. Law Practice Mgmt; mem. ABA, Ariz. State Bar Assn. Jewish. Avocations: computers, automobiles, photography. Office: U Ariz Coll Of Law Tucson AZ 85721-0001

**WOODSIDE, FRANK C., III,** lawyer, educator, physician; b. Glen Ridge, N.J., Apr. 18, 1944. BS, Ohio State U., 1966, JD, 1969; MD, U. Cin., 1973. Diplomate Am. Bd. Legal Medicine, Am. Bd. Forensic Medicine. Mem. Dinsmore & Shohl, Cin.; clin. prof. pediats. U. Cin., 1992—; adj. prof. law U. Cin., 1973—. Editor: Drug Product Liability, 1985—. Fellow Am. Coll. Legal Medicine, Am. Coll. Forensic Examiners, Am. Soc. Hosp. Attys., Soc. Ohio Hosp. Attys.; mem. ABA, FBA, Ohio Bar Assn., Internat. Assn. Def. Counsel, Def. Rsch. Inst. (chmn. drug and med. svc. com. 1988-91), Cin. Bar Assn. Product liability, Professional liability, Personal injury. Office: Dinsmore & Shohl 1900 Chemed Ctr 255 E 5th St Cincinnati OH 45202-4700

**WOODSON, DANNY,** lawyer; b. St. Louis, June 2, 1949; s. William Melvin Woodson and Wanda Jean (Lucas) Bradford; m. Barbara Ann Cook, Aug. 7, 1971; children: Christopher Allen, Timothy Jon. BS, East Tex. State U., 1970; JD, Tex. Tech. U., 1977. Bar: Tex. 1978, U.S. Dist. Ct. (ea. dist.) Tex. 1979. Assoc. Kenley, Boyland, Hawthorne, Star and Coughlin, Longview, Tex., 1978, Florence and Florence, Hughes Springs, Tex., 1978-83; sole practitioner, Mt. Pleasant, Tex., 1983—; adv. bd. mem. Bowie-Cass Mental Health Svcs., Cass County, Tex., 1981; chmn., adv. bd. mem. Couch Phys. Therapy and Rehab. Svcs., Mt. Pleasant, 1994—. Coach Dixie League Baseball, Mt. Pleasant, 1984, 88, 89, Mt. Pleasant Soccer Assn., 1984-85; chmn. legis. com. Mt. Pleasant C. of C., 1984-85; bd. deacons Trinity Bapt. Ch., Mt. Pleasant, 1986-88. Mem. Cass County Bar Assn. (pres. 1981-82), N.E. Tex. Bar Assn., Titus County Bar Assn., Tex. Trial Lawyers Assn., Assn. Trial Lawyers of Am. Baptist. Avocations: travel, softball, sports fan. Family and matrimonial, Personal injury, General civil litigation. Office: PO Box 399 Mount Pleasant TX 75456-0399

**WOODWARD, HALBERT OWEN,** federal judge; b. Coleman, Tex., Apr. 8, 1918; s. Garland A. and Helen (Halbert) W.; m. Dawn Blair, Sept. 28, 1940; children: Halbert Owen, Garland Benton. BBA, U. Tex., 1940, LLB, 1946. Bar: Tex. 1941. Mem. Woodward & Johnson, Coleman, 1949-68; mem. Tex. Hwy. Commn., 1959-68, chmn., 1967-68; judge U.S. Dist. Ct. No. Dist. Tex., 1968—, chief judge, 1977-86, sr. judge; dir. S.W. State Bank, Brownwood, Tex. Bd. dirs. Overall Meml. Hosp., Coleman. Served with USNR, 1942-45. Mem. ABA, Tex. Bar Assn., Am. Judicature Soc., Beta Theta Pi. Office: Fed Bldg C-210 US Courthouse 1205 Texas Ave Lubbock TX 79401-4037*

**WOODWORTH, RAMSEY LLOYD,** lawyer; b. Syracuse, N.Y., Dec. 26, 1941; s. Woodrow Lloyd and Helen (Ramsey) W.; m. Diane Elizabeth McMillion, June 12, 1971; children: Scott, Ashley, Jeffrey. AB, Brown U., 1964; LLM cum laude, Syracuse (N.Y.) U., 1967. Bar: N.Y. 1967, D.C. 1968, U.S. Ct. Appeals (D.C. cir.) 1968. Atty., advisor FCC, Washington, 1967-68; from assoc. to ptnr. Hedrick & Lane, Washington, 1968-82; prin. Wilkes, Artis, Hedrick & Lane, Chartered, Washington, 1982—. Convenor Peace Luth. Ch., Alexandria, 1985-86; pres. Broadcast Pioneers Ednl. Fund, Inc., 1997—. Mem. Fed. Comm. Bar Assn. (exec. com. 1986-89, chair responsibility com. 1984-86, treas. 1989-90, chmn. Fed. Commn. Bar Assn. Found. 1991-93, trustee 1991-94, Univ. Club Washington, Order of Coif. Avocation: swimming. Communications, Administrative and regulatory. Office: Wilkes Artis Hedrick & Lane 1666 K St NW Ste 1100 Washington DC 20006-2897

**WOODY, CLYDE WOODROW,** lawyer; b. Princeton, Tex., Oct. 3, 1920; s. James W. and Emma Mae (Heard) W.; m. Paula Fay Mullen, Aug. 23, 1969; children: Todd, Joe. BS, U. Houston, 1951, JD, 1951; postgrad. St. Mary's U., San Antonio, 1952, U. Colo., 1953. Bar: Tex. 1952, U.S. Ct. Appeals (5th cir.) 1956, U.S. Supreme Ct. 1958, U.S. Ct. Appeals (6th cir.) 1973, U.S. Ct. Appeals (11th cir.) 1981; cert. specialist in criminal law and family law Tex. Bd. Legal Specialization. Pvt. practice law Houston, 1952-66; ptnr., then sr. ptnr. Woody & Rosen, Houston, 1966-80; pvt. practice law, Houston, 1980—; city atty. Southside Pl., Houston, 1955-57; bd. dir. Unitedbank-Houston, Cen. Bank Holding Co., Miami, Fla.; lectr. Bd. dirs. Mossler Found., 1966-70; del. People to People Internat. Citizen Amb. Program, 1988, 91; sect. chmn. State Bar Tex., 1964-65; staff judge adv. N.Am. Air Def. Command, Ent ARB. Capt. U.S. Army, 1941-45, to capt. USAF, 1951-53; PTO, CBI. Mem. Am. Judicature Soc., Nat. Assn. Criminal Def. Lawyers, Tex. Trial Lawyers Assn., Assn. Trial Lawyers Am., ABA, Houston Bar Assn., Tex. Criminal Def. Lawyers Assn., Nat. Transp. Safety Bd. Bar Assn., Phi Delta Phi. Democrat. Methodist. Clubs: University, Texas, (Houston). Contbr. articles to legal jours. Criminal, Family and matrimonial, Federal civil litigation. Home: 731 Brogden Rd Houston TX 77024-3003 Office: PO Box 19028 Houston TX 77224-9028

**WOODY, DONALD EUGENE,** lawyer; b. Springfield, Mo., Mar. 10, 1948; s. Raymond D. and Elizabeth Ellen (Bushnell) W.; m. Ann Louise Ruhl, June 5, 1971; children: Marshall Wittmann, Catherine Elizabeth. BA in Polit. Sci. with honors, U. Mo., 1970, JD, 1973. Bar: Mo. 1973, U.S. Dist. Ct. (we. dist.) Mo. 1973, U.S. Ct. Appeals (8th cir.) 1973, U.S. Supreme Ct. 1987. Assoc. Neale, Newman & Bradshaw, Springfield, 1973-74; ptnr. Taylor, Stafford & Woody, Springfield, 1974-82, Taylor, Stafford, Woody, Cowherd & Clithero, Springfield, 1983-93, Taylor, Stafford, Woody, Clithero & Fitzgerald, Springfield, 1993—. Editor U. Mo. Law Rev., 1973. Chmn. county campaign U.S. senator Thomas Eagleton, Springfield, 1980; committeeman Greene County Dem. Party, Springfield, 1984-86; cons. Children's Home Mayors commn., Springfield, 1985. Mem. ABA, Springfield Metro Bar Assn. (sec. 1977-80, precedure com. 1986, bd. dirs. 1991-93, pres.-elect 1995, pres. 1996), Assn. Trial Lawyers Am., Springfield C. of C. (chmn. performing arts com. 1980-84), Order of Coif, Phi Delta Phi. Avocations: fishing, growing roses, bicycling, running. Federal civil litigation, State civil litigation, Personal injury. Home: 1421 S Ginger Blue Ave Springfield MO 65809-2260 Office: Taylor Stafford Woody Clithero & Fitzgerald 3315 E Ridgeview St Ste 1000 Springfield MO 65804-4083

**WOODY, THOMAS CLIFTON II,** assistant district attorney; b. Portsmouth, Va., Mar. 31, 1962; s. Thomas Clifton Sr. and Jean (Whitehead) W.; m. Sherry Carpenter, Aug. 15, 1981; children: Thomas Clifton III, Seth Chandler, Spencer David. BA, Old Dominion U., 1984; JD, Mercer U., 1987. Bar: Ga. 1987, U.S. Dist. Ct. (mid. dist.) Ga. 1987, U.S. Ct. Appeals (11 cir.) 1987. Assoc. Adams & Hemingway, Macon, Ga., 1987-92; asst. dist. atty. Dist. Atty's. Office-Macon Judicial Cir., Macon, 1992—; lectr. Ga. Coll., Milledgeville, 1992—. Pres. Bibb County Young Reps., Macon, 1986-90; mem. exec. coun. Bibb County Rep. Party, Macon, 1986-92. Mem. Ga. Bar Assn., Macon Bar Assn., Pros. Attys. Coun. Ga., The Federalist Soc. (exec. bd. Ctrl. Ga. Lawyers Divsn.). Republican. Baptist. Avocations: golf, reading, college basketball, baseball. Home: 153 Red Oak Rd Byron GA 31008-6311 Office: Macon Judicial Dist Office of Dist Atty 661 Mulberry St Macon GA 31201-2605

**WOODYSHEK, J. DANIEL,** lawyer; b. Englewood, N.J., May 27, 1948; s. Joseph John and Marjorie (Leahy) W.; m. Alice Ann Murphy; children: David Daniel, Michael Patrick, Danielle. BS cum laude, Marywood Coll., Scranton, Pa., 1976; JD, Boston U., 1979. Bar: Mass. 1980, U.S. Dist. Ct. Mass. 1980. Assoc. Roche, Carens & DeGiacomo, Boston, 1980-83, Shocket, Dockser & Assocs., Boston, 1983-85; ptnr., head real estate dept. Shocket & Dockser, Natick, Mass., 1985—. Active local polit. campaigns. Mem. ABA (conveyance com. 1988—), Mass. Bar Assn. (real property sect.), Mass. Conveyancers Assn., Land Ct. Examiner, Pi Gamma Mu, Lambda Iota Tau, Delta Epsilon Sigma. Democrat. Roman Catholic. Avocations: racquetball, gardening, reading, fishing. Real property, Land use and zoning (including planning), Contracts commercial. Office: Shocket & Dockser PO Box 8007 Natick MA 01760-0050

**WOOL, LEON,** lawyer; b. Chgo., Dec. 10, 1937; s. Irving and Bertha (Kraus) W.; m. Bernadette Elizabeth Meyers, May 7, 1943; children: Louis, Steve, Imily. BS, Drake U., 1960; JD, DePaul U., 1963. Bar: Ill. 1963. Trial atty. Chgo. Trnasit Authority, 1963-67, supr. trial atty., 1967-75, dir. claims dept., 1975-78, mgr. labor rels., 1978-80, mgr. claims dept., 1980-86, assoc. gen. atty., 1986-87, asst. counsel claims and collections, 1988-90, first dep. gen. atty., 1990-98; pvt. practice Chgo., 1998—. Mem. ABA, Ill. Bar Assn., Chgo. Bar Assn., Am. Pub. Transit Assn. Risk Mgmt. Avocations: sports, reading, travel. Fax: (312) 201-9016. General civil litigation, Personal injury, Insurance. Office: 55 W Wacker Dr Chicago IL 60601-1609

**WOOLDRIDGE, WILLIAM CHARLES,** lawyer; b. Miami, Fla., Feb. 24, 1943; s. Clarence Edward and Easter Marguerite (Souders) W.; m. Joyce L. Norton, June 15, 1968; children: William Charles, John Michael. *One son, Chuck, is a doctoral student in Chinese history at Princeton; John works with computers. His wife, descended from New England Havens and Dunklees, earned a graduate degree in patristic Christianity and runs, with Marilyn Robinson, a seminar/retreat business oriented to personal and spiritual growth. His father served as a carrier pilot in the Pacific in World War II. After the Civil War, his great-grandfather, James Wooldridge, disappeared from Lynchburg, Virginia: genealogical work rediscovered him in Turnersville, Texas. First in the line, John Wooldridge, a blacksmith, settled outside Richmond by 1699 and had sixteen grandsons who supported the Revolution.* BA, Harvard U., 1965; LLB, U. Va., 1969. Bar: Va. 1969. Atty. Norfolk and Western Ry. Co., 1973-82; with Norfolk So. Corp., 1982—, v.p. dept. law, 1996—. Pres. John Marshall Found., Richmond, Va., 1992-94; pres. Norfolk Hist. Soc., 1995-96; chair Friends of Chrysler Mus. Hist. Houses, 1997—; bd. dirs. Sta. WHRO, 1997—. Capt. JAGC, U.S. Army, 1969-73. Mem. ABA, Va. Bar Assn. Republican. General corporate, Administrative and regulatory, Antitrust. Office: Norfolk So Corp 3 Commercial Pl Norfolk VA 23510-2108

**WOOLLEY, THOMAS JOSEPH, JR.,** lawyer; b. Atlantic City, N.J., May 11, 1948; s. Thomas Joseph and Inez Kempton (Dunn) W.; m. Patricia L. O'Riley, June 18, 1972; 1 child, Kimberly Erin. BA, Wake Forest U., 1970; JD, U. Fla., 1973. Bar: Fla., U.S. Dist. Ct. (so. dist.) Fla. Pvt. practice Boynton Beach, Fla. Office: 639 E Ocean Ave Ste 428 Boynton Beach FL 33435-5011

**WOOLSON, CHARLES E., JR.,** lawyer; b. Woodbury, N.J., June 6, 1953; s. Charles E. and Alice Woolson; m. Mary Ellen Yoder, June 30, 1986; 1 child, Jennifer E. BA, Temple U., 1975; JD, Widener U., 1977. Bar: N.J., Va., U.S. Dist. Ct. N.J., U.S. Ct. Appeals (3d cir.), U.S. Supreme Ct. Asst. claims atty. Fidelity & Deposit, Richmond, Va., 1978-81; atty. Davidow & Davidow, Millville, N.J., 1981, Montano Summers Mullen Manuel & Owens, Cherry Hill, N.J., 1982-86, Law Offices of Roger Steedle, Absecon, N.J., 1986—. Mem. Atlantic County Rep. Com., 1996—. Mem. Trial Attys. of N.J. (trustee 1996—), N.J. Bar Assn. (spl. com. mcpl. ct. practice). General civil litigation, Insurance, Municipal (including bonds). Office: 122 New Jersey Ave Absecon NJ 08201-2409

**WOOSNAM, RICHARD EDWARD,** venture capitalist, lawyer; b. Anderson, Ind., June 27, 1942; s. Richard Wendelland Ruth (Cleveland) W.; children: Cynthia S., Elizabeth C. BS, Ind. U., 1964, JD, 1967, MBA, 1968. Bar: Ind. 1967, U.S. Dist. Ct. (so. dist.) Ind. 1967. Instr. bus. law Ind. U., Bloomington, 1966-68; assoc. Ferguson, Ferguson & Lloyd, Bloomington, 1967-68; dep. pros. Monroe County (Ind.), Bloomington, 1967-68; tax acct. Price Waterhouse, Phila., 1968-69; v.p., treas. Innovest Group, Inc., Phila., 1969-82, chmn., pres., 1983—; gen. ptnr. Plum Holdings, LLC, 1999—; guest lectr. Wharton Sch. Bus., U. Pa., Ind. U., Bloomington, 1975—; bd. dirs. Capital Mgmt. Corp., Skyworks, Inc., N.Y. Achievement, L.L.C., Innovest Talent Svcs., Inc., Command Corp., World Affairs Coun. of Phila., Fairmount Park Found., Ctr. for Entrepreneurship and Innovation; trustee Pa. Acad. Fine Arts. Mem. ABA, Ind. Bar Assn., Union League of Phila., Sunday Breakfast Club. Home: 70 Shelbourne Ct Wayne PA 19087-5723 Office: 2000 Market St Ste 1400 Philadelphia PA 19103-3214

**WOOTON, WILLIAM ROBERT,** lawyer; b. Providence, Sept. 20, 1944; s. Robert O. and Beulah (Bennett) W.; m. Shirliebeth Wenzel, Aug. 25, 1968; children: William Robert Jr., Richard Bennett, Russell Owen. BBA, Marshall U., 1966; postgrad., Ohio U., 1966-67; JD, W.Va. U., 1971. Bar: U.S. Dist. Ct. (no. and so. dists.) W.Va. 1971, U.S. Ct. Appeals (4th cir.) 1972. Law clk. U.S. Cir. Judge John A. Field, Charleston, W.Va., 1971-72; asst. atty. gen. Atty. Gen. of W.Va., Charleston, 1972-74; asst. prosecuting atty. Raleigh County Prosecuting Atty., Beckley, W.Va., 1974-76; ptnr. Wooton Law Firm, Beckley, 1977—. Del. W.Va. Ho. of Dels., Charleston, 1977-86, 89-90; senator W.Va. Senate, Charleston, 1991—, chmn. jud. com. Col. W. Va. Army N.G. Mem. Rotary. Democrat. Baptist. Office: Drawer A Beckley WV 25802-2800

**WORD, TERRY MULLINS,** lawyer; b. Corpus Christi, Tex., Dec. 30, 1943; s. Terrence Stuart and Leila Elba (Mullins) W.; m. Alice G. Hector, Jan. 27, 1971 (div. 1977); children: Morgan Anna, Zachary Hector; m. Mary Ann L. Rios Garcia, May 28, 1983; children: Jettie Laure, Terrence Rios; 1 stepson, John Jarrett Garcia. B.A. in Econs., Math., U. Tex., 1966, J.D., 1973. Bar: Tex. 1973, N.Mex. 1973, U.S. Dist. Ct. N.Mex. 1973. Ptnr. Stribling, Anderson, Read & Word, Albuquerque, 1973-74; atty. N.Mex.

Pub. Defender, Albuquerque, 1974-76; pvt. practice, Albuquerque, 1976-77; assoc. Richard E. Ransom, P.A., Albuquerque, 1977-83; pres. Terry M. Word, P.C., Albuquerque, 1983—. Workmen's compensation editor The N.Mex. Trial Lawyer, Albuquerque, 1982-84 . Bd. dirs. Big Bros./Big Sisters Albuquerque, 1983—. Served to lt. USN, 1966-70, Vietnam. Fellow Am. Coll. Trial Lawyers; mem. ATLA, N.Mex. Trial Lawyers Assn. (chmn. continuing legal edn. com. 1984-85, treas. 1984-85, bd. dirs. 1984—, pres. elect 1985-86, pres. 1986-87), Am. Bd. Trial Advocates (pres. N.Mex. chpt. 1996-97). Democrat. Episcopalian. Personal injury, Workers' compensation, Civil rights. Home: 6401 Caballero Pkwy NW Albuquerque NM 87107-5635 Office: 500 Tijeras Ave NW Albuquerque NM 87102-3133

**WORENKLEIN, JACOB JOSHUA,** lawyer; b. N.Y.C., Oct. 1, 1948; s. Abraham and Cela (Zyskind) W.; divorced; children: David, Daniel, Laura; m. Cindy Sternkler, Feb. 26, 1995. BA, Columbia U., 1969; MBA, JD, NYU, 1973. Bar: N.Y. 1974. From assoc. to ptnr. Milbank, Tweed, Hadley & McCloy, N.Y.C., 1973-93, chmn. firm planning com., 1988-90, exec. com., 1990-93, sr. advisor to exec. com., 1993-94; mng. dir., group head of global project fin. group Lehman Bros., N.Y.C., 1993-96; mng. dir., head project fin, commodity fin., export fin. Soc. Gen., N.Y.C., 1996-98; mng. dir., global head project and sector fin. Soc. Gen., Paris and N.Y.C., 1998—; mem. investment banking mgmt. com. Lehman Bros., 1993-96; mem. adv. coun. Amoco Power Resources Corp., 1995—; adj. prof. fin. NYU Stern Sch. of Bus. Mem. editl. bd. Jour. Project Fin., 1996—; contbr. articles to profl. jours. Pres. Old Broadway Synagogue, N.Y.C., 1978—; trustee Fedn. Jewish Philanthropies, N.Y.C., 1984-86; bd. overseers United Jewish Appeal-Fedn. Jewish Philanthropies, 1987, chmn. lawyers divsn. major gifts, 1989-91, chmn. lawyers divsn., 1991-93, bd. dirs., 1991-97; trustee Jewish Cmty. Rels. Coun. N.Y., 1995-98, mem. coun. on fgn. rels., 1998—. Mem. Coun. on Fgn. Rels. General corporate, Public utilities. Office: Soc Gen 1221 Avenue Of The Americas New York NY 10020-1001

**WORK, CHARLES ROBERT,** lawyer; b. Glendale, Calif., June 21, 1940; s. Raymond P. and Minna M. (Fricke) W.; m. Linda S. Smith, Oct. 4, 1965 (div.); children: Matthew Keehn, Mary Lucila Landis, Benjamin Reed; m. Veronica A. Haggart, Apr., 1985, 1 child, Andrew Haggart. BA, Wesleyan U., 1962; JD, U. Chgo., 1965; LLM, Georgetown U., 1966. Bar: D.C. 1965, Utah 1965. Asst. U.S. atty. D.C., 1966-73; dep. adminstr. law enforcement assistance adminstrn., U.S. Dept. Justice, 1973-75; ptnr. Peabody, Lambert & Meyers, Washington, 1975-82, McDermott, Will & Emery, Washington, 1982—. Recipient Rockefeller Pub. Service award 1978. Mem. D.C. Bar (pres. 1976-77). Federal civil litigation, State civil litigation, Private international. Office: McDermott Will & Emery 600 13th St NW Fl 12-8 Washington DC 20005-3005

**WORK, MICHAEL JAY,** lawyer; b. Maysville, Ky., Oct. 7, 1946; s. Clarence Lee and Marjorie (Lemon) W.; m. Christine Marion Dignan, Aug. 2, 1969; children: Thomas M., Meghan E., Kristen C. BA, Ohio State U., 1968, JD, 1971. Bar: N.H. 1972, U.S. Dist. Ct. N.H. 1972. Atty., examiner Pub. Utilities Commn. Ohio, Columbus, 1971; criminal justice planner N.H. Gov.'s Commn. on Crime and Delinquency, Concord, 1972-73; assoc. Law Offices of John C. Fairbanks, Newport, N.H., 1973-75; sole practice Newport, N.H., 1975—; mem. adv. bd. Lake Sunapee Bank, Newport, 1980—; mem. N.H. Supreme Ct. Profl. Conduct Commn., Concord, 1981-90. Dir. YMCA Camp Coniston, Inc., Croydon, N.H., 1981—. Named Outstanding Young Man Am., 1978. Mem. ABA, N.H. Bar Assn. (gov. 1982-84), Sullivan County Bar Assn. (pres. 1982), New London Bar Assn. (pres. 1983), Newport C. of C. (pres. 1980), Econ. Corp. Newport, Inc. Democrat. Lodge: Rotary (pres. Newport chpt. 1984-85). Avocations: sports, coin collecting. Real property, Probate, General practice. Home: Burpee Ln PO Box 552 New London NH 03257-0552 Office: 7a Main St PO Box 627 Newport NH 03773-0627

**WORKMAN, MARGARET LEE,** state supreme court justice; b. May 22, 1947; d. Frank Eugene and Mary Emma (Thomas) W.; m. Edward T. Gardner III; children: Lindsay Elizabeth, Christopher Workman, Edward Earnshaw. AB in Polit. Sci., W.Va. U., 1969, JD, 1974. Bar: W.Va. 1974. Asst. counsel to majority, pub. works com. U.S. Senate, Washington, 1974-75; law clk. 13th jud. cir., W.Va. Ct., Charleston, 1975-76, judge, 1981-88; pvt. practice Charleston, 1976-81; justice W.Va. Supreme Ct. Appeals, Charleston, 1989-99, chief justice, 1993, 97. Advance person for Rosalyn Carter, Carter Presdl. Campaign, Atlanta, 1976. Democrat. Episcopalian.

**WORLEY, CHARLES ROBERT,** lawyer; b. Oklahoma City, May 23, 1945; s. Charles Edwin and Evelyn Haste W.; m. Nancy Jean Kouns, June 6, 1970; children: Charles Alan, Megan Riffe. AB in Polit. Sci., U. N.C., 1967, JD, 1970. Bar: N.C. 1970, U.S. Dist. Ct. 1971, U.S. Ct. Appeals (4th cir.) 1972, U.S. Tax Ct. 1989. Atty., shareholder McGuire, Wood, Worley & Bissette, Asheville, N.C., 1971-87; pvt. practice Asheville, 1987—; co-owner Highland Farms Retirement Cmty., Black Mountain, N.C., 1994—. Mem. adv. bd. Salvation Army, Asheville, 1974—; mem. Asheville City Coun., 1991-93, 95-97; mem., chmn. regional water authority Asheville Buncombe & Henderson, 1996—. Recipient Spl. award Land Sky Regional Coun., 1996. Democrat. Presbyterian. Avocations: running, soccer, golfing, hiking. Real property, Estate planning, General corporate. Office: 53 N Market St Ste 101 Asheville NC 28801-2900

**WORLEY, ROBERT WILLIAM, JR.,** lawyer; b. Anderson, Ind., June 13, 1935; s. Robert William and Dorothy Mayhew (Hayler) W.; m. Diana Lynn Matthews, Aug. 22, 1959; children: Nathanael, Hope Hillegas. BS in Chem. Engring., Lehigh U., 1956; LLB, Harvard U., 1960. Bar: Conn. 1960, U.S. Supreme Ct. 1966, Fla. 1977. Assoc. then ptnr. Cummings & Lockwood, Stamford, Conn., 1960-91; gen. counsel Consol. Asset Recover Corp. sub. Chase Manhattan Corp., Bridgeport, Conn., 1991-94; v.p., asst. gen. counsel The Chase Manhattan Bank, N.Y.C., 1994—. Mem. trustees com. on bequests and trusts Lehigh U., 1979—; mem. Conn. Legis. Task Force on Probate Court Sys., 1991-93; chmn. Greenwich Arts Coun., 1981-82; v.p., bd. dirs. Greenwich Choral Soc., 1962-77, 80, mem., 1960-95; bd. dirs. Greenwich Ctr. for Chamber Music, 1981-85, Greenwich Symphony, 1986-89; commr. Greenwich Housing Authority, 1972-77; past mem. Rep. Town Com. Greenwich; mem. bldg. com. for sr. ctr. Greenwich Bd. Selectman, 1980-81. Capt. JAGC, AUS, 1965. Mem. Mem. Conn. Bar Assn. (exec. com. probate sect. 1980), Fla. Bar Assn., Stamford Bar Assn. (sec.), Greenwich Bar Assn., Landmark Club, Harvard Club Boston. Republican. Christian Scientist. Banking, Probate, Estate planning. Home: 316 Sound Beach Ave Old Greenwich CT 06870-1932 Office: The Chase Manhattan Bank Legal Dept 25th Flr 1 Chase Manhattan Plz Fl 25 New York NY 10081-0001

**WORMLEY, CRAIG THOMAS,** lawyer; b. Des Moines, Oct. 8, 1967; s. Thomas Lee and Judith Ann Wormley. BBS, Creighton U., 1990; JD, Thomas Cooley Law Sch., 1993. Bar: Calif. 1996, U.S. Dist. Ct. (ea., so., ctrl. and no. dists.) Calif., U.S. Dist. Ct. (we. dist.) Mich., U.S. Ct. Appeals (6th and 9th cirs.) 1998. Assoc. Schmid & Voiles, L.A., 1994-97; supervising atty. Miller & Assocs., L.A., 1997—. Bd. dirs. Warnborough Coll., Oxford, Eng., 1996—. Mem. ABA (criminal sect.), L.A. County Bar Assn. (sports and industry sects., criminal sect.), Calif. Pub. Defenders Assn., Calif. Assn. for Criminal Justice. Roman Catholic. Criminal. Office: 2530 Wilshire Blvd Santa Monica CA 90403-4616

**WOROBIEC, MICHELE SELIG,** lawyer, law educator; b. Canton, Ohio, Dec. 28, 1966; d. Robert Allen and Sheryl Ann Selig; m. Michael W. Worobiec, July 25, 1992. BS summa cum laude, Ohio State U., 1989, JD, 1996. Bar: Ohio 1996, U.S. Dist. Ct. (so. dist.) Ohio 1996. Program dir. Hons. Ctr. Ohio State U., Columbus, 1990-93; law clk. Wallace & Warner, Columbus, 1994-96, assoc., 1996-97; ptnr. Selig & Hrabcak, Worthington, Ohio, 1997—; adj. prof. Columbus State U., 1997—; presenter in field. Bd. dirs. Morrow County C. of C., Mt. Gilead, Ohio, 1996-97; trustee Rails to Trails, Mt. Gilead, 1996—; ct. apptd. adv. CASA, Columbus, 1995-96. Scholar Ohio State U., 1993-96. Mem. Ohio State Bar Assn., Columbus State Bar Assn., Women Lawyers Franklin County, Morrow County Bar Assn., Ctrl. Ohio Weavers Guild (v.p. 1998—), Phi Beta Kappa. Avocations: horseback riding, boating, handspinning yarn, weaving, skiing. General corporate, Estate planning, Real property. Home: 1475 Light House Rdg Marion OH 43302-8709 Office: Selig & Hrabcak Co LPA 67 E Wilson Bridge Rd Worthington OH 43085-2338

**WORTHINGTON, BRUCE R.,** lawyer. Sr. v.p. and gen. counsel PG&E Corp San Francisco, 1995—. Office: Ste 2400 One Market Spear Tower San Francisco CA 94105

**WORTHINGTON, CAROLE YARD LYNCH,** lawyer; b. Knoxville, Tenn., Aug. 29, 1951; d. Charles R. and Alma (Allred) Yard; m. Robert F. Worthington Jr., Sept. 14, 1996; 1 child, Allison Kathleen. BA, U. Tenn., 1972, JD, 1977. Bar: Tenn. 1977, Ga. 1982. Assoc. Thomas, Leitner, Mann, Warner & Owens, Chattanooga, 1977-78; assoc. Thomas, Mann & Gossett, Chattanooga, 1978-81, ptnr., v.p., 1981-86; ptnr. Grant, Konvalinka & Harrison, P.C., Chattanooga, 1987-96, Carole Lynch Worthington, Atty. at Law, Knoxville, 1996—; sec. Nat. Transp. Rsch. Ctr., Inc.; bd. dirs. CASA, U. Tenn. Alliance of Women Philanthropists. Author: Estate Planning Tennessee Practice, 1992; asst. editor Tenn. Law Rev., 1976-77. Vice chmn. allocations United Way of Cahttanooga, 1985, pilot campaign, 1986; active Jr. League of Chattanooga, 1981-92; mem. alumnae adv. coun. U. Tenn. Coll. Law, 1983-92, dean's cir., 1989—; bd. dirs. Mental Health Assn. Chattanooga Inc., 1986-92, 1st v.p., 1988-89, sec., 1989-92; trustee St. Nicholas Sch., 1992-95. Recipient Alumni Leadership award U. Tenn. Coll. Law, 1988, 92. Fellow Am. Bar Found., Tenn. Bar Found., Chattanooga Bar Found.; mem. ABA (assembly del. 1991-97, 98—, com. on legal aid and indigent defendants 1994-95, select com. of house 1994-96), Chattanooga Bar Assn. (bd. govs. 1982-89, sec.-treas. 1985-86, pres. 1987-88), Tenn. Bar Assn. (vice chair comml. law, banking and bankruptcy 1988-90, unified bar study com. 1990-91, chair bar leadership conf. 1990, editl. bd. Tenn. Bar Jour. 1991-94, long range planning com. 1992-95, 97-99, bd. govs. 1994-96, chair long range planning com. 1995-96, future of bar com. 1998—), Ga. Bar Assn., Nat. Conf. Lawyers and Realtors (ABA del. 1990-92), Nat. Conf. Bar Pres.'s (exec. coun. 1989-92, treas. 1992-93, sec. 1993-94, pres.-elect 1994-95, pres. 1995-96), Tenn. Bd. Profl. Responsibility, Phi Alpha Delta. General corporate, Probate, Securities. Home: 807 Woodland Ct Knoxville TN 37919-6682

**WORTHINGTON, DANIEL GLEN,** lawyer, educator; b. Rexbury, Idaho, Aug. 15, 1957. BA magna cum laude, Brigham Young U., 1982, MEd, 1986, EdD, 1989, JD cum laude, 1989. Bar: Utah 1990. Asst. to assoc. dean students Brigham Young U., 1986-88, cons., 1987-89, mgr. planned giving, tech. cons., 1989-90, adj. prof. law and edn., 1989—; asst. dean students Coll. Eastern Utah, 1985-86; assoc. dean, exec. dir. devel. Porterville Coll. Found., 1990-91; prin. Worthington & Assocs., Provo, Utah, 1991-93; mng. atty., ptnr. Walstad & Babcock, Provo; assoc. dean U. S.D. Sch. Law, 1994-95, exec. v.p. found., 1995—; assoc. v.p., gen. counsel U. Ctrl. Fla. Found., Orlando; adj. faculty Masters of Tax Program, U. Ctrl. Fla., 1995—; sr. cons. Fla. Hosp. and the U. S.D. Bus. Sch., 1997—. Editor-in-chief jour. Edn. & Law Perspectives, 1986-88, co-chair, exec. adv. bd., dir., 1988-91; contbr. articles to profl. jours. Exec. v.p. S.D. Planned Giving Coun., 1994—; nat. assembly del. Nat. Com. on Planned, 1994—. With USAFR, 1982-88. Mem. Supreme Ct. Hist. Soc., Federalist Soc., Nat. Soc. Fund Raising Execs., Phi Kappa Phi. Probate, Alternative dispute resolution, General corporate. Address: 3172 Bothwell Ct Oviedo FL 32765-6597

**WORTHINGTON, SANDRA BOULTON,** lawyer; b. Phila., July 12, 1956; d. Alan Beaumont and Ruth Meyers Worthington; m. Richard A. Sheppard, Apr. 21, 1990; 1 child. BA with high distinction, U. Va., 1978; JD, Temple U., 1983. Bar: Pa. 1983, U.S. Dist. Ct. (ea. dist.) Pa. 1984. Summer clk. Ct. of Common Pleas Montgomery County, Pa., summer 1981; legal intern Peruto, Ryan & Vitullo, Phila., 1982-83; assoc. Michael D. Fioretti Law Office, Phila., 1983-84; founding ptnr. Stocker & Worthington Law Office, Jenkintown, Pa., 1984—; legal counsel Phila. Women's Squash Racquets Assn., 1985—. Mem. Pa. Trial Lawyers Assn., Phila. Trial Lawyers Assn., Pa. Bar Assn., Montgomery County Bar Assn. Avocations: small business consulting, squash, tennis. Personal injury, Family and matrimonial, Consumer commercial. Office: Stocker & Worthington Law Offices 820 Homestead Rd Jenkintown PA 19046-2840

**WORTHY, K(ENNETH) MARTIN,** lawyer; b. Dawson, Ga., Sept. 24, 1920; s. Kenneth Spencer and Jeffrie Pruett (Martin) W.; m. Eleanor Vreeland Blewett, Feb. 15, 1947 (dec. July 1981); children: Jeffrie Martin, William Blewett; m. Katherine Teasley Jackson, June 17, 1983. Student, The Citadel, 1937-39; B.Ph., Emory U., 1941, J.D. with honors, 1947; MBA cum laude, Harvard U., 1943. Bar: Ga. 1947, D.C. 1948. Assoc. Hopkins & Sutter (formerly Hamel & Park), Washington, 1948-51, ptnr., 1952-69, 72-90, sr. counsel, 1991—; asst. gen. counsel Treasury Dept., 1969-72; chief counsel IRS, 1969-72; dir. Beneficial Corp., 1977-96, emeritus, 1996-98; mem. Nat. Coun. Organized Crime, 1970-72; cons. Justice Dept., 1972-74. Author: (with John M. Appleman) Basic Estate Planning, 1957; contbr. articles to profl. jours. Del. Montgomery County Civic Fedn., 1951-61, D.C. Area Health and Welfare Coun., 1960-61; mem. coun. Emory U. Law Sch., 1976—, chmn., 1993-95; trustee Chelsea Sch., 1981—, St. John's Coll., Annapolis, Md. and Santa Fe, 1987-93, 95—, Sherman Found., Newport Beach, Calif., 1991—, Ga. Wilderness Inst., 1997—, chmn. dept. fin. Episcopal Diocese, Washington, 1969-70; fellow Aspen Inst., 1982-92. Capt. AUS, 1943-46, U.S. Army, 1951-52. Recipient Army Commendation Ribbon, 1945, Treasury Exceptional Svc. award and medal, 1972, IRS Commrs. award, 1972, Disting. Alumnus award Emory U., 1992. Fellow Am. Bar Found., Am. Coll. Tax Counsel (bd. regents 1980-88, chmn. 1985-87), Atlantic Coun. (counselor); mem. ABA (coun. taxation sect. 1965-69, 72-75, chmn. 1973-74, del. Nat. Conf. Lawyers and CPAs 1981-87, ho. of dels. 1983-89, chmn. audit com. 1985-90), Fed. Bar Assn. (nat. coun. 1969-72, 77-79), Ga. Bar Assn., D.C. Bar, Am. Law Inst., Nat. Tax Assn., Am. Tax Policy Inst. (trustee 1989-98), Chevy Chase Club, Met. Club, James River Country Club, Sea Island Club, Harvard Club N.Y.C., Phi Delta Theta, Phi Delta Phi, Omicron Delta Kappa. Corporate taxation, Personal income taxation, Government contracts and claims. Home: PO Box 30264 189 W Gascoigne Sea Island GA 31561 Office: Hopkins & Sutter 888 16th St NW Fl 7 Washington DC 20006-4103

**WOUNG, MARGUERITE NATALIE,** lawyer; b. Kingston, Jamaica, Aug. 11, 1965; came to U.S., 1978; d. Maurice Lascelles and Lois (Ogle) W.; m. Kevin Troy Bingham May 27, 1990 (div. Apr. 1998); 1 child, Jordan Nile Bingham. BSLI, Georgetown U., 1986, JD, 1989. Bar: D.C., 1989, U.S. Dist. Ct. D.C., 1991. Assoc. Arter & Hadden, Washington, 1989-91; sr. atty. Tenneco Energy, Houston, 1991-95, counsel, 1995-97; atty. ARCO Pipeline Co., Houston, 1995; sr. counsel El Paso Energy Corp., Houston, 1997-99. Contbg. author: Banks and Thrifts - Government Enforcement and Receivership, 1991. Mem. adv. coun. Houston C.C. Fine Arts Dept., Houston, 1999. Mem. Fed. Energy Bar Assn., D.C. Bar Assn. FERC practice. Office: El Paso Energy Corp 1001 Louisiana St Houston TX 77002-5083

**WOVSANIKER, ALAN,** lawyer, educator; b. Newark, Mar. 19, 1953; s. Harold and Sally (Gooen) W.; m. Susan Orme, Aug. 23, 1987. AB, Brown U., 1974; JD, Harvard U., 1977. Bar: N.J. 1977. Law clk. to presiding judge U.S. Dist. Ct. N.J., Camden, 1977-78; prtnr. Lowenstein Sandler PC, Roseland, N.J., 1978—; adj. prof. Seton Hall Law Sch., 1988-91, Rutgers U. Law Sch., 1989-95; chmn. dist. ethics com. Supreme Ct. Contbr. articles to profl. jours. Mem. exec. com. N.J. chpt. Anti-Defamation League. Mem. Essex County Bar Assn. (trustee 1996-99, chmn. banking law com. 1994-97, chmn. corp. law com. 1999—). Securities, Banking, Mergers and acquisitions. Office: Lowenstein Sandler PC 65 Livingston Ave Ste 2 Roseland NJ 07068-1791

**WOZNIAK, DEBRA GAIL,** lawyer; b. Rockford, Ill., Oct. 3, 1954; d. Richard Michael and Evalyn Louise Wozniak. BA, U. Nebr., 1976, JD, 1979. Bar: Nebr. 1980, Iowa 1980, Ill. 1982. CPCU. Asst. legal counsel Iowa Ho. of Reps., Des Moines, 1980-81; mng. atty. Rapp & Gilliam, Des Moines, 1981; from asst. counsel to counsel and asst. dir. Alliance of Am. Insurers, Schaumburg, Ill., 1981-87; from asst. counsel to counsel StateFarm Ins. Cos., Bloomington, Ill., 1987—. Mem. Nebr. Bar Assn., Iowa Bar Assn. Avocation: antiques. Insurance, Legislative, General corporate. Office: State Farm Ins Cos One State Farm Plz Bloomington IL 61710

**WRAY, ROBERT,** lawyer; s. George and Ann (Moriarty) W.; m. Lila Keogh (dec.); children: Jennifer, Edward, Hillary. BS, Loyola U., 1957; JD, U. Mich., 1960. Bar: D.C., Ill. 1960. Assoc. Hopkins & Sutter, Chgo., 1964-69; gen. counsel Agy. for Internat. Devel., 1969-71; sr. counsel TRW, Inc., 1972-73, Export-Import Bank of the U.S., 1974-79; prin. Robert Wray Assocs., 1979-86; internat. ptnr. Pierson, Ball & Dowd, 1986-87; prin. Robert Wray Assocs., 1988—; spec. counsel Graham & James, 1988-97; of counsel Holland & Knight, Washington, 1997—. Recipient medal of superior honor Dept. of State. Mem. ABA, Fed. Bar Assn., Am. Soc. Internat. Law, Internat. Bar Assn., Coun. for Excellence in Govt., Bretton Woods Com., Met. Club, Talbot Country Club, Annapolis Yacht Club. Aviation, Private international. Office: Holland & Knight 2100 Pennsylvania Ave NW Washington DC 20037-3295

**WRIGHT, BLANDIN JAMES,** lawyer; b. Detroit, Nov. 29, 1947; s. Robert Thomas and Jane Ellen (Blandin) W.; m. Kay Emons Heideman, Aug. 28, 1969; children: Steven Blandin, Martha Kay. BA, U. Mich., 1969; JD, Dickinson Law Sch., 1972; LLM in Taxation, NYU., 1973; MS in Taxation with honors Am. U., 1992. Bar: Pa. 1973, Fla. 1976, U.S. Tax Ct. 1977, D.C. 1979, U.S. Supreme Ct. 1979, Va. 1984, N.Y. 1991. CPA, Tex., Va. Atty. Office Internat. Ops., Nat. Office IRS, Washington, 1973-76; tax dir. Intairdril Ltd., London, 1976-78; tax atty. Allied Chem. Corp., Houston, 1978-79; v.p., gen. counsel Assoc. Oiltools, Inc., London, 1979-82, v.p. taxes, gen. counsel J. Lauritzen (USA), Inc., Charlottesville, Va., 1982-85; sole practice, Charlottesville, 1985-88; ptnr. Richmond & Fishburne, Charlottesville, 1988-90; of counsel, 1990-91; tax counsel Mobil Oil Corp., N.Y.C., 1990, Fairfax, Va., 1990—; officer Pamaco Partnership Mgmt. Corp., Va., 1986-91, CRW Energy Corp., 1986-90, Transp. & Tourism Internat., Inc., 1986—, Hotsprings Assocs., Inc., 1989-91, MDM Hotels, Inc., 1992—, Internat. Shipping & Resorts, Inc., 1992—, United Holdings Ltd., 1993—, Cruise and Resorts Internat., Inc., 1994—; bd. dirs. Blandin J. Wright, P.C., Internat. Shipping Adv. Svcs., Inc.; bd. dirs. T.T.I. Corp. Contbr. articles to profl. jours. Coach Charlottesville Youth Soccer, Baseball and Basketball, 1984-89; coach London Youth Baseball, 1982. Mem. ABA, Fairfax County Bar Assn., Am. Arbitration Assn. (arbitrator 1985—), AICPA, Tex. Soc. CPAs, Va. Soc. CPAs, Farmington Country Club, Beta Gamma Sigma. Roman Catholic. Corporate taxation, Mergers and acquisitions, Oil, gas, and mineral. Home: 4770 Biscayne Blvd Ph G Miami FL 33137-3251 Office: Queen Charlotte Sq 12010 Johns Pl Fairfax VA 22033-4646 also: 3225 Gallows Rd Ste 3a916 Fairfax VA 22037-0001

**WRIGHT, BRADLEY ABBOTT,** lawyer; b. Des Moines, Nov. 24, 1964; s. James Bradley and Carolyn (Abbott) W.; m. Alisa Labut, Aug. 24, 1993; children: Hannah, Alexandra. BA, Miami U., Oxford, Ohio, 1987; JD, Ohio State U., 1990. Bar: Ohio 1990. Assoc. Roetzel & Andress, Akron, Ohio, 1990-97, ptnr., 1997—. Grad. Leadership Akron, 1998; active Big Bros. and Big Sisters, Inc., Akron, United Way of Summit County, Akron. Mem. Akron Bar Assn. (vice chmn./social chmn.), Transp. Lawyers Assn., Def. Rsch. Inst., Assn. for Transp. Law Logistics and Policy, Am. Trucking Assn., Nat. Assn. R.R. Trial Counsel. Transportation, Insurance. Home: 91 N Hayden Pkwy Hudson OH 44236-3157 Office: Roetzel & Andress 222 S Main St Akron OH 44308-1533

**WRIGHT, CALEB MERRILL,** federal judge; b. Georgetown, Del., Oct. 7, 1908; s. William Elwood and Mary Ann (Lynch) W.; m. Katherine McAfee, Nov. 29, 1937; children: Thomas Merrill, William Elwood, Scott McAfee, Victoria. BA, Del. U.; LLB, Yale U., 1933. Bar: Del. 1933. Solo practice Georgetown, 1933-55; U.S. dist. judge Del. Dist., 1955-57, chief judge, 1957-73, sr. judge, 1973—. Mem. Del., Sussex County bar assns., Am. Judicature Soc., Am. Law Inst., Kappa Alpha. Republican. Presbyterian. Club: Wilmington. Home: Cokesbury Village C20 726 Loveville Rd Hockessin DE 19707-1515 Office: US Dist Ct 844 N King St # 34 Wilmington DE 19801-3519

**WRIGHT, CAROL L.,** lawyer, association executive; m. Bruce Allen Murphy; children: Emily P.W., Geoffrey A.W. BA, U. Mass., 1973; JD, Boston U., 1976. Bar: Mass. 1977, Pa. 1978, U.S. Dist. Ct. (mid. dist.) Pa. 1979. Atty. State College, Pa., 1979-87; dir. Prelaw Advising Ctr. Pa. State U., University Park, 1987-97; pres. N.E. Assn. Pre-Law Advisors, Phila., 1995-97; dir. legal studies Lafayette Coll., 1998—; bd. dirs. Pre-Law Advisors Nat. Coun., Durham, N.C., 1994-97, 99—; founder PRE-LAW.COM, 1998. Contbr. articles to profl. jours. Named to Outstanding Young Women in Am., 1984; named a Vol. of Yr., Centre County Coun. Human Svcs., State College, 1987. Mem. ABA, Pa. Bar Assn., Centre County Bar Assn.

**WRIGHT, CHARLES ALAN,** law educator, author; b. Phila., Sept. 3, 1927; s. Charles Adshead and Helen (McCormack) W.; m. Mary Joan Herriott, July 8, 1950 (div. Jan. 1955); 1 child, Charles Edward; m. Eleanor Custis Broyles Clarke, Dec. 17, 1955; children: Henrietta, Cecily; stepchildren: Eleanor Custis Clarke, Margot Clarke. BA, Wesleyan U., Middletown, Conn., 1947; LL.B., Yale U., 1949; LHD (hon.), Episcopal Theol. Sem. S.W., 1992. Bar: Minn. 1951, Tex. 1959. Law clk. to Hon. Charles E. Clark, U.S. Ct. Appeals (2d cir.), New Haven, 1949-50; asst. prof. law U. Minn., Mpls., 1950-53, assoc. prof., 1953-55; assoc. prof. law U. Tex., Austin, 1955-58, prof., 1958-65, McCormick prof., 1965-80, Bates prof., 1980-97; Arthur Goodhart vis. prof. legal sci. Cambridge (Eng.) U., 1990-91, Hayden W. Head regents chair, 1990-91; Charles Alan Wright chair in Fed. Cts. U. Tex., Austin, 1997—; vis. prof. U. Pa., 1959-60. Harvard U., 1964-65, Yale U., 1968-69; vis. fellow Wolfson Coll., Cambridge U., 1984; reporter study div. of jurisdiction between state and fed. cts. Am. Law Inst., 1963-69; mem. adv. com. on civil rules Jud. Conf. U.S., 1961-64, standing com. on rules of practice and proc., 1964-76, 87-93; cons., counsel for Pres., 1973-74; mem. com. on infractions NCAA, 1973-83, chmn., 1978-83, chmn. adminstrv. rev. panel, 1993-94; mem. permanent com for Oliver Wendell Holmes Devise, 1975-83; mem. Commn. on Bicentennial of U.S. Constn., 1985-92. Author: Wright's Minnesota Rules, 1954, Cases on Remedies, 1955, (with C.T. McCormick and J.H. Chadbourn) Cases on Federal Courts, 9th edit., 1992, Handbook of the Law of Federal Courts, 5th edit., 1994, (with H.M. Reasoner) Procedure-The Handmaid of Justice, 1965, Federal Practice and Procedure: Criminal, 3d edit., 19 97, (with A.R. Miller) Federal Practice and Procedure: Civil, 1969-99, 3d edit. (with Miller and E.H. Cooper), 1999, Federal Practice and Procedure: Juriiction and Related Matters, 1975-82, 3rd edit., 1998, (with K.W. Graham and V.J. Gold) Federal Practice and Procedure: Evidence, 1977—; mem. editl. bd. Supreme Ct. Hist. Soc. Yearbook, 1987-93—. Trustee St. Stephen's Episc. Sch., Austin, Tex., 1962-66, St. Andrew's Episc. Sch., Austin, 1971-74, 77-80, 81-84, chmn. bd., 1973-74, 79-80; trustee Capitol Broadcasting Assn., Austin, 1966—, chmn. bd., 1969-90; trustee Austin Symphony Orch., 1966—, mem. exec. com., 1966-70, 72-83, 86—; trustee Austin Choral Union, 1984-90, Austin Lyric Opera Soc., 1986—; bd. dirs. Am. Friends of Cambridge (Eng.) U., 1994—; corr. fellow British Acad., 1999. Recipient Fordham-Stein prize Fordham U., 1997, Learned Hand medal Fed. Bar Co., 1998; hon. fellow Wolfson Coll. Cambridge U., 1986—. Mem. ABA (commn. on standards jud. adminstrn. 1970-77, ho. of dels. 1993—), AAAS, Am. Law Inst. (coun. 1969—, 2d v.p. 1987-88, 1st v.p. 1988-92, pres. 1993—), Am. Bar Found. (Rsch. award 1989), Inst. Jud. Adminstrn., Am. Judicature Soc., Philos. Soc. Tex., Am. Friends Cambridge U. (bd. dirs. 1994—), Country Club, Tarry House Club, Headliners Club, Ridge Harbor Yacht Club, Barton Creek Lakeside Club (Austin), Century Club, Yale Club (N.Y.C.), Mid Ocean Club (Bermuda). Republican. Episcopalian. Avocations: reading and reviewing mysteries, railroads, fishing, coaching Legal Eagles (intramural touch football team). Home: 5304 Western Hills Dr Austin TX 78731-4822 Office: U Tex Sch Law 727 Dean Keeton St Austin TX 78705-3224

**WRIGHT, DANIEL A.,** lawyer; b. Washington, Sept. 30, 1946; s. William L. and Mary J. Wright; m. Deborah J. Wright, Sept. 5, 1981. BA, U. Calif., Davis, 1968; JD, Golden Gate U., 1978; Cert. in Pub. Adminstrn., U. Ala., 1969. Bar: Wash., U.S. Dist. Ct. (we. dist.) Wash. Claims officer Dept. Social and Health Svcs., Olympia, Wash., 1979-85; staff atty. Dept. of Licensing, Olympia, 1985-95; sole practitioner Tumwater, Wash., 1986-96; atty. William B. Pope & Assocs., Olympia, 1996—; adjudicator VA, san Francisco, 1979; law examiner Wash. State Bar Assn., Seattle, 1998—. Asst. scoutmaster Boy Scouts Am., 1990—. Capt. U.S. Army, 1969071, Vietnam. Regional Tng. Program in Pub. Adminstrn. fellow, 1968-69. Mem. Wash. State Bar Assn. (fee dispute arbitration com. 1988-90, com. on professionalism 1998—), Clan Gregor (elections com. Pacific N.W. chpt. 1995—). Avocations: woodworking, auto racing, astronomy. Family and matrimonial, Probate, Administrative and regulatory. Office: William B Pope & Assocs 1605 Cooper Point Rd NW Olympia WA 98502-8325

**WRIGHT, DEBORAH SUE,** lawyer; b. Batesville, Ind., Aug. 26, 1967; d. Charles James and Elaine Marie Bentfield; m. Eric Evan Wright, Dec. 5, 1992. BA, DePauw U., 1989; JD, Valparaiso U., 1992. Bar: Ind. 1992, Wis. 1993. Corp. counsel Hillenbrand Industries, Inc., Batesville, Ind., 1994—. Bd. dirs. Oldenburg (Ind.) Acad., 1995-96. Mem. ABA, Ind. Bar Assn., Wis. Bar Assn., Ripley County (Ind.) Bar Assn. Roman Catholic. Avocations: golf, fishing, waterskiing. General corporate. Office: Hillenbrand Industries Inc 700 State Route 46 E Batesville IN 47006-9137

**WRIGHT, EUGENE ALLEN,** federal judge; b. Seattle, Feb. 23, 1913; s. Elias Allen and Mary (Bailey) W.; m. Esther Ruth Ladley, Mar. 19, 1938; children: Gerald Allen, Meredith Ann Wright Morton. AB, U. Wash., 1935, JD, 1937; LLD, U. Puget Sound, 1984. Bar: Wash. 1937. Assoc. Wright & Wright, Seattle, 1937-54; judge Superior Ct. King County, Wash., 1954-66; v.p., sr. trust officer Pacific Nat. Bank Seattle, 1966-69; sr. judge U.S. Ct. Appeals (9th cir.), Seattle, 1969—; acting municipal judge, Seattle, 1948-52; mem. faculty Nat. Jud. Coll., 1964-72; lectr. Sch. Communications, U. Wash., 1965-66, U. Wash. Law Sch., 1952-74; lectr. appellate judges' seminars, 1973-76, Nat. Law Clks. Inst., La. State U., 1973; chmn. Wash. State Com. on Law and Justice, 1968-69; mem. com. on appellate rules Jud. Conf., 1978-85, mem. com. on courtroom photography, 1983-85, com. jud. ethics, 1984-92, com. Bicentennial of Constn., 1985-87. Author: (with others) The State Trial Judges Book, 1966; also articles; editor: Trial Judges Jour., 1963-66; contbr. articles to profl. jours. Chmn. bd. visitors U. Puget Sound Sch. Law, 1979-84; mem. bd. visitors U. Wash. Sch. Law, 1989—; bd. dirs. Met. YMCA, Seattle, 1955-72; lay reader Episc Ch. Served to lt. col. USAR, 1941-46, col. Res., ret. Decorated Bronze Star, Combat Inf. badge; recipient Army Commendation medal, Disting. Service award U.S. Jr. C. of C., 1948, Disting. Service medal Am. Legion. Fellow Am. Bar Found.; mem. ABA (coun. div. jud. adminstrn. 1971-76), FBA (Disting. Jud. Svc. award 1984), Wash. Bar Assn. (award of merit 1983), Seattle-King County Bar Assn. (Spl. Disting. Svc. award 1984), Appellate Judges Conf., Order of Coif, Wash. Athletic Club, Rainier Club, Masons (33 deg.), Shriners, Delta Upsilon (Disting. Alumni Achievement award 1989), Phi Delta Phi. Office: US Ct Appeals 9th Cir 902 US Courthouse 1010 5th Ave Seattle WA 98104-1195

**WRIGHT, FREDERICK LEWIS, II,** lawyer; b. Roanoke, Va., Sept. 17, 1951; s. Frederick Lewis and Dorothy Marie (Trent) W.; m. Margaret Suzanne Rey, Oct. 16, 1982; children: Lauren Elizabeth, Emily Trent. BA, Ga. State U., 1978; JD, U. Ga., 1981. Bar: Ga. 1982, U.S. Dist. Ct. (no. dist.) Ga. 1984, U.S. Ct. Appeals (11th, 8th and 4th cirs.) 1984, U.S. Supreme Ct. 1990. Law clk. to presiding justice U.S. Ct. Appeals, Atlanta, 1981-82; ptnr. Smith, Currie and Hancock, Atlanta, 1982-96, Vaughn, Wright and Stearns, Atlanta, 1997—. Articles editor Ga. Law Rev., 1980-81. Mem. ABA (forum com. constrn. industry), Assn. Trial Lawyers Am., Fed. Bar Assn., Order of Coif. Methodist. Construction, Environmental, General civil litigation.

**WRIGHT, J. CRAIG,** state supreme court justice; b. Chillicothe, Ohio, June 21, 1929; s. Harry and Marjorie (Riddle) W.; m. Jane LaFollette, Nov. 3, 1951; children: Marjorie Jane, Alice Ann. B.A., U. Ky., 1951; LL.B., Yale U., 1954. Ptnr. Wright, Gilbert & Jones, Columbus, 1957-70; judge Franklin County Common Pleas Ct., 1971-84, adminstrv. and presiding judge, 1980-84; assoc. justice Ohio Supreme Ct., Columbus, 1985-96; with Chester Willcox & Saxbe, Columbus, 1996—. Trustee Columbus Area Coun. on Alcoholism, 1959-83; chmn. bd. House of Hope-Halfway House, Columbus, 1960-68, trustee emeritus; trustee Grace Brethren Ch., Columbus, 1966-81, Worthington Christian Sch., Ohio, 1974-78, St. Anthony's Med. Ctr., Shepherd Hill Hosp. With CIC, U.S. Army, 1955-56. Recipient cert. of excellence Ohio Supreme Ct., 1972-83. Mem. ABA (mem. commn. on impaired lawyers 1988-91, state rep. jud. div. 1975-83), Ohio Bar Assn. (chmn. lawyers assistance com. 1977-84), Ohio Common Pleas Judges Assn. (exec. bd. 1972-83, pres.-elect 1984), Columbus Bar Assn., Am. Judicature Soc., Columbus Country Club, Athletic Club of Columbus. Avocations: golf; duplicate bridge. Office: Chester Willcox & Saxbe 17 S High St Ste 900 Columbus OH 43215-3442*

**WRIGHT, JAMES C.,** lawyer; b. Topeka, Apr. 1, 1938; s. Forest E. and Naomi (Sheafor) W.; m. Judith E. Baker, Sept. 2, 1961 (div. June 1982); children: Lori Batchman, Jeb, Ashley Friend; m. Patricia A. Slider, Apr. 28, 1984; stepsons: Andy, Charlie. BA, Kans. U., 1960; LLB, Washburn U., 1963. Bar: Kans. 1963, U.S. Dist. Ct. Kans. 1963, U.S. Ct. Appeals (10th cir.) 1970. Assoc. Shaw, Hergenreter & Quarnstrom, Topeka, 1963-69; ptnr. Shaw, Hergenreter, Quarnstrom & Wright, Topeka, 1969-81; atty. pvt. practice, Topeka, 1981-86; ptnr. Wright & Shafer, Topeka, 1986—. Bd. dirs., pres. Crittenton Home, Topeka, 1979; bd. dirs. Vol. Ctr., Topeka, 1974-80. Mem. Topeka Bar Assn. (bd. dirs. 1991-95), Topeka Lawyers Club, Topeka Country Club (bd. dirs. 1993-97, pres. 1996), Shawnee Country Club (v.p., bd. dirs. 1974-80), Kans. Golf Assn. (bd. dirs. 1996-98). Avocations: golf, travel. Workers' compensation, Personal injury. Office: Wright & Shafer 4848 SW 21st St Topeka KS 66604-4415

**WRIGHT, J(AMES) LAWRENCE,** lawyer; b. Portland, Oreg., Apr. 12, 1943; s. William A. and Esther M. (Nelson) W.; m. Mary Aileene Roche, June 29, 1968; children: Rachel, Jonathan, Christopher. BBA, Gonzaga U., 1966, JD, 1972; LLM, NYU, 1977. Bar: Wash. 1972, U.S. Ct. Mil. Appeals 1974, U.S. Tax Ct. 1976, U.S. Supreme Ct. 1976. Prin. Halverson & Applegate, P.S., Yakima, Wash., 1972-74, 77—. Mem. St. Elizabeth Hosp. Found., Yakima, 1986-89, Yakima Meml. Hosp. Found., 1990—; pres. fin. bd. St. Paul's Cathedral, Yakima, 1979—; mem. fin. coun. Diocese of Yakima, 1994—; v.p. Apple Tree Racing Assn., 1986-87; bd. dirs. Capital Theatre, Yakima, 1985-95. Capt. U.S. Army, 1966-68, 74-76. Mem. ABA, Wash. Bar Assn., Yakima County Bar Assn., Rotary. Roman Catholic. Avocations: tennis, golf. General corporate, Taxation, general, Estate planning. Office: Halverson & Applegate PS PO Box 22730 311 N 4th St Yakima WA 98901-2427

**WRIGHT, JAMES RALPH,** lawyer; b. Pitts., Jan. 18, 1944; s. Paul J. and Gertrude M. (Stienecker) W.; m. Harriett Ann Howard, Sept. 7, 1968; children: Karen, Cathy. BS, Ohio State U., 1966; JD, George Washington U., 1969. Bar: D.C. 1973, U.S. Dist. Ct. D.C. 1975, U.S. Ct. Appeals (D.C. cir.) 1981. Dir. legal affairs Airport Operators Coun., Internat., Washington, 1969-70; with NAS, Washington, 1970—, staff officer, counsel com. on motor vehicles, 1973-74, staff counsel, 1974-80, gen. counsel, 1980—; exec. dir. Nat. Academies' Corp., a Calif. nonprofit pub. benefit corp., 1986—. Editor, pub. newsletter, 1985-90. Mem. ABA. Office: NAS 2101 Constitution Ave NW Washington DC 20418-0007*

**WRIGHT, JOHN F.,** state supreme court justice. BS, U. Nebr., 1967, JD, 1970. Atty. Wright & Simmons, 1970-84, Wright, Sorensen & Brower, 1984-91; mem., coord. Commn. on Post Secondary Edn., 1991-92; judge Nebr. Ct. Appeals, 1992-94; assoc. justice Nebr. Supreme Ct., 1994—; chmn. bd. dirs. Panhandle Legal Svcs., 1970. Mem. Scottsbluff Bd. Edn., 1980-87, pres., 1984, 86. Served with U.S. Army, 1970, Nebr. N.G., 1970-76. Recipient Friend of Edn. award Scottsbluff Edn. Assn., 1992. Office: Nebr Supreme Ct 2207 State Capitol PO Box 98910 Lincoln NE 68509-8910*

**WRIGHT, JOHN WINFRED,** retired police official, lawyer; b. Salisbury, Md., Apr. 11, 1949; s. Hobart Charles and Margaret Winfred (Wilson) W.; m. Susan Patricia Mason, June 20, 1970; 1 child, Michael John. AA, Catonsville (Md.) Community Coll., 1975; BS, U. Balt., 1978, JD, 1983. Bar: Md. 1983, U.S. Dist. Ct. Md. 1989, U.S. Supreme Ct. 1990, U.S. Ct. Mil. Appeals 1993. Officer Annapolis (Md.) Police Dept., 1970-72, Balt. Police Dept., 1972-74; capt. Annapolis (Md.) Police Dept., 1974-96; cons. Md. Police Tng. Commn., Woodstock, 1984—; adj. faculty Anne Arundel (Md.) C.C., 1991—, Coppin State Coll., Balt., 1992—; lectr. No. Va. Criminal Justice Acad., 1991; judge advocate Alert Internat., 1995—. Recipient Law Enforcement Commendation medal SAR, Annapolis, 1983; recipient commendation Dir. of FBI, Washington, 1984, 91. Mem. Md. State Bar Assn., Anne Arundel County Bar Assn., Chatham County (Ga.) Sheriff's Res., Md. Chiefs Assn. Republican. Presbyterian. Avocations: golf, scuba diving, model railroading. Home: 24 Mary Musgrove Dr Savannah GA 31410-4038 Office: Fortune Personnel Cons 7 E Congress St Ste 712 Savannah GA 31401-3395

**WRIGHT, LAWRENCE A.,** federal judge; b. Stratton, Maine, Dec. 25, 1927; m. Avis Leahy, 1953; children: Michael, David, James, Stephen, Douglas. BA, U. Maine, 1953; JD, Georgetown U., 1956; LLM, Boston U., 1962. Bar: D.C. 1956, Maine 1956, Mass. 1968, Vt. 1971. Sr. trial counsel chief counsel office IRS, Boston, 1958-69; tax commr. State of Vt., 1969-71; ptnr. Gravel, Shea & Wright Ltd., Vt., 1971-84; judge U.S. Tax Ct., Washington, 1984—. Commr. U.S. Battle Monuments Commn., 1982-84. 2d lt. U.S. Army, 1945-48; ret. col. JAG, USAR, 1978. Decorated Legion of Merit, others. Home: 1844 Northbridge Ln Annapolis MD 21401-6575 Office: US Tax Ct 400 2nd St NW Washington DC 20217-0002

**WRIGHT, MINTURN TATUM, III,** lawyer; b. Phila., Aug. 7, 1925; s. Minturn T. and Anna (Moss) W.; m. Nonya R. Stevens, May 11, 1957; children: Minturn T., Richard S., Robert M., Marianne F. BA, Yale U., 1949; LLB, U. Pa., 1952. Bar: Pa. 1953, U.S. Ct. Appeals (3d cir.) 1953, U.S. Supreme Ct. 1962. Law clk. U.S. Ct. Appeals (3d cir.), 1952-53; assoc. Dechert, Price & Rhoads, Phila., 1953-61, ptnr., 1961-95, chmn., 1982-84; bd. dirs. Phila. Contributionship, Vector Security Co. Inc., Cotiga Devel. Co.; vis. prof. U. Pa. Law Sch., 1965-69, 93-97. Contbr. articles to profl. jours. Trustee Acad. Natural Scis. Phila., 1958—, chmn., 1976-81; trustee Hawk Mountain Sanctuary Assn., chmn. bd. dirs., 1992-97; trustee Rare Ctr., Pa. chpt. The Nature Conservancy. Served with U.S. Army, 1943-46. Mem. ABA, Pa. Bar Assn., Phila. Bar Assn., Nat. Coal Lawyers Assn., Eastern Mineral Law Assn. (trustee), Phila. Club, Milldam Club. Episcopalian. Probate, Contracts commercial. Office: Dechert Price & Rhoads 4000 Bell Atlantic Tower 1717 Arch St Philadelphia PA 19103-2793

**WRIGHT, PAUL WILLIAM,** lawyer, oil company executive; b. Jamestown, N.Y., July 7, 1944; s. Julian M. and Ruth (Blake) W.; m. Elizabeth O'Rourke Wright, Nov. 22, 1975; children: Jeffrey, Stephen. BS in Bus. Adminstrn., Georgetown U., 1966, JD, 1969. Bar: Va. 1969, D.C. 1972, Tex. 1973, U.S. Supreme Ct. 1972, La. 1985. Staff atty. Fed. Power Commn. 1969-70; assoc. Wolf & Case, Washington 1970-72; atty. Exxon Corp., Houston, 1973—, chief atty., Houston, 1986-92; sr. staff counsel Exxon Co. Internat.; bd. dirs. of La. Pro Bono-Project, 1986-90. Mem. ABA, Tex. Bar Assn., La. Bar Assn., Va. Bar Assn., D.C. Bar Assn., La. Bar Found. (bd. dirs., sec., treas. 1986-87, v.p. 1987-89, pres. 1989-91). Private international, FERC practice, General civil litigation. Office: Exxon Company Internat 200 Park Ave Florham Park NJ 07932-1094

**WRIGHT, ROBERT JOSEPH,** lawyer; b. Rome, Ga., Dec. 13, 1949; s. Arthur Arley and Maude T. (Lacey) W.; m. Donna Ruth Bishop, Feb. 18, 1972; children: Cynthia Ashley, Laura Christine. BA cum laude, Ga. State U., 1979; JD cum laude, U. Ga., 1983. Bar: GA. 1983, U.S. Dist. Ct. (no. dist.) Ga. 1983, U.S. Dist. Ct. (mid. dist.) Ga. 1985. Assoc. Craig & Gainer, Covington, Ga., 1983-84, Heard, Leverett & Adams, Elberton, Ga., 1984-86; gen. counsel Group Underwriters, Inc., Elberton, 1987—. Editorial staff Ga. Jour. Internat. and Comparative Law, 1981-82. Mem. State Bar Ga. (sec. legal econs. sect. 1987-88, chmn. legal econs. sect. 1988-90), Order of the Coif, Masons, Phi Alpha Delta. Baptist. Insurance, Personal injury, Land use and zoning (including planning). Home: 1030 E Canyon Creek Ct Watkinsville GA 30677-1500

**WRIGHT, ROBERT PAYTON,** lawyer; b. Beaumont, Tex., Feb. 15, 1951; s. Vernon Gerald and Huberta Read (Nunn) W.; m. Sallie Chesnutt Smith, July 16, 1977; children: Payton Cullen, Elizabeth Risher. AB, Princeton U., 1972; JD, Columbia U., 1975. Bar: Tex. 1975. Ptnr. Baker & Botts, L.L.P., Houston, 1975—. Author: The Texas Homebuyer's Manual, 1986. Mem. Am. Coll. Real Estate Lawyers, State Bar Tex. (chmn. coun. real estate, probate, trust law sect. 1994-95), Houston Bar Assn. (chmn. real estate sect. 1989-90), Tex. Coll. Real Estate Lawyers, Houston Real Estate Lawyers Coun., Houston Club (mem. com. young mems. 1987). Episcopalian. Real property, Finance, Environmental.

**WRIGHT, ROBERT ROSS, III,** law educator; b. Ft. Worth, Nov. 20, 1931; m. Susan Webber; children: Robert Ross IV, John, David, Robin. BA cum laude, U. Ark., 1953, JD, 1956; MA (grad. fellow), Duke U., 1954; SJD (law fellow), U. Wis., 1967. Bar: Ark. 1956, U.S. Supreme Ct. 1968, Okla. 1970. Instr. polit. sci. U. Ark., 1955-56; mem. firm Forrest City, Ark., 1956-58; partner firm Norton, Norton & Wright, Forrest City, 1959; asst. gen. counsel, asst. sec. Crossett Co., Ark.; atty. Crossett div. Ga.-Pacific Corp., 1960-63; asst. sec. Pub. Utilities Co., Crossett, Triangle Bag Co., Covington, Ky., 1960-62; mem. faculty law sch. U. Ark., 1963-70; asst. prof., dir. continuing legal edn. and research, then asst. dean U. Ark. (Little Rock div.), 1965-66, prof. law, 1967-70; vis. prof. law U. Iowa, 1969-70; prof. U. Okla., 1970-77; dean U. Okla. (Coll. Law); dir. U. Okla. (Law Center), 1970-76; vis. prof. U. Ark., Little Rock, 1976-77; Donaghey Disting. prof. U. Ark, 1977—; vis. disting. prof. U. Cin., 1983; Ark. commr. Nat. Conf. Commrs. Uniform State Laws, 1967-70; past chmn. Com. Uniform Eminent Domain Code; past mem. Com. Uniform Probate Code, Ark. Gov.'s Ins. Study Commn.; chmn. Gov. Commn. on Uniform Probate Code; chmn. task force joint devel. Hwy. Research Bd.; vice chmn. Okla. Jud. Council, 1970-72, chmn., 1972-75; chmn. Okla. Center Criminal Justice, 1971-76. Author: Arkansas Eminent Domain Digest, 1964, Arkansas Probate Practice System, 1965, The Law of Airspace, 1968, Emerging Concepts in the Law of Airspace, 1969, Cases and Materials on Land Use, 3d edit., 1982, supplement, 1987, 5th edit., 1997, Uniform Probate Code Practice Manual, 1972, Model Airspace Code, 1973, Land Use in a Nutshell, 1978, 2d edit., 1985, 3d edit., 1994, The Arkansas Form Book, 1979, 2d edit., 1988, Zoning Law in Arkansas: A Comparative Analysis, 1980; contbr. numerous articles to legal jours. Mem. Little Rock Planning Commn., 1978-82, chmn., 1982. Named Ark. Man of Year Kappa Sigma, 1958. Fellow Am. Law Inst., Am. Coll. Probate Counsel (acad.); mem. ABA (past chmn., exec. coun. gen. practice, solo and small firm sect., former chmn. new pubs. editl. bd., sect. officers conf., ho. of dels. 1994—, standing com. fed. jud. improvements 1998—), Ark. Bar Assn. (exec. coun. 1985-88, ho. of dels., life mem., chmn. eminent domain code com., past mem. com. new bar ctr., past chmn. preceptorship com., exec. com. young laywers sect.), Okla. Bar Assn. (past vice-chmn. legal internship com., former vice-chmn. gen. practice sect.), Pulaski County Bar Assn., Ark. Bar Found., U. Wis. Alumni Assn., Duke U. Alumni Assn., U. Ark. Alumni Assn., Order of Coif, Phi Beta Kappa, Phi Alpha Delta, Omicron Delta Kappa. Episcopalian. Home: 249 Pleasant Valley Dr Little Rock AR 72212-3170 Office: U Ark Law Sch 1201 Mcalmont St Little Rock AR 72202-5142

**WRIGHT, ROBERT THOMAS, JR.,** lawyer; b. Detroit, Oct. 4, 1946; s. Robert Thomas and Jane Ellen (Blandin) W.; m. Diana Feltman, June 8, 1994; children: Sarah Allison, Jonathan Brian. BA in History and Polit. Sci., U. N.C., 1968; JD, Columbia U., 1974. Bar: Fla. 1974. Assoc. Paul & Thomson, Miami, Fla., 1974-77; assoc. Mershon, Sawyer, Johnston, Dunwoody & Cole, Miami, 1977-81, ptnr., 1981-95; ptnr. Shutts & Bowen, Miami, 1995-98; shareholder Verner, Liipfert, Berhhard, McPherson & Hand, Miami, 1998—. 1st lt. U.S. Army, 1968-71. Mem. ABA, Fla. Bar, Dade County Bar Assn. Avocations: golf, rugby, African cichlids. Federal civil litigation, State civil litigation, Insurance. Home: 11095 SW 84th Ct Miami FL 33156-4311 Office: Verner Lippfert et al 200 S Biscayne Blvd Ste 3100 Miami FL 33131-2310

**WRIGHT, ROGER LANE,** lawyer; b. Blackfoot, Idaho, Aug. 5, 1936; s. Hesden L. and Lois Fern (Chamberlain) W.; children: C. Elyse, Whitney E. Bar: Nev. 1964, U.S. Supreme Ct. 1970. Law clk. to presiding justice Nev. Supreme Ct., Reno, 1964-65; sole practice Reno, 1965—, ret. Mem. scholarships and admissions adv. com. Brigham Young U., 1970-75. Mem. ABA. Nev. Bar Assn., Woshoe County Bar Assn., Assn. Trial Lawyers Assn. Real property, Personal injury, Criminal. Office: PO Box 406 Reno NV 89504-0406

**WRIGHT, SCOTT OLIN,** federal judge; b. Haigler, Nebr., Jan. 15, 1923; s. Jesse H. and Martha I. Wright; m. Shirley Frances Young, Aug. 25, 1972. Student, Central Coll., Fayette, Mo., 1940-42; LLB, U. Mo., Columbia, 1950. Bar: Mo. 1950. City atty. Columbia, 1951-53; pros. atty. Boone County, Mo., 1954-58; practice of law Columbia, 1958-79; U.S. dist. judge Western Dist. Mo., Kansas City, from 1979. Pres. Young Democrats Boone County, 1950, United Fund Columbia, 1965. Served with USN, 1942-43; as aviator USMC, 1943-46. Decorated Air medal. Mem. ABA, Am. Trial Lawyers Assn., Mo. Bar Assn., Mo. Trial Lawyers Assn., Boone County Bar Assn. Unitarian. Clubs: Rockhill Tennis, Woodside Racquet. Lodge: Rotary (pres. Columbia 1965). Office: Charles E Whitaker Courthouse 400 E 9th St Ste 8662 Kansas City MO 64106-2684

**WRIGHT, SUSAN WEBBER,** judge; b. Texarkana, Ark., Aug. 22, 1948; d. Thomas Edward and Betty Jane (Gary) Webber; m. Robert Ross Wright, III, May 21, 1983; 1 child, Robin Elizabeth. BA, Randolph-Macon Woman's Coll., 1970; MPA, U. Ark., 1972, JD with high honors, 1975. Bar: Ark. 1975. Law clk. U.S. Ct. Appeals 8th Circuit, 1975-76; asst. prof. law U. Ark.-Little Rock, 1976-78, assoc. prof., 1978-83, prof., 1983-90, asst. dean, 1976-78; dist. judge U.S. Dist. Ct. (ea. dist.) Ark., Little Rock, 1990—, chief judge, 1998—; vis. assoc. prof. Ohio State U., Columbus, 1981, La. State U., Baton Rouge, 1982-83; mem. adv. com. U.S. Ct. Appeals 8th Circuit, St. Louis, 1983-88. Author: (with R. Wright) Land Use in a Nutshell, 1978, 2d edit., 1985; editor-in-chief Ark. Law Rev., 1975; contbr. articles to profl. jours. Mem. ABA, Ark. Bar Assn., Pulaski County Bar Assn., Am. Law Inst., Ark. Assn. Women Lawyers (v.p. 1977-78), Am. Law Inst. Episcopalian. Office: US District Court 600 W Capitol Ave Ste 520 Little Rock AR 72201-3329

**WRIGHT, THOMAS JON,** lawyer; b. Little Rock, May 27, 1958; s. Robert Derwood and Nina Lou (Hughes) W.; m. Dawn Dynise White, June 16, 1984; 1 child, Rachel. BBA with honors, U. Ark., 1980; JD with high honors, U. Tenn., 1983. Bar: Tenn. 1984, U.S. Dist. Ct. (ea. dist.) Tenn. 1986; U.S. Ct. Appeals (6th cir.) 1990; U.S. Supreme Ct. 1988. Dir. ministry to legal profession Campus Crusade for Christ, Richardson, Tex., 1983-85; law clk. to presiding judge U.S. Dist. Ct. (ea. dist.) Tenn., Greeneville, 1985-86; assoc. Stophel & Stophel, P.C., Chattanooga, 1986-88, Summers, McCrea & Wyatt, P.C., Chattanooga, 1988-91, Dietzen, Atchley & Wright, Chattanooga, 1991—; adj. faculty Chattanooga State Tech. Community Coll., 1991—. Rep. precinct chmn. Hamilton County, Tenn., 1989—, mem. steering com., 1990. Named to Outstanding Young Men of Am., 1988. Mem. ABA (litigation com., ethics com. young lawyers div. 1987-89, pro bono com. 1989—, exec. com. 1988-89), Tenn. Bar Assn., Chattanooga Bar Assn. (pro bono com. 1987-90), Christian Legal Soc. (v.p. Chattanooga chpt. 1989, pres. 1990, dir. legal aid program 1987—), Assn. Trial Lawyers Am., Tenn. Trial Lawyers Assn., Pachyderm Club (bd. dirs. 1987-88, v.p. 1988-89, pres. 1989-90, editor newsletter), Ducks Unltd., Order of Coif, Beta Gamma Sigma. Presbyterian. Avocations: antiques, tennis, hunting, boating. Personal injury, General civil litigation, Workers' compensation. Home: 109 Magnolia Dr Greeneville TN 37743-5430 Office: Dietzen Atchley & Wright 100 W Summer St Greeneville TN 37743-4924

**WRIGHT, THOMAS LAWRENCE, II,** lawyer; b. Borger, Tex., July 20, 1948; s. Thomas Lawrence and Mary Olive Cordellia Jane (Chenoweth) W.; m. Karen Sheffield, Jan. 24, 1976; children: Thomas Lawrence III, Clair Walker. BA, Rice U., 1970; JD, U. Tex., 1974. Bar: Tex. 1975, N.M. 1997, Okla. 1997, Colo. 1998, U.S. Dist. Ct. (we., ea. and so. dists.) Tex., U.S. Dist. Ct. N.Mex., U.S. Dist. Ct. Colo., U.S. Dist. Ct. (we. dist.) Okla., U.S. Ct. Appeals (3d, 4th, 5th, 6th, 7th, 8th, 9th, 10th and 11th cirs.), U.S. Supreme Ct. Atty. El Paso (Tex.) Natural Gas Co., 1979-96; assoc. Law Office Gary Hill, El Paso, 1996—. Mem. Nat. Assn. Criminal Def. Lawyers, Tex. Criminal Def. Lawyers Assn., N.Mex. Assn. Criminal Def. Lawyers. Criminal. Office: Law Office of Gary Hill 1014 N Mesa St Ste 300 El Paso TX 79902-4008

**WRIGHT, VERONICA GIEL,** lawyer; b. Fresno, Calif., Feb. 28, 1955; d. James Cletus Giel and Constance (Steffl) Bittner; m. Raymond Alan Wright, May 3, 1980; children: Virginia Amy, Elizabeth Alana. BA in History, Duquesne U., Pitts., 1976, JD, 1979. Bar: Pa. 1979, U.S. Dist. Ct. (we. dist.) Pa. 1979. Atty. Neighborhood Legal Svcs. Assn., Butler, Pa., 1980—. Bd. dirs. Connoquenessing Valley Elem. Sch. PTO, Zelienople, Pa., 1992-97; leader Girl Scouts, Zelienople, 1994-96. Recipient Pub. Edn. award Pa. Youth Edn. Assn., Zelienople, 1992. Mem. Butler County Bar Assn. Democrat. Roman Catholic. Avocations: gardening, travel. Pension, profit-sharing, and employee benefits, Family and matrimonial. Home: 401 Ziegler Ct Zelienople PA 16063-9717 Office: Neighborhood Legal Svcs 220 S Main St Ste 301 Butler PA 16001-5973

**WRIGHT, WALTER AUGUSTINE, III,** business and corporate lawyer; b. Newton, Mass., Feb. 9, 1957; s. Walter A. Jr. and Charlotte T. (Doucette) W.; m. Elizabeth A. Heger, July 4, 1981; children: John Walter, Gregory, Charlotte, Sarah. BA magna cum laude, Tufts U., 1979, MA in Polit. Sci., 1980; JD magna cum laude, Boston Coll., Newton, 1983. Bar: Mass. 1983, U.S. Dist. Ct. Mass. 1983, U.S. Ct. Appeals (1st cir.) 1983. Owner, mgr. Wright Contracting, Needham, Mass., 1976-81; dir. corp. rels. Gen. Scis. Corp., Needham, 1979-81; assoc. Rich May Bilodeau & Flaherty, P.C., Boston, 1983-90, shareholder, v.p., 1990—, mng. dir., 1998—; chmn. bd. Alberca, Inc., Boston, 1992-93; chmn., pres. MapleCrest Group, Inc., Needham Heights, Mass., 1993—; mng. gen. ptnr. MapleCrest Fund I, Boston, MapleCrest Fund II, Boston; sec. e data resources, inc., Bioshelters, Inc., 1996-98, Environ. Data Resources, Inc., EDR Sanborn, Inc., eData Svcs. Corp., Sanborn Map Co., Inc., Strategis Group, Inc., Strategis Fin. Cons., Inc.; asst. sec. EV Environ., Inc., 1991-95, SRR Solutions, Inc., 1996, Hunter Environ. Svcs., Inc., 1988-91, Weber Group, Inc., Thunder House, Inc., Weber Europe, Ltd.; sec. JTECH Comms., Inc.; cons., investor numerous start-up cos.; mem. IGI, LLC, 1966—; mem. Stonybrook Group I LLC, 1997—. Sec., mem. State Adv. Com. for Spl. Edn.; advisor Mass. Dept. Edn., Boston, 1974-76; mem. Needham Sch. Com., 1978-81; mem. Needham Dem. Town Com.; bd. dirs. Needham Little League, 1993-96; founder, dir. Rookie League, 1993—, Farm League; pastoral coun. St. Bartholomew, 1991-94; dir. Needham Baseball, 1993—; cons. numerous polit. campaigns. Named Exch. Club New England Youth of Yr., 1975; recipient award for dedicated svc. Needham Sch. Com., 1981; honors scholar Tufts U., 1974-80, Adelman scholar, Boston Coll. Law Sch., 1982. Mem. ABA (bus. law sect.), Mass. Bar Assn., Assn. for Corp. Growth, Boston Coll. Club (founding mem.). Roman Catholic. Avocations: venture capital/investment banking, public speaking, political and business consulting, baseball, family. General corporate, Finance, Mergers and acquisitions. Home: 121 Thornton Rd Needham MA 02492-4354 Office: Rich May Bilodeau & Flaherty 294 Washington St Ste 1100 Boston MA 02108-4675

**WRIGHT, WILLIAM EVERARD, JR.,** lawyer; b. New Orleans, Dec. 4, 1949; s. William E. and Claire (Carter) W.; m. Alice Marquez, May 26, 1972; children: Matthew, Caroline. BA, Tulane U., 1971, JD, 1974. Bar: La. 1974. Assoc. Little, Schwartz & Dussom, New Orleans, 1974-76; ptnr. Baldwin & Haspel, New Orleans, 1976-91, Deutsch, Kerrigan & Stiles, New Orleans, 1991—. Mem. La. Bd. Examiners, 1981-84. Mem. ABA (chmn. profl., officers' and dirs. liability law com. 1997-98, constrn. forum), Associated Builders and Contractors (bd. dirs.), La. Bar Assn. (bd. dels. 1985—), New Orleans Bar Assn. (exec. com. 1980-86, officer 1983-86), New Orleans C. of C. Construction, General civil litigation, Professional liability. Home: 700 Eleonore St New Orleans LA 70115-3249 Office: Deutsch Kerrigan & Stiles 755 Magazine St Ste 100 New Orleans LA 70130-3672

**WRIGHT, WYNDELL JOHN,** lawyer; b. N.Y.C., Aug. 30, 1961; s. Jethro Henry and Sylvia (Hillsman) W.; children: Danielle Loraine, Grant Daniel. BA in Econs., U. So. Calif., 1983; JD, Harvard U., 1986. Bar: Calif. 1986. Assoc. Finley, Kumble, L.A., 1986-87, Allen, Matkins et al, L.A., 1987-92; ptnr. Dickson & Wright, L.A., 1992-94; assoc. Ochoa & Sillas, L.A., 1994-95; mng. ptnr. Bedia Murphy & Wright, L.A., 1995-97; prin. W.J. Wright & Assocs., L.A., 1997-98; ptnr. Wright & Mousseau, L.A., 1998—. Exec. dir. Save Our Communities, L.A., 1996—; bd. dirs. West Angeles Cmty. Devel. Corp. Mem. State Bar Calif., Phi Beta Kappa. Real property, Sports, General civil litigation. Office: 3435 Wilshire Blvd Ste 2700 Los Angeles CA 90010-2013

**WROBETZ, DONALD REAY,** lawyer; b. Lewistown, Mont., Apr. 23, 1955; s. Lawrence Stanley and Irene Martha (English) W.; m. Priscilla Ann Eaton, Aug. 26, 1978; children: Kyle Ryan, Kevin Reay, Anne Victoria. BS in Math., Mont. State U., 1978; JD, U. Wyo., 1987. Bar: Wyo. 1987, Colo. 1989, U.S. Dist. Ct. Wyo. 1987, U.S. Dist. Ct. Colo. 1989, U.S. Tax Ct. 1987. Intern Campbell County Atty.'s Office, Gillette, Wyo., 1986; docket atty. Office of Chief Counsel-IRS, Denver, 1987-91, spl. asst. U.S. atty., 1988-91; asst. U.S. atty. U.S. Atty.'s Office, Cheyenne, Wyo., 1991-97; pvt. practice Cheyenne, 1997—. Recipient Bus. Orgn. award Am. Juris Prudence, 1986, 87. Mem. ABA, Wyo. State Bar Assn., Laramie County Bar Assn., Pi Mu Epsilon. Methodist. Avocations: gardening, computers. Bankruptcy, Corporate taxation, Probate. Office: 1603 Capitol Ave Ste 401 Cheyenne WY 82001-4562

**WROBLE, ARTHUR GERARD,** lawyer; b. Taylor, Pa., Jan. 21, 1948; s. Arthur S. and Sophia P. Wroble; m. Mary Ellen Sheehan, Nov. 19, 1977; children: Sophia Ann, Sarah Jean, Stacey Margaret. BSBA with honors, U. fla., 1970, MBA, 1971, JD, 1973. Bar: Fla. 1973, U.S. Ct. Appeals (5th cir.) 1974, U.S. Ct. Appeals (11th cir.) 1981, U.S. Dist. Ct. (so. dist.) Fla. 1974, U.S. Dist. Ct. (mid. dist.) 1982, U.S. Dist. Ct. (no. dist.) Fla. 1986, U.S. Army Ct. Mil. Rev. 1989, U.S. Ct. Mil. Appeals 1990, U.S. Supreme Ct. 1976. Ptnr. Burns, Middleton, Farrell & Faust (now Steel, Hector, Davis, Burns & Middleton), Palm Beach, Fla., 1973-82, Wolf, Block, Schorr & Solis, Cohen, Phila. & West Palm Beach, 1982-87, Scott, Royce, Harris & Bryan, P.A., Palm Beach, 1987-89, Grantham and Wroble, P.A., Lake Worth, 1989-92; prin. Arthur G. Wroble, P.A., West Palm Beach, 1992—; mem. 15th Jud. Cir. Ct. Nominating Commn., 1979-83; mem. U. Fla. Law Ctr. Council, 1981-84, U.S. Magistrate Merit Selection Panel, so. dist. Fla., 1987; mem. adv. bd. alternative sentencing program Palm Beach County Pub. Defender's Office; adj. instr. bus. law Coll. of Boca Raton (now Lynn U.), 1988. Contbr. to profl. jours. Bd. dirs. Palm Glades Girl Scout Coun., 1996—. Served to lt. col. JAG, USAR. Named Eagle Scout, Boy Scouts Am., 1962. Mem. ABA, Fla. Bar (bd. govs. young lawyers sect. 1979-83, bd. govs. 1985-89), Palm Beach County Bar Assn. (pres. young lawyers sect. 1978-79, bd. dirs. 1979-81, sec.-treas. 1981-83, pres. 1984-85), Fla. Bar Found. (bd. dirs. 1990-93), Fla. Assn. Women Lawyers, Fla. Coun. Bar Assn. Pres. (bd. dirs. 1986-92), Guild Cath. Lawyers Diocese Palm Beach, Inc. (pres. 1980-81, bd. dirs. 1981—, Monsignor Jeremiah P. O'Mahoney Outstanding Lawyer award 1993), Legal Aid Soc. Palm Beach County, Inc. (bd. dirs. 1981—), Univ. Fla. Alumni Assn., Palm Beach County Club (pres. 1983-84), Kiwanis (pres. 1980-81, pres. West Palm Beach found. 1989—, dir. 1991—, Citizen of Yr. 1994), KC (grand knight 1978-79). Roman Catholic. General civil litigation, Probate, Real property. Home: 7645 Clarke Rd West Palm Beach FL 33406-8709 Office: 1615 Forum Pl Ste 500 West Palm Beach FL 33401-2318

**WROBLESKI, JEANNE PAULINE,** lawyer; b. Phila., Feb. 14, 1942; d. Edward Joseph and Pauline (Popelak) W.; m. Robert J. Klein, Dec. 3, 1979. BA, Immaculata Coll., 1964; MA, U. Pa., 1966; JD, Temple U., 1975. Bar: Pa. 1975. Pvt. practice law Phila., 1975—; pres. Jeanne Wrobleski & Assocs., LLC, Phila., 1999—; lectr. on bus. law Wharton Sch., Phila. Mem. Commn. on Women and the Legal Profession, 1986-89; v.p. Center City Residents' Assn. Eisenhower Citizen Amb. del. to Soviet Union. Bd. dirs. South St. Dance Co., Women in Transition; bd. dirs., mem. exec. com. Temple Law Alumni; del. to Moscow Conf. on Law and Econ. Coop., 1990; del. to jud. conf. 3d Cir. U.S. Ct. Appeals, 1991; mediator U.S. Dist. Ct. (ea. dist.) Pa., 1996. Rhea Liebman scholar, 1974. Mem. AAUW, ABA, Pa. Bar Assn., Phila. Bar Assn. (chmn. women's rights com. 1986, com. on jud. selection and retention, 1986-87, chmn. appellate cts. com. 1992, bus. cts. task force, com. on bus. litigation), Pa. Acad. Fine Arts, Nat. Mus. Women in the Arts, Am. Judicature Soc., Jagiellonian Law Soc., Lawyers Club, Founders Club, The Cosmopolitan Club, Penn Club, Alpha Psi Omega, Lambda Iota Tau. Democrat. Federal civil litigation, General civil litigation. Office: Jeanne Wrobleski & Assocs LLC Ste 202 2103 Locust St Philadelphia PA 19103-4802

**WROBLEY, RALPH GENE,** lawyer; b. Denver, Sept. 19, 1935; s. Matthew B. and Hedvig (Lyon) W.; m. Madeline C. Kearney, June 13, 1959; children: Kirk Lyon, Eric Lyon, Ann Lyon. BA, Yale U., 1957; JD, U. Chgo., 1962. Bar: Mo. 1962. With Bell Telephone Co., Phila., 1957-59; assoc. Stinson, Mag & Fizzell, Kansas City, Mo., 1962-65, mem. 1965-88; ptnr. Bryan, Cave, McPheeters & McRoberts, Kansas City, 1988-92; (ptnr., exec. com. Blackwell, Sanders, Peper, Martin LLP, 1992—. Bd. dirs. Human Resources Corp., 1971; mem. Civic Coun. Kansas City, 1986—; chmn. Pub. Housing Authority of Kansas City, 1971-74; vice chmn. Mayor's Adv. Commn. on Housing, Kansas City, 1971-74; bd. govs. Citizens Assn., 1965—, vice chmn., 1971-75, chmn., 1978-79; bd. dirs. Coun. on Edn., 1975-81, v.p., 1977-79; bd. dirs., pres. Sam E. and Mary F. Roberts Found., 1974-96; trustee Clearinghouse for Mid Continent Founds., 1977-96, chmn. 1987-89; bd. dirs. Bus. Innovation Ctr., 1984-91, vice-chmn. 1987-91, adv. bd. dirs., 1993—, Midwest Regional Adv. Bd. Inst. Internat. Edn., 1989-93, Internat. Trade Assn., 1989-92, v.p., 1990; former chmn. bd. dir. Mid-Am. Coalition on Healthcare, 1991-95. Mem. Mo. Bar Assn. Republican. Presbyterian (elder). Club: Yale (pres. 1969-71, outstanding mem. award 1967). Mergers and acquisitions, General corporate, Private international. Home: 1015 W 67th Ter Kansas City MO 64113-1942 Office: 2300 Main St Kansas City MO 64108-2416

**WROTEN, WALTER THOMAS,** lawyer; b. Stockton, Calif., Dec. 29, 1950; s. Walter Thomas Wroten and Ellen Amelia (Richards) Israel; m. Georgia Ann Sowers, Jan. 21, 1979 (div. Nov. 1988); m. Mary Alice Ficek, Aug. 1995. AA, Am. River Coll., 1974; BA, U. Calif., Berkeley, 1976; JD, U. No. Calif., 1988. Bar: Calif. 1991, U.S. Dist. Ct. (ea. dist.) Calif. 1991. Pres., CEO Wroten Internat., Sacramento, 1976-83; assoc. Law Office Dan Sullivan, Sacramento, 1991-92; pvt. practice Sacramento, 1992—. Mem. ABA, Am. Trial Lawyers Assn., Calif. Trial Lawyers Assn., Capitol City Trial Lawyers Assn., Sacramento County Bar Assn., San Joaquin County Bar Assn. Democrat. General civil litigation, Personal injury. Office: 901 H St Ste 200 Sacramento CA 95814-1808

**WU, JIMMY C.J.,** lawyer; b. Taipei, Taiwan, Sept. 30, 1962; came to U.S., 1977; s. Allen C.I. and Linda T.Z. Wu. BS, Calif. State U., Hayward, 1989; JD, U. Oreg., 1989; LLM, NYU, 1991. Taxation assoc. Satterlee Stephens Burke & Burke, N.Y.C., 1991-92; internat. assoc. The Justice Firm, Taipei, 1993-94; ct. atty. N.Y. State Supreme Ct., N.Y.C., 1994-97; sole practitioner N.Y.C., 1997—. Mem. Law Rev., U. Oreg. Mem. legal com. San Francisco-Shanghai Sister City Com., 1993-94; mem. DL21, N.Y.C., 1998—. Drerick Bell scholar, 1996; recipient Outstanding Pro Bono and Pub. Svc. N.Y. County Lawyer Assn., 1998. Mem. Rotary Club. Avocations: skiing, golf, rollerblading, rafting. Office: 401 Broadway Fl 25 New York NY 10013-3005 also: 148 Tun-An Rd 7A-3, Taipei Taiwan

**WU, NIPING,** lawyer; b. Shanghai, People's Republic of China, Jan. 2, 1971; came to U.S., 1990; d. Xingkang W.; m. Jing Yan, Aug. 8, 1997. BS summa cum laude, Yale U., 1994, JD, 1997. Bar: N.Y. 1998. Assoc. Cleary, Gottlieb, Steen & Hamilton, N.Y.C., 1997—. Olin fellow Yale U., 1995. Mem. Bar Assn. N.Y.C., Phi Beta Kappa, Tau Beta Pi. Avocations: traveling, watching movies, reading novels. General corporate. Office: Cleary Gottlieb Steen & Hamilton One Liberty Plz New York NY 10006

**WU, ROBIN CHI CHING,** lawyer; b. Guangxi, People's Republic of China, Jan. 6, 1941; came to U.S., 1955; s. Paul S.C. and Janny S.F. (Wong) W. BA, Fordham U., 1964; MA, Columbia U., 1967; LLD, N.Y. Law Sch., 1983. Bar: N.Y. 1983, N.J. 1984. Asst. libr. Fed. Res. Bank N.Y., N.Y.C., 1967-68; asst. dir. rsch. Nat. Rev. mag., N.Y.C., 1968-72, dir. rsch., 1972-79; dir. rsch. TV program Firing Line, N.Y.C., 1972-79; pvt. practice N.Y.C., 1983—. Editor Bridge, 1972, Asian-Am. jour. Mem. N.Y. State Bar Assn., N.Y. County Lawyers Assn., N.J. State Bar Assn. Avocations: reading, writing, movies. General practice, Real property, Contracts commercial. Office: 8 Chatham Sq New York NY 10038-1000

**WU, WILLIAM,** lawyer, dentist; b. Hong Kong, Nov. 29, 1952; s. Hou-I and Mei Ching (Chen) W.; m. Lucia Chiang, Aug. 3, 1980; children: Winona, Eunice, Malinda. BA magna cum laude, SUNY, Buffalo, 1975; DDS, Temple U., 1979, JD cum laude, 1992. Bar: Pa. 1992, N.J. 1993. Pvt. practice dentistry, Phila., 1979—; pvt. practice law, Bryn Mawr, Pa., 1992—. Mem. editl. adv. bd. Dental Econs., 1988-89; contbr. articles to legal and dental jours. Bd. dirs. Asian Am. Coun. Greater Phila., 1980-82, United Comtys. S.W. Phila., 1984-89, Phila. Chinatown Devel. Corp., 1985-89, On-Lok House, residence for elderly, 1986—; mem. adv. bd. Fellowship Commn., Phila., 1981-84; trustee United Way Southeastern Pa., 1987-90; pres. Chinese Benevolent Assn. Greater Phila., 1985—. Health, Professional liability, Contracts commercial. Office: 131 N 9th St Philadelphia PA 19107-2410

**WU, YOLANDA SUNG,** lawyer; b. Radford, Va., June 3, 1967; d. Fa Yueh and Jane C.T. Wu; m. Neil Evan Platt, Oct. 18, 1997. AB, Princeton U., 1989; JD, UCLA, 1994. Bar: N.Y. 1995, U.S. Dist. Ct. (so., ea. and no. dists.) N.Y., U.S. Ct. Appeals (3d, 5th and 10th cirs.), U.S. Supreme Ct. 1998. Staff atty. NOW Legal Def. and Edn. Fund, N.Y.C., 1994—. Mem. ABA, N.Y.C. Bar Assn. (civil rights com. 1997—), Nat. Employment Lawyers Assn., Nat. Coalition for Sex Equity in Edn. Appellate, Civil rights. Office: NOW Legal Def and Edn Fund 395 Hudson St New York NY 10014-3669

**WUKITSCH, DAVID JOHN,** lawyer; b. Schenectady, N.Y., June 7, 1955; s. Julius and Laura (Isabel) W. BA, SUNY, Albany, 1977; MA, Sch. Criminal Justice, 1978; JD, Union U., 1981. Bar: N.Y. 1982, U.S. Dist. Ct. (no. dist. ) N.Y. 1982, U.S. Ct. Appeals (2d cir.) 1986, U.S. Supreme Ct. 1994, U.S. Ct. Appeals (11th cir.) 1999. Law assistant Appellate divsn. N.Y. Supreme Ct., Albany, 1981-83; law clk. to assoc. judge N.Y. Ct. Appeals, Albany, 1983-85; assoc. McNamee, Lochner, Titus & Willaims P.C., Albany, 1985-91, ptnr., 1991—; cons. Police Found., Washington, 1980-81; atty. Town of New Baltimore, N.Y. Author Albany Law Jour. Law and Tech., 1999. Mem. ABA (mem. labor, employement sect.), N.Y. State Bar Assn., Justinian Soc. Republican. Roman Catholic. Labor, Federal civil litigation, Criminal. Office: McNamee Lochner Titus & Williams PC 75 State St Apt 459 Albany NY 12207-2526

**WUKOVICH, GEORGE NICHOLAS,** lawyer; b. Cin., Dec. 29, 1958; s. Nick and Florence M. Wukovich. BA, Miami U., 1982; JD, Case Western Res. U., 1985. Bar: Ohio 1985, U.S. Dist. Ct. (no. dist.) Ohio 1985, U.S. Ct. Appeals (6th cir.) 1986. Locator Chgo. Title Ins. Co., Cleve., 1983; legal intern Weaver, Kolick, Georgeadis & Ernewein Co., LPA, Cleve., 1983-85, Silver & Assocs. Co., LPA, Cleve., 1985; assoc. J. Norman Stark Co., LPA, Cleve., 1985-86, Julian Kahan & Assocs. Co., LPA, Cleve., 1986-97; sole practice Cleve., 1998—. General civil litigation, Personal injury, Criminal. Home and Office: 20312 Lorain Rd Ste 309 Cleveland OH 44126-3472

**WULF, WILLIAM ARTHUR,** lawyer; b. Mpls., Apr. 11, 1945; s. Robert W. and Margaret A. (Rogers) W.; m. Kathleen D. Inzeo, Jan. 4, 1969; children: Robert, Amy, Paula, Maureen. BS in History, U. Wis., 1967; JD, Marquette U., 1971. Bar: Wis. 1971, U.S. Dist. Ct. (we. dist.) Wis. 1971, U.S. Dist. Ct. (ea. dist.) Wis. 1994. Part-time city atty. City of Merrill, 1971-75; assoc. Sazama & Wulf, S.C., Merrill, 1971-79; pvt. practice Merrill, 1979-83; ptnr. Ament, Wulf & Frokjer S.C., Merrill, 1983—; cert. trial specialist Nat. Bd. Trial Advocacy. Past chmn. United Way; bd. dirs. local hosp. found. fund. With USNG, 1969-75. Mem. Nat. Orgn. Social Security Reps., State Bar Wis., Lincoln County Bar Assn. (past sec.-treas., v.p., pres.), Optimists, KC. Roman Catholic. Avocations: skiing, sailing, golf. Personal injury, Workers' compensation, Pension, profit-sharing, and employee benefits. Office: Ament Wulf & Frokjer SC PO Box 626 Merrill WI 54452-0626

**WULFF, ROBERT JOSEPH,** lawyer; b. St. Louis, Aug. 27, 1961. BSEE, U. Mo., Columbia, 1983; JD cum laude, St. Louis U., 1986. Bar: Mo. 1986, U.S. Dist. Ct. (ea. dist.) Mo. 1986, U.S. Ct. Appeals (8th cir.) 1986, Ill. 1987, U.S. Supreme Ct. 1990. Shareholder Amelung, Wulff & Willenbrock, P.C., St. Louis, 1986—. Mem. Mo. Orgn. Def. Lawyers, Bar Assn. Met. St. Louis, Phi Alpha Delta. Insurance, General civil litigation, Product liability. Office: Amelung Wulff & Willenbrock PC 515 Olive St Ste 17 Saint Louis MO 63101-1849

**WUNDER, DAVID HART,** lawyer; b. Argo, Ill., Dec. 6, 1925; s. Mylton Bowerman and Marian Antoinette (Richcreek) W.; m. Shirley May Dahlin, June 10, 1950 (dec. Oct. 1974); children: Rebecca Anne, David Hart II. BA, Wabash Coll., Crawfordsville, Ind., 1950; JD, ITT-Chgo. Kent Coll. Law, 1962. Bar: Ind., U.S. Dist. Ct. (no. and so. dists.) 1985, U.S. Supreme Ct. 1974. Enforcement atty., officer, mgr. Ill. Sec. of State, Chgo., 1963-72; securities commr. Ill. Sec. of State, Springfield, 1972-84; ptnr. Wunder and Wunder, Indpls., 1985—. Sgt. U.S. Army, 1944-46, PTO. Mem. Am. Legion (dist. comdr. 1972), SAR, Soc. Mayflower Descs. Avocations: reading, exercise sports. Bankruptcy, Family and matrimonial, Consumer commercial. Home: 40 W Thompson Rd Indianapolis IN 46217-3558 Office: Wunder and Wunder 4949 Carson Ave # F Indianapolis IN 46227-6603

**WUNSCH, JOHN CARLYLE,** lawyer; b. Chgo., July 30, 1956; s. John K. and Ruth M. (Bennett) W.; m. Mee Ryung Kim, Oct. 1, 1983; children: Justin, Tiffany, Brittany. AB, U. Mich., 1978; JD, DePaul U., 1982. Bar: Ill. 1982, U.S. Dist. Ct. (no. dist.) Ill. 1983, U.S. Ct. Appeals (7th cir.) 1985, U.S. Supreme Ct. 1987. Sr. ptnr. John C. Wunsch, P.C., Chgo., 1985—. Contbr. articles to profl. publs. Mem. ABA, Fed. Bar Assn., Assn. Trial Lawyers Am., Ill. State Bar Assn., Ill. Trial Lawyers Assn., Chgo. Bar Assn. Personal injury, Product liability. Office: 77 W Washington St Ste 1420 Chicago IL 60602-2902

**WUNSCH, KATHRYN SUTHERLAND,** lawyer; b. Tipton, Mo., Jan. 30, 1935; d. Lewis Benjamin and Norene Marie (Wolf) Sutherland; m. Charles Martin Wunsch, Dec. 22, 1956 (div. May 1988); children: Debra Kay, Laura Ellen. AB, Ind. U., 1958, JD summa cum laude, 1977; postgrad., Stanford (Calif.) U., 1977. Bar: Calif. 1977, U.S. Dist. Ct. (no. dist.) Calif. 1977. Founder Wunsch and George, San Francisco, 1989-93, Kathryn Wunsch and Assoc. Counsel, San Francisco, 1993—. Articles editor Ind. U. Law Rev., 1975-76. Mem. ABA, Calif. Bar Assn. (bus. law prof., real property and trusts sect.), San Mateo County Bar Assn., Nat. Assn. Women Bus. Owners (pres. San Francisco chpt. 1992-93), San Francisco Opera Guild, City Club, Phi Beta Kappa (v.p. no. calif. 1995—), Psi Chi. Republican. Avocations: collecting fine art and antiques, theater, opera, gardening, hiking. General corporate, Probate, Real property. Office: Ste 3320 701 Welch Rd Bldg 3320 Palo Alto CA 94304-1705

**WYATT, DEBORAH CHASEN,** lawyer; b. Atlanta, Apr. 19, 1949; d. S.H. and Catherine Jane (Hudlow) Chasen; m. Richard Haste Wyatt, Jr., Feb. 19, 1972; children: Thomas Clayton, William Tyler. Student, Sweet Briar Col., 1968-70; BA, Tufts U., 1971; JD, U. Va., 1978. Bar: Va. 1978, U.S. Dist. Ct. (we. and ea. dists.) Va. 1978, U.S. Ct. Appeals (4th cir.) 1980, U.S. Ct. Appeals (D.C. cir.) 1984, U.S. Supreme Ct. 1983. Assoc. Lowe & Gordon, Charlottesville, Va., 1978-80; partner Wyatt & Rosenfield, Charlottesville, Va., 1980-83, Gordon & Wyatt, Charlottesville, Va., 1984-92, Wyatt & Carter, Charlottesville, Va., 1993—. Mem. ATLA, Va. Coll. Criminal Def. Attys. (bd. dirs. 1997—), Charlottesville-Albemarle Criminal Bar Assn., Charlottesville Bar Assn. Avocations: writing, painting. Criminal, Civil rights, Personal injury. Office: Wyatt and Carter 300 Court Sq Charlottesville VA 22902-5160

**WYATT, JAMES FRANK, III,** lawyer; b. Evanston, Ill., Mar. 19, 1958; s. James Frank Jr. and Rosemary (Slone) W.; m. Edna Wyatt, Oct. 25, 1995; 1 child, Daniel. BS, Vanderbilt U., 1979; JD, Duke U., 1982. Bar: N.C. 1986, U.S. Dist. Ct. (we., mid. and ea. dists.) N.C. 1986, U.S. Ct. Appeals (4th cir.) 1986, Ga. 1983. Clk. to Judge Harold Murphy U.S. Dist. Ct., Rome, Ga., 1982-84; assoc. Cook & Palmour, Summerville, Ga., 1984-86; pvt. practice, Charlotte, N.C., 1986—; mem. Fed. Bar Adv. Coun., N.C., 1996—; spkr. numerous profl. meetings, 1986—. Contbr. numerous articles to law jours. Mem. spkrs.' com. Charlotte Habitat for Humanity, 1991-93; bd. dirs. Davidson (N.C.) Habitat for Humanity, 1992-95. Mem. N.C. Acad. Trial Lawyers (pres. criminal law sect. 1994-95, bd. govs. 1996—). Avocations: cycling, reading, gardening, travel. Criminal, General civil litigation, Personal injury. Office: 435 E Morehead St Charlotte NC 28202-2609

**WYATT, JOHN BRUNDIGE, III,** lawyer, educator; b. Marion, Ohio, Aug. 27, 1953; s. John Brundige Jr. and Mary Elizabeth (Lodwig) W.; children: John Brundige IV, Jacqueline Eva-Marie. Student, U. Madrid, 1974; BA, Findlay Coll., 1975; JD, U. Dayton, Ohio, 1978. Bar: Ohio 1978, U.S. Dist. Ct. (so. dist.) Ohio 1978, U.S. Supreme Ct. 1984, U.S. Ct. Claims 1985, U.S. Ct. Appeals (Fed. cir.) 1988. Staff atty. Dayton Power & Light Co., 1978-82; sr. staff atty. Mead Data Cen. Co., Dayton, 1982-84; pvt. practice Dayton, 1984-90; prof. fin., real estate and law Calif. State Poly. U., Pomona, 1990—; prof. govt. contract law and contract mgmt. Sch. Systems and Logistics, Air Force Inst. Tech., Wright-Patterson AFB, Ohio, 1985-90; adj. prof. govt. contract law Ind. U.-Purdue U., Indpls., 1987-98; adj. asst. prof. bus. law Wright State U., Dayton, 1988-90. Co-author: Government Contract Law, 1986; assoc. editor Govt. Contract Law, 1987, 88. Fellow Nat. Contract Mgmt. Assn.; Outstanding Fellow Natl. Contract Mgmt. Assn., 1994, Natl. Vice Pres., 1998-99, Natl. Contract Mgmt. Assn., mem. ABA, Fed. Bar Assn. (mem. govt. contracts com. 1985-90), Nat. Contract Mgmt. Assn., Nat. Property Mgmt. Assn., Am. Bus. Law Assn., Nat. Property Mgmt. Assn., Am. Bus. Law Assn. (peer reviewer Am. Bus. Law Jour.). Government contracts and claims, Administrative and regulatory, Contracts commercial. Office: Calif State Poly U Dept FRL 3801 W Temple Ave Dept Frl Pomona CA 91768-2557

**WYATT, ROBERT DAVID,** lawyer; b. Palo Alto, Calif., May 25, 1940; s. Francis D. and Dorothy (King) W.; m. Diane Marcia Lomas, Aug. 3, 1963; children: Daniel Adam, Susanna Grace. BA, San Francisco State U., 1964; MA, U. Oreg., 1968, PhD, 1969; JD, U. Calif., Berkeley, 1975. Lectr. dept. English, U. Oreg., Eugene, 1966-69; asst. prof. lit. Drexel U., Phila., 1969-72; ptnr. Bohn & Wyatt, Benicia, Calif.,, also Guam, 1975-79; dept. regional counsel U.S. EPA, San Francisco, 1979-84; spl. counsel Castle & Cooke, Inc., San Francisco, 1984-85; ptnr. Brobeck, Phleger & Harrison, San Francisco, 1986-91, Beveridge & Diamond, San Francisco, 1991—. Mem. ABA, Calif. Bar Assn., D.C. Bar Assn., Guam Bar Assn., Commonwealth of No. Marianas Bar Assn. Environmental. Office: Beveridge & Diamond LLP One Sansome St # 3400 San Francisco CA 94104

**WYATT, ROBERT LEE, IV,** lawyer; b. Las Cruces, N.Mex., Mar. 9, 1964; s. Robert Lee III and Louise Carole (Bard) W.; m. Vicki Harris Wyatt. BS, Southeastern Okla. State U., 1986; JD, U. Okla., 1989. Bar: Okla. 1989, U.S. Dist. Ct. (we. dist.) Okla. 1990, U.S. Ct. Appeals (10th cir.) 1990, U.S. Dist. Ct. (no. dist.) Okla. 1991, U.S. Ct. Appeals (8th cir.) 1991, U.S. Supreme Ct. 1993. Intern Okla. State Bur. Investigation, Oklahoma City, 1988-89, guest lectr., 1989; dep. spl. counsel Gov. of Okla., 1995; atty. Jones & Wyatt, Enid, Okla., 1989—. counsel to Fire Civil Svc. Commn. City of Enid, 1998. Mem. ABA (mem. criminal & litigation sects.), Okla. Bar Assn. (mem. ins., family sect.), Garfield County Bar Assn., Okla. Criminal Def. Lawyers Assn., Nat. Inst. for Trial Advocacy, Nat. Assn. Criminal Defense Lawyers, Phi Delta Phi, Alpha Chi. Democrat. Baptist. Criminal, General civil litigation, Insurance. Home: 2430 Sherwood Dr Enid OK 73703-1512 Office: Jones & Wyatt 114 E Broadway Ave Enid OK 73701-4126

**WYATT, THOMAS CSABA,** lawyer; b. Toronto, Ont., Can., Mar. 19, 1952; came to U.S., 1979; s. Charles Wojatsek and Marietta Marcinkova; m. Helen A. Johnson, Dec. 24, 1979; children: J.P. Max, Stephen M. BA, Bishop's U., 1975; BCL, Mcgill U., 1974; JD, U. San Francisco, 1981; LLM, U. Montreal, 1980. Bar: Que. 1975, Calif. 1982, U.S. Dist. Ct. (no. dist.) Calif. 1982, U.S. Ct. Appeals (9th cir.) 1982. Assoc. counsel Can. Gen. Electric, Montreal, 1975-77; solicitor Du Pont Can., Inc., Montreal, 1977-79; internat. counsel Computerland Corp., Oakland, Calif., 1982-85; sr. counsel Bank of Am., San Francisco, 1985-87, Intel Corp., Santa Clara, Calif., 1987-90; gen. counsel Philips Semiconductors, Sunnyvale, Calif., 1990—; chmn. Flex Force Network Inc., San Francisco, 1996-98; arbitrator Am. Arbitration Assn., San Francisco, 1985—. Mem. Silicon Valley Assn. of Gen. Counsel (chmn. 1998—), Knightly Order of Vitez. Roman Catholic. Avocations: tennis, adventure travel. Contracts commercial, Computer, Intellectual property. Office: Philips Semiconductors Inc 811 E Arques Ave Rm Ms54 Sunnyvale CA 94086-4523

**WYCHE, BRADFORD WHEELER,** lawyer; b. Greenville, S.C., Feb. 22, 1950; s. C. Thomas and Harriet Durham (Smith) W.; m. Carolyn Diane Smock, July 1, 1978; children: Charles Denby Smock, Jessica Kaye. AB in Environ. Sci., Princeton U., 1972; MS in Natural Resource Mgmt., Yale U., 1974; JD, U. Va., 1978. Bar: S.C. 1978, U.S. Dist. Ct. S.C. 1978, U.S. Ct. Appeals (4th cir.) 1978; cert. civil mediator. Ptnr. Wyche, Burgess, Freeman & Parham, Greenville, 1979—. Contbr. articles to profl. jours. Mem. S.C. Gov.'s Coun. on Natural Resources, Columbia, 1983-84, Pendleton Place, Greenville, 1984-88, S.C. Coastal Coun., 1986-95; pres. Warehouse Theatre, Greenville, 1982-83, Greenville's Symphony Assn., 1989-90; chair Greenville Cmty. Found., 1994. Mem. S.C. Bar Assn. (chmn. alternative dispute resolution sect. 1998—), Upstate Mediation Network (pres. 1996), Friends of Reedy River (pres. 1995-98). Avocations: tennis, piano, whitewater kayaking. Environmental, General corporate. Home: 312 Raven Rd Greenville SC 29615-4248 Office: Wyche Burgess Freeman & Parham PO Box 728 44 E Camperdown Way Greenville SC 29601-3591

**WYCHE, MADISON BAKER, III,** lawyer; b. Albany, Ga., Aug. 11, 1947; s. Madison Baker Jr. and Merle (McKemie) W.; m. Marguerite Jernigan Ramage, Aug. 7, 1971; children: Madison Baker IV, James Ramage. BA, Vanderbilt U., 1969, JD, 1972. Bar: Ga. 1972, U.S. Dist. Ct. (mid. dist.) Ga. 1972, U.S. Ct. Appeals (5th cir.) 1973, S.C. 1976, U.S. Dist. Ct. S.C. 1977, U.S. Ct. Appeals (4th cir.) 1977, U.S. Supreme Ct. 1980, U.S. Ct. Appeals (11th cir.) 1981, U.S. Dist. Ct. (no. dist.) Ga. 1995. Assoc. Perry, Walters, Lippitt & Custer, Albany, 1972-76, Thompson, Ogletree & Deakins, Greenville, S.C., 1976-77, Ogletree, Deakins, Smoak & Stewart, Greenville, 1977-80; ptnr. Ogletree, Deakins, Nash, Smoak & Stewart, Greenville, 1980—; bd. dirs. Happy Ho., Inc., Albany. Co-incorporator, sec. State of Tenn. Intercollegiate State Legislature, Nashville, 1967-69; state sec.-treas. Coll. Young Dems., Nashville, 1968; mem. employer and employee rels. com. N.C. Citizens for Bus. and Industry, Raleigh, 1984—; mem. United Way Greenville, vestry Christ Episcopal Ch., Greenville, 1981-85; mem. bd. visitors Clemson U., 1998—. Capt. U.S. Army, 1969-77. Recipient Eagle Scouts award Boy Scouts Am., 1961. Mem. ABA, S.C. Bar Assn. (unauthorized practice of law com. 1977-95, chmn. 1982-92, ho. of dels. 1991-98, nominating com. 1992-95, CLE divsn., chmn., 1997-98, exec. com. 1995—, chmn. seminars subcom. 1995-97), Ga. Bar Assn., Atlanta Bar Assn., Indsl. Rels. Rsch. Assn., S.C. Def. Trial Lawyers Assn., St. Andrews Soc. Upper S.C. (bd. dirs. 1979-81, v.p. 1986-87, pres. 1988-90), Palmetto Soc. (bd. dirs.), Vanderbilt U. Alumni Assn. (pres. S.C. chpt. 1990-95, bd. dirs. 1994—), Rotary (bd. dirs. 1982-84, Paul Harris fellow 1986), Commerce Club of Greenville (bd. dirs. 1990—), Phi Delta Phi. Labor, Environmental, General civil litigation. Office: Ogletree Deakins Nash Smoak & Stewart PO Box 2757 Greenville SC 29602-2757

**WYCKOFF, E. LISK, JR.,** lawyer; b. Middletown, N.J., Jan. 29, 1934; m. Elizabeth Ann Kuphal; children: Jenny Adele, Edward Lisk III, Elizabeth Hannah Longstreet. BA, Duke U., 1955; JD, U. Mich., 1960. Bar: N.Y. 1961, U.S. Dist. Ct. (so. and ea. dists.) N.Y. 1962, U.S. Ct. Appeals (2d cir. 1963), U.S. Tax Ct. 1974. Ptnr. Kramer, Levin, N.Y.C.; lectr. Practising Law Inst., 1970—, World Trade Inst., various profl. and bus. orgns. in U.S. and abroad; spl. counsel N.Y. Bankers Assn., 1974-98; counsel N.Y. State Senate Com. Housing and Urban Renewal, 1969-71, N.Y. State Senate Com. Judiciary, 1963-64, Com. Affairs of the City of N.Y., 1962; mem. N.Y.C. Mayor's Taxi Study Commn., 1967. Directing editor, commentator West's McKinney's Forms on Estates and Trusts, 1974—; mng. editor, 1999; commentator McKinney's Not-For-Profit Corp. law, 1995—; contbr. articles to profl. jours. Bd. dirs. 1652 Wyckoff House and Assn., Inc., 1982—; trustee Soc. for Preservation of L.I. Antiquities, 1988—, N.Y.C. Hist. House Trust, 1993—, Inner-City Scholarship Fund., Inc. 1993—, The Bard Ctr. Bard Coll., 1994—, Goodspeed Opera Co., 1996—, Florence Gris Wold Mus., 1997—; trustee, pres. Homeland Found., 1989—; bd. advisors Wildlife Conservation Soc., 1993—; mem. Concilium Socalium to Vatican Mus., 1991—; papal hon. Knight Commr. of Order of St. Gregory The Great, 1995. Fellow Am. Coll. Trust and Estate Counsel, Am. Bar Found.; mem. ABA (chair com. on internat. property, estate and trust of law sect. real property, probate and trust law, taxation 1991—), Internat. Fiscal Assn., Internat. Bar Assn., N.Y. State Bar Assn. (exec. com. tax sect., chmn. com. income taxation estates and trusts 1976-80, com. internat. estate planning 1980—), Assn. of Bar of City of N.Y., Holland Soc., St. Nicholas Soc., Knickerbocker Club, Racquet and Tennis Club (N.Y.C.), Mashomack Fish and Game Preserve Club (Pine Plains, N.Y.), Essex Yacht Club (Conn.), N.Y. Yacht Club. Avocations: tennis, sailing. General practice, Estate taxation, Non-profit and tax-exempt organizations. Office: Kramer Levin 919 3rd Ave Rm 3802 New York NY 10022-3852

**WYCOFF, WILLIAM MORTIMER,** lawyer; b. Pitts., Jan. 1, 1941; s. William Clyde and Margaret (Shaffer) W.; m. Deborah Seyl, Jan. 25, 1963; children: Ann Richardson, Pieter Claesen. AB, Cornell U., 1963; JD, Northwestern U., 1966. Bar: Pa. 1967, U.S. Ct. Appeals (3d cir.) 1967), U.S. Dist. Ct. (we. dist.) Pa. 1967. Assoc., now ptnr. Thorp Reed and Armstrong, Pitts., 1966—, v.p., gen. counsel, 1989—. Pres. Children's Home Pitts., 1976-78, 86-88, now bd. dirs.; pres. Pressley Ridge Schs., Pitts., 1988-90, now bd. dirs.: pres. Pressley Ridge Found.; pres., bd. dirs. Pitts. Dance Coun., 1991-94; trustee Pitts. Cultural Trust, 1991-94. Fellow Am. Coll. Trial Lawyers; mem. Acad. Trial Lawyers Allegheny County. Avocations: photography, skiing, biking, hiking, golf. Antitrust, General civil litigation, Product liability. Office: Thorp Reed and Armstrong One Riverfront Ctr 20 Stanwix St Ste 900 Pittsburgh PA 15222-4895

**WYDLER, HANS ULRICH,** lawyer, banker, accountant; b. Hamburg, Germany, Nov. 11, 1923; came to U.S., 1927, naturalized, 1932; s. John Joseph and Grethe Adolfine (Heitmann) W.; m. Susan Gail Hart, Sept. 1, 1965; children: Hans Laurence, Steven Courtney. BS, Ohio State U., 1944, BME with honors, 1947; BIE with honors, 1949; MS, MIT, 1948; LLB, Harvard U., 1951. Bar: Mass. 1951; registered profl. engr. Mass. Atty., systems engr., trustee Louis J. Hunter Assocs., Boston, 1951-57; asst. v.p. Chem. Bank, N.Y.C., 1958-64; v.p. Mfrs. Nat. Bank Detroit, 1964-65; sr. v.p. Security Nat. Bank, Huntington, N.Y., 1973-74; internat. and tax atty., acct. Hans U. Wydler, N.Y.C., 1966—; dir. Volume Mdse., Inc., Buning Internat. Inc., 1977-84. With USN, 1944-46. Mem. Acad. Polit. Sci. (life), ABA, N.Y. County Lawyers Assn., ASME. General corporate, Probate, Taxation, general. Home and Office: 945 5th Ave New York NY 10021-2655

**WYLIE, GORDON FRASER,** lawyer; b. Ft. Erie, Ont., Can., Sept. 24, 1949; came to U.S., 1949; m. Ellen Andrea Schwartz, Oct. 14, 1984; children: Andrew, Eric, Rachel, Candance, Matthew. BA cum laude, SUNY, Buffalo, 1976; JD, Bklyn. Law Sch., 1983. Bar: N.Y. 1984. Assoc. Sheft, Wright & Sweeny, N.Y.C., 1983-84, Stroock & Stroock & Lavan, N.Y.C., 1993-94; counsel DW Petroleum, Atlanta, 1984-86; atty. IRS, N.Y.C., 1986-87; sr. atty. N.Y. Ins. Dept., N.Y.C., 1987-93; counsel Guardian Life Ins. Co., N.Y.C., 1994—. 2d lt. U.S. Army, 1967-74, Vietnam. Decorated Silver Star, Bronze Star with three oak leaf clusters, Purple Heart with oak leaf cluster, Air medal with V device; Cross of Gallantry (Vietnam). Mem. N.Y. State Bar Assn., Assn. Bar City N.Y. Administrative and regulatory, General civil litigation, Insurance. Office: Guardian Life Ins Co Law Dept 201 Park Ave S New York NY 10003-1699

**WYLIE, PAUL RICHTER, JR.,** lawyer; b. Dec. 25, 1936; s. Paul Richter and Alice (Dredge) W.; m. Arlene Marie Klem, Mar. 6, 1982; children: Lynne Catherine, John Michael, Thomas Robert. BSChemE, Mont. State U., 1959; JD, Am. U., 1965. Bar: Utah 1978, Calif. 1970, U.S. Supreme Ct. 1971, Mont. 1990. Patent examiner U.S. Patent and Trademark Office, Washington, 1962-64; asst. gen. patent counsel Dart Industries Inc., L.A., 1967-81; pvt. practice L.A., 1981-86, Pacific Palisades, Calif., 1986-90, Bozeman, Mont., 1990—. Mem. ABA, AIChE, Am. Intellectual Property Law Assn., L.a. Intellectual Property Law Assn., Am. Chem. Soc., Licensing Execs. Soc., Tech. Transfer Soc. Patent, Trademark and copyright, Antitrust. Home: 106 Silverwood Dr Bozeman MT 59715-9255 Office: 1805 W Dickerson St Ste 3 Bozeman MT 59715-4131

**WYLIE, WALTER JAY,** lawyer, judge; b. El Centro, Calif., July 20, 1937; s. Robert Oscar and Velda Percival W.; m. Lana Jane Langdon, Mar. 6, 1966; children: Kimberly Anne Wylie McCarthy, Robert Whitacre Wylie. BS, U.S. Naval Acad., 1961; MS, Naval Post Grad. Sch., 1974; JD, U. S.C., 1983. Bar: S.C. 1984, U.S. Dist. Ct. 1987, U.S. Supreme Ct. 1990. Various positions USN, 1961-81; asst. solicitor 15th Cir. Solicitor's Office, Conway and Georgetown, S.C., 1984-85; city atty. City of N. Myrtle Beach, S.C., 1985-86, mcpl. judge, 1993—; assoc. atty. Hudson & Sweeny, Myrtle Beach, S.C., 1986-89; prin. Law Offices Walter J. Wylie, N. Myrtle Beach, 1989—. Co-author: Vietnamese Refugees On Guam, 1976. Mem. NMB Zoning Bd. Appeals, N. Myrtle Beach, 1991-93, Carolina Bays Pky. Com., Myrtle Beach, 1992—. Decorated Bronze Star. Mem. S.C. Bar Assn., Horry County Bar Assn. Avocations: boating, racquetball. Family and matrimonial, Criminal, Personal injury. Office: 112 Ye Olde Kings Hwy North Myrtle Beach SC 29582-3050

**WYNN, CHARLES MILTON,** lawyer; b. Marianna, Fla., Jan. 21, 1953; s. Milton Gerard and Joanne (Wandeck) W.; m. Roberta Lyn Hovanec, Jan. 28, 1977; children: Charles Philip, Michael A. AA, Chipola Jr. Coll., 1972; BA, U. Fla., 1974; JD, Nova U., 1977. Bar: Fla. 1977, U.S. Dist. Ct. (no. dist.) Fla. 1978, U.S. Ct. Appeals (11th cir.) 1981, U.S. Dist. Ct. (mid. dist.) Fla. 1985. Assoc. Herman Laramore Law Offices, Marianna, 1977-78; pvt. practice, Marianna, 1978—; trustee U.S. Bankruptcy Ct., No. Dist. Fla., 1988-90; assoc. pub. defender, Marianna, 1977—; panel trustee U.S. Trustee's Office, Atlanta, 1988-90. Bd. dirs. Jackson County Guidance Clinic, Marianna, 1978-83, Dayspring Christian Acad., Inc., 1993; pres. Bright Start Learning Ctr., Inc., Marianna, 1984; co-founder New Life Family Ch.; mem. Marianna Gideon Camp, 1984—, chmn. Jackson County Freedom Coun., Marianna, 1986; mem. Full Gospel Businessmen's Fellowship, bd. dirs., 1986-87. Mem. Fla. Bar Assn., Panhandle Bar Assn. (pres. 1984), Pub. Defender's Assn., Comml. Law League of Am. (Cert. of Appreciation 1979), Marianna Jaycee's (Membership award 1979), Phi Alpha Delta (v.p. 1985—). Democrat. Avocations: canoeing, fishing. Bankruptcy, Contracts commercial, General corporate. Home: 3086 Watson Dr Marianna FL 32446-2204 Office: PO Box 146 Marianna FL 32447-0146

**WYNN, SIMON DAVID,** lawyer, director; b. London, Nov. 6, 1949; came to U.S., 1980; s. Allan Wynn and Sarah Gilmour; m. Nancy Ellen Anderson; 1 child, Alexander Colin. BA, U. Melbourne, Australia, 1972, LLB, 1973; LLM, U. London, 1974. Bar: N.Y. 1981, U.S. Dist. Ct. (ea. and so. dists.) N.Y. 1981. Lectr. law U. New South Wales, Sydney, Australia, 1975-80; barrister Sydney, 1977-80; rschr. Ctr. for Rsch. in Institutions and Social Policy, N.Y.C., 1980-84; ptnr. Buss & Wynn, N.Y.C., 1985-90; pvt. practice N.Y.C., 1990—; bd. dirs. A.W. Nominees Pty Ltd., Melbourne, 230 W 105 Realty Corp., N.Y.C. Co-author: Racketeering in Legitimate Industry: Two Case Studies, 1983. Arbitrator Sm. Claims Ct., N.Y.C., 1990—. Mem. N.Y. State Bar Assn., N.Y. County Lawyers Assn., Manhattan Soccer Club (treas. 1997—). Avocations: sailing, refereeing soccer. Private international, General corporate, General civil litigation. Home: 230 W 105th St New York NY 10025-3916

**WYNN, STANFORD ALAN,** lawyer; b. Milw., May 9, 1950; s. Sherburn and Marjory (Tarrant) W. BBA, U. Wis., Milw., 1972; JD, Case Western Res. U., 1975; LLM in Taxation, U. Miami, 1976. Bar: Wis. 1975, Fla. 1976. Assoc. Walsh and Simon, Milw., 1976-78; atty., asst. dir. advanced mktg. Northwestern Mut. Life Ins. Co., Milw., 1978—. Author: The Insurance Counselor-Split Dollar Life Insurance, 1991; cons. editor: The Insurance Counselor-The Irrevocable Life Insurance Trust, 1995. Bd. dirs. Waukesha Estate Planning Coun., 1985-86. Estate planning, Estate taxation, Insurance. Office: Northwestern Mut Life Ins Co 720 E Wisconsin Ave Milwaukee WI 53202-4703

**WYNNE, BRIAN DOUGLAS,** lawyer; b. L.A., Oct. 15, 1967; s. Robert Jay and Marlene (Friedman) W.; m. Suzanne Kahn, Aug. 3, 1991; 1 child, Jacob Kahn Wynne. BA, U. Calif., Santa Barbara, 1989; JD, Southwestern U., 1992. Bar: Calif. 1992, U.S. Dist. Ct. (ctrl. dist.) Calif. 1993. Legal extern family law dept. L.A. Superior Ct., L.A., 1992; atty. Trope and Trope, L.A., 1992—. Mem. Beverly Hills Bar Assn., L.A. County Bar Assn. Avocations: golf, skiing, travel. Family and matrimonial, General civil litigation. Office: Trope and Trope 16000 Ventura Blvd Ste 111 Encino CA 91436-2744

**WYNSTRA, NANCY ANN,** lawyer; b. Seattle, June 25, 1941; d. Walter S. and Gaile E. (Cogley) W. BA cum laude, Whitman Coll., 1963; LLB cum laude, Columbia U., 1966. Bar: Wash. 1966, D.C. 1969, Ill. 1979, Pa. 1984. With appellate sect., civil divsn. U. S. Dept. Justice, Washington, 1966-67; TV corr. legal news Stas. WRC, NBC and Stas. WTOP, CBS, Washington, 1967-68; spl. asst. Corp. Counsel Washington, 1968-70; dir. planning and rsch. D.C. Superior Ct., Washington, 1970-78; sp. advisor White house Spl. Action, Office for Drug Abuse Prevention, Washington, 1973-74; fellow Drug Abuse Coun., 1974-75; chief counsel Michael Reese Hosp. and Med. Ctr., Chgo., 1978-83; exec. v.p., gen. counsel Allegheny Health Edn. and Rsch. Found., Pitts., 1983-98; pres., CEO Allegheny Health Svcs. Provider's Ins. CO., Pitts., 1989-98; assoc. prof. Carnegie Mellon U., Sch. Urban and Pub. Affairs, 1985—, Allegheny U. Health Scis., 1991—; cons. to various drug abuse programs, 1971-78, 98—. Author: Fundamentals of Health Law; contbr. articles to profl. jours. Bd. overseers Whitman Coll., 1993—. Mem. ABA, Nat. Health Lawyers Assn. (bd. dirs. 1985-91, 92-97, 97-99, chair publs. com. 1989-91, audit com. 1991-92, treas. 1992-93, 95-96, exec. com. 1992-99, edn. fund com. 1992-93, mem. nominating com. 1992-93, sec. 1993-95, treas. 1995-96, pres.-elect 1996-97, pres. 1997-98), Am. Health Lawyers Assn. (pres. 1997-98, exec. com. 1997-99), Am. Soc. Hosp. Attys., others. Presbyterian. Health, Personal injury, General corporate.

**WYRSCH, JAMES ROBERT,** lawyer, educator, author; b. Springfield, Mo., Feb. 23, 1942; s. Louis Joseph and Jane Elizabeth (Welsh) W.; m. B. Darlene Wyrsch, Oct. 18, 1975; children: Scott, Keith, Mark, Brian, Marcia. BA, U. Notre Dame, 1963; JD, Georgetown U., 1966; LLM, U. Mo., Kansas City, 1972. Bar: Mo. 1966, U.S. Ct. Appeals (8th cir.) 1971, U.S. Supreme Ct. 1972, U.S. Ct. Appeals (10th cir.) 1974, U.S. Ct. Appeals (5th cir.) 1974, U.S. Ct. Mil. & Appeals (5th cir.) 1974, U.S. Ct. Mil. & Appeals (5th cir.) 1974, U.S. Ct. Mil. & Appeals 1978, U.S. Ct. Appeals (6th cir.) 1982, U.S. Ct. Appeals (11th cir.) 1984, U.S. Ct. Appeals (7th cir.) 1986, U.S. Ct. Appeals (4th cir.) 1990, U.S. Ct. Appeals (9th cir.) 1998. Assoc. Wyrsch, Hobbs, Mirakian & Lee P.C. and predecessors, Kansas City, 1970-71; of counsel, 1972-77, ptnr., 1978—, pres., shareholder, 1988—; adj. prof. U. Mo., 1981—; mem. com. instrns. Mo. Supreme Ct. 1983—; mem. cir. ct. adv. com. Jackson COunty, Mo., 1998—; bd. dirs. Kansas City Bar Found. Co-author: Missouri Criminal Trial Practice, 1994; contbr. articles to profl. jours. Capt. U.S. Army, 1966-69. Named to Who's Who in Kansas City Law by Kansas City Bus. Jour., 1991, 94; recipient Joint Svcs. Commendation medal U.S. Army, 1969, U. Mo. Kansas City Svc. award Law Found., 1991-92. Fellow Am. Coll. Trial Lawyers, Am. Bar Found., Mo. Bar Found.; mem. ABA, ATLA, Am. Arbitration Assn. (panel arbitrators), Mo. Bar Assn. (vice-chmn. criminal law com. 1978-79), Kansas City Bar Assn. (chmn. anti-trust com. 1981, chmn. bus. tort, anti-trust, franchise com. 1998), Am. Bd. of Trial Advs. (adv.), Nat. Assn. Criminal Def. Attys., Mo. Assn. Criminal Def. Attys. (sec. 1982), Kansas City Club, Phi Delta Phi, Country Club of Blue Springs. Democrat. Roman Catholic. Criminal, Antitrust. Home: 1501 NE Sunny Creek Ln Blue Springs MO 64014-2044 Office: Wyrsch Hobbs Mirakian & Lee PC 1101 Walnut St Fl 13 Kansas City MO 64106-2134

**WYSHAK, LILLIAN WORTHING,** lawyer; b. N.Y.C., July 19, 1928; d. Emil Michael and Stefanie (Dvorak) Worthing; m. Robert H. Wyshak, 1961 (div. 1986); children: Robin, Susan, Jeanne, Patricia. BS in Acctg., UCLA, 1948, MA in Anthropology, 1971; JD, U. So. Calif., L.A., 1956. Bar: Calif. 1956, U.S. Dist. Ct. (ctrl. dist.) Calif. 1956, U.S. Ct. Appeals (9th cir.) 1967, U.S. Supreme Ct. 1967; cert. specialist in taxation law Calif. Bd. Legal Specialization; lic. real estate broker, Calif. Assoc. Boyle, Bissell & Atwill, Pasadena, Calif., 1956-57, Parker, Milliken, Kohlmeier, L.A., 1957-58; asst. U.S. atty. Tax Div., Office of U.S. Atty., L.A., 1958-62; ptnr. Wyshak & Wyshak, Beverly Hills, Calif., 1963-86; pvt. practice Beverly Hills, Calif., 1986—; referee State Bar Ct., L.A.; arbitrator La. County Bar Dispute Resolution Svcs. Contbr. articles to profl. jours. Trustee U. Redlands, 1972-81. Mem. ABA (civil and criminal tax penalties com. tax sect.), Beta Gamma Sigma, Phi Alpha Delta. Presbyterian. Taxation, general, Estate taxation, Probate.

**WYSKOWSKI, BARBARA JEAN,** lawyer; b. Jersey City, Feb. 20, 1967; d. Robert Louis and Barbara Joan (Dabrowski) W. BA, Rutgers U., New Brunswick, N.J., 1988; JD, Rutgers U., Camden, 1992. Bar: N.J., 1993, U.S. Dist. Ct. N.J., 1993. Law clk. Kevin William Kelly, Esq., Brick, N.J., 1989, Monke & Marriot, Sea Girt, N.J., 1990, Ann Segal, Esq., Voorhees, N.J., 1991; rsch. asst. Sch. Law Rutgers U., Camden, 1991-92; pro bono atty. Ocean-Monmouth Legal Svcs., Toms River, N.J., 1993-94; pvt. practice Manasquan, N.J., 1993—; cons. in field; lectr. in field. Advocate Women Against Abuse, Phila., 1989-90; pres. Amnesty Internat., 1989-92. Mem. ABA, Am. Bankruptcy Inst., Nat. Assn. Consumer Bankruptcy Attys., IWIRC, INSOL Internat., N.J. State Bar Assn. (mem. lawyer to lawyer cons. network 1993-95), Ocean County Bar Assn., So. Monmouth Bd. Realtors. Avocations: surfing, running, skating. Bankruptcy, Real property, Consumer commercial. Home: Royal Court Apts I 5 Wall Rd Spring Lake NJ 07762 Office: 700 Rte 71 & Crescent Pl Sea Girt NJ 08750

**XIFO, LOUISE ELIZABETH,** lawyer; b. Elizabeth, N.J., Sept. 4, 1964; d. Raymond Anthony and Jacqueline H. (McCarthy) X. BA in History and Econs., U. Va., 1986; JD, Seton Hall U., 1989. Bar: N.J. 1989, N.Y. 1990, D.C. 1991. Law editor Commerce Clearing House, Clark, N.J., 1987; legal rschr. Seton Hall U., Newark, 1986-88; law clk. Di Rienzo, Wallerstein & Fellman, P.A., Fanwood, N.J., 1988-89, assoc., 1989—. Vol. Am. Cancer Soc., Elizabeth, 1991—, St. John the Apostle Ch., Linden, N.J., 1986—, Big Bros./Big Sisters, Charlottesville, Va., 1984-86. Mem. ABA (young lawyers div., internat. law sect.), D.C. Bar Assn. (young lawyers div., internat. law sect.), N.J. State Bar Assn. (young lawyers sect., internat. law and orgns. sect. legis. coord.). General civil litigation, Product liability, Insurance. Office: Di Rienzo Wallerstein & Fellman PA 313 South Ave Fanwood NJ 07023-1364

**YABLON, JAY RUSSELL,** lawyer; b. N.Y.C., Jan. 15, 1954; s. Bernard and Muriel D. Yablon; m. Deborah Ann Happ, Aug. 7, 1977; children: Joshua, Paula. BSEE in Computer Sci., MIT, 1976, BS in Polit. Sci., 1976; JD, SUNY, Buffalo, 1979. Bar: U.S. Patent and Trademark Office 1982, N.Y. 1983. Productivity engr. GE, Schenectady, N.Y., 1980-82; sr. sys. engr. Data Gen. Corp., Albany, N.Y., 1982-86; chief counsel N.Y. State Legis. Commn. on Scis. and Tech., Albany, N.Y., 1986-92; exec. dir. N.Y. State Gov.'s Telecom. Exch., Albany, N.Y., 1992-95; founding ptnr. Law Office of Jay R. Yablon, Niskayuna, N.Y., 1995—; U.S. exch. program rep., German Acad. Exch. Svcs., 1992. Committeeperson Niskayuna Dem. Com., 1996-98. Mem. N.Y. State Bar Assn., Schenectady County Bar Assn., Ea. N.Y. Intellectual Property Law Assn., Eta Kappa Nu, Tau Beta Phi, Sigma Psi. Patent, Intellectual property, Trademark and copyright. Home: 910 Northumberland Dr Schenectady NY 12309-2814 Office: Law Office of Jay R Yablon 910 Northumberland Dr Schenectady NY 12309-2814

**YACOB, YOSEF,** lawyer, economist; b. Dire Dawa, Harar, Ethiopia, Nov. 12, 1947; s. Yacob and Egziaraya (Osman) Zanios; m. Betsy Ann Boynton; children: Sarah Ann, Matthew Yosef, Ezra Yosef, Jarred Yosef, Rachel Helen. BA, Linfield Coll., 1971; JD, Lewis and ClarkU., 1974. Bar: Oreg. 1975, U.S. Dist. Ct. Oreg. 1979, U.S. Ct. Appeals (9th cir.) 1980. Rschr. criminal justice State of Oreg., Salem, 1974, sr. administrv. analyst, 1974-76; adjudications specialist, legal counsel, law enforcement coun. Office of the Gov. State of Oregon, Salem, 1976-78; chief administrv. law judge State of Oregon, Milwaukie, 1978-83, dir. hearings, appeals, 1982-84; mng. atty. Hyatt Legal Services, Clakamas, Oreg., 1984-86; pres., sr. ptnr. Yacob & Assocs. P.C., Clackamas, 1986-93; dir. gen. for legal affairs, gen. counsel Ministry of Fgn. Affairs, Govt. of Ethiopia, 1993—. Co-author: Evaluation of Multwomah County District Attorney's High Impact Project, 1978. Avocations: alpine skiing, nordic skiing, water skiing, reading. General civil litigation, Bankruptcy, Family and matrimonial. Office: Yacob & Assocs PC Northwest Legal Svcs 6885 SW Montgomery Way Wilsonville OR 97070-6739

**YACOMELLI, LISA ANNE,** lawyer; b. Denville, N.J., June 17, 1956; m. Patrick D. Sweeney. BA, Seton Hall U., 1978; JD, NYU, 1981; cert. tchr., Royal Acad. London, 1994. Assoc. Morgan, Lewis & Bockius, N.Y.C., 1981-83, Lipkowitz & Plaut, N.Y.C., 1983-85; staff atty. Legal Assistance to Elderly, San Francisco, 1985-87; owner Randolph (N.J.) Dance Arts Ctr., 1988-96. Home: 21 Ford Ct Belle Mead NJ 08502-4529

**YAFFA, ANDREW BRYAN,** lawyer; b. Richmond, Va., May 26, 1966; s. Jack Ber and Phyllis P. Yaffa; m. Romy J. Yaffa, Aug. 17, 1991; children: Ryan, Garrett. BA, U. Richmond, 1988; JD, U. Miami, 1991. Bar: Fla. 1991, U.S. Dist. Ct. (so. dist.) Fla. 1992. Atty. Grossman & Roth, P.A., Miami, 1991—. Mem. ABA, Acad. Fla. Trial Lawyers. Avocations: sports, fishing. Personal injury, Insurance, Product liability. Office: Grossman and Roth PA 2665 S Bayshore Dr Ph 1 Miami FL 33133-5448

**YAFFE, DAVID PHILIP,** lawyer; b. Waukegan, Ill., Jan. 31, 1952; s. Robert M. Yaffe and Ruth David Rickard; m. Deborah Miriam Passow Yaffe, December 26, 1976; children: Andrea, Alicia. BA, Johns Hopkins U., 1974; JD with honors, George Washington U., Washington, 1977. Bar: Va. 1977, D.C. 1978, U.S. Ct. Appeals (4th cir.) 1978, U.S. Ct. Appeals (9th cir.) 1982. Assoc. Duncan & Allen, Washington, 1977-83, ptnr., 1983-96, mng. ptnr., 1988-94; mem. Van Ness Feldman, P.C., Washington, 1996—. Contbr. articles to profl. jours. Nat. chair Second Decade Soc., exec. Alumni Coun., 1996—, Johns Hopkins U., Balt., 1993-94; co-pres. Agudus Achim Congregation, Alexandria, Va., 1993-95. Mem. ABA (sect. on nat. resources, energy and environ. law, vice chmn. energy industry restructuring com. 1993—), Fed. Energy Bar Assn. Avocation: golf. FERC practice, Contracts commercial, Public utilities. Home: 4528 Sleaford Rd Annandale VA 22003-3929

**YAKOWICZ, VINCENT X,** lawyer; b. New Castle, Pa., July 29, 1932; s. Vincent William and Anna (Kahocka) Y.; m. Marlene Brown, Apr. 2, 1977; children: Meredythe, Megan, Michelle. BA in Polit. Sci., Pa. State U., 1953; JD, U. Pa., 1956; postgrad., U. Va., 1968-69. Bar: Pa. 1957, U.S. Dist. Ct. (mid. dist.) Pa. 1962, U.S. Supreme Ct. 1970, U.S. Ct. Appeals (3d cir.) 1983. Asst. atty. gen. Pa. Dept. Revenue, Harrisburg, 1958-59; bur. dir. Pa. Dept. Revenue, 1959-62; dep. atty. gen. State of Pa., Harrisburg, 1962-71; dep. sec. of revenue State of Pa., 1971-74, sec. of revenue, 1974-75, solicitor gen., 1975-78; chief dep. counsel, chief of litigation Pa. Dept. Treasury, Harrisburg, 1979-87; pvt. practice law Harrisburg, 1987—; chief of litigation, Pa. Dept. Ins., 1979; chief tax litigation, Pa. Dept. Justice, 1979; adv. com. Decedent Estate Laws of Joint State Govt. Com.; legal counselor to Pa. Constl. Conv. on Revisions; author, lectr. tax seminars, U. Pa., Pa. Bar Inst. Mem. ABA, Pa. Bar Assn., Lawrence County Bar Assn., Nat. Tax Assn., Nat. Assn. Tax Adminstrs., Fed. Bench-Bar Exec. Com., Nat. Assn. Atty. Gens. (antitrust subcom.), Gov.'s Tax Reform Com., Multi-state Taxation Commn. (chmn. subcom.). General civil litigation, State civil litigation, Constitutional. Home and Office: 227 Oak Knoll Rd New Cumberland PA 17070-2836

**YALE, KENNETH P.,** lawyer, dentist; b. Lincoln, Nebr., Aug. 18, 1956; m. Julia Marie Windsor, Aug. 7, 1982; children: Hilary, Ken, Victoria, George, Lydia. BA, Creighton U., 1978; DDS, U. Md., 1981; JD, Georgetown U., 1988. Bar: Va. 1988. Adminstr., clinician USPHS, Kansas City, Mo., 1981-84; cons. Riggs Nat. Bank, Washington, 1984-85; govt. rels. rep. ADA, Washington, 1985-87; legis. counsel U.S. Senator Simpson, Washington, 1987-89; exec. dir. White House Domestic Policy Coun., Washington, 1989-90; chief of staff White House Sci. Office, Washington, 1990-92; sr. v.p. The Jefferson Group, Washington, 1992-96; pres. Jefferson Healthcare, Washington, 1997-99, Advanced Health Solutions, Rockville, Md., 1999—; instr. Georgetown U., 1984-85. Author: Section on Healthcare, 1988. Policy advisor Presdl. campaign, Washington, 1988, 92, 96. Lt. USPHS, 1981-84. Mem. ABA, ADA. Office: Advanced Health Solutions 10001 Weatherwood Ct Rockville MD 20854-2171

**YALMAN, ANN,** lawyer; b. Boston, June 9, 1948; d. Richard George and Joan (Osterman) Y. BA, Antioch Coll., 1970; JD, NYU, 1973. Trial atty. Fla. Rural Legal Svcs., Immokalee, Fla., 1973-74; staff atty. EEO, Atlanta, 1974-76; pvt. practice Santa Fe, N.Mex., 1976—; probate judge Santa Fe County, 1999—; part time U.S. magistrate, N. Mex., 1988-96. Commr. Met. Water Bd., Santa Fe, 1986-88. Mem. N.Mex. Bar Assn. (commr. Santa Fe chpt. 1983-86). Home: 441 Calle La Paz Santa Fe NM 87501-2821 Office: 304 Catron St Santa Fe NM 87501-1806

**YAMADA, STEPHEN KINICHI,** lawyer, real estate developer; b. Honolulu, July 19, 1946; s. Harold Kiyoshi and Frances Sadako (Uchida) Y.; m. Amy M. Chiemi, Apr. 23, 1965 (div.); 1 child, Tammy Lynn; m. Kwi Nam Kim, Nov. 18, 1984. BA, U. Hawaii, 1968; JD, U. Calif., San Francisco, 1971. Bar: Hawaii 1972, U.S. Dist. Ct. Hawaii 1972, U.S. Ct. Appeals (9th cir.) 1992; lic. real estate broker. Dep. atty. gen. State of Hawaii, Honolulu, 1971-74; pvt. practice law Honolulu, 1974—, pvt. practice real estate, 1975—; real estate developer, 1996; instr. Chaminade U., Honolulu, 1975, owner Sky Sch. Real Estate, Honolulu, 1976. Mem. exploring com. Boy Scouts Am., Honolulu, 1974; second vice chmn. 7th Dem. Dist., Honolulu, 1978. Fellow Hawaii Trial Lawyers Assn.; mem. ABA, ATLA, Hawaii Jaycees (state legal counsel 1976), Full Gospel Businessmen's Fellowship Internat. (chpt. officer), Rotary. Democrat. Avocations: reading, swimming. Pension, profit-sharing, and employee benefits, Workers' compensation, General civil litigation. Office: 1111 Bishop St Ste 504 Honolulu HI 96813-2811

**YAMAKAWA, DAVID KIYOSHI, JR.,** lawyer; b. San Francisco, Jan. 25, 1936; s. David and Shizu (Negishi) Y. BS, U. Calif., Berkeley, 1958, JD, 1963. Bar: Calif. 1964, U.S. Supreme Ct. 1970. Prin. Law Offices David K. Yamakawa Jr., San Francisco, 1964—; dep. dir. Cmty. Action Agy., San Francisco, 1968-69; dir. City Demonsration Agy., San Francisco, 1969-70; mem. adv. coun. Calif. Senate Subcom. on the Disabled, 1982-83, Ctr. for Mental Health Svcs., Substance Abuse and Mental Health Svcs, Adminstrn. U.S. Dept. Health and Human Svcs., 1995-99; chmn. cmty. residential treatment system adv. com. Calif. Dept. Mental Health, 1980-85, San Francisco Human Rights Commn., 1977-80; pres. Legal Assistance to the Elderly, 1981-83; 2d v.p. Nat. Conf. Social Welfare, 1983-89; v.p. Region IX Nat. Mental Health Assn., 1981-83; mem. cmty. partnership bd. Sch. Social Welfare, U. Calif., Berkeley, 1999—. Vice chmn. Mt. Zion Hosp. and Med. Ctr., 1986-88; bd. dirs. United Neighborhood Ctrs. of Am., 1977-83, ARC Bay Area, 1988-91, Goldman Inst. on Aging, 1993-99, v.p. 1994-96, vice-chmn. 1996-99, hon. lifetime dir., exec. com. mem., 1999—; trustee Mt. Zion Med. Ctr. U. Calif., San Francisco, 1993-97, UCSF/Mt. Zion, UCSF Stanford Health Care, 1997—; chmn. bd. trustees United Way Bay Area, 1983-85; CFO Action for Nature, Inc., 1987—; bd. dirs. Ind. sector, 1986-92. Friends of the San Francisco Human Rights Commn., 1980—, CFO, 1980-85, 94—, vice chmn. 1985-94, Father Alfred Boeddeker's La Madre Found., 1982—, v.p. 1994—, Nat. Concilio Am., 1987—, legal coun., 1996—, Hispanic Cmty. Found. of the Bay Area, 1989-98, legal coun., 1989-98, Kimochi, Inc., 1999—; bd. dirs. Non-Profit Svcs., Inc., 1987—, sec. 1987-90; chmn. 1990—; pres. Coun. Internat. Programs, San Francisco, 1987-89, Internat. Inst. San Francisco, 1990-93; mem. citizens adv. com. San Francisco Hotel Tax Fund Grants for the Arts Program, 1991—. Recipient John B. Williams Outstanding Planning and Agy. Rels. vol. award United Way of the Bay Area, 1980, Mortimer Fleishhacker Jr. Outstanding Vol. award Unied Way, 1985, Spl. Recognition award Legal Assistance to the Elderly, 1983, Commendation award Bd. Suprs. City and County of San Francisco, 1983, cert. Honor, 1985, San Francisco Found. award, 1985, 1st Mental Health Awareness award Mental Health Assn., San Francisco, 1990, David Yamakawa Day proclaimed in San Francisco, 1985. Mem. ABA (Liberty Bell award 1986). General practice, Intellectual property, Non-profit and tax-exempt organizations. Office: 582 Market St San Francisco CA 94104-5301

**YAMANO, JOHN Y.,** lawyer; b. Riverside, Calif., Nov. 10, 1959; s. John Yoshiyuki and Junko Yamano; m. Sharon H. Nishi, Apr. 28, 1990. BS in Bus. Adminstrn., U. So. Calif., 1981; JD, U. Calif., Berkeley, 1984. Bar: Calif. 1984, Hawaii 1985, U.S. Dist. Ct. Hawaii 1985, U.S. Ct. Appeals (9th cir.) 1988. Assoc. Case & Lynch, Honolulu, 1984-88, Roeca & Louie, Honolulu, 1988-89; ptnr. McCorriston Miho Miller Mukai, Honolulu, 1989—; bd. dirs. Hawaii Lawyers Care Pro Bono Svcs. Orgn., 1985-91, treas., 1985-87; mem. faculty Legal Seminars, Inc., Honolulu, 1987-96; spkr. in field. Author: Hawaii Motor Vehicle Collision Manual Update, 1994; co-author: Hawaii Motor Vehicle Collision Manual, 1990, Hawaii Tort Liability, 1989. Bd. dirs. Hawaii Parkinson Assn., Honolulu, 1998, v.p., 1999—. Named to Outstanding Young Men of Am., 1998. Mem. ABA, Calif. Bar Assn., Hawaii Bar Assn., Alpha Kappa Psi, Phi Kappa Phi, Beta Gamma Sigma. Avocations: golf, tennis. General civil litigation, Insurance, Constitutional. Office: McCorriston Miho Miller Mukai Five Waterfront Pl 500 Ala Moana Blvd Unit 4 Honolulu HI 96813-4900

**YAMASHIRO, MAUREEN DOROTHY,** lawyer; b. Chgo.. BA, U. Ill., 1982; JD, DePaul U., 1985. Bar: Ill. 1985. Office asst. Cook County State Atty., Chgo., 1985—; mem. adv. coun. domestic violence court. coun. Cook County State Atty., 1997—. Mem. Asian Am. Bar Assn. (bd. dirs. 1987-89),

Chinese Am. Bar Assn., Women's Bar Assn., Ind. Voter Ill./Ind. Precinct. Office: Cook County State's Atty's Office 500 Daley Ctr Chicago IL 60602

**YAMASHITA, WESLEY FARRELL,** lawyer; b. Las Vegas, July 17, 1955; s. Kiyoshi and Mary (Sato) Y.; m. Bonnie Jean Hull, Dec. 28, 1977; children: Nicholas, Nathan, Brent, Amy, Anne. BS cum laude, Brigham Young U., 1978, JD, 1982. CPA, Utah; Bar: Utah 1982, U.S. Dist. Ct. Utah 1982, Nev. 1986, U.S. Dist. Ct. Nev. 1986, U.S. Tax Ct. 1986. Acct. Squire & Co., Orem, Utah, 1981-84; contr., counsel Sommerset Corp., Provo, Utah, 1984-85, Ron Lewis Constrn., Moapa, Nev., 1985; assoc. Mills Gibson & Waite, Las Vegas, 1986-89, Clark Greene & Assocs., Las Vegas, 1989—; mem. supr. com. Moapa Valley Fed. Credit Union, Overton, Nev., 1987-90, chmn., 1993. Author, lectr. course materials Nat. Bus. Inst., 1992—. Scoutmaster, asst. scoutmaster, com. mem. Boy Scouts Am., Boulder Dam Area Coun., 1987—. Mem. ABA, Clark County Bar Assn. Republican. Mem. Ch. of LDS. Avocations: sports, reading. Probate, Estate planning, Estate taxation. Home: PO Box 1355 Overton NV 89040-1355 Office: Clark Greene & Assocs Ltd 3770 Howard Hughes Pkwy Ste 195 Las Vegas NV 89109-0976

**YAMBRUSIC, EDWARD SLAVKO,** lawyer, consultant; b. Conway, Pa., Mar. 9, 1933; s. Michael Misko and Slavica Sylvia (Yambrusic) Y.; m. Natalie Visniak, 1990. *Second generation Croatian American. Father Misko and mother Slavica (Sylvia) born in Ruskovac, Croatia, arrived to the United States 1913 and 1931 respectively. Father, a boiler maker with PRR for 40 years. Mother, a farmer, blue-collar worker, housewife, a beautiful human being who instilled in me the love of God, Country and our beautiful Croatian cultural heritage* BA, Duquesne U., 1957; postgrad. Georgetown U. Law Ctr., 1959-61; JD, U. Balt., 1966; cert. The Hague (Netherlands) Acad. Internat. Law, 1967, 69, diploma Ctr. Study and Research of Internat. Law and Internat. Relations, 1970; PhD in Pub. Internat. Law, Cath. U. Am., 1984. Bar: Md. 1969, U.S. Ct. Customs and Patent Appeals 1972, U.S. Supreme Ct. 1972, U.S. Ct. Internat. Trade 1988. Copyright examiner U.S. Copyright Office, Library of Congress, Washington, 1960-69, atty. adviser Office Register of Copyrights, 1969-98; pvt. practice internat. and immigration law, 1969—; legal counsel Nat. Ethnic Studies Assembly, 1976—, Soc. Fed. Linguists, 1980; pres. AMCRO Internat. Cons., Inc., 1995. Pres. Nat. Confedn. Am. Ethnic Groups, Washington; nat. chmn. Croatian-Am. Bicentennial Com.; nat. chmn. Nat. Pilgrimage of Croatian-Ams. to Nat. Shrine of Immaculate Conception, Washington; v.p. Croatian Acad. Am. Served to capt. U.S. Army, 1957-59. Duquesne U. Tamburitzans scholar, 1953-57; Hague Acad. Internat. Law fellow, 1970. Mem. ABA, Md. Bar Assn., Internat. Law Assn., Internat. Fiscal Assn., Am. Soc. Internat. Law, Croatian Cath. Union Am., Croatian Frat. Union Am. Republican. Roman Catholic. Author: Treaty Interpretation: Theory and Reality, 1987, The Trade-Based Approaches to th Protection of Intellectual Property, 1990; contbr. articles to ofcl. newsletter Nat. Confedn. Am. Ethnic Groups, also legal jours. *Certificate issued by the Librarian of Congress in recognition of 40 years of distinguished service to the people of the United States of America, 1957-98.* Home and Office: 4720 Massachusetts Ave NW Washington DC 20016-2346

**YAMIN, DIANNE ELIZABETH,** judge; b. Danbury, Conn., June 4, 1961; d. Raymond Joseph and Linda May (Bucko) Goetz; m. Robert Joseph Yamin, Sept. 3, 1988; children: Samantha Blythe, Rebecca Anne. AB, Lehigh U., 1983; JD, Mercer U., 1986. Bar: Conn. 1986, U.S. Dist. Ct. Conn. 1989. Lawyer Gerald Hecht & Assocs., Danbury, 1986-92; judge State Conn., Danbury, 1991—; atty. Yamin & Yamin, Danbury, 1992—; chmn. ethics com. Conn. Probate Assembly, 1994—; mem. Conn. Coun. on Adoptions, 1992—, Conn. Probate Assembly, 1991—. Bd. dirs. Big Bros./Big Sisters, Danbury, 1987-94, Conn Brass Soc., Inc., 1991—, Lions Club Danbury, 1993-94, Friends of Tarrywile Park, Inc., Danbury, 1993—, Danbury Music Ctr., 1996—, Hispanic Ctr. Greater Danbury, 1999—. Recipient outstanding young citizen award Conn. Jaycees, 1994, pro bono award Conn. Legal Svcs., 1993; named as one of 21 Young Lawyers Leading Us into the 21st Century, ABA Mag., 1995. Mem. ABA, Conn. Bar Assn., Conn. Health Lawyers Assn., Danbury Bar Assn, Omicron Delta Kappa. Republican. Roman Catholic. Avocations: ballet, volunteerism, travel, outdoor activities. Home: 8 Johnson Dr Danbury CT 06811-2927 Office: 155 Deer Hill Ave Danbury CT 06810-7726

**YAMIN, MICHAEL GEOFFREY,** lawyer; b. N.Y.C., Nov. 10, 1931; s. Michael and Ethel Y.; m. Martina Schaap, Apr. 16, 1961; children: Michael Jeremy, Katrina. AB magna cum laude, Harvard U., 1953, LLB, 1958. Bar: N.Y. 1959, U.S. Dist. Ct. (so. dist.) N.Y., U.S. Dist. Ct. (ea. dist.) N.Y., U.S. Ct. Appeals (2d cir.) 1966, U.S. Supreme Ct. 1967. Assoc. Weil, Gotshal & Manges, N.Y.C., 1958-65; sr. ptnr. Colton, Hartnick, Yamin & Sheresky, N.Y.C., 1966-93; sr. ptnr. Kaufmann, Feiner, Yamin, Gildin & Robbins, LLP, N.Y.C., 1993—. Bd. trustees Gov.'s Com. Scholastic Achievement, 1976—; chmn. Manhattan Community Bd. 6, 1986-88, mem., 1974-88; mem. Manhattan Borough Bd., 1986-88; bd. trustees Rockland County Soc. Prevention of Cruelty to Children, 1979—. Lt. USNR, 1953-55, Korea. Mem. ABA, N.Y. State Bar Assn., Assn. Bar of City of N.Y., Fed. Bar Coun., Am. Fgn. Law Assn. (Am. Branch), Internat. Law Assn., Societe de Legislation Comparee, Internat. Bar Assn. Clubs: Harvard Faculty (Cambridge, Mass.); Harmonie, Harvard (N.Y.C.) (trustee N.Y. Found. 1981—, pres. 1999—, sub-chmn. schs. and scholarships com. 1972-93, bd. mgrs. 1985-88, 93-98, chair house com. 1992-95, v.p. 1995-98, chair comms. com. 1997—), Harvard Alumni Assn. (elected dir. 1995-98). Mergers and acquisitions, General corporate, Private international. Office: 777 3rd Ave New York NY 10017-1401

**YANDLE, STEPHEN THOMAS,** dean; b. Oakland, Calif., Mar. 7, 1947; s. Clyde Thomas and Jane Walker (Hess) Y.; m. Martha Anne Welch, June 26, 1971. BA, U. Va., 1969, JD, 1972. Bar: Va. 1972. Asst. dir. admissions U. Va. Law Sch., Charlottesville, 1972-76; from asst. to assoc. dean Northwestern U. Sch. Law, Chgo., 1976-85; assoc. dean Yale U. Law Sch., New Haven, 1985—; bd. dirs. The Access Group. Commr. New Haven Housing Authority, 1998—. Capt. U.S. Army, 1972. Mem. Law Sch. Admission Coun. (programs, edn. and prelaw com. 1978-84), Assn. Am. Law Schs. (chmn. legal edn. and admissions sect. 1979, nominations com. 1987, chmn. adminstrn. of law schs. sect. 1991), Nat. Assn. for Law Placement (pres. 1984-85, co-chmn. Joint Nat. Assn. com. on placement 1986-88), New Haven Legal Assistance Assn. (bd. dirs., treas. 1992-98). Office: Yale Law Sch Sch Law PO Box 208215 New Haven CT 06520-8215

**YANG, CORA GERMAINE,** lawyer. BA, Williams Coll., 1980; JD, NYU, 1984. Sr. v.p., asst. gen. counsel Diners Club Internat. Ltd., Chgo., 1984—. Fax: 773-380-5796. E-mail: cora.yang@citicorp.com. Private international, Intellectual property. Office: Diners Club International Ltd 8430 W Bryn Mawr Ave Chicago IL 60631-3473

**YANG, PHILLIP SEUNGPIL,** lawyer; b. Seoul, Korea, Aug. 15, 1967; s. Kun Suk and Sung Kil Yang. BS, Cornell U., 1990; JD, Boston Coll., 1993; Cert., Seoul Nat. U., 1997. Bar: N.J. 1993, N.Y. 1994, D.C. 1994, U.S. Dist. Ct. N.J. 1993. Summer law clk. U.S. Ct. Internat. Trade, N.Y.C., 1992; asst. dist. atty. Bronx Dist. Atty.'s Office, N.Y.C., 1993-95; legal counsel Samsung Electronics, Seoul, 1995-97; assoc. Hughes Hubbard and Reed LLP, N.Y.C., 1997—; legal advisor The Bronx Korean Mchts. Assn., 1993—. Mem. Assn. Bar City N.Y. (mem. Asian affairs com. 1997—). General corporate, Intellectual property, Computer. Home: 14615 Booth Memorial Ave Flushing NY 11355-5402 Office: Hughes Hubbard & Reed LLP One Battery Park Plz New York NY 10004

**YANNI, AMY,** lawyer, project director; b. Detroit, Apr. 15, 1954; d. Joseph Donald and Ada Belle (Hodgson) Y.; m. J.R. Ambacher, Dec. 31, 1977 (div. 1984); m. Richard M. Glassman, May 18,, 1996. BA summa cum laude, Framingham State U., 1975; MEd, Boston U., 1979, EdD, 1982; JD, Northeastern U., 1985. Bar: Boston 1985, U.S. Dist. Ct., Mass. 1986. Tchg. fellow Boston U., 1975-78; team leader Spear Edn. Ctr., Framingham, Mass., 1978-80; svc. coord. Dept. Mental Health, Framingham, 1980-82; atty. Serota, Katz, Sasson, & Hoose, Springfield, Mass., 1985-88; staff atty., dir. Americorps Domestic Violence Project W. Mass. Legal Svcs., Pittsfield, 1988—; instr. Women and the Law Berkshire (Mass.) C.C., 1994; bd. dirs. Mass. Bd. Bar Overseas, Boston. Author: Human Service Decision Making, 1982. Mem. adv. bd. HIV/AIDS Law Consortium, Northampton, Mass., 1994—, SAFEPLAN, Hampshire, Franklin, Mass., 1995—; task force Mediation in the Probate Cts., Com. for Gender Equality Mass., 1994. Fellow Mass. Bar Found. Family and matrimonial. Office: We Mass Legal Svcs 127 State St Springfield MA 01103-1944

**YANOFF, LEO,** judge; b. N.Y.C., Sept. 18, 1910; s. William and Rose Yanoff; m. Louise Joseph, Sept. 22, 1935; children: Israel, Ruth. BA, U. Pa., 1930; LLB, Harvard U., 1933. BAr: N.J., U.S. Dist. Ct. N.J. Pres. Jewish Cmty. Coun., Essex County, N.J., 1959-61; judge U.S. Dist. Ct., N.J., 1969-72, County Ct., N.J., 1972-75, Superior Ct., N.J., 1975—; ptnr. Grem & Yanoff, Newark, 1936-61, Fox, Yanoff & Fox, Newark, 1961-69. Author and editor legal materials. Served with U.S. Army, 1943-45. Office: Essex County Courthouse Newark NJ 07102

**YARBOROUGH, CLINTON JOSEPH,** lawyer; b. Ft. Leavenworth, Kans., Dec. 28, 1969; s. William Glenn and Betsy Yarborough; m. Patsy Lee, Aug. 16, 1997. BS, Coll. Charleston, 1991; JD, U. S.C., 1993. Bar: S.C. 1994, Ga. 1995, U.S. Dist. Ct. (so. dist.) S.C. 1995. Title abstractor Woodward, Leventis, Unger, Daves, Herndon & Cothran, Columbia, S.C., 1992-94; for-closure atty. Ronald C. Scott, P.A., Columbia, 1994-95; asst. pub. defender Defender Corp. Aiken County, Aiken, S.C., 1995-98; asst. dist. atty. Toombs Judicial Cir., Thomson, Ga., 1998-99; assoc. Jackson R. Massey & Assocs., P.C., Augusta, Ga., 1999—. Mem. ABA, Sigma Chi,. Roman Catholic. Avocations: archaeology, reading, anthropology, bicycling, forestry. Office: Jackson R Massey & Assocs PC 3643 Walton Way Ext Augusta GA 30909-4507

**YARBROUGH, EDWARD MEACHAM,** lawyer; b. Nashville, Dec. 17, 1943; s. Gurley McTyeire and Miriam (Mefford) Y. BA, Rhodes Coll., 1967; JD, Vanderbilt U., 1973. Bar: Tenn. 1973. Asst. dist. atty. Davidson County, Nashville, 1973-76; ptnr. Hollins, Wagster & Yarbrough, Nashville, 1976—. Chmn. com. Crime Commn., Nashville, 1981-82; mem. task force House Judiciary Com., Nashville, 1984; chmn. Crimestoppers Inc., Nashville, 1983—; trustee United Way, Nashville, 1983—, Belmont U., 1993—, Cumberland Sci. Mus., 1996—; bd. dirs. Big Bros. Inc., Nashville, 1983-85. Served to 1st lt. U.S. Army, 1969-71, Vietnam. Decorated Bronze Star. Fellow Nat. Speleological Soc. (bd. dirs. 1960—); mem. ABA (bd. dirs. 1985), Tenn. Bar Assn., Nashville Bar Assn. (pres. 1983), Tenn. Criminal Def. Lawyers, Nashville Kiwanis (pres. 1992), Richland Country Club, City Club (Nashville). Democrat. Baptist. Avocations: cave exploration, photography, skiing, golf, running. Criminal, State civil litigation, Family and matrimonial. Home: 5230 Granny White Pike Nashville TN 37220-1715 Office: Hollins Wagster & Yarbrough 424 Church St Ste 2210 Nashville TN 37219-2303

**YARBROUGH, FLETCHER LEFTWICH,** lawyer; b. Ruston, La., Oct. 25, 1934; s. Fletcher Leftwich and Bertha Barbara (Bird) Y.; m. Harriett Jean Harris, Dec. 27, 1957; children: John, Matthew, Anne. BA, So. Meth. U., 1957; LLB magna cum laude, Harvard Law Sch., 1960. Sheldon traveling fellow Harvard U., Cambridge, Mass., 1960-61; from assoc. to mng. ptnr. Carrington, Coleman, Sloman & Blumenthal L.L.P. (and predecessors), Dallas, 1961—; lect. So. Meth. U. Sch. Law, Dallas, 1964-66; vis. com. Harvard Law Sch., Cambridge, Mass., 1975-80. Fellow Am. Coll. Trial Lawyers, Am. Bar Found., Tex. Bar Found.; mem. ABA, Am. Law Inst. Federal civil litigation, State civil litigation, Professional liability. Office: Carrington Coleman et al 200 Crescent Ct Ste 1500 Dallas TX 75201-7839

**YARMEY, RICHARD ANDREW,** portfolio manager; b. Kingston, Pa., Aug. 23, 1948; s. Stanley Richard and Rose Mary (Rees) Y.; m. Jeanne Marie Cappelli, Aug. 5, 1972; children: Lynn Rees, Jessica Brett, Kristen Alexandra. BS, U. Scranton, 1970; JD, Cath. U., 1975. Bar: Pa. 1975, D.C. 1976, U.S. Ct. Appeals (5th cir.) 1976, U.S. Tax Ct. 1978, U.S. Ct. Appeals (D.C. cir.) 1980. Contract adjudicator GAO, Washington, 1970-73; program asst. EPA, Washington, 1973; assoc. Sharon, Pierson, et al, Washington, 1975-82; of counsel Pierson, Semmes et al, Washington, 1982-93; prin. Yarmey Capital Mgmt., 1989-95; v.p. investments, sr. portfolio mgr. PNC Advisors, 1995—; fin. cons. various pension plans, individuals and bus. concerns, 1976—; TV panelist, speaker, writer on portfolio mgmt.; instr. fin. mgmt. and investments continuing edn. Wilkes U., Wilkes-Barre. Mem. Pa. Bar Assn., Aircraft Owners and Pilots Assn., Alpha Sigma Nu. Democrat. Avocation: flying. Office: 11 W Market St Wilkes Barre PA 18701-1904 also: One PNC Plz Fifth Ave & Wood St Pittsburgh PA 15265-0001

**YATES, ALFRED GLENN, JR.,** lawyer; b. Sarver, Pa., June 17, 1946; s. Alfred Glenn and Mary Etta (Best) Y.; m. Barbara Jean Lang, June 12, 1982; children: Jennifer Christine, Elizabeth Ann. BA in Philosophy, Coll. William and Mary, 1968; JD, U. Pitts., 1973. Bar: Pa. 1973, U.S. Dist. Ct. (we. dist.) Pa. 1973, U.S. Ct. Appeals (3d cir.) 1984, W.Va. 1987, U.S. Dist. Ct. (so. dist.) W.Va. 1987. Asst. v.p. trust dept. Pitts. Nat. Bank, 1973-79; assoc. Wayman, Irvin & McAuley, Pitts., 1979-80; sole practice, Pitts., 1981—; instr. taxation Robert Morris Coll., Pitts., 1982; founder, dir. Inst. for Corp. Litigation Reform, 1988. Developer (book) Pocket Tax Calculators, 1976—. Legal counsel, founding mem. West Pa. chpt. Lupus Found. Am., Pitts., 1982-91. Served with U.S. Army, 1968-70. Decorated Joint Service Commendation medal. Mem. Pa. Bar Assn., Assn. Trial Lawyers Am. Probate, General civil litigation, Estate planning. Office: 519 Allegheny Bldg 429 Forbes Ave Pittsburgh PA 15219-1622

**YATES, LEIGHTON DELEVAN, JR.,** lawyer; b. Atlanta, Sept. 4, 1946; s. Leighton Delevan and Stella Louise (Hill) Y.; m. Phyllis Jeanne Hummer, Dec. 22, 1968; children: Leighton Delevan III, Lauren Jeanne. BA, Hampden-Sydney Coll., Va., 1968; JD with high honors, U. Fla., 1973. Bar: Fla. 1974, U.S. Dist. Ct. (middle dist.) Fla. 1975. Assoc. Maguire, Voorhis & Wells, P.A., Orlando, Fla., 1974-77, shareholder, 1978-98, dept. chmn., 1985-90; ptnr. Holland & Knight LLP, Orlando, Fla., 1998—; bd. dirs. Hubbard Constrn. Co., Winter Park, Fla., Blythe Constrn. Inc., Charlotte, N.C.; adminstrv. dir. SunTrust Bank, Ctrl. Fla., Orlando, 1990—. Exec. editor U. Fla. Law Rev., 1973. Mem. Fla. Bd. Bar Examiners, 1992-97, vice chmn., 1995-96, chmn. 1996-97; chmn. Ctrl. Fla. Blood Bank, 1995—, vice chmn., 1980-95; chmn. Orlando Opera Co., 1994, pres., 1993. Fellow Am. Bar Found.; mem. ABA, Fla. Bar Assn., Orange County Bar Assn., Univ. Club of Orlando, Country Club of Orlando, Order of the Coif, Omicron Delta Kappa, Phi Kappa Phi. Republican. Presbyterian. Avocations: scuba diving, cycling, music, reading. General corporate, Banking, Securities. Home: 3218 S Osceola Ave Orlando FL 32806-6251 Office: Holland & Knight LLP 200 S Orange Ave Ste 2600 Orlando FL 32801-3449

**YATES, LINDA SNOW,** communications, marketing executive; b. St. Louis, July 20, 1938; d. Robert Anthony Jerrue and June Alberta (Crowder) Armstrong; m. Charles Russell Snow, Nov. 26, 1958 (div. 1979); children: Cathryn Louise, Christopher Armstrong, Heather Highstone, Sean Webster; m. Alan Porter Yates, July 22, 1983. BBA, Auburn U., 1973, MEd, 1975, EdD, 1998. Cert. profl. sec. Div. head placement div. Solutions Group, Atlanta, 1981-83; employment coord. Fulton Fed. Savs., Atlanta, 1983-84; owner, recruiter Data One, Inc., Atlanta, 1984-85; ops. mgr. Talent Tree Temporaries, Atlanta, 1985-87; legal asst., sec. Rice & Keene, Atlanta, 1987-90; legal word processing asst. Kilpatrick & Cody, Atlanta, 1990-94; pres., owner Power Comm., Cashiers, N.C., 1994—; regional coord. S.E. region, regional mktg. rep. WorldConnect Comms., Tulsa; adj. instr. DeKalb Coll., Atlanta, 1980-84, Mercer U., Atlanta, 1981-82; instr. bus. So. Union State Jr. Coll., Valley, Ala., 1974-75; legal sec. Swift, Currie, McGhee & Hiers, Atlanta, 1979-80, Samford, Torbert, Denson & Horsley, Opelika, Ala., 1969-71. Columnist Neon News Flash, 1995. Mem. Paralegal Assn. Beaufort County (charter mem., sec. 1993-94), Women Bus. Owners, Nat. Assn. Pers. Cons., Internat. Soc. Poets (Disting. mem., Internat. Poet of Merit 1996, Internat. Poetry Hall of Fame 1996), Cashiers Writers Group, Phi Delta Kappa, Alpha Xi Delta. Republican. Episcopalian. Avocations: golf, writing, international travel. Office: PO Box 2441 Cashiers NC 28717-2441

**YATES, NORRIS WILLIAM, JR.,** lawyer; b. Alamo Heights, Tex., July 6, 1926; s. Norris William and Maggie Barkley (Curry) Y.; m. Mary Hutchings Spencer, Dec. 30, 1947 (div. Aug. 1949); 1 child, William Spencer; m. Jimmie Carolyn Cook, Sept. 17, 1955; children: Victoria Carolyn Marullo (dec.), Rebecca Elizabeth Yates Bird. BA in Econs., Tex. A&M U., 1950; JD, U. Tex., 1957. Bar: U.S. Ct. of Military Appeals, 1963, U.S. Supreme Ct., 1964, Tex., 1957. Asst. to mgr. rates and tariffs Slick Airways, Inc., San Antonio, 1950; assoc. Beckmann, Stanard, Wood, Barrow & Vance, San Antonio, 1957-60; pvt. practice San Antonio, 1960-67, 83—; asst. criminal dist. atty., chief civil sect. Bexar County Dist. Atty.'s Office, San Antonio, 1967-82; mcpl. ct. judge City of San Antonio, 1966-67. Editor The Subpoena, 1958-59. Exec. com. Bexar County Dem. Party, San Antonio. Cpl. U.S. Army, Airborne Infantry, 1944-46, ETO; 1st lt. USAF, 1951-55, B-29 Bomber Pilot, Korea, lt. col. USAFR, ret. 1978. Decorated Bronze Star medal, combat infantry badge, glider badge, pilot's wings, three battle stars; Eagle Scout. Mem. Daedalians, USAF Pilot Class 52-George Assn. (recording sec.), 307th Bomb Group/Wing Inc. (past pres.), Toastmasters (past pres., Disting. Dist. Gov. 1969-70, Disting. Toastmaster 1984, Presdl. citation 1992), Masons (past master, 32 degree), San Antonio A&M Club (dir.), San Antonio Ret. Officers Assn. (sec.). Democrat. Presbyterian. Avocations: travel, photography. Criminal, Bankruptcy, Probate. Home: 2118 Kenilworth Blvd San Antonio TX 78209-2329

**YATES-CARTER, LYNNE,** lawyer; b. Oakland, Calif., June 1, 1950; d. Charles and Bernice (Rose) Yates; m. William Matthew Carter, July 9, 1972; 1 child, Alexander. BA in English, U. Santa Clara, 1972, JD, 1976. Bar: Calif. 1976, U.S. Dist. Ct. (no. dist.) Calif. Pvt. practice law San Jose, 1976—; judge pro tempore Family Law dept. Santa Clara County Superior Ct., 1979—, spl. master, 1988—, arbitrator in family matters, 1988—; adj. prof. family law Santa Clara U., 1989, 90, 92; lectr. in field. Contbr. articles to profl. jours.; cons./contbr.: California Family Law Service, 1986. Active various polit. and civic orgns. Recipient Resolution of Commendation Santa Clara County Bd. Suprs., 1986. Mem. ABA, Santa Clara County Bar Assn. (conf. of dels. 1984—, sec. 1986, program com. chmn. 1991, Justice Bryl R. salsman award for community svc. 1986, Cert. of Appreciation 1983, 86, family law exec. com.), Am. Acad. Matrimonial Lawyers (past pres. No. Calif. chpt.), Calif. State Bar Assn. (former chair), Calif. Women Lawyers, Friends of Legal Aid. Democrat. Avocations: cooking, reading, gardening. Family and matrimonial. Office: 111 W Saint John St Ste 300 San Jose CA 95113-1104

**YEAGER, CHARLES WILLIAM,** lawyer, newspaper publisher; b. Frederick, Md., Sept. 18, 1921; s. Ralph A. and Ina Jane (Nuckles) Y.; m. Charlotte L. Matthews, Nov. 26, 1958; children: Gretchen A. Murphy, Kristin A. Bridge, Charles W. Yeager Jr., Matthew R. Yeager. BA, W.Va. U., 1943; LLB, U. Va., 1948. Bar: W.Va. 1948, Fla. 1969, U.S. Supreme Ct. 1968. Ptnr. Steptoe & Johnson, Charleston, W.Va., 1948-93; of counsel Rose and Atkinson, Charleston, 1993—. Pub., editor The Nicholas CHronicle. Maj. U.S. Army, 1942-46. Democrat. Office: Nicholas Chronicle 603 Church St Summersville WV 26651-1411

**YEAGER, JORDAN BERSON,** lawyer; b. Phillipsburg, N.J., May 26, 1967; s. H. Robert and Marcia Ellen (Fogel) Y.; m. Kathryn Boockvar, Sept. 24, 1994. BA, Cornell U., 1992; JD, America U., 1989. Bar: Va. 1992, D.C. 1993, Md. 1993, Pa. 1994, U.S. Dist. Ct. D.C., U.S. Dist. Ct. (ea. dist.) Pa., U.S. Dist. Ct. (mid. dist.) Pa. Assoc. Klimaski, Miller & Smith, Washington, 1992-94; sole Jordan Yeager Atty. at Law, Tunkhannock, Pa., 1994-95; assoc. Sugarman & Assocs., Phila., 1995-97; ptnr. Boockvar & Yeager, Bethlehem, Pa., 1997—. Chair Greater Washington Dem. Club, Washington, 1993-94; gen. coord. chief coun. Citizens for New Columbia, Washington, 1993-94. Recipient Alumni award Am. Univ., 1992. Mem. Nat. Lawyers Guild (reg. v.p. 1994-96). Civil rights, Labor, General civil litigation. Office: Boockvar & Yeager 539 Center St Bethlehem PA 18018-5910

**YEAGER, JOSEPH HEIZER, JR.,** lawyer; b. Indpls., Jan. 8, 1957; s. Joseph Heizer and Marilyn Virginia (Hillyard) Y.; m. Candance A. Grass, June 2, 1984; children: Samuel, Henry. AB cum laude, Harvard U., 1979; JD cum laude, Ind. U., 1983. Bar: Ind. 1983, U.S. Dist. Ct., (so. and no. dist.) Ind. 1983, U.S. Ct. Appeals (7th cir.) 1986, U.S. Supreme Ct. 1996. Dir. ops. Penn and Schoen Assocs., N.Y.C., 1979-80; assoc. Baker & Daniels, Indpls., 1983-89, ptnr., 1990—. Bd. dirs. Indpls. Legal Aid Soc., 1990-99, pres. 1992-94; chmn. Indpls. Com. for UNICEF, 1986-91; mem. Indpls. Com. for Fgn. Affairs, 1986-91. Mem. Ind. Bar Assn., Indpls. Bar Assn. (litigation sect. exec. com. 1985-86, 1996—, chair 1999), Cen. Ind. Regional Citizens League (bd. dirs. 1997—). Democrat. Avocation: private pilot. General civil litigation, Insurance, Contracts commercial. Office: Baker & Daniels 300 N Meridian St Ste 2700 Indianapolis IN 46204-1782

**YEAGER, RUTH,** lawyer. Asst. U.S. Atty., Dept. Justice, Tyler, Tex.; chief civil divsn. Dept. Justice, Tyler, 1988—; U.S. Atty., Eastern Dist. Tex., 1993-94. Office: US Attys Office 110 N College Ave Ste 700 Tyler TX 75702-0204

**YEAGER, THOMAS JOSEPH,** lawyer; b. N.Y.C., Apr. 12, 1941; s. Martin Joseph and Anna Marueen (Clarke) Y.; m. Carol Elizabeth Kearns, Aug. 24, 1964; children: Kathleen Elizabeth. BBA, St. John's U., N.Y.C., 1962, JD, 1965. Bar: Fla. 1965, N.Y. 1980, U.S. Dist. Ct. (so. dist.) Fla. 1967, U.S. Ct. Appeals (11th cir.), U.S. Supreme Ct. 1972. Atty./assoc. Nason & Gildan, West Palm Beach, Fla., 1965-67; ptnr., atty. Nason, Gildan & Yeager, West Palm Beach, 1967-70; atty., shareholder, pres. Nason, Gildan, Yeager, Gerson & White, P.A., West Palm Beach, 1970-96, Nason, Yeager, Gerson, White & Lioce, P.A., West Palm Beach, 1996—. Mem. Palm Beach County Bar Assn. (bd. dirs. 1970-73), KC (grand knight, dist. dep. 1968—), Guild Cath. Lawyers of the Diocese of Palm Beach (bd. dirs., pres., Outstanding Cath. Lawyer 1989). Avocations: golf, tennis, snow skiing, reading. State civil litigation, Federal civil litigation, Condemnation. Office: Nason Yeager et al Ste 1200 1645 Palm Beach Lakes Blvd West Palm Beach FL 33401-2214

**YEAGER, THOMAS NELSON,** lawyer, radio personality; b. Laurel, Md., Jan. 18, 1964; s. Thomas Merle and Olivia Lee (Scaggs) Y.; m. Jeanne Michelle MacLeod, June 14, 1997. BA, U. Md., 1986; JD, U. Md., Balt., 1990; grad., Nat. Coll. Dist. Attys., Houston, 1994. Bar: Md. 1990. Law clk. Kent County Circuit Ct., Chestertown, Md., 1990-91; asst. state's atty. Kent County, Chestertown, 1991-96, dep. state's atty., 1996-99; sole practitioner Chestertown, 1995—; radio personality WNAV Radio, Annapolis, Md., 1986-95, WCEI Radio, Easton, Md., 1995—; mem. Gov.'s Exec. Adv. Coun., Balt., 1991-94; ex-officio bd. mem. Crime Solvers of the Upper Eastern Shore, Chestertown, 1996—. Mem. Old Chestertown Neighborhood Assn., 1995—. Mem. Md. State Bar Assn., Kent County Bar Assn., 2d Cir. Bar Assn., Nat. Eagle Scout Assn., KC (dep. grand knight), Chestertown Optimist Club (pres.). Republican. Roman Catholic. Avocations: skiing, rowing, boating. Office: 104 S Cross St Chestertown MD 21620-1514

**YEAZEL, KEITH ARTHUR,** lawyer; b. Fayetteville, N.C., Feb. 14, 1956; s. Russell E. and Barbara E. (Weaver) Y.; m. Deborah M. MacDonald, Aug. 30, 1986. BA, Ohio State U., 1983; JD, Capital U., 1989. Bar: Ohio 1989, U.S. Dist. Ct. (so. dist.) Ohio 1989, U.S. Ct. Appeals (6th cir.) 1990, U.S. Supreme Ct. 1992. Law clk. to judge George C. Smith U.S. Dist. Ct., Columbus, Ohio, 1988-89; prin. Keith A. Yeazel, Atty. at Law, Columbus, 1989—. Mem. ABA, Ohio Bar Assn., Columbus Bar Assn., Nat. Assn. Criminal Def. Lawyers, Ohio Assn. Criminal Def. Lawyers, Order of Curia. Republican. Lutheran. Federal civil litigation, Criminal, Personal injury. Office: 65 S 5th St Columbus OH 43215-4307

**YEDOR, JONATHAN,** lawyer; b. St. Louis, Dec. 26, 1946; s. Harry Mark and Patricia Merle Y. BSBA, U. Mo., 1968; JD, St. Mary's U., 1974. Bar: Tex. 1974, Ill. 1975, U.S. Dist. Ct. (no. dist.) Ill. 1976, U.S. Dist. Ct. (we. dist.) Tex. 1979, U.S. Ct. Appeals (5th cir.) 1989, U.S. Dist. Ct. (no. dist.) Tex. 1998. 1st lt. U.S. Army, 1969-71. General civil litigation, Consumer commercial, Labor. Office: 13750 San Pedro Ste 700 San Antonio TX 78232-4370

**YELENICK, MARY THERESE,** lawyer; b. Denver, May 17, 1954; d. John Andrew and Maesel Joyce (Reed) Y. B.A. magna cum laude, Colo. Coll., 1976; J.D. cum laude, Georgetown U., 1979. Bar: D.C. 1979, U.S. Dist. Ct. D.C. 1980, U.S. Ct. Appeals (D.C. cir.) 1981, N.Y. 1982, U.S. Dist. Ct. (so. and ea. dists.) N.Y. 1982, U.S. Supreme Ct. 1992, U.S. Ct. Appeals (5th cir.) 1995. Law clk. to presiding justices Superior Ct. D.C., 1979-81; ptnr. Chadbourne & Parke, LLP, N.Y.C., 1981—. Editor Jour. of Law and Policy Internat. Bus., 1978-79. Mem. Phi Beta Kappa. Democrat. Roman Catholic. Federal civil litigation, State civil litigation. Home: 310 E 46th St New York NY 10017-3002 Office: Chadbourne & Parke LLP 30 Rockefeller Plz New York NY 10112-0002

**YELLEN, JONATHAN HARRY,** lawyer; b. Buffalo, N.Y., Apr. 18, 1967; s. Richard David and Loretta (Krieger) Y. BA, Amherst (Mass.) Coll., 1989; JD, Columbia (N.Y.) U., 1992; LLM in Tax, Georgetown U., Washington, 1994. Bar: Mass. 1992, N.Y. 1993, D.C. 1993, Calif. 1994. Assoc. Latham & Watkins, Costa Mesa/N.Y.C., Calif., 1994-96, Fried, Frank, Harris, Shriver & Jacobson, N.Y.C., 1996-98; v.p., assoc. gen. counsel Starwood Hotels & Resorts Worldwide, Inc., White Plains, N.Y., 1998—. Mem. Bar Assn. City of N.Y., Univ. Club. Office: Starwood Hotels & Resorts Worldwide Inc 777 Westchester Ave White Plains NY 10604-3520

**YELLIN, MELVIN A.,** lawyer, banker; b. Jan. 23, 1943; s. Samuel and Celia Yellin; children: Nancy Jill, Douglas Matthew; m. Sharon Hodge, June 24, 1983. BA, NYU, 1964, postgrad.in law, 1969; JD, St. John's U., N.Y.C., 1967. Bar: N.Y. 1968. Atty. Eastman Dillon Union Securities, N.Y.C., 1967-68; assoc. Schaeffer Dale Vogel & Tavrow, N.Y.C., 1968-74, ptnr., 1974-75; v.p., counsel, head of domestic group Bankers Trust Co., N.Y.C., 1975—, mng. dir., dep. gen. counsel; chmn. ednl. programs, lectr. seminars for various orgns. including N.Y. State Bankers' Assn., 1980, 83, Monadnock Internat., London, 1983, Banking Law Inst., 1984, Norton Bankruptcy Law and Practice, 1987, Bank Capital Markets Assn. Contbr. articles and chpts. to legal publs. Mem. fund raising com. Save Our Universalist Landmark; mem. exec. com. Bankruptcy Lawyers div. United Jewish Appeal; mem. benefit com. of ann. gala Am. Cancer Soc. Mem. ABA (mem. internat. bankruptcy subcom., bus. bankruptcy com., lectr. programs and instns.), N.Y. State Bar Assn., Assn. of Bar of City of N.Y. (chmn. bankruptcy and corp. reorganization com. 1984-87, lectr. ednl. program 1985), Am. Bankruptcy Inst. (bd. dirs.), Practicing Law Inst. (lectr. ednl. programs 1980-84). Banking, Bankruptcy, General corporate. *

**YELNICK, MARC M(AURICE),** lawyer; b. N.Y.C., Jan. 30, 1947; s. Louis and Jeanne (Friedman) Y.; m. Linda Sherwin, Dec. 20, 1973; children: Sandy, Shauna. BA, Bklyn. Coll., 1967; postgrad., NYU, 1967-70; JD, St. John's U., 1976. Bar: N.Y. 1977, U.S. Dist. Ct. (ea. and so. dists.) N.Y. 1977, U.S. Dist. Ct. (no. dist.) Calif. 1985. Assoc. Billet, Billet & Avirom, N.Y.C., 1977-79, Whitman & Ransom, N.Y.C., 1979-84; sole practice San Mateo, Calif., 1984—. Mem. ABA, Am. Immigration Lawyers Assn. (no. Calif. and N.Y. chpts.). Immigration, naturalization, and customs. Office: 66 Bovet Rd Ste 353 San Mateo CA 94402-3147

**YEOMANS, RUSSELL ALLEN,** lawyer, translator; b. Vancouver, B.C., Can., May 13, 1944; came to U.S., 1951; s. Douglas Allen and Mabel Jean (Maguire) Y.; m. Minako Hara, July 7, 1981; children: Megumi Kay, Ken Douglas. BA, U. Calif., Berkeley, 1966, postgrad.; LLB, U. Ottawa, Ont., Can., 1985; LLM, U. Wash., 1986; postgrad., Hiroshima (Japan) U., York U., Toronto, 1990-92. Bar: N.Y. 1988, Calif. 1992; called to Ont. bar, 1991. Mem. rsch. dept. Japan External Trade Orgn., San Francisco, 1967-69; translator Sec. State, Ottawa, Ont., 1971-73, 84-85; head fgn. trade dept. Tanaka Shoji, Hiroshima, Japan, 1973-76; head tchr. Brit. Japan, Tokyo, 1977-81; fgn. law cons. Tokyo Aoyama Law Office, 1986-88; assoc. Baker & McKenzie, Toronto, 1989-91, L.A., 1991-92; pvt. practice, Rancho Palos Verdes, Calif., 1992-93; ptnr. Sanders and Yeomans, Torrance, Calif., 1993-94; pvt. practice Rancho Palos Verdes, Calif., 1994—; legal adv. Seicho-No-Ie Internat. Hdqs., Tokyo. With USN, 1961-65. Mem. N.Y. State Bar Assn., York Bar Assn., Law Soc. Upper Can., C. of C., Indonesian Bus. Soc., U. Calif. Berkeley Alumni Assn., U. Wash. Law Alumni Assn., Tokyo Can. Club (v.p., pres. 1987-89). General corporate, Private international, Labor. Home: 6746 Los Verdes Dr Palos Verdes Estates CA 90275 Office: 6758 Los Verdes Dr Apt 2 Palos Verdes Peninsula CA 90275-5535

**YERA, EVELIO JESUS,** lawyer, educator; b. Miami, Fla., Mar. 22, 1962; s. Evelio and Marta (Coll) Y.; m. Susan Rachel Lewis, June 11, 1983 (div. Jan. 1986); m. Marta Lucia Salamanca, Nov. 23, 1991. BA, U. Miami, Coral Gables, Fla., 1984, JD, 1987. Bar: Fla. 1988, D.C. 1989, U.S. Ct. Appeals (11th cir.) 1990, U.S. Dist. Ct. (so. dist.) Fla. 1990, U.S. Dist. Ct. (mid. dist.) Fla. 1991. Reference librarian U. Miami Sch. Law, Coral Gables, 1985-87, rsch. instr., 1987-89; law clk. to U.S. Magistrate Fla., 1989-93; in-house counsel Holmes Regional Med. Ctr., 1993—; faculty Barry Univ., 1994—; guest lectr. Miami Dade Community Coll., 1986; mem. faculty Barry U., Miami Shores, Fla., 1988-92. Mem. ABA, Am. Acad. Hosp. Attys. General corporate, Health. Home: PO Box 110324 Miami FL 33111-0324 Office: Holmes Regional Med Ctr 1350 S Hickory St Melbourne FL 32901-3276

**YERKESON, DOUGLAS ALAN,** lawyer; b. Cin., Aug. 12, 1967; s. Richard Douglas and Sally Em (Gatch) Y.; m. Michelle Ann Brueggeman, Sept. 11, 1993. BSME, U. Cin., 1990, JD, 1993. Bar: Ohio 1994, U.S. Patent Trademark Office 1996, U.S. Dist. Ct. (so. dist.) Ohio 1998, U.S. Ct. Appeals (fed. cir.) 1998. Engr. KDI Precision Prod., Inc., Cin., 1990-92; intern U. Cin. Intellectual Property Office, Cin., 1992-93; reference atty. Lexis-Nexis, Dayton, Ohio, 1994-96; assoc. Biebel & French, LPA, Dayton, 1996—. Recipient Jacob D. Cox scholarship U. Cin., 1990-93. Mem. ABA, ASME, Ohio State Bar Assn., Cin. Hist. Soc., Dayton Intellectual Property Law Assn., Dayton Bar Assn., Am. Intellectual Property Law Assn., Am. Railway Engrng. Assn. (pres. U. Cin. chpt. 1990-92, student writing competition award 1992, 93), Intellectual Property Law Soc. (v.p. U. Cin. chpt. 1992-93), Cin. Railroad Club (trustee, v.p. 1995—). Intellectual property, Patent, Trademark and copyright. Home: 6728 Falling Leaves Ct Mason OH 45040-8503 Office: Biebel & French LPA 35 E 1st St Dayton OH 45402-1203

**YERRID, C. STEVEN,** lawyer; b. Charleston, W.Va., Sept. 30, 1949; s. Charles George and Audrey Faye Yerrid; m. Vee West, Aug. 23, 1985. BA in History and Polit. Sci., La. State U., 1971; JD, Georgetown U., 1975. Bar: Fla. 1975, Va. 1975, U.S. Supreme Ct. 1979, D.C. 1984. Aide U.S. Senator Ellender, Washington, 1971-73; lobbyist Am. Hosp. Assn., Washington, 1973-75; ptnr. Holland & Knight, Tampa, Fla., 1975-86; pres. Stagg, Hardy & Yerrid, Tampa, 1986-89, Yerrid, Knopik & Krieger PA, Tampa, 1990—; lobbyist Am. Optometric Assn., 1972-73. Mem. ABA, Va. Bar Assn., D.C. Bar Assn., Fla. Acad. Trial Lawyers (bd. dirs. 1989—), Fla. Bar Assn. (chmn. admiralty law com. 1984-85, bd. cert. com. 1988-91, vice chmn. 1989-91), Southeastern Admiralty Law Inst., Am. Judicature Soc., Assn. Trial Lawyers Am. (sustaining), Am. Bd. Trial Advocates (advocate), Maritime Law Assn. (proctor), Bd. Cert. Civil Trial Lawyers, Nat. Bd. Trial Advocacy, Harbour Island Athletic Club, Centre Club, Tampa Club. Democrat. Avocations: skiing, swimming, fishing. General civil litigation. Office: Yerrid Knopik & Krieger PA 101 E Kennedy Blvd Ste 2160 Tampa FL 33602-5187

**YETTER, R. PAUL,** lawyer; b. Milw., Aug. 5, 1958; s. Richard and Lobelia (Gutierrez) Y.; m. Patricia D. Yetter, May 6, 1983; children: Chris, Mark, Michael, Joseph, Thomas, Andrew, Daniel. BA, U. Tex., El Paso, 1980; JD, Columbia U., 1983. Bar: Tex. 1983, U.S. Dist. Ct. (so., ea., no. and we. dists.) Tex., U.S. Ct. Appeals (5th cir.); bd. cert. in civil trial law and personal injury trial law Tex. Bd. Legal Specialization. Law clk. to Hon. John R. Brown U.S. Ct. Appeals (5th cir.), Houston, 1983-84; assoc. Baker & Botts, L.L.P., Houston, 1984-89, ptnr., 1990-97; name ptnr. Yetter & Warden, L.L.P., Houston, 1997—; chair state judiciary rels. com. State Bar, 1995-96; mem. Funding Parity Task Force, 1995-97; mem. ex officio Jud. Selection Task Force, 1995-97; chair Alliance for Jud. Funding, Inc., 1996—; mem. ex officio contbns. com. Tex. Ctr. for the Judiciary. Contbr. articles to profl. jours. Recipient Presdl. citation State Bar Tex., 1996; Southwestern Legal Found. rsch. fellow. Fellow Tex. Bar Foun., Houston Bar Found. State civil litigation, Federal civil litigation. Office: Yetter & Warden LLP 600 Travis St Ste 3800 Houston TX 77002-2912

**YETTER, RICHARD,** lawyer; b. Phila., Mar. 14, 1929; s. Frederick Jacob and Marie (Kiracher) Y.; m. Loebelia Gutierrez, Feb. 4, 1955; children: Bruce, Tina Marie, Richard Paul, Erich David. BS, Pa. State U., 1951; JD, Marquette U., 1960. Bar: Wis. 1960, U.S. Dist. Ct. (ea. dist.) Wis. 1960, Tex. 1961, U.S. Dist. Ct. (we. dist.) Tex. 1971, U.S. Ct. Appeals (5th cir.) 1972. Adjuster Md. Casualty Co., El Paso, Tex., 1960-62; pres. Richard Yetter & Assocs. Inc., El Paso, 1970-90; sole practitioner, El Paso, 1962-70, 90—; assoc. judge Mcpl. Ct., El Paso, 1967-71; adj. prof. law Webster U., St. Louis. Pres. Pleasantview Home for Sr. Citizens, Inc., 1966-76; state committeeman Tex. Rep. Com., El Paso, 1968-70; chmn. adv. bd. SBA, Lubbock, Tex., Salvation Army, El Paso; life mem. El Paso County Civil Svc. Commn., 1992-96. Served with USAF, 1951-60. Recipient William Booth award Salvation Army, 1997. Mem. Wis. State Bar, Tex. State Bar, El Paso Bar Assn., El Paso Trial Lawyers Assn. (past bd. dirs.), El Paso Probate Bar Assn. (bd. dirs.), Optimist (life, pres. El Paso), Mil. Order World Wars (life). Methodist. Avocation: walking. State civil litigation, Probate. Office: 6070 Gateway Blvd E Ste 501 El Paso TX 79905-2031

**YIN, DOMINIC DAVID,** police officer, educator, lawyer; b. Tokyo, Jan. 3, 1966; came to U.S., 1972; s. Winsor and Helen Yin; m. Kimberly Hyon Kim, Feb. 14, 1996. BA, U. Calif., Berkeley, 1989; JD, UCLA, 1993; MS, San Francisco State U., 1996; postgrad., U. So. Calif., 1998—. Bar: Calif. Atty. JAGC USN, Alexandria, Va., 1991-95; police officer San Francisco Police Dept., 1995—; lectr. Calif. State U., Hayward, 1996—, City Coll. San Francisco, 1999—; instr. San Francisco Police Acad., 1997—; instr. Calif. Specialized Tng., San Luis Obisbo, 1997—. Vol. Chinatown Youth Ctr., San Francisco, 1998. Lt. (j.g.) USNR, 1991-95; 1st lt. Calif. N.G., 1995—. Mem. San Francisco Police Officers Assn. Avocations: reading, travelling, fitness. Home: 652 40th Ave San Francisco CA 94121-2525 Office: 372 7th Ave San Francisco CA 94118-2322

**YIRA, MARKUS CLARENCE,** lawyer; b. St. Croix Falls, Wis., Feb. 6, 1971; s. Robert Gordon and Ruth Elizabeth Yira; m. Dawn Susanne Nelson, June 19, 1993; children: Jordan M., Kaitlin E., Alison M. BA magna cum laude, Hamline U., 1993; JD, William Mitchell Coll. Law, St. Paul, 1996. Bar: Minn. 1996, U.S. Dist. Ct. Minn. 1996, U.S. Ct. Appeals (8th cir.) 1997. Rsch. asst. William Mitchell Coll. Law, 1993-95; assoc. Eckman, Strandness & Egan, P.A., Wayzata, Minn., 1996-99, Lommen, Nelson, Cole & Stageberg, P.A., Mpls., 1999—. Mem. ATLA, Minn. Bar Assn., Minn. Trial Lawyers Assn., Hennepin County Bar Assn., Phi Beta Kappa. Personal injury, Product liability, General civil litigation. Office: Lommen Nelson Cole & Stageberg PA 1800 IDS Ctr 80 S 8th St Minneapolis MN 55402-2100

**YOCKIM, RONALD STEPHEN,** lawyer; b. Williston, N.D., Nov. 3, 1949; s. Daniel and Doris Helene Yockim; m. Christine J. Conroy, Dec. 27, 1980 (div.); children: Daniel, Elizabeth, Katherine. BA, Wartburg Coll., Waverly, Iowa, 1971; MA, Mankato State U., 1975; JD, Lewis and Clark U., 1981. Bar: Oreg. 1981, U.S. Dist. Ct. Oreg. 1982, U.S. Ct. Appeals (9th cir.) 1993, U.S. Ct. Fed. Claims 1993, U.S. Supreme Ct. 1995. Water pollution biologist Wis. DNR, Rhinelander, 1974-75; fisheries biologist Agrl. Rsch. Svc., Beltsville, Md., 1975-78; sole practitioner Portland, Oreg., 1981-84; asst. dir. Oreg. Divsn. State Lands, Salem, 1984-86; corp. counsel D.R. Johnson Lumber Co., Riddle, Oreg., 1986-91; atty. Cegavske, Johnson & Yockim, Roseburg, Oreg., 1991-95; sole practitioner Roseburg, 1995—; bd. dirs. Umpqua Indian Devel., Roseburg, 1993-95; mem. Cow Creek Gaming Commn., Roseburg, 1993-95; mem. Oreg. Rangeland Adv. Com., Salem, 1985-86; mem adv. bd. Roseburg dist. Bur. Land Mgmt., 1992-94. Chmn. Douglas County Water Adv. Bd., Roseburg, 1990-97; bd. dirs. environ. and natural resources sect. Oreg. State Bar, Salem, 1990-91. Democrat. Lutheran. Avocations: mountain climbing, hunting, fishing, tennis. Natural resources, Real property, Administrative and regulatory. Office: 548 SE Jackson St Ste 7 Roseburg OR 97470-4970

**YODER, ROBERT GENE,** lawyer; b. Canton, Ohio, Jan. 27, 1964; s. Eldon A. and Linda F. (Borton) Y.; m. Jill Tennery, May 23, 1992; children: Kasey, Kayleigh, Garrett. AA, Ctrl. Tex. Coll., 1986; BA, Malone Coll., 1991; JD, Cleve. Marshall, 1995. Bar: Ohio 1997; cert. criminal justice specialist, master addictions counselor, chem. dependency counselor III, alcohol and drug counselor. Correctional officer Fed. Bur. Prisons, Oxford, Wis., 1987-88; counselor Massillon (Ohio) Cmty. Hosp., 1991-92, Edwin Shaw Hosp., Akron, Ohio, 1992-93; law clk. Mondello & Levey, Cleve., 1993-94; dir. domestic violence Intercede, Massillon, 1995-97; owner Encourage Program, 1997—; bd. dirs. Children at Risk Empowered, Louisville, Ohio; mem. citizens rev. bd. Family Ct. Divsn., Canton, 1995—. With USAF, 1983-87. Recipient Disting. Svc. award Canton Jaycees, 1996. Mem. Massillon Rotary. Republican. Mennonite. Avocations: softball, golf, karate, travel. Criminal, Family and matrimonial, Juvenile. Home: 5401 Barnhill St Louisville OH 44641-8879 Office: Encourage 116 Cleveland Ave NW Ste 802 Canton OH 44702-1732

**YODICE, JOHN S.,** lawyer; b. Bklyn., June 23, 1932; s. Antonio and Rose (Marcoccio) Y.; m. Barbara Gruenewald, Sept. 1958 (dec.); children: Kathleen, Michael. AB, Bklyn. Coll., 1954; JD, George Washington U., 1959. Bar: D.C. 1959, Md. 1965, U.S. Supreme Ct., 1964. Pvt. practice Washington and Frederick, Md., 1958—. Author: Aviation Lawyers Manual, 1986; contbr. articles to profl. jours. Mem. Aircraft Owners and Pilots Assn. (bd. dirs.), AirSafety Found., Internat. Coun. Aircraft Owners and Pilot Assn., Lawyer Pilots Bar Assn. Avocation: flying. Aviation. Home: 624 4th Pl SW Washington DC 20024-2720 Office: Yodice Assocs 500 E St SW Washington DC 20024-2760

**YODOWITZ, EDWARD J.,** lawyer; b. N.Y.C., 1943. BS, Long Island U., 1965; JD, U. Balt., 1969. Bar: N.Y. 1972. Mem. Skadden, Arps, Slate, Meagher & Flom, L.L.P., N.Y.C.; chmn. seminar Practicing Law Inst., 1984-95; bd. trustees L.I. U., 1990—. Mem. ABA. Federal civil litigation, Securities. Office: Skadden Arps Slate Meagher & Flom 919 3rd Ave New York NY 10022-3902

**YOHN, WILLIAM H(ENDRICKS), JR.,** federal judge; b. Pottstown, Pa., Nov. 20, 1935; s. William H. and Dorothy C. (Cornelius) Y.; m. Jean Louise Kochel, mar. 16, 1963; children: William H. III, Bradley G., Elizabeth J. AB, Princeton U., 1957; JD, Yale U., 1960. Bar: Pa. 1961, U.S. Dist. Ct. D.C. 1961. Ptnr. Wells Campbell Reynier & Yohn, Pottstown, 1961-71; mem., chmn. coms. Pa. House of Reps., Harrisburg, 1968-80; ptnr. Binder Yohn & Kalis, Pottstown, 1971-81; judge Montgomery County Ct. of Common Pleas, Norristown, Pa., 1981-91, U.S. Dist. Ct., ea. dist., Pa., 1991—; asst. D.A., Montgomery County D.A. Office, 1962-65; instr. Am. Inst. of Banking, 1963-66; bd. dirs. Fed. Jud. Ctr. Bd. dirs. Greater Pottstown Drug Abuse Prevention Program, 1970-76, Pottstown Meml. Med. Ctr., 1974-95, chmn., 1984-95; mem. exec. com. Yale LAw Sch. Alumni Assn., 1998—. Cpl. USMCR, 1960-66. Mem. Pa. Bar Assn., Montgomery Bar Assn. (bd. dirs. 1967-70). Republican. Office: US Dist Ct 146130 US Courthouse 601 Market St Philadelphia PA 19106-1713

**YOHO, BILLY LEE,** lawyer; b. Huntington, W.Va., Oct. 24, 1925; s. Wilbert Wiley Yoho Sr. and Nellie Pansy (Bryan) Hawkins; m. Martha Sue Carroll; children: Kevin Richard, Karen Lee; m. Shirley Ann Stone Morris. BA, U. Md., 1950; LLB, U. Md., Balt., 1953. Bar: Md. 1953. Gen. counsel City of College Park, Md., 1959-62; town atty. Town of Colmar Manor, Md., 1956-72; gen. counsel Prince George's Gen. Hosp., Cheverly, Md., 1955-74, MD22 Lions Rsch. Found., Balt., 1965-74; ptnr. Hoyert & Yoho Chartered, Lanham, Md., 1987—. Mem. College Park airport program in saving the oldest airport in the world, 1968. With USN, 1943-47. Mem. ABA, Prince George's County Bar Assn. (pres. 1976-77), Md. Assn. Trial Attys., Lions Clubs Internat. (dist. gov. 1989-90, 1990-98, life mem.), NRA, U. Md. Alumni Assn. Democrat. Presbyterian. Avocation: genealogy, Christian study. General corporate, Family and matrimonial, Personal injury. Home: 5950 Westchester Park Dr College Park MD 20740-2802

**YORK, ALEXANDRA,** lawyer; b. Jersey City, Feb. 9, 1939; d. Daniel Simpson and Regina (Norwich) S. BA, Tulane U., 1960; JD, Fordham U., 1976. Bar: N.Y. 1978, N.J., 1984; U.S. Dist. Ct. (so. and ea. dists.) N.Y. 1978, U.S. Dist. Ct. N.J. 1984, U.S. Ct. Appeals (2d cir.) 1987. Vol. Peace Corps, Philippines, 1961-63; legis. adviser Speaker of the Philippine House of Reps., Manila, 1964; speechwriter Mems. U.S. Congress, Washington, 1965; compliance officer U.S. Equal Employment Opportunity Commn., Washington, 1966-68; cons. N.Y.C. Dept. Consumer Affairs, 1969; cons., speechwriter N.Y.C. Dept. Air Resources, 1970-72; assoc. Shea and Gould, N.Y.C., 1977-79, Leopold Kaplan P.C., N.Y.C., 1980-86; asst. atty. gen. N.Y. State Dept. of Law, N.Y.C., 1987-93; spl. counsel external affairs Congress of Federated States of Micronesia, Pohnpei, 1993-95; del. Federated States of Micronesia Internat. Climate Change Neg., Geneva, 1994; sr. policy adv. Philippine Sen. Com. Environment, 1996-97; cons. Philippine Dept. Environment and Natural Resources, 1996-97; mem., adv. com. environ. law, Practicing Law Inst., N.Y.C., 1991-93; prof. internat. environ. policy, Ateno de Manila U., Philippines, 1996—; ofcl. del. UN Conf. on Environ. and Devel., Rio de Janiero, 1992; spkr. in field. Contbr. articles on internat. environ. law and climate change to profl. jours. Mem. ABA (natural resources sect., energy and environ. sect., internat. law and practice sect. 1990-93, program chair ann. meeting 1991, 92, chair subcom. on Human Rights and Environ., goal IX officer, 1992-93), Assn. of Bar of City of N.Y. (mem. internat. law com. 1990-93, originator spl. com. internat. environ. law 1991, environ. com. 1987-90), Am. Soc. Internat. Law (environ. sect. 1991-92).

**YORK, JAMES MARTIN,** judge; b. Abilene, Tex., Feb. 22, 1939; s. James Orville and Hazel Mae (Martin) Y.; m. Sandra L. Zunker, June 5, 1959 (div. 1967); children: Debra Lynn, James Martin Jr.; m. Nora Darlene Buechman, Nov. 3, 1972; 1 child, Victoria Lee. Student, Baylor U., 1957-60, LLB, 1962. Bar: Tex. 1962; bd. cert. in family law and civil trial law, Tex. Pvt. practice Houston, 1965-94. Sect. editor Baylor Law Rev., 1962. State Rep. primary candidate Rep. Party, Houston, 1970; del.-at-large Rep. State Conv., Houston, 1971; Rep. primary cand. for judge 310th Dist. Ct., 1994; coach Westbury Nat. Little League, Houston, 1967, Voss West Little League, Houston, 1969, 70; apptd. assoc. judge 246th Dist. Ct., 1995. Named Boss of Yr. Houston Assn. Legal Secs., 1973. Mem. Rotary Club of Houston, Inwood Forest Golf Club, Houston Bar Assn., State Bar of Tex., Baylor Alumni Assn., Baylor Lettermen's Assn. Baptist. Avocations: golf, swimming, reading. Office: 246th Dist Ct 7th Fl Family Law Ctr 1115 Congress St Houston TX 77002-1927

**YORK, JOHN C(HRISTOPHER),** lawyer, investment banker; b. Evansville, Ind., Apr. 27, 1946; s. James Edward and Madge (Wease) Y.; m. Judith Anne Carmack, Aug. 24, 1968; children: George Edward Carmack, Charlotte Bayley, Alice Mercer. BA, Vanderbilt U., 1968; JD, Harvard U., 1971. Bar: Ill. 1971, U.S. Dist. Ct. (no. dist.) Ill. 1971. Assoc. firm Mayer Brown & Platt, Chgo., 1971-74; sr. v.p., sec., prin. JMB Realty Corp., Chgo., 1974-84; pres. Robert E. Lend Co. Inc., 1984—, Packard Properties Inc., 1984—; counsel Bell, Boyd & Lloyd, Chgo., 1986—; bd. dirs. McKeever Electric Supply Co., Columbus, 1984—. Bd. dirs. Landmarks Preservation Coun. of Ill., 1972-92, Streeterville Corp., 1986-87, Washington Sq. Health Found., 1985—, Henrotin Hosp., 1976-89; mem. vestry St. Chrysostom's Ch., 1980-92; mem. alumni bd. dirs. Vanderbilt U., 1994—. Mem. ABA, Chgo. Bar Assn., Lambda Alpha Internat., Chgo. Club, Casino Club, Racquet Club. Republican. Episcopalian. Real property, Securities, General corporate. Home: 1242 N Lake Shore Dr Chicago IL 60610-2361 Office: Robert E Lend Co Inc 3 First Nat Plz Ste 2111 Chicago IL 60602

**YORK, STEPHANIE HELAYNE,** law administrator; b. Atlanta, Aug. 6, 1970; d. Harold Morton and Judith Ellen Post; m. John Robert York, May 24, 1998. BS summa cum laude, Ohio U., 1991; JD, U. Akron, 1994. Bar: Ohio 1995, U.S. Dist. Ct. (no. dist.) Ohio 1996, U.S. Ct. Appeals (6th cir.) 1996. Asst. law dir. City of Akron, 1995—. Vol. Hospice of Vis. Nurses, Akron, 1996—. Mem. Ohio State Bar Assn., Akron Bar Assn. (aux. mem. 1995—). Democrat. Jewish. Avocations: tae kwon do, softball, hiking, kick boxing. Office: City of Akron Law Dept 161 S High St Ste 202 Akron OH 44308-1615

**YORK, WENDY C.,** lawyer; b. Kewaunee, Wis., Oct. 12, 1967; d. David James and Joanne Louise Foster. BS in Criminal Justice, Calif. State U., Sacramento, 1989; JD, U. Pacific, 1993. Bar: Calif. 1993, U.S. Ct. Appeals (9th cir.), U.S. Dist. Ct. (ea. dist.) Calif. 1993, U.S. Dist. Ct. (no. dist.) Calif. Assoc. Bolling, Walter & Bawthrop, Sacramento, Calif., 1993-95, Javan, Tenorio & Slater, Sacramento, 1995-97; ptnr. Wendy C. York, PLC, Sacramento, 1997—. Fax: 916-565-8171. Personal injury, State civil litigation. Office: 601 University Ave Ste 110 Sacramento CA 95825-6706

**YORMAK, JONATHON K.,** lawyer; b. N.Y.C., Dec. 13, 1971; s. Stanley S. and Marsha Yormak. BA cum laude, Colby Coll., 1993; JD, Fordham U., 1996. Bar: Fla. 1997, N.Y. 1997. Assoc. Feldman & Gany, N.Y.C., 1996-97, Pryor Cashman Sherman & Flynn LLP, N.Y.C., 1997—. Chmn. Young Profls., The Children's Hearing Inst., N.Y.C., 1996-98. Mem. Bar Assn. of City of N.Y., N.Y. State Bar Assn. (real property law sect. 1997—), Fla. Bar Assn. Real property. Office: Pryor Cashman Sherman & Flynn LLP 410 Park Ave Fl 10 New York NY 10022-4441

**YOSKOWITZ, IRVING BENJAMIN,** merchant banker; b. Bklyn., Dec. 2, 1945; s. Rubin and Jennie Y.; m. Carol L. Magil, Feb. 11, 1973; children: Stephen M., Robert J. BBA, CCNY, 1966; JD, Harvard U., 1969; postgrad., London Sch. Econs., 1971-72. Bar: N.Y. 1970, D.C. 1970, Conn. 1982. Programmer IBM, East Fishkill, N.Y., 1966; systems analyst Office Sec. Def., Washington, 1969-71; assoc. Arnold & Porter, Washington, 1972-73; atty. IBM, 1973-79; regional counsel IBM, Bethesda, Md., to 1979; dep. gen. counsel United Technologies Corp., Hartford, Conn., 1979-81; v.p. and gen. counsel United Technologies Corp., 1981-86, sr. v.p., gen. counsel, 1986-90, exec. v.p., gen. counsel, 1990-98; sr. ptnr. Global Tech. Ptnrs., L.L.C., Washington, 1998—; bd. dirs. BBA Group, PLC, Exec. Risk Inc., Equant, N.V. Mem. editorial bd. Harvard Law Rev., 1968-69. With U.S. Army, 1969-71. Knox fellow, 1971-72. Mem. ABA, Am. Corp. Counsel Assn. (bd. dirs. 1982-85), Assn. Gen. Counsels. Contracts commercial, General corporate, Antitrust. Office: Global Tech Partners LLC 1300 Eye St NW Lowr 220E Washington DC 20005-3320

**YOST, ELLEN G. (ELLEN YOST LAFILI),** lawyer; b. Buffalo, May 30, 1945; d. Irwin Arthur and Sylvia Rosen Ginsberg; m. Louis Lafili; children: Elizabeth Anne, Peter Andrew, Benjamin Lewis Yost. AB, Mt. Holyoke Coll., 1966; JD, SUNY, Buffalo, 1983. Bar: N.Y., U.S. Dist. Ct. (we. dist.) N.Y. 1984. Assoc. Jaeckle, Fleischmann & Mugel, Buffalo, 1983-89, Saperston & Day, P.C., Buffalo, 1989—; ptnr. Griffith & Yost, Buffalo, 1991—. Pres. Buffalo Coun. on World Affairs, 1987-89; bd. dirs. Buffalo World Trade Assn., 1988-90, Legal Svcs. for Elderly, Disabled, Disadvantaged, 1984—. Mem. ABA (co-chair Can. law com. of internat. law and practice sect. 1990-94, vice chair immigration and nationality law com. 1994—, co-chair 1995—, co-chair task force N.Am. Free Trade Agreement 1991-94, immigration coord. com. 1996—, coun. internat. law and practice sect. 1998—), N.Y. State Bar Assn. (chmn. U.S. Can. law com. 1987-89, mem. exec. com. internat. law and practice sect. 1987-89, sec. commn. in internat. trade and transactions 1984-87), Am. Immigration Lawyers' Assn. Jewish. Avocations: travel, skiing, sailing. Immigration, naturalization, and customs, Private international. Office: Griffith & Yost 50 Fountain Plz Buffalo NY 14202-2212 also: Dreve des Renards 4, 1180 Brussels Belgium

**YOST, GERALD B.,** lawyer; b. Harvey, Ill., Dec. 21, 1954; s. Richard Dennis and Marilyn Patricia (Moore) Y.; m. Kay Lynn Benton, Apr. 16, 1977; children: Matthew Brian, Benjamin Gerald, Andrew Richard. BA in Journalsim, Drake U., 1973-76; student, Purdue U., 1975; JD, Hamline U., 1980. Bar: Minn. 1980, U.S. Dist. Ct. Minn. 1980, Wis. 1987. Assoc. Bergman, Street & Ulmen, Mpls., 1980-84; ptnr. Wasserman and Baill, Mpls., 1984-90, Yost, Stephenson & Sanford, Mpls., 1990-95, Yost & Baill LLP, Mpls., 1996—. Editor: Student Osteo. Med. Assn. Publ. mag., 1976; mem. Law Review Hamline U., 1978-80. Active YMCA, St. Paul. Recipient Am. Jurisprudence award, Lawyers Coop. Pub. Co., St. Paul, 1979. Mem. ABA, Minn. State Bar Assn., Wis. Bar Assn., Phi Alpha Delta, Sigma Delta Chi. Avocations: tennis, racquetball, boating and water skiing, jogging. General corporate, Mergers and acquisitions, Real property. Home: 277 Mt Curve Blvd Saint Paul MN 55105-1213 Office: Yost & Baill LLP 2350 One Fin Plz 120 S 6th St Minneapolis MN 55402-1803

**YOSTE, CHARLES TODD,** lawyer; b. Vicksburg, Miss., Nov. 11, 1948; s. Harry M. and Charlene (Todd) Y. BS, Miss. State U., 1971; JD, U. Miss., 1976. Bar: Miss. 1976, U.S. Dist. Ct. Miss. 1976, U.S. Ct. Appeals, 1982. Sole practice, Starkville, Miss., 1976—; city atty. Starkville, Miss., 1979-85, pros. atty., 1977-79, city judge, 1981-82. Candidate for Congress 2d dist. Miss., 1980. Served to capt. U.S. Army, 1971-73. Recipient Outstanding Young Man award Starkville Jaycees, 1980. Mem. ABA, Miss. Bar Assn., Am. Trial Lawyers Assn., Miss. Trial Lawyers Assn. (bd. govs. 1988—), Starkville C. of C. (pres. 1982), Am. Legion. Republican. Roman Catholic. Lodge: Rotary. General practice, Personal injury, Bankruptcy. Home: 902 Montgomery St Starkville MS 39759 Office: PO Box 488 Starkville MS 39760-0488

**YOUNG, ALAN SCOTT,** lawyer, engineer; b. Dallas, Sept. 21, 1960; s. David M. and Rose (Sunshine) Y.; m. Melanie Brown, Feb. 13, 1988; 1 child, Taylor Brianne. BS in Civil Engring., Tex. A&M U., 1984; JD, Tex. Wesleyan U., 1995. Bar: Tex. 1996; registered profl. engr. Tex. Asst. dist. project devel. engr., staff atty. Tex. Dept. of Transp., Dallas, 1984-98; gen. counsel North Tex. Tollway Authority, Dallas, 1998—. Recipient Bronze Key award ABA, 1994. Mem. Dallas Bar Assn., Tex. Inst. Transp. Engrs. Home: 9908 Ridgehaven Dr Dallas TX 75238-2623 Office: NTTA 3015 Raleigh St Dallas TX 75219-1236

**YOUNG, BARNEY THORNTON,** lawyer; b. Chillicothe, Tex., Aug. 10, 1934; s. Bayne and Helen Irene (Thornton) Y.; m. Sarah Elizabeth Taylor, Aug. 31, 1957; children: Jay Thornton, Sarah Elizabeth, Serena Taylor. BA, Yale U., 1955; LLB, U. Tex., 1958. Bar: Tex. 1958. Assoc. Thompson, Knight, Wright & Simmons, Dallas, 1958-65; ptnr. Rain, Harrell, Emery, Young & Doke, Dallas, 1965-87; mem. firm Locke Purnell Rain Harrell (A Profl. Corp.), 1987-98; of counsel Locke, Liddell & Sapp LLP, 1999—. Mem. adv. coun. Dallas Cmty. Chest Trust Fund, Inc., 1964-66; bd. dirs. Mental Health Assn. Dallas County, Inc., 1969-72, Trammell Crow Family Found., 1984-87; trustee Hockaday Sch., Dallas, 1971-77, 90—, chmn., 1994-96, Dallas Zool. Soc., 1986-92, Lamplighter Sch., Dallas, 1976-99, chmn., 1983-86, St. Mark's Sch., Dallas, 1970—, pres., 1976-78, The Found. for Callier Ctr. and Comm. Disorders, 1988-99, Friends of Ctr. for Human Nutrition, 1988—, Shelter Ministries of Dallas Found., 1993—, Dallas Hist. Soc., 1993—; mem. Yale Devel. Bd., 1984-91; 1998—. Fellow Tex. Bar Found., Dallas Bar Found.; mem. ABA, Tex. Bar Assn., Dallas Bar Assn., Am. Judicature Soc., Order of Coif, Phi Beta Kappa, Pi Sigma Alpha, Phi Gamma Delta, Phi Delta Phi, Dallas Country Club., Petroleum Club (Dallas), Yale Club (Dallas, N.Y.C.). General corporate, Mergers and acquisitions, Securities. Home: 6901 Turtle Creek Blvd Dallas TX 75205-1251 Office: Locke Liddell & Sapp LLP 2200 Ross Ave Ste 2200 Dallas TX 75201-2748

**YOUNG, C. CLIFTON,** state supreme court justice; b. Nov. 7, 1922, Lovelock, Nev.; m. Jane Young. BA, U. Nev., 1943; LLB, Harvard U., 1949. Bar: Nev. 1949, U.S. Dist. Ct. Nev. 1950, U.S. Supreme Ct. 1955. Justice Nev. Supreme Ct., Carson City, 1985—, chief justice, 1989-90. Office: Nev Supreme Ct Capitol Complex 201 S Carson St Carson City NV 89701-4702

**YOUNG, DAMON MICHAEL,** lawyer; b. Nashville, Dec. 1, 1940; s. Howard Cecil and Modena Louise Y.; m. Doris Ann Anderson, Aug. 26, 1961; children: Jerri Ann Fitts, Damon Michael Jr. JD, U. Ark., 1965. Bar: Ark., Tex., U.S. Supreme Ct., U.S. Ct. Appeals (8th and 5th cirs.), U.S. Dist. Ct. (ea. and we. dists.) Tex., U.S. Dist. Ct. (ea. & we. dists.) Ark. Assoc. Shaver, Tackett & Jones, Texarkana, Ark., 1964-68; ptnr. Shaver, Tackett, Young & Patton, Texarkana, Ark., 1968-70, Tacket, Young, Patton & Harrelson, Texarkana, Ark., 1970-72, Young & Patton, Texarkana, Ark., 1972-77, Young, Patton & Folsom, Texarkana, Ark., 1977-90; sr. ptnr. Damon Young Law Offices, Texarkana, Ark., 1990-93, Young, Kesterson & Pickett, Texarkana, Ark., 1993-95, Young & Pickett, Texarkana, Ark., 1995—. City atty. City Texarkana, 1965-67; mem. Ark. Ho. of Reps., Little Rock, 1967-70. Fellow Ark. Bar Found., Tex. Bar Found. (life); mem. Texarkana Bar Assn. (pres. 1996-97). Democrat. Episcopalian. Avocations: owning, breeding thoroughbred horses, skiing, hunting, saltwater fishing, flying. Federal civil litigation, Criminal. Home: 2904 Summerhill Rd Texarkana TX 75503 Office: Young & Pickett 4122 Texas Blvd Texarkana TX 75503-3011

**YOUNG, DEBORAH SCHWIND,** lawyer; b. Buffalo, Feb. 28, 1955; d. Richard G. and Rhoda Schwind; m. Thomas Paul Young, May 23, 1981. BA, Dartmouth Coll., 1976; JD, SUNY, Buffalo, 1979. Bar: N.Y. 1980, U.S. Dist. Ct. (we. dist.) N.Y. 1980. Assoc. Harter, Secrest and Emery, Rochester, N.Y., 1979-83; asst. v.p., asst. counsel Chase Lincoln First Bank, Rochester, 1983-85, v.p., sr. counsel, 1985-92; v.p., sr. assoc. counsel The Chase Manhattan Bank, Rochester, 1993-96, v.p., asst. gen. counsel, 1997—. Mem. pension com. Rochester Philharm. Orch., 1983-91; mem. Rochester-Monroe County Youth Bd., 1987-88. Mem. N.Y. Bar Assn. Republican. Lutheran. Banking. Office: The Chase Manhattan Bank 1 Chase Sq Rochester NY 14643-0002

**YOUNG, DONA DAVIS GAGLIANO,** lawyer, insurance executive; b. Bklyn., Jan. 8, 1954; d. Vincent Joseph and Shirley Elizabeth (Davis) Gagliano; m. Roland F. Young III, Aug. 18, 1979; children: Meghan Davis, Wesley Davis, Taylor Davis. BA and MA in Polit. Sci., Drew U., 1976; JD, U. Conn., 1980. Bar: Conn. 1980, U.S. Dist. Ct. Conn. 1980. With Phoenix Home Life Ins. Co., Hartford, Conn., 1980—, asst. v.p. reinsurance adminstrn., 1983-85; 2d v.p., ins. counsel Phoenix Mut. Life Ins. Co., Hartford, Conn., 1985-87, v.p. and asst. gen. counsel, 1987-89; sr. v.p. and gen. counsel Phoenix Home Life Mut. Ins. Co., Hartford, 1989-94; exec. v.p. individual sales and mktg., gen. counsel Phoenix Home Life Mut. Ins. Co., 1994-95, exec. v.p. individual ins. and gen. counsel, 1995—; trustee Hartford Coll. Women; bd. dirs. LIMRA Internat., Sonoco Products Co. Mem. fin. com. Asylum Hill Congl. Ch. Recipient Leadership award Women in Business (New Eng. Coun.), 1994. Mem. ABA, Am. Coun. of Life Ins. (com. on risk classification 1985-88, legis. com. 1989—), Am. Soc. Corp. Secs., Assn. Life Ins. Counsel (bd. govs.), Hartford County Bar Assn., Conn. Bar Assn. Republican. Congregationalist. Insurance, General corporate. Office: Phoenix Home Life Mut Ins 1 American Row Hartford CT 06103-2833

**YOUNG, DOUGLAS HOWARD,** lawyer; b. Bronxville, N.Y., Oct. 16, 1948; s. Joseph Paul and Frances (Lally) Y.; m. Betsy Baker, Apr. 24, 1971; children: Jeffrey D., Kevin C. BA, Gettysburg Coll., 1970; JD magna cum laude, Syracuse U., 1978. Bar: N.Y. 1979, U.S. Dist. Ct. (no. dist.) N.Y. 1979, U.S. Claims Ct. 1992. Ptnr. Melvin & Melvin, Syracuse, N.Y., 1978—; bd. dirs. Onondaga County Legal Svcs. Corp., Syracuse, pres., 1995-96; village atty. Village of Jordan, N.Y., 1980—. Editor Syracuse Law Rev., 1977-78; contbr. articles to profl. jours. Cub scout leader Boy Scouts Am., Syracuse, 1980-81; umpire Liverpool (N.Y.) Little League, Babe Ruth League, 1981-90, Optimists Basketball, Liverpool, 1985-87; coach Babe Ruth Baseball, Liverpool, 1989-90. Capt. USAF, 1971-76. Named Eagle Scout Boy Scouts Am., 1965. Mem. N.Y. State Bar Assn., N.Y.S. Trial Lawyers Assn., Onondaga County Bar Assn. Episcopalian. Avocations: gardening, golf, outdoor hiking. General civil litigation, Condemnation. Home: 4058 Pawnee Dr Liverpool NY 13090-2853 Office: Melvin & Melvin 217 S Salina St Syracuse NY 13202-1390

**YOUNG, DOUGLAS REA,** lawyer; b. L.A., July 21, 1948; s. James Douglas and Dorothy Belle (Rea) Y.; m. Terry Forrest, Jan. 19, 1974; 1 child, Megann Forrest. BA cum laude, Yale U., 1971; JD, U. Calif., Berkeley, 1976. Bar: Calif., 1976, U.S. Dist. Ct. (no. dist.) Calif. 1976, U.S. Ct. Appeals (6th and 9th cirs.) 1977, U.S. Dist. Ct. (ctrl. dist.) Calif. 1979, U.S. Dist. Ct. Hawaii, U.S. Supreme Ct. 1982; cert. specialist in appellate law. Law clk. U.S. Dist. Ct. (no. dist.) Calif., San Francisco, 1976-77; assoc. Farella, Braun & Martel LLP, San Francisco, 1977-82, ptnr., 1983—; spl. master U.S. Dist. Ct. (no. dist.) Calif., 1977-78, 88, 96; mem. Criminal Justice Act Def. Panel no. dist. Calif.; mem. faculty Calif. Continuing Edn. of Bar, Berkeley, 1982—, Nat. Inst. Trial Advocacy, Berkeley, 1984—, Practicing Law Inst., 1988—; adj. prof. Hastings Coll. Advocacy, 1985—; vis. lectr. law Boalt Hall/U. Calif., Berkeley, 1986; judge pro tem San Francisco Mcpl. Ct., 1984—, San Francisco Superior Ct., 1990—. Author: (with Purver and Davis) California Trial Handbook, ed edit., (with Hon. Richard Byrne, Purver and Davis), 3d edit., (with Purver, Davis and Kerper) The Trial Lawyers Book, (with Hon. Eugene Lynch, Taylor, Purver and Davis) California Negotiation and Settlement Handbook; contbr. articles to profl. jours. Bd. dirs. Berkeley Law Found., 1977-78, chmn., 1978-79; bd. dirs. San Francisco Legal Aid Soc., pres., 1993—; bd. dirs. Pub. Interest Clearinghouse, San Francisco, chmn., 1987—, treas., 1988—; chmn. Attys. Task Force for Children, Legal Svcs. for Children, 1987—; mem. State Bar Appreciate Law Adv. Commn., 1994—. Recipient award of appreciation Berkeley Law Found., 1983. Fellow Am. Coll. Trial Lawyers; mem. ABA (Pro Bono Pub. award 1992), San Francisco Bar Assn. (founding chmn. litigation sect. 1988-89, award of appreciation 1989, bd. dirs. 1990-91), Calif. Acad. Appellate Lawyers, McFetridge Am. Inn of Ct. (master), Lawyers Club San Francisco. Democrat. Federal civil litigation, State civil litigation, Criminal. Office: Farella Braun & Martel 235 Montgomery St Ste 3000 San Francisco CA 94104-2902

**YOUNG, GEORGE CRESSLER,** federal judge; b. Cin., Aug. 4, 1916; s. George Philip and Gladys (Cressler) Y.; m. Iris June Hart, Oct. 6, 1951; children: George Cressler, Barbara Ann. A.B., U. Fla., 1938, LL.B., 1940; postgrad., Harvard Law Sch., 1947. Bar: Fla. 1940. Practice in Winter Haven, 1940-41; asso. firm Smathers, Thompson, Maxwell & Dyer, Miami, 1947; adminstrv., legislative asst. to Senator Smathers of Fla., 1948-52; asst. U.S. atty. Jacksonville, 1952; partner firm Knight, Kincaid, Young & Harris, Jacksonville, 1953-61; U.S. dist. judge No., Middle and So. dists. Fla., 1961-73; chief judge Middle Dist., 1973-81, sr. judge, 1981—; Mem. com. on adminstrn. fed. magistrates system Jud. Conf. U.S., 1973-80. Bd. dirs. Jacksonville United Cerebral Palsy Assn., 1953-60. Served to lt. (s.g.) USNR, 1942-46. Mem. Rollins Coll. Alumni Assn. (pres. 1968-69), ABA (spl. com. for adminstrn. criminal justice), Fla. Bar Assn. (gov. 1960-61), Jacksonville Bar Assn. (past pres.), Order of Coif, Fla. Blue Key, Phi Beta Kappa, Phi Kappa Phi, Phi Delta Phi, Sigma Alpha Epsilon. Home: 2424 Shrewsbury Rd Orlando FL 32803-1334 Office: US Dist Ct 635 US Courthouse 80 N Hughey Ave Orlando FL 32801-2278

**YOUNG, HUBERT HOWELL, JR.,** lawyer, real estate investor and developer; b. Franklin, Va., May 30, 1945; s. Hubert Howell and Elizabeth Ann (Davidson) Y.; m. Christine P. Brooks, Dec. 31, 1964; 1 son, Hubert Howell, III. BA, Washington Lee U., 1967, LLB, magna cum laude, 1969. Bar: Va. 1969, U.S. Supreme Ct. 1972, Tex. 1974, U.S. Dist. Ct. Tex. 1974, U.S. Dist. Ct. (ea. dist.) Va. 1980. Assoc., Johnson, Bromberg, Leeds and Riggs, Dallas, 1973-75; gen. counsel Trammel Crow Co., Dallas, 1975-79; sole practice, Suffolk, Va., 1979—; gen. counsel Young Properties, Suffolk, 1979—; dir. Young Properties Devel. Corp., Trammel Crow Investment Corp., Suffolk Broadcasting Corp. Pres. Suffolk (Va.) Found. Trust, 1982-83; vice chmn. Suffolk Coalition for Sr. Citizen Housing, Inc., 1982-83; mem. Suffolk Substance and Abuse and Youth Council, 1982-84; chmn. Suffolk Rep. Party, 1982-85; commr. Med. Coll. Hampton Roads, 1990-96; dir. Va. Symphony, 1991-94. Served as lt. JAG, USN, 1969-73. Designated col. Confederate Army The Lee-Jackson Meml. Inc., 1981. Mem. ABA, Suffolk Bar Assn. (pres. 1994), Property Owners and Mgrs. Assn. (pres. 1995-96). Club: Cedar Point, Town Point, Sports, Ducks Unlimited (Suffolk). General practice, General corporate, Real property. Office: Young Properties 444 N Main St Suffolk VA 23434-4425

**YOUNG, JAMES R.,** corporate lawyer. BA, U. Mich., 1973, JD, 1976. Bar: D.C. 1976. V.p.-regulation, gen. counsel Bell Atlantic Network Svcs., Inc.; v.p., gen. counsel Bell Atlantic Corp., Arlington, Va., 1993—; exec. v.p., gen. counsel Bell Atlantic Corp., N.Y.C. Office: Bell Atlantic Corp 38th Fl 1095 Ave of Americas New York NY 10036*

**YOUNG, JESS WOLLETT,** lawyer; b. San Antonio, Sept. 16, 1926; s. James L. and Zetta (Alonso) Y.; m. Mary Alma Keeter, Apr. 17, 1954 (dec. Dec. 1996); children—Zetta, Imogen. BA, Trinity U., San Antonio, 1957; LLB, St. Mary's U., 1958. Bar: Tex. 1957, U.S. Dist. Ct. (we. dist.) Tex. 1960, U.S. Dist. Ct. (so. dist.) Tex. 1961, U.S. Tax Ct. 1970, U.S. Ct. Appeals (5th cir.) 1981, U.S. Supreme Ct. 1981. Ptnr. Thompson, Thompson, Young & Jones, San Antonio, 1958-63, Moursund, Ball & Young, San Antonio, 1965-73; v.p., dir. Moursund, Ball & Young, Inc., San Antonio, 1973-78; pres., dir. Young & Richards, Inc., San Antonio, 1978-81, Young, Murray & Richards, Inc., San Antonio, 1981-82, Young & Murray, Inc., 1983-87, sole practice, 1987-91, 94—; staff atty., sheriff Bexar County, Tex.; county judge, Bexar County (Tex.), 1964; city atty. City of Olmos Park (Tex.), 1965-70, City of Poteet (Tex.), 1975-76; spl. county judge, Bexar County, 1967. Mem. Tex. State Dem. Exec. Com., 1970-72, Tex. State Rep. Exec. Com., 1984-92, Rep. Precinct committeeman, 1984-92; Dem. precinct committeeman, San Antonio, 1964-76. Served with USNR, 1944-46. Mem. ABA, Tex. Assn. Def. Counsel, Tex. Assn. Bank Counsel, San Antonio Bar Assn., Delta Theta Phi. Episcopalian. Clubs: San Antonio Petroleum, San Antonio Gun (dir. 1958-63, 80-82). Real property, Banking, Administrative and regulatory. Home: 1221 Wiltshire Ave San Antonio TX 78209-6056 Office: 40 NE Loop 410 Ste 210 San Antonio TX 78216-5826

**YOUNG, JOHN ANDREW,** lawyer; b. Corpus Christi, Tex., Nov. 10, 1916; s. Phillip Marvin and Katherine Julia Y.; m. Jane Fife Gallier, Jan. 21, 1950 (dec. 1977); children—Gaffney, Nancy, John, Robert, Patty. B.A., St. Edward's U., Austin, Tex., 1938, LL.D., 1961; student Tex. U. Sch. Law, 1939-41. Bar: Tex. 1940, U.S. Supreme Ct. 1955, U.S. Ct. Appeals (D.C. cir.) 1979, U. D.C. 1978. Chief prosecutor Dist. Atty's. Office, Corpus Christi, 1946-50; county atty. Nueces County (Tex.), Corpus Christi, 1950-51, county judge, 1952-56; mem. 1957-79 Congresses from 14th Tex. dist.; sole practice Washington, 1979—; legal and legis. cons. The Coastal Corp., Houston, 1979—. Contbr. numerous articles and treatises to newspapers and legal jours. Served to lt. cmdr. USN, 1941-45. Recipient Distinguished Service award City of Corpus Christi, 1971, Distinguished Service medal U.S. Fish & Wildlife Service, 1967; numerous plaques of appreciation, 1965-77. Mem. ABA, D.C. Bar Assn., Tex. Bar Assn., Maritime Law Assn. of U.S., Corpus Christi C. of C. (plaques 1965, 76), Delta Theta Phi. Clubs: Chesapeake Country, (Lusby, Md.), Old Dominion Yacht (Alexandria, Va.), Nat. Democratic (Washington). Lodges: K.C., Elks, Eagles, Moose, VFW, DAV, Am. Legion. Admiralty. Home: 1705 N Albemarle St Mc Lean VA 22101-4222 Office: 2000 M St NW Ste 380 Washington DC 20036-3307 Office: 1750 Santa Fe St Corpus Christi TX 78404-1857

**YOUNG, JOHN BYRON,** retired lawyer; b. Bakersfield, Calif., Aug. 10, 1913; s. Lewis James and Gertrude Lorraine (Clark) Y.; m. Helen Beryl Stone, Dec. 26, 1937; children: Sally Jean, Patricia Helen, Lucia Robin. BA, UCLA, 1934; LLB, U. Calif., Berkeley, 1937. Pvt. practice law Hargreaves & Young, later Young Wooldridge, Bakersfield, 1937-40; dep. county counsel County of Kern, Bakersfield, 1940-42; dep. rationing atty. U.S. OPA, Bakersfield and Fresno, Calif., 1942; ptnr. firm Young Wooldridge and predecessors, Bakersfield, 1946-78, assoc. law firm, 1978-91; bd. dirs., legal counsel Kern County Water Assn., Bakersfield, 1953-76. Mem., chmn. Kern County Com. Sch. Dist. Orgn., Bakersfield, 1950s and 60s; mem. Estate Planning Coun. of Bakersfield, 1960-76, pres., 1965-66. Capt. JAGC, U.S. Army, 1943-46. Mem. Kern County Bar Assn. (pres. 1948, Bench and Bar award 1978). Home: 13387 Barbados Way Del Mar CA 92014-3501 Office: Young Wooldridge 1800 30th St Fl 4 Bakersfield CA 93301-1919

**YOUNG, JOHN HARDIN,** lawyer; b. Washington, Apr. 25, 1948; s. John D. and Laura Virginia (Gwathmey) Y.; m. Mary Frances (Farley) Crosby. JD, U. Va., 1973; BCL, Oxford U., Eng., 1976. Bar: Va. 1973, D.C. 1974, U.S. Dist. Ct. (ea. dist.) Va. 1974, U.S. Dist. Ct. D.C. 1974, Internat. Trade Ct. 1974, U.S. Ct. Fed. Claims 1974, U.S. Ct. Appeals (4th, Fed. and D.C. cirs.), U.S. Supreme Ct. 1977, U.S. Dist. Ct. Md. 1989; cert. mediator Va. Supreme Ct. Ptnr. Porter Wright Morris & Arthur, Washington, 1988-92, of counsel, 1992—; gen. counsel The Smoot Corp., 1992—; pvt. practice law, 1973-76, 78-81, 1983-88; spl. counsel Dem. Nat. Com., 1997-99; mem. adv. bd. Antitrust Bull., Jour. Antiturst Law and Econs.; mem. U.S. Sec. State's adv. com. Pvt. internat. Law, 1987-95; chmn. Va. Retirement Sys. Rev. Bd., 1990-94; asst. atty. gen. Commonwealth of Va., 1976-78; mem. master plan task force City of Alexandria, Va., 1987-88, mem. budget and fiscal affairs adv. com., 1989-91; moderator Alexandria Forum, 1993-98, Fedn. Forum/TV Channel 10, 1989-91; gen. counsel CAPAccess, 1992-96. Contbr. articles to profl. jours. and books on litigation, evidence and trial tactics. Gen. counsel Dem. Party of Va., 1993-97, state counsel, 1988-92, state counsel dem. predsl. campaign, 1980-96; counsel Gov. Wilder recount, 1989, Gov. Glendenning recount, 1995; nat. chair DNC Conf. of Dem. Counsel, 1995-97; nat. chair Dem. Nat. Com. Nat. Lawyers Coun., 1998—, mem. exec. com., 1992-97. Mem. ABA (chair 1999-2000, coun. 1986-89, adminstrv. law sect., chmn. trade regulaion and competition com., 1983-86, chair dispute resolution com. 1994-96), Am. Law Inst., George Mason Am. Inn of Ct. (master 1990-99, master emeritus 1999—, counselor 1996-97), Hon. Soc. Mid. Temple U.K., Comml. Bar Assn. U.K. (overseas mem.), Am. Inns of Ct., Temple Bar Found. (founding mem., trustee), Phi Alpha Theta (history honors). Episcopalian. Administrative and regulatory, Federal civil litigation, Computer. Home: 5146 Woodmire Ln Alexandria VA 22311-1301 Office: 5201 Leesburg Pike Ste 1100 Falls Church VA 22041-3268

**YOUNG, JOSEPH H.,** federal judge; b. Hagerstown, Md., July 18, 1922; s. J. Edgar and Mabel K. (Koser) Y.; m. Doris Oliver, Sept. 6, 1947; children: Stephen A., William O., J. Harrison. A.B., Dartmouth Coll., 1948; LL.B., U. Va., 1951. Bar: Md. 1951. Assoc. firm Marbury Miller & Evans, Balt., 1951-52; assoc. firm Piper & Marbury, Balt., 1952-58, ptnr., 1958-71, mng. ptnr., 1968-71; judge U.S. Dist. Ct. Md., from 1971, now sr. judge; instr. Johns Hopkins U. (McCoy Coll.), 1954-62. Bd. dirs. Legal Aid Soc. Balt., 1958-71, CICHA (Health Appeal), 1964-71; bd. dirs. exec. com. Md. div. Am. Cancer Soc., 1958—, chmn. div. bd. dirs. 1969-71, bd. dirs. 1966—, chmn. nat. svcs. com. 1970-73, chmn. exec. com. 1976-77, dir.-at-large 1973-83, vice-chmn. nat. bd. dirs. 1975-77, chmn. nat. bd. 1977-80, chmn. pub. issues com. 1981-83, past officer dir. 1983-90, hon. life mem. 1990—, chmn. world-wide fight com. 1987-90, also mem. trust adv. bd.; mem. oncology adv. coun. Johns Hopkins U.; chmn. com. on campaign orgn. & pub. edn. Internat. Union Contra Cancer, Geneva, Switzerland, 1981-90, mem. fin. com., 1990—, chmn. 1993—, exec. com. 1993—. Decorated Bronze Star, Purple Heart. Recipient Disting. Service Award Am. Cancer Soc., 1983; Dartmouth Coll. Alumni award, 1983; James Ewing Soc. award, 1983. Mem. 4th Circuit Jud. Conf., Assn. Alumni Dartmouth Coll. (pres. 1984-85). Republican. Presbyterian (elder, deacon, trustee). Clubs: Hamilton Street, Rule Day, Lawyers Round Table. Office: US Dist Ct 101 W Lombard St Ste 7B Baltimore MD 21201-2626

**YOUNG, JOSEPH RUTLEDGE, JR.,** lawyer; b. Charleston, S.C., Mar. 28, 1943; s. Joseph Rutledge and Elizabeth Evans (Jenkins) Y.; m. Kathleen Baldwin Kimmell, Aug. 10, 1968; children—Joseph Rutledge, Simons Waring. B.A. with distinction in History, U. Va., 1965, LL.B., 1968. Bar: S.C. 1968, U.S. Dist. Ct. (so. dist.) S.C. 1968, U.S. Ct. Appeals (4th cir.) 1972. Assoc. Young, Clement, Rivers & Tisdale, Charleston, 1970-75, ptnr. 1975—. pres. Cen. R.R. of S.C., 1988—; bd. dirs. So. Nat. Bank of S.C., 1988-95, Branek Bank and Trust Co. of S.C., 1995—. Contbr. articles to profl. jours. Mem. Charleston City Council, 1975-80; v.p. Historic Charleston Found., 1993-95, pres., 1996-98; trustee Middleton Place Found., 1987—, Charleston Day Sch., 1985-91. Served to capt. U.S. Army, 1968-70, Vietnam. Decorated Bronze Star. Fellow Am. Coll. Trial Lawyers; mem. S.C. Bar Assn. (chmn. CLE 1982-84, bd. govs. 1984-88, sec. 1991, treas. 1992-93, pres.-elect 1993-94, pres. 1994-95, exec. com. bd. commrs. on grievances and discipline 1983-86), Am. Bd. Trial Advocates (diplomate), Fedn. Ins. and Corp. Counsel, St. Andrews Soc., St. George's Soc., Preservation Soc., U.S. Supreme Ct. Hist. Soc. (state chmn.), Carolina Yacht Club, Farmington Country Club, Yeamans Hall Club. General civil litigation, Health, Personal injury. Office: Young Clement Rivers & Tisdale 28 Broad St Charleston SC 29401-3070

**YOUNG, KEITH LAWRENCE,** lawyer; b. Chgo., Jan. 15, 1953; s. Lawrence E. and June E. (Verboomen) Y.; m. Wendy A. Kollross; children: Kyle W., Lauren H., Taylor E., Ashley E. BS, Iowa State U., 1974; JD, Ill. Inst. Tech., 1977. Bar: Ill. 1977, U.S. Dist. Ct. (no. dist.) Ill. 1977, U.S. Ct. Appeals (7th cir.) 1977. Pvt. practice law Chgo., 1977—; assoc. Anesi, Ozmon & Lewin, Chgo., 1977-79, James Demos Ltd., Chgo., 1979-80; ptnr. Lambruschi Young & Assocs., Chgo., 1980-87. Mem. ATLA, Ill. Bar Assn., Chgo. Bar Assn., Ill. Trial Lawyers Assn. Personal injury, Product liability. Office: 333 W Wacker Dr Chicago IL 60606-1220

**YOUNG, MICHAEL ANTHONY,** lawyer; b. Lima, Ohio, Sept. 3, 1960; s. William John and Bettye Jean (Day) Y. BS magna cum laude, U. Cen. Fla., 1981; JD with honors, Fla. State U., 1984. Bar: Ga. 1984, Fla. 1985. Assoc. Kilpatrick & Cody, Atlanta, 1984-86, Stokes, Lazarus & Carmichael, Atlanta, 1986-89; pvt. practice, Atlanta, 1989—; jud. intern U.S. Dist. Ct. (no. dist.) Fla., 1984; weekend atty. Atlanta Legal Aid Soc., 1985-86. Rsch. editor Fla. State U. Law Rev., 1982-84; contbr. articles to legal jours. Dir., pres. ChildKind Found. Mem. ABA, Assn. Trial Lawyers of Am., Fla. Bar Assn., Ga. Bar Assn., Atlanta Bar Assn. Avocations: scuba diving, golf, weightlifting. Personal injury, General civil litigation, Labor. Home: 5275 S Trimble Rd NE Atlanta GA 30342-2174 Office: 17 Executive Park Dr NE Ste 440 Atlanta GA 30329-2222

**YOUNG, MICHAEL KENT,** dean, lawyer, educator; b. Sacramento, Nov. 4, 1949; s. Vance Lynn and Ethelyn M. (Sowards) Y.; m. Suzan Kay Stewart, June 1, 1972; children: Stewart, Kathryn, Andrew. BA summa cum laude, Brigham Young U., 1973; JD magna cum laude, Harvard U., 1976. Bar: Calif. 1976, N.Y. 1985. Law clk. to Justice Benjamin Kaplan, Supreme Jud. Ct. Mass., Boston, 1976-77; law clk. to Justice William H. Rehnquist U.S. Supreme Ct., Washington, 1977-78; assoc. prof., prof., Fuyo prof. Japanese law Columbia U., N.Y.C., 1978-98; dir. Ctr. Japanese Legal Studies Ctr. for Korean Legal Studies, N.Y.C., 1985-98; dir. Program Internat. Human Rights and Religious Liberties Columbia U., N.Y.C., 1995-98; dep. legal advisor U.S. Dept. State, Washington, 1989-91, dep. under sec. for econ. affairs, 1991-93, amb. for trade and environ. affairs, 1992-93; dean, prof. of law George Washington U. Sch. of Law, Washington, 1998—; vice chair Commn. on Internat. Freedom of Religion, 1999—; vis. scholar law faculty U. Tokyo, 1978-80, 83; vis. prof. Waseda U., 1989; chmn. bd. advisors Japan Soc.; counsel select subcom. on arms transfers to Bosnia U.S. Ho. of Reps., 1996; mem. steering com. Law Profs. for Dole, 1996; POSCO Rsch. Inst. fellow, 1995-98. Fellow Japan Found., 1979-80; Fulbright fellow, 1983-84. Mem. Coun. Fgn. Rels. Mem. LDS Ch. Avocations: skiing, scuba diving, photography. E-mail: myoung@main.nlc.gwu.edu. Fax: 202-994-5157.

**YOUNG, MICHAEL RICHARD,** lawyer; b. Wiesbaden, Fed. Republic Germany, May 12, 1956; parents Am. Citizens; s. Richard Barton and Janet (Crawford) Y.; m. Leslie Anne Carroll, Aug. 11, 1984. BA, Allegheny Coll., 1978; JD, Duke U., 1981. Bar: N.Y. 1982, U.S. Dist. Ct. (so. and ea. dists.) N.Y. 1982, U.S. Ct. Appeals (9th cir.) 1990, U.S. Supreme Ct. 1994. Assoc. Willkie Farr & Gallagher, N.Y.C., 1981-90, ptnr., 1990—. Rsch. and mng. editor Duke Law Jour., 1980-81. Mem. ABA, Assn. of Bar of City of N.Y. (com. on legal edn. and admission to bar 1983-87), Phi Beta Kappa. Republican. Avocations: sailing, riding. General civil litigation. Home: 645 W End Ave Apt 1A New York NY 10025-7347 Office: Willkie Farr & Gallagher 787 Seventh Ave New York NY 10019-6099

**YOUNG, RANDY WILLIAM,** lawyer; b. Ft. Wayne, Ind., Oct. 19, 1949; s. Robert Arnold and Genevieve Mary (Obert) Y.; m. Julie Maree Brunson, June 16, 1984; children: Maree Elizabeth, Ann Elaine. BBA, U. Notre Dame, 1972; JD, Ind. U., 1975. Bar: Ind. 1975, U.S. Dist. Ct. (no. dist.) Ind. 1976. Law clk. to judge Ind. Ct. Appeals, Indpls., 1975-76; ptnr. Christoff, Cornelius & Young, Ft. Wayne, 1976-80; sole practice Ft. Wayne, 1980—. Recipient Silver Beaver award Boy Scouts Am., 1981, dist. award of Merit, 1985. Mem. Allen County Bar Assn. (treas. 1983-85), Allen County Law Library Assn. (treas. 1980-98). Clubs: St. Vincent Men's (Ft. Wayne), Notre Dame of Ft. Wayne (award of the Yr. 1985). Avocations: scouting, skiing, camping, backpacking. Probate, Family and matrimonial, Personal injury. Home: 2115 Carroll Rd Fort Wayne IN 46818-8908 Office: 202 W Berry St Fort Wayne IN 46802-2273

**YOUNG, ROBERT,** lawyer; b. Forest Hills, N.Y., Apr. 19, 1945; s. Herbert and Sarah Y.; m. Roslyn Patricia Harlan, July 1, 1972. BA, Duke U., 1966; JD, U. S.C., 1969; LLM in Taxation, NYU, 1974. Bar: S.C. 1969; CPA, S.C. Pvt. practice Columbia, S.C., 1974—. Lt. (JAGC) USN, 1969-72. Home: 1312 Greenhill Rd Columbia SC 29206-2810 Office: 1330 Richland St Columbia SC 29201-2522

**YOUNG, ROBERT P.,** state supreme court justice. Bachelor's degree cum laude, Harvard Coll., 1974; JD, Harvard U., 1977. With Dickinson, Wright, Moon, Van Dusen & Freeman, 1977-1992; v.p., corp. sec., gen. counsel AAA Mich., 1992; elected Mich. Ct. Appeals 1st Dist., 1995; justice Mich. Supreme Ct., 1996—. Mem. Mich. Civil Svc. Commn.; bd. trustees Cen. Mich. U. Office: PO Box 30052 Lansing MI 48909*

**YOUNG, ROBERT SHERMAN,** lawyer; b. Salt Lake City, Oct. 26, 1955; s. Sherman C. and Henrietta (Hatch) Y.; m. Laura Brewer, Sept. 19, 1979; children: Sarah, Amy, Emily, Abbie, Clara, Mary. BA in Fin., U. Utah, 1980, JD, 1983. Bar: Utah 1983, U.S. Ct. Appeals (10th cir.) 1987. With Law Offices Davis S. Young & Robert S. Young, Salt Lake City, 1983-85; corp. and gen. counsel Rocky Mountain Helicopters, Provo, Utah, 1985-95; with Prince, Yeates & Geldzahler, Salt Lake City, 1995—. Scoutleader Boy Scouts Am., Salt Lake City, 1992-93; trustee, pres. Brigham Young Family Assn., Salt Lake City, 1995-96. Mem. ABA, Utah Bar Assn., Lawyer-Pilots Bar Assn. (Utah chmn. 1993), Aviation Ins. Assn. (lectr. 1994). Mem. LDS Ch. Avocations: golf, tennis, basketball, travel, home improvement. Aviation, Product liability, General civil litigation. Office: Prince Yeates & Geldzahler City Ctr I 175 E 400 S Ste 900 Salt Lake City UT 84111-2357

**YOUNG, ROGER M.,** lawyer; b. Cass City, Mich., Feb. 15, 1960; s. James William and Joyce (Little) Y.; m. Janice Marie Young, Apr. 13, 1984. BS, Bapt. Coll. Charleston, 1980; JD, U. S.C., 1983; LLD (hon.), U. Charleston, 1992. Bar: S.C. 1983, U.S. Dist. Ct. S.C. 1984. Pvt. practice Charleston, S.C., 1983-95; mcpl. judge City of North Charleston, Charleston, S.C., 1988-90; acting city atty. City of North Charleston, S.C., 1995; mem. S.C. Ho. Reps., 1990-94; equity ct. judge Charleston County, S.C., 1996—; adj. prof. polit. sci. Charleston S. U., 1986. Recipient Order Palmetto Gov. Carroll Campbell, 1994; named Disting. Alumnus of the Yr. Charleston S. U., 1998. Mem. ABA, Am. Judicature Soc., Am. Judges Assn., S.C. Bar Assn. Home: 8121 Greenridge Rd Charleston SC 29406-9769

**YOUNG, ROLAND FREDERIC, III,** lawyer; b. Norway, Maine, Apr. 8, 1954; s. Roland Frederic Jr. and Marylyn May (Bartlett) Y.; m. Dona Davis Gagliano, Aug. 18, 1979; children: Meghan, Wesley, Taylor. AB, Cornell U., 1976; JD, U. Conn., 1979. Bar: Conn. 1979, U.S. Dist. Ct. Conn., U.S. Tax Ct., U.S. Ct. Appeals (2d cir.). Lectr. Hartford (Conn.) Grad. Ctr., Hartford, Conn., 1992—; ptnr. Howard, Kohn, Sprague & FitzGerald, Hartford, Conn., 1984-91, O'Brien, Tanski & Young, Hartford, Conn., 1991—; lectr. Hartford Grad. Ctr., 1991—. Author (seminar booklet) Confidentiality of Med. Records, 1989, Limiting Damages, 1990; co-author (seminar booklet) Med. Malpractice in Conn., 1992; editor Conn. Risk Mgmt. Assn., 1986—. Mem. Am. Acad. Hosp. Attys. (chmn. publs. and programs subcom., tchg. hosps.), Def. Rsch. Inst., Inc., Am. Soc. Law and Medicine, Nat. Assn. Health Law Attys., Am. Coll. Healthcare Execs., Conn. Bar Assn., Conn. Def. Lawyers Assn., Conn. Hosp. Assn., Hartford County Bar Assn. (medico-legal liaison com.). Avocations: tennis, skiing, golf. Federal civil litigation, Health, Personal injury. Office: O'Brien Tanski & Young City Place II 16th Fl Hartford CT 06103

**YOUNG, ROMA SKEEN,** lawyer; b. Vancouver, Wash., Feb. 21, 1950; d. Carroll Hallam and Dorothy Elizabeth (Miller) Skeen; m. Robert Hugh Young, Jr., May 20,1978; children: Matthew Hallam, Brian Robert. BA, Sweetbriar Coll., 1971; JD, Georgetown U., 1978. Bar: Pa. 1978. Mem. staff U.S. Senate Energy Com., Washington, 1972-75; lobbyist Marathon Oil Co., Washington, 1975-78; assoc. Pepper, Hamilton & Scheetz, Phila., 1978-84; assoc. Wolf, Block, Schorr and Solis-Cohen, Phila., 1984-89, ptnr., 1989—. Labor, Real property. Office: Wolf Block Schorr and Solis-Cohen 15th And Chestnut St Fl 12 Philadelphia PA 19102-2625

**YOUNG, RONALD W.,** lawyer, sole practice; b. Fayetteville, W. Va., Oct. 29, 1947; s. Luther J. and Jane Y.; m. Carletta Lynn Clyatt, June 14, 1997; children: Krista, Jason, Malorie. BA, U. So. Fla., 1969; JD, Stetson Coll., 1972. Bar: Fla. 1972, U.S. Dist Ct (mid. dist.) Fla., U.S. Ct. Appeals (11th cir.). Mem. AFTL. Family and matrimonial, Criminal, Personal injury. Office: 200 W Dr M L King Tampa FL 33603

**YOUNG, STEVEN SCOTT,** managing director, writer; b. Chgo., July 10, 1966; s. Richard Allen and Carol Ann (Schellinger) Y. BA, Loyola U., Chgo., 1988; MA, Northwestern U., 1989; postgrad., DePaul U., 1989—. Senate analyst Ill. Senate Rsch. Staff, Chgo., 1986; adminstrv. asst. Cook County Pub. Def., Chgo., 1986-87; investigator Lake County Pub. Def., Waukegan, Ill., 1987-89; v.p. Young Environ. Services, Glenview, Ill., 1988—; mng. dir. Internat. Congress Environ. Profls., Northbrook, Ill, 1986-88, Ill. Acad. Criminology, Chgo., 1986-87. Author: Environmental Law, 1988, (computer program) Criminal Case Tracking System, 1986, Environmental Law Outline, 1991, Environmental Dictionary, 1992, Environmental Auditing, 1994, Clean Air Regulation, 1994, Environmental Crime, 1996, Hazardous Waste Regulation, 1995, Clean Water Regulation, 1998, Environmental Economics, 1998; contbr. articles to profl. jours. Active Young Dems., Northfield Twp., Ill., 1983; bd. dirs. Nat. Registry Environ. Profls., 1989—. Mem. IEEE, ICSA, Soc. for Plastics Engrs., Inter-Am. Bar Assn., Assn. for Computing Machinery. Avocations: sailing, computing, boardgames. Address: 326 Hambletonian Dr Oak Brook IL 60523-2620

**YOUNG, THOMAS PAUL,** lawyer; b. Jamestown, N.Y., Dec. 11, 1955; s. Burdette R. and Ruth Ann (Granquist) Y.; m. Deborah Ann Schwind, May 23, 1981; 1 child, Amanda Marie. BA, SUNY, Geneseo, 1977; JD, Georgetown U., 1980. Bar: N.Y. 1981, U.S. Dist. Ct. (we. dist.) N.Y. 1981. Assoc. Hodgson, Russ, Andrews, Woods & Goodyear, Buffalo, 1980-81; asst. counsel Gannett Co., Inc., Rochester, N.Y., 1982-84; assoc. Underberg & Kessler, Rochester, 1984-91, sr. atty., 1991-98; of counsel Harter, Secrest & Emery LLP, Rochester, 1998—. Mem. Perinton (N.Y.) Rep. Com., 1989—; mem. coun. Bethlehem Luth. Ch., Fairport, N.Y., 1984-90; bd. dirs. Geneseo Found., Inc., 1982—; bd. dirs., sec. Martin Luther Found., Rochester, 1986-89; mem. allocations com. United Way Greater Rochester, 1990-95; mem. zoning bd. appeals, Town of Perinton, N.Y., 1997—. Mem. ABA, N.Y. State Bar Assn. General corporate, Securities, Mergers and acquisitions. Office: Harter Secrest & Emery LLP 700 Midtown Tower Rochester NY 14604-2070

**YOUNG, WILLIAM GLOVER,** federal judge; b. Huntington, N.Y., Sept. 23, 1940; s. Woodhull Benjamin and Margaret Jean (Wilkes) Y.; m. Beverly June Bigelow, Aug. 5, 1967; children: Mark Edward, Jeffrey Woodhull, Todd Russell. AB, Harvard U., 1962, LLB, 1967. Bar: Mass. 1967, U.S. Supreme Ct. 1970. Law clk. to chief justice Supreme Jud. Ct., Mass., 1967-68; spl. asst. atty. gen. Mass., 1969-72, chief legal counsel to gov., 1972-74; asso. firm Bingham, Dana and Gould, Boston, 1968-72; ptnr. Bingham, Dana and Gould, 1975-78; assoc. justice Superior Ct., Commonwealth of Mass., Boston, 1978-85; judge U.S. Dist. Ct. Mass., Boston, 1985—; mem. budget com., 1987—, chmn. economy subcom., 1991—; lectr. part time Harvard Law Sch., 1979-90, Boston Coll. Law Sch., 1968-90, Boston U. Law Sch. Served to capt. U.S. Army, 1962-64. Mem. Am. Law Inst., Mass. Bar Assn., Boston Bar Assn., Harvard Alumni (pres. 1976-77). Office: US Courthouse Rm 5710 US Courthouse Boston MA 02110

**YOUNGBLOOD, ELAINE MICHELE,** lawyer; b. Schenectady, N.Y., Jan. 9, 1944; d. Roy W. and Mary Louise (Read) Ortoleva; m. William Gerald Youngblood, Feb. 14, 1970; children: Flagg Khristian, Megan Michele. BA, Wake Forest Coll., 1965; JD, Albany Law Sch., 1969. Bar: Tex. 1970, U.S. Dist. Ct. (no. dist.) Tex. 1971, U.S. Dist. Ct. (so. dist.) Tex. 1972, Tenn. 1978, U.S. Dist. Ct. (mid. dist.) Tenn. 1978, U.S. Dist. Ct. (we. dist.) Tenn. 1998. Assoc. Fanning & Harper, Dallas, 1969-70, Crocker & Murphy, Dallas, 1970-71, McClure & Burch, Houston, 1972-75, Brown, Bradshaw & Plummer, Houston, 1975-76; ptnr. Seligmann & Youngblood, Nashville, 1977-88; pvt. practice, Nashville, 1988-94; of counsel Ortale, Kelley Herbert & Crawford, 1994—. Contbr. articles to profl. jours. Mem. Comm. for Women in Govt., Dallas, 1969-71, Law Day Com. of Dallas Bar Assn., 1970-71; bd. dirs. Christmas Village, 1999—; vestry Ch. of Advent, 1991. Fellow Nashville Bar Found.; mem. Tex. Bar Assn., Tenn. Bar Assn., Nashville Bar Assn. (fee dispute com. 1990—, vice-chair 1996, chair 1997—, CLE com. 1996—, L.A.W. 1996—, bd. dirs. 1996, treas., 1997, Blvd. Bolt Com. 1996—, publicity, steering com. 1997), Tenn. Trial Lawyers Assn., Phi Beta Pi, Cable Club of Nashville (charter), Davidson County Rep. Women's Club. Republican. Episcopalian. Personal injury, Workers' compensation, Insurance. Address: PO Box 198985 200 Fourth Ave N Fl 3 Noel Pl Nashville TN 37219-8985

**YOUNGDAHL, JAY THOMAS,** lawyer; b. St. Louis, May 29, 1952; s. James Edward and Patricia Ruth (Lucy) Y.; m. Mary Ellen Vogler, Dec. 12, 1981; children: Benjamin Douglass, Colleen Alexandra. BS, U. Houston, 1978; JD, U. Tex., 1980. Bar: Ark. 1981, U.S. Dist. Ct. (ea. and we. dists.) Ark. 1981, U.S. Ct. Appeals (8th, 10th and 11th cirs.) 1981, Ariz. 1992, U.S. Claims Ct. 1992, Tex. 1994. Mng. atty. Youngdahl & Youngdahl, Little Rock, 1981-93; mng. ptnr. Youngdahl & Sadin, PC, Friendswood, Tex., 1993—; adj. instr. Webster Coll., Little Rock, 1983—; adj. prof. U. Ark., Little Rock Sch. of Law, 1988—; mem. Ark. Employment Security Div. Adv. Coun., Little Rock, 1980-97, Gov.'s Workers Compensation Study Com., Little Rock, 1985-86. With U.S. Army, 1972-74. Mem. ABA, Ark. Bar Assn. (chmn. labor law sect. 1983-84), ATLA, Ark. Trial Lawyers Assn., AFL-CIO Lawyers Coordinating Com. (adv. bd.), Acad. Rail Labor Attys., Tex. Trial Lawyers Assn., State Bar Tex. (Pro Bono Coll. 1996). Avocations: running, reading, flying. Labor, Personal injury, Federal civil litigation. Office: Youngdahl & Sadin PC 211 E Parkwood Ave Ste 207 Friendswood TX 77546-5155

**YOUNGER, CANDACE ANNE,** lawyer; b. L.A., Dec. 19, 1968; d. Eric Eberhard Younger and Nina Joyce Webster. BA, Vassar Coll., 1990; JD, UCLA, 1993. Bar: Calif. 1993. Assoc. Hancock, Rothert & Bunshoft, L.A., 1993-95, Manatt, Phelps & Phillips, LLP, L.A., 1995—. Co-chair alumnae/alumni recruiting com. Vassar Coll., L.A., 1993-94; co-chair membership com. MOCA Contemporaries, L.A., 1996-97. Mem. Lawyers Assn. L.A., Beverly Hills Bar Assn. Democrat. Office: Manatt Phelps & Phillips LLP 11355 W Olympic Blvd Los Angeles CA 90064-1614

**YOUNGS, CHRISTOPHER JAY,** lawyer; b. Stuttgart, Germany, Dec. 20, 1956; came to U.S., 1958; s. Jay Rotigel and Nancy (Hazen) Y.; m. Lisa Pepicelli, May 14, 1983; children: Jeffrey Christopher, Marisa Beth. BA cum laude, U. Pitts., 1978, JD, 1982. Bar: Pa. 1982, U.S. Dist. Ct. (we. dist.) Pa. 1982. Assoc. Rosenzweig & Burton, Pitts., 1982-83, Pepicelli, Pepicelli, Watts & Youngs PC, Meadville, Pa., 1983-85; ptnr. Watts, Pepicelli, Youngs & Youngs PC, Meadville, Pa., 1985-90; pres. Pepicelli, Youngs & Youngs, PC, 1990—; solicitor Meadville Parking Authority, French Creek Joint Mcpl. Authority; asst. solicitor to Crawford County. Advisor Crawford County (Pa.) Law Exploring Post, 1986; mem. exec. com. Crawford County Dem. Party. Mem. Pa. Bar Assn., Crawford County Bar Assn., Assn. Trial Lawyers Am., Meadville Area C. of C. (bd. dirs. 1986—, v.p. 1989—, pres. 1991-93), Kiwanis (pres. 1988). Democrat. Avocations: canoeing, fishing, hunting, distance running, working with children and young adults. Workers' compensation, Personal injury, State civil litigation. Home: RR 4 Box 1C Cochranton PA 16314-9729 Office: Pepicelli Youngs & Youngs 363 Chestnut St Meadville PA 16335-3210

**YOUNGSTROM, KAREN DAYKIN,** lawyer; b. Cleve., Mar. 15, 1950; d. Donald R. and Edith (Koster) D.; m. Paul Clarence Youngstrom, Aug. 18, 1973; children: Erica, Christiane, Andrew. BA, Yale U., 1972; JD, Harvard U., 1975. Bar: Ohio 1976. Assoc. Thompson Hine & Flory LLP, Cleve., 1976-84, ptnr., 1984—, area co-chair, 1994—. Mem. ABA (tax sec. employee benefits com.), Midwest Pension and Benefit Conf. (exec. com. 1997—), WEB (founder, past pres.). Pension, profit-sharing, and employee benefits. Home: 14575 Shaker Blvd Shaker Hts OH 44120-1612 Office: Thompson Hine & Flory LLP 3900 Key Ctr 127 Public Sq Cleveland OH 44114-1216

**YOUNSKEVICIUS, ADRIANA,** law librarian; b. Clearwater, Fla., July 5, 1969; d. Robert Edward and Helen Virginia Younskevicius. BA, U. Fla., 1991; MA, U. South Fla., 1994; MBA, U. Bridgeport, 1999. Law libr. Tonkon Torp Galen Marmaduke & Booth, Portland, Oreg., 1994-95; law libr. corp. hdqs. Xerox Corp., Stamford, Conn., 1995-98, head law libr. corp. hdqs., 1998—. Vol. The Hospice of North Ctrl. Fla., Gainesville, Lawyers for Children Am., Stamford, Xerox Cmty. Involvement Program, Stamford. Mem. Am. Assn. Law Librs., Am. Soc. Info. Sci. (hon.), Phi Kappa Phi, Delta Mu Delta. Office: Xerox Corp 800 Long Ridge Rd Stamford CT 06902-1288

**YOVINO, ANTHONY,** lawyer; b. Bklyn., Aug. 15, 1958; s. Sabatiello and Antoinette Yovino; m. Jane E. Pope, July 11, 1981; children: Lauren Elizabeth, Anthony Michael, Andrea Marie. BA cum laude, St. John's U., Jamaica, N.Y., 1980, JD, 1983. Bar: N.Y. 1983, U.S. Dist. Ct. N.Y., U.S. Supreme Ct. Staff atty. Avis Rent A Car, Garden City, N.Y., 1984-86; assoc. atty. Minerva Moloughney D'Agostino, Valley Stream, N.Y., 1983-84, Samuelson & Rieger, Garden City, 1986-93; ptnr. Samuelson Rieger & Yovino, Garden City, 1993—; lectr. in field. Frequent radio show guest Law You Should Know, Garden City, 1992-95; contbr. articles to profl. jours. Pres. local sch. bd., East Rockaway, N.Y., 1995-98. Fellow Am. Acad. Matrimonial Lawyers; mem. N.Y. State Bar Assn. (family law sect.), Nassau County Bar Assn. (matrimonial law com., co-chair ethics com.), Columbia Lawyers Assn., Nassau Lawyers Assn. Avocations: runing, biking, reading. Family and matrimonial, State civil litigation, Appellate. Office: Samuelson Rieger & Yovino 300 Garden City Plz Garden City NY 11530-3302

**YOWELL, GEORGE KENT,** lawyer; b. St. Louis, May 12, 1927; s. John Jasper and Helen Callahan Yowell; m. Joyce McCallum, Sept. 8, 1951; children: John, Susan, Maggie, Liz. BA, U. Colo., 1949; JD, Northwestern U., 1952. Bar: Ill., U.S. Dist. Ct. Ill. 1954, U.S. Ct. Appeals (7th cir.) 1955, U.S. Supreme Ct. 1956. Asst. U.S. atty. U.S. Dist. Ct. (no. dist.) Ill., Chgo., 1954-57, pvt. practice, 1957—. Village atty. Village of Glencoe, Ill., 1970-78, prosecutor, 1963-84; chmn. character and fitness com. First Jud. Dist., Chgo., 1961-71, chmn. profl. responsibility com., 1963-84. Maj. USAR, 1952-64. Mem. Law Club of Chgo., Legal Club of Chgo. General practice, Probate, Real property. Home and Office: 921 Woodbine Ln Northbrook IL 60062-3440

**YU, AIHONG,** lawyer; b. Taiyuan, Shanxi, China, Feb. 19, 1967; came to U.S., 1995; LLB, Peking U., Beijing, China, 1987, LLM, 1990; LLM, U. Chgo., 1996. Bar: N.Y. 1998, China 1993. Lectr. in law U. Internat. Bus. and Econs., Beijing, 1990-95; lawyer China Trade Law Firm, Beijing, 1994-95; assoc. Altheimer & Gray, Chgo., 1997—. Mem. ABA, N.Y. Bar Assn. Avocations: reading, music. General corporate, Private international, Securities. Office: Altheimer & Gray 10 S Wacker Dr Fl 35 Chicago IL 60606-7482

**YU, GENRONG,** lawyer; b. Shanghai, China, Mar. 17, 1949; came to U.S., 1986; s. Fengwu Yu and Fengyin Hu; m. Xinyin Wei, May 4, 1977; 1 child, Mengchao Yu. BA, Anhui (China) Normal U., 1982; LLM in Internat. Econ. and Maritime Law, Shanghai Maritime Inst., Shanghai, 1985; JD, U. Maine, 1989. Bar: N.Y. Asst. atty. Shanghai Lawyers Office for Maritime Affairs, Shanghai, 1985-86; instr. of Law dept. Internat. Shipping Shanghai Maritime Inst., Shanghai, 1985-86; atty. Healy Baillie, N.Y.C., 1989—; resident ptnr. Healy Baillie, Hong Kong, 1994—; farmer Zongpu People's Commune, Anhui Province, China, 1969-70. Contbr. articles to profl. jours. Flutist Orch. of Anhui Huang Mei Opera Troupe, 1970-78. Mem. ABA, Maritime Law Assn. of U.S., Maritime Law Assn. of the People's Republic of China. Admiralty, Contracts commercial, Private international. Home: 110-11 72nd Ave Apt 2C Forest Hills NY 11375-4910 Office: Healy & Baillie 29 Broadway Fl 25 New York NY 10006-3293

**YU, SANDY KYUNG,** lawyer; b. Oct. 21, 1972; d. Chong K. and Young C. Yu. BA, Western Wash. U., 1994; JD, NYU, 1997. Assoc. Seward & Kissel, N.Y.C., 1998—. Recipient Silver medal Jr. Olympics, 1988. Mem. Phi Sigma Alpha. Avocation: tae kwon do. General corporate, Banking, Finance. Office: Seward & Kissel One Battery Park Plaza New York NY 10004

**YUDOF, MARK GEORGE,** law educator, university president; b. Phila., Oct. 30, 1944; s. Jack and Eleanor (Parris) Y.; m. Judith Lynn Gomel, July 11, 1965; children: Seth Adam, Samara Lisa. BA, U. Pa., 1965, LLB, 1968. Bar: Pa. 1970, U.S. Supreme Ct. 1974, U.S. Dist. Ct. (we. dist.) Tex. 1975, U.S. Ct. Appeals (5th cir.) 1976, Tex. 1980. Law clk. to judge U.S. Ct. Appeals (5th cir.), 1968-69; assoc. gen. counsel to ABA study FTC, 1969; rsch. assoc. Harvard Ctr. Law and Edn., 1969-70, sr. staff atty., 1970-71; lectr. Harvard Grad. Sch. Edn., 1970-71; asst. prof. law U. Tex., Austin, 1971-74, prof., 1974—, assoc. dean, 1979-84, James A. Elkins Cent. chmn. in law, 1983-97, dean, 1984-94, exec. v.p., provost, 1994-97, John Jeffers rsch. chair in law, 1991-94; pres. U. Minn., 1997—; of counsel Pennzoil vs. Texaco, 1987. Author: When Government Speaks, 1983 (Scribes Book award 1983, cert. merit ABA 1983), (with others) Educational Policy and the Law, 1992, (with others) Gender Justice, 1986. Mem. Tex. Gov.'s Task Force on Sch. Fin., 1989-90, Tex. Gov.'s Select Com. on Edn., 1988; bd. dirs. Freedom to Read Found., 1989-91; mem. Austin Cable Commn., 1981-84, chmn., 1982; mem. nat. panel on sch. desegregation rsch. Ford Found., 1977-80; mem. state exec. com. Univ. Interscholastic League, 1985-86; bd. dirs. Jewish Children's Regional Svc., 1980-86; mem. Gov.'s Select Task Force on Pub. Edn., 1995; mem. Telecomms. Infrastructure Fund Bd., State of Tex., 1995-97. Recipient Teaching Excellence award, 1975, Most Meritorious Book award Scribes, 1983, Humanitarian award Austin region NCCJ, 1988, Antidefamation League Jurisprudence award, 1991; hon. fellow Queen Mary and Westfield Coll., U. London. Fellow Tex. Bar Found., Am. Bar Found.; mem. Am. Law Inst., Tex. Bar Assn., Assn. Am. Law Schs. (chmn. law and edn. sect. 1983-84, exec. com. 1988-90), Mpls. Club, Minn. Club, Town & Country Club, Minnikahda Club. Avocation: collecting antique maps. Office: U Minn 202 Morrill Hall 100 Church St SE Minneapolis MN 55455-0110

**YUHNKE, ROBERT E.,** lawyer, educator, consultant; b. Buffalo, Dec. 13, 1943; s. Edward L. and Marjorie T. Y.; m. Stephanie Mines; 1 stepdaughter, Rachel Erdman. BS, Canisius Coll., 1965; student, Columbia U., 1968-69; JD, Yale U., 1972. Bar: Pa 1972, U.S. Supreme Ct. 1977, Ill. 1980, Colo. 1981, U.S. Ct. Appeals (D.C., 7th, 9th and 10th cirs.). Spl. asst. atty. gen. Pa. Dept. Environ. Resources, Harrisburg, 1972-78; asst. regional solicitor U.S. Dept. Interior, Denver, 1978-79; pvt. practice Chgo., 1979-80, Boulder, Colo., 1992—; sr. atty. Environ. Def. Fund, Boulder, 1980-92; Founder, treas. DOM Project, Eldorado Springs, Colo., 1993—; adj. prof. environ. law U. Colo. Sch. Law, Boulder, 1998—. Contbr. articles to profl. jours. Tenor Rocky Mountain Chorale, Boulder, 1994—. 1st lt. U.S. Army Res., 1965-68. Avocations: flute, paddling, yoga. trout fishing. Environmental. Office: 2910 County Road 67 Boulder CO 80303-9639

**YUN, EDWARD JOON,** lawyer; b. Seoul, Republic of Korea, Apr. 2, 1969; s. Alex Sanghyum Yun and Lily Sooja Yun. BA, U. Calif., Berkeley, 1992; JD, N.Y. Law Sch., 1995. Bar: N.Y. 1996, U.S. Dist. Ct (so. and ea. dists.) N.Y. 1997. Assoc. Martin, Clearwater & Bell, N.Y.C., 1995-97, Dembin & Assocs., P.C., N.Y.C., 1997—. Contbr. articles to profl. jours. Mem. City Bar Chorus, N.Y.C., 1997—. Mem. ABA, Am. Coll. Legal Medicine (assoc. in law), N.Y. State Bar Assn., Assn. of the Bar of the City of N.Y. Health, General civil litigation, General corporate. Home: 98 Riverside Dr Apt 4A New York NY 10024-5323 Office: Dembin & Assocs PC Ste 1400 225 Broadway Rm 1400 New York NY 10007-3001

**YURASKO, FRANK NOEL,** judge; b. Rahway, N.J., Dec. 22, 1938; s. Frank H. and Estelle (Trudeau) Y.; m. Mary Byrd, July 23, 1966 (dec. 1991); children: Elizabeth Anne, Suzanne, Frank; m. Rosalee Yurasko, May 1997. BA, Brown U., 1960; cert. London Sch. Econs., 1961; student Gray's Inn, London, 1960-61; JD, Yale U., 1964. Bar: N.J. 1964, Fla. 1979, U.S. Dist. Ct. N.J. 1965, U.S. Ct. Appeals (3d cir.) 1980, U.S. Supreme Ct. 1969; cert. civil trial atty., N.J. Judge's law clk. N.J. Dept. Judiciary, Trenton, 1964-66; ptnr. Graham, Yurasko, Golden, Lintner & Rothchild, Somerville, N.J., 1966-80; pvt. practice, Somerville, 1980—; judge Montgomery Twp. (N.J.) Mcpl. Ct., 1973-84; twp. atty. Hillsborough Twp. (N.J.), 1973—; atty. Green Brook (N.J.) Bd. Adjustment, 1973—. Trustee Gill/St. Bernard Sch., Bernardsville, N.J.; mem. alumni bd. trustees Peddie Sch., Hightstown, N.J. Mem. Am. Judicature Soc., N.J. Bar Assn., Fla. Bar Assn., ABA, Somerset County Bar Assn., Mercer County Bar Assn., Assn. Trial Lawyers Am., Trial Attys. N.J., N.J. Fedn. Planning Ofcls., Fed. Bar Assn. Office: PO Box 1041 139 W End Ave Somerville NJ 08876-1809

**YURKO, RICHARD JOHN,** lawyer; b. Ottawa, Ont., Can., Oct. 30, 1953; came to U.S., 1960; s. Michael and Catherine (Ewanishan) Y.; m. Martha S. Faigen, Apr. 18, 1982; children: Nathan, Daniel. AB summa cum laude, Dartmouth Coll., 1975; JD cum laude, Harvard U., 1979. Bar: Mass. 1979, U.S. Dist. Ct. Mass. 1980, U.S. Ct. Appeals (1st cir.) 1980. Law clk. to Judge James L. King, U.S. Dist. Ct. for So. Dist. Fla., Miami, 1979-80; assoc. Bingham, Dana & Gould, Boston, 1980-85; assoc. Widett, Slater & Goldman, P.C., Boston, 1985-87, shareholder, 1987-92, chmn. litigation dept., 1989-91, hiring ptnr., 1992; shareholder Hutchins, Wheeler & Dittmar, Boston, 1992-94, chmn. litigation dept., 1992-94; shareholder Yurko & Perry, P.C., Boston, 1995—. Contbr. articles to legal jours. Mem. ABA, Mass. Bar Assn., Boston Bar Assn. (chmn. antitrust com.), Phi Beta Kappa. General civil litigation, Contracts commercial, Antitrust. Home: 9 Barnstable Rd Wellesley MA 02481-2802 Office: Yurko & Perry P C 100 City Hall Plz Boston MA 02108-2105

**YUSPEH, ALAN RALPH,** lawyer, healthcare company executive; b. New Orleans, June 13, 1949; s. Michel and Rose Fay (Rabenovitz) Y.; m. Janet Horn, June 8, 1975. BA, Yale U., 1971; MBA, Harvard U., 1973; JD, Georgetown U., 1978. Bar: D.C. 1978. Mgmt. cons. McKinsey & Co., Washington, 1973-74; adminstrv. asst., legis. asst. Office of U.S. Senator J. Bennett Johnston, Washington, 1974-78; atty. Shaw, Pittman, Potts & Trowbridge, Washington, 1978-79, Ginsburg, Feldman, Weil and Bress, Washington, 1979-82; gen. counsel Com. on Armed Services-U.S. Senate, Washington, 1982-85; ptnr. Preston, Thorgrimson, Ellis & Holman, Washington, 1985-88, Miller & Chevalier, Washington, 1988-91, Howrey & Simon, Washington, 1991-97; sr. v.p. ethics, compliance and corp. responsibility Columbia/HCA Healthcare Corp., Nashville, 1997—; coord. Def. Industry Initiative on Bus., Ethics and Conduct, 1987-97; bd. dirs. Health Care Compliance Assn. Editor Law and Policy in Internat. Business jour., 1978-79, Nat. Contract Mgmt. Jour., 1988-92; assoc. editor Pub. Contract Law jour., 1987-91. Chmn. bd. of ethics, City of Balt., 1988-96, mem. planning commn., 1996-97; mem. bd. Housing Authority Balt., 1996-97. 1st lt. USAR, 1971-77. E-mail: alan.yuspeh@columbia.net. Government contracts and claims, Health. Home: 1812 South Rd Baltimore MD 21209-4506 Office: Columbia/HCA Healthcare Corp One Park Plaza Nashville TN 37202

**YUSTAS, VINCENT PAUL,** lawyer; b. Paterson, N.J., Apr. 19, 1944; s. Vincent Frank Yustas and Mary Lenora Obel; m. Sue Ann Kavanaugh; children: Judith Leigh, Scott David; m. Mary Nell Hardesty, Sept. 2, 1988. AB in History and Polit. Sci., Seton Hall U., 1966; JD, Rutgers U., Newark, 1970. Bar: N.J. 1970, U.S. Dist. Ct. (ea. dist.) N.J. 1970, U.S. Ct. Mil. Appeals 1976, U.S. Ct. Mil. Rev. 1976, U.S. Supreme Ct. 1976, Ky. 1990, U.S. Dist. Ct. (we. dist.) Ky. 1996, U.S. Ct. Appeals (6th cir.) 1997. Assoc. Law Offices of A.A. Porro, Jr., Lyndhurst, N.J., 1970-91; commd. officer U.S. Army, 1971, advanced through grades to lt. col., ret., 1991; pvt. practice Brandenburg, Ky., 1991-97; chief capital trial unit Ky. Dept. Pub. Advocacy, Frankfort, 1997-98; regional capital conflict atty. Ky. Dept. Pub. Advocacy, Elizabethtown, 1998—. Mem. Ret. Officers Assn. (1st v.p. Ft. Knox chpt. 1991-93), Ret. Army Judge Advs. Roman Catholic. Home: 114 Lakeshore Pkwy Brandenburg KY 40108-9531 Office: Dept Pub Advocacy PO Box 628 Elizabethtown KY 42702-0628

**ZABANAL, EDUARDO OLEGARIO,** lawyer; b. Legazpi City, Albay, The Philippines, Aug. 8, 1952; came to U.S., 1986; s. Jose Agas and Maria Soledad (Olegario) Z.; m. Leorosie Rebodos Nabor, June 18, 1983; children: Shalimar Rosary, Angelica Almira, Regina Tatiana, Lorelei Blossom, Eduardo Olegario. BA, Aquinas U., The Philippines, 1972; BL, U. The Philippines, 1978. Bar: Hawaii 1990, The Philippines 1979, U.S. Dist. Ct. Hawaii 1990. Assoc. Pacis & Reyes, Manila, 1979-86; pvt. practice Honolulu, 1990—. Contbr. articles to profl. jours. Bd. dirs. Kahaluu Neighborhood Bd., Honolulu, 1991-93; active Filipino Coalition for Solidarity, Honolulu, 1991—. Recipient recognition among Disting. Filipinos in Oahu, FIL-AM Courier, 1995. Mem. ABA, Assn. Trial Lawyers Am., Hawaii State Bar Assn., Hawaii Filipino Lawyers Assn., Integrated Bar The Philippines, Philippine Bar Assn., Filipino C. of C. Hawaii. Roman Catholic. Avocations: jogging, travel, reading. Estate planning, Immigration, naturalization, and customs, Personal injury. Home: 1031 Nuuanu Ave Apt 404 Honolulu HI 96817-5602

**ZABEL, SHELDON ALTER,** lawyer, law educator; b. Omaha, Apr. 25, 1941; s. Louis Julius and Anne (Rothenberg) Z.; m. Roberta Jean Butz, May 10, 1975; children: Andrew Louis, Douglas Patrick, Robert Stewart Warren. AB cum laude, Princeton U., 1963; JD cum laude, Northwestern U., 1966. Bar: Ill. 1966, U.S. Supreme Ct. 1976. Law clk. to presiding justice, Ill. Sup. Ct., 1966-67; assoc. Schiff, Hardin & Waite, Chgo., 1967-73, ptnr., 1973—; instr. environ. law Loyola U., Chgo. Mem. bd. dirs. Chgo. Zool. Soc. Mem. ABA, Chgo. Bar Assn., Chgo. Coun. Lawyers, Order of Coif. Jewish. Clubs: Union League, Metropolitan (Chgo.). Avocations: skiing, squash. Environmental, Public utilities. Office: Schiff Hardin & Waite 7200 Sears Tower 233 S Wacker Dr Ste 7200 Chicago IL 60606-6473

**ZABEL, WILLIAM DAVID,** lawyer; b. Omaha, Dec. 14, 1936; s. Louis J. and Anne I. Z.; m. Deborah M. Miller, Oct. 31, 1979; children by previous marriage: Richard, David. AB summa cum laude, Princeton U., 1958; LLB cum laude, Harvard U., 1961. Bar: N.Y. 1961, U.S. Supreme Ct. 1966, Fla. 1975. Ptnr. Schulte Roth & Zabel, N.Y.C., 1969—; ptnr. firm Schulte, Roth

& Zabel, Palm Beach, Fla., 1975—; lectr. Cornell Law Sch., So. Fed. Tax Inst., U. Miami Inst. Estate Planning, Great Plains Tax Inst., Assn. of Bar of City of N.Y., Practising Law Inst., profl. orgns.; N.Y. State adv. com. U.S. Civil Rights Commn., 1969-73; vol. civil rights litigator Lawyers Constl. Def. Com., Miss., summer 1965; bd. dirs. Del. Mgmt. Holdings Inc. Author: Estate Planning for the Large Estate, 1976, Domicile, Wills and Tax Problems of Migrating Clients Transplanted to Florida, 1976, Income, Estate and Gift Tax Consequences of Marital Settlements, 1979, Estate Planning for Interests in a Closely Held Business, 1981, Use of Trusts in Connection with Marital Dissolutions, 1983, Thy Will Be Done?, 1991, The Rich Die Richer - and You Can Too, 1995; Am. editor: The Lawyer, Eng., 1963-66; mem. editl. adv. bd. Trusts and Estates Mag.; contbr. articles to profl. jours. Pres. Merlin Found.; mem. Lymphoma Found., Soros Founds. (Newly Ind. States and the Baltic Republics, Hungary, Romania, Bulgaria and Ctrl. European U.), Open Soc. Fund, Inc., Human Rights Watch/Helsinki, Doctors of World, Winston Found. World Peace, Ottinger Found., David H. Cogan Found., The Picower Med. Rsch. Inst., Lawson Valentine Found., Am. Friends of the Israel Mus., Am. Com. for Weizmann Inst. Sci.; legal counsel Internat. Confedn. Art Dealers; bd. dirs. Tauber Inst., Sakharov Archives, Brandeis U.; trustee The New Sch. for Social Rsch., 1994—; adv. bd. Project on Death in Am.; chmn. Princeton U. Planned Giving Com., 1991—. Recipient Disting. Community Svc. award Brandeis U., 1986, U.S. Masters Squash Team Bronze medal 14th Maccabiah Games, 1993; fellow Brandeis U., 1987—. Fellow Am. Coll. Trust and Estate Coun., Internat. Acad. Estate and Trust Law, N.Y. Bar Found.; mem. ABA, Am. Law Inst., N.Y. State Bar Assn., Assn. of Bar of City of N.Y. (internat. human rights com.), Lawyers Com. for Human Rights (bd. dirs.), Vol. Lawyers for Arts (bd. dirs.), Estate Planning Coun. N.Y.C. (bd. dirs. 1975-79), Fla. Bar Assn., Harmonie Club (pres. 1989-91), Phi Beta Kappa. Probate, Estate taxation, Family and matrimonial. Home: 850 Park Ave New York NY 10021-1845 Office: Schulte Roth & Zabel 900 3rd Ave Fl 19 New York NY 10022-4774 also: Phillips Point W Tower 10th Fl 777 S Flagler Dr West Palm Beach FL 33401-6161

**ZABKA, SVEN PAUL,** lawyer; b. Heide, Germany, May 11, 1971; s. Clifton Thomas and Lieselotte A.M. Zabka. BA cum laude with dept. honors in econs., Union Coll., Schenectady, N.Y., 1993; JD, Emory U., 1996. Bar: Ga. 1996, D.C. 1997. Assoc. Smith, Gambrell & Russell, LLP, Atlanta, 1997—. Mem. Emory Law Rev., 1994. Avocations: water polo, skiing. Non-profit and tax-exempt organizations, Mergers and acquisitions, General corporate. Office: Smith Gambrell & Russell 1230 Peachtree St NE Ste 3100 Atlanta GA 30309-3592

**ZABLE, NORMAN ARNOLD,** lawyer; b. Chgo., July 11, 1934; s. Joseph Irving and Marian (Rosen) Z.; m. Vera Slutzky, June 16, 1963; children: Barak, Brett, Mark. BBA, So. Meth. U., 1955, LLB, 1958. Atty., Dallas, 1958-79; pvt. practice, Dallas, 1979—. Dem. precinct chmn., Dallas, 1978-79; assoc. scoutmaster Boy Scouts Am., Dallas, 1978—. Mem. ABA, State Bar Tex., Dallas Bar Assn., Comml. Law League, Mensa. Democrat. Jewish. Bankruptcy, Contracts commercial, Finance. Office: 5340 Alpha Rd Dallas TX 75240-4318

**ZACHAR, CHRISTOPHER JOSEPH,** lawyer; b. Cedar Rapids, Iowa, Dec. 26, 1964; s. Thomas Joseph and Judith Marie (Smith) Z. BS, Ariz. State U., 1989; JD, U. Ariz., 1992. Bar: Ariz. 1992. Various to law clk. various offices, Chgo., 1989-90, Ariz., 1990-92; ptnr. Zachar & Doughty, P.C., Scottsdale, Ariz., 1992—; futures mgr. Fiesta Bowl, Tempe, 1995. Mem. ATLA, Maricopa County Bar Assn., ABA (student divsn.), Scottsdale Bar Assn. Republican. Avocations: phys. fitness, golf, skiing. State civil litigation, General practice, Personal injury. Office: Zachar & Doughty PC 3509 E Shea Blvd Ste 111 Phoenix AZ 85028-3338 also: 4626 E Shea Blvd # C-200 Phoenix AZ 85028-3071

**ZACHARSKI, DENNIS EDWARD,** lawyer; b. Detroit, Feb. 25, 1951; s. Edward J. and Margaret R. (Cendrowski) Z.; m. Susan G. Foster, Aug. 8, 1975; children: Jeffrey Alan, Lauren Michelle. BBA, U. Mich., 1973; JD, Mich. State U., 1977. Bar: Mich. 1977, U.S. Dist. Ct. (ea. dist.) Mich. 1977, U.S. Dist. Ct. (we. dist.) Mich. 1982, U.S. Supreme Ct. 1988, U.S. Ct. Appeals (6th cir.) 1990, Ohio, 1993. Atty. Lacey & Jones, Birmingham, Mich., 1977—; mediator Mediation Tribunal Assn., Detroit; arbitrator Am. Arbitration Assn., Southfield, Mich. Mem. Oakland County Bar Assn., Assn. Trial Def. Counsel, Mich. Trial Def. Counsel. Avocations: golf, skiing, soccer, tennis, cycling. Insurance, Personal injury, General civil litigation. Office: Lacey & Jones 600 S Adams Rd Ste 300 Birmingham MI 48009-6827

**ZAFFIRO, RICHARD L.,** lawyer; b. Milw.; s. Joseph F. and Therese A. Zaffiro; m. Bethann Burazin, June 7, 1981; children: Andre Richard, Emma Chelsea. BA, Marquette U., 1978; JD, Rutgers U., 1981. Bar: Wis. 1981, U.S. Dist. Ct. (ea. dist.) Wis. 1981, (we. dist.) Wis. 1982, U.S. Ct. Appeals (7th cir.) 1983, U.S. Tax Ct., 1983. Lawyer Alan D. Eisenberg, Milw., 1981-83; pvt. practice Milw., 1984-88; lawyer Am. Family Mut. Ins. Co., Appleton, Wis., 1988—. Mem. Am. Bar Assn., Wis. State Bar Assn. (Young Lawyers Div.), Civil Trial Coun. Wis., Wis. Acad. Trial Lawyers. Fax: 414-784-9117. E-mail: rzaffiro@amfam.com. General civil litigation, Insurance, Criminal. Home: 4261 N 92nd St Milwaukee WI 53222-1617 Office: Am Family Mut Ins Co Milw Legal Dept 440 S Executive Dr Brookfield WI 53201-2927

**ZAGAMI, ANTHONY JAMES,** lawyer; b. Washington, Jan. 19, 1951; s. Placidino and Rosemary Zagami. AA, Prince Georges Community Coll., 1971; BS and Bachelor in Pub. Adminstrn., U. Md., 1973; JD, George Mason U., 1977. Bar: D.C. 1978, U.S. Dist. Ct. D.C. 1979, U.S. Ct. Appeals (D.C. cir.) 1979, U.S. Supreme Ct. 1983. Staff Senate Svc. Dept., Washington, 1968-69; senate engr. Office of the Architect of the Capitol, Washington, 1969-77; sales rep., cons. Zagami Realty Co. and Montgomery Realty Co., 1971-76; with pub. rels. for sales div. Army Times Pub. Co., 1973-74; teaching and rsch. asst. to law prof. George Mason U., 1975-76; asst. to sec. to majority U.S. Senate, Washington, 1977-78, staff asst. ofcl. reporters of debates, 1978-81; gen. counsel Joint Com. on Printing, Washington, 1981-90, U.S. Govt. Printing Office, Washington, 1990—. Bd. dirs. U.S. Senate Credit Union, chmn., Legal Adv. Com., bd. dir. Mem. ABA, FBA (past pres. Capitol Hill chpt.), Nat. Italian-Am. found., U.S. Capitol Hist. Soc., Senate Staff Club, Phi Alpha Phi. Home: PO Box 75154 Washington DC 20013-0154 Office: US Govt Printing Office Office Of Gen Counsel Washington DC 20401-0001

**ZAGEL, JAMES BLOCK,** federal judge; b. Chgo., Mar. 4, 1941; s. Samuel and Ethel (Samuels) Z.; m. Margaret Maxwell, May 27, 1979. BA, U. Chgo., 1962, MA in Philosophy, 1962; JD, Harvard U., 1965. Bar: Ill. 1965, U.S. Dist. Ct. (no. dist.) Ill. 1965, U.S. Supreme Ct. 1970, U.S. Ct. Appeals (7th cir.) 1972. Asst. atty. gen. criminal justice divsn. State of Ill., Springfield, 1970-77; chief prosecuting atty. Ill. Jud. Inquiry Bd., Springfield, 1973-75; exec. dir. Ill. Law Enforcement Commn., Springfield, 1977-79; dir. Ill. Dept. Revenue, Springfield, 1979-80, Ill. Dept. State Police, Springfield, 1980-87; judge U.S. Dist. Ct. (no. dist.) Ill., Chgo., 1987—. Co-author: Criminal Law and Its Administration, 1989, Cases and Comments on Criminal Procedure, 1992. Named Outstanding Young Citizen, Chgo. Jaycees, 1977 ; recipient Disting. Service Merit award Assn. Commerce and Industry, 1983. Mem. Chgo. Bar Assn., Jud. Conf. of U.S. (codes of conduct com. 1987-92). Office: US Dist Ct 219 S Dearborn St Ste 2188 Chicago IL 60604-1801

**ZAGER, STEVEN MARK,** lawyer; b. Memphis, Nov. 16, 1958; s. Jack and Sylvia (Bloomfield) Z.; m. Debra D'Angelo; children: Samantha, Amanda. BA, Vanerbilt U., 1979, JD, 1983. Bar: Tex. 1983, U.S. Dist. Ct. (all dists.) Tex. 1983, U.S. Dist. Ct. Ariz. 1992, U.S. Dist. Ct. (D.C.) 1998, U.S. Ct. Appeals (5th, 6th, and 11th cirs.) 1983, U.S. Ct. Appeals (D.C. cir.) 1991, U.S. Ct. Appeals (Fed. cir.) 1997, U.S. Supreme Ct. 1991. Assoc. Fulbright & Jaworski, Houston, 1983-86; assoc. Weil, Gotshal & Manges, Houston, 1986-90, ptnr., 1990-98, head Houston office litigation sect., 1994-96; ptnr., head Austin office bus. litigation group Brobeck, Phleger & Harrison, Austin, 1998—; adj. prof. U. Houston Sch. Law, 1990-95; mem. nat. adv. bd. NALP, 1996—. Contbr. articles to Tex. Bar Jour., Houston Lawyer. Bd. dirs., mem. exec. com. Alley Theatre, Houston, 1988-96, Tex. Accts. and Lawyers for the Arts, Houston, 1984-88; mem. adv. bd. Montgomery Bell Acad., 1996—. Named Oustanding Young Man in Am., U.S. Jaycees, 1983; recipient Frank J. Scurlock award State Bar Tex., 1991, Outstanding Pro Bono Svc. Mem. ATLA, ABA (litigation sect.), State Bar Tex. (dir. 1997-98), Houston Bar Assn. (sec. 1996-97, v.p. 1997-98, bd. dirs. 1993-96, chair law and arts com. 1994, chair adminstrn. of justice com. 1995, rodeo com. 1997, bd. dirs. 1998, Outstanding Young Lawyer in Houston 1991, Pres.'s award 1996-97, 97-98), Houston Vol. Lawyers Program (bd. dirs. 1997-98, chair 1998), Fed. Bar Assn., Masons. Federal civil litigation, State civil litigation, Computer. Office: Brobeck Phleger & Harrison LLP 111 Congress Ave Ste 2100 Austin TX 78701-4043

**ZAHAROFF, HOWARD GEORGE,** lawyer; b. Bronx, N.Y., Apr. 30, 1951; s. Arthur Charles and Dorothy (Einhorn) Z.; m. Deborah J. Whitehill, Dec. 28, 1975; children: Joshua, Marta, Leah. BA in Philosophy, Lafayette Coll., 1973; MA, Johns Hopkins U., 1975, PhD in Philosophy, 1979; JD, Harvard U., 1980. Bar: Mass. 1980, U.S. Ct. Appeals (1st cir.) 1981, U.S. Dist. Ct. Mass. 1981. Assoc., ptnr., shareholder Brown Rudnick Freed & Gesmer, Boston, 1980-98; ptnr., shareholder Morse, Barnes-Brown & Pendleton, Waltham, Mass., 1998—; trustee Vol. Lawyers for the Arts, Inc., Boston, 1997-99. Contbr. numerous articles to profl. jours. Mem. ABA, Internat. Bar Assn., Boston Bar Assn. (co-chair arts and entertainment law com. 1996-98, co-chair computer and internet law com. 1997-99, co-chair intellectual property sect. 1999—), Computer Law Assn., Copyright Soc. USA, Licensing Execs. Soc., Mass. Software Coun., Nat. Writers Union. Avocations: creative writing, coaching youth soccer. Intellectual property, Computer, Entertainment. Office: Morse Barnes-Brown & Pendleton Waltham MA 02451

**ZAHN, DANIEL ARTHUR,** lawyer; b. Elmhurst, N.Y., Feb. 7, 1957; s. Arthur S. Zahn and Katherine T. Mulvihill; m. Elizabeth A. Quigley, Aug. 2, 1997; 1 child: Christina N. BA, St. John's U., 1980; JD, U. Dayton, 1983. Bar: N.Y. 1985, U.S. Dist. Ct. (ea. and so. dists.) N.Y. 1986, U.S. Ct. Claims 1991, U.S. Ct. Mil. Appeals 1991, U.S. Ct. Appeals (fed. cir.) 1991. U.S. Supreme Ct. 1991. Mem. Suffolk County Legal Aid Soc., Hauppauge, N.Y., 1984-87, CNA Ins. Co., Melville, N.Y., 1987-89; pvt. practice Holbrook, NY, 1989—. Mem. Assn. Trial Lawyers Am., N.Y. State Bar Assn., N.Y. State Trial Lawyer Assn., Suffolk County Bar Assn. Roman Catholic. Avocations: computers, travel, boating. Personal injury. Home: 44 Club Ln Remsenberg NY 11960 Office: Law Offices of Daniel A Zahn PC 1597 Grundy Ave Holbrook NY 11741-2108

**ZAHN, DONALD JACK,** lawyer; b. Oct. 24, 1941; s. Jerome and Clara (Zinsher) Z.; m. Laurie R. Hyman, Aug. 19, 1966; children: Lawrence, Melissa. AB, NYU, 1963; LLB, Union U., 1966; LLM in Taxation, NYU, 1967. Bar: N.Y. 1966, U.S. Dist. Ct. (no. dist.) N.Y. 1966, U.S. Tax Ct. 1969, U.S. Ct. Appeals (2d cir. 1970), Tex. 1972, U.S. Ct. Appeals (5th and 11th cirs.). Assoc. bond, Schoeneck and King, Syracuse, N.Y., 1967-71; ptnr. Haynes and Boone, Dallas, 1971-82, Akin, Gump, Strauss, Hauer & Feld, Dallas, 1982-92; assoc. prof. internat. taxation, fed. income taxation Tex. Wesleyan Sch. Law, Ft. Worth, 1992—; vis. prof. Baylor U. Sch. of Law Fed. Income Taxation, 1995, U. San Diego Sch. of Law Grad. Taxation Program, 1996-98; adj. prof. Sch. Law, So. Meth. U., Dallas, 1972-87, 90-91. Trustee, sec. mem. exec. and fin. com., nominating com. Greenhill Sch., Addison, Tex., 1980-90; trustee, chmn. budget com., mem. fin. com. Jewish Fedn. Greater Dallas, 1978-89; trustee, chmn. Found. Jewish Fedn., Dallas, 1980-89; trustee, v.p., pres. Dallas chpt. Am. Jewish Com., 1980-92; mem. Tex. World Trade Coun., 1986-87, Dallas Mayor's Internat. Com. Mem. State Bar Tex. (sec. 1982-83, chmn. tax sect. 1984-85, newsletter taxation sect. editor 1980-81), Internat. Bar Assn., Internat. Comte (N.Tex. commn.), Southwestern Legal Found. (adv. bd., treas. Internat. and Comparative Law Ctr., lectr. Acad. in Internat. Law), N.Y. State Bar Assn. Jewish. Corporate taxation, Private international, Mergers and acquisitions. Address: 11218 Hillcrest Rd Dallas TX 75230-3501

**ZAHN, RICHARD WILLIAM,** lawyer; b. Richmond, Va., Oct. 1, 1964; s. Richard William and Frances Ellen Z.; m. Kerry Ellen Mahaney, Aug. 7, 1988; children: Ryan William, Allison McKenzie. BA, Washington Lee U., 1986; JD, New Eng. Sch. Law, Boston, 1993. Bar: Va. 1993, U.S. Dist. Ct. (ea. dist.) Va. 1993, U.S. Ct. Appeals (4th cir.) 1994. Law clk. to Hon. John A. MacKenzie U.S. Dist. Ct. (ea. dist.) Va., Norfolk, Va., 1993-94; assoc. Taylor & Walker, P.C., Norfolk, 1994—. Bd. dirs., 2d v.p. Big Bros./Big Sisters of South Hampton Roads, Norfolk, 1996—. Mem. Va. Assn. Def. Attys., Def. Rsch. Inst., Norfolk/Portsmouth Bar Assn. Federal civil litigation, State civil litigation, Insurance. Office: Taylor & Walker PC 555 E Main St Ste 1300 Norfolk VA 23510-2235

**ZAHND, RICHARD H.,** professional sports executive, lawyer; b. N.Y.C., July 22, 1946; s. Hugo and Rose (Genovese) Z.; m. Phyllis Beth Workman, Aug. 13, 1978; children: Andrew Richard, Melissa Dawn. A.B., NYU, 1968, J.D., 1971. Bar: N.Y. 1972. Assoc. Paul, Weiss, Rifkind, Wharton & Garrison, N.Y.C., 1971-74; staff atty. Madison Square Garden Corp., N.Y.C., 1974-75; v.p. legal affairs Madison Square Garden Center, Inc., N.Y.C., 1975-79; v.p., gen. counsel Madison Square Garden Corp., N.Y.C., 1979-86; v.p. N.Y. Knickerbockers Basketball Club, N.Y.C., 1979-86, N.Y. Rangers Hockey Club, N.Y.C., 1979-86; ptnr. Morrison & Foerster, N.Y.C., 1986-91; sr. v.p., gen. counsel NHL Enterprises, L.P., N.Y.C., 1992—. Served to capt. U.S. Army, 1972. John Norton Pomeroy scholar NYU Law Sch., 1969; Mortimer Bishop scholar NYU Law Sch., 1969; Judge Jacob Markowitz scholar NYU Law Sch., 1970; recipient Am. Jurisprudence prize NYU Law Sch., 1969. Episcopalian. Intellectual property, Entertainment, Sports. Office: NHL Enterprises LP Apt 39A 1251 Avenue Of The Americas Fl 46 New York NY 10020-1192

**ZAHORIK, MICHAEL ALAN,** lawyer; b. Rocky River, Ohio, Mar. 22, 1963; s. Donald Jerome and Katherine Barbara (Blonski) Z.; m. Kimberly Sue, June 7, 1987; children: Casey Michael, Jacob Daniel. BA, U. Colo., 1985; JD, U. Denver, 1989. Bar: Colo. 1989, Tex. 1995, U.S. Dist. Ct. Colo. 1991, U.S. Dist. Ct. (no. dist.) Tex. 1995, U.S. Ct. Appeals (10th cir.) 1990, U.S. Ct. Appeals (9th cir.) 1992. Litig. assoc. Brenman, Raskin, Friedlob & Tenenbaum, Denver, 1989-91; sr. litig. assoc. McGeady, Sisneros & Wollins, Denver, 1991-94; v.p. Omni U.S.A., Inc., Houston, 1995-96, exec. v.p./COO, 1996—, gen. counsel, 1994—. Mem. ABA, Tex. Bar Assn., Houston Bar Assn., Colo. Bar Assn., Denver Bar Assn. General corporate, General civil litigation, Mergers and acquisitions. Home: 989 W Princeton Ct Louisville CO 80027-9577 Office: Omni USA Inc 7502 Mesa Dr Houston TX 77028-3524

**ZAHRA, ELLIS E.,** lawyer. V.p., gen. counsel Winn-Dixie Stores Inc., Jacksonville, Fla. Office: Winn-Dixie Stores Inc PO Box B Jacksonville FL 32203-0297

**ZAHRT, WILLIAM DIETRICH, II,** lawyer; b. Dayton, Ohio, July 12, 1944; s. Kenton William and Orpha Catharine (Wagner) Z.; m. Patricia Ann Marek, June 10, 1969; children: Justin William, Alitheia Patricia. BS in Physics, Yale U., 1966, JD, 1969, M of Pub. and Pvt. Mgmt., 1990. Bar: N.Y. 1970, Ohio 1972, Tex. 1982, N.C. 1992, U.S. Ct. Appeals (Fed. cir.) 1977. Assoc. Kenyon & Kenyon, N.Y.C., 1969-71, Biebel, French & Nauman, Dayton, 1971-80; sr. patent atty. Schlumberger Well Svcs., Houston, 1980-82; sole practice Kingwood, Tex., 1982-85, 88-90; patent atty. Shell Oil Co., Houston, 1985-88; sr. patent counsel Raychem Corp., Fuquay-Varina, N.C., 1990-97; asst. gen. counsel Advanced Micro Devices, Sunnyvale, Calif., 1997—. Mem. ABA, Am. Intellectual Property Law Assn., Tex. Bar Assn., Silicon Valley Intellectual Property Law Assn., Dayton Racquet Club, Masons. Anglican. Patent, Trademark and copyright, Intellectual property. Home: 629 Villa Centre Way San Jose CA 95128-5138 Office: PO Box 3453 One AMD Pl Sunnyvale CA 94088

**ZAITZEFF, ROGER MICHAEL,** lawyer; b. Detroit, June 25, 1940; s. Peter and Mary (Fedchenia) Z.; children: Zachary, Natasha, Zoe, Peter. BA with honors and distinction, U. Mich., 1962; MA with distinction, U. Calif., Berkeley, 1963, JD, 1969. Bar: N.Y. 1970, U.S. Dist. Ct. (so. dist.) N.Y. 1975, U.S. Ct. Appeals (2nd cir.) 1975, D.C. 1985. Assoc. Seward & Kissel, N.Y.C., 1969-77, ptnr., 1977-94; ptnr. Latham & Wakins, N.Y.C., 1994—. Contbr. articles to profl. jours. Mem. Tribar Opinion Com., 1990-93. Heller grantee U. Mich., 1962; recipient William Jennings Bryan Prize. Mem. ABA, Internat. Bar Assn., Assn. of Bar of City of N.Y., N.Y. State Bar Found., Southwestern Legal Found. (adv. bd.), N.Y. County Lawyers Assn. (spl. com. legal opinions in comml. transactions), Phi Beta Kappa. Banking, Securities, Finance. Office: Latham & Watkins 885 3rd Ave Fl 9 New York NY 10022-4874

**ZAK, ROBERT JOSEPH,** lawyer; b. Steubenville, Ohio, July 29, 1946; s. Joseph and Pearl (Munyas) Z.; m. Kristy Hubbard Winkler, Sept. 13, 1980; children: Elizabeth Adele, Robert Joseph Jr., Barbara Ann. BS, W.Va. U., 1968, JD, 1975. Bar: W.Va. 1975, U.S. Dist. Ct. (so. dist.) W.Va. 1975, U.S. Dist. Ct. (no. dist.) W.Va. 1989, U.S. Ct. Appeals (4th cir.) 1990. Staff atty. Pub. Svc. Commn. of W.Va., Charleston, 1975-76; assoc. Preiser & Wilson L.C., Charleston, 1976-81, ptnr., 1981-85; sr. ptnr. Zak & Assocs., Charleston, 1985—; hearing examiner W.Va. Bd. Regents, Charleston, 1987-90; spl. asst. atty. gen. State of W.Va., Charleston, 1980-87; chmn. civil svc. commn. City of Charleston, 1987-90; mem. State of W.Va. Worker's Compensation Appeals Bd., Charleston, 1991-97. With U.S. Army, 1969-71, Vietnam. Fellow Am. Acad. Matrimonial Lawyers; mem. Order of Barristers. Republican. Presbyterian. General civil litigation, Personal injury, Family and matrimonial. Office: Zak & Assocs 607 Ohio Ave Charleston WV 25302-2228

**ZAKARIN, KEITH,** lawyer; b. Bklyn., Dec. 24, 1958; s. Leonard Zakarin and Rozlyn Dolling. Student, Mesa Coll., 1979-81; BA in Polit. Sci., U. Calif., San Diego, 1983; JD, U. Calif., Berkeley, 1986. Bar: Calif. 1986, U.S. Dist. Ct. (so., cen., ea. and no. dists.) Calif. 1986, U.S. Tax Ct. 1986, U.S. Ct. Appeals (9th cir.) 1986, U.S. Supreme Ct. 1991. Assoc. Pillsbury, Madison & Sutro, San Diego, 1985-94; ptnr. Booth Banning LLP, San Diego, 1994—. With USN, 1976-81. U. Calif. scholar, San Diego, 1983. Mem. ABA, Calif. Bar Assn., San Diego County Bar Assn., U. Calif. Alumni Assn. Avocations: racquetball, golf. Education and schools, General civil litigation, Appellate. Office: Booth Banning LLP Emerald-Shapery Ctr 402 W Broadway Ste 850 San Diego CA 92101-8574

**ZALENSKI, CHERYL MARIE,** lawyer; b. Wyandotte, Mich., Mar. 8, 1968. BA, Bradley U., 1990; JD, So. Meth. U., 1993. Bar: Mich. 1993. Staff atty. Legal Svcs. Orgn. South Ctrl. Mich., Battle Creek, 1994-98, mng. atty., 1998—. Bd. dirs. Branch County (Mich.) Coalition Against Domestic Violence, 1998—. Mem. ABA, State Bar Mich. (domestic violence com. 1998—), Women Lawyers Assn. Mich. (S.W. region pres. 1997-98, treas. 1998—). Family and matrimonial. Office: Legal Svcs Orgn South Ctrl Mich 70 Michigan Ave E Battle Creek MI 49017-4010

**ZALK, ROBERT H.,** lawyer; b. Albert Lea, Minn., Dec. 1, 1944; s. Donald B. and Juliette J. (Erickson) Z.; m. Ann Lee Anderson, June 21, 1969; children: Amy, Jenna. BA, Carleton Coll., 1966; JD, U. Minn., 1969. Bar: Minn. 1969, U.S. Dist. Ct. Minn. 1969. Atty. Popham, Haik, Schnobrich, Kaufman & Doty, Mpls., 1969-72, No. States Power Co., Mpls., 1972-73, Wright, West & Diessner, Mpls., 1973-84, Fredrikson & Byron P.A., Mpls., 1984-94, Zalk & Assocs., Mpls., 1994-95, Zalk & Wood, Mpls., 1995—. Fellow Am. Acad. Matrimonial Lawyers bd. mgrs. Minn. chpt. 1989-92), Minn. State Bar Assn. (co-chmn. maintenance guideline com. 1991-94), Hennepin County Bar Assn. (co-chmn. family law sect. 1990-91). Family and matrimonial, General civil litigation. Office: Zalk & Wood PA Sunset Ridge Bus Park 5861 Cedar Lake Rd Minneapolis MN 55416-1481

**ZALUTSKY, MORTON HERMAN,** lawyer; b. Schenectady, Mar. 8, 1935; s. Albert and Gertrude (Daffner) Z.; m. Audrey Englebardt, June 16, 1957; children: Jane, Diane, Samuel. BA, Yale U., 1957; JD, U. Chgo., 1960. Bar: Oreg. 1961. Law clk. to presiding judge Oreg. Supreme Ct., 1960-61; assoc. Hart, Davidson, Veazie & Hanlon, 1961-63, Veatch & Lovett, 1963-64, Morrison, Bailey, Dunn, Cohen & Miller, 1964-69; prin. Morton H. Zalutsky, P.C., 1970-76; ptnr. Dahl, Zalutsky, Nichols & Hinson, 1977-79, Zalutsky & Klarquist, P.C., Portland, Oreg., 1980-85, Zalutsky, Klarquist & Johnson, Inc., Portland, 1985-94; Zalutsky & Klarquist, P.C., Portland, 1994—; instr. Portland State U., 1961-64, Northwestern Sch. of Law, 1969-70; assoc. prof. U. Miami Law Sch.; lectr. Practising Law Inst., 1971—, Oreg. State Bar Continuing Legal Edn. Program, 1970, Am. Law Inst.-ABA Continuing Legal Edn. Program, 1973—, 34th, 37th NYU ann. insts. fed. taxation, So. Fed. Tax Inst., U. Miami Inst. Estate Planning, Southwestern Legal Found., Internat. Foun. Employee Benefit Plans, numerous other profl. orgns.; dir. A-E-F-C Pension Plan, 1994—, chair, 1998—. Author: (with others) The Professional Corporation in Oregon, 1970, 82; contbg. author: The Dentist and the Law, 3d edit.; editor-in-chief (retirement plans) Matthew Bender's Federal Tax Service, 1987—; contbr. to numerous publs. in field. Mem. vis. com. U. Chgo. Law Sch., 1986-88. Mem. ABA (vice chair profl. svcs. 1987-89, mem. coun. tax sect. 1985-87, spl. coord. 1980-85), Am. Law Inst., Am. Bar Retirement Assn. (trustee, bd. dirs., vice chair 1990-91, chair 1991-92), Multnomah County Bar Assn., Am. Tax Lawyers (charter mem.), Oreg. Estate Planning Coun. Jewish. Corporate taxation, Pension, profit-sharing, and employee benefits, Estate taxation. Home: 3118 SW Fairmount Blvd Portland OR 97201-1466 Office: 3d Fl 215 SW Washington St Portland OR 97204-2636

**ZAMBITO, PETER J.,** lawyer; b. N.Y.C., Sept. 14, 1935; s. John and Lucy (Mecca) Z.; m. Marguerite C. Ferranti Zambito, July 22, 1961; children: Peter E., Catherine L. BA, St. Bonaventure U., Olean, N.Y., 1957; LLB, Fordham Law Sch., N.Y.C., 1961. Assoc. Haight, Gardner, Poor & Havens, N.Y.C., 1961-67, Daughtery, Ryan, Mahoney, Gellergrino & Giuffra, N.Y.C., 1967-72; ptnr. Daughtery, Ryan, Giuffra, Zambito & Hession, N.Y.C., 1972—; mem. Maritime Law Assn. U.S., N.Y.C., 1961—. Mem., pres. Selection Com. for Sch. Bd. mems., Town of Mamaroneck, N.Y., 1987-88; CCD Tchr. Sts. John & Paul Ch. Larchmont, N.Y., 1986—. Capt. U.S. Army, 1957-64. Named Extraordinary Minister of the Eucharist Sts. John and Paul Roman Cath. Ch. Archdiocese of N.Y., Larchmont, N.Y., 1984—. Roman Catholic. Home: 4 Nancy Ln Larchmont NY 10538-3315 Office: Doughtery Ryan Giuffra Zambito & Hession 131 E 38th St New York NY 10016-2604

**ZAMBOLDI, RICHARD HENRY,** lawyer; b. Kittanning, Pa., Nov. 22, 1941; s. Henry F. and Florence E. (Colligan) Z.; m. Maria Therese Reiser, Aug. 12, 1967; children: Elizabeth M., Richard H. Jr., Margaret B. BBA, St. Bonaventure U., 1963; JD, Villanova U., 1966. Bar: U.S. Dist. Ct. (we. dist.) Pa. 1966, Pa. 1968, U.S. Ct. Appeals (3d cir.) 1970, U.S. Supreme Ct. 1981. Law clk. U.S. Dist. Ct. (we. dist.) Pa., Pitts., 1966-67; atty. Nat. Labor Rels. Bd., Pitts., 1967-68; assoc. Kanehann & McDonald, Allentown, Pa., 1968-69; ptnr. Elderkin Martin Kelly Messina & Zamboldi, Erie, Pa., 1969-90; ptnr. Knox McLaughlin Gornall & Sennett, Erie, 1990—, pres., 1997—; Author (student articles) Villanova Law Rev., 1964-65, editor, 1965-66. Mem. Pa. Bar Assn., Erie County Bar Assn. Republican. Roman Catholic. Labor. Home: 6206 Lake Shore Dr Erie PA 16505-1013 Office: Knox McLaughlin Gornall & Sennett 120 W 10th St Erie PA 16501-1410

**ZAMBORSKY, DONALD A.,** lawyer; b. Allentown, Pa., Dec. 21, 1947; s. Edward J. and Helen A. (Gresko) Z.; m. Joan E. Gallo, July 19, 1969; children: Sonia, Eric, Laura, David. BA, U. Pa., 1969; JD, Villanova U., 1972. Law clk. to Hon. Martin Coyne County Ct., Allentown, Pa., 1972-73; ptnr. Zamborsky & Zamborsky, Allentown, 1973-92; pvt. practice Allentown, 1992-97; ptnr. Tallman, Hudders & Sorrentino, P.C., Allentown, 1998—; mental health rev. officer Lehigh County Ct., Allentown, 1977—; adj. prof. Cedar Crest Coll., Allentown, 1978-93, Pa. State U., Fogelsville, 1978-92. Mem. Lehigh Valley Estate Planning Coun., pres., 1982-83. Mem. Lehigh Country Club (bd. dirs. 1993-97). Roman Catholic. Avocations: golf, paddle tennis. Estate planning, Probate, Estate taxation. Office: 1611 Pond Rd Ste 300 Allentown PA 18104-2258

**ZAMBRI, SALVATORE JOSEPH,** lawyer; b. Brookhaven, N.Y., Oct. 3, 1967; s. Joseph Peter and Mary Rose Zambri; m. Mary Ann Liano, July 28, 1996; children: Samantha Grace, Sophia Rose. BA in Philosophy, Coll. of William and Mary, 1989; JD, George Washington U., 1992. Bar: N.J. 1992, U.S. Dist. Ct. N.J. 1992, D.C. 1993, N.Y. 1993, U.S. Dist. Ct. D.C. 1995, U.S. Dist. Ct. (Md.) 1996, U.S. Ct. Appeals (DC cir.) 1996, U.S. Supreme Ct. 1997. Atty. Koonz, McKenney, Johnson & Regan, Washington, 1992-96; assoc. Regan, Halperin & Long, Washington, 1997-98, ptnr., 1999—; adj. law prof. Cath. U. of Am., Washington, 1998—. Founder Project Smile, Washington, 1998—. Mem. ABA, ATLA, Trial Lawyers Assn. of Met. Washington, Italian-Am. Bar Assn., D.C. Bar Assn., N.J. Bar Assn., N.Y. Bar Assn., Md. Bar Assn. General civil litigation, Personal injury, Product liability. Office: Regan Halperin & Long PLLC # 200 900 19th St NW Ste 200 Washington DC 20006-2105

**ZAMEK, SCOTT,** lawyer; b. Bethpage, N.Y., Feb. 17, 1961; s. Jack and Sandra Z.; m. Alexia Tsunis, June 6, 1987; children: Arielle, Allie. BA, SUNY, Albany, 1983; JD, Yeshiva U., 1986. Bar: N.Y. 1987. Assoc. atty. Gunnigle & Johnson P.C., Port Jefferson, N.Y., 1986-87, John Tsunis, Esq., Hauppauge, N.Y., 1987-90; pvt. practice Melville, N.Y., 1990-96; mng. ptnr. Zamek & Preston LLP, Melville, 1996—. Bd. dirs. Greater Port Jefferson Arts Coun., 1994—; bd. dirs., pres. Royal Ednl. Found., 1997—. Mem. Phi Alpha Delta. Avocations: softball, golf. Real property, Personal injury, General civil litigation. Office: Zamek & Preston LLP 560 Broadhollow Rd Ste 106 Melville NY 11747-3702

**ZAMMIT, JOSEPH PAUL,** lawyer; b. N.Y.C., May 19, 1948; s. John and Farla (Rudolph) Z.; m. Dorothy Therese O'Neill, June 6, 1970; children: Michael, Paul, Brian. AB, Fordham U., 1968; JD, Harvard U., 1971; LLM, NYU, 1974. Bar: N.Y. 1972, U.S. Dist. Ct. (so. and ea. dists.) N.Y. 1973, U.S. Ct. Appeals (2d cir.) 1973, U.S. Supreme Ct. 1978, U.S. Dist. Ct. (no. dist.) N.Y. 1983, U.S. Ct. Appeals (11th cir.) 1987. Assoc. Reavis & McGrath, N.Y.C., 1971-74; asst. prof. law St. John's U., Jamaica, N.Y., 1974-76, assoc. prof., 1976-78; assoc. Reavis & McGrath, N.Y.C., 1978-79, ptnr., 1979-88; ptnr. Fulbright & Jaworski L.L.P. (formerly Fulbright Jaworski & Reavis McGrath), N.Y.C., 1989—; adj. assoc. prof. St. John's U., Jamaica, 1979-83, adj. prof., 1984—; mem. panel computer arbitrators Am. Arbitration Assn., N.Y.C., 1977—. Bd. editors Computer Law Strategist, 1987—; contbr. articles to profl. jours. Mem. ABA, N.Y. State Bar Assn., Assn. of Bar of City of N.Y. (chmn. com. on computer law 1995-98, chmn. comml. liability subcom. 1981-87, fed. cts. com. 1998—), Computer Law Assn., Phi Beta Kappa. General civil litigation, Computer, Contracts commercial. Office: Fulbright & Jaworski LLP 666 5th Ave Fl 31 New York NY 10103-3198

**ZAMORA, STEPHEN,** dean. Dean U. Houston Sch. Law. Office: U Houston Sch Law Houston TX 77204-0001*

**ZAMORANO, ANDRE JORDAN,** lawyer; b. N.Y.C., Mar. 9, 1967; s. Hugo and Angelica Zamorano. BBA, So. Meth. U., 1989; JD, U. Miami, 1992. Bar: Fla. 1992, U.S. Dist. Ct. (so. dist.) Fla. 1992. Atty. Weil Lucia Mandler Croland et al, Miami, Fla., 1993-95, James & Glass Assocs., Miami, 1995-97, Shutts & Bowen, Miami, 1997-98, Verner Liipfert Bernhard McPherson & Hanel, Miami, 1998—. Mem. ABA, Greater Miami C. of C. Republican. General civil litigation. Office: Verner Liipfert et al 200 S Biscayne Blvd Ste 3100 Miami FL 33131-2310

**ZAMORE, JOSEPH DAVID,** lawyer, consultant; b. Bklyn., May 20, 1944; s. Harry and Eleanor (Shientag) Z.; m. Frances S. Zelikow, Nov. 24, 1968; children: Michael Seth, Rachel Anne, Judith Gail. AB with high honors, Brown U., 1966; JD, Columbia U., 1969. Bar: N.Y. 1969; R.I. 1971; U.S. Dist. Ct. R.I. 1971; U.S. Dist. Ct. (so., ea. and no. dists.) N.Y. 1970, Ohio 1971; U.S. Dist. Ct. (no. dist.) Ohio 1971, Fla. 1977; U.S. Dist. Ct. (so. dist.) Fla. 1977, U.S. Ct. Appeals (6th cir.) 1979. Law clk. to U.S. Chief Dist. Judge R.I., 1970-71; assoc. Guren, Merritt, Sogg & Cohen, Cleve., 1971-77; ptnr. Guren, Merritt, Feibel, Sogg & Cohen, Cleve., 1977-82; prin. Joseph D. Zamore Co., L.P.A., Shaker Heights, Ohio, 1982-86; prin. Persky, Shapiro, Zamore, Salim, Arnoff & Nolfi Co., L.P.A., 1986—; mem. adj. faculty Cleve. State U. Sch. Law, 1983—; pres. Telewave Systems, Inc., computer systems and cons., Cleve., 1980-84. Bd. dirs. Am. ORT Fedn., 1983—, exec. com. 1985— ; pres. Cleve. Men's ORT, 1985-87; mem. Shaker Hts. Recreation Bd., 1985-87, vice chmn. 1987. Mem. ABA (chmn. com. bus. torts litigation Litigation Sect. 1979-81, vice-chmn. com. on computers in small law office Gen. Practice Sect. 1982-83, vice chmn. corp., banking and bus. law com. Gen. Practice sect. 1985—), Computer Law Assn., Fla. Bar Assn. (chmn. out-of-state lawyers com. 1981-82), Cuyahoga County Bar Assn. (chmn. corp. law com. 1982-83), Greater Cleve. Bar Assn. (council Sect. on Securities Law 1980-86, chmn. sect. liaison and long-range planning com. 1982-83). Clubs: Oakwood, Masons (Cleve.). Contbr. articles to profl. jours. General corporate, Federal civil litigation, General practice. Office: 1410 Terminal Tower Cleveland OH 44113

**ZAMPARELLI, LEO R.,** lawyer; b. Trenton, N.J., Apr. 17, 1947; s. Leo J. and Bridget Zamparelli; m. Roselynne Fuccello; children: Justin, Nicholas. BA in Polit. Philosophy, Rider U., 1970; JD, Temple U., 1973. Pvt. practice Pa., 1974—, Lawrenceville, N.J., 1983—. Mem. ABA, N.J. State Bar Assn., Pa. Bar Assn., Mercer County Bar Assn., Bucks County Bar Assn., Mercer County C. of C. Office: 1719 Brunswick Pike Lawrenceville NJ 08648-4631

**ZANE, PHILLIP CRAIG,** lawyer; b. N.Y.C., Sept. 25, 1961; s. Martin I.L. and Rosalind Carol (Siegler) Z.; m. Denise Janine Wydra. BA, Pomona Coll., 1983; postgrad., U. Mich., 1985-88; JD cum laude, NYU, 1991. Bar: Ill. 1991, D.C. 1996, U.S. Dist. Ct. (no. dist.) Ill. 1991, U.S. Ct. Appeals (7th cir.) 1994, U.S. Ct. Appeals (8th cir.) 1993, U.S. Ct. Appeals (9th cir.) 1996, U.S. Fed. Cir. Ct. 1994. Assoc. Mayer, Brown & Platt, Chgo., 1991-93; judicial law clerk to Hon. Morris S. Arnold 8th Cir. Ct. Appeals, Little Rock, 1993-94; assoc. Mayer, Brown & Platt, Chgo., 1994-95, Morgan, Lewis & Bockius, Washington, 1996—. Staff editor NYU Rev. of Law and Social Change, 1989-90, critical legal studies editor, 1990-91; editor Sherman Act Almanac, 1998—; contbr. articles to profl. jours. Fellow Thomas J. Watson Found., 1983-84; fgn. lang. area studies fellow U. Mich., Ann Arbor, 1986, 87-88. Mem. ABA (vice chair Sherman Act sect. one com.), Ill. State Bar Assn. (spl. com. on Law Day in Moscow & Kiev 1992). Democrat. Avocation: legal history. Antitrust, Intellectual property, Federal civil litigation. Office: Morgan Lewis & Bockius LLP 1800 M St NW Washington DC 20036-5802

**ZANGRILLI, ALBERT JOSEPH, JR.,** lawyer; b. Pitts., May 3, 1940; s. Albert Joseph and Regina (DeSimone) Z.; m. M. Ursula McKenzie, Aug. 20, 1977; children: Albert J. III, Mary Catherine, Ursula Therese. AB, U. Notre Dame, 1963; MA, Holy Cross Coll., Washington, 1967; JD, Cornell U., 1972. Bar: Pa. 1972, U.S. Dist. Ct. (we. dist.) Pa. 1972, U.S. Ct. Appeals (3d cir.) 1976, U.S. Supreme Ct. 1988. Ptnr. and co-mng. ptnr. Metz, Cook, Welsh & Zangrilli, Pitts., 1981-92; ptnr. Yukevich, Marchetti, Liekar & Zangrilli, PC, Pitts., 1992—; ct. rules com. Allegheny County, Pa., 1974—. Contbr. author: Yearbook of Liturgical Studies, 1964-68. Committeeman Allegheny County Dem. Com., Pitts., 1990—; adv. bd. Notre Dame Club of Pitts., 1990—; mem. Theology Students Com. for Civil Rights, Washington, 1965-66; sec., exec. com. St. Paul Cathedral, 1985—. Mem. ACBA, St. Thomas More Soc. (pres. 1987-89, gov. 1976—), Pitts. Athletic Assn. (dir. 1989-96), Assn. Mcpl. and Sch. Solicitors (bd. dirs.), Irish Centre of Pitts. (dir. 1992-94). Democrat. Roman Catholic. General civil litigation, Land use and zoning (including planning), Municipal (including bonds). Office: Yukevich Marchetti Liekar and Zangrilli One Gateway Ctr Pittsburgh PA 15222

**ZANOT, CRAIG ALLEN,** lawyer; b. Wyandotte, Mich., Nov. 15, 1955; s. Thomas and Faye Blanch (Sperry) Z. AB with distinction, U. Mich., 1977; JD cum laude, Ind. U., 1980. Bar: Ind. 1980, Mich. 1981, U.S. Dist. Ct. (so. dist.) Ind. 1980, U.S. Dist. Ct. (no. dist.) Ind. 1981, U.S. Ct. Appeals (6th cir.) 1985, U.S. Dist. Ct. (ea. dist.) Mich. 1987, U.S. Dist. Ct. (we. dist.) Mich. 1990. Law clk. to presiding justice Allen County Superior Ct, Ft. Wayne, 1980-81; ptnr. Davidson, Breen & Doud P.C., Saginaw, Mich., 1981—. Mem. ABA, Mich. Bar Assn., Ind. Bar Assn., Saginaw County Bar Assn. Roman Catholic. Workers' compensation, Insurance, Personal injury. Home: 547 S Linwood Beach Rd Linwood MI 48634-9432 Office: Davidson Breen & Doud PC 1121 N Michigan Ave Saginaw MI 48602-4762

**ZAPHIRIOU, GEORGE ARISTOTLE,** lawyer, educator; b. July 10, 1919; came to U.S., 1973, naturalized, 1977; s. Aristotle George and Callie Constantine (Economos) Z.; m. Peaches J. Griffin, June 1, 1973; children: Ari, Marie. JD, U. Athens, 1940; LLM, U. London, 1950. Bar: Supreme Ct. Greece 1946, Eng. 1956, Ill. 1975, Va. 1983. Gen. counsel Counties Ship Mgmt. and R & K Ltd., London, 1951-61; lectr., barrister City of London Poly., 1961-73; vis. prof. Ill. Inst. Tech.-Chgo. Kent Coll. Law, 1973-76; pvt. practice Northbrook, Ill., 1976-78; prof. law George Mason U. Sch. Law, 1978-94; prof. law emeritus George Washington U. Sch. Law, 1994—; prof. internat. transactions George Mason U. Internat. Inst., 1992-94; mem. Odin, Feldman & Pittelman P.C., Fairfax, Va., 1994-96; mem. study group on internat. elec. commerce cons. and other pvt. internat. law covs. U.S. Dept. of State. Author: Transfer of Chattels in Private International Law, 1956, U.S. edit., 1981, European Business Law, 1970; co-author: Declining Jurisdiction in Private International Law, 1995; joint editor: Jour. Bus. Law, London, 1962-73; bd. editors Am. Jour. Comp. Law, 1980-94; contbr. articles to law revs. and profl. jours. Mem. ABA (sect. internat. law and practice com. on internat. arbitration), Ill. Bar Assn., Chgo. Bar Assn., Am. Arbitration Assn. (panel of comml. arbitrators), George Mason Am. Inn of Ct. (founder, mem. emeritus). Fax: (301) 984-1164. Alternative dispute resolution, Private international, Contracts commercial. Home: 400 Green Pasture Dr Rockville MD 20852-4233

**ZAPINSKI, ROBERT PAUL,** lawyer; b. Oak Park, Ill., Oct. 24, 1960; s. Norbert J. and Particia Marie (Celeskey) Z.; m. Susan Marie Sullivan, Aug. 10, 1985; children: Andrew, Kevin, Jennifer, Catherine. BS in Criminal Justice, Bradley U., 1982, BS in Psychology, 1982; JD, U. Ill., 1985. Bar: Ill. 1985, U.S. Dist. Ct. (no. dist.) Ill. 1986, U.S. Ct. Appeals (7th cir.) 1987. Law clk. to Hon. Micheal Mihm U.S. Dist. Ct., Peoria, Ill., 1985-94; assoc. Jenner & Block, Chgo., 1984-99, ptnr.; corp. counsel Tenneco Automotive Inc., 1999—. Contbg. author: Insurance Coverage, 1996. Soccer coach Westmont Park Dist., Ill., 1994—. Mem. ABA, Ill. State Bar Assn., Chgo. Bar Assn., Order Coif. Roman Catholic. Avocations: camping, whitewater rafting, kayaking, sports, soccer. General civil litigation, Insurance. Home: 336 Blackhawk Dr Westmont IL 60559-1563 Office: Tenneco Automotive Inc 500 N Field Dr Lake Forest IL 60045-2595

**ZAPPALA, STEPHEN A.,** state supreme court justice; b. 1932; s. Frank and Josephine Zappala. B.A., Duquesne U.; LL.B., Georgetown U., 1958. Bar: Pa. 1958. Solicitor Allegheny County, Pitts., 1974-76; judge Ct. of Common Pleas-Allegheny County, 1980-82; assoc. justice Pa. Supreme Ct., 1982—. Served with U.S. Army. Office: Pa Supreme Ct Ste 616 6 Gateway Ctr Pittsburgh PA 15222*

**ZARCO, ROBERT,** lawyer; b. Havana, Cuba, May 13, 1948; came to U.S., 1961; s. Barouh and Rebecca Zarco; m. Marsha Linda Zarco, Aug. 24, 1985; children: Marissa, Brandon, Sabrina. BA in Econs., Harvard U., 1980; JD, U. Miami, 1985. Bar: Fla., U.S. Dist. Ct. (so. dist.) Fla., U.S. Dist. Ct. Ariz., U.S. Ct. Appeals (11th cir.). Comml. litig. atty. Floyd, Pearson, Richman, Greer, Weil, et al., Miami, Fla., 1985-89; comml. litig. ptnr. Weil, Lucio, Mandler & Crolord, P.A., Miami, Fla., 1989-92; pres., founding ptnr. Zarco & Assocs., P.A., Miami, Fla., 1992—, Zarco & Pardo, P.A., Miami, Fla., 1996—; expert witness Calif. State Legis., Sacramento, 1994, Md. State Legis., Annapolis, 1994, Ariz. State Legis., Phoenix, 1993, Conn. State Legis., Milford, 1993, N.Y. State Legis., L.I., 1993; lectr. Ky. Fried Chicken Ind. Franchises, Atlanta, 1993, Am. Franchisee Assn., Las Vegas, 1994—, 7-Eleven Ind. Franchises, Tucson, Portland, Oreg., Reno, Nev., Valley Forge, N.J., Chgo., Detroit, 1993—, Fla. Restaurant Franchisee Assn., Ft. Lauderdale, 1995, White House Conf. on Small Bus., Washington, 1995, Fla. Bar Assn., Miami, 1996, 97, Beacon Coun. Expo 97, Miami, 1997, Denny's Franchisee Assn., Scottsdale, Ariz., 1997, Am. Franchise Assn., Lake Tahoe, Nev., 1998, TCBY Franchise Assn., Chgo., 1998, Little Caesars' Franchise Assn., Dallas, 1998, Conrad Hilton Coll. Hotel Mgmt., Houston, 1998; numerous TV appearances including CNN, PBS, and CNBC. Lobbyist White House Conf. on Small Bus., Washington, 1995, Fla. House Commerce com. and the Senate Com. on Internat. Trade, Econ. Devel., and Tourism, Tallahassee, 1994; mem. young leadership nat. men's cabinet United Jewish Appeal, 1992-94; mem. new leadership campaign com. commerce and and professions Grtr. Miami Jewish Fedn., Miami, 1995, chmn. missions com., 1992-93, bd. dirs. young leadership coun., 1991-93; bd. dirs. Temple Menorah, Miami, 1986—; mem. budget adv. com. City of Miami Beach, 1987-90. Mem. ATLA, ABA, Am. Franchisee Assn., Fed. Trial Bar Assn., Fla. Bar Assn., Dade County Bar Assn., Cuban Am. BAr Assn., Dade County Trial Lawyers Assn., Acad. Fla. Trial Lawyers. General civil litigation, Franchising, Construction. Office: Zarco & Pardo PA Nationsbank Twr 27th Fl 100 SE 2nd St Ste 2700 Miami FL 33131-2193

**ZARNOWSKI, JAMES DAVID,** lawyer, insurance specialist; b. Freehold, N.J., Feb. 22, 1950; s. Andrew G. and Joan M. (Voltz) Z. B.S., Monmouth Coll., 1972; J.D., Rutgers U., 1977. Bar: N.J. 1977. Prin. research analyst N.J. Dept. Ins., Trenton, 1977-78, project specialist, 1978-79, dir. regulatory affairs, 1987-88; sr. actuarial asst. Chubb & Son, Inc., Short Hills, N.J., 1979-82; sr. research assoc. Am. Ins. Assn., N.Y.C., 1982-84; research mgr., counsel Ind. Ins. Agts. Am., N.Y.C., 1984-87; asst. gen. counsel Reciprocal Mgmt. Corp., Princeton, N.J., 1989—; jr. actuary Crum & Forster Ins. Cos., 1972-74; Active, Rutgers Legal Aid Clinic, 1976-77. N.J. State scholar, 1968-72; Monmouth Bar Found. scholar, 1974, 75, 76. Mem. N.J. Bar Assn., ABA. Insurance, Legislative, Workers' compensation. Home: 28 Ocean Ave Apt 1 Ocean Grove NJ 07756-1712 Office: 103 Carnegie Ctr Ste 300 Princeton NJ 08540-6235

**ZASHIN, ANDREW AARON,** lawyer; b. Cleve., Feb. 7, 1968. AB, Brown U., 1990; JD, Case Western Res. U., 1993. Bar: Ohio 1993, Fla. 1994, D.C. 1995. Atty. Zashin & Rich Co., Cleve., 1993—. Bd. trustees Congregation Beth Am., 1996—; co-chmn. Israel Bonds, Cleve., 1996-98. Family and matrimonial. Office: Zashin & Rich Co CPA 55 Public Sq Ste 1490 Cleveland OH 44113-1998

**ZASHIN, STEPHEN S.,** lawyer; b. Cleve.. BS in Econs., U. Pa., 1991; JD, Case Western Res. U., 1995, MBA, 1995. Bar: Ohio 1995, U.S. Dist. Ct. (no. dist.) Ohio 1996, U.S. Ct. Appeals (6th cir.) 1995. Atty. Duvin, Cahn & Hutton, Cleve., 1995-97, Zashin & Rich Co., L.P.A., Cleve., 1997—. Mem. Law Rev. Labor, Federal civil litigation, State civil litigation. Office: Zashin & Rich Co LPA 55 Public Sq Ste 1490 Cleveland OH 44113-1998

**ZASLOWSKY, DAVID PAUL,** lawyer; b. N.Y.C., Dec. 30, 1960; s. Daniel N. and Rhoda (Sohn) Z.; m. Lisa Ann Freudenberger, Aug. 26, 1982; children: Amanda Lauren, Michael Joel, Steven Ira. BS in Computer/Info. Sci. summa cum laude, Bklyn. Coll., 1981; JD, Yale U., 1984. Bar: N.Y. 1984, N.J. 1984, U.S. Dist. Ct. (so. and ea. dist.) N.Y. 1985, U.S. Dist. Ct. N.J. 1985, U.S. Cir. Ct. (2d cir.) 1992. Assoc. Baker & McKenzie, N.Y.C., 1984-94, ptnr., 1994—. Author: (with others) Federal Civil Practice, 1989, Transnational Litigation in U.S. Federal Courts, 1991, Litigating International Commercial Disputes, 1996. mem. ABA (litigation sect.), N.Y. State Bar Assn. (comml. and fed. litigation sect.), Assn. Bar City N.Y. General civil litigation, Contracts commercial. Office: Baker & McKenzie 805 3rd Ave Fl 29 New York NY 10022-7513

**ZAUDERER, MARK CARL,** lawyer; b. Jan. 26, 1946. BA, Union Coll., 1967; JD, NYU, 1971. Bar: N.Y. 1972. Law clk. U.S. Dist. Ct., Newark, 1971-72; ptnr. Solomon, Zauderer, Ellenhorn, Frischer & Sharp, N.Y.C., 1981—; faculty chmn. Practicing Law Inst. Program., Litigating Comml. Cases up to Trial, N.Y.C. and San Francisco, 1986, faculty mem. Deposition Skills Tng. Program, N.Y., 1986, 88, 89, 90; mem. adv. com. on civil practice to Chief Adminstrn. Judge N.Y. State Ctrs., 1992—; trustee bd. advisors Union Coll., 1993—; chief Judge's Task Force on Comml. Cts., 1995—. Author, moderator practising law inst. satellite TV program Deposition Strategy and Tactics, 1989; contbr. articles to profl. jours. Mem. ABA, N.Y. State Bar Assn. (chmn. program strategy and tactics in bus. and comml. litigation N.Y.C., Buffalo and Rochester, N.Y., 1990, 91, 94, mem. faculty 1992-94), Assn. of Bar of City of N.Y. (com. state cts. superior jurisdiction 1983-87, profl. discipline com. 1987-88, judiciary com. 1988-91, chmn. com. complex civil litigation, comml. and fed. litigation sect., mem. exec. com. 1991—, chair 1996-97), Fed. Bar Coun. (trustee 1998—). Federal civil litigation, State civil litigation. Home: 11 Avon Rd Larchmont NY 10538-1420 Office: 45 Rockefeller Plz New York NY 10111-0100

**ZAUN, ANNE MARIE,** lawyer; b. N.Y.C., Aug. 1, 1949; d. George F. and Clara J. (Varriale) Z.; m. Stephen A. Lokos, Oct. 17, 1987; children: Debra M., Anthony G. BS, Fordham U., 1970; JD cum laude, Seton Hall U., 1979. Assoc. mgr. Prudential Property and Casualty Ins. Co., Woodbridge, N.J., 1972-76; dep. atty. gen. State of N.J., Trenton, 1980-84; staff atty. Knapp & Blejwas, Edison, N.J., 1984-87; dir. legal writing program Law Sch. Seton Hall. U., Newark, 1987-89; prin. Anne M. Zaun, Milltown, N.J., 1989—; adj. prof. paralegal program Middlesex County Coll., 1992—. Mem. N.J. Bar Assn. (elder law sect., family law sect.), Middlesex County Bar Assn. (women's sect., elder law sect.), Latin Am. Parents Assn. (legal counsel). Democrat. Avocations: reading, music, tennis, swimming. Family and matrimonial, Probate, Estate planning. Office: 385 Cranbury Rd East Brunswick NJ 00816

**ZAUZIG, CHARLES J., III,** lawyer; b. Shaw AFB, S.C., June 30, 1953; s. Charles and Barbara (Croft) Z.; m. Linda K., Aug. 30, 1996; children: Michelle, Joseph. BA, Madison Coll., 1975; JD, T.C. Williams Sch. Law, Richmond, Va., 1978. Bar: U.S. Ct. Appeals (4th cir.) 1983, U.S. Supreme Ct. 1983, Va. 1978, U.S. Dist. Ct. (ea. dist.) Va. 1978. Sole practice Woodbridge, Va., 1978-90; ptnr. Nichols, Bergere & Zauzig, Woodbridge, 1990—. Mem. ATLA, Va. Trial Lawyers Assn., Va. State Bar. Personal injury, Product liability. Office: Nichols Bergere & Zauzig 12660 Lake Ridge Dr Woodbridge VA 22192-2335

**ZAVADIL, LAWRENCE MICHAEL,** lawyer; b. Yankton, SD, Dec. 24, 1960; s. Lawrence Raymond and Maryann Zavadil; m. Melissa Lynn McLoughlin, Feb. 3, 1996; children: Lawrence Dalton, Griffin Gunnar. BS in Polit. Sci. and Econs., Kearney State Coll., 1983; JD, U. Nebr., 1987. Bar: Mo. 1987, U.S. Dist. Ct. Mo. 1987, U.S. Ct. Appeals (8th cir.) 1987, Colo. 1987, U.S. Dist. Ct. Colo. 1990, U.S. Ct. Appeals (10th cir.) 1990. Assoc. Stinson, Mag & Fizzell, Kansas City, Mo., 1987-89; assoc. Holme, Roberts & Owen, Denver, 1990-93, sr. assoc., 1993-96, sr. counsel, 1996—. Contbr. chpt. to book, articles to mags.; editor Colorado Lawyer (mag.), Denver, 1995—; exec. editor Nebr. Law Rev., 1986-87. Vol. Jr. Achievement program, Denver, 1998; precinct com. person, Colo. Rep. Party, Denver, 1994—; vol. Eleanor Roosevelt Inst., Denver, 1994-96. Mem. Federalist Soc., South Metro Denver C. of C. Avocations: biking, hiking, kayaking, snowboarding, reading. Contracts commercial. Office: Holme Roberts & Owen 1700 Lincoln St Ste 4100 Denver CO 80203-4541

**ZAVARELLA, GINO PHILLIP,** lawyer; b. Hardin County, Ky., Oct. 31, 1967; s. Gino Phillip and Lillian Ann Zavarella. PhB, Cath. U. Am., 1990, JD, 1995, PhL, 1995. Bar: Ohio 1995, U.S. Dist. Ct. (no. dist.) Ohio 1997, U.S. Ct. Appeals (6th cir.) 1998. Gen. cousnel Maxus Investment Group, Cleve., 1995-97; prin. Gino Savarella, Atty. and Counselor at Law, Cleve., 1997—; bd. dirs. Link Info. Sys. LLC, Cleve.; bd. dirs., cons. Gia USA, Inc., Cleve., 1996—. Roman Catholic. Private international, Contracts commercial, Computer. Office: 28749 Chagrin Blvd Ste 200 Cleveland OH 44122-4544

**ZAVATSKY, MICHAEL JOSEPH,** lawyer; b. Wheeling, W.Va., Dec. 15, 1948; s. Mike and Mary (Mirich) Z.; m. Kathleen Hanson, May 28, 1983; children: David, Emily. BA in Internat. Studies, Ohio State U., 1970; MA in Polit. Sci., U. Hawaii, 1972; JD, U. Cin., 1980. Bar: Ohio 1980, U.S. Dist. Ct. (so. dist.) Ohio 1981, U.S. Ct. Appeals (6th cir.) 1985, U.S. Supreme Ct. 1989. Ptnr. Taft, Stettinius & Hollister, Cin., 1980—; adj. prof. in trial practice and immigration law U. Cin., 1986—. Trustee Internat. Visitors Ctr., Cin., 1984-86; bd. dirs. Cin. Charter Com., 1988-91; bd. dirs., mem. steering com. Leadership Cin., 1994-96. Capt. USAF, 1973-77. William Graham fellow U. Cin., 1979, East West Ctr. fellow U. Hawaii, 1970. Mem ABA, Ohio Bar Assn., Cin. Bar Assn., Am. Immigration Lawyers Assn. (chmn. Ohio chpt. 1987-88, 90-93), Potter Stewart Inn of Ct., Order of Coif. Federal civil litigation, State civil litigation, Immigration, naturalization, and customs. Home: 3820 Eileen Dr Cincinnati OH 45209-2013 Office: 1800 Firstar Tower Cincinnati OH 45202

**ZAVEZ, JOHN PETER,** lawyer; b. New Britain, Conn., Jan. 11, 1959; s. John and Elenore Claffey Zavez; m. Michelle Elizabeth Macken, Aug. 3, 1991; children: Alexis Elenore, Katherine Michelle, Melissa Jane. AB, Harvard U., 1981, JD, 1989. Bar: Mass. 1989. Law clk. U.S. Dist. Ct. Mass., Boston, 1989-90; atty. Sullivan & Worcester, Boston, 1990-96, Berman, DeValerio & Pease, Boston, 1996—. Maj. U.S. Army, 1981—. Decorated Meritorious Svc. medal. Avocations: endurance athletics, military history, military science. Federal civil litigation, General civil litigation, State civil litigation. Office: Berman DeValerio & Pease LLP 1 Liberty Sq Ste 8A Boston MA 02109-4886

**ZAWADSKY, JOHN H.,** lawyer; b. Trenton, N.J., Nov. 4, 1951; s. John P. and Patience H. Zawadsky; m. Linda M. Makholm, Aug. 7, 1976 (div. Jan. 23, 1994); children: Lisa, Daniel, Jayson, Abby; m. Penny L. Vaughan, Aug. 9, 1996. BS, U. Wis., Stevens Point, 1974; JD, U. Wis., 1980. Shareholder Melli, Walker, Pease & Ruhly, S.C., Madison, Wis., 1980-88, Whyte & Hirshboeck, Madison, Wis., 1988-94, Reinhart, Boerner, Van Deuren, Norris & Rieselbach, S.C., Madison and Milw., Wis., 1984—. Co-author: OSHA Guide, 1998; mem. editl. bd. Gempler's, 1995-98. Mem. Madison Club, 1984—, Wis. Postal History Soc., Hartland, 1985—, Madison Arts League; mem. bd. dirs. Dane County Hospice Care, Madison, 1991-95. Recipient Lawyer of Yr. award Epilepsy Found. Dane County, 1994. Mem. State Bar Wis. (labor sect. 1980—), Dane County Bar, Order of Coif. Avocations: trout fishing, archaeology, history, golf. Labor, Administrative and regulatory, Government contracts and claims. Home: 5910 Timber Ridge Trl Madison WI 53711-5182 Office: Reinhart Law Firm 22 E Mifflin St Ste 600 Madison WI 53703-4225

**ZEALEY, SHARON JANINE,** lawyer; b. St. Paul, Aug. 30, 1959; d. Marion Edward and Freddie (Ward) Z. BS, Xavier U. of La., 1981; JD, U. Cin., 1984. Bar: Ohio 1984; U.S. Dist. Ct. (so. dist.) Ohio 1985; U.S. Ct. Appeals (6th cir.) 1990; U.S. Supreme Ct. 1990. Law clk. U.S. Atty. for S. Dist. of Ohio, Cin., 1982; trust adminstr. Star Bank (Formerly FNB), Cin., 1984-86; atty. UAW Legal Svcs., Cin., 1986-88; assoc. Manley, Burke & Fischer, Cin., 1988-91; mng. atty. and dep. atty. gen. Ohio Atty. Gen. Office, Cin., 1991-95; asst. U.S. atty. criminal div. for So. Dist. Ohio U.S. Attys. Office, Cin., 1995-97; United States atty. So. Dist. Ohio, Cin., 1997—; pro bono svc. Pro Srs., 1987-88; mem. merit selection com. U.S. Ct. Appeals 6th Cir., Bankruptcy Ct.; adj. prof. law, civil rights U. Cin. Vol. lawyer for the poor/Pro Bono Panel participant, 1984—; bd. dirs. Seven Hills Neighborhood Houses, Inc., 1989-91; adv. rev. bd. City of Cin. EEOC, 1989-91; mem. Tall Stacks Commn., Cin., 1991-92, Mayor's Commn. on Children, 1992-93, Greater Cin. Found. Task Force on Affordable Homes, 1992; mem. Grace Episcopal Ch., Black Cmty. Crusade for Children, 1994—; vol. legal clinic Allen Temple, 1988-90; trustee, bd. visitors U. Cin. Coll. Law, 1992—; mem. BLAC/CBA Round Table, 1988—. Recipient Law Honor scholarship U. Cin. Coll. Law, 1981. Mem. Black Lawyers Assn. of Cin. (pres. 1989-91), Legal Aid Soc. (sec. 1991-92), ABA, Fed. Bar Assn., Ohio Bar Assn., Nat. Bar Assn. (Mem. of Yr. region VI 1990), Cin. Bar Assn. (trustee 1989-94), Xavier U. Alumni Assn. Democrat. Episcopalian. Fax: 513-684-6385. Office: US Attys Office 100 E 5th St Ste 220 Cincinnati OH 45202-3982*

**ZEBERSKY, EDWARD HERBERT,** lawyer; b. N.Y.C., May 16, 1966; s. Joseph Zebersky and Patricia (Hirst) Leff. BBA, U. Wis., 1988; JD cum laude, U. Miami, Fla., 1991. Bar: Fla. 1991, U.S. Dist. Ct. (so. dist.) Fla. 1992. Prodn. mgr. Toy Biz Inc., N.Y.C., 1988; assoc. Tripp Scott Conklin & Smith PA, Ft. Lauderdale, 1991-93; dir., mng. ptnr. Zebersky, Zebersky & Guilianti, Plantation, Fla., 1993—; dir. Zebersky & Payne, LLP, Plantation, Fla.; cons. Bole Ent Ltd., Oyster Bay, N.Y., 1991-94; staff atty. Broward Lawyers Care, Ft. Lauderdale, 1991—, Fla. Bar Pro Bono Svc., Tallahassee, 1992—, Lawyers for the Arts, Ft. Lauderdale, 1993-94. Deans Honor scholar U. Miami, 1989-9, 90-91. Mem. ATLA, Acad. Fla. Trial Lawyers (chmn. ins. task force, bd. dirs.), Greater Miami Jewish Fedn., Miami Project Cure Paralysis, Order of Coif. Avocations: mountain climbing, fishing, golf. Personal injury, Insurance, Product liability. Office: Zebersky & Payne LLP 3850 Hollywood Blvd Hollywood FL 33021-6748

**ZEDER, FRED M.,** lawyer; b. Detroit, July 20, 1945; s. Fred Monroe and Martha Irene (Blood) Z.; m. Betty Darby, Aug. 10, 1985; children: Margaret, Elizabeth, Aaron. BA in Lit., Arts. and Sci., U. Mich., 1968; JD, Georgetown U., 1972. Bar: Wash. 1972. Assoc. Williams Kastner Gibbs, Seattle, 1972-78; ptnr. Aaron & Zeder, Seattle, 1978-84; shareholder Peterson, Young, Putra, Fletcher & Zeder, Seattle, 1985—. Mem. ATLA, Wash. State Trial Lawyers Assn. (bd. dirs.). Health, Insurance, Product liability. Office: Peterson Young et al 1501 4th Ave Ste 2800 Seattle WA 98101-1664

**ZEDROSSER, JOSEPH JOHN,** lawyer; b. Milw., Jan. 24, 1938; s. Joseph and Rose (Zollner) Z.; m. Antonina Krass, Sept. 6, 1997. AB, Marquette U., 1959; LLB, Harvard U., 1963. Bar: N.Y. 1964, U.S. Dist. Ct. (so. dist.) N.Y. 1966, U.S. Dist. Ct. (ea. dist.) N.Y. 1971, U.S. Ct. Appeals (2d cir.) 1971, U.S. Ct. Appeals (D.C. Cir.) 1975, U.S. Supreme Ct. 1975. Assoc. William G. Mulligan, N.Y.C., 1964-67, Christy, Bauman, Frey and Christy and successors, N.Y.C., 1967-71; dir. community devel. unit Bedford-Stuyvesant Community Legal Svcs. Corp., N.Y.C., 1971-73; assoc. atty. fed. defender svcs. unit Legal Aid Soc., N.Y.C., 1973-74; asst. atty. gen. Environ. Protection Bur., N.Y. State Dept. Law, N.Y.C., 1974-80; regional counsel EPA, N.Y.C., 1980-82; assoc. prof. St. John's U. Sch. Law, N.Y.C., 1982-86; ptnr. Rivkin, Radler, Dunne & Bayh, Uniondale, N.Y., 1986-89, Breed, Abbott & Morgan, N.Y.C., 1989-93, Whitman Breed Abbott & Morgan, N.Y.C., 1993-95; v.p. CPR Inst. for Dispute Resolution, N.Y.C., 1996; sr. investigative counsel com. on investigations, taxation, and gov. ops. N.Y. State Senate, 1998—. Lectr., contbr. to course handbooks for courses sponsored by Practicing Law Inst. and other assns. Lt. USNR, 1965-74, USAR, 1963-65. Mem. ABA, Assn. of Bar of City of N.Y., N.Y. State Bar Assn. (mem. Environ. Law Sect. Exec. Com.), Alpha Sigma Nu. Roman Catholic. Legislative, Environmental, General civil litigation. Home: 45 E End Ave Apt 11F New York NY 10028-7982

**ZEGLIS, JOHN D.,** communications company executive, lawyer. BS, U. Ill., 1969; JD, Harvard U., 1972. Bar; Ill. Sr. v.p., gen. counsel and govt. affairs AT&T, N.Y.C., 1996—, now pres., CEO. Mem. ABA (vice chmn. communications of pub. utility law sect). Office: AT&T 295 N Maple Ave Basking Ridge NJ 07920-1025

**ZEIDMAN, PHILIP FISHER,** lawyer; b. Birmingham, Ala., May 2, 1934; s. Eugene Morris and Ida (Fisher) Z.; m. Nancy Levy, Aug. 19, 1956; children: Elizabeth Miriam, John Fisher (dec.), Jennifer Kahn. BA cum laude, Yale U., 1955; LLB, Harvard U., 1958; postgrad., Grad. Sch. Bus. Adminstrn., 1957-58. Bar: Ala. 1958, Fla. 1960, U.S. Supreme Ct. 1961, D.C. 1968, N.Y. 1981. Trial atty. FTC, 1960-61; staff asst. White House Com. Small Bus., 1961-63; spl. asst. to adminstr. SBA, 1961-63, asst. gen. counsel, 1963-65, gen. counsel, 1965-68; spl. asst. to Vice Pres. of U.S., 1968; govt. rels. mgr. Nat. Alliance Businessmen, 1968; founding prin. Brownstein & Zeidman P.C., Washington, 1968-96; sr. ptnr. Rudnick, Wolfe, Epstien & Zeidman, Washington, 1996—; chmn. grants and benefits com. Adminstrv. Conf. U.S., 1968; chmn. food industry adv. com. Dept. Energy, 1979-81; chmn. distbn. and food merchandising subcom. Alliance to Save Energy, 1978; mem. Pres.'s Commn. on Exec. Exch., 1978-81; gen. counsel Internat. Franchise Assn., Am. Bus. Conf.; spl. counsel Japanese Franchise Assn.; advisor to govts. and internat. orgns.; founder EastEuropeLaw, Ltd., Budapest, Hungary. Editor, author: Survey of Laws and Regulations Affecting International Franchising, 1982, 2nd edit., 1990, Regulation of Buying and Selling a Franchise, 1983, Legal Aspects of Selling and Buying, 1983, 2nd edit., 1991; cons. editor Global Franchising Alert; assoc. editor Jour. of International Franchising Law and Distribution; contbg. editor Legal Times of Washington, 1978-85; mem. adv. bd. Antitrust and Trade Regulation Report for Bur. Nat. Affairs, 1978-85. Mem. young leadership coun. Dem. Nat. Com.; exec. dir. Dem. platform com., 1972; adviser Nat. Presdl. Campaign of Jimmy Carter, 1976; mem. pres.'s adv. com. John F. Kennedy Ctr. for Performing Arts, 1981; chmn. class coun. Yale Class of 1955; mem. adv. bd. Yale U. Sch. Mgmt.; trustee Yale-China Assn., 1983-89; dir. Appleseed Found., 1994—; mem. adv. bd. DeWitt Wallace Ctr. for Comm., Terry Sanford Inst. Pub. Policy, Duke U., 1994-98. With USAF, 1958-60. Recipient Younger Fed. Lawyer award Fed. Bar Assn., 1965; Jonathan Davenport Oratorical award, 1954; William Houston McKim award, 1955. Mem. ABA (chmn. com. on franchising 1977-81), D.C. Bar Assn., Ala. Bar Assn., Fla. Bar Assn., Fed. Bar Assn., Bar Assn. D.C., Internat. Bar Assn. (chmn. internat. franchising com. 1986-90, mem. coun. sect. bus. law 1996—), Am. Intellectual Property Law Assn. (chmn. franchising com. 1987-90), Assn. Yale U. Alumni (class rep.). Antitrust, Franchising. Office: 1201 New York Ave NW Ph Washington DC 20005-3917

**ZEIGER, TIMOTHY DAVID,** lawyer; b. Langdale, Ala., June 22, 1953; s. H. Evan and Gene (Morris) Z.; m. Nancy Kay Willis, Aug. 16, 1975; children: David, Matthew, Karolena, Daniel. BA, Samford U., 1975; JD, Baylor U., 1981. Bar: Tex. 1981, U.S. Dist. Ct. (no. dist.) Tex. 1982, U.S. Ct. Appeals (5th dir.) 1983; cert. in civil trial law and civil appellate law Tex. Bd. Legal Specialization. Assoc. Gassaway Gurley Sheets & Michael, Borger, Tex., 1981-84, ptnr., 1985-88; ptnr. McKinley Dubner Schura & Warner, Dallas, 1988, shareholder, dir., 1989-91; shareholder, dir. McKinney Hinton Ringer LLP, Dallas, 1991-96, McKinley Ringer Zeiger P.C., Dallas, 1996-99, McKinley & Zeiger LLP, Dallas, 1999—. Mem. Nat. Bd. Trial Advocacy (cert. civil trial law). General civil litigation, Appellate. Office: McKinley & Zeiger LLP LB400 10440 N Central Expy Dallas TX 75231-2221

**ZEIGLER, ANN DEPENDER,** lawyer; b. Spokane, Wash., June 7, 1947; d. F. Norman and Dorothy (Wolter) dePender; m. Paul Stewart Zeigler, June 20, 1970; 1 child, Kate Elizabeth. BA magna cum laude, Ft. Wright Coll. Holy Names, Spokane, 1969; MFA in Creative Writing, U. Mont., 1975; JD, U. Houston, 1984. Bar: Tex. 1984. Course adminstr. legal communications U. Houston, 1982-84; assoc. Dula, Shields & Egbert, 1984-87; ind. project atty., 1987; assoc. Dow, Cogburn & Friedman, 1987-90; assoc. bankruptcy sect./avoidance litigation Hughes, Watters & Askanase, Houston, 1990—. Co-editor: Insurance Guide-Arts Nonprofits, 1993, Basic Issues in Estate Planning-Representing the Artist, 1994, Leading the Arts Nonprofit: Duties of Officers and Directors, 1999; contbr. articles to legal jours. Mem. publs. com., writer Tex. Accts. and Lawyers for Arts, Houston, 1988—; mem. Supreme Ct. of Tex. Unauthorized Practice of Law Com., Houston; vol. Houston Lawyers for Hunger Relief, 1988-90. Mem. ABA, State Bar Tex., Houston Bar Assn. (chair law and the arts com. 1996-97, co-chair ann. fiction contest), Can. Bar Assn., Phi Alpha Delta. Democrat. Bankruptcy, Real property, General civil litigation. Home: 4038 Cheena Dr Houston TX 77025-4702 Office: Hughes Watters & Askanase 1415 Louisiana St Fl 37 Houston TX 77002-7360

**ZEIGLER, JUDY ROSE,** law firm administrator; b. Monte Vista, Colo., Aug. 26, 1946; d. Orville Edgar Zeigler and Kathryn Genevieve (Parsons) Duncan. BA, U. Oreg., 1968. Asst. v.p., mgr. staff planning and devel. Rainier Nat. Bank, Seattle, 1979-81, asst. v.p., mgr. staff devel., 1981-83; v.p., mgr. staff planning Blue Cross of Washington and Alaska, Seattle, 1983-85, mgr. market research, 1985-86; pres. Strategies Unltd., Seattle, 1986-96; law firm adminstr. Law Offices of Judith A. Lonnquist P.S., Seattle; workshop presenter Gov.'s Conf. Women on the Move, Seattle, 1984, Women Plus Bus Conf., Seattle, 1984, 85, 86, 88, 89; pres. Natalie Skeels Meml. Found. Trustees, Seattle, 1987-90; co-founder, dir. N.W. Women's Inst., 1995—. Vice chair Blue Ribbon Citizens Task Force of King County Assessor's Office, Seattle, 1984; chair mktg. com. Bellevue Community Coll. Telecommunications Ctr. Task Force, Seattle, 1985-87; mem. Women's Polit. Caucus, Seattle, 1987-88, co-chair fundraising com. Mem. ASTD (pres. Puget Sound chpt. 1984-85), Women's Profl. and Managerial Network (pres. 1987-88), N.W. Women's Law Ctr. (bd. dirs. 1988-90, pres. Leadership Synthesis 1991-92, mem. adv. coun. 1988-96), Internat. Women's Conf. (exec. bd. officer 1991-95), Pacific N.W. Writers Conf. (bd. dirs. 1998—, mem. exec. com. 1999—). Democrat. Avocation: student pilot. Home: 1523 11th Ave W Seattle WA 98119-3204 Office: Law Offices of Judith A Lonnquist PS 1218 3rd Ave Ste 1500 Seattle WA 98101-3021

**ZEITLAN, MARILYN LABB,** lawyer; b. N.Y.C., Sept. 17, 1938; d. Charles and Florence (Geller) Labb; m. Barrett M. Zeitlan, Apr. 14, 1957; children: Adam Scott, Daniel Craig. BA, Queens Coll., 1958, MS, 1970; JD, Hofstra U., 1978. Bar: N.Y. 1979. Tchr. N.Y.C., 1958-61; pvt. practice matrimonial law, Roslyn, N.Y., 1980—. Assoc. editor: Law Rev., Hofstra U., 1977-78; contbr. articles to profl. jours. Commr. East Hills Environ. Commn., 1971-75; co-founder Roslyn Environ. Assn., 1970; v.p. Roslyn LWV, 1974-75. Hofstra Law Sch. fellow, 1976. Mem. Nassau County Bar Assn., N.Y. State Bar Assn., Phi Beta Kappa. Avocation: horseback riding. Family and matrimonial. Office: 1025 Northern Blvd Ste 201 Roslyn NY 11576-1506

**ZELDES, ILYA MICHAEL,** forensic scientist, lawyer; b. Baku, Azerbaidjan, Mar. 15, 1933; came to U.S., 1976; s. Michael B. and Pauline L. (Ainbinder) Z.; m. Emma S. Kryss, Nov. 5, 1957; 1 child, Irina Zeldes Rieser. JD, U. Azerbaidjan, Baku, 1955; PhD in Forensic Scis., U. Moscow, 1969. Expert-criminalist Med. Examiner's Bur., Baku, 1954-57; rsch. assoc. Criminalistics Lab., Moscow, 1958-62; sr. rsch. assoc. All-Union Sci. Rsch. Inst. Forensic Expertise, Moscow, 1962-75; chief forensic scientist S.D. Forensic Lab., Pierre, 1977-93; owner Forensic Scientist's Svcs., Pierre, 1977-93. Author: Physical-Technical Examination, 1968, Complex Examination, 1971, The Problems of Crime, 1981; contbr. numerous articles to profl. publs. in Australia, Austria, Bulgaria, Can., Eng., Germany, Holland, India, Ireland, Israel, Rep. of China, Russia, U.S. and USSR. Mem. Internat. Assn. Identification (rep. S.D. chpt. 1979-93, chmn. forensic lab. analysis subcom. 1991-98), Assn. Firearm and Tool Mark Examiners (emeritus). Avocation: travel. Home: 5735 Foxlake Dr Apt 1 Fort Myers FL 33917-5661

**ZELDES, JACOB DEAN,** lawyer; b. Galesburg, Ill., Dec. 10, 1929; s. Louis Herman and Sophia Ruth (Koren) Z.; m. Nancy S. Zeldes, Aug. 23, 1953; children: Stephen, Kathryn, Amy. BS, U. Wis., 1951; LLB, Yale U., 1957. Bar: Conn. 1957, U.S. Dist. Ct. Conn. 1958, U.S. Ct. Appeals (2nd cir.) 1959, U.S. Supreme Ct. 1960, U.S. Tax Ct. 1966. Ptnr. Zeldes Needle & Cooper PC, Bridgeport, Conn. Lt. (j.g.) USNR, 1951-53, Korea. Fellow Am. Bar Found., Am. Coll. Trial Lawyers; mem. ABA Assn. Profl. Responsibility Lawyers, Conn. Bar Assn. (lawyer to lawyer dispute resolution com., spl. counsel Conn. Ho. of Reps., select com. to investigate impeachment of probate judge 1985), Conn. Trial Lawyers Assn., Assn. Trial Lawyers of Am., Nat. Assn. Criminal Def. Lawyers, Conn. Criminal Def. Lawyers Assn., Bridgeport Bar Assn. Democrat. Jewish. Avocations: swimming, hiking, travel. Criminal, General civil litigation. Office: Zeldes Needle & Cooper PC 1000 Lafayette Blvd Fl 5 Bridgeport CT 06604-4725

**ZELECHIWSKY, BOHDAN JOHN,** lawyer; b. Pottsville, Pa., July 6, 1951; s. Bohdan Stephen and Nadia Z.; m. Chrystyna Hawrylak, Sept. 15, 1978 (div. Jan. 1989); children: Sophia, Adrian; m. Anita Louise Walters, Dec. 5, 1993; children: Roman, Zenia. BA, Moravian Coll., 1973; JD, U. Vt., 1976. Bar: Pa. 1977. Pvt. practice Bethlehem, Pa., 1978—. Coun. mem. Ukranian Orthodox Ch., N.J., 1993. With USMC, 1971-72. Avocations: skiing, biking. Probate, Workers' compensation, General practice.

**ZELENAK, EDWARD MICHAEL,** lawyer, musician; b. Dearborn, Mich., Aug. 26, 1953; s. Edward Patrick and Irene Elaine (Maruska) Z.; m. Angline Rose Cianfarani, May 24, 1986; children: Amelia Mary Rose and Edward Patrick (twins), Elliott William. BA, Wayne State U., 1975, JD, 1977. Bar: Mich. 1977, U.S. Dist. Ct. (ea. dist.) Mich. 1977, 6th Cir. Ct. of Appeals 1987. Leader Ed Zelenak Orch., Lincoln Park, Mich., 1971—; dir. pub. affairs Sta. WDRQ, Southfield, Mich., 1977-83, host talk show, 1978-83; instr. Wayne State Univ., Detroit, 1977-84; pvt. practice, Lincoln Park, 1977—; atty. Cities of Lincoln Park and Southgate (Mich.), 1978—; corr. RKO Network, 1980-83; host talk show United Cable TV Mich., Woodhaven, 1980—, Sta. WXYT, 1988-94; gen. counsel Pat Paulsen for Pres., 1996. Composer, performer (album) C. B. Polka, 1977. Alt. del. Dem. Nat. Conv., Miami, Fla., 1972, mem. staff Dem. Nat. Conv., N.Y.C., 1976; exec. bd. 16th Dist. Dems., Dearborn, 1975-87; gen. counsel First Cath. Slovak Union U.S. and Can., 1988-99, Pat Paulsen for Pres. Campaign, 1996; spl. counsel City of Ecorse, Mich., 1989—; bd. dirs. People's Cmty. Svcs. of Detroit, 1992-98; dir. Downriver Coun. for the Arts, 1997—; mem. Congress on New Urbanism, Seaside Inst. Recipient Commendation Mich. State Senate, 1982; named One of Five Outstanding Young Michiganders, Mich. Jaycees, 1990. Mem. Am. Fedn. Musicians, State Bar Mich., Wayne State U. Law Sch. Alumni Assn. (dir. 1998—), Downriver Bar Assn., Slovak League Am. (nat. dir. 1985—, del. meeting with Vaclav Havel and Alexander Dubcek conf. in Czecho-Slovakia 1990), Wayne State U. Law Alumni Assn. (mem. exec. com.), Slovak Cath. Sokol Club, Slovak Jednota Club, KC (fin. com. Robert Jones chpt. 1987-96), Kiwanis (pres. local chpt. 1981-82). Home: 711 Saint Johns Blvd Lincoln Park MI 48146-4925 Office: 2933 Fort St Lincoln Park MI 48146-2425

**ZELENOCK, KATHERYNE L.,** lawyer; b. Detroit, Aug. 7, 1966; d. Gerald B. and Mary K. Z. BA in Polit. Sci., U. Mich., 1987; JD, U. Notre Dame, 1991. Bar: Mich. 1991, U.S. Dist. Ct. (ea. and we. dists.) Mich. 1991. Atty. Simpson & Berry, Birmingham, Mich., 1991-95; ptnr. Simpson, Zelenock, Birmingham, Mich., 1995—. Vol. counselor Women's Survival Ctr., Pontiac, Mich., 1996—; vol. coach Birmingham Groves High Sch. Mock Trial Team, 1995—. Mem. Notre Dame Club Detroit (dir. 1995—), U. Mich. Alumnae Club Oakland County. Avocations: golf, tennis. Contracts commercial, General corporate, Real property. Office: Simpson Zelenock 260 E Brown St Ste 300 Birmingham MI 48009-6232

**ZELLER, MICHAEL EUGENE,** lawyer; b. Queens, N.Y., June 19, 1967; s. Hans Ludwig and Geri Ann (Schottenstein) Z. BA, Union Coll., 1989; JD, Temple Law Sch., 1992; LLM magna cum laude, U. Hamburg, Germany, 1994. Bar: N.Y. 1992, U.S. Dist. Ct. (so. and ea. dists.) N.Y. 1995, N.C. 1996. Fgn. intern Bryan Gonzalez Vargas y Gonzalez Baz, Mexico City, 1990; student law clk. Hon. Jane Cutler Greenspan, Phila., 1990-91; fgn. clk. DROSTE, Hamburg, 1991, fgn. assoc., translator, 1992-94; freelance translator Charlotte, N.C., 1995—; assoc. internat. and Corp. Law Group of Moore & Van Allen PLLC, Charlotte, 1995—; owner, restaurateur Salad Garden, L.L.C. and Salad Garden Café, L.L.C., 1998-99; vol. atty. Children's Law Ctr. Mem. Charlotte World Affairs Coun., Charlotte Mayor's Internat. Cabinet; bd. dirs. Alemannia Soc., 1996—, Young Affiliates of Mint Mus., 1999—; bd. dirs., pres. Southgate Commons Homeowners Assn., 1998—. Recipient scholarship Fedn. German/Am. Clubs, 1987. Mem. ABA, N.Y. State Bar Assn., N.C. Bar Assn., Mecklenburg County Bar Assn., Gewerblicher Rechtsschutz und Urheberrecht e.V., European Am. Bus. Forum, Am. Translators Assn., Am. Immigration Lawyers Assn. Avocations: singing, theater, golf, fictional writing. Private international, General corporate, Trademark and copyright. Office: 100 N Tryon St Fl 47 Charlotte NC 28202-4000

**ZELLER, RONALD JOHN,** lawyer; b. Phila., Jan. 28, 1940; m. Lucille Bell; children: John, Kevin, Suzanne. BSBA, LaSalle Coll., 1964; JD, Ohio State U., 1967. Bar: Mich. 1968, Fla. 1971. Ptnr. Patton & Kanner, Miami, Fla., 1973-80, of counsel, 1980-89; pres., chief exec. officer Norwegian Cruise Lines, 1980-86; pres. Twenty First Century Mgmt. Group, Inc., Coconut Grove, Fla., 1986-90, Miami Voice Corp., 1990-92; gen. counsel Splty. Mgmt. Co., Delray Beach, Fla., 1992-93, pres., 1994-96; ptnr. Zeller & Keihner, Palm Beach, Fla., 1996—; dep. chmn. Cruise Lines Internat. Assoc., N.Y.C., 1981-85, chmn., 1986. Trustee United Way Dade County, 1981-86; pres. Cath. Charities, Archdiocese of Miami 1976-78, Broward County, 1975-76, Excalibur Devel. Ctrs., Inc., 1973-75; mem. citizens bd. U. Miami; mem. exec. bd. New World Sch. Arts, 1986-87; mem. centennial campaign com. Ohio State U. Coll. Law, 1982-92, also mem. nat. coun.; mem. coun. Pres.'s Assocs., LaSalle U., 1982-87; mem. Fla. Postsecondary Edn. Planning Commn., 1986-87; mem. Cmty. Assns. Inst., 1995—; chmn. exec. com. Maritime Inst., 1997—; mem. utility rev. bd. Village of Wellington, 1997-98; mem. gen. counsel Palm Beach Maritime Mus.; mem. Fla. com. Affirm Thy Friendship Campaign, Ohio State U.; mem. cruise line incentive com. Port of Palm Beach, 1997—. Mem. ABA, Fla. Bar Assn., Maritime Law Assn. (proctor in admiralty), Pres.' Club Ohio State U. Fax: (561) 832-1492. Real property, General corporate, Taxation, general. Office: Zeller & Keinher LLP First Union Bank Bldg # 200 411 S County Rd Palm Beach FL 33480-4440

**ZENTZ, ROBERT,** lawyer; b. Newark, Oct. 14, 1955; s. Robert Jr. and Barbara Cynthia (Sims) Z.; m. Cheryl Ann Kostelac, July 9, 1977; 1 child, erik Hans. AAS, Brookdale C.C., Middletown, N.J., 1982; BA, U. Pitts., 1987, JD, 1990. Bar: Nev. 1991, U.S. Dist. Ct. Nev. 1991, U.S. Ct. Appeals (9th cir.) 1992. Police officer Rutgers U., New Brunswick, N.J., 1980-81, Fanwood (N.J.) Police Dept., 1981-86; atty. Kirshman & Harris, Las Vegas, 1991-95; dep. city atty. City of Henderson, Nev., 1995—. With security police USAF, 1974-79. Lutheran. Avocations: softball, reading. Office: City Atty's Office 243 S Water St Henderson NV 89015-7226

**ZERIN, STEVEN DAVID,** lawyer; b. N.Y.C., Oct. 1, 1953; s. Stanley Robert and Cecilie Paula (Goldberg) Z.; children: Alexander James, J. Oliver. BS, Syracuse U., 1974; JD, St. Johns U., 1977. Bar: N.Y. 1978, U.S. Dist. Ct. (so. dist.) N.Y. 1985, U.S. Supreme Ct. 1986. Assoc. Gladstein & Isaac, N.Y.C., 1981-82, Sperry, Weinberg, Wels, Waldman & Rubenstein, N.Y.C., 1982-85; ptnr. Wels & Zerin, N.Y.C., 1985—. Trustee, mem. bd. govs. Daytop Village. Mem. ABA (exec. mem. and lectr. family law sect.), N.Y. State Bar Assn. (exec. com. family law sect.), Assn. of Bar of City of N.Y. Democrat. Family and matrimonial, Probate, State civil litigation. Home: 12 E 88th St New York NY 10128-0535 Office: Wels & Zerin 600 Madison Ave Fl 22 New York NY 10022-1615

**ZERMAN, ALLAN H.,** lawyer; b. St. Louis, Feb. 3, 1937; s. Jay and Rose (Fadem) Z.; m. Marilyn Sandra Schear, Aug. 24, 1958 (div. 1980); children: Lisa, Laura, Leslie; m. Marilyn Rose House, May 28, 1982. AB, Washington U., St. Louis, 1958, JD, 1960. Bar: Mo. 1960, U.S. Ct. Appeals (8th cir.) 1961, U.S. Supreme Ct. 1972. Pvt. practice Clayton, Mo., 1961—. Capt. USAR, 1960-67. Fellow Am. Acad. Matrimonial Lawyers; mem. Mo. Bar Assn. (contbg. editor jour. 1988—), St. Louis Met. Bar Assn., St. Louis County Bar Assn. Republican. Jewish. Family and matrimonial. Office: 100 S Brentwood Blvd Ste 325 Saint Louis MO 63105-1691

**ZERR, RICHARD KEVIN,** lawyer; b. St. Charles, Mo., Apr. 10, 1949; s. Elmer George and Lillian Grace (Gross) Z.; m. Martha Jo Zerr, Mar. 19, 1969 (div. June 1976); m. Judy Ann Yeager, Aug. 8, 1978; 1 child, Richard Kevin Jr. AB in Polit. Sci., U. Mo., 1971; JD, U. Ark., 1974. Bar: Mo. 1974, U.S. Dist. Ct. (we. dist.) Mo. 1974, U.S. Dist. Ct. (ea. dist.) Mo. 1983, U.S. Ct. Appeals (8th cir.) 1985, U.S. Supreme Ct. 1985. Asst. to pros. atty. County of St. Charles, 1974; magistrate judge City of St. Charles, 1975-78; assoc. judge Cir. Ct., St. Charles, 1979-82; ptnr. Beck, Tiemeyer & Zerr, St. Charles, 1983—; bd. dirs. St. Charles County Police Acad., 1978-88, Legal Svcs. Ea. Mo., 1992—. Bd. dir. St. Charles City-County Libr. Dist., 1991—. Mem. ABA (state chmn. small claims ct. com. 1978-82), Mo. Bar Assn. (bd. govs. 1999—), St. Charles County Bar Assn., Metro. St. Louis Bar Assn., U. Mo. Columbia Alumni Assn. (nat. bd. dirs. 1994—). Democrat. Roman Catholic. Lodge: Kiwanis. Avocation: high sch. and coll. football official. Criminal, Personal injury, Family and matrimonial. Home: 176 Huntington Downs Saint Charles MO 63301-8700 Office: Beck Tiemeyer & Zerr 2777 W Clay St Saint Charles MO 63301-2539

**ZERUNYAN, FRANK VRAM,** lawyer; b. Istanbul, Turkey, Sept. 17, 1959; came to U.S., 1978; s. Jack Hagop and Ayda (Yagupyan) Z.; m. Jody Lynn Forman, May 18, 1986; children: Daniel, Nicole. French Bacalaureat, Coll. Samuel Moorat, Paris, 1978; BA, Calif. State U., Long Beach, 1982; JD, Western State U., Fullerton, Calif., 1985; postgrad., U. Southern Calif., 1988. Bar: Calif. 1989, D.C., 1995, U.S. Dist. Ct. (cen. dist.) Calif. 1989, U.S. Ct. Internat. Trade 1994. V.p. law Internat. Mktg. Alliance, Torrance, Calif., 1985-89; pvt. practice L.A., 1989-92; mng. mem. Yacoubian & Zerunyan, P.C., L.A., 1992-95; mem. Sulmeyer, Kupetz, Baumann & Rothman, L.A., 1995—; instr. law Alex Pilibos Sch., L.A., 1993—; judge pro tem, L.A. Mcpl. Ct. Editor SKB&R Newsletter, 1995—. Bd. dirs. Am. Youth Soccer Orgn., Palos Verdes, Calif., 1995—, referee adminstr., 1995—; bd. dirs., vice-chmn. Daniel Freeman Hosps. Found., 1998—; chmn. scholarship com. Orgn. Istanbul Armenians, Van Nuys, Calif., 1992-94; legal counsel and polity adv. com. Armenian Nat. Com. of Am., Washington, 1993. Mem. ABA, Financial Lawyers Conf. Avocations: golf, soccer, tennis. E-mail: fzerunyan@skbr.com. Real property, Bankruptcy, Contracts commercial. Office: Sulmeyer Kupetz et al 300 S Grand Ave Ste 1400 Los Angeles CA 90071-3124

**ZERVOS, MITRA KAVOUSSI,** lawyer; b. Tehran, Iran, June 17, 1957; came to the U.S., 1975; d. Keyghobad Kavoussi and Katayoon Hormozan; m. George A. Zervos, Apr. 25, 1986; children: E. Daniela, I. Cristina. BS, St. John's U., Queens, N.Y., 1980; BSN, Columbia U., 1983; JD, CUNY, Queens, 1990. Bar: N.J. 1991, U.S. Dist. Ct. N.J. 1991, N.Y. 1992, U.S. Dist. Ct. (ea. dist.) 1992. RN burn unit N.Y. Hosp., N.Y.C., 1983-84; RN ICU VA Hosp., Bklyn., 1984-94; law intern Family Ct., N.Y.C., 1989-90; pvt. practice law Great Neck, N.Y., 1994—. Vol. lawyer Nassau/Suffolk Vol. Lawyers Project, Hempstead, N.Y., 1993—. Zoroastrian. Avocations: skiing, bicycle riding, tennis. Contracts commercial, Health, Probate. Office: 505 Northern Blvd Ste 204 Great Neck NY 11021-5101

**ZICCARDI, DOMENICK,** lawyer; b. Andretta, Italy, May 4, 1946; came to U.S., 1954; s. Vittorio Veneto and Maria Antonia Ziccardi; m. Maria Julia Maneiro; children: Victor, Maria V. BA, Hofstra U., 1968; JD, St. John's U., 1971. Trial atty. Corp. Counsel N.Y.C., 1973-80, chief spl. litigation unit, 1980-97, sr. trial counsel, 1997—. Mem. Columbian Lawyers Assn., Assn. Bar City of N.Y. Avocations: reading, walking, listening to music, writing. Office: Corp Counsel City NY 100 Church St New York NY 10007-2601

**ZICHERMAN, DAVID L.,** lawyer, educator, financial consultant; b. N.Y.C., Oct. 12, 1961. BA in Psychology magna cum laude, W.Va. U., 1984; JD, U. Pitts., 1989, MPIA, 1989. Bar: Del. 1990, Pa. 1990, D.C. 1990. Assoc. Richards, Layton & Finger, Wilmington, Del., 1989-92, Klehr Harrison et al, Phila., 1992-94, Kelly Grimes Pietrangelo & Vakil, P.C., Media, Pa., 1994-97; adj. prof. Widener U. Law Ctr., Wilmington, 1993-95, fin. cons., Merrill Lynch, 1998—. Editor: State Legislation Forum newsletter, 1991-93; editor Delaware County Legal Jour., 1995-97; contbr. chpt. to book, articles to profl. jours. Avocations: sports, photography, creative writing, travel. General civil litigation, Insurance, Administrative and regulatory. Office: Merrill Lynch PO Box 748 Media PA 19063-0748

**ZIEGENHORN, ERIC HOWARD,** lawyer, legal writer; b. Independence, Mo., Oct. 17, 1957. AB in Econs. with honors, U. Mo., 1979; JD, U. Calif., Berkeley, 1983. Bar: Calif. 1983, Kans. 1986, Mo. 1987. Atty. Law Offices of Richard A. Goodman, Oakland, Calif., 1983-86, Lewis, Rice & Fingersh, Overland Park, Kans., 1986-87; pvt. practice, legal writer Kansas City, Mo., 1987—; sr. staff atty. Midland Loan Svcs., 1991-96. Author: (3-vol. set) Missouri Legal Forms, 1992. Mem. Mo. Bar Assn., Calif. Bar Assn. Estate planning, General practice, Real property. Office: 104 Vietnam Veterans Meml Dr Kansas City MO 64111-2301

**ZIEGLER, DONALD EMIL,** federal judge; b. Pitts., Oct. 1, 1936; s. Emil Nicholas and Elizabeth (Barclay) Z.; m. Claudia J. Chermak, May 1, 1965; 1 son, Scott Emil. B.A., Duquesne U., 1958; LL.B., Georgetown U., 1961. Bar: Pa. 1962, U.S. Supreme Ct. 1967. Practice law Pitts., 1962-74; judge Ct. of Common Pleas of Allegheny County, Pa., 1974-78; judge U.S. Dist. Ct. (we. dist.) Pa., Pitts., 1978-94, chief judge, 1994—; mem. Jud. Conf. U.S., 1997—. Treas. Big Bros. of Allegheny County, 1969-74. Mem. ABA, Pa. Bar Assn., Allegheny County Bar Assn., Am. Judicature Soc., St. Thomas More Soc. Democrat. Roman Catholic. Club: Oakmont Country. Office: US Post Office & Courthouse 6th Fl Courtroom 12 7th & Grant Sts Pittsburgh PA 15219

**ZIEGLER, MICHAEL LEWIS,** lawyer; b. N.Y.C., Apr. 27, 1950. BA, SUNY, Albany, 1972; JD, SUNY, Buffalo, 1976; MPH, Columbia U., 1978. Bar: N.Y. 1976. Asst. prof. Columbia U., N.Y.C., 1977-80; ptnr. Epstein Becker & Green, N.Y.C., 1980-88, Bower & Gardner, N.Y.C., 1988-92, LeBoeuf, Lamb, Greene & MacRae, N.Y.C., 1992—; adj. asst. prof. Columbia U., 1980—, adj. assoc. prof. NYU, 1980—; adj. prof. SUNY Coll. Optometry, 1988—. Gen. counsel Ronald MacDonald House of L.I., 1990—; bd. dirs., gen. counsel Care for the Homeless, Inc., 1992—; bd. dirs. Casita Maria. Named disting. adj. prof. grad. sch. pub. adminstrn. NYU, 1986. Mem. Nat. Health Lawyers Assn., N.Y. Acad. Scis., Assn. Bar N.Y.C. Health. Office: LeBoeuf Lamb Greene & MacRae 125 W 55th St New York NY 10019-5369

**ZIERDT, ALYSON KATHLEEN,** lawyer; b. Milw., Feb. 10, 1947; d. Edward Paul and Alyce Ann (Burt) Dietzmann; m. William Henry Zierdt III, July 12, 1991. Student, St. Norbert Coll., West DePere, Wis., 1964-66; BA, U. Wis., Milw., 1969; JD, Marquette U., 1981. Bar: Wis. 1981, U.S. Dist. Ct. (we. and ea. dist.) Wis. 1981, U.S. Ct. Appeals (7th cir.) 1986. Asst. buyer/sales mgr. Boston Store divsn. Federated Dept. Stores, Milw., 1969-71, buyer, dept. mgr., 1971-78; law clk. Warshafsky, Rotter, Tarnoff, Gesler, Reinhardt & Bloch, S.C., Milw., 1979-81, assoc., 1981-86; assoc. Mulcahy & Wherry, S.C., Milw., 1986-89, atty./shareholder, 1989-91; atty./shareholder Davis & Kuelthau, S.C., Milw., 1991-94, Reff Baivier Bermingham Zierdt & Lim, S.C., Oshkosh, Wis., 1994—; mem. dist. III com. Bd. of Atty.'s Profl.

Responsibility, Oshkosh, Fox Valley, 1997—. Author: Wisconsin Trial Practice, 1999 co-author: The Law of Damages in Wisconsin, 1988, 2d edit. 1994-95, 96. Vol. mediator Winnebago Conflict Resolution Ctr., Oshkosh, 1995—, Fond du Lac (Wis.) Conflict Resolution Ctr., 1995—; vols. Irish Fest, Milw., 1990—; bd. dirs. Irish Cultural and Heritage Ctr., Milw., 1994-95; trustee Evergreen Retirement Cmty. Found., Oshkosh, 1995—, Paine Art Ctr. and Arboretum, Oshkosh, 1996—; bd. dirs. TEMPO, Milw., pres., 1987-88, bd. dirs. TEMPO Fox Valley, 1995-98, pres. 1995-97, bd. dirs. TEMPO Internat., 1996-97; bd. dirs., pres. Women's Fund of Oshkosh Cmty. Found., 1998—. Thomas More scholar Marquette U., 1980. Mem. State Bar Wis. (editl. bd. Wis. Lawyer 1988-95, 96—, Wis. Acad. Trial Lawyers (bd. dirs. 1987-90), Assn. for Women Lawyers (bd. dirs. 1984-89, pres. 1987-88), Milw. Bar Assn. (bd. dirs. 1987-88, sec. 1988-91, co-chmn. joint bench and bar cir. ct. com. 1986-88, editor-in-chief Milw. Lawyer 1985-87, chair case mediation com. 1992-94), Oshkosh C. of C. (bd. dirs. 1997—, pres. 1999—), Fond du Lac Yacht Club, Rotary (bd. dirs. Oshkosh S.W. 1998-99). E-mail: akz@rbbzl.com. State civil litigation, Federal civil litigation, Personal injury. Office: Reff Baivier Bermingham Zierdt & Lim SC 217 Ceape Ave PO Box 1190 Oshkosh WI 54903-1190

**ZIKA, PATRICK JOHN,** judge; b. Ottumwa, Iowa, Dec. 14, 1948. AB, U. Notre Dame, 1970; JD, Ind. U., 1973. Judge Alameda County Superior Ct., Oakland, Calif. Office: Alameda County Superior Ct 661 Washington St Oakland CA 94607-3922

**ZILLY, THOMAS SAMUEL,** federal judge; b. Detroit, Jan. 1, 1935; s. George Samuel and Bernice M. (McWhinney) Z.; divorced; children: John, Peter, Paul, Luke; m. Jane Greller Noland, Oct. 8, 1988; stepchildren: Allison Noland, Jennifer Noland. BA, U. Mich., 1956; LLD, Cornell U., 1962. Bar: Wash. 1962, U.S. Ct. Appeals (9th cir.) 1962, U.S. Supreme Ct. 1976. Ptnr. Lane, Powell, Moss & Miller, Seattle, 1962-88; dist. judge U.S. Dist. Ct. (we. dist.) Wash., Seattle, 1988—; judge pro tem Seattle Mcpl. Ct., 1972-80. Contbr. articles to profl. jours. Mem. Cen. Area Sch. Council, Seattle, 1969-70; scoutmaster Thunderbird Dist. council Boy Scouts Am. Seattle, 1976-84; bd. dirs. East Madison YMCA. Served to lt. (j.g.) USN, 1956-59. Recipient Tuahku Dist. Service to Youth award Boy Scouts Am., 1983. Mem. ABA, Wash. State Bar Assn., Seattle-King County Bar Assn. (treas. 1979-80, trustee 1980-83, sec. 1983-84, 2d v.p. 1984-85, 1st v.p. 1985-86, pres. 1986-87). Office: US Dist Ct 410 US Courthouse 1010 5th Ave Seattle WA 98104-1189

**ZIMA, MICHAEL DAVID,** lawyer; b. St Louis, Aug. 13, 1968; s. Marvin Walter Z. BA, U. Mich., 1990; JD, Ind. U., 1993. Atty. Dist. Coun. IRS, Jacksonville, Fla., 1993—. Author: (short story) The Brook, 1994, The Play, 1994. Mem. Ind. State Bar. Avocations: tennis, golf, basketball, water-skiing, writing. Home: 7758 Spindletree Ct Jacksonville FL 32256-5419 Office: Dist Counsel IRS 400 W Bay St Rm 564 Jacksonville FL 32202-4410

**ZIMET, MARC JOSEPH,** lawyer; b. N.Y.C., Oct. 3, 1964; s. John Zimet and JoAnn Beth Polakoff. BBA, S.W. Tex. State U., 1987; JD, U. LaVerne Coll., 1996. Law clk. L.A. City Atty.'s Office, 1993-96; atty. Ward, Kroll & Jampol, Beverly Hills, Calif., 1996—; lectr. L.A. Fair Housing Congress. City coun. mem. San Marcos City Coun. Recipient Am. Jurisprudence award Bancroft-Witney, 1995. Mem. ABA, L.A. County Bar Assn., Calif. State Bar Assn., Phi Kappa Theta (pres. 1985-87). Avocations: skiing, raquetball, boating, cooking. Professional liability, Insurance, General civil litigation. Home: 6209 Pacific Ave Unit 104 Playa Del Rey CA 90293-7551 Office: Ward Kroll & Jampol 9107 Wilshire Blvd Ste 400 Beverly Hills CA 90210-5527

**ZIMMER, JOHN HERMAN,** lawyer; b. Sioux Falls, S.D., Dec. 30, 1922; s. John Francis and Veronica (Berke) Z.; student Augustana Coll., Sioux Falls, 1941-42, Mont. State Coll., 1943; LLB, U. S.D., 1948; m. Deanna Langner, 1976; children by previous marriage: Mary Zimmer Quinlin, Robert Joseph, Judith Maureen Zimmer Rose. Bar: S.D. 1948. Pvt. practice, Turner County, S.D., 1948—; of counsel Zimmer, Duncan & Cole, Parker, S.D., 1992—; states atty. Turner County, 1955-58, 62-64; asst. prof. med. jurisprudence U. S.D.; minority counsel U.S. Senate Armed Services Com. on Strategic and Critical Materials Investigation, 1962-63; chmn. Southeastern Council Govts., 1973-75; mem. U. S.D. Law Sch. adv. council, 1973-74. Chmn. Turner County Rep. Com., 1955-56; mem. S.D. Rep. adv. com., 1959-60; alt. del. Rep. Nat. Conv., 1968; pres. S.D. Easter Seal Soc., 1986-87. Served with AUS, 1943-46; PTO. Decorated Bronze Star, Philippine Liberation ribbon. Mem. ABA, Fed., S.D. (commr. 1954-57) Bar Assns., Assn. Trial Lawyers Am., S.D. Trial Lawyers Assn. (pres. 1967-68), VFW, Am. Legion, Elks, Shriners, Phi Delta Phi. General practice, Administrative and regulatory, Probate. Home: PO Box 640 Parker SD 57053-0640 Office: Zimmer Duncan & Cole Law Bldg PO Box 550 Parker SD 57053-0550

**ZIMMERLY, JAMES GREGORY,** lawyer, physician; b. Longview, Tex., Mar. 25, 1941; s. George James and Irene Gertrude (Kohler) Z.; m. Nancy Carol Zimmerly, June 11, 1966; children: Mark, Scott, Robin; m. Johanna Bross Huffer, Feb. 14, 1991. BA, Gannon Coll., 1962; MD, U. Md., 1966, JD, 1969; MPH, Johns Hopkins U., 1968; LLD (hon.), Gannon U., 1998. Bar: Md. 1970, D.C. 1972, U.S. Ct. Mil. Appeals 1973, U.S. Supreme Ct. 1973. Ptnr. Acquisto, Asplen & Morstein, Ellicott City, Md., 1970—. Chmn. dept. legal medicine Armed Forces Inst. Pathology, 1971-91; prof. George Washington U., 1972-80; adj. prof. law Georgetown U. Law Ctr., 1972—, Antioch Sch. Law, 1977-80; assoc. prof. U. Md. Sch. Medicine, 1973—; mem. sci. adv. bd. Armed Forces Inst. Path., 1997—; cons. Dept. Def., Dept. Justice, HHS, VA, 1971-91. Fellow Am. Acad. Forensic Scis., Am. Coll. Legal Medicine, (pres. 1980-81), Am. Coll. Preventive Medicine; mem. ABA, Md. Bar Assn., Am. Soc. on Law and Medicine, Am. Coll. Emergency Physicians, Md. Med. Soc. Editor: Legal Aspects of Medical Practice, 1978-88, Jour. Legal Medicine, 1975-78, Md. Med. Jour., 1977-88, Lawyers' Med. Ency., 1980-90, chmn. bd. dirs. Baltimore Rh Lab., 1984—; med. dir. Monumental Life Ins. Co., 1994—, Aegon Spl. Markets Group, Inc.; chmn. Am. Coll. Legal Med. Fdn., bd. dirs., 1996—. Personal injury, Health, Insurance. Home: 6300 Old National Pike Bluestone Overlook Boonsboro MD 21713 Office: Monumental Life Ins Co 2 E Chase St Baltimore MD 21202-2559

**ZIMMERMAN, AARON MARK,** lawyer; b. Syracuse, N.Y., Jan. 28, 1953; s. Julius and Sara (Lavine) Z. B.S., Syracuse U., 1974, J.D., 1976. Bar: N.Y. 1977, Pa. 1977, D.C. 1978, S.C. 1978, Fla. 1978, U.S. Dist. Ct. S.C. 1978, U.S. Dist. Ct. (no. dist.) N.Y. Corp. atty., asst. sec. Daniel Internat. Corp., Greenville, S.C., 1977-79; ptnr. Abend, Driscoll & Zimmerman, 1979-81; Zimmerman Law Office, Syracuse, 1981—. Bd. dirs. Syracuse Friends Ametuer Boxing, 1982-92. Mem. Am. Arbitration Assn. (arbitrator), Workers Compensation Com. N.Y. State Bar (exec. com. 1984—), Workers Compensation Assn. of Cen. N.Y. (charter mem., dir., treas. 1980-95), N.Y. State Bar, S.C. State Bar, D.C. State Bar, Fla. State Bar, ABA. Lodge: Masons. Personal injury, Workers' compensation, State civil litigation. Home: 602 Standish Dr Syracuse NY 13224-2018 Office: 117 S State St Syracuse NY 13202-1103

**ZIMMERMAN, D(ONALD) PATRICK,** lawyer; b. Albany, N.Y., Mar. 20, 1942; s. Bernard M. and Helen M. (Eshelman) Z. Student, Lawrenceville Sch., 1960; BA, Rollins Coll., 1964; JD, Dickinson Sch. Law, 1967. Bar: Pa. 1968, U.S. Supreme Ct. 1971. Atty. Legal Aid, 1968-69; pub. defender Lancaster County, Pa., 1969-72; sole practice Lancaster, 1974—; instr. Ct. Common Pleas for Constables, 1976—; solicitor Lancaster County Dep. Sheriff Assn., 1977—, Lancaster County Constable Assn., 1975—; instr. sheriff's dept. Lancaster County for Dep. Sheriffs, 1978-85; of counsel to Dep. Sheriff Assn. Pa., 1979-81; spl. counsel Pa. State Constables Assn., 1981; chmn. Bd. Arbitrators Lancaster County, 1975-81; spl. counsel Legislative Com. to Constable Assn. Pa., 1982. Author: The Pennsylvania Landlord and Tenant Handbook, 1982, revised edit., 1993; editor (with J. Hatfield and A. Taylor) Pennsylvania in Constable Handbook, 1998; contbr. articles to profl. jours. Mem. pastoral coun. St. Anthony's Cath. Ch., 1995-98. Recipient Ofcl. Commendation of Merit, Lancaster County Sheriff's Dept., 1979, Ofcl. Commendation of Merit, F.O.P. State Police Lodge 66, 1985, Disting. Svc. award, 1987, Outstanding Leadership award Lancaster County Constables, 1988, Disting. Svc. award as solicitor, 1998. Mem. ABA, Am. Trial Lawyers Assn., Pa. Bar Assn., Acad. Family Mediators, Lancaster County Bar Assn. Family and matrimonial, Landlord-tenant, Personal injury. Office: 214 E King St Lancaster PA 17602-2977

**ZIMMERMAN, EARL S.,** lawyer; b. Abington, Pa., Jan. 18, 1956; s. Earl Clarence and Grace Estelle Zimmerman; m. Elisabeth Curzan, Sept. 5, 1993. BA, Temple U., 1978; JD, Columbia U., 1992. Profl. musician Phila. and N.Y.C., 1978-89; atty. Rogers & Wells LLP, N.Y.C., 1992—; bd. dirs. 301 East Tenants Assn., N.Y.C., 1995—. Author and lectr. in field. Mem. ABA. Avocations: jazz guitar, listening to classical music, fitness, golf. Securities, Insurance, General corporate. Office: Rogers & Wells LLP 200 Park Ave Fl 8E New York NY 10166-0800

**ZIMMERMAN, JEAN,** lawyer; b. Berkeley, Calif., Dec. 3, 1947; d. Donald Scheel Zimmerman and Phebe Jean (Reed) Doan; m. Gilson Berryman Gray III, Nov. 25, 1982; children: Charles Donald Buffum and Catherine Elisabeth Phebe (twins); stepchildren: Alison Travis, Laura Rebecca, Gilson Berryman. BSBA, U. Md., 1970; JD, Emory U., 1975. Bar: Ga. 1975, D.C. 1976, N.Y. 1980. Asst. mgr. investments FNMA, Washington, 1970-73; assoc. counsel Fuqua Industries Inc., Atlanta, 1976-79; assoc. Sage Gray Todd & Sims, N.Y.C., 1979-84; from assoc. to sr. v.p., gen. counsel, sec. IBJ Whitehall Bank & Trust Co., N.Y.C., 1994—; sr. v.p., gen. counsel, sec., bd. dirs. IBJ Schroder Bus. Credit Corp., N.Y.C., 1996-98, Innovest Capital Mgmt., Inc., N.Y.C., 1997—; sr. v.p., gen. counsel, sec. Innovest Corp., N.Y.C., 1997—; from asst. sec. to sr. v.p., gen. counsel, sec., bd. dirs. IBJ Whitehall Bus. Credit Corp., IBJ Whitehall Capital Corp., IBJ Whitehall Securities, Inc., Delphi Asset Mgmt., Inc., Innovest Asset Mgmt., Inc., N.Y.C., 1997-99; from asst. sec. to v.p., gen. counsel, sec. IBJ Schroder Internat. Bank, Miami, Fla., 1989-98; sr. v.p., gen. counsel, sec. Execution Svcs., N.Y.C., 1991-93. Founder, officer ERA Ga., Atlanta, 1977-79; bd. dirs. Ct. Apptd. Spl. Advs., 1988-94. Named one of Outstanding Atlantans, 1978-79; recipient Disting. Alumni award Emory U. Sch. Law, 1999. Mem. ABA, Assn. of Bar of City of N.Y., Ga. Assn. Women Lawyers (bd. dirs. 1977-79), Am. Soc. Corp. Secs., Inc., LWV, DAR. Banking, Contracts commercial, General corporate. Office: IBJ Whitehall Bank & Trust Co 1 State St New York NY 10004-1417

**ZIMMERMAN, MICHAEL DAVID,** state supreme court justice; b. Chgo., Oct. 21, 1943; s. Elizabeth Porter; m. Lynne Mariani (dec. 1994); children: Evangeline Albright, Alessandra Mariani, Morgan Elisabeth; m. Diane Hamilton, 1998. BS, U. Utah, 1966, JD, 1969. Bar: Calif. 1971, Utah 1978. Law clk. to Chief Justice Warren Earl Burger U.S. Supreme Ct., Washington, 1969-70; assoc. O'Melveny & Myers, L.A., 1970-76; assoc. prof. law U. Utah, 1976-78, adj. prof. law, 1978-84, 89-93; of counsel Kruse, Landa, Zimmerman & Maycock, Salt Lake City, 1978-80; spl. counsel Gov. of Utah, Salt Lake City, 1978-80; ptnr. Watkiss & Campbell, Salt Lake City, 1980-84; assoc. justice Supreme Ct. Utah, Salt Lake City, 1984-93, 98—, chief justice, 1994-98; co-moderator Justice Soc. Program of Snowbird Inst. for Arts and Humanities, 1991, 92, 93, 94, 95, 97, 98; moderator, Tanner lecture panel dept. philosophy U. Utah, 1994; faculty Judging Sci. Program Duke U., 1992, 93; bd. dirs. Conf. of Chief Justices, 1995-98. Note editor: Utah Law Rev., 1968-69; contbr. numerous articles to legal publs. Mem. Project 2000, Coalition for Utah's Future, 1985-96; trustee Hubert and Eliza B. Michael Found., 1994-98, Rowland-Hall St. Mark's Sch., 1997—, Utah Mus. Natural History Found., 1997—; bd. dirs. Summit Inst. for Arts and Humanities, 1998—, Hansen Planetarium, 1998— (chair 1999—). Named Utah State Bar Appellate Ct. Judge of Yr., 1988; recipient Excellence in Ethics award, Ctr. for Study of Ethics, 1994, Disting. Svc. award Utah State Bar, 1998, Individual Achievement award Downtown Alliance, 1998; participant Justice and Soc. Program of Aspen Inst. for Humanistic Studies, 1988, co-moderator, 1989. Fellow Am. Bar Found.; mem. ABA (faculty mem. appellate judges' seminar 1993), Am. Law Inst., Utah Bar Assn., Salt Lake County Bar Assn., Jud. Conf. U.S. (adv. com. civil rules 1985-91), Utah Jud. Coun. (supreme ct. rep. 1986-91, chair 1994-98), Snowbird Inst. for Arts and Humanities (bd. dirs., 1989-96), Am. Inns of Ct. VII, Am. Judicature Soc. (bd. dirs. 1995—), Order of Coif, Phi Kappa Phi. Office: Utah Supreme Ct Box 140210 450 S State St Salt Lake City UT 84114-0210

**ZIMMERMAN, PAULA SUSAN,** lawyer; b. Amarillo, Tex., Feb. 23, 1965; d. Alan J. and Marcia B. Zimmerman; m. Andrew D. Schifrin, June 21, 1998. BA, Tufts U., 1987; JD, Fordham U., 1993. Bar: N.J. 1993, Mass. 1993, N.Y. 1994, U.S. Dist. Ct. Staff atty. U.S. Govt., Dept. IRS, N.Y.C., 1993-94; assoc. Fisher, Fisher & Berger, N.Y.C., 1994-95, Stursberg & Veith, N.Y.C., 1995—. Mem. Hadassah, 1994—; vol. Big Bros./Big Sisters, N.Y.C., 1998—. Mem. ABA, N.Y. State Bar Assn. Real property, General corporate, Securities. Office: Stursberg & Veith 405 Lexington Ave Ste 4949 New York NY 10017-3906

**ZIMMERMAN, ROBERT W.,** lawyer, accountant; b. Bay City, Mich., Apr. 27, 1952; m. Judy A. Zimmerman; children: Mike, Cindy, Brian. BS, Marquette U., 1974, JD, 1977. Bar: Wis., 1977, U.S. Ct. Appeals (7th cir.), U.S. Dist. Ct. (ea., we. dists.) Wis., U.S. Tax Ct.; CPA, Wis. Acct., atty. Arthur Andersen, Milw., 1977-81; atty. Ruder, Ware, Michler & Forester, Wausau, Wis., 1981-88; atty., CPA Mallery & Zimmerman, S.C., Wausau, 1988—. Mem. Small Bus. Coun. C. of C. General corporate, Taxation, general, Estate planning. Office: Mallery & Zimmerman SC 101 Grand Ave Wausau WI 54403-6288

**ZIMMERMAN, WILLIAM IRVING,** lawyer; b. Miami Beach, Fla., Dec. 10, 1952; s. S. Robert Zimmerman and Shirley (Munroe) Neivert; m. Felicia Jo French, children: William, Jason, Cyrina, Hunter. BA, Wesleyan U., 1974; JD, U. Miami, 1978. Bar: Fla. 1978, Hawaii 1991. Lawyer William I. Zimmerman Atty. at Law, Pompano Beach, Fla., 1978-90, Captain Cook, Hawaii, 1991-93; lawyer Van Pernis, Smith & Vancil, Kailua-Kona, Hawaii, 1993—; dir. Families in Transition, Kailua-Kona, Hawaii, 1994-95. Pro bono counsel Protect Kohanaiki Ohana, 1991-99; officer, dir. Green Alert, Kailua-Kona, 1992-93; pro bono atty. Hui Hee Nalu o Kona, 1992-94. Named in Am. Leading Lawyers, 1993-94, Who's Who in Am. Law, 1996-99, Who's Who in the World, 1997-99, Who's Who in Am., 1997-99; recipient Cert. Outstanding Excellence, Families in Transition, 1994-95. Mem. Lymans Surf Classic (atty. 1992-94), Ocean Awareness and Preservation. Avocations: surfing, fishing, swimming, camping, spending quality time with family. Family and matrimonial, General civil litigation, Real property. Home and Office: 75-6150 Alii Dr # 8 Kailua Kona HI 96740-2359

**ZIMMERMANN, ANN MARIE,** lawyer, educator; b. Flint, Mich., July 1, 1963; d. John Fredrick and Maryann Zimmermann; m. David Huerta, Sept. 20, 1998. BA cum laude, U. Mich., 1985; JD, U. San Diego, 1990. Bar: Calif. 1991, U.S. Dist. Ct. (so. dist.) Calif. 1992, U.S. Dist. Ct. (ctrl. dist.) Calif. 1997. Intern Nat. Wildlife Fedn., Washington, 1991-92; atty. L. Brooks Anderholt, El Centro, Calif., 1992—; tchr. bankruptcy Imperial Valley Coll., El Centro, 1998; jud. intern 4th Dist. Ct. Appeal, San Diego, 1989. Mem. San Diego Law Rev., 1980-90. Mem. Imperial County Bar Assn. (bd. dirs. 1992-96, pres. 1998), Imperial Valley Breakfast Rotary Club (charter mem.), Order of Barristers. Avocations: scuba diving, skiing, dancing, reading. Probate, General civil litigation, Consumer commercial. Home: 740 Drew Rd Calexico CA 92231-9711 Office: Anderholt & Storey 654 Main St El Centro CA 92243

**ZIMMETT, MARK PAUL,** lawyer; b. Waukegan, Ill., July 4, 1950; s. Nelson H. Zimmett and Roslyn (Yastrow) Zimmett Grodzin; m. Joan Robin Urken, June 11, 1972; children: Nora Helene, Lili Eleanor. BA, Johns Hopkins U., 1972; JD, NYU, 1975. Bar: N.Y. 1976, U.S. Dist. Ct. (so. and ea. dists.) N.Y. 1976, U.S. Dist. Ct. (no. dist.) Calif. 1980, U.S. Ct. Appeals (2d cir.) 1980, U.S. Supreme Ct. 1981, U.S. Ct. Appeals (5th cir.) 1986, U.S. Ct. Appeals (9th cir.) 1988. Assoc. Shearman & Sterling, N.Y.C., 1975-83, ptnr., 1984-90; adj. assoc. prof. internat. law NYU, 1986-88. Author: Letters of Credit, New York Practice Guide Business and Commercial Law, 1990; contbr. articles to profl. jours. Mem. ABA (subcom. on letters of credit, com. on uniform comml. code sect. bus. law), N.Y. State Bar Assn., Assn. of Bar of City of N.Y., N.Y. County Lawyers Assn. (com. on bus. bankruptcy law), Citizens Union. Democrat. Jewish. Federal civil litigation, State civil litigation, Private international. Office: 126 E 56th St New York NY 10022-3613

**ZIMRING, STUART DAVID,** lawyer; b. L.A., Dec. 12, 1946; s. Martin and Sylvia (Robinson) Z.; m. Eve Axelrad, Aug. 24, 1969 (div. 1981); m. Carol Grenert, May 24, 1981; children: Wendy Lynn Grenert, Joseph Noah, Matthew Kevin Grenert, Dov Shimon. BA in U.S. History, UCLA, 1968, JD, 1971. Bar: Calif. 1972, U.S. Dist. Ct. (cen. dist.) Calif. 1972, U.S. Dist. Ct. (no. dist.) Calif. 1984; U.S. Supreme Ct., 1994; cert. specialist in estate planning, probate and trust law. Assoc. Law Offices Leonard Smith, Beverly Hills, Calif., 1971-73; ptnr. Law Offices Smith & Zimring, Beverly Hills, Calif., 1973-76; assoc. Levin & Ballin, North Hollywood, Calif., 1976-77; prin. Levin, Ballin, Plotkin, Zimring & Goffin, A.P.C., North Hollywood, 1978-91, Law Offices Stuart D. Zimring, North Hollywood, 1991—; lectr. Los Angeles Valley Coll., Van Nuys, Calif., 1974-82. Author: Inter Vivos Trust Trustees Operating Manual, 1994, Durable Powers of Attorney for Health Care--A Practical Approach to an Intimate Document, 1995, Reverse Mortgages--An Update, 1996, Cultural and Religious Concerns in Drafting Advance Directives, 1996. Bd. dirs. Bet Tzedek, Jewish Legal Svcs., L.A., 1975-88, chmn. legal svcs. com., 1978-82; bd. dirs. Brandeis-Bardin Inst., Simi Valley, Calif., 1976-80; bd. dirs. Bur. Jewish Edn., L.A., 1973-88, chmn. com. on parent and family edn., 1985-87; trustee Adat Ari El Synagogue, L.A., 1982—; bd. dirs. Orgn. for the Needs of the Elderly, 1994, 1st v.p. 1995-97, pres., 1997—. Recipient Circle award Juvenile Justice Connection Project, L.A., 1989, Wiley W. Manuel award for pro bono legal svcs., 1994, 95, 96, 97, 98. Fellow Nat. Acad. Elder Law Attys. (pres. So. Calif. chpt. 1997, chair nat. tech. com., nat. bd. dirs. 1997—); mem. State Bar Calif., San Fernando Valley Bar Assn. (trustee 1979-86). Democrat. Avocations: music, collecting wine, travel, photography. Estate planning, Probate, Contracts commercial. Office: 12650 Riverside Dr North Hollywood CA 91607-3421

**ZINK, WALTER EARL, II,** lawyer; b. Lincoln, Nebr., Nov. 20, 1947; s. Walter Earl and Marjorie Ellen (Hull) Z.; m. Carol Ann Thomas, June 26, 1971; children: Walter, Robert, Carmela. BA in Edn., Nebr. Wesleyan U., 1970; JD with distinction, Nebr. Coll. Law, 1974. Bar: Nebr. 1974, U.S. Dist. Ct. Nebr. 1974. Ptnr. Baylor, Evnen, Curtiss, Grimit & Witt, Lincoln, 1974—; adj. prof. law Nebr. Coll. Law, Lincoln, 1978-82; asst. adj. gen. Army, NEARNG. Bd. dirs. Camp Kitaki YMCA, Lincoln, 1980-92. mem. ABA, Nebr. Bar Assn. (vice chmn. young lawyers 1982-83), Fedn. Inst. Corp. Counsel (workers' compensation chair 1995-97), Assn. Def. Trial Attys., Am. Bd. Trial Advocates, Internat. Assn. Indsl. and Accident Bds. and Commns., Internat. Assn. Def. Counsel (past chair employment law and membership com.), N.G. Assn. U.S., Res. Officers Assn. (v.p. Army 1984-85), Hillcrest Country Club (pres. 1994-96), Blue Key, Kappa Delta Pi. Workers' compensation, Insurance, Military. Home: 1420 Broadmoore Dr Lincoln NE 68506-1511 Office: Baylor Evnen Curtiss Grimit & Witt 206 S 13th St Ste 1200 Lincoln NE 68508-2077

**ZINKIN, EPHRAIM ZEV,** lawyer; b. N.Y.C., Mar. 30, 1971; s. Lewis and Rochelle Zinkin; m. Devora Beim, Feb. 19, 1996. BS in Fin., Sy Syms Sch. Bus., N.Y.C., 1993; JD, Benjamin N. Cardozo Sch. Law, N.Y.C., 1996. Bar: N.J. 1996, U.S. Dist. Ct. N.J. 1996, N.Y. 1997. Jud. intern Hon. Alfred N. Wolin, Newark, 1994; legal rsch. asst. United Baseball League, N.Y.C., 1995; bd. agt./intern NLRB, Bklyn., 1995; mediator Bklyn. Mediation Clinic, 1995-96; jud. law clk. Hon. Mark B. Epstein, Superior Ct., Middlesex County, N.J., 1996-97; assoc. Smith Stratton Wise Heher & Brennan, Princeton, N.J., 1997—. Mem. ABA, N.J. Bar Assn., Mercer County Bar Assn., Sports Lawyers Assn. Avocations: softball, wrestling, acting. General civil litigation, Alternative dispute resolution, Environmental. Office: Smith Stratton Wise Heher & Brennan 600 College Rd E Princeton NJ 08540-6636

**ZIOGAS, ROBERT ARISTIDIS,** lawyer; b. Marathia, Evrytania, Greece, June 20, 1959; came to U.S., 1970; s. Aristidis G. and Marika A. (Billios) Z.; m. Ruby Tripodianos; children: Aristidis, Maria. BA, Roanoke Coll., 1982; JD, U. Va., 1985. Bar: Va. 1985, U.S. Dist. Ct. (we. dist., ea. dist.) Va. 1985, U.S. Ct. Appeals (4th cir.) 1986. Assoc. Glenn, Feldmann, Darby & Goodlatte, Roanoke, Va., 1985-91, mem., 1998—. V.p. of bd. dirs. Nat. Conf. Christians and Jews, Roanoke; chmn. alumni steering com. Roanoke Coll., Salem, Va., 1993-98; legal advisor Rep. Com., Botetourt County, Va., 1993-97. Mem. ABA, Def. Rsch. Inst., Va. Bar Assn., Ba. Assn. Def. Attys. Greek Orthodox. General civil litigation, Construction, Insurance. Office: Glenn Feldmann et al PO Box 2887 Roanoke VA 24001-2887

**ZIPKIN, SHELDON LEE,** lawyer, educator; b. Washington, June 10, 1951; s. Sol and Selma (Rumerman) Z.; m. Ellen Linda Reitman, July 1, 1973; children: Saul Moshe, Shana Chaya, Joel Mordechai, Abigail Deborah. Student, Hebrew U., Jerusalem, 1970-71; BA, U. Fla., 1973, MA, Cert. in Urban Studies, 1977; JD, Emory U., 1980. Bar: Ga. 1980, Fla. 1980, U.S. Dist. Ct. (so. dist.) Fla. 1983. Assoc. Gladstone Assocs., Miami, Fla., 1973-75; ptnr. Emory Assocs., Atlanta, 1979-80; dep. consumer adv. Metro Dade County, Miami, 1980-81; asst. pub. defender 11th Jud. Cir., Miami, 1981-83; ptnr. Roth & Zipkin, Miami, 1984-86; pvt. practice, Miami, 1986-87, 88-91; chief consumer litigation sect. Fla. Dept. Legal Affairs, Miami and Tallahassee, 1987-88; ptnr. Roth, Zipkin, Cove & Roth, Miami, 1991-95; pvt. practice law, 1995—; adj. prof. law U. Miami, St. Thomas U., 1998—; pres., chmn. bd. Analytic Prognostication, Inc., Miami, 1988—. Pres., chmn. bd. dirs. Sta. WDNA-FM Pub. Radio, Miami, 1981-82; mem. consumer adv. coun. Fla. Hosp. Cost Containment Bd., Tallahassee, 1988-89. Fellow Soc. for Applied Anthropology; mem. ABA, ATLA, North Dade Bar Assn., Dade County Bar Assn., Fla. Bar Assn. (consumer protection com. 1988—), Omicron Delta Kappa. Democrat. Jewish. Avocations: chess, sailing. General civil litigation, Criminal, General practice. Office: 2020 NE 163rd St N Miami Beach FL 33162-4927

**ZIPP, JOEL FREDERICK,** lawyer; b. Shaker Heights, Ohio, Feb. 12, 1948; s. Jack David and Eleanor Adele Z.; m. Elizabeth Ann Frieden, Dec. 4, 1976; 1 child, Carlyn Leigh. BS, U. Wis., 1970, MS, 1972; JD, Case Western Res. U., 1975. Bar: Ohio 1975, D.C. 1976, U.S. Ct. Claims, 1976, U.S. Ct. Appeals (D.C. cir.) 1976, U.S. Ct. Appeals (5th cir.) 1979, U.S. Ct. Appeals (11th cir.) 1983, U.S. Supreme Ct. 1983. Trial atty. Fed. Energy Regulation Com., Washington, 1975-79, asst. dir. office of enforcement, 1979; assoc. Morley & Caskin, Washington, 1979-80; ptnr. Morley, Caskin & Generelly, Washington, 1981-98; mng. ptnr. Cameron McKenna LLP, Washington, 1998—; gen. counsel, sec. Portland Natural Gas Transmission Sys., 1993—. Notes editor Energy Law Jour., 1990-98; bd. dirs. Found. of the Energy Law Jour., 1999—; contbr. articles to profl. jours. Bd. dirs. Westmoreland Children's Ctr., Washington, 1986-88, Found. of the Energy Law Jour. Smithsonian fellow, 1969. Mem ABA, Fed. Energy Bar Assn. (bd. dirs. 1993-96, past com. chair 1992, 93 ann. meetings, v.p. 1998-99, pres.-elect 1999—). Jewish. Avocations: skiing, running, bicycling. FERC practice, Public utilities, Administrative and regulatory. Home: 9216 Burning Tree Rd Bethesda MD 20817-2251 Office: Cameron McKenna LLP 2175 K St NW Washington DC 20037

**ZIPP, RONALD DUANE,** judge; b. New Braunfels, Tex., Dec. 7, 1946; s. Nolan William and Irene Alyce (Stiba) Z.; children: Robert Andrew, Kristi Nicole; m. Saundra Zipp, Mar. 5, 1989. BBA, Tex. A&M U., 1968; JD St. Mary U., San Antonio, 1971, MA Oxford (Eng.) U., 1997. Bar: Tex. 1971, U.S. Dist. Ct. (so. dist.) Tex. 1972, U.S. Dist. Ct. (we. dist.) Tex. 1974, U.S. Ct. Appeals (5th cir.) 1973, U.S. Supreme Ct. 1974. Assoc. Kelley, Looney, Alexander & Hiester, Edinburg, Tex., 1971-73; ptnr. Pena, McDonald, Prestia & Zipp, Edinburg, 1973-81; sole practice, New Braunfels, 1981-82, 89—; judge Comal County (Tex.) Ct.-at-Law, New Braunfels, 1983—; adj. prof. San Antonio Coll. Author local newspaper column; contbr. articles to profl. jours. Bd. dirs. New Braunfels Cmty. Svcs., 1992—, pres. 1981-83, 97-98, sec. 1994; bd. dirs. Child Welfare, vice-chmn., 1981-82, chmn. 1982-83; dir. Drover-Comal County Fair Assn.; vol. H.O.S.T.S.; vice chmn. Folkfest, 1994, chmn., 1995—; pres. Cmty. Svc. Ctr., 1997; bd. dirs., trustee Sr. Citizens Ctr. & Found.; dir. Comal County Fair Assn; mentor New Braunfels Ind. Sch. Dist.; clergyman and chancellor Anglican Diocese of Southwest. Mem. ABA, Greater New Braunfels C. of C. (legislative com., resources com., heritage com.), Tex. State Jr. Bar (criminal law com. 1975-76), Tex. Criminal Def. Lawyers' Assn. (bd. dirs. 1976-77, mem. various coms.), Tex. Aggie Bar Assn. (charter), Comal County Bar Assn. (past pres.), Comal County A&M Club (pres., treas.), Hidalgo County Bar Assn. (treas. 1972-75), Opa and Kleine Opa of Wurstfest Assn. (chmn. Folkfest), Hidalgo County A&M Club (pres.), Elks, Kiwanis, Lions (sec. 1996, pres. 1997), Phi Delta Phi. Lutheran. Office: 384 Landa St New Braunfels TX 78130-5401

**ZIPS, CRAIG DANNY,** lawyer; b. El Cajon, Calif., Aug. 5, 1970; s. Danny Pat and Patricia Horstead Zips. BS in Bus. Adminstrn., Tex. A&M U., 1993; JD, Tex. Tech. U., 1996. Bar: Tex. Atty. Jenkens & Gilchrist, Dallas, 1996—. Product liability, Consumer commercial, Contracts commercial. Office: Jenkens & Gilchrist 1445 Ross Ave Ste 3200 Dallas TX 75202-2799

**ZISKA, MAURA A.,** lawyer; b. Tampa, Fla., Sept. 23, 1968. BSBA, U. Fla., 1991; JD, St. Thomas Law Sch., 1996. Bar: Fla., U.S. Dist. Ct. (so. dist.) Fla., U.S. Ct. Appeals (11th cir.). Assoc. Adams, Coogler, Watson & Merkel, P.A., West Palm Beach, Fla., 1996—. Active Jr. League. Mem. Fla. Assn. Women Lawyers. Avocation: community service. Personal injury, Professional liability, General civil litigation. Office: Adams Coogler Watson & Merkel Ste 1600 1555 Palm Beach Lakes Blvd West Palm Beach FL 33401-2378

**ZISMAN, BARRY STUART,** lawyer; b. N.Y.C., Sept. 18, 1937; s. Harry and Florence Rita (Tucker) Z.; m. Maureen Frances Brumond, Dec. 30, 1979; children: Michael Glenn, Marlene Ann. AB, Columbia U., 1958, JD, 1961. Bar: D.C. 1962, N.Y. 1965, Tex. 1986, U.S. Dist. Ct. (ea. and so. dists.) N.Y. 1967, U.S. Ct. Appeals (D.C. cir.) 1967, U.S. Dist. Ct. (no. and so. dists.) Tex. 1986, U.S. Ct. Appeals (5th cir.) 1988, U.S. Supreme Ct. 1967. With U.S. Govt., 1962-66; pvt. practice Syosset, N.Y., 1966-71; sr. counsel CBS Inc., N.Y.C., 1972-75; asst. gen. counsel, asst. sec. M. Lowenstein & Sons, N.Y.C., 1975-79; gen. counsel Grumman Allied Indsl. Inc., Bethpage, N.Y., 1979-83; asst. gen. counsel Grumman Corp., Bethpage, 1982-83; sr. atty. FDIC, Dallas, 1984-87; of counsel Arter & Hadden, Dallas, 1987-88, ptnr., 1988; ptnr. Winstead, McGuire, Sechrest & Minick, Dallas, 1988-90, Arter & Hadden, Dallas and Washington, 1990-91, Rubinstein & Perry, Dallas, 1991-94, The Zisman Law Firm, P.C., Dallas, 1994—; advisor in field; vice-chmn. Assn. of Bank and Thrift Receivership Coun. Editor and author: Banks and Thrifts: Government Enforcement and Receivership Law, 1991. With U.S. Army, 1961-62. Banking, General civil litigation, General corporate. Home: 905 Murl Dr Irving TX 75062-4441 Office: 200 Renaissance Pl 714 Jackson St Dallas TX 75202-4548

**ZISSU, MICHAEL JEROME,** lawyer; b. N.Y.C., June 3, 1934; s. Leonard and Ruth Edith (Katz) Z.; m. Maria Theresia Duffner, June 27, 1960 (div. Feb. 1971); children: Audrey Lynn Zissu Hensley, Erik March; m. Patricia Joan Murphy, Feb. 20, 1971 (div. 1977); 1 child, Jacob Royal. AB, Dartmouth Coll., 1956; postgrad., U. Chgo., 1956-58; LLB, New Eng. Law Sch., 1962. Bar: Mass. Supreme Jud. Ct. 1963, N.Y. (app. divsn. 1st. dept.) 1964. Assoc. Zissu, Marcus & Stein, N.Y.C., 1962-68, Regan Goldfarb Powell & Quinn, N.Y.C., 1968-71; ptnr. Zissu & Harris, N.Y.C., 1972-82, Murphy & Zissu, N.Y.C., 1985-96. With U.S. Army, 1958-60. Mem. Assn. of the Bar of the City of N.Y., Copyright Soc. USA. Jewish. Trademark and copyright, Entertainment, General civil litigation. Home: 12800 Vonn Rd Apt 7603 Largo FL 33774-2590 Office: Murphy & Zissu 500 5th Ave New York NY 10110-0002

**ZITANI, GREGORY ANTHONY,** lawyer; b. Aversa, Italy, July 1, 1957; d. Genius Ares and Rosemarie Catherine (Spina) Z.; m. Brenda Louise, June 12, 1990; 1 child, Michael. BS, U. Calif., Berkeley, 1979; JD magna cum laude, California Western U., 1983. Bar: Calif. 1984, Fla. 1999, U.S. Dist. Ct. (so. dist.) Calif. 1984, U.S. Dist. Ct. (no. dist.) Calif. 1991, U.S. Ct. Appeals for the Armed Forces 1991. Pvt. practice Imperial Beach, Calif., 1987-90, San Diego, 1993—; litigation atty. Quintrall & Assocs., San Diego, 1990-92, Haas & Haut, San Diego, 1992-93. Lt. USN, 1983-87. Mem. ABA, San Diego Bar Assn., San Diego Trial Lawyers Assn. Avocations: athletics, coins. General civil litigation, Bankruptcy, Family and matrimonial. Office: James C Fetterman PA 4521 Bee Ridge Rd Ste A Sarasota FL 34233-2517

**ZITO, ROBERT JOHN AMADEUS,** lawyer; b. N.Y.C., Sept. 11, 1956; s. Joseph J. and Phyllis A. (Esposito) Z.; m. Dana Sabine Cole, July 4, 1992. BA, Tulane U., 1978; JD, NYU, 1981. Bar: N.Y. 1985, U.S. Dist. Ct. (so. and ea. dists.) N.Y. 1983, (no. dist.) 1993, U.S. Ct. Appeals (2nd cir.) 1988, U.S. Tax Ct. 1984, U.S. Supreme Ct. 1988. Assoc. LaRossa Cooper, N.Y.C., 1981-85, Spengler Carlson, N.Y.C., 1985-90; ptnr. Zito & Assocs., N.Y.C., 1990-91, Sullivan Donovan, N.Y.C., 1991-93, Tanner Propp & Farber, N.Y.C., 1993—; advisor Ch. of Incarnation, N.Y.C., 1994. Maj. N.Y. Guard, 1991—. Recipient Bklyn. Achievement award The Bklyn. (N.Y.) Dems., 1994, N.Y. Guard Achievement medal, 1995. Mem. ABA, N.Y. Bar Assn., Fed. Bar Coun., Columbian Coun., Ancient Chpt. RAM, Holland Lodge F & AM, Knights Templar. Democrat. Episcopalian. Avocation: musical instruments. Federal civil litigation, Bankruptcy, General civil litigation. Office: Tanner Propp & Farber 99 Park Ave Fl 25 New York NY 10016-1643

**ZITTRAIN, LESTER EUGENE,** lawyer; b. Norfolk, Va., Mar. 27, 1931; s. Leonard and Lee Zittrain; m. Ruth Ann Cohen, Aug. 20, 1957; children: Laura Zittrain Eisenberg, Jeffrey, Jonathan. BA, Washington and Lee U., 1952; JD, U. Va., 1955. Bar: Va. 1955, Pa. 1959, U.S. Supreme Ct. 1970. Ptnr. Zittrain and Zittrain, Pitts., 1958—. Former mem. exec. bd. and trustee Tree of Life Congregation, Pitts. Lt. USN, 1955-58. Fellow Pa. Bar Found. (life); mem. ABA, ATLA, Pa. Bar Assn. (jud. selection reform com., mem. ho. of dels. from Allegheny County), Pa. Assn. Trial Lawyers, Acad. Trial Lawyers Allegheny County (bd. govs. 1981-85, treas. 1986-88), Allegheny County Bar Assn. (judiciary com. 1983-86, chmn. 1986, mem. lawyer ins. com. 1984—, bench-bar conf. com. 1986-88, ct. rules com. 1987—, women in law com. 1988—, law libr. com. 1988—, bd. govs. 1988—, by-laws com. 1990—, chmn. civil litigation sect. 1986, Amram award 1998). Fax: 412-721-2300. Personal injury, General practice. Home: 136 Thornberry Dr Pittsburgh PA 15235-5061 Office: Zittrain & Zittrain 201 Franklin Ctr Profl Bldg 4240 Greensburg Pike Pittsburgh PA 15221-4235

**ZITZMANN, KELLY C.,** lawyer, consultant; b. Doylestown, Pa., Dec. 28, 1968; d. John F. Carr, Jr. and Elaina M. McCartney; m. Oliver A. M. Zitzmann, Oct. 28, 1995. AB, Cornell U., 1990; JD cum laude, Bklyn. Law Sch., 1993. Bar: N.Y. 1994. Assoc. Skadden, Arps, et al., N.Y.C., 1993-97; gen. counsel Erie Plastics, Corry, Pa., 1997-98; pres. Zitzmann Consulting, LLC, New Milford, Conn., 1998—. Recipient Thurgood Marshall award Assn. Bar City N.Y., 1998. Mem. ABA, N.Y. State Bar Assn. Republican. Episcopalian. Avocations: cycling, skiing, scuba diving. General corporate, Contracts commercial, General practice. Office: Zitzmann Consulting LLC 10 Fair Oaks Cir New Milford CT 06776-3860

**ZIVE, GREGG WILLIAM,** judge; b. Chgo., Aug. 9, 1945; s. Simon Louis and Betty Jane (Hansen) Z.; m. Franny Alice Forsman, Sept. 3, 1966; children: Joshua Carleton; m. Lu Ann Zive, June 9, 1974; 1 child, Dana Mary. BA in Journalism, U. Nev., 1967; JD magna cum laude, U. Notre Dame, 1973. Bar: Calif. 1973, Nev. 1976, U.S. Ct. Appeals (9th cir.), U.S. Supreme Ct. Assoc. Gray, Cary, Ames & Frye, San Diego, 1973-75, Breen, Young, Whitehead & Hoy, Reno, 1975-76; ptnr. Hale Lane, Peek, Dennison & Howard, Reno, 1977-90, Lionel, Sawyer & Collins, Reno, 1990-92, Bible, Hoy, Trachok, Wadhams & Zive, 1992-95; U.S. bankruptcy judge Dist. Nev., 1995—; lectr. bus. law U. Nev., 1977—. Note and comment editor Notre Dame, 1972-73; contbr. articles to profl. jours. Bd. dirs. Washoe Youth Found., 1977-81, Jr. Achievement; commr. Washoe County Parks, 1988-95, chmn., 1990; trustee U. Nev., Reno Found., 1986-94, trustee emeritus, 1994—, chmn., 1993, exec. bd., 1991-96; bd. dirs. YMCA Sierra, 1989-95; mem. univ. legis. rels. com., 1986-95; dir. Friends of Libr., 1995—, v.p., 1998; mem. adv. com. Sparks Redevelopment Authority, 1992—; trustee Access to Justice Found., 1998—. 1st lt. U.S. Army, 1968-70. Mem. Calif. Bar Assn., State Nev. Bar Assn. (law related edn. com.), San Diego County Bar Assn., Washoe County Bar Assn. (exec. bd. 1987-93, pres. 1992-93), Nat. Conf. Bankruptcy Judges (bd. govs. 1998—), Am. Bankruptcy Inst., Master Inns Ct., Bruce Thompson Chpt., Am. Judicature Soc., Vol. Lawyers Washoe County (bd. dirs. 1991), Washoe Legal Svc. (bd. dirs. 1992-96, pres. 1996), Soc. Profl. Journalists, U. Nev. Alumni Assn. (coun. 1981-87, pres. 1986-87), Univ. Club (dir., past pres.).

**ZLAKET, THOMAS A.,** state supreme court justice; b. May 30, 1941. AB in Polit. Sci., U. Notre Dame, 1962; LLB, U. Ariz., 1965. Bar: Ariz. 1965, U.S. Dist. Ct. Ariz. 1967, U.S. Ct. Appeals (9th cir.) 1969, Calif. 1976. Atty. Lesher Scruggs Rucker Kimble & Lindamood, Tucson, 1965-68, Maud & Zlaket, 1968-70, Estes Browning Maud and Zlaket, 1970-73, Slutes Estes Zlaket Sakrison & Wasley, 1973-82, Zlaket & Zlaket, 1982-92; judge pro tempore Pima County (Ariz.) Superior Ct., 1983—; justice Ariz. Supreme Ct., 1992, vice chief justice, 1996, chief justice, 1997. Fellow Am. Coll. Trial Lawyers, Am. Bar Found., Ariz. Bar Found.; mem. ABA, Pima County Bar Assn., Am. Bd. Trial Advocates, Ariz. Coll. Trial Advocacy, U. Ariz. Law Coll. Assn., Ariz. Law Rev. Assn. Office: Arizona Supreme Ct 1501 W Washington St Phoenix AZ 85007-3231*

**ZLOCH, WILLIAM J.,** federal judge; b. 1944. Judge U.S. Dist. Ct. (so. dist.) Fla., Ft. Lauderdale, 1985—. Office: US Dist Ct 299 E Broward Blvd Fort Lauderdale FL 33301-1944

**ZLOTNICK, NORMAN LEE,** lawyer; b. Bklyn., Nov. 2, 1947; s. Harry S. and Frances Zlotnick; m. JoAnn L. Zlotnick, Nov. 26, 1976. BA in History, CCNY, 1969; JD, Rutgers U., 1972. Bar: N.J. 1972, U.S. Dist. Ct. N.J. 1972, U.S. Ct. Appeals (3d cir.) 1974, U.S. Supreme Ct. 1976, N.Y. 1990. Assoc. Perskie & Callinan, 1972-77; ptnr. Perskie, Bloom & Zlotnick, P.A., 1977-79, Bloom & Zlotnick, 1979-82, Marione, Biel, Zlotnick & Feinberg, P.A., Atlantic City, 1982—. Contbr. Rutgers-Camden Law Jour. Mem. ABA, ATLA, N.J. Bar Assn., Cape May County Bar Assn., Atlantic County Bar Assn. (N.J. Supreme Ct. spl. ethics master, Atlantic County civil case arbitrator, cert. civil trial atty.). General civil litigation, Contracts commercial, Real property. Office: 3201 Atlantic Ave Atlantic City NJ 08401-6216 Address: 933 Sea Sounds Ave Marmora NJ 08223-1061

**ZOBEL, RYA WEICKERT,** federal judge; b. Germany, Dec. 18, 1931. AB, Radcliffe Coll., 1953; LLB, Harvard U., 1956. Bar: Mass. 1956, U.S. Dist. Ct. Mass., 1956, U.S. Ct. Appeals (1st cir.) 1967. Assoc. Hill & Barlow, Boston, 1967-73; assoc. Goodwin, Procter & Hoar, Boston, 1973-76, ptnr., 1976-79; judge U.S. Dist. Ct. Mass., Boston, 1979—; dir. Fed. Jud. Ctr., Washington, 1995-99. Mem. ABA, Boston Bar Assn., Am. Bar Found., Mass. Bar Assn., Am. Law Inst. Office: Fed Judicial Ctr Thurgood Marshall Fed Bldg One Columbus Cir NE Washington DC 20002

**ZOELLER, D. BRYCE,** lawyer; b. New Albany, Ind., Apr. 12, 1969; s. Richard A. and Janet S. Z.; m. Susan M. Zoeller, Nov. 25, 1995. BA, Ind. U., 1991, JD, 1995. Bar: Ill. 1995, U.S. Dist. Ct. (no. dist.) Ill. 1995, Ind. 1997, U.S. Dist. Ct. (no. and so. dists.) Ind. 1997. Legis. corr. Senator Dan Coats, Washington, 1990; atty. Querrey & Harrow, Chgo., 1995-96, Kightlinger & Gray, Indpls., 1996—. Contbr. articles to profl. jours. Mem. FBA, Ill. Bar Assn., Ind. Bar Assn., Ind. Def. Lawyers Assn., Indpls. Bar Assn., Chgo. Bar Assn., Def. Rsch. Inst. Roman Catholic. Avocations: triathlete, cycling, golfing, running, skiing. Insurance, State civil litigation, Alternative dispute resolution. Office: Kightlinger & Gray 151 N Delaware St Fl 6 Indianapolis IN 46204-2526

**ZOELLICK, ROBERT BRUCE,** political science administrator, lawyer; b. Evergreen Park, Ill., July 25, 1953; s. William T. and Gladys Zoellick; m. Sherry Lynn Ferguson, June 28, 1980. BA with honors, Swarthmore Coll., 1975; M Pub. Policy, JD magna cum laude, Harvard U., 1981. Bar: D.C. 1981. Spl. asst. to asst. atty. gen. criminal div. U.S. Dept. Justice, Washington, 1978-79; pvt. practice law, 1981-82; law clk. to Judge Patricia M. Wald, U.S. Ct. Appeals for D.C. Cir., Washington, 1982-83; v.p., asst. to chmn. and chief exec. officer of bd. Fannie Mae, Washington, 1983-85; from spl. asst. to Dep. Sec., Dep. Asst. Sec. for Fin. Instns. Policy, to counselor to sec. and exec. sec. U.S. Treasury Dept., Washington, 1985-88; counselor of Dept. with rank under sec. U.S. Dept. State, Washington, 1989-92, under sec. for econ. and agrl. affairs, 1991-92; dep. chief of staff, asst. to Pres. White House, Washington, 1992-93; exec. v.p. housing and law Fannie Mae, Washington, 1993-97; Olin prof. nat. security U.S. Naval Acad., 1997-98; pres., CEO-designate Ctr. Strategic & Internat. Studies, Washington, 1998—; bd. dirs. Alliance Capital, Jones Intercable, Said Holdings. Decorated Knight Comdr.'s Cross ( for work on German unification, Germany); recipient Alexander Hamilton award U.S. Treasury Dept., 1988, Disting. Svc. award U.S. State Dept, 1992; fellow Luce Found., Hong Kong, 1980. Mem. D.C. Bar Assn., Phi Beta Kappa.

**ZOELLNER, GEORGE L.,** lawyer; b. Gypsum, Colo., Mar. 23, 1924; s. George W. and Clara Marie Z.; m. Carol M. Lockhart, Mar. 24, 1946; children: Gary W., Georgiana, Rhonda L., Rebecca L. LLB, U. Colo., 1951. Asst. atty. gen. State of Colo., Denver, 1952-66; gen. counsel Denver Water Bd., 1966-77. Staff sgt. USAF and U.S. Army, 1943-46. Mem. Colo. Bar Assn. (mem. bd. govs., professionalism award 1998), Adams County Bar Assn. (past pres., past v.p., past sec.), Aurora Bar Assn. (professionalism award 1998), Elks (life). Home: 462 Oswego St Aurora CO 80010-4754 Office: 12101 E 2nd Ave Ste 206 Aurora CO 80011-8328

**ZOFFER, DAVID B.,** lawyer; b. N.Y.C., 1947. BA, Hofstra U., 1969; JD, Fordham U., 1972. Bar: N.Y. 1973, U.S. Dist. Ct. (so. and ea. dists.) N.Y. 1974, U.S. Ct. Appeals (2d cir.) 1974, U.S. Supreme Ct. 1978; cert. mediator. Asst. dist. atty. frauds bur. N.Y. County Dist. Atty.'s Office, N.Y.C., 1972-76; spl. asst. atty. gen. State of N.Y., N.Y.C., 1976-79; sr. v.p. USAU, Inc. (subs. Gen. Reins. Corp.), N.Y.C., 1979-90; exec. v.p. Internat. Claims and Litig. Mgmt. Group Inc., Chapel Hill, N.C., 1990—; mem. faculty Fordham Crisis Mgmt. Strategies Program, N.Y.C., 1994, 7th Annual Tenn. Corp. Counsel Inst., Nashville, 1999, 5th Annual FICC Litig. Mgmt. Coll., Evanston, Ill., 1999; litig. strategies panelist Am. Trucking Assns., New Orleans, 1998; lectr. in field. Mem. Fordham Urban Law Jour., 1971; contbr. articles to profl. jours. Mem. ABA (moderator and chmn. tort and ins. practice conf. 1997, 98, 99), N.Y. Bar Assn., Fedn. Ins. and Corp. Counsel, Def. Rsch. Inst., Am. Corp. Counsel Assn. (chief legal officers' club 1998—), N.C. Bar Assn. (task force on Multidisciplinary practice), N. Hempstead Country Club, Carolina Club, Pi Gamma Mu. Fax: 919-419-7366. E-mail: dbz@icalmgroup.com. Personal injury, Insurance, Aviation. Home: 150 Meadow Run Dr Chapel Hill NC 27514-7786 Office: ICALM Group 6320 Quadrangle Dr Ste 230 Chapel Hill NC 27514-7815

**ZOGHBY, GUY ANTHONY,** lawyer; b. Mobile, Ala., Sept. 30, 1934; s. Herbert Michael and Laurice (Haik) Z.; m. Verna Madelyn Antoine, Mar. 2, 1957 (dissolved); children: Guy Anthony II, Madelyn A., Gregory M.; m. Judy-ann EcKberg, Jan. 2, 1976. AB in English, Spring Hill Coll., 1955; JD, U. Cin., 1963; cert., U.S. Army JAG Sch., 1964. Bar: Ohio 1963, Ala. 1965, Calif. 1978, Pa. 1988. Advanced through grades to capt. U.S. Army, 1963, various assignments, 1955-63; dep. staff JAG 11th Air Assault Div., Ft. Benning, Ga., 1963-64, 1st Cav. Div., 1964-65; atty. office of v.p. and gen. counsel IBM, Armonk, N.Y., 1965-67, staff atty., 1967-69, sr. atty., 1969-71; regional counsel IBM, Bethesda, Md., 1972-73; corp. staff counsel IBM, London, 1973-77; div. counsel IBM, Armonk, N.Y., 1977-80, mng. atty., 1980-83, group counsel, from 1983; v.p., gen. counsel PPG Industries Inc., Pitts., 1987-93, sr. v.p., gen. counsel, 1994-97; now mediator, arbitrator, Pitts., 1997—; lectr. profl. seminars; co-chmn. corp. counsel com. Nat. Ctr. for St. Cts., 1998—. Editor U. Cin. Law Rev., 1962-63. Bd. dirs. Allegheny ARC, 1989—, Am. Judicature Soc., 1988—, pres., 1993-95; bd. dirs. Pitts. Civic Light Opera, 1992—, Am. Arbitration Assn., 1996—; mem. Am. Law Inst., 1992—, The Duquesne Club, 1988; bd. visitors U. Cin. Coll. Law, 1986—; exec. com. Ctr. for Pub. Resource, 1994—. Decorated Commendation medal with one oak leaf cluster; recipient Lawrence Maxwell prize U. Cin. Mem. Am. Corp. Counsel Assn. (cir. 1982—, exec. com. 1982-88, chmn. 1987—), Assn. Gen. Counsel, Order of Coif. Roman Catholic. Fax: (850) 897-6433. Alternative dispute resolution. Office: 4540 E Highway 20 Ste 9 Niceville FL 32578-9755

**ZOHNY, A. Y.,** law educator, business educator, consultant, international development consultant; b. Cairo, May 13, 1946; s. Younis Zohny and Dawlat Hussein; m. Patricia Trobian, Aug. 20, 1983; 1 child, Josephine. BS, El Shorta Acad., Cairo, 1969; LLB, Ain Shams U., Cairo, 1969; MA in Polit. Sci., Bloomsburg U., 1976; PhD in Pub. and Internat. Affairs, U. Pitts., 1984; LLM, Am. U., 1999. Assoc. prof. European divsn. U. Md., Heidelberg, Fed. Republic of Germany, 1987-88; assoc. prof. bus. adminstrn., dir. Inst. for Internat. Devel. & Strategic Studies Southea. U., Washington, 1988-90; prof. bus. law and bus. adminstrn. Strayer U., Washington, 1990—; CEO, pres. Mid. East Devel. and Sci. Inst., Hanover, Md., 1992—; faculty assoc. Johns Hopkins U., Balt., 1994—; sr. advisor Ednl. Mission Embassy of Saudi Arabia, Washington, 1985-86; internat. devel. cons. World Bank, USDA. Author: (book) Politics, Economics and Dynamics of Development Administration, 1988. Recipient scholarship Bloomsburg U., 1975-76; fellow U. Pitts., 1979-84. Mem. Congress of Polit. Economists, Middle East Inst., World Assn. Law Profs., Am. Soc. Internat. Law. Democrat. Avocations: swimming, horseback riding. Office: Mid East Devel and Sci Inst Inc 2657 Old Annapolis Rd #144 Hanover MD 21076-1288

**ZOIA, ROSE MARIE,** lawyer; b. Independence, Ohio, Mar. 18, 1961; d. Tullio Anthony and Catherine Louise (Angaroni) Z; m. Douglas A. Buescher, Aug. 14, 1993. BA summa cum laude, Ohio U., Athens, 1983; JD cum laude, George Washington U. Law Ctr., Washington, 1987. Bar: Calif. 1988, U.S. Dist. Ct. (no. dist.) Calif. 1988, U.S. Dist. Ct. (ctrl. dist.) Calif. 1993, U.S. Ct. Appeals (9th cir.) 1993. From law clk. to assoc. Senneff & Kelly, Santa Rosa, Calif., 1987-90; pvt. practice Law Office of Rose M. Zoia, Santa Rosa, 1990-93; ptnr. Brandt- Hawley & Zoia, Glen Ellen, Calif., 1993—; vol. settlement conf. panelisr Sonoma County Superior Ct., 1990-95; small claims judge pro tempore, Sonoma County, Mcpl. Ct., 1990—; instr. legal writing, Sonoma State Legal Asst. Program, Rohnert Park, Calif., 1990; speaker and panelist on Calif. Environ Quality Act at seminars and confs. including Nat. Alliance of Preservation Commns.--Calif. Office of Hist. Preservation, Calif. Preservation Found. and U. So. Calif. Sch. of Arch. Grad. Leadership Santa Rosa, 1992—; mem. United Way of Sonoma-Lake Mendocino Counties Comty Allocations Com., 1993-95; pres. YWCA Sonoma County, Santa Rosa, 1993-94, Routes for Youth, Santa Rosa, 1997; appointee Sonoma County Domestic Violence Policy Com., 1996; mem. Sonoma Commn. on the Status of Women, 1998—. Mem. Calif. Bar Assn. (environ. law sect. 1995—), Sonoma County Bar Assn. (pres. 1996), Am. Inn. of Ct (barrister 1997—), Phi Beta Kappa. Democrat. Avocations: sailing, hiking, fitness.

**ZOLA, MICHAEL S.,** lawyer; b. Madison, Wis., Dec. 15, 1942; s. Emanuel and Harriet (Sher) Z.; 1 son, Emanuel David. BS cum laude, U. Wis., 1964; LLB, Columbia U., 1967. Bar: D.C. 1968, Wis. 1968, Calif. 1969, Hawaii 1981, U.S. Dist. Ct. Hawaii 1981, U.S. Dist. Ct. (we. dist.) Wis. 1968, U.S. Dist. Ct. (no. dist.) Calif. 1969, U.S. Ct. Appeals (9th cir.) 1969. Law clk. to judge U.S. Dist. Ct. (we. dist.) Wis., 1967-68; mng. atty. San Francisco Neighborhood Legal Assistance Found., San Francisco, 1968-70; sole practice, Calistoga, Calif., 1970-73; directing atty. Mendocino Legal Services, Ukiah, Calif., 1973-76; state chief of legal services State of Calif., Sacramento, 1976-78, dep. state pub. defender, State of Calif., 1978-79; sole practice, Kailua-Kona, Hawaii, 1980—. Chmn. Mendocino County Dem. Cen. Com., Ukiah, 1975-76; pres. Kona Beth Shalom Congregation, 1991-94; Kona Salvation Army adv. bd., 1993-98. Reginald Heber Smith Poverty Law fellowship, 1968-70. Mem. Hawaii Assn. Criminal Def. Lawyers (bd. dirs. 1989, 91—), Nat. Assn. Criminal Def. Lawyers, Legal Aid Soc. Hawaii (bd. dirs. 1985-86), Rotary Club Kona (pres. 1998-99). Criminal, Family and matrimonial, Personal injury. Office: 75-5744 Alii Dr Ste 223 Kailua Kona HI 96740-1740

**ZOLLINGER, THOMAS TENNANT,** lawyer; b. Louisville, Feb. 13, 1945; s. Robert William and Betty Beatrice (Benkert) Z.; m. Anne Marie Green, April 9, 1993. B.S., Murray State U., 1969; J.D., U. Wyo., 1972. Bar: Wyo. 1972, U.S. Dist. Ct. Wyo. 1972, U.S. Ct. Appeals (10th cir.) 1979, S.D. 1996. Sole practice, Lander, Wyo., 1972-74, Rock Springs, Wyo., 1975—; prosecuting atty. Sweetwater County, 1987-91; surpervising atty. territorial pub. defender St. Croix, U.S. Virgin Island, 1993; sr. asst. pub. defender Wyo., Gillette, Wyo., 1994—, dir. Northern Hills S.D. Public Defender, 1995-97, town atty. Wright, Wyo., sole practice, Gillette, Wyo. Commr. Wyo. State Bar, Cheyenne, 1983-85. Chmn., Sweetwater County central com. Republican Party, 1975-76, state committeeman, 1977-80, 88-91; bd. dirs. S.W. Wyo. Alcohol Rehab. Assn., 1981-87. Mem. Assn. Trial Lawyers Am., ABA, Am. Judicature Soc. Methodist. Lodges: Elks, Eagles. Criminal, Personal injury, Civil rights. Home: PO Box 474 Wright WY 82732-0474 Office: 214 S Gillette Ave Ste 200 Gillette WY 82716-3704

**ZOLTAR, ELIZABETH MARIE,** lawyer; b. Balt., June 30, 1969. BA, U. Md., 1991, JD, 1992. Bar: Md., D.C. Assoc. Werik & Werik, Washington, 1992-99; ptnr. Werik, Werik & Zoltar, Washington, 1999—; part time instr. George Washington U. Contbr. articles to profl. jours. Active United Way. Mem. ABA. Office: Werik Werik & Zoltar 7826 Eastern Ave NW Ste 410 Washington DC 20012

**ZONANA, VICTOR,** lawyer, educator; b. Zagazig, Eqypt, Aug. 28, 1940; s. Isaac A. and Fortunee (Cohen Beyda) Z.; m. Mary Linda Haynie, Aug. 22, 1964; children: David A., Nancy B. Zonana Dickinson. BS in Econs., Hofstra U., 1961; LLB, NYU, 1964, LLM, 1966. Assoc. Kaye, Scholer, Fierman, Hays & Handler, N.Y.C., 1966-69; asst. prof. NYU, 1969-80, adj. prof., 1981—, Charles S. Lyon vis. prof., 1994; dep. tax legis. counsel U.S. Dept. Treasury, 1975-76; cons. to asst. commr. IRS, 1975, office of chief counsel, 1994; counsel, ptnr. Kaye, Scholer, Fierman, Hays & Handler, N.Y.C., 1980-87, Arnold & Porter, N.Y.C., 1988—; prof. Bklyn. Law Sch., 1996—; mem., chmn. adv. bd. NYU Tax Inst. Fellow Am. Coll. Tax Counsel; mem. ABA, N.Y. State Bar Assn. (co-chmn. com. on fgn. activities of U.S. taxpayers, chmn. com. on depreciation and investment credit, co-chmn. com. tax acctg. matters, com. tax policy). Corporate taxation, Private international. Office: Arnold & Porter 399 Park Ave Fl 35 New York NY 10022-4690 also: Bklyn Law Sch 250 Joralemon St Brooklyn NY 11201-3700

**ZOOK, BILL,** lawyer; b. Oak Park, Ill., Mar. 16, 1946; s. William E. and Betty L. (Kane) Z.; m. Sharon Oakley, Sept. 1, 1973; children: Aaron, Justin, Sean. BS in Engrin., U.S. Mil. Acad., 1969; JD, U. Tex., 1976. Bar: Tex. 1977, U.S. Dist. Ct. (we. dist.) Tex. 1979, U.S. Ct. Appeals (5th and 11th cirs.) 1981, U.S. Dist. Ct. (ea. dist.) Tex. 1989; cert. in personal injury trial law and civil trial law Tex. Bd. Legal Specialization. Atty. J. Howard Hayden, PC, Austin, Tex., 1976-77, Law Offices Bob Gibbins, Austin, 1977-81; pvt. practice Austin, 1981-89; atty. McLaughlin, Hutchison & Hunt, Paris, Tex., 1989-91, Ted B. Lyon & Assocs., Mesquite, Tex., 1991—. Capt. U.S. Army, 1969-74. Avocations: sports. General civil litigation, Personal injury, Product liability. Home: 301 Redbird Ln Highland Vill TX 75077-6845 Office: Ted B Lyon & Assocs Ste 525 18601 Lyndon B Johnson Fwy Mesquite TX 75150-5614

**ZORIE, STEPHANIE MARIE,** lawyer; b. Walla Walla, Wash., Mar. 18, 1951; d. Albert Robert and L. Ruth (Land) Z.; m. Francis Benedict Buda, Apr. 18, 1981 (div. 1985). BA, U. Fla., 1974, JD, 1978. Bar: N.Mex. 1991, Fla. 1978, U.S. Dist. Ct. (so. and mid. dists.) Fla. 1979, U.S. Ct. Appeals (5th cir.) 1979, U.S. Tax Ct. 1980, U.S. Ct. Customs and Patent Appeals 1980, U.S. Customs Ct. 1980, U.S. Ct. Mil. Appeals 1980, U.S. Ct. Claims 1981, U.S. Ct. Internat. Trade 1981, U.S. Ct. Appeals (11th cir.) 1981, U.S. Ct. Appeals (fed. cir.) 1982, U.S. Supreme Ct. 1988; cert. civil ct. mediator Fla. Supreme Ct.; cert. family mediator, N.Mex. Assoc. Richard Hardwich, Coral Gables, Fla., 1978-79, Brown, Terrell & Hogan P.A., Jacksonville, Fla., 1979-80, Dorsey, Arnold & Nichols, Jacksonville, Fla., 1980-81; sole practice Jacksonville, Fla., 1981-84; ptnr. Blakeley & Zorie P.A., Orlando, Fla., 1985-86; sole practice Orlando, Fla., 1986—, Santa Fe; owner Coyote Cody Co., 1991. Recipient Rep. Claude Pepper award, 1978. Mem. John Marshall Bar Assn., Spanish-Am. Law Students Assn., Phi Alpha Delta (local sec.-treas. 1978-79). Avocations: water sports, needlework, cooking. Family and matrimonial, Personal injury, State civil litigation. Office: PO Box 2898 Santa Fe NM 87504-2898 also: PO Box 372118 Satellite Beach FL 32937-0118

**ZORNOW, DAVID M.,** lawyer; b. N.Y.C., Mar. 31, 1955; s. Jack and Marion (Gilden) Z.; m. Martha Malkin, July 21, 1985; children: Samuel Morris, Hannah Jane, Ethan Lewis. AB summa cum laude, Harvard U., 1976; JD, Yale U., 1980. Bar: N.Y. 1981, U.S. Ct. Appeals (3d cir.) 1982, U.S. Dist. Ct. (so. dist.) N.Y. 1983, U.S. Ct. Appeals (2d cir.) 1984, U.S. Dist. Ct. D.C. 1989, U.S. Ct. Appeals (D.C. cir.) 1989, U.S. Dist. Ct. Ariz. 1990, U.S. Dist. Ct. (ea. dist.) N.Y. 1993. Law clerk to Judge Herbert J. Stern U.S. Dist. Ct. N.J., Newark, 1980-82; assoc. Kramer Levin Kamin Nessen & Frankel, N.Y.C., 1982-83; asst. U.S. atty. so. dist. N.Y. U.S. Atty.'s Office, N.Y.C., 1983-87; assoc. counsel Office Ind. Counsel-Iran/Contra Investigation, Washington, 1987-89; ptnr. Skadden Arps Slate Meagher & Flom LLP, N.Y.C., 1989—; chmn. N.Y.C. Civilian Complaint Rev. Bd., 1994-96; vis. faculty Trial Advocacy Workshop Harvard Law Sch., Cambridge, Mass., 1988. Mem. ABA (com. on white collar crime), Fed. Bar Coun., Assn. of Bar of City of N.Y., N.Y. Coun. Def. Lawyers. Criminal.

Office: Skadden Arps Slate Meagher & Flom LLP 919 3rd Ave New York NY 10022-3902

**ZORZA, JOAN,** periodical editor, lawyer; b. Boston, July 9, 1941; d. Norman and Zipporah A. Levinson; m. Thomas O. Sherman, July 9, 1961 (div.); m. Richard Zorza, June 2, 1978; children: Derin A., M. Arloc. BA, Boston U., 1962; JD, Boston Coll., 1981. Bar: Mass. 1981, D.C. 1991, N.Y. 1993. Clin. supr. Legal Svcs. Ctr., Harvard Law Sch., Boston, 1981-86; supr. divorce unit Greater Boston Legal Svcs., 1986-90; sr. atty. Nat. Ctr. on Women and Family Law, N.Y.C., 1990-95; editor Domestic Violence Report, N.Y.C., 1995—, Sexual Assault Report, N.Y.C., 1997—; cons. Nat. Coun. Juvenile and Family Ct. Judges, Reno, 1991—; bd. advisors Crime Victims Report, 1997—. Contbr. articles to profl. jours.; mem. editl. bd. Jour. of Aggression, Maltreatment & Trauma, 1997—. Bd. dirs. Nat. Coalition Against Domestic Violence, Denver, 1993—, Coalition of Battered Women's Advocates, N.Y.C., 1995—; pres. bd. dirs. N.Y. State Coalition Against Domestic Violence, Albany, 1995—; mem. adv. bd. Victimization of the Elderly & Disabled. Home and Office: 25 Sutton Pl S Apt 8D New York NY 10022-2462

**ZOTALEY, BYRON LEO,** lawyer; b. Mpls., Mar. 18, 1944; s. Leo John and Tula (Koupis) Z.; m. Theresa L. Cassady, Sept. 7, 1969; children: Nicole, Jason, Krisanthy. BA in Psychology, U. Minn., 1966; MATC, U. St. Thomas, St. Paul, 1968; JD, William Mitchell Coll. of Law, 1970. Bar: Minn. 1970, U.S. Dist. Ct. Minn. 1971, U.S. Ct. Appeals (8th cir.) 1972, U.S. Supreme Ct. 1975. Pres. LeVander, Zotaley & Vander Linden, Mpls., 1970—; arbitrator Minn. No Fault Panel, 1974—; cons. Marthe Properties, Mpls., 1980-90, Theron Properties, Mpls., 1985—. Bd. dirs. Minn. Consumer Alliance, 1994-95; mem. adv. bd. Benilde-St. Margaret's Jr. H.s., 1993-95; v.p. bd. trustees St. Mary's Greek Orthodox Ch. Mpls., 1997—, v.p., 1998, pres., 1999. Mem. ABA, ATLA, Minn. Bar Assn., Hennepin County Bar Assn., Minn. Trial Lawyers Assn. (chmn. Amicus Curiae com. 1980-87, bd. govs. 1982-93, mem. exec. com. 1987-89, emeritus, 1994—). General corporate, Personal injury, Probate. Home: 5504 Parkwood Ln Minneapolis MN 55436-1728 Office: LeVander Zotaley & Vander Linden 720 Northstar W Minneapolis MN 55402

**ZOUHARY, KATHLEEN MAHER,** lawyer; b. Greenville, Ohio, June 28, 1951; d. Thomas Richard and Mary (Brown) Maher; m. Jack Zouhary, Oct. 21, 1978; children: Kathleen Marie, Alexis Jacqueline. BA in Polit. Sci. cum laude, Miami U., Oxford, Ohio, 1973; JD cum laude, U. Notre Dame, 1976. Bar: Ohio 1976. Assoc. Fuller & Henry, Toledo, 1976-81; v.p., gen. counsel St. Luke's Hops., Maumee, Ohio, 1985—. Gen. chmn. Tribute to Women and Industry, Toledo, 1984, honoree, 1982; bd. dirs. Women Involved in Toledo, 1981-83; trustee Toledo Legal Aid Soc., 1977-90, Miami U., Oxford, Ohio, 1998—. Mem. ABA, Am. Health Lawyers Assn., Ohio Bar Assn., Toledo Bar Assn., Miami Presidents Club, St. Luke's Hosp. Pacesetter Club, Phi Beta Kappa. Health. Office: St Luke's Hosp 5901 Monclova Rd Maumee OH 43537-1899

**ZOUMBERIS, NIKITIS,** lawyer; b. Americus, Ga., Aug. 17, 1949; s. Demetrius N. and Bessie B. Zoumberis; m. Patricia Plant, Nov. 27, 1971; children: Stephanie M., Demetrius D. BS, Ga. Southwestern Coll., 1971; MSA, Ga. Coll., 1977; JD, Atlanta Law Sch., 1980. Owner Second Gate Package, Warner Robins, Ga., 1973-85; legal asst. Kathleen Grantham, Warner Robins, 1985-89; assoc. Grentham & Peterson, Warner Robins, 1989; lawyer in pvt. practice Warner Robins, 1989—; instr. Ft. Valley (Ga.) State Coll., 1983-84, Mid. Ga. Tech. Coll., Warner Robins, 1985-89. Atty. Habitat for Humanity, Warner Robins, 1991—. Democrat. Greek Orthodox. Bankruptcy, Family and matrimonial. Home: 111 Chestnut Rd Warner Robins GA 31088-5549 Office: 723 Bernard Dr Warner Robins GA 31093-3063

**ZUBEL, ERIC LOUIS,** lawyer; b. Detroit, Nov. 14, 1943; s. Stanley and Virginia (Poplawski) Z.; m. Catherine Hodges, Oct. 6, 1973; children—Conrad, Roland, Kristin. A.B., U. Mich., 1966; J.D., Golden Gate U., 1971, LLM in Internat. Law, 1998. Bar: Nev. 1973, U.S. Dist. Ct. Nev. 1973, U.S. Ct. Appeals (9th cir.) 1973, U.S. Supreme Ct. 1976. Law clk. to 8th Jud. Ct., Las Vegas, Nev., 1971-73; sole practice, Las Vegas, 1973—. Contbr. articles to profl. jours. Fellow Am. Coll. Trial Lawyers mem. Nev. Trial Lawyers (bd. govs. 1981-83), Am. Trial Lawyers. Federal civil litigation, State civil litigation, Private international. Home: 13 Windcrest Ln South San Francisco CA 94080-7307 Office: 1900 E Flamingo Rd Ste 296 Las Vegas NV 89119-5116

**ZUCCHI, JEFFREY JOSEPH,** lawyer; b. Manitowoc, Wis., Nov. 23, 1966; s. Anthony Joseph and Barbara Jean Zucchi; m. Kathleen Niesen, Aug. 21, 1995; 1 child, Avery Anthony. BA in Philosophy, St. Hobart Colll, DePere, Wis., 1989; JD, No. Ill. U., 1992. Bar: Ill. 1992, U.S. Dist. Ct. (no. dist.) Ill. 1998. Assoc. Law Offices Peter F. Ferracuti, Ottawa, Ill., 1992-96, Donohue & Clark, Ltd., Rockford, Ill., 1996—. Avocations: basketball, tennis, golf. Insurance, Personal injury, Workers' compensation. Home: 3710 Sherbrooke Rd Rockford IL 61114-4955 Office: Donohue & Clark Ltd 124 N Water St Ste 202 Rockford IL 61107-3959

**ZUCKER, CLAUDIA JOY,** lawyer; b. Butler, Pa., Feb. 7, 1961; d. Gerald A. and Sylvia R. Zucker; m. Humberto A. Morrell; 1 child, Gabriela Sabrina Morrell Zucker. BA in Polit. Sci., Boston Coll., 1984; JD, Boston U., 1988. Bar: Va. 1991, U.S. Dist. Ct. Va., U.S. Ct. Appeals (4th cir.) 1994. Law clk. U.S. Dept. of Justice, Boston, 1982-83; gen. counsel Conf. of State Bank Examiners, Washington, 1989-90; pvt. practice Arlington, Va., 1992—; lectr. in field; expert interviewee Dubai Internat. Satellite T.V. Contbr. (weekly columns) La Nacion, 1994-97, Cronica, 1993-94, (monthly column) ABC Mag., 1992-96, also articles to France-Amerique. Mem. new leadership com. Weitzmann Inst. Sci., Washington, 1997-98, Israel Bonds, Bethesda, Md., 1997-98. Mem. Iberian C. of C., City Club. Avocations: skiing, dancing, travel, scuba diving. Family and matrimonial, Immigration, naturalization, and customs, Juvenile. Office: 2300 Clarendon Blvd Arlington VA 22201-3367

**ZUCKER, HOWARD,** lawyer; b. N.Y.C., June 21, 1952; s. Morris Milton and Sarah Shirley (Spector) Z.; m. Lynn Carol Bierschenk; children: Lauren Heather, Erica Rachael, Monica Juliet. Student, London Sch. Econs., 1973; BS in Econs. summa cum laude, U. Pa., 1973, JD, 1977. Bar: N.Y. 1978. Ptnr. Hawkins, Delafield & Wood, N.Y.C., 1977—. Author: ABCs of Housing Bonds, 5th edit., 1993. Mem. ABA (chmn. pub. fin. com. of state and local govt. law sect. 1996-98), N.Y. State Bar Assn., Nat. Assn. Bond Lawyers (bd. dirs. 1994—, pres.-elect 1998-99, pres. 1999—), Omicron Delta Epsilon. Municipal (including bonds), State and local taxation, Securities. Office: Hawkins Delafield & Wood 67 Wall St Fl 11 New York NY 10005-3155

**ZUCKERBROD, MARTIN,** lawyer; b. Bklyn., Dec. 13, 1930; s. Samuel and Fanny Z.; m. Elaine L. Schatten, July 3, 1954; children: Stewart L., Gary M., Todd A. BA, Bklyn. Coll., 1952; JD, Columbia U., 1954. Ptnr. Zuckerbrod & Taubenfeld, Cedarhurst, N.Y., 1959—; arbitrator Small Claims Assessment Rev. Bd., Mineola, N.Y., 1981—; hearing officer U.S. Dist. Ct. (ea. dist.) N.Y., N.Y.C., 1987—; bd. dirs. Cornerstone Realty Income Trust, Richmond, Va., Next Generation Mktg., Inc., Manhasset, N.Y. Pres. Peninsula Counseling Ctr., 1998—; bd. dirs. 200 E 36th Owners Corp., 1986—, 21 N. Chatsworth Owners Corp., 1986—. With U.S. Army, 1954-56. Family and matrimonial, Real property. Office: Zuckerbrod & Taubenfeld PO Box 488 Cedarhurst NY 11516-0488

**ZUCKERMAN, HERBERT LAWRENCE,** lawyer; b. Newark, June 11, 1928; s. David and Adele Zuckerman; m. Janet Albert, Sept. 10, 1950; children: Julia, Elizabeth, William. BSBA, Lehigh U., 1949; JD, rutgers U., 1953. Acct. Zuckerman & Black, Newark, 1949-56; pvt. practice law Newark, 1956-71; ptnr. Zuckerman, Aronson & Horn, Newark, 1971-81; ptnr., v.p. Sills Cummis, Newark, 1981-98, sr.counsel, 1998—. Bd. dirs. Am. Jewish Com., 1990—; vol. The Hospice, Glen Ridge, N.J., 1985—. Fellow Coll. of Tax Counsel; mem. ABA, N.J. Bar Assn., Fed. Bar Assn., Essex County Bar Assn., Mental Health Assn. (bd. dirs. 1997—). Avocations: tennis, music, theater, opera, reading. Taxation, general, Estate taxation, State and local taxation. Office: Sills Cummis 1 Riverfront Plz Fl 10 Newark NJ 07102-5400

**ZUCKERMAN, LANDON ROY,** lawyer; b. Bklyn., Apr. 22, 1928; s. Samuel and Minna Z.; m. Marilyn Gold, July 18, 1951; children: Harold, Laurie, David, Judith. LLB, Bklyn. Coll., 1949, LLM, 1955. Bar: U.S. Dist. Ct. (ea. dist.) N.Y. 1949. Ptnr. Zuckerman & Powers, Bay Shore, N.Y. 1st lt. U.S. Army, 1952-53, Korea. Mem. Am. Trial Lawyers Assn., Suffolk County Bar Assn., Nassau County Bar Assn. General civil litigation, State civil litigation, Federal civil litigation. Office: Zuckerman & Powers 1622 Brentwood Rd Bay Shore NY 11706-3231

**ZUCKERMAN, PAUL HERBERT,** lawyer; b. Bklyn., Mar. 7, 1935; s. Max B. and Minnie (Mendelson) Z.; m. Sara Shiffman, Aug. 25, 1963; children: David Isaac, Daniel Mark. BS in Econs., Wharton Sch., U. Pa., 1957; MBA in Corp. Fin., NYU, 1964; JD, Bklyn. Law Sch., 1967. Bar: N.Y. 1968, U.S. Dist. Ct. (so. and ea. dists.) N.Y. 1975, U.S. Tax Ct. 1977, U.S. Ct. Appeals (2d cir.) 1972, U.S. Supreme Ct. 1973. Security analyst U.S. Trust Co., N.Y.C., 1962-66; sr. security analyst CNA Mgmt. Rsch. Corp., N.Y.C., 1966-71, mgr. dept. investment rsch., 1971-73; sole practice N.Y.C., 1973—; speaker and writer in field; radio, TV appearances. Bd. trustees Sutton Place Synogogue. Served to lt. (j.g.) USN, 1957-60. Mem. Assn. Bar City N.Y., Wharton Bus. Sch. (N.Y.C.). Estate planning, Probate, General corporate. Office: 19 W 44th St Suite 518 New York NY 10036

**ZUCKERMAN, RICHARD ENGLE,** lawyer, law educator; b. Yonkers, N.Y., Aug. 2, 1945; s. Julius and Roslyn (Ehrlich) Z.; m. Denise Ellen Spoon, July 14, 1968; children: Julie Ann, Lindsay Beth. BA, U. Mich., 1967; JD cum laude, Southwestern U., 1974. Bar: Calif. 1974, Mich. 1976, Nev. 1986, U.S. Dist. Ct. (ea. and we. dists.) Mich. 1977, U.S. Ct. Appeals (6th cir.) 1977, U.S. Ct. Appeals (9th cir.) 1982, U.S. Ct. Appeals 2d and 7th cirs.) 1994, U.S. Tax Ct. 1980, U.S. Supreme Ct. 1985. Spl. atty. organized crime and racketeering sect. U.S. Dept. Justice, Detroit, 1974-77; sr. ptnr. Raymond, Rupp, Wienberg, Stone & Zuckerman, P.C., Troy, Mich., 1977-87; sr. ptnr. Honigman, Miller, Schwartz & Cohn, Detroit, 1987—, chair litigation dept., 1996—; adj. prof. Detroit Coll. Law, 1978-98, bd. dirs., 1999—; mem. Mich. Atty. Grievance Commn. (Mich. supreme ct. appointee), 1995—; trustee Detroit Metropolitan Bar Found., 1999—. Served to lt. USN, 1967-71, Vietnam. Mem. ABA (grand jury com. criminal justice sect.), Fed. Bar Assn. (chmn. criminal law sect. Detroit chpt. 1985-90, bd. dirs. 1985-94, co-chair criminal def. com. 1990-95), Knollwood Country Club (West Bloomfield, Mich.), Std. Club, Am. Inns Ct. (master of bench 1995-97). Republican. Jewish. Criminal, Federal civil litigation. Office: Honigman Miller Schwartz & Cohn 2290 First National Bldg Detroit MI 48226

**ZUCKERMAN, RICHARD KARL,** lawyer; b. Bay Shore, N.Y., Feb. 23, 1960; s. Jack Irwin and Dorothy Ann (Sugarman) Z.; m. Jackie Lynn Lachow, Aug. 25, 1984. BA summa cum laude, SUNY, Stony Brook, 1981; JD, Columbia U., 1984. Bar: N.Y. 1985, U.S. Dist. Ct. (ea. and so. dists.) N.Y. 1987. Assoc. Rains & Pogrebin, P.C., Mineola, N.Y., 1984-91, ptnr., 1992—. Editor: Discipline and Discharge in Arbitration, 1998; contbg. author: N.Y. State Public Sector Law and Employment Law, 1998; contbr. articles to profl. newsletters. Chairperson ann. fund. SUNY, Stony Brook, 1986-91, bd. dirs. Alumni Assn., 1990-96. Mem. ABA, N.Y. State Bar Assn. (chair labor and employment law sect. com. on govt. employee rels. law 1998—, chair mcpl. law sect., employment rels. com. 1998—, mem. exec. com. labor and employment law sect.), Nassau County Bar Assn. Labor, Education and schools. Home: 3187 Ann St Baldwin NY 11510-4509 Office: Rains & Pogrebin PC 210 Old Country Rd Ste 12 Mineola NY 11501-4288

**ZUETEL, KENNETH ROY, JR.,** lawyer; b. L.A., Apr. 5, 1954; s. Kenneth Roy Sr. and Adelle Francis (Avant) Z.; m. Cheryl Kay Morse, May 29, 1976; children: Bryan, Jarid, Christopher, Lauren. BA, San Diego State U., 1974; JD, U. San Diego, 1978. Bar: Calif. 1978 U.S. Ct. Appeals (9th cir.) 1979, U.S. Dist. Ct. (ctrl. dist.) Calif. 1979, U.S. Dist. Ct. (so. and no. dists.) Calif. 1980, U.S. Dist. Ct. (ea. dist.) 1981. Clk. to fed. Judge Martin Pence U.S. Dist. Ct. Hawaii, Honolulu, 1978-79; assoc. litigation Buchalter, Nemer, L.A., 1979-83, Thelen, Marrin, L.A., 1983-88; ptnr. Zuetel & Tomlinson, Pasadena, Calif., 1988—; superior ct. arbitrator L.A. Superior Ct., 1982-90, superior ct. settlement officer, 1988-93; judge pro temp L.A. Mcpl. Ct., 1983—, L.A. Superior Ct., 1989—; guest lectr. Loyola U. Sch. Law, 1986-95; CEB lectr. Author: Civil Procedure Before Trial, 1992; cons. editor: Cal. Civ. Proc., 1992; contbr. articles to profl. jours. Recipient Recognition award L.A. (Calif.) Bd. Suprs., 1988. Mem. State Bar Calif. (mem. adv. com. continuing edn. 1985-88, trial practice subcom. 1985-88, disciplinary examiner 1986), Los Angeles County Bar Assn. (chair trial atty. project 1982-83, mem. L.A. del. conf. of dels. 1986-96, chair L.A. de. conf. of dels. 1995, exec. com. barristers 1984-88, superior ct. com. 1985-88, civil practice com. 1992-94, exec. com. litigation sect. 1989-90), Pasadena Bar Assn., Inns of Ct. (barrister L.A. chpt. 1991-92), Phi Beta Kappa, Phi Kappa Phi, Phi Alpha Theta, Pi Sigma Alpha. Republican. Presbyterian. General civil litigation, Health. Home: 567 Willow Springs Ln Glendora CA 91741-2974 Office: Zuetel & Tomlinson 180 S Lake Ave Ste 540 Pasadena CA 91101-2666

**ZUHDI, NABIL (BILL),** lawyer, litigator, consultant, producer; b. N.Y.C., June 8, 1955; s. Nazih and Lamya Zuhdi; child from previous marriage: Noah; m. Darla L. Boyd, May 19, 1984. BS, U. Ctrl. Okla., 1979; JD, U. Okla., 1982. Bar: Okla. 1982, U.S. Dist. Ct. (we. dist.) Okla. 1982, U.S. Ct. Appeals (10th cir.) 1989, U.S. Supreme Ct. 1990, Tex. 1991, U.S. Dist. Ct. (no. dist.) Tex. 1998. Assoc. Linn & Helms, Oklahoma City, 1982-85; ptnr. Zuhdi & Denum, Oklahoma City, 1985-87; assoc. Law Firm Darrell Keith, Ft. Worth, 1994; pvt. practice Oklahoma City, 1987—; pres. Zuhdi Entertainment Group, Inc., Okla. City, 1986—, Amerisphere, Inc., Okla. City, 1996—, criminal justice act panel We. Dist. Okla., 1985—, spl. death penalty habeas corpus panel, 1998, criminal justice act voluntary panel No. Dist. Tex., 1998. Producer: (concerts) Frank Sinatra, Julio Igleas. Patron Okla. Heart Ctr., Oklahoma City, 1994—. Mem. ABA, ATLA, State Bar Tex., Oklahoma Bar Assn., Oklahoma County Bar Assn., Phi Alpha Delta, Alpha Chi. Republican. Avocations: boxing, film, prodr. of concerts including Frank Sinatra and others. Federal civil litigation, Criminal, Personal injury. Office: PO Box 1077 Oklahoma City OK 73101-1077

**ZUKERMAN, LARRY WILLIAM,** lawyer; b. Pitts., Nov. 11, 1960; s. Robert Allen and Marlene (Maysels) Z.; m. Norma Friedman, July 8, 1990; children: Matthew, Shayna, Dara. BA, Washington & Jefferson Coll., 1982; JD, Case Western U., 1985. Bar: Ohio 1985, U.S. Dist. Ct. (no. dist.) Ohio 1985, U.S. Ct. Appeals (6th cir.) 1988, U.S. Supreme Ct. 1993. Atty. Greene & Hennenberg, Cleve., 1985-91; ptnr. Hennenberg Stuplinski & Zukerman, Cleve., 1991-93; proprieter Zukerman & Assocs., Cleve., 1993-96; mng. ptnr., shareholder Zukerman & Daiker Co. L.P.A., Cleve., 1996—; law dir., chief prosecutor Village of Moreland Hills (Ohio), 1996-98; adj. prof., trustee Case Western Res. U., Cleve., 1996—. Vice-chair Nat. Israel Bonds Orgn., 1996—; bd. dirs. Solomon Schechter Day Sch., 1996—, Cleve. ORT, 1997—. Mem. ABA, Assn. Trial Lawyers Am., Ohio Assn. Criminal Def. Lawyers (v.p. 1996-98), Cleve. Acad. Trial Lawyers, Ohio State Bar Assn. (coun. dels. 1994-96), Cuyahoga Bar Assn. (judicial selection com. 1992—), Nat. Assn. Criminal Def. Lawyers, Cleve. Bar Assn. (trustee, chair criminal law sect. 1994-95, vice chair fee dispute/arbitration com. 1992—, chair profl. ethics com. 1990-91), Cuyahoga Criminal Def. Lawyers Assn. (v.p. 1998-99, pres.-elect 1999—). Democrat. Jewish. Avocations: travel, skiing. Criminal, Municipal (including bonds), Personal injury. Office: Zukerman & Daiker Co LPA 2000 E 9th St Ste 700 Cleveland OH 44115-1301

**ZUKERMAN, MICHAEL,** lawyer; b. Bklyn., Oct. 3, 1940; s. Charles Morris and Gertrude Ethel Zukerman; m. Claire J. Goldsmith, June 25, 1961 (div. 1986); children: Steven, Amy; m. Elaine DeMasi, Nov. 21, 1986; children: Jaclyn, Laura. BS, U. Fla., 1961; LLB, St. John's U., 1964; LLM, NYU, 1966. Bar: N.Y. 1965, Pa. 1983, U.S. Tax Ct. 1984. Credit analyst, loan officer Franklin Nat. Bank, 1964-66; assoc. Jaffin, Schneider, Kimmel & Galpeer, N.Y.C., 1966-67; ptnr. Zukerman, Licht & Friedman and predecessors, N.Y.C., 1967-79, Baskin & Sears, P.C., N.Y.C., 1979-85, Graubard, Moskowitz, Dannett, Horowitz & Mollen, N.Y.C., 1985-86, Gersten, Savage, Kaplowitz & Zukerman, N.Y.C., 1986-89; of counsel Olsham, Grundman, Frome & Rosenzweig, N.Y.C., 1990-95, Graham & James, N.Y.C., 1995—; pres. Ptnrs. Credit Corp., 1988-93; exec. v.p. Brookhill Group, 1986-89; pres. First Ptnrs. Credit Corp., N.Y.C., 1988-93, exec. v.p. Brookhill Group, 1986-88; bd. dirs. Interjurist LTD, internat. law firm, Dames Moore/Brookhill LLC; mng. dir. Colebrook Capital Corp., 1996—, Salem Realty Capital LLC, 1997—. Contbg. editor Real Estate Taxation and Acctg., 1988-93; lectr. on various subjects, 1986—. Contbr. articles to profl. jours. Trustee Temple Beth Torah, Melville, N.Y., 1972-80, YMHA Suffolk County, Hauppague, N.Y., 1980-85; bd. dirs. Dayton Mgmt. Corp., 1974—, Suffolk Jewish Cmty. Planning Bd., Hauppague, 1982-85, Congregation Bnai Elohim, 1994, 2nd v.p., 1995; co-chmn. bus. adv. coun. Town of Greenburgh, 1992. Mem. ABA. Real property, General corporate, Securities. Home: 500 E 77th St New York NY 10162-0025 Office: Graham & James 885 3rd Ave Fl 24 New York NY 10022-4834

**ZUKERNICK, HARRY,** lawyer; b. N.Y.C., Nov. 25, 1905; s. Jacob and Becky (Meltz) Z.; m. Susan Brower, July 31, 1929; 1 son, Michael. BBA, CCNY, 1926; LLB, Bklyn. Law Sch., 1929. Bar: N.Y. 1930, Fla. 1935, U.S. Ct. Appeals (5th cir.) 1947, U.S. Supreme Ct. 1948. Pvt. practice, N.Y.C., 1930-35 Miami Beach, Fla., 1935—; chmn. dist. welfare bd. State of Fla. Mem. pres.'s council Brandeis U.; pres. Miami Beach Lodge, B'nai B'rith; founder Grtr. Miami Jewish Fedn.; trustee Fla. Region Anti-Defamation League. Mem. ABA, Fla. Bar (chmn. real property, probate and trust law sect., bd. govs.), Dade County Bar Assn., Miami Beach Bar Assn. (pres. 1950, merit award 1964), Bklyn. Law Sch. Alumni Assn. (pres. Fla. chpt.), Council Bar Assn. Pres. Fla. (Outstanding Past Local Bar Assn. Pres. award 1981), Miami Beach Civic League (pres. 1940), Anti-Defamation League (nat. vice chmn. deferred gifts com.). Author chpts. in law books. Office: 169 Lincoln Rd Ste 216 Miami Beach FL 33139-2047

**ZULAUF, JON ROBERT,** lawyer; b. Ann Arbor, Mich., Nov. 20, 1950. BA, Emory U., 1973; JD, U. Ga., 1976. With Finegold & Zulauf, Seattle, 1985-98, Zulauf & Chambliss, Seattle, 1998—. Mem. Wash. Assn. Criminal Def. Lawyers (pres.). Office: Finegold & Zulauf Tower Bldg 13th Fl 1809 7th Ave Seattle WA 98101-1393

**ZULLO, PETER FRANK,** lawyer; b. Chgo., Aug. 2, 1953; m. Monica Ann Murphy, Feb. 26, 1983; children: Kyla Marie, Peter Frank. Student St. Olaf Coll., 1971-73; B.A. in Sociology, U. Ill., 1975; J.D., John Marshall Law Sch., 1979. Bar: Ill. 1979, U.S. Dist. Ct. (no. dist.) Ill. 1982. Gen. counsel United Pharmacy Ptnrs., Inc. Mem. ABA, DRI, IDC, ISBA, CBA, Justinian Soc. Roman Catholic. Office: Sweeney & Riman 2 N La Salle St # 10 Chicago IL 60602-3702

**ZURAV, DAVID BERNARD,** lawyer; b. NYC, NY, Apr. 21, 1926; s. Irwin and Ida (Levine) Z.; m. Frances Stalford, Mar. 18, 1951; children: Ilene, Edward. BS in Econs., U. Pa., 1950; LLB, Rutgers U., 1953. Bar: N.J. 1953, N.Y. 1984. U.S. Ct. Appeals (3d. cir.) 1990, U.S. Supreme Ct. 1957. Pvt. prac. Union, NJ, 1953-70, 71—; ptnr. Zurav & Myers, Union, NJ, 1970-71; atty. Springfield Twshp. PLanning Bd., 1961-79, Union Twshp. Planning Bd., Union, NJ, 1975-81; spl. couns. NJ Dept Transp., 1970; dir., gen couns. Brunswick Capital Corp., Hillside, NJ, 1966-70; gen. couns. Met. N.J. Home Builders Assn., 1980-94; asst. cty. couns. Union Cty., NJ, 1982-88. Mem. adv. bd. 1st N.J. Bank Union, 1966-73, Union Cty. Freeholder, 1968-71. With USNR 1944-46. Republican Mcpl. chmn., Springfield, N.J., 1967-68. Fellow Amer. Acad. AMtrimonial Lawyers (cert. arbitrator, mem. N.J. state bd. mgrs. 1985-87, v.p. 1987-89, pres. elect 1989-90, pres. 1990-91); mem. Union Cty. Bar Assn. (chmn. jud. appointments com.) Essex Cty. Bar Assn., N.J. Inst. Mcpl. Attys., N.J. Home Builders Assn. (dir. 1982-94), Union Twshp. C. of C. (dir. 1980-88, v.p. 1983-87, pres. 1987-94), Am. Arbitration Assn. (nat. panel arbitrators), Lawyers Club Union (past pres.). Family and matrimonial, Land use and zoning (including planning), Real property.

**ZURBRIGGEN, JEFFREY MICHAEL,** lawyer, educator; b. Duluth, Minn., Mar. 7, 1971; s. Edward Michael and Darlene Elvera Zurbriggen; m. Susan Marie Herp, May 29, 1993; 1 child, Abigail Marie. BS in Mgmt., Ariz. State U., 1992, JD, 1994, MBA, 1997. Bar: Ariz. 1995, U.S. Dist. Ct. Ariz. 1996, U.S. Ct. Appeals (9th cir.) 1996. Mgr. Joe Fortune Floor Finishing, Inc., Phoenix, Ariz., 1987-94; legal asst. to pvt. attys. Tempe, Ariz., 1993-95; pvt. practice Tempe, 1995—; prof. Ariz. Sch. Paralegals, Phoenix, 1998. Mem. Nat. Assn. of Counsel for Children, Ariz. State Bar Assn. (juvenile law sect.). Avocations: family, tae kwan do, snow skiing, water skiing, camping. Criminal, Juvenile, Family and matrimonial. Office: # 118-217 6340 S Rural Rd Tempe AZ 85283-2930

**ZWACK, HENRY FRANCIS,** lawyer; b. Bronx, N.Y., Dec. 5, 1952; s. Frank and Maria (Mohos) Z.; m. Laura M. Giumarra, Oct. 28, 1984. BA, Siena Coll., 1975; JD, Albany Law Sch., 1978. Bar: N.Y. 1979, U.S. Dist. Ct. (no. dist.) N.Y. 1979, U.S. Supreme Ct. 1988. Pvt. practice law Stephentown, N.Y., 1979—. Fireman Stephentown Vol. Fire Dept., 1972—, emergency med. technician, 1980—; counsel to Senator Owen H. Johnson civil svcs. N.Y. State Senate, Albany, 1979-80-89, social svcs., Albany, 1980-89; active environ. conservation, 1989-95; scoutmaster Troop 518 Boy Scouts Am., Stephentown, 1983-85; legislator Rensselaer County, N.Y., 1986-95; dep. minority leader Rensselaer County Legis., 1990-93, chmn. legislature, 1994-95, exec., 1996—. Named Fireman of Yr. Stephentown Vol. Fire Dept., 1984. Mem. ABA, N.Y. State Bar Assn., Rensselaer County Bar Assn., Stephentown Rod and Gun Club. Republican. Roman Catholic. Avocation: hunting. General practice, Legislative, Real property. Home: Madden Rd Stephentown NY 12168-9743 Office: 272 Main St Stephentown NY 12168-9701

**ZWEBEN, MURRAY,** lawyer, consultant; b. Elizabeth, N.J., May 9, 1930; s. Jacob and Anna (Katz) Z.; m. Elaine Tinkelman, Nov. 22, 1950 (div. Apr. 1974); children: M. Lisa, Marc Samuel, John Eric, Harry T.; m. Anne Waggoner, Apr. 23, 1974; 1 child, Suzanne Grady. BS, Albany (N.Y.) State U., 1952, MS, 1953; LLB, George Washington U., 1959. Sec. to parliamentarian U.S. Senate, Washington, 1956-59, asst. parliamentarian, 1963-75, parliamentarian, 1975-81, parliamentarian emeritus, 1983—; law clk. U.S. Claims Ct., Washington, 1959-60; atty. Columbia Gas Systems, N.Y.C., 1960-63; pvt. practice, Washington, 1981-84; cons. atty. Nossaman, Guthner, Knox & Elliott, Washington, 1984-86, of counsel, 1986-, Elliott, Zweben & Steelman, Washington, 1986-90, Elliott & Zweben, Washington, 1990-96. Lt. USN, 1953-56. Avocation: tennis. Legislative. Home: 4010 Highwood Ct NW Washington DC 20007-2131 Office: The Homer Bldg #370 S 601 13th St NW Washington DC 20005-3807

**ZWICK, SHELLY CRITTENDON,** lawyer; b. Cin., Dec. 27, 1941; d. Kenneth Shelby and Rosa Henrietta (Ruda) Crittendon; m. Peter Ronald Zwick, July 6, 1963. BA, Stetson U., Deland, Fla., 1963; JD, La. State U., 1976. Bar: La. 1977, U.S. Dist. Ct. (mid. dist.) La. 1977, U.S. Ct. Appeals (5th cir.) 1979, (11th cir.) 1981, U.S. Dist. Ct. (ea. dist.) La. 1988, (we. dist.) La. 1988, U.S. Supreme Ct. 1990. Asst. U.S. atty. mid. dist. Dept. Justice, Baton Rouge, 1978-84, chief civil div., 1981-84; magistrate U.S. Cts., Baton Rouge, 1984-86; ptnr. Roy, Kiesel, Aaron, Tucker & Zwick, Baton Rouge, 1986-90; dir. affirmative action Calif. State U., San Marcos, 1992-94; vol. lawyer San Diego North County Mcpl. Ct.; adj. prof. La. State U., Baton Rouge, 1987-90, lectr., 1979-90, La. State Police, Baton Rouge, 1980-84. Contbr. articles to profl. jour. Recipient Disting. Alumni award Stetson U., 1985. Mem. Fed. Bar Assn., La. State Bar Assn., Nat. Assn. Coll. and Univ. Attys., Am. Assn. for Affirmative Action, Dean Henry George McMahon Inn of Ct. Episcopalian. Education and schools, Alternative dispute resolution. Home: 849 N Rios Ave Solana Beach CA 92075-1269

**ZWICKER, JOSEPH H.,** lawyer; b. N.Y.C.; s. Leopold and Barbara Zwicker; m. Marguerite P. Jones, May 16, 1998. BA, Columbia Coll., 1983; JD, NYU, 1987. Clk. to Judge Max Rosenn U.S. Ct. Appeals (3d cir.), Wilkes-Barre, Pa., 1987-88; assoc. Depevoife & Plimpton, N.Y.C., 1988-91; staff atty. Mass. Correctional League Svcs., Boston, 1992-95; assoc. Choate, Hall & Stewart, Boston, 1995—. Vol. Nat. Conf. for Comty. and Justice, Boston, 1998. Mem. ABA (internat. human rights sect., Brookline Human Rels. Com. (assoc.). General civil litigation, Civil rights. Home: 3 Gorham Ave Brookline MA 02445-6824 Office: 53 State St Boston MA 02109-2804

**ZYCHICK, JOEL DAVID,** lawyer; b. Cleve., June 23, 1954; s. Eugene K. and Myra (Rotblatt) Z. BBA, George Washington U., 1976; JD, Case Western Res. U., 1979; LLM in Taxation, NYU, 1979. Bar: Ohio 1979, N.Y.

1985, D.C. 1985, U.S. Tax Ct. 1980, U.S. Ct. Claims 1980, U.S. Ct. Appeals (fed. cir.) 1982. Assoc. Jones, Day, Reavis & Pogue, Cleve., 1980-83, Milbank, Tweed, Hadley & McCloy, N.Y.C., 1983-85; ptnr. Hertzog, Calamari & Gleason, N.Y.C., 1986-98; pres., CEO, GETKO Group, Inc., Westbury, N.Y.; gen. counsel, dir. The Egg Factory, LLC, Va.; participating dir. mgmt. decision lab. NYU; contbg. articles to profl. jours. Dir. Northside Ctr. for Child Devel., N.Y.C. Mem. ABA (sec., tax sect., nominating com., former chmn. sales and fin. trans. com., past vice chmn. regulations com. govt. submissions), N.Y. State Bar Assn. Avocations: hiking, music, traveling. E-mail: ztax@aol.com. Corporate taxation, Personal income taxation, General corporate. Home: PO Box 1097 Amagansett NY 11930-1097 Office: GETKO Group Inc 115 N Service Rd Westbury NY 11568-1707

**ZYCHOWICZ, RALPH CHARLES,** lawyer; b. Toledo, Mar. 22, 1948; s. Ralph Stanley and Sophia Imelda (Sliwinski) Z. BS, U.S. Mil. Acad., 1970; JD, U. Toledo, 1978. Bar: Ohio 1979, U.S. Dist. Ct. (no. dist.) Ohio 1979. Commd. 2d lt. U.S. Army, 1970, advanced through grades to capt., 1973, resigned, 1975; lt. col. USAR, 1975—; criminal prosecutor Lucas County, Ohio, 1980-82; civil law staff atty., prosecutor's office Lucas County, 1982—; asst. law dir. City of Oregon, Ohio, 1983-87; in-house counsel Zychowicz Sausage Factory, Inc. Maumee, Ohio, 1980—. Appt. mem. Ottawa-Jermain Park Bd., 1987-94, Downtown Toledo Cmty. Bd., 1992—. Mem. ABA, VFW, Ohio Bar Assn., Toledo Bar Assn., Res. Officers Assn., La Grange Bus. and Profl. Assn. (v.p. 1981-84), West Toledo Exch. (bd. dirs. 1981-82). Roman Catholic. Avocations: bicycling, English horseback riding, golf. Home: 2155 Chadbury Ln Toledo OH 43614-1122 Office: Lucas County Prosecutor County Courthouse Toledo OH 43624

# Fields of Practice Index

## ADMINISTRATIVE AND REGULATORY

### UNITED STATES

#### ALABAMA

**Birmingham**
Gale, Fournier Joseph, III
Henry, James Fred
**Mobile**
Brooker, Norton William, Jr.
Murchison, David Roderick
**Montgomery**
Gooden, Pamela Joyce
Laurie, Robin Garrett
Lawson, Thomas Seay, Jr.
Nelms, K. Anderson
Prestwood, Alvin Tennyson

#### ALASKA

**Anchorage**
Linxwiler, James David

#### ARIZONA

**Flagstaff**
Gliege, John Gerhardt
**Phoenix**
Arbetman, Jeffrey Farrell
Chanen, Steven Robert
Johnston, Logan Truax, III
Lieberman, Marc R(obert)
Lubin, Stanley
Mousel, Craig Lawrence
O'Steen, Van
Ryan, D. Jay
Schermer, Beth
**Scottsdale**
Buri, Charles Edward
**Tucson**
Corey, Barry Martin
Glaser, Steven Jay

#### ARKANSAS

**Fort Smith**
Carrick, Paula Strecker
**Little Rock**
Gibson, Calvin Roe
Mackey, Diane Stoakes
**Pocahontas**
Throesch, David

#### CALIFORNIA

**Carmel**
Heisinger, James Gordon, Jr.
**Carmichael**
Halpenny, Diana Doris
**Costa Mesa**
Putman, Philip A.
**Irvine**
Ristau, Kenneth Eugene, Jr.
**Los Angeles**
Bogaard, William Joseph
Burke, Robert Bertram
Burkholder, John Allen
Carr, Willard Zeller, Jr.
Girard, Robert David
Hogeboom, Robert Wood
Memel, Sherwin Leonard
Olivas, Daniel A.
Peters, Aulana Louise
Rothman, Michael Judah
Sands, Velma Ahda
Snyder, Arthur Kress
Van de Kamp, John Kalar
Wolf, Lawrence
**Martinez**
Williams, Charles Judson
**Millbrae**
Rosenthal, Herbert Marshall
**Mission Viejo**
Ruben, Audrey H. Zweig
**Northridge**
Van Der Wal, Jeanne Huber
**Oakland**
Cotter, Edward Francis, Jr.
**Pomona**
Wyatt, John Brundige, III
**Rosemead**
Danner, Bryant Craig
**Sacramento**
Keiner, Christian Mark
Micheli, Christopher Michael
**San Diego**
Dawe, James Robert
Peterson, Paul Ames
**San Francisco**
DeMuro, Paul Robert
Dryvynsyde, Geoffrey Beresford
Hernandez, Gary A.
Odgers, Richard William
Tobin, James Michael
**Santa Barbara**
Israel, Barry John
**Santa Monica**
Winograde, Audrey
**Torrance**
Pierno, Anthony Robert
**Tustin**
Kraft, Henry R.
**Woodland Hills**
Fields, Brian Jay

#### COLORADO

**Boulder**
Anuta, Karl Frederick
Nichols, Robert William
**Breckenridge**
Katz, Jeri Beth
**Broomfield**
Sissel, George Allen
**Colorado Springs**
White, Deborah Sue Youngblood
**Denver**
Adkins, Roy Allen
Blum, Gary Bernard
Christopher, Daniel Roy
Goldberg, Gregory Eban
Kahn, Benjamin Alexander
McManus, Richard Griswold, Jr.
Norton, Gale Ann
Pope, David Bruce
Rockwood, Linda Lee
**Longmont**
Lyons, Richard Newman, II
**Pueblo**
Farley, Thomas T.

#### CONNECTICUT

**Greenwich**
Cantor, Samuel C.
**Hartford**
Flynn, Brendan Thomas
Knickerbocker, Robert Platt, Jr.
Newman, John David
Space, Theodore Maxwell
**Manchester**
Gaines, Robert Martin
**Middletown**
Adams, Richard Glen
**New Haven**
Babbin, Jeffrey R.
**Newington**
Gutis, Mark Philip
**Stamford**
Barreca, Christopher Anthony
Harrison, Michael

#### DELAWARE

**Wilmington**
Baldwin, Glen S.
Kirk, Richard Dillon
Waisanen, Christine M.

#### DISTRICT OF COLUMBIA

**Washington**
Adams, Lee Stephen
Allan, Richmond Frederick
Allen, William Hayes
Baran, Jan Witold
Barnard, Robert C.
Barnes, Donald Michael
Basseches, Robert Treinis
Bebchick, Leonard Norman
Beck, David Charles
Beisner, John Herbert
Bercovici, Martin William
Beresford, Douglas Lincoln
Bernstein, Mitchell Harris
Berrington, Craig Anthony
Berry, Max Nathan
Berryman, Richard Byron
Bierman, James Norman
Blair, Robert Allen
Blake, Jonathan Dewey
Bloch, Stuart Marshall
Borkowski, John Joseph
Brewster, Christopher Ralph
Brinkmann, Robert Joseph
Burt, Jeffrey Amsterdam
Camp, John Clayton
Chierichella, John W.
Clark, Jeffrey Bossert
Close, David Palmer
Cobbs, Nicholas Hammer
Collins, Daniel Francis
Colman, Richard Thomas
Cortese, Alfred William, Jr.
Coursen, Christopher Dennison
Cox, Kenneth Allen
Czarra, Edgar F., Jr.
Daly, Joseph Patrick
Danas, Andrew Michael
Dennis, Warren Lewis
Devall, James Lee
Ellicott, John LeMoyne
Elrod, Eugene Richard
Englert, Roy Theodore, Jr.
Ferguson, John R.
Fisher, Bart Steven
Fisher, Benjamin Chatburn
Flagg, Ronald Simon
Flannery, Ellen Joanne
Freedman, Walter
Freeman, Milton Victor
Gellhorn, Ernest Albert Eugene
Ginsburg, Charles David
Glitzenstein, Eric Robert
Golden, Gregg Hannan Stewart
Goldstein, Michael B.
Grady, Gregory
Grier, Phillip Michael
Guy, Gary Edward
Hammerman, Edward Scott
Harrison, Marion Edwyn
Hastings, Douglas Alfred
Heckman, Jerome Harold
Helfer, Michael Stevens
Henke, Michael John
Heron, Julian Briscoe, Jr.
Hirrel, Michael John
Hobelman, Carl Donald
Hobson, James Richmond
Hollis, Sheila Slocum
Holmstead, Jeffrey Ralph
Holtz, Edgar Wolfe
Hoppel, Robert Gerald, Jr.
Horn, Charles M.
Horne, Michael Stewart
Howard, Jeffrey Hjalmar
Hynes, Terence Michael
Johnson, Philip McBride
Johnson, Richard Tenney
Johnson, Shirley Z.
Journey, Drexel Dahlke
Kiddoo, Jean Lynn
Kiley, Edward John
Kirsch, Laurence Stephen
Kissel, Peter Charles
Knauer, Leon Thomas
Kovacs, William Lawrence
Kramer, William David
Kriesberg, Simeon M.
La Force, Pierre Joseph
Lamm, Carolyn Beth
Langworthy, Lucinda Minton
Latham, Weldon Hurd
Leary, Thomas Barrett
Leibold, Arthur William, Jr.
Leonard, Will Ernest, Jr.
Lesar, James Hiram
Levin, Michael Henry
Lim, Joseph Edward
Lobel, Martin
Luce, Gregory M.
MacDougall, Gordon Pier
Mailander, William Stephen
Mann, Donegan
Mannina, George John, Jr.
Mapes, William Rodgers, Jr.
Mayer, Neal Michael
McCormick, Walter Bernard, Jr.
McKinney, James DeVaine, Jr.
McReynolds, Mary Armilda
Michaels, Gary David
Miller, John T., Jr.
Miller, Randy E.
Mishkin, Barbara Friedman
Mitchell, Carol Ann
Moates, G. Paul
Mode, Paul J., Jr.
Murphy, Emalee Godsey
Murry, Harold David, Jr.
Navarro, Bruce Charles
Odom, Thomas H.
Paper, Lewis J.
Pearce, Cary Jack
Penn-Jenkins, Monique Lorae
Pickering, John Harold
Pollard, Michael Ross
Rabinovitz, Joel A.
Ramey, Carl Robert
Raul, Alan Charles
Raymond, David Walker
Rehm, John Bartram
Rice, Paul Jackson
Roach, Arvid Edward, II
Roberts, Michael James
Roderer, David William
Roll, David Lee
Rose, Jonathan Chapman
Rosenthal, Steven Siegmund
Rubel, Eric A.
Schafrick, Frederick Craig
Sellers, John W.
Simons, Barbara M.
Sloame, Stuart C.
Sommer, Alphonse Adam, Jr.
Stayin, Randolph John
Sundermeyer, Michael S.
Sweeney, Eileen Patricia
Taylor, Richard Powell
Temko, Stanley Leonard
Timmer, Barbara
Trager, Michael David
Violante, Joseph Anthony
Waite, Frederick Paul
Wald, Robert Lewis
Waldron, Jonathan Kent
Weissman, William R.
Wilde, Jinhee Kim
Wilderotter, James Arthur
Williams, Thomas Raymond
Wine, L. Mark
Wolff, Elroy Harris
Woodworth, Ramsey Lloyd
Zipp, Joel Frederick

#### FLORIDA

**Boca Raton**
Lesnick, Irving Isaac
Wichinsky, Glenn Ellis
**Boynton Beach**
Babler, Wayne E.
**Bradenton**
Barnebey, Mark Patrick
**Clearwater**
Fine, A(rthur) Kenneth
McCormack, John Robert
**Daytona Beach**
Watts, C. Allen
**Islamorada**
Mattson, James Stewart
**Jacksonville**
Grogan, Michael Kevin
**Lake Buena Vista**
Schmudde, Lee Gene
**Lake Worth**
Kreidler, Frank Allan
**Miami**
Fleming, Joseph Z.
Hartman, Douglas Cole
Horn, Mark
Kuehne, Benedict P.
Maher, Stephen Trivett
Quirantes, Albert M.
Wheeler, Harold Austin, Sr.
**North Palm Beach**
Koffler, Warren William
**Orlando**
Downie, Robert Collins, II
Leonhardt, Frederick Wayne
Sheaffer, William Jay
Sims, Roger W.
**Palm Beach Gardens**
Silverman, Thomas Nelson
**Saint Petersburg**
Glass, Roy Leonard
Kiefner, John Robert, Jr.
**Sarasota**
Janney, Oliver James
Patten, Brenda L.
**St Petersburg**
Hudkins, John W.
**Tallahassee**
Barnett, Martha Walters
Booth, Edgar Charles
Cummings, Frederic Alan
Curtin, Lawrence N.
Mang, Douglas Arthur
Matthews, Frank Edward
Neal, Austin Baylor
Underwood, R. Michael
**Tampa**
Fernandez, Frances Garcia
Lamb, Bruce Douglas
Pellett, Jon Michael
Stiles, Mary Ann
**West Palm Beach**
Wagner, Arthur Ward, Jr.
**Winter Park**
Goldsmith, Karen Lee

#### GEORGIA

**Atlanta**
Boynton, Frederick George
Brecher, Armin G.
Brown, John Robert
Campbell, Charles Edward
McAlpin, Kirk Martin
Prince, David Cannon
Remar, Robert Boyle
Rusher, Derwood H., II
**Valdosta**
Council, Pauline Carter

#### HAWAII

**Honolulu**
Fujiyama, Rodney Michio
Sumida, Gerald Aquinas
**Kula**
Rohlfing, Frederick William

#### IDAHO

**Boise**
Barber, Phillip Mark
Hoagland, Samuel Albert

#### ILLINOIS

**Aurora**
Lowe, Ralph Edward
**Chicago**
Baer, John Richard Frederick
Baker, Bruce Jay
Bleiweiss, Shell J.
Blume, Paul Chiappe
Brown, Steven Spencer
Burditt, George Miller, Jr.
DeVries, James Howard
Donohoe, Jerome Francis
Eggert, Russell Raymond
Forcade, Billy Stuart
Gillio, Vickie Ann
Gordon, James S.
Head, Patrick James
Herman, Stephen Charles
Hester, Thomas Patrick
Hoffman, Valerie Jane
Hoover, R. Sam
Hunt, Lawrence Halley, Jr.
Levine, Laurence Harvey
Maher, Francesca Marciniak
Mangum, Ronald Scott
Meyer, J. Theodore
Montgomery, Julie-April
Saunders, George Lawton, Jr.
Schoonhoven, Ray James
Simon, Seymour
Smith, Arthur B., Jr.
**Des Plaines**
Davis, Larry Allen
Kotelman, Laura Mary
**Hoffman Estates**
Walpole, James R.
**Long Grove**
Obert, Paul Richard
**Northbrook**
Dilling, Kirkpatrick Wallwick
**O'Fallon**
Koebel, Delmar Oliver
**Rockford**
Rudy, Elmer Clyde
**Schaumburg**
Vitale, James Drew
**Springfield**
Artman, Eric Alan
Draper, Carl R.
Hanley, William Stanford
Rominger, M. Kyle
**Wilmette**
Frick, Robert Hathaway
Simon, Thelma Brook
**Winnetka**
Bishop, Mahlon Lee

#### INDIANA

**Evansville**
Hayes, Philip Harold
**Indianapolis**
Allen, David James
Boyko, Ihor Nestor
Bush, Robert Bradford
Carney, Joseph Buckingham
Miller, David Anthony
Price, Phillip Vincent
**Merrillville**
Brenman, Stephen Morris

#### IOWA

**Davenport**
Shaw, Elizabeth Orr
**Des Moines**
Bannister, T(homas) Scott
Berry, Jan Vance
Crook, Charles Samuel, III
Graziano, Craig Frank
Tipton, Sheila Kay

#### KANSAS

**Topeka**
Dimmitt, Lawrence Andrew
**Westwood**
Devlin, James Richard

#### KENTUCKY

**Lexington**
Beshear, Steven L.
Murphy, Richard Vanderburgh
**Louisville**
Cowan, Frederic Joseph
Northern, Richard
Pettyjohn, Shirley Ellis
Sandler, David Bruce
Sommer, Mark F.

#### LOUISIANA

**Baton Rouge**
Burland, James S.
Gonzales, Edward Joseph, III
**La Place**
Cicet, Donald James
**Metairie**
Hardy, Ashton Richard
**New Orleans**
Gelpi, C. James (Jim Gelpi)
Lombardo Trostorff, Danielle Maria
Thornton, Lucie Elizabeth
**Saint Francisville**
Eldredge, George Badge

#### MAINE

**Augusta**
Bickerman, Peter Bruce
**Portland**
Ingalls, Everett Palmer, III
Lehman, Kenneth William

#### MARYLAND

**Baltimore**
Gutierrez, Maria Cristina
Jenkins, Robert Rowe
McGarvey, Jack F(rancis)
Redden, Roger Duffey
Sfekas, Stephen James
**Bethesda**
Abrams, Stanley David
Eisen, Eric Anshel
English, William deShay
Goldstein, James Bruce
Goodwin, Robert Cronin
Herman, Stephen Allen
Pankopf, Arthur, Jr.
**Bowie**
Lucchi, Leonard Louis
**North Potomac**
Lehman, Leonard
**Potomac**
Meyer, Lawrence George
Reback, Richard Neal

**Rockville**
Pensinger, John Lynn
**Towson**
Conwell, John Fredrick

### MASSACHUSETTS

**Ashfield**
Pepyne, Edward Walter
**Boston**
Blake, Tamra A.
Gargiulo, Andrea W.
Graceffa, John Philip
**Framingham**
Freeman, Kathleen Jane
**Holyoke**
Ferriter, Maurice Joseph
**Ludlow**
Mondry, Paul Michael
**Marblehead**
Lundregan, William Joseph
**Springfield**
Burke, Michael Henry
Gelinas, Robert Albert
**Worcester**
Moschos, Demitrios Mina

### MICHIGAN

**Ann Arbor**
Anderson, Austin Gothard
**Bloomfield Hills**
Norris, John Hart
**Detroit**
Babcock, Charles Witten, Jr.
Calkins, Stephen
Gold, Kenneth Craig
Gottschalk, Thomas A.
Mamat, Frank Trustick
Targan, Holli Hart
**Lansing**
Katz-Crank, Sherry L.
Marvin, David Edward Shreve
**Mount Pleasant**
Lynch, John Joseph
**Warren**
Bridenstine, Louis Henry, Jr.

### MINNESOTA

**Eagan**
O'Connor, Michael William
**Edina**
Burk, Robert S.
**Minneapolis**
Bras, Robert W.
Coyne, Dennis Michael
Franzen, Douglas John
French, John Dwyer
Johnson, G. Robert
Keppel, William James
Marshall, Siri Swenson

### MISSISSIPPI

**Brandon**
Chatham, Lloyd Reeve
**Hattiesburg**
Davis-Morris, Angela Elizabeth
**Jackson**
Chinn, Mark Allan
Fuselier, Louis Alfred
Hemleben, Scott P.
Martinez, Eduardo Vidal
Mosley, Deanne Marie
Wise, Robert Powell
**Laurel**
Cline, Lee Williamson
**Ridgeland**
Anderson, James Michael

### MISSOURI

**Hazelwood**
Purvines, Verne Ewald, Jr.
**Jefferson City**
Craft, John Charles
Graham, Christopher
Martin, Cathleen A.
Tettlebaum, Harvey M.
**Kansas City**
Bevan, Robert Lewis
Cross, William Dennis
Franke, Linda Frederick
Satterlee, Terry Jean
**Platte City**
Cozad, John Condon
**Saint Louis**
Brostron, Judith Curran
Gilhousen, Brent James
Sullivan, Edward Lawrence
Watters, Richard Donald
Withers, W. Wayne
**Salem**
Mitchell, Austin L.
**Springfield**
Penninger, William Holt, Jr.

### MONTANA

**Billings**
Sites, James Philip
**Helena**
Nazaryk, Paul Alan
**Missoula**
Loring, Emilie
Tuholske, Jack R.

### NEBRASKA

**Lincoln**
Hewitt, James Watt
**Omaha**
Lee, Dennis Patrick

### NEVADA

**Carson City**
Crowell, Robert Lamson
**Las Vegas**
Brown, Joseph Wentling
Curran, William P.
Faiss, Robert Dean
Fink, Gordon Ian
Jost, Richard Frederic, III
Larsen, Paul Edward
Lovell, Carl Erwin, Jr.
Nozero, Elizabeth Catherine

### NEW HAMPSHIRE

**Concord**
Miller, Timmie Maine
**Manchester**
Wells, Robert Alfred

### NEW JERSEY

**Bridgewater**
Conroy, Robert John
Schoppmann, Michael Joseph
**East Hanover**
Davidson, Anne Stowell
**Hackensack**
Navatta, Anna Paula
**Kenilworth**
Berkowite, Jeffrey
Wasman, Jane G.
**Lawrenceville**
Beyer, Vicki Woody
**Montville**
Wolk, Stuart Rodney
**Newark**
Chaplin, Dolcey Elizabeth
Cummis, Clive Sanford
Milita, Martin Joseph
**Pluckemin**
Ames, Marc L.
**Princeton**
Picco, Steven Joseph
Souter, Sydney Scull
Szwalbenest, Benedykt Jan
**Roseland**
Vanderbilt, Arthur T., II
**Secaucus**
McNamara, Patrick James
**Somerville**
Laskey, James Howard
**Springfield**
Mytelka, Arnold Krieger
**Summit**
Pearlmutter, Fredi L.
**Trenton**
Pellecchia, John Michael
**Vauxhall**
Ross, Mark Samuel
**Woodbridge**
Goldenberg, Steven Saul
Marcy, Eric John

### NEW MEXICO

**Albuquerque**
Barela, Jonathan Lewis
Pezzillo, Brian James
Thompson, Rufus E.
**Farmington**
Echols, Douglas Allen
Gurley, Curtis Raymond
**Santa Fe**
Coffield, Conrad Eugene
Cohen, David Saul

### NEW YORK

**Albany**
Barsamian, J(ohn) Albert
Bogdan, Edward Andrew, Jr.
Bougen, Harriet Sandra
Feller, Robert H.
Fernandez, Hermes A., III
Hanna, John, Jr.
Piedmont, Richard Stuart
Provorny, Frederick Alan
Ruzow, Daniel Arthur
Teitelbaum, Steven Usher
Weiss, Leonard Arye
**Ardsley On Hudson**
Stein, Milton Michael
**Armonk**
Walsh, David James
**Brooklyn**
Jacobson, Barry Stephen
**Hauppauge**
Saminsky, Robert L.
**Irvington**
Bonomi, John Gurnee
**Larchmont**
Berridge, George Bradford
**Le Roy**
Harner, Timothy R.
**Mineola**
Rossen, Jordan
**New York**
Abrams, Robert
Allen, Leon Arthur, Jr.
Block, William Kenneth
Buchman, M. Abraham
Butterklee, Neil Howard
Cicconi, James William
Clapman, Peter Carlyle
Davidson, Sheila Kearney
Douchkess, George
Drucker, Jacquelin F.
Edozien, Margaret Ekwutozia
Fleischman, Edward Hirsh
Ginsberg, Ernest
Gottlieb, Paul Mitchel
Gotts, Ilene Knable
Hall, Robert Turnbull, III
Handler, Arthur M.
Iyeki, Marc Hideo
Jacobson, Jerold Dennis
Kandel, William Lloyd
Lacovara, Philip Allen
Lederer, Karen F.
Lupkin, Stanley Neil
Malawsky, Donald N.
Margulis, Howard Lee
Miller, Richard Allan
Miller, Sam Scott
Moak, Roger Martin
Most, Jack Lawrence
Naftalis, Gary Philip
Nolan, Terrance Joseph, Jr.
Oliensis, Sheldon
Piscitelli, Peter
Sack, Edward J.
Sangerman, Jay J.
Semaya, Francine Levitt
Shaw, Melvin Robert
Sidamon-Eristoff, Constantine
Stack, Jane Marcia
Stewart, David Robert
Teicher, Martin
Webb, Morrison DeSoto
White, Katherine Patricia
Wylie, Gordon Fraser
**Newburgh**
Marcus, Michelle S.
**Rochester**
George, Richard Neill
**Rye**
Varona, Daniel Robert
**Smithtown**
Dowis, Lenore
**Uniondale**
Joslin, Lana Ellen
**White Plains**
Taft, Nathaniel Belmont

### NORTH CAROLINA

**Charlotte**
Essaye, Anne Elizabeth
**Durham**
Markham, Charles Buchanan
**Fairview**
Rhynedance, Harold Dexter, Jr.
**Greensboro**
Koonce, Neil Wright
**Pittsboro**
Hubbard, Thomas Edwin (Tim Hubbard)
**Raleigh**
Allen, Noel Lee
Dixon, Wright Tracy, Jr.
Kapp, Michael Keith
Thomas, Jason Selig
Wilson, Robert Lee, Jr.

### NORTH DAKOTA

**Bismarck**
Hinman, Michael J.
Klemin, Lawrence R.

### OHIO

**Cincinnati**
McClain, William Andrew
O'Reilly, James Thomas
**Cleveland**
Binford, Gregory Glenn
Burchmore, David Wegner
Schabes, Alan Elliot
Utrata, Carl Ignatius
**Columbus**
Deal, John Charles
Eftimoff, Katerina
Graff, Douglas Eric
Maynard, Robert Howell
Morgan, Dennis Richard
Taylor, Joel Sanford
**Dayton**
Cameron, Ken
Kinlin, Donald James
**Dublin**
Bennett, Steven Alan
Blaugrund, David Scott
**Geneva**
Epstein, Sherry Stein
**Howard**
Lee, William Johnson
**Lancaster**
Libert, Donald Joseph
**Marysville**
Howard, Lowell Bennett, Jr.
**Portsmouth**
Gerlach, Franklin Theodore
**Toledo**
McGinn, Barbara Ann
**Westlake**
Kolick, Daniel Joseph

### OKLAHOMA

**Edmond**
Loving, Susan Brimer
Ryan, Gregory J.
**Moore**
Pipkin, William A.
**Oklahoma City**
Allen, Robert Dee
Decker, Michael Lynn
Harris, Allen Keith
Legg, William Jefferson
Taliaferro, Henry Beauford, Jr.
**Tulsa**
Bowman, David Wesley
Estill, John Staples, Jr.

### OREGON

**Canby**
Thalhofer, Paul Terrance
**Portland**
Baxendale, James Charles Lewis
Dotten, Michael Chester
Geil, John Clinton
Sadler, Richard Lawrence
**Roseburg**
Yockim, Ronald Stephen

### PENNSYLVANIA

**Bala Cynwyd**
Gotanda, Brenda Hustis
**Bethlehem**
Barnette, Curtis Handley
**Blue Bell**
Grayson, Zachary Louis
Settle, Eric Lawrence
Teklits, Joseph Anthony
**Clarion**
Pope, Henry Ray, Jr.
**Harrisburg**
Barto, Charles O., Jr.
Burcat, Joel Robin
Cline, Andrew Haley
Kury, Franklin Leo
Schmidt, Thomas Bernard, III
Van Zile, Philip Taylor, III
**Media**
Zicherman, David L.
**Newtown**
Vosik, Wayne Gilbert
**Philadelphia**
Collings, Robert L.
Dabrowski, Doris Jane
Fineman, S. David
Kemler, R(obert) Michael
Kendall, Robert Louis, Jr.
Myers, Kenneth Raymond
Pickering, Gretchen Anderson
Reiss, John Barlow
Stevens, Mark A.
**Pipersville**
Sigety, Charles Edward
**Pittsburgh**
Bleier, Michael E.
Conley, Martha Richards
DeForest, Walter Pattison, III
Klodowski, Harry Francis, Jr.
Leibowitz, Marvin
Pfeifer, Gregory J.
Ross-Ray, Frances Ann
**Scranton**
Pocius, James Edward
**Yardley**
Hamberg, Gilbert Lee

### RHODE ISLAND

**Newport**
Nelligan, Kenneth Egan
**Providence**
Germani, Elia
Southgate, (Christina) Adrienne Graves
**Wakefield**
Rothschild, Donald Phillip

### SOUTH CAROLINA

**Charleston**
Cannon, Hugh
**Columbia**
Carpenter, Charles Elford, Jr.
Givens, Edwin D.
Harvey, Jonathan Matthew
Ready, William Alva, III
Scott, Ronald Charles
**Mount Pleasant**
Whitten, Beatrice Ehrenberg

### SOUTH DAKOTA

**Parker**
Zimmer, John Herman
**Sioux Falls**
Clapper, Jeffrey Curtis

### TENNESSEE

**Chattanooga**
Edge, Kathryn Reed
**Cleveland**
Kilby, Marcia Annette
**Hendersonville**
McCaleb, Joe Wallace
**Kingsport**
Pierce, Phylis Mise
**Nashville**
Fraley, Mark Thomas
Penny, William Lewis

### TEXAS

**Austin**
Anderson, Richard Michael
Brim, Jefferson Kearney, III
Cloudt, Jim B.
Colburn, Stuart Dale
Cortez, Hernan Glenn
Cunningham, Judy Marie
Davis, Creswell Dean
Demond, Walter Eugene
Donley, Dennis W.
Drummond, Eric Hubert
Gallo, A. Andrew
Golemon, Ronald Kinnan
Hale, Louis Dewitt
Heath, Claude Robert
McDaniel, Myra Atwell
Moss, Bill Ralph
Nevola, Roger Paul
Patman, Philip Franklin
Roan, Forrest Calvin, Jr.
Schwartz, Leonard Jay
Stephen, John Erle
Strauser, Robert Wayne
Warren, Jessica Mendes
**Dallas**
Barlow, W. P., Jr.
Beard, Bruce E.
Courtney Westfall, Constance
Douglass, Frank Russell
Hamby, Robert Kevin
Staley, Joseph Hardin, Jr.
**Diboll**
Ericson, Roger Delwin
**Fort Worth**
Eubank, Christina
**Houston**
Eiland, Gary Wayne
Friedman, J. Kent
Rozzell, Scott Ellis
Salch, Steven Charles
**McAllen**
Jarvis, Robert Glenn
**San Antonio**
Brito, Maria Teresa
Cruse, Rex Beach, Jr.
Lutter, Charles William, Jr.
Young, Jess Wollett
**Spring**
Hearn-Haynes, Theresa
**Wichita Falls**
Helton, Robert Moore

### UTAH

**Provo**
Abbott, Charles Favour
**Salt Lake City**
Heaton, Jon C.
Holbrook, Donald Benson
Jensen, Dallin W.
Mills, Lawrence

### VERMONT

**Rutland**
George, Alan Barry

### VIRGINIA

**Alexandria**
Dokurno, Anthony David
Fugate, Wilbur Lindsay
Pugh, William Wallace
Walkup, Charlotte Lloyd
Walkup, Homer Allen
**Arlington**
Carbaugh, John Edward, Jr.
Cohen, Sheldon Irwin
Morris, Roy Leslie
Wong, Richard Lee
**Fairfax**
Abrams, Sheri
**Falls Church**
Kirk, Dennis Dean
Young, John Hardin
**Great Falls**
Smith, John Anthony
**Manassas**
Platt, Leslie A.
**Mc Lean**
Anthony, Joan Caton
Byrnes, William Joseph
Herge, J. Curtis
Ingersoll, William Boley
Kennedy, Cornelius Bryant
Olson, William Jeffrey
Rau, Lee Arthur
Shepard, Julian Leigh
Stephens, William Theodore
**Norfolk**
Corcoran, Andrew Patrick, Jr.
Johnson, William H.
Wooldridge, William Charles
**Norton**
Shortridge, Judy Beth
**Reston**
Reicin, Eric David
**Richmond**
Baron, Mark
Freeman, George Clemon, Jr.
Grey, Robert J.
Watts, Stephen Hurt, II
**Vienna**
Barger, Kathleen Carson
Hagberg, Chris Eric
**Virginia Beach**
Layton, Garland Mason

### WASHINGTON

**Olympia**
Wright, Daniel A.
**Seattle**
Blom, Daniel Charles
Dolan, Andrew Kevin
Dussault, William Leonard Ernest
Eberhard, Eric Drake
Endriss, Marilyn Jean
Freeman, Antoinette Rosefeldt
Kinsey, Ronald C., Jr.
Rosen, Jon Howard
**Spokane**
Weatherhead, Leslie R.

### WEST VIRGINIA

**Bluefield**
Kantor, Isaac Norris

### WISCONSIN

**Colby**
Nikolay, Frank Lawrence
**Madison**
Fleischli, George Robert
Hansen, John Alton
Toman, William Joseph
Zawadsky, John H.
**Milwaukee**
Bachhuber, Michael Joseph
Fitzgerald, Kevin Gerard
Friebert, Robert Howard
Kennedy, John Patrick
Scrivner, Thomas William

### WYOMING

**Cheyenne**
Hickey, Paul Joseph

### TERRITORIES OF THE UNITED STATES

### PUERTO RICO

**San Juan**
Pierluisi, Pedro R.

### MILITARY ADDRESSES OF THE UNITED STATES

### PACIFIC

**FPO**
Blazewick, Robert B.

### ENGLAND

**London**
Kingham, Richard Frank

### ADDRESS UNPUBLISHED

Anderson, Jon Eric
Andrews, David Ralph
Babbin, Jed Lloyd
Blount, David Laurence
Boersig, Thomas Charles, Jr.

Hall, Pike, Jr.

### MAINE

**Portland**
McHold, Sharon Lawrence

### MARYLAND

**Baltimore**
Bell, Venetia Darlene
McWilliams, John Michael
Wescott, Laurence Stewart
**Brookeville**
Johns, Warren LeRoi
**Gaithersburg**
Massengill, Alan Durwood
**North Potomac**
Meiselman, Alyson
**Rockville**
Zaphiriou, George Aristotle
**Silver Spring**
Viertel, George Joseph

### MASSACHUSETTS

**Boston**
Ristuben, Karen R.
**Cambridge**
Esher, Jacob Aaron
**Maynard**
Weiss, Andrew Richard
**Newton**
Tennant, Doris Fay
**Northampton**
Thomas, Margot Eva
**Pittsfield**
Simons, William W.
**Stow**
Golder, Leonard Howard
**Worcester**
Deiana, Robert Vincent

### MICHIGAN

**Birmingham**
Morganroth, Fred
**Grand Rapids**
Iverson, Dale Ann

### MINNESOTA

**Minneapolis**
Berg, Jeffrey A.
Biglow, Robert R.
Jensen, Darrell Alf
Johnson, Paul Owen
Martinson, Bradley James
Saunders, Pamela Ruth
**Saint Louis Park**
Nightingale, Tracy Irene
**Saint Paul**
Awsumb, Robert Ardin
Noonan, James C.

### MISSISSIPPI

**Jackson**
Rosenblatt, Stephen Woodburn

### MISSOURI

**Chesterfield**
Ross, Richard Lee
**Higginsville**
Ver Dught, ElGene Clark
**Jefferson City**
Easley, Glenn Edward
**Kansas City**
Sauer, Elisabeth Ruth
**Saint Louis**
Buckley, Eugene Kenyon
Chackes, Kenneth Michael

### MONTANA

**Billings**
Toole, Bruce Ryan
**Kalispell**
Kaufman, Leonard Lee

### NEVADA

**Las Vegas**
Chrisman, James Paul
**Reno**
Simmons, Terry Allan

### NEW JERSEY

**Hackensack**
Goldsamt, Bonnie Blume
Spiegel, Linda F.
**Liberty Corner**
Spierer, Howard
**Newark**
Thompson, Paul Brower
**Princeton**
Wood, Joshua Warren, III
Zinkin, Ephraim Zev
**Rutherford**
Henschel, John James
**Short Hills**
Schell, Norka M.
**Somerville**
Dreier, William Alan

### NEW MEXICO

**Albuquerque**
Ricks, J. Brent

### NEW YORK

**Albany**
Weiss, Leonard Arye
**Buffalo**
Pearson, Paul David
**Malden Bridge**
Benton, Edward Henry
**New City**
Abel, Steven L.
**New York**
Aibel, Howard J.
Berger, Vivian Olivia
Bernstein, Michael Irwin
Clemente, Robert Stephen
Cohen, Donald N.
Davidson, Robert Bruce
DeCarlo, Donald Thomas
Drucker, Jacquelin F.
D'Ull, Walter
Freyer, Dana Hartman
Gans, Walter Gideon
Hochman, Stephen Allen
Hoffman, David Nathaniel
Matus, Wayne Charles
McDonell, Neil Edwin
Menack, Steven Boyd
Milmed, Paul Kussy
Rothstein, Amy Lone
Rovine, Arthur William
Savitt, Susan Schenkel
Schiffer, Larry Philip
Schindler, Steven Roy
Smoak, Evan Lewis
Tinnion, Antoine
**Uniondale**
Eilen, Howard Scott
**Valley Stream**
Levine, Marilyn Markovich

### NORTH CAROLINA

**Charlotte**
Campbell, Hugh Brown, Jr.
**Fayetteville**
Ruppe, Arthur Maxwell
**Hickory**
Farthing, Edwin Glenn
**New Bern**
Stoller, David Allen
**Raleigh**
Tucker, Sherry E.
Verdon, Jane Kathryn
**Winston Salem**
Motsinger, John Kings

### OHIO

**Akron**
Woodley, Ann E.
**Cambridge**
Nicolozakes, William Angelo
**Cincinnati**
Lawrence, James Kaufman Lebensburger
**Cleveland**
Skulina, Thomas Raymond
**Columbus**
Mendel, David Phillip
**Dayton**
Chema, Susan Russell
**Wilmington**
Buckley, Frederick Jean

### OKLAHOMA

**Oklahoma City**
Conner, Leslie Lynn, Jr.
Pendell, Terry Ashley
**Tulsa**
Ballard, Elizabeth Ann
Fell, Riley Brown
McCann, James Patrick
Riggs, M. David
Siegel, Nancy Jane

### OREGON

**Bend**
Costello, Don Owen
**Salem**
Gangle, Sandra Smith

### PENNSYLVANIA

**Philadelphia**
Adams, Arlin Marvin
Berger, Harold
Blumstein, Edward
Jamison, Judith Jaffe
Mullinix, Edward Wingate
**Pittsburgh**
MacBeth, Lynn Ellen
Ubinger, John W., Jr.
**Plymouth**
Musto, Joseph John

### SOUTH CAROLINA

**Columbia**
Richardson, Donald V.
**Greenville**
Bernstein, Barry Joel

### TENNESSEE

**Knoxville**
Campbell, Robert Roe
Murphree, Sharon Ann
Vines, William Dorsey
**Memphis**
Williams, J. Maxwell
**Nashville**
Conner, Lewis Homer, Jr.
Gannon, John Sexton
Jackson, Kenneth Monroe

### TEXAS

**Arlington**
Dowdy, John Vernard, Jr.
**Austin**
Davis, Robert Larry
Gammage, Robert Alton (Bob Gammage)
Graham, Samuel R.
Saltmarsh, Sara Elizabeth
Terry, Craig Robert
White, Michael Lee
**Corpus Christi**
Coover, Ann E.
Johnson, John Lynn
**Dallas**
Frick, John Michael
Greiner, Mary Louise
Hodges, Charles Robert
Mighell, Kenneth John
Roberts, Ronald
**Fort Worth**
Dushman, Lowell Edward
Johns, Deborah Ann Henry
Shannon, Joe, Jr.
**Houston**
Butler, Randall Edward
Fisher, Donald Elton, Jr.
Kientz, Val William
Moroney, Linda L. S.
Prestridge, Pamela Adair
Schwartz, Brenda Keen
Shurn, Peter Joseph, III
**New Braunfels**
Pfeuffer, Robert Tug
**Plano**
Hand, Randall Eugene
**Richardson**
Hubbard, Carolyn Marie
**San Antonio**
Javore, Gary William

### UTAH

**Sandy**
Western, Marion Wayne

### VERMONT

**Concord**
Norsworthy, Elizabeth Krassovsky

### VIRGINIA

**Harrisonburg**
Wallinger, M(elvin) Bruce
**Portsmouth**
Lavin, Barbara Hofheins
**Richmond**
Merhige, Robert Reynold, Jr.
**Vienna**
Titus, Bruce Earl

### WASHINGTON

**Bellevue**
Sebris, Robert, Jr.
**Mountlake Terrace**
Field, Kathleen Cottrell
**Seattle**
Blair, M. Wayne
Cavanaugh, Michael Everett
Cutler, Philip Edgerton
Loftus, Thomas Daniel
Wagoner, David Everett
**Spokane**
Winston, Robert W., Jr.
**Tacoma**
Teller, Stephen Aiden

### WEST VIRGINIA

**Huntington**
Bagley, Charles Frank, III

### WISCONSIN

**Elm Grove**
Gorske, Robert Herman
**Milwaukee**
Michelstetter, Stanley Hubert
Nelson, Roy Hugh, Jr.
Voss, Kenneth Erwin

### IRAN

**Teheran**
Westberg, John Augustin

### ADDRESS UNPUBLISHED

Bandy, Jack D.
Boersig, Thomas Charles, Jr.
Deric, Arthur Joseph
Dickstein, Michael Ethan
Dubuc, Carroll Edward
Glanzer, Mona Naomi
Harris, Janine Diane
Hetrick, Brenda Drendel
Hornthal, Louis Philip, Jr.
Kahn, Laurence Michael
Reath, George, Jr.
Siemon, Joyce Marilyn
Silver, Carol Ruth

---

## ANTITRUST

---

## UNITED STATES

### ALABAMA

**Birmingham**
Alexander, James Patrick
Givhan, Robert Marcus
Hardin, Edward Lester, Jr.
Hinton, James Forrest, Jr.
Long, Thad Gladden
Lynn, George Gambrill
Stabler, Lewis Vastine, Jr.

### ARIZONA

**Phoenix**
Allen, Robert Eugene Barton
Beggs, Harry Mark
Bouma, John Jacob
Carlock, George Read
Galbut, Martin Richard
Klausner, Jack Daniel
Price, Charles Steven
**Scottsdale**
Titus, Jon Alan

### ARKANSAS

**Little Rock**
Anderson, Philip Sidney
Creasman, William Paul

### CALIFORNIA

**Alameda**
Birren, Jeffrey Emmett
**Anaheim**
Lieb, John Stevens
**Burbank**
Campbell, L. Cooper
Cunningham, Robert D.
**Carlsbad**
McCracken, Steven Carl
**Cupertino**
Maddux, Parker Ahrens
**Los Altos**
Weir, Robert H.
**Los Angeles**
Baker, Robert Kenneth
Belleville, Philip Frederick
Cohen, Cynthia Marylyn
Fine, Richard Isaac
Fredman, Howard S
Hanson, John J.
Hufstedler, Shirley Mount (Mrs. Seth M. Hufstedler)
Varner, Carlton A.
von Kalinowski, Julian Onesime
Woodland, Irwin Francis
**Menlo Park**
Fairman, Marc P.
**Mill Valley**
Judson, Philip Livingston
**Modesto**
Mussman, William Edward
**Palo Alto**
Cohen, Nancy Mahoney
**Rancho Santa Fe**
Cary, Frederick Albert
**San Diego**
Lewin, Jeffrey David
Schuck, Carl Joseph
**San Francisco**
Allen, Paul Alfred
Bertain, G(eorge) Joseph, Jr.
Campbell, Scott Robert
Davis, Anthony Edward
Gelhaus, Robert Joseph
Haas, Richard
Hockett, Christopher Burch
Mussman, William Edward, III
Odgers, Richard William
Raven, Robert Dunbar
Robin, Kenneth David
Salomon, Darrell Joseph
**San Jose**
Anderson, Edward Virgil
Blasgen, Sharon Walther
**San Marcos**
Dixon, William Cornelius
**Walnut Creek**
Epstein, Judith Ann
Pagter, Carl Richard
**Woodside**
Martin, Joseph, Jr.
Lessy, Roy Paul, Jr.
Loevinger, Lee
McDavid, Janet Louise
McDiarmid, Robert Campbell
Melamed, Arthur Douglas
Michael, Helen Katherine
Miller, John T., Jr.
Moates, G. Paul
Pearce, Cary Jack
Pfeiffer, Margaret Kolodny
Podgorsky, Arnold Bruce
Pollard, Michael Ross
Pugh, Keith E., Jr.
Rivlin, Lewis Allen
Roll, David Lee
Rosengren, Paul Gregory
Shenefield, John Hale
Smith, Brian William
Temko, Stanley Leonard
Timberg, Sigmund
Townsend, John Michael
Vakerics, Thomas Vincent
Wald, Robert Lewis
Weiss, Mark Anschel
Whiting, Richard Albert
Wilson, Gary Dean
Wolff, Elroy Harris
Yoskowitz, Irving Benjamin
Zane, Phillip Craig
Zeidman, Philip Fisher

### COLORADO

**Broomfield**
Sissel, George Allen
**Denver**
Harris, Dale Ray
Hill, Robert F.
Hjelmfelt, David Charles
Miller, Gale Timothy
Thomasch, Roger Paul
Timmins, Edward Patrick

### CONNECTICUT

**Avon**
Wiechmann, Eric Watt
**Hartford**
Dennis, Anthony James
Veltrop, James D.
**New Haven**
Belt, David Levin
Murphy, William Robert
**Stamford**
Critelli, Michael J.
Huth, William Edward
**Wilton**
Blankmeyer, Kurt Van Cleave

### DELAWARE

**Wilmington**
Baldwin, Glen S.
Magee, Thomas Hugh

### DISTRICT OF COLUMBIA

**Washington**
Altschul, Michael F.
Applebaum, Harvey Milton
Atwood, James R.
Barnard, Robert C.
Barnes, Donald Michael
Bickel, David Robert
Blumenfeld, Jeffrey
Bowe, Richard Welbourn
Boyle, Timothy Edward
Brame, Joseph Robert, III
Bray, John Martin
Burchfield, Bobby Roy
Calderwood, James Albert
Colman, Richard Thomas
Denger, Michael L.
Dickstein, Sidney
Englert, Roy Theodore, Jr.
Ewing, Ky Pepper, Jr.
Ferguson, John R.
Fogel, J(oan) Cathy
Funkhouser, Robert Bruce
Gellhorn, Ernest Albert Eugene
Gold, Peter Frederick
Goodman, Alfred Nelson
Granger, David Ireland
Haines, Terry L.
Heckman, Jerome Harold
Henke, Michael John
Hills, Carla Anderson
Howard, Jeffrey Hjalmar
Hynes, Terence Michael
Jacobsen, Raymond Alfred, Jr.
Jetton, C. Loring, Jr.
Johnson, Shirley Z.
Kilburn, Edwin Allen
Kiley, Edward John
Klarfeld, Peter James
Lavelle, Joseph P.
Leary, Thomas Barrett

### FLORIDA

**Alachua**
Gaines, Weaver Henderson
**Boca Raton**
Kassner, Herbert Seymore
Kauffman, Alan Charles
**Boynton Beach**
Babler, Wayne E.
**Coral Gables**
Weissenborn, Sheridan Kendall
**Miami**
Armstrong, James Louden, III
Hall, Andrew Clifford
Houlihan, Gerald John
Kearns, John W.
Nachwalter, Michael
Nagin, Stephen E.
Winship, Blaine H.
**Orlando**
Subin, Eli Harold
**Tampa**
Gifford, Donald Arthur

### GEORGIA

**Atlanta**
Doyle, Michael Anthony
Genberg, Ira
Gladden, Joseph Rhea, Jr.
Grady, Kevin E.
Harrison, Bryan Guy
Killorin, Robert Ware
Lotito, Nicholas Anthony
Rhodes, Thomas Willard
Rusher, Derwood H., II
**Marietta**
Stein, Julie Lynne

### HAWAII

**Honolulu**
Char, Vernon Fook Leong

### IDAHO

**Boise**
Baird, Denise Colleen
Holleran, John W.

### ILLINOIS

**Barrington**
Lee, William Marshall
**Chicago**
Baker, James Edward Sproul
Donner, Ted A.
Eimer, Nathan Philip
Esrick, Jerald Paul
Fahner, Tyrone C.
Fogel, Joseph Lewis
Franch, Richard Thomas
Gordon, James S.
Gustman, David Charles
Harrold, Bernard
Horn, Richard Leslie
Howell, R(obert) Thomas, Jr.
Hunter, James Galbraith, Jr.
Hyman, Michael Bruce
Johnson, Douglas Wells
Johnson, Lael Frederic
Kempf, Donald G., Jr.
King, Michael Howard
Kuhns, Thomas O.
Linklater, William Joseph
Lipnick, Stanley Melvin
Luning, Thomas P.
Lynch, John Peter
Michaels, Richard Edward
Montgomery, William Adam
Rankin, James Winton
Saunders, George Lawton, Jr.
Silberman, Alan Harvey
Simon, Seymour
**Deerfield**
Staubitz, Arthur Frederick
**Dekalb**
Tucker, Watson Billopp
**Park Ridge**
LaRue, Paul Hubert
**Prospect Heights**
Leopold, Mark F.
**Wheaton**
Beckley, James Emmett

### INDIANA

**Elkhart**
Breckenridge, Franklin Eugene
**Indianapolis**
Knebel, Donald Earl
McTurnan, Lee Bowes

### IOWA
**Newton**
Bennett, Edward James

### KANSAS
**Olathe**
Logan, Samuel Price

### KENTUCKY
**Louisville**
Reed, John Squires, II
**Newport**
Siverd, Robert Joseph

### LOUISIANA
**Metairie**
Kutcher, Robert A.
**New Orleans**
Fraiche, Donna DiMartino
Masinter, Paul James

### MAINE
**Brunswick**
Owen, H. Martyn
**Portland**
Haddow, James Buchanan

### MARYLAND
**Baltimore**
Wilson, Thomas Matthew, III
**Potomac**
Meyer, Lawrence George
**Rockville**
Wagshal, Jerome Stanley

### MASSACHUSETTS
**Boston**
Downs, J. Anthony
Gans, Nancy Freeman
Yurko, Richard John
**Framingham**
Gould, Rodney Elliott
**Springfield**
Dibble, Francis Daniel, Jr.

### MICHIGAN
**Ann Arbor**
Britton, Clarold Lawrence
**Detroit**
Boonstra, Mark Thomas
Calkins, Stephen
Gottschalk, Thomas A.
Krsul, John Aloysius, Jr.
Langs, Edward F(orrest)
**Franklin**
Kessler, Philip Joel
**Grand Rapids**
Smith, H(arold) Lawrence
**Grosse Pointe**
Avant, Grady, Jr.
**Monroe**
Lipford, Rocque Edward
**Muskegon**
Nehra, Gerald Peter

### MINNESOTA
**Crystal**
Reske, Steven David
**Minneapolis**
Clary, Bradley G.
Duncan, Richard Alan
French, John Dwyer
Hagstrom, Richard Michael
Long, James Jay
Paulsrud, Eric David
Preus, Christian Andrew
Silver, Alan Irving
Sippel, William Leroy
**Saint Paul**
Mahoney, Kathleen Mary
Ursu, John Joseph

### MISSISSIPPI
**Jackson**
Henegan, John C(lark)

### MISSOURI
**Clayton**
Schwartz, Theodore Frank
**Kansas City**
Cross, William Dennis
Egan, Charles Joseph, Jr.
Eiszner, James Richard, Jr.
Holt, Ronald Lee
Marquette, I. Edward
Paul, Richard Monroe, III
Woods, Curtis E(ugene)
Wyrsch, James Robert
**Saint Louis**
Berendt, Robert Tryon
Clear, John Michael
Ellis, Dorsey Daniel, Jr.
Estes, Royce Joe
Joerling, Dale Raymond
Luberda, George Joseph
Pickle, Robert Douglas
Wiehl, James George
Wolff, Frank Pierce, Jr.

### MONTANA
**Bozeman**
Wylie, Paul Richter, Jr.

### NEW JERSEY
**Chester**
Hanson, Eugene Paul
**Florham Park**
Laulicht, Murray Jack
**Iselin**
Dornbusch, Arthur A., II
Goodman, Barry S.
**Kenilworth**
Hoffman, John Fletcher
**Livingston**
Grace, Thomas Edward
**Madison**
Connors, Joseph Conlin
**Morristown**
Whitmer, Frederick Lee
**Newark**
Dreyfuss, Stephen Lawrence
Simon, David Robert
Weber, Scott Louis
**Parsippany**
Donovan, Richard Edward
**Somerville**
Laskey, James Howard
**Summit**
Benjamin, Jeff
**Wayne**
Cupka, Brian Joseph

### NEW MEXICO
**Albuquerque**
Bardacke, Paul Gregory
Wertheim, John V.

### NEW YORK
**Buffalo**
Halpern, Ralph Lawrence
Mucci, Gary Louis
**Corning**
Hauselt, Denise Ann
**Garden City**
Posch, Robert John, Jr.
**Mineola**
Lynn, Robert Patrick, Jr.
**New York**
Altieri, Peter Louis
Arquit, Kevin James
Axinn, Stephen Mark
Barrett, David A.
Barthold, Walter
Bialo, Kenneth Marc
Boes, Lawrence William
Briggs, Taylor Rastrick
Clary, Richard Wayland
Cooper, Michael Anthony
Dallas, William Moffit, Jr.
Einhorn, Harold
Epstein, Michael Alan
Foster, David Lee
Fraser, Brian Scott
Freeman, Robert E.
Gallagher, Brian John
Getzoff, Steven B.
Goldey, Mark H.
Gotts, Ilene Knable
Greenwald, Harold
Heller, Robert Martin
Holley, Steven Lyon
Holman, Bud George
Hurlock, James Bickford
Jackson, Thomas Gene
Jackson, William Eldred
Joffe, Robert David
Karmali, Rashida Alimahomed
King, Henry Lawrence
Kleinberg, Norman Charles
Knight, Robert Huntington
Kobak, James Benedict, Jr.
Larkin, Leo Paul, Jr.
Lieberman, Ellen
Madsen, Stephen Stewart
Malina, Michael
Malkin, Michael M.
Maneker, Morton M.
McGuire, Eugene Guenard
McMahon, James Charles
Meiklejohn, Donald Stuart
Mentz, Barbara Antonello
Miller, Gordon David
Moyer, Jay Edward
Nolan, Richard Edward
Norfolk, William Ray
Orr, Dennis Patrick
Paul, James William
Pelster, William Charles
Pepper, Allan Michael
Pfeffer, David H.
Primps, William Guthrie
Quinlan, Guy Christian
Reinthaler, Richard Walter
Reynolds, Michael Timothy
Rich, R(obert) Bruce
Rifkind, Robert S(inger)
Ringel, Dean
Rothman, Dennis Michael
Salman, Robert Ronald
Skirnick, Robert Andrew
Spivack, Gordon Bernard
Steuer, Richard Marc
Stewart, David Robert
Stoll, Neal Richard
Struve, Guy Miller
Supino, Anthony Martin
Taylor, Job, III
Thackeray, Jonathan E.
Urowsky, Richard J.
Vig, Vernon Edward
Warden, John L.
Weinschel, Alan Jay
**Oyster Bay**
Gaffney, Mark William
**Peconic**
Mitchell, Robert Everitt
**Pleasantville**
Soden, Paul Anthony
**Rochester**
Braunsdorf, Paul Raymond
**Sleepy Hollow**
Andrew, Leonard DeLessio

### NORTH CAROLINA
**Charlotte**
Allred, John Thompson
Clodfelter, Daniel Gray
Murchison, Bradley Duncan
**Fairview**
Rhynedance, Harold Dexter, Jr.
**Hendersonville**
Hull, J(ames) Richard
**Raleigh**
Allen, Noel Lee
**Wilmington**
Jones, Lucian Cox

### OHIO
**Canton**
Davila, Edwin
**Cincinnati**
Hill, Thomas Clark
**Cleveland**
Collin, Thomas James
Hoerner, Robert Jack
Rains, M. Neal
Weller, Charles David
**Dayton**
Faruki, Charles Joseph
Ireland, D. Jeffrey
Rapp, Gerald Duane
Saul, Irving Isaac
**Lancaster**
Libert, Donald Joseph
**Toledo**
Wicklund, David Wayne

### OREGON
**Portland**
Anderson, Mark Alexander
Hurd, Paul Gemmill

### PENNSYLVANIA
**Kennett Square**
Partnoy, Ronald Allen
**Lancaster**
Nast, Dianne Martha
**Malvern**
Quay, Thomas Emery
**Moon Township**
Lipson, Barry J.
**Philadelphia**
Berger, David
Bissell, Rolin Plumb
Caldwell, John Warwick
Calvert, Jay H., Jr.
Cohen, David Louis
Elkins, S. Gordon
Grady, Thomas Michael
Harkins, John Graham, Jr.
Haviland, Donald Edward, Jr.
Kastenberg, Stephen Joel
Kendall, Robert Louis, Jr.
Kessler, Alan Craig
Kitchenoff, Robert Samuel
Kohn, Harold Elias
Mack, Wayne A.
Mannino, Edward Francis
Schneider, Richard Graham
Shestack, Jerome Joseph
Toll, Seymour Irving
**Pittsburgh**
Drake, Edwin P.
Gutnick, H. Yale
Hague, Paul Christian
Hickton, David John
O'Connor, Edward Gearing
Schmidt, Edward Craig
Van Kirk, Thomas L.
Wycoff, William Mortimer
**Wayne**
Wilson, Bruce Brighton
**York**
Markowitz, Lewis Harrison

### RHODE ISLAND
**Barrington**
Soutter, Thomas Douglas
**Providence**
Medeiros, Matthew Francis

### SOUTH CAROLINA
**Columbia**
Day, Richard Earl
**Greenville**
Phillips, Joseph Brantley, Jr.

### TENNESSEE
**Chattanooga**
Bryan, Rosemarie Luise
**Nashville**
Blumstein, Andrée Kahn
Douse, Steven Carl
Riley, Steven Allen

### TEXAS
**Austin**
Stephen, John Erle
Sudarshan, Arvind Jewett
**Corpus Christi**
Evans, Allene Delories
**Dallas**
Beane, Jerry Lynn
Frisbie, Curtis Lynn, Jr.
Harrison, Orrin Lea, III
Hunt, Amy Katherine
Kearney, Douglas Charles
Kroemer, John Albert
Marquardt, Robert Richard
McAtee, David Ray
McGowan, Patrick Francis
McNamara, Anne H.
Miers, Harriet E.
Portman, Susan Newell
Price, John Aley
**Diboll**
Ericson, Roger Delwin
**Fort Worth**
Mack, Theodore
**Houston**
Barnett, Edward William
Brantley, John Randolph
Carter, John Loyd
Chavez, John Anthony
Cotton, James Alexendre
Devlin, Francis James
Dillon, Clifford Brien
Garten, David Burton
Irvine, Lynda Myska
Jaasma, Keith Duane
Lynch, John Edward, Jr.
Mai, Mark F.
McEvily, Daniel Vincent Sean
Owens, Betty Ruth
Reasoner, Harry Max
Schwartz, Charles Walter
Skoller, Ronald Aaron
Van Fleet, George Allan
**San Antonio**
Orr, Cynthia Hujar
Wachsmuth, Robert William

### UTAH
**Salt Lake City**
Holbrook, Donald Benson
Karrenberg, Thomas Richard
Lavitt, Kathy A.

### VIRGINIA
**Alexandria**
Fugate, Wilbur Lindsay
**Arlington**
Kelly, John James
**Manassas**
Mitchell, William Graham Champion
**Mc Lean**
Kennedy, Cornelius Bryant
Rau, Lee Arthur
**Norfolk**
Wooldridge, William Charles
**Richmond**
Carrell, Daniel Allan
Riopelle, Brian Charles
Walsh, James Hamilton

### WASHINGTON
**Seattle**
Gandara, Daniel
Gould, Ronald Murray
Gray, Marvin Lee, Jr.
Hough, Mark Mason
Ruddy, James W.
Sandler, Michael David
Van Kampen, Al
**Tacoma**
Malanca, Albert Robert

### WEST VIRGINIA
**Morgantown**
Fusco, Andrew G.

### WISCONSIN
**Marinette**
Anuta, Michael Joseph
**Milwaukee**
Kennedy, John Patrick
Levit, William Harold, Jr.
Martin, Quinn William
Wiley, Edwin Packard
**Wausau**
Haarmann, Bruce Donald

### TERRITORIES OF THE UNITED STATES

### PUERTO RICO
**San Juan**
Antonetti-Zequeira, Salvador

### ADDRESS UNPUBLISHED
Avery, James Thomas, III
Beukema, John Frederick
Blumenthal, William
Braun, Jerome Irwin
Davidson, Barry Rodney
Gass, Raymond William
Harris, Richard Eugene Vassau
Krivoshia, Eli, Jr.
Lea, Lorenzo Bates
Lecocke, Suzanne Elizabeth
McCobb, John Bradford, Jr.
Murchison, David Claudius
Newman, Carol L.
Pratt, Robert Windsor
Quillen, Cecil Dyer, Jr.
Serota, James Ian
Springer, Paul David
Stern, John Jules
Streicker, James Richard
Tapley, James Leroy
Tone, Philip Willis
Tubman, William Charles
Walker, Craig Michael

## APPELLATE

### UNITED STATES

### ALABAMA
**Montgomery**
Sanders-Cochran, Rachel Deanna
**Rainbow City**
Stover, Jay Elton

### ALASKA
**Anchorage**
Jensen, Jill Ellen

### ARIZONA
**Phoenix**
Doran, John Alan
Ulrich, Paul Graham
**Sierra Vista**
Borowiec, William Matthew
**Tucson**
Errico, Melissa
Lesher, Stephen Harrison

### ARKANSAS
**Fayetteville**
Kester, Charles Melvin

### CALIFORNIA
**Albany**
Chazin, Seth Paul
**Beverly Hills**
Amado, Honey Kessler
**Costa Mesa**
Putman, Philip A.
**El Segundo**
Blair, Janyce Keiko Imata
**Fresno**
Clegg, Trevor Clement
Wells, Gary B.
**Huntington Beach**
Guerin, John Joseph
**Irvine**
Dannemeyer, Bruce William
Hensley, William Michael
Toledano, James
**Laguna Hills**
Mathews, Stanton Terry
**Long Beach**
Tikosh, Mark Axente
**Los Angeles**
Barth, Karen Ann
Boydston, Brian D.
Coleman, Richard Michael
Horowitz, Edward Jay
Mc Adam, Patrick Michael
Mintz, Ronald Steven
Nordlinger, Stephanie G.
Pesta, Ben W., II
Scholtz, Kenneth P.
**Mill Valley**
Grantland, Brenda
**Novato**
Bien, Elliot Lewis
Cleek, Robert Joseph
**Oakland**
Leung, Jacqueline Jordan
**Pasadena**
Ashley-Farrand, Margalo
Link, James S.
**Pleasanton**
Elstead, John Clifton
**Redwood City**
Inama, Christopher Roy
**Sacramento**
Eickmeyer, Evan
Keiner, Christian Mark
**San Diego**
Curran, Michaela C.
McFall, James Alan
Mongan, Anthony David
Zakarin, Keith
**San Francisco**
Brantner, Paula Ann
Dryvynsyde, Geoffrey Beresford
Malcheski, Kim
Richmond, Diana
Seabolt, Richard L.
Utrecht, Paul F.
Wendell Hsu, Linda Sharon
**San Jose**
Simpson, Mary Kathleen
**San Rafael**
Roth, Hadden Wing
**Santa Barbara**
Fox, Herb
**Santa Monica**
Genego, William Joseph
Weatherup, Roy Garfield
**Santa Rosa**
Hillberg, Marylou Elin
**Van Nuys**
Imre, Christina Joanne
**Ventura**
Bray, Laurack Doyle

### COLORADO
**Denver**
Drake, Christopher Todd
Kahn, Benjamin Alexander
Krulewitch, Beth Lee
Low, Andrew M.
Nemiron, Ronald H.
Rhodes, Ralph Beauford
Sabey, Mark L.
Willett, Jonathan S.
**Englewood**
Campbell, Darrel Lee
**Thornton**
Liberman, David Israel

### CONNECTICUT
**Brookfield**
Secola, Joseph Paul
**New Haven**
Babbin, Jeffrey R.
Cox, Barbara Lynne
Geisler, Thomas Milton, Jr.

### DISTRICT OF COLUMBIA
**Washington**
Blume, Joshua Shai
Braga, Stephen Louis
Clark, Jeffrey Bossert
Cooper, Clement Theodore
Dowdey, Landon Gerald
Englert, Roy Theodore, Jr.
Gellhorn, Ernest Albert Eugene
Greenberger, I. Michael
Guy, Gary Edward
Kent, M. Elizabeth
Kissel, Peter Charles
Koontz, Glen Franklin
Loevinger, Lee
McGuire, Andrew Philip
McKinney, James DeVaine, Jr.
Miller, Nory
Moffitt, William Benjamin
Neurock, Mitchel
Odom, Thomas H.
Penn-Jenkins, Monique Lorae
Pierson, W. DeVier
Schafrick, Frederick Craig
Waite, Frederick Paul
Wasserman, Michael Francis

### FLORIDA
**Bartow**
Stevenson, Robin Howard

Sutton, Debra J.
**Clearwater**
Silberman, Morris
**Coral Gables**
Metcalfe, Olga
**Fort Lauderdale**
Bogenschutz, J. David
Hester, Julia A.
Lundt, Eric L.
Mitchell, Shelley Marie
Seligman, Guy Jaime
**Fort Myers**
Peet, Maria Lara
**Hollywood**
Tannen, Ricki Lewis
**Jacksonville**
Allen, William Lee
Korn, Michael Jeffrey
**Lakeland**
Senn, Stephen Russell
**Miami**
Berger, Steven R.
Blum, Bambi G.
Curtis, Karen Haynes
Eaton, Joel Douglas
Hauser, Helen Ann
Mehta, Eileen Rose
Rashkind, Paul Michael
Scherker, Elliot H.
Segor, Joseph Charles
Silvers, Marcia Jean
**N Miami Beach**
MacIvor, Catherine J.
**North Miami Beach**
Franklin, Barry Scott
**Ocala**
Crabtree, John Granville
**Orlando**
Hernandez, H(ermes) Manuel
Kehoe, Terrence Edward
Russ, James Matthias
**Palm Bch Gdns**
Cox, Jack Schramm
**Palm Beach Gardens**
Graham, Marjorie Gadarian
**Saint Pete Beach**
Milham, Julee Lynn
**Sarasota**
Garland, Richard Roger
Silverman, Susan Joy
**Spring Hill**
Shaw, Ray
**Tallahassee**
McNeely, Robert A.
Traynham, Jerry Glenn
**Tampa**
Carbone, Edward John
Castillo, Daniel L.
Pellett, Jon Michael
Steele, Rebecca Harrison
**West Palm Beach**
Kreusler-Walsh, Jane Ann
Spillias, Kenneth George

### GEORGIA

**Athens**
Byers, Rhonda Leann
Houser, Ronald Edward
**Atlanta**
Davies, Caleb, IV
Henwood, William Scott
**Columbus**
Hicks, Deron Ray
**Decatur**
Guest, Abbi Taylor

### ILLINOIS

**Belleville**
Hamilton, Harriet Homsher
**Chicago**
Anderson, Eric Daniel
Ellbogen, Andrew D.
Hoffa, Thomas Edward
Kroll, Barry Lewis
Leyhane, Francis John, III
Loew, Jonathan L.
Murphy-Petros, Melissa Aniela
Rappaport, Bret Andrew
Sarauskas, Paul Justas
Tenenbaum, J. Samuel
Van Demark, Ruth Elaine
**Columbia**
Gutknecht, Timothy Arthur
**Effingham**
Siemer, Martin W.
**Evanston**
DeWolfe, Ruthanne K. S.
**Minooka**
Lab, Charles Edward
**Oak Park**
Armstrong, Gene Lyndon
**Peoria**
Bell, Gregory S.
**Wheaton**
Stein, Lawrence A.
**Wilmette**
Lieberman, Eugene
Simon, Thelma Brook

### INDIANA

**Anderson**
Cage, Christopher Allen
**Indianapolis**
Arceneaux, Adam
Small, Mark Eugene
**Terre Haute**
Coleson, Richard Eugene

### IOWA

**Des Moines**
Finley, Kerry A.
Graziano, Craig Frank

### KENTUCKY

**Lexington**
Conner, Tonya Sue
**Louisville**
Clay, Richard H.C.
Morgan-White, Stephanie Lynn
**Providence**
Bock, Valerie L.

### LOUISIANA

**Baton Rouge**
Avant, Daniel L.
**Lafayette**
Morgan, Glenn L.
**Lake Charles**
Elliot, N. Frank
Miller, Frank C., III
**Leesville**
Smith, Simeon Christie, IV
**New Orleans**
Futrell, John Maurice
Grundmeyer, Douglas Lanaux
**Shreveport**
Hall, Pike, Jr.

### MARYLAND

**Abingdon**
Wolf, Martin Eugene
**Baltimore**
Howell, Harley Thomas
Wilson, Thomas Matthew, III

### MASSACHUSETTS

**Boston**
Drogin, Susan F.
Epstein, Elaine May
Gabovitch, William
Gaynor, Martin F., III
Glaser, Lenore Meryl
Honegger, Andrew Alan
Ritvo, Elizabeth Ann
**Cambridge**
Bowman, Judith Farris
**Salem**
Rogal, James London

### MICHIGAN

**Bloomfield Hills**
Hintzen, Erich Heinz
**Detroit**
Kostovski, Suzanna
Mengel, Christopher Emile
Walsh, James Joseph
**Southfield**
Jacobs, John Patrick
Tombers, Evelyn Charlotte

### MINNESOTA

**Minneapolis**
Anderson, Alan Marshall
Borger, John Philip
Miller, Michael Thomas
Williams, Maureen
**Saint Paul**
Pastoor, Maria K.
**Wayzata**
Geng, Thomas W.

### MISSISSIPPI

**Jackson**
Burkes, Jennifer Parkinson
Northington, Hiawatha
**Pascagoula**
Heidelberg, James Hinkle

### MISSOURI

**Kansas City**
Deacy, Thomas Edward, Jr.
Gaddy, William Brian
Larson, Thomas Roy
Paul, Richard Monroe, III
**Saint Louis**
Marks, Murry Aaron
Michenfelder, Albert A.
Newman, Charles A.
Schroeder, Mary Patricia

### NEVADA

**Carson City**
Johnson, Erik Reid
**Reno**
Cornell, Richard Farnham

### NEW HAMPSHIRE

**Manchester**
Cazden, Elizabeth
Middleton, Jack Baer

### NEW JERSEY

**Cherry Hill**
Fols, Stacy Alison
Spielberg, Joshua Morris
**Hackensack**
Rubenstein, Jay D.
**Lawrenceville**
Blumstein, Jeffrey Phillip
**Morristown**
Rich, Michael Louis
**Newark**
Brenner, John Finn
**Rocky Hill**
Console, Dale Elizabeth
**Tenafly**
Vort, Robert A.
**Weehawken**
Silber, Alan

### NEW YORK

**Albany**
Weiss, Leonard Arye
**Buffalo**
Isenberg, Andrew Brian
**Cape Vincent**
Stiefel, Linda Shields
**Garden City**
Yovino, Anthony
**Ithaca**
Pinnisi, Michael Donato
**Mineola**
Dachs, Jonathan A.
Wilson, George J.
**New York**
Axelrad, Alexis Sarah
Benakis, George James
Berger, Vivian Olivia
Boes, Lawrence William
Bondy, Joseph Aaron
Dean, Robert Stuart
Felder, Raoul Lionel
Kastner, Menachem J.
Landau, James Kenneth
Levy, Herbert Monte
Raab, Sheldon
Rogoff, Jeffrey Scott
Scialabba, Donald Joseph
Shear, Andrew Charles
Vogel, Michael Scott
Weinberg, Steven Lewis
Wu, Yolanda Sung
**Newburgh**
Mishkin, Kathleen Anne
**Pomona**
Fisch, Edith L.
**Rochester**
Affronti, Francis Christopher
Glickman, Philip S.
Regan, John Manning, Jr.
**Seneca Falls**
Porter, James Scott
**Syracuse**
Cirando, John Anthony
**White Plains**
D'Aloise, Lawrence T., Jr.

### NORTH CAROLINA

**Fayetteville**
Parish, James Riley
**Greensboro**
Carmack, Amie Flowers
**Wilmington**
Nunalee, Mary Margaret McEachern

### OHIO

**Cincinnati**
Hust, Bruce Kevin
**Cleveland**
Fitzgerald, Timothy John
Krueger, Jeffrey W.
Osborne, Frank R.
Spade, Eric F.
**Columbus**
Chappelear, Stephen Eric
Depascale, Diane Kappeler
Spencer, Scott W.
**Wellston**
Oths, Joseph Anthony

### OKLAHOMA

**Oklahoma City**
Callahan, Kelley Charles
**Tulsa**
Anderson, William Carl
Clark, Joseph Francis, Jr.
Crawford, B(urnett) Hayden
Morley, Randal Dean

### OREGON

**Portland**
Berger, Leland Roger
Cross, Daniel Albert
Darnall, Darleen R.
Gottlieb, Ira Leonard
Johnson, Mark Andrew
Shorr, Scott Alden

### PENNSYLVANIA

**Allentown**
Stevens, Timothy Towles
**Conway**
Krebs, Robert Alan
**Glenside**
Mermelstein, Jules Joshua
**Norristown**
Andrews, Cheri D.
**Philadelphia**
Adams, Arlin Marvin
Fennell, Daniel Joseph, II
Phillips, Dorothy Kay
Solano, Carl Anthony
Wittels, Barnaby Caesar
**Pittsburgh**
Greene, Korry Alden
Tucker, Richard Blackburn, III
**Reading**
Rethore, Kevin Watt

### RHODE ISLAND

**Providence**
Jones, Lauren Evans

### SOUTH CAROLINA

**Charleston**
Lady, James Edward

### TENNESSEE

**Nashville**
Cornell, Helen Loftin
Trent, John Thomas, Jr.

### TEXAS

**Austin**
Cloudt, Jim B.
Gammage, Robert Alton (Bob Gammage)
Heath, Claude Robert
Hicks, Renea
Saltmarsh, Sara Elizabeth
Schulze, Eric William
Sultan, Frederick William, IV
**Beaumont**
Cobb, Bruce Wayne
**College Station**
Kennady, Emmett Hubbard, III
**Corpus Christi**
Shackelford, Patricia Ann
**Dallas**
Blount, Charles William, III
Freytag, Sharon Nelson
Gegen, Theresa Mary
Goren, John Alan
Honea, Floyd Franklin
May, Michelle April
Pruessner, David Morgan
Robinson, Kimberly Marie
Rucker, R.D.
Sloman, Marvin Sherk
Zeiger, Timothy David
**El Paso**
Broaddus, John Morgan, III
Collins, William Coldwell
Hughes, Steven Lee
**Fort Worth**
Nelson, Edward Reese, III
Tatum, Stephen Lyle
**Galveston**
Vie, George William, III
**Houston**
Ailts, Evelyn Tonia
Beck, Lauren Lynn
Carver, Teresa Ann
Crews, Glenna England
Gilbert, Keith Thomas
Harris, Warren Wayne
Owens, Betty Ruth
Peddie, Collyn Ann
Rigby, Robert Glen
Van Kerrebrook, Mary Alice
**Mason**
Johnson, Rufus Winfield
**San Antonio**
Aoki, Zachary Burke
Higdon, James Noel
Orr, Cynthia Hujar
Richardson, Joel Glenn
**Sugar Land**
Clennan, John Joseph
**Tyler**
Thames, E. Glenn, Jr.
**Waco**
Mackenzie, Charles Alfred

### UTAH

**Salt Lake City**
Turner, Shawn Dennis

### VERMONT

**Montpelier**
Putter, David Seth
**Sharon**
Thrasher, John Edwin

### VIRGINIA

**Mc Lean**
Anthony, Joan Caton
Byrnes, William Joseph
Peet, Richard Clayton
**Richmond**
Nagle, David Edward
Spencer, Anthony George
**Spotsylvania**
Pugh, Randall Scott

### WASHINGTON

**Bellingham**
Buri, Philip James
**Seattle**
Brower, Joshua Christopher Allen
Cutler, Philip Edgerton
Goodnight, David R.
Novotny, Patricia Susan
Roche, Robert Joseph
Rummage, Stephen Michael

### WISCONSIN

**Madison**
Heffernan, Michael Stewart
Provis, Timothy Alan
**West Allis**
Redding, Joseph E.

### WYOMING

**Cheyenne**
Scorsine, John Magnus
**Jackson**
Noble, Heather

### ADDRESS UNPUBLISHED

Albin, Barry G.
Arencibia, Raul Antonio
Beasley, James W., Jr.
Berger, Marc Joseph
Beukema, John Frederick
DeLaFuente, Charles
Kittrell, Pamela R.
Logan, James Kenneth
Markle, Robert
Mugridge, David Raymond
Newman, Carol L.
O'Connor, Kathleen Mary
O'Dell, Joan Elizabeth
Ostergaard, Joni Hammersla
Pagano, Eugene Salvatore Rooney
Pannill, William Presley
Rench, Stephen Charles
Siemon, Joyce Marilyn
Vinar, Benjamin

## AVIATION

### UNITED STATES

### ALABAMA

**Birmingham**
DeGaris, Annesley Hodges
**Mobile**
Roedder, William Chapman, Jr.

### ALASKA

**Anchorage**
Powell, James M.
Wagstaff, Robert Hall

### ARIZONA

**Phoenix**
Brewer, John Brian
Toone, Thomas Lee
**Tucson**
McNeill, Frederick Wallace

### ARKANSAS

**Little Rock**
Bohannon, Charles Tad

### CALIFORNIA

**Cambria**
Stotter, James, II
**Laguna Hills**
Mathews, Stanton Terry
**Long Beach**
Behar, Jeffrey Steven
Johnson, Philip Leslie
**Los Angeles**
Aristei, J. Clark
Downey, William J., III
Foley, Martin James
Greaves, John Allen
Hedlund, Paul James
Pascotto, Alvaro
Steinbrecher, Alan K.
**Monterey**
Bomberger, Russell Branson
**Pleasanton**
Elstead, John Clifton
**Redwood City**
Coddington, Clinton Hays
**San Francisco**
Truett, Harold Joseph, III (Tim Truett)
**San Mateo**
Dworkin, Michael Leonard
**San Rafael**
Axelrod, Peter
**Santa Cruz**
Damon, Richard Everett
**Santa Monica**
Bower, Allan Maxwell
Hofer, Stephen Robert
McGovern, David Carr

### COLORADO

**Denver**
Byrne, Thomas J.

### CONNECTICUT

**East Hartford**
Kerrigan, Vanessa Griffith
**Hartford**
Karpe, Brian Stanley
**Stratford**
McDonough, Sandra Martin

### DISTRICT OF COLUMBIA

**Washington**
Broadus, Charlsa Dorsantres
Cobbs, Nicholas Hammer
Devall, James Lee
Johnson, Richard Tenney
Littell, Richard Gregory
Mendelsohn, Allan Irving
Pogue, L(loyd) Welch
Roberts, Michael James
Schafrick, Frederick Craig
Trinder, Rachel Bandele
Wilder, William Randell
Wray, Robert
Yodice, John S.

### FLORIDA

**Coral Gables**
Hoffman, Carl H(enry)
**Daytona Beach**
Hassell, Frank Bradley, Sr.
**Deerfield Beach**
Daugherty, Walter Emory
**Jupiter**
Mallory, Earl K.
**Melbourne**
Trachtman, Jerry H.
**Miami**
Andrews, Mary Ruth
Avera, Troy G., Jr.
Becerra, Robert John
Marks, Steven Craig
Podhurst, Aaron Samuel
**Ocala**
Sommer, Robert George
**Saint Petersburg**
Pedata, Martin Anthony

### GEORGIA

**Atlanta**
Harkey, Robert Shelton
Strauss, Robert David
**Tucker**
Armstrong, Edwin Alan

### HAWAII

**Honolulu**
Char, Vernon Fook Leong
Moore, Willson Carr, Jr.

### IDAHO

**Boise**
Furey, Patrick Dennis

### ILLINOIS

**Chicago**
Adler, John William, Jr.
Collins, Glenn
Cunningham, Craig Carnell
Durkin, Albert Eugene
Geiman, J. Robert
Goodman, Ann Paton

Graber, Patrick Matthew
Kennelly, John Jerome
McCabe, Charles Kevin
Pullano, Richard L.
Rapoport, David E.
Sundvall, Sheila A.

**Rosemont**
Richter, Paul David

### LOUISIANA

**Lafayette**
Keaty, Robert Burke

**Metairie**
Ellefson, Vance E.

### MARYLAND

**Baltimore**
Ferguson, Robert L., Jr.

### MASSACHUSETTS

**Boston**
Sarrouf, Camille Francis

### MICHIGAN

**East Lansing**
Joseph, Raymond

**Farmington**
Torpey, Scott Raymond

**Springport**
McKay, M. Dale

### MINNESOTA

**Saint Paul**
Levinson, Kenneth S.

### MISSISSIPPI

**Jackson**
Ferrell, Wayne Edward, Jr.

### NEVADA

**Reno**
Hibbs, Loyal Robert

### NEW HAMPSHIRE

**Keene**
Heed, Peter W.

### NEW JERSEY

**Princeton**
Brennan, William Joseph, III

### NEW MEXICO

**Albuquerque**
Dorr, Roderick A.

**Questa**
Lamb, Margaret Weldon

### NEW YORK

**Buffalo**
Ross, Christopher Theodore

**Garrison**
Donnelly, Daniel Patrick

**New York**
Adler, Charles David
Barry, Desmond Thomas, Jr.
Bowers, William Charles
Clemen, John Douglas
Furniss, Peter Glenn
Mentz, Lawrence
Nordquist, Stephen Glos
Pantelopoulos, Nicholas Evan
Perrone, Joseph Joseph
Stefano, Joseph M.

### NORTH CAROLINA

**Chapel Hill**
Zoffer, David B.

**Charlotte**
Gordon, David Stott

### NORTH DAKOTA

**Crosby**
Forsgren, F. Leslie

**Fargo**
Solberg, Wayne O.

### OHIO

**Cleveland**
Schloss, John P.

**Warren**
Keating, Daniel Gerard

### OREGON

**Astoria**
Haskell, Donald McMillan

**Portland**
DeChaine, Dean Dennis

### PENNSYLVANIA

**Chadds Ford**
Lamonaca, Joseph Michael

**Philadelphia**
Heintz, Paul Capron

**Valley Forge**
Corchin, Mark Alan

### SOUTH CAROLINA

**Greenville**
Phillips, Joseph Brantley, Jr.

### TENNESSEE

**Knoxville**
Arnett, Foster Deaver

**Nashville**
Dundon, Thomas H.

### TEXAS

**Austin**
Byrd, Linward Tonnett
Furman, James Housley
Gibbins, Bob
Papadakis, Myron Philip

**Dallas**
Fitzmaurice, Edward Joseph, Jr.
Howie, John Robert
Parker, James Francis

**Fort Worth**
Sheehan, Edward Michael

**Houston**
Rigby, Robert Glen

**Lindale**
Anderson, Lawrence Worthington

**San Antonio**
Guess, James David

### UTAH

**Salt Lake City**
Young, Robert Sherman

### VERMONT

**Shelburne**
Kurrelmeyer, Louis Hayner

### VIRGINIA

**Falls Church**
Van Oeveren, Edward Lanier

**Norfolk**
Bishop, Bruce Taylor

### WASHINGTON

**Seattle**
Walters, Dennis H.
Williams, J. Vernon

### WEST VIRGINIA

**Charleston**
Heiskell, Edgar Frank, III

### WISCONSIN

**Marinette**
Anuta, Michael Joseph

**Milwaukee**
Gray, Sidney

### ADDRESS UNPUBLISHED

Bailey, Francis Lee
Dubuc, Carroll Edward
O'Connor, Kathleen Mary
Wallach, Steven Ernst

---

## BANKING. *See also* Commercial.

---

### UNITED STATES

### ALABAMA

**Birmingham**
Brooke, William Wade
Davis, Timothy Donald
Greenwood, P. Nicholas
Maynard, George Fleming

**Mobile**
Lott, Victor H., Jr.

**Montgomery**
Waters, Michael D.

### ARIZONA

**Oro Valley**
Robinson, Bernard Leo

**Phoenix**
Craig, Laurie Baker
Dunipace, Ian Douglas

### ARKANSAS

**Conway**
Brazil, William Clay

**Little Rock**
Jiles, Gary D.

**Pine Bluff**
Strode, Joseph Arlin

### CALIFORNIA

**Carlsbad**
Kelsall, Samuel, V

**Downey**
Bear, Henry Louis

**Los Angeles**
Biele, Hugh Irving
Clark, R(ufus) Bradbury
Farrar, Stanley F.
Francis, Merrill Richard
Fredman, Howard S
Geiger, Roy Stephen
Gyemant, Robert Ernest
Ibekwe, Edebeatu
Levine, Thomas Jeffrey Pello
Marcus, Stephen Howard
Millard, Neal Steven
Miller, Craig Dana
Morgenthaler, Alisa Marie
Share, Richard Hudson
Thoren-Peden, Deborah Suzanne
Weg, Howard Jay
Weinman, Glenn Alan

**Menlo Park**
Crandall, Nelson David, III

**Pasadena**
Linstedt, Walter Griffiths
Logan, Francis Dummer

**Pomona**
Lunsford, Jeanne Denise

**San Diego**
Shippey, Sandra Lee

**San Francisco**
Block, David Jeffrey
Casillas, Mark
Faye, Richard Brent
Haley, Peter C.
Halloran, Michael James
Shepherd, John Michael
Smith, Robert Michael
Stroup, Stanley Stephenson

**Santa Barbara**
Cappello, A. Barry

### COLORADO

**Denver**
Jacobs, Ronald Hedstrom
Moye, John Edward
Otten, Arthur Edward, Jr.
Stockmar, Ted P.

**Fort Collins**
Gast, Richard Shaeffer
Rogers, Garth Winfield

**Littleton**
Keely, George Clayton

### CONNECTICUT

**Glastonbury**
Schroth, Peter W(illiam)

**Hartford**
Bouton, William Wells, III
Lotstein, James Irving
Rome, Donald Lee

**New Haven**
Craig, William Emerson

**Stamford**
Padilla, James Earl
Rose, Richard Loomis

**Waterbury**
Wolfe, Harriet Munrett

**Westport**
Burns, Paul Edward

### DELAWARE

**Claymont**
Rollins, Gene A.

**Dover**
Twilley, Joshua Marion

**Wilmington**
Salinger, Frank Max

### DISTRICT OF COLUMBIA

**Washington**
Adams, Lee Stephen
Bellinger, John Bellinger, III
Bruemmer, Russell John
Clark, Paul Thomas
Cope, John R(obert)
Cumberland, William Edwin
Daly, Joseph Patrick
Debevoise, Eli Whitney, II
Dennis, Warren Lewis
Dolan, Edward Charles
Gonzalez, Edward
Hanas, Stephen Michael
Helfer, Michael Stevens
Horn, Charles M.
Hyde, Howard Laurence
Kaufman, Thomas Frederick
Klein, Michael Roger
Lehr, Dennis James
Leibold, Arthur William, Jr.
Levenson, Alan Bradley
Lucas, Steven Mitchell
Lybecker, Martin Earl
More, John Herron
Murphy, Sean Patrick
Overman, Dean Lee
Policy, Vincent Mark
Rainbolt, John Vernon, II
Roderer, David William
Smith, Brian William
Timmer, Barbara
Weinstein, Harris
Weiss, Mark Anschel
Wolff, Paul Martin

### FLORIDA

**Altamonte Springs**
Hoogland, Robert Frederics
Rudisill, Robert Mack, Jr.

**Coconut Grove**
Arboleya, Carlos Joaquin

**Fort Lauderdale**
Heidgerd, Frederick Cay

**Fort Myers**
Harrison, Simon M.

**Jacksonville**
Christian, Gary Irvin
Hodge, James Edward
Kent, John Bradford
Sadler, Luther Fuller, Jr.

**Jasper**
McCormick, John Hoyle

**Key West**
Smith, Wayne LaRue

**Miami**
Berley, David Richard
Coffey, Kendall Brindley
Garrett, Richard G.
Landy, Burton Aaron
Miller, James M.
Muñiz, Nicolas Jose
Murai, Rene Vicente
Paul, Robert
Roddenberry, Stephen Keith
Stanley, Sherry A.

**Naples**
Bornmann, Carl Malcolm
Gebhardt, Robert Charles

**North Palm Beach**
Koffler, Warren William

**Orlando**
Christiansen, Patrick T.
Higgins, Robert Frederick
Jontz, Jeffry Robert
Yates, Leighton Delevan, Jr.

**Palm Beach**
Grogan, Robert Harris

**Panama City**
Byrne, Robert William

**Plantation**
Buck, Thomas Randolph

**Saint Petersburg**
Harrell, Roy G., Jr.
Lyman, Curtis Lee, Jr.

**Sarasota**
Walters, Joel W.

**Tampa**
Gardner, J. Stephen
McBride, William Howard, Jr.
Roberson, Bruce H.

**West Palm Beach**
James, Keith Alan

**Winter Park**
Hadley, Ralph Vincent, III

### GEORGIA

**Atlanta**
Baker, Anita Diane
Barker, Clayton Robert, III
Carpenter, David Allan
Collins, Steven M.
Cornwell, William John
Crews, William Edwin
Dobbs, C. Edward
Johnson, Benjamin F(ranklin), III
Kessler, Richard Paul, Jr.
Moeling, Walter Goos, IV
Scibilia, Joseph Logan
Sibley, James Malcolm

**Canton**
Hasty, William Grady, Jr.

**Cuthbert**
Bowles, Jesse Groover

**Gainesville**
Gilliam, Steven Philip, Sr.

**Norcross**
Morochnik, Paul J.

**Savannah**
Shawe, Mark Thackeray

**Zebulon**
Watson, Forrest Albert, Jr.

### HAWAII

**Honolulu**
Lau, Jeffrey Daniel
Mirikitani, Richard Kiyoshi
Nakata, Gary Kenji
Okinaga, Lawrence Shoji
Wong, Reuben Sun Fai

### ILLINOIS

**Bloomington**
Stevens, John Nickless

**Chicago**
Anderson, Eric Daniel
Baker, Bruce Jay
Bridewell, David Alexander
Burke, Edmund Patrick, Sr.
Burke, Richard William
Cohen, Melanie Rovner
Conlon, Steven Denis
Duric, Nicholas M.
Field, Robert Edward
Franklin, Christine Carroll
Hanson, Ronald William
Hurwitz, Joel Michael
Jacobson, Ronald H.
Jock, Paul F., II
Kaufman, Andrew Michael
Kohn, William Irwin
Lind, Jon Robert
Malkin, Cary Jay
McCrohon, Craig
Prochnow, Herbert Victor, Jr.
Reum, James Michael

**Deerfield**
Bartlett, Robert William

**Du Quoin**
Atkins, Aaron Ardene

**Gurnee**
Southern, Robert Allen

**Highland Park**
Tabin, Seymour

**Hoffman Estates**
Kelly, Anastasia Donovan

**Marengo**
Franks, Herbert Hoover

**Springfield**
Walbaum, Robert C.

**Watseka**
Tungate, James Lester

**Wheaton**
Stein, Lawrence A.

### INDIANA

**Fowler**
Kepner, Rex William

**Indianapolis**
Kleiman, Mary Margaret
Talesnick, Stanley
Welch, William

**Lagrange**
Schultess, LeRoy Kenneth

### IOWA

**Davenport**
Skora, Susan Sundman

**Iowa City**
Downer, Robert Nelson

### KANSAS

**Coffeyville**
Kirby, William Roy

**Overland Park**
Butler, James Glenn, Jr.
Cohen, Barton Pollock

### KENTUCKY

**Benton**
Johnson, Martin Wolfe

**Bowling Green**
Catron, Stephen Barnard
Goad, Frank Roark

**Glasgow**
Gardner, Woodford Lloyd, Jr.

**Lexington**
Byrne, Walter Robbins, Jr.
McClelland, Denise H.
Scott, Joseph Mitchell, Jr.

**Louisville**
Fenton, Thomas Conner
Maggiolo, Allison Joseph

### LOUISIANA

**Baton Rouge**
Cutshaw, James Michael

**Farmerville**
Earle, Robert Ray

**New Orleans**
Butler, Peter Joseph
McMillan, Lee Richards, II

**Shreveport**
Cox, John Thomas, Jr.

### MAINE

**Portland**
Hirshon, Robert Edward

**Yarmouth**
Webster, Peter Bridgman

### MARYLAND

**Annapolis**
Michaelson, Benjamin, Jr.

**Baltimore**
Haines, Thomas W. W.
Wasserman, Richard Leo

**Bethesda**
Chapman, Gerald Frederick

**Ellicott City**
McElroy, David Carleton

**Kensington**
Mathias, Joseph Marshall

**New Market**
Gabriel, Eberhard John

**Potomac**
Gingold, Dennis Marc

**Rockville**
Kochanski, David Majlech

### MASSACHUSETTS

**Arlington**
Keshian, Richard

**Boston**
Ayoub, Paul Joseph
Blumenreich, Gene Arnold
Bornheimer, Allen Millard
Cherwin, Joel Ira
Coukos, Stephen John
Fischer, Eric Robert
Kyle, Amy Lynn
Loria, Martin A.
McDonald, John Barry, Jr.
O'Brien, Duncan Thomas
Parker, Christopher William
Read, Nicholas Cary
Smith, Edwin Eric
Van, Peter

**Framingham**
Gatlin, Michael Gerard

**Greenfield**
Blanker, Alan Harlow

**Lincoln**
Gnichtel, William Van Orden

**Worcester**
Baldiga, Joseph Hilding

### MICHIGAN

**Ann Arbor**
Fineman, Gary Lee

**Detroit**
Callahan, John William (Bill Callahan)
Lardner, Cynthia Marie-Martinovich
Lawrence, John Kidder
Rohr, Richard David
Targan, Holli Hart
Williams, J. Bryan

**Kalamazoo**
Gordon, Edgar George

**Muskegon**
Fauri, Eric Joseph

### MINNESOTA

**Duluth**
Nys, John Nikki

**Eden Prairie**
Nilles, John Michael

**Fridley**
Savelkoul, Donald Charles

**Minneapolis**
Leonard, Brian Francis

**Saint Paul**
Winthrop, Sherman

### MISSISSIPPI

**Clarksdale**
Chaffin, William Michael

**Gulfport**
Harral, John Menteith

**Jackson**
Allen, Leigh Briscoe, III
Barnett, Robert Glenn
Hammond, Frank Jefferson, III

### MISSOURI

**Hannibal**
Welch, Joseph Daniel

**Kansas City**
Ayers, Jeffrey David
Bevan, Robert Lewis
Deacy, Thomas Edward, Jr.
Dolson, Edward M.
Frisbie, Charles
Graham, Harold Steven
Miller, Richard William

**Macon**
Parkinson, Paul K.

**Saint Louis**
DeHaven, Michael Allen
Graham, Robert Clare, III
Inkley, John James, Jr.
McNearney, John Patrick
Poscover, Maury B.
Willard, Gregory Dale

### MONTANA

**Kalispell**
Robinson, Calvin Stanford

**Missoula**
Bender, Ronald Andrew

**Ronan**
Grainey, Philip J.

**NEBRASKA**

**Lincoln**
Guthery, John M.
Perry, Edwin Charles
**Omaha**
Bracht, David Leo
Hamann, Deryl Frederick
**Valentine**
O'Kief, W. Gerald

**NEVADA**

**Las Vegas**
Eisner, Elliott Roy

**NEW HAMPSHIRE**

**Manchester**
Stebbins, Henry Blanchard

**NEW JERSEY**

**Atlantic City**
Feinberg, Jack
**Bernardsville**
Maher, Gary Laurence
**Bridgewater**
Kosten, Jeffrey Thomas
**East Brunswick**
Cosner, Alan G.
**Linwood**
Frisch, David Bruce
**Montvale**
Beattie, James Raymond
**Morristown**
Kandravy, John
O'Grady, Dennis Joseph
**Newark**
Radin, Steven S.
**Princeton**
Beimfohr, Douglas Alan
Szwalbenest, Benedykt Jan
**Red Bank**
Barnes, Bray B.
DuPont, Michael Richard
Rogers, Lee Jasper
**Roseland**
McMahon, Edward Richard
Wovsaniker, Alan
**Summit**
Woller, James Alan
**Trenton**
Frost, Barry Warren
**Union**
Greenstein, Richard Henry
**Verona**
Tobia, Ronald Lawrence
**Wayne**
Long, Lucinda Parshall
**Woodbridge**
Hoberman, Stuart A.

**NEW MEXICO**

**Albuquerque**
Threet, Martin Edwin
Ussery, Albert Travis
**Clovis**
Skarda, Lynell Griffith
**Farmington**
Echols, Douglas Allen

**NEW YORK**

**Bronxville**
Veneruso, James John
**Brooklyn**
Kelleher, Terence L.
Rice, Thomas O'Connor
**Buffalo**
Struble, Michelle Leigh
**Clifton Park**
Hayes, Norman Robert, Jr.
**Garden City**
Bishar, John Joseph, Jr.
Golden, Christopher Anthony
Licatesi, Anthony Joseph
Tucker, William P.
**Hudson**
Howard, Andrew Baker
**Larchmont**
Berridge, George Bradford
**Le Roy**
Whiting, Reid A.
**Long Island City**
Wanderman, Susan Mae
**Lowville**
Snyder, Donald Edward, Jr.
**Mount Kisco**
Edelstein, Peter Michael
**New York**
Armstrong, James Sinclair
Bergan, Philip James
Bernstein, Donald Scott
Boynton, James Stephen
Broude, Mark Allen
Bruenner, Eric William
Caytas, Ivo George
Chen, Wesley
Christenfeld, Alan M.
Cohen, Henry Rodgin
Colleran, Robert T.
Corbin, Sol Neil
Das, Kalyan
De Leon, Albert Vernon
Diamond, Joseph
Fawer, Mark S.
Fernandez, Jose Walfredo
Fewell, Charles Kenneth, Jr.
Garber, Robert Edward
Garfinkel, Neil B.
Genova, Diane Melisano
Ginsberg, Ernest
Gooch, Anthony Cushing
Greene, Ira S.
Grew, Robert Ralph
Gross, Richard Benjamin
Guynn, Randall David
Hauser, Rita Eleanore Abrams
Higgs, John H.
Hill, Joseph C.
Jong, James C. (Chuanping Zhang)
Junius, Andreas Gretus
Kelly, Thomas Michael
Knight, Townsend Jones
Kraemer, Lillian Elizabeth
Krivoy, Clara
Lane, Arthur Alan
Lee, In-Young
Lee, Robert Edward, Jr.
Lindauer, Erik D.
Lindsay, George Peter
Lynch, Luke Daniel, Jr.
MacRae, Cameron Farquhar, III
Maney, Michael Mason
Markel, Gregory Arthur
Mavrides, Michael Fotios
McDavid, William Henry
Miller, Neil Scott
Minsky, Bruce William
Myerson, Toby Salter
Nissenbaum, David
Nocera, John Anthony
O'Connor, William Matthew
Phillips, Pamela Kim
Pollack, Stanley P.
Prentice, Eugene Miles, III
Quale, Andrew Christopher, Jr.
Quillen, Cecil Dyer, III
Quinn, Linda C.
Rachlin, Leila
Radon, Jenik Richard
Ring, Renee Etheline
Robinson, Irwin Jay
Rocklen, Kathy Hellenbrand
Rosenblum, William F., Jr.
Ross, Michael Aaron
Russo, Thomas Anthony
Schleimer, Karen Beth
Schwab, Terrance W.
Semaya, Francine Levitt
Setrakian, Berge
Sheehan, Robert C.
Spencer, David Eric
Thaler, Craig H.
Toumey, Donald Joseph
Trott, Dennis C(harles)
Wiseman, Michael Martin
Wolfe, James Ronald
Worley, Robert William, Jr.
Yu, Sandy Kyung
Zaitzeff, Roger Michael
Zimmerman, Jean
**Rochester**
Brown, Peter Ogden
Galbraith, Robert Lyell, Jr.
Groschadl, Paul Stephen
Lundback, Staffan Bengt Gunnar
Willett, Thomas Edward
Young, Deborah Schwind
**Staten Island**
Hall, John George
**Syracuse**
Ackerman, Kenneth Edward
Barclay, H(ugh) Douglas
Hubbard, Peter Lawrence
**White Plains**
Serchuk, Ivan

**NORTH CAROLINA**

**Charlotte**
Bryce, Teresa Audrey
Bush, F. Brad
McDermott, Christopher Manning
Taylor, David Brooke
Walls, George Rodney
**Greensboro**
Davis, Herbert Owen
**Murphy**
Bata, Rudolph Andrew, Jr.
**Raleigh**
Carlton, Alfred Pershing, Jr.
Jernigan, John Lee
**Wilmington**
Jones, Lucian Cox
Kaufman, James Jay
McCauley, Cleyburn Lycurgus
**Winston Salem**
Herring, Jerone Carson
Loughridge, John Halsted, Jr.

**OHIO**

**Cincinnati**
Coffey, Thomas William
Rubin, Robert Samuel
**Cleveland**
Chilcote, Lee A.
Lawniczak, James Michael
Lear, S. Michael
Owendoff, Stephen Peter
Singerman, Paul Joseph
Stevens, Thomas Charles
**Columbus**
Deal, John Charles
Frasier, Ralph Kennedy
Fultz, Robert Edward
Pigman, Jack Richard
**Dayton**
McSwiney, Charles Ronald
**Dublin**
Bennett, Steven Alan
**Hamilton**
Meyers, Pamela Sue
**Rocky River**
Grady, Francis Xavier
**Springfield**
Pedraza, Miguel A., Jr.
**Troy**
Utrecht, James David
**Upper Sandusky**
Fox, Mary Ellen
**Warren**
McGeough, Robert Saunders

**OKLAHOMA**

**Jones**
Dean, Bill Verlin, Jr.
**Kingfisher**
Logsdon, Harold L.
**Muskogee**
Robinson, Adelbert Carl
**Oklahoma City**
Beech, Johnny Gale
Britton, James Edward
Elder, James Carl
Kenney, Herbert King
Leeviraphan, Americ (Eric Leeviraphan)
Wilson, Julia Ann Yother

**OREGON**

**Lake Oswego**
Byczynski, Edward Frank
**Portland**
Rasmussen, Richard Robert

**PENNSYLVANIA**

**Allison Park**
Ries, William Campbell
**Erie**
Mosier, David Michael
**Exton**
Teti, Louis N.
**King Of Prussia**
Beausang, Michael Francis, Jr.
**Morrisville**
Golding, Gilbert James
**New Castle**
Palmer, Allen L.
**Philadelphia**
Auten, David Charles
Barnum, Jeanne Schubert
Berger, Lawrence Howard
De Simone, Dominic J.
Doran, William Michael
Esser, Carl Eric
Genkin, Barry Howard
Hunter, James Austen, Jr.
Loveless, George Group
Maxey, David Walker
**Pittsburgh**
Bleier, Michael E.
Chamberlain, Denise Kay
Dell, Ernest Robert
Gold, Harold Arthur
Messner, Robert Thomas
Todd, Thomas
**Reading**
Kline, Sidney DeLong, Jr.
**Scranton**
Henkelman, Willard Max
**Warren**
Ristau, Mark Moody
**Washington**
Posner, David S.
**Williamsport**
Holland, Fred Anthony
Knecht, William L.

**RHODE ISLAND**

**Providence**
Furness, Peter John
McGowan, Matthew J.
**Warwick**
Gazerro, G. John, Jr.

**SOUTH CAROLINA**

**Charleston**
Warren, John Hertz, III
**Columbia**
Currin, Robert Graves, Jr.
Johnson, Lawrence Wilbur, Jr.
**Hartsville**
DeLoach, Harris E(ugene), Jr.
**Myrtle Beach**
Barnett, Michael James

**TENNESSEE**

**Chattanooga**
Edge, Kathryn Reed
**Memphis**
Walsh, Thomas James, Jr.
**Nashville**
Eisen, Steven Jeffrey
Farris, Frank Mitchell, Jr.

**TEXAS**

**Austin**
Bauer, Sydney Meade
**Brownsville**
Fleming, Tommy Wayne
**Bryan**
Bond, Randall Scott
Strong, Stephen Andrew
**Carthage**
Dowd, Steven Milton
**Cat Spring**
Conner, Warren Wesley
**Dallas**
Barlow, W. P., Jr.
Beuttenmuller, Rudolf William
Bishop, Bryan Edwards
Freedman, Randall Lee
Harvey, James Clement
Kearney, Douglas Charles
Laves, Alan Leonard
True, Roy Joe
White, James Richard
Zisman, Barry Stuart
**Fort Worth**
Ratliff, William D., III
**Houston**
Block, Nelson R(ichard)
Bridges, David Manning
Judice, Kenneth R.
Mark, Daniel Lee
Melamed, Richard
Miller, Robert Daniel
Orton, John Stewart
Stuart, Walter Bynum, IV
**Hurst**
Casey, David Robert
**La Porte**
Askins, Knox Winfred
**Liberty**
Wheat, John Nixon
**Marshall**
Gilstrap, James Rodney
**Midland**
Truitt, Robert Ralph, Jr.
**Panhandle**
Neal, A. Curtis
**Plainview**
Lafont, William Harold
**Richardson**
Olson, Dennis Oliver
**San Antonio**
Young, Jess Wollett
**Sherman**
Freels, Jesse Saunders, Jr.
**Spring**
Hagerman, John David
**Tyler**
Lake, David Alan
**Weslaco**
Pomerantz, Jerald Michael

**UTAH**

**Saint George**
Gallian, Russell Joseph
**Salt Lake City**
Kent, Dale R.

**VERMONT**

**Brattleboro**
Dunn, David Norman

**VIRGINIA**

**Alexandria**
Elsberg, David Donald
**Charlottesville**
Hodous, Robert Power
**Falls Church**
Christman, Bruce Lee
Jennings, Thomas Parks
**Mc Lean**
Toole, John Harper
Walton, Edmund Lewis, Jr.
**Norfolk**
Stackhouse, Robert Clinton
**Richmond**
Buford, Robert Pegram
Jones, Reginald Nash
Northup, Stephen A.
Rainey, Gordon Fryer, Jr.
**Roanoke**
Densmore, Douglas Warren
**Sterling**
McBarnette, Bruce Olvin

**WASHINGTON**

**Seattle**
Kuhrau, Edward W.
Mucklestone, Peter John
Tune, James Fulcher

**WEST VIRGINIA**

**Huntington**
McGuire, J(ames) Grant
**New Martinsville**
Hill, Philip Bonner
**Wheeling**
Gardill, James Clark

**WISCONSIN**

**Appleton**
Hartzheim, Charles John
**Madison**
Petershack, Richard Eugene
Shea, Jeremy Charles
**Milwaukee**
Adashek, James Lewis
Friedman, James Dennis
Wiley, Edwin Packard
**Monroe**
Ewald, Rex Alan
**Pewaukee**
Engel, John Charles
**Racine**
Dye, William Ellsworth
**Sun Prairie**
Eustice, Francis Joseph

**WYOMING**

**Casper**
Lowe, Robert Stanley
**Cheyenne**
Dyekman, Gregory Chris

**TERRITORIES OF THE UNITED STATES**

**PUERTO RICO**

**San Juan**
Vallone, Ralph, Jr.

**ENGLAND**

**London**
Brownwood, David Owen

**ADDRESS UNPUBLISHED**

Carmody, Richard Patrick
Cherney, Andrew Knox
Cion, Judith Ann
Crook, Donald Martin
Forst, John Kelly
Freeman, Russell Adams
Funnell, Kevin Joseph
Hanson, Fred B.
Harman, Wallace Patrick
Holloway, Hiliary Hamilton
Jacobs, Alan
Johnson, Leonard Hjalma
Jolley, R. Gardner
Long, Charles Thomas
Marker, Marc Linthacum
Riddle, Michael Lee
Rohrer, George John
Rounsaville, Guy, Jr.
Shambaugh, Stephen Ward
Skal, Debra Lynn
Watson, John Michael
Weil, Peter Henry
Yellin, Melvin A.

## BANKRUPTCY. *See also* Commercial.

**UNITED STATES**

**ALABAMA**

**Birmingham**
Benton, Lee Rimes
Dortch, Clarence, III
Stuckenschneider, James Theodore, II
**Enterprise**
Price, Robert Allan
**Huntsville**
Baxter, James Thomas, III
Blair, Edward Eugene
Burton, Hilary Coleman
**Tuscaloosa**
Crain, Annette Brashier

**ALASKA**

**Anchorage**
Johnson, Brent Allen
Willard-Jones, Donna C.

**ARIZONA**

**Flagstaff**
Cowser, Danny Lee
**Phoenix**
Chenal, Thomas Kevin
Hover, John Charles
Lee, Richard H(arlo)
Norris, Benjamin R.
**Tempe**
Palmer, Janice Maude
**Tucson**
Polan, David Jay

**ARKANSAS**

**Camden**
Ives, Daniel Delbert
**Corning**
Manatt, Scott
**Fayetteville**
Nobles, Ethan Christopher
Stacy, Burton E., Jr.
**Fort Smith**
Foster, M. Shannon
**Harrison**
Inman-Campbell, Gail
**Little Rock**
Hughes, Steven Jay
**Searcy**
Hughes, Teresa Lee

**CALIFORNIA**

**Anaheim**
Fleming, Richard Alfred
**Bakersfield**
Gardner, D. Max
**Carpinteria**
Kump, Kary Ronald
**Chino Hills**
Radcliffe, William Louis
**Downey**
Schauf, Carolyn Jane
**El Cajon**
Graf, Sheryl Susan
**Encinitas**
Williams, Michael Edward
**Encino**
Kent, Thomas Edward
**Fresno**
Clegg, Trevor Clement
**La Crescenta**
McNally, Gerald, Jr.
**Los Angeles**
Biele, Hugh Irving
Brickwood, Susan Callaghan
Cohen, Cynthia Marylyn
Davidson, Jeffrey H.
Francis, Merrill Richard
Gilhuly, Peter Martin
Gubner, Adam Lance
Gyemant, Robert Ernest
Huben, Brian David
Kessler, Joan Blumenstein
Leibow, Ronald Louis
Maizel, Samuel Ruven
Merola, Frank A.
Roney, John Harvey
Samuels, Joel Gregory
Sands, Velma Ahda
Weg, Howard Jay
Zerunyan, Frank Vram
**Modesto**
Leong, Linda S.
**Newport Beach**
Molseed, Michael Clyde
Wolf, Alan Steven
**Oakland**
Allen, Jeffrey Michael
Mannis, Estelle Claire
**Orangevale**
King, Franklin Weaver
**Palm Springs**
Parry, Paul Stewart
**Palo Alto**
Kent, Edward Angle, Jr.
**Pasadena**
Katzman, Harvey Lawrence
**Pleasanton**
Opperwall, Stephen Gabriel
**Sacramento**
Felderstein, Steven Howard
**San Diego**
Catherwood, Kathryn M.S.
Godone-Maresca, Lillian
Shapiro, Philip Alan
**San Francisco**
Kerner, Michael Philip
Stinnett, Terrance Lloyd

**Syracuse**
Ackerman, Kenneth Edward
Bidwell, Mark Edward
Dove, Jeffrey Austin
Hubbard, Peter Lawrence
**Troy**
Marinstein, Elliott F.
**Westbury**
Hurst, Margaret Anne
**White Plains**
Balaber-Strauss, Barbara
Posner, Martin Louis

### NORTH CAROLINA

**Charlotte**
Clodfelter, Daniel Gray
**Durham**
Carpenter, Charles Francis
Craven, James Braxton, III
Petersen, Elisabeth Saranec
**Greenville**
Flanagan, Michael Perkins
**New Bern**
Ward, Thomas Monroe
**Oxford**
Burnette, Sarah Katherine
**Winston Salem**
Schollander, Wendell Leslie, Jr.

### NORTH DAKOTA

**Bismarck**
Rosenberg, Max D.

### OHIO

**Akron**
Lammert, Thomas Edward
**Bexley**
Kamin-Meyer, Tami
**Canfield**
Beck, James Hayes
**Cincinnati**
Bibus, Thomas William
Bissinger, Mark Christian
Candito, Joseph
Coffey, Thomas William
Hayden, William Taylor
**Cleveland**
Arnoff, Fred Jay
Eisen, Saul
Felty, Kriss Delbert
Foote, Richard Charles
Helbling, Lauren A.
Lawniczak, James Michael
**Columbus**
Kauffman, Ronald P.
Pigman, Jack Richard
Schaeffer, Matthew Thomas
Sidman, Robert John
Swetnam, Daniel Richard
**Greenville**
Finnarn, Theodore Ora
**Kent**
Nome, William Andreas
**Massillon**
Breyfogle, Edwin Howard
**Toledo**
Wicklund, David Wayne
**Warren**
Buzulencia, Michael Douglas
**Worthington**
Minton, Harvey Steiger

### OKLAHOMA

**Muskogee**
Williams, Betty Outhier
**Oklahoma City**
Buckles, Joseph Aaron, II
Gibson, Keith Russell
Kline, Timothy Deal
Leeviraphan, Americ (Eric Leeviraphan)
Schwabe, George Blaine, III
**Tulsa**
Abrahamson, A. Craig
Clark, Gary Carl
Eliot, Theodore Quentin
Hardcastle, Heath E.
Haynie, Tony Wayne
Moffett, J. Denny
Pataki, Leonard Ignatius
Tomlins, Neal Edward

### OREGON

**Bend**
Erwin, Lawrence Warde
**Portland**
Anderson, Herbert Hatfield
Waggoner, James Clyde
**Wilsonville**
Yacob, Yosef

### PENNSYLVANIA

**Abington**
Budman, Alan David
**Blue Bell**
Siedzikowski, Henry Francis
**Brookville**
Smith, Sharon Louise
**Center Valley**
Smillie, Douglas James
**Donora**
Miller, David A.
**Drexel Hill**
West, Kenneth Edward
**Franklin**
Greenfield, James Milton
**Harrisburg**
Imblum, Gary Joseph
Tyler, Brian Joseph
Warshaw, Allen Charles
**Huntingdon**
Covell, Robert Martin
**Kng Of Prussa**
Noonan, Gregory Robert
**Lehighton**
Schwab, William G.
**Mc Murray**
Brzustowicz, John Cinq-Mars
**Monongahela**
Black, Blane Alan
**Morrisville**
Glosser, Harry John, Jr.
Golding, Gilbert James
**Philadelphia**
Aaron, Kenneth Ellyot
Berger, David
Bloom, Michael Anthony
Bressler, Barry E.
Flame, Andrew Jay
Gordesky, Morton
Gough, John Francis
Loveless, George Group
McKeon, Jami Wintz
Ramsey, Natalie D.
Schorling, William Harrison
Tractenberg, Craig R.
**Pittsburgh**
Aderson, Sanford M.
Calairo, Donald Robert
Chamberlain, Denise Kay
Conti, Joy Flowers
Davis, Lewis U., Jr.
Fieschko, Joseph Edward, Jr.
Grego, Samuel Robert
Helmrich, Joel Marc
Hollinshead, Earl Darnell, Jr.
Kelleher, William Eugene, Jr.
Leibowitz, Marvin
Murdoch, David Armor
Peduto, Mark B.
**Warren**
Ristau, Mark Moody
**Williamsport**
Knecht, William L.
**Yardley**
Hamberg, Gilbert Lee

### RHODE ISLAND

**Providence**
Furness, Peter John
McGowan, Matthew J.
Salvadore, Mal Andrew

### SOUTH CAROLINA

**Charleston**
Steadman, Richard Anderson, Jr.
**Columbia**
Johnson, Lawrence Wilbur, Jr.
**Hartsville**
Blake, Daniel L.
**Myrtle Beach**
Breen, David Hart

### TENNESSEE

**Brentwood**
Easter, Timothy Lee
**Chattanooga**
North, Harold Lebron, Jr.
Ragan, Charles Oliver, Jr.
Weems, Kyle Richard
**Jackson**
Latimer, Timothy B.
**Memphis**
Harpster, James Erving
Matthews, Paul Aaron
Philip, John B.
**Nashville**
Baugh, Mark Anthony
Harris, James Harold, III
Kelley, James Russell
Nevin, Ronald Kent

### TEXAS

**Abilene**
Boone, Celia Trimble
**Austin**
Hampton, Charles Edwin
**Bryan**
Steelman, Frank (Sitley)
**Corpus Christi**
Herin, David V.
McMillen, James Thomas
**Dallas**
Burke, William Temple, Jr.
Campbell, David Lee
Farquhar, Robert Michael
Houser, Barbara J.
Johnson, James Joseph Scofield
Nolan, John Michael
Palmer, Philip Isham, Jr.
Phelan, Robin Eric
Portman, Glenn Arthur
Riley, Peter James
Zable, Norman Arnold
**Denton**
Waage, Mervin Bernard
**El Paso**
Mott, H. Christopher
**Fort Worth**
Mack, Theodore
Morton, Deborah Burwell
Tillman, Karen Sue
**Houston**
Banks, John Robert, Jr.
Barnett, Stephanie Blair
Caddy, Michael Douglas
Crews, Glenna England
McDaniel, Jarrel Dave
Minor, Sterling Arthur
Prestridge, Pamela Adair
Ray, Hugh Massey, Jr.
Sheinfeld, Myron M.
Stephens, Delia Marie Lucky
Zeigler, Ann dePender
**Kingwood**
Demuth, C. Jeanne
**Lubbock**
Crowson, James Lawrence
**Mc Kinney**
Pederson, Janet Claire
**Mcallen**
McLeaish, Robert Burns
**Midland**
Truitt, Robert Ralph, Jr.
**Odessa**
Rouse, Randall Lyle
**Richardson**
Olson, Dennis Oliver
**San Antonio**
Biery, Evelyn Hudson
Burham, Cynthia Faye
Williamson, Deborah Daywood
Yates, Norris William, Jr.
**Sherman**
Freels, Jesse Saunders, Jr.
**Sulphur Springs**
Froneberger, Joel Douglas
**Tyler**
Patterson, Donald Ross
**Wichita Falls**
Todd, Richard D. R.
Williams, Steven Mark

### UTAH

**Midvale**
Johnson, Howard Price
**Salt Lake City**
Atkin, Gary Eugene
Lochhead, Robert Bruce

### VERMONT

**Bethel**
Obuchowski, Raymond Joseph
**Brattleboro**
Dunn, David Norman

### VIRGINIA

**Alexandria**
Paul, Adam Craig
Peyton, Gordon Pickett
**Arlington**
McAlevy, Vincent William
**Chesapeake**
Lascara, Dominic Paul
**Danville**
Goodman, Lewis Elton, Jr.
**Hopewell**
Clark, Bruce Arlington, Jr.
**Newport News**
Nachman, Erwin B(ehr)
**Norfolk**
Harrell, Charles Lydon, Jr.
Johnson, William H.
Reeves, Ross Campbell
Stackhouse, Robert Clinton
**Norton**
Shortridge, Michael L.
**Richmond**
Buffenstein, Allan S.
Call, Susan Hope
Street, Walter Scott, III
**Roanoke**
Bromm, Frederick Whittemore
Douthat, James Fielding
**Virginia Beach**
Spitzli, Donald Hawkes, Jr.

### WASHINGTON

**Grandview**
Maxwell, John Edward
**Kennewick**
Hames, William Lester
**Maple Valley**
Engle, David Scott
**Seattle**
Bergstedt, Anders Spencer
Cullen, Jack Joseph
Guy, Andrew A.
Jackson, Dillon Edward
Mueller, Daniel Edward
Sandman, Irvin W(illis)
Shulkin, Jerome
**Spokane**
Boyden, Bruce Robert
Esposito, Joseph Anthony
**Yakima**
Mathieu, Richard Louis

### WEST VIRGINIA

**Charleston**
Cannon-Ryan, Susan Kaye
**Martinsburg**
Scales, Cinda L.
**Wheeling**
Riley, Arch Wilson, Jr.

### WISCONSIN

**Kenosha**
Losey, Mary A.
**Madison**
Walsh, David Graves
**Milwaukee**
Adashek, James Lewis
Blain, Peter Charles
Sturm, William Charles
**Oshkosh**
Swanson, Paul G.

### WYOMING

**Cheyenne**
Wrobetz, Donald Reay
**Rawlins**
DeHerrera, Juan Leo
**Riverton**
Girard, Nettabell

### CHINA

**Hong Kong**
Allen, Richard Marlow

### ADDRESS UNPUBLISHED

Carmody, Richard Patrick
Choslovsky, William
Crown, Nancy Elizabeth
Gewertz, Martin Anson
Hughes, Deborah Ann
Jackman, James David
Perlman, Richard Brian
Perlstein, William James
Putney, Wainscott Walker
Sager, Daniel Ian
Seifert, Stephen Wayne
Simon, Barry Philip
Smock, James F.
Weil, Peter Henry
Wharton, James Carl
Williams, Thomas Arthur
Yellin, Melvin A.

## CIVIL LITIGATION, FEDERAL

### UNITED STATES

### ALABAMA

**Anniston**
Woodrow, Randall Mark
**Birmingham**
Alexander, James Patrick
Baker, Beverly Poole
Benton, Lee Rimes
Gardner, William F.
Hollis, Louie Andrew
Max, Rodney Andrew
Newton, Alexander Worthy
Stabler, Lewis Vastine, Jr.
Wiggins, Robert L.
**Gadsden**
Spray, Vann Allan
**Huntsville**
Steakley, Roderic G
Stephens, (Holman) Harold
**Mobile**
Byrne, Bradley Roberts
Philips, Abe L., Jr.
Pierce, Donald Fay
Rogers, Jannea Suzanne
**Montgomery**
Prestwood, Alvin Tennyson
Sanders-Cochran, Rachel Deanna
**Talladega**
Gaines, Ralph Dewar, Jr.

### ALASKA

**Anchorage**
Fortier, Samuel John
Hayes, George Nicholas

### ARIZONA

**Phoenix**
Balitis, John James, Jr.
Beggs, Harry Mark
Bivens, Donald Wayne
Cohen, Ronald Jay
Coleman, George Joseph, III (Jay Coleman)
Condo, James Robert
Corson, Kimball Jay
Daughton, Donald
Grant, Merwin Darwin
Leonard, Jeffrey S.
Petitti, Michael Joseph, Jr.
Ulrich, Paul Graham
Wall, Donald Arthur
**Rio Rico**
Ryan, John Duncan
**Tucson**
Conn, Deanna
Dickey, Harrison Gaslin, III
Hyams, Harold
Meehan, Michael Joseph
Polan, David Jay
Willis, Jeffrey Lynn

### ARKANSAS

**Benton**
Ellis, George Dawlin
**Corning**
Manatt, Scott
**Fort Smith**
Foster, M. Shannon
**Jonesboro**
Bristow, Bill Wayne
**Little Rock**
Anderson, Philip Sidney
Dillahunty, Wilbur Harris
Ervin, Edie Renee
Griffin, William Mell, III
Jones, Stephen Witsell
Lavey, John Thomas

### CALIFORNIA

**Aptos**
Garrison, Melissa Lyn
**Burbank**
Litvack, Sanford Martin
**Burlingame**
Cotchett, Joseph Winters
**Carlsbad**
Kelsall, Samuel, V
McCracken, Steven Carl
**Costa Mesa**
Guilford, Andrew John
**Culver City**
Pavitt, William Hesser, Jr.
**Danville**
Candland, D. Stuart
**Encino**
Shtofman, Robert Scott
**Irvine**
Gauntlett, David Allan
McInnis, Terrence Reilly
Muller, Edward Robert
Rudolph, George Cooper
Toledano, James
**Laguna Hills**
Reinglass, Michelle Annette
**Long Beach**
Nikas, Richard John
Walker, Timothy Lee
**Los Angeles**
Baker, Robert Kenneth
Barack, Deborah Elise
Barrett, Jane Hayes
Belleville, Philip Frederick
Bodkin, Henry Grattan, Jr.
Bressan, Paul Louis
Fine, Richard Isaac
Franceschi, Ernest Joseph, Jr.
Grebow, Arthur Jeffrey
Gyemant, Robert Ernest
Handzlik, Jan Lawrence
Heller, Philip
Highberger, William Foster
Hufstedler, Shirley Mount (Mrs. Seth M. Hufstedler)
Hutchins, Robert Bruce
Jacques, Nigel Edward
Lauchengco, Jose Yujuico, Jr.
Levine, Jerome Lester
Manning, Steven Donald
McDermott, Thomas John, Jr.
Miller, Louis R., III
Miller, Milton Allen
Morganstern, Myrna Dorothy
Mosk, Richard Mitchell
Muhlbach, Robert Arthur
Newell, Robert Melvin
Newman, Michael Rodney
Niles, John Gilbert
Noble, Richard Lloyd
Nocas, Andrew James
Packard, Robert Charles
Perlis, Michael Fredrick
Peters, Aulana Louise
Pollock, John Phleger
Rutter, Marshall Anthony
Samuels, Joel Gregory
Selwood, Pierce Taylor
Simons, Bernard Philip
Straw, Lawrence Joseph, Jr.
Strong, George Gordon, Jr.
von Kalinowski, Julian Onesime
Walcher, Alan Ernest
Williams, Lee Dwain
**Menlo Park**
Dyer, Charles Arnold
**Middletown**
Downing, James Christie
**Mill Valley**
Judson, Philip Livingston
**Modesto**
Mussman, William Edward
**Newport Beach**
Calcagnie, Kevin Frank
Dito, John Allen
Friedland, Michael Keith
Mandel, Maurice, II
Martens, Don Walter
Millar, Richard William, Jr.
Price, Stuart Winston
Wagner, John Leo
Willard, Robert Edgar
**Oakland**
Bjork, Robert David, Jr.
**Orinda**
Perez, Richard Lee
**Oxnard**
Gerber, David A.
Regnier, Richard Adrian
**Palm Desert**
Singer, Gerald Michael
**Palm Springs**
Kimberling, John Farrell
**Palo Alto**
Bridges, Andrew Phillip
Furbush, David Malcolm
Pasahow, Lynn H(arold)
Sands, Michael Arthur
**Pasadena**
Tanner, Dee Boshard
**Rancho Santa Fe**
Cary, Frederick Albert
**Redwood City**
Coddington, Clinton Hays
**Richmond**
Straus, Douglas Charles
**Sacramento**
Duggan, Jennifer E.
Schleicher, Estelle Ann
**San Diego**
Buzunis, Constantine Dino
Castellanos, Richard Henry
Chenoweth, Jenny K.
Clark, David Robert
Klinedinst, John David
Lewin, Jeffrey David
Petix, Stephen Vincent
Schuck, Carl Joseph
Schulz, Peter Jon
Udell, Lei (Lisa) Karen
Weaver, Michael James
**San Francisco**
Bertain, G(eorge) Joseph, Jr.
Finberg, James Michael
Gelhaus, Robert Joseph
Goode, Barry Paul
Haas, Richard
Herlihy, Thomas Mortimer
Johns, Richard Seth Ellis
Kern, John McDougall
Ladar, Jerrold Morton
Levit, Victor Bert
Meadows, John Frederick
Patula, Rodney Richard
Raven, Robert Dunbar
Renfrew, Charles Byron
Robertson, J. Martin
Roethe, James Norton
Rosenthal, Kenneth W.
Rubin, Michael
Shin, Chang Shik
Suter, Ben
Traynor, John Michael
Venning, Robert Stanley
Young, Douglas Rea
**San Jose**
Alexander, Richard
Cobey, Christopher Earle
**San Mateo**
Sayad, Pamela Miriam
**Santa Ana**
Ingalsbe, William James
Ultimo, Paul Joseph
**Universal Cty**
Peter, Arnold Philimon

**Van Nuys**
Haile, Lawrence Barclay
**Ventura**
Bray, Laurack Doyle

## COLORADO

**Aurora**
Flicker, Howard
**Boulder**
Leh, Christopher Marshall
Purvis, John Anderson
Ward, Denitta Dawn
**Carbondale**
Wohl, Kenneth Allan
**Castle Rock**
Robinson, Michael Allen
**Colorado Springs**
LeHouillier, Patric Jaymes
**Denver**
Abramovitz, Michael John
Anderson, Alan Wendell
Appel, Garry Richard
Bader, Gerald Louis, Jr.
Bain, James William
Christopher, Daniel Roy
Daily, Richard W.
Duffy, William J.
Featherstone, Bruce Alan
Hilbert, Otto Karl, II
Hill, Robert F.
Hjelmfelt, David Charles
Hoffman, Daniel Steven
Holme, Howard Kelley
Jonsen, Eric R.
Law, John Manning
Lindquist-Kleissler, Arthur
Macaulay, Christopher Todd
Marquess, Lawrence Wade
McFarland, Matthew Gabriel
Miller, Gale Timothy
Roesler, John Bruce
Samuels, Donald L.
Starrs, Elizabeth Anne
Stuart, Mary Hurley
Thomasch, Roger Paul
Tisdale, Douglas Michael
Ulrich, Theodore Albert
Wedgle, Richard Jay
Wheeler, Malcolm Edward
Widmann, Edward Healy
Wilcox, Martha Anne
Wollins, David Hart
**Englewood**
Branney, Joseph John
Karr, David Dean
**Fort Collins**
Brown, Ronald Laming
**Golden**
Carney, Deborah Leah Turner
**Littleton**
Spelts, Richard John

## CONNECTICUT

**Bloomfield**
Mawhinney, Kent D.
**Bridgeport**
Mitchell, Robert Burdette
**Greenwich**
Fogarty, James Robert
**Hartford**
Blumenthal, Jeffrey Michael
Dempsey, Edward Joseph
Dowling, Vincent John
Elliot, Ralph Gregory
Fain, Joel Maurice
Kainen, Burton
Pepe, Louis Robert
Sussman, Mark Richard
Tanski, James Michael
Taylor, Allan Bert
Veltrop, James D.
Young, Roland Frederic, III
**Madison**
Clendenen, William Herbert, Jr.
**Milford**
Sagarin, J. Daniel
**New Haven**
Belt, David Levin
Cox, Barbara Lynne
Geisler, Thomas Milton, Jr.
Gildea, Brian Michael
Murphy, William Robert
Reiner, Leona Hudak
Secola, Carl A., Jr.
**North Haven**
Walsh, Kevin Peter
**Norwalk**
Jacobs, Mark Randolph
**Southport**
Pickerstein, Harold James
**Stamford**
Hamlin, John Wadsworth
Margolis, Emanuel
Rosenberg, Burton Stuart
Thompson, Frank J(oseph)
**Westport**
Burns, Paul Edward
Razzano, Pasquale Angelo
**Windsor**
Molitor, Karen Ann
Smith, Spencer Thomas

## DELAWARE

**Wilmington**
Green, James Samuel
Holzman, James L(ouis)
Klayman, Barry Martin
Laster, J. Travis
Macel, Stanley Charles, III

## DISTRICT OF COLUMBIA

**Washington**
Allen, William Hayes
Altschul, Michael F.
Ambrose, Myles Joseph
Atwood, James R.
Auerbach, Jeffrey Ira
Augustini, Michael Charles
Baran, Jan Witold
Barnes, Donald Michael
Barrett, Jane Frances
Bebchick, Leonard Norman
Beisner, John Herbert
Bergner, Jane Cohen
Best, Judah
Beyer, Wayne Cartwright
Blumenfeld, Jeffrey
Bonner, Walter Joseph
Braga, Stephen Louis
Bray, John Martin
Bruton, James Asa, III
Burt, Jeffrey Amsterdam
Calderwood, James Albert
Carr, Lawrence Edward, Jr.
Chabot, Philip Louis, Jr.
Chafetz, Marc Edward
Cheston, Sheila Carol
Clagett, Brice McAdoo
Clarke, John O'Brien, Jr.
Coates, Melanie Diana
Cobb, Ty
Cohen, Louis Richard
Colman, Richard Thomas
Cooter, Dale A.
Cortese, Alfred William, Jr.
Cummings, Frank
Cymrot, Mark Alan
Czarra, Edgar F., Jr.
Danas, Andrew Michael
Denger, Michael L.
Dennis, Warren Lewis
Dinan, Donald Robert
Doumar, George R. A.
Dowdey, Landon Gerald
Esposito, Joseph Paul
Esslinger, John Thomas
Evans, Thomas William
Ewing, Ky Pepper, Jr.
Falk, James Harvey, Sr.
Ferguson, John R.
Fisher, Raymond Corley
Flagg, Ronald Simon
Flowe, Carol Connor
Fogel, J(oan) Cathy
Foster, C(harles) Allen
Frost, Edmund Bowen
Geneson, David Franklin
Geniesse, Robert John
Gibson, Kumiki S.
Ginsburg, Charles David
Glitzenstein, Eric Robert
Golden, Gregg Hannan Stewart
Grady, Gregory
Greenberger, I. Michael
Greenebaum, Leonard Charles
Grier, Phillip Michael
Guerrieri, Joseph, Jr.
Hansen, Mark Charles
Harris, Scott Blake
Hassett, Joseph Mark
Haynes, William J(ames), II
Hefferon, Thomas Michael
Hefter, Laurence Roy
Helfer, Michael Stevens
Henke, Michael John
Hirrel, Michael John
Isbell, David Bradford
Israel, Deborah Jean
Jacobsen, Raymond Alfred, Jr.
Jacobson, Richard Lee
Janis, N. Richard
Kirsch, Laurence Stephen
Klein, Michael Roger
Koontz, Glen Franklin
Kramer, Andrew Michael
La Force, Pierre Joseph
Lamm, Carolyn Beth
Lange, William Michael
Larroca, Raymond G.
Lavelle, Joseph P.
Lear, Richard Edwin
Leary, Thomas Barrett
Lessy, Roy Paul, Jr.
Lettow, Charles Frederick
Lewis, David John
Lewis, William Henry, Jr.
Liebman, Ronald Stanley
Linn, Richard
Lobel, Martin
Loeffler, Robert Hugh
Luce, Gregory M.
Luskin, Robert David
Mailander, William Stephen
McDavid, Janet Louise
McDiarmid, Robert Campbell
McReynolds, Mary Armilda
Medaglia, Mary-Elizabeth
Melamed, Arthur Douglas
Michaels, Gary David
Mortenson, R. Stan
Murry, Harold David, Jr.
Myers, James R.
Nace, Barry John
Newman, Elizabeth L.
O'Neil, Thomas Francis, III
O'Sullivan, Lynda Troutman
Paper, Lewis J.
Patten, Thomas Louis
Peters, Frederick Whitten
Pfeiffer, Margaret Kolodny
Pickering, John Harold
Pollak, Stephen John
Pollock, Stacy Jane
Povich, David
Price, Griffith Baley, Jr.
Pugh, Keith E., Jr.
Quarles, James Linwood, III
Rabinovitz, Joel A.
Roach, Arvid Edward, II
Roll, David Lee
Rose, Jonathan Chapman
Rosenthal, Ilene Goldstein
Rosenthal, Steven Siegmund
Rubel, Eric A.
Sandor, Lawrence Paul
Sayler, Robert Nelson
Schor, Laurence
Schropp, James Howard
Sellers, John W.
Shapiro, George Howard
Shenefield, John Hale
Sloame, Stuart C.
Spaeder, Roger Campbell
Stephens, Andrew Russell
Stuart, Pamela Bruce
Sundermeyer, Michael S.
Sung, Lawrence M.
Taylor, William Woodruff, III
Tegfeldt, Jennifer Ann
Teichler, Stephen Lin
Tomar, Richard Thomas
Tompert, James Emil
Tompkins, Joseph Buford, Jr.
Trager, Michael David
Tufaro, Richard Chase
Vardaman, John Wesley
Villa, John Kazar
Wasserman, Michael Francis
Waxman, Seth Paul
Weisgall, Jonathan Michael
Weissman, William R.
Wilder, Roland Percival, Jr.
Wilder, William Randell
Williams, Thomas Raymond
Wilson, Gary Dean
Wine, L. Mark
Wolff, Elroy Harris
Wolff, Paul Martin
Work, Charles Robert
Zane, Phillip Craig

## FLORIDA

**Bartow**
Pansler, Karl Frederick
**Boca Raton**
Comisky, Ian Michael
Kauffman, Alan Charles
**Boynton Beach**
Babler, Wayne E.
**Clearwater**
Simms, John Seth
**Coconut Grove**
McAmis, Edwin Earl
**Coral Gables**
Chonin, Neil Harvey
Keedy, Christian David
Lott, Leslie Jean
Weissenborn, Sheridan Kendall
**Fort Lauderdale**
Stankee, Glen Allen
**Gainesville**
Kaimowitz, Gabe Hillel
**Hialeah**
Dominik, Jack Edward
**Hollywood**
Goodrich, Robert Forester
**Jacksonville**
Bradford, Dana Gibson, II
Ceballos, M(ichael) Alan
Gabel, George DeSaussure, Jr.
Moseley, James Francis
O'Neal, Michael Scott, Sr.
Pillans, Charles Palmer, III
**Key Biscayne**
Burnbaum, Michael William
**Lakeland**
Schott, Clifford Joseph
Senn, Stephen Russell
**Longboat Key**
Pulvermacher, Louis Cecil
**Maitland**
Edwards, James Alfred
**Marianna**
Brooten, Kenneth Edward, Jr.
**Miami**
Armstrong, James Louden, III
Becerra, Robert John
Blackburn, Roger Lloyd
Blumberg, Edward Robert
Brown, Lewis Nathan
Burstein, Bernardo
Clark, James Kendall
Coberly, Jennifer Rae
Cohen, Jeffrey Michael
Curtis, Karen Haynes
Eaton, Joel Douglas
Ferrell, Milton Morgan, Jr.
Hall, Andrew Clifford
Houlihan, Gerald John
Lipcon, Charles Roy
Lipton, Paul R.
McHale, Michael John
Miller, Raymond Vincent, Jr.
Mody, Renu Noor
Nachwalter, Michael
Nagin, Stephen E.
Sotorrio, Rene Alberto
Weinger, Steven Murray
Winship, Blaine H.
Wright, Robert Thomas, Jr.
**Naples**
Crehan, Joseph Edward
**North Miami**
Malman, Myles Henry
**Ocala**
Briggs, Randy Robert
Crabtree, John Granville
**Orlando**
Allen, William Riley
Brodersen, Daniel N.
Dempsey, Bernard Hayden, Jr.
Eagan, William Leon
Hernandez, H(ermes) Manuel
Losey, Ralph Colby
Motes, Carl Dalton
Noah, Douglas True
Parrish, Sidney Howard
Reinhart, Richard Paul
Wilson, William Berry
**Pensacola**
Gaines, Robert Pendleton
Windham, John Franklin
**Port Saint Lucie**
Hoey, William Edward
**Saint Petersburg**
Kiefner, John Robert, Jr.
**Sarasota**
Kirtley, William Thomas
**Sebring**
Trombley, Michael Jerome
**Stuart**
Harvin, Wesley Reid
**Tallahassee**
Booth, Edgar Charles
Boyd, Joseph Arthur, Jr.
Collette, Charles T. (Chip Collette)
Davis, William Howard
Gievers, Karen A.
Mang, Douglas Arthur
Schreiber, Charles Joseph, Jr.
**Tampa**
Alley, John-Edward
Boos, Robert Walter, II
Buell, Mark Paul
Butler, Paul Bascomb, Jr.
Davis, David Earl
DeVaney, Donna Brookes
Fulton, Robert Maurice
Gifford, Donald Arthur
Kelly, Thomas Paine, Jr.
Lau, Mary Applegate
Munoz, Shane Thomas
Stagg, Clyde Lawrence
Thomas, Wayne Lee
Vessel, Robert Leslie
**West Palm Beach**
Djokic, Walter Henry
Holland, William Meredith
Norton, William Alan
Yeager, Thomas Joseph
**Winter Park**
Ackert, T(errence) W(illiam)

## GEORGIA

**Athens**
Tolley, Edward Donald
**Atlanta**
Appley, Elizabeth Joan
Blank, A(ndrew) Russell
Booth, Gordon Dean, Jr.
Boynton, Frederick George
Calvert, Matthew James
Doyle, Michael Anthony
Duffey, William Simon, Jr.
Farnham, Clayton Henson
Fellows, Henry David, Jr.
Fleming, Julian Denver, Jr.
Gladden, Joseph Rhea, Jr.
González, Carlos A.
Grady, Kevin E.
Hopkins, George Mathews Marks
Hunt, John Robert
Killorin, Edward Wylly
Kneisel, Edmund M.
Ortiz, Jay Richard Gentry
Paquin, Jeffrey Dean
Prince, David Cannon
Remar, Robert Boyle
Rochelle, Dudley Cecile
Seacrest, Gary Lee
Smith, Grant B.
Spalten, David Elliot
Stanhope, William Henry
Stone, Matthew Peter
Sweeney, Neal James
Tewes, R. Scott
**Augusta**
Cooney, William J.
**Jonesboro**
Vail, Bruce Ronald
**Macon**
Ennis, Edgar William, Jr.
**Marietta**
Ingram, George Conley
**Norcross**
Anderson, Albert Sydney, III
**Savannah**
Forbes, Morton Gerald
Ladson, M. Brice
Lancaster, Miriam Diemmer
Painter, Paul Wain, Jr.
Ratterree, Ryburn Clay
**Statesboro**
Snipes, Daniel Brent
**Winder**
McLemore, Michael Kerr

## HAWAII

**Honolulu**
Bail, Lisa A.
Cassiday, Benjamin Buckles, III
Chuck, Walter G(oonsun)
Dezzani, David John
Fukumoto, Leslie Satsuki
Gelber, Don Jeffrey
Hart, Brook
Kunkel, Daniel James
Lawson, William Homer
Potts, Dennis Walker
Robinson, Stacey Mukai
Wong, James Thomas

## ILLINOIS

**Belleville**
Churchill, Allen Delos
Coghill, William Thomas, Jr.
Marlen, Matthew James
Menges, Eugene Clifford
**Bridgeport**
Stout, James Dudley
**Champaign**
Rawles, Edward Hugh
**Chicago**
Adelman, Stanley Joseph
Baker, James Edward Sproul
Banta, Don Arthur
Barnett, William A.
Bashwiner, Steven Lacelle
Bellah, Kenneth David
Berenzweig, Jack Charles
Berghoff, Paul Henry
Bernstein, Stuart
Boies, Wilber H.
Bresnahan, Arthur Stephen
Brown, Steven Spencer
Bruner, Stephen C.
Burditt, George Miller, Jr.
Burke, Dennis J.
Burke, John Michael
Burke, Thomas Joseph, Jr.
Cederoth, Richard Alan
Chemers, Robert Marc
Cherney, James Alan
Chestnut, John William
Cipolla, Carl Joseph
Cole, Jeffrey
Coulson, William Roy
Cunningham, Thomas Justin
Daley, Michael Joseph
Ditkowsky, Kenneth K.
Elden, Gary Michael
Fahner, Tyrone C.
Fennell, Monica Ann
Flaxman, Kenneth N.
Fleischmann, Thomas Joseph
Formeller, Daniel Richard
Franch, Richard Thomas
Frew, Stephen B.
Geiman, J. Robert
George, John Martin, Jr.
Geren, Gerald S.
Gordon, James S.
Griffith, Donald Kendall
Hall, Joan M.
Halloran, Michael John
Hanson, Ronald William
Harrington, James Timothy
Head, Patrick James
Hecht, Frank Thomas
Helt, Christopher William
Hilliard, David Craig
Horn, Richard Leslie
Hunter, James Galbraith, Jr.
Jacover, Jerold Alan
Karon, Sheldon
Katz, Harold Ambrose
Kennelly, John Jerome
King, Michael Howard
Knuepfer, Robert Claude, Jr.
Kohn, Shalom L.
Komie, Stephen Mark
Kozak, John W.
Krupka, Robert George
Kuhns, Thomas O.
Levine, Laurence Harvey
Linklater, William Joseph
Lyerla, Bradford Peter
Lynch, John Peter
Manzo, Edward David
Marick, Michael Miron
Mason, Henry Lowell, III
McConnell, James Guy
Mendelson, Alan Conrad
Meyer, John Albert
Millner, Robert B.
Molo, Steven Francis
Montgomery, William Adam
Mulroy, Thomas Robert, Jr.
Murray, Daniel Charles
Nash, Gordon Bernard, Jr.
Novotny, David Joseph
Oberhardt, William Patrick
Palmer, Robert Towne
Parkhurst, Beverly Susler
Parson, Jason A.
Partridge, Mark Van Buren
Pattishall, Beverly Wyckliffe
Pavalon, Eugene Irving
Pelton, Russell Meredith, Jr.
Perrin, James Kirk
Potter, Richard Clifford
Rankin, James Winton
Redman, Clarence Owen
Redmond, Richard Anthony
Richmond, William Patrick
Richter, Tobin Marais
Romanyak, James Andrew
Roper, Harry Joseph
Rovell, Michael Jay
Rupert, Donald William
Saunders, Terry Rose
Smith, Arthur B., Jr.
Smith, Stephen Edward
Sparks, Kenneth Franklin
Spector, David M.
Spiotto, James Ernest
Spognardi, Mark Anthony
Sternstein, Allan J.
Torshen, Jerome Harold
Van Demark, Ruth Elaine
Von Mandel, Michael Jacques
Wemple, Peter Holland
Wick, Lawrence Scott
Witwer, Samuel Weiler, Jr.
Wohlreich, Jack Jay
Wolf, Neal Lloyd
**Danville**
Blan, Kennith William, Jr.
**Deerfield**
Birmingham, William Joseph
Scott, Theodore R.
**Hinsdale**
Farrug, Eugene Joseph, Sr.
**Kenilworth**
Dixon, Carl Franklin
**Kewanee**
McRae, Donald James
**Lake Forest**
Emerson, William Harry
**Libertyville**
DeSanto, James John
**Lincolnshire**
Galatz, Henry Francis
**Lombard**
O'Shea, Patrick Joseph
**Monee**
Bohlen, Christopher Wayne
**Northbrook**
Dilling, Kirkpatrick Wallwick
**Oak Brook**
Farnell, Alan Stuart
Ring, Leonard M.
**Park Ridge**
LaRue, Paul Hubert
**Peoria**
Slevin, John A.
Winget, Walter Winfield
**Prospect Heights**
Leopold, Mark F.
**Rockford**
Mateer, Don Metz
**Saint Charles**
Hines, Suzanne
**Schaumburg**
Rudd, Donnie
**Willowbrook**
Walton, Stanley Anthony, III
**Winnetka**
Theis, William Harold

## INDIANA

**Beech Grove**
Brown, Richard Lawrence
**Bloomington**
Applegate, Karl Edwin
**Carmel**
Newman, Mary Lynn Canmann
**Columbus**
Fairchild, Raymond Francis
**Crown Point**
Stevens, William J.
**Evansville**
Berger, Charles Lee
Bodkin, Robert Thomas
**Fort Wayne**
Harants, Stephen John
**Hammond**
Ruman, Saul I.
**Indianapolis**
Albright, Terrill D.
Badger, David Harry
Baker, Tim A.
Conour, William Frederick
Daniel, Melvin Randolph
Elberger, Ronald Edward
Karwath, Bart Andrew
Kashani, Hamid Reza
Knauer, James A.
Knebel, Donald Earl
McNeil, Andrew M.
McTurnan, Lee Bowes
Montross, W. Scott
Reuben, Lawrence Mark
Rudolf, Steven George
Tabler, Bryan G.
**Lafayette**
Layden, Charles Max
**Merrillville**
Dignam, Robert James
**Schererville**
Anast, Nick James
**Seymour**
Pardieck, Roger Lee
**South Bend**
Myers, James Woodrow, III
**Terre Haute**
Coleson, Richard Eugene
Newmeyer, Robert J.
Willard, Glenn Mark
**Valparaiso**
Evans, Larry G.

## IOWA

**Davenport**
Lathrop, Roger Alan
**Des Moines**
Belin, David William
Frederici, C. Carleton
Krull, Curtis Jay
Logan, Thomas Joseph
Phipps, David Lee
Tully, Robert Gerard
**Marshalltown**
Brooks, Patrick William
**Sioux City**
Mayne, Wiley Edward
Nymann, P. L.

## KANSAS

**Lenexa**
McCreary, Lynn S.
**Olathe**
Logan, Samuel Price
**Overland Park**
Keplinger, (Donald) Bruce
Sampson, William Roth
Starrett, Frederick Kent
Waxse, David John
**Prairie Vlg**
Stanton, Roger D.
**Shawnee Mission**
Badgerow, John Nicholas
Sparks, Billy Schley
**Topeka**
Dimmitt, Lawrence Andrew
Hamilton, John Richard
Justus, Jo Lynne
Schroer, Gene Eldon
Sebelius, Keith Gary
**Wichita**
Bostwick, Donald W.
Fisher, Randall Eugene
Kennedy, Joseph Winston

## KENTUCKY

**Bowling Green**
Rudloff, William Joseph
**Eddyville**
Story, James Eddleman
**Florence**
Busald, E. André
**Lexington**
Fryman, Virgil Thomas, Jr.
Turley, Robert Joe
**Louisville**
Bishop, Robert Whitsitt
Chauvin, Leonard Stanley, Jr.
Cohen, Edwin Louis
Dolt, Frederick Corrance
Guethlein, William O.
Ogburn, John Denis
Reed, John Squires, II
Stavros, Peter James
**Newport**
Siverd, Robert Joseph

## LOUISIANA

**Alexandria**
Everett, Stephen Edward
**Baton Rouge**
Donnan, Susan L.
LeClere, David Anthony
Watson, Craig Sterling
**Lafayette**
Bernard, Barton Willis
Davidson, James Joseph, III
**Lake Charles**
Cagney, Nanette Heath
Davidson, Van Michael, Jr.
Parkerson, Hardy Martell
Veron, J. Michael
**Leesville**
Smith, Simeon Christie, III
**Metairie**
Butcher, Bruce Cameron
Haygood, John Warren
Kastl, Dian Evans
Kutcher, Robert A.
**New Orleans**
Bordelon, Alvin Joseph, Jr.
Buckley, Samuel Olliphant, III
Gertler, Meyer H.
Grant, Arthur Gordon, Jr.
Harris, Thorne D., III
Herman, Russ Michel
Jones, Philip Kirkpatrick, Jr.
Kelly, William James, III
Kupperman, Stephen Henry
Leger, Walter John, Jr.
McGlone, Michael Anthony
Perez, Luis Alberto
Rosen, William Warren
Smith, Ralph E.
Whitney, John Franklin
**Shreveport**
Smith, Brian David
**Slidell**
Shamis, Edward Anthony, Jr.

## MAINE

**Augusta**
Bickerman, Peter Bruce
**Bangor**
Haddow, Jon Andrew
**Freeport**
Lea, Lola Stendig
**Portland**
Amory, Daniel
Culley, Peter William
Germani, Elizabeth A.
Groff, Joseph Halsey, III
Lancaster, Ralph Ivan, Jr.
Marjerison, Thomas Sydney

## MARYLAND

**Annapolis**
Lillard, John Franklin, III
**Baltimore**
Baker, William Parr
Carbine, James Edmond
Crowe, Thomas Leonard
Dubé, Lawrence Edward, Jr.
Golomb, George Edwin
Himeles, Martin Stanley, Jr.
Howell, Harley Thomas
Kramer, Paul R.
Nazarian, Douglas Richard Miller
Ohly, D. Christopher
Pappas, George Frank
Radding, Andrew
Schochor, Jonathan
Sfekas, Stephen James
Walker, Irving Edward
Weltchek, Robert Jay
White, George Wendell, Jr.
**Bethesda**
Karp, Ronald Alvin
**Chevy Chase**
Weiss, Harlan Lee
**Parkville**
Hill, Milton King, Jr.
**Patuxent River**
Fitzhugh, David Michael
**Phoenix**
Schlenger, Robert Purnell
**Potomac**
Meyer, Lawrence George
Mullenbach, Linda Herman
Reback, Richard Neal
**Rockville**
Dugan, John R.
Pensinger, John Lynn
Steren, Marc Nathan
Wagshal, Jerome Stanley
**Salisbury**
Clarke, Wm. A. Lee, III
**Silver Spring**
Gagliardo, Thomas James
**Takoma Park**
Browning, Deborah Lea
**Towson**
Hansen, Christopher Agnew
**Upper Marlboro**
Wallace, Sean Daniel

## MASSACHUSETTS

**Boston**
Carpenter, Robert Brent
Carroll, James Edward
Costa, Michael R.
Curley, Robert Ambrose, Jr.
Dignan, Thomas Gregory, Jr.
Dillon, James Joseph
Felter, John Kenneth
Gaynor, Martin F., III
Gelb, Richard Mark
Hieken, Charles
Kavanaugh, James Francis, Jr.
Lacovara, Kirsten Marie
Lindley, James David
Lukey, Joan A.
Macauley, William Francis
MacFarlane, Maureen Anne
Meyer, Andrew C., Jr.
Moriarty, George Marshall
Naughton, Edward Joseph
Neuner, George William
Oetheimer, Richard A.
O'Neill, Timothy P.
Parker, Christopher William
Reece, Laurence Hobson, III
Rose, Alan Douglas
Stoner, Wayne Lee
Sullivan, Edward Michael
Trimmier, Roscoe, Jr.
Zavez, John Peter
**Brookline**
Houlihan, F(rancis) Robert, Jr.
**Lexington**
Glovsky, Susan G. L.
**Medford**
Berman, David
**Weston**
Haas, Jacqueline Crawford

## MICHIGAN

**Ann Arbor**
Britton, Clarold Lawrence
DeVine, Edmond Francis
**Big Rapids**
Clarke, Alan William
**Bingham Farms**
Moffitt, David Louis
**Bloomfield Hills**
Googasian, George Ara
Mucha, John, III
Pappas, Edward Harvey
Rader, Ralph Terrance
Vocht, Michelle Elise
Weinstein, William Joseph
**Dearborn**
Currier, Gene Mark
**Detroit**
Andreoff, Christopher Andon
Budaj, Steven T.
Bushnell, George Edward, Jr.
Callahan, John William (Bill Callahan)
Christiansen, Roy Hvidkaer
Longhofer, Ronald Stephen
Monsanto, Raphael Angel
Rassel, Richard Edward
Saxton, William Marvin
Smith, James Albert
Taweel, A. Tony
Walsh, James Joseph
Zuckerman, Richard Engle
**East Lansing**
Joseph, Raymond
**Elk Rapids**
Palmer, Thomas Earl
**Flint**
Hart, Clifford Harvey
**Fort Gratiot**
Carson, Robert William
**Franklin**
Kessler, Philip Joel
Pritchard, Clyde Basil
**Grand Rapids**
Kara, Paul Mark
Litton, Randall Gale
**Harbor Springs**
Turner, Lester Nathan
**Holland**
Bidol, James Alexander
**Kalamazoo**
Plaszczak, Roman Thaddeus
**Lansing**
Baker, Frederick Milton, Jr.
Coey, David Conrad
Fink, Joseph Allen
Kritselis, William Nicholas
Nurkiewicz, Dennis John, Jr.
Rasmusson, Thomas Elmo
**Midland**
Battle, Leonard Carroll
**Northville**
Leavitt, Martin Jack
**Southfield**
Fieger, Geoffrey Nels
Forrest, Robert Edwin
Jacobs, John Patrick
Morganroth, Mayer
**Troy**
Alber, Phillip George
Lenihan, Robert Joseph, II
Ponitz, John Allan

## MINNESOTA

**Anoka**
Beens, Richard Albert
**Crystal**
Reske, Steven David
**Duluth**
Thibodeau, Thomas Raymond
**Golden Valley**
Hagglund, Clarance Edward
**Minneapolis**
Bras, Robert W.
Ciresi, Michael Vincent
D'Aquila, Barbara Jean
French, John Dwyer
Hanson, Bruce Eugene
Hanson, Kent Bryan
Jarpe, Geoffrey Pellas
Keppel, William James
Magnuson, Roger James
Mansfield, Seymour J.
McGunnigle, George Francis
Meller, Robert Louis, Jr.
Muirhead, Douglas James
Saeks, Allen Irving
Shroyer, Thomas Jerome
Sippel, William Leroy
Sortland, Paul Allan
Tanick, Marshall Howard
Woods, Robert Edward
**New Brighton**
Krueger, William James
**Saint Paul**
Allison, John Robert
Seymour, Mary Frances

## MISSISSIPPI

**Clarksdale**
Cocke, John Hartwell
Merkel, Charles Michael
**Greenville**
Hafter, Jerome Charles
**Hernando**
Maddox, Nancy McCraine
**Jackson**
Bullock, James N.
Clark, David Wright
Hemleben, Scott P.
Henegan, John C(lark)
Hewes, George Poindexter, III
Pyle, Luther Arnold
Wise, Sherwood Willing
**Kosciusko**
Pickle, L. Scott

## MISSOURI

**Clayton**
Schwartz, Theodore Frank
**Kansas City**
Abele, Robert Christopher
Beck, William G.
Beckett, Theodore Charles
Berson, Susan A.
Bradshaw, Jean Paul, II
Clarke, Milton Charles
Cowden, John William
Cross, William Dennis
Eiszner, James Richard, Jr.
Healy, Michael Patrick
Helder, Jan Pleasant, Jr.
Holt, Ronald Lee
Hopkins, William Carlisle, II
Housh, Tedrick Addison, III
Hubbell, Ernest
Johnson, Mark Eugene
Levings, Theresa Lawrence
Lolli, Don R(ay)
Martucci, William Christopher
McManus, James William
Morefield, Richard Watts
Palmer, Dennis Dale
Price, James Tucker
Redmond, Christopher John
Schult, Thomas P.
Wirken, James Charles
Woods, Curtis E(ugene)
**Saint Louis**
Bonacorsi, Mary Catherine
Breidenbach, Robert A.
Brown, Paul Sherman
Carr, Gary Thomas
Clear, John Michael
Collins, James Slade, II
Conran, Joseph Palmer
DeWoskin, Alan Ellis
Douaihy, Toni Patricia
Floyd, Walter Leo
Gianoulakis, John Louis
Gilhousen, Brent James
Hempstead, Gerard Francis
Hunt, Jeffrey Brian
Kortenhof, Joseph Michael
Lucchesi, Lionel Louis
Moore, McPherson Dorsett
Rabbitt, Daniel Thomas, Jr.
Rice, Canice Timothy, Jr.
Sandberg, John Steven
Sestric, Anthony James
Smith, Arthur Lee
Sneeringer, Stephen Geddes
Spooner, Jack Bernard
Tierney, Betty Thorne
**Springfield**
McDonald, William Henry
Myers, Ronald Lynn
Woody, Donald Eugene

## MONTANA

**Billings**
Malee, Thomas Michael

## NEBRASKA

**Grand Island**
Busick, Denzel Rex
**Lincoln**
Colleran, Kevin
Stine, Margaret Elizabeth
**Omaha**
Brownrigg, John Clinton
Dolan, James Vincent
Lamson, William Maxwell, Jr.
Riley, William Jay

## NEVADA

**Las Vegas**
England, Kathleen Jane
Galane, Morton Robert
Graham, Robert Chase
Zubel, Eric Louis

## NEW HAMPSHIRE

**Concord**
Hodes, Paul William
Johnson, Robert Veiling, II
**Hollis**
Lumbard, Eliot Howland
**Manchester**
Damon, Claudia Cords
Richards, Thomas H.
Walker, Jeremy Thomas
**Portsmouth**
Volk, Kenneth Hohne
**West Lebanon**
Isaacs, Robert Charles

## NEW JERSEY

**Audubon**
Montano, Arthur
**Cherry Hill**
Feldman, Arnold H.
Garrigle, William Aloysius
Korin, Joel Benjamin
**Collingswood**
Kole, Janet Stephanie
**Cranford**
De Luca, Thomas George
**East Brunswick**
Eder, Todd Brandon
**Edison**
Lavigne, Lawrence Neil
**Florham Park**
Charme, Stephen Mark
**Franklin Lakes**
Hector, Bruce John
**Hackensack**
Usatine, Warren Alan
**Haddonfield**
Fuoco, Philip Stephen
**Hammonton**
Picariello, Pasquale
**Kenilworth**
Hoffman, John Fletcher
**Lambertville**
Peluso, Matthew A.
**Lawrenceville**
Blumstein, Jeffrey Phillip
**Madison**
Huettner, Richard Alfred
**Millburn**
Biebelberg, Keith N.
**Morristown**
Bartkus, Robert Edward
Donaldson, Craig John
Fenske, Karl Arthur
Humick, Thomas Charles Campbell
McDonough, Joseph Richard
Newman, John Merle
Samay, Z. Lance
Szuch, Clyde Andrew
Whitmer, Frederick Lee
**Newark**
Cahn, Jeffrey Barton
Cummis, Clive Sanford
Dreyfuss, Stephen Lawrence
Feldman, Elda Beylerian
Herman, Ross Neil
Jacobs, Andrew Robert
McGuire, William B(enedict)
Muscato, Andrew
Rak, Lorraine Karen
Simon, David Robert
Thompson, Paul Brower
**Parsippany**
Kallmann, Stanley Walter
**Princeton**
Lampert, Michael A.
**Red Bank**
Duggan, John Peter
**Rochelle Park**
Knopf, Barry Abraham
**Roseland**
Garrod, Jeffrey Mead
McMahon, Edward Richard
Saloman, Mark Andrew
Schwartz, Andrea B.
**Saddle Brook**
Pearlman, Peter Steven
**Ship Bottom**
Shackleton, Richard James
**Short Hills**
Marshall, John Patrick
**Trenton**
Bilder, Marshall D.
Williams, Barbara June
**West Orange**
Gordon, Harrison J.
**Woodcliff Lake**
Sneirson, Marilyn

## NEW MEXICO

**Albuquerque**
Bardacke, Paul Gregory
Bohnhoff, Henry M.
Branch, Turner Williamson
Fish, Paul Mathew
McBride, Thomas John
Messersmith, Lanny Dee
Roehl, Jerrald J.
Threet, Martin Edwin
**Farmington**
Gurley, Curtis Raymond
**Santa Fe**
Burton, John Paul (Jack Burton)
Cunningham, David Fratt
McClaugherty, Joe L.
Schwarz, Michael

## NEW YORK

**Albany**
Jehu, John Paul
Linnan, James Daniel
Powers, John Kieran
Wallender, Michael Todd
Wukitsch, David John
**Armonk**
Quinn, James W.
**Bay Shore**
Zuckerman, Landon Roy
**Binghamton**
Gouldin, David Millen
**Bronx**
Calamari, Andrew M.
**Brooklyn**
DeMarco, Anthony J., Jr.
Swain, Laura Taylor
**Buffalo**
Brown, Jerrold Stanley
Goldstein, Brian Alan
Halpern, Ralph Lawrence
Herdzik, Arthur Alan
Manning, Kenneth Alan
Mattar, Lawrence Joseph
Sampson, John David
**Canaan**
Pennell, William Brooke
**East Meadow**
Hyman, Montague Allan
**Floral Park**
Friedman, Jon George
**Garden City**
Kaplan, Joel Stuart
Kleinberg, Howard Bruce
Kroll, Martin N.
**Getzville**
DiNardo, Joseph
**Glen Cove**
Mills, Charles Gardner
**Hamburg**
Killeen, Henry Walter
**Hornell**
Pulos, William Whitaker
**Huntington**
German, June Resnick

**Islip**
Baker, Lloyd Harvey
**Jericho**
Rehbock, Richard Alexander
**Jordan**
McCabe, Matthew Clark
**Malone**
Nichols, Joseph Patrick
**Mayville**
Dolan, John F.
**Mineola**
Agoglia, Emmet John
Block, Martin
Braid, Frederick Donald
Kelly, Edward Joseph
Lynn, Robert Patrick, Jr.
Monaghan, Peter Gerard
Plastaras, Thomas Edward
Wilson, George J.
**Mount Kisco**
Curran, Maurice Francis
**New City**
Marcus, Robert Bruce
**New Hyde Park**
Levine, Kimberly Anne
**New York**
Adams, Ludwig Howard
Amabile, John Louis
Amsterdam, Mark Lemle
Axinn, Stephen Mark
Barenholtz, Celia Goldwag
Bazerman, Steven Howard
Beatie, Russel Harrison, Jr.
Behrendt, John Thomas
Benedict, James Nelson
Bentley, Anthony Miles
Beranbaum, John A.
Berman, Tony
Bezanson, Thomas Edward
Bialo, Kenneth Marc
Bizar, Irving
Bodovitz, James Philip
Bosses, Stevan J.
Bradley, E. Michael
Briggs, Taylor Rastrick
Brill, Haydn J.
Broder, Eric Jason
Brown, Peter Megargee
Buchwald, Don David
Burrows, Michael Donald
Caputo, Nicholas Raymond
Carter, James Hal, Jr.
Cashman, Gideon
Cayea, Donald Joseph
Chan, Lai Lee
Clary, Richard Wayland
Cohen, Anne Elizabeth
Cohen, Robert Stephan
Cole, Charles Dewey, Jr.
Coleman, Jerome P.
Coll, John Peter, Jr.
Cook, Michael Lewis
Cooper, Michael Anthony
Cunha, Mark Geoffrey
Daichman, Jeffrey Howard
Dallas, William Moffit, Jr.
Davidson, Robert Bruce
DeOrchis, Vincent Moore
Dopf, Glenn William
Dunne, Gerard Francis
Eisman, Clyde Jay
Elsen, Sheldon Howard
Feldberg, Michael Svetkey
Fink, Robert Steven
Finnerty, Joseph Gregory, III
Fiske, Robert Bishop, Jr.
Fitzpatrick, Joseph Mark
Flamm, Leonard N(athan)
Fletcher, Anthony L.
Flintoft, Gerald James
Folkenflik, Max
Foster, David Lee
Frankel, Sandor
Fraser, Brian Scott
Fredericks, William Curtis
Freeman, David John
Freeman, Robert E.
Frisch, Harry David
Futterman, Stanley Norman
Gallagher, Brian John
Garfinkel, Barry Herbert
Garvey, Christopher John
Gerber, Robert Evan
Gitter, Max
Glekel, Jeffrey Ives
Goetz, Peter
Gold, Richard L.
Goldberg, Jay
Gray, Glenn Oliver
Greenawalt, William Sloan
Greenspon, Robert Alan
Grisi, James Robert
Gruen, Michael Stephan
Habian, Bruce George
Haig, Robert Leighton
Halperin, Kyle Mallary
Harris, Joel B(ruce)
Hartmann, Carl Joseph
Hathaway, Gerald Thomas
Haynes, Jean Reed
Hecht, Charles Joel
Heller, Robert Martin
Hennessy, Mickee M.
Hirsch, Jerome S.
Hollyer, A(rthur) Rene
Hritz, George F.
Iannuzzi, John Nicholas
Isquith, Fred Taylor
Jackson, Thomas Gene
Jacob, Edwin J.
Jacobson, Jeffrey Eli
Jannuzzo, Jeffrey Anthony
Joffe, Robert David
Joseph, Gregory Paul
Kandel, William Lloyd
Kaplan, Lawrence I.
Karmali, Rashida Alimahomed
Katz, Jerome Charles
Kazanjian, John Harold
Keneally, Kathryn Marie
Kidd, John Edward
Kimelman, Steven
Kimm, Michael S.
King, Henry Lawrence
Klein, Martin I.
Klein, William, II
Kobak, James Benedict, Jr.
Koegel, William Fisher
Kohn, Jeffrey Ira
Kramer, Daniel Jonathan
Krane, Steven Charles
Krasner, Daniel Walter
Kuh, Richard Henry
Kurland, Paul Carl
Lacovara, Philip Allen
Lacy, Robinson Burrell
Landau, James Kenneth
Langer, Bruce Alden
Lanza, Robert John
Larkin, Leo Paul, Jr.
Lauer, Eliot
Lederer, Karen F.
Lee, Jerome G.
Leiman, Eugene A.
Levin, Roger Michael
Levine, Alan
Lupert, Leslie Allan
Lustig, David Carl, III
Madrid, Andres N.
Malina, Michael
Mandelker, Lawrence Arthur
Maneker, Morton M.
Maney, Michael Mason
Markel, Gregory Arthur
Martone, Patricia Ann
Mayesh, Jay Philip
McCormack, Howard Michael
McGahren, Richard George
Mentz, Barbara Antonello
Mentz, Lawrence
Miller, Richard Allan
Moerdler, Charles Gerard
Morris, John E.
Moy, Mary Anastasia
Muccia, Joseph William
Mullaney, Thomas Joseph
Munzer, Stephen Ira
Muskin, Victor Philip
Naftalis, Gary Philip
Newman, Lawrence Walker
Nolan, Richard Edward
O'Connor, William Matthew
Olick, Arthur Seymour
Oliensis, Sheldon
Owen, Richard Knowles
Pepper, Allan Michael
Phillips, Anthony Francis
Pickholz, Jason R.
Primps, William Guthrie
Quinn, Timothy Charles, Jr.
Raylesberg, Alan Ira
Reich, Larry Sam
Reinthaler, Richard Walter
Reiter, Allen Gary
Rich, R(obert) Bruce
Rifkind, Robert S(inger)
Ringel, Dean
Rivera, Walter
Robertson, Edwin David
Rosensaft, Menachem Zwi
Rosenzweig, Charles Leonard
Rothman, Dennis Michael
Rothstein, Amy Lone
Rovine, Arthur William
Rubin, Howard Jeffrey
Saldana, Adrienne L.
Savitt, Susan Schenkel
Schaffer, Seth Andrew
Schmidt, Charles Edward
Schochet, Ira A.
Schwab, Harold Lee
Schwartz, Barry Fredric
Seidel, Selvyn
Shanman, James Alan
Shapiro, Stanley K.
Shaughnessy, James Michael
Shollenberger, Elizabeth Ann
Short, Skip
Siegel, Charles
Skirnick, Robert Andrew
Sladkus, Harvey Ira
Smiley, Guy Ian
Smith, Robert Everett
Smoak, Evan Lewis
Sperber, Joseph John, IV
Stathis, Nicholas John
Stoll, Neal Richard
Stratton, Walter Love
Sugarman, Robert P.
Sweeney, John Francis
Swire, James Bennett
Taylor, Job, III
Thackeray, Jonathan E.
Tilewick, Robert
Toplitz, George Nathan
Urowsky, Richard J.
Vandenberg, Raymond Leonard, Jr.
Vyskocil, Mary Kay
Wagner, Michael G.
Weinberger, Harold Paul
Weiner, Stephen L.
Weiss, Jonathan Arthur
Wells, Joshua Joseph
Witkin, Eric Douglas
Wohl, Ronald Gene
Wolff, Kurt Jakob
Yelenick, Mary Therese
Yodowitz, Edward J.
Zauderer, Mark Carl
Zimmett, Mark Paul
Zito, Robert John Amadeus
**Newburgh**
Mishkin, Kathleen Anne
**Oneonta**
Scarzafava, John Francis
**Oyster Bay**
Gaffney, Mark William
**Rochester**
Andolina, Lawrence J.
Braunsdorf, Paul Raymond
Dolin, Lonny H.
Geiger, Alexander
Law, Michael R.
Leclair, Paul Lucien
Moore, James Conklin
Reed, James Alexander, Jr.
Smith, Jules Louis
**Rye**
Goldstein, Peter Dobkin
**Sands Point**
Busner, Philip H.
Hoynes, Louis LeNoir, Jr.
**Scarsdale**
King, Robert Lucien
**Schenectady**
DeLorenzo, Paul E.
**Southampton**
Lopez, David
**Staten Island**
Howard, Davis Jonathan
**Syracuse**
Cherundolo, John Charles
Copani, Anthony Frank
DiLorenzo, Louis Patrick
Gerber, Edward F.
Muldoon, James Raymond
**Troy**
Jones, E. Stewart, Jr.
**Uniondale**
Rivkin, John Lawrence
**Waterford**
Novotny, F. Douglas
**White Plains**
Dannenberg, Richard Bruce
Doyle, Dennis Thomas
Halpern, Philip Morgan
Morell, Philip M.
Pickard, John Allan

### NORTH CAROLINA

**Asheville**
Cogburn, Max Oliver
Davis, Roy Walton, Jr.
**Charlotte**
Allred, John Thompson
Bell, Paul Buckner
**Durham**
Craven, James Braxton, III
**Fairview**
Rhynedance, Harold Dexter, Jr.
**Greensboro**
Carmack, Amie Flowers
McGinn, Max Daniel
**Raleigh**
Jolly, John Russell, Jr.
Sasser, Jonathan Drew
**Tabor City**
Jorgensen, Ralph Gubler
**Wilmington**
Baldwin, Charles Selden, IV
Hinson, Reid Garrett
Seagle, J. Harold
**Winston Salem**
Barnhill, Henry Grady, Jr.
Dahl, Tyrus Vance, Jr.

### NORTH DAKOTA

**Bismarck**
Gilbertson, Joel Warren

### OHIO

**Akron**
Ruport, Scott Hendricks
Tipping, Harry A.
Woodley, Ann E.
**Avon Lake**
Kitchen, Charles William
**Cincinnati**
Cioffi, Michael Lawrence
Cissell, James Charles
Cunningham, Pierce Edward
Dornette, W(illiam) Stuart
Frantz, Robert Wesley
Fuchs, Jack Frederick
Holschuh, John David, Jr.
Kammerer, Matthew Paul
Lugbill, Ann
McClain, William Andrew
Shea, Joseph William, III
Smith, Sheila Marie
Stalf, Dale Anthony
Zavatsky, Michael Joseph
**Cleveland**
Alexandersen, Kevin Carl
Bell, Steven Dennis
Boles, Edgar Howard, II
Cohan, Michael Charles
Collin, Thomas James
Dauchot, Luke Lucien
Fisher, Thomas Edward
Goldfarb, Bernard Sanford
Hoerner, Robert Jack
Kelly, Dennis Michael
Kelly, Sandra M.
Kramer, Edward George
Leiken, Earl Murray
Lowe, James Allison
Mc Cartan, Patrick Francis
Moore, Kenneth Cameron
Norman, Forrest Alonzo
Satola, James William
Skulina, Thomas Raymond
Spade, Eric F.
Toohey, Brian Frederick
Zamore, Joseph David
Zashin, Stephen S.
**Columbus**
Bartemes, Amy Straker
Berliner, Alan Frederick
Briggs, Marjorie Crowder
Ferguson, Gerald Paul
Frye, Richard Arthur
Hollenbaugh, H(enry) Ritchey
Hutson, Jeffrey Woodward
Sidman, Robert John
Spencer, Scott W.
Thompson, Harold Lee
Warner, Charles Collins
Whipps, Edward Franklin
Yeazel, Keith Arthur
**Dayton**
Faruki, Charles Joseph
Hollingsworth, Jonathan
Ireland, D. Jeffrey
Saul, Irving Isaac
Wightman, Ann
**Dublin**
Coco, Mark Steven
**Fairborn**
Roach, B. Randall
**Lakewood**
Traci, Donald Philip
**Toledo**
Anspach, Robert Michael
Dane, Stephen Mark

### OKLAHOMA

**Antlers**
Stamper, Joe Allen
**Enid**
Gungoll, Bradley A.
McNaughton, Alexander Bryant
**Muskogee**
Williams, Betty Outhier
**Oklahoma City**
Buckles, Joseph Aaron, II
Featherly, Henry Frederick
Hughes, Carl Douglas
Kenney, John Arthur
Paul, William George
Woods, Harry Arthur, Jr.
Zuhdi, Nabil (Bill)
**Tulsa**
Beustring, Glenn Roland
Biolchini, Robert Fredrick
Brewster, Clark Otto
Davis, G. Reuben
Eagan, Claire Veronica
Eldridge, Richard Mark
Eliot, Theodore Quentin
Haynie, Tony Wayne
Jackman, J. Warren
Kincaid, James Lewis
Luthey, Graydon Dean, Jr.
Matthies, Mary Constance T.
Pataki, Leonard Ignatius
Strecker, David Eugene
**Vinita**
Linscott, Michael S.

### OREGON

**Eugene**
Lowry, Robert Dudley
**Medford**
Deatherage, William Vernon
O'Connor, Karl William (Goodyear Johnson)
Thierolf, Richard Burton, Jr.
**Portland**
Bakkensen, John Reser
Campbell, James, VII
Eakin, Margaretta Morgan
Hurd, Paul Gemmill
Martson, William Frederick, Jr.
Moore, Thomas Scott
Shorr, Scott Alden
Sullivan, Dana Louise
Troutwine, Gayle Leone
**Salem**
Haselton, Rick Thomas

### PENNSYLVANIA

**Allentown**
McGinley, Paul Anthony, Jr.
**Altoona**
Serbin, Richard Martin
**Bethlehem**
Barnette, Curtis Handley
**Blue Bell**
Lawrence, Gerald, Jr.
Siedzikowski, Henry Francis
Teklits, Joseph Anthony
**Clarks Summit**
Beemer, John Barry
**Erie**
Wingerter, John Raymond
**Fort Washington**
Daller, Morton F.
**Harrisburg**
Ward, William Francis
**Lancaster**
Lewis, Alvin Bower, Jr.
Nast, Dianne Martha
**Langhorne**
Ely, Wayne Arlen
**Ligonier**
Walters, Gomer Winston
**New Hope**
Baldi, Robert Otjen
**Newtown**
Godwin, Robert Anthony
**Philadelphia**
Barrett, John J(ames), Jr.
Berger, David
Berger, Harold
Binder, David Franklin
Bissell, Rolin Plumb
Brown, William Hill, III
Carroll, Thomas Colas
Chanin, Bernard
Collins, Todd Stowe
Cooney, J(ohn) Gordon, Jr.
Cramer, Harold
Damsgaard, Kell Marsh
Dennis, Edward S(pencer) G(ale), Jr.
Donohue, John Patrick
Durant, Marc
Epstein, Alan Bruce
Fiebach, H. Robert
Garcia, Rudolph
Gordesky, Morton
Hangley, William Thomas
Harkins, John Graham, Jr.
Haviland, Donald Edward, Jr.
Kemler, R(obert) Michael
Kessler, Alan Craig
Kitchenoff, Robert Samuel
Klein, Howard Bruce
Kohn, Harold Elias
Kraeutler, Eric
Lowery, William Herbert
Mack, Wayne A.
Madva, Stephen Alan
Martin-Boyan, Annemarie
Mathes, Stephen Jon
McBride, James Francis
McKeon, Jami Wintz
Milbourne, Walter Robertson
Milone, Francis Michael
Monheit, Herbert
Mullinix, Edward Wingate
O'Connor, Patrick J.
Ossip, Michael J.
Parry, William DeWitt
Powell, Charles Law
Rainville, Christina
Ramsey, Natalie D.
Resnick, Stephanie
Savage, Timothy Joseph
Scher, Howard Dennis
Sheils, Denis Francis
Sigmond, Richard Brian
Smith, John Francis, III
Stuart, Glen R(aymond)
Suddath, Thomas Howle, Jr.
Toll, Seymour Irving
Wrobleski, Jeanne Pauline
**Pipersville**
Carr, Stephen Kerry
**Pittsburgh**
Acheson, Amy J.
Baicker-McKee, Steven F.
Baldauf, Kent Edward
Beachler, Edwin Harry, III
Blenko, Walter John, Jr.
Brown, James Benton
Candris, Laura A.
Christof, Joseph S. D., II
Cohen, David R.
Cohen, Robert (Avram)
Conley, William Vance
Donahoe, Daniel Brennen
Forsyth, Andrew Watson, III
Gutnick, H. Yale
Hall, K. Mark
Hull, John Daniel, IV
Hurnyak, Christina Kaiser
Jones, Craig Ward
Klett, Edwin Lee
Lerach, Richard Fleming
Litman, Roslyn Margolis
McConomy, James Herbert
McGinley, John Regis, Jr.
McKenna, J. Frank, III
Murray, Philip Joseph, III
Ober, Russell John, Jr.
O'Connor, Edward Gearing
Raynovich, George, Jr.
Rostek, Nancy Elizabeth
Schmidt, Edward Craig
Sherry, John Sebastian
Stroyd, Arthur Heister
Ulven, Mark Edward
Van Kirk, Thomas L.
**Plymouth Meeting**
Bracaglia, Thomas Paul
**Reading**
Turner, David Eldridge
**Scranton**
Howley, James McAndrew
**Southeastern**
Husick, Lawrence Alan
**Stroudsburg**
Catina, Janet K.

### RHODE ISLAND

**Newport**
Scheck, Frank Foetisch
**Providence**
Blish, John Harwood
Greenwood, Charles
Kacir, Barbara Brattin
Medeiros, Matthew Francis
Parks, Albert Lauriston

### SOUTH CAROLINA

**Charleston**
Bernstein, Robert Alan
Darling, Stephen Edward
Dominick, Paul Allen
Glass, Benjamin Philip
Kahn, Ellis Irvin
Laddaga, Beth Jane
Solomon, Cindi Anne
**Columbia**
Babcock, Keith Moss
Barnes, Robert Bryan
Rawl, A. Victor, Jr.
Sheftman, Howard Stephen
**Greenville**
Ferguson, Donald Littlefield
Gallivan, Henry Mills
Laws, James Terry
White, Daniel Bowman
**Hilton Head Island**
Carter, Stephen Edward
McKay, John Judson, Jr.
**Kiawah Island**
Jacobson, Stephen Wayne
**Myrtle Beach**
Leiter, John M.

### SOUTH DAKOTA

**Pierre**
Gerdes, David Alan
**Webster**
Burke, John William

### TENNESSEE

**Chattanooga**
Campbell, Paul, III
Cooper, Gary Allan
Dennis, Tricia I.
Moore, Hugh Jacob, Jr.
**Collierville**
Scroggs, Larry Kenneth
**Hendersonville**
McCaleb, Joe Wallace
**Kingsport**
Mason, Donald F., Jr.
**Knoxville**
Fox, James Erwin
Hagood, Lewis Russell
Sanger, Herbert Shelton, Jr.
**Lookout Mountain**
Leitner, Paul Revere
**Memphis**
Carr, Oscar Clark, III
Clark, Ross Bert, II
Garts, James Rufus, Jr.
Hancock, Jonathan Cromwell
Noel, Randall Deane

Sossaman, William Lynwood
Turner, Kay Farese
Warren, Keith Ashley
Wilder, James Sampson, III

**Nashville**
Hildebrand, Donald Dean
Knowles, Emmitt Clifton
Phillips, W. Alan

**Sewanee**
Pierce, Donna L.

**Signal Mountain**
Leitner, Gregory Marc

## TEXAS

**Abilene**
Suttle, Stephen Hungate

**Arlington**
Jensen, John Robert

**Austin**
Lochridge, Lloyd Pampell, Jr.
Ludlum, James S.
Mallios, George James
Schwartz, Leonard Jay
Sudarshan, Arvind Jewett
Zager, Steven Mark

**Beaumont**
Black, Robert Allen
Freeman, Mark Allan

**Brownsville**
Jordan, John Joseph
Weisfeld, Sheldon

**Corpus Christi**
Elizondo, Luis A.

**Dallas**
Acker, Rodney
Atwood, Roy Tress
Austin, Ann Sheree
Babcock, Charles Lynde, IV
Baggett, Steven Ray
Barnett, Barry Craig
Beane, Jerry Lynn
Bickel, John W., II
Biermacher, Kenneth Wayne
Burkett, Joe Wylie
Case, Thomas Louis
Coleman, Robert Winston
Conant, Allah B., Jr.
Evans, Roger
Falk, Robert Hardy
Figari, Ernest Emil, Jr.
Freytag, Sharon Nelson
Frick, John Michael
Frisbie, Curtis Lynn, Jr.
Govett, Brett Christopher
Harrison, Orrin Lea, III
Hartnett, Thomas Robert, III
Henderson, David Allen
Jones, James Alton
Kearney, Douglas Charles
Keithley, Bradford Gene
Kirby, Le Grand Carney, III
Lynn, Barbara Michele
McAtee, David Ray
Mc Elhaney, John Hess
McGarry, Charles William
McGowan, Patrick Francis
Medford, Leane Capps
Mow, Robert Henry, Jr.
Palmer, Philip Isham, Jr.
Palter, John Theodore
Perez, Daniel Francisco
Price, John Aley
Ringle, Brett Adelbert
Roberts, Scott Raymond
Scuro, Joseph E., Jr.
Sides, Jack Davis, Jr.
Valdez, Frances Valdez
Yarbrough, Fletcher Leftwich

**Diboll**
Moss, Logan Vansen

**El Paso**
Gordon, Norman James
Howell, Mark Franklin
Malone, Daniel Robert
Mott, H. Christopher

**Fort Worth**
Chappell, David Franklin
Dean, Beale
Elliott, Frank Wallace
Hart, John Clifton
Mack, Theodore
Randolph, Robert McGehee
Rutherford, Jay K.
Streck, Frederick Louis, III
Watson, Robert Francis

**Friendswood**
Youngdahl, Jay Thomas

**Houston**
Amdur, Arthur R.
Aschermann, Mark L.
Bayko, Emil Thomas
Behrmann, Lawrence James
Beirne, Martin Douglas
Blair, Graham Kerin (Kerry Blair)
Boswell, John Howard
Brinson, Gay Creswell, Jr.
Cagle, Stephen Henderson
Caldwell, Rodney Kent
Carr, Edward A.
Chavez, John Anthony
Craig, Robert Mark, III
Crinion, Gregory Paul
De La Garza, Charles H.
Durham, William Andrew
Engerrand, Kenneth G.
Essmyer, Michael Martin
Fladung, Richard Denis
Fleming, George Matthews
Forlano, Frederick Peter
Gonynor, Francis James
Hamel, Lee
Jordan, Charles Milton
Kean, James Campbell
Kelly, Hugh Rice
Ketchand, Robert Lee
Krieger, Paul Edward
Lawhon, Susan Harvin
Leach, Sydney Minturn
Lopez, David Tiburcio
Mallia, Michael Patrick
Martin, Christopher W.
McKinney, Carolyn Jean
Michaels, Kevin Richard
Norman, Richard Eugene
Peddie, Collyn Ann
Pettiette, Alison Yvonne
Ray, Hugh Massey, Jr.
Reasoner, Harry Max
Rowland, Robert Alexander, III
Sales, James Bohus
Schwartz, Charles Walter
Secrest, Ronald Dean
Shurn, Peter Joseph, III
Sikora, Tomasz Jacek
Spence, W. Ross
Stuart, Walter Bynum, IV
Susman, Morton Lee
Tran, Minh Quang
Wallis, Olney Gray
Waska, Ronald Jerome
Woody, Clyde Woodrow
Yetter, R. Paul

**Irving**
Freiling, Don Rynn

**Kaufman**
Legg, Reagan Houston

**Mesquite**
Daniels, Russell Howard

**Midland**
Estes, Andrew Harper

**San Antonio**
Biery, Evelyn Hudson
Johnson, Edward Michael
Moynihan, John Bignell

**Sherman**
Harrison, Richard Edward

**Spring**
McGregor, Martin Luther, Jr.

**Sweetwater**
Jones, Charles Eric, Jr.

**Texarkana**
Young, Damon Michael

**Tyler**
George, Samuel Mills
Kent, Don Wayne

**Victoria**
Tipton, Drew B.

## UTAH

**Salt Lake City**
Anderson, Craig W.
Christensen, Patricia Anne Watkins
Clark, Robert Stokes
Colessides, Nick John
Erickson, David Belnap
Holbrook, Donald Benson
Lochhead, Robert Bruce
Orton, R. Willis
Scofield, David Willson

## VERMONT

**Norwich**
Lundquist, Weyman Ivan

**Sharon**
Thrasher, John Edwin

**Shelburne**
Kurrelmeyer, Louis Hayner

**Stowe**
Davison, Robert P., Jr.

## VIRGINIA

**Abingdon**
McElroy, Howard Chowning

**Alexandria**
Carter, Richard Dennis
Drennan, Joseph Peter
Georges, Peter John
Green, James Francis
Phan, Nhat D.
Pugh, William Wallace
Sherk, George William
Tompkins, Michael William
Toothman, John William

**Arlington**
Collins, Philip Reilly
Dunham, Frank Willard
Kaufman, Jeffrey Hugh
Kelly, John James
Laughlin, James Harold, Jr.
Rowan, Robert Allen

**Fairfax**
Chapman, Edmund Whyte

**Falls Church**
Gorenstein, Charles
Kirk, Dennis Dean
Van Oeveren, Edward Lanier
Young, John Hardin

**Great Falls**
Railton, William Scott
Smith, John Anthony

**Lynchburg**
Burnette, Ralph Edwin, Jr.

**Mc Lean**
Harrison, John Edwards
Kennedy, Cornelius Bryant
Mason, Thomas Owen
Raley, Charles Edward

**McLean**
Bredehoft, John Michael

**Norfolk**
Clark, Morton Hutchinson
Corcoran, Andrew Patrick, Jr.
Sims, Hunter W., Jr.
Zahn, Richard William

**Norton**
Shortridge, Michael L.

**Richmond**
Bing, Richard McPhail
Brooks, Robert Franklin, Sr.
Hall, Stephen Charles
Landin, David Craig
McElligott, James Patrick, Jr.
Northup, Stephen A.
Riopelle, Brian Charles
Tashjian-Brown, Eva S(usan)

**Roanoke**
Harris, Bayard Easter
Jennings, James Wilson, Jr.
Skolrood, Robert Kenneth
Tegenkamp, Gary Elton

**Springfield**
Chappell, Milton Leroy

**Vienna**
Razzano, Frank Charles

**Virginia Beach**
Clark, Donald H.
Dumville, S(amuel) Lawrence
Gray, Jeffrey Hugh
Hajek, Francis Paul

## WASHINGTON

**Bellingham**
Anderson, David Bowen

**Everett**
Ferguson, Royce Allan, Jr.

**Seattle**
Bagshaw, Bradley Holmes
Bateman, Heidi S.
Bishin, William Robert
Bringman, Joseph Edward
Caryl, Michael R.
Corning, Nicholas F.
Dunham, Douglas Spence
Estes, Stewart Andrew
Fredericksen, Scott L.
Freedman, Bart Joseph
Gandara, Daniel
Gibbons, Steven Van
Gould, Ronald Murray
Gray, Marvin Lee, Jr.
Groff, David Clark, Jr.
Larson, Linda R.
Leed, Roger Melvin
McConaughy, Bennet Alan
McKay, Michael Dennis
McKinstry, Ronald Eugene
Mines, Michael
Reardon, Mark William
Schumacher, Scott Alan
Schwartz, Irwin H.
Squires, William Randolph, III
Tallman, Richard C.
Webber, James Carl

**Spokane**
Smythe, Andrew Campbell
Weatherhead, Leslie R.

**Tacoma**
Mungia, Salvador Alejo, Jr.

## WEST VIRGINIA

**Charleston**
Bell, Harry Fullerton, Jr.
Cowan, John Joseph
Neely, Richard

**Moundsville**
Artimez, John Edward, Jr.

**Wheeling**
Hill, Barry Morton

## WISCONSIN

**La Crosse**
Ablan, Michael C.

**Madison**
Bruchs, Amy O'Brien
Coaty, Thomas Jerome
Hildebrand, Daniel Walter
Skilton, John Singleton

**Milwaukee**
Brown, Thomas Edward
Croak, Francis R.
Finerty, John Daniel, Jr.
Fishbach, Nathan A.
Fuller, Henry Chester, Jr.
Habush, Robert Lee
Kennedy, John Patrick
Levit, William Harold, Jr.
Melin, Robert Arthur
Puerner, Paul Raymond
Robinson, Richard Russell
Terschan, Frank Robert
Titley, Robert L.

**Oshkosh**
Zierdt, Alyson Kathleen

**Racine**
Gasiorkiewicz, Eugene Anthony

## WYOMING

**Casper**
Bostwick, Richard Raymond
Combs, W(illiam) Henry, III

**Cheyenne**
Dyekman, Gregory Chris
Rosenthal, Michael Bruce

**Cody**
Stradley, Richard Lee

**Jackson**
Noble, Heather
Schuster, Robert Parks
Shockey, Gary Lee

**Wheatland**
Hunkins, Raymond Breedlove

## TERRITORIES OF THE UNITED STATES

## PUERTO RICO

**San Juan**
Vallone, Ralph, Jr.

## VIRGIN ISLANDS

**Christiansted**
Hart, Thomas Hughson, III

## FRANCE

**Lyon**
Dahling, Gerald Vernon

## ADDRESS UNPUBLISHED

Anderson, David Alan
Arencibia, Raul Antonio
Bersin, Alan Douglas
Blevins, Jeffrey Alexander
Bloom, Charles Joseph
Blumenthal, William
Braun, Jerome Irwin
Brumbaugh, John Moore
Burton, Richard Jay
Bush, Wendell Earl
Davidson, Barry Rodney
Dubuc, Carroll Edward
Eaton, Larry Ralph
Elster, J. Robert
Erlebacher, Arlene Cernik
Ettinger, Joseph Alan
Freedlander, Barrett Walter
Fridkin, Jeffrey David
Futter, Victor
Gilster, Peter Stuart
Goddard, Claude Philip, Jr.
Golder, Frederick Thomas
Gomez, David Frederick
Hall, John Hopkins
Hampson, Robert George
Harris, Janine Diane
Harvitt, Adrianne Stanley
Heins, Samuel David
Heise, John Irvin, Jr.
Henry, DeLysle Leon
Hogan, Richard Phillips
Howard, Christopher Holm
Howard, John Wayne
Hunt, Merrill Roberts
Kessler, Todd Lance
Lepp, Gerald Peter
Levin, William Edward
Locke, John Howard
Mann, Michael B.
Murchison, David Claudius
O'Donnell, Martin J.
Ogden, David William
Pannill, William Presley
Pereyra-Suarez, Charles Albert
Reid, Benjamine
Reminger, Richard Thomas
Robbins, Frank Edward
Roche, Thomas Garrett
Roe, Michael Flinn
Saxon, John David
Schlei, Norbert Anthony
Schulman, Steven Gary
Schwartzman, James Charles
Serota, James Ian
Smouse, H(ervey) Russell
Smyth, Jeffrey A.
Souder, Susan
Speaker, Susan Jane
Spiegel, Jayson Leslie
Springer, Paul David
Stack, Beatriz de Greiff
Stern, John Jules
Stout, Gregory Stansbury
Sussman, Howard S(ivin)
Thornton, John W., Sr.
Tone, Philip Willis
Torregrossa, Joseph Anthony
Twardy, Stanley Albert, Jr.
Wilson, Hugh Steven

# CIVIL LITIGATION, GENERAL

## UNITED STATES

## ALABAMA

**Andalusia**
Albritton, William Harold, IV

**Anniston**
Klinefelter, James Louis

**Bessemer**
Freeman, V(ernie) Edward, II

**Birmingham**
Akers, Ottie Clay
Bloomston, Brett Michael
Boardman, Mark Seymour
Brown, Stephen Edward
Christ, Chris Steve
Cohan, Michael Joseph
Crook, Ronald R.
Gale, Fournier Joseph, III
Givhan, Robert Marcus
Hardin, Edward Lester, Jr.
Harris, George Bryan
Henry, James Fred
Hinton, James Forrest, Jr.
Knight, William Collins, Jr.
Long, Thad Gladden
Lynn, George Gambrill
Nettles, Bert Sheffield
Norris, Rick D.
Oliver, Thomas L., II
Scherf, John George, IV
Simmons Scott, Vanessa Ann
Stelzenmuller, Cyril Vaughn
Timberlake, Marshall
Waldrep, Charlie David
Wettermark, James Hart

**Clayton**
Jackson, Lynn Robertson

**Dadeville**
Oliver, John Percy, II

**Decatur**
Hammond, Stephen Van

**Dothan**
Derrick, Raymond Todd
Hogg, David Kenneth
Morris, Joseph Anthony

**Enterprise**
Fuller, Mark Everett

**Eutaw**
Ford, Byron Todd

**Fayette**
Chambless, Ricky Thomas

**Florence**
Case, Basil Timothy

**Gadsden**
Cornett, Bradley Williams
Davis, Thomas E.
Kimberley, David Alan
Roberts, Michael Lee

**Guntersville**
McLaughlin, Jeffrey Rex

**Huntsville**
Baxter, James Thomas, III
Richardson, Patrick William
Watson, S.A.

**Mobile**
Beckish, Richard Michael
Coley, F(ranklin) Luke, Jr.
Harris, Benjamin Harte, Jr.
Janecky, John Franklin
Lyons, George Sage
Minus, Joseph J., Jr.
Roedder, William Chapman, Jr.
Satterwhite, Harry Vincent

**Montgomery**
Duncan, Priscilla Black
Esdale, R. Graham, Jr.
Gooden, Pamela Joyce
Laurie, Robin Garrett
Lawson, Thomas Seay, Jr.
Lunt, Jennifer Lee
McFadden, Frank Hampton
Nelms, K. Anderson
Nix, H.E., Jr. (Chip Nix)
Smith, Maury Drane

**Moulton**
Dutton, Mark Anthony

**Tuscaloosa**
Blume, Nettie Lynn
Crain, Annette Brashier
Davis, Kenneth Dudley
Smith, James Dwight
Williams, Roger Courtland

## ALASKA

**Anchorage**
Anderson, Lloyd Vincent
Dickson, Robert Jay
Ealy, Jonathan Bruce
Evans, Charles Graham
Flynn, Charles P.
Jensen, Jill Ellen
Powell, James M.
Weddle, Randall Jay
Wonnell, Thomas Burke

**Fairbanks**
Covell, Kenneth

**Juneau**
Sonneman, Joseph Abram

**Kodiak**
Jamin, Matthew Daniel
Ott, Andrew Eduard

## ARIZONA

**Flagstaff**
Stoops, Daniel J.

**Phoenix**
Allen, Robert Eugene Barton
Bodney, David Jeremy
Bouma, John Jacob
Brandon, George Ian
Brecher, Allison Leigh
Brewer, John Brian
Brockelman, Kent
Carlock, George Read
Chenal, Thomas Kevin
Condo, James Robert
Forshey, Timothy Allan
Galbut, Martin Richard
Gerity, Michael E.
Goldstein, Stuart Wolf
Harris, Ray Kendall
Harrison, Mark Isaac
Henderson, James Forney
Hover, John Charles
Johnston, Logan Truax, III
Keilp, Joe
Klausner, Jack Daniel
Lee, Richard H(arlo)
Lemberg, Frederic Gary
Lieberman, Marc R(obert)
Lindholm, Donald Wayne
Luikens, Thomas Gerard
Marable, Sidney Thomas
Marks, Merton Eleazer
Maynard, Daniel Dwight
Moehle, Carm Robert
Nelson, Timothy Andrew
Nichols-Young, Stephanie
Norris, Benjamin R.
Postal, David Ralph
Preston, Bruce Marshall
Richards, Charles Franklin, Jr.
Richman, Stephen Edward
Rose, David L.
Rosenthal, Jay P.
Seamons, Quinton Frank
Smith, Gretchen Nicole
Smock, Timothy Robert
Susman, Alan Howard
Torrens, Daniel
Turk, Andrew Borders
Wilcox, Debra Kay
Winthrop, Lawrence Fredrick

**Prescott**
Gose, Richard Vernie

**Rio Rico**
Ryan, John Duncan

**Scottsdale**
Buri, Charles Edward

**Tempe**
Barnes, Jennifer Reon
Bucklin, Leonard Herbert

**Tucson**
Baldwin, Howard
Berlat, William Leonard
Blackman, Jeffrey William
Burton, Stephen David
D'Antonio, James Joseph
Davis, Richard
Dickey, Harrison Gaslin, III
Esposito, Joseph Louis
Lesher, Stephen Harrison
MacBan, Laura Vaden
Rollins, Michael F.
Willis, Jeffrey Lynn

## ARKANSAS

**Arkadelphia**
Turner, Otis Hawes

**Blytheville**
Fendler, Oscar

**Bryant**
Jackson, James Ralph

**Crossett**
Hubbell, Billy James

**Fayetteville**
Bumpass, Ronald Eugene
McIvor, Marcia Lynn
Smith, Raymond Carroll
Stacy, Burton E., Jr.
Wall, John David

**Hot Springs National Park**
Sanders, Michael Edward

**Jonesboro**
Deacon, John C.
Ledbetter, Joseph Michael

**Little Rock**
Heuer, Sam Tate
Hope, Ronald Arthur
Jiles, Gary D.
Julian, Jim Lee

**Monticello**
Gibson, Charles Clifford, III

**North Little Rock**
McGough, Phillip Allan

## CALIFORNIA

**Alamo**
Davis, Walter Lee
Madden, Palmer Brown

**Auburn**
Litchfield, Robert Latta, Jr.

**Bakersfield**
Karcher, Steven Michael
Lynch, Craig M.

**Belvedere Tiburon**
Buell, Edward Rick, II

**Berkeley**
De Goff, Victoria Joan
Pyle, Walter K.

**Beverly Hills**
Amado, Honey Kessler
Kirkland, John C.
Litwak, Glenn Tod
Rondeau, Charles Reinhardt
Shacter, David Mervyn
Zimet, Marc Joseph

**Burbank**
Litvack, Sanford Martin

**Burlingame**
Narayan, Beverly Elaine

**Calabasas**
Nagle, Robert E.

**Cambria**
Stotter, James, II

**Canoga Park**
Gordon, Jerome

**Carlsbad**
Kelsall, Samuel, V
Koehnke, Phillip Eugene
McCracken, Steven Carl
Villavicencio, Dennis (Richard)

**Carmel**
Varga, S. Gary

**Chatsworth**
Laukenmann, Christopher Bernd

**Chico**
Fuller, David Ralph

**Chula Vista**
Swift, Jack H.

**Citrus Heights**
Marman, Joseph H.

**Claremont**
Ferguson, C. Robert
Gray, Paul Bryan

**Costa Mesa**
Boyer, David Dyer
Long, Susan
Shallenberger, Garvin F.

**Cupertino**
Jelinch, Frank Anthony
Maddux, Parker Ahrens
Van Der Walde, Paul D.

**Davis**
Henderson, Mark Gordy

**Del Mar**
Seitman, John Michael

**Downey**
Duzey, Robert Lindsey

**El Centro**
Zimmermann, Ann Marie

**Encino**
Kent, Thomas Edward
Magidsohn, Herman Edward
Mittenthal, Peter A.
Sperber, David Sol
Terterian, George
Wynne, Brian Douglas

**Escondido**
Barraza, Horacio

**Fallbrook**
Leehey, Paul Wade

**Fremont**
Chou, Yung-Ming

**Fresno**
Clegg, Trevor Clement
DeMaria, Anthony Nicholas
Jamison, Daniel Oliver
Renberg, Michael Loren

**Fullerton**
Moerbeek, Stanley Leonard

**Glendale**
Bright, James Stephen
MacDonald, Kirk Stewart

**Indio**
De Salva, Christopher Joseph

**Irvine**
Ashley, Fred Turner
Callahan, Robert Edward
Carpenter, Scott Rockwell
Dannemeyer, Bruce William
Desai, Aashish Y.
Hamann, Howard Evans
Hensley, William Michael
McInnis, Terrence Reilly
Miller, Richard Wayne
Petrasich, John Moris
Rorty, Bruce Vail
Thompson, Donald Mizelle

**La Canada Flintridge**
Stell, Joseph

**La Jolla**
Eischen, James John, Jr.
Philp, P. Robert, Jr.

**Lafayette**
Lustig, Norman I.

**Long Beach**
Lodwick, Michael Wayne
Roberts, James Donzil
Tikosh, Mark Axente

**Los Angeles**
Adler, Erwin Ellery
Barrett, Jane Hayes
Boydston, Brian D.
Bringardner, John Michael
Brogan, Kevin Herbert
Burns, Marvin Gerald
Byrd, Christine Waterman Swent
Cain, Patrick Joseph
Cathcart, Robert James
Cohen, Cynthia Marylyn
Coleman, Richard Michael
Cornwell, Donald Lee
Craigie, Alex William
Dawson, Norma Ann
Dean, Jon
Desario, Daniel J.
Early, Eric Peter
Field, Richard Clark
Fredman, Howard S
Gallegos, Esteban Guillermo
Garcia-Barron, Gerard Lionel
Geibelson, Michael Aaron
Genga, John Michael
Gould, Howard Neal
Gould, Julian Saul
Gravelle, Douglas Arthur
Grimwade, Richard Llewellyn
Heller, Philip
Herron, Vincent H.
Huben, Brian David
Hutchins, Robert Bruce
Hutt, Laurence Jeffrey
Jacques, Nigel Edward
Johnson, Willie Dan
Kessler, Joan Blumenstein
King, Victor I.
Kolber, Richard A.
Korduner, Debra Lynn
Lamison, Eric Ross
Langberg, Barry Benson
Lange, Joseph Jude Morgan
Lebovits, Moses
Lipton, Jack Philip
Maizel, Samuel Ruven
Marcus, Stephen Howard
Mc Adam, Patrick Michael
McDermott, Thomas John, Jr.
Miller, Louis R., III
Miller, Milton Allen
Montgomery, James Issac, Jr.
Morgenthaler, Alisa Marie
Nordlinger, Stephanie G.
Ogbogu, Cecilia Ify
Olivas, Daniel A.
Pasich, Kirk Alan
Peters, Aulana Louise
Popowitz, Neil Michael
Renner, John Robert
Robinett, Timothy Douglas
Rothman, Frank
Rothman, Michael Judah
Sayas, Conrado Joe
Scholtz, Kenneth P.
Schulman, Robert S.
Schuyler, Rob Rene
Scoular, Robert Frank
Shapiro, Robert Leslie
Simons, Bernard Philip
Sonnett, Anthony Evan
Steinbrecher, Alan K.
Tackowiak, Bruce Joseph
Van de Kamp, John Kalar
Vertun, Alan Stuart
von Kalinowski, Julian Onesime
Whitaker, Ronald Stephen
Windham, Timothy Ray
Winfrey, Diana Lee
Woodland, Irwin Francis
Wright, Wyndell John

**Los Gatos**
Seligmann, William Robert

**Manhattan Beach**
Baer, Joseph Richard

**Menlo Park**
Coats, William Sloan, III
Fairman, Marc P.

**Mill Valley**
Nemir, Donald Philip

**Millbrae**
Agosta, Steven S.
Pliska, Edward William

**Modesto**
Bagley, Shana Angela

**Monterey Park**
Groce, Ewin Petty

**Napa**
Kuntz, Charles Powers
Meyers, David W.

**Newark**
Bernard, Steven Martin

**Newport Beach**
Abendroth, Douglas William
Arnold, Larry Millard
Calcagnie, Kevin Frank
Carman, Ernest Day
Dito, John Allen
Glass, Geoffrey Theodore
Johnson, Thomas Webber, Jr.
Lopez, Ramon Rossi
Merring, Robert Alan

**Oakland**
Allen, Jeffrey Michael
Anton, John M.
Beninati, Nancy Ann
Berry, Phillip Samuel
Drexel, Baron Jerome
Mannis, Estelle Claire
Mendelson, Steven Earle
Nishi, Jin
Patton, Roger William

**Oxnard**
Gerber, David A.
McGinley, James Duff

**Palm Springs**
FitzGerald, John Edward, III
Kimberling, John Farrell

**Palo Alto**
Haile, Elster Sharon

**Pasadena**
Adsit, John Michael
Doyle, John C.
Epstein, Bruce Howard
Zuetel, Kenneth Roy, Jr.

**Piedmont**
McCormick, Timothy Brian Beer

**Pleasanton**
Harding, John Edward
Scott, G. Judson, Jr.

**Point Richmond**
Alexander, Richard John

**Rancho Mirage**
Reuben, Don Harold

**Rancho Palos Verdes**
Wall, Thomas Edward

**Redondo Beach**
Hachmeister, John H.

**Redwood City**
Emanuel, Todd Powell
Givens, Richard Donald
Inama, Christopher Roy

**Rodeo**
Wagner, Eric Roland

**Sacramento**
Bleckley, Jeanette A.
Brookman, Anthony Raymond
Cahill, Virginia Arnoldy
Daniel, Lance
Eickmeyer, Evan
Foster, Douglas Taylor
Greiner, James Ralph
Heller, Donald Herbert
Houpt, James Edward
Martorano, Rebekka Ruth
Mendoza, Joanna R.
Van Dermyden, Sue Ann
Wroten, Walter Thomas

**San Bernardino**
Prince, Timothy Peter

**San Diego**
Adelman, Marc D.
Admire, Duane A.
Brave, Georgine Frances
Brown, LaMar Bevan
Brownlie, Robert William
Cannon, Gary Curtis
Castellanos, Richard Henry
Clark, David Robert
Clark, Grant Lawrence
Curran, Michaela C.
Detisch, Donald W.
Emge, Derek John
Estep, Arthur Lee
Fazio, James Vincent, III
Frantz, William Michael
Frasch, Brian Bernard
Getz, David H.
Guinn, Stanley Willis
Guinn, Susan Lee
Hamer, Mark Harris
Holmes, Karen Anderson
Hutcheson, J(ames) Sterling
Iredale, Eugene Gerald
Lathrop, Mitchell Lee
Lory, Loran Steven
Margolis, Anita Joy
Mortier, Raymond David
Norris, David Baxter
Noziska, Charles Brant
O'Nell, William E.
Robinson, Shawn Michael
Schwartz, Jeffrey Scott
Shelton, Dorothy Diehl Rees
Smigliani, Suzanne Lovelace
Sooy, Richard R.
Stevens, Todd Frederick
Udell, Lei (Lisa) Karen
Vakili, Alidad
Von Passenheim, John B.
Weaver, Michael James
Weidner, Lauren Finder
Zakarin, Keith

**San Francisco**
Alexander, Mary Elsie
Allen, Paul Alfred
Arbuthnot, Robert Murray
Aronovsky, Ronald George
Berning, Paul Wilson
Bertain, G(eorge) Joseph, Jr.
Bleich, Jeffrey Laurence
Boutin, Peter Rucker
Brayer, Janet
Briscoe, John
Callison, Russell James
Chao, Cedric C.
Christopher, Thomas Van
Cicala, Conte Carmelo
Danoff, Eric Michael
Donovan, Charles Stephen
Dunn, Robert Lawrence
Freeman, Tom M.
Haley, Peter C.
Hill, Richard Paul
Hockett, Christopher Burch
Johns, Richard Seth Ellis
Kane, Robert F.
Kang, Helen Haekyong
Links, Robert David
Lombardi, David Ennis, Jr.
Malone, Michael Glen
Martin, Jay R.
Mazhari, Niloufar
Mussman, William Edward, III
Ogilby, Barry Ray
Reding, John Anthony
Rice, Denis Timlin
Richardson, Daniel Ralph
Riley, Benjamin Kneeland
Robin, Kenneth David
Roethe, James Norton
Rosen, Sanford Jay
Salomon, Sheila M.
Samad-Salameh, Alia Fahmi
Scarlett, Randall H.
Seabolt, Richard L.
Sharp, Stefanie Teresa
Slavitt, Howard Alan
Smith, Robert Michael
Staring, Graydon Shaw
Utrecht, Paul F.
Venning, Robert Stanley
Weber, Arnold I.
Weiner, Jody Carl
Wendell Hsu, Linda Sharon
Wolf, Carl
Wolf, Lillian F.
Woodard, Heather Anne

**San Jose**
Bennion, David Jacobsen
Boccardo, James Frederick
Bramer, Lisan Hung
Cummins, Charles Fitch, Jr.
Dresser, William Charles
Hernández, Fernando Vargas
McManis, James
Nielsen, Christian Bayard
Patton, David Alan

**San Marino**
Tomich, Lillian

**San Mateo**
Slabach, Stephen Hall

**San Rafael**
Bloomfield, Neil Jon
Fairbairn, Sydney Elise
Farley, Margaret M.
Freitas, David Prince
Huffman, Jared William
Madow, James Sheldon
Roth, Hadden Wing

**Santa Ana**
Dillard, John Martin
Douville, Louise M.
Fraser, Robert William
Frost, Winston Lyle
Heckler, Gerard Vincent
McCarron, Andrew
Patt, Herbert Jacob
Shelton, Ralph Conrad

**Santa Barbara**
Ah-Tye, Kirk Thomas
Cappello, A. Barry
Delaughter, Jerry L.
Fox, Herb
Hellman, Michael David
Metzinger, Timothy Edward
Moncharsh, Philip Isaac
Pyle, Kurt H.

**Santa Cruz**
Campos, Victor Manuel
Damon, Richard Everett
Redenbacher, Gary

**Santa Monica**
Bower, Allan Maxwell
McGovern, David Carr
Pizzulli, Francis Cosmo Joseph
Ringler, Jerome Lawrence
Wong, Elizabeth Anne

**Santa Rosa**
Clement, Clayton Emerson
McCutchan, B. Edward, Jr.

**Sherman Oaks**
Hartzfeld, Howard Alexander, Jr.

**Simi Valley**
Gruen, Evelyn Jeanette

**Stockton**
Malm, Scott

**Thousand Oaks**
Dougherty, Gerard Michael

**Tiburon**
Bremer, William Richard

**Torrance**
Johnson, Einar William

**Tracy**
Hay, Dennis Lee

**Tustin**
Dao, Hanh D.
Gaughan, John Stephen
Kraft, Henry R.

**Universal Cty**
Gentino, Robert E.

**Van Nuys**
Mikesell, Richard Lyon

**Walnut Creek**
Clark, Michael Patrick
Horner, Clifford R.
Leone, Louis Anthony
Lucchese, David Ross
Rathjen, Jon Laurence
Schreiber, John T.
Wood, Steven Noel Housley

**Weaverville**
Correll, Joanna Rae

**Woodland Hills**
Comroe, Eugene W.
DeSantis, Richard A.
Glicker, Brian Irving
Murphy, Robert Eugene

**Yuba City**
Doughty, Mark Anthony
Santana, Jesse Isaias

## COLORADO

**Arvada**
Carney, T. J

**Aspen**
Bernstein, Jeremy Marshall
Shipp, Dan Shackelford

**Boulder**
Bellac, Patricia Sharman
Cope, Joseph Adams
Enwall, Michael R.
Garlin, Alexander
Gordon, Glen Frank
Pineau, John Kenneth

**Canon City**
McDermott, John Arthur

**Cherry Hl Vlg**
Kerwin, Mary Ann Collins

**Colorado Springs**
Crizer, Celeste Lisanne
Donohoe, John Joseph
Graski, Diana
Harris, Stephen Donnell
Kennedy, Richard Joseph
McCready, Guy Michael
Pressman, Glenn Spencer
Purvis, Randall W. B.
Sheffield, Alden Daniel, Jr.
White, Deborah Sue Youngblood

**Denver**
Avery, James William
Beatty, Michael L.
Breitenstein, Peter Frederic
Ceriani, Gary James
Christopher, Daniel Roy
Das, Arun
Deikman, Eugene Lawrence
DeSisto, John Anthony
Dowdle, Patrick Dennis
Drake, Christopher Todd
Dunn, Randy Edwin
Fink, Steven D.
Finn, John Stephen
Fowler, Daniel McKay
Gallegos, Larry Duayne
Green, Jersey Michael-Lee
Hagen, Glenn W(illiam)
Hamel, Fred Meade
Harris, Dale Ray
Hensen, Stephen Jerome
Hix, Andrea Noel
Horowitz, Robert M.
Jonsen, Eric R.
Kahn, Benjamin Alexander
Kaplan, David S.
Karp, Sander Neil
Kelso, Donald Iain Junor
Kintzele, John Alfred
Lindquist-Kleissler, Arthur
Livingston, Randall Murch
London, David L.
Low, Andrew M.
Macaulay, Christopher Todd
Malatesta, Mary Anne
Mann, Stuart D.
Martin, Raymond Walter
McPherson, Gary Lee
Merritts, Jack Michael
Mumaugh, Brian Michael
Munteanu, Victor John
Nesland, James Edward
Palmeri, John M.
Robinson, Warren A. (Rip Robinson)
Samour, Carlos A.
Savitz, David Barry
Shore, Heather Field
Smith, Daniel Timothy
Spillane, John Michael
Theune, Philipp Charles
Timmins, Edward Patrick
Tomlinson, Warren Leon
Vriesman, Todd L.
Wheeler, Malcolm Edward
Willett, Jonathan S.
Wollins, David Hart

**Englewood**
Burg, Michael S.
Campbell, Darrel Lee
Rediger, Richard Kim
Wheeler, Karen Hannah

**Fort Collins**
Redder, Thomas Joseph

**Frisco**
McElyea, Monica Sergent

**Golden**
Snead, Kathleen Marie

**Greenwood Village**
Underhill, Joanne Parsons

**Lakewood**
Jacobson, Dennis John

**Littleton**
Ballantine, Beverly Neblett
Benkert, Joseph Philip, Jr.
Minckley, Carla Beth

**Lone Tree**
Kaplan, Marc J.

**Manassa**
Garcia, Castelar Medardo

**Manitou Springs**
Slivka, Michael Andrew

**Pagosa Springs**
Kelly, Reid Browne

**Pueblo**
O'Conner, Loretta Rae

**Thornton**
Liberman, David Israel

## CONNECTICUT

**Avon**
Wiechmann, Eric Watt

**Bridgeport**
Arons, Mark David
Shepro, Daniel
Zeldes, Jacob Dean

**Brookfield**
Secola, Joseph Paul

**Danbury**
Dornfeld, Sharon Wicks

**Fairfield**
Burke, William Milton
Denniston, Brackett Badger, III
Rosenstein, Sheila Kovaleski

**Hamden**
Bershtein, Herman Sammy

**Hartford**
Berlage, Jan Ingham
Bonee, John Leon, III
Donnell, Brian James
Harrington, Christopher Michael
Holtman, Donald Richard
Kesten, Linda Ann
Orth, Paul William
Space, Theodore Maxwell

**Madison**
Hollo, Leslie Stephen

**Manchester**
Eldergill, Kathleen

**Meriden**
Lowry, Houston Putnam

**Milford**
Smith, Brian William

**Monroe**
Beck, Dana Kendall

**New Haven**
Babbin, Jeffrey R.
Belt, David Levin
Carty, Paul Vernon
Gallagher, William F.
Sosensky, Steven C.
Todd, Erica Weyer

**New London**
Reardon, Robert Ignatius, Jr.
Woods, Kerin Margaret

**New Milford**
Guendelsberger, Robert Joseph

**North Haven**
Cella, Carl Edward
Walsh, Kevin Peter

**Norwalk**
Feinstein, Stephen Michael
Lang, Jules
**Simsbury**
Houlihan, Charles Daniel, Jr.
**Southport**
Pickerstein, Harold James
Sanetti, Stephen Louis
**Stamford**
Casper, Stewart Michael
Kweskin, Edward Michael
Mayerson Cannella, Renee
**Torrington**
Leard, David Carl
**West Hartford**
Connors, Susan Ann
Swerdloff, Mark Harris
**Woodbridge**
Cousins, William Joseph

## DELAWARE

**Dover**
Guerke, I. Barry
Stone, F. L. Peter
**Wilmington**
Burnett, James F.
Eppes, Sharon Marie
Goldman, Michael David
Julian, J. R.
Katzenstein, Robert John
Kulesza, Joseph Dominick, Jr.
Macel, Stanley Charles, III
Saville, Yvonne Takvorian
Semple, James William
Smith, Craig Bennett

## DISTRICT OF COLUMBIA

**Washington**
Abrahams, Daniel B.
Baine, Kevin T.
Barnett, Robert Bruce
Beck, David Charles
Beresford, Douglas Lincoln
Bernabei, Lynne Ann
Boss, Lenard Barrett
Boyle, Timothy Edward
Broadus, Charlsa Dorsantres
Broas, Timothy Michael
Buckley, John Joseph, Jr.
Burchfield, Bobby Roy
Canfield, Edward Francis
Carome, Patrick Joseph
Carter, William Joseph
Casey, Bernard J.
Charles, Robert Bruce
Chierichella, John W.
Cihon, Christopher Michael
Cooper, Clement Theodore
Cope, John R(obert)
Craig, Gregory Bestor
Denison, Mary Boney
Deso, Robert Edward, Jr.
Dolan, Edward Charles
Dorsen, David M(ilton)
Duhig, Diane
Duross, Charles Edward, IV
English, Caroline Turner
Fisher, Raymond Corley
Frank, Arthur J.
Frantz, David Joseph
Friedlander, Lisa L.
Fuller, Vincent J.
Funkhouser, Robert Bruce
Gelb, Joseph Donald
Gibson, Kumiki S.
Goldfarb, Ronald Lawrence
Hansen, Mark Charles
Hassett, Joseph Mark
Hoge, Chris
Jetton, C. Loring, Jr.
Jones, Allen, Jr.
Kendall, David E.
Kent, M. Elizabeth
Kilburn, Edwin Allen
Klarfeld, Peter James
Kofman, Stephanie Wank
Levine, Steven Mark
Lim, Joseph Edward
Liss, Jeffrey F.
Martin, Ralph Drury
Marvin, Charles Rodney, Jr.
McDaniels, William E.
McGuire, Andrew Philip
Mendelsohn, Allan Irving
Michael, Helen Katherine
Miller, Nory
Mode, Paul J., Jr.
Moore, Diane Preston
Moses, Alfred Henry
Murphy, Sean Patrick
Pierson, W. DeVier
Podgorsky, Arnold Bruce
Pollock, Stacy Jane
Renner, Curtis Shotwell
Rizzo, James Gerard
Rustad, Jeannine
Salsbury, Michael
Schaumberg, Tom Michael
Shaffer, David James
Sherman, Lawrence Jay
Stein, Cheryl Denise
Taylor, William Woodruff, III
Thaler, Paul Sanders
Tompert, James Emil
Watson, Thomas C.
Weinstein, Harris
Wilk, Adam Ross
Wilson, Charles Haven
Wolff, Paul Martin
Zambri, Salvatore Joseph

## FLORIDA

**Bartow**
Pansler, Karl Frederick
Stevenson, Robin Howard
Sutton, Debra J.
**Boca Raton**
Barwell, Cindy Ann
Beber, Robert H.
Dudley, Everett Haskell, Jr.
Feldman, Donald
Haverman, Daniel Lipman
Horn, Douglas Michael
Nussbaum, Howard Jay
Silver, Barry Morris
Willis, John Alexander
**Bradenton**
Plews, Dennis James
Shapiro, Richard Michael
**Clearwater**
Berman, Elihu H.
Carlson, Edward D.
Coleman, Jeffrey Peters
Silberman, Morris
Swope, Scott Paul
**Coconut Grove**
Freeman, Lewis Bernard
**Coral Gables**
Buell, Rodd Russell
Coleman, Roderick Flynn
Feiler, Michael Benjamin
Fournaris, Theodore J.
Hoffman, Carl H(enry)
Kaplan, Eli
Mellinger, Robert Louis
**Crawfordville**
Bass, Donna Blackwell
**Dade City**
Brock, P. Hutchison, II
**Daytona Beach**
Hassell, Frank Bradley, Sr.
Politis, Michael John
**Delray Beach**
Weitzman, Linda Sue
**Dunedin**
Felos, George James
**Fort Lauderdale**
Beck, Wendy Lynn
Cornell, G(eorge) Ware, Jr.
Cubit, William Aloysius
Fischer, Carey Michael
Futch, Lynn
Heath, Thomas Clark
Heidgerd, Frederick Cay
Hoines, David Alan
James, Gordon, III
Kreizinger, Loreen I.
Lundt, Eric L.
Mager, Scott Alan
Rodriguez, Carlos Augusto
Stalions, William C.
Strickland, Wilton L.
Turner, Hugh Joseph, Jr.
Wich, Donald Anthony, Jr.
**Fort Myers**
Cipriano, Gene Ralph
Harrison, Simon M.
Peet, Maria Lara
**Gainesville**
Kurrus, Thomas William
Mercadante, Stephen G.
Varela, Laura Joan
**Gulf Breeze**
Jester, William David
**Hollywood**
Goodrich, Robert Forester
**Jacksonville**
Allen, Dudley Dean
Allen, William Lee
Alterman, Leonard Mayer
Bradford, Dana Gibson, II
Brock, Lindsey Cook, III
Bullock, Bruce Stanley
Coker, Howard C.
Dunkle, Kurt Hughes
Hamilton, Lawrence Joseph
Hollon, John Oaks
Judas, Suzanne Meyer
Korn, Michael Jeffrey
Liles, Rutledge Richardson
McCorvey, John Harvard, Jr.
Milton, Joseph Payne
Pope, Shawn Hideyoshi
Wachs, Alan Scott
White, Edward Alfred
**Jupiter**
Houser, Stephen Douglas Barlow, III
Mallory, Earl K.
**Key West**
Brihammar, B. Niklas
Smith, Wayne LaRue
**Lake Worth**
Kreidler, Frank Allan
**Lakeland**
Artigliere, Ralph
Knowlton, Kevin Charles
Sanoba, Gregory A.
Schott, Clifford Joseph
**Longwood**
Simon, James Lowell
**Maitland**
Bailey, Michael Keith
**Margate**
Shooster, Frank Mallory
**Miami**
Acosta, Julio Cesar
Armstrong, James Louden, III
Aronberg, David Andrew
Beasley, Joseph Wayne
Berger, Steven R.
Blackburn, Roger Lloyd
Boren, Barry Marc
Brennan, J. Lorraine
Bronis, Stephen J.
Cabanas, Oscar Jorge
Castillo, Angel, Jr.
Coll, Norman Alan
Critchlow, Richard H.
Curtis, Karen Haynes
Cusack, James Wesley
de la Fe, Ernesto Juan
Dougan, Stacey Pastel
Edwards, Thomas Ashton
Feinberg, Dyanne Elyce
Fiore, Robert J.
Fitzgerald, Joseph Michael, Jr.
Freud, John Sigmund
Hartz, Steven Edward Marshall
Hauser, Helen Ann
Hickey, John Heyward
Johnson, Alise M.
Korchin, Judith Miriam
Lanza, Christopher F.
Leone, Dennis Dean
Leslie, Richard McLaughlin
Levine, Robert Jeffrey
Maher, Stephen Trivett
Matthews, Joseph Michael
Miller, James M.
Mody, Renu Noor
Osman, Edith Gabriella
Payne, R.W., Jr.
Picazio, Kim Lowry
Prego, Mayda
Russell, Patrick
Santoro, Thomas Mead
Scherker, Elliot H.
Segall, Norman S.
Silvers, Marcia Jean
Solomon, Michael Bruce
Stansell, Leland Edwin, Jr.
Touby, Kathleen Anita
Vento, M. Thérèse
Weinger, Steven Murray
Zamorano, Andre Jordan
Zarco, Robert
**Miami Beach**
Cesarano, Michael Chapman
Fuller, Lawrence Arthur
Ryce, Donald Theodore
**N Miami Beach**
MacIvor, Catherine J.
Zipkin, Sheldon Lee
**Naples**
Blakely, John T.
Cardillo, John Pollara
Doyle, Robert Eugene, Jr.
**New Smyrna Beach**
Kolodinsky, Richard Hutton
**North Miami Beach**
Franklin, Barry Scott
Snihur, William Joseph, Jr.
**Ocala**
McCall, Wayne Charles
Spivey, Stephen Dale
**Orlando**
Bitner, Richard H.
Blackwell, Bruce Beuford
Collie, Kathryn Kaye
Handley, Leon Hunter
Hartley, Carl William, Jr.
Higgins, Robert Frederick
Hurt, Jennings Laverne, III
Johnson, Kraig Nelson
Jontz, Jeffry Robert
Kelaher, James Peirce
Kolin, Lawrence Howard
Lou Pendás, Luzardo
Marcus, Lee Warren
Metz, Larry Edward
Morgan, Mary Ann
Nadeau, Robert Bertrand, Jr.
Nelson, Frederick Herbert
Palmer, William D.
Paul, David Aaron
Peterson, David Eugene
Sawicki, Stephen Craig
Spoonhour, James Michael
Subin, Eli Harold
Wagner, Lynn Edward
**Palm Beach Gardens**
Pumphrey, Gerald Robert
Whalen, Jeanmarie
**Palm Harbor**
Lentz, Harold James
**Panama City**
Fensom, James B.
**Pensacola**
Baker, William Costello, Jr.
Green, James R.
Kelly, John Barry, II
McKenzie, James Franklin
Soloway, Daniel Mark
**Plantation**
Koltnow, H. Robert
**Pompano Beach**
Shulmister, M(orris) Ross
**Pt Charlotte**
Jones, Phillip Jeffrey
**Saint Petersburg**
Battaglia, Brian Peter
Henniger, David Thomas
Hickman, James K.
Keane, Michael J.
Mann, Sam Henry, Jr.
Pedata, Martin Anthony
Ross, Howard Philip
Wahl, Robert James
**Sanford**
Partlow, James Justice
**Sarasota**
Christopher, William Garth
Garland, Richard Roger
Goldsmith, Stanley Alan
Lamia, Christine Edwards
Shults, Thomas Daniel
Zitani, Gregory Anthony
**South Miami**
Carnesoltas, Ana-Maria
**Stuart**
Harvin, Wesley Reid
Lako, Charles Michael, Jr.
McManus, Frank Shields
Ponsoldt, William Raymond, Jr.
**Tallahassee**
Barley, John Alvin
Connor, Kenneth Luke
Johnson, Fred Mack
Kitchen, E.C. Deeno
Miller, Gregory R.
Schreiber, Charles Joseph, Jr.
Sheffield, Frank Elwyn
Underwood, R. Michael
Varn, Wilfred Claude
**Tampa**
Apgar, Kenneth Edward
Aye, Walter Edwards
Bardi, Henry J.
Barker, Chris A(llen)
Berkowitz, Herbert Mattis
Boos, Robert Walter, II
Campbell, Richard Bruce
Castello, Joe, Jr.
Colton, Roberta Ann
Cunningham, Anthony Willard
Davis, Kirk Stuart
DeVaney, Donna Brookes
Elligett, Raymond Thomas, Jr.
Fernandez, Ricardo Antonio
Fulton, Robert Maurice
Gordon, Jeffrey
Hahn, William Edward
Hoyt, Brooks Pettingill
Huneycutt, Alice Ruth
Knopik, Christopher Scott
Lamb, Bruce Douglas
MacDonald, Thomas Cook, Jr.
Mandelbaum, Samuel Robert
McClurg, Douglas P.
McQuigg, John Dolph
Neumaier, Mark Adam
Nutter, Robert Heinrich
Olson, John Karl
Robinson, John William, IV
Sanders, L. Gray
Steiner, Geoffrey Blake
Taub, Theodore Calvin
Tripp, Paul Wayne
Turmel, Stacey Lynn
Vogt, Martha Diane
Yerrid, C. Steven
**Tavernier**
Jabro, John A.
**West Palm Beach**
Barnhart, Forrest Gregory
Ciotoli, Eugene L.
Gildan, Phillip Clarke
Gordon, Robert E.
Hicks, James Hermann
Kamen, Michael Andrew
Kornspan, Susan Fleischner
Moffet, Kenneth William
Mrachek, Lorin Louis
Norton, William Alan
Posgay, Matthew Nichols
Quattlebaum, Guy Elliot
Rosenberg, Robin L.
Spillias, Kenneth George
Wagner, Arthur Ward, Jr.
Wroble, Arthur Gerard
Ziska, Maura A.
**Winter Park**
Aikin, Wendy Lise
Goldsmith, Karen Lee

## GEORGIA

**Albany**
Cannon, William E., Jr.
Eidson, Patrick Samuel
**Alpharetta**
Singer, Randy Darrell
**Athens**
Elkins, Robert Neal
**Atlanta**
Barton, Thomas McCarty
Bates, Beverly Bailey
Beckham, Walter Hull, III
Bramlett, Jeffrey Owen
Brown, John Robert
Bruckner, William J.
Cahalan, Scott David
Calvert, Matthew James
Campbell, Charles Edward
Campbell, Jennifer Katze
Carpenter, David Allan
Cheeley, Robert David
Chenevert, Donald James, Jr.
Chilivis, Nickolas Peter
Collins, Donnell Jawan
Collins, Steven M.
Cornwell, William John
Corry, Robert Emmett
Croft, Terrence Lee
Crumpler, Joan Gale
Denham, Vernon Robert, Jr.
Devins, Robert Sylvester
Eidson, James Anthony
England, John Melvin
Ethridge, Robert Michael
Fellows, Henry David, Jr.
Genberg, Ira
Griffin, Harry Leigh
Hagan, James Walter
Harrison, Bryan Guy
Haubenreich, John Gilman
Hunt, John Robert
Jackson, Terry D.
Janney, Donald Wayne
Jester, Carroll Gladstone
Johnson, Benjamin F(ranklin), III
Jones, Evan Wier
Jordan, Paul Rodgers, III
Killorin, Robert Ware
Koplan, Andrew Bennet
Lindsey, Edward Harman, Jr.
Manley, David Bott, III
Mathis, Benton J., Jr.
Matthews, James B., III
Mayfield, William Scott
McAlpin, Kirk Martin
Medlin, Charles McCall
Miller, Janise Luevenia Monica
Owens, L. Dale
Paquin, Jeffrey Dean
Pombert, Jeffrey Lawrence
Rhodes, Thomas Willard
Stamps, Thomas Paty
Steel, John Deaton
Tate, Edwin Arthur
Williamson, James Robert, Jr.
Wilson, Roger Calvin
Young, Michael Anthony
**Augusta**
Williams, William James
**Canton**
Hasty, William Grady, Jr.
**College Park**
Stokes, Arch Yow
**Columbus**
Harp, John Anderson
Lasseter, Earle Forrest
McGlamry, Max Reginald
**Cuthbert**
Bowles, Jesse Groover
**Decatur**
Apolinsky, Stephen Douglas
O'Connell, John James, Jr.
**Fitzgerald**
Hughes, (Terry) Chris(topher)
**Homerville**
Helms, Catherine Harris
**Jonesboro**
Teske, Steven Cecil
**Macon**
Cleveland, Blair Knox
Cole, John Prince
Cranford, James Michael
Grant, George Clarence
**Mcdonough**
Meadows, Rod G.
**Metter**
Doremus, Ogden
**Nashville**
Ellis, Robert Bryan, Jr.
**Rincon**
Carellas, Theodore T.
**Rome**
Brinson, Robert Maddox
**Savannah**
Aderhold, Kathleen
Gannam, Michael Joseph
Mason, Kirby Gould
Muller, Peter Deppish
Painter, Paul Wain, Jr.
Stabell, Edward Reidar, III
**Statesboro**
Brogdon, W.M. "Rowe"
**Swainsboro**
Edenfield, James Franklin
**Valdosta**
Bass, Jay Michael
Copeland, Roy Wilson
Lawrence, Matthew Russell
**Zebulon**
Galloway, Newton Monroe

## HAWAII

**Honolulu**
Ando, Russell Hisashi
Chin, Stephanie Anne
Chu, Harold
Deaver, Phillip Lester
Dwyer, John Ryan, Jr.
Edmunds, John Sanford
Fong, Peter C. K.
Godbey, Robert Carson
Grande, Thomas Robert
Hart, Brook
Heller, Ronald Ian
Ichinose, Susan M.
Kawachika, James Akio
Kohn, Robert
Lau, Jeffrey Daniel
Minkin, David Justin
Mirikitani, Andrew Kotaro
Moore, Willson Carr, Jr.
O'Neill, Ralph James
Pyun, Matthew Sung Kwan
Reinke, Stefan Michael
Robinson, Stacey Mukai
Sato, Glenn Kenji
Sekiya, Gerald Yoshinori
Sumida, Kevin P.H.
Wong, Reuben Sun Fai
Woo, Christopher
Yamada, Stephen Kinichi
Yamano, John Y.
**Kailua Kona**
Fagundes, Joseph Marvin, III
Zimmerman, William Irving
**Koloa**
Blair, Samuel Ray
**Lihue**
Valenciano, Randal Grant Bolosan
**Makawao**
Barrad, Catherine Marie
**Wailuku**
Green, Eve Marie
Jenkins, Brian Rennert

## IDAHO

**Boise**
Desler, Peter
Furey, Patrick Dennis
Green, Cumer L.
Hall, Richard Edgar
Hoagland, Samuel Albert
Kristensen, Debora Kathleen
Lombardi, David Richard
Noack, Harold Quincy, Jr.
Runft, John L.
Scanlan, Kevin J.
Thomas, Eugene C.
**Hailey**
Hogue, Terry Glynn
**Idaho Falls**
Whittier, Monte Ray
**Pocatello**
Nye, W. Marcus W.
**Twin Falls**
Hohnhorst, John Charles

## ILLINOIS

**Belleville**
Boyle, Richard Edward
Churchill, Allen Delos
Neville, James Edward
**Bloomington**
Bragg, Michael Ellis
Varney, Robert T.
**Carol Stream**
Handley, Robert
**Champaign**
Harden, Richard Russell
**Chicago**
Adelman, Stanley Joseph
Adler, John William, Jr.
Anagnost, Themis John
Anderson, Eric Daniel
Argeros, Anthony George
Aronovitz, Cory Jay
Augustynski, Adam J.
Banta, Don Arthur
Becker, Theodore Michaelson
Belz, Edwin J.
Benak, James Donald
Blatt, Richard Lee
Brand, Mark
Brice, Roger Thomas
Burke, Edmund Patrick, Sr.
Burke, William Joseph

Burns, Terrence Michael
Byrne, Katharine Crane
Cannizzaro, Sam F.
Cazares, Jorge V.
Collins, Glenn
Connelly, Mary Jo
Cunningham, Craig Carnell
Daley, Michael Joseph
Daniels, John Draper
Daniels, Keith Byron, Jr.
Davis, Scott Jonathan
Dombrowski, Gerald Michael
Donner, Ted A.
Duric, Nicholas M.
Edelman, Bernard Paul
Eggert, Russell Raymond
Eimer, Nathan Philip
Elden, Gary Michael
Ellbogen, Andrew D.
Enright, Thomas Michael
Esrick, Jerald Paul
Fennell, Monica Ann
Ferrini, James Thomas
Filpi, Robert Alan
Fogel, Joseph Lewis
Ford, Michael W.
Formeller, Daniel Richard
Fox, Elaine Saphier
Frank, Jay Allan
Franklin, Christine Carroll
Frazen, Mitchell Hale
French, Timothy A.
Frew, Stephen B.
Geraldson, Raymond I., Jr.
Giampietro, Wayne Bruce
Gilford, Steven Ross
Goodman, Ann Paton
Gordon, Gilbert Wayne
Graber, Patrick Matthew
Gustman, David Charles
Halloran, Michael John
Harrold, Bernard
Heilmann, David Michael
Henry, Brian Thomas
Henry, Kenneth Alan
Herman, Stephen Charles
Hoffa, Thomas Edward
Hoover, R. Sam
Howe, Jonathan Thomas
Howser, Richard Glen
Hyman, Michael Bruce
Iwan, Lori E.
Jordan, Susan Patricia
Kallianis, James H., Jr.
Kamerick, Eileen Ann
Kaminsky, Richard Alan
Karnes, Evan Burton, II
Kempf, Donald G., Jr.
Kikoler, Stephen Philip
Kim, Michael Charles
Kresse, William Joseph
Krivicich, John Augustine
Kunkle, William Joseph, Jr.
Kurfirst, Leonard Stanley
Lederleitner, Joseph Benedict
Lien, John Donovan
Liggio, Carl Donald
Lipnick, Stanley Melvin
Luning, Thomas P.
Lynch, John James
Marsh, Weston W.
McFadden, Monica Elizabeth
McNerney, Joseph James
Molo, Steven Francis
Montgomery, William Adam
Moran, John Thomas, Jr.
Murphy, Edward J.
Neumeier, Matthew Michael
Nora, Gerald Ernest
Nordgren, Gerald Paul
Novak, Mark
O'Hagan, Kevin Michael
Olavarria, Frank J.
Parkhurst, Beverly Susler
Pitzer, Jeff Scott
Podlewski, Joseph Roman, Jr.
Price, Paul L.
Pugh, Stephen Henry, Jr.
Rappaport, Bret Andrew
Roberson, G. Gale, Jr.
Rothstein, Jonathan Alan
Rovell, Michael Jay
Rubin, Jeffry Mark
Sarauskas, Paul Justas
Saunders, Terry Rose
Schmall, Steven Todd
Shank, William O.
Shipley, Robert Allen
Simon, Seymour
Smith, Stephen Edward
Snyder, Jean Maclean
Stick, Michael Alan
Stiegel, Michael Allen
Sundvall, Sheila A.
Suskin, Howard Steven
Tenenbaum, J. Samuel
Thomson, George Ronald
Tucker, Bowen Hayward
Van Tine, Matthew Eric
Vranicar, Michael Gregory
Ward, Michael W.
Weaver, Timothy Allan
Wilcox, Mark Dean
Wood, Allison Lorraine
Wool, Leon

**Chicago Heights**
Wigell, Raymond George

**Columbia**
Gutknecht, Timothy Arthur

**Decatur**
Ansbro, James Michael
Jones, Steven Gary

**Deerfield**
Rollin, Kenneth B.

**Dekalb**
Tucker, Watson Billopp

**Des Plaines**
Jacobs, William Russell, II

**East Alton**
Tobin, Gregory Michael

**Elgin**
Childers, John Aaron
Karayannis, Marios Nicholas
Roeser, Ronald O.

**Elk Grove**
Hale, Jennifer Ansbro

**Elmhurst**
Berry, James Frederick

**Evanston**
Smith, Mark Steven

**Flossmoor**
Gevers, Marcia Bonita

**Franklin Park**
Motta, Robert Michael

**Hinsdale**
De Rose, John Patrick
Imbierowicz, Angela
O'Brien, Donald Joseph

**Hoffman Est**
Schaefer, Alan Charles

**Joliet**
Boyer, Andrew Ben
Copeland, Charlene Carole
Klukas, Elizabeth Ann

**Kankakee**
Marek, James Dennis

**La Grange**
Kerr, Alexander Duncan, Jr.

**Lake Forest**
Zapinski, Robert Paul

**Libertyville**
Mihelic, Kristin Tavia

**Lincolnshire**
Giza, David Alan

**Mattoon**
Corn, Stephen Leslie

**Morton Grove**
Klunder, Scott Ross

**Mundelein**
Ackley, Robert O.

**Naperville**
Levy, Steven Barry

**Oak Brook**
Oldfield, E. Lawrence
Washburn, John James

**Oak Park**
Armstrong, Gene Lyndon

**Oakbrook Terrace**
LaForte, George Francis, Jr.

**Palos Heights**
Jasinski, George John

**Park Ridge**
Bellas, George Steven
Tinaglia, Michael Lee

**Peoria**
Bell, Gregory S.
Bertschy, Timothy L.
Prusak, Maximilian Michael
Urban, Charles J.

**Rock Island**
Lousberg, Peter Herman
Wallace, Franklin Sherwood

**Rockford**
Fredrickson, Robert Alan
Hunsaker, Richard Kendall
Ohlander, Jan H.
Rouleau, Mark A.

**Rolling Meadows**
Sullivan, Terry

**Rosemont**
Richter, Paul David

**Saint Charles**
Clancy Boles, Susan

**Schaumburg**
Gardner, Caryn Sue

**South Holland**
Olofsson, Daniel Joel
Scott, Edward Aloysius

**Springfield**
Feldman, Howard William
Hanley, William Stanford
Heckenkamp, Robert Glenn
Narmont, John Stephen
Reed, Robert Phillip
Thornton, Joseph Philip

**Streator**
Mohan, John J.

**Sycamore**
Smith, Peter Thomas

**Urbana**
Kearns, James Cannon
Moore, David Robert

**Wauconda**
Malik, Thomas Warren

**Wheaton**
Beckley, James Emmett
Butt, Edward Thomas, Jr.
May, Frank Brendan, Jr.

**Wilmette**
Griffith, James D.

## INDIANA

**Angola**
Blosser, David John

**Avilla**
Stephens, James F.

**Bedford**
McSoley, Patrick Shannon

**Danville**
Baldwin, Jeffrey Kenton

**Evansville**
Barber, Steven Thomas
Hayes, Philip Harold
Knight, Jeffrey Lin
Sauvey, David R.

**Fort Wayne**
Clark, Jeffrey A.
James, Ronald Eugene

**Franklin**
Johnson, Russell A.

**Indianapolis**
Albright, Terrill D.
Arceneaux, Adam
Barrett, David Olan
Blythe, James David, II
Caress, Timothy Charles
Carney, Joseph Buckingham
Carr, David J.
Conour, William Frederick
Due, Danford Royce
Fuller, Samuel Ashby
Hill, Douglas Jennings
Kautzman, John Fredrick
Leitch, Ryan L.
Loiseau, Richard
Love, Jennifer Stephens
McTurnan, Lee Bowes
Moffatt, Michael Alan
Mortier, Jeffrey James
Padgett, Gregory Lee
Paris, Timothy John
Peters, Stephen Jay
Petersen, James Leo
Price, Henry J.
Scaletta, Phillip Ralph, III
Tinsley, Nancy Grace
Wampler, Robert Joseph
Whitney, Larry Gene
Yeager, Joseph Heizer, Jr.

**Indianpolis**
Holtzlander, Stephanie Franco

**Jeffersonville**
Harris, Ronald Dean

**Knox**
Gudeman, Leroy Dennis

**Kokomo**
Bayliff, Edgar W.

**Lafayette**
Bumbleburg, Joseph Theodore
Garwood, Cynthia Lynn

**Merrillville**
Miller, Richard Allen
Steele, Kevin Edward

**South Bend**
Murphy, Patrick David
Reinke, William John

**Terre Haute**
Bopp, James, Jr.
Bough, Bradley A.
Kesler, John A.

**Valparaiso**
Gioia, Daniel August

## IOWA

**Ames**
Sotak, Ronald Michael

**Cedar Rapids**
Squires, Vernon Pellett

**Creston**
Kenyon, Arnold Oakley, III

**Davenport**
Lane, Gary M.

**Decorah**
Belay, Stephen Joseph

**Des Moines**
Conlin, Roxanne Barton
Crook, Charles Samuel, III
Eaton, Jay
Finley, Kerry A.
Phipps, David Lee
Sisk, Gregory Charles
Voigts, L.R.
Wanek, Jerrold

**Dubuque**
Hammer, David Lindley

**Estherville**
Mohn, Maynard Martin

**Iowa City**
Hayek, John William

**Johnston**
Leitner, David Larry

**Marshalltown**
Lorenz, William Joseph

**Mount Pleasant**
Vance, Michael Charles

**Newton**
Dalen, DuWayne John

**Sioux City**
Bottaro, Timothy Shanahan

**Vinton**
Mossman, Mark E.

**Webster City**
Karr, Richard Lloyd

## KANSAS

**Fort Scott**
Short, Forrest Edwin

**Garden City**
Loyd, Ward Eugene

**Hays**
Toepfer, Thomas Lyle

**Kansas City**
Holbrook, Reid Franklin
Jurcyk, John Joseph, Jr.

**Lawrence**
Krogh, Richard Alan

**Leawood**
Dvorak, Richard Dee
Shetlar, James R.

**Lenexa**
Bigus, Edward Lowell
Gould, Robert P.
Myers, Ross S
Scott, Robert Gene

**Olathe**
Branham, Melanie J.
Logan, Samuel Price

**Overland Park**
Gunnison, Mark Steven
Knopp, Timothy John
Level, Kurt Alan
Smith, Daniel Lynn
Smith, Edwin Dudley
Smith, Jill Galbreath
Vratil, John Logan

**Paola**
Arnett, Debra Jean

**Shawnee Mission**
Badgerow, John Nicholas
Wetzler, Richard S.

**Topeka**
Frost, Brian Standish
Lawson, Christopher Patrick

**Wichita**
Arabia, Paul
Bostwick, Donald W.
Franklin, Joni Jeanette
Grace, Brian Guiles
Hite, Richard C.
Jones, Gary Kenneth
Liebau, Judd Alan
Willis, Shari Renee Lyne

## KENTUCKY

**Bowling Green**
Brennenstuhl, Henry Brent
Darrell, Barton David
Sparks, David Thomas

**Covington**
Crout, Daniel Wesley
Stepner, Donald Leon

**Crestwood**
Ray, Ronald Dudley

**Florence**
Brown, Stuart P.
Busald, E. André

**Glasgow**
Gardner, Woodford Lloyd, Jr.

**Hazard**
Rose, Danny

**Henderson**
Hamilton, Curtis James, II

**Lexington**
Bagby, Glen Stovall
Beshear, Steven L.
Breeding, Carl Wayne
Campbell, Joe Bill
Conner, Tonya Sue
Cox, Walter Clay Jr.
Curtz, Chauncey S.R.
Ecabert, Peter Leo
Garmer, William Robert
Hiestand, Sheila Patricia
Matl, Lois Tudor
Miller, Harry B(enjamin)
Rich, William Hagood Bellinger
Turley, Robert Joe

**London**
Keller, John Warren

**Louisville**
Ballantine, Douglas Cain
Ballantine, John Tilden
Blaine, Steven Robert
Clay, Richard H.C.
Cowan, Frederic Joseph
Edwards, Steven Alan
Ethridge, Larry Clayton
Furman, C. Dean
Grossman, H. Philip
Humphreys, Gene Lynn
Keeney, Steven Harris
Manly, Samuel
McAdam, Thomas Anthony, III
Morreau, James Earl, Jr.
Orberson, William Baxter
Sales, Kenneth L.
Sandler, David Bruce
Schecter, Benjamin Seth
Swyers, Walter John, Jr.
Talbott, Ben Johnson, Jr.
Valenti, Michael A.

**Newport**
Halloran, Brian Paul

**Paducah**
Nickell, Christopher Shea

**Paintsville**
Massengale, Roger Lee

**Pineville**
Lawson, Susan Coleman

**Providence**
Bock, Valerie L.

**Richmond**
Martin, James Neal

**Shepherdsville**
Givhan, Thomas Bartram

**Versailles**
Jones, Tracy Webb

## LOUISIANA

**Alexandria**
Pharis, James Andrew, Jr.

**Baton Rouge**
Avant, Daniel L.
Ferguson, James Curtis
Giglio, Steven Rene
Gonzales, Edward Joseph, III
Holliday, James Sidney, Jr.
Ray, Betty Jean G.
Robinson, Bert Kris
Scobee, H. Evans
Sledge, L. D.
Walsh, Milton O'Neal
Wittenbrink, Jeffrey Scott

**Bunkie**
McKay, Dan Boies, Jr.

**Covington**
Reynolds, Richard Louis

**Hammond**
Ross, Kenneth L.

**Hessmer**
Jeansonne, Mark Anthony

**Lafayette**
Beyer, Jennifer Elmer
Landry, Michael W.
Morgan, Glenn L.
Myers, Stephen Hawley
Nehrbass, Jennifer Stuller
Ottinger, Patrick S.
Roy, James Parkerson
Swift, John Goulding

**Lake Charles**
Judice, Gregory Van
Miller, Frank C., III
Monk, William Boyce
Veron, J. Michael

**Metairie**
Album, Jerald Lewis
Butcher, Bruce Cameron
Gauthier, Celeste Anne
Haygood, John Warren
Milazzo, Thomas Gregory
Recile, George B.
Senter, Mark Seymour

**Natchitoches**
Seaman, Charles Wilson

**New Orleans**
Abaunza, Donald Richard
Barnett, William Michael
Benjamin, Jack Charles
Bordelon, Alvin Joseph, Jr.
Burr, Timothy Fuller
Butler, Peter Joseph
Christovich, Alvin Richard, Jr.
Clarke, Shaun G.
Curtis, Martha Young
David, Robert Jefferson
Dwyer, Ralph Daniel, Jr.
Eustis, Richmond Minor
Exnicios, Val Patrick
Fierke, Thomas Garner
Gelpi, C. James (Jim Gelpi)
Grundmeyer, Douglas Lanaux
Hammond, Peirce Aldridge, II
Hearin, Robert Matlock, Jr.
Herman, Fred L.
Hoffman, Donald Alfred
Irwin, James Burke, V
Lang, Susan Gail
Levin, Richard Barry
Masinter, Paul James
Molony, Michael Janssens, Jr.
Pearce, John Y.
Perry, Brian Drew, Sr.
Pugh, William Whitmell Hill
Redmann, John William
Rodriguez, Antonio Jose
Roux, Kermit Louis, III
Sinor, Howard Earl, Jr.
Stag, Michael Gregory
Steinberg, Sylvan Julian
Thomas, Joseph Winand
Waltzer, Joel Reuben
Wright, William Everard, Jr.

**Ruston**
Oakley, Tracy L.

**Shreveport**
Achee, Roland Joseph
Carmody, Arthur Roderick, Jr.
Clark, James E.
Fortson, James Leon, Jr.
Hall, Pike, Jr.
Politz, Nyle Anthony

**Slidell**
D'Antonio, Guy Joseph
Hammond, Margaret

## MAINE

**Augusta**
Bickerman, Peter Bruce
McKee, Walter Frederic

**Bangor**
Gilbert, Charles E., III
Gould, Edward Ward
Woodcock, John Alden

**Bass Harbor**
Ervin, Spencer

**Brunswick**
Lamothe, Arthur J.

**Freeport**
Lea, Lola Stendig

**Fryeburg**
Weimer, Gregory Aloyisius

**Hallowell**
Smith, Jeffrey Allen

**Kennebunk**
Clifford, Peter
Libby, Gene Roger

**Portland**
Bennett, Jeffrey
Brogan, Jonathan William
Culley, Peter William
Dinan, Christopher Charles
Groff, Joseph Halsey, III
Hansel, Gregory Paul
Hirshon, Robert Edward
Lehman, Kenneth William
Martin, Michael Keith
Monaghan, Matthew John
Quinn, Thomas Joseph
Whiting, Stephen Clyde

**S Portland**
Mooers, Daniel William

**Sanford**
Nadeau, Robert Maurice Auclair

## MARYLAND

**Abingdon**
Wolf, Martin Eugene

**Annapolis**
Burns, B. Darren
Evans, William Davidson, Jr.
Ferris, William Michael
Nash, Brian Joseph
Rutland, David Lee
Wharton, James T.

**Baltimore**
Black, Herbert Allen
Burch, Francis Boucher, Jr.
Christianson, Charles Anthony Patrick
Ellin, Marvin
Ferguson, Robert L., Jr.
Gillece, James Patrick, Jr.
Hafets, Richard Jay
Himeles, Martin Stanley, Jr.
Joseph, Charles Ian
Kandel, Nelson Robert
Kandel, Peter Thomas
King, David Paul
Knuckey, Kenneth Scott
Lynch, Timothy Cronin
McGarvey, Jack F(rancis)
Messina, Bonnie Lynn
Nazarian, Douglas Richard Miller
Powell, Roger Norman
Russo, Michael Natale, Jr.
Shuster, David Jonathan
Sloane, Marc K.
Tiller, Steven Edward
Vice, LaVonna Lee
White, George Wendell, Jr.

**Bel Air**
Crocker, Michael Pue
Miller, Max Dunham, Jr.

**Bethesda**
Chapman, Gerald Frederick
Eisen, Eric Anshel
Moss, Stephen Edward
Nelson, William Eugene
Poppleton, Miller John

**Chevy Chase**
Montedonico, Joseph
**College Park**
Neal, Edward Garrison
**Gaithersburg**
Pearlstein, Brian K.
Plave, Erica Frohman
**Greenbelt**
Greenwald, Andrew Eric
**Hagerstown**
Moylan, Dana
**Lanham Seabrook**
McCarthy, Kevin John
**Laurel**
Barr, June Hatton
**Lexington Park**
Lacer, Alfred Antonio
**Ocean City**
Ayres, Guy Robins, III
Grech, Christopher Alan
Harrison, Joseph George, Jr.
Wimbrow, Peter Ayers, III
**Oxon Hill**
Serrette, Cathy Hollenberg
**Riverdale**
Turkheimer, Paul Adam
**Rockville**
Armstrong, Kenneth
Cromwell, James Julian
Doyle, Thomas Edward
Fogleman, Christopher Curtis
Litteral, Daniel Pace
McGaukian, Rachel Theora
McGuire, Edward David, Jr.
**Silver Spring**
Viertel, George Joseph
**Stevensville**
Ronayne, Donald Anthony
**Sykesville**
Bartolini, Daniel John
**Taneytown**
Shoemaker, Daniel W.
**Towson**
Lalumia, Matthew Paul
Vettori, Paul Marion

## MASSACHUSETTS

**Amherst**
Howland, Richard Moulton
**Andover**
Thorn, Andrea Papp
**Boston**
Alves, Emanuel
Ballard, Nancer H.
Berry, Janis Marie
Blank, Garry Neal
Brick, Howard Andrew
Brody, Richard Eric
Buell, Barbara Hayes
Burns, Thomas David
Carpenter, Robert Brent
Carroll, James Edward
Casby, Robert William
Cashore, Amy C.
Coffey, James Francis
Cramer, Jennifer Goldenson
Cunha, John Henry, Jr.
Deutsch, Stephen B.
Downs, J. Anthony
Drogin, Susan F.
Ellis, Fredric Lee
Epstein, Elaine May
Fahy, Joseph Thomas
Feinberg, Robert I(ra)
Fishman, Kenneth Jay
Gans, Nancy Freeman
Gargiulo, Andrea W.
Goscinak, Virginia Casey
Gossels, Claus Peter Rolf
Graham, John Joseph
Guberman, David Aaron
Harding, Ronald Evan
Honegger, Andrew Alan
Jones, Jeffrey Foster
Kaler, Robert Joseph
Kavanaugh, James Francis, Jr.
Kutchin, Edward David
Lanckton, Arthur Van Cleve
Licata, Arthur Frank
Looney, William Francis, Jr.
Lund, Theodore Anton
Lyons, Nance
McKittrick, Neil Vincent
Morgera, Vincent D.
Moriarty, George Marshall
Murray, Philip Edmund, Jr.
Oetheimer, Richard A.
O'Neill, Philip Daniel, Jr.
Poss, Stephen Daniel
Rafferty, Edson Howard
Ramsey, James E.
Reardon, Frank Emond
Redlich, Marc
Rikleen, Sander A.
Ritvo, Elizabeth Ann
Sager, Steven Travis
Sarrouf, Camille Francis
Saturley, Ellen McLaughlin
Seidel, Rebecca Suzanne
Spelfogel, Scott David
Sullivan, Edward Michael
Swain, Philip C., Jr.
Sykes, Tracy Allan
Testa, Richard Joseph
Yurko, Richard John
Zavez, John Peter
Zwicker, Joseph H.
**Burlington**
Graves, Robert
**Canton**
Bauer, Gene Marc
**Charlestown**
DuLaurence, Henry J., III
**Chelmsford**
Grossman, Debra A.
Lerer, Neal M.
**Concord**
O'Brien, James Freeman
**Danvers**
Christopher, John Anthony
**Duxbury**
Goldman, Eric Scot
**Foxboro**
Cohen, Harold
**Greenfield**
Berson, Mark Ira
**Holyoke**
Sarnacki, Michael Thomas
**Hyannis**
McLaughlin, Edward Francis, Jr.
**Medford**
Berman, David
**Natick**
Marr, David E
**Newburyport**
Murphy, Lawrence John
**Newton**
Peterson, Osler Leopold
**Norwell**
O'Sullivan, James Michael
**Norwood**
Gorski, Ronald William
Salvatore, David Anthony
**Orleans**
Chaplin, Ansel Burt
**Quincy**
Motejunas, Gerald William
**Salem**
Del Vecchio, Debra Anne
Rogal, James London
**Somerville**
Belfort, David Ernst
**South Easton**
Finn, Anne-Marie
**Springfield**
Dibble, Francis Daniel, Jr.
Low, Terrence Allen
Markey, Patrick Joseph
Nicolai, Paul Peter
Ryan, Phyllis Paula
**Wakefield**
Lucas, Robert Frank
**Waltham**
Malone, Steven C.
**Worcester**
Chandler, Burton
Deiana, Robert Vincent
DePaolo, John P.
Donnelly, James Corcoran, Jr.
Maciolek, John Richard
Reitzell, William R.
Uhl, Christopher Martin
Weinstein, Jordan Harvey

## MICHIGAN

**Adrian**
Kralick, Richard Louis
**Ann Arbor**
DeVine, Edmond Francis
Ellmann, Douglas Stanley
Ferris, Donald William, Jr.
Joscelyn, Kent Buckley
McDaniel, Timothy Ellis
Niehoff, Leonard Marvin
Patti, Anthony Peter
**Bingham Farms**
Fershtman, Julie Ilene
**Birmingham**
Bank, Mark Albert
Delin, Sylvia Kaufman
Polzin, Charles Henry
Zacharski, Dennis Edward
**Bloomfield Hills**
Baumkel, Mark S.
Butters, Frederick Francis
Cranmer, Thomas William
Cunningham, Gary H.
Lehman, Richard Leroy
Mucha, John, III
**Charlevoix**
Telgenhof, Allen Ray
**Dearborn**
Demorest, Mark Stuart
**Detroit**
Ankers, Norman C.
Benjamin, Gary Adams
Boonstra, Mark Thomas
Branigan, Thomas Patrick
Christiansen, Roy Hvidkaer
Foley, Thomas John
Gottschalk, Thomas A.
Kostovski, Suzanna
Lenga, J. Thomas
Mamat, Frank Trustick
Nix, Robert Royal, II
Norris, Megan Pinney
Pope, Harold D.
Rassel, Richard Edward
Rooney, Scott William
Stern, Mark Alan
Taweel, A. Tony
Wagner, Brian J.
Walsh, James Joseph
**East Lansing**
Stroud, Ted William
**Eastpointe**
Ionetz, Ronald George
**Eaton Rapids**
Nolan, Lawrence Patrick
**Ecorse**
Rhoads, Carl Lynn
**Farmingtn Hls**
Bernstein, Stephen Richard
Stokes, Joelynn Towanda
**Farmington**
Lebow, Michael Jeffrey
Torpey, Scott Raymond
**Farmington Hills**
Beamer, Dirk Allen
Gross, Lynn Westfall
Hampton, William Peck
Weiss, Leon Jeffrey
**Flint**
Edmunds, Michael Winterton
Hart, Clifford Harvey
Henneke, Edward George
**Grand Rapids**
Blackwell, Thomas Francis
Boer, Roger William
Elve, Daniel Leigh
Gibson, Lori Lynn
Gillis, Geoffrey Lawrence
Iverson, Dale Ann
Jack, William Wilson, Jr.
Jennette, Noble Stevenson, III
Prasher, Gregory George
Roth, Michael John
**Grosse Pointe**
Carey, Raymond J.
Goss, James William
McIntyre, Anita Grace Jordan
**Holland**
Moritz, John Reid
**Jackson**
Klaasen, Terry John
**Kalamazoo**
Hatch, Hazen van den Berg
**Lansing**
Canady, Mark Howard
Fink, Joseph Allen
Schlinker, John Crandall
Shafer, Stuart Robert
Stackable, Frederick Lawrence
**Madison Heights**
Szczesny, Ronald William
**Manistee**
Simon, Stephanie Eden
**Muskegon**
Van Leuven, Robert Joseph
**Okemos**
Platsis, George James
**Petoskey**
Erhart, James Nelson
Powers, Bridget Brown
**Plymouth**
Haynes, Richard Terry
Morgan, Donald Crane
**Saginaw**
Concannon, Andrew Donnelly
**Saint Clair Shores**
Shehan, Wayne Charles
**Saint Joseph**
Butzbaugh, Alfred M.
Butzbaugh, Elden W., Jr.
**South Haven**
Waxman, Sheldon Robert
**Southfield**
Baughman, Leonora Knoblock
Cohen, H. Adam
Gold, Gordon Stanford
MacLean, Joseph Curran
Mazey, Larry William
Moloughney, Kevin Patrick
Morganroth, Mayer
Sullivan, Robert Emmet, Jr.
Taravella, Christopher Anthony
**Suttons Bay**
Robb, Dean Allen, Sr.
**Trenton**
Counard, Allen Joseph
**Troy**
Burnard, George Willard
Gullen, Christopher Roy
Olson, Edward M.
Schroeder, Douglas Jay
Wells, Steven W.

## MINNESOTA

**Albert Lea**
Savelkoul, Donald Wayne
**Bemidji**
Woodke, Robert Allen
**Bloomington**
Boedigheimer, Robert David
Jackson, Renee Leone
Wilson, Rebecca Lynn
**Brooklyn Center**
Neff, Fred Leonard
Thompson, Jeffrey Charles
**Burnsville**
McGrath, Daniel Scott
**Eagan**
Peotter, Sara Jo
**Edina**
Ashley, James Patrick
**Erskine**
Taylor, Richard Charles
**Hallock**
Malm, Roger Charles
**Hawley**
Baer, Zenas
**Hopkins**
Hunter, Donald Forrest
**Minneapolis**
Adams, Thomas Lewis
Anderson, Alan Marshall
Baillie, James Leonard
Barnard, Allen Donald
Bland, J(ohn) Richard
Blanton, W. C.
Bodas, Margie Ruth
Borger, John Philip
Bruner, Philip Lane
Christensen, Robert Paul
Clary, Bradley G.
Cole, Phillip Allen
Coyne, Dennis Michael
Dietzen, Christopher J.
Erstad, Leon Robert
Faricy, John Hartnett, Jr.
Gant, Jesse, III
Gill, Richard Lawrence
Hagstrom, Richard Michael
Hinderaker, John Hadley
Hogen-Kind, Vanya S.
Jarpe, Geoffrey Pellas
Jensen, Darrell Alf
Johannsen, Marc Alan
Klosowski, Thomas Kenneth
Kunert, Paul Charles
Laurie, Gerald Tenzer
Long, James Jay
Luong, Phong Minh
Magarian, Edward Brian
Manning, William Henry
Mansfield, Seymour J.
Martinson, Bradley James
McGunnigle, George Francis
McNamara, Michael John
Meshbesher, Ronald I.
Messerly, Chris Alan
Morgan, Richard George
Paulsrud, Eric David
Perl, Justin Harley
Pluimer, Edward J.
Plunkett, Stephen Oliver
Reichert, Brent Larry
Reinhart, Robert Rountree, Jr.
Rochlin, Davis Samuel
Roe, Roger Rolland
Schermer, Judith Kahn
Silver, Alan Irving
Strothman, John Henry
Vander Weide, Vernon Jay
Voss, Barry Vaughan
Woods, Robert Edward
Yira, Markus Clarence
Zalk, Robert H.
**Minnetonka**
Brennan, Sidney L.
Freeman, Gerald Russell
Martell, Saundra Adkins
**Moorhead**
Cahill, Steven James
**Saint Cloud**
Hughes, Kevin John
**Saint Louis Park**
Rothenberg, Elliot Calvin
**Saint Paul**
Awsumb, Robert Ardin
Bell, Robert Charles
Fabel, Thomas Lincoln
King, Lawrence R.
Patient, Robert J.
Seymour, Mary Frances
**South Saint Paul**
O'Reilly, Ann Catherine
**Wayzata**
Reutiman, Robert William, Jr.

## MISSISSIPPI

**Ashland**
Robinson, David Lee
**Biloxi**
Miller, William Carl
Pritchard, Thomas Alexander
**Brandon**
Obert, Keith David
**Brookhaven**
Doty, Sally Burchfield
**Columbus**
Geeslin, Gary Lloyd
**Drew**
Holladay, Robert Lawson
**Gulfport**
Allen, Harry Roger
Foster, James (Jay) R.
Harral, John Menteith
Hatten, W. Edward, Jr.
Warren, Anne Schaefer
Westbrook, William V.
**Hattiesburg**
Jernigan, Jay Lawrence
**Hernando**
Neyman, Joseph David, Jr.
**Jackson**
Boackle, K.F.
Burch, Donald Victor
Burkes, Jennifer Parkinson
Corlew, John Gordon
Holbrook, Frank Malvin
Langford, James Jerry
McCullough, James Altus, II
McLeod, Gia Nicole
O'Mara, James Wright
Scales, Clarence Ray
**Lumberton**
Tonry, Richard Alvin
**Mc Comb**
Starrett, Keith
**Ocean Springs**
Lawson-Jowett, Mary Juliet
Pattison, Daphne Lynn
**Oxford**
Freeland, John Hale
**Ridgeland**
Giuffrida, Noel Peter
Humphreys, Kevin Lee
**Tupelo**
Clayton, Claude F., Jr.
Edwards, John Max, Jr.
Moffett, T(errill) K(ay)
**Winona**
Reid, William Joseph

## MISSOURI

**Branson**
Anglen, Randall S.
**Cape Girardeau**
Rith, David J., II
**Chesterfield**
McLaughlin, Kevin Thomas
**Clayton**
Clarkin, E. Thomas
Fluhr, Steven Solomon
Klein, Jerry A.
**Hannibal**
Terrell, James Daniel
**Jackson**
Waldron, Kenneth Lynn
**Jefferson City**
Martin, Cathleen A.
**Kansas City**
Beckerman, Dale Lee
Beckett, Theodore Cornwall
Brake, Timothy L.
Cartmell, Thomas Philip
Conner, John Shull
Cowden, John William
Davis, Donald Lee
Deacy, Thomas Edward, Jr.
Doherty, Brian John
Eldridge, Truman Kermit, Jr.
Foster, Mark Stephen
Fox, Byron Neal
Gaddy, William Brian
Gould, Michael Alan
Helder, Jan Pleasant, Jr.
Herron, Donald Patrick
Holt, Ronald Lee
Horn, Robert Allen
Joyce, Michael Patrick
Larson, Thomas Roy
Lewandowski, Alex Michael
Lotven, Howard Lee
Martucci, William Christopher
Mayer, David Mathew
McManus, James William
Mikkelson, Eric T.
Miller, Richard William
Modin, Richard F.
Molzen, Christopher John
Newsom, James Thomas
Norton, John Hise
O'Neill, Thomas Tyrone
Palmer, Dennis Dale
Paul, Richard Monroe, III
Sands, Darry Gene
Sauer, Elisabeth Ruth
Sharp, Rex Arthur
Shay, David E.
Siro, Rik Neal
Smith, R(onald) Scott
Smithson, Lowell Lee
Stoup, Arthur Harry
Tamburini, Michael Mario
Tyler, John E., III
Vranicar, Gregory Leonard
**Liberty**
Sayles, Cathy A.
**Marshall**
Peterson, William Allen
**Mexico**
Hagan, Ann P.
**Saint Joseph**
Koerner, Wendell Edward, Jr.
Sokol, Ronald Mark
Taylor, Michael Leslie
**Saint Louis**
Barken, Bernard Allen
Berendt, Robert Tryon
Boggs, Beth Clemens
Bossi, Mark Vincent
Burke, Thomas Michael
Corrigan, Ann Phillips
Evans, William Wallace
Floyd, Walter Leo
Fournie, Raymond Richard
Gilroy, Tracy Anne Hunsaker
Greenberg, Karen Alane
Haar, Robert Theodore
Hellmuth, Theodore Henning
Huck, Richard Felix, III
Joerling, Dale Raymond
Klobasa, John Anthony
Komen, Leonard
Kraft, Carl David
Luberda, George Joseph
Massey, Raymond Lee
McCarter, W. Dudley
McDaniel, James Edwin
Menghini, Henry Dave
Michenfelder, Albert A.
Myre, Donald Paul
Newman, Charles A.
Ramirez, Anthony Benjamin
Riggio, Nicholas Joseph, Sr.
Rubenstein, Sarah Wright
Schaberg, John Irvin
Schramm, Paul Howard
Shalowitz, Howard A.
Suess, Jeffrey Karl
Switzer, Frederick Michael, III
Tierney, Betty Thorne
Vandover, Samuel Taylor
Walsh, Joseph Leo, III
Will, Robert John
Wulff, Robert Joseph
**Springfield**
Clithero, Monte Paul
Conway, Ronald Anthony
FitzGerald, Kevin Michael
Greene, Robert Lee
**Webster Groves**
Crowell, George Bradford

## MONTANA

**Billings**
Beiswanger, Gary Lee
Cromley, Brent Reed
Hanson, Norman
Krogh, Harlan B.
Malee, Thomas Michael
Toole, Bruce Ryan
**Bozeman**
Conover, Richard Corrill
Madden, William Lee, Jr.
Nelson, Steven Dwayne
**Great Falls**
Seidlitz, John E.
**Havre**
Richardson, Kathleen Harris
**Helena**
Morrison, John Martin
**Kalispell**
Heckathorn, I. James
**Livingston**
Jovick, Robert L.
**Missoula**
Bender, Ronald Andrew
Mudd, John O.
Poore, James Albert, III
Vannatta, Shane Anthony
Williams, Mark Shelton F.

## NEBRASKA

**Columbus**
Milbourn, Douglas Ray
**Lincoln**
Blake, William George
Guthery, John M.
Mussman, David C.
O'Brien, Patrick Thomas
Rowe, David Winfield
Sapp, Susan Kubert
Stine, Margaret Elizabeth
**Norfolk**
McGough, James Kingsley

**Omaha**
Fitzgerald, James Patrick
Gaines, Tyler Belt
Lamson, William Maxwell, Jr.
Martin, Elaine M.
Riley, William Jay
Schmitt, David Jon
Walsh, Thomas John, Sr.

**York**
Stephens, Bruce Edward

## NEVADA

**Carson City**
King, Patrick Owen
Wilson, James Edward, Jr.

**Incline Village**
Skinner, Gregory Sala

**Las Vegas**
Albright, George Mark
Chrisman, James Paul
Geihs, Frederick Siegfried
Kirsch, Lynn
Lefebvre, Alan J.
Mahan, James Cameron
Martini, Alyssa Ann
Nohrden, Patrick Thomas
Parry, Stanley Warren
Pitegoff, Jeffrey I.
Throne, Dawn Renee

**Reno**
Bader, Angela Marie
Hardy, Del
Hayward, Daniel Thomas
Hibbs, Loyal Robert
Hill, Earl McColl
Hornbeck, David Arthur
Kent, Stephen Smiley
Richards, Paul A.
Shaffer, Wayne Alan

## NEW HAMPSHIRE

**Concord**
Irwin, Lauren Simon

**Dover**
Catalfo, Alfred, Jr. (Alfio Catalfo)

**Exeter**
Beckett, William Henry Miller

**Henniker**
Foley, David N.

**Manchester**
Middleton, Jack Baer
Nixon, David L.

**Nashua**
Brown, Kenneth Mackinnon
Jette, Ernest Arthur
Kerrigan, Timothy George
Raudonis, Valerie Christine

**Newington**
Lewis, John Michael

**North Conway**
Cooper, Randall F.

**Plymouth**
Hopkins, William Hayes

**Portsmouth**
Doleac, Charles Bartholomew
Lown, Bradley Merrill
Watson, Thomas Roger
Wolowitz, David

**Salem**
Notaris, Mary

## NEW JERSEY

**Absecon**
Woolson, Charles E., Jr.

**Atlantic City**
Baylinson, Christopher Michael
Brown, Christopher Arthur
Zlotnick, Norman Lee

**Bernardsville**
Forzani, Rinaldo, III
Maher, Gary Laurence

**Bridgewater**
Conroy, Robert John
Kosten, Jeffrey Thomas

**Brigantine**
Kokes, Alois Harold

**Chatham**
Krovatin, Gerald

**Chatham Township**
Manning, Victoria Anne

**Cherry Hill**
DeVoto, Louis Joseph
Fols, Stacy Alison
Thomas, Robert F.
Tomar, William

**Chester**
Hanson, Eugene Paul

**Clark**
Barr, Jon-Henry

**Collingswood**
Martin, Burchard V.

**Denville**
Greene, Steven K.

**East Brunswick**
Schreiber, Jeffrey
Tharney, Laura Christine

**East Hanover**
Kayser, Kenneth Wayne
Wilson, Deanne Marie

**Edison**
Homisak, Theresa
Rothenberg, Adam Leigh
Wong, Linda

**Elizabeth**
Budanitsky, Sander

**Englewood Cliffs**
Fredericks, Barry Irwin

**Fairfield**
Denes, Richard Ford

**Fanwood**
Xifo, Louise Elizabeth

**Florham Park**
Chase, Eric Lewis
Haber, Karin Duchin
Laulicht, Murray Jack
Wright, Paul William

**Fort Lee**
Macri, Marcantonio Dominic

**Freehold**
Brown, Sanford Donald
McLean, Gary P.
Scenna, Michele Carton

**Glen Rock**
Markey, Brian Michael

**Hackensack**
Bialkowski, Stephen Walter
Chagaris, Arthur N.
Fede, Andrew Thomas
Flor, Patrick John
Gallucci, Michael A.
Haworth, Gregory Robert
Horowitz, Donald
Jacobs, Lawrence H.
Spiegel, Linda F.

**Haddonfield**
Heuisler, Charles William

**Highland Park**
Alman, Emily Arnow
Michaels, Jennifer Alman

**Hoboken**
Curley, John Joseph

**Iselin**
Goodman, Barry S.

**Kearny**
Brady, Lawrence Peter

**Kenilworth**
Cohen, Edward Arthur
Wasman, Jane G.

**Lawrenceville**
Argiropoulos, Anthony
Benesch, Katherine

**Lebanon**
Johnstone, Irvine Blakeley, III

**Liberty Corner**
Spierer, Howard

**Linden**
Falk, Lauren Weissman

**Little Egg Harbor Township**
Rumpf, Brian E.

**Livingston**
Nagel, Bruce H.

**Millburn**
Diamond, Richard Scott

**Moorestown**
Caniglia, Lawrence S.
Kearney, John Francis, III

**Morris Plains**
Pluciennik, Thomas Casimir

**Morristown**
Geppert, John Gustave
Gladstone, Robert Albert
Halasz, Paul J.
Kreindler, Peter Michael
Milsteon, Rachelle H. (Shelly Milsteon)
O'Grady, Dennis Joseph
Rich, Michael Louis
Rose, Robert Gordon
Sperling, Joy Harmon
Szuch, Clyde Andrew

**Mount Holly**
Mintz, Jeffry Alan

**New Providence**
Marris, Joan Banan

**Newark**
Brenner, John Finn
Cahn, Jeffrey Barton
Callahan, Patrick Michael
Creenan, Katherine Heras
Garde, John Charles
Gouraige, Hervé
Laura, Anthony Joseph
Loprete, Michael D.
Mattson, Leroy Harry
Rak, Lorraine Karen
Siegal, Joel Davis
Siegal, Ronny Jo
Slavitt, Ben J.
Thompson, Paul Brower
Weber, Scott Louis

**North Haledon**
Harrington, Kevin Paul

**Paramus**
Giantonio, Clifford John

**Park Ridge**
Takashima, Hideo

**Parsippany**
Asserson, Brian Michael
Donovan, Richard Edward
Haney, James Kevin
Kummer, Richard Edward, Jr.
Whipkey, Lisa J.

**Phillipsburg**
Jones, Bruce Alan

**Pitman**
Powell, J. R.

**Princeton**
Bergman, Edward Jonathan
Brennan, William Joseph, III
Lampert, Michael A.
Lewin, Ross Allen
Souter, Sydney Scull
Sutphin, William Taylor
Zinkin, Ephraim Zev

**Red Bank**
Allegra, Peter Alexander
Auerbach, Philip Gary
Duggan, John Peter
Halfacre, Michael Ian
Warshaw, Michael Thomas

**River Vale**
Lotito, Joseph Daniel

**Roseland**
Bennett, John K.
Clemente, Mark Andrew
Kenny, George James
LaVecchia, John B.
Nathan, Edward Singer
Robinson, Richard S.
Saloman, Mark Andrew
Sarasohn, Peter Radin
Smith, Wendy Hope

**Rutherford**
Henschel, John James

**Scotch Plains**
Hayes, Lewis Mifflin, Jr.

**Secaucus**
Castano, Gregory Joseph
Glassen, James Warren

**Short Hills**
Kaye, Marc Mendell

**Shrewsbury**
Hopkins, Charles Peter, II

**Somerset**
Robinson, Patricia Snyder

**Somerville**
Dreier, William Alan
Miller, Charles William, III

**South Amboy**
Moskovitz, Stuart Jeffrey

**Springfield**
Mytelka, Arnold Krieger

**Stirling**
Michels, Kevin Howard

**Stone Harbor**
Taylor, Robert Lee

**Succasunna**
Gates, Marshall L.

**Tenafly**
Vort, Robert A.

**Toms River**
Leone, Stephan Robert

**Trenton**
Bilder, Marshall D.
Harbeck, Dorothy Anne
Pellecchia, John Michael

**Union**
Mark, Michael David

**Vineland**
O'Neill, Joseph Dean

**Weehawken**
Hayden, Joseph A., Jr.
Silber, Alan

**West Atlantic City**
Sinderbrand, David I.

**Westfield**
Nicolai, Donald F.
Schmidt, John H., Jr.

**Westwood**
McGuirl, Robert Joseph

**Woodbridge**
Golden, Daniel Lewis
Goldenberg, Steven Saul

**Woodbury**
Celano, Peter J., Jr.

**Woodcliff Lake**
DeVita, Danielle
Shulman, Frederic M.

## NEW MEXICO

**Albuquerque**
Barela, Jonathan Lewis
Beach, Arthur O'Neal
Bova, Vincent Arthur, Jr.
Bregman, Jacqueline De Oliveira
Bregman, Sam
Carrico, Michael Layne
Caruso, Mark John
Dorr, Roderick A.
Hanna, Robert Cecil
Hollis, John Lee
Lombardi, Curtis Jay
Lopez, Floyd William
Martinez, David Brian
Pezzillo, Brian James
Romero, Jeff
Shane, Richard J.
Simon, Robert S.
Thompson, Rufus E.
Wertheim, John V.

**Carlsbad**
Bruton, Charles Clinton

**Deming**
Sherman, Frederick Hood
Turner, Robert F.

**Farmington**
Hale, J. Kevin
Moeller, Floyd Douglas

**Hobbs**
Stout, Lowell

**Las Cruces**
Sandenaw, Thomas Arthur, Jr.

**Roswell**
Kraft, Richard Lee
Romero, Freddie Joseph

**Santa Fe**
Bienvenu, John Charles
Brannen, Jeffrey Richard
Casey, Patrick Anthony
Cohen, David Saul
Culbert, Peter Van Horn
Herr, Bruce
Pound, John Bennett

## NEW YORK

**Albany**
Alessi, Robert Joseph
Case, Forrest N., Jr.
Couch, Leslie Franklin
Couch, Mark Woodworth
Fanciullo, William Patrick
Ganz, Robert E.
Greagan, William Joseph
Laird, Edward DeHart, Jr.
Pozner, Louis-Jack
Rohan, Brian Patrick
Whalen, Colleen Hiser

**Albion**
Lyman, Nathan Marquis

**Amherst**
Jones, E. Thomas

**Amsterdam**
Sise, Robert J.

**Bay Shore**
Zuckerman, Landon Roy

**Binghamton**
Gates, Gregory Ansel
Kramer, Philip Joseph

**Bronx**
Aris, Joram Jehudah

**Bronxville**
Fuller, David Otis, Jr.

**Brooklyn**
Blank, Helene E.
Fallek, Andrew Michael
Held, Marc Jason
Reichman, Adelle E.

**Buffalo**
Armstrong, James F.
Bermingham, Joseph Daniel
Curran, Patrick Barton
Feuerstein, Alan Ricky
Freedman, Bernard Benjamin
Freedman, Maryann Saccomando
Gallman, Ryan Lance
Garvey, James Anthony
Hayes, J. Michael
Isenberg, Andrew Brian
Jasen, Matthew Joseph
Kieffer, James Marshall
Magavern, James L.
Manning, Kenneth Alan
Merriman, Kevin Thomas
Murphy, Edward J., III
Murray, Glenn Edward
Possé, Olga Alicia

**Central Islip**
Bronstein, Richard M.

**Corning**
Hauselt, Denise Ann

**De Witt**
Dunn, Mark L.

**Delhi**
Hamilton, John Thomas, Jr.
Hartmann, James M.

**Delmar**
Galvin, Madeline Sheila

**Flushing**
Bernstein, Barry Selwyn

**Garden City**
Balkan, Kenneth J.
Beck, Leland S.
DaSilva, Willard H.
Di Mascio, John Philip
Fischoff, Gary Charles
Kroll, Martin N.
Wimpfheimer, Steven

**Garrison**
Donnelly, Daniel Patrick

**Granite Spgs**
Stokes, Harry McKinney

**Great Neck**
Samanowitz, Ronald Arthur

**Hempstead**
Furey, James Michael
Kane, Donald Vincent

**Hicksville**
Giuffré, John Joseph

**Highland**
Murphy, Sean

**Hollis**
Jairam, Khelanand Vishvaykanand

**Howard Beach**
Hernandez-Gonzalez, Gloria Maria

**Hudson**
Howard, Andrew Baker

**Huntington**
DeMartin, Charles Peter

**Ithaca**
Mulvey, Richard Ignatius
Pinnisi, Michael Donato

**Jamestown**
DeAngelo, Charles Salvatore

**Lake Success**
Lee, Brian Edward

**Long Beach**
Solomon, Robert H.

**Long Island City**
Risi, Joseph John

**Malone**
Grue, Thomas Andrew

**Manhasset**
Kashanian, Shahriar

**Mayville**
Dolan, John F.

**Melville**
Adler, Kenneth
Zamek, Scott

**Mineola**
Bartol, Ernest Thomas

**New City**
Fenster, Robert David

**New Rochelle**
Staple, Irwin

**New Windsor**
Ventry, Catherine Valerie

**New York**
Adler, Derek J.T.
Aloe, Paul Hubschman
Altieri, Peter Louis
Appel, Albert M.
Aquila, Albert
Aron, Roberto
Bainton, J(ohn) Joseph
Banner, Robert Alan
Barrett, David A.
Barthold, Walter
Beatty, Andrew Hyland
Beinin, William J.
Belnick, Mark Alan
Benakis, George James
Berger, Michael Gary
Berland, Sanford Neil
Berman, Tony
Bern, Marc Jay
Bicks, Peter Andrews
Blair, James Newell
Blinken, Sally S.
Bloom, Robert Avrum
Bluestone, Andrew Lavoott
Boddie, Reginald Alonzo
Bodovitz, James Philip
Boes, Lawrence William
Bonacquist, Harold Frank, Jr.
Borker, Wallace Jacob
Bortnick, Blaine H.
Bradford, Elizabeth
Broder, Eric Jason
Brollesy, Hany Sayed
Brooks, Kermitt Jerome
Brown, Peter Megargee
Burke, Kathleen Mary
Burrows, Michael Donald
Butterfield, Toby Michael John
Butterman, Jay Ronald
Caputo, Nicholas Raymond
Carley, John Halliday
Carling, Francis
Carlinsky, Michael Barry
Castellitto, Mario
Clemen, John Douglas
Clement, Daniel Evan
Cohen, Anne Elizabeth
Cohen, Donald N.
Cohen, Lisa C.
Colfin, Bruce Elliott
Coll, John Peter, Jr.
Conboy, Kenneth
Connuck, Eric S.
Crane, Roger Ryan, Jr.
Cuneo, Donald Lane
Cunha, Mark Geoffrey
Dankner, Jay Warren
David, Reuben
Davidson, George Allan
Davis, Deborah Lynn
Davis, Michael S.
Dean, Jay Douglas
Dehn, Francis Xavier
Derzaw, Richard Lawrence
DeWeil, Dawn Susan
di Domenico, Philip
Donoyan, Gary Leon
Dropkin, Charles Edward
Eakins, William Shannon
Effel, Laura
Elkins, David Mark
Faizakoff, Daniel Benjamin
Faust, Jonathan Jay
Feig, Edward Steven
Fern, Carole Lynn
Field, David Anthony
Finnerty, Joseph Gregory, Jr.
Fleischman, Keith Martin
Franklin, Gary Lawrence
Fredericks, William Curtis
Freyer, Dana Hartman
Friedland, Shelly Leah
Gadsden, James
Ganz, Howard Laurence
Garland, Sylvia Dillof
Gerstmann, Elan
Gesmer, Ellen Frances
Getnick, Neil Victor
Gillikin, Virginia
Gilman, Scott
Gioiella, Russell Michael
Goetz, Peter
Gold, Richard L.
Goldey, Mark H.
Goldstein, Howard Sheldon
Golomb, Barry
Gordon, Evan L.
Graifman, Brian Dale
Grassi, Joseph F.
Greathead, R. Scott
Green, Eric Howard
Green, Lawrence Rodman
Greenberg, Philip Alan
Greenhill, Jonathan Seth
Greenman, Frederick F., Jr.
Gropper, Allan Louis
Grunewald, Raymond Bernhard
Haig, Robert Leighton
Handler, Arthur M.
Hennessy, Mickee M.
Hershman, Scott Edward
Hicks, J. Portis
Hirshowitz, Melvin Stephen
Hoff, Jonathan M(orind)
Holman, Bud George
Hopper, Walter Everett
Houlihan, Christopher Michael
Hynes, Patricia
Jackson, Raymond Sidney, Jr.
Jackson, William Eldred
Jacobs, Hara Kay
Jacqueney, Stephanie A(lice)
Jaffe, Mark M.
Janowitz, James Arnold
Johnson, Christopher Paul
Kamaiko, Laurie Ann
Kamien, Kalvin
Kaplan, Steven Mark
Karmel, Philip Elias
Karson, Barry M.
Kasowitz, Marc Elliot
Katz, Jerome Charles
Katz, Seth Alan
Kilsch, Gunther H.
Kim, Helen Byung-son
Kimler, Andrew A.
Kirschner, Kenneth Harold
Kittay, David R.
Klapper, Molly
Kleinberg, Norman Charles
Kolker, Lawrence Paul
Korn, Monroe J.
Kostelanetz, Boris
Kresky, Harry
Landron, Michel John
Lauer, Andrew Jay
Laufer, Jacob
LeBlang, Skip Alan
Levander, Andrew Joshua
Levin, Michael Joseph
Levine, Ronald Jay
Levinson, Paul Howard
Levy, Herbert Monte
Lichten, Rachel Gordon
Liss, Norman
Livingston, Judith A.
London, Ira D.
Lowenbraun, Solomon M.
Lund, Daniel P.
Lupkin, Stanley Neil
MacGregor, Meichelle R.
Madsen, Stephen Stewart
Mandell, Mitchell Gregory
Mannheimer, Michael Jay
Marantz, Neil G.
Marcus, Todd Barry
Margulis, Howard Lee
Matus, Wayne Charles
McCabe, Monica Petraglia
McDonell, Neil Edwin
McGahren, Richard George
McGrath, Christopher Thomas
McMahon, Dennis C.

Meiklejohn, Donald Stuart
Meister, Robert Allen
Mermelstein, Edward A.
Milmed, Paul Kussy
Mitchell, C. MacNeil
Moore, Thomas Ronald (Lord Bridestowe)
Moran, Edward Kevin
Motola, David Henry
Moyer, Jay Edward
Munzer, Stephen Ira
Newman, Fredric Samuel
Nocera, John Anthony
Nonna, John Michael
Norfolk, William Ray
Oberman, Michael Stewart
O'Brien, John Graham
O'Connell, Margaret Sullivan
O'Dell, Charlene Anne Audrey
Oechler, Henry John, Jr.
Orden, Stewart L.
Owen, Robert Dewit
Packard, Stephen Michael
Pantelopoulos, Nicholas Evan
Pappachen, George V., Jr.
Paul, James William
Pfeffer, Robert E.
Polishook, Lewis A.
Raab, Sheldon
Reiter, Allen Gary
Reynolds, Michael Timothy
Reynolds, Timothy Gerard
Rivera, Walter
Rodes, Leonard Anthony
Rogers, Theodore Otto, Jr.
Rogoff, Jeffrey Scott
Romano, Edgar Ness
Rosen, Eric Alan
Roth, Barbara M.
Rotstein, Andrew David
Rubin, Herbert
Russotti, Philip Anthony
Sahid, Joseph Robert
Sallay, Tibor
Salman, Robert Ronald
Samson, Martin Harris
Santana, Robert Rafael
Schallert, Edwin Glenn
Schiesel, Steven
Schiffer, Larry Philip
Schindler, Steven Roy
Schoenfeld, Steven Russell
Schwartz, Barry Steven
Schwartz, James Evan
Schwarz, Frederick August Otto, Jr.
Seiff, Eric A.
Shampanier, Judith Michele
Shapiro, Stanley K.
Shaw, Robert Bernard
Sherman, Jonathan Henry
Sigmond, Carol Ann
Silverman, Arthur Charles
Simmons, Peter Lawrence
Sommers, George R.
Sperber, Joseph John, IV
Stavis, Roger Lee
Stein, Tracy A.
Steuer, Richard Marc
Stewart, Charles Evan
Stratton, Walter Love
Stringer, Ronald E.
Struve, Guy Miller
Sugarman, Robert P.
Teicher, Martin
Tigue, John J., Jr.
Tilewick, Robert
Tinnion, Antoine
Tritter, Daniel F.
Ueno, Takemi
Vandenberg, Raymond Leonard, Jr.
Vassallo, John A.
Vitkowsky, Vincent Joseph
Vladeck, Judith Pomarlen
Vogel, Bernard Henry
Vogel, Michael Scott
Vullo, Maria Therese
Vyskocil, Mary Kay
Walder, Noeleen Gwynaeth
Wallach, Eric Jean
Walpin, Gerald
Walton, Robert Prentiss
Warden, John L.
Way, Brian H.
Weddle, Justin Seth
Weinberg, Steven Lewis
Weinschel, Alan Jay
Weinstock, Gregg D.
Weiser, Martin Jay
Westin, David Lawrence
Wexelbaum, Michael
Wiggin, Thomas Byron
Williams Umlauf, Natalie R.
Wisehart, Arthur McKee
Witherwax, Charles Halsey
Witmeyer, John Jacob, III
Wohl, Ronald Gene
Wylie, Gordon Fraser
Wynn, Simon David
Young, Michael Richard
Yun, Edward Joon
Zammit, Joseph Paul
Zaslowsky, David Paul
Zedrosser, Joseph John
Zissu, Michael Jerome
Zito, Robert John Amadeus

**Newburgh**
Liberth, Richard Francis
Mishkin, Kathleen Anne

**Niagara Falls**
Anton, Ronald David
Berrigan, Patrick Joseph

**Nyack**
Seidler, B(ernard) Alan

**Oyster Bay**
Griffin, James Alfred
Press, Michael S.

**Patchogue**
Esteve, Edward V.
Weisberg, David Charles

**Perry**
Kelly, Michael Joseph

**Pittsford**
Finucane, Leo Gerard

**Pleasant Valley**
Vasti, Thomas Francis, III

**Purchase**
Kolbrener, Jonathan

**Riverhead**
Liccione, Maureen T.
Maggipinto, V. Anthony
Shane, Suzanne V.

**Rochester**
Gross, Bryon William
Kelly, Paul Donald
Lapine, Felix Victor
Leclair, Paul Lucien
Massare, Edward John
Mayka, Stephen Paul
Micca, Louis Joseph
Moore, James Conklin
Palermo, Anthony Robert
Regan, John Manning, Jr.
Relin, Leonard
Schwarz, Stephen George
Smith, Jules Louis
Stiller, Sharon Paula
Thomas, Jacqueline Marie
Walsh, Thomas F.

**Salamanca**
Brady, Thomas Carl

**Scarsdale**
Keeffe, John Arthur
Sabadie, Francisca Alejandra
Sheehan, Larry John
Sweeney, John J(oseph)

**Schenectady**
Galvin, Christine M.
Lewis, Kirk McArthur
Wickerham, Richard Dennis

**Sherburne**
Joyce, Stephen P.

**Smithtown**
Spellman, Thomas Joseph, Jr.

**South Ozone Park**
Narain, Camy Tribeni

**Staten Island**
Casella, Ralph Philip
Howard, Davis Jonathan

**Syracuse**
Bottar, Anthony Samuel
Burstein, Alan Stuart
Copani, Anthony Frank
Dove, Jeffrey Austin
Engel, Richard Lee
Greene, Arthur M.
Johnson, Eric Gates
Mathews, Daniel Francis, III
Mathewson, George Atterbury
McGinty, Elizabeth Caryl
Paquette, Steven A.
Traylor, Robert Arthur
Young, Douglas Howard

**Troy**
Finkel, Sanford Norman

**Uniondale**
Cassidy, David Michael
Eilen, Howard Scott
Joslin, Lana Ellen
Kotula, Michael Anthony
Paciullo, Maria Maestranzi

**Valley Stream**
Blakeman, Bruce Arthur

**Wantagh**
Dwyer, Diane Marie

**West Harrison**
Johnson, Craig Edward

**Westbury**
Nogee, Jeffrey Laurence

**White Plains**
Bader, Izaak Walton
Downes, James J.
Doyle, Dennis Thomas
Greenspan, Leon Joseph
Greenspan, Michael Evan
Halpern, Philip Morgan
Keane, Thomas J.
Merran, Harold
O'Rourke, Richard Lynn
Ryan, Robert Davis
Weingarden, Mitchell Ian

**Woodbury**
Taub, Linda Marsha

## NORTH CAROLINA

**Asheville**
Leake, Larry Bruce

**Cary**
Glass, Fred Stephen

**Charlotte**
Brotherton, Allen C.
Campbell, Hugh Brown, Jr.
Chesson, Calvin White
Gage, Gaston Hemphill
Harris, Richard Foster, III
Klein, Paul Ira
Lynch, Craig Taylor
Newitt, John Garwood, Jr.
Ogburn, Thomas Lynn, III
Shiau, H. Lin
Vinroot, Richard Allen
Wyatt, James Frank, III

**Durham**
Carpenter, Charles Francis
Cheek, Lewis Alexander
Conner, James Leon, II
Pollard, Edward Neal

**Fayetteville**
Britton, Rebecca Johnson
Newman, Roger

**Greensboro**
Clark, David McKenzie
Cline, Todd Wakefield
Harris, Terrill Johnson
Kobrin, Thomas Barstow
Sperling, Mack

**Greenville**
Hopf, James Fredrik
Kiess, Stephen David

**Hickory**
Cagle, Joe Neal

**High Point**
Baker, Walter Wray, Jr.
Floyd, Kimberly Hayes
Griffin, Robert Gerard

**New Bern**
Kellum, Norman Bryant, Jr.
Stoller, David Allen
Ward, Thomas Monroe

**Oxford**
Burnette, James Thomas
Burnette, Sarah Katherine

**Raleigh**
Dixon, Wright Tracy, Jr.
Ellis, Lester Neal, Jr.
Gaskins, Eura DuVal, Jr.
Jolly, John Russell, Jr.
Kapp, Michael Keith
Kenyon, Rosemary Gill
Madden, John Dale
Millberg, John C.
Stallings, Joseph Henry
Thomas, Jason Selig
Thomas, Mark Stanton
Wetsch, Laura Johnson

**Rockingham**
Futrell, Stephan Ray

**Smithfield**
Schulz, Bradley Nicholas

**Wilmington**
Johnston, Sharon A.

**Winston Salem**
Kelly, James Howard, Jr.

## NORTH DAKOTA

**Bismarck**
Edin, Charles Thomas
Klemin, Lawrence R.
Strutz, William A.

**Dickinson**
Ficek, Vince H.
Greenwood, Mark Lawrence

**Grand Forks**
Cilz, Douglas Arthur
Clapp, Richard Allen
Morley, Patrick Robert

**Mandan**
Bair, Bruce B.

**Minot**
Backes, Jon William

## OHIO

**Akron**
Breen, Kevin J.
Djordjevic, Michael M.
Lammert, Thomas Edward
Lombardi, Frederick McKean
Minney, R. Brent
Parker, Christopher Lee
Quirk, Frank Edward
Swing, Christopher Frederick

**Batavia**
Ostendarp, Gary David
Pattison, George Edgar
Rosenhoffer, Chris

**Beachwood**
Mintz, Carl A.

**Beavercreek**
Stadnicar, Joseph William

**Bucyrus**
McBride, Gordon Scott

**Cambridge**
Nicolozakes, William Angelo

**Canton**
Costa, Carol Ann
Davila, Edwin
Lindamood, John Beyer

**Chardon**
Newman, Paul A.

**Cincinnati**
Ashdown, Charles Coster
Bissinger, Mark Christian
Bloemer, Donna Michelle
Broderick, Dennis John
Burke, Timothy Michael
Chesley, Stanley Morris
Cioffi, Michael Lawrence
Cohen, Edward
Faller, Susan Grogan
Frantz, Robert Wesley
Fuchs, Jack Frederick
Holschuh, John David, Jr.
Kamp, David Paul
Knabe, Bruce David
Lugbill, Ann
Lutz, James Gurney
Lydon, Deborah Ruth
Melville, Charles Hartley
Randolph, Jerome C.
Richards, Gates Thornton
Rose, Donald McGregor
Scacchetti, David J.
Shea, Joseph William, III
Terp, Thomas Thomsen
Trauth, Joseph Louis, Jr.
Vander Laan, Mark Alan
Whalen, James Lawrence
Whitaker, Glenn Virgil

**Cleveland**
Alexandersen, Kevin Carl
Bacon, Brett Kermit
Berns, Sheldon
Billington, Glenn Earle
Boukis, Kenneth
Casarona, Robert B.
Chandler, Everett Alfred
Cohn, Mark Barry
Daiker, Paul B.
Duncan, Ed Eugene
Fitzgerald, Timothy John
Franey, Martin Thomas
Gabinet, Sarah Joan
Gerlack, Lisa Marie
Goldberg, James R.
Gray, R. Benton
Havens, Hunter Scott
Hofelich, James Albert
Keller, C. Reynolds
Kelly, Dennis Michael
Krueger, Jeffrey W.
La Rue, Edward Rice
Lear, S. Michael
Lentz, Mary A.
Liber, John (Douglas)
Markus, Stephen Allan
Norman, Forrest Alonzo
Nyerges, George Ladislaus
O'Neill, Mark
Osborne, Frank R.
Piscitelli, Frank E., Jr.
Pohl, Michael A.
Rains, M. Neal
Satola, James William
Schaefer, David Arnold
Spade, Eric F.
Stavnicky, Michael Ross
Szaller, James Francis
Weller, Charles David
Wilsman, James Michael
Wukovich, George Nicholas

**Columbus**
Acker, Frederick Wayne
Arnold, Gayle Edward
Ayers, James Cordon
Barclay, Craig Douglas
Binning, J. Boyd
Briggs, Marjorie Crowder
Brown, Jeffrey Monet
Caborn, David Arthur
Cavalaris, Nicholas Curtis
Chappelear, Stephen Eric
D'Aurora, Jack
Draper, Gerald Linden
Eblin, Robert L.
Eftimoff, Katerina
Frye, Richard Arthur
Gittes, Frederick M.
Hardymon, David Wayne
Kilgore, Terry Lee
Kloss, William Darrell, Jr.
Kurtz, Charles Jewett, III
Matan, Eugene Louis
McDermott, Kevin R.
Neuman, Todd Howard
Plymale, Ronald E.
Pryor, David W.
Ray, Frank Allen
Ryan, Joseph W., Jr.
Schaeffer, Matthew Thomas
Scott, David Matthew
Silverman, Perry Raynard
Smallwood, Carl Demouy
Sprader, Bobbie S.
Swetnam, Daniel Richard
Taylor, Joel Sanford
Todaro, Frank Edward
Warner, Charles Collins
Woods, William Hunt

**Dayton**
Baggott, Thomas McCann
Cameron, Ken
Chema, Susan Russell
Faruki, Charles Joseph
Hollingsworth, Jonathan
Krebs, Leo Francis
Rudwall, David Fuller
Segreti, Albert Mark, Jr.
Tucker, Michael Lane

**Dublin**
Tenuta, Luigia

**Fairborn**
Miles, David R.

**Findlay**
Kentris, George Lawrence
Rakestraw, Gregory Allen

**Fremont**
Albrechta, Joseph Francis

**Ironton**
Collier, James Bruce

**Jackson**
Lewis, Richard M.

**Kenton**
Tudor, John Martin

**Lakewood**
Traci, Donald Philip

**Lima**
Jacobs, Ann Elizabeth

**Miamisburg**
Anzman, Mark Charles

**North Olmsted**
Dorchak, Thomas J.

**Poland**
Vasvari, Thomas M.

**Risingsun**
Buchanan, J. Vincent Marino

**Saint Marys**
Huber, William Evan

**Sandusky**
Bailey, K. Ronald

**Springfield**
Catanzaro, Michael A.

**Toledo**
Baker, Richard Southworth
Cooper, Emily K.
Miller, Barbara Kaye
Pletz, Thomas Gregory
Wicklund, David Wayne

**Twinsburg**
Carr, Adam E.

**Warren**
Hawley, William Lee

**Wilmington**
Buckley, Frederick Jean

**Youngstown**
Blair, Richard Bryson
Bolton, Stephen Timothy
Melnick, Robert Russell
Messenger, James Louis

## OKLAHOMA

**Ardmore**
Bahner, S. Brent

**Bartlesville**
Benedict, Anthony Wayne

**Edmond**
Lester, Andrew William
Ryan, Gregory J.

**Enid**
Gungoll, Bradley A.
Jones, Stephen
Wyatt, Robert Lee, IV

**Norman**
Talley, Richard Bates

**Oklahoma City**
Christiansen, Mark D.
Coats, Andrew Montgomery
Cook, Russell Austin
Cunningham, Stanley Lloyd
Enis, Thomas Joseph
Epperson, Kraettli Quynton
Fitch, Brent E.
Gibson, Keith Russell
Gordon, Kevin Dell
High, David Royce
Kouri, Harry J., III
Lindsey, Lori Dawn
Looney, Robert Dudley
Margo, Robert Cravens
Necco, Alexander David
Nesbitt, Charles Rudolph
Rinehart, William James
Schuster, E. Elaine
Tompkins, Raymond Edgar
White, Joe E., Jr.
Wilson, Julia Ann Yother

**Sapulpa**
Lane, Tom Cornelius

**Seminole**
Choate, John

**Stilwell**
Morton, Kathryn R.

**Stroud**
Swanson, Robert Lee

**Tulsa**
Anderson, William Carl
Arrington, John Leslie, Jr.
Bright, Thomas Lynn
Clark, Joseph Francis, Jr.
Clark, Wendell W.
Cooper, Richard Casey
Crawford, B(urnett) Hayden
Daniel, Samuel Phillips
Davis, G. Reuben
Eagan, Claire Veronica
Eliot, Theodore Quentin
Hardcastle, Heath E.
Haynie, Tony Wayne
Herrold, David Henry
Jackman, J. Warren
Kincaid, James Lewis
La Sorsa, William George
McCann, James Patrick
McGonigle, Richard Thomas
Riggs, M. David
Sterling, Timothy F.

**Vinita**
Curnutte, Mark William
Johnston, Oscar Black, III

## OREGON

**Bend**
Costello, Don Owen

**Canby**
Thalhofer, Paul Terrance

**Corvallis**
Heinrich, Steven Allan
Ringo, Robert Gribble

**Eugene**
Horn, John Harold
Hutchinson, Stephen Aloysius

**Grants Pass**
Baker, Lindi L.
Day, Gregory Thomas
Preslar, Holly Ann

**Hillsboro**
Tyner, John Joseph, III

**La Grande**
Joseph, Steven Jay

**Lincoln City**
Elliott, Scott

**Portland**
Byrne, Gregory William
Coreson, Latricia Kadene
Dailey, Dianne K.
Darnall, Darleen R.
De Meo, Antonia M.
Duden, Paul Russell
Geil, John Clinton
Hart, John Edward
Hummel, Holly Jane
James, Christopher
Kennedy, Jack Leland
Kennedy, Michael Dean
Lacey, Henry Bernard
Larsen, Daniel Patrick
Maloney, Robert E., Jr.
Martson, William Frederick, Jr.
Meyer, Paul Richard
Moore, Thomas Scott
Palmer, Wayne Darwin
Rayburn, Ralph F.
Rieke, Forrest Neill
Ruess, Brian Knight
Sadler, Richard Lawrence
Sand, Thomas Charles
Savage, John William
Shinn, Michael Robert
Swider, Robert Arthur

**Redmond**
Welborn, Gordon Lee

**Salem**
Pacheco, Michael Mauro
Walsh, Richard Michael

**Springfield**
Wilson, Virgil James, III

**Wilsonville**
Yacob, Yosef

## PENNSYLVANIA

**Allentown**
Albright, Mark Preston
Dower, Harry Allen
Stevens, Timothy Towles

**Bala Cynwyd**
Olley, Michael Joseph

**Bethlehem**
Bush, Raymond George
Yeager, Jordan Berson

**Blue Bell**
Grayson, Zachary Louis

**Bryn Mawr**
Frumer, Richard J.

**Butler**
Biondi, John Michael

**Camp Hill**
Adler, Theodore Arthur

**Carlisle**
Turo, Ron

**Doylestown**
Elliott, Richard Howard

Karsch, Jay Harris
**Easton**
Brown, Robert Carroll
Noel, Nicholas, III
**Elkins Park**
Nemeroff, Robert Howard
**Glenside**
Mellon, Thomas S.
**Greensburg**
Gounley, Dennis Joseph
McDowell, Michael David
**Greenville**
Rowley, George Hardy
**Harrisburg**
Burcat, Joel Robin
Cline, Andrew Haley
Cunningham, Jordan Daniel
Downey, Brian Patrick
Husic, Yvonne M.
Kaylor, Cynthia Anne
Lappas, Spero Thomas
Mark, Timothy Ivan
McGuire, Jeffrey Thomas
Sadlock, Richard Alan
Schmidt, Thomas Bernard, III
Simpson, Kathryn Lease
Stefanon, Anthony
Warshaw, Allen Charles
Wolfgang, Jayson Richard
**Hilltown**
Hetherington, John Joseph
**Hollidaysburg**
Pfaff, Robert James
**Horsham**
Troy, Richard Hershey
**Jenkintown**
McNally, John Bernard
**Johnstown**
Kaharick, Jerome John
**King Of Prussia**
DeMaria, Joseph Carminus
**Kingston**
Meyer, Martin Jay
**Lancaster**
Golin, Charles
McGuire, Kendra Diane
Roda, Joseph Francis
**Lansdowne**
Kyriazis, Arthur John (Athanasios Ioannis Kyriazis)
**Mc Murray**
Brzustowicz, John Cinq-Mars
**Media**
Berman, Bernard Mayer
Blake, David Gordon
D'Amico, Andrew J.
DiOrio, Robert Michael
Ewing, Robert Clark
Firkser, Robert M.
Zicherman, David L.
**Morrisville**
Glosser, Harry John, Jr.
**Narberth**
Malloy, Martin Gerard
**New Castle**
Natale, Frank Anthony, II
**New Cumberland**
Yakowicz, Vincent X
**New Hope**
Baldi, Robert Otjen
**Newtown**
Kardos, Mel D.
Kopil, Thomas Edward
**Norristown**
Andrews, Cheri D.
Folmar, Larry John
Oliver, James John
**Oakmont**
Medonis, Robert Xavier
**Philadelphia**
Aris, John Lynnwood
Armenti, Joseph Rocco
Barnum, Jeanne Schubert
Baum, E. Harris
Best, Franklin Luther, Jr.
Bochetto, George Alexander
Bogutz, Jerome Edwin
Bressler, Barry E.
Butterworth, David Gardner
Calvert, Jay H., Jr.
Cannon, John, III
Carpey, Stuart A.
Chanin, Bernard
Chiacchiere, Mark Dominic
Connor, Joseph Patrick, III
Cooney, J(ohn) Gordon, Jr.
Cooper, Brad
Cullen, Raymond T.
D'Angelo, Christopher Scott
Devlin, John Gerard
Diamond, Paul Steven
Donner, Henry Jay
Falcao, Linda Phyllis
Fennell, Daniel Joseph, II
Fickler, Arlene
Fine, Stephanie Beth
Fineman, S. David
Flame, Andrew Jay
Ginsberg, David M.
Goldberg, Joseph
Gray, Edward Anthony
Hagan, Mary Ann
Hamilton, Michael Alan
Hamilton, Perrin C.
Hanselmann, Fredrick Charles
Hanzelik, Carl Harold
Hoffman, Alan Jay
Hoyle, Lawrence Truman, Jr.
Ivey, Stephen David
Jurewicz, Richard Michael
Kastenberg, Stephen Joel
Kupperman, Louis Brandeis
Lawn, Timothy Regis
Litt, H. Allen
Mannino, Edward Francis
Mannino, Robert John
Martillotti, Gerard Jacob
McNamara, John C.
Miller, Leslie Anne
Mishkin, Jeremy David
Mundy, James Francis
Murphy, Daniel Ignatius
Ominsky, Andrew Michael
Pace, Samuel J., Jr.
Pasek, Jeffrey Ivan
Rainone, Michael Carmine
Reilly, Marie Sambor
Resnick, Stephanie
Rosenbaum, Marcia F.
Rosenthal, Brian David
Samuel, Ralph David
Schildt, Steven Joseph
Schneider, Richard Graham
Shapiro, Mathieu Jode
Sheils, Denis Francis
Spivack, Gerald W.
Viletto, Harold Ernst
Wellington, Ralph Glenn
Whinston, Stephen Alan
Wrobleski, Jeanne Pauline
**Pittsburgh**
Alberty, Michael Charles
Arnold, Roy William
Bass, John A.
Belliveau, James Dennis
Bogut, John Carl, Jr.
Botta, Frank Charles
Braszo, John J.
Breault, Theodore Edward
Cohen, David R.
Conlon, Raymond Joseph
Corbett, Thomas Wingett, Jr.
Crawford, Karen Shichman
DeForest, Walter Pattison, III
Donahoe, Daniel Brennen
Esposito, Cheryl Lynne
Greene, Korry Alden
Grego, Samuel Robert
Hague, Paul Christian
Hickton, David John
Hornak, Mark Raymond
Karaffa, Michael Alan, Sr.
Kelleher, William Eugene, Jr.
Klodowski, Harry Francis, Jr.
Lee, Victoria
Matzus, Jason Eric
Miller, James Robert
Morgan, John Joseph, Jr.
Mulvihill, Keithley D.
Nerone, Michael F.
Owen, Jeffrey Randall
Perry, Jon Robert
Pfeifer, Gregory J.
Picadio, Anthony Peter
Purcupile, John Stephen
Rostek, Nancy Elizabeth
Salpietro, Frank Gugliotta
Schooley, Elizabeth Walter
Scully, Erik Vincent
Tarasi, Louis Michael, Jr.
Trower, William Kevin
Tucker, Richard Blackburn, III
Tungate, David E.
Wycoff, William Mortimer
Yates, Alfred Glenn, Jr.
Zangrilli, Albert Joseph, Jr.
**Pocono Pines**
Hardiman, Therese Anne
**Punxsutawney**
Lorenzo, Nicholas Francis, Jr.
**Reading**
Rethore, Kevin Watt
**Reynoldsville**
Wheeler, Mark Andrew, Sr.
**Scranton**
Burke, Henry Patrick
Cowley, Michael C.
Howley, James McAndrew
Sposito, James Anthony
Wenzel, Francis George, Jr.
**Sharon**
Kosmowski, Audra Michele
**Shavertown**
Malak, Paul John
**State College**
Nollau, Lee Gordon
**Sunbury**
Saylor, Charles Horace
**Valley Forge**
Corchin, Mark Alan
**Warendale**
Jacobs, Richard Louis
**Warminster**
Corr, Martin Joseph
**Warrendale**
Micale, Frank Jude
**Washington**
Curran, M(ichael) Scot
Mitchell, Clark A.
**Wayne**
Griffith, Edward, II
**West Chester**
Sommer, Jeffrey Robert
**Wilkes Barre**
Lach, Joseph Andrew
**York**
Markowitz, Lewis Harrison
Senft, John L.

## RHODE ISLAND

**Cranston**
Walsh, Leatrice D.
**Providence**
Burrows, Richard Henry
Dana, Mark William
Devereaux, William P.
Donnelly, Kevin William
Esposito, Dennis Harry
Gianfrancesco, Anthony Joseph
Glavin, Kevin Charles
Handy, Seth Howland
Jones, Lauren Evans
Kersh, DeWitte Talmadge, Jr.
MacFadyen, John Archibald, III
McElroy, Michael Robert
Medeiros, Matthew Francis
Mulhearn, Christopher Michael
Ratcliffe, J. Richard
Resmini, Ronald Joseph
Totten, R. Bart
**Warwick**
McGair, Joseph J.
Reilly, John B.
**Woonsocket**
Koutsogiane, Phillip Charles

## SOUTH CAROLINA

**Camden**
Furman, Hezekiah Wyndol Carroll
**Charleston**
Barker, Douglas Alan
Cooke, Morris Dawes, Jr.
Helms, William Collier, III
Hood, Robert Holmes
Lady, James Edward
Leath, William Jefferson, Jr.
Novak, Karl Eric
Patrick, Charles William, Jr.
Thompson, Joseph Durant
Waring, Bradish J.
Young, Joseph Rutledge, Jr.
**Columbia**
Blanton, Hoover Clarence
Carpenter, Charles Elford, Jr.
Gibbes, William Holman
Givens, Edwin D.
Meyer, Patricia R.
Morrison, Stephen George
Rawl, A. Victor, Jr.
Richardson, Donald V.
Strom, J. Preston, Jr.
**Greenville**
Christophillis, Constantine S.
Farry, Michael Allen
Ferguson, Donald Littlefield
James, William Richard
Johnson, Matthew Kinard
Pitts, Michael Stuart
Wyche, Madison Baker, III
**Hampton**
Runyan, Charles Alan
**Hilton Head**
Laughlin, Drew Alan
**Hilton Head Island**
Carter, Stephen Edward
**Johnsonville**
Poston, Ellerby Delance
**Kingstree**
Jenkinson, William Eldridge, III
**Mount Pleasant**
Swanson, Shane Eric
**Myrtle Beach**
Barnett, Michael James
Breen, David Hart
Leiter, John M.
**N Charleston**
Joye, Mark Christopher
Wigger, Jarrel L.
**Pawleys Island**
Daniel, J. Reese
**Spartanburg**
Anthony, Kenneth C., Jr.
Vega, Matthew Anthony
**Summerville**
Mortimer, Rory Dixon
**Walterboro**
Harvin, L(ucius) Scott

## SOUTH DAKOTA

**Rapid City**
Connot, Mark Jeffrey
**Sioux Falls**
Clapper, Jeffrey Curtis
Nelson, Robert R.
Orr, Rick W.

## TENNESSEE

**Brentwood**
Easter, Timothy Lee
**Chattanooga**
Adams, Morgan Goodpasture
Akers, Samuel Lee
Bryan, Rosemarie Luise
Burnette, Harry Forbes
Campbell, Paul, Jr.
Cirina, Angela Marie
Eason, Marcia Jean
Helton, Thomas Oswald
James, Stuart Fawcett
Moore, Hugh Jacob, Jr.
Newton, Michael David
North, Harold Lebron, Jr.
Simonds, Timothy Ray
Vital, Patricia Best
Weidlich, Paul Scott
**Dresden**
Herron, Roy Brasfield
**Greeneville**
Welch, Lawrence Andrew, Jr.
Wright, Thomas Jon
**Jackson**
Phillips, Marty Roy
**Johnson City**
Jenkins, Ronald Wayne
King, Robert Lewis
**Kingsport**
Hull, E. Patrick
**Knoxville**
Arnett, Foster Deaver
Campbell, Robert Roe
Coleman, Gregory Frederic
Conrad, Frederick Larue, Jr.
Cremins, William Carroll
Giordano, Lawrence Francis
Houser, Timothy Curtis
Murphree, Sharon Ann
Murray, Rebecca Brake
Roach, Jon Gilbert
Schwamm, Virginia Ann
Vines, William Dorsey
Walter, Glenn Richard
Ward, Kenneth Wayne
Wedekind, David N.
Wheeler, John Watson
White, Edward Gibson, II
**Lawrenceburg**
Plant, Paul Brunson
**Memphis**
Allen, Newton Perkins
Barna, James Francis
Bennett, Richard D.
Bland, James Theodore, Jr.
Branson, John R.
David, Monroe Steven
Davis, Earl Prichard (Pat Davis)
Fonville, Harold Wayne, II
Gentry, Gavin Miller
Hancock, Jonathan Cromwell
Matthews, Paul Aaron
McLean, Robert Alexander
Morgan, Colby Shannon, Jr.
Pfrommer, Michael Paul
Philip, John B.
Rutledge, Roger Keith
Schuler, Walter E.
Summers, James Branson
Veazey, Gary Eugene
Walsh, Thomas James, Jr.
Witthauer, Robert Taylor
**Nashville**
Blumstein, Andrée Kahn
Bramlett, Paul Kent
Cantrell, Luther E., Jr.
Clayton, Daniel Louis
Conner, Lewis Homer, Jr.
Cooney, Charles Hayes
Cornell, Helen Loftin
Douse, Steven Carl
Dundon, Thomas H.
Dyer, Sue McClure
Harris, Alvin Louis
Hunt, Sean Antone
Lowell, Roland M.
Phillips, Bruce Harold
Riley, Steven Allen
Spining, W. Carl
Wayland, R. Eddie
**Paris**
Rose, Todd Alan
**White House**
Ruth, Bryce Clinton, Jr.

## TEXAS

**Abilene**
Boone, Celia Trimble
**Addison**
Martens, Dan E.
**Alvin**
Hewitt, Otto D., III
**Amarillo**
Burnette, Susan Lynn
Hand, Matthew Henry
Isern, Kevin Anthony
Lara, Art B., Jr.
**Arlington**
Campbell, William Lee
**Austin**
Allison, James Purney
Brothers, D. Douglas
Connolly, Carla Garcia
Davis, Creswell Dean
Davis, David Murrel
Donley, Dennis W.
Drolla, John Casper Dodt, Jr.
Furman, James Housley
Gallo, A. Andrew
Gammage, Robert Alton (Bob Gammage)
Greig, Brian Strother
Hager, Julie-Ann
Hampton, Charles Edwin
Hicks, Renea
Hill, Melissa Clute (Lisa Hill)
Lochridge, Lloyd Pampell, Jr.
McCullough, Frank Witcher, III
Schaffer, Dean Aaron
Shapiro, David L.
Smith, Peyton Noble
Sudarshan, Arvind Jewett
Sultan, Frederick William, IV
Tice, Laurie Dietrich
Warren, Jessica Mendes
Wilson, James William
**Bastrop**
Van Gilder, Derek Robert
**Beaumont**
Bragg, J. J.
Cobb, Bruce Wayne
Dowell, James Dale
Newton, John Wharton, III
Scofield, Louis M., Jr.
**Boerne**
Deegear, James Otis, III
**Brownfield**
Moore, Bradford L.
**Brownsville**
Cowen, Michael Raphael
Ray, Mary Louise Ryan
**Brownwood**
Steele, Todd Bennett
**Bryan**
Michel, C. Randall
**Cleveland**
Campbell, Selaura Joy
**College Station**
Kennady, Emmett Hubbard, III
**Corpus Christi**
Anthony, James Lloyd
Laws, Gordon Derby
Leon, Rolando Luis
Martinez, Diana Marie
Shackelford, Patricia Ann
**Corsicana**
Sodd, Glenn
**Dallas**
Acker, Rodney
Appenzeller, Phillip Carl, Jr.
Baggett, Steven Ray
Bennett, Paul William
Bickel, John W., II
Bonesio, Woodrow Michael
Bryant, David
Case, Thomas Louis
Clardy, Thelma Sanders
Clark, Robert Murel, Jr.
Cobb, William Dowell, Jr.
Conant, Allah B., Jr.
Crain, Gayla Campbell
Cromartie, Eric Ross
Crotty, Robert Bell
Curry, Gregory William
Davenport, James Kent
Davis, Derek Shane
Dicus, Brian George
Douglass, Frank Russell
Eaton, Michael William
Elkind, Laura Peterson
Ellis, Alfred Wright (Al Ellis)
Garcia Barron, Ramiro
Gibson, John Wheat
Glazer, Rachelle Hoffman
Goodwin, R. Brad
Grimmer, Stephen Andrew
Hackney, Hugh Edward
Hardwick, Martha Josephine
Hawkins, Scott Alexis
Henry, Vic Houston
Henvey, John William
Holmes, James Hill, III
Honea, Floyd Franklin
Hoskins, Sonya Denise
Hranitzky, Rachel Robyn
Hunt, Amy Katherine
James, Walter D., III
Johnson, James Joseph Scofield
Johnston, Coyt Randal
Jones, Grier Patterson
Joseph, Marc Ward
Keegan, Karen Ann
Kirby, Le Grand Carney, III
Kroemer, John Albert
Leach, James Glover
Lotzer, Gerald Balthazar
Lynn, Barbara Michele
Maguire, Kevin Jerome
Malorzo, Thomas Vincent
Malouf, Edward Wayne
McCreary, David Sean
McDonald, Michael Scott
Mc Elhaney, John Hess
McKennon, Richard Otey
Miers, Harriet E.
Mighell, Kenneth John
Pruessner, David Morgan
Ravji, Aamer
Rittenberry, Kelly Culhane
Roberts, Scott Raymond
Robinson, Kimberly Marie
Schening, Judith Anne
Skibell, Arthur
Sloman, Marvin Sherk
Stinnett, Mark Allan
Turley, Linda
Vangelisti, Richard J.
Washington, Karen Roberts
Wewers, Mark Eric
Zeiger, Timothy David
Zisman, Barry Stuart
**El Paso**
Broaddus, John Morgan, III
Collins, William Coldwell
Cox, Sanford Curtis, Jr.
Dickey, John M.
Ingram, Temple Byrn, Jr.
Leachman, Russell DeWitt
Lipson, Myer Jack
McDonald, Charles Edward
Moffeit, Michael Paul
Provenghi, Ruggero
Strahan, Jeffery V.
Torkildson, Thomas Miles
**Fort Worth**
Berenson, William Keith
Brender, Art
Cleveland, Joseph F., Jr.
Cottongame, W. Brice
Dean, Beale
Emerson, Douglas Theodore
Griffith, Richard Lattimore
Johnston, Michael Wayne
Langenheim, Roger Allen
Law, Thomas Hart
Lemons, Keith David
Litke, Jennifer Holland
Moses, Shayne Daniel
Mullanax, Milton Greg
Nelson, Edward Reese, III
Randolph, Robert McGehee
Rice, Bradley Harold
Sharpe, James Shelby
Sheehan, Edward Michael
Tatum, Stephen Lyle
Tillman, Karen Sue
**Galveston**
Kilgore, Jeffrey Harper
Neves, Kerry Lane
**Harlingen**
Pope, William L.
**Henderson**
Adkison, Ron
**Hillsboro**
Aufill, Bennett Brantley, III
**Houston**
Aarons-Holder, Charmaine Michele
Agosto, Benny, Jr.
Altsuler, Kent
Amann, Leslie Kiefer
Bailey, Stephen Robert
Banks, John Robert, Jr.
Barnett, Edward William
Barnett, Stephanie Blair
Bell, Robert Christopher
Benesh, William Stephen
Bradie, Peter Richard
Brown, David Hurst
Brown, Kelly D.
Carmody, James Albert
Carstarphen, Edward Morgan, III
Carter, John Loyd
Chapman, Patricia Gayle
Cohen, Jay I.
Conway, Sharon Elizabeth
Cooney, James Patrick
Countiss, Richard Neil
Crowley, David James
Dampier, Harold Dean, Jr.
Del Valle, Teresa Jones
Dijkman, Christiana
Edwards, Blaine Douglass
Ekwem, Robertson M.
England, Rudy Alan
Farnsworth, T. Brooke
Fox, Jan Woodward
Frels, Kelly
Garten, David Burton
Griffin, Marilyn Otteman
Grossberg, Marc Elias
Hanks, George Carol, Jr.
Hanson, Jerry Clinton
Heggen, Ivar Nelson
Holloway, Gordon Arthur

Ivey, Jack Todd
Junell, William Edward, Jr.
Ketchand, Robert Lee
Kientz, Val William
Knutson, Sam Houston
Krock, Kenneth Michael
Kruse, Charles Thomas
Lapin, Robert E.
Lawhon, Susan Harvin
Love, Scott Anthony
Lynch, John Edward, Jr.
McDaniel, Jarrel Dave
McEvily, Daniel Vincent Sean
Montgomery, Kendall Charles
Moreland, Mary Louise
Moroney, Linda L. S.
Nations, Howard Lynn
O'Neill, Alice Jane
Owens, Betty Ruth
Pamphilis, Constantine Z.
Pappas, Daniel C.
Pate, Stephen Patrick
Prestridge, Pamela Adair
Pruitt, Robert Randall
Raley, John Wesley, III
Rambo, Rick Lynn
Ransom, Clifton Louis, Jr.
Reasoner, Barrett Hodges
Rhodes, George Frederick, Jr.
Rigby, Robert Glen
Roach, Robert Michael, Jr.
Samuelson, Douglas Allen
Sears, Terry H.
Sikora, Tomasz Jacek
Sitzes, Madeline D'ree Penton
Skoller, Ronald Aaron
Spain, H. Daniel
Spence, W. Ross
Stephens, Delia Marie Lucky
Tavormina, John William
Towns, William Roy
Turek, Douglas D.
Van Fleet, George Allan
Van Kerrebrook, Mary Alice
Walton, Dan Gibson
Wesely, Nathan
Wojciechowski, Marc James
Zahorik, Michael Alan
Zeigler, Ann dePender

**Humble**
Frazier, William Sumpter

**Irving**
Beach, Charles Addison
Bradley, Jean Marie
Freiling, Don Rynn

**Killeen**
Carlson, Craig W.

**Lamesa**
Saleh, John

**League City**
Chudleigh, G. Stephen

**Lindale**
Anderson, Lawrence Worthington

**Longview**
Beckworth, Lindley Gary, Jr.
Stevens, Scott English
Welge, Jack Herman, Jr.

**Lubbock**
Cobb, David Randall
Harrell, Walter Hugh

**Mcallen**
Alvarez, Adolfo, Jr.
Carrera, Victor Manuel
Dyer, J.W.

**Mesquite**
Zook, Bill

**Midland**
Fletcher, Richard Royce

**Mount Pleasant**
Woodson, Danny

**Odessa**
Hendrick, Benard Calvin, VII

**Orange**
Dugas, Louis, Jr.

**Pecos**
Weinacht, John William

**Plainview**
Lafont, William Harold

**Plano**
Hand, Randall Eugene

**Rusk**
Guy, Steve R.

**San Antonio**
Anderson, Bruce Edwin
Aoki, Zachary Burke
Armstrong, William Tucker, III
Barnhill, Donald Earl
Countryman, Thomas Arthur
Cumpian, Joe G.
Drought, James L.
Higdon, James Noel
Maloney, Patrick, Sr.
McFarlen, Gerald Dale
Montgomery, James Edward, Jr.
Munsinger, Harry L.
Patrick, Dane Herman
Pipkin, Marvin Grady
Wachsmuth, Robert William
Wallis, Ben Alton, Jr.
Welmaker, Forrest Nolan
West, David Blair
Yedor, Jonathan

**Sherman**
Freels, Jesse Saunders, Jr.
Harrison, Richard E.

**Spring**
Loomis, Wendell Sylvester

**Sugar Land**
Aldrich, Lovell W(eld)
Greer, Raymond White
Poock, Steven Doyle
West, S. Scott

**Teague**
Smith, William Lafayette, Jr.

**Temple**
Cuba, Benjamin James

**Texarkana**
Poff, Franklin Albright, Jr.
Potter, David Jimmie

**The Woodlands**
Schlacks, Stephen Mark

**Tyler**
Bryan, Christian E.
Thames, E. Glenn, Jr.
Vickery, Ronald Stephen

**Waco**
Bostwick, Frederick deBurlo, III
Mackenzie, Charles Alfred

## UTAH

**Logan**
Jenkins, James C.

**Park City**
Kennicott, James W.

**Provo**
Abbott, Charles Favour
Jeffs, M. Dayle

**Salt Lake City**
Anderson, Robert Monte
Anderson, Ross Carl
Barker, Ronald C.
Beckstead, John Alexander
Burton, H(ubert) Dickson
Butler, Cass C.
Clark, Robert Stokes
Davies, Glen Ensign
Deamer, Michael Lynn
Henriksen, C. Richard, Jr.
Humpherys, LeGrande Rich
Karrenberg, Thomas Richard
Lambert, Dale John
Larsen, Lynn Beck
Linebaugh, Kent B.
McIntosh, James Albert
Orton, R. Willis
Purser, Donald Joseph
Rasmussen, Thomas Val, Jr.
Reeder, F. Robert
Rogers, Jon H.
Scofield, David Willson
Tateoka, Reid
Turner, Shawn Dennis
Wagner, Mark Alan
Young, Robert Sherman

**Woods Cross**
Weiler, Todd David

## VERMONT

**Berlin**
Craddock, Stephen James

**Brattleboro**
Munzing, Richard Harry

**Burlington**
Blackwood, Eileen Morris
Davis, Christopher Lee
Roy, Christopher Denis
Sartore, John Thornton

**Montpelier**
Putter, David Seth

**Norwich**
McGee, P. Scott

**Rutland**
Faignant, John Paul
Vreeland, Neal C.

**Saint Albans**
Appel, Kenneth Mark
Bugbee, Jesse D.

**Saint Johnsbury**
Palmer, Bruce C.

**Stowe**
Davison, Robert P., Jr.

**Woodstock**
Dagger, William Carson

## VIRGINIA

**Abingdon**
Conway, Berry Leslie, II

**Alexandria**
Battle, Timothy Joseph
Costello, Daniel Brian
Delaney, Raighne C.
Hirschkop, Philip Jay
Isaacs, Dorothy Ann
Kiyonaga, John Cady
Rogers, L. Lawton, III
Toothman, John William

**Annandale**
Dunkum, Betty Lee

**Arlington**
Cutler, Miriam
Fowler, David Lucas

**Bristol**
Arrington, James Edgar, Jr.
Minor, Steven Ray

**Charlottesville**
Kendall, Gary Wheeler
McKay, John Douglas
Robinette, Christopher John

**Fairfax**
Baird, Charles Bruce
Britton, Matthew Joseph
Downey, Richard Lawrence
Dwornik, Frances Pierson
Field, David Ellis
Joshi, Michael
Keith, John A.C.
Lash, Richard Anthony
Murray, Michael Patrick
Stanley, William Martin

**Fredericksburg**
Jones, Owaiian Maurice

**Front Royal**
Napier, Ronald Lewis

**Glen Allen**
Urelius, Shawn Renea
Ware, Henry Neill, Jr.

**Hampton**
Long, Robert Elliott

**Harrisonburg**
Ledbetter, Melisa Gay
Wallinger, M(elvin) Bruce

**Lawrenceville**
Bain, C. Ridley

**Lebanon**
Compton, Carnis Eugene

**Leesburg**
Saunders, Richard R.

**Lynchburg**
Packert, G(ayla) Beth

**Manassas**
Hancock, Alton Guy
Locklin, Kevin Lee
McGolrick, J. Edward, Jr.

**Martinsville**
Smith, Fred Dempsey, Jr.

**Mc Lean**
Cochran, Stephen Grey
Erickson, John Richard
Sparks, Robert Ronold, Jr.

**Midlothian**
Tuttle, Roger Lewis

**Newport News**
Martin, Terrence Keech
Meade, Steven A.

**Norfolk**
Davis, Terry Hunter, Jr.
Devine, William Franklin
Harrell, Charles Lydon, Jr.
Johnson, William H.
McCaa, James Cureton, III
Pearson, John Y., Jr.
Rashkind, Alan Brody
Sacks, Stewart Jonathan

**Norton**
Earls, Donald Edward
Jessee, Roy Mark

**Portsmouth**
Miller, Joseph Aaron
Moody, Willard James, Sr.

**Reston**
Bredehoft, Elaine Charlson

**Richmond**
Angelidis, Stephen Alexander
Bing, Richard McPhail
Boyd, B(everley) Randolph
Carrell, Daniel Allan
Ellis, Andrew Jackson, Jr.
Hall, Stephen Charles
Hicks, C. Flippo
King, William H., Jr.
Levit, Jay J(oseph)
Merhige, Robert Reynold, Jr.
O'Toole, Deborah Shea
Pollard, Henry Robinson, IV
Porter, Kirby Hugh
Robinson, John Victor
Ross, David Lee
Rudlin, David Alan
Spahn, Gary Joseph
Spencer, Anthony George
Street, Walter Scott, III
Walsh, James Hamilton
Whitlock, Julie Marie

**Roanoke**
Barnhill, David Stan
Bullington, David Bingham
Densmore, Douglas Warren
Hale, Lance Mitchell
Harbert, Guy M., III
Hylton, Myles Talbert
Jennings, James Wilson, Jr.
McGarry, Richard Lawrence
Mundy, Gardner Marshall
Ziogas, Robert Aristidis

**Spotsylvania**
Pugh, Randall Scott

**Stafford**
Locklear, W. Ross

**Sterling**
Babirak, Milton Edward, Jr.

**Vienna**
Titus, Bruce Earl

**Virginia Beach**
Buzard, David Andrew
Clark, Donald H.
Dumville, S(amuel) Lawrence
Gray, Jeffrey Hugh
Moore, Michael Calvin
Swope, Richard McAllister

**Winchester**
Adams, Nate Lavinder, III

**Wise**
Rogers, Leonard David

## WASHINGTON

**Aberdeen**
Brown, James Marston

**Anacortes**
Osborn, Gerald T.

**Auburn**
Gibson, Landon Mack, III

**Bainbridge Is**
Otorowski, Christopher Lee

**Bellevue**
Landau, Felix

**Bellingham**
Britain, James Edward
Raas, Daniel Alan

**Centralia**
Tiller, Laurel Lee

**East Wenatchee**
Lacy, Steven C.

**Everett**
Dewell, Julian C.

**Federal Way**
Pratum, Michael James

**Gig Harbor**
Thompson, Ronald Edward

**Grandview**
Maxwell, John Edward

**Mount Vernon**
Sjostrom, Craig David

**Port Orchard**
Crawford, William Matterson

**Seattle**
Block, Steven William
Boman, Marc Allen
Collins, Theodore John
Cunningham, Joel Dean
Easter, Scott Beyer
Ferrer, Rafael Douglas Paul
Franke, Patrick Joseph
Fredericksen, Scott L.
Freedman, Bart Joseph
Goodnight, David R.
Guy, Andrew A.
Hamilton, Henry Kerr
Hillman, Roger Lewis
Hollon, Gregory J.
Hough, Mark Mason
Johnson, Bruce Edward Humble
Krohn, Gary John
Lassman, Iro Richard
Lemly, Thomas Adger
Linn, Brian James
Longfelder, Lawrence Lee
Lundgren, Gail M.
Marshall, David Stanley
McCoid, Nancy Katherine
McConaughy, Bennet Alan
McCune, Philip Spear
McKinstry, Ronald Eugene
Paul, Thomas Frank
Perey, Ron
Pettigrew, Edward W.
Roche, Robert Joseph
Rummage, Stephen Michael
Salter, Andrew H.
Sandler, Michael David
Thomas, Jeffrey Walton
Turner, Duncan Calvert
Walters, Dennis H.
Wayne, Robert Jonathan
Whitson, Lish

**Spokane**
Allen, Keller Wayne
Annis, Eugene Irwin
Lineberger, Peter Saalfield
Luciani, Thomas Richard
Olson, James Warren
Smith, Brad Edward
Smythe, Andrew Campbell
Symmes, William Daniel

**Tacoma**
Felker, Robert Stratton
Krueger, James A.
Maichel, Jack J.
Malanca, Albert Robert

**Walla Walla**
Mitchell, Michael Sherman
Monahan, Richard F.

**Winthrop**
Eklund, Paul G.

## WEST VIRGINIA

**Beckley**
Sayre, Floyd McKinley, III

**Bluefield**
Evans, Wayne Lewis
Henderson, Susan Ellen Fortune

**Buckhannon**
McCauley, David W.

**Charleston**
Brown, James Knight
Ciccarello, Arthur T.
Crislip, Stephen Ray
Douglas, Robert Edward
Fisher, Michael Matthew
Hicks, Elliot Gene
Michelson, Gail Ida
Neely, Richard
Powell, J(ames) C(orbley)
Teare, John Richard, Jr.
Victorson, Michael Bruce
Zak, Robert Joseph

**Fairmont**
Brandfass, Robert Lee

**Huntington**
McGuire, J(ames) Grant

**Martinsburg**
Rose, Laura Rauch

**Morgantown**
Fusco, Andrew G.
Kimble, Kelly Jean

**Parkersburg**
Full, Robert Witmer

**Princeton**
White, Benjamin Ballard, Jr.

**Weirton**
Makricostas, Dean George

**Wellsburg**
Bell, Charles D.

## WISCONSIN

**Baraboo**
Vesely, Tori Ann

**Brookfield**
Benson, Scott Michael
Zaffiro, Richard L.

**Deerfield**
Pappas, David Christopher

**Green Bay**
Barker, April Rockstead
Burnett, Ralph George
Thompson, John Mortimer

**Kaukauna**
Curry, Irving Gregg, III

**Lake Geneva**
Olson, John Olmstead

**Madison**
Anderson, Michael Steven
Blanchard, Brian Wheatley
Coaty, Thomas Jerome
Hansen, John Alton
Peterson, H. Dale
Schmid, John Henry, Jr.
Schooler, Steven James
Skilton, John Singleton
Stoddard, Glenn McDonald
Tomaselli, Anthony Allen

**Milwaukee**
Bachhuber, Michael Joseph
Beightol, Scott Christopher
Bohren, Michael Oscar
Carroll, Douglas James
Daily, Frank J(erome)
Decker, John Robert
Ehlinger, Ralph Jerome
Fishbach, Nathan A.
Fredericks, James Matthew
Friebert, Robert Howard
Gimbel, Franklyn M.
Hodan, Patrick John
Margolis, Marvin Allen
Marquis, William Oscar
McCarty, William Edward
McClure, Thomas James
Nelson, Roy Hugh, Jr.
O'Neill, Kevin Edgeworth
Pindyck, Bruce Eben
Scoptur, Paul Joseph
Terschan, Frank Robert
Trecek, Timothy Scott
Van Grunsven, Paul Robert
Williams, Clay Rule

**Mosinee**
Schira, Diana Rae

**Oshkosh**
Wilde, William Richard

**Osseo**
Feltes, Charles Victor

**Racine**
Rudebusch, Alice Ann

**Rhinelander**
Saari, John William, Jr.

**River Falls**
Krueger, Stuart James

**Sheboygan**
Darrow, Dwight Daniel

**Washburn**
Nordling, H.G.

**Waukesha**
Gesler, Alan Edward
Ward, James A.

**Wausau**
Connell, James Bernard
Weber, Richard J.
Wolf, Kevin Earl

## WYOMING

**Casper**
Day, Stuart Reid
Hjelmstad, William David
Shumate, Roger Eugene

**Cheyenne**
Hickey, Paul Joseph
Kehl, Larry Bryan

**Rawlins**
DeHerrera, Juan Leo

**Riverton**
Hursh, John R.

**Sheridan**
Cannon, Kim Decker

## TERRITORIES OF THE UNITED STATES

## PUERTO RICO

**San Juan**
Antonetti-Zequeira, Salvador
Pierluisi, Pedro R.

**Vega Baja**
Arraiza, Manuel F.

## VIRGIN ISLANDS

**St Croix**
Welcome, Patricia

## MEXICO

**Cuernavaca**
Foss, George B., Jr.

**Tijuana**
Berger, Jaime Benjamin

## GEORGIA

**Tbilisi**
Swann, Barbara

## ADDRESS UNPUBLISHED

Adams, Samuel Franklin
Alfrey, Thomas Neville
Arencibia, Raul Antonio
Bailey, Francis Lee
Barnier, David John
Baxter-Smith, Gregory John
Beasley, James W., Jr.
Beldock, Myron
Bell, John William
Bell, Troy Nathan
Berger, Marc Joseph
Beukema, John Frederick
Blount, David Laurence
Blume, James Donald
Bondi, Harry Gene
Boone, Richard Winston, Sr.
Braun, Jerome Irwin
Brodsky, David M.
Brown, Jay W.
Brumbaugh, John Moore
Brush, Kirkland L.
Burcham, Randall Parks
Bush, Robert G., III
Cash, Michelle Hoogendam
Chang, Deborah
Choslovsky, William
Coletti, Julie A.
Connell, William D.
Connors, Kevin Charles
Coviello, Frank Joseph
Craven, Robert Emmett
Di Carlo, Patrick Connors
Dickstein, Michael Ethan
Dolce, Julia Wagner
Dow, William F.
Farley, Barbara Suzanne
Feazell, Vic
Fischer, David Jon
Fleischman, Herman Israel
Foreman, Lee David
Forster, Clifford
Foster, Cindy Cooper
Frank, Jeffrey Michael
Freedlander, Barrett Walter
Gates, Pamela Sue
Giovanniello, Joseph, Jr.
Goddard, Claude Philip, Jr.
Grutman, Jewel Humphrey
Hall, John Hopkins
Harman, Wallace Patrick
Harvey, Marc Sean
Hetrick, Brenda Drendel
Higginbotham, John Taylor
Higginson, Carla Jean
Holmes, Michael Gene
Hornthal, Louis Philip, Jr.
Hubbard, Michael James
Kapnick, Richard Bradshaw
Kennedy, Vekeno

Killeen, Michael John
Klein, Linda Ann
Knuth, Eric Joseph
Krelstein, Ronald Douglas
Lestelle, Terrence Jude
Levinson, Kenneth Lee
Lipsman, Richard Marc
Mains, Steve Alan
Martin, Thomas MacDonald
Mathieu, Michelle Elise
McCormick, Homer L., Jr.
McCray, Douglas Gerald
McDonald, Sandra K.
McFerrin, James Hamil
McKay, John
McKenzie, Curtis David
McNeil Staudenmaier, Heidi Loretta
Milberg, Melinda Sharon
Miller, Frank William
Missan, Richard Sherman
Monsees, Timothy William
Nadelson, Eileen Nora
Neuhaus, Joseph Emanuel
Newman, Carol L.
Norman, Albert George, Jr.
Olsen, Kenneth Allen
Pagano, Eugene Salvatore Rooney
Paul, Richard Wright
Peterson, Stephen D.
Phillips, Florence Tsu
Pucillo, Anthony Ernest
Quillen, Cecil Dyer, Jr.
Redmond, Lawrence Craig
Rench, Stephen Charles
Roe, Michael Flinn
Ross, Catherine Jane
Schild, Raymond Douglas
Schor, Suzi
Schroeder, Edward James
Schultz, Dennis Bernard
Seifert, Stephen Wayne
Shaner, Leslie Ann
Shapiro, Edwin Stanley
Shigley, Kenneth Lowell
Shutt, Nekki
Siporin, Sheldon
Smallwood, John Daniel
Smith, Ronald Ehlbert
Smock, James F.
Smyth, Jeffrey A.
Speaker, Susan Jane
Spiegel, Jayson Leslie
Streicker, James Richard
Tone, Philip Willis
Turen, Barbara Ellen
Vale, Victor John Eugene, II
Walner, Robert Joel
Wessel, Peter
White, John Joseph, III
Wigler, Andrew Jeffrey
Wright, Frederick Lewis, II

## CIVIL LITIGATION, STATE

### UNITED STATES

#### ALABAMA

**Anniston**
Woodrow, Randall Mark
**Birmingham**
Benton, Lee Rimes
Harris, George Bryan
Hollis, Louie Andrew
Kracke, Robert Russell
Max, Rodney Andrew
Newton, Alexander Worthy
Stabler, Lewis Vastine, Jr.
**Cullman**
Poston, Beverly Paschal
**Decatur**
McWhorter, Robert Tweedy, Jr.
**Demopolis**
Dinning, Woodford Wyndham, Jr.
**Eutaw**
Ford, Byron Todd
**Gadsden**
Spray, Vann Allan
**Hartford**
Eldridge, William Phillip
**Huntsville**
Stephens, (Holman) Harold
**Mobile**
Byrne, Bradley Roberts
Rogers, Jannea Suzanne
**Moulton**
Dutton, Mark Anthony
**Sheffield**
Hamby, Gene Malcolm, Jr.
**Talladega**
Gaines, Ralph Dewar, Jr.
**Tuscumbia**
Hunt, James L.

#### ALASKA

**Anchorage**
Ealy, Jonathan Bruce
Hayes, George Nicholas
**Sitka**
Graham, David Antony

#### ARIZONA

**Phoenix**
Balitis, John James, Jr.
Beggs, Harry Mark
Cohen, Ronald Jay
Coleman, George Joseph, III (Jay Coleman)
Corson, Kimball Jay
Cummings, Frederick Michael
Daughton, Donald
Grant, Merwin Darwin
Lasee, Mark Edward
Leonard, Jeffrey S.
Petitti, Michael Joseph, Jr.
Ulrich, Paul Graham
Wall, Donald Arthur
Zachar, Christopher Joseph
**Prescott**
Goodman, Mark N.
**Scottsdale**
Smith, David Burnell
**Sierra Vista**
Borowiec, William Matthew
**Surprise**
Hayes, Ray, Jr.
**Tempe**
Palmer, Janice Maude
**Tucson**
Bergin, Jeffrey Thomas
Willis, Jeffrey Lynn
**Yuma**
Hossler, David Joseph

#### ARKANSAS

**Benton**
Ellis, George Dawlin
**Corning**
Manatt, Scott
**Harrison**
Pinson, Jerry D.
**Jonesboro**
Bristow, Bill Wayne
**Little Rock**
Dillahunty, Wilbur Harris
Ervin, Edie Renee
Griffin, William Mell, III
**Newport**
Howard, Steven Gray
**Walnut Ridge**
Mullen, William David
**West Memphis**
Weisburd, Everard J.

#### CALIFORNIA

**Aptos**
Garrison, Melissa Lyn
**Auburn**
Lyon, Bruce Arnold
**Bakersfield**
Kind, Kenneth Wayne
**Belvedere**
Loube, Irving
**Beverly Hills**
Jaffe, F. Filmore
Juno, Cynthia
**Burbank**
Ajalat, Sol Peter
**Burlingame**
Cotchett, Joseph Winters
**Campbell**
Castello, Raymond Vincent
**Carpinteria**
Kump, Kary Ronald
**Costa Mesa**
Frieden, Clifford E.
Guilford, Andrew John
**Daly City**
Boccia, Barbara
**Encinitas**
Williams, Michael Edward
**Encino**
Cadwell, David Robert
**Fresno**
Fischbach, Donald Richard
Nunes, Frank M.
Ramirez, Frank Tenorio
**Glendale**
Kazanjian, Phillip Carl
Martinetti, Ronald Anthony
**Grass Valley**
Bell, Joseph James
**Hanford**
Snyder, Thom
**Huntington Beach**
Garrels, Sherry Ann
**Irvine**
Cahill, Richard Frederick
Rudolph, George Cooper
Specter, Richard Bruce
Toledano, James
Vermes, L. Robert
**King City**
Bolles, Donald Scott
**Laguna Hills**
Reinglass, Michelle Annette
**Larkspur**
Katz, Richard Leonard
**Long Beach**
Blumberg, John Philip
**Los Angeles**
Adler, Erwin Ellery
Bell, Wayne Steven
Belleville, Philip Frederick
Bodkin, Henry Grattan, Jr.
Bressan, Paul Louis
Fine, Richard Isaac
Goldie, Ron Robert
Grebow, Arthur Jeffrey
Grush, Julius Sidney
Handzlik, Jan Lawrence
Heller, Philip
Hufstedler, Shirley Mount (Mrs. Seth M. Hufstedler)
Hutchins, Robert Bruce
Irving, Jeanne Ellen
Jacques, Nigel Edward
Jalbuena, Arnel Babiera
Lawton, Eric
Levine, Jerome Lester
Liebhaber, Jack Mitchell
Lurvey, Ira Harold
Manning, Steven Donald
McDermott, Thomas John, Jr.
Miller, Louis R., III
Mosk, Richard Mitchell
Murray, Anthony
Newell, Robert Melvin
Newman, Michael Rodney
Niles, John Gilbert
Nocas, Andrew James
Packard, Robert Charles
Pollock, John Phleger
Renner, John Robert
Robison, William Robert
Selwood, Pierce Taylor
Snyder, Arthur Kress
Straw, Lawrence Joseph, Jr.
Strong, George Gordon, Jr.
Tepper, R(obert) Bruce, Jr.
Walcher, Alan Ernest
White, Susan Page
Williams, Lee Dwain
**Malibu**
Pilling, George William
**Martinez**
Williams, Charles Judson
**Menlo Park**
Dyer, Charles Arnold
**Middletown**
Downing, James Christie
**Mill Valley**
Georgeson, Adamont Nicholas
Judson, Philip Livingston
**Modesto**
Mussman, William Edward
Schrimp, Roger Martin
**Monterey**
Feavel, Patrick McGee
**Newport Beach**
Cordova, Ron
Dito, John Allen
McEvers, Duff Steven
Millar, Richard William, Jr.
Milman, Alyssa Ann
Mirabel, Farrah
Price, Stuart Winston
Willard, Robert Edgar
**Oakland**
Bjork, Robert David, Jr.
McCarthy, Steven Michael
Trowbridge, Jeffery David
**Oceanside**
Ferrante, R. William
**Orinda**
Perez, Richard Lee
Resneck, William Allan
**Oxnard**
Regnier, Richard Adrian
**Palm Desert**
Reinhardt, Benjamin Max
**Palm Springs**
Caruthers, Dennis Michael
Kimberling, John Farrell
**Palo Alto**
Sands, Michael Arthur
**Pasadena**
Algorri, Mark Steven
Brenner, Anita Susan
Telleria, Anthony F.
**Pleasant Hill**
Weiss, Edward Abraham
**Redwood City**
Coddington, Clinton Hays
**Richmond**
Straus, Douglas Charles
**Riverside**
McKinney, Dan George
**Rodeo**
Wagner, Eric Roland
**Sacramento**
Brazier, John Richard
Brookman, Anthony Raymond
Callahan, Gary Brent
Duggan, Jennifer E.
Portello, William Leslie, III
Schleicher, Estelle Ann
York, Wendy C.
**San Bernardino**
Brittain, Gregory W.
**San Diego**
Appleton, Richard Newell
Buzunis, Constantine Dino
Castellanos, Richard Henry
Chenoweth, Jenny K.
Christensen, Charles Brophy
Klinedinst, John David
Lewin, Jeffrey David
Lotkin, Adam H.
Mongan, Anthony David
Roseman, Charles Sanford
Sceper, Duane Harold
Schuck, Carl Joseph
Schulz, Peter Jon
Speckman, David Leon
Udell, Lei (Lisa) Karen
Vancho, Janine
Weaver, Michael James
**San Fernando**
Lynch, Kevin G.
**San Francisco**
Goode, Barry Paul
Herlihy, Thomas Mortimer
Higgins, Valerie Jan
Howe, Drayton Ford, Jr.
Kern, John McDougall
Ladar, Jerrold Morton
Levit, Victor Bert
Raven, Robert Dunbar
Traynor, John Michael
Truett, Harold Joseph, III (Tim Truett)
Venning, Robert Stanley
Young, Douglas Rea
**San Jose**
Cobey, Christopher Earle
Hannon, Timothy Patrick
Liccardo, Salvador A.
Stutzman, Thomas Chase, Sr.
**San Mateo**
Sayad, Pamela Miriam
**San Pedro**
Stephenson, Michael Murray
**Santa Ana**
Harvey, Margot Marie
Ingalsbe, William James
Ultimo, Paul Joseph
**Santa Barbara**
Bauer, Marvin Agather
Willey, Charles Wayne
**Santa Clarita**
Kotler, Richard Lee
**Santa Monica**
Kanner, Gideon
Weatherup, Roy Garfield
**Seaside**
Weingarten, Saul Myer
**Sherman Oaks**
Joyce, Stephen Michael
**Tustin**
Madory, Richard Eugene
**Universal Cty**
Peter, Arnold Philimon
**Van Nuys**
Haile, Lawrence Barclay
Imre, Christina Joanne
**Ventura**
Borrell, Mark Steven
Gartner, Harold Henry, III
Milne, Gary E.
**Victorville**
Kennedy, Jeanne Elizabeth
**Visalia**
Crowe, Daniel Walston
McKinney, Russell Raymond
**Walnut Creek**
Medak, Walter Hans
Pinkerton, Albert Duane, II
Skaggs, Sanford Merle
**West Covina**
Ebiner, Robert Maurice
**Woodland Hills**
Robertson, Alexander, IV

#### COLORADO

**Aspen**
McGrath, J. Nicholas
**Aurora**
Flicker, Howard
**Boulder**
Leh, Christopher Marshall
Purvis, John Anderson
**Breckenridge**
Katz, Jeri Beth
**Castle Rock**
Robinson, Michael Allen
**Colorado Springs**
LeHouillier, Patric Jaymes
MacDougall, Malcolm Edward
**Delta**
Wendt, John Arthur Frederic, Jr.
**Denver**
Aisenberg, Bennett S.
Anderson, Alan Wendell
Bain, James William
Bryans, Richard W.
Cox, William Vaughan
Daily, Richard W.
DeLaney, Herbert Wade, Jr.
Ehrlich, Stephen Richard
Featherstone, Bruce Alan
Garcia, Anthony J.
Hoffman, Daniel Steven
Law, John Manning
Macaulay, Christopher Todd
McFarland, Matthew Gabriel
Miller, Gale Timothy
Quiat, Marshall
Rhodes, Ralph Beauford
Samuels, Donald L.
Sedlak, Joseph Anthony, III
Starrs, Elizabeth Anne
Stuart, Mary Hurley
Thomasch, Roger Paul
Wedgle, Richard Jay
Widmann, Edward Healy
**Englewood**
Branney, Joseph John
**Fort Collins**
Brown, Ronald Laming
**Frisco**
Helmer, David Alan
**Golden**
Carney, Deborah Leah Turner
**Littleton**
Carleno, Harry Eugene
Spelts, Richard John
**Pueblo**
Geisel, Henry Jules

#### CONNECTICUT

**Bloomfield**
Mawhinney, Kent D.
**Bridgeport**
Meehan, Richard Thomas, Jr.
Osis, Daiga Guntra
Williams, Ronald Doherty
**Fairfield**
LaFollette, Ernest Carlton
**Greenwich**
Fogarty, James Robert
**Hartford**
Blumenthal, Jeffrey Michael
Elliot, Ralph Gregory
Fain, Joel Maurice
Pepe, Louis Robert
Sussman, Mark Richard
Tanski, James Michael
**Madison**
Clendenen, William Herbert, Jr.
**Middletown**
Adams, Richard Glen
**Milford**
Sagarin, J. Daniel
**New Haven**
Ajello, Michael John
Cox, Barbara Lynne
Geisler, Thomas Milton, Jr.
Murphy, William Robert
Secola, Carl A., Jr.
**Norwich**
Masters, Barbara J.
**Stafford Springs**
Paradiso, F. Joseph
**Stamford**
Livolsi, Frank William, Jr.
**Trumbull**
Brennan, Daniel Edward, Jr.
**Willimantic**
Lombardo, Michael John
**Wilton**
Silverman, Melvin J.

#### DELAWARE

**Wilmington**
Carey, Wayne John
Green, James Samuel
Kimmel, Morton Richard
Klayman, Barry Martin
Laster, J. Travis
Schlusser, Robert Elmer

#### DISTRICT OF COLUMBIA

**Washington**
Bellinger, Edgar Thomson
Bonner, Walter Joseph
Burch, John Thomas, Jr.
Coates, Melanie Diana
Cooter, Dale A.
Esposito, Joseph Paul
Evans, Thomas William
Fisher, Raymond Corley
Gibson, Kumiki S.
Hassett, Joseph Mark
Kuder, Armin Ulrich
Liebman, Ronald Stanley
Medaglia, Mary-Elizabeth
Nace, Barry John
Paper, Lewis J.
Policy, Vincent Mark
Potenza, Joseph Michael
Tompert, James Emil
Tompkins, Joseph Buford, Jr.
Tufaro, Richard Chase
Work, Charles Robert

#### FLORIDA

**Altamonte Springs**
Heindl, Phares Matthews
**Boca Raton**
Feldman, Joel Harvey
Golis, Paul Robert
Kauffman, Alan Charles
Retamar, Richard E.
**Brandon**
Curry, Clifton Conrad, Jr.
Tittsworth, Clayton (Magness)
**Clearwater**
Durand, Jean-Paul
Simms, John Seth
**Coconut Grove**
McAmis, Edwin Earl
**Coral Gables**
Anthony, Andrew John
Chonin, Neil Harvey
Coleman, Roderick Flynn
David, George A.
Fuentes-Cid, Pedro Jose
Hengber, Gregory Paul
Keedy, Christian David
Weissenborn, Sheridan Kendall
**Crestview**
Duplechin, D. James
**Fort Lauderdale**
Bunnell, George Eli
Di Giulian, Bruno L.
Haliczer, James Solomon
Krathen, David Howard
Nyce, John Daniel
Rose, Norman
Santa Maria, Diana
**Gainesville**
Mollica, Salvatore Dennis
Pugh, David Edward
**Hollywood**
London, Jack Edward
**Jacksonville**
Bradford, Dana Gibson, II
Cowles, Robert Lawrence
Gabel, George DeSaussure, Jr.
Oberdier, Ronald Ray
O'Neal, Michael Scott, Sr.
Pillans, Charles Palmer, III
**Key Biscayne**
Burnbaum, Michael William
**Key West**
Davila, Gregory David
**Lake Mary**
Loe, Brian Robert
**Lake Wales**
White, Norman
**Lakeland**
Martin, Michael David
**Longboat Key**
Pulvermacher, Louis Cecil
**Maitland**
Edwards, James Alfred
**Melbourne**
Trachtman, Jerry H.
**Miami**
Blumberg, Edward Robert
Brown, Lewis Nathan
Burstein, Bernardo
Clark, James Kendall
Coffey, Kendall Brindley
Cohen, Jeffrey Michael
Critchlow, Richard H.
Davis, Jeffrey Robert
Eaton, Joel Douglas
Ferrell, Milton Morgan, Jr.
Gander, Deborah J.
Glickman, Fred Elliott
Hall, Andrew Clifford
Hall, Miles Lewis, Jr.
Hochman, Alan Robert
Kearns, John W.
Kreutzer, Franklin David
Leibowitz, Mark A.
Lipton, Paul R.
Miller, Raymond Vincent, Jr.
Nachwalter, Michael
Nelson, Richard M.
Rogers, Harvey DeLano
Scremin, Anthony James
Segor, Joseph Charles
Smith, Samuel Stuart
Starr, Ivar Miles
Wiseheart, Malcolm Boyd, Jr.
Wright, Robert Thomas, Jr.
**Naples**
Cimino, Richard Dennis
Gebhardt, Robert Charles
**North Miami Beach**
Cain, May Lydia

**Ocala**
Briggs, Randy Robert
**Orlando**
Allen, William Riley
Cohen, David Sacks
Cullen, Kim Michael
deBeaubien, Hugo H.
Dempsey, Bernard Hayden, Jr.
Downie, Robert Collins, II
Eagan, William Leon
Losey, Ralph Colby
Motes, Carl Dalton
Noah, Douglas True
Parrish, Sidney Howard
Reinhart, Richard Paul
Wasson, Karen Reed
Weiss, Christopher John
Wilson, William Berry
**Palm Beach Gardens**
Hayes, Neil John
**Pensacola**
Duke, Thomas Harrison
Gaines, Robert Pendleton
Levin, David Harold
Windham, John Franklin
**Port Saint Lucie**
Hoey, William Edward
**Ruskin**
Norse, Kristin A.
**Saint Petersburg**
Allen, John Thomas, Jr.
Blews, William Frank
Glass, Roy Leonard
Holland, Troy Whitzhurst
**Sarasota**
Blucher, Paul Arthur
Phillips, Elvin Willis
Rossi, William Matthew
**Sebring**
Trombley, Michael Jerome
**Stuart**
Harvin, Wesley Reid
**Sun City Center**
Balkany, Caron Lee
**Tallahassee**
Anderson, Bruce Paige
Davis, William Howard
Gievers, Karen A.
Schreiber, Charles Joseph, Jr.
**Tampa**
Boos, Robert Walter, II
Butler, Paul Bascomb, Jr.
Davis, David Earl
DeVaney, Donna Brookes
Guerra, Rolando Gilberto, Jr.
Halliday, Stanley Grant
Kelly, Mark Patrick
Kelly, Thomas Paine, Jr.
Ramey, Mark S.
Salem, Albert McCall, Jr.
Somers, Clifford Louis
Stagg, Clyde Lawrence
Thomas, Wayne Lee
**Valrico**
Carlucci, Paul Pasquale
**West Palm Beach**
Chopin, Susan Gardiner
Djokic, Walter Henry
Eyler, Bonnie
Farina, John
Holland, William Meredith
Hudson, Lise Lyn
Koons, Stephen Robert
Norton, William Alan
Nugent, Paul Allen
O'Flarity, James P.
Shapero, Bertram Malcolm
Wearn, James McCartney
Yeager, Thomas Joseph
**Winter Park**
Ackert, T(errence) W(illiam)

## GEORGIA

**Athens**
Tolley, Edward Donald
**Atlanta**
Blank, A(ndrew) Russell
Boynton, Frederick George
Collins, Donnell Jawan
Doyle, Michael Anthony
Duffey, William Simon, Jr.
Farnham, Clayton Henson
Fleming, Julian Denver, Jr.
Paquin, Jeffrey Dean
Seacrest, Gary Lee
Smith, Grant B.
Stone, Matthew Peter
Wellon, Robert G.
**Columbus**
Patrick, James Duvall, Jr.
**Cumming**
Mantagna, Michael
**Decatur**
Mears, Michael
Skinner, William French Cochran, Jr.
**Fayetteville**
Johnson, Donald Wayne
**Hazlehurst**
Elder, Lamar Alexander, Jr.
**Macon**
Dozier, Lester Zack
Elliott, James Sewell
**Marietta**
Ingram, George Conley
**Mcdonough**
Crumbley, R. Alex
**Newnan**
Franklin, Bruce Walter
**Norcross**
Morochnik, Paul J.
**Savannah**
Ladson, M. Brice
Ratterree, Ryburn Clay
**Snellville**
Giallanza, Charles Philip
**Statesboro**
Stone, Ralph Kenny
**Tucker**
Armstrong, Edwin Alan
Polstra, Larry John
**Winder**
McLemore, Michael Kerr
Stell, John Elwin, Jr.

## HAWAII

**Honolulu**
Chuck, Walter G(oonsun)
Dezzani, David John
Fukumoto, Leslie Satsuki
Iwai, Wilfred Kiyoshi
Kobayashi, Bert Takaaki, Jr.
Kunkel, Daniel James
Lawson, William Homer
Potts, Dennis Walker
Taylor, Carroll Stribling
Turbin, Richard
Wong, James Thomas

## IDAHO

**Lewiston**
Tait, John Reid

## ILLINOIS

**Aurora**
Dreyer, John Edward
**Belleville**
Churchill, Allen Delos
Coghill, William Thomas, Jr.
Menges, Eugene Clifford
**Champaign**
Rawles, Edward Hugh
**Chicago**
Adelman, Stanley Joseph
Baker, James Edward Sproul
Bellah, Kenneth David
Biebel, Paul Philip, Jr.
Boies, Wilber H.
Bresnahan, Arthur Stephen
Burdelik, Thomas L.
Burditt, George Miller, Jr.
Burke, Dennis J.
Burke, John Michael
Burke, Thomas Joseph, Jr.
Chemers, Robert Marc
Cherney, James Alan
Cipolla, Carl Joseph
Cole, Jeffrey
Ditkowsky, Kenneth K.
Dombrowski, Gerald Michael
Fennell, Monica Ann
Fina, Paul Joseph
Forcade, Billy Stuart
Franch, Richard Thomas
Griffith, Donald Kendall
Hall, Joan M.
Halloran, Michael John
Harrington, James Timothy
Hecht, Frank Thomas
Hunter, James Galbraith, Jr.
Katz, Harold Ambrose
Kennelly, John Jerome
Kroll, Barry Lewis
Leyhane, Francis John, III
Marick, Michael Miron
Marszalek, John Edward
Mason, Henry Lowell, III
McConnell, James Guy
Mendelson, Alan Conrad
Meyer, John Albert
Miller, Douglas Andrew
Montgomery, Julie-April
Mulroy, Thomas Robert, Jr.
Nash, Gordon Bernard, Jr.
Novotny, David Joseph
Palmer, Robert Towne
Parson, Jason A.
Pattishall, Beverly Wyckliffe
Pavalon, Eugene Irving
Pelton, Russell Meredith, Jr.
Perrin, James Kirk
Redmond, Richard Anthony
Richmond, William Patrick
Richter, Tobin Marais
Romanyak, James Andrew
Schulte, Bruce John
Schwartzberg, Hugh Joel
Tefft, Steven M.
Torshen, Jerome Harold
Van Demark, Ruth Elaine
Walsh, Robert Patrick, Jr.
Wemple, Peter Holland
Witwer, Samuel Weiler, Jr.
**Danville**
Blan, Kennith William, Jr.
**Elgin**
Carbary, Jonathan Leigh
Flanagan, Leo M., Jr.
**Elmhurst**
Kordik, Daniel Joseph
**Elmwood Park**
Spina, Anthony Ferdinand
**Geneva**
Skaar, James Douglas
**Hinsdale**
Farrug, Eugene Joseph, Sr.
**Inverness**
Victor, Michael Gary
**Joliet**
Miller, Randal J.
Ozmon, Laird Michael
**Kewanee**
McRae, Donald James
**Lake Forest**
Emerson, William Harry
**Libertyville**
DeSanto, James John
**Mattoon**
Horsley, Jack Everett
**Monee**
Bohlen, Christopher Wayne
**Mount Carroll**
Leemon, John Allen
**Mount Vernon**
Harvey, Morris Lane
**Oak Brook**
Ring, Leonard M.
**Oakbrook Terrace**
Bashaw, Steven Bradley
**Palatine**
Runes, Kenneth Alan
**Peoria**
Slevin, John A.
Winget, Walter Winfield
**Princeton**
Johnson, Watts Carey
**Rockford**
Mateer, Don Metz
**Schaumburg**
Rudd, Donnie
Shapiro, Edwin Henry
**Skokie**
Greenspan, Jeffrey Dov
Plotnick, Paul William
**Springfield**
Artman, Eric Alan
**Waukegan**
Decker, David Alfred
**Wheaton**
Cunningham, William Francis
**Willowbrook**
Walton, Stanley Anthony, III
**Winnetka**
Krucks, William Norman
Theis, William Harold
**Woodstock**
Kell, Vette Eugene

## INDIANA

**Beech Grove**
Brown, Richard Lawrence
**Carmel**
Newman, Mary Lynn Canmann
**Columbus**
Fairchild, Raymond Francis
Harrison, Patrick Woods
**Crown Point**
Stevens, William J.
**Elkhart**
Wicks, Charles Carter
**Evansville**
Berger, Charles Lee
Bodkin, Robert Thomas
Clouse, John Daniel
**Fort Wayne**
Harants, Stephen John
Pope, Mark Andrew
**Fowler**
Woods, Dennis Lynn
**Franklin**
Jones, Tom George
**Hammond**
Ruman, Saul I.
Voelker, Louis William, III
**Indianapolis**
Daniel, Melvin Randolph
Elberger, Ronald Edward
Grinnan, Gloria Katherine
Karwath, Bart Andrew
Koch, Edna Mae
Lisher, John Leonard
Montross, W. Scott
Schreckengast, William Owen
Wellnitz, Craig Otto
Zoeller, D. Bryce
**Kokomo**
Russell, Richard Lloyd
**Lafayette**
Layden, Charles Max
**Lebanon**
Donaldson, John Weber
**Marion**
Ryan, Patrick Nelson
**Seymour**
Pardieck, Roger Lee
**Shelbyville**
McNeely, James Lee
**South Bend**
Myers, James Woodrow, III
Sopko, Thomas Clement
**Warsaw**
Rigdon, Jay Alden

## IOWA

**Davenport**
Halligan, Kevin Leo
Lathrop, Roger Alan
**Des Moines**
Baybayan, Ronald Alan
Doyle, Richard Henry, IV
Duckworth, Marvin E.
Foxhoven, Jerry Ray
Frederici, C. Carleton
Logan, Thomas Joseph
Murray, William Michael (Mike Murray)
Tully, Robert Gerard
**Iowa City**
Spies, Leon Fred
**Keokuk**
Hoffman, James Paul
**Sioux City**
Mayne, Wiley Edward

## KANSAS

**Emporia**
Helbert, Michael Clinton
**Garden City**
Pierce, Ricklin Ray
**Lyons**
Hodgson, Arthur Clay
**Overland Park**
Keplinger, (Donald) Bruce
Starrett, Frederick Kent
**Shawnee Mission**
Sparks, Billy Schley
**Topeka**
Hamilton, John Richard
Justus, Jo Lynne
Schroer, Gene Eldon
**Winfield**
Krusor, Mark William

## KENTUCKY

**Bowling Green**
Rudloff, William Joseph
**Covington**
Lawrence, Richard Dean
Wolnitzek, Stephen Dale
**Danville**
Clay, James Franklin
**Florence**
Busald, E. André
**Lexington**
Fryman, Virgil Thomas, Jr.
Turley, Robert Joe
**Louisville**
Baker, H. Nicholas
Bishop, Robert Whitsitt
Brown, Bonnie Maryetta
Chauvin, Leonard Stanley, Jr.
Davidson, Scott Allen
Dolt, Frederick Corrance
Guethlein, William O.
Karageorge, Thomas George
Ogburn, John Denis
**Paris**
Budden, Harry Edward, Jr.

## LOUISIANA

**Baton Rouge**
Donnan, Susan L.
Jones, Keith Dunn
**Kenner**
Todaro, Laura Jean
**Lafayette**
Bernard, Barton Willis
Davidson, James Joseph, III
Saloom, Kaliste Joseph, Jr.
**Lake Charles**
Parkerson, Hardy Martell
Veron, J. Michael
**Leesville**
Smith, Simeon Christie, III
**Metairie**
Haygood, John Warren
**New Orleans**
Bordelon, Alvin Joseph, Jr.
Buckley, Samuel Olliphant, III
Gertler, Meyer H.
Herman, Russ Michel
Kelly, William James, III
Kupperman, Stephen Henry
Lowe, Robert Charles
Rosen, William Warren
Thomas, Joseph Winand
Wheeler, V.M., III
Whitney, John Franklin
**Shreveport**
Rigby, Kenneth
**Slidell**
Shamis, Edward Anthony, Jr.
Singletary, Alvin D.
**Thibodaux**
Clement, Leslie Joseph, Jr.

## MAINE

**Bangor**
Haddow, Jon Andrew
**Hallowell**
Crawford, Linda Sibery
**Portland**
Germani, Elizabeth A.
Lancaster, Ralph Ivan, Jr.
Marjerison, Thomas Sydney
Rundlett, Ellsworth Turner, III

## MARYLAND

**Annapolis**
Perkins, Roger Allan
**Baltimore**
Bell, Venetia Darlene
Byrd, Ronald Dicky
Carbine, James Edmond
Crowe, Thomas Leonard
Gilbert, Blaine Louis
Golomb, George Edwin
Howell, Harley Thomas
Kallina, Emanuel John, II
Kleid, Wallace
Kramer, Paul R.
Kuryk, David Neal
Pappas, George Frank
Radding, Andrew
Schochor, Jonathan
Summers, Thomas Carey
Weltchek, Robert Jay
White, William Nelson
**Bethesda**
Karp, Ronald Alvin
**Chevy Chase**
Weiss, Harlan Lee
**Ellicott City**
Silverstein, Fred Howard
**Gaithersburg**
Santa Maria, Philip Joseph, III
**Laytonsville**
McDowell, Donna Schultz
**Parkville**
Hill, Milton King, Jr.
**Rockville**
Dugan, John R.
Moul, Robert Gemmill, II
Thompson, James Lee
Van Grack, Steven
Wagshal, Jerome Stanley
**Salisbury**
Clarke, Wm. A. Lee, III
**Towson**
Hansen, Christopher Agnew
**Upper Marlboro**
Wallace, Sean Daniel
**Wheaton**
Kirchman, Charles Vincent

## MASSACHUSETTS

**Andover**
Lakin, John Francis
**Boston**
Abraham, Nicholas Albert
Carpenter, Robert Brent
Costa, Michael R.
Curley, Robert Ambrose, Jr.
Dillon, James Joseph
Felter, John Kenneth
Gaynor, Martin F., III
Gelb, Richard Mark
Halström, Frederic Norman
Hamelburg, Gerald A.
Kavanaugh, James Francis, Jr.
Krulewich, Leonard M.
Lacovara, Kirsten Marie
Lindley, James David
Lukey, Joan A.
Macauley, William Francis
MacFarlane, Maureen Anne
Meyer, Andrew C., Jr.
Moriarty, George Marshall
O'Neill, Timothy P.
Packenham, Richard Daniel
Reece, Laurence Hobson, III
Trimmier, Roscoe, Jr.
Urquhart, Stephen E.
Zavez, John Peter
**Brighton**
Gilden, James William
**Brookline**
Houlihan, F(rancis) Robert, Jr.
**Burlington**
Feeley, Kelly A.
Graves, Robert
**Framingham**
Gaffin, Gerald Eliot
**Medford**
Berman, David
**New Bedford**
Murray, Robert Fox
**Newton**
Monahan, Marie Terry
**Pittsfield**
Simons, William W.
**Wellesley**
Goglia, Charles A., Jr.
**West Yarmouth**
Gens, Richard Howard
**Winchester**
La Rosa, Lillian J.

## MICHIGAN

**Ann Arbor**
Britton, Clarold Lawrence
DeVine, Edmond Francis
**Battle Creek**
Blaske, E. Robert
**Bay City**
Kennedy, Brian Melville
**Big Rapids**
Clarke, Alan William
**Birmingham**
Cunningham, James Patrick
**Bloomfield Hills**
Googasian, George Ara
Mucha, John, III
Pappas, Edward Harvey
Vocht, Michelle Elise
Weinstein, William Joseph
**Brighton**
Nielsen, Neal D.
**Dearborn**
Currier, Gene Mark
**Detroit**
Andreoff, Christopher Andon
Bushnell, George Edward, Jr.
Christiansen, Roy Hvidkaer
Gilbert, Ronald Rhea
Leuchtman, Stephen Nathan
Longhofer, Ronald Stephen
Mengel, Christopher Emile
Saxton, William Marvin
Tucciarone, Enrico Gregory
**Flint**
Hart, Clifford Harvey
Wheaton, Robin Lee
**Holland**
Bidol, James Alexander
**Kalamazoo**
Plaszczak, Roman Thaddeus
**Lansing**
Baker, Frederick Milton, Jr.
Coey, David Conrad
Rasmusson, Thomas Elmo
**Midland**
Battle, Leonard Carroll
**Mount Clemens**
Stepek, Mark William
**Owosso**
Johnson, James Randall
**Pontiac**
Pierson, William George
**Rapid City**
Ring, Ronald Herman
**Romeo**
Clark, Mark Lee
**Saginaw**
McGraw, Patrick John
**Saint Joseph**
Gleiss, Henry Weston
**Southfield**
Bereznoff, Gregory Michael
Fieger, Geoffrey Nels
Jacobs, John Patrick
May, Alan Alfred
Schwartz, Robert H.
Thurswell, Gerald Elliott
Tyler, David Malcolm
**Troy**
Alber, Phillip George
Kruse, John Alphonse

## MINNESOTA

**Anoka**
Beens, Richard Albert
**Bemidji**
Baer, H. Carl, III
**Duluth**
Thibodeau, Thomas Raymond

**Golden Valley**
Hagglund, Clarance Edward
**Minneapolis**
Ciresi, Michael Vincent
D'Aquila, Barbara Jean
Degnan, John Michael
Hanson, Bruce Eugene
Hanson, Kent Bryan
Jarpe, Geoffrey Pellas
Jepsen, William E.
Kempf, Douglas Paul
Lazar, Raymond Michael
McGunnigle, George Francis
Meller, Robert Louis, Jr.
Meyer, Paul T.
Shroyer, Thomas Jerome
Sortland, Paul Allan
Tanick, Marshall Howard
**New Brighton**
Krueger, William James
**Saint Cloud**
Provinzino, John C.
**Saint Paul**
Allison, John Robert
Gehan, Mark William
Seymour, Mary Frances
Trojack, John Edward

## MISSISSIPPI

**Gulfport**
Pettey, William Hall, Jr.
**Hernando**
Maddox, Nancy McCraine
**Jackson**
Clark, David Wright
Hewes, George Poindexter, III
Mitchell, Meade Westmoreland
Pyle, Luther Arnold

## MISSOURI

**Ballwin**
Gunn, Michael Peter
**Clayton**
Schwartz, Theodore Frank
**Columbia**
Dannov, Fred
Schwabe, John Bennett, II
**Excelsior Springs**
Berrey, Robert Wilson, III
**Higginsville**
Ver Dught, ElGene Clark
**Independence**
Minton, Kent W.
Terry, Jack Chatterson
**Kansas City**
Beckett, Theodore Charles
Clarke, Milton Charles
Cowden, John William
Helder, Jan Pleasant, Jr.
Hopkins, William Carlisle, II
Housh, Tedrick Addison, III
Hubbell, Ernest
Jackson, James B.
Johnson, Mark Eugene
Lolli, Don R(ay)
Moore, Diana Dowell
Morefield, Richard Watts
Price, James Tucker
Schult, Thomas P.
Wirken, James Charles
**Keytesville**
Wheeler, James Julian
**Lees Summit**
Walsh, Thomas Joseph
**Saint Ann**
Johnson, Harold Gene
**Saint Louis**
Beach, Douglas Ryder
Brown, Paul Sherman
Burns, Mark Gardner
Carr, Gary Thomas
Collins, James Slade, II
Conran, Joseph Palmer
DeWoskin, Alan Ellis
Douaihy, Toni Patricia
Floyd, Walter Leo
Kortenhof, Joseph Michael
Rabbitt, Daniel Thomas, Jr.
Rice, Canice Timothy, Jr.
Sestric, Anthony James
Sneeringer, Stephen Geddes
Spooner, Jack Bernard
**Springfield**
McDonald, William Henry
Woody, Donald Eugene

## MONTANA

**Butte**
Harrington, James Patrick
**Kalispell**
Lerner, Alan Jay

## NEBRASKA

**Cozad**
McKeone, Mark R.
**Grand Island**
Busick, Denzel Rex
**Lincoln**
Colleran, Kevin
Cope, Thom K.
Swihart, Fred Jacob
**Omaha**
Brownrigg, John Clinton
Lee, Dennis Patrick
Riley, William Jay

## NEVADA

**Gardnerville**
Terzich, Milos
**Las Vegas**
England, Kathleen Jane
Stoberski, Michael Edward
Zubel, Eric Louis
**Reno**
Kladney, David
Santos, Herbert Joseph, Jr.

## NEW HAMPSHIRE

**Concord**
Johnson, Robert Veiling, II
**Hollis**
Lumbard, Eliot Howland
**Manchester**
Damon, Claudia Cords
**Portsmouth**
Tober, Stephen Lloyd

## NEW JERSEY

**Atlantic City**
Markwardt, John James
**Audubon**
Montano, Arthur
**Brigantine**
Kokes, Alois Harold
**Cherry Hill**
Garrigle, William Aloysius
Korin, Joel Benjamin
**Clark**
Farina, Mario G.
**Clifton**
Palma, Nicholas James
**Collingswood**
Kole, Janet Stephanie
**Cranford**
De Luca, Thomas George
McCreedy, Edwin James
**East Brunswick**
Eder, Todd Brandon
**Edison**
Lavigne, Lawrence Neil
**Florham Park**
Calabrese, Arnold Joseph
Charme, Stephen Mark
**Gibbsboro**
Ferreri, Vito Richard
**Hackensack**
Greenberg, Steven Morey
Masi, John Roger
Pollinger, William Joshua
Schuber, William Patrick
Usatine, Warren Alan
**Hackettstown**
Mulligan, Elinor Patterson
**Haddonfield**
Andres, Kenneth G., Jr.
**Jersey City**
D'Alessandro, Daniel Anthony
**Kearny**
Brady, Lawrence Peter
**Kendall Park**
Fisch, Joseph
**Kenilworth**
Hoffman, John Fletcher
**Lambertville**
Peluso, Matthew A.
**Lawrenceville**
Blumstein, Jeffrey Phillip
**Livingston**
Burns, Susie
**Medford**
Timban, Demetrio Sunga
**Metuchen**
Frizell, David J.
**Millburn**
Biebelberg, Keith N.
**Moorestown**
Polansky, Steven Jay
**Morristown**
Bartkus, Robert Edward
Fenske, Karl Arthur
Humick, Thomas Charles Campbell
McDonough, Joseph Richard
Newman, John Merle
Rosenthal, Meyer L(ouis)
Samay, Z. Lance
Szuch, Clyde Andrew
**Newark**
Barrett, Virginia M.
Cummis, Clive Sanford
Herman, Ross Neil
Jacobs, Andrew Robert
Madden, Edward George, Jr.
McGuire, William B(enedict)
Muscato, Andrew
Rak, Lorraine Karen
Simon, David Robert
**Northfield**
Broome, Henry George, Jr.
Cohen, Barry David
**Ocean**
Maul, Donna L.
**Parsippany**
Doherty, Robert Christopher
Gallagher, Jerome Francis, Jr.
Hansbury, Stephan Charles
Kallmann, Stanley Walter
Rothstadt, Garry Sigmund
**Princeton**
Lampert, Michael A.
**Red Bank**
Duggan, John Peter
**Rochelle Park**
Knopf, Barry Abraham
**Roseland**
Garrod, Jeffrey Mead
McMahon, Edward Richard
Schenkler, Bernard
Schwartz, Andrea B.
Smith, Dennis Jay
**Saddle Brook**
Pearlman, Peter Steven
**Ship Bottom**
Shackleton, Richard James
**Short Hills**
Marshall, John Patrick
**Springfield**
Kahn, Eric G.
**Succasunna**
Correale, Robert D.
**Trenton**
Gogo, Gregory
**Warren**
Kraus, Steven Gary
**West Orange**
Gordon, Harrison J.
Kantowitz, Jeffrey Leon
Serviss, Daniel Marc
**Westfield**
Phillips, John C.
**Westmont**
Pozzuoli-Buecker, Renee M.
**Wildwood**
Gould, Alan I.
**Woodbury**
Adler, Lewis Gerard
**Woodcliff Lake**
Pollak, Cathy Jane
Sneirson, Marilyn

## NEW MEXICO

**Albuquerque**
Bardacke, Paul Gregory
Branch, Turner Williamson
Crollett, Richard Jacques
Hale, Timothy S.
McBride, Thomas John
Threet, Martin Edwin
**Farmington**
Gurley, Curtis Raymond
**Santa Fe**
Cunningham, David Fratt
Hallmark, Bruce Cullen, Jr.
McClaugherty, Joe L.
Schwarz, Michael
Zorie, Stephanie Marie

## NEW YORK

**Albany**
Linnan, James Daniel
Powers, John Kieran
**Amherst**
Vinal, Jeanne Marie
**Armonk**
Quinn, James W.
**Bay Shore**
Zuckerman, Landon Roy
**Bethpage**
Carlen, Leon C.
**Binghamton**
Gouldin, David Millen
**Bronx**
Fraiden, Norman Arthur
**Brooklyn**
DeMarco, Anthony J., Jr.
Nicholson, Michael
Roth, Pamela Susan
**Buffalo**
Brown, Jerrold Stanley
Canale, John F.
Goldberg, Neil A.
Herdzik, Arthur Alan
Mattar, Lawrence Joseph
Pajak, David Joseph
Sampson, John David
Smith, Carrie Lynette
Stachowski, Michael Joseph
Vinal, Gregory Michael
**Canaan**
Pennell, William Brooke
**Carmel**
Grossman, Victor G.
**Catskill**
Kingsley, John Piersall
**Central Valley**
Levinson, David Lawrence
**Chestnut Ridge**
Burns, Richard Owen
**Commack**
Steindler, Walter G.
**Dansville**
Vogel, John Walter
**Delhi**
Schimmerling, Thomas Emile
**East Meadow**
Weiss, Adam William
**Elmsford**
Mevec, Edward Robert
**Flushing**
Ginsberg, Jerome Maurice
**Garden City**
Corleto, Raymond Anthony
Kaplan, Joel Stuart
Yovino, Anthony
**Getzville**
DiNardo, Joseph
**Glens Falls**
Caffry, John W.
**Gouverneur**
Leader, Robert John
**Great Neck**
Gilbert, Theodore
Salzman, Stanley P.
**Hempstead**
Raab, Ira Jerry
**Highland**
Nardone, Richard
**Hornell**
Pulos, William Whitaker
**Islip**
Baker, Lloyd Harvey
**Ithaca**
Patte, George David, Jr.
**Jackson Heights**
Casanova, Lorenzo
**Jericho**
Corso, Frank Mitchell
**Jordan**
McCabe, Matthew Clark
**Lake Grove**
Melbardis, Wolfgang Alexander
**Malone**
Nichols, Joseph Patrick
**Mayville**
Dolan, John F.
**Mineola**
Block, Martin
Braid, Frederick Donald
Fowler, David Thomas
Kelly, Edward Joseph
Lynn, Robert Patrick, Jr.
Monaghan, Peter Gerard
Plastaras, Thomas Edward
Sandback, William Arthur
Wilson, George J.
**Mohegan Lake**
Stokes, Ron
**Mount Kisco**
Curran, Maurice Francis
**New Hyde Park**
Ezersky, William Martin
Jensen, Richard Currie
Levine, Kimberly Anne
**New York**
Amabile, John Louis
Amsterdam, Mark Lemle
Barenholtz, Celia Goldwag
Beatie, Russel Harrison, Jr.
Benedict, James Nelson
Bezanson, Thomas Edward
Bizar, Irving
Bradley, E. Michael
Brecker, Jeffrey Ross
Brill, Haydn J.
Broder, Eric Jason
Brown, Peter Megargee
Buchwald, Don David
Burrows, Michael Donald
Caputo, Nicholas Raymond
Cashman, Gideon
Cohen, Robert Stephan
Cole, Charles Dewey, Jr.
Coll, John Peter, Jr.
Costikyan, Edward N.
Daichman, Jeffrey Howard
Dallas, William Moffit, Jr.
Damashek, Philip Michael
Dopf, Glenn William
Eiseman, Neal Martin
Eisman, Clyde Jay
Elsen, Sheldon Howard
Faillace, Charles Kenneth
Feder, Saul E.
Feffer, Joanna Wahl
Feldberg, Michael Svetkey
Fiske, Robert Bishop, Jr.
Fletcher, Anthony L.
Folkenflik, Max
Frankel, Sandor
Futterman, Stanley Norman
Gallagher, Timothy D.
Garfield, Martin Richard
Garfinkel, Barry Herbert
Garland, Sylvia Dillof
Garvey, Christopher John
Gerber, Robert Evan
Gitter, Max
Goldstein, Kenneth B.
Gray, Glenn Oliver
Greenawalt, William Sloan
Gruen, Michael Stephan
Gurfein, Richard Alan
Habian, Bruce George
Haig, Robert Leighton
Halperin, Kyle Mallary
Harris, Joel B(ruce)
Haynes, Jean Reed
Heisler, Stanley Dean
Hennessy, Mickee M.
Hirsch, Jerome S.
Hirshowitz, Melvin Stephen
Hollyer, A(rthur) Rene
Hritz, George F.
Iannuzzi, John Nicholas
Isquith, Fred Taylor
Jacob, Edwin J.
Jacobowitz, Harold Saul
Jacobson, Sandra W.
Joseph, Gregory Paul
Kahn, Alan Edwin
Kaplan, Lawrence I.
Katz, Jerome Charles
Kelmachter, Leslie Debra
Kimelman, Steven
Koegel, William Fisher
Kronman, Carol Jane
Kuh, Richard Henry
Kurland, Paul Carl
Kushel, Glenn Elliot
Landau, James Kenneth
Langer, Bruce Alden
Lederer, Karen F.
Lesman, Michael Steven
Lesser, William Melville
Levine, Melvin Charles
Loscalzo, Anthony Joseph
Lupert, Leslie Allan
Lustig, David Carl, III
Mandelker, Lawrence Arthur
Maneker, Morton M.
Mantel, Allan David
Mayesh, Jay Philip
McGahren, Richard George
McGrath, Christopher Thomas
Muccia, Joseph William
Mullaney, Thomas Joseph
Muskin, Victor Philip
Neff, Michael Alan
Nolan, Richard Edward
North, Steven Edward
O'Connor, William Matthew
O'Leary, Michael Thomas
Oliensis, Sheldon
Owen, Richard Knowles
Pepper, Allan Michael
Phillips, Anthony Francis
Pickholz, Jason R.
Quinn, Timothy Charles, Jr.
Raylesberg, Alan Ira
Reich, Larry Sam
Reiter, Allen Gary
Rifkind, Robert S(inger)
Rikon, Michael
Rivera, Walter
Rosenberg, Gary Marc
Rosenzweig, Theodore B.
Rothman, Bernard
Rothman, Dennis Michael
Salvan, Sherwood Allen
Schechter, Howard
Schwab, Harold Lee
Schwartz, Leonard
Shanman, James Alan
Shaughnessy, James Michael
Shollenberger, Elizabeth Ann
Simon, Michael Scott
Sladkus, Harvey Ira
Smiley, Guy Ian
Smith, Robert Everett
Smoak, Evan Lewis
Sperber, Joseph John, IV
Stratton, Walter Love
Swiedler, Alan M.
Toplitz, George Nathan
Vandenberg, Raymond Leonard, Jr.
Weinberger, Harold Paul
Weiner, Stephen L.
Weinstock, Gregg D.
Weltz, Paul Martin
Witkin, Eric Douglas
Wolff, Kurt Jakob
Yelenick, Mary Therese
Zauderer, Mark Carl
Zerin, Steven David
Zimmett, Mark Paul
**Newburgh**
Milligram, Steven Irwin
**Oneonta**
Burns, Brian Douglas
Scarzafava, John Francis
**Oyster Bay**
Gaffney, Mark William
Robinson, Edward T., III
**Patchogue**
Tona, Thomas
**Poughkeepsie**
Sproat, Christine A.
**Riverhead**
Kelley, Christopher Donald
Twomey, Thomas A., Jr.
**Rochester**
Braunsdorf, Paul Raymond
Dolin, Lonny H.
Geiger, Alexander
Harris, Wayne Manley
Inclima, Charles P.
Law, Michael R.
Leclair, Paul Lucien
Moore, James Conklin
Reed, James Alexander, Jr.
**Rome**
Rizzo, James S.
**Roslyn Heights**
Tannenbaum, Richard Neil
**Rye**
Goldstein, Peter Dobkin
**Sands Point**
Busner, Philip H.
**Saratoga Springs**
Harper, David Alexander
**Scarsdale**
King, Robert Lucien
**Syracuse**
Cherundolo, John Charles
Gerber, Edward F.
Givas, Thomas Peter
Zimmerman, Aaron Mark
**Waterford**
Novotny, F. Douglas
**White Plains**
Dannenberg, Richard Bruce
Doyle, Dennis Thomas
Halpern, Philip Morgan
Kalish, Daniel A.
Morell, Philip M.
Nesci, Vincent Peter
Nolletti, James Joseph
Pohlmann, William Howard
Weiss, Terri Lynn
**Yonkers**
Connors, James Patrick

## NORTH CAROLINA

**Asheville**
Cogburn, Max Oliver
Davis, Roy Walton, Jr.
Frue, William Calhoun
**Blowing Rock**
Corlett, Edward Stanley, III
**Cary**
Cromer, Charles Lemuel
Montgomery, Charles Harvey
**Charlotte**
Bragg, Ellis Meredith, Jr.
Eve, Robert Michael, Jr.
**Greensboro**
Carmack, Amie Flowers
Harrington, Ellis Jackson, Jr.
**Greenville**
Romary, Peter John Michael
**High Point**
Aldridge, Bryant Taylor, Jr.
**Hillsborough**
Cheshire, Lucius McGehee
**Kinston**
Braswell, Edwin Maurice, Jr.
**Lillington**
Edwards, Charlene Vernell
**Newton**
Cutchin, John Franks
**Raleigh**
Becton, Charles L.
Hunter, Richard Samford, Jr.
Jolly, John Russell, Jr.
Parker, John Hill
Sasser, Jonathan Drew
Verdon, Jane Kathryn
**Roxboro**
King, Ronnie Patterson
**Tabor City**
Jorgensen, Ralph Gubler
**Wilmington**
Hinson, Reid Garrett
**Winston Salem**
Barnhill, Henry Grady, Jr.
Durham, Richard Monroe

## NORTH DAKOTA

**Bismarck**
Harms, Robert Wayne

**Dickinson**
Greenwood, Dann E.

## OHIO

**Akron**
Ruport, Scott Hendricks
Tipping, Harry A.
Weitendorf, Kurt Robert
Woodley, Ann E.
**Avon Lake**
Kitchen, Charles William
**Bowling Green**
Hanna, Martin Shad
**Celina**
Faber, Keith L.
**Cincinnati**
Cunningham, Pierce Edward
Davis, Robert Lawrence
Dornette, W(illiam) Stuart
Fuchs, Jack Frederick
Kammerer, Matthew Paul
Morrisroe, Donald Patrick
Shea, Joseph William, III
Stalf, Dale Anthony
Zavatsky, Michael Joseph
**Cleveland**
Alexandersen, Kevin Carl
Birne, Kenneth Andrew
Boles, Edgar Howard, II
Carter, Daniel Paul
Climaco, Michael Louis
Cohan, Michael Charles
Dauchot, Luke Lucien
Jeffers, John William
Kelly, Dennis Michael
LaFond, Thomas Joseph
Leiken, Earl Murray
Mc Cartan, Patrick Francis
Moore, Kenneth Cameron
Perella, Marie Louise
Spero, Keith Erwin
Stavnicky, Michael Ross
Weiss, Leon Alan
Zashin, Stephen S.
**Columbus**
Barnes, Belinda Sue
Bartemes, Amy Straker
Belton, John Thomas
Berliner, Alan Frederick
Cline, Richard Allen
Drexel, Ray Phillips
Ferguson, Gerald Paul
Hollenbaugh, H(enry) Ritchey
Hutson, Jeffrey Woodward
Kauffman, Ronald P.
Starkoff, Alan Gary
Whipps, Edward Franklin
**Dayton**
Roberts, Brian Michael
Saul, Irving Isaac
Schneble, Alfred William, III
Wightman, Ann
**Dublin**
Coco, Mark Steven
**Eaton**
Thomas, James William
**Findlay**
Kostyo, John Francis
**Hamilton**
Bressler, H.J.
**Jefferson**
Geary, Michael Philip
**Logan**
Kernen, Will
**Mansfield**
Carto, David Draffan
**Ravenna**
Giulitto, Paula Christine
**Toledo**
Morgan, James Edward
**Warren**
Kafantaris, George Nicholas
White, Martin Fred
**Westlake**
Kolick, Daniel Joseph
**Wooster**
Kennedy, Charles Allen

## OKLAHOMA

**Antlers**
Stamper, Joe Allen
**Bartlesville**
Huchteman, Ralph Douglas
**Broken Arrow**
Frieze, H(arold) Delbert
**Durant**
McPheron, Alan Beaumont
**Enid**
Gungoll, Bradley A.
McNaughton, Alexander Bryant
**Muskogee**
Williams, Betty Outhier
**Oklahoma City**
Beech, Johnny Gale
Featherly, Henry Frederick
Kenney, John Arthur
Paul, William George
Woods, Harry Arthur, Jr.
**Tulsa**
Abrahamson, A. Craig
Beustring, Glenn Roland
Brewster, Clark Otto
Cowdery, Allen Craig
Davis, G. Reuben
Eagan, Claire Veronica
Eldridge, Richard Mark
Jackman, J. Warren
Luthey, Graydon Dean, Jr.
**Vinita**
Linscott, Michael S.

## OREGON

**Brookings**
Hinton, Floyd
**Clackamas**
Gibson, K(enneth) William
**Coquille**
Lounsbury, Steven Richard
**Eugene**
Owens, A(rnold) Dean
**Medford**
Deatherage, William Vernon
Mansfield, William Amos
**Oregon City**
Jonasson, William Bradford
**Portland**
Bakkensen, John Reser
Bayless, Richard Vern
Eakin, Margaretta Morgan
Martson, William Frederick, Jr.
Moore, Thomas Scott
Troutwine, Gayle Leone
**Salem**
Haselton, Rick Thomas

## PENNSYLVANIA

**Allentown**
Brown, Robert Wayne
**Altoona**
Serbin, Richard Martin
**Beaver**
Petrush, John Joseph
**Bensalem**
Hoffa, Robert Alan
**Blue Bell**
Lawrence, Gerald, Jr.
**Bryn Mawr**
Hankin, Mitchell Robert
**Butler**
Stepanian, Leo McElligott
**Clarks Summit**
Beemer, John Barry
**Doylestown**
Gathright, Howard T.
**Erie**
Wingerter, John Raymond
**Feasterville Trevose**
Osterhout, Richard Cadwallader
**Fort Washington**
Daller, Morton F.
**Glenside**
Mermelstein, Jules Joshua
**Harrisburg**
Barto, Charles O., Jr.
Maleski, Cynthia Maria
Sadlock, Richard Alan
Ward, William Francis
**Hazleton**
Schiavo, Pasco Louis
**Hollidaysburg**
Pfaff, Robert James
**Indiana**
Barbor, John Howard
Kauffman, Thomas Andrew
**King Of Prussia**
Dorfman, Frederick Niles
**Lancaster**
Lewis, Alvin Bower, Jr.
**Lansdale**
Kline, David Benjamin
**Meadville**
Barrett, Bruce Alan
Youngs, Christopher Jay
**New Cumberland**
Yakowicz, Vincent X
**New Hope**
Baldi, Robert Otjen
**Newtown**
Godwin, Robert Anthony
**Norristown**
Scheffler, Stuart Jay
**Penns Park**
Itkoff, David F.
**Philadelphia**
Barrett, John J(ames), Jr.
Binder, David Franklin
Brown, William Hill, III
Cooney, J(ohn) Gordon, Jr.
Damsgaard, Kell Marsh
Fiebach, H. Robert
Fodera, Leonard V.
Garcia, Rudolph
Gordesky, Morton
Haviland, Donald Edward, Jr.
Kormes, John Winston
Lawson, William Thomas, III
Mathes, Stephen Jon
McBride, James Francis
Milbourne, Walter Robertson
Milone, Francis Michael
Parry, William DeWitt
Phillips, Dorothy Kay
Powell, Charles Law
Savage, Timothy Joseph
Scher, Howard Dennis
Sheils, Denis Francis
Topel, David Louis
**Pittsburgh**
Acheson, Amy J.
Aronson, Mark Berne
Beachler, Edwin Harry, III
Cohen, Robert (Avram)
Conley, William Vance
Donahoe, Daniel Brennen
Hurnyak, Christina Kaiser
Jones, Craig Ward
King, Peter J.
Klein, Joel Aaron
Klett, Edwin Lee
Lerach, Richard Fleming
Litman, Roslyn Margolis
McConomy, James Herbert
McGinley, John Regis, Jr.
Ober, Russell John, Jr.
O'Connor, Edward Gearing
Rostek, Nancy Elizabeth
Sherry, John Sebastian
Stroyd, Arthur Heister
Ulven, Mark Edward
**Plymouth Meeting**
Bracaglia, Thomas Paul
**Pottsville**
Tamulonis, Frank Louis, Jr.
**Reading**
Turner, David Eldridge
**Scranton**
Howley, James McAndrew
**Sharon**
Dill, William Allen
**Stroudsburg**
Catina, Janet K.
**Uniontown**
Roskovensky, Vincent Joseph, II
**Washington**
Curran, M(ichael) Scot
O'Dell, Debbie
**White Oak**
Pribanic, Victor Hunter

## RHODE ISLAND

**Providence**
Blish, John Harwood
Greenwood, Charles
Miller, Samuel Aaron
Parks, Albert Lauriston
**Warwick**
Gazerro, G. John, Jr.

## SOUTH CAROLINA

**Aiken**
Pearce, Richard Lee
**Charleston**
Darling, Stephen Edward
Dominick, Paul Allen
Glass, Benjamin Philip
Kahn, Ellis Irvin
Spitz, Hugo Max
Steadman, Richard Anderson, Jr.
**Columbia**
Babcock, Keith Moss
Cooper, Robert Gordon
Sheftman, Howard Stephen
**Georgetown**
Goude, Charles Reuben
**Greenville**
Ferguson, Donald Littlefield
Gallivan, Henry Mills
Laws, James Terry
White, Daniel Bowman
**Hilton Head Island**
McKay, John Judson, Jr.
**Myrtle Beach**
Leiter, John M.
**Summerville**
Mortimer, Rory Dixon

## SOUTH DAKOTA

**Webster**
Burke, John William

## TENNESSEE

**Chattanooga**
Akers, Samuel Lee
Campbell, Paul, III
Cooper, Gary Allan
Johnson, John Walter, III
**Collierville**
Scroggs, Larry Kenneth
**Knoxville**
Ailor, Earl Starnes
Bailey, Bridget
Hagood, Lewis Russell
London, James Harry
**Lookout Mountain**
Leitner, Paul Revere
**Martin**
Gearin, Kent Farrell
**Memphis**
Carr, Oscar Clark, III
Garts, James Rufus, Jr.
Noel, Randall Deane
Turner, Kay Farese
Wilder, James Sampson, III
**Nashville**
Knowles, Emmitt Clifton
Midgett, James Clayton, Jr.
Turner, Robert Joseph
Yarbrough, Edward Meacham
**Sewanee**
Pierce, Donna L.

## TEXAS

**Abilene**
Suttle, Stephen Hungate
**Addison**
Geary, Joseph William
**Amarillo**
McDougall, Gerald Duane
**Arlington**
Jensen, John Robert
Rosenberry, William Kenneth
**Austin**
Colburn, Stuart Dale
Hernandez, Mack Ray
Lione, John Gabriel, Jr.
Ludlum, James S.
Mallios, George James
McDaniel, Myra Atwell
Zager, Steven Mark
**Brownsville**
Jordan, John Joseph
**Brownwood**
Bell, William Woodward
**Carthage**
Dowd, Steven Milton
**College Station**
Hoelscher, Michael Ray
**Corpus Christi**
Alberts, Harold
Chesney, Brent Jackson
Elizondo, Luis A.
Herin, David V.
**Dallas**
Atwood, Roy Tress
Babcock, Charles Lynde, IV
Baggett, Steven Ray
Barnett, Barry Craig
Beane, Jerry Lynn
Bickel, John W., II
Biermacher, Kenneth Wayne
Blount, Charles William, III
Branson, Frank Leslie, III
Burkett, Joe Wylie
Callahan, Tena Toye
Coleman, Robert Winston
Conant, Allah B., Jr.
Curry, Gregory William
Dunnill, William Connor
Eaton, Michael William
Evans, Roger
Figari, Ernest Emil, Jr.
Freytag, Sharon Nelson
Frick, John Michael
Govett, Brett Christopher
Harrison, Orrin Lea, III
Hartnett, Thomas Robert, III
Hartnett, Will Ford
Hoskins, Sonya Denise
King, Ira Thomas
Lynn, Barbara Michele
May, Michelle April
McAtee, David Ray
Medford, Leane Capps
Mow, Robert Henry, Jr.
Mueller, Mark Christopher
Palter, John Theodore
Ringle, Brett Adelbert
Roberts, Scott Raymond
Scuro, Joseph E., Jr.
Sides, Jack Davis, Jr.
Siegel, Mark Jordan
Yarbrough, Fletcher Leftwich
**Diboll**
Moss, Logan Vansen
**Edinburg**
Peña, Aaron, Jr.
**El Paso**
Gordon, Norman James
Howell, Mark Franklin
Malone, Daniel Robert
Yetter, Richard
**Farmersville**
Seward, Richard Bevin
**Fort Worth**
Ablon, Karen Herrick
Chappell, David Franklin
Crumley, John Walter
Dean, Beale
Elliott, Frank Wallace
Harcrow, E. Earl
Hart, John Clifton
Randolph, Robert McGehee
Rutherford, Jay K.
**Garland**
Irby, Holt
**Hallettsville**
Baber, Wilbur H., Jr.
**Hico**
Peterson, Martin Lee
**Houston**
Aschermann, Mark L.
Bayko, Emil Thomas
Behrmann, Lawrence James
Beirne, Martin Douglas
Blair, Graham Kerin (Kerry Blair)
Boswell, John Howard
Brinson, Gay Creswell, Jr.
Cagle, Stephen Henderson
Carr, Edward A.
Clawater, Wayne
Coleman, Bryan Douglas
Cook, Eugene Augustus
Couch, Steve Earl
Craig, Robert Mark, III
Crinion, Gregory Paul
Dampier, Harold Dean, Jr.
Fleming, George Matthews
Forlano, Frederick Peter
Gilbert, Keith Thomas
Hamel, Lee
Hatchett, Cynthia M.
Horrigan, Joseph Stewart
Jordan, Charles Milton
Kean, James Campbell
Kelly, Hugh Rice
Ketchand, Robert Lee
Kline, Allen Haber, Jr.
Krebs, Arno William, Jr.
Lawhon, Susan Harvin
Mallia, Michael Patrick
Martin, Christopher W.
Michaels, Kevin Richard
Peddie, Collyn Ann
Ray, Hugh Massey, Jr.
Reasoner, Harry Max
Rowland, Robert Alexander, III
Sales, James Bohus
Secrest, Ronald Dean
Spence, W. Ross
Susman, Morton Lee
Sutter, J. Douglas
Wallis, Olney Gray
Waska, Ronald Jerome
Yetter, R. Paul
**Hurst**
Casey, David Robert
**Irving**
Freiling, Don Rynn
**Jacksonville**
Thrall, Gordon Fish
**Kaufman**
Legg, Reagan Houston
**Killeen**
Roberts, Burk Austin
**Lufkin**
Garrison, Pitser Hardeman
**Mc Kinney**
Roessler, P. Dee
**Mcallen**
McLeaish, Robert Burns
**Midland**
Estes, Andrew Harper
Truitt, Robert Ralph, Jr.
**Paris**
Standifer, Rick M.
**Richardson**
Olson, Dennis Oliver
**San Antonio**
Labay, Eugene Benedict
Maloney, Marynell
Valadez, Robert Allen
Wennermark, John David
**Sherman**
Harrison, Richard Edward
**Spring**
Hagerman, John David
**Sugar Land**
Aldrich, Lovell W(eld)
**Sweetwater**
Jones, Charles Eric, Jr.
**Tyler**
George, Samuel Mills

## UTAH

**Ogden**
Sullivan, Kevin Patrick
**Park City**
Fay, John Farrell
**Salt Lake City**
Anderson, Craig W.
Christensen, Patricia Anne Watkins
Colessides, Nick John
Erickson, David Belnap
Kent, Dale R.
Orton, R. Willis

## VERMONT

**Brattleboro**
Corum, Jesse Maxwell, IV
**Montpelier**
Storrow, Charles Fiske
**Norwich**
Lundquist, Weyman Ivan

## VIRGINIA

**Abingdon**
McElroy, Howard Chowning
**Alexandria**
Carter, Richard Dennis
Stone, Steven David
Tompkins, Michael William
**Chesapeake**
Brown, John Wayne
**Fairfax**
Arnold, William McCauley
**Great Falls**
Preston, Charles George
**Lynchburg**
Burnette, Ralph Edwin, Jr.
**Mc Lean**
Church, Randolph Warner, Jr.
Harrison, John Edwards
Walton, Edmund Lewis, Jr.
**Newport News**
Sarfan, Edward I.
**Norfolk**
Zahn, Richard William
**Petersburg**
Shell, Louis Calvin
Spero, Morton Bertram
**Radford**
Davis, Richard Waters
Turk, James Clinton, Jr.
**Richmond**
Allen, Wilbur Coleman
Brooks, Robert Franklin, Sr.
Hall, Stephen Charles
Northup, Stephen A.
**Roanoke**
Bromm, Frederick Whittemore
Tegenkamp, Gary Elton
**Vienna**
Razzano, Frank Charles
**Virginia Beach**
Clark, Donald H.
Hajek, Francis Paul

## WASHINGTON

**Bellevue**
Cowan, Douglas Leo
Lawyer, David James
**Centralia**
Buzzard, Steven Ray
**Everett**
Ferguson, Royce Allan, Jr.
Johnson, Richard Bruce
**Lynnwood**
Kastle, David Anthony
**Olympia**
Gentry, Fred Dee
**Renton**
Swanson, Arthur Dean
**Seattle**
Bagshaw, Bradley Holmes
Bateman, Heidi S.
Bishin, William Robert
Bringman, Joseph Edward
Caryl, Michael R.
Cornell, Kenneth Lee
Corning, Nicholas F.
Dunham, Douglas Spence
Gandara, Daniel
Leed, Roger Melvin
McKay, Michael Dennis
Merkle, Alan Ray
Mines, Michael
Sayre, Matt Melvin Mathias
Tuffley, Francis Douglas
Walter, Michael Charles
Webber, James Carl
Wechsler, Mary Heyrman
**Spokane**
Anderson, Robert Edward
**Tacoma**
Mungia, Salvador Alejo, Jr.
Novasky, Robert William
Seinfeld, Lester
**Tukwila**
Gouras, Mark Steven

## WEST VIRGINIA

**Charleston**
Bell, Harry Fullerton, Jr.
Cowan, John Joseph
Kiblinger, Cindy Jo
Neely, Richard
**Moundsville**
Artimez, John Edward, Jr.
**Romney**
Saville, Royce Blair

**Wheeling**
Hill, Barry Morton

### WISCONSIN

**Appleton**
Murray, John Daniel
**Beaver Dam**
Becker, Eric L.
**Black River Falls**
Lister, Thomas Edward
**De Pere**
Cerminara, Laura Mary
**Green Bay**
Grzeca, Michael (Gerard)
**Janesville**
Kopp, Mark David
**La Crosse**
Sleik, Thomas Scott
**Madison**
Hildebrand, Daniel Walter
**Milwaukee**
Connolly, L. William
Finerty, John Daniel, Jr.
Fishbach, Nathan A.
Gaines, Irving David
Habush, Robert Lee
Levit, William Harold, Jr.
McCormick, David Joseph
Melin, Robert Arthur
Reardon, James Patrick
Robinson, Richard Russell
**Oshkosh**
Curtis, George Warren
Zierdt, Alyson Kathleen
**Rhinelander**
Eckert, Michael Louis

### WYOMING

**Casper**
Bostwick, Richard Raymond
Combs, W(illiam) Henry, III
**Cheyenne**
Dyekman, Gregory Chris
Godfrey, Paul Bard
Rosenthal, Michael Bruce
**Cody**
Webster, C. Edward, II
**Jackson**
Schuster, Robert Parks
Shockey, Gary Lee

### ADDRESS UNPUBLISHED

Adams, Thomas Lawrence
Arber, Howard Bruce
Atkinson, Sheridan Earle
Bailey, J. Dennis
Bersin, Alan Douglas
Blevins, Jeffrey Alexander
Block, Jessica
Bouvier, Marshall Andre
Brandes, Joel R.
Brumbaugh, John Moore
Burton, Richard Jay
Carney, Donald Francis, Jr.
Cohen, Anita Marilyn
Dow, William F.
Elster, J. Robert
Erlebacher, Arlene Cernik
Fekete, George Otto
Fowler, Flora Daun
Freedlander, Barrett Walter
Fridkin, Jeffrey David
Gomez, David Frederick
Hall, John Hopkins
Hampson, Robert George
Heins, Samuel David
Hoffman, Alan Craig
Hogan, Richard Phillips
Horn, Andrew Warren
Howard, John Wayne
Hunt, Merrill Roberts
Johnson, Richard Wesley
Jolley, R. Gardner
Kellerman, Edwin
Kessler, Todd Lance
Klein, Beth Morrison
Leventhal, Howard G.
Locke, John Howard
Maloney, John William
Martin, Robert James
Pannill, William Presley
Pereyra-Suarez, Charles Albert
Reid, Benjamine
Reminger, Richard Thomas
Roche, Thomas Garrett
Saliterman, Richard Arlen
Samalin, Edwin
Sanders, Alan Mark
Saxon, John David
Sheahan, Joseph D.
Smouse, H(ervey) Russell
Smyth, Jeffrey A.
Souder, Susan
Speaker, Susan Jane
Sperry, Martin Jay
Stern, John Jules
Stout, Gregory Stansbury
Thornton, John W., Sr.
Torregrossa, Joseph Anthony
Vinar, Benjamin
Watson, John Michael
Weeks, Tresi Lea

---

## CIVIL RIGHTS

### UNITED STATES

### ALABAMA

**Birmingham**
Burnside, Cynthia Grace
Coleman, John James, III
Waldrep, Charlie David
Wiggins, Robert L.
**Huntsville**
Simpson, Shannon Smith
**Montgomery**
Conley, Charles Swinger
Prestwood, Alvin Tennyson

### ALASKA

**Anchorage**
Goldberg, Robert M.
**Fairbanks**
Schendel, William Burnett

### ARIZONA

**Phoenix**
Rosenthal, Jay P.
**Tucson**
Bainton, Denise Marlene
Esposito, Joseph Louis

### ARKANSAS

**Fayetteville**
Kester, Charles Melvin
**Little Rock**
Boe, Myron Timothy
Johnson, Michael Dennis
Jones, Stephen Witsell
Lavey, John Thomas

### CALIFORNIA

**Alamo**
Davis, Walter Lee
**Beverly Hills**
Juno, Cynthia
**Camarillo**
Schulner, Keith Alan
**Encino**
Kaufman, Albert I.
**Irvine**
Ashley, Fred Turner
**Lafayette**
Lustig, Norman I.
**Los Angeles**
Feigen, Brenda S.
Manning, Steven Donald
Mintz, Ronald Steven
Muoneke, Anthony
**Mill Valley**
Grantland, Brenda
**Newport Beach**
Carman, Ernest Day
Mandel, Maurice, II
**Oakland**
Burris, John Leonard
Drexel, Baron Jerome
Lomhoff, Peter George
Patton, Roger William
Wallace, Elaine Wendy
**Oxnard**
Heredia, F. Samuel
**Rancho Santa Fe**
Cary, Frederick Albert
**Sacramento**
Duggan, Jennifer E.
Martorano, Rebekka Ruth
Palmer, Floyd James
**San Francisco**
Brantner, Paula Ann
Rubin, Michael
Samad-Salameh, Alia Fahmi
Wolf, Lillian F.
**San Rafael**
Huffman, Jared William
**San Ramon**
Siegel, Jeffrey Roy
**Venice**
Schanes, Christine Elise
**Walnut Creek**
Leone, Louis Anthony

### COLORADO

**Carbondale**
Wohl, Kenneth Allan
**Denver**
Bove, Mark Stephen
Burke, Marlin W.
Karp, Sander Neil
Martin, Raymond Walter
Nathan, J(ay) Andrew
Nier, Harry K.
Roesler, John Bruce
**Englewood**
Breeskin, Michael Wayne
McClung, Merle Steven
**Pagosa Springs**
Kelly, Reid Browne

### CONNECTICUT

**Bridgeport**
Mitchell, Robert Burdette
**Hartford**
Dempsey, Edward Joseph
**Manchester**
Eldergill, Kathleen
**New Haven**
Dodge, Mannette Antill
**Stamford**
Margolis, Emanuel
Spitzer, Vlad Gerard

### DELAWARE

**Wilmington**
Shearin, Kathryn Kay

### DISTRICT OF COLUMBIA

**Washington**
Bernabei, Lynne Ann
Beyer, Wayne Cartwright
Bruner, Paul Daniel
Christensen, Karen Kay
Colapinto, David Keith
Duhig, Diane
Germain, Regina
Katsurinis, Stephen Avery
Kramer, Andrew Michael
Levine, Steven Mark
Newman, Elizabeth L.
Schmidt, Richard Marten, Jr.
Shaffer, David James
Sherman, Lawrence Jay
Sloame, Stuart C.
Wilson, Charles Haven

### FLORIDA

**Boca Raton**
Silver, Barry Morris
**Coral Gables**
Feiler, Michael Benjamin
Rodriguez, Lourdes A. de los Angeles
**Deerfield Beach**
Slavin, Edward A., Jr.
**Fort Lauderdale**
Cornell, G(eorge) Ware, Jr.
**Gainesville**
Kaimowitz, Gabe Hillel
**Jacksonville**
Grogan, Michael Kevin
**Lakeland**
Senn, Stephen Russell
**Margate**
Shooster, Frank Mallory
**Miami**
Cohen, Ronald J.
Kurzban, Ira Jay
Maher, Stephen Trivett
Sarnoff, Marc David
**Orlando**
Collie, Kathryn Kaye
Nelson, Frederick Herbert
Noah, Douglas True
**Palm Bay**
Tietig, Edward Chester
**Panama City**
Stone, Michel Leon
**Pensacola**
Kelly, John Barry, II
Soloway, Daniel Mark
**Saint Petersburg**
Escarraz, Enrique, III
**Stuart**
Watson, Robert James
**Tallahassee**
Booth, Edgar Charles
Minnick, Bruce Alexander
Traynham, Jerry Glenn
**Tampa**
Brudny, Peter J.
Munoz, Shane Thomas
**West Palm Beach**
Hoch, Rand
Holland, William Meredith
Rosenberg, Robin L.

### GEORGIA

**Atlanta**
Boisseau, Richard Robert
Bramlett, Jeffrey Owen
González, Carlos A.
Hill, Sonia Elizabeth
**Columbus**
Hicks, Deron Ray
**Decatur**
Pankey, Larry Allen
**Savannah**
Lancaster, Miriam Diemmer

### HAWAII

**Honolulu**
Schweigert, Jack F.

### ILLINOIS

**Chicago**
Brice, Roger Thomas
Farber, Bernard John
Flaxman, Kenneth N.
Gillio, Vickie Ann
Halprin, Rick
Hecht, Frank Thomas
Helt, Christopher William
Hubbard, Elizabeth Louise
Joyce, Sarah Elizabeth
Mastandrea, Linda Lee
McFadden, Monica Elizabeth
Null, Michael Elliot
O'Hagin, Zarina Eileen Suarez
Peters, Kevin Richard
Rothstein, Jonathan Alan
**Elmhurst**
Amato, Theresa Ann
**Evanston**
DeWolfe, Ruthanne K. S.
**Hinsdale**
De Rose, John Patrick
**Oak Park**
Redleaf, Diane Lynn
**Springfield**
Draper, Carl R.
Feldman, Howard William

### INDIANA

**Fort Wayne**
Baker, Carl Leroy
**Indianapolis**
Baker, Tim A.
Bush, Robert Bradford
Kashani, Hamid Reza
Klaper, Martin Jay
Nettles, Gaylon James
Rodeheffer, Brenda Franklin
**Merrillville**
Dignam, Robert James
**Terre Haute**
Willard, Glenn Mark

### IOWA

**Cedar Rapids**
Squires, Vernon Pellett
**Des Moines**
Conlin, Roxanne Barton
**Mason City**
Kinsey, Robert Stanleigh, III

### KANSAS

**Olathe**
DeWitt, Anthony Louis
**Overland Park**
Waxse, David John
**Shawnee Mission**
Badgerow, John Nicholas
**Topeka**
Pigg, James Steven
Sebelius, Keith Gary
Wisler, James Lynn
**Wichita**
Arabia, Paul

### KENTUCKY

**Frankfort**
Bias, Dana G.
**Lexington**
Hiestand, Sheila Patricia
**Louisville**
Morton, Donna Theresa

### LOUISIANA

**Alexandria**
Everett, Stephen Edward
**Baton Rouge**
Ferguson, James Curtis
**New Orleans**
Desmond, Susan Fahey
Dwyer, Ralph Daniel, Jr.

### MAINE

**Portland**
Connolly, Thomas Joseph

### MARYLAND

**Ocean City**
Wimbrow, Peter Ayers, III
**Owings Mills**
Granat, Richard Stuart
**Silver Spring**
Carter, Glenn Thomas
Gagliardo, Thomas James
McDermitt, Edward Vincent

### MASSACHUSETTS

**Boston**
Brody, Richard Eric
Hrones, Stephen Baylis
Lindley, James David
Neumeier, Richard L.
Zwicker, Joseph H.
**Newton Center**
Soifer, Aviam
**Springfield**
Markey, Patrick Joseph
**Woburn**
Karshbaum, Bonnie L.

### MICHIGAN

**Ann Arbor**
McHugh, Richard Walker
Mullkoff, Douglas Ryan
**Detroit**
Heenan, Cynthia
Leuchtman, Stephen Nathan
Nemeth, Patricia Marie
Norris, Megan Pinney
Posner, Alan B.
Santo, Ronald Joseph
**Flint**
Edmunds, Michael Winterton
**Grand Rapids**
Gibson, Lori Lynn
Kara, Paul Mark
Savickas, Stephen Anthony
**Grosse Pointe**
Carey, Raymond J.
**Lansing**
Schlinker, John Crandall
**Muskegon**
Van Leuven, Robert Joseph
**Okemos**
Schneider, Karen Bush
**Royal Oak**
Gordon, Deborah Leigh
**Saint Clair Shores**
Danielson, Gary R.
**South Haven**
Waxman, Sheldon Robert
**Troy**
Burnard, George Willard

### MINNESOTA

**Minneapolis**
Bolter, Howard Lee
Corwin, Gregg Marlowe
Gant, Jesse, III
Rubenstein, Andrea Fichman
Schermer, Judith Kahn

### MISSISSIPPI

**Biloxi**
Miller, William Carl
**Brookhaven**
Doty, Sally Burchfield
**Gulfport**
Hatten, W. Edward, Jr.
**Hernando**
Maddox, Nancy McCraine
**Jackson**
Fuselier, Louis Alfred
**Oxford**
Lewis, Ronald Wayne

### MISSOURI

**Chesterfield**
McLaughlin, Kevin Thomas
**Kansas City**
Beckerman, Dale Lee
**Lake Saint Louis**
Callahan, Robert John, Jr.
**Saint Charles**
Green, Joseph Libory
**Saint Louis**
Chestnut, Kathi Lynne
Martin, Arthur Joseph
Meehan, John Justin
**Springfield**
Hedrick, Peggy Shepherd

### NEBRASKA

**Lincoln**
Cope, Thom K.
**Omaha**
Gleason, James Mullaney

### NEW HAMPSHIRE

**Concord**
Irwin, Lauren Simon

### NEW JERSEY

**Cherry Hill**
Schall, Richard Miller
**Hackensack**
Latimer, Stephen Mark
**Haddonfield**
Fuoco, Philip Stephen
**Hammonton**
Picariello, Pasquale
**Madison**
Rabkin, Peggy Ann
**Newark**
Barrett, Virginia M.
Weinberg, Shelley Ann
**Pluckemin**
Ames, Marc L.
**Salem**
Petrin, Helen Fite
**Somerset**
Robinson, Patricia Snyder
**Somerville**
Fleischer, Steven H.
**Warren**
Gargano, Francine Ann
**Woodbridge**
Marcy, Eric John

### NEW MEXICO

**Albuquerque**
Hale, Timothy S.
Nichols, Carolyn M.
Salvador, Vernon William
Word, Terry Mullins
**Carlsbad**
Bruton, Charles Clinton
**Las Cruces**
Sandenaw, Thomas Arthur, Jr.
**Santa Fe**
Bienvenu, John Charles
Farber, Steven Glenn
Herr, Bruce
Schwarz, Michael
Vigil, Carol Jean
**Tijeras**
Berry, Dawn Bradley

### NEW YORK

**Albany**
Cook, Gavin A.
Gray, William J.
Mishler, Mark Sean
**Bronx**
Wolf, Robert Thomas
**Buffalo**
Feuerstein, Alan Ricky
**Floral Park**
Chatoff, Michael Alan
**Garden City**
Lilly, Thomas Joseph
**Glen Cove**
Mills, Charles Gardner
**Huntington**
German, June Resnick
Levitan, Katherine D.
**Kew Gardens**
Reichel, Aaron Israel
**Mineola**
Millman, Bruce Russell
Rossen, Jordan
**New York**
Birnbaum, Julian R.
Boddie, Reginald Alonzo
Bondy, Joseph Aaron
Chan, Lai Lee
Diamond, David Howard
Flamm, Leonard N(athan)
Fleischman, Keith Martin
Goldberg, Suzanne Beth
Gross, Ari Michael
Hirozawa, Kent Y.
Kennedy, Michael John
Kresky, Harry
Orden, Stewart L.
Shaffer, Donald
Shen, Michael
Sommers, George R.
Stack, Jane Marcia
Watson, Kipp Elliott
Wiggin, Thomas Byron
Wisehart, Arthur McKee
Wu, Yolanda Sung
**Rochester**
Andolina, Lawrence J.
**Rome**
Rizzo, James S.

### NORTH CAROLINA

**Charlotte**
Rockey, Arlaine
**Durham**
Fisher, Stewart Wayne
Loflin, Thomas Franklin, III
**Fayetteville**
Britton, Rebecca Johnson
**Greensboro**
McGinn, Max Daniel
**Hickory**
Farthing, Edwin Glenn
**Raleigh**
Sasser, Jonathan Drew
Wetsch, Laura Johnson

**Winston Salem**
Dahl, Tyrus Vance, Jr.

OHIO

**Cincinnati**
Hornberger, Lee
Smith, Sheila Marie
**Cleveland**
Friedman, Avery S.
Goddard, Richard Patrick
Kramer, Edward George
**Columbus**
Gellman, Susan Beth
Gittes, Frederick M.
Pressley, Fred G., Jr.
**Dayton**
Hollingsworth, Jonathan
Smiley, Charles Adam, Jr.
**Toledo**
Dane, Stephen Mark
Griffin, Sharon L.

OKLAHOMA

**Edmond**
Lester, Andrew William
Loving, Susan Brimer
**Oklahoma City**
Court, Leonard
Leeviraphan, Americ (Eric Leeviraphan)
**Tulsa**
Coulter, Jean Walpole
Matthies, Mary Constance T.

OREGON

**Grants Pass**
Lansing, Mark Alexander
**Lincoln City**
Elliott, Scott
**Portland**
Blitz, Charles Akin
Shinn, Michael Robert
Sullivan, Dana Louise
**Tigard**
Lowry, David Burton

PENNSYLVANIA

**Bethlehem**
Yeager, Jordan Berson
**Conshohocken**
Gutkin, Arthur Lee
**Easton**
Noel, Nicholas, III
**Forty Fort**
Cosgrove, Joseph Matthias
**Harrisburg**
Music, Yvonne M.
Lappas, Spero Thomas
Warshaw, Allen Charles
**Johnstown**
Kaharick, Jerome John
**Philadelphia**
Cohen, Jonathan Morley
Epstein, Alan Bruce
Falcao, Linda Phyllis
Fodera, Leonard V.
Goldberg, Joseph
Krampf, John Edward
McHugh, James Joseph
Pasek, Jeffrey Ivan
Rainville, Christina
Reilly, Marie Sambor
Satinsky, Barnett
Whinston, Stephen Alan
**Pittsburgh**
Denys, Sylvia
Lyncheski, John E.
Pushinsky, Jon
Schooley, Elizabeth Walter
**Williamsport**
Dohrmann, Jeffrey Charles

RHODE ISLAND

**Providence**
Smith, Robert Ellis

SOUTH CAROLINA

**Charleston**
McCormick, Karen Elizabeth
**Columbia**
Hancock, Harriet Daniels
**Port Royal**
Newman, Jared Sullivan
**Spartanburg**
Ballard, Wade Edward
Vega, Matthew Anthony

SOUTH DAKOTA

**Sioux Falls**
Hattervig, Karen Ann

TENNESSEE

**Memphis**
Barna, James Francis
Smith, Joseph Philip
Warren, Keith Ashley
**Nashville**
Barrett, George Edward
Lyon, Philip K(irkland)
**Pigeon Forge**
Powell, Russell Alan

TEXAS

**Alvin**
Hewitt, Otto D., III
**Austin**
Brim, Jefferson Kearney, III
Hamilton, Dagmar Strandberg
Heath, Claude Robert
Krueger, William Wayne, III
Ludlum, James S.
Schulze, Eric William
**Beaumont**
Newton, John Wharton, III
**Dallas**
Cloutman, Edward Bradbury, III
Jones, James Alton
McKennon, Richard Otey
Washington, Karen Roberts
**Edinburg**
Peña, Aaron, Jr.
**El Paso**
McDonald, Charles Edward
**Eldorado**
Kosub, James Albert
**Fort Worth**
Gwinn, D. Lee
**Galveston**
Vie, George William, III
**Houston**
Krock, Kenneth Michael
**Lubbock**
Williams, Anthony Jerome
**Mesquite**
Daniels, Russell Howard
**Orange**
Dugas, Louis, Jr.
**San Antonio**
Armstrong, William Tucker, III
Maloney, Marynell
Moynihan, John Bignell
**Victoria**
Tipton, Drew B.
**Waco**
Bostwick, Frederick deBurlo, III

UTAH

**Salt Lake City**
Anderson, Ross Carl
Lambert, Dale John

VERMONT

**Sharon**
Thrasher, John Edwin

VIRGINIA

**Annandale**
Dunkum, Betty Lee
**Bristol**
Minor, Steven Ray
**Charlottesville**
Wyatt, Deborah Chasen
**McLean**
Bredehoft, John Michael
**Norfolk**
Breit, Jeffrey Arnold
Drescher, John Webb
**Reston**
Bredehoft, Elaine Charlson
**Richmond**
Baron, Mark
Hill, Oliver White, Sr.
Nagle, David Edward
Tashjian-Brown, Eva S(usan)
**Roanoke**
Harris, Bayard Easter
Skolrood, Robert Kenneth
**Virginia Beach**
Swope, Richard McAllister
Thornton, Joel Hamilton

WASHINGTON

**Bellevue**
Lawyer, David James
**East Wenatchee**
Lacy, Steven C.
**Everett**
Dewell, Julian C.
Mestel, Mark David
**Seattle**
Endriss, Marilyn Jean
Estes, Stewart Andrew
Kline, Daniel Adam
Linn, Brian James
Needle, Jeffrey Lowell
Rosen, Jon Howard
**Tacoma**
Teller, Stephen Aiden

WEST VIRGINIA

**Charleston**
Teare, John Richard, Jr.

WISCONSIN

**Madison**
MacDougall, Priscilla Ruth
Provis, Timothy Alan
Schooler, Steven James
Stix, Sally Ann
**Milwaukee**
Beightol, Scott Christopher
Bohren, Michael Oscar

WYOMING

**Gillette**
Zollinger, Thomas Tennant

ENGLAND

**London**
Green, Richard

ADDRESS UNPUBLISHED

Beldock, Myron
Broadus, Joseph Edward
Campos-Orrego, Nora Patricia
D'Agusto, Karen Rose
Forster, Clifford
Foster, Cindy Cooper
Franke, Ann Harriet
Goldberg, Scot Dale
Golder, Frederick Thomas
McCray, Douglas Gerald
Rusnak, Susan E.
Shattuck, Cathie Ann
Sulton, Anne Thomas
Tietig, Lisa Kuhlman
Twanmoh, Valerie Hurley

**COLLECTIONS.** *See* **Commercial, consumer.**

**COMMERCIAL FINANCING.** *See* **Commercial, contracts.**

## COMMERCIAL, CONSUMER

UNITED STATES

ALABAMA

**Birmingham**
Christ, Chris Steve
**Dothan**
Hogg, David Kenneth
**Huntsville**
Baxter, James Thomas, III
**Mobile**
Armstrong, Gordon Gray, III
Beckish, Richard Michael
**Montgomery**
Sanders-Cochran, Rachel Deanna
**Tuscaloosa**
Davis, Kenneth Dudley

ALASKA

**Anchorage**
Evans, Charles Graham
Lekisch, Peter Allen

ARIZONA

**Phoenix**
Arbetman, Jeffrey Farrell
Clarke, David Alan
Wilcox, Debra Kay
**Prescott**
Goodman, Mark N.

ARKANSAS

**Fayetteville**
Pettus, E. Lamar
**Harrison**
Inman-Campbell, Gail
**Nashville**
Graves, James Clements

CALIFORNIA

**Bakersfield**
Karcher, Steven Michael
**Costa Mesa**
Frieden, Clifford E.
Grogan, Virginia S.
**Del Mar**
Seitman, John Michael
**Dixon**
Levin, Roy C.
**El Centro**
Zimmermann, Ann Marie
**Long Beach**
Greenberg, Bruce A.
Rothschild, Toby James
**Los Angeles**
Barth, Karen Ann
Gilhuly, Peter Martin
Kundinger, Mathew Hermann
Levine, Thomas Jeffrey Pello
Marcus, Stephen Howard
Norris, Floyd Hamilton
Porter, Verna Louise
Robinett, Timothy Douglas
Share, Richard Hudson
**Modesto**
Leong, Linda S.
**Orange**
Bennett, William Perry
**Palo Alto**
Kent, Edward Angle, Jr.
Small, Jonathan Andrew
**Pleasant Hill**
Weiss, Edward Abraham
**Pleasanton**
Opperwall, Stephen Gabriel
**Riverside**
Briskin, Boyd Edward
**Sacramento**
Stone, Peter Robert
**San Diego**
Catherwood, Kathryn M.S.
Cohen, Philip Meyer
Guinn, Stanley Willis
Tow, L. Michelle
**San Francisco**
Sharp, Stefanie Teresa
**San Jose**
Hannon, Timothy Patrick
**Santa Barbara**
Cappello, A. Barry
Hellman, Michael David
**Santa Cruz**
Joseph, Irwin H.
**Tracy**
Hay, Dennis Lee
**Tustin**
Gaughan, John Stephen

COLORADO

**Arvada**
Kreis, Elizabeth Susan
**Colorado Springs**
Gefreh, Paul Thomas
**Denver**
Burkhardt, Donald Malcolm
DeMuth, Alan Cornelius
Finesilver, Jay Mark
Temple, Dana A.
**Englewood**
McClung, Merle Steven
**Golden**
Arp, Randall Craig
**Pueblo**
Kogovsek, Daniel Charles

CONNECTICUT

**Hartford**
Flynn, Brendan Thomas
Harrington, Christopher Michael
**Madison**
Clendenen, William Herbert, Jr.
**New Haven**
Ajello, Michael John
Skalka, Douglas Scott
Wiznia, Carolann Kamens
**West Hartford**
Swerdloff, Ileen Pollock

DELAWARE

**Wilmington**
Joseph, Michael Brandes
Salinger, Frank Max

DISTRICT OF COLUMBIA

**Washington**
Brewster, Christopher Ralph
Cohen, Nelson Craig
Genz, Michael Andrew
Hefferon, Thomas Michael
McIntyre, Douglas Carmichael, II
Wilk, Adam Ross

FLORIDA

**Altamonte Springs**
Hoogland, Robert Frederics
**Clearwater**
Doudna, Heather Lynn
**Daytona Beach**
Dunagan, Walter Benton
**Delray Beach**
Kravetz, David Hubert
**Fernandina Beach**
Manson, Keith Alan Michael
**Fort Lauderdale**
Stalions, William C.
**Hollywood**
London, Jack Edward
**Jacksonville**
Coker, Howard C.
Hamilton, Lawrence Joseph
**Miami**
Freud, John Sigmund
Hartz, Steven Edward Marshall
Podhurst, Aaron Samuel
Russell, Patrick
Stein, Allan Mark
**North Miami Beach**
Hankin, Sandra H.
Sugerman, Karen Beth
**Ocala**
Hatch, John D.
**Orlando**
Ashby, Kimberly A.
Christiansen, Patrick T.
Peterson, David Eugene
**Palm Harbor**
Summers-Powell, Alan
**Panama City**
Byrne, Robert William
**Saint Petersburg**
Hickman, James K.
**Tamarac**
Bumgardner, Donna Lee Arrington
**Tampa**
Anton, S. David
Davis, David Earl
Roberson, Bruce H.
**West Palm Beach**
Cooper, Margaret Leslie
Laing, Robert Scott

GEORGIA

**Atlanta**
Chenevert, Donald James, Jr.
Kessler, Richard Paul, Jr.
**Dublin**
Warren, Johnny Wilmer
**Marietta**
Smith, Jere Crews, Jr.
**Norcross**
Winkler, Allen Warren

HAWAII

**Honolulu**
Ando, Russell Hisashi
Dang, Marvin S. C.
Lobdell, Henry Raymond
Minkin, David Justin
Pyun, Matthew Sung Kwan
Sato, Glenn Kenji
Tharp, James Wilson
**Wailuku**
Kinaka, William Tatsuo

ILLINOIS

**Belleville**
Volmert, Deborah Jean
**Champaign**
Hall, Guy Charles
**Chicago**
Arvey, James Terrence
Berkoff, Mark Andrew
Hoseman, Daniel
Kawitt, Alan
Neumeier, Matthew Michael
Wood, Allison Lorraine
**Moline**
Cleaver, William Lehn
**Oak Brook**
Washburn, John James
**Palos Heights**
Swanson, Warren Lloyd
**Paris**
Bell, Allen Andrew, Jr.
**Prospect Heights**
Mancini, Rose C.

INDIANA

**Crawfordsville**
Donaldson, Steven Bryan
**Evansville**
Jewell, John J.
**Fort Wayne**
Clark, Jeffrey A.
Gehring, Ronald Kent
**Indianapolis**
Hammel, John Wingate
Hebenstreit, Michael Joseph
Loiseau, Richard
Watson, Richard Prather
Wellnitz, Craig Otto
Wunder, David Hart

IOWA

**Davenport**
Phelps, Robert J.
**Des Moines**
Wanek, Jerrold
Watson, Phil
**Estherville**
Mohn, Maynard Martin

KANSAS

**Arkansas City**
Templar, Ted Mac
**Lawrence**
Karlin, Calvin Joseph

KENTUCKY

**Fort Thomas**
Whalen, Paul Lewellin
**Grayson**
Caummisar, Robert Lee
**Lexington**
Cox, Walter Clay Jr.
Rich, William Hagood Bellinger
**Louisville**
Friedman, Hal Daniel
**New Castle**
Brammell, William Hartman
**Pikeville**
Johnson, Lon M., Jr.
**Russellville**
Wilson, Elizabeth Davis
**Versailles**
Dunlap, Tavner Branham

LOUISIANA

**Baton Rouge**
Ray, Betty Jean G.
**Lake Charles**
Everett, John Prentis, Jr.
**New Orleans**
Barnett, William Michael
Curtis, Charles Thach, Jr.
Duggins, David Dryden
Forman, William Harper, Jr.
Levin, Richard Barry
Madera, Carmen Soria
Roux, Kermit Louis, III
**Opelousas**
Sandoz, William Charles
**Ville Platte**
Coreil, C. Brent

MARYLAND

**Baltimore**
Erwin, H. Robert
Shuster, David Jonathan
Wilson, Dana Michelle Sirkis
**Bel Air**
Wilson, Christian Burhenn
**Lutherville**
Fascetta, Christopher M.
**New Market**
Gabriel, Eberhard John
**Owings Mills**
Wolf, Cyd Beth
**Rockville**
Kochanski, David Majlech
Margulies, Laura Jacobs

MASSACHUSETTS

**Amesbury**
Swartz, Mark Lee
**Boston**
Bankowski, Carolyn Ann
Bodoff, Joseph Samuel Uberman
Krulewich, Leonard M.
Read, Nicholas Cary

MICHIGAN

**Ann Arbor**
Fineman, Gary Lee
**Birmingham**
Harms, Steven Alan
**Detroit**
Pope, Harold D.
Rochkind, Louis Philipp
**Farmington Hills**
Cuttner, David Allan
**Grand Rapids**
Mears, Patrick Edward

MINNESOTA

**Austin**
Bodensteiner, William Leo
**Minneapolis**
Leonard, Brian Francis
Ventres, Daniel Brainerd, Jr.
Weil, Cass Sargent
**Wayzata**
Reutiman, Robert William, Jr.

MISSISSIPPI

**Bay Springs**
Shoemaker, Bobby Lynn
**Columbus**
Sanders, David Lawrence
**Gulfport**
Pate, William August

**Jackson**
Eicher, Donald E., III
McCullough, James Altus, II
Wise, Robert Powell
**Pascagoula**
Roberts, David Ambrose

### MISSOURI

**Joplin**
Lonardo, Charles Henry
**Kansas City**
Gould, Michael Alan
Joyce, Michael Patrick
**Lexington**
Giorza, John C.
**Saint Louis**
Bloom, Allen Jerry
Breidenbach, Robert A.
Kramer, Donald Burton
Riggio, Nicholas Jospeh, Sr.
Willard, Gregory Dale

### MONTANA

**Great Falls**
Larsen, Dirk Herbert

### NEBRASKA

**Kearney**
Voigt, Steven Russell
**Omaha**
Lee, Dennis Patrick

### NEVADA

**Las Vegas**
Pitegoff, Jeffrey I.
**Reno**
Broili, Robert Howard
Chubb, Janet L.

### NEW JERSEY

**Cherry Hill**
Thomas, Robert F.
**Hackensack**
Gallucci, Michael A.
**Iselin**
Gupta, Rajat Kumar
**Lakewood**
Bielory, Abraham Melvin
**Linden**
Falk, Lauren Weissman
**Morristown**
Sperling, Joy Harmon
**Parsippany**
Gallagher, Jerome Francis, Jr.
**Ridgewood**
Trocano, Russell Peter
**Roseland**
Nathan, Edward Singer
**Sea Girt**
Wyskowski, Barbara Jean
**Summit**
Jarvis, Percy Alton, Jr.
**Westfield**
Nicolai, Donald F.
**Westmont**
Pozzuoli-Buecker, Renee M.

### NEW MEXICO

**Albuquerque**
Bova, Vincent Arthur, Jr.

### NEW YORK

**Baldwin**
Naranjo, Carolyn R.
**Buffalo**
Isenberg, Andrew Brian
**Cornwall**
Obremski, Charles Peter
**East Northport**
Ryesky, Kenneth H.
**Garden City**
Golden, Christopher Anthony
Kleinberg, Howard Bruce
**Great Neck**
Salzman, Stanley P.
**Mineola**
Bekritsky, Bruce Robert
Berman, Eric M.
**New York**
Birn, Harold M.
Censor, Martin A.
Reynard, Muriel Joyce
**Rochester**
Lustig, Douglas James
Rasmussen, David L.
**Scarsdale**
Sabadie, Francisca Alejandra
**Slingerlands**
Rhodes-Devey, Michael
**Syosset**
Upton, Arthur Edward
**Syracuse**
Gingold, Harlan Bruce
Givas, Thomas Peter
Melnicoff, Joel Niesen
**Troy**
Marinstein, Elliott F.

### NORTH CAROLINA

**Charlotte**
Buckley, Charles Robinson, III
Ogburn, Thomas Lynn, III
**Durham**
Carpenter, Charles Francis
Petersen, Elisabeth Saranec
**Greensboro**
Galloway, Hunter Henderson, III
Glover, Durant Murrell
Kobrin, Thomas Barstow
**Wilmington**
Johnston, Sharon A.

### NORTH DAKOTA

**Bismarck**
Rosenberg, Max D.

### OHIO

**Akron**
Breen, Kevin J.
**Bexley**
Kamin-Meyer, Tami
**Cincinnati**
Vogel, Cedric Wakelee
**Cleveland**
Eisen, Saul
Felty, Kriss Delbert
Helbling, Lauren A.
Krueger, Jeffrey W.
**Columbus**
Drexel, Ray Phillips
Frasier, Ralph Kennedy
Mancuso, Anthony O.
Robinson, Randal D.
Silverman, Perry Raynard
**Dayton**
Liberman, Scott A.
**Massillon**
Breyfogle, Edwin Howard
**Shaker Heights**
Cherchiglia, Dean Kenneth

### OKLAHOMA

**Oklahoma City**
Gibson, Keith Russell
Pardue, Wallace David, Jr.
Schwabe, George Blaine, III
**Stilwell**
Morton, Kathryn R.
**Tulsa**
Herrold, David Henry

### OREGON

**Brookings**
Hinton, Floyd
**Portland**
Lacey, Henry Bernard
Waggoner, James Clyde

### PENNSYLVANIA

**Abington**
Budman, Alan David
**Allentown**
Feinberg, Gregg Michael
McGrail-Szabo, Sharon Joan
**Canonsburg**
Kurowski, Charles Edward
**Conway**
Krebs, Robert Alan
**Doylestown**
Goldman, William Lewis, Sr.
**Harrisburg**
Lighty, Fredrick W.
Tyler, Brian Joseph
**Jenkintown**
Worthington, Sandra Boulton
**Lemoyne**
Stewart, Richard Williams
**Philadelphia**
Culhane, John Langdon
Flame, Andrew Jay
Lipshutz, Robert Murray
Morris, John Whelchel
Sweeney, Clayton Anthony, Jr.
Tumola, Thomas Joseph
Wittels, Barnaby Caesar
**Pittsburgh**
Calairo, Donald Robert
Helmrich, Joel Marc
Messner, Robert Thomas

### RHODE ISLAND

**Cranston**
Coletti, John Anthony
Walsh, Leatrice D.
**Providence**
McGowan, Matthew J.

### SOUTH CAROLINA

**Charleston**
Bernstein, Robert Alan
Hood, Robert Holmes
**Columbia**
Cooper, Robert Gordon
Johnson, Lawrence Wilbur, Jr.
**West Columbia**
Applegate, William Russell

### SOUTH DAKOTA

**Sioux Falls**
Johnson, Richard Arlo
Nelson, Robert R.

### TENNESSEE

**Dresden**
Herron, Roy Brasfield
**Knoxville**
Conrad, Frederick Larue, Jr.
**Memphis**
Noel, Randall Deane
Peppel, Howard Rex
Witthauer, Robert Taylor

### TEXAS

**Austin**
McCullough, Frank Witcher, III
**Bryan**
Bond, Randall Scott
Michel, C. Randall
**Corpus Christi**
McMillen, James Thomas
**Dallas**
Bonesio, Woodrow Michael
Freedman, Randall Lee
Hranitzky, Rachel Robyn
Zips, Craig Danny
**El Paso**
Ingram, Temple Byrn, Jr.
**Fort Worth**
Johnston, Michael Wayne
Sartain, James Edward
**Houston**
Aschermann, Mark L.
Banks, John Robert, Jr.
Diaz-Arrastia, George Ravelo
Ivey, Jack Todd
Judice, Kenneth R.
Rhodes, George Frederick, Jr.
**Hurst**
Casey, David Robert
**Mcallen**
McLeaish, Robert Burns
**Richmond**
Slone, Charles R.
**San Antonio**
Javore, Gary William
Yedor, Jonathan
**Sugar Land**
Greer, Raymond White
Poock, Steven Doyle
**Sweetwater**
Jones, Charles Eric, Jr.
**Tyler**
Patterson, Donald Ross
**Weslaco**
Pomerantz, Jerald Michael

### UTAH

**Salt Lake City**
Kent, Dale R.
Rogers, Jon H.

### VERMONT

**Bethel**
Obuchowski, Raymond Joseph
**Burlington**
Gravel, John Cook

### VIRGINIA

**Alexandria**
Paul, Adam Craig
**Arlington**
Walker, Woodrow Wilson
**Falls Church**
Redmond, Robert
**Spotsylvania**
Pugh, Randall Scott
**Winchester**
Adams, Nate Lavinder, III

### WASHINGTON

**Bellingham**
Raas, Daniel Alan
**Kennewick**
Hames, William Lester
**Olympia**
Walker, Francis Joseph
**Seattle**
Diggs, Bradley C.
Mucklestone, Peter John
Mueller, Daniel Edward
**Spokane**
Michaelsen, Howard Kenneth

### WEST VIRGINIA

**Charleston**
Cannon-Ryan, Susan Kaye
Cline, Michael Robert
Michelson, Gail Ida
**Fairmont**
Cohen, Richard Paul
Stanton, George Patrick, Jr.

### WISCONSIN

**Milwaukee**
Rotter, Emanuel Norman
Sturm, William Charles
**Pewaukee**
Engel, John Charles
**Racine**
Dye, William Ellsworth
**Wausau**
Deffner, Roger L.

### ADDRESS UNPUBLISHED

Caquatto, Norma Madeline
Collins, James Francis
Gewertz, Martin Anson
Gold, Mitchell M.
Hardcastle, Robert Thomas
Horn, Andrew Warren
Martin, Robert James
Rodenburg, Clifton Glenn
Siebert, William Alan
Skal, Debra Lynn
Toms, Frederic E.

## COMMERCIAL, CONTRACTS

### UNITED STATES

### ALABAMA

**Birmingham**
Brooke, William Wade
Burnside, Cynthia Grace
Cornelius, Walter Felix
Cornett, Wendy Love
Stewart, Joseph Grier
Trimmier, Charles Stephen, Jr.
**Demopolis**
Dinning, Woodford Wyndham, Jr.
**Mobile**
Johnston, Neil Chunn
Loveless, Ralph Peyton
Quina, Marion Albert, Jr.
Roedder, William Chapman, Jr.
**Montgomery**
Duncan, Priscilla Black

### ALASKA

**Anchorage**
Ginder, Peter Craig
Gorski, James Michael
Owens, Robert Patrick
Perkins, Joseph John, Jr.

### ARIZONA

**Chandler**
Markey, James Kevin
**Mesa**
Guffey, Douglas Oliver
**Phoenix**
Clarke, David Alan
Coppersmith, Sam
Hover, John Charles
Lasee, Mark Edward
Luikens, Thomas Gerard
Olson, Kevin Lory
Postal, David Ralph
Susman, Alan Howard
Turk, Andrew Borders
White, Nancy Lee
**Scottsdale**
Angle, Margaret Susan
Marhoffer, David
**Tempe**
Vanderpoel, James Robert
**Tucson**
Burton, Stephen David

### ARKANSAS

**Crossett**
Hubbell, Billy James
**Little Rock**
Cearley, Robert M., Jr.
Creasman, William Paul
Riordan, Deborah Truby
**Pine Bluff**
Strode, Joseph Arlin
**Searcy**
Hannah, R. Craig

### CALIFORNIA

**Antioch**
Richards, Gerald Thomas
**Auburn**
Lyon, Bruce Arnold
**Buena Park**
Kehrli, David P.
**Calabasas**
Weiss, Sherman David
**Carmel**
Varga, S. Gary
**Clovis**
Simmons, Robert Jacob
**Cypress**
Olschwang, Alan Paul
**Encinitas**
Williams, Michael Edward
**Encino**
Kent, Thomas Edward
Magidsohn, Herman Edward
**Fremont**
Chou, Yung-Ming
**Glendale**
MacDonald, Kirk Stewart
**Irvine**
Hurst, Charles Wilson
**La Jolla**
Eischen, James John, Jr.
**Los Angeles**
Allan, Michael Lee
Ariel, Frank Y.
Biele, Hugh Irving
Burkholder, John Allen
Camp, James Carroll
Davidson, Jeffrey H.
Desario, Daniel J.
Forster, Jonathan Shawn
Francis, Merrill Richard
Geiger, Roy Stephen
Gould, Howard Neal
Gubner, Adam Lance
Hahn, Elliott Julius
Hayes, Byron Jackson, Jr.
Huben, Brian David
Ibekwe, Edebeatu
Kessler, Joan Blumenstein
Kundinger, Mathew Hermann
Kupietzky, Moshe J.
Leibow, Ronald Louis
Marshall, Arthur K.
Popowitz, Neil Michael
Samuels, Joel Gregory
Share, Richard Hudson
Weg, Howard Jay
Weinman, Glenn Alan
Zerunyan, Frank Vram
**Marina Dl Rey**
Seiden, Andy
**Mill Valley**
Georgeson, Adamont Nicholas
**Modesto**
Leong, Linda S.
**Napa**
Meibeyer, Charles William, Jr.
**Newark**
Bernard, Steven Martin
**Newport Beach**
Barclay, John Allen
Hancock, S. Lee
**North Hollywood**
Zimring, Stuart David
**Northridge**
Van Der Wal, Jeanne Huber
**Oakland**
Leslie, Robert Lorne
Loving, Deborah June Pierre
**Orangevale**
King, Franklin Weaver
**Palm Springs**
FitzGerald, John Edward, III
**Palo Alto**
Hasko, Judith Ann
Nycum, Susan Hubbell
**Pasadena**
Linstedt, Walter Griffiths
**Pleasanton**
Straff, Donna Evelyn
**Pomona**
Wyatt, John Brundige, III
**Redondo Beach**
Michael, Geoffrey Palmer
**Richmond**
Straus, Douglas Charles
**Riverside**
Nassar, William Michael
**Sacramento**
Felderstein, Steven Howard
Stone, Peter Robert
**San Bernardino**
Brittain, Gregory W.
**San Clemente**
Geyser, Lynne M.
**San Diego**
Catherwood, Kathryn M.S.
Clark, Grant Lawrence
Copley, Rocky K.
Emge, Derek John
Mayer, James Hock
Smith, Norman Leslie
Speckman, David Leon
Tow, L. Michelle
Vakili, Alidad
**San Francisco**
Collas, Juan Garduño, Jr.
Diamond, Philip Ernest
Finck, Kevin William
Fleischmann, Roger Justice
Gillmar, Stanley Frank
Hinman, Harvey DeForest
Kallgren, Edward Eugene
Kimport, David Lloyd
Meador, Ross DeShong
Seabolt, Richard L.
Sharp, Stefanie Teresa
Shin, Chang Shik
Strauss, Philip Reed
Stroup, Stanley Stephenson
Teitler, Harold Herman
**San Jose**
Blasgen, Sharon Walther
Bramer, Lisan Hung
Chacon, Gerald Gilbert
**San Mateo**
Bhatnagar, Mary Elizabeth
Dworkin, Michael Leonard
**San Pedro**
DeWitt, Brian Leigh
**San Ramon**
Freed, Kenneth Alan
**Santa Barbara**
Metzinger, Timothy Edward
**Santa Clara**
Kaner, Cem
**Santa Cruz**
Atchison, Rodney Raymond
Joseph, Irwin H.
**Santa Monica**
Homeier, Michael George
**Santa Rosa**
McCutchan, B. Edward, Jr.
**Sherman Oaks**
Hartzfeld, Howard Alexander, Jr.
**Stockton**
Malm, Scott
**Sunnyvale**
Ludgus, Nancy Lucke
Wyatt, Thomas Csaba
**Temecula**
Thompson, Susannah Elizabeth
**Thousand Oaks**
Tenner, Erin K.
**Tracy**
Hay, Dennis Lee
**Tustin**
Dao, Hanh D.
**Universal Cty**
Gentino, Robert E.
**Venice**
Schanes, Christine Elise
**Walnut Creek**
Sohnen, Harvey

### COLORADO

**Arvada**
Carney, T. J
**Aspen**
Shulman, Harry
**Boulder**
Earnest, G. Lane
Ward, Denitta Dawn
**Denver**
Burkhardt, Donald Malcolm
Cox, William Vaughan
Daily, Richard W.
Dean, James Benwell
DeSisto, John Anthony
Finn, John Stephen
Gallegos, Larry Duayne
Hamel, Fred Meade
Horowitz, Robert M.
Keatinge, Robert Reed
Kirchhoff, Bruce C.
Lutz, John Shafroth
Mauro, Richard Frank
McPherson, Gary Lee
Molling, Charles Francis
Moye, John Edward
Pollack, Howard Jay
Temple, Dana A.
Ulrich, Theodore Albert
Zavadil, Lawrence Michael
**Englewood**
Gognat, Richard J.
Katz, Michael Jeffery
**Grand Junction**
Mayberry, Herbert Sylvester

### CONNECTICUT

**Brooklyn**
Dune, Steve Charles

**Danbury**
Bassett, Robert Andrews
**Darien**
Flanagan, Mari Jo Florio
**East Hartford**
Kerrigan, Vanessa Griffith
**Groton**
Kehoe, Thomas Joseph
**Hartford**
Alleyne, Julie Sudhir
Beck, Henry M., Jr.
Donnell, Brian James
Feigenbaum, Barry S.
Flynn, Brendan Thomas
Rome, Donald Lee
**Madison**
Hollo, Leslie Stephen
**Manchester**
Gaines, Robert Martin
**Meriden**
Lowry, Houston Putnam
**Middletown**
Quattro, Mark Henry
**Milford**
Berchem, Robert Lee, Sr.
**Monroe**
Beck, Dana Kendall
**New Haven**
Peabody, Bruce R.
Skalka, Douglas Scott
Sosensky, Steven C.
Stankewich, Paul Joseph
**New Milford**
Zitzmann, Kelly C.
**Ridgefield**
Sherman, Harold
**Stamford**
Gold, Steven Michael
Huth, William Edward
Lois, Dale Joseph
Padilla, James Earl
Rose, Richard Loomis
**Weatogue**
Greenlaw, Dawn Sharon
**Westport**
LoMonte, Douglas Edward
**Wilton**
Blankmeyer, Kurt Van Cleave

### DELAWARE

**Claymont**
Rollins, Gene A.
**Wilmington**
Boudreaux, Gerald Joseph
Carey, Wayne John
Cummings, Stacey L.
Durante, Charles Joseph
Gundersen, Mark Jonathan
Kristol, Daniel Marvin
Morris, Kenneth Donald
Patton, James Leeland, Jr.
Semple, James William

### DISTRICT OF COLUMBIA

**Washington**
Babby, Lon S.
Bodansky, Robert Lee
Canfield, Edward Francis
Dickerman, Dorothea Wilhelmina
Feinstein, Nathan B.
Flowe, Benjamin Hugh, Jr.
Goergen, Michael James
Greif, Joseph
Hanas, Stephen Michael
Harrison, Earl David
Hellbeck, Eckhard Robert
Israel, Deborah Jean
Konselman, Douglas Derek
Longstreet, Susan Cannon
Lowell, H. Bret
Mazo, Mark Elliott
Overman, Dean Lee
Roberts, Jared Ingersoll
Samuelson, Kenneth Lee
Tavallali, Jalal Chaicar
Tufaro, Richard Chase
Weiner, Kenneth Brian
Weiss, Arnold Hans
Yoskowitz, Irving Benjamin

### FLORIDA

**Altamonte Springs**
Rudisill, Robert Mack, Jr.
Salfi, Dominick Joseph
**Boca Raton**
Buckstein, Mark Aaron
Kornberg, Joel Barry
Nussbaum, Howard Jay
**Clearwater**
Coleman, Jeffrey Peters
Silberman, Morris
**Clewiston**
Gonzalez, Francisco Javier
**Coral Gables**
Pallot, Joseph Wedeles
**Coral Springs**
Polin, Alan Jay
**Delray Beach**
Weitzman, Linda Sue
**Dunedin**
Felos, George James
**Fort Lauderdale**
Bustamante, Nestor
Lipnack, Martin I.
Tripp, Norman Densmore
**Jacksonville**
Alterman, Leonard Mayer
Christian, Gary Irvin
Dunkle, Kurt Hughes
Gooding, David Michael
Held, Edwin Walter, Jr.
Hodge, James Edward
Kent, John Bradford
Legler, Mitchell Wooten
Prom, Stephen George
**Key West**
Smith, Wayne LaRue
**Lakeland**
Harris, Christy Franklin
**Lauderhill**
Berry, Carl David, Jr.
**Marianna**
Wynn, Charles Milton
**Miami**
Baena, Scott Louis
Coberly, Jennifer Rae
Coffey, Kendall Brindley
Feinberg, Dyanne Elyce
Furnari, Doreen S.
Gomez, Ivan A.
Granata, Linda M.
Gutierrez, Renaldy Jose
Hoffman, Larry J.
Martinez-Cid, Ricardo
McHale, Michael John
Mendelson, Victor Howard
Murai, Rene Vicente
Osman, Edith Gabriella
Pennington, John Wesley, III
Schuette, Charles A.
Schwartz, Martin A.
Segall, Norman S.
Stanley, Sherry A.
Stein, Allan Mark
Touby, Richard
**Miami Beach**
Thomas, Lola Bohn
**Naples**
Emerson, John Williams, II
**North Palm Beach**
Coyle, Dennis Patrick
**Orlando**
Buhaly Ibold, Catherine
Dierking, John Randall
Hartley, Carl William, Jr.
Leonhardt, Frederick Wayne
Pleus, Robert J., Jr.
Weiss, Christopher John
**Palm Bay**
Balog, Douglas Allan
Howard, Marilyn Hoey
**Palm Beach**
Grogan, Robert Harris
**Punta Gorda**
Cherry, Paul Stephen
**Saint Petersburg**
Ross, Howard Philip
**Sarasota**
Christopher, William Garth
Goldsmith, Stanley Alan
Walters, Joel W.
**Tallahassee**
Barley, John Alvin
Boge, Samantha
Cummings, Frederic Alan
**Tampa**
Colton, Roberta Ann
Heyck, Joseph Giraud, Jr.
Mandelbaum, Samuel Robert
McBride, William Howard, Jr.
Olson, John Karl
Pacheco, Felipe Ramon
Schwenke, Roger Dean
Teblum, Gary Ira
Whatley, Jacqueline Beltram
**Tavernier**
Lupino, James Samuel
**West Palm Beach**
Aron, Jerry E.
Cooper, Margaret Leslie
James, Keith Alan
Laing, Robert Scott
Shapero, Bertram Malcolm
**Winter Park**
Ackert, T(errence) W(illiam)
Hadley, Ralph Vincent, III

### GEORGIA

**Alpharetta**
Linder, Harvey Ronald
**Atlanta**
Bates, Beverly Bailey
Calhoun, Scott Douglas
Cargill, Robert Mason
Crews, William Edwin
Hinchey, John William
Jester, Carroll Gladstone
Jones, Glower Whitehead
Kelly, James Michael
Koplan, Andrew Bennet
Liss, Matthew Martin
Stamps, Thomas Paty
Strauss, Robert David
Veal, Rex R.
Williams, Neil, Jr.
**Marietta**
Ahlstrom, Michael Joseph
Smith, Jere Crews, Jr.
Stein, Julie Lynne
**Norcross**
Winkler, Allen Warren
**Perry**
Geiger, James Norman
**Roswell**
Mimms, Thomas Bowman, Jr.
**Savannah**
Shawe, Mark Thackeray

### HAWAII

**Honolulu**
Asai-Sato, Carol Yuki
Chin, Stephanie Anne
Chu, Harold
Dwyer, John Ryan, Jr.
Gay, E(mil) Laurence
Ichinose, Susan M.
Lau, Eugene Wing Iu
Mirikitani, Richard Kiyoshi
Sato, Glenn Kenji
**Paia**
Richman, Joel Eser

### IDAHO

**Boise**
Baird, Denise Colleen
Hickman, Lori A. DeMond
Rowe, John R.
Runft, John L.
Wood, Troy James
**Coeur D Alene**
Davis, Dennis Milan
**Idaho Falls**
Avery, John Orval
**Twin Falls**
Hohnhorst, John Charles
Tolman, Steven Kay

### ILLINOIS

**Abbott Park**
Brock, Charles Marquis
**Alton**
Durr, Malcolm Daniel
**Buffalo Grove**
Greenspon, Susan Jean
**Chicago**
Anderson, J. Trent
Baer, John Richard Frederick
Brand, Mark
Burke, Edmund Patrick, Sr.
Cohen, Melanie Rovner
Cunningham, Thomas Justin
Dashow, Jules
Dondanville, Patricia
Fazio, Peter Victor, Jr.
Field, Robert Edward
Frank, Jay Allan
French, Timothy A.
Harris, Linda Chaplik
Henry, Robert John
Hoffman, Douglas Raymond
Hoseman, Daniel
Jacobson, Ronald H.
Johnson, Douglas Wells
Kagan, Andrew Besdin
Karnes, Evan Burton, II
Kohn, William Irwin
Kozlowski, Kimberly Frances
Krakauer, Bryan
Laidlaw, Andrew R.
Lapin, Andrew William
LeBaron, Charles Frederick, Jr.
Lemberis, Theodore Thomas
Loew, Jonathan L.
Mandel, Reid Alan
Mehlman, Mark Franklin
Mertes, Arthur Edward
Miller, Paul J.
Millner, Robert B.
Moltz, Marshall Jerome
Murray, Daniel Richard
Nachman, Norman Harry
Pallasch, B. Michael
Peterson, Ronald Roger
Proctor, Edward George
Rohrman, Douglass Frederick
Touhy, John M.
Wahlen, Edwin Alfred
Weil, Andrew L.
White, Linda Diane
Wolf, Neal Lloyd
**Elgin**
Roeser, Ronald O.
**Libertyville**
Mihelic, Kristin Tavia
**Lincolnshire**
Giza, David Alan
**Long Grove**
Obert, Paul Richard
**Moline**
Cleaver, William Lehn
**Oakbrook Terrace**
Bashaw, Steven Bradley
Fenech, Joseph Charles
**Palatine**
Roti, Thomas David
**Park Ridge**
Bellas, George Steven
**Peoria**
Atterbury, Robert Rennie, III
**Rock Island**
Lousberg, Peter Herman
**Springfield**
Rabin, Avrum Mark

### INDIANA

**Avilla**
Stephens, James F.
**Bloomington**
Williams, Cynthia Anne
**Elkhart**
Breckenridge, Franklin Eugene
**Evansville**
Harrison, Joseph Heavrin
**Fort Wayne**
Clark, Jeffrey A.
**Highland**
Fine, William Irwin
**Indianapolis**
Abrams, Jeffrey Alan
Carlberg, James Edwin
Kessler, Susan D.
Kleiman, Mary Margaret
Knauer, James A.
Miller, David Anthony
Talesnick, Stanley
Vandivier, Blair Robert
Yeager, Joseph Heizer, Jr.
**Merrillville**
Brenman, Stephen Morris
**Portage**
Henke, Robert John
**Schererville**
Anast, Nick James
**South Bend**
Hall, Thomas Jennings
Reinke, William John

### IOWA

**Des Moines**
Bannister, T(homas) Scott
Eaton, Jay
**Sioux City**
Madsen, George Frank

### KANSAS

**Hutchinson**
Chalfant, William Young
**Kansas City**
Peters, Daniel Wade
**Lawrence**
Hoeflich, Michael Harlan
**Overland Park**
Anderson, Steven Robert
Cohen, Barton Pollock
Glasser, Philip Russell
Herman, Robert Stephen
Knopp, Timothy John
Vratil, John Logan
**Shawnee Mission**
Shank, Suzanne Adams

### KENTUCKY

**Bowling Green**
Catron, Stephen Barnard
**Lexington**
Curtz, Chauncey S.R.
McClelland, Denise H.
Scott, Joseph Mitchell, Jr.
**Louisville**
Fenton, Thomas Conner
Friedman, Hal Daniel
Halbleib, Walter Thomas
Humphreys, Gene Lynn
Macdonald, Lenna Ruth
Shaikun, Michael Gary
Vincenti, Michael Baxter

### LOUISIANA

**Baton Rouge**
Anderson, Lawrence Robert, Jr.
Richards, Marta Alison
**Lafayette**
Myers, Stephen Hawley
Ottinger, Patrick S.
**Lake Charles**
Everett, John Prentis, Jr.
Norman, Rick Joseph
**Metairie**
Hardy, Ashton Richard
Kutcher, Robert A.
**New Orleans**
Curtis, Charles Thach, Jr.
Hoffman, Robert Dean, Jr.
Miller, Gary H.
Perez, Luis Alberto
Raphael, David Coleman
Rumage, Joseph Paul, Jr.
Steeg, Moise S., Jr.
Steinberg, Sylvan Julian
Waechter, Arthur Joseph, Jr.
Wedig, Regina Scotto
**Shreveport**
Bryant, J(ames) Bruce

### MAINE

**Portland**
Amory, Daniel
Bennett, Jeffrey
Martin, Michael Keith
Ray, David P.
Stauffer, Eric P.

### MARYLAND

**Baltimore**
Baker, William Parr
Kandel, Nelson Robert
Knuckey, Kenneth Scott
Kuryk, David Neal
Mogol, Alan Jay
Russo, Michael Natale, Jr.
Wasserman, Richard Leo
**Bethesda**
Bregman, Douglas M.
Chapman, Gerald Frederick
Goodwin, Robert Cronin
Herman, Stephen Allen
Himelfarb, Stephen Roy
Poppleton, Miller John
Scully, Roger Tehan
**Gaithersburg**
Godwin, Richard Jeffrey
Phillips, Leo Harold, Jr.
**Lexington Park**
Lacer, Alfred Antonio
**Ocean City**
Harrison, Joseph George, Jr.
**Rockville**
Fogleman, Christopher Curtis
Herzog, Carolyn Beth
Zaphiriou, George Aristotle
**Westminster**
Blakeslee, Wesley Daniel

### MASSACHUSETTS

**Boston**
Aresty, Jeffrey M.
Bankowski, Carolyn Ann
Bodoff, Joseph Samuel Uberman
Cataldo, Alexander Lawrence
Dello Iacono, Paul Michael
Hester, Patrick Joseph
Huang, Thomas Weishing
Kyle, Amy Lynn
Lamb, Kevin Thomas
Levine, Steven B.
O'Brien, Duncan Thomas
Read, Nicholas Cary
Schoenfeld, Barbara Braun
Shapiro, Sandra
Shure, Andrew F.
Smith, Edwin Eric
Snyder, John Gorvers
Tarbet, David W.
Van, Peter
Yurko, Richard John
**Cambridge**
Esher, Jacob Aaron
**Chestnut Hill**
Bursley, Kathleen A.
**Concord**
O'Brien, James Freeman
**Framingham**
Gatlin, Michael Gerard
Meltzer, Jay H.
**Manchester**
Rumpf, Pierre Cameron
**Natick**
Woodyshek, J. Daniel
**Newton Highlands**
Gans, Steven H.
**Pembroke**
Schacter, Stacey Jay
**Somerville**
Brown, Peter Mason
**Springfield**
Nicolai, Paul Peter
**Wellesley**
Marx, Peter A.
**Worcester**
Baldiga, Joseph Hilding
Chernin, Russell Scott
Joyce, James Joseph, Jr.
Weinstein, Jordan Harvey

### MICHIGAN

**Ann Arbor**
Ellmann, Douglas Stanley
Valenti, Dennis R.
**Battle Creek**
Karre, Nelson Thomas
**Birmingham**
Harms, Steven Alan
Zelenock, Katheryne L.
**Bloomfield Hills**
Berlow, Robert Alan
Cunningham, Gary H.
Dawson, Stephen Everette
**Clinton Township**
Theut, C. Peter
**Detroit**
Branigan, Thomas Patrick
Candler, James Nall, Jr.
Carroll, Michael Dennis
Darlow, Julia Donovan
Dunn, William Bradley
Langs, Edward F(orrest)
Lardner, Cynthia Marie-Martinovich
Nix, Robert Royal, II
Pirtle, H(arold) Edward
Rochkind, Louis Philipp
Targan, Holli Hart
Thorpe, Norman Ralph
**Farmington Hills**
Ciampa, Jeffrey Nelson
Haliw, Andrew Jerome, III
**Flint**
Edmunds, Michael Winterton
Powers, Edward Herbert
**Grand Rapids**
Curtin, Timothy John
Engbers, James Arend
Gillis, Geoffrey Lawrence
**Lansing**
Burlingame, Stephen Lee
Moody, Kevin Joseph
**Muskegon**
Fauri, Eric Joseph
Nehra, Gerald Peter
**Plymouth**
Koroi, Mark Michael
**Port Huron**
Wallace, Matthew Mark
**Southfield**
Baughman, Leonora Knoblock
Jacobs, John E.
**Taylor**
Hirsch, David L.
**Traverse City**
Smith, Louis Adrian
**Troy**
Berman, Leonard Keith

### MINNESOTA

**Austin**
Schneider, Mahlon C.
**Benson**
Wilcox, Donald Alan
**Edina**
Gurstel, Norman Keith
**Hopkins**
Hunter, Donald Forrest
**Minneapolis**
Baillie, James Leonard
Forrest, Bradley Albert
Frecon, Alain
Kelley, Shane Richard
Moore, Terry Mason
Neumeyer, Susan Lee
Opdahl, Clark Donald
Reilly, George
Rochlin, Davis Samuel
Rude, Brian William
Strothman, John Henry
Weil, Cass Sargent
**Saint Cloud**
Hughes, Kevin John
**Saint Paul**
Rebane, John T.
Van Zomeren, Barbara Ruth

### MISSISSIPPI

**Greenville**
Hafter, Jerome Charles
**Gulfport**
Westbrook, William V.
Wetzel, James K.
**Jackson**
Boackle, K.F.
Grant, Russell Porter, Jr.
Holbrook, Frank Malvin
Montagnet, O. Stephen
O'Mara, James Wright
Rosenblatt, Stephen Woodburn
Tohill, Jim Barnette

### MISSOURI

**Brentwood**
Timm, Walter William
**Chesterfield**
Pollihan, Thomas Henry

**Columbia**
Mays, William Gay, II
**Kansas City**
Frisbie, Charles
Gaines, Robert Darryl
Hill, John Brian
Lewandowski, Alex Michael
Lolli, Don R(ay)
Mordy, James Calvin
Stoup, Arthur Harry
**Saint Louis**
Bossi, Mark Vincent
Brickey, James Nelson
Cook, Thomas Alfred Ashley
DeHaven, Michael Allen
Duesenberg, Richard William
Engel, Richard W., Jr.
Goldenhersh, Robert Stanley
Hetlage, Robert Owen
Komen, Leonard
Leontsinis, George John
Lowther, Thomas Edward
Poscover, Maury B.
Sullivan, Edward Lawrence
**Saint Peters**
Goss, J. Bradford
**West Plains**
Brill, Newton Clyde

## MONTANA

**Missoula**
Vannatta, Shane Anthony

## NEBRASKA

**Cozad**
McKeone, Mark R.
**Omaha**
Fitzgerald, James Patrick
Rouse, Michael Adams

## NEVADA

**Las Vegas**
Albright, George Mark
Eisner, Elliott Roy
Graham, Robert Chase
Mahan, James Cameron
Nozero, Elizabeth Catherine
Singer, Michael Howard

## NEW HAMPSHIRE

**Concord**
Richmond, Tanya Goff
**Nashua**
Goodwin, Rolf Ervine
**Plymouth**
Clark, R. Thomas
**Portsmouth**
Doleac, Charles Bartholomew

## NEW JERSEY

**Atlantic City**
Markwardt, John James
Zlotnick, Norman Lee
**Audubon**
Watson, Mark Henry
**Bridgewater**
DeFranceschi, Gary M.
Kosten, Jeffrey Thomas
**Budd Lake**
Webb, John Gibbon, III
**Cliffside Park**
Diktas, Christos James
**Clinton**
Kennedy, Harold Edward
**Edison**
Applebaum, Charles
**Hackensack**
Bialkowski, Stephen Walter
Greenberg, Steven Morey
**Iselin**
Oriolo, Joseph Michael
**Kenilworth**
Berkowite, Jeffrey
**Linwood**
Frisch, David Bruce
**Livingston**
Burns, Susie
Kuller, Jonathan Mark
**Lyndhurst**
Lasky, David
**Metuchen**
Vercammen, Kenneth Albert
**Moorestown**
Caniglia, Lawrence S.
**Morristown**
Aspero, Benedict Vincent
Donaldson, Craig John
Greenapple, Steven Bruce
Massey, Henry Nelson
Platt, Gary R.
Rosenthal, Meyer L(ouis)
**New Providence**
Bronstein, Glen Max
**Newark**
Day, Edward Francis, Jr.
Long, Reginald Alan
Muscato, Andrew
Neuer, Philip David
Smith, Frederick Theodore
**Parsippany**
Chobot, John Charles
Prague, Ronald Jay
Rothstadt, Garry Sigmund
Sesso, George
**Princeton**
Atkins, Thomas Herman
Beimfohr, Douglas Alan
**Ramsey**
Ogden, John Hamilton
**River Vale**
Falcon, Raymond Jesus, Jr.
**Roseland**
Harris, Allan Michael
Nathan, Edward Singer
Schenkler, Bernard
Schwartz, Andrea B.
Smith, Dennis Jay
Vaiden, Kristi L.
**Roselle Park**
Tancs, Linda Ann
**Saddle River**
Bastedo, Wayne Webster
**Scotch Plains**
Hayes, Lewis Mifflin, Jr.
**Short Hills**
Fast, Kenneth H.
**Somerset**
Green, Jeffrey C.
**South Amboy**
Moskovitz, Stuart Jeffrey
**Teaneck**
Kaplan, Howard M(ark)
**Trenton**
Frost, Barry Warren
Strassberg, Jonathan Elliot
**Union**
Suplee, Katherine Ann
**Voorhees**
Harris, Glenn Anthony
**Warren**
Rana, Harminderpal Singh
**Wayne**
Cupka, Brian Joseph
Long, Lucinda Parshall
**Wildwood**
Gould, Alan I.
**Woodbridge**
Falk, Kenneth B.
**Woodcliff Lake**
Klein, Marilyn Yaffe
Shulman, Frederic M.

## NEW MEXICO

**Albuquerque**
Hanna, Robert Cecil
Moughan, Peter Richard, Jr.
Rager, Rudolph Russell
**Santa Fe**
Burton, John Paul (Jack Burton)

## NEW YORK

**Armonk**
Moskowitz, Stuart Stanley
**Bronxville**
Veneruso, James John
**Brooklyn**
Kelleher, Terence L.
Nicholson, Michael
Nuccio, Paul Vincent
Reichman, Adelle E.
Rice, Thomas O'Connor
**Buffalo**
Bond, Jill Kawa
Cramer, Mark Kenley
Nichols, F(rederick) Harris
Oppenheimer, Randolph Carl
Ritchie, Stafford Duff, II
Struble, Michelle Leigh
**Cedarhurst**
Taubenfeld, Harry Samuel
**Clifton Park**
Hayes, Norman Robert, Jr.
**Corning**
Hauselt, Denise Ann
**Croton On Hudson**
Hoffman, Paul Shafer
**Dunkirk**
Woodbury, Robert Charles
**Floral Park**
Catanzano, Raymond Augustine
**Flushing**
Chang, Lee-Lee
Deerson, Adele Shapiro
**Garden City**
Mastaglio, Peter James
**Glens Falls**
Pontiff, Paul E.
**Great Neck**
Rockowitz, Noah Ezra
Zervos, Mitra Kavoussi
**Hauppauge**
Silberling, Stephen Pierce
**Hillsdale**
Lunde, Asbjorn Rudolph
**Howard Beach**
Hernandez-Gonzalez, Gloria Maria
**Jackson Heights**
Casanova, Lorenzo
**Jericho**
Rehbock, Richard Alexander
**Long Beach**
Solomon, Robert H.
**Long Island City**
Barnholdt, Terry Joseph, Jr.
Risi, Joseph John
**Malverne**
Benigno, Thomas Daniel
**Mount Kisco**
Edelstein, Peter Michael
**New Hyde Park**
Richman, Theodore Charles
**New York**
Aron, Roberto
Axelrod, Charles Paul
Beltre, Luis Oscar
Bendes, Barry Jay
Berk, Brian D.
Bernstein, Bernard
Bernstein, Donald Scott
Berzow, Harold Steven
Bianco, S. Anthony
Bidwell, James Truman, Jr.
Bloomer, Harold Franklin, Jr.
Bluestone, Andrew Lavoott
Bowers, William Charles
Bradford, Elizabeth
Brooks, Kermitt Jerome
Broude, Mark Allen
Browne, Jeffrey Francis
Bruenner, Eric William
Butterklee, Neil Howard
Chaitman, Helen Davis
Chen, Wesley
Cho, Tai Yong
Christenfeld, Alan M.
Clapman, Peter Carlyle
Clement, Daniel Evan
Cowan, Wallace Edgar
Cowen, Edward S.
Dale, Margaret A.
Das, Kalyan
Derzaw, Richard Lawrence
di Domenico, Philip
Dienes, Louis Robert
Dodge, Jonathan Karel
Dolan, Patrick Daniel
Dropkin, Charles Edward
Dugan, Terrence Lee
Edozien, Margaret Ekwutozia
Feder, Saul E.
Feit, David Jonathan
Fernandez, Jose Walfredo
Filler, Ronald Howard
Finnegan, Hugh Patrick
Gadsden, James
Ganz, David L.
Gates, Peter P.
Gelfman, Peter Trustman
Getzoff, Steven B.
Gibbs, L(ippman) Martin
Goebel, William Horn
Gooch, Anthony Cushing
Goodkind, E. Robert
Granoff, Gary Charles
Greene, Ira S.
Greenspon, Robert Alan
Grosz, Morton Eric
Herbst, Todd L.
Herz, Andrew Lee
Hirshfield, Stuart
Jaglom, Andre Richard
Jiménez, Emilio
Kamien, Kalvin
Kaminsky, Judith A.
Kaplan, Steven Mark
Karson, Barry M.
Kasowitz, Marc Elliot
Katsos, Barbara Helene
Kinney, Stephen Hoyt, Jr.
Koblenz, Michael Robert
Kojevnikov, Boris Oleg
Kornreich, Edward Scott
Lalla, Thomas Rocco, Jr.
Lee, In-Young
Lee, Thomas Dongho
Lefkowitz, Howard N.
Levitsky, Asher Samuel
Lieberman, Nancy Ann
Lighter, Lawrence
Lindauer, Erik D.
Lindsay, George Peter
Lutringer, Richard Emil
MacRae, Cameron Farquhar, III
Mann, Philip Roy
Mantle, Raymond Allan
Marcus, Todd Barry
McMahon, Dennis C.
Melnik, Selinda A.
Menack, Steven Boyd
Michigan, Alan
Miller, Neil Scott
Modlin, Howard S.
Motola, David Henry
Newman, Lawrence Walker
O'Rorke, James Francis, Jr.
Owen, Robert Dewit
Perlberger, Ralph
Phillips, Pamela Kim
Pollack, Stanley P.
Rachlin, Leila
Rogers, Danforth William
Rosen, Eric Alan
Ross, Otho Bescent
Sacks, Karen Goldfarb
Satovsky, Stacey Yael
Savell, Polly Carolyn
Schaab, Arnold J.
Scheler, Brad Eric
Schoenfeld, Steven Russell
Schwab, Terrance W.
Schwartz, James Evan
Setrakian, Berge
Sheikh, Kemal A.
Shelby, Jerome
Sher, Michael Lee
Shih, Michael Ming-Yu
Silverberg, Jay L.
Smagula, John William
Sobel, Jay
Stefano, Joseph M.
Swiedler, Alan M.
Teiman, Richard B.
Urban, Lisa Breier
Urquia, Rafael, II
Wald, Bernard Joseph
Walton, Robert Prentiss
Westin, David Lawrence
Wexelbaum, Michael
White, Katherine Patricia
Wise, Aaron Noah
Wolff, Kurt Jakob
Wu, Robin Chi Ching
Yu, Genrong
Zammit, Joseph Paul
Zaslowsky, David Paul
Zimmerman, Jean
**Nyack**
Cember, M. Nathan
**Oneida**
Campanie, Samuel John
**Orangeburg**
Seaman, Robert E., III
**Pleasantville**
Soden, Paul Anthony
**Poughkeepsie**
Brenner, Marshall Leib
Constantino, James Peter
**Purchase**
Sharpe, Robert Francis, Jr.
**Rego Park**
Feijoo, John
**Rochester**
Galbraith, Robert Lyell, Jr.
Griffin, Shawn Michael
Mayka, Stephen Paul
Micca, Louis Joseph
Rasmussen, David L.
**Schenectady**
Sciocchetti, Paul Vincent
**Syracuse**
Ackerman, Kenneth Edward
Bogart, William Harry
Bruno, Richard Thomas
Dove, Jeffrey Austin
Frank, Jennifer Karen
Givas, Thomas Peter
Hubbard, Peter Lawrence
**Uniondale**
Paciullo, Maria Maestranzi
**Walden**
Gubits, David Barry
**White Plains**
Balaber-Strauss, Barbara
Rosenberg, Michael
Weingarden, Mitchell Ian

## NORTH CAROLINA

**Cary**
Taylor, Marvin Edward, Jr.
**Chapel Hill**
Hultquist, Steven John
**Charlotte**
Barbery, Paul Saunders
Chesson, Calvin White
Eve, Robert Michael, Jr.
Lynch, Craig Taylor
McDermott, Christopher Manning
Murchison, Bradley Duncan
Pansegrau, Phaedra Renée
Whelpley, David B., Jr.
**Greensboro**
Walker, Edward Garrett
**Hendersonville**
Hull, J(ames) Richard
**Raleigh**
Gaskins, Eura DuVal, Jr.
Harazin, William Dennis
Jernigan, John Lee
**Wilmington**
Jones, Lucian Cox
Kaufman, James Jay
**Winston Salem**
Coffey, Larry B(ruce)
Ventura, Bruce Anthony

## NORTH DAKOTA

**Bismarck**
Rosenberg, Max D.
**Grand Forks**
Morley, Patrick Robert

## OHIO

**Akron**
Lammert, Thomas Edward
Lombardi, Frederick McKean
**Beachwood**
Sobel, Jonathan F.
**Beavercreek**
Stadnicar, Joseph William
**Canton**
Brannen, John Howard
Davila, Edwin
Fitzpatrick, Lauren Elaine
Putman, Timothy Joseph
**Cincinnati**
Arango, Emilio
Ashdown, Charles Coster
Broderick, Dennis John
Case, Douglas Manning
Coffey, Thomas William
Hayden, William Taylor
Melville, Charles Hartley
Rubin, Robert Samuel
Strauss, William Victor
**Cleveland**
Arnoff, Fred Jay
Bacon, Brett Kermit
Baxter, Howard H.
Boukis, Kenneth
Groetzinger, Jon, Jr.
Kahn, Scott H.
Lawniczak, James Michael
Osborne, Frank R.
Pallam, John James
Zavarella, Gino Phillip
**Columbus**
Acker, Frederick Wayne
Buchenroth, Stephen Richard
Deal, John Charles
Fultz, Robert Edward
Joseph, John James
Kurtz, Charles Jewett, III
Robinson, Randal D.
Schaeffer, Matthew Thomas
Sidman, Robert John
Sully, Ira Bennett
**Dayton**
Chernesky, Richard John
Kinlin, Donald James
Krygowski, Walter John
Nicholson, Mark William
**Delaware**
Deavers, Maribeth
**Findlay**
Kostyo, John Francis
**Hamilton**
Meyers, Pamela Sue
**Miamisburg**
Battles, John Martin
Niemeyer, Jonathan David
**Piqua**
Davis, Dale Gordon
**Shaker Heights**
Cherchiglia, Dean Kenneth
**Toledo**
Gouttiere, John P.
**Warren**
Buzulencia, Michael Douglas
Hawley, William Lee
McGeough, Robert Saunders
**Wooster**
Haught, Sharon Kay

## OKLAHOMA

**Bartlesville**
Roff, Alan Lee
**Broken Arrow**
Frieze, H(arold) Delbert
**Norman**
Talley, Richard Bates
**Oklahoma City**
Barth, J. Edward
Britton, James Edward
Elder, James Carl
Kenney, Herbert King
Schwabe, George Blaine, III
**Tulsa**
Bowman, David Wesley
Chandler, Ronald Jay
Herrold, David Henry
Hilsabeck, Michael D.
Marlar, Donald Floyd
Tomlins, Neal Edward
**Walters**
Flanagan, Michael Charles

## OREGON

**Ashland**
Shaw, Barry N.
**Beaverton**
Robertson, Douglas Stuart
**Cannon Beach**
Hillestad, Charles Andrew
**Grants Pass**
Lansing, Mark Alexander
**Portland**
Bayless, Richard Vern
De Meo, Antonia M.
Eakin, Margaretta Morgan
Kennedy, Michael Dean
Norby, Mark Alan
Smith, Douglas Dean
Weiner, David P.

## PENNSYLVANIA

**Allentown**
Brown, Robert Wayne
**Berwyn**
Huggler, David H.
**Bristol**
Kashkashian, Arsen
**Bryn Mawr**
Hankin, Mitchell Robert
**Center Valley**
Smillie, Douglas James
**Franklin**
Greenfield, James Milton
**Harrisburg**
Sullivan, John Cornelius, Jr.
**Horsham**
Eisenberg, Steven Keith
Minihan, John Edward
**Jenkintown**
Ormsby, Charles William, Jr.
**Kennett Square**
Partnoy, Ronald Allen
**Lancaster**
Byler, William Bryan
Caminero, Rafael
**Lansdale**
Walper, Robert Andrew
**Media**
Humphrey, Carlos M.
Lipton, Robert Stephen
**Philadelphia**
Aaron, Kenneth Ellyot
Barnum, Jeanne Schubert
Baum, E. Harris
Bochetto, George Alexander
Coyne, Charles Cole
Cross, Milton H.
Denmark, William Adam
Dennis, Andre L.
Finkelstein, Joseph Simon
Ginsberg, David M.
Lawson, William Thomas, III
Liu, Diana Chua
Ominsky, Andrew Michael
Powell, Charles Law
Rainone, Michael Carmine
Schorling, William Harrison
Shapiro, Mathieu Jode
Tractenberg, Craig R.
Wright, Minturn Tatum, III
Wu, William
**Pittsburgh**
Arnold, Roy William
Brown, David Ronald
Crawford, Karen Shichman
Fiore, Kevin John
Grego, Samuel Robert
Hartman, Ronald G.
Kalil, David Thomas
Kelleher, William Eugene, Jr.
Lee, Victoria
Lucas, Robert Mark
McConomy, James Herbert
McKenna, J. Frank, III
Munsch, Richard John
Murdoch, David Armor
Tungate, David E.
Vater, Charles J.
von Waldow, Arnd N.
**Reading**
DiSibio, Carol Lynn Kridler
**Richboro**
Van Blunk, Henry Edward
**Warren**
Ristau, Mark Moody
**Washington**
Posner, David S.
**Wayne**
Spiess, F. Harry, Jr.
**West Chester**
Osborn, John Edward
**Wilkes Barre**
Roth, Eugene
Ufberg, Murray
**Williamsport**
Holland, Fred Anthony
**York**
Perry, Ronald

### RHODE ISLAND

**Providence**
Berkelhammer, Robert Bruce
Furness, Peter John
Salvadore, Guido Richard
**Wakefield**
Rothschild, Donald Phillip
**West Warwick**
Nota, Kenneth Joseph
**Westerly**
Nardone, William Andrew
**Woonsocket**
Moffatt, Thomas Swift

### SOUTH CAROLINA

**Blythewood**
Edwards, Van Everette, III
**Charleston**
Webb, Richard Craig
**Columbia**
Caulk, Glen Paul
Currin, Robert Graves, Jr.
**Kingstree**
Jenkinson, William Eldridge, III
**Mount Pleasant**
Laddaga, Lawrence Alexander

### TENNESSEE

**Brentwood**
Provine, John C.
**Chattanooga**
North, Harold Lebron, Jr.
Simonds, Timothy Ray
**Collierville**
Rogers, Gordon Keith, Jr.
**Kingsport**
Flanary, James Lee
**Memphis**
Fonville, Harold Wayne, II
Matthews, Paul Aaron
Peppel, Howard Rex
Spore, Richard Roland, III
Waddell, Phillip Dean
**Nashville**
Harris, Alvin Louis
Oldfield, Russell Miller
**Parsons**
Petrey, R. Claybourne, Jr.

### TEXAS

**Austin**
Bauer, Sydney Meade
Borden, Diana Kimball
Hernandez, Mack Ray
Owen, Jack Edward, Jr.
**Beaumont**
Johnson, Leanne
**Brownfield**
Moore, Bradford L.
**Brownsville**
Fleming, Tommy Wayne
**Bryan**
Strong, Stephen Andrew
**Corpus Christi**
Anthony, James Lloyd
Dohse, Roberta Shellum
Locke, William Henry
**Dallas**
Broussard, Peter O.
Buchanan, Robert Graham, Jr.
Burke, William Temple, Jr.
Campbell, David Lee
Clark, Robert Murel, Jr.
England, Austin Hinds
Freedman, Randall Lee
Helfand, Marcy Caren
Hunter, Robert Frederick
Joseph, Marc Ward
Marquardt, Robert Richard
Palter, John Theodore
Portman, Glenn Arthur
Portman, Susan Newell
Sears, Ruth Ann
Thau, William Albert, Jr.
True, Roy Joe
Zable, Norman Arnold
Zips, Craig Danny
**El Paso**
Ingram, Temple Byrn, Jr.
Lipson, Myer Jack
**Fort Worth**
Gwinn, D. Lee
Langenheim, Roger Allen
Moses, Shayne Daniel
Rice, Bradley Harold
Sartain, James Edward
**Garland**
Irby, Holt
**Henderson**
Adkison, Ron
**Houston**
Benesh, William Stephen
Bily, Kirkland Jarrard
Block, Nelson R(ichard)
Bradie, Peter Richard
Bridges, David Manning
Brinsmade, Lyon Louis
Carmody, James Albert
Chandler, George Francis, III
Clark, John A., Jr.
Cogan, John P.
Collins, Susan E.
Crews, Glenna England
Ewen, Pamela Binnings
Farnsworth, T. Brooke
Fisher, Donald Elton, Jr.
Harris, Warren Wayne
Heinrich, Timothy John
Kurz, Thomas Patrick
McDaniel, Jarrel Dave
Melamed, Richard
Montgomery, Kendall Charles
O'Donnell, Lawrence, III
Orton, John Stewart
Pappas, Daniel C.
Pruitt, Robert Randall
Ragazzo, Corina-Maria
Stuart, Walter Bynum, IV
Sutter, J. Douglas
Turek, Douglas D.
Williams, Percy Don
Wojciechowski, Marc James
**Killeen**
Kleff, Pierre Augustine, Jr.
**Mcallen**
Dyer, J.W.
**Midland**
Martin, C. D.
**New Braunfels**
Nolte, Melvin, Jr.
**Rockwall**
Holt, Charles William, Jr.
**San Antonio**
Bailey, Maryann George
Becker, Douglas Wesley
Fisher, Eric A.
Montgomery, James Edward, Jr.
Munsinger, Harry L.
Trotter, Richard Clayton
West, David Blair
**Spring**
Hagerman, John David
Loomis, Wendell Sylvester
**Wichita Falls**
Batson, David Warren

### UTAH

**Logan**
Honaker, Jimmie Joe
**Pleasant Grove**
Merritt, Laramie Dee
**Salt Lake City**
Barker, Ronald C.
Beckstead, John Alexander
Henriksen, C. Richard, Jr.
Hunt, George Andrew
Jones, Ken Paul
Jones, Michael Frank
Lochhead, Robert Bruce
Ockey, Ronald J.
Reeder, F. Robert
Rogers, Jon H.
**Sandy**
Western, Marion Wayne

### VERMONT

**Brattleboro**
Dunn, David Norman
**Burlington**
Baker, Robert W., Jr.
Cole, Leigh Polk
Judge, Walter E.
Rushford, Robert Howard
**Randolph Center**
Casson, Richard Frederick
**Rutland**
Vreeland, Neal C.
**Saint Albans**
Bugbee, Jesse D.
**Woodstock**
Dagger, William Carson

### VIRGINIA

**Alexandria**
Toothman, John William
**Annandale**
Yaffe, David Philip
**Arlington**
Kauffman, Thomas Richard
Walker, Woodrow Wilson
**Bristol**
Arrington, James Edgar, Jr.
**Charlottesville**
McKay, John Douglas
Robinette, Christopher John
**Chesapeake**
Tinkham, James Jeffrey
**Fairfax**
Downey, Richard Lawrence
Sanderson, Douglas Jay
**Falls Church**
Jennings, Thomas Parks
Nunes, Morris A.
**Fredericksburg**
Sheffield, Walter Jervis
**Glen Allen**
Ware, Henry Neill, Jr.
**Mc Lean**
Friedlander, Jerome Peyser, II
Goolrick, Robert Mason
Toole, John Harper
**Newport News**
Meade, Steven A.
**Norfolk**
Devine, William Franklin
Parker, Richard Wilson
Reeves, Ross Campbell
Waldo, Joseph Thomas
**Reston**
Spath, Gregg Anthony
**Richmond**
Angelidis, Stephen Alexander
Bing, Richard McPhail
Pollard, Henry Robinson, IV
**Roanoke**
Bromm, Frederick Whittemore
Bullington, David Bingham
Douthat, James Fielding

### WASHINGTON

**Bellevue**
Gulick, Peter VanDyke
**Bellingham**
Buri, Philip James
Packer, Mark Barry
**Issaquah**
Benoliel, Joel
**Port Angeles**
Gay, Carl Lloyd
**Redmond**
Merrill, Michael Gordon
Scowcroft, Jerome Chilwell
**Seattle**
Abelite, Jahnis John
Cullen, Jack Joseph
Cutler, Philip Edgerton
Diamond, Josef
Ferrer, Rafael Douglas Paul
Franke, Patrick Joseph
Gibbons, Steven Van
Graham, Stephen Michael
Guedel, William Gregory
Guy, Andrew A.
Hamilton, Henry Kerr
Krohn, Gary John
Mucklestone, Peter John
Pettigrew, Edward W.
Sandman, Irvin W(illis)
Shulkin, Jerome
Steinberg, Jack
Tune, James Fulcher
**Spokane**
Cerutti, Patrick Bernard
Esposito, Joseph Anthony
**Tacoma**
Beale, Robert Lyndon
Seinfeld, Lester
**Yakima**
Larson, Paul Martin

### WEST VIRGINIA

**Charleston**
Brown, James Knight
Cannon-Ryan, Susan Kaye
**Martinsburg**
Martin, Clarence Eugene, III
**Parkersburg**
Full, Robert Witmer

### WISCONSIN

**Beloit**
Blakely, Robert George
**Chippewa Falls**
Hunt, Heather M.
**Kohler**
Sheedy, Kathleen Ann
**Madison**
Boucher, Joseph W(illiam)
Croake, Paul Allen
Peterson, H. Dale
Walsh, David Graves
**Milwaukee**
Adashek, James Lewis
Bohren, Michael Oscar
Hatch, Michael Ward
Levine, Herbert
Martin, Quinn William
Rintelman, Donald Brian
Roge, Bret Alan
**Neenah**
Birtch, Grant Eacrett
**Sun Prairie**
Eustice, Francis Joseph
**Viroqua**
Jenkins, David Lynn
**Wausau**
Haarmann, Bruce Donald
Wolf, Kevin Earl

### WYOMING

**Riverton**
Girard, Nettabell

### TERRITORIES OF THE UNITED STATES

### PUERTO RICO

**San Juan**
Rodriguez-Diaz, Juan E.

### MEXICO

**Tijuana**
Berger, Jaime Benjamin

### CHINA

**Hong Kong**
Allen, Richard Marlow

### ENGLAND

**London**
Harrell, Michael P.

### FRANCE

**Lyon**
Dahling, Gerald Vernon
**Paris**
Rawlings, Boynton Mott

### JAPAN

**Tokyo**
Hunter, Larry Dean

### SAUDI ARABIA

**Riyadh**
Taylor, Frederick William, Jr. (Fritz Taylor)

### ZIMBABWE

**Harare**
Wood Kahari, Brenda Marie

### ADDRESS UNPUBLISHED

Berry, Robert Worth
Bloom, Charles Joseph
Brodhead, David Crawmer
Cadigan, Richard Foster
Canoff, Karen Huston
Carmody, Richard Patrick
Chong-Spiegel, Ginger Geroma
Choukas-Bradley, James Richard
Clabaugh, Elmer Eugene, Jr.
Coletti, Julie A.
Contino, Richard Martin
Cornish, Jeannette Carter
Dakin, Karl Jonathan
Durgom-Powers, Jane Ellyn
Edwards, William Thomas, Jr.
Feldman, Richard David
Finkelstein, Marcia Lyn
Funnell, Kevin Joseph
Gale, Connie R(uth)
Gewertz, Martin Anson
Gora, Daniel Martin
Hagerman, Michael Charles
Holden, Mary Gayle Reynolds
Jamieson, Michael Lawrence
Jessop, Jeanette Wanless
Jolley, R. Gardner
Kahn, Laurence Michael
Kingston, Andrew Brownell
Kordons, Uldis
Krivoshia, Eli, Jr.
Landy, Lisa Anne
Lerner, Harry
Levine, Solomon L.
Marker, Marc Linthacum
Mewhinney, Len Everette
Nadelson, Eileen Nora
O'Donnell, Michael R.
Oliver, Samuel William, Jr.
Painton, Russell Elliott
Pratt, Robert Windsor
Pucillo, Anthony Ernest
Reath, George, Jr.
Rodenburg, Clifton Glenn
Samuels, Janet Lee
Schultz, Dennis Bernard
Seifert, Stephen Wayne
Stevens, Rhea Christina
Stone, Andrew Grover
Tattersall, Hargreaves Victor, III
Tobin, Paul Xavier
Voight, Elizabeth Anne
von Sauers, Joseph F.
Watson, John Michael
Weil, Peter Henry

## COMMUNICATIONS

### UNITED STATES

### ALABAMA

**Birmingham**
Akers, Ottie Clay

### ARIZONA

**Phoenix**
Bodney, David Jeremy
Henderson, James Forney
Silverman, Alan Henry
**Tucson**
Meehan, Michael Joseph

### ARKANSAS

**Little Rock**
Riordan, Deborah Truby

### CALIFORNIA

**Los Angeles**
Kenoff, Jay Stewart
**Sacramento**
Foster, Douglas Taylor
**San Diego**
Eger, John Mitchell
Jackson, Roni D.
**San Francisco**
Bertram, Phyllis Ann
Thompson, Robert Charles
Tobin, James Michael

### COLORADO

**Boulder**
Nichols, Robert William
**Denver**
Adkins, Roy Allen
Dunn, Randy Edwin
Finesilver, Jay Mark
Quiat, Marshall
**Englewood**
DeMuth, Laurence Wheeler, Jr.
Steele, Elizabeth Meyer
**Littleton**
Benkert, Joseph Philip, Jr.

### CONNECTICUT

**Darien**
Beach, Stephen Holbrook
**Hartford**
Knickerbocker, Robert Platt, Jr.
**Stamford**
Apfelbaum, Marc

### DISTRICT OF COLUMBIA

**Washington**
Altschul, Michael F.
Beisner, John Herbert
Bercovici, Martin William
Besozzi, Paul Charles
Blake, Jonathan Dewey
Blumenfeld, Jeffrey
Borkowski, John Joseph
Brinkmann, Robert Joseph
Carome, Patrick Joseph
Christensen, Karen Kay
Coursen, Christopher Dennison
Cox, Kenneth Allen
Friedlander, Lisa L.
Haines, Terry L.
Hammerman, Edward Scott
Harris, Scott Blake
Heckman, Jerome Harold
Hirrel, Michael John
Hobson, James Richmond
Holtz, Edgar Wolfe
Kiddoo, Jean Lynn
Knauer, Leon Thomas
Marks, Richard Daniel
McKey, Arthur Duncan
McReynolds, Mary Armilda
Michaels, Gary David
Rabinovitz, Joel A.
Ramey, Carl Robert
Ray, Tamber
Russo, Roy R.
Salsbury, Michael
Schmidt, Richard Marten, Jr.
Shapiro, George Howard
Silverman, David Malanos
Spector, Phillip Louis
Tannenwald, Peter
Vaughn-Carrington, Debra Miller
Wiley, Richard Emerson
Woodworth, Ramsey Lloyd

### FLORIDA

**Jacksonville**
Dornan, Kevin William
**Palm Bay**
Howard, Marilyn Hoey

### GEORGIA

**Atlanta**
Keck, Richard Paul
McCloud, Robert Olmsted, Jr.
Meyerson, Amy Lin
Muller, William Manning

### ILLINOIS

**Chicago**
Chudzinski, Mark Adam
Cortes, William Patrick
LeBaron, Charles Frederick, Jr.
Peterson, Bradley Laurits
Sennet, Charles Joseph
Ward, Michael W.
**Springfield**
Thornton, Joseph Philip

### INDIANA

**Indianapolis**
Barrett, David Olan

### IOWA

**Des Moines**
Fisher, Thomas George

### KANSAS

**Westwood**
Devlin, James Richard

### KENTUCKY

**Louisville**
Cowan, Frederic Joseph

### LOUISIANA

**Metairie**
Hardy, Ashton Richard
**Shreveport**
Bryant, J(ames) Bruce

### MAINE

**Augusta**
Donahue, Joseph Gerald

### MARYLAND

**Bethesda**
Goldstein, James Bruce
**Towson**
Conwell, John Fredrick

### MASSACHUSETTS

**Boston**
Tarbet, David W.
**Brookline**
Burnstein, Daniel
**Framingham**
Heng, Gerald C. W.

### MICHIGAN

**Kalamazoo**
Crocker, Patrick David
**Lansing**
Marvin, David Edward Shreve
**Troy**
Wells, Steven W.

### MINNESOTA

**Duluth**
Burns, Richard Ramsey
**Minneapolis**
Reilly, George
Tanick, Marshall Howard
**Saint Louis Park**
Rothenberg, Elliot Calvin

### MISSISSIPPI

**Jackson**
Martinez, Eduardo Vidal

### MISSOURI

**Chesterfield**
Denneen, John Paul
**Kansas City**
Miller, Richard William
**Saint Louis**
Schaberg, John Irvin

### NEVADA

**Las Vegas**
Fink, Gordon Ian

### NEW JERSEY

**Florham Park**
Chase, Eric Lewis
**Franklin Lakes**
Lagdameo-Hogan, Maria-Elena
**Liberty Corner**
Spierer, Howard
**Livingston**
Grace, Thomas Edward
**Roseland**
Vaiden, Kristi L.
**Saddle River**
Bastedo, Wayne Webster
**Warren**
Quinn, Thomas Gerard

### NEW YORK

**East Syracuse**
Atkins, Theresa

**New York**
Bender, John Charles
Briskman, Louis Jacob
Fry, Morton Harrison, II
Jacqueney, Stephanie A(lice)
Joffe, Robert David
Mathus, David L.
McCarthy, Robert Emmett
Savell, Polly Carolyn
Sutter, Laurence Brener
Telsey, Suzanne Lisa
Thackeray, Jonathan E.
Webb, Morrison DeSoto
Welt, Philip Stanley

### OKLAHOMA

**Oklahoma City**
Allen, Robert Dee

### OREGON

**Beaverton**
Fulsher, Allan Arthur
**Portland**
Hinkle, Charles Frederick

### PENNSYLVANIA

**Blue Bell**
Grayson, Zachary Louis
**Clearfield**
Falvo, Mark Anthony
**Philadelphia**
Bogutz, Jerome Edwin
DeBunda, Salvatore Michael
Henry, Ragan Augustus
Solano, Carl Anthony
**Shavertown**
Ostroski, Raymond B.

### TENNESSEE

**Nashville**
Wayland, R. Eddie

### TEXAS

**Austin**
Drummond, Eric Hubert
Smith, Jeffrey Carlin
Stephen, John Erle
**Dallas**
Beard, Bruce E.
Elkind, Laura Peterson
Sears, Ruth Ann

### VIRGINIA

**Arlington**
Morris, Roy Leslie
**Charlottesville**
McKay, John Douglas
**Fairfax**
Baird, Charles Bruce
**Mc Lean**
Byrnes, William Joseph
Shepard, Julian Leigh
**Norfolk**
Ryan, Louis Farthing
**Roanoke**
Barnhill, David Stan
Glenn, Robert Eastwood
**Vienna**
Barger, Kathleen Carson

### WASHINGTON

**Bellevue**
Waldbaum, Alan G.
**Seattle**
Gustafson, Alice Fairleigh

### WISCONSIN

**Madison**
Tomaselli, Anthony Allen
Walsh, David Graves

### CANADA

### ONTARIO

**Brampton**
Allen, Clive Victor

### ADDRESS UNPUBLISHED

Katz, Roberta R.
Killeen, Michael John
Lyons, Patrice Ann
Norman, Albert George, Jr.
Polsky, Howard David
Price, Steven
Pullen, Richard Owen
Wilson, Michael B(ruce)

## COMPUTER

### UNITED STATES

### ARIZONA

**Phoenix**
Bivens, Donald Wayne
Harris, Ray Kendall
**Tempe**
Vanderpoel, James Robert
**Tucson**
Conn, Deanna

### ARKANSAS

**Fayetteville**
Wall, John David

### CALIFORNIA

**Cupertino**
Naylor, Brian Thomas
Simon, Nancy Ruth
**Los Angeles**
Chan, Thomas Tak-Wah
Strong, George Gordon, Jr.
**Menlo Park**
Coats, William Sloan, III
**Mountain View**
Koehler, Fritz K.
**Orinda**
Perez, Richard Lee
**Palo Alto**
Bridges, Andrew Phillip
Daunt, Jacqueline Ann
Laurie, Ronald Sheldon
Nycum, Susan Hubbell
Wilson, Thomas Russell
**Pasadena**
Brenner, Anita Susan
**Redwood City**
Cole, George Stuart
**San Francisco**
Green, Philip R.
Richardson, Daniel Ralph
**San Jose**
Blasgen, Sharon Walther
Goldstein, Robin
**Santa Clara**
Kaner, Cem
**Sunnyvale**
Wyatt, Thomas Csaba
**Tustin**
Sun, Raymond Chi-Chung

### COLORADO

**Boulder**
Cypser, Darlene Ann
**Broomfield**
Hogle, Sean Sherwood
**Denver**
Anderson, Alan Wendell
Dorr, Robert Charles
**Fort Collins**
Fromm, Jeffery Bernard

### CONNECTICUT

**Darien**
Beach, Stephen Holbrook
**Stamford**
Gold, Steven Michael

### DISTRICT OF COLUMBIA

**Washington**
Bancroft, Judith Gail
Greif, Joseph
Haines, Terry L.
Hoffmann, Martin Richard
Jacobs, Harvey S.
Johnson, David Reynold
Lazar, Dale Steven
Marks, Richard Daniel
Marvin, Charles Rodney, Jr.
McKey, Arthur Duncan
Peters, Frederick Whitten
Rosenthal, Ilene Goldstein

### FLORIDA

**Fort Lauderdale**
Austin, Scott Raymond
**Jacksonville**
Miller, Carla Dorothy
**Melbourne**
Ballantyne, Richard Lee
**Orlando**
Losey, Ralph Colby
**Tallahassee**
Miller, Morris Henry

### GEORGIA

**Atlanta**
Arkin, Robert David
Baker, Anita Diane
Harrison, Bryan Guy
Hassett, Robert William
Meyerson, Amy Lin
Quittmeyer, Peter Charles
Somers, Fred Leonard, Jr.

### IDAHO

**Boise**
Baird, Denise Colleen

### ILLINOIS

**Chicago**
Lorenzen, Donald Robert
Lyerla, Bradford Peter
Maher, David Willard
McCrohon, Craig
McGuigan, Philip Palmer
Parkhurst, Beverly Susler
Peterson, Bradley Laurits
Potter, Richard Clifford
Smedinghoff, Thomas J.
Wanke, Ronald Lee
**Palatine**
Roti, Thomas David
**Skokie**
Sitrick, David Howard
**Urbana**
Fitz-Gerald, Roger Miller

### INDIANA

**Indianapolis**
Dutton, Stephen James
Kashani, Hamid Reza
Koeller, Robert Marion

### KANSAS

**Overland Park**
Cole, Roland Jay

### KENTUCKY

**Lexington**
McCoy, D. Chad

### LOUISIANA

**Metairie**
Kastl, Dian Evans
**New Orleans**
Harris, Thorne D., III

### MAINE

**Portland**
Stauffer, Eric P.

### MARYLAND

**Baltimore**
Ritter, Jeffrey Blake
**Bethesda**
Weinberger, Alan David
**Rockville**
Dennis, Benjamin Franklin, III
Patrick, Philip Howard

### MASSACHUSETTS

**Billerica**
Pellegrin, Gilles George
**Boston**
Blumenreich, Gene Arnold
Chow, Stephen Y(ee)
Fischer, Mark Alan
Honig, Stephen Michael
Kyros, Konstantine William
Lev, Avi Meir
Livingston, Mary Counihan
Mullare, T(homas) Kenwood, Jr.
Reece, Laurence Hobson, III
Sopel, George C.
Storer, Thomas Perry
**Brookline**
Burnstein, Daniel
**Pembroke**
Schacter, Stacey Jay
**Springfield**
Maidman, Stephen Paul
**Waltham**
Barnes-Brown, Peter Newton
Zaharoff, Howard George
**Wellesley**
Marx, Peter A.
**Westborough**
Chapin, Barry W.

### MICHIGAN

**Farmington**
Legg, Michael William

### MINNESOTA

**Minneapolis**
McDonald, Daniel William
McNeil, Mark Sanford

### MISSOURI

**Kansas City**
Marquette, I. Edward
**Saint Louis**
Chervitz, David Howard

### NEVADA

**Reno**
Ryan, Robert Collins

### NEW HAMPSHIRE

**Manchester**
Coolidge, Daniel Scott

### NEW JERSEY

**Liberty Corner**
Edwards, Robert Nelson
**Ridgewood**
Harris, Micalyn Shafer
**Roseland**
Vaiden, Kristi L.
**Roselle Park**
Tancs, Linda Ann
**Somerville**
Miller, Charles William, III
**Springfield**
Katz, Jeffrey Harvey
**Westfield**
Hrycak, Michael Paul
**Woodbridge**
Harris, Brett Rosenberg
Schaff, Michael Frederick
**Woodbury**
Adler, Lewis Gerard

### NEW YORK

**Albany**
Ganz, Robert E.
**Albion**
Lyman, Nathan Marquis
**Croton On Hudson**
Hoffman, Paul Shafer
**Long Island City**
Wanderman, Susan Mae
**Mineola**
Ryan, Marianne Elizabeth
**New York**
Bandon, William Edward, III
Bendes, Barry Jay
Black, Louis Engleman
Colamarino, Katrin Belenky
Connolly, Kevin Jude
De Leon, Albert Vernon
Einhorn, David Allen
Epstein, Michael Alan
Halket, Thomas D(aniel)
Hooker, Wade Stuart, Jr.
Jinnett, Robert Jefferson
Jun, Meeka
Kinney, Stephen Hoyt, Jr.
Lefkowitz, Howard N.
Macioce, Frank Michael
Mathus, David L.
Matus, Wayne Charles
Prochnow, Thomas Herbert
Ross, Otho Bescent
Samson, Martin Harris
Spiegel, Jerrold Bruce
Taylor, Job, III
Weisburd, Steven I.
Woods, Christopher John
Yang, Phillip Seungpil
Zammit, Joseph Paul
**Poughkeepsie**
Taphorn, Joseph Bernard
**Rochester**
Fiandach, Edward Louis
**Rome**
Burstyn, Harold Lewis
**Sleepy Hollow**
Andrew, Leonard DeLessio
**Uniondale**
Gracin, Hank

### NORTH CAROLINA

**Charlotte**
Abelman, Henry Moss
Linker, Raymond Otho, Jr.

### OHIO

**Cleveland**
Stovsky, Michael David
Zavarella, Gino Phillip
**Dayton**
Nicholson, Mark William
**Dublin**
Emmert, Steven Michael
**Miamisburg**
Battles, John Martin
**North Canton**
Dettinger, Warren Walter

### OKLAHOMA

**Seminole**
Choate, John

### OREGON

**Portland**
Swider, Robert Arthur

### PENNSYLVANIA

**Allentown**
Albright, Mark Preston
**Malvern**
Carr, Christopher C.
**Media**
Lipton, Robert Stephen
**Newtown**
Simkanich, John Joseph
**Philadelphia**
Culhane, John Langdon
King, David Roy
**Pittsburgh**
Baicker-McKee, Steven F.
Colen, Frederick Haas
Salpietro, Frank Gugliotta
Silverman, Arnold Barry
Tungate, David E.

### RHODE ISLAND

**Providence**
Totten, R. Bart

### SOUTH CAROLINA

**Charleston**
Ray, Paul DuBose
**Columbia**
Morrison, Stephen George

### TEXAS

**Austin**
Borden, Diana Kimball
Laughead, James Marshall
Livingston, Ann Chambliss
Miller, John Eddie
Zager, Steven Mark
**Beaumont**
Cavaliere, Frank Joseph
**Dallas**
Farquhar, Robert Michael
Hammond, Herbert J.
**Houston**
Hyland, Stephen James
Winer, Stephen I.
**Plano**
Hand, Randall Eugene
**San Antonio**
Aoki, Zachary Burke

### UTAH

**Salt Lake City**
Ockey, Ronald J.
Wagner, Mark Alan

### VERMONT

**Burlington**
Baker, Robert W., Jr.

### VIRGINIA

**Alexandria**
Wieder, Bruce Terrill
**Arlington**
Dennison, Donald Lee
Doyle, Gerard Francis
**Chesapeake**
North, Kenneth E(arl)
**Fairfax**
Baird, Charles Bruce
Gordon, Gail Kimberly
**Falls Church**
Greigg, Ronald Edwin
Young, John Hardin
**Mc Lean**
Bardack, Paul Roitman

### WASHINGTON

**Bellevue**
Gadre, Aniruddha Rudy
Oratz, Lisa T.
**Seattle**
Goto, Bruce T.
Kelly, Kevin Francis
Lavery, Liam Burgess
Prentke, Richard Ottesen
Reardon, Mark William

### WISCONSIN

**Milwaukee**
Marcus, Richard Steven

### CANADA

### ONTARIO

**Toronto**
Chester, Robert Simon George

### ADDRESS UNPUBLISHED

Fernandez, Dennis Sunga
Fischer, David Jon
Hagerman, Michael Charles
Krone, Paula H.
Lyons, Patrice Ann
Mahallati, Narges Nancy
McCobb, John Bradford, Jr.
Pear, Charles E., Jr.
Peters, William James
Stone, Andrew Grover
Tokars, Fredric William
Wilson, Michael B(ruce)

## CONDEMNATION

### UNITED STATES

### ALASKA

**Anchorage**
Weinig, Richard Arthur

### CALIFORNIA

**Irvine**
Dannemeyer, Bruce William
**La Jolla**
Eischen, James John, Jr.
**Los Angeles**
Brogan, Kevin Herbert
Salvaty, Benjamin Benedict
**Oakland**
Hausrath, Les A.
**Sacramento**
Mooney, Donald B.
**San Diego**
Detisch, Donald W.
Endeman, Ronald Lee
**San Jose**
Boccardo, James Frederick
**Santa Monica**
Kanner, Gideon
**Santa Rosa**
Clement, Clayton Emerson
**Walnut Creek**
Skaggs, Sanford Merle

### COLORADO

**Colorado Springs**
Sheffield, Alden Daniel, Jr.
**Denver**
Bryans, Richard W.
Rufien, Paul Charles

### CONNECTICUT

**Willimantic**
Lombardo, Michael John

### FLORIDA

**Boca Raton**
Golis, Paul Robert
Siemon, Charles L.
**Brandon**
Curry, Clifton Conrad, Jr.
**Jacksonville**
Allen, William Lee
**Miami**
Beasley, Joseph Wayne
**Orlando**
Harris, Gordon H.
Spoonhour, James Michael
**Saint Petersburg**
Battaglia, Brian Peter
Holland, Troy Whitzhurst
**Sarasota**
Blucher, Paul Arthur
Shults, Thomas Daniel
**Tallahassee**
Varn, Wilfred Claude
**Tampa**
Buell, Mark Paul
**West Palm Beach**
Yeager, Thomas Joseph

### GEORGIA

**Atlanta**
Janney, Donald Wayne
**Smyrna**
Seigler, Michael Edward

### HAWAII

**Honolulu**
Bunn, Robert Burgess

### ILLINOIS

**Chicago**
Redmond, Richard Anthony
**Marion**
Powless, Kenneth Barnett

### INDIANA

**Indianapolis**
Daniel, Melvin Randolph
**Merrillville**
Miller, Richard Allen

### KANSAS

**Topeka**
Hamilton, John Richard

KENTUCKY
**Louisville**
Cohen, Edwin Louis
Schecter, Benjamin Seth

LOUISIANA
**Alexandria**
Pharis, James Andrew, Jr.
**Gretna**
Stumpf, Harry Charles
**Lafayette**
Davidson, James Joseph, III

MARYLAND
**Bel Air**
Crocker, Michael Pue

MASSACHUSETTS
**Boston**
Fahy, Joseph Thomas
Levine, Julius Byron
Saturley, Ellen McLaughlin
**Hyannis**
McLaughlin, Edward Francis, Jr.
**Worcester**
Bassett, Edward Caldwell, Jr.
Maciolek, John Richard

MICHIGAN
**Brighton**
Nielsen, Neal D.
**Detroit**
Ankers, Norman C.
Richardson, Ralph Herman
**Muskegon**
Briggs, John Mancel, III
**Okemos**
Platsis, George James
**Saginaw**
Martin, Walter
**Saint Joseph**
Gleiss, Henry Weston
**Southfield**
Cohen, H. Adam

MINNESOTA
**Minneapolis**
Barnard, Allen Donald
Dietzen, Christopher J.
**Saint Paul**
Spencer, David James

MISSOURI
**Kansas City**
Jackson, James B.
Smithson, Lowell Lee
Tyler, John E., III
**Saint Louis**
Gilroy, Tracy Anne Hunsaker
Riggio, Nicholas Jospeh, Sr.

NEBRASKA
**Lincoln**
Blake, William George

NEW HAMPSHIRE
**Concord**
Morris, James Edgar

NEW JERSEY
**Hoboken**
Curley, John Joseph
**Moorestown**
Hardt, Frederick William
**Morristown**
Gladstone, Robert Albert
**Teaneck**
Rosenblum, Edward G.
**Toms River**
Leone, Stephan Robert

NEW YORK
**Garden City**
Wimpfheimer, Steven
**New York**
Rikon, Michael
**Poughkeepsie**
Wallace, Herbert Norman
**Syracuse**
Young, Douglas Howard

NORTH CAROLINA
**Durham**
King, William Oliver
**Graham**
Walker, Daniel Joshua, Jr.
**Raleigh**
Davis, Thomas Hill, Jr.

OHIO
**Cleveland**
Satola, James William
**Columbus**
Kurtz, Charles Jewett, III

OKLAHOMA
**Oklahoma City**
Allen, Robert Dee
Rinehart, William James
**Tulsa**
McGonigle, Richard Thomas

OREGON
**Portland**
Maloney, Robert E., Jr.

SOUTH CAROLINA
**Columbia**
Babcock, Keith Moss

TEXAS
**Corsicana**
Sodd, Glenn
**Dallas**
Purnell, Charles Giles
Staley, Joseph Hardin, Jr.
**San Antonio**
Hartnett, Dan Dennis
Wallis, Ben Alton, Jr.

VIRGINIA
**Leesburg**
Minchew, John Randall
**Richmond**
Ellis, Andrew Jackson, Jr.

WEST VIRGINIA
**Charleston**
Douglas, Robert Edward
Kauffelt, James David

WISCONSIN
**Wausau**
Weber, Richard J.

ADDRESS UNPUBLISHED
Barry, David F.
Bell, Asa Lee, Jr.
Davidson, Barry Rodney
McCormick, Homer L., Jr.

## CONSTITUTIONAL

UNITED STATES

ALABAMA
**Birmingham**
Hopkins, Harry L.

ARIZONA
**Phoenix**
Henderson, James Forney

CALIFORNIA
**Berkeley**
Ogg, Wilson Reid
**Los Angeles**
Bringardner, John Michael
**Mission Viejo**
Leathers, Stephen Kelly
**Newport Beach**
Abendroth, Douglas William
Mandel, Maurice, II
**Palm Desert**
Spirtos, Nicholas George
**Rancho Mirage**
Reuben, Don Harold
**San Francisco**
Hill, Richard Paul
Hilton, Stanley Goumas
**Santa Cruz**
Brennan, Enda Thomas
**Santa Monica**
Pizzulli, Francis Cosmo Joseph

COLORADO
**Colorado Springs**
McCready, Guy Michael
**Denver**
Nier, Harry K.
Norton, Gale Ann

DISTRICT OF COLUMBIA
**Washington**
Baine, Kevin T.
Beyer, Wayne Cartwright
Brame, Joseph Robert, III
Burchfield, Bobby Roy
Cihon, Christopher Michael
Clark, Jeffrey Bossert
Dowdey, Landon Gerald
Mathias, Charles McCurdy
Miller, Nory
Odom, Thomas H.
Ramey, Carl Robert
Shapiro, George Howard
Stephens, Andrew Russell
Waxman, Seth Paul
Wilson, Charles Haven

FLORIDA
**Boca Raton**
Kassner, Herbert Seymore
**Daytona Beach**
Watts, C. Allen
**Deerfield Beach**
Levitan, David M(aurice)
**Fort Lauderdale**
Benjamin, James Scott
**Gainesville**
Kaimowitz, Gabe Hillel
**Hollywood**
Tannen, Ricki Lewis
**Miami**
Fitzgerald, Joseph Michael, Jr.
Horn, Mark
Rashkind, Paul Michael
**Orlando**
Mason, Steven Gerald
Nelson, Frederick Herbert
**Palm Bay**
Tietig, Edward Chester
**Sarasota**
Blucher, Paul Arthur
**Tallahassee**
Collette, Charles T. (Chip Collette)
**Tampa**
MacKay, John William
Thomas, Gregg Darrow

GEORGIA
**Alpharetta**
Singer, Randy Darrell
**Atlanta**
Bird, Wendell Raleigh
Bramlett, Jeffrey Owen
Schroeder, Eric Peter
Tewes, R. Scott
**Tucker**
Wheeler, Edd Dudley

HAWAII
**Honolulu**
Yamano, John Y.

IDAHO
**Boise**
Kristensen, Debora Kathleen

ILLINOIS
**Chicago**
Flaxman, Kenneth N.
Giampietro, Wayne Bruce
Null, Michael Elliot
Wade, Edwin Lee
**Evanston**
DeWolfe, Ruthanne K. S.
**Joliet**
Lenard, George Dean
**Naperville**
Heap, Robert A.
**Oregon**
Cargerman, Alan William
**Wilmette**
Simon, Thelma Brook

INDIANA
**Indianapolis**
Korin, Offer
**Terre Haute**
Bopp, James, Jr.
Coleson, Richard Eugene
Newmeyer, Robert J.
Willard, Glenn Mark

IOWA
**Des Moines**
Fisher, Thomas George, Jr.

KANSAS
**Hutchinson**
Chalfant, William Young
**Wichita**
Ayres, Ted Dean

KENTUCKY
**Eddyville**
Story, James Eddleman
**Frankfort**
Bias, Dana G.
**Louisville**
Manly, Samuel

LOUISIANA
**Baton Rouge**
Anderson, Lawrence Robert, Jr.
Riddick, Winston Wade, Sr.
**Lafayette**
Willard, David Charles
**Lake Charles**
Cagney, Nanette Heath

MARYLAND
**Bethesda**
Goldstone, Mark Lewis
**Silver Spring**
McDermitt, Edward Vincent

MASSACHUSETTS
**Boston**
Looney, William Francis, Jr.
Nugent, Alfred Emanuel

MICHIGAN
**Ann Arbor**
McHugh, Richard Walker
Niehoff, Leonard Marvin
**Bloomfield Hills**
Cumbey, Constance Elizabeth
**Detroit**
Budaj, Steven T.
Furton, Joseph Rae, Jr.
Heenan, Cynthia
**Southfield**
Sullivan, Robert Emmet, Jr.
**Ypsilanti**
Shapiro, Douglas Bruce

MINNESOTA
**Crystal**
Reske, Steven David
**Saint Louis Park**
Rothenberg, Elliot Calvin

MISSISSIPPI
**Jackson**
Maron, David F.

MISSOURI
**Kansas City**
Bryant, Richard Todd

NEBRASKA
**Omaha**
Rock, Harold L.
Runge, Patrick Richard

NEVADA
**Las Vegas**
Larsen, Paul Edward

NEW HAMPSHIRE
**Plymouth**
Clark, R. Thomas

NEW JERSEY
**Warren**
Gargano, Francine Ann

NEW MEXICO
**Albuquerque**
Salvador, Vernon William

NEW YORK
**Albany**
Gray, William J.
Jehu, John Paul
**Brooklyn**
Lewis, Felice Flanery
**Campbell Hall**
Stone, Peter George
**New York**
Bamberger, Michael Albert
Conboy, Kenneth
Cooper, Sonja Jean Muller
Davidson, George Allan
Glekel, Jeffrey Ives
Kresky, Harry
Levy, Herbert Monte
Sherman, Jonathan Henry
Shientag, Florence Perlow
Sommers, George R.
**Rego Park**
Jain, Lalit K.
**White Plains**
Pickard, John Allan

OHIO
**Cleveland**
La Rue, Edward Rice
Perris, Terrence George
**Columbus**
Gellman, Susan Beth
Martin, Paige Arlene
McDermott, Kevin R.
**Toledo**
Iorio, Theodore
**Youngstown**
Melnick, Robert Russell

OKLAHOMA
**Edmond**
Lester, Andrew William
**Oklahoma City**
Angel, Steven Michael

OREGON
**Oregon City**
Hingson, John Henry, III
**Portland**
Berger, Leland Roger
Byrne, Gregory William
Hinkle, Charles Frederick

PENNSYLVANIA
**Forty Fort**
Cosgrove, Joseph Matthias
**Glenside**
Mermelstein, Jules Joshua
**New Cumberland**
Yakowicz, Vincent X
**Philadelphia**
Adams, Arlin Marvin
Dennis, Andre L.
Diamond, Paul Steven
Hamilton, Perrin C.
Shapiro, Mathieu Jode
**Pittsburgh**
Pushinsky, Jon

TENNESSEE
**Fayetteville**
Dickey, John Harwell
**Knoxville**
Fels, Charles Wentworth Baker
**Pigeon Forge**
Powell, Russell Alan

TEXAS
**Austin**
Bray, Austin Coleman, Jr.
Hamilton, Dagmar Strandberg
Weddington, Sarah Ragle
**Dallas**
Gibson, John Wheat
**Eldorado**
Kosub, James Albert
**Fort Worth**
Sharpe, James Shelby
**Galveston**
Vie, George William, III
**Wichita Falls**
Helton, Robert Moore

VERMONT
**Burlington**
McKearin, Robert R.
Volk, Paul S.
**Montpelier**
Putter, David Seth

VIRGINIA
**Alexandria**
Hirschkop, Philip Jay
**Annandale**
Dunkum, Betty Lee
**Fairfax**
Murray, Michael Patrick
**Fredericksburg**
Glessner, Thomas Allen
**Mc Lean**
Peet, Richard Clayton
Rhyne, Charles Sylvanus
Sparks, Robert Ronold, Jr.
**Richmond**
Freeman, George Clemon, Jr.
Ryland, Walter H.
**Roanoke**
Skolrood, Robert Kenneth
**Virginia Beach**
Thornton, Joel Hamilton

WASHINGTON
**Bellevue**
Lawyer, David James
**Edmonds**
Conom, Tom Peter
**Seattle**
Johnson, Bruce Edward Humble
Tucker, Kathryn Louise
**Tacoma**
Gersch, Charles Frant

WISCONSIN
**West Bend**
Fincke, Waring Roberts

GEORGIA
**Tbilisi**
Swann, Barbara

ADDRESS UNPUBLISHED
Albin, Barry G.
Boyd, Thomas Marshall
DeLaFuente, Charles
Deric, Arthur Joseph
Grutman, Jewel Humphrey
Howard, John Wayne
Markle, Robert
Morgan, James Evan
Ogden, David William
Ross, Catherine Jane
Rusnak, Susan E.
Shutt, Nekki
Siporin, Sheldon
Tietig, Lisa Kuhlman
Twardy, Stanley Albert, Jr.

## CONSTRUCTION

UNITED STATES

ALABAMA
**Birmingham**
Goodrich, Thomas Michael
**Eufaula**
Twitchell, E(rvin) Eugene
**Montgomery**
McFadden, Frank Hampton
Wood, James Jerry

ALASKA
**Anchorage**
Dickson, Robert Jay
Evans, Charles Graham
Kreger, Michael E.
Willard-Jones, Donna C.

ARIZONA
**Phoenix**
Beeghley, Steven Ray
Brecher, Allison Leigh
Richman, Stephen Edward
Ryan, D. Jay
Susman, Alan Howard
**Tucson**
Dickey, Harrison Gaslin, III

CALIFORNIA
**Bakersfield**
Stead, Calvin Rudi
**Berkeley**
Pyle, Walter K.
**Carlsbad**
Koehnke, Phillip Eugene
**Costa Mesa**
Long, Susan
**Fresno**
Renberg, Michael Loren
**Glendale**
MacDonald, Kirk Stewart
**Irvine**
Suojanen, Wayne William
**La Jolla**
Philp, P. Robert, Jr.
**Long Beach**
Behar, Jeffrey Steven
Walker, Timothy Lee
**Los Angeles**
Bayard, Michael John
Cathcart, Robert James
Craigie, Alex William
Drozin, Garth Matthew
Kamine, Bernard Samuel
Lawton, Eric
Lund, James Louis
Moloney, Stephen Michael
Pieper, Darold D.
Robison, William Robert
**Los Gatos**
Sweet, Jonathan Justin
**Marina Dl Rey**
Smolker, Gary Steven
**Monarch Beach**
Luttrell, William Harvey
**Newport Beach**
Dillion, Gregory Lee
Fleming, Dawn DeAnn
McGee, James Francis
Smithson, David Matthew
**Oakland**
Leslie, Robert Lorne
**Palo Alto**
Baum, Donald Hiram
**Redondo Beach**
Hachmeister, John H.

**CONSUMER CREDIT.** *See* **Commercial, consumer.**

**CONTRACTS.** *See* **Commercial, contracts.**

## CORPORATE, GENERAL

### UNITED STATES

#### ALABAMA

**Foley**
Leatherbury, Gregory Luce, Jr.
**Guntersville**
McLaughlin, Jeffrey Rex
**Huntsville**
Ludwig, Scott Edward
**Mobile**
Lott, Victor H., Jr.
Lyons, George Sage
Murchison, David Roderick
Quina, Marion Albert, Jr.
**Montgomery**
Gregory, William Stanley
Waters, Michael D.
Wood, James Jerry
**Northport**
Allen, Randy Lee
**Opelika**
Hand, Benny Charles, Jr.

## ALASKA

**Anchorage**
Fortier, Samuel John
Lekisch, Peter Allen
Mahoney, F. Steven
Stanley, James Troy
Willard-Jones, Donna C.

## ARIZONA

**Carefree**
Rooney, Michael James
**Chandler**
Markey, James Kevin
**Kingman**
Basinger, Richard Lee
**Oro Valley**
Robinson, Bernard Leo
**Phoenix**
Bauman, Frederick Carl
Bixby, David Michael
Case, David Leon
Chanen, Steven Robert
Chauncey, Tom Webster, II
Clarke, David Alan
Coppersmith, Sam
Curzon, Thomas Henry
Dunipace, Ian Douglas
Forshey, Timothy Allan
Hay, John Leonard
King, Jack A.
Le Clair, Douglas Marvin
Lieberman, Marc R(obert)
Madden, Paul Robert
Maledon, Michael Brien
Mangum, John K.
Marable, Sidney Thomas
Martori, Joseph Peter
Mousel, Craig Lawrence
Moya, Patrick Robert
Nivica, Gjon Nelson, Jr.
Olson, Kevin Lory
Perry, Lee Rowan
Pidgeon, Steven D.
Pietzsch, Michael Edward
Quayle, Marilyn Tucker
Rosen, Sidney Marvin
Schermer, Beth
Seamons, Quinton Frank
Thompson, Terence William
Tomback, Jay Loren
Williams, Quinn Patrick
**Scottsdale**
Berry, Charles Richard
Peshkin, Samuel David
**Tempe**
Evans, Lawrence Jack, Jr.
**Tucson**
Berlat, William Leonard
Glaser, Steven Jay
Hanshaw, A. Alan
Levitan, Roger Stanley
Stewart, Hugh W.
Stirton, Charles Paul
Tindall, Robert Emmett

## ARKANSAS

**Fayetteville**
Bumpass, Ronald Eugene
Pettus, E. Lamar
**Jonesboro**
Womack, Tom D.
**Little Rock**
Anderson, Philip Sidney
Campbell, George Emerson
Haley, John Harvey
Knight, David Arceneaux
Marshall, William Taylor
Nelson, Edward Sheffield
Skokos, Theodore C., Jr.
**Newport**
Thaxton, Marvin Dell
**Pine Bluff**
Ramsay, Louis Lafayette, Jr.
**Warren**
Claycomb, Hugh Murray

## CALIFORNIA

**Auburn**
Moglen, Leland Louis
**Bakersfield**
Tornstrom, Robert Ernest
**Belvedere**
Loube, Irving
**Berkeley**
Woodhouse, Thomas Edwin
**Beverly Hills**
Bordy, Michael Jeffrey
Kite, Richard Lloyd
Rosky, Burton Seymour
Russell, Irwin Emanuel
**Buena Park**
Kehrli, David P.
**Burbank**
Noddings, Sarah Ellen
**Burlingame**
Spyros, Nicholas L., Jr.
Telleen, L. Michael
**Calabasas**
Nagle, Robert E.
Weiss, Sherman David
**Chatsworth**
Laukenmann, Christopher Bernd
**Claremont**
Ferguson, C. Robert
**Costa Mesa**
Schaaf, Douglas Allan
**Cupertino**
Naylor, Brian Thomas
**Cypress**
Olschwang, Alan Paul
**Downey**
Bear, Henry Louis
Tompkins, Dwight Edward
**Encino**
McDonough, Patrick Joseph
**Fremont**
Chou, Yung-Ming
Kitta, John Noah
**Fresno**
Ewell, A. Ben, Jr.
Jensen, Douglas Blaine
**Fullerton**
Apke, Thomas Michael
**Glendale**
Ball, James Herington
**Hanford**
Snyder, Thom
**Huntington Beach**
Armstrong, Alan Leigh
**Irvine**
Bastiaanse, Gerard C.
Gay, William Tolin
Muller, Edward Robert
Weissbard, Samuel Held
**La Crescenta**
McNally, Gerald, Jr.
**La Jolla**
Caplan, Allen
**Los Altos**
Bell, Richard G.
**Los Angeles**
Allan, Michael Lee
Allred, Gloria Rachel
Apfel, Gary
Argue, John Clifford
Baker, Robert Kenneth
Barnes, Willie R.
Basile, Paul Louis, Jr.
Bell, Wayne Steven
Blencowe, Paul Sherwood
Boston, Derrick Osmond
Brown, Avery R.
Cahill, Michael Edward
Call, Merlin Wendell
Camp, James Carroll
Carlson, Robert Edwin
Carrey, Neil
Carter, Bret Robert
Castro, Leonard Edward
Clark, R(ufus) Bradbury
Costales, Marco Daniel
Davis, J. Alan
De Brier, Donald Paul
Gilhuly, Peter Martin
Girard, Robert David
Golay, Frank H., Jr.
Goldie, Ron Robert
Gravelle, Douglas Arthur
Grush, Julius Sidney
Haakh, Gilbert Edward
Hahn, Elliott Julius
Hatch, Hilary Joy
Hayes, Byron Jackson, Jr.
Hogeboom, Robert Wood
Hsu, Julie L.
Kim, Edward K.
Klein, Raymond Maurice
Kupietzky, Moshe J.
Lappen, Timothy
Lesser, Joan L.
Levin, Evanne Lynn
Levine, Jerome Lester
May, Lawrence Edward
Mc Adam, Patrick Michael
McNeil, Malcolm Stephen
Miller, Craig Dana
Molleur, Richard Raymond
Noble, Richard Lloyd
Parker, Catherine Marie
Pircher, Leo Joseph
Power, John Bruce
Reid, Donna Lake
Richardson, Douglas Fielding
Roney, John Harvey
Schuyler, Rob Rene
Shilling, Monica Jill
Shultz, John David
Stauber, Ronald Joseph
Synn, Gordon
Tackowiak, Bruce Joseph
Vertun, Alan Stuart
Weinman, Glenn Alan
Williams, Lee Dwain
Winfrey, Diana Lee
**Malibu**
Hanson, Gary A.
**Manhattan Beach**
Guimera, Irene Mermelstein
**Menlo Park**
Crandall, Nelson David, III
Gunderson, Robert Vernon, Jr.
McLain, Christopher M.
Sauers, William Dale
Walsh, Tara Jane
**Mill Valley**
Nemir, Donald Philip
**Monte Sereno**
Allan, Lionel Manning
**Morgan Hill**
Foster, John Robert
**Mountain View**
Koehler, Fritz K.
Montgomery, John Bishop
**Newport Beach**
Black, William Rea
Cano, Kristin Maria
Fleming, Dawn DeAnn
Hancock, S. Lee
Milman, Alyssa Ann
Terner, Andor David
**Northridge**
Van Der Wal, Jeanne Huber
**Novato**
Obninsky, Victor Peter
**Oakland**
Bewley, Peter David
Trowbridge, Jeffery David
Webster, William Hodges
**Oceanside**
Ferrante, R. William
**Orange**
Sawdei, Milan A.
**Orangevale**
King, Franklin Weaver
**Oxnard**
Arnold, Gary D.
**Pacific Palisades**
Flattery, Thomas Long
Lagle, John Franklin
**Palo Alto**
Cohen, Nancy Mahoney
Daunt, Jacqueline Ann
Donnally, Robert Andrew
Huskins, Michael Louis
Lesser, Henry
Nopar, Alan Scott
Phair, Joseph Baschon
Pohlen, Patrick Alan
Whaley, James Thaddeus
Wunsch, Kathryn Sutherland
**Palos Verdes Peninsula**
Yeomans, Russell Allen
**Pasadena**
Armour, George Porter
Katzman, Harvey Lawrence
Morris, Gary Wayne
O'Neill, J. Norman, Jr.
Talt, Alan R.
van Schoonenberg, Robert G.
**Pleasanton**
Straff, Donna Evelyn
**Pomona**
Bausch, Janet Jean
Lunsford, Jeanne Denise
**Rancho Mirage**
Goldie, Ray Robert
**Redondo Beach**
Mercant, Jon Jeffry
**Riverside**
Chang, Janice May
Nassar, William Michael
**Sacramento**
Foster, Douglas Taylor
Uranga, Jose Navarette
**Saint Helena**
Marvin, Monica Louise Wolf
**San Clemente**
Geyser, Lynne M.
**San Diego**
Admire, Duane A.
Bilstad, Blake Timothy
Cannon, Gary Curtis
Chatroo, Arthur Jay
Denniston, John Alexander
Dorne, David J.
Dostart, Paul Joseph
Gartrell, P. Garth
Jackson, Roni D.
Kelly, Karla Rosemarie
Mayer, James Hock
O'Malley, James Terence
Pineda, Dayna Jayne
Shippey, Sandra Lee
Strauss, Steven Marc
Vakili, Alidad
**San Francisco**
Allen, Paul Alfred
Baker, Cameron
Block, Maureen Shanghnessy
Burden, James Ewers
Campbell, Scott Robert
Collas, Juan Garduño, Jr.
Devine, Antoine Maurice
Diamond, Philip Ernest
Evers, William Dohrmann
Faye, Richard Brent
Finck, Kevin William
Fleisher, Steven M.
Halloran, Michael James
Henderson, Dan Fenno
Kallgren, Edward Eugene
Larson, John William
Latta, Thomas Albert
La Vine, Robert L.
Levie, Mark Robert
Ludemann, Doreen Ann
Lynch, Timothy Jeremiah-Mahoney
Mann, Bruce Alan
McGuckin, John Hugh, Jr.
Meyerson, Ivan D.
Olejko, Mitchell J.
Palmer, Venrice Romito
Renfrew, Charles Byron
Rice, Denis Timlin
Shepherd, John Michael
Silk, Thomas
Tobin, James Michael
Weiner, Jody Carl
Whitehead, David Barry
Wild, Nelson Hopkins
**San Jose**
Bebb, Richard S.
Doan, Xuyen Van
Gonzales, Daniel S.
Jorgensen, Norman Eric
Kraw, George Martin
**San Luis Obispo**
Collins, Mary Elizabeth
**San Marino**
Tomich, Lillian
**San Mateo**
Mandel, Martin Louis
Slabach, Stephen Hall
**San Rafael**
Keegin, Stafford Warwick
**San Ramon**
Davis, John Albert
**Santa Ana**
McCarron, Andrew
**Santa Clara**
Denten, Christopher Peter
**Santa Monica**
Focht, Michael Harrison, Jr.
Hofer, Stephen Robert
Homeier, Michael George
**Santa Rosa**
Adams, Delphine Szyndrowski
**Sunnyvale**
Ludgus, Nancy Lucke
**Temecula**
Rosenstein, Robert Bryce
**Thousand Oaks**
Tenner, Erin K.
**Tiburon**
Bauch, Thomas Jay
**Toluca Lake**
Runquist, Lisa A.
**Torrance**
Crane, Kathleen D.
Petillon, Lee Ritchey
Pierno, Anthony Robert
Sarkisian, Alan Herbert
Wilson, Karen LeRohl
**Tustin**
Dao, Hanh D.
**Universal City**
Coupe, James Warnick
**Vernon**
Smith, Lawrence Ronald
**Visalia**
Crowe, John T.
**Walnut Creek**
Baker, Roy Gordon, Jr.
Clark, Sherry Walker
Deming, Bruce Robert
Epstein, Judith Ann
Nolan, David Charles
Pagter, Carl Richard
Wood, Steven Noel Housley
**Westlake Vlg**
Vinson, William Theodore
**Woodside**
Martin, Joseph, Jr.
**Yorba Linda**
Ward, Robert Richard

## COLORADO

**Aspen**
Peirce, Frederick Fairbanks
Peterson, Brooke Alan
**Aurora**
Stauffer, Scott William
**Boulder**
Earnest, G. Lane
**Broomfield**
Sissel, George Allen
**Castle Rock**
Bell, Brian Mayes
Procopio, Joseph Guydon
**Colorado Springs**
Benson, John Scott
Gaddis, Larry Roy
Palermo, Norman Anthony
**Crested Butte**
Renfrow, Jay Royce
**Delta**
Wendt, John Arthur Frederic, Jr.
**Denver**
Bader, Gerald Louis, Jr.
Bryans, Richard W.
Callison, James William
Campbell, William J.
Christy, Cynthia Ullem
Dean, James Benwell
Dunn, Randy Edwin
Goldberg, Gregory Eban
Groom, David A.
Hagen, Glenn W(illiam)
Irwin, R. Robert
Jones, Richard Michael
Keatinge, Robert Reed
Kirchhoff, Bruce C.
Kuhn, Gretchen
Mauro, Richard Frank
McMichael, Donald Earl
McPherson, Gary Lee
Molling, Charles Francis
Moye, John Edward
Munteanu, Victor John
Oakes, Susan Leigh
Otten, Arthur Edward, Jr.
Peloquin, Louis Omer
Potter, Gary Thomas
Scott, Peter Bryan
Shannon, Malcolm Lloyd, Jr.
Shore, Heather Field
Spiegleman, John G.
Stockmar, Ted P.
**Durango**
Sherman, Lester Ivan
**Englewood**
Ambrose, Arlen S.
Brett, Stephen M.
Choi, Jay Junekun
DeMuth, Laurence Wheeler, Jr.
Gognat, Richard J.
Katz, Michael Jeffery
Lidstone, Herrick Kenley, Jr.
McClung, Merle Steven
Schilken, Bruce A.
Steele, Elizabeth Meyer
Wiegand, Robert, II
**Evergreen**
Coriden, Michael Warner
**Fort Collins**
Gast, Richard Shaeffer
**Grand Junction**
Mayberry, Herbert Sylvester
**Littleton**
Keely, George Clayton
Ross, William Robert
**Longmont**
Lyons, Richard Newman, II
**Lyons**
Brown, Michael DeWayne

## CONNECTICUT

**Brooklyn**
Dune, Steve Charles
**Danbury**
Bassett, Robert Andrews
Geoghan, Joseph Edward
**Darien**
Beach, Stephen Holbrook
**East Hartford**
Kerrigan, Vanessa Griffith
**Enfield**
Berger, Robert Bertram
**Farmington**
McCann, John Joseph
**Greenwich**
Auerbach, Ernest Sigmund
Raimondi, Josephine Ann
Storms, Clifford Beekman
**Groton**
Kehoe, Thomas Joseph
**Guilford**
Thomas, David Robert
**Hartford**
Alleyne, Julie Sudhir
Beck, Henry M., Jr.
Bernier, Marcel J.
Bouton, William Wells, III
Cain, George Harvey
Coyle, Michael Lee
Cullina, William Michael
Del Negro, John Thomas
Dennis, Anthony James
Feigenbaum, Barry S.
Lloyd, Alex
Lotstein, James Irving
Martocchio, Louis Joseph
Middlebrook, Stephen Beach
Milliken, Charles Buckland
Quinn, Andrew Peter, Jr.
Reilly, Edward Anthony, Jr.
Richter, Donald Paul
Smith, Richard Stanley, Jr.
Young, Dona Davis Gagliano
**New Canaan**
Bennett, James H.
**New Haven**
Dodge, Mannette Antill
Gollaher, Merton G
Peabody, Bruce R.
Stankewich, Paul Joseph
**New London**
Johnstone, Philip MacLaren
**New Milford**
Zitzmann, Kelly C.
**Old Greenwich**
Klemann, Gilbert Lacy, II
**Rowayton**
Raikes, Charles FitzGerald
**Southport**
Moore, Roy Worsham, III
Sanetti, Stephen Louis
**Stamford**
Apfelbaum, Marc
Barreca, Christopher Anthony
Bello, Christopher Robert
Critelli, Michael J.
Della Rocco, Kenneth Anthony
Dupont, Wesley David
Gold, Steven Michael
Harrison, Michael
Lois, Dale Joseph
Strone, Michael Jonathan
**Trumbull**
Auerbach, Hillel Joshua
**Waterbury**
Chase, Robert L.
Malaspina, Mark J.
Wolfe, Harriet Munrett
**Weatogue**
Greenlaw, Dawn Sharon
**West Hartford**
Nereberg, Eliot Joel
**Westbrook**
Dundas, Philip Blair, Jr.
**Westport**
Jacobs, Jeffrey Lee
**Wilton**
Blankmeyer, Kurt Van Cleave
**Windsor**
Lerman, Kenneth Brian
Molitor, Karen Ann
**Winsted**
Finch, Frank Herschel, Jr.

## DELAWARE

**Claymont**
Rollins, Gene A.
**Dover**
Stone, F. L. Peter
**Wilmington**
Burnett, James F.
Carey, Wayne John
Goldman, Michael David
Gundersen, Mark Jonathan
Holzman, James L(ouis)
Kirk, Richard Dillon
Laster, J. Travis
Morris, Kenneth Donald
Patton, James Leeland, Jr.
Rudge, Howard J.
Smith, Craig Bennett
Stoltzfus, James Allen
Togman, Leonard S.
Welch, Edward P.

## DISTRICT OF COLUMBIA

**Washington**
Bancroft, Judith Gail
Barnett, Robert Bruce
Barr, Michael Blanton
Bebchick, Leonard Norman
Berryman, Richard Byron
Bill, Arthur Henry
Bisceglie, Anthony Patrick
Blair, Robert Allen
Bodansky, Robert Lee
Boone, Theodore Sebastian
Bowe, Richard Welbourn
Browne, Richard Cullen

Canfield, Edward Francis
Cannon, Dean Hollingsworth
Caplan, Corina Ruxandra
Caplin, Mortimer Maxwell
Chanin, Michael Henry
Cohen, Louis Richard
Craft, Robert Homan, Jr.
Daly, Joseph Patrick
Debevoise, Eli Whitney, II
Dickstein, Sidney
Dye, Alan Page
Ellicott, John LeMoyne
Falk, James Harvey, Sr.
Feuerstein, Donald Martin
Finkelstein, Jay Gary
Fontheim, Claude G.B.
Frank, Arthur J.
Freedman, Walter
Freeman, Milton Victor
Ginsburg, Charles David
Goldson, Amy Robertson
Granger, David Ireland
Grier, Phillip Michael
Halvorson, Newman Thorbus, Jr.
Hastings, Douglas Alfred
Hobelman, Carl Donald
Hockenberry, John Fedden
Hoffmann, Martin Richard
Holtz, Edgar Wolfe
Hyde, Howard Laurence
Isbell, David Bradford
Jacobs, Harvey S.
Jones, Allen, Jr.
Klein, Michael Roger
Kohn, Dexter Morton
Kroll, Milton Paul
Lanam, Linda Lee
Landfield, Richard
Lange, William Michael
Latham, Weldon Hurd
Lavine, Henry Wolfe
Lybecker, Martin Earl
Mailander, William Stephen
McMillan, James Gardner
Meer, Cary Jesse
Miller, Gay Davis
Molenkamp, Jack A.
Moses, Alfred Henry
Muir, J. Dapray
Nauheim, Stephen Alan
Nelson, Robert Louis
Norris, Lawrence Geoffrey
Overman, Dean Lee
Pogue, L(loyd) Welch
Rabekoff, Elise Jane
Rafferty, James Gerard
Raymond, David Walker
Riley, Daniel Joseph
Rosengren, Paul Gregory
Sayler, Robert Nelson
Schmidt, William Arthur, Jr.
Schropp, James Howard
Silver, Sidney J.
Smith, Brian William
Sommer, Alphonse Adam, Jr.
Stromberg, Jean Wilbur Gleason
Strong, Carter
Tavallali, Jalal Chaicar
Taylor, Richard Powell
Timmer, Barbara
Trimble, Sandra Ellingson
Trinder, Rachel Bandele
Vaughn-Carrington, Debra Miller
Watson, Thomas C.
Wilderotter, James Arthur
Wilson, Bruce Sandness
Wolf, Maurice
Yoskowitz, Irving Benjamin

### FLORIDA

**Alachua**
Gaines, Weaver Henderson
**Altamonte Springs**
Harding, Calvin Fredrick, Jr.
**Auburndale**
Haff, Tula Michele
**Boca Grande**
Brock, Mitchell
**Boca Raton**
Beber, Robert H.
Beck, Jan Scott
Buckstein, Mark Aaron
Horn, Douglas Michael
Kornberg, Joel Barry
Lesnick, Irving Isaac
Nussbaum, Howard Jay
Reinstein, Joel
Wichinsky, Glenn Ellis
**Casselberry**
Campbell, John Michael
**Clearwater**
Doudna, Heather Lynn
Durand, Jean-Paul
Fine, A(rthur) Kenneth
Gifford, Janet Lynn
Swope, Scott Paul
**Clewiston**
Gonzalez, Francisco Javier
**Coconut Grove**
Arboleya, Carlos Joaquin
**Coral Gables**
Mitchell, David Benjamin
Pallot, Joseph Wedeles
**Daytona Beach**
Davidson, David John
**Fort Lauderdale**
Beck, Wendy Lynn
Behr, Ralph Steven
Cole, James Otis
Golden, E(dward) Scott
King, Robert Lee
Mastronardi, Corinne Marie
Platner, Michael Gary
Schneider, Laz Levkoff
**Fort Myers**
Sutherlund, David Arvid
**Hobe Sound**
Simpson, Russell Gordon
**Hollywood**
Singer, Bernard Alan
Weisman, David
**Jacksonville**
Braddock, Donald Layton
Dornan, Kevin William
Held, Edwin Walter, Jr.
Kelso, Linda Yayoi
Kent, John Bradford
Lee, Lewis Swift
Legler, Mitchell Wooten
Manning, G(erald) Stephen
Ringel, Fred Morton
Sadler, Luther Fuller, Jr.
**Jupiter**
Kennedy, Loan Bui
**Lake Buena Vista**
Schmudde, Lee Gene
**Lakeland**
Harris, Christy Franklin
**Lauderhill**
Berry, Carl David, Jr.
**Marianna**
Wynn, Charles Milton
**Melbourne**
Ballantyne, Richard Lee
Yera, Evelio Jesus
**Miami**
Alonso, Antonio Enrique
Barrett, John Richard
Berley, David Richard
Berritt, Harold Edward
Betz, Gilbert Calvin
Bronis, Stephen J.
Cassel, Marwin Shepard
Chabrow, Penn Benjamin
Dougan, Stacey Pastel
Dreize, Livia Rebbeka
Edwards, Thomas Ashton
Feinsmith, Paul Lowell
Fishman, Lewis Warren
Fontes, J. Mario F., Jr.
Friedman, Nicholas R.
Fucci, Rick James
Furnari, Doreen S.
Glickman, Fred Elliott
Granata, Linda M.
Gross, Leslie Jay
Grossman, Robert Louis
Gutierrez, Renaldy Jose
Hall, Miles Lewis, Jr.
Hoffman, Larry J.
Jacobson, Bernard
Klein, Peter William
Kurzer, Martin Joel
Landy, Burton Aaron
Martinez-Cid, Ricardo
McGuigan, Thomas Richard
Mendelson, Victor Howard
Merrill, George Vanderneth
Mudd, John Philip
Murai, Rene Vicente
Murphy, Timothy James
Paul, Robert
Pearlman, Michael Allen
Pozo-Diaz, Martha del Carmen
Roddenberry, Stephen Keith
Samole, Myron Michael
Short, Eugene Maurice, Jr.
Silber, Norman Jules
Touby, Richard
Villasana, George Anthony
Weiner, Lawrence
Whitlow, James Adams
**Miami Beach**
Thomas, Lola Bohn
**Naples**
Bornmann, Carl Malcolm
Budd, David Glenn
**New Port Richey**
Focht, Theodore Harold
**North Miami**
Moreno, Christine Margaret
**North Miami Beach**
Snihur, William Joseph, Jr.
**North Palm Beach**
Coyle, Dennis Patrick
**Ocala**
Haldin, William Carl, Jr.
Hatch, John D.
Sommer, Robert George
**Orlando**
Blackford, Robert Newton
Buhaly Ibold, Catherine
Capouano, Albert D.
Chong, Stephen Chu Ling
Conti, Louis Thomas Moore
Dierking, John Randall
Extein, Mark Charles
Hendry, Robert Ryon
Ioppolo, Frank S., Jr.
Lowndes, John Foy
Pierce, John Gerald (Jerry Pierce)
Popp, Gregory Allan
Rush, Fletcher Grey, Jr.
Stuart, Alice Melissa
Whitehill, Clifford Lane
Yates, Leighton Delevan, Jr.
**Oviedo**
Worthington, Daniel Glen
**Palm Bay**
Balog, Douglas Allan
**Palm Beach**
Grogan, Robert Harris
Keihner, Bruce William
Tabernilla, Armando Alejandro
Tarone, Theodore T.
Zeller, Ronald John
**Palm Beach Gardens**
Brams, Jeffrey Brent
Olson, Carl Eric
**Palm Coast**
Conner, Timothy James
**Pensacola**
Huston, Gary William
**Pinellas Park**
Blacklidge, Raymond Mark
**Plantation**
Buck, Thomas Randolph
**Redington Shores**
Christ, Earle L.
**Saint Augustine**
Atter, Helen Sofge
**Saint Petersburg**
DiFilippo, Fernando, Jr.
Georges, Richard Martin
Gross, Alan Marc
Lewis, Mark Russell, Sr.
Ross, Howard Philip
**Sarasota**
Davis, Louis Poisson, Jr.
Fetterman, James Charles
Herb, F(rank) Steven
Janney, Oliver James
Kirtley, William Thomas
Moore, John Leslie
**St Petersburg**
Hudkins, John W.
**Tallahassee**
Miller, John Samuel, Jr.
Miller, Morris Henry
Neal, Austin Baylor
**Tampa**
Burgess, Bryan Scott
Doliner, Nathaniel Lee
Farrior, J. Rex, Jr.
Grammig, Robert James
McBride, William Howard, Jr.
O'Neill, Albert Clarence, Jr.
Roberson, Bruce H.
**Tavernier**
Lupino, James Samuel
**West Palm Beach**
Callahan, Richard Paul
Gildan, Phillip Clarke
James, Keith Alan
O'Brien, Thomas George, III
Stuber, James Arthur
**Winter Haven**
Rignanese, Cynthia Crofoot
**Winter Park**
Goldsmith, Karen Lee
Livingston, Edward Michael

### GEORGIA

**Alpharetta**
Hoenig, Gerald Jay
Linder, Harvey Ronald
**Athens**
Bryant, Everett Clay, Jr.
Davis, Claude-Leonard
**Atlanta**
Andros, James Harry
Baker, Anita Diane
Barker, Clayton Robert, III
Barkoff, Rupert Mitchell
Brecher, Armin G.
Bridges, Louis Emerson, III
Bruckner, William J.
Calhoun, Scott Douglas
Cargill, Robert Mason
Chisholm, Tommy
Coleman, Sean Joseph
Drucker, Michael Stuart
Durrett, James Frazer, Jr.
Fiorentino, Carmine
Fortin, Raymond D.
Ganz, Charles David
Gladden, Joseph Rhea, Jr.
Greer, Bernard Lewis, Jr.
Harkey, Robert Shelton
Howell, Arthur
Isaf, Fred Thomas
Kelley, James Francis
Kelly, James Michael
Kelly, James Patrick
Killorin, Edward Wylly
Kohn, Robert Alexander
Levy, David
Luther, Donald William
Manley, David Bott, III
McCloud, Robert Olmsted, Jr.
Meyerson, Amy Lin
Moderow, Joseph Robert
Moeling, Walter Goos, IV
Morgan, Charles Russell
Moss, Raymond Lloyd
Ortiz, Jay Richard Gentry
Peterzell, Betsy Vance
Pless, Laurance Davidson
Pombert, Jeffrey Lawrence
Pryor, Shepherd Green, III
Quittmeyer, Peter Charles
Schilling, Laura K.
Scibilia, Joseph Logan
Sibley, James Malcolm
Smith, Lawrence A.
Somers, Fred Leonard, Jr.
Stallings, Ronald Denis
Verska, Kimberly Anne
Williams, Joel Cash
Williams, Neil, Jr.
Zabka, Sven Paul
**Augusta**
Lee, Lansing Burrows, Jr.
**Carrollton**
Park, Kelley Barrett
**Dunwoody**
Callison, James W.
Tramonte, James Albert
**Jonesboro**
Teske, Steven Cecil
Vail, Bruce Ronald
**Macon**
Cole, John Prince
Elliott, James Sewell
**Marietta**
Ahlstrom, Michael Joseph
**Mcdonough**
Meadows, Rod G.
**Norcross**
Hasbrouck, Catherine O'Malley
**Saint Simons Island**
Kunda, Preston B.
**Savannah**
Hirsberg, David M.

### HAWAII

**Honolulu**
Asai-Sato, Carol Yuki
Bourgoin, David L.
Char, Vernon Fook Leong
Cuskaden, Everett
Fujiyama, Rodney Michio
Gay, E(mil) Laurence
Ichikawa, Robert K.
Ingersoll, Richard King
Miller, Clifford Joel
Mirikitani, Richard Kiyoshi
Nakata, Gary Kenji
Okinaga, Lawrence Shoji
Reber, David James
Rohrer, Reed Beaver
Sumida, Gerald Aquinas
Suzuki, Norman Hitoshi
Tharp, James Wilson
**Kahului**
Richardson, Robert Allen
**Wailuku**
Judge, James Robert

### IDAHO

**Boise**
Arnold, Rebecca Williams
Hess, Jeffery L.
Hickman, Lori A. DeMond
Holleran, John W.
Marcus, Craig Brian
Runft, John L.
Thomas, Eugene C.
Wood, Troy James
**Idaho Falls**
Simmons, John G.
Whittier, Monte Ray

### ILLINOIS

**Abbott Park**
Brock, Charles Marquis
**Alton**
Durr, Malcolm Daniel
Hoagland, Karl King, Jr.
**Belleville**
Mathis, Patrick Bischof
**Bloomington**
Wozniak, Debra Gail
**Broadview**
Baer, Luke
**Buffalo Grove**
Greenspon, Susan Jean
Israelstam, Alfred William
Kole, Julius S.
**Chicago**
Anderson, J. Trent
Baker, Bruce Jay
Berolzheimer, Karl
Boardman, Robert A.
Bockelman, John Richard
Bryant, Jacqueline Shim
Burgdoerfer, Jerry
Cascino, Anthony Elmo, Jr.
Cass, Neil Earl
Chudzinski, Mark Adam
Clinton, Edward Xavier
Collins, Glenn
Cross, Chester Joseph
Davis, Scott Jonathan
Docksey, John Ross
Doetsch, Douglas Allen
Dondanville, Patricia
Donohoe, Jerome Francis
Dunn, Edwin Rydell
Dunn, Kenneth Carl
Edelman, Bernard Paul
Esrick, Jerald Paul
Farrell, Thomas Dinan
Fein, Roger Gary
Felsenthal, Steven Altus
Filpi, Robert Alan
Friedli, Helen Russell
Gerstein, Mark Douglas
Goldman, Michael P.
Gray, Steven Joseph
Grossberg, David Alan
Hand, Gary S.
Harris, Linda Chaplik
Head, Patrick James
Henning, Joel Frank
Henry, Robert John
Hester, Thomas Patrick
Hoffman, Douglas Raymond
Hollins, Mitchell Leslie
Howell, R(obert) Thomas, Jr.
Hubbard, Elizabeth Louise
Hurwitz, Joel Michael
Huston, Steven Craig
Jock, Paul F., II
Johnson, Gary Thomas
Johnson, Lael Frederic
Johnson, Tige Christopher
Kamerick, Eileen Ann
Kaufman, Andrew Michael
Knuepfer, Robert Claude, Jr.
Kolmin, Kenneth Guy
Kozlowski, Kimberly Frances
Kramm, Deborah Lucille
Ladd, Jeffrey Raymond
Lang, Gordon, Jr.
Lauderdale, Katherine Sue
LeBaron, Charles Frederick, Jr.
Levin, Michael David
Liggio, Carl Donald
Lind, Jon Robert
Lowinger, Frederick Charles
Lubin, Donald G.
Maher, Francesca Marciniak
Malkin, Cary Jay
Malovany, Howard
Mandler, Thomas Yale
Mangum, Ronald Scott
Manzoni, Charles R., Jr.
Marvel, Kenneth Robert
McCrohon, Craig
McMahon, Thomas Michael
Mertes, Arthur Edward
Meyers, Joel G.
Michaels, Richard Edward
Michod, Charles Louis, Jr.
Miller, John Leed
Miller, Paul J.
Munzer, Cynde Hirschtick
Murdock, Charles William
Nachman, Norman Harry
Niehoff, Philip John
O'Leary, Daniel Vincent, Jr.
Pallasch, B. Michael
Para, Gerard Albert
Peterson, Bradley Laurits
Polk, Lee Thomas
Proctor, Edward George
Redman, Clarence Owen
Reicin, Ronald Ian
Rhind, James Thomas
Roberson, G. Gale, Jr.
Robson, Douglas Spears
Rubin, Jeffrey Mark
Rudnick, William Alan
Ruiz, Michele Ilene
Schneider, Robert E., II
Shank, William O.
Shindler, Donald A.
Siegel, Howard Jerome
Sigal, Michael Stephen
Silets, Harvey Marvin
Smedinghoff, Thomas J.
Sprowl, Charles Riggs
Stambler, Olga
Stone, Bertram Allen
Swibel, Steven Warren
Thomas, Stephen Paul
Timmer, Stephen Blaine
Vranicar, Michael Gregory
Wade, Edwin Lee
Wahlen, Edwin Alfred
Wander, Herbert Stanton
Weil, Andrew L.
Wilson, Roger Goodwin
Winkler, Charles Howard
York, John C(hristopher)
Yu, Aihong
**Chicago Heights**
Wigell, Raymond George
**Decatur**
Ansbro, James Michael
Greenleaf, John L., Jr.
Kenney, Frederic Lee
Reising, Richard P.
**Deerfield**
Abbey, G(eorge) Marshall
Cutchins, Clifford Armstrong, IV
Gaither, John F.
Oettinger, Julian Alan
Rollin, Kenneth B.
Staubitz, Arthur Frederick
**Elgin**
Flanagan, Leo M., Jr.
**Franklin Park**
Blanchard, Eric Alan
**Gurnee**
Southern, Robert Allen
**Highland Park**
Kupferberg, Lloyd Sherman
Nyberg, William Arthur
Tabin, Seymour
**Hinsdale**
Diamant, William
O'Brien, Donald Joseph
**Hoffman Estates**
Kelly, Anastasia Donovan
**Joliet**
Boyer, Andrew Ben
**Kenilworth**
Dixon, Carl Franklin
**La Grange**
Kerr, Alexander Duncan, Jr.
**Lansing**
Hill, Philip
**Lincolnshire**
Giza, David Alan
**Long Grove**
Obert, Paul Richard
**Mount Prospect**
Cohn, Bradley M.
**North Chicago**
de Lasa, José M.
**Northbrook**
Irons, Spencer Ernest
Lapin, Harvey I.
Pollak, Jay Mitchell
Sernett, Richard Patrick
Teichner, Bruce A.
**Oak Brook**
Farnell, Alan Stuart
Getz, Herbert A.
Johnson, Grant Lester
La Petina, Gary Michael
Oldfield, E. Lawrence
**Oak Lawn**
Tucker, Berry Kenneth
**Oakbrook Terrace**
Fenech, Joseph Charles
O'Brien, Walter Joseph, II
**Palatine**
Roti, Thomas David
**Park Ridge**
Hegarty, Mary Frances
**Peoria**
Atterbury, Robert Rennie, III
Winget, Walter Winfield
**Prospect Heights**
Mancini, Rose C.
**Rockford**
Brassfield, Eugene Everett
Johnson, Thomas Stuart
Rudy, Elmer Clyde
**Rolling Meadows**
Sullivan, Michael D.
**Saint Charles**
Hines, Suzanne
**Schaumburg**
Graft, William Christopher
Vitale, James Drew
**Schiller Park**
Congalton, Christopher William
**Skokie**
Gopman, Howard Z.
**Springfield**
Cullen, Mark Kenneth
Thornton, Joseph Philip
Walbaum, Robert C.
**Taylorville**
Austin, Daniel William
**Vernon Hills**
Gaus Ehning, Michele B.
**Wheaton**
May, Frank Brendan, Jr.
**Wilmette**
Frick, Robert Hathaway

**Winnetka**
Ryan, Robert Jeffers
**Wonder Lake**
McNamara, Joseph Burk

## INDIANA

**Angola**
Blosser, David John
**Batesville**
Wright, Deborah Sue
**Bloomington**
Mann, Robert David
**Elkhart**
Breckenridge, Franklin Eugene
Cawley, John Arnold, Jr.
Harman, John Royden
Hesser, Randall Gary
Like, Steven
Thorne, William Albert
Whitmer, J. A.
**Evansville**
Baugh, Jerry Phelps
Harrison, Joseph Heavrin
Knight, Jeffrey Lin
Wallace, Keith M.
**Fort Wayne**
Lawson, Jack Wayne
Pope, Mark Andrew
Shoaff, Thomas Mitchell
**Frankfort**
Appleton, Alan B.
**Greenwood**
Bekes, Gregory E.
**Indianapolis**
Barrett, David Olan
Blythe, James David, II
Carlberg, James Edwin
Comer, Jerome Edward
Culp, Charles William
Dorocke, Lawrence Francis
Dutton, Clarence Benjamin
Dutton, Stephen James
Fuller, Samuel Ashby
Haycox, Rolanda Moore
Heerens, Joseph Robert
Henderson, Eugene Leroy
Kappes, Philip Spangler
Koeller, Robert Marion
Nettles, Gaylon James
Patrick, William Bradshaw
Russell, David Williams
Springer, Marilee J.
Strain, James Arthur
Tabler, Bryan G.
Tuchman, Steven Leslie
Vandivier, Blair Robert
Watson, Richard Prather
Whitney, Larry Gene
**Lafayette**
Branigin, Roger D., Jr.
**Lagrange**
Schultess, LeRoy Kenneth
**Merrillville**
Hites, Earle Floyd
**Muncie**
Dennis, Ralph Emerson, Jr.
**Noblesville**
Fleck, (Kevin) Sean
**Schererville**
Anast, Nick James
**South Bend**
Carey, John Leo
Hall, Thomas Jennings
Lambert, George Robert
Mintz, Richard L.

## IOWA

**Burlington**
Hoth, Steven Sergey
**Davenport**
Shaw, Elizabeth Orr
**Des Moines**
Bannister, T(homas) Scott
Belin, David William
Brown, Paul Edmondson
Carroll, Frank James
Neumann, Gordon Richard, Jr.
Simpson, Lyle Lee
Tipton, Sheila Kay
**Grinnell**
Munyon, Wendy Nelson
**Iowa City**
Downer, Robert Nelson
Thomas, Randall Stuart
**Mason City**
Winston, Harold Ronald
**Muscatine**
Coulter, Charles Roy
Lande, Roger L.
**Newton**
Bennett, Edward James
**Sioux City**
Klass, Marvin Joseph
Madsen, George Frank

## KANSAS

**Garden City**
Pierce, Ricklin Ray
**Hutchinson**
Swearer, William Brooks
**Kansas City**
Andersen, Anton Chris
Peters, Daniel Wade
**Leawood**
Snyder, Willard Breidenthal
**Overland Park**
Anderson, Steven Robert
Bohm, Jack Nelson
Bunn, G. Peter, III
Ellis, Jeffrey Orville
Glasser, Philip Russell
Westerhaus, Douglas Bernard
**Salina**
Owens, William Dean
**Shawnee Mission**
Shank, Suzanne Adams
**Topeka**
Frost, Brian Standish
Lawson, Christopher Patrick
Rainey, William Joel
Snyder, Brock Robert
**Westwood**
Devlin, James Richard
**Wichita**
Arabia, Paul
Depew, Spencer Long
Steele, Thomas Lee
Stephenson, Richard Ismert
Stewart, Kenneth Parsons

## KENTUCKY

**Bowling Green**
Catron, Stephen Barnard
**Covington**
Gilliland, John Campbell, II
**Lexington**
Basconi, Pamela Bray
Byrne, Walter Robbins, Jr.
Terry, Joseph H.
**Louisville**
Anderson, P. Richard
Buckaway, William Allen, Jr.
Furman, C. Dean
Griffith, C. Laurie
Halbleib, Walter Thomas
Keeney, Steven Harris
Luber, Thomas J(ulian)
Macdonald, Lenna Ruth
Mellen, Francis Joseph, Jr.
Morreau, James Earl, Jr.
Morris, Benjamin Hume
Northern, Richard
Reed, D. Gary
Smith, Trevor A.
Talbott, Ben Johnson, Jr.
Valenti, Michael A.
Welsh, Alfred John
**Newport**
Siverd, Robert Joseph
**Owensboro**
Miller, James Monroe
**Paducah**
Treece, Randy Lionel
**Pineville**
Lawson, Susan Coleman

## LOUISIANA

**Baton Rouge**
Block, Mitchell Stern
Cutshaw, James Michael
Holliday, James Sidney, Jr.
Richards, Marta Alison
**Covington**
Shinn, Clinton Wesley
**Gretna**
Fadaol, Robert Frederick
**Hammond**
Ross, Kenneth L.
**Lafayette**
Breaux, Paul Joseph
**Lake Charles**
Judice, Gregory Van
Norman, Rick Joseph
**Metairie**
Senter, Mark Seymour
**Monroe**
Curry, Robert Lee, III
**New Orleans**
Abbott, Hirschel Theron, Jr.
Beahm, Franklin D.
Bronfin, Fred
Coleman, James Julian, Jr.
Downing, Carl Seldon
Fierke, Thomas Garner
Herman, Fred L.
Katz, Morton Howard
Martinez, Andrew Tredway
Perez, Luis Alberto
Raphael, David Coleman
Roux, Kermit Louis, III
Simon, H(uey) Paul
Title, Peter Stephen
Vickery, Eugene Benton, Jr.
Waechter, Arthur Joseph, Jr.
**Saint Francisville**
Eldredge, George Badge
**Shreveport**
Cox, John Thomas, Jr.
Hardtner, Quintin Theodore, III
Jeter, Katherine Leslie Brash
Roberts, Robert, III
Skinner, Michael David
**Sulphur**
Sumpter, Dennis Ray
**West Monroe**
Caldwell, Douglas Cody

## MAINE

**Brunswick**
Owen, H. Martyn
**Freeport**
Lea, Lola Stendig
**Portland**
Haddow, James Buchanan
Harlan, Wendy Jill
Ingalls, Everett Palmer, III
Tierney, Kevin Joseph
**Yarmouth**
Webster, Peter Bridgman

## MARYLAND

**Baltimore**
Bruner, William Gwathmey, III
Chernow, Jeffrey Scott
Cook, Bryson Leitch
Curran, Robert Bruce
Dopkin, Mark Dregant
Haines, Thomas W. W.
Kandel, Peter Thomas
Mogol, Alan Jay
Moser, M(artin) Peter
Ritter, Jeffrey Blake
Robinson, Zelig
Russo, Michael Natale, Jr.
Scriggins, Larry Palmer
Wheatley, Charles Henry, III
**Bel Air**
Miller, Max Dunham, Jr.
**Bethesda**
Goldstone, Mark Lewis
Hagberg, Viola Wilgus
Himelfarb, Stephen Roy
Levy, Leonard Joel
Menaker, Frank H., Jr.
Robinson, Jean Marie
Weinberger, Alan David
**Brookeville**
Johns, Warren LeRoi
**Burtonsville**
Covington, Marlow Stanley
**College Park**
Yoho, Billy Lee
**Columbia**
Gelfman, Richard David
Maseritz, Guy B.
**Crofton**
Doherty, Daniel Joseph, III
Norman, David Joseph
**Ellicott City**
Silverstein, Fred Howard
**Gaithersburg**
Phillips, Leo Harold, Jr.
Plave, Erica Frohman
**Greenbelt**
Jackley, Michael Dano
**Lexington Park**
Lacer, Alfred Antonio
**Lutherville**
Fascetta, Christopher M.
**Lutherville Timonium**
Freeland, Charles
**New Market**
Gabriel, Eberhard John
**North Potomac**
Brandsdorfer, Mark Michael
**Potomac**
Gingold, Dennis Marc
Peter, Phillips Smith
**Riverdale**
Billingsley, Lance W.
**Rockville**
Herzog, Carolyn Beth
Katz, Steven Martin
Patrick, Philip Howard
Roberts, Christopher Chalmers
Steren, Marc Nathan
Teller, Howard Barry
**Silver Spring**
Priest, Troy Alfred-Wiley
Quinlan, William Allen
Stempler, Michael
**Towson**
Lutz, Randall Matthew
Miller, Herbert H.
Winter, Leslie Antone
**Upperco**
McMahon, Richard Michael, Sr.
**Westminster**
Staples, Lyle Newton

## MASSACHUSETTS

**Billerica**
Fraser, Everett MacKay
**Boston**
Abraham, Nicholas Albert
Auerbach, Joseph
Ayoub, Paul Joseph
Bernhard, Alexander Alfred
Bines, Harvey Ernest
Blank, Garry Neal
Bloch, Donald Martin
Boger, Kenneth Snead
Bohnen, Michael J.
Borenstein, Milton Conrad
Bornheimer, Allen Millard
Cekala, Chester
Chambers, Margaret Warner
Chase, Thomas Charles
Cherwin, Joel Ira
Christodoulo, George Evans
Coffey, James Francis
Connors, Donald Louis
Coukos, Stephen John
DeAgazio, Christopher Richard
Dello Iacono, Paul Michael
DeRensis, Paul
Elfman, Eric Michael
Engel, David Lewis
Fischer, Eric Robert
Frankenheim, Samuel
Garcia, Adolfo Ramon
Goldman, Richard Harris
Greenblatt, Martin Elliott
Greer, Gordon Bruce
Haddad, Ernest Mudarri
Halligan, Brendan Patrick
Hester, Patrick Joseph
Hines, Edward Francis, Jr.
Honig, Stephen Michael
Jones, Sheldon Atwell
Jordan, Alexander Joseph, Jr.
Kane, Stephen Michael
Korb, Kenneth Allan
Kutchin, Edward David
Matzka, Michael Alan
McDonald, John Barry, Jr.
Milder, Forrest David
Mooney, Michael Edward
O'Neill, Philip Daniel, Jr.
Patterson, John de la Roche, Jr.
Redlich, Marc
Rosenbloom, Thomas Adam
Rowe, Larry Jordan
Sager, Steven Travis
Saltiel, David M.
Schoenfeld, Barbara Braun
Shure, Andrew F.
Snyder, John Gorvers
Soden, Richard Allan
Sopel, George C.
Spelfogel, Scott David
Stokes, James Christopher
Storer, Thomas Perry
Testa, Richard Joseph
Thibeault, George Walter
Trevett, Kenneth Parkhurst
Weaver, Paul David
Williams, Robert Dana
Wright, Walter Augustine, III
**Brookline**
Alban, Ludwig
Goldenberg, Stephen Bernard
**Cambridge**
Bellamy, Werten F. W., Jr.
Connors, Frank Joseph
Gonson, S. Donald
Wirth, Peter
**Canton**
Bauer, Gene Marc
**Danvers**
Eisenhauer, Wayne Harold
**Everett**
Root, Carole A.Z.
**Framingham**
Meltzer, Jay H.
**Greenfield**
Blanker, Alan Harlow
**Haverhill**
Spurling, Dennis Michael
**Holden**
Price, Robert DeMille
**Holyoke**
Ferriter, Maurice Joseph
**Lexington**
D'Avignon, Roy Joseph
**Lincoln**
Schwartz, Edward Arthur
**Lowell**
Curtis, James Theodore
**Natick**
Grassia, Thomas Charles
**New Bedford**
Hurwitz, Barrett Alan
**Newton**
Glazer, Donald Wayne
Horbaczewski, Henry Zygmunt
**Newton Highlands**
Gans, Steven H.
**Northampton**
Offner, Daniel O'Connell
**Norwood**
Gorski, Ronald William
**Somerville**
Brown, Peter Mason
**Springfield**
Fialky, Gary Lewis
Nicolai, Paul Peter
Weiss, Ronald Phillip
**Waltham**
Barnes-Brown, Peter Newton
**Wellesley**
Goglia, Charles A., Jr.
Marx, Peter A.
**Westborough**
Frank, Jacob
**Weston**
Haas, Jacqueline Crawford
**Westwood**
Eastman, Jennifer
**Williamstown**
Filson, J. Adam
**Worcester**
Chandler, Burton
Donnelly, James Corcoran, Jr.
Joyce, James Joseph, Jr.
Longden, Robert Edward, Jr.
Lougee, David Louis
Silver, Marvin S.

## MICHIGAN

**Ada**
Mc Callum, Charles Edward
**Ann Arbor**
Dew, Thomas Edward
Fineman, Gary Lee
Keppelman, Nancy
Pierce, Richard William
**Battle Creek**
Kelly, Janet Langford
**Birmingham**
Bick, Robert Steven
Gold, Edward David
Zelenock, Katheryne L.
**Bloomfield Hills**
Berlow, Robert Alan
Callow, Thomas Edward
Kasischke, Louis Walter
Meyer, George Herbert
Norris, John Hart
Wellman, David Joseph
Wilson, Cynthia Diane
**Dearborn**
Demorest, Mark Stuart
**Detroit**
Babcock, Charles Witten, Jr.
Breach, David Andrew
Brustad, Orin Daniel
Bushnell, George Edward, Jr.
Calkins, Stephen
Darlow, Julia Donovan
Deason, Herold McClure
Deron, Edward Michael
Kamins, John Mark
Krsul, John Aloysius, Jr.
Lewand, F. Thomas
McKim, Samuel John, III
Myers, Rodman Nathaniel
Pearce, Harry Jonathan
Phillips, Elliott Hunter
Richardson, Ralph Herman
Rohr, Richard David
Shaevsky, Mark
Thoms, David Moore
Williams, J. Bryan
Wisner, Cynthia Ficke
**East Lansing**
Castellani, Edward Joseph
Platt, David M.
Story, Monte Robert
**Elk Rapids**
Palmer, Thomas Earl
**Farmington**
Brody, Jay Howard
Legg, Michael William
**Farmington Hills**
Ciampa, Jeffrey Nelson
Haliw, Andrew Jerome, III
**Flint**
Pelavin, Michael Allen
**Franklin**
Kessler, Philip Joel
**Grand Haven**
Johnson, Todd Alan
**Grand Rapids**
Boer, Roger William
Dugan, Robert John
Engbers, James Arend
Hogan, Thomas Patrick
Prasher, Gregory George
Titley, Larry J.
**Grosse Pointe**
Avant, Grady, Jr.
Cobau, John Reed
Hindelang, Robert Louis
**Grosse Pointe Woods**
Darke, Richard Francis
**Ishpeming**
Steward, James Brian
**Jackson**
Curtis, Philip James
**Kalamazoo**
Borsos, Robert Bruce
Deming, Stuart Hayden
Durham, Sidney Down
Gordon, Edgar George
**Lansing**
Burlingame, Stephen Lee
Ewert, Quentin Albert
Gallagher, Byron Patrick, Jr.
**Livonia**
Hoffman, Barry Paul
**Marquette**
Jessup, James R.
**Monroe**
Lipford, Rocque Edward
**Muskegon**
Nehra, Gerald Peter
**Northville**
Leavitt, Martin Jack
**Owosso**
Johnson, James Randall
**Plymouth**
Morgan, Donald Crane
**Saint Clair Shores**
Stevens, Clark Valentine
**Shelby**
Law, Roger Alan
**Southfield**
Dawson, Dennis Ray
Jacobs, John E.
Kaplow, Robert David
Klein, Coleman Eugene
Labe, Robert Brian
Levine, Jeffrey Barry
Nykanen, David Edward
Schwartz, Robert H.
Silber, Albert J.
**Sturgis**
Dresser, Raymond H., Jr.
**Troy**
Akhtar, Sher M.
Chapman, Conrad Daniel
Dillon, Joseph Francis
Haron, David Lawrence
Lenihan, Robert Joseph, II
Olson, Edward M.
Ponitz, John Allan
**Walled Lake**
Seglund, Bruce Richard
**Warren**
Bridenstine, Louis Henry, Jr.

## MINNESOTA

**Albert Lea**
Savelkoul, Donald Wayne
**Bloomington**
Broeker, John Milton
**Duluth**
Nys, John Nikki
**Eden Prairie**
Nilles, John Michael
**Fridley**
Savelkoul, Donald Charles
**Grand Rapids**
Licke, Wallace John
**Hopkins**
Hunter, Donald Forrest
**Minneapolis**
Al, Marc Andre
Andrews, Albert O'Beirne, Jr.
Bergerson, David Raymond
Chester, Stephanie Ann
Duran, Stanley John
Erhart, John Joseph
Frecon, Alain
Freeman, Todd Ira
Grayson, Edward Davis
Greener, Ralph Bertram
Hasselquist, Maynard Burton
Hergott, Daniel Weldon
Hibbs, John Stanley
Houston, John R.
Ingber, Marvin C.
Kaplan, Sheldon
Kelley, Shane Richard
Kennedy, Steven Charles
Laitinen, Sari K.M.
Lofstrom, Mark D.
Marshall, Siri Swenson
McNamara, Michael John
McNeil, Mark Sanford
Mellum, Gale Robert
Nelson, Gary Michael
Neumeyer, Susan Lee
Opdahl, Clark Donald
Radmer, Michael John
Reilly, George
Rude, Brian William
Sanner, Royce Norman
Skare, Robert Martin
Stageberg, Roger V.
Strothman, John Henry
Towey, Edward Andrew

Vander Weide, Vernon Jay
Witort, Janet Lee
Yost, Gerald B.
Zotaley, Byron Leo
**Minnetonka**
Lubben, David J.
**Moorhead**
Guy, William Lewis, III
**Rochester**
Orwoll, Gregg S. K.
Seeger, Ronald L.
**Saint Paul**
Bernick, Alan E.
Devgun, Dharminder Singh
Dietz, Charlton Henry
Maffei, Rocco John
Margoles, Alan D.
Rebane, John T.
Ursu, John Joseph
Van Zomeren, Barbara Ruth
Winthrop, Sherman

### MISSISSIPPI

**Bay Saint Louis**
Bernstein, Joseph
**Brookhaven**
Doty, Sally Burchfield
**Columbus**
Gholson, Hunter Maurice
**Diamondhead**
Reddien, Charles Henry, II
**Greenville**
Hafter, Jerome Charles
**Gulfport**
Westbrook, William V.
**Jackson**
Clark, David Wright
Corlew, John Gordon
Martinez, Eduardo Vidal
Wise, Sherwood Willing
**Ridgeland**
Humphreys, Kevin Lee

### MISSOURI

**Brentwood**
Timm, Walter William
**Chesterfield**
Coffin, Richard Keith
Fagerberg, Roger Richard
Hier, Marshall David
Pollihan, Thomas Henry
**Clayton**
Mohrman, Henry J(oe), Jr.
**Cuba**
Lange, C. William
**Hazelwood**
Purvines, Verne Ewald, Jr.
**Hillsboro**
Howald, John William
**Kansas City**
Ball, Owen Keith, Jr.
Bartunek, Robert R(ichard), Jr.
Brenneman, Gerald Wayne
Brous, Thomas Richard
Carman, Steven F.
Egan, Charles Joseph, Jr.
Gaines, Robert Darryl
Gorman, Gerald Warner
Graham, Harold Steven
Holewinski, Paul Patrick
Howes, Brian Thomas
Kaplan, Eliot Lawrence
Kaufman, Michelle Stark
Kitchin, John Joseph
Margolin, Abraham Eugene
Mikkelson, Eric T.
Murguia, Ramon
Newcom, Jennings Jay
Reaves, Craig Charles
Seigfreid, James Thomas
Seitter, David Charles
Shughart, Donald Louis
Sparks, Stephen Stone
Voran, Joel Bruce
Willy, Thomas Ralph
Wrobley, Ralph Gene
**Lamar**
Geddie, Rowland Hill, III
**Liberty**
Sayles, Cathy A.
**Macon**
Parkinson, Paul K.
**Saint Charles**
Beck, Rudy Dale
**Saint Louis**
Anderson, Anthony LeClaire
Armstrong, Owen Thomas
Arnold, Fred English
Barken, Bernard Allen
Behrens, Brian Charles
Boggs, Beth Clemens
Brickler, John Weise
Bryan, Henry C(lark), Jr.
Chasnoff, Jules
Cook, Thomas Alfred Ashley
Cullen, James D.
DeHaven, Michael Allen
Dorwart, Donald Bruce
Duesenberg, Richard William
Elbert, Charles Steiner
Engel, Richard W., Jr.
Estes, Royce Joe
Graham, Robert Clare, III
Gunn, James F.
Hille, Robert John
Inkley, John James, Jr.
Kauffman, William Ray
Lattinville, Robert Henry
Leontsinis, George John
Lowther, Thomas Edward
Luberda, George Joseph
McCracken, Ellis W., Jr.
Metcalfe, Walter Lee, Jr.
Neville, James Morton
Paster, Robert W.
Peper, Christian Baird
Pickle, Robert Douglas
Poscover, Maury B.
Rose, Albert Schoenburg
Schoene, Kathleen Snyder
Schramm, Paul Howard
Tierney, Michael Edward
Van Cleve, William Moore
Wagner, Raymond Thomas, Jr.
Watson-Wesley, Denise J.
Watters, Richard Donald
Winning, John Patrick
Withers, W. Wayne
Wolff, Frank Pierce, Jr.
**Springfield**
Greene, Robert Lee
Penninger, William Holt, Jr.
Shantz, Debra Mallonee

### MONTANA

**Billings**
Beiswanger, Gary Lee
**Butte**
Bartlett, Edward
**Great Falls**
Berry, Anders Taylor
**Kalispell**
Robinson, Calvin Stanford
**Missoula**
George, Alexander Andrew

### NEBRASKA

**Falls City**
Halbert, Richard Lewis
**Lincoln**
Crosby, Robert Berkey
Hewitt, James Watt
Ludtke, David Allen
**Omaha**
Barmettler, Joseph John
Blunk, Christian Raymond
Burke, Thomas Raymond
Dolan, James Vincent
Hamann, Deryl Frederick
Hohman, David Michael
Kozlik, Michael David
Martin, Elaine M.
Minter, Gregory Byron
Moylan, James Harold
Rock, Harold L.
Rouse, Michael Adams
von Bernuth, Carl W.
Vosburg, Bruce David

### NEVADA

**Carson City**
Crowell, Robert Lamson
**Incline Village**
Skinner, Gregory Sala
**Las Vegas**
Brewer, John Nelson
Brown, Joseph Wentling
Burnett, Gary Boyd
Geihs, Frederick Siegfried
Lovell, Carl Erwin, Jr.
Nozero, Elizabeth Catherine
Singer, Michael Howard
Wilson, Joseph Morris, III
**Reno**
Fletcher, Douglas Charles
Jeppson, Roger Wayne
Kelly, Brian Coleman
Olechny, Steven John
Oskam, Gerard Lambert
Richards, Paul A.

### NEW HAMPSHIRE

**Hampton**
DuChene, Todd Michael
**Laconia**
Martin, Willard Gordon, Jr.
**Manchester**
Chamberlain, Douglas Reginald
Dastin, Robert Earl
Monson, John Rudolph
**Nashua**
Goodwin, Rolf Ervine
Snow, Robert Brian
**Newport**
Budnitz, Arron Edward
**Portsmouth**
DeGrandpre, Charles Allyson

### NEW JERSEY

**Audubon**
Watson, Mark Henry
**Bridgewater**
DeFranceschi, Gary M.
Snyder, Deborah Ann
**Budd Lake**
Webb, John Gibbon, III
**Camden**
Furey, John J.
Lario, Frank M., Jr.
**Cherry Hill**
Moleski, Anthony G.
Shapiro, Richard Allen
**Clifton**
Sudol, Walter Edward
**Clinton**
Kennedy, Harold Edward
**Cranbury**
Iatesta, John Michael
**Dumont**
Schuster, Steven Vincent
**East Hanover**
Davidson, Anne Stowell
**Edgewater**
Virelli, Louis James, Jr.
**Elizabeth**
Budanitsky, Sander
**Far Hills**
Corash, Richard
**Florham Park**
Calabrese, Arnold Joseph
**Fort Lee**
Cox, Melvin Monroe
LaRocca, Nicholas Joseph
**Franklin Lakes**
Galiardo, John William
Hector, Bruce John
**Freehold**
McLean, Gary P.
**Hackensack**
Greenberg, Steven Morey
Masi, John Roger
**Hackettstown**
Israels, Michael Jozef
**Iselin**
Dornbusch, Arthur A., II
Oriolo, Joseph Michael
**Jersey City**
Lawatsch, Frank Emil, Jr.
**Lawrenceville**
Dahl, Michael Bruce
Kline, Michael J.
Rudy, James Francis Xavier
Silk, Allen M.
**Lebanon**
Johnstone, Irvine Blakeley, III
**Liberty Corner**
Edwards, Robert Nelson
**Livingston**
Grace, Thomas Edward
**Lyndhurst**
Lasky, David
**Madison**
Connors, Joseph Conlin
**Medford**
Gruccio-Thorman, Lillian Joan
**Metuchen**
Convery, Samuel Vincent, Jr.
**Montclair**
Franges, Anne King
**Montvale**
Ulrich, Robert Gardner
**Montville**
Wolk, Stuart Rodney
**Morris Plains**
Johnson, Gregory L.
**Morristown**
Aspero, Benedict Vincent
Gillen, James Robert
Greenapple, Steven Bruce
Humick, Thomas Charles Campbell
Kandravy, John
Kreindler, Peter Michael
Massey, Henry Nelson
Rich, Michael Louis
Schwarz, Kent Louis
Sherman, Sandra Brown
Smith, J. Edward
**New Brunswick**
Scott, David Rodick
**Newark**
Creenan, Katherine Heras
Knee, Stephen H.
Rosmarin, Susan Gresser
**Oakland**
Goldenberg, Eva J.
**Park Ridge**
Takashima, Hideo
**Parsippany**
Chobot, John Charles
Prague, Ronald Jay
**Pitman**
Cloues, Edward Blanchard, II
**Princeton**
Atkins, Thomas Herman
Beimfohr, Douglas Alan
Carlis, Brian Alexander
Glogoff, David Louis
Mattessich, Richard Stephen
Mulchinock, David Steward
**Ramsey**
Ogden, John Hamilton
**Ridgewood**
Harris, Micalyn Shafer
**River Vale**
Falcon, Raymond Jesus, Jr.
**Roseland**
Chapman, Philip Lan Rence
Harris, Allan Michael
Osvald-Mruz, Christine
Starr, Ira M.
**Saddle Brook**
Pearlman, Peter Steven
**Saddle River**
Bastedo, Wayne Webster
Nordlund, William Chalmers
**Scotch Plains**
Hayes, Lewis Mifflin, Jr.
**Secaucus**
Castano, Gregory Joseph
Fitzpatrick, Harold Francis
Holt, Michael Bartholomew
**Somerset**
Green, Jeffrey C.
Macey, Scott J.
**South Orange**
Kassoff, Mitchell Jay
**Springfield**
Steinberg, Jeffrey Marc
**Stirling**
Michels, Kevin Howard
**Summit**
Benjamin, Jeff
Woller, James Alan
**Teaneck**
Diamond, Stanley
**Tetersboro**
Marier, Raymond Conrad
**Union**
Greenstein, Richard Henry
Suplee, Katherine Ann
**Warren**
Hasl, Hannelore Vera Margarete
**Wayne**
Cupka, Brian Joseph
Dockry, Kathleen A.
**Weehawken**
Fleischer, Elizabeth B.
**West Orange**
Goldberg, Leonard Marvin
Mandelbaum, Barry Richard
**Westfield**
Gutterman, Alan J.
**Whitehouse Station**
McDonald, Mary M.
**Woodbridge**
Falk, Kenneth B.
Harris, Brett Rosenberg
Hoberman, Stuart A.
Schaff, Michael Frederick
**Woodcliff Lake**
Nachtigal, Patricia

### NEW MEXICO

**Albuquerque**
Adams, Mark Kildee
Bregman, Sam
Haltom, B(illy) Reid
Lombardi, Curtis Jay
Mueller, Diane Mayne
Pezzillo, Brian James
Rager, Rudolph Russell
Roehl, Jerrald J.
Schuler, Alison Kay
Simon, Robert S.
Thiel, Albert Nicholas, Jr.
Ussery, Albert Travis
**Santa Fe**
Pound, John Bennett

### NEW YORK

**Albany**
Gosdeck, Thomas Joseph
Hyde, Carol Ann
Provorny, Frederick Alan
Rohan, Brian Patrick
Stanton, Victoria Mead
Wallender, Michael Todd
**Armonk**
Moskowitz, Stuart Stanley
**Auburn**
Wolczyk, Joseph Michael
**Batavia**
Saleh, David John
**Bedford**
Atkins, Ronald Raymond
**Bethpage**
Lemle, Robert Spencer
**Binghamton**
Gerhart, Eugene Clifton
**Bronx**
Balka, Sigmund Ronell
Calamari, Andrew M.
Margid, Leonard
**Brooklyn**
Edwards, Arthur Aden
Karmel, Roberta Segal
Rice, Thomas O'Connor
Villa, James Gerard
**Buffalo**
Bailey, Thomas Charles
Cramer, Mark Kenley
Friedman, Scott Edward
Greene, Robert Michael
Halpern, Ralph Lawrence
Ivancic, Gregory Thomas
Jasen, Matthew Joseph
Lippes, Gerald Sanford
Mattar, Lawrence Joseph
McElvein, Thomas Irving, Jr.
Mucci, Gary Louis
Nichols, F(rederick) Harris
Oppenheimer, Randolph Carl
Schulz, Paul John
**Campbell Hall**
Stone, Peter George
**Canandaigua**
Sorce, David Samuel
**Carle Place**
Smolev, Terence Elliot
**Carmel**
Laporte, Cloyd, Jr.
Lowe, E(dwin) Nobles
**Clarence**
Dec, Francis P.
**Clifton Park**
Hayes, Norman Robert, Jr.
Lazarow, Martin Sidney
**Corning**
Ughetta, William Casper
**Dunkirk**
Woodbury, Robert Charles
**Elmhurst**
Lapinski, Alexander J.
**Floral Park**
Catanzano, Raymond Augustine
**Forest Hills**
Greenberg, Robert Jay
**Garden City**
Bishar, John Joseph, Jr.
Breslin, Eileen Mary
Kestenbaum, Harold Lee
Posch, Robert John, Jr.
Scarfone, John A.
**Glen Cove**
Shields, Craig M.
**Glens Falls**
McMillen, Robert Stewart
**Goshen**
Joseph, Alan Lloyd
**Great Neck**
Gastwirth, Stuart Lawrence
Luckman, Gregg A.
Rockowitz, Noah Ezra
**Hamburg**
Glose, Herbert James
Hargesheimer, Elbert, III
**Hauppauge**
Silberling, Stephen Pierce
**Hillsdale**
Lunde, Asbjorn Rudolph
**Hollis**
Testani, Rosa Anna
**Holtsville**
Goldner, Leonard Howard
**Huntington**
DeMartin, Charles Peter
**Jamaica**
Biehl, Kathy Anne
Dickerson, Claire Moore
Gonzalez-Perez, Ramon Horacio
**Jamestown**
Beckstrom, Charles G.
**Jericho**
Corso, Frank Mitchell
**Le Roy**
Harner, Timothy R.
**Lowville**
Snyder, Donald Edward, Jr.
**Malden Bridge**
Benton, Edward Henry
**Manhasset**
Fletcher, James Harry
Lester, David S.
**Manlius**
Sarofeen, Michael Joseph
**Middletown**
Kossar, Ronald Steven
**Mount Kisco**
Edelstein, Peter Michael
**N Syracuse**
Kasouf, Joseph Chickery
**New City**
Fenster, Robert David
**New Hyde Park**
Richman, Theodore Charles
**New Rochelle**
Gunning, Francis Patrick
Stevens, Roger Ross
**New York**
Aibel, Howard J.
Ames, John Lewis
Amhowitz, Harris J.
Andresen, Malcolm
Atkins, Peter Allan
Axelrod, Charles Paul
Bab, Andrew Laurance
Backman, Gerald Stephen
Baker, Mark Robert
Bamberger, Michael Albert
Bandon, William Edward, III
Bannister, J. Alan
Barnabeo, Susan Patricia
Barrett, William L. D.
Bartlett, Joseph Warren
Barton, Roger E.
Baumgardner, John Ellwood, Jr.
Beck, Andrew James
Beckman, Michael
Beebe, Walter H.
Behrendt, John Thomas
Beinecke, Candace Krugman
Beller, Gary A.
Bender, John Charles
Bergreen, Morris Harvey
Bergtraum, Howard Michael
Bernstein, Bernard
Bertoni, Fernando Raul
Berzow, Harold Steven
Beshar, Robert Peter
Bialkin, Kenneth Jules
Bickford, Nathaniel Judson
Bidwell, James Truman, Jr.
Black, Louis Engleman
Blackman, Kenneth Robert
Boehner, Leonard Bruce
Borker, Wallace Jacob
Brandrup, Douglas Warren
Brauner, David A.
Brecher, Howard Arthur
Breinin, Bartley James
Breslow, Stephanie R.
Briggs, Taylor Rastrick
Bring, Murray H.
Briskman, Louis Jacob
Brooks, Gene C.
Brown, Meredith M.
Browne, Jeffrey Francis
Bruenner, Eric William
Brumm, James Earl
Bryan, Barry Richard
Burak, H(oward) Paul
Bushnell, George Edward, III
Butler, Samuel Coles
Calvey, Brian J.
Cannell, John Redferne
Cashman, Gideon
Chasey, Jacqueline
Chilstrom, Robert Meade
Cho, Tai Yong
Cleland, Edward Gordon
Cogan, Sarah Edwards
Cohen, Edward Herschel
Cohen, Hollace T.
Cohen, Howard Marvin
Colamarino, Katrin Belenky
Colleran, Robert T.
Connor, John Thomas, Jr.
Cooper, Stephen Herbert
Corbin, Sol Neil
Cotter, James Michael
Cowan, Wallace Edgar
Cowen, Edward S.
Cranney, Marilyn Kanrek
Crawshaw, Donald R.
Davidson, Sheila Kearney
Davis, Gordon J.
De Leon, Albert Vernon
Derwin, Jordan
Derzaw, Richard Lawrence
Detjen, David Wheeler
Diaz-Granados, Rafael Andres
Dienes, Louis Robert
Dlugoff, Marc Alan
Dodge, Jonathan Karel
Donald, Norman Henderson, III
Dorado, Marianne Gaertner
Dropkin, Charles Edward
Dubin, James Michael
Duffy, Edmund Charles
Dunham, Wolcott Balestier, Jr.
Dunkin, Ellen R.
Eiseman, Neal Martin
Eisenberg, Viviane
Estes, Richard Martin
Farrow, Sallie
Feig, Edward Steven
Feit, Glenn M.
Fernicola, Gregory Anthony
Feuerstein, Bernard A.
Fewell, Charles Kenneth, Jr.
Finkelstein, Allen Lewis
Fisher, Ann Bailen
Fishman, Fred Norman

Fortenbaugh, Samuel Byrod, III
Fraidin, Stephen
Frank, Lloyd
Frazza, George S.
French, John, III
Fried, Donald David
Friedman, Bart
Friedman, Jeffrey Lawrence
Friedman, Samuel Selig
Friss, Warren Edward
Gambro, Michael S.
Gans, Walter Gideon
Garber, Robert Edward
Garvey, Richard Anthony
Gates, Peter P.
Gelfman, Peter Trustman
Getnick, Neil Victor
Gettner, Alan Frederick
Giancarlo, J. Christopher
Gibbs, L(ippman) Martin
Gilioli, Eric Lawrence
Ginsberg, Ernest
Gluck, Marshall J.
Glusband, Steven Joseph
Goldberg, Michael Edward
Golden, Howard Ira
Goldstein, Howard Sheldon
Golomb, Barry
Goodkind, E. Robert
Grader, Scott Paul
Graham, Christopher Francis
Grant, Stephen Allen
Greenberg, Philip Alan
Greenslade, George Alfred
Greenstein, Karen Anne
Greenwald, David Jeffrey
Greenwald, Harold
Greilsheimer, William Henry
Grew, Robert Ralph
Gross, Richard Benjamin
Grosz, Morton Eric
Gruen, Michael Stephan
Haddad, Mark Anthony
Haje, Peter Robert
Halket, Thomas D(aniel)
Hamel, Rodolphe
Hart, Joseph Thomas Campbell
Hartmann, Carl Joseph
Haythe, Thomas Madison
Hecht, Charles Joel
Heleniak, David William
Hendry, Andrew Delaney
Henryson, Herbert, II
Herold, Karl Guenter
Hersh, Robert Michael
Herzeca, Lois Friedman
Hiden, Robert Battaile, Jr.
Hirsch, Barry
Hirsch, Daniel
Hochman, Stephen Allen
Hoffman, Alan S.
Houlihan, Christopher Michael
Howe, Edwin A(lberts), Jr.
Howe, Richard Rives
Hsiao, Monica Lo-Ching
Hurlock, James Bickford
Hutton, G. Thompson
Jacobson, Leon Irwin
Jaffe, Mark M.
Jaglom, Andre Richard
Jefferies, Jack P.
Jenner, Eva Catherine
Jinnett, Robert Jefferson
Johnson, Lynne A.
Jones, Douglas W.
Kalat, Peter Anthony
Kane, Alice Theresa
Kanter, Stacy J.
Kaplan, Carl Eliot
Kaplan, Mark Norman
Karpe, Mark Ark
Katz, Gary M.
Katz, Ronald Scott
Kaufman, Robert Max
Kelly, Thomas Michael
Kelly, W. Michael
Kensington, Costa Nicholas
Kern, George Calvin, Jr.
Kessel, Mark
Kirkland, Galen D.
Kirman, Igor
Klapper, Molly
Kleckner, Robert George, Jr.
Knight, Robert Huntington
Koblenz, Michael Robert
Kobrin, Lawrence Alan
Komaroff, Stanley
Krieger, Sanford
Krinsly, Stuart Z.
Krivoy, Clara
Krouse, George Raymond, Jr.
Krylov, Nikolai
Kumble, Steven Jay
Lalla, Thomas Rocco, Jr.
Landau, Walter Loeber
Landes, Robert Nathan
Lane, Arthur Alan
Laremont, Anita Webb
Larose, Lawrence Alfred
LeFevre, David E.
Lefkowitz, Howard N.
Leonard, Edwin Deane
Levin, Ezra Gurion
Levin, Roger Michael
Levitsky, Asher Samuel
Lewis, Edwin Leonard, III
Li, Donna Dongli
Lieberman, Nancy Ann
Lowenfels, Lewis David
Lund, Daniel P.
Lutringer, Richard Emil
Lutzker, Elliot Howard
Lynch, Luke Daniel, Jr.
Macioce, Frank Michael
Maghiar, Livia L.
Mahan, (Daniel) Dulany, Jr.
Mantle, Raymond Allan
Margolin, Jesse
Margulis, Michael Henry
Marks, Ramon Paul
Marks, Theodore Lee
Martinez, Jose, Jr.
Mathus, David L.
Matteson, William Bleecker
McCarthy, Robert Emmett
McCurrach, Duncan C.
McDavid, William Henry
McGuire, Eugene Guenard
McMeen, Elmer Ellsworth, III
McSloy, Steven Paul
Meer, Jesse Ross
Mestres, Ricardo Angelo, Jr.
Meyer, Matthew J.
Meyering, Christopher P.
Michel, Clifford Lloyd
Milgrim, Roger Michael
Miller, Paul S(amuel)
Miller, Sam Scott
Minsky, Bruce William
Moak, Roger Martin
Mock, Eric V.
Modlin, Howard S.
Most, Jack Lawrence
Mullman, Michael S.
Munsell, James Frederick
Myerson, Toby Salter
Nance, Allan Taylor
Nash, Paul LeNoir
Nathan, Andrew Jonathan
Newman, Fredric Samuel
Nimetz, Matthew
Nissenbaum, David
Norwitz, Trevor S.
Orol, Elliot S.
Pack, Leonard Brecher
Paladino, Daniel R.
Papernik, Joel Ira
Park, Sang Hyuk
Passer-Muslin, Juliette Mayabelle
Pavia, George M.
Pellecchio, Ralph L.
Peragine, Paul Francis
Perkins, Roswell Burchard
Perlberger, Ralph
Pettibone, Peter John
Pisano, Vincent James
Prashker, Audrey Eve
Prem, F. Herbert, Jr.
Prentice, Eugene Miles, III
Purcell, John Joseph, III
Quinn, Linda C.
Rabb, Bruce
Rachlin, Leila
Radey, Dona Lynn
Radon, Jenik Richard
Rankin, Clyde Evan, III
Rawson, Richard J.
Ray, Jeanne Cullinan
Reid, Edward Snover, III
Ressa, Gregory John
Ring, Renee Etheline
Robinson, Irwin Jay
Robinson, John Kelly
Rocklen, Kathy Hellenbrand
Rodman, Leroy Eli
Rogers, Danforth William
Rosen, Richard Lewis
Rosenberg, Marc S.
Rosenblum, Scott S.
Rosenblum, William F., Jr.
Rosenzweig, Charles Leonard
Ross, Matthew
Roth, Paul Norman
Rubin, Herbert
Rubinstein, Frederic Armand
Rusmisel, Stephen R.
Russo, Thomas Anthony
Ryan, J. Richard
Sacks, Karen Goldfarb
Saft, Stuart Mark
Sallay, Tibor
Sargent, James Cunningham
Sastow, Gary Saul
Satovsky, Stacey Yael
Saunders, Mark A.
Schaab, Arnold J.
Scherr, Stephanie Lynn
Schizer, Zevie Baruch
Schleimer, Karen Beth
Schmidt, Daniel Edward, IV
Schmidt, Joseph W.
Schmitt, John Patrick
Schneider, Harold Lawrence
Schorr, Brian Lewis
Schulte, Stephen John
Schuur, Robert George
Schwartz, Carol Vivian
Seifert, Thomas Lloyd
Seward, George Chester
Shapiro, Aleena Rieger
Shecter, Howard L.
Sheehan, Robert C.
Shenker, Joseph C.
Sher, Michael Lee
Sheridan, Peter N.
Siegel, Charles
Siegel, Jeffrey Norton
Silkenat, James Robert
Siller, Stephen I.
Silverberg, Jay L.
Silvermintz, Michael B.
Slezak, Edward M.
Smith, Robert Everett
Sorkin, David James
Spanbock, Maurice Samuel
Spatt, Robert Edward
Spencer, David Eric
Sperling, Allan George
Spiegel, Jerrold Bruce
Squire, Walter Charles
Steinbach, Harold I.
Steinberg, Howard Eli
Stephenson, Alan Clements
Stewart, Charles Evan
Strom, Milton Gary
Sulger, Francis Xavier
Swiedler, Alan M.
Taylor, John Chestnut, III
Teiman, Richard B.
Tengi, Frank R.
Terrell, J. Anthony
Tract, Marc Mitchell
Tran, Julie Hoan
Trott, Dennis C(harles)
Tse, Charles Yung Chang
Underberg, Mark Alan
Urquia, Rafael, II
Van Gundy, Gregory Frank
Vig, Vernon Edward
Vogel, Bernard Henry
Wald, Bernard Joseph
Wallin, James Peter
Wang, Albert Huai-En
Waterman, William, Jr.
Webb, Morrison DeSoto
Weiner, Earl David
Welikson, Jeffrey Alan
Whitman, Charles S., III
Wiegley, Roger Douglas
Wilder, Charles Willoughby
Wilson, Edward N.
Wise, Aaron Noah
Witmeyer, John Jacob, III
Wolf, Gary Wickert
Wolfe, James Ronald
Wolson, Craig Alan
Worenklein, Jacob Joshua
Wu, Niping
Wydler, Hans Ulrich
Wynn, Simon David
Yamin, Michael Geoffrey
Yang, Phillip Seungpil
Yu, Sandy Kyung
Yun, Edward Joon
Zimmerman, Earl S.
Zimmerman, Jean
Zimmerman, Paula Susan
Zuckerman, Paul Herbert
Zukerman, Michael

**Niagara Falls**
Berrigan, Patrick Joseph

**Oswego**
Greene, Stephen Craig

**Peconic**
Mitchell, Robert Everitt

**Pleasantville**
Ahrensfeld, Thomas Frederick
Soden, Paul Anthony

**Poughkeepsie**
Millman, Jode Susan

**Purchase**
Sharpe, Robert Francis, Jr.

**Riverhead**
Maggipinto, V. Anthony
Shane, Suzanne V.

**Rochester**
Adair, Donald Robert
Brovitz, Richard Stuart
Doyle, Justin P
Groschadl, Paul Stephen
Harris, Wayne Manley
Lundback, Staffan Bengt Gunnar
Willett, Thomas Edward
Young, Thomas Paul

**Rye**
Dixon, Paul Edward
Roberts, Thomas Alba
Varona, Daniel Robert

**Sands Point**
Hoynes, Louis LeNoir, Jr.

**Saratoga Springs**
Capozzola, Theresa A.

**Scarsdale**
Crawford, Homer
Keeffe, John Arthur

**Schenectady**
Buso, Eduardo L.
Thiele, Leslie Kathleen Larsen

**Sleepy Hollow**
Andrew, Leonard DeLessio

**Smithtown**
Pruzansky, Joshua Murdock

**Snyder**
Genrich, Willard Adolph

**Southampton**
Lopez, David

**Spring Valley**
Graifman, Gary Steven

**Suffern**
Stack, Daniel

**Syracuse**
Barclay, H(ugh) Douglas
Bruno, Richard Thomas
Bullock, Stephen C.
Engel, Richard Lee
Evans, Thomas S.
Hayes, David Michael
Rivette, Francis Robert
Sager, Jonathan Ward
Wladis, Mark Neil

**Uniondale**
Paciullo, Maria Maestranzi

**Watertown**
Militello, Samuel Philip

**Westbury**
Zychick, Joel David

**White Plains**
Balaber-Strauss, Barbara
Berlin, Alan Daniel
Feder, Robert
Hecker, Robert J.
Rosenberg, Michael
Serchuk, Ivan
Shin, Helen
Silverberg, Steven Mark
Vogel, Howard Stanley

**Yonkers**
Clark, Celia Rue

## NORTH CAROLINA

**Asheville**
Hamilton, Jackson Douglas
Worley, Charles Robert

**Burlington**
Slayton, John Howard

**Cary**
Gannon, Christopher J. I.
Taylor, Marvin Edward, Jr.

**Charlotte**
Abelman, Henry Moss
Barbery, Paul Saunders
Belthoff, Richard Charles, Jr.
Bernstein, Mark R.
Bryce, Teresa Audrey
Chesson, Calvin White
Claytor, William Mimms
Culbreth, James Harold, Jr.
Gage, Gaston Hemphill
McBryde, Neill Gregory
McDermott, Christopher Manning
Murchison, Bradley Duncan
Newitt, John Garwood, Jr.
Pansegrau, Phaedra Renée
Preston, James Young
Shiau, H. Lin
Taylor, David Brooke
Walker, Clarence Wesley
Walls, George Rodney
Zeller, Michael Eugene

**Cherryville**
Huffstetler, Palmer Eugene

**Durham**
Welborn, Reich Lee

**Elizabeth City**
Riley, John Frederick

**Fayetteville**
Townsend, William Jackson

**Greensboro**
Davis, Herbert Owen
Gabriel, Richard Weisner
Hopkins, John David
Koonce, Neil Wright

**Hendersonville**
Hull, J(ames) Richard

**Hickory**
Cagle, Joe Neal

**High Point**
Ashcraft, David Bee

**Morganton**
Simpson, Daniel Reid

**Raleigh**
Carruth, Paul
Geil, John McIntosh
Graham, William Edgar, Jr.
Gwyn, William Blair, Jr.
Harazin, William Dennis
Hargrove, Wade Hampton
Jernigan, John Lee
Markoff, Brad Steven
Reinhard, Steven Ira
Stallings, Joseph Henry
Tucker, Sherry E.
Wilson, Robert Lee, Jr.

**Salisbury**
Porter, J. Andrew

**Wilmington**
Gibson, Frank Byron, Jr.
McCauley, Cleyburn Lycurgus

**Winston Salem**
Barnhardt, Zeb Elonzo, Jr.
Early, James H., Jr.
Herring, Jerone Carson
Ingersoll, Marc W.
Loughridge, John Halsted, Jr.
Motsinger, John Kings
Schollander, Wendell Leslie, Jr.
Ventura, Bruce Anthony

## NORTH DAKOTA

**Bismarck**
Hinman, Michael J.

**Minot**
Backes, Jon William

## OHIO

**Akron**
Allan, Ronald Curtis
Cox, Steven St. Leger
Harvie, Crawford Thomas
Mohler, Robert E.
Quirk, Frank Edward
Rooney, George Willard

**Athens**
Gall, Robert Jay

**Canfield**
Beck, James Hayes

**Canton**
Brannen, John Howard
Haupt, Fred Jerry
Putman, Timothy Joseph

**Cincinnati**
Arango, Emilio
Case, Douglas Manning
Cobey, John Geoffrey
Evans, James E.
Flanagan, John Anthony
Fleming, Lisa L.
Hayden, William Taylor
Heldman, Paul W.
Henderson, Stephen Paul
Kenrich, John Lewis
Kite, William McDougall
Lindberg, Charles David
Neumark, Michael Harry
Olson, Robert Wyrick
Petrie, Bruce Inglis
Porter, Robert Carl, Jr.
Schwab, Nelson, Jr.
Silvers, Jane Fink
Vander Laan, Mark Alan
Wagner, Barbara
Wales, Ross Elliot

**Cleveland**
Arnoff, Fred Jay
Band, Jordan Clifford
Baxter, Howard H.
Billington, Glenn Earle
Blackford, Jason Collier
Braverman, Herbert Leslie
Coyle, Martin Adolphus, Jr.
Donahue, Charles Bertrand, II
Ebert, Gary Andrew
Falsgraf, William Wendell
Farah, Benjamin Frederick
Furber, Philip Craig
Gherlein, Gerald Lee
Groetzinger, Jon, Jr.
Kelly, Sandra M.
Koblenz, N(orman) Herschel
Langer, Carlton Earl
Markus, Stephen Allan
Mc Cartan, Patrick Francis
McKee, Thomas Frederick
Owendoff, Stephen Peter
Pearlman, Samuel Segel
Posteraro, David Robert
Pyke, John Secrest, Jr.
Schabes, Alan Elliot
Schneider, David Miller
Singerman, Paul Joseph
Sogg, Wilton Sherman
Stavnicky, Michael Ross
Stellato, Louis Eugene
Stevens, Thomas Charles
Stovsky, Michael David
Trevor, Leigh Barry
Utrata, Carl Ignatius
Waldeck, John Walter, Jr.
Zamore, Joseph David

**Columbus**
Anderson, Jon Mac
Balthaser, James Harvey
Brinkman, Dale Thomas
Casey, John Frederick
Darling, Stanton Girard
D'Aurora, Jack
Dunlay, Catherine Telles
Emens, J. Richard
Frasier, Ralph Kennedy
Fried, Samuel
Kington, John Anthony
McConnaughey, George Carlton, Jr.
Postlewaite, William Neal, Sr.
Robins, Ronald Albert, Jr.
Scott, David Matthew
Spencer, Scott W.
Starkoff, Alan Gary
Summer, Fred A.
Tarpy, Thomas Michael
Vorys, Arthur Isaiah
Willcox, Roderick Harrison
Wolper, Beatrice Emens

**Dayton**
Booth, Michael A.
Chernesky, Richard John
Furry, Richard Logan
Lamme, Kathryn Anne
Liberman, Scott A.
McSwiney, Charles Ronald
Nicholson, Mark William
Rapp, Gerald Duane
Schneble, Alfred William, III
Schwartz, Richard Anthony
Teeters, Bruce A.
Tweel, Donna Shank
Watts, Steven Richard

**Dublin**
Bennett, Steven Alan
Emmert, Steven Michael
Inzetta, Mark Stephen

**Elyria**
Sarkar, Neil Steven

**Geneva**
Epstein, Sherry Stein

**Grove City**
Dodd, Jerry Lee

**Hamilton**
Meyers, Pamela Sue

**Jefferson**
Lemire, Jerome Albert

**Kenton**
Tudor, John Martin

**Lancaster**
Libert, Donald Joseph

**Massillon**
Netzly, Dwight H.

**Maumee**
Kline, James Edward

**Miamisburg**
Niemeyer, Jonathan David

**Milford**
Kushner, Gordon Peter

**Mount Vernon**
Rose, Kim Matthew

**N Royalton**
Jungeberg, Thomas Donald

**North Canton**
Dettinger, Warren Walter

**Piqua**
Davis, Dale Gordon

**Richfield**
Calise, Nicholas James

**Rocky River**
Grady, Francis Xavier

**Shaker Heights**
Cherchiglia, Dean Kenneth

**Solon**
Fouts, Douglas Robert

**Springfield**
Barnett, Hugh

**Tipp City**
Arenstein, Gilbert Gregory

**Toledo**
O'Connell, Maurice Daniel
Rollison, Gerardo Roy
Strobel, Martin Jack
Webb, Thomas Irwin, Jr.

**Troy**
Bazler, Frank Ellis

**Twinsburg**
Hill, Thomas Allen

**Warren**
Letson, William Normand
McGeough, Robert Saunders

**Westlake**
Reichard, William Edward

**Wickliffe**
Crehore, Charles Aaron
Kidder, Fred Dockstater

**Worthington**
Minton, Harvey Steiger
Worobiec, Michele Selig

**Youngstown**
Lenga, Robert Allen
Messenger, James Louis

## OKLAHOMA

**Bartlesville**
Benedict, Anthony Wayne
Roff, Alan Lee

**Cherokee**
Mitchell, Allan Edwin

**Norman**
Talley, Richard Bates

**Oklahoma City**
Barth, J. Edward
High, David Royce
Kenney, Herbert King
Kirschner, Jonna Dee Kauger
McBride, Kenneth Eugene
Mock, Randall Don
Paliotta, Armand
Pardue, Wallace David, Jr.
Paul, William George
Rockett, D. Joe
Schuster, E. Elaine

Stanley, Brian Jordan
Steinhorn, Irwin Harry
Williams, Teresa Ann Goode
Wilson, Julia Ann Yother
**Stroud**
Swanson, Robert Lee
**Tulsa**
Arrington, John Leslie, Jr.
Barnes, Deborah Browers
Biolchini, Robert Fredrick
Bowman, David Wesley
Chandler, Ronald Jay
Cooper, Richard Casey
Davenport, Gerald Bruce
Estill, John Staples, Jr.
Gaberino, John Anthony, Jr.
Hickman, Frank Robert
Hilsabeck, Michael D.
Huffman, Robert Allen, Jr.
Kenney, Bruce Allen
Kihle, Donald Arthur
Mackey, Steven R.
Marlar, Donald Floyd
Moffett, J. Denny
Tomlins, Neal Edward

### OREGON

**Ashland**
Fine, J. David
Shaw, Barry N.
**Beaverton**
Robertson, Douglas Stuart
**Eugene**
Anderson, Bruce Hamilton
Gallagher, Donald Avery, Jr.
Pilcher, Debra Evelyn
**Lebanon**
Kuntz, Joel Dubois
**Portland**
Abravanel, Allan Ray
Anderson, Mark Alexander
Baxendale, James Charles Lewis
Bayless, Richard Vern
Culpepper, David Charles
Hanna, Harry Mitchell
Hendricks, Stephen
Hurd, Paul Gemmill
King, Christy Olson
Krahmer, Donald Leroy, Jr.
Meyer, Paul Richard
Norby, Mark Alan
Richardson, Jay
Sadler, Richard Lawrence
Smith, Douglas Dean
Weiler, Mary Pauline

### PENNSYLVANIA

**Allentown**
Agger, James H.
Feinberg, Gregg Michael
Frank, Bernard
McGinley, Paul Anthony, Jr.
**Aston**
Newton, John Edward, Jr.
**Bala Cynwyd**
Kane-Vanni, Patricia Ruth
Lasak, John Joseph
Lee, Rotan Edward
**Bethlehem**
Barnette, Curtis Handley
**Blue Bell**
Barron, Harold Sheldon
**Bradford**
Hauser, Christopher George
**Devon**
Graf, Bayard Mayhew
**Exton**
Hedges, Donald Walton
**Franklin Center**
Harvey, Alice Elease
**Gibsonia**
Heilman, Carl Edwin
**Grove City**
McBride, Milford Lawrence, Jr.
**Harrisburg**
Boswell, William Douglas
Fritz, Martin Andrew
**Havertown**
Donohue, Robert John
**Holtwood**
Campbell, Paul Gary
**Horsham**
Eisenberg, Steven Keith
Troy, Richard Hershey
**Jenkintown**
Michie, Daniel Boorse, Jr.
Ormsby, Charles William, Jr.
Robbins, Jack Winton
**Johnstown**
Glosser, William Louis
**Kennett Square**
Partnoy, Ronald Allen
**King Of Prussia**
Breslin, Michael Francis
**Lancaster**
Duroni, Charles Eugene
Golin, Charles
Lewis, Alvin Bower, Jr.
**Langhorne**
Lynch, James Edward
**Lansdale**
Pearlstine, Neal R.
Walper, Robert Andrew
**Lehighton**
Schwab, William G.
**Lewistown**
Levin, Allen Joseph
**Malvern**
Cameron, John Clifford
Quay, Thomas Emery
**Marietta**
Shumaker, Harold Dennis
**Mc Murray**
Brzustowicz, John Cinq-Mars
**Media**
Humphrey, Carlos M.
Mardinly, Peter Alan
Rainer, G. Bradley
**Milton**
Davis, Preston Lindner
**Moon Township**
Lipson, Barry J.
**Morrisville**
Dobin, Edward I.
**Mount Pleasant**
Johnson, Michael A.
**New Castle**
Lynch, Paul Patrick
**Norristown**
Aman, George Matthias, III
Milner, Kenneth Paul
**Oakmont**
Medonis, Robert Xavier
**Philadelphia**
Agran, Raymond Daniel
Baum, E. Harris
Berger, Lawrence Howard
Bogutz, Jerome Edwin
Bonovitz, Sheldon M.
Briscoe, Jack Clayton
Chiacchiere, Mark Dominic
Chimples, George
Clark, William H., Jr.
Cohen, David Louis
Cooper, Wendy Fein
Coyne, Charles Cole
Cramer, Harold
Cross, Milton H.
DeBunda, Salvatore Michael
Del Raso, Joseph Vincent
Doran, William Michael
Drake, William Frank, Jr.
Feder, Steven J.
Gadon, Steven Franklin
Gagne, William Roderick
Goldberg, Marvin Allen
Goldman, Gary Craig
Goldman, Jerry Stephen
Gough, John Francis
Grady, Thomas Michael
Greenstein, J. Richard
Hennessy, Joseph H.
Henry, Ragan Augustus
Hunter, Jack Duval
Hunter, James Austen, Jr.
Krzyzanowski, Richard L(ucien)
Liu, Diana Chua
Loveless, George Group
Loverdi, Rosemary J.
Luongo, Stephen Earle
Malloy, Michael P.
O'Brien, William Jerome, II
Pauciulo, John William
Pillion, Michael Leith
Promislo, Daniel
Reiss, John Barlow
Subak, John Thomas
Tumola, Thomas Joseph
Wert, Robert Clifton
Wolff, Deborah H(orowitz)
**Pittsburgh**
Aaron, Marcus, II
Aderson, Sanford M.
Alberty, Michael Charles
Barnes, James Jerome
Blume, Peter Keefe
Boswell, William Paret
Conti, Joy Flowers
Davis, Lewis U., Jr.
Dell, Ernest Robert
Drake, Edwin P.
Hardie, James Hiller
Harff, Charles Henry
Helmrich, Joel Marc
Hess, Emerson Garfield
Hildreth, Gary R.
Holsinger, John Paul
Johnson, Stephen W.
Kalil, David Thomas
Lefkowitz, Alan Zoel
Letwin, Jeffrey William
McCabe, Lawrence James
McGuire, Matthew Francis
McKee, Ralph Dyer, Jr.
Messer, Susan J.
Messner, Robert Thomas
Murdoch, David Armor
Nevin, Hugh Williamson, Jr.
Newlin, William Rankin
Nute, Leslie F.
Owen, Jeffrey Randall
Pugliese, Robert Francis
Sandman, Dan D.
Shuman, Joseph Duff
Stepanian, Steven Arvid, II
Sutton, William Dwight
Todd, Stephan Kent
Todd, Thomas
Walton, Jon David
Whyte, Kevin J.
Wilkinson, James Allan
**Radnor**
Boardman, Harold Frederick, Jr.
**Reading**
DiSibio, Carol Lynn Kridler
Ober, Paul Russell
Scianna, Russell William
**Saint Davids**
Preston, Robert F.
**Sharon**
Ekker, Henry Mayer
**Shavertown**
Malak, Paul John
Ostroski, Raymond B.
**Southampton**
Benz, William J.
**Valley Forge**
Bovaird, Brendan Peter
Posner, Ernest Gary
**Wayne**
Donnella, Michael Andre
Kalogredis, Vasilios J.
Wilson, Bruce Brighton
**West Chester**
Osborn, John Edward
**Wilkes Barre**
Roth, Eugene
Ufberg, Murray
**Williamsport**
Ertel, Allen Edward
Kane, Joseph Patrick
**Wormleysburg**
Cherewka, Michael
**Wyndmoor**
Starr, Harold Page
**York**
Benn, Niles S.
Pell, Daniel Max

### RHODE ISLAND

**Barrington**
Soutter, Thomas Douglas
**Newport**
McConnell, David Kelso
**Pawtucket**
Belliveau, Kathrin Pagonis
Kranseler, Lawrence Michael
**Providence**
Berkelhammer, Robert Bruce
Carlotti, Stephen Jon
Donnelly, Kevin William
Kacir, Barbara Brattin
Kean, John Vaughan
McMahon, Raymond John
Salvadore, Guido Richard
**Warwick**
Battle, Leslie Anne Elizabeth
**West Warwick**
Nota, Kenneth Joseph
**Westerly**
Hennessy, Dean McDonald

### SOUTH CAROLINA

**Aiken**
Alan, Matthew W. A.
**Charleston**
Cannon, Hugh
Clement, Robert Lebby, Jr.
Cooke, Morris Dawes, Jr.
Warren, John Hertz, III
Webb, Richard Craig
**Columbia**
Marchant, Bristow
Unger, Richard Mahlon
**Greenville**
Dana, Frank J., III
Dobson, Robert Albertus, III
Edwards, Harry LaFoy
Phillips, Joseph Brantley, Jr.
Wyche, Bradford Wheeler
**Greenwood**
Nexsen, Julian Jacobs, Jr.
**Hartsville**
DeLoach, Harris E(ugene), Jr.
**Hilton Head Island**
Hagoort, Thomas Henry
Rose, William Shepard, Jr.
Scarminach, Charles Anthony
**Mount Pleasant**
Swanson, Shane Eric
**Rock Hill**
Alford, Duncan Earl
Hardin, James Carlisle, III
**Salem**
Everett, C(harles) Curtis
**Summerville**
Mortimer, Rory Dixon

### SOUTH DAKOTA

**Sioux Falls**
Van Demark, Richard Edward

### TENNESSEE

**Brentwood**
Provine, John C.
Schreiber, Kurt Gilbert
**Chattanooga**
Durand, Whitney
Durham, J(oseph) Porter, Jr.
Levine, James Howard
Weems, Kyle Richard
**Greeneville**
Bell, William Hall
**Knoxville**
Campbell, Robert Roe
Howard, Lewis Spilman
McCall, Jack Humphreys, Jr.
Sanger, Herbert Shelton, Jr.
Worthington, Carole Yard Lynch
**Memphis**
Buhler, Lynn Bledsoe
David, Monroe Steven
Friedman, Robert Michael
Gentry, Gavin Miller
Jackson, Thomas Francis, III
Jalenak, James Bailey
Masterson, Kenneth Rhodes
Morgan, Colby Shannon, Jr.
Rawlins, Donald R.
Rutledge, Roger Keith
Schuler, Walter E.
Spore, Richard Roland, III
Tate, Stonewall Shepherd
Waddell, Phillip Dean
**Nashville**
Anderson, Charles Hill
Berry, William Wells
Bingham, Pamela Mary Muir
Carr, Davis Haden
Eisen, Steven Jeffrey
Farris, Frank Mitchell, Jr.
Freeman, James Atticus, III
Jackson, Kenneth Monroe
Kelley, James Russell
Lowell, Roland M.
Mayden, Barbara Mendel
Mefford, R. Douglas
Oldfield, Russell Miller
Sidwell, Susan Von Brock
Spining, W. Carl
Tuke, Robert Dudley
Turner, Robert Joseph

### TEXAS

**Abilene**
Whitten, C. G.
**Arlington**
Dowdy, John Vernard, Jr.
Pierson, Grey
**Austin**
Borden, Diana Kimball
Donley, Dennis W.
Gangstad, John Erik
Laughead, James Marshall
Lione, John Gabriel, Jr.
Roan, Forrest Calvin, Jr.
Schrauff, Christopher Wesley
Smith, Jeffrey Carlin
**Beaumont**
Cavaliere, Frank Joseph
**Brownfield**
Moore, Bradford L.
**Brownsville**
Ray, Mary Louise Ryan
**Dallas**
Agnich, Richard John
Beard, Bruce E.
Beuttenmuller, Rudolf William
Bivans, Roger Wayne
Blachly, Jack Lee
Blount, Charles William, III
Broussard, Peter O.
Buchanan, Robert Graham, Jr.
Burke, William Temple, Jr.
Coleman, Russell Forester
Crain, Christina Melton
Crowley, James Worthington
England, Austin Hinds
Feld, Alan David
Fishman, Edward Marc
Garcia Barron, Ramiro
Glendenning, Don Mark
Godfrey, Cullen Michael
Hamby, Robert Kevin
Hunter, Robert Frederick
Irwin, Ivan, Jr.
Joseph, Marc Ward
Kennedy, Marc J.
King, Jeffrey P.
Leach, James Glover
Malorzo, Thomas Vincent
Marquardt, Robert Richard
McNamara, Anne H.
Mears, Rona Robbins
Menges, John Kenneth, Jr.
Meyer, Ferdinand Charles, Jr.
Moore, Marilyn Payne
Moore, Richard George
Morrison, David Eugene
Parker, James Francis
Pleasant, James Scott
Rice, Darrel Alan
Riley, Peter James
Roberts, David Mace
Scott, John Roland
Sears, Ruth Ann
Solomon, Mark S.
Spears, Robert Fields
Swanson, Wallace Martin
True, Roy Joe
Veach, Robert Raymond, Jr.
Young, Barney Thornton
Zisman, Barry Stuart
**Diboll**
Ericson, Roger Delwin
**El Paso**
Hedrick, Mark
Smith, Tad Randolph
**Farmersville**
Seward, Richard Bevin
**Fort Worth**
Carr, Thomas Eldridge
Collins, Whitfield James
Curry, Donald Robert
Fanous, Nikki Hobert
Light, Russell Jeffers
Sartain, James Edward
Sheehan, Edward Michael
Watson, Robert Francis
**Garland**
Guldi, Rebecca Elizabeth
**Georgetown**
Bryce, William Delf
**Houston**
Anderson, Eric Severin
Bader, Gregory Vincent
Bech, Douglas York
Becher, Andrew Clifford
Beirne, Martin Douglas
Bily, Kirkland Jarrard
Bland, John L.
Born, Dawn Slater
Brantley, John Randolph
Brentin, John Olin
Brinsmade, Lyon Louis
Brown, Michael Lance
Callegari, William A., Jr.
Carter, Daniel Roland
Clark, John A., Jr.
Cohen, Jay I.
Cooper, Thomas Randolph
Cotton, James Alexandre
Craig, Robert Mark, III
Duffy, Stephen William
Eastin, Keith E.
Eckman, David Walter
Engerrand, Kenneth G.
Ewen, Pamela Binnings
Finch, Michael Paul
Fisher, Donald Elton, Jr.
Forbes, Arthur Lee, III
Goldman, Nathan Carliner
Harrington, Bruce Michael
Hartrick, Janice Kay
Heinrich, Randall Wayne
Kelly, William Franklin, Jr.
Khan, Lori Jean
Kurz, Thomas Patrick
Lamme, Thomas Robert
Landry, Brenda Marguerite
Lee, William Gentry
Love, Jeffrey Benton
Mai, Mark F.
Marlow, Orval Lee, II
Minor, Sterling Arthur
Murphy, Ewell Edward, Jr.
Myers, Franklin
Nacol, Mae
O'Donnell, Lawrence, III
Oldham, J. Thomas
O'Toole, Austin Martin
Parker, Dallas Robert
Plaeger, Frederick Joseph, II
Pruitt, Robert Randall
Sanchez, Manuel
Sapp, Walter William
Schneller, John, IV
Shaddix, James W.
Simmons, Stephen Judson
Still, Charles Henry
Taten, Bruce Malcolm
Tran, Minh Quang
Valentine, Michael John
Weberpal, Michael Andrew
Williams, Percy Don
Winer, Stephen I.
Zahorik, Michael Alan
**Irving**
French, Colin Val
Glober, George Edward, Jr.
**Kaufman**
Legg, Reagan Houston
**La Porte**
Askins, Knox Winfred
**Lubbock**
Crowson, James Lawrence
**Missouri City**
Hodges, Jot Holiver, Jr.
**Panhandle**
Neal, A. Curtis
**Richardson**
Jeffreys, Albert Leonidas
**San Antonio**
Becker, Douglas Wesley
Biery, Evelyn Hudson
Bramble, Ronald Lee
Fisher, Eric A.
Lippoldt, Darin Michael
Lutter, Charles William, Jr.
Pipkin, Marvin Grady
**Temple**
Cuba, Benjamin James
Pickle, Jerry Richard
**Tyler**
Killough, J. Scott
**Waco**
Page, Jack Randall
**Wichita Falls**
Todd, Richard D. R.

### UTAH

**Ogden**
Mecham, Glenn Jefferson
**Salt Lake City**
Atkin, Gary Eugene
Headman, Arlan Osmond, Jr.
Heaton, Jon C.
Jones, Michael Frank
Ockey, Ronald J.
Sine, Wesley Franklin
**Spanish Fork**
Ashworth, Brent Ferrin

### VERMONT

**Burlington**
Baker, Robert W., Jr.
Cole, Leigh Polk
Gravel, John Cook
**Montpelier**
Bland, Richard Norman
**Randolph Center**
Casson, Richard Frederick
**Rutland**
Taylor, A. Jeffry
**Taftsville**
Johnson, Philip Martin

### VIRGINIA

**Alexandria**
Beach, Barbara Purse
Higgins, Mary Celeste
Klewans, Samuel N.
Paturis, E. Michael
**Arlington**
Fowler, David Lucas
Kelly, John James
McCorkindale, Douglas Hamilton
Morgens, Warren Kendall
Schwartz, Philip
Welty, Charles Douglas
**Charlottesville**
Caccese, Michael Stephen
Hodous, Robert Power
Stroud, Robert Edward
**Chesapeake**
Lascara, Dominic Paul
Tinkham, James Jeffrey
**Danville**
Regan, Michael Patrick
**Fairfax**
Bloomquist, Dennis Howard
Chapman, Edmund Whyte
Downey, Richard Lawrence
Dwornik, Frances Pierson
Kear, Maria Martha Ruscitella
Lash, Richard Anthony
Maiwurm, James John
Murray, Michael Patrick
**Falls Church**
Duesenberg, Robert H.
Halagao, Avelino Garabiles
Jennings, Thomas Parks
Nunes, Morris A.
Ward, Joe Henry, Jr.
**Glen Allen**
Urelius, Shawn Renea
**Great Falls**
Preston, Charles George
Rath, Francis Steven
**Hampton**
McNider, James Small, III
**Herndon**
Afshar, Carolyn McKinney
**Lynchburg**
Davies, Arthur B(everly), III
Whitesell, Darryl Duane
**Mc Lean**
Brown, Thomas Cartmel, Jr.
Church, Randolph Warner, Jr.
Goolrick, Robert Mason
Greene, Timothy Geddes
LeSourd, Nancy Susan Oliver

Maloof, Farahe Paul
Morris, James Malachy
Rau, Lee Arthur
Stephens, William Theodore
Walton, Edmund Lewis, Jr.
Weiss, Rhett Louis

**McLean**
Djinis, Stephanie Ann
Houle, Jeffrey Robert

**Newport News**
Kamp, Arthur Joseph, Jr.
Segall, James Arnold

**Norfolk**
Best, Charles William, Jr.
Poston, Anita Owings
Reeves, Ross Campbell
Stackhouse, Robert Clinton
Tolmie, Donald McEachern
Wooldridge, William Charles

**Reston**
Reicin, Eric David

**Richmond**
Belcher, Dennis Irl
Buffenstein, Allan S.
Buford, Robert Pegram
Carrell, Daniel Allan
Denny, Collins, III
Elmore, Edward Whitehead
Goodpasture, Philip Henry
Grey, Robert J.
Jones, Reginald Nash
Mezzullo, Louis Albert
Minardi, Richard A., Jr.
Musick, Robert Lawrence, Jr.
Perkins, Jon Scott
Rainey, Gordon Fryer, Jr.
Robinson, John Victor
Rucker, Douglas Pendleton, Jr.
Ryland, Walter H.
Starke, Harold E., Jr.
Weis, Laura Visser

**Roanoke**
Bates, Harold Martin
Densmore, Douglas Warren
Glenn, Robert Eastwood

**Sterling**
Babirak, Milton Edward, Jr.

**Suffolk**
Young, Hubert Howell, Jr.

**Vienna**
McCabe, Thomas Edward
Randolph, Christopher Craven

**Virginia Beach**
Layton, Garland Mason

### WASHINGTON

**Bellevue**
Gulick, Peter VanDyke
Medved, Robert Allen
Morie, G. Glen
Parsons, James Bowne
Sullivan, James Jerome
Waldbaum, Alan G.

**Issaquah**
Benoliel, Joel
Sterling, Michael Erwin

**Montesano**
Stewart, James Malcolm

**Seattle**
Albright, Douglas Eaton
Blair, M. Wayne
Blom, Daniel Charles
Brooks, Julie Anne
Canavor, Frederick Charles, Jr.
Collins, Theodore John
Comstock, Brian Lloyd
Creim, Jerry Alan
DeForest, Stephen Elliott
Diamond, Josef
Diggs, Bradley C.
Ebell, C(ecil) Walter
Ferrer, Rafael Douglas Paul
Franke, Patrick Joseph
Graham, Stephen Michael
Hilpert, Edward Theodore, Jr.
Hoffman, Mark Frederick
Hough, Mark Mason
Jackson, Dillon Edward
Judson, C(harles) James (Jim Judson)
Kelly, Kevin Francis
Malone, Thomas William
Palmer, Douglas S., Jr.
Pym, Bruce Michael
Rieke, Paul Victor
Ruddy, James W.
Shulkin, Jerome
Tune, James Fulcher
Whitford, Joseph P.
Williams, J. Vernon

**Silverdale**
Wildsmith, Quentin

**Spokane**
Cerutti, Patrick Bernard

**Tacoma**
Barcus, Benjamin Franklin
Krueger, James A.

**Walla Walla**
Hayner, Herman Henry

**Yakima**
Wright, J(ames) Lawrence

### WEST VIRGINIA

**Charleston**
George, Larry Wayne

**Fairmont**
Brandfass, Robert Lee

**Huntington**
Colburn, James Allan
McGuire, J(ames) Grant

**Martinsburg**
Martin, Clarence Eugene, III

**Morgantown**
Fusco, Andrew G.
Ringer, Darrell Wayne

**Wheeling**
Gardill, James Clark

### WISCONSIN

**Appleton**
Hartzheim, Charles John
Thenell, Heather Jo

**Elkhorn**
Sweet, Lowell Elwin

**Elm Grove**
Gorske, Robert Herman

**Janesville**
Finman-Pince, Terry J.

**Kohler**
Sheedy, Kathleen Ann

**La Crosse**
Ablan, Michael C.

**Lake Geneva**
McCormack, Joanne Marie

**Madison**
Anderson, Michael Steven
Boucher, Joseph W(illiam)
Brewster, Francis Anthony
Burish, Mark Dennis
Hanson, David James
Nora, Wendy Alison
Pellino, Charles Edward, Jr.
Peterson, H. Dale
Robison, John S.
Shea, Jeremy Charles
Toman, William Joseph

**Manitowoc**
Muchin, Arden Archie

**Marinette**
Anuta, Michael Joseph

**Milwaukee**
Bliss, Richard Jon
Bratt, Herbert Sidney
Bremer, John M.
Donahue, John Edward
Ehlinger, Ralph Jerome
Ericson, James Donald
Friedman, James Dennis
Galanis, John William
Grebe, Michael W.
Iding, Allan Earl
LaBudde, Roy Christian
Levine, Herbert
Lombard, Benjamin G.
Loots, Robert James
Marcus, Richard Steven
Martin, Quinn William
McGaffey, Jere D.
Mulcahy, Charles Chambers
Pindyck, Bruce Eben
Reardon, Timothy P.
Rice, Shawn G.
Rintelman, Donald Brian
Skipper, Walter John
Williams, Clay Rule

**New Berlin**
Schober, Thomas Gregory

**Park Falls**
Marvin, Janet L.

**Pewaukee**
Engel, John Charles

**Racine**
Coates, Glenn Richard
Crawford, Timothy Patrick
Du Rocher, James Howard
Dye, William Ellsworth
Hart, Robert Camillus
Smith, Stephen James

**Sun Prairie**
Eustice, Francis Joseph

**Wausau**
Ware, G. Lane
Zimmerman, Robert W.

**Wauwatosa**
Alexander, Robert Gardner

### WYOMING

**Casper**
Gray, Jan Charles
Lowe, Robert Stanley

**Cheyenne**
McKinley, John Clark

### TERRITORIES OF THE UNITED STATES

### PUERTO RICO

**San Juan**
Pierluisi, Pedro R.
Rodriguez-Diaz, Juan E.
Vallone, Ralph, Jr.

### CANADA

### ONTARIO

**Toronto**
Chester, Robert Simon George

### AUSTRALIA

**Sydney**
Brown, John Thomas

### CHINA

**Hong Kong**
Allen, Richard Marlow
Scown, Michael John
Shinkle, John Thomas

### ENGLAND

**London**
Brownwood, David Owen
Gates, Stephen Frye
Smith, Jerry Leon
White, Walter Hiawatha, Jr.

### FRANCE

**Courbevoie**
Herzog, Brigitte

**Paris**
Rawlings, Boynton Mott

### JAPAN

**Tokyo**
Hunter, Larry Dean

### SAUDI ARABIA

**Riyadh**
Taylor, Frederick William, Jr. (Fritz Taylor)

### ADDRESS UNPUBLISHED

Adams, Samuel Franklin
Agraz, Francisco Javier, Sr.
Anderson, Geoffrey Allen
Andreozzi, Louis Joseph
Atkinson, Sheridan Earle
Avery, James Thomas, III
Ayres, Caroline Patricia
Banks, Robert Sherwood
Bartz, David John
Baxter-Smith, Gregory John
Berman, Joshua Mordecai
Berry, Robert Worth
Bloom, Barry Marshall
Bouvier, Marshall Andre
Brashear, William Ronald
Brodhead, David Crawmer
Brody, Nancy Louise
Burcham, Randall Parks
Burlingame, John Hunter
Cadigan, Richard Foster
Cannon, Gayle Elizabeth
Canoff, Karen Huston
Cattani, Maryellen B.
Christiansen, Eric Robert
Chuman, Frank Fujio
Cion, Judith Ann
Coleman, John Michael
Coleman, Robert Lee
Collins, James Francis
Colton, Sterling Don
Contino, Richard Martin
Cornish, Jeannette Carter
Crook, Donald Martin
Crowe, James Joseph
Crown, Nancy Elizabeth
Davey, Gerard Paul
Denaro, Charles Thomas
Duffy, James F.
Durgom-Powers, Jane Ellyn
Feuvrel, Sidney Leo, Jr.
Finkelstein, Marcia Lyn
Fischer, David Charles
Fischer, David Jon
Francis, Patricia Ann
Frankel, James Burton
Friedman, Tod H.
Futter, Victor
Gale, Connie R(uth)
Gass, Raymond William
Giovanniello, Joseph, Jr.
Gordon, David Zevi
Greenberg, Ronald David
Griffin, Campbell Arthur, Jr.
Gutman, Richard Edward
Haber, Joel Abba
Hackett, Wesley Phelps, Jr.
Hanson, Fred B.
Harmon, Gail McGreevy
Harris, Janine Diane
Hausman, Bruce
Heider, Jon Vinton
Heise, John Irvin, Jr.
Helweg, M. Diana
Holden, Mary Gayle Reynolds
Holloway, Hiliary Hamilton
Holmes, Charles Everett
Holtzmann, Howard Marshall
Hubbard, Michael James
Hunt, Ronald Forrest
Jacobs, Alan
Jamieson, Michael Lawrence
Johnson, Leonard Hjalma
Jones, Clifford Aaron, Sr.
Katz, Roberta R.
Kiefer, Karen LaVerne
Kingston, Andrew Brownell
Kordons, Uldis
Krivoshia, Eli, Jr.
Krutter, Forrest Nathan
Lea, Lorenzo Bates
Leibowitt, Sol David
Lerner, Harry
Lewitus, Marla Berman
Lieb, Charles Herman
Liftin, John Matthew
Lightstone, Ronald
Linde, Maxine Helen
Logan, James Kenneth
Long, Charles Thomas
Loomie, Edward Raphael
Mahallati, Narges Nancy
Martin, James William
Mayer, James Joseph
Mayersohn, Arnold Linn, Jr.
McIntosh, Rhodina Covington
McLendon, Susan Michelle
Mercer, Edwin Wayne
Mewhinney, Len Everette
Meyer, Max Earl
Meyerson, Stanley Phillip
Millimet, Erwin
Missan, Richard Sherman
Moylan, James Joseph
Murphy, Jo Anne
Nadelson, Eileen Nora
Natcher, Stephen Darlington
Newman, Sanders David
Nunalee, Thomas Hervey, IV
Oates, Carl Everette
O'Brien, James Edward
O'Dell, Joan Elizabeth
Oliver, Samuel William, Jr.
Painton, Russell Elliott
Palizzi, Anthony N.
Patrick, Victor Phillip
Patton, James Richard, Jr.
Porter, Michael Pell
Powers, Elizabeth Whitmel
Price, Steven
Quigley, Leonard Vincent
Rawls, Frank Macklin
Reath, George, Jr.
Rivera, Oscar R.
Rosenn, Harold
Rossel-Jones, Mary Louise
Rounsaville, Guy, Jr.
Ruhm, Thomas Francis
Rutland, John Dudley
Saliterman, Richard Arlen
Samuels, Janet Lee
Schild, Raymond Douglas
Schlei, Norbert Anthony
Shaffer, Richard James
Shambaugh, Stephen Ward
Silverberg, Mark Victor
Simon, Barry Philip
Smock, James F.
Springer, Paul David
Stephenson, Barbera Wertz
Stickney, John Moore
Stone, Edward Herman
Surratt, John Richard
Tanaka, Jeannie E.
Tapley, James Leroy
Tattersall, Hargreaves Victor, III
Taub, Cathy Ellen
Terry, John Hart
Tobin, Paul Xavier
Tolins, Roger Alan
Torgerson, Larry Keith
Tubman, William Charles
Tupper, Kent Phillip
Vale, Victor John Eugene, II
Voight, Elizabeth Anne
Wagner, Michael Duane
Walker, A. Harris
Walker, John Sumpter, Jr.
Walner, Robert Joel
Williams, William John, Jr.
Wilson, Hugh Steven
Wilson, Rhys Thaddeus
Wynstra, Nancy Ann
Yellin, Melvin A.

---

**CREDITOR.** *See* **Commercial, consumer.**

---

## CRIMINAL

### UNITED STATES

### ALABAMA

**Atmore**
Hartley, Wade Leon

**Birmingham**
Alford, Margie Searcy
Bloomston, Brett Michael
Christ, Chris Steve
Dodd, Hiram, Jr.
Dortch, Clarence, III
Thompson, Charles Amos

**Cullman**
Poston, Beverly Paschal

**Dothan**
Hogg, David Kenneth

**Florence**
Case, Basil Timothy

**Foley**
Dasinger, Thomas Edgar

**Gadsden**
Callis, Clifford Louis, Jr.

**Hartford**
Eldridge, William Phillip

**Huntsville**
Burton, Hilary Coleman

**Mobile**
Armstrong, Gordon Gray, III
Beckish, Richard Michael
Coley, F(ranklin) Luke, Jr.
Rogers, Jannea Suzanne

**Montgomery**
Lunt, Jennifer Lee
Smith, Maury Drane

**Moulton**
Dutton, Mark Anthony

**Tuscaloosa**
Blume, Nettie Lynn
Smith, James Dwight

**Tuscumbia**
Hunt, James L.

### ALASKA

**Anchorage**
Butler, Rex Lamont
Fleischer, Hugh William
Jensen, Jill Ellen
Ross, Wayne Anthony
Wonnell, Thomas Burke

**Bethel**
Valcarce, Jim J.

**Fairbanks**
Covell, Kenneth

**Juneau**
Sonneman, Joseph Abram

**Sitka**
Graham, David Antony

### ARIZONA

**Flagstaff**
Cowser, Danny Lee

**Phoenix**
Florence, Henry John
Forshey, Timothy Allan
Keilp, Joe
Klahr, Gary Peter
Maynard, Daniel Dwight
O'Driscoll, Cornelius Joseph
Rose, David L.
Song Ong, Roxanne Kay
Thompson, Joel Erik
Woods, Grant

**Scottsdale**
Smith, David Burnell

**Tempe**
Zurbriggen, Jeffrey Michael

**Tucson**
Blackman, Jeffrey William
Gonzales, Richard Joseph
Hirsh, Robert Joel
McNeill, Frederick Wallace

### ARKANSAS

**Fayetteville**
Kester, Charles Melvin
Poore, Shannon Leigh
VanWinkle, John Ragan

**Little Rock**
Files, Jason Daniel
Heuer, Sam Tate
Johnson, Michael Dennis

**Marion**
Fogleman, John Nelson

**Nashville**
Graves, James Clements

**North Little Rock**
McGough, Phillip Allan

**Pocahontas**
Throesch, David

**Walnut Ridge**
Mullen, William David

### CALIFORNIA

**Albany**
Chazin, Seth Paul

**Berkeley**
Pyle, Walter K.
Van Winkle, Wesley Andrew

**Beverly Hills**
Bear, Jeffrey Lewis
Marino, Nina
Steinberger, Jeffrey Wayne

**Burlingame**
Chase, Steven Alan

**Cameron Park**
Weiner, Dain Pascal

**Costa Mesa**
Meyer, Paul Seth

**El Cajon**
Graf, Sheryl Susan

**El Segundo**
Blair, Janyce Keiko Imata

**Fairfield**
Honeychurch, Denis Arthur

**Fresno**
Bailey, Howard William (Bill Bailey)
Ramirez, Frank Tenorio

**Glendale**
Toscano, Oscar Ernesto
Unger, Charles Joseph

**Huntington Beach**
Garrels, Sherry Ann

**Indio**
De Salva, Christopher Joseph

**Inglewood**
Lee, Michael Hal

**La Jolla**
Caplan, Allen

**Laguna Beach**
Simons, Barry Thomas

**Long Beach**
Poland, Richard L.

**Los Angeles**
Berman, Myles Lee
Byrd, Christine Waterman Swent
Desario, Daniel J.
Garber, Albert Caesar
Garcia-Barron, Gerard Lionel
Handzlik, Jan Lawrence
Kupperman, Henry John
Lauchengco, Jose Yujuico, Jr.
Mintz, Ronald Steven
Murray, Anthony
Pesta, Ben W., II
Rozanski, Stanley Howard
Shapiro, Robert Leslie
Wolf, Lawrence

**Marina Del Rey**
Freed, Evan Phillip
Murphy, Tamela Jayne

**Mill Valley**
Grantland, Brenda

**Millbrae**
Pliska, Edward William

**Mission Viejo**
Leathers, Stephen Kelly

**Monterey**
Newhouse, James Howard

**Newport Beach**
Cordova, Ron

**Oakland**
Burris, John Leonard
Patton, Roger William
Thompson Stanley, Trina

**Orange**
Avdeef, Thomas
Besser, Barry I.

**Palm Desert**
Spirtos, Nicholas George

**Palmdale**
Reichman, Dawn Leslie

**Palo Alto**
Goldman, Mara Kapelovitz

**Paramount**
Hall, Howard Harry

**Pasadena**
Brenner, Anita Susan
Telleria, Anthony F.

**Rancho Palos Verdes**
Swank, Damon Raynard

**Redwood City**
Emanuel, Todd Powell
Inama, Christopher Roy

**Riverside**
Schwartz, Bernard Julian

**Roseville**
Bedore, Jess C.

**Sacramento**
Daniel, Lance
Greiner, James Ralph
Heller, Donald Herbert
Schleicher, Estelle Ann
Wishek, Michael Bradley

**San Diego**
Brown, Douglas Colton
Curran, Michaela C.

Iredale, Eugene Gerald
Sevilla, Charles Martin
Shelton, Dorothy Diehl Rees

**San Francisco**
Bondoc, Rommel
Bruen, James A.
Bryan, Robert Russell
Chao, Cedric C.
Cohn, Nathan
Forsythe, Janet Winifred
Ladar, Jerrold Morton
Malcheski, Kim
Philipsborn, John Timothy
Russoniello, Joseph Pascal
Young, Douglas Rea

**San Jose**
Duell-Cazes, Tracy Leigh
McManis, James

**Santa Ana**
Fraser, Robert William
Harley, Robison Dooling, Jr.
Ultimo, Paul Joseph

**Santa Cruz**
Brennan, Enda Thomas
Campos, Victor Manuel
Chang, Peter Asha, Jr.

**Santa Monica**
English, Charles Royal
Genego, William Joseph
Hirsch, Richard Gary
Winogr00ade, Audrey
Wormley, Craig Thomas

**Santa Rosa**
Hillberg, Marylou Elin

**Seal Beach**
Porter, Joseph Edward, III

**Tiburon**
Bremer, William Richard

**Ukiah**
Nelson, David Eugene

**Ventura**
Borrell, Mark Steven
Bray, Laurack Doyle
Schwartz, Robert Irwin

**Weaverville**
Correll, Joanna Rae

**West Hollywood**
Finstad, Suzanne Elaine

**Woodland**
Melton, Barry

**Yuba City**
McCaslin, Leon
Santana, Jesse Isaias

## COLORADO

**Boulder**
Enwall, Michael R.
Garlin, Alexander
Hale, Daniel Cudmore
Pineau, John Kenneth

**Breckenridge**
Katz, Jeri Beth

**Castle Rock**
Robinson, Michael Allen

**Colorado Springs**
Barnes, Thomas Arthur, Jr.
Crizer, Celeste Lisanne
Dean, Lawrence Kenyon
Donohoe, John Joseph
Fisher, Robert Scott
Galka, Lawrence S.
Link, Gary Steven
Salley, George Henry, III
Walker, Jonathan Lee

**Denver**
Abramovitz, Michael John
Anstine, Glen Roscoe
Cantor, Darren R.
Deikman, Eugene Lawrence
Ehrlich, Stephen Richard
Finck, Barry Russell
Garcia, Anthony J.
Graf, Gregory C.
Kaplan, David S.
Krulewitch, Beth Lee
Malatesta, Mary Anne
Nesland, James Edward
Pearman, Shaun
Pluss, Edward Allen
Rhodes, Ralph Beauford
Savitz, David Barry
Schauer, Tone Terjesen
Sedlak, Joseph Anthony, III
Skok, Paul Joseph
Smith, Daniel Timothy
Springer, Jeffrey Alan
Willett, Jonathan S.

**Fort Collins**
Redder, Thomas Joseph

**Frisco**
McElyea, Monica Sergent

**Grand Junction**
Nugent, Edward James, III

**Lakewood**
Jacobson, Dennis John
Lawler, Richard Allen

**Littleton**
Spelts, Richard John

**Manassa**
Garcia, Castelar Medardo

**Pueblo**
O'Conner, Loretta Rae

## CONNECTICUT

**Bridgeport**
Meehan, Richard Thomas, Jr.
Zeldes, Jacob Dean

**Brookfield**
Dittmar, Dawn Marie

**Danbury**
Arconti, Richard David

**Fairfield**
Denniston, Brackett Badger, III

**Hartford**
Bennett, Jessie F.
Foden, Maria Luisa de Castro
Karpe, Brian Stanley

**New Haven**
Carty, Paul Vernon

**Norwalk**
Feinstein, Stephen Michael

**Ridgefield**
Foster, Julie Irene

**Southport**
Pickerstein, Harold James

**Stamford**
Margolis, Emanuel

**Waterbury**
Marano, Richard Michael

**West Hartford**
Morrissey, Ellen C.

## DELAWARE

**Wilmington**
Bartley, Brian James
Malik, John Stephen
Wier, Richard Royal, Jr.

## DISTRICT OF COLUMBIA

**Washington**
Ambrose, Myles Joseph
Barrett, Jane Frances
Best, Judah
Bisceglie, Anthony Patrick
Bonner, Walter Joseph
Boss, Lenard Barrett
Braga, Stephen Louis
Bray, John Martin
Broas, Timothy Michael
Bruton, James Asa, III
Buckley, John Joseph, Jr.
Chafetz, Marc Edward
Charles, Robert Bruce
Christensen, Karen Kay
Cobb, Ty
Craig, Gregory Bestor
Doyle, Austin Joseph
English, Caroline Turner
Feffer, Gerald Alan
Fuller, Vincent J.
Geneson, David Franklin
Geniesse, Robert John
Goldfarb, Ronald Lawrence
Greenebaum, Leonard Charles
Hansen, Mark Charles
Janis, N. Richard
Kendall, David E.
Kent, M. Elizabeth
Koontz, Glen Franklin
Larroca, Raymond G.
Liebman, Ronald Stanley
Luskin, Robert David
Martin, Ralph Drury
McDaniels, William E.
McGuire, Andrew Philip
Moffitt, William Benjamin
Mortenson, R. Stan
O'Neil, Thomas Francis, III
Patten, Thomas Louis
Peters, Frederick Whitten
Povich, David
Salsbury, Michael
Sellers, John W.
Spaeder, Roger Campbell
Stein, Cheryl Denise
Stuart, Pamela Bruce
Sundermeyer, Michael S.
Taylor, William Woodruff, III
Tompkins, Joseph Buford, Jr.
Vardaman, John Wesley
Waxman, Seth Paul
Weinstein, Martin James

## FLORIDA

**Altamonte Springs**
Gunewardene, Roshani Mala
Laurence, Steven Lamar

**Bartow**
Stevenson, Robin Howard

**Boca Raton**
Comisky, Ian Michael

**Clearwater**
Cheek, Michael Carroll

**Coconut Grove**
Denaro, Gregory
Joffe, David Jonathon

**Coral Gables**
Cano, Mario Stephen

**Daytona Beach**
Neitzke, Eric Karl
Politis, Michael John

**Fernandina Beach**
Manson, Keith Alan Michael

**Fort Lauderdale**
Behr, Ralph Steven
Benjamin, James Scott
Bogenschutz, J. David
Bustamante, Nestor
Dutko, Michael Edward
Harris, Jeffrey Mark
Henderson, Carol
Hester, Julia A.
Imperato, Gabriel Louis
Pascal, Robert Albert
Rodriguez, Carlos Augusto
Sale, David Todd
Schreiber, Alan Hickman
Seligman, Guy Jaime

**Fort Myers**
Cipriano, Gene Ralph
Peet, Maria Lara

**Gainesville**
DeThomasis, Craig Constantine
Kurrus, Thomas William
Mollica, Salvatore Dennis

**Hollywood**
Hartman, Honey

**Jacksonville**
Ceballos, M(ichael) Alan
Hardesty, W. Marc
Link, Robert James
McBurney, Charles Walker, Jr.
Miller, Carla Dorothy
Pillans, Charles Palmer, III

**Key Biscayne**
Burnbaum, Michael William

**Key West**
Davila, Gregory David
Eden, Nathan E.

**Lake Alfred**
Slaughter, Marshall Glenn

**Lake Worth**
Kreidler, Frank Allan

**Largo**
Trevena, John Harry

**Longwood**
McLatchey, Russell Francis

**Maitland**
Gabel, Michael Wayne

**Melbourne**
Ollinger, George Edward, III

**Miami**
Batista, Alberto Victor
Becerra, Robert John
Black, Roy
Blecher, Jonathan Burton
Bombino, Isabel Pinera
Bronis, Stephen J.
Cohen, Eric Martin
Cusack, James Wesley
de Leon, Ruben L.
Ferrell, Milton Morgan, Jr.
Hartman, Douglas Cole
Hartz, Steven Edward Marshall
Hirsch, Milton Charles
Horn, Mark
Houlihan, Gerald John
Jorgensen, Lauren
Kreisberg, Steven E.
Kritzer, Glenn Bruce
Kuehne, Benedict P.
Pena, Guillermo Enrique
Poston, Rebekah Jane
Quirantes, Albert M.
Rashkind, Paul Michael
Rogers, Harvey DeLano
Rothman, David Bill
Rust, Robert Warren
Scremin, Anthony James
Silvers, Marcia Jean
Sotorrio, Rene Alberto
Tarkoff, Michael Harris
Weinstein, Alan Edward

**Naples**
Cardillo, John Pollara

**North Miami**
Malman, Myles Henry

**North Miami Beach**
Cain, May Lydia
Ginsberg, Alan
Zipkin, Sheldon Lee

**Orlando**
Barnes, Susan Elizabeth
Brodersen, Daniel N.
deBeaubien, Hugo H.
Dempsey, Bernard Hayden, Jr.
Dicembre, Michael Dominick
Hernandez, H(ermes) Manuel
Kehoe, Terrence Edward
Mason, Steven Gerald
Russ, James Matthias
Sheaffer, William Jay

**Palm Beach Gardens**
Auerbach, Paul Ira

**Panama City**
Allan, Sher L.
Patterson, Christopher Nida
Stone, Michel Leon
Sutton, Pamela Dru

**Pensacola**
Griffith, Michael John

**Pt Charlotte**
Jones, Phillip Jeffrey

**Punta Gorda**
Cherry, Paul Stephen
Price, Pine Scott

**Saint Petersburg**
Russo, Frank
Scott, Kathryn Fenderson
Wadley, W. Thomas

**Sarasota**
Burzynski, Martin Andrew
Byrd, L(awrence) Derek
Shults, Thomas Daniel

**South Miami**
Carnesoltas, Ana-Maria

**Stuart**
Belanger, Robert Eugene
Watson, Robert James

**Tallahassee**
Kitchen, E.C. Deeno
Miller, Gregory R.
Morphonios, Dean B.
Sheffield, Frank Elwyn

**Tampa**
Castillo, Daniel L.
Givens, Stann William
Halliday, Stanley Grant
Hernandez, Daniel Mario
MacKay, John William
Medina, Omar F.
Neaves, Nancy J.
Nutter, Robert Heinrich
Polli, Robert Paul
Steiner, Geoffrey Blake
Suarez, Eddie A.
Tirella, David Theodore
Young, Ronald W.

**Tavernier**
Jabro, John A.

**West Palm Beach**
Dubiner, Michael
Vilchez, Victoria Anne

## GEORGIA

**Americus**
Cooper, Cecilia Marie

**Athens**
Byers, Rhonda Leann
Houser, Ronald Edward

**Atlanta**
Allen, Denise
Arbes, Jake
Bernstein, Brenda Joy
Billington, Barry E.
Chilivis, Nickolas Peter
Devins, Robert Sylvester
England, John Melvin
Feldman, Monroe Joseph
Head, William Carl
Lotito, Nicholas Anthony
Miller, Janise Luevenia Monica
Morris, Bruce H.
Mull, Gale W.
Pilcher, James Brownie
Scott, Mark Anthony
Thompson, Larry Dean
Whitley, Joe Dally
Womack, Mary Pauline

**Augusta**
Sibley, Sam B., Jr.

**Barnesville**
Kennedy, Harvey John, Jr.

**Blue Ridge**
Rosenberg, David Michael

**Brunswick**
Gough, Kevin Robert

**Cartersville**
Pope, Robert Daniel

**Columbus**
Dodgen, Andrew Clay
Shelnutt, John Mark

**Cumming**
Mantagna, Michael

**Darien**
Coppage, James Robert
Jenkins, Olney Dale

**Decatur**
Goddard, Ross Millard, Jr.
Guest, Abbi Taylor
O'Connell, John James, Jr.

**Douglas**
Sims, Rebecca Littleton

**Fitzgerald**
Hughes, (Terry) Chris(topher)

**Gainesville**
Hester, Francis (Frank) Bartow, III

**Homerville**
Helms, Catherine Harris

**Jasper**
Marger, Edwin

**Jonesboro**
Teske, Steven Cecil

**Lawrenceville**
Harrison, Samuel Hughel

**Macon**
Cranford, James Michael

**Marietta**
Cox, Reed Elbredge

**Nashville**
Ellis, Robert Bryan, Jr.

**Riverdale**
Terry, Pandora Elaine

**Savannah**
Morrell, Diane Marie

**Tucker**
Polstra, Larry John

**Valdosta**
Bass, Jay Michael
Bright, Joseph Converse
Edwards, Edith Martha
Lawrence, Matthew Russell

## HAWAII

**Honolulu**
Cassiday, Benjamin Buckles, III
Cedillos, Steve H.
Edmunds, John Sanford
Gillin, Malvin James, Jr.
Hart, Brook
Pallett, James McCormack
Schweigert, Jack F.
Shigetomi, Keith Shigeo
Weight, Michael Anthony

**Kailua Kona**
Miller, Frank Lewis
Zola, Michael S.

**Lihue**
Valenciano, Randal Grant Bolosan

## IDAHO

**Boise**
Derr, Allen R.

**Caldwell**
Orr, Debra Ann

**Ketchum**
Elkins, Brian Edward

## ILLINOIS

**Arlington Heights**
Blomquist, Ernest Richard, III

**Aurora**
Camic, David Edward
Mateas, Kenneth Edward

**Barrington**
Tobin, Dennis Michael

**Buffalo Grove**
Kole, Julius S.

**Carbondale**
Clemons, John Robert

**Chicago**
Barnett, William A.
Cole, Jeffrey
Coulson, William Roy
Fanone, John R.
Farber, Bernard John
Farina, James L.
Halprin, Rick
Hoffa, Thomas Edward
Hooks, William Henry
King, Michael Howard
Komie, Stephen Mark
Kunkle, William Joseph, Jr.
Kurz, Jerry Bruce
Lassar, Scott R.
Linklater, William Joseph
Makowski-Rivera, Donna
McNerney, Joseph James
Meyer, John Albert
Molo, Steven Francis
Moran, John Thomas, Jr.
Murray, Daniel Charles
Nash, Gordon Bernard, Jr.
Nora, Gerald Ernest
Null, Michael Elliot
Olavarria, Frank J.
Peters, Kevin Richard
Pitzer, Jeff Scott
Roustan, Yvon Dominique
Rovell, Michael Jay
Silets, Harvey Marvin
Smith, Ronald Charles
Stone, Howard Lawrence
Theobald, Edward Robert
Tobin, Craig Daniel

**Chicago Heights**
Wigell, Raymond George

**Collinsville**
Freeman, David Ralph

**Danville**
McFetridge, John David

**Decatur**
Vigneri, Joseph William

**Des Plaines**
Davis, Larry Allen

**Eureka**
Harrod, Daniel Mark

**Franklin Park**
Motta, Robert Michael

**Galesburg**
Butts, Cyril William, Jr.
McCrery, David Neil, III

**Hinsdale**
De Rose, John Patrick

**Homewood**
Getty, Gerald Winkler

**Joliet**
Egan, James E.
Lenard, George Dean

**Lombard**
O'Shea, Patrick Joseph

**Oregon**
Cargerman, Alan William

**Palos Heights**
Taylor, Joseph Henry

**Rockford**
Rouleau, Mark A.

**Rolling Meadows**
Sullivan, Terry

**Schaumburg**
Wilke, Barbara R.

**Skokie**
Plotnick, Paul William

**South Holland**
Olofsson, Daniel Joel

**Urbana**
Moore, David Robert
Piland, John Charles

**Vandalia**
Lawinger, Jane M.

**Wheaton**
Fawell, Blanche Hill

**Winnetka**
Theis, William Harold

## INDIANA

**Anderson**
Cage, Christopher Allen
Woodruff, Randall Lee

**Brazil**
Deal, James Edward

**Crown Point**
Stevens, William J.

**Decatur**
Sheets, Thomas Wade

**Evansville**
Clouse, John Daniel

**Fort Wayne**
Fleck, John R.

**Fowler**
Woods, Dennis Lynn

**Franklin**
Gholston, Robert M.
Johnson, Russell A.
Jones, Tom George

**Gary**
Lewis, Robert Lee

**Greenfield**
Dobbins, Caryl Dean

**Indianapolis**
Kautzman, John Fredrick
Pinkus, I(rving) Marshall
Small, Mark Eugene

**Lagrange**
Schultess, LeRoy Kenneth

**Lebanon**
Donaldson, John Weber

**Marion**
Ryan, Patrick Nelson

**Portage**
Germann, Gary Stephen
Henke, Robert John

**Shelbyville**
Baldwin, Kelley Yeager
Lisher, James Richard

**South Bend**
Galso, Ernest Peter Gabriel
Horn, George Edward, Jr.

**Terre Haute**
Kesler, John A.

**Waynetown**
Dicks, Sarah Houston

## IOWA

**Ames**
Sotak, Ronald Michael

**Creston**
Kenyon, Arnold Oakley, III

**Davenport**
Phelps, Robert J.

**Des Moines**
Branstad, Christine Ellen
Fisher, Thomas George, Jr.
Foxhoven, Jerry Ray
Krull, Curtis Jay

**Iowa City**
Spies, Leon Fred

**Marshalltown**
Lorenz, William Joseph

## KANSAS

**Cottonwood Falls**
North, William T.
**Fort Scott**
Short, Forrest Edwin
**Garden City**
Pierce, Ricklin Ray
**Lawrence**
Krogh, Richard Alan
**Leawood**
Dvorak, Richard Dee
**Lenexa**
Bigus, Edward Lowell
**Olathe**
Branham, Melanie J.
**Topeka**
Moots, Jeffrey Alan
Schultz, Richard Allen
**Wichita**
Robinson, G. Craig
**Winfield**
Krusor, Mark William

## KENTUCKY

**Covington**
Crout, Daniel Wesley
**Eddyville**
Story, James Eddleman
**Florence**
Bogucki, Raymond Spencer
Brown, Stuart P.
**Frankfort**
Bias, Dana G.
Chadwick, Robert
**Glasgow**
Dickinson, Temple
**Hazard**
Rose, Danny
**Lexington**
Conner, Tonya Sue
Fryman, Virgil Thomas, Jr.
Shouse, William Chandler
**Louisa**
Carter, Robert Philip, Sr.
**Louisville**
Manly, Samuel
Smith, T.J.
Wade, Jeffrey Lee
**Newport**
Halloran, Brian Paul
**Richmond**
Martin, James Neal

## LOUISIANA

**Alexandria**
Everett, Stephen Edward
Perkins, Alvin Bruce, II
**Baton Rouge**
Boren, James Edgar
Dixon, Jerome Wayne
Gonzales, Edward Joseph, III
**Bunkie**
McKay, Dan Boies, Jr.
**Chalmette**
Ginart, Michael Charles, Jr.
**Covington**
Paddison, David Robert
**Farmerville**
Earle, Robert Ray
**Gretna**
Marino, Joseph Anthony, III
**Houma**
Stewart, Craig Henry
**Lafayette**
Boustany, Alfred Frem
Morgan, Glenn L.
Nehrbass, Jennifer Stuller
Willard, David Charles
**Lake Charles**
Cagney, Nanette Heath
Sanchez, Walter Marshall
**Leesville**
Smith, Simeon Christie, IV
**New Orleans**
Clarke, Shaun G.
**River Ridge**
Kelly, Quentin Patrick
**Ruston**
Oakley, Tracy L.
**Shreveport**
Goorley, Richard Carl
Skinner, Michael David
**Slidell**
Hammond, Margaret

## MAINE

**Augusta**
McKee, Walter Frederic
**Bangor**
Greif, Arthur John
**Bath**
Regan, Richard Robert
**Kennebunk**
Clifford, Peter
Libby, Gene Roger
**Portland**
Chapman, John Whitaker
Connolly, Thomas Joseph
Groff, Joseph Halsey, III
Marjerison, Thomas Sydney
Schwartz, Stephen Jay
**Waterville**
Sandy, Robert Edward, Jr.

## MARYLAND

**Baltimore**
Crowe, Thomas Leonard
Eisenberg, Bruce Alan
Gillece, James Patrick, Jr.
Gutierrez, Maria Cristina
Himeles, Martin Stanley, Jr.
King, David Paul
Kramer, Paul R.
Nazarian, Douglas Richard Miller
Ohly, D. Christopher
Radding, Andrew
Snyder, Mark Allen
Tousey, Robert Ryan
**Bethesda**
Goldstone, Mark Lewis
**College Park**
Neal, Edward Garrison
**Darnestown**
Kasunic, Robert Joyce
**Glen Burnie**
Cole, Ronald Clark
**Ocean City**
Grech, Christopher Alan
Wimbrow, Peter Ayers, III
**Oxon Hill**
Serrette, Cathy Hollenberg
**Potomac**
Mullenbach, Linda Herman
**Rockville**
Jaffe, Matthew Ely
Lamari, Joseph Paul
Moul, Robert Gemmill, II
Segal, Gary L.
Van Grack, Steven
**Salisbury**
Clarke, Wm. A. Lee, III
**Silver Spring**
McDermitt, Edward Vincent
**Stevensville**
Ronayne, Donald Anthony
**Sykesville**
Bartolini, Daniel John

## MASSACHUSETTS

**Andover**
Lakin, John Francis
**Arlington**
Kelleher, D. Ring
**Barnstable**
Ryley, Arthur Charles
**Boston**
Benzan, John Patrick
Berry, Janis Marie
Brick, Howard Andrew
Campbell, Richard P.
Carroll, James Edward
Cunha, John Henry, Jr.
Egbert, Richard Michael
Fishman, Kenneth Jay
Glaser, Lenore Meryl
Hrones, Stephen Baylis
Lacovara, Kirsten Marie
Levine, Julius Byron
Looney, William Francis, Jr.
McKittrick, Neil Vincent
Nugent, Alfred Emanuel
Rose, Alan Douglas
Sultan, James Lehman
Sweda, Edward Leon, Jr.
**Brighton**
Gilden, James William
**Brockton**
Belinsky, Ilene Beth
**Buckland**
Shauger, Susan Joyce
**Cambridge**
Ta, Tai Van
**Chestnut Hill**
Lowinger, Lazar
**Concord**
O'Brien, James Freeman
**Danvers**
Christopher, John Anthony
**Duxbury**
Goldman, Eric Scot
**Foxboro**
Cohen, Harold
**Framingham**
Gaffin, Gerald Eliot
**Gloucester**
O'Reilly, Edward Joseph
**Hyannis**
McLaughlin, Edward Francis, Jr.
**Ipswich**
Gonick, Richard S.
**Newburyport**
Murphy, Lawrence John
**Peabody**
Papanickolas, Emmanuel N.
**Quincy**
Syat, Scott Mitchell
**Revere**
Cipoletta, James Joseph
**Salem**
Andrews, John
Del Vecchio, Debra Anne
Sellers, Jill Suzanne
**Springfield**
Klyman, Andrew Michael
Maidman, Stephen Paul
**West Yarmouth**
Gens, Richard Howard
**Weston**
Haas, Jacqueline Crawford
**Worcester**
Gribouski, James Joseph
Uhl, Christopher Martin

## MICHIGAN

**Ann Arbor**
Ferris, Donald William, Jr.
Mullkoff, Douglas Ryan
**Bay City**
Kennedy, Brian Melville
**Big Rapids**
Clarke, Alan William
**Bloomfield Hills**
Cranmer, Thomas William
**Brighton**
Nielsen, Neal D.
**Burton**
Breczinski, Michael Joseph
**Charlevoix**
Telgenhof, Allen Ray
**Coldwater**
Colbeck, J. Richard
**Dearborn**
Gardner, Gary Edward
**Detroit**
Andreoff, Christopher Andon
Kostovski, Suzanna
Pirtle, H(arold) Edward
Richardson, Ralph Herman
Taylor, William Edward
Wagner, Brian J.
Zuckerman, Richard Engle
**Eastpointe**
Ionetz, Ronald George
**Ecorse**
Rhoads, Carl Lynn
**Farmington**
Lebow, Michael Jeffrey
**Farmington Hills**
Reagle, Jack Evan
Weiss, Leon Jeffrey
**Flint**
Wheaton, Robin Lee
**Franklin**
Pritchard, Clyde Basil
**Grand Rapids**
Elve, Daniel Leigh
Roth, Michael John
Savickas, Stephen Anthony
**Harbor Beach**
Schumacher, Dawn Kristi Ann
**Inkster**
Bullock, Steven Carl
**Ishpeming**
Andriacchi, Dominic Francis
**Jackson**
Barton, Bruce Andrew
Jacobs, Wendell Early, Jr.
**Lansing**
Kronzek, Charles Michael
Nurkiewicz, Dennis John, Jr.
Rasmusson, Thomas Elmo
Shafer, Stuart Robert
**Mount Clemens**
Ososki-Slanec, Darra
Stepek, Mark William
**Redford**
Philippart, Howard Louis, Jr.
**Saint Clair Shores**
Shehan, Wayne Charles
**South Haven**
Waxman, Sheldon Robert
**Southfield**
Forrest, Robert Edwin
Gold, Gordon Stanford
Morganroth, Mayer
**Sterling Heights**
Girdwood, Derik Renard
**Troy**
McGinnis, Thomas Michael
Morgan, Michael Vincent
Schroeder, Douglas Jay

## MINNESOTA

**Albert Lea**
Savelkoul, Donald Wayne
**Anoka**
Beens, Richard Albert
Ostroot, Timothy Vincent
**Bemidji**
Kief, Paul Allan
**Brooklyn Center**
Neff, Fred Leonard
**Eagan**
O'Connor, Michael William
**Edina**
Weber, Gail Mary
**Hawley**
Baer, Zenas
**Mankato**
Manahan, James Hinchon
**Maplewood**
Beck, Bruce Lennart
Nemo, Anthony James
Stiles, Debra Jean
**Minneapolis**
Magarian, Edward Brian
Magnuson, Roger James
McNamara, Michael John
Meshbesher, Ronald I.
Oleisky, Robert Edward
Spaeth, Nicholas John
Tolin, Stefan A.
Voss, Barry Vaughan
Westphal, James Phillip
Williams, Maureen
**Saint Cloud**
Provinzino, John C.
Seifert, Luke Michael
Walz, Gregory Stephen
**Saint Paul**
Duckstad, Jon R.
Malone, Robert Gerard
**South Saint Paul**
O'Reilly, Ann Catherine

## MISSISSIPPI

**Bay Springs**
Shoemaker, Bobby Lynn
**Biloxi**
Miller, William Carl
**Drew**
Holladay, Robert Lawson
**Gloster**
Davis, Cynthia D'Ascenzo
**Hattiesburg**
Adelman, Michael Schwartz
Davis-Morris, Angela Elizabeth
**Jackson**
McLeod, Gia Nicole
Scales, Clarence Ray
**Lumberton**
Tonry, Richard Alvin
**Ocean Springs**
Pattison, Daphne Lynn
**Oxford**
Lewis, Ronald Wayne
Smith, Kent Elliot
**Pascagoula**
Roberts, David Ambrose
**Ridgeland**
Giuffrida, Noel Peter
**Starkville**
Drungole, Paula Elaine

## MISSOURI

**Branson**
Anglen, Randall S.
**Cape Girardeau**
Lowes, Albert Charles
Rith, David J., II
**Columbia**
Aulgur, Robert Davis
Dannov, Fred
Mays, William Gay, II
Moore, Mitchell Jay
Murray, Robert Arthur
**Hannibal**
Curl, Jeffrey Robert
**Hermann**
Kell, Scott K.
**Hillsboro**
Guberman, Ted
Pyatt, Joyce A.
**Independence**
Kerr, J. Martin
**Joplin**
Lonardo, Charles Henry
**Kansas City**
Bradshaw, Jean Paul, II
Carter, J. Denise
Eiszner, James Richard, Jr.
Fox, Byron Neal
Gaddy, William Brian
Handley, Gerald Matthew
Joyce, Michael Patrick
Laurans, Jonathan Louis
Lotven, Howard Lee
Rogers, Charles Myers
Salmon, Steven Brett
White, F(loyd) Al
Wyrsch, James Robert
**Keytesville**
Wheeler, James Julian
**Rogersville**
LeCompte, Charles Martin
**Saint Charles**
Carmichael, James Edward
Green, Joseph Libory
Zerr, Richard Kevin
**Saint Louis**
Haar, Robert Theodore
Liberman, Keith Gordon
Marks, Murry Aaron
Meehan, John Justin
Pleban, Sarah Shelledy
Ramirez, Anthony Benjamin
Shalowitz, Howard A.
Warren, Russell Allen
Wines, Lawrence Eugene
**Springfield**
Conway, Ronald Anthony
Groce, Steven Fred
**Webster Groves**
Crowell, George Bradford

## MONTANA

**Bozeman**
Nelson, Steven Dwayne
**Kalispell**
Nardi, Stephen J.

## NEBRASKA

**Fremont**
Eskey, Leo Joseph
Line, William Gunderson
**Kearney**
Voigt, Steven Russell
**Lincoln**
Swihart, Fred Jacob
**Neligh**
Doerr, Jeffrey Mark
**Norfolk**
McGough, James Kingsley
**Omaha**
Fabian, Emil Michelle
Frank, Julie Ann
Gutowski, Michael Francis
Kelly, Christopher Edward
Runge, Patrick Richard

## NEVADA

**Carson City**
Johnson, Erik Reid
Wilson, James Edward, Jr.
**Gardnerville**
Jackson, Mark Bryan
**Las Vegas**
Bell, Stewart Lynn
Myers, Andrew S.
**Reno**
Cornell, Richard Farnham
Dunn, Larry K.
Wright, Roger Lane

## NEW HAMPSHIRE

**Concord**
Hodes, Paul William
**Dover**
Catalfo, Alfred, Jr. (Alfio Catalfo)
**Henniker**
Foley, David N.
**Keene**
Bell, John Andrew
Heed, Peter W.
**Manchester**
Bruzga, Paul Wheeler
**Nashua**
Snow, Robert Brian
**Portsmouth**
Mason, J. William L.
**Wolfeboro Falls**
Hawthorne, Stan

## NEW JERSEY

**Brigantine**
Kokes, Alois Harold
**Chatham**
Krovatin, Gerald
**Cherry Hill**
Korin, Joel Benjamin
**Clark**
Barr, Jon-Henry
Farina, Mario G.
**Clifton**
Feinstein, Miles Roger
Palma, Nicholas James
**Denville**
Caivano, Anthony P.
Greene, Steven K.
**East Hanover**
Kayser, Kenneth Wayne
**Elizabeth**
Kuhrt, Richard Lee
**Englewood Cliffs**
Fredericks, Barry Irwin
**Fairfield**
Bilinkas, Edward J.
Denes, Richard Ford
**Flemington**
Miller, Louis H.
Weinblatt, Seymour Solomon
**Freehold**
Lomurro, Donald Michael
McLean, Gary P.
**Hackensack**
Flor, Patrick John
Horowitz, Donald
Latimer, Stephen Mark
Mullin, Patrick Allen
Neary, Brian Joseph
**Haddon Heights**
Cipparone, Rocco C., Jr.
D'Alfonso, Mario Joseph
**Haddonfield**
Fuoco, Philip Stephen
**Linden**
Littman, David Bernard
**Marlton**
Cavallo, Frank P., Jr.
**Metuchen**
Eugene, John
Vercammen, Kenneth Albert
**Millburn**
Biebelberg, Keith N.
**Morris Plains**
Pluciennik, Thomas Casimir
**Morristown**
Bograd, Sandra Lynn
Cocca, Anthony
**Newark**
Gouraige, Hervé
Herman, Ross Neil
Jacobs, Andrew Robert
Lazzaro, Clifford Emanuel
Mintz, Robert A.
**Northfield**
Day, Christopher Mark
**Ocean**
Weisberg, Adam Jon
**Old Bridge**
Downs, Thomas Edward, IV
**Plainfield**
Grayson, Russell Wayne
**Red Bank**
Allegra, Peter Alexander
Auerbach, Philip Gary
Halfacre, Michael Ian
**Ridgewood**
Seigel, Jan Kearney
**Secaucus**
Glassen, James Warren
**South Plainfield**
Scialabba, Damian Angelo
**Spring Lake**
Anderson, James Francis
**Springfield**
Katz, Jeffrey Harvey
**Succasunna**
Correale, Robert D.
Gates, Marshall L.
**Union City**
Navarrete, Yolanda
**Vineland**
O'Neill, Joseph Dean
**Warren**
Hurley, Lawrence Joseph
**Weehawken**
Hayden, Joseph A., Jr.
Silber, Alan
**Westfield**
Hrycak, Michael Paul
**Woodbridge**
Marcy, Eric John
**Woodbury Heights**
Heim, Thomas George

## NEW MEXICO

**Alamogordo**
Atkins, Spencer Bert
**Albuquerque**
Duarte, Leroy Wilson
Lopez, Floyd William
Nichols, Carolyn M.
**Farmington**
Titus, Victor Allen
**Santa Fe**
Cunningham, David Fratt
Farber, Steven Glenn
Marlowe, Mary Louise

## NEW YORK

**Albany**
Barsamian, J(ohn) Albert
Collins, George Vincent, III
Devine, Eugene Peter

Donohue, Brian E.
Dulin, Thomas N.
Fanciullo, William Patrick
Gray, William J.
Mishler, Mark Sean
Wukitsch, David John
**Albion**
Church, Sanford Allan
**Batavia**
Saleh, David John
**Bellmore**
Sachs, Eric
**Binghamton**
Gates, Gregory Ansel
**Briarcliff Manor**
Rosen, Paul Maynard
**Bronx**
Bigelow, Robert Wilson
**Brooklyn**
DeMarco, Arthur J., Jr.
Edwards, Arthur Aden
Jacobson, Barry Stephen
Kamins, Barry Michael
Kavowras, Mona
Roth, Pamela Susan
**Buffalo**
Murray, Glenn Edward
Possé, Olga Alicia
Ross, Christopher Theodore
Schreck, Robert J.
**Caledonia**
Litteer, Harold Hunter, Jr.
**Canandaigua**
Winthrop, Griffith Joel
**Carle Place**
Mulhern, Edwin Joseph
**Carmel**
Grossman, Victor G.
**Central Islip**
Bronstein, Richard M.
**Central Valley**
Levinson, David Lawrence
**Delhi**
Hartmann, James M.
**East Northport**
Juliano, John Louis
**Elmira**
O'Mara, Thomas Fellers
**Floral Park**
Friedman, Jon George
**Forest Hills**
Addabbo, Dominic Lucian
**Garden City**
Druker, James Owen
Hausch, Adrienne Louise Flipse
**Geneva**
Mirras, Michael John
**Goshen**
Joseph, Alan Lloyd
**Hamburg**
Gaughan, Dennis Charles
**Hawthorne**
Medina, Luis Anibal
**Hempstead**
Kane, Donald Vincent
**Herkimer**
Kirk, Patrick Laine
**Hudson Falls**
Martindale, Daniel S.
**Islandia**
Buckley, Terrence Patrick
**Jericho**
Rehbock, Richard Alexander
**Kew Gardens**
Nizin, Leslie S.
Schechter, Donald Robert
**Mayfield**
McAuliffe, J. Gerard
**Mineola**
Daniels, John Hill
Galison, Edward
Gulotta, Frank Andrew, Jr.
Levine, David I.
Marinello, Salvatore John
Michelen, Oscar
Naclerio, Gregory J.
Rubine, Robert Samuel
Sandback, William Arthur
**Mohegan Lake**
Stokes, Ron
**New Hyde Park**
Ezersky, William Martin
**New Windsor**
Ventry, Catherine Valerie
**New York**
Adler, Charles David
Aiello, Robert John
Amsterdam, Mark Lemle
Aron, Roberto
Barenholtz, Celia Goldwag
Belnick, Mark Alan
Beltre, Luis Oscar
Berger, Michael Gary
Berger, Vivian Olivia
Bondy, Joseph Aaron
Bradley, E. Michael
Buchwald, Don David
Castellitto, Mario
Checkman, Neil Bruce
Dean, Robert Stuart
Di Chiara, Gerald J.
Edelbaum, Philip R.
Elsen, Sheldon Howard
Feldberg, Michael Svetkey
Fink, Robert Steven
Fiske, Robert Bishop, Jr.
Fogelnest, Robert
Frankel, Sandor
Gerstmann, Elan
Getnick, Neil Victor
Gioiella, Russell Michael
Glekel, Jeffrey Ives
Goldberg, Jay
Goldman, Lawrence Saul
Greenfield, Scott H.
Grunewald, Raymond Bernhard
Hershman, Scott Edward
Hopper, Walter Everett
Hynes, Patricia
Iannuzzi, John Nicholas
Javier, Ramon Emilio
Johnson, Christopher Paul
Joseph, Michael P.
Katz, Seth Alan
Kedia, Sarita
Keneally, Kathryn Marie
Kennedy, Michael John
Kimelman, Steven
Kostelanetz, Boris
Kuh, Richard Henry
Lauer, Eliot
Laufer, Jacob
Lerner, Max Kasner
Levander, Andrew Joshua
Levine, Alan
Levinson, Paul Howard
London, Ira D.
Lupert, Leslie Allan
Lupkin, Stanley Neil
McGeady, Paul Joseph
Naftalis, Gary Philip
Necheles, Susan R.
Orden, Stewart L.
Pfeffer, Robert E.
Pickholz, Jason R.
Raylesberg, Alan Ira
Scheiman, Eugene R.
Seiff, Eric A.
Seligman, Frederick
Shaw, Melvin Robert
Shear, Andrew Charles
Shientag, Florence Perlow
Smith, Morton Alan
Stavis, Roger Lee
Supino, Anthony Martin
Tigue, John J., Jr.
Walpin, Gerald
Weddle, Justin Seth
Weiner, Stephen L.
Wiggin, Thomas Byron
Zornow, David M.
**North Syracuse**
Wallace, John Paul
**Northport**
Valente, Douglas
**Nyack**
Seidler, B(ernard) Alan
**Oneonta**
Burns, Brian Douglas
Rothermel, Richard Allan
**Patchogue**
Esteve, Edward V.
Feuer, Paul Robert
**Purchase**
Lytton, William B(ryan)
**Rochester**
Andolina, Lawrence J.
Barr, Culver Kent
Fiandach, Edward Louis
Hinman, James Stuart
Jacobson, Peter A.
Lapine, Felix Victor
Murante, David Alan
Nesser, Joseph George
Rosner, Leonard Allen
Servis, William George
**Rockaway Park**
Mulvaney, James E.
**Rome**
Domenico, Calvin J., Jr.
**Saratoga Springs**
Harper, David Alexander
**Scarsdale**
King, Robert Lucien
Sheehan, Larry John
**Schenectady**
DeLorenzo, Paul E.
Mueller, Philip Winfield
**Seneca Falls**
Porter, James Scott
**Staten Island**
Battiste, Paul A.
**Syracuse**
Gerber, Edward F.
Mathews, Daniel Francis, III
Paquette, Steven A.
Rosenthal, Kate
**Troy**
Frost, Jerome Kenneth
Jones, E. Stewart, Jr.
**Tupper Lake**
Hayes, Jeremiah Michael
**Valley Stream**
Isaacs, Leonard Bernard
**Wantagh**
Dwyer, Diane Marie
**Wappingers Falls**
O'Neil, D. James
**Watertown**
Marsh, Leonard Roy
**White Plains**
Fufidio, George E.
Greenspan, Leon Joseph
Greenspan, Michael Evan
Pickard, John Allan
Pohlmann, William Howard
**Yonkers**
Rubeo, Stephen Vincent

### NORTH CAROLINA

**Burnsville**
Howell, Dennis Lee
**Cary**
Cromer, Charles Lemuel
**Charlotte**
Brackett, Martin Luther, Jr.
Brotherton, Allen C.
Wyatt, James Frank, III
**Durham**
Craven, James Braxton, III
Hill, Marcus Edison
Loflin, Thomas Franklin, III
**Emerald Isle**
Lincoln, Michael Powell
**Fayetteville**
Newman, Roger
Parish, James Riley
**Greensboro**
Lloyd, Charles Allen
North, H. Davis, III
Oakley, Joel Neese
**Greenville**
Clark, John Graham, III
Conner, Ernest Lee, Jr.
Romary, Peter John Michael
**Lillington**
Edwards, Charlene Vernell
**Murphy**
MacFarlan, John Howard
**Newton**
Cutchin, John Franks
**Oxford**
Burnette, James Thomas
**Raleigh**
Ansley, James Ronald
Collins, G. Bryan, Jr.
Hall, John Thomas
Suhr, Paul Augustine
Verdon, Jane Kathryn
**Roxboro**
King, Ronnie Patterson
**Wilkesboro**
Gray, William Campbell

### NORTH DAKOTA

**Dickinson**
Ficek, Vince H.
Greenwood, Mark Lawrence
**Grand Forks**
Arnason, Joel Frederick
Seaworth, Mary Ellen

### OHIO

**Ada**
Streib, Victor Lee
**Akron**
Cody, Daniel Schaffner
Glinsek, Gerald John
Mohler, Robert E.
Mullen, Thomas Terry
**Barnesville**
Jefferis, Paul Bruce
**Batavia**
Pattison, George Edgar
**Bowling Green**
Hanna, Martin Shad
**Canton**
Yoder, Robert Gene
**Cincinnati**
Cissell, James Charles
Fingerman, Albert R.
Frank, William Nelson
Hust, Bruce Kevin
Scacchetti, David J.
Sims, Victor Dwayne
Whitaker, Glenn Virgil
**Cleveland**
Bell, Steven Dennis
Casarona, Robert B.
Chandler, Everett Alfred
Daiker, Paul B.
DeVan, Mark Roy
Incorvaia, Santo Thomas
La Rue, Edward Rice
Lear, S. Michael
Wukovich, George Nicholas
Zukerman, Larry William
**Columbus**
Belton, John Thomas
Binning, J. Boyd
Cline, Richard Allen
Depascale, Diane Kappeler
Donahey, Richard Sterling, Jr.
Hollenbaugh, H(enry) Ritchey
Ketcham, Richard Scott
Kilgore, Terry Lee
Mancuso, Anthony O.
Meyers, Gregory William
Tyack, Thomas Michael
Wolery, Don Edward
Wonnell, Harold Edward
Yeazel, Keith Arthur
**Dayton**
Cole, Dana Keith
Holz, Michael Harold
Posey, Terry Wayne
Smiley, Charles Adam, Jr.
**Eaton**
Bennett, Gray Weston
Thomas, James William
**Elyria**
Illner, Michael Douglas
**Fairborn**
Miles, David R.
**Findlay**
Kentris, George Lawrence
**Lebanon**
Diehl, Thomas James
**Leetonia**
Shelar, Richard Clyde
**Lima**
Kluge, William Frederick
**Mansfield**
Carto, David Draffan
Wolf, Marcus Alan
**Marion**
Slagle, James William
**Medina**
Hanwell, Robert Michael
**Miamisburg**
Anzman, Mark Charles
**New Philadelphia**
Mastin, Scott Joseph
**Risingsun**
Buchanan, J. Vincent Marino
**Salem**
Slack, Mark Robert
**Sandusky**
Bailey, K. Ronald
**Springfield**
Lagos, James Harry
**Steubenville**
Noble, Frank Wesley, Jr.
**Toledo**
Morgan, James Edward
Rice, Kollin Lawrence
St. Clair, Donald David
**Warren**
Keating, Daniel Gerard
Swauger, Terry Allen
White, Martin Fred
**Wooster**
Kennedy, Charles Allen
**Xenia**
Chappars, Timothy Stephen

### OKLAHOMA

**Cherokee**
Mitchell, Allan Edwin
**Enid**
Gill, Amber McLaughlin
Jones, Stephen
Wyatt, Robert Lee, IV
**Moore**
Pipkin, William A.
**Norman**
Chesley, Patrick J.
McFall, Sara Weer
**Oklahoma City**
Burton, Catherine Marie
Ferguson, Steven E.
Henry, David Patrick
Hughes, Carl Douglas
White, Joe E., Jr.
Zuhdi, Nabil (Bill)
**Sallisaw**
George, Steve Daniel
**Sayre**
Brooks, David Eugene
**Tulsa**
Brewster, Clark Otto
Hickman, Frank Robert
La Sorsa, William George
Morley, Randal Dean
Nigh, Robert Russell, Jr.
**Vinita**
Johnston, Oscar Black, III
**Yukon**
Hixson, Wendell Mark

### OREGON

**Ashland**
Jarvis, Barbara Anne
**Canby**
Thalhofer, Paul Terrance
**Eugene**
Halpern, John (Michael), Jr.
**Grants Pass**
Day, Gregory Thomas
Preslar, Holly Ann
**Hillsboro**
Tyner, John Joseph, III
**Medford**
O'Connor, Karl William (Goodyear Johnson)
**Newport**
Greco, Guy Benjamin
Strever, Kevin Kirk
**Ontario**
Rader, Diane Cecile
**Oregon City**
Hingson, John Henry, III
Jonasson, William Bradford
**Portland**
Bender, Laurie
Berger, Leland Roger
Birmingham, Patrick Michael
Cross, Daniel Albert
Rieke, Forrest Neill
Sellers, Marc Kellogg
**Roseburg**
Cremer, Richard Anthony
**Vale**
Carlson, David Rusco

### PENNSYLVANIA

**Birchrunville**
McClean, James Allen, Jr.
**Bryn Mawr**
Frumer, Richard J.
**Carlisle**
Turo, Ron
**Clarks Summit**
Beemer, John Barry
**Conshohocken**
Gutkin, Arthur Lee
**Doylestown**
Hoopes, Robert Patrick
**Du Bois**
Blakley, Benjamin Spencer, III
**Erie**
Williams, Dennis Vaughn
**Forty Fort**
Cosgrove, Joseph Matthias
**Frackville**
Domalakes, Paul George
**Harrisburg**
Curcillo, Joseph A., III
Lappas, Spero Thomas
Ward, William Francis
**Indiana**
Kauffman, Thomas Andrew
**Jenkintown**
McNally, John Bernard
**Johnstown**
Kaharick, Jerome John
**Kingston**
Urbanski, Stephen Karl
**Lancaster**
MacDonald, Richard Barry
Minney, Michael Jay
Pyfer, John Frederick, Jr.
**Lansdowne**
Kyriazis, Arthur John (Athanasios Ioannis Kyriazis)
**Lebanon**
Burkett, Loreen Marae
Keys, Robert Barr, Jr.
**Meadville**
Barrett, Bruce Alan
**Media**
Malloy, Michael Joseph
**Mercer**
Kochems, Robert Gregory
**New Castle**
Mangino, Matthew Thomas
**New Kensington**
Joseph, Daniel
**Newtown**
Kardos, Mel D.
**Norristown**
Gregg, John Pennypacker
**Philadelphia**
Armenti, Joseph Rocco
Caravasos, NiaLena
Carroll, Thomas Colas
Dennis, Edward S(pencer) G(ale), Jr.
Diamond, Paul Steven
Durant, Marc
Hoffman, Alan Jay
Ivey, Stephen David
Klein, Howard Bruce
Kraeutler, Eric
Lawson, William Thomas, III
Lipshutz, Robert Murray
Love, William Allan
Morris, John Whelchel
Rainville, Christina
Reiff, Jeffrey Marc
Savage, Timothy Joseph
Shmukler, Stanford
Siegel, Bernard Louis
Suddath, Thomas Howle, Jr.
Sweeney, Clayton Anthony, Jr.
Wittels, Barnaby Caesar
Wolf, Bruce
**Pittsburgh**
Bogut, John Carl, Jr.
Conley, William Vance
Corbett, Thomas Wingett, Jr.
Karaffa, Michael Alan, Sr.
King, Peter J.
Klein, Joel Aaron
Larson, Mark Adam
Pollock, Jeffrey Lawrence
Reich, Samuel Joseph
Terra, Sharon Ecker
Tully, Bernard Michael
**Pottstown**
Bauer, Paul Anthony, III
**Reynoldsville**
Wheeler, Mark Andrew, Sr.
**Saint Marys**
Daghir, George Nejm
**Scranton**
Sposito, James Anthony
**State College**
Nollau, Lee Gordon
**Stroudsburg**
Catina, Janet K.
**Tannersville**
Love, Mark Steven
**Trevose**
McEvilly, James Patrick, Jr.
**Uniontown**
Roskovensky, Vincent Joseph, II
**Washington**
O'Dell, Debbie
**White Oak**
Pribanic, Victor Hunter
**Williamsport**
Dohrmann, Jeffrey Charles
Rudinski, Michael J.
**York**
Pell, Daniel Max

### RHODE ISLAND

**Coventry**
Szarek, Milton Louis
**Providence**
Crilline, John Francis
Dana, Mark William
Devereaux, William P.
MacFadyen, John Archibald, III
Ratcliffe, J. Richard
Tramonti, John, Jr.
**West Warwick**
Pollock, Bruce Gerald

### SOUTH CAROLINA

**Camden**
Furman, Hezekiah Wyndol Carroll
**Charleston**
Swope, Denise Grainger
**Columbia**
Harvey, Jonathan Matthew
Strom, J. Preston, Jr.
Swerling, Jack Bruce
**Greenville**
James, William Richard
Talley, Michael Frank
**Hartsville**
Blake, Daniel L.
**Johnsonville**
Poston, Ellerby Delance
**Kingstree**
Jenkinson, William Eldridge, III
**North Myrtle Beach**
Wylie, Walter Jay
**Port Royal**
Newman, Jared Sullivan
**Seneca**
Sires, Norman Gruber, Jr.
**Summerville**
Hardee-Thomas, Marva A.
**Walterboro**
Harvin, L(ucius) Scott
**Winnsboro**
Goode, Kenneth George

### SOUTH DAKOTA

**Sioux Falls**
Johnson, Richard Arlo

### TENNESSEE

**Brentwood**
Easter, Timothy Lee
**Bristol**
Slaughter, Frank L., Jr.
**Chattanooga**
Bryan, Rosemarie Luise
Moore, Hugh Jacob, Jr.
Thompson, Neal Lewis
**Clarksville**
Smith, Gregory Dale
**Cookeville**
Qualls, Steven Daniel
**Fayetteville**
Dickey, John Harwell
**Kingsport**
Flanary, James Lee
**Knoxville**
Fels, Charles Wentworth Baker
Giordano, Lawrence Francis
Oberman, Steven
Routh, John William
**Martin**
Gearin, Kent Farrell
**Memphis**
Friedman, Robert Michael
Garts, James Rufus, Jr.
Grubb, Steven Cochran
McDaniel, Mark Steven
Veazey, Gary Eugene
**Nashville**
Burkett, Gerald Arthur
Butler, Jack A.
Dundon, Thomas H.
Lane, William Arthur
McNally, Patrick T.
Yarbrough, Edward Meacham
**Shelbyville**
Bramlett, Brenda Susan
**Springfield**
Wilks, Larry Dean
**Trenton**
Harrell, Limmie Lee, Jr.
**White House**
Ruth, Bryce Clinton, Jr.

### TEXAS

**Amarillo**
Isern, Kevin Anthony
McDougall, Gerald Duane
**Austin**
Dudley, Todd Steven
Shapiro, David L.
Stockard, Janet Louise
**Beaumont**
Lawrence, Edward Jack, III
**Boerne**
Deegear, James Otis, III
Reppeto, William M., III
**Brownsville**
Weisfeld, Sheldon
**Brownwood**
Steele, Todd Bennett
**Bryan**
Bond, Randall Scott
**Canton**
White, Jeffery Howell
**Corpus Christi**
Chesney, Brent Jackson
Miller, Carroll Gerard, Jr. (Gerry Miller)
**Dallas**
Booth, John W. (Bill Booth)
Branson, Frank Leslie, III
Burnham, Jim
Fitzmaurice, Edward Joseph, Jr.
Gioffredi, John M.
Grant, Deandra Michelle
Lenox, Roger Shawn
McCreary, David Sean
Miller, Deborah Slye
Rucker, R.D.
Scuro, Joseph E., Jr.
Sommers, Conrad Hoyle
Udashen, Robert Nathan
**Edinburg**
Hunter, Jack Duval, II
**El Paso**
Leachman, Russell DeWitt
Wright, Thomas Lawrence, II
**Fort Worth**
Alford, Barry James
Dickson, Victor Paul
Emerson, Douglas Theodore
Evans, Lance T.
Westfall, Gregory Burke
**Hico**
Peterson, Martin Lee
**Hillsboro**
Aufill, Bennett Brantley, III
**Houston**
Barnett, Stephanie Blair
Bell, Robert Christopher
Berg, David Howard
Disher, David Alan
Ekwem, Robertson M.
Essmyer, Michael Martin
Fox, Jan Woodward
Hamel, Lee
McCormack, David Richard
Susman, Morton Lee
Wallis, Olney Gray
Waska, Ronald Jerome
Wheelan, R(ichelieu) E(dward)
Willi, James Norman
Woody, Clyde Woodrow
**Humble**
Frazier, William Sumpter
**Longview**
Holmes, Clifton Lee (Scrappy Holmes)
Komorowski, Michele
**Lubbock**
Trowers, Teresa Cardenas
Williams, Anthony Jerome
**Mason**
Johnson, Rufus Winfield
**Mc Kinney**
Roessler, P. Dee
**Mcallen**
Alvarez, Adolfo, Jr.
Connors, Joseph Aloysius, III
**Midland**
Frost, Wayne N.
**New Braunfels**
Clark, Mark Adrian
**Odessa**
Wilson, Kevin Lang
**Orange**
Dugas, Louis, Jr.
**Plainview**
Lafont, William Harold
**San Antonio**
Orr, Cynthia Hujar
Raign, Michael Stephen
Yates, Norris William, Jr.
**San Marcos**
Maysel, Kyle Wayne
**Sulphur Springs**
Froneberger, Joel Douglas
**Texarkana**
Young, Damon Michael
**Victoria**
Serrata, Lidia
**Wichita Falls**
Williams, Steven Mark

### UTAH

**Ogden**
Gorman, Deirdre A.
Kaufman, Steven Michael
Sullivan, Kevin Patrick
**Salt Lake City**
Mooney, Jerome Henri
Rasmussen, Thomas Val, Jr.

### VERMONT

**Berlin**
Craddock, Stephen James
**Brattleboro**
Corum, Jesse Maxwell, IV
Reid, David G.
**Burlington**
Davis, Christopher Lee
Volk, Paul S.
**Middlebury**
Hill, Cindy Ellen
**Norwich**
McGee, P. Scott
**Rutland**
Harnett, Matt
**Stowe**
Davison, Robert P., Jr.

### VIRGINIA

**Abingdon**
Conway, Berry Leslie, II
**Alexandria**
Kiyonaga, John Cady
**Arlington**
Dunham, Frank Willard
Packett, Larry French
**Ashland**
Allen, Russell Earl
**Charlottesville**
Wyatt, Deborah Chasen
**Chesapeake**
Brown, John Wayne
**Coles Point**
Rager, Susan Godman
**Culpeper**
DeJarnette, Elliott Hawes
**Fairfax**
Britton, Matthew Joseph
Collins, Charles Edward, Jr.
Field, David Ellis
Joshi, Michael
McGowan, James Francis, III
Rieger, Michael Ira
Stanley, William Martin
**Fredericksburg**
Jones, Owaiian Maurice
**Front Royal**
Napier, Ronald Lewis
**Hampton**
Boester, Robert Alan
**Hillsville**
McGrady, Jonathan L.
**Lebanon**
Compton, Carnis Eugene
**Leesburg**
Biberaj, Buta
**Lynchburg**
Angel, James Joseph
Light, William Randall
Packert, G(ayla) Beth
**Manassas**
Hancock, Alton Guy
**Newport News**
Hankins, Timothy Howard
Sarfan, Edward I.
Saunders, Bryan Leslie
**Norfolk**
Sims, Hunter W., Jr.
Sutton, Paul Eugene, II
**Norton**
Earls, Donald Edward
**Orange**
Wilkinson, Richard K.
**Petersburg**
Spero, Morton Bertram
**Portsmouth**
Sayer, Darell Lee
**Radford**
Turk, James Clinton, Jr.
**Richmond**
Hauck, David Leahigh
Porter, Kirby Hugh
Spencer, Anthony George
**Roanoke**
Hale, Lance Mitchell
Hylton, Myles Talbert
**Virginia Beach**
Holmes, William James
McGraw, Frank William, Jr.
Moore, Michael Calvin
Schafer, Gerard Thomas Roger
**Waynesboro**
Jones, Linda Schorsch
**Wytheville**
Baird, Thomas Bryan, Jr.

### WASHINGTON

**Anacortes**
Osborn, Gerald T.
**Clarkston**
Kernan, Tina Lynn
Ledgerwood, Thomas L.
**Edmonds**
Conom, Tom Peter
**Everett**
Chamberlin, Harvey H.
Ferguson, Royce Allan, Jr.
Mestel, Mark David
**Mount Vernon**
Moser, C. Thomas
**Port Orchard**
Crawford, William Matterson
**Seattle**
Canavor, Frederick Charles, Jr.
Gonick, Peter B.
Grantham, Gene M.
Hollon, Gregory J.
Marshall, David Stanley
McKay, Michael Dennis
Novotny, Patricia Susan
Schumacher, Scott Alan
Schwartz, Irwin H.
Takahashi, Steven Shigeru
Tallman, Richard C.
Valerio, Pat J
Wayne, Robert Jonathan
**Spokane**
Rodrigues, Daryl Anthony
Weatherhead, Leslie R.
**Tacoma**
Barcus, Benjamin Franklin
Gersch, Charles Frant
Peters, Frank August
Walker, E. Allen

### WEST VIRGINIA

**Bluefield**
Henderson, Susan Ellen Fortune
**Charleston**
Ciccarello, Arthur T.
Cline, Michael Robert
Cowan, John Joseph
Deitzler, Harry G.
Michelson, Gail Ida
**Fairmont**
Martino, Gary James
**Huntington**
Stapleton, John Warren
**Morgantown**
Ringer, Darrell Wayne
**Parkersburg**
Powell, Eric Karlton
**Princeton**
Bell, Rebecca Morgan
**Saint Albans**
McKittrick, William David Parrish
**Wheeling**
Wilmoth, William David

### WISCONSIN

**Brookfield**
Zaffiro, Richard L.
**Colby**
Nikolay, Frank Lawrence
**Elkhart Lake**
Melowski, Dennis Michael
**Germantown**
Statkus, Jerome Francis
**Kenosha**
Constant, Terry Lynn
**Lake Geneva**
Olson, John Olmstead
**Little Chute**
Cornett, Paul Michael, Sr.
**Madison**
Blanchard, Brian Wheatley
Coaty, Thomas Jerome
Halloran, Thomas Giuld
Kelly, T. Christopher
Kuemmel, Joseph Kenneth
Pellino, Charles Edward, Jr.
Provis, Timothy Alan
Wood, Tracey A.
**Menomonie**
Steans, Phillip Michael
**Merrill**
Rogers, James Thomas
**Milwaukee**
Brown, Thomas Edward
Connolly, L. William
Gimbel, Franklyn M.
Marquis, William Oscar
McClure, Thomas James
O'Neill, Kevin Edgeworth
Orzel, Michael Dale
Stellman, L. Mandy
**Oshkosh**
Curtis, George Warren
**Portage**
Kohlwey, Jane Ellen
**Racine**
Hoelzel, Sally Ann
**Washburn**
Nordling, H.G.
**Wausau**
Connell, James Bernard
Drengler, William Allan John
**Wauwatosa**
Bonneson, Paul Garland
**West Allis**
Redding, Joseph E.
**West Bend**
Fincke, Waring Roberts

### WYOMING

**Casper**
Miller, Corinne
**Cheyenne**
Scorsine, John Magnus
**Gillette**
Zollinger, Thomas Tennant
**Jackson**
Goody, William Keith
Spence, Gerald Leonard
**Rawlins**
DeHerrera, Juan Leo
**Worland**
Richins, Kent Alan
Sweeny, Wendy Press

### TERRITORIES OF THE UNITED STATES

### PUERTO RICO

**Vega Baja**
Arraiza, Manuel F.

### MILITARY ADDRESSES OF THE UNITED STATES

### PACIFIC

**FPO**
Blazewick, Robert B.

### ADDRESS UNPUBLISHED

Abrahams, Samuel
Albin, Barry G.
Atwood, Jack McLean
Babbin, Jed Lloyd
Bailey, Francis Lee
Bartz, David John
Beldock, Myron
Bondi, Harry Gene
Brodsky, David M.
Brush, Kirkland L.
Cacciatore, Ronald Keith
Chesnutt, Marcus Wilkes
Ching, Louis Michael
Cohen, Anita Marilyn
Craven, Robert Emmett
Crebbin, Anthony Micek
Dorrier, Lindsay Gordon, Jr.
Dow, William F.
Eagen, William James
Ettinger, Joseph Alan
Evans, G. Anne
Feazell, Vic
Feuvrel, Sidney Leo, Jr.
Foreman, Lee David
Garry, John Thomas, II
Gianotti, Ernest F.
Goldberg, Scot Dale
Gregory, Rick Dean
Hickey, Timothy Andrew
Hornblass, Jerome
Johnson, Richard Wesley
Krelstein, Ronald Douglas
Leventhal, Howard G.
Liu, Albert Jingion
Mann, Michael B.
Martin, Thomas MacDonald
Mugridge, David Raymond
Nash, Melvin Samuel
Naughton, John Alexander
Pauca, Janet Frances
Pereyra-Suarez, Charles Albert
Putney, Wainscott Walker
Redmond, Lawrence Craig
Reeder, Robert Harry
Rench, Stephen Charles
Roche, Thomas Garrett
Schor, Suzi
Schwartzman, James Charles
Siebert, William Alan
Smouse, H(ervey) Russell
Stein, Daniel Jeremiah
Stout, Gregory Stansbury
Streicker, James Richard
Sussman, Howard S(ivn)
Tokars, Fredric William
Twardy, Stanley Albert, Jr.
Walsh, Gerry O'Malley
Wessel, Peter

---

**DEBTOR-CREDITOR.** *See* **Commercial, consumer.**

---

**DIVORCE.** *See* **Family.**

---

## EDUCATION AND SCHOOLS

### UNITED STATES

### ALABAMA

**Anniston**
Klinefelter, James Louis

### ARIZONA

**Phoenix**
Ullman, James A.
**Tucson**
Bainton, Denise Marlene
Corey, Barry Martin

### CALIFORNIA

**Berkeley**
Harris, Michael Gene
**Carmichael**
Halpenny, Diana Doris
**Claremont**
Vera, Ronald Thomas
**Los Alamitos**
Peters, Samuel Anthony
**Los Angeles**
Lipton, Jack Philip
**Malibu**
Hanson, Gary A.
**Pleasanton**
Hearey, Elizabeth Berle
**Pomona**
Lunsford, Jeanne Denise
**Sacramento**
Keiner, Christian Mark
**San Diego**
Zakarin, Keith
**San Francisco**
Davis, Roland Chenoweth
Links, Robert David
**San Rafael**
Farley, Margaret M.
**Santa Barbara**
Ah-Tye, Kirk Thomas
**Santa Cruz**
Redenbacher, Gary
**Solana Beach**
Zwick, Shelly Crittendon
**Walnut Creek**
Leone, Louis Anthony

### COLORADO

**Commerce City**
Trujillo, Lorenzo A.
**Denver**
Otten, Arthur Edward, Jr.
Roesler, John Bruce
**Englewood**
Breeskin, Michael Wayne
Cunningham, Samuel Scot
**Longmont**
Lyons, Richard Newman, II
**Pueblo**
Farley, Thomas T.

### CONNECTICUT

**Hartford**
Kemp, Wendi J.
**New Haven**
Choate, Edward Lee

### DISTRICT OF COLUMBIA

**Washington**
Goldstein, Michael B.
Medalie, Susan Diane
Portnoy, Elliott Ivan
Ward, Nicholas Donnell

### FLORIDA

**Miami**
Santoro, Thomas Mead
**Naples**
Rawson, Marjorie Jean
**Plantation**
Buck, Thomas Randolph
**Sarasota**
Fetterman, James Charles
**Tampa**
Burgess, Bryan Scott
MacDonald, Thomas Cook, Jr.

### GEORGIA

**Athens**
Davis, Claude-Leonard
**Atlanta**
González, Carlos A.

### HAWAII

**Honolulu**
Boas, Frank
**Kahului**
Richardson, Robert Allen

### IDAHO

**Boise**
Green, Cumer L.

### ILLINOIS

**Champaign**
Miller, Harold Arthur
**Chicago**
Cazares, Jorge V.
Gillio, Vickie Ann
Himes, A. Lynn
Joyce, Sarah Elizabeth
Mastandrea, Linda Lee
O'Hagin, Zarina Eileen Suarez
**Dekalb**
Davidson, Kenneth Lawrence
**East Alton**
Boyle, Patrick Otto
**Evanston**
Weston, Michael C.
**Lincolnshire**
Galatz, Henry Francis

### INDIANA

**Dyer**
DeGuilio, Jon E.
**Indianapolis**
Nettles, Gaylon James

### KANSAS

**Garden City**
Loyd, Ward Eugene
**Hutchinson**
Swearer, William Brooks
**Iola**
Toland, John Robert
**Overland Park**
Vratil, John Logan
**Wichita**
Ayres, Ted Dean

### KENTUCKY

**Benton**
Johnson, Martin Wolfe

**Covington**
Wolnitzek, Stephen Dale

### LOUISIANA

**Baton Rouge**
Nelson, David K.
**Jennings**
Miller, Ruth Loyd
**Shreveport**
Prestridge, Rogers Meredith

### MAINE

**Yarmouth**
Webster, Peter Bridgman

### MARYLAND

**Annapolis**
Burns, B. Darren
**Rockville**
Gordon, Joan Irma
Litteral, Daniel Pace
**Takoma Park**
Browning, Deborah Lea

### MASSACHUSETTS

**Boston**
Felter, John Kenneth
Garrett, Karen Ann
Gondek, Diana Stasia
Gossels, Claus Peter Rolf
Jones, Jeffrey Foster
Lyons, Paul Vincent
Rose, Alan Douglas
**Braintree**
McNulty, Michelle Allaire
**Medford**
Jacobs, Mary Lee
**South Hadley**
Sheridan, Daniel Joseph

### MICHIGAN

**Detroit**
Furton, Joseph Rae, Jr.
**Grand Rapids**
Elve, Daniel Leigh
**Harbor Springs**
Turner, Lester Nathan

### MINNESOTA

**Minneapolis**
Wille, Karin L.

### MISSISSIPPI

**Tupelo**
Edwards, John Max, Jr.

### MISSOURI

**Kansas City**
Sands, Darry Gene
**Saint Louis**
Chackes, Kenneth Michael
Gianoulakis, John Louis
Kauffman, William Ray

### MONTANA

**Missoula**
Loring, Emilie

### NEBRASKA

**Lincoln**
Perry, Edwin Charles
Sapp, Susan Kubert

### NEW HAMPSHIRE

**Concord**
Irwin, Lauren Simon

### NEW JERSEY

**Clifton**
Pincus, Sheldon Howard
**Edison**
Wong, Linda
**Freehold**
Brown, Sanford Donald
**Marlton**
Cavallo, Frank P., Jr.
**New Brunswick**
Scott, David Rodick
**Pitman**
Powell, J. R.
**Somerville**
Bernstein, Eric Martin
**Trenton**
Williams, Barbara June

### NEW MEXICO

**Albuquerque**
Carrico, Michael Layne
**Las Cruces**
Martin, Connie Ruth

### NEW YORK

**Albany**
Danziger, Peter
Girvin, James Edward
Jehu, John Paul
**Briarcliff Manor**
Rosen, Paul Maynard
**Brooklyn**
Castro, Sonia Mendez
**Buffalo**
Goldstein, Bruce A.
**Fayetteville**
Alderman, Judith Lorraine
**Floral Park**
Chatoff, Michael Alan
**Garden City**
Ehrlich, Jerome Harry
**Keeseville**
Turetsky, Aaron
**Mineola**
Millman, Bruce Russell
Pogrebin, Bertrand B.
Zuckerman, Richard Karl
**Mount Kisco**
Curran, Maurice Francis
**New York**
Aiello, Robert John
Bear, Larry Alan
Ebert, Michael
Josephson, William Howard
Liss, Norman
Nolan, Terrance Joseph, Jr.
Schaffer, Seth Andrew
**Northport**
Gross, John H.
**Oneonta**
Burns, Brian Douglas
**Pearl River**
Riley, James Kevin
**Riverhead**
Shane, Suzanne V.
**Schenectady**
Levine, Sanford Harold
**White Plains**
Longo, Ronald Anthony

### NORTH CAROLINA

**Charlotte**
Campbell, Hugh Brown, Jr.
**Gastonia**
Garland, James Boyce
**Hillsborough**
Martin, Harry Corpening
**Raleigh**
Kurz, Mary Elizabeth

### OHIO

**Akron**
Minney, R. Brent
**Cincinnati**
Hornberger, Lee
**Cleveland**
Lentz, Mary A.
**Columbus**
Sims, August Charles
**Lima**
Kluge, William Frederick
**Toledo**
Pletz, Thomas Gregory
**Youngstown**
Messenger, James Louis

### OKLAHOMA

**El Reno**
Grantham, Robert Edward

### PENNSYLVANIA

**Bangor**
Spry, Donald Francis, II
**Harrisburg**
Husic, Yvonne M.
**Lansdale**
Sultanik, Jeffrey Ted
**Lehigh Valley**
Marles, Blake Curtis
**Lumberville**
McGuckin, Ronald V.
**Norristown**
Rees, Thomas Dynevor
**Philadelphia**
Brier, Bonnie Susan

### RHODE ISLAND

**Providence**
Keeney, Thomas Critchfield
Long, Nicholas Trott

### TENNESSEE

**Kingsport**
Hull, E. Patrick
**Memphis**
deWitt, Charles Benjamin, III
Smith, Joseph Philip
**Nashville**
Torrey, Claudia Olivia

### TEXAS

**Abilene**
Robinson, Vianei Lopez
**Austin**
Brim, Jefferson Kearney, III
Hale, Louis Dewitt
Hanner, Karl Tiger
Schulze, Eric William
**Beaumont**
Lawrence, Edward Jack, III
**El Paso**
Hughes, Steven Lee
**Fort Worth**
Carr, Thomas Eldridge
Law, Thomas Hart
**Houston**
Diaz-Arrastia, George Ravelo
Frels, Kelly
McEvily, Daniel Vincent Sean
Moroney, Linda L. S.
**Pearland**
Bittick, Peggy Sue

### UTAH

**Ogden**
Mecham, Glenn Jefferson

### VERMONT

**Burlington**
Blackwood, Eileen Morris
McKearin, Robert R.
Roy, Christopher Denis

### VIRGINIA

**Alexandria**
Stone, Steven David
**Mc Lean**
Bardack, Paul Roitman
**Richmond**
Ross, David Lee
Ryland, Walter H.

### WASHINGTON

**Bellevue**
Hannah, Lawrence Burlison
**Seattle**
Warner, Charles Ford
**Spokane**
Winston, Robert W., Jr.

### WEST VIRGINIA

**Huntington**
Ransbottom, Jennifer Dickens
**Morgantown**
Kimble, Kelly Jean

### WISCONSIN

**Milwaukee**
Olivieri, José Alberto
**Monroe**
Kittelsen, Rodney Olin
**Oshkosh**
Williams, Edward J.

### WYOMING

**Casper**
Day, Stuart Reid

### ADDRESS UNPUBLISHED

Anderson, Jon Eric
D'Agusto, Karen Rose
Fink, Norman Stiles
Franke, Ann Harriet
Hornthal, Louis Philip, Jr.
Mann, Richard Lynn
Miller, Frank William
Smith, Ronald Ehlbert

## EMINENT DOMAIN. *See* Condemnation.

## ENERGY, FERC PRACTICE

### UNITED STATES

### ARIZONA

**Phoenix**
Nelson, Douglas Clarence

### CALIFORNIA

**Los Angeles**
Rothman, Frank
Woodland, Irwin Francis
**San Francisco**
Ogilby, Barry Ray

### COLORADO

**Denver**
Beatty, Michael L.

### DISTRICT OF COLUMBIA

**Washington**
Beresford, Douglas Lincoln
Betts, Kirk Howard
Calderwood, James Albert
Collins, Daniel Francis
Downs, Clark Evans
Egan, Joseph Richard
Elrod, Eugene Richard
Feldman, Roger David
Fogel, J(oan) Cathy
Grady, Gregory
Grenier, Edward Joseph, Jr.
Guy, Gary Edward
Hobelman, Carl Donald
Hollis, Sheila Slocum
Journey, Drexel Dahlke
Kelly, Frank Xavier, Jr.
Kissel, Peter Charles
Lange, William Michael
Loeffler, Robert Hugh
Mann, Donegan
Mapes, William Rodgers, Jr.
Martin, Jay Griffith
Mathis, John Prentiss
McDiarmid, Robert Campbell
McKinney, James DeVaine, Jr.
Miller, John T., Jr.
Penn-Jenkins, Monique Lorae
Simons, Barbara M.
Zipp, Joel Frederick

### ILLINOIS

**Chicago**
Fazio, Peter Victor, Jr.
Meyer, J. Theodore
**Lake Forest**
Emerson, William Harry

### KANSAS

**Wichita**
Bostwick, Donald W.

### LOUISIANA

**Shreveport**
Hetherwick, Gilbert Lewis

### MAINE

**Augusta**
Donahue, Joseph Gerald

### MARYLAND

**Bethesda**
Eisen, Eric Anshel
Herman, Stephen Allen
Rivkin, Steven Robert

### MASSACHUSETTS

**Boston**
Hester, Patrick Joseph

### MISSISSIPPI

**Laurel**
Cline, Lee Williamson

### NEW HAMPSHIRE

**Concord**
Moffett, Howard Mackenzie

### NEW JERSEY

**Florham Park**
Wright, Paul William
**Saddle River**
Nordlund, William Chalmers
**Woodcliff Lake**
Getler, Janine A.

### NEW YORK

**New York**
Allen, Leon Arthur, Jr.
Butterklee, Neil Howard
Hall, Robert Turnbull, III
Margulis, Howard Lee
Meyering, Christopher P.
**Rochester**
George, Richard Neill

### OKLAHOMA

**Oklahoma City**
Harris, Allen Keith
Taliaferro, Henry Beauford, Jr.

### OREGON

**Portland**
Baxendale, James Charles Lewis
Dotten, Michael Chester

### PENNSYLVANIA

**Lancaster**
Caminero, Rafael
**Philadelphia**
Brown, Baird
**Pittsburgh**
Holsinger, John Paul

### RHODE ISLAND

**Providence**
Southgate, (Christina) Adrienne Graves

### TEXAS

**Dallas**
Armour, James Lott
Keithley, Bradford Gene
**Houston**
Hartrick, Janice Kay
Kruse, Charles Thomas
Morgan, Richard Greer
Rocan, Jacquelyne Marie
Ryan, Thomas William
Woung, Marguerite Natalie

### VERMONT

**Rutland**
Werle, Mark Fred

### VIRGINIA

**Alexandria**
Sczudlo, Walter Joseph
**Annandale**
Yaffe, David Philip
**Richmond**
Watts, Stephen Hurt, II

### WASHINGTON

**Tacoma**
Waldo, James Chandler

### ADDRESS UNPUBLISHED

Choukas-Bradley, James Richard
Flood, James J(oseph), Jr.
Sweeney, Kevin Michael
Tanenbaum, Jay Harvey
Terry, John Hart

## ENERGY, NUCLEAR POWER

### UNITED STATES

### ALABAMA

**Birmingham**
Robin, Theodore Tydings, Jr.

### CONNECTICUT

**Hartford**
Knickerbocker, Robert Platt, Jr.

### DISTRICT OF COLUMBIA

**Washington**
Edgar, George Lukens
Egan, Joseph Richard
Langworthy, Lucinda Minton
Lessy, Roy Paul, Jr.
Mathis, John Prentiss
Ruddy, Frank

### MARYLAND

**Gaithersburg**
Godwin, Richard Jeffrey
**Saint Michaels**
Brown, Omer Forrest, II

### MASSACHUSETTS

**Boston**
Dignan, Thomas Gregory, Jr.

### NEW YORK

**Dunkirk**
Woodbury, Robert Charles
**New York**
Hayes, Gerald Joseph

### NORTH CAROLINA

**Cary**
Glass, Fred Stephen

### OKLAHOMA

**Fairview**
Schoeppel, James

### TENNESSEE

**Oak Ridge**
Pearman, Joel Edward

### VERMONT

**Randolph Center**
Casson, Richard Frederick

### VIRGINIA

**Lynchburg**
Elliott, James Ward
**Richmond**
Roach, Edgar Mayo, Jr.

### ADDRESS UNPUBLISHED

Buffington, John Victor
Doub, William Offutt
Fetzer, Mark Stephen

## ENTERTAINMENT

### UNITED STATES

### ALABAMA

**Huntsville**
Blair, Edward Eugene

### ARIZONA

**Phoenix**
Lubin, Stanley
Mousel, Craig Lawrence
Silverman, Alan Henry

### CALIFORNIA

**Beverly Hills**
Donaldson, Michael Cleaves
Holmes, Henry W.
Litwak, Glenn Tod
Ramer, Bruce M.
Rondeau, Charles Reinhardt
Russell, Irwin Emanuel
Steinberger, Jeffrey Wayne
**Burbank**
Campbell, L. Cooper
Noddings, Sarah Ellen
**Century City**
Davis, Donald G(lenn)
**Encinitas**
Nemeth, Valerie Ann
**Encino**
Shtofman, Robert Scott
**Huntington Beach**
Guerin, John Joseph
**Irvine**
Specter, Richard Bruce
**Los Angeles**
Biederman, Donald Ellis
Branca, John Gregory
Cooper, Jay Leslie
Davis, J. Alan
Dean, Jon
Demoff, Marvin Alan
Diamond, Stanley Jay
Early, Eric Peter
Feigen, Brenda S.
Gallegos, Esteban Guillermo
Genga, John Michael
Kenoff, Jay Stewart
Korduner, David Jerome
Langberg, Barry Benson
Lenkov, Jeffrey Myles
Levin, Evanne Lynn
Lurvey, Ira Harold
Palazzo, Robert P.
Pascotto, Alvaro
Pasich, Kirk Alan
Robertson, Hugh Duff
Synn, Gordon
Venable, Giovan Harbour
White, Susan Page
**Marina Del Rey**
Murphy, Tamela Jayne
Seiden, Andy

**Oakland**
Loving, Deborah June Pierre
**Pacific Palisades**
Verrone, Patric Miller
**Palm Desert**
Singer, Gerald Michael
**San Diego**
Von Passenheim, John B.
**San Francisco**
Makiyama, Hiroe Ruby
Peter, Laura Anne
Weiner, Jody Carl
**San Mateo**
Mandel, Martin Louis
**Santa Ana**
Lane, Dominick V.
Shelton, Ralph Conrad
**Santa Clarita**
Kotler, Richard Lee
**Santa Cruz**
Brennan, Enda Thomas
**Santa Monica**
Homeier, Michael George
Pizzulli, Francis Cosmo Joseph
**Seal Beach**
Porter, Joseph Edward, III
**Sherman Oaks**
Joyce, Stephen Michael
**Tarzana**
Godino, Marc Lawrence
**Universal City**
Coupe, James Warnick

**West Hollywood**
Finstad, Suzanne Elaine

COLORADO

**Denver**
Horowitz, Robert M.

CONNECTICUT

**Windsor**
Molitor, Karen Ann

DISTRICT OF COLUMBIA

**Washington**
Barnett, Robert Bruce
Goldson, Amy Robertson
O'Connor, Charles P.
Vaughn-Carrington, Debra Miller

FLORIDA

**Altamonte Springs**
Harding, Calvin Fredrick, Jr.
**Clearwater**
Weidemeyer, Carleton Lloyd
**Fort Lauderdale**
Benjamin, James Scott
**Lauderhill**
Berry, Carl David, Jr.
**Miami**
Friedman, Richard Nathan
Kolback, Kimberly Dawn
Whitlow, James Adams
**Orlando**
Kolin, Lawrence Howard
Lang, Thomas Frederick
**Palm Harbor**
Deckelman, Arthur D.
**Saint Pete Beach**
Milham, Julee Lynn
**Tallahassee**
McNeely, Robert A.
**West Palm Beach**
Finley, Chamdler R.

GEORGIA

**Atlanta**
Coleman, Sean Joseph
Croone, Eric
Hassett, Robert William
Koplan, Andrew Bennet
Muller, William Manning
Smith, Jeffrey Michael

HAWAII

**Honolulu**
Pallett, James McCormack

IDAHO

**Boise**
Rowe, John R.

ILLINOIS

**Chicago**
Aronovitz, Cory Jay
Hoffman, Valerie Jane
Kurz, Jerry Bruce
Lauderdale, Katherine Sue
Marvel, Kenneth Robert
Materre, Gloria Leann
Mattes, Barry A.
Rubin, E(rwin) Leonard
Sennet, Charles Joseph
Snyder, Jean Maclean
**Oak Brook**
Misna, Kathryn Kimura
**Roselle**
Bassitt, Janet Louise

INDIANA

**Indianapolis**
Carr, David J.
Elberger, Ronald Edward

LOUISIANA

**Lacombe**
Price, Lionel Franklin
**Shreveport**
Bryant, J(ames) Bruce

MARYLAND

**Baltimore**
Gilbert, Blaine Louis
Hopps, Raymond, Jr.
Katz, Lawrence Edward

MASSACHUSETTS

**Boston**
Carberry, Kenneth Anthony
Fischer, Mark Alan
Geismer, Alan Stearn, Jr.
Kassler, Haskell A.
Kyros, Konstantine William
Larson, Olive Elizabeth
**Northampton**
Fierst, Frederick Udell
Offner, Daniel O'Connell
**Springfield**
Miller, J(ohn) Wesley, III
**Waltham**
Zaharoff, Howard George

MICHIGAN

**Bloomfield Hills**
Wilson, Cynthia Diane

MINNESOTA

**Minneapolis**
Street, Erica Catherine
Voss, Barry Vaughan

MISSOURI

**Kansas City**
Kitchin, John Joseph
Seigfreid, James Thomas
**Saint Louis**
Fournie, Raymond Richard
Watson-Wesley, Denise J.

NEBRASKA

**Omaha**
Castello, David A.

NEVADA

**Las Vegas**
Larsen, Paul Edward

NEW HAMPSHIRE

**Concord**
Hodes, Paul William

NEW JERSEY

**Maplewood**
Joseph, Susan B.
**Morristown**
Schwartz, Howard J.
**Red Bank**
Rogers, Lee Jasper
**Roseland**
Robinson, Richard S.
**Secaucus**
Rideout, Joi Huckaby

NEW YORK

**Bethpage**
Lemle, Robert Spencer
**Buffalo**
Runfola, Ross Thomas
**Garden City**
Critelli, Christopher William
Posch, Robert John, Jr.
**Great Neck**
Luckman, Gregg A.
**Kew Gardens**
Schechter, Donald Robert
**Mineola**
Berman, Eric M.
**New York**
Ames, John Lewis
Barnabeo, Susan Patricia
Berger, Michael Gary
Berk, Brian D.
Bicks, Peter Andrews
Bomser, Alan H.
Butterfield, Toby Michael John
Butterman, Jay Ronald
Colfin, Bruce Elliott
Collyer, Michael
Cooper, Stephanie R.
Dehn, Francis Xavier
Dretzin, David
Eisenberg, Viviane
Farber, Donald Clifford
Fry, Morton Harrison, II
Goldberg, David
Green, Richard George
Grossman, Stacy Jill
Hartnick, Alan J.
Hathaway, Gerald Thomas
Huston, Barry Scott
Indursky, Arthur
Jacobson, Jeffrey Eli
Jacqueney, Stephanie A(lice)
Janowitz, James Arnold
Krieger, Sanford
Laufer, Jacob
LeFevre, David E.
Levinson, Paul Howard
Lighter, Lawrence
Lonner, Jonathan Ari
Martinez, Jose, Jr.
McCabe, Monica Petraglia
McCarthy, Robert Emmett
Pack, Leonard Brecher
Papernik, Joel Ira
Rozan, Alain
Ryan, J. Richard
Saldana, Adrienne L.
Salman, Robert Ronald
Schmitt, John Patrick
Seligman, Delice
Sendroff, Mark D.
Spanbock, Maurice Samuel
Taylor, John Chestnut, III
Tormey, John Joseph, III
Tritter, Daniel F.
Watanabe, Roy Noboru
Zahnd, Richard H.
Zissu, Michael Jerome
**Poughkeepsie**
Millman, Jode Susan
**Rochester**
Twietmeyer, Don Henry
**Roslyn Heights**
Dieguez, Richard Peter
**White Plains**
Castrataro, Barbara Ann

NORTH CAROLINA

**Charlotte**
Shiau, H. Lin
**Greensboro**
Cline, Todd Wakefield
**Wilmington**
Nunalee, Mary Margaret McEachern

OHIO

**Columbus**
Mendel, David Phillip

OKLAHOMA

**Norman**
Fairbanks, Robert Alvin
**Oklahoma City**
Briggs, M. Courtney
Hanna, Terry Ross

PENNSYLVANIA

**Clearfield**
Falvo, Mark Anthony
**Franklin Center**
Harvey, Alice Elease
**Lansdowne**
Kyriazis, Arthur John (Athanasios Ioannis Kyriazis)
**Philadelphia**
Berger, Harold
DeBunda, Salvatore Michael
Reiff, Jeffrey Marc
**Pittsburgh**
Gutnick, H. Yale
Pollock, Jeffrey Lawrence
Reich, Samuel Joseph
Stepanian, Steven Arvid, II

RHODE ISLAND

**Cranston**
Cervone, Anthony Louis

TENNESSEE

**Knoxville**
Bailey, Bridget
**Memphis**
Monypeny, David Murray
Moore, Dwight Terry
**Nashville**
Bramlett, Paul Kent
Harris, James Harold, III
Lyon, Philip K(irkland)
Phillips, Bruce Harold
Phillips, W. Alan

TEXAS

**Austin**
Terry, Craig Robert
**Dallas**
Gunnstaks, C. Luke
Hammond, Herbert J.
McGarry, Charles William
**Irving**
French, Colin Val
**Longview**
Beckworth, Lindley Gary, Jr.

UTAH

**Salt Lake City**
Mooney, Jerome Henri

VIRGINIA

**Culpeper**
Dulaney, Richard Alvin
**Mount Vernon**
Spiegel, H. Jay
**Richmond**
Goodpasture, Philip Henry

WASHINGTON

**Bellevue**
Gadre, Aniruddha Rudy
**Seattle**
Bergstedt, Anders Spencer
Sussman, Neil A.

WISCONSIN

**Milwaukee**
Stomma, Peter Christopher

ADDRESS UNPUBLISHED

Feazell, Vic
Goldstein, Glenn Alan
Gordon, Kenneth Ira
Hall-Barron, Deborah
Harris, James T.
Harvey, Marc Sean
Higginbotham, John Taylor
Kantrowitz, Susan Lee
Lightstone, Ronald
McLendon, Susan Michelle
Meyerson, Stanley Phillip
O'Connor, Edward Vincent, Jr.
Saunders, Lonna Jeanne
Schor, Suzi
Siporin, Sheldon
Smith, Jeanette Elizabeth
von Sauers, Joseph F.

## ENVIRONMENTAL

UNITED STATES

ALABAMA

**Birmingham**
Alford, Margie Searcy
Gale, Fournier Joseph, III
Palmer, Robert Leslie
Robin, Theodore Tydings, Jr.
Timberlake, Marshall
**Magnolia Springs**
Kuykendall, Frederick Thurman, III
**Mobile**
Johnston, Neil Chunn
Pierce, Donald Fay

ALASKA

**Anchorage**
Flynn, Charles P.
Linxwiler, James David
Owens, Robert Patrick
**Kodiak**
Ott, Andrew Eduard

ARIZONA

**Flagstaff**
Gliege, John Gerhardt
**Phoenix**
Jorden, Douglas Allen
Kramer, Robert J.
Matheson, Alan Adams, Jr.
Nelson, Douglas Clarence
Storey, Lee A.
Wolf, G. Van Velsor, Jr.
**Tempe**
Shimpock, Kathy Elizabeth

ARKANSAS

**Little Rock**
Julian, Jim Lee
Mackey, Diane Stoakes

CALIFORNIA

**Beverly Hills**
Bordy, Michael Jeffrey
**China Lake**
Hatley, Rodney James
**Claremont**
Vera, Ronald Thomas
**Fremont**
Cummings, John Patrick
**Glendale**
Bright, James Stephen
**Grass Valley**
Bell, Joseph James
**Los Angeles**
Chin, Llewellyn Philip
Gravelle, Douglas Arthur
Lewand, Kimberly Ellen
Molleur, Richard Raymond
Moyer, Craig Alan
Olivas, Daniel A.
Rutter, Marshall Anthony
Straw, Lawrence Joseph, Jr.
Tepper, R(obert) Bruce, Jr.
**Moraga**
Kilbourne, George William
**Newport Beach**
McGee, James Francis
Smithson, David Matthew
Wagner, John Leo
**Palo Alto**
Cohen, Nancy Mahoney
**Pleasanton**
MacDonald, Peter David
**Redwood City**
Givens, Richard Donald
**Rosemead**
Danner, Bryant Craig
**Sacramento**
Cahill, Virginia Arnoldy
Mooney, Donald B.
Robbins, Stephen J. M.
Taber, Kelley Morgan
Uranga, Jose Navarette
**San Diego**
Brownlie, Robert William
Dawe, James Robert
Getz, David H.
Peterson, Paul Ames
**San Francisco**
Alexander, Mary Elsie
Aronovsky, Ronald George
Bruen, James A.
Goode, Barry Paul
Haughton, Brian Stephens
Infelise, Robert Donald
Kang, Helen Haekyong
Malone, Michael Glen
Moser, David E.
Ogilby, Barry Ray
Reding, John Anthony
Robertson, J. Martin
Robin, Kenneth David
Scarlett, Randall H.
Thompson, Robert Charles
Wyatt, Robert David
**Santa Barbara**
Metzinger, Timothy Edward
**Walnut Creek**
Steele, Dwight Cleveland

COLORADO

**Boulder**
Cypser, Darlene Ann
Fenster, Herbert Lawrence
Gray, William R.
Yuhnke, Robert E.
**Colorado Springs**
Harris, Stephen Donnell
**Denver**
Arfmann, Dennis L.
DeSisto, John Anthony
Duffy, William J.
Featherstone, Bruce Alan
Freeman, Deborah Lynn
Goldberg, Gregory Eban
Grant, Patrick Alexander
Holme, Howard Kelley
Martz, Clyde Ollen
McKenna, Frederick Gregory
Merritts, Jack Michael
Norton, Gale Ann
Pope, David Bruce
Ray, Bruce David
Rockwood, Linda Lee
Sayre, John Marshall
Schindler, Ronald Irvin
Shepherd, John Frederic
**Englewood**
Wheeler, Karen Hannah
**Evergreen**
Coriden, Michael Warner
**Golden**
Hughes, Marcia Marie
Snead, Kathleen Marie

CONNECTICUT

**Hartford**
Buck, Gurdon Hall
Davis, Andrew Neil
Merriam, Dwight Haines
Sussman, Mark Richard
Sylvester, Kathryn Rose
**Plainville**
Anderson, William Carl
**Stamford**
Eckweiler, Karl Terrance

DELAWARE

**Wilmington**
Kirk, Richard Dillon
Klayman, Barry Martin
Malinowski, Andrea V.
Rice, Vernon Rawl
Waisanen, Christine M.

DISTRICT OF COLUMBIA

**Washington**
Ayres, Richard Edward
Barnard, Robert C.
Barrett, Jane Frances
Bernstein, Mitchell Harris
Browne, Richard Cullen
Cannon, Dean Hollingsworth
Carr, Lawrence Edward, Jr.
Condrell, William Kenneth
Edmondson, Paul William
Ewing, Ky Pepper, Jr.
Faron, Robert Steven
Frost, Edmund Bowen
Geneson, David Franklin
Glitzenstein, Eric Robert
Guerry, William
Haynes, William J(ames), II
Hollis, Sheila Slocum
Holmstead, Jeffrey Ralph
Howard, Jeffrey Hjalmar
Jones, Theodore Lawrence
Keiner, Suellen Terrill
Kirsch, Laurence Stephen
Kovacs, William Lawrence
Langworthy, Lucinda Minton
Lettow, Charles Frederick
Levin, Michael Henry
Lewis, William Henry, Jr.
Liss, Jeffrey F.
Littell, Richard Gregory
Mannina, George John, Jr.
Martin, Jay Griffith
McCrum, Robert Timothy
McKey, Arthur Duncan
Mills, Kevin Paul
Raul, Alan Charles
Rizzo, James Gerard
Roberts, Jared Ingersoll
Rose, Jonathan Chapman
Ruddy, Frank
Schiffbauer, William G.
Sherer, Samuel Ayers
Stephens, Andrew Russell
Stoll, Richard G(iles)
Vardaman, John Wesley
Waldron, Jonathan Kent
Weissman, William R.
Wine, L. Mark

FLORIDA

**Coral Gables**
Thornton, John William, Sr.
**Daytona Beach**
Watts, C. Allen
**Fort Lauderdale**
Hopen, Richard Martin
**Islamorada**
Mattson, James Stewart
**Jacksonville**
Dornan, Kevin William
Manning, G(erald) Stephen
**Lake Buena Vista**
Schmudde, Lee Gene
**Lakeland**
Martin, Michael David
**Miami**
Butler, John Thomas
Coll, Norman Alan
Fleming, Joseph Z.
Halsey, Douglas Martin
Jorgensen, Lauren
Prego, Mayda
**Miami Lakes**
Sharett, Alan Richard
**Naples**
Humphreville, John David
**Orlando**
Chotas, Elias Nicholas
Downie, Robert Collins, II
Sims, Roger W.
**Palm Bay**
Tietig, Edward Chester
**Saint Petersburg**
Harrell, Roy G., Jr.
**Sarasota**
Janney, Oliver James
Patten, Brenda L.
**Tallahassee**
Curtin, Lawrence N.
DeFoor, J. Allison, II
Matthews, Frank Edward
**Tampa**
Brown, Enola T.
Elliggett, Raymond Thomas, Jr.
Schwenke, Roger Dean

GEORGIA

**Atlanta**
Bridges, Louis Emerson, III
Denham, Vernon Robert, Jr.
Draper, Stephen Elliot
Killorin, Robert Ware
Medlin, Charles McCall
Ortiz, Jay Richard Gentry
Owens, L. Dale
Phillips, William Russell, Sr.
Stokes, James Sewell
Williams, Joel Cash
**Macon**
Ennis, Edgar William, Jr.
**Marietta**
Nowland, James Ferrell
**Metter**
Doremus, Ogden

HAWAII

**Honolulu**
Bail, Lisa A.
Lombardi, Dennis M.
Pallett, James McCormack

IDAHO

**Boise**
Turcke, Paul Andrew

ILLINOIS

**Chicago**
Bleiweiss, Shell J.
Drumke, Michael William

**San Antonio**
Labay, Eugene Benedict
**Wichita Falls**
Todd, Richard D. R.

### UTAH

**Logan**
Honaker, Jimmie Joe
**Midvale**
Dahl, Everett E.
**Salt Lake City**
Davies, Glen Ensign
Deisley, David Lee
Dragoo, Denise Ann
Kirkham, John Spencer

### VERMONT

**Burlington**
Schroeder, William Wayne
**Middlebury**
Hill, Cindy Ellen
**Montpelier**
Storrow, Charles Fiske
**Norwich**
Lundquist, Weyman Ivan
**Saint Johnsbury**
Palmer, Bruce C.

### VIRGINIA

**Alexandria**
Sherk, George William
**Fairfax**
Chapman, Edmund Whyte
**Fort Lee**
Baker, Loren Leonard
**Glen Allen**
Urelius, Shawn Renea
**Lynchburg**
Elliott, James Ward
**Mc Lean**
Mason, Thomas Owen
**Norfolk**
Parker, Richard Wilson
**Richmond**
Freeman, George Clemon, Jr.
Landin, David Craig
Pomeroy, Christopher Donald
Rudlin, David Alan

### WASHINGTON

**Bellevue**
Medved, Robert Allen
**Everett**
Dewell, Julian C.
**Olympia**
Miller, Allen Terry, Jr.
**Seattle**
Aramburu, John Richard
Eberhard, Eric Drake
Eustis, Jeffrey Murdock
Freedman, Bart Joseph
Goeltz, Thomas A.
Haggard, Joel Edward
Jensen, Howard Fernando
Kilbane, Thomas M.
Larson, Linda R.
Leed, Roger Melvin
McCune, Philip Spear
McKinstry, Ronald Eugene
Mullaney, Patrick Joseph
Salter, Andrew H.
Walters, Dennis H.
Wilson, Richard Randolph
**Spokane**
Annis, Eugene Irwin
**Tacoma**
Densley, James Albert
Goodstein, Robert I.
Waldo, James Chandler

### WEST VIRGINIA

**Charleston**
George, Larry Wayne
Victorson, Michael Bruce
**Fairview**
Bunner, Patricia Andrea
**Morgantown**
Bunner, William Keck

### WISCONSIN

**Elkhorn**
Leibsle, Robert Carl
**Madison**
Rankin, Gene Raymond
Stoddard, Glenn McDonald
**Milwaukee**
Croak, Francis R.
Fredericks, James Matthew
**West Bend**
Fincke, Waring Roberts

### WYOMING

**Cheyenne**
Godfrey, Paul Bard
**Sheridan**
Cannon, Kim Decker

### TERRITORIES OF THE UNITED STATES

### VIRGIN ISLANDS

**Christiansted**
Hart, Thomas Hughson, III

### ADDRESS UNPUBLISHED

Andrews, David Ralph
Arnold, Craig Anthony (Tony Arnold)
Ayres, Caroline Patricia
Blount, David Laurence
Braud, Rene S.
Connell, William D.
Eaton, Larry Ralph
Fetzer, Mark Stephen
Garner, Mary Martin
Gates, Pamela Sue
Gerwin, Leslie Ellen
Hampson, Robert George
Jones, David Edwin
Lippes, Richard James
Miskimin, Alice Schwenk
Reynolds, H. Gerald
Russo, Donna Marie
Sampson, David Synnott
Toole, William Walter
Wright, Frederick Lewis, II
Wright, Robert Payton

---

## ESTATE PLANNING. *See also* Probate; Taxation, estate.

---

### UNITED STATES

### ALABAMA

**Birmingham**
Foster, Arthur Key, Jr.
Hughes, James Donald
**Decatur**
Blackburn, John Gilmer
**Foley**
Leatherbury, Gregory Luce, Jr.
**Huntsville**
Ludwig, Scott Edward
Potter, Ernest Luther
**Mobile**
Armbrecht, William Henry, III
Brock, Glen Porter, Jr.
Holland, Lyman Faith, Jr.
**Montgomery**
Kirtland, Michael Arthur

### ALASKA

**Anchorage**
Johnson, Brent Allen
**Fairbanks**
Rice, Julian Casavant

### ARIZONA

**Mesa**
Gunderson, Brent Merrill
**Phoenix**
Case, David Leon
Ehmann, Anthony Valentine
Hiller, Neil Howard
Lowry, Edward Francis, Jr.
Olsen, Alfred Jon
Rosen, Sidney Marvin
Sliger, Herbert Jacquemin, Jr.
Tomback, Jay Loren
**Scottsdale**
Burris, Donald J.
Franz, J. Noland
Roberts, Jean Reed
Swartz, Melvin Jay
**Surprise**
Hayes, Ray, Jr.
**Tucson**
Adamson, Larry Robertson
Farsjo, Fred A.
Levitan, Roger Stanley
**Yuma**
Hunt, Gerald Wallace

### ARKANSAS

**Fort Smith**
Moore, Patrick Neill
**Jonesboro**
Ledbetter, Joseph Michael
**Little Rock**
Haught, William Dixon
Skokos, Theodore C., Jr.
Stockburger, Jean Dawson
**Pine Bluff**
Harrelson, F(rederick) Daniel
**Warren**
Claycomb, Hugh Murray

### CALIFORNIA

**Anaheim**
Ross, Roger Scott
**Auburn**
Litchfield, Robert Latta, Jr.
**Beverly Hills**
Rosky, Burton Seymour
Shacter, David Mervyn
**Camarillo**
Dunlevy, William Sargent
Pugh, Francis Leo
Van Conas, Kendall Ashleigh
**Campbell**
Desmarais, Michael George
Temmerman, Robert Eugene, Jr.
**Cerritos**
Sarno, Maria Erlinda
**Davis**
Henderson, Mark Gordy
**Downey**
Tompkins, Dwight Edward
**Fresno**
Wells, Gary B.
**Fullerton**
Roberts, Mark Scott
**Glendale**
Green, Norman Harry
**Grass Valley**
Hawkins, Richard Michael
**Healdsburg**
Jonas, Gail E.
**Huntington Beach**
Armstrong, Alan Leigh
**Indian Wells**
Smith, Byron Owen
**Irvine**
Hilker, Walter Robert, Jr.
**Laguna Hills**
Tepper, Nancy Boxley
**Lancaster**
Bianchi, David Wayne
**Los Altos**
Weir, Robert H.
**Los Angeles**
Anderson, William Augustus
Antin, Michael
Basile, Paul Louis, Jr.
Campbell, Jennifer L.
Carter, Bret Robert
Cohan, John Robert
Gallo, Jon Joseph
Livadary, Paul John
May, Lawrence Edward
Mitchell, Michael Charles
Palliari, Richard M.
Pollock, John Phleger
Rae, Matthew Sanderson, Jr.
Schuyler, Rob Rene
Weiser, Frank Alan
**Mill Valley**
Dyer, Gregory Clark
**Monterey**
Gaver, Frances Rouse
Johnson, Mark Harold
**Morgan Hill**
Foster, John Robert
**Newport Beach**
Copenbarger, Lloyd Gaylord
Wexler, Danniel Justin
**North Fork**
Flanagan, James Henry, Jr.
**North Hollywood**
Kreger, Melvin Joseph
Zimring, Stuart David
**Oceanside**
Ferrante, R. William
**Oxnard**
O'Hearn, Michael John
**Palo Alto**
Haile, Elster Sharon
**Palos Verdes Estates**
Toftness, Cecil Gillman
**Pasadena**
Brown, Lorne James
Klein, Jill
Morris, Gary Wayne
Talt, Alan R.
**Redondo Beach**
Mercant, Jon Jeffry
**Riverside**
Chang, Janice May
**Sacramento**
Goodart, Nan L.
Mueller, Virginia Schwartz
**Saint Helena**
Marvin, Monica Louise Wolf
**San Carlos**
Raye-Wong, Catherine
**San Diego**
Hofflund, Paul
Payne, Margaret Anne
Sceper, Duane Harold
Sullivan, Michelle Cornejo
White, Edith Jean
**San Francisco**
Guggenhime, Richard Johnson
Haynes, William Ernest
Hellman, Theodore Albert, Jr.
Howe, Drayton Ford, Jr.
Kerner, Michael Philip
Major, Hugh Geoffrey
Stephenson, Charles Gayley
Wild, Nelson Hopkins
**San Jose**
Bebb, Richard S.
Cummins, Charles Fitch, Jr.
**San Leandro**
Newacheck, David John
**San Luis Obispo**
Dorsi, Stephen Nathan
**San Mateo**
Bhatnagar, Mary Elizabeth
Fox, Audrey Braker
Slabach, Stephen Hall
**San Pedro**
DeWitt, Brian Leigh
**San Rafael**
Drexler, Kenneth
**San Ramon**
Siegel, Jeffrey Roy
**Santa Barbara**
Ambrecht, John Ward
Egenolf, Robert F.
Willey, Charles Wayne
**Santa Monica**
Axe, Norman Gold
Landay, Andrew Herbert
**Torrance**
Crane, Kathleen D.
Finer, William A.
Moore, Christopher Minor
**Walnut Creek**
Baker, Roy Gordon, Jr.
**Yorba Linda**
Ward, Robert Richard
**Yuba City**
Doughty, Mark Anthony

### COLORADO

**Boulder**
Gamm, Gordon Julius
Hundley, Laura S.
**Colorado Springs**
Benson, John Scott
Keene, Kenneth Paul
Kendall, Phillip Alan
Palermo, Norman Anthony
**Commerce City**
Trujillo, Lorenzo A.
**Crested Butte**
Renfrow, Jay Royce
**Denver**
Ash, Walter Brinker
Atlass, Theodore Bruce
Christianssen, Kenneth Gordon
Crow, Nancy Rebecca
Frederiksen, Paul Asger
Gelt, Theodore Zvi
Graf, Gregory C.
Hodges, Joseph Gilluly, Jr.
McMichael, Donald Earl
Olsen, M. Kent
Potter, Gary Thomas
Schmidt, L(ail) William, Jr.
Scott, Peter Bryan
Smead, Burton Armstrong, Jr.
Van Devander, Charles Wayne
**Durango**
Sherman, Lester Ivan
**Englewood**
Carraher, John Bernard
Schilken, Bruce A.
**Lakewood**
Thome, Dennis Wesley
**Littleton**
Eberhardt, Gretchen Ann
**Ouray**
Johnson, Christian Kent
**Parker**
Greenberg, Morton Paul
**Pueblo**
O'Callaghan, Robert Patrick
**Rocky Ford**
Mendenhall, Harry Barton
**Wheat Ridge**
Brant, John Getty

### CONNECTICUT

**Bridgeport**
Flynn, Walter Andrew
**Colchester**
Broder, Joseph Arnold
**Danbury**
Tuozzolo, John Joseph
**Hartford**
Appel, Robert Eugene
Bernier, Marcel J.
McKone, Thomas Christopher
Pinney, Sidney Dillingham, Jr.
Richter, Donald Paul
Toro, Amalia Maria
**New Haven**
Carr, Cynthia
**New London**
Johnstone, Philip MacLaren
**North Haven**
Gradoville, Robert Thomas
**South Windsor**
Hale, Kathryn Scholle
**Stamford**
Daniels, Daniel Lloyd
Gilman, Derek
Himmelreich, David Baker
Sarner, Richard Alan
**Waterbury**
Chase, Robert L.
Dost, Mark W.
**West Hartford**
Storm, Robert Warren
**Westport**
Kosakow, James Matthew
Saxl, Richard Hildreth

### DELAWARE

**Wilmington**
Cooch, Edward W(ebb), Jr.
Grossman, Jerome Kent
Reiver, Joanna
Sawyer, H(arold) Murray, Jr.
Tigani, Bruce William

### DISTRICT OF COLUMBIA

**Washington**
Bergner, Jane Cohen
Bixler, John Mourer
Coughlin, Thomas A.
Damico, Nicholas Peter
Doyle, Austin Joseph
Faley, R(ichard) Scott
Gonzalez, Edward
Hoge, Chris
Kohn, Dexter Morton
McCoy, Jerry Jack
Plaine, Lloyd Leva
Rafferty, Catherine Mary
Silver, Sidney J.
Ward, Nicholas Donnell
Wofford, Cindy Lynn

### FLORIDA

**Bay Harbor Is**
Patrick, Marty
**Boca Raton**
Reinstein, Joel
**Boynton Beach**
Armstrong, Jack Gilliland
**Bradenton**
Lopacki, Edward Joseph, Jr.
St. Paul, Alexandra De La Vergne
**Casselberry**
Campbell, John Michael
**Clearwater**
Bonner, John Ryckman
Gulecas, James Frederick
Hogan, Elwood
Weidemeyer, Carleton Lloyd
**Coral Springs**
Polin, Alan Jay
**Deerfield Beach**
Lenoff, Michele Malka
**Fort Lauderdale**
Cox, James Clifton
Golden, E(dward) Scott
Hess, George Franklin, II
Katz, Thomas Owen
**Gainesville**
Rosenblatt, Howard Marshall
Tillman, Michael Gerard
**Hollywood**
Singer, Bernard Alan
**Jacksonville**
Ball, Haywood Moreland
Cooke, Alexander Hamilton
Getman, Willard Etheridge
**Jupiter**
Click, David Forrest
**Key West**
Fohrman, Darryl
**Lake Placid**
Haile, John Sanders
**Lakeland**
Harris, Christy Franklin
Koren, Edward Franz
Martin, Michael David
**Miami**
Chabrow, Penn Benjamin
Dribin, Michael A.
Glickman, Fred Elliott
Gomez, Ivan A.
Gordon, Howard W.
Hall, Miles Lewis, Jr.
Lancaster, Kenneth G.
Merrill, George Vanderneth
Rust, Robert Warren
Scheer, Mark Jeffrey
Short, Eugene Maurice, Jr.
Weiner, Lawrence
**N Miami Beach**
Slewett, Robert David
**Naples**
Cimino, Richard Dennis
Galvin, Daniel Leo
Lile, Laird Andrew
Rigor, Bradley Glenn
Westman, Carl Edward
**North Miami**
Moreno, Christine Margaret
**Ocala**
Haldin, William Carl, Jr.
Thompson, Raymond Edward
**Orlando**
Ibanez, Silvia Safille
Lefkowitz, Ivan Martin
**Palm Beach**
Rampell, Paul
Tarone, Theodore T.
**Pensacola**
Huston, Gary William
**Plantation**
Singer, Joseph K.
**Port Orange**
Anthony, Gayle Deanna
**Pt Charlotte**
Levin, Allen Jay
**Redington Shores**
Christ, Earle L.
**Saint Petersburg**
Lyman, Curtis Lee, Jr.
**Sarasota**
Conetta, Tami Foley
Kimbrough, Robert Averyt
**Sebring**
Trombley, Michael Jerome
**Tallahassee**
Dariotis, Terrence Theodore
**Tampa**
Ellwanger, Thomas John
Farrior, J. Rex, Jr.
Gonzalez, Alan Francis
Russo, Ronald John
Salem, Albert McCall, Jr.
**Venice**
Gaylor, William E., III
**Wellington**
Ladwig, Patti Heidler
**West Palm Beach**
Bertles, James Billet
Grantham, Kirk Pinkerton
Lampert, Michael Allen
Tanzer, Jed Samuel
**Wilton Manors**
Daly, Susan Mary
**Winter Haven**
Rignanese, Cynthia Crofoot

### GEORGIA

**Athens**
Bryant, Everett Clay, Jr.
**Atlanta**
Bird, Francis Marion, Jr.
Bloodworth, A(bert) W(illiam) Franklin
Calhoun, Scott Douglas
Durrett, James Frazer, Jr.
Edee, James Philip
Hoffman, Michael William
Lamon, Harry Vincent, Jr.
Salo, Ann Sexton Distler
Schilling, Laura K.
**Augusta**
Lee, Lansing Burrows, Jr.
**Doraville**
Gerstein, Joe Willie
**Savannah**
Dickey, David Herschel
Hirsberg, David M.

### HAWAII

**Honolulu**
Bunn, Robert Burgess
Gerson, Mervyn Stuart
Larsen, David Coburn
Miyasaki, Shuichi
Zabanal, Eduardo Olegario
**Kihei**
Burns, Richard Gordon
**Wailuku**
Bodden, Thomas Andrew

### IDAHO

**Boise**
Erickson, Robert Stanley
Gwartney, Tore Beal
**Caldwell**
Kerrick, David Ellsworth
**Idaho Falls**
Avery, John Orval
**Moscow**
Bielenberg, Leonard Herman
Wakefield, Robert

**Long Island City**
Risi, Joseph John
**Manlius**
Sarofeen, Michael Joseph
**Melville**
Burke, Richard James
**Miller Place**
Lucivero, Lucretia M.
**Mineola**
Bartol, Ernest Thomas
Stein, Rita
**Nanuet**
Waldorf, Geraldine Polack
**New Hyde Park**
Rose, Elihu Isaac
**New York**
Ashton, Robert W.
Barasch, Mal Livingston
Beebe, Walter H.
Bergreen, Morris Harvey
Black, James Isaac, III
Boehner, Leonard Bruce
Brandrup, Douglas Warren
Brauner, David A.
Coon, Robert Morell, Jr.
Crary, Miner Dunham, Jr.
Donovan, Maureen Driscoll
Evans, Douglas Hayward
Gelb, Judith Anne
Goodkind, E. Robert
Guth, Paul C.
Hader, Cheryl Elizabeth
Heineman, Andrew David
Herbst, Abbe Ilene
Hewitt, Richard Gilbert
Hirschson, Linda Benjamin
Hull, Philip Glasgow
Jasper, Seymour
Johnson, Bruce Carlton
Karan, Paul Richard
Kartiganer, Joseph
Kavoukjian, Michael Edward
Kirkland, Galen D.
Kitay, Harvey Robert
Lingelbach, Albert Lane
Martin, Malcolm Elliot
Materna, Joseph Anthony
McGrath, Thomas J.
Miller, Jill Lee
Molnar, Lawrence
Moore, Thomas Ronald (Lord Bridestowe)
Muhlstock, Arthur C.
Paul, Herbert Morton
Posner, Louis Joseph
Rabunski, Alan E.
Radin, Sam
Rafalowicz, Joseph
Robinson, Barbara Paul
Rom, Judith R.
Rubenstein, Joshua Seth
Rubin, Jane Lockhart Gregory
Rubinstein, Kenneth
Sangerman, Jay J.
Saufer, Isaac Aaron
Schlesinger, Sanford Joel
Sederbaum, Arthur David
Shapiro, Aleena Rieger
Spanbock, Maurice Samuel
Spero, C. Michael
Terry, Frederick Arthur, Jr.
Valente, Peter Charles
Warner, Jeannette Sloan
Weltz, Paul Martin
Wimpfheimer, Michael Clark
Worley, Robert William, Jr.
Zuckerman, Paul Herbert
**Niagara Falls**
Truex, Shelley Anne
**Oneonta**
Konstanty, James E.
**Oyster Bay**
Bernstein, Jacob
**Patchogue**
Weisberg, David Charles
**Pearl River**
Riley, James Kevin
**Pelham**
Hanrahan, Michael G.
**Poughkeepsie**
Haven, Milton M.
**Riverhead**
Twomey, Thomas A., Jr.
**Rochester**
Brovitz, Richard Stuart
Brown, Peter Ogden
Buckley, Michael Francis
Clifford, Eugene Thomas
Colby, William Michael
Corcoran, Christopher Holmes
Fero, Dean John
Gross, Bryon William
Harter, Ralph Millard Peter
O'Toole, Martin William
Palermo, Anthony Robert
Trevett, Thomas Neil
Twietmeyer, Don Henry
**Rome**
McMahon, Richard H.
**Roslyn Heights**
Dieguez, Richard Peter
**Scarsdale**
Keeffe, John Arthur
**Schenectady**
McCartney, Brian Palmer
Suprunowicz, Michael Robert
Wickerham, Richard Dennis
**Somers**
Cowles, Frederick Oliver
**Syracuse**
Cambs, Denise P.
**White Plains**
Danziger, Joel Bernard
Gjertsen, O. Gerard
Markowitz, Linda Wishnick
McQuaid, John Gaffney
**Yonkers**
Clark, Celia Rue

## NORTH CAROLINA

**Asheville**
Branch, John Wells (Jack Twig)
Lavelle, Brian Francis David
Lawrence, Betty Tenn
Worley, Charles Robert
**Black Mountain**
Le Van, Nolan Gerald
**Chapel Hill**
Crassweller, Robert Doell
Herman-Giddens, Gregory
**Charlotte**
Claytor, William Mimms
Edwards, Mark Brownlow
McBryde, Neill Gregory
Preston, James Young
Wood, William McBrayer
**Emerald Isle**
Lincoln, Michael Powell
**Gastonia**
Garland, James Boyce
**Goldsboro**
Hine, John C.
**High Point**
Griffin, Robert Gerard
**Jamestown**
Schmitt, William Allen
**Monroe**
Love, Walter Bennett, Jr.
**Raleigh**
Byrd, Stephen Timothy
**Salisbury**
Porter, J. Andrew
**Wilmington**
Gibson, Frank Byron, Jr.
**Winston Salem**
Edwards, Robert Leon
Ingersoll, Marc W.

## NORTH DAKOTA

**Fargo**
Vogel, Charles Nicholas
**Grand Forks**
Cilz, Douglas Arthur
**Mandan**
Bair, Bruce B.

## OHIO

**Athens**
Gall, Robert Jay
**Beavercreek**
Stier, Charles Herman, Jr.
**Berea**
Jolles, Janet Kavanaugh Pilling
**Bucyrus**
Neff, Robert Clark, Sr.
**Canton**
Haupt, Fred Jerry
**Cincinnati**
Buechner, Robert William
Crouse, Rebecca Ann
Hoffheimer, Daniel Joseph
Kite, William McDougall
Neltner, Michael Martin
Petrie, Bruce Inglis
Ryan, James Joseph
Schwab, Nelson, Jr.
Silvers, Jane Fink
Strauss, William Victor
Whalen, James Lawrence
**Cleveland**
Braverman, Herbert Leslie
Donahue, Charles Bertrand, II
Ebert, Gary Andrew
Farah, Benjamin Frederick
Furber, Philip Craig
Hochman, Kenneth George
Nudelman, Sidney
Sogg, Wilton Sherman
Weiss, Leon Alan
**Columbus**
Anderson, Jon Mac
Balthaser, James Harvey
Casey, John Frederick
Emens, J. Richard
Goulder, Diane Kessler
Kauffman, Ronald P.
Kington, John Anthony
Martin, Paige Arlene
Willcox, Roderick Harrison
Wolper, Beatrice Emens
**Dayton**
Conway, Mark Allyn
Johnson, C. Terry
Pietz, Lynne Pepi
Roberts, Brian Michael
**Greenville**
Finnarn, Theodore Ora
**Oak Harbor**
Robertson, Jerry D.
**Painesville**
Cooper, Linda Dawn
**Perrysburg**
Hartsel, Norman Clyde
**Saint Clairsville**
Hanlon, Lodge L.
**Salem**
Bowman, Scott McMahan
**Solon**
Fouts, Douglas Robert
**Springfield**
Barnett, Hugh
**Tipp City**
Arenstein, Gilbert Gregory
**Toledo**
Nicholson, Brent Bentley
**Warren**
Kearney, Patricia Ann
Letson, William Normand
**Wellston**
Oths, Joseph Anthony
**Westerville**
Westervelt, Charles Ephraim, Jr.
**Westlake**
Reichard, William Edward
**Willoughby**
Greene, Ralph Vernon
**Worthington**
Minton, Harvey Steiger
Worobiec, Michele Selig
**Youngstown**
Lenga, Robert Allen

## OKLAHOMA

**Cherokee**
Hadwiger, Mickey J.
**Cushing**
Draughon, Scott Wilson
**Edmond**
Kamp, Randall William
**Fairview**
Schoeppel, James
**Idabel**
Shaw, Donald Ray
**Muskogee**
Frix, Paige Lane
Robinson, Adelbert Carl
**Oklahoma City**
Mock, Randall Don
Ross, William Jarboe
**Tulsa**
Bowles, Margo La Joy
Clark, Gary Carl
Crawford, B(urnett) Hayden
Hatfield, Jack Kenton
Marlar, Donald Floyd
Taliaferro, Bruce Owen
Unruh, Robert James
**Vinita**
Curnutte, Mark William

## OREGON

**Corvallis**
Morris, Gretchen Reynolds
**Eugene**
Cooper, Michael Lee
Owens, A(rnold) Dean
Thompson, Edward P.
**La Grande**
Joseph, Steven Jay
**Oregon City**
Hill, Gary D.
**Pendleton**
Rew, Lawrence B.
**Portland**
Bauer, Henry Leland
Christensen, Darin S.
Froebe, Gerald Allen
Klarquist, Kenneth Stevens, Jr.
Lee, Laurie Neilson
Reisman, Joanne
Strader, Timothy Richards
Tremaine, H. Stewart

## PENNSYLVANIA

**Allentown**
Coe, Ilse G.
Frank, Bernard
Zamborsky, Donald A.
**Berwyn**
Gadsden, Christopher Henry
Huffaker, John Boston
**Bethlehem**
Bush, Raymond George
**Clarion**
O'Neil, Kenton R.
**Doylestown**
Gathright, Howard T.
Wagner, Joseph Hagel
**Harrisburg**
Cicconi, Christopher M.
Imblum, Gary Joseph
Sullivan, John Cornelius, Jr.
**Haverford**
Frick, Benjamin Charles
**Horsham**
Eisenberg, Steven Keith
**Jenkintown**
Robbins, Jack Winton
**Lancaster**
Byler, William Bryan
Kraybill, J(ames) Elvin
**Lansdale**
Pearlstine, Neal R.
**Lehigh Valley**
Harris, Judith A.
**Lock Haven**
Snowiss, Alvin L.
**Media**
Rainer, G. Bradley
**Middletown**
Pannebaker, James Boyd
**Milton**
Davis, Preston Lindner
**Murrysville**
Kemp, Kathleen Nagy
**Nazareth**
Reed, Gregory Russell
**Norristown**
Harp, Chadwick Allen
**Philadelphia**
Abramowitz, Robert Leslie
Bonovitz, Sheldon M.
Briscoe, Jack Clayton
Chimples, George
Deming, Frank Stout
Denmark, William Adam
Gagne, William Roderick
Gillis, Richard Moffitt, Jr.
Goldman, Jerry Stephen
Greenstein, J. Richard
Jamison, Judith Jaffe
Kaier, Edward John
Kaufman, David Joseph
Lombard, John James, Jr.
Mirabello, Francis Joseph
Rainone, Michael Carmine
Schneider, Pam Horvitz
Speyer, Debra Gail
Wilf, Mervin M.
**Pittsburgh**
Anderson, Lea E.
Connell, Janice T.
Daniel, Robert Michael
Dodson, F. Brian
Forsyth, Andrew Watson, III
Houston, William McClelland
Kabala, Edward John
MacBeth, Lynn Ellen
Peduto, Mark B.
Ummer, James Walter
Vater, Charles J.
Yates, Alfred Glenn, Jr.
**Reading**
Linton, Jack Arthur
**Sharon**
Ekker, Henry Mayer
Kosmowski, Audra Michele
**Venetia**
Breslin, Elvira Madden
**Washington**
Key, Susan Mondik
**Wayne**
Spiess, F. Harry, Jr.
**West Chester**
DeVlieger, Tracy Blake
Rolfe, John L.
**Williamsport**
Kane, Joseph Patrick
**Wormleysburg**
Cherewka, Michael

## RHODE ISLAND

**Providence**
Hastings, Edwin H(amilton)
Salvadore, Guido Richard
**Warwick**
Goldman, Steven Jason

## SOUTH CAROLINA

**Charleston**
Branham, C. Michael
Ray, Paul DuBose
**Columbia**
Bailey, George Screven
Gibbes, William Holman
**Greenville**
Dobson, Robert Albertus, III
Edwards, Harry LaFoy
Walters, Johnnie McKeiver
**Newberry**
Senn, Lisa Robinson
**Rock Hill**
Hardin, James Carlisle, III

## TENNESSEE

**Chattanooga**
Durand, Whitney
**Collierville**
Rogers, Gordon Keith, Jr.
**Knoxville**
Ailor, Earl Starnes
Bly, Robert Maurice
Gentry, Mack A.
**Memphis**
Autry, Edward Thomas
Cook, August Joseph
Jalenak, James Bailey
Patton, Charles Henry
Tate, Stonewall Shepherd
**Nashville**
Farris, Frank Mitchell, Jr.
Skoney, Lesa Hartley
Turner, Robert Joseph

## TEXAS

**Amarillo**
Burnette, Susan Lynn
**Arlington**
Willey, Stephen Douglas
**Austin**
Bloomquist, Amy Peterson
Dougherty, John Chrysostom, III
Helman, Stephen Jody
Lock, John Richard
Osborne, Duncan Elliott
**Beaumont**
Cavaliere, Frank Joseph
**Borger**
Edmonds, Thomas Leon
**Canton**
Sanders, Bobby Lee
**Corpus Christi**
Davis, Martin Clay
**Dallas**
Crain, Christina Melton
Dicus, Brian George
Owens, Rodney Joe
Phelps, Robert Frederick, Jr.
Smith, Frank Tupper
Stephens, Marjorie Johnsen
Turner, Elizabeth Ruth
**El Paso**
Hedrick, Mark
Marshall, Richard Treeger
Sanders, Amy Stewart
**Fort Worth**
Collins, Whitfield James
Gwinn, D. Lee
Mullanax, Milton Greg
Phillips, Robert James, Jr.
Tilley, Rice M(atthews), Jr.
Tracy, J. David
Whitney, William Bernard
**Georgetown**
Wilkerson, James Neill
**Houston**
Amann, Leslie Kiefer
Brentin, John Olin
Brown, Stephen Smiley
Cenatiempo, Michael J.
Collins, Susan E.
Crocker, Charles Allan
Eastland, S. Stacy
Friedman, J. Kent
Hatchett, Cynthia M.
Jeske, Charles Matthew
Koenig, Rodney Curtis
Minor, Sterling Arthur
Schwartzel, Charles Boone
Shearer, Dean Paul
Stewart, Pamela L.
Touchy, Deborah K. P.
Valentine, Michael John
**Hurst**
Leach, Terry Ray
**Jacksonville**
Cummins, Michael Wayne
**Longview**
Crowson, David Lee
**Panhandle**
Neal, A. Curtis
**Richardson**
Conkel, Robert Dale
**San Angelo**
Carter, James Alfred
Noelke, Henry Tolbert (Hal Noelke)
**San Antonio**
Goldsmith, Richard Elsinger
Veitch, Thomas Harold
**Tyler**
Killough, J. Scott
**Waco**
Page, Jack Randall
**Weatherford**
Akers, Charles Benjamin
Westenhover, Gary Floyd
**Wichita Falls**
Goff, Robert William, Jr.

## UTAH

**Park City**
Kennicott, James W.
**Salt Lake City**
Adams, Joseph Keith

## VERMONT

**Saint Albans**
Bugbee, Jesse D.
**South Royalton**
Prye, Steven Marvell
**Taftsville**
Johnson, Philip Martin

## VIRGINIA

**Alexandria**
McClure, Roger John
**Arlington**
Welty, Charles Douglas
**Ashburn**
Gold, George Myron
**Charlottesville**
Edwards, James Edwin
Kudravetz, David Waller
Middleditch, Leigh Benjamin, Jr.
**Christiansburg**
Spence, Helen Jean
**Culpeper**
DeJarnette, Elliott Hawes
**Fairfax**
Abrams, Sheri
Spitzberg, Irving Joseph, Jr.
**Falls Church**
Ward, Joe Henry, Jr.
**Lynchburg**
Davies, Arthur B(everly), III
Whitesell, Darryl Duane
**Madison**
Coates, Frederick Ross
**Martinsville**
Frith, Douglas Kyle
**Mc Lean**
Aucutt, Ronald David
**Nellysford**
Vandenburgh, Beverly Ann
**Norfolk**
Best, Charles William, Jr.
Knight, Montgomery, Jr.
Poston, Anita Owings
**Petersburg**
Baskervill, Charles Thornton
**Richmond**
Addison, David Dunham
Aghdami, Farhad
Horsley, Waller Holladay
Mezzullo, Louis Albert
Musick, Robert Lawrence, Jr.
Starke, Harold E., Jr.
Stevens, C. Daniel
**Roanoke**
Bates, Harold Martin
**Sterling**
Babirak, Milton Edward, Jr.
Blair, Richard Eugene
**Vienna**
Callahan, Timothy J.

## WASHINGTON

**Bellevue**
Hand, Bruce George
McCutcheon, James Edward, III
Parsons, James Bowne
Scaringi, Michael Joseph
Sullivan, James Jerome
Treacy, Gerald Bernard, Jr.
**Bellingham**
Packer, Mark Barry
**Issaquah**
Hammerly, Mary Leverenz
Sterling, Michael Erwin
**Montesano**
Stewart, James Malcolm
**Pasco**
Ungerecht, Todd Edward
**Seattle**
Andreasen, Steven W.
Bergstedt, Anders Spencer
Blais, Robert Howard
Cavin, Clark
Gores, Thomas C.
Hilpert, Edward Theodore, Jr.
Lombard, John Cutler
Malone, Thomas William
Olver, Michael Lynn
Thomas, Jeffrey Walton
**Silverdale**
Wildsmith, Quentin
**Spokane**
Michaelsen, Howard Kenneth

Riherd, John Arthur
Sayre, Richard Layton

**Tacoma**
Krueger, James A.
Novasky, Robert William

**Yakima**
Larson, Paul Martin
Wright, J(ames) Lawrence

### WEST VIRGINIA

**New Martinsville**
Hill, Philip Bonner

**Wheeling**
Gardill, James Clark
Gompers, Joseph Alan

### WISCONSIN

**Appleton**
Drescher, Kathleen Ebben
Hartzheim, Charles John
Thenell, Heather Jo

**Beaver Dam**
Becker, Eric L.

**Chippewa Falls**
Hunt, Heather M.

**Cross Plains**
Moretti, Jay Donald

**Delavan**
Weber, Laura Ann

**Janesville**
Williams, Mary Beth

**Lake Geneva**
McCormack, Joanne Marie
Olson, John Olmstead

**Madison**
Burish, Mark Dennis
Mannis, Valerie Sklar
Roberson, Linda
Wilcox, Michael Wing

**Middleton**
Berman, Ronald Charles

**Milwaukee**
Iding, Allan Earl
LaBudde, Roy Christian
Loots, Robert James
Nelson, Randy Scott
Peltin, Sherwin Carl
Voss, Kenneth Erwin
Wynn, Stanford Alan

**Portage**
Bennett, David Hinkley

**Racine**
Coates, Glenn Richard
Crawford, Timothy Patrick

**Rhinelander**
Reese, Kirk David

**Salem**
Edenhofer, Carl R.

**Waukesha**
Ward, James A.

**Wausau**
Zimmerman, Robert W.

**Wauwatosa**
Alexander, Robert Gardner

### WYOMING

**Sheridan**
Lonabaugh, Ellsworth Eugene

### ADDRESS UNPUBLISHED

Asmar, Laila Michelle
Bailin, Deborah M.
Bergkvist, Thomas A.
Bloom, Barry Marshall
Buechel, William Benjamin
Canan, Michael James
Carney, Donald Francis, Jr.
Eagen, William James
Edwards, Daniel Paul
Edwards, William Thomas, Jr.
Egan, Alece Blanche
Emry, Frederic Grant
Fanning, Nita Kissel
Fiala, David Marcus
Fink, Norman Stiles
Fogel, Adelaide Forst
Garry, John Thomas, II
Gora, Daniel Martin
Gray, Brian Mark
Green, Harland Norton
Hackett, Wesley Phelps, Jr.
Hardcastle, Robert Thomas
Kaitz, Haskell A.
Keister, Jean Clare
Logan, James Kenneth
Matheny, Mary Jane
McGinty, Brian Donald
Merrill, Abel Jay
Meyerson, Stanley Phillip
Mitchell, William D.
Neilson, Benjamin Reath
Nunalee, Thomas Hervey, IV
O'Brien, Charles H.
Peterson, Howard Cooper
Reber, Joseph E.
Reiche, Frank Perley
Rohrer, George John
Schroeder, Edward James
Shariff, Vivian Rodriguez
Shook, Ann Jones
Silver, Carol Ruth
Smith, Ronald Ehlbert
Solkoff, Jerome Ira
Stack, Beatriz de Greiff
Stevens, Rhea Christina
Stickney, John Moore
Stone, Edward Herman
Sweeney, Deidre Ann
Weisman, Paul Howard
Williams, Thomas Arthur

## FAMILY AND MATRIMONIAL

### UNITED STATES

### ALABAMA

**Anniston**
Bailey, Gordon Freeborn, Jr.

**Atmore**
Hartley, Wade Leon

**Birmingham**
Stuckenschneider, James Theodore, II

**Cullman**
Poston, Beverly Paschal

**Demopolis**
Dinning, Woodford Wyndham, Jr.

**Dothan**
Waddell, John Emory

**Enterprise**
Price, Robert Allan

**Florence**
Schuessler, Cindy Sandlin

**Foley**
Dasinger, Thomas Edgar

**Gadsden**
Callis, Clifford Louis, Jr.

**Hartford**
Eldridge, William Phillip

**Huntsville**
Blair, Edward Eugene
Burton, Hilary Coleman
Potter, Ernest Luther

**Mobile**
McKnight, Charles Noel

**Montgomery**
Gooden, Pamela Joyce
Lunt, Jennifer Lee
Nelms, K. Anderson
Smith, Maury Drane

**Tuscaloosa**
Blume, Nettie Lynn

### ALASKA

**Anchorage**
Johnson, Brent Allen
Ross, Wayne Anthony
Wonnell, Thomas Burke

**Fairbanks**
Rice, Julian Casavant

**Juneau**
Davis, Gerald Kenneth, Jr.

**Kodiak**
Jamin, Matthew Daniel

### ARIZONA

**Flagstaff**
Cowser, Danny Lee

**Glendale**
Bellah, C. Richard

**Phoenix**
Coghlan, Carol Lynn
Lindholm, Donald Wayne
Rose, David L.

**Tempe**
Palmer, Janice Maude
Zurbriggen, Jeffrey Michael

**Tucson**
Bolt, John Robert
Errico, Melissa
Miller, Michael Douglas
Polan, David Jay
Samet, Dee-Dee

**Yuma**
Hossler, David Joseph

### ARKANSAS

**Fayetteville**
McIvor, Marcia Lynn
Nobles, Ethan Christopher
Poore, Shannon Leigh

**Fort Smith**
Foster, M. Shannon

**Little Rock**
Files, Jason Daniel
Heuer, Sam Tate
Hope, Ronald Arthur
Smith, Anne Orsi

**Nashville**
Graves, James Clements

**Searcy**
Hughes, Teresa Lee

**Van Buren**
Gant, Horace Zed

**West Helena**
Bell, Amy Clifton

**West Memphis**
Weisburd, Everard J.

### CALIFORNIA

**Anaheim**
Fleming, Richard Alfred

**Bakersfield**
Farr, G(ardner) Neil

**Beverly Hills**
Amado, Honey Kessler
Anteau, Ronald W.
Horwin, Leonard
Jaffe, F. Filmore

**Burlingame**
Kuehn, Barbara Jean

**Calabasas**
Rosenberg, Florence Pessah

**Camarillo**
Van Conas, Kendall Ashleigh

**Chino Hills**
Radcliffe, William Louis

**Corte Madera**
Edgemon, Pauline Diane

**Downey**
Schauf, Carolyn Jane

**El Cajon**
Graf, Sheryl Susan

**Encino**
Kaufman, Albert I.
Wynne, Brian Douglas

**Fallbrook**
Leehey, Paul Wade

**Fullerton**
Parsons, Rodney Hunter

**Glendale**
Toscano, Oscar Ernesto

**Glendora**
Stettner, Pamela Panasiti

**Grass Valley**
Bell, Joseph James

**Healdsburg**
Jonas, Gail E.

**Hermosa Beach**
Roberts, Laurel Lee

**Indian Wells**
Criste, Virginia Spiegel

**Irvine**
Callahan, Robert Edward

**King City**
Bolles, Donald Scott

**Lafayette**
Michelsen, Diane

**Lancaster**
Bianchi, David Wayne

**Los Alamitos**
Lia, James Douglas

**Los Angeles**
Allred, Gloria Rachel
Glavin, William Patrick, IV
Gould, Julian Saul
Grebow, Arthur Jeffrey
Kane, Paula
Lurvey, Ira Harold
Mudie, F. Patricia
Newell, Robert Melvin
Ogbogu, Cecilia Ify
Rutter, Marshall Anthony
Weaver, Donna Beck

**Malibu**
Pilling, George William

**Modesto**
Reed, Betty Ann

**Napa**
Burke, Patrick William

**Newport Beach**
Bernauer, Thomas A.
Cordova, Ron
Molseed, Michael Clyde
Schilling, John Russell

**Novato**
Cleek, Robert Joseph
Portman, Mark E.

**Oakland**
Mc Elwain, Lester Stafford
Thompson Stanley, Trina

**Ontario**
Perri, Audrey Ann

**Orange**
Batchelor, James Kent
Bennett, William Perry
Besser, Barry I.
Green, Carolyn F.
McNamara, Eileen

**Palm Springs**
Parry, Paul Stewart

**Palmdale**
Reichman, Dawn Leslie

**Palo Alto**
Stringer, Nanette Schulze

**Palos Verdes Peninsula**
Bryan, Sharon Ann

**Pasadena**
Ashley-Farrand, Margalo
Chan, Daniel Chung-Yin

**Pleasanton**
Staley, John Fredric

**Rancho Cordova**
Lynch, Robert Berger

**Redwood City**
Silvestri, Philip Salvatore

**Riverside**
Briskin, Boyd Edward
Sklar, Wilford Nathanield

**Sacramento**
Bleckley, Jeanette A.
Burton, Randall James
Jacobs, H. Vincent
Mueller, Virginia Schwartz

**San Diego**
Brave, Georgine Frances
Brown, Barbara Fletcher
Godone-Maresca, Lillian
Harf, Cynthia Minette
Kremer, Matthew Markus
Margolis, Anita Joy
Morris, Sandra Joan
Sullivan, Michelle Cornejo

**San Francisco**
MacGowan, Eugenia
MacLeod, Norman
Major, Hugh Geoffrey
Mosk, Susan Hines
Musser, Sandra G.
Richmond, Diana
Stotter, Lawrence Henry
Teitler, Harold Herman

**San Jose**
Duell-Cazes, Tracy Leigh
Katzman, Irwin
Simpson, Mary Kathleen
Stutzman, Thomas Chase, Sr.
Yates-Carter, Lynne

**San Mateo**
Fox, Audrey Braker
Miller, Ruth Rymer

**San Pedro**
Stephenson, Michael Murray

**San Rafael**
Greene, Fredrica Kertz

**Santa Ana**
Knox Rios, Delilah Jane
Shelton, Ralph Conrad

**Santa Clarita**
Kotler, Richard Lee

**Seaside**
Weingarten, Saul Myer

**Sunnyvale**
Vorreiter, Patricia Joan

**Temecula**
Thompson, Susannah Elizabeth

**Thousand Oaks**
Dougherty, Gerard Michael
Garcia, Raymond Arthur

**Torrance**
Moore, Christopher Minor
Stark, Jeffrey Rozelle

**Vacaville**
Myhre, Deanna Shirley

**Visalia**
Shirk, Jennifer Conn

**Walnut Creek**
Rathjen, Jon Laurence

**Westlake Vlg**
Ellicott, Vernon L.

### COLORADO

**Arvada**
Kreis, Elizabeth Susan

**Aspen**
Bernstein, Jeremy Marshall

**Aurora**
Schilling, Edwin Carlyle, III

**Boulder**
Enwall, Michael R.

**Cherry Hl Vlg**
Kerwin, Mary Ann Collins

**Colorado Springs**
Adams, Deborah Rowland
Cross, Thomas Robert
Dean, Lawrence Kenyon
Donohoe, John Joseph
Evans, Paul Vernon
Fisher, Robert Scott
Garvert, Melinda Lee
Graski, Diana
Rahaman, Vincent N.
Salley, George Henry, III
Swift, Stephen Hyde

**Delta**
Wendt, John Arthur Frederic, Jr.

**Denver**
Bonin, Albert M.
Finck, Barry Russell
Fink, Steven D.
Frederiksen, Paul Asger
Graf, Gregory C.
Kaplan, David S.
Leibowitz, Paul H.
McDowell, Karen Ann
McGuane, Frank L., Jr.
Quiat, Marshall
Robinson, Warren A. (Rip Robinson)
Schauer, Tone Terjesen
Wedgle, Richard Jay

**Englewood**
Ambrose, Arlen S.
Bolocofsky, David N.

**Florence**
Davis, Allyn Whitney

**Fort Morgan**
Higinbotham, Jacquelyn Joan

**Golden**
Arp, Randall Craig
Hughes, Marcia Marie

**Grand Junction**
Hermundstad, Sara Sexson
Nugent, Edward James, III

**Greeley**
Bodine, Joseph Ira

**Lakewood**
Jacobson, Dennis John
Lawler, Richard Allen

**Littleton**
Carleno, Harry Eugene
Eberhardt, Gretchen Ann
Truhlar, Doris Broaddus

**Lone Tree**
Kaplan, Marc J.

**Pueblo**
Geisel, Henry Jules

### CONNECTICUT

**Bridgeport**
Meehan, Richard Thomas, Jr.
Osis, Daiga Guntra

**Brookfield**
Dittmar, Dawn Marie

**Danbury**
Dornfeld, Sharon Wicks

**Fairfield**
Rosenstein, Sheila Kovaleski

**Greenwich**
Schoonmaker, Samuel Vail, III

**Hartford**
Cantor, Donald Jerome
Foden, Maria Luisa de Castro
Holtman, Donald Richard
Kesten, Linda Ann
Martocchio, Louis Joseph
Spear, H(enry) Dyke N(ewcome), Jr.

**New Canaan**
Barndollar, Livia DeFilippis
Jaffe, Sari Blonder
Tirelli, Linda Marie

**New Haven**
Greenfield, James Robert
Reiner, Leona Hudak

**North Haven**
Morytko, Jeremiah Joseph

**Norwich**
Masters, Barbara J.

**Ridgefield**
Foster, Julie Irene
Fricke, Richard John

**Rocky Hill**
DiCara, Phyllis M.

**South Windham**
Asselin, John Thomas

**South Windsor**
Gerlt, Wayne Christopher
Hale, Kathryn Scholle

**Stamford**
Kweskin, Edward Michael

**Stratford**
Berlin, Patricia
McDonough, Sandra Martin

**West Hartford**
Connors, Susan Ann
Morrissey, Ellen C.
Nereberg, Eliot Joel
Swerdloff, Ileen Pollock
Swerdloff, Mark Harris

**Westport**
Dimes, Edwin Kinsley
Swiggart, Carolyn Clay
Wisser, Ellen

### DELAWARE

**Newark**
McCann, Richard Stephen

**Wilmington**
Boudart, Mary Cecile
Eppes, Sharon Marie
Kulesza, Joseph Dominick, Jr.
Shearin, Kathryn Kay

### DISTRICT OF COLUMBIA

**Washington**
Ain, Sanford King
Hoge, Chris
Karpinski, Irena Izabella
Kuder, Armin Ulrich
May, Christopher
Richards, Suzanne V.
Wofford, Cindy Lynn

### FLORIDA

**Altamonte Springs**
Laurence, Steven Lamar

**Aventura**
Butter, Stephen H.

**Bartow**
Sutton, Debra J.

**Boca Raton**
Feldman, Joel Harvey
Greenberg, Susan Ellen

**Bradenton**
St. Paul, Alexandra De La Vergne
Scheult, Malcolm McDonald Richardson

**Clearwater**
Berman, Elihu H.
Free, E. LeBron
Simms, John Seth

**Coral Gables**
Cano, Mario Stephen
Chonin, Neil Harvey
Fletcher, Paul Gerald
Gary, Thomas
Leinoff, Andrew Morris
Metcalfe, Olga
Mitchell, David Benjamin
Pastoriza, Julio

**Daytona Beach**
Dunagan, Walter Benton
Neitzke, Eric Karl

**Fort Lauderdale**
Brawer, Marc Harris
Browner, Julius Harvey
Brydger, Gordon Charles
Di Giulian, Bruno L.
Finkel, Barry I.
Glantz, Wendy Newman
Kirschbaum, Joel Leon
Mars, Burton H.
Mastronardi, Corinne Marie
Mitchell, Shelley Marie
Nyce, John Daniel
Sanders, Dale R.

**Fort Myers**
Dalton, Anne
Finman, Sheldon Eliot

**Gainesville**
Pugh, David Edward

**Hallandale**
Sackrin, Cindy Dawn

**Hollywood**
Fischler, Shirley Balter

**Jacksonville**
Gooding, David Michael
Kendrick, Darryl D.

**Jupiter**
Brophy, Gilbert Thomas

**Key West**
Brihammar, B. Niklas

**Lake Alfred**
Slaughter, Marshall Glenn

**Lake Mary**
Loe, Brian Robert

**Marianna**
Brooten, Kenneth Edward, Jr.

**Merritt Island**
Church, Glenn J.

**Miami**
Batista, Alberto Victor
Betz, Gilbert Calvin
Bombino, Isabel Pinera
de Leon, Ruben L.
Dienstag, Cynthia Jill
Dreize, Livia Rebbeka
Milstein, Richard Craig
Osman, Edith Gabriella
Perez-Abreu, Javier
Picazio, Kim Lowry
Pruna, Laura Maria
Samole, Myron Michael
Segall, Norman S.
Vogelsang, Beth Tyler
Weinstein, Alan Edward

**Naples**
Rawson, Marjorie Jean
Rocuant, Paul A.

**New Port Richey**
Strand, Arnelle Marie

**North Miami Beach**
Franklin, Barry Scott
Lechtman, Michael Lowell
MacIvor, Catherine J.
Sugerman, Karen Beth

**Orlando**
Blackwell, Bruce Beuford
deBeaubien, Hugo H.
Heskin, Keersten Lee
**Palatka**
Baldwin, Allen Adail
**Palm Beach Gardens**
Auerbach, Paul Ira
Kahn, David Miller
**Panama City**
Allan, Sher L.
Sutton, Pamela Dru
**Pensacola**
Griffith, Michael John
Levin, David Harold
**Plantation**
Singer, Joseph K.
**Port Orange**
Anthony, Gayle Deanna
**Punta Gorda**
Bell, Peter A.
**Ruskin**
Norse, Kristin A.
**Saint Augustine**
Poole, Sharon Alexandra
**Saint Petersburg**
Lee, Patricia Marie
Schultz, G. Robert
Scott, Kathryn Fenderson
**Sanford**
Partlow, James Justice
**Sarasota**
Byrd, L(awrence) Derek
Zitani, Gregory Anthony
**Shalimar**
Petermann, Tonya C.
**South Miami**
Carnesoltas, Ana-Maria
**Tallahassee**
McNeely, Robert A.
Morphonios, Dean B.
Sheffield, Frank Elwyn
**Tamarac**
Bumgardner, Donna Lee Arrington
**Tampa**
Anton, S. David
Catlin, Catherine M.
Givens, Stann William
Halliday, Stanley Grant
Hernandez, Daniel Mario
Kelly, Mark Patrick
Neumaier, Mark Adam
Real, Catherine Williams
Russo, Ronald John
Stalnaker, Lance Kuebler
Thatcher, Matthew Eugene
Turmel, Stacey Lynn
Young, Ronald W.
**West Palm Beach**
Chopin, Susan Gardiner
Dubiner, Michael
Hicks, James Hermann
Hudson, Lise Lyn
O'Flarity, James P.
Vilchez, Victoria Anne
**Winter Park**
Aikin, Wendy Lise

## GEORGIA

**Americus**
Cooper, Cecilia Marie
**Atlanta**
Allen, Denise
Berryman, Randall Scott
Billington, Barry E.
Callner, Bruce Warren
Cooper, Lawrence Allen
Devins, Robert Sylvester
Ethridge, Robert Michael
Miller, Janise Luevenia Monica
Mull, Gale W.
Stoner, Michael Alan
Wellon, Robert G.
**Augusta**
Williams, William James
**Barnesville**
Kennedy, Harvey John, Jr.
**Blue Ridge**
Rosenberg, David Michael
**Brunswick**
Gough, Kevin Robert
**Columbus**
Dodgen, Andrew Clay
Grogan, Lynn Langley
Shelnutt, John Mark
**Cumming**
Mantagna, Michael
**Dalton**
Bolling, Walter Harrison, Jr.
**Decatur**
Skinner, William French Cochran, Jr.
**Douglas**
Sims, Rebecca Littleton
**Jasper**
Marger, Edwin
**Lawrenceville**
Harrison, Samuel Hughel
**Mcdonough**
Crumbley, R. Alex
**Nashville**
Ellis, Robert Bryan, Jr.
**Riverdale**
Terry, Pandora Elaine
**Savannah**
Aderhold, Kathleen
**Snellville**
Giallanza, Charles Philip
**Tucker**
Polstra, Larry John
**Valdosta**
Council, Pauline Carter
Edwards, Edith Martha
**Warner Robins**
Zoumberis, Nikitis

## HAWAII

**Honolulu**
Adaniya, Kevin Seisho
Cedillos, Steve H.
Cuskaden, Everett
Fong, Leslie Kaleiopu Wah Cheong
**Kailua Kona**
Miller, Frank Lewis
Zimmerman, William Irving
Zola, Michael S.
**Lihue**
Valenciano, Randal Grant Bolosan
**Makawao**
Barrad, Catherine Marie
**Wailuku**
Kinaka, William Tatsuo

## IDAHO

**Boise**
Gwartney, Tore Beal
**Burley**
Barrus, Alfred Emery
**Caldwell**
Orr, Debra Ann
**Hailey**
Hogue, Terry Glynn
**Idaho Falls**
Avery, John Orval
**Moscow**
Wakefield, Robert

## ILLINOIS

**Alton**
Bohne, Edward Daniel
**Arlington Heights**
Massucci, Raymond R.
**Aurora**
Mateas, Kenneth Edward
**Belleville**
Grueninger, Daniel J.
Johnston, John Joseph
**Chicago**
Auerbach, Marshall Jay
Bolaños, Anita Marie
Cannizzaro, Sam F.
Davis, Muller
Frank, Jay Allan
Grant, Burton Fred
Grant, Joan Carolyn
Grund, David Ira
Hubbard, Elizabeth Louise
Kirsh, Sanford
Komie, Stephen Mark
Lehrer, Julius Marshall
Minton, Michael Harry
Muller, Kurt Alexander
Nordgren, Gerald Paul
Pimentel, Julio Gumeresindo
Pritikin, James B.
Schiller, Donald Charles
Stein, Arnold Bruce
**Decatur**
Vigneri, Joseph William
**Des Plaines**
Jacobs, William Russell, II
**Elgin**
Flanagan, Leo M., Jr.
**Eureka**
Harrod, Daniel Mark
**Flossmoor**
Gevers, Marcia Bonita
**Galesburg**
Butts, Cyril William, Jr.
McCrery, David Neil, III
**Joliet**
Egan, James E.
**Momence**
Engels, Patricia Louise
**Mount Carroll**
Leemon, John Allen
**Mount Vernon**
Harvey, Morris Lane
**Mundelein**
Ackley, Robert O.
**Naperville**
Hittle, Kathleen J.
**Northfield**
Gelfman, Stuart G.
**Palatine**
Runes, Kenneth Alan
**Park Ridge**
Wasko, Steven E.
**Peoria**
Urban, Charles J.
**Princeton**
Johnson, Watts Carey
**Rock Island**
Lousberg, Peter Herman
Wallace, Franklin Sherwood
**Schaumburg**
Wilke, Barbara R.
**South Holland**
Olofsson, Daniel Joel
**Springfield**
Draper, Carl R.
Narmont, John Stephen
Schmidt, Amy K.
**Vandalia**
Lawinger, Jane M.
**Waukegan**
Gurewitz, Thomas Mark
**Wheaton**
DaRosa, Ronald Anthony
**Wheeling**
Kulinsky, Lois
**Wilmette**
Lieberman, Eugene

## INDIANA

**Anderson**
Cage, Christopher Allen
**Avilla**
Stephens, James F.
**Crawfordsville**
Donaldson, Steven Bryan
**Decatur**
Sheets, Thomas Wade
**Elkhart**
Wicks, Charles Carter
**Evansville**
Clouse, John Daniel
**Fort Wayne**
Troyer, Tracy Lynn
Young, Randy William
**Franklin**
Gholston, Robert M.
**Gary**
Lewis, Robert Lee
**Hammond**
Kohl, Jacquelyn Marie
**Indianapolis**
Blythe, James David, II
Gaddy, Maureen
Grinnan, Gloria Katherine
Hebenstreit, Michael Joseph
Pennamped, Bruce Michael
Pinkus, I(rving) Marshall
Reed, James A.
Reinert, Cynthia
Sherman, Stephen Michael
Spence, Steven Allen
Woods, Joseph Reid
Wunder, David Hart
**Kokomo**
Russell, Richard Lloyd
**Lafayette**
Garwood, Cynthia Lynn
**Lebanon**
Donaldson, John Weber
**Portage**
Germann, Gary Stephen
**Rushville**
Morning, Leigh Suzanne
**Shelbyville**
Baldwin, Kelley Yeager
**South Bend**
Galso, Ernest Peter Gabriel
Sopko, Thomas Clement
**Valparaiso**
Gioia, Daniel August
**Warsaw**
Rigdon, Jay Alden
Walmer, James L.
**Waynetown**
Dicks, Sarah Houston

## IOWA

**Adair**
Fisher, Martin Louis
**Cedar Rapids**
Willems, Daniel Wayne
**Charles City**
Troge, Ann Marie
**Council Blfs**
Rodenburg, John A.
**Decorah**
Belay, Stephen Joseph
**Des Moines**
Baybayan, Ronald Alan
Schadle, William James
Shoff, Patricia Ann
**Indianola**
Ouderkirk, Mason James
**Iowa City**
Klockau, Lori Lee
Trca, Randy Ernest
**Newton**
Dalen, DuWayne John
**Sioux City**
Giles, William Jefferson, III

## KANSAS

**Kansas City**
Andersen, Anton Chris
**Lawrence**
Brown, David James
**Lenexa**
Bigus, Edward Lowell
**Overland Park**
Bunn, G. Peter, III
Short, Joel Bradley
**Paola**
Arnett, Debra Jean
**Shawnee Mission**
Gastl, Eugene Francis
Wetzler, Richard S.
**Topeka**
Frost, Brian Standish
Hejtmanek, Danton Charles
**Wichita**
Casey, Paula Kidd
Robinson, G. Craig
Wilson, T. Michael
**Winfield**
Krusor, Mark William

## KENTUCKY

**Bowling Green**
Sparks, David Thomas
**Fort Mitchell**
Wietholter, Thomas Andrew
**Fort Thomas**
Whalen, Paul Lewellin
**Grayson**
Caummisar, Robert Lee
**Henderson**
Hamilton, Curtis James, II
**Lexington**
Bagby, Glen Stovall
Goldman, Elisabeth Paris
Matl, Lois Tudor
Miller, Harry B(enjamin)
**Louisa**
Carter, Robert Philip, Sr.
**Louisville**
Brown, Bonnie Maryetta
Fuchs, Olivia Anne Morris
Gowin, Richard Bryan
Karageorge, Thomas George
McAdam, Thomas Anthony, III
Morgan-White, Stephanie Lynn
Morton, Donna Theresa
Smith, Trevor A.
Spalding, Catherine
Stone, Thomas Kendall
Storment, Harold Lloyd
Straw-Boone, Melanie
Wade, Jeffrey Lee
Welch, Louise Bridgman
**Paducah**
Sanderson, Cynthia Ellen
**Paris**
Budden, Harry Edward, Jr.
**Russellville**
Wilson, Elizabeth Davis
**Somerset**
Harlan, Jane Ann
**Versailles**
Dunlap, Tavner Branham

## LOUISIANA

**Alexandria**
Perkins, Alvin Bruce, II
**Baton Rouge**
Gibbs, Deborah P.
Taylor, John McKowen
Wittenbrink, Jeffrey Scott
**Covington**
Paddison, David Robert
**Kenner**
Todaro, Laura Jean
**Lafayette**
Johnson, Helen Scott
Nehrbass, Jennifer Stuller
**Lake Charles**
Ortego, Jim
Sanchez, Walter Marshall
**Mandeville**
Tranchina, Frank Peter, Jr.
**Metairie**
Miles, Terri
**Monroe**
Creed, Christian Carl
**Natchitoches**
Seaman, Charles Wilson
**New Orleans**
Levin, Richard Barry
Lowe, Robert Charles
Madera, Carmen Soria
Morris, Edith Henderson
**Shreveport**
Fortson, James Leon, Jr.
Rigby, Kenneth
**Thibodaux**
Clement, Leslie Joseph, Jr.

## MAINE

**Bangor**
Ebitz, Elizabeth Kelly
**Lewiston**
Peters, Thomas P., II
**Waterville**
Sandy, Robert Edward, Jr.

## MARYLAND

**Annapolis**
Ferris, William Michael
Perkins, Roger Allan
**Baltimore**
Cohen, Hyman K.
Hendler, Michael G.
Kleid, Wallace
Thomas, Daniel French
**Bel Air**
Gintling, Karen Janette
**Bethesda**
Moss, Stephen Edward
Strickler, Scott Michael
**Brooklandville**
Rosenzweig, Janice Popick
**Chestertown**
Mowell, George Mitchell
**Chevy Chase**
Groner, Beverly Anne
**College Park**
Yoho, Billy Lee
**Easton**
Blades, G(ene) Granville
**Ellicott City**
Henry, Edwin Maurice, Jr.
Silverstein, Fred Howard
**Gaithersburg**
Massengill, Alan Durwood
Pearlstein, Brian K.
**Glen Burnie**
Cole, Ronald Clark
**Hagerstown**
Marks, Russell Robert
Moylan, Dana
Schneider, Arthur
**Hanover**
Carter, Candy Lorraine
**North Potomac**
Meiselman, Alyson
**Owings Mills**
Silverman, Steven D.
**Oxon Hill**
Serrette, Cathy Hollenberg
**Rockville**
Dennis, Benjamin Franklin, III
Jaffe, Matthew Ely
Lamari, Joseph Paul
Segal, Gary L.
**Silver Spring**
Dunn, John Benjamin
**Taneytown**
Shoemaker, Daniel W.
**Towson**
Campion, Renée

## MASSACHUSETTS

**Amherst**
Howland, Richard Moulton
**Barnstable**
Ryley, Arthur Charles
**Boston**
Cherny, David Edward
Craven, Terry Marie
Epstein, Elaine May
Geismer, Alan Stearn, Jr.
Gossels, Claus Peter Rolf
Hailey, Hans Ronald
Kassler, Haskell A.
Larson, Olive Elizabeth
Packenham, Richard Daniel
Perera, Lawrence Thacher
Sweeney, Paul John
**Bradford**
Cox, William Donald, Jr.
**Brighton**
Gilden, James William
**Brockton**
Belinsky, Ilene Beth
**Burlington**
Feeley, Kelly A.
Graves, Robert
**Cambridge**
Bowman, Judith Farris
**Chelmsford**
Grossman, Debra A.
**Greenfield**
Berson, Mark Ira
**Lowell**
Lawton, Thomas Edward, Jr.
**Natick**
Marr, David E
**Newton**
Monahan, Marie Terry
Tennant, Doris Fay
**Salem**
Andrews, John
Marks, Scott Charles
**South Hamilton**
Campbell, Diana Butt
**Springfield**
Dibble, Francis Daniel, Jr.
Yanni, Amy
**Winchester**
La Rosa, Lillian J.
**Woburn**
Karshbaum, Bonnie L.
**Worcester**
Leb, Clara Silvia
Moschos, Michael Christos

## MICHIGAN

**Adrian**
Kralick, Richard Louis
**Battle Creek**
Fisher, James A.
Zalenski, Cheryl Marie
**Birmingham**
Bank, Mark Albert
Cunningham, James Patrick
Delin, Sylvia Kaufman
Gold, Edward David
Morganroth, Fred
Sater, Nazli G.
**Bloomfield Hills**
Barnhart, Katherine Louise
Gornbein, Henry Seidel
Victor, Richard Steven
**Coldwater**
Colbeck, J. Richard
**Dearborn**
Gardner, Gary Edward
**Detroit**
Prather, Kenneth Earl
**East Lansing**
Casey, Nan Elizabeth
**Eastpointe**
Ionetz, Ronald George
**Farmingtn Hls**
Bernstein, Stephen Richard
Maloney, Vincent John
Stokes, Joelynn Towanda
**Farmington Hills**
Hampton, William Peck
Reagle, Jack Evan
**Flint**
Cooley, Richard Eugene
**Grand Rapids**
Boer, Roger William
Borja, Arthur
Jennette, Noble Stevenson, III
**Grosse Pointe**
McIntyre, Anita Grace Jordan
**Holland**
Moritz, John Reid
Murphy, Max Ray
**Inkster**
Bullock, Steven Carl
**Ishpeming**
Andriacchi, Dominic Francis
**Jackson**
Jacobs, Wendell Early, Jr.
**Kalamazoo**
Durham, Sidney Down
**Lansing**
Kronzek, Charles Michael
Nurkiewicz, Dennis John, Jr.
Shafer, Stuart Robert
**Manistee**
Simon, Stephanie Eden
**Mount Clemens**
Stepek, Mark William
**Okemos**
Barton, Judith Marie
**Petoskey**
Erhart, James Nelson
**Saginaw**
Suffety, Hamed William, Jr.
**Saint Clair Shores**
Shehan, Wayne Charles
**Southfield**
Davis-Yancey, Gwendolyn
Gold, Gordon Stanford
Martina, Carlo Jack
**Suttons Bay**
Johnson, Darryl Todd

## NORTH CAROLINA

**Cary**
Montgomery, Charles Harvey
**Charlotte**
Brackett, Martin Luther, Jr.
Bragg, Ellis Meredith, Jr.
Hatcher, James Gregory
Rockey, Arlaine
**Durham**
King, William Oliver
**Fayetteville**
Brady, B(arbara) Dianne
Townsend, William Jackson
**Greenville**
Clark, John Graham, III
Conner, Ernest Lee, Jr.
**Lillington**
Edwards, Charlene Vernell
**Murphy**
MacFarlan, John Howard
**Newton**
Cutchin, John Franks
**Oxford**
Burnette, Sarah Katherine
**Raleigh**
Ansley, James Ronald
Parker, John Hill
**Winston Salem**
Motsinger, John Kings

## NORTH DAKOTA

**Bismarck**
Harms, Robert Wayne
**Dickinson**
Greenwood, Dann E.
**Grand Forks**
Seaworth, Mary Ellen

## OHIO

**Akron**
Finan, Christine Denise
Glinsek, Gerald John
Mullen, Thomas Terry
**Athens**
Hedges, Richard Houston
**Barnesville**
Jefferis, Paul Bruce
**Bellevue**
Smith, Ronald R.
**Bucyrus**
McBride, Gordon Scott
**Canton**
Costa, Carol Ann
Yoder, Robert Gene
**Cincinnati**
Bibus, Thomas William
Candito, Joseph
Moskowitz, James Howard
Sims, Victor Dwayne
Whalen, James Lawrence
**Cleveland**
Akers-Parry, Deborah
Cahn, James
Daiker, Paul B.
Gabinet, Sarah Joan
Kapp, C. Terrence
Kraemer, Lisa Russert
LaFond, Thomas Joseph
Palkovitz, Herbert
Perella, Marie Louise
Spero, Keith Erwin
Wilsman, James Michael
Wolf, Marshall Jay
Zashin, Andrew Aaron
**Columbus**
Depascale, Diane Kappeler
Donahey, Richard Sterling, Jr.
Elsass, Tobias Harold
Jewett, James Michael
Juhola, Michael Duane
Koblentz, Robert Alan
Tyack, Thomas Michael
Whipps, Edward Franklin
Wolery, Don Edward
**Dayton**
Blaschak, Thomas R.
Goelz, Robert Dean
Mues, Robert Leighton
Posey, Terry Wayne
Tucker, Michael Lane
**Eaton**
Bennett, Gray Weston
**Elyria**
Illner, Michael Douglas
Kovacs, John Joseph
**Fairborn**
Miles, David R.
**Findlay**
Rakestraw, Gregory Allen
**Garfield Hts**
Demer, Margaret E.
**Georgetown**
Hornschemeier, Patrick
**Hamilton**
Bressler, H.J.
**Jackson**
Lewis, Richard M.
**Jefferson**
Geary, Michael Philip
**Mansfield**
Wolf, Marcus Alan
**Medina**
Hanwell, Robert Michael
**New Philadelphia**
Mastin, Scott Joseph
**North Olmsted**
Dorchak, Thomas J.
**Painesville**
Cooper, Linda Dawn
**Ravenna**
Giulitto, Paula Christine
**Saint Marys**
Huber, William Evan
**Salem**
Slack, Mark Robert
**Shaker Heights**
Adrine, Herbert A.
**Springfield**
Catanzaro, Michael A.
Lagos, James Harry
**Toledo**
Cooper, Emily K.
Griffin, Sharon L.
Skotynsky, Walter John
**Upper Sandusky**
Fox, Mary Ellen
**Van Wert**
Gordon, Scott R.
**Westerville**
Lancione, Bernard Gabe
**Wooster**
Kennedy, Charles Allen
**Youngstown**
Briach, George Gary

## OKLAHOMA

**Bartlesville**
Huchteman, Ralph Douglas
Thomas, Linda S.
**Durant**
McPheron, Alan Beaumont
**El Reno**
Grantham, Robert Edward
**Enid**
Gill, Amber McLaughlin
**Idabel**
Shaw, Donald Ray
**Moore**
Pipkin, William A.
**Norman**
McFall, Sara Weer
**Oklahoma City**
Ferguson, Steven E.
Henry, David Patrick
Necco, Alexander David
**Sayre**
Brooks, David Eugene
**Stilwell**
Morton, Kathryn R.
**Tulsa**
Abrahamson, A. Craig
Clark, Wendell W.
Daniel, Samuel Phillips
Hood, William Wayne, Jr.
La Sorsa, William George
Raynolds, William F., II
Steltzlen, Janelle Hicks
Sutton, Jonathan Mark
**Vinita**
Johnston, Oscar Black, III
**Yukon**
Hixson, Wendell Mark

## OREGON

**Ashland**
Jarvis, Barbara Anne
**Brookings**
Hinton, Floyd
**Corvallis**
Heinrich, Steven Allan
**Eugene**
Owens, A(rnold) Dean
**Grants Pass**
Day, Gregory Thomas
Preslar, Holly Ann
**Oregon City**
Hill, Gary D.
Jonasson, William Bradford
McFarland, Carol Anne
**Portland**
Bender, Laurie
Beshears, Charles Daniel, III
Gottlieb, Ira Leonard
Johnson, Mark Andrew
Palmer, Wayne Darwin
Reisman, Joanne
Williams, Sharon A.
**Roseburg**
Cremer, Richard Anthony
**Wilsonville**
Yacob, Yosef

## PENNSYLVANIA

**Bangor**
Spry, Donald Francis, II
**Beaver**
Ledebur, Linas Vockroth, Jr.
**Bensalem**
Kirk, Barbara M.
**Butler**
Paulisick, Gerri Volchko
Wright, Veronica Giel
**Canonsburg**
Kurowski, Charles Edward
**Carlisle**
Baird, Lindsay Dare
**Chadds Ford**
Lamonaca, Joseph Michael
**Devon**
Graf, Bayard Mayhew
**Donora**
Miller, David A.
**Dover**
Krug, Rob Alan
**Doylestown**
Bolla, William Joseph
Goldman, William Lewis, Sr.
Hoopes, Robert Patrick
**Du Bois**
Blakley, Benjamin Spencer, III
**Enola**
Sheaffer, Cindy Elaine
Sheetz, Ralph Albert
**Erie**
Williams, Dennis Vaughn
**Exton**
Ashton, Mark Randolph
**Feasterville Trevose**
Osterhout, Richard Cadwallader
**Fort Washington**
Hess, Lawrence Eugene, Jr.
**Girard**
Steadman, James Robert
**Harrisburg**
Cunningham, Jordan Daniel
Howett, John Charles, Jr.
Imblum, Gary Joseph
Kaylor, Cynthia Anne
Miles, Patricia Ann
**Hatboro**
John, Robert McClintock
**Holtwood**
Campbell, Paul Gary
**Huntingdon**
Covell, Robert Martin
**Jenkintown**
Worthington, Sandra Boulton
**Kingston**
Meyer, Martin Jay
Urbanski, Stephen Karl
**Lancaster**
Pyfer, John Frederick, Jr.
Zimmerman, D(onald) Patrick
**Langhorne**
Hillje, Barbara Brown
**Lebanon**
Burkett, Loreen Marae
Keys, Robert Barr, Jr.
**Lewistown**
Levin, Allen Joseph
**Lumberville**
McGuckin, Ronald V.
**Media**
Berman, Bernard Mayer
DiOrio, Robert Michael
Ewing, Robert Clark
Meloni, Kathryn Ann
Tomlinson, Herbert Weston
**Mercer**
Kochems, Robert Gregory
McConnell, Mary Ann
**Milford**
Siegel, Arthur Bernard
**Monroeville**
Cohen, Laura
**Murrysville**
Kemp, Kathleen Nagy
**New Castle**
Palmer, Allen L.
**Norristown**
Gregg, John Pennypacker
Mirabile, Carolyn Rose
**Philadelphia**
Blumstein, Edward
Cooper, Brad
Fioretti, Michael D.
Kormes, John Winston
Patrick, Paula Antoinette
Phillips, Dorothy Kay
Shmukler, Stanford
Wolf, Bruce
**Pittsburgh**
Alberty, Michael Charles
Anderson, Lea E.
Chase, Norma
Goldberg, Mark Joel
Gubinsky, Mark Kevin
Isabella, Mary Margaret
King, Peter J.
Klein, Joel Aaron
MacBeth, Lynn Ellen
Mahood, James Edward
Pollock, David Samuel
Pollock, Jeffrey Lawrence
Reich, Samuel Joseph
Schooley, Elizabeth Walter
**Pocono Pines**
Hardiman, Therese Anne
**Reynoldsville**
Wheeler, Mark Andrew, Sr.
**Scranton**
Sposito, James Anthony
**Sharon**
Ekker, Henry Mayer
**State College**
Sinclair, I.B.
**Trevose**
Fanning, Eleanor
**Washington**
O'Dell, Debbie
**Waynesburg**
Webb, Jane Marie
**Wexford**
Fall, Robert J.
**Wilkes Barre**
Dalessandro, Sherry Ann
**Yardley**
Lieberson, Jay B.

## RHODE ISLAND

**Cranston**
Loffredo, Pasco Frank
Walsh, Leatrice D.
**Pawtucket**
Marran, Joseph Edward, Jr.
**Providence**
Greenwood, Charles
Kersh, DeWitte Talmadge, Jr.
Lombardi, Valentino Dennis

## SOUTH CAROLINA

**Camden**
Jacobs, Rolly Warren
**Charleston**
McCormick, Karen Elizabeth
Swope, Denise Grainger
**Columbia**
Hancock, Harriet Daniels
Lester, Ken Harrison
Sheftman, Howard Stephen
**Georgetown**
Goude, Charles Reuben
**Greenville**
Bernstein, Barry Joel
**Mount Pleasant**
Whitten, Beatrice Ehrenberg
**Newberry**
Senn, Lisa Robinson
**North Myrtle Beach**
Wylie, Walter Jay
**Seneca**
Sires, Norman Gruber, Jr.
**Summerville**
Hardee-Thomas, Marva A.
Prettyman, Howard Cross, Jr.
**Sumter**
McDougall, John Olin
**West Columbia**
Applegate, William Russell

## SOUTH DAKOTA

**Sioux Falls**
Hattervig, Karen Ann
Johnson, Richard Arlo

## TENNESSEE

**Chattanooga**
Adams, Morgan Goodpasture
**Cookeville**
Lytal, Scott Lee
Qualls, Steven Daniel
**Erwin**
Shults-Davis, Lois Bunton
**Knoxville**
Cremins, William Carroll
Schwamm, Virginia Ann
**Martin**
Gearin, Kent Farrell
**Memphis**
Blanton, Darrell Drew
Branson, John R.
Dykes, Lillian Elise Levy
Lait, Hayden David
Philip, John B.
Rice, George Lawrence, III (Larry Rice)
Turner, Kay Farese
**Nashville**
Boyd, Mary Olert
Cobb, Stephen A.
Conner, Lewis Homer, Jr.
Lane, William Arthur
Nevin, Ronald Kent
Yarbrough, Edward Meacham
**Rogersville**
Skelton, Mark Albert
**Shelbyville**
Bramlett, Brenda Susan
**Springfield**
Richter, Lisa Sherrill
**White House**
Ruth, Bryce Clinton, Jr.

## TEXAS

**Abilene**
Boone, Celia Trimble
**Addison**
Geary, Joseph William
**Amarillo**
Lara, Art B., Jr.
**Arlington**
Campbell, William Lee
Rosenberry, William Kenneth
**Austin**
Piper, James Walter
Saltmarsh, Sara Elizabeth
Scates, Jennifer Ann
Shapiro, David L.
Terry, Craig Robert
Weddington, Sarah Ragle
**Beaumont**
Lawrence, Edward Jack, III
**Bellaire**
Soffar, William Douglas
**Boerne**
Reppeto, William M., III
**Bryan**
Steelman, Frank (Sitley)
**Canton**
White, Jeffery Howell
**Cat Spring**
Conner, Warren Wesley
**Cleveland**
Campbell, Selaura Joy
**College Station**
Borman, Channa Erin
Hoelscher, Michael Ray
**Corpus Christi**
Chesney, Brent Jackson
Johnson, John Lynn
Turpin, John Russell, Jr.
**Dallas**
Broussard, Peter O.
Callahan, Tena Toye
Clardy, Thelma Sanders
Eaton, Michael William
Fitzmaurice, Edward Joseph, Jr.
Gunnstaks, C. Luke
Hodges, Charles Robert
May, Michelle April
McCrory, Tom M., III
McCurley, Mary Johanna
Miller, Deborah Slye
Roberts, Steven Dillon
Sommers, Conrad Hoyle
Vanden Eykel, Ike
Verner, Jimmy Lynn, Jr.
**Denton**
Eames, Robert Newton
**El Paso**
Collins, William Coldwell
Torkildson, Thomas Miles
**Fort Worth**
Fischel, Robert Oscar
Johns, Deborah Ann Henry
O'Neal, Dale, Jr.
Paddock, Michael Buckley
Shannon, Joe, Jr.
**Grapevine**
Franks, Jon Michael
**Houston**
Behrmann, Lawrence James
Burg, Brent Lawrence
Cook, Eugene Augustus
Crowley, David James
Disher, David Alan
Eckman, David Walter
Fabio, Thea Marie
Fason, Rita Miller
Gagnon, Stewart Walter
Michael, Charles Joseph
Newman, Bobby King
Oldham, J. Thomas
O'Neill, Alice Jane
Ongert, Steven Walter
Pesikoff, Bette Schein
Ransom, Clifton Louis, Jr.
Schwartz, Brenda Keen
Sitzes, Madeline D'ree Penton
Woody, Clyde Woodrow
**Hurst**
Marling, Lynwood Bradley
**Jacksonville**
Thrall, Gordon Fish
**Killeen**
Roberts, Burk Austin
**League City**
Chudleigh, G. Stephen
**Longview**
Komorowski, Michele
Welge, Jack Herman, Jr.
**Lubbock**
Trowers, Teresa Cardenas
**Mc Kinney**
Roessler, P. Dee
**Mcallen**
Alvarez, Adolfo, Jr.
**Midland**
Frost, Wayne N.
**Mount Pleasant**
Woodson, Danny
**New Braunfels**
Clark, Mark Adrian
**Richardson**
Hubbard, Carolyn Marie
**San Antonio**
Cabezas-Gil, Rosa M.
Cumpian, Joe G.
Higdon, James Noel
O'Keeffe, Cynthia Grisham
Spence, Craig H.
Tharp, Christine M.
**San Marcos**
Maysel, Kyle Wayne
**Sugar Land**
Greer, Raymond White
**Tyler**
George, Samuel Mills
**Victoria**
Serrata, Lidia
**Waco**
Hall, Donald Orell
Villarreal, Fernando Marin
**Wharton**
Roades, John Leslie
**Yoakum**
Kvinta, Charles J.

## UTAH

**Midvale**
Johnson, Howard Price
**Ogden**
Kaufman, Steven Michael
**Salt Lake City**
Sine, Wesley Franklin

## VERMONT

**Brattleboro**
Corum, Jesse Maxwell, IV
**Burlington**
Volk, Paul S.
**Middlebury**
Reiff, Helen Hayslette
**Norwich**
McGee, P. Scott
**Rutland**
Dardeck, Stephen A.
Harnett, Matt
**White River Junction**
Davis, Emily S.

## VIRGINIA

**Alexandria**
Cassell, Richard Emmett
Isaacs, Dorothy Ann
**Arlington**
Cutler, Miriam
Malone, William Grady
McAlevy, Vincent William
Phillips, Stanton Earl
Schwartz, Philip
Zucker, Claudia Joy
**Ashland**
Allen, Russell Earl
**Bristol**
Alan, Sondra Kirschner
**Chesapeake**
Leftwich, James Asbury, Jr.
**Coles Point**
Rager, Susan Godman
**Fairfax**
Colten, Richard J.
Sanderson, Douglas Jay
**Fredericksburg**
Glessner, Thomas Allen
Jones, Owaiian Maurice
**Front Royal**
Napier, Ronald Lewis
**Glen Allen**
Batzli, Terrence Raymond
**Hillsville**
McGrady, Jonathan L.
**Lawrenceville**
Bain, C. Ridley
**Lebanon**
Compton, Carnis Eugene

**Leesburg**
Biberaj, Buta
Saunders, Richard R.
**Lynchburg**
Packert, G(ayla) Beth
**Manassas**
Hammond, Patricia Flood
**Mc Lean**
Cochran, Stephen Grey
Szabo, Valerie
**Newport News**
Hankins, Timothy Howard
Nachman, Erwin B(ehr)
Segall, James Arnold
**Norfolk**
Sutton, Paul Eugene, II
**Petersburg**
Baskervill, Charles Thornton
Spero, Morton Bertram
**Portsmouth**
Lavin, Barbara Hofheins
Sayer, Darell Lee
**Richmond**
Butler, Donald K.
Call, Susan Hope
Cook, Deanna Dworakowski
**Roanoke**
Mundy, Gardner Marshall
**Springfield**
Virk, Rachel Lewis
**Stafford**
Locklear, W. Ross
**Sterling**
Blair, Richard Eugene
**Virginia Beach**
Holmes, William James
McGraw, Frank William, Jr.
Spitzli, Donald Hawkes, Jr.
**Waynesboro**
Jones, Linda Schorsch

### WASHINGTON

**Auburn**
Gibson, Landon Mack, III
**Bellevue**
Hand, Bruce George
Landau, Felix
**Clarkston**
Kernan, Tina Lynn
**Grandview**
Maxwell, John Edward
**Issaquah**
Hammerly, Mary Leverenz
**Kent**
Ahern, Theresa M.
**Lynnwood**
Kastle, David Anthony
**Maple Valley**
Engle, David Scott
**Moses Lake**
Black, Barbara Jean
**Mount Vernon**
Sjostrom, Craig David
**Mountlake Terrace**
Field, Kathleen Cottrell
**Olympia**
Wright, Daniel A.
**Port Orchard**
Crawford, William Matterson
Shiers, Frank Abram
**Seattle**
Abelite, Jahnis John
Anderson, Wolfgang Richter
Novotny, Patricia Susan
Pritchard, Llewelyn G.
Steinberg, Jack
Wechsler, Mary Heyrman
**Spokane**
Anderson, Robert Edward
Cooper, R(obert) Maurice
Lineberger, Peter Saalfield
Rodrigues, Daryl Anthony
**Tacoma**
Walker, E. Allen
**Tukwila**
Gouras, Mark Steven
**Yakima**
Mathieu, Richard Louis

### WEST VIRGINIA

**Bluefield**
Kantor, Isaac Norris
**Charleston**
Zak, Robert Joseph
**Gassaway**
Jones, Jeniver James
**Huntington**
Ransbottom, Jennifer Dickens
Stapleton, John Warren
**Martinsburg**
Scales, Cinda L.
**Princeton**
Bell, Rebecca Morgan
Griffith, Mary E.

### WISCONSIN

**Baraboo**
Vesely, Tori Ann
**Beloit**
Blakely, Robert George
**Cross Plains**
Moretti, Jay Donald
**Deerfield**
Pappas, David Christopher
**Delafield**
Hausman, C. Michael
**Elkhorn**
Eberhardt, Daniel Hugo
**Elm Grove**
Kaestner, Richard Darwin
**Janesville**
Finman-Pince, Terry J.
Kopp, Mark David
**Kenosha**
Constant, Terry Lynn
Losey, Mary A.
**La Crosse**
Sleik, Thomas Scott
**Madison**
Heffernan, Michael Stewart
Kuemmel, Joseph Kenneth
MacDougall, Priscilla Ruth
Mannis, Valerie Sklar
Roberson, Linda
**Mauston**
Hollenbeck, Fred Drury
**Milwaukee**
Kohn, Valorie
Loeb, Leonard L.
Margolis, Marvin Allen
McCarty, William Edward
Meldman, Clifford Kay
O'Neill, Kevin Edgeworth
Orzel, Michael Dale
Peckerman, Bruce Martin
Stellman, L. Mandy
**Mosinee**
Schira, Diana Rae
**Park Falls**
Marvin, Janet L.
**Racine**
Crawford, Gerald Marcus
Hoelzel, Sally Ann
**Reedsburg**
Gorsuch, Sandra Cardo
**Shawano**
Habeck, James Roy
**Sheboygan**
Darrow, Dwight Daniel
Wasserman, Sylvia Katz
**Union Grove**
Stern, Walter Wolf, III
**Wausau**
Drengler, William Allan John
Molinaro, Thomas J.
Strande, Jeffrey Jay
**Wauwatosa**
Bonneson, Paul Garland

### WYOMING

**Casper**
Hjelmstad, William David
Miller, Corinne
**Cheyenne**
Frentheway, John E.
Steiner, Linda Jo
**Worland**
Sweeny, Wendy Press

### TERRITORIES OF THE UNITED STATES

### PUERTO RICO

**Ponce**
Leon-Sotomayor, Jose Rafael

### TRUST TERRITORY OF PACIFIC ISLANDS

**Palau**
Barden, Kenneth Eugene

### ADDRESS UNPUBLISHED

Abrahams, Samuel
Arber, Howard Bruce
Brandes, Joel R.
Bush, Robert G., III
Caquatto, Norma Madeline
Cohen, Anita Marilyn
Coryell, Frank
Eagen, William James
Eayrs, Sonja Trom
Egan, Alece Blanche
Evans, G. Anne
Fanning, Nita Kissel
Fayette, Kathleen Owens
Feldman, Richard David
Fowler, Flora Daun
Gourvitz, Elliot Howard
Hibbert, David Wilson
Hickey, Timothy Andrew
Hinds, Robert Taylor, Jr.
Janecek, Jeanette Mary
Karp, David Barry
Keister, Jean Clare
Kjos, Victoria Ann
Kolodny, Stephen Arthur
LaForest, Lana Jean
Lazor, John Adam
Leventhal, Howard G.
Maloney, John William
Marr, Jack Wayne
Martin, Robert James
Matheny, Mary Jane
McAlhany, Toni Anne
Naughton, John Alexander
O'Connor, Edward Vincent, Jr.
Pahides, Ann-Marie MacDonald
Pauca, Janet Frances
Perlman, Richard Brian
Phillips, Florence Tsu
Rosenn, Harold
Sager, Daniel Ian
Shaner, Leslie Ann
Smallwood, John Daniel
Tanenbaum, Jay Harvey
Vale, Victor John Eugene, II
Vamos, Florence M.
Walsh, Gerry O'Malley
Wigler, Andrew Jeffrey
Zurav, David Bernard

## FINANCE

### UNITED STATES

### ALABAMA

**Birmingham**
Greenwood, P. Nicholas
Martin, Arthur Lee, Jr.

### ALASKA

**Anchorage**
Wohlforth, Eric Evans

### ARIZONA

**Mesa**
Guffey, Douglas Oliver
**Phoenix**
Bauman, Frederick Carl
Bixby, David Michael
James, Charles E., Jr.
Perry, Lee Rowan
White, Nancy Lee
**Tempe**
Chander, Anupam

### ARKANSAS

**Little Rock**
Nelson, Edward Sheffield

### CALIFORNIA

**Camarillo**
Cayley, Susan Nicole
**Costa Mesa**
Caldwell, Courtney Lynn
**Irvine**
Creatura, Mark A.
Farrell, Teresa Joanning
**Los Angeles**
Carlson, Robert Edwin
Leibow, Ronald Louis
Lesser, Joan L.
Robertson, Hugh Duff
Shilling, Monica Jill
**Marina Dl Rey**
Smolker, Gary Steven
**Newport Beach**
Wolf, Alan Steven
**Orange**
Sawdei, Milan A.
**Redondo Beach**
Michael, Geoffrey Palmer
**San Diego**
O'Malley, James Terence
Shippey, Sandra Lee
**San Francisco**
Burden, James Ewers
Casillas, Mark
Latta, Thomas Albert
Levie, Mark Robert
Ludemann, Doreen Ann
Palmer, Venrice Romito
**San Luis Obispo**
Collins, Mary Elizabeth
**Universal City**
Coupe, James Warnick
**Vernon**
Smith, Lawrence Ronald

### COLORADO

**Castle Rock**
Procopio, Joseph Guydon
**Denver**
Dolan, Brian Thomas
Gallegos, Larry Duayne
Spiegleman, John G.
**Englewood**
Cunningham, Samuel Scot

### CONNECTICUT

**Farmington**
Levy, Coleman Bertram
**Guilford**
Thomas, David Robert
**Hartford**
Gitlin, Richard Alan
Reilly, Edward Anthony, Jr.
**New Haven**
Craig, William Emerson
**Stamford**
Herling, Michael James
**Westbrook**
Dundas, Philip Blair, Jr.

### DISTRICT OF COLUMBIA

**Washington**
Bruemmer, Russell John
Caplan, Corina Ruxandra
Chanin, Michael Henry
Cumberland, William Edwin
Dickerman, Dorothea Wilhelmina
Downs, Clark Evans
Fanone, Joseph Anthony
Feldman, Roger David
Finkelstein, Jay Gary
Henck, Charles Seymour
Hu, Patrick Haiping
Lehr, Dennis James
Levin, Michael Henry
Molenkamp, Jack A.
Pogue, L(loyd) Welch
Rogers, George Christopher
Trimble, Sandra Ellingson
Weiner, Kenneth Brian
Wilson, Bruce Sandness

### FLORIDA

**Coral Gables**
Kaplan, David Louis
**Gainesville**
Rosenblatt, Howard Marshall
**Jacksonville**
Slade, Thomas Bog, III
**Miami**
Alvarez-Farré, Emilio José
Gross, Leslie Jay
Merrill, George Vanderneth
Pearson, John Edward
**Orlando**
Salzman, Gary Scott
Stewart, Harry A.
Stuart, Alice Melissa
**Tallahassee**
Reid, Robert C.
**West Palm Beach**
Angeloff, Carl
Holt, Richard Duane
Rosen, Marvin Shelby

### GEORGIA

**Atlanta**
Crews, William Edwin
Keck, Richard Paul
McNeill, Thomas Ray
Moeling, Walter Goos, IV
Peterzell, Betsy Vance
Schulte, Jeffrey Lewis
Scibilia, Joseph Logan
Stallings, Ronald Denis
Strauss, Robert David
Veal, Rex R.

### HAWAII

**Honolulu**
Lau, Eugene Wing Iu

### ILLINOIS

**Chicago**
Boardman, Robert A.
Crawford, Dewey Byers
Doetsch, Douglas Allen
Dondanville, Patricia
Hand, Gary S.
Jacobson, Ronald H.
Johnson, Gary Thomas
Kaufman, Andrew Michael
Lang, Gordon, Jr.
Majers, Elizabeth Louise
Malkin, Cary Jay
McGuigan, Philip Palmer
Mehlman, Mark Franklin
Pugh, Stephen Henry, Jr.
Reum, James Michael
Stambler, Olga
**Franklin Park**
Blanchard, Eric Alan

### INDIANA

**Lafayette**
Branigin, Roger D., Jr.

### KENTUCKY

**Louisville**
Halbleib, Walter Thomas
Maggiolo, Allison Joseph

### LOUISIANA

**Metairie**
Ostendorf, Lance Stephen
**New Orleans**
Wheeler, V.M., III

### MARYLAND

**Baltimore**
Scriggins, Larry Palmer
**Bethesda**
Gottlieb, Jonathan W.
**Silver Spring**
Hannan, Myles

### MASSACHUSETTS

**Boston**
Bornheimer, Allen Millard
Clark, Jennifer Babbin
Cohn, Andrew Howard
Duffy, James Francis, III
Jordan, Alexander Joseph, Jr.
Kamborian, Lisbeth N.
Krasnow, Jordan Philip
Kyle, Amy Lynn
Levine, Steven B.
Masud, Robert
McDonald, John Barry, Jr.
O'Brien, Duncan Thomas
Schoenfeld, Barbara Braun
Soden, Richard Allan
Sopel, George C.
Stokes, James Christopher
Wright, Walter Augustine, III
**Cambridge**
Wirth, Peter
**Lincoln**
Gnichtel, William Van Orden
**Newton**
Glazer, Donald Wayne
**Springfield**
Santopietro, Albert Robert

### MICHIGAN

**Detroit**
Rentenbach, Paul Robert
Rohr, Richard David
**Grosse Pointe**
Barrows, Ronald Thomas

### MINNESOTA

**Minneapolis**
Duran, Stanley John
Laitinen, Sari K.M.
Parsons, Charles Allan, Jr.
Potuznik, Charles Laddy
Saunders, Jeffrey N.
**Saint Paul**
Levinson, Kenneth S.

### MISSISSIPPI

**Jackson**
Johnson, Mark Wayne

### MISSOURI

**Kansas City**
Ayers, Jeffrey David
Graham, Harold Steven
Hindman, Larrie C.
Holewinski, Paul Patrick
**Saint Louis**
Gillis, John Lamb, Jr.
Lowther, Thomas Edward
Mersman, Richard Kendrick, III
Watson-Wesley, Denise J.

### NEBRASKA

**Omaha**
Bracht, David Leo

### NEVADA

**Reno**
Oskam, Gerard Lambert

### NEW JERSEY

**Cranbury**
Iatesta, John Michael
**Edison**
Lijoi, Peter Bruno
**Morristown**
Gillen, James Robert
Smith, J. Edward
**Newark**
Knee, Stephen H.
**Princeton**
Wood, Joshua Warren, III
**Ridgewood**
Harris, Micalyn Shafer
**Woodbridge**
Hoberman, Stuart A.

### NEW MEXICO

**Albuquerque**
Haltom, B(illy) Reid
Moise, Steven Kahn

### NEW YORK

**Baldwin**
Naranjo, Carolyn R.
**Hamburg**
Glose, Herbert James
**Long Beach**
Solomon, Robert H.
**Long Island City**
Alimaras, Gus
**New York**
Altschuler, Fredric Lawrence
Andersen, Richard Esten
Barnett, Gary
Bear, Larry Alan
Bergan, Philip James
Bertoni, Fernando Raul
Bickford, Nathaniel Judson
Bliwise, Lester Martin
Bloomer, Harold Franklin, Jr.
Brewer, William Dane
Brooks, Gene C.
Burgweger, Francis Joseph Dewes, Jr.
Bushnell, George Edward, III
Calvey, Brian J.
Cannell, John Redferne
Caytas, Ivo George
Chilstrom, Robert Meade
Clemente, Robert Stephen
Crawshaw, Donald R.
Das, Kalyan
Devers, Peter Dix
Diaz-Granados, Rafael Andres
Dolan, Patrick Daniel
Drucker, Richard Allen
Dugan, Terrence Lee
Effel, Laura
Faulkner, Andrew Montgomery
Fawer, Mark S.
Feit, David Jonathan
Fernicola, Gregory Anthony
Finnegan, Hugh Patrick
Fishman, Fred Norman
Forry, John Ingram
Furniss, Peter Glenn
Genova, Diane Melisano
Granoff, Gary Charles
Grosz, Morton Eric
Hanson, Stephen Philip
Healy, Walter F. X.
Higgs, John H.
Hirsch, Barry
Hoffman, Alan S.
Hooker, Wade Stuart, Jr.
Howard, Susanne C.
Janowitz, James Arnold
Jiménez, Emilio
Junius, Andreas Gretus
Kaplan, Carl Eliot
Kelly, Daniel Grady, Jr.
Kelly, W. Michael
Kensington, Costa Nicholas
Krouse, George Raymond, Jr.
Laurenson, Edwin Charles
Lee, Thomas Dongho
Li, Donna Dongli
Li, Rebecca Jia
Lindsay, George Peter
Macan, William Alexander, IV
Maghiar, Livia L.
McDavid, William Henry
Mock, Eric V.
Nahm, Nathan Ihru
Nissenbaum, David
Nordquist, Stephen Glos
Novikoff, Harold Stephen
Orol, Elliot S.
O'Rorke, James Francis, Jr.
Passer-Muslin, Juliette Mayabelle
Paul, Robert Carey
Pellecchio, Ralph L.
Rabb, Bruce
Rom, Judith R.
Rosendahl, Roger Wayne
Ross, Michael Aaron
Scheler, Brad Eric
Schmidt, Joseph W.
Schmitt, John Patrick
Schorr, Brian Lewis
Seward, George Chester
Shea, Edward Emmett
Silkenat, James Robert
Sperling, Allan George
Stefano, Joseph M.
Stein, Stephen William
Sulger, Francis Xavier
Terrell, J. Anthony
Thaler, Craig H.
Welt, Philip Stanley
Wiegley, Roger Douglas
Wilson, Edward N.
Wiseman, Michael Martin
Wolfe, James Ronald

Yu, Sandy Kyung
Zaitzeff, Roger Michael
**Orangeburg**
Seaman, Robert E., III
**Rochester**
Adair, Donald Robert
**Syracuse**
Bullock, Stephen C.
**White Plains**
Hecker, Robert J.
Shin, Helen

### NORTH CAROLINA

**Charlotte**
Bush, F. Brad
Taylor, David Brooke
Whelpley, David B., Jr.
**Greensboro**
Hopkins, John David
**Raleigh**
Fricke, David Robert
Gwyn, William Blair, Jr.
Homick, Daniel John
Huggard, John Parker
Markoff, Brad Steven
Miller, Jeffrey D.

### OHIO

**Cincinnati**
Heldman, James Gardner
Wagner, Barbara
**Cleveland**
Brown, Harry M.
Chilcote, Lee A.
Hogg, James Stuart
Pearlman, Samuel Segel
Stanton, R. Thomas
Waldeck, John Walter, Jr.
**Columbus**
Darling, Stanton Girard
Pigman, Jack Richard
Summer, Fred A.
Tannous, Robert Joseph
**Dayton**
McSwiney, Charles Ronald

### OKLAHOMA

**Oklahoma City**
Johnson, Robert Max
**Tulsa**
Hilborne, Thomas George, Jr.

### OREGON

**Ashland**
Shaw, Barry N.
**Beaverton**
Fulsher, Allan Arthur
**Portland**
Rasmussen, Richard Robert

### PENNSYLVANIA

**Bala Cynwyd**
Lee, Rotan Edward
**Berwyn**
Huggler, David H.
**Bradford**
Hauser, Christopher George
**Gibsonia**
Heilman, Carl Edwin
**Gladwyne**
Booth, Harold Waverly
**Harrisburg**
Cicconi, Christopher M.
**Philadelphia**
Auten, David Charles
Cooney, John Gordon
De Simone, Dominic J.
Dombrowski, Raymond Edward, Jr.
Doran, William Michael
Flanagan, Joseph Patrick, Jr.
Jones, Robert Jeffries
Malloy, Michael P.
Mason, Theodore W.
Stuntebeck, Clinton A.
**Pittsburgh**
Adelkoff, Steven J.
Barnes, James Jerome
Brown, Ronald James
Ehrenwerth, David Harry
Gold, Harold Arthur
Newlin, William Rankin
Purtell, Lawrence Robert
**Venetia**
Brewer, Christopher
**Wyndmoor**
Starr, Harold Page

### SOUTH CAROLINA

**Hilton Head Island**
Hagoort, Thomas Henry

### TENNESSEE

**Knoxville**
McCall, Jack Humphreys, Jr.
**Memphis**
Buhler, Lynn Bledsoe
**Nashville**
Carr, Davis Haden

### TEXAS

**Austin**
Hollen, Theodore Thomas
Rider, Brian Clayton
**Corpus Christi**
Locke, William Henry
**Dallas**
Coleman, Russell Forester
Hamby, Robert Kevin
Harvey, James Clement
Helfand, Marcy Caren
Kipp, John Theodore
Laves, Alan Leonard
Roberts, Harry Morris, Jr.
St. Claire, Frank Arthur
Veach, Robert Raymond, Jr.
White, James Richard
Zable, Norman Arnold
**El Paso**
Smith, Tad Randolph
**Euless**
Paran, Mark Lloyd
**Houston**
Bilger, Bruce R.
Ewen, Pamela Binnings
Gover, Alan Shore
O'Toole, Austin Martin
Weber, Fredric Alan

### VIRGINIA

**Arlington**
Morris, Roy Leslie
**Falls Church**
Christman, Bruce Lee
**Mc Lean**
Weiss, Rhett Louis
**Newport News**
Kamp, Arthur Joseph, Jr.
**Richmond**
Bush, Thomas Norman
Perkins, Jon Scott
Rainey, Gordon Fryer, Jr.

### WASHINGTON

**Seattle**
Hoffman, Mark Frederick
Kuhrau, Edward W.
Ruddy, James W.
Tousley, Russell Frederick
Whitford, Joseph P.

### WISCONSIN

**Madison**
Nora, Wendy Alison
Petershack, Richard Eugene
**Milwaukee**
Galanis, John William
Hatch, Michael Ward

### CHINA

**Hong Kong**
Scown, Michael John

### ENGLAND

**London**
Smith, Jerry Leon

### ADDRESS UNPUBLISHED

Brodhead, David Crawmer
Cassidy, M. Sharon
Cherney, Andrew Knox
Collins, James Francis
Colton, Sterling Don
Contino, Richard Martin
Francis, Patricia Ann
Gutman, Richard Edward
Howell, Donald Lee
Hubbard, Michael James
Johanson, David Richard
Kibler, Rhoda Smith
Murphy, Jo Anne
Newman, Sanders David
O'Brien, Charles H.
O'Brien, James Edward
Patrick, Victor Phillip
Pear, Charles E., Jr.
Pratt, Robert Windsor
Pusateri, Lawrence Xavier
Ruhm, Thomas Francis
Shaffer, Richard James
Smoke, Richard Edwin
Wallison, Frieda K.
Wright, Robert Payton

## FRANCHISING

### UNITED STATES

### ALABAMA

**Huntsville**
Steakley, Roderic G
**Mobile**
Satterwhite, Harry Vincent

### ARIZONA

**Phoenix**
Hay, John Leonard
Ullman, James A.
Williams, Quinn Patrick

### CALIFORNIA

**Los Angeles**
Barnes, Willie R.
**Newport Beach**
Barclay, John Allen
**Palo Alto**
Nopar, Alan Scott
**Pasadena**
Adsit, John Michael
**Pleasanton**
Straff, Donna Evelyn
**San Ramon**
Freed, Kenneth Alan

### DISTRICT OF COLUMBIA

**Washington**
Klarfeld, Peter James
Lowell, H. Bret
McDavid, Janet Louise
Williams, Thomas Raymond
Zeidman, Philip Fisher

### FLORIDA

**Miami**
Leone, Dennis Dean
Zarco, Robert
**Orlando**
Blaher, Neal Jonathan
Chong, Stephen Chu Ling
**Palm Beach Gardens**
Brams, Jeffrey Brent

### GEORGIA

**Atlanta**
Barkoff, Rupert Mitchell
McNeill, Thomas Ray
**Augusta**
Cooney, William J.

### ILLINOIS

**Chicago**
Baer, John Richard Frederick
Johnson, Douglas Wells
Lambert, Kim Anita
Lapin, Andrew William
Para, Gerard Albert
**Northbrook**
Pollak, Jay Mitchell

### INDIANA

**Indianapolis**
Petersen, James Leo

### LOUISIANA

**Baton Rouge**
Ferguson, James Curtis
**New Orleans**
Butler, Peter Joseph

### MARYLAND

**Baltimore**
Chernow, Jeffrey Scott
Wilson, Thomas Matthew, III
**Crofton**
Norman, David Joseph

### MICHIGAN

**Bloomfield Hills**
Foley, Sally Lee

### MINNESOTA

**Minneapolis**
Long, James Jay
Pluimer, Edward J.

### MISSOURI

**Kansas City**
Culp, Donald Allen
Dolson, Edward M.
Kaufman, Michelle Stark
Palmer, Dennis Dale
**Saint Louis**
Anderson, Anthony LeClaire

### NEW JERSEY

**Florham Park**
Chase, Eric Lewis
**Parsippany**
Asserson, Brian Michael
**Red Bank**
Barnes, Bray B.
**Short Hills**
Schell, Norka M.
**South Orange**
Kassoff, Mitchell Jay

### NEW YORK

**Buffalo**
Bailey, Thomas Charles
**Garden City**
Kestenbaum, Harold Lee
**New York**
Rosen, Richard Lewis
**Purchase**
Joyce, Joseph James

### NORTH CAROLINA

**Greenville**
Kiess, Stephen David
**Morganton**
Simpson, Daniel Reid
**Raleigh**
Kapp, Michael Keith
**Winston Salem**
Schollander, Wendell Leslie, Jr.

### OHIO

**Cincinnati**
Lutz, James Gurney
**Columbus**
Buchenroth, Stephen Richard

### OKLAHOMA

**Oklahoma City**
Britton, James Edward
**Tulsa**
Slicker, Frederick Kent

### OREGON

**Lake Oswego**
Byczynski, Edward Frank
**Portland**
Smith, Douglas Dean

### PENNSYLVANIA

**Blue Bell**
Siedzikowski, Henry Francis
**Norristown**
Milner, Kenneth Paul
**Philadelphia**
Briscoe, Jack Clayton
Mack, Wayne A.
Tractenberg, Craig R.
**Pittsburgh**
Owen, Jeffrey Randall

### TENNESSEE

**Nashville**
Habermann, Ted Richard

### TEXAS

**Dallas**
Rittenberry, Kelly Culhane
**Houston**
Devlin, Francis James
Simmons, Stephen Judson

### WISCONSIN

**Milwaukee**
Marcus, Richard Steven

### TERRITORIES OF THE UNITED STATES

### PUERTO RICO

**San Juan**
Antonetti-Zequeira, Salvador

### ADDRESS UNPUBLISHED

Cannon, Gayle Elizabeth
Davey, Gerard Paul
Glickman, Gladys

## GENERAL PRACTICE

### UNITED STATES

### ALABAMA

**Atmore**
Hartley, Wade Leon
**Birmingham**
Cicio, Anthony Lee
Cohan, Michael Joseph
Cornelius, Walter Felix
Kracke, Robert Russell
Thompson, Charles Amos
**Clanton**
Jackson, John Hollis, Jr.
Karn, David B.
**Enterprise**
Fuller, Kenneth T.
**Fairhope**
Dorgan, James Richard
**Fayette**
Chambless, Ricky Thomas
**Florence**
Schuessler, Cindy Sandlin
**Gadsden**
Davis, Thomas E.
**Huntsville**
Potter, Ernest Luther
**Mobile**
Armbrecht, William Henry, III
Ballard, Michael Eugene
Coley, F(ranklin) Luke, Jr.
Loveless, Ralph Peyton
Lyons, George Sage
Philips, Abe L., Jr.
**Muscle Shoals**
Riley, Anthony Dale
**Tuscaloosa**
Williams, Roger Courtland
**Tuscumbia**
Hunt, James L.

### ALASKA

**Anchorage**
Breckberg, Robert Lee
Goldberg, Robert M.
**Juneau**
Davis, Gerald Kenneth, Jr.
**Kodiak**
Ott, Andrew Eduard

### ARIZONA

**Glendale**
Bellah, C. Richard
**Phoenix**
Coghlan, Carol Lynn
Goldstein, Stuart Wolf
Zachar, Christopher Joseph
**Tempe**
Evans, Lawrence Jack, Jr.
**Tucson**
Baldwin, Howard
Blackman, Jeffrey William
Gonzales, Richard Joseph
McNeill, Frederick Wallace
Tindall, Robert Emmett

### ARKANSAS

**Blytheville**
Fendler, Oscar
**Camden**
Ives, Daniel Delbert
**Conway**
Brazil, William Clay
**Fayetteville**
Pearson, Charles Thomas, Jr.
**Harrison**
Inman-Campbell, Gail
Pinson, Jerry D.
**Hot Springs National Park**
Sanders, Michael Edward
**Jonesboro**
Deacon, John C.
**Little Rock**
Hughes, Steven Jay
Ryan, Donald Sanford
Sherman, William Farrar
**Marion**
Fogleman, John Nelson
**Mena**
Thrailkill, Daniel B.
**Newport**
Howard, Steven Gray
Thaxton, Marvin Dell
**Van Buren**
Gant, Horace Zed
**Walnut Ridge**
Mullen, William David
**West Helena**
Bell, Amy Clifton

### CALIFORNIA

**Alameda**
Birren, Jeffrey Emmett
**Antioch**
Richards, Gerald Thomas
**Berkeley**
Ogg, Wilson Reid
**Beverly Hills**
Horwin, Leonard
Jaffe, F. Filmore
Juno, Cynthia
**Burbank**
Ajalat, Sol Peter
**Cambria**
Stotter, James, II
**Canoga Park**
Gordon, Jerome
**Carmel Valley**
Mullally, David Smart
**Cerritos**
Sarno, Maria Erlinda
**Del Mar**
Seitman, John Michael
**Encino**
Smith, Selma Moidel
**Fresno**
Bailey, Howard William (Bill Bailey)
**Hermosa Beach**
Roberts, Laurel Lee
**King City**
Bolles, Donald Scott
**Los Alamitos**
Lia, James Douglas
Peters, Samuel Anthony
**Los Angeles**
Ariel, Frank Y.
De Brier, Donald Paul
Van de Kamp, John Kalar
Winfrey, Diana Lee
**Malibu**
Pilling, George William
**Millbrae**
Agosta, Steven S.
**Monarch Beach**
Luttrell, William Harvey
**Mount Shasta**
Armstrong, Kenneth
**Napa**
Burke, Patrick William
**Newport Beach**
Carman, Ernest Day
**North Fork**
Flanagan, James Henry, Jr.
**Novato**
Lewin, Werner Siegfried, Jr.
Obninsky, Victor Peter
**Oakland**
Trowbridge, Jeffery David
**Orange**
Stagner, Robert Dean
**Pacific Palisades**
Margolis, Benjamin Robert
**Pacifica**
Dye, David Alan
**Palm Desert**
Reinhardt, Benjamin Max
**Palo Alto**
Donnally, Robert Andrew
**Pasadena**
Fellman, Gerry Louis
**Pleasanton**
Harding, John Edward
**Rancho Cordova**
Lynch, Robert Berger
**Sacramento**
Brazier, John Richard
Giguiere, Michele Louise
**Saint Helena**
Marvin, Monica Louise Wolf
**San Diego**
Hofflund, Paul
Schwartz, Jeffrey Scott
Shapiro, Philip Alan
Von Passenheim, John B.
**San Francisco**
Cohn, Nathan
Enersen, Burnham
Haas, Richard
Kane, Robert F.
Yamakawa, David Kiyoshi, Jr.
**San Jose**
Hannon, Timothy Patrick
Klay, Anna Nettie
Trapp, David James
**San Rafael**
Drexler, Kenneth
**Santa Ana**
Fraser, Robert William
**Santa Barbara**
Delaughter, Jerry L.
Falstrom, Kenneth Edward
**Seaside**
Weingarten, Saul Myer
**Sherman Oaks**
Joyce, Stephen Michael
**Sunnyvale**
McReynolds, Stephen Paul
**Tustin**
Kraft, Henry R.
**Visalia**
Crowe, John T.
**Walnut Creek**
Pinkerton, Albert Duane, II
**West Hollywood**
Finstad, Suzanne Elaine

### COLORADO

**Arvada**
Kreis, Elizabeth Susan
**Aspen**
Peterson, Brooke Alan
Schumacher, Barry Lee
Shipp, Dan Shackelford

**Colorado Springs**
Evans, Paul Vernon
Graski, Diana
**Commerce City**
Trujillo, Lorenzo A.
**Denver**
Fink, Steven D.
Frederiksen, Paul Asger
Slaninger, Frank Paul
**Florence**
Davis, Allyn Whitney
**Fort Collins**
Brown, Ronald Laming
Redder, Thomas Joseph
**Frisco**
Helmer, David Alan
**Greeley**
Bodine, Joseph Ira
**Greenwood Village**
Underhill, Joanne Parsons
**Highlands Ranch**
Mierzwa, Joseph William
**Lakewood**
Mielke, Donald Earl
**Littleton**
Truhlar, Doris Broaddus
**Pueblo**
Geisel, Henry Jules
O'Conner, Loretta Rae

## CONNECTICUT

**Bethel**
Medvecky, Thomas Edward
Murray, Gwen E.
**Branford**
Hanchuruck, Stephen Paul
**Bridgeport**
Arons, Mark David
**Canaan**
Capecelatro, Mark John
**Colchester**
Broder, Joseph Arnold
**Fairfield**
Rosenstein, Sheila Kovaleski
**Hartford**
Bonee, John Leon, III
Foden, Maria Luisa de Castro
Gale, John Quentin
**Monroe**
Beck, Dana Kendall
**New Haven**
Choate, Edward Lee
Sabetta, Paul M.
Wiznia, Carolann Kamens
**New London**
Wilson, Thomas Buck
**New Milford**
Zitzmann, Kelly C.
**Newington**
Gutis, Mark Philip
**Norwalk**
Feinstein, Stephen Michael
Lang, Jules
**Old Greenwich**
Klemann, Gilbert Lacy, II
**Ridgefield**
Fricke, Richard John
**Rocky Hill**
DiCara, Phyllis M.
**South Windsor**
Gerlt, Wayne Christopher
**Stafford Springs**
Paradiso, F. Joseph
**Stamford**
Livolsi, Frank William, Jr.
Richichi, Joseph
Spitzer, Vlad Gerard
**Stratford**
Berlin, Patricia
O'Rourke, James Louis
**Trumbull**
Brennan, Daniel Edward, Jr.
**Wallingford**
Galligan, Matthew G.
**Waterbury**
Marano, Richard Michael
**West Hartford**
Morrissey, Ellen C.
Storm, Robert Warren
Swerdloff, Ileen Pollock
**Westport**
Cramer, Allan P.
Dimes, Edwin Kinsley
Swiggart, Carolyn Clay
Wisser, Ellen
**Wilton**
Adams, Thomas Tilley
**Windsor**
Morelli, Carmen
**Winsted**
Finch, Frank Herschel, Jr.

## DELAWARE

**Wilmington**
Boudart, Mary Cecile
Kulesza, Joseph Dominick, Jr.

## DISTRICT OF COLUMBIA

**Washington**
Burch, John Thomas, Jr.
Close, David Palmer
Deso, Robert Edward, Jr.
Donegan, Charles Edward
Feuerstein, Donald Martin
Goldson, Amy Robertson
Granger, David Ireland
Greenebaum, Leonard Charles
Harrison, Marion Edwyn
Jones, Allen, Jr.
Lim, Joseph Edward
Mann, Lawrence Moses
Murry, Harold David, Jr.
Perry, Rotraud Mezger
Richards, Suzanne V.
Scriven, Wayne Marcus
Thaler, Paul Sanders
Wald, Robert Lewis
Wilk, Adam Ross

## FLORIDA

**Altamonte Springs**
Salfi, Dominick Joseph
**Auburndale**
Haff, Tula Michele
**Boca Raton**
Barwell, Cindy Ann
Dudley, Everett Haskell, Jr.
**Clearwater**
Weidemeyer, Carleton Lloyd
**Coral Gables**
Mellinger, Robert Louis
**Crawfordville**
Bass, Donna Blackwell
**Delray Beach**
Kravetz, David Hubert
**Fort Lauderdale**
Nyce, John Daniel
**Fort Myers**
Dalton, Anne
**Fort Myers Beach**
Cotter, Richard Timothy
**Hollywood**
Wolis, Kenneth Arnold
**Jacksonville**
Alterman, Leonard Mayer
Kendrick, Darryl D.
**Jupiter**
Brophy, Gilbert Thomas
Gumson, Adam S.
**Key West**
Fohrman, Darryl
**Longboat Key**
Pulvermacher, Louis Cecil
**Miami**
Amber, Laurie Kaufman
Barrett, John Richard
Coberly, Jennifer Rae
Hirsch, Milton Charles
Kearns, John W.
Milstein, Richard Craig
Pennington, John Wesley, III
Rogers, Harvey DeLano
Samole, Myron Michael
Silber, Norman Jules
Starr, Ivar Miles
Touby, Richard
**Miami Beach**
Arbuz, Joseph Robert
**Milton**
Stoudenmire, William Ward
**Naples**
Bornmann, Carl Malcolm
Cimino, Richard Dennis
Crehan, Joseph Edward
Westman, Carl Edward
**North Miami Beach**
Cain, May Lydia
Zipkin, Sheldon Lee
**Orlando**
Cohen, David Sacks
Harris, Gordon H.
**Palatka**
Baldwin, Allen Adail
**Palm Beach Gardens**
Pumphrey, Gerald Robert
**Palm Coast**
Conner, Timothy James
**Palm Harbor**
Deckelman, Arthur D.
**Panama City**
Allan, Sher L.
**Punta Gorda**
Cherry, Paul Stephen
Price, Pine Scott
**Ruskin**
Norse, Kristin A.
**Saint Augustine**
Poole, Sharon Alexandra
**Saint Petersburg**
Allen, John Thomas, Jr.
Wilson, Darryl Cedric
**Tallahassee**
Anderson, Bruce Paige
Roland, Raymond William
Varn, Wilfred Claude
**Tampa**
Salem, Albert McCall, Jr.
**West Palm Beach**
Callahan, Richard Paul
Chopin, Susan Gardiner
Nugent, Paul Allen
Wearn, James McCartney
**Winter Springs**
Fernandez, William Warren, Sr.

## GEORGIA

**Athens**
Barrow, John J.
**Atlanta**
Cavin, Kristine Smith
Fiorentino, Carmine
Jordan, Paul Rodgers, III
Kelly, James Patrick
Mull, Gale W.
Pless, Laurance Davidson
Pryor, Shepherd Green, III
Stoner, Michael Alan
**Barnesville**
Kennedy, Harvey John, Jr.
**Columbus**
Patrick, James Duvall, Jr.
**Conyers**
Moore, Garland Curtis
**Darien**
Coppage, James Robert
**Decatur**
Edwards, Boykin, Jr.
Goddard, Ross Millard, Jr.
**Dublin**
Warren, Johnny Wilmer
**Fitzgerald**
Hughes, (Terry) Chris(topher)
**Hamilton**
Byrd, Gary Ellis
**Hazlehurst**
Elder, Lamar Alexander, Jr.
**Macon**
Cole, John Prince
Elliott, James Sewell
**Marietta**
Ahlstrom, Michael Joseph
Bentley, Fred Douglas, Sr.
Ingram, George Conley
**Perry**
Geiger, James Norman
**Savannah**
Aderhold, Kathleen
Gannam, Michael Joseph
Morrell, Diane Marie
**Statesboro**
Stone, Ralph Kenny
**Stone Mountain**
Weiman, Enrique Watson
**Swainsboro**
Edenfield, James Franklin
**Tucker**
Wheeler, Edd Dudley
**Valdosta**
Cork, Robert Lander

## HAWAII

**Honolulu**
Chuck, Walter G(oonsun)
Fong, Peter C. K.
Iwai, Wilfred Kiyoshi
Pyun, Matthew Sung Kwan
**Kahului**
Richardson, Robert Allen
**Kailua Kona**
Martin, William Charles
**Kihei**
Burns, Richard Gordon
**Wailuku**
Barbin, Ryther Lynn

## IDAHO

**Boise**
Desler, Peter
Hoagland, Samuel Albert
Noack, Harold Quincy, Jr.
**Hailey**
Hogue, Terry Glynn
**Lewiston**
Tait, John Reid
**Twin Falls**
Berry, L. Clyel

## ILLINOIS

**Alton**
Struif, L. James
**Barrington**
Reilly, Francis X.
**Batavia**
Drendel, Kevin Gilbert
**Belleville**
Waller, Paul Pressley, Jr.
**Bridgeport**
Stout, James Dudley
**Buffalo Grove**
Israelstam, Alfred William
**Carbondale**
Habiger, Richard J.
**Champaign**
Hall, Guy Charles
**Chicago**
Anagnost, Themis John
Augustynski, Adam J.
Bernstein, Charles Bernard
Chin, Davis
Ditkowsky, Kenneth K.
Filpi, Robert Alan
Frano, Andrew Joseph
Gordon, Theodora
Henning, Joel Frank
Howe, Jonathan Thomas
Knox, James Marshall
Kresse, William Joseph
Nora, Gerald Ernest
Reicin, Ronald Ian
Saunders, George Lawton, Jr.
Schmall, Steven Todd
Schuyler, Daniel Merrick
Serritella, James Anthony
Smith, Leo Emmet
Touhy, John M.
Vranicar, Michael Gregory
**Collinsville**
Evers, William C., III
**Columbia**
Gutknecht, Timothy Arthur
**Crystal Lake**
Franz, William Mansur
**Danville**
McFetridge, John David
**Des Plaines**
Davis, Larry Allen
**East Alton**
Boyle, Patrick Otto
**Elmhurst**
Kordik, Daniel Joseph
**Elmwood Park**
Spina, Anthony Ferdinand
**Galva**
Massie, Michael Earl
**Geneseo**
Palmgren, Nadine R.
**Genoa**
Cromley, Jon Lowell
**Hinsdale**
O'Brien, Donald Joseph
**Hoopeston**
Manion, Paul Thomas
**Monticello**
Rhoades, Dana Christine
**Morton Grove**
Klunder, Scott Ross
**Naperville**
Heap, Robert A.
Hittle, Kathleen J.
Kelly, Kathryn L.
**Northbrook**
Irons, Spencer Ernest
Yowell, George Kent
**Oak Brook**
Oldfield, E. Lawrence
**Oregon**
Cargerman, Alan William
**Palatine**
Runes, Kenneth Alan
**Palos Heights**
Matug, Alexander Peter
**Paris**
Bell, Allen Andrew, Jr.
Burkybile, Karen L.
**Peoria**
Tomlin, James Milton
**Princeton**
Johnson, Watts Carey
**Rockford**
Johnson, Thomas Stuart
**Skokie**
Gilbert, Howard E.
**South Holland**
Scott, Edward Aloysius
**Streator**
Harrison, Frank Joseph
Mohan, John J.
**Watseka**
Tungate, James Lester
**Waukegan**
Bairstow, Richard Raymond
Gurewitz, Thomas Mark
**West Frankfort**
Riva, David Michael
**Wheaton**
Malm, John Joseph
**Wheeling**
Kulinsky, Lois
**Wilmette**
Griffith, James D.
**Winnetka**
Ryan, Robert Jeffers
**Wonder Lake**
McNamara, Joseph Burk
**Woodhull**
Ciaccio, Karin McLaughlin
**Woodstock**
Kell, Vette Eugene

## INDIANA

**Anderson**
Woodruff, Randall Lee
**Bloomington**
Applegate, Karl Edwin
**Brazil**
Deal, James Edward
**Crawfordsville**
Donaldson, Steven Bryan
**Danville**
Baldwin, Jeffrey Kenton
**Decatur**
Sheets, Thomas Wade
**Dyer**
DeGuilio, Jon E.
**Elkhart**
Whitmer, J. A.
**Evansville**
Barber, Steven Thomas
Knight, Jeffrey Lin
**Fowler**
Kepner, Rex William
Weist, William Bernard
Woods, Dennis Lynn
**Franklin**
Gholston, Robert M.
**Hammond**
Kohl, Jacquelyn Marie
**Hobart**
Longer, William John
**Indianapolis**
Grinnan, Gloria Katherine
Kautzman, John Fredrick
Reuben, Lawrence Mark
Rothbaum, Sandra Lazarus
Sherman, Stephen Michael
Watson, Richard Prather
Woods, Joseph Reid
**Jeffersonville**
Harris, Ronald Dean
**La Porte**
Lewis, Daniel Edwin
**Merrillville**
Irak, Joseph S.
**New Castle**
Schiesswohl, Cynthia Rae Schlegel
**Rushville**
Morning, Leigh Suzanne
**Shelbyville**
Harrold, Dennis Edward
Lisher, James Richard
**South Bend**
Hammerschmidt, Bruce C.
Sopko, Thomas Clement
**Terre Haute**
Bitzegaio, Harold James
Kesler, John A.
**Warsaw**
Rigdon, Jay Alden
Walmer, James L.

## IOWA

**Burlington**
Hoth, Steven Sergey
**Cedar Rapids**
Richards, Allan Max
**Charles City**
Troge, Ann Marie
**Davenport**
Halligan, Kevin Leo
Phelps, Robert J.
**Dayton**
Ferguson, V. Keith
**Des Moines**
Baybayan, Ronald Alan
Schadle, William James
**Iowa City**
Bergan, Marsha Ann
Hayek, John William
**Marshalltown**
Geffe, Kent Lyndon
Lorenz, William Joseph
**Mason City**
Winston, Harold Ronald
**Mount Pleasant**
Vance, Michael Charles
**Vinton**
Mossman, Mark E.
**Wapello**
Hicklin, Edwin Anderson

## KANSAS

**Arkansas City**
Templar, Ted Mac
**Cottonwood Falls**
North, William T.
**Garden City**
Loyd, Ward Eugene
**Hays**
Toepfer, Thomas Lyle
**Hugoton**
Nordling, Bernard Erick
**Hutchinson**
Chalfant, William Young
**Iola**
Toland, John Robert
**Lawrence**
Brown, David James
Smith, Glee Sidney, Jr.
**Lincoln**
Marshall, Susan
**Lyons**
Hodgson, Arthur Clay
**Olathe**
Branham, Melanie J.
**Overland Park**
Bunn, G. Peter, III
Glasser, Philip Russell
Knopp, Timothy John
**Paola**
Arnett, Debra Jean
**Salina**
Owens, William Dean
**Shawnee Mission**
Sparks, Billy Schley
**Syracuse**
Gale, Robert Harrison, Jr.
**Topeka**
Aadalen, David Kevin
Schultz, Richard Allen
Snyder, Brock Robert
**Wichita**
Liebau, Judd Alan
Robinson, G. Craig

## KENTUCKY

**Albany**
Cross, David Martin
**Covington**
Crout, Daniel Wesley
**Danville**
Clay, James Franklin
**Florence**
Frohlich, Anthony William
**Frankfort**
Chadwick, Robert
**Glasgow**
Gardner, Woodford Lloyd, Jr.
**Grayson**
Caummisar, Robert Lee
**Lebanon**
Higdon, Frederick Alonzo
**Lexington**
Hickey, John King
Rich, William Hagood Bellinger
**Louisa**
Carter, Robert Philip, Sr.
**Louisville**
Osterhage, Lawrence Edward
Pettyjohn, Shirley Ellis
**New Castle**
Brammell, William Hartman
**Newport**
Halloran, Brian Paul
**Owensboro**
Miller, James Monroe
**Paris**
Budden, Harry Edward, Jr.
**Pikeville**
Johnson, Lon M., Jr.
**Pineville**
Lawson, Susan Coleman
**Richmond**
Martin, James Neal
**Scottsville**
Secrest, James Seaton, Sr.
**Shelbyville**
Igleheart, Ted Lewis
**Shepherdsville**
Flaherty, Robert Patrick
Givhan, Thomas Bartram
**Somerset**
Harlan, Jane Ann
Prather, John Gideon, Jr.

## LOUISIANA

**Baton Rouge**
Gibbs, Deborah P.
Moreno, Richard Dale
**Hessmer**
Jeansonne, Mark Anthony

**Lafayette**
Boustany, Alfred Frem
**Lake Charles**
McHale, Robert Michael
Norman, Rick Joseph
**Metairie**
Miles, Terri
**New Orleans**
Fields, Timmy Lee
Gelpi, C. James (Jim Gelpi)
Hammond, Peirce Aldridge, II
Harris, Thorne D., III
Lowe, Robert Charles
Perry, Brian Drew, Sr.
Rosen, William Warren
**Shreveport**
Hetherwick, Gilbert Lewis
**Slidell**
Singletary, Alvin D.
**Thibodaux**
Clement, Leslie Joseph, Jr.

### MAINE

**Bangor**
Gilbert, Charles E., III
**Bass Harbor**
Ervin, Spencer
**Brunswick**
Lamothe, Arthur J.
**Farmington**
Holman, Joseph Frederick
**Hallowell**
Smith, Jeffrey Allen
**Portland**
Rundlett, Ellsworth Turner, III
**S Portland**
Berry, Henry Newhall, III
**Sanford**
Nadeau, Robert Maurice Auclair
**Waterville**
Sandy, Robert Edward, Jr.

### MARYLAND

**Annapolis**
Lillard, John Franklin, III
**Baltimore**
Baker, William Parr
Cohen, Hyman K.
Ferro, Elizabeth Krams
Kandel, Nelson Robert
Kandel, Peter Thomas
Powell, Roger Norman
**Bethesda**
Brown, Thomas Philip, III
Morgan, Jo Valentine, Jr.
Moss, Stephen Edward
Nelson, William Eugene
Sheble, Walter Franklin
**Brookeville**
Johns, Warren LeRoi
**Chestertown**
Mowell, George Mitchell
**Columbia**
Gelfman, Richard David
**Crofton**
Doherty, Daniel Joseph, III
**Ellicott City**
Henry, Edwin Maurice, Jr.
**Frederick**
Sica, John
**Glen Burnie**
Smith, John Stanley
**Hagerstown**
Berkson, Jacob Benjamin
**Hanover**
Carter, Candy Lorraine
**Kensington**
Mathias, Joseph Marshall
**Laurel**
Barr, June Hatton
**Laytonsville**
McDowell, Donna Schultz
**North Potomac**
Brandsdorfer, Mark Michael
**Ocean City**
Grech, Christopher Alan
**Owings Mills**
Silverman, Steven D.
**Rockville**
Avery, Bruce Edward
Jaffe, Matthew Ely
Thompson, James Lee
**Silver Spring**
Viertel, George Joseph
**Sykesville**
Bartolini, Daniel John
**Taneytown**
Shoemaker, Daniel W.
**Wheaton**
Kirchman, Eric Hans

### MASSACHUSETTS

**Amherst**
Howland, Richard Moulton
**Ashfield**
Pepyne, Edward Walter
**Boston**
Berman, Martin Samuel
Bozza, Mario
Fahy, Joseph Thomas
Gargiulo, Andrea W.
Graham, John Joseph
Lyons, Nance
McAuliffe, Rosemary
Nardone, Glenn A.
Nugent, Alfred Emanuel
Perera, Lawrence Thacher
Politi, Stephen Michael
Redlich, Marc
Weaver, Paul David
**Bradford**
Cox, William Donald, Jr.
**Brookline**
Dow, Joseph Sheffield
Houlihan, F(rancis) Robert, Jr.
Lipson, Roger Russell
**Buckland**
Shauger, Susan Joyce
**Burlington**
Feeley, Kelly A.
**Cambridge**
Ta, Tai Van
**Chestnut Hill**
Lowinger, Lazar
**Everett**
Root, Carole A.Z.
**Fitchburg**
DiPace, Steven B.
**Framingham**
Heng, Gerald C. W.
**Lowell**
Curtis, James Theodore
**Ludlow**
Mondry, Paul Michael
**Manchester**
Rumpf, Pierre Cameron
**Marblehead**
Lundregan, William Joseph
**Milford**
Murray, Brian William
**New Bedford**
Hurwitz, Barrett Alan
Mathieu, Thomas Joseph
**Newburyport**
Murphy, Lawrence John
**Newton**
Stern, Edward Mayer
**Norwood**
Salvatore, David Anthony
**Orleans**
Chaplin, Ansel Burt
**Pittsfield**
Doyle, Anthony Peter
**Quincy**
Motejunas, Gerald William
**Rockland**
Auton, Linda May Eisenschmidt
**Salem**
Marks, Scott Charles
Sellers, Jill Suzanne
**Springfield**
Maidman, Stephen Paul
**West Springfield**
Ely, John P.
**Westfield**
Angell, James Edward

### MICHIGAN

**Ada**
Johnson, Byron John
**Ann Arbor**
Ellmann, William Marshall
McDaniel, Timothy Ellis
**Battle Creek**
Fisher, James A.
**Birmingham**
Delin, Sylvia Kaufman
**Burton**
Breczinski, Michael Joseph
**Detroit**
Johnson, Cynthia L(e) M(ae)
Mengel, Christopher Emile
**Eaton Rapids**
Nolan, Lawrence Patrick
**Farmington Hills**
Reagle, Jack Evan
**Fenton**
Hildner, Phillips Brooks, II
**Flint**
Powers, Edward Herbert
**Grand Haven**
Johnson, Todd Alan
**Grosse Pointe**
Johnson, Edward Carl
**Harbor Springs**
Turner, Lester Nathan
**Holland**
Murphy, Max Ray
**Ishpeming**
Andriacchi, Dominic Francis
**Jackson**
Barton, Bruce Andrew
Jacobs, Wendell Early, Jr.
**Muskegon**
Houghtaling, Chris Allen
**Plymouth**
Koroi, Mark Michael
**Rapid City**
Ring, Ronald Herman
**Redford**
Philippart, Howard Louis, Jr.
**Rochester Hls**
Diehl, Richard Paul
**Romeo**
Clark, Mark Lee
**Suttons Bay**
Johnson, Darryl Todd
**Traverse City**
Smith, Louis Adrian
**Troy**
Berman, Leonard Keith
Coe, Richard Thomas
Schroeder, Douglas Jay
**Ypsilanti**
Barr, John Monte

### MINNESOTA

**Bemidji**
Kief, Paul Allan
Woodke, Robert Allen
**Chanhassen**
Peterson, Steven A.
**Cottage Grove**
O'Gorman, Patricia Ann
**Eagan**
Peotter, Sara Jo
**Fergus Falls**
Bigwood, Robert William
**Grand Rapids**
Licke, Wallace John
**Hallock**
Malm, Roger Charles
**Kenyon**
Peterson, Franklin Delano
**Minneapolis**
Kempf, Douglas Paul
Martinson, Bradley James
**Minnetonka**
Brennan, Sidney L.
Freeman, Gerald Russell
**Pine River**
Swanson, Bradley Dean
**Rochester**
Baker, Gail Dyer
Murakami, Steven Kiyoshi
Seeger, Ronald L.
**Saint Paul**
Jacobs, Stephen Louis
Trojack, John Edward
**Shoreview**
Bertelsen, Michael William
**Willmar**
Hulstrand, George Eugene
**Winthrop**
Engwall, Gregory Bond
**Woodbury**
Baumann, Craig William

### MISSISSIPPI

**Bay Saint Louis**
Bernstein, Joseph
**Bay Springs**
Shoemaker, Bobby Lynn
**Clarksdale**
Twiford, H. Hunter, III
**Columbus**
Geeslin, Gary Lloyd
Sanders, David Lawrence
**Gloster**
Davis, Cynthia D'Ascenzo
**Gulfport**
Pate, William August
**Jackson**
Chadwick, Vernon Henry
Pyle, Luther Arnold
**Kosciusko**
Pickle, L. Scott
**Mc Comb**
Starrett, Keith
**Pascagoula**
Roberts, David Ambrose
**Raymond**
Moss, Jack Gibson
**Ridgeland**
Giuffrida, Noel Peter
**Starkville**
Yoste, Charles Todd
**Tupelo**
Moffett, T(errill) K(ay)

### MISSOURI

**Bethany**
Moulthrop, Roscoe Emmett
**Cape Girardeau**
McManaman, Kenneth Charles
**Chesterfield**
Coffin, Richard Keith
**Columbia**
Parrigin, Elizabeth Ellington
**Cuba**
Lange, C. William
**Hannibal**
Welch, Joseph Daniel
**Independence**
Terry, Jack Chatterson
Watkins, Susan Gail
**Joplin**
Guillory, Jeffery Michael
**Kansas City**
Carter, J. Denise
Laurans, Jonathan Louis
O'Neill, Thomas Tyrone
White, F(loyd) Al
Ziegenhorn, Eric Howard
**Keytesville**
Wheeler, James Julian
**Lees Summit**
Walsh, Thomas Joseph
**Lexington**
Giorza, John C.
**Saint Ann**
Johnson, Harold Gene
**Saint Charles**
Dorsey, Richard P., III
**Saint Louis**
Barken, Bernard Allen
Beach, Douglas Ryder
Blanke, Richard Brian
Bloom, Allen Jerry
DeWoskin, Alan Ellis
Duesenberg, Richard William
Neill, Joseph Vincent
Shalowitz, Howard A.
Switzer, Frederick Michael, III
**Salem**
Mitchell, Austin L.
**Sedalia**
Rice, James Briggs, Jr.
**Springfield**
Hedrick, Peggy Shepherd
**Union**
Schroeder, Matthew A.

### MONTANA

**Billings**
Cromley, Brent Reed
Schleusner, Clifford Edward
**Bozeman**
Nelson, Steven Dwayne
**Great Falls**
Larsen, Dirk Herbert
**Kalispell**
Leatzow, Millicent Anne (Penny Leatzow)
**Missoula**
Anderson, Clare Eberhart

### NEBRASKA

**Aurora**
Whitney, Charles Leroy
**Falls City**
Halbert, Richard Lewis
**Fremont**
Line, William Gunderson
**Holdrege**
Klein, Michael Clarence
**Humboldt**
Fankhauser, Allen
**Lincoln**
Brown, Mark Charles
Crosby, Robert Berkey
McClain, Richard Douglas
O'Brien, Patrick Thomas
**Omaha**
Buzzello, Eileen Reilly
Gutowski, Michael Francis
**Valentine**
O'Kief, W. Gerald
**York**
Stephens, Bruce Edward

### NEVADA

**Las Vegas**
Brown, Joseph Wentling
Goldberg, Aubrey
**Reno**
Davenport, Brian Lynn

### NEW HAMPSHIRE

**Concord**
Johnson, Robert Veiling, II
**Lebanon**
Trunzo, Thomas Harold, Jr.
**Manchester**
Bruzga, Paul Wheeler
Nixon, David L.
**Nashua**
Jette, Ernest Arthur
**Newport**
Budnitz, Arron Edward
Shklar, Michael Charles
Work, Michael Jay
**North Conway**
Rader, Philip Spendelow
**Portsmouth**
Lefebvre, Albert Paul Conrad
McGee, John Paul, Jr.
Tober, Stephen Lloyd
**Salem**
Notaris, Mary
**Seabrook**
Ganz, Mary Keohan
**Woodsville**
Bruno, Kevin Robert

### NEW JERSEY

**Bloomfield**
Lordi, Katherine Mary
**Boonton**
Bucco, Anthony Mark
Walzer, James Harvey
**Brick**
Tivenan, Charles Patrick
**Camden**
Lario, Frank M., Jr.
**Cedar Grove**
Stickel, Frederick George, III
**Cherry Hill**
Shapiro, Richard Allen
**Clark**
Barr, Jon-Henry
**Cliffside Park**
Diktas, Christos James
**Clifton**
Pincus, Sheldon Howard
Sudol, Walter Edward
**East Brunswick**
Tharney, Laura Christine
**Edison**
Fink, Edward Murray
**Elmwood Park**
Mangano, Louis
**Freehold**
Scenna, Michele Carton
**Gibbsboro**
Ferreri, Vito Richard
**Glen Rock**
Markey, Brian Michael
**Hackensack**
Bar-Nadav, Meiron
Fede, Andrew Thomas
Gallucci, Michael A.
Goldsamt, Bonnie Blume
**Haddon Heights**
D'Alfonso, Mario Joseph
**Haddonfield**
Cohen, Diane Berkowitz
**Hammonton**
Tarver, Margaret Leggett
**Highland Park**
Michaels, Jennifer Alman
**Hillsdale**
Hodinar, Michael
**Holmdel**
Monteiro, Ricardo J.
**Jersey City**
D'Alessandro, Daniel Anthony
Signorile, Vincent Anthony
Talafous, Joseph John, Sr.
**Kendall Park**
Fisch, Joseph
**Liberty Corner**
Apruzzese, Vincent John
**Linden**
Littman, David Bernard
**Little Egg Harbor Township**
Rumpf, Brian E.
**Manahawkin**
Privetera, Lora Marie
**Metuchen**
Eugene, John
**Morristown**
Geppert, John Gustave
Samay, Z. Lance
**Mount Laurel**
Schmoll, Harry F., Jr.
**Neptune**
Ronan, James Michael, Jr.
**Oakland**
Goldenberg, Eva J.
**Parsippany**
Doherty, Robert Christopher
**Paulsboro**
Fichera, Lewis Carmen
**Pilesgrove Township**
Crouse, Farrell R.
**Piscataway**
Wilson, Abraham
**Princeton**
Bergman, Edward Jonathan
**Ridgewood**
Boardman, Michael Neil
Trocano, Russell Peter
**River Vale**
Lotito, Joseph Daniel
**Roseland**
Smith, Dennis Jay
**Salem**
Petrin, Helen Fite
**Sea Girt**
Crispi, Michele Marie
**Secaucus**
Castano, Gregory Joseph
Holt, Michael Bartholomew
**Somerset**
Green, Jeffrey C.
**South Plainfield**
Santoro, Frank Anthony
Scialabba, Damian Angelo
**Spring Lake**
Anderson, James Francis
Pandolfe, John Thomas, Jr.
**Springfield**
Katz, Jeffrey Harvey
**Stone Harbor**
Taylor, Robert Lee
**Succasunna**
Correale, Robert D.
**Union**
Rosenberg, A. Irving
**Vauxhall**
Ross, Mark Samuel
**Verona**
Slattery, Jill Sheridan
**Warren**
Rana, Harminderpal Singh
**West Orange**
Cuozzi, William F., Jr.
**Woodbury**
Primas, Emmett E., Jr.
**Woodbury Heights**
Heim, Thomas George
**Woodcliff Lake**
Getler, Janine A.
**Woodcliff Lk**
Pollak, Cathy Jane
**Wyckoff**
Spizziri, John Anthony

### NEW MEXICO

**Albuquerque**
Addis, Richard Barton
Duarte, Leroy Wilson
Lopez, Floyd William
Shaw, Mark Howard
**Carlsbad**
Byers, Matthew T(odd)
**Clovis**
Skarda, Lynell Griffith
**Deming**
Turner, Robert F.
**Farmington**
Moeller, Floyd Douglas
**Rio Rancho**
Perls, N. Lynn
**Roswell**
Bassett, John Walden, Jr.
**Santa Fe**
Coffield, Conrad Eugene
Hallmark, Bruce Cullen, Jr.

### NEW YORK

**Albany**
Bramley, Bruce C.
Devine, Eugene Peter
Pozner, Louis-Jack
**Amherst**
Diakos, Maria Louise
Jones, E. Thomas
Murray, William Michael
Vinal, Jeanne Marie
**Auburn**
Gunger, Richard William
**Batavia**
Saleh, David John
**Bellmore**
Sachs, Eric
**Bethpage**
Sanna, Richard Jeffrey
**Binghamton**
Beck, Stephanie G.
**Bronx**
Glynn, James Martin
Lynch, Thom
**Bronxville**
Fuller, David Otis, Jr.

Wiacek, Bruce Edward
**Brooklyn**
Erlitz, Stephen W.
Lewis, Felice Flanery
Nuccio, Paul Vincent
**Buffalo**
Freedman, Maryann Saccomando
Nichols, F(rederick) Harris
Ritchie, Stafford Duff, II
Vinal, Gregory Michael
**Caledonia**
Litteer, Harold Hunter, Jr.
**Clarence**
Dec, Francis P.
**Commack**
Somer, Stanley Jerome
**Corning**
Becraft, Charles D., Jr.
**Dansville**
Vogel, John Walter
**Delmar**
Cavanaugh, John Joseph, Jr.
Galvin, Madeline Sheila
**Douglaston**
Salvo, Joseph Aldo
**Elma**
Markello, Jeffrey Philip
**Elmhurst**
Lapinski, Alexander J.
**Floral Park**
Cardalena, Peter Paul, Jr.
**Flushing**
Deerson, Adele Shapiro
**Garden City**
Ehrlich, Jerome Harry
Kreger-Grella, Cheryl Leslie
Tucker, William P.
**Glens Falls**
Caffry, John W.
**Gouverneur**
Heller, Sanders D.
Leader, Robert John
**Great Neck**
Gilbert, Theodore
Wershals, Paul L.
**Groton**
Henry, James Richard
**Guilderland**
Sills, Nancy Mintz
Werlin-Gorenstein, Barbara Carol
**Hamburg**
Hargesheimer, Elbert, III
**Harrison**
Hertz, Natalie Zucker
**Hauppauge**
Knispel, Howard Edward
**Hawthorne**
Medina, Luis Anibal
**Hempstead**
Raab, Ira Jerry
**Hicksville**
Snowe, Alan Martin
**Highland**
Murphy, Sean
**Houghton**
Brautigam, David Clyde
**Hudson**
Thiemann, Kevin Barry
**Huntington**
German, June Resnick
Levitan, Katherine D.
Munson, Nancy Kay
**Ithaca**
Mulvey, Richard Ignatius
**Jamaica**
Biehl, Kathy Anne
Gonzalez-Perez, Ramon Horacio
**Jamestown**
DeAngelo, Charles Salvatore
**Keeseville**
Turetsky, Aaron
**Kew Gardens**
Reichel, Aaron Israel
Ross, Robert A.
Schechter, Donald Robert
**Le Roy**
Whiting, Reid A.
**Lockport**
Brodsky, Felice Adrienne
Penney, Charles Rand
**Long Beach**
Levine, Samuel Milton
**Mahopac**
Sequeira, Manuel Alexandre, Jr.
**Manhasset**
Taylor, Donald Adams
**Melville**
Carroll, Diane C.
**Middletown**
Kossar, Ronald Steven
**Mineola**
Gulotta, Frank Andrew, Jr.
Jones, Lawrence Tunnicliffe
Kral, William George
Levine, David I.
Monaghan, Peter Gerard
Stein, Rita
Vargas, Diana Monica
**Mount Vernon**
Fischbach, Robert
**New Hartford**
McKennan, John T.
**New Rochelle**
DiMarco, Frank Paul
Staple, Irwin
**New York**
Adams, Daniel Nelson
Aloe, Paul Hubschman
Annenberg, Norman
Bearak, Corey B(ecker)
Beinin, William J.
Berland, Sanford Neil
Beshar, Robert Peter
Bianco, S. Anthony
Birn, Harold M.
Boddie, Reginald Alonzo
Brandrup, Douglas Warren
Censor, Martin A.
Cooper, Stephanie R.
Costikyan, Edward N.
Feder, Saul E.
Felder, Raoul Lionel
Feldkamp, John Calvin
Friedman, Elaine Florence
Glanstein, Eleanor Elovich
Gluck, Marshall J.
Goldey, Mark H.
Green, Eric Howard
Greenhill, Jonathan Seth
Grossman, Stacy Jill
Gulino, Frank
Hart, Joseph Thomas Campbell
Haythe, Thomas Madison
Hollyer, A(rthur) Rene
Javier, Ramon Emilio
Kaplan, Lawrence I.
Katsos, Barbara Helene
Kirberger, Elizabeth
Klein, Martin I.
Koerner, Gregory O.
Lande, David Steven
Landron, Michel John
Lane, Arthur Alan
Liss, Norman
Lowenbraun, Solomon M.
Marks, Theodore Lee
Middendorf, Henry Stump, Jr.
Minsky, Bruce William
Morganstern, Gerald H.
Neff, Michael Alan
Quinn, Timothy Charles, Jr.
Sallay, Tibor
Salvan, Sherwood Allen
Sarzin, Evan
Sastow, Gary Saul
Seligman, Frederick
Strougo, Robert Isaac
Thompson, Katherine Genevieve
Tormey, John Joseph, III
Wexelbaum, Michael
Wimpfheimer, Michael Clark
Wu, Robin Chi Ching
Wyckoff, E. Lisk, Jr.
**Niagara Falls**
Hanesian, Shavasp
**North Syracuse**
Wallace, John Paul
**Northport**
Valente, Douglas
**Oneida**
Campanie, Samuel John
**Orchard Park**
Sullivan, Mortimer Allen, Jr.
**Oyster Bay**
Griffin, James Alfred
**Patchogue**
Feuer, Paul Robert
**Pelham**
Hanrahan, Michael G.
**Perry**
Kelly, Michael Joseph
**Port Chester**
Levin, Jeffrey L.
**Potsdam**
Ballan, Steven G.
**Poughkeepsie**
Braswell, Bruce Wayne
Brenner, Marshall Leib
Dietz, Robert Barron
Haven, Milton M.
Wallace, Herbert Norman
**Riverhead**
Kelley, Christopher Donald
Liccione, Maureen T.
**Rochester**
Argento, Victoria M(arie)
Fero, Dean John
Hinman, James Stuart
Massare, Edward John
Palermo, Anthony Robert
Rosner, Leonard Allen
Servis, William George
**Rockville Centre**
Lerner, Steven Paul
**Rome**
Griffith, Emlyn Irving
**Ronkonkoma**
Moss, Francine Hope
**Roslyn Heights**
Dieguez, Richard Peter
Tannenbaum, Richard Neil
**S Richmond Hl**
Goldsmith, Michael Lawrence
**Sands Point**
Busner, Philip H.
**Scarsdale**
Salwen, Joan C.
**Schoharie**
Duncombe, Raynor Bailey
**Scottsville**
Williams, Henry Ward, Jr.
**Sea Cliff**
McGill, Gilbert William
**Seagate**
Levitt, Sidney Bernard
**Smithtown**
Dowis, Lenore
**South Ozone Park**
Narain, Camy Tribeni
**South Richmond Hill**
Scheich, John F.
**Southampton**
Platt, Harold Kirby
**Staten Island**
Ferranti, Thomas, Jr.
Miller, Claire Cody
**Stephentown**
Zwack, Henry Francis
**Syracuse**
Bidwell, Mark Edward
Butler, John Edward
Dwyer, James Francis
Engel, Richard Lee
Kram, Richard Corey
Mathewson, George Atterbury
Paquette, Steven A.
Pinsky, Bradley M.
Rivette, Francis Robert
**Tupper Lake**
Hayes, Jeremiah Michael
Johnson, David Wesley
**Utica**
Brennan, John Joseph
**Walden**
Gubits, David Barry
**Wappingers Falls**
Haynes, Paul R.
**Waterford**
Glavin, A. Rita Chandellier (Mrs. James Henry Glavin, III)
Glavin, James Henry, III
**Watertown**
Marsh, Leonard Roy
**White Plains**
Levine, Steven Jon
**Yonkers**
Rubeo, Stephen Vincent

## NORTH CAROLINA

**Asheville**
Cogburn, Max Oliver
**Burnsville**
Howell, Dennis Lee
**Chapel Hill**
Crassweller, Robert Doell
**Charlotte**
Barbery, Paul Saunders
Bragg, Ellis Meredith, Jr.
Buckley, Charles Robinson, III
Harris, Hugh Stanley, Jr.
Harris, Richard Foster, III
Li, Benjamin Min
Vinroot, Richard Allen
**Gastonia**
Garland, James Boyce
**Hickory**
Farthing, Edwin Glenn
**Hillsborough**
Cheshire, Lucius McGehee
**Kannapolis**
Griggs, Farrar O'Neal
**Pittsboro**
Riggsbee, Lunday Adams
**Raleigh**
Kurz, Mary Elizabeth
**Roanoke Rapids**
Crew, William Lunsford
**Rowland**
Price, Robert Ernest
**Salisbury**
Porter, J. Andrew
**Wilmington**
Nunalee, Mary Margaret McEachern

## NORTH DAKOTA

**Fargo**
Solberg, Wayne O.
**Grand Forks**
Arnason, Joel Frederick
Widdel, John Earl, Jr.

## OHIO

**Akron**
Jalbert, Michael Joseph
Nolfi, Edward Anthony
**Barnesville**
Jefferis, Paul Bruce
**Batavia**
Rosenhoffer, Chris
**Bellevue**
Smith, Ronald R.
**Brecksville**
McBride, Judith Bliss
**Bucyrus**
Neff, Robert Clark, Sr.
Skropits, Amy Elizabeth
**Carrollton**
Childers, John Charles
**Chillicothe**
Boulger, William Charles
**Cincinnati**
Broderick, Dennis John
Cutler, Nancy Jane
Fingerman, Albert R.
Hoffheimer, Daniel Joseph
Hust, Bruce Kevin
Schwab, Nelson, Jr.
Sims, Victor Dwayne
Tranter, Terence Michael
Vogel, Cedric Wakelee
**Cleveland**
Boukis, Kenneth
Boyko, Christopher Allan
Chandler, Everett Alfred
Currivan, John Daniel
Goldfarb, Bernard Sanford
LaFond, Thomas Joseph
Perella, Marie Louise
Sanislo, Paul Steve
Schneider, David Miller
Zamore, Joseph David
**Columbus**
Casey, John Frederick
Cline, Richard Allen
Drexel, Ray Phillips
Matan, Eugene Louis
Wonnell, Harold Edward
**Dayton**
Davis, G(iles) Jack
Holz, Michael Harold
Mues, Robert Leighton
**Dublin**
Blaugrund, David Scott
Tenuta, Luigia
**Eaton**
Bennett, Gray Weston
**Findlay**
Kostyo, John Francis
Rakestraw, Gregory Allen
**Howard**
Lee, William Johnson
**Jefferson**
Geary, Michael Philip
**Kent**
Nome, William Andreas
**Leetonia**
Shelar, Richard Clyde
**Lima**
Jacobs, Ann Elizabeth
**Logan**
Kernen, Will
**London**
Rolfes, James Walter, Sr.
**Maumee**
Moore, Everett Daniel
**Mc Connelsville**
Dye, Ralph Dean, Jr.
**Medina**
Hanwell, Robert Michael
**Mount Vernon**
Rose, Kim Matthew
**Newark**
Untied, Wesley Kyle
**North Olmsted**
Dorchak, Thomas J.
**Painesville**
Cooper, Linda Dawn
**Pepper Pike**
Soukup, Christopher Earl
**Saint Marys**
Huber, William Evan
Kemp, Barrett George
**Salem**
Slack, Mark Robert
**Solon**
Fouts, Douglas Robert
**Springfield**
Martin, David MacCoy
Wilt, Valerie Rae
**Tiffin**
Huth, Lester Charles
**Toledo**
St. Clair, Donald David
Skotynsky, Walter John
**Troy**
Bazler, Frank Ellis
Utrecht, James David
**Upper Sandusky**
Fox, Mary Ellen
**Van Wert**
Gordon, Scott R.
**Warren**
Keating, Daniel Gerard
Swauger, Terry Allen
**Wellston**
Oths, Joseph Anthony
**Westerville**
Lancione, Bernard Gabe
**Wilmington**
Schutt, Walter Eugene
**Youngstown**
Ausnehmer, John Edward
Briach, George Gary
Jeren, John Anthony, Jr.

## OKLAHOMA

**Antlers**
Stamper, Joe Allen
**Bartlesville**
Thomas, Linda S.
**Cherokee**
Mitchell, Allan Edwin
**Edmond**
Loving, Susan Brimer
**Enid**
Martin, Michael Rex
**Idabel**
Shaw, Donald Ray
**Kingfisher**
Baker, Thomas Edward
Logsdon, Harold L.
**Mcalester**
Cornish, Richard Pool
**Oklahoma City**
Boston, William Clayton
Conner, Leslie Lynn, Jr.
Lindsey, Lori Dawn
Nesbitt, Charles Rudolph
Rinehart, William James
Ross, William Jarboe
White, Joe E., Jr.
**Poteau**
Sanders, Douglas Warner, Jr.
**Sayre**
Brooks, David Eugene
**Stroud**
Swanson, Robert Lee
**Tulsa**
Cowdery, Allen Craig
Kellough, William C.
Morley, Randal Dean
Unruh, Robert James
**Yukon**
Hixson, Wendell Mark

## OREGON

**Corvallis**
Heinrich, Steven Allan
**Eugene**
Cooper, Michael Lee
DuPriest, Douglas Millhollen
Hutchinson, Stephen Aloysius
**Florence**
Clark, David Lewis
**Grants Pass**
Baker, Lindi L.
**Mcminnville**
Thompson, Robert Samuel
**Medford**
Mansfield, William Amos
Thierolf, Richard Burton, Jr.
**Ontario**
Rader, Diane Cecile
**Oregon City**
McFarland, Carol Anne
**Portland**
Beshears, Charles Daniel, III
Jenks, George Milan
O'Brien, Kathleen

## PENNSYLVANIA

**Abington**
Budman, Alan David
**Allentown**
Feinberg, Gregg Michael
**Bangor**
Ceraul, David James
**Butler**
Pater, Michael John
Paulisick, Gerri Volchko
Stepanian, Leo McElligott
**Carlisle**
Baird, Lindsay Dare
**Clearfield**
Falvo, Mark Anthony
**Doylestown**
Bolla, William Joseph
Elliott, Richard Howard
Goldman, William Lewis, Sr.
**Du Bois**
Blakley, Benjamin Spencer, III
**Duncansville**
Kemps, Loreen Marie
**Enola**
Sheetz, Ralph Albert
**Erie**
Adair, Evan Edward
**Feasterville Trevose**
Osterhout, Richard Cadwallader
**Fort Washington**
Hess, Lawrence Eugene, Jr.
**Frackville**
Domalakes, Paul George
**Harrisburg**
Boswell, William Douglas
Kendall, Keith Edward
Maleski, Cynthia Maria
**Hatboro**
John, Robert McClintock
Nicholson, Bruce Allen
**Havertown**
Donohue, Robert John
**Hazleton**
Schiavo, Pasco Louis
**Hilltown**
Hetherington, John Joseph
**Holtwood**
Campbell, Paul Gary
**Jenkintown**
Robbins, Jack Winton
**Jersey Shore**
Flayhart, Martin Albert
**Johnstown**
Glosser, William Louis
**Kingston**
Meyer, Martin Jay
**Kng Of Prussa**
Noonan, Gregory Robert
**Lancaster**
Duroni, Charles Eugene
MacDonald, Richard Barry
Pyfer, John Frederick, Jr.
**Langhorne**
Lynch, James Edward
**Lumberville**
McGuckin, Ronald V.
**Mc Keesport**
Kessler, Steven Fisher
**Meadville**
Barrett, Bruce Alan
**Monongahela**
Black, Blane Alan
**Morrisville**
Glosser, Harry John, Jr.
**Narberth**
Mezvinsky, Edward M.
**New Castle**
Mangino, Matthew Thomas
**Newtown**
Godwin, Robert Anthony
**Philadelphia**
Cohen, David Louis
Fine, Stephanie Beth
Hoffman, Alan Jay
O'Brien, William Jerome, II
Wolf, Bruce
**Pittsburgh**
Aronson, Mark Berne
Bogut, John Carl, Jr.
Litman, Roslyn Margolis
Lucas, Robert Mark
McKee, Ralph Dyer, Jr.
McLaughlin, John Sherman
Morgan, John Joseph, Jr.
Purcupile, John Stephen
Pushinsky, Jon
Terra, Sharon Ecker
Trower, William Kevin
Zittrain, Lester Eugene
**Pottsville**
Jones, Joseph Hayward
**Punxsutawney**
Long, Jesse Paul
**Reading**
Scianna, Russell William
**Richboro**
Van Blunk, Henry Edward
**Rydal**
Friedman, Ralph David
**Saint Marys**
Daghir, George Nejm
**Scranton**
Wilson, Charles Frank
**Trevose**
Fanning, Eleanor
McEvilly, James Patrick, Jr.
**Uniontown**
Roskovensky, Vincent Joseph, II
**Wallingford**
DePaul, Anthony Kenneth

**Washington**
Key, Susan Mondik
**Wayne**
Spiess, F. Harry, Jr.
**Waynesboro**
Maxwell, LeRoy Stevenson
**Waynesburg**
Webb, Jane Marie
**Wexford**
Fall, Robert J.
**Wilkes Barre**
Dalessandro, Sherry Ann
**Yardley**
Lieberson, Jay B.
**York**
Hoffmeyer, William Frederick

### RHODE ISLAND

**Coventry**
Szarek, Milton Louis
**Cranston**
Coletti, John Anthony
**Newport**
McConnell, David Kelso
**Pawtucket**
Kranseler, Lawrence Michael
**Providence**
Demopulos, Harold William
Esposito, Dennis Harry
Gianfrancesco, Anthony Joseph
Long, Nicholas Trott
McElroy, Michael Robert
Tammelleo, A. David
**Warwick**
McGair, Joseph J.
**West Warwick**
Pollock, Bruce Gerald

### SOUTH CAROLINA

**Aiken**
Pearce, Richard Lee
**Camden**
Furman, Hezekiah Wyndol Carroll
Jacobs, Rolly Warren
**Charleston**
Bernstein, Robert Alan
Clement, Robert Lebby, Jr.
Gailliard, Robert Lee
Garrett, Gordon Henderson
**Columbia**
Hancock, Harriet Daniels
**Gaffney**
Rhoden, William Gary
**Georgetown**
Goude, Charles Reuben
**Greenville**
Talley, Michael Frank
**Hartsville**
DeLoach, Harris E(ugene), Jr.
**Hilton Head Island**
Scarminach, Charles Anthony
**Kingstree**
McFadden, Helen Tyler
**Newberry**
Senn, Lisa Robinson
**Seneca**
Sires, Norman Gruber, Jr.
**Summerville**
Prettyman, Howard Cross, Jr.
**Walterboro**
Boensch, Arthur Cranwell

### SOUTH DAKOTA

**Parker**
Zimmer, John Herman

### TENNESSEE

**Athens**
Guinn, Charles Clifford, Jr.
**Bristol**
Hillman, Shelton B., Jr.
Massengill, Myers Newton
Slaughter, Frank L., Jr.
**Chattanooga**
Ragan, Charles Oliver, Jr.
Vital, Patricia Best
**Church Hill**
Frazier, Steven Carl
**Clarksville**
Smith, Gregory Dale
**Dresden**
Herron, Roy Brasfield
**Etowah**
Parker, Eugene LeRoy, III
**Jackson**
Latimer, Timothy B.
Womack, Charles Raymond
**Kingsport**
Mason, Donald F., Jr.
**Knoxville**
Conrad, Frederick Larue, Jr.
Giordano, Lawrence Francis
Routh, John William
**Lawrenceburg**
Plant, Paul Brunson
**Memphis**
Allen, Newton Perkins
Blanton, Darrell Drew
David, Monroe Steven
Jackson, Thomas Francis, III
Lait, Hayden David
Manire, James McDonnell
McDaniel, Mark Steven
Moore, Dwight Terry
Rutledge, Roger Keith
**Nashville**
Cantrell, Luther E., Jr.
Fraley, Mark Thomas
Torrey, Claudia Olivia
**Newport**
Bell, John Alton
**Rogersville**
Skelton, Mark Albert
**South Pittsburg**
Ables, Charles Robert
**Springfield**
Richter, Lisa Sherrill
**Trenton**
Harrell, Limmie Lee, Jr.

### TEXAS

**Addison**
Martens, Dan E.
**Arlington**
Campbell, William Lee
**Austin**
Drolla, John Casper Dodt, Jr.
Hale, Louis Dewitt
Kerr, Stanley Munger
Weddington, Sarah Ragle
**Bellaire**
Soffar, William Douglas
**Boerne**
Reppeto, William M., III
**Borger**
Pace, Rosa White
**Brownsville**
Fleming, Tommy Wayne
**Brownwood**
Bell, William Woodward
**Canton**
Sanders, Bobby Lee
**Cleveland**
Campbell, Selaura Joy
**College Station**
Borman, Channa Erin
**Corpus Christi**
Alberts, Harold
Herin, David V.
**Dallas**
Ellsworth-Ungerman, Betty Marie
Levin, Hervey Phillip
Mueller, Mark Christopher
Parker, James Francis
Purnell, Charles Giles
Ringle, Brett Adelbert
Sloman, Marvin Sherk
**El Paso**
Broaddus, John Morgan, III
Villalobos, Raul
**Farmersville**
Seward, Richard Bevin
**Fort Worth**
Emerson, Douglas Theodore
Fischel, Robert Oscar
Mullanax, Milton Greg
Paddock, Michael Buckley
Phillips, Robert James, Jr.
**Garland**
Irby, Holt
**Georgetown**
Bryce, William Delf
**Greenville**
Morris, Leah Curtis
**Hico**
Peterson, Martin Lee
**Houston**
Bradie, Peter Richard
Caddy, Michael Douglas
Callegari, William A., Jr.
Cooper, Thomas Randolph
Cornelius, James Russell
Eckman, David Walter
Fabio, Thea Marie
Forbes, Arthur Lee, III
Gutheinz, Joseph Richard
Pesikoff, Bette Schein
Plaeger, Frederick Joseph, II
Shead, William C.
Williams, Percy Don
**Killeen**
Kleff, Pierre Augustine, Jr.
**Lampasas**
Harvey, Leigh Kathryn
**Lubbock**
Teel, Robert E.
**Lufkin**
Garrison, Pitser Hardeman
**Midland**
Frost, Wayne N.
**Missouri City**
Hodges, Jot Holiver, Jr.
**Odessa**
Corzine, Darrell W.
**Pearland**
Bittick, Peggy Sue
**Pecos**
Weinacht, John William
**Richardson**
Jeffreys, Albert Leonidas
**Round Mountain**
Moursund, Albert Wadel, III
**Rusk**
Guy, Steve R.
**San Angelo**
Moeller, Galen Ashley
**San Antonio**
Cumpian, Joe G.
Farmer, William David
Richardson, Joel Glenn
Spence, Craig H.
Wallis, Ben Alton, Jr.
Welmaker, Forrest Nolan
**San Benito**
Cordova, Adolfo Enrique
**Spring**
Loomis, Wendell Sylvester
**Texarkana**
Potter, David Jimmie
**Waco**
Hall, Donald Orell
Villarreal, Fernando Marin
**Wharton**
Roades, John Leslie
**Wichita Falls**
Helton, Robert Moore

### UTAH

**Salt Lake City**
McConkie, Oscar Walter
Scofield, David Willson
**Woods Cross**
Weiler, Todd David

### VERMONT

**Dorset**
O'Toole, Kevin Michael
**Middlebury**
Deppman, John C.
**Saint Albans**
Appel, Kenneth Mark

### VIRGINIA

**Alexandria**
Beach, Barbara Purse
Costello, Daniel Brian
**Arlington**
Packett, Larry French
Walker, Woodrow Wilson
**Ashland**
d'Evegnee, Charles Paul
**Bristol**
Alan, Sondra Kirschner
**Charlottesville**
Wilson, Lester Arnauld, III
**Chester**
Gray, Charles Robert
**Coles Point**
Rager, Susan Godman
**Danville**
Conway, French Hoge
**Fairfax**
Stanley, William Martin
**Falls Church**
Baskin, William Maxwell, Sr.
Crews, Grasty, II
Kirk, Dennis Dean
Redmond, Robert
**Hopewell**
Clark, Bruce Arlington, Jr.
**Leesburg**
Biberaj, Buta
**Lynchburg**
Angel, James Joseph
Light, William Randall
**Mc Lean**
Friedlander, Jerome Peyser, II
Morris, James Malachy
Rhyne, Charles Sylvanus
**Newport News**
Martin, Terrence Keech
Saunders, Bryan Leslie
**Orange**
Wilkinson, Richard K.
**Portsmouth**
Lavin, Barbara Hofheins
**Providence Forge**
Richardson, William Winfree, III
**Richmond**
Angelidis, Stephen Alexander
Call, Susan Hope
Hill, Oliver White, Sr.
**Springfield**
Chappell, Milton Leroy
**Stafford**
Locklear, W. Ross
**Suffolk**
Young, Hubert Howell, Jr.
**Tazewell**
Whitesell, Eric Dwight
**Virginia Beach**
Spitzli, Donald Hawkes, Jr.
**Williamsburg**
Twiford, Alice Kate
**Winchester**
Adams, Nate Lavinder, III

### WASHINGTON

**Bellevue**
Scaringi, Michael Joseph
**Bellingham**
Britain, James Edward
**Centralia**
Buzzard, Steven Ray
**Clarkston**
Kernan, Tina Lynn
Ledgerwood, Thomas L.
**Everett**
Johnson, Richard Bruce
**Federal Way**
Pratum, Michael James
**Montesano**
Stewart, James Malcolm
**Port Orchard**
Shiers, Frank Abram
**Seattle**
Cavin, Clark
Dunham, Douglas Spence
Ellis, James Reed
Lombard, John Cutler
Mueller, Daniel Edward
Pritchard, Llewelyn G.
Sayre, Matt Melvin Mathias
Steinberg, Jack
**Selah**
Ring, Lucile Wiley
**Spokane**
Anderson, Robert Edward
Olson, James Warren
**Tacoma**
Felker, Robert Stratton
Hostnik, Charles Rivoire
**Walla Walla**
Mitchell, Michael Sherman

### WEST VIRGINIA

**Beckley**
Kennedy, David Tinsley
Sayre, Floyd McKinley, III
**Bluefield**
Henderson, Susan Ellen Fortune
**Charleston**
Douglas, Robert Edward
**Fairmont**
Martino, Gary James
**Fairview**
Bunner, Patricia Andrea
**Gassaway**
Jones, Jeniver James
**Huntington**
Colburn, James Allan
**Morgantown**
Bunner, William Keck
**Parkersburg**
Full, Robert Witmer
**Romney**
Saville, Royce Blair
**Weirton**
Makricostas, Dean George
**Wellsburg**
Bell, Charles D.
**Wheeling**
Gompers, Joseph Alan

### WISCONSIN

**Adams**
Screnock, Paul Steven
**Appleton**
Drescher, Kathleen Ebben
**Colby**
Nikolay, Frank Lawrence
**De Pere**
Cerminara, Laura Mary
**Deerfield**
Pappas, David Christopher
**Germantown**
Statkus, Jerome Francis
**Little Chute**
Cornett, Paul Michael, Sr.
**Mauston**
Hollenbeck, Fred Drury
**Milwaukee**
Donahue, John Edward
Friebert, Robert Howard
Giese, Heiner
McClure, Thomas James
Michelstetter, Stanley Hubert
Orzel, Michael Dale
Reiske, Peter Francis
Rotter, Emanuel Norman
**Monroe**
Ewald, Rex Alan
Kittelsen, Rodney Olin
**Osseo**
Feltes, Charles Victor
**Park Falls**
Marvin, Janet L.
**Portage**
Bennett, David Hinkley
**Racine**
Feil, Frank J., Jr.
**Sheboygan**
Wasserman, Sylvia Katz
**Wausau**
Connell, James Bernard
Deffner, Roger L.
Drengler, William Allan John

### WYOMING

**Casper**
Miller, Corinne
**Cheyenne**
Scorsine, John Magnus
**Riverton**
Girard, Nettabell
**Worland**
Richins, Kent Alan
Sweeny, Wendy Press

### MEXICO

**Cuernavaca**
Foss, George B., Jr.

### ADDRESS UNPUBLISHED

Atkinson, Sheridan Earle
Barry, David F.
Boner, Eleanor Katz
Brashear, William Ronald
Burgess, Hayden Fern (Poka Laenui)
Connors, Kevin Charles
Coryell, Frank
Easterling, Charles Armo
Fayette, Kathleen Owens
Fleischman, Herman Israel
Fowler, Flora Daun
Garry, John Thomas, II
Goodrich, Jeffrey Mark
Hall, Joan Torrens
Hanson, Avarita Laurel
Hardcastle, Robert Thomas
Hawes, Sue
Hetrick, Brenda Drendel
Huenergardt, Darrel J.
Johnson, Elizabeth Diane Long
Jorgensen, Erik Holger
Levinson, Kenneth Lee
Lieb, Charles Herman
Mangler, Robert James
Martin, Thomas MacDonald
McAlhany, Toni Anne
McDonald, Bradley G.
Natcher, Stephen Darlington
Olsen, Kenneth Allen
Perlman, Richard Brian
Perry, George Williamson
Rawls, Frank Macklin
Regenstreif, Herbert
Rosenn, Harold
Sager, Daniel Ian
Saliterman, Richard Arlen
Schroeder, Edward James
Shaner, Leslie Ann
Slipski, Ronald Edward
Smallwood, John Daniel
Stevens, Rhea Christina
Sussman, Howard S(ivin)
Terry, John Hart
Vamos, Florence M.
Walsh, Gerry O'Malley
Weinmann, Richard Adrian
Wharton, Hugh Davis, III
Wigler, Andrew Jeffrey
Zelechiwsky, Bohdan John

## GOVERNMENT CONTRACTS AND CLAIMS

### UNITED STATES

### ALABAMA

**Enterprise**
Fuller, Mark Everett
**Huntsville**
Steakley, Roderic G

### ALASKA

**Anchorage**
Kreger, Michael E.

### ARIZONA

**Phoenix**
Wilcox, Debra Kay

### CALIFORNIA

**California City**
Friedl, Rick
**Los Altos**
Bell, Richard G.
**Los Angeles**
Burkholder, John Allen
Kamine, Bernard Samuel
Pieper, Darold D.
Scoular, Robert Frank
Victorino, Louis D.
Walcher, Alan Ernest
**Manhattan Beach**
Guimera, Irene Mermelstein
**Oakland**
Leslie, Robert Lorne
Wallace, Elaine Wendy
**Pomona**
Bausch, Janet Jean
Wyatt, John Brundige, III
**Redwood City**
Wilhelm, Robert Oscar
**Riverside**
Graves, Patrick Lee
**Sacramento**
Shelley, Susanne Mary
**San Diego**
Clark, Grant Lawrence
Underwood, Anthony Paul
**San Francisco**
Russoniello, Joseph Pascal
**Santa Clara**
Wehde, Albert Edward
**Sherman Oaks**
Crump, Gerald Franklin
**Torrance**
Wilson, Karen LeRohl
**Westlake Vlg**
Vinson, William Theodore

### COLORADO

**Boulder**
Fenster, Herbert Lawrence
**Denver**
McKenna, Frederick Gregory
Rufien, Paul Charles

### CONNECTICUT

**Manchester**
Gaines, Robert Martin
**Waterbury**
Muroff, Elena Marie

### DISTRICT OF COLUMBIA

**Washington**
Abrahams, Daniel B.
Burch, John Thomas, Jr.
Charles, Robert Bruce
Chierichella, John W.
Cope, John R(obert)
Dembling, Paul Gerald
Falk, James Harvey, Sr.
Falk, John Mansfield
Groner, Samuel Brian
Haynes, William J(ames), II
Hoffmann, Martin Richard
Hoppel, Robert Gerald, Jr.
Johnson, Richard Tenney
Kessler, Judd Lewis
Latham, Weldon Hurd
Marvin, Charles Rodney, Jr.
Mishkin, Barbara Friedman
Mitchell, Roy Shaw
Ness, Andrew David
Neurock, Mitchel
O'Sullivan, Lynda Troutman
Patten, Thomas Louis
Portnoy, Elliott Ivan
Riley, Daniel Joseph
Rosenthal, Steven Siegmund
Schmidt, William Arthur, Jr.
Schor, Laurence
Sherzer, Harvey Gerald
Stouck, Jerry
Violante, Joseph Anthony
Weinstein, Martin James
Worthy, K(enneth) Martin

### FLORIDA

**Fort Lauderdale**
Conklin, Howard Lawrence
Futch, Lynn
**Fort Myers Beach**
Shenko, William Edward, Jr.
**Jacksonville**
Halverson, Steven Thomas
**Jasper**
McCormick, John Hoyle
**Miami**
Mehta, Eileen Rose

**Sarasota**
Phillips, Elvin Willis
**St Petersburg**
Hudkins, John W.
**Tampa**
Campbell, Richard Bruce

GEORGIA

**Atlanta**
Cahalan, Scott David
Heady, Eugene Joseph
Sweeney, Neal James

HAWAII

**Fort Shafter**
Feighny, Michael Louis

ILLINOIS

**Chicago**
Bruner, Stephen C.
Van Tine, Matthew Eric

INDIANA

**Brazil**
Deal, James Edward
**Lafayette**
O'Connell, Lawrence B.
**Rushville**
Morning, Leigh Suzanne

KENTUCKY

**Crestwood**
Ray, Ronald Dudley
**Fort Thomas**
Whalen, Paul Lewellin
**Lexington**
Beshear, Steven L.
**Louisville**
Ethridge, Larry Clayton
**Versailles**
Jones, Tracy Webb

LOUISIANA

**Baton Rouge**
Ray, Betty Jean G.
**Lafayette**
Gideon, Kyle Liney
**Lake Charles**
Davidson, Van Michael, Jr.
**New Orleans**
Brian, A(lexis) Morgan, Jr.
Fierke, Thomas Garner

MARYLAND

**Bethesda**
Hagberg, Viola Wilgus
Menaker, Frank H., Jr.
**Patuxent River**
Fitzhugh, David Michael
**Rockville**
Mitchell, Charles F.
Pensinger, John Lynn
**Silver Spring**
Quinlan, William Allen
Stempler, Michael

MASSACHUSETTS

**Carlisle**
Hensleigh, Howard Edgar

MICHIGAN

**Detroit**
Fellrath, Richard Frederic
Lewand, F. Thomas
Thorpe, Norman Ralph
**Farmington Hills**
Birnkrant, Sherwin Maurice
**Rochester Hls**
Diehl, Richard Paul
**Taylor**
Hirsch, David L.

MINNESOTA

**Minneapolis**
Bruner, Philip Lane
**Minnetonka**
Martell, Saundra Adkins
**Saint Paul**
Maffei, Rocco John

MISSISSIPPI

**Jackson**
Mosley, Deanne Marie

MISSOURI

**Jefferson City**
Craft, John Charles
**Kansas City**
White, Jerusha Lynn
**Saint Louis**
Carr, Gary Thomas

NEVADA

**Las Vegas**
Kirsch, Lynn

NEW HAMPSHIRE

**Etna**
Mitrano, Peter Paul

NEW JERSEY

**Fort Monmouth**
Desai, Jignasa
**New Providence**
Bronstein, Glen Max
**Newark**
Chaplin, Dolcey Elizabeth
Mintz, Robert A.

NEW YORK

**Albany**
Couch, Leslie Franklin
Fernandez, Hermes A., III
**Brooklyn**
Nicholson, Michael
**New Rochelle**
Stevens, Roger Ross
**New York**
Grassi, Joseph F.
Kannry, Jack Stephen
Kaufman, Stephen Herscu
Laremont, Anita Webb
Madden, John Patrick
Toplitz, George Nathan
**Upton**
Atney, Irene P.

NORTH CAROLINA

**Charlotte**
Sink, Robert C.

NORTH DAKOTA

**Grand Forks**
Hand, James Stanley

OHIO

**Columbus**
Haught, Jack Gregg
Liggett, Luther LeRoy, Jr.
**Fairborn**
Roach, B. Randall
**Grove City**
Dodd, Jerry Lee
**Marion**
Slagle, James William

PENNSYLVANIA

**Camp Hill**
Adler, Theodore Arthur
**Harrisburg**
Cline, Andrew Haley
Van Zile, Philip Taylor, III
**Philadelphia**
Reiter, Joseph Henry
**Reading**
DiSibio, Carol Lynn Kridler

RHODE ISLAND

**Newport**
Nelligan, Kenneth Egan

SOUTH CAROLINA

**Aiken**
Alan, Matthew W. A.

SOUTH DAKOTA

**Sioux Falls**
Hattervig, Karen Ann

TENNESSEE

**Knoxville**
Fox, James Erwin
**Nashville**
Cobb, Stephen A.
Jackson, Kenneth Monroe
Knowles, Emmitt Clifton
Thornton, Guilford F., Jr.
Yuspeh, Alan Ralph
**Oak Ridge**
Pearman, Joel Edward

TEXAS

**Amarillo**
McDougall, Gerald Duane
**Dallas**
Crowley, James Worthington
Doke, Marshall J., Jr.
**Houston**
Eiland, Gary Wayne
**San Antonio**
Barnhill, Donald Earl

UTAH

**Salt Lake City**
Larsen, Lynn Beck

VIRGINIA

**Annandale**
Gaberman, Harry
**Arlington**
Doyle, Gerard Francis
Fowler, David Lucas
**Falls Church**
Duesenberg, Robert H.
**Fort Lee**
Baker, Loren Leonard
**Lynchburg**
Elliott, James Ward
**Mc Lean**
Love, Michael Kenneth
Mason, Thomas Owen
Olson, William Jeffrey
Raley, Charles Edward
**Petersburg**
Rosenstock, Louis Anthony, III
**Roanoke**
Wilson, Douglas Downes
**Vienna**
Barger, Kathleen Carson
Hagberg, Chris Eric
McCabe, Thomas Edward
Randolph, Christopher Craven

WASHINGTON

**Pasco**
Ungerecht, Todd Edward
**Richland**
Rither, Alan Craig
**Seattle**
Boman, Marc Allen
Collins, Theodore John
Freeman, Antoinette Rosefeldt
Groff, David Clark, Jr.
Guedel, William Gregory
Merkle, Alan Ray
Reardon, Mark William
Tallman, Richard C.
**Tacoma**
Waldo, James Chandler

WEST VIRGINIA

**Charleston**
Lane, Charlotte

WISCONSIN

**Madison**
Zawadsky, John H.

MILITARY ADDRESSES OF THE UNITED STATES

PACIFIC

**APO**
Gordon, Carey Nathaniel

IRAN

**Teheran**
Westberg, John Augustin

ADDRESS UNPUBLISHED

Babbin, Jed Lloyd
Goddard, Claude Philip, Jr.
Hoffman, Ira Eliot
Kiefer, Karen LaVerne
McIntosh, Rhodina Covington
Protigal, Stanley Nathan
Stone, Andrew Grover
Turen, Barbara Ellen
Wilson, Michael B(ruce)
Wittig, Raymond Shaffer

## HEALTH

UNITED STATES

ALABAMA

**Bessemer**
Jones, Stephen M.
**Birmingham**
Givhan, Robert Marcus
Henry, James Fred
Martin, Arthur Lee, Jr.
**Mobile**
Pierce, Donald Fay

ALASKA

**Anchorage**
Dickson, Robert Jay

ARIZONA

**Mesa**
Guffey, Douglas Oliver
**Phoenix**
Barclay, Steven Calder
Bixby, David Michael
Johnston, Logan Truax, III
Leinen, Amy Lynn
Pietzsch, Michael Edward
Price, Charles Steven
Quayle, Marilyn Tucker
Schermer, Beth
Thompson, Terence William
**Tucson**
Baldwin, Howard
Hanshaw, A. Alan
Kaucher, James William

ARKANSAS

**Fayetteville**
Bumpass, Ronald Eugene
**Fort Smith**
Carrick, Paula Strecker
**Little Rock**
Mackey, Diane Stoakes
Marshall, William Taylor
**Rogers**
Myers, Dane Jacob

CALIFORNIA

**Berkeley**
Harris, Michael Gene
**Fresno**
Jamison, Daniel Oliver
**Irvine**
Thompson, Donald Mizelle
**Los Angeles**
Carrey, Neil
Girard, Robert David
Maizel, Samuel Ruven
Memel, Sherwin Leonard
Windham, Timothy Ray
**Mill Valley**
Duke, George F.
**Oakland**
Cotter, Edward Francis, Jr.
**Oxnard**
McGinley, James Duff
**Pasadena**
Zuetel, Kenneth Roy, Jr.
**San Diego**
Kelly, Karla Rosemarie
**San Francisco**
DeMuro, Paul Robert
Fleisher, Steven M.
Kern, John McDougall
Olejko, Mitchell J.
**San Jose**
Hurwitz, Michael A.
Towery, James E.
**Santa Barbara**
Ah-Tye, Kirk Thomas
**Santa Monica**
Focht, Michael Harrison, Jr.
**Walnut Creek**
Clark, Sherry Walker
**Woodland Hills**
Fields, Brian Jay

COLORADO

**Boulder**
Caulfield, Sharon Elizabeth
Earnest, G. Lane
**Denver**
Blum, Gary Bernard
McManus, Richard Griswold, Jr.
Sabey, Mark L.
Stewart, Ellen Elizabeth
**Englewood**
Gipstein, Milton Fivenson
**Fort Morgan**
Higinbotham, Jacquelyn Joan
**Loveland**
Kaufman, William George
**Pueblo**
Farley, Thomas T.

CONNECTICUT

**Hartford**
Blumenthal, Jeffrey Michael
Del Negro, John Thomas
Dennis, Anthony James
Lloyd, Alex
Lyons, Charles Malaher
Newman, John David
Space, Theodore Maxwell
Young, Roland Frederic, III
**Manchester**
Horwitz, Melvin
**Middletown**
Quattro, Mark Henry
**New Haven**
Birnbaum, Irwin Morton
Gollaher, Merton G
**Waterbury**
Muroff, Elena Marie

DELAWARE

**Wilmington**
Martin, William Joseph, III
Rodgers, Stephen John

DISTRICT OF COLUMBIA

**Washington**
Beck, David Charles
Broas, Timothy Michael
Flannery, Ellen Joanne
Ford, Gary Manning
Hastings, Douglas Alfred
Kuder, Armin Ulrich
Luce, Gregory M.
McAnaney, Kevin George
Mishkin, Barbara Friedman
Navarro, Bruce Charles
Nilles, Kathleen Mary
O'Neil, Thomas Francis, III
Pollard, Michael Ross
Rabecs, Robert Nicholas
Schiffbauer, William G.
Temko, Stanley Leonard

FLORIDA

**Boca Raton**
Kornberg, Joel Barry
**Daytona Beach**
Davidson, David John
**Fort Lauderdale**
Haliczer, James Solomon
Imperato, Gabriel Louis
Perling, Lester J.
**Jacksonville**
Korn, Michael Jeffrey
Prom, Stephen George
**Lakeland**
Knowlton, Kevin Charles
**Melbourne**
Yera, Evelio Jesus
**Miami**
Fishman, Lewis Warren
Kurzer, Martin Joel
Mudd, John Philip
Quirantes, Albert M.
Weinger, Steven Murray
**Miami Lakes**
Sharett, Alan Richard
**Naples**
Berning, Randall Karl
**Orlando**
Bitner, Richard H.
**Saint Petersburg**
Battaglia, Brian Peter
**Sarasota**
Garland, Richard Roger
Lumpkin, Douglas Boozer
Moore, John Leslie
**Tallahassee**
Miller, Morris Henry
**Tampa**
Burgess, Bryan Scott
Davis, Kirk Stuart
Fernandez, Frances Garcia
Lamb, Bruce Douglas
Pellett, Jon Michael
Watson, Roberta Casper
**West Palm Beach**
Eyler, Bonnie

GEORGIA

**Atlanta**
Brown, John Robert
Grady, Kevin E.
Horace, Donald
Kelly, James Patrick
Schroder, Jack Spalding, Jr.
Stewart, Jeffrey B.
Sullivan, Terrance Charles
**Mcdonough**
Meadows, Rod G.

IDAHO

**Boise**
Fields, Richard Charles
Lombardi, David Richard

ILLINOIS

**Barrington**
Tobin, Dennis Michael
**Champaign**
Hall, Guy Charles
**Chicago**
Bleiweiss, Shell J.
Cherney, James Alan
Corpuz, Marcelo Navarro, III
Geiman, J. Robert
Gutstein, Solomon
Hoover, R. Sam
Kagan, Andrew Besdin
Kopelman, Ian Stuart
Kurfirst, Leonard Stanley
Ladd, Jeffrey Raymond
Lorenzen, Donald Robert
Mangum, Ronald Scott
Parson, Jason A.
Polk, Lee Thomas
Rankin, James Winton
Reed, Keith Allen
Schuyler, Daniel Merrick
Staab, Michael Joseph
Stone, Howard Lawrence
Wilson, Roger Goodwin
Wohlreich, Jack Jay
**Evanston**
Weston, Michael C.
**Inverness**
Victor, Michael Gary
**Mattoon**
Horsley, Jack Everett
**North Chicago**
de Lasa, José M.
**Northbrook**
Dilling, Kirkpatrick Wallwick
**Springfield**
Morse, Saul Julian

INDIANA

**Hammond**
Diamond, Eugene Christopher
**Indianapolis**
Haycox, Rolanda Moore
Horn, Brenda Sue
Kemper, James Dee
Reddy, Lakshmi Yeddula
Render, John Clifford
**Merrillville**
Hites, Earle Floyd
**South Bend**
Hammerschmidt, Bruce C.

KANSAS

**Kansas City**
Holbrook, Reid Franklin
Peters, Daniel Wade
**Overland Park**
Ellis, Jeffrey Orville
**Prairie Vlg**
Stanton, Roger D.
**Topeka**
Lawson, Christopher Patrick

KENTUCKY

**Covington**
Gilliland, John Campbell, II
**Lexington**
Basconi, Pamela Bray
**Louisville**
Ament, Mark Steven
Edwards, Steven Alan
Morton, Donna Theresa
Reed, D. Gary

LOUISIANA

**Alexandria**
Alexius, Frederick Bernard
**Baton Rouge**
LeClere, David Anthony
Riddick, Winston Wade, Sr.
Scobee, H. Evans
**Hammond**
Matheny, Tom Harrell
**Lafayette**
Breaux, Paul Joseph
**Lake Charles**
Clements, Robert W.
**Metairie**
Ford, Robert David
**New Orleans**
Aiken, Tonia Dandry
Beahm, Franklin D.
David, Robert Jefferson
Fraiche, Donna DiMartino
Lombardo Trostorff, Danielle Maria
Steinberg, Sylvan Julian
**Shreveport**
Prestridge, Rogers Meredith

MAINE

**Bangor**
Sighinolfi, Paul Henry
**Hallowell**
Crawford, Linda Sibery
**Portland**
Harlan, Wendy Jill
Lehman, Kenneth William

MARYLAND

**Annapolis**
Nash, Brian Joseph
**Baltimore**
King, David Paul
McGarvey, Jack F(rancis)
Moser, M(artin) Peter
Sfekas, Stephen James
Wheatley, Charles Henry, III
Zimmerly, James Gregory
**Brooklandville**
Rosenzweig, Janice Popick
**Chevy Chase**
Montedonico, Joseph
**Columbia**
Barton, Ellen Louise

**Silver Spring**
Priest, Troy Alfred-Wiley
**Towson**
Lutz, Randall Matthew

### MASSACHUSETTS

**Boston**
Blumenreich, Gene Arnold
Costa, Michael R.
Haddad, Ernest Mudarri
Lanckton, Arthur Van Cleve
Murray, Philip Edmund, Jr.
Reardon, Frank Emond
Reardon, Thomas Michael
Ristuben, Karen R.
Trevett, Kenneth Parkhurst
**Canton**
Bauer, Gene Marc
**Greenfield**
Berson, Mark Ira
**Newton**
Isselbacher, Rhoda Solin
**Rockland**
Auton, Linda May Eisenschmidt
**Shrewsbury**
Cantu, Tina-Marie
**West Yarmouth**
Gens, Richard Howard
**Weston**
McDaniel, James Alan
**Worcester**
Donnelly, James Corcoran, Jr.

### MICHIGAN

**Ann Arbor**
Muraski, Anthony Augustus
**Detroit**
Johnson, Cynthia L(e) M(ae)
Wisner, Cynthia Ficke
**East Lansing**
Casey, Nan Elizabeth
**Grand Rapids**
Jack, William Wilson, Jr.
**Owosso**
Johnson, James Randall
**Southfield**
Schwartz, Robert H.
Shpiece, Michael Ronald
**Traverse City**
Christopherson, James A.

### MINNESOTA

**Bloomington**
Broeker, John Milton
**Hallock**
Malm, Roger Charles
**Minneapolis**
Hanson, Bruce Eugene
Hibbs, John Stanley
Konezny, Jeryn Ann-Hall
Saunders, Pamela Ruth
Struthers, Margo S.

### MISSISSIPPI

**Greenville**
Martin, Andrew Ayers
**Jackson**
Simmons, Heber Sherwood, III

### MISSOURI

**Cape Girardeau**
Blaes, Stephen Mathias
**Jefferson City**
Tettlebaum, Harvey M.
**Kansas City**
Brous, Thomas Richard
Kaufman, Michelle Stark
Toll, Perry Mark
**Saint Louis**
Brostron, Judith Curran
Gunn, James F.
Schoene, Kathleen Snyder
Watters, Richard Donald
Wiehl, James George

### NEBRASKA

**Omaha**
Burke, Thomas Raymond

### NEVADA

**Carson City**
King, Patrick Owen
**Las Vegas**
Brown, Patricia Leonard
Myers, Andrew S.

### NEW HAMPSHIRE

**Concord**
Moffett, Howard Mackenzie

### NEW JERSEY

**Berlin**
Goldstein, Benjamin
**Bridgewater**
Conroy, Robert John
Schoppmann, Michael Joseph
**East Hanover**
Davidson, Anne Stowell
**Hackensack**
Bar-Nadav, Meiron
Jacobs, Lawrence H.
**Kenilworth**
Berkowitz, Jeffrey
**Kinnelon**
Kossl, Thomas Leonard
**Lawrenceville**
Benesch, Katherine
Kline, Michael J.
Rudy, James Francis Xavier
**Metuchen**
Frizell, David J.
**Morristown**
Cocca, Anthony
**Newark**
Gouraige, Hervé
Mintz, Robert A.
**Parsippany**
Donovan, Richard Edward
**Teaneck**
Diamond, Stanley
**Tetersboro**
Marier, Raymond Conrad
**Westfield**
Nicolai, Donald F.
**Woodbridge**
Schaff, Michael Frederick

### NEW MEXICO

**Santa Fe**
Pound, John Bennett

### NEW YORK

**Albany**
Bougen, Harriet Sandra
Fernandez, Hermes A., III
Hyde, Carol Ann
Sciocchetti, Nancy
**Bronxville**
Recabo, Jaime Miguel
**Buffalo**
Curran, Patrick Barton
Goldstein, Bruce A.
Greene, Robert Michael
Magavern, James L.
**Flushing**
Kotcher, Shirley J. W.
**Garden City**
Scarfone, John A.
**Great Neck**
Zervos, Mitra Kavoussi
**Lido Beach**
Billauer, Barbara Pfeffer
**Manhasset**
Lester, David S.
**Mineola**
Naclerio, Gregory J.
**New York**
Appel, Albert M.
Burke, Kathleen Mary
Cohen, Joshua Robert
Diamond, David Howard
Gluck, Marshall J.
Gray, Glenn Oliver
Hanover, Richard
Hoffman, David Nathaniel
Huston, Barry Scott
Jacobson, Jerold Dennis
Kaufman, Robert Max
Kornreich, Edward Scott
Pappachen, George V., Jr.
Paul, Eve W.
Regan, Susan Ginsberg
Sacks, Karen Goldfarb
Sastow, Gary Saul
Schaffer, Seth Andrew
Scherzer, Mark P.
Shaw, Melvin Robert
Weiss, Jonathan Arthur
Yun, Edward Joon
Ziegler, Michael Lewis
**Schenectady**
Sokolow, Lloyd Bruce
**Syracuse**
Pinsky, Bradley M.
**White Plains**
Burkett, Bradford C.

### NORTH CAROLINA

**Cary**
Glass, Fred Stephen
**Charlotte**
Essaye, Anne Elizabeth
Klein, Paul Ira
**Greensboro**
Harris, Terrill Johnson
**Greenville**
Kiess, Stephen David
**Raleigh**
Simpson, Steven Drexell
Wilson, Robert Lee, Jr.
**Wilmington**
Kaufman, James Jay

### NORTH DAKOTA

**Minot**
Backes, Jon William

### OHIO

**Athens**
Hedges, Richard Houston
**Canton**
Haupt, Fred Jerry
**Cincinnati**
Lydon, Deborah Ruth
Markesberg, Maria Saba
Wales, Ross Elliot
**Cleveland**
Binford, Gregory Glenn
Brown, Harry M.
Koblenz, N(orman) Herschel
Schabes, Alan Elliot
Weller, Charles David
**Columbus**
Dunlay, Catherine Telles
Graff, Douglas Eric
Maloon, Jerry L.
**Howard**
Lee, William Johnson
**Maumee**
Zouhary, Kathleen Maher
**Toledo**
Rollison, Gerardo Roy

### OKLAHOMA

**Cushing**
Draughon, Scott Wilson
**Oklahoma City**
Gordon, Kevin Dell
Hanna, Terry Ross
Harris, Allen Keith
Williams, Teresa Ann Goode
**Tulsa**
Burkett, Teresa Meinders
Coulter, Jean Walpole
Gaberino, John Anthony, Jr.
Kellough, William C.

### OREGON

**Eugene**
Lowry, Robert Dudley
**Portland**
Anderson, Herbert Hatfield
Hart, John Edward
Weiler, Mary Pauline
**Salem**
Bauer, Keith Jay

### PENNSYLVANIA

**Aston**
Newton, John Edward, Jr.
**Bala Cynwyd**
Covner, Ellen B.
Kane-Vanni, Patricia Ruth
**Blue Bell**
Settle, Eric Lawrence
**Camp Hill**
Gray, Kimberly S.
**Harrisburg**
Barto, Charles O., Jr.
Maleski, Cynthia Maria
Quigley, Robert Andrew
**Lancaster**
McGuire, Kendra Diane
**Malvern**
Cameron, John Clifford
**Philadelphia**
Brier, Bonnie Susan
Calvert, Jay H., Jr.
Cramer, Harold
Esser, Carl Eric
Falcao, Linda Phyllis
Flanagan, Joseph Patrick, Jr.
Kemler, R(obert) Michael
Kraeutler, Eric
Lowery, William Herbert
Luongo, Stephen Earle
Reiss, John Barlow
Rosenbaum, Marcia F.
Topel, David Louis
Wu, William
**Pittsburgh**
Conti, Joy Flowers
Geeseman, Robert George
Horty, John Francis
Hough, Thomas Henry Michael
Kabala, Edward John
Lyncheski, John E.
Thurman, Andrew Edward
Wilkinson, James Allan
**Plymouth**
Musto, Joseph John
**Wayne**
Kalogredis, Vasilios J.

### RHODE ISLAND

**Providence**
Germani, Elia
Mulhearn, Christopher Michael
Tammelleo, A. David

### SOUTH CAROLINA

**Charleston**
Young, Joseph Rutledge, Jr.
**Columbia**
Ready, William Alva, III
Scott, Ronald Charles
Strong, Franklin Wallace, Jr.
**Mount Pleasant**
Laddaga, Lawrence Alexander

### SOUTH DAKOTA

**Pierre**
Gerdes, David Alan
**Sioux Falls**
Nelson, Robert R.

### TENNESSEE

**Chattanooga**
Vital, Patricia Best
**Johnson City**
King, Robert Lewis
**Knoxville**
Arnett, Foster Deaver
**Memphis**
Chafetz, Samuel David
Gentry, Gavin Miller
Schuler, Walter E.
Spore, Richard Roland, III
**Nashville**
Blumstein, Andrée Kahn
Dyer, Sue McClure
Mefford, R. Douglas
Penny, William Lewis
Riley, Steven Allen
Torrey, Claudia Olivia
Tuke, Robert Dudley
Yuspeh, Alan Ralph

### TEXAS

**Abilene**
Robinson, Vianei Lopez
**Austin**
Davis, Creswell Dean
Schaffer, Dean Aaron
Smith, Peyton Noble
**Burleson**
Johnstone, Deborah Blackmon
**Corpus Christi**
Shackelford, Patricia Ann
**Dallas**
Davis, Derek Shane
Gerberding Cowart, Greta Elaine
Greiner, Mary Louise
King, Jeffrey P.
Lipton, Matthew Conan
**Fort Worth**
Griffith, Richard Lattimore
Harcrow, E. Earl
Hayes, Larry B.
Moore, Randall D.
**Greenville**
Morris, Leah Curtis
**Harlingen**
Pope, William L.
**Houston**
Blackshear, A. T., Jr.
Eiland, Gary Wayne
Johnson, James Harold
Towns, William Roy
**San Antonio**
Countryman, Thomas Arthur
Cruse, Rex Beach, Jr.
**Temple**
Pickle, Jerry Richard
**Tyler**
Lake, David Alan
**Victoria**
Serrata, Lidia

### UTAH

**Salt Lake City**
Erickson, David Belnap
Lavitt, Kathy A.

### VIRGINIA

**Alexandria**
Carter, Richard Dennis
Klewans, Samuel N.
**Arlington**
Mossinghoff, Gerald Joseph
**Chesapeake**
Leftwich, James Asbury, Jr.
**Manassas**
Platt, Leslie A.
**Mc Lean**
Brown, Thomas Cartmel, Jr.
**Midlothian**
Tuttle, Roger Lewis
**Norfolk**
Poston, Anita Owings
**Richmond**
Ross, David Lee
**Roanoke**
Lemon, William Jacob

### WASHINGTON

**Seattle**
Albright, Douglas Eaton
Dolan, Andrew Kevin
Easter, Scott Beyer
Hutcheson, Mark Andrew
Tucker, Kathryn Louise
Van Kampen, Al
Williams, Rebecca Lynn
Zeder, Fred M.
**Spokane**
Connolly, K. Thomas
Riherd, John Arthur

### WEST VIRGINIA

**Bluefield**
Evans, Wayne Lewis
**Fairmont**
Brandfass, Robert Lee
**Wheeling**
Riley, Arch Wilson, Jr.
Wilmoth, William David

### WISCONSIN

**Janesville**
Finman-Pince, Terry J.
**Madison**
Hanson, David James
Robison, John S.
**Milwaukee**
Ehlinger, Ralph Jerome
Friedman, James Dennis
Rice, Shawn G.
Van Grunsven, Paul Robert

### ENGLAND

**London**
Green, Richard
Kingham, Richard Frank
White, Walter Hiawatha, Jr.

### ADDRESS UNPUBLISHED

Boggs, Judith Susan
Boone, Richard Winston, Sr.
Burgess, Hayden Fern (Poka Laenui)
Cazalas, Mary Rebecca Williams
Deric, Arthur Joseph
Dikeou, George Demetrios
Gerwin, Leslie Ellen
Hausman, Bruce
Howard, Christopher Holm
Kellerman, Edwin
Knight, Faith Tanya
McFerrin, James Hamil
McLendon, Susan Michelle
Reynolds, H. Gerald
Thornton, John W., Sr.
Wimmer, Nancy T.
Wynstra, Nancy Ann

## IMMIGRATION, NATURALIZATION, AND CUSTOMS

### UNITED STATES

### ARIZONA

**Mesa**
Gunderson, Brent Merrill
**Phoenix**
Song Ong, Roxanne Kay

### CALIFORNIA

**Costa Mesa**
Putman, Philip A.
**Fremont**
Cummings, John Patrick
**Los Angeles**
Jalbuena, Arnel Babiera
Parker, Catherine Marie
**Marina Dl Rey**
Freed, Evan Phillip
**Monterey Park**
Groce, Ewin Petty
**Pasadena**
Chan, Daniel Chung-Yin
**San Diego**
Snaid, Leon Jeffrey
**San Jose**
Doan, Xuyen Van
**San Mateo**
Yelnick, Marc M(aurice)
**Sherman Oaks**
Gotcher, James Ronald
**Studio City**
Miller, Charles Maurice
**Torrance**
Sarkisian, Alan Herbert

### COLORADO

**Denver**
Chandler, Kimberley Ann
Das, Arun
**Englewood**
Simmons, David Norman

### CONNECTICUT

**New Haven**
Gildea, Brian Michael
**Westport**
Sporn, Judith Beryl

### DISTRICT OF COLUMBIA

**Washington**
Ambrose, Myles Joseph
Bryant, Ann Lake
Duross, Charles Edward, IV
Engel, Tala
Germain, Regina
Karpinski, Irena Izabella
Labovitz, Priscilla
Mitchell, Carol Ann
Stern, Elizabeth Espin

### FLORIDA

**Altamonte Springs**
Gunewardene, Roshani Mala
**Boca Raton**
Law, Ellen Marie
**Coral Gables**
Cano, Mario Stephen
Rodriguez, Lourdes A. de los Angeles
**Deerfield Beach**
Daugherty, Walter Emory
**Fort Lauderdale**
Caulkins, Charles S.
Pascal, Robert Albert
Schrader, Robert George
**Gainesville**
White, Jill Carolyn
**Miami**
Dreize, Livia Rebbeka
Kuehne, Benedict P.
Kurzban, Ira Jay
Murphy, Timothy James
Poston, Rebekah Jane
Pruna, Laura Maria
Rabenseifner, Hanna Camille
**North Miami**
Forman, Kenneth Alan
**Orlando**
Johnson, Kraig Nelson
Neff, A. Guy
**Tallahassee**
Davis, William Howard
**West Palm Beach**
Finley, Chamdler R.
Stuber, James Arthur

### GEORGIA

**Atlanta**
Colussy, Susan Eileen Hillick
Schock, Robert Christopher

### HAWAII

**Honolulu**
Ichikawa, Robert K.
Ma, Alan Wai-Chuen
Oldenburg, Ronald Troy
Zabanal, Eduardo Olegario
**Wailuku**
Barbin, Ryther Lynn

### ILLINOIS

**Chicago**
Bristol, Douglas
Helt, Christopher William
Meltzer, Robert Craig
Paprocki, Thomas John
Spiegel, Robert Ira
**Lincolnwood**
Birg, Yuri M.
**Wheaton**
Fawell, Blanche Hill

### INDIANA

**Indianapolis**
Loiseau, Richard
Tuchman, Steven Leslie
**New Castle**
Schiesswohl, Cynthia Rae Schlegel

### IOWA

**Des Moines**
Fisher, Thomas George, Jr.

Wright, Robert Thomas, Jr.
Yaffa, Andrew Bryan
**Miami Beach**
Arbuz, Joseph Robert
Fuller, Lawrence Arthur
**Ocala**
Hatch, John D.
Musleh, Victor Joseph, Jr.
**Orlando**
Brown, Janet Lynn
Heskin, Keersten Lee
Hurt, Jennings Laverne, III
Kolin, Lawrence Howard
Lou Pendás, Luzardo
Marcus, Lee Warren
Metz, Larry Edward
Williams, Donald Neal
**Palm Beach**
Gavigan, James Copley
**Palm Beach Gardens**
Hayes, Neil John
Whalen, Jeanmarie
**Panama City**
Fensom, James B.
**Pensacola**
Buchanan, Virginia Marie
Duke, Thomas Harrison
Echsner, Stephen Herre
McKenzie, James Franklin
**Pinellas Park**
Blacklidge, Raymond Mark
**Port Saint Lucie**
Hoey, William Edward
**Saint Petersburg**
Blews, William Frank
Georges, Richard Martin
Holland, Troy Whitzhurst
**Sarasota**
Groseclose, Lynn Hunter
**Tallahassee**
Johnson, Fred Mack
Mang, Douglas Arthur
Neal, Austin Baylor
Roland, Raymond William
**Tampa**
Barbas, Stephen Michael
Bardi, Henry J.
Barker, Chris A(llen)
Berkowitz, Herbert Mattis
Brudny, Peter J.
Butler, Paul Bascomb, Jr.
Elligett, Raymond Thomas, Jr.
Guerra, Rolando Gilberto, Jr.
Gunn, Lee Delton, IV
Hardy, Paul Duane
Mandelbaum, Samuel Robert
Ramey, Mark S.
Rawls, R. Steven
Somers, Clifford Louis
Stiles, Mary Ann
Thatcher, Matthew Eugene
Townsend, Byron Edwin
**Tavares**
Johnson, Terri Sue
**Valrico**
Carlucci, Paul Pasquale
**West Palm Beach**
McAfee, William James
Moffet, Kenneth William
Posgay, Matthew Nichols
Quattlebaum, Guy Elliot

## GEORGIA

**Atlanta**
Barksdale, Michael Scott
Chalker, Ronald Franklin
Collins, Donnell Jawan
Corry, Robert Emmett
Crumpler, Joan Gale
Eckl, William Wray
Farnham, Clayton Henson
Feldman, Monroe Joseph
Gannon, Mark Stephen
Glaser, Arthur Henry
Haubenreich, John Gilman
Jester, Carroll Gladstone
Jones, Eric S.
Killorin, Edward Wylly
Kneisel, Edmund M.
Lindsey, Edward Harman, Jr.
Medlin, Charles McCall
Seacrest, Gary Lee
Stanhope, William Henry
Sullivan, Terrance Charles
Tate, Edwin Arthur
**Brunswick**
Gough, Kevin Robert
**Columbus**
Hicks, Deron Ray
**Decatur**
Apolinsky, Stephen Douglas
Edwards, Boykin, Jr.
**Douglas**
Hayes, Dewey
**Macon**
Cleveland, Blair Knox
Dozier, Lester Zack
**Marietta**
Fielkow, Arnold David
**Savannah**
Bowman, Catherine McKenzie
Forbes, Morton Gerald
Stabell, Edward Reidar, III
**Smyrna**
Seigler, Michael Edward
**Swainsboro**
Edenfield, James Franklin
**Valdosta**
Lawrence, Matthew Russell
Smith, John Holder, Jr.
**Watkinsville**
Wright, Robert Joseph
**Winder**
Stell, John Elwin, Jr.

## HAWAII

**Honolulu**
Boggs, Steven Eugene
Crumpton, Charles Whitmarsh
Fong, Peter C. K.
Kawachika, James Akio
Kaya, Randall Y.
Komeya, Geoffrey Kimo Sanshiro
Kunkel, Daniel James
Lobdell, Henry Raymond
Minkin, David Justin
Mirikitani, Andrew Kotaro
O'Neill, Ralph James
Reinke, Stefan Michael
Robinson, Stacey Mukai
Sumida, Kevin P.H.
Yamano, John Y.
**Kailua Kona**
Martin, William Charles

## IDAHO

**Boise**
Fields, Richard Charles
Hall, Richard Edgar
**Coeur D Alene**
Vernon, Craig K.
**Lewiston**
Aherin, Darrel William
**Twin Falls**
Lezamiz, John T.
Tolman, Steven Kay

## ILLINOIS

**Barrington**
Cass, Robert Michael
**Belleville**
Coghill, William Thomas, Jr.
**Bloomington**
Barrientes, John Charles
Bragg, Michael Ellis
Varney, Robert T.
Wozniak, Debra Gail
**Chicago**
Adler, John William, Jr.
Bellah, Kenneth David
Blatt, Richard Lee
Blume, Paul Chiappe
Bresnahan, Arthur Stephen
Burdelik, Thomas L.
Cascino, Anthony Elmo, Jr.
Chemers, Robert Marc
Daniels, John Draper
Daniels, Keith Byron, Jr.
Dombrowski, Gerald Michael
Donner, Ted A.
Drumke, Michael William
Elden, Gary Michael
Enright, Thomas Michael
Fanone, John R.
Ferrini, James Thomas
Franklin, Christine Carroll
Frazen, Mitchell Hale
Gilford, Steven Ross
Goldman, Michael P.
Goodman, Ann Paton
Gosain, Vineet
Graber, Patrick Matthew
Griffith, Donald Kendall
Heilmann, David Michael
Hooks, William Henry
Johnson, Richard Fred
Jordan, Susan Patricia
Kallianis, James H., Jr.
Kawitt, Alan
Kroll, Barry Lewis
Leyhane, Francis John, III
Luning, Thomas P.
Lynch, John James
Marick, Michael Miron
McCabe, Charles Kevin
Miller, Douglas Andrew
Novotny, David Joseph
Nugent, Lori S.
O'Leary, Daniel Vincent, Jr.
Palmer, Robert Towne
Rubin, Jeffrey Mark
Sarauskas, Paul Justas
Shipley, Robert Allen
Spector, David M.
Tefft, Steven M.
Thomson, George Ronald
Torshen, Jerome Harold
Vojcanin, Sava Alexander
Walsh, Robert Patrick, Jr.
Wilcox, Mark Dean
Wilson, Roger Goodwin
Wool, Leon
**Danville**
Devens, Charles J.
**Decatur**
Kenney, Frederic Lee
**Dekalb**
Davidson, Kenneth Lawrence
**Des Plaines**
Kotelman, Laura Mary
**Edwardsville**
Gorman, James Edward
**Elgin**
Childers, John Aaron
**Glen Ellyn**
O'Connell, Daniel James
**Lake Forest**
Zapinski, Robert Paul
**Libertyville**
Mihelic, Kristin Tavia
**Northbrook**
Ihm, Stephen Lawrence
**Oak Brook**
La Petina, Gary Michael
**Peoria**
Prusak, Maximilian Michael
**Rock Island**
VanDerGinst, Dennis Allen
**Rockford**
Fredrickson, Robert Alan
Hunsaker, Richard Kendall
Zucchi, Jeffrey Joseph
**Schaumburg**
Vitale, James Drew
**Springfield**
Hanley, William Stanford
Heckenkamp, Robert Glenn
Morse, Saul Julian
**Urbana**
Kearns, James Cannon
Moore, David Robert
**Wheaton**
Butt, Edward Thomas, Jr.
Cunningham, William Francis

## INDIANA

**Bloomington**
Mann, Robert David
**Carmel**
Newman, Mary Lynn Canmann
**Fort Wayne**
Baker, Carl Leroy
Harants, Stephen John
Pope, Mark Andrew
**Indianapolis**
Due, Danford Royce
Hammel, John Wingate
Haycox, Rolanda Moore
Henderson, Eugene Leroy
Koch, Edna Mae
Lisher, John Leonard
Peters, Stephen Jay
Schreckengast, William Owen
Townsend, John Frederick, Jr.
Yeager, Joseph Heizer, Jr.
Zoeller, D. Bryce
**Merrillville**
Steele, Kevin Edward
**Shelbyville**
Harrold, Dennis Edward
McNeely, James Lee
**South Bend**
Lambert, George Robert
Norton, Sally Pauline
**Terre Haute**
Bough, Bradley A.

## IOWA

**Des Moines**
Brown, Paul Edmondson
Duckworth, Marvin E.
Narber, Gregg Ross
Phipps, David Lee
**Dubuque**
Hammer, David Lindley
**Grinnell**
Munyon, Wendy Nelson
**Johnston**
Leitner, David Larry
**Marshalltown**
Brooks, Patrick William
**Sioux City**
Bottaro, Timothy Shanahan
Mayne, Wiley Edward
**Webster City**
Karr, Richard Lloyd

## KANSAS

**Fort Scott**
Reynolds, Zackery E.
**Lenexa**
Myers, Ross S
**Mcpherson**
Berthelsen, Richard Glen
**Overland Park**
Ellis, Jeffrey Orville
Gunnison, Mark Steven
**Shawnee Mission**
Shank, Suzanne Adams
**Wichita**
Willis, Shari Renee Lyne

## KENTUCKY

**Bowling Green**
Brennenstuhl, Henry Brent
Darrell, Barton David
Goad, Frank Roark
Rudloff, William Joseph
Sparks, David Thomas
**Covington**
Stepner, Donald Leon
Wolnitzek, Stephen Dale
**Elizabethtown**
Bell, Jason B.
**Lexington**
Campbell, Joe Bill
Vimont, Richard Elgin
**London**
Keller, John Warren
**Louisville**
Ballantine, John Tilden
Davidson, Scott Allen
Furman, C. Dean
Ogburn, John Denis
Orberson, William Baxter
Osbourn, Mark A.
Reed, D. Gary
Shanks, C.A. Dudley
Straw-Boone, Melanie
Weiss, Allan
**Paintsville**
Massengale, Roger Lee

## LOUISIANA

**Alexandria**
Pearce, Mark Douglas
**Baton Rouge**
Dixon, Jerome Wayne
Jones, Keith Dunn
Riddick, Winston Wade, Sr.
Walsh, Milton O'Neal
**Gretna**
Fadaol, Robert Frederick
**Lafayette**
Beyer, Jennifer Elmer
Dartez, Shannon Seiler
Gideon, Kyle Liney
Judice, Marc Wayne
Swift, John Goulding
**Lake Charles**
Judice, Gregory Van
**Metairie**
Ellefson, Vance E.
Ford, Robert David
McMahon, Robert Albert, Jr.
Milazzo, Thomas Gregory
Ostendorf, Lance Stephen
**New Orleans**
Abaunza, Donald Richard
Brian, A(lexis) Morgan, Jr.
Courington, Kaye Newton
Curtis, Martha Young
Eustis, Richmond Minor
Futrell, John Maurice
Hammond, Peirce Aldridge, II
Irwin, James Burke, V
Lang, Susan Gail
Pugh, William Whitmell Hill
Rice, Winston Edward
Schoemann, Rudolph Robert
Sinnott, John William
Smith, Ralph E.
Sutterfield, James Ray
Vickery, Eugene Benton, Jr.
**Shreveport**
Smith, Brian David

## MAINE

**Bangor**
Haddow, Jon Andrew
Woodcock, John Alden
**Fryeburg**
Weimer, Gregory Aloyisus
**Portland**
Dinan, Christopher Charles
Germani, Elizabeth A.
Haddow, James Buchanan
Hirshon, Robert Edward
Lancaster, Ralph Ivan, Jr.
Ray, David P.
Tierney, Kevin Joseph
Whiting, Stephen Clyde

## MARYLAND

**Baltimore**
Ebersole, Jodi Kay
Ferguson, Robert L., Jr.
Messina, Bonnie Lynn
Shortridge, Deborah Green
Shuster, David Jonathan
White, William Nelson
Zimmerly, James Gregory
**Bel Air**
Crocker, Michael Pue
**Burtonsville**
Covington, Marlow Stanley
**Chevy Chase**
Weiss, Harlan Lee
**Columbia**
Barton, Ellen Louise
**Hagerstown**
Moylan, Dana
**Parkville**
Hill, Milton King, Jr.
**Rockville**
Armstrong, Kenneth
Dugan, John R.
McGaukian, Rachel Theora
Steren, Marc Nathan
**Silver Spring**
Lipshultz, Leonard L.
**Towson**
Hansen, Christopher Agnew

## MASSACHUSETTS

**Boston**
Alves, Emanuel
Ballard, Nancer H.
Burns, Thomas David
Carberry, Kenneth Anthony
DeRensis, Paul
Dolan, James Boyle, Jr.
Feinberg, Robert I(ra)
Graceffa, John Philip
Halström, Frederic Norman
Lanckton, Arthur Van Cleve
Livingston, Mary Counihan
Neumeier, Richard L.
Ramsey, James E.
Seidel, Rebecca Suzanne
Urquhart, Stephen E.
**Chelmsford**
Lerer, Neal M.
**Duxbury**
Goldman, Eric Scot
**Norwood**
Gorski, Ronald William
**Quincy**
Motejunas, Gerald William
**South Easton**
Finn, Anne-Marie
**Springfield**
Burkett, Lawrence V.
Markey, Patrick Joseph
**Waltham**
Malone, Steven C.
**Worcester**
Balko, George Anthony, III

## MICHIGAN

**Adrian**
Kralick, Richard Louis
**Ann Arbor**
Goethel, Stephen B.
McDaniel, Timothy Ellis
**Bingham Farms**
Fershtman, Julie Ilene
Toth, John Michael
**Birmingham**
Zacharski, Dennis Edward
**Bloomfield Hills**
Lehman, Richard Leroy
Wilson, Cynthia Diane
**Dearborn**
Bernhard, Christine A.
Currier, Gene Mark
**Detroit**
Gilbert, Ronald Rhea
Smith, James Albert
Tucciarone, Enrico Gregory
**East Lansing**
Joseph, Raymond
**Flint**
Henneke, Edward George
Knecht, Timothy Harry
**Grand Rapids**
Andersen, David Charles
Roth, Michael John
Spies, Frank Stadler
Vander Laan, Allan C.
**Lansing**
Baker, Frederick Milton, Jr.
Canady, Mark Howard
Fink, Joseph Allen
Kritselis, William Nicholas
Moody, Kevin Joseph
**Plymouth**
Haynes, Richard Terry
**Pontiac**
Pierson, William George
**Saginaw**
Chasnis, John Alex
McGraw, Patrick John
Zanot, Craig Allen
**Southfield**
Gordon, Louis
MacLean, Joseph Curran
McLellan, Dale J.
Shpiece, Michael Ronald
Tombers, Evelyn Charlotte
**Trenton**
Counard, Allen Joseph
**Troy**
Kruse, John Alphonse
**West Bloomfield**
Meyer, Philip Gilbert

## MINNESOTA

**Edina**
Ashley, James Patrick
Vukelich, John Edward
**Erskine**
Taylor, Richard Charles
**Golden Valley**
Hagglund, Clarance Edward
**Minneapolis**
Al, Marc Andre
Barrett, Michael D.
Degnan, John Michael
Erstad, Leon Robert
Faricy, John Hartnett, Jr.
Fitch, Raymond William
Gant, Jesse, III
Greener, Ralph Bertram
Hagstrom, Richard Michael
Hektner, Candice Elaine
Johnson, Paul Owen
Kunert, Paul Charles
Muirhead, Douglas James
Plunkett, Stephen Oliver
Preus, Christian Andrew
Reichert, Brent Larry
Sanner, Royce Norman
Taylor, Michael George
Witort, Janet Lee
**Moorhead**
Cahill, Steven James
**Saint Paul**
Awsumb, Robert Ardin
Bell, Robert Charles
Dunn, James Francis

## MISSISSIPPI

**Brandon**
Obert, Keith David
**Clarksdale**
Chaffin, William Michael
**Gulfport**
Allen, Harry Roger
Dukes, James Otis
Foster, James (Jay) R.
Harral, John Menteith
**Jackson**
Bullock, James N.
Holbrook, Frank Malvin
Langford, James Jerry
Mitchell, Meade Westmoreland
**Meridian**
Eppes, Walter W., Jr.
**Oxford**
Smith, Kent Elliot
**Pascagoula**
Hunter, John Leslie
**Ridgeland**
Humphreys, Kevin Lee
**Tupelo**
Edwards, John Max, Jr.

## MISSOURI

**Cape Girardeau**
Lowes, Albert Charles
Rith, David J., II
**Clayton**
Clarkin, E. Thomas
**Hannibal**
Terrell, James Daniel
**Hazelwood**
Purvines, Verne Ewald, Jr.
**Hermann**
Kell, Scott K.
**Jefferson City**
Craft, John Charles
**Kansas City**
Abele, Robert Christopher
Beckerman, Dale Lee
Brenneman, Gerald Wayne
Bryant, Richard Todd
Conner, John Shull
Doherty, Brian John
Franke, Linda Frederick
Herron, Donald Patrick
Horn, Robert Allen
Hursh, Lynn Wilson
Levings, Theresa Lawrence
Milton, Chad Earl
Modin, Richard F.
Sauer, Elisabeth Ruth
Sharp, Rex Arthur
Shay, David E.
Todd, Stephen Max

**Mexico**
Hagan, Ann P.
**Platte City**
Cozad, John Condon
**Saint Louis**
Banstetter, Robert J.
Boggs, Beth Clemens
Brown, Paul Sherman
Burns, Mark Gardner
Chestnut, Kathi Lynne
Evans, William Wallace
Galganski, Terry James
Huck, Richard Felix, III
Johnson, Weldon Neal
Kraft, Carl David
McDaniel, James Edwin
Myre, Donald Paul
Reeg, Kurtis Bradford
Schaberg, John Irvin
Susman, Robert M(ark)
Vandover, Samuel Taylor
Wulff, Robert Joseph
**Springfield**
Clithero, Monte Paul
Myers, Ronald Lynn
Penninger, William Holt, Jr.

## MONTANA

**Billings**
Lodders, Ronald R.
**Great Falls**
George, Michael Joseph
**Helena**
Morrison, John Martin
**Kalispell**
Heckathorn, I. James
Lerner, Alan Jay
**Missoula**
Williams, Mark Shelton F.
**Whitefish**
Gersh, Judah M.

## NEBRASKA

**Grand Island**
Busick, Denzel Rex
**Lincoln**
Zink, Walter Earl, II
**Omaha**
Brownrigg, John Clinton
Gleason, James Mullaney
Schmitt, David Jon
Walsh, Thomas John, Sr.

## NEVADA

**Las Vegas**
Albright, George Mark
Kiraly, Michele Ann
Martini, Alyssa Ann
**Reno**
Bader, Angela Marie
Hayward, Daniel Thomas
Kladney, David

## NEW HAMPSHIRE

**Concord**
Miller, Timmie Maine
**Nashua**
Kerrigan, Timothy George

## NEW JERSEY

**Absecon**
Woolson, Charles E., Jr.
**Atlantic City**
Brown, Christopher Arthur
Wallen, Kate Rabassa
**Bernardsville**
Forzani, Rinaldo, III
**Cherry Hill**
Garrigle, William Aloysius
**Collingswood**
Martin, Burchard V.
**East Hanover**
Wilson, Deanne Marie
**Edison**
Billek, Maxwell L.
**Fanwood**
Xifo, Louise Elizabeth
**Hackensack**
Chagaris, Arthur N.
Haworth, Gregory Robert
Pollinger, William Joshua
Reed, Jonathan Seth
**Hamilton**
Chase, Daniel E.
**Keyport**
Colmant, Andrew Robert
**Maplewood**
Joseph, Susan B.
**Moorestown**
Polansky, Steven Jay
**Morris Plains**
Pluciennik, Thomas Casimir
**Morristown**
Gillen, James Robert
**Newark**
Callahan, Patrick Michael
Feldman, Elda Beylerian
Garde, John Charles
Madden, Edward George, Jr.
Mattson, Leroy Harry
McGuire, William B(enedict)
Radin, Steven S.
**North Haledon**
Harrington, Kevin Paul
**Paramus**
Giantonio, Clifford John
**Parsippany**
Asserson, Brian Michael
Kallmann, Stanley Walter
Sesso, George
**Princeton**
Brennan, William Joseph, III
Lewin, Ross Allen
Zarnowski, James David
**Roseland**
Clemente, Mark Andrew
LaVecchia, John B.
Saloman, Mark Andrew
Smith, Wendy Hope
**Rutherford**
Henschel, John James
**Short Hills**
Kaye, Marc Mendell
**Shrewsbury**
Hopkins, Charles Peter, II
**Summit**
Pearlmutter, Fredi L.
**Trenton**
Strassberg, Jonathan Elliot
Williams, Barbara June
**Voorhees**
Harris, Glenn Anthony
Kueny, Bernard E., III
**Warren**
Kraus, Steven Gary
**West Orange**
Bottitta, Joseph Anthony

## NEW MEXICO

**Albuquerque**
Beach, Arthur O'Neal
Roehl, Jerrald J.
Shane, Richard J.
Thompson, Rufus E.
**Las Cruces**
Sandenaw, Thomas Arthur, Jr.
**Roswell**
Haines, Thomas David, Jr.
**Santa Fe**
Culbert, Peter Van Horn

## NEW YORK

**Albany**
Laird, Edward DeHart, Jr.
Stanton, Victoria Mead
**Armonk**
Walsh, David James
**Baldwin**
Verdirame, Peter J.
**Binghamton**
Gerhart, Eugene Clifton
**Bronx**
Marchese, Matthew
**Buffalo**
Armstrong, James F.
Behr, Laurence Donald
Canale, John F.
Goldberg, Neil A.
Herdzik, Arthur Alan
Kieffer, James Marshall
Merriman, Kevin Thomas
Smith, Carrie Lynette
**East Meadow**
Weiss, Adam William
**Flushing**
Kotcher, Shirley J. W.
**Garden City**
Balkan, Kenneth J.
Corleto, Raymond Anthony
**Harrison**
Sloane, Marilyn Austern
**Hawthorne**
Traub, Richard Kenneth
**Hempstead**
Furey, James Michael
**Manhasset**
Kashanian, Shahriar
**Melville**
Adler, Kenneth
Schoenfeld, Michael P.
**Mineola**
Agoglia, Emmet John
Dachs, Jonathan A.
Fowler, David Thomas
Kelly, Shawn Paul
Kral, William George
**N Syracuse**
Kasouf, Joseph Chickery
**New City**
Marcus, Robert Bruce
**New York**
Barry, Desmond Thomas, Jr.
Castellitto, Mario
Cayea, Donald Joseph
Clemen, John Douglas
Cohen, Joshua Robert
Colleran, Robert T.
Connuck, Eric S.
Corbett, Patrick James
Corso, Victor Paul
Cucci, Gardenia Paola
Cunha, Mark Geoffrey
Davis, Michael S.
DeCarlo, Donald Thomas
DeOrchis, Vincent Moore
Devers, Peter Dix
Diamond, Joseph
Dopf, Glenn William
Dunham, Wolcott Balestier, Jr.
Farrow, Sallie
Finnerty, Joseph Gregory, III
Foster, David Lee
Franklin, Gary Lawrence
Gallagher, Timothy D.
Garber, Robert Edward
Graham, Jesse Japhet, II
Greenhill, Jonathan Seth
Gulino, Frank
Halperin, Kyle Mallary
Hayden, Raymond Paul
Hayes, Gerald Joseph
Hernandez, Jacqueline Charmaine
Hersh, Robert Michael
Hirsch, Daniel
Jacobowitz, Harold Saul
Jacobson, Leon Irwin
Kamaiko, Laurie Ann
Kazanjian, John Harold
Kelly, Thomas Michael
Klapper, Molly
Kleinberg, Norman Charles
Koerner, Gregory O.
Kroll, Sol
Kushel, Glenn Elliot
LeBlang, Skip Alan
Leiman, Eugene A.
Lesman, Michael Steven
Lesser, William Melville
Lewis, David Robert
Lynch, Luke Daniel, Jr.
Markel, Gregory Arthur
McCormack, Howard Michael
McCormick, Hugh Thomas
Mentz, Lawrence
Mitchell, C. MacNeil
Moak, Roger Martin
Moran, Edward Kevin
Morris, John E.
Nocera, John Anthony
Nonna, John Michael
O'Brien, John Graham
O'Connell, Margaret Sullivan
O'Leary, Michael Thomas
Olick, Arthur Seymour
Packard, Stephen Michael
Pappachen, George V., Jr.
Polishook, Lewis A.
Primps, William Guthrie
Quinlan, Guy Christian
Rejan, Jeffrey Neil
Reynolds, Timothy Gerard
Riley, Scott C.
Rogoff, Jeffrey Scott
Scherzer, Mark P.
Schiesel, Steven
Schiffer, Larry Philip
Schmidt, Charles Edward
Schmidt, Daniel Edward, IV
Seitelman, Mark Elias
Semaya, Francine Levitt
Shanman, James Alan
Short, Skip
Smith, James Walker
Squire, Walter Charles
Tract, Marc Mitchell
Vyskocil, Mary Kay
Weiser, Martin Jay
Witherwax, Charles Halsey
Wylie, Gordon Fraser
Zimmerman, Earl S.
**Newburgh**
Milligram, Steven Irwin
**Patchogue**
Tona, Thomas
**Purchase**
Kolbrener, Jonathan
**Rochester**
Heyman, Sidney
Reed, James Alexander, Jr.
Thomas, Jacqueline Marie
**Rye**
Varona, Daniel Robert
**Smithtown**
Spellman, Thomas Joseph, Jr.
**Staten Island**
Howard, Davis Jonathan
**Syracuse**
Greene, Arthur M.
Sager, Jonathan Ward
**Uniondale**
Cassidy, David Michael
Kotula, Michael Anthony
Rivkin, John Lawrence
**West Hempstead**
Klebanoff, Stanley Milton
**White Plains**
Keane, Thomas J.
Klein, Paul E.
Merran, Harold
Taft, Nathaniel Belmont
**Yonkers**
Connors, James Patrick

## NORTH CAROLINA

**Asheville**
Chidnese, Patrick N.
Davis, Roy Walton, Jr.
Leake, Larry Bruce
**Blowing Rock**
Corlett, Edward Stanley, III
**Chapel Hill**
Zoffer, David B.
**Charlotte**
Harris, Hugh Stanley, Jr.
Holden, C. Byron
**Greensboro**
Agapion, Bill
**Kinston**
Braswell, Edwin Maurice, Jr.
**Marion**
Burgin, Charles Edward
**Raleigh**
Coats, David Stebbins
Dixon, Wright Tracy, Jr.
Hunter, Richard Samford, Jr.
Madden, John Dale
Millberg, John C.
Robinson, William C.
**Rockingham**
Futrell, Stephan Ray
**Smithfield**
Schulz, Bradley Nicholas
**Wilmington**
Johnston, Sharon A.
**Winston Salem**
Dahl, Tyrus Vance, Jr.
Kelly, James Howard, Jr.
Osborn, Malcolm Everett

## NORTH DAKOTA

**Bismarck**
Edin, Charles Thomas
Gilbertson, Joel Warren
Strutz, William A.
**Grand Forks**
Clapp, Richard Allen

## OHIO

**Akron**
Mullen, Thomas Terry
Parker, Christopher Lee
Wright, Bradley Abbott
**Aurora**
Hermann, Philip J.
**Batavia**
Ostendarp, Gary David
**Canton**
Lindamood, John Beyer
**Celina**
Faber, Keith L.
**Cincinnati**
Hill, Thomas Clark
Knabe, Bruce David
Neltner, Michael Martin
**Cleveland**
Carter, Daniel Paul
Condeni, Joseph Anthony
Duncan, Ed Eugene
Maher, Edward Joseph
Nicholas, Joseph Frederick, Jr.
Norman, Forrest Alonzo
Pohl, Michael A.
Schneider, David Miller
Toohey, Brian Frederick
Wood, Robert Alexander
**Columbus**
Barnes, Belinda Sue
Berliner, Alan Frederick
Briggs, Marjorie Crowder
Brown, Jeffrey Monet
Draper, Gerald Linden
Mann, William Craig
Ryan, Joseph W., Jr.
Vorys, Arthur Isaiah
Woods, William Hunt
**East Liverpool**
Davis, William J.
**Independence**
Rutter, Robert Paul
**N Royalton**
Jungeberg, Thomas Donald
**Toledo**
Tuschman, James Marshall
**Twinsburg**
Carr, Adam E.
**Warren**
Hawley, William Lee
**Youngstown**
Blair, Richard Bryson
Bolton, Stephen Timothy
Melnick, Robert Russell

## OKLAHOMA

**Ardmore**
Bahner, S. Brent
**Enid**
Wyatt, Robert Lee, IV
**Jones**
Dean, Bill Verlin, Jr.
**Oklahoma City**
Babb, Donald Lynn
Callahan, Kelley Charles
Cunningham, Ryan Yerger
Gordon, Kevin Dell
Looney, Robert Dudley
Margo, Robert Cravens
**Tulsa**
Atkinson, Michael Pearce
Ballard, Elizabeth Ann
Clark, Joseph Francis, Jr.
Sterling, Timothy F.
**Vinita**
Linscott, Michael S.

## OREGON

**Astoria**
Haskell, Donald McMillan
**Coquille**
Lounsbury, Steven Richard
**Eugene**
Carlson, Charles David
Lowry, Robert Dudley
**Medford**
Deatherage, William Vernon
**Portland**
Dailey, Dianne K.
Kennedy, Jack Leland
**Salem**
Bauer, Keith Jay

## PENNSYLVANIA

**Allentown**
McGrail-Szabo, Sharon Joan
**Bala Cynwyd**
Kane-Vanni, Patricia Ruth
**Bensalem**
Hoffa, Robert Alan
**Bethel Park**
Bobrowsky, Kim Russell
**Butler**
Biondi, John Michael
**Exton**
Amaral Ryan, Rosa Olinda
**Gladwyne**
Booth, Harold Waverly
**Glenside**
Mellon, Thomas S.
**Greenville**
Rowley, George Hardy
**Harrisburg**
Hafer, Joseph Page
Mark, Timothy Ivan
**Hollidaysburg**
Pfaff, Robert James
**King Of Prussia**
Beausang, Michael Francis, Jr.
DeMaria, Joseph Carminus
**Lancaster**
Roda, Joseph Francis
**Lansdale**
Kline, David Benjamin
**Media**
Blake, David Gordon
Zicherman, David L.
**Narberth**
Malloy, Martin Gerard
**Newtown**
Vosik, Wayne Gilbert
**Norristown**
Scheffler, Stuart Jay
**Penns Park**
Itkoff, David F.
**Philadelphia**
Aaron, Kenneth Ellyot
Aris, John Lynnwood
Best, Franklin Luther, Jr.
Connor, Joseph Patrick, III
Cooper, Brad
DeLuca, Anthony R.
Devlin, John Gerard
Elkins, S. Gordon
Fineman, S. David
Garcia, Rudolph
German, Edward Cecil
Goldberg, Marvin Allen
Hamilton, Michael Alan
Hanselmann, Fredrick Charles
Horn, Robert F.
Lieberman, Joel M.
Lowery, William Herbert
McNamara, John C.
Milbourne, Walter Robertson
Palmer, Richard Ware
Resnick, Stephanie
Schildt, Steven Joseph
Viletto, Harold Ernst
Wagner, Thomas Joseph
**Pittsburgh**
Bochicchio, Vito Salvatore
Cohen, David R.
Keenan, C. Robert, III
Leonard, Arthur J.
Loch, Robert Anthony
McKenzie, Thomas James
Mulvihill, Keithley D.
Nerone, Michael F.
Ober, Russell John, Jr.
Salpietro, Frank Gugliotta
Sherry, John Sebastian
von Waldow, Arnd N.
**Reading**
Turner, David Eldridge
**Scranton**
Pocius, James Edward
Wenzel, Francis George, Jr.
**Warendale**
Jacobs, Richard Louis
**Warminster**
Corr, Martin Joseph
**Wayne**
Griffith, Edward, II

## RHODE ISLAND

**Providence**
Burrows, Richard Henry
Devereaux, William P.
**Warwick**
Battle, Leslie Anne Elizabeth
Reilly, John B.

## SOUTH CAROLINA

**Charleston**
Cooke, Morris Dawes, Jr.
Thompson, Joseph Durant
Waring, Bradish J.
**Columbia**
Carpenter, Charles Elford, Jr.
Jones, Hartwell Kelley, Jr.
Kelly, D. Michael
**Greenville**
Farry, Michael Allen
Johnson, Matthew Kinard
Pitts, Michael Stuart

## SOUTH DAKOTA

**Pierre**
Gerdes, David Alan
**Rapid City**
Connot, Mark Jeffrey
**Sioux Falls**
Orr, Rick W.

## TENNESSEE

**Chattanooga**
Campbell, Paul, Jr.
Campbell, Paul, III
Cirina, Angela Marie
Cooper, Gary Allan
Copeland, Floyd Dean
Eason, Marcia Jean
Hays, Melissa Padgett
Simonds, Timothy Ray
**Johnson City**
Jenkins, Ronald Wayne
**Kingsport**
Hull, E. Patrick
**Knoxville**
Bailey, Bridget
Coleman, Gregory Frederic
Johnson, Steven Boyd
London, James Harry
Walter, Glenn Richard
Ward, Kenneth Wayne
Wedekind, David N.
Wheeler, John Watson
White, Edward Gibson, II
**Lawrenceburg**
Plant, Paul Brunson
**Memphis**
Russell, James Franklin
Witthauer, Robert Taylor
**Nashville**
Anderson, Charles Hill
Freeman, James Atticus, III
Midgett, James Clayton, Jr.
Tudor, Bynum Ellsworth, III
Youngblood, Elaine Michele

## TEXAS

**Amarillo**
Hand, Matthew Henry
**Austin**
Barnes, Natasha Lynn
Hager, Julie-Ann
Krueger, William Wayne, III
Roan, Forrest Calvin, Jr.
Schaffer, Dean Aaron

Schrauff, Christopher Wesley
Staelin, Earl Hudson
**Baytown**
Linebaugh, Daniel Bruce
**Beaumont**
Dowell, James Dale
Scofield, Louis M., Jr.
**Brownsville**
Jordan, John Joseph
**Bryan**
Michel, C. Randall
**Corpus Christi**
Anthony, James Lloyd
Elizondo, Luis A.
Evans, Allene Delories
Fancher, Rick
Leon, Rolando Luis
**Dallas**
Balido, Carlos A.
Bennett, Paul William
Brandt, Edward Newman
Brown, James Earle
Cobb, William Dowell, Jr.
Davenport, James Kent
Doyle, Mark Anthony
Dunnill, William Connor
Ellis, Alfred Wright (Al Ellis)
Glazer, Rachelle Hoffman
Goodwin, R. Brad
Henry, Vic Houston
Hranitzky, Rachel Robyn
Ivey, John Kemmerer
Keegan, Karen Ann
King, Ira Thomas
Leach, James Glover
Lotzer, Gerald Balthazar
Pruessner, David Morgan
Rittenberry, Kelly Culhane
Roberts, Ronald
Roberts, Steven Dillon
Spear, James Hodges
Weitzel, J. Dennis
**El Paso**
Dickey, John M.
Oaxaca, Juan Roberto
**Fort Worth**
Cottongame, W. Brice
Dent, Edward Dwain
Dushman, Lowell Edward
Hart, John Clifton
Johnston, Michael Wayne
Jones, Gregory G.
Paddock, Michael Buckley
Shannon, Joe, Jr.
Tatum, Stephen Lyle
Wagner, James Peyton
**Houston**
Bluestein, Edwin A., Jr.
Brown, David Hurst
Carver, Teresa Ann
Coleman, Bryan Douglas
Couch, Steve Earl
Durham, William Andrew
Heggen, Ivar Nelson
Knutson, Sam Houston
Krebs, Arno William, Jr.
Love, Scott Anthony
Martin, Christopher W.
Pate, Stephen Patrick
Rambo, Rick Lynn
Sorrels, Randall Owen
Toney, William David, II
Vickery, Edward Downtain
Wojciechowski, Marc James
**Irving**
Bradley, Jean Marie
**Killeen**
Carlson, Craig W.
**Lindale**
Anderson, Lawrence Worthington
**Longview**
Stevens, Scott English
**Midland**
Fletcher, Richard Royce
**Odessa**
Corzine, Darrell W.
Hendrick, Benard Calvin, VII
**Paris**
Standifer, Rick M.
**San Antonio**
Farmer, William David
Guevara, Roger
Henry, Peter York
Johnson, Edward Michael
McFarlen, Gerald Dale
Patrick, Dane Herman
Scalise-Qubrosi, Celeste
Shiely, Gerald Lawrence
Veitch, Thomas Harold
**Sherman**
Harrison, Richard E.
**Temple**
Pickle, Jerry Richard
**Texarkana**
Poff, Franklin Albright, Jr.
**The Woodlands**
Schlacks, Stephen Mark
**Tyler**
Kent, Don Wayne
Vickery, Ronald Stephen
**Wichita Falls**
Altman, William Kean

### UTAH

**Park City**
Fay, John Farrell
**Provo**
Jeffs, M. Dayle
**Salt Lake City**
Butler, Cass C.
Deamer, Michael Lynn
Humpherys, LeGrande Rich
Larson, Bryan A.
Nebeker, Stephen Bennion
Purser, Donald Joseph

### VERMONT

**Burlington**
Sartore, John Thornton
**Montpelier**
Bland, Richard Norman
**Rutland**
Faignant, John Paul
O'Rourke, William Andrew, III
Werle, Mark Fred
**Saint Johnsbury**
Palmer, Bruce C.
**Springfield**
Boxer, Andrew Carey

### VIRGINIA

**Abingdon**
McElroy, Howard Chowning
**Alexandria**
Battle, Timothy Joseph
Summers, Alicia Lehnes
**Culpeper**
Dulaney, Richard Alvin
**Fairfax**
Bardott, Heather Kathleen
**Hampton**
Boester, Robert Alan
**Harrisonburg**
Ledbetter, Melisa Gay
**Lynchburg**
Burnette, Ralph Edwin, Jr.
**Norfolk**
Davis, Terry Hunter, Jr.
McCaa, James Cureton, III
Rashkind, Alan Brody
Zahn, Richard William
**Norton**
Shortridge, Judy Beth
**Radford**
Davis, Richard Waters
**Richmond**
Allen, Wilbur Coleman
Ellis, Andrew Jackson, Jr.
Hauck, David Leahigh
Spahn, Gary Joseph
Street, Walter Scott, III
**Roanoke**
Austin, J. Rudy
Harbert, Guy M., III
Ziogas, Robert Aristidis
**Virginia Beach**
Dumville, S(amuel) Lawrence
Moore, Michael Calvin
Swope, Richard McAllister
**Wytheville**
Baird, Thomas Bryan, Jr.

### WASHINGTON

**Everett**
Bacetich, Dominic Lee
**Gig Harbor**
Malarchick, Timothy Paul
**Longview**
Barlow, John Aden
**Mercer Island**
Gosanko, Gary Nicolas
**Olympia**
Gentry, Fred Dee
Hoglund, John Andrew
**Renton**
Swanson, Arthur Dean
**Seattle**
Blom, Daniel Charles
Diamond, Maria Sophia
Easter, Scott Beyer
Field, Harold Basil
Hillman, Roger Lewis
Lassman, Iro Richard
Loftus, Thomas Daniel
Mines, Michael
Soderland, Douglas R.
Tuffley, Francis Douglas
Walter, Michael Charles
Whitehead, James Fred, III
Zeder, Fred M.
**Spokane**
Annis, Eugene Irwin
Bunch, Jeffrey R.
Luciani, Thomas Richard
Pontarolo, Michael Joseph
Riherd, John Arthur
Smith, Brad Edward
Smythe, Andrew Campbell
Symmes, William Daniel
**Walla Walla**
Monahan, Richard F.
**Yakima**
Mathieu, Richard Louis

### WEST VIRGINIA

**Charleston**
Bell, Harry Fullerton, Jr.
Brennaman, Sandra Lee
Fisher, Michael Matthew
**Huntington**
Bagley, Charles Frank, III
**Morgantown**
Kimble, Kelly Jean
**Princeton**
White, Benjamin Ballard, Jr.
**Wheeling**
Wilmoth, William David

### WISCONSIN

**Appleton**
Lonergan, Kevin
**Brookfield**
Palmersheim, Richard J.
Zaffiro, Richard L.
**Elm Grove**
Miracle, Dale Neil
**Green Bay**
Barker, April Rockstead
Grzeca, Michael (Gerard)
Thompson, John Mortimer
**Madison**
Croake, Paul Allen
Schmid, John Henry, Jr.
Toman, William Joseph
**Mequon**
Tolan, David J.
**Milwaukee**
Bremer, John M.
Carroll, Douglas James
Esser, Christine D.
Fitzgerald, Kevin Gerard
Fredericks, James Matthew
Gaines, Irving David
Galanis, John William
Quirk, Michael L.
Wynn, Stanford Alan
**Oshkosh**
Wilde, William Richard
**Rhinelander**
Eckert, Michael Louis
Saari, John William, Jr.
**Wausau**
Haarmann, Bruce Donald
Strande, Jeffrey Jay

### WYOMING

**Cheyenne**
Argeris, George John
Kehl, Larry Bryan
McKinley, John Clark
**Sheridan**
Lonabaugh, Ellsworth Eugene

### TERRITORIES OF THE UNITED STATES

### VIRGIN ISLANDS

**St Croix**
Welcome, Patricia

### ADDRESS UNPUBLISHED

Anderson, David Alan
Bandy, Jack D.
Bell, John William
Berman, Richard Bruce
Brown, Jay W.
Chong-Spiegel, Ginger Geroma
Denaro, Charles Thomas
Dick, Sheryl Lynn
Dikeou, George Demetrios
DiSalvo, Theodore L.
Eaton, Larry Ralph
Fekete, George Otto
Gingras, John Richard
Grady, Maureen Frances
Gregory, Rick Dean
Griffith, Steven Franklin, Sr.
Iannacone, Randolph Frank
Kennedy, Vekeno
Klausman, Glenn
Klein, Judah B.
Krutter, Forrest Nathan
Levinson, Kenneth Lee
Levy, David
Massey, Kathleen Marie Oates
Mathieu, Michelle Elise
McDonald, Sandra K.
O'Connor, Kathleen Mary
Radogno, Joseph Anthony
Rosseel-Jones, Mary Louise
Russo, Donna Marie
Shigley, Kenneth Lowell
Sperry, Martin Jay
Spiegel, Jayson Leslie
Vinar, Benjamin
Weeks, Tresi Lea
Wells, Wayne Alton
Wimmer, Nancy T.

## INTELLECTUAL PROPERTY

### UNITED STATES

### ALABAMA

**Birmingham**
Hinton, James Forrest, Jr.
Long, Thad Gladden
Ramsey, David Wade

### ARIZONA

**Phoenix**
Allen, Robert Eugene Barton
Brecher, Allison Leigh
Corson, Kimball Jay
Gerity, Michael E.
Harris, Ray Kendall
Maynard, Daniel Dwight
Meschkow, Jordan M.
Sutton, Samuel J.
**Tempe**
Shimpock, Kathy Elizabeth
Vanderpoel, James Robert
**Tucson**
Conn, Deanna

### ARKANSAS

**Pine Bluff**
Strode, Joseph Arlin

### CALIFORNIA

**Aptos**
Garrison, Melissa Lyn
**Beverly Hills**
Donaldson, Michael Cleaves
Litwak, Glenn Tod
**Burbank**
Campbell, L. Cooper
Noddings, Sarah Ellen
**Burlingame**
Spyros, Nicholas L., Jr.
**Claremont**
Ansell, Edward Orin
**Costa Mesa**
Stone, Samuel Beckner
**Culver City**
Pavitt, William Hesser, Jr.
**Cupertino**
Naylor, Brian Thomas
Simon, Nancy Ruth
**Encinitas**
Nemeth, Valerie Ann
**La Jolla**
Karlen, Peter Hurd
**Los Angeles**
Barrett, Jane Hayes
Biederman, Donald Ellis
Chan, Thomas Tak-Wah
Dean, Jon
Feigen, Brenda S.
Foley, Martin James
Genga, John Michael
Immerman, William Joseph
Kenoff, Jay Stewart
Kindred, Alan M.
Kupperman, Henry John
Lamison, Eric Ross
Levin, Evanne Lynn
Scoular, Robert Frank
Synn, Gordon
**Marina Dl Rey**
Seiden, Andy
**Menlo Park**
Coats, William Sloan, III
Dodson, Gerald Paul
Halluin, Albert Price
**Monterey**
Bomberger, Russell Branson
**Mountain View**
Koehler, Fritz K.
**Newport Beach**
Friedland, Michael Keith
Knobbe, Louis Joseph
Merring, Robert Alan
Mirabel, Farrah
Rowlett, Robert Duane
**Pacific Palisades**
Flattery, Thomas Long
**Palo Alto**
Hasko, Judith Ann
Postner, Marya A.
Sands, Michael Arthur
Small, Jonathan Andrew
Wilson, Thomas Russell
**Pasadena**
van Schoonenberg, Robert G.
**Redwood City**
Cole, George Stuart
**Riverside**
Nassar, William Michael
**Sacramento**
Mendoza, Joanna R.
**San Diego**
Bilstad, Blake Timothy
Chatroo, Arthur Jay
Denniston, John Alexander
Fawcett, Robroy Ronald
Lathrop, Mitchell Lee
Michels, Dirk
Pineda, Dayna Jayne
Preston, David Raymond
Smith, Norman Leslie
Strauss, Steven Marc
Underwood, Anthony Paul
**San Francisco**
Bleich, Jeffrey Laurence
Davis, Anthony Edward
Green, Philip R.
Meador, Ross DeShong
Peter, Laura Anne
Reding, John Anthony
Richardson, Daniel Ralph
Riley, Benjamin Kneeland
Salomon, Darrell Joseph
Shin, Chang Shik
Slavitt, Howard Alan
Tong, Peter P.
Traynor, John Michael
Yamakawa, David Kiyoshi, Jr.
**San Jose**
Anderson, Edward Virgil
Jorgensen, Norman Eric
McManis, James
**Santa Clara**
Kaner, Cem
**Santa Cruz**
Damon, Richard Everett
**Saratoga**
Stephens, Lawrence Keith
**Sunnyvale**
Wyatt, Thomas Csaba
Zahrt, William Dietrich, II
**Ventura**
English, Woodrow Douglas
**Vista**
Talpalatsky, Sam

### COLORADO

**Boulder**
Miller, Jonathan Lewis
**Broomfield**
Hogle, Sean Sherwood
**Denver**
Jonsen, Eric R.
Schindler, Ronald Irvin

### CONNECTICUT

**Danbury**
Leuzzi, Paul William
**Groton**
Kehoe, Thomas Joseph
**Hartford**
Berlage, Jan Ingham
Veltrop, James D.
**New Haven**
De Lio, Anthony Peter
**Stamford**
Carten, Francis Noel
Kelly, Michael John

### DELAWARE

**Wilmington**
Boudreaux, Gerald Joseph
Devine, Donn
Frank, George Andrew
Goldstein, Jack Charles
Huntley, Donald Wayne
Macel, Stanley Charles, III
Magee, Thomas Hugh
Parsons, Donald Francis

### DISTRICT OF COLUMBIA

**Washington**
Bancroft, Judith Gail
Cantor, Herbert I.
Dinan, Donald Robert
Hockenberry, John Fedden
Liss, Jeffrey F.
Loevinger, Lee
McDaniels, William E.
Pfeiffer, Margaret Kolodny
Price, Griffith Baley, Jr.
Quarles, James Linwood, III
Ray, Tamber
Rosenthal, Ilene Goldstein
Ryan, John William
Schaumberg, Tom Michael
Silverman, David Malanos
Sung, Lawrence M.
Wilson, Gary Dean
Zane, Phillip Craig

### FLORIDA

**Boca Raton**
Horn, Douglas Michael
Schwartz, Kenneth Jeffrey
**Casselberry**
Campbell, John Michael
**Clearwater**
Hopen, Anton John
**Coral Gables**
Lott, Leslie Jean
**Fort Lauderdale**
Kubler, Frank Lawrence
**Gainesville**
McLeod, Christine Quillian
**Hialeah**
Dominik, Jack Edward
**Miami**
Buchenhorner, Michael Joseph
Burstein, Bernardo
Kolback, Kimberly Dawn
Nagin, Stephen E.
**Naples**
Werder, Horst Heinrich
**Palm Bay**
Howard, Marilyn Hoey
**Saint Petersburg**
Wilson, Darryl Cedric
**Tampa**
Pettis, David Wilson, Jr.
Thomas, Gregg Darrow
**Wilton Manors**
Daly, Susan Mary

### GEORGIA

**Atlanta**
Fleming, Julian Denver, Jr.
Hassett, Robert William
Luther, Donald William
Owens, L. Dale
Quittmeyer, Peter Charles
Spalten, David Elliot
**Decatur**
Middleton, James Boland
**Dunwoody**
Tramonte, James Albert

### HAWAII

**Honolulu**
Godbey, Robert Carson

### IDAHO

**Boise**
Hickman, Lori A. DeMond
Scanlan, Kevin J.

### ILLINOIS

**Chicago**
Altman, Louis
Benak, James Donald
Cederoth, Richard Alan
Chestnut, John William
Chin, Davis
DeVries, James Howard
Elliott, Thomas Clark, Jr.
Geraldson, Raymond I., Jr.
Hilliard, David Craig
Horn, Richard Leslie
Karon, Sheldon
Lorenzen, Donald Robert
Manzo, Edward David
Norek, Joan I.
Oberhardt, William Patrick
Rupert, Donald William
Shurtleff, John Howard
Shurtz, Steven Park
Smedinghoff, Thomas J.
Smith, Gregory Michael
Snyder, Jean Maclean
Wesley, William Matthew
Wick, Lawrence Scott
Yang, Cora Germaine
**Oak Brook**
Mlsna, Kathryn Kimura
**Saint Charles**
Hines, Suzanne
**Urbana**
Berns, Michael Andrew

### INDIANA

**Indianapolis**
Knebel, Donald Earl
Taylor, Jay Gordon
Tinsley, Nancy Grace
**Merrillville**
Kinney, Richard Gordon

### IOWA

**Des Moines**
Fisher, Thomas George

### KANSAS

**Overland Park**
Sampson, William Roth

## INTERNATIONAL, PRIVATE

Blake, Jonathan Dewey
Boone, Theodore Sebastian
Bregman, Arthur Randolph
Buechner, Jack W(illiam)
Burt, Jeffrey Amsterdam
Chanin, Michael Henry
Cheston, Sheila Carol
Clagett, Brice McAdoo
Cole, Robert Theodore
Craig, Gregory Bestor
Cymrot, Mark Alan
Danas, Andrew Michael
Debevoise, Eli Whitney, II
Denison, Mary Boney
Devall, James Lee
Dinan, Donald Robert
Donohoe, Charles Richard
Ellicott, John LeMoyne
Falk, John Mansfield
Faron, Robert Steven
Fishburne, Benjamin P., III
Fisher, Bart Steven
Flowe, Benjamin Hugh, Jr.
Fontheim, Claude G.B.
Geniesse, Robert John
Gold, Peter Frederick
Harris, Scott Blake
Harrison, Earl David
Harrison, Marion Edwyn
Hellbeck, Eckhard Robert
Heron, Julian Briscoe, Jr.
Hu, Patrick Haiping
Ives, Stephen Bradshaw, Jr.
Jetton, C. Loring, Jr.
Karpinski, Irena Izabella
Kassinger, Theodore William
Kessler, Judd Lewis
Knauer, Leon Thomas
Kramer, William David
Kriesberg, Simeon M.
La Force, Pierre Joseph
Lamm, Carolyn Beth
Landfield, Richard
Larroca, Raymond G.
Lavine, Henry Wolfe
Leonard, Will Ernest, Jr.
Linowitz, Sol Myron
Lucas, Steven Mitchell
Malia, Gerald Aloysius
Mathias, Charles McCurdy
Mazo, Mark Elliott
Mendelsohn, Allan Irving
Mendelsohn, Martin
Miller, Randy E.
Mirvahabi, Farin
Mitchell, Carol Ann
Mitchell, Roy Shaw
More, John Herron
Norberg, Charles Robert
Pearce, Cary Jack
Pomeroy, Harlan
Price, Daniel Martin
Rainbolt, John Vernon, II
Raul, Alan Charles
Rehm, John Bartram
Riley, Daniel Joseph
Ruddy, Frank
Schaumberg, Tom Michael
Sherzer, Harvey Gerald
Spector, Phillip Louis
Stayin, Randolph John
Stuart, Pamela Bruce
Tavallali, Jalal Chaicar
Timberg, Sigmund
Townsend, John Michael
Trinder, Rachel Bandele
Vakerics, Thomas Vincent
Verrill, Charles Owen, Jr.
Waite, Frederick Paul
Waldron, Jonathan Kent
Weinstein, Martin James
Weiss, Arnold Hans
Weiss, Mark Anschel
Wilde, Jinhee Kim
Wolf, Maurice
Work, Charles Robert
Wray, Robert

## FLORIDA

**Boca Grande**
Brock, Mitchell
**Clearwater**
Durand, Jean-Paul
**Deerfield Beach**
Daugherty, Walter Emory
**Fort Lauderdale**
Barnard, George Smith
Pascal, Robert Albert
Schrader, Robert George
Turner, Hugh Joseph, Jr.
**Hialeah**
Dominik, Jack Edward
**Hobe Sound**
Simpson, Russell Gordon
**Miami**
Alvarez-Farré, Emilio José
Berley, David Richard
Boren, Barry Marc
Castillo, Angel, Jr.
Ersek, Gregory Joseph Mark
Fontes, J. Mario F., Jr.
Gutierrez, Renaldy Jose
Hudson, Robert Franklin, Jr.
Jacobson, Bernard
Landy, Burton Aaron
Muñiz, Nicolas Jose
Murphy, Timothy James
Paul, Robert
Pearlman, Michael Allen
Poston, Rebekah Jane
Pruna, Laura Maria
Short, Eugene Maurice, Jr.
Sotorrio, Rene Alberto
**Naples**
Emerson, John Williams, II
Werder, Horst Heinrich
**North Palm Beach**
Koffler, Warren William
**Orlando**
Hendry, Robert Ryon
Ioppolo, Frank S., Jr.
Johnson, Kraig Nelson
Neff, A. Guy
**Palm Beach**
Keihner, Bruce William
**Palm Beach Gardens**
Brams, Jeffrey Brent
Olson, Carl Eric
**Sarasota**
Partoyan, Garo Arakel
**Tampa**
Bierley, John Charles
Dyal, Lucius Mahlon, Jr.
Grammig, Robert James
**West Palm Beach**
Hill, Thomas William, Jr.
Stuber, James Arthur

## GEORGIA

**Atlanta**
Barker, Clayton Robert, III
Booth, Gordon Dean, Jr.
Cargill, Robert Mason
Greer, Bernard Lewis, Jr.
Keck, Richard Paul
Kelley, James Francis
Kohn, Robert Alexander
Muller, William Manning
Schock, Robert Christopher
Verska, Kimberly Anne
Wilson, Roger Calvin

## HAWAII

**Honolulu**
Boas, Frank
Bourgoin, David L.
Cassiday, Benjamin Buckles, III
Ingersoll, Richard King
Miller, Clifford Joel
Sumida, Gerald Aquinas

## ILLINOIS

**Abbott Park**
Brock, Charles Marquis
**Aurora**
Marchetti, Marilyn H.
**Barrington**
Cass, Robert Michael
**Chicago**
Blatt, Richard Lee
Burgdoerfer, Jerry
Chudzinski, Mark Adam
Cortes, William Patrick
DeVries, James Howard
Docksey, John Ross
Doetsch, Douglas Allen
Farrell, Thomas Dinan
Hoffman, Douglas Raymond
Hunt, Lawrence Halley, Jr.
Johnson, Tige Christopher
Kamerick, Eileen Ann
Knuepfer, Robert Claude, Jr.
Lemberis, Theodore Thomas
Marroquin-Merino, Victor Miguel
McLees, John Alan
Meltzer, Robert Craig
Michaels, Richard Edward
O'Leary, Daniel Vincent, Jr.
Pallasch, B. Michael
Partridge, Mark Van Buren
Potter, Richard Clifford
Prochnow, Herbert Victor, Jr.
Rizowy, Carlos Guillermo
Smith, Stephen Edward
Stevenson, Adlai Ewing, III
Thomas, Stephen Paul
Timmer, Stephen Blaine
Yang, Cora Germaine
Yu, Aihong
**Deerfield**
Staubitz, Arthur Frederick
**Naperville**
Larson, Mark Edward, Jr.
**North Chicago**
de Lasa, José M.
**Northbrook**
Ihm, Stephen Lawrence
Teichner, Bruce A.
**Oakbrook Ter**
Fenech, Joseph Charles
**Peoria**
Atterbury, Robert Rennie, III

## INDIANA

**Indianapolis**
Heerens, Joseph Robert
Kessler, Susan D.
Russell, David Williams
**Lafayette**
O'Connell, Lawrence B.

## IOWA

**Burlington**
Hoth, Steven Sergey

## KENTUCKY

**Louisville**
Anderson, P. Richard
Northern, Richard
Welsh, Alfred John

## LOUISIANA

**Metairie**
Ostendorf, Lance Stephen
**New Orleans**
Jones, Philip Kirkpatrick, Jr.
Perry, Brian Drew, Sr.
Rice, Winston Edward

## MAINE

**Castine**
Wiswall, Frank Lawrence, Jr.

## MARYLAND

**Baltimore**
Black, Herbert Allen
Ohly, D. Christopher
Ritter, Jeffrey Blake
Robinson, Zelig
**Bethesda**
English, William deShay
Goodwin, Robert Cronin
Scully, Roger Tehan
**Brookeville**
Fobe, Nicholas M(atthew)
**Gaithersburg**
Phillips, Leo Harold, Jr.
**North Potomac**
Lehman, Leonard
**Rockville**
Zaphiriou, George Aristotle

## MASSACHUSETTS

**Billerica**
Pellegrin, Gilles George
**Boston**
Aresty, Jeffrey M.
Bernhard, Alexander Alfred
Bines, Harvey Ernest
Browne, Aidan Francis
Chow, Stephen Y(ee)
Garcia, Adolfo Ramon
Graham, John Joseph
Greer, Gordon Bruce
Huang, Thomas Weishing
Kaler, Robert Joseph
Kelakos, George M.
Kopelman, Leonard
Licata, Arthur Frank
Masud, Robert
Menoyo, Eric Felix
O'Neill, Philip Daniel, Jr.
Sager, Steven Travis
Stokes, James Christopher
Thibeault, George Walter
Trevisani, Robert Armand
**Brookline**
Burnstein, Daniel
**Cambridge**
Gonson, S. Donald
Ta, Tai Van
**Canton**
Fuller, Robert L(eander)
**Carlisle**
Hensleigh, Howard Edgar
**Haverhill**
Spurling, Dennis Michael
**Lexington**
D'Avignon, Roy Joseph
**Lincoln**
Gnichtel, William Van Orden
**Nantucket**
Lobl, Herbert Max
**Waltham**
Barnes-Brown, Peter Newton

## MICHIGAN

**Ada**
Mc Callum, Charles Edward
**Ann Arbor**
Muraski, Anthony Augustus
**Birmingham**
Elsman, James Leonard, Jr.
Eydelshteyn, Simon Mark
**Clinton Township**
Theut, C. Peter
**Detroit**
Darlow, Julia Donovan
Lawrence, John Kidder
Thorpe, Norman Ralph
**Grosse Pointe**
Hindelang, Robert Louis
**Grosse Pointe Woods**
Darke, Richard Francis
**Kalamazoo**
Deming, Stuart Hayden
**Troy**
Dillon, Joseph Francis

## MINNESOTA

**Minneapolis**
Bras, Robert W.
Frecon, Alain
Hasselquist, Maynard Burton
Lofstrom, Mark D.
McNeil, Mark Sanford
Sippel, William Leroy
**Saint Paul**
Devgun, Dharminder Singh
Dordell, Timothy Paul
Maffei, Rocco John
Oh, Matthew InSoo

## MISSOURI

**Chesterfield**
Hier, Marshall David
**Clayton**
Mohrman, Henry J(oe), Jr.
**Kansas City**
Redmond, Christopher John
Socarras, Michael Peter
Wrobley, Ralph Gene
**Saint Louis**
Leontsinis, George John

## NEVADA

**Las Vegas**
Zubel, Eric Louis
**Reno**
Olechny, Steven John

## NEW HAMPSHIRE

**Portsmouth**
Volk, Kenneth Hohne

## NEW JERSEY

**Budd Lake**
Webb, John Gibbon, III
**Cherry Hill**
Moleski, Anthony G.
**Clifton**
Sudol, Walter Edward
**Clinton**
Kennedy, Harold Edward
**Florham Park**
Wright, Paul William
**Fort Lee**
Cox, Melvin Monroe
**Franklin Lakes**
Lagdameo-Hogan, Maria-Elena
**Kenilworth**
Wasman, Jane G.
**Keyport**
Colmant, Andrew Robert
**Kinnelon**
Kossl, Thomas Leonard
**Livingston**
Watson, Stephen Allison, III
**Newark**
Dreyfuss, Stephen Lawrence
**Princeton**
Atkins, Thomas Herman
Glogoff, David Louis
**Ramsey**
Ogden, John Hamilton
**Short Hills**
Marshall, John Patrick
**Warren**
Hasl, Hannelore Vera Margarete
Kasper, Horst Manfred
**Woodbridge**
Golden, Daniel Lewis

## NEW MEXICO

**Albuquerque**
Hanna, Robert Cecil
Messersmith, Lanny Dee
Schoen, Stevan Jay
Schuler, Alison Kay

## NEW YORK

**Albany**
Hanna, John, Jr.
**Albion**
Lyman, Nathan Marquis
**Armonk**
Walsh, David James
**Auburn**
Wolczyk, Joseph Michael
**Bridgehampton**
Cummings, Richard M.
**Brooklyn**
Villa, James Gerard
**Buffalo**
Yost, Ellen G. (Ellen Yost Lafili)
**Canaan**
Pennell, William Brooke
**Floral Park**
Friedman, Jon George
**Hillsdale**
Lunde, Asbjorn Rudolph
**Jamaica**
Dickerson, Claire Moore
Gonzalez-Perez, Ramon Horacio
**Larchmont**
Berridge, George Bradford
**Malden Bridge**
Benton, Edward Henry
**Mineola**
Vargas, Diana Monica
**New York**
Allen, Leon Arthur, Jr.
Allen, Phillip Stephen
Andersen, Richard Esten
Behrendt, John Thomas
Beinecke, Candace Krugman
Bernstein, Bernard
Bertoni, Fernando Raul
Bickford, Nathaniel Judson
Bidwell, James Truman, Jr.
Bloomer, Harold Franklin, Jr.
Breitenecker, Rudiger
Brumm, James Earl
Bryan, Barry Richard
Burak, H(oward) Paul
Carpenter, Randle Burt
Carter, James Hal, Jr.
Chilstrom, Robert Meade
Cho, Tai Yong
Clapman, Peter Carlyle
Cohen, Howard Marvin
Connor, John Thomas, Jr.
Cooper, Stephen Herbert
Corso, Victor Paul
Cuneo, Donald Lane
Davidson, Robert Bruce
Detjen, David Wheeler
Diaz-Granados, Rafael Andres
di Domenico, Philip
Dlugoff, Marc Alan
Duffy, Edmund Charles
Edelman, Paul Sterling
Edozien, Margaret Ekwutozia
Essien, Victor Kwesi
Fernandez, Jose Walfredo
Fewell, Charles Kenneth, Jr.
Fleischman, Edward Hirsh
Fogelnest, Robert
Forry, John Ingram
Fredericks, Wesley Charles, Jr.
Freyer, Dana Hartman
Furniss, Peter Glenn
Gallagher, Brian John
Gans, Walter Gideon
Ganz, David L.
Garfinkel, Barry Herbert
Gettner, Alan Frederick
Giancarlo, J. Christopher
Gilioli, Eric Lawrence
Gill, Patrick David
Goldman, Richard Lurie
Gooch, Anthony Cushing
Grant, Stephen Allen
Greenspon, Robert Alan
Greenwald, Harold
Greilsheimer, William Henry
Gustafson, Albert Katsuaki
Haddad, Mark Anthony
Halket, Thomas D(aniel)
Hamel, Rodolphe
Harris, Joel B(ruce)
Hauser, Rita Eleanore Abrams
Hayden, Raymond Paul
Hayes, Gerald Joseph
Herold, Karl Guenter
Hicks, J. Portis
Higgs, John H.
Hill, Joseph C.
Hirsch, Daniel
Howe, Edwin A(lberts), Jr.
Hritz, George F.
Hurlock, James Bickford
Jackson, William Eldred
Jannuzzo, Jeffrey Anthony
Jefferies, Jack P.
Johnson, Lynne A.
Johnson, Stephen Patrick Howard
Jones, Douglas W.
Jong, James C. (Chuanping Zhang)
Kalat, Peter Anthony
Katsos, Barbara Helene
Katz, Gary M.
Kies, David M.
King, Henry Lawrence
Kirberger, Elizabeth
Knight, Robert Huntington
Knight, Townsend Jones
Kojevnikov, Boris Oleg
Komaroff, Stanley
Kreitzman, Ralph J.
Krikorian, Van Z.
Krivoy, Clara
Krylov, Nikolai
Larose, Lawrence Alfred
Leckie, Gavin Frederick
Lee, In-Young
Lee, Thomas Dongho
LeFevre, David E.
Li, Donna Dongli
Li, Rebecca Jia
Lutringer, Richard Emil
MacRae, Cameron Farquhar, III
Madden, John Patrick
Marks, Ramon Paul
Matteson, William Bleecker
McDonell, Neil Edwin
Melnik, Selinda A.
Michel, Clifford Lloyd
Milgrim, Roger Michael
Molnar, Lawrence
Muskin, Victor Philip
Nahm, Nathan Ihru
Nathan, Andrew Jonathan
Newman, Lawrence Walker
Nimetz, Matthew
Oliner, Martin
Orol, Elliot S.
Osborn, Donald Robert
Parker, Bret I.
Passer-Muslin, Juliette Mayabelle
Paul, Robert Carey
Pavia, George M.
Perkins, Roswell Burchard
Perlberger, Ralph
Pettibone, Peter John
Pierce, Morton Allen
Polishook, Lewis A.
Prashker, Audrey Eve
Prem, F. Herbert, Jr.
Prentice, Eugene Miles, III
Quale, Andrew Christopher, Jr.
Quillen, Cecil Dyer, III
Rabb, Bruce
Radon, Jenik Richard
Rankin, Clyde Evan, III
Rosendahl, Roger Wayne
Rosensaft, Menachem Zwi
Rosenzweig, Charles Leonard
Rovine, Arthur William
Rozan, Alain
Rubin, Herbert
Sassoon, Andre Gabriel
Saunders, Mark A.
Savell, Polly Carolyn
Schaab, Arnold J.
Schwab, Terrance W.
Schwartz, Carol Vivian
Seidel, Selvyn
Setrakian, Berge
Seward, George Chester
Shea, Edward Emmett
Shecter, Howard L.
Sheikh, Kemal A.
Sher, Michael Lee
Short, Skip
Silkenat, James Robert
Snitow, Charles
Stein, Stephen William
Thalacker, Arbie Robert
Tran, Julie Hoan
Tse, Charles Yung Chang
Urquia, Rafael, II
Van Praag, Alan
Vig, Vernon Edward
Vitkowsky, Vincent Joseph
Wald, Bernard Joseph
Wallin, James Peter
Wang, Albert Huai-En
Weiner, Earl David
Westin, David Lawrence
Wise, Aaron Noah
Wynn, Simon David
Yamin, Michael Geoffrey
Yu, Genrong
Zimmett, Mark Paul
Zonana, Victor
**Oneida**
Campanie, Samuel John
**Oyster Bay**
Coates, Winslow Shelby, Jr.
**Port Chester**
Levin, Jeffrey L.
**Purchase**
Joyce, Joseph James
**Rochester**
Blyth, John E.
**Schenectady**
Thiele, Leslie Kathleen Larsen
**Somers**
Cowles, Frederick Oliver
**Syracuse**
Bogart, William Harry
Fitzpatrick, James David
**Uniondale**
Carnesi, Kenneth Brian
**Upton**
Atney, Irene P.
**Westbury**
Nogee, Jeffrey Laurence
**White Plains**
Shin, Helen

Klahr, Gary Peter
**Tempe**
Zurbriggen, Jeffrey Michael

ARKANSAS

**Fayetteville**
McIvor, Marcia Lynn
Poore, Shannon Leigh
**Little Rock**
Smith, Anne Orsi

CALIFORNIA

**Albany**
Chazin, Seth Paul
**Fresno**
Bailey, Howard William (Bill Bailey)
**Hanford**
Snyder, Thom
**La Jolla**
Caplan, Allen
**Laguna Beach**
Simons, Barry Thomas
**Los Angeles**
Glavin, William Patrick, IV
Wolf, Lawrence
**Oakland**
Thompson Stanley, Trina
**Rancho Palos Verdes**
Swank, Damon Raynard
**San Diego**
Lory, Loran Steven
**San Francisco**
Malcheski, Kim
**Santa Monica**
English, Charles Royal
Winograde, Audrey
**Santa Rosa**
Hillberg, Marylou Elin
**Vacaville**
Myhre, Deanna Shirley
**Visalia**
Shirk, Jennifer Conn
**Woodland**
Melton, Barry

COLORADO

**Colorado Springs**
Barnes, Thomas Arthur, Jr.
Dean, Lawrence Kenyon
Link, Gary Steven
**Englewood**
Bolocofsky, David N.

CONNECTICUT

**Branford**
Hanchuruck, Stephen Paul
**Danbury**
Dornfeld, Sharon Wicks
**Ridgefield**
Sherman, Harold

DISTRICT OF COLUMBIA

**Washington**
Genz, Michael Andrew

FLORIDA

**Bradenton**
Seheult, Malcolm McDonald Richardson
**Coconut Grove**
Joffe, David Jonathon
**Coral Gables**
Metcalfe, Olga
**Fort Lauderdale**
Hester, Julia A.
**Gainesville**
Mollica, Salvatore Dennis
**Jacksonville**
McBurney, Charles Walker, Jr.
**Lake Alfred**
Slaughter, Marshall Glenn
**Longwood**
McLatchey, Russell Francis
**West Palm Beach**
Vilchez, Victoria Anne

GEORGIA

**Athens**
Byers, Rhonda Leann
**Decatur**
Guest, Abbi Taylor

HAWAII

**Honolulu**
Shigetomi, Keith Shigeo

IDAHO

**Caldwell**
Orr, Debra Ann

ILLINOIS

**Belleville**
Grueninger, Daniel J.
**Carbondale**
Clemons, John Robert
**Chicago**
Muller, Kurt Alexander
Tucker, Bowen Hayward
**Mundelein**
Ackley, Robert O.
**Oak Lawn**
Tucker, Berry Kenneth

INDIANA

**Indianapolis**
Gaddy, Maureen
**Lafayette**
Garwood, Cynthia Lynn
**Waynetown**
Dicks, Sarah Houston

IOWA

**Charles City**
Troge, Ann Marie
**Des Moines**
Lawyer, Vivian Jury

KENTUCKY

**Louisville**
Spalding, Catherine
Welch, Louise Bridgman

LOUISIANA

**Baton Rouge**
Dixon, Jerome Wayne
**La Place**
Cicet, Donald James
**Lafayette**
Saloom, Kaliste Joseph, Jr.
**Metairie**
Miles, Terri

MARYLAND

**Towson**
Campion, Renée

MASSACHUSETTS

**Barnstable**
Ryley, Arthur Charles
**Boston**
Craven, Terry Marie
**Newton**
Stern, Edward Mayer
**South Hamilton**
Campbell, Diana Butt

MICHIGAN

**Farmingtn Hls**
Maloney, Vincent John
**Mount Clemens**
Ososki-Slanec, Darra
**Muskegon**
Houghtaling, Chris Allen
**Saginaw**
Suffety, Hamed William, Jr.
**Sterling Heights**
Girdwood, Derik Renard

MINNESOTA

**Minneapolis**
Born, Suzanne
Oleisky, Robert Edward
**Rochester**
Baker, Gail Dyer

MISSOURI

**Columbia**
Aulgur, Robert Davis
Murray, Robert Arthur
**Saint Louis**
Pleban, Sarah Shelledy

NEBRASKA

**Fremont**
Eskey, Leo Joseph
**Omaha**
Frank, Julie Ann
Kelly, Christopher Edward

NEVADA

**Carson City**
Johnson, Erik Reid

NEW HAMPSHIRE

**Newport**
Shklar, Michael Charles

NEW JERSEY

**Blackwood**
Bloch, Stefanie Z.
**Clark**
Farina, Mario G.

NEW MEXICO

**Farmington**
Hale, J. Kevin

NEW YORK

**Fayetteville**
Alderman, Judith Lorraine
**Flushing**
Gerson, Nancy L.
**Mineola**
Bekritsky, Bruce Robert
**New Rochelle**
Malach, Herbert John
**New York**
Rothberg, Glenda Fay Morris
Vachss, Andrew Henry
**Niagara Falls**
Truex, Shelley Anne
**Scarsdale**
Salwen, Joan C.
**Seneca Falls**
Porter, James Scott
**Watertown**
Sovie, Susan Anne

NORTH CAROLINA

**Charlotte**
Rockey, Arlaine
**Pittsboro**
Riggsbee, Lunday Adams
**Raleigh**
Ansley, James Ronald
Hall, John Thomas

NORTH DAKOTA

**Grand Forks**
Anderson, Damon Ernest

OHIO

**Ada**
Streib, Victor Lee
**Akron**
Finan, Christine Denise
**Bowling Green**
Huffman, Diane Rausch
**Bucyrus**
Skropits, Amy Elizabeth
**Canton**
Yoder, Robert Gene
**Dayton**
Smiley, Charles Adam, Jr.
**Toledo**
Griffin, Sharon L.

OKLAHOMA

**Bartlesville**
Thomas, Linda S.
**Enid**
Gill, Amber McLaughlin
**Norman**
Chesley, Patrick J.

OREGON

**Portland**
Bender, Laurie
Cross, Daniel Albert
Williams, Sharon A.

PENNSYLVANIA

**Carlisle**
Baird, Lindsay Dare
**Lancaster**
MacDonald, Richard Barry
**Lebanon**
Burkett, Loreen Marae
**Mercer**
Kochems, Robert Gregory
**Monroeville**
Cohen, Laura
**Philadelphia**
Love, William Allan
Sweeney, Clayton Anthony, Jr.
**Wallingford**
DePaul, Anthony Kenneth
**Williamsport**
Rudinski, Michael J.

RHODE ISLAND

**Providence**
Germani, Elia

TENNESSEE

**Clarksville**
Smith, Gregory Dale
**Fayetteville**
Dickey, John Harwell
**Knoxville**
Schwamm, Virginia Ann
**Nashville**
Burkett, Gerald Arthur
Clark, Nannette
**South Pittsburg**
Ables, Charles Robert

TEXAS

**Austin**
Dudley, Todd Steven
**Canton**
White, Jeffery Howell
**Dallas**
Callahan, Tena Toye
**Fort Worth**
Evans, Lance T.
**Hurst**
Marling, Lynwood Bradley
**Longview**
Komorowski, Michele
**San Antonio**
Richardson, Joel Glenn
**San Marcos**
Maysel, Kyle Wayne

UTAH

**Salt Lake City**
Rasmussen, Thomas Val, Jr.

VIRGINIA

**Arlington**
Packett, Larry French
Zucker, Claudia Joy
**Ashland**
Allen, Russell Earl
**Christiansburg**
Spence, Helen Jean
**Fairfax**
Collins, Charles Edward, Jr.
**Newport News**
Saunders, Bryan Leslie
**Virginia Beach**
McGraw, Frank William, Jr.
**Waynesboro**
Jones, Linda Schorsch
**Williamsburg**
Twiford, Alice Kate

WASHINGTON

**Lynnwood**
Kastle, David Anthony
**Seattle**
Linn, Brian James
Marshall, David Stanley

WEST VIRGINIA

**Huntington**
Ransbottom, Jennifer Dickens
**Parkersburg**
Powell, Eric Karlton
**Princeton**
Griffith, Mary E.

WISCONSIN

**Madison**
Wood, Tracey A.
**Milwaukee**
Stellman, L. Mandy
**Portage**
Kohlwey, Jane Ellen
**Racine**
Hoelzel, Sally Ann

WYOMING

**Cheyenne**
Frentheway, John E.

ADDRESS UNPUBLISHED

Brandes, Joel R.
Brush, Kirkland L.
Fayette, Kathleen Owens
Hickey, Timothy Andrew
Kleinberg, Judith G.
Pauca, Janet Frances
Ross, Catherine Jane
Shattuck, Cathie Ann

---

## LABOR. *See also* Workers' compensation; Pension.

---

UNITED STATES

ALABAMA

**Birmingham**
Alexander, James Patrick
Baker, Beverly Poole
Brown, Stephen Edward
Burnside, Cynthia Grace
Coleman, John James, III
Gardner, William F.
Hopkins, Harry L.
Stelzenmuller, Cyril Vaughn
Thornton, Wendy Nix
Wiggins, Robert L.
**Eufaula**
Twitchell, E(rvin) Eugene
**Huntsville**
Simpson, Shannon Smith
**Mobile**
Byrne, Bradley Roberts
**Montgomery**
Duncan, Priscilla Black
Rodgers, Karen Sampson

ALASKA

**Anchorage**
Fleischer, Hugh William
Flynn, Charles P.
Goldberg, Robert M.
**Fairbanks**
Covell, Kenneth
Schendel, William Burnett

ARIZONA

**Flagstaff**
Currey, Rebecca S.
**Phoenix**
Arbetman, Jeffrey Farrell
Balitis, John James, Jr.
Brockelman, Kent
Doran, John Alan
Kelly, David Andrew
Lubin, Stanley
Petitti, Michael Joseph, Jr.
Wall, Donald Arthur
**Tempe**
Shimpock, Kathy Elizabeth
**Tucson**
Bainton, Denise Marlene
Esposito, Joseph Louis
Kaucher, James William

ARKANSAS

**Fayetteville**
Dill Chadick, Terri
**Hot Springs National Park**
Sanders, Michael Edward
**Little Rock**
Boe, Myron Timothy
Creasman, William Paul
Gibson, Calvin Roe
Gunter, Russell Allen
Jiles, Gary D.
Jones, Stephen Witsell
Lavey, John Thomas
Miller, William Scott

CALIFORNIA

**Belvedere Tiburon**
Buell, Edward Rick, II
**Beverly Hills**
Florence, Kenneth James
**Carmichael**
Halpenny, Diana Doris
**Glendale**
Martinetti, Ronald Anthony
**Irvine**
Ashley, Fred Turner
Desai, Aashish Y.
Ristau, Kenneth Eugene, Jr.
Rorty, Bruce Vail
Thompson, Donald Mizelle
**Lafayette**
Lustig, Norman I.
**Laguna Hills**
Reinglass, Michelle Annette
**Los Altos**
Bell, Richard G.
**Los Angeles**
Allred, Gloria Rachel
Bell, Wayne Steven
Bodnar, Alexandra A.
Bressan, Paul Louis
Carr, Willard Zeller, Jr.
Cornwell, Donald Lee
Foley, Martin James
Highberger, William Foster
Korduner, David Jerome
Lipton, Jack Philip
Moloney, Stephen Michael
Silbergeld, Arthur F.
Thoren-Peden, Deborah Suzanne
Whitaker, Ronald Stephen
**Newport Beach**
Black, William Rea
Hagen, Catherine B.
**Oakland**
Beninati, Nancy Ann
Burnison, Boyd Edward
Wallace, Elaine Wendy
**Orange**
Stagner, Robert Dean
**Palm Springs**
FitzGerald, John Edward, III
**Palos Verdes Peninsula**
Yeomans, Russell Allen
**Pasadena**
Klein, Jill
**Pleasanton**
Hearey, Elizabeth Berle
**Pomona**
Bausch, Janet Jean
**Sacramento**
Gillan, Kayla J.
Martorano, Rebekka Ruth
Palmer, Floyd James
Shelley, Susanne Mary
Van Dermyden, Sue Ann
**San Diego**
Bleiler, Charles Arthur
Hon, Donald Allen
Shaw, Lee Charles
White, Edith Jean
**San Francisco**
Berkowitz, Alan Robert
Boutin, Peter Rucker
Brantner, Paula Ann
Brayer, Janet
Davis, Roland Chenoweth
Fastiff, Wesley J.
Gelhaus, Robert Joseph
Hill, Richard Paul
Hilton, Stanley Goumas
Mazhari, Niloufar
Mosk, Susan Hines
Rubin, Michael
Samad-Salameh, Alia Fahmi
Wolf, Lillian F.
**San Jose**
Bohn, Robert Herbert
Cobey, Christopher Earle
**San Rafael**
Huffman, Jared William
**Santa Barbara**
Pyle, Kurt H.
**Stockton**
Malm, Scott
**Torrance**
Johnson, Einar William
Smith, Michael Cordon
**Universal Cty**
Peter, Arnold Philimon
**Walnut Creek**
Clark, Sherry Walker
Sohnen, Harvey
Steele, Dwight Cleveland

COLORADO

**Boulder**
Bellac, Patricia Sharman
Caulfield, Sharon Elizabeth
Leh, Christopher Marshall
Ward, Denitta Dawn
**Canon City**
McDermott, John Arthur
**Carbondale**
Wohl, Kenneth Allan
**Denver**
Bove, Mark Stephen
Burke, Marlin W.
Das, Arun
Kelso, Donald Iain Junor
Marquess, Lawrence Wade
Martin, Raymond Walter
McManus, Richard Griswold, Jr.
Mumaugh, Brian Michael
Nosler, Michael D.
Sabey, Mark L.
Stuart, Mary Hurley
Temple, Dana A.
Timmins, Edward Patrick
Tomlinson, Warren Leon
**Englewood**
Breeskin, Michael Wayne
Ewing, Mary Arnold
McReynolds, Gregg Clyde
**Golden**
Snead, Kathleen Marie
**Littleton**
Ballantine, Beverly Neblett
**Pagosa Springs**
Kelly, Reid Browne
**Placerville**
Reagan, Harry Edwin, III

CONNECTICUT

**Bridgeport**
Mitchell, Robert Burdette
**Fairfield**
LaFollette, Ernest Carlton
**Glastonbury**
Rintoul, David Skinner
**Hartford**
Cullina, William Michael
Dempsey, Edward Joseph
Kainen, Burton
Kemp, Wendi J.
Lyons, Charles Malaher
O'Donnell, Edward Francis, Jr.
Orth, Paul William
**Manchester**
Eldergill, Kathleen
**New Canaan**
Baker, George Walter
**New Haven**
Choate, Edward Lee

**Roseland**
Bennett, John K.
Foster, M. Joan
Glassman, Jerold Erwin
Hinsdale, Beth A.
Sarasohn, Peter Radin
**Somerset**
Macey, Scott J.
Robinson, Patricia Snyder
**Somerville**
Bernstein, Eric Martin
**Toms River**
Berman, Michael Barry
**Verona**
Tobia, Ronald Lawrence
**Warren**
Gerard, Stephen Stanley
Hurley, Lawrence Joseph
**Westfield**
Schmidt, John H., Jr.
**Woodbridge**
Rosenberg, Jodi L.
**Woodcliff Lake**
Sneirson, Marilyn

## NEW MEXICO

**Albuquerque**
Hollis, John Lee
Romero, Jeff
Thiel, Albert Nicholas, Jr.
**Las Cruces**
Neumann, Rita
**Santa Fe**
Herr, Bruce

## NEW YORK

**Albany**
Barsamian, J(ohn) Albert
Bramley, Bruce C.
Couch, Mark Woodworth
Devine, Eugene Peter
Ganz, Robert E.
Girvin, James Edward
Mishler, Mark Sean
Wukitsch, David John
**Bronxville**
Wiacek, Bruce Edward
**Brooklyn**
Fallek, Andrew Michael
Swain, Laura Taylor
**Buffalo**
Bond, Jill Kawa
Brydges, Thomas Eugene
Cohen, Jeremy V.
Odza, Randall M.
Oppenheimer, Randolph Carl
Pearce, Mark Gaston
Salisbury, Eugene W.
**Chappaqua**
Whittlesey, John Williams
**Chestnut Ridge**
Burns, Richard Owen
**Cutchogue**
O'Connell, Francis Joseph
**Floral Park**
Cardalena, Peter Paul, Jr.
**Garden City**
Ehrlich, Jerome Harry
Fishberg, Gerard
Lilly, Thomas Joseph
Schwarz, Carl A., Jr.
**Howard Beach**
Hernandez-Gonzalez, Gloria Maria
**Jamestown**
Beckstrom, Charles G.
DeAngelo, Charles Salvatore
**Mineola**
Braid, Frederick Donald
Chaikin, Bonnie Patricia
Millman, Bruce Russell
Pogrebin, Bertrand B.
Rossen, Jordan
Sandback, William Arthur
Zuckerman, Richard Karl
**New Hyde Park**
Levine, Kimberly Anne
**New York**
Altieri, Peter Louis
Bassen, Ned Henry
Beranbaum, John A.
Bernstein, Michael Irwin
Bianco, S. Anthony
Birnbaum, Julian R.
Bortnick, Blaine H.
Bradford, Elizabeth
Brand, Irving
Brooks, Kermitt Jerome
Budd, Thomas Witbeck
Carling, Francis
Chan, Lai Lee
Coleman, Jerome P.
Crook, Jennifer Marie
Derwin, Jordan
Diamond, David Howard
Dichner, Ellen
Dretzin, David
Drucker, Jacquelin F.
Duff, William Brandon
Effel, Laura
Flamm, Leonard N(athan)
Friedman, Eugene Stuart
Friedman, Jeffrey Lawrence
Futterman, Stanley Norman
Ganz, Howard Laurence
Glanstein, Joel Charles
Grisi, James Robert
Hartmann, Carl Joseph
Hathaway, Gerald Thomas
Hirozawa, Kent Y.
Jacobson, Jerold Dennis
Kalomiris, Errika
Kandel, William Lloyd
Kimler, Andrew A.
Kiok, Joan Stern
Kirschner, Kenneth Harold
Kohn, Jeffrey Ira
Kolko, Hanan B.
Lanza, Robert John
Lauer, Andrew Jay
Levin, Roger Michael
Lichten, Rachel Gordon
McMahon, James Charles
Miller, Gordon David
Moerdler, Charles Gerard
Murphy, James Gilmartin
Nolan, Terrance Joseph, Jr.
Oechler, Henry John, Jr.
Pack, Leonard Brecher
Paul, James William
Peikes, Lawrence David
Pompa, Renata
Putney, Laura Lea
Rogers, Theodore Otto, Jr.
Roth, Barbara M.
Rubin, Howard Jeffrey
Safon, David Michael
Saldana, Adrienne L.
Savitt, Susan Schenkel
Schreffler, Neil Franklin
Seham, Martin Charles
Shen, Michael
Shinevar, Peter O'Neil
Silverstein, Harlan Jay
Stack, Jane Marcia
Steigman, Meredith Lee
Stein, Tracy A.
Stock, Alice Beth
Vladeck, Judith Pomarlen
Wallach, Eric Jean
Watanabe, Roy Noboru
Watson, Kipp Elliott
Weiss, Jonathan Arthur
Winzenreid, James Ernest
Wisehart, Arthur McKee
Witkin, Eric Douglas
**Niagara Falls**
Berrigan, Patrick Joseph
**Northport**
Gross, John H.
**Queensbury**
McCann, Bernard Thomas
**Rochester**
Smith, Jules Louis
Stiller, Sharon Paula
Wild, Robert Warren
**Sands Point**
Hoynes, Louis LeNoir, Jr.
**Saratoga Springs**
Goldberger, Franklin Henry
**Staten Island**
Casella, Ralph Philip
**Syracuse**
DiLorenzo, Louis Patrick
Gaal, John
King, Bernard T.
Sager, Jonathan Ward
**Valley Stream**
Levine, Marilyn Markovich
**White Plains**
Longo, Ronald Anthony
Tsamis, Donna Robin
Weingarden, Mitchell Ian

## NORTH CAROLINA

**Charlotte**
Allred, John Thompson
Belthoff, Richard Charles, Jr.
**Cherryville**
Huffstetler, Palmer Eugene
**Durham**
Fisher, Stewart Wayne
**Greensboro**
Cline, Todd Wakefield
Kobrin, Thomas Barstow
McGinn, Max Daniel
Sperling, Mack
**High Point**
Sheahan, Robert Emmett
**Raleigh**
Davis, Thomas Hill, Jr.
Kenyon, Rosemary Gill
Kurz, Mary Elizabeth
Wetsch, Laura Johnson
**Winston Salem**
Early, James H., Jr.

## OHIO

**Akron**
Jalbert, Michael Joseph
Minney, R. Brent
Rooney, George Willard
Tipping, Harry A.
**Athens**
Hedges, Richard Houston
**Beachwood**
Mintz, Carl A.
**Cincinnati**
Adams, Deborah Susan
Finnigan, John Julius, Jr.
Hornberger, Lee
Lawrence, James Kaufman Lebensburger
Lugbill, Ann
Morrisroe, Donald Patrick
Smith, Sheila Marie
**Cleveland**
Duvin, Robert Phillip
Goddard, Richard Patrick
Goldfarb, Bernard Sanford
Gray, R. Benton
Kainec, Lisa Anne
Leiken, Earl Murray
Lentz, Mary A.
Markus, Stephen Allan
Miller, Clinton J., III
Oberdank, Lawrence Mark
Pace, Stanley Dan
Pallam, John James
Ross, Harold Anthony
Ruf, H(arold) William, Jr.
Strimbu, Victor, Jr.
Utrata, Carl Ignatius
Zashin, Stephen S.
**Columbus**
Bartemes, Amy Straker
Eblin, Robert L.
Gellman, Susan Beth
Gittes, Frederick M.
Haught, Jack Gregg
Morgan, Dennis Richard
Pressley, Fred G., Jr.
Tarpy, Thomas Michael
Warner, Charles Collins
**Dayton**
Davis, G(iles) Jack
Lamme, Kathryn Anne
**Delaware**
Deavers, Maribeth
**Dublin**
Blaugrund, David Scott
Coco, Mark Steven
Emmert, Steven Michael
**Elyria**
Sarkar, Neil Steven
**Fairborn**
Roach, B. Randall
**N Royalton**
Jungeberg, Thomas Donald
**Springfield**
Pedraza, Miguel A., Jr.
**Toledo**
Dane, Stephen Mark
Iorio, Theodore
Miller, Barbara Kaye
O'Connell, Maurice Daniel
Rice, Kollin Lawrence
**Warren**
Kafantaris, George Nicholas

## OKLAHOMA

**Cushing**
Draughon, Scott Wilson
**Mustang**
Denton, Michael David, Jr.
**Oklahoma City**
Angel, Steven Michael
Court, Leonard
Pendell, Terry Ashley
Puckett, Tony Greg
Van Dyke, Peter Tyson
**Sapulpa**
Lane, Tom Cornelius
**Tulsa**
Barnes, Deborah Browers
Bright, Thomas Lynn
Burkett, Teresa Meinders
Matthies, Mary Constance T.
Mattson, Lynn Paul
Pataki, Leonard Ignatius
Strecker, David Eugene

## OREGON

**Medford**
O'Connor, Karl William (Goodyear Johnson)
**Portland**
Blitz, Charles Akin
Jernstedt, Kenneth Elliott
Rayburn, Ralph F.
Sullivan, Dana Louise

## PENNSYLVANIA

**Allentown**
Albright, Mark Preston
**Bala Cynwyd**
Gotanda, Brenda Hustis
**Bethlehem**
Bush, Raymond George
Yeager, Jordan Berson
**Blue Bell**
Teklits, Joseph Anthony
**Conshohocken**
Gutkin, Arthur Lee
**Erie**
Zamboldi, Richard Henry
**Greensburg**
McDowell, Michael David
**Harrisburg**
Kendall, Keith Edward
Quigley, Robert Andrew
**Langhorne**
Ely, Wayne Arlen
**Lansdale**
Sultanik, Jeffrey Ted
**New Castle**
Babb, Alfred Ward
Flannery, Harry Audley
Natale, Frank Anthony, II
**Norristown**
Rees, Thomas Dynevor
**Oakdale**
Brendel, John S.
**Philadelphia**
Abrams, Nancy
Baccini, Laurance Ellis
Bernard, John Marley
Bildersee, Robert Alan
Brown, William Hill, III
Dabrowski, Doris Jane
Dichter, Mark S.
Epstein, Alan Bruce
Gilberg, Kenneth Roy
Goldman, Gary Craig
Goldman, Jeffrey E.
Hagan, Mary Ann
Halber, Lori Elizabeth
Krampf, John Edward
Mannino, Robert John
McEldrew, James Joseph, III
Milone, Francis Michael
O'Reilly, Timothy Patrick
Ossip, Michael J.
Pasek, Jeffrey Ivan
Reisman, Jason Eric
Satinsky, Barnett
Sigmond, Richard Brian
Smith, John Francis, III
Stewart, Robert Forrest, Jr.
Whiteside, William Anthony, Jr.
Young, Roma Skeen
**Pittsburgh**
Bellisario, Domenic Anthony
Botta, Frank Charles
Brown, James Benton
Candris, Laura A.
DeForest, Walter Pattison, III
Denys, Sylvia
Dugan, John F.
Hill, John Howard
Hornak, Mark Raymond
Hough, Thomas Henry Michael
Keenan, C. Robert, III
Lyncheski, John E.
Murray, Philip Joseph, III
Orsatti, Ernest Benjamin
Scheinholtz, Leonard Louis
**Reading**
Decker, Kurt Hans
**Sewickley**
Grigsby, Robert S.
Jackson, Velma Louise
**Washington**
Chaban, Lawrence Richard
**York**
Senft, John L.

## RHODE ISLAND

**Pawtucket**
Belliveau, Kathrin Pagonis
**Providence**
Keeney, Thomas Critchfield
Long, Nicholas Trott
Parks, Albert Lauriston
**Wakefield**
Rothschild, Donald Phillip

## SOUTH CAROLINA

**Charleston**
Glass, Benjamin Philip
**Greenville**
Griggs, Wade Garney, III
Wyche, Madison Baker, III
**Johnsonville**
Poston, Ellerby Delance
**Spartanburg**
Ballard, Wade Edward
Vega, Matthew Anthony

## TENNESSEE

**Chattanooga**
Burnette, Harry Forbes
Helton, Thomas Oswald
Phillips, John Bomar
**Kingsport**
Mason, Donald F., Jr.
**Knoxville**
Hagood, Lewis Russell
Walter, Glenn Richard
**Memphis**
Barna, James Francis
Bennett, Richard D.
Clark, Ross Bert, II
Dykes, Lillian Elise Levy
Hancock, Jonathan Cromwell
McGrew, Anne Elizabeth
Sossaman, William Lynwood
Summers, James Branson
Warren, Keith Ashley
**Nashville**
Anderson, Charles Hill
Barrett, George Edward
Baugh, Mark Anthony
Douse, Steven Carl
Gannon, John Sexton
Lyon, Philip K(irkland)
Tudor, Bynum Ellsworth, III
Wayland, R. Eddie

## TEXAS

**Abilene**
Robinson, Vianei Lopez
**Austin**
Brothers, D. Douglas
Connolly, Carla Garcia
Greig, Brian Strother
Hill, Melissa Clute (Lisa Hill)
Schwartz, Leonard Jay
Tice, Laurie Dietrich
**Beaumont**
Hambright, Robert John
**Carrollton**
Riggs, Arthur Jordy
**Corpus Christi**
Carnahan, Robert Narvell
**Dallas**
Austin, Ann Sheree
Barnes, Hershell Louis, Jr.
Case, Thomas Louis
Cloutman, Edward Bradbury, III
Crain, Gayla Campbell
England, Austin Hinds
Evans, Roger
Gegen, Theresa Mary
Hackney, Hugh Edward
Jones, James Alton
McDonald, Michael Scott
Mebus, Robert Gwynne
Valdez, Frances Valdez
Washington, Karen Roberts
Wewers, Mark Eric
**El Paso**
Hughes, Steven Lee
Malone, Daniel Robert
Oaxaca, Juan Roberto
Strahan, Jeffery V.
**Eldorado**
Kosub, James Albert
**Fairfield**
McKinney, Rozanne Moore
**Fort Worth**
Brender, Art
Eubank, Christina
Maher, Patrick Joseph
Rutherford, Jay K.
**Friendswood**
Youngdahl, Jay Thomas
**Houston**
Bader, Gregory Vincent
Bircher, Edgar Allen
Callegari, William A., Jr.
Dijkman, Christiana
Frels, Kelly
Jaasma, Keith Duane
Krock, Kenneth Michael
Lopez, David Tiburcio
McKinney, Carolyn Jean
Roven, John David
Ryan, Thomas William
Sears, Ross Allen, II
Shaddix, James W.
Turek, Douglas D.
Valetutto, David Michael
Vaughn, Kathryn Sue
Wesely, Nathan
**Longview**
Jones, Christopher Don
**McAllen**
Jarvis, Robert Glenn
**Odessa**
Rouse, Randall Lyle
**Pearland**
Bittick, Peggy Sue
**San Antonio**
Barnhill, Donald Earl
Bettac, Robert Edward
Moynihan, John Bignell
Putman, (James) Michael
Yedor, Jonathan
**Victoria**
Tipton, Drew B.

## UTAH

**Salt Lake City**
Burton, H(ubert) Dickson
Lavitt, Kathy A.
**Woods Cross**
Weiler, Todd David

## VERMONT

**Burlington**
Blackwood, Eileen Morris
McKearin, Robert R.

## VIRGINIA

**Arlington**
Cohen, Sheldon Irwin
**Bristol**
Minor, Steven Ray
Wise, Donald Edward
**Christiansburg**
Spence, Helen Jean
**Fairfax**
Dwornik, Frances Pierson
McGowan, James Francis, III
**Fort Lee**
Baker, Loren Leonard
**Great Falls**
Railton, William Scott
**Harrisonburg**
Wallinger, M(elvin) Bruce
**Herndon**
Afshar, Carolyn McKinney
**Mc Lean**
Bredehoft, John Michael
Erickson, John Richard

**Portsmouth**
Moody, Willard James, Sr.
**Reston**
Reicin, Eric David
**Richmond**
Baron, Mark
Levit, Jay J(oseph)
Marstiller, Philip S.
McElligott, James Patrick, Jr.
Nagle, David Edward
O'Toole, Deborah Shea
Tashjian-Brown, Eva S(usan)
Whitlock, Julie Marie
**Roanoke**
Harris, Bayard Easter
Larson, Bruce Robert
Wilson, Douglas Downes
**Springfield**
Chappell, Milton Leroy
**Vienna**
Hagberg, Chris Eric

## WASHINGTON

**Bellevue**
Hannah, Lawrence Burlison
Sebris, Robert, Jr.
**Bellingham**
Garrett, Deborra Elizabeth
**Federal Way**
Pratum, Michael James
**Redmond**
Merrill, Michael Gordon
**Seattle**
Bendich, Judith Ellen
Cavanaugh, Michael Everett
DeForest, Stephen Elliott
Elliott, Clifton Langsdale
Endriss, Marilyn Jean
Fredericksen, Scott L.
Freeman, Antoinette Rosefeldt
Gustafson, Alice Fairleigh
Hearn, Holly Michelle
Hutcheson, Mark Andrew
Lemly, Thomas Adger
Needle, Jeffrey Lowell
Rosen, Jon Howard
Squires, William Randolph, III
Turner, Duncan Calvert
Webber, James Carl
**Spokane**
Allen, Keller Wayne
Conrad, Charles Thomas
Winston, Robert W., Jr.
**Tacoma**
Condon, David Bruce
Teller, Stephen Aiden
**Winthrop**
Eklund, Paul G.

## WEST VIRGINIA

**Charleston**
Dissen, James Hardiman
Roles, Forrest Hansbury
Teare, John Richard, Jr.
Wolfe, Roger Allen

## WISCONSIN

**Hudson**
Lundeen, Bradley Curtis

**La Crosse**
Sleik, Thomas Scott
**Madison**
Brewster, Francis Anthony
Bruchs, Amy O'Brien
Fleischli, George Robert
Kelly, T. Christopher
MacDougall, Priscilla Ruth
Stix, Sally Ann
Stoddard, Glenn McDonald
Zawadsky, John H.
**Manitowoc**
Muchin, Arden Archie
**Milwaukee**
Beightol, Scott Christopher
Finerty, John Daniel, Jr.
Gimbel, Franklyn M.
Hawks, Timothy Edward
Kern, David Bernard
Levy, Alan M.
Michelstetter, Stanley Hubert
Mulcahy, Charles Chambers
Olivieri, José Alberto
Scrivner, Thomas William
**Oshkosh**
Williams, Edward J.
**Union Grove**
Stern, Walter Wolf, III
**Wausau**
Wolf, Kevin Earl

### WYOMING

**Casper**
Shumate, Roger Eugene

### ADDRESS UNPUBLISHED

Anderson, Jon Eric
Andreozzi, Louis Joseph
Bartz, David John
Berger, Marc Joseph
Blevins, Jeffrey Alexander
Branstetter, Cecil Dewey, Sr.
Broadus, Joseph Edward
Bush, Wendell Earl
Campos-Orrego, Nora Patricia
Cash, Michelle Hoogendam
Cohen, Seymour
Dickstein, Michael Ethan
Foster, Cindy Cooper
Franke, Ann Harriet
Gass, Raymond William
Glanzer, Mona Naomi
Golder, Frederick Thomas
Gomez, David Frederick
Gora, Daniel Martin
Hagerman, Michael Charles
Holmes, Michael Gene
Kennedy, Thomas J.
Killeen, Michael John
Kleiman, Bernard
Kruse, Pamela Jean
McFarland, Robert Edwin
Milberg, Melinda Sharon
Miller, Frank William
Mitchell, William D.
Rodenburg, Clifton Glenn
Rusnak, Susan E.
Sapp, John Raymond
Saxon, John David
Slipski, Ronald Edward
Stack, Beatriz de Greiff
Tietig, Lisa Kuhlman
Torkildson, Raymond Maynard
Treacy, Vincent Edward
Twanmoh, Valerie Hurley
Valois, Robert Arthur
Wagner, Michael Duane
Weinmann, Richard Adrian
White, Richard Clarence

## LAND USE AND ZONING

### UNITED STATES

### ALASKA

**Anchorage**
Stanley, James Troy

### ARIZONA

**Phoenix**
Jorden, Douglas Allen
Thompson, Joel Erik
**Sun City**
Hauer, James Albert

### CALIFORNIA

**Burlingame**
Fogarty, Janet E.
**Claremont**
Ferguson, C. Robert
**Costa Mesa**
Caldwell, Courtney Lynn
**Irvine**
Hurst, Charles Wilson
**Los Angeles**
Burns, Marvin Gerald
Lewand, Kimberly Ellen
Salvaty, Benjamin Benedict
Tepper, R(obert) Bruce, Jr.
Weiser, Frank Alan
**Los Gatos**
Seligmann, William Robert
**Newark**
Bernard, Steven Martin
**Oakland**
Hausrath, Les A.
**Pleasanton**
MacDonald, Peter David
**Sacramento**
Robbins, Stephen J. M.
Taber, Kelley Morgan
**San Diego**
Dawe, James Robert
Witt, John William
**San Francisco**
Briscoe, John
Haughton, Brian Stephens
Robertson, J. Martin
**San Jose**
Gonzales, Daniel S.
**Walnut Creek**
Skaggs, Sanford Merle

### COLORADO

**Aspen**
McGrath, J. Nicholas
Shulman, Harry
**Denver**
Grimshaw, Thomas Tollin
Petros, Raymond Louis, Jr.
Spillane, John Michael
**Englewood**
Campbell, Darrel Lee

### CONNECTICUT

**Bridgeport**
Wolf, Austin Keith
**Burlington**
Bauer, Charles Widmayer
**Derby**
Cohen, James E.
**Hartford**
Buck, Gurdon Hall
Davis, Andrew Neil
Merriam, Dwight Haines
**Stamford**
Richichi, Joseph
**Wilton**
Adams, Thomas Tilley
Healy, James Casey
Silverman, Melvin J.

### DELAWARE

**Wilmington**
Brosseit, A. Kimberly Rockwell
Devine, Donn
Waisanen, Christine M.

### DISTRICT OF COLUMBIA

**Washington**
Edmondson, Paul William
Glasgow, Norman Milton
Rosenberg, Ruth Helen Borsuk
Rustad, Jeannine
Sherer, Samuel Ayers

### FLORIDA

**Bradenton**
Barnebey, Mark Patrick
**Fort Lauderdale**
Moss, Stephen B.
**Indian Harbor Beach**
Tasker, Molly Jean
**Islamorada**
Mattson, James Stewart
**Jacksonville**
Ansbacher, Barry B.
Manning, G(erald) Stephen
**Lutz**
Hayes, Timothy George
**Miami**
Mehta, Eileen Rose
Scherker, Elliot H.
**Naples**
Anderson, R(obert) Bruce
Humphreville, John David
**Orlando**
Chotas, Elias Nicholas
Stewart, Harry A.
**Palm Beach Gardens**
Edgar, Charles Wesley, III
**Punta Gorda**
Haymans, Michael P.
**Sarasota**
Patten, Brenda L.
**Tampa**
Sparkman, Steven Leonard
Taub, Theodore Calvin
Tripp, Paul Wayne
**West Palm Beach**
Sklar, William Paul
**Winter Park**
Cool, Dwight I.

### GEORGIA

**Albany**
Cannon, William E., Jr.
**Atlanta**
Stokes, James Sewell
**Watkinsville**
Wright, Robert Joseph

### HAWAII

**Honolulu**
Kupchak, Kenneth Roy
Lombardi, Dennis M.
**Kula**
Rohlfing, Frederick William
**Wailuku**
Jenkins, Brian Rennert

### IDAHO

**Boise**
Arnold, Rebecca Williams
**Coeur D Alene**
Davis, Dennis Milan

### ILLINOIS

**Chicago**
Arvey, James Terrence
Ungaretti, Richard Anthony
**Elmhurst**
Berry, James Frederick
**Lake Forest**
Covington, George Morse
**Oak Brook**
Warnock, William Reid
**Skokie**
Greenspan, Jeffrey Dov
**Winnetka**
Davis, Chester R., Jr.

### INDIANA

**Fort Wayne**
Lawson, Jack Wayne
**Lafayette**
Bumbleburg, Joseph Theodore
**Muncie**
Kelly, Eric Damian

### KENTUCKY

**Lexington**
Murphy, Richard Vanderburgh

### LOUISIANA

**New Orleans**
Morton, James Russell
Villavaso, Stephen Donald
**Slidell**
D'Antonio, Guy Joseph

### MAINE

**Fryeburg**
Weimer, Gregory Aloyisus

### MARYLAND

**Abingdon**
Wolf, Martin Eugene
**Baltimore**
Dopkin, Mark Dregant
**Bethesda**
Abrams, Stanley David
**Chestertown**
Mowell, George Mitchell
**Frederick**
Sica, John

### MASSACHUSETTS

**Boston**
Connors, Donald Louis
Hamilton, John Dayton, Jr.
Hawkey, G. Michael
Krasnow, Jordan Philip
Shapiro, Sandra
**Dennis Port**
Singer, Myer R(ichard)
**Natick**
Marr, David E
Woodyshek, J. Daniel
**Newton**
Bernard, Michael Mark
**Norwood**
Salvatore, David Anthony
**Revere**
Cipoletta, James Joseph
**Williamstown**
Filson, J. Adam

### MICHIGAN

**Bingham Farms**
Moffitt, David Louis
**East Lansing**
Stroud, Ted William
**Farmington Hills**
Birnkrant, Sherwin Maurice
Hampton, William Peck
**Grand Rapids**
Jennette, Noble Stevenson, III
**Kalamazoo**
Bauckham, John Henry
**Lansing**
Canady, Mark Howard
**Petoskey**
Smith, Wayne Richard
**Saginaw**
Beer, Louis Delamare
**Southfield**
Nykanen, David Edward
Sullivan, Robert Emmet, Jr.

### MINNESOTA

**Eagan**
O'Connor, Michael William
**Minneapolis**
Barnard, Allen Donald
Jensen, Darrell Alf
Steinwall, Susan Deborah
Thorson, Steven Greg

### MISSOURI

**Kansas City**
Gardner, Brian E.
Moore, Stephen James
Watts, James Dariel
**Saint Louis**
Mersman, Richard Kendrick, III
Michenfelder, Albert A.

### NEVADA

**Las Vegas**
Curran, William P.
Parry, Stanley Warren

### NEW HAMPSHIRE

**Concord**
Morris, James Edgar
**Exeter**
Donahue, Michael Joseph
**Laconia**
Giere, John Patrick

### NEW JERSEY

**Atlantic City**
Baylinson, Christopher Michael
Brown, Christopher Arthur
**Boonton**
Bucco, Anthony Mark
**Cedar Grove**
Stickel, Frederick George, III
**Edison**
Applebaum, Charles
**Fair Lawn**
Hirschklau, Morton
**Freehold**
Brown, Sanford Donald
**Hackensack**
Duus, Gordon Cochran
Navatta, Anna Paula
**Iselin**
Kracht, Richard William
**Metuchen**
Convery, Samuel Vincent, Jr.
**Montclair**
Conrad, David Williams
**Montvale**
Beattie, James Raymond
**Montville**
Buzak, Edward Joseph
**Moorestown**
Hardt, Frederick William
**Morristown**
Platt, Gary R.
**Newark**
Deutsch, Stuart Lewis
Neuer, Philip David
**Newton**
Cox, William Martin
**Nutley**
Feigenbaum, Larry Seth
**Parsippany**
Silverstein, Robert Selnick
Whipkey, Lisa J.
**Phillipsburg**
Jones, Bruce Alan
**Plainfield**
Dowling, Joan E.
**Princeton**
Moore, Kevin John
Sutphin, William Taylor
**Springfield**
Grayson, Bette Rita
Kurzweil, Bette Grayson
Mytelka, Arnold Krieger
**Union**
Greenstein, Richard Henry
**West Orange**
Kantowitz, Jeffrey Leon
Mandelbaum, Barry Richard
**Westfield**
Phillips, John C.
**Westwood**
Regan, Robert Terrence
**Willingboro**
Guest, Brian Milton
**Woodcliff Lake**
DeVita, Danielle
**Wyckoff**
Spizziri, John Anthony

### NEW YORK

**Albany**
Feller, Robert H.
Ruzow, Daniel Arthur
**Amherst**
Murray, William Michael
**Hudson**
Palmateer, Lee Allen
**Melville**
Rathkopf, Daren Anthony
**Mineola**
Goldstein, Sheldon Mark
**New York**
Armstrong, James Sinclair
Davis, Gordon J.
Kafin, Robert Joseph
Marcus, Norman
Piscitelli, Peter
Sidamon-Eristoff, Constantine
**Rochester**
Walsh, Thomas F.
**Rome**
Rizzo, James S.
**Schenectady**
McCartney, Brian Palmer
**Syracuse**
Gilligan, Kevin Michael
McGinty, Elizabeth Caryl

### NORTH CAROLINA

**Cary**
Montgomery, Charles Harvey
**Chapel Hill**
Brower, David John
**Greensboro**
Walker, Edward Garrett

### OHIO

**Akron**
Schrader, Alfred Eugene
Swing, Christopher Frederick
**Cincinnati**
Ashdown, Charles Coster
Bonhaus, Laurence Allen
Burke, Timothy Michael
Cutler, Nancy Jane
Mara, Timothy Gerald
Trauth, Joseph Louis, Jr.
**Cleveland**
Berns, Sheldon
**Columbus**
Neuman, Todd Howard
**Toledo**
McGinn, Barbara Ann

### OKLAHOMA

**Oklahoma City**
Epperson, Kraettli Quynton

### OREGON

**Eugene**
DuPriest, Douglas Millhollen
**Portland**
Firestone, Gary
Hribernick, Paul R.
**Salem**
Lien, Wallace Wayne

### PENNSYLVANIA

**Bryn Mawr**
Broseman, George W.
**Norristown**
Folmar, Larry John
Rees, Thomas Dynevor
**Philadelphia**
Brooman, David J.
**Pipersville**
Sigety, Charles Edward
**Pittsburgh**
Zangrilli, Albert Joseph, Jr.
**Reading**
Ober, Paul Russell
**Uniontown**
Leskinen, Steve Peter

### RHODE ISLAND

**Providence**
Smith, Robert Ellis
**Westerly**
Nardone, William Andrew

### SOUTH CAROLINA

**Charleston**
Lady, James Edward
Robinson, Neil Cibley, Jr.
**Columbia**
Caulk, Glen Paul
**Greenwood**
Nexsen, Julian Jacobs, Jr.

### TENNESSEE

**Parsons**
Petrey, R. Claybourne, Jr.

### TEXAS

**Houston**
Wall, Kenneth E., Jr.
**Mcallen**
Darling, James Edward

### VERMONT

**Burlington**
Roy, Christopher Denis
Rushford, Robert Howard
**Middlebury**
Hill, Cindy Ellen
**Rutland**
Facey, John Abbott, III

### VIRGINIA

**Alexandria**
Beach, Barbara Purse
**Fairfax**
Stearns, Frank Warren
**Leesburg**
Minchew, John Randall
**Richmond**
Bates, John Wythe, III
**Roanoke**
Douthat, James Fielding

### WASHINGTON

**Bellevue**
Boespflug, John Francis, Jr.
**Bellingham**
Buri, Philip James
**Mount Vernon**
Moser, C. Thomas
**Olympia**
Miller, Allen Terry, Jr.
**Seattle**
Aramburu, John Richard
Brower, Joshua Christopher Allen
Eustis, Jeffrey Murdock
Goeltz, Thomas A.
Haggard, Joel Edward
Jensen, Howard Fernando
Larson, Linda R.
McCune, Philip Spear
Mullaney, Patrick Joseph
Murray, Michael Kent
Simpson, Jennifer Lynn
Wilson, Richard Randolph
**Tacoma**
Densley, James Albert
Harlow, Angelia DeAn
**Wenatchee**
Aylward, J. Patrick

### WEST VIRGINIA

**Charleston**
George, Larry Wayne

### WISCONSIN

**Elkhorn**
Leibsle, Robert Carl
**Madison**
Rankin, Gene Raymond
**Milwaukee**
Rieselbach, Allen Newman
**Oshkosh**
Williams, Edward J.
**Waukesha**
Macy, John Patrick

### MEXICO

**Cuernavaca**
Foss, George B., Jr.

### ADDRESS UNPUBLISHED

Arnold, Craig Anthony (Tony Arnold)
Bateman, David Alfred
Higginson, Carla Jean
Miskimin, Alice Schwenk
Siegel, Sarah Ann
Zurav, David Bernard

## LANDLORD-TENANT. *See also* Commercial.

### UNITED STATES

#### ALABAMA

**Birmingham**
Cornett, Wendy Love
Theibert, Richard Wilder
**Montgomery**
Franco, Ralph Abraham

#### ARIZONA

**Scottsdale**
Marhoffer, David

#### CALIFORNIA

**Burlingame**
Fogarty, Janet E.
**Canoga Park**
Gordon, Jerome
**Irvine**
Farrell, Teresa Joanning
**Long Beach**
Rothschild, Toby James
**Los Angeles**
McBirney, Bruce Henry
Porter, Verna Louise
**Placentia**
Evans, Winthrop Shattuck
**Riverside**
Chang, Janice May
**Sacramento**
Giguiere, Michele Louise
**San Diego**
Frasch, Brian Bernard
Tow, L. Michelle
**San Francisco**
Brayer, Janet
**Santa Ana**
Arghavani, Firoozeh (Fay)
**Torrance**
Johnson, Einar William
**Victorville**
Kennedy, Jeanne Elizabeth
**Walnut Creek**
Horner, Clifford R.

#### COLORADO

**Aspen**
Peirce, Frederick Fairbanks
**Lakewood**
Lawler, Richard Allen

#### CONNECTICUT

**Bloomfield**
Mark, Henry Allen
**Clinton**
Hershatter, Richard Lawrence
**Hartford**
Sylvester, Kathryn Rose
**New Haven**
Ajello, Michael John
**Waterbury**
Muroff, Elena Marie

#### DELAWARE

**Wilmington**
Kristol, Daniel Marvin

#### DISTRICT OF COLUMBIA

**Washington**
Genz, Michael Andrew
Loewinger, Kenneth Jeffery

#### FLORIDA

**Boca Raton**
Barwell, Cindy Ann
**Hollywood**
Weisman, David
**Jacksonville**
Wachs, Alan Scott
**Miami**
Feinsmith, Paul Lowell
Wiseheart, Malcolm Boyd, Jr.
**Orlando**
Ashby, Kimberly A.
**West Palm Beach**
Layman, David Michael
**Winter Park**
Cool, Dwight I.

#### GEORGIA

**Atlanta**
Foreman, Edward Rawson
Womack, Mary Pauline
**Valdosta**
Smith, John Holder, Jr.

#### HAWAII

**Wailuku**
Kinaka, William Tatsuo

#### ILLINOIS

**Chicago**
Bernstein, Charles Bernard
Dodds, Frances Alison
Kawitt, Alan
Magner, Michele Geralyn
Meyers, Joel G.
Moltz, Marshall Jerome
Ungaretti, Richard Anthony
Ungerleider, Robert Norman
White, Linda Diane

#### INDIANA

**Evansville**
Jewell, John J.
**Indianapolis**
Abrams, Jeffrey Alan
Dorocke, Lawrence Francis
Grayson, John Allan

#### KENTUCKY

**Louisville**
Vincenti, Michael Baxter

#### LOUISIANA

**Baton Rouge**
Block, Mitchell Stern
Moreno, Richard Dale

#### MARYLAND

**Bel Air**
Wilson, Christian Burhenn
**Bethesda**
Bregman, Douglas M.
**Silver Spring**
Hannan, Myles

#### MASSACHUSETTS

**Boston**
Berman, Martin Samuel
Bloch, Donald Martin
Hawkey, G. Michael
Saltiel, David M.
**Brookline**
Lipson, Roger Russell
**Manchester**
Rumpf, Pierre Cameron
**Rockland**
Auton, Linda May Eisenschmidt
**Salem**
Wasserman, Stephen Alan

#### MICHIGAN

**Bloomfield Hills**
Berlow, Robert Alan
Dawson, Stephen Everette
**Detroit**
Candler, James Nall, Jr.

#### MINNESOTA

**Minneapolis**
Jensch, Charles Campbell
**Saint Paul**
Spencer, David James

#### MISSOURI

**Independence**
Watkins, Susan Gail
**Saint Louis**
Klamer, Jane Ferguson

#### NEW JERSEY

**Florham Park**
Haber, Karin Duchin
**Hackensack**
Navatta, Anna Paula
**Medford**
Timban, Demetrio Sunga
**Parsippany**
Silverstein, Robert Selnick
**Short Hills**
Fast, Kenneth H.

#### NEW YORK

**Chittenango**
Baum, Peter Alan
**Commack**
Somer, Stanley Jerome
**Jericho**
Beal, Carol Ann
**Mineola**
Vogel, Jennifer Lyn
**New York**
Bentley, Anthony Miles
Davis, Deborah Lynn
Finkelstein, Daniel
Gesmer, Ellen Frances
Goldstein, Kenneth B.
Intriligator, Marc Steven
Kastner, Menachem J.
Levine, Melvin Charles
Rahm, David Alan
Rosenberg, Gary Marc
Sanseverino, Raymond Anthony
Schechter, Howard
Schwartz, Barry Steven
Shollenberger, Elizabeth Ann
Simon, Michael Scott
Uram, Gerald Robert
Urban, Lisa Breier
Vernon, Darryl Mitchell
Willinger, Lowell D.
**Newburgh**
Bernz, David
**Port Washington**
Adler, Edward Andrew Koeppel
**Snyder**
Genrich, Willard Adolph

#### NORTH CAROLINA

**Greensboro**
Agapion, Bill

#### OHIO

**Cleveland**
Kramer, Edward George
Schloss, John P.
**Columbus**
Joseph, John James
**Pepper Pike**
Soukup, Christopher Earl
**Youngstown**
Galip, Ronald George

#### OKLAHOMA

**Oklahoma City**
Johnson, Robert Max

#### OREGON

**Cannon Beach**
Hillestad, Charles Andrew
**Portland**
Jenks, George Milan

#### PENNSYLVANIA

**Lancaster**
Zimmerman, D(onald) Patrick
**Philadelphia**
Bressler, Barry E.
Goldman, Gary Craig
Pillion, Michael Leith
**Pittsburgh**
Hartman, Ronald G.

#### TEXAS

**Austin**
Owen, Jack Edward, Jr.
**Dallas**
Fishman, Edward Marc
Hawkins, Scott Alexis
Roberts, Harry Morris, Jr.
Stewart, Robb P.
**Fort Worth**
Fanous, Nikki Hobert
Johns, Deborah Ann Henry
**Houston**
Davis, Martha Algenita Scott

#### UTAH

**Salt Lake City**
Jones, Ken Paul

#### VIRGINIA

**Fairfax**
Kear, Maria Martha Ruscitella
**Richmond**
Bates, John Wythe, III

#### WASHINGTON

**Spokane**
Smith, Brad Edward

#### WISCONSIN

**Milwaukee**
Rotter, Emanuel Norman

#### ADDRESS UNPUBLISHED

Assael, Michael
Chong-Spiegel, Ginger Geroma
Mayersohn, Arnold Linn, Jr.
Rivera, Oscar R.

## LEGISLATIVE

### UNITED STATES

#### ALABAMA

**Mobile**
Murchison, David Roderick

#### ARIZONA

**Phoenix**
Barclay, Steven Calder
Wolf, G. Van Velsor, Jr.
**Scottsdale**
Angle, Margaret Susan

#### ARKANSAS

**Little Rock**
Sherman, William Farrar

#### CALIFORNIA

**Camarillo**
Lingl, James Peter
**Encino**
McDonough, Patrick Joseph
**Los Angeles**
Memel, Sherwin Leonard
**Oakland**
Cotter, Edward Francis, Jr.
**Sacramento**
Micheli, Christopher Michael

#### COLORADO

**Denver**
McLain, William Allen
Quinn, Michael S.
**Lakewood**
Mielke, Donald Earl
**Littleton**
Ross, William Robert
**Lyons**
Brown, Michael DeWayne

#### CONNECTICUT

**Danbury**
Winfree, Gregory Dainard
**Greenwich**
Cantor, Samuel C.
Trotta, Frank P., Jr.
**New Haven**
Dodge, Mannette Antill

#### DELAWARE

**Wilmington**
Boswell, David A.
Salinger, Frank Max

#### DISTRICT OF COLUMBIA

**Washington**
Ator, Lloyd George, Jr.
Besozzi, Paul Charles
Boone, Theodore Sebastian
Brewster, Christopher Ralph
Brinkmann, Robert Joseph
Buechner, Jack W(illiam)
Cernicky, Ann Hardman
Chabot, Philip Louis, Jr.
Clark, Paul Thomas
Corman, James C.
Cortese, Alfred William, Jr.
Coursen, Christopher Dennison
Dietz, Robert Sheldon
Falk, John Mansfield
Fontheim, Claude G.B.
Gold, Peter Frederick
Goldstein, Michael B.
Heron, Julian Briscoe, Jr.
Johnson, Shirley Z.
Jones, Theodore Lawrence
Katsurinis, Stephen Avery
Kautter, David John
Kennedy, Jerry Wayne
Kovacs, William Lawrence
Kramer, William David
Lanam, Linda Lee
Lobel, Martin
Lopatin, Alan G.
Mannina, George John, Jr.
McCormick, Walter Bernard, Jr.
McMillan, James Gardner
Mendelsohn, Martin
Navarro, Bruce Charles
Raymond, David Walker
Rehm, John Bartram
Richmond, David Walker
Rivlin, Lewis Allen
Sacher, Steven Jay
Schiffbauer, William G.
Spector, Phillip Louis
Stayin, Randolph John
Sweeney, Eileen Patricia
Violante, Joseph Anthony
Waris, Michael, Jr.
Weisgall, Jonathan Michael
Zweben, Murray

#### FLORIDA

**Fort Lauderdale**
Conklin, Howard Lawrence
**Indian Harbor Beach**
Tasker, Molly Jean
**Jacksonville**
Halverson, Steven Thomas
**Pinellas Park**
Blacklidge, Raymond Mark
**Tallahassee**
Barnett, Martha Walters
Curtin, Lawrence N.
Matthews, Frank Edward

#### GEORGIA

**Atlanta**
Appley, Elizabeth Joan
**Conyers**
Moore, Garland Curtis
**Dunwoody**
Callison, James W.

#### HAWAII

**Honolulu**
Mirikitani, Andrew Kotaro
Suzuki, Norman Hitoshi
**Kula**
Rohlfing, Frederick William

#### IDAHO

**Boise**
Barber, Phillip Mark
Thomas, Eugene C.

#### ILLINOIS

**Bloomington**
Wozniak, Debra Gail
**Chicago**
Aronovitz, Cory Jay
Blume, Paul Chiappe
Miller, John Leed
**Des Plaines**
Kotelman, Laura Mary
**Northbrook**
Ihm, Stephen Lawrence
**Springfield**
Artman, Eric Alan
Morse, Saul Julian

#### INDIANA

**Danville**
Baldwin, Jeffrey Kenton
**Indianapolis**
Allen, David James
Miller, David Anthony

#### IOWA

**Des Moines**
Brown, Paul Edmondson

#### LOUISIANA

**Baton Rouge**
Burland, James S.
Cutshaw, James Michael

#### MARYLAND

**Baltimore**
Wheatley, Charles Henry, III
**Bethesda**
English, William deShay
Pankopf, Arthur, Jr.
Sheble, Walter Franklin
**Bowie**
Lucchi, Leonard Louis
**Potomac**
Redding, Robert Ellsworth

#### MASSACHUSETTS

**Boston**
Sears, John Winthrop
Sweda, Edward Leon, Jr.
**Stow**
Golder, Leonard Howard

#### MICHIGAN

**Okemos**
Barton, Judith Marie

#### MINNESOTA

**Minneapolis**
Franzen, Douglas John

#### MISSISSIPPI

**Jackson**
Johnson, Mark Wayne

#### MISSOURI

**Kansas City**
Bevan, Robert Lewis

#### MONTANA

**Helena**
Watson, Rebecca Wunder
**Missoula**
Mudd, John O.

#### NEBRASKA

**Lincoln**
Crosby, Robert Berkey
**Omaha**
Moylan, James Harold

#### NEVADA

**Las Vegas**
Faiss, Robert Dean

#### NEW HAMPSHIRE

**Concord**
Miller, Timmie Maine

#### NEW JERSEY

**Dumont**
Schuster, Steven Vincent
**Liberty Corner**
McDermott, Frank Xavier
**Newark**
Milita, Martin Joseph
**Princeton**
Zarnowski, James David
**Trenton**
Pellecchia, John Michael

#### NEW MEXICO

**Albuquerque**
Barela, Jonathan Lewis
**Santa Fe**
Carpenter, Richard Norris

#### NEW YORK

**Albany**
Bogdan, Edward Andrew, Jr.
Gosdeck, Thomas Joseph
Ruggeri, Robert Edward
**Buffalo**
Pajak, David Joseph
**Floral Park**
Chatoff, Michael Alan
**Garden City**
Ungar, Robert Arthur
**Lancaster**
Walsh, J(ohn) B(ronson)
**New York**
Bear, Larry Alan
Bearak, Corey B(ecker)
Derwin, Jordan
Ganz, David L.
Mandelker, Lawrence Arthur
McGeady, Paul Joseph
Miller, Sam Scott
Piscitelli, Peter
Sack, Edward J.
Stringer, Ronald E.
Zedrosser, Joseph John
**Queensbury**
McCann, Bernard Thomas
**Stephentown**
Zwack, Henry Francis

#### NORTH CAROLINA

**Cary**
Cromer, Charles Lemuel

#### NORTH DAKOTA

**Grand Forks**
Hand, James Stanley

#### OHIO

**Columbus**
Haught, Jack Gregg
Liggett, Luther LeRoy, Jr.
Morgan, Dennis Richard
Shumate, Alex

#### OREGON

**Portland**
Weiler, Mary Pauline

#### PENNSYLVANIA

**Newtown**
Vosik, Wayne Gilbert
**Philadelphia**
Wagner, Thomas Joseph
**Pittsburgh**
Hull, John Daniel, IV

#### SOUTH CAROLINA

**Columbia**
Givens, Edwin D.

#### TENNESSEE

**Chattanooga**
Walker, Robert Kirk
**Nashville**
Thornton, Guilford F., Jr.

#### TEXAS

**Austin**
Allison, James Purney
Bray, Austin Coleman, Jr.
Cunningham, Judy Marie
Strauser, Robert Wayne
White, Michael Lee
**Dallas**
Barlow, W. P., Jr.

**Houston**
Devlin, Francis James
Miller, Robert Daniel
**Lubbock**
Crowson, James Lawrence

### UTAH

**Salt Lake City**
McConkie, Oscar Walter

### VIRGINIA

**Alexandria**
Campbell, Thomas Douglas
Sczudlo, Walter Joseph
Stone, Steven David
**Arlington**
Carbaugh, John Edward, Jr.
Collins, Philip Reilly
Kauffman, Thomas Richard
Laughlin, James Harold, Jr.
McDermott, Francis Owen
Wong, Richard Lee
**Charlottesville**
Cohen, Edwin Samuel
**Dunn Loring**
Melton, Michael Eric
**Fairfax**
Golden, Wilson
**Fredericksburg**
Glessner, Thomas Allen
**Manassas**
Platt, Leslie A.
**Mc Lean**
Bardack, Paul Roitman
Greene, Timothy Geddes
Ingersoll, William Boley
Peet, Richard Clayton
Shepard, Julian Leigh
Stephens, William Theodore
**Richmond**
Grey, Robert J.
Jones, Reginald Nash

### WASHINGTON

**Pasco**
Ungerecht, Todd Edward
**Seattle**
Eberhard, Eric Drake

### WISCONSIN

**Madison**
Bremer, Howard Walter
**Milwaukee**
Hodan, Patrick John

### ADDRESS UNPUBLISHED

Boyd, Thomas Marshall
Dikeou, George Demetrios
Doub, William Offutt
Hanzlik, Rayburn DeMara
Kibler, Rhoda Smith
Klapper, Gail Heitler
Perlstein, William James
Protigal, Stanley Nathan
Reeder, James Arthur
Schoor, Michael Mercier
Wittig, Raymond Shaffer

## LIBEL

### UNITED STATES

### ARIZONA

**Phoenix**
Bodney, David Jeremy
Chauncey, Tom Webster, II
Silverman, Alan Henry

### ARKANSAS

**Fayetteville**
VanWinkle, John Ragan

### CALIFORNIA

**Los Angeles**
Langberg, Barry Benson
**Newport Beach**
Abendroth, Douglas William
**Rancho Mirage**
Reuben, Don Harold
**Sacramento**
Houpt, James Edward
**Walnut Creek**
Epstein, Judith Ann

### COLORADO

**Denver**
Low, Andrew M.

### CONNECTICUT

**Hartford**
Elliot, Ralph Gregory

### DELAWARE

**Wilmington**
Green, James Samuel

### DISTRICT OF COLUMBIA

**Washington**
Baine, Kevin T.
Carome, Patrick Joseph
Dorsen, David M(ilton)
Horne, Michael Stewart
Isbell, David Bradford
Pickering, John Harold
Schmidt, Richard Marten, Jr.

### FLORIDA

**Fort Lauderdale**
Custer, Andy M.
**Hollywood**
Tannen, Ricki Lewis
**Jacksonville**
Judas, Suzanne Meyer
**Miami**
Vento, M. Thérèse
**Tampa**
Alley, John-Edward
Thomas, Gregg Darrow

### GEORGIA

**Atlanta**
Glaser, Arthur Henry
Schroeder, Eric Peter

### HAWAII

**Honolulu**
Dezzani, David John

### IDAHO

**Boise**
Kristensen, Debora Kathleen

### ILLINOIS

**Chicago**
Cazares, Jorge V.
Gilford, Steven Ross
Moran, John Thomas, Jr.
Rubin, E(rwin) Leonard
Sennet, Charles Joseph
Touhy, John M.
**Waukegan**
Rizzo, John Joseph

### MARYLAND

**Baltimore**
Mullady, Raymond George, Jr.

### MASSACHUSETTS

**Boston**
Ritvo, Elizabeth Ann
**Springfield**
Gross, Steven Ronald

### MICHIGAN

**Ann Arbor**
Niehoff, Leonard Marvin
**Detroit**
Rassel, Richard Edward

### MINNESOTA

**Minneapolis**
Borger, John Philip
Magnuson, Roger James
Paulsrud, Eric David

### MISSISSIPPI

**Jackson**
Henegan, John C(lark)

### MISSOURI

**Kansas City**
Milton, Chad Earl

### NEVADA

**Las Vegas**
Faiss, Robert Dean
Galane, Morton Robert

### NEW JERSEY

**Cherry Hill**
Fols, Stacy Alison

### NEW YORK

**Albany**
Danziger, Peter
**Buffalo**
Schreck, Robert J.
**Campbell Hall**
Stone, Peter George
**Glen Cove**
Mills, Charles Gardner
**Hamburg**
Killeen, Henry Walter
**New York**
Abelman, Arthur F.
Bamberger, Michael Albert
Cayea, Donald Joseph
Daichman, Jeffrey Howard
Dehn, Francis Xavier
Deutsch, Andrew L.
Green, Richard George
Jun, Meeka
Kennedy, Michael John
Larkin, Leo Paul, Jr.
Nemerov, Jeffrey Arnold
Ringel, Dean
Robertson, Edwin David
Scheiman, Eugene R.
Schwartz, Renee Gerstler
Sherman, Jonathan Henry
**Purchase**
Lytton, William B(ryan)

### NORTH CAROLINA

**Marion**
Burgin, Charles Edward

### OHIO

**Cincinnati**
Faller, Susan Grogan
**Toledo**
Pletz, Thomas Gregory
**Youngstown**
Bolton, Stephen Timothy

### OREGON

**Portland**
Hinkle, Charles Frederick

### PENNSYLVANIA

**Harrisburg**
Sullivan, John Cornelius, Jr.
**Philadelphia**
Beasley, James Edwin
Kohn, Harold Elias
McHugh, James Joseph
Mishkin, Jeremy David
Shestack, Jerome Joseph
Solano, Carl Anthony
Toll, Seymour Irving
**Pittsburgh**
Hornak, Mark Raymond
**York**
Benn, Niles S.

### RHODE ISLAND

**Providence**
Smith, Robert Ellis

### SOUTH CAROLINA

**Charleston**
Norris, Charles R.

### TENNESSEE

**Chattanooga**
Phillips, John Bomar

### TEXAS

**Beaumont**
Black, Robert Allen
Thomas, Brett Scott
**Dallas**
Babcock, Charles Lynde, IV
Elkind, Laura Peterson
Mc Elhaney, John Hess
**Fort Worth**
Sharpe, James Shelby
**Houston**
Pamphilis, Constantine Z.
Rhodes, George Frederick, Jr.
**San Antonio**
Trotter, Richard Clayton

### VIRGINIA

**Hampton**
Long, Robert Elliott
Smith, Stephen M.
**Norfolk**
Sims, Hunter W., Jr.
**Richmond**
Rudlin, David Alan

### WASHINGTON

**Seattle**
Johnson, Bruce Edward Humble

### WISCONSIN

**Green Bay**
Barker, April Rockstead

### CANADA

### ONTARIO

**Toronto**
Chester, Robert Simon George

### GEORGIA

**Tbilisi**
Swann, Barbara

### ADDRESS UNPUBLISHED

Bloom, Charles Joseph
DeLaFuente, Charles
Grutman, Jewel Humphrey
Kapnick, Richard Bradshaw
Saunders, Lonna Jeanne

**MALPRACTICE.** *See* **Personal injury.**

## MERGERS AND ACQUISITIONS

### UNITED STATES

### ALABAMA

**Birmingham**
Baker, David Remember
Grant, Walter Matthews
Rotch, James E.
Stewart, Joseph Grier

### ALASKA

**Anchorage**
Gorski, James Michael

### ARIZONA

**Chandler**
Markey, James Kevin
**Phoenix**
Bauman, Frederick Carl
Curzon, Thomas Henry
Maledon, Michael Brien
Moya, Patrick Robert
Theobald, Scott M.

### ARKANSAS

**Little Rock**
Knight, David Arceneaux

### CALIFORNIA

**Buena Park**
Kehrli, David P.
**Burlingame**
Spyros, Nicholas L., Jr.
Telleen, L. Michael
**Camarillo**
Cayley, Susan Nicole
**Glendale**
Ball, James Herington
**Irvine**
Gay, William Tolin
**Los Angeles**
Apfel, Gary
Blencowe, Paul Sherwood
Bogaard, William Joseph
Boston, Derrick Osmond
Brown, Avery R.
Costales, Marco Daniel
Farrar, Stanley F.
Forster, Jonathan Shawn
Haakh, Gilbert Edward
Hatch, Hilary Joy
Hsu, Julie L.
Kim, Edward K.
Klein, Raymond Maurice
Miller, Craig Dana
Shilling, Monica Jill
Shultz, John David
**Menlo Park**
Sauers, William Dale
**Newport Beach**
Black, William Rea
Cano, Kristin Maria
Terner, Andor David
**Oakland**
Bewley, Peter David
**Palo Alto**
Daunt, Jacqueline Ann
Laurie, Ronald Sheldon
Lesser, Henry
Nopar, Alan Scott
Phair, Joseph Baschon
Pohlen, Patrick Alan
Whaley, James Thaddeus
**San Diego**
Michels, Dirk
Sapin, Craig P.
**San Francisco**
Baker, Cameron
Block, David Jeffrey
DeMuro, Paul Robert
Evers, William Dohrmann
Forsythe, Janet Winifred
Larson, John William
Mann, Bruce Alan
Shepherd, John Michael
Wood, Robert Warren
**San Jose**
Bebb, Richard S.
Chacon, Gerald Gilbert
**San Luis Obispo**
Collins, Mary Elizabeth
**San Ramon**
Freed, Kenneth Alan
**Santa Clara**
Denten, Christopher Peter
**Saratoga**
Stephens, Lawrence Keith
**Vernon**
Smith, Lawrence Ronald
**Walnut Creek**
Deming, Bruce Robert

### COLORADO

**Denver**
Dean, James Benwell
Groom, David A.
Levine, Ronald Raymond
Oakes, Susan Leigh
Peloquin, Louis Omer
Ruppert, John Lawrence
Terry, Ward Edgar, Jr.
**Englewood**
Gognat, Richard J.
Lidstone, Herrick Kenley, Jr.
**Littleton**
Keely, George Clayton

### CONNECTICUT

**Darien**
Flanagan, Mari Jo Florio
**Farmington**
Levy, Coleman Bertram
McCann, John Joseph
**Greenwich**
Raimondi, Josephine Ann
**Hartford**
Bernier, Marcel J.
Cain, George Harvey
Davis, Andrew Neil
Lotstein, James Irving
Reilly, Edward Anthony, Jr.
Smith, Richard Stanley, Jr.
**New Haven**
Gollaher, Merton G
**Stamford**
Della Rocco, Kenneth Anthony
Dupont, Wesley David
Herling, Michael James
**Weston**
Cohen, Fred Howard

### DELAWARE

**Wilmington**
Baldwin, Glen S.
Burnett, James F.
Goldman, Michael David
Gundersen, Mark Jonathan
Stoltzfus, James Allen

### DISTRICT OF COLUMBIA

**Washington**
Bierman, James Norman
Bill, Arthur Henry
Bowe, Richard Welbourn
Bruemmer, Russell John
Czarra, Edgar F., Jr.
Fishburne, Benjamin P., III
Hockenberry, John Fedden
Jacobsen, Raymond Alfred, Jr.
Konselman, Douglas Derek
Mazo, Mark Elliott
McHugh, Richard Patrick
Pugh, Keith E., Jr.
Rafferty, James Gerard
Repper, George Robert
Ryan, Joseph
Strong, Carter

### FLORIDA

**Altamonte Springs**
Rudisill, Robert Mack, Jr.
**Boca Raton**
Beck, Jan Scott
**Fort Lauderdale**
Austin, Scott Raymond
Platner, Michael Gary
**Hobe Sound**
Simpson, Russell Gordon
**Jacksonville**
Lee, Lewis Swift
**Miami**
Alvarez-Farré, Emilio José
Ersek, Gregory Joseph Mark
Friedman, Richard Nathan
Grossman, Robert Louis
McGuigan, Thomas Richard
Pearlman, Michael Allen
Villasana, George Anthony
Whitlow, James Adams
**Orlando**
Capouano, Albert D.
Collard, Stacey Lee
Conti, Louis Thomas Moore
Heinle, Richard Alan
**Palm Beach**
Tabernilla, Armando Alejandro
**Sarasota**
Moore, John Leslie
**Tampa**
Doliner, Nathaniel Lee
**West Palm Beach**
O'Brien, Thomas George, III

### GEORGIA

**Atlanta**
Andros, James Harry
Arkin, Robert David
Bruckner, William J.
Coleman, Sean Joseph
Kelley, James Francis
Kelly, James Michael
McNeill, Thomas Ray
Morgan, Charles Russell
Moss, Raymond Lloyd
Peterzell, Betsy Vance
Pless, Laurance Davidson
Schulte, Jeffrey Lewis
Stewart, Jeffrey B.
Verska, Kimberly Anne
Zabka, Sven Paul
**Dunwoody**
Tramonte, James Albert

### HAWAII

**Honolulu**
Reber, David James

### ILLINOIS

**Aurora**
Marchetti, Marilyn H.
**Chicago**
Ackerman, David Paul
Anderson, J. Trent
Brown, Gregory K.
Burke, Richard William
Cortes, William Patrick
Crawford, Dewey Byers
Davis, Scott Jonathan
Docksey, John Ross
Dunn, Edwin Rydell
Dunn, Kenneth Carl
Fein, Roger Gary
Friedli, Helen Russell
Gerstein, Mark Douglas
Grossberg, David Alan
Harris, Linda Chaplik
Howell, R(obert) Thomas, Jr.
Johnson, Tige Christopher
Kaplan, Jared
Kempf, Donald G., Jr.
Kopelman, Ian Stuart
Lowinger, Frederick Charles
Malovany, Howard
Marroquin-Merino, Victor Miguel
McGuigan, Philip Palmer
McLees, John Alan
Mertes, Arthur Edward
O'Hagan, Kevin Michael
Reum, James Michael
Rizowy, Carlos Guillermo
Rudnick, William Alan
Rudo, Saul E.
Scogland, William Lee
Wander, Herbert Stanton
**Deerfield**
Gaither, John F.
**Highland Park**
Nyberg, William Arthur
**Hoffman Estates**
Walpole, James R.
**Northbrook**
Sernett, Richard Patrick
**Springfield**
Cullen, Mark Kenneth

### INDIANA

**Indianapolis**
Henderson, Eugene Leroy
Strain, James Arthur

### IOWA

**Des Moines**
Neumann, Gordon Richard, Jr.
**Iowa City**
Thomas, Randall Stuart

### KENTUCKY

**Lexington**
Terry, Joseph H.
**Louisville**
Ament, Mark Steven
Anderson, P. Richard
Mellen, Francis Joseph, Jr.

### LOUISIANA

**New Orleans**
Downing, Carl Seldon
McMillan, Lee Richards, II

### MAINE

**Portland**
Stauffer, Eric P.
Tierney, Kevin Joseph

## MARYLAND

**Baltimore**
Robinson, Zelig
**Bethesda**
Menaker, Frank H., Jr.
**Rockville**
Roberts, Christopher Chalmers

## MASSACHUSETTS

**Boston**
Anderson, Arthur Irvin
Auerbach, Joseph
Bohnen, Michael J.
Coukos, Stephen John
Greenblatt, Martin Elliott
Halligan, Brendan Patrick
Kane, Stephen Michael
Mullare, T(homas) Kenwood, Jr.
Patterson, John de la Roche, Jr.
Poss, Stephen Daniel
Rosenbloom, Thomas Adam
Trevisani, Robert Armand
Williams, Robert Dana
Wright, Walter Augustine, III
**Cambridge**
Gonson, S. Donald
**Lexington**
D'Avignon, Roy Joseph
**Newton**
Horbaczewski, Henry Zygmunt
**Springfield**
Fialky, Gary Lewis
Weiss, Ronald Phillip
**Worcester**
Joyce, James Joseph, Jr.
Lougee, David Louis

## MICHIGAN

**Ada**
Johnson, Byron John
Mc Callum, Charles Edward
**Ann Arbor**
Valenti, Dennis R.
**Birmingham**
Bick, Robert Steven
**Bloomfield Hills**
Wellman, David Joseph
**Detroit**
Deason, Herold McClure
Lawrence, John Kidder
Rentenbach, Paul Robert
**Farmington Hills**
Ciampa, Jeffrey Nelson

## MINNESOTA

**Minneapolis**
Bergerson, David Raymond
Duran, Stanley John
Erhart, John Joseph
Houston, John R.
Kaplan, Sheldon
Kelley, Shane Richard
Konezny, Jeryn Ann-Hall
Mellum, Gale Robert
Nelson, Gary Michael
Opdahl, Clark Donald
Saunders, Jeffrey N.
Stageberg, Roger V.
Yost, Gerald B.
**Saint Paul**
Devgun, Dharminder Singh
Dordell, Timothy Paul
Rebane, John T.

## MISSISSIPPI

**Jackson**
Allen, Leigh Briscoe, III

## MISSOURI

**Chesterfield**
Denneen, John Paul
**Kansas City**
Ball, Owen Keith, Jr.
Brenneman, Gerald Wayne
Dolson, Edward M.
Newcom, Jennings Jay
Seitter, David Charles
Wrobley, Ralph Gene
**Saint Louis**
Cook, Thomas Alfred Ashley
Dorwart, Donald Bruce
Gillis, John Lamb, Jr.
Kuhlmann, Fred Mark
Tierney, Michael Edward
**Springfield**
Starnes, James Wright

## NEVADA

**Las Vegas**
Brewer, John Nelson
**Reno**
Olechny, Steven John

## NEW HAMPSHIRE

**Hampton**
DuChene, Todd Michael

## NEW JERSEY

**Fort Lee**
Cox, Melvin Monroe
**Iselin**
Oriolo, Joseph Michael
**Jersey City**
Lawatsch, Frank Emil, Jr.
**Lawrenceville**
Dahl, Michael Bruce
Rudy, James Francis Xavier
**Morristown**
Greenapple, Steven Bruce
Kandravy, John
Massey, Henry Nelson
**Newark**
Vajtay, Stephen Michael, Jr.
**Pitman**
Cloues, Edward Blanchard, II
**Roseland**
Osvald-Mruz, Christine
Wovsaniker, Alan
**Somerset**
Macey, Scott J.
**Woodbridge**
Falk, Kenneth B.
**Woodcliff Lake**
Klein, Marilyn Yaffe

## NEW YORK

**Buffalo**
Cramer, Mark Kenley
Lippes, Gerald Sanford
Schulz, Paul John
**Garden City**
Breslin, Eileen Mary
**Le Roy**
Harner, Timothy R.
**New York**
Allen, Phillip Stephen
Atkins, Peter Allan
Bab, Andrew Laurance
Backman, Gerald Stephen
Baker, Mark Robert
Bannister, J. Alan
Barre, Erwan
Beinecke, Candace Krugman
Bialkin, Kenneth Jules
Boynton, James Stephen
Breinin, Bartley James
Brewer, William Dane
Brown, Meredith M.
Burak, H(oward) Paul
Bushnell, George Edward, III
Butler, Samuel Coles
Calvey, Brian J.
Cogan, Sarah Edwards
Cohen, Howard Marvin
Cotter, James Michael
Crawshaw, Donald R.
Detjen, David Wheeler
Dorado, Marianne Gaertner
Dubin, James Michael
Dunn, M(orris) Douglas
Feit, Glenn M.
Fishman, Fred Norman
Fogg, Blaine Viles
Fortenbaugh, Samuel Byrod, III
Fraidin, Stephen
Fredericks, Wesley Charles, Jr.
Fried, Donald David
Friedman, Samuel Selig
Garvey, Richard Anthony
Gettner, Alan Frederick
Giancarlo, J. Christopher
Gilioli, Eric Lawrence
Grader, Scott Paul
Greenstein, Karen Anne
Greenwald, David Jeffrey
Haje, Peter Robert
Hanson, Stephen Philip
Haythe, Thomas Madison
Healy, Walter F. X.
Heleniak, David William
Heller, Robert Martin
Hendry, Andrew Delaney
Henryson, Herbert, II
Hiden, Robert Battaile, Jr.
Hill, Joseph C.
Hochman, Stephen Allen
Hoff, Jonathan M(orind)
Holley, Steven Lyon
Howe, Richard Rives
Hsiao, Monica Lo-Ching
Hutton, G. Thompson
Jenner, Eva Catherine
Johnson, Lynne A.
Junius, Andreas Gretus
Katz, Ronald Scott
Kelly, Daniel Grady, Jr.
Kern, George Calvin, Jr.
Kessel, Mark
Kies, David M.
Kirman, Igor
Klein, Alan M.
Klein, William, II
Komaroff, Stanley
Landau, Walter Loeber
Landes, Robert Nathan
Larose, Lawrence Alfred
Laurenson, Edwin Charles
Leonard, Edwin Deane
Levin, Ezra Gurion
Lewis, Edwin Leonard, III
Margulis, Michael Henry
McCurrach, Duncan C.
Mestres, Ricardo Angelo, Jr.
Meyer, Matthew J.
Morphy, James Calvin
Mullman, Michael S.
Myerson, Toby Salter
Nahm, Nathan Ihru
Nance, Allan Taylor
Nash, Paul LeNoir
Norfolk, William Ray
Norwitz, Trevor S.
Park, Sang Hyuk
Perkins, Roswell Burchard
Phillips, Pamela Kim
Pierce, Morton Allen
Pisano, Vincent James
Prashker, Audrey Eve
Quale, Andrew Christopher, Jr.
Radey, Dona Lynn
Rawson, Richard J.
Reid, Edward Snover, III
Richey, Kent Ramon
Robinson, John Kelly
Rogers, Danforth William
Rosenberg, Marc S.
Rosenblum, Scott S.
Rosoff, William L.
Roth, Paul Norman
Rubinstein, Frederic Armand
Rusmisel, Stephen R.
Schmidt, Joseph W.
Schneider, Harold Lawrence
Schorr, Brian Lewis
Schwartz, Barry Fredric
Seifert, Thomas Lloyd
Serota, Susan Perlstadt
Shecter, Howard L.
Sheehan, Robert C.
Sheikh, Kemal A.
Siegel, Jeffrey Norton
Siller, Stephen I.
Slezak, Edward M.
Sorkin, David James
Spatt, Robert Edward
Thalacker, Arbie Robert
Toumey, Donald Joseph
Tract, Marc Mitchell
Tran, Julie Hoan
Tse, Charles Yung Chang
Vlahakis, Patricia
Warden, John L.
Welikson, Jeffrey Alan
Wiegley, Roger Douglas
Yamin, Michael Geoffrey
**Rochester**
Adair, Donald Robert
Doyle, Justin P
Young, Thomas Paul
**Rye**
Roberts, Thomas Alba
**Southampton**
Lopez, David
**Suffern**
Stack, Daniel
**Syracuse**
Bullock, Stephen C.
**White Plains**
Burkett, Bradford C.
Serchuk, Ivan

## NORTH CAROLINA

**Charlotte**
Bernstein, Mark R.
Culbreth, James Harold, Jr.
McBryde, Neill Gregory
Newitt, John Garwood, Jr.
Whelpley, David B., Jr.
**Greensboro**
Davis, Herbert Owen
Hopkins, John David
**High Point**
Ashcraft, David Bee
**Raleigh**
Byrd, Stephen Timothy
Geil, John McIntosh
Gwyn, William Blair, Jr.
Miller, Jeffrey D.
Powell, Durwood Royce
**Winston Salem**
Coffey, Larry B(ruce)
Gunter, Michael Donwell

## OHIO

**Akron**
Allan, Ronald Curtis
**Cincinnati**
Henderson, Stephen Paul
Lindberg, Charles David
Olson, Robert Wyrick
**Cleveland**
Band, Jordan Clifford
Blackford, Jason Collier
Donahue, Charles Bertrand, II
Fryt, Michael David
Hogg, James Stuart
Langer, Carlton Earl
Pyke, John Secrest, Jr.
Trevor, Leigh Barry
**Columbus**
Bowen, John Wesley Edward, IV
Brinkman, Dale Thomas
Robins, Ronald Albert, Jr.
Tannous, Robert Joseph
Vorys, Arthur Isaiah
**Dayton**
Furry, Richard Logan
Lamme, Kathryn Anne
Schwartz, Richard Anthony
Teeters, Bruce A.
Tweel, Donna Shank
**Miamisburg**
Niemeyer, Jonathan David
**Richfield**
Calise, Nicholas James
**Rocky River**
Grady, Francis Xavier
**Toledo**
Webb, Thomas Irwin, Jr.
**Wickliffe**
Kidder, Fred Dockstater

## OKLAHOMA

**Oklahoma City**
Rockett, D. Joe
Tytanic, Christopher Alan
**Tulsa**
Davenport, Gerald Bruce
Slicker, Frederick Kent

## OREGON

**Beaverton**
Fulsher, Allan Arthur
**Eugene**
Gallagher, Donald Avery, Jr.
Thompson, Edward P.
**Lake Oswego**
Wilson, Jeffrey Dale
**Portland**
Denecke, David Rockey
James, Christopher
Krahmer, Donald Leroy, Jr.

## PENNSYLVANIA

**Blue Bell**
Barron, Harold Sheldon
**Exton**
Hedges, Donald Walton
**Franklin Center**
Harvey, Alice Elease
**Harrisburg**
Cicconi, Christopher M.
**Philadelphia**
Agran, Raymond Daniel
Clark, William H., Jr.
Cooney, John Gordon
Dombrowski, Raymond Edward, Jr.
Feder, Steven J.
Genkin, Barry Howard
Gough, John Francis
Grady, Thomas Michael
Hennessy, Joseph H.
King, David Roy
Malloy, Michael P.
Promislo, Daniel
Strasbaugh, Wayne Ralph
Stuntebeck, Clinton A.
**Pittsburgh**
Aderson, Sanford M.
Bleier, Michael E.
Drake, Edwin P.
Hardie, James Hiller
Hildreth, Gary R.
Lefkowitz, Alan Zoel
Messer, Susan J.
Newlin, William Rankin
Pandit, Amy Indravadan
Pollack, David L.
Purtell, Lawrence Robert
Shuman, Joseph Duff
Todd, Thomas
Whyte, Kevin J.
Wilkinson, James Allan
**Saint Davids**
Preston, Robert F.
**Shavertown**
Malak, Paul John
Ostroski, Raymond B.
**Valley Forge**
Bovaird, Brendan Peter
**Wilkes Barre**
Roth, Eugene

## RHODE ISLAND

**Pawtucket**
Kranseler, Lawrence Michael
**Providence**
Donnelly, Kevin William
**Woonsocket**
Moffatt, Thomas Swift

## SOUTH CAROLINA

**Charleston**
Clement, Robert Lebby, Jr.
**Hilton Head Island**
Hagoort, Thomas Henry
**Salem**
Everett, C(harles) Curtis

## TENNESSEE

**Chattanooga**
Copeland, Floyd Dean
Durham, J(oseph) Porter, Jr.
Edge, Kathryn Reed
Levine, James Howard
**Knoxville**
Howard, Lewis Spilman
**Memphis**
Chafetz, Samuel David
**Nashville**
Anderson, Lauren Wirthlin
Carr, Davis Haden
Mayden, Barbara Mendel
Sidwell, Susan Von Brock

## TEXAS

**Austin**
Gangstad, John Erik
Smith, Jeffrey Carlin
**Dallas**
Bishop, Bryan Edwards
Feld, Alan David
Kipp, John Theodore
Laves, Alan Leonard
Menges, John Kenneth, Jr.
Morrison, David Eugene
Rice, Darrel Alan
Solomon, Mark S.
Spears, Robert Fields
Swanson, Wallace Martin
Young, Barney Thornton
Zahn, Donald Jack
**Garland**
Guldi, Rebecca Elizabeth
**Houston**
Bech, Douglas York
Becher, Andrew Clifford
Bilger, Bruce R.
Bily, Kirkland Jarrard
Bland, John L.
Born, Dawn Slater
Duffy, Stephen William
Finch, Michael Paul
Gover, Alan Shore
Grace, James Martin, Jr.
Heinrich, Randall Wayne
Heinrich, Timothy John
Johnson, James Harold
Lawson, Ben F.
Lee, William Gentry
Mai, Mark F.
Mark, Daniel Lee
Myers, Franklin
O'Donnell, Lawrence, III
O'Toole, Austin Martin
Schneller, John, IV
Sheinfeld, Myron M.
Snowden, Barry Howard
Still, Charles Henry
Taten, Bruce Malcolm
Zahorik, Michael Alan
**San Antonio**
Lippoldt, Darin Michael
**Wichita Falls**
Batson, David Warren

## UTAH

**Salt Lake City**
Brown, Charles R.

## VERMONT

**Rutland**
George, Alan Barry

## VIRGINIA

**Arlington**
McCorkindale, Douglas Hamilton
**Charlottesville**
Stroud, Robert Edward
**Chesapeake**
Tinkham, James Jeffrey
**Dunn Loring**
Melton, Michael Eric
**Fairfax**
Maiwurm, James John
Wright, Blandin James
**Manassas**
Mitchell, William Graham Champion
**Mc Lean**
Olsen, Robert Eric
**Richmond**
Bush, Thomas Norman
Goodpasture, Philip Henry
Perkins, Jon Scott
**Virginia Beach**
Purcell, Brian Christopher

## WASHINGTON

**Seattle**
Albright, Douglas Eaton
Comstock, Brian Lloyd
Creim, Jerry Alan
Kilbane, Thomas M.
Pym, Bruce Michael

## WISCONSIN

**Milwaukee**
Bliss, Richard Jon
Lombard, Benjamin G.
Loots, Robert James
Reardon, Timothy P.
Rice, Shawn G.
Rintelman, Donald Brian
Skipper, Walter John
**New Berlin**
Schober, Thomas Gregory
**Racine**
Coates, Glenn Richard

## BELGIUM

**Brussels**
Parker, Donald Samuel

## ENGLAND

**London**
Harrell, Michael P.
Smith, Jerry Leon

## ADDRESS UNPUBLISHED

Berman, Joshua Mordecai
Blumenthal, William
Cattani, Maryellen B.
Cherney, Andrew Knox
Crook, Donald Martin
Fischer, David Charles
Francis, Patricia Ann
Hanzlik, Rayburn DeMara
Johanson, David Richard
Lewitus, Marla Berman
Mewhinney, Len Everette
Meyer, Max Earl
Millimet, Erwin
O'Brien, James Edward
Oliver, Samuel William, Jr.
Patrick, Victor Phillip
Tattersall, Hargreaves Victor, III
Voight, Elizabeth Anne
Wilson, Hugh Steven
Wilson, Rhys Thaddeus

---

# MILITARY

---

## UNITED STATES

## ALABAMA

**Birmingham**
Norris, Robert Wheeler

## ARKANSAS

**Little Rock**
Sherman, William Farrar

## CALIFORNIA

**China Lake**
Hatley, Rodney James
**San Diego**
Brown, Douglas Colton
**Santa Ana**
Harley, Robison Dooling, Jr.
**Sherman Oaks**
Crump, Gerald Franklin

## COLORADO

**Aurora**
Schilling, Edwin Carlyle, III

## DISTRICT OF COLUMBIA

**Washington**
Neurock, Mitchel

## FLORIDA

**Fernandina Beach**
Manson, Keith Alan Michael

## GEORGIA

**Decatur**
Goddard, Ross Millard, Jr.

## HAWAII

**Fort Shafter**
Feighny, Michael Louis

## INDIANA

**Lawrenceburg**
Ewan, William Kenneth

## KENTUCKY

**Lexington**
Hickey, John King

### LOUISIANA
**New Orleans**
Forman, William Harper, Jr.

### MARYLAND
**Annapolis**
Ferris, William Michael
**Rockville**
Avery, Bruce Edward

### MISSOURI
**Jefferson City**
Graham, Christopher
**Kansas City**
White, F(loyd) Al

### NEBRASKA
**Lincoln**
Zink, Walter Earl, II

### NEW YORK
**New York**
Issler, Harry

### NORTH CAROLINA
**Charlotte**
Gordon, David Stott
**Raleigh**
Huggard, John Parker

### OHIO
**Dayton**
Kinlin, Donald James

### PENNSYLVANIA
**Philadelphia**
Shmukler, Stanford
Wert, Robert Clifton

### SOUTH CAROLINA
**Columbia**
Strong, Franklin Wallace, Jr.
**Greenville**
Bernstein, Barry Joel

### TENNESSEE
**Memphis**
Peppel, Howard Rex
**Newport**
Bell, John Alton

### TEXAS
**Dallas**
Spear, James Hodges
**Killeen**
Carlson, Craig W.
**Mason**
Johnson, Rufus Winfield

### VIRGINIA
**Alexandria**
Walkup, Homer Allen
**Arlington**
Cohen, Sheldon Irwin
**Fairfax**
McGowan, James Francis, III
**Sterling**
McBarnette, Bruce Olvin
**Virginia Beach**
Buzard, David Andrew
Holmes, William James

### WISCONSIN
**Wausau**
Long, Jerome Allen

### MILITARY ADDRESSES OF THE UNITED STATES

### PACIFIC
**FPO**
Blazewick, Robert B.

### ADDRESS UNPUBLISHED
Crebbin, Anthony Micek

## MUNICIPAL (include BONDS)

### UNITED STATES

### ALABAMA
**Birmingham**
Foster, Arthur Key, Jr.
Johnson, Joseph H., Jr.
**Montgomery**
Gregory, William Stanley

### ALASKA
**Anchorage**
Wohlforth, Eric Evans

### ARIZONA
**Flagstaff**
Gliege, John Gerhardt
**Phoenix**
James, Charles E., Jr.

### ARKANSAS
**Little Rock**
Bohannon, Charles Tad
Campbell, George Emerson

### CALIFORNIA
**Claremont**
Vera, Ronald Thomas
**Fresno**
Jensen, Douglas Blaine
**Los Angeles**
Richardson, Douglas Fielding
Watson, Glenn Robert
**Napa**
Meyers, David W.
**Oakland**
Webster, William Hodges
**San Diego**
Witt, John William
**Sherman Oaks**
Crump, Gerald Franklin

### COLORADO
**Denver**
Coyne, Robert Patrick
Grimshaw, Thomas Tollin

### CONNECTICUT
**Burlington**
Bauer, Charles Widmayer

### DISTRICT OF COLUMBIA
**Washington**
Henck, Charles Seymour
Journey, Drexel Dahlke
Ryan, Joseph
Samuelson, Kenneth Lee

### FLORIDA
**Bradenton**
Barnebey, Mark Patrick
**Coral Gables**
Kaplan, David Louis
**Jacksonville**
Slade, Thomas Bog, III
**Miami**
Johnson, Alise M.
Jorgensen, Lauren
**Orlando**
Collard, Stacey Lee
Lang, Thomas Frederick
**Plant City**
Buchman, Kenneth William
**Tallahassee**
Reid, Robert C.
**West Palm Beach**
Kornspan, Susan Fleischner
Spillias, Kenneth George
Wearn, James McCartney

### GEORGIA
**Atlanta**
Mobley, John Homer, II
Stallings, Ronald Denis
**Jonesboro**
Vail, Bruce Ronald
**Peachtree City**
Ott, Stephen Douglas

### IDAHO
**Boise**
Turcke, Paul Andrew

### ILLINOIS
**Aurora**
McCleary, Scott Fitzgerald
**Batavia**
Drendel, Kevin Gilbert
**Chicago**
Gray, Steven Joseph
Hummel, Gregory William
Jester, Jack D.
Ladd, Jeffrey Raymond
Pitt, George
Spiotto, James Ernest
**Crystal Lake**
Thoms, Jeannine Aumond
**Peoria**
Bell, Gregory S.
**Skokie**
Greenspan, Jeffrey Dov

### INDIANA
**Indianapolis**
Horn, Brenda Sue
**Lafayette**
O'Connell, Lawrence B.

### KANSAS
**Overland Park**
Gaar, Norman Edward
**Shawnee Mission**
Wetzler, Richard S.
**Topeka**
Wolfe, Philip Brannon

### KENTUCKY
**Benton**
Johnson, Martin Wolfe
**Fort Mitchell**
Wietholter, Thomas Andrew
**Louisville**
Maggiolo, Allison Joseph
McAdam, Thomas Anthony, III

### LOUISIANA
**Baton Rouge**
Richards, Marta Alison
**Lake Charles**
McHale, Robert Michael
**New Orleans**
Beck, William Harold, Jr.
Cornelius, O. Ray
Judell, Harold Benn

### MAINE
**Brunswick**
Owen, H. Martyn

### MARYLAND
**Baltimore**
Redden, Roger Duffey
**Ocean City**
Ayres, Guy Robins, III
**Riverdale**
Billingsley, Lance W.

### MASSACHUSETTS
**Boston**
DeRensis, Paul
Kopelman, Leonard
**Braintree**
McNulty, Michelle Allaire
**Danvers**
Christopher, John Anthony
**Holyoke**
Ferriter, Maurice Joseph
**Newton**
Bernard, Michael Mark
**Revere**
Cipoletta, James Joseph
**Worcester**
Moschos, Demitrios Mina

### MICHIGAN
**Birmingham**
Polzin, Charles Henry
**Detroit**
Deason, Herold McClure
Kamins, John Mark
Lewand, F. Thomas
**Flint**
Cooley, Richard Eugene
**Kalamazoo**
Bauckham, John Henry
**Manistee**
Simon, Stephanie Eden
**Romeo**
Clark, Mark Lee
**Southfield**
Lowther, Charles Michael
**Suttons Bay**
Johnson, Darryl Todd
**Traverse City**
Judson, Charles B.
**Walled Lake**
Seglund, Bruce Richard

### MINNESOTA
**Minneapolis**
Thorson, Steven Greg
**Saint Paul**
Bell, Robert Charles
**South Saint Paul**
O'Reilly, Ann Catherine

### MISSOURI
**Clayton**
Fluhr, Steven Solomon
**Kansas City**
Lotven, Howard Lee
Moore, Stephen James
Sparks, Stephen Stone
**Saint Louis**
Brickler, John Weise
**Springfield**
Starnes, James Wright

### NEBRASKA
**Omaha**
Barmettler, Joseph John

### NEVADA
**Las Vegas**
Jost, Richard Frederic, III

### NEW HAMPSHIRE
**North Conway**
Cooper, Randall F.

### NEW JERSEY
**Absecon**
Woolson, Charles E., Jr.
**Barrington**
Guice, Stephen W.
**Berlin**
Gattuso, Dina
**Bernardsville**
Maher, Gary Laurence
**Boonton**
Bucco, Anthony Mark
**Clifton**
Mohammed, Sohail
**Flemington**
Ligorano, Michael Kenneth
**Hackensack**
Dario, Ronald Anthony
Fede, Andrew Thomas
**Hackettstown**
Israels, Michael Jozef
**Iselin**
Kracht, Richard William
**Marlton**
Cavallo, Frank P., Jr.
**Montville**
Buzak, Edward Joseph
**Roseland**
Vanderbilt, Arthur T., II
**Secaucus**
Fitzpatrick, Harold Francis
**Shrewsbury**
Baxter, Gregory Stephen
**Somerville**
Bernstein, Eric Martin
**Westwood**
Regan, Robert Terrence

### NEW MEXICO
**Farmington**
Echols, Douglas Allen

### NEW YORK
**Albany**
Girvin, James Edward
**Amherst**
Murray, William Michael
**Buffalo**
Magavern, James L.
McElvein, Thomas Irving, Jr.
**Cedarhurst**
Taubenfeld, Harry Samuel
**Garden City**
Kroll, Martin N.
**Ithaca**
Theisen, Henry William
**Jamesport**
Cardinale, Philip John
**Kingston**
Maier, John, III
**Mineola**
Chaikin, Bonnie Patricia
**New York**
Bach, Thomas Handford
Collinson, Dale Stanley
Josephson, William Howard
Miller, Arthur Madden
Molinaro, Valerie Ann
Zucker, Howard
**Oneonta**
Konstanty, James E.
**Orangeburg**
Rivet, Diana Wittmer
**Pearl River**
Riley, James Kevin
**Poughkeepsie**
Sproat, Christine A.
**Rochester**
Griffin, Shawn Michael
**Salamanca**
Brady, Thomas Carl
**Syracuse**
Dwyer, James Francis
Gilligan, Kevin Michael
**White Plains**
Nolletti, James Joseph

### NORTH CAROLINA
**Charlotte**
Buckley, Charles Robinson, III
**Raleigh**
Carlton, Alfred Pershing, Jr.
Fricke, David Robert

### OHIO
**Akron**
Schrader, Alfred Eugene
**Cincinnati**
Burke, Timothy Michael
**Cleveland**
Boyko, Christopher Allan
Climaco, Michael Louis
Currivan, John Daniel
Ebert, Gary Andrew
Incorvaia, Santo Thomas
Kramer, Eugene Leo
Zukerman, Larry William
**Columbus**
Bowen, John Wesley Edward, IV
**Dayton**
Krygowski, Walter John

### OKLAHOMA
**Tulsa**
Hilborne, Thomas George, Jr.

### OREGON
**Portland**
Abravanel, Allan Ray
Blitz, Charles Akin
Firestone, Gary

### PENNSYLVANIA
**Bala Cynwyd**
Lee, Rotan Edward
**Bangor**
Ceraul, David James
**Chester**
Cartisano, Linda Ann
**Elkins Park**
Nemeroff, Robert Howard
**Erie**
Adair, Evan Edward
**Lansdale**
Sultanik, Jeffrey Ted
**Lehigh Valley**
Marles, Blake Curtis
**Morrisville**
Dobin, Edward I.
**Norristown**
Aman, George Matthias, III
**Philadelphia**
Jones, Robert Jeffries
Mason, Theodore W.
**Pittsburgh**
Brown, Ronald James
Loch, Robert Anthony
Lynch, Victor K.
Zangrilli, Albert Joseph, Jr.
**Pocono Pines**
Hardiman, Therese Anne
**West Chester**
Sommer, Jeffrey Robert

### RHODE ISLAND
**Newport**
McConnell, David Kelso
**Providence**
Handy, Seth Howland
Salvadore, Mal Andrew

### TENNESSEE
**Athens**
Guinn, Charles Clifford, Jr.
**Knoxville**
Roach, Jon Gilbert
**Memphis**
Fonville, Harold Wayne, II
**Nashville**
Bingham, Pamela Mary Muir
Trent, John Thomas, Jr.

### TEXAS
**Austin**
Krueger, William Wayne, III
**Beaumont**
Cobb, Bruce Wayne
**Dallas**
Austin, Ann Sheree
Horton, Paul Bradfield
Kobdish, George Charles
**Houston**
Anderson, Eric Severin
Wall, Kenneth E., Jr.
Weber, Fredric Alan
**Tyler**
Green, Jay Nelson
**Waco**
Bracken, William Earl, Jr.

### UTAH
**Pleasant Grove**
Merritt, Laramie Dee

### VERMONT
**Rutland**
Bloomer, William John
Facey, John Abbott, III

### VIRGINIA
**Roanoke**
Tegenkamp, Gary Elton

### WASHINGTON
**Seattle**
Ellis, James Reed
Estes, Stewart Andrew
Gottlieb, Daniel Seth
Simpson, Jennifer Lynn
Spitzer, Hugh D.
Thomas, Elizabeth
Walter, Michael Charles

### WISCONSIN
**Janesville**
Kopp, Mark David
**Little Chute**
Cornett, Paul Michael, Sr.
**Milwaukee**
Levy, Alan M.
**Shawano**
Habeck, James Roy
**Waukesha**
Macy, John Patrick
**Wausau**
Weber, Richard J.

### ADDRESS UNPUBLISHED
Choukas-Bradley, James Richard
Howell, Donald Lee
Mangler, Robert James
Miskimin, Alice Schwenk
Ostergaard, Joni Hammersla
Pahides, Ann-Marie MacDonald
Siegel, Sarah Ann
Wittebort, Robert John, Jr.

## NATIVE AMERICAN

### UNITED STATES

### ALASKA
**Anchorage**
Fortier, Samuel John

### ARIZONA
**Phoenix**
Storey, Lee A.

### DISTRICT OF COLUMBIA
**Washington**
Nilles, Kathleen Mary

### FLORIDA
**West Palm Beach**
Kamen, Michael Andrew

### IDAHO
**Moscow**
Wakefield, Robert

### MASSACHUSETTS
**Boston**
Craven, Terry Marie

### MICHIGAN
**Lansing**
Moody, Kevin Joseph

### MINNESOTA
**Minneapolis**
Duncan, Richard Alan
Hogen-Kind, Vanya S.
Moore, Terry Mason

### MONTANA
**Missoula**
Poore, James Albert, III
**Whitefish**
Gersh, Judah M.

### NEW MEXICO
**Albuquerque**
Slade, Lynn Heyer
**Carlsbad**
Bruton, Charles Clinton
**Farmington**
Hale, J. Kevin

**NEW YORK**
**New York**
McSloy, Steven Paul
**Slingerlands**
Rhodes-Devey, Michael
**Syracuse**
Frank, Jennifer Karen

**OKLAHOMA**
**Welling**
Carter-White, Kathy Jean

**OREGON**
**Bend**
Costello, Don Owen
**Medford**
Thierolf, Richard Burton, Jr.
**Portland**
Geil, John Clinton
**Salem**
Pacheco, Michael Mauro

**TEXAS**
**Dallas**
Ivey, John Kemmerer

**WASHINGTON**
**Bellingham**
Raas, Daniel Alan
**Seattle**
Ebell, C(ecil) Walter
Jonsson, Jon Marvin
**Tacoma**
Hostnik, Charles Rivoire

**WISCONSIN**
**Rice Lake**
Bichler, Howard Joseph

**ADDRESS UNPUBLISHED**
McNeil Staudenmaier, Heidi Loretta
Tupper, Kent Phillip

## NATURAL RESOURCES

**UNITED STATES**

**ALABAMA**
**Northport**
Allen, Randy Lee

**ALASKA**
**Anchorage**
Perkins, Joseph John, Jr.

**ARIZONA**
**Phoenix**
Carlock, George Read
Ferguson, Fred Ernest, Jr.
Kramer, Robert J.
Matheson, Alan Adams, Jr.
Nelson, Douglas Clarence

**CALIFORNIA**
**Los Angeles**
Lewand, Kimberly Ellen
**Sacramento**
Taber, Kelley Morgan
**San Francisco**
Moser, David E.

**COLORADO**
**Boulder**
Anuta, Karl Frederick
Cope, Joseph Adams
**Colorado Springs**
Harris, Stephen Donnell
**Denver**
Dolan, Brian Thomas
Duffy, William J.
Schindler, Ronald Irvin
Shepherd, John Frederic
Stockmar, Ted P.

**DISTRICT OF COLUMBIA**
**Washington**
Chabot, Philip Louis, Jr.
McCrum, Robert Timothy

**GEORGIA**
**Atlanta**
Draper, Stephen Elliot

**IDAHO**
**Boise**
Turcke, Paul Andrew

**KENTUCKY**
**Lexington**
Breeding, Carl Wayne
Curtz, Chauncey S.R.

**LOUISIANA**
**Lafayette**
Durio, William Henry

**MICHIGAN**
**Southfield**
Gotthelf, Beth
**Traverse City**
Quandt, Joseph Edward

**MINNESOTA**
**Minneapolis**
Blanton, W. C.
Johnson, G. Robert

**MISSOURI**
**Saint Louis**
Sullivan, Edward Lawrence

**MONTANA**
**Butte**
Bartlett, Edward
**Helena**
Nazaryk, Paul Alan
Watson, Rebecca Wunder
**Missoula**
Tuholske, Jack R.

**NEW MEXICO**
**Albuquerque**
Ausherman, Larry Price
Slade, Lynn Heyer
**Santa Fe**
Carpenter, Richard Norris

**NEW YORK**
**Syracuse**
Malmsheimer, Robert William

**OHIO**
**Columbus**
Maynard, Robert Howell

**OKLAHOMA**
**Oklahoma City**
Tytanic, Christopher Alan
**Tulsa**
Tobey, Rayanne Griffin
**Welling**
Carter-White, Kathy Jean

**OREGON**
**Portland**
Lacey, Henry Bernard
**Roseburg**
Yockim, Ronald Stephen

**PENNSYLVANIA**
**Pittsburgh**
Kalil, David Thomas

**TENNESSEE**
**Knoxville**
Howard, Lewis Spilman

**TEXAS**
**Houston**
Skoller, Ronald Aaron
**Midland**
Martin, C. D.
**San Antonio**
Eyster, Charles Richard

**UTAH**
**Salt Lake City**
Barusch, Lawrence Roos
Davies, Glen Ensign
Deisley, David Lee
Dragoo, Denise Ann
Jensen, Dallin W.
Kirkham, John Spencer

**VIRGINIA**
**Mc Lean**
Anthony, Joan Caton
**Richmond**
Denny, Collins, III

**WASHINGTON**
**Seattle**
Thomas, Elizabeth

**ADDRESS UNPUBLISHED**
Steinberger, Richard Lynn

## NON-PROFIT AND TAX-EXEMPT ORGANIZATIONS

**UNITED STATES**

**ALABAMA**
**Bessemer**
Jones, Stephen M.

**CALIFORNIA**
**Los Angeles**
Bringardner, John Michael
Costales, Marco Daniel
**Newport Beach**
Copenbarger, Lloyd Gaylord
**Oakland**
Webster, William Hodges
**Orange**
Bennett, William Perry
**Rancho Mirage**
Goldie, Ray Robert
**San Diego**
Dostart, Paul Joseph
**San Francisco**
Fleisher, Steven M.
Olejko, Mitchell J.
Yamakawa, David Kiyoshi, Jr.
**Toluca Lake**
Runquist, Lisa A.

**COLORADO**
**Boulder**
Cypser, Darlene Ann
**Denver**
Hodges, Joseph Gilluly, Jr.
**Lakewood**
Thome, Dennis Wesley

**DISTRICT OF COLUMBIA**
**Washington**
Coughlin, Thomas A.
Dye, Alan Page
Edmondson, Paul William
Frantz, David Joseph
Frost, Edmund Bowen
McCoy, Jerry Jack
Medalie, Susan Diane
Nelson, Robert Louis
Schmidt, William Arthur, Jr.
Watkins, Charles Morgan

**FLORIDA**
**Lake Worth**
Stafford, Shane Ludwig
**Miami**
Mody, Renu Noor
**Saint Petersburg**
DiVito, Joseph Anthony

**GEORGIA**
**Atlanta**
Bird, Wendell Raleigh
Pombert, Jeffrey Lawrence
Zabka, Sven Paul

**HAWAII**
**Kihei**
Burns, Richard Gordon

**IDAHO**
**Boise**
Klein, Edith Miller

**ILLINOIS**
**Chicago**
Dodds, Frances Alison
Howe, Jonathan Thomas
Paprocki, Thomas John
Ungerleider, Robert Norman
**Schaumburg**
Gardner, Caryn Sue

**INDIANA**
**Terre Haute**
Bopp, James, Jr.

**KANSAS**
**Kansas City**
Case, Rosemary Podrebarac
**Leawood**
Snyder, Willard Breidenthal
**Overland Park**
Cole, Roland Jay
**Wichita**
Stewart, Kenneth Parsons

**KENTUCKY**
**Louisville**
Buckaway, William Allen, Jr.
Griffith, C. Laurie

**MASSACHUSETTS**
**Boston**
Clymer, John Howard
Haddad, Ernest Mudarri
Rowe, Larry Jordan
**Maynard**
Weiss, Andrew Richard

**MICHIGAN**
**Detroit**
Phillips, Elliott Hunter
**East Lansing**
Castellani, Edward Joseph
**Grand Rapids**
Iverson, Dale Ann

**MINNESOTA**
**Minneapolis**
Greener, Ralph Bertram
Konezny, Jeryn Ann-Hall
Moore, Terry Mason
Wille, Karin L.

**MISSOURI**
**Kansas City**
Langworthy, Robert Burton
Tyler, John E., III
Vranicar, Gregory Leonard
Willy, Thomas Ralph
**Saint Louis**
Baum, Gordon Lee
Van Cleve, William Moore
Wolff, Frank Pierce, Jr.

**NEW HAMPSHIRE**
**Manchester**
Dastin, Robert Earl

**NEW JERSEY**
**Princeton**
Carlis, Brian Alexander

**NEW YORK**
**Brooklyn**
Castro, Sonia Mendez
**Hamburg**
Glose, Herbert James
**Harrison**
Sloane, Marilyn Austern
**New York**
Ashton, Robert W.
Davidson, George Allan
Dunkin, Ellen R.
Finch, Edward Ridley, Jr.
Gates, Peter P.
Jefferies, Jack P.
Kaufman, Robert Max
Kirschner, Kenneth Harold
Kobrin, Lawrence Alan
Kornreich, Edward Scott
Malkin, Michael M.
Mann, Pamela A.
Margolin, Jesse
Morganstern, Gerald H.
Neuwirth, Gloria S.
Paul, Eve W.
Regan, Susan Ginsberg
Reynolds, Michael Timothy
Rubin, Jane Lockhart Gregory
Sabalja, Lorraine
Small, Jonathan Andrew
Wyckoff, E. Lisk, Jr.
**Syracuse**
Evans, Thomas S.
**Westbury**
Hurst, Margaret Anne

**NORTH CAROLINA**
**Raleigh**
Simpson, Steven Drexell

**OHIO**
**Akron**
Allan, Ronald Curtis
Cox, Steven St. Leger
**Cincinnati**
Crouse, Rebecca Ann
**Cleveland**
Leavitt, Jeffrey Stuart
**Springfield**
Harkins, Daniel Conger
**Wilmington**
Schutt, Walter Eugene

**PENNSYLVANIA**
**Berwyn**
Gadsden, Christopher Henry
**Philadelphia**
Berger, Lawrence Howard
Heintz, Paul Capron
Nofer, George Hancock
**Pittsburgh**
Johnson, Robert Alan
Pollack, David L.
**Venetia**
Breslin, Elvira Madden

**SOUTH DAKOTA**
**Rapid City**
Thatcher, Anna Marie

**TENNESSEE**
**Chattanooga**
Walker, Robert Kirk

**TEXAS**
**Austin**
Osborne, Duncan Elliott
**Dallas**
King, Jeffrey P.
**Fort Worth**
West, Robert Grady
**Richardson**
Hubbard, Carolyn Marie

**VIRGINIA**
**Charlottesville**
Caccese, Michael Stephen
Middleditch, Leigh Benjamin, Jr.
**Mc Lean**
Herge, J. Curtis
LeSourd, Nancy Susan Oliver
Olson, William Jeffrey
**Portsmouth**
Tynch, David Ray

**WASHINGTON**
**Seattle**
Hanson, William Lewis

**WISCONSIN**
**Madison**
Brewster, Francis Anthony
**Milwaukee**
Melin, Robert Arthur

**ADDRESS UNPUBLISHED**
Fink, Norman Stiles
Kleinberg, Judith G.
Sulton, Anne Thomas
Wharton, Hugh Davis, III

## OIL, GAS, AND MINERAL

**UNITED STATES**

**ALABAMA**
**Decatur**
Hammond, Stephen Van
**Mobile**
Armbrecht, William Henry, III
Brooker, Norton William, Jr.
Harris, Benjamin Harte, Jr.
**Northport**
Allen, Randy Lee

**ALASKA**
**Anchorage**
Linxwiler, James David
Perkins, Joseph John, Jr.

**ARIZONA**
**Prescott**
Gose, Richard Vernie

**CALIFORNIA**
**Bakersfield**
Lynch, Craig M.
Tornstrom, Robert Ernest
**Glendale**
Bright, James Stephen
**Los Angeles**
Moyer, Craig Alan
Watson, Glenn Robert
**Pasadena**
Armour, George Porter
**San Francisco**
Hinman, Harvey DeForest

**COLORADO**
**Denver**
Irwin, R. Robert
Jones, Richard Michael
Kirchhoff, Bruce C.
Kuhn, Gretchen
Martz, Clyde Ollen
Merritts, Jack Michael
Pope, David Bruce
Shannon, Malcolm Lloyd, Jr.
Shepherd, John Frederic

**DISTRICT OF COLUMBIA**
**Washington**
Allan, Richmond Frederick
Martin, Jay Griffith
Teichler, Stephen Lin
Wilde, Jinhee Kim

**ILLINOIS**
**Bridgeport**
Stout, James Dudley
**Chicago**
Marroquin-Merino, Victor Miguel
**Pinckneyville**
Johnson, Don Edwin
**Wilmette**
Frick, Robert Hathaway

**INDIANA**
**Indianapolis**
Boyko, Ihor Nestor

**KANSAS**
**Hugoton**
Nordling, Bernard Erick
**Olathe**
Lowe, Roy Goins
**Wichita**
Depew, Spencer Long

**LOUISIANA**
**Alexandria**
Alexius, Frederick Bernard
**Baton Rouge**
Johnson, Joseph Clayton, Jr.
Taylor, John McKowen
**Jennings**
Miller, Ruth Loyd
**Lafayette**
Durio, William Henry
Mansfield, James Norman, III
Ottinger, Patrick S.
**Lake Charles**
Monk, William Boyce
Shaddock, William Edward, Jr.
**New Orleans**
Johnson, Beth Exum
Morton, James Russell
Pearce, John Y.
**Shreveport**
Roberts, Robert, III

**MICHIGAN**
**Bloomfield Hills**
Norris, John Hart
**Gaylord**
Topp, Susan Hlywa
**Mount Pleasant**
Lynch, John Joseph

**MISSISSIPPI**
**Jackson**
Eicher, Donald E., III
Grant, Russell Porter, Jr.
Hughes, Byron William
Presson, William Russell

**MONTANA**
**Billings**
Hanson, Norman
**Great Falls**
Overfelt, Clarence Lahugh

**NEVADA**
**Reno**
Jeppson, Roger Wayne

**NEW MEXICO**
**Albuquerque**
Adams, Mark Kildee
Addis, Richard Barton
Haltom, B(illy) Reid
Moise, Steven Kahn
**Santa Fe**
Coffield, Conrad Eugene

**NEW YORK**
**Babylon**
Hennelly, Edmund Paul
**Gouverneur**
Heller, Sanders D.
**New York**
Meyering, Christopher P.
Owen, Robert Dewit
Stein, Stephen William
**Olean**
Heyer, John Henry, II
**Oyster Bay**
Griffin, James Alfred
**Watertown**
Militello, Samuel Philip
**White Plains**
Berlin, Alan Daniel

**NORTH DAKOTA**
**Crosby**
Forsgren, F. Leslie

**OHIO**
**Jefferson**
Lemire, Jerome Albert

## PATENT

### VERMONT

**Essex Junction**
Walsh, Robert Anthony

### VIRGINIA

**Alexandria**
Georges, Peter John
Phan, Nhat D.
Wendel, Charles Allen
Wieder, Bruce Terrill
**Arlington**
Dennison, Donald Lee
Hogue, Dale Curtis, Sr.
Landry, Walter Joseph
Laughlin, James Harold, Jr.
Litman, Richard Curtis
Mossinghoff, Gerald Joseph
Rowan, Robert Allen
Scafetta, Joseph, Jr.
Swift, Stephen Christopher
**Dunn Loring**
Melton, Michael Eric
**Falls Church**
Brady, Rupert Joseph
Gorenstein, Charles
Greigg, Ronald Edwin
Kondracki, Edward John
**Great Falls**
Railton, William Scott
**Hampton**
Hammerle, Kurt Georg
**Mount Vernon**
Spiegel, H. Jay
**Nellysford**
Vandenburgh, Beverly Ann

### WISCONSIN

**Madison**
Bremer, Howard Walter
**Milwaukee**
Fuller, Henry Chester, Jr.
Puerner, Paul Raymond
Stomma, Peter Christopher

### FRANCE

**Lyon**
Dahling, Gerald Vernon

### THE NETHERLANDS

**Manstruchts**
Woods, Thomas Fabian

### ADDRESS UNPUBLISHED

Adams, Thomas Lawrence
Amberg, Stanley Louis
Antolin, Stanislav
Beck, Stuart Edwin
Fernandez, Dennis Sunga
Fiorito, Edward Gerald
Gilster, Peter Stuart
Gray, Brian Mark
Harris, James T.
Hogan, Charles Marshall
Jester, Michael Henry
Lecocke, Suzanne Elizabeth
O'Donnell, Martin J.
Peters, R. Jonathan
Phelan, Charles Scott
Protigal, Stanley Nathan
Robbins, Frank Edward
Sprung, Arnold

## PENSION, PROFIT-SHARING, AND EMPLOYEE BENEFITS

### UNITED STATES

### ALABAMA

**Birmingham**
Cullen, William Zachary
Hughes, James Donald
Simmons Scott, Vanessa Ann
**Muscle Shoals**
Riley, Anthony Dale

### ARIZONA

**Phoenix**
Ehmann, Anthony Valentine
Hiller, Neil Howard
Pietzsch, Michael Edward
Sliger, Herbert Jacquemin, Jr.
**Tucson**
Tretschok, Dale Deege

### ARKANSAS

**Fort Smith**
Moore, Patrick Neill
**Searcy**
Hughes, Teresa Lee

### CALIFORNIA

**Elverta**
Betts, Barbara Lang
**Fallbrook**
Leehey, Paul Wade
**Glendale**
Wax, Harold Wilfred
**Los Angeles**
Carrey, Neil
Highberger, William Foster
**Novato**
Cleek, Robert Joseph
**Pacific Palisades**
Dean, Ronald Glenn
**Sacramento**
Gillan, Kayla J.
**San Diego**
Atcherley, Linda Francesca
Gartrell, P. Garth
Shaw, Lee Charles
**San Francisco**
Davis, Roland Chenoweth
Foster, David Scott
Gibson, Virginia Lee
**San Jose**
Kraw, George Martin
Kraw, Sarah Kenyon
**Sunnyvale**
Ludgus, Nancy Lucke

### COLORADO

**Boulder**
Bellac, Patricia Sharman
**Colorado Springs**
Pring, Cynthia Marie
**Denver**
Crow, Nancy Rebecca
Marquess, Lawrence Wade
O'Toole, Neil D.
**Fort Morgan**
Higinbotham, Jacquelyn Joan
**Placerville**
Reagan, Harry Edwin, III

### CONNECTICUT

**Hartford**
Cullina, William Michael
McKone, Thomas Christopher
**New London**
Woods, Kerin Margaret
**North Haven**
Gradoville, Robert Thomas
**Stamford**
Moore, Peggy Braden
Rosenberg, Burton Stuart
Strone, Michael Jonathan
**Trumbull**
Czajkowski, Frank Henry
**Westport**
LoMonte, Douglas Edward

### DELAWARE

**Wilmington**
Martin, William Joseph, III

### DISTRICT OF COLUMBIA

**Washington**
Cummings, Frank
Damico, Nicholas Peter
Faley, R(ichard) Scott
Fleeman, Mary Grace
Flowe, Carol Connor
Ford, Gary Manning
Goldsmith, Willis Jay
Hennessy, Ellen Anne
Kautter, David John
Konselman, Douglas Derek
Lopatin, Alan G.
Mackiewicz, Edward Robert
McHugh, Richard Patrick
Miller, Evan
Oliphant, Charles Frederick, III
Quintiere, Gary Gandolfo
Roach, Arvid Edward, II
Sacher, Steven Jay
Stauffer, Ronald Eugene
Tawshunsky, Alan Neal
Watkins, Charles Morgan
Wilder, Roland Percival, Jr.

### FLORIDA

**Bradenton**
Lopacki, Edward Joseph, Jr.
**Fort Lauderdale**
Caulkins, Charles S.
Ruback, Alan Steven
**Miami**
Cohen, Ronald J.
**North Miami Beach**
Ginsberg, Alan
**Oldsmar**
Hirschman, Sherman Joseph
**Orlando**
Heskin, Keersten Lee
Lefkowitz, Ivan Martin
**Saint Petersburg**
Escarraz, Enrique, III
**Tampa**
O'Neill, Albert Clarence, Jr.
Robinson, John William, IV
Steele, Rebecca Harrison
Watson, Roberta Casper
**Tavares**
Johnson, Terri Sue
**West Palm Beach**
Levy, Jonathan Todd

### GEORGIA

**Albany**
Patterson, Rudolph N.
**Atlanta**
Brecher, Armin G.
Lamon, Harry Vincent, Jr.
**Carrollton**
Park, Kelley Barrett
**Dallas**
Williams, Gary Randall

### HAWAII

**Honolulu**
Maloney, John T., Jr.
Rohrer, Reed Beaver
Yamada, Stephen Kinichi

### IDAHO

**Coeur D Alene**
Garbrecht, Louis
**Idaho Falls**
Simmons, John G.

### ILLINOIS

**Alton**
Bohne, Edward Daniel
**Aurora**
Marchetti, Marilyn H.
**Chicago**
Ackerman, David Paul
Braitman, Barry H.
Brown, Gregory K.
Chandler, Kent, Jr.
Corday, Lane Allan
Daley, Susan Jean
Greenfield, Michael C.
Kaplan, Jared
Kelly, Peter McClorey, II
Kopelman, Ian Stuart
Menson, Richard L.
Miller, Stephen Ralph
Polk, Lee Thomas
Rizzo, Ronald Stephen
Scogland, William Lee
Shepherd, Stewart Robert
Spognardi, Mark Anthony
**Park Ridge**
Tinaglia, Michael Lee
**Peoria**
Higgs, David Lawrence
**Riverside**
Kubiczky, Stephen Ralph
**Winnetka**
Bishop, Mahlon Lee

### INDIANA

**Elkhart**
Like, Steven
**Indianapolis**
Boldt, Michael Herbert
Culp, Charles William
Karwath, Bart Andrew
Kemper, James Dee
Price, Phillip Vincent

### IOWA

**Des Moines**
Narber, Gregg Ross
**Muscatine**
Nepple, James Anthony
**Sioux City**
Nymann, P. L.
**West Des Moines**
Begleiter, Ronni Frankel

### KANSAS

**Topeka**
Rainey, William Joel

### KENTUCKY

**Fort Mitchell**
Beetem, A. Page
**Lexington**
Bryson, Arthur Joseph
**Louisville**
Gilman, Sheldon Glenn
Hallenberg, Robert Lewis

### LOUISIANA

**Lafayette**
Edwards, Christopher Alan
**New Orleans**
Martinez, Andrew Tredway

### MAINE

**Bangor**
Ebitz, Elizabeth Kelly
**Portland**
O'Brien, Murrough Hall
Pooler, Delia Bridget

### MARYLAND

**Baltimore**
Adkins, Edward James
Bruner, William Gwathmey, III
Curran, Robert Bruce
Dubé, Lawrence Edward, Jr.
Jenkins, Robert Rowe

### MASSACHUSETTS

**Boston**
Miller, Wayne Hamilton
**Framingham**
Felper, David Michael
**Needham**
Coleman, Richard William
**Newburyport**
Maslen, David Peter

### MICHIGAN

**Ann Arbor**
Keppelman, Nancy
Stevenson, Robert Bruce
**Bloomfield Hills**
Callow, Thomas Edward
**Detroit**
Brustad, Orin Daniel
Neydon, Ann Elizabeth
Phillips, Elliott Hunter
Rastigue, Kerry Ann
**Grand Rapids**
Titley, Larry J.
**Jackson**
Curtis, Philip James
**Lansing**
Deprez, Deborah Ann
**Muskegon**
McKendry, John H., Jr.
**Southfield**
Hamlar, Portia Yvonne Trenholm
McClow, Roger James
Shpiece, Michael Ronald
**Troy**
Kinney, Gregory Hoppes

### MINNESOTA

**Duluth**
Burns, Richard Ramsey
**Minneapolis**
Freeman, Todd Ira
Nelson, Richard Arthur
Vanhove, Lorri Kay
**Rochester**
Jacobsen, Van Paul
**Saint Cloud**
Provinzino, John C.
**Saint Paul**
Hitesman, Darcy L.

### MISSISSIPPI

**Jackson**
Black, D(eWitt) Carl(isle), Jr.

### MISSOURI

**Columbia**
Crepeau, Dewey Lee
**Kansas City**
Brous, Thomas Richard
Fershee, Susan Joyce
Toll, Perry Mark
**Kirkwood**
Sweeney, Robert Kevin
**Saint Louis**
Armstrong, Owen Thomas
Farnam, Thomas Campbell
Kandel, Alan Harold
Kuhlmann, Fred Mark
Marks, Murry Aaron
Rataj, Edward William

### NEVADA

**Las Vegas**
Brown, Patricia Leonard
Greene, Addison Kent

### NEW HAMPSHIRE

**Manchester**
Chamberlain, Douglas Reginald

### NEW JERSEY

**Camden**
Furey, John J.
**Florham Park**
Witman, Leonard Joel
**Kenilworth**
Cohen, Edward Arthur
**Lawrenceville**
Beyer, Vicki Woody
**Mc Afee**
Fogel, Richard
**Morristown**
Doyle, David Perrie
**Newark**
Weinberg, Shelley Ann
**Paulsboro**
Fichera, Lewis Carmen
**South Orange**
Delo, Ellen Sanderson
**Warren**
Gerard, Stephen Stanley

### NEW MEXICO

**Albuquerque**
Lieuwen, John N.
Ramo, Roberta Cooper
**Carlsbad**
Diamond, Jeffrey Brian
**Deming**
Sherman, Frederick Hood

### NEW YORK

**Albany**
Flory, Judith A.
**Bronx**
Lynch, Thom
Verrelli, Anthony Louis
**Brooklyn**
Bitterman, Gregory Val
Levy, Samuel Robert
Swain, Laura Taylor
**Buffalo**
Newman, Stephen Michael
Salisbury, Eugene W.
Schulz, Paul John
**Chappaqua**
Whittlesey, John Williams
**Cutchogue**
O'Connell, Francis Joseph
**Flushing**
Schwartz, Estar Alma
**Garden City**
Lilly, Thomas Joseph
Schwarz, Carl A., Jr.
**Glens Falls**
McMillen, Robert Stewart
**Harrison**
Sloane, Marilyn Austern
**Huntington**
Hochberg, Ronald Mark
**Jamestown**
Beckstrom, Charles G.
**Kingston**
Ellison, Patricia Lee
**Lockport**
Brodsky, Felice Adrienne
**Long Island City**
Wanderman, Susan Mae
**Mineola**
Pogrebin, Bertrand B.
**New York**
Battaglia, John Joseph
Bergman, Robert Ira
Budd, Thomas Witbeck
Carling, Francis
Collins, Adrian Anthony
Cooper, Sonja Jean Muller
David, Reuben
Donovan, Maureen Driscoll
Duff, William Brandon
Dunkin, Ellen R.
Estes, Richard Martin
Friedman, Eugene Stuart
Glanstein, Joel Charles
Grisi, James Robert
Hardy, Robert Paul
Hirozawa, Kent Y.
Kolko, Hanan B.
Kroll, Arthur Herbert
Leibowitz, Nadine S.
Moore, Donald Francis
Nassau, Michael Jay
Pompa, Renata
Ray, Jeanne Cullinan
Rom, Judith R.
Serota, Susan Perlstadt
Shinevar, Peter O'Neil
Simone, Joseph R.
Steigman, Meredith Lee
Thompson, Loran Tyson
Wagner, Michael G.
Watanabe, Roy Noboru
**Oneonta**
Hill, Peter Waverly
**Rego Park**
Jain, Lalit K.
**Rochester**
Colby, William Michael
Wild, Robert Warren
**Rockville Centre**
Lerner, Steven Paul
**Syracuse**
King, Bernard T.
**White Plains**
Danziger, Joel Bernard
Klein, Paul E.
Lalli, Michael Anthony
Taft, Nathaniel Belmont

### NORTH CAROLINA

**Asheville**
Gantt, David
**Charlotte**
Culbreth, James Harold, Jr.
**Goldsboro**
Fuller, Robert E., Jr.
**Hickory**
Ingle, John David
**Raleigh**
Thomas, Mark Stanton
**Tarboro**
O'Malley, Susan Marie
**Winston Salem**
Gunter, Michael Donwell

### NORTH DAKOTA

**Fargo**
Vogel, Charles Nicholas

### OHIO

**Cleveland**
Leavitt, Jeffrey Stuart
Youngstrom, Karen Daykin
**Columbus**
Ciriaco, Anthony Charles
Goulder, Diane Kessler
Kusma, Kyllikki
Tarpy, Thomas Michael
**Hamilton**
Gattermeyer, Daniel J.
**Marysville**
Howard, Lowell Bennett, Jr.
**Warren**
Letson, William Normand
**Westlake**
Reichard, William Edward
**Youngstown**
Wellman, Thomas Peter

### OKLAHOMA

**Bartlesville**
Huchteman, Ralph Douglas
**Norman**
Fairbanks, Robert Alvin
**Tulsa**
Bright, Thomas Lynn
Coulter, Jean Walpole

### OREGON

**Portland**
Froebe, Gerald Allen
Klarquist, Kenneth Stevens, Jr.
Richardson, Jay
Zalutsky, Morton Herman
**Tigard**
Lowry, David Burton

### PENNSYLVANIA

**Allentown**
Dower, Harry Allen
**Allison Park**
Ries, William Campbell
**Butler**
Wright, Veronica Giel
**Erie**
Mosier, David Michael
**Norristown**
Mirabile, Carolyn Rose
**Philadelphia**
Abramowitz, Robert Leslie
Abrams, Nancy
Bernard, John Marley
Bildersee, Robert Alan
Cannon, John, III
Dabrowski, Doris Jane
Drake, William Frank, Jr.
Fox, Gregory John
Gadon, Steven Franklin
Gilberg, Kenneth Roy
Glassmoyer, Thomas Parvin
Kastenberg, Stephen Joel
Krampf, John Edward
Lichtenstein, Robert Jay
O'Reilly, Timothy Patrick
Rudolph, Andrew J.
Sigmond, Richard Brian
Thomas, Lowell Shumway, Jr.
Whiteside, William Anthony, Jr.
Wilf, Mervin M.
**Pittsburgh**
Candris, Laura A.
Fieschko, Joseph Edward, Jr.
Geeseman, Robert George
Johnson, Robert Alan
Kabala, Edward John
Scheinholtz, Leonard Louis
**Reading**
Linton, Jack Arthur

Medak, Walter Hans
Sohnen, Harvey
**West Covina**
Ebiner, Robert Maurice
**Westlake Village**
Vititoe, James Wilson
**Woodland Hills**
Comroe, Eugene W.
Glicker, Brian Irving
Koep, Richard Michael
**Yorba Linda**
Ward, Robert Richard
**Yuba City**
Doughty, Mark Anthony
McCaslin, Leon
Santana, Jesse Isaias

## COLORADO

**Aspen**
Bernstein, Jeremy Marshall
Shipp, Dan Shackelford
**Aurora**
Flicker, Howard
**Boulder**
Garlin, Alexander
Gordon, Glen Frank
Gray, William R.
Hale, Daniel Cudmore
Hult, Stephanie Smith
Purvis, John Anderson
**Canon City**
McDermott, John Arthur
**Colorado Springs**
Barnes, Thomas Arthur, Jr.
Crizer, Celeste Lisanne
Evans, Paul Vernon
Fisher, Robert Scott
Kennedy, Richard Joseph
LeHouillier, Patric Jaymes
McCready, Guy Michael
Pressman, Glenn Spencer
Pring, Cynthia Marie
Salley, George Henry, III
Swift, Stephen Hyde
**Denver**
Aisenberg, Bennett S.
Avery, James William
Burkhardt, Donald Malcolm
Deikman, Eugene Lawrence
DeLaney, Herbert Wade, Jr.
de Marino, Thomas John
Drake, Christopher Todd
Ehrlich, Stephen Richard
Fowler, Daniel McKay
Hoffman, Daniel Steven
Karp, Sander Neil
Kaye, Bruce Jeffrey
Keithley, Roger Lee
Kintzele, John Alfred
Krulewitch, Beth Lee
Leibowitz, Paul H.
Mann, Stuart D.
Miller, J(ohn) Kent
Nathan, J(ay) Andrew
O'Toole, Neil D.
Robinson, Warren A. (Rip Robinson)
Samour, Carlos A.
Sarney, Saul Richard
Sedlak, Joseph Anthony, III
Skok, Paul Joseph
Slaninger, Frank Paul
Springer, Jeffrey Alan
Travis, Todd Andrew
Widmann, Edward Healy
Wilcox, Martha Anne
**Englewood**
Branney, Joseph John
Burg, Michael S.
Ewing, Mary Arnold
Gipstein, Milton Fivenson
Karr, David Dean
Nixon, Scott Sherman
Wheeler, Karen Hannah
**Frisco**
McElyea, Monica Sergent
**Golden**
Carney, Deborah Leah Turner
**Greeley**
Conway, Rebecca Ann Koppes
**Littleton**
Eberhardt, Gretchen Ann
Eberhardt, Robert Schuler, Jr.
**Lone Tree**
Kaplan, Marc J.
**Manassa**
Garcia, Castelar Medardo
**Manitou Springs**
Slivka, Michael Andrew
**Vail**
Telepas, George Peter

## CONNECTICUT

**Bethel**
Murray, Gwen E.
**Bridgeport**
Arons, Mark David
Feldman, David Scott
Mulcahey, Garie Jean
Osis, Daiga Guntra
Williams, Ronald Doherty
**Brookfield**
Dittmar, Dawn Marie
Secola, Joseph Paul
**Colchester**
Broder, Joseph Arnold
**Danbury**
Arconti, Richard David
**Fairfield**
Burke, William Milton
**Hamden**
Bershtein, Herman Sammy
**Hartford**
Fain, Joel Maurice
Gale, John Quentin
Harrington, Christopher Michael
Karpe, Brian Stanley
Kesten, Linda Ann
Martocchio, Louis Joseph
Tanski, James Michael
Toro, Amalia Maria
Young, Roland Frederic, III
**Madison**
Hollo, Leslie Stephen
**Manchester**
Horwitz, Melvin
**Middletown**
Poliner, Bernard
**New Canaan**
Tirelli, Linda Marie
**New Haven**
Carty, Paul Vernon
Forino, Alfred Paul
Gallagher, William F.
Sabetta, Paul M.
Secola, Carl A., Jr.
Todd, Erica Weyer
**New London**
Reardon, Robert Ignatius, Jr.
Wilson, Thomas Buck
Woods, Kerin Margaret
**New Milford**
Guendelsberger, Robert Joseph
**Newington**
Borowy, Frank Rhine
**North Haven**
Cella, Carl Edward
Morytko, Jeremiah Joseph
**South Windham**
Asselin, John Thomas
**Stamford**
Casper, Stewart Michael
Filan, Patrick J.
Mayerson Cannella, Renee
**Stratford**
O'Rourke, James Louis
**Torrington**
Leard, David Carl
Wall, Robert Anthony, Jr.
**Waterbury**
Marano, Richard Michael
**Watertown**
Del Buono, John Angelo
**West Hartford**
Connors, Susan Ann
Swerdloff, Mark Harris
**Westport**
Cramer, Allan P.
**Willimantic**
Lombardo, Michael John
**Windsor**
Morelli, Carmen

## DELAWARE

**Dover**
Guerke, I. Barry
Jones, R. Brandon
**Wilmington**
Bartley, Brian James
Boswell, David A.
Cummings, Stacey L.
Eppes, Sharon Marie
Erisman, James A.
Heyden, Michael C.
Kimmel, Morton Richard
Morris, Kenneth Donald
Ralston, Robert W.
Ramunno, L. Vincent
Saville, Yvonne Takvorian
Wier, Richard Royal, Jr.

## DISTRICT OF COLUMBIA

**Washington**
Broadus, Charlsa Dorsantres
Carter, William Joseph
Cernicky, Ann Hardman
Frank, Arthur J.
Frantz, David Joseph
Gelb, Joseph Donald
Gelb, Roger Kenneth
Janis, N. Richard
Levine, Steven Mark
Long, Victor Earl
Mann, Lawrence Moses
Martin, Ralph Drury
McIntyre, Douglas Carmichael, II
Moore, Diane Preston
Nace, Barry John
Olender, Jack Harvey
Povich, David
Scriven, Wayne Marcus
Walker, Betty Stevens
Wilson, Michael Moureau
Zambri, Salvatore Joseph

## FLORIDA

**Altamonte Springs**
Heindl, Phares Matthews
**Bartow**
Pansler, Karl Frederick
**Boca Raton**
Feldman, Donald
Haverman, Daniel Lipman
Kitzes, William Fredric
Law, Ellen Marie
Retamar, Richard E.
Silver, Barry Morris
Willis, John Alexander
**Bradenton**
Plews, Dennis James
Shapiro, Richard Michael
**Brandon**
Curry, Clifton Conrad, Jr.
**Bushnell**
Hagin, T. Richard
**Clearwater**
Berman, Elihu H.
Carlson, Edward D.
Free, E. LeBron
**Coconut Grove**
Joffe, David Jonathon
**Coral Gables**
Anthony, Andrew John
Buell, Rodd Russell
David, George A.
Fournaris, Theodore J.
Friedman, Marvin Ross
Fuentes-Cid, Pedro Jose
Hengber, Gregory Paul
Hoffman, Carl H(enry)
Kaplan, Eli
Mellinger, Robert Louis
Thornton, John William, Sr.
**Crestview**
Duplechin, D. James
**Dade City**
Brock, P. Hutchison, II
**Daytona Beach**
Neitzke, Eric Karl
**Dunedin**
Felos, George James
**Fort Lauderdale**
Bunnell, George Eli
Cubit, William Aloysius
Custer, Andy M.
Fischer, Carey Michael
Haliczer, James Solomon
Heath, Thomas Clark
James, Gordon, III
Korthals, Candace Durbin
Kramish, Marc Eric
Krathen, David Howard
Kreizinger, Loreen I.
Pomeroy, Gregg Joseph
Rodriguez, Carlos Augusto
Rose, Norman
Roselli, Richard Joseph
Sale, David Todd
Santa Maria, Diana
Sherman, Richard Allen
Strickland, Wilton L.
Wich, Donald Anthony, Jr.
**Gainesville**
Kurrus, Thomas William
Mercadante, Stephen G.
Varela, Laura Joan
**Hobe Sound**
Buetens, Eric D.
**Hollywood**
London, Jack Edward
Wolis, Kenneth Arnold
Zebersky, Edward Herbert
**Indian Harbor Beach**
Burger, Robert Theodore
**Jacksonville**
Allen, Dudley Dean
Bullock, Bruce Stanley
Ceballos, M(ichael) Alan
Coker, Howard C.
Cramer, Jeffrey Allen
Ehrlich, Raymond
Eikner, Tod Bayard
Gooding, David Michael
Hardesty, W. Marc
Hollon, John Oaks
Kendrick, Darryl D.
Liles, Rutledge Richardson
Link, Robert James
McCorvey, John Harvard, Jr.
Miller, Carla Dorothy
Milton, Joseph Payne
Oberdier, Ronald Ray
O'Neal, Michael Scott, Sr.
Phillips, Mary Kleyla
Pope, Shawn Hideyoshi
Reed, Ronald Ernst
White, Edward Alfred
**Jaxville Bch**
Howell, Jay Charlton
**Jupiter**
Houser, Stephen Douglas Barlow, III
Mallory, Earl K.
**Key West**
Brihammar, B. Niklas
Eden, Nathan E.
**Lake Wales**
White, Norman
**Lake Worth**
Stafford, Shane Ludwig
**Lakeland**
Artigliere, Ralph
Schott, Clifford Joseph
**Longwood**
McLatchey, Russell Francis
**Lutz**
Epperson, Joel Rodman
**Maitland**
Bailey, Michael Keith
Gabel, Michael Wayne
**Margate**
Shooster, Frank Mallory
**Melbourne**
Cacciatore, Sammy Michel
Ollinger, George Edward, III
Trachtman, Jerry H.
**Merritt Island**
Church, Glenn J.
**Miami**
Acosta, Julio Cesar
Andrews, Mary Ruth
Batista, Alberto Victor
Baumberger, Charles Henry
Blackburn, Roger Lloyd
Blumberg, Edward Robert
Bombino, Isabel Pinera
Brennan, J. Lorraine
Cabanas, Oscar Jorge
Chasin, Keith A.
Clark, James Kendall
Cohen, Jeffrey Michael
Davis, Jeffrey Robert
de la Fe, Ernesto Juan
de Leon, Ruben L.
Fiore, Robert J.
Fox, Gary Devenow
Gander, Deborah J.
Ginsberg, Marc Robert
Greenberg, Stewart Gary
Hecker, Leslie Faye
Hickey, John Heyward
Hochman, Alan Robert
Kritzer, Glenn Bruce
Lanza, Christopher F.
Leibowitz, Mark A.
Leslie, Richard McLaughlin
Lipcon, Charles Roy
Marks, Steven Craig
Miller, Raymond Vincent, Jr.
Moore, Michael T.
Payne, R.W., Jr.
Picazio, Kim Lowry
Podhurst, Aaron Samuel
Sarnoff, Marc David
Scremin, Anthony James
Solomon, Michael Bruce
Stansell, Leland Edwin, Jr.
Touby, Kathleen Anita
Valle, Laurence Francis
Vogelsang, Beth Tyler
Yaffa, Andrew Bryan
**Miami Beach**
Arbuz, Joseph Robert
Cohen, Karen Beth
Fuller, Lawrence Arthur
**Naples**
Blakely, John T.
Cardillo, John Pollara
Crehan, Joseph Edward
Rocuant, Paul A.
**New Smyrna Beach**
Kolodinsky, Richard Hutton
**North Miami Beach**
Ginsberg, Alan
Lechtman, Michael Lowell
**Ocala**
Briggs, Randy Robert
McCall, Wayne Charles
Musleh, Victor Joseph, Jr.
**Orlando**
Allen, William Riley
Bitner, Richard H.
Blackwell, Bruce Beuford
Cullen, Kim Michael
Eidson, Frank M.
Handley, Leon Hunter
Hurt, Jennings Laverne, III
Kelaher, James Peirce
Kest, John Marshall
Marcus, Lee Warren
Mooney, Thomas Robert
Morgan, Mary Ann
Parrish, Sidney Howard
Paul, David Aaron
Sawicki, Stephen Craig
Wasson, Karen Reed
Williams, Donald Neal
**Palm Beach**
Gavigan, James Copley
**Palm Beach Gardens**
Whalen, Jeanmarie
**Panama City**
Fensom, James B.
Stone, Michel Leon
Sutton, Pamela Dru
**Panama City Beach**
Kapp, John Paul
**Pensacola**
Baker, William Costello, Jr.
Buchanan, Virginia Marie
Duke, Thomas Harrison
Echsner, Stephen Herre
Green, James R.
Griffith, Michael John
Levin, David Harold
Marsh, William Douglas
McKenzie, James Franklin
Soloway, Daniel Mark
**Punta Gorda**
Price, Pine Scott
**Saint Petersburg**
Allen, John Thomas, Jr.
Blews, William Frank
Glass, Roy Leonard
Gustafson, James William, Jr. ()
Lee, Patricia Marie
Mann, Sam Henry, Jr.
McKeown, H. Mary
Scott, Kathryn Fenderson
Wadley, W. Thomas
**Sarasota**
Byrd, L(awrence) Derek
Groseclose, Lynn Hunter
Lumpkin, Douglas Boozer
**Stuart**
Lako, Charles Michael, Jr.
McManus, Frank Shields
Watson, Robert James
**Sun City Center**
Balkany, Caron Lee
**Tallahassee**
Connor, Kenneth Luke
Fonvielle, Charles David
Gievers, Karen A.
Kitchen, E.C. Deeno
Miller, John Samuel, Jr.
Roland, Raymond William
**Tampa**
Apgar, Kenneth Edward
Barbas, Stephen Michael
Bardi, Henry J.
Berkowitz, Herbert Mattis
Brudny, Peter J.
Buell, Mark Paul
Carbone, Edward John
Cunningham, Anthony Willard
Fernandez, Frances Garcia
Fernandez, Ricardo Antonio
Givens, Stann William
Gordon, Jeffrey
Guerra, Rolando Gilberto, Jr.
Gunn, Lee Delton, IV
Hahn, William Edward
Hernandez, Daniel Mario
Kelly, Mark Patrick
Kelly, Thomas Paine, Jr.
Knopik, Christopher Scott
MacKay, John William
Medina, Omar F.
Morgenstern, Dennis Michael
Nutter, Robert Heinrich
Oehler, Richard Dale
Ramey, Mark S.
Rawls, R. Steven
Reyes, Lillian Jenny
Somers, Clifford Louis
Steiner, Geoffrey Blake
Tirella, David Theodore
Townsend, Byron Edwin
Vessel, Robert Leslie
Young, Ronald W.
**Tavares**
Johnson, Terri Sue
**Tavernier**
Jabro, John A.
Lupino, James Samuel
**Valrico**
Carlucci, Paul Pasquale
**West Palm Beach**
Barnhart, Forrest Gregory
Ciotoli, Eugene L.
Djokic, Walter Henry
Eyler, Bonnie
Flanagan, L. Martin
Gordon, Robert E.
Hicks, James Hermann
Koons, Stephen Robert
Laing, Robert Scott
Levy, Jonathan Todd
McAfee, William James
Nugent, Paul Allen
Quattlebaum, Guy Elliot
Wagner, Arthur Ward, Jr.
Ziska, Maura A.
**Winter Park**
Aikin, Wendy Lise

## GEORGIA

**Albany**
Eidson, Patrick Samuel
Patterson, Rudolph N.
**Athens**
Barrow, John J.
Elkins, Robert Neal
**Atlanta**
Allen, Denise
Bates, Beverly Bailey
Beckham, Walter Hull, III
Billington, Barry E.
Blank, A(ndrew) Russell
Brooks, Wilbur Clinton
Campbell, Jennifer Katze
Chalker, Ronald Franklin
Cheeley, Robert David
Cooper, Lawrence Allen
Cornwell, William John
Corry, Robert Emmett
Davis, E. Marcus
Eckl, William Wray
England, John Melvin
Feldman, Monroe Joseph
Fiorentino, Carmine
Gannon, Mark Stephen
Glaser, Arthur Henry
Hagan, James Walter
Haubenreich, John Gilman
Head, William Carl
Holder, Thomas Lee
Jones, Eric S.
Jones, Evan Wier
Lindsey, Edward Harman, Jr.
Matthews, James B., III
Mayfield, William Scott
McAlpin, Kirk Martin
Morris, Bruce H.
Pilcher, James Brownie
Steel, John Deaton
Stoner, Michael Alan
Sullivan, Terrance Charles
Wellon, Robert G.
Womack, Mary Pauline
Young, Michael Anthony
**Blue Ridge**
Rosenberg, David Michael
**Canton**
Hasty, William Grady, Jr.
**Carrollton**
Tisinger, David H.
**Cartersville**
Pope, Robert Daniel
**Columbus**
Dodgen, Andrew Clay
Harp, John Anderson
Lasseter, Earle Forrest
McGlamry, Max Reginald
Patrick, James Duvall, Jr.
Shelnutt, John Mark
**Dalton**
Bolling, Walter Harrison, Jr.
**Darien**
Coppage, James Robert
Jenkins, Olney Dale
**Decatur**
Apolinsky, Stephen Douglas
Edwards, Boykin, Jr.
Henry, Wendell S.
O'Connell, John James, Jr.
Pankey, Larry Allen
**Douglas**
Hayes, Dewey
**Fayetteville**
Johnson, Donald Wayne
**Gainesville**
Gilliam, Steven Philip, Sr.
**Homerville**
Helms, Catherine Harris
**Macon**
Bennett, Thomas Wesley
Cranford, James Michael
Dozier, Lester Zack
Grant, George Clarence
**Marietta**
Fielkow, Arnold David
Nowland, James Ferrell
**Newnan**
Franklin, Bruce Walter
**Peachtree City**
Ott, Stephen Douglas
**Rincon**
Carellas, Theodore T.
**Riverdale**
Terry, Pandora Elaine
**Rome**
Brinson, Robert Maddox
**Savannah**
Ladson, M. Brice
Lorberbaum, Ralph Richard
Morrell, Diane Marie
**Snellville**
Giallanza, Charles Philip
**Statesboro**
Brogdon, W.M. "Rowe"
Snipes, Daniel Brent
**Tucker**
Armstrong, Edwin Alan

**Valdosta**
Bright, Joseph Converse
Copeland, Roy Wilson
Smith, John Holder, Jr.
**Watkinsville**
Wright, Robert Joseph

### HAWAII

**Honolulu**
Boggs, Steven Eugene
Crumpton, Charles Whitmarsh
Cuskaden, Everett
Edmunds, John Sanford
Fong, Leslie Kaleiopu Wah Cheong
Fritz, Collin Martin
Fukumoto, Leslie Satsuki
Gillin, Malvin James, Jr.
Grande, Thomas Robert
Kawachika, James Akio
Kaya, Randall Y.
Kohn, Robert
Komeya, Geoffrey Kimo Sanshiro
Kotada, Kelly Kenichi
Lawson, William Homer
Lobdell, Henry Raymond
Moore, Willson Carr, Jr.
Potts, Dennis Walker
Sekiya, Gerald Yoshinori
Shigetomi, Keith Shigeo
Sumida, Kevin P.H.
Turbin, Richard
Umebayashi, Clyde Satoru
Wong, James Thomas
Zabanal, Eduardo Olegario
**Kailua Kona**
Miller, Frank Lewis
Zola, Michael S.
**Koloa**
Blair, Samuel Ray
**Makawao**
Barrad, Catherine Marie
**Wailuku**
Green, Eve Marie

### IDAHO

**Boise**
Derr, Allen R.
Hall, Richard Edgar
Lombardi, David Richard
Marcus, Craig Brian
**Caldwell**
Kerrick, David Ellsworth
**Coeur D Alene**
Vernon, Craig K.
**Idaho Falls**
Whittier, Monte Ray
**Lewiston**
Aherin, Darrel William
**Twin Falls**
Berry, L. Clyel
Lezamiz, John T.
Tolman, Steven Kay
Webb, Curtis Randall

### ILLINOIS

**Alton**
Struif, L. James
Talbert, Hugh Mathis
**Belleville**
Boyle, Richard Edward
Hamilton, Harriet Homsher
Heiligenstein, Christian E.
Johnston, John Joseph
Marlen, Matthew James
Menges, Eugene Clifford
Neville, James Edward
Ripplinger, George Raymond, Jr.
Urban, Donald Wayne
**Bloomington**
Bragg, Michael Ellis
Kelly, Timothy William
**Carol Stream**
Handley, Robert
**Champaign**
Harden, Richard Russell
Rawles, Edward Hugh
**Chicago**
Argeros, Anthony George
Berg, William Gerard
Bristol, Douglas
Burdelik, Thomas L.
Burke, Dennis J.
Burke, John Michael
Burke, William Joseph
Burns, Terrence Michael
Byrne, Katharine Crane
Cannizzaro, Sam F.
Cavenagh, Timothy Joseph
Cipolla, Carl Joseph
Connelly, Mary Jo
Corday, Lane Allan
Costello, James Paul
Durkin, Albert Eugene
Ellis, Stuart L.
Enright, Thomas Michael
Farina, James L.
Ferrini, James Thomas
Fina, Paul Joseph
Fleischmann, Thomas Joseph
Frazen, Mitchell Hale
Glenn, Cleta Mae
Gordon, Gilbert Wayne
Gordon, Theodora
Griffin, Lawrence Joseph
Henry, Brian Thomas
Howser, Richard Glen
Iwan, Lori E.
Johnson, Jennifer Jerit
Johnson, Richard Fred
Knox, James Marshall
Kremin, David Keith
Kroll, Jeffrey Joseph
Kunkle, William Joseph, Jr.
Laatsch, Gary Kenneth
Lederleitner, Joseph Benedict
Lowery, Timothy J.
Marsh, Weston W.
Marszalek, John Edward
Mattes, Barry A.
McCabe, Charles Kevin
McConnell, James Guy
McFadden, Monica Elizabeth
Mendelson, Alan Conrad
Miller, Douglas Andrew
Mullen, Michael T.
Napleton, Robert Joseph
Novak, Mark
Olavarria, Frank J.
Pach, Lisa Anne
Pavalon, Eugene Irving
Pimentel, Julio Gumeresindo
Pollock, Bradley Neil
Pullano, Richard L.
Rapoport, David E.
Richmond, William Patrick
Rogers, William John
Roustan, Yvon Dominique
Schaffner, Howard
Shipley, Robert Allen
Tassone, Bruno Joseph
Tefft, Steven M.
Theobald, Edward Robert
Tobin, Craig Daniel
Walsh, Robert Patrick, Jr.
Weaver, Timothy Allan
Wemple, Peter Holland
Wohlreich, Jack Jay
Wool, Leon
Wunsch, John Carlyle
Young, Keith Lawrence
**Danville**
Blan, Kennith William, Jr.
Devens, Charles J.
McFetridge, John David
**Decatur**
Ansbro, James Michael
Jones, Deanne Fortna
**Des Plaines**
Jacobs, William Russell, II
**East Alton**
Tobin, Gregory Michael
**Edwardsville**
Carlson, Jon Gordon
Gorman, James Edward
**Elgin**
Carbary, Jonathan Leigh
Childers, John Aaron
Karayannis, Marios Nicholas
**Elmhurst**
Kordik, Daniel Joseph
**Evanston**
Smith, Mark Steven
**Franklin Park**
Motta, Robert Michael
**Galesburg**
McCrery, David Neil, III
**Hinsdale**
Avgeris, George Nicholas
Farrug, Eugene Joseph, Sr.
**Homewood**
Getty, Gerald Winkler
**Hoopeston**
Manion, Paul Thomas
**Joliet**
Klukas, Elizabeth Ann
Miller, Randal J.
Ozmon, Laird Michael
**Kankakee**
Marek, James Dennis
**Libertyville**
DeSanto, James John
Rallo, Douglas
**Lincolnwood**
Birg, Yuri M.
**Lombard**
O'Shea, Patrick Joseph
**Mattoon**
Corn, Stephen Leslie
Horsley, Jack Everett
**Minooka**
Lab, Charles Edward
**Monee**
Bohlen, Christopher Wayne
**Morris**
Belt, Scott M.
**Mount Vernon**
Harvey, Morris Lane
**Naperville**
Levy, Steven Barry
**Oak Brook**
Ring, Leonard M.
Washburn, John James
**Oak Lawn**
Tucker, Berry Kenneth
**Oakbrook Terrace**
LaForte, George Francis, Jr.
**Palos Heights**
Jasinski, George John
**Paris**
Pearman, John Stewart
**Peoria**
O'Brien, Daniel Robert
Prusak, Maximilian Michael
Slevin, John A.
**Rock Island**
VanDerGinst, Dennis Allen
**Rockford**
Brassfield, Eugene Everett
Fredrickson, Robert Alan
Mateer, Don Metz
Ohlander, Jan H.
Rouleau, Mark A.
Sullivan, Peter Thomas, III
Zucchi, Jeffrey Joseph
**Roselle**
Dobra, Charles William
**Rosemont**
Richter, Paul David
Willens, Matthew Lyle
**Saint Charles**
Clancy Boles, Susan
**Skokie**
Gilbert, Howard E.
**South Holland**
Scott, Edward Aloysius
**Springfield**
Heckenkamp, Robert Glenn
**Waukegan**
Decker, David Alfred
Henrick, Michael Francis
Rizzo, John Joseph
**Wheaton**
Cunningham, William Francis
Malm, John Joseph
**Woodstock**
Kell, Vette Eugene

### INDIANA

**Anderson**
Woodruff, Randall Lee
**Bedford**
McSoley, Patrick Shannon
**Bloomington**
Applegate, Karl Edwin
Nunn, Ken
**Columbus**
Fairchild, Raymond Francis
Harrison, Patrick Woods
**Elkhart**
Wicks, Charles Carter
**Evansville**
Berger, Charles Lee
Bodkin, Robert Thomas
**Fort Wayne**
Young, Randy William
**Franklin**
Jones, Tom George
**Gary**
Lewis, Robert Lee
**Greenfield**
Dobbins, Caryl Dean
**Hammond**
Ruman, Saul I.
**Indianapolis**
Caress, Timothy Charles
Cline, Lance Douglas
Conour, William Frederick
Due, Danford Royce
Hammel, John Wingate
Hovde, F. Boyd
Hovde, Frederick Russell
Koch, Edna Mae
Lisher, John Leonard
Love, Jennifer Stephens
Montross, W. Scott
Mortier, Jeffrey James
Pinkus, I(rving) Marshall
Price, Henry J.
Reddy, Lakshmi Yeddula
Schreckengast, William Owen
Sherman, Stephen Michael
Small, Mark Eugene
Spence, Steven Allen
Townsend, John Frederick, Jr.
Wellnitz, Craig Otto
Whitney, Larry Gene
Woods, Joseph Reid
**Indianpolis**
Holtzlander, Stephanie Franco
**Jeffersonville**
Harris, Ronald Dean
Henderson, Joan Blust
**Kokomo**
Bayliff, Edgar W.
Harrigan, Daniel Joseph
Russell, Richard Lloyd
**Lafayette**
Layden, Charles Max
**Merrillville**
Irak, Joseph S.
Miller, Richard Allen
**Portage**
Germann, Gary Stephen
Henke, Robert John
**Seymour**
Gill, W(alter) Brent
Pardieck, Roger Lee
**Shelbyville**
Harrold, Dennis Edward
**South Bend**
Galso, Ernest Peter Gabriel
Horn, George Edward, Jr.
Myers, James Woodrow, III
Norton, Sally Pauline
**Terre Haute**
Bough, Bradley A.
Fleschner, G. Steven
**Valparaiso**
Gioia, Daniel August

### IOWA

**Adair**
Fisher, Martin Louis
**Ames**
Sotak, Ronald Michael
**Cedar Rapids**
O'Brien, David A.
Willems, Daniel Wayne
Wilson, Robert Foster
**Creston**
Kenyon, Arnold Oakley, III
**Davenport**
Bush, Michael Kevin
Halligan, Kevin Leo
Lane, Gary M.
Lathrop, Roger Alan
Liebbe, Michael William
**Des Moines**
Branstad, Christine Ellen
Conlin, Roxanne Barton
Cortese, Joseph Samuel, II
Cutler, Charles Edward
Doyle, Richard Henry, IV
Foxhoven, Jerry Ray
Hermann, Robin L.
Krull, Curtis Jay
Lawyer, Vivian Jury
Logan, Thomas Joseph
Murray, William Michael (Mike Murray)
Schadle, William James
Tully, Robert Gerard
Werner, Thomas M.
**Indianola**
Ouderkirk, Mason James
**Iowa City**
Spies, Leon Fred
Trca, Randy Ernest
**Johnston**
Leitner, David Larry
**Keokuk**
Hoffman, James Paul
**Marshalltown**
Brooks, Patrick William
Geffe, Kent Lyndon
**Mason City**
Kinsey, Robert Stanleigh, III
**Newton**
Dalen, DuWayne John
**Sioux City**
Bottaro, Timothy Shanahan
Giles, William Jefferson, III

### KANSAS

**Emporia**
Helbert, Michael Clinton
**Fort Scott**
Hudson, Leigh Carleton
Reynolds, Zackery E.
Short, Forrest Edwin
**Kansas City**
Greenbaum, Frederick Joel
Holbrook, Reid Franklin
Jurcyk, John Joseph, Jr.
**Lawrence**
Krogh, Richard Alan
**Leawood**
Dvorak, Richard Dee
Shetlar, James R.
**Lenexa**
Gould, Robert P.
Rappard, Gary Donald
**Olathe**
DeWitt, Anthony Louis
**Overland Park**
Gunnison, Mark Steven
Keplinger, (Donald) Bruce
Level, Kurt Alan
Smith, Daniel Lynn
Smith, Edwin Dudley
Starrett, Frederick Kent
**Shawnee Mission**
Wells, Samuel Jay
**Topeka**
Hejtmanek, Danton Charles
Pigg, James Steven
Schroer, Gene Eldon
Snyder, Brock Robert
Wisler, James Lynn
Wright, James C.
**Wichita**
Badger, Ronald Kay
Fisher, Randall Eugene
Franklin, Joni Jeanette
Grace, Brian Guiles
Jones, Gary Kenneth
Stalcup, Randy Stephen

### KENTUCKY

**Bowling Green**
Brennenstuhl, Henry Brent
**Covington**
Lawrence, Richard Dean
Stepner, Donald Leon
**Danville**
Clay, James Franklin
**Elizabethtown**
Bell, Jason B.
**Florence**
Bogucki, Raymond Spencer
**Fort Mitchell**
Beetem, A. Page
Wietholter, Thomas Andrew
**Glasgow**
Dickinson, Temple
**Henderson**
Hamilton, Curtis James, II
**Lexington**
Campbell, Joe Bill
Garmer, William Robert
Masterton, Lucinda Cronin
Shouse, William Chandler
**Louisville**
Baker, H. Nicholas
Ballantine, John Tilden
Edwards, Steven Alan
Faller, Rhoda Dianne Grossberg
Grossman, H. Philip
Morreau, James Earl, Jr.
Orberson, William Baxter
Osterhage, Lawrence Edward
Sales, Kenneth L.
Shanks, C.A. Dudley
Smith, T.J.
Spalding, Catherine
Storment, Harold Lloyd
Talbott, Ben Johnson, Jr.
Wade, Jeffrey Lee
Welsh, Alfred John
**Paducah**
Nickell, Christopher Shea
**Paintsville**
Massengale, Roger Lee
**Providence**
Bock, Valerie L.
**Russellville**
Wilson, Elizabeth Davis
**Shepherdsville**
Givhan, Thomas Bartram
**Somerset**
Prather, John Gideon, Jr.

### LOUISIANA

**Alexandria**
Alexius, Frederick Bernard
Arsenault, Gary Joseph
Bolen, James Aubrey, Jr.
Perkins, Alvin Bruce, II
**Baton Rouge**
Andrews, Brandon Scott
Gibbs, Deborah P.
Giglio, Steven Rene
Jones, Keith Dunn
Robinson, Bert Kris
Sledge, L. D.
Watson, Craig Sterling
Wittenbrink, Jeffrey Scott
**Chalmette**
Ginart, Michael Charles, Jr.
**Covington**
Paddison, David Robert
**Farmerville**
Earle, Robert Ray
**Hessmer**
Jeansonne, Mark Anthony
**Houma**
Lirette, Danny Joseph
Stewart, Craig Henry
**Jefferson**
Conino, Joseph Aloysius
**Lacombe**
Price, Lionel Franklin
**Lafayette**
Bostany, Alfred Frem
Curtis, Lawrence Neil
Dartez, Shannon Seiler
Edwards, Christopher Alan
Hutchens, Charles Kenneth
Judice, Marc Wayne
Keaty, Robert Burke
Landry, Michael W.
Lemoine, Gano D., Jr.
Roy, James Parkerson
Simien, Clyde Ray
Willard, David Charles
**Lake Charles**
Clements, Robert W.
McHale, Robert Michael
Sanchez, Walter Marshall
Townsley, Todd Alan
Watson, Wells
**Leesville**
Smith, Simeon Christie, III
Smith, Simeon Christie, IV
**Metairie**
Album, Jerald Lewis
Gauthier, Celeste Anne
Recile, George B.
**Monroe**
Creed, Christian Carl
**Natchitoches**
Seaman, Charles Wilson
**New Orleans**
Aiken, Tonia Dandry
Allen, F(rank) C(linton), Jr.
Ates, J. Robert
Benjamin, Jack Charles
Bruno, Frank Silvo
Burr, Timothy Fuller
Christovich, Alvin Richard, Jr.
David, Robert Jefferson
Exnicios, Val Patrick
Fields, Timmy Lee
Gay, Esmond Phelps
Hearin, Robert Matlock, Jr.
Herman, Fred L.
Herman, Russ Michel
Hoffman, Donald Alfred
Irwin, James Burke, V
Katz, Morton Howard
Lang, Susan Gail
Leger, Walter John, Jr.
McGlone, Michael Anthony
Rawls, John D.
Redmann, John William
Riess, George Febiger
Rumage, Joseph Paul, Jr.
Schoemann, Rudolph Robert
Shuey, James Frank
Sinnott, John William
Snellings, Daniel Breard
Thomas, Joseph Winand
Thornton, Lucie Elizabeth
Waltzer, Joel Reuben
**Opelousas**
Sandoz, William Charles
**River Ridge**
Kelly, Quentin Patrick
**Shreveport**
Clark, James E.
Fortson, James Leon, Jr.
Politz, Nyle Anthony
Rigby, Kenneth
Smith, Brian David
**Slidell**
D'Antonio, Guy Joseph
Hammond, Margaret
Shamis, Edward Anthony, Jr.
**Sulphur**
Sumpter, Dennis Ray
**Ville Platte**
Coreil, C. Brent

### MAINE

**Augusta**
McKee, Walter Frederic
**Bangor**
Ebitz, Elizabeth Kelly
Gilbert, Charles E., III
Gould, Edward Ward
Greif, Arthur John
Woodcock, John Alden
**Bath**
Regan, Richard Robert
**Hallowell**
Crawford, Linda Sibery
Smith, Jeffrey Allen
**Kennebunk**
Libby, Gene Roger
**Lewiston**
Peters, Thomas P., II
**Portland**
Brogan, Jonathan William
Connolly, Thomas Joseph
Dinan, Christopher Charles
Martin, Michael Keith
Monaghan, Matthew John
Pooler, Delia Bridget
Quinn, Thomas Joseph
Rundlett, Ellsworth Turner, III
Schwartz, Stephen Jay
Whiting, Stephen Clyde
**S Portland**
Mooers, Daniel William
**Sanford**
Nadeau, Robert Maurice Auclair

**Topsham**
MacAdam, James Joseph

## MARYLAND

**Annapolis**
Levin, David Alan
Nash, Brian Joseph
Wharton, James T.

**Baltimore**
Byrd, Ronald Dicky
Christianson, Charles Anthony Patrick
Cohen, Hyman K.
DeVries, Donald Lawson, Jr.
Ebersole, Jodi Kay
Eisenberg, Bruce Alan
Ellin, Marvin
Gutierrez, Maria Cristina
Jenkins, Robert Rowe
Joseph, Charles Ian
Katz, Lawrence Edward
Kuryk, David Neal
Lynch, Timothy Cronin
Rosenberg, David A.
Sack, Sylvan Hanan
Schochor, Jonathan
Shortridge, Deborah Green
Snyder, Mark Allen
Summers, Thomas Carey
Tousey, Robert Ryan
Vice, LaVonna Lee
Weltchek, Robert Jay
White, George Wendell, Jr.
White, William Nelson
Zimmerly, James Gregory

**Bel Air**
Gintling, Karen Janette

**Bethesda**
Himelfarb, Stephen Roy
Karp, Ronald Alvin
Strickler, Scott Michael

**Bowie**
Lucchi, Leonard Louis

**Burtonsville**
Covington, Marlow Stanley

**Chevy Chase**
Montedonico, Joseph

**College Park**
Neal, Edward Garrison
Yoho, Billy Lee

**Columbia**
Barton, Ellen Louise

**Gaithersburg**
Massengill, Alan Durwood
Santa Maria, Philip Joseph, III

**Glen Burnie**
Cole, Ronald Clark
Smith, John Stanley

**Greenbelt**
Greenwald, Andrew Eric

**Hagerstown**
Berkson, Jacob Benjamin
Marks, Russell Robert
Schneider, Arthur

**Lanham Seabrook**
McCarthy, Kevin John

**Laytonsville**
McDowell, Donna Schultz

**Riverdale**
Turkheimer, Paul Adam

**Rockville**
Armstrong, Kenneth
Avery, Bruce Edward
Doyle, Thomas Edward
Fogleman, Christopher Curtis
Lamari, Joseph Paul
Michael, Robert Roy
Segal, Gary L.
Van Grack, Steven

**Silver Spring**
Lipshultz, Leonard L.

**Stevensville**
Ronayne, Donald Anthony

**Westminster**
Blakeslee, Wesley Daniel

## MASSACHUSETTS

**Andover**
Bucci, Kathleen Elizabeth
Lakin, John Francis

**Arlington**
Kelleher, D. Ring

**Boston**
Berry, Janis Marie
Blank, Garry Neal
Bozza, Mario
Brody, Richard Eric
Burns, Thomas David
Carney, Gerard Barry
Casby, Robert William
Cunha, John Henry, Jr.
Curley, Robert Ambrose, Jr.
Dolan, James Boyle, Jr.
Edwards, Richard Lansing
Ellis, Fredric Lee
Feinberg, Robert I(ra)
Fishman, Kenneth Jay
Goscinak, Virginia Casey
Hailey, Hans Ronald
Halström, Frederic Norman
Hamelburg, Gerald A.
Harding, Ronald Evan
Hrones, Stephen Baylis
Levine, Julius Byron
Liapis, Georgia P.
Licata, Arthur Frank
Lumsden, Diana J.
McKittrick, Neil Vincent
Meyer, Andrew C., Jr.
Morgera, Vincent D.
Murray, Philip Edmund, Jr.
Neumeier, Richard L.
O'Neill, Timothy P.
Rafferty, Edson Howard
Reed, Barry C., Jr.
Ristuben, Karen R.
Sarrouf, Camille Francis
Schafer, Steven Harris
Urquhart, Stephen E.

**Braintree**
Riccio, Frank Joseph

**Brockton**
Belinsky, Ilene Beth

**Brookline**
Dow, Joseph Sheffield
Nayor, Charles Francis

**Charlestown**
DuLaurence, Henry J., III

**Chelmsford**
Grossman, Debra A.
Lerer, Neal M.

**Chestnut Hill**
Lowinger, Lazar

**Foxboro**
Cohen, Harold

**Framingham**
Gaffin, Gerald Eliot

**Holyoke**
Sarnacki, Michael Thomas

**Ipswich**
Gonick, Richard S.

**Lexington**
Nason, Leonard Yoshimoto

**Milford**
Murray, Brian William

**New Bedford**
Murray, Robert Fox

**Newton**
Peterson, Osler Leopold

**North Andover**
Barbagallo, Ralph A.

**Peabody**
Papanickolas, Emmanuel N.

**Pittsfield**
Doyle, Anthony Peter

**Quincy**
Syat, Scott Mitchell

**Salem**
Andrews, John
Marks, Scott Charles
Sellers, Jill Suzanne
Wasserman, Stephen Alan

**Somerset**
Sabra, Steven Peter

**South Easton**
Finn, Anne-Marie

**Springfield**
Burke, Michael Henry
Gelinas, Robert Albert
Low, Terrence Allen
Ryan, Phyllis Paula

**Stow**
Golder, Leonard Howard

**Wakefield**
Lucas, Robert Frank

**Waltham**
Malone, Steven C.

**Woburn**
Karshbaum, Bonnie L.

**Worcester**
Balko, George Anthony, III
Bassett, Edward Caldwell, Jr.
Gribouski, James Joseph
Reitzell, William R.
Weinstein, Jordan Harvey

## MICHIGAN

**Ann Arbor**
Ferris, Donald William, Jr.
Goethel, Stephen B.
Patti, Anthony Peter

**Auburn Hills**
DeAgostino, Thomas M.

**Battle Creek**
Blaske, E. Robert

**Bay City**
Kennedy, Brian Melville

**Bingham Farms**
Goren, Steven Eliot
Toth, John Michael

**Birmingham**
Elsman, James Leonard, Jr.
Zacharski, Dennis Edward

**Bloomfield Hills**
Baumkel, Mark S.
Googasian, George Ara
Lehman, Richard Leroy
Victor, Richard Steven
Weinstein, William Joseph

**Coldwater**
Colbeck, J. Richard

**Detroit**
Benjamin, Gary Adams
Budaj, Steven T.
Foley, Thomas John
Gilbert, Ronald Rhea
Glotta, Ronald Delon
Leuchtman, Stephen Nathan
Phillips, Dwight Wilburn
Posner, Alan B.
Prather, Kenneth Earl
Taweel, A. Tony
Tucciarone, Enrico Gregory

**East Lansing**
Stroud, Ted William

**Eaton Rapids**
Nolan, Lawrence Patrick

**Farmingtn Hls**
Maloney, Vincent John

**Farmington Hills**
Gregory, Russell
Weiss, Leon Jeffrey

**Flint**
Knecht, Timothy Harry
Wheaton, Robin Lee

**Fort Gratiot**
Carson, Robert William

**Grand Rapids**
Andersen, David Charles
Blackwell, Thomas Francis
Jack, William Wilson, Jr.
Savickas, Stephen Anthony
Spies, Frank Stadler
Vander Laan, Allan C.

**Holland**
Bidol, James Alexander
Moritz, John Reid

**Kalamazoo**
Halpert, Richard Lee
Hatch, Hazen van den Berg
Plaszczak, Roman Thaddeus

**Lansing**
Coey, David Conrad
Deprez, Deborah Ann
Kritselis, William Nicholas
Kronzek, Charles Michael
Stackable, Frederick Lawrence

**Madison Heights**
Szczesny, Ronald William

**Muskegon**
Van Leuven, Robert Joseph

**Okemos**
Platsis, George James

**Petoskey**
Erhart, James Nelson

**Plymouth**
Haynes, Richard Terry
Koroi, Mark Michael

**Pontiac**
Pierson, William George

**Rapid City**
Ring, Ronald Herman

**Redford**
Philippart, Howard Louis, Jr.

**Royal Oak**
Gordon, Deborah Leigh

**Saginaw**
Chasnis, John Alex
Concannon, Andrew Donnelly
Martin, Walter
McGraw, Patrick John
Zanot, Craig Allen

**Saint Joseph**
Butzbaugh, Elden W., Jr.
Gleiss, Henry Weston

**Southfield**
Bereznoff, Gregory Michael
Fieger, Geoffrey Nels
Goodman, Barry Joel
Gordon, Louis
Jaffa, Jonathan Mark
Lipton, William
Martina, Carlo Jack
Mazey, Larry William
McClow, Roger James
Moloughney, Kevin Patrick
Ornstein, Alexander Thomas
Thurswell, Gerald Elliott
Tyler, David Malcolm
Weiner, Ronald Allen

**Springport**
McKay, M. Dale

**Sterling Heights**
Hartkop, Jeffrey Wells

**Suttons Bay**
Robb, Dean Allen, Sr.

**Trenton**
Counard, Allen Joseph

**Troy**
Kruse, John Alphonse
Ponitz, John Allan
Sachs, Ralph Gordon

**Walled Lake**
Connelly, Thomas Joseph

**West Bloomfield**
Meyer, Philip Gilbert

**Ypsilanti**
Shapiro, Douglas Bruce

## MINNESOTA

**Anoka**
Malzahn, Mark William

**Bemidji**
Baer, H. Carl, III
Woodke, Robert Allen

**Bloomington**
Boedigheimer, Robert David

**Burnsville**
McGrath, Daniel Scott

**Cambridge**
Parker, Robert Samuel

**Duluth**
Thibodeau, Thomas Raymond

**Edina**
Vukelich, John Edward
Weber, Gail Mary

**Erskine**
Taylor, Richard Charles

**Hawley**
Baer, Zenas

**Mankato**
Manahan, James Hinchon

**Maple Grove**
Saville, Derric James

**Maplewood**
Nemo, Anthony James

**Minneapolis**
Adams, Thomas Lewis
Barrett, Michael D.
Biglow, Robert R.
Bland, J(ohn) Richard
Christensen, Robert Paul
Cuellar, Norbert
Degnan, John Michael
Fitch, Raymond William
Jepsen, William E.
Johnson, Paul Owen
Laurie, Gerald Tenzer
Luong, Phong Minh
Manning, William Henry
Meshbesher, Ronald I.
Messerly, Chris Alan
Muirhead, Douglas James
Roe, Roger Rolland
Sortland, Paul Allan
Tatone, Kathy
Tolin, Stefan A.
Westphal, James Phillip
Yira, Markus Clarence
Zotaley, Byron Leo

**Minnetonka**
Brennan, Sidney L.
Freeman, Gerald Russell

**Moorhead**
Cahill, Steven James

**New Brighton**
Krueger, William James

**New Ulm**
Lowther, Patrick Alan

**Rochester**
Murakami, Steven Kiyoshi
Orwoll, Gregg S. K.

**Saint Cloud**
Seifert, Luke Michael
Walz, Gregory Stephen

**Saint Louis Park**
Flom, Katherine S.
Nightingale, Tracy Irene

**Saint Paul**
Amdahl, Faith A.
Duckstad, Jon R.
Dunn, James Francis
Engebretson, Andrew Peter
King, Lawrence R.
Krug, Michael Steven
Patient, Robert J.

**Wayzata**
Geng, Thomas W.
Reutiman, Robert William, Jr.

**Winona**
Borman, John

## MISSISSIPPI

**Batesville**
Cook, William Leslie, Jr.

**Biloxi**
O'Barr, Bobby Gene, Sr.
Pritchard, Thomas Alexander

**Brandon**
Chatham, Lloyd Reeve

**Clarksdale**
Chapman, Ralph E.
Cocke, John Hartwell
Merkel, Charles Michael

**Drew**
Holladay, Robert Lawson

**Gulfport**
Allen, Harry Roger
Dukes, James Otis
Foster, James (Jay) R.
Pate, William August
Wetzel, James K.

**Hattiesburg**
Adelman, Michael Schwartz
Jernigan, Jay Lawrence

**Hernando**
Brown, William A.
Neyman, Joseph David, Jr.

**Jackson**
Bullock, James N.
Burch, Donald Victor
Burkes, Jennifer Parkinson
Chinn, Mark Allan
Ferrell, Wayne Edward, Jr.
Northington, Hiawatha
Scales, Clarence Ray
Simmons, Heber Sherwood, III

**Lumberton**
Tonry, Richard Alvin

**Ocean Springs**
Lawson-Jowett, Mary Juliet
Luckey, Alwyn Hall
Pattison, Daphne Lynn

**Oxford**
Howorth, Andrew Kincannon
Smith, Kent Elliot

**Pascagoula**
Heidelberg, James Hinkle
Hunter, John Leslie

**Southaven**
Branan, Debra Pace

**Starkville**
Drungole, Paula Elaine
Yoste, Charles Todd

**Tupelo**
Clayton, Claude F., Jr.

**Winona**
Reid, William Joseph

## MISSOURI

**Branson**
Anglen, Randall S.

**Cape Girardeau**
Lowes, Albert Charles

**Clayton**
Clarkin, E. Thomas
Fluhr, Steven Solomon
Klein, Jerry A.
Ritter, Robert Thornton

**Columbia**
Moore, Mitchell Jay
Schwabe, John Bennett, II

**Hannibal**
Curl, Jeffrey Robert

**Hillsboro**
Guberman, Ted
Pyatt, Joyce A.

**Jackson**
Waldron, Kenneth Lynn

**Joplin**
Guillory, Jeffery Michael

**Kansas City**
Bartimus, James Russell
Beckett, Theodore Cornwall
Borel, Steven James
Brake, Timothy L.
Cartmell, Thomas Philip
Davis, Donald Lee
Dymer, Marilyn
Herron, Donald Patrick
Hopkins, William Carlisle, II
Hubbell, Ernest
Hursh, Lynn Wilson
Koelling, Thomas Winsor
Mayer, David Mathew
McManus, James William
Molzen, Christopher John
Moore, Diana Dowell
Morefield, Richard Watts
Murguia, Ramon
Norton, John Hise
O'Neill, Thomas Tyrone
Redfearn, Paul L., III
Salmon, Steven Brett
Sharp, Rex Arthur
Siro, Rik Neal
Smith, R(onald) Scott
Stoup, Arthur Harry
Vandever, William Dirk
Wirken, James Charles

**Lake Saint Louis**
Callahan, Robert John, Jr.

**Lees Summit**
Cownie, Willian Garry

**Mexico**
Hagan, Ann P.

**Rolla**
Hickle, William Earl

**Saint Ann**
Johnson, Harold Gene

**Saint Charles**
Carmichael, James Edward
Green, Joseph Libory
Zerr, Richard Kevin

**Saint Joseph**
Koerner, Wendell Edward, Jr.
Taylor, Michael Leslie

**Saint Louis**
Baldwin, Brent Winfield
Baum, Gordon Lee
Blanke, Richard Brian
Brostron, Judith Curran
Burke, Thomas Michael
Burns, Mark Gardner
Collins, James Slade, II
Cox, Dallas Wendell, Jr.
Ellis, Dorsey Daniel, Jr.
Evans, William Wallace
Fournie, Raymond Richard
Greenberg, Karen Alane
Hempstead, Gerard Francis
Hunt, Jeffrey Brian
Johnson, Weldon Neal
Kell, John Mark
Kolker, Scott Lee
Liberman, Keith Gordon
Meehan, John Justin
Myre, Donald Paul
Neill, Joseph Vincent
Ramirez, Anthony Benjamin
Rice, Canice Timothy, Jr.
Sandberg, John Steven
Schroeder, Mary Patricia
Spooner, Jack Bernard
Suess, Jeffrey Karl
Susman, Robert M(ark)
Vandover, Samuel Taylor
Walsh, Joseph Leo, III
Webb Anderson, JoAnn Marie
Williams, Theodore Joseph, Jr.
Wines, Lawrence Eugene

**Sedalia**
Rice, James Briggs, Jr.

**Springfield**
Clithero, Monte Paul
Conway, Ronald Anthony
Crites, Richard Don
FitzGerald, Kevin Michael
Groce, Steven Fred
McDonald, William Henry
Myers, Ronald Lynn
Van Pelt, Fred Richard
Woody, Donald Eugene

## MONTANA

**Billings**
Krogh, Harlan B.
Lodders, Ronald R.
Malee, Thomas Michael

**Butte**
Harrington, James Patrick

**Great Falls**
Baker, Lynn Dale
George, Michael Joseph
Overfelt, Clarence Lahugh
Seidlitz, John E.

**Helena**
Morrison, John Martin

**Kalispell**
Heckathorn, I. James
Lerner, Alan Jay

**Livingston**
Jovick, Robert L.

**Missoula**
Anderson, Clare Eberhart
Morales, Julio K.

## NEBRASKA

**Columbus**
Milbourn, Douglas Ray

**Cozad**
McKeone, Mark R.

**Holdrege**
Klein, Michael Clarence

**Lincoln**
Guthery, John M.
Mussman, David C.
Swihart, Fred Jacob

**Norfolk**
McGough, James Kingsley

**Omaha**
Banwo, Opeolu
Blunk, Christian Raymond
Castello, David A.
Cuddigan, Timothy John
Fellman, Richard Mayer
Gleason, James Mullaney
Gutowski, Michael Francis
Schmidt, Kathleen Marie
Schmitt, David Jon
Walsh, Thomas John, Sr.

## NEVADA

**Carson City**
McCarthy, Ann Price
Wilson, James Edward, Jr.

**Gardnerville**
Jackson, Mark Bryan
Terzich, Milos

**Henderson**
Dobberstein, Eric

**Incline Village**
Skinner, Gregory Sala

**Las Vegas**
Bell, Stewart Lynn
Brattain, Richard Howard
Galatz, Neil Gilbert
Geihs, Frederick Siegfried
Goldberg, Aubrey
Kiraly, Michele Ann
Lovell, Carl Erwin, Jr.
Lucas, Craig John
Mainor, W. Randall
Pitegoff, Jeffrey I.
Schwartz, Daniel Leonard
Van Alfen, Scott B.
**Reno**
Bader, Angela Marie
Hardy, Del
Kent, Stephen Smiley
Kladney, David
Manson, Gary Lyle
Santos, Herbert Joseph, Jr.
Shaffer, Wayne Alan
Whitbeck, Jill Karla
Wright, Roger Lane

## NEW HAMPSHIRE

**Concord**
Mekeel, Robert K.
Richmond, Tanya Goff
**Gorham**
Cote, Thomas Jacques
**Keene**
Bell, John Andrew
Gardner, Eric Raymond
Heed, Peter W.
**Manchester**
Bruzga, Paul Wheeler
Daley, Terrence Joseph
Damon, Claudia Cords
Dugan, Kevin F.
Middleton, Jack Baer
Nixon, David L.
**Nashua**
Brown, Kenneth Mackinnon
Jette, Ernest Arthur
Snow, Robert Brian
**Newington**
Lewis, John Michael
**North Conway**
Cooper, Randall F.
**Portsmouth**
Lown, Bradley Merrill
Mason, J. William L.
Tober, Stephen Lloyd
Watson, Thomas Roger
Wolowitz, David

## NEW JERSEY

**Atlantic City**
Feinberg, Jack
Targan, Donald Gilmore
Wallen, Kate Rabassa
**Audubon**
Montano, Arthur
**Barrington**
Guice, Stephen W.
**Berlin**
Goldstein, Benjamin
**Bernardsville**
Forzani, Rinaldo, III
**Blackwood**
Bloch, Stefanie Z.
**Brick**
Tivenan, Charles Patrick
**Chatham**
Fried, David M.
**Cherry Hill**
DeVoto, Louis Joseph
Feldman, Arnold H.
Spielberg, Joshua Morris
Tomar, William
**Clifton**
Palma, Nicholas James
**Cranford**
McCreedy, Edwin James
**Denville**
Caivano, Anthony P.
Greene, Steven K.
**East Brunswick**
Cosner, Alan G.
Eder, Todd Brandon
**Edison**
Billek, Maxwell L.
Homisak, Theresa
Lavigne, Lawrence Neil
Rothenberg, Adam Leigh
**Elizabeth**
Kuhrt, Richard Lee
**Fairfield**
Denes, Richard Ford
**Flemington**
Miller, Louis H.
Weinblatt, Seymour Solomon
**Freehold**
Lomurro, Donald Michael
**Gloucester City**
Ford, Mark William
**Hackensack**
Bar-Nadav, Meiron
Dario, Ronald Anthony
Gerlanc, Glenn Marc
Jacobs, Lawrence H.
Masi, John Roger
Pollinger, William Joshua
**Haddon Heights**
Cipparone, Rocco C., Jr.
D'Alfonso, Mario Joseph
**Haddonfield**
Andres, Kenneth G., Jr.
**Hamilton**
Chase, Daniel E.
**Hillsdale**
Hodinar, Michael
**Jersey City**
Grossman, Randy
**Kearny**
Brady, Lawrence Peter
**Kenilworth**
Finn, Jerry Martin
**Lawrenceville**
Benesch, Katherine
**Lebanon**
Johnstone, Irvine Blakeley, III
**Little Egg Harbor Township**
Rumpf, Brian E.
**Livingston**
Harris, Brian Craig
Nagel, Bruce H.
Rinsky, Joel Charles
**Medford**
Evans, Jan Roger
**Metuchen**
Vercammen, Kenneth Albert
**Moorestown**
Kearney, John Francis, III
Polansky, Steven Jay
**Morristown**
Cocca, Anthony
**Mount Holly**
Algeo, Annemarie
Mintz, Jeffry Alan
**Mount Laurel**
Schmoll, Harry F., Jr.
**New Providence**
Marris, Joan Banan
**Newark**
Cooner, David James
Lazzaro, Clifford Emanuel
**North Haledon**
Harrington, Kevin Paul
**Northfield**
Broome, Henry George, Jr.
Cohen, Barry David
Day, Christopher Mark
**Ocean**
Weisberg, Adam Jon
**Paramus**
Giantonio, Clifford John
**Parsippany**
Doherty, Robert Christopher
**Paterson**
de la Carrera, Miguel Antonio
**Pilesgrove Township**
Crouse, Farrell R.
**Pitman**
Powell, J. R.
**Plainfield**
Grayson, Russell Wayne
**Red Bank**
Allegra, Peter Alexander
Auerbach, Philip Gary
DuPont, Michael Richard
Halfacre, Michael Ian
Warshaw, Michael Thomas
**Ridgewood**
Baxter, George T.
Seigel, Jan Kearney
**Rochelle Park**
Knopf, Barry Abraham
**Roseland**
Clemente, Mark Andrew
Smith, Wendy Hope
**Short Hills**
Kaye, Marc Mendell
**Shrewsbury**
Hopkins, Charles Peter, II
**Somerville**
Fleischer, Steven H.
**South Plainfield**
Scialabba, Damian Angelo
**Springfield**
Kahn, Eric G.
**Succasunna**
Gates, Marshall L.
**Teaneck**
Kaplan, Howard M(ark)
**Trenton**
Gogo, Gregory
Harbeck, Dorothy Anne
Kahn, Edward Stanton
**Union City**
Navarrete, Yolanda
**Warren**
Kraus, Steven Gary
**Wayne**
Gelman, Jon Leonard
**West Atlantic City**
Sinderbrand, David I.
**West Orange**
Bottitta, Joseph Anthony
Gordon, Harrison J.
**Westfield**
Phillips, John C.
**Westmont**
Tonogbanua, A. Robert
**Westwood**
McGuirl, Robert Joseph
**Woodbury**
Celano, Peter J., Jr.
**Woodbury Heights**
Heim, Thomas George

## NEW MEXICO

**Albuquerque**
Beach, Arthur O'Neal
Cargo, David Francis
Caruso, Mark John
Crollett, Richard Jacques
Dorr, Roderick A.
Duarte, Leroy Wilson
Martinez, David Brian
Moughan, Peter Richard, Jr.
Patterson, Cynthia J.
Ricks, J. Brent
Romero, Jeff
Thiel, Albert Nicholas, Jr.
Wertheim, John V.
Word, Terry Mullins
**Carlsbad**
Diamond, Jeffrey Brian
**Clovis**
Doerr, Stephen
**Deming**
Sherman, Frederick Hood
Turner, Robert F.
**Farmington**
Moeller, Floyd Douglas
Titus, Victor Allen
**Hobbs**
Stout, Lowell
**Las Cruces**
Palacios, Pedro Pablo
**Roswell**
Haines, Thomas David, Jr.
Kraft, Richard Lee
Romero, Freddie Joseph
**Santa Fe**
Brannen, Jeffrey Richard
Casey, Patrick Anthony
Culbert, Peter Van Horn
Farber, Steven Glenn
Marlowe, Mary Louise
McClaugherty, Joe L.
Murphy, Dennis Patrick
Zorie, Stephanie Marie

## NEW YORK

**Albany**
Case, Forrest N., Jr.
Collins, George Vincent, III
Donohue, Brian E.
Dulin, Thomas N.
Fanciullo, William Patrick
Laird, Edward DeHart, Jr.
Linnan, James Daniel
Napierski, Eugene Edward
Powers, John Kieran
Santola, Daniel Ralph
Whalen, Colleen Hiser
**Amherst**
Vinal, Jeanne Marie
**Astoria**
Bender, Michael Seth
**Attica**
Dadd, Margaret Baggot
**Baldwin**
Verdirame, Peter J.
**Bellmore**
Sachs, Eric
**Bethpage**
Carlen, Leon C.
Sanna, Richard Jeffrey
**Binghamton**
Gates, Gregory Ansel
Gouldin, David Millen
Kramer, Philip Joseph
**Bronx**
Aris, Joram Jehudah
Fraiden, Norman Arthur
Marchese, Matthew
Verrelli, Anthony Louis
Wolf, Robert Thomas
**Brooklyn**
Blank, Helene E.
Braude, Jacob
Chesley, Stephen Robert
Held, Marc Jason
Martin, Jack
Nuccio, Paul Vincent
Roth, Pamela Susan
**Buffalo**
Behr, Laurence Donald
Bermingham, Joseph Daniel
Canale, John F.
Curran, Patrick Barton
Feuerstein, Alan Ricky
Freedman, Bernard Benjamin
Garvey, James Anthony
Goldberg, Neil A.
Goldstein, Brian Alan
Goldstein, Bruce A.
Hayes, J. Michael
Jasen, Matthew Joseph
Kieffer, James Marshall
Kirkpatrick, James W.
Murphy, Edward J., III
Possé, Olga Alicia
Ross, Christopher Theodore
Sampson, John David
Smith, Carrie Lynette
Stachowski, Michael Joseph
Szanyi, Kevin Andrew
Vinal, Gregory Michael
**Caledonia**
Litteer, Harold Hunter, Jr.
**Camillus**
Endieveri, Anthony Frank
**Carle Place**
Mulhern, Edwin Joseph
Seiden, Steven Jay
**Chestnut Ridge**
Burns, Richard Owen
**Dansville**
Vogel, John Walter
**De Witt**
Dunn, Mark L.
**Delhi**
Hamilton, John Thomas, Jr.
Schimmerling, Thomas Emile
**Delmar**
Cavanaugh, John Joseph, Jr.
**Dunkirk**
Spann, James J., Jr.
**East Meadow**
Weiss, Adam William
**East Northport**
Juliano, John Louis
**Elma**
Markello, Jeffrey Philip
**Elmira**
Daubner, Susan Moore
**Elmsford**
Mevec, Edward Robert
**Fairport**
Capanna, Paloma A.
**Farmingdale**
O'Brien, Joan Susan
**Flushing**
Bernstein, Barry Selwyn
Gerson, Nancy L.
Ginsberg, Jerome Maurice
Kotcher, Shirley J. W.
Schwartz, Estar Alma
**Forest Hills**
Addabbo, Dominic Lucian
**Garden City**
Beck, Leland S.
Corleto, Raymond Anthony
Hausch, Adrienne Louise Flipse
Licatesi, Anthony Joseph
Ungar, Robert Arthur
**Hauppauge**
Saminsky, Robert L.
**Hempstead**
Furey, James Michael
Kane, Donald Vincent
Raab, Ira Jerry
**Hicksville**
Giuffré, John Joseph
**Highland**
Nardone, Richard
**Holbrook**
Zahn, Daniel Arthur
**Hornell**
Pulos, William Whitaker
**Hudson**
Howard, Andrew Baker
Palmateer, Lee Allen
**Huntington**
DeMartin, Charles Peter
**Islandia**
Buckley, Terrence Patrick
**Ithaca**
Mulvey, Richard Ignatius
**Jericho**
Corso, Frank Mitchell
**Kew Gardens**
Reichel, Aaron Israel
Ross, Robert A.
**Lake Grove**
Melbardis, Wolfgang Alexander
**Lake Success**
Lee, Brian Edward
**Latham**
Brearton, James Joseph
**Lido Beach**
Billauer, Barbara Pfeffer
**Mahopac**
Sequeira, Manuel Alexandre, Jr.
**Malone**
Grue, Thomas Andrew
**Manhasset**
Kashanian, Shahriar
**Mayfield**
McAuliffe, J. Gerard
**Melville**
Schoenfeld, Michael P.
Zamek, Scott
**Miller Place**
Lucivero, Lucretia M.
**Mineola**
Agoglia, Emmet John
Block, Martin
Dachs, Jonathan A.
Fowler, David Thomas
Kelly, Edward Joseph
Kelly, Shawn Paul
Kral, William George
Michelen, Oscar
Plastaras, Thomas Edward
Rubine, Robert Samuel
**N Syracuse**
Kasouf, Joseph Chickery
**New City**
Marcus, Robert Bruce
**New Hartford**
McKennan, John T.
**New Hyde Park**
Ezersky, William Martin
Jensen, Richard Currie
**New York**
Aiello, Robert John
Aquila, Albert
Barton, Roger E.
Beinin, William J.
Bergman, Robert Ira
Bern, Marc Jay
Bloom, Robert Avrum
Bluestone, Andrew Lavoott
Brecker, Jeffrey Ross
Chase, Edward Thornton
Coffinas, Eleni
Cohen, Joshua Robert
Colbert, Douglas Marc
Cooper, Sonja Jean Muller
Corbett, Patrick James
Damashek, Philip Michael
Dankner, Jay Warren
DeWeil, Dawn Susan
Edelman, Paul Sterling
Faillace, Charles Kenneth
Gallagher, Timothy D.
Garfield, Martin Richard
Gillikin, Virginia
Gilman, Scott
Ginsberg, Robert Michael
Gioiella, Russell Michael
Goldsmith, Gerald P.
Graham, Jesse Japhet, II
Green, Eric Howard
Gross, Ari Michael
Grunewald, Raymond Bernhard
Gulino, Frank
Gurfein, Richard Alan
Habian, Bruce George
Hanover, Richard
Hernandez, Jacqueline Charmaine
Hirschhorn, Herbert Herman
Huston, Barry Scott
Issler, Harry
Jacobowitz, Harold Saul
Kamaiko, Laurie Ann
Kelmachter, Leslie Debra
Kilsch, Gunther H.
Koerner, Gregory O.
Kushel, Glenn Elliot
Lantier, Brendan John
LeBlang, Skip Alan
Leiman, Eugene A.
Lesman, Michael Steven
Lesser, William Melville
Lewis, David Robert
Livingston, Judith A.
Loscalzo, Anthony Joseph
Lowenbraun, Solomon M.
Lustig, David Carl, III
Mackauf, Stephen Henry
Marber, Paul Andrew
McGrane, Virginia Laura
McGrath, Christopher Thomas
McMahon, Dennis C.
Mermelstein, Edward A.
Moran, Edward Kevin
Morris, John E.
Motola, David Henry
Nemerov, Jeffrey Arnold
Nevins, Arthur Gerard, Jr.
North, Steven Edward
O'Brien, John Graham
O'Connell, Margaret Sullivan
O'Leary, Michael Thomas
Orr, Dennis Patrick
Pappas, Chris
Pecoraro, Steven John
Rejan, Jeffrey Neil
Relkin, Ellen
Ritter, Ann L.
Romano, Edgar Ness
Rosenzweig, Theodore B.
Ruger, James Richard
Russotti, Philip Anthony
Salvan, Sherwood Allen
Schiesel, Steven
Schreffler, Neil Franklin
Schwartz, Leonard
Scialabba, Donald Joseph
Seitelman, Mark Elias
Shapiro, Stanley K.
Singer, Jeffrey
Smiley, Guy Ian
Strober, Eric Saul
Subin, Florence
Tessler, Robert Louis
Watson, Kipp Elliott
Weinstock, Gregg D.
Weiser, Martin Jay
Weitz, Harvey
Wohl, Ronald Gene
**Newburgh**
Milligram, Steven Irwin
Reisenman, Debra Jill
**Oneonta**
Harlem, Richard Andrew
Konstanty, James E.
Rothermel, Richard Allan
Scarzafava, John Francis
**Ossining**
Daly, William Joseph
**Patchogue**
Feuer, Paul Robert
Tona, Thomas
Weisberg, David Charles
**Pittsford**
Finucane, Leo Gerard
**Pleasant Valley**
Vasti, Thomas Francis, III
**Poughkeepsie**
Kranis, Michael David
LaRose, Keith Vernon
Sproat, Christine A.
**Purchase**
Kolbrener, Jonathan
**Rego Park**
Feijoo, John
**Rhinebeck**
Melley, Steven Michael
**Rochester**
Dolin, Lonny H.
Fiandach, Edward Louis
Geiger, Alexander
Heyman, Sidney
Jacobson, Peter A.
Kelly, Paul Donald
Law, Michael R.
Massare, Edward John
Micca, Louis Joseph
Nesser, Joseph George
Regan, John Manning, Jr.
Schwarz, Stephen George
Thomas, Jacqueline Marie
Trevett, Thomas Neil
**Rome**
Domenico, Calvin J., Jr.
**S Richmond Hl**
Goldsmith, Michael Lawrence
**Salamanca**
Brady, Thomas Carl
**Saratoga Springs**
Dorsey, James Baker
**Schenectady**
DeLorenzo, Paul E.
Galvin, Christine M.
Kouray, Athena C.
Taub, Eli Irwin
**Smithtown**
Spellman, Thomas Joseph, Jr.
**South Richmond Hill**
Scheich, John F.
**Syracuse**
Bogart, William Harry
Bottar, Anthony Samuel
Butler, John Edward
Cherundolo, John Charles
Copani, Anthony Frank
Frank, Jennifer Karen
Greene, Arthur M.
Johnson, Eric Gates
King, Bernard T.
Mathews, Daniel Francis, III
McGinty, Elizabeth Caryl
Melnicoff, Joel Niesen
Rivette, Francis Robert
Rothschild, Martin Jay
Zimmerman, Aaron Mark
**Troy**
Finkel, Sanford Norman
Frost, Jerome Kenneth
Jones, E. Stewart, Jr.
**Tupper Lake**
Hayes, Jeremiah Michael
**Valley Stream**
Isaacs, Leonard Bernard

**West Hempstead**
Klebanoff, Stanley Milton
**White Plains**
D'Aloise, Lawrence T., Jr.
Downes, James J.
Fufidio, George E.
Kalish, Daniel A.
Keane, Thomas J.
Levine, Steven Jon
Morell, Philip M.
Nesci, Vincent Peter
Nolletti, James Joseph
Ryan, Robert Davis
**White Stone**
Uris, Alan M.
**Yonkers**
Connors, James Patrick

## NORTH CAROLINA

**Asheville**
Chidnese, Patrick N.
Gantt, David
Leake, Larry Bruce
**Blowing Rock**
Corlett, Edward Stanley, III
**Burnsville**
Howell, Dennis Lee
**Chapel Hill**
Zoffer, David B.
**Charlotte**
Brackett, Martin Luther, Jr.
Brotherton, Allen C.
Campbell, Clair Gilliland
Eve, Robert Michael, Jr.
Harris, Hugh Stanley, Jr.
Holden, C. Byron
Klein, Paul Ira
Wyatt, James Frank, III
**Durham**
Cheek, Lewis Alexander
Fisher, Stewart Wayne
King, William Oliver
Loflin, Thomas Franklin, III
Markham, Charles Buchanan
**Fayetteville**
Brady, B(arbara) Dianne
Britton, Rebecca Johnson
Townsend, William Jackson
**Greensboro**
Clark, David McKenzie
Donaldson, Arthur Joseph
Gabriel, Richard Weisner
Harrington, Ellis Jackson, Jr.
Koonce, Neil Wright
**Greenville**
Clark, John Graham, III
Hopf, James Fredrik
Romary, Peter John Michael
**Hickory**
Ingle, John David
**High Point**
Aldridge, Bryant Taylor, Jr.
Baker, Walter Wray, Jr.
Floyd, Kimberly Hayes
**Jamestown**
Schmitt, William Allen
**Marion**
Burgin, Charles Edward
**New Bern**
Kellum, Norman Bryant, Jr.
**Oxford**
Burnette, James Thomas
**Pittsboro**
Hubbard, Thomas Edwin (Tim Hubbard)
**Raleigh**
Becton, Charles L.
Hunter, Richard Samford, Jr.
Madden, John Dale
Millberg, John C.
Robinson, William C.
Shyllon, Prince E.N.
Suhr, Paul Augustine
Teague, Charles Woodrow
**Rockingham**
Futrell, Stephan Ray
**Roxboro**
King, Ronnie Patterson
**Smithfield**
Schulz, Bradley Nicholas
**Tarboro**
O'Malley, Susan Marie
**Wilmington**
Seagle, J. Harold
**Winston Salem**
Durham, Richard Monroe
Early, James H., Jr.
Kelly, James Howard, Jr.

## NORTH DAKOTA

**Bismarck**
Gilbertson, Joel Warren
Harms, Robert Wayne
Strutz, William A.
**Dickinson**
Ficek, Vince H.
Greenwood, Dann E.
Greenwood, Mark Lawrence
**Grand Forks**
Arnason, Joel Frederick
Morley, Patrick Robert
Seaworth, Mary Ellen

## OHIO

**Akron**
Cody, Daniel Schaffner
Djordjevic, Michael M.
Glinsek, Gerald John
Parker, Christopher Lee
Schrader, Alfred Eugene
Weitendorf, Kurt Robert
**Aurora**
Hermann, Philip J.
**Batavia**
Ostendarp, Gary David
**Beachwood**
Sobel, Jonathan F.
**Beavercreek**
Stadnicar, Joseph William
**Bellevue**
Smith, Ronald R.
**Bowling Green**
Hanna, Martin Shad
**Bucyrus**
McBride, Gordon Scott
**Canton**
Firestone, Eric A.
Huryn, Christopher Michael
**Celina**
Faber, Keith L.
**Chillicothe**
Boulger, William Charles
**Cincinnati**
Braden, Roger Newman
Chesley, Stanley Morris
Cohen, Edward
Davis, Robert Lawrence
Finnigan, John Julius, Jr.
Gehrig, Michael Ford
Goldberg, John A.
Holschuh, John David, Jr.
Kamp, David Paul
Lutz, James Gurney
Lydon, Deborah Ruth
Mara, Timothy Gerald
Morrisroe, Donald Patrick
Neltner, Michael Martin
Scacchetti, David J.
Stalf, Dale Anthony
Waite, Jeffrey C.
Whitaker, Glenn Virgil
Woodside, Frank C., III
**Cleveland**
Alcox, Patrick Joseph
Bacon, Brett Kermit
Birne, Kenneth Andrew
Climaco, Michael Louis
Cohn, Mark Barry
Condeni, Joseph Anthony
DeVan, Mark Roy
Duncan, Ed Eugene
Gerlack, Lisa Marie
Goldberg, James R.
Gruhin, Michael H.
Havens, Hunter Scott
Hofelich, James Albert
Incorvaia, Santo Thomas
Jeffers, John William
Krawczak, Kenneth Francis
Liber, John (Douglas)
Lowe, James Allison
Maher, Edward Joseph
Marvar, Raymond James
Nyerges, George Ladislaus
O'Neill, Mark
Piscitelli, Frank E., Jr.
Pohl, Michael A.
Rua, M. Jane
Sanislo, Paul Steve
Schloss, John P.
Spero, Keith Erwin
Szaller, James Francis
Tosti, Jeanne Marie
Weinberger, Peter Henry
Wukovich, George Nicholas
Zukerman, Larry William
**Columbus**
Alton, John Marshall
Arnold, Gayle Edward
Ayers, James Cordon
Barclay, Craig Douglas
Barnes, Belinda Sue
Belton, John Thomas
Binning, J. Boyd
Chappelear, Stephen Eric
Donahey, Richard Sterling, Jr.
Juhola, Michael Duane
Kilgore, Terry Lee
Maloon, Jerry L.
Mancuso, Anthony O.
Mann, William Craig
Martin, Paige Arlene
Mendel, David Phillip
Nemeth, John Charles
Plymale, Ronald E.
Radnor, Alan T.
Ray, Frank Allen
Scott, David Matthew
Silverman, Perry Raynard
Sprader, Bobbie S.
Starkoff, Alan Gary
Thompson, Harold Lee
Todaro, Frank Edward
Tripp, Thomas Neal
Tyack, Thomas Michael
Vickery, Byron Lamar
Wolery, Don Edward
Wonnell, Harold Edward
Yezzel, Keith Arthur
**Dayton**
Baggott, Thomas McCann
Cole, Dana Keith
Davis, G(iles) Jack
Krebs, Leo Francis
Mues, Robert Leighton
Posey, Terry Wayne
Rudwall, David Fuller
Salyer, David Ronald
Schneble, Alfred William, III
Segreti, Albert Mark, Jr.
Sutton, Richard Stansbury
Tucker, Michael Lane
**East Liverpool**
Davis, William J.
**Elyria**
Kovacs, John Joseph
**Findlay**
Kentris, George Lawrence
**Fremont**
Albrechta, Joseph Francis
**Hamilton**
Bressler, H.J.
Gattermeyer, Daniel J.
**Independence**
Rutter, Robert Paul
**Jackson**
Lewis, Richard M.
**Lakewood**
Traci, Donald Philip
**Lebanon**
Diehl, Thomas James
**Lima**
Jacobs, Ann Elizabeth
**Lorain**
Levin, Arnold Sampson
**Mansfield**
Carto, David Draffan
**Miamisburg**
Anzman, Mark Charles
**Middletown**
Allen, Patrick William
**New Philadelphia**
Mastin, Scott Joseph
**Newark**
Meyer, Christopher Richard
**Poland**
Vasvari, Thomas M.
**Portsmouth**
Gerlach, Franklin Theodore
**Ravenna**
Giulitto, Paula Christine
**Sandusky**
Bailey, K. Ronald
**Springfield**
Lagos, James Harry
**Steubenville**
Noble, Frank Wesley, Jr.
**Toledo**
Barone, Guy T.
Rice, Kollin Lawrence
St. Clair, Donald David
Skiver, Stephen Allen
Tuschman, James Marshall
**Troy**
Utrecht, James David
**Twinsburg**
Carr, Adam E.
**Warren**
Kafantaris, George Nicholas
Newendop, Paul William
Swauger, Terry Allen
White, Martin Fred
**Westerville**
Lancione, Bernard Gabe
**Westlake**
Kolick, Daniel Joseph
**Xenia**
Chappars, Timothy Stephen
**Youngstown**
Ausnehmer, John Edward
Blair, Richard Bryson
Carlin, Clair Myron
Jeren, John Anthony, Jr.

## OKLAHOMA

**Edmond**
Ryan, Gregory J.
**Enid**
McNaughton, Alexander Bryant
**Midwest City**
Howell, James F.
**Mustang**
Denton, Michael David, Jr.
**Norman**
Chesley, Patrick J.
Fairbanks, Robert Alvin
McFall, Sara Weer
**Oklahoma City**
Babb, Donald Lynn
Cunningham, Ryan Yerger
Ferguson, Steven E.
Fitch, Brent E.
Henry, David Patrick
Hughes, Carl Douglas
Kouri, Harry J., III
Lindsey, Lori Dawn
Margo, Robert Cravens
Simpson, Michael Wayne
Zuhdi, Nabil (Bill)
**Ponca City**
Northcutt, Clarence Dewey
**Sapulpa**
Lane, Tom Cornelius
**Tulsa**
Atkinson, Michael Pearce
Beustring, Glenn Roland
Eldridge, Richard Mark
Riggs, M. David
Sterling, Timothy F.
Sutton, Jonathan Mark

## OREGON

**Albany**
Kryger, Jon David
**Bend**
Erwin, Lawrence Warde
**Central Point**
Richardson, Dennis Michael
**Clackamas**
Gibson, K(enneth) William
**Coquille**
Lounsbury, Steven Richard
**Corvallis**
Ringo, Robert Gribble
**Eugene**
Carlson, Charles David
Cooper, Michael Lee
Halpern, John (Michael), Jr.
Hutchinson, Stephen Aloysius
**Grants Pass**
Lansing, Mark Alexander
**Hillsboro**
Tyner, John Joseph, III
**Lincoln City**
Elliott, Scott
**Medford**
Mansfield, William Amos
**Newport**
Greco, Guy Benjamin
Strever, Kevin Kirk
**Ontario**
Rader, Diane Cecile
**Portland**
Beshears, Charles Daniel, III
Bovarnick, Paul Simon
Hart, John Edward
Hendricks, Stephen
Hummel, Holly Jane
Kennedy, Jack Leland
Kennedy, Michael Dean
Reisman, Joanne
Rieke, Forrest Neill
Robinowitz, Charles
Ruess, Brian Knight
Savage, John William
Schuster, Philip Frederick, II
Shinn, Michael Robert
Sokol, Larry Nides
Swanson, Leslie Martin, Jr.
Swider, Robert Arthur
Troutwine, Gayle Leone
**Redmond**
Welborn, Gordon Lee
**Salem**
Bauer, Keith Jay
Hittle, David William
Pacheco, Michael Mauro
Roy, Matthew Lansing
Walsh, Richard Michael
**Springfield**
Wilson, Virgil James, III
**Tigard**
Lowry, David Burton

## PENNSYLVANIA

**Allentown**
Altemose, Mark Kenneth
**Altoona**
Serbin, Richard Martin
**Bala Cynwyd**
Covner, Ellen B.
Olley, Michael Joseph
**Beaver**
Petrush, John Joseph
**Bethel Park**
Bobrowsky, Kim Russell
**Birchrunville**
McClean, James Allen, Jr.
**Butler**
Stepanian, Leo McElligott
**Clarion**
Pope, Henry Ray, Jr.
**Conway**
Krebs, Robert Alan
**Donora**
Miller, David A.
**Doylestown**
Hoopes, Robert Patrick
Karsch, Jay Harris
**Drexel Hill**
West, Kenneth Edward
**Easton**
Brown, Robert Carroll
**Elkins Park**
Nemeroff, Robert Howard
**Erie**
Bernard, Bruce William
Williams, Dennis Vaughn
Wingerter, John Raymond
**Exton**
Amaral Ryan, Rosa Olinda
**Glenside**
Mellon, Thomas S.
**Harrisburg**
Angino, Richard Carmen
Cunningham, Jordan Daniel
Hafer, Joseph Page
Kaylor, Cynthia Anne
Lighty, Fredrick W.
Mark, Timothy Ivan
McGuire, Jeffrey Thomas
Melillo, Joseph Michael
Sadlock, Richard Alan
Stefanon, Anthony
**Hazleton**
Schiavo, Pasco Louis
**Indiana**
Bell, Paul Anthony, II
Kauffman, Thomas Andrew
**Jenkintown**
McNally, John Bernard
Worthington, Sandra Boulton
**Johnstown**
Glosser, William Louis
**King Of Prussia**
Dorfman, Frederick Niles
**Kittanning**
Petrosky, Robert
**Lancaster**
Hall, Thomas W.
Roda, Joseph Francis
Zimmerman, D(onald) Patrick
**Langhorne**
Lynch, James Edward
**Lansdale**
Kline, David Benjamin
**Lebanon**
Keys, Robert Barr, Jr.
**Leola**
Eaby, Christian Earl
**Lock Haven**
Miceli, Frank S.
Rosamilia, Charles R.
**Mc Keesport**
Kessler, Steven Fisher
**Meadville**
Youngs, Christopher Jay
**Media**
Berman, Bernard Mayer
Blake, David Gordon
D'Amico, Andrew J.
DiOrio, Robert Michael
Farber, Howard
Firkser, Robert M.
Mackrides, William Charles
Malloy, Michael Joseph
Meloni, Kathryn Ann
Tomlinson, Herbert Weston
**Middletown**
Pannebaker, James Boyd
**Monongahela**
Black, Blane Alan
**Narberth**
Metter, Ronald Elliot
**New Castle**
Babb, Alfred Ward
Natale, Frank Anthony, II
Sapienza, Charles Pat, Jr.
**New Kensington**
Joseph, Daniel
**Newtown**
Kardos, Mel D.
Kopil, Thomas Edward
**Norristown**
Brophy, Thomas Andrew
Oliver, James John
Scheffler, Stuart Jay
**Penns Park**
Itkoff, David F.
**Philadelphia**
Aris, John Lynnwood
Armenti, Joseph Rocco
Beasley, James Edwin
Beech, Kristen Lee
Binder, David Franklin
Blumstein, Edward
Brigham, Martin Kenneth
Buccino, Ernest John, Jr.
Carpey, Stuart A.
Chiacchiere, Mark Dominic
Clinton, Michael W.
Cohen, Jonathan Morley
Coleman, Robert J.
Collings, Robert L.
Connor, Joseph Patrick, III
Feinberg, Jack E.
German, Edward Cecil
Ginsberg, David M.
Goldberg, Joseph
Goldberg, Marvin Allen
Gray, Edward Anthony
Hanselmann, Fredrick Charles
Heslin, Gary Phillip
Horn, Robert F.
Kormes, John Winston
Kunnel, Joseph Mathew
Lawn, Timothy Regis
Lieberman, Joel M.
Lipshutz, Robert Murray
Litt, H. Allen
Martillotti, Gerard Jacob
Martin-Boyan, Annemarie
McBride, James Francis
McEldrew, James Joseph, III
McHugh, James Joseph
Messa, Joseph Louis, Jr.
Miller, Leslie Anne
Mishkin, Jeremy David
Monheit, Herbert
Mundy, James Francis
Ominsky, Alan Jay
Pace, Samuel J., Jr.
Parry, William DeWitt
Patrick, Paula Antoinette
Patton, Peter Mark
Perry, Sherryl Rosenbaum
Reiff, Jeffrey Marc
Reilly, Marie Sambor
Rhoads, Nancy Glenn
Rosenbaum, Marcia F.
Rosenthal, Brian David
Samuel, Ralph David
Seidel, Richard Stephen
Spivack, Gerald W.
Topel, David Louis
**Pipersville**
Carr, Stephen Kerry
**Pittsburgh**
Bass, John A.
Beachler, Edwin Harry, III
Bellisario, Domenic Anthony
Belliveau, James Dennis
Bochicchio, Vito Salvatore
Braszo, John J.
Breault, Theodore Edward
Cohen, Robert (Avram)
Conlon, Raymond Joseph
Crawford, Karen Shichman
Esposito, Cheryl Lynne
Fieschko, Joseph Edward, Jr.
Gigler, Daniel Richard
Greene, Korry Alden
Hurnyak, Christina Kaiser
Leonard, Arthur J.
Matzus, Jason Eric
McKenzie, Thomas James
Meyers, Jerry Ivan
Miller, James Robert
Mills, Edward James
Perry, Jon Robert
Schmidt, Edward Craig
Tarasi, Louis Michael, Jr.
Terra, Sharon Ecker
Todd, Stephan Kent
Tully, Bernard Michael
Wertkin, Robin Stuart
Wise, Roger Lambert
Zittrain, Lester Eugene
**Plymouth Meeting**
Bracaglia, Thomas Paul
**Pottsville**
Tamulonis, Frank Louis, Jr.
**Punxsutawney**
Lorenzo, Nicholas Francis, Jr.
**Rydal**
Friedman, Ralph David
**Scranton**
Cowley, Michael C.
O'Malley, Todd J.
Wenzel, Francis George, Jr.
Wilson, Charles Frank
**Sewickley**
Grigsby, Robert S.
**Southampton**
Benz, William J.
**Spring City**
Mayerson, Hy
**State College**
Nollau, Lee Gordon
**Sunbury**
Saylor, Charles Horace
**Swarthmore**
Ullman, Roger Roland
**Tannersville**
Love, Mark Steven
**Trevose**
Fanning, Eleanor

McEvilly, James Patrick, Jr.
**Uniontown**
Leskinen, Steve Peter
**Valley Forge**
Corchin, Mark Alan
**Warendale**
Jacobs, Richard Louis
**Warminster**
Corr, Martin Joseph
**Warrendale**
Micale, Frank Jude
**Washington**
Curran, M(ichael) Scot
Mitchell, Clark A.
Richman, Stephen I.
**Wayne**
Griffith, Edward, II
**White Oak**
Pribanic, Victor Hunter
**Wilkes Barre**
Lach, Joseph Andrew
**Williamsport**
Dohrmann, Jeffrey Charles
Ertel, Allen Edward
**Yardley**
Lieberson, Jay B.
**York**
Markowitz, Lewis Harrison
Pell, Daniel Max

## RHODE ISLAND

**Cranston**
Cervone, Anthony Louis
Loffredo, Pasco Frank
**Pawtucket**
Marran, Joseph Edward, Jr.
Vacca, Anthony
**Providence**
Cosentino, Robert J(ohn)
Demopulos, Harold William
Gianfrancesco, Anthony Joseph
Glavin, Kevin Charles
Jones, Lauren Evans
Kacir, Barbara Brattin
Kersh, DeWitte Talmadge, Jr.
McElroy, Michael Robert
Miller, Samuel Aaron
Resmini, Ronald Joseph
Tammelleo, A. David
**West Warwick**
Pollock, Bruce Gerald
**Woonsocket**
Koutsogiane, Phillip Charles

## SOUTH CAROLINA

**Aiken**
Pearce, Richard Lee
**Anderson**
Krause, Steven Michael
**Charleston**
Bell, James Lee
Bluestein, S. Scott
Hahn, H. Blair
Helms, William Collier, III
Hood, Robert Holmes
Kahn, Ellis Irvin
Laddaga, Beth Jane
Patrick, Charles William, Jr.
Spitz, Hugo Max
Swope, Denise Grainger
Thompson, Joseph Durant
Young, Joseph Rutledge, Jr.
**Columbia**
Blanton, Hoover Clarence
Cooper, Robert Gordon
Harvey, Jonathan Matthew
Jones, Hartwell Kelley, Jr.
Kelly, D. Michael
Meyer, Patricia R.
Richardson, Donald V.
**Greenville**
Christian, Warren Harold, Jr.
Christophillis, Constantine S.
Hagood, William Milliken, III
Johnson, Matthew Kinard
Talley, Michael Frank
**Hampton**
Runyan, Charles Alan
**Hartsville**
Blake, Daniel L.
**Hilton Head Island**
Carter, Stephen Edward
McKay, John Judson, Jr.
**Kingstree**
McFadden, Helen Tyler
**Langley**
Bell, Robert Morrall
**Myrtle Beach**
Breen, David Hart
**N Charleston**
Joye, Mark Christopher
Wigger, Jarrel L.
**North Myrtle Beach**
Wylie, Walter Jay
**Pawleys Island**
Daniel, J. Reese
**Spartanburg**
Anthony, Kenneth C., Jr.
**Summerville**
Hardee-Thomas, Marva A.
**Walterboro**
Harvin, L(ucius) Scott
**West Columbia**
Applegate, William Russell
**Winnsboro**
Goode, Kenneth George

## SOUTH DAKOTA

**Rapid City**
Connot, Mark Jeffrey
**Sioux Falls**
Clapper, Jeffrey Curtis
Orr, Rick W.
**Webster**
Burke, John William

## TENNESSEE

**Bristol**
Hillman, Shelton B., Jr.
Massengill, Myers Newton
Slaughter, Frank L., Jr.
**Chattanooga**
Adams, Morgan Goodpasture
Burnette, Harry Forbes
Cirina, Angela Marie
Dennis, Tricia I.
James, Stuart Fawcett
Johnson, John Walter, III
Newton, Michael David
Ragan, Charles Oliver, Jr.
Thompson, Neal Lewis
**Etowah**
Parker, Eugene LeRoy, III
**Greeneville**
Welch, Lawrence Andrew, Jr.
Wright, Thomas Jon
**Jackson**
Drew, Gayden, IV
Nicks, Paul Todd
Phillips, Marty Roy
**Johnson City**
King, Robert Lewis
Meade, Evan McDaniel
**Kingsport**
Flanary, James Lee
**Knoxville**
Cremins, William Carroll
Fox, James Erwin
Houser, Timothy Curtis
Johnson, Steven Boyd
London, James Harry
Oberman, Steven
Ownby, Jere Franklin, III
Routh, John William
Vines, William Dorsey
Waite, David Ernest
White, Edward Gibson, II
**Lookout Mountain**
Leitner, Paul Revere
**Memphis**
Branson, John R.
Davis, Earl Prichard (Pat Davis)
Dykes, Lillian Elise Levy
Friedman, Robert Michael
Grubb, Steven Cochran
Harvey, Albert C.
Lait, Hayden David
McDaniel, Mark Steven
Pfrommer, Michael Paul
Rice, George Lawrence, III (Larry Rice)
Veazey, Gary Eugene
Wilder, James Sampson, III
**Nashville**
Barrow, Clisby Hall
Bramlett, Paul Kent
Butler, Jack A.
Cantrell, Luther E., Jr.
Clayton, Daniel Louis
Cooney, Charles Hayes
Day, John Arthur
Freeman, James Atticus, III
Hildebrand, Donald Dean
Hunt, Sean Antone
Lane, William Arthur
Midgett, James Clayton, Jr.
Parker, Mary Ann
Youngblood, Elaine Michele
**Newport**
Bell, John Alton
**Paris**
Rose, Todd Alan
**Rogersville**
Skelton, Mark Albert
**Shelbyville**
Bramlett, Brenda Susan
**Springfield**
Wilks, Larry Dean
**Trenton**
Harrell, Limmie Lee, Jr.

## TEXAS

**Alvin**
Hewitt, Otto D., III
**Amarillo**
Isern, Kevin Anthony
Lara, Art B., Jr.
**Arlington**
Hubby, Bert Gorman
Jensen, John Robert
Smythe, Peter Christian
**Austin**
Allison, James Purney
Barnes, Natasha Lynn
Brothers, D. Douglas
Byrd, Linward Tonnett
Connolly, Carla Garcia
Cortez, Hernan Glenn
Davis, David Murrel
Furman, James Housley
Gibbins, Bob
Hager, Julie-Ann
Mallios, George James
Pena, Richard
Pluymen, Bert W.
Probus, Michael Maurice, Jr.
Smith, Peyton Noble
Staelin, Earl Hudson
**Baytown**
Linebaugh, Daniel Bruce
**Beaumont**
Black, Robert Allen
Bragg, J. J.
Dowell, James Dale
Dryden, Woodson E.
Ferguson, Paul F., Jr.
Johnson, Leanne
Newton, John Wharton, III
Scofield, Louis M., Jr.
Sutton, Brian Dale
Thomas, Brett Scott
**Bellaire**
Soffar, William Douglas
**Belton**
Sleeth, David Thompson
**Boerne**
Deegear, James Otis, III
**Brownsville**
Cowen, Michael Raphael
**Brownwood**
Steele, Todd Bennett
**Bryan**
Goss, Jay Bryan
**Burleson**
Johnstone, Deborah Blackmon
**Canton**
Sanders, Bobby Lee
**College Station**
Borman, Channa Erin
Hoelscher, Michael Ray
**Corpus Christi**
Carnahan, Robert Narvell
Fancher, Rick
Laws, Gordon Derby
Leon, Rolando Luis
Martinez, Diana Marie
Miller, Carroll Gerard, Jr. (Gerry Miller)
**Corsicana**
Sodd, Glenn
**Dallas**
Balido, Carlos A.
Biermacher, Kenneth Wayne
Booth, John W. (Bill Booth)
Brandt, Edward Newman
Branson, Debbie Dudley
Branson, Frank Leslie, III
Brown, James Earle
Burns, Sandra
Davis, Derek Shane
Doyle, Mark Anthony
Dunnill, William Connor
Ellis, Alfred Wright (Al Ellis)
Girards, James Edward
Glazer, Rachelle Hoffman
Goodwin, R. Brad
Gunnstaks, C. Luke
Harkey, John D., Jr.
Hawkins, Scott Alexis
Henvey, John William
Holmes, James Hill, III
Howie, John Robert
Johnston, Coyt Randal
Kemp, Jeffrey Winslow
Lenox, Roger Shawn
Malouf, Edward Wayne
McCreary, David Sean
McCrory, Tom M., III
McKennon, Richard Otey
Mighell, Kenneth John
Miller, Deborah Slye
Ravji, Aamer
Roberts, Steven Dillon
Siegel, Mark Jordan
Smith, Larry Francis
Spear, James Hodges
Stinnett, Mark Allan
Sutherland, Shirley M.
Terry, David William
Turley, Linda
Weitzel, J. Dennis
Wileman, George Robert
**De Soto**
Boyanton, Janet Shafer
**Diboll**
Moss, Logan Vansen
**Edinburg**
Peña, Aaron, Jr.
**El Paso**
Boyaki, Walter L.
Dickey, John M.
Fogel, Lark House
Gordon, Norman James
Marshall, Richard Treeger
Moffeit, Michael Paul
Oaxaca, Juan Roberto
Provenghi, Ruggero
Torkildson, Thomas Miles
Villalobos, Raul
**Fort Worth**
Ablon, Karen Herrick
Berenson, William Keith
Brender, Art
Chappell, David Franklin
Cleveland, Joseph F., Jr.
Cottongame, W. Brice
Dent, Edward Dwain
Dushman, Lowell Edward
Fischel, Robert Oscar
Griffith, Richard Lattimore
Harcrow, E. Earl
Hayes, Larry B.
Jones, Gregory G.
Lemons, Keith David
Moore, Randall D.
Stewart, Mark Steven
Streck, Frederick Louis, III
Wagner, James Peyton
Wallach, David Michael
Westfall, Gregory Burke
**Friendswood**
Youngdahl, Jay Thomas
**Galveston**
Kilgore, Jeffrey Harper
Neves, Kerry Lane
**Grapevine**
Glenn, David Milton
**Houston**
Agosto, Benny, Jr.
Berg, David Howard
Berger, Barry Stuart
Boswell, John Howard
Brinson, Gay Creswell, Jr.
Butler, Randall Edward
Caddy, Michael Douglas
Carver, Teresa Ann
Chapman, Patricia Gayle
Clawater, Wayne
Coleman, Bryan Douglas
Cooney, James Patrick
Couch, Steve Earl
Countiss, Richard Neil
Crowley, David James
Dampier, Harold Dean, Jr.
Dijkman, Christiana
Ekwem, Robertson M.
Essmyer, Michael Martin
Fisher, Guy G.
Fisher, Wayne
Fitzgerald, William Terry
Fleming, George Matthews
Fox, Jan Woodward
Fromm, Eva Maria
Gonzalez-Lecaroz, J.A.
Griffin, Marilyn Otteman
Haden, Charles McIntyre
Hanson, Jerry Clinton
Harris, Warren Wayne
Heggen, Ivar Nelson
Holloway, Gordon Arthur
Honsaker, Mark Llewellyn
Ivey, Jack Todd
Kientz, Val William
Kline, Allen Haber, Jr.
Knutson, Sam Houston
Krebs, Arno William, Jr.
Lapin, Robert E.
Love, Scott Anthony
Mallia, Michael Patrick
Michael, Charles Joseph
Montgomery, Kendall Charles
Nacol, Mae
Nations, Howard Lynn
Newman, Bobby King
Norman, Richard Eugene
O'Neill, Alice Jane
Ongert, Steven Walter
Pamphilis, Constantine Z.
Pate, Stephen Patrick
Perdue, Jim Mac
Pettiette, Alison Yvonne
Pitts, Gary Benjamin
Raley, John Wesley, III
Riddle, Don Ramon
Roach, Robert Michael, Jr.
Sales, James Bohus
Samuelson, Douglas Allen
Sears, Ross Allen, II
Sitzes, Madeline D'ree Penton
Sorrels, Randall Owen
Spain, H. Daniel
Stephens, Delia Marie Lucky
Sutter, J. Douglas
Tavormina, John William
Toney, William David, II
Valetutto, David Michael
Vickery, Edward Downtain
Walter, Teri A.
**Humble**
Frazier, William Sumpter
**Katy**
Fudge, Edward William
**Longview**
Holmes, Clifton Lee (Scrappy Holmes)
Jones, Christopher Don
McMahon, Mark Preston
Stevens, Scott English
**Lubbock**
Cobb, David Randall
Harrell, Walter Hugh
Teel, Robert E.
Trowers, Teresa Cardenas
Williams, Anthony Jerome
**Mcallen**
Carrera, Victor Manuel
**Mesquite**
Zook, Bill
**Midland**
Fletcher, Richard Royce
**Mount Pleasant**
Woodson, Danny
**New Braunfels**
Clark, Mark Adrian
**Odessa**
Hendrick, Benard Calvin, VII
Wilson, Kevin Lang
**Paris**
Standifer, Rick M.
**Pecos**
Weinacht, John William
**Plano**
Robinson, Timothy Stephen
**Rockwall**
Holt, Charles William, Jr.
**Rowlett**
Lyon, Robert Charles
**Rusk**
Guy, Steve R.
**San Angelo**
Moeller, Galen Ashley
**San Antonio**
Anderson, Bruce Edwin
Bailey, Maryann George
Branton, James LaVoy
Brito, Maria Teresa
Cabezas-Gil, Rosa M.
Countryman, Thomas Arthur
Farmer, William David
Guevara, Roger
Henry, Peter York
Maisel, Margaret Rose Meyer
Maloney, Marynell
Maloney, Patrick, Sr.
McFarlen, Gerald Dale
Munsinger, Harry L.
Patrick, Dane Herman
Putman, (James) Michael
Rhodes, Jesse Thomas, III
Spence, Craig H.
Trotter, Richard Clayton
Valadez, Robert Allen
Weed, Ray Arnold
Welmaker, Forrest Nolan
Wennermark, John David
**San Benito**
Cordova, Adolfo Enrique
**Sherman**
Harrison, Richard E.
Harrison, Richard Edward
**Spring**
Hearn-Haynes, Theresa
**Sugar Land**
Aldrich, Lovell W(eld)
West, S. Scott
**Sulphur Springs**
Froneberger, Joel Douglas
**Teague**
Smith, William Lafayette, Jr.
**Texarkana**
Potter, David Jimmie
**Tyler**
Ellis, Donald Lee
Green, Jay Nelson
Kent, Don Wayne
Thames, E. Glenn, Jr.
Vickery, Ronald Stephen
**Uvalde**
Kerby, Yale Leland
**Waco**
Hall, Donald Orell
**Wharton**
Roades, John Leslie
**Wichita Falls**
Altman, William Kean
Williams, Steven Mark

## UTAH

**Logan**
Jenkins, James C.
**Midvale**
Johnson, Howard Price
**Ogden**
Gorman, Deirdre A.
Kaufman, Steven Michael
Sullivan, Kevin Patrick
**Provo**
Abbott, Charles Favour
**Salt Lake City**
Anderson, Ross Carl
Atkin, Gary Eugene
Barker, Ronald C.
Dewsnup, Ralph L.
Henriksen, C. Richard, Jr.
Humpherys, LeGrande Rich
Lambert, Dale John
Larson, Bryan A.
Linebaugh, Kent B.
McIntosh, James Albert
Nebeker, Stephen Bennion
Purser, Donald Joseph
Sine, Wesley Franklin
**Sandy**
Bush, Rex Curtis

## VERMONT

**Barre**
FitzGerald, Geoffrey M.
**Berlin**
Craddock, Stephen James
**Brattleboro**
Munzing, Richard Harry
Reid, David G.
**Burlington**
Davis, Christopher Lee
Sartore, John Thornton
**Montpelier**
Bland, Richard Norman
**Rutland**
Dardeck, Stephen A.
Faignant, John Paul
Harnett, Matt
O'Rourke, William Andrew, III
**Saint Albans**
Appel, Kenneth Mark

## VIRGINIA

**Abingdon**
Conway, Berry Leslie, II
**Alexandria**
Battle, Timothy Joseph
Cassell, Richard Emmett
Drennan, Joseph Peter
Green, James Francis
Hirschkop, Philip Jay
Isaacs, Dorothy Ann
Summers, Alicia Lehnes
**Annandale**
Hovis, Robert Houston, III
**Arlington**
Dunham, Frank Willard
Malone, William Grady
McAlevy, Vincent William
**Ashburn**
Gold, George Myron
**Bristol**
Arrington, James Edgar, Jr.
**Charlottesville**
Chandler, Lawrence Bradford, Jr.
Wyatt, Deborah Chasen
**Chesapeake**
Brown, John Wayne
**Chester**
Gray, Charles Robert
**Culpeper**
Dulaney, Richard Alvin
**Danville**
Conway, French Hoge
**Fairfax**
Bardott, Heather Kathleen
Field, David Ellis
Joshi, Michael
Keith, John A.C.
**Falls Church**
Halagao, Avelino Garabiles
Redmond, Robert
Van Oeveren, Edward Lanier
**Fredericksburg**
Allen, Edward Lefebvre
Sheffield, Walter Jervis
**Hampton**
Boester, Robert Alan
Long, Robert Elliott
Smith, Stephen M.
**Hillsville**
McGrady, Jonathan L.
**Hopewell**
Marks, Bryant Mayes, Jr.
**Lynchburg**
Angel, James Joseph
Light, William Randall
**Manassas**
Hammond, Patricia Flood
Hancock, Alton Guy
Locklin, Kevin Lee
**Martinsville**
Frith, Douglas Kyle
Smith, Fred Dempsey, Jr.
**Mc Lean**
Cochran, Stephen Grey

Friedlander, Jerome Peyser, II
Santoni, Cynthia Lee
**Midlothian**
Tuttle, Roger Lewis
**Newport News**
Hankins, Timothy Howard
Hatten, Robert Randolph
Martin, Terrence Keech
Sarfan, Edward I.
Segall, James Arnold
**Norfolk**
Breit, Jeffrey Arnold
Brydges, James Edward
Davis, Terry Hunter, Jr.
Drescher, John Webb
Gorry, James A., III
McCaa, James Cureton, III
Rashkind, Alan Brody
Sutton, Paul Eugene, II
**Norton**
Earls, Donald Edward
Jessee, Roy Mark
Shortridge, Judy Beth
Shortridge, Michael L.
**Petersburg**
Shell, Louis Calvin
**Portsmouth**
Bangel, Herbert K.
Blachman, Michael Joel
Miller, Joseph Aaron
Moody, Willard James, Sr.
Sayer, Darell Lee
**Radford**
Davis, Richard Waters
Turk, James Clinton, Jr.
**Reston**
Bredehoft, Elaine Charlson
Hall, Robert Taggart
**Richmond**
Allen, Wilbur Coleman
Boyd, B(everley) Randolph
Cantor, Irvin Victor
Landin, David Craig
Spahn, Gary Joseph
Tronfeld, Jay
**Roanoke**
Bullington, David Bingham
Hylton, Myles Talbert
Krasnow, Jeffrey Harry
McGarry, Richard Lawrence
Mundy, Gardner Marshall
**Virginia Beach**
Buzard, David Andrew
Hajek, Francis Paul
Schafer, Gerard Thomas Roger
**Woodbridge**
Zauzig, Charles J., III

### WASHINGTON

**Aberdeen**
Brown, James Marston
**Anacortes**
Osborn, Gerald T.
**Bainbridge Is**
Otorowski, Christopher Lee
**Bellevue**
Landau, Felix
**Bellingham**
Anderson, David Bowen
Britain, James Edward
Garrett, Deborra Elizabeth
**Centralia**
Buzzard, Steven Ray
**Clarkston**
Ledgerwood, Thomas L.
**Edmonds**
Conom, Tom Peter
**Everett**
Bacetich, Dominic Lee
Johnson, Richard Bruce
Mestel, Mark David
**Gig Harbor**
Thompson, Ronald Edward
**Hoquiam**
Jones, Garth Lewis
Kahler, Ray William
Kessler, Keith Leon
**Kennewick**
Hames, William Lester
**Longview**
Barlow, John Aden
**Maple Valley**
Engle, David Scott
**Mercer Island**
Gosanko, Gary Nicolas
**Mount Vernon**
Moser, C. Thomas
**Mountlake Terrace**
Field, Kathleen Cottrell
**Olympia**
Gentry, Fred Dee
Hoglund, John Andrew
**Port Orchard**
Becker, Andrew N.
**Renton**
Barber, Mark Edward
Swanson, Arthur Dean
**Richland**
Barr, Carlos Harvey
**Seattle**
Caryl, Michael R.
Clement, William Scott
Cornell, Kenneth Lee
Corning, Nicholas F.
Cunningham, Joel Dean
Davis, Susan Rae
Diamond, Maria Sophia
Field, Harold Basil
Grantham, Gene M.
Jonsson, Jon Marvin
Kline, Daniel Adam
Kohles, David Allan
Kraft, Robert Morris
Lassman, Iro Richard
Loftus, Thomas Daniel
Longfelder, Lawrence Lee
Lundgren, Gail M.
McCoid, Nancy Katherine
Needle, Jeffrey Lowell
Olver, Michael Lynn
Perey, Ron
Peterson, Jan Eric
Richdale, David Allen
Rogers, James Steven
Scott, Brian David
Tinker, Gregg Lynn
Tuffley, Francis Douglas
Warner, Charles Ford
Wayne, Robert Jonathan
Whitehead, James Fred, III
Whitson, Lish
**Spokane**
Bunch, Jeffrey R.
Conrad, Charles Thomas
Harbaugh, Daniel Paul
Luciani, Thomas Richard
Olson, James Warren
Pontarolo, Michael Joseph
Rodrigues, Daryl Anthony
**Tacoma**
Barcus, Benjamin Franklin
Condon, David Bruce
Felker, Robert Stratton
Hostnik, Charles Rivoire
Maichel, Jack J.
Peters, Frank August
Walker, E. Allen
**Walla Walla**
Mitchell, Michael Sherman
Monahan, Richard F.

### WEST VIRGINIA

**Beckley**
Stacy, Don Matthew
**Bluefield**
Evans, Wayne Lewis
Kantor, Isaac Norris
**Charleston**
Brennaman, Sandra Lee
Ciccarello, Arthur T.
Cline, Michael Robert
Crislip, Stephen Ray
Deitzler, Harry G.
Heiskell, Edgar Frank, III
Kiblinger, Cindy Jo
McKowen, Laurie Garrigan
Powell, J(ames) C(orbley)
Zak, Robert Joseph
**Fairmont**
Martino, Gary James
Stanton, George Patrick, Jr.
**Fairview**
Bunner, Patricia Andrea
**Huntington**
Colburn, James Allan
Stapleton, John Warren
**Martinsburg**
Martin, Clarence Eugene, III
Rose, Laura Rauch
Scales, Cinda L.
**Morgantown**
Ringer, Darrell Wayne
**Moundsville**
Artimez, John Edward, Jr.
**Parkersburg**
Powell, Eric Karlton
**Princeton**
Bell, Rebecca Morgan
Griffith, Mary E.
White, Benjamin Ballard, Jr.
**Saint Albans**
McKittrick, William David Parrish
**Weirton**
Makricostas, Dean George
**Wheeling**
Hill, Barry Morton

### WISCONSIN

**Appleton**
Lonergan, Kevin
Murray, John Daniel
**Black River Falls**
Lister, Thomas Edward
**De Pere**
Cerminara, Laura Mary
**Delafield**
Hausman, C. Michael
**Elm Grove**
Miracle, Dale Neil
**Green Bay**
Burnett, Ralph George
Grzeca, Michael (Gerard)
Thompson, John Mortimer
**Janesville**
McDonald, Patrick K.
**Kenosha**
Constant, Terry Lynn
**Madison**
Kelly, T. Christopher
Kuemmel, Joseph Kenneth
McCusker, William LaValle
Schooler, Steven James
Steingass, Susan
**Mauston**
Hollenbeck, Fred Drury
**Menomonie**
Steans, Phillip Michael
**Merrill**
Wulf, William Arthur
**Milwaukee**
Daily, Frank J(erome)
Dentice, M. Angela
Foley, Stephen Patrick
Gray, Sidney
Habush, Robert Lee
Kmiec, Steven Gerard
Leffler, Michael D.
Marquis, William Oscar
McCarty, William Edward
McCormick, David Joseph
Quirk, Michael L.
Reardon, James Patrick
Reis, Werner Adam
Scoptur, Paul Joseph
Slavik, Donald Harlan
Terschan, Frank Robert
Trecek, Timothy Scott
Van Grunsven, Paul Robert
**Monona**
Murphy, Donald James
**Mosinee**
Schira, Diana Rae
**Oshkosh**
Curtis, George Warren
Wilde, William Richard
Zierdt, Alyson Kathleen
**Osseo**
Feltes, Charles Victor
**Portage**
Bennett, David Hinkley
**Racine**
Feil, Frank J., Jr.
Gasiorkiewicz, Eugene Anthony
Rudebusch, Alice Ann
**Rhinelander**
Eckert, Michael Louis
Saari, John William, Jr.
**River Falls**
Krueger, Stuart James
**Salem**
Edenhofer, Carl R.
**Sheboygan**
Darrow, Dwight Daniel
**Waukesha**
Gesler, Alan Edward
Hoefle, Paul Ryan
**Wausau**
Gray, Robert Joseph
Molinaro, Thomas J.
**Wauwatosa**
Bonneson, Paul Garland

### WYOMING

**Casper**
Bostwick, Richard Raymond
Combs, W(illiam) Henry, III
Day, Stuart Reid
Shumate, Roger Eugene
**Cheyenne**
Argeris, George John
Kehl, Larry Bryan
Rosenthal, Michael Bruce
**Gillette**
Zollinger, Thomas Tennant
**Jackson**
Noble, Heather
Shockey, Gary Lee
Spence, Gerald Leonard
**Wheatland**
Hunkins, Raymond Breedlove

### ADDRESS UNPUBLISHED

Alfrey, Thomas Neville
Atwood, Jack McLean
Ayres, Caroline Patricia
Bailey, J. Dennis
Bandy, Jack D.
Bell, Asa Lee, Jr.
Bell, John William
Berman, Richard Bruce
Bondi, Harry Gene
Boone, Richard Winston, Sr.
Bouvier, Marshall Andre
Brown, Jay W.
Burris, Steven Michael
Bush, Robert G., III
Chang, Deborah
Chesnutt, Marcus Wilkes
Coviello, Frank Joseph
Craven, Robert Emmett
D'Agusto, Karen Rose
Davis, Mark Warden
Deane, Ruth M.
DiSalvo, Theodore L.
Dolce, Julia Wagner
Embry, Stephen Creston
Ettinger, Joseph Alan
Evans, G. Anne
Fanning, Nita Kissel
Fekete, George Otto
Feuvrel, Sidney Leo, Jr.
Fleischman, Herman Israel
Gingras, John Richard
Goldberg, Scot Dale
Grady, Maureen Frances
Gregory, Rick Dean
Griffith, Steven Franklin, Sr.
Grutz, James Arthur
Harrington, Donald Francis
Hibbert, David Wilson
Hoffman, Alan Craig
Hogan, Richard Phillips
Horn, Andrew Warren
Hunt, Merrill Roberts
Iannacone, Randolph Frank
Johnson, Richard Wesley
Karp, David Barry
Kellerman, Edwin
Kjos, Victoria Ann
Klausman, Glenn
Klein, Linda Ann
Knuth, Eric Joseph
Krelstein, Ronald Douglas
Lestelle, Terrence Jude
Lippes, Richard James
Locke, John Howard
Maloney, John William
Mann, Michael B.
Massey, Kathleen Marie Oates
McAlhany, Toni Anne
McCallister, John Wilson
McCray, Douglas Gerald
McDonald, Sandra K.
Monsees, Timothy William
Mugridge, David Raymond
Nash, Melvin Samuel
Otten, Wesley Paul
Pafford, John Walter
Phillips, Florence Tsu
Puttock, John Lawrence
Rawls, Frank Macklin
Reminger, Richard Thomas
Rosseel-Jones, Mary Louise
Samalin, Edwin
Sanders, Alan Mark
Schaeffer, Herbert D.
Schwartzman, James Charles
Sheahan, Joseph D.
Shigley, Kenneth Lowell
Siebel, Brian J.
Smith, Patricia A.
Sperry, Martin Jay
Tanenbaum, Jay Harvey
Toms, Frederic E.
Tupper, Kent Phillip
Weeks, Tresi Lea
Weill, (Lige) Harry, Sr.
Wells, Wayne Alton
Wessel, Peter
Wharton, James Carl
White, John Joseph, III
Wynstra, Nancy Ann

## PROBATE. *See also* Estate planning; Taxation, estate.

### UNITED STATES

### ALABAMA

**Athens**
Plunk, John Matthew
**Birmingham**
Cicio, Anthony Lee
Foster, Arthur Key, Jr.
Gamble, Joseph Graham, Jr.
Stuckenschneider, James Theodore, II
Thompson, Charles Amos
**Clayton**
Jackson, Lynn Robertson
**Decatur**
McWhorter, Robert Tweedy, Jr.
**Dothan**
Waddell, John Emory
**Florence**
Schuessler, Cindy Sandlin
**Guntersville**
McLaughlin, Jeffrey Rex
**Huntsville**
Richardson, Patrick William
**Mobile**
Ballard, Michael Eugene
Brock, Glen Porter, Jr.
Holland, Lyman Faith, Jr.
McKnight, Charles Noel
**Montgomery**
Franco, Ralph Abraham
Howell, Allen Windsor
Kirtland, Michael Arthur
**Muscle Shoals**
Riley, Anthony Dale

### ALASKA

**Anchorage**
Ginder, Peter Craig
**Kodiak**
Jamin, Matthew Daniel

### ARIZONA

**Kingman**
Basinger, Richard Lee
**Mesa**
Gunderson, Brent Merrill
**Phoenix**
Lowry, Edward Francis, Jr.
Mangum, John K.
Martori, Joseph Peter
Olsen, Alfred Jon
Sliger, Herbert Jacquemin, Jr.
**Portal**
Beumler, Henry Weber
**Scottsdale**
Franz, J. Noland
Roberts, Jean Reed
Swartz, Melvin Jay
**Tucson**
Farsjo, Fred A.
Stewart, Hugh W.
Stirton, Charles Paul
**Yuma**
Hunt, Gerald Wallace

### ARKANSAS

**Blytheville**
Fendler, Oscar
**Fayetteville**
Smith, Raymond Carroll
**Jonesboro**
Womack, Tom D.
**Little Rock**
Haught, William Dixon
Stockburger, Jean Dawson
**North Little Rock**
McGough, Phillip Allan
**Pine Bluff**
Harrelson, F(rederick) Daniel
Ramsay, Louis Lafayette, Jr.
**Russellville**
Simmons, Scott Michael
**Van Buren**
Gant, Horace Zed
**Warren**
Claycomb, Hugh Murray
**West Memphis**
Weisburd, Everard J.

### CALIFORNIA

**Anaheim**
Fleming, Richard Alfred
Ross, Roger Scott
**Antioch**
Richards, Gerald Thomas
**Berkeley**
Ogg, Wilson Reid
Ross, Julia
**Beverly Hills**
Rosky, Burton Seymour
**Camarillo**
Van Conas, Kendall Ashleigh
**Campbell**
Castello, Raymond Vincent
Desmarais, Michael George
Temmerman, Robert Eugene, Jr.
**Chula Vista**
Swift, Jack H.
**Davis**
Henderson, Mark Gordy
**Downey**
Bear, Henry Louis
Schauf, Carolyn Jane
**El Centro**
Zimmermann, Ann Marie
**Elverta**
Betts, Barbara Lang
**Fresno**
Sherr, Morris Max
**Fullerton**
Roberts, Mark Scott
**Glendale**
Green, Norman Harry
**Grass Valley**
Hawkins, Richard Michael
**Hayward**
Smith, John Kerwin
**Hermosa Beach**
Roberts, Laurel Lee
**Huntington Beach**
Armstrong, Alan Leigh
Guerin, John Joseph
**Indian Wells**
Smith, Byron Owen
**Irvine**
Hilker, Walter Robert, Jr.
**La Canada Flintridge**
Stell, Joseph
**La Jolla**
Shannahan, William Paul
**Laguna Hills**
Tepper, Nancy Boxley
**Lancaster**
Bianchi, David Wayne
**Los Angeles**
Anderson, William Augustus
Antin, Michael
Call, Merlin Wendell
Campbell, Jennifer L.
Cohan, John Robert
Gallo, Jon Joseph
Garber, Albert Caesar
Gould, Julian Saul
Grim, Douglas Paul
Livadary, Paul John
Marshall, Arthur K.
Mitchell, Michael Charles
Nordlinger, Stephanie G.
Norris, Floyd Hamilton
Rae, Matthew Sanderson, Jr.
**Mill Valley**
Dyer, Gregory Clark
**Modesto**
Reed, Betty Ann
**Monterey**
Bomberger, Russell Branson
Gaver, Frances Rouse
Johnson, Mark Harold
**Morgan Hill**
Foster, John Robert
**Napa**
Burke, Patrick William
**Newport Beach**
Copenbarger, Lloyd Gaylord
Wexler, Danniel Justin
**North Hollywood**
Kreger, Melvin Joseph
Zimring, Stuart David
**Novato**
Obninsky, Victor Peter
**Oakland**
Depper, Estelle M.
Mc Elwain, Lester Stafford
**Palm Desert**
Reinhardt, Benjamin Max
**Palo Alto**
Miller, Michael Patiky
Wunsch, Kathryn Sutherland
**Palos Verdes Estates**
Toftness, Cecil Gillman
**Pasadena**
Ashley-Farrand, Margalo
Brown, Lorne James
Fellman, Gerry Louis
Katzman, Harvey Lawrence
Klein, Jill
**Placentia**
Evans, Winthrop Shattuck
**Rancho Cordova**
Lynch, Robert Berger
**Redondo Beach**
Mercant, Jon Jeffry
**Riverside**
Briskin, Boyd Edward
**Sacramento**
Burton, Randall James
Goodart, Nan L.
Mueller, Virginia Schwartz
**San Carlos**
Raye-Wong, Catherine
**San Clemente**
Fisher, Myron R.
**San Diego**
Hansotte, Louis Bernard
Hofflund, Paul
Payne, Margaret Anne
**San Fernando**
Lynch, Kevin G.
**San Francisco**
Guggenhime, Richard Johnson
Hellman, Theodore Albert, Jr.
Higgins, Valerie Jan
MacLeod, Norman
Major, Hugh Geoffrey
Selvig, Jettie Pierce
Silk, Thomas
Stephenson, Charles Gayley
Utrecht, Paul F.
Weber, Arnold I.
Whitehead, David Barry
Wild, Nelson Hopkins
**San Marino**
Tomich, Lillian

**San Mateo**
Fox, Audrey Braker
**Santa Ana**
Patt, Herbert Jacob
**Santa Barbara**
Ambrecht, John Ward
**Santa Cruz**
Campos, Victor Manuel
**Santa Monica**
Axe, Norman Gold
Landay, Andrew Herbert
**Sunnyvale**
Vorreiter, Patricia Joan
**Thousand Oaks**
Garcia, Raymond Arthur
Trover, Ellen Lloyd
**Torrance**
Moore, Christopher Minor
**Tustin**
Gaughan, John Stephen
Posey, Janette Robison
**Ukiah**
Sager, Madeline Dean
**Visalia**
Crowe, Daniel Walston
**Walnut Creek**
Baker, Roy Gordon, Jr.
**West Covina**
Ebiner, Robert Maurice

## COLORADO

**Boulder**
Gamm, Gordon Julius
Hundley, Laura S.
**Cherry Hl Vlg**
Kerwin, Mary Ann Collins
**Colorado Springs**
Gaddis, Larry Roy
Keene, Kenneth Paul
Kendall, Phillip Alan
Kennedy, Richard Joseph
Link, Gary Steven
Purvis, Randall W. B.
**Denver**
Ash, Walter Brinker
Atlass, Theodore Bruce
Christianssen, Kenneth Gordon
Hodges, Joseph Gilluly, Jr.
McMichael, Donald Earl
Olsen, M. Kent
Potter, Gary Thomas
Quiat, Gerald M.
Schauer, Tone Terjesen
Schmidt, L(ail) William, Jr.
Scott, Peter Bryan
**Englewood**
Carraher, John Bernard
Schilken, Bruce A.
**Lakewood**
Thome, Dennis Wesley
**Littleton**
Ballantine, Beverly Neblett
Carleno, Harry Eugene
Eberhardt, Robert Schuler, Jr.
Minckley, Carla Beth
**Loveland**
Kaufman, William George
**Ouray**
Johnson, Christian Kent
**Pueblo**
O'Callaghan, Robert Patrick
**Rocky Ford**
Mendenhall, Harry Barton
**Wheat Ridge**
Brant, John Getty

## CONNECTICUT

**Bethel**
Medvecky, Thomas Edward
**Burlington**
Bauer, Charles Widmayer
**Canaan**
Capecelatro, Mark John
**Clinton**
Hershatter, Richard Lawrence
**Derby**
Cohen, James E.
**Enfield**
Berger, Robert Bertram
**Hartford**
Berall, Frank Stewart
Bonee, John Leon, III
Gale, John Quentin
Milliken, Charles Buckland
Pinney, Sidney Dillingham, Jr.
Toro, Amalia Maria
**New Haven**
Wiznia, Carolann Kamens
**Ridgefield**
Foster, Julie Irene
Sherman, Harold
**Rocky Hill**
DiCara, Phyllis M.
**Simsbury**
Main, Philip David
**Southport**
Moore, Roy Worsham, III
**Stamford**
Daniels, Daniel Lloyd
Gilman, Derek
Sarner, Richard Alan
**Trumbull**
Auerbach, Hillel Joshua
**Wallingford**
Galligan, Matthew G.
**Waterbury**
Dost, Mark W.
**Watertown**
Del Buono, John Angelo
**Westport**
Kosakow, James Matthew
Saxl, Richard Hildreth
Swiggart, Carolyn Clay
**Wilton**
Adams, Thomas Tilley
**Windsor**
Morelli, Carmen

## DELAWARE

**Dover**
Jones, R. Brandon
Twilley, Joshua Marion
**Newark**
McCann, Richard Stephen
**Wilmington**
Cooch, Edward W(ebb), Jr.
Durante, Charles Joseph
Reiver, Joanna
Sawyer, H(arold) Murray, Jr.
Schlusser, Robert Elmer

## DISTRICT OF COLUMBIA

**Washington**
Bellinger, Edgar Thomson
Bixler, John Mourer
Cernicky, Ann Hardman
Close, David Palmer
Damico, Nicholas Peter
Freedman, Walter
Kohn, Dexter Morton
Pearlstein, Paul Davis
Perry, Rotraud Mezger
Plaine, Lloyd Leva
Rafferty, Catherine Mary
Richards, Suzanne V.
Ward, Nicholas Donnell

## FLORIDA

**Altamonte Springs**
Laurence, Steven Lamar
**Auburndale**
Haff, Tula Michele
**Boca Raton**
Berlin, Mark A.
Carlile, Robert Toy
Dudley, Everett Haskell, Jr.
Wichinsky, Glenn Ellis
**Boynton Beach**
Armstrong, Jack Gilliland
**Bradenton**
Lopacki, Edward Joseph, Jr.
**Brandon**
Tittsworth, Clayton (Magness)
**Clearwater**
Bonner, John Ryckman
Free, E. LeBron
Gulecas, James Frederick
Hogan, Elwood
Jirotka, George M.
Swope, Scott Paul
**Coral Gables**
Fletcher, Paul Gerald
**Deerfield Beach**
Lenoff, Michele Malka
Levitan, David M(aurice)
**Fort Lauderdale**
Beck, Wendy Lynn
Browner, Julius Harvey
Gardner, Russell Menese
Heidgerd, Frederick Cay
Hess, George Franklin, II
Hoines, David Alan
Katz, Thomas Owen
King, Robert Lee
Moss, Stephen B.
**Fort Myers**
Cipriano, Gene Ralph
**Fort Myers Beach**
Cotter, Richard Timothy
Shenko, William Edward, Jr.
**Gainesville**
Rosenblatt, Howard Marshall
**Hobe Sound**
Buetens, Eric D.
**Hollywood**
Fischler, Shirley Balter
Wolis, Kenneth Arnold
**Jacksonville**
Ball, Haywood Moreland
Cooke, Alexander Hamilton
Getman, Willard Etheridge
Lee, Lewis Swift
**Jasper**
McCormick, John Hoyle
**Jupiter**
Brophy, Gilbert Thomas
Click, David Forrest
**Key West**
Fohrman, Darryl
**Lake Placid**
Haile, John Sanders
**Lakeland**
Koren, Edward Franz
**Lutz**
Hayes, Timothy George
**Miami**
Amber, Laurie Kaufman
Barrett, John Richard
Cassel, Marwin Shepard
Dribin, Michael A.
Formoso, Marika Gulyas
Gordon, Howard W.
Greenleaf, Walter Franklin
Hartman, Douglas Cole
Kreutzer, Franklin David
Lancaster, Kenneth G.
Milstein, Richard Craig
Skolnick, S. Harold
Smith, Samuel Stuart
Weiner, Lawrence
**Miami Beach**
Brodie, Ronald
**Naples**
Blakely, John T.
Budd, David Glenn
Lile, Laird Andrew
Westman, Carl Edward
**New Port Richey**
Strand, Arnelle Marie
**North Miami Beach**
Slewett, Robert David
Snihur, William Joseph, Jr.
**North Palm Beach**
Daniels, Bruce Joel
**Ocala**
Thompson, Raymond Edward
**Orlando**
Ibanez, Silvia Safille
Rush, Fletcher Grey, Jr.
**Oviedo**
Worthington, Daniel Glen
**Palatka**
Baldwin, Allen Adail
**Palm Beach Gardens**
Auerbach, Paul Ira
Kahn, David Miller
**Palm Harbor**
Summers-Powell, Alan
**Panama City**
Byrne, Robert William
**Plantation**
Koltnow, H. Robert
**Pompano Beach**
Shulmister, M(orris) Ross
**Pt Charlotte**
Levin, Allen Jay
**Punta Gorda**
Bell, Peter A.
**Redington Shores**
Christ, Earle L.
**Saint Petersburg**
DiVito, Joseph Anthony
Gross, Alan Marc
Lewis, Mark Russell, Sr.
Lyman, Curtis Lee, Jr.
Mann, Sam Henry, Jr.
Wilsey, Steven M.
**Sanford**
Smith, Vicki Lynn
**Sarasota**
Conetta, Tami Foley
Kimbrough, Robert Averyt
**Sebastian**
Lulich, Steven
**Sebring**
McCollum, James Fountain
**Spring Hill**
Shaw, Ray
**Stuart**
Lako, Charles Michael, Jr.
**Tallahassee**
Boyd, Joseph Arthur, Jr.
Dariotis, Terrence Theodore
**Tampa**
Castillo, Daniel L.
Ellwanger, Thomas John
Farrior, J. Rex, Jr.
Gardner, J. Stephen
Heyck, Joseph Giraud, Jr.
Oehler, Richard Dale
Pacheco, Felipe Ramon
Stalnaker, Lance Kuebler
Steele, Rebecca Harrison
Turmel, Stacey Lynn
**Venice**
Gaylor, William E., III
**West Palm Beach**
Bertles, James Billet
Farina, John
Grantham, Kirk Pinkerton
Kamen, Michael Andrew
Shapero, Bertram Malcolm
Wroble, Arthur Gerard

## GEORGIA

**Albany**
Patterson, Rudolph N.
**Americus**
Cooper, Cecilia Marie
**Atlanta**
Bird, Francis Marion, Jr.
Bloodworth, A(lbert) W(illiam) Franklin
Edee, James Philip
Howell, Arthur
Salo, Ann Sexton Distler
Schilling, Laura K.
Sibley, James Malcolm
**Augusta**
Cooney, William J.
Lee, Lansing Burrows, Jr.
Williams, William James
**Columbus**
Johnson, Walter Frank, Jr.
**Dallas**
Williams, Gary Randall
**Doraville**
Gerstein, Joe Willie
**Douglas**
Sims, Rebecca Littleton
**Hamilton**
Byrd, Gary Ellis
**Savannah**
Dickey, David Herschel
Gannam, Michael Joseph
**Valdosta**
Cork, Robert Lander

## HAWAII

**Honolulu**
Dang, Marvin S. C.
Gerson, Mervyn Stuart
Larsen, David Coburn
Rohrer, Reed Beaver
Roth, Randall W.
Suzuki, Norman Hitoshi
Taylor, Carroll Stribling
**Kailua Kona**
Martin, William Charles
**Wailuku**
Bodden, Thomas Andrew

## IDAHO

**Boise**
Derr, Allen R.
Erickson, Robert Stanley
Marcus, Craig Brian
**Idaho Falls**
Eskelson, Scott P.
**Moscow**
Bielenberg, Leonard Herman

## ILLINOIS

**Alton**
Bohne, Edward Daniel
**Aurora**
Lowe, Ralph Edward
**Batavia**
Drendel, Kevin Gilbert
**Belleville**
Waller, Paul Pressley, Jr.
**Bloomington**
Stevens, John Nickless
**Calumet City**
Scullion, Kevin Peter
**Chicago**
Acker, Frederick George
Bernstein, Charles Bernard
Bockelman, John Richard
Bridewell, David Alexander
Brown, Alan Crawford
Cross, Chester Joseph
English, John Dwight
Gelman, Andrew Richard
Gordon, Theodora
Gutstein, Solomon
Harrington, Carol A.
Herpe, David A.
Kresse, William Joseph
Lehrer, Julius Marshall
Lutter, Paul Allen
Martin, Siva
Nicolaides, Mary
Nordgren, Gerald Paul
Schar, Stephen L.
Schwartzberg, Hugh Joel
Spain, Richard Colby
Sprowl, Charles Riggs
Stone, Bertram Allen
Swaney, Thomas Edward
Trio, Edward Alan
Trost, Eileen Bannon
**Collinsville**
Evers, William C., III
**Crystal Lake**
Thoms, Jeannine Aumond
**Du Quoin**
Atkins, Aaron Ardene
**Effingham**
Siemer, Martin W.
**Geneseo**
Brown, Mabel Welton
**Genoa**
Cromley, Jon Lowell
**Glenview**
Marmet, Gottlieb John
**Hinsdale**
Diamant, William
**Joliet**
Teas, Richard Harper
**Kewanee**
McRae, Donald James
**Monticello**
Rhoades, Dana Christine
Tracy, William Francis, II
**Mount Carroll**
Leemon, John Allen
**Murphysboro**
McCann, Maurice Joseph
**Naperville**
Erickson, Diane Quinn
Kelly, Kathryn L.
**Northbrook**
Pollak, Jay Mitchell
Yowell, George Kent
**Northfield**
Gelfman, Stuart G.
**O'Fallon**
Koebel, Delmar Oliver
**Oakbrook Terrace**
O'Brien, Walter Joseph, II
**Palos Heights**
Matug, Alexander Peter
**Paris**
Fruin, Roger Joseph
**Park Ridge**
Bellas, George Steven
Hegarty, Mary Frances
**Peoria**
Coletta, Ralph John
Tomlin, James Milton
**Pinckneyville**
Johnson, Don Edwin
**Skokie**
Kahn, Bert L.
**Springfield**
Rabin, Avrum Mark
Reed, Robert Phillip
Walbaum, Robert C.
**Streator**
Harrison, Frank Joseph
Mohan, John J.
**Taylorville**
Austin, Daniel William
**Watseka**
Tungate, James Lester
**Wauconda**
Malik, Thomas Warren
**Waukegan**
Bairstow, Richard Raymond
**West Frankfort**
Riva, David Michael
**Wheeling**
Kulinsky, Lois
**Winchester**
Mann, Richard Evans
**Winnetka**
Abell, David Robert
Barnard, Morton John
Ryan, Robert Jeffers
**Woodhull**
Ciaccio, Karin McLaughlin

## INDIANA

**Bloomington**
Tackitt, Sylvan Wright
**Brazil**
Berry, Margaret Anne
**Columbus**
Crump, Francis Jefferson, III
**Elkhart**
Cawley, John Arnold, Jr.
**Evansville**
Baugh, Jerry Phelps
**Fort Wayne**
Fink, Thomas Michael
Gehring, Ronald Kent
James, Ronald Eugene
Troyer, Tracy Lynn
Young, Randy William
**Fowler**
Kepner, Rex William
Weist, William Bernard
**Greenfield**
Dobbins, Caryl Dean
**Hammond**
Kohl, Jacquelyn Marie
**Highland**
Fine, William Irwin
**Hobart**
Longer, William John
**Indianapolis**
Carlock, Mahlon Waldo, II (Steve Carlock)
Dutton, Clarence Benjamin
Fuller, Samuel Ashby
Leitch, Ryan L.
Lowe, Louis Robert, Jr.
Padgett, Gregory Lee
Patrick, William Bradshaw
Price, Phillip Vincent
Rothbaum, Sandra Lazarus
Warren, Bradford Lloyd
**Knox**
Gudeman, Leroy Dennis
**La Porte**
Lewis, Daniel Edwin
**Lafayette**
Branigin, Roger D., Jr.
**Lawrenceburg**
Ewan, William Kenneth
**Marion**
Ryan, Patrick Nelson
**Merrillville**
Brenman, Stephen Morris
**Muncie**
Dennis, Ralph Emerson, Jr.
**Noblesville**
Fleck, (Kevin) Sean
**Shelbyville**
Lisher, James Richard

## IOWA

**Algona**
Handsaker, Jerrold Lee
**Burlington**
Beckman, David
**Cedar Falls**
Rolinger, Mark Stephen
**Cedar Rapids**
Wilson, Robert Foster
**Council Blfs**
Rodenburg, John A.
**Davenport**
Skora, Susan Sundman
**Des Moines**
Schuling, Mark Richard
Watson, Phil
**Indianola**
Ouderkirk, Mason James
**Iowa City**
Downer, Robert Nelson
**Mason City**
Heiny, James Ray
Winston, Harold Ronald
**Mount Pleasant**
Vance, Michael Charles
**Muscatine**
Coulter, Charles Roy
**Parkersburg**
Lawler, Thomas Albert
**Sioux City**
Klass, Marvin Joseph
**Vinton**
Mossman, Mark E.
**Webster City**
Hemingway, Whitley Maynard
**West Des Moines**
Begleiter, Ronni Frankel

## KANSAS

**Arkansas City**
Templar, Ted Mac
**Hays**
Toepfer, Thomas Lyle
**Hugoton**
Nordling, Bernard Erick
**Hutchinson**
Swearer, William Brooks
**Iola**
Toland, Clyde William
Toland, John Robert
**Kansas City**
Case, Rosemary Podrebarac
**Lawrence**
Brown, David James
Gage, John Cutter
Smith, Glee Sidney, Jr.
**Lenexa**
Rappard, Gary Donald
**Lincoln**
Marshall, Susan
**Lyons**
Hodgson, Arthur Clay
**Olathe**
Haskin, J. Michael
Lowe, Roy Goins

**Overland Park**
Bohm, Jack Nelson
**Salina**
Conner, Fred L.
**Shawnee Mission**
Gastl, Eugene Francis
**Topeka**
Aadalen, David Kevin
Barnes, Tom R., II
Fisher, David Hugh
Hejtmanek, Danton Charles
**Wichita**
Badger, Ronald Kay
Stewart, Kenneth Parsons

## KENTUCKY

**Lebanon**
Higdon, Frederick Alonzo
**Lexington**
Bagby, Glen Stovall
Bagby, William Rardin
Bryson, Arthur Joseph
Miller, Harry B(enjamin)
**Louisville**
Baker, H. Nicholas
Buckaway, William Allen, Jr.
Chauvin, Leonard Stanley, Jr.
Duffy, Martin Patrick
Fuchs, Olivia Anne Morris
Gilman, Sheldon Glenn
Hallenberg, Robert Lewis
Henry, Kelly Sue
Noe, Randolph
Pettyjohn, Shirley Ellis
Stone, Thomas Kendall
Storment, Harold Lloyd
**Paducah**
Treece, Randy Lionel
**Scottsville**
Secrest, James Seaton, Sr.
**Somerset**
Prather, John Gideon, Jr.

## LOUISIANA

**Baton Rouge**
Blitzer, Sidney Milton, Jr.
LeClere, David Anthony
**Covington**
Reynolds, Richard Louis
Shinn, Clinton Wesley
**Gretna**
Fadaol, Robert Frederick
Stumpf, Harry Charles
**Hammond**
Ross, Kenneth L.
**Jefferson**
Conino, Joseph Aloysius
**Lafayette**
Durio, William Henry
Mansfield, James Norman, III
**Lake Charles**
Shaddock, William Edward, Jr.
**Metairie**
Sherman, David Robert
**New Orleans**
Barnett, William Michael
Carman, Laura Junge
Curtis, Charles Thach, Jr.
Johnson, Beth Exum
Lemann, Thomas Berthelot
Steeg, Moise S., Jr.
Stone, Saul
Vickery, Eugene Benton, Jr.
Wedig, Regina Scotto
**Shreveport**
Hardtner, Quintin Theodore, III
**Slidell**
Singletary, Alvin D.
**Ville Platte**
Coreil, C. Brent
**West Monroe**
Caldwell, Douglas Cody

## MAINE

**Bath**
Regan, Richard Robert
**Farmington**
Holman, Joseph Frederick
**Lewiston**
Peters, Thomas P., II
**Portland**
Cowan, Caspar Frank
Hunt, David Evans
Klebe, Kurt Edward
LeBlanc, Richard Philip
Schwartz, Stephen Jay

## MARYLAND

**Annapolis**
Michaelson, Benjamin, Jr.
**Baltimore**
Heisler, John Charles
Lewis, Alexander Ingersoll, III
Mitchell, Hugh Allen, Jr.
Potts, Bernard
**Bethesda**
Morgan, Jo Valentine, Jr.
Strickler, Scott Michael
**Bowie**
Bagaria, Gail Farrell
**Brookeville**
Fobe, Nicholas M(atthew)
**Crofton**
Doherty, Daniel Joseph, III
**Laurel**
Barr, June Hatton
**Lutherville**
Mc Kenney, Walter Gibbs, Jr.
**Rockville**
Katz, Steven Martin
**Silver Spring**
Dunn, John Benjamin
**Towson**
Lalumia, Matthew Paul
Miller, Herbert H.

**Wheaton**
Kirchman, Charles Vincent

## MASSACHUSETTS

**Amesbury**
Swartz, Mark Lee
**Arlington**
Keshian, Richard
**Boston**
Chapin, Melville
Cherny, David Edward
Clymer, John Howard
Goldman, Richard Harris
Hamann, Charles Martin
Menoyo, Eric Felix
Perera, Lawrence Thacher
Sears, John Winthrop
Smith, Clark Robinson
Sullivan, Edward Michael
Sweeney, Paul John
Woodburn, Ralph Robert, Jr.
**Bradford**
Cox, William Donald, Jr.
**Brookline**
Alban, Ludwig
Goldenberg, Stephen Bernard
**Chatham**
Popkin, Alice Brandeis
**Danvers**
Eisenhauer, Wayne Harold
**Fitchburg**
DiPace, Steven B.
**Ludlow**
Mondry, Paul Michael
**Needham**
Cox, Gilbert W., Jr.
**New Bedford**
Hurwitz, Barrett Alan
Mathieu, Thomas Joseph
**Newton**
Isselbacher, Rhoda Solin
Monahan, Marie Terry
**Northampton**
Thomas, Margot Eva
**Norwell**
O'Sullivan, James Michael
**Palmer**
Auchter, John Richard
**Pittsfield**
Doyle, Anthony Peter
**Plymouth**
Barreira, Brian Ernest
**South Hamilton**
Campbell, Diana Butt
**Springfield**
Fialky, Gary Lewis
McCarthy, Charles Francis, Jr.
**Tewksbury**
Dulchinos, Peter
**Wakefield**
Lucas, Robert Frank
**Wellesley**
Riley, Michael Hylan
**West Chatham**
Rowley, Glenn Harry
**West Springfield**
Ely, John P.
**Westfield**
Angell, James Edward
Pollard, Frank Edward
**Weston**
Schwartz, Edward Lester
**Winchester**
La Rosa, Lillian J.
**Worcester**
Erskine, Matthew Forbes
Leb, Clara Silvia
**Yarmouth Port**
Brown, Robert G.
Paquin, Thomas Christopher

## MICHIGAN

**Ann Arbor**
Dew, Thomas Edward
Ellmann, William Marshall
Petoskey, Elizabeth M.
**Battle Creek**
Schoder, Wendell Louis
**Birmingham**
Sweeney, Thomas Frederick
**Bloomfield Hills**
Kirk, John MacGregor
Snavely, Gordon Alden
**Center Line**
Litch, John Michael
**Detroit**
Mecoli Kamp, Carla Marie
Miller, George DeWitt, Jr.
Rasmussen, Douglas John
**East Lansing**
Platt, David M.
Story, Monte Robert
**Farmington Hills**
Gross, Lynn Westfall
Stokes, Joelynn Towanda
**Fenton**
Hildner, Phillips Brooks, II
**Flint**
Henneke, Edward George
Pelavin, Michael Allen
**Grand Ledge**
Smith, Terry J.
**Grand Rapids**
Davis, Henry Barnard, Jr.
Prasher, Gregory George
**Grosse Pointe**
Cobau, John Reed
**Harbor Beach**
Schumacher, Dawn Kristi Ann
**Ishpeming**
Steward, James Brian
**Jackson**
Barton, Bruce Andrew
Curtis, Philip James

**Kalamazoo**
Gordon, Edgar George
**Lansing**
Gallagher, Byron Patrick, Jr.
Stackable, Frederick Lawrence
**Mount Clemens**
Ososki-Slanec, Darra
**Muskegon**
Houghtaling, Chris Allen
**Niles**
Stone, Donald P.
**Petoskey**
Powers, Bridget Brown
Smith, Wayne Richard
**Saginaw**
Martin, Walter
**Southfield**
May, Alan Alfred
Silber, Albert J.
**Sturgis**
Dresser, Raymond H., Jr.
**Troy**
Coe, Richard Thomas
McGinnis, Thomas Michael

## MINNESOTA

**Benson**
Wilcox, Donald Alan
**Cambridge**
Parker, Robert Samuel
**Chanhassen**
Peterson, Steven A.
**Fergus Falls**
Bigwood, Robert William
**Kenyon**
Peterson, Franklin Delano
**Maplewood**
Beck, Bruce Lennart
**Minneapolis**
Biglow, Robert R.
Brand, Steve Aaron
Chester, Stephanie Ann
Rachie, Cyrus
Saeks, Allen Irving
Vanhove, Lorri Kay
Ventres, Judith Martin
Zotaley, Byron Leo
**Moorhead**
Guy, William Lewis, III
**Pine River**
Swanson, Bradley Dean
**Roseville**
Heitler, Perrie Nanette
**Saint Paul**
Grayson, Richard A.
Jacobs, Stephen Louis
Noonan, James C.
Trojack, John Edward
**Shoreview**
Bertelsen, Michael William
**Willmar**
Hulstrand, George Eugene
**Winthrop**
Engwall, Gregory Bond
**Woodbury**
Baumann, Craig William

## MISSISSIPPI

**Jackson**
Chadwick, Vernon Henry
Presson, William Russell
**Oxford**
Howorth, Andrew Kincannon
**Raymond**
Moss, Jack Gibson

## MISSOURI

**Ballwin**
Gunn, Michael Peter
**Chesterfield**
Fagerberg, Roger Richard
**Columbia**
Parrigin, Elizabeth Ellington
**Independence**
Minton, Kent W.
**Kansas City**
Clarke, Milton Charles
Dicus, Stephen Howard
Gorman, Gerald Warner
Langworthy, Robert Burton
Marvin, Wendy Byers
Moffat, Marian MacIntyre
Murguia, Ramon
Reaves, Craig Charles
Setzler, Edward Allan
Tanner, Eric Benson
Voran, Joel Bruce
**Lake Saint Louis**
Callahan, Robert John, Jr.
**Lexington**
Giorza, John C.
**Marshall**
Peterson, William Allen
**Rock Port**
Mulvania, Walter Lowell
**Saint Charles**
Beck, Rudy Dale
**Saint Louis**
Bloom, Allen Jerry
Boardman, Richard John
Bryan, Henry C(lark), Jr.
Burcke, Joseph Robert
Chasnoff, Jules
Cullen, James D.
Greenfield, Milton, Jr.
Greenley, Beverly Jane
Hille, Robert John
Klobasa, John Anthony
Lane, Frank Joseph, Jr.
Paster, Robert W.
Redd, Charles Appleton
Schroeder, Mary Patricia
Sherby, Kathleen Reilly
Warren, Russell Allen
**Springfield**
Dickey, Samuel Stephens

**West Plains**
Brill, Newton Clyde

## MONTANA

**Billings**
Schleusner, Clifford Edward
Thompson, James William
**Great Falls**
Larsen, Dirk Herbert
**Missoula**
George, Alexander Andrew
Morales, Julio K.
Spangler, John Thomas
**Ronan**
Grainey, Philip J.

## NEBRASKA

**Aurora**
Whitney, Charles Leroy
**Hildreth**
Jelkin, John Lamoine
**Lincoln**
Brown, Mark Charles
McClain, Richard Douglas
O'Brien, Patrick Thomas
**Omaha**
Burke, Thomas Raymond
Gaines, Tyler Belt
Moylan, James Harold
Schmidt, Kathleen Marie
**York**
Stephens, Bruce Edward

## NEVADA

**Carson City**
Crowell, Robert Lamson
**Las Vegas**
Chesnut, Carol Fitting
Dawson, John E.
Graham, Robert Chase
Greene, Addison Kent
Gubler, John Gray
Oshins, Steven Jeffrey
Van Alfen, Scott B.
Yamashita, Wesley Farrell
**Reno**
Broili, Robert Howard
Davenport, Brian Lynn
Hibbs, Loyal Robert
Manson, Gary Lyle

## NEW HAMPSHIRE

**Concord**
McDonald, Joseph F., III
**Exeter**
Jones, Daniel W.
**Laconia**
Martin, Willard Gordon, Jr.
**Lancaster**
Goss, Steven Bryant
**Manchester**
Mullikin, Anu Radha
Wells, Robert Alfred
**Nashua**
Raudonis, Valerie Christine
**Newport**
Work, Michael Jay
**Plymouth**
Deachman, Ross Varick
Sawyer, Leonard Sylvester
**Portsmouth**
DeGrandpre, Charles Allyson
Lefebvre, Albert Paul Conrad
Money, Kenneth F., Jr.
**Woodsville**
Bruno, Kevin Robert

## NEW JERSEY

**Bayonne**
Olsen, Mary Ann
**Bedminster**
Donegan, Joseph Michael
**Camden**
Lario, Frank M., Jr.
**East Brunswick**
Zaun, Anne Marie
**Edison**
Nagle, Claire Waller
**Florham Park**
LeVine, Walter Daniel
**Hackensack**
Knee, Peggy Sheahan
Schuber, William Patrick
Weiner, Samuel
**Hackettstown**
Hudacek, Daniel Andrew
Mulligan, Elinor Patterson
**Hammonton**
Tarver, Margaret Leggett
**Highland Park**
Alman, Emily Arnow
Feld, Franklin Fred
**Hillsdale**
Hodinar, Michael
**Jersey City**
Talafous, Joseph John, Sr.
**Lakewood**
Bielory, Abraham Melvin
**Livingston**
Hock, Frederick Wyeth
Rosenberg, Paul I.
**Medford**
Gruccio-Thorman, Lillian Joan
**Metuchen**
Eugene, John
**Montclair**
Conrad, David Williams
**Moorestown**
Begley, Thomas D., Jr.
**Morristown**
Aspero, Benedict Vincent
Neff, Robert Carey
Sweeney, John Lawrence
**Mount Laurel**
Schmoll, Harry F., Jr.

**Newark**
Day, Edward Francis, Jr.
Long, Reginald Alan
**Paulsboro**
Fichera, Lewis Carmen
**Pompton Plains**
Ludemann, Cathie Jane
**Princeton**
Mulchinock, David Steward
Sutphin, William Taylor
Ufford, Charles Wilbur, Jr.
**Salem**
Petrin, Helen Fite
**South Orange**
Kamens, Harold
**South Plainfield**
Santoro, Frank Anthony
**Sparta**
Schupp, Anastasia Luka
**Summit**
Jarvis, Percy Alton, Jr.
**Union**
Rosenberg, A. Irving
**Vauxhall**
Ross, Mark Samuel
**West Orange**
Goldberg, Leonard Marvin
Laves, Benjamin Samuel
**Westfield**
Gutterman, Alan J.
**Willingboro**
Guest, Brian Milton
**Woodcliff Lake**
Getler, Janine A.

## NEW MEXICO

**Albuquerque**
Bova, Vincent Arthur, Jr.
Gorman, Robert Dennis
Keleher, Michael Lawrence
Messersmith, Lanny Dee
Moughan, Peter Richard, Jr.
Ramo, Roberta Cooper
Schoen, Stevan Jay
Tomita, Susan K.
**Carlsbad**
Byers, Matthew T(odd)
**Clovis**
Skarda, Lynell Griffith
**Las Cruces**
Martin, Connie Ruth
Palacios, Pedro Pablo
**Roswell**
Bassett, John Walden, Jr.
**Santa Fe**
Hickey, John Miller

## NEW YORK

**Albany**
Piedmont, Richard Stuart
**Amherst**
Allen, Lisa Joan
Jones, E. Thomas
**Babylon**
Garvey, Jane Roberts
**Ballston Spa**
Brown, Ifigenia Theodore
**Bedford**
Atkins, Ronald Raymond
**Binghamton**
Beck, Stephanie G.
Peyton, Walter Burdette
**Bronx**
Aris, Joram Jehudah
**Brooklyn**
Erlitz, Stephen W.
Lewis, Felice Flanery
**Buffalo**
Gardner, Sue Shaffer
Newman, Stephen Michael
Pearson, Paul David
Seggio-Ball, Josephine
**Canandaigua**
Winthrop, Griffith Joel
**Cape Vincent**
Stiefel, Linda Shields
**Carmel**
Lowe, E(dwin) Nobles
**Cortlandt Mnr**
Galella, Joseph Peter
**Delmar**
Galvin, Madeline Sheila
**Dobbs Ferry**
Juettner, Diana D'Amico
**Douglaston**
Salvo, Joseph Aldo
**Floral Park**
Goldman, Alan Barry
**Flushing**
Chang, Lee-Lee
**Forest Hills**
Greenberg, Robert Jay
**Garden City**
Hand, Stephen Block
Haskel, Jules J.
Kreger-Grella, Cheryl Leslie
**Geneva**
Brind, David Hutchison
**Getzville**
DiNardo, Joseph
**Glens Falls**
Baker, Carl TenEyck
Pontiff, Paul E.
**Gouverneur**
Heller, Sanders D.
**Great Neck**
Gastwirth, Stuart Lawrence
Wershals, Paul L.
Zervos, Mitra Kavoussi
**Groton**
Henry, James Richard
**Guilderland**
Sills, Nancy Mintz

**Harrison**
Hertz, Natalie Zucker
**Hicksville**
Giuffré, John Joseph
Snowe, Alan Martin
**Houghton**
Brautigam, David Clyde
**Huntington**
Munson, Nancy Kay
**Ithaca**
Theisen, Henry William
**Jamaica**
Biehl, Kathy Anne
**Jamesport**
Cardinale, Philip John
**Jericho**
Beal, Carol Ann
Hecht, Donald Stuart
**Kew Gardens**
Adler, David Neil
**Kingston**
Ellison, Patricia Lee
**Larchmont**
Engel, Ralph Manuel
**Latham**
Brearton, James Joseph
**Lawrence**
Goldstein, Irwin Melvin
**Long Island City**
Alimaras, Gus
**Manhasset**
Fletcher, James Harry
**Melville**
Burke, Richard James
**Miller Place**
Lucivero, Lucretia M.
**Mineola**
Bartol, Ernest Thomas
Daniels, John Hill
Jones, Lawrence Tunnicliffe
**Mohegan Lake**
Stokes, Ron
**Montour Falls**
Argetsinger, Cameron R.
**Nanuet**
Waldorf, Geraldine Polack
**New Hartford**
McKennan, John T.
**New Rochelle**
DiMarco, Frank Paul
**New York**
Annenberg, Norman
Barasch, Mal Livingston
Black, James Isaac, III
Blinken, Sally S.
Bloom, Robert Avrum
Christensen, Henry, III
Coon, Robert Morell, Jr.
Crary, Miner Dunham, Jr.
Donovan, Maureen Driscoll
DuLaux, Russell Frederick
Eakins, William Shannon
Evans, Douglas Hayward
Field, David Anthony
Friedman, Elaine Florence
Gelb, Judith Anne
Goldman, Richard Lurie
Guth, Paul C.
Hader, Cheryl Elizabeth
Herbst, Abbe Ilene
Hewitt, Richard Gilbert
Hirschson, Linda Benjamin
Hirshowitz, Melvin Stephen
Hopper, Walter Everett
Hull, Philip Glasgow
Jacob, Shalom
Jasper, Seymour
Johnson, Bruce Carlton
Kahn, Alan Edwin
Karan, Paul Richard
Kartiganer, Joseph
Katsoris, Constantine Nicholas
Kavoukjian, Michael Edward
Kitay, Harvey Robert
Klipstein, Robert Alan
Knight, Townsend Jones
Kroll, Arthur Herbert
Kronman, Carol Jane
Lande, David Steven
Lee, Robert Edward, Jr.
Lerner, Max Kasner
Lingelbach, Albert Lane
Mandel, Patricia C.
Martin, Malcolm Elliot
Materna, Joseph Anthony
McCaffrey, Carlyn Sundberg
McGrath, Thomas J.
Miller, Jill Lee
Molnar, Lawrence
Moore, Donald Francis
Muhlstock, Arthur C.
Neuwirth, Gloria S.
O'Neil, John Joseph
Osborn, Donald Robert
Oxman, David Craig
Rabunski, Alan E.
Rafalowicz, Joseph
Robinson, Barbara Paul
Rodman, Leroy Eli
Rogers, Theodore Otto, Jr.
Rosenberg, Jerome Roy
Rubenstein, Joshua Seth
Sabalja, Lorraine
Sangerman, Jay J.
Saufer, Isaac Aaron
Schizer, Zevie Baruch
Schlesinger, Sanford Joel
Sederbaum, Arthur David
Shipper, David W.
Spero, C. Michael
Stringer, Ronald E.
Subin, Florence
Tricarico, Joseph Archangelo
Valente, Peter Charles
Worley, Robert William, Jr.
Wydler, Hans Ulrich
Zabel, William David
Zerin, Steven David
Zuckerman, Paul Herbert
**Niagara Falls**
Hanesian, Shavasp
Levine, David Ethan
**Northport**
Bialla, Rowley
**Nyack**
Seidler, B(ernard) Alan
**Oneonta**
Harlem, Richard Andrew
Hill, Peter Waverly
**Ossining**
Daly, William Joseph
**Oswego**
Greene, Stephen Craig
**Oyster Bay**
Bernstein, Jacob
Robinson, Edward T., III
**Pelham**
Hanrahan, Michael G.
**Penfield**
Farber, Sidney Theodore
**Perry**
Kelly, Michael Joseph
**Pomona**
Fisch, Edith L.
**Poughkeepsie**
Dietz, Robert Barron
Reed, Thomas A.
**Purchase**
Gioffre, Bruno Joseph
**Queensbury**
Sleight, Virginia Mae
**Riverhead**
Maggipinto, V. Anthony
**Rochester**
Barr, Culver Kent
Brown, Peter Ogden
Buckley, Michael Francis
Clifford, Eugene Thomas
Corcoran, Christopher Holmes
Harris, Wayne Manley
Harter, Ralph Millard Peter
O'Toole, Martin William
Servis, William George
**Rockville Centre**
Lerner, Steven Paul
**Rome**
Griffith, Emlyn Irving
McMahon, Richard H.
**S Richmond Hl**
Goldsmith, Michael Lawrence
**Saratoga Springs**
Capozzola, Theresa A.
**Schenectady**
Kouray, Athena C.
Suprunowicz, Michael Robert
Wickerham, Richard Dennis
**Seagate**
Levitt, Sidney Bernard
**Smithtown**
Pruzansky, Joshua Murdock
**South Richmond Hill**
Scheich, John F.
**Southampton**
Platt, Harold Kirby
**Staten Island**
Ferranti, Thomas, Jr.
Hall, John George
**Syosset**
Upton, Arthur Edward
**Syracuse**
Butler, John Edward
Cambs, Denise P.
Cirando, John Anthony
Traylor, Robert Arthur
Wladis, Mark Neil
**Troy**
Marinstein, Elliott F.
**Wappingers Falls**
Haynes, Paul R.
**Westbury**
Nogee, Jeffrey Laurence
**White Plains**
Kurzman, Robert Graham
Markowitz, Linda Wishnick
McQuaid, John Gaffney

## NORTH CAROLINA

**Asheville**
Branch, John Wells (Jack Twig)
Frue, William Calhoun
Lavelle, Brian Francis David
Lawrence, Betty Tenn
**Boone**
Brown, Wade Edward
**Chapel Hill**
Crassweller, Robert Doell
Herman-Giddens, Gregory
**Charlotte**
Edwards, Mark Brownlow
Wood, William McBrayer
**Elizabeth City**
Riley, John Frederick
**Goldsboro**
Fuller, Robert E., Jr.
Hine, John C.
**Graham**
Walker, Daniel Joshua, Jr.
**Greensboro**
Gabriel, Richard Weisner
Glover, Durant Murrell
**High Point**
Griffin, Robert Gerard
**Jamestown**
Schmitt, William Allen
**Kannapolis**
Griggs, Farrar O'Neal
**Monroe**
Love, Walter Bennett, Jr.
**Murphy**
Bata, Rudolph Andrew, Jr.
**Raleigh**
Carruth, Paul
Huggard, John Parker
**Winston Salem**
Edwards, Robert Leon

## NORTH DAKOTA

**Crosby**
Forsgren, F. Leslie
**Fargo**
Vogel, Charles Nicholas
**Grand Forks**
Widdel, John Earl, Jr.
**Mandan**
Bair, Bruce B.

## OHIO

**Akron**
Holloway, Donald Phillip
Mohler, Robert E.
**Athens**
Gall, Robert Jay
**Batavia**
Rosenhoffer, Chris
**Beachwood**
Sobel, Jonathan F.
**Beavercreek**
Stier, Charles Herman, Jr.
**Berea**
Jolles, Janet Kavanaugh Pilling
**Bowling Green**
Huffman, Diane Rausch
**Bucyrus**
Neff, Robert Clark, Sr.
**Carrollton**
Childers, John Charles
**Chillicothe**
Boulger, William Charles
**Cincinnati**
Bibus, Thomas William
Buechner, Robert William
Candito, Joseph
Cissell, James Charles
Davis, Robert Lawrence
Fingerman, Albert R.
Frank, William Nelson
Hoffheimer, Daniel Joseph
Knabe, Bruce David
Mara, Timothy Gerald
Moskowitz, James Howard
Porter, Robert Carl, Jr.
Vogel, Cedric Wakelee
**Cleveland**
Alcox, Patrick Joseph
Billington, Glenn Earle
Boyko, Christopher Allan
Braverman, Herbert Leslie
Falsgraf, William Wendell
Farah, Benjamin Frederick
Foote, Richard Charles
Furber, Philip Craig
Hochman, Kenneth George
Maher, Edward Joseph
Nudelman, Sidney
Nyerges, George Ladislaus
Sharp, Robert Weimer
Steiger, Sheldon Gerald
Weiss, Leon Alan
**Columbus**
Albert, Robert Hamilton
Anderson, Jon Mac
Darling, Stanton Girard
Elsass, Tobias Harold
Jewett, James Michael
Juhola, Michael Duane
Postlewaite, William Neal, Sr.
Sims, August Charles
Sully, Ira Bennett
**Dayton**
Baggott, Thomas McCann
Blaschak, Thomas R.
Conway, Mark Allyn
Johnson, C. Terry
Krebs, Leo Francis
Pietz, Lynne Pepi
Roberts, Brian Michael
**Garfield Hts**
Demer, Margaret E.
**Georgetown**
Hornschemeier, Patrick
**Greenville**
Finnarn, Theodore Ora
**Ironton**
Collier, James Bruce
**Kent**
Nome, William Andreas
**Kenton**
Tudor, John Martin
**Leetonia**
Shelar, Richard Clyde
**Lima**
Kluge, William Frederick
**Lorain**
Levin, Arnold Sampson
**Massillon**
Netzly, Dwight H.
**Maumee**
Moore, Everett Daniel
**Mc Connelsville**
Dye, Ralph Dean, Jr.
**Mount Vernon**
Rose, Kim Matthew
**Newark**
Hite, David L.
Untied, Wesley Kyle
**Oak Harbor**
Robertson, Jerry D.
**Parma Heights**
Pojman, Paul J.
**Perrysburg**
Hartsel, Norman Clyde
**Saint Clairsville**
Hanlon, Lodge L.
**Salem**
Bowman, Scott McMahan
**Shaker Heights**
Adrine, Herbert A.
**Springfield**
Martin, David MacCoy
**Steubenville**
Noble, Frank Wesley, Jr.
**Tipp City**
Arenstein, Gilbert Gregory
**Toledo**
Gouttiere, John P.
Morgan, James Edward
Nicholson, Brent Bentley
**Warren**
Kearney, Patricia Ann
**Westerville**
Westervelt, Charles Ephraim, Jr.
**Willoughby**
Greene, Ralph Vernon
**Wilmington**
Buckley, Frederick Jean
Schutt, Walter Eugene
**Youngstown**
Briach, George Gary
Lenga, Robert Allen

## OKLAHOMA

**Cherokee**
Hadwiger, Mickey J.
**Durant**
McPheron, Alan Beaumont
**Edmond**
Kamp, Randall William
**Enid**
Musser, William Wesley, Jr.
**Kingfisher**
Baker, Thomas Edward
**Mcalester**
Cornish, Richard Pool
**Oklahoma City**
Conner, Leslie Lynn, Jr.
High, David Royce
Necco, Alexander David
Pendell, Terry Ashley
Ross, William Jarboe
Schuster, E. Elaine
**Ponca City**
Northcutt, Clarence Dewey
**Tulsa**
Blackstock, LeRoy
Bowles, Margo La Joy
Clark, Gary Carl
Cowdery, Allen Craig
Hatfield, Jack Kenton
Steltzlen, Janelle Hicks
**Vinita**
Curnutte, Mark William
**Walters**
Flanagan, Michael Charles

## OREGON

**Beaverton**
Cyr, Steven Miles
**Corvallis**
Morris, Gretchen Reynolds
**Eugene**
Horn, John Harold
Thompson, Edward P.
**Oregon City**
McFarland, Carol Anne
**Portland**
Bauer, Henry Leland
Jenks, George Milan
Kamin, Scott Allan
Klarquist, Kenneth Stevens, Jr.
Lee, Laurie Neilson
Strader, Timothy Richards

## PENNSYLVANIA

**Allentown**
Coe, Ilse G.
Zamborsky, Donald A.
**Berwyn**
Gadsden, Christopher Henry
**Brookville**
Smith, Sharon Louise
**Butler**
Pater, Michael John
Paulisick, Gerri Volchko
**Clarion**
O'Neil, Kenton R.
Pope, Henry Ray, Jr.
**Devon**
Graf, Bayard Mayhew
**Dover**
Krug, Rob Alan
**Doylestown**
Elliott, Richard Howard
Wagner, Joseph Hagel
**Enola**
Sheaffer, Cindy Elaine
Sheetz, Ralph Albert
**Erie**
Adair, Evan Edward
**Fort Washington**
Hess, Lawrence Eugene, Jr.
**Franklin**
Greenfield, James Milton
**Girard**
Steadman, James Robert
**Gradyville**
Harvey, Edmund Lukens
**Greensburg**
Gounley, Dennis Joseph
**Grove City**
McBride, Milford Lawrence, Jr.
**Harrisburg**
Boswell, William Douglas
**Hatboro**
John, Robert McClintock
Nicholson, Bruce Allen
**Haverford**
Frick, Benjamin Charles
**Havertown**
Donohue, Robert John
**Indiana**
Barbor, John Howard
Bell, Paul Anthony, II
**Jenkintown**
Michie, Daniel Boorse, Jr.
**King Of Prussia**
Breslin, Michael Francis
DeMaria, Joseph Carminus
**Kittanning**
Petrosky, Robert
**Lancaster**
Golin, Charles
Kraybill, J(ames) Elvin
McGuire, Kendra Diane
**Langhorne**
Hillje, Barbara Brown
**Lemoyne**
Stewart, Richard Williams
**Lock Haven**
Snowiss, Alvin L.
**Marietta**
Shumaker, Harold Dennis
**Mc Keesport**
Kessler, Steven Fisher
**Media**
Farber, Howard
Firkser, Robert M.
Mackrides, William Charles
Mardinly, Peter Alan
Tomlinson, Herbert Weston
**Mercer**
McConnell, Mary Ann
**Middletown**
Pannebaker, James Boyd
**Milton**
Davis, Preston Lindner
**Monroeville**
Cohen, Laura
**Murrysville**
Kemp, Kathleen Nagy
**Nazareth**
Reed, Gregory Russell
**New Castle**
Babb, Alfred Ward
Lynch, Paul Patrick
**Norristown**
Andrews, Cheri D.
Folmar, Larry John
**Philadelphia**
Best, Franklin Luther, Jr.
Cooper, Wendy Fein
Deming, Frank Stout
Gillis, Richard Moffitt, Jr.
Hagan, Mary Ann
Hamilton, Perrin C.
Heintz, Paul Capron
Jamison, Judith Jaffe
Kaier, Edward John
Kaufman, David Joseph
Lombard, John James, Jr.
Mirabello, Francis Joseph
Murphy, Daniel Ignatius
Nofer, George Hancock
Schneider, Pam Horvitz
Speyer, Debra Gail
Wolff, Deborah H(orowitz)
Wright, Minturn Tatum, III
**Pittsburgh**
Aaron, Marcus, II
Anderson, Lea E.
Brown, David Ronald
Connell, Janice T.
Daniel, Robert Michael
Hess, Emerson Garfield
Hollinshead, Earl Darnell, Jr.
Houston, William McClelland
Isabella, Mary Margaret
McGuire, Matthew Francis
McKee, Ralph Dyer, Jr.
McLaughlin, John Sherman
Peduto, Mark B.
Scully, Erik Vincent
Sutton, William Dwight
Ummer, James Walter
Vater, Charles J.
Yates, Alfred Glenn, Jr.
**Pottstown**
Evans, Robert Whiteside, III
**Pottsville**
Jones, Joseph Hayward
**Punxsutawney**
Long, Jesse Paul
**Reading**
Kline, Sidney DeLong, Jr.
**Scranton**
Burke, Henry Patrick
Henkelman, Willard Max
**Sewickley**
Jackson, Velma Louise
**Sharon**
Dill, William Allen
**Southampton**
Benz, William J.
**Swarthmore**
Ullman, Roger Roland
**Uniontown**
Leskinen, Steve Peter
**Verona**
Chisnell, Janice Hoffman
**Washington**
Key, Susan Mondik
**Waynesboro**
Maxwell, LeRoy Stevenson
**West Chester**
DeVlieger, Tracy Blake
Rolfe, John L.
Sommer, Jeffrey Robert
**Wexford**
Fall, Robert J.
**York**
Hoffmeyer, William Frederick

## RHODE ISLAND

**Coventry**
Szarek, Milton Louis
**Pawtucket**
Marran, Joseph Edward, Jr.
Vacca, Anthony
**Providence**
Demopulos, Harold William
Hastings, Edwin H(amilton)
Kean, John Vaughan
McMahon, Raymond John
Mulhearn, Christopher Michael

**Warwick**
Gazerro, G. John, Jr.
Goldman, Steven Jason
**Woonsocket**
Koutsogiane, Phillip Charles

### SOUTH CAROLINA

**Charleston**
Branham, C. Michael
Ray, Paul DuBose
**Columbia**
Gibbes, William Holman
Unger, Richard Mahlon
**Greenville**
Dana, Frank J., III
Smock, C(arolyn) Diane
Walters, Johnnie McKeiver
**Mount Pleasant**
Whitten, Beatrice Ehrenberg
**Pawleys Island**
Daniel, J. Reese
**Rock Hill**
Alford, Duncan Earl
Hardin, James Carlisle, III
**Sumter**
Reynolds, William MacKenzie, Jr.

### SOUTH DAKOTA

**Parker**
Zimmer, John Herman

### TENNESSEE

**Bristol**
Massengill, Myers Newton
**Chattanooga**
Akers, Samuel Lee
Walker, Robert Kirk
Weems, Kyle Richard
**Church Hill**
Frazier, Steven Carl
**Collierville**
Rogers, Gordon Keith, Jr.
**Erwin**
Shults-Davis, Lois Bunton
**Jackson**
Womack, Charles Raymond
**Knoxville**
Ailor, Earl Starnes
Roach, Jon Gilbert
Worthington, Carole Yard Lynch
**Memphis**
Allen, Newton Perkins
Autry, Edward Thomas
Bland, James Theodore, Jr.
Davis, Earl Prichard (Pat Davis)
Harpster, James Erving
Jackson, Thomas Francis, III
Patton, Charles Henry
Tate, Stonewall Shepherd
**Nashville**
Berry, William Wells
Boyd, Mary Olert
Cornell, Helen Loftin
Nevin, Ronald Kent
Skoney, Lesa Hartley
Spining, W. Carl
Trautman, Herman Louis
**Union City**
Graham, Hardy Moore

### TEXAS

**Addison**
Geary, Joseph William
Martens, Dan E.
**Amarillo**
Burnette, Susan Lynn
**Arlington**
Dowdy, John Vernard, Jr.
**Austin**
Bloomquist, Amy Peterson
Dougherty, John Chrysostom, III
Graham, Samuel R.
Helman, Stephen Jody
Hernandez, Mack Ray
Hollen, Theodore Thomas
Kerr, Stanley Munger
**Ballinger**
Grindstaff, Everett James
**Bellaire**
Jacobus, Charles Joseph
**Borger**
Pace, Rosa White
**Brownsville**
Ray, Mary Louise Ryan
**Bryan**
Steelman, Frank (Sitley)
**Cat Spring**
Conner, Warren Wesley
**Corpus Christi**
Alberts, Harold
Davis, Martin Clay
Dohse, Roberta Shellum
Turpin, John Russell, Jr.
**Dallas**
Burns, Sandra
Clardy, Thelma Sanders
Crain, Christina Melton
Dicus, Brian George
Hartnett, Will Ford
Jones, Grier Patterson
Phelps, Robert Frederick, Jr.
Skibell, Arthur
Smith, Frank Tupper
Sommers, Conrad Hoyle
**De Soto**
Boyanton, Janet Shafer
**Edinburg**
Looney, Cullen Rogers
**El Paso**
Cox, Sanford Curtis, Jr.
Hedrick, Mark
Marshall, Richard Treeger
Moffeit, Michael Paul
Sanders, Amy Stewart
Yetter, Richard
**Fort Worth**
Carr, Thomas Eldridge
Collins, Whitfield James
Crumley, John Walter
Law, Thomas Hart
Ratliff, William D., III
Tilley, Rice M(atthews), Jr.
West, Robert Grady
Whitney, William Bernard
**Georgetown**
Bryce, William Delf
Wilkerson, James Neill
**Hallettsville**
Baber, Wilbur H., Jr.
**Houston**
Amann, Leslie Kiefer
Brown, Michael Lance
Brown, Stephen Smiley
Cenatiempo, Michael J.
Collins, Susan E.
Crocker, Charles Allan
Eastland, S. Stacy
Fabio, Thea Marie
Fallis, Norma Eleanor
Fason, Rita Miller
Forlano, Frederick Peter
Griffin, Marilyn Otteman
Hatchett, Cynthia M.
Horrigan, Joseph Stewart
Jeske, Charles Matthew
Koenig, Rodney Curtis
Pesikoff, Bette Schein
Schwartzel, Charles Boone
Shearer, Dean Paul
Stewart, Pamela L.
Touchy, Deborah K. P.
**Hurst**
Leach, Terry Ray
**Jacksonville**
Cummins, Michael Wayne
Thrall, Gordon Fish
**La Porte**
Askins, Knox Winfred
**Liberty**
Wheat, John Nixon
**Longview**
Crowson, David Lee
Welge, Jack Herman, Jr.
**Lubbock**
Barnhill, Robert Edwin, III
Harrell, Walter Hugh
Teel, Robert E.
**Lufkin**
Garrison, Pitser Hardeman
**Marshall**
Gilstrap, James Rodney
**New Braunfels**
Nolte, Melvin, Jr.
Pfeuffer, Robert Tug
**Richardson**
Jeffreys, Albert Leonidas
**Richmond**
Slone, Charles R.
**San Angelo**
Carter, James Alfred
Moeller, Galen Ashley
**San Antonio**
Cabezas-Gil, Rosa M.
Ross, James Ulric
Veitch, Thomas Harold
Yates, Norris William, Jr.
**Tyler**
Hadden, Arthur Roby
**Uvalde**
Kerby, Yale Leland
**Weatherford**
Akers, Charles Benjamin
Westenhover, Gary Floyd
**Wichita Falls**
Goff, Robert William, Jr.
**Yoakum**
Kvinta, Charles J.

### UTAH

**Salt Lake City**
Adams, Joseph Keith

### VERMONT

**Burlington**
Gravel, John Cook
**Dorset**
O'Toole, Kevin Michael
**Middlebury**
Reiff, Helen Hayslette
**Rutland**
Bloomer, William John
**South Royalton**
Prye, Steven Marvell
**Woodstock**
Sincerbeaux, Robert Abbott

### VIRGINIA

**Alexandria**
Peyton, Gordon Pickett
**Arlington**
Collins, Philip Reilly
Malone, William Grady
Welty, Charles Douglas
**Ashburn**
Gold, George Myron
**Bristol**
Alan, Sondra Kirschner
**Charlottesville**
Edwards, James Edwin
Middleditch, Leigh Benjamin, Jr.
**Danville**
Conway, French Hoge
Goodman, Lewis Elton, Jr.
**Fairfax**
Spitzberg, Irving Joseph, Jr.
**Falls Church**
Baskin, William Maxwell, Sr.
Crews, Grasty, II
**Fredericksburg**
Sheffield, Walter Jervis
**Lynchburg**
Davies, Arthur B(everly), III
**Madison**
Coates, Frederick Ross
**Mc Lean**
Herge, J. Curtis
Morris, James Malachy
**Newport News**
Nachman, Erwin B(ehr)
**Norfolk**
Knight, Montgomery, Jr.
**Petersburg**
Baskervill, Charles Thornton
**Providence Forge**
Richardson, William Winfree, III
**Richmond**
Addison, David Dunham
Aghdami, Farhad
Belcher, Dennis Irl
Buffenstein, Allan S.
Hill, Oliver White, Sr.
Horsley, Waller Holladay
Stevens, C. Daniel
Warthen, Harry Justice, III
**Roanoke**
Lemon, William Jacob
**Vienna**
Callahan, Timothy J.

### WASHINGTON

**Bellevue**
Hand, Bruce George
McCutcheon, James Edward, III
Treacy, Gerald Bernard, Jr.
**Bremerton**
Cunningham, Gary Allen
**Centralia**
Tiller, Laurel Lee
**Issaquah**
Hammerly, Mary Leverenz
**Olympia**
Walker, Francis Joseph
Wright, Daniel A.
**Port Angeles**
Gay, Carl Lloyd
**Port Orchard**
Shiers, Frank Abram
**Seattle**
Abelite, Jahnis John
Andreasen, Steven W.
Blais, Robert Howard
Cavin, Clark
Dussault, William Leonard Ernest
Gores, Thomas C.
Hanson, William Lewis
Jonsson, Jon Marvin
Lombard, John Cutler
Olver, Michael Lynn
Rieke, Paul Victor
Sayre, Matt Melvin Mathias
**Spokane**
Cooper, R(obert) Maurice
Sayre, Richard Layton
**Tacoma**
Peters, Frank August
Seinfeld, Lester
**Walla Walla**
Hayner, Herman Henry

### WEST VIRGINIA

**Wheeling**
Gompers, Joseph Alan

### WISCONSIN

**Adams**
Screnock, Paul Steven
**Beaver Dam**
Becker, Eric L.
**Delavan**
Weber, Laura Ann
**Elkhorn**
Eberhardt, Daniel Hugo
Sweet, Lowell Elwin
**Elm Grove**
Kaestner, Richard Darwin
**Hales Corners**
Case, Karen Ann
**Janesville**
Williams, Mary Beth
**La Crosse**
Ablan, Michael C.
**Madison**
Burish, Mark Dennis
Kuehling, Robert Warren
Pitzner, Richard William
Roberson, Linda
Wilcox, Michael Wing
**Manitowoc**
Muchin, Arden Archie
**Milwaukee**
Bratt, Herbert Sidney
Dencker, Lester J.
Gray, Sidney
Iding, Allan Earl
Margolis, Marvin Allen
Nelson, Randy Scott
Peltin, Sherwin Carl
Quirk, Michael L.
Reiske, Peter Francis
**Monroe**
Kittelsen, Rodney Olin
**Neenah**
Birtch, Grant Eacrett
**Port Washington**
Check, Melvin Anthony
**Racine**
Crawford, Gerald Marcus
Du Rocher, James Howard
Feil, Frank J., Jr.
**Reedsburg**
Gorsuch, Sandra Cardo
**Rhinelander**
Reese, Kirk David
**Shawano**
Habeck, James Roy
**Sheboygan**
Wasserman, Sylvia Katz
**Waukesha**
Ward, James A.

### WYOMING

**Casper**
Hjelmstad, William David
**Cheyenne**
Wrobetz, Donald Reay
**Cody**
Stradley, Richard Lee
**Laramie**
Smith, Thomas Shore

### TERRITORIES OF THE UNITED STATES

### PUERTO RICO

**Ponce**
Leon-Sotomayor, Jose Rafael

### ADDRESS UNPUBLISHED

Abrahams, Samuel
Adams, Samuel Franklin
Ansley, Shepard Bryan
Asmar, Laila Michelle
Barry, David F.
Bergkvist, Thomas A.
Bertram, Manya M.
Brashear, William Ronald
Buechel, William Benjamin
Burcham, Randall Parks
Caquatto, Norma Madeline
Carney, Donald Francis, Jr.
Clabaugh, Elmer Eugene, Jr.
Connors, Kevin Charles
Coryell, Frank
Deane, Ruth M.
Dolce, Julia Wagner
Dorrier, Lindsay Gordon, Jr.
Duncan, Nora Kathryn
Easterling, Charles Armo
Edwards, William Thomas, Jr.
Emry, Frederic Grant
Engelhardt, John Hugo
Farley, Barbara Suzanne
Fiala, David Marcus
Frank, Jeffrey Michael
Frankel, James Burton
Gooch, Robert Francis
Green, Harland Norton
Grutz, James Arthur
Hanson, Fred B.
Harris, Morton Allen
Higginson, Carla Jean
Huenergardt, Darrel J.
Janecek, Jeanette Mary
Jones, Clifford Aaron, Sr.
Jorgensen, Erik Holger
Kaitz, Haskell A.
LaForest, Lana Jean
Lazor, John Adam
Loomie, Edward Raphael
Mann, Robert Paul
Martin, James William
Matheny, Mary Jane
Meier, Matthew Hamilton
Meli, Salvatore Andrew
Merrill, Abel Jay
Milberg, Melinda Sharon
Neilson, Benjamin Reath
O'Brien, Charles H.
O'Connor, Edward Vincent, Jr.
O'Dell, Joan Elizabeth
Reber, Joseph E.
Reiche, Frank Perley
Schild, Raymond Douglas
Shapiro, Edwin Stanley
Shariff, Vivian Rodriguez
Shook, Ann Jones
Silverberg, Mark Victor
Solkoff, Jerome Ira
Stone, Edward Herman
Surratt, John Richard
Sweeney, Deidre Ann
Weill, (Lige) Harry, Sr.
Wharton, Hugh Davis, III
Williams, Thomas Arthur
Wyshak, Lillian Worthing
Zelechiwsky, Bohdan John

## PRODUCT LIABILITY

### UNITED STATES

### ALABAMA

**Birmingham**
Crook, Ronald R.
DeGaris, Annesley Hodges
Fox, Anthony N.
Harris, George Bryan
Norris, Rick D.
Wettermark, James Hart
**Gadsden**
Cornett, Bradley Williams
Kimberley, David Alan
Roberts, Michael Lee
**Magnolia Springs**
Kuykendall, Frederick Thurman, III
**Mobile**
Carwie, Annette McDermott
**Montgomery**
Boone, LaBarron N.
Esdale, R. Graham, Jr.
McGowin, William Claude

### ALASKA

**Anchorage**
Anderson, Lloyd Vincent
Wagstaff, Robert Hall

### ARIZONA

**Phoenix**
Begam, Robert George
Condo, James Robert
Cummings, Frederick Michael
Gerity, Michael E.
Keane, William Timothy
Marks, Merton Eleazer
Norris, Raymond Michael
O'Driscoll, Cornelius Joseph
Plattner, Richard Serber
Smith, Gretchen Nicole
Studnicki, Adam A.
Van Wagner, Albert Edwin, Jr.
**Tempe**
Barnes, Jennifer Reon
**Tucson**
Davis, Richard
Osborne, John Edwards
Shultz, Silas Harold

### ARKANSAS

**Arkadelphia**
Turner, Otis Hawes
**Bryant**
Jackson, James Ralph
**Little Rock**
Cearley, Robert M., Jr.
Ervin, Edie Renee
Pryor, Kathryn Ann
Taylor, Sammye Lou

### CALIFORNIA

**Anaheim**
Randall, James Grafton
**Beverly Hills**
Bear, Jeffrey Lewis
**Citrus Heights**
Marman, Joseph H.
**Cupertino**
Svalya, Phillip Gordon
**Downey**
Duzey, Robert Lindsey
**Escondido**
Barraza, Horacio
**Fresno**
DeMaria, Anthony Nicholas
Runyon, Brett L.
**Irvine**
Hamann, Howard Evans
Miller, Richard Wayne
Suojanen, Wayne William
**Long Beach**
Johnson, Philip Leslie
**Los Angeles**
Angelo, Christopher Edmond
Aristei, J. Clark
Barth, Karen Ann
Craigie, Alex William
Downey, William J., III
Field, Richard Clark
Greaves, John Allen
Hedlund, Paul James
Lebovits, Moses
Muoneke, Anthony
Sayas, Conrado Joe
Sonnett, Anthony Evan
Steinbrecher, Alan K.
**Manhattan Beach**
Baer, Joseph Richard
**Newport Beach**
Wentworth, Theodore Sumner
**Oakland**
Berry, Phillip Samuel
Ivary, Eric Henry
**Orinda**
Noah, Paul Randall
**Oxnard**
McGinley, James Duff
**Pasadena**
Algorri, Mark Steven
Doyle, John C.
**Redondo Beach**
Hachmeister, John H.
**Sacramento**
Blackman, David Michael
Mendoza, Joanna R.
**San Bernardino**
Prince, Timothy Peter
**San Diego**
Brown, LaMar Bevan
Copley, Rocky K.
Guinn, Susan Lee
Huston, Kenneth Dale
McClellan, Craig Rene
Mongan, Anthony David
Petix, Stephen Vincent
**San Francisco**
Arbuthnot, Robert Murray
Bruen, James A.
Dryden, Robert Eugene
Fergus, Gary Scott
Fleischmann, Roger Justice
Ray, Jennifer Smith
Salomon, Sheila M.
Strauss, Philip Reed
Walker, Walter Herbert, III
Woodard, Heather Anne
**San Jose**
Alexander, Richard
Bennion, David Jacobsen
Bohn, Robert Herbert
Liccardo, Salvador A.
Nielsen, Christian Bayard
**Santa Barbara**
Kallman, Kristofer
Simpson, Curtis Chapman, III
**Santa Monica**
Bower, Allan Maxwell
McGovern, David Carr
Peters, Thomas Harry
Ringler, Jerome Lawrence
Wong, Elizabeth Anne
**Walnut Creek**
Blackburn, Michael Philip
Everson, Martin Joseph
Pagter, Carl Richard
**Woodland Hills**
Comroe, Eugene W.

### COLORADO

**Aspen**
Shulman, Harry
**Boulder**
Fenster, Herbert Lawrence
Gordon, Glen Frank
Gray, William R.

**Colorado Springs**
Pressman, Glenn Spencer
Walker, Jonathan Lee
**Denver**
Byrne, Thomas J.
Kaye, Bruce Jeffrey
Malatesta, Mary Anne
Palmeri, John M.
Samour, Carlos A.
Shore, Heather Field
Wheeler, Malcolm Edward
**Englewood**
Nixon, Scott Sherman

### CONNECTICUT

**Avon**
Wiechmann, Eric Watt
**Bridgeport**
Feldman, David Scott
**Hamden**
Bershtein, Herman Sammy
**Middletown**
Poliner, Bernard
**New London**
Reardon, Robert Ignatius, Jr.
**North Haven**
Walsh, Kevin Peter
**Southport**
Sanetti, Stephen Louis
**Stamford**
Eckweiler, Karl Terrance
Filan, Patrick J.
**Trumbull**
Czajkowski, Frank Henry

### DELAWARE

**Wilmington**
Cummings, Stacey L.
Julian, J. R.

### DISTRICT OF COLUMBIA

**Washington**
Augustini, Michael Charles
Casey, Bernard J.
Doumar, George R. A.
Duross, Charles Edward, IV
Flannery, Ellen Joanne
Gelb, Joseph Donald
Lewis, David John
Long, Victor Earl
Michael, Helen Katherine
Pollock, Stacy Jane
Renner, Curtis Shotwell
Rice, Paul Jackson
Rizzo, James Gerard
Rubel, Eric A.
Wasserman, Michael Francis
Zambri, Salvatore Joseph

### FLORIDA

**Bradenton**
Plews, Dennis James
**Bushnell**
Hagin, T. Richard
**Coral Gables**
Fournaris, Theodore J.
Friedman, Marvin Ross
**Fort Lauderdale**
Fischer, Carey Michael
Heath, Thomas Clark
James, Gordon, III
Kramish, Marc Eric
Lundt, Eric L.
Pomeroy, Gregg Joseph
Roselli, Richard Joseph
Santa Maria, Diana
Sherman, Richard Allen
Strickland, Wilton L.
Turner, Hugh Joseph, Jr.
**Hollywood**
Zebersky, Edward Herbert
**Jacksonville**
Bullock, Bruce Stanley
Cowles, Robert Lawrence
Eikner, Tod Bayard
Link, Robert James
Reed, Ronald Ernst
**Maitland**
Edwards, James Alfred
**Melbourne**
Cacciatore, Sammy Michel
**Miami**
Brady, Steven Michael
Cabanas, Oscar Jorge
Coll, Norman Alan
Davis, Jeffrey Robert
Fox, Gary Devenow
Golden, John Dennis
Greenberg, Stewart Gary
Marks, Steven Craig
Payne, R.W., Jr.
Yaffa, Andrew Bryan
**Ocala**
Crabtree, John Granville
Spivey, Stephen Dale
**Orlando**
Metz, Larry Edward
**Pensacola**
Green, James R.
Marsh, William Douglas
**Saint Petersburg**
Gustafson, James William, Jr. ()
**Sarasota**
Herb, F(rank) Steven
**Tallahassee**
Connor, Kenneth Luke
Fonvielle, Charles David
**Tampa**
Apgar, Kenneth Edward
Cunningham, Anthony Willard
Fernandez, Ricardo Antonio
Fulton, Robert Maurice
Gunn, Lee Delton, IV
Knopik, Christopher Scott
Morgenstern, Dennis Michael
Vogt, Martha Diane
**West Palm Beach**
Barnhart, Forrest Gregory
Flanagan, L. Martin
Levy, Jonathan Todd
Moffet, Kenneth William
Posgay, Matthew Nichols

### GEORGIA

**Albany**
Cannon, William E., Jr.
**Alpharetta**
Singer, Randy Darrell
**Athens**
Barrow, John J.
**Atlanta**
Brooks, Wilbur Clinton
Calvert, Matthew James
Cheeley, Robert David
Cooper, Lawrence Allen
Crumpler, Joan Gale
Eckl, William Wray
Eidson, James Anthony
Hagan, James Walter
Head, William Carl
Jones, Evan Wier
Rusher, Derwood H., II
Steel, John Deaton
Wilson, Roger Calvin
**Carrollton**
Tisinger, David H.
**Cartersville**
Pope, Robert Daniel
**Columbus**
Harp, John Anderson
Lasseter, Earle Forrest
McGlamry, Max Reginald
**Macon**
Grant, George Clarence
**Newnan**
Franklin, Bruce Walter
**Rome**
Brinson, Robert Maddox
**Savannah**
Forbes, Morton Gerald
**Statesboro**
Brogdon, W.M. "Rowe"
Snipes, Daniel Brent
**Valdosta**
Bright, Joseph Converse

### HAWAII

**Honolulu**
Bail, Lisa A.
Kaya, Randall Y.
Komeya, Geoffrey Kimo Sanshiro
**Koloa**
Blair, Samuel Ray
**Wailuku**
Green, Eve Marie

### IDAHO

**Boise**
Furey, Patrick Dennis
**Lewiston**
Aherin, Darrel William
**Pocatello**
Nye, W. Marcus W.
**Twin Falls**
Lezamiz, John T.
Webb, Curtis Randall

### ILLINOIS

**Alton**
Talbert, Hugh Mathis
**Belleville**
Boyle, Richard Edward
Heiligenstein, Christian E.
Marlen, Matthew James
Ripplinger, George Raymond, Jr.
**Champaign**
Harden, Richard Russell
**Chicago**
Argeros, Anthony George
Berg, William Gerard
Brand, Mark
Burke, Thomas Joseph, Jr.
Burke, William Joseph
Cavenagh, Timothy Joseph
Costello, James Paul
Daniels, John Draper
Durkin, Albert Eugene
Ellbogen, Andrew D.
Fanone, John R.
Formeller, Daniel Richard
Griffin, Lawrence Joseph
Howser, Richard Glen
Iwan, Lori E.
Johnson, Jennifer Jerit
Krivicich, John Augustine
Kroll, Jeffrey Joseph
Marszalek, John Edward
Mulroy, Thomas Robert, Jr.
Murphy, Edward J.
Napleton, Robert Joseph
Neumeier, Matthew Michael
Novak, Mark
O'Hagan, Kevin Michael
Pach, Lisa Anne
Perrin, James Kirk
Pollock, Bradley Neil
Price, Paul L.
Pullano, Richard L.
Rapoport, David E.
Rogers, William John
Rohrman, Douglass Frederick
Stiegel, Michael Allen
Sundvall, Sheila A.
Tucker, Bowen Hayward
Weaver, Timothy Allan
Wunsch, John Carlyle
Young, Keith Lawrence
**Decatur**
Jones, Deanne Fortna
**Edwardsville**
Carlson, Jon Gordon
**Glen Ellyn**
O'Connell, Daniel James
**Joliet**
Klukas, Elizabeth Ann
**Libertyville**
Rallo, Douglas
**Morris**
Belt, Scott M.
**Palos Heights**
Jasinski, George John
**Paris**
Pearman, John Stewart
**Prospect Heights**
Leopold, Mark F.
**Rock Island**
VanDerGinst, Dennis Allen
**Rockford**
Sullivan, Peter Thomas, III
**Rosemont**
Willens, Matthew Lyle
**Saint Charles**
Clancy Boles, Susan
**Wheaton**
Butt, Edward Thomas, Jr.

### INDIANA

**Bloomington**
Nunn, Ken
**Indianapolis**
Arceneaux, Adam
Caress, Timothy Charles
Hovde, F. Boyd
Hovde, Frederick Russell
Mortier, Jeffrey James
Petersen, James Leo
Price, Henry J.
Tinsley, Nancy Grace
Townsend, John Frederick, Jr.
**Indianpolis**
Holtzlander, Stephanie Franco
**Seymour**
Gill, W(alter) Brent
**South Bend**
Horn, George Edward, Jr.
**Valparaiso**
Evans, Larry G.

### IOWA

**Des Moines**
Cortese, Joseph Samuel, II

### KANSAS

**Fort Scott**
Reynolds, Zackery E.
**Overland Park**
Sampson, William Roth

### KENTUCKY

**Lexington**
Garmer, William Robert
**Louisville**
Clay, Richard H.C.
Sales, Kenneth L.

### LOUISIANA

**Alexandria**
Bolen, James Aubrey, Jr.
Pearce, Mark Douglas
**Baton Rouge**
Andrews, Brandon Scott
LeBlanc, J. Burton, IV
Scobee, H. Evans
**Lafayette**
Bass, William Morris
Lemoine, Gano D., Jr.
Swift, John Goulding
**Metairie**
Ford, Robert David
Gauthier, Celeste Anne
McMahon, Robert Albert, Jr.
Milazzo, Thomas Gregory
**New Orleans**
Allen, F(rank) C(linton), Jr.
Ates, J. Robert
Bruno, Frank Silvo
Christovich, Alvin Richard, Jr.
Courington, Kaye Newton
Gay, Esmond Phelps
Gertler, Meyer H.
Grant, Arthur Gordon, Jr.
Masinter, Paul James
Moore, Blaine Augusta
Riess, George Febiger
Shuey, James Frank
Sinnott, John William

### MAINE

**Portland**
Brogan, Jonathan William
Culley, Peter William
Quinn, Thomas Joseph

### MARYLAND

**Annapolis**
Rutland, David Lee
Wharton, James T.
**Baltimore**
Bartlett, James Wilson, III
Burch, Francis Boucher, Jr.
Christianson, Charles Anthony Patrick
DeVries, Donald Lawson, Jr.
Digges, Edward S(imms), Jr.
Erwin, H. Robert
Joseph, Charles Ian
Mullady, Raymond George, Jr.
**Greenbelt**
Greenwald, Andrew Eric
**Lanham Seabrook**
McCarthy, Kevin John
**Phoenix**
Schlenger, Robert Purnell
**Rockville**
Michael, Robert Roy
**Silver Spring**
Lipshultz, Leonard L.

### MASSACHUSETTS

**Boston**
Campbell, Richard P.
Casby, Robert William
Cashore, Amy C.
Dillon, James Joseph
Dolan, James Boyle, Jr.
Edwards, Richard Lansing
Ellis, Fredric Lee
Goscinak, Virginia Casey
Lumsden, Diana J.
Rafferty, Edson Howard
Ramsey, James E.
Reed, Barry C., Jr.
Schafer, Steven Harris
Seidel, Rebecca Suzanne
**Worcester**
Balko, George Anthony, III
Bassett, Edward Caldwell, Jr.

### MICHIGAN

**Ann Arbor**
Joscelyn, Kent Buckley
**Auburn Hills**
DeAgostino, Thomas M.
**Bingham Farms**
Goren, Steven Eliot
**Birmingham**
Elsman, James Leonard, Jr.
**Bloomfield Hills**
Baumkel, Mark S.
Hintzen, Erich Heinz
**Detroit**
Babcock, Charles Witten, Jr.
Branigan, Thomas Patrick
Foley, Thomas John
Lenga, J. Thomas
Pope, Harold D.
Posner, Alan B.
Rooney, Scott William
Wagner, Brian J.
**Farmington**
Torpey, Scott Raymond
**Grand Rapids**
Blackwell, Thomas Francis
Borja, Arthur
Spies, Frank Stadler
Vander Laan, Allan C.
**Madison Heights**
Szczesny, Ronald William
**Saginaw**
Chasnis, John Alex
**Saint Joseph**
Butzbaugh, Elden W., Jr.
**Southfield**
Gordon, Louis
Jaffa, Jonathan Mark
Tombers, Evelyn Charlotte
Tyler, David Malcolm
**Sterling Heights**
Hartkop, Jeffrey Wells
**Suttons Bay**
Robb, Dean Allen, Sr.
**Ypsilanti**
Shapiro, Douglas Bruce

### MINNESOTA

**Austin**
Schneider, Mahlon C.
**Edina**
Ashley, James Patrick
**Maplewood**
Nemo, Anthony James
**Minneapolis**
Christensen, Robert Paul
Gill, Richard Lawrence
Hanson, Kent Bryan
Hinderaker, John Hadley
Klosowski, Thomas Kenneth
LeNeave, Cortney Scott
Manning, William Henry
Morgan, Richard George
Plunkett, Stephen Oliver
Reichert, Brent Larry
Roe, Roger Rolland
Yira, Markus Clarence
**Saint Louis Park**
Flom, Katherine S.
**Saint Paul**
Allison, John Robert
Dunn, James Francis
King, Lawrence R.
Krug, Michael Steven
Ursu, John Joseph
**Winona**
Borman, John

### MISSISSIPPI

**Brandon**
Obert, Keith David
**Clarksdale**
Chapman, Ralph E.
Merkel, Charles Michael
**Hattiesburg**
Jernigan, Jay Lawrence
**Jackson**
Corlew, John Gordon
Hewes, George Poindexter, III
Langford, James Jerry
Montagnet, O. Stephen
Northington, Hiawatha
**Ocean Springs**
Luckey, Alwyn Hall
**Tupelo**
Clayton, Claude F., Jr.
**Winona**
Reid, William Joseph

### MISSOURI

**Kansas City**
Abele, Robert Christopher
Bartimus, James Russell
Breneman, Diane Marie
Cartmell, Thomas Philip
Doherty, Brian John
Eldridge, Truman Kermit, Jr.
Horn, Robert Allen
Hursh, Lynn Wilson
Larson, Thomas Roy
Levings, Theresa Lawrence
Mayer, David Mathew
Modin, Richard F.
Newsom, James Thomas
Norton, John Hise
Redfearn, Paul L., III
Smith, R(onald) Scott
Socarras, Michael Peter
Triplett, Timothy Wayne
**Rolla**
Hickle, William Earl
**Saint Joseph**
Koerner, Wendell Edward, Jr.
Sokol, Ronald Mark
**Saint Louis**
Baldwin, Brent Winfield
Hesse, Margaret Ann
Kell, John Mark
Rabbitt, Daniel Thomas, Jr.
Reeg, Kurtis Bradford
Suess, Jeffrey Karl
Walsh, Joseph Leo, III
Williams, Theodore Joseph, Jr.
Wines, Lawrence Eugene
Wulff, Robert Joseph
**Springfield**
FitzGerald, Kevin Michael

### MONTANA

**Billings**
Lodders, Ronald R.
**Great Falls**
George, Michael Joseph

### NEBRASKA

**Omaha**
Cuddigan, Timothy John

### NEVADA

**Las Vegas**
Galatz, Neil Gilbert
Mainor, W. Randall
Stoberski, Michael Edward
**Reno**
Hayward, Daniel Thomas
Shaffer, Wayne Alan
Whitbeck, Jill Karla

### NEW HAMPSHIRE

**Concord**
Mekeel, Robert K.
**Keene**
Gardner, Eric Raymond
**Manchester**
Richards, Thomas H.
**Nashua**
Brown, Kenneth Mackinnon

### NEW JERSEY

**Chatham**
Fried, David M.
**Cherry Hill**
DeVoto, Louis Joseph
**Collingswood**
Martin, Burchard V.
**Edison**
Rothenberg, Adam Leigh
**Fanwood**
Xifo, Louise Elizabeth
**Hackensack**
Gerlanc, Glenn Marc
**Haddonfield**
Andres, Kenneth G., Jr.
**Hamilton**
Chase, Daniel E.
**Livingston**
Harris, Brian Craig
Nagel, Bruce H.
**Moorestown**
Kearney, John Francis, III
**Morristown**
Bromberg, Myron James
**Newark**
Barrett, Virginia M.
Brenner, John Finn
Callahan, Patrick Michael
Cooner, David James
Garde, John Charles
Laura, Anthony Joseph
Pollock, Jeffrey Morrow
Smith, Frederick Theodore
Weber, Scott Louis
**Northfield**
Cohen, Barry David
**Plainfield**
Grayson, Russell Wayne
**Ship Bottom**
Shackleton, Richard James
**Somerville**
Dreier, William Alan
Miller, Charles William, III
**Trenton**
Bilder, Marshall D.
**Voorhees**
Kueny, Bernard E., III
**Warren**
Quinn, Thomas Gerard
**Wayne**
Gelman, Jon Leonard
**West Atlantic City**
Sinderbrand, David I.
**Westwood**
McGuirl, Robert Joseph

### NEW MEXICO

**Albuquerque**
Caruso, Mark John
**Clovis**
Doerr, Stephen
**Santa Fe**
Brannen, Jeffrey Richard
Casey, Patrick Anthony
Murphy, Dennis Patrick

### NEW YORK

**Albany**
Case, Forrest N., Jr.
Danziger, Peter
Greagan, William Joseph
Napierski, Eugene Edward

Santola, Daniel Ralph
**Astoria**
Bender, Michael Seth
**Bronx**
Fraiden, Norman Arthur
Wolf, Robert Thomas
**Brooklyn**
Blank, Helene E.
Chesley, Stephen Robert
Fallek, Andrew Michael
Martin, Jack
**Buffalo**
Armstrong, James F.
Bermingham, Joseph Daniel
Bond, Jill Kawa
Hayes, J. Michael
Szanyi, Kevin Andrew
**Camillus**
Endieveri, Anthony Frank
**Elmsford**
Mevec, Edward Robert
**Farmingdale**
O'Brien, Joan Susan
**Flushing**
Schwartz, Estar Alma
**Garrison**
Donnelly, Daniel Patrick
**Granite Spgs**
Stokes, Harry McKinney
**Hudson**
Palmateer, Lee Allen
**Lake Success**
Lee, Brian Edward
**Melville**
Schoenfeld, Michael P.
**Mineola**
Kelly, Shawn Paul
**New Hyde Park**
Jensen, Richard Currie
**New York**
Aquila, Albert
Bainton, J(ohn) Joseph
Beatty, Andrew Hyland
Berland, Sanford Neil
Bern, Marc Jay
Bezanson, Thomas Edward
Brecker, Jeffrey Ross
Chase, Edward Thornton
Cohen, Anne Elizabeth
Dankner, Jay Warren
DeWeil, Dawn Susan
Faizakoff, Daniel Benjamin
Finnerty, Joseph Gregory, Jr.
Garfield, Martin Richard
Garvey, Christopher John
Getzoff, Steven B.
Gray, Joanne Maria
Green, Lawrence Rodman
Gross, Ari Michael
Gurfein, Richard Alan
Hart, Joseph Thomas Campbell
Hernandez, Jacqueline Charmaine
Holman, Bud George
Jacob, Edwin J.
Johnson, Christopher Paul
Kasowitz, Marc Elliot
Kazanjian, John Harold
Levine, Ronald Jay
Lewis, David Robert
Lewis, Edwin Leonard, III
Mannheimer, Michael Jay
Marber, Paul Andrew
Mayesh, Jay Philip
Mitchell, C. MacNeil
Nemerov, Jeffrey Arnold
Newman, Fredric Samuel
Rejan, Jeffrey Neil
Relkin, Ellen
Roth, Barbara M.
Russotti, Philip Anthony
Schwab, Harold Lee
Scialabba, Donald Joseph
Seitelman, Mark Elias
Sheridan, Peter N.
Singer, Jeffrey
Smith, James Walker
Strober, Eric Saul
Teicher, Martin
Tessler, Robert Louis
Williams Umlauf, Natalie R.
**Newburgh**
Liberth, Richard Francis
**Poughkeepsie**
LaRose, Keith Vernon
**Rochester**
Schwarz, Stephen George
**Saratoga Springs**
Dorsey, James Baker
**Scarsdale**
Sweeney, John J(oseph)
**Schenectady**
Galvin, Christine M.
Kouray, Athena C.
Lewis, Kirk McArthur
**Syracuse**
Bottar, Anthony Samuel
Rothschild, Martin Jay
**White Plains**
D'Aloise, Lawrence T., Jr.
Ryan, Robert Davis

### NORTH CAROLINA

**Charlotte**
Gage, Gaston Hemphill
**Greensboro**
Donaldson, Arthur Joseph
**Pittsboro**
Hubbard, Thomas Edwin (Tim Hubbard)
**Raleigh**
Teague, Charles Woodrow
**Winston Salem**
Barnhill, Henry Grady, Jr.
Maready, William Frank

### NORTH DAKOTA

**Grand Forks**
Clapp, Richard Allen

### OHIO

**Akron**
Weitendorf, Kurt Robert
**Aurora**
Hermann, Philip J.
**Canton**
Lindamood, John Beyer
**Cincinnati**
Chesley, Stanley Morris
Kammerer, Matthew Paul
Kamp, David Paul
Woodside, Frank C., III
**Cleveland**
Baughman, R(obert) Patrick
Condeni, Joseph Anthony
Gerlack, Lisa Marie
Goldberg, James R.
Havens, Hunter Scott
Jeffers, John William
Lowe, James Allison
Marvar, Raymond James
Schaefer, David Arnold
**Columbus**
Alton, John Marshall
Brown, Jeffrey Monet
Hardymon, David Wayne
Kloss, William Darrell, Jr.
Mann, William Craig
Nemeth, John Charles
Radnor, Alan T.
Ray, Frank Allen
Todaro, Frank Edward
**Dayton**
Salyer, David Ronald
**East Liverpool**
Davis, William J.
**Fremont**
Albrechta, Joseph Francis
**Middletown**
Allen, Patrick William
**Newark**
Meyer, Christopher Richard
**Poland**
Vasvari, Thomas M.
**Toledo**
Anspach, Robert Michael
Barone, Guy T.
**Warren**
Newendop, Paul William
**Youngstown**
Carlin, Clair Myron

### OKLAHOMA

**Mustang**
Denton, Michael David, Jr.
**Oklahoma City**
Babb, Donald Lynn
Callahan, Kelley Charles
Coats, Andrew Montgomery
Fitch, Brent E.
Looney, Robert Dudley
Woods, Harry Arthur, Jr.
**Tulsa**
Atkinson, Michael Pearce
Ballard, Elizabeth Ann

### OREGON

**Central Point**
Richardson, Dennis Michael
**Corvallis**
Ringo, Robert Gribble
**Eugene**
Carlson, Charles David
**Portland**
Duden, Paul Russell
Maloney, Robert E., Jr.
Ruess, Brian Knight
Swanson, Leslie Martin, Jr.
**Salem**
Roy, Matthew Lansing
**Springfield**
Wilson, Virgil James, III

### PENNSYLVANIA

**Allentown**
Altemose, Mark Kenneth
**Bala Cynwyd**
Olley, Michael Joseph
**Bethel Park**
Bobrowsky, Kim Russell
**Easton**
Brown, Robert Carroll
**Fort Washington**
Daller, Morton F.
**Harrisburg**
Angino, Richard Carmen
Downey, Brian Patrick
Melillo, Joseph Michael
Schmidt, Thomas Bernard, III
Stefanon, Anthony
**Lancaster**
Hall, Thomas W.
Nast, Dianne Martha
**Leola**
Eaby, Christian Earl
**Narberth**
Metter, Ronald Elliot
**New Castle**
Sapienza, Charles Pat, Jr.
**Newtown**
Kopil, Thomas Edward
**Norristown**
Brophy, Thomas Andrew
Oliver, James John
**Philadelphia**
Barrett, John J(ames), Jr.
Brigham, Martin Kenneth
Clinton, Michael W.
Cohen, Jonathan Morley
Coleman, Robert J.
Cullen, Raymond T.
Damsgaard, Kell Marsh
D'Angelo, Christopher Scott
Elkins, S. Gordon
Feinberg, Jack E.
Fickler, Arlene
Gray, Edward Anthony
Jurewicz, Richard Michael
Lawn, Timothy Regis
Madva, Stephen Alan
Mannino, Robert John
Martillotti, Gerard Jacob
Martin-Boyan, Annemarie
McNamara, John C.
Messa, Joseph Louis, Jr.
Monheit, Herbert
Morris, John Whelchel
Mundy, James Francis
Patton, Peter Mark
Perry, Sherryl Rosenbaum
Samuel, Ralph David
Seidel, Richard Stephen
Spivack, Gerald W.
**Pittsburgh**
Belliveau, James Dennis
Gigler, Daniel Richard
Matzus, Jason Eric
Miller, James Robert
Nerone, Michael F.
Perry, Jon Robert
von Waldow, Arnd N.
Wertkin, Robin Stuart
Wise, Roger Lambert
Wycoff, William Mortimer
**Sewickley**
Grigsby, Robert S.
**Spring City**
Mayerson, Hy
**Warrendale**
Micale, Frank Jude
**West Point**
Anderson, Margret Elizabeth
**Wilkes Barre**
Lach, Joseph Andrew

### RHODE ISLAND

**Pawtucket**
Belliveau, Kathrin Pagonis
**Providence**
Glavin, Kevin Charles

### SOUTH CAROLINA

**Anderson**
Krause, Steven Michael
**Charleston**
Bell, James Lee
Darling, Stephen Edward
Hahn, H. Blair
Laddaga, Beth Jane
Norris, Charles R.
Patrick, Charles William, Jr.
Ritter, Ann
Solomon, Cindi Anne
Tuck, Thomas Christopher
Waring, Bradish J.
**Columbia**
Morrison, Stephen George
**N Charleston**
Joye, Mark Christopher
**Spartanburg**
Anthony, Kenneth C., Jr.

### TENNESSEE

**Chattanooga**
Campbell, Paul, Jr.
James, Stuart Fawcett
**Jackson**
Nicks, Paul Todd
Phillips, Marty Roy
**Knoxville**
Murray, Rebecca Brake
Ownby, Jere Franklin, III
Waite, David Ernest
Ward, Kenneth Wayne
**Memphis**
Harvey, Albert C.
Summers, James Branson
Walsh, Thomas James, Jr.
**Nashville**
Barrow, Clisby Hall
Parker, Mary Ann
**Paris**
Rose, Todd Alan
**Springfield**
Wilks, Larry Dean

### TEXAS

**Arlington**
Smythe, Peter Christian
**Austin**
Byrd, Linward Tonnett
Gibbins, Bob
Papadakis, Myron Philip
Probus, Michael Maurice, Jr.
Staelin, Earl Hudson
**Baytown**
Linebaugh, Daniel Bruce
**Beaumont**
Bragg, J. J.
Ferguson, Paul F., Jr.
Sutton, Brian Dale
Thomas, Brett Scott
**Brownsville**
Cowen, Michael Raphael
**Burleson**
Johnstone, Deborah Blackmon
**Corpus Christi**
Carnahan, Robert Narvell
Evans, Allene Delories
Fancher, Rick
Laws, Gordon Derby
Martinez, Diana Marie
**Dallas**
Booth, John W. (Bill Booth)
Brown, James Earle
Henvey, John William
Holmes, James Hill, III
Howie, John Robert
Ivey, John Kemmerer
Kemp, Jeffrey Winslow
Lotzer, Gerald Balthazar
Maguire, Kevin Jerome
Schening, Judith Anne
Smith, Larry Francis
Stinnett, Mark Allan
Terry, David William
Turley, Linda
Zips, Craig Danny
**Fort Worth**
Ablon, Karen Herrick
Cleveland, Joseph F., Jr.
Hayes, Larry B.
Jones, Gregory G.
Moore, Randall D.
Wagner, James Peyton
Wallach, David Michael
**Galveston**
Neves, Kerry Lane
**Grapevine**
Glenn, David Milton
**Houston**
Benesh, William Stephen
Berger, Barry Stuart
Butler, Randall Edward
Carstarphen, Edward Morgan, III
Clawater, Wayne
Fisher, Guy G.
Fitzgerald, William Terry
Hanson, Jerry Clinton
Holloway, Gordon Arthur
Lapin, Robert E.
Nations, Howard Lynn
Norman, Richard Eugene
Perdue, Jim Mac
Pettiette, Alison Yvonne
Roach, Robert Michael, Jr.
Roven, John David
Sorrels, Randall Owen
Spain, H. Daniel
Valetutto, David Michael
**Longview**
Jones, Christopher Don
**Lubbock**
Cobb, David Randall
**Mesquite**
Zook, Bill
**Rowlett**
Lyon, Robert Charles
**San Antonio**
Branton, James LaVoy
Guess, James David
Montgomery, James Edward, Jr.
Putman, (James) Michael
Shiely, Gerald Lawrence
Valadez, Robert Allen
Weed, Ray Arnold
**San Benito**
Cordova, Adolfo Enrique
**Sugar Land**
West, S. Scott
**Tyler**
Bryan, Christian E.
**Waco**
Bostwick, Frederick deBurlo, III
**Wichita Falls**
Altman, William Kean

### UTAH

**Park City**
Fay, John Farrell
**Salt Lake City**
Nebeker, Stephen Bennion
Young, Robert Sherman

### VERMONT

**Burlington**
Judge, Walter E.
**Rutland**
Werle, Mark Fred
**Springfield**
Boxer, Andrew Carey

### VIRGINIA

**Charlottesville**
Barnes, Mary Ann
Kendall, Gary Wheeler
**Glen Allen**
Ware, Henry Neill, Jr.
**Hampton**
Smith, Stephen M.
**Manassas**
Mitchell, William Graham Champion
**McLean**
Djinis, Stephanie Ann
**Norfolk**
Bishop, Bruce Taylor
Brydges, James Edward
Drescher, John Webb
Gorry, James A., III
Pearson, John Y., Jr.
**Norton**
Jessee, Roy Mark
**Reston**
Hall, Robert Taggart
**Richmond**
Cantor, Irvin Victor
Hauck, David Leahigh
King, William H., Jr.
Marstiller, Philip S.
Walsh, James Hamilton
**Roanoke**
Harbert, Guy M., III
Jennings, James Wilson, Jr.
Krasnow, Jeffrey Harry
McGarry, Richard Lawrence
**Woodbridge**
Zauzig, Charles J., III

### WASHINGTON

**Hoquiam**
Kahler, Ray William
Kessler, Keith Leon
**Renton**
Barber, Mark Edward
**Richland**
Barr, Carlos Harvey
**Seattle**
Clement, William Scott
Cunningham, Joel Dean
Kraft, Robert Morris
Lundgren, Gail M.
Paul, Thomas Frank
Peterson, Jan Eric
Richdale, David Allen
Roche, Robert Joseph
Rogers, James Steven
Scott, Brian David
Tinker, Gregg Lynn
Whitson, Lish
Zeder, Fred M.
**Spokane**
Symmes, William Daniel
**Tacoma**
Maichel, Jack J.
Novasky, Robert William

### WEST VIRGINIA

**Charleston**
Brennaman, Sandra Lee
Deitzler, Harry G.
Heiskell, Edgar Frank, III
Hicks, Elliot Gene
Kiblinger, Cindy Jo
Powell, J(ames) C(orbley)
**Saint Albans**
McKittrick, William David Parrish

### WISCONSIN

**Appleton**
Lonergan, Kevin
Murray, John Daniel
**Green Bay**
Burnett, Ralph George
**Madison**
Anderson, Michael Steven
Hansen, John Alton
McCusker, William LaValle
Skilton, John Singleton
**Menomonie**
Steans, Phillip Michael
**Milwaukee**
Brown, Thomas Edward
Carroll, Douglas James
Daily, Frank J(erome)
Hodan, Patrick John
Kmiec, Steven Gerard
McCormick, David Joseph
Slavik, Donald Harlan
**Monona**
Murphy, Donald James
**Salem**
Edenhofer, Carl R.
**Waukesha**
Gesler, Alan Edward
Hoefle, Paul Ryan

### WYOMING

**Cheyenne**
Argeris, George John
**Jackson**
Spence, Gerald Leonard
**Sheridan**
Cannon, Kim Decker

### TERRITORIES OF THE UNITED STATES

### VIRGIN ISLANDS

**Christiansted**
Hart, Thomas Hughson, III

### ADDRESS UNPUBLISHED

Bell, Troy Nathan
Chang, Deborah
Connell, William D.
Coviello, Frank Joseph
Davis, Mark Warden
DiSalvo, Theodore L.
Embry, Stephen Creston
Erlebacher, Arlene Cernik
Gingras, John Richard
Grady, Maureen Frances
Iannacone, Randolph Frank
Kennedy, Vekeno
Klein, Beth Morrison
Knuth, Eric Joseph
Markle, Robert
Mathieu, Michelle Elise
McCallister, John Wilson
Monsees, Timothy William
Otten, Wesley Paul
Paul, Richard Wright
Reid, Benjamine
Roe, Michael Flinn
Siebel, Brian J.
Smith, Patricia A.
Wallach, Steven Ernst

## PROFESSIONAL LIABILITY

### UNITED STATES

### ALABAMA

**Birmingham**
Nettles, Bert Sheffield
Oliver, Thomas L., II
**Mobile**
Waldrop, Norman Erskine, Jr.

### ARIZONA

**Phoenix**
Bouma, John Jacob
Coleman, George Joseph, III (Jay Coleman)
Cummings, Frederick Michael
Gama, J. Richard
Harrison, Mark Isaac
Leinen, Amy Lynn
Smock, Timothy Robert
**Tempe**
Bucklin, Leonard Herbert
**Tucson**
Bergin, Jeffrey Thomas
MacBan, Laura Vaden
Rollins, Michael F.

### CALIFORNIA

**Anaheim**
Mazurek, Mike E.

**Beverly Hills**
Zimet, Marc Joseph
**Cupertino**
Svalya, Phillip Gordon
**Danville**
Candland, D. Stuart
**Encino**
Tannenbaum, Jack Joseph
**Irvine**
Rorty, Bruce Vail
**Los Angeles**
Drozin, Garth Matthew
Geibelson, Michael Aaron
Grimwade, Richard Llewellyn
Irving, Jeanne Ellen
King, Victor I.
Lange, Joseph Jude Morgan
Lebovits, Moses
Lee, Henry
Miller, Bruce Norman
**Newport Beach**
Pores, Joel Michael
**Oakland**
Ivary, Eric Henry
McCarthy, Steven Michael
Nishi, Jin
**Oxnard**
Heredia, F. Samuel
**Roseville**
Bedore, Jess C.
**Sacramento**
Birney, Philip Ripley
Hassan, Allen Clarence
**San Diego**
Emge, Derek John
Hutcheson, J(ames) Sterling
Sooy, Richard R.
Speckman, David Leon
Sussman, Nancy
Weidner, Lauren Finder
Wolfe, Deborah Ann
**San Francisco**
Carnes, Thomas Mason
**San Jose**
Ellard, Geroge William
Towery, James E.
**Santa Monica**
Peters, Thomas Harry
Saunders, Jennifer Kay
**Sherman Oaks**
Feldman, Phillip
**Thousand Oaks**
Richelson, Harvey
**Visalia**
Shirk, Jennifer Conn
**Walnut Creek**
Lucchese, David Ross
**Westlake Village**
Vititoe, James Wilson

### COLORADO

**Denver**
Avery, James William
Bove, Mark Stephen
Hensen, Stephen Jerome
Miller, J(ohn) Kent
Nemiron, Ronald H.
Palmeri, John M.
Sarney, Saul Richard
Starrs, Elizabeth Anne
Wilcox, Martha Anne
**Englewood**
Gipstein, Milton Fivenson
Nixon, Scott Sherman
**Greenwood Village**
Underhill, Joanne Parsons

### CONNECTICUT

**Bridgeport**
Mulcahey, Garie Jean
**New Haven**
Forino, Alfred Paul

### DELAWARE

**Wilmington**
Erisman, James A.

### DISTRICT OF COLUMBIA

**Washington**
Marks, Andrew H.
Mortenson, R. Stan
Villa, John Kazar

### FLORIDA

**Coral Gables**
Coleman, Roderick Flynn
Feiler, Michael Benjamin
**Dade City**
Brock, P. Hutchison, II
**Jacksonville**
Cowles, Robert Lawrence
Ehrlich, Raymond
**Miami**
Fox, Gary Devenow
Leibowitz, Mark A.
**New Smyrna Beach**
Kolodinsky, Richard Hutton
**North Miami Beach**
Lechtman, Michael Lowell
**Orlando**
Motes, Carl Dalton
Wasson, Karen Reed
**Pensacola**
Buchanan, Virginia Marie
**Saint Petersburg**
Gustafson, James William, Jr. ()
**Sarasota**
Groseclose, Lynn Hunter
**Sebastian**
Lulich, Steven
**Tallahassee**
Fonvielle, Charles David
**Tampa**
Hahn, William Edward
Morgenstern, Dennis Michael
**West Palm Beach**
Ciotoli, Eugene L.
Hudson, Lise Lyn
Koons, Stephen Robert
Ziska, Maura A.

### GEORGIA

**Atlanta**
Barksdale, Michael Scott
Matthews, James B., III
Smith, Jeffrey Michael
Spalten, David Elliot
**Macon**
Bennett, Thomas Wesley
**Peachtree City**
Ott, Stephen Douglas
**Savannah**
Stabell, Edward Reidar, III

### IDAHO

**Boise**
Scanlan, Kevin J.

### ILLINOIS

**Belleville**
Neville, James Edward
Ripplinger, George Raymond, Jr.
**Chicago**
Cavenagh, Timothy Joseph
Costello, James Paul
Daniels, Keith Byron, Jr.
Fleischmann, Thomas Joseph
Fogel, Joseph Lewis
George, John Martin, Jr.
Henry, Brian Thomas
Hooks, William Henry
Lynch, John James
McNerney, Joseph James
Napleton, Robert Joseph
Pollock, Bradley Neil
Rieger, Mitchell Sheridan
Wilcox, Mark Dean
**Naperville**
Levy, Steven Barry
**Urbana**
Kearns, James Cannon

### INDIANA

**Hammond**
Voelker, Louis William, III
**Indianapolis**
Hill, Douglas Jennings
Hovde, F. Boyd
Wampler, Robert Joseph
**Merrillville**
Dignam, Robert James

### IOWA

**Des Moines**
Cutler, Charles Edward
Finley, Kerry A.
Hermann, Robin L.

### KANSAS

**Fort Scott**
Hudson, Leigh Carleton
**Overland Park**
Smith, Edwin Dudley

### KENTUCKY

**Louisville**
Ballantine, Douglas Cain
Davidson, Scott Allen

### LOUISIANA

**Alexandria**
Bolen, James Aubrey, Jr.
**Lafayette**
Bass, William Morris
**New Orleans**
Beahm, Franklin D.
Wright, William Everard, Jr.

### MARYLAND

**Annapolis**
Rutland, David Lee
**Baltimore**
Bartlett, James Wilson, III
DeVries, Donald Lawson, Jr.
Ebersole, Jodi Kay
Shortridge, Deborah Green
Summers, Thomas Carey
Vice, LaVonna Lee
**Riverdale**
Turkheimer, Paul Adam
**Rockville**
Michael, Robert Roy

### MASSACHUSETTS

**Boston**
Saturley, Ellen McLaughlin
Schafer, Steven Harris
**Worcester**
Deiana, Robert Vincent

### MICHIGAN

**Auburn Hills**
DeAgostino, Thomas M.
**Bingham Farms**
Toth, John Michael
**Bloomfield Hills**
Butters, Frederick Francis
**Saginaw**
Concannon, Andrew Donnelly
**Southfield**
Jaffa, Jonathan Mark
Moloughney, Kevin Patrick

### MINNESOTA

**Minneapolis**
Bland, J(ohn) Richard
Cole, Phillip Allen
Messerly, Chris Alan
Saeks, Allen Irving
Towey, Edward Andrew
**Winona**
Borman, John

### MISSISSIPPI

**Clarksdale**
Cocke, John Hartwell
**Gulfport**
Dukes, James Otis
**Jackson**
Simmons, Heber Sherwood, III
**Meridian**
Eppes, Walter W., Jr.

### MISSOURI

**Kansas City**
Healy, Michael Patrick
Koelling, Thomas Winsor
Moore, Diana Dowell
**Saint Joseph**
Sokol, Ronald Mark
**Saint Louis**
Baldwin, Brent Winfield
Haar, Robert Theodore
Hesse, Margaret Ann

### NEBRASKA

**Columbus**
Milbourn, Douglas Ray

### NEVADA

**Las Vegas**
Stoberski, Michael Edward

### NEW HAMPSHIRE

**Keene**
Gardner, Eric Raymond

### NEW JERSEY

**Atlantic City**
Feinberg, Jack
**Berlin**
Goldstein, Benjamin
**Chatham**
Fried, David M.
**Cranford**
McCreedy, Edwin James
**Denville**
Caivano, Anthony P.
**Freehold**
Lomurro, Donald Michael
**Hackensack**
Reed, Jonathan Seth
**Haddonfield**
Heuisler, Charles William
**Hammonton**
Picariello, Pasquale
**Iselin**
Goodman, Barry S.
**Morristown**
Bromberg, Myron James
**New Providence**
Marris, Joan Banan
**Springfield**
Kahn, Eric G.

### NEW MEXICO

**Albuquerque**
Bohnhoff, Henry M.
Franse, R(ichard) Nelson
Martinez, David Brian
McBride, Thomas John
Patterson, Cynthia J.

### NEW YORK

**Baldwin**
Verdirame, Peter J.
**Buffalo**
Behr, Laurence Donald
**Camillus**
Endieveri, Anthony Frank
**Fairport**
Capanna, Paloma A.
**Garden City**
Balkan, Kenneth J.
Beck, Leland S.
**Islandia**
Buckley, Terrence Patrick
**New York**
Faillace, Charles Kenneth
Finnerty, Joseph Gregory, Jr.
Hoffman, David Nathaniel
Kilsch, Gunther H.
Kramer, Daniel Jonathan
Nevins, Arthur Gerard, Jr.
Ross, Matthew
Scheiman, Eugene R.
Smith, James Walker
**Syracuse**
Johnson, Eric Gates

### NORTH CAROLINA

**Winston Salem**
Maready, William Frank

### OHIO

**Akron**
Djordjevic, Michael M.
**Cincinnati**
Woodside, Frank C., III
**Cleveland**
Fitzgerald, Timothy John
Gray, R. Benton
O'Neill, Mark
**Columbus**
Alton, John Marshall
Arnold, Gayle Edward
Caborn, David Arthur
Draper, Gerald Linden
Maloon, Jerry L.
Nemeth, John Charles
Plymale, Ronald E.
Smallwood, Carl Demouy
Thompson, Harold Lee
**Dayton**
Cameron, Ken
Rudwall, David Fuller
**Youngstown**
Carlin, Clair Myron

### OREGON

**Portland**
Savage, John William
**Redmond**
Welborn, Gordon Lee

### PENNSYLVANIA

**Easton**
Noel, Nicholas, III
**Exton**
Amaral Ryan, Rosa Olinda
**Harrisburg**
Angino, Richard Carmen
McGuire, Jeffrey Thomas
Quigley, Robert Andrew
Simpson, Kathryn Lease
**Lancaster**
Hall, Thomas W.
**Langhorne**
Ely, Wayne Arlen
**Norristown**
Brophy, Thomas Andrew
**Philadelphia**
Beech, Kristen Lee
Bochetto, George Alexander
Donner, Henry Jay
Feinberg, Jack E.
Fodera, Leonard V.
Mannino, Edward Francis
McCarron, Jeffrey Baldwin
Messa, Joseph Louis, Jr.
Mullinix, Edward Wingate
Pace, Samuel J., Jr.
Perry, Sherryl Rosenbaum
Rosenthal, Brian David
Schildt, Steven Joseph
Seidel, Richard Stephen
Wu, William
**Pittsburgh**
Mills, Edward James
Mulvihill, Keithley D.

### SOUTH CAROLINA

**Charleston**
Norris, Charles R.

### TENNESSEE

**Chattanooga**
Eason, Marcia Jean
**Johnson City**
Jenkins, Ronald Wayne
Meade, Evan McDaniel
**Knoxville**
Waite, David Ernest

### TEXAS

**Arlington**
Smythe, Peter Christian
**Austin**
Hanna, Jett Lowell
Moss, Bill Ralph
Probus, Michael Maurice, Jr.
**Dallas**
Bennett, Paul William
Cobb, William Dowell, Jr.
Coleman, Robert Winston
Govett, Brett Christopher
Hunt, Amy Katherine
Johnston, Coyt Randal
Kemp, Jeffrey Winslow
Lenox, Roger Shawn
Mow, Robert Henry, Jr.
Smith, Larry Francis
Weitzel, J. Dennis
Wileman, George Robert
Yarbrough, Fletcher Leftwich
**El Paso**
McDonald, Charles Edward
**Fort Worth**
Wallach, David Michael
**Grapevine**
Glenn, David Milton
**Houston**
Bailey, Stephen Robert
Conway, Sharon Elizabeth
Samuelson, Douglas Allen
Sears, Ross Allen, II
Toney, William David, II
Van Fleet, George Allan
Walton, Dan Gibson
**Odessa**
Rouse, Randall Lyle
**San Antonio**
Branton, James LaVoy
Rhodes, Jesse Thomas, III
Shiely, Gerald Lawrence
**Teague**
Smith, William Lafayette, Jr.
**Tyler**
Green, Jay Nelson

### VERMONT

**Rutland**
Taylor, A. Jeffry

### VIRGINIA

**Alexandria**
Tompkins, Michael William
**Annandale**
Hovis, Robert Houston, III
**Norfolk**
Brydges, James Edward
Pearson, John Y., Jr.
**Reston**
Hall, Robert Taggart
**Roanoke**
Krasnow, Jeffrey Harry

### WASHINGTON

**Renton**
Barber, Mark Edward
**Seattle**
Bringman, Joseph Edward
Gould, Ronald Murray
Hillman, Roger Lewis
Longfelder, Lawrence Lee
McCoid, Nancy Katherine
Peterson, Jan Eric
Tinker, Gregg Lynn
Tucker, Kathryn Louise
Turner, Duncan Calvert

### WEST VIRGINIA

**Charleston**
Crislip, Stephen Ray
Fisher, Michael Matthew

### WISCONSIN

**Brookfield**
Palmersheim, Richard J.
**Milwaukee**
Sceptur, Paul Joseph
**River Falls**
Krueger, Stuart James
**Waukesha**
Hoefle, Paul Ryan

### ADDRESS UNPUBLISHED

Bailey, J. Dennis
Block, Jessica
Hall-Barron, Deborah
Harris, Richard Eugene Vassau
Howard, Christopher Holm
Klein, Beth Morrison
Otten, Wesley Paul
Paul, Richard Wright

---

**PROPERTY DAMAGE.** *See* **Personal injury.**

---

## PROPERTY, REAL

### UNITED STATES

### ALABAMA

**Athens**
Plunk, John Matthew
**Birmingham**
Cornelius, Walter Felix
Cornett, Wendy Love
Davis, Timothy Donald
Maynard, George Fleming
Ramsey, David Wade
Theibert, Richard Wilder
**Clayton**
Jackson, Lynn Robertson
**Dadeville**
Oliver, John Percy, II
**Decatur**
McWhorter, Robert Tweedy, Jr.
**Fayette**
Chambless, Ricky Thomas
**Foley**
Leatherbury, Gregory Luce, Jr.
**Huntsville**
Richardson, Patrick William
**Mobile**
Brooker, Norton William, Jr.
Holland, Lyman Faith, Jr.
Johnston, Neil Chunn
Lott, Victor H., Jr.
Loveless, Ralph Peyton
**Montgomery**
Conley, Charles Swinger
Franco, Ralph Abraham
**Sheffield**
Hamby, Gene Malcolm, Jr.

### ALASKA

**Anchorage**
Ginder, Peter Craig
Gorski, James Michael
Lekisch, Peter Allen
Nosek, Francis John
Stanley, James Troy

### ARIZONA

**Carefree**
Rooney, Michael James
**Kingman**
Basinger, Richard Lee
**Phoenix**
Chauncey, Tom Webster, II
Coppersmith, Sam
Craig, Laurie Baker
Ferguson, Fred Ernest, Jr.
Jorden, Douglas Allen
Klausner, Jack Daniel
Kramer, Robert J.
Lasee, Mark Edward
Lee, Richard H(arlo)
Lemberg, Frederic Gary
Lowry, Edward Francis, Jr.
Mangum, John K.
Matheson, Alan Adams, Jr.
May, Bruce Barnett
Moehle, Carm Robert
Perry, Lee Rowan
Postal, David Ralph
Storey, Lee A.
**Prescott**
Goodman, Mark N.
Gose, Richard Vernie
**Scottsdale**
Berry, Charles Richard
Marhoffer, David
Titus, Jon Alan
**Sun City**
Hauer, James Albert
**Tucson**
D'Antonio, James Joseph
Farsjo, Fred A.

Hanshaw, A. Alan
Miller, Michael Douglas
Stirton, Charles Paul

## ARKANSAS

**Fayetteville**
Pearson, Charles Thomas, Jr.
Pettus, E. Lamar
**Little Rock**
Campbell, George Emerson
Gibson, Calvin Roe
Haley, John Harvey
Hughes, Steven Jay
Miller, William Scott
Riordan, Deborah Truby
**Mena**
Thrailkill, Daniel B.
**Monticello**
Gibson, Charles Clifford, III
**Newport**
Howard, Steven Gray
Thaxton, Marvin Dell
**Searcy**
Hannah, R. Craig

## CALIFORNIA

**Anaheim**
Ross, Roger Scott
**Auburn**
Litchfield, Robert Latta, Jr.
Lyon, Bruce Arnold
Moglen, Leland Louis
**Bakersfield**
Karcher, Steven Michael
Kind, Kenneth Wayne
Lynch, Craig M.
**Belvedere**
Loube, Irving
**Berkeley**
Ross, Julia
**Beverly Hills**
Bordy, Michael Jeffrey
Horwin, Leonard
Kite, Richard Lloyd
Nicholas, Frederick M.
**Burlingame**
Fogarty, Janet E.
**California City**
Friedl, Rick
**Camarillo**
Dunlevy, William Sargent
**Carmel**
Heisinger, James Gordon, Jr.
Varga, S. Gary
**Costa Mesa**
Boyer, David Dyer
Caldwell, Courtney Lynn
Frieden, Clifford E.
**Elverta**
Betts, Barbara Lang
**Encinitas**
Forrester, Kevin Kreg
**Fremont**
Kitta, John Noah
**Fresno**
Ewell, A. Ben, Jr.
Jensen, Douglas Blaine
Nunes, Frank M.
**Fullerton**
Apke, Thomas Michael
Moerbeek, Stanley Leonard
**Glendale**
Ball, James Herington
**Hayward**
Smith, John Kerwin
**Huntington Beach**
Garrels, Sherry Ann
**Irvine**
Carpenter, Scott Rockwell
Farrell, Teresa Joanning
Hurst, Charles Wilson
Kaminsky, Larry Michael
Petrasich, John Moris
Weissbard, Samuel Held
**La Canada Flintridge**
Stell, Joseph
**Los Angeles**
Argue, John Clifford
Brogan, Kevin Herbert
Burns, Marvin Gerald
Camp, James Carroll
Carter, Bret Robert
Cathcart, Robert James
Chin, Llewellyn Philip
Forster, Jonathan Shawn
Geiger, Roy Stephen
Goldie, Ron Robert
Gould, Howard Neal
Grim, Douglas Paul
Grush, Julius Sidney
Hayes, Byron Jackson, Jr.
Hutt, Laurence Jeffrey
Ibekwe, Edebeatu
Klein, Raymond Maurice
Lappen, Timothy
Lesser, Joan L.
Lund, James Louis
May, Lawrence Edward
McBirney, Bruce Henry
Millard, Neal Steven
Miller, Bruce Norman
Pircher, Leo Joseph
Popowitz, Neil Michael
Porter, Verna Louise
Robertson, Hugh Duff
Robison, William Robert
Sheppard, Thomas Richard
Snyder, Arthur Kress
Stauber, Ronald Joseph
Strickstein, Herbert Jerry
Venable, Giovan Harbour
Watson, Glenn Robert
Wright, Wyndell John
Zerunyan, Frank Vram
**Los Gatos**
Seligmann, William Robert
Sweet, Jonathan Justin
**Manhattan Beach**
Guimera, Irene Mermelstein
**Marina Dl Rey**
Smolker, Gary Steven
**Menlo Park**
Sauers, William Dale
Walsh, Tara Jane
**Mill Valley**
Georgeson, Adamont Nicholas
Nemir, Donald Philip
**Mount Shasta**
Armstrong, Kenneth
**Napa**
Meibeyer, Charles William, Jr.
Meyers, David W.
**Newport Beach**
Arnold, Larry Millard
Barclay, John Allen
McEvers, Duff Steven
McGee, James Francis
Molseed, Michael Clyde
Willard, Robert Edgar
Wolf, Alan Steven
**Oakland**
Allen, Jeffrey Michael
Hausrath, Les A.
Mannis, Estelle Claire
**Orange**
Parker, Charles Edward
Sawdei, Milan A.
**Oxnard**
Arnold, Gary D.
**Pacific Palisades**
Lagle, John Franklin
**Palo Alto**
Baum, Donald Hiram
Donnally, Robert Andrew
Wunsch, Kathryn Sutherland
**Pasadena**
Epstein, Bruce Howard
Linstedt, Walter Griffiths
Morris, Gary Wayne
Talt, Alan R.
**Piedmont**
McCormick, Timothy Brian Beer
**Pleasant Hill**
Weiss, Edward Abraham
**Pleasanton**
Staley, John Fredric
**Rancho Mirage**
Goldie, Ray Robert
**Rancho Santa Fe**
Freeberg, Eric Olafur
**Redwood City**
Givens, Richard Donald
**Riverside**
Darling, Scott Edward
Graves, Patrick Lee
McKinney, Dan George
**Sacramento**
Cahill, Virginia Arnoldy
Giguiere, Michele Louise
Mooney, Donald B.
Robbins, Stephen J. M.
Waks, Stephen Harvey
**San Bernardino**
Brittain, Gregory W.
**San Clemente**
Geyser, Lynne M.
**San Diego**
Asaro, V. Frank
Clark, David Robert
Detisch, Donald W.
Dorne, David J.
Frasch, Brian Bernard
Hansotte, Louis Bernard
O'Malley, James Terence
Peterson, Paul Ames
Strauss, Steven Marc
**San Francisco**
Briscoe, John
Burden, James Ewers
Diamond, Philip Ernest
Enersen, Burnham
Gillmar, Stanley Frank
Haughton, Brian Stephens
Johns, Richard Seth Ellis
Kimport, David Lloyd
La Vine, Robert L.
Mosk, Susan Hines
Riley, Benjamin Kneeland
Suter, Ben
**San Jose**
Gonzales, Daniel S.
Hernández, Fernando Vargas
Stutzman, Thomas Chase, Sr.
**San Luis Obispo**
Dorsi, Stephen Nathan
**San Pedro**
DeWitt, Brian Leigh
**San Rafael**
Bloomfield, Neil Jon
Fairbairn, Sydney Elise
**Santa Ana**
Beasley, Oscar Homer
Frost, Winston Lyle
Knox Rios, Delilah Jane
McCarron, Andrew
**Santa Barbara**
Egenolf, Robert F.
Fox, Herb
Willey, Charles Wayne
**Santa Cruz**
Atchison, Rodney Raymond
**Santa Monica**
Hofer, Stephen Robert
**Santa Rosa**
Adams, Delphine Szyndrowski
Clement, Clayton Emerson
McCutchan, B. Edward, Jr.
**South Lake Tahoe**
Bates, David Allen
**Tiburon**
Stolman, Marc Daniel
**Torrance**
Finer, William A.
**Ukiah**
Sager, Madeline Dean
**Van Nuys**
Mikesell, Richard Lyon
**Visalia**
Crowe, Daniel Walston
**Walnut Creek**
Horner, Clifford R.
Starr, Marvin Blake
Wood, Steven Noel Housley
**Westlake Vlg**
Kennedy, Jeff Grant
**Windsor**
Greiner, Robert Philip
**Woodland Hills**
DeSantis, Richard A.
Robertson, Alexander, IV

## COLORADO

**Arvada**
Carney, T. J
**Aspen**
McGrath, J. Nicholas
Peirce, Frederick Fairbanks
Peterson, Brooke Alan
Schumacher, Barry Lee
**Boulder**
Anuta, Karl Frederick
**Colorado Springs**
Benson, John Scott
Everson, Steven Lee
Gaddis, Larry Roy
MacDougall, Malcolm Edward
Palermo, Norman Anthony
Purvis, Randall W. B.
Sheffield, Alden Daniel, Jr.
**Crested Butte**
Renfrow, Jay Royce
**Denver**
Bader, Gerald Louis, Jr.
Christy, Cynthia Ullem
DeMuth, Alan Cornelius
Dowdle, Patrick Dennis
Finesilver, Jay Mark
Foster, Erik Koehler
Freeman, Deborah Lynn
Grant, Patrick Alexander
Grimshaw, Thomas Tollin
Hamel, Fred Meade
Irwin, R. Robert
Jacobs, Ronald Hedstrom
Kuhn, Gretchen
Mann, Stuart D.
Martz, Clyde Ollen
Molling, Charles Francis
Munteanu, Victor John
Pearman, Shaun
Petros, Raymond Louis, Jr.
Pollack, Howard Jay
Quiat, Gerald M.
Rufien, Paul Charles
Sayre, John Marshall
Shannon, Malcolm Lloyd, Jr.
Slaninger, Frank Paul
Spiegleman, John G.
Spillane, John Michael
Tisdale, Douglas Michael
**Durango**
Sherman, Lester Ivan
**Englewood**
Ambrose, Arlen S.
Choi, Jay Junekun
Katz, Michael Jeffery
**Florence**
Davis, Allyn Whitney
**Fort Collins**
Gast, Richard Shaeffer
Rogers, Garth Winfield
**Frisco**
Helmer, David Alan
**Lakewood**
Mielke, Donald Earl
**Loveland**
Kaufman, William George
**Pueblo**
O'Callaghan, Robert Patrick
**Rocky Ford**
Mendenhall, Harry Barton
**Thornton**
Liberman, David Israel

## CONNECTICUT

**Avon**
Godbout, Arthur Richard, Jr.
**Bethel**
Medvecky, Thomas Edward
Murray, Gwen E.
**Bloomfield**
Mark, Henry Allen
**Branford**
Hanchuruck, Stephen Paul
**Bridgeport**
Wolf, Austin Keith
**Canaan**
Capecelatro, Mark John
**Danbury**
Murray, Stephen James
Tuozzolo, John Joseph
**Derby**
Cohen, James E.
**Enfield**
Berger, Robert Bertram
**Fairfield**
Burke, William Milton
**Farmington**
Harvey, Elton Bartlett, III
Levy, Coleman Bertram
Mandell, Joel
**Guilford**
Thomas, David Robert
**Hartford**
Buck, Gurdon Hall
Merriam, Dwight Haines
Sylvester, Kathryn Rose
**Middletown**
Adams, Richard Glen
Quattro, Mark Henry
**Milford**
Berchem, Robert Lee, Sr.
**New Canaan**
Bennett, James H.
**New Haven**
Craig, William Emerson
Peabody, Bruce R.
Sabetta, Paul M.
Stankewich, Paul Joseph
**New London**
Johnstone, Philip MacLaren
**Newington**
Borowy, Frank Rhine
**Norwalk**
Lang, Jules
**Norwich**
Masters, Barbara J.
**Ridgefield**
Fricke, Richard John
**Simsbury**
Main, Philip David
**South Windsor**
Gerlt, Wayne Christopher
Hale, Kathryn Scholle
**Southport**
Moore, Roy Worsham, III
**Stafford Springs**
Paradiso, F. Joseph
**Stamford**
Della Rocco, Kenneth Anthony
Kweskin, Edward Michael
Lois, Dale Joseph
Richichi, Joseph
Strone, Michael Jonathan
**Stratford**
Berlin, Patricia
McDonough, Sandra Martin
**Wallingford**
Galligan, Matthew G.
**Waterbury**
Chase, Robert L.
**West Hartford**
Nereberg, Eliot Joel
**Westport**
Cramer, Allan P.
Dimes, Edwin Kinsley
Saxl, Richard Hildreth
**Wilton**
Healy, James Casey
Silverman, Melvin J.
**Windsor**
Lerman, Kenneth Brian
**Winsted**
Finch, Frank Herschel, Jr.

## DELAWARE

**Dover**
Jones, R. Brandon
Twilley, Joshua Marion
**Newark**
McCann, Richard Stephen
**Wilmington**
Brosseit, A. Kimberly Rockwell
Kristol, Daniel Marvin
Sawyer, H(arold) Murray, Jr.
Tigani, Bruce William

## DISTRICT OF COLUMBIA

**Washington**
Ain, Sanford King
Allan, Richmond Frederick
Bloch, Stuart Marshall
Bodansky, Robert Lee
Brenner, Janet Maybin Walker
Cooper, Clement Theodore
Cumberland, William Edwin
Dickerman, Dorothea Wilhelmina
Edson, Charles Louis
Glasgow, Norman Milton
Hanas, Stephen Michael
Harrison, Earl David
Jacobs, Harvey S.
Kaufman, Thomas Frederick
Landfield, Richard
Lane, Bruce Stuart
Loewinger, Kenneth Jeffery
Longstreet, Susan Cannon
McIntyre, Douglas Carmichael, II
Moses, Alfred Henry
Nauheim, Stephen Alan
Nichols, Henry Eliot
Norstrand, Hans Peter
Osnos, David Marvin
Pearlstein, Paul Davis
Policy, Vincent Mark
Rabekoff, Elise Jane
Rosenberg, Ruth Helen Borsuk
Samuelson, Kenneth Lee

## FLORIDA

**Altamonte Springs**
Harding, Calvin Fredrick, Jr.
Hoogland, Robert Frederics
**Bay Harbor Is**
Patrick, Marty
**Boca Raton**
Carlile, Robert Toy
Feldman, Joel Harvey
Kassner, Herbert Seymore
Schwartz, Kenneth Jeffrey
Siemon, Charles L.
**Bradenton**
St. Paul, Alexandra De La Vergne
**Brandon**
Tittsworth, Clayton (Magness)
**Clearwater**
Coleman, Jeffrey Peters
Gifford, Janet Lynn
Hogan, Elwood
Jirotka, George M.
**Clewiston**
Gonzalez, Francisco Javier
**Coconut Grove**
Arboleya, Carlos Joaquin
**Coral Gables**
Fletcher, Paul Gerald
Pastoriza, Julio
**Coral Springs**
Polin, Alan Jay
**Daytona Beach**
Dunagan, Walter Benton
**Deerfield Beach**
Lenoff, Michele Malka
**Delray Beach**
Weitzman, Linda Sue
**Fort Lauderdale**
Browner, Julius Harvey
Gardner, Russell Menese
Golden, E(dward) Scott
King, Robert Lee
Mars, Burton H.
Moss, Stephen B.
Tripp, Norman Densmore
Wich, Donald Anthony, Jr.
**Fort Myers**
Dalton, Anne
Harrison, Simon M.
**Fort Myers Beach**
Cotter, Richard Timothy
Shenko, William Edward, Jr.
**Hobe Sound**
Buetens, Eric D.
**Hollywood**
Fischler, Shirley Balter
Weisman, David
**Jacksonville**
Ansbacher, Barry B.
Ball, Haywood Moreland
Braddock, Donald Layton
Christian, Gary Irvin
Cooke, Alexander Hamilton
Getman, Willard Etheridge
Hodge, James Edward
Mikals, John Joseph
Scheu, William E.
**Jupiter**
Click, David Forrest
**Key West**
Davila, Gregory David
**Lake Mary**
Loe, Brian Robert
**Lake Placid**
Haile, John Sanders
**Lakeland**
Kittleson, Henry Marshall
McClurg, E. Vane
Sanoba, Gregory A.
**Lutz**
Hayes, Timothy George
**Miami**
Alonso, Antonio Enrique
Amber, Laurie Kaufman
Betz, Gilbert Calvin
Cassel, Marwin Shepard
de la Fe, Ernesto Juan
Edwards, Thomas Ashton
Feinsmith, Paul Lowell
Formoso, Marika Gulyas
Friedman, Nicholas R.
Garrett, Richard G.
Gross, Leslie Jay
Lancaster, Kenneth G.
Martinez-Cid, Ricardo
Mudd, John Philip
Pearson, John Edward
Pozo-Diaz, Martha del Carmen
Rabenseifner, Hanna Camille
Schuette, Charles A.
Schwartz, Martin A.
Silber, Norman Jules
Stanley, Sherry A.
Starr, Ivar Miles
Wheeler, Harold Austin, Sr.
Wiseheart, Malcolm Boyd, Jr.
**Miami Beach**
Thomas, Lola Bohn
**N Miami Beach**
Slewett, Robert David
**Naples**
Budd, David Glenn
Emerson, John Williams, II
Gebhardt, Robert Charles
Humphreville, John David
Mac'Kie, Pamela S.
**North Miami**
Moreno, Christine Margaret
**North Palm Beach**
Daniels, Bruce Joel
**Ocala**
Haldin, William Carl, Jr.
Sommer, Robert George
Thompson, Raymond Edward
**Orlando**
Buhaly Ibold, Catherine
Chong, Stephen Chu Ling
Chotas, Elias Nicholas
Christiansen, Patrick T.
Cohen, David Sacks
Davidson, Richard Dodge
Eagan, William Leon
Extein, Mark Charles
Gray, J. Charles
Hartley, Carl William, Jr.
Hendry, Robert Ryon
Leonhardt, Frederick Wayne
Lowndes, John Foy
Neff, A. Guy
Pierce, John Gerald (Jerry Pierce)
Pleus, Robert J., Jr.
Popp, Gregory Allan
Rush, Fletcher Grey, Jr.
Salzman, Gary Scott
Stewart, Harry A.

**Palm Beach**
Keihner, Bruce William
Rampell, Paul
Tarone, Theodore T.
Zeller, Ronald John
**Palm Beach Gardens**
Cox, Jack Schramm
Edgar, Charles Wesley, III
Kahn, David Miller
Pumphrey, Gerald Robert
**Palm Coast**
Conner, Timothy James
**Plant City**
Buchman, Kenneth William
**Pt Charlotte**
Levin, Allen Jay

**Grand Rapids**
Anderson, Jonathan Walfred
Davis, Henry Barnard, Jr.
Dugan, Robert John
Hogan, Thomas Patrick
**Grosse Pointe**
Barrows, Ronald Thomas
Cobau, John Reed
Johnson, Edward Carl
McIntyre, Anita Grace Jordan
**Grosse Pointe Woods**
Darke, Richard Francis
**Harbor Beach**
Schumacher, Dawn Kristi Ann
**Ishpeming**
Steward, James Brian
**Jackson**
Klaasen, Terry John
**Kalamazoo**
Bauckham, John Henry
**Lansing**
Burlingame, Stephen Lee
Gallagher, Byron Patrick, Jr.
**Livonia**
Cote, Jennifer Wanty
**Mount Pleasant**
Lynch, John Joseph
**Muskegon**
Briggs, John Mancel, III
**Okemos**
Barton, Judith Marie
**Petoskey**
Powers, Bridget Brown
Smith, Wayne Richard
**Plymouth**
Morgan, Donald Crane
**Port Huron**
Wallace, Matthew Mark
**Saginaw**
Beer, Louis Delamare
**Shelby**
Law, Roger Alan
**Southfield**
Davis-Yancey, Gwendolyn
Gotthelf, Beth
Jacobs, John E.
Nykanen, David Edward
Silber, Albert J.
**Traverse City**
Judson, Charles B.
Quandt, Joseph Edward
**Troy**
Haron, David Lawrence
Olson, Edward M.
**Walled Lake**
Connelly, Thomas Joseph
**West Bloomfield**
Tobin, Bruce Howard

## MINNESOTA

**Benson**
Wilcox, Donald Alan
**Chanhassen**
Peterson, Steven A.
**Fergus Falls**
Bigwood, Robert William
**Maple Grove**
Saville, Derric James
**Maplewood**
Beck, Bruce Lennart
**Minneapolis**
Brehl, James William
Cohen, Earl Harding
Hergott, Daniel Weldon
Jensch, Charles Campbell
Kempf, Douglas Paul
Parsons, Charles Allan, Jr.
Skare, Robert Martin
Steinwall, Susan Deborah
Thorson, Steven Greg
Ventres, Daniel Brainerd, Jr.
Witort, Janet Lee
Yost, Gerald B.
**New Ulm**
Lowther, Patrick Alan
**Roseville**
Heitler, Perrie Nanette
**Saint Paul**
Jacobs, Stephen Louis
Spencer, David James
Winthrop, Sherman
**Willmar**
Hulstrand, George Eugene
**Winthrop**
Engwall, Gregory Bond
**Woodbury**
Baumann, Craig William

## MISSISSIPPI

**Clarksdale**
Chaffin, William Michael
**Gulfport**
Hatten, W. Edward, Jr.
Pettey, William Hall, Jr.
Warren, Anne Schaefer
**Hernando**
Brown, William A.
Neyman, Joseph David, Jr.
**Jackson**
Boackle, K.F.
Chadwick, Vernon Henry
Eicher, Donald E., III
Grant, Russell Porter, Jr.
Hammond, Frank Jefferson, III
Hughes, Byron William
Presson, William Russell
Tohill, Jim Barnette
**Kosciusko**
Pickle, L. Scott
**Oxford**
Howorth, Andrew Kincannon
**Raymond**
Moss, Jack Gibson
**Southaven**
Branan, Debra Pace

## MISSOURI

**Brentwood**
Timm, Walter William
**Chesterfield**
Coffin, Richard Keith
Pollihan, Thomas Henry
**Clayton**
Ritter, Robert Thornton
**Columbia**
Mays, William Gay, II
**Hermann**
Kell, Scott K.
**Hillsboro**
Howald, John William
**Kansas City**
Carman, Steven F.
Dicus, Stephen Howard
Frisbie, Charles
Hill, John Brian
Hindman, Larrie C.
Howes, Brian Thomas
Jackson, James B.
Moore, Stephen James
Mulvihill, Joseph James
Randall, Evan Levy
Satterlee, Terry Jean
Sparks, Stephen Stone
Todd, Stephen Max
Watts, James Dariel
Ziegenhorn, Eric Howard
**Rock Port**
Mulvania, Walter Lowell
**Saint Louis**
Arnold, Fred English
Behrens, Brian Charles
Boardman, Richard John
Chasnoff, Jules
Chung, Eric C.
Cullen, James D.
Elbert, Charles Steiner
Gilroy, Tracy Anne Hunsaker
Goldenhersh, Robert Stanley
Graham, Robert Clare, III
Hellmuth, Theodore Henning
Hetlage, Robert Owen
Inkley, John James, Jr.
Klamer, Jane Ferguson
McNearney, John Patrick
Mersman, Richard Kendrick, III
Winning, John Patrick
**Saint Peters**
Goss, J. Bradford
**Springfield**
Groce, Steven Fred
**Union**
Schroeder, Matthew A.
**West Plains**
Brill, Newton Clyde

## MONTANA

**Billings**
Beiswanger, Gary Lee
Hanson, Norman
Schleusner, Clifford Edward
**Kalispell**
Kaufman, Leonard Lee
**Livingston**
Jovick, Robert L.
**Ronan**
Grainey, Philip J.

## NEBRASKA

**Aurora**
Whitney, Charles Leroy
**Hildreth**
Jelkin, John Lamoine
**Lincoln**
Blake, William George
Brown, Mark Charles
McClain, Richard Douglas
**Omaha**
Barmettler, Joseph John
Rouse, Michael Adams

## NEVADA

**Gardnerville**
Terzich, Milos
**Las Vegas**
Burnett, Gary Boyd
Curran, William P.
Eisner, Elliott Roy
Mahan, James Cameron
Parry, Stanley Warren
Swanson, Kelly Hansen
**Reno**
Fletcher, Douglas Charles
Hill, Earl McColl
Marshall, Robert William
Simmons, Terry Allan
Wright, Roger Lane

## NEW HAMPSHIRE

**Concord**
Morris, James Edgar
**Exeter**
Donahue, Michael Joseph
Jones, Daniel W.
**Hooksett**
Rogers, David John
**Laconia**
Giere, John Patrick
**Lancaster**
Goss, Steven Bryant
**Lebanon**
Trunzo, Thomas Harold, Jr.
**Manchester**
Stebbins, Henry Blanchard
**Nashua**
Goodwin, Rolf Ervine
**Newport**
Work, Michael Jay
**Plymouth**
Deachman, Ross Varick
Sawyer, Leonard Sylvester
**Portsmouth**
Lefebvre, Albert Paul Conrad
Lown, Bradley Merrill
**Woodsville**
Bruno, Kevin Robert

## NEW JERSEY

**Atlantic City**
Baylinson, Christopher Michael
Markwardt, John James
Zlotnick, Norman Lee
**Barrington**
Guice, Stephen W.
**Boonton**
Walzer, James Harvey
**Brick**
Tivenan, Charles Patrick
**Cherry Hill**
Amodeo, Tina Nielsen
**Cliffside Park**
Diktas, Christos James
**Clifton**
Mohammed, Sohail
**Cranbury**
Iatesta, John Michael
**East Brunswick**
Fried, Richard F.
**East Hanover**
Kayser, Kenneth Wayne
**Edison**
Applebaum, Charles
Fink, Edward Murray
Lijoi, Peter Bruno
**Fair Lawn**
Hirschklau, Morton
**Far Hills**
Corash, Richard
**Flemington**
Ligorano, Michael Kenneth
**Florham Park**
Calabrese, Arnold Joseph
**Franklin Lakes**
Lagdameo-Hogan, Maria-Elena
**Glen Rock**
Markey, Brian Michael
**Hackensack**
Duus, Gordon Cochran
Schuber, William Patrick
**Highland Park**
Feld, Franklin Fred
**Hoboken**
Curley, John Joseph
**Iselin**
Gupta, Rajat Kumar
Kracht, Richard William
**Jersey City**
D'Alessandro, Daniel Anthony
Guarini, Frank J.
Talafous, Joseph John, Sr.
**Kendall Park**
Fisch, Joseph
**Lakewood**
Bielory, Abraham Melvin
**Linden**
Falk, Lauren Weissman
**Linwood**
Frisch, David Bruce
**Livingston**
Kuller, Jonathan Mark
Rinsky, Joel Charles
**Maplewood**
Joseph, Susan B.
**Mc Afee**
Fogel, Richard
**Medford**
Gruccio-Thorman, Lillian Joan
Timban, Demetrio Sunga
**Metuchen**
Convery, Samuel Vincent, Jr.
Frizell, David J.
**Montclair**
Conrad, David Williams
Franges, Anne King
**Montvale**
Beattie, James Raymond
**Moorestown**
Ewan, David E.
Hardt, Frederick William
**Morristown**
Pantel, Glenn Steven
Platt, Gary R.
Rosenthal, Meyer L(ouis)
**Newark**
Day, Edward Francis, Jr.
Lazzaro, Clifford Emanuel
Long, Reginald Alan
Neuer, Philip David
Slavitt, Ben J.
Tous, Raul F.
**Old Bridge**
Downs, Thomas Edward, IV
**Parsippany**
Hansbury, Stephan Charles
Silverstein, Robert Selnick
**Piscataway**
Wilson, Abraham
**Plainfield**
Dowling, Joan E.
**Pompton Plains**
Ludemann, Cathie Jane
**Princeton**
Moore, Kevin John
Souter, Sydney Scull
**Red Bank**
Rogers, Lee Jasper
**Ridgewood**
Boardman, Michael Neil
**River Vale**
Meyer, Grace Tomanelli
**Roseland**
Chapman, Philip Lan Rence
Starr, Ira M.
**Sea Girt**
Crispi, Michele Marie
Wyskowski, Barbara Jean
**Secaucus**
McNamara, Patrick James
**Short Hills**
Fast, Kenneth H.
**Shrewsbury**
Baxter, Gregory Stephen
**South Orange**
Kassoff, Mitchell Jay
**South Plainfield**
Santoro, Frank Anthony
**Sparta**
Schupp, Anastasia Luka
**Springfield**
Grayson, Bette Rita
Kurzweil, Bette Grayson
Steinberg, Jeffrey Marc
**Stone Harbor**
Taylor, Robert Lee
**Summit**
Jarvis, Percy Alton, Jr.
Woller, James Alan
**Teaneck**
Diamond, Stanley
**Toms River**
Leone, Stephan Robert
**Trenton**
Kahn, Edward Stanton
Strassberg, Jonathan Elliot
**Union**
Mark, Michael David
Rosenberg, A. Irving
**Wayne**
Long, Lucinda Parshall
**West Orange**
Bottitta, Joseph Anthony
Mandelbaum, Barry Richard
**Westfield**
Gutterman, Alan J.
**Westwood**
Regan, Robert Terrence
**Willingboro**
Guest, Brian Milton
**Woodbury**
Celano, Peter J., Jr.

## NEW MEXICO

**Albuquerque**
Bregman, Jacqueline De Oliveira
Bregman, Sam
Gorman, Robert Dennis
Keleher, Michael Lawrence
Moise, Steven Kahn
Rager, Rudolph Russell
Ramo, Roberta Cooper
Ricks, J. Brent
Schoen, Stevan Jay
Simon, Robert S.
Ussery, Albert Travis
**Las Cruces**
Martin, Connie Ruth
**Roswell**
Bassett, John Walden, Jr.
**Santa Fe**
Abeles, Richard Alan
Burton, John Paul (Jack Burton)
**Seneca**
Monroe, Kendyl Kurth

## NEW YORK

**Albany**
Gosdeck, Thomas Joseph
Piedmont, Richard Stuart
**Albion**
Church, Sanford Allan
**Amherst**
Diakos, Maria Louise
**Attica**
Dadd, Margaret Baggot
**Auburn**
Wolczyk, Joseph Michael
**Ballston Spa**
Brown, Ifigenia Theodore
**Bethpage**
Sanna, Richard Jeffrey
**Binghamton**
Peyton, Walter Burdette
**Briarcliff Manor**
Rosen, Paul Maynard
**Bridgehampton**
Cummings, Richard M.
**Bronx**
Crescenzi, Armando A.
Marchese, Matthew
Margid, Leonard
Verrelli, Anthony Louis
**Bronxville**
Veneruso, James John
**Brooklyn**
Chesley, Stephen Robert
Edwards, Arthur Aden
Held, Marc Jason
Kelleher, Terence L.
Levy, Samuel Robert
Reichman, Adelle E.
**Buffalo**
Bailey, Thomas Charles
Mucci, Gary Louis
Murphy, Edward J., III
Ritchie, Stafford Duff, II
Seggio-Ball, Josephine
**Carmel**
Lowe, E(dwin) Nobles
**Cedarhurst**
Taubenfeld, Harry Samuel
Zuckerbrod, Martin
**Chittenango**
Baum, Peter Alan
**Clifton Park**
Lazarow, Martin Sidney
**Commack**
Somer, Stanley Jerome
**Corning**
Becraft, Charles D., Jr.
**Cornwall**
Obremski, Charles Peter
**Cortlandt Mnr**
Galella, Joseph Peter
**Delhi**
Hamilton, John Thomas, Jr.
**Dobbs Ferry**
Juettner, Diana D'Amico
Maiocchi, Christine
**Douglaston**
Salvo, Joseph Aldo
**East Meadow**
Adler, Ira Jay
Hyman, Montague Allan
**Elmsford**
Wagner, Gary Ted
**Floral Park**
Catanzano, Raymond Augustine
Goldman, Alan Barry
**Flushing**
Chang, Lee-Lee
**Forest Hills**
Addabbo, Dominic Lucian
**Garden City**
DaSilva, Willard H.
Fischoff, Gary Charles
Golden, Christopher Anthony
Kestenbaum, Harold Lee
Licatesi, Anthony Joseph
Tucker, William P.
Wimpfheimer, Steven
**Geneva**
Brind, David Hutchison
**Glens Falls**
McMillen, Robert Stewart
**Goshen**
Joseph, Alan Lloyd
**Great Neck**
Gastwirth, Stuart Lawrence
Luckman, Gregg A.
Samanowitz, Ronald Arthur
Wershals, Paul L.
**Greenvale**
Halper, Emanuel B(arry)
**Groton**
Henry, James Richard
**Hicksville**
Snowe, Alan Martin
**Hollis**
Jairam, Khelanand Vishvaykanand
**Houghton**
Brautigam, David Clyde
**Hudson Falls**
Martindale, Daniel S.
**Huntington**
Munson, Nancy Kay
**Ithaca**
Theisen, Henry William
**Jamesport**
Cardinale, Philip John
**Le Roy**
Whiting, Reid A.
**Little Neck**
Gaffner, David Lewis
**Lockport**
Kennedy, Stephen Charles
**Long Beach**
Levine, Samuel Milton
**Long Island City**
Alimaras, Gus
Barnholdt, Terry Joseph, Jr.
**Lowville**
Snyder, Donald Edward, Jr.
**Mahopac**
Sequeira, Manuel Alexandre, Jr.
**Malverne**
Benigno, Thomas Daniel
**Manhasset**
Lester, David S.
**Melville**
Burke, Richard James
D'Angelo-Mayer, Ida
Zamek, Scott
**Middletown**
Kossar, Ronald Steven
**Mineola**
Daniels, John Hill
Galison, Edward
Goldstein, Sheldon Mark
Jones, Lawrence Tunnicliffe
Levine, David I.
**Montour Falls**
Argetsinger, Cameron R.
**New City**
Fenster, Robert David
**New Rochelle**
DiMarco, Frank Paul
Gunning, Francis Patrick
**New York**
Abelman, Arthur F.
Adler, Arthur S.
Alden, Steven Michael
Altschuler, Fredric Lawrence
Andresen, Malcolm
Beckman, Michael
Benakis, George James
Black, James Isaac, III
Bliwise, Lester Martin
Block, William Kenneth
Brauner, David A.
Briedis, Robert A.
Broadwin, Joseph Louis
Browdy, Joseph Eugene
Burgweger, Francis Joseph Dewes, Jr.
Chen, Wesley
Colbert, Douglas Marc
Cuiffo, Frank Wayne
Davis, Deborah Lynn
Davis, Gordon J.
Devers, Peter Dix
Diamond, Bernard Robin
Donoyan, Gary Leon
Dugan, Terrence Lee
DuLaux, Russell Frederick
D'Ull, Walter
Fawer, Mark S.
Feffer, Joanna Wahl
Feit, David Jonathan
Finkelstein, Allen Lewis
Finnegan, Hugh Patrick
Garfinkel, Neil B.
Goebel, William Horn

Golden, Howard Ira
Goldstein, Charles Arthur
Graham, Christopher Francis
Granoff, Gary Charles
Greene, Andrea Leigh
Grew, Robert Ralph
Grossman, Sanford
Gustafson, Albert Katsuaki
Handlin, Joseph Jason
Herbst, Todd L.
Herz, Andrew Lee
Howard, Susanne C.
Howe, Edwin A(lberts), Jr.
Ingram, Samuel William, Jr.
Intriligator, Marc Steven
Kalomiris, Erika
Karmel, Philip Elias
Kastner, Menachem J.
Katz, Seth Alan
Kaufman, Stephen Herscu
Kirkland, Galen D.
Kobrin, Lawrence Alan
Kreitzman, Ralph J.
Kuklin, Anthony Bennett
Kumble, Steven Jay
Lee, Robert Edward, Jr.
Leibowitz, Nadine S.
Levine, Melvin Charles
Levy, Mark Allan
Mandel, Patricia C.
Marantz, Neil G.
Marcus, Norman
Marks, Theodore Lee
Michigan, Alan
Miller, Neil Scott
Moerdler, Charles Gerard
Morganstern, Gerald H.
Mullman, Michael S.
Munzer, Stephen Ira
Nance, Allan Taylor
Nathan, Andrew Jonathan
Neveloff, Jay A.
O'Rorke, James Francis, Jr.
Paul, Robert Carey
Peragine, Paul Francis
Rahm, David Alan
Ressa, Gregory John
Richards, David Alan
Richey, Kent Ramon
Rikon, Michael
Robinson, Irwin Jay
Rosen, Richard Lewis
Rosenberg, Gary Marc
Saft, Stuart Mark
Sanseverino, Raymond Anthony
Sarzin, Evan
Schechter, Howard
Schleimer, Karen Beth
Schwartz, Barry Steven
Schwartz, James Evan
Seifert, Thomas Lloyd
Shaikh-Bahai, Carrie Anne
Shenker, Joseph C.
Shipper, David W.
Silverman, Arthur Charles
Silvermintz, Michael B.
Simon, Michael Scott
Sobel, Jay
Steinbach, Harold I.
Strauss, Gary Joseph
Strougo, Robert Isaac
Tsismenakis, Vasilia Helen A.
Uram, Gerald Robert
Urban, Lisa Breier
Vernon, Darryl Mitchell
Viener, John D.
Vogel, Bernard Henry
Warner, Jeannette Sloan
Willinger, Lowell D.
Wimpfheimer, Michael Clark
Wu, Robin Chi Ching
Yormak, Jonathon K.
Zimmerman, Paula Susan
Zukerman, Michael
**Newburgh**
Bernz, David
Grobstein, Gene Lawrence
**Niagara Falls**
Hanesian, Shavasp
Levine, David Ethan
**Northport**
Bialla, Rowley
**Nyack**
Cember, M. Nathan
**Olean**
Heyer, John Henry, II
**Oneonta**
Harlem, Richard Andrew
**Orangeburg**
Rivet, Diana Wittmer
**Oswego**
Greene, Stephen Craig
**Oyster Bay**
Bernstein, Jacob
Robinson, Edward T., III
**Patchogue**
Esteve, Edward V.
**Penfield**
Farber, Sidney Theodore
**Pittsford**
Finucane, Leo Gerard
**Port Chester**
Levin, Jeffrey L.
**Port Washington**
Adler, Edward Andrew Koeppel
**Poughkeepsie**
Braswell, Bruce Wayne
Brenner, Marshall Leib
Dietz, Robert Barron
Kranis, Michael David
Reed, Thomas A.
Wallace, Herbert Norman
**Purchase**
Gioffre, Bruno Joseph
**Queensbury**
Sleight, Virginia Mae
**Riverhead**
Twomey, Thomas A., Jr.
**Rochester**
Argento, Victoria M(arie)
Barr, Culver Kent
Blyth, John E.
Brovitz, Richard Stuart
Clifford, Eugene Thomas
Corcoran, Christopher Holmes
Galbraith, Robert Lyell, Jr.
Griffin, Shawn Michael
Lundback, Staffan Bengt Gunnar
Lustig, Douglas James
Relin, Leonard
Trevett, Thomas Neil
**Rome**
Griffith, Emlyn Irving
McMahon, Richard H.
**Saratoga Springs**
Capozzola, Theresa A.
Harper, David Alexander
**Scarsdale**
Sabadie, Francisca Alejandra
**Schenectady**
McCartney, Brian Palmer
Sciocchetti, Paul Vincent
Sokolow, Lloyd Bruce
**Seagate**
Levitt, Sidney Bernard
**Slingerlands**
Rhodes-Devey, Michael
**Smithtown**
Pruzansky, Joshua Murdock
**Snyder**
Genrich, Willard Adolph
**Southampton**
Platt, Harold Kirby
**Spring Valley**
Graifman, Gary Steven
**Staten Island**
Ferranti, Thomas, Jr.
Hall, John George
Miller, Claire Cody
**Stephentown**
Zwack, Henry Francis
**Syosset**
Upton, Arthur Edward
**Syracuse**
Bruno, Richard Thomas
Cirando, John Anthony
Dwyer, James Francis
Fitzpatrick, James David
Mathewson, George Atterbury
Melnicoff, Joel Niesen
Pinsky, Bradley M.
Regan, Paul Michael
Traylor, Robert Arthur
**Uniondale**
Carnesi, Kenneth Brian
**Valley Stream**
Blakeman, Bruce Arthur
**Walden**
Gubits, David Barry
**Wappingers Falls**
Haynes, Paul R.
O'Neil, D. James
**West Hempstead**
Klebanoff, Stanley Milton
**White Plains**
Feder, Robert
Gjertsen, O. Gerard
Hecker, Robert J.
O'Rourke, Richard Lynn
Posner, Martin Louis
Rosenberg, Michael
Silverberg, Steven Mark
Topol, Robin April Levitt
**Woodbury**
Taub, Linda Marsha
**Yonkers**
Rubeo, Stephen Vincent

## NORTH CAROLINA

**Asheville**
Frue, William Calhoun
Worley, Charles Robert
**Boone**
Brown, Wade Edward
**Charlotte**
Bryce, Teresa Audrey
Bush, F. Brad
Lynch, Craig Taylor
Sink, Robert C.
**Durham**
Welborn, Reich Lee
**Elizabeth City**
Riley, John Frederick
**Emerald Isle**
Lincoln, Michael Powell
**Greensboro**
Agapion, Bill
Galloway, Hunter Henderson, III
Glover, Durant Murrell
Walker, Edward Garrett
**Hickory**
Cagle, Joe Neal
**Kannapolis**
Griggs, Farrar O'Neal
**Monroe**
Love, Walter Bennett, Jr.
**Murphy**
Bata, Rudolph Andrew, Jr.
MacFarlan, John Howard
**New Bern**
Ward, Thomas Monroe
**Pittsboro**
Riggsbee, Lunday Adams
**Raleigh**
Cameron, Christie Speir
Carruth, Paul
Fricke, David Robert
Homick, Daniel John
Reinhard, Steven Ira
Safran, Perry Renfrow
Shyllon, Prince E.N.
Tucker, Sherry E.
**Rowland**
Price, Robert Ernest

## NORTH DAKOTA

**Bismarck**
Edin, Charles Thomas
Klemin, Lawrence R.
**Grand Forks**
Widdel, John Earl, Jr.

## OHIO

**Batavia**
Pattison, George Edgar
**Beavercreek**
Stier, Charles Herman, Jr.
**Bowling Green**
Huffman, Diane Rausch
**Bucyrus**
Skropits, Amy Elizabeth
**Canfield**
Beck, James Hayes
**Canton**
Fitzpatrick, Lauren Elaine
Putman, Timothy Joseph
**Carrollton**
Childers, John Charles
**Chardon**
Newman, Paul A.
**Cincinnati**
Bonhaus, Laurence Allen
Cobey, John Geoffrey
Cunningham, Pierce Edward
Heldman, James Gardner
Naylor, Paul Donald
Petrie, Bruce Inglis
Rubin, Robert Samuel
Strauss, William Victor
Trauth, Joseph Louis, Jr.
**Cleveland**
Band, Jordan Clifford
Chilcote, Lee A.
Felty, Kriss Delbert
Kahn, Scott H.
Owendoff, Stephen Peter
Pearlman, Samuel Segel
Singerman, Paul Joseph
Waldeck, John Walter, Jr.
**Columbus**
Albert, Robert Hamilton
Buchenroth, Stephen Richard
D'Aurora, Jack
Elsass, Tobias Harold
Fultz, Robert Edward
Graff, Douglas Eric
Jewett, James Michael
Joseph, John James
Kington, John Anthony
Pryor, David W.
Sully, Ira Bennett
Tripp, Thomas Neal
**Dayton**
Holz, Michael Harold
Liberman, Scott A.
**Dublin**
Inzetta, Mark Stephen
**Eaton**
Thomas, James William
**Elyria**
Kovacs, John Joseph
**Garfield Hts**
Demer, Margaret E.
**Georgetown**
Hornschemeier, Patrick
**Logan**
Kernen, Will
**Lorain**
Levin, Arnold Sampson
**Maumee**
Moore, Everett Daniel
**Newark**
Untied, Wesley Kyle
**Pepper Pike**
Soukup, Christopher Earl
**Piqua**
Davis, Dale Gordon
**Salem**
Bowman, Scott McMahan
**Springfield**
Martin, David MacCoy
Pedraza, Miguel A., Jr.
**Toledo**
Barone, Guy T.
Gouttiere, John P.
Skotynsky, Walter John
**Twinsburg**
Hill, Thomas Allen
**Warren**
Buzulencia, Michael Douglas
Kearney, Patricia Ann
**Wooster**
Haught, Sharon Kay
**Worthington**
Worobiec, Michele Selig
**Youngstown**
Burdman, B. Richard
Galip, Ronald George

## OKLAHOMA

**Broken Arrow**
Frieze, H(arold) Delbert
**Cherokee**
Hadwiger, Mickey J.
**El Reno**
Grantham, Robert Edward
**Enid**
Musser, William Wesley, Jr.
**Fairview**
Schoeppel, James
**Jones**
Dean, Bill Verlin, Jr.
**Muskogee**
Frix, Paige Lane
Robinson, Adelbert Carl
**Oklahoma City**
Barth, J. Edward
Elder, James Carl
Epperson, Kraettli Quynton
Johnson, Robert Max
Kallstrom, James David
McBride, Kenneth Eugene
Stanley, Brian Jordan
**Tulsa**
Blackstock, LeRoy
Chandler, Ronald Jay
Clark, Wendell W.
Hilsabeck, Michael D.
Huffman, Robert Allen, Jr.
Mackey, Steven R.
Steltzlen, Janelle Hicks
Unruh, Robert James
**Walters**
Flanagan, Michael Charles

## OREGON

**Bend**
Erwin, Lawrence Warde
**Cannon Beach**
Hillestad, Charles Andrew
**Eugene**
DuPriest, Douglas Millhollen
Gallagher, Donald Avery, Jr.
Horn, John Harold
**Grants Pass**
Baker, Lindi L.
**La Grande**
Joseph, Steven Jay
**Lake Oswego**
Byczynski, Edward Frank
**Pendleton**
Rew, Lawrence B.
**Portland**
Anderson, Herbert Hatfield
Bauer, Henry Leland
Byrne, Gregory William
Chevis, Cheryl Ann
Coreson, Latricia Kadene
Denecke, David Rockey
Fassetto, Eugene A.
Frassetto, Eugene A.
Hanna, Harry Mitchell
Hummel, Holly Jane
James, Christopher
Kamin, Scott Allan
Schuster, Philip Frederick, II
Waggoner, James Clyde
Weiner, David P.
**Roseburg**
Yockim, Ronald Stephen
**Salem**
Lien, Wallace Wayne

## PENNSYLVANIA

**Allentown**
Brown, Robert Wayne
McGinley, Paul Anthony, Jr.
**Bala Cynwyd**
Lasak, John Joseph
**Bangor**
Ceraul, David James
**Berwyn**
Huggler, David H.
**Bradford**
Hauser, Christopher George
**Bristol**
Kashkashian, Arsen
**Brookville**
Smith, Sharon Louise
**Bryn Mawr**
Broseman, George W.
Hankin, Mitchell Robert
**Butler**
Pater, Michael John
**Dover**
Krug, Rob Alan
**Doylestown**
Bolla, William Joseph
Gathright, Howard T.
Wagner, Joseph Hagel
**Drexel Hill**
West, Kenneth Edward
**Erie**
Bernard, Bruce William
**Exton**
Teti, Louis N.
**Gibsonia**
Heilman, Carl Edwin
**Girard**
Steadman, James Robert
**Greensburg**
Gounley, Dennis Joseph
**Grove City**
McBride, Milford Lawrence, Jr.
**Harrisburg**
Fritz, Martin Andrew
Kury, Franklin Leo
**Hatboro**
Nicholson, Bruce Allen
**Huntingdon**
Covell, Robert Martin
**Indiana**
Barbor, John Howard
Bell, Paul Anthony, II
**Jenkintown**
Michie, Daniel Boorse, Jr.
Ormsby, Charles William, Jr.
**Kittanning**
Petrosky, Robert
**Lancaster**
Byler, William Bryan
Kraybill, J(ames) Elvin
Minney, Michael Jay
**Lansdale**
Pearlstine, Neal R.
Walper, Robert Andrew
**Lehigh Valley**
Marles, Blake Curtis
**Lehighton**
Schwab, William G.
**Lewistown**
Levin, Allen Joseph
**Lock Haven**
Miceli, Frank S.
Rosamilia, Charles R.
Snowiss, Alvin L.
**Marietta**
Shumaker, Harold Dennis
**Media**
D'Amico, Andrew J.
Ewing, Robert Clark
Mackrides, William Charles
Mardinly, Peter Alan
**Mercer**
McConnell, Mary Ann
**Milford**
Siegel, Arthur Bernard
**Mount Pleasant**
Johnson, Michael A.
**New Castle**
Mangino, Matthew Thomas
Palmer, Allen L.
**Norristown**
Milner, Kenneth Paul
**Philadelphia**
Auten, David Charles
Butterworth, David Gardner
Cross, Milton H.
Culhane, John Langdon
Davis, C. VanLeer, III
Denmark, William Adam
De Simone, Dominic J.
Finkelstein, Joseph Simon
Goldberg, Richard Robert
Hunter, James Austen, Jr.
Keene, John Clark
Kupperman, Louis Brandeis
Liu, Diana Chua
Loverdi, Rosemary J.
Maxey, David Walker
Miller, Henry Franklin
O'Brien, William Jerome, II
Pauciulo, John William
Pollack, Michael
Stevens, Mark A.
Young, Roma Skeen
**Pipersville**
Sigety, Charles Edward
**Pittsburgh**
Adelkoff, Steven J.
Aronson, Mark Berne
Brown, David Ronald
Ehrenwerth, David Harry
Fiore, Kevin John
Gold, Harold Arthur
Hartman, Ronald G.
Hess, Emerson Garfield
Hollinshead, Earl Darnell, Jr.
Holsinger, John Paul
Leonard, Arthur J.
Letwin, Jeffrey William
Messer, Susan J.
Raynovich, George, Jr.
Stepanian, Steven Arvid, II
**Pottstown**
Evans, Robert Whiteside, III
**Reading**
Kline, Sidney DeLong, Jr.
**Richboro**
Van Blunk, Henry Edward
**Rydal**
Friedman, Ralph David
**Scranton**
Burke, Henry Patrick
Cowley, Michael C.
Henkelman, Willard Max
**Swarthmore**
Ullman, Roger Roland
**Wallingford**
DePaul, Anthony Kenneth
**Washington**
Posner, David S.
**Waynesboro**
Maxwell, LeRoy Stevenson
**Waynesburg**
Webb, Jane Marie
**Wilkes Barre**
Ufberg, Murray
**Williamsport**
Holland, Fred Anthony
Kane, Joseph Patrick
Knecht, William L.
**York**
Benn, Niles S.
Hoffmeyer, William Frederick

## RHODE ISLAND

**Cranston**
Coletti, John Anthony
Loffredo, Pasco Frank
**Providence**
Berkelhammer, Robert Bruce
Carlotti, Stephen Jon
Cosentino, Robert J(ohn)
Lombardi, Valentino Dennis
Salvadore, Mal Andrew
**Westerly**
Nardone, William Andrew

## SOUTH CAROLINA

**Camden**
Jacobs, Rolly Warren
**Charleston**
Garrett, Gordon Henderson
Robinson, Neil Cibley, Jr.
Steadman, Richard Anderson, Jr.
Warren, John Hertz, III
**Columbia**
Caulk, Glen Paul
Currin, Robert Graves, Jr.
Marchant, Bristow
Scott, Ronald Charles
Unger, Richard Mahlon
**Greenville**
Dana, Frank J., III
Edwards, Harry LaFoy
Laws, James Terry
Riley, Edward Patterson, Jr.
**Greenwood**
Nexsen, Julian Jacobs, Jr.
**Hilton Head**
Laughlin, Drew Alan
**Hilton Head Island**
Scarminach, Charles Anthony
**Myrtle Beach**
Barnett, Michael James
**Rock Hill**
Alford, Duncan Earl

**Summerville**
Prettyman, Howard Cross, Jr.
**Sumter**
Reynolds, William MacKenzie, Jr.

### SOUTH DAKOTA

**Sioux Falls**
Van Demark, Richard Edward

### TENNESSEE

**Bristol**
Hillman, Shelton B., Jr.
**Church Hill**
Frazier, Steven Carl
**Cookeville**
Qualls, Steven Daniel
**Erwin**
Shults-Davis, Lois Bunton
**Jackson**
Latimer, Timothy B.
**Memphis**
deWitt, Charles Benjamin, III
Jalenak, James Bailey
Kirk, Robert S.
Waddell, Phillip Dean
Webb, Kathleen Rochford
**Nashville**
Trent, John Thomas, Jr.
**Parsons**
Petrey, R. Claybourne, Jr.
**Union City**
Graham, Hardy Moore

### TEXAS

**Addison**
Turner, Bruce Edward
**Arlington**
Pierson, Grey
Rosenberry, William Kenneth
**Austin**
Bauer, Sydney Meade
Davis, Robert Larry
Drolla, John Casper Dodt, Jr.
Hollen, Theodore Thomas
Lione, John Gabriel, Jr.
Nevola, Roger Paul
Owen, Jack Edward, Jr.
Rider, Brian Clayton
Schrauff, Christopher Wesley
**Ballinger**
Grindstaff, Everett James
**Baytown**
Kennamer, John Harold
**Bellaire**
Jacobus, Charles Joseph
**Bryan**
Strong, Stephen Andrew
**Carthage**
Dowd, Steven Milton
**Corpus Christi**
Locke, William Henry
Turpin, John Russell, Jr.
**Dallas**
Beuttenmuller, Rudolf William
Buchanan, Robert Graham, Jr.
Davis, Gregg C.
Fishman, Edward Marc
Harvey, James Clement
Helfand, Marcy Caren
Hoskins, Sonya Denise
Levin, Hervey Phillip
McDonald, Scott K.
Moore, Richard George
Mueller, Mark Christopher
Nolan, John Michael
Pleasant, James Scott
Portman, Glenn Arthur
Roberts, Harry Morris, Jr.
St. Claire, Frank Arthur
Skibell, Arthur
Stewart, Robb P.
Swanson, Wallace Martin
Thau, William Albert, Jr.
White, James Richard
**El Paso**
Cox, Sanford Curtis, Jr.
Lipson, Myer Jack
Provenghi, Ruggero
**Euless**
Paran, Mark Lloyd
**Fort Worth**
Fanous, Nikki Hobert
Phillips, Robert James, Jr.
Ratliff, William D., III
West, Robert Grady
**Houston**
Anderson, Doris Ehlinger
Brown, Stephen Smiley
Cohen, Jay I.
Heinrich, Timothy John
Judice, Kenneth R.
Marlow, Orval Lee, II
Melamed, Richard
Miller, Robert Daniel
Orton, John Stewart
Sears, Terry H.
Simmons, Stephen Judson
Snowden, Barry Howard
Walter, Teri A.
White, Letitia H.
Zeigler, Ann dePender
**Killeen**
Kleff, Pierre Augustine, Jr.
**League City**
Chudleigh, G. Stephen
**Liberty**
Wheat, John Nixon
**Marshall**
Gilstrap, James Rodney
**Midland**
Chappell, Clovis Gillham, Jr.
**Missouri City**
Hodges, Jot Holiver, Jr.
**New Braunfels**
Nolte, Melvin, Jr.
Pfeuffer, Robert Tug
**Odessa**
Corzine, Darrell W.
**Richardson**
Davis, M. G.
**Richmond**
Slone, Charles R.
**Rockwall**
Holt, Charles William, Jr.
**San Angelo**
Noelke, Henry Tolbert (Hal Noelke)
**San Antonio**
Barton, James Cary
Hartnett, Dan Dennis
Pipkin, Marvin Grady
Young, Jess Wollett
**Spring**
Hearn-Haynes, Theresa
Hendricks, Randal Arlan
**Sugar Land**
Clennan, John Joseph
Poock, Steven Doyle
**Temple**
Cuba, Benjamin James
**Tyler**
Hadden, Arthur Roby
Lake, David Alan
**Uvalde**
Kerby, Yale Leland
**Weslaco**
Pomerantz, Jerald Michael
**Yoakum**
Kvinta, Charles J.

### UTAH

**Logan**
Honaker, Jimmie Joe
Jenkins, James C.
**Midvale**
Dahl, Everett E.
**Ogden**
Mecham, Glenn Jefferson
**Park City**
Kennicott, James W.
**Pleasant Grove**
Merritt, Laramie Dee
**Provo**
Jeffs, M. Dayle
**Saint George**
Gallian, Russell Joseph
**Salt Lake City**
Anderson, Robert Monte
Barusch, Lawrence Roos
Brown, Charles R.
Colessides, Nick John
Cornaby, Kay Sterling
Dragoo, Denise Ann
Headman, Arlan Osmond, Jr.
Heaton, Jon C.
Hunt, George Andrew
Jensen, Dallin W.
Jones, Ken Paul
Jones, Michael Frank
Kirkham, John Spencer
McIntosh, James Albert

### VERMONT

**Burlington**
Rushford, Robert Howard
Schroeder, William Wayne
**Dorset**
O'Toole, Kevin Michael
**Middlebury**
Reiff, Helen Hayslette
**Rutland**
Dardeck, Stephen A.
Facey, John Abbott, III
**Taftsville**
Johnson, Philip Martin
**Woodstock**
Dagger, William Carson

### VIRGINIA

**Alexandria**
Costello, Daniel Brian
Elsberg, David Donald
McClure, Roger John
Sherk, George William
**Charlottesville**
Kudravetz, David Waller
**Chesapeake**
Lascara, Dominic Paul
**Chester**
Connelly, Colin Charles
**Culpeper**
DeJarnette, Elliott Hawes
**Danville**
Goodman, Lewis Elton, Jr.
**Fairfax**
Bloomquist, Dennis Howard
Kear, Maria Martha Ruscitella
Keith, John A.C.
Sanderson, Douglas Jay
Stearns, Frank Warren
**Falls Church**
Baskin, William Maxwell, Sr.
Christman, Bruce Lee
Goldrosen, Donald Norman
Nunes, Morris A.
**Great Falls**
Preston, Charles George
**Lawrenceville**
Bain, C. Ridley
**Leesburg**
Minchew, John Randall
**Madison**
Coates, Frederick Ross
**Martinsville**
Frith, Douglas Kyle
**Mc Lean**
Ingersoll, William Boley
Maloof, Farahe Paul
Toole, John Harper
Weiss, Rhett Louis
**Newport News**
Kamp, Arthur Joseph, Jr.
**Norfolk**
Harrell, Charles Lydon, Jr.
Parker, Richard Wilson
Sacks, Stewart Jonathan
Waldo, Joseph Thomas
**Providence Forge**
Richardson, William Winfree, III
**Reston**
Spath, Gregg Anthony
**Richmond**
Bates, John Wythe, III
Boyd, B(everley) Randolph
Pollard, Henry Robinson, IV
Rucker, Douglas Pendleton, Jr.
Swartz, Charles Robert
Weis, Laura Visser
**Roanoke**
Glenn, Robert Eastwood
Lemon, William Jacob
**Suffolk**
Young, Hubert Howell, Jr.
**Virginia Beach**
Layton, Garland Mason
**Wise**
Rogers, Leonard David
**Wytheville**
Baird, Thomas Bryan, Jr.

### WASHINGTON

**Bellevue**
Gulick, Peter VanDyke
Scaringi, Michael Joseph
Sullivan, James Jerome
**Bellingham**
Packer, Mark Barry
**Bremerton**
Cunningham, Gary Allen
**Centralia**
Tiller, Laurel Lee
**Gig Harbor**
Thompson, Ronald Edward
**Issaquah**
Benoliel, Joel
**Mount Vernon**
Sjostrom, Craig David
**Olympia**
Miller, Allen Terry, Jr.
**Port Angeles**
Gay, Carl Lloyd
**Seattle**
Bateman, Heidi S.
Blair, M. Wayne
Brower, Joshua Christopher Allen
Cornell, Kenneth Lee
Creim, Jerry Alan
Cullen, Jack Joseph
Eustis, Jeffrey Murdock
Goeltz, Thomas A.
Haggard, Joel Edward
Jensen, Howard Fernando
Kilbane, Thomas M.
Krohn, Gary John
Kuhrau, Edward W.
Murray, Michael Kent
Palmer, Douglas S., Jr.
Richdale, David Allen
Rieke, Paul Victor
Thorne, David W.
Tousley, Russell Frederick
Williams, J. Vernon
Wilson, Richard Randolph
**Spokane**
Cooper, R(obert) Maurice
Esposito, Joseph Anthony
Lineberger, Peter Saalfield
Michaelsen, Howard Kenneth
**Tacoma**
Beale, Robert Lyndon
Goodstein, Robert I.
Harlow, Angelia DeAn
**Tukwila**
Gouras, Mark Steven
**Wenatchee**
Aylward, J. Patrick
**Yakima**
Larson, Paul Martin

### WEST VIRGINIA

**Beckley**
Sayre, Floyd McKinley, III
**Fairmont**
Stanton, George Patrick, Jr.
**Gassaway**
Jones, Jeniver James
**Morgantown**
Bunner, William Keck
**New Martinsville**
Hill, Philip Bonner
**Romney**
Saville, Royce Blair
**Wheeling**
Riley, Arch Wilson, Jr.

### WISCONSIN

**Adams**
Screnock, Paul Steven
**Appleton**
Drescher, Kathleen Ebben
**Beloit**
Blakely, Robert George
**Brookfield**
Benson, Scott Michael
**Chippewa Falls**
Hunt, Heather M.
**Cross Plains**
Moretti, Jay Donald
**Delavan**
Weber, Laura Ann
**Elkhorn**
Eberhardt, Daniel Hugo
Leibsle, Robert Carl
Sweet, Lowell Elwin
**Janesville**
Williams, Mary Beth
**Kohler**
Sheedy, Kathleen Ann
**Lake Geneva**
McCormack, Joanne Marie
**Madison**
Kuehling, Robert Warren
Petershack, Richard Eugene
Rankin, Gene Raymond
Shea, Jeremy Charles
**Milwaukee**
Bratt, Herbert Sidney
Bremer, John M.
Decker, John Robert
Dencker, Lester J.
Gaines, Irving David
Giese, Heiner
Hatch, Michael Ward
Levine, Herbert
Reiske, Peter Francis
Rieselbach, Allen Newman
Roge, Bret Alan
**Neenah**
Birtch, Grant Eacrett
**New Berlin**
Schober, Thomas Gregory
**Port Washington**
Check, Melvin Anthony
**Racine**
Crawford, Timothy Patrick
Du Rocher, James Howard
**Reedsburg**
Gorsuch, Sandra Cardo
**Viroqua**
Jenkins, David Lynn
**Washburn**
Nordling, H.G.
**Wausau**
Deffner, Roger L.

### WYOMING

**Cody**
Webster, C. Edward, II
**Laramie**
Smith, Thomas Shore
**Sheridan**
Lonabaugh, Ellsworth Eugene
**Worland**
Richins, Kent Alan

### TERRITORIES OF THE UNITED STATES

### PUERTO RICO

**Ponce**
Leon-Sotomayor, Jose Rafael

### AUSTRALIA

**Sydney**
Brown, John Thomas

### GREECE

**Athens**
Vakrinos, Theodore Christos

### ADDRESS UNPUBLISHED

Ansley, Shepard Bryan
Arber, Howard Bruce
Arnold, Craig Anthony (Tony Arnold)
Assael, Michael
Bateman, David Alfred
Buffington, John Victor
Campbell, Pollyann S.
Cazalas, Mary Rebecca Williams
Clabaugh, Elmer Eugene, Jr.
Colton, Sterling Don
Crown, Nancy Elizabeth
Deane, Ruth M.
Edwards, Daniel Paul
Engelhardt, John Hugo
Feldman, Richard David
Fetzer, Mark Stephen
Finkelstein, Marcia Lyn
Fogel, Adelaide Forst
Frankel, James Burton
Friedman, Tod H.
Funnell, Kevin Joseph
Garner, Mary Martin
Gooch, Robert Francis
Gordon, David Zevi
Griffith, Steven Franklin, Sr.
Hackett, Wesley Phelps, Jr.
Harman, Wallace Patrick
Higginbotham, John Taylor
Holtzschue, Karl Bressem
Hybl, William Joseph
Jessop, Jeanette Wanless
Johnson, Leonard Hjalma
Jorgensen, Erik Holger
Keister, Jean Clare
Klein, Judah B.
LaForest, Lana Jean
Levine, Solomon L.
Loomie, Edward Raphael
Mann, Richard Lynn
Martin, James William
Mayersohn, Arnold Linn, Jr.
McCormick, Homer L., Jr.
McGinty, Brian Donald
McIntosh, Rhodina Covington
Meli, Salvatore Andrew
Missan, Richard Sherman
Mitlak, Stefany (Lynn)
Naughton, John Alexander
Nunalee, Thomas Hervey, IV
Oates, Carl Everette
Pahides, Ann-Marie MacDonald
Pear, Charles E., Jr.
Peterson, Howard Cooper
Poliakoff, Gary A.
Riddle, Michael Lee
Rivera, Oscar R.
Rohrer, George John
Samalin, Edwin
Shaffer, Richard James
Siebert, William Alan
Siegel, Sarah Ann
Silver, Carol Ruth
Silverberg, Mark Victor
Solkoff, Jerome Ira
Stephenson, Barbera Wertz
Torgerson, Larry Keith
Wharton, James Carl
White, Kendred Alan
Wittebort, Robert John, Jr.
Wright, Robert Payton
Zurav, David Bernard

---

**REAL ESTATE DEVELOPMENT.** *See* **Property, real.**

---

**SALES OF GOODS.** *See* **Commercial, contracts.**

---

## SECURITIES

### UNITED STATES

### ALABAMA

**Birmingham**
Baker, David Remember
Johnson, Joseph H., Jr.
Rotch, James E.
Wilson, James Charles, Jr.
**Montgomery**
Waters, Michael D.

### ARIZONA

**Phoenix**
Bivens, Donald Wayne
Chanen, Steven Robert
Curzon, Thomas Henry
Dunipace, Ian Douglas
Galbut, Martin Richard
James, Charles E., Jr.
Madden, Paul Robert
Maledon, Michael Brien
Moya, Patrick Robert
Olson, Kevin Lory
Pidgeon, Steven D.
Price, Charles Steven
Seamons, Quinton Frank
Theobald, Scott M.
Thompson, Terence William
Williams, Quinn Patrick
**Scottsdale**
Berry, Charles Richard
Titus, Jon Alan
**Tempe**
Chander, Anupam
**Tucson**
Meehan, Michael Joseph

### ARKANSAS

**Little Rock**
Knight, David Arceneaux

### CALIFORNIA

**Burlingame**
Narayan, Beverly Elaine
Telleen, L. Michael
**Camarillo**
Cayley, Susan Nicole
**Carlsbad**
Koehnke, Phillip Eugene
Villavicencio, Dennis (Richard)
**Century City**
Davis, Donald G(lenn)
**Costa Mesa**
Grogan, Virginia S.
**Cupertino**
Maddux, Parker Ahrens
**Irvine**
Creatura, Mark A.
Hensley, William Michael
**Los Angeles**
Apfel, Gary
Barnes, Willie R.
Blencowe, Paul Sherwood
Bogaard, William Joseph
Boston, Derrick Osmond
Cahill, Michael Edward
Carlson, Robert Edwin
Castro, Leonard Edward
Farrar, Stanley F.
Golay, Frank H., Jr.
Haakh, Gilbert Edward
Hatch, Hilary Joy
Hsu, Julie L.
Kim, Edward K.
Morganstern, Myrna Dorothy
Noble, Richard Lloyd
Power, John Bruce
Richardson, Douglas Fielding
Shultz, John David
**Menlo Park**
Crandall, Nelson David, III
Fairman, Marc P.
Gunderson, Robert Vernon, Jr.
**Monte Sereno**
Allan, Lionel Manning
**Mountain View**
Montgomery, John Bishop
**Newport Beach**
Cano, Kristin Maria
Hancock, S. Lee
Terner, Andor David
**Oakland**
Bewley, Peter David
**Pacific Palisades**
Lagle, John Franklin
**Palo Alto**
Furbush, David Malcolm
Huskins, Michael Louis
Lesser, Henry
Phair, Joseph Baschon
Pohlen, Patrick Alan
Whaley, James Thaddeus
**Pasadena**
van Schoonenberg, Robert G.
**San Diego**
Bilstad, Blake Timothy
Brownlie, Robert William
Denniston, John Alexander
Frantz, William Michael
Hamer, Mark Harris
**San Francisco**
Aronovsky, Ronald George

Block, David Jeffrey
Block, Maureen Shanghnessy
Boutin, Peter Rucker
Campbell, Scott Robert
Casillas, Mark
Christopher, Thomas Van
Devine, Antoine Maurice
Evers, William Dohrmann
Faye, Richard Brent
Finberg, James Michael
Halloran, Michael James
Hockett, Christopher Burch
Larson, John William
Latta, Thomas Albert
Levie, Mark Robert
Mann, Bruce Alan
Martin, Jay R.
Palmer, Venrice Romito
Rice, Denis Timlin
Suter, Ben
Whitehead, David Barry

**San Rafael**
Keegin, Stafford Warwick

**San Ramon**
Davis, John Albert

**Tarzana**
Godino, Marc Lawrence

**Toluca Lake**
Runquist, Lisa A.

**Torrance**
Petillon, Lee Ritchey

**Walnut Creek**
Deming, Bruce Robert

**Woodland Hills**
DeSantis, Richard A.

### COLORADO

**Castle Rock**
Bell, Brian Mayes

**Denver**
Campbell, William J.
Ceriani, Gary James
Hilbert, Otto Karl, II
Hill, Robert F.
Keithley, Roger Lee
Kelso, Donald Iain Junor
Levine, Ronald Raymond
Lutz, John Shafroth
Mauro, Richard Frank
Oakes, Susan Leigh
Quinn, Michael S.
Terry, Ward Edgar, Jr.
Wollins, David Hart

**Englewood**
Brett, Stephen M.
Lidstone, Herrick Kenley, Jr.
Wagner, David James
Wiegand, Robert, II

**Littleton**
Minckley, Carla Beth

### CONNECTICUT

**Bridgeport**
McCrory, Anne O.

**Danbury**
Bassett, Robert Andrews

**Fairfield**
Denniston, Brackett Badger, III

**Greenwich**
Raimondi, Josephine Ann

**Hartford**
Beck, Henry M., Jr.
Bouton, William Wells, III
Cain, George Harvey
Smith, Richard Stanley, Jr.

**Milford**
Sagarin, J. Daniel

**Stamford**
Bello, Christopher Robert
Dupont, Wesley David
Herling, Michael James

**Waterbury**
Wolfe, Harriet Munrett

**Weston**
Cohen, Fred Howard

**Windsor**
Lerman, Kenneth Brian

### DELAWARE

**Wilmington**
Smith, Craig Bennett
Stoltzfus, James Allen

### DISTRICT OF COLUMBIA

**Washington**
Bill, Arthur Henry
Chafetz, Marc Edward
Clark, Paul Thomas
Cohen, Louis Richard
Craft, Robert Homan, Jr.
Dickstein, Sidney
Feuerstein, Donald Martin
Finkelstein, Jay Gary
Flagg, Ronald Simon
Freeman, Milton Victor
Greenberger, I. Michael
Horn, Charles M.
Hu, Patrick Haiping
Hyde, Howard Laurence
Jacobson, Richard Lee
Johnson, Philip McBride
Kroll, Milton Paul
Lehr, Dennis James
Levenson, Alan Bradley
Lucas, Steven Mitchell
Lybecker, Martin Earl
McMillan, James Gardner
Meer, Cary Jesse
Molenkamp, Jack A.
More, John Herron
Muir, J. Dapray
Murphy, Sean Patrick
Quarles, James Linwood, III
Rainbolt, John Vernon, II
Rosengren, Paul Gregory
Ryan, Joseph
Sandor, Lawrence Paul
Schropp, James Howard
Stromberg, Jean Wilbur Gleason
Strong, Carter
Trager, Michael David
Trimble, Sandra Ellingson
Unger, Peter Van Buren
Wenner, Charles Roderick
Wilson, Bruce Sandness

### FLORIDA

**Boca Raton**
Buckstein, Mark Aaron

**Fort Lauderdale**
Austin, Scott Raymond
Platner, Michael Gary
Schneider, Laz Levkoff

**Jacksonville**
Kelso, Linda Yayoi
Liles, Rutledge Richardson
Sadler, Luther Fuller, Jr.
Slade, Thomas Bog, III

**Laud By Sea**
Hasenauer, Judith Anne

**Melbourne**
Ollinger, George Edward, III

**Miami**
Berritt, Harold Edward
Critchlow, Richard H.
Ersek, Gregory Joseph Mark
Feinberg, Dyanne Elyce
Fontes, J. Mario F., Jr.
Friedman, Richard Nathan
Furnari, Doreen S.
Garrett, Richard G.
Granata, Linda M.
Grossman, Robert Louis
Hoffman, Larry J.
Jacobson, Bernard
Klein, Peter William
McGuigan, Thomas Richard
Mendelson, Victor Howard
Miller, James M.
Roddenberry, Stephen Keith
Villasana, George Anthony

**New Port Richey**
Focht, Theodore Harold

**North Palm Beach**
Coyle, Dennis Patrick

**Ocala**
Spivey, Stephen Dale

**Orlando**
Blackford, Robert Newton
Blaher, Neal Jonathan
Collard, Stacey Lee
Heinle, Richard Alan
Ioppolo, Frank S., Jr.
Nadeau, Robert Bertrand, Jr.
Pierce, John Gerald (Jerry Pierce)
Stuart, Alice Melissa
Yates, Leighton Delevan, Jr.

**Palm Beach**
Tabernilla, Armando Alejandro

**Saint Petersburg**
DiFilippo, Fernando, Jr.
Kiefner, John Robert, Jr.

**Sarasota**
Kirtley, William Thomas

**Stuart**
Ponsoldt, William Raymond, Jr.

**Tallahassee**
Minnick, Bruce Alexander
Underwood, R. Michael

**Tampa**
Barker, Chris A(llen)
Grammig, Robert James
Teblum, Gary Ira

**West Palm Beach**
O'Brien, Thomas George, III

### GEORGIA

**Atlanta**
Arkin, Robert David
Beckham, Walter Hull, III
Collins, Steven M.
Ganz, Charles David
Grayson, Neil Estridge
Greer, Bernard Lewis, Jr.
Isaf, Fred Thomas
Morgan, Charles Russell
Moss, Raymond Lloyd
Prince, David Cannon
Schulte, Jeffrey Lewis
Stewart, Jeffrey B.
Williams, Neil, Jr.

**Norcross**
Hasbrouck, Catherine O'Malley

### HAWAII

**Honolulu**
Gay, E(mil) Laurence
Reber, David James

### ILLINOIS

**Chicago**
Bashwiner, Steven Lacelle
Berolzheimer, Karl
Boardman, Robert A.
Burgdoerfer, Jerry
Clinton, Edward Xavier
Conlon, Steven Denis
Crawford, Dewey Byers
Cunningham, Craig Carnell
Donohoe, Jerome Francis
Dunn, Edwin Rydell
Dunn, Kenneth Carl
Fahner, Tyrone C.
Fein, Roger Gary
Friedli, Helen Russell
George, John Martin, Jr.
Gerstein, Mark Douglas
Goldman, Michael P.
Gray, Steven Joseph
Henry, Robert John
Hollins, Mitchell Leslie
Huston, Steven Craig
Hyman, Michael Bruce
Jock, Paul F., II
Johnson, Gary Thomas
Johnson, Lael Frederic
Kallianis, James H., Jr.
Kolmin, Kenneth Guy
Lang, Gordon, Jr.
Levin, Michael David
Liggio, Carl Donald
Lind, Jon Robert
Maher, Francesca Marciniak
Malovany, Howard
Manzoni, Charles R., Jr.
Marvel, Kenneth Robert
Miller, Paul J.
Murdock, Charles William
Niehoff, Philip John
Rhind, James Thomas
Roberson, G. Gale, Jr.
Ruiz, Michele Ilene
Sigal, Michael Stephen
Suskin, Howard Steven
Thomas, Stephen Paul
Wander, Herbert Stanton
Weil, Andrew L.
Winkler, Charles Howard
York, John C(hristopher)
Yu, Aihong

**Deerfield**
Cutchins, Clifford Armstrong, IV
Gaither, John F.
Oettinger, Julian Alan

**Dekalb**
Tucker, Watson Billopp

**Franklin Park**
Blanchard, Eric Alan

**Gurnee**
Southern, Robert Allen

**Highland Park**
Nyberg, William Arthur

**Naperville**
Larson, Mark Edward, Jr.

**Northbrook**
Teichner, Bruce A.

**Oak Brook**
Farnell, Alan Stuart
Getz, Herbert A.

**Schiller Park**
Congalton, Christopher William

**Skokie**
Gopman, Howard Z.

**Springfield**
Cullen, Mark Kenneth

**Wheaton**
Beckley, James Emmett

### INDIANA

**Indianapolis**
Dutton, Stephen James
Kleiman, Mary Margaret
Koeller, Robert Marion
Lowe, Louis Robert, Jr.
Padgett, Gregory Lee
Strain, James Arthur
Welch, William

### IOWA

**Des Moines**
Neumann, Gordon Richard, Jr.

**Iowa City**
Thomas, Randall Stuart

**Newton**
Bennett, Edward James

### KANSAS

**Overland Park**
Gaar, Norman Edward

**Prairie Vlg**
Stanton, Roger D.

**Topeka**
Rainey, William Joel

### KENTUCKY

**Lexington**
McClelland, Denise H.

### LOUISIANA

**New Orleans**
Kupperman, Stephen Henry
McMillan, Lee Richards, II
Whitney, John Franklin

### MARYLAND

**Baltimore**
Burch, Francis Boucher, Jr.
Chernow, Jeffrey Scott
Lynch, Timothy Cronin
Scriggins, Larry Palmer

**Bethesda**
Rivkin, Steven Robert

**Columbia**
Maseritz, Guy B.

**Rockville**
Roberts, Christopher Chalmers

### MASSACHUSETTS

**Andover**
Thorn, Andrea Papp

**Boston**
Anderson, Arthur Irvin
Auerbach, Joseph
Bines, Harvey Ernest
Boger, Kenneth Snead
Bohnen, Michael J.
Chambers, Margaret Warner
Chase, Thomas Charles
Christodoulo, George Evans
Drogin, Susan F.
Duffy, James Francis, III
Engel, David Lewis
Fischer, Eric Robert
Gans, Nancy Freeman
Garcia, Adolfo Ramon
Greenblatt, Martin Elliott
Halligan, Brendan Patrick
Honig, Stephen Michael
Jones, Sheldon Atwell
Jordan, Alexander Joseph, Jr.
Kane, Stephen Michael
Korb, Kenneth Allan
Masud, Robert
Matzka, Michael Alan
Poss, Stephen Daniel
Rikleen, Sander A.
Rosenbloom, Thomas Adam
Rowe, Larry Jordan
Soden, Richard Allan
Thibeault, George Walter
Williams, Robert Dana

**Cambridge**
Wirth, Peter

**Framingham**
Meltzer, Jay H.

**Newton**
Glazer, Donald Wayne

**Springfield**
Gross, Steven Ronald

**Weston**
McDaniel, James Alan

**Worcester**
Lougee, David Louis

### MICHIGAN

**Battle Creek**
Kelly, Janet Langford

**Birmingham**
Bick, Robert Steven

**Charlevoix**
Telgenhof, Allen Ray

**Detroit**
Boonstra, Mark Thomas
Breach, David Andrew
Kamins, John Mark
Rentenbach, Paul Robert
Rooney, Scott William
Shaevsky, Mark

**Grosse Pointe**
Avant, Grady, Jr.
Johnson, Edward Carl

**Southfield**
Ornstein, Alexander Thomas

### MINNESOTA

**Minneapolis**
Bergerson, David Raymond
Cole, Phillip Allen
Houston, John R.
Kennedy, Steven Charles
Laitinen, Sari K.M.
Mellum, Gale Robert
Nelson, Gary Michael
Pluimer, Edward J.
Potuznik, Charles Laddy
Radmer, Michael John
Sanner, Royce Norman
Saunders, Jeffrey N.
Stageberg, Roger V.
Vander Weide, Vernon Jay
Woods, Robert Edward

**Minnetonka**
Lubben, David J.

**Saint Paul**
Boehnen, David Leo

### MISSOURI

**Chesterfield**
Denneen, John Paul
Hier, Marshall David
Ross, Richard Lee

**Kansas City**
Ayers, Jeffrey David
Ball, Owen Keith, Jr.
Carman, Steven F.
Healy, Michael Patrick
Holewinski, Paul Patrick
Newcom, Jennings Jay

**Lamar**
Geddie, Rowland Hill, III

**Saint Louis**
Brickler, John Weise
Clear, John Michael
Conran, Joseph Palmer
Gillis, John Lamb, Jr.
Pickle, Robert Douglas
Schoene, Kathleen Snyder
Smith, Arthur Lee
Sneeringer, Stephen Geddes
Tierney, Michael Edward
Wagner, Raymond Thomas, Jr.

**Springfield**
Starnes, James Wright

### MONTANA

**Great Falls**
Berry, Anders Taylor

### NEBRASKA

**Omaha**
Blunk, Christian Raymond
Ellsworth, John David
Hohman, David Michael
Minter, Gregory Byron
Rock, Harold L.
von Bernuth, Carl W.
Vosburg, Bruce David

### NEVADA

**Las Vegas**
Brewer, John Nelson

**Reno**
Oskam, Gerard Lambert

### NEW HAMPSHIRE

**Hampton**
DuChene, Todd Michael

### NEW JERSEY

**Camden**
Furey, John J.

**Cherry Hill**
Moleski, Anthony G.

**Chester**
Hanson, Eugene Paul

**Jersey City**
Lawatsch, Frank Emil, Jr.

**Lawrenceville**
Dahl, Michael Bruce
Kline, Michael J.

**Liberty Corner**
Edwards, Robert Nelson

**Lyndhurst**
Lasky, David

**Morristown**
Smith, J. Edward

**Princeton**
Carlis, Brian Alexander
Glogoff, David Louis
Mattessich, Richard Stephen
Szwalbenest, Benedykt Jan

**Roseland**
Osvald-Mruz, Christine
Starr, Ira M.
Wovsaniker, Alan

**Weehawken**
Fleischer, Elizabeth B.

### NEW MEXICO

**Albuquerque**
Schuler, Alison Kay

**Seneca**
Monroe, Kendyl Kurth

### NEW YORK

**Ardsley On Hudson**
Stein, Milton Michael

**Armonk**
Moskowitz, Stuart Stanley

**Brooklyn**
Karmel, Roberta Segal

**Buffalo**
Lippes, Gerald Sanford

**Canandaigua**
Sorce, David Samuel

**Garden City**
Breslin, Eileen Mary

**Glen Cove**
Shields, Craig M.

**Great Neck**
Rockowitz, Noah Ezra

**Hollis**
Testani, Rosa Anna

**Holtsville**
Goldner, Leonard Howard

**New Rochelle**
Gunning, Francis Patrick

**New York**
Adler, Derek J.T.
Armstrong, James Sinclair
Atkins, Peter Allan
Axelrod, Charles Paul
Axinn, Stephen Mark
Bach, Thomas Handford
Backman, Gerald Stephen
Baker, Mark Robert
Bannister, J. Alan
Barnett, Gary
Barrett, David A.
Barrett, William L. D.
Bartlett, Joseph Warren
Beck, Andrew James
Beckman, Michael
Bendes, Barry Jay
Benedict, James Nelson
Bergan, Edmund Paul, Jr.
Bergan, Philip James
Bergtraum, Howard Michael
Bialkin, Kenneth Jules
Bicks, Peter Andrews
Bizar, Irving
Blackman, Kenneth Robert
Bodovitz, James Philip
Boehner, Leonard Bruce
Borker, Wallace Jacob
Boynton, James Stephen
Breinin, Bartley James
Breslow, Stephanie R.
Brewer, William Dane
Brooks, Gene C.
Brown, Meredith M.
Browne, Jeffrey Francis
Bryan, Barry Richard
Butler, Samuel Coles
Carlinsky, Michael Barry
Caytas, Ivo George
Clemente, Robert Stephen
Cogan, Sarah Edwards
Cohen, Donald N.
Cohen, Edward Herschel
Cohen, Hollace T.
Conboy, Kenneth
Connor, John Thomas, Jr.
Cooper, Michael Anthony
Cooper, Stephen Herbert
Corbin, Sol Neil
Cotter, James Michael
Cowan, Wallace Edgar
Crane, Roger Ryan, Jr.
Cranney, Marilyn Kanrek
Davidson, Sheila Kearney
Dodge, Jonathan Karel
Dorado, Marianne Gaertner
Drucker, Richard Allen
Dubin, James Michael
Duffy, Edmund Charles
D'Ull, Walter
Dunham, Wolcott Balestier, Jr.
Dunn, M(orris) Douglas
Edwards, Christine Annette
Elkins, David Mark
Farrow, Sallie
Fass, Peter Michael
Feig, Edward Steven
Feit, Glenn M.
Fernicola, Gregory Anthony
Feuerstein, Bernard A.
Filler, Ronald Howard
Finch, Edward Ridley, Jr.
Finkel, Miriam Jo
Finnerty, Joseph Gregory, III
Fisher, Ann Bailen
Fleischman, Edward Hirsh
Fleischman, Keith Martin
Folkenflik, Max
Fortenbaugh, Samuel Byrod, III
Frank, Lloyd
Fraser, Brian Scott
Fredericks, Wesley Charles, Jr.
Fredericks, William Curtis
Fried, Donald David
Friedman, Bart
Friedman, Jeffrey Lawrence
Friedman, Samuel Selig
Frisch, Harry David
Gambro, Michael S.
Garvey, Richard Anthony

Glusband, Steven Joseph
Goldberg, Michael Edward
Gottlieb, Paul Mitchel
Grader, Scott Paul
Grant, Stephen Allen
Greenawalt, William Sloan
Greenslade, George Alfred
Greenwald, David Jeffrey
Greilsheimer, William Henry
Gross, Richard Benjamin
Guynn, Randall David
Haddad, Mark Anthony
Haje, Peter Robert
Hanson, Stephen Philip
Healy, Walter F. X.
Hecht, Charles Joel
Hendry, Andrew Delaney
Henryson, Herbert, II
Hersh, Robert Michael
Hershman, Scott Edward
Herzeca, Lois Friedman
Hiden, Robert Battaile, Jr.
Higel, F. Eugene
Hirsch, Barry
Hirsch, Jerome S.
Hoff, Jonathan M(orind)
Hoffman, Alan S.
Holley, Steven Lyon
Howe, Richard Rives
Hutton, G. Thompson
Hynes, Patricia
Isquith, Fred Taylor
Iyeki, Marc Hideo
Jenner, Eva Catherine
Jiménez, Emilio
Jones, Douglas W.
Kanter, Stacy J.
Kaplan, Carl Eliot
Kaplan, Mark Norman
Karpe, Mark Ark
Katz, Ronald Scott
Kelly, Daniel Grady, Jr.
Kensington, Costa Nicholas
Kern, George Calvin, Jr.
Kessel, Mark
Kies, David M.
Kinney, Stephen Hoyt, Jr.
Klein, Alan M.
Klein, William, II
Knoll, Alan M.
Koblenz, Michael Robert
Kolker, Lawrence Paul
Kramer, Daniel Jonathan
Krasner, Daniel Walter
Krieger, Sanford
Krouse, George Raymond, Jr.
Lacovara, Philip Allen
Landau, Walter Loeber
Landes, Robert Nathan
Laurenson, Edwin Charles
Leonard, Edwin Deane
Levander, Andrew Joshua
Levin, Ezra Gurion
Levitsky, Asher Samuel
Li, Rebecca Jia
Lieberman, Ellen
Lowenfels, Lewis David
Lutzker, Elliot Howard
Macioce, Frank Michael
Maghiar, Livia L.
Malawsky, Donald N.
Marcus, Todd Barry
Margulis, Michael Henry
Maynard, Natasha C.
McCurrach, Duncan C.
McGuire, Eugene Guenard
McMeen, Elmer Ellsworth, III
Meiklejohn, Donald Stuart
Meister, Robert Allen
Mentz, Barbara Antonello
Mestres, Ricardo Angelo, Jr.
Michel, Clifford Lloyd
Miller, Arthur Madden
Miller, Richard Allan
Mock, Eric V.
Modlin, Howard S.
Morphy, James Calvin
Morris, Edward William, Jr.
Muccia, Joseph William
Mullaney, Thomas Joseph
Munsell, James Frederick
Nash, Paul LeNoir
Nimetz, Matthew
Nordquist, Stephen Glos
Norwitz, Trevor S.
Orr, Dennis Patrick
Papernik, Joel Ira
Park, Sang Hyuk
Pellecchio, Ralph L.
Pettibone, Peter John
Pierce, Morton Allen
Pisano, Vincent James
Pompa, Renata
Purcell, John Joseph, III
Quillen, Cecil Dyer, III
Quinn, Linda C.
Raab, Sheldon
Radey, Dona Lynn
Ray, Jeanne Cullinan
Reid, Edward Snover, III
Reinthaler, Richard Walter
Richey, Kent Ramon
Ring, Renee Etheline
Robertson, Edwin David
Robinson, John Kelly
Rocklen, Kathy Hellenbrand
Rosenberg, Marc S.
Rosenblum, Scott S.
Rosenblum, William F., Jr.
Ross, Matthew
Roth, Paul Norman
Rothstein, Amy Lone
Rubinstein, Frederic Armand
Rusmisel, Stephen R.
Russo, Thomas Anthony
Sargent, James Cunningham
Saunders, Mark A.
Schallert, Edwin Glenn
Scherr, Stephanie Lynn
Schizer, Zevie Baruch
Schmidt, Daniel Edward, IV
Schneider, Harold Lawrence
Schochet, Ira A.
Schonfeld, Joel
Schulte, Stephen John
Schuur, Robert George
Schwartz, Barry Fredric
Shaev, David
Shenker, Joseph C.
Siegel, Charles
Siegel, Jeffrey Norton
Siller, Stephen I.
Skirnick, Robert Andrew
Slezak, Edward M.
Smagula, John William
Sorkin, David James
Spatt, Robert Edward
Sperling, Allan George
Steinberg, Howard Eli
Stephenson, Alan Clements
Stewart, Charles Evan
Stewart, David Robert
Strom, Milton Gary
Strougo, Robert Isaac
Sugarman, Robert P.
Sulger, Francis Xavier
Supino, Anthony Martin
Terrell, J. Anthony
Thalacker, Arbie Robert
Toumey, Donald Joseph
Tricarico, Joseph Archangelo
Underberg, Mark Alan
Urowsky, Richard J.
Viener, John D.
Vlahakis, Patricia
Wallin, James Peter
Walpin, Gerald
Wang, Albert Huai-En
Welikson, Jeffrey Alan
Whitman, Charles S., III
Wilson, Edward N.
Wiseman, Michael Martin
Wolf, Gary Wickert
Wolson, Craig Alan
Yodowitz, Edward J.
Zaitzeff, Roger Michael
Zimmerman, Earl S.
Zimmerman, Paula Susan
Zucker, Howard
Zukerman, Michael

**Orangeburg**
Seaman, Robert E., III

**Oyster Bay**
Press, Michael S.

**Peconic**
Mitchell, Robert Everitt

**Purchase**
Sharpe, Robert Francis, Jr.

**Rochester**
Doyle, Justin P
Willett, Thomas Edward
Young, Thomas Paul

**Rye**
Goldstein, Peter Dobkin
Roberts, Thomas Alba

**Suffern**
Stack, Daniel

**Uniondale**
Eilen, Howard Scott
Gracin, Hank

**White Plains**
Bader, Izaak Walton
Burkett, Bradford C.
Dannenberg, Richard Bruce
Vogel, Howard Stanley

### NORTH CAROLINA

**Burlington**
Slayton, John Howard

**Charlotte**
Holmquist, Michael G.
Walker, Clarence Wesley

**Durham**
Welborn, Reich Lee

**Greensboro**
Clark, David McKenzie

**Raleigh**
Carlton, Alfred Pershing, Jr.
Homick, Daniel John
Markoff, Brad Steven
Miller, Jeffrey D.
Powell, Durwood Royce

**Winston Salem**
Barnhardt, Zeb Elonzo, Jr.

### OHIO

**Canton**
Brannen, John Howard

**Chagrin Falls**
Streicher, James Franklin

**Cincinnati**
Evans, James E.
Heldman, James Gardner
Heldman, Paul W.
Kite, William McDougall
Olson, Robert Wyrick
Wagner, Barbara

**Cleveland**
Blackford, Jason Collier
Hogg, James Stuart
Langer, Carlton Earl
McKee, Thomas Frederick
Pyke, John Secrest, Jr.
Stevens, Thomas Charles
Stovsky, Michael David

**Columbus**
Bowen, John Wesley Edward, IV
Brinkman, Dale Thomas
Dunlay, Catherine Telles
Fried, Samuel
McDermott, Kevin R.
Neuman, Todd Howard
Robins, Ronald Albert, Jr.
Summer, Fred A.
Tannous, Robert Joseph

**Dayton**
Furry, Richard Logan
Schwartz, Richard Anthony
Teeters, Bruce A.
Watts, Steven Richard

**Maumee**
Kline, James Edward

**Richfield**
Calise, Nicholas James

**Toledo**
Webb, Thomas Irwin, Jr.

**Wickliffe**
Kidder, Fred Dockstater

### OKLAHOMA

**Oklahoma City**
Derrick, Gary Wayne
Kirschner, Jonna Dee Kauger
Paliotta, Armand
Rockett, D. Joe
Steinhorn, Irwin Harry

**Tulsa**
Barnes, Deborah Browers
Biolchini, Robert Fredrick
Kihle, Donald Arthur
Luthey, Graydon Dean, Jr.
Slicker, Frederick Kent

### OREGON

**Lake Oswego**
Wilson, Jeffrey Dale

**Portland**
Krahmer, Donald Leroy, Jr.
Sand, Thomas Charles
Shorr, Scott Alden

### PENNSYLVANIA

**Allison Park**
Ries, William Campbell

**Blue Bell**
Barron, Harold Sheldon

**Exton**
Hedges, Donald Walton

**Horsham**
Troy, Richard Hershey

**Philadelphia**
Agran, Raymond Daniel
Bissell, Rolin Plumb
Clark, William H., Jr.
Collins, Todd Stowe
Cooney, John Gordon
Del Raso, Joseph Vincent
Drake, William Frank, Jr.
Esser, Carl Eric
Feder, Steven J.
Genkin, Barry Howard
Hangley, William Thomas
Harkins, John Graham, Jr.
Hoyle, Lawrence Truman, Jr.
Jones, Robert Jeffries
King, David Roy
Pauciulo, John William
Promislo, Daniel
Shestack, Jerome Joseph
Speyer, Debra Gail
Stuntebeck, Clinton A.
Wellington, Ralph Glenn
Whinston, Stephen Alan

**Pittsburgh**
Arnold, Roy William
Barnes, James Jerome
Blume, Peter Keefe
Brown, Ronald James
Connell, Janice T.
Davis, Lewis U., Jr.
Ehrenwerth, David Harry
Hardie, James Hiller
Harff, Charles Henry
Johnson, Stephen W.
Klett, Edwin Lee
Lefkowitz, Alan Zoel
Letwin, Jeffrey William
McCabe, Lawrence James
Pandit, Amy Indravadan
Purtell, Lawrence Robert
Shuman, Joseph Duff

**Wyndmoor**
Starr, Harold Page

### RHODE ISLAND

**Providence**
Carlotti, Stephen Jon

**Woonsocket**
Moffatt, Thomas Swift

### SOUTH CAROLINA

**Charleston**
Dominick, Paul Allen

**Mount Pleasant**
Swanson, Shane Eric

**Salem**
Everett, C(harles) Curtis

### TENNESSEE

**Chattanooga**
Copeland, Floyd Dean
Durham, J(oseph) Porter, Jr.
Levine, James Howard

**Knoxville**
McCall, Jack Humphreys, Jr.
Worthington, Carole Yard Lynch

**Memphis**
Buhler, Lynn Bledsoe
Chafetz, Samuel David
Rawlins, Donald R.

**Nashville**
Anderson, Lauren Wirthlin
Eisen, Steven Jeffrey
Mayden, Barbara Mendel
Mefford, R. Douglas
Sidwell, Susan Von Brock
Tuke, Robert Dudley

### TEXAS

**Austin**
Gangstad, John Erik
Laughead, James Marshall

**Dallas**
Acker, Rodney
Bishop, Bryan Edwards
Bivans, Roger Wayne
Blachly, Jack Lee
Coleman, Russell Forester
Feld, Alan David
Glendenning, Don Mark
Irwin, Ivan, Jr.
Kipp, John Theodore
Kirby, Le Grand Carney, III
McNamara, Anne H.
Menges, John Kenneth, Jr.
Moore, Marilyn Payne
Morrison, David Eugene
Pleasant, James Scott
Portman, Susan Newell
Rice, Darrel Alan
Roberts, David Mace
Solomon, Mark S.
Spears, Robert Fields
Veach, Robert Raymond, Jr.
Young, Barney Thornton

**El Paso**
Smith, Tad Randolph

**Euless**
Paran, Mark Lloyd

**Fort Worth**
Watson, Robert Francis

**Garland**
Guldi, Rebecca Elizabeth

**Houston**
Anderson, Eric Severin
Bech, Douglas York
Becher, Andrew Clifford
Bell, Robert Christopher
Bland, John L.
Born, Dawn Slater
Brantley, John Randolph
Carter, John Loyd
Cotton, James Alexandre
England, Rudy Alan
Finch, Michael Paul
Garten, David Burton
Grace, James Martin, Jr.
Heinrich, Randall Wayne
Johnson, James Harold
Kelly, William Franklin, Jr.
Kurz, Thomas Patrick
Lamme, Thomas Robert
Landry, Brenda Marguerite
Lee, William Gentry
Mark, Daniel Lee
Myers, Franklin
Parker, Dallas Robert
Sapp, Walter William
Schwartz, Charles Walter
Still, Charles Henry
Taten, Bruce Malcolm
Weber, Fredric Alan
Winer, Stephen I.

**San Antonio**
Johnson, Edward Michael
Lippoldt, Darin Michael
Lutter, Charles William, Jr.

### UTAH

**Salt Lake City**
Headman, Arlan Osmond, Jr.
Karrenberg, Thomas Richard

### VERMONT

**Concord**
Norsworthy, Elizabeth Krassovsky

### VIRGINIA

**Arlington**
McCorkindale, Douglas Hamilton
Morgens, Warren Kendall

**Charlottesville**
Caccese, Michael Stephen

**Fairfax**
Maiwurm, James John

**Mc Lean**
Olsen, Robert Eric

**McLean**
Houle, Jeffrey Robert

**Oakton**
Vernava, Anthony Michael

**Richmond**
Buford, Robert Pegram
Canup, James W.C.
Minardi, Richard A., Jr.

**Sterling**
McBarnette, Bruce Olvin

**Vienna**
McCabe, Thomas Edward
Randolph, Christopher Craven
Razzano, Frank Charles

**Virginia Beach**
Gray, Jeffrey Hugh

### WASHINGTON

**Bellevue**
Morie, G. Glen
Parsons, James Bowne

**Seattle**
Barker, William W.
Brooks, Julie Anne
Comstock, Brian Lloyd
Graham, Stephen Michael
Hoffman, Mark Frederick
Parsons, A. Peter
Pym, Bruce Michael
Rummage, Stephen Michael
Whitford, Joseph P.

**Tacoma**
Malanca, Albert Robert

### WISCONSIN

**Milwaukee**
Lombard, Benjamin G.
Skipper, Walter John
Williams, Clay Rule

**Wausau**
Ware, G. Lane

### ENGLAND

**London**
Brownwood, David Owen
Gates, Stephen Frye

### HONG KONG

**Hong Kong**
Shinkle, John Thomas

### JAPAN

**Tokyo**
Hunter, Larry Dean

### ADDRESS UNPUBLISHED

Anderson, Geoffrey Allen
Asmar, Laila Michelle
Avery, James Thomas, III
Beasley, James W., Jr.
Berman, Joshua Mordecai
Bersin, Alan Douglas
Boersig, Thomas Charles, Jr.
Brodsky, David M.
Burlingame, John Hunter
Cassidy, M. Sharon
Cattani, Maryellen B.
Christiansen, Eric Robert
Cion, Judith Ann
Davey, Gerard Paul
Dennin, Timothy J.
Duffy, James F.
Edwards, Daniel Paul
Fischer, David Charles
Forst, John Kelly
Futter, Victor
Gale, Connie R(uth)
Giovanniello, Joseph, Jr.
Goldberg, Joel Henry
Gordon, David Zevi
Gordon, Kenneth Ira
Griffin, Campbell Arthur, Jr.
Gutman, Richard Edward
Harvitt, Adrianne Stanley
Heath, Charles Dickinson
Hunt, Ronald Forrest
Jacobs, Alan
Jamieson, Michael Lawrence
Lewitus, Marla Berman
Liftin, John Matthew
Long, Charles Thomas
Millimet, Erwin
Morgan, James Evan
Moylan, James Joseph
Murphy, Jo Anne
Natcher, Stephen Darlington
Newman, Sanders David
Painton, Russell Elliott
Porter, Michael Pell
Powers, Elizabeth Whitmel
Ruhm, Thomas Francis
Samuels, Janet Lee
Schulman, Steven Gary
Skal, Debra Lynn
Tanaka, Jeannie E.
Tobin, Paul Xavier
Tubman, William Charles
Wagner, Michael Duane
Walker, Craig Michael
Wallison, Frieda K.
Walner, Robert Joel
Williams, William John, Jr.
Williamson, Edwin Dargan
Wilson, Rhys Thaddeus
Wittebort, Robert John, Jr.

---

**SOCIAL SECURITY.** *See* **Pension.**

---

## SPORTS

### UNITED STATES

### ALABAMA

**Opelika**
Hand, Benny Charles, Jr.

### ARKANSAS

**Russellville**
Simmons, Scott Michael

### CALIFORNIA

**Encinitas**
Forrester, Kevin Kreg

**Encino**
Mittenthal, Peter A.

**Irvine**
Callahan, Robert Edward
Specter, Richard Bruce

**Los Angeles**
Demoff, Marvin Alan
Hutt, Laurence Jeffrey
Reid, Donna Lake
Wright, Wyndell John

**Marina Del Rey**
Murphy, Tamela Jayne

**San Diego**
Robinson, Shawn Michael

**San Francisco**
Bertram, Phyllis Ann

### COLORADO

**Denver**
Hilbert, Otto Karl, II

**Lyons**
Brown, Michael DeWayne

### CONNECTICUT

**Stamford**
Tepper, Jacqueline Gail

### DISTRICT OF COLUMBIA

**Washington**
Babby, Lon S.
Osnos, David Marvin

### FLORIDA

**Daytona Beach**
Gewirtz, Jeffrey Brian

**Fort Lauderdale**
Mastronardi, Corinne Marie

**North Miami**
Malman, Myles Henry

**Orlando**
Lang, Thomas Frederick

**Tampa**
Carbone, Edward John

### GEORGIA

**Atlanta**
Drucker, Michael Stuart

**Marietta**
Fielkow, Arnold David

**Saint Simons Island**
Kunda, Preston B.

### ILLINOIS

**Chicago**
Gordon, Gilbert Wayne
Kurz, Jerry Bruce

**Northbrook**
Bronner, James Russell

### KANSAS

**Wichita**
Liebau, Judd Alan

### KENTUCKY

**Lexington**
Terry, Joseph H.

### MAINE

**Portland**
Judge, Janet Patricia

### MARYLAND

**Rockville**
Doyle, Thomas Edward

**Upperco**
McMahon, Richard Michael, Sr.

### MASSACHUSETTS

**Boston**
Carney, Gerard Barry

**Natick**
Grassia, Thomas Charles

**Newton Highlands**
Gans, Steven H.

**Shrewsbury**
Cantu, Tina-Marie

### MICHIGAN

**Farmingtn Hls**
Bernstein, Stephen Richard

### MINNESOTA

**Eagan**
Peotter, Sara Jo

### MISSOURI

**Kansas City**
Kitchin, John Joseph

**Saint Louis**
Lattinville, Robert Henry

### MONTANA

**Billings**
Krogh, Harlan B.

### NEW MEXICO

**Albuquerque**
Franse, R(ichard) Nelson

### NEW YORK

**Buffalo**
Ivancic, Gregory Thomas

**Geneva**
Mirras, Michael John

**New York**
Feffer, Joanna Wahl
Freeman, Robert E.
Friss, Warren Edward
Ganz, Howard Laurence
Kelly, W. Michael
Krane, Steven Charles
Moyer, Jay Edward
Orlinsky, Ethan George
Zahnd, Richard H.

### NORTH CAROLINA

**Charlotte**
Thigpen, Richard Elton, Jr.

### OHIO

**Cincinnati**
Dornette, W(illiam) Stuart

### OKLAHOMA

**Oklahoma City**
Beech, Johnny Gale

### PENNSYLVANIA

**Harrisburg**
Fritz, Martin Andrew

### RHODE ISLAND

**Cranston**
Cervone, Anthony Louis

**Providence**
Burrows, Richard Henry

### SOUTH CAROLINA

**Charleston**
Webb, Richard Craig

### TEXAS

**Austin**
Hanner, Karl Tiger

**Dallas**
Roberts, Ronald

**Fort Worth**
Nelson, Edward Reese, III

**Spring**
Hendricks, Randal Arlan

### ADDRESS UNPUBLISHED

Choslovsky, William
Weisman, Paul Howard

## TAXATION, CORPORATE

### UNITED STATES

### ALABAMA

**Decatur**
Blackburn, John Gilmer

**Huntsville**
Ludwig, Scott Edward

**Montgomery**
Proctor, David Ray

### ALASKA

**Anchorage**
Mahoney, F. Steven

### ARIZONA

**Phoenix**
Derdenger, Patrick
Ehmann, Anthony Valentine
Everett, James Joseph
Le Clair, Douglas Marvin
Martori, Joseph Peter
Olsen, Alfred Jon

**Scottsdale**
Peshkin, Samuel David
Simonson, Michael

### ARKANSAS

**Jonesboro**
Womack, Tom D.

**Little Rock**
Marshall, William Taylor
Miller, William Scott

### CALIFORNIA

**Costa Mesa**
Goldstein, Michael Gerald
Schaaf, Douglas Allan

**Fullerton**
Apke, Thomas Michael

**Larkspur**
Greenberg, Myron Silver

**Los Angeles**
Anderson, Charles David
Baram, Art
Coleman, Rexford Lee
Friedman, Simon
Grim, Douglas Paul
Moffett, Martin Lee
Palazzo, Robert P.
Pircher, Leo Joseph
Sheppard, Thomas Richard

**Palo Alto**
Klotsche, John Chester

**San Francisco**
Howe, Drayton Ford, Jr.
Klott, David Lee
Silk, Thomas
Spiegel, Hart Hunter
Wood, Robert Warren

**San Rafael**
Keegin, Stafford Warwick

**Santa Clara**
Denten, Christopher Peter

**Santa Cruz**
Schalk, Robert Partridge

**Tarzana**
Balkin, Jeffrey Gilbert

### COLORADO

**Aspen**
Schumacher, Barry Lee

**Aurora**
Stauffer, Scott William

**Denver**
Callison, James William
Keatinge, Robert Reed
Rich, Robert Stephen
Ruppert, John Lawrence
Terry, Ward Edgar, Jr.

**Englewood**
Wiegand, Robert, II

**Parker**
Greenberg, Morton Paul

### CONNECTICUT

**Darien**
Dale, Erwin Randolph

**Fairfield**
LaFollette, Ernest Carlton

**Hartford**
Coyle, Michael Lee
Lloyd, Alex
Lyon, James Burroughs

**Plainville**
Anderson, William Carl

**Westport**
Sheiman, Ronald Lee

### DELAWARE

**Wilmington**
Baumann, Julian Henry, Jr.
Grossman, Jerome Kent

### DISTRICT OF COLUMBIA

**Washington**
Ator, Lloyd George, Jr.
Berrington, Craig Anthony
Birnkrant, Henry Joseph
Blair, David Belmont
Caplin, Mortimer Maxwell
Chapoton, John Edgar
Cole, Robert Theodore
Davidson, Daniel Morton
DiFronzo, Michael A.
Fleeman, Mary Grace
Ginsburg, Martin David
Greif, Joseph
Gutman, Harry Largman
Halvorson, Newman Thorbus, Jr.
Hawkins, Edward Jackson
Heffernan, James Vincent
Kahn, Edwin Leonard
Lane, Bruce Stuart
Magee, John B.
McHugh, Richard Patrick
Nauheim, Stephen Alan
Oosterhuis, Paul William
Paul, William McCann
Rafferty, James Gerard
Richmond, David Walker
Silver, Sidney J.
Stauffer, Ronald Eugene
Waris, Michael, Jr.
Worthy, K(enneth) Martin

### FLORIDA

**Boca Raton**
Beck, Jan Scott
Reinstein, Joel

**Fort Lauderdale**
Stankee, Glen Allen

**Miami**
Hudson, Robert Franklin, Jr.
Klein, Peter William
Muñiz, Nicolas Jose
Ruffner, Charles Louis
Scheer, Mark Jeffrey
Simmons, Sherwin Palmer
Stiver, Charles Ellwood, Jr.
Weinstein, Andrew H.

**Miami Beach**
Brodie, Ronald

**Oldsmar**
Hirschman, Sherman Joseph

**Orlando**
Conti, Louis Thomas Moore
Lefkowitz, Ivan Martin
Whitehill, Clifford Lane

**Tampa**
Barton, Bernard Alan, Jr.
LaCasse, James Phillip
Levine, Jack Anton
Teblum, Gary Ira

### GEORGIA

**Atlanta**
Cook, Philip Carter
Ganz, Charles David

### HAWAII

**Honolulu**
Galati, Vito
Ingersoll, Richard King
Miyasaki, Shuichi

### IDAHO

**Boise**
Erickson, Robert Stanley

### ILLINOIS

**Calumet City**
Scullion, Kevin Peter

**Chicago**
Ackerman, David Paul
Banoff, Sheldon Irwin
Bowen, Stephen Stewart
Kanter, Burton Wallace
Kaplan, Jared
McKenzie, Robert Ernest
McLees, John Alan
Pinsky, Michael S.
Rizzo, Ronald Stephen
Shepherd, Stewart Robert
Swibel, Steven Warren
Truskowski, John Budd
Von Mandel, Michael Jacques
Witt, Alan Michael

**Glenview**
Marmet, Gottlieb John

**Lake Forest**
Palmer, Ann Therese Darin

**Naperville**
Larson, Mark Edward, Jr.

**Northbrook**
Lapin, Harvey I.

### INDIANA

**Indianapolis**
Kemper, James Dee
Ponder, Lester McConnico
Springer, Marilee J.

**South Bend**
Carey, John Leo

### IOWA

**Burlington**
Beckman, David

**Des Moines**
Carroll, Frank James
Narber, Gregg Ross

### KANSAS

**Wichita**
Sorensen, Harvey R.

### KENTUCKY

**Louisville**
Gilman, Sheldon Glenn
Lavelle, Charles Joseph

### LOUISIANA

**Metairie**
Sherman, David Robert

**New Orleans**
Benjamin, Edward Bernard, Jr.
Nuzum, Robert Weston
Simon, H(uey) Paul
Stone, Saul

### MAINE

**Ellsworth**
Sang, Peter Bennett

### MARYLAND

**Baltimore**
Adkins, Edward James
Cook, Bryson Leitch
Curran, Robert Bruce

**Bethesda**
Robinson, Jean Marie

**Cambridge**
Robbins, Vernon Earl

**Greenbelt**
Jackley, Michael Dano

**Lutherville Timonium**
Freeland, Charles

**Potomac**
Peter, Phillips Smith

**Rockville**
De Jong, David Samuel

### MASSACHUSETTS

**Boston**
Bernhard, Alexander Alfred
Cutler, Arnold Robert
Elfman, Eric Michael
Gabovitch, William
Metzer, Patricia Ann
Milder, Forrest David
Miller, Wayne Hamilton
Mooney, Michael Edward
Ritt, Roger Merrill
Trevisani, Robert Armand

**Canton**
Fuller, Robert L(eander)

**Nantucket**
Lobl, Herbert Max

**Springfield**
Clarke, David Gordon
Gelinas, Robert Albert

### MICHIGAN

**Bloomfield Hills**
Kasischke, Louis Walter
Solomon, Mark Raymond
Wellman, David Joseph

**Detroit**
Thoms, David Moore

**Grand Rapids**
Oetting, Roger H.

**Grosse Pointe**
Hindelang, Robert Louis

**Lansing**
Bahs, Jess Allen

**Saint Clair Shores**
Stevens, Clark Valentine

**Southfield**
Kippert, Robert John, Jr.

**Sturgis**
Dresser, Raymond H., Jr.

**Troy**
Chapman, Conrad Daniel

**West Bloomfield**
Tobin, Bruce Howard

### MINNESOTA

**Minneapolis**
Kaplan, Sheldon

**Saint Paul**
Bernick, Alan E.
Geis, Jerome Arthur

### MISSOURI

**Kansas City**
Kaplan, Eliot Lawrence

**Saint Louis**
Brickey, James Nelson
Burton, Earl Gillespie, III
Farnam, Thomas Campbell
Kuhlmann, Fred Mark
Venker, Thomas Edward
Wiehl, James George

### MONTANA

**Missoula**
George, Alexander Andrew

### NEBRASKA

**Omaha**
Ellsworth, John David
Littlejohn, Kent Oscar

### NEVADA

**Las Vegas**
Wilson, Joseph Morris, III

### NEW HAMPSHIRE

**Hanover**
Harvey, Nicholas D. N., Jr.

**Manchester**
Chamberlain, Douglas Reginald
Sanborn, Von Eric

### NEW JERSEY

**Boonton**
Massler, Howard Arnold

**Jersey City**
Feder, Arthur A.

**Livingston**
Rosenberg, Paul I.

**Morristown**
Fishman, Richard Glenn

**Newark**
O'Connor Quinn, Deirdre
Vajtay, Stephen Michael, Jr.

**Plainsboro**
Gorrin, Eugene

**Princeton**
Wood, Joshua Warren, III

**South Orange**
Delo, Ellen Sanderson
Kamens, Harold

**West Orange**
Richmond, Harold Nicholas

**Woodbridge**
Lepelstat, Martin L.

### NEW MEXICO

**Albuquerque**
Lieuwen, John N.

**Seneca**
Monroe, Kendyl Kurth

### NEW YORK

**Albany**
Koff, Howard Michael

**Carle Place**
Smolev, Terence Elliot

**Eastchester**
Katz, Kenneth Arthur

**Glens Falls**
Pontiff, Paul E.

**Manlius**
Sarofeen, Michael Joseph

**New York**
Adams, Daniel Nelson
Adams, Ludwig Howard
Agranoff, Gerald Neal
Aidinoff, M(erton) Bernard
Allen, Phillip Stephen
Amdur, Martin Bennett
Andersen, Richard Esten
Bergtraum, Howard Michael
Bowers, William Charles
Brandman, Scott Lewis
Cleland, Edward Gordon
Cliff, Walter Conway
Collins, Adrian Anthony
Collinson, Dale Stanley
Faber, Peter Lewis
Ferguson, Milton Carr, Jr.
Finkelstein, Stuart M.
Forry, John Ingram
Ganz, Marc David
Gardner, Stephen David
Garfunkel, Alan J.
Goldman, Richard Lurie
Hirschfeld, Michael
Jacobson, Leon Irwin
Jassy, Everett Lewis
Kalish, Arthur
Koch, Edward Richard
Kroll, Arthur Herbert
Kurtz, Jerome
Leckie, Gavin Frederick
Levy, Mark Allan
Lipsky, Burton G.
Macan, William Alexander, IV
MacLean, Babcock
Margolin, Jesse
McCormick, Hugh Thomas
Newman, Scott David
Osborn, Donald Robert
Paul, Herbert Morton
Phillips, Barnet, IV
Rosen, Matthew A.
Sicular, David R.
Small, Jonathan Andrew
Solomon, Andrew P.
Spencer, David Eric
Tengi, Frank R.
Thompson, Loran Tyson
Viener, John D.
White, Harry Edward, Jr.
Whoriskey, Robert Donald
Zonana, Victor

**Rochester**
Kraus, Sherry Stokes

**Scarsdale**
Macchia, Vincent Michael

**Syracuse**
Stack, Gerald Francis

**Westbury**
Zychick, Joel David

**White Plains**
Danziger, Joel Bernard
Klein, Paul E.
Lalli, Michael Anthony
Vogel, Howard Stanley

### NORTH CAROLINA

**Asheville**
Hamilton, Jackson Douglas

**Burlington**
Slayton, John Howard

**Goldsboro**
Hine, John C.

**Raleigh**
Geil, John McIntosh
Powell, Durwood Royce
Simpson, Steven Drexell

**Wilmington**
McCauley, Cleyburn Lycurgus

**Winston Salem**
Gunter, Michael Donwell
Osborn, Malcolm Everett

### OHIO

**Cincinnati**
Buechner, Robert William
Flanagan, John Anthony
Ryan, James Joseph

**Cleveland**
Doris, Alan S(anford)
Fryt, Michael David
Perris, Terrence George

**Columbus**
Fried, Samuel
Goulder, Diane Kessler
Kusma, Kyllikki

**Dayton**
Hitter, Joseph Ira

**Grove City**
Dodd, Jerry Lee

**Maumee**
Kline, James Edward

**Springfield**
Harkins, Daniel Conger

**Warren**
Aley, Charles R.

**Youngstown**
Burdman, B. Richard
Matune, Frank Joseph

### OKLAHOMA

**Muskogee**
Frix, Paige Lane

**Oklahoma City**
Kornfeld, Julian Potash

Paliotta, Armand

OREGON

**Beaverton**
Cyr, Steven Miles
**Lebanon**
Kuntz, Joel Dubois
**Portland**
Chevis, Cheryl Ann
Culpepper, David Charles
Richardson, Jay
Strader, Timothy Richards
Tremaine, H. Stewart
Zalutsky, Morton Herman

PENNSYLVANIA

**Bala Cynwyd**
Odell, Herbert
**Philadelphia**
Bernard, John Marley
Bildersee, Robert Alan
Comfort, Robert Dennis
Davis, C. VanLeer, III
Dombrowski, Raymond Edward, Jr.
Fisher, Solomon
Flaster, Richard Joel
Frank, Barry H.
Gadon, Steven Franklin
Lichtenstein, Robert Jay
Strasbaugh, Wayne Ralph
Thomas, Lowell Shumway, Jr.
**Pittsburgh**
Boocock, Stephen William
Dell, Ernest Robert
Dodson, F. Brian
Hitt, Leo N.
Phillips, Larry Edward
**Spring House**
Rosoff, William A.
**York**
Perry, Ronald

RHODE ISLAND

**Providence**
Olsen, Hans Peter
Reilly, Charles James

SOUTH CAROLINA

**Columbia**
Bailey, George Screven

TENNESSEE

**Memphis**
Cook, August Joseph
**Nashville**
Kelley, James Russell

TEXAS

**Dallas**
Hughes, Vester Thomas, Jr.
Jenkins, John Richard, III
Kerridge, Ronald David
McLean, Susan Ralston
Nihill, Julian Dumontiel
Pingree, Bruce Douglas
Willingham, Clark Suttles
Zahn, Donald Jack
**El Paso**
Mott, H. Christopher
**Houston**
Blackshear, A. T., Jr.
Estes, Carl Lewis, II
Looper, Donald Ray
Salch, Steven Charles
Seymour, Barbara Laverne
Stryker, Steven Charles
Weberpal, Michael Andrew
Wells, Benjamin Gladney
**Midland**
Arizaga, Lavora Spradlin
**San Antonio**
Ross, James Ulric
**Waco**
Jackson, Leah Witcher

UTAH

**Salt Lake City**
Barusch, Lawrence Roos
Woodland, Steven Dee

VERMONT

**Burlington**
Schroeder, William Wayne

VIRGINIA

**Alexandria**
Klewans, Samuel N.
Paturis, E. Michael
Sczudlo, Walter Joseph
**Arlington**
McDermott, Francis Owen
Susko, Carol Lynne
**Charlottesville**
Cohen, Edwin Samuel
Stroud, Robert Edward
**Fairfax**
Bloomquist, Dennis Howard
Wright, Blandin James
**Falls Church**
Ward, Joe Henry, Jr.
**Hampton**
McNider, James Small, III
**Oakton**
Vernava, Anthony Michael
**Portsmouth**
Tynch, David Ray
**Richmond**
Bush, Thomas Norman
Canup, James W.C.
Howell, George Cook, III
Magette, Kurt Robert
Mezzullo, Louis Albert
Minardi, Richard A., Jr.
**Roanoke**
Bates, Harold Martin
**Virginia Beach**
Frantz, Thomas Richard
Purcell, Brian Christopher

WASHINGTON

**Bellevue**
Medved, Robert Allen
**Seattle**
Beyer, Garrett Joseph
Minorchio, James W.
**Spokane**
Connolly, K. Thomas

WISCONSIN

**Hales Corners**
Case, Karen Ann
**Madison**
Boucher, Joseph W(illiam)
Pitzner, Richard William
**Milwaukee**
McGaffey, Jere D.
Meldman, Robert Edward
Reardon, Timothy P.
Roge, Bret Alan
**Slinger**
Gonyo, Jeffrey Myron

WYOMING

**Cheyenne**
Wrobetz, Donald Reay

TURKEY

**Camkaya**
Wales, Gwynne Huntington

ADDRESS UNPUBLISHED

Aikman, Albert Edward
Bailin, Deborah M.
Bost, Thomas Glen
Grange, Janet Lenore
Greenberg, Ronald David
Harris, Morton Allen
Heath, Charles Dickinson
Levy, David
Maeder, Gary William
Marinis, Thomas Paul, Jr.
Meier, Matthew Hamilton
Pustilnik, David Daniel
Richardson, John Carroll
Rothman, Howard Joel
Tolins, Roger Alan

## TAXATION, ESTATE. *See also* Estate planning; Probate.

UNITED STATES

ALABAMA

**Decatur**
Blackburn, John Gilmer
**Montgomery**
Kirtland, Michael Arthur

ARIZONA

**Phoenix**
Everett, James Joseph
**Scottsdale**
Franz, J. Noland
Simonson, Michael
Swartz, Melvin Jay
**Tucson**
Adamson, Larry Robertson

ARKANSAS

**Fort Smith**
Moore, Patrick Neill
**Little Rock**
Haught, William Dixon
**Pine Bluff**
Harrelson, F(rederick) Daniel
**Russellville**
Simmons, Scott Michael

CALIFORNIA

**Campbell**
Temmerman, Robert Eugene, Jr.
**Costa Mesa**
Goldstein, Michael Gerald
**Fresno**
Sherr, Morris Max
**Grass Valley**
Hawkins, Richard Michael
**Indian Wells**
Smith, Byron Owen
**Indio**
De Salva, Christopher Joseph
**Irvine**
Hilker, Walter Robert, Jr.
**Laguna Hills**
Tepper, Nancy Boxley
**Larkspur**
Greenberg, Myron Silver
**Los Angeles**
Anderson, William Augustus
Call, Merlin Wendell
Campbell, Jennifer L.
Cohan, John Robert
Gallo, Jon Joseph
Livadary, Paul John
Mitchell, Michael Charles
Norris, Floyd Hamilton
Rae, Matthew Sanderson, Jr.
**Monterey**
Gaver, Frances Rouse
**Newport Beach**
Wexler, Danniel Justin
**Palo Alto**
Miller, Michael Patiky
**Palos Verdes Estates**
Toftness, Cecil Gillman
**Pasadena**
Brown, Lorne James
**Riverside**
Darling, Scott Edward
**Sacramento**
Goodart, Nan L.
**San Carlos**
Raye-Wong, Catherine
**San Diego**
Payne, Margaret Anne
**San Francisco**
Hellman, Theodore Albert, Jr.
Stephenson, Charles Gayley
**Santa Barbara**
Ambrecht, John Ward
**Santa Monica**
Landay, Andrew Herbert
**Simi Valley**
Gruen, Evelyn Jeanette
**Thousand Oaks**
Trover, Ellen Lloyd

COLORADO

**Boulder**
Hundley, Laura S.
**Colorado Springs**
Keene, Kenneth Paul
Kendall, Phillip Alan
**Denver**
Ash, Walter Brinker
Atlass, Theodore Bruce
Christianssen, Kenneth Gordon
Gelt, Theodore Zvi
Olsen, M. Kent
Schmidt, L(ail) William, Jr.
Smead, Burton Armstrong, Jr.
**Englewood**
Carraher, John Bernard
**Littleton**
Eberhardt, Robert Schuler, Jr.
**Ouray**
Johnson, Christian Kent
**Wheat Ridge**
Brant, John Getty

CONNECTICUT

**Hartford**
Appel, Robert Eugene
Berall, Frank Stewart
Pinney, Sidney Dillingham, Jr.
**Stamford**
Daniels, Daniel Lloyd
Himmelreich, David Baker
Sarner, Richard Alan
**Waterbury**
Dost, Mark W.
**Westport**
Kosakow, James Matthew
Sheiman, Ronald Lee

DELAWARE

**Wilmington**
Reiver, Joanna
Schlusser, Robert Elmer
Shearin, Kathryn Kay

DISTRICT OF COLUMBIA

**Washington**
Bixler, John Mourer
Coughlin, Thomas A.
Gutman, Harry Largman
Heffernan, James Vincent
Kahn, Edwin Leonard
McCoy, Jerry Jack
Plaine, Lloyd Leva
Rafferty, Catherine Mary

FLORIDA

**Boynton Beach**
Armstrong, Jack Gilliland
**Clearwater**
Gulecas, James Frederick
**Deerfield Beach**
Levitan, David M(aurice)
**Fort Lauderdale**
Barnard, George Smith
Cox, James Clifton
Gardner, Russell Menese
**Jacksonville**
Braddock, Donald Layton
Donahoo, Thomas Mitchell
**Miami**
Dribin, Michael A.
Gordon, Howard W.
Rust, Robert Warren
Simmons, Sherwin Palmer
Weinstein, Andrew H.
**Naples**
Lile, Laird Andrew
**Palm Beach Gardens**
Silverman, Thomas Nelson
**Saint Petersburg**
Wilsey, Steven M.
**Sarasota**
Conetta, Tami Foley
**Tampa**
Ellwanger, Thomas John
Gonzalez, Alan Francis
**Venice**
Gaylor, William E., III
**West Palm Beach**
Bertles, James Billet

GEORGIA

**Atlanta**
Bloodworth, A(lbert) W(illiam) Franklin
Edee, James Philip
Jackson, Terry D.
Liss, Matthew Martin

HAWAII

**Honolulu**
Gerson, Mervyn Stuart
Larsen, David Coburn
Miyasaki, Shuichi

IDAHO

**Moscow**
Bielenberg, Leonard Herman

ILLINOIS

**Chicago**
Acker, Frederick George
Brown, Alan Crawford
Cass, Neil Earl
Chiles, Stephen Michael
Cross, Chester Joseph
Dashow, Jules
English, John Dwight
Gelman, Andrew Richard
Harrington, Carol A.
Herpe, David A.
Kanter, Burton Wallace
Schar, Stephen L.
Spain, Richard Colby
Sprowl, Charles Riggs
Swaney, Thomas Edward
Trost, Eileen Bannon
Witt, Alan Michael
**Geneva**
Skaar, James Douglas
**Joliet**
Teas, Richard Harper
**Monticello**
Tracy, William Francis, II
**Naperville**
Kelly, Kathryn L.
**Peoria**
Higgs, David Lawrence
**Winnetka**
Abell, David Robert
Barnard, Morton John

INDIANA

**Carmel**
Jewell, George Benson
**Fort Wayne**
Fink, Thomas Michael
**Indianapolis**
Carlock, Mahlon Waldo, II (Steve Carlock)
Hetzner, Marc Andrew
Kissel, Richard Oliver, II
Patrick, William Bradshaw
Ponder, Lester McConnico

IOWA

**Cedar Falls**
Rolinger, Mark Stephen
**Des Moines**
Campbell, Bruce Irving

KANSAS

**Iola**
Toland, Clyde William
**Lawrence**
Smith, Glee Sidney, Jr.
**Wichita**
Peare, Dan C.
Sorensen, Harvey R.

KENTUCKY

**Louisville**
Duffy, Martin Patrick
Fuchs, Olivia Anne Morris
Henry, Kelly Sue
Noe, Randolph

LOUISIANA

**Baton Rouge**
Blitzer, Sidney Milton, Jr.
**New Orleans**
Benjamin, Edward Bernard, Jr.
Carman, Laura Junge
Keller, Thomas Clements
Lemann, Thomas Berthelot
McDaniel, Donald Hamilton

MAINE

**Boothbay Harbor**
Griffin, Carl Russell, III
**Ellsworth**
Sang, Peter Bennett
**Portland**
Klebe, Kurt Edward
LeBlanc, Richard Philip

MARYLAND

**Baltimore**
Cook, Bryson Leitch
Heisler, John Charles
Kallina, Emanuel John, II
Lewis, Alexander Ingersoll, III
Mitchell, Hugh Allen, Jr.
**Bethesda**
Lewis, Myron Bruce
**Cambridge**
Robbins, Vernon Earl
**Rockville**
De Jong, David Samuel

MASSACHUSETTS

**Boston**
Chapin, Melville
Hamann, Charles Martin
Menoyo, Eric Felix
Metzer, Patricia Ann
Smith, Clark Robinson
Woodburn, Ralph Robert, Jr.
**Holden**
Price, Robert DeMille
**Plymouth**
Barreira, Brian Ernest
**Stoughton**
Gabovitch, Steven Alan
**Wellesley**
Riley, Michael Hylan
**West Chatham**
Rowley, Glenn Harry
**Worcester**
DePaolo, John P.
Erskine, Matthew Forbes
Silver, Marvin S.

MICHIGAN

**Ann Arbor**
Dew, Thomas Edward
Petoskey, Elizabeth M.
**Bingham Farms**
Sommerfeld, David William
**Birmingham**
Sweeney, Thomas Frederick
**Bloomfield Hills**
Kirk, John MacGregor
**Detroit**
Miller, George DeWitt, Jr.
**Saint Clair Shores**
Joslyn, Robert Bruce
**Southfield**
Labe, Robert Brian
**West Bloomfield**
Tobin, Bruce Howard

MINNESOTA

**Minneapolis**
Brand, Steve Aaron
Ingber, Marvin C.

MISSISSIPPI

**Columbus**
Gholson, Hunter Maurice

MISSOURI

**Independence**
Moore, Lee Alan
**Kansas City**
Bartunek, Robert R(ichard), Jr.
Marvin, Wendy Byers
Setzler, Edward Allan
Tanner, Eric Benson
**Saint Charles**
Beck, Rudy Dale
**Saint Louis**
Burton, Earl Gillespie, III
Greenfield, Milton, Jr.
Lane, Frank Joseph, Jr.
Lowenhaupt, Charles Abraham
Redd, Charles Appleton
Sherby, Kathleen Reilly

MONTANA

**Billings**
Thompson, James William
**Havre**
Moog, Mary Ann Pimley
**Missoula**
Spangler, John Thomas

NEBRASKA

**Omaha**
Kozlik, Michael David

NEVADA

**Las Vegas**
Dawson, John E.
Oshins, Steven Jeffrey
Yamashita, Wesley Farrell
**Reno**
Kelly, Brian Coleman

NEW HAMPSHIRE

**Concord**
McDonald, Joseph F., III
**Hanover**
Harvey, Nicholas D. N., Jr.
**Manchester**
Mullikin, Anu Radha
**Portsmouth**
Money, Kenneth F., Jr.

NEW JERSEY

**Bedminster**
Donegan, Joseph Michael
**Boonton**
Massler, Howard Arnold
**Edison**
Nagle, Claire Waller
**Hackensack**
Deener, Jerome Alan
**Hackettstown**
Hudacek, Daniel Andrew
Israels, Michael Jozef
**Jersey City**
Feder, Arthur A.
**Livingston**
Rosenberg, Paul I.
**Morristown**
Hapward, Curt Matthew
Neff, Robert Carey
**Newark**
Levin, Simon
Zuckerman, Herbert Lawrence
**Princeton**
Ufford, Charles Wilbur, Jr.
**West Orange**
Laves, Benjamin Samuel
**Woodbridge**
Lepelstat, Martin L.

NEW MEXICO

**Albuquerque**
Lieuwen, John N.
Tomita, Susan K.
**Santa Fe**
Hallmark, Bruce Cullen, Jr.

NEW YORK

**Albany**
Flory, Judith A.
**Babylon**
Garvey, Jane Roberts
**Bedford**
Atkins, Ronald Raymond
**Buffalo**
Gardner, Sue Shaffer

**Eastchester**
Katz, Kenneth Arthur
**Elmira**
Daubner, Susan Moore
**Garden City**
Hand, Stephen Block
Haskel, Jules J.
**Glens Falls**
Baker, Carl TenEyck
**Huntington**
Hochberg, Ronald Mark
**Kew Gardens**
Adler, David Neil
**Larchmont**
Engel, Ralph Manuel
**Lawrence**
Goldstein, Irwin Melvin
**Manhasset**
Fletcher, James Harry
**Mineola**
Brush, Louis Frederick
**Montour Falls**
Argetsinger, Cameron R.
**Nanuet**
Waldorf, Geraldine Polack
**New Hyde Park**
Rose, Elihu Isaac
**New York**
Ashton, Robert W.
Barasch, Mal Livingston
Bergreen, Morris Harvey
Christensen, Henry, III
Coon, Robert Morell, Jr.
Crary, Miner Dunham, Jr.
DuLaux, Russell Frederick
Eakins, William Shannon
Evans, Douglas Hayward
Finch, Edward Ridley, Jr.
Gelb, Judith Anne
Hader, Cheryl Elizabeth
Herbst, Abbe Ilene
Hewitt, Richard Gilbert
Hirschson, Linda Benjamin
Hull, Philip Glasgow
Johnson, Bruce Carlton
Karan, Paul Richard
Kartiganer, Joseph
Katsoris, Constantine Nicholas
Kavoukjian, Michael Edward
Klipstein, Robert Alan
Leckie, Gavin Frederick
Lingelbach, Albert Lane
Lipsky, Burton G.
Martin, Malcolm Elliot
Materna, Joseph Anthony
McGrath, Thomas J.
Miller, Jill Lee
Muhlstock, Arthur C.
Neuwirth, Gloria S.
Newman, Scott David
Radin, Sam
Rafalowicz, Joseph
Robinson, Barbara Paul
Rodman, Leroy Eli
Rubenstein, Joshua Seth
Rubinstein, Kenneth
Sabalja, Lorraine
Saufer, Isaac Aaron
Schlesinger, Sanford Joel
Sederbaum, Arthur David
Spero, C. Michael
Tsismenakis, Vasilia Helen A.
Valente, Peter Charles
Warner, Jeannette Sloan
Whoriskey, Robert Donald
Wyckoff, E. Lisk, Jr.
Zabel, William David
**Northport**
Bialla, Rowley
**Pearl River**
Meyer, Irwin Stephan
**Poughkeepsie**
Haven, Milton M.
**Rochester**
Buckley, Michael Francis
Harter, Ralph Millard Peter
O'Toole, Martin William
**Scarsdale**
Macchia, Vincent Michael
**Schenectady**
Suprunowicz, Michael Robert
**Syracuse**
Cambs, Denise P.
Stack, Gerald Francis
**White Plains**
Kurzman, Robert Graham
Pohlmann, William Howard

### NORTH CAROLINA

**Chapel Hill**
Herman-Giddens, Gregory
**Charlotte**
Edwards, Mark Brownlow
Wood, William McBrayer

### OHIO

**Berea**
Jolles, Janet Kavanaugh Pilling
**Cincinnati**
Crouse, Rebecca Ann
**Cleveland**
Hochman, Kenneth George
Nudelman, Sidney
**Columbus**
Postlewaite, William Neal, Sr.
Willcox, Roderick Harrison
**Dayton**
Conway, Mark Allyn
Johnson, C. Terry
**Oak Harbor**
Robertson, Jerry D.
**Parma Heights**
Pojman, Paul J.
**Perrysburg**
Hartsel, Norman Clyde
**Saint Clairsville**
Hanlon, Lodge L.
**Springfield**
Harkins, Daniel Conger
**Westerville**
Westervelt, Charles Ephraim, Jr.
**Willoughby**
Greene, Ralph Vernon

### OKLAHOMA

**Enid**
Musser, William Wesley, Jr.
**Oklahoma City**
Kornfeld, Julian Potash

### OREGON

**Beaverton**
Cyr, Steven Miles
**Corvallis**
Morris, Gretchen Reynolds
**Portland**
Lee, Laurie Neilson
Zalutsky, Morton Herman

### PENNSYLVANIA

**Allentown**
Zamborsky, Donald A.
**Clarion**
O'Neil, Kenton R.
**Haverford**
Frick, Benjamin Charles
**Philadelphia**
Deming, Frank Stout
Flaster, Richard Joel
Frank, Barry H.
Glassmoyer, Thomas Parvin
Kaier, Edward John
Kaufman, David Joseph
Lombard, John James, Jr.
Nofer, George Hancock
Schneider, Pam Horvitz
**Pittsburgh**
Daniel, Robert Michael
Dodson, F. Brian
Houston, William McClelland
Phillips, Larry Edward
**Punxsutawney**
Long, Jesse Paul
**Reading**
Linton, Jack Arthur
**Verona**
Chisnell, Janice Hoffman
**West Chester**
DeVlieger, Tracy Blake
Rolfe, John L.

### SOUTH CAROLINA

**Charleston**
Branham, C. Michael

### TENNESSEE

**Knoxville**
Bly, Robert Maurice
**Memphis**
Autry, Edward Thomas
Patton, Charles Henry
**Nashville**
Berry, William Wells
Trautman, Herman Louis
**Union City**
Graham, Hardy Moore

### TEXAS

**Addison**
Turner, Bruce Edward
**Arlington**
Willey, Stephen Douglas
**Austin**
Bloomquist, Amy Peterson
Dougherty, John Chrysostom, III
Helman, Stephen Jody
Lock, John Richard
Osborne, Duncan Elliott
**Dallas**
Hughes, Vester Thomas, Jr.
Jenkins, John Richard, III
McLean, Susan Ralston
Owens, Rodney Joe
Phelps, Robert Frederick, Jr.
Smith, Frank Tupper
Willingham, Clark Suttles
**El Paso**
Sanders, Amy Stewart
**Houston**
Brentin, John Olin
Cenatiempo, Michael J.
Crocker, Charles Allan
Eastland, S. Stacy
Friedman, J. Kent
Jeske, Charles Matthew
Koenig, Rodney Curtis
Schwartzel, Charles Boone
Shearer, Dean Paul
**Hurst**
Leach, Terry Ray
**Lubbock**
Barnhill, Robert Edwin, III
**Midland**
Arizaga, Lavora Spradlin
**San Antonio**
Goldsmith, Richard Elsinger
**Weatherford**
Akers, Charles Benjamin
Westenhover, Gary Floyd
**Wichita Falls**
Goff, Robert William, Jr.

### UTAH

**Midvale**
Dahl, Everett E.
**Salt Lake City**
Adams, Joseph Keith

### VERMONT

**South Royalton**
Prye, Steven Marvell
**Woodstock**
Sincerbeaux, Robert Abbott

### VIRGINIA

**Alexandria**
McClure, Roger John
Paturis, E. Michael
**Charlottesville**
Edwards, James Edwin
**Mc Lean**
Aucutt, Ronald David
**Richmond**
Aghdami, Farhad
Belcher, Dennis Irl
Horsley, Waller Holladay
Stevens, C. Daniel
Warthen, Harry Justice, III
**Vienna**
Callahan, Timothy J.
**Virginia Beach**
Frantz, Thomas Richard

### WASHINGTON

**Bellevue**
Treacy, Gerald Bernard, Jr.
**Olympia**
Walker, Francis Joseph
**Seattle**
Gores, Thomas C.
Minorchio, James W.

### WISCONSIN

**Appleton**
Thenell, Heather Jo
**Madison**
Nora, Wendy Alison
Pitzner, Richard William
Wilcox, Michael Wing
**Milwaukee**
Dencker, Lester J.
McGaffey, Jere D.
Nelson, Randy Scott
Wynn, Stanford Alan
**Racine**
Smith, Stephen James

### WYOMING

**Cody**
Stradley, Richard Lee

### ADDRESS UNPUBLISHED

Bailin, Deborah M.
Baxter-Smith, Gregory John
Bergkvist, Thomas A.
Buechel, William Benjamin
Gooch, Robert Francis
Green, Harland Norton
Kahan, Rochelle Liebling
Kaitz, Haskell A.
Merrill, Abel Jay
Mintz, M. J.
Reber, Joseph E.
Reiche, Frank Perley
Stickney, John Moore
Stuart, Michael George
Surratt, John Richard
Sweeney, Deidre Ann
Weill, (Lige) Harry, Sr.
Wyshak, Lillian Worthing

## TAXATION, GENERAL

### UNITED STATES

### ALABAMA

**Birmingham**
Hughes, James Donald
Savage, Kay Webb
**Mobile**
Ballard, Michael Eugene
Brock, Glen Porter, Jr.

### ALASKA

**Anchorage**
Mahoney, F. Steven

### ARIZONA

**Phoenix**
Case, David Leon
Derdenger, Patrick
Hiller, Neil Howard
Tomback, Jay Loren
**Tucson**
Levitan, Roger Stanley
**Yuma**
Hunt, Gerald Wallace

### ARKANSAS

**Little Rock**
Bohannon, Charles Tad
Haley, John Harvey
Skokos, Theodore C., Jr.

### CALIFORNIA

**Camarillo**
Pugh, Francis Leo
**China Lake**
Hatley, Rodney James
**Fresno**
Sherr, Morris Max
Wells, Gary B.
**Glendale**
Green, Norman Harry
**La Crescenta**
McNally, Gerald, Jr.
**La Jolla**
Shannahan, William Paul
**Larkspur**
Maier, Peter Klaus
**Los Altos**
Weir, Robert H.
**Los Angeles**
Anderson, Charles David
Antin, Michael
Argue, John Clifford
Baram, Art
Basile, Paul Louis, Jr.
Friedman, Simon
Wasserman, William Phillip
**Modesto**
Schrimp, Roger Martin
**North Hollywood**
Kreger, Melvin Joseph
**Oxnard**
Arnold, Gary D.
**Redondo Beach**
Michael, Geoffrey Palmer
**San Diego**
Dorne, David J.
Dostart, Paul Joseph
Guinn, Stanley Willis
Harf, Cynthia Minette
Sapin, Craig P.
**San Francisco**
Daily, Frederick William
Foster, David Scott
Freud, Nicholas S.
Haynes, William Ernest
Kerner, Michael Philip
La Vine, Robert L.
**San Jose**
Chacon, Gerald Gilbert
**San Rafael**
Bloomfield, Neil Jon
**Santa Barbara**
Egenolf, Robert F.
**Santa Cruz**
Schalk, Robert Partridge
**Torrance**
Crane, Kathleen D.
Finer, William A.

### COLORADO

**Colorado Springs**
Everson, Steven Lee
**Denver**
Abramovitz, Michael John
Callison, James William
Crow, Nancy Rebecca
Groom, David A.
Rich, Robert Stephen

### CONNECTICUT

**Bridgeport**
Flynn, Walter Andrew
**Hartford**
Del Negro, John Thomas
Milliken, Charles Buckland
**New Haven**
Carr, Cynthia
**North Haven**
Gradoville, Robert Thomas
**Stamford**
Gilman, Derek
**Westport**
Jacobs, Jeffrey Lee
LoMonte, Douglas Edward

### DELAWARE

**Wilmington**
Baumann, Julian Henry, Jr.
Durante, Charles Joseph
Grossman, Jerome Kent
Martin, William Joseph, III
Tigani, Bruce William
Togman, Leonard S.

### DISTRICT OF COLUMBIA

**Washington**
Bergner, Jane Cohen
Bickel, David Robert
Birnkrant, Henry Joseph
Blair, David Belmont
Bruton, James Asa, III
Caplin, Mortimer Maxwell
Chapoton, John Edgar
Condrell, William Kenneth
Davidson, Daniel Morton
DiFronzo, Michael A.
Doyle, Austin Joseph
Dye, Alan Page
Faley, R(ichard) Scott
Fleeman, Mary Grace
Gonzalez, Edward
Hawkins, Edward Jackson
Henck, Charles Seymour
Kyhos, Thomas Flynn
Mann, Donegan
Nilles, Kathleen Mary
Oliphant, Charles Frederick, III
Osnos, David Marvin
Pomeroy, Harlan
Sterrett, Samuel Black
Waris, Michael, Jr.
Watkins, Charles Morgan

### FLORIDA

**Boca Raton**
Comisky, Ian Michael
**Fort Lauderdale**
Hoines, David Alan
Katz, Thomas Owen
**Hollywood**
Singer, Bernard Alan
**Jacksonville**
Donahoo, Thomas Mitchell
**Lakeland**
Koren, Edward Franz
**Miami**
Chabrow, Penn Benjamin
Gomez, Ivan A.
Kurzer, Martin Joel
Simmons, Sherwin Palmer
Stiver, Charles Ellwood, Jr.
Wheeler, Harold Austin, Sr.
**Orlando**
Capouano, Albert D.
Ibanez, Silvia Safille
**Palm Beach**
Zeller, Ronald John
**Palm Beach Gardens**
Silverman, Thomas Nelson
**Pensacola**
Huston, Gary William
**Plantation**
Singer, Joseph K.
**Saint Petersburg**
Gross, Alan Marc
**Tallahassee**
Reid, Robert C.
**Tampa**
Aye, Walter Edwards
Barton, Bernard Alan, Jr.
Doliner, Nathaniel Lee
Humphries, J. Bob
Levine, Jack Anton
O'Neill, Albert Clarence, Jr.
Russo, Ronald John
**West Palm Beach**
Lampert, Michael Allen

### GEORGIA

**Atlanta**
Andros, James Harry
Cook, Philip Carter
Durrett, James Frazer, Jr.
Hackett, Stanley Hailey
Hoffman, Michael William
Jackson, Terry D.
Lamon, Harry Vincent, Jr.
**Dallas**
Williams, Gary Randall
**Doraville**
Gerstein, Joe Willie
**Savannah**
Dickey, David Herschel
**Smyrna**
Seigler, Michael Edward

### HAWAII

**Honolulu**
Galati, Vito
Heller, Ronald Ian
Roth, Randall W.

### IDAHO

**Boise**
Green, Cumer L.
**Idaho Falls**
Simmons, John G.

### ILLINOIS

**Belleville**
Mathis, Patrick Bischof
**Chicago**
Banoff, Sheldon Irwin
Barnett, William A.
Chin, Davis
Conlon, Steven Denis
Felsenthal, Steven Altus
Kanter, Burton Wallace
Kolmin, Kenneth Guy
Mandel, Reid Alan
Menson, Richard L.
Pinsky, Michael S.
Rudo, Saul E.
Silets, Harvey Marvin
Tassone, Bruno Joseph
Truskowski, John Budd
Von Mandel, Michael Jacques
Ward, Michael W.
Winkler, Charles Howard
**Evanston**
Weston, Michael C.
**Lake Forest**
Palmer, Ann Therese Darin
**Lisle**
Fortier, Robert Frederic
**Rolling Meadows**
Sullivan, Michael D.
**Wonder Lake**
McNamara, Joseph Burk

### INDIANA

**Indianapolis**
Comer, Jerome Edward
Hetzner, Marc Andrew
Kappes, Philip Spangler
Kissel, Richard Oliver, II
Springer, Marilee J.

### IOWA

**Algona**
Handsaker, Jerrold Lee
**Cedar Rapids**
Richards, Allan Max
**Des Moines**
Campbell, Bruce Irving
Schuling, Mark Richard
**Marshalltown**
Geffe, Kent Lyndon
**Muscatine**
Nepple, James Anthony
**Parkersburg**
Lawler, Thomas Albert

### KANSAS

**Lincoln**
Marshall, Susan
**Onaga**
Stallard, Wayne Minor
**Wichita**
Sorensen, Harvey R.

### KENTUCKY

**Lebanon**
Higdon, Frederick Alonzo
**Lexington**
Bagby, William Rardin
**Louisville**
Lavelle, Charles Joseph
Luber, Thomas J(ulian)
Sommer, Mark F.

**LOUISIANA**
**Lafayette**
Myers, Stephen Hawley
**Monroe**
Curry, Robert Lee, III
**New Orleans**
Abbott, Hirschel Theron, Jr.
Keller, Thomas Clements
McDaniel, Donald Hamilton
Nuzum, Robert Weston

**MAINE**
**Portland**
Hunt, David Evans

**MARYLAND**
**Baltimore**
Potts, Bernard
**Bethesda**
Lewis, Myron Bruce
**Lutherville**
Mc Kenney, Walter Gibbs, Jr.
**Rockville**
Teller, Howard Barry
**Westminster**
Staples, Lyle Newton

**MASSACHUSETTS**
**Boston**
Cutler, Arnold Robert
Hines, Edward Francis, Jr.
Larson, Olive Elizabeth
Metzer, Patricia Ann
Ritt, Roger Merrill
Solet, Maxwell David
**Cambridge**
Connors, Frank Joseph
**Framingham**
Heng, Gerald C. W.
**Newburyport**
Maslen, David Peter
**Springfield**
Clarke, David Gordon

**MICHIGAN**
**Ann Arbor**
Keppelman, Nancy
**Birmingham**
Sweeney, Thomas Frederick
**Bloomfield Hills**
Callow, Thomas Edward
Kasischke, Louis Walter
Solomon, Mark Raymond
**Detroit**
Deron, Edward Michael
Rasmussen, Douglas John
Wisner, Cynthia Ficke
**East Lansing**
Castellani, Edward Joseph
**Farmington**
Brody, Jay Howard
**Grand Rapids**
Oetting, Roger H.
**Grosse Pointe**
Goss, James William
**Lansing**
Bahs, Jess Allen
**Saint Joseph**
Butzbaugh, Alfred M.
**Southfield**
Forrest, Robert Edwin
Kippert, Robert John, Jr.
Klein, Coleman Eugene
Levine, Jeffrey Barry
**Troy**
Dillon, Joseph Francis

**MINNESOTA**
**Minneapolis**
Andrews, Albert O'Beirne, Jr.
Erhart, John Joseph
Hibbs, John Stanley

**MISSISSIPPI**
**Jackson**
Black, D(eWitt) Carl(isle), Jr.
Hammond, Frank Jefferson, III
Maron, David F.

**MISSOURI**
**Chesterfield**
Fagerberg, Roger Richard
**Clayton**
Mohrman, Henry J(oe), Jr.
**Kansas City**
Bartunek, Robert R(ichard), Jr.
Berson, Susan A.
Egan, Charles Joseph, Jr.
Gorman, Gerald Warner
Kaplan, Eliot Lawrence
Mikkelson, Eric T.
Prugh, William Byron
Voran, Joel Bruce
**Saint Charles**
Dorsey, Richard P., III
**Saint Louis**
Goldenhersh, Robert Stanley
Greenley, Beverly Jane
Rose, Albert Schoenburg
Venker, Thomas Edward
Wagner, Raymond Thomas, Jr.
**Salem**
Mitchell, Austin L.

**MONTANA**
**Kalispell**
Kaufman, Leonard Lee

**NEBRASKA**
**Lincoln**
Ludtke, David Allen
**Omaha**
Gaines, Tyler Belt
Littlejohn, Kent Oscar

**NEVADA**
**Las Vegas**
Singer, Michael Howard

**NEW HAMPSHIRE**
**Laconia**
Giere, John Patrick

**NEW JERSEY**
**Florham Park**
LeVine, Walter Daniel
Witman, Leonard Joel
**Hackensack**
Deener, Jerome Alan
Knee, Peggy Sheahan
Mullin, Patrick Allen
Weiner, Samuel
**Highland Park**
Feld, Franklin Fred
**Jersey City**
Feder, Arthur A.
Guarini, Frank J.
**Lawrenceville**
Silk, Allen M.
**Morristown**
Doyle, David Perrie
Fishman, Richard Glenn
Hapward, Curt Matthew
Schwarz, Kent Louis
Sherman, Sandra Brown
Sweeney, John Lawrence
**New Brunswick**
Shirtz, Joseph Frank
**Newark**
Costenbader, Charles Michael
Levin, Simon
O'Connor Quinn, Deirdre
Vajtay, Stephen Michael, Jr.
Zuckerman, Herbert Lawrence
**Princeton**
Mulchinock, David Steward
**Wayne**
Sabino, William
**West Orange**
Goldberg, Leonard Marvin
Richmond, Harold Nicholas

**NEW MEXICO**
**Albuquerque**
Gorman, Robert Dennis
Loubet, Jeffrey W.
**Santa Fe**
Hickey, John Miller

**NEW YORK**
**Albany**
Hyde, Carol Ann
Teitelbaum, Steven Usher
**Brooklyn**
Levy, Samuel Robert
**Buffalo**
Ivancic, Gregory Thomas
**Clifton Park**
Lazarow, Martin Sidney
**East Northport**
Ryesky, Kenneth H.
**Floral Park**
Goldman, Alan Barry
**Hauppauge**
Silberling, Stephen Pierce
**New York**
Adams, Ludwig Howard
Aidinoff, M(erton) Bernard
Andresen, Malcolm
Battaglia, John Joseph
Black, Louis Engleman
Brecher, Howard Arthur
Collinson, Dale Stanley
Dlugoff, Marc Alan
Estes, Richard Martin
Fass, Peter Michael
Ferguson, Milton Carr, Jr.
Fink, Robert Steven
Finkelstein, Stuart M.
Ganz, Marc David
Gardner, Stephen David
Hirschfeld, Michael
Infanti, Anthony C.
Keneally, Kathryn Marie
Kitay, Harvey Robert
Kolbe, Karl William, Jr.
Kurtz, Jerome
Loengard, Richard Otto, Jr.
Lynn, Leslie Robin
MacLean, Babcock
Mahan, (Daniel) Dulany, Jr.
Moore, Thomas Ronald (Lord Bridestowe)
Oliner, Martin
Peragine, Paul Francis
Phillips, Barnet, IV
Posner, Louis Joseph
Rabunski, Alan E.
Rosen, Matthew A.
Serota, Susan Perlstadt
Shapiro, Aleena Rieger
Shipper, David W.
Sicular, David R.
Smith, Morton Alan
Solomon, Andrew P.
Surkin, Dean Leslie
Thompson, Loran Tyson
Tigue, John J., Jr.
White, Harry Edward, Jr.
Whoriskey, Robert Donald
Wydler, Hans Ulrich
**Pearl River**
Meyer, Irwin Stephan
**Poughkeepsie**
Constantino, James Peter
**Rego Park**
Jain, Lalit K.
**Rochester**
Colby, William Michael
Kraus, Sherry Stokes
Twietmeyer, Don Henry
Wild, Robert Warren
**Syracuse**
Stack, Gerald Francis
Wladis, Mark Neil
**White Plains**
Berlin, Alan Daniel
Greenspan, Leon Joseph
Lalli, Michael Anthony
**Yonkers**
Clark, Celia Rue

**NORTH CAROLINA**
**Asheville**
Hamilton, Jackson Douglas
Lavelle, Brian Francis David
**Charlotte**
Preston, James Young
Thigpen, Richard Elton, Jr.
**Durham**
Boles, Richard Joseph
**Raleigh**
Byrd, Stephen Timothy
**Tabor City**
Jorgensen, Ralph Gubler
**Winston Salem**
Edwards, Robert Leon
Ingersoll, Marc W.

**NORTH DAKOTA**
**Grand Forks**
Cilz, Douglas Arthur

**OHIO**
**Akron**
Cox, Steven St. Leger
**Cincinnati**
Faller, Susan Grogan
Flanagan, John Anthony
Frank, William Nelson
Neumark, Michael Harry
Porter, Robert Carl, Jr.
Ryan, James Joseph
Silvers, Jane Fink
**Cleveland**
Cohn, Mark Barry
Currivan, John Daniel
Doris, Alan S(anford)
Koblenz, N(orman) Herschel
Sharp, Robert Weimer
Sogg, Wilton Sherman
**Columbus**
Albert, Robert Hamilton
Balthaser, James Harvey
**Dayton**
Hitter, Joseph Ira
**Massillon**
Netzly, Dwight H.
**Toledo**
Nicholson, Brent Bentley
**Youngstown**
Matune, Frank Joseph

**OKLAHOMA**
**Edmond**
Kamp, Randall William
**Enid**
Jones, Stephen
**Oklahoma City**
Buckles, Joseph Aaron, II
Hanna, Terry Ross
Kornfeld, Julian Potash
Mock, Randall Don
**Tulsa**
Blackstock, LeRoy
Moffett, J. Denny

**OREGON**
**Portland**
Christensen, Darin S.
Culpepper, David Charles
Froebe, Gerald Allen
Hanna, Harry Mitchell
Kamin, Scott Allan
Sellers, Marc Kellogg

**PENNSYLVANIA**
**Bala Cynwyd**
Odell, Herbert
**Berwyn**
Huffaker, John Boston
**Erie**
Mosier, David Michael
**Exton**
Teti, Louis N.
**King Of Prussia**
Beausang, Michael Francis, Jr.
Breslin, Michael Francis
Noonan, Gregory Robert
**Lehigh Valley**
Harris, Judith A.
**Norristown**
Harp, Chadwick Allen
**Philadelphia**
Bonovitz, Sheldon M.
Brier, Bonnie Susan
Chimples, George
Comfort, Robert Dennis
Cooper, Wendy Fein
Fisher, Solomon
Frank, Barry H.
Glassmoyer, Thomas Parvin
Goldman, Jerry Stephen
Greenstein, J. Richard
Lichtenstein, Robert Jay
Rudolph, Andrew J.
Sparrow, Ruth S.
Strasbaugh, Wayne Ralph
Wilf, Mervin M.
Wolff, Deborah H(orowitz)
**Pittburg**
Montgomery, Richard C.
**Pittsburgh**
Boocock, Stephen William
Forsyth, Andrew Watson, III
Geeseman, Robert George
Hitt, Leo N.
Nevin, Hugh Williamson, Jr.
Pollack, David L.
Scully, Erik Vincent
Ummer, James Walter
**Pottsville**
Jones, Joseph Hayward
**Reading**
Scianna, Russell William
**Venetia**
Breslin, Elvira Madden
**Wormleysburg**
Cherewka, Michael
**York**
Perry, Ronald

**RHODE ISLAND**
**Providence**
Kean, John Vaughan
**Warwick**
Goldman, Steven Jason

**SOUTH CAROLINA**
**Greenville**
Dobson, Robert Albertus, III
Walters, Johnnie McKeiver
**Hilton Head Island**
Rose, William Shepard, Jr.

**TENNESSEE**
**Knoxville**
Gentry, Mack A.
**Memphis**
Bland, James Theodore, Jr.
Monypeny, David Murray
**Nashville**
Skoney, Lesa Hartley
Trautman, Herman Louis

**TEXAS**
**Austin**
Cloudt, Jim B.
**Dallas**
Brewer, David Madison
Gerberding Cowart, Greta Elaine
Jenkins, John Richard, III
Kerridge, Ronald David
McLean, Susan Ralston
Nolan, John Michael
Owens, Rodney Joe
Stephens, Marjorie Johnsen
Wilson, Claude Raymond, Jr.
**Fort Worth**
Tilley, Rice M(atthews), Jr.
Tracy, J. David
**Houston**
Grossberg, Marc Elias
Hull, Robert Joe
Lamme, Thomas Robert
Schneller, John, IV
Sheinfeld, Myron M.
Touchy, Deborah K. P.
Valentine, Michael John
Wells, Benjamin Gladney
**Irving**
French, Colin Val
**Jacksonville**
Cummins, Michael Wayne
**Kingwood**
Demuth, C. Jeanne
**San Antonio**
Cruse, Rex Beach, Jr.
Goldsmith, Richard Elsinger
**Tyler**
Killough, J. Scott
**Waco**
Jackson, Leah Witcher
Page, Jack Randall

**UTAH**
**Salt Lake City**
Brown, Charles R.
Deamer, Michael Lynn
Turner, Shawn Dennis
Woodland, Steven Dee

**VIRGINIA**
**Arlington**
McDermott, Francis Owen
Susko, Carol Lynne
**Lynchburg**
Whitesell, Darryl Duane
**Mc Lean**
Aucutt, Ronald David
Houle, Jeffrey Robert
**Nellysford**
Vandenburgh, Beverly Ann
**Norfolk**
Knight, Montgomery, Jr.
**Portsmouth**
Tynch, David Ray
**Richmond**
Addison, David Dunham
Canup, James W.C.
Denny, Collins, III
Magette, Kurt Robert
Starke, Harold E., Jr.
**Roanoke**
Hale, Lance Mitchell
**Virginia Beach**
Purcell, Brian Christopher
**Williamsburg**
Twiford, Alice Kate

**WASHINGTON**
**Bellevue**
McCutcheon, James Edward, III
**Issaquah**
Sterling, Michael Erwin
**Seattle**
Judson, C(harles) James (Jim Judson)
Malone, Thomas William
Schumacher, Scott Alan
Sussman, Neil A.
**Yakima**
Wright, J(ames) Lawrence

**WISCONSIN**
**Madison**
Croake, Paul Allen
Pellino, Charles Edward, Jr.
Robison, John S.
**Middleton**
Berman, Ronald Charles
**Milwaukee**
Peltin, Sherwin Carl
**Wausau**
Zimmerman, Robert W.

**TERRITORIES OF THE UNITED STATES**

**PUERTO RICO**
**San Juan**
Rodriguez-Diaz, Juan E.

**ADDRESS UNPUBLISHED**
Bloom, Barry Marshall
Clark, Donald Otis
Grange, Janet Lenore
Harmon, Gail McGreevy
Jessop, Jeanette Wanless
Levy, David
Lipsman, Richard Marc
Meier, Matthew Hamilton
Meyer, Max Earl
Mintz, M. J.
Morgan, Timi Sue
Peterson, Howard Cooper
Putney, Wainscott Walker
Rothman, Howard Joel
Segel, Karen Lynn Joseph
Shariff, Vivian Rodriguez
Stuart, Michael George
Tokars, Fredric William
Torgerson, Larry Keith
Wyshak, Lillian Worthing

## TAXATION, PERSONAL INCOME

**UNITED STATES**

**ALABAMA**
**Birmingham**
Savage, Kay Webb
**Montgomery**
Proctor, David Ray

**ARIZONA**
**Phoenix**
Everett, James Joseph
**Scottsdale**
Simonson, Michael
**Tucson**
Adamson, Larry Robertson

**CALIFORNIA**
**Beverly Hills**
Kite, Richard Lloyd
**Costa Mesa**
Schaaf, Douglas Allan
**Glennville**
Walton, Lewis R.
**Larkspur**
Greenberg, Myron Silver
**Los Angeles**
Baram, Art
Palazzo, Robert P.
Sheppard, Thomas Richard
**Palo Alto**
Miller, Michael Patiky
**Sacramento**
Waks, Stephen Harvey
**San Diego**
Harf, Cynthia Minette
Sapin, Craig P.
**San Francisco**
Heng, Donald James, Jr.
Wood, Robert Warren
**San Leandro**
Newacheck, David John
**Santa Cruz**
Schalk, Robert Partridge
**Santa Monica**
Axe, Norman Gold
**Temecula**
Rosenstein, Robert Bryce

**COLORADO**
**Aurora**
Stauffer, Scott William
**Colorado Springs**
Everson, Steven Lee
**Denver**
Ruppert, John Lawrence
Smead, Burton Armstrong, Jr.
**Parker**
Greenberg, Morton Paul

**CONNECTICUT**
**Danbury**
Tuozzolo, John Joseph
**Darien**
Dale, Erwin Randolph
**Hartford**
Appel, Robert Eugene
Lyon, James Burroughs
**Stamford**
Himmelreich, David Baker
**Trumbull**
Auerbach, Hillel Joshua
**Westport**
Sheiman, Ronald Lee

**DELAWARE**
**Wilmington**
Baumann, Julian Henry, Jr.

### DISTRICT OF COLUMBIA
**Washington**
Birnkrant, Henry Joseph
Chapoton, John Edgar
Davidson, Daniel Morton
Ginsburg, Martin David
Gutman, Harry Largman
Hawkins, Edward Jackson
Heffernan, James Vincent
Kahn, Edwin Leonard
Kautter, David John
Paul, William McCann
Wofford, Cindy Lynn
Worthy, K(enneth) Martin

### FLORIDA
**Boca Raton**
Berlin, Mark A.
**Fort Lauderdale**
Barnard, George Smith
Hess, George Franklin, II
**Jacksonville**
Donahoo, Thomas Mitchell
**Miami**
Ruffner, Charles Louis
Stiver, Charles Ellwood, Jr.
Weinstein, Andrew H.
**Miami Beach**
Brodie, Ronald
**Oldsmar**
Hirschman, Sherman Joseph
**Sarasota**
Davis, Louis Poisson, Jr.
**Tampa**
Levine, Jack Anton
**West Palm Beach**
Tanzer, Jed Samuel

### ILLINOIS
**Calumet City**
Scullion, Kevin Peter
**Chicago**
Banoff, Sheldon Irwin
Brown, Steven Spencer
Chandler, Kent, Jr.
Dashow, Jules
Lutter, Paul Allen
Mandel, Reid Alan
McKenzie, Robert Ernest
Stone, Howard Lawrence
Swibel, Steven Warren
Trio, Edward Alan
Truskowski, John Budd
**Glenview**
Marmet, Gottlieb John
**Northbrook**
Bronner, James Russell
**Schaumburg**
Colombik, Richard Michael
**Skokie**
Kahn, Bert L.

### INDIANA
**Carmel**
Jewell, George Benson
**Indianapolis**
Ponder, Lester McConnico
Warren, Bradford Lloyd

### IOWA
**Mason City**
Heiny, James Ray
**Webster City**
Hemingway, Whitley Maynard

### KENTUCKY
**Versailles**
Dunlap, Tavner Branham

### LOUISIANA
**Metairie**
Sherman, David Robert
**New Orleans**
Hoffman, Robert Dean, Jr.

### MAINE
**Ellsworth**
Sang, Peter Bennett
**Portland**
Cowan, Caspar Frank

### MARYLAND
**Baltimore**
Adkins, Edward James
**Bethesda**
Lewis, Myron Bruce
**Cambridge**
Robbins, Vernon Earl
**Lutherville Timonium**
Freeland, Charles
**Rockville**
De Jong, David Samuel

### MASSACHUSETTS
**Boston**
Elfman, Eric Michael
Milder, Forrest David
Mooney, Michael Edward
Ritt, Roger Merrill
**Springfield**
Clarke, David Gordon
**Stoughton**
Gabovitch, Steven Alan

### MICHIGAN
**Flint**
Pelavin, Michael Allen
**Grand Rapids**
Oetting, Roger H.
**Saint Clair Shores**
Joslyn, Robert Bruce
**Southfield**
Kaplow, Robert David

### MINNESOTA
**Minneapolis**
Vanhove, Lorri Kay
Ventres, Judith Martin
**Saint Paul**
Geis, Jerome Arthur

### MISSOURI
**Independence**
Moore, Lee Alan
**Saint Louis**
Farnam, Thomas Campbell
Lowenhaupt, Charles Abraham

### MONTANA
**Havre**
Moog, Mary Ann Pimley

### NEBRASKA
**Hildreth**
Jelkin, John Lamoine
**Omaha**
Ellsworth, John David

### NEW HAMPSHIRE
**Laconia**
Martin, Willard Gordon, Jr.

### NEW JERSEY
**Boonton**
Massler, Howard Arnold
**Hackensack**
David, Theodore Martin
**Plainsboro**
Gorrin, Eugene
**South Orange**
Kamens, Harold

### NEW MEXICO
**Albuquerque**
Messinger, J. Henry

### NEW YORK
**Albany**
Koff, Howard Michael
**Babylon**
Garvey, Jane Roberts
**Eastchester**
Katz, Kenneth Arthur
**Garden City**
Druker, James Owen
**Latham**
Brearton, James Joseph
**Lawrence**
Goldstein, Irwin Melvin
**Mineola**
Brush, Louis Frederick
**New Hyde Park**
Rose, Elihu Isaac
**New York**
Agranoff, Gerald Neal
Amdur, Martin Bennett
Christensen, Henry, III
Cleland, Edward Gordon
Collins, Adrian Anthony
Garfunkel, Alan J.
Hirschfeld, Michael
Jassy, Everett Lewis
Kahn, Alan Edwin
Kalish, Arthur
Katsoris, Constantine Nicholas
Koch, Edward Richard
Kurtz, Jerome
Levy, Mark Allan
Lipsky, Burton G.
Macan, William Alexander, IV
MacLean, Babcock
Miller, Arthur Madden
Newman, Scott David
Paul, Herbert Morton
Phillips, Barnet, IV
Rosen, Matthew A.
Rosenberg, Jerome Roy
Small, Jonathan Andrew
Tengi, Frank R.
White, Harry Edward, Jr.
**Pearl River**
Meyer, Irwin Stephan
**Rochester**
Kraus, Sherry Stokes
**Scarsdale**
Macchia, Vincent Michael
**Westbury**
Zychick, Joel David

### NORTH CAROLINA
**Winston Salem**
Osborn, Malcolm Everett

### OHIO
**Cleveland**
Doris, Alan S(anford)
Leavitt, Jeffrey Stuart
Perris, Terrence George
**Columbus**
Kusma, Kyllikki
**Parma Heights**
Pojman, Paul J.
**Warren**
Aley, Charles R.

### OKLAHOMA
**Tulsa**
Hatfield, Jack Kenton
Taliaferro, Bruce Owen

### OREGON
**Lebanon**
Kuntz, Joel Dubois
**Portland**
Christensen, Darin S.

### PENNSYLVANIA
**Bala Cynwyd**
Odell, Herbert
**Berwyn**
Huffaker, John Boston
**Philadelphia**
Comfort, Robert Dennis
Fisher, Solomon
Gillis, Richard Moffitt, Jr.
Mirabello, Francis Joseph
Thomas, Lowell Shumway, Jr.
**Pittsburgh**
Phillips, Larry Edward
**Spring House**
Rosoff, William A.
**Venetia**
Brewer, Christopher
**Verona**
Chisnell, Janice Hoffman

### RHODE ISLAND
**Providence**
Olsen, Hans Peter
Reilly, Charles James

### SOUTH CAROLINA
**Columbia**
Bailey, George Screven

### TENNESSEE
**Memphis**
Cook, August Joseph

### TEXAS
**Austin**
Lock, John Richard
**Borger**
Pace, Rosa White
**Dallas**
Hughes, Vester Thomas, Jr.
Pingree, Bruce Douglas
Willingham, Clark Suttles
Wilson, Claude Raymond, Jr.
**Houston**
Blackshear, A. T., Jr.
Disher, David Alan
Estes, Carl Lewis, II
Grossberg, Marc Elias
Stewart, Pamela L.
Wheelan, R(ichelieu) E(dward)
**Kingwood**
Demuth, C. Jeanne
**Lubbock**
Barnhill, Robert Edwin, III
**Midland**
Arizaga, Lavora Spradlin
**Richardson**
Conkel, Robert Dale
**San Antonio**
Ross, James Ulric
**Spring**
Hendricks, Randal Arlan
**Waco**
Jackson, Leah Witcher

### VIRGINIA
**Charlottesville**
Cohen, Edwin Samuel
Kudravetz, David Waller
**Richmond**
Magette, Kurt Robert
**Virginia Beach**
Frantz, Thomas Richard

### WASHINGTON
**Seattle**
Birmingham, Richard Joseph

### WISCONSIN
**Hales Corners**
Case, Karen Ann
**Milwaukee**
LaBudde, Roy Christian
Meldman, Robert Edward
**Racine**
Smith, Stephen James
**Slinger**
Gonyo, Jeffrey Myron
**Viroqua**
Jenkins, David Lynn

### TURKEY
**Camkaya**
Wales, Gwynne Huntington

### ADDRESS UNPUBLISHED
Assael, Michael
Bost, Thomas Glen
Fiala, David Marcus
Grange, Janet Lenore
Maeder, Gary William
Marinis, Thomas Paul, Jr.
Morgan, Timi Sue
Phelan, Charles Scott
Shook, Ann Jones
Souder, Susan
Weisman, Paul Howard

## TAXATION, STATE AND LOCAL

### UNITED STATES

### ALABAMA
**Montgomery**
Gregory, William Stanley
Proctor, David Ray

### ARIZONA
**Phoenix**
Derdenger, Patrick
Le Clair, Douglas Marvin

### CALIFORNIA
**Costa Mesa**
Goldstein, Michael Gerald
**Los Angeles**
Anderson, Charles David
Polley, Terry Lee
**Sacramento**
Micheli, Christopher Michael
**San Francisco**
Dunn, Robert Lawrence
Martin, Jay R.
Spiegel, Hart Hunter
**San Leandro**
Newacheck, David John
**Tarzana**
Balkin, Jeffrey Gilbert

### COLORADO
**Denver**
McLain, William Allen

### CONNECTICUT
**Hartford**
Berall, Frank Stewart
Coyle, Michael Lee
Lyon, James Burroughs

### DISTRICT OF COLUMBIA
**Washington**
Drabkin, Murray
Halvorson, Newman Thorbus, Jr.

### FLORIDA
**Fort Lauderdale**
Stankee, Glen Allen
**Jacksonville**
Ringel, Fred Morton
**Miami**
Korchin, Judith Miriam
Ruffner, Charles Louis
**Orlando**
Spoonhour, James Michael
**Tallahassee**
Barnett, Martha Walters
**Tampa**
Barton, Bernard Alan, Jr.
Hoyt, Brooks Pettingill

### GEORGIA
**Atlanta**
Hoffman, Michael William
McArthur, John William, Jr.
**Decatur**
Mears, Michael

### HAWAII
**Honolulu**
Galati, Vito
Heller, Ronald Ian

### IDAHO
**Idaho Falls**
Eskelson, Scott P.

### ILLINOIS
**Chicago**
Griffin, Lawrence Joseph
Michod, Charles Louis, Jr.
Montgomery, Julie-April
Peterson, Ronald Roger
**Rockford**
Rudy, Elmer Clyde

### INDIANA
**Indianapolis**
Hendrickson, Thomas Atherton

### IOWA
**Des Moines**
Schuling, Mark Richard

### KANSAS
**Topeka**
Wolfe, Philip Brannon

### KENTUCKY
**Louisville**
Luber, Thomas J(ulian)
Sommer, Mark F.

### LOUISIANA
**New Orleans**
Keller, Thomas Clements
Nuzum, Robert Weston

### MASSACHUSETTS
**Boston**
Hines, Edward Francis, Jr.
Politi, Stephen Michael
Solet, Maxwell David
**Canton**
Fuller, Robert L(eander)

### MICHIGAN
**Detroit**
McKim, Samuel John, III
**Lansing**
Bahs, Jess Allen
**Southfield**
Kippert, Robert John, Jr.

### MINNESOTA
**Saint Paul**
Bernick, Alan E.
Geis, Jerome Arthur

### MISSISSIPPI
**Jackson**
Johnson, Mark Wayne

### MISSOURI
**Kansas City**
Howes, Brian Thomas
Prugh, William Byron
**Saint Louis**
Armstrong, Owen Thomas

### MONTANA
**Billings**
Sites, James Philip

### NEBRASKA
**Omaha**
Kozlik, Michael David

### NEVADA
**Las Vegas**
Wilson, Joseph Morris, III

### NEW JERSEY
**Cherry Hill**
Thomas, Robert F.
**Fair Lawn**
Hirschklau, Morton
**Hamilton**
Haushalter, Harry
**Newark**
Costenbader, Charles Michael
Levin, Simon
Zuckerman, Herbert Lawrence
**River Vale**
Lotito, Joseph Daniel
**South Orange**
Delo, Ellen Sanderson
**Teaneck**
Rosenblum, Edward G.

### NEW MEXICO
**Albuquerque**
Loubet, Jeffrey W.

### NEW YORK
**Albany**
Koff, Howard Michael
Teitelbaum, Steven Usher
**East Meadow**
Hyman, Montague Allan
**Mineola**
Brush, Louis Frederick
**New York**
Agranoff, Gerald Neal
Block, William Kenneth
Brandman, Scott Lewis
Faber, Peter Lewis
Garfunkel, Alan J.
Koch, Edward Richard
Newman, Glenn
Rosenberg, Jerome Roy
Zucker, Howard

### NORTH CAROLINA
**Charlotte**
Thigpen, Richard Elton, Jr.

### OHIO
**Beachwood**
Mintz, Carl A.
**Cleveland**
Kramer, Eugene Leo
**Dayton**
Hitter, Joseph Ira
**Warren**
Aley, Charles R.
**Youngstown**
Matune, Frank Joseph

### OKLAHOMA
**Oklahoma City**
Legg, William Jefferson

### OREGON
**Portland**
Chevis, Cheryl Ann

### PENNSYLVANIA
**Philadelphia**
Davis, C. VanLeer, III
Tumola, Thomas Joseph
**Pittsburgh**
Boocock, Stephen William

### RHODE ISLAND
**Providence**
Olsen, Hans Peter
Reilly, Charles James

### TENNESSEE
**Nashville**
Bingham, Pamela Mary Muir

### TEXAS
**Austin**
Cunningham, Judy Marie
McDaniel, Myra Atwell
**Dallas**
Bonesio, Woodrow Michael
Wilson, Claude Raymond, Jr.
**Houston**
Hull, Robert Joe
Sears, Terry H.
Seymour, Barbara Laverne
Van Kerrebrook, Mary Alice
Wall, Kenneth E., Jr.
**Mcallen**
Darling, James Edward
**San Angelo**
Carter, James Alfred
**San Antonio**
Hartnett, Dan Dennis

### VIRGINIA
**Arlington**
Susko, Carol Lynne

**Hampton**
McNider, James Small, III

WASHINGTON

**Seattle**
Hilpert, Edward Theodore, Jr.
Judson, C(harles) James (Jim Judson)

WISCONSIN

**Waukesha**
Macy, John Patrick

ADDRESS UNPUBLISHED

Blume, James Donald
Bost, Thomas Glen
Harris, Richard Eugene Vassau
Maeder, Gary William
Morgan, Timi Sue
Rothman, Howard Joel
Ryan, James Frederick

## TOXIC TORT

UNITED STATES

ALABAMA

**Birmingham**
Knight, William Collins, Jr.
Palmer, Robert Leslie

ARIZONA

**Phoenix**
Turk, Andrew Borders
Woods, Terrence Patrick

ARKANSAS

**Little Rock**
Taylor, Sammye Lou

CALIFORNIA

**Bakersfield**
Stead, Calvin Rudi
**Fresno**
Runyon, Brett L.
**Irvine**
Suojanen, Wayne William
**Moraga**
Kilbourne, George William
**San Diego**
McFall, James Alan
**San Francisco**
Fergus, Gary Scott
**San Jose**
Alexander, Richard
**Westlake Village**
Vititoe, James Wilson

CONNECTICUT

**Danbury**
Winfree, Gregory Dainard

DISTRICT OF COLUMBIA

**Washington**
Renner, Curtis Shotwell
Watson, Thomas C.

FLORIDA

**Deerfield Beach**
Slavin, Edward A., Jr.
**Miami Beach**
Cohen, Karen Beth
**Tampa**
Rawls, R. Steven

GEORGIA

**Atlanta**
Denham, Vernon Robert, Jr.

ILLINOIS

**Chicago**
Byrne, Katharine Crane
Drumke, Michael William
Ford, Michael W.
Johnson, Jennifer Jerit
Kuhns, Thomas O.
Sparks, Kenneth Franklin
**Elgin**
Karayannis, Marios Nicholas
**Oak Park**
Birkbeck, A.J. Koerts

KANSAS

**Olathe**
DeWitt, Anthony Louis

KENTUCKY

**Lexington**
Masterton, Lucinda Cronin

LOUISIANA

**Baton Rouge**
LeBlanc, J. Burton, IV
Nelson, David K.
**Lake Charles**
Elliot, N. Frank
Parkerson, Hardy Martell
Watson, Wells
**New Orleans**
Courington, Kaye Newton
Curtis, Martha Young
Exnicios, Val Patrick
Moore, Blaine Augusta
**Shreveport**
Politz, Nyle Anthony

MARYLAND

**Baltimore**
Mullady, Raymond George, Jr.
Sack, Sylvan Hanan

MASSACHUSETTS

**Boston**
Graceffa, John Philip
**Salem**
Wasserman, Stephen Alan

MICHIGAN

**Southfield**
McLellan, Dale J.

MINNESOTA

**Minneapolis**
Faricy, John Hartnett, Jr.
Tolin, Stefan A.

MISSISSIPPI

**Pascagoula**
Heidelberg, James Hinkle

MISSOURI

**Kansas City**
Beck, William G.
Koelling, Thomas Winsor
**Saint Louis**
Reeg, Kurtis Bradford

NEVADA

**Reno**
Whitbeck, Jill Karla

NEW JERSEY

**Cherry Hill**
Spielberg, Joshua Morris
**Jersey City**
Grossman, Randy
**Newark**
Laura, Anthony Joseph
Rosmarin, Susan Gresser
Smith, Frederick Theodore
**Parsippany**
Haney, James Kevin
**Voorhees**
Kueny, Bernard E., III
**Warren**
Quinn, Thomas Gerard
**Westmont**
Tonogbanua, A. Robert

NEW MEXICO

**Albuquerque**
Carrico, Michael Layne

NEW YORK

**Buffalo**
Merriman, Kevin Thomas
Szanyi, Kevin Andrew
**New York**
Faizakoff, Daniel Benjamin
Kelmachter, Leslie Debra
Riley, Scott C.
Ruger, James Richard
Strober, Eric Saul
Vogel, Michael Scott

NORTH CAROLINA

**Durham**
Conner, James Leon, II
**Winston Salem**
Grubbs, Robert Howard
Maready, William Frank

OHIO

**Cleveland**
Krawczak, Kenneth Francis

OREGON

**Portland**
Duden, Paul Russell

PENNSYLVANIA

**Philadelphia**
Fickler, Arlene
Hoyle, Lawrence Truman, Jr.
Madva, Stephen Alan
**Pittsburgh**
Gigler, Daniel Richard
Lerach, Richard Fleming
Mills, Edward James
Tarasi, Louis Michael, Jr.
**Washington**
Richman, Stephen I.

SOUTH CAROLINA

**Charleston**
Solomon, Cindi Anne

TEXAS

**Arlington**
Hubby, Bert Gorman
**Beaumont**
Johnson, Leanne
**Dallas**
James, Walter D., III
**Houston**
Carstarphen, Edward Morgan, III
Edwards, Blaine Douglass
Fisher, Guy G.
Fromm, Eva Maria
Perdue, Jim Mac
Roven, John David
Towns, William Roy
**San Antonio**
Rhodes, Jesse Thomas, III
**Texarkana**
Poff, Franklin Albright, Jr.

VIRGINIA

**Norfolk**
Bishop, Bruce Taylor
Gorry, James A., III
**Portsmouth**
Miller, Joseph Aaron
**Richmond**
King, William H., Jr.

WASHINGTON

**Hoquiam**
Kahler, Ray William

WEST VIRGINIA

**Huntington**
Bagley, Charles Frank, III

TERRITORIES OF THE UNITED STATES

VIRGIN ISLANDS

**St Croix**
Welcome, Patricia

ADDRESS UNPUBLISHED

Bell, Troy Nathan
Gates, Pamela Sue
Keltner, Cecil Green

## TRADEMARK AND COPYRIGHT

UNITED STATES

ALABAMA

**Birmingham**
Ramsey, David Wade

ARIZONA

**Phoenix**
Meschkow, Jordan M.
Sutton, Samuel J.
Ullman, James A.
**Scottsdale**
Barbee, Joe Ed

CALIFORNIA

**Anaheim**
Lieb, John Stevens
**Claremont**
Ansell, Edward Orin
**Costa Mesa**
Stone, Samuel Beckner
**Encinitas**
Nemeth, Valerie Ann
**Irvine**
Weissenberger, Harry George
**La Jolla**
Karlen, Peter Hurd
**Los Angeles**
Allan, Michael Lee
Cornwell, Donald Lee
Gallegos, Esteban Guillermo
Green, William Porter
Immerman, William Joseph
Kindred, Alan M.
Lenkov, Jeffrey Myles
**Newport Beach**
Knobbe, Louis Joseph
Martens, Don Walter
Rowlett, Robert Duane
**Oxnard**
Gerber, David A.
**Palo Alto**
Bridges, Andrew Phillip
Nycum, Susan Hubbell
Pasahow, Lynn H(arold)
**San Francisco**
Forsythe, Janet Winifred
Green, Philip R.
Smegal, Thomas Frank, Jr.
**San Jose**
Goldstein, Robin
**San Luis Obispo**
Dorsi, Stephen Nathan
**Santa Ana**
Lane, Dominick V.
**Sunnyvale**
Zahrt, William Dietrich, II
**Tustin**
Sun, Raymond Chi-Chung
**Ventura**
Arant, Eugene Wesley
English, Woodrow Douglas

COLORADO

**Boulder**
Miller, Jonathan Lewis
**Broomfield**
Hogle, Sean Sherwood
**Denver**
Dorr, Robert Charles
Samuels, Donald L.
Weinstein, David Akers
**Fort Collins**
Fromm, Jeffery Bernard

CONNECTICUT

**New Haven**
Carlson, Dale Lynn
De Lio, Anthony Peter
**Stamford**
Carten, Francis Noel
Kelly, Michael John
Thompson, Frank J(oseph)
**Westport**
Razzano, Pasquale Angelo
**Windsor**
Smith, Spencer Thomas

DELAWARE

**Wilmington**
Goldstein, Jack Charles
Huntley, Donald Wayne

DISTRICT OF COLUMBIA

**Washington**
Browne, Richard Cullen
Cantor, Herbert I.
DeGrandi, Joseph Anthony
Denison, Mary Boney
Donohoe, Charles Richard
Goodman, Alfred Nelson
Hefter, Laurence Roy
Hobbs, J. Timothy, Sr.
Israel, Deborah Jean
Kessler, Edward J.
Lazar, Dale Steven
Linn, Richard
Lowell, H. Bret
Marks, Richard Daniel
Mathias, Charles McCurdy
Myers, James R.
Potenza, Joseph Michael
Price, Griffith Baley, Jr.
Repper, George Robert
Ryan, John William
Shapiro, Nelson Hirsh
Silverman, David Malanos
Tegfeldt, Jennifer Ann
Timberg, Sigmund

FLORIDA

**Clearwater**
Hopen, Anton John
**Coral Gables**
Lott, Leslie Jean
**Gainesville**
McLeod, Christine Quillian
**Longwood**
Simon, James Lowell
**Miami**
Boren, Barry Marc
Buchenhorner, Michael Joseph
Castillo, Angel, Jr.
**Miami Beach**
Cesarano, Michael Chapman
**Naples**
Werder, Horst Heinrich
**Orlando**
Blaher, Neal Jonathan
**Saint Petersburg**
Pedata, Martin Anthony
**Sanibel**
Liljequist, Jon Leon
**Sarasota**
Partoyan, Garo Arakel
**Tampa**
Pettis, David Wilson, Jr.
**Winter Park**
Livingston, Edward Michael

GEORGIA

**Atlanta**
Campbell, Jennifer Katze
Drucker, Michael Stuart
Hetsko, Jeffrey Francis
Hopkins, George Mathews Marks
Schroeder, Eric Peter
**Norcross**
Anderson, Albert Sydney, III

ILLINOIS

**Barrington**
Lee, William Marshall
**Chicago**
Altman, Louis
Berenzweig, Jack Charles
Berghoff, Paul Henry
Coolley, Ronald B.
Geraldson, Raymond I., Jr.
Geren, Gerald S.
Hilliard, David Craig
Huston, Steven Craig
Jacover, Jerold Alan
Kozak, John W.
Kramm, Deborah Lucille
Krupka, Robert George
Maher, David Willard
Mason, Henry Lowell, III
Norek, Joan I.
Partridge, Mark Van Buren
Pattishall, Beverly Wyckliffe
Provenzano, Ronald Casper
Roper, Harry Joseph
Rubin, E(rwin) Leonard
Shulman, Alvin David
Shurtleff, John Howard
Smith, Gregory Michael
Sternstein, Allan J.
Wanke, Ronald Lee
Wick, Lawrence Scott
**Deerfield**
Birmingham, William Joseph
Scott, Theodore R.
**Lansing**
Hill, Philip
**Northbrook**
Sernett, Richard Patrick
**Urbana**
Berns, Michael Andrew
Fitz-Gerald, Roger Miller

INDIANA

**Indianapolis**
Badger, David Harry
**Merrillville**
Kinney, Richard Gordon

IOWA

**Cedar Rapids**
Squires, Vernon Pellett
**Hull**
DeKoster, Lucas J(ames)

KANSAS

**Lenexa**
Scott, Robert Gene
**Overland Park**
Cole, Roland Jay

KENTUCKY

**Louisville**
Blaine, Steven Robert
**Mayfield**
Phipps, Robert Maurice

LOUISIANA

**Lafayette**
Domingue, C. Dean
**Metairie**
Kastl, Dian Evans
**New Orleans**
Keaty, Thomas St. Paul, II

MARYLAND

**Baltimore**
Hopps, Raymond, Jr.
**Potomac**
Troffkin, Howard Julian

MASSACHUSETTS

**Boston**
Cramer, Jennifer Goldenson
Fischer, Mark Alan
Hieken, Charles
Kaler, Robert Joseph
Lambert, Gary Ervery
Loginov, William Alex
Naughton, Edward Joseph
Neuner, George William
Swain, Philip C., Jr.
Weaver, Paul David
**Chestnut Hill**
Bursley, Kathleen A.
**Framingham**
Kriegsman, Edward Michael
**Lexington**
Glovsky, Susan G. L.
**Somerville**
Brown, Peter Mason
**Springfield**
Miller, J(ohn) Wesley, III
**Tewksbury**
Dulchinos, Peter

MICHIGAN

**Ann Arbor**
Patti, Anthony Peter
Pierce, Richard William
**Bloomfield Hills**
Foley, Sally Lee
Meyer, George Herbert
Rader, Ralph Terrance
**Grand Rapids**
Litton, Randall Gale
Smith, H(arold) Lawrence
**Southfield**
Taravella, Christopher Anthony
**Troy**
Cantor, Bernard Jack

MINNESOTA

**Apple Valley**
Huusko, Gary Lawrence
**Minneapolis**
Lofstrom, Mark D.
McDonald, Daniel William
Sawicki, Zbigniew Peter
Street, Erica Catherine
Tufte, Brian N.

MISSOURI

**Chesterfield**
Michaels, Martha A.
**Kansas City**
Marquette, I. Edward
Milton, Chad Earl
Woods, Curtis E(ugene)
**Saint Louis**
Chervitz, David Howard
Corrigan, Ann Phillips
Evans, Lawrence E.
Forsman, Alpheus Edwin
Lucchesi, Lionel Louis
Moore, McPherson Dorsett

MONTANA

**Bozeman**
Conover, Richard Corrill
Wylie, Paul Richter, Jr.
**Missoula**
Vannatta, Shane Anthony

NEBRASKA

**Omaha**
Jondle, Robert John

NEVADA

**Reno**
Ryan, Robert Collins

NEW JERSEY

**Edgewater**
Virelli, Louis James, Jr.
**Englewood Cliffs**
Fredericks, Barry Irwin
**Madison**
Huettner, Richard Alfred
**Morristown**
Schwartz, Howard J.
Whitmer, Frederick Lee
**Newark**
Cahn, Jeffrey Barton
**Warren**
Kasper, Horst Manfred
**Wayne**
Awerdick, John Holmes
**Westfield**
Bobis, Daniel Harold
**Woodbridge**
Plevy, Arthur L.

NEW YORK

**Croton On Hudson**
Hoffman, Paul Shafer
**Huntington**
Robinson, Kenneth Patrick
**Kingston**
Maier, John, III

## TRANSPORTATION



**TRIAL.** *See* **Civil Litigation; Criminal.**

**TRUSTS.** *See* **Probate.**

## UTILITIES, PUBLIC

**MASSACHUSETTS**

**Boston**
Anderson, Arthur Irvin
Jones, Jeffrey Foster

**Weston**
McDaniel, James Alan

**MICHIGAN**

**Detroit**
Smith, James Albert

**Lansing**
Ewert, Quentin Albert
Marvin, David Edward Shreve

**MINNESOTA**

**Minneapolis**
LeVander, Harold Powrie, Jr.

**MISSISSIPPI**

**Bay Saint Louis**
Bernstein, Joseph

**Jackson**
Wise, Sherwood Willing

**Meridian**
Eppes, Walter W., Jr.

**MISSOURI**

**Kansas City**
Breneman, Diane Marie
Mordy, James Calvin
Triplett, Timothy Wayne

**Saint Louis**
Smith, Arthur Lee

**NEBRASKA**

**Omaha**
Dolan, James Vincent

**NEVADA**

**Reno**
Marshall, Robert William

**NEW JERSEY**

**Roseland**
Vanderbilt, Arthur T., II

**Somerville**
Laskey, James Howard

**Woodbridge**
Goldenberg, Steven Saul

**NEW MEXICO**

**Santa Fe**
Carpenter, Richard Norris
Cohen, David Saul

**NEW YORK**

**Albany**
Alessi, Robert Joseph

**New York**
Birn, Harold M.
Dunn, M(orris) Douglas
McMeen, Elmer Ellsworth, III
Schuur, Robert George
Schwartz, Renee Gerstler
Seham, Martin Charles
White, Katherine Patricia
Wolf, Gary Wickert
Worenklein, Jacob Joshua

**Rochester**
George, Richard Neill

**NORTH CAROLINA**

**Charlotte**
Walker, Clarence Wesley

**Raleigh**
Hargrove, Wade Hampton

**NORTH DAKOTA**

**Bismarck**
Hinman, Michael J.

**OHIO**

**Cincinnati**
Finnigan, John Julius, Jr.

**Columbus**
McConnaughey, George Carlton, Jr.
Ryan, Joseph W., Jr.

**Dayton**
Chernesky, Richard John

**Newark**
Hite, David L.

**OKLAHOMA**

**Kingfisher**
Logsdon, Harold L.

**Tulsa**
Arrington, John Leslie, Jr.
Gaberino, John Anthony, Jr.
Huffman, Robert Allen, Jr.

**OREGON**

**Portland**
Dotten, Michael Chester
Fell, James F.

**PENNSYLVANIA**

**Butler**
Biondi, John Michael

**Greensburg**
McDowell, Michael David

**New Castle**
Flannery, Harry Audley

**Philadelphia**
Kendall, Robert Louis, Jr.
Myers, Kenneth Raymond
Satinsky, Barnett
Stuart, Glen R(aymond)

**Pittsburgh**
Boswell, William Paret
Munsch, Richard John

**Wayne**
Donnella, Michael Andre

**Yardley**
Hamberg, Gilbert Lee

**RHODE ISLAND**

**Providence**
Southgate, (Christina) Adrienne Graves

**TENNESSEE**

**Athens**
Guinn, Charles Clifford, Jr.

**Knoxville**
Sanger, Herbert Shelton, Jr.

**Memphis**
Williams, J. Maxwell

**Nashville**
Thornton, Guilford F., Jr.

**TEXAS**

**Austin**
Anderson, Richard Michael
Cortez, Hernan Glenn
Demond, Walter Eugene
Drummond, Eric Hubert

**Dallas**
Meyer, Ferdinand Charles, Jr.

**Houston**
Gover, Alan Shore
Hartrick, Janice Kay
Kelly, Hugh Rice
Morgan, Richard Greer
Rozzell, Scott Ellis

**UTAH**

**Salt Lake City**
Reeder, F. Robert

**VERMONT**

**Montpelier**
Storrow, Charles Fiske

**Rutland**
George, Alan Barry
Taylor, A. Jeffry

**VIRGINIA**

**Annandale**
Yaffe, David Philip

**Richmond**
Flippen, Edward L.
Roach, Edgar Mayo, Jr.
Watts, Stephen Hurt, II

**WASHINGTON**

**Seattle**
Thomas, Elizabeth

**Tacoma**
Densley, James Albert

**WEST VIRGINIA**

**Charleston**
Kauffelt, James David
Lane, Charlotte

**WISCONSIN**

**Elm Grove**
Gorske, Robert Herman

**Madison**
Hanson, David James

**WYOMING**

**Cheyenne**
Godfrey, Paul Bard
Hickey, Paul Joseph

**ADDRESS UNPUBLISHED**

Branstetter, Cecil Dewey, Sr.
Buffington, John Victor
Doub, William Offutt
Heath, Charles Dickinson
Hittle, Larry Glenn
Howell, Donald Lee
Mayer, James Joseph
Norman, Albert George, Jr.
Ostergaard, Joni Hammersla
Polsky, Howard David
Powers, Elizabeth Whitmel
Pullen, Richard Owen

---

**WATER.** *See* **Property, real.**

---

**WILLS.** *See* **Probate.**

---

**WORKERS' COMPENSATION.** *See also* **Labor; Personal injury.**

---

**UNITED STATES**

**ALABAMA**

**Andalusia**
Albritton, William Harold, IV

**Anniston**
Burgess, Timothy Christopher

**Birmingham**
Brown, Stephen Edward
Coleman, John James, III
Cullen, William Zachary
McAtee, James Stuart
Oliver, Thomas L., II
Thornton, Wendy Nix

**Dadeville**
Oliver, John Percy, II

**Dothan**
Morris, Joseph Anthony

**Huntsville**
Simpson, Shannon Smith

**Mobile**
Harris, Benjamin Harte, Jr.
Janecky, John Franklin

**Montgomery**
Wood, James Jerry

**ALASKA**

**Anchorage**
Weddle, Randall Jay

**Juneau**
Davis, Gerald Kenneth, Jr.

**ARIZONA**

**Flagstaff**
Currey, Rebecca S.

**Phoenix**
Weiss, Stephen L.
Wilmer, Charles Mark

**Tucson**
McNamara, Patrick Robert
Samet, Dee-Dee
Tretschok, Dale Deege
Waterman, David Moore

**ARKANSAS**

**Fayetteville**
Wall, John David

**CALIFORNIA**

**Anaheim**
Mazurek, Mike E.

**Beverly Hills**
Nagel, Stuart

**California City**
Friedl, Rick

**Chico**
Lenzi, Albert James, Jr.

**Daly City**
Boccia, Barbara

**Dixon**
Levin, Roy C.

**Encino**
Magidsohn, Herman Edward

**Glendale**
Kaplan, Kenneth J.
Wax, Harold Wilfred

**Irvine**
Vermes, L. Robert

**Los Angeles**
Hinden, Barry Harris
Johnson, Willie Dan

**Oakland**
Heywood, Robert Gilmour
Russo, Frank D.

**Orinda**
Resneck, William Allan

**Oxnard**
Beckwith, Michael V.

**Palm Springs**
Caruthers, Dennis Michael

**Pleasant Hill**
Gearheart, Mark Edwin
Otis, Roy James

**Riverside**
Sklar, Wilford Nathanield

**Sacramento**
Hassan, Allen Clarence

**San Diego**
Atcherley, Linda Francesca
Cohen, Philip Meyer

**San Francisco**
Mazhari, Niloufar
Selvig, Jettie Pierce

**San Jose**
Beauzay, Victor H(ilton)
Clark, William Frederick

**Santa Rosa**
Meechan, Rick James

**Seal Beach**
Weitzman, Marc Herschel

**Yuba City**
McCaslin, Leon

**COLORADO**

**Colorado Springs**
Pring, Cynthia Marie

**Denver**
Burke, Marlin W.
de Marino, Thomas John
Kintzele, John Alfred
Leibowitz, Paul H.
O'Toole, Neil D.

**Englewood**
Ewing, Mary Arnold
McReynolds, Gregg Clyde
Rediger, Richard Kim

**Greeley**
Conway, Rebecca Ann Koppes

**CONNECTICUT**

**Bridgeport**
Feldman, David Scott

**Middletown**
Poliner, Bernard

**New Milford**
Guendelsberger, Robert Joseph

**South Windham**
Asselin, John Thomas

**Stamford**
Casper, Stewart Michael
Moore, Peggy Braden

**Stratford**
O'Rourke, James Louis

**Torrington**
Leard, David Carl

**Watertown**
Del Buono, John Angelo

**Westport**
Wisser, Ellen

**Woodbridge**
Cousins, William Joseph

**DELAWARE**

**Wilmington**
Bartley, Brian James
Ralston, Robert W.
Saville, Yvonne Takvorian

**DISTRICT OF COLUMBIA**

**Washington**
Groner, Samuel Brian

**FLORIDA**

**Altamonte Springs**
Heindl, Phares Matthews

**Bushnell**
Hagin, T. Richard

**Clearwater**
Carlson, Edward D.

**Crestview**
Duplechin, D. James

**Jacksonville**
Cramer, Jeffrey Allen
Hardesty, W. Marc
McCorvey, John Harvard, Jr.
Pope, Shawn Hideyoshi

**Lake Worth**
Williams, Charles August

**Merritt Island**
Church, Glenn J.

**Miami**
Lanza, Christopher F.
Segor, Joseph Charles
Valle, Laurence Francis

**Ocala**
Musleh, Victor Joseph, Jr.

**Orlando**
Dietz, Robert Lee
Eidson, Frank M.
Mooney, Thomas Robert

**Palm Beach Gardens**
Hayes, Neil John

**Pensacola**
Windham, John Franklin

**Saint Petersburg**
Escarraz, Enrique, III

**Tampa**
Barbas, Stephen Michael
Hayes, Audrey Dawn
McQuigg, John Dolph
Medina, Omar F.
Sanders, L. Gray
Stiles, Mary Ann
Townsend, Byron Edwin

**West Palm Beach**
Hoch, Rand

**GEORGIA**

**Atlanta**
Chalker, Ronald Franklin
Gannon, Mark Stephen
Holder, Thomas Lee
Jones, Eric S.

**Douglas**
Hayes, Dewey

**Fayetteville**
Johnson, Donald Wayne

**Gainesville**
Gilliam, Steven Philip, Sr.

**Marietta**
Cox, Reed Elbredge

**Savannah**
Bowman, Catherine McKenzie
Lorberbaum, Ralph Richard
Mason, Kirby Gould

**Valdosta**
Bass, Jay Michael

**HAWAII**

**Honolulu**
Fong, Leslie Kaleiopu Wah Cheong
Kotada, Kelly Kenichi
Turbin, Richard
Umebayashi, Clyde Satoru
Yamada, Stephen Kinichi

**IDAHO**

**Coeur D Alene**
Garbrecht, Louis

**Lewiston**
Tait, John Reid

**Twin Falls**
Berry, L. Clyel

**ILLINOIS**

**Aurora**
Loats, J. Timothy

**Belleville**
Heiligenstein, Christian E.

**Bloomington**
Lapan, Roger Don

**Chicago**
Corday, Lane Allan
Ellis, Stuart L.
Haskins, Charles Gregory, Jr.
Kane, Arthur O.
Knox, James Marshall
Mattes, Barry A.
Menchetti, David Barry

**Danville**
Devens, Charles J.

**Decatur**
Jones, Deanne Fortna

**Elgin**
Carbary, Jonathan Leigh

**Hoopeston**
Manion, Paul Thomas

**Joliet**
Miller, Randal J.

**Libertyville**
Rallo, Douglas

**Marengo**
Franks, Herbert Hoover

**Mattoon**
Corn, Stephen Leslie

**Paris**
Pearman, John Stewart

**Peoria**
Ferrari, Gary John
O'Brien, Daniel Robert

**Rockford**
Hunsaker, Richard Kendall
Sullivan, Peter Thomas, III

Zucchi, Jeffrey Joseph

**Vandalia**
Lawinger, Jane M.

**Waukegan**
Rizzo, John Joseph

**Winnetka**
Krucks, William Norman

**INDIANA**

**Fort Wayne**
James, Ronald Eugene

**Kokomo**
Harrigan, Daniel Joseph

**South Bend**
Norton, Sally Pauline

**IOWA**

**Cedar Rapids**
O'Brien, David A.
Wilson, Robert Foster

**Davenport**
Liebbe, Michael William

**Des Moines**
Branstad, Christine Ellen
Cortese, Joseph Samuel, II
Crook, Charles Samuel, III
Cutler, Charles Edward
Duckworth, Marvin E.
Murray, William Michael (Mike Murray)
Shoff, Patricia Ann
Werner, Thomas M.

**Keokuk**
Hoffman, James Paul

**Mason City**
Kinsey, Robert Stanleigh, III

**Webster City**
Karr, Richard Lloyd

**KANSAS**

**Emporia**
Helbert, Michael Clinton

**Fort Scott**
Hudson, Leigh Carleton

**Kansas City**
Andersen, Anton Chris
Greenbaum, Frederick Joel

**Leawood**
Shetlar, James R.

**Lenexa**
Gould, Robert P.
Rappard, Gary Donald
Scott, Robert Gene

**Overland Park**
McGrath, Patrick Edward
Smith, Daniel Lynn
Smith, Jill Galbreath

**Shawnee Mission**
Gastl, Eugene Francis
Wells, Samuel Jay

**Topeka**
Wisler, James Lynn
Wright, James C.

**Wichita**
Fisher, Randall Eugene
Franklin, Joni Jeanette
Jones, Gary Kenneth
Stalcup, Randy Stephen

**KENTUCKY**

**Bowling Green**
Darrell, Barton David
Goad, Frank Roark

**Fort Mitchell**
Beetem, A. Page

**Lexington**
Hiestand, Sheila Patricia
Matl, Lois Tudor

**Louisville**
Osterhage, Lawrence Edward
Weiss, Allan

**Paducah**
Nickell, Christopher Shea

**LOUISIANA**

**Alexandria**
Arsenault, Gary Joseph

**Lafayette**
Curtis, Lawrence Neil
Dartez, Shannon Seiler
Landry, Michael W.

**New Orleans**
Snellings, Daniel Breard

**MAINE**

**Bangor**
Gould, Edward Ward
Sighinolfi, Paul Henry

**Brunswick**
Lamothe, Arthur J.

**Portland**
Chapman, John Whitaker
Monaghan, Matthew John
Pooler, Delia Bridget

**Topsham**
MacAdam, James Joseph

**MARYLAND**

**Baltimore**
Kleid, Wallace
Snyder, Mark Allen
Tousey, Robert Ryan

**Bel Air**
Gintling, Karen Janette

**Hagerstown**
Schneider, Arthur

**Rockville**
Galiher, Richard Wilkinson, Jr.

**MASSACHUSETTS**

**Boston**
Carney, Gerard Barry

**Framingham**
Felper, David Michael

**Lexington**
Nason, Leonard Yoshimoto
**Peabody**
Papanickolas, Emmanuel N.
**Salem**
Del Vecchio, Debra Anne
**Somerset**
Sabra, Steven Peter
**Somerville**
Belfort, David Ernst
**South Hadley**
Sheridan, Daniel Joseph
**Springfield**
Low, Terrence Allen
**Worcester**
Reitzell, William R.

### MICHIGAN

**Detroit**
Glotta, Ronald Delon
Phillips, Dwight Wilburn
**Farmington Hills**
Cuttner, David Allan
**Fort Gratiot**
Carson, Robert William
**Grand Rapids**
Stadler, James Robert
**Lansing**
Deprez, Deborah Ann
**Saginaw**
Zanot, Craig Allen
**Southfield**
May, Alan Alfred
Mazey, Larry William
Ornstein, Alexander Thomas
**Springport**
McKay, M. Dale

### MINNESOTA

**Bemidji**
Baer, H. Carl, III
**Minneapolis**
Barrett, Michael D.
Bodas, Margie Ruth
Cuellar, Norbert
Fitch, Raymond William
Hektner, Candice Elaine
**Rochester**
Jacobsen, Van Paul
**Saint Cloud**
Seifert, Luke Michael
**Saint Paul**
Cassidy, Edward Q.
Engebretson, Andrew Peter
Krug, Michael Steven

### MISSISSIPPI

**Batesville**
Cook, William Leslie, Jr.
**Biloxi**
O'Barr, Bobby Gene, Sr.
Pritchard, Thomas Alexander
**Hattiesburg**
Adelman, Michael Schwartz
**Hernando**
Brown, William A.
**Jackson**
Burch, Donald Victor
**Oxford**
Freeland, John Hale
**Ridgeland**
Anderson, James Michael

### MISSOURI

**Cape Girardeau**
McManaman, Kenneth Charles
**Clayton**
Klein, Jerry A.
**Columbia**
Crepeau, Dewey Lee
Schwabe, John Bennett, II
**Hillsboro**
Guberman, Ted
**Jefferson City**
Easley, Glenn Edward
**Joplin**
Guillory, Jeffery Michael
**Kansas City**
Franke, Linda Frederick
**Marshall**
Peterson, William Allen
**Saint Louis**
Burke, Thomas Michael
Gallen, James Michael
Greenberg, Karen Alane
Kell, John Mark
Kolker, Scott Lee
Neill, Joseph Vincent
Susman, Robert M(ark)
**Sedalia**
Rice, James Briggs, Jr.
**Springfield**
Crites, Richard Don
Greene, Robert Lee

### MONTANA

**Butte**
Harrington, James Patrick
**Great Falls**
Overfelt, Clarence Lahugh
Seidlitz, John E.
**Missoula**
Morales, Julio K.

### NEBRASKA

**Holdrege**
Klein, Michael Clarence
**Lincoln**
Atwood, Raymond Percival, Jr.
Zink, Walter Earl, II
**Omaha**
Castello, David A.
Cuddigan, Timothy John
Fellman, Richard Mayer

### NEVADA

**Las Vegas**
Goldberg, Aubrey
Lucas, Craig John
Schwartz, Daniel Leonard
**Reno**
Santos, Herbert Joseph, Jr.

### NEW HAMPSHIRE

**Concord**
Mekeel, Robert K.
**Hooksett**
Rogers, David John
**Manchester**
Daley, Terrence Joseph
**Newington**
Lewis, John Michael
**Plymouth**
Hopkins, William Hayes
**Portsmouth**
Mason, J. William L.

### NEW JERSEY

**Elizabeth**
Kuhrt, Richard Lee
**Gloucester City**
Ford, Mark William
**Hackensack**
Gerlanc, Glenn Marc
**Jersey City**
Grossman, Randy
**Kenilworth**
Finn, Jerry Martin
**Lawrenceville**
Beyer, Vicki Woody
**Medford**
Evans, Jan Roger
**Metuchen**
Brause, Fred S., Jr.
**Moorestown**
Caniglia, Lawrence S.
**Newark**
Mattson, Leroy Harry
Weinberg, Shelley Ann
**Northfield**
Day, Christopher Mark
**Ocean**
Weisberg, Adam Jon
**Princeton**
Zarnowski, James David
**Toms River**
Berman, Michael Barry
**Trenton**
Gogo, Gregory
**Wayne**
Gelman, Jon Leonard
**Woodbridge**
Rosenberg, Jodi L.

### NEW MEXICO

**Albuquerque**
Cargo, David Francis
Crollett, Richard Jacques
Hale, Timothy S.
Word, Terry Mullins
**Farmington**
Titus, Victor Allen
**Hobbs**
Stout, Lowell
**Roswell**
Haines, Thomas David, Jr.
Romero, Freddie Joseph

### NEW YORK

**Chappaqua**
Whittlesey, John Williams
**Farmingdale**
O'Brien, Joan Susan
**Hauppauge**
Saminsky, Robert L.
**Lockport**
Syraski, Tina Louise
**New Windsor**
Ventry, Catherine Valerie
**New York**
Bergman, Robert Ira
DeCarlo, Donald Thomas
Douchkess, George
Lauer, Andrew Jay
Leibowitz, Nadine S.
Loscalzo, Anthony Joseph
Nevins, Arthur Gerard, Jr.
Owen, Richard Knowles
Romano, Edgar Ness
Shen, Michael
Steigman, Meredith Lee
Wagner, Michael G.
**Niagara Falls**
Levine, David Ethan
**Oneonta**
Hill, Peter Waverly
Rothermel, Richard Allan
**Rochester**
Gross, Bryon William
**Schenectady**
Taub, Eli Irwin
**Syracuse**
Zimmerman, Aaron Mark

### NORTH CAROLINA

**Asheville**
Chidnese, Patrick N.
Gantt, David
**Charlotte**
Harris, Richard Foster, III
**Durham**
Markham, Charles Buchanan
**Fayetteville**
Newman, Roger
**Hickory**
Ingle, John David
**High Point**
Aldridge, Bryant Taylor, Jr.
Floyd, Kimberly Hayes
**Raleigh**
Shyllon, Prince E.N.
Teague, Charles Woodrow
**Tarboro**
O'Malley, Susan Marie
**Winston Salem**
Durham, Richard Monroe

### OHIO

**Akron**
Jalbert, Michael Joseph
**Cincinnati**
Cohen, Edward
Waite, Jeffrey C.
**Cleveland**
Alcox, Patrick Joseph
Baughman, R(obert) Patrick
Birne, Kenneth Andrew
Duber, Michael Joseph
Gruhin, Michael H.
Krawczak, Kenneth Francis
Sanislo, Paul Steve
Steiger, Sheldon Gerald
**Columbus**
Ayers, James Cordon
Butler, Robert Anthony
Smallwood, Carl Demouy
Sprader, Bobbie S.
Tripp, Thomas Neal
**Dayton**
Piercy, James R.
Sutton, Richard Stansbury
**Hamilton**
Gattermeyer, Daniel J.
**Portsmouth**
Gerlach, Franklin Theodore
**Toledo**
Baker, Richard Southworth
Iorio, Theodore
**Warren**
Newendop, Paul William
**Youngstown**
Ausnehmer, John Edward
Jeren, John Anthony, Jr.
Wellman, Thomas Peter

### OKLAHOMA

**Oklahoma City**
Featherly, Henry Frederick
Kouri, Harry J., III
Simpson, Michael Wayne
**Tulsa**
McGonigle, Richard Thomas
Strecker, David Eugene
Sutton, Jonathan Mark
Taliaferro, Bruce Owen

### OREGON

**Albany**
Kryger, Jon David
**Newport**
Greco, Guy Benjamin
**Portland**
Bovarnick, Paul Simon
Robinowitz, Charles
Schuster, Philip Frederick, II
**Salem**
Hittle, David William
Roy, Matthew Lansing
Walsh, Richard Michael

### PENNSYLVANIA

**Allentown**
Altemose, Mark Kenneth
McGrail-Szabo, Sharon Joan
**Beaver**
Petrush, John Joseph
**Camp Hill**
Merlo, Perry David
**Erie**
Bernard, Bruce William
**Frackville**
Domalakes, Paul George
**Harrisburg**
Cook, Thomas S.
Hafer, Joseph Page
Kendall, Keith Edward
**King Of Prussia**
Dorfman, Frederick Niles
**Leola**
Eaby, Christian Earl
**Lock Haven**
Miceli, Frank S.
Rosamilia, Charles R.
**Meadville**
Youngs, Christopher Jay
**Media**
Farber, Howard
Malloy, Michael Joseph
Meloni, Kathryn Ann
**Mount Pleasant**
Johnson, Michael A.
**Narberth**
Malloy, Martin Gerard
**New Castle**
Flannery, Harry Audley
Sapienza, Charles Pat, Jr.
**New Kensington**
Joseph, Daniel
**Philadelphia**
Brigham, Martin Kenneth
Fine, Stephanie Beth
Heslin, Gary Phillip
Kunnel, Joseph Mathew
Ossip, Michael J.
Patrick, Paula Antoinette
Prim, Joseph Anthony
**Pittsburgh**
Bochicchio, Vito Salvatore
Braszo, John J.
Breault, Theodore Edward
Conley, Martha Richards
Keenan, C. Robert, III
Leibowitz, Marvin
Loch, Robert Anthony
McKenzie, Thomas James
**Pottsville**
Tamulonis, Frank Louis, Jr.
**Punxsutawney**
Lorenzo, Nicholas Francis, Jr.
**Scranton**
O'Malley, Todd J.
Pocius, James Edward
Wilson, Charles Frank
**Sharon**
Dill, William Allen
Kosmowski, Audra Michele
**Washington**
Chaban, Lawrence Richard
Mitchell, Clark A.
Richman, Stephen I.
**Wilkes Barre**
Dalessandro, Sherry Ann
**York**
Senft, John L.

### RHODE ISLAND

**Providence**
Cosentino, Robert J(ohn)

### SOUTH CAROLINA

**Anderson**
Krause, Steven Michael
**Charleston**
Garrett, Gordon Henderson
Spitz, Hugo Max
**Columbia**
Blanton, Hoover Clarence
Bluestein, Margaret Miles
Kelly, D. Michael
Meyer, Patricia R.
**Greenville**
Christian, Warren Harold, Jr.
Christophillis, Constantine S.
Farry, Michael Allen
Gallivan, Henry Mills
**Kingstree**
McFadden, Helen Tyler
**Langley**
Bell, Robert Morrall
**N Charleston**
Wigger, Jarrel L.
**Winnsboro**
Goode, Kenneth George

### TENNESSEE

**Chattanooga**
Dennis, Tricia I.
Johnson, John Walter, III
Newton, Michael David
Thompson, Neal Lewis
**Etowah**
Parker, Eugene LeRoy, III
**Greeneville**
Welch, Lawrence Andrew, Jr.
Wright, Thomas Jon
**Jackson**
Drew, Gayden, IV
Nicks, Paul Todd
**Johnson City**
Meade, Evan McDaniel
**Knoxville**
Houser, Timothy Curtis
Johnson, Steven Boyd
Murray, Rebecca Brake
Ownby, Jere Franklin, III
Wedekind, David N.
Wheeler, John Watson
**Memphis**
Grubb, Steven Cochran
Pfrommer, Michael Paul
Russell, James Franklin
**Nashville**
Baugh, Mark Anthony
Butler, Jack A.
Clayton, Daniel Louis
Cooney, Charles Hayes
Hardison Reisner, Sarah Castle
Hildebrand, Donald Dean
Youngblood, Elaine Michele

### TEXAS

**Austin**
Colburn, Stuart Dale
Pena, Richard
Pluymen, Bert W.
**Corpus Christi**
Johnson, John Lynn
**Dallas**
Balido, Carlos A.
Doyle, Mark Anthony
Levin, Hervey Phillip
**El Paso**
Fogel, Lark House
**Fort Worth**
Stewart, Mark Steven
Streck, Frederick Louis, III
**Galveston**
Kilgore, Jeffrey Harper
**Harlingen**
Pope, William L.
**Houston**
Michael, Charles Joseph
Pitts, Gary Benjamin
**Longview**
Holmes, Clifton Lee (Scrappy Holmes)
McMahon, Mark Preston
**San Antonio**
Brito, Maria Teresa
Henry, Peter York
Maisel, Margaret Rose Meyer
Wennermark, John David

### VERMONT

**Barre**
FitzGerald, Geoffrey M.
**Brattleboro**
Munzing, Richard Harry
**Rutland**
O'Rourke, William Andrew, III
**Springfield**
Boxer, Andrew Carey

### VIRGINIA

**Alexandria**
Cassell, Richard Emmett
Green, James Francis
**Ashland**
d'Evegnee, Charles Paul
**Bristol**
Wise, Donald Edward
**Charlottesville**
Kendall, Gary Wheeler
**Fairfax**
Bardott, Heather Kathleen
**Hopewell**
Marks, Bryant Mayes, Jr.
**Newport News**
Hatten, Robert Randolph
**Richmond**
O'Toole, Deborah Shea

### WASHINGTON

**Richland**
Barr, Carlos Harvey
**Seattle**
Kohles, David Allan
Scott, Brian David
Warner, Charles Ford
**Spokane**
Bunch, Jeffrey R.
Harbaugh, Daniel Paul
Pontarolo, Michael Joseph
**Tacoma**
Condon, David Bruce

### WEST VIRGINIA

**Beckley**
Stacy, Don Matthew
**Fairmont**
Cohen, Richard Paul
**Martinsburg**
Rose, Laura Rauch

### WISCONSIN

**Baraboo**
Vesely, Tori Ann
**Black River Falls**
Lister, Thomas Edward
**Delafield**
Hausman, C. Michael
**Hudson**
Lundeen, Bradley Curtis
**Madison**
Bruchs, Amy O'Brien
McCusker, William LaValle
Schmid, John Henry, Jr.
**Merrill**
Wulf, William Arthur
**Milwaukee**
Kmiec, Steven Gerard
Reardon, James Patrick
**Racine**
Rudebusch, Alice Ann
**Rhinelander**
Reese, Kirk David
**Union Grove**
Stern, Walter Wolf, III
**Wausau**
Gray, Robert Joseph
Long, Jerome Allen
Molinaro, Thomas J.
Strande, Jeffrey Jay

### ADDRESS UNPUBLISHED

Berman, Richard Bruce
Branstetter, Cecil Dewey, Sr.
Dixon, Edward Kenneth
Easterling, Charles Armo
Embry, Stephen Creston
Grutz, James Arthur
Harrington, Donald Francis
Hibbert, David Wilson
Hoffman, Alan Craig
Keltner, Cecil Green
Locke, Laurence S.
McFerrin, James Hamil
Rosen, Stephen Leslie
Slipski, Ronald Edward
Wells, Wayne Alton
Zelechiwsky, Bohdan John

## OTHER

### UNITED STATES

### ALABAMA

**Birmingham**
Norris, Robert Wheeler *Ethics*
Small, Clarence Merilton, Jr.
**Mobile**
Hannan, David Carroll
**Montgomery**
Eubanks, Ronald W.

### ALASKA

**Anchorage**
Jones, Thomas Brooks

### ARIZONA

**Phoenix**
McRae, Hamilton Eugene, III
Mulvihill, David Brian
**Scottsdale**
Roberts, Jean Reed *Elder*

### CALIFORNIA

**El Segundo**
Van Dam, Margot Nicole *Media*
**Los Angeles**
Bonner, Robert Cleve
Link, George Hamilton
Morganstern, Myrna Dorothy *Election*
**Oakland**
Lomhoff, Peter George *Elder*

**Sacramento**
Day, James McAdam, Jr.
Perschbacher, Debra Bassett
**San Francisco**
Davies, Paul Lewis, Jr.
Gibson, Virginia Lee *Fiduciary*
Millstein, David J.
**Santa Monica**
Prewoznik, Jerome Frank

### COLORADO

**Denver**
Cockrell, Richard Carter

### DISTRICT OF COLUMBIA

**Washington**
Auerbach, Jeffrey Ira *Biotechnology*
Bell, James Frederick
Bishop, James Dodson
Cheston, Sheila Carol *Election*
Johnson, Philip McBride *Commodities*
Meer, Cary Jesse *Commodities*
Millhauser, Marguerite Sue
Pollak, Mark A.
Rill, James Franklin
Simpson, John M.

### FLORIDA

**Aventura**
Fishman, Barry Stuart
**Fort Lauderdale**
Conklin, Howard Lawrence *Trade*
**Fort Myers**
Fisher, Michael Bruce
**Lady Lake**
Clements, Allen, Jr.
**Leesburg**
Austin, Robert Eugene, Jr.
**Miami**
Seitz, Patricia Ann
**Orlando**
Durie, Jack Frederick, Jr.
**Saint Petersburg**
Hadsall, John D.
**Sarasota**
Wise, Warren Roberts
**Tallahassee**
DeFoor, J. Allison, II *Technology*
Holcomb, Lyle Donald, Jr.
**Tampa**
Hapner, Elizabeth Lynn

### GEORGIA

**Atlanta**
Alexander, Kent B.
**Marietta**
Stein, Julie Lynne *Advertising*

### ILLINOIS

**Carbondale**
Habiger, Richard J. *Elder*
**Chicago**
Early, Bert Hylton
Getzendanner, Susan
Nicolaides, Mary *Elder*
Nissen, William John *Commodities*
Timmer, Stephen Blaine *Art*
Wine-Banks, Jill Susan
**Galva**
Massie, Michael Earl *Agriculture*
**Pittsfield**
Burrows, Cecil J.
**Skokie**
Sitrick, David Howard *Biotechnology*
**Wheaton**
Fawell, Blanche Hill *Election*

### INDIANA

**New Castle**
Schiesswohl, Cynthia Rae Schlegel *Religion*
**Terre Haute**
Newmeyer, Robert J. *Election*

### IOWA

**Cedar Rapids**
Richards, Allan Max *Agriculture*
**Des Moines**
Hoffmann, Michael Richard
Tyler, Paul Richard
Wine, Donald Arthur
**Spirit Lake**
Larson, David Christopher

### KANSAS

**Topeka**
Holmes, Richard Winn

### KENTUCKY

**Lexington**
Vimont, Richard Elgin *Equine*

### MARYLAND

**Bowie**
Bagaria, Gail Farrell *Elder*
**Frederick**
Sica, John *Agriculture*

### MASSACHUSETTS

**Belmont**
Simpson, Russell Avington
**Boston**
Jones, Sheldon Atwell *Investment*
Kassler, Haskell A. *Election*
Vestner, Eliot N., Jr.
**Framingham**
Gould, Rodney Elliott *Travel*
**Springfield**
Miller, J(ohn) Wesley, III *Art*
Sweeney, Kevin Michael

### MICHIGAN

**Detroit**
Charla, Leonard Francis *Art*
Hanson, Victor G. *Maritime*
**Farmington Hills**
Birnkrant, Sherwin Maurice *Municipal (excluding bonds)*
**Jackson**
Brunner, James Edwin
**Owosso**
Shulaw, Richard A.

### MINNESOTA

**Edina**
Lillehaug, David Lee
**Minneapolis**
Dayton, Charles Kelly
**Rochester**
Somsen, Henry Northrop
**Saint Paul**
Duckstad, Jon R. *Mental health*

### MISSOURI

**Saint Louis**
Terschluse, Val

### NEBRASKA

**Omaha**
Caporale, D. Nick

### NEVADA

**Las Vegas**
Chesnut, Carol Fitting *Elder*

### NEW JERSEY

**Jersey City**
Guarini, Frank J. *Trade*
**Moorestown**
Begley, Thomas D., Jr. *Elder*
Slemmer, Carl Weber, Jr.
**Morristown**
Pollock, Stewart Glasson
**Newark**
Simmons, Peter
**Pompton Plains**
Ludemann, Cathie Jane *Elder*
**Somerset**
Magness, Michael Kenneth
**Trenton**
Harbeck, Dorothy Anne *Election*
**Wayne**
Awerdick, John Holmes *Advertising*

### NEW YORK

**Goshen**
Owen, Joseph Gabriel
**Granite Spgs**
Stokes, Harry McKinney *Equine*
**Huntington**
Robinson, Kenneth Patrick *Technology*
**Jericho**
Hecht, Donald Stuart *Elder*
**Merrick**
Heller, Fred Ira *Media*
**New York**
Birnbaum, Sheila L.
Davis, Evan Anderson
Filler, Ronald Howard *Commodities*
Fleischer, Arthur, Jr.
Freund, Fred A.
Glusband, Steven Joseph *Commodities*
Goldsmith, Gerald P. *Election*
Greenbaum, Jeffrey Alan *Advertising*
Kailas, Leo George *Commodities*
Kassebaum, John Philip *Art*
McGoldrick, John Lewis
Parkinson, Thomas Ignatius, Jr.
Resor, Stanley Rogers
Reynard, Muriel Joyce *Advertising*
Seligman, Delice *Art*
Vernon, Darryl Mitchell *Animal welfare*

### NORTH CAROLINA

**Charlotte**
Claytor, William Mimms *Elder*
**Raleigh**
Hargrove, Wade Hampton *Media*

### OHIO

**Columbus**
Petro, James Michael
Pryor, David W. *Agriculture*
Woods, William Hunt *Fidelity and surety*
**Dayton**
Pietz, Lynne Pepi *Elder*

### OREGON

**Pendleton**
Rew, Lawrence B. *Agriculture*

### PENNSYLVANIA

**Bensalem**
Hoffa, Robert Alan *Equine*
**Chadds Ford**
Bainbridge, John Seaman
**Hilltown**
Hetherington, John Joseph *Elder*
**Langhorne**
Hillje, Barbara Brown *Elder*
**Media**
Rainer, G. Bradley *Ethics*
**Philadelphia**
Bloom, Michael Anthony *Ethics*
**Pittsburgh**
Simpson, Craig Evan

### RHODE ISLAND

**Little Compton**
Caron, Wilfred Rene

### SOUTH CAROLINA

**Greenville**
Simmons, Charles Bedford, Jr.

### TENNESSEE

**Knoxville**
Lloyd, Francis Leon, Jr.
**Nashville**
May, Joseph Leserman (Jack May)

### TEXAS

**Austin**
Bray, Austin Coleman, Jr. *Election*
Moss, Bill Ralph *Ethics*
**Dallas**
Miers, Harriet E. *Trade*
**De Soto**
Boyanton, Janet Shafer *Elder*
**Houston**
Chavez, John Anthony *Trade*
Fallis, Norma Eleanor *Animal welfare*
Gilbert, Keith Thomas *Election*
**San Antonio**
Hardy, Harvey Louchard
Sakai, Peter A.

### UTAH

**Salt Lake City**
Gardiner, Lester Raymond, Jr.
Linebaugh, Kent B. *Equine*

### VIRGINIA

**Alexandria**
Carlson, J(ohn) Philip
Rubin, Burton Jay
Schroeder, James White
Wilner, Morton Harrison
**Chesapeake**
North, Kenneth E(arl) *Religion*

### WASHINGTON

**Seattle**
Dussault, William Leonard Ernest *Mental health*
Kelly, Kevin Francis *Biotechnology*
Lybeck, Kevin Lee *Surety*
Parsons, A. Peter *Technology*
**Spokane**
Sayre, Richard Layton *Elder*

### WISCONSIN

**Milwaukee**
Noelke, Paul
Sanfilippo, Jon Walter

### ADDRESS UNPUBLISHED

Amberg, Stanley Louis *Trade*
Baughn, Alfred Fairhurst
Coliver, Norman
Crawford, Muriel Laura
Fowler, Donald Raymond
Givens, Richard Ayres
Gold, Harold
Harvitt, Adrianne Stanley *Commodities*
Hedien, Colette Johnston
Lackland, John
Lardent, Esther Ferster
Moylan, James Joseph *Commodities*
Pawlik, James David
Perrin, Edward Patterson
Redmond, Lawrence Craig *Election*
Regenstreif, Herbert *Religion*
Smoke, Richard Edwin *Investment*
Turnheim, Joy Karen
Walker, Craig Michael *Technology*
Wimmer, Nancy T. *Elder*

# Professional Index

## ARBITRATION AND MEDIATION

### UNITED STATES

#### ALABAMA

**Birmingham**
Bird, John Commons
Furman, Howard

#### ALASKA

**Anchorage**
Anderson, Kathleen Gay

#### CALIFORNIA

**Arcadia**
Mc Cormack, Francis Xavier
**Lancaster**
Finch, Susan Chloë
**Long Beach**
Feinberg, Cheryl Lackman
**Los Angeles**
Adler, Sara
Delahunty, Jane Goodman
**Petaluma**
Castagnola, George Joseph, Jr.
**Rancho Palos Verdes**
Brigden, Ann Schwartz
**Rolling Hills Estates**
Rumbaugh, Charles Earl
**Saint Helena**
Robertson, William Abbott
**Santa Monica**
Costello, Edward J., Jr.
**Santa Rosa**
Henderson, Joe H.
**Stanford**
Mann, J. Keith
**Van Nuys**
Arabian, Armand

#### COLORADO

**Boulder**
Meyrich, Steven
**Colorado Springs**
Carol, Joan
**Denver**
Carrigan, Jim R.

#### FLORIDA

**Clearwater**
Bairstow, Frances Kanevsky
**Jacksonville**
Hair, Mattox S.
**Miami**
Canner, Gary F.
**Ormond Beach**
Barker, Robert Osborne (Bob Barker)
**Palm Beach**
Brett-Major, Lin
**Sarasota**
Stephens, Paula Christine (Polly)

#### GEORGIA

**Atlanta**
Ordover, Abraham Philip
Schowalter, Deborah

#### ILLINOIS

**Antioch**
Heyl, Erica Lynn

#### LOUISIANA

**Metairie**
Stern, Lynne Rothschild

#### MAINE

**Richmond**
Ogilvie, Gail

#### MARYLAND

**Greenbelt**
Jascourt, Hugh D.

#### MASSACHUSETTS

**Brookline**
Ellis, Sharon Henderson
**Weston**
Lashman, L. Edward

#### MICHIGAN

**Dearborn**
Kahn, Mark Leo
**Lansing**
Burns, Marshall Shelby
**Northville**
Hariri, V. M.
**Southfield**
Gordon, Arnold Mark

#### MINNESOTA

**Minneapolis**
Hoffman, John Richard
**Saint Cloud**
Lalor, Edward David Darrell

#### MISSOURI

**Kansas City**
Clark, Charles Edward

#### NEW JERSEY

**Berlin**
Marmero, Franc J(oseph) H(enry)

#### NEW MEXICO

**Ruidoso**
Martines, Sue B.

#### NEW YORK

**Albany**
Selchick, Jeffrey Mark
**Carle Place**
Dubinsky, Donna
**New Hartford**
Chapin, Mary Q.
**New York**
Hallingby, Jo Davis
**Oneida**
Sullivan, Robert F.

#### PENNSYLVANIA

**Elkins Park**
Dickstein, Joan Borteck

#### SOUTH CAROLINA

**Saint Helena Island**
Scoville, Laurence McConway, Jr.

#### TEXAS

**Dallas**
Leeper, Harold Harris

#### VIRGINIA

**Fairfax**
Scott, Robert William
**Lynchburg**
Healy, Joseph Francis, Jr.
**Manassas**
Weimer, Peter Dwight

#### WISCONSIN

**Fish Creek**
Henke, Robert John

#### ADDRESS UNPUBLISHED

Ashe, Bernard Flemming
Baker, Patricia (Jean)
Gaunt, Janet Lois
Harbus, Richard
Keeley, Michael Glenn
Monsma, Robbie Elizabeth

## EDUCATION

### UNITED STATES

#### ALABAMA

**Birmingham**
Riegert, Robert Adolf
Weeks, Arthur Andrew
**Mobile**
Campbell, Robert Craig, III
**Orange Beach**
Adams, Daniel Fenton
**Tuscaloosa**
Randall, Kenneth C.

#### ARIZONA

**Scottsdale**
Starr, Isidore
**Tempe**
Matheson, Alan Adams
Spritzer, Ralph Simon
Teson, Fernando Roberto
White, Patricia Denise
**Tucson**
Fortman, Marvin
Massaro, Toni Marie
Woods, Winton D.

#### ARKANSAS

**Fayetteville**
Copeland, John Dewayne
Jones, Louis, Jr. (Bucky Jones)
**Little Rock**
Paulson, Terry Clayton
Wright, Robert Ross, III

#### CALIFORNIA

**Aliso Viejo**
Llorente, Alex Jeronimo
**Anaheim**
Williams, Parham Henry, Jr.
**Berkeley**
Berring, Robert Charles, Jr.
Hetland, John Robert
Kadish, Sanford Harold
Kay, Herma Hill
Messinger, Sheldon L(eopold)
Moran, Rachel
Samuelson, Pamela
Scheiber, Harry N.
**Beverly Hills**
Shire, Harold Raymond
**Camarillo**
Long, Andre Edwin
**Claremont**
Gann, Pamela Brooks
**Costa Mesa**
Reich, Peter Lester
**Cypress**
Katz, Cherol Bobby
**Davis**
Bartosic, Florian
Glennon, Michael John
Johnson, Kevin Raymond
Oakley, John Bilyeu
Perschbacher, Rex Robert
Wolk, Bruce Alan
**Fullerton**
Bakken, Gordon Morris
Frizell, Samuel
**La Jolla**
Siegan, Bernard Herbert
**Larkspur**
Ratner, David Louis
**Los Angeles**
Abrams, Norman
Arlen, Jennifer Hall
Bice, Scott Haas
Blumberg, Grace Ganz
Capron, Alexander Morgan
Follick, Edwin Duane
Jordan, Robert Leon
Mandel, Joseph David
Pugsley, Robert Adrian
Raeder, Myrna Sharon
Sumner, James DuPre, Jr.
Varat, Jonathan D.
**Malibu**
Phillips, Ronald Frank
**Menlo Park**
Wegner, Judith Welch
**Monterey**
Kadushin, Karen D.
**Newport Beach**
Naffah, Eli A.
**Pacific Palisades**
Schwartz, Murray Louis
**Pomona**
Palmer, Robert Alan
**Sacramento**
Landsberg, Brian Keith
Malloy, Michael Patrick
Wile, Philip Hodges
**San Diego**
Brooks, Roy Lavon
Cohn, Marjorie F.
Fellmeth, Robert Charles
Paupp, Terrence Edward
Rai, Arti K.
Ryan, Barry Thomas
Smith, Steven Ray
**San Francisco**
Amar, Vikram David
Donnici, Peter Joseph
Folberg, Harold Jay
Kane, Mary Kay
Lee, Richard Diebold
McKelvey, Judith Grant
Wong, Francisco Raimundo
**Santa Clara**
Alexander, George Jonathon
Blawie, James Louis
**Stanford**
Babcock, Barbara Allen
Bagley, Constance Elizabeth
Brest, Paul A.
Donohue, John Joseph
Rhode, Deborah Lynn
Sullivan, Kathleen M.
Williams, Howard Russell
**Stockton**
Armstrong, Victoria Elizabeth
**Walnut**
McKee, Catherine Lynch
**Woodland Hills**
Barrett, Robert Matthew

#### COLORADO

**Boulder**
Bruff, Harold Hastings
DuVivier, Katharine Keyes
Fiflis, Ted James
Vigil, Daniel Agustin
**Denver**
Nanda, Ved Prakash
Rich, Ben Arthur
Walker, Timothy Blake
**Greeley**
Shadwick, Gerald
**U S A F Academy**
Center, Charles R.

#### CONNECTICUT

**Derby**
McEvoy, Sharlene Ann
**Hamden**
Bix, Brian
Margulies, Martin B.
Robinson, Toni
**Hartford**
Blumberg, Phillip Irvin
Macgill, Hugh C.
Wolfson, Nicholas
**New Haven**
Ackerman, Bruce Arnold
Ellickson, Robert Chester
Fiss, Owen M.
Freed, Daniel Josef
Goldstein, Abraham Samuel
Hansmann, Henry Baethke
Kronman, Anthony Townsend
Priest, George L.
Rose-Ackerman, Susan
Simon, John Gerald
Wedgwood, Ruth
Yandle, Stephen Thomas
**New London**
Dupont, Ralph Paul
**Storrs Mansfield**
Tucker, Edwin Wallace
**Torrington**
Lippincott, Walter Edward

#### DISTRICT OF COLUMBIA

**Washington**
Aaronson, David Ernest
Anderson, John Bayard
Barron, Jerome Aure
Bradlow, Daniel David
Carter, Barry Edward
Elliott, Edwin Donald, Jr.
Firestone, Charles Morton
Friedenthal, Jack H.
Goldblatt, Steven Harris
Goldschmid, Harvey Jerome
Gostin, Lawrence
Guttman, Egon
Jamar, Steven Dwight
Katzmann, Robert Allen
Kovacic, William Evan
Milstein, Elliott Steven
Provost, James H(arrison)
Rabb, Harriet Schaffer
Raskin, Jamin Ben
Rohner, Ralph John
Saltzburg, Stephen Allan
Silecchia, Lucia Ann
Sohn, Louis Bruno
Starrs, James Edward
Strand, Joan H.
Tigar, Michael Edward
Treanor, William Michael
Vazquez, Carlos Manuel
Wallace, Don, Jr.
Weiss, Edith Brown
Wilmarth, Arthur Edward, Jr.

#### FLORIDA

**Coral Gables**
Rosenn, Keith Samuel
**Deland**
Pearce, Richard Warren
**Fort Lauderdale**
Jarvis, Robert Mark
Joseph, Paul R
Mintz, Joel Alan
**Fort Myers**
Zeldes, Ilya Michael
**Gainesville**
Freeland, James M. Jackson
Matasar, Richard Allan
**Jupiter**
del Russo, Alessandra Luini
**Miami**
Beckham, Walter Hull, Jr.
Matthews, Douglas Eugene
**North Miami**
Batavia, Andrew I.
Bonham-Yeaman, Doria
**Opa Locka**
Light, Alfred Robert
**Saint Augustine**
Poland, Richard Clayton
**Saint Petersburg**
Carrere, Charles Scott
Elson, Charles Myer
Jacob, Bruce Robert
**Sarasota**
Wagner, Wenceslas Joseph
**Tallahassee**
D'Alemberte, Talbot (Sandy D'Alemberte)
**Tarpon Springs**
Mann, Robert Trask

#### GEORGIA

**Athens**
Beaird, James Ralph
Huszagh, Fredrick Wickett
Shipley, David Elliott
Spurgeon, Edward Dutcher
**Atlanta**
Cooper, James Russell
Hunter, Howard Owen
Knowles, Marjorie Fine
Landau, Michael B.
Marvin, Charles Arthur
Podgor, Ellen Sue
Witte, John, Jr.
**Macon**
Dessem, R. Lawrence
**Stockbridge**
Rehberger, Robert Lee

#### HAWAII

**Honolulu**
Bloede, Victor Carl
Callies, David Lee
Iijima, Chris K.
Miller, Richard Sherwin

#### IDAHO

**Moscow**
Vincenti, Sheldon Arnold

#### ILLINOIS

**Champaign**
Kindt, John Warren, Sr.
Mc Cord, John Harrison
Mengler, Thomas M.
Nowak, John E.
Stone, Victor J.
**Chicago**
Appel, Nina Schick
Baird, Douglas Gordon
Bannister, Shelley Ashley
Bennett, Robert William
Cassel, Douglass Watts, Jr.
Elwin, James William, Jr.
Garth, Bryant Geoffrey
Hablutzel, Nancy Zimmerman
Hablutzel, Philip Norman
Hermann, Donald Harold James
Herzog, Fred F.
Hillman, Jordan Jay
Hopkins, Kevin L.
Kerstetter, Wayne Arthur
Landes, William M.
McCormack, John Leo
Meltzer, Bernard David
Monahan, Marie Adornetto
Morris, Norval
O'Malley, John Daniel
Palm, Gary Howard
Presser, Stephen Bruce
Schulhofer, Stephen Joseph
Shoenberger, Allen Edward
Steinman, Joan Ellen
Stone, Geoffrey Richard
Stone, Randolph Noel
Van Zandt, David E.
**De Kalb**
Schneider, Daniel Max
**Highland Park**
Ruder, David Sturtevant
**Saint Charles**
Alfini, James Joseph
**Springfield**
Ford, Nancy L.
Spielman, Bethany June
**Wilmette**
Atkinson, Jeff John Frederick

#### INDIANA

**Bloomington**
Aman, Alfred Charles, Jr.
Cate, Fred Harrison
Dilts, Jon Paul
Hughes, Sarah Jane
O'Leary, Rosemary
Palmer, Judith Grace
Shreve, Gene Russell
**Fort Wayne**
Spielman, Kim Morgan
**Indianapolis**
Falender, Debra Ann
Funk, David Albert
Krotoszynski, Ronald James, Jr.
Polston, Ronald Wayne
**Muncie**
Ervin, Mark Alan
**Notre Dame**
Gunn, Alan
Link, David Thomas
**Valparaiso**
Hires, Jack Merle
**West Lafayette**
Scaletta, Phillip Jasper

#### IOWA

**Des Moines**
Begleiter, Martin David
Edwards, John Duncan
**Grinnell**
Osgood, Russell King
**Iowa City**
Hines, N. William
Wing, Adrien Katherine

#### KANSAS

**Lawrence**
Turnbull, H. Rutherford, III
**Topeka**
Concannon, James M.
Elrod, Linda Diane Henry

#### KENTUCKY

**Alexandria**
Rini, Alice Gertrude
**Fort Thomas**
Short, David Carlos
**Highland Heights**
Brewer, Edward Cage, III
Jones, William Rex
Seaver, Robert Leslie

**Lexington**
Fowler, Michael Ross
Michael, Douglas Charles
Oberst, Paul
Schwemm, Robert G.

### LOUISIANA

**Baton Rouge**
Bowers, James Winfield
Ghetti, Michelle Ward
Lamonica, P(aul) Raymond
Schroeder, Leila Obier
**New Orleans**
Abriel, Evangeline G.
Childress, Steven Alan
Kramer, John Robert
Osakwe, Christopher
Palmer, Vernon Valentine
Ponoroff, Lawrence
Sherman, Edward Francis

### MAINE

**Lewiston**
Kessler, Mark Allen

### MARYLAND

**Baltimore**
Anderson, José F.
Herr, Stanley Sholom
Milio, Louis Romolo
**Hanover**
Zohny, A. Y.

### MASSACHUSETTS

**Amherst**
Katsh, M. Ethan
Mazor, Lester Jay
**Andover**
Boumil, Marcia Mobilia
**Boston**
Abrams, Roger Ian
Bae, Frank S. H.
Carter, T(homas) Barton
Cass, Ronald Andrew
Davis, Wendy Beth
Daynard, Richard Alan
Frankel, Tamar
Freehling, Daniel Joseph
Gordon, Wendy Jane
Hall, David
Marks, Stephen Paul
Nolan, John Joseph
Park, William Wynnewood
Scharf, Michael Paul
Whitters, James Payton, III
**Cambridge**
Aldave, Barbara Bader
Andrews, William Dorey
Bok, Derek
Clark, Robert Charles
Dershowitz, Alan Morton
Fisher, Roger Dummer
Fried, Charles
Glendon, Mary Ann
Kaplow, Louis
Kaufman, Andrew Lee
Miller, Arthur Raphael
Patton, Bruce M.
Ray, Stephen Alan
Schauer, Frederick Franklin
Steiner, Henry Jacob
von Mehren, Arthur Taylor
Warren, Elizabeth
**Chestnut Hill**
Garvey, John Hugh
**Medford**
Salacuse, Jeswald William
**Newton**
Coquillette, Daniel Robert
Huber, Richard Gregory
**North Dartmouth**
Conward, Cynthia Mae
**Worcester**
Harris, William Theodore, Jr.

### MICHIGAN

**Ann Arbor**
Allen, Layman Edward
Bollinger, Lee Carroll
Duquette, Donald Norman
Kamisar, Yale
Lehman, Jeffrey Sean
Reed, John Wesley
St. Antoine, Theodore Joseph
White, James Boyd
**Detroit**
Lamborn, LeRoy Leslie
**East Lansing**
Bitensky, Susan Helen
Starnes, Cynthia
**Grosse Pointe Park**
Centner, Charles William
**Lansing**
Latovick, Paula R(ae)
Rooney, John Philip
Stockmeyer, Norman Otto, Jr.

### MINNESOTA

**Minneapolis**
Gardebring, Sandra S.
Kilbourn, William Douglas, Jr.
Sullivan, E. Thomas
Yudof, Mark George
**Saint Paul**
Daly, Joseph Leo
Failinger, Marie Anita
Jones, C. Paul
Kirwin, Kenneth Francis

### MISSISSIPPI

**Jackson**
West, Carol Catherine
**University**
Abbott, Guthrie Turner

### MISSOURI

**Columbia**
Peth, Howard Allen
Westbrook, James Edwin
**Kansas City**
Cooper, Corinne
Popper, Robert
**Saint Louis**
Bernstein, Merton Clay
Flagg, Barbara Jean
Keating, Daniel Louis
Levin, Ronald Mark
Needham, Carol Ann
Seligman, Joel

### NEBRASKA

**Lincoln**
Milligan, Cynthia Hardin
**Omaha**
Forbes, Franklin Sim

### NEVADA

**Las Vegas**
Goodwin, John Robert
Morgan, Richard J.

### NEW HAMPSHIRE

**Exeter**
Vogelman, Lawrence Allen
**Hanover**
Prager, Susan Westerberg
**Nashua**
Post, Ruth-Ellen

### NEW JERSEY

**Cherry Hill**
Dunfee, Thomas Wylie
**Montclair**
Mullins, Margaret Ann Frances
**New Brunswick**
Martin, Shannon E.
Stamato, Linda Ann Lautenschlaeger
**Newark**
Blumrosen, Alfred William
Blumrosen, Ruth Gerber
Burt, Jacquelyn Jean-Marie
Defeis, Elizabeth Frances
Reams, Bernard Dinsmore, Jr.
**West Orange**
Askin, Marilyn

### NEW YORK

**Albany**
Miccio, G. Kristian
Sponsler, Thomas H.
Sprow, Howard Thomas
Unger, Gere Nathan
**Brooklyn**
Graham, Arnold Harold
Remington, Clark A.
Sebok, Anthony James
Wexler, Joan G.
**Buffalo**
Pitegoff, Peter Robert
Scales-Trent, Judy
**Corning**
Avagliano, Francis Anthony
**Flushing**
Farago, John Michael
**Hempstead**
Agata, Burton C.
Rabinowitz, Stuart
**Huntington**
Pratt, George Cheney
**Ithaca**
Alexander, Gregory Stewart
Barcelo, John James, III
Clermont, Kevin Michael
Cramton, Roger Conant
Eisenberg, Theodore
Wolfram, Charles William
**Jamaica**
Helldorfer, Bernard George
**Neponsit**
Re, Edward Domenic
**New York**
Abramovsky, Abraham
Bell, Derrick Albert
Black, Barbara Aronstein
Chapnick, Ellen P.
Chiang, Yung Frank
Cunningham, Lawrence Aloysius
Dorsen, Norman
Duffy, John Fitzgerald
Eisgruber, Christopher L.
Estreicher, Samuel
Eustice, James Samuel
Farnsworth, E(dward) Allan
Fine, Toni Michele
First, Harry
Golick, Toby
Grad, Frank Paul
Greenawalt, Robert Kent
Greenberg, Jack
Greenberger, Howard Leroy
Guggenheim, Martin Franklin
Hellawell, Robert
Henkin, Louis
Hill, Alfred
Kaden, Lewis B.
Kernochan, John Marshall
King, Lawrence Philip
Leebron, David Wayne
Liebman, Lance Malcolm
Marcus, Maria Lenhoff
Mundheim, Robert Harry
Parsons, Inga Lorraine
Redlich, Norman
Rigolosi, Elaine La Monica
Rubino, Victor Joseph
Sandler, Ross
Schmertz, Eric Joseph
Schwartz, William
Sexton, John Edward
Siegel, Stanley
Stewart, Richard Burleson
Strauss, Peter L(ester)
Teclaff, Ludwik Andrzej
Wellington, Harry Hillel
**Staten Island**
Gatti, John Gabriel
**Syracuse**
Hancock, Stewart F., Jr.
Micale, Frederick J.
**White Plains**
Ottinger, Richard Lawrence
Robinson, Nicholas Adams
Sloan, F(rank) Blaine
Stein, Ralph Michael

### NORTH CAROLINA

**Buies Creek**
Whichard, Willis Padgett
**Chapel Hill**
Daye, Charles Edward
Nichol, Gene Ray, Jr.
**Columbus**
Bell, Mildred Bailey
**Cullowhee**
Wilson, LeVon Edward
**Durham**
Chambers, Julius LeVonne
Dellinger, Walter Estes, III
Havighurst, Clark Canfield
Joyner, Irving L.
**Greensboro**
Swan, George Steven
**Jacksonville**
Switzer, Robert Earl
**Raleigh**
Schwab, Carol Ann
**Winston Salem**
Foy, Herbert Miles, III
Walker, George Kontz
Walsh, Robert K.

### NORTH DAKOTA

**Grand Forks**
Ahlen, Michael J.

### OHIO

**Akron**
Coleman, Malina
**Bowling Green**
Holmes, Robert Allen
**Cincinnati**
Carro, Jorge Luis
Christenson, Gordon A.
Tomain, Joseph Patrick
**Cleveland**
Korngold, Gerald
Sharpe, Calvin William
Walsh, Charles Michael
**Columbus**
Bahls, Steven Carl
Burns, Robert Edward
Daicoff, Susan (Susan Daicoff Baskin)
Jost, Timothy Stoltzfus
Williams, Gregory Howard
**Dayton**
Kapp, Marshall Barry
**Toledo**
Quick, Albert Thomas

### OKLAHOMA

**Tulsa**
Belsky, Martin Henry
Stockwell, Lance

### OREGON

**Eugene**
Frohnmayer, David Braden
**Portland**
Bernstine, Daniel O'Neal
Kanter, Stephen
Rudnick, Rebecca Sophie
**Salem**
Nafziger, James Albert Richmond

### PENNSYLVANIA

**Bala Cynwyd**
Strazzella, James Anthony
**Carlisle**
Romero, Victor Carreon
**Carnegie**
Nemeth, Charles Paul
**Devon**
Garbarino, Robert Paul
**Harrisburg**
Diehm, James Warren
Sheldon, J. Michael
**Philadelphia**
Aronstein, Martin Joseph
Boss, Amelia Helen
Burbank, Stephen Bradner
Darby, Karen Sue
Diver, Colin S.
Leech, Noyes Elwood
Levin, A. Leo
Pollard, Dennis Bernard
Reinstein, Robert J.
Summers, Clyde Wilson
**Pittsburgh**
Frolik, Lawrence Anton
Greeno, John Gordon
Jordan, Sandra Dickerson
Nordenberg, Mark Alan
Pois, Joseph
Rosen, Richard David
Shane, Peter Milo
**Scranton**
Cimini, Joseph Fedele
**Upper Darby**
Hudiak, David Michael
**Villanova**
Sargent, Mark A.
Termini, Roseann Bridget
**Wynnewood**
Phillips, Almarin

### RHODE ISLAND

**Bristol**
Bogus, Carl Thomas
Kogan, Bruce Ivan
**Providence**
Lipsey, Howard Irwin

### SOUTH CAROLINA

**Columbia**
Haimbaugh, George Dow, Jr.
McCullough, Ralph Clayton, II
Rouse, LeGrand Ariail, II
Seamon, Richard Henry

### TENNESSEE

**Knoxville**
Galligan, Thomas C., Jr.
Phillips, Jerry Juan
Wirtz, Richard Stanley
**Livingston**
Roberts, John M.
**Martin**
Ogg, Elton Jerald, Jr.
**Memphis**
Davis, Frederick Benjamin
Kritchevsky, Barbara Ann
Pickard, Howard Brevard
**Nashville**
Syverud, Kent Douglas

### TEXAS

**Austin**
Jentz, Gaylord Adair
Sharlot, M. Michael
Sutton, John F., Jr.
Wright, Charles Alan
**Dallas**
Attanasio, John Baptist
Bromberg, Alan Robert
Busbee, Kline Daniel, Jr.
Cooper, Steven Mark
Elkins-Elliott, Kay
Galvin, Charles O'Neill
Garner, Bryan Andrew
Lowe, John Stanley
Winship, Peter
**Fort Worth**
Ingram, Denny Ouzts, Jr.
**Houston**
Douglas, James Matthew
Douglass, John Jay
Graving, Richard John
Marsel, Robert Steven
Moya, Olga Lydia
Skolnick, Malcolm Harris
Zamora, Stephen
**Lubbock**
Skillern, Frank Fletcher
**Plano**
Hemingway, Richard William
**Pottsboro**
Thomas, Ann Van Wynen
**San Antonio**
Castleberry, James Newton, Jr.
Juárez, José Roberto, Jr.
Schlueter, David Arnold
**Waco**
Toben, Bradley J. B.

### UTAH

**Provo**
Fleming, Joseph Clifton, Jr.
Hansen, H. Reese
Thomas, David Albert
**Salt Lake City**
Teitelbaum, Lee E.
**Sandy**
Joslin, Gary James

### VERMONT

**South Royalton**
Doria, Anthony Notarnicola

### VIRGINIA

**Alexandria**
Phillips, Karen Borlaug
**Arlington**
Anthony, Robert Armstrong
Parker, Jeffrey Scott
**Blacksburg**
Jensen, Walter Edward
**Charlottesville**
Alford, Neill Herbert, Jr.
Ellett, John Spears, II
Kitch, Edmund Wells
Martin, David Alan
Meador, Daniel John
Menefee, Samuel Pyeatt
O'Brien, David Michael
O'Neil, Robert Marchant
Scott, Robert Edwin
Whitehead, John Wayne
**Earlysville**
Grattan, George Gilmer, IV
**Grundy**
Kintzer, Gail Ann
**Leesburg**
Phillips, John T., II
**Lexington**
Grunewald, Mark Howard
Kirgis, Frederic Lee
Sullivan, Barry
**Norfolk**
Achampong, Francis Kofi
**Richmond**
Reveley, Walter Taylor, III
Small, Daniel Priestley
**Springfield**
Gawalt, Gerard W(ilfred)
**Virginia Beach**
Hernandez, Michael Vincent
Jones, Robert Griffith
Kerr, Gerald Lee, III
Kohm, Lynne Marie
Tuskey, John P.
**Williamsburg**
Marcus, Paul

### WASHINGTON

**Pullman**
Michaelis, Karen Lauree
**Seattle**
Hjorth, Roland L.
Perry, Timothy A.
Price, John Richard
Stoebuck, William Brees

### WISCONSIN

**Madison**
Baldwin, Gordon Brewster
Davis, Kenneth Boone, Jr.
Foster, George William, Jr.
**Milwaukee**
Barnes, Alison
Eisenberg, Howard Bruce
Geske, Janine Patricia
Grenig, Jay Edward
Kircher, John Joseph
**Oshkosh**
Mars, Joan Rosemary

### WYOMING

**Kemmerer**
Sundar, Vijendra

### TERRITORIES OF THE UNITED STATES

### PUERTO RICO

**San Juan**
Ramos, Carlos E.

### ENGLAND

**London**
Montgomery, John Warwick

### ADDRESS UNPUBLISHED

Areen, Judith Carol
Bernard, Donald Ray
Bork, Robert Heron
DeMitchell, Terri Ann
Dutile, Fernand Neville
Feerick, John David
Freedman, Monroe Henry
Goldstein, Joseph
Green, Carol H.
Hazard, Geoffrey Cornell, Jr.
Heymann, Philip Benjamin
Lichter-Heath, Laurie Jean
Lungren, John Howard
Manne, Henry Girard
Matheson, Scott Milne, Jr.
McCarthy, J. Thomas
Merrifield, Leroy Sorenson
Ramsey, Henry, Jr.
Rasmussen, Wayne Roger
Reidenberg, Joel R.
Rhame, Harold Ellis, Jr.
Rodriguez-Orellana, Manuel
Schlueter, Linda Lee
Tso, Tom
Wiehl, Lis W.
Young, Michael Kent

## FINANCE AND REAL ESTATE

### UNITED STATES

### CALIFORNIA

**Los Angeles**
Bradshaw, Carl John
Chan, David Ronald
**Newport Beach**
Harley, Halvor Larson
**Norco**
Knöbel, David Harold
**San Mateo**
Brugger, Joern-Eric Walter

### CONNECTICUT

**Hartford**
Wilder, Michael Stephen
**Stamford**
Fignar, Eugene Michael

### DISTRICT OF COLUMBIA

**Washington**
Bourgault, Dennis Paul
Butler, Steven Irwin
Shihata, Ibrahim Fahmy Ibrahim

### FLORIDA

**Dade City**
Johnson, Hjalma Eugene

### GEORGIA

**Augusta**
Snellings, Ross Schley
**Columbus**
Loudermilk, Joey M.

### ILLINOIS

**Chicago**
DeMoss, Jon W.
Goldberg, Sherman I.
Powell, Barry L.
**Deerfield**
Lifschultz, Phillip
**Northbrook**
McCabe, Michael J.
Pike, Robert William
**Wilmette**
Rosenbaum, Martin Michael

### INDIANA

**Indianapolis**
Ritz, Stephen Mark
Sokolov, Richard Saul

### KANSAS

**Shawnee Mission**
Gregory, Lewis Dean

### MARYLAND

**Silver Spring**
Grubbs, Donald Shaw, Jr.

Apperson, Bernard James
Arbit, Terry Steven
Berger, Melvin Gerald
Bohlke, Gary Lee
Born, Brooksley Elizabeth
Bracete, Juan Manuel
Bradley, Amelia Jane
Bradley, Leigh A.
Brick, Barrett Lee
Bromm, Susan Elizabeth
Brookshire, James Earl
Burgess, David
Burson, Charles W.
Calhoun-Senghor, Keith
Carver, George Allen, Jr.
Chabot, Elliot Charles
Chang, Ta-Tung Jacob
Coleman, William Thaddeus, III
Conner, Michael Timothy
Crosby, William Duncan, Jr.
Cruden, John Charles
Crump, Ronald Cordell
Damus, Robert George
Dewey, Anne Elizabeth Marie
Dingfelder, Justin
Disheroon, Fred Russell
Donilon, Thomas E.
Doyle, Justin Emmett
Duncan, John Dean, Jr.
Dunn, Herbert Irvin
Edelman, Alan Irwin
Eder, Elaine AnnMarie
Effros, Robert Carlton
Elcano, Mary S.
Elliot, Cameron Robert
Enzel, David H.
Eriksen, Richard Eugene
Etters, Ronald Milton
Ferren, John Maxwell
Flannery, John Philip
Fogarty, John Patrick Cody
Fong, Phyllis Kamoi
Forrest, Herbert Emerson
Fortuno, Victor M.
Fox, James Edward, Jr.
Frankle, Edward Alan
Freije, Philip Charles
Gable, Edward Brennan, Jr.
Gallup, David M.
Gay, Bonnie Lewis
Glaser, Howard B.
Gleichman, Norman M.
Glynn, Marilyn
Godwin, Kimberly Ann
Gordon, Robert M.
Gorelick, Jamie Shona
Gorman, Thomas O(rlo)
Gottlieb, James Rubel
Greene, Philip James
Greenstone, Adam Franklin
Hansen, Kenneth
Hargraves, Dirck Antony
Harris, Patricia Ann
Haythe, Winston McDonald
Hendry, Nancy H.
Hirsch, Michael
Holder, Eric H.
Hollis, Andre Dale
Horn, Joseph Peter
Iscoe, Craig Steven
Jeweler, Robin
Joseph, Robert George
Kacoyanis, Dennis Charles
Katz, John W.
Katzen, Sally
Kendall, Paul F.
Kennard, William Earl
Kennedy, Colleen Mary
Kimmitt, Robert Michael
Kittrie, Orde F.
Klothen, Kenneth
Konwinski, Lisa Michele
Kosarin, Jonathan Henry
Kroener, William Frederick, III
Laster, Gail W.
Leary, Mary Lou
Leshy, John D.
Levin, Edward M.
Levinson, Peter Joseph
Lewis, Wilma Antoinette
Lietzau, William Kendall
Lurensky, Marcia Adele
Lyons, Francis Xavier
Maco, Paul Stephen
Madden, Jerome Anthony
Mamalian, Paul
Marburg-Goodman, Jeffrey Emil
Margolis, Eugene
Martin, Stephen Russell, II
Mastromarco, Dan Ralph
Mates, Carol Maxine
Mays, Janice Ann
McClellan, Donald William, Jr.
McIntyre, Carl Henry, Jr.
McKinney, Linda Otani
McNamara, Robert M., Jr.
Mehle, Roger W.
Metz, Craig Huseman
Miller, Judith A.
Miller, Kerry Lee
Mixter, Christian John
Moore, Stephanie Y.
Morse, M. Howard
Murphy, C. Westbrook
Newkirk, Thomas Charles
Nitze, William Albert
Noble, Lawrence Mark
Nolan, David Brian
Noonan, Michael Dennis
Ohman, Earl R., Jr.
Oman, Ralph
O'Meara, John J.
O'Sullivan, Judith Roberta
Page, Edward John
Panebianco, Thomas
Patton, John Michael
Phillips, Cyrus Eastman, IV
Pincus, Andrew J.
Pluta, Tom
Poppler, Doris Swords
Preston, Stephen W.
Pryce, Jeffrey Fremont
Pulley, Lewis Carl
Ragland, Robert Allen
Raimo, Bernard (Bernie Raimo)
Rawls, Charles Richardson
Reback, Joyce Ellen
Reno, Janet
Robinson, James Kenneth
Rodemeyer, Michael Leonard, Jr.
Roetzel, Danny Nile
Roosevelt, James, Jr.
Rosenberg, Lawrence David
Roth, Alan J.
Rusch, Jonathan Jay
Rush, Henri Francis
Russell, Michael James
Schapiro, Mary
Schlitt, Lyn M.
Schwartzman, Andrew Jay
Scott, Betsy Sue
Sessions, Jefferson Beauregard, III
Shaheen, Michael Edmund, Jr.
Shapiro, Michael Henry
Sharfman, Stephen
Shotwell, Charles Bland
Siler, J. Bernard
Smith, Dwight Chichester, III
Smyth, Paul Burton
Solano, Henry L.
Solomon, Rodney Jeff
Spotila, John T.
Stern, Gerald Mann
Stevens, Paul Schott
Stewart, C. Gregory
Stewart, David Pentland
Stillman, Elinor Hadley
Straser, Richard Alan
Stuart, Raymond Wallace
Stucky, Jean Seibert
Stucky, Scott Wallace
Sullivan, Mary Anne
Suter, William Kent
Svab, Stephen
Swenson, Diane Kay
Swerdzewski, Joseph
Thompson, Mozelle Willmont
Udall, Thomas
Wagner, Brenda Carol
Waldman, Daniel
Weeks, Rhoda Lethea
Weissenborn, Anne Adkins
Wilchins, Howard Martin
Willcox, Breckinridge Long
Williams, Julie Lloyd
Williams, Mark Colburn
Winston, Judith Ann
Wright, James Ralph
Yambrusic, Edward Slavko
Zagami, Anthony James

### FLORIDA

**Bartow**
Cury, Bruce Paul
Mars, Richard Donald
**Boynton Beach**
Kune, Bernard Jack
**Bradenton**
Angulo, Charles Bonin
Gould, Bret Adam
**Clearwater**
Falkner, William Carroll
Tragos, George Euripedes
**Fort Lauderdale**
Cobb, James Abernethy, Jr.
Lautenschlager, Tracy Haub
Shein, Michael
Stapleton, John Owen
**Gainesville**
Anderson, Gregg Alan
Huszar, Arlene Celia
**Hialeah**
Gross, Richard Wilson
**Jacksonville**
Arpen, Tracey I., Jr.
Carlson, Raymond Howard
Still, Lisa Stotsbery
**Live Oak**
Peters, Lee Ira, Jr.
**Miami**
de Leon, John Louis
Henderson, Kelly James
Keating, Stephen John
Kurzweil, Vivianne V.
Langer, Sharon Lynne
Lastra, Carlos Mariano
Meltz, Jonathan Scott
Ronzetti, Thomas A. Tucker
Rosen, Howard Robert
Scott, Thomas Emerson, Jr.
Serralta, Gedety Nayets
Tamen, Frank H.
Tifford, Arthur W.
**New Port Richey**
Muck, Stacey Lynn
**Ocala**
Lockshin, Lori
**Orlando**
Gold, I. Randall
**Panama City**
Dingus, Jonathan Wesley
**Pensacola**
Johnson, Rodney Marcum
**Saint Augustine**
Ansbacher, Sidney Franklyn
**Saint Petersburg**
Comparetto, Anthony J.
**Sanford**
Hastings, Thomas Warren
**Shalimar**
Grinsted, Albert Hugh, III
**Tallahassee**
Butterworth, Robert A.
Hall, Judith Dougherty
Herskovitz, S(am) Marc
Kerns, David Vincent
Marshall, Marilyn Josephine
Martin, Paul Jeffrey
Menser, Mark Christopher
Olenick, Michael Haskel
Patterson, Michael P.
Simmons, Karen Denise
Thiele, Herbert William Albert
Whitney, Enoch Jonathan
**Tampa**
Becker, Alison Lea
Govern, Kevin Hugh
Scionti, Michael Joseph
Wilson, Charles R.
**Tequesta**
Kay, Richard Broughton
**West Palm Beach**
Brannon, Dave Lee
Damico, Paul Anthony
Giles, Edward Lee
Karmelin, Ira D.
Penalta, C. Richard
Rizzardi, Keith William
Selfridge, Gordon Phillip

### GEORGIA

**Atlanta**
Baker, Thurbert E.
Dion, Alan
Liebes, Cindy Ann
Martin, James Francis
Murphy, Richard Patrick
Raby, Kenneth Alan
Ricks, Joycia Camilla
Whaley, Nancy Jean
**Augusta**
Yarborough, Clinton Joseph
**Bainbridge**
Warr, John Arthur
**Douglasville**
Anderson, Jill Lynn
Ballew, Jeffrey Lynn
**Gainesville**
Deal, Jason J.
**Macon**
Aderhold, H. Randolph
Duke, Miriam D. Wansley
Martin, Beverly
Scarbary, Otis Lee
Woody, Thomas Clifton II
**Marietta**
Pearlberg, Irvan A.
**Savannah**
Dixon, Harry D., Jr. (Donnie Dixon)
**Stone Mountain**
Bowers, Michael Joseph
**Valdosta**
Talley, George Tyler

### HAWAII

**Honolulu**
Alm, Steve
Bronster, Margery S
Cowan, Stuart Marshall
Moroney, Michael John
Stacey, Richard Wayne
Stapleton, Carolyn Louise
Tanaka, Leila Chiyako
**Kaneohe**
Donahoe, Peter Aloysius

### IDAHO

**Boise**
Lance, Alan George
Richardson, Betty H.
**Idaho Falls**
Shindurling, Jon J.
**Twin Falls**
Hansen, John Joseph

### ILLINOIS

**Aledo**
Heintz, Baron Strum
**Chicago**
Abt, Ralph Edwin
Acosta, Sergio Enrique
Bizot, John Eric
Bodenstein, Ira
Burns, James B.
Gallanis, Kathryn Ann
Jackowiak, Patricia
Jaconetty, Thomas Anthony
Jones, Sandra Yvonne
Kerycznskyj, Leo Ihor
Krakowski, Richard John
Kuczwara, Thomas Paul
MacCarthy, Terence Francis
Mansfield, Karen Lee
Mikva, Abner Joseph
Norek, Frances Therese
Redmond, Darlene Leola
Richmond, James G.
Rosso, Christine Hehmeyer
Sklamberg, Robert Joseph
Sprovieri, Connie R.
Taren, Jeffrey Lynn
Triplett, Austin Henry
Tryban, Esther Elizabeth
Yamashiro, Maureen Dorothy
Zullo, Peter Frank
**Danville**
Aldag, Jeffrey Noel
**Elgin**
Moltz, Martin Paul
**Fairview Heights**
Grace, (Walter) Charles
**Glen Ellyn**
Hudson, Dennis Lee
**Joliet**
Guzman, Matthew Lopez
**Macomb**
Myers, Richard P.
**Normal**
Spears, Larry Jonell
**Oak Park**
Sengpiehl, Paul Marvin
**Peoria**
Lyons, Kevin W.
Sergey, James Adam
**Princeton**
Henneberry, Michael L.
**Skokie**
Pfannkuche, Christopher Edward Koenig
**Springfield**
Dodge, James William
Easum, Nancy G.
Hulin, Frances C.
Johnson, Jenifer L.
Myers-Wilkins, Crystal Ann
Ryan, James E.
**Waukegan**
Fix, Patricia Sowinski
**Westchester**
Matuga, Edward Anthony

### INDIANA

**Anderson**
Eisele, John Eugene
**Columbus**
Carter, Pamela Lynn
**Connersville**
Kuntz, William Henry
**Dyer**
Capp, David A.
**Evansville**
Miller, Daniel Raymond
**Franklin**
Hamner, Lance Dalton
**Indianapolis**
King, J. Bradley
Knight, Margarett Lee
McCarthy, Kevin Bart
Modisett, Jeffrey A.
Stewart, Judith A.
Williams, Raifael Worley
**Lafayette**
Gerde, Carlyle Noyes (Cy Gerde)
**Munster**
Amber, Douglas George
**New Albany**
Faith, Stanley O.
**Valparaiso**
Soliday, Matthew D.

### IOWA

**Cedar Rapids**
Flitz, James Henry
**Council Bluffs**
Greiner, Mark L.
**Des Moines**
Anderson, Melissa A.
Burns, Bernard John, III
Flaherty, Daniel Lee
Hansen, Christina Flores
Kelly, Edwin Frost
Miller, Thomas J.
Nickerson, Don C.
Ovrom, Eliza Jane
Smith, Neal Edward
**Dubuque**
Ernst, Daniel Pearson
**Rockwell City**
Meth-Farrington, Tina Marie
**Waterloo**
Hinton, Charles Franklin
Rapp, Stephen John

### KANSAS

**Belleville**
Grace, Brian Vincent
**Erie**
Creitz, Daniel Dale
**Hutchinson**
O'Neal, Michael Ralph
**Kansas City**
Coleman, Thomas
Dunlay, F. Charles
**Olathe**
Cowles, John Emerson
Gyllenborg, Scott Christie
Snowbarger, Vince
**Topeka**
Stovall, Carla Jo
**Wichita**
Dickgrafe, Sharon Louise
Randels, Ed L.
Williams, Jackie N.
Winkler, Dana John

### KENTUCKY

**Danville**
McClure, George Morris, III
**Elizabethtown**
Yustas, Vincent Paul
**Fort Campbell**
Weicker, Raymond, III
**Frankfort**
Chandler, Albert Benjamin III
Gillig, John Stephenson
Sonego, Ian G.
**Hickman**
Langford, Timothy Andrew
**Lexington**
Famularo, Joseph L.
**Louisville**
Barr, James Houston, III
Smith, R(obert) Michael
Troop, (Walter) Michael
**Munfordville**
Lang, George Edward
**Newport**
Patton, Robert Charles

### LOUISIANA

**Baton Rouge**
Byrd, Patricia
Callaghan, Kathleen Richard
Hymel, L(ezin) J(oseph)
Ieyoub, Richard Phillip
Parks, James William, II
**Lafayette**
Cloutier, Monique Legendre
Marx, Gregory Paul
Mickel, Joseph Thomas
**Marksville**
Riddle, Charles Addison, III
**New Orleans**
Davis, Darlene Rose
Jordan, Eddie J.
Ortique, Revius Oliver, Jr.

### MAINE

**Augusta**
Ketterer, Andrew
Wake, Robert Alan
**Portland**
Dilworth, George Thayer
McCloskey, Jay P.

### MARYLAND

**Annapolis Junction**
Woodard, Mark Davis
**Baltimore**
Battaglia, Lynne Ann
Carey, Eleanor Mackey
Coleman, Louis Kress
Cooper, Ellen Schiff
Curran, J. Joseph, Jr.
De shields-Minnis, Tarra R.
Fili, Denise M.
Fried, Arthur
Lilly, John Richard, II
**Bethesda**
Gosliner, Michael L.
Robertson, Paul Joseph
Rubin, Allan Avrom
**Bowie**
Lower, Philip Edward
**Chestertown**
Yeager, Thomas Nelson
**College Park**
Anderson, Laura Elisabeth
**Ellicott City**
Closson, Walter Franklin
**Gaithersburg**
McCann, Joseph Leo
**Hyattsville**
Rummel, Edgar Ferrand
Spiegel, Robert Alan
**Kensington**
Dauster, William Gary
**Patuxent River**
Lundstrom, Thomas John
**Rockville**
Cusumano, Leanne
Cyr, Karen D.
Essex, Maureen Frances
Friedman, Eric S.
Frye, Roland Mushat, Jr.
Rheinstein, Peter Howard
Via, Patricia Prestigiacomo
Wilder, Sharon Beth
Yale, Kenneth P.
**Silver Spring**
Ryan, Miles Francis, III
**Solomons**
Whitaker, Mary Fernan
**Towson**
Comeau, Michael Gerard
**Upper Marlboro**
Creech, Jay Heyward
Manico, William M.
**Wheaton**
Kelly, Patricia Ann

### MASSACHUSETTS

**Boston**
Casper, Denise Jefferson
Donahue, Charlotte Mary
Gilfix, Suzanne Glick
Guild, Irene Lillian
Hoover, David Carlson
Katzmann, Gary Stephen
Knopf, Amy Susan
McCourt, Joyce Elise
Messuri, Nicholas Joseph
Norris, Charles Head
Sears, Douglas Warren
Shea, Megan Carroll
Stern, Donald Kenneth
Wild, Victor Allyn
**Brockton**
Holmes, Jeanne L.
**Holyoke**
Brunault-McGuinness, Andrea Louise
**Natick**
Savage, James Cathey, III
**Newton**
Conte, Anthony R.
**Plymouth**
Sullivan, John Arthur
**Sandwich**
Troy, Robert Sweeney, Sr.
**Springfield**
Reilly, Thomas F.
Susse, Sandra Slone

### MICHIGAN

**Ann Arbor**
Krislov, Marvin
**Bay City**
Duggan, Patrick O'Neill
**Centreville**
Thistlethwaite, William H.
**Detroit**
Dones-Carson, Kathie Denise
Frazer, Marilee Helen
Green, Saul A.
Parker, Ross Gail
Quinn, John Peter
**Flint**
Beltz, Charles Robert
**Grand Rapids**
Allen, Robert B.
Dettmer, Michael Hayes
LaVille, Daniel Michael
**Hastings**
Crowley, Dale Alan
**Lansing**
Granholm, Jennifer Mulhern
Haggerty, William Francis
Przekop-Shaw, Susan
**Livonia**
Fisher, Michael Ernest
**Midland**
Donker, Norman Wayne
**Monroe**
Werner, Cheryl E.
**Mount Clemens**
Jackson, Nicholas Miller
**Pontiac**
O'Brien, John Newell, II

**Sterling Heights**
Novak, Joseph Anthony
**Traverse City**
Black, Martha L.

## MINNESOTA

**Austin**
Leighton, Robert Joseph
**Cloquet**
Skare, Thomas M.
**Hallock**
Hane, Jeffrey W.
**Minneapolis**
Coloma, Maria Lourdes Claris
Genia, James Michael
Jones, B. Todd
Munic, Martin Daniel
**Rochester**
Canan, Thomas Michael
**Saint Louis Park**
Paschke, Jerry Bryan
**Saint Paul**
Casey, Susan Anne
Conney, Carl M.
Hatch, Mike
Street, James J.
Villaume, Frank Eugene, III
**Winona**
Sonneman, Karl Walter

## MISSISSIPPI

**Greenwood**
Franklin, Webb
**Grenada**
Hill, Clyde Vernon, Jr.
**Hattiesburg**
Riley, Thomas Jackson
**Holly Springs**
Belk, Fred M., Jr.
**Jackson**
Lee, Leslie Staehle
Moize, Jerry Dee
Moore, Mike
Phillips, George Landon
Pigott, Brad
**Laurel**
Hedgepeth, Curtis Grant
**Oxford**
Buchanan, Calvin D. (Buck Buchanan)
Dawson, Thomas Winter
**Parchman**
Norris, James Marshall
**Tylertown**
Mord, Irving Conrad, II

## MISSOURI

**Chesterfield**
Wiegers, Edward G.
**Clayton**
Livergood, Robert Frank
**Farmington**
Pratte, Geoffrey Lynn
**Independence**
Lashley, Curtis Dale
**Jefferson City**
Bruce, Theodore Allen
Burgess, Breck Kristen
McCoy, James M.
Nixon, Jeremiah W. (Jay Nixon)
Pritchett, Michael Eugene Cook
**Kansas City**
Depew, Chauncey Mitchell, III
Hill, Stephen L., Jr.
Laue, Brant Mitchell
Mortimer, Anita Louise
**Liberty**
Norris, Donald Terry
Sims, Karen Ann
**Saint Louis**
Banks, Eric Kendall
Dowd, Edward L., Jr.
Fredericks, Henry Jacob
Gangle, Margaret Ellen
Geiler, Jane Buchanan
O'Malley, Kevin Francis
Tutt, Louise Thompson
**Springfield**
Leonard, Michelle Nahon

## MONTANA

**Belgrade**
Brown, Robert Warren
**Billings**
Gallinger, Lorraine D.
Matteucci, Sherry Scheel
Robbins, Dale Robert
**Butte**
McCarthy, Bernard Francis
**Helena**
Gersovitz, Jeremy
Mazurek, Joseph P.
**Livingston**
Becker, Bruce Erwin
**Superior**
Donovan, Michael Shaun

## NEBRASKA

**Columbus**
Schumacher, Paul Maynard
**Fremont**
Gill, Lyle Bennett
**Grand Island**
Piccolo, Gerard Anthony
**Kearney**
Kelley, Michael Eugene
**Lincoln**
Arterburn, David K.
Bancroft, Webb Ernest
Stenberg, Donald B.
**Omaha**
Conboy, Martin James
Crouchley, Daniel Gerard
Cryne, Robert Francis
Monaghan, Thomas Justin

## NEVADA

**Carson City**
Del Papa, Frankie Sue
Rodefer, Jeffrey Robert
**Henderson**
Zentz, Robert
**Las Vegas**
Bersi, Ann
Goodman, Oscar Baylin
Landreth, Kathryn E.
**Reno**
Pinkerton, C(harles) Frederick
**Yerington**
Schlegelmilch, John Paul

## NEW HAMPSHIRE

**Concord**
Gagnon, Paul Michael
McLaughlin, Philip T.
Topham, Lee Evans

## NEW JERSEY

**Camden**
Misci, John A., Jr.
Morris, Leah McGarry
**Cherry Hill**
Copsetta, Norman George
**Elizabeth**
Kabak, Douglas Thomas
**Flemington**
Skarpetowski, Carol
**Hackensack**
Caminiti, Donald Angelo
D'Alessandro, Dianne Marie
**Harrison**
Gilmore, Jean Linda
**Jersey City**
De Julio, Lois A.
**Lawrenceville**
Stark, Albert Maxwell
**Livingston**
Celentano, Leslie Zyto
**Morristown**
Fletcher, Michael S.
**Newark**
Douglas, Ollis, Jr.
Goldberg, Glenn D.
Hochberg, Faith S.
Larosiliere, Jean Darly Martin
Laurino, Robert Dennis
Martin, James Hanley
O'Dowd, Patricia Jean
Vachier, Caroline
**North Caldwell**
Friedman, Richard I(rwin)
**Paterson**
Bellomo, Salvatore
**Peapack**
McConnell, Marianne
**Princeton**
Balint, Ellen Barney
Meiser, Kenneth Edward
**Spring Lake**
Shaw, Charles Franklin, III
**Toms River**
Farley, Terrence P.
**Trenton**
Gusler, Kathleen Mary
Hill, Robyn Marcella
Hurd, Douglas Herold
Jacobson, Mary Carol
Jones, Dale Edwin
McCauley, Brian Charles
Metzger, John Mackay
Mroz, Richard S.
Nason, Judith A.
Parker, Robin Robert
Scully, Thomas Francis
Sivolella, John Joseph
Smith, John Joseph
Warren, Stewart David
Webster Cobb, Deirdré Louise
**Union City**
Rondon, Edania Cecilia

## NEW MEXICO

**Albuquerque**
Altwies, Julie Noreen
Kelly, John J.
McCue, Stephen Patrick
**Clovis**
Wilson, James Gwynn
**Gallup**
Allan, Robert Olav
**Hobbs**
Reagan, Gary Don
**Santa Fe**
Madrid, Patricia Ann

## NEW YORK

**Albany**
Buchanan, George Howard
Buldrini, George James
Devine, John Michael
Koczaja, Joseph Stanley
Kramer, Steven J.
Lefkowitz, Jerome
Spitzer, Eliot
**Ballston Spa**
Rider, Mark McMaster
**Bath**
Squires, Jeffrey E.
**Bronx**
MacDonald, Angelo Gerard
Mitchell, Guy Hamilton
**Bronxville**
Falvey, Patrick Joseph
**Brooklyn**
Gray, Carol A.
Herzog, Lester Barry
Lynch, Loretta B.
Mandel, Susan L.
Margolin, Frederick A.
Miles, Gavin Wentworth
Philip, Amanda
Shay, Madeline Lee Brummer
Stamboulidis, George Alexander
Twersky, Jonathan
**Buffalo**
Martoche, Salvatore Richard
NeMoyer, Patrick H.
O'Donnell, Denise Ellen
Schwegler, Lawrence M.
Tobe, Susan Bring
**Cortland**
Howe, Karen Louise
**Delmar**
Eldridge, Douglas Alan
**Fort Edward**
Cullen, Kathleen Joy
**Goshen**
Stockburger, Susan Zlomke
**Hancock**
Sienko, Leonard Edward Jr.
**Hauppauge**
Robinson, Derrick Jeffrey
**Huntington**
Selkirk, Alexander MacDonald, Jr.
**Kew Gardens**
Ford, Bernadette K.
Lomp, Peter Vincent
**Kingston**
Kellar, Norman
**Latham**
Conway, Robert George, Jr.
**Little Neck**
Walsh, Sean M.
**Mayville**
Subjack, James Patrick
**Mineola**
Kunken, Kenneth James
**Nassau**
Moldoff, William Morris
**New York**
Baez, Julio A.
Barton, Robin Lisa
Brieger, George
Buchbinder, Darrell Bruce
Burgman, Dierdre Ann
Carter, Zachary W.
Clark, John Holley, III
Clark, William J.
Cremer, Leon Earl
DeCuzzi, James
Dodell, Sue Ellen
Esperon, Rosaria Rodriguez
Feinmark, Phyllis S. Kaplan
Fortain, Renee Therese
Frey, Andrew Lewis
Friedlander, Mark
Graham, Jul Eliot
Grant Bruce, Darlene Camille
Halloran, John Joseph, Jr.
Hanson, Jean Elizabeth
Hilf, Michael Gary
Kmiotek-Welsh, Jacqueline
Kostelny, Albert Joseph, Jr.
LaCaprucia, Cynthia Marie
Lodico, Yvonne C.
Loprest, Frank James Jr.
Lord, Barbara Joanni
Mangia, Angelo James
Mayer, Carl Joseph
Merris, Donna Rose
Minkowitz, Martin
Minuse, Catherine Jean
Morgenthau, Robert Morris
Morris, Cecelia G.
Nguyen, Paul Dung Quoc
Pinczower, Kenneth Ephraim
Rachlin, Alan Sanders
Raisler, Kenneth Mark
Rivellese, Vincent Woodrow
Rootenberg, Sharyn Michele
Rosenberg, Jonathan S.
Samuel, Raphael
Schweitzer, Melvin L.
Scott, Sarah Alice
Spillane, Dennis Kevin
Steiner, David Miller
Strassberg, Richard Mark
Ulrey, Prescott David
Van Eysden, Inga
Waldman, Seymour Morton
Weprin, Barry Alan
White, Mary Jo
Willer, Rebecca Sharon
Ziccardi, Domenick
**Niagara Falls**
Cantlon, James Daniel
**Oceanside**
Satran, Edward Saul
**Oswego**
Sullivan, John Thomas, Jr.
**Peekskill**
Rubenfeld, Leonard
**Pierrepont Manor**
Rosenberg, Peter David
**Rochester**
Johnson, Christopher George
Pilato, Louis Peter
**Saratoga Springs**
Sipperly, Peter C.
**Schenectady**
Camino, George J.
Van Dyke, Henry Joseph
**Seneca Falls**
Bove, Emil J., Jr.
**Shokan**
Schwartzberg, Paul David
**Staten Island**
Bryk, William Michael
**Syracuse**
Bodow, Wayne R.
Fitzpatrick, William John
French, Daniel J.
Gozzi, Joanna
Stevens, Betsy L.
Voninski, John R.
**Watervliet**
Hilts, Earl T.
**White Plains**
Bender, Steven A.
Pirro, Jeanine Ferris

## NORTH CAROLINA

**Asheville**
Wilson, Susan Elizabeth
**Charlotte**
Calloway, Mark T.
Davis, William Maxie, Jr.
Penn, Philip Julian
**Greensboro**
Holton, Walter Clinton, Jr.
**Lenoir**
Flaherty, David Thomas, Jr.
**Lexington**
Kurtz, Andrea Sloane
**Monroe**
Parker, Michael Dean
**New Bern**
Hicks, Donald Cade, III
Overholt, Hugh Robert
**Raleigh**
Blackburn, James B., III
Cole, Janice McKenzie
Dean, Christine Witcover
Easley, Michael F.
Givens, George Franklin
Hirsch, Alan Seth
**Washington**
Rader, Steven Palmer
**Whiteville**
Wood, William Edward

## NORTH DAKOTA

**Bismarck**
Heitkamp, Heidi
Huey, David W.
**Cooperstown**
Ratcliffe, Phyllis Ann
**Fargo**
Schneider, John Thomas

## OHIO

**Akron**
York, Stephanie Helayne
**Athens**
McCarthy, George P.
**Cincinnati**
Halpert, Douglas Joshua
Kaminski, Gerald Francis
Morthorst, Michael Edward
Scheve, Thomas John
Wang, Charleston Cheng-Kung
Zealey, Sharon Janine
**Cleveland**
Dever, Veronica McNamara
Grabow, Raymond John
Laster Mays, Anita
Robiner, Donald Maxwell
Sweeney, Emily Margaret
**Columbus**
Adler, Allen Paul
Aukland, Duncan Dayton
Barber, Barbara Lenise
Chavers, Dane Carroll
Chesley-Lahm, Diane
Hale, Harland Hanna
La Cour, Louis Bernard
Laughlin-Schopis, Susan Kay
Lindsey, Thomas Kenneth
Maser, Douglas James
Mentel, Michael Christopher
Montgomery, Betty Dee
Rennick, Kyme Elizabeth Wall
**Dayton**
Bunn, Randall J.
Lockhart, Gregory Gordon
**Fairborn**
Mayer, Michael A.
**Hamilton**
Kennedy, Sharon Lee
**Lancaster**
Vandervoort, Terre Lynne
**Miamisburg**
Fobes, Ronald L.
**Minerva**
Martin, Robert Dale
**Painesville**
Bell, Janette Moore
Campbell, Margaret Susan
**Shaker Heights**
Ondrey Gruber, William Michael
**Toledo**
Bates, Julia Reinberger
Kuhn, Jeffrey Craig
Zychowicz, Ralph Charles
**Westerville**
Helvey, Edward Douglas

## OKLAHOMA

**El Reno**
McCurdy, Gary Dean
**Fort Sill**
Livingston, Douglas Mark
**Muskogee**
Gallant, Jeffrey Andrew
Green, Bruce
**Oklahoma City**
Edmondson, William Andrew
Gatewood, Tela Lynne
Keating, Francis Anthony, II
Parrott, Nancy Sharon
Roth, James Anthony
Ryan, Patrick M.
Tuck-Richmond, Doletta Sue
**Sapulpa**
Gardner, Dale Ray
**Tulsa**
Huckin, William Price, Jr.
Knorr, Stephen James
Lewis, Stephen C.

## OREGON

**Eugene**
Fitzgerald, William Emil
Hoar, Sean Bennett
**Mcminnville**
Berry, Bradley Carl
**Portland**
Balmer, Thomas Ancil
Edmonds, Thomas H.
Leineweber, Robert J.
Olson, Kristine
Sponsler, Thomas Clyde
Uhle, William K.
**Salem**
Bulkley, Robert De Groff, Jr.
Myers, Hardy
**Springfield**
DePuy, Walter Albert, Jr.

## PENNSYLVANIA

**Bellefonte**
Arnold, J. Karen
**Blue Bell**
Vukelich, Milo Michael
**Butler**
McLean, Patricia Jo
**Chester**
Kaufman, Mark Alan
**Diamond Park**
DiGiacomo, Paula Cosenza
**Doylestown**
Hall, Peter C.
Mazaheri, Tina
Rubenstein, Alan Morris
**Harrisburg**
Anderson, Janice Lee
Barasch, David M.
Fisher, D. Michael
Frye, Mary Catherine
Preski, Brian Joseph
Sacks, Diana L.
Teplitz, Robert Forman
**Hollidaysburg**
Fecik, Shelley Ann
**Norristown**
Williamson, Ronald Thomas
**Philadelphia**
Carlin, Kevin Francis Christopher
Creagan, David John
Guyton, Odell
Mack, Debra K.
Mundis, Daryl Alan
Panek, Edward S., Jr.
Stiles, Michael
Swarns, Christina Allison
Tichenor, James Lee
Weaver, Sandjai
Wolfe, J. Matthew
**Pittsburgh**
Brysh, Paul John
Gabriel, Brian Pierce
Kelly, Linda L.
Kornreich, Alida J.
Litman, Harry Peter
Novara, Michael J.
Orie, Jane Clare
**Pottsville**
Bushinski, Stephen John
**Somerset**
Barkman, Jon Albert
**Washington**
Makel, Dennis Michael
**West Chester**
McAteer, Melanie
**Wind Gap**
Filingo, Michael Anthony

## RHODE ISLAND

**Newport**
Judge, Brian
**Providence**
Clifford, Sidney, Jr.
Curran, Margaret E.

## SOUTH CAROLINA

**Charleston**
Bennett, John Henry, Jr.
**Columbia**
Condon, Charles Molony
Handel, Richard Craig
Josey, Jon Rene
McLeod, Walton James
Woodington, Kenneth P.
**Conway**
Suggs, Michael Edward
**Greenville**
Foulke, Edwin Gerhart, Jr.
Mauldin, John Inglis
McKinney, Ronald W.
**Hardeeville**
Johnson, Darrell Thomas, Jr.
**Seneca**
Fleming, Mack Gerald

## SOUTH DAKOTA

**Huron**
Keller, Mary Garvey
**Pierre**
Barnett, Mark William
Braun, David Lee
Wald, Sherri Sundem
**Sioux Falls**
McBride, Ted
Schreier, Karen Elizabeth

## TENNESSEE

**Crossville**
Marlow, James Allen
**Dandridge**
Miller, Edward C.
**Huntsville**
Galloway, John W., Jr.
**Knoxville**
Christenbury, Edward Samuel
Creekmore, David Dickason
Francis, Shannon Claire
Goggin, Wendy
Kirkpatrick, Carl Kimmel
Marquand, Brent Richard
**Mc Minnville**
Potter, Clement Dale
**Memphis**
Coleman, Veronica Freeman

Steinhauer, Gillian
Terry, Joseph Ray, Jr.
**Nashville**
Adkins, Nanci Cherry Pugh
Anderson, Robert Charles
Hill, Jeffrey Lee
Himmelreich, David Merrill
Keenan, John Raymond
Martin, Henry Alan
McDonald, Michael Eugene
Milam, Roger Arling
Summers, Paul
Tarkington, Amy Leigh
Walkup, John Knox
Waterhouse, Rachel L.
**Newport**
Bunnell, John Blake
**Powell**
Hyman, Roger David

### TEXAS

**Abilene**
Tomme, Curtis Rabon
**Arlington**
Rogers, Jean Gregory
**Austin**
Cornyn, John
Dukes, Katharine Lee
Greene, John Joseph
Head, Ben Thomas
Jeffords, Edward Alan
Pemberton, Robert Harnson
Troilo, Arthur, III
**Beaumont**
Bradford, J. Michael
**Brenham**
Mueller, Renee Ann
**Bryan**
Miller, Thomas Eugene
**Dallas**
Coggins, Paul Edward, Jr.
Harlan, Peter Llewellyn
Hartt, Grover, III
Hytken, Louise Parks
Kohl, Kathleen Allison Barnhart
Morris, Audrey M.
Young, Alan Scott
**Eden**
Campbell, Bill
**Edinburg**
Talbot, Mark Mitchell
**Fort Worth**
Bosser, Steven John
Harper, Vesta Tamora
Tracy, Barbara Marie
**Houston**
An, Yong Jun
Babcock, Jeffery Alan
Blackmon, Willie Edward Boney
DeAtley, James Harry
Fellers, Rhonda Gay
Fleming, Michael Paul
Hu, Daniel David
Mosbacker, Mervyn
Womack, Guy Lee
**Irving**
Colbert, Kathryn Hendon
**Laredo**
Davis, Jason Murray
**Lubbock**
Davis, Jimmy Frank
**Mineola**
Bruce, Robert Denton
**San Antonio**
Blagg, James W.
Cathey, M. Elizabeth
Durbin, Richard Louis, Jr.
Frigerio, Charles Straith
Priest, Melissa Lenore
Sessions, William Steele
**Tyler**
Yeager, Ruth
**Wichita Falls**
Walker, Randall Wayne

### UTAH

**Ogden**
Richards, Maurice
Thompson, Laura Kaye
**Salt Lake City**
Graham, Jan
Loveless, A. Scott
Schwendiman, Dave J.
Warner, Paul M.
**Tooele**
Jeppesen, Alan Karl
**Vernal**
Judd, Dennis L.

### VERMONT

**Burlington**
Shattuck, Gary G.
Tetzlaff, Charles Robert
**Manchester**
Mount, Joe Horn
**Montpelier**
Malley, J. Wallace, Jr.
Sorrell, William H.
**Saint Johnsbury**
Sipples, Kyle C.

### VIRGINIA

**Alexandria**
Abell, Richard Bender
Fahey, Helen F.
Kinzler, Peter
Kotlarchuk, Ihor O. E.
Rossi, Eugene Joseph
**Arlington**
Fries, Kenneth Eugene
Goans, Judy Winegar
McGinley, Nancy Elizabeth
Monroe, Carl Dean, III
Retson, Nicholas Philip
Smith, John Michael
Williams, Henry Newton
**Blackstone**
Allen, Jeffrey Rodgers
**Bowling Green**
Long, Clarence Dickinson, III
**Boydton**
White-Hurst, John Marshall
**Cedar Bluff**
Cooke, Hugh Shannon
**Chesapeake**
Parr, Nancy Grace
**Danville**
Martin, James Chandler
**Fairfax**
Hopson, Everett George
**Fairfax Station**
Bishop, Alfred Chilton, Jr.
**Falls Church**
Morris, Dee Dodson
Skoler, Daniel Lawrence
Winzer, P.J.
**Hampton**
Schon, Alan Wallace
**Harrisonburg**
Landes, Angela Hochmeister
**Mc Lean**
Mater, Maud
Noonan, Jean
**Mineral**
Whitlock, Willie Walker
**Newport News**
Robinson, Willard Montellous, Jr.
**Norfolk**
Metcalfe, James Ashford
**Palmyra**
Perrin, Sarah Ann
**Petersburg**
Burns, Cassandra Stroud
**Pulaski**
McCarthy, Thomas James, Jr.
**Richmond**
Earley, Mark Lawrence
Flannagan, Benjamin Collins, IV
Gilmore, James Stuart, III
Lucyk, Gregory E.
MacIlroy, John Whittington
McFarlane, Walter Alexander
Miller, Stephen Wiley
Phillips, Elizabeth Jason
Pollard, Overton Price
Thro, William Eugene
**Roanoke**
Crouch, Robert P., Jr.
**Spotsylvania**
Neely, William F.
**Sterling**
Brittigan, Robert Lee
**Virginia Beach**
Ventker, David Neil
**Yorktown**
Hackworth, William Michael

### WASHINGTON

**Everett**
Brudvik, Jacalyn Dean
Knutzen, Raymond Edward
**Kelso**
Baur, Susan Irene
**Olympia**
Boothby, Carol Ann
Carlson, Susan Marie
Edmondson, Frank Kelley, Jr.
Freimund, Jeffrey A. O.
Roe, Charles Barnett
Welsh, John Beresford, Jr.
**Port Hadlock**
Baril, Lynda Katherine
**Renton**
Chess, Faye Rosalind
Thompson, George Lewis
**Seattle**
Hunter, Theodore Paul
King, William Kimble, Jr.
McDonald, Brian Martin
Pflaumer, Katrina C.
Prezyna, Ann Elizabeth
Russell, Robie George
Voget, Jane J.
White, Thomas S.
**Spokane**
Ames, Edward Jay
Clarke, Judy
Connelly, James P.
Hayashi, Arthur
Hirschel, Rebecca L.
Lister, Stephanie Joyce
**Tacoma**
Frohmader, Frederick Oliver
George, Nicholas
Kouklis, John C.
**Vancouver**
Dodds, Michael Bruce
**Wenatchee**
Vandegrift, Lee Bartlett

### WEST VIRGINIA

**Charleston**
Betts, Rebecca A.
Kilmer, Douglas Aaron
Mc Graw, Darrell Vivian, Jr.
**Fayetteville**
Rees, James Brennan
**Huntington**
Qualls, Alvie Edward, II
**Sutton**
Martin, William Clinton
**Wheeling**
Godwin, David

### WISCONSIN

**Appleton**
Metropulos, Mitchell James
**Brookfield**
Flaherty, Karen Janet
**De Pere**
Matyas, David John
**Eau Claire**
Frank, John LeRoy
**Janesville**
Jablonski, Raymond Leo
**Keshena**
Kussel, William Ferdinand, Jr.
**Madison**
Chesnik, Constance Mary
Cronin, Kevin Brian
Doyle, James E(dward)
Lautenschlager, Peggy Ann
Moriarty, Richard Briles
Potter, Kevin
**Milwaukee**
Dallosto, Raymond Michael
Dick, Terése Margaret
Laughter, Ron D.
Schneider, Thomas Paul
Stephens, Marla Jean
Wall, Joseph R.
**Montello**
Dufour, Richard Joseph
**Waukesha**
Hanson, Jason David

### WYOMING

**Cheyenne**
Freudenthal, David D.
Romero, Francisco Leandro
Woodhouse, Gay Vanderpoel
**Worland**
Berryman, Larry Brent

### TERRITORIES OF THE UNITED STATES

### AMERICAN SAMOA

**Pago Pago**
Aumoeualogo, Soli Salanoa
Mailo, Toetagata Albert

### GUAM

**Agana**
Black, Frederick A.
Tock, Joseph

### PUERTO RICO

**San Juan**
Gil, Guillermo

### VIRGIN ISLANDS

**Charlotte Amalie**
Hurd, James A., Jr.

### MILITARY ADDRESSES OF THE UNITED STATES

### EUROPE

**APO**
Lederer, Max Donald, Jr.

### CANADA

### ONTARIO

**Ottawa**
Buchanan, John MacLennan

### ENGLAND

**Beverley**
Edles, Gary Joel

### ADDRESS UNPUBLISHED

Altman, Barbara Jean Friedman
Berg, Hans Fredrik
Block, Richard Raphael
Booher, Alice Ann
Cambrice, Robert Louis
Campbell, John William
Capps, James Leigh, II
Carpenter, Susan Karen
Cohen-Gallet, Bonnie Robin
Cologne, Gordon Bennett
Condra, Allen Lee
Craig, Vicki Rene
Curtin, Kevin Gerard
Darr, Carol C.
Dietel, James Edwin
Eastwood, Mary
Fihn, Jeffrey Glaser
Gibson, Paula Lauren
Grab, Frederick Charles
Gregoire, Christine O.
Hallyburton, Margaret D.
Harms, John Kevin
Honigman, Steven
Housh, Tedrick Addison, Jr.
Izzo, John A.
Jallins, Richard David
Jochner, Michele Melina
Knepper, Kathleen N.
Kubo, Edward Hachiro, Jr.
Lachcik, Nancy Lou Marshall
Lundy, Sheila Edwards
Maroney, Thomas J.
Marr, Carmel Carrington
McCormick, David Arthur
McDowell, Margaret Holmes
McFadden, Nancy Elizabeth
McGraw, Warren Randolph, II
McManus, Martin Joseph
Metcalfe, Robert Davis, III
Metzger, Jeffrey Paul
Miller, Steven Richard
Murray, Fred F.
Nathanson, David J.
Paranzino, Michael
Patterson, Robert Dewey
Preston, Colleen Ann
Prozan, Michael William
Rae, John Joseph
Ray, Paula Marie
Reilly, Edward Francis, Jr.
Ruschky, Eric William
Samotin, Nancy
Sanders, Dennis Carl
Shaffert, Kurt
Smith, Deirdre O'Meara
Spencer, Billie Jane
Steptoe, Mary Lou
Thornbury, William Mitchell
Whitehouse, Sheldon
Wilburn, Mary Nelson
York, Alexandra

## INDUSTRY

### UNITED STATES

### ALABAMA

**Birmingham**
Rubright, James Alfred

### ARKANSAS

**Little Rock**
Gardner, Kathleen D.

### DISTRICT OF COLUMBIA

**Washington**
Moore, Robert Madison
Thompson, Richard Leon

### FLORIDA

**Ponte Vedra Beach**
Fiorentino, Thomas Martin

### IDAHO

**Boise**
Saldin, Thomas R.

### ILLINOIS

**Glenview**
Hudnut, Stewart Skinner

### INDIANA

**Indianapolis**
Greer, Charles Eugene
King, J. B.

### KANSAS

**Overland Park**
Callahan, Michael Thomas

### MICHIGAN

**Benton Harbor**
Hopp, Daniel Frederick

### MINNESOTA

**Saint Paul**
Cohen, Robert

### NEBRASKA

**Omaha**
Rohde, Bruce C.

### NEW JERSEY

**New Brunswick**
Fine, Roger Seth
**New Providence**
Thompson, Holley Marker

### NEW YORK

**Binghamton**
Farley, Daniel W.
**New York**
Konney, Paul Edward

### OKLAHOMA

**Oklahoma City**
Horner, Russell Grant, Jr.

### TENNESSEE

**Bristol**
Macione, Kyle Pritchett

### TEXAS

**San Antonio**
McCoy, Reagan Scott

### VIRGINIA

**Richmond**
Rudnick, Alan A.

### ADDRESS UNPUBLISHED

Crawford, William Walsh
Jackson, Robbi Jo
Ormasa, John

## JUDICIAL ADMINISTRATION

### UNITED STATES

### ALABAMA

**Ashland**
Ingram, Kenneth Frank
**Birmingham**
Acker, William Marsh, Jr.
Blackburn, Sharon Lovelace
Clemon, U. W.
Ferguson, Ralph Alton, Jr. (Sonny Ferguson)
Goldstein, Debra Holly
Guin, Junius Foy, Jr.
Hancock, James Hughes
Lynne, Seybourn Harris
Nelson, Edwin L.
Pointer, Sam Clyde, Jr.
Propst, Robert Bruce
Shores, Janie Ledlow
Smith, Edward Samuel
**Florence**
Smith, Larry Mack
**Gadsden**
Sledge, James Scott
**Mobile**
Butler, Charles Randolph, Jr.
Cox, Emmett Ripley
Hand, William Brevard
Howard, Alex T., Jr.
McCall, Daniel Thompson, Jr.
Pittman, Virgil
Thomas, Daniel Holcombe
**Montgomery**
Albritton, William Harold, III
Almon, Reneau Pearson
Brown, Jean Williams
Carnes, Edward E.
Cook, Ralph D.
De Ment, Ira
Dubina, Joel Fredrick
Godbold, John Cooper
Hobbs, Truman McGill
Hooper, Perry Ollie
Houston, James Gorman, Jr.
Johnstone, Douglas Inge
Kennedy, (Henry) Mark
Lyons, Champ, Jr.
Maddox, Alva Hugh
Steele, Rodney Redfearn
Thompson, Myron H.
Varner, Robert Edward
**Tuscaloosa**
See, Harold Frend

### ALASKA

**Anchorage**
Branson, Albert Harold (Harry Branson)
Bryner, Alexander O.
Carpeneti, Walter L.
Compton, Allen T.
Eastaugh, Robert L.
Fabe, Dana Anderson
Fitzgerald, James Michael
Holland, H. Russel
Sedwick, John W.
Singleton, James Keith
von der Heydt, James Arnold
**Fairbanks**
Kleinfeld, Andrew Jay

### ARIZONA

**Bisbee**
Holland, Robert Dale
**Phoenix**
Broomfield, Robert Cameron
Canby, William Cameron, Jr.
Carroll, Earl Hamblin
Carter, James Edward
Copple, William Perry
Ehrlich, Susan Anne
Feldman, Stanley George
Hardy, Charles Leach
Hicks, Bethany Gribben
Jones, Charles E.
Martone, Frederick J.
McGregor, Ruth Van Roekel
McNamee, Stephen M.
Rosenblatt, Paul Gerhardt
Schroeder, Mary Murphy
Silverman, Barry G.
Strand, Roger Gordon
Weisenburger, Theodore Maurice
Zlaket, Thomas A.
**Tucson**
Bilby, Richard Mansfield
Browning, William Docker
Marquez, Alfredo C.
Roll, John McCarthy
**Window Rock**
Austin, Raymond Darrel

### ARKANSAS

**Batesville**
Harkey, John Norman
**Conway**
Hays, Steele
**El Dorado**
Barnes, Harry F.
**Fayetteville**
Hendren, Jimm Larry
Waters, H. Franklin
**Little Rock**
Arnold, Morris Sheppard
Arnold, Richard Sheppard
Arnold, W. H. (Dub Arnold)
Corbin, Donald L.
Eisele, Garnett Thomas
Glaze, Thomas A.
Imber, Annabelle Clinton
Marshall, Linda Kaye
Reasoner, Stephen M.
Roaf, Andree Layton
Rogers, Judith M.
Roy, Elsijane Trimble
Smith, Lavenski R. (Vence)
Thornton, Ray
Wilson, William R., Jr.
Woods, Henry
Wright, Susan Webber

### CALIFORNIA

**Fort Bragg**
Lehan, Jonathan Michael
**Fresno**
Beck, Dennis L.
Coyle, Robert Everett
Crocker, Myron Donovan
Petrucelli, James Michael
Wanger, Oliver Winston
**Fullerton**
Prickett, Gregory L.
**Glendale**
Early, Alexander Rieman, III
**Long Beach**
Gasper, Robert W.
Tucker, Marcus Othello
**Los Angeles**
Alarcon, Arthur Lawrence
Armstrong, Orville
Baird, Lourdes G.
Bufford, Samuel Lawrence
Byrne, William Matthew, Jr.
Collins, Audrey B.
Cooper, Candace DeCarol
Curry, Daniel Arthur
Fenning, Lisa Hill
Fleming, Macklin
Gembacz, Gilbert Thaddeus
Hatter, Terry Julius, Jr.
Hupp, Harry L.
Ideman, James M.
Ito, Lance Allan
Kelleher, Robert Joseph
Keller, William D.

Kenyon, David V.
Letts, J. Spencer
Lew, Ronald S. W.
Manella, Nora M.
Marshall, Consuelo Bland
Masterson, William A.
Norris, William Albert
Paez, Richard A.
Pfaelzer, Mariana R.
Rafeedie, Edward, Sr.
Rea, William J.
Real, Manuel Lawrence
Stephens, Albert Lee, Jr.
Takasugi, Robert Mitsuhiro
Tevrizian, Dickran M., Jr.
Troost, Frank William
Waters, Laughlin Edward
Williams, David Welford
Wilson, Stephen Victor

**Modesto**
Siefkin, Susan Deeble

**Oakland**
Armstrong, Saundra Brown
Cline, Wilson Ettason
Jensen, D. Lowell
Newsome, Randall Jackson
Wilken, Claudia
Zika, Patrick John

**Pasadena**
Boochever, Robert
Fernandez, Ferdinand Francis
Goodwin, Alfred Theodore
Hall, Cynthia Holcomb
Johnson, Barbara Jean
Kozinski, Alex
Nelson, Dorothy Wright (Mrs. James F. Nelson)
Rymer, Pamela Ann
Tashima, Atsushi Wallace
Wardlaw, Kim A.M.

**Pleasanton**
Helm, Hugh Barnett

**Pomona**
Moore, S. Clark

**Ramona**
Jordan, David Francis, Jr.

**Rancho Cucamonga**
Irons, Sue E. Frayle

**Riverside**
Timlin, Robert J.

**Sacramento**
Burrell, Garland E., Jr.
Dahl, Loren Silvester
Garcia, Edward J.
Gilmoor, Richard H.
Karlton, Lawrence K.
Kolkey, Daniel Miles
Levi, David F.
Moulds, John F.
Schwartz, Milton Lewis
Van Camp, Brian Ralph

**San Carlos**
Cohn, Melvin E.

**San Diego**
Bowie, Peter Wentworth
Brewster, Rudi Milton
Enright, William Benner
Gilliam, Earl B.
Gonzalez, Irma Elsa
Harutunian, Albert T(heodore), III
Huff, Marilyn L.
Jones, Napoleon A., Jr.
Keep, Judith N.
Lewis, Gerald Jorgensen
Nielsen, Leland C.
Rhoades, John Skylstead, Sr.
Schwartz, Edward J.
Thompson, David Renwick
Thompson, Gordon, Jr.
Turrentine, Howard Boyd
Wallace, J. Clifford

**San Fernando**
Schwab, Howard Joel

**San Francisco**
Anderson, Carl West
Baxter, Marvin Ray
Brown, Janice Rogers
Browning, James Robert
Chesney, Maxine M.
Chin, Ming
Conti, Samuel
George, Ronald M.
Henderson, Thelton Eugene
Illston, Susan Y.
Jarvis, Donald Bertram
Kennard, Joyce L.
Kline, John Anthony
Mosk, Stanley
Noonan, John T., Jr.
Orrick, William Horsley, Jr.
Patel, Marilyn Hall
Schwarzer, William W
Sneed, Joseph Tyree, III
Walker, Vaughn R.
Werdegar, Kathryn Mickle

**San Jose**
Ingram, William Austin
Panelli, Edward Alexander
Stewart, Melinda Jane
Ware, James W.
Whyte, Ronald M.
Williams, Spencer Mortimer

**San Marino**
Mortimer, Wendell Reed, Jr.

**Santa Ana**
Barr, James Norman
Colaw, Thierry Patrick
Ferguson, Warren John
Stotler, Alicemarie Huber
Taylor, Gary L.
Wilkinson, Randell L.

**Santa Barbara**
Aldisert, Ruggero John

**Santa Monica**
Collins, Patricia Lynne
Vega, Benjamin Urbizo

**Solana Beach**
Watson, Jack Crozier

**South Lake Tahoe**
Kingsbury, Suzanne Nelson

**Studio City**
Lasarow, William Julius

**Van Nuys**
Kolostian, Richard George, Sr.
Mohr, Anthony James

**Woodland Hills**
Mund, Geraldine
Pregerson, Harry

### COLORADO

**Central City**
Rodgers, Frederic Barker

**Denver**
Babcock, Lewis Thornton
Bender, Michael Lee
Ebel, David M.
Felter, Edwin Lester, Jr.
Hobbs, Gregory James, Jr.
Kane, John Lawrence, Jr.
Kirshbaum, Howard M.
Kourlis, Rebecca Love
Lucero, Carlos
Martinez, Alex
Matsch, Richard P.
McWilliams, Robert Hugh
Mullarkey, Mary J.
Nottingham, Edward Willis, Jr.
Porfilio, John Carbone
Rice, Nancy E.
Rovira, Luis Dario
Satter, Raymond Nathan
Scott, Gregory Kellam
Sparr, Daniel Beattie
Stacy, Richard A.
Vollack, Anthony F.
Weinshienk, Zita Leeson

**Englewood**
Coffman, Penelope Dalton
Erickson, William Hurt

**Fort Collins**
Gandy, Hoke Conway

**Golden**
Demlow, James Carl
Jackson, Richard Brooke

**Hotchkiss**
Ela, William MacHarg

### CONNECTICUT

**Bridgeport**
Eginton, Warren William

**Danbury**
Cutsumpas, Lloyd
Yamin, Dianne Elizabeth

**Fairfield**
Lumbard, Joseph Edward, Jr.

**Guilford**
Ross, Michael Frederick

**Hartford**
Berdon, Robert Irwin
Bieluch, William Charles
Borden, David M.
Callahan, Robert Jeremiah
Chatigny, Robert Neil
Droney, Christopher F.
Dupont, Antoinette L.
Katz, Joette
Killian, Robert Kenneth, Jr.
Newman, Jon O.
Norcott, Fleming L., Jr.
Palmer, Richard N.
Peters, Ellen Ash
Schaller, Barry R.
Shea, David Michael
Sullivan, William J.
Thompson, Alvin W.

**Middlebury**
McDonald, Francis Michael

**New Britain**
Meskill, Thomas J.

**New Haven**
Arterton, Janet Bond
Burns, Ellen Bree
Cabranes, José Alberto
Calabresi, Guido
Dorsey, Peter Collins
Walker, John Mercer, Jr.
Winter, Ralph Karl, Jr.

**Waterbury**
Glass, Robert Davis
Goettel, Gerard Louis

### DELAWARE

**Dover**
Hartnett, Maurice A., III

**Georgetown**
Holland, Randy James

**Wilmington**
Balick, Helen Shaffer
Berger, Carolyn
Farnan, Joseph James, Jr.
Jacobs, Jack Bernard
Latchum, James Levin
Longobardi, Joseph J.
McKelvie, Roderick R.
Robinson, Sue L(ewis)
Roth, Jane Richards
Schwartz, Murray Merle
Stapleton, Walter King
Veasey, Eugene Norman
Walsh, Joseph Thomas
Wright, Caleb Merrill

### DISTRICT OF COLUMBIA

**Washington**
Archer, Glenn LeRoy, Jr.
Bayly, John Henry, Jr.
Beddow, Richard Harold
Beghe, Renato
Belson, James Anthony
Bernstein, Edwin S.
Blair, Warren Emerson
Breyer, Stephen Gerald
Bryant, William B.
Bryson, William Curtis
Buckley, James Lane
Burnett, Arthur Louis, Sr.
Chabot, Herbert L.
Chiechi, Carolyn Phyllis
Clevenger, Raymond C., III
Cohen, Mary Ann
Colvin, John O.
Couvillion, David Irvin
Cowen, Wilson
Cox, Walter Thompson, III
Crawford, Susan Jean
Edwards, Harry T.
Farley, John Joseph, III
Farrell, Michael W.
Flannery, Thomas Aquinas
Friedman, Daniel Mortimer
Gajarsa, Arthur J.
Gallagher, George R.
Garland, Merrick Brian
Gasch, Oliver
Gerber, Joel
Gibson, Reginald Walker
Gierke, Herman Fredrick, III
Ginsburg, Douglas Howard
Ginsburg, Ruth Bader
Glickman, Stephen
Goldberg, Stanley Joshua
Green, Joyce Hens
Green, June Lazenby
Greene, Harold H.
Hamblen, Lapsley Walker, Jr.
Harris, Stanley S.
Heifetz, Alan William
Henderson, Karen LeCraft
Holdaway, Ronald M.
Horn, Marian Blank
Ivers, Donald Louis
Jackson, Thomas Penfield
Jacobs, Julian I.
Johnson, Norma Holloway
Kennedy, Anthony McLeod
Kern, John Worth, III
King, Warren R.
Kline, Norman Douglas
Kramer, Kenneth Bentley
Lamberth, Royce C.
Laro, David
Lourie, Alan David
Mack, Julia Cooper
Margolis, Lawrence Stanley
Marvel, L. Paige
Mayer, Haldane Robert
Michel, Paul Redmond
Miller, Christine Odell Cook
Nangle, John Francis
Nebeker, Frank Quill
Newman, Pauline
Nims, Arthur Lee, III
Oberdorfer, Louis F.
O'Connor, Sandra Day
Parr, Carolyn Miller
Penn, John Garrett
Plager, S. Jay
Pryor, William C.
Rader, Randall Ray
Randolph, Arthur Raymond
Raum, Arnold
Rehnquist, William Hubbs
Reid, Inez Smith
Rich, Giles Sutherland
Robertson, James
Robinson, Aubrey Eugene, Jr.
Robinson, Wilkes Coleman
Rogers, Judith W.
Ruiz, Vanessa
Scalia, Antonin
Schall, Alvin Anthony
Schwelb, Frank Ernest
Sentelle, David Bryan
Smith, Roy Philip
Sporkin, Stanley
Steadman, John Montague
Steinberg, Jonathan Robert
Stevens, John Paul
Sullivan, Eugene Raymond
Swift, Stephen Jensen
Tatel, David Stephen
Terry, John Alfred
Thomas, Clarence
Tidwell, Moody Rudolph
Turner, James Thomas
Urbina, Ricardo M.
Vasquez, Juan Flores
Wagner, Annice McBryde
Wagner, Curtis Lee, Jr.
Wald, Patricia McGowan
Washington, Eric
Weinstein, Diane Gilbert
Whalen, Laurence J.
White, Byron R.
Williams, Stephen Fain
Wright, Lawrence A.
Zobel, Rya Weickert

### FLORIDA

**Belleair**
Blackmar, Charles Blakey

**Clearwater**
Peters, Robert Timothy

**Daytona Beach**
Rouse, Robert Kelly, Jr.

**Deland**
Sanders, Edwin Perry Bartley

**Fort Lauderdale**
Gonzalez, Jose Alejandro, Jr.
Roettger, Norman Charles, Jr.
Zloch, William J.

**Gainesville**
Paul, Maurice M.

**Jacksonville**
Black, Susan Harrell
Fryefield, Peter Jay
Hill, James Clinkscales
Hodges, William Terrell
Melton, Howell Webster, Sr.
Moore, John Henry, II
Nimmons, Ralph Wilson, Jr.
Schlesinger, Harvey Erwin
Tjoflat, Gerald Bard

**Key Biscayne**
Kraft, C. William, Jr.

**Merritt Island**
Johnson, Clarence Traylor, Jr.

**Miami**
Atkins, C(arl) Clyde
Barkett, Rosemary
Brown, Stephen Thomas
Cristol, A. Jay
Davis, Edward Bertrand
Fay, Peter Thorp
Freeman, Gill Sherryl
Friedman, Ronald Michael
Gold, Alan Stephen
Graham, Donald Lynn
Hague, Andrew Stuart
Highsmith, Shelby
Hoeveler, William M.
Karlan, Sandy Ellen
Kehoe, James W.
King, James Lawrence
Marcus, Stanley
Moore, Kevin Michael
Nesbitt, Lenore Carrero
Rosinek, Jeffrey
Ungaro-Benages, Ursula Mancusi

**Orlando**
Conway, Anne Callaghan
Fawsett, Patricia Combs
Sharp, George Kendall
Young, George Cressler

**Pensacola**
Collier, Lacey Alexander
Vinson, C. Roger

**Perry**
Bean, James Roy

**Saint Petersburg**
Grube, Karl Bertram
Roney, Paul H(itch)

**Tallahassee**
Anstead, Harry Lee
Grimes, Stephen Henry
Harding, Major Best
Kahn, Charles Jules, Jr.
Kogan, Gerald
Lewis, R. Fred
Overton, Benjamin Frederick
Pariente, Barbara J.
Quince, Peggy A.
Shaw, Leander Jerry, Jr.
Siegendorf, Arden M.
Stafford, William Henry, Jr.
Webster, Peter David
Wells, Charles Talley

**Tampa**
Adams, Henry Lee, Jr.
Bucklew, Susan Cawthon
Corcoran, Clement Timothy, III
Dail, Joseph Garner, Jr.
Kovachevich, Elizabeth Anne
Menendez, Manuel, Jr.
Merryday, Steven D.

**West Palm Beach**
Cohen, Stephen M(artin)
Eschbach, Jesse Ernest
Farmer, Gary Michael
Hurley, Daniel T. K.
Lindsey, Hubert Rolane
Paine, James Carriger
Ryskamp, Kenneth Lee
Scheiner, Howard

### GEORGIA

**Albany**
Sands, W. Louis

**Atlanta**
Benham, Robert
Birch, Stanley Francis, Jr.
Camp, Jack Tarpley, Jr.
Carley, George H.
Carnes, Julie Elizabeth
Cooper, Clarence
Deane, Richard H., Jr.
Edmondson, James Larry
Evans, Orinda D.
Fletcher, Norman S.
Forrester, J. Owen
Freeman, Richard Cameron
Henderson, Albert John
Hines, Preston Harris
Hull, Frank Mays
Hunstein, Carol
Hunt, Willis B., Jr.
Kravitch, Phyllis A.
Moore, Thelma Wyatt
Murphy, Margaret Hackett
O'Kelley, William Clark
Sears, Leah J.
Shoob, Marvin H.
Thompson, Hugh P
Tidwell, George Ernest
Ward, Horace Taliaferro

**Augusta**
Allgood, Robert Lynell
Bowen, Dudley Hollingsworth, Jr.

**Brunswick**
Alaimo, Anthony A.

**Cleveland**
Barrett, David Eugene

**Columbus**
Elliott, James Robert
Laney, John Thomas, III

**Decatur**
Carriere, Edward E., Jr.

**Fayetteville**
Pierce, Sharon Irene

**Fort Valley**
Lee, Laurens Conway

**Hapeville**
McCord, Robert Bryan

**Jefferson**
Gray, Jerry Clinton

**Lawrenceville**
Iannazzone, Joseph Charles
Reeves, Gene

**Macon**
Anderson, Robert Lanier, III
Fitzpatrick, Duross
Hershner, Robert Franklin, Jr.
Owens, Wilbur Dawson, Jr.
Phillips, J(ohn) Taylor

**Rome**
Murphy, Harold Loyd
Vining, Robert Luke, Jr.

**Savannah**
Edenfield, Berry Avant
Moore, William Theodore, Jr.

**Statesboro**
Martin, Faye Sanders

### HAWAII

**Honolulu**
Acoba, Simeon Rivera, Jr.
Choy, Herbert Young Cho
Ezra, David Alan
Kay, Alan Cooke
King, Samuel Pailthorpe
Klein, Robert Gordon
Levinson, Steven Henry
Moon, Ronald T. Y.
Nakayama, Paula Aiko
Pence, Martin
Ramil, Mario R.

**Wailuku**
McNish, Douglas Scott

### IDAHO

**Boise**
Kidwell, Wayne L.
Lodge, Edward James
McDevitt, Charles Francis
Nelson, Thomas G.
Silak, Cathy R.
Trott, Stephen Spangler
Walters, Jesse Raymond, Jr.

### ILLINOIS

**Belleville**
Ferguson, John Marshall
Kernan, Stephen Michael, Sr.
Stevens, C. Glenn

**Benton**
Foreman, James Louis
Gilbert, J. Phil

**Chicago**
Alesia, James H(enry)
Andersen, Wayne R.
Aspen, Marvin Edward
Barliant, Ronald
Bauer, William Joseph
Berman, Andrew Harris
Bilandic, Michael A.
Castillo, Ruben
Conlon, Suzanne B.
Cousins, William, Jr.
Cudahy, Richard D.
Duff, Brian Barnett
Easterbrook, Frank Hoover
Fairchild, Thomas E.
Flaum, Joel Martin
Freeman, Charles E.
Funderburk, Raymond
Gettleman, Robert William
Grady, John F.
Hart, William Thomas
Holderman, James F., Jr.
Kanne, Michael Stephen
Kocoras, Charles Petros
Leighton, George Neves
Leikin, Mitchell
Leinenweber, Harry D.
Lindberg, George W.
Marovich, George M.
McMorrow, Mary Ann G.
Moran, James Byron
Morrissey, George Michael
Nickels, John L.
Nordberg, John Albert
Norgle, Charles Ronald, Sr.
Pallmeyer, Rebecca Ruth
Pell, Wilbur Frank, Jr.
Plunkett, Paul Edmund
Posner, Richard Allen
Rovner, Ilana Kara Diamond
Shadur, Milton I.
Sonderby, Susan Pierson
Squires, John Henry
Toles, Edward Bernard
Williams, Ann Claire
Zagel, James Block

**East Saint Louis**
Beatty, William Louis
Riley, Paul E.
Stiehl, William D.

**Edwardsville**
Crowder, Barbara Lynn

**Elgin**
Kirkland, Alfred Younges, Sr.

**Fairview Heights**
Harrison, Moses W., II

**Hennepin**
Bumgarner, James McNabb

**Joliet**
Bertani-Tomczak, Amy M.

**Kankakee**
Bradshaw Elliott, Kathy

**Naperville**
Homer, Thomas J.

**Peoria**
Heiple, James Dee
McDade, Joe Billy
Mihm, Michael Martin

**Pontiac**
Glennon, Charles Edward

**Rockford**
Reinhard, Philip G.

**Springfield**
Lessen, Larry Lee
Miller, Benjamin K.
Mills, Richard Henry
Wood, Harlington, Jr.

**Urbana**
Baker, Harold Albert

**Waukegan**
Brady, Terrence Joseph

**Wheaton**
Ferguson, William I.

**Wilmette**
Bowman, George Arthur, Jr.

### INDIANA

**Boonville**
Aylsworth, Robert Reed
Campbell, Edward Adolph

**Evansville**
Capshaw, Tommie Dean
Liberty, Arthur Andrew

**Fort Wayne**
Bobay, Craig John
Lee, William Charles

**Hammond**
Dywan, Jeffery Joseph
Lozano, Rudolpho
Moody, James T(yne)
Rodovich, Andrew Paul

**Indianapolis**
Barker, Sarah Evans
Boehm, Theodore Reed
Dickson, Brent E(llis)
Dillin, S. Hugh
Fisher, Thomas Graham
Givan, Richard Martin
Hamilton, David F.
McKinney, Larry J.
Price, John Louis
Selby, Myra Consetta
Shepard, Randall Terry
Sullivan, Frank, Jr.
Tinder, John Daniel
**Jeffersonville**
Barthold, Clementine B.
**Kokomo**
Stein, Eleanor Bankoff
**Lagrange**
Brown, George E.
**South Bend**
Brueseke, Harold Edward
Manion, Daniel Anthony
Miller, Robert L., Jr.
Ripple, Kenneth Francis
Sharp, Allen

## IOWA

**Algona**
Andreasen, James Hallis
**Cedar Rapids**
Hansen, David Rasmussen
Mc Manus, Edward Joseph
Melloy, Michael J.
**Chariton**
Stuart, William Corwin
**Council Bluffs**
Peterson, Richard William
**Davenport**
Neuman, Linda Kinney
**Des Moines**
Cady, Mark S.
Carter, James H.
Fagg, George Gardner
Harris, K. David
Larson, Jerry Leroy
Lavorato, Louis A.
Longstaff, Ronald E.
McGiverin, Arthur A.
Snell, Bruce M., Jr.
Ternus, Marsha K.
Vietor, Harold Duane
Wolle, Charles Robert
**Sioux City**
O'Brien, Donald Eugene
**West Des Moines**
Miller, Theodore Hillis

## KANSAS

**Kansas City**
Lungstrum, John W.
VanBebber, George Thomas
Vratil, Kathryn Hoefer
**Lawrence**
Briscoe, Mary Beck
Tacha, Deanell Reece
**Leavenworth**
Stanley, Arthur Jehu, Jr.
**Olathe**
Chipman, Marion Walter
**Topeka**
Abbott, Bob
Allegrucci, Donald Lee
Cox, Joseph Lawrence
Crow, Sam Alfred
Davis, Robert Edward
Larson, Edward
Lockett, Tyler Charles
Macnish, James Martin, Jr.
Marquardt, Christel Elisabeth
McFarland, Kay Eleanor
Pusateri, James Anthony
Rogers, Richard Dean
Saffels, Dale Emerson
Six, Fred N.
**Wichita**
Brown, Wesley Ernest

## KENTUCKY

**Ashland**
Wilhoit, Henry Rupert, Jr.
**Bowling Green**
Huddleston, Joseph Russell
**Campbellsville**
Phillips, Connie Sullivan
**Elizabethtown**
Cooper, William S.
**Frankfort**
Graves, John William
Hood, Joseph M.
Johnstone, Martin E.
Lambert, Joseph Earl
Stephens, Robert F.
Stumbo, Janet Lynn
Wintersheimer, Donald Carl
**Lexington**
Forester, Karl S.
Keller, James
Varellas, Sandra Motte
**London**
Coffman, Jennifer B.
Siler, Eugene Edward, Jr.
Unthank, G. Wix
**Louisville**
Allen, Charles Mengel
Boggs, Danny Julian
Heyburn, John Gilpin, II
Martin, Boyce Ficklen, Jr.
Roberts, J. Wendell
Simpson, Charles R., III
Strause, Randall Scott
**Madisonville**
Spain, Thomas B.
**Paducah**
Johnstone, Edward Huggins
Russell, Thomas B.
**Richmond**
Chenault, James Stouffer

**Wickliffe**
Shadoan, William Lewis

## LOUISIANA

**Alexandria**
Little, F. A., Jr.
**Baton Rouge**
Kelley, Timothy Edward
Parker, John Victor
Polozola, Frank Joseph
**Covington**
Fitzsimmons, Brady Michael
**Franklinton**
Burris, William Joseph
**Gretna**
McManus, Clarence Elburn
Wicker, Thomas Carey, Jr.
**Lafayette**
Davis, William Eugene
Doherty, Rebecca Feeney
Duhe, John Malcolm, Jr.
Haik, Richard T., Sr.
Melançon, Tucker Lee
Putnam, Richard Johnson
Shaw, John Malach
**Lake Charles**
Hunter, Edwin Ford, Jr.
Trimble, James T., Jr.
**Marksville**
Spruill, Kerry Lyndon
**New Orleans**
Beer, Peter Hill
Berrigan, Helen Ginger
Calogero, Pascal Frank, Jr.
Clement, Edith Brown
Dennis, James Leon
Duplantier, Adrian Guy
Duval, Stanwood Richardson, Jr.
Fallon, Eldon E.
Feldman, Martin L. C.
Johnson, Bernette J.
Kimball, Catherine D.
Knoll, Jeannette Theriot
Lemmon, Harry Thomas
Livaudais, Marcel, Jr.
Marcus, Walter F., Jr.
McNamara, A. J.
Mentz, Henry Alvan, Jr.
Mitchell, Lansing Leroy
Porteous, G. Thomas, Jr.
Schwartz, Charles, Jr.
Sear, Morey Leonard
Traylor, Chet D.
Victory, Jeffrey Paul
Wiener, Jacques Loeb, Jr.
**Ponchatoula**
Kuhn, James E.
**Shreveport**
Payne, Roy Steven
Politz, Henry Anthony
Stagg, Tom
Stewart, Carl E.
Walter, Donald Ellsworth

## MAINE

**Auburn**
Clifford, Robert William
**Bangor**
Brody, Morton Aaron
Rudman, Paul Lewis
**Bath**
Field, Joseph Hooper
**Portland**
Alexander, Donald G.
Bradford, Carl O.
Calkins, Susan W.
Carter, Gene
Coffin, Frank Morey
Dana, Howard H., Jr.
Glassman, Caroline Duby
Hornby, David Brock
Lipez, Kermit V.
McKusick, Vincent Lee
Saufley, Leigh Ingalls
**Rockland**
Collins, Samuel W., Jr.

## MARYLAND

**Annapolis**
Cathell, Dale Roberts
Eldridge, John Cole
**Baltimore**
Bell, Robert M.
Black, Walter Evan, Jr.
Derby, Ernest Stephen
Garbis, Marvin Joseph
Goetz, Clarence Edward
Harvey, Alexander, II
Legg, Benson Everett
Levin, Marshall Abbott
Maletz, Herbert Naaman
Motz, Diana Gribbon
Motz, John Frederick
Murnaghan, Francis Dominic, Jr.
Nickerson, William Milnor
Niemeyer, Paul Victor
Northrop, Edward Skottowe
Quarles, William Daniel
Rodowsky, Lawrence Francis
Sfekas, James Stephen
Smalkin, Frederic N.
Young, Joseph H.
**Greenbelt**
Chasanow, Deborah K.
Messitte, Peter Jo
Williams, Alexander, Jr.
**Rockville**
McAuliffe, John F.
Raker, Irma Steinberg
**Towson**
Eyler, James R.
Wilner, Alan M.
**Upper Marlboro**
Chasanow, Howard Stuart

## MASSACHUSETTS

**Boston**
Abrams, Ruth Ida
Aldrich, Bailey
Boudin, Michael
Bowler, Marianne Bianca
Bownes, Hugh Henry
Campbell, Levin Hicks
Connolly, Thomas Edward
Garrity, Wendell Arthur, Jr.
Gertner, Nancy
Greaney, John M.
Harrington, Edward F.
Ireland, Roderick L.
Keeton, Robert Ernest
Lasker, Morris E.
Lindsay, Reginald Carl
Lynch, Neil L(awrence)
Lynch, Sandra Lea
Marshall, Margaret Hilary
Mazzone, A. David
Nelson, David S.
O'Connor, Francis Patrick
O'Toole, George A., Jr.
Saris, Patti Barbara
Selya, Bruce Marshall
Skinner, Walter Jay
Stearns, Richard Gaylore
Tauro, Joseph Louis
Wolf, Mark Lawrence
Woodlock, Douglas Preston
Young, William Glover
**Holyoke**
Donohue, Michael Joseph
**Longmeadow**
Keady, George Cregan, Jr.
**Newton**
Wilkins, Herbert Putnam
**Pittsfield**
Koenigs, Rita Scales
Sacco, Rudolph Augustine
**Springfield**
Crampton, Rebekah Jean
Freedman, Frank Harlan
Ponsor, Michael Adrian
**Worcester**
Gorton, Nathaniel M.

## MICHIGAN

**Ann Arbor**
Hackett, Barbara (Kloka)
Pepe, Steven Douglas
**Bay City**
Churchill, James Paul
Cleland, Robert Hardy
**Birmingham**
La Plata, George
**Bloomfield Hills**
Kaufman, Ira Gladstone
**Charlotte**
Eveland, Thomas Shaw
**Dearborn**
Runco, William Joseph
**Detroit**
Adams, Lydia Cecile
Borman, Paul David
Boyle, Patricia Jean
Clay, Eric L.
Corrigan, Maura Denise
Duggan, Patrick James
Edmunds, Nancy Garlock
Feikens, John
Friedman, Bernard Alvin
Gilmore, Horace Weldon
Graves, Ray Reynolds
Keith, Damon Jerome
Kelly, Marilyn
Kennedy, Cornelia Groefsema
Levin, Charles Leonard
Lloyd, Leona Loretta
Rosen, Gerald Ellis
Ryan, James Leo
Szymanski, David J.
Taylor, Anna Diggs
Woods, George Edward
**East Lansing**
Bladen, Edwin Mark
**Flint**
Gadola, Paul V.
Washington, Valdemar Luther
**Glen Arbor**
Newblatt, Stewart Albert
**Grand Rapids**
Bell, Robert Holmes
Brenneman, Hugh Warren, Jr.
Hillman, Douglas Woodruff
Miles, Wendell A.
Quist, Gordon Jay
**Grayling**
Davis, Alton Thomas
**Kalamazoo**
Enslen, Richard Alan
**Kentwood**
Kelly, William Garrett
**Lansing**
Brickley, James H.
Cavanagh, Michael Francis
Hoffman, Harvey John
Mallett, Conrad LeRoy, Jr.
McKeague, David William
Spence, Howard Tee Devon
Suhrheinrich, Richard Fred
Taylor, Clifford Woodworth
Young, Robert P.
**Mason**
Harrison, Michael Gregory
**Pontiac**
Tyner, Deborah G.
**Port Huron**
Keyes, Allen E.
**Saint Clair Shores**
Hausner, John Herman
Ryan, Harold Martin
**Saint Joseph**
Fields, John Norris
**Traverse City**
Weaver, Elizabeth A.

## MINNESOTA

**Albert Lea**
Broberg, James E.
Sturtz, William Rosenberg
**Anoka**
Quinn, R. Joseph

**Duluth**
Sweetland, Heather Leigh
**Minneapolis**
Aldrich, Stephen Charles
Amdahl, Douglas Kenneth
Arthur, Lindsay Grier
Davis, Michael J.
Doty, David Singleton
Lebedoff, Jonathan Galanter
MacLaughlin, Harry Hunter
Murphy, Diana E.
Rosenbaum, James Michael
**Minnetonka**
Rogers, James Devitt
**Rochester**
Keith, Alexander Macdonald
**Saint Cloud**
Nierengarten, Roger Joseph
**Saint Paul**
Alsop, Donald Douglas
Anderson, Paul Holden
Anderson, Russell A.
Blatz, Kathleen Ann
Coyne, Mary Jeanne
Kishel, Gregory Francis
Kyle, Richard House
Lancaster, Joan Erickson
Lay, Donald Pomeroy
Loken, James Burton
Page, Alan Cedric
Renner, Robert George
Stringer, Edward Charles
Tomljanovich, Esther M.
Willis, Bruce Donald

## MISSISSIPPI

**Aberdeen**
Davidson, Glen Harris
Senter, Lyonel Thomas, Jr.
**Fulton**
Mills, Michael Paul
**Gulfport**
Russell, Dan M., Jr.
**Hattiesburg**
Pickering, Charles W., Sr.
**Jackson**
Banks, Fred Lee, Jr.
Barbour, William H., Jr.
Barksdale, Rhesa Hawkins
Cobb, Kay B.
Jolly, E. Grady
Lee, Tom Stewart
McRae, Charles R.
Payne, Mary Libby
Pittman, Edwin Lloyd
Prather, Lenore Loving
Smith, James W., Jr.
Sullivan, Michael David
Waller, William Lowe, Jr.
Wingate, Henry Travillion
**Natchez**
Bramlette, David C., III
**Oxford**
Biggers, Neal Brooks, Jr.

## MISSOURI

**Farmington**
Pennoyer, James Esten
**Jefferson City**
Benton, W. Duane
Covington, Ann K.
Holstein, John Charles
Knox, William Arthur
Limbaugh, Stephen Nathaniel, Jr.
Price, William Ray, Jr.
Robertson, Edward D., Jr.
White, Ronnie L.
Wolff, Michael A.
**Kansas City**
Bartlett, D. Brook
Bowman, Pasco Middleton, II
Gaitan, Fernando J., Jr.
Gibson, Floyd Robert
Gibson, John Robert
Hunter, Elmo Bolton
Koger, Frank Williams
Sachs, Howard F(rederic)
Whipple, Dean
Wright, Scott Olin
**Saint Louis**
Barta, James Joseph
Filippine, Edward Louis
Gaertner, Gary M.
Hamilton, Jean Constance
Jackson, Carol E.
Limbaugh, Stephen Nathaniel
McMillian, Theodore
Seiler, James Elmer
Shaw, Charles Alexander
Stohr, Donald J.
**Springfield**
Clark, Russell Gentry

## MONTANA

**Billings**
Shanstrom, Jack D.
Thomas, Sidney R.
**Circle**
McDonough, Russell Charles
**Great Falls**
Hatfield, Paul Gerhart
**Hamilton**
Langton, Jeffrey H.
**Helena**
Gray, Karla Marie
Harrison, John Conway
Hunt, William E., Sr.
Leaphart, W. William
Lovell, Charles C.
Nelson, James C
Regnier, James
Trieweiler, Terry Nicholas
Turnage, Jean A.

## NEBRASKA

**Lincoln**
Beam, Clarence Arlen
Connolly, William M.
Gerrard, John M.
Hastings, William Charles
Hendry, John
Kopf, Richard G.
McCormack, Michael
Miller-Lerman, Lindsey
Stephan, Kenneth C.
Urbom, Warren Keith
White, C. Thomas
Wright, John F.
**Omaha**
Cambridge, William G.
Hartigan, John Dawson, Jr.
Shanahan, Thomas M.
Strom, Lyle Elmer
**Seward**
Rouse, Gerald Edward

## NEVADA

**Carson City**
Agosti, Deborah
Becker, Nancy Anne
Gunderson, Elmer Millard
Leavitt, Myron E.
Maupin, Bill
Rose, Robert E(dgar)
Springer, Charles Edward
Young, C. Clifton
**Las Vegas**
George, Lloyd D.
Jones, Steven Emrys
Parraguirre, Ronald David
Pro, Philip Martin
Steffen, Thomas Lee
**Reno**
Brunetti, Melvin T.
Hagen, David Warner
Hug, Procter Ralph, Jr.
McKibben, Howard D.
Reed, Edward Cornelius, Jr.

## NEW HAMPSHIRE

**Concord**
Barbadoro, Paul J.
Brock, David Allen
Broderick, John T., Jr.
Devine, Shane
DiClerico, Joseph Anthony, Jr.
Horton, Sherman D., Jr.
Johnson, William R.
McAuliffe, Steven James
Stahl, Norman H.
Thayer, W(alter) Stephen, III
**Nashua**
Barry, William Henry, Jr.

## NEW JERSEY

**Atlantic City**
Lashman, Shelley Bortin
**Basking Ridge**
Griffin, Bryant Wade
**Camden**
Brotman, Stanley Seymour
Irenas, Joseph Eron
Rodriguez, Joseph H.
Simandle, Jerome B.
**Elizabeth**
Spatola, Jo-Anne Buccinna
**Freehold**
Newman, James Michael
**Hackensack**
Cipollone, Anthony Dominic
Stein, Gary S.
**Jersey City**
Connors, Richard F.
**Morristown**
Schreiber, Sidney M.
**New Brunswick**
Ferencz, Bradley
**Newark**
Ackerman, Harold A.
Alito, Samuel Anthony, Jr.
Barry, Maryanne Trump
Bassler, William G.
Bissell, John W.
Chesler, Stanley Richard
Debevoise, Dickinson Richards
Garth, Leonard I.
Lechner, Alfred James, Jr.
Lifland, John C.
Politan, Nicholas H.
Wolin, Alfred M.
Yanoff, Leo
**Paterson**
Reiss, Sidney H.
**Red Bank**
O'Hern, Daniel Joseph
**Somerville**
Yurasko, Frank Noel
**Trenton**
Brown, Garrett Edward, Jr.
Cooper, Mary Little
Cowen, Robert E.
Gindin, William Howard
Greenberg, Morton Ira
Long, Virginia
Poritz, Deborah T.
Thompson, Anne Elise
Verniero, Peter
**Warren**
Coleman, James H., Jr.

## NEW MEXICO

**Albuquerque**
Conway, John E.
Dal Santo, Diane
Hansen, Curtis LeRoy
Knowles, Richard John
Mechem, Edwin Leard
Parker, James Aubrey
**Las Cruces**
Bratton, Howard Calvin
**Lordsburg**
Richins, Norma Jean
**Los Lunas**
Pope, John William
**Roswell**
Baldock, Bobby Ray
**Santa Fe**
Baca, Joseph Francis
Campos, Santiago E.

Franchini, Gene Edward
Kaufman, Bruce Eric
Kelly, Paul Joseph, Jr.
Maes, Petra Jimenez
Minzner, Pamela B.
Serna, Patricio
Vazquez, Martha Alicia
Yalman, Ann

### NEW YORK

**Albany**
Bellacosa, Joseph W.
Kaye, Judith Smith
Meader, John Daniel
Miner, Roger Jeffrey
Smith, Ralph Wesley, Jr.
Wesley, Richard C.
**Binghamton**
McAvoy, Thomas James
Regenbogen, Adam
**Bronx**
Bamberger, Phylis Skloot
Barone, John A.
Price, Richard Lee
Sonberg, Michael Robert
**Brooklyn**
Ambrosio, Michael Angelo
Amon, Carol Bagley
Dearie, Raymond Joseph
Glasser, Israel Leo
Gleeson, John
Hurley, Denis R.
Johnson, Sterling, Jr.
Korman, Edward R.
Levy, Robert Morris
Nickerson, Eugene H.
Raggi, Reena
Reichbach, Gustin Lewis
Ryan, Leonard Eames
Sifton, Charles Proctor
Trager, David G.
Weinstein, Jack Bertrand
**Buffalo**
Arcara, Richard Joseph
Curtin, John T.
Elfvin, John Thomas
Kaufman, Adam D.
Skretny, William Marion
**Catskill**
Lalor, Daniel Kevin
**Central Islip**
Blydenburgh, Donald Richard
**Farmingdale**
Lavallee, George
**Fresh Meadows**
Nisnewitz, David Zalman
**Hauppauge**
Wexler, Leonard D.
**Jamaica**
Grayshaw, James Raymond
**Lake George**
Austin, John DeLong
**Little Valley**
Himelein, Larry M.
**Mineola**
Burstein, Beatrice S.
**New Rochelle**
Jamieson, Linda Susan
**New York**
Aquilino, Thomas Joseph, Jr.
Batts, Deborah A.
Blinder, Albert Allan
Buchwald, Naomi Reice
Carman, Gregory Wright
Carter, Robert Lee
Cedarbaum, Miriam Goldman
Chin, Denny
Ciparick, Carmen Beauchamp
DiCarlo, Dominick L.
Duffy, Kevin Thomas
Edelstein, David Northon
Feinberg, Wilfred
Francis, James Clark, IV
Freedman, Helen Edelstein
Griesa, Thomas Poole
Haight, Charles Sherman, Jr.
Jacobs, Dennis
Jurow, George
Kaplan, Lewis A.
Kearse, Amalya Lyle
Keenan, John Fontaine
Klein, Harold S(herman)
Knapp, Whitman
Koeltl, John George
Kram, Shirley Wohl
Kramer, Raymond E.
Leisure, Peter Keeton
Leval, Pierre Nelson
Lowe, Mary Johnson
Maas, Frank
Martin, John Sherwood, Jr.
McLaughlin, Joseph Michael
Motley, Constance Baker (Mrs. Joel Wilson Motley)
Mukasey, Michael B.
Musgrave, R. Kenton
Owen, Richard
Patterson, Robert Porter, Jr.
Pollack, Milton
Preska, Loretta A.
Sack, Robert David
Sand, Leonard B.
Schwartz, Allen G.
Sklar, Stanley Lawrence
Smith, George Bundy
Sotomayor, Sonia
Sprizzo, John Emilio
Stackhouse, John E.H.
Stein, Sidney H.
Straub, Chester John
Titone, Vito Joseph
Vassilakis, Theodore
Ward, Robert Joseph
Watson, James Lopez
Williams, Milton Lawrence
Wood, Kimba M.
**Niagara Falls**
Koshian, Jacqueline Marie
**Oswego**
Jansen, Lambertus
**Penn Yan**
Falvey, W(illiam) Patrick
**Plattsburgh**
Feinberg, Robert Julian
**Poughkeepsie**
Dolan, Thomas Joseph
Rosenblatt, Albert Martin
**Rochester**
Campbell, Vincent Bernard
Larimer, David George
Schwartz, John Robert
Telesca, Michael Anthony
Van Graafeiland, Ellsworth Alfred
**Rome**
Simons, Richard Duncan
**Sag Harbor**
Pierce, Lawrence Warren
**Schenectady**
Levine, Howard Arnold
**Staten Island**
Meyer, M. Holt
**Syracuse**
McCurn, Neal Peters
Munson, Howard G.
Pooler, Rosemary S.
Scullin, Frederick James, Jr.
Wells, Peter Nathaniel
**Uniondale**
Boyle, E. Thomas
Mishler, Jacob
Platt, Thomas Collier, Jr.
Seybert, Joanna
Spatt, Arthur Donald
**Utica**
Cardamone, Richard J.
**White Plains**
Brieant, Charles La Monte
Conner, William Curtis
Ellerby, James Edward, Jr.
Hardin, Adlai Stevenson, Jr.
McMahon, Colleen
West, Joseph King
**Yonkers**
Edlitz, Sandra B.

### NORTH CAROLINA

**Asheville**
Thornburg, Lacy Herman
**Charlotte**
Mullen, Graham C.
Potter, Robert Daniel
Voorhees, Richard Lesley
**Elizabeth City**
Boyle, Terrence W.
**Greensboro**
Bullock, Frank William, Jr.
Gordon, Eugene Andrew
Osteen, William L., Sr.
Tilley, Norwood Carlton, Jr.
**Greenville**
Howard, Malcolm Jones
**Morganton**
Ervin, Samuel James, III
**Raleigh**
Britt, W. Earl
Brown, James Joseph
Denson, Alexander Bunn
Eagles, Sidney Smith, Jr.
Freeman, Franklin Edward, Jr.
Frye, Henry E.
Lake, I. Beverly, Jr.
Martin, John Charles
Martin, Mark D.
Mitchell, Burley Bayard, Jr.
Orr, Robert F.
Parker, Sarah Elizabeth
Small, Alden Thomas
Wainwright, George
Webb, John
**Wilmington**
Fox, James Carroll
**Winston Salem**
Beaty, James Arthur, Jr.
Eliason, Russell Allen
Erwin, Richard Cannon, Sr.
Ward, Hiram Hamilton

### NORTH DAKOTA

**Bismarck**
Conmy, Patrick A.
Erickstad, Ralph John
Jorgensen, Donald LeRoy
Kapsner, Carol Ronning
Maring, Mary Muehlen
Neumann, William Allen
Sandstrom, Dale Vernon
VandeWalle, Gerald Wayne
Van Sickle, Bruce Marion
**Fargo**
Bright, Myron H.
Magill, Frank John
Webb, Rodney Scott
**Minot**
Kerian, Jon Robert

### OHIO

**Akron**
Bell, Samuel H.
Contie, Leroy John, Jr.
Dowd, David D., Jr.
**Athens**
Lavelle, William Ambrose
**Bellefontaine**
O'Connor, Mark S.
**Cincinnati**
Beckwith, Sandra Shank
Black, Robert L., Jr.
Engel, Albert Joseph
Jones, Nathaniel Raphael
Karam, Ernest
Nelson, David Aldrich
Painter, Mark Philip
Perlman, Burton
Spiegel, S. Arthur
Weber, Herman Jacob
**Cleveland**
Aldrich, Ann
Baxter, Randolph
Kilbane, Anne L.
Krupansky, Robert Bazil
Manos, John M.
Matia, Paul Ramon
Moore, Karen Nelson
Oliver, Solomon, Jr.
Porter, James Morris
Wells, Lesley B.
White, George W.
**Columbus**
Calhoun, Donald Eugene, Jr.
Cole, Ransey Guy, Jr.
Cook, Deborah L.
Douglas, Andrew
Graham, James Lowell
Holschuh, John David
Kinneary, Joseph Peter
La Salle, Lawrence Joseph
Leach, Russell
Miller, Nodine
Moyer, Thomas J.
Norris, Alan Eugene
Pfeifer, Paul E.
Resnick, Alice Robie
Sargus, Edmund A., Jr.
Sellers, Barbara Jackson
Smith, George Curtis
Stratton, Evelyn Lundberg
Sweeney, Asher William
Sweeney, Francis E.
Wright, J. Craig
**Dayton**
Knapp, James Ian Keith
Merz, Michael
Petzold, John P.
**Lisbon**
Dailey, Coleen Hall
**Lucasville**
Reno, Ottie Wayne
**Marion**
Rogers, Richard Michael
**Medina**
Batchelder, Alice M.
**Middletown**
Powell, Stephen Walter
**Newton Falls**
Old, Thomas Leigh
**Sandusky**
Lawson, Michael
Stacey, James Allen
**Toledo**
Carr, James Gray
Potter, John William
**Van Wert**
Walters, Sumner J.

### OKLAHOMA

**Atoka**
Gabbard, (James) Douglas, II
**Guthrie**
Brooks, Larry Roger
**Muskogee**
Seay, Frank Howell
**Oklahoma City**
Alley, Wayne Edward
Bohanon, Luther L.
Cauthron, Robin J.
Hargrave, Rudolph
Henry, Robert Harlan
Hodges, Ralph B.
Holloway, William Judson, Jr.
Irwin, Pat
Lavender, Robert Eugene
Leonard, Timothy Dwight
Lumpkin, Gary Leonard
Opala, Marian P(eter)
Russell, David L.
Simms, Robert D.
Summers, Hardy
Thompson, Ralph Gordon
Towery, Curtis Kent
Watt, Joseph Michael
West, Lee Roy
Wilson, Alma
**Seminole**
Snow, Gary Paul
**Tulsa**
Brett, Thomas Rutherford
Cook, Harold Dale
Ellison, James Oliver
Frizzell, Gregory Kent
Kern, Terry C.
Seymour, Stephanie Kulp
Taylor, Joe Clinton
Turnbull, E. R. (Ned Turnbull)

### OREGON

**Eugene**
Hogan, Michael R(obert)
**Portland**
Belloni, Robert Clinton
Burns, James M.
Fisher, Ann L.
Frye, Helen Jackson
Graber, Susan P.
Haggerty, Ancer Lee
Higdon, Polly Susanne
Hubel, Dennis James
Hyatt, Dan Richard
Jones, Robert Edward
King, Garr Michael
Leavy, Edward
Marsh, Malcolm F.
O'Scannlain, Diarmuid Fionntain
Panner, Owen M.
Redden, James Anthony
Roth, Phillip Joseph
Skopil, Otto Richard, Jr.
Todd, Steven A.
Unis, Richard L.
**Saint Helens**
Shera Taylor, Diana Marie
**Salem**
Carson, Wallace Preston, Jr.
Durham, Robert Donald, Jr.
Kulongoski, Theodore Ralph
Leeson, Susan M.
Linder, Virginia Lynn
Peterson, Edwin J.
Riggs, R. William
Russell, Maurice Lloyd
Van Hoomissen, George Albert

### PENNSYLVANIA

**Allentown**
Cahn, Edward N.
Platt, William Henry
**Doylestown**
Rufe, Cynthia Marie
**Easton**
Van Antwerpen, Franklin Stuart
**Erie**
McLaughlin, Sean J.
Mencer, Glenn Everell
Nygaard, Richard Lowell
**Harrisburg**
Caldwell, William Wilson
Rambo, Sylvia H.
Saylor, Thomas G.
**Johnstown**
Getty, Charles A.
Smith, David Brooks
**Lancaster**
Nickel, George Wall, Jr.
**Orwigsburg**
Troutman, E. Mac
**Philadelphia**
Angell, M(ary) Faith
Bartle, Harvey, III
Bechtle, Louis Charles
Becker, Edward Roy
Broderick, Raymond Joseph
Brody, Anita Blumstein
Buckwalter, Ronald Lawrence
Castille, Ronald D.
Dalzell, Stewart
Ditter, J. William, Jr.
DuBois, Jan Ely
Fullam, John P.
Gawthrop, Robert Smith, III
Giles, James T.
Green, Clifford Scott
Hutton, Herbert J.
Jaffe, Paul Lawrence
Joyner, J(ames) Curtis
Katz, Marvin
Kelly, James McGirr
Kelly, Robert F.
Ludwig, Edmund Vincent
McGlynn, Joseph Leo, Jr.
McKee, Theodore A.
Newcomer, Clarence Charles
Nigro, Russell M.
O'Neill, Thomas Newman, Jr.
Padova, John R.
Pollak, Louis Heilprin
Reed, Lowell A., Jr.
Rendell, Marjorie O.
Robreno, Eduardo C.
Scholl, David Allen
Scirica, Anthony Joseph
Shapiro, Norma Sondra Levy
Sloviter, Dolores Korman
Van Artsdalen, Donald West
Waldman, Jay Carl
Weiner, Charles R.
Yohn, William H(endricks), Jr.
**Pittsburgh**
Ambrose, Donetta W.
Bloch, Alan Neil
Brosky, John G.
Cappy, Ralph Joseph
Cohill, Maurice Blanchard, Jr.
Colville, Robert E.
Diamond, Gustave
Fitzgerald, Judith Klaswick
Flaherty, John Paul, Jr.
Lally-Green, Maureen Ellen
Lee, Donald John
Lewis, Timothy K.
Mansmann, Carol Los
O'Reilly, Timothy Patrick
Sensenich, Ila Jeanne
Skwaryk, Robert Francis
Standish, William Lloyd
Weis, Joseph Francis, Jr.
Zappala, Stephen A.
Ziegler, Donald Emil
**Scranton**
Conaboy, Richard Paul
Kosik, Edwin Michael
Nealon, William Joseph, Jr.
O'Malley, Carlon Martin
Vanaskie, Thomas Ignatius
**Uniontown**
Franks, William J.
**Washington**
Mc Cune, Barron Patterson
**Waynesburg**
Nalitz, William Robert
**West Conshohocken**
Newman, Sandra Schultz
**Wilkes Barre**
Rosenn, Max
Schwartz, Roger Alan
**Williamsport**
McClure, James Focht, Jr.
Muir, Malcolm
**York**
Cassimatis, Emanuel Andrew

### RHODE ISLAND

**Hope Valley**
Williams, Frank J.
**North Providence**
Caldarone, Thomas J., Jr.
**Providence**
Bourcier, John Paul
Flanders, Robert G., Jr.
Goldberg, Maureen McKenna
Hagopian, Jacob
Lagueux, Ronald Rene
Lederberg, Victoria
Lisi, Mary M.
Ragosta, Vincent A.F.
Torres, Ernest C.
Weisberger, Joseph Robert
**Westerly**
Newman, Edward Henry

### SOUTH CAROLINA

**Aiken**
Huff, Thomas E.
Simons, Charles Earl, Jr.
**Anderson**
Anderson, George Ross, Jr.
**Charleston**
Blatt, Solomon, Jr.
Hawkins, Falcon Black, Jr.
Norton, David C.
**Columbia**
Anderson, Joseph Fletcher, Jr.
Bristow, Walter James, Jr.
Chapman, Robert Foster
Finney, Ernest Adolphus, Jr.
Hamilton, Clyde Henry
Perry, Matthew J., Jr.
Shedd, Dennis W.
Toal, Jean Hoefer
**Florence**
Currie, Cameron McGowan
Houck, Charles Weston
**Greenville**
Herlong, Henry Michael, Jr.
Smith, Willie Tesreau, Jr.
Traxler, William Byrd, Jr.
Wilkins, William Walter, Jr.
**Greenwood**
Moore, James E.
**Marion**
Waller, John Henry, Jr.
**Myrtle Beach**
Harwell, David Walker
**Orangeburg**
Williams, Karen Johnson
**Spartanburg**
Burnett, E. C., III

### SOUTH DAKOTA

**Pierre**
Amundson, Robert A.
Gilbertson, David
Konenkamp, John K.
Miller, Robert Arthur
Sabers, Richard Wayne
**Rapid City**
Battey, Richard Howard
Bogue, Andrew Wendell
**Sioux Falls**
Jones, John Bailey
Piersol, Lawrence L.
Wollman, Roger Leland

### TENNESSEE

**Chattanooga**
Barker, William M.
Edgar, R(obert) Allan
Franks, Herschel Pickens
**Cleveland**
Puckett, Lawrence Howard
**Greeneville**
Hull, Thomas Gray
**Jackson**
Todd, James Dale
**Johnson City**
Kiener, John Leslie
**Kingsport**
Beck, Ronald Jerry
McLellan, John Sidney, III
**Knoxville**
Anderson, Edward Riley
Jarvis, James Howard, II
Jordan, Robert Leon
Murrian, Robert Phillip
**Memphis**
Allen, James Henry
Brown, Bailey
Gibbons, Julia Smith
Gilman, Ronald Lee
Holder, Janice Marie
McCalla, Jon P.
McRae, Robert Malcolm, Jr.
Turner, Jerome
Wellford, Harry Walker
**Nashville**
Birch, Adolpho A., Jr.
Brown, Joe Blackburn
Daughtrey, Martha Craig
Drowota, Frank F., III
Echols, Robert L.
Higgins, Thomas A.
Merritt, Gilbert Stroud
Nixon, John Trice
Reid, Lyle
Wiseman, Thomas Anderton, Jr.
**Newport**
Porter, James Kenneth
**Pigeon Forge**
Brackett, Colquitt Prater, Jr.
**Signal Mountain**
Cooper, Robert Elbert
**Smyrna**
Coats, Christopher Dale

### TEXAS

**Alice**
Saenz, L. Arnoldo
**Amarillo**
Johnson, Philip Wayne
Robinson, Mary Lou
**Austin**
Abbott, Greg Wayne
Baird, Charles F.
Baker, James A.
Benavides, Fortunato Pedro (Pete Benavides)
Coronado, Santiago Sybert (Jim Coronado)
Enoch, Craig Trively
Garwood, William Lockhart
Gonzales, Alberto R.
Gonzalez, Raul A.
Hankinson, Deborah G.
Hecht, Nathan Lincoln
Johnson, Cheryl Ann
Justice, William Wayne
Keller, Sharon Faye
Maloney, Frank
Mansfield, Stephen W.
McCormick, Michael Jerry
Meyers, Lawrence Edward
Nowlin, James Robertson
O'Neill, Harriet

Overstreet, Morris L.
Owen, Priscilla Richman
Perkins, Robert Anton
Phillips, Thomas Royal
Pope, Andrew Jackson, Jr. (Jack Pope)
Reavley, Thomas Morrow
Sparks, Sam
Spector, Rose

**Bastrop**
Eskew, Benton

**Beaumont**
Cobb, Howell
Heartfield, Thad
Schell, Richard A.

**Bellaire**
Martin, John Randolph

**Brady**
Jordan, Vernon Murray

**Brazoria**
Germany, Garvin Holt, Jr.

**Brownsville**
Vela, Filemon B.

**Bryan**
Smith, Steven Lee

**Corpus Christi**
Brazell, Ida Hernandez
Head, Hayden Wilson, Jr.
Jack, Janis Graham

**Dallas**
Buchmeyer, Jerry
Chae, Don B.
Fish, A. Joe
Fitzwater, Sidney Allen
Higginbotham, Patrick Errol
Kendall, Joe
Leonie, Andrew Drake, III
Lewis, Marilea Whatley
Maloney, Robert B.
Moyé, Eric Vaughn
Sanders, Harold Barefoot, Jr.
Solis, Jorge Antonio
Stewart, Wesley Holmgreen

**Del Rio**
Thurmond, George Murat

**Edinburg**
Hinojosa, Federico Gustavo, Jr.

**El Paso**
Briones, David
Dinsmoor, Robert Davidson
Hudspeth, Harry Lee
Peca, Peter Samuel

**Fort Worth**
Mahon, Eldon Brooks
McBryde, John Henry
Means, Terry Robert
Rodgers, James Daniel
Tillman, Massie Monroe
Wallace, Steven Charles

**Galveston**
Kent, Samuel B.

**Houston**
Amidei, Maurice Eneas
Champagne, Debra
Christopher, Tracy Elizabeth Kee
DeMoss, Harold Raymond, Jr.
Gilmore, Vanessa D.
Harmon, Melinda Furche
Hittner, David
Hoyt, Kenneth M.
Hughes, Lynn Nettleton
Jones, Edith Hollan
King, Carolyn Dineen
Krocker, Jan
Lake, Sim
Lanford, Norman Eugene
Rainey, John David
Rendon, Josefina Muniz
Rosenthal, Lee H.
Schwarz, Paul Winston
Smith, Jerry Edwin
Sondock, Ruby Kless
Werlein, Ewing, Jr.
York, James Martin

**Humble**
Lawrence, Thomas Eugene

**Laredo**
Kazen, George Philip

**Longview**
Martin, William Clifford, III

**Lubbock**
Cummings, Sam R.
Woodward, Halbert Owen

**Mcallen**
Hinojosa, Ricardo H.

**Midland**
Furgeson, William Royal

**New Braunfels**
Zipp, Ronald Duane

**Richmond**
Elliott, Brady Gifford

**Rusk**
Hassell, Morris William

**San Angelo**
Sutton, John Ewing

**San Antonio**
Biery, Fred
Clark, Leif Michael
Duncan, Sarah Baker
Garcia, Hipolito Frank (Hippo Garcia)
Garcia, Orlando Luis
Garza, Emilio M(iller)
King, Ronald Baker
Luitjen, Mark Randal
Suttle, Dorwin Wallace
Tanne, Martha B.

**Sherman**
Brown, Paul Neeley

**Temple**
Clawson, James F., Jr.
Skelton, Byron George

**Texarkana**
Folsom, David

**Tomball**
Vaccaro, Charles G.

**Tyler**
DeVasto, Diane V.
Guthrie, Judith K.
Kent, Cynthia Stevens
Parker, Robert M.
Rogers, Randall Lee

Steger, William Merritt

**Waco**
Smith, Walter S., Jr.

### UTAH

**Murray**
Robinson, Richard Spencer, II

**Provo**
Bullock, J(ames) Robert
Harding, Ray Murray, Jr.
Schofield, Anthony Wayne
Stott, Gary Don

**Salt Lake City**
Anderson, Stephen Hale
Clark, Glen Edward
Durham, Christine Meaders
Greene, John Thomas
Hall, Gordon R.
Howe, Richard Cuddy
Jenkins, Bruce Sterling
McKay, Monroe Gunn
Murphy, Michael R.
Rigtrup, Kenneth
Russon, Leonard H.
Sam, David
Stewart, Isaac Daniel, Jr.
Wilkins, Michael Jon
Winder, David Kent
Zimmerman, Michael David

### VERMONT

**Brattleboro**
Murtha, J. Garvan
Oakes, James L.

**Burlington**
Parker, Fred I.

**Manchester**
Gagliardi, Lee Parsons

**Montpelier**
Dooley, John Augustine, III
Gibson, Ernest Willard, III
Johnson, Denise Reinka
Morse, James L.
Skoglund, Marilyn

**Waterbury Center**
Amestoy, Jeffrey Lee

**Woodstock**
Billings, Franklin Swift, Jr.

### VIRGINIA

**Abingdon**
Widener, Hiram Emory, Jr.
Williams, Glen Morgan

**Alexandria**
Brinkema, Leonie Milhomme
Bryan, Albert V., Jr.
Cacheris, James C.
Ellis, Thomas Selby, III
Hilton, Claude Meredith
Luttig, J. Michael

**Annandale**
Hollis, Daryl Joseph

**Charlottesville**
Crigler, B. Waugh
Hogshire, Edward Leigh
Michael, James Harry, Jr.
Wilkinson, James Harvie, III

**Chesterfield**
Davis, Bonnie Christell
Gill, Herbert Cogbill

**Clifton**
Gales, Robert Robinson

**Covington**
Lacy, Elizabeth Bermingham
Stephenson, Roscoe Bolar, Jr.

**Danville**
Kiser, Jackson L.

**Fairfax**
Williams, Marcus Doyle

**Falls Church**
Barton, Robert L., Jr.

**King George**
Revercomb, Horace Austin, III

**Manassas**
Van Broekhoven, Rollin Adrian

**Norfolk**
Adams, David Huntington
Bonney, Hal James, Jr.
Clarke, J. Calvitt, Jr.
Doumar, Robert George
Jackson, Raymond A.
Morgan, Henry Coke, Jr.
Prince, William Taliaferro
Smith, Rebecca Beach

**Pennington Gap**
Kinser, Cynthia D.

**Richmond**
Carrico, Harry Lee
Compton, Asbury Christian
Hassell, Leroy Rountree, Sr.
Keenan, Barbara Milano
King, Robert Bruce
Payne, Robert E.
Poff, Richard Harding
Russell, Charles Stevens
Spencer, James R.
Tice, Douglas Oscar, Jr.
Whiting, Henry H.
Williams, Richard Leroy

**Roanoke**
Turk, James Clinton

**Salem**
Koontz, Lawrence L., Jr.
Pearson, Henry Clyde

### WASHINGTON

**Bellevue**
Andersen, James A.

**Ephrata**
Fitterer, Richard Clarence

**Everett**
Bowden, George Newton
Castleberry, Ronald LeRoy

**Mercer Island**
Noe, James Alva

**Mount Vernon**
Meyer, John Michael

**Olympia**
Alexander, Gerry L.
Durham, Barbara
Guy, Richard P.
Harrison, William Alan
Ireland, Faith
Johnson, Charles William
Sanders, Richard Browning
Smith, Charles Z.

**Seattle**
Beezer, Robert Renaut
Coughenour, John Clare
Dimmick, Carolyn Reaber
Dwyer, William L.
Farris, Jerome
Fletcher, Betty B.
Mc Govern, Walter T.
McKeown, Mary Margaret
Pekelis, Rosselle
Rothstein, Barbara Jacobs
Wright, Eugene Allen
Zilly, Thomas Samuel

**Spokane**
Nielsen, William Fremming
Quackenbush, Justin Lowe
Sweeney, Dennis Joseph

**Tacoma**
Bryan, Robert J.
Burgess, Franklin Douglas

**Yakima**
McDonald, Alan Angus
Suko, Lonny Ray

### WEST VIRGINIA

**Bluefield**
Faber, David Alan

**Charleston**
Brewer, Lewis Gordon
Copenhaver, John Thomas, Jr.
Davis, Robin Jean
Goodwin, Joseph R.
Haden, Charles Harold, II
Hallanan, Elizabeth V.
Kiss, Robert
Knapp, Dennis Raymond
Marland, Melissa Kaye
Maynard, Elliott
McGraw, Warren Randolph
McHugh, Thomas Edward
Michael, M. Blane
Starcher, Larry Victor
Wilson, Robert Bryan

**Clarksburg**
Keeley, Irene Patricia Murphy

**Elkins**
Maxwell, Robert Earl

**Union**
Sprouse, James Marshall

**Williamson**
Thornsbury, Michael

### WISCONSIN

**Appleton**
Bayorgeon, James Thomas

**Madison**
Abrahamson, Shirley Schlanger
Bablitch, William A.
Bradley, Ann Walsh
Crabb, Barbara Brandriff
Crooks, N(eil) Patrick
Heffernan, Nathan Stewart
Martin, Robert David
Prosser, David Thomas, Jr.
Shabaz, John C.
Wilcox, Jon P.

**Milwaukee**
Curran, Thomas J.
Evans, Terence Thomas
Gordon, Myron L.
Randa, Rudolph Thomas
Reynolds, John W.
Shapiro, James Edward
Stadtmueller, Joseph Peter

### WYOMING

**Casper**
Downes, William F.

**Cheyenne**
Barrett, James Emmett
Brimmer, Clarence Addison
Brorby, Wade
Golden, T. Michael
Hill, William U.
Johnson, Alan Bond
Lehman, Larry L.
Macy, Richard J.
Taylor, William Al
Thomas, Richard Van

**Cody**
Patrick, H. Hunter

**Wheatland**
Mickelsen, Einer Bjegaard

### TERRITORIES OF THE UNITED STATES

### GUAM

**Agana**
Cruz, Benjamin Joseph Franquez
Lamorena, Alberto C., III
Manibusan, Joaquin V.E., Jr.
Siguenza, Peter Charles, Jr.
Unpingco, John Walter Sablan

**Barrigada**
Diaz, Ramon Valero

**Hagatna**
Maraman, Katherine Ann
Weeks, Janet Healy

### NORTHERN MARIANA ISLANDS

**Saipan**
Dela Cruz, Jose Santos
Munson, Alex Robert

### PUERTO RICO

**Hato Rey**
Cerezo, Carmen Consuelo
Laffitte, Hector Manuel

**San Juan**
Acosta, Raymond Luis
Alonso-Alonso, Rafael
Andreu-Garcia, Jose Antonio
Casellas, Salvador E.
Corrada del Rio, Baltasar
de Rodon, Miriam Naveira
Dominguez, Daniel R.
Fusté, José Antonio
Fuster, Jaime B.
Gierbolini-Ortiz, Gilberto
Hernandez-Denton, Federico
Negron-Garcia, Antonio S.
Pieras, Jaime, Jr.
Rebollo-Lopez, Francisco
Torruella, Juan R.

### VIRGIN ISLANDS

**Charlotte Amalie**
Barnard, Geoffrey W.

**Christiansted**
Finch, Raymond Lawrence
Resnick, Jeffrey Lance

**Saint Thomas**
Caffee, Lorren Dale
Moore, Thomas Kail

### CANADA

### ONTARIO

**Ottawa**
Muldoon, Francis Creighton

### THE NETHERLANDS

**The Hague**
Aldrich, George Hoover
Allison, Richard Clark

### ADDRESS UNPUBLISHED

Aaroe, Paul Morris
Askey, William Hartman
Avery, Emerson Roy, Jr.
Bertelsman, William Odis
Bierce, James Malcolm
Boyle, Francis Joseph
Brown, Robert Laidlaw
Bunton, Lucius Desha, III
Butzner, John Decker, Jr.
Callow, Keith McLean
Callow, William Grant
Castagna, William John
Ceci, Louis J.
Clark, Thomas Alonzo
Clinton, Sam Houston
Cochran, George Moffett
Coffey, John Louis
Cohn, Avern Levin
Cole, Betty Lou McDonel Shelton (Mrs. Dewey G. Cole, Jr.)
Cook, Julian Abele, Jr.
Cyr, Conrad Keefe
Daugherty, Frederick Alvin
Davis, Marguerite Herr
Day, Roland Bernard
Dolliver, James Morgan
Dunn, Melvin Edward
Eaton, Joe Oscar
Edwards, Ninian Murry
Fadeley, Edward Norman
Fahrnbruch, Dale E.
Fenster, Sidney J.
Fisk, Merlin Edgar
Flynn, Peter Anthony
Garibaldi, Marie Louise
Gieringer, Raymond E.
Gillette, W. Michael
Golden, Elliott
Grant, Isabella Horton
Griffin, Robert Paul
Grimes, William Alvan
Haltom, Elbert Bertram, Jr.
Handler, Alan B.
Hawkins, Michael Daly
Hayek, Carolyn Jean
Hightower, Jack English
Hogan, Thomas Francis
Horton, Odell
Howard, George, Jr.
Johnson, Byron Jerald
Joiner, Charles Wycliffe
Karwacki, Robert Lee
Kauger, Yvonne
Keyko, David Andrew
Klein, Harriet Farber
Lee, Dan M.
Levine, Beryl Joyce
Liacos, Paul Julian
Lively, Pierce
Madsen, Barbara A
Magnuson, Paul Arthur
Mai, Harold Leverne
Matthews, Warren Wayne
McClure, Ann Crawford
McKee, Roger Curtis
Meschke, Herbert Leonard
Metzner, Charles Miller
Meyer, Louis B.
Montgomery, Seth David
Moore, Daniel Alton, Jr.
Muecke, Charles Andrew (Carl Muecke)
Murray, Florence Kerins
Nesbit, Phyllis Schneider
Newbern, William David
Newman, Theodore Roosevelt, Jr.
Perez-Gimenez, Juan Manuel
Phillips, James Dickson, Jr.
Rabin, Gilbert
Ramsey, Edward Lawrence
Reinhardt, Stephen Roy
Rice, Walter Herbert
Roberts, James L., Jr.
Ross, Donald Roe
Roszkowski, Stanley Julian
Saeta, Philip Max
Sarokin, H. Lee
Schroeder, Gerald Frank
Schultz, Louis William
Shearing, Miriam
Sheldon, Michael Richard
Shubb, William Barnet
Silberman, Laurence Hirsch
Smith, Fern M.
Smith, Loren Allan
Sognier, John Woodward
Souter, David Hackett
Stahl, Madonna
Staker, Robert Jackson
Stamp, Frederick Pfarr, Jr.
Stanton, Louis Lee
Steinmetz, Donald Walter
Sweet, Robert Workman
Talmadge, Philip Albert
Tesmer, Louise M.
Thomas, Herman
Trout, Linda Copple
Utter, Robert French
Vollmer, Richard Wade
Wathen, Daniel Everett
Weber, Fred J.
White, Helene Nita
Wiggins, Charles Edward
Wood, Diane Pamela
Workman, Margaret Lee
Zive, Gregg William

## LIBRARY

### UNITED STATES

### ALABAMA

**Birmingham**
Sinclair, Julie Moores Williams

### ARKANSAS

**Fayetteville**
Ahlers, Glen-Peter, Sr.

### CALIFORNIA

**Fairfield**
Moore, Marianna Gay

**Los Angeles**
Iamele, Richard Thomas

**Oakland**
Stromme, Gary L.

**Sacramento**
David, Shirley Hart

### COLORADO

**Denver**
Schroeder, Merrie Jo

### CONNECTICUT

**Stamford**
Younskevicius, Adriana

**Vernon Rockville**
Purnell, Oliver James, III

### DISTRICT OF COLUMBIA

**Washington**
Goldberg, Jolande Elisabeth
Leiter, Richard Allen
Mahar, Ellen Patricia
McGuirl, Marlene Dana Callis
Pursley, Ricky Anthony
Sheeler, Harva Lee

### FLORIDA

**Atlantic Beach**
Bruno, Lisa

**Jacksonville**
Sheng, Jack Tse-liang

**Miami**
Mahnk, Karen

**Opa Locka**
Citron, Beatrice Sally

**Orlando**
Diefenbach, Dale Alan

**Tallahassee**
Hebenthal, M(argareta) Elaine

### GEORGIA

**Athens**
Puckett, Elizabeth Ann

**Atlanta**
Schein, Julia Ruth

**Smyrna**
Cavallini, Donna Francesca

### ILLINOIS

**Carbondale**
Matthews, Elizabeth Woodfin

**Chicago**
Lefco, Kathy Nan
Patterson, Patricia Anne

**Springfield**
Larison, Brenda Irene

### INDIANA

**Notre Dame**
Payne, Lucy Ann Salsbury

### IOWA

**Des Moines**
Robertson, Linda Lou

### MASSACHUSETTS

**Boston**
Wellington, Carol Strong

**Cambridge**
Duckett, Joan

**Greenfield**
Lee, Marilyn (Irma) Modarelli

**Leominster**
Lambert, Lyn Dee

**Sherborn**
Borgeson, Earl Charles

**Winthrop**
Brown, Patricia Irene

### MICHIGAN

**Grand Rapids**
Calvin, Mary Lou

**Lansing**
Studwell, Roberta Frances

**Pittsburgh**
Reich, Deborah Ziskind *public relations and legal marketing executive*

### RHODE ISLAND

**Providence**
Castelnovo, Annie Teresa *legal nurse consultant*

**Westerly**
Matarese, Lauren A. *police officer, lawyer*

### SOUTH DAKOTA

**Sioux Falls**
Haas, Joseph Alan *court administrator, lawyer*

### TENNESSEE

**Cleveland**
Rhodes, Arthur Delano *benefits administrator*

**Kingsport**
Kindle, Judith O. *court reporter*

### TEXAS

**Austin**
Porter, Charles, Jr. *writer, mediator, business executive*

**Dallas**
Lanio, Kimberley DiGiacobbe *lawyer, legal recruiter*

**El Paso**
Miller, Roger Wayne *court reporter*

**Huntsville**
Stowe, Charles Robinson Beecher *management consultant, educator, lawyer*

**Richardson**
Clark, Daniel *law researcher*

**San Antonio**
Johnson, Katherine Anne *health research administrator, lawyer*
Kehl, Randall Herman *executive, consultant, lawyer*

**Sinton**
Miller, Josephine Welder *legal administrator*

**Waco**
Thomson, Basil Henry, Jr. *lawyer, university general counsel*

### UTAH

**Brigham City**
McCullough, Edward Eugene *patent agent, inventor*

### VIRGINIA

**Alexandria**
Montague, Robert Latane, III *lawyer*
Siemens, Terrance Lee *patent executive*

**Fairfax**
Blackman, Paul H. *criminologist, political scientist*

**Lynchburg**
Cox, Herbert David *lawyer*

**Mc Lean**
Stewart, James Kevin *judicial administrator, management technology consultant*

**Rustburg**
Hughes, Deborah Enoch *circuit court clerk*

### WASHINGTON

**Seattle**
Leitzke, Randy Lee *law firm executive, accountant*
Stearns, Susan Tracey *lighting design company executive, lawyer*

### WISCONSIN

**Madison**
Barnick, Helen *retired judicial clerk*
Crowe, Patricia Mary *family court commissioner*

### WYOMING

**Douglas**
Bunn, Dorothy Irons *court reporter*

### ADDRESS UNPUBLISHED

Anderson, Pamela Sue *contract compliance analyst*
Casella, Peter F(iore) *patent and licensing executive*
Dancy, Bonita Joyce *lawyer*
David, Marilyn Hattie *lawyer, retired military officer*
Erwin, Judith Ann (Judith Ann Peacock) *writer, photographer, lawyer*
Ferguson, Whitworth, III *consulting company executive*
Hoffman, Darnay Robert *management consultant*
Kelepecz, Betty Patrice *protective services official, lawyer*
Landon, William J. *intelligence officer*
Renfro, William Leonard *futurist, lawyer, inventor, entrepreneur*
Rivers, Kenneth Jay *retired judicial administrator, consultant*
Rodenberg-Roberts, Mary Patricia *advocacy services administrator, lawyer*
Schneider, Patricia J. *court reporter*
Skaggs, Kathy Cheryl *writer, consultant*
Sobocinski, Joseph S. *federal law enforcement agent*
Wims, Travis Martin *lawyer*
Winchell, William Olin *mechanical engineer, educator, lawyer*

## PARAPROFESSIONAL

### UNITED STATES

### ALABAMA

**Birmingham**
Cade, Gregory Andrews

### ARKANSAS

**De Queen**
Melancon, Sybil O.

**Pine Bluff**
Moon, Deborah Joan

### CALIFORNIA

**Altadena**
Vaughan, Audrey Judd

**Arcadia**
Forward, Dorothy Elizabeth

**Lafayette**
Randick, Marlys Ann

**Long Beach**
Boccia Rosado, Ann Marie
Breaux, Dawn Croft

**Los Angeles**
Arbit, Beryl Ellen
Arnkraut, Joe
Wilson, Mable Jean

**Monterey**
Salow, Cynthia Louise

**Pasadena**
Guynes, Verta Corina

**Sacramento**
Willis, Dawn Louise

**San Francisco**
Edwards, Priscilla Ann

**Santa Barbara**
Nelson, Sonja Bea

**Santa Rosa**
Hinton, Rhetta Ann

### COLORADO

**Boulder**
LaVelle, Betty Sullivan Dougherty

**Denver**
Gustus, Stacey A.

**Pueblo**
White, Rodney Curtis

### CONNECTICUT

**Bridgeport**
Green, Sonya Yvette

**Danbury**
Keenan, Linda Lee

### DELAWARE

**Dover**
Rivard, Debra Lynn

**New Castle**
Brzoska, Denise Jeanne

### DISTRICT OF COLUMBIA

**Washington**
Pollock, Melany Tawanda
Townsend, Brian Douglas

### FLORIDA

**Hialeah**
Canes, Carmen Dahlia

**Miami**
Colbert, Dia Teresa

**Orlando**
Kidd, Pamela Sue

**Safety Harbor**
Slevin, Patrick Jeremiah

**West Palm Beach**
Beelner, Ken Phillip

### GEORGIA

**Atlanta**
Smith, Eleanor Van Law

**Valdosta**
Steinberg, Teresa Sherwood

### ILLINOIS

**Chicago**
Eileraas, Karina Astrid

**Glen Ellyn**
Barrett, Carolyn Hernly

**Rock Island**
Tank, Sharon Rae

### INDIANA

**Carmel**
Richards, Barbara L.

**Highland**
Forsythe, Randall Newman

**Indianapolis**
Wallace, Edna Marie

**South Bend**
Knepp, Virginia Lee Hahn

### KANSAS

**Leawood**
Johnston, Jocelyn Stanwell

### LOUISIANA

**Metairie**
Quidd, David Andrew

**Shreveport**
Fisher, Elizabeth Blair

**Slidell**
Eiermann-Wegener, Darlene Mae

### MARYLAND

**Baltimore**
Garnes-Thomas, Terri Diana

**Suitland**
Bea, Barbara Ann

### MASSACHUSETTS

**Andover**
Newell, Keith Douglas

**Boston**
Daniels, Tracy Ellen
Hunt, Cynthia Ann

### MINNESOTA

**Minnetrista**
Black, Pamela Wynne

### MISSISSIPPI

**Tupelo**
Lukas, Joseph Frank

### MISSOURI

**Camdenton**
Clark, Mark Jeffrey

**Washington**
Schmelz, Brenda Lea

### MONTANA

**Great Falls**
Speer, John Elmer

### NEW JERSEY

**Haddonfield**
Willis, Beth Anne

**Hopatcong**
Falconer, Thomas Robert

**Trenton**
Smith, George Joseph

### NEW MEXICO

**Albuquerque**
Miller, Gardner Hartmann

### NEW YORK

**Buffalo**
Mahony, Karen Elizabeth

**Crugers**
Walther, Zerita

**Garden City**
Caputo, Kathryn Mary
McCann, Louise Mary

**New York**
Bordoff, Jason Eric

### NORTH CAROLINA

**Cary**
Stell, Camille Stuckey

**Charlotte**
Beatty, Tina Marie

**Durham**
Burrows, Virginia Moore

**Raleigh**
Kaufman, Sarah Hall

**Salisbury**
Trexler, Wynn Ridenhour

### NORTH DAKOTA

**Minot**
Sundby, Connie L.

### OHIO

**Cleveland**
Stith, Beverly Jean

**Columbus**
Larzelere, Kathy Lynn Heckler

**Saint Clairsville**
Cook, LeAnn Cecilia

### OKLAHOMA

**Oklahoma City**
Elwell, Celia Candace

### OREGON

**La Grande**
Larsen-Hill, Di Lyn

### PENNSYLVANIA

**Hershey**
Kaylor, Gay L.

**Philadelphia**
Pollard, Caroline Pray

**Pittsburgh**
Long-Eberhardt, Cordova Jacqueline

**Uniontown**
Fox, Susan E.

### SOUTH CAROLINA

**Columbia**
McQuillan, Barbara Glatz
Wilson, Karen Wilkerson

### TENNESSEE

**Harriman**
Thacker, Penny Ann

**Knoxville**
Midkiff, Kimberly Ann

### TEXAS

**Amarillo**
Hayes, Karla Lavon

**Dallas**
Flood, Joan Moore
Matos, Jose Ricardo

**Fort Worth**
Reedom, James Patrick

**Grand Prairie**
Avery, Reigh Kessen

**Houston**
Cope-Gibbs, Amy Michelle
Hancock, Mary Jane
Larson, Peter L.
Rucker, Valerie Lynn

### UTAH

**Manti**
Petersen, Benton Lauritz

**Salt Lake City**
Balthaser, Anita Young

### VIRGINIA

**Boissevain**
Welch-McKay, Dawn Renee

**Fairfax**
Belcher, Christine Victoria

**Richmond**
Anderson, Patricia Coulter

### WASHINGTON

**Seattle**
Tessier, Dennis Medward

### WEST VIRGINIA

**Wellsburg**
Viderman, Linda Jean

### ADDRESS UNPUBLISHED

Kaufman, Helene
Moore, Betty Jo
Moreno, Patricia Frazier
Myhand, Wanda Reshel
Schmidt, Stephanie
Snell, Lori B.
Taylor, Deborah Ann
Trent, Clyde Nathaniel
Vetter, Joanne Reiniger